S0-DTB-828

Peterson's Graduate Programs in the Physical Sciences, Mathematics, Agricultural Sciences, the Environment & Natural Resources

2005

Book 4

THOMSON PETERSON'S™

Australia • Canada • Mexico • Singapore • Spain • United Kingdom • United States

Abou... Peterson's

Tho...son's (www.petersons.com) is a leading provider of education information and advice, with books and online re...using on education search, test preparation, and financial aid. Its Web site offers searchable databases and i...ools for contacting educational institutions, online practice tests and instruction, and planning tools for securing ...aid. Thomson Peterson's serves 110 million education consumers annually.

...more information, contact Thomson Peterson's, 2000 Lenox Drive, Lawrenceville, ...J 08648; 800-338-3282; or find us on the World Wide Web at www.petersons.com/about.

Editor: Fern A. Oram; Production Editor: Susan W. Dilts; Copy Editors: Bret Bollman, Jim Colbert, Michele N. Firestone, Michael Haines, Sally Ross, Jill C. Schwartz, Pam Sullivan, Valerie Bolus Vaughan; Research Project Manager: Peter Delaney; Research Associates: Marie Leach, Kristina Moran; Programmer: John Raba; Manufacturing Manager: Ray Golaszewski; Composition Manager: Linda M. Williams; Client Relations Representatives: Mimi Kaufman, Lois Regina Milton, Mary Ann Murphy, Jim Swinarski, Eric Wallace.

ISSN 1093-8443
ISBN 0-7689-1390-X

Printed in the United States of America

10 9 8 7 6 5 4 3 2 1 07 06 05

Thirty-ninth Edition

A NOTE FROM THE PETERSON'S EDITORS

The six volumes of *Peterson's Graduate and Professional Programs*, the only annually updated reference work of its kind, provide wide-ranging information on the graduate and professional programs offered by accredited colleges and universities in the United States, U.S. territories, and Canada and by those institutions outside the United States that are accredited by U.S. accrediting bodies. More than 42,000 individual academic and professional programs at more than 2,000 institutions are listed. *Peterson's Graduate and Professional Programs* have been used for almost forty years by prospective graduate and professional students, placement counselors, faculty advisers, and all others interested in postbaccalaureate education.

Book 1: *Graduate & Professional Programs: An Overview*, contains information on institutions as a whole, while Books 2 through 6 are devoted to specific academic and professional fields.

Book 2: *Graduate Programs in the Humanities, Arts & Social Sciences*

Book 3: *Graduate Programs in the Biological Sciences*

Book 4: *Graduate Programs in the Physical Sciences, Mathematics, Agricultural Sciences, the Environment & Natural Resources*

Book 5: *Graduate Programs in Engineering & Applied Sciences*

Book 6: *Graduate Programs in Business, Education, Health, Information Studies, Law & Social Work*

The books may be used individually or as a set. For example, if you have chosen a field of study but do not know what institution you want to attend or if you have a college or university in mind but have not chosen an academic field of study, the best place to begin is Book 1.

Book 1 presents several directories to help you identify programs of study that might interest you; you can then research those programs further in Books 2 through 6. The *Directory of Graduate and Professional Programs by Field* lists the 457 fields for which there are program directories in Books 2 through 6 and gives the names of those institutions that offer graduate degree programs in each.

For geographical or financial reasons, you may be interested in attending a particular institution and will want to know what it has to offer. You should turn to the *Directory of Institutions and Their Offerings*, which lists the degree programs available at each institution, again, in the 457 academic and professional fields for which Books 2 through 6 have program directories. As in the *Directory of Graduate and Professional Programs by Field*, the level of degrees offered is also indicated.

All books in the series include advice on graduate education, including topics such as admissions tests, financial aid, and accreditation. **The Graduate Adviser** includes two essays and information about accreditation. The first essay, "The Admissions Process," discusses general admission requirements, admission tests, factors to consider when selecting a graduate school or program, when and how to apply, and how admission decisions are made. Special information for international students and tips for minority students are also included. The second essay, "Financial Support," is an overview of the broad range of support available at the graduate level. Fellowships, scholarships, and grants; assistantships and internships; federal and private loan programs, as well as Federal Work-Study; and the GI bill are detailed. This essay concludes with advice on applying for need-based financial aid. "Accreditation and Accrediting Agencies" gives information on accreditation and its purpose and lists first institutional accrediting agencies and then specialized accrediting agencies relevant to each volume's specific fields of study.

With information on more than 42,000 graduate programs in 457 disciplines, *Peterson's Graduate and Professional Programs* give you all the information you need about the programs that are of interest to you in three formats: **Profiles** (capsule summaries of basic information), **Announcements** (information that an institution or program wants to emphasize, written by administrators), and **In-Depth Descriptions** (also written by administrators, with more expansive information than the **Profiles**, emphasizing different aspects of their programs). By using these various formats of program information, coupled with **Appendixes** and **Indexes** covering directories and subject areas for all six books, you will find that these guides provide the most comprehensive, accurate, and up-to-date graduate study information available.

Thomson Peterson's publishes a full line of resources to help you with any information you need to guide you through the graduate admissions process. Peterson's publications can be found at your local bookstore, library, and high school guidance office—or visit us on the Web at www.petersons.com.

Colleges and universities will be pleased to know that Thomson Peterson's helped you in your selection. Admissions staff members are more than happy to answer questions, address specific problems, and help in any way they can. The editors at Peterson's wish you great success in your graduate program search!

THE GRADUATE ADVISER

The Admissions Process

Generalizations about graduate admissions practices are not always helpful because each institution has its own set of guidelines and procedures. Nevertheless, some broad statements can be made about the admissions process that may help you plan your strategy.

General Requirements

Graduate schools and departments have requirements that applicants for admission must meet. Typically, these requirements include undergraduate transcripts (which provide information about undergraduate grade point average and course work applied toward a major), admission test scores, and letters of recommendation. Most graduate programs also ask for an essay or personal statement that describes your personal reasons for seeking graduate study. In some fields, such as art and music, portfolios or auditions may be required in addition to other evidence of talent. Some institutions require that the applicant have an undergraduate degree in the same subject as the intended graduate major.

Most institutions evaluate each applicant on the basis of the applicant's total record, and the weight accorded any given factor varies widely from institution to institution and from program to program.

Admission Tests

The major testing program used in graduate admissions is the Graduate Record Examinations (GRE) testing program, sponsored by the GRE Board and administered by Educational Testing Service, Princeton, New Jersey.

The Graduate Record Examinations testing program consists of a General Test and eight Subject Tests. The General Test measures verbal reasoning, quantitative reasoning, and analytical writing skills. It is offered as a computer-adaptive test (CAT) in the United States, Canada, and many other countries. In the CAT, the computer determines which question to present next by adjusting to your previous responses. Paper-based General Test administrations are offered in some parts of the world.

The computer-adaptive General Test consists of a 30-minute verbal section, a 45-minute quantitative section, and a 75-minute analytical writing section. In addition, an unidentified verbal or quantitative section that doesn't count toward a score may be included and an identified research section that is not scored may also be included.

The paper-based General Test consists of two 30-minute verbal sections, two 30-minute quantitative sections, and a 75-minute analytical writing section. In addition, an unidentified verbal or quantitative section that doesn't count toward a score may be included.

The Subject Tests measure achievement and assume undergraduate majors or extensive background in the following eight disciplines:

- Biochemistry, Cell and Molecular Biology
- Biology
- Chemistry
- Computer Science
- Literature in English
- Mathematics
- Physics
- Psychology

The Subject Tests are available at regularly scheduled paper-based administrations at test centers around the world. Testing time is approximately 2 hours and 50 minutes. You can obtain more information about the GRE tests by visiting the GRE Web site at www.gre.org or consulting the *GRE Information and Registration Bulletin.* The *Bulletin* can be obtained at many undergraduate colleges. You can also download it from the GRE Web site or obtain it by contacting Graduate Record Examinations, Educational Testing Service, PO Box 6000, Princeton, NJ 08541-6000, telephone 1-609-771-7670.

If you expect to apply for admission to a program that requires any of the GRE tests, you should select a test date well in advance of the application deadline. Scores on the computer-adaptive General Test are reported within ten to fifteen days; scores on the paper-based General Test and the Subject Tests are reported within six weeks.

Another testing program, the Miller Analogies Test (MAT), is administered at more than 600 Controlled Testing Centers in the United States, Canada, and other countries. The MAT computer-based test is now available in select areas. For information, call 800-211-8378. Testing time is 50 minutes. The test consists of 100 partial analogies. You can obtain the *Candidate Information Booklet,* which contains a list of test centers and instructions for taking the test from http://www.tpcweb.com/mat/index.htm or by calling The Psychological Corporation at 1-800-622-3231.

Check the specific requirements of the programs to which you are applying.

Factors Involved in Selecting a Graduate School or Program

Selecting a graduate school and a specific program of study is a complex matter. Quality of the faculty; program and course offerings; the nature, size, and location of the institution; admission requirements; cost; and the availability of financial assistance are among the many factors that affect one's choice of institution. Other considerations are job placement and achievements of the program's graduates and the institution's resources, such as libraries, laboratories, and computer facilities. If you are to make the best possible choice, you need to learn as much as you can about the schools and programs you are considering before you apply.

The following steps may help you narrow your choices.

- Talk to alumni of the programs or institutions you are considering to get their impressions of how well they were prepared for work in their fields of study.
- Remember that graduate school requirements change, so be sure to get the most up-to-date information possible.
- Talk to department faculty and the graduate adviser at your undergraduate institution. They often have information about programs of study at other institutions.
- Visit the Web sites of the graduate schools in which you are interested to request a graduate catalog. Contact the department chair in your chosen field of study for additional information about the department and the field.
- Visit as many campuses as possible. Call ahead for an appointment with the graduate adviser in your field of interest and be sure to check out the facilities and talk to students.

When and How to Apply

You should begin the application process at least one year before you expect to begin your graduate study. Find out the application deadline for each institution (many are provided in the profile section of this volume). Go to the institution Web site and find out if you can apply online. If not, request a paper application form. Fill out this form thoroughly and neatly. Assume that the school needs all the information it is requesting and that the admissions officer will be sensitive to the neatness and overall quality of what you submit. Do not supply more information than the school requires.

The institution may ask at least one question that will require a three- or four-paragraph answer. Compose your response on the assumption that the admissions officer is interested in both what you think and how you express yourself. Keep your statement brief and to the point, but, at the same time, include all pertinent information about your past experiences and your educational goals. Individual statements vary greatly in style and content, which helps admissions officers to differentiate among applicants. Many graduate departments give considerable weight to the statement in making their admissions decisions, so be sure to take the time to prepare a thoughtful and concise statement.

If recommendations are a part of the admissions requirements, carefully choose the individuals you ask to write them. It is generally best to ask current or former professors to write the recommendations, provided they are able to attest to your intellectual ability and motivation for doing the work required of a graduate student. It is advisable to provide stamped, preaddressed envelopes to people being asked to submit recommendations on your behalf.

Completed applications, including references and transcripts and admission test scores, should be received at the institution by the specified date.

Be advised that institutions do not usually make admissions decisions until all materials have been received. Enclose a self-addressed postcard with your application, requesting confirmation of receipt. Allow at least 10 days for the return of the postcard before making further inquiries.

If you plan to apply for financial support, it is imperative that you file your application early.

How Admission Decisions Are Made

The program you apply to is directly involved in the admissions process. Although the final decision is usually made by the graduate dean (or an associate) or by the faculty admissions committee, recommendations from faculty members in your intended field are important. At some institutions, an interview is incorporated into the decision process.

A Special Note for International Students

In addition to the steps already described, there are some special considerations for international students who intend to apply for graduate study in the United States. All graduate schools require an indication of competence in English. The purpose of the Test of English as a Foreign Language (TOEFL) is to evaluate the English proficiency of people who are nonnative speakers of English and want to study at colleges and universities where English is the language of instruction. The TOEFL is administered by Educational Testing Service (ETS) under the general direction of a policy board established by the College Board and the Graduate Record Examinations Board.

The TOEFL is administered as a computer-based test throughout most of the world and is available year-round by appointment only. It is not necessary to have previous computer experience to take the test. The test consists of four sections—listening, reading, structure, and writing. Total testing time is approximately 4 hours.

The TOEFL is offered in the paper-based format in areas of the world where computer-based testing is not available. The paper-based TOEFL consists of three sections—listening comprehension, structure and written expression, and reading comprehension. Testing time is approximately 3 hours. The Test of Written English (TWE) is also given. TWE is a 30-minute essay that measures the examinee's ability to compose in English. Examinees receive a TWE score separate from their TOEFL score. The *Information Bulletin* contains information on local fees and registration procedures.

A new TOEFL (the next generation TOEFL) that assesses the four basic language skills, listening, reading, writing, and speaking, will be administered for the first time in September 2005. The new test will be administered via the Internet at secure, official test centers. Testing time will be approximately 4 hours. Because the next generation TOEFL will include a speaking section, the TSE will no longer be needed.

Additional information and registration materials are available from TOEFL Services, Educational Testing Service, P.O. Box 6151, Princeton, New Jersey 08541-6151. Telephone: 1-609-771-7100. E-mail: toefl@ets.org. World Wide Web: http://www.toefl.org.

International students should apply especially early because of the number of steps required to complete the admissions process. Furthermore, many United States graduate schools have a limited number of spaces for international students, and many more students apply than the schools can accommodate.

International students may find financial assistance from institutions very limited. The U.S. government requires international applicants to submit a certification of support, which is a statement attesting to the applicant's financial resources. In addition, international students *must* have health insurance coverage.

Tips for Minority Students

Indicators of a university's values in terms of diversity are found both in its recruitment programs and its resources directed to student success. Important questions: Does the institution vigorously recruit minorities for its graduate programs? Is there funding available to help with the costs associated with visiting the school? Are minorities represented in the institution's brochures or Web site or on their faculty rolls? What campus-based resources or services (including assistance in locating housing or career counseling and placement) are available? Is funding available to members of underrepresented groups?

At the program level, it is particularly important for minority students to investigate the "climate" of a program under consideration. How many minority students are enrolled and how many have graduated? What opportunities are there to work with diverse faculty and mentors whose research interests match yours? How are conflicts resolved or concerns addressed? How interested are faculty in building strong and supportive relations with students? "Climate" concerns should be addressed by posing questions to various individuals, including faculty members, current students, and alumni.

Information is also available through various organizations, such as the Hispanic Association of Colleges and Universities (HACU), and publications, such as *Black Issues in Higher Education* and *Hispanic Outlook* magazine. There are also books devoted to this topic, such as *The Multicultural Student's Guide to Colleges* by Robert Mitchell.

Financial Support

The range of financial support at the graduate level is very broad. The following descriptions will give you a general idea of what you might expect and what will be expected of you as a financial support recipient.

Fellowships, Scholarships, and Grants

These are usually outright awards of a few hundred to many thousands of dollars with no service to the institution required in return. Fellowships and scholarships are usually awarded on the basis of merit and are highly competitive. Grants are made on the basis of financial need or special talent in a field of study. Many grants not only cover tuition, fees, and supplies but also include stipends for living expenses with allowances for dependents. However, the terms of each grant should be examined because some do not permit recipients to supplement their income with outside work. Fellowships, scholarships, and grants may vary in the number of years for which they are awarded.

In addition to the availability of these funds at the university or program level, many excellent fellowship programs are available at the national level and may be applied for before and during enrollment in a graduate program. A listing of many of these programs can be found at the Council of Graduate Schools' Web site: http://www.cgsnet.org/ResourcesForStudents/fellowships.htm.

Assistantships and Internships

Many graduate students receive financial support through assistantships, particularly involving teaching or research duties. It is important to recognize that such appointments should not be simply employment relationships but rather should constitute an integral and important part of a student's graduate education. As such, the appointments should be accompanied by strong faculty mentoring and increasingly responsible apprenticeship experiences (these are often lacking for teaching assistantships). The specific nature of these appointments in a given program should be considered in selecting that graduate program.

TEACHING ASSISTANTSHIPS

These usually provide a salary and full or partial tuition remission and may also provide health benefits. Unlike fellowships, scholarships, and grants, which require no service to the institution, teaching assistantships require recipients to provide the institution with a specific amount of undergraduate teaching, ideally related to the student's field of study. Some teaching assistants are limited to grading papers, compiling bibliographies, taking notes, or monitoring laboratories. At some graduate schools, teaching assistants must carry lighter course loads than regular full-time students.

RESEARCH ASSISTANTSHIPS

These are very similar to teaching assistantships in the manner in which financial assistance is provided. The difference is that recipients are given basic research assignments in their disciplines rather than teaching responsibilities. The work required is normally related to the student's field of study; in most instances, the assistantship supports the student's thesis or dissertation research.

ADMINISTRATIVE INTERNSHIPS

These are similar to assistantships in application of financial assistance funds, but the student is given an assignment on a part-time basis, usually as a special assistant with one of the university's administrative offices. The assignment may not necessarily be directly related to the recipient's discipline.

RESIDENCE HALL AND COUNSELING ASSISTANTSHIPS

These assistantships are frequently assigned to graduate students in psychology, counseling, and social work. Duties can vary from being available in a dean's office for a specific number of hours for consultation with undergraduates to living in campus residences and being responsible for both counseling and administrative tasks or advising student activity groups. Residence hall assistantships sometimes include room and board in addition to tuition and stipends.

Health Insurance

The availability and affordability of health insurance is an important issue and one that should be considered in an applicant's choice of institution and program. While often included with assistantships and fellowships, this is not always the case and, even if provided, the benefits may be limited. It is important to note that the U.S. government requires international students to have health insurance.

The GI Bill

This provides financial assistance for students who are veterans of the United States armed forces. If you are a veteran, contact your local Veterans Administration office to determine your eligibility and to get full details about benefits. There are a number of programs that offer educational benefits to current military enlistees. Some states have tuition assistance programs for members of the National Guard. Contact the VA office at the college for more information.

Federal Work-Study Program (FWS)

Employment is another way some students finance their graduate studies. The federally funded Federal Work-Study Program provides eligible students with employment opportunities, usually in public and private nonprofit organizations. Federal funds pay up to 75 percent of the wages, with the remainder paid by the employing agency. FWS is available to graduate students who demonstrate financial need. Not all schools have these funds, and some only award them to undergraduates. Each school sets its application deadline and work-study earnings limits. Wages vary and are related to the type of work done.

Loans

Many graduate students borrow to finance their graduate programs when other sources of assistance (which do not have to be repaid) prove insufficient. You should always read and understand the terms of any loan program before submitting your application.

FEDERAL LOANS

Federal Stafford Loans. The Federal Stafford Loan Program offers government-sponsored, low-interest loans to students through a private lender such as a bank, credit union, or savings and loan association.

There are two components of the Federal Stafford Loan program. Under the *subsidized* component of the program, the federal government pays the interest on the loan while you are enrolled in graduate school on at least a half-time basis. Under the *unsubsidized* component of the program, you pay the interest on the loan from the day proceeds are issued. Eligibility for the federal subsidy is based on demonstrated financial need as determined by the financial aid office from the information you provide on the Free Application for Federal Student Aid (FAFSA). A cosigner is not required, since the loan is not based on creditworthiness.

Although *unsubsidized* Federal Stafford Loans may not be as desirable as *subsidized* Federal Stafford Loans from the student's perspective, they are a useful source of support for those who may not qualify for the subsidized loans or who need additional financial assistance.

Graduate students may borrow up to $18,500 per year through the Stafford Loan Program, up to a cumulative maximum of $138,500, including undergraduate borrowing. This may include up to $8500 in Subsidized Stafford Loans annually, depending on eligibility, up to a cumulative maximum of $65,500, including undergraduate borrowing. The amount of the loan borrowed through the *unsubsidized* Stafford Program equals the total amount of the loan (as much $18,500) minus your eligibility for a Subsidized Stafford Loan (as much as $8500). You may borrow up to the cost of the school in which you are enrolled or will attend, minus estimated financial assistance from other federal, state, and private sources, up to a maximum of $18,500.

The interest rate for the Federal Stafford Loans varies annually and is set every July. The rate during in-school, grace, and deferment periods is based on the 91-Day U.S. Treasury Bill rate plus 1.7 percent, capped at 8.25 percent. The rate during repayment is based on the 91-Day U.S. Treasury Bill rate plus 2.3 percent, capped at 8.25 percent. The 2004–05 rate during repayment is 3.37 percent.

Two fees may be deducted from the loan proceeds upon disbursement: a guarantee fee of up to 1 percent, which is deposited in an insurance pool to ensure repayment to the lender if the borrower defaults, and a federally mandated 3 percent origination fee, which is used to offset the administrative cost of the Federal Stafford Loan Program.

Under the *subsidized* Federal Stafford Loan Program, repayment begins six months after your last enrollment on at least a half-time basis. Under the *unsubsidized* program, repayment of interest begins within thirty days from disbursement of the loan proceeds, and repayment of the principal begins six months after your last enrollment on at least a half-time basis. Some borrowers may choose to defer interest payments while they are in school. The accrued interest is added to the loan balance when the borrower begins repayment. There are several repayment options.

Federal Direct Loans. Some schools participate in the Department of Education's William D. Ford Direct Lending Program instead of the Federal Stafford Loan Program. The two programs are essentially the same except that with the Direct Loans, schools themselves provide the loans with funds from the federal government. Terms and interest rates are virtually the same except that there are a few additional repayment options with Federal Direct Loans.

Federal Perkins Loans. The Federal Perkins Loan is available to students demonstrating financial need and is administered directly by the school. Not all schools have these funds, and some may award them to undergraduates only. Eligibility is determined from the information you provide on the FAFSA. The school will notify you of your eligibility.

Eligible graduate students may borrow up to $6000 per year, up to a maximum of $40,000, including undergraduate borrowing (even if your previous Perkins Loans have been repaid). The interest rate for Federal Perkins Loans is 5 percent, and no interest accrues while you remain in school at least half-time. There are no guarantee, loan, or disbursement fees. Repayment begins nine months after your last enrollment on at least a half-time basis and may extend over a maximum of ten years with no prepayment penalty.

Deferring Your Federal Loan Repayments. If you borrowed under the Federal Stafford Loan Program or the Federal Perkins Loan Program for previous undergraduate or graduate study, your repayments may be deferred when you return to graduate school, depending on when you borrowed and under which program.

There are other deferment options available if you are temporarily unable to repay your loan. Information about these deferments is provided at your entrance and exit interviews. If you believe you are eligible for a deferment of your loan repayments, you must contact your lender to complete a deferment form. The deferment must be filed prior to the time your repayment is due, and it must be refiled when it expires if you remain eligible for deferment at that time.

SUPPLEMENTAL (PRIVATE) LOANS

Many lending institutions offer supplemental loan programs and other financing plans, such as the ones described here, to students seeking additional assistance in meeting their educational expenses. Some loan programs target all types of graduate students; others are designed specifically for business, law, or medical students. In addition, you can use private loans not specifically designed for education to help finance your graduate degree.

If you are considering borrowing through a supplemental or private loan program, you should carefully consider the terms and be sure to "read the fine print." Check with the program sponsor for the most current terms that will be applicable to the amounts you intend to borrow for graduate study. Most supplemental loan programs for graduate study offer unsubsidized, credit-based loans. In general, a credit-ready borrower is one who has a satisfactory credit history or no credit history at all. A creditworthy borrower generally must pass a credit test to be eligible to borrow or act as a cosigner for the loan funds.

Many supplemental loan programs have a minimum annual loan limit and a maximum annual loan limit. Some offer amounts equal to the cost of attendance minus any other aid you will receive for graduate study. If you are planning to borrow for several years of graduate study, consider whether there is a cumulative or aggregate limit on the amount you may borrow. Often this cumulative or aggregate limit will include any amounts you borrowed and have not repaid for undergraduate or previous graduate study.

The combination of the annual interest rate, loan fees, and the repayment terms you choose will determine how much you will repay over time. Compare these features in combination before you decide which loan program to use. Some loans offer interest rates that are adjusted monthly, some quarterly, some annually. Some offer interest rates that are lower during the in-school, grace, and deferment periods, and then increase when you begin repayment. Most programs include a loan "origination" fee, which is usually deducted from the principal amount you receive when the loan is disbursed, and must be repaid along with the interest and other principal when you graduate, withdraw from school, or drop below half-time study. Sometimes the loan fees are reduced if you borrow with a qualified cosigner. Some programs allow you to defer interest and/or principal payments while you are enrolled in graduate school. Many programs allow you to capitalize your interest payments; the interest due on your loan is added to the outstanding balance of your loan, so you don't have to repay immediately, but this increases the amount you owe. Other programs allow you to pay the interest as you go, which reduces the amount you later have to repay.

Some examples of supplemental programs follow.

CitiAssist Loans. Offered by Citibank, these no-fee loans help graduate students fill the gap between the financial aid they receive and the money they need for school. Visit www.studentloan.com for more loan information from Citibank.

EXCEL Loan. This program, sponsored by Nellie Mae, is designed for students who are not ready to borrow on their own and wish to borrow with a creditworthy cosigner. Visit www.nelliemae.com for more information.

Key Alternative Loan. This loan can bridge the gap between education costs and traditional funding. Visit www.keybank.com for more information.

Graduate Access Loan. Sponsored by the Access Group, this is for graduate students enrolled at least half-time. The Web site is www.accessgroup.com.

Signature Student Loan. A loan program for students who are enrolled at least half-time, this is sponsored by Sallie Mae. Visit www.salliemae.com for more information.

Applying for Need-Based Financial Aid

Schools that award federal and institutional financial assistance based on need will require you to complete the FAFSA and, in some cases, an institutional financial aid application.

If you are applying for federal student assistance, you must complete the FAFSA. A service of the U.S. Department of Education, it is free to all applicants. You must send the FAFSA to the address listed in the FAFSA instructions (a self-addressed envelope is provided) or you can apply online at http://www.fafsa.ed.gov.

After your FAFSA information has been processed, you will receive a Student Aid Report (SAR). If you provided an e-mail address on the FAFSA, this will be sent to you electronically; otherwise, it will be mailed to your home address.

Follow the instructions on the SAR if you need to correct information reported on your original application. If your situation changes after you file your FAFSA, contact your financial aid officer to discuss amending your information. You can also appeal your financial aid award if you have extenuating circumstances.

If you would like more information on federal student financial aid, visit the FAFSA Web site or download *The Student Guide 2005–2006* at http://studentaid.ed.gov/students/publications/student_guide/index.html.

The U.S. Department of Education also has a toll-free number for questions concerning federal student aid programs. The number is 1-800-4-FED AID (1-800-433-3243). If you are hearing impaired, call toll-free, 1-800-730-8913.

Summary

Remember that these are generalized statements about financial assistance at the graduate level. Because each institution allots its aid differently, you should communicate directly with the school and the specific department of interest to you. It is not unusual, for example, to find that an endowment vested within a specific department supports one or more fellowships. You may fit its requirements and specifications precisely.

Accreditation and Accrediting Agencies

Colleges and universities in the United States, and their individual academic and professional programs, are accredited by nongovernmental agencies concerned with monitoring the quality of education in this country. Agencies with both regional and national jurisdictions grant accreditation to institutions as a whole, while specialized bodies acting on a nationwide basis—often national professional associations—grant accreditation to departments and programs in specific fields.

Institutional and specialized accrediting agencies share the same basic concerns: the purpose an academic unit—whether university or program—has set for itself and how well it fulfills that purpose, the adequacy of its financial and other resources, the quality of its academic offerings, and the level of services it provides. Agencies that grant institutional accreditation take a broader view, of course, and examine university-wide or college-wide services with which a specialized agency may not concern itself.

Both types of agencies follow the same general procedures when considering an application for accreditation. The academic unit prepares a self-evaluation, focusing on the concerns mentioned above and usually including an assessment of both its strengths and weaknesses; a team of representatives of the accrediting body reviews this evaluation, visits the campus, and makes its own report; and finally, the accrediting body makes a decision on the application. Often, even when accreditation is granted, the agency makes a recommendation regarding how the institution or program can improve. All institutions and programs are also reviewed every few years to determine whether they continue to meet established standards; if they do not, they may lose their accreditation.

Accrediting agencies themselves are reviewed and evaluated periodically by the U.S. Department of Education and the Council for Higher Education Accreditation (CHEA). Recognized agencies adhere to certain standards and practices, and their authority in matters of accreditation is widely accepted in the educational community.

This does not mean, however, that accreditation is a simple matter, either for schools wishing to become accredited or for students deciding where to apply. Indeed, in certain fields the very meaning and methods of accreditation are the subject of a good deal of debate. For their part, those applying to graduate school should be aware of the safeguards provided by regional accreditation, especially in terms of degree acceptance and institutional longevity. Beyond this, applicants should understand the role that specialized accreditation plays in their field, as this varies considerably from one discipline to another. In certain professional fields, it is necessary to have graduated from a program that is accredited in order to be eligible for a license to practice, and in some fields the federal government also makes this a hiring requirement. In other disciplines, however, accreditation is not as essential, and there can be excellent programs that are not accredited. In fact, some programs choose not to seek accreditation, although most do.

Institutions and programs that present themselves for accreditation are sometimes granted the status of candidate for accreditation, or what is known as "preaccreditation." This may happen, for example, when an academic unit is too new to have met all the requirements for accreditation. Such status signifies initial recognition and indicates that the school or program in question is working to fulfill all requirements; it does not, however, guarantee that accreditation will be granted.

Institutional Accrediting Agencies—Regional

MIDDLE STATES ASSOCIATION OF COLLEGES AND SCHOOLS
Accredits institutions in Delaware, District of Columbia, Maryland, New Jersey, New York, Pennsylvania, Puerto Rico, and the Virgin Islands.
Jean Avnet Morse, Executive Director
Commission on Higher Education
3624 Market Street
Philadelphia, Pennsylvania 19104
Telephone: 215-662-5606
Fax: 215-662-5501
E-mail: jmorse@msache.org
World Wide Web: www.msache.org

NEW ENGLAND ASSOCIATION OF SCHOOLS AND COLLEGES
Accredits institutions in Connecticut, Maine, Massachusetts, New Hampshire, Rhode Island, and Vermont.
Charles M. Cook, Director
Commission on Institutions of Higher Education
209 Burlington Road
Bedford, Massachusetts 01730
Telephone: 781-271-0022
Fax: 781-271-0950
E-mail: ccook@neasc.org
World Wide Web: www.neasc.org

NORTH CENTRAL ASSOCIATION OF COLLEGES AND SCHOOLS
Accredits institutions in Arizona, Arkansas, Colorado, Illinois, Indiana, Iowa, Kansas, Michigan, Minnesota, Missouri, Nebraska, New Mexico, North Dakota, Ohio, Oklahoma, South Dakota, West Virginia, Wisconsin, and Wyoming.
Steven D. Crow, Executive Director
The Higher Learning Commission
30 North LaSalle Street, Suite 2400
Chicago, Illinois 60602
Telephone: 312-263-0456
Fax: 312-263-7462
E-mail: scrow@hlcommission.org
World Wide Web: www.ncacihe.org

NORTHWEST COMMISSION ON COLLEGES AND UNIVERSITIES
Accredits institutions in Alaska, Idaho, Montana, Nevada, Oregon, Utah, and Washington.
Sandra E. Elman, Executive Director
8060 165th Avenue, NE, Suite 100
Redmond, Washington 98052
Telephone: 425-558-4224
Fax: 425-376-0596
E-mail: selman@nwccu.org
World Wide Web: www.nwccu.org

SOUTHERN ASSOCIATION OF COLLEGES AND SCHOOLS
Accredits institutions in Alabama, Florida, Georgia, Kentucky, Louisiana, Mississippi, North Carolina, South Carolina, Tennessee, Texas, and Virginia.
James T. Rogers, Executive Director
Commission on Colleges
1866 Southern Lane
Decatur, Georgia 30033
Telephone: 404-679-4500
Fax: 404-679-4558
E-mail: jrogers@sacscoc.org
World Wide Web: www.sacscoc.org

WESTERN ASSOCIATION OF SCHOOLS AND COLLEGES
Accredits institutions in California, Guam, and Hawaii.
Ralph A. Wolff, Executive Director
The Senior College Commission
985 Atlantic Avenue, Suite 100
Alameda, California 94501
Telephone: 510-748-9001

Fax: 510-748-9797
E-mail: rwolff@wascsenior.org
World Wide Web: www.wascweb.org/senior

Institutional Accrediting Agencies—Other

ACCREDITING COUNCIL FOR INDEPENDENT COLLEGES AND SCHOOLS
Steven A. Eggland, Executive Director
750 First Street, NE, Suite 980
Washington, DC 20002
Telephone: 202-336-6780
Fax: 202-842-2593
E-mail: steve@acics.org
World Wide Web: www.acics.org

DISTANCE EDUCATION AND TRAINING COUNCIL
Accrediting Commission
Michael P. Lambert, Executive Director
1601 18th Street, NW
Washington, DC 20009
Telephone: 202-234-5100
Fax: 202-332-1386
E-mail: mike@detc.org
World Wide Web: www.detc.org

Specialized Accrediting Agencies

[Only Book 1 of *Peterson's Graduate and Professional Programs* includes the complete list of specialized accrediting groups recognized by the U.S. Department of Education and the Council on Higher Education Accreditation (CHEA). The lists in Books 2, 4, 5, and 6 are abridged, and there are no such recognized specialized accrediting bodies for the programs in Book 3.]

FORESTRY
Michael T. Goergen Jr.
Executive Vice President and CEO
Society of American Foresters
5400 Grosvenor Lane
Bethesda, Maryland 20814
Telephone: 301-897-8720
Fax: 301-897-3690
E-mail: goergenm@safnet.org
World Wide Web: www.safnet.org

How to Use These Guides

As you identify the particular programs and institutions that interest you, you can use both Book 1 and the specialized volumes (Books 2–6) to obtain detailed information—Book 1 for information on the institutions overall and Books 2 through 6 for details about the individual graduate units and their degree programs.

Books 2 through 6 are divided into sections that contain one or more directories devoted to programs in a particular field. If you do not find a directory devoted to your field of interest in a specific book, consult *Directories and Subject Areas in Books 2–6* (located at the end of each volume). After you have identified the correct book, consult the *Directories and Subject Areas in This Book* index, which shows (as does the more general directory) what directories cover subjects not specifically named in a directory or section title. This index in Book 2, for example, will tell you that if you are interested in sculpture, you should see the directory entitled Art/Fine Arts. The Art/Fine Arts entry will direct you to the proper page.

Books 2 through 6 have a number of general directories. These directories have entries for the largest unit at an institution granting graduate degrees in that field. For example, the general Engineering and Applied Sciences directory in Book 5 consists of **Profiles** for colleges, schools, and departments of engineering and applied sciences.

General directories are followed by other directories, or sections, in Books 2, 3, 5, and 6 that give more detailed information about programs in particular areas of the general field that has been covered. The general Engineering and Applied Sciences directory, in the previous example, is followed by nineteen sections with directories in specific areas of engineering, such as Chemical Engineering, Industrial/Management Engineering, and Mechanical Engineering.

Because of the broad nature of many fields, any system of organization is bound to involve a certain amount of overlap. Environmental studies, for example, is a field whose various aspects are studied in several types of departments and schools. Readers interested in such studies will find information on relevant programs in Book 3 under Ecology and Environmental Biology; in Book 4 under Environmental Management and Policy and Natural Resources; in Book 5 under Energy Management and Policy and Environmental Engineering; and in Book 6 under Environmental and Occupational Health. To help you find all of the programs of interest to you, the introduction to each section of Books 2 through 6 includes, if applicable, a paragraph suggesting other sections and directories with information on related areas of study.

Directory of Institutions with Programs in the Physical Sciences, Mathematics, Agricultural Sciences, the Environment & Natural Resources

This directory lists institutions in alphabetical order and includes beneath each name the academic fields in the physical sciences, mathematics, agricultural sciences, the environment, and natural resources in which each institution offers graduate programs. The degree level in each field is also indicated, provided that the institution has supplied that information in response to *Thomson Peterson's Annual Survey of Graduate and Professional Institutions*. An *M* indicates that a master's degree program is offered; a *D* indicates that a doctoral degree program is offered; a *P* indicates that the first professional degree is offered; an *O* signifies that other advanced degrees (e.g., certificates or specialist degrees) are offered; and an * (asterisk) indicates that an **In-Depth Description** and/or **Announcement** is located in this volume. See the index, *In-Depth Descriptions and Announcements*, for the specific page number.

Profiles of Academic and Professional Programs in Books 2–6

Each section of **Profiles** has a table of contents that lists the Program Directories, **Announcements**, and **In-Depth Descriptions**. Program Directories consist of the **Profiles** of programs in the relevant fields, with **Announcements** following if programs have chosen to include them. **Cross-Discipline Announcements**, if any programs have chosen to submit such entries, and **In-Depth Descriptions**, which are more individualized statements, again if programs have chosen to submit them, are also listed.

The **Profiles** found in the 457 directories in Books 2 through 6 provide basic data about the graduate units in capsule form for quick reference. To make these directories as useful as possible, **Profiles** are generally listed for an institution's smallest academic unit within a subject area. In other words, if an institution has a College of Liberal Arts that administers many related programs, the **Profile** for the individual program (e.g., Program in History), not the entire College, appears in the directory.

There are some programs that do not fit into any current directory and are not given individual **Profiles**. The directory structure is reviewed annually in order to keep this number to a minimum and to accommodate major trends in graduate education.

The following outline describes the **Profile** information found in the guides and explains how best to use that information. Any item that does not apply to or was not provided by a graduate unit is omitted from its listing. The format of the **Profiles** is constant, making it easy to compare one institution with another and one program with another. A description of the information in the **Profiles** in Books 2 through 6 follows; the Book 1 **Profile** description is found immediately preceding the **Profiles** in Book 1.

Identifying Information. The institution's name, in boldface type, is followed by a complete listing of the administrative structure for that field of study. (For example, University of Akron, Buchtel College of Arts and Sciences, Department of Mathematical Sciences and Statistics, Program in Mathematics.) The last unit listed is the one to which all information in the **Profile** pertains. The institution's city, state, and zip code follow.

Offerings. Each field of study offered by the unit is listed with all postbaccalaureate degrees awarded. Degrees that are not preceded by a specific concentration are awarded in the general field listed in the unit name. Frequently, fields of study are broken down into subspecializations, and those appear following the degrees awarded; for example, "Offerings in secondary education (M.Ed.), including English education, mathematics education, science education." Students enrolled in the M.Ed. program would be able to specialize in any of the three fields mentioned.

Professional Accreditation. Some **Profiles** indicate whether a program is professionally accredited. Because it is possible for a program to receive or lose professional accreditation at any time, students entering fields in which accreditation is important to a career should verify the status of programs by contacting either the chairperson or the appropriate accrediting association.

Jointly Offered Degrees. Explanatory statements concerning programs that are offered in cooperation with other institutions are included in the list of degrees offered. This occurs most commonly on a regional basis (for example, two state universities offering a cooperative Ph.D. in special education) or where the specialized nature of the institutions encourages joint efforts (a J.D./M.B.A. offered by a law school at an institution with no formal business programs and an institution with a business school but lacking a law school). Only programs that are truly cooperative are listed; those involving only limited course work at another institution are not. Interested students should contact the heads of such units for further information.

Part-Time and Evening/Weekend Programs. When information regarding the availability of part-time or evening/weekend study appears in the **Profile**, it means that students are able to earn a degree exclusively through such study.

Postbaccalaureate Distance Learning Degrees. A postbaccalaureate distance learning degree program signifies that course requirements can be fulfilled with minimal or no on-campus study.

Faculty. Figures on the number of faculty members actively involved with graduate students through teaching or research are separated into full- and part-time as well as men and women whenever the information has been supplied.

Students. Figures for the number of students enrolled in graduate and professional programs pertain to the semester of highest enrollment from the 2003–04 academic year. These figures are broken down into full- and part-time and men and women whenever the data have been supplied. Information on the number of matriculated students enrolled in the unit who are members of a minority group or are international students appears here. The average age of the matriculated students is followed by the number of applicants, the percentage accepted, and the number enrolled for fall 2003.

Degrees Awarded. The number of degrees awarded in the calendar year is listed, as is the percentage of students in those degree programs who entered university research/teaching, business/industry, or government service or continued full-time study. Many doctoral programs offer a terminal master's degree if students leave the program after completing only part of the requirements for a doctoral degree; that is indicated here. All degrees are classified into one of four types: master's, doctoral, first professional, and other advanced degrees. A unit may award one or several degrees at a given level; however, the data are only collected by type and may therefore represent several different degree programs.

Median Time to Degree. If provided, information on the median amount of time required to earn the degree for full-time and part-time students is listed here. Also provided is the percentage of students who began their doctoral program in 1995 and received their degree in eight years or less.

Degree Requirements. The information in this section is also broken down by type of degree, and all information for a degree level pertains to all degrees of that type unless otherwise specified. Degree requirements are collected in a simplified form to provide some very basic information on the nature of the program and on foreign language, thesis or dissertation, comprehensive exam, and registration requirements. Many units also provide a short list of additional requirements, such as fieldwork or an internship. No information is listed on the number of courses or credits required for completion or whether a minimum or maximum number of years or semesters is needed. For complete information on graduation requirements, contact the graduate school or program directly.

Entrance Requirements. Entrance requirements are broken down into the four degree levels of master's, doctoral, first professional, and other advanced degrees. Within each level, information may be provided in two basic categories, entrance exams and other requirements. The entrance exams are identified by the standard acronyms used by the testing agencies, unless they are not well known. Other entrance requirements are quite varied, but they often contain an undergraduate or graduate grade point average (GPA). Unless otherwise stated, the GPA is calculated on a 4.0 scale and is listed as a minimum required for admission. Additional exam requirements/recommendations for international students may be listed here. Application deadlines for domestic and international students, the application fee, and whether electronic applications are accepted may be listed here. Note that the deadline should be used for reference only; these dates are subject to change, and students interested in applying should contact the graduate unit directly about application procedures and deadlines.

Expenses. The typical cost of study for the 2003–04 academic year is given in two basic categories, tuition and fees. Cost of study may be quite complex at a graduate institution. There are often sliding scales for part-time study, a different cost for first-year students, and other variables that make it impossible to completely cover the cost of study for each graduate program. To provide the most usable information, figures are given for full-time study for a full year where available and for part-time study in terms of a per-unit rate (per credit, per semester hour, etc.). Occasionally, variances may be noted in tuition and fees for reasons such as the type of program, whether courses are taken during the day or evening, whether courses are at the master's or doctoral level, or other institution-specific reasons. Expenses are usually subject to change; for exact costs at any given time, contact your chosen schools and programs directly. Keep in mind that the tuition of Canadian institutions is usually given in Canadian dollars.

Financial Support. This section contains data on the number of awards administered by the institution and given to graduate students during the 2003–04 academic year. The first figure given represents the total number of students receiving financial support enrolled in that unit. If the unit has provided information on graduate appointments, these are broken down into three major categories: *fellowships* give money to graduate students to cover the cost of study and living expenses and are not based on a work obligation or research commitment, *research assistantships* provide stipends to graduate students for assistance in a formal research project with a faculty member, and *teaching assistantships* provide stipends to graduate students for teaching or for assisting faculty members in teaching undergraduate classes. Within each category, figures are given for the total number of awards, the average yearly amount per award, and whether full or partial tuition reimbursements are awarded. In addition to graduate appointments, the availability of several other financial aid sources is covered in this section. *Tuition waivers* are routinely part of a graduate appointment, but units sometimes waive part or all of a student's tuition even if a graduate appointment is not available. *Federal Work-Study* is made available to students who demonstrate need and meet the federal guidelines; this form of aid normally includes 10 or more hours of work per week in an office of the institution. *Institutionally sponsored loans* are low-interest loans available to graduate students to cover both educational and living expenses. *Career-related internships* or *fieldwork* offer money to students who are participating in a formal off-campus research project or practicum. Grants, scholarships, traineeships, unspecified assistantships, and other awards may also be noted. The availability of financial support to part-time students is also indicated here.

Some programs list the financial aid application deadline and the forms that need to be completed for students to be eligible for financial awards. There are two forms: FAFSA, the Free Application for Federal Student Aid, which is required for federal aid, and the PROFILE®.

Faculty Research. Each unit has the opportunity to list several keyword phrases describing the current research involving faculty members and graduate students. Space limitations prevent the unit from listing complete information on all research programs. The total expenditure for funded research from the previous academic year may also be included.

Unit Head and Application Contact. The head of the graduate program for each unit is listed with academic title and telephone and fax numbers and e-mail address if available. In addition to the unit head, many graduate programs list a separate contact for application and admission information, which follows the listing for the unit head. If no unit head or application contact is given, you should contact the overall institution for information on graduate admissions.

Announcements and In-Depth Descriptions

The **Announcements** and **In-Depth Descriptions** are supplementary insertions submitted by deans, chairs, and other administrators who wish to offer an additional, more individualized statement to readers. A number of graduate school and program administrators have attached **Announcements** to the end of their **Profile** listings. In them you will find information that an institution or program wants to emphasize. The **In-Depth Descriptions** are by their very nature more expansive and flexible than the **Profiles**, and the administrators who have written them may emphasize different aspects of their programs. All of these **In-Depth Descriptions** are organized in the same way (with the exception of a few that describe research and training opportunities instead of degree programs), and in each one you will find information on the same basic topics, such as programs of study, research facilities, tuition and fees, financial aid, and application procedures. If an institution or program has submitted an **In-Depth Description**, a boldface cross-reference appears below its **Profile**. As with the **Announcements**, all of the **In-Depth Descriptions** in the guides have been submitted by choice; the absence of an **Announcement** or **In-Depth Description** does not reflect any type of editorial judgment on the part of Thomson Peterson's and their presence in the guides should not be taken as an indication of status, quality, or approval. Statements regarding a university's objectives and accomplishments are a reflection of its own beliefs and are not the opinions of the Thomson Peterson's editors.

Cross-Discipline Announcements

In addition to the regular directories that present **Profiles** of programs in each field of study, many sections in Books 2 through 6 contain special notices under the heading **Cross-Discipline Announcements**. Appearing at the end of many **Profile** sections, these **Cross-Discipline Announcements** inform you about programs that you may find of interest described in a different section. A biochemistry department, for example, may place a notice under **Cross-Discipline Announcements** in the Chemistry section (Book 4) to alert chemistry students to their current description in the Biochemistry section of Book 3. **Cross-Discipline Announcements**, also written by administrators to highlight their programs, will be helpful to you not only in finding out about programs in fields related to your own but also in locating departments that are actively recruiting students with a specific undergraduate major.

Appendixes

This section contains two appendixes. The first, *Institutional Changes Since the 2004 Edition*, lists institutions that have closed, moved, merged, or changed their name or status since the last edition of the guides. The second, *Abbreviations Used in the Guides*, gives abbreviations of degree names, along with what those abbreviations stand for. These appendixes are identical in all six volumes of *Peterson's Graduate and Professional Programs*.

Indexes

There are three indexes presented here. The first index, *In-Depth Descriptions and Announcements*, gives page references for all programs that have chosen to place **In-Depth Descriptions** and **Announcements** in this volume. It is arranged alphabetically by institution; within institutions, the arrangement is alphabetical by subject area. It is not an index to all programs in the book's directories of **Profiles**; readers must refer to the directories themselves for **Profile** information on programs that have not submitted the additional, more individualized statements. The second index, *Directories and Subject Areas in Books 2–6*, gives book references for the directories in Books 2-6, for example, "Industrial Design—Book 2," and also includes cross-references for subject area names not used in the directory structure, for example, "Computing Technology (see Computer Science)." The third index, *Directories and Subject Areas in This Book*, gives page references for the directories in this volume and cross-references for subject area names not used in this volume's directory structure.

Data Collection Procedures

The information published in the directories and **Profiles** of all the books is collected through *Thomson Peterson's Annual Survey of Graduate and Professional Institutions*. The survey is sent each spring to more than 2,000 institutions offering postbaccalaureate degree programs, including accredited institutions in the United States, U.S. territories, and Canada and those institutions outside the United States that are accredited by U.S. accrediting bodies. Deans and other administrators complete these surveys, providing information on programs in the 457 academic and professional fields covered in the guides as well as overall institutional information. Peterson's staff then goes over each returned survey carefully and verifies or revises responses after further research and discussion with administrators at the institutions. While every effort has been made to ensure the accuracy and completeness of the data, information is sometimes unavailable or changes occur after publication deadlines. All usable information received in time for publication has been included. The omission of any particular item from a directory or **Profile** signifies either that the item is not applicable to the institution or program or that information was not available. **Profiles** of programs scheduled to begin during the 2004–05 academic year cannot, obviously, include statistics on enrollment or, in many cases, the number of faculty members. If no usable data were submitted by an institution, its name, address, and program name appear in order to indicate the availability of graduate work.

Criteria for Inclusion in This Guide

To be included in this guide, an institution must have full accreditation or be a candidate for accreditation (preaccreditation) status by an institutional or specialized accrediting body recognized by the U.S. Department of Education or the Council for Higher Education Accreditation (CHEA). Institutional accrediting bodies, which review each institution as a whole, include the six regional associations of schools and colleges (Middle States, New England, North Central, Northwest, Southern, and Western), each of which is responsible for a specified portion of the United States and its territories. Other institutional accrediting bodies are national in scope and accredit specific kinds of institutions (e.g., Bible colleges, independent colleges, and rabbinical and Talmudic schools). Program registration by the New York State Board of Regents is considered to be the equivalent of institutional accreditation, since the board requires that all programs offered by an institution meet its standards before recognition is granted. A Canadian institution must be chartered and authorized to grant degrees by the provincial government, affiliated with a chartered institution, or accredited by a recognized U.S. accrediting body. This guide also includes institutions outside the United States that are accredited by these U.S. accrediting bodies. There are recognized specialized or professional accrediting bodies in more than fifty different fields, each of which is authorized to accredit institutions or specific programs in its particular field. For specialized institutions that offer programs in one field only, we designate this to be the equivalent of institutional accreditation. A full explanation of the accrediting process and complete information on recognized institutional (regional and national) and specialized accrediting bodies can be found online at www.chea.org or at www.ed.gov/offices/OPE/accreditation/index.html.

DIRECTORY OF INSTITUTIONS WITH PROGRAMS IN THE PHYSICAL SCIENCES, MATHEMATICS, AGRICULTURAL SCIENCES, THE ENVIRONMENT & NATURAL RESOURCES

ACADIA UNIVERSITY
Applied Mathematics M
Chemistry M
Geology M
Statistics M

ADELPHI UNIVERSITY
Environmental Management and Policy M

AIR FORCE INSTITUTE OF TECHNOLOGY
Applied Mathematics M,D
Applied Physics M,D
Astrophysics M,D
Environmental Management and Policy M
Optical Sciences M,D
Planetary and Space Sciences M,D

ALABAMA AGRICULTURAL AND MECHANICAL UNIVERSITY
Agricultural Sciences—General M,D
Agronomy and Soil Sciences M,D
Animal Sciences M,D
Applied Physics M,D
Environmental Sciences M,D
Food Science and Technology M,D
Optical Sciences M,D
Physics M,D
Plant Sciences M,D

ALABAMA STATE UNIVERSITY
Mathematics M,O

ALASKA PACIFIC UNIVERSITY
Environmental Sciences M

ALBANY STATE UNIVERSITY
Water Resources M

ALCORN STATE UNIVERSITY
Agricultural Sciences—General M
Agronomy and Soil Sciences M
Animal Sciences M

AMERICAN UNIVERSITY
Chemistry M
Environmental Management and Policy M,D,O
Environmental Sciences M
Mathematics M
Physics O
Statistics M,O

ANDREWS UNIVERSITY
Mathematics M

ANGELO STATE UNIVERSITY
Agricultural Sciences—General M
Animal Sciences M

ANTIOCH NEW ENGLAND GRADUATE SCHOOL
Environmental Management and Policy M,D*
Environmental Sciences M,D*

ANTIOCH UNIVERSITY SEATTLE
Environmental Management and Policy M

APPALACHIAN STATE UNIVERSITY
Applied Physics M
Mathematics M

ARIZONA STATE UNIVERSITY
Applied Mathematics M,D
Astronomy M,D
Biostatistics M,D
Chemistry M,D
Computational Sciences M,D
Mathematics M,D
Physics M,D
Statistics M,D

ARIZONA STATE UNIVERSITY EAST
Environmental Management and Policy M

ARKANSAS STATE UNIVERSITY
Agricultural Sciences—General M,O
Chemistry M,O
Environmental Sciences D
Mathematics M

ARKANSAS TECH UNIVERSITY
Fish, Game, and Wildlife Management M

AUBURN UNIVERSITY
Agricultural Sciences—General M,D
Agronomy and Soil Sciences M,D
Animal Sciences M,D
Applied Mathematics M,D
Aquaculture M,D
Chemistry M,D
Fish, Game, and Wildlife Management M,D
Food Science and Technology M,D
Forestry M,D
Geology M*
Horticulture M,D
Hydrology M,D
Mathematics M,D
Physics M,D*
Statistics M,D

BALL STATE UNIVERSITY
Chemistry M
Geology M
Geosciences M
Mathematics M
Natural Resources M
Physics M
Statistics M

BARD COLLEGE
Environmental Management and Policy M,O*

BAYLOR UNIVERSITY
Chemistry M,D*
Environmental Management and Policy M
Geology M,D
Geosciences M,D
Limnology M,D
Mathematics M,D
Physics M,D
Statistics M,D

BEMIDJI STATE UNIVERSITY
Environmental Management and Policy M

BERNARD M. BARUCH COLLEGE OF THE CITY UNIVERSITY OF NEW YORK
Mathematical and Computational Finance M*
Statistics M

BOISE STATE UNIVERSITY
Environmental Management and Policy M
Geology M
Geophysics M,D
Geosciences M

BOSTON COLLEGE
Chemistry M,D
Geology M
Geophysics M
Inorganic Chemistry M,D
Mathematics M
Organic Chemistry M,D
Physical Chemistry M,D
Physics M,D

BOSTON UNIVERSITY
Astronomy M,D
Biostatistics M,D
Chemistry M,D
Environmental Management and Policy M,O
Geosciences M,D
Mathematical and Computational Finance M,D
Mathematics M,D
Photonics M,D
Physics M,D*

BOWLING GREEN STATE UNIVERSITY
Astronomy M
Chemistry M,D*
Geology M
Mathematics M,D,O*
Physics M
Statistics M,D,O

BRADLEY UNIVERSITY
Chemistry M

BRANDEIS UNIVERSITY
Chemistry M,D
Inorganic Chemistry M,D
Mathematics M,D*
Organic Chemistry M,D
Physical Chemistry M,D
Physics M,D

BRIGHAM YOUNG UNIVERSITY
Agricultural Sciences—General M,D
Agronomy and Soil Sciences M
Analytical Chemistry M,D
Animal Sciences M
Astronomy M,D
Chemistry M,D*
Fish, Game, and Wildlife Management M,D
Food Science and Technology M
Geology M
Horticulture M
Inorganic Chemistry M,D
Mathematics M,D
Organic Chemistry M,D
Physical Chemistry M,D
Physics M,D
Plant Sciences M
Statistics M

BROCK UNIVERSITY
Chemistry M
Geosciences M
Physics M

BROOKLYN COLLEGE OF THE CITY UNIVERSITY OF NEW YORK
Applied Physics M,D
Chemistry M,D
Geology M,D
Mathematics M,D
Physics M,D

BROWN UNIVERSITY
Applied Mathematics M,D*
Biostatistics M,D
Chemistry M,D
Environmental Management and Policy M
Geosciences M,D
Mathematics M,D
Physics M,D

BRYN MAWR COLLEGE
Chemistry M,D
Mathematics M,D
Physics M,D

BUCKNELL UNIVERSITY
Chemistry M
Mathematics M

BUFFALO STATE COLLEGE, STATE UNIVERSITY OF NEW YORK
Chemistry M

CALIFORNIA INSTITUTE OF TECHNOLOGY
Applied Mathematics M,D
Applied Physics M,D
Astronomy D
Chemistry M,D
Computational Sciences M,D
Geochemistry M,D
Geology M,D
Geophysics M,D
Mathematics D
Physics D
Planetary and Space Sciences M,D

CALIFORNIA POLYTECHNIC STATE UNIVERSITY, SAN LUIS OBISPO
Agricultural Sciences—General M
Forestry M
Mathematics M

CALIFORNIA STATE POLYTECHNIC UNIVERSITY, POMONA
Agricultural Sciences—General M
Animal Sciences M
Applied Mathematics M
Chemistry M
Food Science and Technology M
Mathematics M

CALIFORNIA STATE UNIVERSITY, BAKERSFIELD
Geology M
Hydrology M

CALIFORNIA STATE UNIVERSITY, CHICO
Environmental Sciences M
Geology M
Geosciences M
Hydrology M

CALIFORNIA STATE UNIVERSITY, FRESNO
Agricultural Sciences—General M
Animal Sciences M
Chemistry M
Food Science and Technology M
Geology M
Marine Sciences M
Mathematics M
Physics M
Plant Sciences M

CALIFORNIA STATE UNIVERSITY, FULLERTON
Analytical Chemistry M
Applied Mathematics M
Chemistry M
Environmental Management and Policy M
Environmental Sciences M
Geochemistry M
Geology M
Inorganic Chemistry M
Mathematics M
Organic Chemistry M
Physical Chemistry M
Physics M
Statistics M

CALIFORNIA STATE UNIVERSITY, HAYWARD
Chemistry M
Geology M
Marine Sciences M
Mathematics M
Statistics M

CALIFORNIA STATE UNIVERSITY, LONG BEACH
Applied Mathematics M,D,O
Chemistry M
Geology M
Mathematics M
Physics M

CALIFORNIA STATE UNIVERSITY, LOS ANGELES
Analytical Chemistry M
Applied Mathematics M
Chemistry M
Geology M
Inorganic Chemistry M
Mathematics M
Organic Chemistry M
Physical Chemistry M
Physics M

CALIFORNIA STATE UNIVERSITY, MONTEREY BAY
Marine Sciences M

CALIFORNIA STATE UNIVERSITY, NORTHRIDGE
Chemistry M
Geology M
Mathematics M
Physics M

CALIFORNIA STATE UNIVERSITY, SACRAMENTO
Chemistry M
Marine Sciences M
Mathematics M
Statistics M

CALIFORNIA STATE UNIVERSITY, SAN BERNARDINO
Mathematics M

CALIFORNIA STATE UNIVERSITY, SAN MARCOS
Mathematics M

CALIFORNIA UNIVERSITY OF PENNSYLVANIA
Geosciences M

CARLETON UNIVERSITY
Chemistry M,D
Geosciences M,D
Mathematics M,D
Physics M,D

CARNEGIE MELLON UNIVERSITY
Chemistry M,D*
Computational Sciences M,D
Mathematical and Computational Finance M,D
Mathematics M,D
Physics D
Statistics M,D*

CASE WESTERN RESERVE UNIVERSITY
Analytical Chemistry M,D
Applied Mathematics M,D
Astronomy M,D
Biostatistics M,D
Chemistry M,D
Geology M,D
Geosciences M,D
Inorganic Chemistry M,D
Mathematics M,D
Organic Chemistry M,D
Physical Chemistry M,D
Physics M,D
Statistics M,D

THE CATHOLIC UNIVERSITY OF AMERICA
Acoustics M,D
Chemistry M
Physics M,D

CENTRAL CONNECTICUT STATE UNIVERSITY
Chemistry M
Geosciences M
Mathematics M
Physics M
Statistics M

CENTRAL EUROPEAN UNIVERSITY
Environmental Management and Policy M,D

CENTRAL MICHIGAN UNIVERSITY
Chemistry M
Mathematics M,D
Physics M

CENTRAL MISSOURI STATE UNIVERSITY
Agricultural Sciences—General M
Applied Mathematics M
Mathematics M

CENTRAL WASHINGTON UNIVERSITY
Chemistry M
Environmental Management and Policy M
Geology M
Mathematics M

CHAPMAN UNIVERSITY
Food Science and Technology M

CHICAGO STATE UNIVERSITY
Mathematics M

CHRISTOPHER NEWPORT UNIVERSITY
Applied Physics M
Environmental Sciences M
Physics M

CITY COLLEGE OF THE CITY UNIVERSITY OF NEW YORK
Atmospheric Sciences M,D
Chemistry M,D
Environmental Sciences M,D
Geosciences M,D
Mathematics M
Physics M,D*

CLAREMONT GRADUATE UNIVERSITY
Applied Mathematics M,D
Computational Sciences M,D
Mathematics M,D
Statistics M,D

CLARK ATLANTA UNIVERSITY
Applied Mathematics M
Chemistry M,D
Inorganic Chemistry M,D
Organic Chemistry M,D
Physical Chemistry M,D
Physics M

CLARKSON UNIVERSITY
Analytical Chemistry M,D
Chemistry M,D
Environmental Sciences M,D
Inorganic Chemistry M,D
Mathematics M,D
Organic Chemistry M,D
Physical Chemistry M,D
Physics M,D

CLARK UNIVERSITY
Chemistry M,D
Environmental Management and Policy M
Physics M,D

CLEMSON UNIVERSITY
Agricultural Sciences—General M,D
Applied Mathematics M,D
Aquaculture M,D
Astronomy M,D
Astrophysics M,D
Atmospheric Sciences M,D
Chemistry M,D
Computational Sciences M,D
Environmental Management and Policy M,D
Environmental Sciences M,D
Fish, Game, and Wildlife Management M,D
Food Science and Technology M,D
Forestry M,D
Hydrology M
Mathematics M,D
Physics M,D
Statistics M,D

CLEVELAND STATE UNIVERSITY
Analytical Chemistry M,D
Applied Mathematics M
Chemistry M,D
Condensed Matter Physics M
Environmental Management and Policy M
Environmental Sciences M,D
Geology M,D
Inorganic Chemistry M,D
Mathematics M
Optical Sciences M
Organic Chemistry M,D
Physical Chemistry M,D
Physics M

COASTAL CAROLINA UNIVERSITY
Marine Sciences M

COLLEGE OF CHARLESTON
Environmental Sciences M
Mathematics M

COLLEGE OF STATEN ISLAND OF THE CITY UNIVERSITY OF NEW YORK
Chemistry D
Environmental Sciences M

COLLEGE OF THE ATLANTIC
Environmental Management and Policy M

THE COLLEGE OF WILLIAM AND MARY
Chemistry M
Computational Sciences M
Marine Sciences M,D
Physics M,D

COLORADO SCHOOL OF MINES
Applied Physics M,D
Chemistry M,D
Environmental Sciences M,D
Geochemistry M,D,O
Geology M,D,O
Geophysics M,D,O
Geosciences M,D,O
Hydrology M,D,O
Mathematics M,D
Physics M,D

COLORADO STATE UNIVERSITY
Agricultural Sciences—General M,D
Agronomy and Soil Sciences M,D
Animal Sciences M,D
Atmospheric Sciences M,D
Chemistry M,D
Environmental Management and Policy M,D
Fish, Game, and Wildlife Management M,D
Food Science and Technology M,D
Forestry M,D
Geology M,D
Geosciences M,D
Horticulture M,D
Hydrology M,D
Mathematics M,D
Natural Resources M,D
Physics M,D
Plant Sciences M,D
Range Science M,D
Statistics M,D
Water Resources M,D

COLUMBIA UNIVERSITY
Applied Mathematics M,D,O
Applied Physics M,D,O*
Astronomy M,D
Atmospheric Sciences M,D*
Biostatistics M,D
Chemistry M,D
Environmental Management and Policy M*
Geochemistry M,D
Geodetic Sciences M,D
Geophysics M,D
Geosciences M,D
Inorganic Chemistry M,D
Mathematics M,D*
Meteorology M
Oceanography M,D
Optical Sciences M,D,O
Organic Chemistry M,D
Physical Chemistry M,D
Physics M,D
Planetary and Space Sciences M,D
Plasma Physics M,D,O
Statistics M,D

COLUMBUS STATE UNIVERSITY
Environmental Sciences M

CONCORDIA UNIVERSITY (CANADA)
Chemistry M,D
Environmental Management and Policy O
Mathematics M,D

CONVERSE COLLEGE
Chemistry M,O

CORNELL UNIVERSITY
Agronomy and Soil Sciences M,D
Analytical Chemistry D
Animal Sciences M,D
Applied Mathematics M,D*
Applied Physics M,D
Astronomy D
Astrophysics D
Atmospheric Sciences M,D
Biometrics M,D
Chemistry D*
Computational Sciences M,D
Environmental Management and Policy M,D
Environmental Sciences M,D
Fish, Game, and Wildlife Management M,D
Food Science and Technology M,D
Forestry M,D
Geochemistry M,D
Geology M,D*
Geophysics M,D
Geosciences M,D
Horticulture M,D
Hydrology M,D
Inorganic Chemistry D
Limnology D
Marine Sciences M,D
Mathematics D
Mineralogy M,D
Natural Resources M,D
Oceanography D
Organic Chemistry D
Physical Chemistry D
Physics M,D
Planetary and Space Sciences D
Plant Sciences M,D
Statistics M,D
Theoretical Chemistry D
Theoretical Physics M,D

CREIGHTON UNIVERSITY
Atmospheric Sciences M
Physics M

DALHOUSIE UNIVERSITY
Agricultural Sciences—General M
Applied Mathematics M,D
Chemistry M,D
Environmental Management and Policy M
Food Science and Technology M,D
Geosciences M,D
Marine Affairs M
Mathematics M,D
Oceanography M,D
Physics M,D
Statistics M,D

DARTMOUTH COLLEGE
Astronomy M,D
Chemistry D
Geosciences M,D
Mathematics D*
Physics M,D

DELAWARE STATE UNIVERSITY
Chemistry M
Mathematics M
Physics M

DEPAUL UNIVERSITY
Applied Physics M
Chemistry M
Mathematics M*
Physics M
Statistics M

DOWLING COLLEGE
Mathematics M

DREXEL UNIVERSITY
Biostatistics M,D
Chemistry M,D
Environmental Management and Policy M
Environmental Sciences M,D
Food Science and Technology M,D
Mathematics M,D
Physics M,D

DUKE UNIVERSITY
Chemistry D
Environmental Management and Policy M,D*
Environmental Sciences M,D
Forestry M,D
Geology M,D
Marine Affairs M,D
Marine Sciences M,D*
Mathematics D
Natural Resources M,D*
Physics D
Statistics D
Water Resources M,D

DUQUESNE UNIVERSITY
Chemistry M,D*
Environmental Management and Policy M,O
Environmental Sciences M,O
Mathematics M

EAST CAROLINA UNIVERSITY
Applied Mathematics M
Chemistry M
Environmental Management and Policy D
Geology M
Marine Affairs D
Mathematics M
Physics M,D*

EASTERN ILLINOIS UNIVERSITY
Chemistry M
Mathematics M

EASTERN KENTUCKY UNIVERSITY
Chemistry M
Geology M,D
Mathematics M

EASTERN MICHIGAN UNIVERSITY
Chemistry M*
Mathematics M
Physics M
Statistics M

EASTERN NEW MEXICO UNIVERSITY
Chemistry M
Mathematics M

EASTERN WASHINGTON UNIVERSITY
Geology M
Mathematics M

EAST TENNESSEE STATE UNIVERSITY
Chemistry M
Mathematics M

ÉCOLE POLYTECHNIQUE DE MONTRÉAL
Applied Mathematics M,D
Mathematics M,D
Optical Sciences M,D,O

EMORY UNIVERSITY
Biostatistics M,D*
Chemistry D
Mathematics M,D*
Physics D

EMPORIA STATE UNIVERSITY
Chemistry M
Geosciences M
Mathematics M
Physics M

THE EVERGREEN STATE COLLEGE
Environmental Management and Policy M*

FAIRFIELD UNIVERSITY
Mathematics M

FAIRLEIGH DICKINSON UNIVERSITY, COLLEGE AT FLORHAM
Chemistry M

FAYETTEVILLE STATE UNIVERSITY
Mathematics M

FISK UNIVERSITY
Chemistry M
Physics M

FLORIDA AGRICULTURAL AND MECHANICAL UNIVERSITY
Animal Sciences M
Chemistry M
Environmental Sciences M,D
Food Science and Technology M
Physics M,D
Plant Sciences M

FLORIDA ATLANTIC UNIVERSITY
Applied Mathematics M,D
Chemistry M,D
Environmental Sciences M
Geology M
Mathematics M,D
Physics M,D

FLORIDA GULF COAST UNIVERSITY
Environmental Management and Policy M
Environmental Sciences M

FLORIDA INSTITUTE OF TECHNOLOGY
Applied Mathematics M,D
Chemistry M,D
Environmental Management and Policy M,D
Environmental Sciences M,D*
Marine Affairs M,D
Marine Sciences M,D
Meteorology M,D
Oceanography M,D*
Physics M,D

Florida Institute of Technology (continued)
- Planetary and Space Sciences M,D

FLORIDA INTERNATIONAL UNIVERSITY
- Chemistry M,D*
- Environmental Management and Policy M
- Environmental Sciences M
- Geosciences M,D
- Mathematics M
- Physics M,D
- Statistics M

FLORIDA STATE UNIVERSITY
- Analytical Chemistry M,D
- Applied Mathematics M,D
- Chemistry M,D*
- Food Science and Technology M,D
- Geology M,D
- Geophysics D
- Inorganic Chemistry M,D
- Mathematical and Computational Finance M,D
- Mathematics M,D
- Meteorology M,D
- Oceanography M,D*
- Organic Chemistry M,D
- Physical Chemistry M,D
- Physics M,D*
- Statistics M,D

FORT HAYS STATE UNIVERSITY
- Geology M

FORT VALLEY STATE UNIVERSITY
- Animal Sciences M

FRAMINGHAM STATE COLLEGE
- Food Science and Technology M*

FRIENDS UNIVERSITY
- Environmental Management and Policy M

FROSTBURG STATE UNIVERSITY
- Fish, Game, and Wildlife Management M

FURMAN UNIVERSITY
- Chemistry M

GEORGE MASON UNIVERSITY
- Applied Physics M
- Chemistry M
- Computational Sciences M,D,O*
- Environmental Management and Policy M,D
- Environmental Sciences M,D
- Mathematics M
- Physics M
- Statistics M

GEORGETOWN UNIVERSITY
- Analytical Chemistry M,D
- Biostatistics M
- Chemistry M,D
- Inorganic Chemistry M,D
- Organic Chemistry M,D
- Physical Chemistry M,D
- Theoretical Chemistry M,D

THE GEORGE WASHINGTON UNIVERSITY
- Analytical Chemistry M,D
- Applied Mathematics M,D
- Biostatistics M,D
- Chemistry M,D
- Environmental Management and Policy M,D
- Geology M,D
- Geosciences M,D
- Inorganic Chemistry M,D
- Mathematics M,D
- Organic Chemistry M,D
- Physical Chemistry M,D
- Physics M,D
- Statistics M,D

GEORGIA INSTITUTE OF TECHNOLOGY
- Applied Mathematics M,D
- Atmospheric Sciences M,D
- Chemistry M,D
- Environmental Management and Policy M,D
- Environmental Sciences M,D
- Geochemistry M,D
- Geophysics M,D
- Geosciences M,D*
- Hydrology M,D
- Mathematical and Computational Finance M,D
- Mathematics M,D
- Natural Resources M,D
- Physics M,D*
- Statistics M,D

GEORGIAN COURT UNIVERSITY
- Mathematics M,O

GEORGIA SOUTHERN UNIVERSITY
- Mathematics M

GEORGIA STATE UNIVERSITY
- Astronomy D
- Chemistry M,D
- Geology M
- Geosciences M
- Mathematics M
- Physics M,D

GOVERNORS STATE UNIVERSITY
- Analytical Chemistry M

GRADUATE SCHOOL AND UNIVERSITY CENTER OF THE CITY UNIVERSITY OF NEW YORK
- Chemistry D
- Environmental Sciences D
- Geosciences D
- Mathematics D
- Physics D

HAMPTON UNIVERSITY
- Applied Mathematics M
- Chemistry M
- Physics M,D

HARDIN-SIMMONS UNIVERSITY
- Environmental Management and Policy M

HARVARD UNIVERSITY
- Applied Mathematics M,D
- Applied Physics M,D
- Astronomy M,D
- Astrophysics M,D
- Biostatistics M,D
- Chemistry M,D*
- Environmental Management and Policy M,O
- Environmental Sciences M,D
- Forestry M
- Geosciences M,D*
- Inorganic Chemistry M,D
- Mathematics M,D
- Organic Chemistry M,D
- Physical Chemistry M,D
- Physics M,D*
- Planetary and Space Sciences M,D
- Statistics M,D
- Theoretical Physics M,D

HOFSTRA UNIVERSITY
- Applied Mathematics M
- Mathematics M

HOWARD UNIVERSITY
- Analytical Chemistry M,D
- Applied Mathematics M,D
- Atmospheric Sciences M,D
- Chemistry M,D
- Environmental Sciences M,D
- Inorganic Chemistry M,D
- Mathematics M,D
- Organic Chemistry M,D
- Physical Chemistry M,D
- Physics M,D

HUMBOLDT STATE UNIVERSITY
- Environmental Sciences M
- Natural Resources M

HUNTER COLLEGE OF THE CITY UNIVERSITY OF NEW YORK
- Applied Mathematics M
- Environmental Sciences M,O
- Geosciences M,O
- Mathematics M
- Physics M,D

ICR GRADUATE SCHOOL
- Astrophysics M
- Geology M
- Geophysics M

IDAHO STATE UNIVERSITY
- Chemistry M
- Environmental Sciences M
- Geology M,O
- Geophysics M,O
- Geosciences M,O
- Hydrology M,O
- Mathematics M,D*
- Physics M*

ILLINOIS INSTITUTE OF TECHNOLOGY
- Analytical Chemistry M,D
- Applied Mathematics M,D
- Chemistry M,D
- Environmental Management and Policy M,D
- Food Science and Technology M
- Inorganic Chemistry M,D
- Organic Chemistry M,D
- Physical Chemistry M,D
- Physics M,D

ILLINOIS STATE UNIVERSITY
- Agricultural Sciences—General M
- Chemistry M
- Hydrology M
- Mathematics M

INDIANA STATE UNIVERSITY
- Geosciences M,D
- Mathematics M

INDIANA UNIVERSITY BLOOMINGTON
- Analytical Chemistry M,D
- Applied Mathematics M,D
- Astronomy M,D
- Astrophysics D
- Chemistry M,D
- Environmental Sciences M,D*
- Geochemistry M,D
- Geology M,D
- Geophysics M,D
- Geosciences M,D
- Inorganic Chemistry M,D
- Mathematics M,D
- Mineralogy M,D
- Optical Sciences M,D
- Physical Chemistry M,D
- Physics M,D*
- Statistics M,D

INDIANA UNIVERSITY OF PENNSYLVANIA
- Applied Mathematics M
- Chemistry M
- Mathematics M
- Physics M

INDIANA UNIVERSITY–PURDUE UNIVERSITY FORT WAYNE
- Applied Mathematics M
- Mathematics M

INDIANA UNIVERSITY–PURDUE UNIVERSITY INDIANAPOLIS
- Applied Mathematics M,D
- Chemistry M,D
- Geology M
- Mathematics M,D
- Physics M,D
- Statistics M,D

INDIANA UNIVERSITY SOUTH BEND
- Applied Mathematics M

INSTITUTO TECNOLÓGICO Y DE ESTUDIOS SUPERIORES DE MONTERREY, CAMPUS CIUDAD DE MÉXICO
- Environmental Sciences M,D

INSTITUTO TECNOLÓGICO Y DE ESTUDIOS SUPERIORES DE MONTERREY, CAMPUS ESTADO DE MÉXICO
- Environmental Management and Policy M,D

INSTITUTO TECNOLÓGICO Y DE ESTUDIOS SUPERIORES DE MONTERREY, CAMPUS IRAPUATO
- Environmental Management and Policy M,D

INSTITUTO TECNOLÓGICO Y DE ESTUDIOS SUPERIORES DE MONTERREY, CAMPUS MONTERREY
- Agricultural Sciences—General M,D
- Chemistry M,D
- Organic Chemistry M,D
- Statistics M,D

INTER AMERICAN UNIVERSITY OF PUERTO RICO, SAN GERMÁN CAMPUS
- Applied Mathematics M
- Environmental Sciences M

IOWA STATE UNIVERSITY OF SCIENCE AND TECHNOLOGY
- Agricultural Sciences—General M,D
- Agronomy and Soil Sciences M,D
- Animal Sciences M,D
- Applied Mathematics M,D
- Applied Physics M,D
- Astronomy M,D
- Astrophysics M,D
- Biostatistics M,D
- Chemistry M,D
- Computational Sciences M,D
- Condensed Matter Physics M,D
- Environmental Management and Policy M,D
- Fish, Game, and Wildlife Management M,D
- Food Science and Technology M,D*
- Forestry M,D
- Geology M,D
- Geosciences M,D
- Horticulture M,D
- Mathematics M,D
- Meteorology M,D
- Natural Resources M,D
- Physics M,D
- Statistics M,D
- Water Resources M,D

JACKSON STATE UNIVERSITY
- Chemistry M,D
- Environmental Sciences M,D
- Mathematics M

JACKSONVILLE STATE UNIVERSITY
- Mathematics M

JOHN CARROLL UNIVERSITY
- Chemistry M
- Mathematics M
- Physics M

THE JOHNS HOPKINS UNIVERSITY
- Applied Mathematics M,D
- Applied Physics M,O
- Astronomy D
- Biostatistics M,D
- Chemistry M,D
- Environmental Management and Policy M
- Geochemistry M,D
- Geology M,D
- Geophysics M,D
- Mathematics M,D
- Oceanography M,D
- Physics D*
- Planetary and Space Sciences M,D
- Statistics M,D
- Water Resources M,D

KANSAS STATE UNIVERSITY
- Agricultural Sciences—General M,D
- Agronomy and Soil Sciences M,D
- Analytical Chemistry M,D
- Animal Sciences M,D
- Chemistry M,D
- Environmental Management and Policy M
- Food Science and Technology M,D
- Geology M
- Horticulture M,D
- Inorganic Chemistry M,D
- Mathematics M,D
- Organic Chemistry M,D
- Physical Chemistry M,D
- Physics M,D
- Range Science M,D
- Statistics M,D

KEAN UNIVERSITY
- Computational Sciences M
- Environmental Management and Policy M
- Mathematics M
- Statistics M

KENT STATE UNIVERSITY
- Analytical Chemistry M,D
- Applied Mathematics M,D
- Chemistry M,D*
- Geology M,D*
- Inorganic Chemistry M,D
- Mathematics M,D*
- Organic Chemistry M,D
- Physical Chemistry M,D
- Physics M,D*

KENTUCKY STATE UNIVERSITY
- Aquaculture M

KUTZTOWN UNIVERSITY OF PENNSYLVANIA
- Mathematics M

LAKEHEAD UNIVERSITY
- Chemistry M
- Forestry M
- Geology M
- Mathematics M
- Physics M
- Statistics M

LAMAR UNIVERSITY
- Chemistry M
- Environmental Management and Policy M,D
- Mathematics M

LAURENTIAN UNIVERSITY
- Applied Physics M
- Chemistry M
- Geology M

LEHIGH UNIVERSITY
- Applied Mathematics M,D
- Chemistry M,D*
- Environmental Sciences M,D*

Geology M,D
Geosciences M,D
Mathematics M,D*
Photonics M,D
Physics M,D*
Statistics M

LEHMAN COLLEGE OF THE CITY UNIVERSITY OF NEW YORK

Mathematics M
Plant Sciences D

LOMA LINDA UNIVERSITY

Biostatistics M
Geology M

LONG ISLAND UNIVERSITY, BROOKLYN CAMPUS

Chemistry M

LONG ISLAND UNIVERSITY, C.W. POST CAMPUS

Applied Mathematics M
Environmental Management and Policy M
Mathematics M

LOUISIANA STATE UNIVERSITY AND AGRICULTURAL AND MECHANICAL COLLEGE

Agricultural Sciences—General M,D
Agronomy and Soil Sciences M,D
Animal Sciences M,D
Astronomy M,D
Astrophysics M,D
Chemistry M,D
Environmental Management and Policy M
Environmental Sciences M,D
Fish, Game, and Wildlife Management M,D
Food Science and Technology M,D
Forestry M,D
Geology M,D
Geophysics M,D
Horticulture M,D
Marine Affairs M,D
Mathematics M,D
Natural Resources M,D*
Oceanography M,D
Physics M,D
Statistics M

LOUISIANA STATE UNIVERSITY HEALTH SCIENCES CENTER

Biometrics M

LOUISIANA TECH UNIVERSITY

Chemistry M
Computational Sciences M,D
Mathematics M
Physics M,D
Statistics M

LOYOLA MARYMOUNT UNIVERSITY

Environmental Sciences M

LOYOLA UNIVERSITY CHICAGO

Chemistry M,D
Mathematics M
Statistics M

MARQUETTE UNIVERSITY

Analytical Chemistry M,D
Chemistry M,D
Inorganic Chemistry M,D
Mathematics M,D
Organic Chemistry M,D
Physical Chemistry M,D
Statistics M,D

MARSHALL UNIVERSITY

Chemistry M
Environmental Sciences M
Mathematics M
Physics M

MARYWOOD UNIVERSITY

Food Science and Technology M

MASSACHUSETTS COLLEGE OF PHARMACY AND HEALTH SCIENCES

Chemistry M,D

MASSACHUSETTS INSTITUTE OF TECHNOLOGY

Atmospheric Sciences M,D
Chemistry D
Computational Sciences D
Environmental Sciences M,D,O
Geochemistry M,D
Geology M,D
Geophysics M,D
Geosciences M,D
Hydrology M,D,O
Inorganic Chemistry D
Mathematics D
Oceanography M,D,O
Organic Chemistry M,D,O
Physical Chemistry D
Physics D
Planetary and Space Sciences M,D
Plasma Physics M,D,O

MCGILL UNIVERSITY

Agricultural Sciences—General M,D,O
Agronomy and Soil Sciences M,D
Animal Sciences M,D
Atmospheric Sciences M,D
Biostatistics M,D,O
Chemistry M,D
Fish, Game, and Wildlife Management M,D
Food Science and Technology M,D
Forestry M,D
Geosciences M,D,O
Mathematics M,D
Meteorology M,D
Natural Resources M,D
Oceanography M,D
Physics M,D
Planetary and Space Sciences M,D,O
Plant Sciences M,D
Statistics M,D

MCMASTER UNIVERSITY

Analytical Chemistry M,D
Astrophysics M,D
Chemistry M,D
Geochemistry M,D
Geology M,D
Geosciences M,D
Inorganic Chemistry M,D
Mathematics M,D
Organic Chemistry M,D
Physical Chemistry M,D
Physics M,D
Statistics M,D

MCNEESE STATE UNIVERSITY

Chemistry M,D
Environmental Sciences M,D
Mathematics M
Statistics M

MEDICAL COLLEGE OF WISCONSIN

Biostatistics D*

MEDICAL UNIVERSITY OF SOUTH CAROLINA

Biometrics M,D
Biostatistics M,D

MEMORIAL UNIVERSITY OF NEWFOUNDLAND

Aquaculture M
Chemistry M,D
Computational Sciences M
Environmental Sciences M
Fish, Game, and Wildlife Management M
Food Science and Technology M,D
Geology M,D
Geophysics M,D
Geosciences M,D
Marine Affairs M,D
Marine Sciences M
Mathematics M,D
Natural Resources M
Oceanography M,D
Physics M,D
Statistics M,D

MIAMI UNIVERSITY

Analytical Chemistry M,D
Chemistry M,D
Environmental Sciences M
Geology M,D
Inorganic Chemistry M,D
Mathematics M*
Organic Chemistry M,D
Physical Chemistry M,D
Physics M
Statistics M

MICHIGAN STATE UNIVERSITY

Agricultural Sciences—General M,D
Agronomy and Soil Sciences M,D
Animal Sciences M,D
Applied Mathematics M,D
Astronomy M,D
Astrophysics M,D
Chemistry M,D
Environmental Management and Policy M,D
Environmental Sciences M,D
Fish, Game, and Wildlife Management M,D
Food Science and Technology M,D
Forestry M,D
Geology M,D
Geosciences M,D
Horticulture M,D
Mathematics M,D
Physical Chemistry M,D
Physics M,D*
Plant Sciences M,D
Statistics M,D

MICHIGAN TECHNOLOGICAL UNIVERSITY

Chemistry M,D*
Computational Sciences D*
Environmental Management and Policy M*
Forestry M,D*
Geology M,D*
Geophysics M*
Mathematics M,D*
Physics M,D*

MIDDLE TENNESSEE STATE UNIVERSITY

Chemistry M,D
Mathematics M

MINNESOTA STATE UNIVERSITY MANKATO

Astronomy M
Chemistry M
Environmental Sciences M
Mathematics M
Physics M
Statistics M

MISSISSIPPI COLLEGE

Chemistry M
Mathematics M

MISSISSIPPI STATE UNIVERSITY

Agricultural Sciences—General M,D
Agronomy and Soil Sciences M,D
Animal Sciences M
Chemistry M,D
Fish, Game, and Wildlife Management M
Food Science and Technology M,D
Forestry M
Geosciences M
Mathematics M,D
Physics M,D
Plant Sciences M,D
Statistics M,D

MONTANA STATE UNIVERSITY–BOZEMAN

Agricultural Sciences—General M,D
Animal Sciences M,D
Chemistry M,D
Environmental Management and Policy M,D
Environmental Sciences M,D
Fish, Game, and Wildlife Management M,D
Geosciences M,D
Mathematics M,D
Natural Resources M,D
Physics M,D
Plant Sciences M,D
Range Science M,D
Statistics M,D

MONTANA TECH OF THE UNIVERSITY OF MONTANA

Geochemistry M
Geology M
Geosciences M
Hydrology M

MONTCLAIR STATE UNIVERSITY

Applied Mathematics M,O
Chemistry M
Environmental Management and Policy M,D*
Environmental Sciences M,D,O
Geosciences M,O
Mathematics M
Statistics M,O
Water Resources M,O

MONTEREY INSTITUTE OF INTERNATIONAL STUDIES

Environmental Management and Policy M

MORGAN STATE UNIVERSITY

Chemistry M
Mathematics M
Physics M

MOUNT ALLISON UNIVERSITY

Chemistry M

MOUNT SINAI SCHOOL OF MEDICINE OF NEW YORK UNIVERSITY

Biometrics D
Biostatistics D

MURRAY STATE UNIVERSITY

Agricultural Sciences—General M
Chemistry M
Geosciences M
Marine Sciences M
Mathematics M

NAROPA UNIVERSITY

Environmental Management and Policy M

NATIONAL TECHNOLOGICAL UNIVERSITY

Environmental Management and Policy M

NAVAL POSTGRADUATE SCHOOL

Acoustics M,D
Mathematics M,D
Meteorology M,D
Oceanography M,D
Physics M,D

NEW JERSEY INSTITUTE OF TECHNOLOGY

Applied Mathematics M
Applied Physics M,D
Chemistry M,D
Computational Sciences M
Environmental Management and Policy M,D
Environmental Sciences M,D
Mathematics D
Statistics M

NEW MEXICO HIGHLANDS UNIVERSITY

Chemistry M
Environmental Management and Policy M

NEW MEXICO INSTITUTE OF MINING AND TECHNOLOGY

Applied Mathematics M,D
Astrophysics M,D
Atmospheric Sciences M,D
Chemistry M,D
Environmental Sciences M,D
Geochemistry M,D
Geology M,D
Geophysics M,D
Geosciences M,D
Hydrology M,D
Mathematical Physics M,D
Mathematics M,D
Physics M,D

NEW MEXICO STATE UNIVERSITY

Agricultural Sciences—General M,D
Agronomy and Soil Sciences M,D
Animal Sciences M,D
Astronomy M,D
Chemistry M,D
Fish, Game, and Wildlife Management M
Geology M
Horticulture M,D
Mathematics M,D
Physics M,D
Plant Sciences M
Range Science M,D
Statistics M

NEW YORK INSTITUTE OF TECHNOLOGY

Environmental Management and Policy M,O

NEW YORK MEDICAL COLLEGE

Biostatistics M

NEW YORK UNIVERSITY

Chemistry M,D*
Mathematical and Computational Finance M,D
Mathematics M,D*
Physics M,D
Statistics M,D

NICHOLLS STATE UNIVERSITY

Applied Mathematics M
Mathematics M

NORFOLK STATE UNIVERSITY

Optical Sciences M

NORTH CAROLINA AGRICULTURAL AND TECHNICAL STATE UNIVERSITY

Agricultural Sciences—General M
Chemistry M
Environmental Sciences M
Plant Sciences M

NORTH CAROLINA CENTRAL UNIVERSITY

Chemistry M
Geosciences M

North Carolina Central University (continued)

Mathematics M

NORTH CAROLINA STATE UNIVERSITY

Agricultural Sciences—General M,D
Agronomy and Soil Sciences M,D
Animal Sciences M,D
Applied Mathematics M,D
Atmospheric Sciences M,D
Biometrics M,D
Chemistry M,D
Fish, Game, and Wildlife Management M
Food Science and Technology M,D
Forestry M,D
Geosciences M,D*
Horticulture M,D
Marine Sciences M,D
Mathematical and Computational Finance M*
Mathematics M,D
Meteorology M,D
Natural Resources M
Oceanography M,D
Physics M,D
Statistics M,D

NORTH DAKOTA STATE UNIVERSITY

Agricultural Sciences—General M,D
Agronomy and Soil Sciences M,D
Animal Sciences M,D
Applied Mathematics M,D
Chemistry M,D
Environmental Management and Policy M,D
Environmental Sciences M,D
Food Science and Technology M,D
Mathematics M,D
Physics M,D
Plant Sciences M,D
Range Science M,D
Statistics M,D

NORTHEASTERN ILLINOIS UNIVERSITY

Chemistry M
Environmental Management and Policy M
Geosciences M
Mathematics M

NORTHEASTERN UNIVERSITY

Analytical Chemistry M,D
Chemistry M,D*
Inorganic Chemistry M,D
Mathematics M,D*
Organic Chemistry M,D
Physical Chemistry M,D
Physics M,D*

NORTHERN ARIZONA UNIVERSITY

Applied Physics M
Chemistry M
Environmental Management and Policy M,O
Environmental Sciences M,D
Forestry M,D
Geology M
Geosciences M
Mathematics M
Statistics M

NORTHERN ILLINOIS UNIVERSITY

Chemistry M,D
Geology M,D
Mathematics M,D
Physics M,D
Statistics M

NORTHERN MICHIGAN UNIVERSITY

Chemistry M

NORTHWESTERN UNIVERSITY

Applied Mathematics M,D*
Astronomy M,D
Astrophysics M,D
Chemistry D
Geology M,D
Geosciences M,D
Mathematics D
Physics M,D
Statistics M,D

NORTHWEST MISSOURI STATE UNIVERSITY

Agricultural Sciences—General M

NOVA SCOTIA AGRICULTURAL COLLEGE

Agricultural Sciences—General M
Agronomy and Soil Sciences M
Animal Sciences M
Aquaculture M
Environmental Management and Policy M
Environmental Sciences M
Food Science and Technology M
Horticulture M
Water Resources M

NOVA SOUTHEASTERN UNIVERSITY

Environmental Sciences M
Marine Affairs M
Marine Sciences M
Oceanography D*

OAKLAND UNIVERSITY

Applied Mathematics M
Chemistry M,D
Environmental Sciences M,D
Mathematics M
Physics M,D
Statistics M,D,O

OGI SCHOOL OF SCIENCE & ENGINEERING AT OREGON HEALTH & SCIENCE UNIVERSITY

Environmental Management and Policy M,D
Environmental Sciences M,D*
Mathematical and Computational Finance M,D,O

THE OHIO STATE UNIVERSITY

Agricultural Sciences—General M,D
Agronomy and Soil Sciences M,D
Animal Sciences M,D
Astronomy M,D
Atmospheric Sciences M,D
Biostatistics D
Chemistry M,D
Environmental Sciences M,D
Food Science and Technology M,D
Geodetic Sciences M,D
Geology M,D
Horticulture M,D
Mathematics M,D*
Natural Resources M,D
Optical Sciences M,D
Physical Chemistry M,D
Physics M,D
Statistics M,D

OHIO UNIVERSITY

Environmental Management and Policy M
Environmental Sciences M
Geochemistry M
Geology M
Geophysics M
Hydrology M
Mathematics M,D
Physics M,D*

OKLAHOMA STATE UNIVERSITY

Agricultural Sciences—General M,D
Agronomy and Soil Sciences M,D
Animal Sciences M,D
Applied Mathematics M,D
Chemistry M,D
Environmental Sciences M,D
Food Science and Technology M,D
Forestry M
Geology M
Horticulture M,D
Mathematics M,D*
Natural Resources M,D
Photonics M,D*
Physics M,D
Plant Sciences D
Statistics M,D

OLD DOMINION UNIVERSITY

Analytical Chemistry M
Chemistry M
Mathematics M,D
Oceanography M,D
Organic Chemistry M
Physical Chemistry M
Physics M,D

OREGON HEALTH & SCIENCE UNIVERSITY

Biostatistics M

OREGON STATE UNIVERSITY

Agricultural Sciences—General M,D
Agronomy and Soil Sciences M,D
Analytical Chemistry M,D
Animal Sciences M,D
Atmospheric Sciences M,D
Biometrics M,D
Chemistry M,D
Environmental Management and Policy M,D
Environmental Sciences M,D
Fish, Game, and Wildlife Management M,D
Food Science and Technology M,D
Forestry M,D
Geology M,D
Geophysics M,D
Geosciences M,D
Horticulture M,D
Inorganic Chemistry M,D
Marine Affairs M
Marine Sciences M
Mathematics M,D
Oceanography M,D
Organic Chemistry M,D
Physical Chemistry M,D
Physics M,D*
Range Science M,D
Statistics M,D

PACE UNIVERSITY, WHITE PLAINS CAMPUS

Environmental Sciences M*

PAPER SCIENCE AND ENGINEERING PROGRAM

Chemistry M,D
Mathematics M,D
Physics M,D

THE PENNSYLVANIA STATE UNIVERSITY HARRISBURG CAMPUS OF THE CAPITAL COLLEGE

Environmental Sciences M

THE PENNSYLVANIA STATE UNIVERSITY UNIVERSITY PARK CAMPUS

Acoustics M,D
Agricultural Sciences—General M,D
Agronomy and Soil Sciences M,D
Animal Sciences M,D
Applied Mathematics M,D
Astronomy M,D
Astrophysics M,D
Chemistry M,D*
Environmental Management and Policy M
Environmental Sciences M
Fish, Game, and Wildlife Management M,D
Food Science and Technology M,D
Forestry M,D
Geochemistry M,D
Geology M,D
Geophysics M,D
Geosciences M,D*
Horticulture M,D
Mathematics M,D*
Meteorology M,D
Physics M,D*
Statistics M,D

PITTSBURG STATE UNIVERSITY

Applied Physics M
Chemistry M
Mathematics M
Physics M

POLYTECHNIC UNIVERSITY, BROOKLYN CAMPUS

Chemistry M,D
Environmental Sciences M
Mathematics M,D
Physics M,D

POLYTECHNIC UNIVERSITY, LONG ISLAND GRADUATE CENTER

Chemistry M,D

POLYTECHNIC UNIVERSITY OF PUERTO RICO

Environmental Management and Policy M

POLYTECHNIC UNIVERSITY, WESTCHESTER GRADUATE CENTER

Chemistry M
Mathematical and Computational Finance M,O

PONTIFICAL CATHOLIC UNIVERSITY OF PUERTO RICO

Chemistry M

PORTLAND STATE UNIVERSITY

Chemistry M,D
Environmental Management and Policy M,D
Environmental Sciences M,D
Geology M,D
Mathematics M,D,O
Physics M,D

PRAIRIE VIEW A&M UNIVERSITY

Agricultural Sciences—General M
Agronomy and Soil Sciences M
Animal Sciences M
Chemistry M
Mathematics M

PRESCOTT COLLEGE

Environmental Management and Policy M

PRINCETON UNIVERSITY

Applied Mathematics M,D*
Applied Physics M,D
Astrophysics D
Atmospheric Sciences D
Chemistry M,D*
Computational Sciences D
Environmental Management and Policy M,D
Geology D
Geophysics D
Geosciences D
Mathematical Physics D
Mathematics D
Oceanography D
Photonics D
Physical Chemistry M,D
Physics D
Plasma Physics D
Statistics M,D

PURDUE UNIVERSITY

Agricultural Sciences—General M,D
Agronomy and Soil Sciences M,D
Analytical Chemistry M,D
Animal Sciences M,D
Aquaculture M,D
Atmospheric Sciences M,D
Chemistry M,D
Environmental Management and Policy M,D
Fish, Game, and Wildlife Management M,D
Food Science and Technology M,D
Forestry M,D*
Geosciences M,D
Horticulture M,D
Inorganic Chemistry M,D
Mathematical and Computational Finance M,D
Mathematics M,D*
Natural Resources M,D
Organic Chemistry M,D
Physical Chemistry M,D
Physics M,D
Statistics M,D*

PURDUE UNIVERSITY CALUMET

Mathematics M

QUEENS COLLEGE OF THE CITY UNIVERSITY OF NEW YORK

Chemistry M
Environmental Sciences M
Geology M
Mathematics M
Physics M

QUEEN'S UNIVERSITY AT KINGSTON

Chemistry M,D
Geology M,D
Mathematics M,D
Physics M,D
Statistics M,D

RADFORD UNIVERSITY

Geosciences M

RENSSELAER POLYTECHNIC INSTITUTE

Acoustics M
Analytical Chemistry M,D
Applied Mathematics M
Applied Physics M,D
Astrophysics M,D
Chemistry M,D
Environmental Management and Policy M,D
Environmental Sciences M,D
Geochemistry M,D
Geology M,D
Geophysics M,D
Geosciences M,D
Inorganic Chemistry M,D
Mathematics M,D
Organic Chemistry M,D
Physical Chemistry M,D
Physics M,D
Statistics M

RHODE ISLAND COLLEGE

Mathematics M,O

RICE UNIVERSITY

Applied Mathematics M,D
Applied Physics M,D
Astronomy M,D
Biostatistics M,D
Chemistry M,D
Computational Sciences M,D
Environmental Management and Policy M
Environmental Sciences M,D
Geophysics M
Geosciences M,D
Inorganic Chemistry M,D
Mathematical and Computational Finance M,D
Mathematics M,D
Organic Chemistry M,D
Physical Chemistry M,D
Physics M,D

Statistics M,D

RIVIER COLLEGE
Mathematics M

ROCHESTER INSTITUTE OF TECHNOLOGY
Applied Mathematics M
Chemistry M
Environmental Management and Policy M
Optical Sciences M,D
Statistics M,O

ROOSEVELT UNIVERSITY
Chemistry M
Mathematics M

ROSE-HULMAN INSTITUTE OF TECHNOLOGY
Optical Sciences M

ROWAN UNIVERSITY
Mathematics M

ROYAL MILITARY COLLEGE OF CANADA
Chemistry M,D
Environmental Sciences M,D
Mathematics M
Physics M

ROYAL ROADS UNIVERSITY
Environmental Management and Policy M

RUTGERS, THE STATE UNIVERSITY OF NEW JERSEY, CAMDEN
Chemistry M
Mathematics M

RUTGERS, THE STATE UNIVERSITY OF NEW JERSEY, NEWARK
Analytical Chemistry M,D
Applied Physics M,D
Chemistry M,D
Computational Sciences M
Environmental Sciences M,D
Geology M
Inorganic Chemistry M,D
Mathematics D
Organic Chemistry M,D
Physical Chemistry M,D

RUTGERS, THE STATE UNIVERSITY OF NEW JERSEY, NEW BRUNSWICK/ PISCATAWAY
Analytical Chemistry M,D
Animal Sciences M,D
Applied Mathematics M,D
Atmospheric Sciences M,D
Biostatistics M,D
Chemistry M,D*
Condensed Matter Physics M,D
Environmental Sciences M,D
Food Science and Technology M,D
Geology M,D
Horticulture M,D
Inorganic Chemistry M,D
Mathematics M,D
Oceanography M,D*
Organic Chemistry M,D
Physical Chemistry M,D
Physics M,D*
Plant Sciences M,D
Statistics M,D
Theoretical Physics M,D
Water Resources M,D

SACRED HEART UNIVERSITY
Chemistry M

ST. CLOUD STATE UNIVERSITY
Environmental Management and Policy M
Mathematics M

ST. FRANCIS XAVIER UNIVERSITY
Chemistry M
Geology M
Geosciences M
Physics M

ST. JOHN'S UNIVERSITY (NY)
Applied Mathematics M
Chemistry M
Mathematics M
Statistics M
Theoretical Physics M,O

SAINT JOSEPH COLLEGE
Chemistry M

SAINT JOSEPH'S UNIVERSITY
Environmental Management and Policy M

SAINT LOUIS UNIVERSITY
Biostatistics M
Chemistry M
Geophysics M,D
Geosciences M,D
Mathematics M,D
Meteorology M,D

SAINT MARY-OF-THE-WOODS COLLEGE
Environmental Management and Policy M

SAINT MARY'S UNIVERSITY
Astronomy M

SAINT MARY'S UNIVERSITY OF MINNESOTA
Environmental Management and Policy M,O

SAINT XAVIER UNIVERSITY
Mathematics M

SALEM STATE COLLEGE
Mathematics M

SAM HOUSTON STATE UNIVERSITY
Agricultural Sciences—General M
Chemistry M
Computational Sciences M
Mathematics M
Physics M
Statistics M

SAN DIEGO STATE UNIVERSITY
Applied Mathematics M
Astronomy M
Biometrics D
Biostatistics M,D
Chemistry M,D
Computational Sciences M,D
Geology M
Mathematics M,D
Physics M
Statistics M

SAN FRANCISCO STATE UNIVERSITY
Astrophysics M
Chemistry M
Environmental Management and Policy M
Geosciences M
Mathematics M
Physics M

SAN JOSE STATE UNIVERSITY
Chemistry M
Environmental Management and Policy M
Geology M
Marine Sciences M
Mathematics M
Meteorology M
Physics M

SANTA CLARA UNIVERSITY
Applied Mathematics M

SAVANNAH STATE UNIVERSITY
Marine Sciences M

THE SCRIPPS RESEARCH INSTITUTE
Chemistry D

SETON HALL UNIVERSITY
Analytical Chemistry M,D
Chemistry M,D*
Inorganic Chemistry M,D
Organic Chemistry M,D
Physical Chemistry M,D

SHIPPENSBURG UNIVERSITY OF PENNSYLVANIA
Environmental Management and Policy M

SIMON FRASER UNIVERSITY
Applied Mathematics M,D
Chemistry M,D
Environmental Management and Policy M,D
Geosciences M
Mathematics M,D
Physical Chemistry M,D
Physics M,D
Statistics M,D

SLIPPERY ROCK UNIVERSITY OF PENNSYLVANIA
Environmental Management and Policy M

SMITH COLLEGE
Chemistry M

SOUTH DAKOTA SCHOOL OF MINES AND TECHNOLOGY
Atmospheric Sciences M,D*
Chemistry M,D
Environmental Sciences D
Geology M,D
Physics M,D
Water Resources D

SOUTH DAKOTA STATE UNIVERSITY
Agricultural Sciences—General M,D
Agronomy and Soil Sciences M,D
Analytical Chemistry M,D
Animal Sciences M,D
Atmospheric Sciences D*
Chemistry M,D
Environmental Sciences D
Fish, Game, and Wildlife Management M,D
Inorganic Chemistry M,D
Mathematics M
Organic Chemistry M,D
Physical Chemistry M,D
Physics M
Plant Sciences M,D
Water Resources D

SOUTHEAST MISSOURI STATE UNIVERSITY
Chemistry M
Environmental Management and Policy M
Geosciences M
Mathematics M

SOUTHERN CONNECTICUT STATE UNIVERSITY
Chemistry M
Mathematics M

SOUTHERN ILLINOIS UNIVERSITY CARBONDALE
Agricultural Sciences—General M
Agronomy and Soil Sciences M
Animal Sciences M
Chemistry M,D*
Environmental Sciences D*
Forestry M
Geology M,D
Horticulture M
Mathematics M,D*
Physics M
Plant Sciences M
Statistics M,D

SOUTHERN ILLINOIS UNIVERSITY EDWARDSVILLE
Chemistry M
Environmental Sciences M
Mathematics M
Physics M
Statistics M

SOUTHERN METHODIST UNIVERSITY
Applied Mathematics M,D
Chemistry M
Computational Sciences M,D
Environmental Sciences M,D
Geology M,D
Geophysics M,D
Mathematics M,D
Physics M,D
Statistics M,D

SOUTHERN OREGON UNIVERSITY
Mathematics M

SOUTHERN UNIVERSITY AND AGRICULTURAL AND MECHANICAL COLLEGE
Agricultural Sciences—General M
Analytical Chemistry M
Chemistry M
Environmental Sciences M
Forestry M
Inorganic Chemistry M
Mathematics M
Organic Chemistry M
Physical Chemistry M
Physics M

SOUTHWEST MISSOURI STATE UNIVERSITY
Agricultural Sciences—General M
Agronomy and Soil Sciences M
Chemistry M
Environmental Management and Policy M

Geology M
Geosciences M
Mathematics M
Plant Sciences M

STANFORD UNIVERSITY
Applied Physics M,D
Chemistry D*
Computational Sciences M,D
Environmental Management and Policy M
Environmental Sciences M,D,O
Geophysics M,D
Geosciences M,D,O
Mathematical and Computational Finance M,D
Mathematics M,D
Physics D
Statistics M,D

STATE UNIVERSITY OF NEW YORK AT BINGHAMTON
Analytical Chemistry M,D
Applied Physics M
Chemistry M,D
Geology M,D
Inorganic Chemistry M,D
Mathematics M,D
Organic Chemistry M,D
Physical Chemistry M,D
Physics M
Statistics M,D

STATE UNIVERSITY OF NEW YORK AT NEW PALTZ
Chemistry M
Geology M
Mathematics M

STATE UNIVERSITY OF NEW YORK AT OSWEGO
Chemistry M

STATE UNIVERSITY OF NEW YORK COLLEGE AT BROCKPORT
Computational Sciences M
Mathematics M*

STATE UNIVERSITY OF NEW YORK COLLEGE AT CORTLAND
Mathematics M

STATE UNIVERSITY OF NEW YORK COLLEGE AT FREDONIA
Chemistry M

STATE UNIVERSITY OF NEW YORK COLLEGE AT ONEONTA
Geosciences M

STATE UNIVERSITY OF NEW YORK COLLEGE AT POTSDAM
Mathematics M

STATE UNIVERSITY OF NEW YORK COLLEGE OF ENVIRONMENTAL SCIENCE AND FORESTRY
Chemistry M,D
Environmental Management and Policy M,D
Environmental Sciences M,D
Fish, Game, and Wildlife Management M,D
Forestry M,D
Hydrology M,D
Natural Resources M,D
Organic Chemistry M,D
Plant Sciences M,D
Water Resources M,D

STEPHEN F. AUSTIN STATE UNIVERSITY
Chemistry M
Environmental Sciences M
Forestry M,D
Geology M
Mathematics M
Physics M
Statistics M

STEVENS INSTITUTE OF TECHNOLOGY
Analytical Chemistry M,D,O
Applied Mathematics M,D
Chemistry M,D,O
Marine Affairs M
Mathematics M,D
Organic Chemistry M,D,O
Physical Chemistry M,D,O
Physics M,D,O
Statistics M,O

STONY BROOK UNIVERSITY, STATE UNIVERSITY OF NEW YORK
Applied Mathematics M,D*
Atmospheric Sciences M,D*
Chemistry M,D*

Stony Brook University, State University of New York (continued)
- Environmental Management and Policy M,O*
- Geosciences M,D*
- Marine Sciences M,D*
- Mathematics M,D*
- Physics M,D*
- Planetary and Space Sciences M,D
- Statistics M,D

SUL ROSS STATE UNIVERSITY
- Animal Sciences M
- Chemistry M
- Fish, Game, and Wildlife Management M
- Geology M*
- Range Science M

SYRACUSE UNIVERSITY
- Chemistry M,D
- Geology M,D
- Mathematics M,D
- Physics M,D
- Statistics M

TARLETON STATE UNIVERSITY
- Agricultural Sciences—General M
- Animal Sciences M
- Environmental Sciences M
- Mathematics M

TAYLOR UNIVERSITY
- Environmental Sciences M

TEMPLE UNIVERSITY
- Applied Mathematics M,D
- Chemistry M,D*
- Computational Sciences M,D
- Geology M
- Mathematics M,D
- Physics M,D*
- Statistics M,D

TENNESSEE STATE UNIVERSITY
- Agricultural Sciences—General M,D
- Chemistry M
- Mathematics M

TENNESSEE TECHNOLOGICAL UNIVERSITY
- Chemistry M
- Environmental Sciences D*
- Fish, Game, and Wildlife Management M
- Mathematics M

TEXAS A&M INTERNATIONAL UNIVERSITY
- Mathematics M
- Physics M

TEXAS A&M UNIVERSITY
- Agricultural Sciences—General M,D
- Agronomy and Soil Sciences M,D
- Animal Sciences M,D
- Applied Physics M,D
- Chemistry M,D*
- Fish, Game, and Wildlife Management M,D
- Food Science and Technology M,D
- Forestry M,D
- Geology M,D
- Geophysics M,D
- Horticulture M,D
- Hydrology M,D
- Mathematics M,D
- Meteorology M,D
- Natural Resources M,D
- Oceanography M,D
- Physics M,D
- Plant Sciences M,D
- Range Science M,D
- Statistics M,D

TEXAS A&M UNIVERSITY AT GALVESTON
- Marine Sciences M

TEXAS A&M UNIVERSITY–COMMERCE
- Agricultural Sciences—General M
- Chemistry M
- Geosciences M
- Mathematics M
- Physics M

TEXAS A&M UNIVERSITY–CORPUS CHRISTI
- Environmental Sciences M

TEXAS A&M UNIVERSITY–KINGSVILLE
- Agricultural Sciences—General M,D
- Agronomy and Soil Sciences M,D
- Animal Sciences M
- Chemistry M
- Fish, Game, and Wildlife Management M,D
- Geology M
- Mathematics M
- Plant Sciences M,D
- Range Science M

TEXAS CHRISTIAN UNIVERSITY
- Astronomy D
- Astrophysics D
- Chemistry M,D
- Environmental Sciences M
- Geology M
- Geosciences M
- Mathematics M
- Physics D

TEXAS SOUTHERN UNIVERSITY
- Chemistry M
- Mathematics M

TEXAS STATE UNIVERSITY-SAN MARCOS
- Applied Mathematics M
- Chemistry M
- Environmental Management and Policy M
- Fish, Game, and Wildlife Management M
- Mathematics M
- Physics M

TEXAS TECH UNIVERSITY
- Agricultural Sciences—General M,D
- Agronomy and Soil Sciences M,D
- Animal Sciences M,D
- Applied Physics M,D
- Atmospheric Sciences M,D
- Chemistry M,D
- Environmental Management and Policy D
- Environmental Sciences M,D
- Fish, Game, and Wildlife Management M,D
- Food Science and Technology M,D
- Geosciences M,D
- Horticulture M,D
- Mathematics M,D
- Physics M,D
- Plant Sciences M,D
- Range Science M,D

TEXAS WOMAN'S UNIVERSITY
- Chemistry M
- Food Science and Technology M,D
- Mathematics M

TOWSON UNIVERSITY
- Applied Mathematics M
- Environmental Management and Policy M
- Environmental Sciences M,O

TRENT UNIVERSITY
- Chemistry M
- Environmental Management and Policy M,D
- Physics M

TROY UNIVERSITY
- Environmental Management and Policy M

TUFTS UNIVERSITY
- Analytical Chemistry M,D
- Biostatistics M,D
- Chemistry M,D*
- Environmental Management and Policy M,D,O
- Environmental Sciences M,D
- Inorganic Chemistry M,D
- Mathematics M,D
- Organic Chemistry M,D
- Physical Chemistry M,D
- Physics M,D

TULANE UNIVERSITY
- Applied Mathematics M,D
- Biostatistics M,D
- Chemistry M,D
- Geology M,D*
- Mathematics M,D
- Physics M,D
- Statistics M,D

TUSKEGEE UNIVERSITY
- Agricultural Sciences—General M
- Agronomy and Soil Sciences M
- Animal Sciences M
- Chemistry M
- Environmental Sciences M
- Food Science and Technology M
- Plant Sciences M

UNIVERSIDAD DE LAS AMÉRICAS–PUEBLA
- Food Science and Technology M

UNIVERSIDAD DEL TURABO
- Environmental Management and Policy M

UNIVERSIDAD METROPOLITANA
- Environmental Management and Policy M

UNIVERSITÉ DE MONCTON
- Astronomy M
- Chemistry M
- Food Science and Technology M
- Mathematics M
- Physics M

UNIVERSITÉ DE MONTRÉAL
- Chemistry M,D
- Environmental Management and Policy O
- Mathematics M,D
- Physics M,D
- Statistics M,D

UNIVERSITÉ DE SHERBROOKE
- Chemistry M,D
- Environmental Sciences M,O
- Mathematics M,D
- Physics M,D

UNIVERSITÉ DU QUÉBEC À CHICOUTIMI
- Environmental Management and Policy M
- Geosciences M
- Mineralogy D

UNIVERSITÉ DU QUÉBEC À MONTRÉAL
- Atmospheric Sciences M,D,O
- Chemistry M
- Environmental Sciences M,D
- Geology M,D,O
- Geosciences M,D,O
- Mathematics M,D
- Meteorology M,D,O
- Mineralogy M,D,O
- Natural Resources M,D,O

UNIVERSITÉ DU QUÉBEC À RIMOUSKI
- Fish, Game, and Wildlife Management M,O
- Marine Affairs M
- Oceanography M,D

UNIVERSITÉ DU QUÉBEC À TROIS-RIVIÈRES
- Chemistry M
- Environmental Sciences M,D
- Mathematics M

UNIVERSITÉ DU QUÉBEC, INSTITUT NATIONAL DE LA RECHERCHE SCIENTIFIQUE
- Environmental Management and Policy M,D
- Geosciences M,D
- Hydrology M,D

UNIVERSITÉ LAVAL
- Agricultural Sciences—General M,D,O
- Agronomy and Soil Sciences M,D
- Animal Sciences M,D
- Chemistry M,D
- Environmental Management and Policy M,D
- Environmental Sciences M,D
- Food Science and Technology M,D
- Forestry M,D
- Geodetic Sciences M,D
- Geology M,D
- Geosciences M,D
- Mathematics M,D
- Oceanography D
- Physics M,D
- Statistics M

UNIVERSITY AT ALBANY, STATE UNIVERSITY OF NEW YORK
- Atmospheric Sciences M,D
- Biometrics M,D
- Chemistry M,D
- Environmental Management and Policy M
- Environmental Sciences M
- Geology M,D
- Geosciences M,D
- Mathematics M,D
- Physics M,D
- Statistics M,D,O

UNIVERSITY AT BUFFALO, THE STATE UNIVERSITY OF NEW YORK
- Biostatistics M,D
- Chemistry M,D
- Geology M,D
- Mathematics M,D
- Physics M,D

THE UNIVERSITY OF AKRON
- Applied Mathematics M,D
- Chemistry M,D
- Food Science and Technology M
- Geology M
- Geophysics M
- Geosciences M
- Mathematics M
- Physics M
- Statistics M

THE UNIVERSITY OF ALABAMA
- Applied Mathematics M,D
- Chemistry M,D*
- Geology M,D
- Mathematics M,D
- Physics M,D
- Statistics M,D

THE UNIVERSITY OF ALABAMA AT BIRMINGHAM
- Applied Mathematics M,D
- Biometrics M,D
- Biostatistics M,D
- Chemistry M,D
- Mathematics M,D
- Physics M,D

THE UNIVERSITY OF ALABAMA IN HUNTSVILLE
- Applied Mathematics M,D
- Atmospheric Sciences M,D
- Chemistry M
- Environmental Sciences M,D
- Mathematics M,D
- Optical Sciences D
- Physics M,D

UNIVERSITY OF ALASKA ANCHORAGE
- Environmental Sciences M

UNIVERSITY OF ALASKA FAIRBANKS
- Astrophysics M,D
- Atmospheric Sciences M,D
- Chemistry M,D
- Environmental Management and Policy M
- Environmental Sciences M,D
- Fish, Game, and Wildlife Management M,D
- Geology M,D
- Geophysics M,D
- Limnology M,D
- Marine Sciences M,D*
- Mathematics M,D
- Oceanography M,D
- Physics M,D
- Statistics M,D

UNIVERSITY OF ALBERTA
- Agricultural Sciences—General M,D
- Agronomy and Soil Sciences M,D
- Applied Mathematics M,D,O
- Astrophysics M,D
- Biostatistics M,D,O
- Chemistry M,D
- Condensed Matter Physics M,D
- Environmental Management and Policy M,D
- Environmental Sciences M,D
- Forestry M,D
- Geophysics M,D
- Geosciences M,D
- Mathematical and Computational Finance M,D,O
- Mathematical Physics M,D,O
- Mathematics M,D,O
- Natural Resources M,D
- Physics M,D
- Statistics M,D,O

THE UNIVERSITY OF ARIZONA
- Agricultural Sciences—General M,D
- Agronomy and Soil Sciences M,D
- Animal Sciences M,D
- Applied Mathematics M,D*
- Applied Physics M
- Astronomy M,D
- Atmospheric Sciences M,D
- Chemistry M,D
- Environmental Management and Policy M
- Environmental Sciences M,D
- Fish, Game, and Wildlife Management M,D
- Forestry M,D
- Geosciences M,D
- Hydrology M,D
- Mathematics M,D
- Natural Resources M,D
- Optical Sciences M,D
- Physics M,D
- Planetary and Space Sciences M,D*
- Plant Sciences M,D
- Range Science M,D
- Water Resources M,D

UNIVERSITY OF ARKANSAS
- Agricultural Sciences—General M,D

Agronomy and Soil Sciences M,D
Animal Sciences M,D
Applied Physics M,D
Chemistry M,D
Food Science and Technology M,D
Geology M
Horticulture M
Mathematics M,D
Photonics M,D
Physics M,D
Plant Sciences D
Statistics M

UNIVERSITY OF ARKANSAS AT LITTLE ROCK
Applied Mathematics M
Chemistry M
Statistics M

UNIVERSITY OF ARKANSAS AT MONTICELLO
Forestry M
Natural Resources M

THE UNIVERSITY OF BRITISH COLUMBIA
Agricultural Sciences—General M,D
Agronomy and Soil Sciences M,D
Animal Sciences M,D
Applied Mathematics M,D
Atmospheric Sciences M,D
Chemistry M,D
Environmental Management and Policy M,D
Food Science and Technology M,D
Forestry M,D
Geology M,D
Geophysics M,D
Marine Sciences M,D
Mathematics M,D
Oceanography M,D
Physics M,D
Plant Sciences M,D
Statistics M,D

UNIVERSITY OF CALGARY
Analytical Chemistry M,D
Astronomy M,D
Chemistry M,D
Environmental Management and Policy M,D
Geology M,D
Geophysics M,D
Inorganic Chemistry M,D
Mathematics M,D
Organic Chemistry M,D
Physical Chemistry M,D
Physics M,D
Statistics M,D
Theoretical Chemistry M,D

UNIVERSITY OF CALIFORNIA, BERKELEY
Applied Mathematics D
Astrophysics D
Biostatistics M,D
Chemistry M,D
Environmental Management and Policy M,D*
Environmental Sciences M,D
Forestry M,D
Geology M,D
Geophysics M,D
Mathematics M,D
Physics D
Range Science M
Statistics M,D

UNIVERSITY OF CALIFORNIA, DAVIS
Agricultural Sciences—General M
Agronomy and Soil Sciences M,D
Animal Sciences M
Applied Mathematics M,D
Atmospheric Sciences M,D
Biostatistics M,D
Chemistry M,D
Environmental Sciences M,D
Food Science and Technology M,D
Geology M,D
Horticulture M
Hydrology M,D
Mathematics M,D
Physics M,D
Statistics M,D

UNIVERSITY OF CALIFORNIA, IRVINE
Chemistry M,D
Environmental Management and Policy M,D
Geosciences M,D
Mathematics M,D
Physics M,D

UNIVERSITY OF CALIFORNIA, LOS ANGELES
Astronomy M,D
Astrophysics M,D
Atmospheric Sciences M,D
Biometrics M,D*
Biostatistics M,D
Chemistry M,D
Environmental Sciences D*
Geochemistry M,D*
Geology M,D*
Geophysics M,D
Geosciences M,D
Mathematics M,D
Physics M,D*
Planetary and Space Sciences M,D
Statistics M,D

UNIVERSITY OF CALIFORNIA, RIVERSIDE
Agronomy and Soil Sciences M,D*
Chemistry M,D*
Environmental Sciences M,D
Geology M,D*
Mathematics M,D
Physics M,D
Plant Sciences M,D
Statistics M,D

UNIVERSITY OF CALIFORNIA, SAN DIEGO
Applied Mathematics M,D
Applied Physics M,D
Chemistry M,D*
Geology M,D
Marine Sciences M,D
Mathematics M,D
Oceanography M,D
Photonics M,D
Physics M,D
Statistics M,D

UNIVERSITY OF CALIFORNIA, SAN FRANCISCO
Chemistry D*

UNIVERSITY OF CALIFORNIA, SANTA BARBARA
Applied Mathematics M
Chemistry M,D
Computational Sciences M,D
Environmental Management and Policy M,D
Environmental Sciences M,D*
Geology M,D
Geophysics M,D
Marine Sciences M,D
Mathematics M,D
Physics D
Statistics M,D

UNIVERSITY OF CALIFORNIA, SANTA CRUZ
Applied Mathematics M,D
Astronomy D
Astrophysics D
Chemistry M,D
Environmental Management and Policy D
Geosciences M,D
Marine Sciences M,D
Mathematics M,D
Physics M,D

UNIVERSITY OF CENTRAL ARKANSAS
Mathematics M

UNIVERSITY OF CENTRAL FLORIDA
Chemistry M
Mathematics M,D
Optical Sciences M,D,O
Physics M,D
Statistics M

UNIVERSITY OF CENTRAL OKLAHOMA
Applied Mathematics M
Applied Physics M
Chemistry M
Mathematics M
Statistics M

UNIVERSITY OF CHICAGO
Applied Mathematics M,D
Astronomy M,D
Astrophysics M,D
Atmospheric Sciences M,D
Chemistry D
Environmental Management and Policy M,D
Environmental Sciences M,D
Geology M,D
Geophysics M,D
Geosciences M,D
Mathematical and Computational Finance M
Mathematics M,D
Physics M,D
Planetary and Space Sciences M,D
Statistics M,D

UNIVERSITY OF CINCINNATI
Analytical Chemistry M,D
Applied Mathematics M,D
Biostatistics M,D
Chemistry M,D
Environmental Sciences M,D
Geology M,D
Inorganic Chemistry M,D
Mathematics M,D
Organic Chemistry M,D
Physical Chemistry M,D
Physics M,D
Statistics M,D

UNIVERSITY OF COLORADO AT BOULDER
Applied Mathematics M,D
Astrophysics M,D
Atmospheric Sciences M,D
Chemistry M,D
Environmental Management and Policy M,D
Geology M,D
Geophysics M,D
Mathematical Physics M,D
Mathematics M,D
Oceanography M,D
Optical Sciences M,D
Physical Chemistry M,D
Physics M,D
Plasma Physics M,D

UNIVERSITY OF COLORADO AT COLORADO SPRINGS
Applied Mathematics M
Environmental Sciences M

UNIVERSITY OF COLORADO AT DENVER
Applied Mathematics M,D
Chemistry M
Computational Sciences D
Environmental Sciences M
Mathematics M

UNIVERSITY OF COLORADO HEALTH SCIENCES CENTER
Biometrics M,D

UNIVERSITY OF CONNECTICUT
Agricultural Sciences—General M,D
Agronomy and Soil Sciences M,D
Animal Sciences M,D
Applied Mathematics M,D
Chemistry M,D
Environmental Management and Policy M,D
Geology M,D
Marine Sciences M,D
Mathematical and Computational Finance M,D
Mathematics M,D
Natural Resources M,D
Oceanography M,D
Physics M,D*
Plant Sciences M,D
Statistics M,D

UNIVERSITY OF DAYTON
Applied Mathematics M
Chemistry M
Optical Sciences M
Physics M

UNIVERSITY OF DELAWARE
Agricultural Sciences—General M,D
Agronomy and Soil Sciences M,D
Applied Mathematics M,D
Astronomy M,D
Atmospheric Sciences D
Chemistry M,D
Environmental Management and Policy M,D*
Food Science and Technology M,D*
Geology M,D*
Horticulture M,D
Marine Affairs M,D
Marine Sciences M,D
Mathematics M,D*
Oceanography M,D
Physics M,D
Plant Sciences M,D
Statistics M

UNIVERSITY OF DENVER
Applied Mathematics M
Chemistry M,D
Environmental Management and Policy M
Mathematics M,D
Physics M,D

UNIVERSITY OF DETROIT MERCY
Chemistry M
Mathematics M

UNIV
Agricult
Agronomy
Animal Scie
Applied Math
Aquaculture
Astronomy
Chemistry
Fish, Game, and Wi
Management
Food Science and Tech
Forestry
Geology
Geosciences
Horticulture
Limnology
Marine Sciences
Mathematics
Natural Resources
Physics
Plant Sciences
Statistics M,D
Water Resources M,D

UNIVERSITY OF GEORGIA
Agricultural Sciences—General M,D
Agronomy and Soil Sciences M,D
Analytical Chemistry M,D
Animal Sciences M,D
Applied Mathematics M,D
Astronomy M,D
Chemistry M,D
Food Science and Technology M,D
Forestry M,D
Geology M,D
Horticulture M,D
Inorganic Chemistry M,D
Marine Sciences M,D
Mathematics M,D
Natural Resources M,D
Oceanography M,D
Organic Chemistry M,D
Physical Chemistry M,D
Physics M,D
Statistics M,D

UNIVERSITY OF GUAM
Environmental Sciences M

UNIVERSITY OF GUELPH
Agricultural Sciences—General M,D,O
Agronomy and Soil Sciences M,D
Animal Sciences M,D
Applied Mathematics M,D
Aquaculture M
Atmospheric Sciences M,D
Chemistry M,D
Environmental Management and Policy M,D
Environmental Sciences M,D
Food Science and Technology M,D
Horticulture M,D
Mathematics M,D
Natural Resources M,D
Physics M,D
Statistics M,D

UNIVERSITY OF HAWAII AT MANOA
Agricultural Sciences—General M,D*
Animal Sciences M
Astronomy M,D
Chemistry M,D
Environmental Management and Policy M,D
Food Science and Technology M
Geochemistry M,D
Geology M,D
Geophysics M,D
Horticulture M,D
Hydrology M,D
Mathematics M,D
Meteorology M,D
Natural Resources M,D
Oceanography M,D
Physics M,D
Planetary and Space Sciences M,D
Plant Sciences M,D

UNIVERSITY OF HOUSTON
Applied Mathematics M,D
Chemistry M,D*
Geology M,D
Geophysics M,D
Mathematics M,D
Physics M,D

UNIVERSITY OF HOUSTON–CLEAR LAKE
Chemistry M
Environmental Management and Policy M
Environmental Sciences M
Mathematics M

M
M
M,D*
M,D*
M,D*
M,D
M,D*
M*
ife
M,D*
Technology M*
M,D*
M,D*
M
M
tics M,D*
s M,D*
Sciences M,D
nge Science M,D*
Statistics M*

UNIVERSITY OF ILLINOIS AT CHICAGO
Applied Mathematics M,D
Biostatistics M,D
Chemistry M,D
Geochemistry M,D
Geology M,D
Geophysics M,D
Geosciences M,D
Hydrology M,D
Mathematics M,D*
Mineralogy M,D
Physics M,D
Statistics M,D
Water Resources M,D

UNIVERSITY OF ILLINOIS AT SPRINGFIELD
Environmental Management and Policy M

UNIVERSITY OF ILLINOIS AT URBANA–CHAMPAIGN
Agricultural Sciences—General M,D
Agronomy and Soil Sciences M,D
Animal Sciences M,D
Applied Mathematics M,D
Astronomy M,D
Atmospheric Sciences M,D
Chemistry M,D
Environmental Sciences M,D
Food Science and Technology M,D
Geochemistry M,D
Geology M,D
Geophysics M,D
Geosciences M,D
Mathematics M,D
Natural Resources M,D
Physics M,D
Statistics M,D

THE UNIVERSITY OF IOWA
Applied Mathematics D
Astronomy M
Biostatistics M,D
Chemistry M,D
Computational Sciences D
Geosciences M,D
Mathematics M,D
Physics M,D
Statistics M,D,O*

UNIVERSITY OF KANSAS
Applied Mathematics M,D
Astronomy M,D
Chemistry M,D
Environmental Sciences M,D
Geology M,D
Mathematics M,D
Physics M,D*
Statistics M,D
Water Resources M,D

UNIVERSITY OF KENTUCKY
Agricultural Sciences—General M,D
Agronomy and Soil Sciences M,D
Animal Sciences M,D
Astronomy M,D
Chemistry M,D
Forestry M
Geology M,D
Mathematics M,D
Physics M,D
Plant Sciences M
Statistics M,D

THE UNIVERSITY OF LETHBRIDGE
Agricultural Sciences—General M,D
Chemistry M,D
Environmental Sciences M,D
Mathematics M,D
Physics M,D

UNIVERSITY OF LOUISIANA AT LAFAYETTE
Geology M
Mathematics M,D
Physics M

UNIVERSITY OF LOUISIANA AT MONROE
Chemistry M
Geosciences M

UNIVERSITY OF LOUISVILLE
Analytical Chemistry M,D
Applied Mathematics M,D
Biostatistics M,D
Chemistry M,D
Inorganic Chemistry M,D
Mathematics M,D
Organic Chemistry M,D
Physical Chemistry M,D
Physics M

UNIVERSITY OF MAINE
Agricultural Sciences—General M,D
Agronomy and Soil Sciences M,D
Animal Sciences M
Chemistry M,D
Environmental Management and Policy M,D
Environmental Sciences M,D
Fish, Game, and Wildlife Management M,D
Food Science and Technology M,D
Forestry M,D
Geology M,D
Geosciences M,D
Horticulture M
Marine Affairs M
Marine Sciences M,D
Mathematics M
Natural Resources M,D
Oceanography M,D
Physics M,D
Plant Sciences M,D

UNIVERSITY OF MANITOBA
Agricultural Sciences—General M,D
Agronomy and Soil Sciences M,D
Animal Sciences M,D
Chemistry M,D
Computational Sciences M
Environmental Management and Policy M,D
Food Science and Technology M
Geology M,D
Geophysics M,D
Horticulture M,D
Mathematics M,D
Physics M,D
Statistics M,D

UNIVERSITY OF MARYLAND
Environmental Sciences M,D
Marine Sciences M,D*

UNIVERSITY OF MARYLAND, BALTIMORE COUNTY
Applied Mathematics M,D
Applied Physics M,D
Atmospheric Sciences M,D
Chemistry M,D*
Environmental Sciences M,D
Marine Sciences M,D
Optical Sciences M,D
Physics M,D
Statistics M,D

UNIVERSITY OF MARYLAND, COLLEGE PARK
Agricultural Sciences—General P,M,D
Agronomy and Soil Sciences M,D
Analytical Chemistry M,D
Animal Sciences M,D
Applied Mathematics M,D
Astronomy M,D
Chemistry M,D
Environmental Sciences M,D
Food Science and Technology M,D
Geology M,D*
Horticulture D
Inorganic Chemistry M,D
Marine Sciences M,D
Mathematics M,D
Meteorology M,D
Natural Resources M,D
Organic Chemistry M,D
Physical Chemistry M,D
Physics M,D*
Statistics M,D

UNIVERSITY OF MARYLAND EASTERN SHORE
Agricultural Sciences—General M
Environmental Sciences M,D
Food Science and Technology M
Marine Sciences M,D

UNIVERSITY OF MARYLAND UNIVERSITY COLLEGE
Environmental Management and Policy M,O

UNIVERSITY OF MASSACHUSETTS AMHERST
Agronomy and Soil Sciences M,D
Animal Sciences M,D
Applied Mathematics M
Astronomy M,D
Chemistry M,D
Fish, Game, and Wildlife Management M,D
Food Science and Technology M,D
Forestry M,D
Geosciences M,D
Mathematics M,D
Physics M,D
Plant Sciences M,D
Statistics M,D

UNIVERSITY OF MASSACHUSETTS BOSTON
Applied Physics M
Chemistry M
Environmental Sciences M,D
Marine Sciences D

UNIVERSITY OF MASSACHUSETTS DARTMOUTH
Chemistry M
Marine Sciences M,D
Physics M

UNIVERSITY OF MASSACHUSETTS LOWELL
Applied Mathematics M,D
Applied Physics M,D
Chemistry M,D
Computational Sciences M,D
Environmental Management and Policy M,D,O
Environmental Sciences M,D,O
Mathematics M,D
Optical Sciences M,D
Physics M,D

UNIVERSITY OF MEDICINE AND DENTISTRY OF NEW JERSEY
Environmental Sciences D

THE UNIVERSITY OF MEMPHIS
Applied Mathematics M,D
Chemistry M,D
Geology M,D
Geophysics M,D
Geosciences M,D
Mathematics M,D
Physics M
Statistics M,D

UNIVERSITY OF MIAMI
Atmospheric Sciences M,D
Chemistry M,D
Environmental Management and Policy M,D
Fish, Game, and Wildlife Management M,D
Geology M,D
Geophysics M,D
Inorganic Chemistry M,D
Marine Affairs M
Marine Sciences M,D
Mathematics M,D
Meteorology M,D*
Oceanography M,D
Organic Chemistry M,D
Physical Chemistry M,D
Physics M,D*
Statistics M,D

UNIVERSITY OF MICHIGAN
Analytical Chemistry D
Applied Physics D
Astronomy M,D
Atmospheric Sciences M,D
Biostatistics M,D
Chemistry D
Environmental Management and Policy M,D
Forestry M,D,O
Geochemistry M,D
Geology M,D
Inorganic Chemistry D
Mathematics M,D
Mineralogy M,D
Natural Resources M,D,O
Oceanography M,D
Organic Chemistry D
Physical Chemistry D
Physics M,D*
Planetary and Space Sciences M,D
Statistics M,D

UNIVERSITY OF MICHIGAN–DEARBORN
Applied Mathematics M
Computational Sciences M
Environmental Sciences M

UNIVERSITY OF MINNESOTA, DULUTH
Applied Mathematics M*
Chemistry M
Computational Sciences M
Geology M*
Physics M*

UNIVERSITY OF MINNESOTA, TWIN CITIES CAMPUS
Agricultural Sciences—General M,D
Agronomy and Soil Sciences M,D
Animal Sciences M,D
Astronomy M,D
Astrophysics M,D
Biostatistics M,D
Chemistry M,D
Computational Sciences M,D
Environmental Management and Policy M,D
Fish, Game, and Wildlife Management M,D
Food Science and Technology M,D
Forestry M,D
Geology M,D
Geophysics M,D
Mathematics M,D
Physics M,D
Plant Sciences M,D
Statistics M,D
Water Resources M,D

UNIVERSITY OF MISSISSIPPI
Chemistry M,D
Computational Sciences M,D
Mathematics M,D
Physics M,D

UNIVERSITY OF MISSOURI–COLUMBIA
Agricultural Sciences—General M,D
Agronomy and Soil Sciences M,D
Analytical Chemistry M,D
Animal Sciences M,D
Applied Mathematics M
Astronomy M,D
Atmospheric Sciences M,D
Chemistry M,D
Fish, Game, and Wildlife Management M,D
Food Science and Technology M,D
Forestry M,D
Geology M,D
Horticulture M,D
Inorganic Chemistry M,D
Mathematics M,D
Organic Chemistry M,D
Physical Chemistry M,D
Physics M,D
Statistics M,D

UNIVERSITY OF MISSOURI–KANSAS CITY
Analytical Chemistry M,D
Chemistry M,D
Geology M,D
Geosciences M,D
Inorganic Chemistry M,D
Mathematics M,D
Organic Chemistry M,D
Physical Chemistry M,D
Physics M,D
Statistics M,D

UNIVERSITY OF MISSOURI–ROLLA
Applied Mathematics M
Chemistry M,D
Geochemistry M,D
Geology M,D
Geophysics M,D
Hydrology M,D
Mathematics M,D
Physics M,D
Water Resources M,D

UNIVERSITY OF MISSOURI–ST. LOUIS
Applied Mathematics M,D,O
Applied Physics M,D
Astrophysics M,D
Chemistry M,D
Environmental Management and Policy M,D,O
Inorganic Chemistry M,D
Mathematics M,D,O
Organic Chemistry M,D
Physical Chemistry M,D
Physics M,D

THE UNIVERSITY OF MONTANA–MISSOULA
Analytical Chemistry M,D
Chemistry M,D
Environmental Management and Policy M,D
Environmental Sciences M*
Fish, Game, and Wildlife Management M,D
Forestry M,D
Geology M,D
Inorganic Chemistry M,D
Mathematics M,D

Natural Resources M,D
Organic Chemistry M,D
Physical Chemistry M,D

UNIVERSITY OF NEBRASKA AT OMAHA

Mathematics M

UNIVERSITY OF NEBRASKA–LINCOLN

Agricultural Sciences—General M,D
Agronomy and Soil Sciences M,D
Analytical Chemistry M,D
Animal Sciences M,D
Astronomy M,D
Biometrics M
Chemistry M,D
Food Science and Technology M,D
Geosciences M,D
Horticulture M,D
Inorganic Chemistry M,D
Mathematics M,D
Natural Resources M,D
Organic Chemistry M,D
Physical Chemistry M,D
Physics M,D
Statistics M,D

UNIVERSITY OF NEVADA, LAS VEGAS

Applied Mathematics M
Chemistry M
Environmental Sciences M,D
Geosciences M,D
Mathematics M
Physics M,D
Statistics M
Water Resources M

UNIVERSITY OF NEVADA, RENO

Agricultural Sciences—General M,D
Animal Sciences M
Atmospheric Sciences M,D
Chemistry M,D
Environmental Management and Policy M
Environmental Sciences M,D
Geochemistry M,D,O
Geology M,D,O
Geophysics M,D,O
Hydrology M,D
Mathematics M
Physical Chemistry D
Physics M,D

UNIVERSITY OF NEW BRUNSWICK FREDERICTON

Chemistry M,D
Forestry M,D
Geodetic Sciences M,D,O
Geology M,D
Hydrology M,D
Mathematics M,D
Physics M,D
Statistics M,D
Water Resources M,D

UNIVERSITY OF NEW BRUNSWICK SAINT JOHN

Environmental Management and Policy M

UNIVERSITY OF NEW HAMPSHIRE

Agronomy and Soil Sciences M
Animal Sciences M,D
Applied Mathematics M,D
Atmospheric Sciences M,D
Chemistry M,D
Environmental Management and Policy M*
Fish, Game, and Wildlife Management M
Forestry M
Geochemistry M
Geology M
Geosciences M
Hydrology M
Mathematics M,D
Natural Resources D
Oceanography M,D
Physics M,D
Statistics M,D
Water Resources M

UNIVERSITY OF NEW HAVEN

Environmental Sciences M

UNIVERSITY OF NEW MEXICO

Chemistry M,D
Geosciences M,D
Mathematics M,D
Optical Sciences M,D
Physics M,D
Planetary and Space Sciences M,D
Statistics M,D
Water Resources M

UNIVERSITY OF NEW ORLEANS

Chemistry M,D
Geology M

Geophysics M
Mathematics M
Physics M,D

THE UNIVERSITY OF NORTH CAROLINA AT CHAPEL HILL

Astronomy M,D
Astrophysics M,D
Atmospheric Sciences M,D
Biostatistics M,D
Chemistry M,D
Environmental Management and Policy M,D
Environmental Sciences M,D
Geology M,D
Marine Sciences M,D
Mathematics M,D*
Physics M,D
Statistics M,D

THE UNIVERSITY OF NORTH CAROLINA AT CHARLOTTE

Applied Mathematics M,D
Applied Physics M,D
Chemistry M
Geosciences M
Mathematical and Computational Finance M
Mathematics M,D*
Optical Sciences M,D

THE UNIVERSITY OF NORTH CAROLINA AT GREENSBORO

Chemistry M
Mathematics M

THE UNIVERSITY OF NORTH CAROLINA AT WILMINGTON

Chemistry M
Geology M
Geosciences M
Marine Sciences M
Mathematics M

UNIVERSITY OF NORTH DAKOTA

Atmospheric Sciences M
Chemistry M,D
Fish, Game, and Wildlife Management M,D
Geology M,D
Geosciences M,D
Mathematics M
Physics M,D
Planetary and Space Sciences M

UNIVERSITY OF NORTHERN BRITISH COLUMBIA

Environmental Management and Policy M,D
Mathematics M,D
Natural Resources M,D

UNIVERSITY OF NORTHERN COLORADO

Chemistry M,D
Geosciences M
Mathematics M,D

UNIVERSITY OF NORTHERN IOWA

Chemistry M
Environmental Sciences M
Mathematics M

UNIVERSITY OF NORTH FLORIDA

Mathematics M
Statistics M

UNIVERSITY OF NORTH TEXAS

Chemistry M,D
Environmental Sciences M,D
Mathematics M,D
Physics M,D

UNIVERSITY OF NORTH TEXAS HEALTH SCIENCE CENTER AT FORT WORTH

Biostatistics M,D

UNIVERSITY OF NOTRE DAME

Applied Mathematics M,D
Chemistry M,D
Geosciences M,D
Inorganic Chemistry M,D
Mathematics M,D*
Organic Chemistry M,D
Physical Chemistry M,D
Physics D*

UNIVERSITY OF OKLAHOMA

Astrophysics M,D
Chemistry M,D
Environmental Sciences M,D
Geology M,D
Geophysics M
Mathematics M,D*
Meteorology M,D
Natural Resources M,D
Physics M,D

Water Resources M,D

UNIVERSITY OF OKLAHOMA HEALTH SCIENCES CENTER

Biostatistics M,D

UNIVERSITY OF OREGON

Chemistry M,D
Environmental Management and Policy M,D*
Geology M,D
Mathematics M,D
Physics M,D

UNIVERSITY OF OTTAWA

Chemistry M,D
Geosciences M,D
Mathematics M,D
Physics M,D
Statistics M,D

UNIVERSITY OF PENNSYLVANIA

Astrophysics M,D
Biostatistics M,D
Chemistry M,D
Environmental Management and Policy M
Geology M,D
Mathematics M,D
Physics M,D
Statistics M,D

UNIVERSITY OF PITTSBURGH

Applied Mathematics M,D
Biostatistics M,D
Chemistry M,D*
Environmental Management and Policy M
Geology M,D
Mathematical and Computational Finance M,D
Mathematics M,D
Physics M,D*
Planetary and Space Sciences M,D
Statistics M,D

UNIVERSITY OF PRINCE EDWARD ISLAND

Chemistry M

UNIVERSITY OF PUERTO RICO, MAYAGÜEZ CAMPUS

Agricultural Sciences—General M
Agronomy and Soil Sciences M
Animal Sciences M
Applied Mathematics M
Chemistry M
Computational Sciences M
Food Science and Technology M
Geology M
Horticulture M
Marine Sciences M,D*
Mathematics M
Oceanography M,D
Physics M
Statistics M

UNIVERSITY OF PUERTO RICO, MEDICAL SCIENCES CAMPUS

Biostatistics M

UNIVERSITY OF PUERTO RICO, RÍO PIEDRAS

Applied Physics M,D
Chemistry M,D*
Mathematics M,D
Physical Chemistry M,D
Physics M,D

UNIVERSITY OF REGINA

Analytical Chemistry M,D
Chemistry M,D
Geology M
Inorganic Chemistry M,D
Mathematics M,D
Organic Chemistry M,D
Physical Chemistry M,D
Physics M,D
Statistics M,D

UNIVERSITY OF RHODE ISLAND

Animal Sciences M
Applied Mathematics M,D
Aquaculture M
Chemistry M,D
Environmental Management and Policy M,D
Fish, Game, and Wildlife Management M,D
Food Science and Technology M,D
Geosciences M
Marine Affairs M,D
Mathematics M,D
Natural Resources M,D
Oceanography M,D
Physics M,D

UN

Astro
Biostat
Chemist
Geology
Geoscience
Mathematics
Optical Science
Physics
Statistics

UNIVERSITY OF ST.

Environmental Managem
and Policy

UNIVERSITY OF SAN DIEG

Geosciences
Marine Affairs
Marine Sciences

UNIVERSITY OF SAN FRANCISCO

Chemistry
Environmental Management and Policy M

UNIVERSITY OF SASKATCHEWAN

Agricultural Sciences—General M,D
Agronomy and Soil Sciences M,D
Animal Sciences M,D
Chemistry M,D
Food Science and Technology M,D
Geology M,D,O
Mathematics M,D
Physics M,D
Plant Sciences M,D
Statistics M,D

THE UNIVERSITY OF SCRANTON

Chemistry M

UNIVERSITY OF SOUTH ALABAMA

Marine Sciences M,D
Mathematics M

UNIVERSITY OF SOUTH CAROLINA

Astronomy M,D
Biostatistics M,D
Chemistry M,D
Environmental Management and Policy M
Environmental Sciences M,D
Geology M,D
Geosciences M,D
Marine Sciences M,D
Mathematics M,D
Physics M,D*
Statistics M,D,O

THE UNIVERSITY OF SOUTH DAKOTA

Chemistry M
Mathematics M

UNIVERSITY OF SOUTHERN CALIFORNIA

Applied Mathematics M,D
Biometrics M
Biostatistics M,D*
Chemistry M,D
Geosciences M,D
Marine Sciences D
Mathematics M,D
Oceanography D
Physical Chemistry D
Physics M,D
Statistics M

UNIVERSITY OF SOUTHERN MAINE

Statistics M

UNIVERSITY OF SOUTHERN MISSISSIPPI

Analytical Chemistry M,D
Astronomy M
Chemistry M,D
Food Science and Technology M,D
Geology M
Hydrology M,D
Inorganic Chemistry M,D
Marine Sciences M,D
Mathematics M
Organic Chemistry M,D
Physical Chemistry M,D
Physics M

UNIVERSITY OF SOUTH FLORIDA

Analytical Chemistry M,D
Applied Mathematics M,D
Biostatistics M,D
Chemistry M,D
Computational Sciences M,D
Environmental Management and Policy M,D
Environmental Sciences M,D
Geology M,D

M,D
M,D
M,D*
M,D
M,D
M,D
M,D
M,D

NNESSEE

General M,D
M,D
M,D
cs M,D
M,D
Management M,D
e, and Wildlife
ement M
cience and Technology M,D
try M
ology M,D
orticulture M
Inorganic Chemistry M,D
Mathematics M,D
Organic Chemistry M,D
Physical Chemistry M,D
Physics M,D
Statistics M,D
Theoretical Chemistry M,D

THE UNIVERSITY OF TENNESSEE AT CHATTANOOGA

Environmental Sciences M

THE UNIVERSITY OF TENNESSEE AT MARTIN

Food Science and Technology M

THE UNIVERSITY OF TENNESSEE SPACE INSTITUTE

Applied Mathematics M
Physics M,D

THE UNIVERSITY OF TEXAS AT ARLINGTON

Chemistry M,D*
Environmental Sciences M,D
Geology M,D
Geosciences M,D
Mathematics M,D
Physics M,D

THE UNIVERSITY OF TEXAS AT AUSTIN

Analytical Chemistry M,D
Applied Mathematics M,D
Astronomy M,D
Chemistry M,D
Computational Sciences M,D
Environmental Management and Policy M
Geology M,D
Geosciences M,D
Inorganic Chemistry M,D
Marine Sciences M,D*
Mathematics M,D
Organic Chemistry M,D
Physical Chemistry M,D
Physics M,D*
Statistics M

THE UNIVERSITY OF TEXAS AT DALLAS

Applied Mathematics M,D
Chemistry M,D
Geosciences M,D
Mathematics M,D*
Physics M,D
Statistics M,D

THE UNIVERSITY OF TEXAS AT EL PASO

Chemistry M
Environmental Sciences M,D
Geology M,D
Geophysics M
Mathematics M
Physics M
Statistics M

THE UNIVERSITY OF TEXAS AT SAN ANTONIO

Applied Mathematics M
Chemistry M
Environmental Sciences M,D
Geology M,D
Statistics M

THE UNIVERSITY OF TEXAS AT TYLER

Chemistry M
Mathematics M

THE UNIVERSITY OF TEXAS HEALTH SCIENCE CENTER AT HOUSTON

Biometrics M,D*

THE UNIVERSITY OF TEXAS OF THE PERMIAN BASIN

Geology M

THE UNIVERSITY OF TEXAS–PAN AMERICAN

Mathematics M

UNIVERSITY OF THE DISTRICT OF COLUMBIA

Mathematics M

UNIVERSITY OF THE INCARNATE WORD

Mathematics M

UNIVERSITY OF THE SCIENCES IN PHILADELPHIA

Chemistry M,D

UNIVERSITY OF TOLEDO

Analytical Chemistry M,D
Applied Mathematics M,D
Chemistry M,D*
Environmental Sciences D*
Geology M,D
Geosciences M,D
Inorganic Chemistry M,D
Mathematics M,D*
Organic Chemistry M,D
Physical Chemistry M,D
Physics M,D*
Statistics M,D

UNIVERSITY OF TORONTO

Astronomy M,D
Chemistry M,D
Forestry M,D
Geology M,D
Mathematics M,D
Physics M,D
Statistics M,D

UNIVERSITY OF TULSA

Chemistry M
Geology M
Geosciences M,D
Mathematics M

UNIVERSITY OF UTAH

Biostatistics M,D
Chemistry M,D
Geology M,D
Geophysics M,D
Mathematics M,D*
Meteorology M,D
Physical Chemistry M,D
Physics M,D
Statistics M

UNIVERSITY OF VERMONT

Agricultural Sciences—General M,D
Agronomy and Soil Sciences M,D
Animal Sciences M,D
Biostatistics M
Chemistry M,D
Environmental Management and Policy M,D
Fish, Game, and Wildlife Management M
Forestry M
Geology M
Mathematics M,D
Physics M
Plant Sciences M,D
Statistics M
Water Resources M

UNIVERSITY OF VICTORIA

Applied Mathematics M,D
Astronomy M,D
Astrophysics M,D
Chemistry M,D
Condensed Matter Physics M,D
Geochemistry M,D
Geology M,D
Geophysics M,D
Geosciences M,D
Mathematics M,D
Oceanography M,D
Physics M,D
Statistics M,D
Theoretical Physics M,D

UNIVERSITY OF VIRGINIA

Astronomy M,D
Chemistry M,D
Environmental Sciences M,D
Mathematics M,D
Physics M,D
Statistics M,D

UNIVERSITY OF WASHINGTON

Applied Mathematics M,D
Applied Physics M,D
Astronomy M,D
Atmospheric Sciences M,D
Biostatistics M,D
Chemistry M,D
Environmental Management and Policy M,D*
Fish, Game, and Wildlife Management M,D
Forestry M,D
Geology M,D
Geophysics M,D
Horticulture M,D
Hydrology M,D
Marine Affairs M
Mathematics M,D
Oceanography M,D
Physics M,D
Statistics M,D

UNIVERSITY OF WATERLOO

Applied Mathematics M,D
Biostatistics M,D
Chemistry M,D
Environmental Management and Policy M
Geosciences M,D
Mathematics M,D
Physics M,D
Statistics M,D

THE UNIVERSITY OF WESTERN ONTARIO

Applied Mathematics M,D
Astronomy M,D
Biostatistics M,D
Chemistry M,D
Environmental Sciences M,D
Geology M,D
Geophysics M,D
Geosciences M,D
Mathematics M,D
Physics M,D
Plant Sciences M,D
Statistics M,D

UNIVERSITY OF WEST FLORIDA

Marine Affairs M
Mathematics M
Statistics M

UNIVERSITY OF WINDSOR

Chemistry M,D
Geosciences M,D
Mathematics M,D
Physics M,D
Statistics M,D

UNIVERSITY OF WISCONSIN–GREEN BAY

Environmental Management and Policy M
Environmental Sciences M

UNIVERSITY OF WISCONSIN–LA CROSSE

Marine Sciences M

UNIVERSITY OF WISCONSIN–MADISON

Agricultural Sciences—General M,D
Agronomy and Soil Sciences M,D
Animal Sciences M,D
Astronomy D
Atmospheric Sciences M,D
Biometrics M
Chemistry M,D
Environmental Management and Policy M,D
Environmental Sciences M,D
Food Science and Technology M,D
Forestry M,D
Geology M,D
Geophysics M,D
Horticulture M,D
Limnology M,D
Marine Sciences M,D
Mathematics M,D
Oceanography M,D
Physics M,D
Plant Sciences M,D
Statistics M,D
Water Resources M

UNIVERSITY OF WISCONSIN–MILWAUKEE

Chemistry M,D
Geology M,D
Mathematics M,D
Physics M,D

UNIVERSITY OF WISCONSIN–OSHKOSH

Physics M

UNIVERSITY OF WISCONSIN–RIVER FALLS

Agricultural Sciences—General M

UNIVERSITY OF WISCONSIN–STEVENS POINT

Natural Resources M

UNIVERSITY OF WISCONSIN–STOUT

Food Science and Technology M

UNIVERSITY OF WYOMING

Agricultural Sciences—General M,D
Agronomy and Soil Sciences M,D
Animal Sciences M,D
Atmospheric Sciences M,D
Chemistry M,D
Food Science and Technology M
Geology M,D
Geophysics M,D
Mathematics M,D
Natural Resources M,D
Range Science M,D
Statistics M,D
Water Resources M,D

UTAH STATE UNIVERSITY

Agricultural Sciences—General M,D
Agronomy and Soil Sciences M,D
Animal Sciences M,D
Applied Mathematics M,D
Chemistry M,D*
Environmental Management and Policy M,D
Fish, Game, and Wildlife Management M,D
Food Science and Technology M,D
Forestry M,D
Geology M
Mathematics M,D
Meteorology M,D
Natural Resources M
Physics M,D
Plant Sciences M,D
Range Science M,D
Statistics M,D

VANDERBILT UNIVERSITY

Analytical Chemistry M,D
Astronomy M,D
Chemistry M,D*
Environmental Management and Policy M,D
Geology M
Inorganic Chemistry M,D
Mathematics M,D
Organic Chemistry M,D
Physical Chemistry M,D
Physics M,D
Theoretical Chemistry M,D

VASSAR COLLEGE

Chemistry M

VERMONT LAW SCHOOL

Environmental Management and Policy M

VILLANOVA UNIVERSITY

Chemistry M*
Mathematics M
Statistics M

VIRGINIA COMMONWEALTH UNIVERSITY

Applied Mathematics M
Applied Physics M
Biostatistics M,D
Chemistry M,D
Environmental Management and Policy M
Environmental Sciences M
Mathematics M,O
Physics M
Statistics M,O

VIRGINIA POLYTECHNIC INSTITUTE AND STATE UNIVERSITY

Agricultural Sciences—General M,D
Agronomy and Soil Sciences M,D
Animal Sciences M,D
Applied Mathematics M,D
Applied Physics M,D
Chemistry M,D
Computational Sciences D
Environmental Sciences M,D
Fish, Game, and Wildlife Management M,D
Food Science and Technology M,D
Forestry M,D
Geology M,D
Geophysics M,D
Horticulture M,D
Mathematical Physics M,D
Mathematics M,D
Natural Resources M,D
Physics M,D
Statistics M,D

VIRGINIA STATE UNIVERSITY

Mathematics M
Physics M

WAKE FOREST UNIVERSITY

Analytical Chemistry M,D
Chemistry M,D
Inorganic Chemistry M,D
Mathematics M
Organic Chemistry M,D
Physical Chemistry M,D

Physics M,D*

WASHINGTON STATE UNIVERSITY

Agricultural Sciences—General M,D
Agronomy and Soil Sciences M,D
Analytical Chemistry M,D
Animal Sciences M,D
Chemistry M,D
Environmental Sciences M,D*
Food Science and Technology M,D
Geology M,D
Horticulture M,D
Inorganic Chemistry M,D
Mathematics M,D*
Natural Resources M,D
Organic Chemistry M,D
Physical Chemistry M,D
Physics M,D

WASHINGTON STATE UNIVERSITY TRI-CITIES

Chemistry M
Environmental Sciences M

WASHINGTON STATE UNIVERSITY VANCOUVER

Environmental Sciences M

WASHINGTON UNIVERSITY IN ST. LOUIS

Chemistry M,D
Computational Sciences D
Geochemistry M,D
Geology M,D
Geophysics M,D
Geosciences M,D
Mathematics M,D
Physics M,D*
Planetary and Space Sciences M,D
Statistics M,D

WAYNE STATE UNIVERSITY

Applied Mathematics M,D
Chemistry M,D
Food Science and Technology M,D,O
Geology M
Mathematics M,D
Physics M,D
Statistics M,D

WEBSTER UNIVERSITY

Environmental Management and Policy M,D

WESLEYAN UNIVERSITY

Astronomy M
Chemistry M,D*
Geosciences M
Inorganic Chemistry M,D
Mathematics M,D*
Organic Chemistry M,D
Physical Chemistry M,D
Physics M,D*
Theoretical Chemistry M,D

WESLEY COLLEGE

Environmental Sciences M

WEST CHESTER UNIVERSITY OF PENNSYLVANIA

Astronomy M
Chemistry M
Geology M
Mathematics M

WESTERN CAROLINA UNIVERSITY

Chemistry M
Mathematics M

WESTERN CONNECTICUT STATE UNIVERSITY

Environmental Sciences M
Geosciences M
Mathematics M
Planetary and Space Sciences M

WESTERN ILLINOIS UNIVERSITY

Chemistry M
Mathematics M
Physics M

WESTERN KENTUCKY UNIVERSITY

Agricultural Sciences—General M
Chemistry M
Geology M
Mathematics M

WESTERN MICHIGAN UNIVERSITY

Applied Mathematics M
Biostatistics M
Chemistry M,D
Computational Sciences M
Geology M,D
Geosciences M
Mathematics M,D
Physics M,D
Statistics M,D

WESTERN WASHINGTON UNIVERSITY

Chemistry M
Environmental Sciences M
Geology M
Mathematics M

WEST TEXAS A&M UNIVERSITY

Agricultural Sciences—General M,D
Animal Sciences M
Chemistry M
Environmental Sciences M
Mathematics M
Plant Sciences M

WEST VIRGINIA UNIVERSITY

Agricultural Sciences—General M,D
Agronomy and Soil Sciences M,D
Analytical Chemistry M,D
Animal Sciences M,D
Applied Mathematics M,D
Applied Physics M,D
Chemistry M,D
Condensed Matter Physics M,D
Environmental Management and Policy M,D
Fish, Game, and Wildlife Management M
Food Science and Technology M,D
Forestry M,D
Geology M,D
Geophysics M,D
Horticulture M
Hydrology M,D
Inorganic Chemistry M,D
Mathematics M,D
Natural Resources D
Organic Chemistry M,D
Physical Chemistry M,D
Physics M,D
Plant Sciences M,D
Plasma Physics M,D
Statistics M,D
Theoretical Chemistry M,D
Theoretical Physics M,D

WICHITA STATE UNIVERSITY

Applied Mathematics M,D
Chemistry M,D
Environmental Sciences M
Geology M
Mathematics M,D
Physics M
Statistics M,D

WILKES UNIVERSITY

Mathematics M

WILLIAM PATERSON UNIVERSITY OF NEW JERSEY

Limnology M

WINTHROP UNIVERSITY

Mathematics M

WOODS HOLE OCEANOGRAPHIC INSTITUTION

Geochemistry M,D,O
Geophysics M,D,O
Oceanography M,D,O*

WORCESTER POLYTECHNIC INSTITUTE

Applied Mathematics M,D,O

Sta

WRIG

Applied
Chemistry
Environme
and Policy
Environmental
Geochemistry
Geology
Geophysics
Hydrology
Mathematics
Physics
Statistics

YALE UNIVERSITY

Applied Mathematics
Applied Physics
Astronomy
Biostatistics
Chemistry
Computational Sciences
Environmental Management and Policy M,D
Environmental Sciences M,D
Forestry M,D*
Geochemistry D
Geology D*
Geophysics D
Geosciences D
Inorganic Chemistry D
Mathematics M,D
Meteorology D
Mineralogy D
Oceanography D
Organic Chemistry D
Physical Chemistry D
Physics D*
Statistics M,D

YORK UNIVERSITY

Applied Mathematics M,D
Astronomy M,D
Chemistry M,D
Environmental Management and Policy M,D
Geosciences M,D
Mathematics M,D
Physics M,D
Planetary and Space Sciences M,D
Statistics M,D

YOUNGSTOWN STATE UNIVERSITY

Chemistry M
Environmental Management and Policy M,O
Mathematics M

ACADEMIC AND PROFESSIONAL PROGRAMS IN THE PHYSICAL SCIENCES

Section 1
Astronomy and Astrophysics

This section contains a directory of institutions offering graduate work in astronomy and astrophysics, followed by in-depth entries submitted by institutions that chose to prepare detailed program descriptions. Additional information about programs listed in the directory but not augmented by an in-depth entry may be obtained by writing directly to the dean of a graduate school or chair of a department at the address given in the directory.

For programs offering related work, see also in this book Geosciences, Meteorology and Atmospheric Sciences, and Physics. In Book 3, see Biological and Biomedical Sciences and Biophysics; and in Book 5, see Aerospace/Aeronautical Engineering, Energy and Power Engineering (Nuclear Engineering), Engineering and Applied Sciences, and Mechanical Engineering and Mechanics.

CONTENTS

Program Directories

In-Depth Descriptions

See:

Astronomy

...llege, College of Liberal Arts and Sciences, Depart- ... AZ 85287. Offers MNS, MS, PhD. *Degree requirements:* ...en exams; for doctorate, thesis/dissertation. *Entrance* ...ctorate, GRE. *Expenses:* Tuition, state resident: full-time ... hour. Tuition, nonresident: full-time $12,228; part-time $510 ...87; $22 per semester. Part-time tuition and fees vary accord- ...*arch:* Electromagnetic interaction of hadrons, investigation of ... activity of various elements formed in fission processes; phase

...raduate School of Arts and Sciences, Department of Astronomy, ...fers MA, PhD. *Students:* 29 full-time (15 women), 2 part-time; includes 1 ...ndian/Alaska Native), 9 international. Average age 27. 76 applicants, 39% ...lled. In 2003, 5 master's, 2 doctorates awarded. Terminal master's awarded ...etion of doctoral program. *Degree requirements:* For master's, one foreign ...is or alternative, comprehensive exam, registration; for doctorate, one foreign ...esis/dissertation, comprehensive exam, registration. *Entrance requirements:* For ...nd doctorate, GRE General Test, GRE Subject Test (physics), 3 letters of ...endation. Additional exam requirements/recommendations for international students: ...ed—TOEFL (minimum score 550 paper-based; 213 computer-based). *Application ...line:* For fall admission, 1/15 for domestic students, 1/15 for international students. ...plication fee: $60. *Expenses:* Tuition: Full-time $28,512; part-time $891 per credit hour. *...inancial support:* In 2003–04, 31 students received support, including 1 fellowship (averaging $15,500 per year), 19 research assistantships (averaging $15,000 per year), 8 teaching assistantships (averaging $15,000 per year); Federal Work-Study and unspecified assistantships also available. Support available to part-time students. Financial award application deadline: 1/15; financial award applicants required to submit FAFSA. *Unit head:* Harlan E. Spence, Chairman, 617-353-7412, Fax: 617-353-6463, E-mail: spence@bu.edu. *Application contact:* Kristin M. Sacca, Department Administrator, 617-363-2625, Fax: 617-353-5704, E-mail: ksacca@bu.edu.

Bowling Green State University, Graduate College, College of Arts and Sciences, Department of Physics and Astronomy, Bowling Green, OH 43403. Offers physics (MAT, MS); physics and astronomy (MAT). *Faculty:* 8 full-time. *Students:* 8 full-time (1 woman), 12 part-time (9 women), 6 international. Average age 32. 21 applicants, 62% accepted, 4 enrolled. In 2003, 5 degrees awarded. *Degree requirements:* For master's, thesis or alternative. *Entrance requirements:* For master's, GRE General Test. Additional exam requirements/recommendations for international students: Required—TOEFL. Application fee: $30. Electronic applications accepted. *Expenses:* Tuition, state resident: part-time $436 per hour. Tuition, nonresident: part-time $768 per hour. *Financial support:* In 2003–04, 7 teaching assistantships with full tuition reimbursements (averaging $10,242 per year) were awarded; research assistantships with full tuition reimbursements, career-related internships or fieldwork, institutionally sponsored loans, and unspecified assistantships also available. Financial award applicants required to submit FAFSA. *Faculty research:* Computational physics, solid-state physics, materials science, theoretical physics. *Unit head:* Dr. John Laird, Chair, 419-372-7244. *Application contact:* Dr. Lewis Fulcher, Graduate Coordinator, 419-372-2635.

Brigham Young University, Graduate Studies, College of Physical and Mathematical Sciences, Department of Physics and Astronomy, Provo, UT 84602-1001. Offers physics (MS, PhD); physics and astronomy (PhD). Part-time programs available. *Faculty:* 31 full-time (0 women). *Students:* 24 full-time (11 women), 12 part-time (3 women); includes 5 minority (4 Asian Americans or Pacific Islanders, 1 Hispanic American). Average age 28. 19 applicants, 37% accepted, 7 enrolled. In 2003, 11 master's, 1 doctorate awarded. Terminal master's awarded for partial completion of doctoral program. *Median time to degree:* Master's–2.3 years full-time; doctorate–7.25 years full-time. Of those who began their doctoral program in fall 1995, 100% received their degree in 8 years or less. *Degree requirements:* For master's, thesis/dissertation, registration; for doctorate, thesis/dissertation, comprehensive exam, registration. *Entrance requirements:* For master's and doctorate, GRE Subject Test (physics), minimum GPA of 3.0 in last 60 hours. Additional exam requirements/recommendations for international students: Required—TOEFL (minimum score 550 paper-based; 213 computer-based). *Application deadline:* For fall admission, 1/15 priority date for domestic students, 1/15 priority date for international students. Application fee: $50. Electronic applications accepted. *Expenses:* Tuition: Part-time $221 per hour. *Financial support:* In 2003–04, 2 fellowships with full tuition reimbursements (averaging $15,000 per year), 8 research assistantships with full tuition reimbursements (averaging $15,000 per year), 18 teaching assistantships with full tuition reimbursements (averaging $15,000 per year) were awarded. Career-related internships or fieldwork, institutionally sponsored loans, and tuition waivers (partial) also available. Support available to part-time students. Financial award application deadline: 1/15. *Faculty research:* Acoustics; astrophysics; atomic, molecular, and optical physics; plasma; theoretical and mathematical physics. Total annual research expenditures: $807,360. *Unit head:* Dr. Scott D. Sommerfeldt, Graduate Coordinator, 801-422-2205, Fax: 801-422-0553, E-mail: scott_sommerfeldt@byu.edu. *Application contact:* Dr. Ross L. Spencer, Graduate Coordinator, 801-422-2341, Fax: 801-422-0553, E-mail: graduatep_physics@byu.edu.

California Institute of Technology, Division of Physics, Mathematics and Astronomy, Department of Astronomy, Pasadena, CA 91125-0001. Offers PhD. *Degree requirements:* For doctorate, one foreign language, thesis/dissertation, candidacy and final exams. *Entrance requirements:* For doctorate, GRE General Test, GRE Subject Test. Additional exam requirements/recommendations for international students: Required—TOEFL. *Faculty research:* Observational and theoretical astrophysics, cosmology, radio astronomy, solar physics.

Case Western Reserve University, School of Graduate Studies, Department of Astronomy, Cleveland, OH 44106. Offers MS, PhD. Part-time programs available. *Faculty:* 3 full-time, 1 part-time/adjunct (0 women). *Students:* 7 applicants, 0% accepted. In 2003, 1 degree awarded. *Degree requirements:* For doctorate, thesis/dissertation. *Entrance requirements:* For master's and doctorate, GRE General Test, GRE Subject Test (physics). Additional exam requirements/recommendations for international students: Required—TOEFL. *Application deadline:* Applications are processed on a rolling basis. Application fee: $50. *Expenses:* Tuition: Full-time $26,900. *Financial support:* Fellowships, research assistantships available. *Faculty research:* Ground-based optical astronomy, high- and low-dispersion spectroscopy, theoretical astrophysics, galactic structure. *Unit head:* R. Earle Luck, Chairman, 216-368-6697, Fax: 216-368-5406, E-mail: luck@fafnir.astr.cwru.edu. *Application contact:* Linda Day, Department Assistant, 216-368-3728, Fax: 216-368-5406, E-mail: lmd3@po.cwru.edu.

Clemson University, Graduate School, College of Engineering and Science, Department of Physics and Astronomy, Program in Physics, Clemson, SC 29634. Offers astronomy and astrophysics (MS, PhD); atmospheric physics (MS, PhD); biophysics (MS, PhD). Part-time programs available. *Students:* 40 full-time (11 women), 5 part-time; includes 1 minority (African American), 19 international. 59 applicants, 53% accepted, 8 enrolled. In 2003, 7 master's, 5 doctorates awarded. Terminal master's awarded for partial completion of doctoral program. *Degree requirements:* For master's, thesis or alternative; for doctorate, thesis/dissertation. *Entrance requirements:* For master's and doctorate, GRE General Test. Additional exam requirements/recommendations for international students: Required—TOEFL. *Application deadline:* For fall admission, 2/15 for domestic students. Applications are processed on a rolling basis. Application fee: $40. *Expenses:* Tuition, state resident: full-time $7,432. Tuition, nonresident: full-time $14,732. *Financial support:* Fellowships, research assistantships, teaching assistantships available. Financial award application deadline: 6/1; financial award applicants required to submit FAFSA. *Faculty research:* Radiation physics, solid-state physics, nuclear physics, radar and lidar studies of atmosphere. *Unit head:* Dr. Brad Myer, Head, 864-656-5320. *Application contact:* Dr. Miguel Larsen, Coordinator, 864-656-5309, Fax: 864-656-0805, E-mail: milarsen@clemson.edu.

Columbia University, Graduate School of Arts and Sciences, Division of Natural Sciences, Department of Astronomy, New York, NY 10027. Offers M Phil, MA, PhD. Part-time programs available. *Faculty:* 9 full-time, 2 part-time/adjunct. *Students:* 14 full-time (5 women), 1 part-time; includes 1 minority (Asian American or Pacific Islander), 5 international. Average age 30. 47 applicants, 19% accepted. In 2003, 1 degree awarded. *Degree requirements:* For doctorate, thesis/dissertation. *Entrance requirements:* For master's and doctorate, GRE General Test, major in astronomy or physics. Additional exam requirements/recommendations for international students: Required—TOEFL. Application fee: $75. *Expenses:* Tuition: Full-time $14,820. *Financial support:* Fellowships, teaching assistantships, Federal Work-Study and institutionally sponsored loans available. Support available to part-time students. Financial award application deadline: 1/5; financial award applicants required to submit FAFSA. *Faculty research:* Theoretical astrophysics, x-ray astronomy, radio astronomy. *Unit head:* David Helfand, Chair, 212-854-3278, Fax: 212-854-8121. *Application contact:* Information Contact, 212-854-6850, Fax: 212-854-8121.

Cornell University, Graduate School, Graduate Fields of Arts and Sciences, Field of Astronomy and Space Sciences, Ithaca, NY 14853-0001. Offers astronomy (PhD); astrophysics (PhD); general space sciences (PhD); infrared astronomy (PhD); planetary studies (PhD); radio astronomy (PhD); radiophysics (PhD); theoretical astrophysics (PhD). *Faculty:* 28 full-time. *Students:* 31 full-time (11 women), 16 international. 103 applicants, 21% accepted, 6 enrolled. In 2003, 2 doctorates awarded. *Degree requirements:* For doctorate, thesis/dissertation, comprehensive exam. *Entrance requirements:* For doctorate, GRE General Test, GRE Subject Test (physics), 3 letters of recommendation. Additional exam requirements/recommendations for international students: Required—TOEFL (minimum score 600 paper-based; 250 computer-based). *Application deadline:* For fall admission, 1/15 for domestic students. Application fee: $60. Electronic applications accepted. *Expenses:* Tuition: Full-time $28,630. One-time fee: $50 full-time. *Financial support:* In 2003–04, 30 students received support, including 8 fellowships with full tuition reimbursements available, 14 research assistantships with full tuition reimbursements available, 8 teaching assistantships with full tuition reimbursements available; institutionally sponsored loans, scholarships/grants, health care benefits, tuition waivers (full and partial), and unspecified assistantships also available. Financial award applicants required to submit FAFSA. *Faculty research:* Observational astrophysics, planetary sciences, cosmology, instrumentation, gravitational astrophysics. *Unit head:* Director of Graduate Studies, 607-255-4341. *Application contact:* Graduate Field Assistant, 607-255-4341, E-mail: oconnor@astro.cornell.edu.

Dartmouth College, School of Arts and Sciences, Department of Physics and Astronomy, Hanover, NH 03755. Offers MS, PhD. *Faculty:* 11 full-time (3 women). *Students:* 32 full-time (11 women); includes 1 minority (African American), 13 international. Average age 25. 251 applicants, 14% accepted, 13 enrolled. In 2003, 2 master's, 5 doctorates awarded. Terminal master's awarded for partial completion of doctoral program. *Degree requirements:* For master's and doctorate, thesis/dissertation. *Entrance requirements:* For master's and doctorate, GRE General Test, GRE Subject Test. Additional exam requirements/recommendations for international students: Required—TOEFL. *Application deadline:* For fall admission, 2/1 for domestic students. Application fee: $15. *Expenses:* Tuition: Full-time $28,965. *Financial support:* In 2003–04, 32 students received support, including fellowships with full tuition reimbursements available (averaging $18,528 per year), research assistantships with full tuition reimbursements available (averaging $18,528 per year); institutionally sponsored loans, scholarships/grants, and tuition waivers (full) also available. *Faculty research:* Matter physics, plasma and beam physics, space physics, astronomy, cosmology. Total annual research expenditures: $2.4 million. *Unit head:* Mary K. Hudson, Chair, 603-646-0350, Fax: 603-646-1446, E-mail: mary.k.hudson@dartmouth.edu. *Application contact:* Jean Blandin, Administrative Assistant, 603-646-2854, Fax: 603-646-1446, E-mail: jean.blandin@dartmouth.edu.

Georgia State University, College of Arts and Sciences, Department of Physics and Astronomy, Program in Astronomy, Atlanta, GA 30303-3083. Offers PhD. *Degree requirements:* For doctorate, 2 foreign languages, thesis/dissertation, exam. *Entrance requirements:* For doctorate, GRE General Test, GRE Subject Test. Additional exam requirements/recommendations for international students: Required—TOEFL. Electronic applications accepted. *Faculty research:* Extragalactic photometry, theoretical astrophysics, young stellar objects.

Harvard University, Graduate School of Arts and Sciences, Department of Astronomy, Cambridge, MA 02138. Offers astronomy (AM, PhD); astrophysics (AM, PhD). *Degree requirements:* For doctorate, thesis/dissertation, paper, research project, teaching 2 semesters. *Entrance requirements:* For master's, GRE General Test; for doctorate, GRE General Test, GRE Subject Test (physics). Additional exam requirements/recommendations for international students: Required—TOEFL. Electronic applications accepted. *Expenses:* Tuition: Full-time $26,066. Full-time tuition and fees vary according to program and student level. *Faculty research:* Atomic and molecular physics, electromagnetism, solar physics, nuclear physics, fluid dynamics.

Indiana University Bloomington, Graduate School, College of Arts and Sciences, Department of Astronomy, Bloomington, IN 47405. Offers astronomy (MA, PhD); astrophysics (PhD). PhD offered through the University Graduate School. Part-time programs available. *Faculty:* 8 full-time (3 women). *Students:* 10 full-time (2 women), 6 part-time (1 woman), 4 international. Average age 25. In 2003, 4 master's, 1 doctorate awarded. Terminal master's awarded for partial completion of doctoral program. *Degree requirements:* For master's, thesis, oral exam; for doctorate, thesis/dissertation, written qualifying exam. *Entrance requirements:* For master's and doctorate, GRE General Test, GRE Subject Test (physics), BA or BS in science. Additional exam requirements/recommendations for international students: Required—TOEFL. *Application deadline:* For fall admission, 1/15 priority date for domestic students, 12/15 priority date for international students; for spring admission, 9/1 priority date for domestic students, 9/1 priority date for international students. Applications are processed on a rolling basis. Application fee: $45 ($55 for international students). Electronic applications accepted. *Expenses:* Tuition, state resident: full-time $4,908; part-time $205 per credit. Tuition, nonresident: full-time $14,298; part-time $596 per credit. Required fees: $661. Tuition and fees vary according to campus/location and program. *Financial support:* In 2003–04, 2 fellowships, 2 research assistantships (averaging $12,000 per year), 7 teaching assistantships (averaging $11,000 per year) were awarded. Federal Work-Study and tuition waivers (full and partial) also available. Support available to part-time students. Financial award application deadline: 5/2. *Faculty research:* Galaxies and cosmology, stellar astronomy, cataclysmic variables, high-energy astrophysics, globular clusters. *Unit head:* Dr. R. Kent Honeycutt, Chair, 812-855-6912, Fax: 812-855-8725, E-mail: honey@astro.indiana.edu. *Application contact:* Brenda Records, Secretary, 812-855-6912, Fax: 812-855-8725, E-mail: brecords@indiana.edu.

Iowa State University of Science and Technology, Graduate College, College of Liberal Arts and Sciences, Department of Physics and Astronomy, Ames, IA 50011. Offers applied physics (MS, PhD); astrophysics (MS, PhD); condensed matter physics (MS, PhD); high energy physics (MS, PhD); nuclear physics (MS, PhD); physics (MS, PhD). Part-time programs available. *Faculty:* 45 full-time, 4 part-time/adjunct. *Students:* 83 full-time (12 women), 5 part-time; includes 1 minority (Hispanic American), 66 international. 174 applicants, 59% accepted, 31 enrolled. In 2003, 3 master's, 4 doctorates awarded. Terminal master's awarded for partial completion of doctoral program. *Median time to degree:* Master's–2.9 years full-time; doctorate–7.1 years full-time. *Degree requirements:* For master's, thesis (for some programs); for doctorate, thesis/dissertation. *Entrance requirements:* For master's and doctorate, GRE General Test, GRE Subject Test (physics). Additional exam requirements/recommendations for international students: Required—TOEFL (paper score 550; computer score 213) or IELTS (score 6.5). *Application deadline:* For fall admission, 2/15 priority date for domestic students, 2/15 priority date for international students; for spring admission, 10/15 for domestic students, 10/15 for international students. Applications are processed on a rolling basis. Application fee: $30 ($70 for international students). Electronic applications accepted. Tuition, nonresident: part-time $560 per credit. Required fees: $38 per unit. *Financial support:* In 2003–04, 38 research assistantships with full tuition reimbursements (averaging $17,400 per year), 42 teaching assistantships with full tuition reimbursements (averaging $17,400 per year) were awarded. Fellowships, Federal Work-Study, institutionally sponsored loans, scholarships/grants, health care benefits, and unspecified assistantships also available. Support available to part-time students. Financial award application deadline: 2/15. *Faculty research:* Condensed-matter physics, including superconductivity and new materials; high-energy and nuclear physics; astronomy and astrophysics; atmospheric and environmental physics. Total annual research expenditures: $8.8 million. *Unit head:* Dr. Eli Rosenberg, Chair, 515-294-5441, Fax: 515-294-6027, E-mail: phys_astro@iastate.edu. *Application contact:* Dr. Steven Kawaler, Director of Graduate Education, 515-294-9728, E-mail: phys_astro@iastate.edu.

The Johns Hopkins University, Zanvyl Krieger School of Arts and Sciences, Henry A. Rowland Department of Physics and Astronomy, Baltimore, MD 21218-2699. Offers astronomy (PhD); physics (PhD). *Faculty:* 32 full-time (3 women), 1 part-time/adjunct (0 women). *Students:* 104 full-time (26 women); includes 5 minority (1 African American, 1 American Indian/Alaska Native, 2 Asian Americans or Pacific Islanders, 1 Hispanic American), 49 international. Average age 25. 384 applicants, 26% accepted, 32 enrolled. In 2003, 16 doctorates awarded. *Median time to degree:* Doctorate–6.5 years full-time. Of those who began their doctoral program in fall 1995, 75% received their degree in 8 years or less. *Degree requirements:* For doctorate, thesis/dissertation, comprehensive exam, registration. *Entrance requirements:* For doctorate, GRE General Test, GRE Subject Test. Additional exam requirements/recommendations for international students: Required—TOEFL (minimum score 600 paper-based; 250 computer-based). *Application deadline:* For fall admission, 1/15 priority date for domestic students, 1/15 priority date for international students. Application fee: $55. Electronic applications accepted. *Expenses:* Tuition: Full-time $28,730; part-time $1,490 per course. Part-time tuition and fees vary according to course load, campus/location and program. *Financial support:* In 2003–04, 17 fellowships (averaging $2,500 per year), 63 research assistantships with full tuition reimbursements (averaging $19,333 per year), 40 teaching assistantships with full tuition reimbursements (averaging $14,500 per year) were awarded. Career-related internships or fieldwork, Federal Work-Study, institutionally sponsored loans, and tuition waivers (full and partial) also available. Financial award application deadline: 4/15; financial award applicants required to submit FAFSA. *Faculty research:* High-energy physics, condensed-matter astrophysics, particle and experimental physics, physics theory. Total annual research expenditures: $27 million. *Unit head:* Dr. Jonathan A. Bagger, Chair, 410-516-7346, Fax: 410-516-7239, E-mail: bagger@jhu.edu. *Application contact:* Carmelita D. King, Academic Affairs Administrator, 410-516-7344, Fax: 410-516-7239, E-mail: jazzy@pha.jhu.edu.

See in-depth description on page 373.

Louisiana State University and Agricultural and Mechanical College, Graduate School, College of Basic Sciences, Department of Physics and Astronomy, Baton Rouge, LA 70803. Offers astronomy (PhD); astrophysics (PhD); physics (MS, PhD). *Faculty:* 36 full-time (2 women), 3 part-time/adjunct (0 women). *Students:* 58 full-time (13 women), 1 (woman) part-time; includes 3 minority (2 Asian Americans or Pacific Islanders, 1 Hispanic American), 33 international. Average age 28. 69 applicants, 32% accepted, 13 enrolled. In 2003, 7 master's, 10 doctorates awarded. Terminal master's awarded for partial completion of doctoral program. *Degree requirements:* For master's, thesis or alternative; for doctorate, thesis/dissertation. *Entrance requirements:* For master's and doctorate, GRE General Test, minimum GPA of 3.0. Additional exam requirements/recommendations for international students: Required—TOEFL (minimum score 550 paper-based; 213 computer-based). *Application deadline:* For fall admission, 1/25 priority date for domestic students, 5/15 priority date for international students. Applications are processed on a rolling basis. Application fee: $25. Electronic applications accepted. *Expenses:* Tuition, state resident: part-time $337 per hour. Tuition, nonresident: part-time $577 per hour. *Financial support:* In 2003–04, 15 students received support, including 5 fellowships (averaging $18,000 per year), 28 research assistantships with partial tuition reimbursements available (averaging $18,041 per year), 23 teaching assistantships with partial tuition reimbursements available (averaging $19,196 per year); institutionally sponsored loans and unspecified assistantships also available. Financial award application deadline: 3/15; financial award applicants required to submit FAFSA. *Faculty research:* Experimental and theoretical atomic, nuclear, particle, cosmic-ray, low-temperature, and condensed-matter physics. Total annual research expenditures: $4.9 million. *Unit head:* Dr. Roger McNeil, Chair, 225-578-2261, Fax: 225-578-5855, E-mail: mcneil@phys.lsu.edu. *Application contact:* Dr. James Matthews, Graduate Adviser, 225-578-8598, Fax: 225-578-5855, E-mail: jmatth5@lsu.edu.

Michigan State University, Graduate School, College of Natural Science, Department of Physics and Astronomy, East Lansing, MI 48824. Offers astrophysics and astronomy (MS, PhD); physics (MS, PhD). *Faculty:* 52 full-time (2 women). *Students:* 128 full-time (21 women), 5 part-time; includes 5 minority (1 American Indian/Alaska Native, 3 Asian Americans or Pacific Islanders, 1 Hispanic American), 72 international. Average age 28. 291 applicants, 6% accepted. In 2003, 27 master's, 13 doctorates awarded. *Degree requirements:* For master's, qualifying exam, thesis optional; for doctorate, thesis/dissertation, qualifying exam, comprehensive exam. *Entrance requirements:* For master's and doctorate, minimum GPA of 3.0 in science/math courses, course work equivalent to a major in physics or astronomy, 3 letters of recommendation. Additional exam requirements/recommendations for international students: Required—TOEFL (minimum score 550 paper-based; 213 computer-based), Michigan State University ELT (85), Michigan ELAB (83). *Application deadline:* For fall admission, 1/15 for domestic students; for spring admission, 9/30 for domestic students. Application fee: $50. Electronic applications accepted. *Expenses:* Tuition, state resident: part-time $291 per hour. Tuition, nonresident: part-time $589 per hour. *Financial support:* In 2003–04, 14 fellowships with tuition reimbursements (averaging $7,077 per year), 18 research assistantships with tuition reimbursements (averaging $13,681 per year), 39 teaching assistantships with tuition reimbursements (averaging $12,741 per year) were awarded. Financial award applicants required to submit FAFSA. *Faculty research:* Nuclear and accelerator physics, high-energy physics, condensed-matter physics, astrophysics and astronomy, biophysics. Total annual research expenditures: $4.8 million. *Unit head:* Dr. Wolfgang Bauer, Chairperson, 517-355-9200 Ext. 2015, Fax: 517-355-4500. *Application contact:* Dr. S. D. Mahanti, Director of Graduate Studies, 517-355-9200 Ext. 2303, Fax: 517-355-4500, E-mail: mahanti@pa.msu.edu.

See in-depth description on page 381.

Minnesota State University Mankato, College of Graduate Studies, College of Science, Engineering and Technology, Department of Physics and Astronomy, Mankato, MN 56001. Offers MS, MT. *Faculty:* 7 full-time (1 woman). *Students:* 4 full-time (3 women), 3 part-time (1 woman). Average age 34. In 2003, 1 degree awarded. *Degree requirements:* For master's, one foreign language, thesis or alternative, comprehensive exam. *Entrance requirements:* For master's, minimum GPA of 3.0 during previous 2 years. *Application deadline:* For fall admission, 7/9 for domestic students; for spring admission, 11/27 for domestic students. Applications are processed on a rolling basis. Application fee: $40. *Expenses:* Tuition, state resident: part-time $226 per credit hour. Tuition, nonresident: part-time $339 per credit hour. Tuition and fees vary according to reciprocity agreements. *Financial support:* Research assistantships, teaching assistantships with full tuition reimbursements, Federal Work-Study and unspecified assistantships available. Support available to part-time students. Financial award application deadline: 3/15; financial award applicants required to submit FAFSA. *Unit head:* Dr. Sandford Schuster, Chairperson, 507-389-5743. *Application contact:* Joni Roberts, Admissions Coordinator, 507-389-5244, Fax: 507-389-5974, E-mail: grad@mankato.msus.edu.

New Mexico State University, Graduate School, College of Arts and Sciences, Department of Astronomy, Las Cruces, NM 88003-8001. Offers MS, PhD. Part-time programs available. *Faculty:* 8 full-time (2 women), 2 part-time/adjunct (0 women). *Students:* 22 full-time (9 women), 3 part-time (1 woman); includes 2 minority (1 Asian American or Pacific Islander, 1 Hispanic American), 8 international. Average age 27. 27 applicants, 19% accepted, 5 enrolled. In 2003, 1 degree awarded. Terminal master's awarded for partial completion of doctoral program. *Degree requirements:* For master's and doctorate, thesis/dissertation. *Entrance requirements:* For master's and doctorate, GRE General Test, GRE Subject Test (advanced physics). Additional exam requirements/recommendations for international students: Required—TOEFL. *Application deadline:* For fall admission, 2/10 priority date for domestic students, 2/10 priority date for international students. Applications are processed on a rolling basis. Application fee: $30 ($50 for international students). Electronic applications accepted. *Expenses:* Tuition, state resident: full-time $2,670; part-time $151 per credit. Tuition, nonresident: full-time $10,596; part-time $481 per credit. Required fees: $954. *Financial support:* In 2003–04, 9 research assistantships with tuition reimbursements, 11 teaching assistantships with partial tuition reimbursements were awarded. Fellowships with partial tuition reimbursements, scholarships/grants and unspecified assistantships also available. Financial award application deadline: 3/1. *Faculty research:* Planetary systems, accreting binary stars, stellar populations, galaxies, interstellar medium. *Unit head:* Dr. Reinirus Walterbos, Head, 505-646-4438, Fax: 505-646-1602, E-mail: rwalterb@nmsu.edu. *Application contact:* James Murphy, Assistant Professor, 505-646-5333, Fax: 505-646-1602, E-mail: murphy@nmsu.edu.

Northwestern University, The Graduate School, Judd A. and Marjorie Weinberg College of Arts and Sciences, Department of Physics and Astronomy, Evanston, IL 60208. Offers astrophysics (PhD); physics (MS, PhD). Admissions and degrees offered through The Graduate School. Terminal master's awarded for partial completion of doctoral program. *Degree requirements:* For doctorate, thesis/dissertation, qualifying exam. *Entrance requirements:* For doctorate, GRE General Test, GRE Subject Test. Additional exam requirements/recommendations for international students: Required—TOEFL. *Faculty research:* Nuclear and particle physics, condensed-matter physics, nonlinear physics, astrophysics.

The Ohio State University, Graduate School, College of Mathematical and Physical Sciences, Department of Astronomy, Columbus, OH 43210. Offers MS, PhD. *Faculty:* 20. *Students:* 24 full-time (5 women), 10 international. 75 applicants, 15% accepted. In 2003, 6 degrees awarded. *Degree requirements:* For master's and doctorate, thesis/dissertation, comprehensive exam. *Entrance requirements:* For master's and doctorate, GRE General Test, GRE Subject Test (physics), minimum GPA of 2.7. Additional exam requirements/recommendations for international students: Required—TOEFL. *Application deadline:* For fall admission, 8/15 for domestic students. Applications are processed on a rolling basis. Application fee: $40 ($50 for international students). *Expenses:* Tuition, state resident: full-time $7,233. Tuition, nonresident: full-time $18,489. *Financial support:* Fellowships, research assistantships, teaching assistantships, Federal Work-Study and institutionally sponsored loans available. Support available to part-time students. *Unit head:* Dr. Patrick S. Osmer, Chair, 614-292-2022, Fax: 614-292-2928, E-mail: osmer.1@osu.edu. *Application contact:* Dr. Kristen Sellgren, Graduate Studies Committee Chair, 614-292-5850, Fax: 614-292-2928, E-mail: sellgren.1@osu.edu.

The Pennsylvania State University University Park Campus, Graduate School, Eberly College of Science, Department of Astronomy and Astrophysics, State College, University Park, PA 16802-1503. Offers MS, PhD. *Students:* 30 full-time (8 women); includes 2 minority (both Hispanic Americans), 15 international. *Entrance requirements:* For master's and doctorate, GRE General Test. Application fee: $45. *Unit head:* Dr. Lawrence W. Ramsey, Head, 814-865-0418, Fax: 814-863-3399, E-mail: lwr@psu.edu.

Rice University, Graduate Programs, Wiess School of Natural Sciences, Department of Physics and Astronomy, Houston, TX 77251-1892. Offers physics (MA); physics and astronomy (MS, PhD). *Faculty:* 46 full-time (3 women). *Students:* 90 full-time (12 women), 2 part-time (1 woman); includes 11 minority (1 African American, 3 Asian Americans or Pacific Islanders, 7 Hispanic Americans), 46 international. Average age 28. 169 applicants, 36% accepted, 24 enrolled. In 2003, 7 master's awarded, leading to continued full-time study 71%; 10 doctorates awarded. *Median time to degree:* Doctorate–7 years full-time. Of those who began their doctoral program in fall 1995, 50% received their degree in 8 years or less. *Degree requirements:* For master's and doctorate, thesis/dissertation. *Entrance requirements:* For master's and doctorate, GRE General Test, GRE Subject Test (physics), minimum GPA of 3.0. Additional exam requirements/recommendations for international students: Required—TOEFL (minimum score 600 paper-based; 250 computer-based). *Application deadline:* For fall admission, 2/1 for domestic students, 2/1 for international students. Applications are processed on a rolling basis. Application fee: $35. Electronic applications accepted. *Expenses:* Tuition: Full-time $19,700; part-time $1,096 per hour. *Financial support:* In 2003–04, 24 fellowships with full tuition reimbursements (averaging $21,000 per year), 68 research assistantships with full tuition reimbursements (averaging $21,000 per year) were awarded. Tuition waivers (full and partial) also available. *Faculty research:* Atomic, solid-state, and molecular physics; biophysics; medium- and high-energy physics, magnetospheric physics, planetary atmospheres, astrophysics. Total annual research expenditures: $6.6 million. *Unit head:* Dr. F. Barry Dunning, Acting Chairman, 713-348-3544, Fax: 713-348-4510, E-mail: fbd@rice.edu. *Application contact:* Bridgitt G. Ayers, Graduate Program Director, 713-348-6348, Fax: 713-348-4150, E-mail: physgrad@rice.edu.

Saint Mary's University, Faculty of Science, Department of Astronomy and Physics, Halifax, NS B3H 3C3, Canada. Offers M Sc. Part-time programs available. *Degree requirements:* For master's, thesis. *Entrance requirements:* For master's, honors degree. Additional exam requirements/recommendations for international students: Required—TOEFL. *Faculty research:* Young stellar objects, interstellar medium, star clusters, galactic structure, early-type galaxies.

San Diego State University, Graduate and Research Affairs, College of Sciences, Department of Astronomy, San Diego, CA 92182. Offers MS. *Students:* 4 full-time (2 women), 14 part-time (3 women); includes 3 minority (2 African Americans, 1 Hispanic American), 1 international. Average age 30. 17 applicants, 53% accepted, 4 enrolled. In 2003, 2 degrees awarded. *Degree requirements:* For master's, thesis. *Entrance requirements:* For master's, GRE General Test. Additional exam requirements/recommendations for international students: Required—TOEFL. *Application deadline:* For fall admission, 5/1 for domestic students, 5/1 for international students; for spring admission, 11/1 for domestic students, 10/1 for international students. Applications are processed on a rolling basis. Application fee: $55. Electronic applications accepted. Tuition, nonresident: part-time $282 per unit. Required fees: $1,349; $875 per year. *Financial support:* In 2003–04, 2 research assistantships were awarded. Financial award applicants required to submit FAFSA. *Faculty research:* CCD, classical and dwarf novae, photometry, interactive binaries. Total annual research expenditures: $183,088. *Unit head:* Paul B. Etzel, Chair, 619-594-6169, Fax: 619-594-1413, E-mail: etzel@sciences.sdsu.edu. *Application contact:* William Welsh, Graduate Coordinator, 619-594-2288, Fax: 619-594-1413, E-mail: wwelsh@mail.sdsu.edu.

Texas Christian University, College of Science and Engineering, Department of Physics and Astronomy, Fort Worth, TX 76129-0002. Offers physics (PhD), including astrophysics, business, physics. Part-time and evening/weekend programs available. *Degree requirements:* For doctorate, thesis/dissertation, qualifying exams. *Entrance requirements:* For doctorate, GRE General Test. Additional exam requirements/recommendations for international students: Required—TOEFL. *Application deadline:* For fall admission, 3/1 for domestic students; for spring admission, 12/1 for domestic students. Applications are processed on a rolling basis. Application fee: $0. *Expenses:* Tuition: Part-time $640 per credit hour. Tuition and fees vary according to program. *Financial support:* Fellowships, teaching assistantships available. Financial award application deadline: 3/1. *Unit head:* Dr. C. Magnus Rittby, Chairperson, 817-257-7375, E-mail: m.rittby@tcu.edu. *Application contact:* Dr. Bonnie Melhart, Associate Dean, College of Science and Engineering, E-mail: b.melhart@tcu.edu.

Université de Moncton, Faculty of Science, Department of Physics and Astronomy, Moncton, NB E1A 3E9, Canada. Offers M Sc. *Degree requirements:* For master's, thesis. *Entrance*

Astronomy

Université de Moncton (continued)
requirements: For master's, proficiency in French. Electronic applications accepted. *Faculty research:* Thin films, optical properties, solar selective surfaces, microgravity and photonic materials.

The University of Arizona, Graduate College, College of Science, Department of Astronomy, Tucson, AZ 85721. Offers MS, PhD. *Degree requirements:* For doctorate, thesis/dissertation. *Entrance requirements:* For master's and doctorate, GRE General Test, GRE Subject Test. Additional exam requirements/recommendations for international students: Required—TOEFL. *Expenses:* Tuition, state resident: part-time $196 per unit. Tuition, nonresident: part-time $326 per unit. *Faculty research:* Astrophysics, submillimeter astronomy, infrared astronomy, NICMOS, SIRTF.

University of Calgary, Faculty of Graduate Studies, Faculty of Science, Department of Physics and Astronomy, Calgary, AB T2N 1N4, Canada. Offers M Sc, PhD. Part-time programs available. *Faculty:* 22 full-time (1 woman), 12 part-time/adjunct (0 women). *Students:* 39 full-time (8 women), 3 part-time (2 women). Average age 28. 50 applicants, 46% accepted, 13 enrolled. In 2003, 4 master's, 1 doctorate awarded. *Degree requirements:* For master's, thesis; for doctorate, thesis/dissertation, oral candidacy exam, written qualifying exam. *Entrance requirements:* For master's and doctorate, GRE General Test, GRE Subject Test. Additional exam requirements/recommendations for international students: Required—TOEFL (minimum score 550 paper-based; 213 computer-based). *Application deadline:* For fall admission, 3/1 for domestic students, 3/1 for international students; for winter admission, 7/1 for domestic students. Applications are processed on a rolling basis. Application fee: $60. Electronic applications accepted. Tuition, nonresident: full-time $4,765. Tuition and fees vary according to degree level, program and student level. *Financial support:* Fellowships with full and partial tuition reimbursements, research assistantships, teaching assistantships, institutionally sponsored loans available. Financial award application deadline: 2/1. *Faculty research:* Astronomy and astrophysics, mass spectrometry, atmospheric physics, space physics, medical physics. Total annual research expenditures: $4.6 million. *Unit head:* Dr. R. B. Hicks, Head, 403-220-5385, Fax: 403-289-3331, E-mail: hicks@ucalgary.ca. *Application contact:* Dr. R. I. Thompson, Chairman, Graduate Affairs, 403-220-5407, Fax: 403-289-3331, E-mail: gradinfo@ucalgary.ca.

University of California, Los Angeles, Graduate Division, College of Letters and Science, Department of Physics and Astronomy, Program in Astronomy, Los Angeles, CA 90095. Offers MAT, MS, PhD. *Degree requirements:* For doctorate, thesis/dissertation, oral and written qualifying exams. *Entrance requirements:* For master's, GRE General Test, GRE Subject Test (physics), minimum GPA of 3.0; for doctorate, GRE General Test, GRE Subject Test (physics), minimum undergraduate GPA of 3.0. Electronic applications accepted. Tuition, nonresident: full-time $12,245. Required fees: $6,318.

University of California, Santa Cruz, Division of Graduate Studies, Division of Physical and Biological Sciences, Program in Astronomy and Astrophysics, Santa Cruz, CA 95064. Offers PhD. *Faculty:* 23 full-time (3 women). *Students:* 25 full-time (10 women); includes 2 minority (1 African American, 1 Asian American or Pacific Islander), 2 international. 137 applicants, 23% accepted, 7 enrolled. In 2003, 5 doctorates awarded. *Median time to degree:* Doctorate–7 years full-time. *Degree requirements:* For doctorate, one foreign language, thesis/dissertation, qualifying exam. *Entrance requirements:* For doctorate, GRE General Test, GRE Subject Test. *Application deadline:* For fall admission, 1/15 for domestic students. Application fee: $60. Tuition, nonresident: full-time $12,492. *Financial support:* Fellowships, research assistantships, teaching assistantships, Federal Work-Study and institutionally sponsored loans available. Financial award application deadline: 1/15. *Faculty research:* Stellar structure and evolution, stellar spectroscopy, the interstellar medium, galactic structure, external galaxies and quasars. *Unit head:* Dr. Stephen Thorsett, Chairperson, 831-459-2976, E-mail: thorsett@ucolick.ucsc.edu. *Application contact:* James M. Moore, Graduate Admissions, Director, 831-459-2301, Fax: 831-459-4843, E-mail: gradadm@ucsc.edu.

University of Chicago, Division of the Physical Sciences, Department of Astronomy and Astrophysics, Chicago, IL 60637-1513. Offers SM, PhD. *Faculty:* 33 full-time (2 women), 4 part-time/adjunct (0 women). *Students:* 28 full-time (6 women); includes 10 minority (7 Asian Americans or Pacific Islanders, 3 Hispanic Americans). Average age 26. In 2003, 8 master's, 2 doctorates awarded. Terminal master's awarded for partial completion of doctoral program. *Degree requirements:* For master's, candidacy exam; for doctorate, thesis/dissertation, dissertation for publication. *Entrance requirements:* For doctorate, GRE General Test, GRE Subject Test, minimum GPA of 3.0. Additional exam requirements/recommendations for international students: Required—TOEFL (minimum score 600 paper-based; 250 computer-based). *Application deadline:* For fall admission, 12/28 priority date for domestic students, 12/28 priority date for international students. Application fee: $55. Electronic applications accepted. *Financial support:* In 2003–04, 28 students received support, including fellowships (averaging $4,250 per year), research assistantships with full tuition reimbursements available (averaging $19,800 per year), teaching assistantships with full tuition reimbursements available (averaging $19,800 per year); career-related internships or fieldwork, Federal Work-Study, institutionally sponsored loans, and tuition waivers (partial) also available. Financial award application deadline: 12/28. *Faculty research:* Quasi-stellar object absorption lines, fluid dynamics, interstellar matter, particle physics, cosmology. *Unit head:* Angela Olinto, Chairman, 773-702-8203, Fax: 773-702-8212. *Application contact:* Laticia Rebeles, Admissions Officer, 773-702-9808, Fax: 773-702-8212, E-mail: lrebeles@oddjob.uchicago.edu.

University of Delaware, College of Arts and Sciences, Joint Graduate Program of Department of Physics and Astronomy and Bartol Research Institute, Newark, DE 19716. Offers physics (MA, MS, PhD). Part-time programs available. *Faculty:* 21 full-time (2 women), 3 part-time/adjunct (1 woman). *Students:* 70 full-time (15 women), 2 part-time; includes 3 minority (2 African Americans, 1 Asian American or Pacific Islander), 55 international. Average age 26. 134 applicants, 34% accepted, 24 enrolled. In 2003, 4 master's, 5 doctorates awarded. Terminal master's awarded for partial completion of doctoral program. *Degree requirements:* For master's and doctorate, thesis/dissertation. *Entrance requirements:* For master's and doctorate, GRE General Test, GRE Subject Test. *Application deadline:* For fall admission, 7/1 for domestic students. Application fee: $60. Electronic applications accepted. *Expenses:* Tuition, state resident: full-time $5,890; part-time $327 per credit. Tuition, nonresident: full-time $15,420; part-time $857 per credit. Required fees: $968. *Financial support:* In 2003–04, 70 students received support, including 2 fellowships with full tuition reimbursements available (averaging $11,000 per year), 27 research assistantships with full tuition reimbursements available (averaging $18,000 per year), 25 teaching assistantships with full tuition reimbursements available (averaging $18,000 per year); career-related internships or fieldwork, Federal Work-Study, institutionally sponsored loans, and corporate sponsorships also available. Financial award application deadline: 3/1. *Faculty research:* Magnetoresistance and magnetic materials, ultrafast optical phenomena, superfluidity, elementary particle physics, stellar atmospheres and interiors. Total annual research expenditures: $2.6 million. *Unit head:* Dr. George Hadjipanayis, Chair, 302-831-3361. *Application contact:* Dr. John Xiao, Information Contact, 302-831-1995, E-mail: grad.physics@udel.edu.

University of Florida, Graduate School, College of Liberal Arts and Sciences, Department of Astronomy, Gainesville, FL 32611. Offers MS, PhD. *Faculty:* 29. *Students:* 25 full-time (15 women), 2 part-time; includes 4 minority (2 Asian Americans or Pacific Islanders, 2 Hispanic Americans), 6 international. In 2003, 8 master's, 3 doctorates awarded. Terminal master's awarded for partial completion of doctoral program. *Degree requirements:* For master's, thesis (terminal MS); for doctorate, one foreign language, thesis/dissertation. *Entrance requirements:* For master's and doctorate, GRE General Test, minimum GPA of 3.0. Additional exam requirements/recommendations for international students: Required—TOEFL (minimum score 550 paper-based; 213 computer-based). *Application deadline:* For fall admission, 1/31 for domestic students. Applications are processed on a rolling basis. Application fee: $30. Electronic applications accepted. *Expenses:* Tuition, state resident: part-time $205 per credit hour. Tuition, nonresident: part-time $775 per credit hour. *Financial support:* In 2003–04, 25 students received support, including 12 fellowships (averaging $16,000 per year), 4 research assistantships (averaging $7,000 per year), 10 teaching assistantships (averaging $8,000 per year); tuition waivers (full) and unspecified assistantships also available. Financial award application deadline: 1/31. *Faculty research:* Cosmology, photometry, variable and binary stars, dynamical solar system astronomy, infrared. Total annual research expenditures: $575,000. *Unit head:* Dr. Stanley F. Dermott, Chairman, 352-392-2052 Ext. 203, Fax: 352-392-5089, E-mail: dermott@astro.ufl.edu. *Application contact:* Dr. John P. Oliver, Coordinator, 352-392-2052 Ext. 206, Fax: 352-392-5089, E-mail: oliver@astro.ufl.edu.

University of Georgia, Graduate School, College of Arts and Sciences, Department of Physics and Astronomy, Athens, GA 30602. Offers physics (MS, PhD). *Faculty:* 21 full-time (0 women). *Students:* 28 full-time (5 women), 2 part-time (1 woman); includes 3 minority (1 African American, 1 American Indian/Alaska Native, 1 Asian American or Pacific Islander), 18 international. 74 applicants, 19% accepted. In 2003, 4 master's, 2 doctorates awarded. *Degree requirements:* For master's, thesis; for doctorate, one foreign language, thesis/dissertation. *Entrance requirements:* For master's and doctorate, GRE General Test. *Application deadline:* For fall admission, 7/1 for domestic students; for spring admission, 11/15 for domestic students. Application fee: $50. Electronic applications accepted. *Expenses:* Tuition, state resident: part-time $161 per hour. Tuition, nonresident: part-time $690 per hour. One-time fee: $435 part-time. *Financial support:* Fellowships, research assistantships, teaching assistantships, unspecified assistantships available. *Unit head:* Dr. Heinz-Bernd Schüttler, Head, 706-542-2485, Fax: 706-542-2492, E-mail: hbs@physast.uga.edu. *Application contact:* Dr. F. Todd Baker, Graduate Coordinator, 706-542-0979, Fax: 706-542-2492, E-mail: tbaker@physast.uga.edu.

University of Hawaii at Manoa, Graduate Division, Colleges of Arts and Sciences, College of Natural Sciences, Department of Physics and Astronomy, Honolulu, HI 96822. Offers MS, PhD. *Faculty:* 66 full-time (4 women), 4 part-time/adjunct (1 woman). *Students:* 57 full-time (19 women), 3 part-time; includes 5 minority (1 African American, 3 Asian Americans or Pacific Islanders, 1 Hispanic American), 21 international. 156 applicants, 29% accepted, 17 enrolled. *Median time to degree:* Master's–4 years full-time; doctorate–7 years full-time. *Degree requirements:* For master's, qualifying exam or thesis; for doctorate, thesis/dissertation, oral comprehensive and qualifying exams. *Entrance requirements:* For master's and doctorate, GRE General Test, GRE Subject Test. *Application deadline:* For fall admission, 1/15 for domestic students, 1/15 for international students. Application fee: $50. *Expenses:* Tuition, state resident: full-time $4,464; part-time $186 per credit hour. Tuition, nonresident: full-time $10,608; part-time $442 per credit hour. Tuition and fees vary according to program. *Financial support:* In 2003–04, 37 research assistantships (averaging $18,849 per year), 16 teaching assistantships (averaging $15,222 per year) were awarded. *Unit head:* Dr. Michael Peters, Chairperson, 808-956-7087, Fax: 808-956-7107. *Application contact:* Dr. Gareth Wynn-Williams, Graduate Chair, 808-956-8807, Fax: 808-956-9580, E-mail: wynnwill@ifa.hawaii.edu.

University of Illinois at Urbana–Champaign, Graduate College, College of Liberal Arts and Sciences, Department of Astronomy, Champaign, IL 61820. Offers MS, PhD. *Faculty:* 13 full-time (1 woman), 1 part-time/adjunct (0 women). *Students:* 26 full-time (10 women), 20 international. 55 applicants, 5% accepted, 3 enrolled. In 2003, 3 master's, 1 doctorate awarded. *Degree requirements:* For doctorate, thesis/dissertation. *Entrance requirements:* For master's and doctorate, GRE General Test, GRE Subject Test, minimum GPA of 3.0. *Application deadline:* For fall admission, 2/15 for domestic students. Applications are processed on a rolling basis. Application fee: $40 ($50 for international students). Electronic applications accepted. *Expenses:* Tuition, state resident: full-time $6,692. Tuition, nonresident: full-time $18,692. *Financial support:* In 2003–04, 1 fellowship, 13 research assistantships, 10 teaching assistantships were awarded. Financial award application deadline: 2/15. *Unit head:* Lewis E. Snyder, Chair, 217-333-5530, Fax: 217-244-7638, E-mail: lesnyder@uiuc.edu. *Application contact:* Carol Stickrod, Administrative Assistant, 217-333-5537, Fax: 217-244-7638, E-mail: cas@astro.uiuc.edu.

The University of Iowa, Graduate College, College of Liberal Arts and Sciences, Department of Physics and Astronomy, Program in Astronomy, Iowa City, IA 52242-1316. Offers MS. *Students:* 4 applicants, 25% accepted, 0 enrolled. In 2003, 1 degree awarded. *Degree requirements:* For master's, exam, thesis optional. *Entrance requirements:* For master's, GRE General Test, GRE Subject Test, minimum GPA of 3.0. Additional exam requirements/recommendations for international students: Required—TOEFL (minimum score 550 paper-based; 213 computer-based). *Application deadline:* For fall admission, 4/1 for domestic students, 4/1 for international students. Applications are processed on a rolling basis. Application fee: $50 ($75 for international students). Electronic applications accepted. *Expenses:* Tuition, state resident: full-time $5,038. Tuition, nonresident: full-time $15,072. Tuition and fees vary according to course load and program. *Financial support:* Fellowships, research assistantships, teaching assistantships available. Financial award applicants required to submit FAFSA. *Unit head:* Thomas Boggess, Chair, Department of Physics and Astronomy, 319-335-1688, Fax: 319-335-1753.

University of Kansas, Graduate School, College of Liberal Arts and Sciences, Department of Physics and Astronomy, Lawrence, KS 66045. Offers computational physics and astronomy (MS); physics (MS, PhD). *Faculty:* 30. *Students:* 35 full-time (11 women), 7 part-time (3 women); includes 2 minority (1 Asian American or Pacific Islander, 1 Hispanic American), 20 international. Average age 29. 69 applicants, 39% accepted, 8 enrolled. In 2003, 3 master's, 6 doctorates awarded. *Median time to degree:* Master's–3 years full-time; doctorate–5.5 years full-time. *Degree requirements:* For master's, thesis (for some programs); for doctorate, thesis/dissertation, comprehensive exam. *Entrance requirements:* Additional exam requirements/recommendations for international students: Required—TOEFL; Recommended—TSE. *Application deadline:* For fall admission, 3/1 priority date for domestic students, 3/1 priority date for international students; for spring admission, 10/1 priority date for domestic students, 10/1 priority date for international students. Applications are processed on a rolling basis. Application fee: $55 ($60 for international students). Electronic applications accepted. *Expenses:* Tuition, state resident: full-time $3,745. Tuition, nonresident: full-time $10,075. Required fees: $574. *Financial support:* In 2003–04, 27 research assistantships with full and partial tuition reimbursements (averaging $12,097 per year), 21 teaching assistantships with full and partial tuition reimbursements (averaging $12,864 per year) were awarded. Financial award application deadline: 3/1. *Faculty research:* Condensed-matter, cosmology, elementary particles, nuclear physics, space physics. Total annual research expenditures: $3.1 million. *Unit head:* Dr. Stephen J. Sanders, Chair, 785-864-4626, Fax: 785-864-5262. *Application contact:* Patricia Marvin, Graduate Admission Specialist, 785-864-4626, Fax: 785-864-5262, E-mail: physics@ku.edu.

See in-depth description on page 413.

University of Kentucky, Graduate School, Graduate School Programs from the College of Arts and Sciences, Program in Physics and Astronomy, Lexington, KY 40506-0032. Offers MS, PhD. *Faculty:* 32 full-time (2 women). *Students:* 53 full-time (14 women), 16 part-time (4 women); includes 1 minority (Asian American or Pacific Islander), 53 international. 104 applicants, 48% accepted, 20 enrolled. In 2003, 3 master's, 3 doctorates awarded. *Degree requirements:* For master's, thesis optional; for doctorate, thesis/dissertation, comprehensive exam. *Entrance requirements:* For master's, GRE General Test, minimum undergraduate GPA of 2.5; for doctorate, GRE General Test, minimum graduate GPA of 3.0. Additional exam requirements/recommendations for international students: Required—TOEFL (minimum score 550 paper-based; 213 computer-based). *Application deadline:* For fall admission, 7/18 for domestic students, 2/1 for international students. Applications are processed on a rolling basis. Application fee: $35 ($45 for international students). *Expenses:* Tuition, state resident: full-time $4,975; part-time $261 per credit hour. Tuition, nonresident: full-time $12,315; part-time $668 per credit hour. *Financial support:* Fellowships, research assistantships, teaching assistantships, Federal Work-Study, institutionally sponsored loans, and unspecified assistantships available. Support available to part-time students. *Faculty research:* Astrophysics, active galactic nuclei, interstellar masses, and radio astronomy; atomic physics, Rydbert atoms, and electron scattering; TOF spectroscopy, hyperon interactions and muons; solid-state, STM, charge-density waves, fulleneues, and 1-dimensional systems; particle theory, lattice gauge theory, quark, and skyrmion models. Total annual research expenditures: $3.1 million. *Unit head:* Dr. Thomas Troland, Director of Graduate Studies, 859-257-8620, Fax: 859-323-2846, E-mail: troland@asta.pa.uky.edu. *Application contact:* Dr. Brian Jackson, Associate Dean, 859-257-4905, Fax: 859-323-1928.

University of Maryland, College Park, Graduate Studies and Research, College of Computer, Mathematical and Physical Sciences, Department of Astronomy, College Park, MD 20742. Offers MS, PhD. Part-time and evening/weekend programs available. *Faculty:* 63 full-time (12 women), 8 part-time/adjunct (4 women). *Students:* 31 full-time (18 women), 7 part-time (2 women); includes 3 minority (1 African American, 1 Asian American or Pacific Islander, 1 Hispanic American), 9 international. 83 applicants, 31% accepted. In 2003, 3 master's, 3 doctorates awarded. Terminal master's awarded for partial completion of doctoral program. *Median time to degree:* Of those who began their doctoral program in fall 1995, 50% received their degree in 8 years or less. *Degree requirements:* For master's, written exam, thesis optional; for doctorate, thesis/dissertation, research project. *Entrance requirements:* For master's, GRE General Test, GRE Subject Test, minimum GPA of 3.0, 3 letters of recommendation; for doctorate, GRE General Test, GRE Subject Test. *Application deadline:* For fall admission, 1/1 for domestic students, 2/1 for international students; for spring admission, 10/1 for domestic students, 6/1 for international students. Applications are processed on a rolling basis. Application fee: $50. Electronic applications accepted. *Expenses:* Tuition, state resident: part-time $349 per credit hour. Tuition, nonresident: part-time $602 per credit hour. *Financial support:* In 2003–04, fellowships with full tuition reimbursements (averaging $2,875 per year), research assistantships with tuition reimbursements (averaging $18,274 per year), teaching assistantships with tuition reimbursements (averaging $12,658 per year) were awarded. Career-related internships or fieldwork, Federal Work-Study, and scholarships/grants also available. Support available to part-time students. Financial award applicants required to submit FAFSA. *Faculty research:* Solar radio astronomy, plasma and high-energy astrophysics, galactic and extragalactic astronomy. Total annual research expenditures: $14.7 million. *Unit head:* Dr. Lee Mundy, Chair, 301-405-1508, Fax: 301-314-9067. *Application contact:* Trudy Lindsey, Director, Graduate Enrollment Management Services, 301-405-4190, Fax: 301-314-9305, E-mail: tlindsey@gradschool.umd.edu.

University of Massachusetts Amherst, Graduate School, College of Natural Sciences and Mathematics, Department of Astronomy, Amherst, MA 01003. Offers MS, PhD. Part-time programs available. *Faculty:* 13 full-time (0 women). *Students:* 16 full-time (5 women), 6 part-time (1 woman); includes 1 minority (Asian American or Pacific Islander), 15 international. Average age 28. 57 applicants, 35% accepted, 5 enrolled. In 2003, 2 master's, 1 doctorate awarded. Terminal master's awarded for partial completion of doctoral program. *Degree requirements:* For doctorate, thesis/dissertation. *Entrance requirements:* For master's and doctorate, GRE General Test, GRE Subject Test. Additional exam requirements/recommendations for international students: Required—TOEFL (minimum score 530 paper-based; 197 computer-based). *Application deadline:* For fall admission, 2/1 priority date for domestic students, 2/1 priority date for international students; for spring admission, 10/1 for domestic students, 10/1 for international students. Applications are processed on a rolling basis. Application fee: $40 ($50 for international students). *Expenses:* Tuition, state resident: full-time $1,320; part-time $110 per credit. Tuition, nonresident: full-time $4,969; part-time $414 per credit. Required fees: $2,626 per term. Tuition and fees vary according to course load. *Financial support:* In 2003–04, research assistantships with full tuition reimbursements (averaging $10,724 per year), teaching assistantships with full tuition reimbursements (averaging $10,037 per year) were awarded. Fellowships with full tuition reimbursements, career-related internships or fieldwork, Federal Work-Study, scholarships/grants, traineeships, and unspecified assistantships also available. Support available to part-time students. Financial award application deadline: 2/1. *Unit head:* Dr. Ronald Snell, Director, 413-545-2194, Fax: 413-545-4223, E-mail: snell@astro.umass.edu. *Application contact:* Dr. Donald Candela, Chair, Admissions Committee, 413-545-2407, E-mail: candela@phast.umass.edu.

University of Michigan, Horace H. Rackham School of Graduate Studies, College of Literature, Science, and the Arts, Department of Astronomy, Ann Arbor, MI 48109. Offers MS, PhD. *Faculty:* 9 full-time (1 woman). *Students:* 18 full-time (9 women); includes 6 minority (3 Asian Americans or Pacific Islanders, 3 Hispanic Americans). Average age 24. 71 applicants, 18% accepted, 5 enrolled.Terminal master's awarded for partial completion of doctoral program. *Median time to degree:* Master's–2 years full-time; doctorate–3 years full-time. *Degree requirements:* For master's, comprehensive exam, registration; for doctorate, thesis/dissertation, oral defense of dissertation, preliminary exam. *Entrance requirements:* For master's and doctorate, GRE General Test, GRE Subject Test. *Application deadline:* For fall admission, 2/1 for domestic students. Applications are processed on a rolling basis. Application fee: $55. Electronic applications accepted. *Expenses:* Tuition, state resident: full-time $7,463. Tuition, nonresident: full-time $13,913. Full-time tuition and fees vary according to course load, degree level and program. *Financial support:* In 2003–04, 4 fellowships with full tuition reimbursements (averaging $18,656 per year), 8 research assistantships with full tuition reimbursements (averaging $18,656 per year), 5 teaching assistantships with full tuition reimbursements (averaging $18,656 per year) were awarded. Institutionally sponsored loans and health care benefits also available. Financial award application deadline: 2/1. *Faculty research:* Radio astronomy, interstellar medium, stellar evolution, dynamics of stellar systems, gravitational lensing. Total annual research expenditures: $973,000. *Unit head:* Dr. Douglas O. Richstone, Chair, 734-764-3440, Fax: 734-763-6317, E-mail: dor@umich.edu. *Application contact:* Kelly Alber-Drake, Administrative Associate, 734-764-3440, Fax: 734-763-6317, E-mail: kalberdr@umich.edu.

University of Minnesota, Twin Cities Campus, Graduate School, Institute of Technology, School of Physics and Astronomy, Department of Astronomy, Minneapolis, MN 55455-0213. Offers astrophysics (MS, PhD). Terminal master's awarded for partial completion of doctoral program. *Degree requirements:* For master's, thesis optional; for doctorate, thesis/dissertation. *Entrance requirements:* For master's and doctorate, GRE General Test, GRE Subject Test. *Expenses:* Tuition, state resident: full-time $3,681; part-time $614 per credit. Tuition, nonresident: full-time $7,231; part-time $1,205 per credit. *Faculty research:* Evolution of stars and galaxies; the interstellar medium; cosmology; observational, optical, infrared, and radio astronomy; computational astrophysics.

University of Missouri–Columbia, Graduate School, College of Arts and Sciences, Department of Physics and Astronomy, Columbia, MO 65211. Offers MS, PhD. *Faculty:* 23 full-time (4 women). *Students:* 27 full-time (5 women), 6 part-time (1 woman), 21 international. In 2003, 1 master's, 5 doctorates awarded. Terminal master's awarded for partial completion of doctoral program. *Degree requirements:* For doctorate, one foreign language, thesis/dissertation. *Entrance requirements:* For master's and doctorate, GRE General Test, minimum GPA of 3.0. *Application deadline:* For fall admission, 4/15 for domestic students. Applications are processed on a rolling basis. Application fee: $45 ($60 for international students). *Expenses:* Tuition, state resident: full-time $5,205. Tuition, nonresident: full-time $14,058. *Financial support:* Research assistantships, teaching assistantships, institutionally sponsored loans available. *Unit head:* Dr. H. R. Chandrasekhar, Director of Graduate Studies, 573-882-6086, E-mail: chandra@missouri.edu.

University of Nebraska–Lincoln, Graduate College, College of Arts and Sciences, Department of Physics and Astronomy, Lincoln, NE 68588. Offers astronomy (MS, PhD); physics (MS, PhD). *Degree requirements:* For master's, thesis optional; for doctorate, thesis/dissertation, comprehensive exam. *Entrance requirements:* For master's and doctorate, GRE General Test. Additional exam requirements/recommendations for international students: Required—TOEFL (minimum score 550 paper-based; 213 computer-based). Electronic applications accepted. *Faculty research:* Electromagnetics of solids and thin films, photoionization, ion collisions with atoms, molecules and surfaces, nanostructures.

The University of North Carolina at Chapel Hill, Graduate School, College of Arts and Sciences, Department of Physics and Astronomy, Chapel Hill, NC 27599. Offers physics (MS, PhD). *Faculty:* 31 full-time (3 women), 7 part-time/adjunct (1 woman). *Students:* 65 full-time (21 women). Average age 26. 200 applicants, 21% accepted, 19 enrolled. In 2003, 8 master's, 6 doctorates awarded. Terminal master's awarded for partial completion of doctoral program. *Median time to degree:* Master's–3 years full-time; doctorate–6 years full-time. *Degree requirements:* For master's, comprehensive exam, registration; for doctorate, thesis/dissertation, comprehensive exam, registration. *Entrance requirements:* For master's and doctorate, GRE General Test, minimum GPA of 3.0. *Application deadline:* For fall admission, 1/1 for domestic students. Application fee: $60. Electronic applications accepted. *Expenses:* Tuition, state resident: full-time $3,163. Tuition, nonresident: full-time $15,161. *Financial support:* In 2003–04, 2 fellowships with full tuition reimbursements (averaging $14,000 per year), 31 research assistantships with full tuition reimbursements (averaging $18,600 per year), 38 teaching assistantships with full tuition reimbursements (averaging $13,950 per year) were awarded. Federal Work-Study, scholarships/grants, health care benefits, and unspecified assistantships also available. Financial award application deadline: 3/1. *Faculty research:* Observational astronomy, fullerenes, polarized beams, nanotubes, nucleosynthesis in stars and supernovae, superstring theory, ballistic transport in semiconductors, gravitation. Total annual research expenditures: $5.5 million. *Unit head:* Dr. Bruce W. Carney, Chairman, 919-962-2079, Fax: 919-962-8205, E-mail: bruce@physics.unc.edu. *Application contact:* Prof. Thomas B. Clegg, Director of Graduate Admissions, 919-843-8168, Fax: 919-962-0480, E-mail: clegg@physics.unc.edu.

University of Rochester, The College, Arts and Sciences, Department of Physics and Astronomy, Rochester, NY 14627-0250. Offers physics (MA, MS, PhD); physics and astronomy (PhD). Part-time programs available. *Faculty:* 28. *Students:* 134 full-time (23 women); includes 7 minority (2 African Americans, 2 Asian Americans or Pacific Islanders, 3 Hispanic Americans), 70 international. 487 applicants, 15% accepted, 33 enrolled. In 2003, 11 master's, 8 doctorates awarded. Terminal master's awarded for partial completion of doctoral program. *Degree requirements:* For master's, thesis (for some programs), comprehensive exam; for doctorate, thesis/dissertation, qualifying exam, comprehensive exam. *Entrance requirements:* For master's and doctorate, GRE General Test. Additional exam requirements/recommendations for international students: Required—TOEFL. *Application deadline:* For fall admission, 2/1 for domestic students. Application fee: $25. *Expenses:* Tuition: Part-time $880 per credit hour. Required fees: $522. *Financial support:* Fellowships, research assistantships, teaching assistantships, tuition waivers (full and partial) available. Financial award application deadline: 2/1. *Unit head:* Arie Bodek, Chair, 585-275-4351. *Application contact:* Barbara Warren, Graduate Program Secretary, 585-275-4351.

See in-depth description on page 431.

University of South Carolina, The Graduate School, College of Science and Mathematics, Department of Physics and Astronomy, Columbia, SC 29208. Offers IMA, MAT, MS, PMS, PhD. IMA and MAT offered in cooperation with the College of Education. Part-time programs available. *Faculty:* 24 full-time (2 women), 1 part-time/adjunct (0 women). *Students:* 46 full-time (8 women); includes 4 minority (all African Americans), 26 international. Average age 28. 52 applicants, 73% accepted, 18 enrolled. In 2003, 6 master's awarded, leading to continued full-time study 50%, business/industry 50%; 1 doctorate awarded, leading to university research/teaching 100%. Terminal master's awarded for partial completion of doctoral program. *Median time to degree:* Master's–2.5 years full-time; doctorate–2 years full-time. *Degree requirements:* For master's, thesis, comprehensive exam, registration; for doctorate, one foreign language, thesis/dissertation, comprehensive exam, registration. *Entrance requirements:* For master's and doctorate, GRE General Test, GRE Subject Test. Additional exam requirements/recommendations for international students: Required—TOEFL (minimum score 570 paper-based; 230 computer-based). *Application deadline:* For fall admission, 8/1 priority date for domestic students, 8/1 priority date for international students. Applications are processed on a rolling basis. Application fee: $40. Electronic applications accepted. *Expenses:* Tuition, state resident: part-time $308 per hour. Tuition, nonresident: part-time $655 per hour. *Financial support:* In 2003–04, 41 students received support, including 4 fellowships with full tuition reimbursements available (averaging $20,727 per year), 13 research assistantships (averaging $19,000 per year), 24 teaching assistantships (averaging $16,000 per year); Federal Work-Study and unspecified assistantships also available. Support available to part-time students. *Faculty research:* Condensed matter, intermediate-energy nuclear physics, foundations of quantum mechanics, astronomy/astrophysics. Total annual research expenditures: $2.5 million. *Unit head:* Dr. Fred Myhrer, Chair, 803-777-4121, Fax: 803-777-3065, E-mail: myhrer@sc.edu. *Application contact:* Dr. Chaden Djalali, Director of Graduate Studies, 803-777-8104, Fax: 803-777-3065, E-mail: djalali@sc.edu.

See in-depth description on page 433.

University of Southern Mississippi, Graduate School, College of Science and Technology, Department of Physics and Astronomy, Hattiesburg, MS 39406-0001. Offers MS. *Faculty:* 2 full-time (0 women). *Students:* 2 full-time (both women); includes 1 minority (Asian American or Pacific Islander) Average age 27. 6 applicants, 67% accepted, 4 enrolled. In 2003, 1 degree awarded. *Degree requirements:* For master's, thesis, comprehensive exam. *Entrance requirements:* For master's, GRE General Test, minimum GPA of 2.75 in last 60 hours. Additional exam requirements/recommendations for international students: Required—TOEFL. *Application deadline:* For fall admission, 8/6 for domestic students. Applications are processed on a rolling basis. Application fee: $25. *Expenses:* Tuition, state resident: part-time $1,967 per semester. Tuition, nonresident: part-time $4,376 per semester. *Financial support:* Teaching assistantships with full tuition reimbursements, Federal Work-Study available. Financial award application deadline: 3/15. *Faculty research:* Polymers, atomic physics, fluid mechanics, liquid crystals, refractory materials. *Unit head:* Dr. Joe B. Whitehead, Chair, 601-266-4934, Fax: 601-266-5149.

The University of Texas at Austin, Graduate School, College of Natural Sciences, Department of Astronomy, Austin, TX 78712-1111. Offers MA, PhD. *Entrance requirements:* For master's and doctorate, GRE General Test, GRE Subject Test (physics). Additional exam requirements/recommendations for international students: Required—TOEFL. Electronic applications accepted. *Faculty research:* Stars, interstellar medium, galaxies, planetary astronomy, cosmology.

University of Toronto, School of Graduate Studies, Physical Sciences Division, Department of Astronomy, Toronto, ON M5S 1A1, Canada. Offers M Sc, PhD. Part-time programs available. *Faculty:* 25 full-time (1 woman). *Students:* 25 full-time (8 women), 8 international. 29 applicants, 45% accepted. In 2003, 5 master's, 3 doctorates awarded. *Degree requirements:* For doctorate, thesis/dissertation, qualifying exam, thesis defense. *Entrance requirements:* For master's, minimum B average, bachelor's degree in astronomy or equivalent, 3 letters of reference; for doctorate, GRE General Test and Subject Test in physics (strongly recommended), minimum B+ average, master's degree in astronomy or equivalent, or demonstrated research competance, 3 letters of reference. Application fee: $90 Canadian dollars. Tuition, nonresident: full-time $4,185. International tuition: $10,739 full-time. *Financial support:* In 2003–04, teaching assistantships (averaging $4,000 Canadian dollars per year). *Unit head:* P. G. Martin, Chair, 416-978-2016, Fax: 416-971-2026, E-mail: chair@astro.utoronto.ca. *Application contact:* Lillian Lanca, Secretary, 416-978-2016, Fax: 416-946-7287, E-mail: grad.admit@astro.utoronto.ca.

University of Victoria, Faculty of Graduate Studies, Faculty of Science, Department of Physics and Astronomy, Victoria, BC V8W 2Y2, Canada. Offers astronomy and astrophysics (M Sc, PhD); condensed matter physics (M Sc, PhD); medical physics (M Sc, PhD); nuclear and particle studies (M Sc, PhD); ocean physics (M Sc, PhD); theoretical physics (M Sc, PhD).

Astronomy

University of Victoria (continued)
Degree requirements: For master's, thesis/dissertation, registration; for doctorate, thesis/dissertation, comprehensive exam, registration. *Entrance requirements:* Additional exam requirements/recommendations for international students: Required—TOEFL (minimum score 575 paper-based; 213 computer-based). *Faculty research:* Old stellar populations; observational cosmology and large scale structure; cp violation; atlas.

University of Virginia, College and Graduate School of Arts and Sciences, Department of Astronomy, Charlottesville, VA 22903. Offers MS, PhD. *Faculty:* 15 full-time (0 women). *Students:* 23 full-time (5 women); includes 1 minority (Asian American or Pacific Islander), 9 international. Average age 26. 55 applicants, 38% accepted, 6 enrolled. In 2003, 2 degrees awarded. *Degree requirements:* For master's, one foreign language, thesis; for doctorate, variable foreign language requirement, thesis/dissertation. *Entrance requirements:* For master's and doctorate, GRE General Test, GRE Subject Test. Additional exam requirements/recommendations for international students: Recommended—TOEFL (minimum score 630 paper-based). *Application deadline:* For fall admission, 7/15 for domestic students; for spring admission, 2/1 for domestic students. Applications are processed on a rolling basis. Application fee: $40. Electronic applications accepted. *Expenses:* Tuition, state resident: full-time $6,476. Tuition, nonresident: full-time $18,534. Required fees: $1,380. *Financial support:* Application deadline: 1/15; *Unit head:* Robert T. Rood, Chairman, 434-924-7494, Fax: 434-924-3104. *Application contact:* Peter C. Brunjes, Associate Dean for Graduate Programs and Research, 434-924-7184, Fax: 434-924-6737, E-mail: grad-a-s@virginia.edu.

University of Washington, Graduate School, College of Arts and Sciences, Department of Astronomy, Seattle, WA 98195. Offers MS, PhD. Terminal master's awarded for partial completion of doctoral program. *Degree requirements:* For doctorate, thesis/dissertation. *Entrance requirements:* For master's and doctorate, GRE General Test, GRE Subject Test, minimum GPA of 3.0. Additional exam requirements/recommendations for international students: Required—TOEFL. *Faculty research:* Solar system dust, space astronomy, high-energy astrophysics, galactic and extragalactic astronomy, stellar astrophysics.

The University of Western Ontario, Faculty of Graduate Studies, Physical Sciences Division, Department of Physics and Astronomy, Program in Astronomy, London, ON N6A 5B8, Canada. Offers M Sc, PhD. Terminal master's awarded for partial completion of doctoral program. *Degree requirements:* For master's, thesis optional; for doctorate, thesis/dissertation, comprehensive exam. *Entrance requirements:* For master's, GRE Physics Test, honors B Sc degree, minimum B average (Canadian), A—(international); for doctorate, M Sc degree, minimum B average (Canadian), A—(international). Additional exam requirements/recommendations for international students: Required—TOEFL (minimum score 580 paper-based; 237 computer-based). *Faculty research:* Observational and theoretical astrophysics spectroscopy, photometry, spectro-polarimetry, variable stars, cosmology.

University of Wisconsin–Madison, Graduate School, College of Letters and Science, Department of Astronomy, Madison, WI 53706-1380. Offers PhD. *Degree requirements:* For doctorate, thesis/dissertation, comprehensive exam. *Entrance requirements:* For doctorate, GRE General Test, GRE Subject Test (physics), bachelor's degree in related field. Additional exam requirements/recommendations for international students: Required—TOEFL. Electronic applications accepted. Tuition, area resident: Full-time $7,593; part-time $476 per credit. Tuition, nonresident: full-time $22,824; part-time $1,430 per credit. Required fees: $292; $38 per credit. Part-time tuition and fees vary according to course load and reciprocity agreements. *Faculty research:* Kinematics, evolution of galaxies, cosmic distance, scale and large-scale structures, interstellar intergalactic medium, star formation and evolution, solar system chemistry and dynamics.

Vanderbilt University, Graduate School, Department of Physics and Astronomy, Nashville, TN 37240-1001. Offers astronomy (MS); physics (MA, MAT, MS, PhD). *Degree requirements:* For master's, thesis; for doctorate, thesis/dissertation, final and qualifying exams. *Entrance requirements:* For master's, GRE General Test; for doctorate, GRE General Test, GRE Subject Test. Electronic applications accepted. *Expenses:* Tuition: Part-time $1,155 per semester hour. Required fees: $1,538. *Faculty research:* Experimental and theoretical physics, free electron laser, living-state physics, heavy-ion physics, nuclear structure.

Wesleyan University, Graduate Programs, Department of Astronomy, Middletown, CT 06459-0260. Offers MA. *Faculty:* 2 full-time (0 women). *Students:* 5 full-time (4 women), 1 international. Average age 23. In 2003, 1 degree awarded. *Degree requirements:* For master's, thesis. *Entrance requirements:* For master's, GRE General Test, GRE Subject Test. *Application deadline:* For fall admission, 3/1 for domestic students. Applications are processed on a rolling basis. Application fee: $0. *Expenses:* Tuition: Full-time $22,338. Required fees: $20. *Financial support:* In 2003–04, 3 teaching assistantships were awarded. Financial award application deadline: 4/15; financial award applicants required to submit FAFSA. *Faculty research:* Observational-theoretical astronomy and astrophysics. *Unit head:* John Salzer, Chairman, 860-685-3672. *Application contact:* Linda Shettleworth, Information Contact, 860-685-2130, E-mail: shettleworth@wesleyan.edu.

West Chester University of Pennsylvania, Graduate Studies, College of Arts and Sciences, Department of Geology and Astronomy, West Chester, PA 19383. Offers physical science (MA). Part-time and evening/weekend programs available. *Students:* 6 full-time (3 women), 6 part-time (2 women). Average age 33. 7 applicants, 86% accepted. In 2003, 4 degrees awarded. *Degree requirements:* For master's, thesis optional. *Entrance requirements:* For master's, GRE General Test, interview. *Application deadline:* For fall admission, 4/15 for domestic students; for spring admission, 10/15 for domestic students. Applications are processed on a rolling basis. Application fee: $35. *Expenses:* Tuition, state resident: full-time $5,518; part-time $307 per credit. Tuition, nonresident: full-time $8,830; part-time $491 per credit. Required fees: $902; $52 per credit. One-time fee: $35 part-time. *Financial support:* In 2003–04, 1 research assistantship with full tuition reimbursement (averaging $5,000 per year) was awarded; unspecified assistantships also available. Support available to part-time students. Financial award application deadline: 2/15; financial award applicants required to submit FAFSA. *Faculty research:* Developing and using a meteorological data station. *Unit head:* Dr. Gil Wiswall, Chair, 610-436-2727. *Application contact:* Dr. Steven Good, Information Contact, 610-436-2203, E-mail: sgood@wcupa.edu.

Yale University, Graduate School of Arts and Sciences, Department of Astronomy, New Haven, CT 06520. Offers MS, PhD. *Degree requirements:* For doctorate, thesis/dissertation. *Entrance requirements:* For doctorate, GRE General Test, GRE Subject Test (physics). *Expenses:* Tuition: Full-time $25,600; part-time $6,400 per term.

York University, Faculty of Graduate Studies, Faculty of Pure and Applied Science, Program in Physics and Astronomy, Toronto, ON M3J 1P3, Canada. Offers M Sc, PhD. Part-time and evening/weekend programs available. *Degree requirements:* For master's, thesis or alternative; for doctorate, thesis/dissertation. *Entrance requirements:* For master's, minimum B+ average. Electronic applications accepted. Tuition, area resident: Full-time $5,431; part-time $905 per term. Tuition, nonresident: part-time $1,987 per term. International tuition: $11,918 full-time. Required fees: $287. Tuition and fees vary according to program.

Astrophysics

Air Force Institute of Technology, Graduate School of Engineering and Management, Department of Engineering Physics, Dayton, OH 45433-7765. Offers applied physics (MS, PhD); electro-optics (MS, PhD); materials science (PhD); nuclear engineering (MS, PhD); space physics (MS). *Accreditation:* ABET (one or more programs are accredited). Part-time programs available. *Degree requirements:* For master's and doctorate, thesis/dissertation. *Entrance requirements:* For master's and doctorate, GRE General Test, minimum GPA of 3.0, U.S. citizenship. *Faculty research:* High-energy lasers, space physics, nuclear weapon effects, semiconductor physics.

Clemson University, Graduate School, College of Engineering and Science, Department of Physics and Astronomy, Program in Physics, Clemson, SC 29634. Offers astronomy and astrophysics (MS, PhD); atmospheric physics (MS, PhD); biophysics (MS, PhD). Part-time programs available. *Students:* 40 full-time (11 women), 5 part-time; includes 1 minority (African American), 19 international. 59 applicants, 53% accepted, 8 enrolled. In 2003, 7 master's, 5 doctorates awarded. Terminal master's awarded for partial completion of doctoral program. *Degree requirements:* For master's, thesis or alternative; for doctorate, thesis/dissertation. *Entrance requirements:* For master's and doctorate, GRE General Test. Additional exam requirements/recommendations for international students: Required—TOEFL. *Application deadline:* For fall admission, 2/15 for domestic students. Applications are processed on a rolling basis. Application fee: $40. *Expenses:* Tuition, state resident: full-time $7,432. Tuition, nonresident: full-time $14,732. *Financial support:* Fellowships, research assistantships, teaching assistantships available. Financial award application deadline: 6/1; financial award applicants required to submit FAFSA. *Faculty research:* Radiation physics, solid-state physics, nuclear physics, radar and lidar studies of atmosphere. *Unit head:* Dr. Brad Myer, Head, 864-656-5320. *Application contact:* Dr. Miguel Larsen, Coordinator, 864-656-5309, Fax: 864-656-0805, E-mail: milarsen@clemson.edu.

Cornell University, Graduate School, Graduate Fields of Arts and Sciences, Field of Astronomy and Space Sciences, Ithaca, NY 14853-0001. Offers astronomy (PhD); astrophysics (PhD); general space sciences (PhD); infrared astronomy (PhD); planetary studies (PhD); radio astronomy (PhD); radiophysics (PhD); theoretical astrophysics (PhD). *Faculty:* 28 full-time. *Students:* 31 full-time (11 women), 16 international. 103 applicants, 21% accepted, 6 enrolled. In 2003, 2 doctorates awarded. *Degree requirements:* For doctorate, thesis/dissertation, comprehensive exam. *Entrance requirements:* For doctorate, GRE General Test, GRE Subject Test (physics), 3 letters of recommendation. Additional exam requirements/recommendations for international students: Required—TOEFL (minimum score 600 paper-based; 250 computer-based). *Application deadline:* For fall admission, 1/15 for domestic students. Application fee: $60. Electronic applications accepted. *Expenses:* Tuition: Full-time $28,630. One-time fee: $50 full-time. *Financial support:* In 2003–04, 30 students received support, including 8 fellowships with full tuition reimbursements available, 14 research assistantships with full tuition reimbursements available, 8 teaching assistantships with full tuition reimbursements available; institutionally sponsored loans, scholarships/grants, health care benefits, tuition waivers (full and partial), and unspecified assistantships also available. Financial award applicants required to submit FAFSA. *Faculty research:* Observational astrophysics, planetary sciences, cosmology, instrumentation, gravitational astrophysics. *Unit head:* Director of Graduate Studies, 607-255-4341. *Application contact:* Graduate Field Assistant, 607-255-4341, E-mail: oconnor@astro.cornell.edu.

Harvard University, Graduate School of Arts and Sciences, Department of Astronomy, Cambridge, MA 02138. Offers astronomy (AM, PhD); astrophysics (AM, PhD). *Degree requirements:* For doctorate, thesis/dissertation, paper, research project, teaching 2 semesters. *Entrance requirements:* For master's, GRE General Test; for doctorate, GRE General Test, GRE Subject Test (physics). Additional exam requirements/recommendations for international students: Required—TOEFL. Electronic applications accepted. *Expenses:* Tuition: Full-time $26,066. Full-time tuition and fees vary according to program and student level. *Faculty research:* Atomic and molecular physics, electromagnetism, solar physics, nuclear physics, fluid dynamics.

ICR Graduate School, Graduate Programs, Santee, CA 92071. Offers astro/geophysics (MS); biology (MS); geology (MS); science education (MS). Part-time programs available. *Faculty:* 6 full-time (0 women), 4 part-time/adjunct (1 woman). *Students:* 11 full-time (6 women), 18 part-time (9 women); includes 3 minority (2 African Americans, 1 Asian American or Pacific Islander). Average age 41. In 2003, 4 degrees awarded, leading to university research/teaching 50%, business/industry 50%. *Median time to degree:* Master's–4.6 years full-time. *Degree requirements:* For master's, thesis (for some programs), comprehensive exam (for some programs). *Entrance requirements:* For master's, bachelor's degree in science or science education, minimum GPA of 3.0 (undergraduate). *Application deadline:* Applications are processed on a rolling basis. Application fee: $30. *Expenses:* Tuition: Full-time $1,800; part-time $150 per unit. *Financial support:* In 2003–04, 25 students received support. *Faculty research:* Age of the earth, limits of variation, catastrophe, optimum methods for teaching. Total annual research expenditures: $200,000. *Unit head:* Kenneth B. Cumming, Dean, 619-448-0900, Fax: 619-448-3469. *Application contact:* Dr. Jack Kriege, Registrar, 619-448-0900 Ext. 6016, Fax: 619-448-3469, E-mail: jkriege@icr.org.

Indiana University Bloomington, Graduate School, College of Arts and Sciences, Department of Astronomy, Program in Astrophysics, Bloomington, IN 47405. Offers PhD. *Students:* 5 full-time (0 women), 2 part-time, 2 international. Average age 24. *Degree requirements:* For doctorate, thesis/dissertation, written qualifying exam. *Entrance requirements:* For doctorate, GRE General Test, GRE Subject Test (physics), BA or BS in science. Additional exam requirements/recommendations for international students: Required—TOEFL. *Application deadline:* For fall admission, 1/15 priority date for domestic students, 12/15 priority date for international students; for spring admission, 9/1 priority date for domestic students, 9/1 priority date for international students. Applications are processed on a rolling basis. Application fee: $45 ($55 for international students). Electronic applications accepted. *Expenses:* Tuition, state resident: full-time $4,908; part-time $205 per credit. Tuition, nonresident: full-time $14,298; part-time $596 per credit. Required fees: $661. Tuition and fees vary according to campus/location and program. *Financial support:* In 2003–04, research assistantships (averaging $12,000 per year), teaching assistantships (averaging $11,000 per year) were awarded. Financial award application deadline: 5/2. *Faculty research:* Nuclear astrophysics, cosmic-ray physics, astrophysical fluid dynamics, active galactic nuclei, high-energy astrophysics. *Application contact:* Brenda Records, Secretary, 812-855-6912, Fax: 812-855-8725, E-mail: brecords@indiana.edu.

Iowa State University of Science and Technology, Graduate College, College of Liberal Arts and Sciences, Department of Physics and Astronomy, Ames, IA 50011. Offers applied physics (MS, PhD); astrophysics (MS, PhD); condensed matter physics (MS, PhD); high energy physics (MS, PhD); nuclear physics (MS, PhD); physics (MS, PhD). Part-time programs available. *Faculty:* 45 full-time, 4 part-time/adjunct. *Students:* 83 full-time (12 women), 5 part-time; includes 1 minority (Hispanic American), 66 international. 174 applicants, 59% accepted, 31 enrolled. In 2003, 3 master's, 4 doctorates awarded. Terminal master's awarded for partial completion of doctoral program. *Median time to degree:* Master's–2.9 years full-time; doctorate–7.1 years full-time. *Degree requirements:* For master's, thesis (for some programs); for doctorate, thesis/dissertation. *Entrance requirements:* For master's and doctorate, GRE General Test, GRE Subject Test (physics). Additional exam requirements/recommendations for international students: Required—TOEFL (paper score 550; computer score 213) or IELTS (score 6.5). *Application deadline:* For fall admission, 2/15 priority date for domestic students, 2/15 priority date for international students; for spring admission, 10/15 for domestic students, 10/15 for international students. Applications are processed on a rolling basis. Application fee: $30 ($70 for international students). Electronic applications accepted. Tuition, nonresident: part-time $560 per credit. Required fees: $38 per unit. *Financial support:* In 2003–04, 38 research assistantships with full tuition reimbursements (averaging $17,400 per year), 42 teaching assistantships with full tuition reimbursements (averaging $17,400 per year) were awarded. Fellowships, Federal Work-Study, institutionally sponsored loans, scholarships/grants, health care benefits, and unspecified assistantships also available. Support available to part-time students. Financial award application deadline: 2/15. *Faculty research:* Condensed-matter physics, including superconductivity and new materials; high-energy and nuclear physics; astronomy and astrophysics; atmospheric and environmental physics. Total annual research expenditures: $8.8 million. *Unit head:* Dr. Eli Rosenberg, Chair, 515-294-5441, Fax: 515-294-6027, E-mail: phys_astro@iastate.edu. *Application contact:* Dr. Steven Kawaler, Director of Graduate Education, 515-294-9728, E-mail: phys_astro@iastate.edu.

Louisiana State University and Agricultural and Mechanical College, Graduate School, College of Basic Sciences, Department of Physics and Astronomy, Baton Rouge, LA 70803. Offers astronomy (PhD); astrophysics (PhD); physics (MS, PhD). *Faculty:* 36 full-time (2 women), 3 part-time/adjunct (0 women). *Students:* 58 full-time (13 women), 1 (woman) part-time; includes 3 minority (2 Asian Americans or Pacific Islanders, 1 Hispanic American), 33 international. Average age 28. 69 applicants, 32% accepted, 13 enrolled. In 2003, 7 master's, 10 doctorates awarded. Terminal master's awarded for partial completion of doctoral program. *Degree requirements:* For master's, thesis or alternative; for doctorate, thesis/dissertation. *Entrance requirements:* For master's and doctorate, GRE General Test, minimum GPA of 3.0. Additional exam requirements/recommendations for international students: Required—TOEFL (minimum score 550 paper-based; 213 computer-based). *Application deadline:* For fall admission, 1/25 priority date for domestic students, 5/15 priority date for international students. Applications are processed on a rolling basis. Application fee: $25. Electronic applications accepted. *Expenses:* Tuition, state resident: part-time $337 per hour. Tuition, nonresident: part-time $577 per hour. *Financial support:* In 2003–04, 15 students received support, including 5 fellowships (averaging $18,000 per year), 28 research assistantships with partial tuition reimbursements available (averaging $18,041 per year), 23 teaching assistantships with partial tuition reimbursements available (averaging $19,196 per year); institutionally sponsored loans and unspecified assistantships also available. Financial award application deadline: 3/15; financial award applicants required to submit FAFSA. *Faculty research:* Experimental and theoretical atomic, nuclear, particle, cosmic-ray, low-temperature, and condensed-matter physics. Total annual research expenditures: $4.9 million. *Unit head:* Dr. Roger McNeil, Chair, 225-578-2261, Fax: 225-578-5855, E-mail: mcneil@phys.lsu.edu. *Application contact:* Dr. James Matthews, Graduate Adviser, 225-578-8598, Fax: 225-578-5855, E-mail: jmatth5@lsu.edu.

McMaster University, School of Graduate Studies, Faculty of Science, Department of Physics and Astronomy, Hamilton, ON L8S 4M2, Canada. Offers astrophysics (PhD); medical physics and applied radiation sciences (M Sc, PhD), including health and radiation physics (M Sc), medical physics; physics (PhD). Part-time programs available. *Degree requirements:* For master's, thesis or alternative; for doctorate, thesis/dissertation, comprehensive exam. *Entrance requirements:* For master's and doctorate, minimum B+ average. Additional exam requirements/recommendations for international students: Required—TOEFL (minimum score 550 paper-based; 213 computer-based). *Faculty research:* Condensed matter, astrophysics, nuclear, medical, nonlinear dynamics.

Michigan State University, Graduate School, College of Natural Science, Department of Physics and Astronomy, East Lansing, MI 48824. Offers astrophysics and astronomy (MS, PhD); physics (MS, PhD). *Faculty:* 52 full-time (2 women). *Students:* 128 full-time (21 women), 5 part-time; includes 5 minority (1 American Indian/Alaska Native, 3 Asian Americans or Pacific Islanders, 1 Hispanic American), 72 international. Average age 28. 291 applicants, 6% accepted. In 2003, 27 master's, 13 doctorates awarded. *Degree requirements:* For master's, qualifying exam, thesis optional; for doctorate, thesis/dissertation, qualifying exam, comprehensive exam. *Entrance requirements:* For master's and doctorate, minimum GPA of 3.0 in science/math courses, course work equivalent to a major in physics or astronomy, 3 letters of recommendation. Additional exam requirements/recommendations for international students: Required—TOEFL (minimum score 550 paper-based; 213 computer-based), Michigan State University ELT (85), Michigan ELAB (83). *Application deadline:* For fall admission, 1/15 for domestic students; for spring admission, 9/30 for domestic students. Application fee: $50. Electronic applications accepted. *Expenses:* Tuition, state resident: part-time $291 per hour. Tuition, nonresident: part-time $589 per hour. *Financial support:* In 2003–04, 14 fellowships with tuition reimbursements (averaging $7,077 per year), 18 research assistantships with tuition reimbursements (averaging $13,681 per year), 39 teaching assistantships with tuition reimbursements (averaging $12,741 per year) were awarded. Financial award applicants required to submit FAFSA. *Faculty research:* Nuclear and accelerator physics, high-energy physics, condensed-matter physics, astrophysics and astronomy, biophysics. Total annual research expenditures: $4.8 million. *Unit head:* Dr. Wolfgang Bauer, Chairperson, 517-355-9200 Ext. 2015, Fax: 517-355-4500. *Application contact:* Dr. S. D. Mahanti, Director of Graduate Studies, 517-355-9200 Ext. 2303, Fax: 517-355-4500, E-mail: mahanti@pa.msu.edu.

See in-depth description on page 381.

New Mexico Institute of Mining and Technology, Graduate Studies, Department of Physics, Socorro, NM 87801. Offers astrophysics (MS, PhD); atmospheric physics (MS, PhD); instrumentation (MS); mathematical physics (PhD). *Faculty:* 14 full-time (2 women), 19 part-time/adjunct (2 women). *Students:* 19 full-time (5 women), 2 part-time (1 woman); includes 2 minority (1 Asian American or Pacific Islander, 1 Hispanic American), 3 international. Average age 28. 21 applicants, 5 enrolled. In 2003, 1 master's, 3 doctorates awarded. *Degree requirements:* For master's, thesis optional; for doctorate, thesis/dissertation. *Entrance requirements:* For master's, GRE General Test; for doctorate, GRE General Test, GRE Subject Test. Additional exam requirements/recommendations for international students: Required—TOEFL (minimum score 540 paper-based; 207 computer-based). *Application deadline:* For fall admission, 3/1 for domestic students; for spring admission, 6/1 for domestic students. Applications are processed on a rolling basis. Application fee: $16 ($30 for international students). *Expenses:* Tuition, state resident: full-time $2,276; part-time $126 per credit. Tuition, nonresident: full-time $9,170; part-time $509 per credit. Required fees: $924; $27 per credit. $214 per term. Part-time tuition and fees vary according to course load. *Financial support:* In 2003–04, 10 research assistantships (averaging $14,242 per year), 10 teaching assistantships with full and partial tuition reimbursements (averaging $9,600 per year) were awarded. Fellowships, Federal Work-Study, institutionally sponsored loans, and unspecified assistantships also available. Financial award application deadline: 3/1; financial award applicants required to submit CSS PROFILE or FAFSA. *Faculty research:* Cloud physics, stellar and extragalactic processes. *Unit head:* Dr. Kenneth Minschwaner, Chairman, 505-835-5226, Fax: 505-835-5707, E-mail: krm@kestrel.nmt.edu. *Application contact:* Dr. David B. Johnson, Dean of Graduate Studies, 505-835-5513, Fax: 505-835-5476, E-mail: graduate@nmt.edu.

Northwestern University, The Graduate School, Judd A. and Marjorie Weinberg College of Arts and Sciences, Department of Physics and Astronomy, Evanston, IL 60208. Offers astrophysics (PhD); physics (MS, PhD). Admissions and degrees offered through The Graduate School. Terminal master's awarded for partial completion of doctoral program. *Degree requirements:* For doctorate, thesis/dissertation, qualifying exam. *Entrance requirements:* For doctorate, GRE General Test, GRE Subject Test. Additional exam requirements/recommendations for international students: Required—TOEFL. *Faculty research:* Nuclear and particle physics, condensed-matter physics, nonlinear physics, astrophysics.

The Pennsylvania State University University Park Campus, Graduate School, Eberly College of Science, Department of Astronomy and Astrophysics, State College, University Park, PA 16802-1503. Offers MS, PhD. *Students:* 30 full-time (8 women); includes 2 minority (both Hispanic Americans), 15 international. *Entrance requirements:* For master's and doctorate, GRE General Test. Application fee: $45. *Unit head:* Dr. Lawrence W. Ramsey, Head, 814-865-0418, Fax: 814-863-3399, E-mail: lwr@psu.edu.

Princeton University, Graduate School, Department of Astrophysical Sciences, Princeton, NJ 08544-1019. Offers astrophysical sciences (PhD); plasma physics (PhD). *Faculty:* 16 full-time (2 women), 1 part-time/adjunct (0 women). *Students:* 38 full-time (4 women), 16 international. 63 applicants, 21% accepted, 3 enrolled. In 2003, 5 degrees awarded, leading to university research/teaching 33%, continued full-time study 67%. *Median time to degree:* Doctorate–5.8 years full-time. Of those who began their doctoral program in fall 1995, 100% received their degree in 8 years or less. *Degree requirements:* For doctorate, thesis/dissertation. *Entrance requirements:* For doctorate, GRE General Test, GRE Subject Test (physics). Additional exam requirements/recommendations for international students: Required—TOEFL (minimum score 600 paper-based; 250 computer-based). *Application deadline:* For fall admission, 12/31 for domestic students, 12/1 for international students. Application fee: $80 ($55 for international students). Electronic applications accepted. *Expenses:* Tuition: Full-time $29,910. Required fees: $810. *Financial support:* In 2003–04, 4 fellowships with full tuition reimbursements (averaging $16,105 per year), 4 research assistantships with full tuition reimbursements (averaging $30,963 per year), 1 teaching assistantship with full tuition reimbursement (averaging $32,500 per year) were awarded. Federal Work-Study and institutionally sponsored loans also available. Financial award application deadline: 1/2. *Faculty research:* Theoretical astrophysics, cosmology, galaxy formation, galactic dynamics, interstellar and intergalactic matter. Total annual research expenditures: $2.6 million. *Unit head:* Prof. James M. Stone, Dean of Graduate Studies, 609-258-3815, Fax: 609-258-1020, E-mail: jstone@astro.princeton.edu. *Application contact:* Janice Yip, Director of Graduate Admissions, 609-258-3034, Fax: 609-258-6180, E-mail: gsadmit@princeton.edu.

Rensselaer Polytechnic Institute, Graduate School, School of Science, Department of Physics, Applied Physics and Astronomy, Troy, NY 12180-3590. Offers physics (MS, PhD). *Faculty:* 23 full-time (3 women), 2 part-time/adjunct (0 women). *Students:* 45 full-time (9 women); includes 22 minority (all Asian Americans or Pacific Islanders), 39 international. Average age 28. 101 applicants, 12% accepted. In 2003, 10 master's, 13 doctorates awarded. *Degree requirements:* For doctorate, thesis/dissertation. *Entrance requirements:* For master's and doctorate, GRE General Test, GRE Subject Test. Additional exam requirements/recommendations for international students: Required—TOEFL (minimum score 600 paper-based; 250 computer-based). *Application deadline:* For fall admission, 1/15 for domestic students; for spring admission, 10/1 priority date for domestic students. Applications are processed on a rolling basis. Application fee: $45. Electronic applications accepted. *Expenses:* Tuition: Full-time $27,700; part-time $1,320 per credit. Required fees: $1,470. *Financial support:* In 2003–04, 2 fellowships with tuition reimbursements (averaging $25,000 per year), 19 research assistantships with tuition reimbursements (averaging $18,700 per year), 22 teaching assistantships with tuition reimbursements (averaging $19,000 per year) were awarded. Career-related internships or fieldwork and institutionally sponsored loans also available. Financial award application deadline: 2/1. *Faculty research:* Astrophysics, condensed matter, nuclear physics, optics, physics education. Total annual research expenditures: $3.6 million. *Unit head:* Dr. G. C. Wang, Chair, 518-276-8387, Fax: 518-276-6680, E-mail: wangg@rpi.edu. *Application contact:* Dr. Toh-Ming Lu, Chair, Graduate Recruitment Committee, 518-276-8391, Fax: 518-276-6680, E-mail: mcquade@rpi.edu.

San Francisco State University, Division of Graduate Studies, College of Science and Engineering, Department of Physics and Astronomy, San Francisco, CA 94132-1722. Offers physics (MS). Part-time programs available. *Faculty:* 10 full-time (4 women), 6 part-time/adjunct (0 women). *Students:* 52 full-time (12 women), 10 part-time (4 women). 19 applicants, 74% accepted, 12 enrolled. In 2003, 11 degrees awarded. *Median time to degree:* Master's–2 years full-time, 3 years part-time. *Degree requirements:* For master's, thesis, registration. *Entrance requirements:* For master's, minimum GPA of 2.5 in last 60 units. Additional exam requirements/recommendations for international students: Required—TOEFL (minimum score 550 paper-based; 213 computer-based). *Application deadline:* For fall admission, 5/1 for domestic students, 4/2 for international students; for spring admission, 11/15 for domestic students. Applications are processed on a rolling basis. Application fee: $55. Electronic applications accepted. *Expenses:* Tuition, state resident: part-time $871 per unit. Tuition, nonresident: part-time $1,093 per unit. *Financial support:* In 2003–04, 35 students received support, including research assistantships (averaging $10,000 per year), teaching assistantships with partial tuition reimbursements available (averaging $8,500 per year); career-related internships or fieldwork, Federal Work-Study, institutionally sponsored loans, and tuition waivers (partial) also available. Financial award application deadline: 3/1. *Faculty research:* Quark search, thin-films, dark matter detection, search for planetary systems, low temperature. Total annual research expenditures: $500,000. *Unit head:* Dr. James Lockhart, Chair, 415-338-1659, E-mail: lockhart@stars.sfsu.edu. *Application contact:* Dr. Susan Lea, Graduate Coordinator, 415-338-1691, E-mail: lea@stars.sfsu.edu.

Texas Christian University, College of Science and Engineering, Department of Physics and Astronomy, Fort Worth, TX 76129-0002. Offers physics (PhD), including astrophysics, business, physics. Part-time and evening/weekend programs available. *Degree requirements:* For doctorate, thesis/dissertation, qualifying exams. *Entrance requirements:* For doctorate, GRE General Test. Additional exam requirements/recommendations for international students: Required—TOEFL. *Application deadline:* For fall admission, 3/1 for domestic students; for spring admission, 12/1 for domestic students. Applications are processed on a rolling basis. Application fee: $0. *Expenses:* Tuition: Part-time $640 per credit hour. Tuition and fees vary according to program. *Financial support:* Fellowships, teaching assistantships available. Financial award application deadline: 3/1. *Unit head:* Dr. C. Magnus Rittby, Chairperson, 817-257-7375, E-mail: m.rittby@tcu.edu. *Application contact:* Dr. Bonnie Melhart, Associate Dean, College of Science and Engineering, E-mail: b.melhart@tcu.edu.

University of Alaska Fairbanks, College of Science, Engineering and Mathematics, Department of Physics, Fairbanks, AK 99775-7520. Offers atmospheric science (MS, PhD); physics (MS, PhD); space physics (MS, PhD). Part-time programs available. Terminal master's awarded for partial completion of doctoral program. *Degree requirements:* For master's, thesis or alternative, comprehensive exam, registration; for doctorate, one foreign language, thesis/dissertation, comprehensive exam, registration. *Entrance requirements:* For master's and doctorate, GRE General Test, GRE Subject Test. Additional exam requirements/recommendations for international students: Required—TOEFL. Electronic applications accepted. *Faculty research:* Atmospheric and ionospheric radar studies, space plasma theory, magnetospheric dynamics, space weather and auroral studies, turbulence and complex systems.

University of Alberta, Faculty of Graduate Studies and Research, Department of Physics, Edmonton, AB T6G 2E1, Canada. Offers astrophysics (M Sc, PhD); condensed matter (M Sc, PhD); geophysics (M Sc, PhD); medical physics (M Sc, PhD); subatomic physics (M Sc, PhD). *Faculty:* 36 full-time (3 women), 7 part-time/adjunct (0 women). *Students:* 56 full-time (6 women), 16 part-time (2 women), 25 international. 85 applicants, 35% accepted. In 2003, 7 master's, 10 doctorates awarded. *Degree requirements:* For master's and doctorate, thesis/dissertation. *Entrance requirements:* For master's and doctorate, minimum GPA of 7.0 on a 9.0 scale. Additional exam requirements/recommendations for international students: Required—TOEFL. *Application deadline:* For fall admission, 2/15 for domestic students. Applications are processed on a rolling basis. Tuition charges are reported in Canadian dollars. Tuition, nonresident: full-time $3,921 Canadian dollars. International tuition: $7,113 Canadian dollars full-time. *Financial support:* In 2003–04, 45 students received support, including 6 fellowships with

Astrophysics

University of Alberta (continued)
partial tuition reimbursements available, 40 teaching assistantships; research assistantships, career-related internships or fieldwork, institutionally sponsored loans, and scholarships/grants also available. Financial award application deadline: 2/15. *Faculty research:* Cosmology, astroparticle physics, high-intermediate energy, magnetism, superconductivity. Total annual research expenditures: $3.1 million. *Unit head:* Dr. Richard Sydora, Associate Chair, 780-492-1072, E-mail: assoc-chair@phys.ualberta.ca. *Application contact:* Lynn Chandler, Program Advisor, 780-492-1072, Fax: 780-492-0714, E-mail: lynn@phys.ualberta.ca.

University of California, Berkeley, Graduate Division, College of Letters and Science, Department of Astronomy, Berkeley, CA 94720-1500. Offers astrophysics (PhD). *Faculty:* 17 full-time (2 women), 2 part-time/adjunct (0 women). *Students:* 33 (11 women); includes 3 minority (2 African Americans, 1 American Indian/Alaska Native) 6 international. 148 applicants, 9% accepted, 4 enrolled. In 2003, 3 degrees awarded. *Median time to degree:* Doctorate–6 years full-time. *Degree requirements:* For doctorate, thesis/dissertation, qualifying exam. *Entrance requirements:* For doctorate, GRE General Test, GRE Subject Test, minimum GPA of 3.0. *Application deadline:* For fall admission, 1/5 for domestic students. Application fee: $60. International tuition: $12,491 full-time. Required fees: $5,484. *Financial support:* In 2003–04, fellowships with full tuition reimbursements (averaging $21,000 per year), research assistantships with full tuition reimbursements (averaging $21,000 per year), teaching assistantships with full tuition reimbursements (averaging $21,000 per year) were awarded. Scholarships/grants, health care benefits, tuition waivers (full), and unspecified assistantships also available. Financial award application deadline: 12/19. *Faculty research:* Theory, cosmology, radio astronomy, extra solar planets, infrared instrumentation. *Unit head:* Dr. Donald Backer, Chair.

University of California, Los Angeles, Graduate Division, College of Letters and Science, Department of Earth and Space Sciences, Program in Geophysics and Space Physics, Los Angeles, CA 90095. Offers MS, PhD. *Degree requirements:* For master's, comprehensive exams or thesis; for doctorate, thesis/dissertation, oral and written qualifying exams. *Entrance requirements:* For master's, GRE General Test, minimum GPA of 3.0; for doctorate, GRE General Test, minimum undergraduate GPA of 3.0. Electronic applications accepted. Tuition, nonresident: full-time $12,245. Required fees: $6,318.

University of California, Santa Cruz, Division of Graduate Studies, Division of Physical and Biological Sciences, Program in Astronomy and Astrophysics, Santa Cruz, CA 95064. Offers PhD. *Faculty:* 23 full-time (3 women). *Students:* 25 full-time (10 women); includes 2 minority (1 African American, 1 Asian American or Pacific Islander), 2 international. 137 applicants, 23% accepted, 7 enrolled. In 2003, 5 doctorates awarded. *Median time to degree:* Doctorate–7 years full-time. *Degree requirements:* For doctorate, one foreign language, thesis/dissertation, qualifying exam. *Entrance requirements:* For doctorate, GRE General Test, GRE Subject Test. *Application deadline:* For fall admission, 1/15 for domestic students. Application fee: $60. Tuition, nonresident: full-time $12,492. *Financial support:* Fellowships, research assistantships, teaching assistantships, Federal Work-Study and institutionally sponsored loans available. Financial award application deadline: 1/15. *Faculty research:* Stellar structure and evolution, stellar spectroscopy, the interstellar medium, galactic structure, external galaxies and quasars. *Unit head:* Dr. Stephen Thorsett, Chairperson, 831-459-2976, E-mail: thorsett@ucolick.ucsc.edu. *Application contact:* James M. Moore, Graduate Admissions, Director, 831-459-2301, Fax: 831-459-4843, E-mail: gradadm@ucsc.edu.

University of Chicago, Division of the Physical Sciences, Department of Astronomy and Astrophysics, Chicago, IL 60637-1513. Offers SM, PhD. *Faculty:* 33 full-time (2 women), 4 part-time/adjunct (0 women). *Students:* 28 full-time (6 women); includes 10 minority (7 Asian Americans or Pacific Islanders, 3 Hispanic Americans). Average age 26. In 2003, 8 master's, 2 doctorates awarded. Terminal master's awarded for partial completion of doctoral program. *Degree requirements:* For master's, candidacy exam; for doctorate, thesis/dissertation, dissertation for publication. *Entrance requirements:* For doctorate, GRE General Test, GRE Subject Test, minimum GPA of 3.0. Additional exam requirements/recommendations for international students: Required—TOEFL (minimum score 600 paper-based; 250 computer-based). *Application deadline:* For fall admission, 12/28 priority date for domestic students, 12/28 priority date for international students. Application fee: $55. Electronic applications accepted. *Financial support:* In 2003–04, 28 students received support, including fellowships (averaging $4,250 per year), research assistantships with full tuition reimbursements available (averaging $19,800 per year), teaching assistantships with full tuition reimbursements available (averaging $19,800 per year); career-related internships or fieldwork, Federal Work-Study, institutionally sponsored loans, and tuition waivers (partial) also available. Financial award application deadline: 12/28. *Faculty research:* Quasi-stellar object absorption lines, fluid dynamics, interstellar matter, particle physics, cosmology. *Unit head:* Angela Olinto, Chairman, 773-702-8203, Fax: 773-702-8212. *Application contact:* Laticia Rebeles, Admissions Officer, 773-702-9808, Fax: 773-702-8212, E-mail: lrebeles@oddjob.uchicago.edu.

University of Colorado at Boulder, Graduate School, College of Arts and Sciences, Department of Astrophysical and Planetary Sciences, Boulder, CO 80309. Offers astrophysical and geophysical fluid dynamics (MS, PhD); astrophysics (MS, PhD); plasma physics (MS, PhD). *Faculty:* 17 full-time (1 woman). *Students:* 70 full-time (22 women), 21 part-time (8 women); includes 6 minority (3 Asian Americans or Pacific Islanders, 3 Hispanic Americans), 9 international. Average age 28. 103 applicants, 50% accepted. In 2003, 7 master's, 12 doctorates awarded. Terminal master's awarded for partial completion of doctoral program. *Degree requirements:* For master's, thesis or alternative, comprehensive exam; for doctorate, one foreign language, thesis/dissertation. *Entrance requirements:* For master's and doctorate, GRE General Test, GRE Subject Test. *Application deadline:* For fall admission, 3/1 for domestic students. Applications are processed on a rolling basis. Application fee: $50 ($60 for international students). *Expenses:* Tuition, state resident: full-time $2,122. Tuition, nonresident: full-time $9,754. Tuition and fees vary according to course load and program. *Financial support:* In 2003–04, 6 fellowships (averaging $17,509 per year), 23 research assistantships (averaging $15,762 per year), 20 teaching assistantships (averaging $17,065 per year) were awarded. Tuition waivers (full) also available. Support available to part-time students. Financial award application deadline: 2/1. *Faculty research:* Stellar and extragalactic astrophysics cosmology, space astronomy, planetary science. Total annual research expenditures: $30.6 million. *Unit head:* J. Michael Shull, Chair, 303-492-8915, Fax: 303-492-3822, E-mail: mshull@casa.colorado.edu. *Application contact:* Graduate Program Assistant, 303-492-8914, Fax: 303-492-3822, E-mail: admin@aps.colorado.edu.

University of Minnesota, Twin Cities Campus, Graduate School, Institute of Technology, School of Physics and Astronomy, Department of Astronomy, Minneapolis, MN 55455-0213. Offers astrophysics (MS, PhD). Terminal master's awarded for partial completion of doctoral program. *Degree requirements:* For master's, thesis optional; for doctorate, thesis/dissertation. *Entrance requirements:* For master's and doctorate, GRE General Test, GRE Subject Test. *Expenses:* Tuition, state resident: full-time $3,681; part-time $614 per credit. Tuition, nonresident: full-time $7,231; part-time $1,205 per credit. *Faculty research:* Evolution of stars and galaxies; the interstellar medium; cosmology; observational, optical, infrared, and radio astronomy; computational astrophysics.

University of Missouri–St. Louis, Graduate School, College of Arts and Sciences, Department of Physics and Astronomy, St. Louis, MO 63121-4499. Offers applied physics (MS); astrophysics (MS); physics (PhD). Part-time and evening/weekend programs available. *Faculty:* 14 full-time (0 women). *Students:* 9 full-time (2 women), 10 part-time (3 women); includes 1 minority (Asian American or Pacific Islander), 5 international. Average age 25. In 2003, 3 master's, 1 doctorate awarded. Terminal master's awarded for partial completion of doctoral program. *Degree requirements:* For master's, thesis optional; for doctorate, thesis/dissertation. *Entrance requirements:* For master's and doctorate, GRE General Test. Additional exam requirements/recommendations for international students: Required—TOEFL (minimum score 550 paper-based; 213 computer-based). *Application deadline:* For fall admission, 4/1 for domestic students; for spring admission, 12/1 priority date for domestic students. Applications are processed on a rolling basis. Application fee: $35 ($40 for international students). Electronic applications accepted. *Expenses:* Tuition, state resident: part-time $237 per credit hour. Tuition, nonresident: part-time $639 per credit hour. Required fees: $10 per credit hour. *Financial support:* In 2003–04, 1 research assistantship with full and partial tuition reimbursement (averaging $6,750 per year), 9 teaching assistantships with full and partial tuition reimbursements (averaging $12,978 per year) were awarded. Fellowships with full tuition reimbursements, career-related internships or fieldwork also available. *Faculty research:* Biophysics, atomic physics, nonlinear dynamics, materials science. *Unit head:* Dr. Ricardo Flores, Director of Graduate Studies, 314-516-5931, Fax: 314-516-6152, E-mail: graduate@newton.umsl.edu. *Application contact:* 314-516-5458, Fax: 314-516-5310, E-mail: gradadm@umsl.edu.

The University of North Carolina at Chapel Hill, Graduate School, College of Arts and Sciences, Department of Physics and Astronomy, Chapel Hill, NC 27599. Offers physics (MS, PhD). *Faculty:* 31 full-time (3 women), 7 part-time/adjunct (1 woman). *Students:* 65 full-time (21 women). Average age 26. 200 applicants, 21% accepted, 19 enrolled. In 2003, 8 master's, 6 doctorates awarded. Terminal master's awarded for partial completion of doctoral program. *Median time to degree:* Master's–3 years full-time; doctorate–6 years full-time. *Degree requirements:* For master's, comprehensive exam, registration; for doctorate, thesis/dissertation, comprehensive exam, registration. *Entrance requirements:* For master's and doctorate, GRE General Test, minimum GPA of 3.0. *Application deadline:* For fall admission, 1/1 for domestic students. Application fee: $60. Electronic applications accepted. *Expenses:* Tuition, state resident: full-time $3,163. Tuition, nonresident: full-time $15,161. *Financial support:* In 2003–04, 2 fellowships with full tuition reimbursements (averaging $14,000 per year), 31 research assistantships with full tuition reimbursements (averaging $18,600 per year), 38 teaching assistantships with full tuition reimbursements (averaging $13,950 per year) were awarded. Federal Work-Study, scholarships/grants, health care benefits, and unspecified assistantships also available. Financial award application deadline: 3/1. *Faculty research:* Observational astronomy, fullerenes, polarized beams, nanotubes, nucleosynthesis in stars and supernovae, superstring theory, ballistic transport in semiconductors, gravitation. Total annual research expenditures: $5.5 million. *Unit head:* Dr. Bruce W. Carney, Chairman, 919-962-2079, Fax: 919-962-8205, E-mail: bruce@physics.unc.edu. *Application contact:* Prof. Thomas B. Clegg, Director of Graduate Admissions, 919-843-8168, Fax: 919-962-0480, E-mail: clegg@physics.unc.edu.

University of Oklahoma, Graduate College, College of Arts and Sciences, Department of Physics and Astronomy, Norman, OK 73019-0390. Offers astrophysics (MS, PhD); physics (MS, PhD). Part-time programs available. *Faculty:* 29 full-time (4 women), 1 part-time/adjunct (0 women). *Students:* 50 full-time (15 women), 3 part-time (1 woman); includes 6 minority (2 African Americans, 3 American Indian/Alaska Native, 1 Asian American or Pacific Islander), 27 international. Average age 26. 28 applicants, 100% accepted, 9 enrolled. In 2003, 4 master's, 5 doctorates awarded. Terminal master's awarded for partial completion of doctoral program. *Degree requirements:* For master's, thesis or alternative, departmental qualifying exam; for doctorate, thesis/dissertation, comprehensive, departmental qualifying, oral, and written exams. *Entrance requirements:* For master's and doctorate, GRE General Test, GRE Subject Test, previous course work in physics. Additional exam requirements/recommendations for international students: Required—TOEFL (minimum score 600 paper-based; 250 computer-based). *Application deadline:* For fall admission, 3/1 for domestic students. Application fee: $25 ($75 for international students). *Expenses:* Tuition, state resident: full-time $2,774; part-time $116 per credit hour. Tuition, nonresident: full-time $9,571; part-time $399 per credit hour. Required fees: $953; $33 per credit hour. Full-time tuition and fees vary according to course level, course load and program. *Financial support:* In 2003–04, 10 students received support, including 3 fellowships with full tuition reimbursements available (averaging $4,333 per year), 26 research assistantships with partial tuition reimbursements available (averaging $13,733 per year), 29 teaching assistantships with partial tuition reimbursements available (averaging $12,533 per year); Federal Work-Study, scholarships/grants, health care benefits, tuition waivers (full), and unspecified assistantships also available. Financial award application deadline: 3/1; financial award applicants required to submit FAFSA. *Faculty research:* Atomic, molecular, and chemical physics; high energy, solid state and applied physics, astrophysics. Total annual research expenditures: $3.9 million. *Unit head:* Dr. Ryan Doezema, Chair, 405-325-3961, Fax: 405-325-7557, E-mail: rdoezema@ou.edu. *Application contact:* Sonya Brindle, Curriculum Advisor, 405-325-3961 Ext. 36127, Fax: 405-325-7557, E-mail: brindle@mail.ou.edu.

University of Pennsylvania, School of Arts and Sciences, Graduate Group in Physics and Astronomy, Philadelphia, PA 19104. Offers medical physics (MS); physics (PhD). Part-time programs available. *Faculty:* 43 full-time (4 women), 28 part-time/adjunct (3 women). *Students:* 89 full-time (17 women), 4 part-time (1 woman); includes 3 minority (1 Asian American or Pacific Islander, 2 Hispanic Americans), 41 international. 465 applicants, 9% accepted, 13 enrolled. In 2003, 29 master's, 6 doctorates awarded. *Degree requirements:* For doctorate, thesis/dissertation, oral, preliminary, and final exams. *Entrance requirements:* For doctorate, GRE General Test, GRE Subject Test (recommended). Additional exam requirements/recommendations for international students: Required—TOEFL; Recommended—TSE. *Application deadline:* For fall admission, 12/1 for domestic students. Application fee: $70. Electronic applications accepted. *Expenses:* Tuition: Full-time $28,040; part-time $3,550 per course. Required fees: $1,750; $214 per course. Tuition and fees vary according to degree level, program and student level. *Financial support:* Fellowships, research assistantships, teaching assistantships, institutionally sponsored loans available. Financial award application deadline: 12/15. *Faculty research:* Astrophysics, condensed matter experiment, condensed matter theory, particle experiment, particle theory. Total annual research expenditures: $7.3 million. *Application contact:* Patricia Rea, Coordinator for Admissions, 215-573-5816, Fax: 215-573-8068, E-mail: gdasadmis@sas.upenn.edu.

University of Victoria, Faculty of Graduate Studies, Faculty of Science, Department of Physics and Astronomy, Victoria, BC V8W 2Y2, Canada. Offers astronomy and astrophysics (M Sc, PhD); condensed matter physics (M Sc, PhD); medical physics (M Sc, PhD); nuclear and particle studies (M Sc, PhD); ocean physics (M Sc, PhD); theoretical physics (M Sc, PhD). *Degree requirements:* For master's, thesis/dissertation, registration; for doctorate, thesis/dissertation, comprehensive exam, registration. *Entrance requirements:* Additional exam requirements/recommendations for international students: Required—TOEFL (minimum score 575 paper-based; 213 computer-based). *Faculty research:* Old stellar populations; observational cosmology and large scale structure; cp violation; atlas.

Section 2
Chemistry

This section contains a directory of institutions offering graduate work in chemistry, followed by in-depth entries submitted by institutions that chose to prepare detailed program descriptions. Additional information about programs listed in the directory but not augmented by an in-depth entry may be obtained by writing directly to the dean of a graduate school or chair of a department at the address given in the directory.

For programs offering related work, see also in this book Geosciences and Physics. In Book 3, see Biological and Biomedical Sciences, Biochemistry, Biophysics, Nutrition, and Pharmacology and Toxicology; in Book 5, see Engineering and Applied Sciences; Agricultural Engineering; Chemical Engineering; Geological, Mineral/Mining, and Petroleum Engineering; Materials Sciences and Engineering; and Pharmaceutical Engineering; and in Book 6, see Pharmacy and Pharmaceutical Sciences.

CONTENTS

Analytical Chemistry

Brigham Young University, Graduate Studies, College of Physical and Mathematical Sciences, Department of Chemistry and Biochemistry, Provo, UT 84602-1001. Offers analytical chemistry (MS, PhD); biochemistry (MS, PhD); inorganic chemistry (MS, PhD); organic chemistry (MS, PhD); physical chemistry (MS, PhD). *Faculty:* 34 full-time (2 women). *Students:* 90 full-time (56 women); includes 2 minority (1 Asian American or Pacific Islander, 1 Hispanic American), 61 international. Average age 31. 103 applicants, 54% accepted, 23 enrolled. In 2003, 6 master's, 6 doctorates awarded. *Median time to degree:* Master's–2.8 years full-time. Of those who began their doctoral program in fall 1995, 100% received their degree in 8 years or less. *Degree requirements:* For master's, thesis, registration; for doctorate, thesis/dissertation, degree qualifying exam. *Entrance requirements:* For master's, pass 1 (biochemistry), 4 (chemistry) of 5 area exams, GRE General Test, minimum GPA of 3.0 in last 60 hours; for doctorate, pass 1 (biochemistry) or 4 (chemistry) of 5 area exams, GRE General Test, minimum GPA of 3.0 in last 60 hours. Additional exam requirements/recommendations for international students: Required—TOEFL, TWE. *Application deadline:* For fall admission, 2/1 priority date for domestic students, 2/1 priority date for international students. Applications are processed on a rolling basis. Application fee: $50. Electronic applications accepted. *Expenses:* Tuition: Part-time $221 per hour. *Financial support:* In 2003–04, 90 students received support, including 12 fellowships with full tuition reimbursements available (averaging $18,400 per year), 37 research assistantships with full tuition reimbursements available (averaging $18,400 per year), 30 teaching assistantships with full tuition reimbursements available (averaging $18,300 per year); institutionally sponsored loans, scholarships/grants, health care benefits, tuition waivers (full), and unspecified assistantships also available. Financial award application deadline: 2/1. *Faculty research:* Separation science, molecular recognition, organic synthesis and biomedical application, biochemistry and molecular biology, molecular spectroscopy. Total annual research expenditures: $2.7 million. *Unit head:* Dr. Francis R. Nordmeyer, Chair, 801-422-3667, Fax: 801-422-0153, E-mail: fran_nordmeyer@byu.edu. *Application contact:* Dr. Noel L. Owen, Graduate Coordinator, 801-422-2973, Fax: 801-422-0153, E-mail: chemgrad@byu.edu.

See in-depth description on page 97.

California State University, Fullerton, Graduate Studies, College of Natural Science and Mathematics, Department of Chemistry and Biochemistry, Fullerton, CA 92834-9480. Offers analytical chemistry (MS); biochemistry (MS); geochemistry (MS); inorganic chemistry (MS); organic chemistry (MS); physical chemistry (MS). Part-time programs available. *Faculty:* 17 full-time (5 women), 17 part-time/adjunct. *Students:* 21 full-time (9 women), 23 part-time (11 women); includes 19 minority (1 African American, 9 Asian Americans or Pacific Islanders, 9 Hispanic Americans), 8 international. Average age 28. 49 applicants, 61% accepted, 20 enrolled. In 2003, 5 degrees awarded. *Degree requirements:* For master's, thesis, departmental qualifying exam. *Entrance requirements:* For master's, minimum GPA of 2.5 in last 60 units, major in chemistry or related field. Application fee: $55. Tuition, nonresident: part-time $282 per unit. Required fees: $889 per semester. *Financial support:* Teaching assistantships, career-related internships or fieldwork, Federal Work-Study, institutionally sponsored loans, and scholarships/grants available. Support available to part-time students. Financial award application deadline: 3/1. *Unit head:* Dr. Robert Belloli, Chair, 714-278-3621. *Application contact:* Dr. Gregory Williams, Adviser, 714-278-2170.

California State University, Los Angeles, Graduate Studies, College of Natural and Social Sciences, Department of Chemistry and Biochemistry, Los Angeles, CA 90032-8530. Offers analytical chemistry (MS); biochemistry (MS); chemistry (MS); inorganic chemistry (MS); organic chemistry (MS); physical chemistry (MS). Part-time and evening/weekend programs available. *Faculty:* 15 full-time, 12 part-time/adjunct. *Students:* 12 full-time (6 women), 11 part-time (7 women); includes 11 minority (2 African Americans, 5 Asian Americans or Pacific Islanders, 4 Hispanic Americans), 5 international. In 2003, 5 degrees awarded. *Degree requirements:* For master's, one foreign language. *Entrance requirements:* Additional exam requirements/recommendations for international students: Required—TOEFL. *Application deadline:* For fall admission, 6/30 for domestic students; for spring admission, 2/1 for domestic students. Applications are processed on a rolling basis. Application fee: $55. Tuition, nonresident: part-time $188 per unit. Required fees: $2,477. *Financial support:* Federal Work-Study available. Support available to part-time students. Financial award application deadline: 3/1. *Faculty research:* Intercalation of heavy metal, carborane chemistry, conductive polymers and fabrics, titanium reagents, computer modeling and synthesis. *Unit head:* Dr. Wayne Tikkanen, Chair, 323-343-2300.

Case Western Reserve University, School of Graduate Studies, Department of Chemistry, Cleveland, OH 44106. Offers analytical chemistry (MS, PhD); inorganic chemistry (MS, PhD); organic chemistry (MS, PhD); physical chemistry (MS, PhD). Part-time programs available. *Faculty:* 22 full-time (2 women). *Students:* 64 full-time (18 women), 27 part-time (9 women); includes 2 minority (both Asian Americans or Pacific Islanders), 69 international. Average age 27. 483 applicants, 9% accepted, 18 enrolled. In 2003, 5 master's, 13 doctorates awarded. Terminal master's awarded for partial completion of doctoral program. *Degree requirements:* For doctorate, thesis/dissertation. *Entrance requirements:* For master's and doctorate, GRE General Test, GRE Subject Test. Additional exam requirements/recommendations for international students: Required—TOEFL. *Application deadline:* Applications are processed on a rolling basis. Application fee: $50. *Expenses:* Tuition: Full-time $26,900. *Financial support:* In 2003–04, 77 students received support, including 53 research assistantships, 20 teaching assistantships. *Faculty research:* Electrochemistry, synthetic chemistry, chemistry of life process, spectroscopy, kinetics. *Unit head:* Lawrence Sayre, Chairman, 216-368-3622, Fax: 216-368-3006, E-mail: lms3@case.edu. *Application contact:* Zedeara Diaz, Graduate Admissions, 216-368-3621, Fax: 216-368-3006, E-mail: zcd@case.edu.

Clarkson University, Graduate School, School of Arts and Sciences, Department of Chemistry, Potsdam, NY 13699. Offers analytical chemistry (MS, PhD); inorganic chemistry (MS, PhD); organic chemistry (MS, PhD); physical chemistry (MS, PhD). *Faculty:* 11 full-time (2 women). *Students:* 31 full-time (12 women); includes 3 minority (2 African Americans, 1 Asian American or Pacific Islander), 14 international. Average age 28. 45 applicants, 67% accepted. In 2003, 4 master's, 1 doctorate awarded. *Median time to degree:* Master's–2.5 years full-time; doctorate–4 years full-time, 6 years part-time. *Degree requirements:* For doctorate, thesis/dissertation, departmental qualifying exam. *Entrance requirements:* For master's, GRE. Additional exam requirements/recommendations for international students: Required—TOEFL. *Application deadline:* For fall admission, 5/15 for domestic students; for spring admission, 10/15 priority date for domestic students. Applications are processed on a rolling basis. Application fee: $25 ($35 for international students). *Expenses:* Tuition: Full-time $19,272; part-time $803 per credit. Tuition and fees vary according to course load. *Financial support:* In 2003–04, 23 students received support, including 2 fellowships (averaging $22,000 per year), 9 research assistantships (averaging $18,000 per year), 12 teaching assistantships (averaging $18,000 per year); scholarships/grants and tuition waivers (partial) also available. *Faculty research:* Particle adhesion phenomena, airborne radon, ceramic materials, materials processing, chemical kinetics. Total annual research expenditures: $1.3 million. *Unit head:* Dr. Phillip A. Christiansen, Division Head, 315-268-6669, Fax: 315-268-6610, E-mail: pac@clarkson.edu. *Application contact:* Donna Brockway, Assistant to Dean/Foreign Student Advisor, 315-268-6447, Fax: 315-268-7994, E-mail: brockway@clarkson.edu.

Cleveland State University, College of Graduate Studies, College of Arts and Sciences, Department of Chemistry, Cleveland, OH 44115. Offers analytical chemistry (MS, PhD); clinical chemistry (MS, PhD); clinical/bioanalytical (PhD); inorganic chemistry (MS); organic chemistry (MS); physical chemistry (MS); structural analysis (MS, PhD). Part-time and evening/weekend programs available. *Faculty:* 16 full-time (1 woman), 3 part-time/adjunct (1 woman). *Students:* 44 full-time (21 women), 23 part-time (9 women); includes 3 minority (1 African American, 1 Asian American or Pacific Islander, 1 Hispanic American), 29 international. Average age 33. 30 applicants, 23% accepted, 2 enrolled. In 2003, 6 master's, 1 doctorate awarded. *Degree requirements:* For master's, thesis (for some programs); for doctorate, thesis/dissertation. *Entrance requirements:* For master's and doctorate, GRE General Test, GRE Subject Test. Additional exam requirements/recommendations for international students: Required—TOEFL (minimum score 525 paper-based; 197 computer-based). *Application deadline:* For fall admission, 1/15 priority date for domestic students, 1/15 priority date for international students. Applications are processed on a rolling basis. Application fee: $30. Electronic applications accepted. Tuition, area resident: Full-time $8,258; part-time $344 per credit hour. Tuition, nonresident: full-time $16,352; part-time $681 per credit hour. *Financial support:* In 2003–04, 37 students received support, including fellowships (averaging $16,000 per year), 19 research assistantships with full tuition reimbursements available (averaging $16,000 per year), 18 teaching assistantships with full tuition reimbursements available (averaging $15,000 per year) Financial award application deadline: 1/15. *Faculty research:* Trace metal analysis in biological systems, application of HPLC/LPCC to clinical systems, synthetic organic and inorganic chemistry, molecular structure determinations, structure-function relationships of factor Va, MALDI-TOF based DNA sequencing, spectroscopic studies of chemical and biochemical phenomena, novel electro-optic tunable filters (AOTFs) to explore biological systems. Total annual research expenditures: $1 million. *Unit head:* Dr. Stan Duraj, Chair, 216-687-2454, Fax: 216-687-9298, E-mail: s.duraj@csuohio.edu. *Application contact:* Richelle P. Emery, Administrative Coordinator, 216-687-2457, Fax: 216-687-9298, E-mail: r.emery@csuohio.edu.

Cornell University, Graduate School, Graduate Fields of Arts and Sciences, Field of Chemistry and Chemical Biology, Ithaca, NY 14853-0001. Offers analytical chemistry (PhD); bio-organic chemistry (PhD); biophysical chemistry (PhD); chemical biology (PhD); chemical physics (PhD); inorganic chemistry (PhD); materials chemistry (PhD); organic chemistry (PhD); organometallic chemistry (PhD); physical chemistry (PhD); polymer chemistry (PhD); theoretical chemistry (PhD). *Faculty:* 37 full-time. *Students:* 174 full-time (70 women); includes 22 minority (4 African Americans, 10 Asian Americans or Pacific Islanders, 8 Hispanic Americans), 57 international. 371 applicants, 35% accepted, 42 enrolled. In 2003, 22 doctorates awarded. *Degree requirements:* For doctorate, thesis/dissertation, comprehensive exam. *Entrance requirements:* For doctorate, GRE General Test, GRE Subject Test (chemistry), 3 letters of recommendation. Additional exam requirements/recommendations for international students: Required—TOEFL (minimum score 600 paper-based; 250 computer-based). *Application deadline:* For fall admission, 1/10 for domestic students. Application fee: $60. Electronic applications accepted. *Expenses:* Tuition: Full-time $28,630. One-time fee: $50 full-time. *Financial support:* In 2003–04, 162 students received support, including 28 fellowships with full tuition reimbursements available, 77 research assistantships with full tuition reimbursements available, 57 teaching assistantships with full tuition reimbursements available; institutionally sponsored loans, scholarships/grants, health care benefits, tuition waivers (full and partial), and unspecified assistantships also available. Financial award applicants required to submit FAFSA. *Faculty research:* Analytical, organic, inorganic, physical, materials, chemical biology. *Unit head:* Director of Graduate Studies, 607-255-4139, Fax: 607-255-4137. *Application contact:* Graduate Field Assistant, 607-255-4139, Fax: 607-255-4137, E-mail: chemgrad@cornell.edu.

See in-depth description on page 105.

Florida State University, Graduate Studies, College of Arts and Sciences, Department of Chemistry and Biochemistry, Tallahassee, FL 32306. Offers analytical chemistry (MS, PhD); biochemistry (MS, PhD); chemical physics (MS, PhD); inorganic chemistry (MS, PhD); organic chemistry (MS, PhD); physical chemistry (MS, PhD). Part-time programs available. *Faculty:* 30 full-time (6 women), 4 part-time/adjunct (2 women). *Students:* 142 full-time (46 women); includes 18 minority (9 African Americans, 1 American Indian/Alaska Native, 6 Asian Americans or Pacific Islanders, 2 Hispanic Americans), 51 international. Average age 25. 410 applicants, 15% accepted, 39 enrolled. In 2003, 9 master's, 11 doctorates awarded. Terminal master's awarded for partial completion of doctoral program. *Median time to degree:* Master's–3.5 years full-time; doctorate–5 years full-time. Of those who began their doctoral program in fall 1995, 72% received their degree in 8 years or less. *Degree requirements:* For master's, thesis (for some programs), cumulative and diagnostic exams, comprehensive exam (for some programs); for doctorate, thesis/dissertation, cumulative and diagnostic exams. *Entrance requirements:* For master's and doctorate, GRE General Test, minimum B average in undergraduate course work. Additional exam requirements/recommendations for international students: Required—TOEFL (minimum score 515 paper-based; 213 computer-based). *Application deadline:* For fall admission, 4/15 priority date for domestic students, 4/15 priority date for international students. Applications are processed on a rolling basis. Application fee: $20. Electronic applications accepted. *Expenses:* Tuition, state resident: part-time $196 per credit hour. Tuition, nonresident: part-time $731 per credit hour. Part-time tuition and fees vary according to campus/location. *Financial support:* In 2003–04, 2 fellowships with tuition reimbursements (averaging $15,000 per year), 54 research assistantships with tuition reimbursements (averaging $18,000 per year), 76 teaching assistantships with tuition reimbursements (averaging $18,000 per year) were awarded. Career-related internships or fieldwork, Federal Work-Study, institutionally sponsored loans, and traineeships also available. Financial award application deadline: 2/15; financial award applicants required to submit FAFSA. *Faculty research:* Spectroscopy, computational chemistry, nuclear chemistry, separations, synthesis. *Unit head:* Dr. Naresh Dalal, Chairman, 850-644-3398, Fax: 850-644-8281. *Application contact:* Dr. Oliver Steinbock, Chair, Graduate Admissions Committee, 888-525-9286, Fax: 850-644-8281, E-mail: gradinfo@chem.fsu.edu.

See in-depth description on page 115.

Georgetown University, Graduate School of Arts and Sciences, Department of Chemistry, Washington, DC 20057. Offers analytical chemistry (MS, PhD); biochemistry (MS, PhD); chemical physics (MS, PhD); inorganic chemistry (MS, PhD); organic chemistry (MS, PhD); physical chemistry (MS, PhD); theoretical chemistry (MS, PhD). Terminal master's awarded for partial completion of doctoral program. *Degree requirements:* For master's, thesis (for some programs), qualifying exam; for doctorate, thesis/dissertation, comprehensive exam. *Entrance requirements:* For master's and doctorate, GRE General Test. Additional exam requirements/recommendations for international students: Required—TOEFL.

The George Washington University, Columbian College of Arts and Sciences, Department of Chemistry, Washington, DC 20052. Offers analytical chemistry (MS, PhD); inorganic chemistry (MS, PhD); materials science (MS, PhD); organic chemistry (MS, PhD); physical chemistry (MS, PhD). Part-time and evening/weekend programs available. *Faculty:* 7 full-time (1 woman). *Students:* 16 full-time (6 women), 11 part-time (6 women); includes 4 minority (2 African Americans, 1 Asian American or Pacific Islander, 1 Hispanic American), 11 international. 39 applicants, 95% accepted. In 2003, 3 master's, 2 doctorates awarded. Terminal master's awarded for partial completion of doctoral program. *Degree requirements:* For master's, thesis or alternative, comprehensive exam; for doctorate, thesis/dissertation, general exam. *Entrance requirements:* For master's and doctorate, GRE General Test, interview, minimum GPA of 3.0. Additional exam requirements/recommendations for international students: Required—TOEFL (minimum score 550 paper-based; 213 computer-based). *Application deadline:* For fall admission, 2/1 priority date for domestic students, 2/1 priority date for international students; for spring admission, 10/1 priority date for domestic students, 10/1 priority date for international students. Applications are processed on a rolling basis. Application fee: $60. Electronic applications accepted. *Expenses:* Tuition: Part-time $876 per credit. Required fees: $1 per credit. Tuition and fees vary according to campus/location. *Financial support:* In 2003–04, fellowships with tuition reimbursements (averaging $10,000 per year), teaching assistantships with tuition reimbursements (averaging $5,000 per year) were awarded. Research assistantships, Federal Work-Study also available. Financial award application deadline: 2/1. *Unit head:* Dr. Michael King, Chair, 202-994-6488. *Application contact:* Information Contact, E-mail: gwchem@www.gwu.edu.

Governors State University, College of Arts and Sciences, Program in Analytical Chemistry, University Park, IL 60466-0975. Offers MS. Part-time and evening/weekend programs available. *Faculty:* 5 full-time (2 women). *Students:* 19 (11 women). Average age 33. In 2003, 7 degrees awarded. *Degree requirements:* For master's, thesis or alternative. *Application deadline:* For fall admission, 7/15 for domestic students; for spring admission, 11/10 for domestic students. Applications are processed on a rolling basis. Application fee: $25. *Expenses:* Tuition, state resident: part-time $130 per semester hour. Tuition, nonresident: part-time $390 per semester hour. Required fees: $15 per semester hour. *Financial support:* Research assistantships, career-related internships or fieldwork, Federal Work-Study, institutionally sponsored loans, and scholarships/grants available. Support available to part-time students. Financial award application deadline: 5/1. *Faculty research:* Electrochemistry, photochemistry, spectrochemistry, biochemistry. *Unit head:* Dr. Roger Oden, Dean, College of Arts and Sciences, 708-534-4101.

Howard University, Graduate School of Arts and Sciences, Department of Chemistry, Washington, DC 20059-0002. Offers analytical chemistry (MS, PhD); atmospheric (MS, PhD); biochemistry (MS, PhD); environmental (MS, PhD); inorganic chemistry (MS, PhD); organic chemistry (MS, PhD); physical chemistry (MS, PhD); polymer chemistry (MS, PhD). Part-time programs available. *Degree requirements:* For master's, one foreign language, thesis, teaching experience, comprehensive exam, registration; for doctorate, 2 foreign languages, thesis/dissertation, teaching experience, comprehensive exam, registration. *Entrance requirements:* For master's, GRE General Test, minimum GPA of 2.7; for doctorate, GRE General Test, minimum GPA of 3.0. *Faculty research:* Stratospheric aerosols, liquid crystals, polymer coatings, terrestrial and extraterrestrial atmospheres, amidogen reaction.

Illinois Institute of Technology, Graduate College, College of Science and Letters, Department of Biological, Chemical and Physical Sciences, Chemistry Division, Chicago, IL 60616-3793. Offers analytical chemistry (M Ch, MS, PhD); chemistry (M Chem); inorganic chemistry (MS, PhD); materials and chemical synthesis (M Ch); organic chemistry (MS, PhD); physical chemistry (MS, PhD); polymer chemistry (MS, PhD). Part-time and evening/weekend programs available. Postbaccalaureate distance learning degree programs offered (no on-campus study). *Faculty:* 4 full-time (0 women), 2 part-time/adjunct (0 women). *Students:* 14 full-time (7 women), 32 part-time (18 women); includes 7 minority (1 African American, 4 Asian Americans or Pacific Islanders, 2 Hispanic Americans), 17 international. Average age 32. 94 applicants, 68% accepted, 7 enrolled. In 2003, 14 master's, 2 doctorates awarded. Terminal master's awarded for partial completion of doctoral program. *Degree requirements:* For master's, thesis (for some programs), comprehensive exam; for doctorate, thesis/dissertation, comprehensive exam. *Entrance requirements:* For master's and doctorate, GRE General Test, minimum undergraduate GPA of 3.0. Additional exam requirements/recommendations for international students: Required—TOEFL (minimum score 550 paper-based; 213 computer-based). *Application deadline:* For fall admission, 5/1 for domestic students, 5/1 for international students; for spring admission, 10/15 for domestic students, 10/15 for international students. Applications are processed on a rolling basis. Application fee: $40. Electronic applications accepted. *Expenses:* Tuition: Part-time $628 per credit. Tuition and fees vary according to course load and program. *Financial support:* In 2003–04, 11 students received support, including 1 fellowship with full tuition reimbursement available, 9 research assistantships with full tuition reimbursements available (averaging $15,000 per year), 7 teaching assistantships with full tuition reimbursements available (averaging $15,000 per year); Federal Work-Study, institutionally sponsored loans, scholarships/grants, and tuition waivers (partial) also available. Support available to part-time students. Financial award application deadline: 3/1; financial award applicants required to submit FAFSA. *Faculty research:* Organic and inorganic chemistry, polymers research, physical chemistry, analytical chemistry. *Unit head:* Kenneth Stagliano, Associate Chair, 312-567-3428, Fax: 312-567-3494, E-mail: stagliano@iit.edu. *Application contact:* Kelly A. Cherwin, Director of Graduate Outreach, 312-567-7974, Fax: 312-567-3494, E-mail: inquiry.grad@iit.edu.

Indiana University Bloomington, Graduate School, College of Arts and Sciences, Department of Chemistry, Bloomington, IN 47405. Offers analytical chemistry (PhD); biological chemistry (PhD); chemistry (MAT, MS); inorganic chemistry (PhD); physical chemistry (PhD). PhD offered through the University Graduate School. *Faculty:* 29 full-time (2 women). *Students:* 95 full-time (30 women), 51 part-time (16 women); includes 9 minority (3 African Americans, 4 Asian Americans or Pacific Islanders, 2 Hispanic Americans), 52 international. Average age 26. 309 applicants, 41% accepted. In 2003, 4 master's, 23 doctorates awarded. Terminal master's awarded for partial completion of doctoral program. *Degree requirements:* For master's and doctorate, thesis/dissertation. *Entrance requirements:* For master's and doctorate, GRE General Test, GRE Subject Test. Additional exam requirements/recommendations for international students: Required—TOEFL. *Application deadline:* For fall admission, 1/15 priority date for domestic students, 12/15 priority date for international students; for spring admission, 9/1 priority date for domestic students, 9/1 priority date for international students. Applications are processed on a rolling basis. Application fee: $45 ($55 for international students). *Expenses:* Tuition, state resident: full-time $4,908; part-time $205 per credit. Tuition, nonresident: full-time $14,298; part-time $596 per credit. Required fees: $661. Tuition and fees vary according to campus/location and program. *Financial support:* In 2003–04, 23 fellowships with full tuition reimbursements (averaging $15,091 per year), 57 research assistantships with full tuition reimbursements (averaging $14,844 per year), 78 teaching assistantships with full tuition reimbursements (averaging $15,588 per year) were awarded. Federal Work-Study and institutionally sponsored loans also available. *Faculty research:* Synthesis of complex natural products, organic reaction mechanisms, organic electrochemistry, transitive-metal chemistry, solid-state and surface chemistry. Total annual research expenditures: $7.7 million. *Unit head:* Dr. Gary M. Hieftje, Chairperson, 812-855-6239, Fax: 812-855-8300, E-mail: cemchair@indiana.edu. *Application contact:* Dr. Jack K. Crandall, Chairperson of Admissions, 812-855-2068, Fax: 812-855-8300, E-mail: chemgrad@indiana.edu.

Kansas State University, Graduate School, College of Arts and Sciences, Department of Chemistry, Manhattan, KS 66506. Offers analytical chemistry (MS); chemistry (PhD); inorganic chemistry (MS); organic chemistry (MS); physical chemistry (MS). *Faculty:* 15 full-time (2 women). *Students:* 51 full-time (17 women); includes 1 minority (African American), 33 international. 71 applicants, 20% accepted, 14 enrolled. In 2003, 1 master's, 7 doctorates awarded. Terminal master's awarded for partial completion of doctoral program. *Degree requirements:* For master's and doctorate, thesis/dissertation. *Entrance requirements:* For master's and doctorate, GRE, minimum GPA of 3.0. Additional exam requirements/recommendations for international students: Required—TOEFL. *Application deadline:* For fall admission, 2/1 for domestic students; for spring admission, 10/1 for domestic students. Applications are processed on a rolling basis. Application fee: $0 ($25 for international students). *Expenses:* Tuition, state resident: part-time $155 per credit hour. Tuition, nonresident: part-time $428 per credit hour. Required fees: $11 per credit hour. *Financial support:* In 2003–04, 23 research assistantships (averaging $15,648 per year), 26 teaching assistantships with full tuition reimbursements (averaging $17,890 per year) were awarded. Fellowships, institutionally sponsored loans and scholarships/grants also available. Support available to part-time students. Financial award application deadline: 3/1; financial award applicants required to submit FAFSA. *Faculty research:* Computational, environmental and materials, nanoscale, natural products, theoretical chemistry. Total annual research expenditures: $2.8 million. *Unit head:* Peter M. A. Sherwood, Head, 785-532-6665, Fax: 785-532-6666, E-mail: escachem@ksu.edu. *Application contact:* Robert Hammaker, Director, 785-532-1454, Fax: 785-532-6666, E-mail: rmh3008@ksu.edu.

Kent State University, College of Arts and Sciences, Department of Chemistry, Kent, OH 44242-0001. Offers analytical chemistry (MS, PhD); biochemistry (MS, PhD); chemistry (MA, MS, PhD); inorganic chemistry (MS, PhD); organic chemistry (MS, PhD); physical chemistry (MS, PhD). Terminal master's awarded for partial completion of doctoral program. *Degree requirements:* For master's and doctorate, thesis/dissertation, comprehensive exam, registration. *Entrance requirements:* For master's and doctorate, placement exam, GRE General Test, GRE Subject Test (recommended), minimum GPA of 2.75. Additional exam requirements/recommendations for international students: Required—TOEFL (minimum score 575 paper-based; 230 computer-based). Electronic applications accepted. *Expenses:* Tuition, state resident: part-time $334 per hour. Tuition, nonresident: part-time $627 per hour. *Faculty research:* Biological chemistry, materials chemistry, molecular spectroscopy.

See in-depth description on page 119.

Marquette University, Graduate School, College of Arts and Sciences, Department of Chemistry, Milwaukee, WI 53201-1881. Offers analytical chemistry (MS, PhD); bioanalytical chemistry (MS, PhD); biophysical chemistry (MS, PhD); chemical physics (MS, PhD); inorganic chemistry (MS, PhD); organic chemistry (MS, PhD); physical chemistry (MS, PhD). Part-time programs available. *Faculty:* 19 full-time (2 women), 2 part-time/adjunct (0 women). *Students:* 44 full-time (17 women), 4 part-time (1 woman); includes 1 minority (African American), 36 international. Average age 31. 37 applicants, 32% accepted, 8 enrolled. In 2003, 1 master's, 1 doctorate awarded. Terminal master's awarded for partial completion of doctoral program. *Degree requirements:* For master's, comprehensive exam; for doctorate, thesis/dissertation, cumulative exams. *Entrance requirements:* For master's and doctorate, GRE Subject Test. Additional exam requirements/recommendations for international students: Required—TOEFL. Application fee: $40. *Expenses:* Tuition: Full-time $10,080; part-time $630 per credit. Tuition and fees vary according to program. *Financial support:* In 2003–04, 3 research assistantships, 27 teaching assistantships were awarded. Fellowships, Federal Work-Study, institutionally sponsored loans, scholarships/grants, and tuition waivers (full and partial) also available. Support available to part-time students. Financial award application deadline: 2/15. *Faculty research:* Inorganic complexes, laser Raman spectroscopy, organic synthesis, chemical dynamics, biophysiology. Total annual research expenditures: $586,915. *Unit head:* Dr. Charles Wilkie, Chairman, 414-288-7065, Fax: 414-288-7066. *Application contact:* Dr. Mark Steinmetz, Director of Graduate Studies, 414-288-7374, Fax: 414-288-7066.

McMaster University, School of Graduate Studies, Faculty of Science, Department of Chemistry, Hamilton, ON L8S 4M2, Canada. Offers analytical chemistry (M Sc, PhD); chemical physics (M Sc, PhD); chemistry (M Sc, PhD); inorganic chemistry (M Sc, PhD); organic chemistry (M Sc, PhD); physical chemistry (M Sc, PhD); polymer chemistry (M Sc, PhD). Part-time programs available. Terminal master's awarded for partial completion of doctoral program. *Degree requirements:* For master's, thesis/dissertation; for doctorate, thesis/dissertation, comprehensive exam. *Entrance requirements:* For master's, minimum B+ average. Additional exam requirements/recommendations for international students: Required—TOEFL (minimum score 550 paper-based; 213 computer-based).

Miami University, Graduate School, College of Arts and Sciences, Department of Chemistry and Biochemistry, Oxford, OH 45056. Offers analytical chemistry (MS, PhD); biochemistry (MS, PhD); chemical education (MS, PhD); chemistry (MS, PhD); inorganic chemistry (MS, PhD); organic chemistry (MS, PhD); physical chemistry (MS, PhD). Part-time programs available. *Faculty:* 22 full-time (2 women). *Students:* 45 full-time (16 women), 1 part-time; includes 2 minority (both Asian Americans or Pacific Islanders), 21 international. 131 applicants, 98% accepted, 13 enrolled. In 2003, 4 master's, 4 doctorates awarded. *Degree requirements:* For master's, thesis, final exam; for doctorate, thesis/dissertation, final exams, comprehensive exam. *Entrance requirements:* For master's, minimum undergraduate GPA of 3.0 during previous 2 years or 2.75 overall; for doctorate, minimum undergraduate GPA of 2.75, 3.0 graduate. Additional exam requirements/recommendations for international students: Required—TOEFL, TWE. *Application deadline:* For fall admission, 3/1 priority date for domestic students, 3/1 priority date for international students. Applications are processed on a rolling basis. Application fee: $35. Electronic applications accepted. Tuition, area resident: Full-time $9,346. International tuition: $19,924 full-time. Full-time tuition and fees vary according to course level and campus/location. *Financial support:* In 2003–04, 22 fellowships with full tuition reimbursements (averaging $16,813 per year), 3 research assistantships with full tuition reimbursements (averaging $16,813 per year), 17 teaching assistantships with full tuition reimbursements (averaging $18,934 per year) were awarded. Federal Work-Study, tuition waivers (full), and unspecified assistantships also available. Financial award application deadline: 3/1. *Unit head:* Dr. Chris Makaroff, Chair, 513-529-2813. *Application contact:* Dr. Michael Crowder, Director of Graduate Studies, 513-529-2813, Fax: 513-529-5715, E-mail: chemistry@muohio.edu.

Northeastern University, College of Arts and Sciences, Department of Chemistry and Chemical Biology, Boston, MA 02115-5096. Offers analytical chemistry (PhD); chemistry (MS, PhD); inorganic chemistry (PhD); organic chemistry (PhD); physical chemistry (PhD). Part-time and evening/weekend programs available. *Faculty:* 17 full-time (2 women), 3 part-time/adjunct (0 women). *Students:* 46 full-time (23 women), 29 part-time (17 women). Average age 28. 113 applicants, 37% accepted. In 2003, 12 master's, 10 doctorates awarded. Terminal master's awarded for partial completion of doctoral program. *Degree requirements:* For master's, thesis (for some programs); for doctorate, thesis/dissertation, qualifying exam in specialty area. *Entrance requirements:* Additional exam requirements/recommendations for international students: Required—TOEFL. *Application deadline:* For fall admission, 4/15 for domestic students. Applications are processed on a rolling basis. Application fee: $50. Electronic applications accepted. *Expenses:* Tuition: Part-time $790 per credit hour. Tuition and fees vary according to course load and program. *Financial support:* In 2003–04, 27 research assistantships with tuition reimbursements (averaging $16,000 per year) were awarded; fellowships with tuition reimbursements, teaching assistantships with tuition reimbursements, career-related internships or fieldwork, tuition waivers (partial), and unspecified assistantships also available. Financial award application deadline: 4/15; financial award applicants required to submit FAFSA. *Faculty research:* Electron transfer, theoretical chemical physics, analytical biotechnology, mass spectrometry, materials chemistry. Total annual research expenditures: $250,000. *Unit head:* Dr. Graham Jones, Chairman, 617-373-2822, Fax: 617-373-8795, E-mail: chemistry-grad-info@neu.edu. *Application contact:* Dr. Pam Mabrouk, Chair, Graduate Admissions Committee, 617-373-2383, Fax: 617-373-8795, E-mail: chemistry-grad-info@neu.edu.

See in-depth description on page 133.

Old Dominion University, College of Sciences, Program in Chemistry, Norfolk, VA 23529. Offers analytical chemistry (MS); biochemistry (MS); clinical chemistry (MS); environmental chemistry (MS); organic chemistry (MS); physical chemistry (MS). Part-time and evening/weekend programs available. *Faculty:* 15 full-time (4 women). *Students:* 6 full-time (3 women), 9 part-time (5 women); includes 1 minority (Asian American or Pacific Islander), 3 international. Average age 30. 19 applicants, 74% accepted. In 2003, 2 degrees awarded. *Degree requirements:* For master's, thesis, comprehensive exam. *Entrance requirements:* For master's, GRE General Test, minimum GPA of 3.0 in major, 2.5 overall. Additional exam requirements/recommendations for international students: Required—TOEFL. *Application deadline:* For fall admission, 7/1 for domestic students; for spring admission, 11/1 for domestic students. Applications are processed on a rolling basis. Application fee: $30. *Expenses:* Tuition, state resident: part-time $235 per credit hour. Tuition, nonresident: part-time $603 per credit hour. Part-time tuition and fees vary according to campus/location. *Financial support:* In 2003–04, research assistantships with tuition reimbursements (averaging $15,000 per year), teaching assistantships with tuition reimbursements (averaging $15,000 per year) were awarded. Fellowships, career-related internships or fieldwork and scholarships/grants also available. Financial award application deadline: 2/15; financial award applicants required to submit FAFSA. *Faculty research:* Organic and trace metal biogeochemistry, materials chemistry, bioanalytical chemistry, computational chemistry. Total annual research expenditures: $854,968. *Unit head:* Dr. John R. Donat, Graduate Program Director, 757-683-4098, Fax: 757-683-4628, E-mail: chemgpd@odu.edu.

Oregon State University, Graduate School, College of Science, Department of Chemistry, Corvallis, OR 97331. Offers analytical chemistry (MS, PhD); chemistry (MA, MAIS); inorganic chemistry (MS, PhD); nuclear and radiation chemistry (MS, PhD); organic chemistry (MS, PhD); physical chemistry (MS, PhD). Part-time programs available. *Faculty:* 30 full-time (5 women). *Students:* 63 full-time (22 women), 1 part-time; includes 5 minority (3 Asian Americans or Pacific Islanders, 2 Hispanic Americans), 29 international. Average age 28. In 2003, 3

Analytical Chemistry

Oregon State University (continued)

master's, 13 doctorates awarded. Terminal master's awarded for partial completion of doctoral program. *Degree requirements:* For master's and doctorate, one foreign language, thesis/dissertation. *Entrance requirements:* For master's and doctorate, minimum GPA of 3.0 in last 90 hours. Additional exam requirements/recommendations for international students: Required—TOEFL. *Application deadline:* For fall admission, 3/1 for domestic students. Applications are processed on a rolling basis. Application fee: $50. *Expenses:* Tuition, state resident: full-time $8,139; part-time $301 per credit. Tuition, nonresident: full-time $14,376; part-time $532 per credit. Required fees: $1,227. *Financial support:* Fellowships, research assistantships, teaching assistantships, institutionally sponsored loans available. Support available to part-time students. Financial award application deadline: 2/1. *Faculty research:* Solid state chemistry, enzyme reaction mechanisms, structure and dynamics of gas molecules, chemiluminescence, nonlinear optical spectroscopy. *Unit head:* Dr. John C. Westall, Chair, 541-737-2591, Fax: 541-737-2062, E-mail: john.westall@orst.edu. *Application contact:* Carolyn Brumley, Graduate Secretary, 541-737-6707, Fax: 541-737-2062, E-mail: carolyn.brumley@orst.edu.

Purdue University, Graduate School, School of Science, Department of Chemistry, West Lafayette, IN 47907. Offers analytical chemistry (MS, PhD); biochemistry (MS, PhD); chemical education (MS, PhD); inorganic chemistry (MS, PhD); organic chemistry (MS, PhD); physical chemistry (MS, PhD). *Accreditation:* NCATE (one or more programs are accredited). Terminal master's awarded for partial completion of doctoral program. *Degree requirements:* For master's and doctorate, thesis/dissertation. *Entrance requirements:* Additional exam requirements/recommendations for international students: Required—TOEFL. Electronic applications accepted.

Rensselaer Polytechnic Institute, Graduate School, School of Science, Department of Chemistry and Chemical Biology, Troy, NY 12180-3590. Offers analytical chemistry (MS, PhD); biochemistry (MS, PhD); inorganic chemistry (MS, PhD); organic chemistry (MS, PhD); physical chemistry (MS, PhD); polymer chemistry (MS, PhD). Part-time and evening/weekend programs available. *Faculty:* 20 full-time (4 women). *Students:* 58 full-time (25 women), 3 part-time (2 women); includes 40 minority (2 African Americans, 37 Asian Americans or Pacific Islanders, 1 Hispanic American), 36 international. Average age 24. 102 applicants, 29% accepted, 19 enrolled. In 2003, 9 master's, 9 doctorates awarded. Terminal master's awarded for partial completion of doctoral program. *Median time to degree:* Of those who began their doctoral program in fall 1995, 100% received their degree in 8 years or less. *Degree requirements:* For master's, thesis (for some programs), registration; for doctorate, thesis/dissertation, comprehensive exam, registration. *Entrance requirements:* For master's, GRE General Test, GRE Subject Test (strongly recommended); for doctorate, GRE General Test, GRE Subject Test (chemistry or biochemistry strongly recommended). Additional exam requirements/recommendations for international students: Required—TOEFL (minimum score 600 paper-based). *Application deadline:* For fall admission, 2/1 for domestic students; for spring admission, 11/15 for domestic students. Applications are processed on a rolling basis. Application fee: $45. Electronic applications accepted. *Expenses:* Tuition: Full-time $27,700; part-time $1,320 per credit. Required fees: $1,470. *Financial support:* In 2003–04, 59 students received support, including 1 fellowship with full tuition reimbursement available (averaging $25,000 per year), 25 research assistantships with full tuition reimbursements available (averaging $18,000 per year), 30 teaching assistantships with full tuition reimbursements available (averaging $18,000 per year); institutionally sponsored loans and tuition waivers (full and partial) also available. Financial award application deadline: 2/1. *Faculty research:* Synthetic polymer and biopolymer chemistry, physical chemistry of polymeric systems, bioanalytical chemistry, synthetic and computational drug design, protein folding and protein design. Total annual research expenditures: $1.9 million. *Unit head:* Dr. Ronald A. Bailey, Acting Chair, 518-276-4856, Fax: 518-276-4887, E-mail: bailer@rpi.edu. *Application contact:* Beth E. McGraw, Department Admissions Assistant, 518-276-6456, Fax: 518-276-4887, E-mail: mcgrae@rpi.edu.

Rutgers, The State University of New Jersey, Newark, Graduate School, Program in Chemistry, Newark, NJ 07102. Offers analytical chemistry (MS, PhD); biochemistry (MS, PhD); inorganic chemistry (MS, PhD); organic chemistry (MS, PhD); physical chemistry (MS, PhD). Part-time and evening/weekend programs available. *Faculty:* 22 full-time (5 women). *Students:* 19 full-time (9 women), 35 part-time (12 women); includes 28 minority (3 African Americans, 25 Asian Americans or Pacific Islanders). 107 applicants, 31% accepted, 8 enrolled. In 2003, 4 master's, 6 doctorates awarded. Terminal master's awarded for partial completion of doctoral program. *Degree requirements:* For master's, cumulative exams, thesis optional; for doctorate, thesis/dissertation, exams, research proposal. *Entrance requirements:* For master's and doctorate, GRE General Test, minimum undergraduate B average. Additional exam requirements/recommendations for international students: Required—TOEFL. *Application deadline:* For fall admission, 7/1 for domestic students; for spring admission, 12/1 for domestic students. Applications are processed on a rolling basis. Application fee: $50. Electronic applications accepted. *Expenses:* Tuition, state resident: full-time $10,030. Tuition, nonresident: full-time $14,202. *Financial support:* In 2003–04, 35 students received support, including 6 fellowships with full tuition reimbursements available, 20 teaching assistantships with full tuition reimbursements available (averaging $14,300 per year); Federal Work-Study and institutionally sponsored loans also available. Financial award application deadline: 3/1. *Faculty research:* Medicinal chemistry, natural products, isotope effects, biophysics and biorganic approaches to enzyme mechanisms, organic and organometallic synthesis. *Unit head:* Prof. W. Philip Huskey, Chairman and Program Director, 973-353-5741, Fax: 973-353-1264, E-mail: huskey@andromeda.rutgers.edu.

Rutgers, The State University of New Jersey, New Brunswick/Piscataway, Graduate School, Program in Chemistry and Chemical Biology, New Brunswick, NJ 08901-1281. Offers analytical chemistry (MS, PhD); biological chemistry (PhD); chemistry education (MST); inorganic chemistry (MS, PhD); organic chemistry (MS, PhD); physical chemistry (MS, PhD). Part-time and evening/weekend programs available. Terminal master's awarded for partial completion of doctoral program. *Degree requirements:* For master's, thesis or alternative, exam, comprehensive exam, registration; for doctorate, thesis/dissertation, cumulative exams, 1 year residency, comprehensive exam, registration. *Entrance requirements:* For master's and doctorate, GRE General Test, GRE Subject Test. Additional exam requirements/recommendations for international students: Required—TOEFL. Electronic applications accepted. *Expenses:* Tuition, state resident: full-time $10,030. Tuition, nonresident: full-time $14,202. *Faculty research:* Biophysical organic/bioorganic, inorganic/bioinorganic, theoretical, and solid-state/surface chemistry.

See in-depth description on page 141.

Seton Hall University, College of Arts and Sciences, Department of Chemistry and Biochemistry, South Orange, NJ 07079-2694. Offers analytical chemistry (MS, PhD); biochemistry (MS, PhD); chemistry (MS); inorganic chemistry (MS, PhD); organic chemistry (MS, PhD); physical chemistry (MS, PhD). Part-time and evening/weekend programs available. Terminal master's awarded for partial completion of doctoral program. *Degree requirements:* For master's, formal seminar, thesis optional; for doctorate, thesis/dissertation, annual seminars, comprehensive exam. *Entrance requirements:* For master's, undergraduate major in chemistry or related field with minimum 30 credits in chemistry, including 2 semesters of physical chemistry; for doctorate, oral matriculation exam based on proposed doctoral research, minimum GPA of 3.0 in course distribution requirements, formal seminar. Additional exam requirements/recommendations for international students: Required—TOEFL. *Faculty research:* DNA metal reactions; chromatography; bioinorganic, biophysical, organometallic, polymer chemistry; heterogeneous catalyst.

South Dakota State University, Graduate School, College of Arts and Science and College of Agriculture and Biological Sciences, Department of Chemistry, Brookings, SD 57007. Offers analytical chemistry (MS, PhD); biochemistry (MS, PhD); chemistry (MS, PhD); inorganic chemistry (MS, PhD); organic chemistry (MS, PhD); physical chemistry (MS, PhD). *Degree requirements:* For master's, thesis, oral exam; for doctorate, thesis/dissertation, preliminary oral and written exams, research tool. *Entrance requirements:* For master's, bachelor's degree in chemistry or equivalent. Additional exam requirements/recommendations for international students: Required—TOEFL. *Faculty research:* Environmental chemistry, computational chemistry, organic synthesis and photochemistry, novel material development and characterization.

Southern University and Agricultural and Mechanical College, Graduate School, College of Sciences, Department of Chemistry, Baton Rouge, LA 70813. Offers analytical chemistry (MS); biochemistry (MS); environmental sciences (MS); inorganic chemistry (MS); organic chemistry (MS); physical chemistry (MS). *Degree requirements:* For master's, thesis. *Entrance requirements:* For master's, GMAT or GRE General Test. Additional exam requirements/recommendations for international students: Required—TOEFL. *Faculty research:* Synthesis of macrocyclic ligands, latex accelerators, anticancer drugs, biosensors, absorption isotheums, isolation of specific enzymes from plants.

State University of New York at Binghamton, Graduate School, School of Arts and Sciences, Department of Chemistry, Binghamton, NY 13902-6000. Offers analytical chemistry (PhD); chemistry (MA, MS); inorganic chemistry (PhD); organic chemistry (PhD); physical chemistry (PhD). Part-time programs available. Terminal master's awarded for partial completion of doctoral program. *Degree requirements:* For master's, thesis or alternative, oral exam, seminar presentation; for doctorate, thesis/dissertation, cumulative exams. *Entrance requirements:* For master's and doctorate, GRE General Test, GRE Subject Test. Additional exam requirements/recommendations for international students: Required—TOEFL. Electronic applications accepted.

Stevens Institute of Technology, Graduate School, School of Applied Sciences and Liberal Arts, Department of Chemistry and Chemical Biology, Hoboken, NJ 07030. Offers chemistry (MS, PhD, Certificate), including analytical chemistry, chemical biology, chemical physiology (Certificate), instrumental analysis (Certificate), organic chemistry (MS, PhD), physical chemistry (MS, PhD), polymer chemistry. Part-time and evening/weekend programs available. Terminal master's awarded for partial completion of doctoral program. *Degree requirements:* For master's, thesis or alternative; for doctorate, one foreign language, thesis/dissertation; for Certificate, project or thesis. *Entrance requirements:* Additional exam requirements/recommendations for international students: Required—TOEFL. Electronic applications accepted.

Tufts University, Graduate School of Arts and Sciences, Department of Chemistry, Medford, MA 02155. Offers analytical chemistry (MS, PhD); bioorganic chemistry (MS, PhD); environmental chemistry (MS, PhD); inorganic chemistry (MS, PhD); organic chemistry (MS, PhD); physical chemistry (MS, PhD). *Faculty:* 13 full-time, 1 part-time/adjunct. *Students:* 56 (24 women); includes 6 minority (1 African American, 4 Asian Americans or Pacific Islanders, 1 Hispanic American) 22 international. 66 applicants, 56% accepted, 17 enrolled. In 2003, 4 master's, 6 doctorates awarded. Terminal master's awarded for partial completion of doctoral program. *Degree requirements:* For master's and doctorate, thesis/dissertation. *Entrance requirements:* For master's and doctorate, GRE General Test, GRE Subject Test. Additional exam requirements/recommendations for international students: Required—TOEFL (minimum score 600 paper-based; 213 computer-based), TSE. *Application deadline:* For fall admission, 2/1 for domestic students, 12/30 for international students; for spring admission, 10/15 for domestic students, 9/15 for international students. Applications are processed on a rolling basis. Application fee: $60. Electronic applications accepted. *Expenses:* Tuition: Full-time $29,949. *Financial support:* Research assistantships with full and partial tuition reimbursements, teaching assistantships with full and partial tuition reimbursements, Federal Work-Study, scholarships/grants, and tuition waivers (partial) available. Financial award application deadline: 2/1; financial award applicants required to submit FAFSA. *Unit head:* Mary Jane Shultz, Chair, 617-627-3477, Fax: 617-627-3443. *Application contact:* Arthur Utz, Information Contact, 617-627-3441, Fax: 617-627-3443.

See in-depth description on page 153.

University of Calgary, Faculty of Graduate Studies, Faculty of Science, Department of Chemistry, Calgary, AB T2N 1N4, Canada. Offers analytical chemistry (M Sc, PhD); applied chemistry (M Sc, PhD); inorganic chemistry (M Sc, PhD); organic chemistry (M Sc, PhD); physical chemistry (M Sc, PhD); polymer chemistry (M Sc, PhD); theoretical chemistry (M Sc, PhD). *Faculty:* 29 full-time (6 women), 1 part-time/adjunct (0 women). *Students:* 74 full-time (29 women). Average age 25. 130 applicants, 20% accepted. In 2003, 12 master's, 6 doctorates awarded. *Degree requirements:* For master's, thesis; for doctorate, thesis/dissertation, candidacy exam. *Entrance requirements:* For master's, minimum GPA of 3.0; for doctorate, honors degree minimum GPA of 3.7, minimum GPA of 3.3. Additional exam requirements/recommendations for international students: Required—TOEFL (minimum score 580 paper-based; 237 computer-based). *Application deadline:* For fall admission, 12/1 for domestic students. Applications are processed on a rolling basis. Application fee: $60. Electronic applications accepted. Tuition, nonresident: full-time $4,765. Tuition and fees vary according to degree level, program and student level. *Financial support:* In 2003–04, research assistantships (averaging $11,000 per year), teaching assistantships (averaging $6,221 per year) were awarded. Fellowships, scholarships/grants also available. Financial award application deadline: 12/1. *Faculty research:* Chemical analysis, chemical dynamics, synthesis theory, polymer, applied chemistry. *Unit head:* Dr. Brian Keay, Head, 403-220-6252, E-mail: gradinfo@chem.ucalgary.ca.

University of Cincinnati, Division of Research and Advanced Studies, McMicken College of Arts and Sciences, Department of Chemistry, Cincinnati, OH 45221. Offers analytical chemistry (MS, PhD); biochemistry (MS, PhD); inorganic chemistry (MS, PhD); organic chemistry (MS, PhD); physical chemistry (MS, PhD); polymer chemistry (MS, PhD); sensors (PhD). Part-time and evening/weekend programs available. Terminal master's awarded for partial completion of doctoral program. *Degree requirements:* For master's, thesis optional; for doctorate, thesis/dissertation, comprehensive exam, registration. *Entrance requirements:* For master's and doctorate, GRE General Test. Additional exam requirements/recommendations for international students: Required—TOEFL (minimum score 580 paper-based; 237 computer-based); Recommended—TSE(minimum score 50). Electronic applications accepted. *Faculty research:* Biomedical chemistry, laser chemistry, surface science, chemical sensors, synthesis.

University of Georgia, Graduate School, College of Arts and Sciences, Department of Chemistry, Athens, GA 30602. Offers analytical chemistry (MS, PhD); inorganic chemistry (MS, PhD); organic chemistry (MS, PhD); physical chemistry (MS, PhD). *Faculty:* 26 full-time (2 women). *Students:* 130 full-time (43 women). 160 applicants, 29% accepted, 36 enrolled. In 2003, 3 master's, 17 doctorates awarded. Terminal master's awarded for partial completion of doctoral program. *Median time to degree:* Of those who began their doctoral program in fall 1995, 100% received their degree in 8 years or less. *Degree requirements:* For master's, thesis; for doctorate, one foreign language, thesis/dissertation. *Entrance requirements:* For master's and doctorate, GRE General Test. Additional exam requirements/recommendations for international students: Required—TOEFL (minimum score 213 computer-based), TSE(minimum score 50). *Application deadline:* For fall admission, 7/1 for domestic students; for spring admission, 11/15 for domestic students. Application fee: $50. Electronic applications accepted. *Expenses:* Tuition, state resident: part-time $161 per hour. Tuition, nonresident: part-time $690 per hour. One-time fee: $435 part-time. *Financial support:* Fellowships, research assistantships, teaching assistantships, unspecified assistantships available. *Unit head:* Dr. John L. Stickney, Head, 706-542-2726, Fax: 706-542-9454, E-mail: stickney@chem.uga.edu. *Application contact:* Dr. Donald Kurtz, Information Contact, 706-542-2010, Fax: 706-542-9454, E-mail: kurtz@chem.uga.edu.

University of Louisville, Graduate School, College of Arts and Sciences, Department of Chemistry, Louisville, KY 40292-0001. Offers analytical chemistry (MS, PhD); biochemistry (MS, PhD); chemical physics (PhD); inorganic chemistry (MS, PhD); organic chemistry (MS, PhD); physical chemistry (MS, PhD). *Students:* 48 full-time (19 women), 13 part-time (5 women); includes 4 minority (1 African American, 1 Asian American or Pacific Islander, 2 Hispanic Americans), 27 international. Average age 27. In 2003, 7 master's, 1 doctorate awarded. *Degree requirements:* For master's, thesis/dissertation; for doctorate, thesis/

dissertation, comprehensive exam. *Entrance requirements:* For master's and doctorate, GRE General Test. Additional exam requirements/recommendations for international students: Required—TOEFL. *Application deadline:* Applications are processed on a rolling basis. Application fee: $50. *Expenses:* Tuition, state resident: full-time $4,842. Tuition, nonresident: full-time $13,338. *Financial support:* In 2003–04, 30 teaching assistantships (averaging $14,000 per year) were awarded. *Unit head:* Dr. George R. Pack, Chair, 502-852-6798, Fax: 502-852-8149, E-mail: george.pack@louisville.edu.

University of Maryland, College Park, Graduate Studies and Research, College of Life Sciences, Department of Chemistry and Biochemistry, Chemistry Program, College Park, MD 20742. Offers analytical chemistry (MS, PhD); inorganic chemistry (MS, PhD); organic chemistry (MS, PhD); physical chemistry (MS, PhD). Part-time and evening/weekend programs available. *Students:* 89 full-time (46 women), 4 part-time (2 women); includes 6 minority (2 African Americans, 2 Asian Americans or Pacific Islanders, 2 Hispanic Americans), 39 international. 141 applicants, 19% accepted. In 2003, 16 degrees awarded. Terminal master's awarded for partial completion of doctoral program. *Median time to degree:* Of those who began their doctoral program in fall 1995, 33% received their degree in 8 years or less. *Degree requirements:* For master's, thesis optional; for doctorate, thesis/dissertation, 2 seminar presentations, oral exam. *Entrance requirements:* For master's, GRE General Test, GRE Subject Test (recommended), minimum GPA of 3.1, 3 letters of recommendation; for doctorate, GRE General Test, GRE Subject Test (recommended), minimum GPA of 3.1. *Application deadline:* For fall admission, 5/1 for domestic students, 2/1 for international students; for spring admission, 10/1 for domestic students, 6/1 for international students. Applications are processed on a rolling basis. Application fee: $50. Electronic applications accepted. *Expenses:* Tuition, state resident: part-time $349 per credit hour. Tuition, nonresident: part-time $602 per credit hour. *Financial support:* Fellowships, research assistantships, teaching assistantships with partial tuition reimbursements available. Financial award applicants required to submit FAFSA. *Faculty research:* Environmental chemistry, nuclear chemistry, lunar and environmental analysis, x-ray crystallography. *Application contact:* Trudy Lindsey, Director, Graduate Enrollment Management Services, 301-405-4190, Fax: 301-314-9305, E-mail: tlindsey@gradschool.umd.edu.

University of Michigan, Horace H. Rackham School of Graduate Studies, College of Literature, Science, and the Arts, Department of Chemistry, Ann Arbor, MI 48109. Offers analytical chemistry (PhD); chemical biology (PhD); inorganic chemistry (PhD); material chemistry (PhD); organic chemistry (PhD); physical chemistry (PhD). *Faculty:* 50 full-time (10 women), 3 part-time/adjunct (0 women). *Students:* 213 full-time (101 women); includes 20 minority (5 African Americans, 1 American Indian/Alaska Native, 9 Asian Americans or Pacific Islanders, 5 Hispanic Americans), 64 international. Average age 26. 310 applicants, 56% accepted, 58 enrolled. In 2003, 27 degrees awarded. *Degree requirements:* For doctorate, thesis/dissertation, oral defense of dissertation, organic cumulative proficiency exams. *Entrance requirements:* For doctorate, GRE General Test, GRE Subject Test (recommended), statement of prior research. Additional exam requirements/recommendations for international students: Required—TOEFL. *Application deadline:* For fall admission, 1/15 priority date for domestic students, 1/15 priority date for international students. Applications are processed on a rolling basis. Application fee: $60 ($75 for international students). Electronic applications accepted. *Expenses:* Tuition, state resident: full-time $7,463. Tuition, nonresident: full-time $13,913. Full-time tuition and fees vary according to course load, degree level and program. *Financial support:* In 2003–04, 10 fellowships with full tuition reimbursements (averaging $20,000 per year), 70 research assistantships with full tuition reimbursements (averaging $19,000 per year), 120 teaching assistantships with full tuition reimbursements (averaging $20,000 per year) were awarded. Financial award applicants required to submit FAFSA. *Faculty research:* Biological catalysis, protein engineering, chemical sensors, de novo metalloprotein design, supramolecular architecture. Total annual research expenditures: $8 million. *Unit head:* Dr. William R. Roush, Chair, 734-763-9681, Fax: 734-647-4847, E-mail: roush@umich.edu. *Application contact:* Linda Deitert, Assistant Director Graduate Studies, 734-764-7278, Fax: 734-647-4865, E-mail: chemadmissions@umich.edu.

University of Missouri–Columbia, Graduate School, College of Arts and Sciences, Department of Chemistry, Columbia, MO 65211. Offers analytical chemistry (MS, PhD); inorganic chemistry (MS, PhD); organic chemistry (MS, PhD); physical chemistry (MS, PhD). *Faculty:* 20 full-time (4 women). *Students:* 58 full-time (21 women), 36 part-time (7 women); includes 5 minority (1 African American, 1 American Indian/Alaska Native, 3 Asian Americans or Pacific Islanders), 51 international. In 2003, 7 master's, 7 doctorates awarded. *Degree requirements:* For master's, thesis; for doctorate, one foreign language, thesis/dissertation. *Entrance requirements:* For master's and doctorate, GRE General Test, minimum GPA of 3.0. *Application deadline:* For fall admission, 4/1 for domestic students; for winter admission, 11/1 for domestic students. Applications are processed on a rolling basis. Application fee: $45 ($60 for international students). *Expenses:* Tuition, state resident: full-time $5,205. Tuition, nonresident: full-time $14,058. *Financial support:* Research assistantships, teaching assistantships, institutionally sponsored loans available. *Unit head:* Dr. Silvia S. Jurisson, Director of Graduate Studies, 573-882-2107, E-mail: jurissons@missouri.edu.

University of Missouri–Kansas City, College of Arts and Sciences, Department of Chemistry, Kansas City, MO 64110-2499. Offers analytical chemistry (MS, PhD); inorganic chemistry (MS, PhD); organic chemistry (MS, PhD); physical chemistry (MS, PhD); polymer chemistry (MS, PhD). PhD offered through the School of Graduate Studies. Part-time and evening/weekend programs available. *Faculty:* 11 full-time (1 woman), 1 part-time/adjunct (0 women). *Students:* Average age 30. 56 applicants, 46% accepted. In 2003, 1 master's awarded. *Median time to degree:* Master's–1 year full-time, 1 year part-time; doctorate–5 years full-time. *Degree requirements:* For master's, thesis (for some programs); for doctorate, thesis/dissertation. *Entrance requirements:* For master's, equivalent of American Chemical Society approved bachelor's degree in chemistry; for doctorate, GRE General Test, equivalent of American Chemical Society approved bachelor's degree in chemistry. Additional exam requirements/recommendations for international students: Required—TOEFL (minimum score 580 paper-based; 237 computer-based), TWE. *Application deadline:* For fall and spring admission, 4/15; for winter admission, 10/15 for domestic students. Applications are processed on a rolling basis. Application fee: $25. *Financial support:* In 2003–04, 1 fellowship with partial tuition reimbursement (averaging $18,156 per year), 9 research assistantships with partial tuition reimbursements (averaging $17,632 per year), 16 teaching assistantships with partial tuition reimbursements (averaging $16,416 per year) were awarded. Federal Work-Study, institutionally sponsored loans, and scholarships/grants also available. Support available to part-time students. Financial award application deadline: 2/15. *Faculty research:* Molecular spectroscopy, characterization and synthesis of materials and compounds, computational chemistry, natural products, drug delivery systems and anti-tumor agents. Total annual research expenditures: $551,743. *Unit head:* Dr. Jerry Jean, Chairperson, 816-235-2280, Fax: 816-235-5502, E-mail: jeany@umkc.edu. *Application contact:* Dr. Kathleen Y. Kilway, Graduate Recruiting Committee, 816-235-2289, Fax: 816-235-5502, E-mail: kilwayk@umkc.edu.

The University of Montana–Missoula, Graduate School, College of Arts and Sciences, Department of Chemistry, Missoula, MT 59812-0002. Offers chemistry (MS, PhD), including environmental/analytical chemistry, inorganic chemistry, organic chemistry, physical chemistry; chemistry teaching (MST). *Faculty:* 16 full-time (2 women). *Students:* 26 full-time (5 women), 12 part-time (6 women), 10 international. 25 applicants, 44% accepted, 6 enrolled. In 2003, 2 master's, 4 doctorates awarded. Terminal master's awarded for partial completion of doctoral program. *Degree requirements:* For master's, thesis (for some programs); for doctorate, thesis/dissertation. *Entrance requirements:* For master's and doctorate, GRE General Test. Additional exam requirements/recommendations for international students: Required—TOEFL (minimum score 575 paper-based; 230 computer-based). *Application deadline:* For fall admission, 2/15 for domestic students. Applications are processed on a rolling basis. Application fee: $45. *Expenses:* Tuition, state resident: full-time $1,848; part-time $221 per credit. Tuition, nonresident: full-time $4,880; part-time $333 per credit. Required fees: $2,200. *Financial support:* In 2003–04, 13 research assistantships with tuition reimbursements (averaging $14,000 per year), 12 teaching assistantships with full tuition reimbursements (averaging $14,000 per year) were awarded. Federal Work-Study, scholarships/grants, and unspecified assistantships also available. Financial award application deadline: 3/1; financial award applicants required to submit FAFSA. *Faculty research:* Reaction mechanisms and kinetics, inorganic and organic synthesis, analytical chemistry, natural products. Total annual research expenditures: $789,952. *Unit head:* Dr. Edward Rosenberg, Chair, 406-243-4022, Fax: 406-243-4227.

University of Nebraska–Lincoln, Graduate College, College of Arts and Sciences, Department of Chemistry, Lincoln, NE 68588. Offers analytical chemistry (PhD); chemistry (MS); inorganic chemistry (PhD); organic chemistry (PhD); physical chemistry (PhD). *Degree requirements:* For master's, one foreign language, departmental qualifying exam, thesis optional; for doctorate, one foreign language, thesis/dissertation, departmental qualifying exams, comprehensive exam. *Entrance requirements:* For master's and doctorate, GRE. Additional exam requirements/recommendations for international students: Required—TOEFL (minimum score 550 paper-based; 213 computer-based). Electronic applications accepted. *Faculty research:* Bioorganic and bioinorganic chemistry, biophysical and bioanalytical chemistry, structure-function of DNA and proteins, organometallics, mass spectrometry.

University of Regina, Faculty of Graduate Studies and Research, Faculty of Science, Department of Chemistry and Biochemistry, Regina, SK S4S 0A2, Canada. Offers analytical chemistry (M Sc, PhD); biochemistry (M Sc, PhD); inorganic chemistry (M Sc, PhD); organic chemistry (M Sc, PhD); physical chemistry (M Sc, PhD). Part-time programs available. *Faculty:* 9 full-time (2 women), 2 part-time/adjunct (1 woman). *Students:* 7 full-time (4 women), 4 part-time (1 woman). 12 applicants. In 2003, 3 degrees awarded. *Degree requirements:* For master's and doctorate, thesis/dissertation, departmental qualifying exam. *Entrance requirements:* For master's and doctorate, GRE. Additional exam requirements/recommendations for international students: Required—TOEFL. *Application deadline:* For fall admission, 1/1 for domestic students; for winter admission, 7/1 for domestic students. Applications are processed on a rolling basis. Application fee: $60. *Expenses:* Tuition, state resident: part-time $130 per credit hour. Tuition and fees vary according to course load and program. *Financial support:* In 2003–04, 4 fellowships, 1 research assistantship, 3 teaching assistantships were awarded. Scholarships/grants also available. Financial award application deadline: 6/15. *Faculty research:* Organic synthesis, organic oxidations, ionic liquids theoretical/computational chemistry, protein biochemistry/biophysics, environmental analytical, photophysical/photochemistry. *Unit head:* Dr. Andrew G. Wee, Head, 306-585-4767, Fax: 306-585-4894, E-mail: chem.chair@uregina.ca. *Application contact:* Teri Dibble, Office Administrator, 306-585-4146, Fax: 306-585-4894, E-mail: teri.dibble@uregina.ca.

University of Southern Mississippi, Graduate School, College of Science and Technology, Department of Chemistry and Biochemistry, Hattiesburg, MS 39406-0001. Offers analytical chemistry (MS, PhD); biochemistry (MS, PhD); inorganic chemistry (MS, PhD); organic chemistry (MS, PhD); physical chemistry (MS, PhD). *Faculty:* 8 full-time (1 woman). *Students:* 27 full-time (17 women), 1 part-time; includes 14 minority (4 African Americans, 1 American Indian/Alaska Native, 9 Asian Americans or Pacific Islanders). Average age 27. 29 applicants, 45% accepted, 10 enrolled. In 2003, 1 master's, 7 doctorates awarded. *Degree requirements:* For master's and doctorate, thesis/dissertation, comprehensive exam. *Entrance requirements:* For master's, GRE General Test, minimum GPA of 2.75 in last 60 hours; for doctorate, GRE General Test, minimum GPA of 3.5. Additional exam requirements/recommendations for international students: Required—TOEFL. *Application deadline:* For fall admission, 8/6 for domestic students. Applications are processed on a rolling basis. Application fee: $25. *Expenses:* Tuition, state resident: part-time $1,967 per semester. Tuition, nonresident: part-time $4,376 per semester. *Financial support:* Fellowships, research assistantships with full tuition reimbursements, teaching assistantships with full tuition reimbursements, Federal Work-Study and institutionally sponsored loans available. Support available to part-time students. Financial award application deadline: 3/15. *Faculty research:* Plant biochemistry, photo chemistry, polymer chemistry, x-ray analysis, enzyme chemistry. *Unit head:* Dr. Robert Bateman, Chair, 601-266-4701. *Application contact:* Dr. Gordon Cannon, Information Contact, 601-266-4702.

University of South Florida, College of Graduate Studies, College of Arts and Sciences, Department of Chemistry, Tampa, FL 33620-9951. Offers analytical chemistry (MS, PhD); biochemistry (MS, PhD); inorganic chemistry (MS, PhD); organic chemistry (MS, PhD); physical chemistry (MS, PhD); polymer chemistry (PhD). Part-time programs available. *Faculty:* 26 full-time (8 women), 1 (woman) part-time/adjunct. *Students:* 75 full-time (34 women), 11 part-time (4 women); includes 14 minority (3 African Americans, 3 Asian Americans or Pacific Islanders, 8 Hispanic Americans), 30 international. 75 applicants, 37% accepted, 17 enrolled. In 2003, 3 master's, 6 doctorates awarded. Terminal master's awarded for partial completion of doctoral program. *Degree requirements:* For master's, thesis; for doctorate, 2 foreign languages, thesis/dissertation, colloquium. *Entrance requirements:* For master's and doctorate, GRE General Test, minimum GPA of 3.0 in last 30 hours of chemistry course work, letters of recommendation (3). Additional exam requirements/recommendations for international students: Required—TOEFL (minimum score 550 paper-based; 213 computer-based), TSE(minimum score 50). *Application deadline:* For fall admission, 5/1 priority date for domestic students, 3/1 priority date for international students; for spring admission, 10/1 priority date for domestic students, 8/1 priority date for international students. Applications are processed on a rolling basis. Application fee: $30. Electronic applications accepted. *Financial support:* In 2003–04, 74 students received support, including 3 fellowships with partial tuition reimbursements available (averaging $18,500 per year), 13 research assistantships with partial tuition reimbursements available (averaging $18,500 per year), 58 teaching assistantships with partial tuition reimbursements available (averaging $18,500 per year); career-related internships or fieldwork, institutionally sponsored loans, scholarships/grants, and unspecified assistantships also available. Financial award application deadline: 6/30. *Faculty research:* Synthesis, bio-organic chemistry, bioinorganic chemistry, environmental chemistry, NMR. Total annual research expenditures: $1.6 million. *Unit head:* Michael Zaworotko, Chairperson, 813-974-4129, Fax: 813-974-1731. *Application contact:* Dr. Julie Harmon, Graduate Director, 813-974-3397, Fax: 813-974-3203, E-mail: harmon@chuma1.cas.usf.edu.

The University of Tennessee, Graduate School, College of Arts and Sciences, Department of Chemistry, Knoxville, TN 37996. Offers analytical chemistry (MS, PhD); chemical physics (PhD); environmental chemistry (MS, PhD); inorganic chemistry (MS, PhD); organic chemistry (MS, PhD); physical chemistry (MS, PhD); polymer chemistry (MS, PhD); theoretical chemistry (PhD). Part-time programs available. Terminal master's awarded for partial completion of doctoral program. *Degree requirements:* For master's and doctorate, thesis/dissertation. *Entrance requirements:* For master's and doctorate, GRE General Test, minimum GPA of 2.7. Additional exam requirements/recommendations for international students: Required—TOEFL. Electronic applications accepted.

The University of Texas at Austin, Graduate School, College of Natural Sciences, Department of Chemistry and Biochemistry, Austin, TX 78712-1111. Offers analytical chemistry (MA, PhD); biochemistry (MA, PhD); inorganic chemistry (MA, PhD); organic chemistry (MA, PhD); physical chemistry (MA, PhD). *Entrance requirements:* For master's and doctorate, GRE General Test.

University of Toledo, Graduate School, College of Arts and Sciences, Department of Chemistry, Toledo, OH 43606-3390. Offers analytical chemistry (MS, PhD); biological chemistry (MS, PhD); inorganic chemistry (MS, PhD); organic chemistry (MS, PhD); physical chemistry (MS, PhD). Part-time programs available. *Students:* 46 full-time (21 women), 9 part-time (4 women); includes 4 minority (3 African Americans, 1 Hispanic American), 31 international. Average age 27. 23 applicants, 87% accepted. In 2003, 3 master's, 5 doctorates awarded. *Degree requirements:* For master's and doctorate, thesis/dissertation. *Entrance requirements:* For master's and doctorate, GRE General Test, GRE Subject Test. Additional exam requirements/recommendations for international students: Required—TOEFL. *Application deadline:* For fall admission, 8/1 for domestic students. Applications are processed on a rolling basis. Application fee: $40. Electronic applications accepted. Tuition, area resident: Part-time $3,817 per semester. *Expenses:* Tuition, state resident: part-time $8,177 per semester. Required fees:

Analytical Chemistry

University of Toledo (continued)

$502 per semester. *Financial support:* In 2003–04, 4 research assistantships, 47 teaching assistantships were awarded. Fellowships, Federal Work-Study and institutionally sponsored loans also available. Support available to part-time students. Financial award application deadline: 4/1; financial award applicants required to submit FAFSA. *Faculty research:* Enzymology, materials chemistry, crystallography, theoretical chemistry. *Unit head:* Dr. Alan Pinkerton, Chair, 419-530-2109, Fax: 419-530-4033, E-mail: apinker@uoft02.utoledo.edu.

See in-depth description on page 179.

Vanderbilt University, Graduate School, Department of Chemistry, Nashville, TN 37240-1001. Offers analytical chemistry (MAT, MS, PhD); inorganic chemistry (MAT, MS, PhD); organic chemistry (MAT, MS, PhD); physical chemistry (MAT, MS, PhD); theoretical chemistry (MAT, MS, PhD). *Degree requirements:* For master's, thesis or alternative; for doctorate, thesis/dissertation, area, qualifying, and final exams. *Entrance requirements:* For master's and doctorate, GRE General Test, GRE Subject Test (recommended). Additional exam requirements/recommendations for international students: Required—TOEFL. Electronic applications accepted. *Expenses:* Tuition: Part-time $1,155 per semester hour. Required fees: $1,538. *Faculty research:* Chemical synthesis; mechanistic, theoretical, bioorganic, analytical, and spectroscopic chemistry.

See in-depth description on page 185.

Wake Forest University, Graduate School, Department of Chemistry, Winston-Salem, NC 27109. Offers analytical chemistry (MS, PhD); inorganic chemistry (MS, PhD); organic chemistry (MS, PhD); physical chemistry (MS, PhD). Part-time programs available. *Faculty:* 15 full-time (2 women). *Students:* 32 full-time (15 women), 1 part-time; includes 2 minority (both African Americans), 13 international. Average age 28. 34 applicants, 38% accepted, 5 enrolled. In 2003, 4 master's, 2 doctorates awarded. *Degree requirements:* For master's, one foreign language, thesis, comprehensive exam, registration; for doctorate, 2 foreign languages, thesis/dissertation, comprehensive exam, registration. *Entrance requirements:* For master's and doctorate, GRE General Test. Additional exam requirements/recommendations for international students: Required—TOEFL (minimum score 213 computer-based). *Application deadline:* For fall admission, 1/15 for domestic students, 1/15 for international students. Application fee: $25. Electronic applications accepted. *Expenses:* Tuition: Full-time $26,500. *Financial support:* In 2003–04, 32 students received support, including 1 fellowship with full tuition reimbursement available (averaging $19,500 per year), 11 research assistantships with full tuition reimbursements available (averaging $17,500 per year), 17 teaching assistantships with full tuition reimbursements available (averaging $17,500 per year); scholarships/grants and tuition waivers (full and partial) also available. Support available to part-time students. Financial award application deadline: 1/15; financial award applicants required to submit FAFSA. *Unit head:* Dr. Dilip Kondepudi, Director, 336-758-5131, Fax: 336-758-4656, E-mail: dilip@wfu.edu.

Washington State University, Graduate School, College of Sciences, Department of Chemistry, Pullman, WA 99164. Offers analytical chemistry (MS, PhD); biological systems (MS, PhD); inorganic chemistry (MS, PhD); organic chemistry (MS, PhD); physical chemistry (MS, PhD). *Faculty:* 22 full-time (3 women). *Students:* 37 full-time (17 women), 1 part-time; includes 3 minority (2 Asian Americans or Pacific Islanders, 1 Hispanic American), 10 international. Average age 25. 48 applicants, 58% accepted, 12 enrolled. In 2003, 3 master's, 1 doctorate awarded. Terminal master's awarded for partial completion of doctoral program. *Median time to degree:* Master's–2.8 years full-time; doctorate–5 years full-time. *Degree requirements:* For master's, oral exam, teaching experience, thesis optional; for doctorate, thesis/dissertation, oral exam, written exam, comprehensive exam. *Entrance requirements:* For master's and doctorate, GRE General Test, minimum GPA of 3.0, 3 letters of recommendation. *Application deadline:* For fall admission, 3/1 for domestic students; for spring admission, 10/1 priority date for domestic students. Applications are processed on a rolling basis. Application fee: $35. *Expenses:* Tuition, state resident: full-time $6,278; part-time $314 per hour. Tuition, nonresident: full-time $15,514; part-time $765 per hour. Required fees: $444. Full-time tuition and fees vary according to campus/location, program and student level. Part-time tuition and fees vary according to course load. *Financial support:* In 2003–04, 13 research assistantships with full and partial tuition reimbursements (averaging $17,000 per year), 23 teaching assistantships with full and partial tuition reimbursements (averaging $17,000 per year) were awarded. Fellowships, career-related internships or fieldwork, Federal Work-Study, institutionally sponsored loans, scholarships/grants, health care benefits, unspecified assistantships, and summer support also available. Financial award application deadline: 4/1; financial award applicants required to submit FAFSA. *Faculty research:* Environmental chemistry, materials chemistry, radio chemistry, bio-organic, computational chemistry. Total annual research expenditures: $1.9 million. *Unit head:* Dr. Ralph Yount, Chair, 509-335-1516, Fax: 509-335-8867, E-mail: yount@wsu.edu. *Application contact:* Sue B. Clark, Chair, Admissions Committee, 509-335-8866, Fax: 509-335-8867, E-mail: carrie@wsu.edu.

West Virginia University, Eberly College of Arts and Sciences, Department of Chemistry, Morgantown, WV 26506. Offers analytical chemistry (MS, PhD); inorganic chemistry (MS, PhD); organic chemistry (MS, PhD); physical chemistry (MS, PhD); theoretical chemistry (MS, PhD). Part-time programs available. Postbaccalaureate distance learning degree programs offered (no on-campus study). *Faculty:* 14 full-time (1 woman), 5 part-time/adjunct (3 women). *Students:* 45 full-time (15 women), 3 part-time (2 women); includes 1 minority (Hispanic American), 26 international. Average age 28. 84 applicants, 58% accepted, 11 enrolled. In 2003, 5 master's, 3 doctorates awarded. Terminal master's awarded for partial completion of doctoral program. *Degree requirements:* For master's and doctorate, thesis/dissertation, registration. *Entrance requirements:* For master's, GRE General Test, GRE Subject Test (recommended), minimum GPA of 2.5; for doctorate, GRE General Test, GRE Subject Test (recommended), minimum GPA of 2.75. Additional exam requirements/recommendations for international students: Required—TOEFL. *Application deadline:* For fall admission, 3/1 for domestic students. Applications are processed on a rolling basis. Application fee: $50. Electronic applications accepted. *Expenses:* Tuition, state resident: full-time $4,332. Tuition, nonresident: full-time $12,442. *Financial support:* In 2003–04, fellowships (averaging $2,000 per year), research assistantships with full tuition reimbursements (averaging $13,000 per year), teaching assistantships with full tuition reimbursements (averaging $12,000 per year) were awarded. Tuition waivers (full and partial) also available. Financial award application deadline: 2/1; financial award applicants required to submit FAFSA. *Faculty research:* Analysis of proteins, drug interactions, solids and effluents by advanced separation methods; electro-chemistry, mass spectrometry and atomic spectrometry; development of new synthetic strategies for complex organic molecules; synthesis and structural characterization of metal complexes for polymerization catalysis; nonmagnetic resonance studies of amorphous solids. *Unit head:* Dr. Harry O. Finklea, Chair, 304-293-3435 Ext. 6408, Fax: 304-293-4904, E-mail: harry.finklea@mail.wvu.edu.

Chemistry

Acadia University, Faculty of Pure and Applied Science, Department of Chemistry, Wolfville, NS B4P 2R6, Canada. Offers M Sc. *Students:* Average age 26. 8 applicants, 0% accepted. In 2003, 1 degree awarded. *Degree requirements:* For master's, thesis. *Entrance requirements:* For master's, GRE. Additional exam requirements/recommendations for international students: Required—TOEFL. *Application deadline:* For fall admission, 2/1 for domestic students. Application fee: $50. Electronic applications accepted. *Expenses:* Tuition, state resident: full-time $5,611. *Financial support:* In 2003–04, 1 teaching assistantship (averaging $8,000 per year) was awarded. Financial award application deadline: 2/1. *Faculty research:* Atmospheric chemistry, chemical kinetics, bioelectrochemistry of proteins, organosilicon dewdrimers, self assembling monolayers. *Unit head:* Dr. John M. Roscoe, Head, 902-585-1353, Fax: 902-585-1114, E-mail: john.roscoe@acadiau.ca. *Application contact:* Avril Bird, Secretary, 902-585-1242, Fax: 902-585-1114, E-mail: avril.bird@acadiau.ca.

American University, College of Arts and Sciences, Department of Chemistry, Program in Chemistry, Washington, DC 20016-8001. Offers MS. *Students:* 6 full-time (4 women), 23 part-time (13 women); includes 7 minority (4 African Americans, 3 Asian Americans or Pacific Islanders), 10 international. Average age 29. *Degree requirements:* For master's, thesis, comprehensive exam. *Entrance requirements:* For master's, GRE, minimum GPA of 3.0. *Application deadline:* For fall admission, 2/1 for domestic students; for spring admission, 10/1 priority date for domestic students. Applications are processed on a rolling basis. Application fee: $50. *Expenses:* Tuition: Full-time $15,786; part-time $877 per credit hour. Required fees: $300. Tuition and fees vary according to course load and program. *Financial support:* In 2003–04, 28 students received support, including fellowships with full tuition reimbursements available (averaging $14,500 per year), research assistantships with full tuition reimbursements available (averaging $8,500 per year), teaching assistantships with full tuition reimbursements available (averaging $8,500 per year); career-related internships or fieldwork, Federal Work-Study, scholarships/grants, and traineeships also available. Financial award application deadline: 2/1.

Arizona State University, Graduate College, College of Liberal Arts and Sciences, Department of Chemistry and Biochemistry, Tempe, AZ 85287. Offers MNS, MS, PhD. *Degree requirements:* For master's, thesis; for doctorate, one foreign language, thesis/dissertation. *Entrance requirements:* For master's and doctorate, GRE. Additional exam requirements/recommendations for international students: Required—TOEFL, TSE. *Expenses:* Tuition, state resident: full-time $3,708; part-time $194 per credit hour. Tuition, nonresident: full-time $12,228; part-time $510 per credit hour. Required fees: $87; $22 per semester. Part-time tuition and fees vary according to program. *Faculty research:* Meteorite chemistry, structure of biopolymers, electron microprobe analysis of air pollutants, x-ray crystallography.

Arkansas State University, Graduate School, College of Sciences and Mathematics, Department of Chemistry and Physics, Jonesboro, State University, AR 72467. Offers chemistry (MS); chemistry education (MSE, SCCT). *Accreditation:* NCATE (one or more programs are accredited). Part-time programs available. *Faculty:* 6 full-time (1 woman). *Students:* Average age 30. *Degree requirements:* For master's, thesis or alternative, comprehensive exam. *Entrance requirements:* For master's, GRE General Test or MAT, appropriate bachelor's degree; for SCCT, GRE General Test or MAT, interview, master's degree. Additional exam requirements/recommendations for international students: Required—TOEFL (minimum score 213 computer-based). *Application deadline:* For fall admission, 7/1 for domestic students; for spring admission, 11/15 priority date for domestic students. Applications are processed on a rolling basis. Application fee: $15 ($25 for international students). Electronic applications accepted. *Expenses:* Tuition, state resident: full-time $2,844; part-time $158 per hour. Tuition, nonresident: full-time $7,200; part-time $400 per hour. Required fees: $644; $33 per hour. $25 per semester. Tuition and fees vary according to course load. *Financial support:* Teaching assistantships, career-related internships or fieldwork, Federal Work-Study, scholarships/grants available. Support available to part-time students. Financial award application deadline: 7/1; financial award applicants required to submit FAFSA. *Unit head:* Dr. Bao-An Li, Interim Chair, 870-972-3086, Fax: 870-972-3089, E-mail: bali@astate.edu.

Auburn University, Graduate School, College of Sciences and Mathematics, Department of Chemistry, Auburn University, AL 36849. Offers MS, PhD. Part-time programs available. *Faculty:* 20 full-time (0 women). *Students:* 43 full-time (16 women), 16 part-time (6 women); includes 4 minority (2 African Americans, 1 American Indian/Alaska Native, 1 Asian American or Pacific Islander), 38 international. 65 applicants, 46% accepted. In 2003, 1 master's, 11 doctorates awarded. *Degree requirements:* For master's, thesis (for some programs); for doctorate, thesis/dissertation, oral and written exams. *Entrance requirements:* For master's and doctorate, GRE General Test. *Application deadline:* For fall admission, 7/7 for domestic students; for spring admission, 11/24 for domestic students. Applications are processed on a rolling basis. Application fee: $25 ($50 for international students). Electronic applications accepted. *Expenses:* Tuition, state resident: part-time $175 per credit hour. Tuition, nonresident: part-time $525 per credit hour. *Financial support:* Fellowships, research assistantships, teaching assistantships available. Financial award application deadline: 3/15. *Unit head:* Dr. J. Howard Hargis, Head, 334-844-4043, Fax: 334-844-4043, E-mail: hargijh@mail.auburn.edu.

Ball State University, Graduate School, College of Sciences and Humanities, Department of Chemistry, Muncie, IN 47306-1099. Offers MA, MS. *Faculty:* 12. *Students:* 3 full-time (0 women), 9 part-time (6 women), 2 international. Average age 22. 9 applicants, 67% accepted, 4 enrolled. In 2003, 4 degrees awarded. *Entrance requirements:* For master's, GRE General Test. Application fee: $25 ($35 for international students). *Expenses:* Tuition, state resident: full-time $5,748. Tuition, nonresident: full-time $14,166. *Financial support:* In 2003–04, 9 research assistantships with full tuition reimbursements (averaging $9,460 per year) were awarded. Financial award application deadline: 3/1. *Faculty research:* Synthetic and analytical chemistry, biochemistry, theoretical chemistry. *Unit head:* Dr. Robert Morris, Chair, 765-285-8060, Fax: 765-285-2351.

Baylor University, Graduate School, College of Arts and Sciences, Department of Chemistry and Biochemistry, Waco, TX 76798. Offers chemistry (MS, PhD). Part-time programs available. *Faculty:* 14 full-time (2 women). *Students:* 44 full-time (13 women); includes 1 minority (Hispanic American), 26 international. In 2003, 1 master's, 5 doctorates awarded. Terminal master's awarded for partial completion of doctoral program. *Degree requirements:* For master's, thesis/dissertation; for doctorate, thesis/dissertation, comprehensive exam. *Entrance requirements:* For master's and doctorate, GRE General Test, GRE Subject Test. Additional exam requirements/recommendations for international students: Required—TOEFL. *Application deadline:* For fall admission, 8/1 for domestic students. Applications are processed on a rolling basis. Application fee: $25. *Expenses:* Tuition: Part-time $698 per hour. *Financial support:* In 2003–04, 20 students received support; fellowships, research assistantships, teaching assistantships, Federal Work-Study, institutionally sponsored loans, and tuition waivers (full) available. Support available to part-time students. *Unit head:* Dr. Marianna Busch, Chair, 254-710-3311, Fax: 254-710-2403, E-mail: marianna_busch@baylor.edu. *Application contact:* Dr. Carlos Manzanares, Director of Graduate Studies, 254-710-4247, Fax: 254-710-2403, E-mail: carlos_manzanares@baylor.edu.

See in-depth description on page 93.

Boston College, Graduate School of Arts and Sciences, Department of Chemistry, Chestnut Hill, MA 02467-3800. Offers biochemistry (PhD); inorganic chemistry (PhD); organic chemistry (PhD); physical chemistry (PhD); science education (MST). MST is offered through the School of Education for secondary school science teaching. Part-time programs available. *Students:* 95 full-time (31 women); includes 12 minority (2 African Americans, 7 Asian Americans or Pacific Islanders, 3 Hispanic Americans), 22 international. 285 applicants, 24% accepted, 14 enrolled. In 2003, 2 master's, 13 doctorates awarded. *Degree requirements:* For doctorate, thesis/dissertation, qualifying exam. *Entrance requirements:* For doctorate, GRE General Test, GRE Subject Test. Additional exam requirements/recommendations for international students: Required—TOEFL (minimum score 550 paper-based; 213 computer-based). *Application deadline:* For fall admission, 1/2 for domestic students. Application fee: $60. Electronic applications accepted. *Expenses:* Tuition: Part-time $810 per credit. *Financial support:* Fellowships with full tuition reimbursements, research assistantships with full tuition reimbursements, teaching assistantships with full tuition reimbursements, Federal Work-Study available. Support available to part-time students. Financial award application deadline: 3/1; financial award applicants required to submit FAFSA. *Unit head:* Dr. David McFadden, Chairperson, 617-552-3605, E-mail: david.mcfadden@bc.edu. *Application contact:* Dr. John Fourkas, Information Contact, 617-552-3605, Fax: 617-552-0833, E-mail: john.fourkas@bc.edu.

Boston University, Graduate School of Arts and Sciences, Department of Chemistry, Boston, MA 02215. Offers MA, PhD. *Students:* 106 full-time (46 women), 1 (woman) part-time; includes 5 minority (1 African American, 3 Asian Americans or Pacific Islanders, 1 Hispanic American), 64 international. Average age 27. 265 applicants, 31% accepted, 25 enrolled. In 2003, 6 master's, 7 doctorates awarded. Terminal master's awarded for partial completion of doctoral program. *Degree requirements:* For master's, one foreign language, registration; for doctorate, one foreign language, thesis/dissertation, comprehensive exam, registration. *Entrance requirements:* For master's and doctorate, GRE General Test, GRE Subject Test (recommended), 3 letters of recommendation. Additional exam requirements/recommendations for international students: Required—TOEFL (minimum score 550 paper-based; 213 computer-based). *Application deadline:* For fall admission, 7/1 for domestic students, 7/1 for international students; for spring admission, 10/15 for domestic students, 10/15 for international students. Application fee: $60. *Expenses:* Tuition: Full-time $28,512; part-time $891 per credit hour. *Financial support:* In 2003–04, 102 students received support, including 4 fellowships with full tuition reimbursements available (averaging $15,500 per year), 62 research assistantships with full tuition reimbursements available (averaging $15,000 per year), 40 teaching assistantships with full tuition reimbursements available (averaging $15,000 per year); Federal Work-Study, scholarships/grants, and tuition waivers (full) also available. Support available to part-time students. Financial award application deadline: 1/15; financial award applicants required to submit FAFSA. *Unit head:* Thomas D. Tullius, Chairman, 617-353-2482, Fax: 617-353-6466, E-mail: tullius@bu.edu. *Application contact:* Kevin F. Burgoyne, Academic Administrator, 617-353-2503, Fax: 617-353-6466, E-mail: burgoyne@bu.edu.

Bowling Green State University, Graduate College, College of Arts and Sciences, Center for Photochemical Sciences, Bowling Green, OH 43403. Offers PhD. *Faculty:* 12. *Students:* 50 full-time (21 women); includes 1 minority (Asian American or Pacific Islander), 48 international. Average age 27. 33 applicants, 48% accepted, 9 enrolled. In 2003, 7 degrees awarded. *Degree requirements:* For doctorate, thesis/dissertation, comprehensive exam. *Entrance requirements:* For doctorate, GRE General Test. Additional exam requirements/recommendations for international students: Required—TOEFL. *Application deadline:* For fall admission, 1/1 for domestic students. Application fee: $30. Electronic applications accepted. *Expenses:* Tuition, state resident: part-time $436 per hour. Tuition, nonresident: part-time $768 per hour. *Financial support:* In 2003–04, 13 research assistantships with full tuition reimbursements (averaging $16,907 per year), 34 teaching assistantships with full tuition reimbursements (averaging $12,296 per year) were awarded. Federal Work-Study, tuition waivers (full), and unspecified assistantships also available. Financial award applicants required to submit FAFSA. *Faculty research:* Laser-initiated photopolymerization, spectroscopic and kinetic studies, optoelectronics of semiconductor multiple quantum wells, electron transfer processes, carotenoid pigments. *Unit head:* Dr. Douglas C. Neckers, Executive Director, 419-372-2033. *Application contact:* Dr. Phil Castellano, Graduate Program Coordinator, 419-372-2809, Fax: 419-372-0366.

See in-depth description on page 95.

Bowling Green State University, Graduate College, College of Arts and Sciences, Department of Chemistry, Bowling Green, OH 43403. Offers MAT, MS. Part-time programs available. *Faculty:* 14 full-time. *Students:* 13 full-time (5 women), 1 part-time, 11 international. Average age 27. 28 applicants, 29% accepted, 4 enrolled. In 2003, 8 degrees awarded. *Degree requirements:* For master's, thesis or alternative. *Entrance requirements:* For master's, GRE General Test. Additional exam requirements/recommendations for international students: Required—TOEFL. *Application deadline:* Applications are processed on a rolling basis. Application fee: $30. Electronic applications accepted. *Expenses:* Tuition, state resident: part-time $436 per hour. Tuition, nonresident: part-time $768 per hour. *Financial support:* In 2003–04, 1 research assistantship with full tuition reimbursement (averaging $10,500 per year), 11 teaching assistantships with full tuition reimbursements (averaging $8,381 per year) were awarded. Federal Work-Study, tuition waivers (full), and unspecified assistantships also available. Financial award applicants required to submit FAFSA. *Faculty research:* Organic, inorganic, physical, and analytical chemistry; biochemistry; surface science. *Unit head:* Dr. Michael Dgawa, Chair, 419-372-2033. *Application contact:* Tom Kinstle, Graduate Program Coordinator, 419-372-2658, Fax: 419-372-0366.

Bradley University, Graduate School, College of Liberal Arts and Sciences, Department of Chemistry and Biochemistry, Peoria, IL 61625-0002. Offers MS. Part-time and evening/weekend programs available. *Students:* 1 applicant, 0% accepted, 0 enrolled. *Degree requirements:* For master's, thesis, comprehensive exam. *Entrance requirements:* Additional exam requirements/recommendations for international students: Required—TOEFL (minimum score 550 paper-based; 213 computer-based). *Application deadline:* For fall admission, 7/1 for domestic students; for spring admission, 11/1 for domestic students. Applications are processed on a rolling basis. Application fee: $40. *Expenses:* Tuition: Part-time $460 per semester hour. Tuition and fees vary according to course load. *Financial support:* Scholarships/grants and tuition waivers (partial) available. Financial award application deadline: 3/1. *Unit head:* Dr. Kurt Field, Chairperson, 309-677-3024. *Application contact:* Dr. Kristi McQuade, Graduate Coordinator, 309-677-3022, E-mail: mcquade@bradley.edu.

Brandeis University, Graduate School of Arts and Sciences, Department of Chemistry, Waltham, MA 02454-9110. Offers inorganic chemistry (MS, PhD); organic chemistry (MS, PhD); physical chemistry (MS, PhD). *Faculty:* 18 full-time (3 women). *Students:* 39 full-time (20 women), 1 (woman) part-time; includes 2 minority (1 Asian American or Pacific Islander, 1 Hispanic American), 32 international. Average age 25. 114 applicants, 5% accepted. In 2003, 8 master's, 5 doctorates awarded. Terminal master's awarded for partial completion of doctoral program. *Degree requirements:* For master's, 1 year of residency; for doctorate, one foreign language, thesis/dissertation, 3 years of residency, 2 seminars, qualifying exams. *Entrance requirements:* For master's and doctorate, GRE General Test, resumé, letters of recommendation. Additional exam requirements/recommendations for international students: Required—TOEFL (minimum score 600 paper-based; 250 computer-based). *Application deadline:* For fall admission, 1/15 for domestic students. Applications are processed on a rolling basis. Application fee: $60. Electronic applications accepted. *Expenses:* Tuition: Full-time $28,999; part-time $4,867 per course. Required fees: $175. *Financial support:* In 2003–04, 20 fellowships (averaging $20,000 per year), 21 research assistantships (averaging $20,000 per year), 18 teaching assistantships (averaging $20,000 per year) were awarded. Institutionally sponsored loans and scholarships/grants also available. Financial award application deadline: 4/15; financial award applicants required to submit CSS PROFILE or FAFSA. *Faculty research:* Oscillating chemical reactions, molecular recognition systems, protein crystallography, synthesis of natural product spectroscopy and magnetic resonance. Total annual research expenditures: $1,900. *Unit head:* Dr. Thomas C. Pochapsky, Chair, 781-736-2559, Fax: 781-736-2516, E-mail: pochapsky@brandeis.edu. *Application contact:* Charlotte Haygazian, Graduate Admissions Secretary, 781-736-2500, Fax: 781-736-2516, E-mail: chemadm@brandeis.edu.

Brigham Young University, Graduate Studies, College of Physical and Mathematical Sciences, Department of Chemistry and Biochemistry, Provo, UT 84602-1001. Offers analytical chemistry (MS, PhD); biochemistry (MS, PhD); inorganic chemistry (MS, PhD); organic chemistry (MS, PhD); physical chemistry (MS, PhD). *Faculty:* 34 full-time (2 women). *Students:* 90 full-time (56 women); includes 2 minority (1 Asian American or Pacific Islander, 1 Hispanic American), 61 international. Average age 31. 103 applicants, 54% accepted, 23 enrolled. In 2003, 6 master's, 6 doctorates awarded. *Median time to degree:* Master's–2.8 years full-time. Of those who began their doctoral program in fall 1995, 100% received their degree in 8 years or less. *Degree requirements:* For master's, thesis, registration; for doctorate, thesis/dissertation, degree qualifying exam. *Entrance requirements:* For master's, pass 1 (biochemistry), 4 (chemistry) of 5 area exams, GRE General Test, minimum GPA of 3.0 in last 60 hours; for doctorate, pass 1 (biochemistry) or 4 (chemistry) of 5 area exams, GRE General Test, minimum GPA of 3.0 in last 60 hours. Additional exam requirements/recommendations for international students: Required—TOEFL, TWE. *Application deadline:* For fall admission, 2/1 priority date for domestic students, 2/1 priority date for international students. Applications are processed on a rolling basis. Application fee: $50. Electronic applications accepted. *Expenses:* Tuition: Part-time $221 per hour. *Financial support:* In 2003–04, 90 students received support, including 12 fellowships with full tuition reimbursements available (averaging $18,400 per year), 37 research assistantships with full tuition reimbursements available (averaging $18,400 per year), 30 teaching assistantships with full tuition reimbursements available (averaging $18,300 per year); institutionally sponsored loans, scholarships/grants, health care benefits, tuition waivers (full), and unspecified assistantships also available. Financial award application deadline: 2/1. *Faculty research:* Separation science, molecular recognition, organic synthesis and biomedical application, biochemistry and molecular biology, molecular spectroscopy. Total annual research expenditures: $2.7 million. *Unit head:* Dr. Francis R. Nordmeyer, Chair, 801-422-3667, Fax: 801-422-0153, E-mail: fran_nordmeyer@byu.edu. *Application contact:* Dr. Noel L. Owen, Graduate Coordinator, 801-422-2973, Fax: 801-422-0153, E-mail: chemgrad@byu.edu.

See in-depth description on page 97.

Brock University, Graduate Studies and Research, Faculty of Mathematics and Science, Department of Chemistry, St. Catharines, ON L2S 3A1, Canada. Offers M Sc. Part-time programs available. *Degree requirements:* For master's, thesis. *Entrance requirements:* For master's, honors B Sc in chemistry. Additional exam requirements/recommendations for international students: Required—TOEFL. *Faculty research:* Inorganic, organic, analytical, theoretical, and physical chemistry.

Brooklyn College of the City University of New York, Division of Graduate Studies, Department of Chemistry, Brooklyn, NY 11210-2889. Offers applied chemistry (MA); chemistry (MA, PhD). The department offers courses at Brooklyn College that are creditable toward the CUNY doctoral degree. Part-time programs available. *Students:* 2 full-time (1 woman), 18 part-time (8 women); includes 9 minority (4 African Americans, 4 Asian Americans or Pacific Islanders, 1 Hispanic American), 4 international. 11 applicants, 45% accepted, 3 enrolled. *Degree requirements:* For master's, one foreign language, thesis or alternative. *Entrance requirements:* For master's, 2 letters of recommendation. Additional exam requirements/recommendations for international students: Required—TOEFL. *Application deadline:* For fall admission, 3/1 for domestic students, 2/1 for international students; for spring admission, 11/1 for domestic students, 10/1 for international students. Application fee: $50. *Expenses:* Tuition, state resident: full-time $5,440; part-time $230 per credit. Tuition, nonresident: full-time $10,200; part-time $425 per credit. Required fees: $280; $103 per term. *Financial support:* Teaching assistantships, Federal Work-Study, institutionally sponsored loans, and scholarships/grants available. Support available to part-time students. Financial award application deadline: 5/1; financial award applicants required to submit FAFSA. Total annual research expenditures: $25,000. *Unit head:* Dr. Malgorzata Ciszkowska, Chairperson, 718-951-5458, E-mail: malgcisz@brooklyn.cuny.edu. *Application contact:* Michael Lovaglio, Assistant Director of Graduate Admissions, 718-951-5001, E-mail: adminqry@brooklyn.cuny.edu.

Brown University, Graduate School, Department of Chemistry, Providence, RI 02912. Offers biochemistry (PhD); chemistry (Sc M, PhD). *Degree requirements:* For master's, thesis; for doctorate, one foreign language, thesis/dissertation, cumulative exam.

Bryn Mawr College, Graduate School of Arts and Sciences, Department of Chemistry, Bryn Mawr, PA 19010-2899. Offers MA, PhD. *Faculty:* 8. *Students:* 4 full-time (3 women), 7 part-time (3 women); includes 1 minority (Asian American or Pacific Islander), 3 international. 15 applicants, 60% accepted, 4 enrolled. In 2003, 3 degrees awarded. *Degree requirements:* For master's, one foreign language, thesis, registration; for doctorate, 2 foreign languages, thesis/dissertation, comprehensive exam, registration. *Entrance requirements:* For master's and doctorate, GRE General Test, GRE Subject Test. Additional exam requirements/recommendations for international students: Required—TOEFL (minimum score 600 paper-based; 250 computer-based). *Application deadline:* For fall admission, 1/15 for domestic students, 1/15 for international students. Application fee: $30. *Expenses:* Tuition: Full-time $24,540; part-time $4,150 per unit. One-time fee: $60 part-time. *Financial support:* Research assistantships with full tuition reimbursements, teaching assistantships with partial tuition reimbursements, Federal Work-Study, scholarships/grants, and tuition waivers (partial) available. Support available to part-time students. Financial award application deadline: 1/15. *Unit head:* Dr. Susan White, Chair, 610-526-5104, E-mail: swhite@brynmawr.edu. *Application contact:* Lea R. Miller, Secretary, 610-526-5072, Fax: 610-526-5076, E-mail: lrmiller@brynmawr.edu.

Bucknell University, Graduate Studies, College of Arts and Sciences, Department of Chemistry, Lewisburg, PA 17837. Offers MA, MS. Part-time programs available. *Degree requirements:* For master's, thesis. *Entrance requirements:* For master's, GRE General Test, GRE Subject Test, minimum GPA of 2.8. Additional exam requirements/recommendations for international students: Required—TOEFL.

Buffalo State College, State University of New York, Graduate Studies and Research, Faculty of Natural and Social Sciences, Department of Chemistry, Buffalo, NY 14222-1095. Offers chemistry (MA); secondary education (MS Ed), including chemistry. *Accreditation:* NCATE (one or more programs are accredited). Part-time and evening/weekend programs available. *Faculty:* 8 full-time (2 women), 1 part-time/adjunct (0 women). *Students:* Average age 30. 9 applicants, 33% accepted, 2 enrolled. In 2003, 2 degrees awarded. *Degree requirements:* For master's, thesis (for some programs), project. *Entrance requirements:* For master's, minimum GPA of 2.6, New York teaching certificate (MS Ed). Additional exam requirements/recommendations for international students: Required—TOEFL (minimum score 550 paper-based; 213 computer-based). *Application deadline:* For fall admission, 5/1 for domestic students; for spring admission, 10/1 priority date for domestic students. Applications are processed on a rolling basis. Application fee: $50. *Expenses:* Tuition, state resident: full-time $2,550; part-time $213 per credit hour. Tuition, nonresident: full-time $4,208; part-time $351 per credit hour. Required fees: $17 per credit hour. *Financial support:* In 2003–04, fellowships with full tuition reimbursements (averaging $7,000 per year), 4 research assistantships with partial tuition reimbursements (averaging $6,000 per year) were awarded. Federal Work-Study and unspecified assistantships also available. Support available to part-time students. Financial award application deadline: 3/1; financial award applicants required to submit FAFSA. *Unit head:* Dr. Zeki Y. Al-Saigh, Chairperson, 716-878-5204, Fax: 716-878-4028, E-mail: alsaigzy@buffalostate.edu.

California Institute of Technology, Division of Chemistry and Chemical Engineering, Program in Chemistry, Pasadena, CA 91125-0001. Offers MS, PhD. *Faculty:* 25 full-time (3 women). *Students:* 230 full-time (69 women). Average age 24. 488 applicants, 30% accepted, 50 enrolled. In 2003, 5 master's, 29 doctorates awarded. Terminal master's awarded for partial completion of doctoral program. *Degree requirements:* For master's and doctorate, thesis/dissertation. *Application deadline:* For fall admission, 1/1 for domestic students. Application fee: $0. Electronic applications accepted. *Financial support:* In 2003–04, 230 students received support, including 47 fellowships, 66 research assistantships, 125 teaching assistant-

Chemistry

California Institute of Technology (continued)

ships; Federal Work-Study, institutionally sponsored loans, scholarships/grants, traineeships, health care benefits, and unspecified assistantships also available. Financial award application deadline: 1/1. *Faculty research:* Genetic structure and gene expression, organic synthesis, reagents and mechanisms, homogeneous and electrochemical catalysis. *Unit head:* Dr. Douglas C. Rees, Executive Officer, 626-395-8393, Fax: 626-744-9524, E-mail: dcrees@caltech.edu. *Application contact:* Dian Buchness, Graduate Secretary, 626-395-6110, Fax: 626-568-8824, E-mail: dianb@its.caltech.edu.

California State Polytechnic University, Pomona, Academic Affairs, College of Science, Program in Chemistry, Pomona, CA 91768-2557. Offers MS. Part-time programs available. *Students:* 11 full-time (3 women), 5 part-time (1 woman); includes 10 minority (6 Asian Americans or Pacific Islanders, 4 Hispanic Americans), 2 international. Average age 27. 21 applicants, 43% accepted, 3 enrolled. In 2003, 7 degrees awarded. *Degree requirements:* For master's, thesis. *Entrance requirements:* For master's, GRE General Test. *Application deadline:* For fall admission, 5/1 for domestic students; for winter admission, 10/15 for domestic students; for spring admission, 1/20 for domestic students. Applications are processed on a rolling basis. Application fee: $55. Electronic applications accepted. Tuition, nonresident: full-time $6,016; part-time $188 per unit. Required fees: $2,256. *Financial support:* In 2003–04, 2 students received support. Career-related internships or fieldwork, Federal Work-Study, and institutionally sponsored loans available. Support available to part-time students. Financial award application deadline: 3/2; financial award applicants required to submit FAFSA. *Unit head:* Dr. Michael L. Keith, Graduate Coordinator, 909-869-3662, E-mail: mlkeith@csupomona.edu.

California State University, Fresno, Division of Graduate Studies, College of Science and Mathematics, Department of Chemistry, Fresno, CA 93740-8027. Offers MS. Part-time programs available. *Degree requirements:* For master's, thesis or alternative. *Entrance requirements:* For master's, GRE General Test, minimum GPA of 2.5. Additional exam requirements/recommendations for international students: Required—TOEFL. Electronic applications accepted. *Faculty research:* Genetics, viticulture, DNA, soils, molecular modeling.

California State University, Fullerton, Graduate Studies, College of Natural Science and Mathematics, Department of Chemistry and Biochemistry, Fullerton, CA 92834-9480. Offers analytical chemistry (MS); biochemistry (MS); geochemistry (MS); inorganic chemistry (MS); organic chemistry (MS); physical chemistry (MS). Part-time programs available. *Faculty:* 17 full-time (5 women), 17 part-time/adjunct. *Students:* 21 full-time (9 women), 23 part-time (11 women); includes 19 minority (1 African American, 9 Asian Americans or Pacific Islanders, 9 Hispanic Americans), 8 international. Average age 28. 49 applicants, 61% accepted, 20 enrolled. In 2003, 5 degrees awarded. *Degree requirements:* For master's, thesis, departmental qualifying exam. *Entrance requirements:* For master's, minimum GPA of 2.5 in last 60 units, major in chemistry or related field. Application fee: $55. Tuition, nonresident: part-time $282 per unit. Required fees: $889 per semester. *Financial support:* Teaching assistantships, career-related internships or fieldwork, Federal Work-Study, institutionally sponsored loans, and scholarships/grants available. Support available to part-time students. Financial award application deadline: 3/1. *Unit head:* Dr. Robert Belloli, Chair, 714-278-3621. *Application contact:* Dr. Gregory Williams, Adviser, 714-278-2170.

California State University, Hayward, Academic Programs and Graduate Studies, College of Science, Department of Chemistry, Hayward, CA 94542-3000. Offers biochemistry (MS); chemistry (MS). *Students:* 7 full-time (3 women), 12 part-time (5 women); includes 13 minority (2 African Americans, 10 Asian Americans or Pacific Islanders, 1 Hispanic American), 3 international. 8 applicants, 50% accepted. *Degree requirements:* For master's, comprehensive exam or thesis. *Entrance requirements:* For master's, minimum GPA of 2.5 in field during previous 2 years. Additional exam requirements/recommendations for international students: Required—TOEFL (minimum score 550 paper-based; 213 computer-based). *Application deadline:* For fall admission, 5/31 for domestic students, 2/29 for international students; for winter admission, 9/30 for domestic students. Applications are processed on a rolling basis. Application fee: $55. Electronic applications accepted. Tuition, nonresident: part-time $188 per unit. Required fees: $560 per quarter hour. *Financial support:* Career-related internships or fieldwork, Federal Work-Study, and institutionally sponsored loans available. Support available to part-time students. Financial award application deadline: 3/2. *Unit head:* Dr. Richard Luibrand, Chair, 510-885-3452. *Application contact:* Jennifer Cason, Graduate Program Coordinator/ Operations Analyst, 510-885-3286, Fax: 510-885-4777, E-mail: jcason@csuhayward.edu.

California State University, Long Beach, Graduate Studies, College of Natural Sciences, Department of Chemistry and Biochemistry, Long Beach, CA 90840. Offers biochemistry (MS); chemistry (MS). Part-time programs available. *Students:* 20 full-time (9 women), 13 part-time (4 women); includes 20 minority (1 African American, 17 Asian Americans or Pacific Islanders, 2 Hispanic Americans), 1 international. Average age 28. 50 applicants, 46% accepted, 10 enrolled. In 2003, 4 degrees awarded. *Degree requirements:* For master's, thesis, departmental qualifying exam. *Application deadline:* For fall admission, 7/1 for domestic students; for spring admission, 12/1 for domestic students. Applications are processed on a rolling basis. Application fee: $55. Electronic applications accepted. Tuition, nonresident: part-time $282 per unit. Required fees: $504 per semester. *Financial support:* Research assistantships, teaching assistantships, Federal Work-Study, institutionally sponsored loans, scholarships/grants, and unspecified assistantships available. Financial award application deadline: 3/2. *Faculty research:* Enzymology, organic synthesis, molecular modeling, environmental chemistry, reaction kinetics. *Unit head:* Dr. Douglas D. McAbee, Chair, 562-985-4941, Fax: 562-985-2315, E-mail: dmcabee@csulb.edu. *Application contact:* Dr. Lijuan Li, Graduate Coordinator, 562-985-5068, Fax: 562-985-2315, E-mail: lli@csulb.edu.

California State University, Los Angeles, Graduate Studies, College of Natural and Social Sciences, Department of Chemistry and Biochemistry, Major in Chemistry, Los Angeles, CA 90032-8530. Offers MS. *Students:* 11 full-time (5 women), 10 part-time (6 women); includes 11 minority (2 African Americans, 5 Asian Americans or Pacific Islanders, 4 Hispanic Americans), 5 international. In 2003, 1 degree awarded. *Degree requirements:* For master's, one foreign language. *Entrance requirements:* Additional exam requirements/recommendations for international students: Required—TOEFL. *Application deadline:* For fall admission, 6/30 for domestic students; for spring admission, 2/1 for domestic students. Applications are processed on a rolling basis. Application fee: $55. Tuition, nonresident: part-time $188 per unit. Required fees: $2,477. *Financial support:* Application deadline: 3/1. *Faculty research:* Transition-metal chemistry, electrochemistry, chromatography, computer modeling of reactions. *Unit head:* Dr. Wayne Tikkanen, Chair, Department of Chemistry and Biochemistry, 323-343-2300.

California State University, Northridge, Graduate Studies, College of Science and Mathematics, Department of Chemistry, Northridge, CA 91330. Offers MS. *Faculty:* 13 full-time, 11 part-time/adjunct. *Students:* 7 full-time (5 women), 20 part-time (15 women); includes 8 minority (5 Asian Americans or Pacific Islanders, 3 Hispanic Americans), 8 international. Average age 30. 27 applicants, 59% accepted. In 2003, 4 degrees awarded. *Degree requirements:* For master's, thesis. *Entrance requirements:* For master's, GRE General Test or minimum GPA of 2.5. Additional exam requirements/recommendations for international students: Required—TOEFL. *Application deadline:* For fall admission, 11/30 for domestic students. Application fee: $55. Required fees: $1,327; $853 per year. *Financial support:* Teaching assistantships available. Support available to part-time students. Financial award application deadline: 3/1. *Unit head:* Dr. Sandor Reichman, Chair, 818-677-3381. *Application contact:* Dr. Francis L. Harris, Graduate Coordinator, 818-677-3371.

California State University, Sacramento, Graduate Studies, College of Natural Sciences and Mathematics, Department of Chemistry, Sacramento, CA 95819-6048. Offers MS. Part-time programs available. *Students:* 1 full-time (0 women), 13 part-time (7 women); includes 4 minority (all Hispanic Americans) *Degree requirements:* For master's, thesis or alternative, departmental qualifying exam, writing proficiency exam. *Entrance requirements:* For master's, minimum GPA of 2.5 during previous 2 years, BA in chemistry or equivalent. Additional exam requirements/recommendations for international students: Required—TOEFL. *Application deadline:* For fall admission, 5/1 for domestic students; for spring admission, 11/1 for domestic students. Application fee: $55. *Expenses:* Tuition, state resident: full-time $2,256. Tuition, nonresident: full-time $10,716. *Financial support:* Career-related internships or fieldwork and Federal Work-Study available. Support available to part-time students. Financial award application deadline: 3/1. *Unit head:* Dr. James Hill, Chair, 916-278-6684, Fax: 916-278-4986.

Carleton University, Faculty of Graduate Studies, Faculty of Science, Department of Chemistry, Ottawa, ON K1S 5B6, Canada. Offers M Sc, PhD. *Degree requirements:* For master's, thesis/dissertation; for doctorate, thesis/dissertation, comprehensive exam. *Entrance requirements:* For master's, honors degree; for doctorate, M Sc. Additional exam requirements/ recommendations for international students: Required—TOEFL. *Application deadline:* Applications are processed on a rolling basis. Application fee: $60 Canadian dollars. *Expenses:* Tuition, state resident: part-time $2,052 per term. Tuition, nonresident: part-time $4,266 per term. Full-time tuition and fees vary according to course load, degree level and program. *Financial support:* Fellowships, research assistantships, teaching assistantships, institutionally sponsored loans, scholarships/grants, and unspecified assistantships available. *Faculty research:* Bioorganic chemistry, analytical toxicology, theoretical and physical chemistry, inorganic chemistry. *Unit head:* G. W. Buchanan, Chair, 613-520-2600 Ext. 3840, Fax: 613-520-3749, E-mail: cns@carleton.ca. *Application contact:* P.R. Sundararajan, Associate Chair, Graduate Studies, 613-520-2600 Ext. 3605, Fax: 613-520-3749, E-mail: cns@carleton.ca.

Carnegie Mellon University, Mellon College of Science, Department of Chemistry, Pittsburgh, PA 15213-3891. Offers chemical instrumentation (MS); chemistry (MS, PhD); colloids, polymers and surfaces (MS); polymer science (MS). Part-time programs available. Terminal master's awarded for partial completion of doctoral program. *Degree requirements:* For doctorate, thesis/dissertation, departmental qualifying and oral exams, teaching experience. *Entrance requirements:* For master's, GRE General Test; for doctorate, GRE General Test, GRE Subject Test. Additional exam requirements/recommendations for international students: Required—TOEFL. Electronic applications accepted. *Expenses:* Tuition: Full-time $28,200; part-time $392 per unit. Required fees: $220. *Faculty research:* Physical and theoretical chemistry, chemical synthesis, biophysical/bioinorganic chemistry.

See in-depth description on page 101.

Case Western Reserve University, School of Graduate Studies, Department of Chemistry, Cleveland, OH 44106. Offers analytical chemistry (MS, PhD); inorganic chemistry (MS, PhD); organic chemistry (MS, PhD); physical chemistry (MS, PhD). Part-time programs available. *Faculty:* 22 full-time (2 women). *Students:* 64 full-time (18 women), 27 part-time (9 women); includes 2 minority (both Asian Americans or Pacific Islanders), 69 international. Average age 27. 483 applicants, 9% accepted, 18 enrolled. In 2003, 5 master's, 13 doctorates awarded. Terminal master's awarded for partial completion of doctoral program. *Degree requirements:* For doctorate, thesis/dissertation. *Entrance requirements:* For master's and doctorate, GRE General Test, GRE Subject Test. Additional exam requirements/recommendations for international students: Required—TOEFL. *Application deadline:* Applications are processed on a rolling basis. Application fee: $50. *Expenses:* Tuition: Full-time $26,900. *Financial support:* In 2003–04, 77 students received support, including 53 research assistantships, 20 teaching assistantships. *Faculty research:* Electrochemistry, synthetic chemistry, chemistry of life process, spectroscopy, kinetics. *Unit head:* Lawrence Sayre, Chairman, 216-368-3622, Fax: 216-368-3006, E-mail: lms3@case.edu. *Application contact:* Zedeara Diaz, Graduate Admissions, 216-368-3621, Fax: 216-368-3006, E-mail: zcd@case.edu.

The Catholic University of America, School of Arts and Sciences, Department of Chemistry, Washington, DC 20064. Offers MS. Part-time programs available. *Faculty:* 6 full-time (3 women), 1 part-time/adjunct (0 women). *Students:* Average age 29. 3 applicants, 33% accepted, 1 enrolled. *Degree requirements:* For master's, one foreign language, thesis or alternative, comprehensive exam. *Entrance requirements:* For master's, GRE General Test, GRE Subject Test, 3 letters of recommendation. Additional exam requirements/recommendations for international students: Required—TOEFL (minimum score 580 paper-based; 237 computer-based). *Application deadline:* For fall admission, 2/1 for domestic students; for spring admission, 11/15 priority date for domestic students. Applications are processed on a rolling basis. Application fee: $55. Electronic applications accepted. *Expenses:* Tuition: Full-time $23,600; part-time $895 per credit hour. Required fees: $1,040; $270 per term. One-time fee: $175 part-time. Part-time tuition and fees vary according to campus/location and program. *Financial support:* Fellowships, research assistantships, teaching assistantships, career-related internships or fieldwork, Federal Work-Study, institutionally sponsored loans, scholarships/grants, and tuition waivers (full and partial) available. Support available to part-time students. Financial award application deadline: 2/1; financial award applicants required to submit FAFSA. *Faculty research:* Theoretical chemistry; bioinorganic chemistry; chemical kinetics; synthetic organic chemistry; inorganic, bio-organic, and physical organic chemistry. *Unit head:* Dr. Greg Brewer, Chair, 202-319-5385, Fax: 202-319-5381, E-mail: brewer@cua.edu.

Central Connecticut State University, School of Graduate Studies, School of Arts and Sciences, Department of Chemistry, New Britain, CT 06050-4010. Offers natural science chemistry (MS). Part-time and evening/weekend programs available. *Faculty:* 9 full-time (1 woman), 2 part-time/adjunct (1 woman). *Students:* 1 (woman) full-time, 1 (woman) part-time. Average age 37. 19 applicants, 63% accepted, 10 enrolled. *Degree requirements:* For master's, thesis or alternative, comprehensive exam. *Entrance requirements:* For master's, minimum GPA of 2.7. Additional exam requirements/recommendations for international students: Required—TOEFL. *Application deadline:* For fall admission, 8/10 for domestic students; for spring admission, 12/10 for domestic students. Applications are processed on a rolling basis. Application fee: $50. *Expenses:* Tuition, state resident: full-time $3,298. Tuition, nonresident: full-time $9,190. *Financial support:* Research assistantships, teaching assistantships, Federal Work-Study available. Financial award application deadline: 3/15; financial award applicants required to submit FAFSA. *Unit head:* Dr. Timothy Shine, Coordinator, 860-832-2675.

Central Michigan University, College of Graduate Studies, College of Science and Technology, Department of Chemistry, Mount Pleasant, MI 48859. Offers chemistry (MS); teaching chemistry (MA). *Accreditation:* NCATE (one or more programs are accredited). *Faculty:* 17 full-time (2 women). *Students:* 4 full-time (2 women), 13 part-time (7 women). Average age 28. In 2003, 9 degrees awarded. *Degree requirements:* For master's, thesis or alternative. *Application deadline:* Applications are processed on a rolling basis. Application fee: $35 ($45 for international students). *Expenses:* Tuition, state resident: part-time $200 per credit hour. Tuition, nonresident: part-time $397 per credit hour. *Financial support:* In 2003–04, 7 research assistantships with tuition reimbursements, 6 teaching assistantships with tuition reimbursements were awarded. Fellowships with tuition reimbursements, career-related internships or fieldwork and Federal Work-Study also available. Financial award application deadline: 3/7. *Faculty research:* Biochemistry, analytical and organic-inorganic chemistry, polymer chemistry. *Unit head:* Dr. James Falender, Chairperson, 989-774-3981, Fax: 989-774-3883, E-mail: falen1jr@cmich.edu.

Central Washington University, Graduate Studies, Research and Continuing Education, College of the Sciences, Department of Chemistry, Ellensburg, WA 98926. Offers MS. Part-time programs available. *Faculty:* 8 full-time (4 women). *Students:* 3 full-time (1 woman), 1 international. 1 applicant, 100% accepted, 1 enrolled. In 2003, 1 degree awarded. *Degree requirements:* For master's, thesis. *Entrance requirements:* For master's, GRE General Test, minimum GPA of 3.0. Additional exam requirements/recommendations for international students: Required—TOEFL (minimum score 550 paper-based; 213 computer-based). *Application deadline:* For fall admission, 4/1 for domestic students; for winter admission, 10/1 for domestic students; for spring admission, 1/1 for domestic students. Applications are processed on a rolling basis. Application fee: $35. *Expenses:* Tuition, state resident: part-time $183 per credit. Tuition, nonresident: part-time $381 per credit. Required fees: $369. *Financial support:* In 2003–04, 1 research assistantship with partial tuition reimbursement, 2 teaching assistantships with partial tuition reimbursements (averaging $7,120 per year) were awarded. Career-related internships or fieldwork and Federal Work-Study also available. Financial award application deadline: 3/1; financial award applicants required to submit FAFSA. *Unit head:* Dr. Martha Kurtz, Chair, 509-963-2811, Fax: 509-963-1050. *Application contact:* Barbara Sisko, Office Assistant, Graduate Studies, Research and Continuing Education, 509-963-3103, Fax: 509-963-1799, E-mail: masters@cwu.edu.

City College of the City University of New York, Graduate School, College of Liberal Arts and Science, Division of Science, Department of Chemistry, Program in Chemistry, New York, NY 10031-9198. Offers MA, PhD. *Students:* 14 applicants, 43% accepted, 3 enrolled. In 2003, 2 degrees awarded. Terminal master's awarded for partial completion of doctoral program. *Degree requirements:* For doctorate, one foreign language, thesis/dissertation. *Entrance requirements:* For doctorate, GRE. Additional exam requirements/recommendations for international students: Required—TOEFL. *Application deadline:* For fall admission, 5/1 for domestic students; for spring admission, 11/1 for domestic students. Application fee: $40. *Expenses:* Tuition, state resident: full-time $5,440; part-time $230 per credit. Tuition, nonresident: part-time $425 per credit. Required fees: $63 per semester. *Financial support:* Federal Work-Study available. Financial award application deadline: 6/1. *Faculty research:* Laser spectroscopy, bioorganic chemistry, polymer chemistry and crystallography, electroanalytical chemistry, ESR of metal clusters. *Unit head:* Neil McKelvie, MA Adviser, 212-650-6062.

Clark Atlanta University, School of Arts and Sciences, Department of Chemistry, Atlanta, GA 30314. Offers inorganic chemistry (MS, PhD); organic chemistry (MS, PhD); physical chemistry (MS, PhD); science education (DA). Part-time programs available. *Degree requirements:* For master's, one foreign language, thesis, comprehensive exam; for doctorate, 2 foreign languages, thesis/dissertation, cumulative exam. *Entrance requirements:* For master's, GRE General Test, minimum GPA of 2.5; for doctorate, GRE General Test, GRE Subject Test, minimum graduate GPA of 3.0.

Clarkson University, Graduate School, School of Arts and Sciences, Department of Chemistry, Potsdam, NY 13699. Offers analytical chemistry (MS, PhD); inorganic chemistry (MS, PhD); organic chemistry (MS, PhD); physical chemistry (MS, PhD). *Faculty:* 11 full-time (2 women). *Students:* 31 full-time (12 women); includes 3 minority (2 African Americans, 1 Asian American or Pacific Islander), 14 international. Average age 28. 45 applicants, 67% accepted. In 2003, 4 master's, 1 doctorate awarded. *Median time to degree:* Master's–2.5 years full-time; doctorate–4 years full-time, 6 years part-time. *Degree requirements:* For doctorate, thesis/dissertation, departmental qualifying exam. *Entrance requirements:* For master's, GRE. Additional exam requirements/recommendations for international students: Required—TOEFL. *Application deadline:* For fall admission, 5/15 for domestic students; for spring admission, 10/15 priority date for domestic students. Applications are processed on a rolling basis. Application fee: $25 ($35 for international students). *Expenses:* Tuition: Full-time $19,272; part-time $803 per credit. Tuition and fees vary according to course load. *Financial support:* In 2003–04, 23 students received support, including 2 fellowships (averaging $22,000 per year), 9 research assistantships (averaging $18,000 per year), 12 teaching assistantships (averaging $18,000 per year); scholarships/grants and tuition waivers (partial) also available. *Faculty research:* Particle adhesion phenomena, airborne radon, ceramic materials, materials processing, chemical kinetics. Total annual research expenditures: $1.3 million. *Unit head:* Dr. Phillip A. Christiansen, Division Head, 315-268-6669, Fax: 315-268-6610, E-mail: pac@clarkson.edu. *Application contact:* Donna Brockway, Assistant to Dean/Foreign Student Advisor, 315-268-6447, Fax: 315-268-7994, E-mail: brockway@clarkson.edu.

Clark University, Graduate School, Department of Chemistry, Worcester, MA 01610-1477. Offers MA, PhD. *Faculty:* 10 full-time (2 women), 2 part-time/adjunct (1 woman). *Students:* 17 full-time (6 women), 1 part-time, 14 international. Average age 29. 31 applicants, 39% accepted, 1 enrolled. In 2003, 1 master's, 1 doctorate awarded. Terminal master's awarded for partial completion of doctoral program. *Degree requirements:* For master's, thesis or alternative; for doctorate, one foreign language, thesis/dissertation. *Entrance requirements:* For master's and doctorate, GRE General Test. Additional exam requirements/recommendations for international students: Required—TOEFL. *Application deadline:* For fall admission, 2/15 for domestic students. Applications are processed on a rolling basis. Application fee: $40. *Expenses:* Tuition: Full-time $26,700. *Financial support:* In 2003–04, fellowships with tuition reimbursements (averaging $18,000 per year), 4 research assistantships with full tuition reimbursements (averaging $18,000 per year), 12 teaching assistantships with full tuition reimbursements (averaging $18,000 per year) were awarded. Tuition waivers (full) also available. *Faculty research:* Nuclear chemistry, molecular biology. Total annual research expenditures: $463,300. *Unit head:* Dr. Mark Turnbull, Chair, 508-793-7116. *Application contact:* Evike Boudreau, Department Secretary, 508-793-7116, Fax: 508-793-8861, E-mail: chemistry@clarku.edu.

Clemson University, Graduate School, College of Engineering and Science, Department of Chemistry, Clemson, SC 29634. Offers MS, PhD. *Students:* 101 full-time (33 women), 3 part-time (1 woman); includes 8 minority (4 African Americans, 1 American Indian/Alaska Native, 2 Asian Americans or Pacific Islanders, 1 Hispanic American), 39 international. Average age 25. 87 applicants, 60% accepted, 26 enrolled. In 2003, 4 master's, 14 doctorates awarded. *Degree requirements:* For master's and doctorate, one foreign language, thesis/dissertation. *Entrance requirements:* For master's and doctorate, GRE General Test. Additional exam requirements/recommendations for international students: Required—TOEFL. *Application deadline:* For fall admission, 6/1 for domestic students. Application fee: $40. *Expenses:* Tuition, state resident: full-time $7,432. Tuition, nonresident: full-time $14,732. *Financial support:* Fellowships, research assistantships, teaching assistantships, unspecified assistantships available. Financial award applicants required to submit FAFSA. *Faculty research:* Fluorine chemistry, organic synthetic methods and natural products, metal and non-metal clusters, analytical spectroscopies, polymers. Total annual research expenditures: $1 million. *Unit head:* Dr. Luis Echegoyen, Chair, 864-656-5017, Fax: 864-656-6613, E-mail: luis@clemson.edu. *Application contact:* Dr. Stephen Creager, Graduate Coordinator, 864-656-4995, Fax: 864-656-6613, E-mail: screage@clemson.edu.

Cleveland State University, College of Graduate Studies, College of Arts and Sciences, Department of Chemistry, Cleveland, OH 44115. Offers analytical chemistry (MS, PhD); clinical chemistry (MS, PhD); clinical/bioanalytical (PhD); inorganic chemistry (MS); organic chemistry (MS); physical chemistry (MS); structural analysis (MS, PhD). Part-time and evening/weekend programs available. *Faculty:* 16 full-time (1 woman), 3 part-time/adjunct (1 woman). *Students:* 44 full-time (21 women), 23 part-time (9 women); includes 3 minority (1 African American, 1 Asian American or Pacific Islander, 1 Hispanic American), 29 international. Average age 33. 30 applicants, 23% accepted, 2 enrolled. In 2003, 6 master's, 1 doctorate awarded. *Degree requirements:* For master's, thesis (for some programs); for doctorate, thesis/dissertation. *Entrance requirements:* For master's and doctorate, GRE General Test, GRE Subject Test. Additional exam requirements/recommendations for international students: Required—TOEFL (minimum score 525 paper-based; 197 computer-based). *Application deadline:* For fall admission, 1/15 priority date for domestic students, 1/15 priority date for international students. Applications are processed on a rolling basis. Application fee: $30. Electronic applications accepted. Tuition, area resident: Full-time $8,258; part-time $344 per credit hour. Tuition, nonresident: full-time $16,352; part-time $681 per credit hour. *Financial support:* In 2003–04, 37 students received support, including fellowships (averaging $16,000 per year), 19 research assistantships with full tuition reimbursements available (averaging $16,000 per year), 18 teaching assistantships with full tuition reimbursements available (averaging $15,000 per year) Financial award application deadline: 1/15. *Faculty research:* Trace metal analysis in biological systems, application of HPLC/LPCC to clinical systems, synthetic organic and inorganic chemistry, molecular structure determinations, structure-function relationships of factor Va, MALDI-TOF based DNA sequencing, spectroscopic studies of chemical and biochemical phenomena, novel electro-optic tunable filters (AOTFs) to explore biological systems. Total annual research expenditures: $1 million. *Unit head:* Dr. Stan Duraj, Chair, 216-687-2454, Fax: 216-687-9298, E-mail: s.duraj@csuohio.edu. *Application contact:* Richelle P. Emery, Administrative Coordinator, 216-687-2457, Fax: 216-687-9298, E-mail: r.emery@csuohio.edu.

College of Staten Island of the City University of New York, Graduate Programs, Program in Polymer Chemistry, Staten Island, NY 10314-6600. Offers PhD. *Degree requirements:* For doctorate, one foreign language, thesis/dissertation. *Entrance requirements:* For doctorate, GRE. *Application deadline:* For fall admission, 12/1 for domestic students. Applications are processed on a rolling basis. Application fee: $50. *Expenses:* Tuition, state resident: full-time $5,440; part-time $230 per credit. Tuition, nonresident: full-time $10,200; part-time $425 per credit. Required fees: $154 per semester. Tuition and fees vary according to course load. *Financial support:* In 2003–04, fellowships with partial tuition reimbursements (averaging $15,000 per year), research assistantships with partial tuition reimbursements (averaging $15,000 per year), teaching assistantships with partial tuition reimbursements (averaging $15,000 per year) were awarded. Tuition waivers (partial) also available. Total annual research expenditures: $721,240. *Unit head:* Dr. Nan–Loh Yang, Coordinator, 718-982-3920, Fax: 718-982-3910, E-mail: yang@postbox.csi.cuny.edu.

The College of William and Mary, Faculty of Arts and Sciences, Department of Chemistry, Williamsburg, VA 23187-8795. Offers MA, MS. *Faculty:* 16 full-time (3 women), 2 part-time/adjunct (1 woman). *Students:* 4 full-time (1 woman), 1 part-time, 4 international. Average age 24. 15 applicants, 40% accepted, 4 enrolled. In 2003, 4 degrees awarded. *Degree requirements:* For master's, thesis (for some programs), comprehensive exam. *Entrance requirements:* For master's, GRE General Test, minimum GPA of 2.5. *Application deadline:* For fall admission, 1/15 for domestic students. Applications are processed on a rolling basis. Application fee: $30. *Expenses:* Tuition, state resident: full-time $4,858; part-time $222 per credit hour. Tuition, nonresident: full-time $16,440; part-time $618 per credit hour. Required fees: $2,674. Tuition and fees vary according to program. *Financial support:* In 2003–04, 1 research assistantship with full tuition reimbursement (averaging $12,700 per year), 3 teaching assistantships with full tuition reimbursements (averaging $12,700 per year) were awarded. Financial award application deadline: 5/1; financial award applicants required to submit FAFSA. *Faculty research:* Organic, inorganic, physical, polymer and analytic chemistry; biochemistry. Total annual research expenditures: $586,520. *Unit head:* Dr. Gary Rice, Chair, 757-221-2540, Fax: 757-221-2715. *Application contact:* Dr. Christopher J. Abelt, Graduate Director, 757-221-2551, Fax: 757-221-2715, E-mail: cjabel@wm.edu.

Colorado School of Mines, Graduate School, Department of Chemistry and Geochemistry, Program in Chemistry, Golden, CO 80401-1887. Offers applied chemistry (PhD); chemistry (MS). Part-time programs available. *Students:* 1 full-time (0 women). *Degree requirements:* For master's, thesis/dissertation; for doctorate, thesis/dissertation, comprehensive exam. *Entrance requirements:* For master's and doctorate, GRE General Test. Additional exam requirements/recommendations for international students: Required—TOEFL (minimum score 550 paper-based; 213 computer-based). *Application deadline:* For fall admission, 12/1 priority date for domestic students, 12/1 priority date for international students; for spring admission, 5/1 priority date for domestic students, 5/1 priority date for international students. Application fee: $45. *Expenses:* Tuition, state resident: full-time $5,700; part-time $285 per credit hour. Tuition, nonresident: full-time $19,040; part-time $952 per credit hour. Required fees: $733. *Financial support:* In 2003–04, fellowships with full tuition reimbursements (averaging $12,500 per year), research assistantships with full tuition reimbursements (averaging $10,000 per year), 2 teaching assistantships with full tuition reimbursements (averaging $10,000 per year) were awarded. Scholarships/grants and unspecified assistantships also available. Financial award applicants required to submit FAFSA. *Application contact:* G. Mike Reimer, Professor, 303-273-3505, Fax: 303-273-3629, E-mail: mreimer@mines.edu.

Colorado State University, Graduate School, College of Natural Sciences, Department of Chemistry, Fort Collins, CO 80523-0015. Offers MS, PhD. Part-time programs available. *Faculty:* 27 full-time (4 women). *Students:* Average age 27. 506 applicants, 16% accepted, 26 enrolled. In 2003, 5 master's, 12 doctorates awarded. Terminal master's awarded for partial completion of doctoral program. *Median time to degree:* Master's–3 years part-time; doctorate–7 years part-time. Of those who began their doctoral program in fall 1995, 100% received their degree in 8 years or less. *Degree requirements:* For master's and doctorate, thesis/dissertation. *Entrance requirements:* For master's and doctorate, GRE General Test, minimum GPA of 3.0. Additional exam requirements/recommendations for international students: Required—TOEFL. *Application deadline:* For fall admission, 3/1 for domestic students; for spring admission, 8/15 for domestic students. Applications are processed on a rolling basis. Application fee: $50. Electronic applications accepted. *Expenses:* Tuition, state resident: full-time $4,156. Tuition, nonresident: full-time $14,762. Required fees: $205. Tuition and fees vary according to course load, campus/location, program and reciprocity agreements. *Financial support:* In 2003–04, fellowships with full tuition reimbursements (averaging $7,222 per year), research assistantships with full tuition reimbursements (averaging $18,000 per year), teaching assistantships with full tuition reimbursements (averaging $18,000 per year) were awarded. Unspecified assistantships also available. *Faculty research:* Analytical chemistry, inorganic chemistry, organic chemistry, physical chemistry, materials and biological chemistry. Total annual research expenditures: $6.7 million. *Unit head:* Anthony K. Rappé, Chairman, 970-491-6292, Fax: 970-491-1801, E-mail: rappe@lamar.colostate.edu. *Application contact:* Dr. Bruce Parkinson, Chairman, Graduate Admissions Committee, 970-491-0504, Fax: 970-491-1801, E-mail: chemgrad@lamar.colostate.edu.

Columbia University, Graduate School of Arts and Sciences, Division of Natural Sciences, Department of Chemistry, New York, NY 10027. Offers chemical physics (M Phil, PhD); inorganic chemistry (M Phil, MS, PhD); organic chemistry (M Phil, MS, PhD). *Faculty:* 17 full-time. *Students:* 115 full-time (35 women). Average age 27. 452 applicants, 20% accepted. In 2003, 13 master's, 20 doctorates awarded. *Degree requirements:* For master's, comp exams (MS); foreign language, teaching experience, oral/written exams (M Phil); for doctorate, one foreign language, thesis/dissertation. *Entrance requirements:* For master's and doctorate, GRE General Test, GRE Subject Test. Additional exam requirements/recommendations for international students: Required—TOEFL. Application fee: $75. *Expenses:* Tuition: Full-time $14,820. *Financial support:* Fellowships, teaching assistantships, Federal Work-Study and institutionally sponsored loans available. Support available to part-time students. Financial award application deadline: 1/5; financial award applicants required to submit FAFSA. *Faculty research:* Biophysics. *Unit head:* Bruce Berne, Chair, 212-854-2186, Fax: 212-932-1289.

Concordia University, School of Graduate Studies, Faculty of Arts and Science, Department of Chemistry and Biochemistry, Montréal, QC H3G 1M8, Canada. Offers chemistry (M Sc, PhD). *Students:* 62 full-time, 6 part-time. In 2003, 14 master's, 3 doctorates awarded. *Degree requirements:* For master's and doctorate, thesis/dissertation. *Entrance requirements:* For master's, honors degree in chemistry; for doctorate, M Sc in biochemistry, biology, or chemistry. *Application deadline:* For fall admission, 6/1 for domestic students; for winter admission, 10/1 for domestic students; for spring admission, 4/1 for domestic students. Application fee: $50. *Expenses:* Tuition, state resident: full-time $2,140. Tuition, nonresident: full-time $4,190. International tuition: $8,449 full-time. Tuition and fees vary according to course load, degree level and program. *Financial support:* Teaching assistantships available. *Faculty research:* Bioanalytical, bio-organic, and inorganic chemistry; materials and solid-state chemistry. *Unit head:* Dr. Marcus Lawrence, Chair, 514-848-2424 Ext. 3355, Fax: 514-848-2868. *Application contact:* Dr. Cameron Skinner, Director, 514-848-2424 Ext. 3341, Fax: 514-848-2868.

Converse College, Department of Education, Spartanburg, SC 29302-0006. Offers early childhood education (MAT); education (MAT, Ed S), including administration and supervision (Ed S), curriculum and instruction (Ed S), marriage and family therapy (Ed S); elementary education (M Ed, MAT); gifted education (M Ed); leadership (M Ed); liberal arts (MLA), including English (M Ed, MLA), history, political science; secondary education (M Ed, MAT), including biology (MAT), chemistry (MAT), English (M Ed, MLA), English (MAT), mathematics, natural sciences (M Ed), social sciences (M Ed), social studies (MAT); special education (M Ed, MAT), including educable mental disabilities (MAT), learning disabilities (MAT), special education (M Ed). Part-time and evening/weekend programs available. *Faculty:* 57 full-time (30 women), 4 part-time/adjunct (3 women). *Students:* 77 full-time (52 women), 868 part-time (704 women). Average age 35. In 2003, 215 master's, 25 other advanced degrees awarded.

Chemistry

Converse College (continued)

Entrance requirements: For master's, PRAXIS II, minimum GPA of 2.75; for Ed S, GRE or MAT, minimum GPA of 3.0. *Application deadline:* Applications are processed on a rolling basis. Application fee: $35. Electronic applications accepted. *Expenses:* Tuition: Part-time $260 per credit hour. *Financial support:* In 2003–04, 500 students received support; research assistantships, career-related internships or fieldwork and scholarships/grants available. Support available to part-time students. Financial award applicants required to submit FAFSA. *Faculty research:* Motivation, classroom management, predictors of success in classroom teaching, sex equity in public education, gifted research. Total annual research expenditures: $50,000. *Unit head:* Dr. Thomas R. McDaniel, Acting Dean, 864-596-9082, Fax: 864-596-9221, E-mail: thomas.mcdaniel@converse.edu.

Cornell University, Graduate School, Graduate Fields of Arts and Sciences, Field of Chemistry and Chemical Biology, Ithaca, NY 14853-0001. Offers analytical chemistry (PhD); bio-organic chemistry (PhD); biophysical chemistry (PhD); chemical biology (PhD); chemical physics (PhD); inorganic chemistry (PhD); materials chemistry (PhD); organic chemistry (PhD); organometallic chemistry (PhD); physical chemistry (PhD); polymer chemistry (PhD); theoretical chemistry (PhD). *Faculty:* 37 full-time. *Students:* 174 full-time (70 women); includes 22 minority (4 African Americans, 10 Asian Americans or Pacific Islanders, 8 Hispanic Americans), 57 international. 371 applicants, 35% accepted, 42 enrolled. In 2003, 22 doctorates awarded. *Degree requirements:* For doctorate, thesis/dissertation, comprehensive exam. *Entrance requirements:* For doctorate, GRE General Test, GRE Subject Test (chemistry), 3 letters of recommendation. Additional exam requirements/recommendations for international students: Required—TOEFL (minimum score 600 paper-based; 250 computer-based). *Application deadline:* For fall admission, 1/10 for domestic students. Application fee: $60. Electronic applications accepted. *Expenses:* Tuition: Full-time $28,630. One-time fee: $50 full-time. *Financial support:* In 2003–04, 162 students received support, including 28 fellowships with full tuition reimbursements available, 77 research assistantships with full tuition reimbursements available, 57 teaching assistantships with full tuition reimbursements available; institutionally sponsored loans, scholarships/grants, health care benefits, tuition waivers (full and partial), and unspecified assistantships also available. Financial award applicants required to submit FAFSA. *Faculty research:* Analytical, organic, inorganic, physical, materials, chemical biology. *Unit head:* Director of Graduate Studies, 607-255-4139, Fax: 607-255-4137. *Application contact:* Graduate Field Assistant, 607-255-4139, Fax: 607-255-4137, E-mail: chemgrad@cornell.edu.

See in-depth description on page 105.

Dalhousie University, Faculty of Graduate Studies, College of Arts and Science, Faculty of Science, Department of Chemistry, Halifax, NS B3H 4R2, Canada. Offers M Sc, PhD. Part-time programs available. *Faculty:* 26 full-time (3 women), 10 part-time/adjunct (2 women). *Students:* 74 full-time (27 women); includes 28 minority (6 African Americans, 8 Asian Americans or Pacific Islanders, 14 Hispanic Americans), 3 international. Average age 25. 150 applicants, 21% accepted, 19 enrolled. In 2003, 6 master's, 4 doctorates awarded. Terminal master's awarded for partial completion of doctoral program. *Median time to degree:* Master's–2 years full-time; doctorate–4 years full-time. Of those who began their doctoral program in fall 1995, 100% received their degree in 8 years or less. *Degree requirements:* For master's and doctorate, thesis/dissertation. *Entrance requirements:* For master's and doctorate, GRE Subject Test (non-U.S. or Canadian). Additional exam requirements/recommendations for international students: Required—TOEFL (minimum score 580 paper-based; 237 computer-based). *Application deadline:* For fall admission, 6/1 priority date for domestic students, 4/1 priority date for international students; for winter admission, 11/15 for domestic students; for spring admission, 2/28 for domestic students. Applications are processed on a rolling basis. Application fee: $70. *Financial support:* In 2003–04, fellowships with full tuition reimbursements (averaging $10,980 per year), teaching assistantships (averaging $2,850 per year) were awarded. Scholarships/grants also available. Financial award application deadline: 4/15. *Faculty research:* Analytical, inorganic, organic, physical, and theoretical chemistry. Total annual research expenditures: $2.5 million. *Unit head:* Dr. R. J. Boyd, Chair, 902-494-3707, Fax: 902-494-1310, E-mail: russell.boyd@dal.ca. *Application contact:* Dr. D. J. Burnell, Graduate Coordinator, 902-494-3306, Fax: 902-494-1310, E-mail: jean.burnell@dal.ca.

Dartmouth College, School of Arts and Sciences, Department of Chemistry, Hanover, NH 03755. Offers PhD. *Faculty:* 12 full-time (3 women). *Students:* 43 full-time (18 women); includes 4 minority (1 American Indian/Alaska Native, 2 Asian Americans or Pacific Islanders, 1 Hispanic American), 19 international. Average age 26. 240 applicants, 14% accepted, 15 enrolled. In 2003, 6 degrees awarded. *Degree requirements:* For doctorate, thesis/dissertation, departmental qualifying exams. *Entrance requirements:* For doctorate, GRE General Test, GRE Subject Test. Additional exam requirements/recommendations for international students: Required—TOEFL. *Application deadline:* For fall admission, 1/15 for domestic students. Application fee: $25. Electronic applications accepted. *Expenses:* Tuition: Full-time $28,965. *Financial support:* In 2003–04, 43 students received support, including fellowships with full tuition reimbursements available (averaging $18,528 per year), research assistantships with full tuition reimbursements available (averaging $18,528 per year); Federal Work-Study, institutionally sponsored loans, scholarships/grants, traineeships, tuition waivers (full), and unspecified assistantships also available. *Faculty research:* Organic and polymer synthesis, bioinorganic chemistry, magnetic resonance parameters. Total annual research expenditures: $1.6 million. *Unit head:* Dr. Joseph J. BelBruno, Chair, 603-646-2501. *Application contact:* Deborah Carr, Administrative Assistant, 603-646-2501, Fax: 603-646-3946, E-mail: deborah.a.carr@dartmouth.edu.

Delaware State University, Graduate Programs, Department of Chemistry, Dover, DE 19901-2277. Offers applied chemistry (MS); chemistry (MS). Part-time and evening/weekend programs available. *Entrance requirements:* For master's, GRE, minimum GPA of 3.0 in major, 2.75 overall. Electronic applications accepted. *Faculty research:* Chemiluminescence, environmental chemistry, forensic chemistry, heteropoly anions anti-cancer and antiviral agents, low temperature infrared studies of lithium salts.

DePaul University, College of Liberal Arts and Sciences, Department of Chemistry, Chicago, IL 60604-2287. Offers biochemistry (MS); chemistry (MS); polymer chemistry and coatings technology (MS). Part-time and evening/weekend programs available. *Faculty:* 11 full-time (4 women), 4 part-time/adjunct (1 woman). *Students:* 7 full-time (2 women), 13 part-time (4 women); includes 4 minority (1 African American, 1 Asian American or Pacific Islander, 2 Hispanic Americans), 1 international. Average age 27. 6 applicants, 100% accepted, 4 enrolled. In 2003, 2 degrees awarded, leading to business/industry 100%. *Degree requirements:* For master's, thesis (for some programs), oral exam for selected programs. *Entrance requirements:* For master's, BS in chemistry or equivalent. Additional exam requirements/recommendations for international students: Required—TOEFL (minimum score 590 paper-based; 243 computer-based). *Application deadline:* For fall admission, 7/15 for domestic students, 5/1 for international students; for winter admission, 11/15 for domestic students; for spring admission, 2/15 for domestic students. Applications are processed on a rolling basis. Application fee: $35. Electronic applications accepted. *Expenses:* Tuition: Part-time $395 per hour. *Financial support:* In 2003–04, 4 students received support, including 6 teaching assistantships with tuition reimbursements available (averaging $8,000 per year) Financial award application deadline: 4/1. *Faculty research:* Polymers, DNA sequencing, computational chemistry, water pollution, diffusion kinetics. Total annual research expenditures: $30,000. *Unit head:* Dr. Wendy S. Wolbach, Chair, 773-325-7420, Fax: 773-325-7421, E-mail: wwolbach@condor.depaul.edu. *Application contact:* Marion Blackmon, Director of Graduate Admissions, 773-325-7885, Fax: 773-325-7311, E-mail: mblackmo@depaul.edu.

Drexel University, College of Arts and Sciences, Department of Chemistry, Philadelphia, PA 19104-2875. Offers MS, PhD. Part-time programs available. Terminal master's awarded for partial completion of doctoral program. *Degree requirements:* For master's, thesis optional; for doctorate, one foreign language, thesis/dissertation. *Entrance requirements:* For master's and doctorate, GRE. Additional exam requirements/recommendations for international students: Required—TOEFL, TSE (financial award applicants for teaching assistantships). Electronic applications accepted. *Faculty research:* Inorganic, analytical, organic, physical, and atmospheric polymer chemistry.

Duke University, Graduate School, Department of Chemistry, Durham, NC 27708. Offers PhD. *Faculty:* 20 full-time. *Students:* 101 full-time (42 women); includes 5 minority (1 African American, 1 American Indian/Alaska Native, 3 Asian Americans or Pacific Islanders), 51 international. 289 applicants, 21% accepted, 16 enrolled. In 2003, 12 doctorates awarded. *Degree requirements:* For doctorate, one foreign language, thesis/dissertation. *Entrance requirements:* For doctorate, GRE General Test, GRE Subject Test (recommended). Additional exam requirements/recommendations for international students: Required—IELT (preferred) or TOEFL. *Application deadline:* For fall admission, 12/31 for domestic students. Application fee: $75. *Expenses:* Tuition: Full-time $23,280; part-time $835 per unit. *Financial support:* Fellowships, research assistantships, teaching assistantships available. Financial award application deadline: 12/31. *Unit head:* Richard MacPhail, Director of Graduate Studies, 919-660-1546, Fax: 919-660-1607, E-mail: dgs@chem.duke.edu.

Duquesne University, Bayer School of Natural and Environmental Sciences, Department of Chemistry and Biochemistry, Pittsburgh, PA 15282-0001. Offers biochemistry (MS, PhD); chemistry (MS, PhD). Part-time and evening/weekend programs available. *Faculty:* 16 full-time (2 women), 2 part-time/adjunct (both women). *Students:* 39 full-time (23 women), 6 part-time (1 woman), 22 international. Average age 27. 28 applicants, 46% accepted, 8 enrolled. In 2003, 4 master's, 5 doctorates awarded, leading to university research/teaching 80%. Terminal master's awarded for partial completion of doctoral program. *Median time to degree:* Master's–3.7 years full-time; doctorate–5 years full-time. Of those who began their doctoral program in fall 1995, 75% received their degree in 8 years or less. *Degree requirements:* For master's, thesis (for some programs), registration; for doctorate, thesis/dissertation, registration. *Entrance requirements:* For master's and doctorate, GRE General Test. Additional exam requirements/recommendations for international students: Required—TOEFL, TSE. *Application deadline:* For fall admission, 2/15 for domestic students; for spring admission, 10/1 priority date for domestic students. Applications are processed on a rolling basis. Application fee: $40. *Expenses:* Contact institution. Tuition and fees vary according to degree level and program. *Financial support:* In 2003–04, 1 fellowship with full and partial tuition reimbursement (averaging $20,000 per year), 10 research assistantships with full tuition reimbursements (averaging $17,600 per year), 26 teaching assistantships with full tuition reimbursements (averaging $17,600 per year) were awarded. Institutionally sponsored loans, scholarships/grants, tuition waivers (partial), and unspecified assistantships also available. Financial award application deadline: 5/1; financial award applicants required to submit FAFSA. *Faculty research:* Computational physical chemistry, bioinorganic chemistry, analytical chemistry, biophysics, synthetic organic chemistry. Total annual research expenditures: $616,534. *Unit head:* Dr. Jeffry Madura, Chair, 412-396-6341, Fax: 412-396-5683, E-mail: madura@duq.edu. *Application contact:* Mary Ann Quinn, Assistant to the Dean Graduate Affairs, 412-396-6339, Fax: 412-396-4881, E-mail: gradinfo@duq.edu.

See in-depth description on page 109.

East Carolina University, Graduate School, Thomas Harriot College of Arts and Sciences, Department of Chemistry, Greenville, NC 27858-4353. Offers MS. Part-time programs available. *Faculty:* 14 full-time (1 woman). *Students:* 9 full-time (3 women), 5 part-time (2 women); includes 5 minority (3 African Americans, 1 Asian American or Pacific Islander, 1 Hispanic American), 3 international. Average age 26. 7 applicants, 57% accepted. In 2003, 5 degrees awarded. *Degree requirements:* For master's, one foreign language, thesis, comprehensive exam. *Entrance requirements:* For master's, GRE General Test. Additional exam requirements/recommendations for international students: Required—TOEFL. *Application deadline:* For fall admission, 6/1 for domestic students; for spring admission, 10/15 for domestic students. Applications are processed on a rolling basis. Application fee: $50. *Expenses:* Tuition, state resident: full-time $1,991; part-time $249 per hour. Tuition, nonresident: full-time $12,232; part-time $1,529 per hour. Required fees: $1,221; $153 per hour. *Financial support:* Teaching assistantships, Federal Work-Study available. Financial award application deadline: 6/1. *Faculty research:* Organometallic, natural-product syntheses; chemometrics; electroanalytical method development; microcomputer adaptations for handicapped students. *Unit head:* Dr. Art Rodriguez, Director of Graduate Studies, 252-328-6228, Fax: 252-328-6210, E-mail: rodrigueza@mail.ecu.edu. *Application contact:* Dr. Paul D. Tschetter, Interim Dean of Graduate School, 252-328-6012, Fax: 252-328-6071, E-mail: gradschool@mail.ecu.edu.

Eastern Illinois University, Graduate School, College of Sciences, Department of Chemistry, Charleston, IL 61920-3099. Offers MS. *Faculty:* 13 full-time (2 women). In 2003, 6 degrees awarded. *Degree requirements:* For master's, thesis. *Entrance requirements:* For master's, GRE General Test. *Application deadline:* For fall admission, 7/31 for domestic students. Applications are processed on a rolling basis. Application fee: $30. *Expenses:* Tuition, state resident: part-time $125 per semester hour. Tuition, nonresident: part-time $375 per semester hour. Required fees: $53 per semester hour. $698 per semester. *Financial support:* In 2003–04, 8 research assistantships with tuition reimbursements (averaging $6,300 per year), teaching assistantships with tuition reimbursements (averaging $6,300 per year) were awarded. *Unit head:* Dr. Doug Klarup, Chairperson, 217-581-6227, E-mail: cfdgk@eiu.edu.

Eastern Kentucky University, The Graduate School, College of Arts and Sciences, Department of Chemistry, Richmond, KY 40475-3102. Offers MS. Part-time and evening/weekend programs available. *Faculty:* 13 full-time (5 women). *Students:* 6 full-time (4 women), 1 (woman) part-time; includes 1 minority (Asian American or Pacific Islander), 2 international. 14 applicants, 64% accepted, 6 enrolled. In 2003, 3 degrees awarded. *Entrance requirements:* For master's, GRE General Test, minimum GPA of 2.5. Application fee: $0. *Expenses:* Tuition, state resident: full-time $3,550; part-time $197 per credit. Tuition, nonresident: full-time $9,752; part-time $542 per credit. *Financial support:* Research assistantships, teaching assistantships, Federal Work-Study available. Support available to part-time students. *Faculty research:* Organic synthesis, surface chemistry, inorganic chemistry, analytical chemistry. Total annual research expenditures: $370,328. *Unit head:* Dr. Alan Schick, Chair, 859-622-1456, Fax: 859-622-8197.

Eastern Michigan University, Graduate School, College of Arts and Sciences, Department of Chemistry, Ypsilanti, MI 48197. Offers MS, MS/PhD. Evening/weekend programs available. *Faculty:* 18 full-time. *Students:* 4 full-time (3 women), 25 part-time (12 women); includes 2 minority (both American Indian/Alaska Native), 11 international. Average age 24. *Degree requirements:* For master's, thesis. *Entrance requirements:* For master's, GRE General Test. Additional exam requirements/recommendations for international students: Required—TOEFL. *Application deadline:* For fall admission, 5/15 for domestic students. Applications are processed on a rolling basis. Application fee: $30. *Expenses:* Tuition, state resident: full-time $4,324. Tuition, nonresident: full-time $8,769. Required fees: $496. Tuition and fees vary according to course level. *Financial support:* In 2003–04, research assistantships with full tuition reimbursements (averaging $8,950 per year), teaching assistantships with full tuition reimbursements (averaging $8,950 per year) were awarded. Fellowships, career-related internships or fieldwork, Federal Work-Study, and institutionally sponsored loans also available. Support available to part-time students. Financial award application deadline: 3/15; financial award applicants required to submit FAFSA. *Unit head:* Dr. Wade Tornquist, Head, 734-487-0106. *Application contact:* Dr. Krish Rengan, Coordinator, 734-487-0106.

Announcement: The Department of Chemistry offers comprehensive programs leading to a professional MS degree. Specializations include analytical, biochemical, inorganic, organic, physical, polymer, radiochemical, and toxicological areas. The professional degree program prepares students for work as industrial chemists and for doctoral study; a high percentage of MS graduates join PhD programs at top universities. Among the major items of equipment available are research-quality Fourier Transform IR; NMR spectrometer; a GC-MS and an LC-MS; gas chromatographs; ultracentrifuges; DNA sequencer; PCR thermal cyclers; automated peptide synthesizer; and lyophilizer. The new library provides a vast array of state-of-the-art facilities and technologies. An active weekly seminar program featuring a number of outside speakers also contributes to a better awareness of recent research developments.

Eastern New Mexico University, Graduate School, College of Liberal Arts and Sciences, Department of Physical Sciences, Portales, NM 88130. Offers chemistry (MS). Part-time programs available. *Faculty:* 4 full-time (0 women). *Students:* 2 full-time (both women), 11 part-time (4 women), 12 international. Average age 26. 5 applicants, 40% accepted. In 2003, 1 degree awarded. *Degree requirements:* For master's, field exam, thesis optional. *Entrance requirements:* For master's, minimum GPA of 2.5. *Application deadline:* For fall admission, 8/20 for domestic students. Applications are processed on a rolling basis. Application fee: $10. Electronic applications accepted. *Expenses:* Tuition, state resident: full-time $2,064; part-time $86 per credit hour. Tuition, nonresident: full-time $7,620; part-time $318 per credit hour. Required fees: $29 per credit hour. *Financial support:* In 2003–04, 1 research assistantship (averaging $7,700 per year), 12 teaching assistantships (averaging $7,700 per year) were awarded. Fellowships, career-related internships or fieldwork and Federal Work-Study also available. Support available to part-time students. Financial award application deadline: 3/1. *Faculty research:* Synfuel, electrochemistry, protein chemistry. *Unit head:* Dr. Newton Hilliard, Graduate Coordinator, 505-562-2463, E-mail: newton.hilliard@enmu.edu.

East Tennessee State University, School of Graduate Studies, College of Arts and Sciences, Department of Chemistry, Johnson City, TN 37614. Offers MS. Part-time and evening/weekend programs available. *Faculty:* 9 full-time (1 woman). *Students:* 13 full-time (6 women), 6 part-time; includes 2 minority (1 African American, 1 Asian American or Pacific Islander), 9 international. Average age 29. 23 applicants, 43% accepted, 6 enrolled. In 2003, 2 degrees awarded. *Degree requirements:* For master's, thesis, comprehensive exam. *Entrance requirements:* For master's, GRE. Additional exam requirements/recommendations for international students: Required—TOEFL (minimum score 550 paper-based; 213 computer-based). *Application deadline:* For fall admission, 7/15 for domestic students; for spring admission, 11/1 for domestic students. Applications are processed on a rolling basis. Application fee: $25 ($35 for international students). *Expenses:* Tuition, state resident: part-time $222 per hour. Tuition, nonresident: part-time $344 per hour. Required fees: $264 per hour. *Financial support:* In 2003–04, 9 teaching assistantships with full tuition reimbursements (averaging $8,000 per year) were awarded; research assistantships with full tuition reimbursements, Federal Work-Study and institutionally sponsored loans also available. Financial award application deadline: 7/1; financial award applicants required to submit FAFSA. *Faculty research:* Development of luminescence techniques for chemical analysis, new functional materials and biosensor technology, synthesis of theoretically significant organic molecules and synthetic metals, synthesis and characterization of mixed valence complexes of transition metals, synthesis and study of phosphatase enzyme models. Total annual research expenditures: $12,500. *Unit head:* Dr. Jeffrey G. Wardeska, Interim Chair, 423-439-4367, Fax: 423-439-5835, E-mail: rd1jeff@etsu.edu.

Emory University, Graduate School of Arts and Sciences, Department of Chemistry, Atlanta, GA 30322-1100. Offers PhD. *Faculty:* 20 full-time (1 woman). *Students:* 160 full-time (71 women); includes 18 minority (6 African Americans, 7 Asian Americans or Pacific Islanders, 5 Hispanic Americans), 92 international. 245 applicants, 37% accepted, 42 enrolled. In 2003, 13 doctorates awarded. *Degree requirements:* For doctorate, thesis/dissertation, comprehensive exam. *Entrance requirements:* For doctorate, GRE General Test. Additional exam requirements/recommendations for international students: Required—TOEFL. *Application deadline:* For fall admission, 1/20 for domestic students. Application fee: $50. Electronic applications accepted. *Expenses:* Tuition: Part-time $1,115 per hour. Required fees: $5 per hour. $125 per term. *Financial support:* In 2003–04, 80 fellowships were awarded; research assistantships, teaching assistantships, Federal Work-Study, institutionally sponsored loans, and scholarships/grants also available. Financial award application deadline: 1/20; financial award applicants required to submit FAFSA. *Faculty research:* Organometallic synthesis and catalysis, synthesis of natural products, x-ray crystallography, mass spectrometry, analytical neurochemistry. Total annual research expenditures: $5.1 million. *Unit head:* Dr. Joel Bowman, Chairman, 404-727-6585. *Application contact:* Dr. Vince Conticello, Director of Graduate Studies, 404-727-2779, Fax: 404-727-6586, E-mail: gradchem@emory.edu.

Emporia State University, School of Graduate Studies, College of Liberal Arts and Sciences, Department of Physical Sciences, Emporia, KS 66801-5087. Offers chemistry (MS); earth science (MS); physical science (MS); physics (MS). *Faculty:* 18 full-time (2 women), 1 (woman) part-time/adjunct. *Students:* 2 full-time (0 women), 21 part-time (6 women); includes 1 minority (African American), 2 international. 1 applicant, 100% accepted, 1 enrolled. In 2003, 3 degrees awarded. *Degree requirements:* For master's, comprehensive exam or thesis. *Entrance requirements:* For master's, written exam, appropriate undergraduate degree. Additional exam requirements/recommendations for international students: Required—TOEFL. *Application deadline:* For fall admission, 8/15 for domestic students. Applications are processed on a rolling basis. Application fee: $30 ($75 for international students). Electronic applications accepted. *Expenses:* Tuition, state resident: full-time $2,640; part-time $110 per credit hour. Tuition, nonresident: full-time $8,454; part-time $352 per credit hour. Required fees: $576; $35 per credit hour. Tuition and fees vary according to campus/location. *Financial support:* In 2003–04, 3 research assistantships (averaging $6,225 per year), 5 teaching assistantships with full tuition reimbursements (averaging $6,225 per year) were awarded. Federal Work-Study, institutionally sponsored loans, health care benefits, and unspecified assistantships also available. Financial award application deadline: 3/15; financial award applicants required to submit FAFSA. *Faculty research:* Bredigite, larnite, and dicalcium silicates–Marble Canyon. *Unit head:* Dr. DeWayne Backhus, Chair, 620-341-5330, Fax: 620-341-6055, E-mail: backhusd@emporia.edu.

Fairleigh Dickinson University, College at Florham, Maxwell Becton College of Arts and Sciences, Department of Chemistry and Geological Sciences, Program in Chemistry, Madison, NJ 07940-1099. Offers MS. *Students:* 22 full-time (8 women), 8 part-time (4 women). Average age 26. 59 applicants, 49% accepted, 15 enrolled. In 2003, 8 degrees awarded. *Application deadline:* Applications are processed on a rolling basis. Application fee: $40. *Expenses:* Tuition: Part-time $700 per credit. *Unit head:* Dr. William Fordham, Chair, Department of Chemistry and Geological Sciences, 973-443-8747, Fax: 973-443-8766, E-mail: fordham@fdu.edu.

Fisk University, Graduate Programs, Department of Chemistry, Nashville, TN 37208-3051. Offers MA. *Degree requirements:* For master's, thesis, comprehensive exam. *Entrance requirements:* For master's, GRE General Test, minimum GPA of 3.0. *Faculty research:* Environmental studies, lithium compound synthesis, HIU compound synthesis.

Florida Agricultural and Mechanical University, Division of Graduate Studies, Research, and Continuing Education, College of Arts and Sciences, Department of Chemistry, Tallahassee, FL 32307-3200. Offers MS. *Faculty:* 15 full-time (1 woman). *Students:* 9 full-time (5 women), 4 part-time (2 women); all minorities (12 African Americans, 1 Asian American or Pacific Islander). In 2003, 9 degrees awarded. *Degree requirements:* For master's, thesis optional. *Entrance requirements:* For master's, GRE General Test, minimum GPA of 3.0. *Application deadline:* For fall admission, 5/18 for domestic students, 12/18 for international students; for spring admission, 11/12 for domestic students, 5/12 for international students. Application fee: $20. *Expenses:* Tuition, state resident: part-time $192 per credit. Tuition, nonresident: part-time $727 per credit. Tuition and fees vary according to course load. *Unit head:* Dr. Maurice Edington, Chairperson, 850-599-3638, Fax: 740-561-2388.

Florida Atlantic University, Charles E. Schmidt College of Science, Department of Chemistry and Biochemistry, Boca Raton, FL 33431-0991. Offers MS, MST, PhD. Part-time programs available. *Faculty:* 13 full-time (2 women). *Students:* 51 full-time (25 women), 9 part-time (4 women); includes 12 minority (2 African Americans, 4 Asian Americans or Pacific Islanders, 6 Hispanic Americans), 20 international. Average age 32. 34 applicants, 44% accepted, 12 enrolled. In 2003, 2 master's, 1 doctorate awarded. Terminal master's awarded for partial completion of doctoral program. *Degree requirements:* For master's, thesis/dissertation; for doctorate, thesis/dissertation, comprehensive exam. *Entrance requirements:* For master's, GRE General Test, minimum GPA of 3.0; for doctorate, GRE, minimum GPA of 3.0. Additional exam requirements/recommendations for international students: Required—TOEFL. *Application deadline:* For fall admission, 7/1 priority date for domestic students, 2/15 priority date for international students; for winter admission, 11/1 for domestic students; for spring admission, 4/1 for domestic students. Applications are processed on a rolling basis. Application fee: $30. *Expenses:* Tuition, state resident: full-time $3,777. Tuition, nonresident: full-time $13,953. *Financial support:* In 2003–04, 2 research assistantships with full tuition reimbursements (averaging $14,000 per year), 24 teaching assistantships with full tuition reimbursements (averaging $14,000 per year) were awarded. Fellowships, Federal Work-Study also available. *Faculty research:* Polymer synthesis and characterization, spectroscopy, geochemistry, environmental chemistry, biomedical chemistry. Total annual research expenditures: $1.2 million. *Unit head:* Dr. Gregg B. Fields, Chair, 561-297-2093, Fax: 561-297-2759, E-mail: fieldsg@fau.edu. *Application contact:* Dr. Salvatore D. Lepore, Professor, 561-297-0330, Fax: 561-297-2759, E-mail: slepore@fau.edu.

Florida Institute of Technology, Graduate Programs, College of Science and Liberal Arts, Department of Chemistry, Melbourne, FL 32901-6975. Offers MS, PhD. Part-time programs available. *Faculty:* 11 full-time (2 women). *Students:* 11 full-time (7 women), 5 part-time (2 women); includes 1 minority (African American), 11 international. Average age 30. 23 applicants, 61% accepted, 3 enrolled. In 2003, 1 master's, 1 doctorate awarded. Terminal master's awarded for partial completion of doctoral program. *Degree requirements:* For master's, thesis, oral defense of thesis; for doctorate, one foreign language, thesis/dissertation, oral defense of dissertation, dissertation research publishable to standards, comprehensive exam, registration. *Entrance requirements:* For master's, minimum GPA of 3.0; for doctorate, minimum GPA of 3.2, resumé, letters of recommendation (3), statement of objectives. Additional exam requirements/recommendations for international students: Required—TOEFL (minimum score 550 paper-based; 213 computer-based). *Application deadline:* Applications are processed on a rolling basis. Application fee: $50. Electronic applications accepted. *Expenses:* Tuition: Part-time $745 per credit. *Financial support:* In 2003–04, 2 research assistantships with full and partial tuition reimbursements (averaging $18,200 per year), 22 teaching assistantships with full and partial tuition reimbursements (averaging $17,712 per year) were awarded. Fellowships with full and partial tuition reimbursements, career-related internships or fieldwork and tuition remissions also available. Financial award application deadline: 3/1; financial award applicants required to submit FAFSA. *Faculty research:* Energy storage applications, marine and organic chemistry, stereochemistry, medicinal chemistry, environmental chemistry. Total annual research expenditures: $456,667. *Unit head:* Dr. Michael W. Babich, Department Head, 321-674-8046, Fax: 321-674-8951, E-mail: babich@fit.edu. *Application contact:* Carolyn P. Farrior, Director of Graduate Admissions, 321-674-7118, Fax: 321-723-9468, E-mail: cfarrior@fit.edu.

Florida International University, College of Arts and Sciences, Department of Chemistry, Miami, FL 33199. Offers chemistry (MS, PhD); forensic science (MS). Part-time and evening/weekend programs available. *Faculty:* 22 full-time (2 women). *Students:* 49 full-time (30 women), 19 part-time (10 women); includes 21 minority (5 African Americans, 4 Asian Americans or Pacific Islanders, 12 Hispanic Americans), 21 international. Average age 31. 96 applicants, 33% accepted, 16 enrolled. In 2003, 19 master's, 1 doctorate awarded. *Degree requirements:* For master's and doctorate, thesis/dissertation. *Entrance requirements:* For master's and doctorate, GRE General Test. Additional exam requirements/recommendations for international students: Required—TOEFL. *Application deadline:* For fall admission, 4/1 for domestic students; for spring admission, 10/1 for domestic students. Applications are processed on a rolling basis. Application fee: $20. *Expenses:* Tuition, state resident: part-time $202 per credit. Tuition, nonresident: part-time $771 per credit. Required fees: $112 per semester. *Financial support:* Research assistantships, teaching assistantships, Federal Work-Study, institutionally sponsored loans, and tuition waivers (full and partial) available. Support available to part-time students. Financial award application deadline: 4/1. *Faculty research:* Organic synthesis and reaction catalysis, environmental chemistry, molecular beam studies, organic geochemistry, bioinorganic and organometallic chemistry. *Unit head:* Dr. Stanislaw Wnuk, Chairperson, 305-348-2606, Fax: 305-348-3772, E-mail: stanislaw.wnuk@fiu.edu.

See in-depth description on page 113.

Florida State University, Graduate Studies, College of Arts and Sciences, Department of Chemistry and Biochemistry, Tallahassee, FL 32306. Offers analytical chemistry (MS, PhD); biochemistry (MS, PhD); chemical physics (MS, PhD); inorganic chemistry (MS, PhD); organic chemistry (MS, PhD); physical chemistry (MS, PhD). Part-time programs available. *Faculty:* 30 full-time (6 women), 4 part-time/adjunct (2 women). *Students:* 142 full-time (46 women); includes 18 minority (9 African Americans, 1 American Indian/Alaska Native, 6 Asian Americans or Pacific Islanders, 2 Hispanic Americans), 51 international. Average age 25. 410 applicants, 15% accepted, 39 enrolled. In 2003, 9 master's, 11 doctorates awarded. Terminal master's awarded for partial completion of doctoral program. *Median time to degree:* Master's–3.5 years full-time; doctorate–5 years full-time. Of those who began their doctoral program in fall 1995, 72% received their degree in 8 years or less. *Degree requirements:* For master's, thesis (for some programs), cumulative and diagnostic exams, comprehensive exam (for some programs); for doctorate, thesis/dissertation, cumulative and diagnostic exams. *Entrance requirements:* For master's and doctorate, GRE General Test, minimum B average in undergraduate course work. Additional exam requirements/recommendations for international students: Required—TOEFL (minimum score 515 paper-based; 213 computer-based). *Application deadline:* For fall admission, 4/15 priority date for domestic students, 4/15 priority date for international students. Applications are processed on a rolling basis. Application fee: $20. Electronic applications accepted. *Expenses:* Tuition, state resident: part-time $196 per credit hour. Tuition, nonresident: part-time $731 per credit hour. Part-time tuition and fees vary according to campus/location. *Financial support:* In 2003–04, 2 fellowships with tuition reimbursements (averaging $15,000 per year), 54 research assistantships with tuition reimbursements (averaging $18,000 per year), 76 teaching assistantships with tuition reimbursements (averaging $18,000 per year) were awarded. Career-related internships or fieldwork, Federal Work-Study, institutionally sponsored loans, and traineeships also available. Financial award application deadline: 2/15; financial award applicants required to submit FAFSA. *Faculty research:* Spectroscopy, computational chemistry, nuclear chemistry, separations, synthesis. *Unit head:* Dr. Naresh Dalal, Chairman, 850-644-3398, Fax: 850-644-8281. *Application contact:* Dr. Oliver Steinbock, Chair, Graduate Admissions Committee, 888-525-9286, Fax: 850-644-8281, E-mail: gradinfo@chem.fsu.edu.

See in-depth description on page 115.

Furman University, Graduate Division, Department of Chemistry, Greenville, SC 29613. Offers MS. *Faculty:* 5 full-time (1 woman). *Students:* 8 full-time (2 women). Average age 25. 3 applicants, 100% accepted, 3 enrolled. In 2003, 1 degree awarded, leading to continued full-time study 100%. *Median time to degree:* Master's–2 years full-time. *Degree requirements:* For master's, thesis, comprehensive exam. *Entrance requirements:* For master's, GRE General Test, GRE Subject Test. *Application deadline:* For fall admission, 8/1 for domestic students, 8/1 for international students; for winter admission, 12/1 for domestic students; for spring admission, 2/1 for domestic students. Applications are processed on a rolling basis. Application fee: $40. *Expenses:* Tuition: Part-time $244 per credit hour. *Financial support:* In 2003–04, 8 students received support, including 8 fellowships (averaging $4,984 per year); research assistantships, scholarships/grants and unspecified assistantships also available. Financial award application deadline: 8/1. *Faculty research:* Computer-assisted chemical analysis, DNA-metal interactions, laser-initiated reactions, nucleic acid chemistry and biochemistry. *Unit head:* Dr. Lon B. Knight, Professor, 864-294-3372, Fax: 864-294-3559, E-mail: lon.knight@furman.edu. *Application contact:* Myra Crumley, 864-294-2056, Fax: 864-294-3559, E-mail: myra.crumley@furman.edu.

George Mason University, College of Arts and Sciences, Department of Chemistry, Fairfax, VA 22030. Offers MS. *Faculty:* 19 full-time (3 women), 5 part-time/adjunct (2 women). *Students:* 3

Chemistry

George Mason University (continued)
full-time (1 woman), 14 part-time (6 women); includes 4 minority (2 African Americans, 1 American Indian/Alaska Native, 1 Asian American or Pacific Islander), 1 international. Average age 34. 16 applicants, 88% accepted, 2 enrolled. In 2003, 2 degrees awarded. *Degree requirements:* For master's, thesis or alternative. *Entrance requirements:* For master's, GRE General Test, minimum GPA of 3.0 in last 60 hours. *Application deadline:* For fall admission, 5/1 for domestic students; for spring admission, 11/1 for domestic students. Application fee: $60. Electronic applications accepted. *Expenses:* Tuition, state resident: full-time $4,398. Tuition, nonresident: full-time $14,952. Required fees: $1,482. *Financial support:* Research assistantships available. Support available to part-time students. Financial award application deadline: 3/1; financial award applicants required to submit FAFSA. *Unit head:* Gregory Foster, Chairperson, 703-993-1081, Fax: 703-993-1070, E-mail: gfoster@gmu.edu.

Georgetown University, Graduate School of Arts and Sciences, Department of Chemistry, Washington, DC 20057. Offers analytical chemistry (MS, PhD); biochemistry (MS, PhD); chemical physics (MS, PhD); inorganic chemistry (MS, PhD); organic chemistry (MS, PhD); physical chemistry (MS, PhD); theoretical chemistry (MS, PhD). Terminal master's awarded for partial completion of doctoral program. *Degree requirements:* For master's, thesis (for some programs), qualifying exam; for doctorate, thesis/dissertation, comprehensive exam. *Entrance requirements:* For master's and doctorate, GRE General Test. Additional exam requirements/recommendations for international students: Required—TOEFL.

The George Washington University, Columbian College of Arts and Sciences, Department of Chemistry, Washington, DC 20052. Offers analytical chemistry (MS, PhD); inorganic chemistry (MS, PhD); materials science (MS, PhD); organic chemistry (MS, PhD); physical chemistry (MS, PhD). Part-time and evening/weekend programs available. *Faculty:* 7 full-time (1 woman). *Students:* 16 full-time (6 women), 11 part-time (6 women); includes 4 minority (2 African Americans, 1 Asian American or Pacific Islander, 1 Hispanic American), 11 international. 39 applicants, 95% accepted. In 2003, 3 master's, 2 doctorates awarded. Terminal master's awarded for partial completion of doctoral program. *Degree requirements:* For master's, thesis or alternative, comprehensive exam; for doctorate, thesis/dissertation, general exam. *Entrance requirements:* For master's and doctorate, GRE General Test, interview, minimum GPA of 3.0. Additional exam requirements/recommendations for international students: Required—TOEFL (minimum score 550 paper-based; 213 computer-based). *Application deadline:* For fall admission, 2/1 priority date for domestic students, 2/1 priority date for international students; for spring admission, 10/1 priority date for domestic students, 10/1 priority date for international students. Applications are processed on a rolling basis. Application fee: $60. Electronic applications accepted. *Expenses:* Tuition: Part-time $876 per credit. Required fees: $1 per credit. Tuition and fees vary according to campus/location. *Financial support:* In 2003–04, fellowships with tuition reimbursements (averaging $10,000 per year), teaching assistantships with tuition reimbursements (averaging $5,000 per year) were awarded. Research assistantships, Federal Work-Study also available. Financial award application deadline: 2/1. *Unit head:* Dr. Michael King, Chair, 202-994-6488. *Application contact:* Information Contact, E-mail: gwchem@www.gwu.edu.

Georgia Institute of Technology, Graduate Studies and Research, College of Sciences, School of Chemistry and Biochemistry, Atlanta, GA 30332-0001. Offers MS, MS Chem, PhD. Terminal master's awarded for partial completion of doctoral program. *Degree requirements:* For master's, thesis (for some programs); for doctorate, thesis/dissertation. *Entrance requirements:* For master's and doctorate, GRE General Test, GRE Subject Test, minimum GPA of 2.7. Additional exam requirements/recommendations for international students: Required—TOEFL. Electronic applications accepted. *Expenses:* Tuition, state resident: part-time $1,925 per semester. Tuition, nonresident: part-time $7,700 per semester. Required fees: $434 per semester. Full-time tuition and fees vary according to program. *Faculty research:* Inorganic, organic, physical, and analytical chemistry.

Georgia State University, College of Arts and Sciences, Department of Chemistry, Atlanta, GA 30303-3083. Offers MS, PhD. Part-time programs available. *Faculty:* 18 full-time (5 women), 2 part-time/adjunct (1 woman). *Students:* 62 full-time (38 women), 10 part-time (6 women); includes 39 minority (15 African Americans, 19 Asian Americans or Pacific Islanders, 5 Hispanic Americans). 61 applicants, 36% accepted. In 2003, 12 master's, 7 doctorates awarded. Terminal master's awarded for partial completion of doctoral program. *Degree requirements:* For master's, one foreign language, thesis or alternative, exam; for doctorate, one foreign language, thesis/dissertation, exam. *Entrance requirements:* For master's, GRE General Test, departmental supplemental form; for doctorate, GRE General Test. Additional exam requirements/recommendations for international students: Required—TOEFL. *Application deadline:* For fall admission, 8/1 for domestic students; for spring admission, 12/1 for domestic students. Applications are processed on a rolling basis. Application fee: $25. Electronic applications accepted. *Financial support:* In 2003–04, fellowships (averaging $18,000 per year), research assistantships (averaging $16,800 per year), teaching assistantships (averaging $16,800 per year) were awarded. Career-related internships or fieldwork, Federal Work-Study, institutionally sponsored loans, tuition waivers (partial), and unspecified assistantships also available. Support available to part-time students. Financial award applicants required to submit FAFSA. *Faculty research:* DNA, AIDS, drug design, biothermodynamics, biological electron transfer and NMR applied to biochemical systems. Total annual research expenditures: $2.4 million. *Unit head:* Dr. Alfons A. Baumstark, Chair, 404-651-1716, Fax: 404-651-1416, E-mail: chealb@panther.gsu.edu. *Application contact:* Rashid Mosley, Graduate Coordinator, 404-651-1664, Fax: 404-651-1416, E-mail: chegsc@langate.gsu.edu.

Graduate School and University Center of the City University of New York, Graduate Studies, Program in Chemistry, New York, NY 10016-4039. Offers PhD. *Faculty:* 64 full-time (5 women). *Students:* 124 full-time (51 women); includes 16 minority (8 African Americans, 4 Asian Americans or Pacific Islanders, 4 Hispanic Americans), 88 international. Average age 31. 80 applicants, 43% accepted, 21 enrolled. In 2003, 11 degrees awarded. *Degree requirements:* For doctorate, one foreign language, thesis/dissertation. *Entrance requirements:* For doctorate, GRE General Test, GRE Subject Test. *Application deadline:* For fall admission, 4/15 for domestic students. Application fee: $50. *Expenses:* Tuition, state resident: part-time $2,435 per semester. Tuition, nonresident: part-time $475 per credit. *Financial support:* In 2003–04, 79 students received support, including 78 fellowships, 1 teaching assistantship; research assistantships, career-related internships or fieldwork, Federal Work-Study, institutionally sponsored loans, and tuition waivers (full and partial) also available. Financial award application deadline: 2/1; financial award applicants required to submit FAFSA. *Unit head:* Dr. Gerald Koeppl, Executive Officer, 212-817-8136, Fax: 212-817-1507, E-mail: gkoeppl@gc.cuny.edu.

Hampton University, Graduate College, Department of Chemistry, Hampton, VA 23668. Offers MS. Part-time and evening/weekend programs available. *Degree requirements:* For master's, thesis. *Entrance requirements:* For master's, GRE General Test.

Harvard University, Graduate School of Arts and Sciences, Committee on Chemical Physics, Cambridge, MA 02138. Offers chemical physics (PhD); chemistry (AM); physics (AM). *Degree requirements:* For doctorate, one foreign language, thesis/dissertation, cumulative exams. *Entrance requirements:* For master's, GRE General Test; for doctorate, GRE General Test, GRE Subject Test. Additional exam requirements/recommendations for international students: Required—TOEFL. *Expenses:* Tuition: Full-time $26,066. Full-time tuition and fees vary according to program and student level.

Harvard University, Graduate School of Arts and Sciences, Department of Chemistry and Chemical Biology, Cambridge, MA 02138. Offers biochemical chemistry (AM, PhD); inorganic chemistry (AM, PhD); organic chemistry (AM, PhD); physical chemistry (AM, PhD). *Degree requirements:* For doctorate, thesis/dissertation, cumulative exams. *Entrance requirements:* For master's, GRE General Test; for doctorate, GRE General Test, GRE Subject Test. Additional exam requirements/recommendations for international students: Required—TOEFL. *Expenses:* Tuition: Full-time $26,066. Full-time tuition and fees vary according to program and student level.

See in-depth description on page 117.

Howard University, Graduate School of Arts and Sciences, Department of Chemistry, Washington, DC 20059-0002. Offers analytical chemistry (MS, PhD); atmospheric (MS, PhD); biochemistry (MS, PhD); environmental (MS, PhD); inorganic chemistry (MS, PhD); organic chemistry (MS, PhD); physical chemistry (MS, PhD); polymer chemistry (MS, PhD). Part-time programs available. *Degree requirements:* For master's, one foreign language, thesis, teaching experience, comprehensive exam, registration; for doctorate, 2 foreign languages, thesis/dissertation, teaching experience, comprehensive exam, registration. *Entrance requirements:* For master's, GRE General Test, minimum GPA of 2.7; for doctorate, GRE General Test, minimum GPA of 3.0. *Faculty research:* Stratospheric aerosols, liquid crystals, polymer coatings, terrestrial and extraterrestrial atmospheres, amidogen reaction.

Idaho State University, Office of Graduate Studies, College of Arts and Sciences, Department of Chemistry, Pocatello, ID 83209. Offers MNS, MS. MS students must enter as undergraduates. *Faculty:* 10 full-time (2 women). *Students:* 1 full-time (0 women). Average age 22. In 2003, 3 degrees awarded. *Degree requirements:* For master's, one foreign language, thesis (for some programs), comprehensive exam, registration. *Entrance requirements:* For master's, GRE General Test, minimum GPA of 3.0 in all upper division classes. Additional exam requirements/recommendations for international students: Required—TOEFL (minimum score 550 paper-based; 213 computer-based). *Application deadline:* For fall admission, 7/1 priority date for domestic students, 7/1 priority date for international students; for spring admission, 12/1 priority date for domestic students, 12/1 priority date for international students. Applications are processed on a rolling basis. Application fee: $35. *Expenses:* Tuition, state resident: part-time $205 per credit. Tuition, nonresident: full-time $6,600; part-time $300 per credit. Required fees: $4,108. One-time fee: $35 full-time. *Financial support:* Research assistantships, teaching assistantships with full and partial tuition reimbursements, Federal Work-Study available. Financial award application deadline: 1/1. *Faculty research:* Natural product synthesis, solar energy devices, low temperature plasma, chemometrics. Total annual research expenditures: $149,345. *Unit head:* Dennis Strommen, Chair, 208-282-4444, Fax: 208-282-4373, E-mail: graddean@isu.edu.

Idaho State University, Office of Graduate Studies, Department of Interdisciplinary Studies, Pocatello, ID 83209. Offers biology (MNS); chemistry (MNS); general interdisciplinary (M Ed, MA); geology (MNS); mathematics (MNS); physics (MNS); waste management and environmental science (MS). Part-time programs available. *Students:* 3 full-time, 337 part-time; includes 7 minority (1 African American, 1 Asian American or Pacific Islander, 5 Hispanic Americans). Average age 45. In 2003, 7 degrees awarded. *Degree requirements:* For master's, thesis optional. *Entrance requirements:* For master's, GRE General Test or MAT, minimum GPA of 3.0. Additional exam requirements/recommendations for international students: Required—TOEFL (minimum score 550 paper-based; 213 computer-based). *Application deadline:* For fall admission, 7/1 priority date for domestic students, 7/1 priority date for international students; for spring admission, 12/1 priority date for domestic students, 12/1 priority date for international students. Applications are processed on a rolling basis. Application fee: $35. *Expenses:* Tuition, state resident: part-time $205 per credit. Tuition, nonresident: full-time $6,600; part-time $300 per credit. Required fees: $4,108. One-time fee: $35 full-time. *Financial support:* Research assistantships, teaching assistantships, career-related internships or fieldwork, Federal Work-Study, scholarships/grants, and tuition waivers (full and partial) available. Support available to part-time students. Financial award application deadline: 1/1. Total annual research expenditures: $1.7 million. *Unit head:* Dr. Edwin House, Chief Research Officer/Department Chair, 208-282-2714, Fax: 208-282-4529.

Illinois Institute of Technology, Graduate College, College of Science and Letters, Department of Biological, Chemical and Physical Sciences, Chemistry Division, Chicago, IL 60616-3793. Offers analytical chemistry (M Ch, MS, PhD); chemistry (M Chem); inorganic chemistry (MS, PhD); materials and chemical synthesis (M Ch); organic chemistry (MS, PhD); physical chemistry (MS, PhD); polymer chemistry (MS, PhD). Part-time and evening/weekend programs available. Postbaccalaureate distance learning degree programs offered (no on-campus study). *Faculty:* 4 full-time (0 women), 2 part-time/adjunct (0 women). *Students:* 14 full-time (7 women), 32 part-time (18 women); includes 7 minority (1 African American, 4 Asian Americans or Pacific Islanders, 2 Hispanic Americans), 17 international. Average age 32. 94 applicants, 68% accepted, 7 enrolled. In 2003, 14 master's, 2 doctorates awarded. Terminal master's awarded for partial completion of doctoral program. *Degree requirements:* For master's, thesis (for some programs), comprehensive exam; for doctorate, thesis/dissertation, comprehensive exam. *Entrance requirements:* For master's and doctorate, GRE General Test, minimum undergraduate GPA of 3.0. Additional exam requirements/recommendations for international students: Required—TOEFL (minimum score 550 paper-based; 213 computer-based). *Application deadline:* For fall admission, 5/1 for domestic students, 5/1 for international students; for spring admission, 10/15 for domestic students, 10/15 for international students. Applications are processed on a rolling basis. Application fee: $40. Electronic applications accepted. *Expenses:* Tuition: Part-time $628 per credit. Tuition and fees vary according to course load and program. *Financial support:* In 2003–04, 11 students received support, including 1 fellowship with full tuition reimbursement available, 9 research assistantships with full tuition reimbursements available (averaging $15,000 per year), 7 teaching assistantships with full tuition reimbursements available (averaging $15,000 per year); Federal Work-Study, institutionally sponsored loans, scholarships/grants, and tuition waivers (partial) also available. Support available to part-time students. Financial award application deadline: 3/1; financial award applicants required to submit FAFSA. *Faculty research:* Organic and inorganic chemistry, polymers research, physical chemistry, analytical chemistry. *Unit head:* Kenneth Stagliano, Associate Chair, 312-567-3428, Fax: 312-567-3494, E-mail: stagliano@iit.edu. *Application contact:* Kelly A. Cherwin, Director of Graduate Outreach, 312-567-7974, Fax: 312-567-3494, E-mail: inquiry.grad@iit.edu.

Illinois State University, Graduate School, College of Arts and Sciences, Department of Chemistry, Normal, IL 61790-2200. Offers MS. *Faculty:* 20 full-time (5 women). *Students:* 36 full-time (14 women), 7 part-time (3 women); includes 4 minority (3 African Americans, 1 Asian American or Pacific Islander), 7 international. 17 applicants, 94% accepted. In 2003, 12 degrees awarded. *Degree requirements:* For master's, thesis. *Entrance requirements:* For master's, GRE General Test, minimum GPA of 2.6 in last 60 hours. *Application deadline:* Applications are processed on a rolling basis. Application fee: $30. *Expenses:* Tuition, state resident: full-time $3,322; part-time $138 per hour. Tuition, nonresident: full-time $6,922; part-time $288 per hour. Required fees: $974; $41 per hour. *Financial support:* In 2003–04, 8 research assistantships (averaging $14,270 per year), 23 teaching assistantships (averaging $7,478 per year) were awarded. Tuition waivers (full) and unspecified assistantships also available. Financial award application deadline: 4/1. *Faculty research:* Enhancing college preparation in middle school math and science, isotopic perturbations in aromatic character and new annulene conformers. Total annual research expenditures: $376,614. *Unit head:* Dr. C. Frank Shaw, Chairperson, 309-438-7661.

Indiana University Bloomington, Graduate School, College of Arts and Sciences, Department of Chemistry, Bloomington, IN 47405. Offers analytical chemistry (PhD); biological chemistry (PhD); chemistry (MAT, MS); inorganic chemistry (PhD); physical chemistry (PhD). PhD offered through the University Graduate School. *Faculty:* 29 full-time (2 women). *Students:* 95 full-time (30 women), 51 part-time (16 women); includes 9 minority (3 African Americans, 4 Asian Americans or Pacific Islanders, 2 Hispanic Americans), 52 international. Average age 26. 309 applicants, 41% accepted. In 2003, 4 master's, 23 doctorates awarded. Terminal master's awarded for partial completion of doctoral program. *Degree requirements:* For master's and doctorate, thesis/dissertation. *Entrance requirements:* For master's and doctorate, GRE General Test, GRE Subject Test. Additional exam requirements/recommendations for international students: Required—TOEFL. *Application deadline:* For fall admission, 1/15 priority date for domestic students, 12/15 priority date for international students; for spring admission, 9/1 priority date for domestic students, 9/1 priority date for international students. Applications are processed on a rolling basis. Application fee: $45 ($55 for international students). *Expenses:* Tuition, state resident: full-time $4,908; part-time $205 per credit. Tuition, nonresident: full-time $14,298; part-time $596 per credit. Required fees: $661. Tuition and fees vary according to campus/location and program. *Financial support:* In 2003–04, 23 fellowships with full tuition reimbursements (averaging $15,091 per year), 57 research assistantships with full tuition reimbursements (averaging $14,844 per year), 78 teaching assistantships with full tuition reimbursements (averaging $15,588 per year) were awarded. Federal Work-Study and institutionally sponsored loans also available. *Faculty research:* Synthesis of complex natural products, organic reaction mechanisms, organic electrochemistry, transitive-metal chemistry, solid-state and surface chemistry. Total annual research expenditures: $7.7 million. *Unit head:* Dr. Gary M. Hieftje, Chairperson, 812-855-6239, Fax: 812-855-8300, E-mail: cemchair@indiana.edu. *Application contact:* Dr. Jack K. Crandall, Chairperson of Admissions, 812-855-2068, Fax: 812-855-8300, E-mail: chemgrad@indiana.edu.

Indiana University of Pennsylvania, Graduate School and Research, College of Natural Sciences and Mathematics, Department of Chemistry, Program in Chemistry, Indiana, PA 15705-1087. Offers MA, MS. Part-time programs available. *Faculty:* 14 full-time (5 women). *Students:* 6 full-time (0 women), 2 part-time, 3 international. Average age 28. 9 applicants, 67% accepted. In 2003, 2 degrees awarded. *Degree requirements:* For master's, thesis optional. *Entrance requirements:* For master's, 2 letters of recommendation. Additional exam requirements/recommendations for international students: Required—TOEFL. *Application deadline:* For fall admission, 7/1 for domestic students; for spring admission, 11/1 for domestic students. Applications are processed on a rolling basis. Application fee: $30. *Expenses:* Tuition, state resident: full-time $5,518; part-time $307 per credit. Tuition, nonresident: full-time $8,830; part-time $491 per credit. Required fees: $31 per credit. $111 per semester. Tuition and fees vary according to degree level. *Financial support:* In 2003–04, 5 research assistantships with full and partial tuition reimbursements (averaging $5,660 per year) were awarded. Financial award application deadline: 3/15; financial award applicants required to submit FAFSA. *Unit head:* Dr. Lawrence Kupchella, Graduate Coordinator, 724-357-5702, E-mail: lkup@iup.edu.

Indiana University–Purdue University Indianapolis, School of Science, Department of Chemistry, Indianapolis, IN 46202-2896. Offers MS, PhD, MD/PhD. Part-time and evening/weekend programs available. *Faculty:* 10 full-time (2 women). *Students:* 10 full-time (6 women), 31 part-time (18 women); includes 5 minority (2 African Americans, 1 American Indian/Alaska Native, 1 Asian American or Pacific Islander, 1 Hispanic American), 4 international. Average age 27. In 2003, 12 degrees awarded. Terminal master's awarded for partial completion of doctoral program. *Degree requirements:* For master's, thesis (for some programs); for doctorate, thesis/dissertation. *Entrance requirements:* For master's and doctorate, minimum GPA of 3.0. Additional exam requirements/recommendations for international students: Required—TOEFL, GRE (international applicants). *Application deadline:* Applications are processed on a rolling basis. Application fee: $45 ($55 for international students). *Expenses:* Tuition, state resident: full-time $4,658; part-time $194 per credit. Tuition, nonresident: full-time $13,444; part-time $560 per credit. Required fees: $571. Tuition and fees vary according to campus/location and program. *Financial support:* In 2003–04, 2 fellowships with partial tuition reimbursements (averaging $16,800 per year), 9 research assistantships with partial tuition reimbursements (averaging $16,800 per year), 16 teaching assistantships with partial tuition reimbursements (averaging $16,800 per year) were awarded. Career-related internships or fieldwork, institutionally sponsored loans, tuition waivers (partial), and co-op positions also available. Financial award application deadline: 3/1. *Faculty research:* Analytical, biological, inorganic, organic, and physical chemistry. Total annual research expenditures: $1.6 million. *Unit head:* Dr. David J. Malik, Chair, 317-274-6872, Fax: 317-274-4701, E-mail: malik@chem.iupui.edu. *Application contact:* Eric Long, Information Contact, 317-274-6888, Fax: 317-274-4701, E-mail: long@chem.iupui.edu.

Instituto Tecnológico y de Estudios Superiores de Monterrey, Campus Monterrey, Graduate and Research Division, Program in Natural and Social Sciences, Monterrey, , Mexico. Offers biotechnology (MS); chemistry (MS, PhD); communications (MS); education (MA). Part-time programs available. *Degree requirements:* For master's and doctorate, one foreign language, thesis/dissertation. *Entrance requirements:* For master's, PAEG; for doctorate, PAEG, master's degree in related field. Additional exam requirements/recommendations for international students: Required—TOEFL. *Faculty research:* Cultural industries, mineral substances, bioremediation, food processing, CQ in industrial chemical processing.

Iowa State University of Science and Technology, Graduate College, College of Liberal Arts and Sciences, Department of Chemistry, Ames, IA 50011. Offers MS, PhD. *Faculty:* 32 full-time. *Students:* 179 full-time (63 women), 7 part-time (3 women); includes 5 minority (3 Asian Americans or Pacific Islanders, 2 Hispanic Americans), 95 international. 80 applicants, 46% accepted, 33 enrolled. In 2003, 7 master's, 17 doctorates awarded. *Median time to degree:* Master's–3.5 years full-time; doctorate–5.7 years full-time. *Degree requirements:* For master's and doctorate, thesis/dissertation. *Entrance requirements:* Additional exam requirements/recommendations for international students: Required—GRE General Test, TOEFL (paper score 570; computer score 230) or IELTS (score 6.5). *Application deadline:* For fall admission, 2/1 priority date for domestic students, 2/1 priority date for international students. Applications are processed on a rolling basis. Application fee: $30 ($70 for international students). Electronic applications accepted. Tuition, nonresident: part-time $560 per credit. Required fees: $38 per unit. *Financial support:* In 2003–04, 121 research assistantships with full and partial tuition reimbursements (averaging $20,940 per year), 42 teaching assistantships with full and partial tuition reimbursements (averaging $20,940 per year) were awarded. Fellowships, scholarships/grants, health care benefits, and unspecified assistantships also available. *Unit head:* Dr. Gordon Miller, Chair, 515-294-7871, Fax: 515-294-0105, E-mail: chemgrad@iastate.edu. *Application contact:* Information Contact, 800-521-2436, E-mail: chemgrad@iastate.edu.

Jackson State University, Graduate School, School of Science and Technology, Department of Chemistry, Jackson, MS 39217. Offers MS, PhD. Part-time and evening/weekend programs available. *Degree requirements:* For master's and doctorate, thesis/dissertation, comprehensive exam. *Entrance requirements:* For master's, GRE General Test; for doctorate, MAT. Additional exam requirements/recommendations for international students: Required—TOEFL. *Faculty research:* Electrochemical and spectroscopic studies on charge transfer and energy transfer processes, spectroscopy of trapped molecular ions, respirable mine dust.

John Carroll University, Graduate School, Department of Chemistry, University Heights, OH 44118-4581. Offers MS. Part-time and evening/weekend programs available. *Faculty:* 8 full-time (1 woman), 1 part-time/adjunct (0 women). *Students:* Average age 28. In 2003, 2 degrees awarded. *Median time to degree:* Master's–2.5 years full-time. *Degree requirements:* For master's, research essay or thesis. *Entrance requirements:* For master's, bachelor's degree in chemistry. *Application deadline:* For fall admission, 8/1 for domestic students; for spring admission, 12/15 for domestic students. Applications are processed on a rolling basis. Application fee: $25 ($35 for international students). Electronic applications accepted. *Expenses:* Tuition: Part-time $600 per semester hour. Tuition and fees vary according to program. *Financial support:* In 2003–04, teaching assistantships with tuition reimbursements (averaging $9,000 per year); institutionally sponsored loans, tuition waivers (partial), and summer research support also available. *Faculty research:* Protein–nucleic acid interactions, protein-surface interactions, butyllithium compounds, copper proteins, magnetic materials. Total annual research expenditures: $45,000. *Unit head:* Dr. Paul R. Challen, Chairperson, 216-397-4793, Fax: 216-397-1791, E-mail: pchallen@jcu.edu. *Application contact:* Dr. Michael A. Nichols, Associate Professor, 216-397-4796, Fax: 216-397-1791, E-mail: mnichols@jcu.edu.

The Johns Hopkins University, Zanvyl Krieger School of Arts and Sciences, Department of Chemistry, Baltimore, MD 21218-2699. Offers MA, PhD. *Faculty:* 18 full-time (2 women). *Students:* 113 full-time (53 women); includes 8 minority (4 African Americans, 1 American Indian/Alaska Native, 2 Asian Americans or Pacific Islanders, 1 Hispanic American), 30 international. Average age 25. 181 applicants, 47% accepted, 29 enrolled. In 2003, 12 master's, 14 doctorates awarded. Terminal master's awarded for partial completion of doctoral program. *Degree requirements:* For master's, oral exam; for doctorate, thesis/dissertation, oral exams. *Entrance requirements:* For master's and doctorate, GRE General Test, GRE Subject Test. *Application deadline:* For fall admission, 1/15 for domestic students; for spring admission, 11/15 for domestic students. Applications are processed on a rolling basis. Application fee: $55. Electronic applications accepted. *Expenses:* Tuition: Full-time $28,730; part-time $1,490 per course. Part-time tuition and fees vary according to course load, campus/location and program. *Financial support:* In 2003–04, 97 fellowships, 55 research assistantships, 43 teaching assistantships were awarded. Federal Work-Study and institutionally sponsored loans also available. Financial award application deadline: 4/15; financial award applicants required to submit FAFSA. Total annual research expenditures: $6.8 million. *Unit head:* Dr. Paul J. Dagdigian, Chair, 410-516-7444, Fax: 410-516-8420. *Application contact:* Judith Dandro, Academic Program Coordinator, 410-516-5250, Fax: 410-516-8420, E-mail: chem.grad.adm@jhu.edu.

Kansas State University, Graduate School, College of Arts and Sciences, Department of Chemistry, Manhattan, KS 66506. Offers analytical chemistry (MS); chemistry (PhD); inorganic chemistry (MS); organic chemistry (MS); physical chemistry (MS). *Faculty:* 15 full-time (2 women). *Students:* 51 full-time (17 women); includes 1 minority (African American), 33 international. 71 applicants, 20% accepted, 14 enrolled. In 2003, 1 master's, 7 doctorates awarded. Terminal master's awarded for partial completion of doctoral program. *Degree requirements:* For master's and doctorate, thesis/dissertation. *Entrance requirements:* For master's and doctorate, GRE, minimum GPA of 3.0. Additional exam requirements/recommendations for international students: Required—TOEFL. *Application deadline:* For fall admission, 2/1 for domestic students; for spring admission, 10/1 for domestic students. Applications are processed on a rolling basis. Application fee: $0 ($25 for international students). *Expenses:* Tuition, state resident: part-time $155 per credit hour. Tuition, nonresident: part-time $428 per credit hour. Required fees: $11 per credit hour. *Financial support:* In 2003–04, 23 research assistantships (averaging $15,648 per year), 26 teaching assistantships with full tuition reimbursements (averaging $17,890 per year) were awarded. Fellowships, institutionally sponsored loans and scholarships/grants also available. Support available to part-time students. Financial award application deadline: 3/1; financial award applicants required to submit FAFSA. *Faculty research:* Computational, environmental and materials, nanoscale, natural products, theoretical chemistry. Total annual research expenditures: $2.8 million. *Unit head:* Peter M. A. Sherwood, Head, 785-532-6665, Fax: 785-532-6666, E-mail: escachem@ksu.edu. *Application contact:* Robert Hammaker, Director, 785-532-1454, Fax: 785-532-6666, E-mail: rmh3008@ksu.edu.

Kent State University, College of Arts and Sciences, Department of Chemistry, Kent, OH 44242-0001. Offers analytical chemistry (MS, PhD); biochemistry (MS, PhD); chemistry (MA, MS, PhD); inorganic chemistry (MS, PhD); organic chemistry (MS, PhD); physical chemistry (MS, PhD). Terminal master's awarded for partial completion of doctoral program. *Degree requirements:* For master's and doctorate, thesis/dissertation, comprehensive exam, registration. *Entrance requirements:* For master's and doctorate, placement exam, GRE General Test, GRE Subject Test (recommended), minimum GPA of 2.75. Additional exam requirements/recommendations for international students: Required—TOEFL (minimum score 575 paper-based; 230 computer-based). Electronic applications accepted. *Expenses:* Tuition, state resident: part-time $334 per hour. Tuition, nonresident: part-time $627 per hour. *Faculty research:* Biological chemistry, materials chemistry, molecular spectroscopy.

See in-depth description on page 119.

Lakehead University, Graduate Studies, Faculty of Social Sciences and Humanities, Department of Chemistry, Thunder Bay, ON P7B 5E1, Canada. Offers M Sc. Part-time and evening/weekend programs available. *Degree requirements:* For master's, thesis, oral examination. *Entrance requirements:* For master's, minimum B+ average. Additional exam requirements/recommendations for international students: Required—TOEFL. *Faculty research:* Physical inorganic chemistry, photochemistry, physical chemistry.

Lamar University, College of Graduate Studies, College of Arts and Sciences, Department of Chemistry and Physics, Beaumont, TX 77710. Offers chemistry (MS). Part-time programs available. *Faculty:* 6 full-time (0 women). *Students:* 13 full-time (2 women), 3 part-time (1 woman), 13 international. Average age 25. 20 applicants, 75% accepted, 7 enrolled. In 2003, 2 degrees awarded, leading to university research/teaching 25%, continued full-time study50%, business/industry 25%. *Median time to degree:* Master's–2 years full-time. *Degree requirements:* For master's, thesis, practicum. *Entrance requirements:* For master's, GRE General Test, minimum GPA of 2.5 in last 60 hours. Additional exam requirements/recommendations for international students: Required—TOEFL, TWE, TSE. *Application deadline:* For fall admission, 8/1 for domestic students, 7/1 for international students; for spring admission, 12/1 for domestic students, 11/1 for international students. Applications are processed on a rolling basis. Application fee: $25 ($50 for international students). *Expenses:* Tuition, state resident: part-time $170 per semester hour. Tuition, nonresident: part-time $351 per semester hour. Required fees: $174 per semester hour. One-time fee: $10 part-time. *Financial support:* In 2003–04, 6 students received support, including 5 teaching assistantships with partial tuition reimbursements available (averaging $9,000 per year); tuition waivers (partial) and unspecified assistantships also available. Financial award application deadline: 4/1. *Faculty research:* Environmental chemistry, surface chemistry, polymer chemistry, organic synthesis, computational chemistry. Total annual research expenditures: $750,000. *Unit head:* Dr. Richard S. Lumpkin, Chair, 409-880-8267, Fax: 409-880-8270, E-mail: lumpkines@hal.lamar.edu.

Laurentian University, School of Graduate Studies and Research, Programme in Chemistry and Biochemistry, Sudbury, ON P3E 2C6, Canada. Offers M Sc. Part-time programs available. *Degree requirements:* For master's, thesis or alternative. *Entrance requirements:* For master's, honors degree with minimum second class. *Faculty research:* Cell cycle checkpoints, kinetic modeling, toxicology to metal stress, quantum chemistry, biogeochemistry metal speciation.

Lehigh University, College of Arts and Sciences, Department of Chemistry, Bethlehem, PA 18015-3094. Offers MS, DA, PhD. Part-time programs available. Postbaccalaureate distance learning degree programs offered (no on-campus study). *Faculty:* 13 full-time (2 women), 2 part-time/adjunct (1 woman). Terminal master's awarded for partial completion of doctoral program. *Degree requirements:* For master's, seminar, thesis optional; for doctorate, thesis/dissertation, 2 seminars, comprehensive exam, registration. *Entrance requirements:* For master's and doctorate, GRE General Test, bachelor's degree in chemistry or related field. Additional exam requirements/recommendations for international students: Required—TOEFL (minimum score 550 paper-based; 213 computer-based), TSE; Recommended—TWE. *Application deadline:* For fall admission, 7/15 priority date for domestic students, 7/15 priority date for international students; for winter admission, 12/30 for domestic students; for spring admission, 4/30 for domestic students. Applications are processed on a rolling basis. Application fee: $50. Electronic applications accepted. *Expenses:* Tuition: Full-time $16,920; part-time $940 per credit hour. Required fees: $200. Tuition and fees vary according to degree level and program. *Financial support:* Research assistantships with full tuition reimbursements, teaching assistantships available. Financial award application deadline: 1/15. *Faculty research:* Surfaces and interfaces, polymers, drug conjugates, organo-metallics. *Unit head:* Dr. Robert H. Flowers, Chairman, Fax: 610-758-6536. *Application contact:* Dr. James E. Roberts, Graduate Coordinator, 610-758-4841, Fax: 610-758-6536, E-mail: jer1@lehigh.edu.

See in-depth description on page 123.

Long Island University, Brooklyn Campus, Richard L. Conolly College of Liberal Arts and Sciences, Department of Chemistry, Brooklyn, NY 11201-8423. Offers MS. Part-time and evening/weekend programs available. *Faculty:* 10 full-time. *Students:* 7 full-time (2 women), 7 part-time (3 women); includes 11 minority (5 African Americans, 5 Asian Americans or Pacific Islanders, 1 Hispanic American). 11 applicants, 55% accepted, 4 enrolled. In 2003, 5 degrees awarded. *Degree requirements:* For master's, thesis or alternative. *Entrance*

Chemistry

Long Island University, Brooklyn Campus (continued)
requirements: For master's, 2 letters of recommendation. Additional exam requirements/recommendations for international students: Required—TOEFL (minimum score 500 paper-based; 173 computer-based). *Application deadline:* Applications are processed on a rolling basis. Application fee: $30. Electronic applications accepted. *Expenses:* Tuition: Part-time $658 per credit. *Financial support:* In 2003–04, teaching assistantships with full tuition reimbursements (averaging $7,000 per year); fellowships, scholarships/grants also available. Support available to part-time students. Financial award application deadline: 8/1; financial award applicants required to submit FAFSA. *Faculty research:* Clinical chemistry, free radicals, heats of hydrogenation. *Unit head:* Dr. Azzedine Bensalem, Chair, 718-488-1208. *Application contact:* Edward Dettling, Director of Graduate Admissions, 718-488-1011, Fax: 718-797-2399, E-mail: admissions@brooklyn.liu.edu.

Louisiana State University and Agricultural and Mechanical College, Graduate School, College of Basic Sciences, Department of Chemistry, Baton Rouge, LA 70803. Offers MS, PhD. Part-time programs available. *Faculty:* 29 full-time (3 women), 1 part-time/adjunct. *Students:* 140 full-time (66 women), 4 part-time (3 women); includes 36 minority (33 African Americans, 2 Asian Americans or Pacific Islanders, 1 Hispanic American), 69 international. Average age 28. 76 applicants, 39% accepted, 22 enrolled. In 2003, 4 master's, 9 doctorates awarded. Terminal master's awarded for partial completion of doctoral program. *Degree requirements:* For master's, thesis (for some programs); for doctorate, thesis/dissertation, general exam. *Entrance requirements:* For master's and doctorate, GRE General Test, minimum GPA of 3.0. Additional exam requirements/recommendations for international students: Required—TOEFL (minimum score 550 paper-based; 213 computer-based). *Application deadline:* For fall admission, 3/1 priority date for domestic students, 5/15 priority date for international students; for spring admission, 8/1 for domestic students, 10/15 for international students. Applications are processed on a rolling basis. Application fee: $25. Electronic applications accepted. *Expenses:* Tuition, state resident: part-time $337 per hour. Tuition, nonresident: part-time $577 per hour. *Financial support:* In 2003–04, 33 students received support, including 24 fellowships (averaging $22,426 per year), 52 research assistantships with partial tuition reimbursements available (averaging $21,807 per year), 62 teaching assistantships with partial tuition reimbursements available (averaging $20,844 per year); unspecified assistantships also available. Financial award application deadline: 7/1; financial award applicants required to submit FAFSA. *Faculty research:* Free radicals, bioinorganic chemistry, polymers, synthesis, spectroscopy. Total annual research expenditures: $6.4 million. *Unit head:* Dr. Luigi Marzilli, Chair, 225-578-7623, Fax: 225-578-3458, E-mail: lmarzil@lsu.edu. *Application contact:* Dr. Steven Watkins, Director of Graduate Studies, 225-578-3359, Fax: 225-578-3458, E-mail: swatkins@lsu.edu.

Louisiana Tech University, Graduate School, College of Engineering and Science, Department of Chemistry, Ruston, LA 71272. Offers MS. Part-time programs available. *Degree requirements:* For master's, thesis. *Entrance requirements:* For master's, GRE General Test, minimum GPA of 3.0 in last 60 hours. Additional exam requirements/recommendations for international students: Required—TOEFL. *Expenses:* Tuition, state resident: full-time $3,120. Tuition, nonresident: full-time $9,120. Tuition and fees vary according to course load. *Faculty research:* Vibrational spectroscopy, quantum studies of chemical reactions, enzyme kinetics, synthesis of transition metal compounds, NMR spectrometry.

Loyola University Chicago, Graduate School, Department of Chemistry, Chicago, IL 60611-2196. Offers MS, PhD. Part-time and evening/weekend programs available. *Faculty:* 15 full-time (4 women). *Students:* 27 full-time (13 women), 8 part-time (4 women); includes 3 Asian Americans or Pacific Islanders, 2 Hispanic Americans, 12 international. Average age 33. 66 applicants, 30% accepted. In 2003, 3 master's, 4 doctorates awarded. Terminal master's awarded for partial completion of doctoral program. *Degree requirements:* For master's and doctorate, thesis/dissertation. *Entrance requirements:* For master's and doctorate, GRE General Test, GRE Subject Test. Additional exam requirements/recommendations for international students: Required—TOEFL. *Application deadline:* For fall admission, 8/1 for domestic students; for spring admission, 12/1 for domestic students. Application fee: $40. Electronic applications accepted. *Expenses:* Tuition: Part-time $578 per credit hour. Tuition and fees vary according to course level and program. *Financial support:* In 2003–04, 13 fellowships with full tuition reimbursements (averaging $19,600 per year), 3 research assistantships with full tuition reimbursements (averaging $15,000 per year), 16 teaching assistantships with full tuition reimbursements (averaging $14,300 per year) were awarded. Federal Work-Study, scholarships/grants, traineeships, and unspecified assistantships also available. Support available to part-time students. Financial award application deadline: 2/1; financial award applicants required to submit FAFSA. *Faculty research:* Magnetic resonance of membrane/protein systems, organometallic catalysis, novel synthesis of natural products. Total annual research expenditures: $682,510. *Unit head:* Dr. David Crumrine, Chair, 773-508-3114, Fax: 773-508-3086. *Application contact:* Dr. Daniel Graham, Graduate Program Director, 773-508-3169, Fax: 773-508-3086.

Marquette University, Graduate School, College of Arts and Sciences, Department of Chemistry, Milwaukee, WI 53201-1881. Offers analytical chemistry (MS, PhD); bioanalytical chemistry (MS, PhD); biophysical chemistry (MS, PhD); chemical physics (MS, PhD); inorganic chemistry (MS, PhD); organic chemistry (MS, PhD); physical chemistry (MS, PhD). Part-time programs available. *Faculty:* 19 full-time (2 women), 2 part-time/adjunct (0 women). *Students:* 44 full-time (17 women), 4 part-time (1 woman); includes 1 minority (African American), 36 international. Average age 31. 37 applicants, 32% accepted, 8 enrolled. In 2003, 1 master's, 1 doctorate awarded. Terminal master's awarded for partial completion of doctoral program. *Degree requirements:* For master's, comprehensive exam; for doctorate, thesis/dissertation, cumulative exams. *Entrance requirements:* For master's and doctorate, GRE Subject Test. Additional exam requirements/recommendations for international students: Required—TOEFL. Application fee: $40. *Expenses:* Tuition: Full-time $10,080; part-time $630 per credit. Tuition and fees vary according to program. *Financial support:* In 2003–04, 3 research assistantships, 27 teaching assistantships were awarded. Fellowships, Federal Work-Study, institutionally sponsored loans, scholarships/grants, and tuition waivers (full and partial) also available. Support available to part-time students. Financial award application deadline: 2/15. *Faculty research:* Inorganic complexes, laser Raman spectroscopy, organic synthesis, chemical dynamics, biophysiology. Total annual research expenditures: $586,915. *Unit head:* Dr. Charles Wilkie, Chairman, 414-288-7065, Fax: 414-288-7066. *Application contact:* Dr. Mark Steinmetz, Director of Graduate Studies, 414-288-7374, Fax: 414-288-7066.

Marshall University, Academic Affairs Division, Graduate College, College of Science, Department of Chemistry, Huntington, WV 25755. Offers MS. *Faculty:* 9 full-time (2 women). *Students:* 9 full-time (3 women), 1 (woman) part-time, 3 international. Average age 26. In 2003, 2 degrees awarded. *Degree requirements:* For master's, thesis. Tuition, area resident: Part-time $1,730 per semester. *Expenses:* Tuition, state resident: part-time $3,295 per semester. Tuition, nonresident: part-time $5,003 per semester. *Financial support:* Career-related internships or fieldwork available. *Unit head:* Dr. Daniel Babb, Chairperson, 304-696-2430, E-mail: babb@marshall.edu. *Application contact:* Information Contact, 304-746-1900, Fax: 304-746-1902, E-mail: services@marshall.edu.

Massachusetts College of Pharmacy and Health Sciences, Graduate Studies, Program in Chemistry, Boston, MA 02115-5896. Offers MS, PhD. *Faculty:* 7 full-time (0 women). *Students:* 9 full-time (5 women), 1 (woman) part-time, 7 international. Average age 24. 11 applicants, 73% accepted, 4 enrolled. In 2003, 2 degrees awarded. Terminal master's awarded for partial completion of doctoral program. *Degree requirements:* For master's, thesis, oral defense of thesis; for doctorate, one foreign language, thesis/dissertation, oral defense of dissertation, qualifying exam, comprehensive exam, registration. *Entrance requirements:* For master's and doctorate, GRE General Test, minimum QPA of 3.0. Additional exam requirements/recommendations for international students: Required—TOEFL (minimum score 600 paper-based; 230 computer-based). *Application deadline:* For fall admission, 3/1 for domestic students. Application fee: $70. *Expenses:* Tuition: Full-time $22,000; part-time $690 per credit hour. *Financial support:* In 2003–04, 8 students received support, including 8 teaching assistantships with full tuition reimbursements available (averaging $11,000 per year); fellowships with partial tuition reimbursements available, research assistantships with partial tuition reimbursements available, tuition waivers (partial) and unspecified assistantships also available. Financial award application deadline: 3/1. *Faculty research:* Analytical chemistry, medicinal chemistry, organic chemistry, neurochemistry. Total annual research expenditures: $30,000. *Unit head:* Mehdi Boroujerdi, Dean, 617-732-2939, E-mail: divisionofgraduatestudies@mcphs.edu. *Application contact:* Richard Kivior, Coordinator of Graduate Admissions, 617-732-2986, Fax: 617-732-2801, E-mail: admissions@mcp.edu.

Massachusetts Institute of Technology, School of Science, Department of Chemistry, Cambridge, MA 02139-4307. Offers biological chemistry (PhD, Sc D); inorganic chemistry (PhD, Sc D); organic chemistry (PhD, Sc D); physical chemistry (PhD, Sc D). *Faculty:* 31 full-time (6 women). *Students:* 253 full-time (85 women), 7 part-time (5 women); includes 34 minority (8 African Americans, 17 Asian Americans or Pacific Islanders, 9 Hispanic Americans), 81 international. Average age 26. 573 applicants, 25% accepted, 54 enrolled. In 2003, 28 doctorates awarded. *Degree requirements:* For doctorate, thesis/dissertation, comprehensive exam. *Entrance requirements:* For doctorate, GRE General Test. Additional exam requirements/recommendations for international students: Required—TOEFL (minimum score 577 paper-based; 233 computer-based). *Application deadline:* For fall admission, 12/15 for domestic students, 12/15 for international students. Application fee: $70. Electronic applications accepted. *Expenses:* Tuition: Full-time $29,400. Required fees: $200. *Financial support:* In 2003–04, 50 fellowships with tuition reimbursements, 167 research assistantships with tuition reimbursements (averaging $23,760 per year), 59 teaching assistantships with tuition reimbursements (averaging $18,270 per year) were awarded. Career-related internships or fieldwork, Federal Work-Study, institutionally sponsored loans, scholarships/grants, health care benefits, and unspecified assistantships also available. *Faculty research:* Synthetic organic chemistry, enzymatic reaction mechanisms, inorganic and organometallic spectroscopy, high resolution NMR spectroscopy. Total annual research expenditures: $20.7 million. *Unit head:* Prof. Stephen J. Lippard, Head, 617-253-1801, Fax: 617-258-0241. *Application contact:* Susan Brighton, Graduate Administrator, 617-253-1845, Fax: 617-258-0241, E-mail: brighton@mit.edu.

McGill University, Faculty of Graduate and Postdoctoral Studies, Faculty of Science, Department of Chemistry, Montréal, QC H3A 2T5, Canada. Offers M Sc, PhD. *Faculty:* 29 full-time (4 women). *Students:* 98 full-time, 1 part-time. 113 applicants, 45% accepted, 26 enrolled. In 2003, 8 master's, 15 doctorates awarded. *Degree requirements:* For master's and doctorate, thesis/dissertation. *Entrance requirements:* For master's, minimum GPA of 3.0. Additional exam requirements/recommendations for international students: Required—TOEFL. *Application deadline:* For fall admission, 3/1 for domestic students. Applications are processed on a rolling basis. Application fee: $60 Canadian dollars. Tuition, area resident: Full-time $1,668. *Expenses:* Tuition, state resident: full-time $4,173. Tuition, nonresident: full-time $9,468. Required fees: $1,081. *Financial support:* Stipends available. *Unit head:* Masad Damha, Director of Graduate Studies, 514-398-7552, Fax: 514-398-3797, E-mail: masad.damha@mcgill.ca. *Application contact:* Chantal Marotte, Graduate Studies Coordinator, 514-398-6941, Fax: 514-398-3797, E-mail: chantal.marotte@mcgill.ca.

McMaster University, School of Graduate Studies, Faculty of Science, Department of Chemistry, Hamilton, ON L8S 4M2, Canada. Offers analytical chemistry (M Sc, PhD); chemical physics (M Sc, PhD); chemistry (M Sc, PhD); inorganic chemistry (M Sc, PhD); organic chemistry (M Sc, PhD); physical chemistry (M Sc, PhD); polymer chemistry (M Sc, PhD). Part-time programs available. Terminal master's awarded for partial completion of doctoral program. *Degree requirements:* For master's, thesis/dissertation; for doctorate, thesis/dissertation, comprehensive exam. *Entrance requirements:* For master's, minimum B+ average. Additional exam requirements/recommendations for international students: Required—TOEFL (minimum score 550 paper-based; 213 computer-based).

McNeese State University, Graduate School, College of Science, Department of Biological and Environmental Sciences and Department of Chemistry, Program in Environmental and Chemical Sciences, Lake Charles, LA 70609. Offers MS. Evening/weekend programs available. *Degree requirements:* For master's, thesis or alternative, comprehensive exam. *Entrance requirements:* For master's, GRE General Test.

McNeese State University, Graduate School, College of Science, Department of Chemistry, Lake Charles, LA 70609. Offers chemistry (PhD); environmental and chemical sciences (MS, PhD). Evening/weekend programs available. *Degree requirements:* For master's, thesis or alternative, comprehensive exam. *Entrance requirements:* For master's, GRE General Test. *Faculty research:* Environmental studies, carotenoids, polymers, chemical education.

Memorial University of Newfoundland, School of Graduate Studies, Department of Chemistry, St. John's, NL A1C 5S7, Canada. Offers chemistry (M Sc, PhD); instrumental analysis (M Sc). Part-time programs available. *Students:* 36 full-time, 4 part-time. 63 applicants, 14% accepted, 8 enrolled. In 2003, 6 master's, 4 doctorates awarded. *Degree requirements:* For master's, thesis, research seminar, American Chemical Society Exam; for doctorate, thesis/dissertation, seminars, oral thesis defense, American Chemical Society Exam, comprehensive exam. *Entrance requirements:* For master's, B Sc or honors degree in chemistry (preferred); for doctorate, master's degree in chemistry or honors bachelor's degree. *Application deadline:* Applications are processed on a rolling basis. Application fee: $40. Electronic applications accepted. Tuition and fees charges are reported in Canadian dollars. *Expenses:* Tuition, state resident: part-time $733 Canadian dollars per semester. Tuition, nonresident: part-time $953 Canadian dollars per semester. Required fees: $194 Canadian dollars per year. Tuition and fees vary according to degree level and program. *Financial support:* Fellowships, research assistantships, teaching assistantships available. *Faculty research:* Analytical/environmental chemistry; medicinal electrochemistry; inorganic, marine, organic, physical, and theoretical/computational chemistry, environmental science and instrumental analysis. *Unit head:* Dr. Robert Davis, Head, 709-737-8772, Fax: 709-737-3702, E-mail: rdavis@mun.ca. *Application contact:* Dr. Peter Pickup, Graduate Officer, 709-737-8657, Fax: 709-737-3702, E-mail: gradchem@mun.ca.

Miami University, Graduate School, College of Arts and Sciences, Department of Chemistry and Biochemistry, Oxford, OH 45056. Offers analytical chemistry (MS, PhD); biochemistry (MS, PhD); chemical education (MS, PhD); chemistry (MS, PhD); inorganic chemistry (MS, PhD); organic chemistry (MS, PhD); physical chemistry (MS, PhD). Part-time programs available. *Faculty:* 22 full-time (2 women). *Students:* 45 full-time (16 women), 1 part-time; includes 2 minority (both Asian Americans or Pacific Islanders), 21 international. 131 applicants, 98% accepted, 13 enrolled. In 2003, 4 master's, 4 doctorates awarded. *Degree requirements:* For master's, thesis, final exam; for doctorate, thesis/dissertation, final exams, comprehensive exam. *Entrance requirements:* For master's, minimum undergraduate GPA of 3.0 during previous 2 years or 2.75 overall; for doctorate, minimum undergraduate GPA of 2.75, 3.0 graduate. Additional exam requirements/recommendations for international students: Required—TOEFL, TWE. *Application deadline:* For fall admission, 3/1 priority date for domestic students, 3/1 priority date for international students. Applications are processed on a rolling basis. Application fee: $35. Electronic applications accepted. Tuition, area resident: Full-time $9,346. International tuition: $19,924 full-time. Full-time tuition and fees vary according to course level and campus/location. *Financial support:* In 2003–04, 22 fellowships with full tuition reimbursements (averaging $16,813 per year), 3 research assistantships with full tuition reimbursements (averaging $16,813 per year), 17 teaching assistantships with full tuition reimbursements (averaging $18,934 per year) were awarded. Federal Work-Study, tuition waivers (full), and unspecified assistantships also available. Financial award application deadline: 3/1. *Unit head:* Dr. Chris Makaroff, Chair, 513-529-2813. *Application contact:* Dr. Michael Crowder, Director of Graduate Studies, 513-529-2813, Fax: 513-529-5715, E-mail: chemistry@muohio.edu.

Michigan State University, Graduate School, College of Natural Science, Department of Chemistry, East Lansing, MI 48824. Offers chemical physics (PhD); chemistry (MS, PhD); chemistry-environmental toxicology (PhD); computational chemistry (MS). *Faculty:* 33 full-time (4 women). *Students:* 205 full-time (93 women), 6 part-time (3 women); includes 5 minority (2 African Americans, 1 American Indian/Alaska Native, 2 Hispanic Americans), 132 international. Average age 27. 192 applicants, 50% accepted. In 2003, 13 master's, 18 doctorates awarded. *Degree requirements:* For master's, thesis optional; for doctorate, thesis/dissertation, oral defense of dissertation, comprehensive exam. *Entrance requirements:* For master's, GRE General Test, bachelor's degree in chemistry, coursework in chemistry, physics, and calculus, 3 letters of recommendation; for doctorate, GRE General Test, minimum GPA of 3.0; bachelor's or master's degree in chemistry, coursework in chemistry, physics, and calculus; 3 letters of recommendation. Additional exam requirements/recommendations for international students: Required—TOEFL (minimum score 550 paper-based; 213 computer-based), Michigan State University ELT (85), Michigan ELAB (83). *Application deadline:* For fall admission, 12/23 for domestic students. Application fee: $50. Electronic applications accepted. *Expenses:* Tuition, state resident: part-time $291 per hour. Tuition, nonresident: part-time $589 per hour. *Financial support:* In 2003–04, 34 fellowships with tuition reimbursements (averaging $2,720 per year), 95 research assistantships with tuition reimbursements (averaging $14,460 per year), 118 teaching assistantships (averaging $14,354 per year) were awarded. Financial award applicants required to submit FAFSA. *Faculty research:* Analytical chemistry, inorganic and organic chemistry, nuclear chemistry, physical chemistry, theoretical and computational chemistry. Total annual research expenditures: $8.7 million. *Unit head:* Dr. John L. McCracken, Chairperson, 517-355-9715 Ext. 092, Fax: 517-353-1793, E-mail: chemdept@cem.msu.edu. *Application contact:* Dr. Gregory L. Baker, Director of Admissions, 517-355-9715 Ext. 343, Fax: 517-353-1793, E-mail: gradoff@cem.msu.edu.

Michigan Technological University, Graduate School, College of Sciences and Arts, Department of Chemistry, Houghton, MI 49931-1295. Offers MS, PhD. Part-time programs available. *Faculty:* 16 full-time (3 women). *Students:* 30 full-time (15 women), 3 part-time (1 woman), 27 international. Average age 30. 66 applicants, 23% accepted, 7 enrolled. In 2003, 2 master's, 2 doctorates awarded. *Degree requirements:* For master's, comprehensive exam, registration; for doctorate, thesis/dissertation, comprehensive exam, registration. *Entrance requirements:* Additional exam requirements/recommendations for international students: Required—TOEFL. *Application deadline:* For fall admission, 3/15 for domestic students. Applications are processed on a rolling basis. Application fee: $40 ($45 for international students). Electronic applications accepted. Tuition, nonresident: full-time $9,552; part-time $398 per credit. Required fees: $768. *Financial support:* In 2003–04, 2 fellowships with full tuition reimbursements (averaging $13,500 per year), 2 research assistantships with full tuition reimbursements (averaging $8,950 per year), 26 teaching assistantships with full tuition reimbursements (averaging $8,950 per year) were awarded. Career-related internships or fieldwork, Federal Work-Study, institutionally sponsored loans, scholarships/grants, traineeships, unspecified assistantships, and co-op also available. Support available to part-time students. Financial award application deadline: 3/1; financial award applicants required to submit FAFSA. *Faculty research:* Physical chemistry, inorganic chemistry, organic chemistry, polymer chemistry, analytical chemistry, biochemistry. Total annual research expenditures: $186,051. *Unit head:* Dr. Pushpalatha Murthy, Chair, 906-487-2094, Fax: 906-487-2061, E-mail: ppmurthy@mtu.edu. *Application contact:* Celine Grace, Office Assistant 5, 906-487-2048, Fax: 906-487-2061.

Announcement: The Department of Chemistry offers graduate programs leading to the Master of Science (MS) and Doctor of Philosophy (PhD) degrees in chemistry. Students work with faculty mentors to conduct and publish research in diverse fields of chemistry. The department maintains modern instrumentation and computing facilities, which are available to all graduate students. Multidisciplinary work is encouraged and opportunities for collaboration exist across the MTU campus.

See in-depth description on page 125.

Middle Tennessee State University, College of Graduate Studies, College of Basic and Applied Sciences, Department of Chemistry, Murfreesboro, TN 37132. Offers chemistry (MS, DA); natural science (MS). *Faculty:* 24. *Students:* Average age 33. 5 applicants, 100% accepted. In 2003, 3 master's, 1 doctorate awarded. *Degree requirements:* For master's, one foreign language, thesis, comprehensive exam; for doctorate, thesis/dissertation, comprehensive exam. *Entrance requirements:* For master's and doctorate, GRE General Test. Additional exam requirements/recommendations for international students: Required—TOEFL (minimum score 525 paper-based; 195 computer-based). *Application deadline:* For fall admission, 8/1 for domestic students. Applications are processed on a rolling basis. Application fee: $25. Electronic applications accepted. *Expenses:* Tuition, state resident: full-time $4,206. Tuition, nonresident: full-time $12,138. *Financial support:* In 2003–04, 17 students received support; teaching assistantships, institutionally sponsored loans available. Support available to part-time students. Financial award application deadline: 5/1; financial award applicants required to submit FAFSA. *Faculty research:* Chemical education, computational chemistry and visualization, materials science and surface modifications, biochemistry, antibiotics and leukemia, environmental chemistry and toxicology. Total annual research expenditures: $21,622. *Unit head:* Dr. Earl F. Pearson, Chair, 615-898-2956, Fax: 615-898-5182, E-mail: epearson@mtsu.edu.

Minnesota State University Mankato, College of Graduate Studies, College of Science, Engineering and Technology, Department of Chemistry and Geology, Mankato, MN 56001. Offers chemistry (MA, MS). *Faculty:* 9 full-time (2 women). *Students:* Average age 27. *Degree requirements:* For master's, one foreign language, thesis or alternative, departmental qualifying exam, comprehensive exam. *Entrance requirements:* For master's, minimum GPA of 2.75 during previous 2 years. Additional exam requirements/recommendations for international students: Required—TOEFL (minimum score 550 paper-based). *Application deadline:* For fall admission, 7/9 for domestic students; for spring admission, 11/27 for domestic students. Applications are processed on a rolling basis. Application fee: $40. *Expenses:* Tuition, state resident: part-time $226 per credit hour. Tuition, nonresident: part-time $339 per credit hour. Tuition and fees vary according to reciprocity agreements. *Financial support:* Research assistantships, teaching assistantships with full tuition reimbursements, career-related internships or fieldwork, Federal Work-Study, and institutionally sponsored loans available. Support available to part-time students. Financial award application deadline: 3/15; financial award applicants required to submit FAFSA. *Unit head:* Jeff Pribyl, Chairperson, 507-389-1963. *Application contact:* Joni Roberts, Admissions Coordinator, 507-389-5244, Fax: 507-389-5974, E-mail: grad@mankato.msus.edu.

Mississippi College, Graduate School, College of Arts and Sciences, Program in Combined Sciences, Department of Chemistry, Clinton, MS 39058. Offers MCS.

Mississippi State University, College of Arts and Sciences, Department of Chemistry, Mississippi State, MS 39762. Offers MS, PhD. *Faculty:* 16 full-time (3 women). *Students:* 30 full-time (9 women), 4 part-time (2 women), 27 international. Average age 30. 74 applicants, 14% accepted, 4 enrolled. In 2003, 3 degrees awarded. Terminal master's awarded for partial completion of doctoral program. *Degree requirements:* For master's and doctorate, thesis/dissertation, comprehensive oral or written exam. *Entrance requirements:* For master's and doctorate, minimum GPA of 2.75. Additional exam requirements/recommendations for international students: Required—TOEFL. *Application deadline:* For fall admission, 7/1 for domestic students; for spring admission, 11/1 for domestic students. Applications are processed on a rolling basis. Application fee: $25 for international students. *Expenses:* Tuition, state resident: full-time $3,874; part-time $215 per hour. Tuition, nonresident: full-time $8,780; part-time $488 per hour. International tuition: $9,105 full-time. Tuition and fees vary according to course load. *Financial support:* In 2003–04, 5 research assistantships with full tuition reimbursements (averaging $12,221 per year), 20 teaching assistantships with full tuition reimbursements (averaging $11,427 per year) were awarded. Federal Work-Study, institutionally sponsored loans, scholarships/grants, and unspecified assistantships also available. Financial award applicants required to submit FAFSA. *Faculty research:* Spectroscopy, fluorometry, NMR, organic and inorganic synthesis, electrochemistry. Total annual research expenditures: $1.2 million. *Unit head:* Dr. Keith T. Mead, Head, 662-325-3584, Fax: 662-325-1618, E-mail: kmead@ra.msstate.edu. *Application contact:* Diane D. Wolfe, Director of Admissions, 662-325-2224, Fax: 662-325-7360, E-mail: admit@admissions.msstate.edu.

Montana State University–Bozeman, College of Graduate Studies, College of Letters and Science, Department of Chemistry and Biochemistry, Bozeman, MT 59717. Offers biochemistry (MS, PhD); chemistry (MS, PhD). Part-time programs available. *Faculty:* 15 full-time (3 women), 17 part-time/adjunct (10 women). *Students:* 1 (woman) full-time, 50 part-time (12 women), 8 international. Average age 28. 22 applicants, 95% accepted, 15 enrolled. In 2003, 7 master's, 6 doctorates awarded. *Degree requirements:* For master's, thesis (for some programs), comprehensive exam, registration; for doctorate, thesis/dissertation, comprehensive exam, registration. *Entrance requirements:* For master's and doctorate, GRE General Test. Additional exam requirements/recommendations for international students: Required—TOEFL (minimum score 550 paper-based; 213 computer-based). *Application deadline:* For fall admission, 7/15 priority date for domestic students, 5/15 priority date for international students; for spring admission, 12/1 priority date for domestic students, 10/1 priority date for international students. Applications are processed on a rolling basis. Application fee: $50. Electronic applications accepted. *Expenses:* Tuition, state resident: full-time $3,907; part-time $163 per credit. Tuition, nonresident: full-time $12,383; part-time $516 per credit. Required fees: $890; $445 per term. Tuition and fees vary according to course load and program. *Financial support:* In 2003–04, 50 students received support, including 29 research assistantships with full tuition reimbursements available (averaging $18,500 per year), 21 teaching assistantships with full tuition reimbursements available (averaging $18,000 per year); health care benefits and unspecified assistantships also available. Financial award application deadline: 3/1; financial award applicants required to submit FAFSA. *Faculty research:* Natural products synthesis, bio-and nano-materials chemistry, gas-phase and gas surface reaction dynamics, mass spectrometry, enzyme structure and mechanism. Total annual research expenditures: $4.6 million. *Unit head:* Dr. Paul Grieco, Head, 406-994-4801, Fax: 406-994-5407, E-mail: grieco@chemistry.montana.edu.

Montclair State University, The Graduate School, College of Science and Mathematics, Department of Chemistry and Biochemistry, Upper Montclair, NJ 07043-1624. Offers chemistry (MS), including biochemistry. Part-time and evening/weekend programs available. *Faculty:* 11 full-time (2 women). *Students:* 3 full-time (0 women), 15 part-time (6 women); includes 3 minority (1 African American, 1 Asian American or Pacific Islander, 1 Hispanic American), 2 international. 13 applicants, 69% accepted, 7 enrolled. In 2003, 18 degrees awarded. *Degree requirements:* For master's, comprehensive exam. *Entrance requirements:* For master's, GRE General Test, 24 undergraduate credits in chemistry, 2 letters of recommendation. Additional exam requirements/recommendations for international students: Required—TOEFL (minimum score 550 paper-based; 213 computer-based). *Application deadline:* Applications are processed on a rolling basis. Application fee: $60. Electronic applications accepted. *Expenses:* Tuition, state resident: full-time $8,771; part-time $323 per credit. Tuition, nonresident: full-time $10,365; part-time $470 per credit. Required fees: $42 per credit. Tuition and fees vary according to degree level and program. *Financial support:* In 2003–04, 3 research assistantships with full tuition reimbursements (averaging $5,000 per year) were awarded; Federal Work-Study, scholarships/grants, and unspecified assistantships also available. Support available to part-time students. Financial award application deadline: 3/1; financial award applicants required to submit FAFSA. *Unit head:* Dr. Marc Kasner, Chair, 973-655-7121. *Application contact:* Dr. Mark Whitener, Adviser, 973-655-7166, E-mail: whitenerm@mail.montclair.edu.

Morgan State University, School of Graduate Studies, School of Computer, Mathematical, and Natural Sciences, Department of Biology, Interdisciplinary Program in Science, Baltimore, MD 21251. Offers science (MS), including biology, chemistry, physics. *Students:* 14; includes 11 minority (all African Americans), 3 international. In 2003, 2 degrees awarded. *Degree requirements:* For master's, thesis, comprehensive exam. *Entrance requirements:* For master's, GRE, minimum GPA of 2.5. Additional exam requirements/recommendations for international students: Required—TOEFL (minimum score 550 paper-based; 213 computer-based). *Application deadline:* For fall admission, 2/1 for domestic students; for spring admission, 10/1 for domestic students. Applications are processed on a rolling basis. Application fee: $0. *Expenses:* Tuition, state resident: part-time $215 per credit hour. Tuition, nonresident: part-time $409 per credit hour. Required fees: $48 per credit hour. *Application contact:* Dr. James E. Waller, Admissions and Programs Officer, 443-885-3185, Fax: 443-885-8226, E-mail: jwaller@moac.morgan.edu.

Mount Allison University, Faculty of Science, Department of Chemistry, Sackville, NB E4L 1E4, Canada. Offers M Sc. *Degree requirements:* For master's, thesis. *Entrance requirements:* For master's, honors degree in chemistry. *Faculty research:* Biophysical chemistry of model biomembranes, organic synthesis, fast-reaction kinetics, physical chemistry of micelles.

Murray State University, College of Science, Engineering and Technology, Department of Chemistry, Murray, KY 42071-0009. Offers MAT, MS. Part-time programs available. *Degree requirements:* For master's, thesis (for some programs). *Entrance requirements:* For master's, GRE General Test. Additional exam requirements/recommendations for international students: Required—TOEFL.

New Jersey Institute of Technology, Office of Graduate Studies, College of Science and Liberal Arts, Department of Chemistry and Environmental Science, Program in Chemistry, Newark, NJ 07102. Offers MS, PhD. Part-time and evening/weekend programs available. *Students:* 7 full-time (4 women), 9 part-time (3 women); includes 7 minority (3 African Americans, 4 Asian Americans or Pacific Islanders), 5 international. Average age 32. 42 applicants, 33% accepted, 3 enrolled. In 2003, 2 degrees awarded. *Degree requirements:* For doctorate, thesis/dissertation. *Entrance requirements:* For master's, GRE General Test; for doctorate, GRE General Test, minimum graduate GPA of 3.5. *Application deadline:* For fall admission, 6/5 for domestic students; for spring admission, 10/15 for domestic students. Applications are processed on a rolling basis. Application fee: $50. Electronic applications accepted. *Expenses:* Tuition, state resident: full-time $9,620; part-time $520 per credit. Tuition, nonresident: full-time $13,542; part-time $715 per credit. Tuition and fees vary according to course load. *Financial support:* Fellowships with full and partial tuition reimbursements, research assistantships with full and partial tuition reimbursements, teaching assistantships with full and partial tuition reimbursements, career-related internships or fieldwork, Federal Work-Study, institutionally sponsored loans, and unspecified assistantships available. Financial award application deadline: 3/15. *Faculty research:* Medical instrumentation, prosthesis design, biodegradation of hazardous waste, orthopedic biomechanics, image processing. *Application contact:* Kathryn Kelly, Director of Admissions, 973-596-3300, Fax: 973-596-3461, E-mail: admissions@njit.edu.

New Mexico Highlands University, Graduate Studies, College of Arts and Sciences, Department of Natural Sciences, Las Vegas, NM 87701. Offers applied chemistry (MS); biology (MS); environmental science and management (MS). Part-time programs available. *Faculty:* 11 full-time (3 women), 6 part-time/adjunct (2 women). *Students:* 21 full-time (9 women), 12 part-time (7 women). Average age 30. 30 applicants, 70% accepted, 11 enrolled. In 2003, 5 degrees awarded. *Degree requirements:* For master's, thesis, comprehensive exam, registration. *Entrance requirements:* For master's, minimum undergraduate GPA of 3.0. Additional exam requirements/recommendations for international students: Required—TOEFL (minimum score 540 paper-based; 207 computer-based). *Application deadline:* For fall admission, 8/1 for domestic students. Applications are processed on a rolling basis. Application fee: $15. *Expenses:* Tuition, state resident: full-time $2,328; part-time $97 per hour. Tuition, nonresident: full-time $9,672. One-time fee: $50 full-time; $20 part-time. *Financial support:* In 2003–04, 13 students received support, including 13 teaching assistantships (averaging $11,500 per year); research assistantships with full and partial tuition reimbursements available, Federal Work-Study, institutionally sponsored loans, scholarships/grants, and unspecified assistantships also available. Support available to part-time students. Financial award application deadline: 3/1. *Unit head:* Dr. Ken Bentson, Director. *Application contact:* Dr. Linda S. LaGrange, Dean of Graduate Studies, 505-454-3194, Fax: 505-454-3558, E-mail: lagrange_l@nmhu.edu.

New Mexico Institute of Mining and Technology, Graduate Studies, Department of Chemistry, Socorro, NM 87801. Offers biochemistry (MS); chemistry (MS); environmental chemistry (PhD); explosives technology and atmospheric chemistry (PhD). Part-time programs available.

Chemistry

New Mexico Institute of Mining and Technology (continued)

Faculty: 9 full-time (1 woman), 4 part-time/adjunct (1 woman). *Students:* 14 full-time (6 women), 11 international. Average age 28. 20 applicants, 5 enrolled. In 2003, 1 degree awarded. *Degree requirements:* For master's and doctorate, thesis/dissertation. *Entrance requirements:* For master's, GRE General Test; for doctorate, GRE General Test, GRE Subject Test. Additional exam requirements/recommendations for international students: Required—TOEFL (minimum score 540 paper-based; 207 computer-based). *Application deadline:* For fall admission, 3/1 for domestic students; for spring admission, 6/1 priority date for domestic students. Applications are processed on a rolling basis. Application fee: $16 ($30 for international students). Electronic applications accepted. *Expenses:* Tuition, state resident: full-time $2,276; part-time $126 per credit. Tuition, nonresident: full-time $9,170; part-time $509 per credit. Required fees: $924; $27 per credit. $214 per term. Part-time tuition and fees vary according to course load. *Financial support:* In 2003–04, 6 research assistantships (averaging $5,492 per year), 13 teaching assistantships with full and partial tuition reimbursements (averaging $10,384 per year) were awarded. Fellowships, Federal Work-Study, institutionally sponsored loans, and unspecified assistantships also available. Financial award application deadline: 3/1; financial award applicants required to submit CSS PROFILE or FAFSA. *Faculty research:* Organic, analytical, environmental, and explosives chemistry. *Unit head:* Dr. Tanja Pietrass, Chairman, 505-835-5586, Fax: 505-835-5364, E-mail: tanja@nmt.edu. *Application contact:* Dr. David B. Johnson, Dean of Graduate Studies, 505-835-5513, Fax: 505-835-5476, E-mail: graduate@nmt.edu.

New Mexico State University, Graduate School, College of Arts and Sciences, Department of Chemistry and Biochemistry, Las Cruces, NM 88003-8001. Offers MS, PhD. Part-time programs available. *Faculty:* 19 full-time (1 woman), 2 part-time/adjunct (0 women). *Students:* 48 full-time (13 women), 4 part-time (1 woman); includes 7 minority (1 American Indian/Alaska Native, 6 Hispanic Americans), 33 international. Average age 29. 55 applicants, 55% accepted, 8 enrolled. In 2003, 1 master's, 3 doctorates awarded. *Degree requirements:* For master's and doctorate, thesis/dissertation. *Entrance requirements:* For master's and doctorate, GRE, BS in chemistry or biochemistry, minimum GPA of 3.0. Additional exam requirements/recommendations for international students: Required—TOEFL. *Application deadline:* For fall admission, 7/1 for domestic students; for spring admission, 11/1 for domestic students. Applications are processed on a rolling basis. Application fee: $30 ($50 for international students). *Expenses:* Tuition, state resident: full-time $2,670; part-time $151 per credit. Tuition, nonresident: full-time $10,596; part-time $481 per credit. Required fees: $954. *Financial support:* In 2003–04, 15 research assistantships, 31 teaching assistantships were awarded. Fellowships, career-related internships or fieldwork and Federal Work-Study also available. Support available to part-time students. Financial award application deadline: 3/1. *Faculty research:* Clays, surfaces, and water structure; electroanalytical and environmental chemistry; organometallic synthesis and organobiomimetics; molecular genetics and enzymology of stress; spectroscopy and reaction kinetics. *Unit head:* Dr. Aravamudan Gopalan, Head, 505-646-5877, Fax: 505-646-2649, E-mail: agopalan@nmsu.edu. *Application contact:* Dr. James Herndon, Associate Professor, Chemistry, 505-646-2738, Fax: 505-646-2649.

New York University, Graduate School of Arts and Science, Department of Chemistry, New York, NY 10012-1019. Offers MS, PhD. *Faculty:* 23 full-time (1 woman), 3 part-time/adjunct. *Students:* 80 full-time (28 women), 4 part-time (1 woman); includes 7 minority (1 African American, 5 Asian Americans or Pacific Islanders, 1 Hispanic American), 60 international. Average age 29. 196 applicants, 21% accepted. In 2003, 8 master's, 16 doctorates awarded. *Degree requirements:* For master's, thesis or alternative; for doctorate, one foreign language, thesis/dissertation. *Entrance requirements:* For master's and doctorate, GRE General Test, GRE Subject Test. Additional exam requirements/recommendations for international students: Required—TOEFL, TSE. *Application deadline:* For fall admission, 1/4 for domestic students. Application fee: $75. *Expenses:* Tuition: Full-time $22,056; part-time $919 per credit. Required fees: $1,664; $49 per credit. Tuition and fees vary according to course load and program. *Financial support:* Fellowships with tuition reimbursements, research assistantships with tuition reimbursements, teaching assistantships with tuition reimbursements, institutionally sponsored loans and teaching fellowships available. Financial award application deadline: 1/4; financial award applicants required to submit FAFSA. *Faculty research:* Biomolecular chemistry, theoretical and computational chemistry, physical chemistry, nanotechnology, bio-organic chemistry. *Unit head:* Nicholas Geacintov, Chairman, 212-998-8400, Fax: 212-995-4203. *Application contact:* Mark Tuckerman, Director of Graduate Studies, 212-998-8400, Fax: 212-260-7905, E-mail: grad.chem@nyu.edu.

See in-depth description on page 129.

North Carolina Agricultural and Technical State University, Graduate School, College of Arts and Sciences, Department of Chemistry, Greensboro, NC 27411. Offers MS. Part-time and evening/weekend programs available. *Degree requirements:* For master's, thesis or alternative, qualifying exam, comprehensive exam. *Entrance requirements:* For master's, GRE General Test, minimum GPA of 3.0. *Faculty research:* Tobacco pesticides.

North Carolina Central University, Division of Academic Affairs, College of Arts and Sciences, Department of Chemistry, Durham, NC 27707-3129. Offers MS. *Faculty:* 7 full-time (1 woman), 4 part-time/adjunct (1 woman). *Students:* 6 full-time (4 women), 5 part-time (2 women); all minorities (10 African Americans, 1 Asian American or Pacific Islander). Average age 30. 4 applicants, 100% accepted, 3 enrolled. In 2003, 1 degree awarded. *Degree requirements:* For master's, one foreign language, thesis, comprehensive exam. *Entrance requirements:* For master's, GRE, minimum GPA of 3.0 in major, 2.5 overall. Additional exam requirements/recommendations for international students: Required—TOEFL. *Application deadline:* For fall admission, 8/1 for domestic students. Application fee: $30. *Expenses:* Tuition, state resident: full-time $3,366. Tuition, nonresident: full-time $12,872. *Financial support:* Career-related internships or fieldwork, Federal Work-Study, institutionally sponsored loans, and unspecified assistantships available. Support available to part-time students. Financial award application deadline: 5/1; financial award applicants required to submit FAFSA. *Unit head:* Dr. Wendell W. Wilkerson, Chairperson, 919-560-6462, Fax: 919-560-5135, E-mail: wwilkerson@wpo.nccu.edu. *Application contact:* Dr. Mattie Moss, Dean, 919-560-6368, Fax: 919-530-5361, E-mail: mmoss@wpo.nccu.edu.

North Carolina State University, Graduate School, College of Physical and Mathematical Sciences, Department of Chemistry, Raleigh, NC 27695. Offers MCH, MS, PhD. Part-time programs available. *Faculty:* 32 full-time (5 women), 15 part-time/adjunct (2 women). *Students:* 114 full-time (50 women), 11 part-time (3 women); includes 24 minority (15 African Americans, 8 Asian Americans or Pacific Islanders, 1 Hispanic American), 36 international. Average age 29. 203 applicants, 29% accepted. In 2003, 5 master's, 11 doctorates awarded. Terminal master's awarded for partial completion of doctoral program. *Degree requirements:* For master's, thesis (for some programs); for doctorate, thesis/dissertation. *Entrance requirements:* For master's and doctorate, GRE General Test, minimum GPA of 3.0. *Application deadline:* For fall admission, 6/25 for domestic students, 3/1 for international students; for spring admission, 11/25 for domestic students, 7/15 for international students. Applications are processed on a rolling basis. Application fee: $45. *Expenses:* Tuition, state resident: part-time $396 per hour. Tuition, nonresident: part-time $1,895 per hour. *Financial support:* In 2003–04, 5 fellowships with tuition reimbursements (averaging $8,371 per year), 105 research assistantships with tuition reimbursements (averaging $6,709 per year) were awarded. Teaching assistantships with tuition reimbursements, career-related internships or fieldwork also available. Financial award application deadline: 3/1. *Faculty research:* Biological chemistry, electrochemistry, organic/inorganic materials, natural products, organometallics. Total annual research expenditures: $4.5 million. *Unit head:* Dr. Bruce M. Novak, Head, 919-515-4563, Fax: 919-515-5079, E-mail: bruce_novak@ncsu.edu. *Application contact:* Dr. Edmond F. Bowden, Director of Graduate Programs, 919-515-7069, Fax: 919-515-5079, E-mail: gradinfo@chemdept.ncsu.edu.

North Dakota State University, The Graduate School, College of Science and Mathematics, Department of Chemistry, Fargo, ND 58105. Offers biochemistry (MS, PhD); chemistry (MS, PhD). *Faculty:* 14 full-time (0 women), 1 part-time/adjunct (0 women). *Students:* 32 full-time (9 women), 16 international. Average age 24. 40 applicants, 53% accepted, 8 enrolled. In 2003, 1 master's awarded, leading to business/industry 100%, 5 doctorates awarded, leading to business/industry 100%. Terminal master's awarded for partial completion of doctoral program. *Degree requirements:* For master's and doctorate, thesis/dissertation. *Entrance requirements:* For master's and doctorate, GRE. Additional exam requirements/recommendations for international students: Required—TOEFL (minimum score 600 paper-based). *Application deadline:* For fall admission, 6/1 for domestic students. Applications are processed on a rolling basis. Application fee: $35 ($50 for international students). Tuition, nonresident: full-time $4,071. Required fees: $493. *Financial support:* In 2003–04, 3 fellowships with tuition reimbursements (averaging $19,000 per year), 15 research assistantships with tuition reimbursements (averaging $19,000 per year), 17 teaching assistantships with tuition reimbursements (averaging $19,000 per year) were awarded. Federal Work-Study, institutionally sponsored loans, and scholarships/grants also available. Financial award application deadline: 4/15. *Faculty research:* Analytical, syntheticorganic, inorganic, physical, and theoretical chemistry. Total annual research expenditures: $1.6 million. *Unit head:* Dr. John Hershberger, Chair, 701-231-8225, Fax: 701-231-8831, E-mail: john.hershberger@ndsu.nodak.edu. *Application contact:* Dr. Seth Rasmussen, Chair, Graduate Admissions, 701-231-8747, Fax: 701-231-8831, E-mail: seth.rasmussen@ndsu.nodak.edu.

Northeastern Illinois University, Graduate College, College of Arts and Sciences, Department of Chemistry, Program in Chemistry, Chicago, IL 60625-4699. Offers MS. Part-time and evening/weekend programs available. *Degree requirements:* For master's, final exam or thesis. *Entrance requirements:* For master's, minimum B average 2 semesters chemistry; 2 semesters calculus, organic chemistry, physical chemistry, and physics; 1 semester analytic chemistry; minimum GPA 2.75. *Faculty research:* Liquid chromatographic separation of pharmaceuticals, Diels-Alder reaction products, organogermanium chemistry, mass spectroscopy.

Northeastern University, College of Arts and Sciences, Department of Chemistry and Chemical Biology, Boston, MA 02115-5096. Offers analytical chemistry (PhD); chemistry (MS, PhD); inorganic chemistry (PhD); organic chemistry (PhD); physical chemistry (PhD). Part-time and evening/weekend programs available. *Faculty:* 17 full-time (2 women), 3 part-time/adjunct (0 women). *Students:* 46 full-time (23 women), 29 part-time (17 women). Average age 28. 113 applicants, 37% accepted. In 2003, 12 master's, 10 doctorates awarded. Terminal master's awarded for partial completion of doctoral program. *Degree requirements:* For master's, thesis (for some programs); for doctorate, thesis/dissertation, qualifying exam in specialty area. *Entrance requirements:* Additional exam requirements/recommendations for international students: Required—TOEFL. *Application deadline:* For fall admission, 4/15 for domestic students. Applications are processed on a rolling basis. Application fee: $50. Electronic applications accepted. *Expenses:* Tuition: Part-time $790 per credit hour. Tuition and fees vary according to course load and program. *Financial support:* In 2003–04, 27 research assistantships with tuition reimbursements (averaging $16,000 per year) were awarded; fellowships with tuition reimbursements, teaching assistantships with tuition reimbursements, career-related internships or fieldwork, tuition waivers (partial), and unspecified assistantships also available. Financial award application deadline: 4/15; financial award applicants required to submit FAFSA. *Faculty research:* Electron transfer, theoretical chemical physics, analytical biotechnology, mass spectrometry, materials chemistry. Total annual research expenditures: $250,000. *Unit head:* Dr. Graham Jones, Chairman, 617-373-2822, Fax: 617-373-8795, E-mail: chemistry-grad-info@neu.edu. *Application contact:* Dr. Pam Mabrouk, Chair, Graduate Admissions Committee, 617-373-2383, Fax: 617-373-8795, E-mail: chemistry-grad-info@neu.edu.

See in-depth description on page 133.

Northern Arizona University, Graduate College, College of Arts and Sciences, Department of Chemistry, Flagstaff, AZ 86011. Offers MS. Part-time programs available. *Students:* 13 full-time (7 women), 2 part-time (1 woman); includes 5 minority (2 American Indian/Alaska Native, 2 Asian Americans or Pacific Islanders, 1 Hispanic American). Average age 27. 13 applicants, 31% accepted. In 2003, 6 degrees awarded. *Degree requirements:* For master's, thesis. *Application deadline:* For fall admission, 3/1 for domestic students. Applications are processed on a rolling basis. Application fee: $45. *Expenses:* Tuition, state resident: full-time $5,103. Tuition, nonresident: full-time $12,623. *Financial support:* In 2003–04, 9 research assistantships were awarded; fellowships, teaching assistantships, Federal Work-Study and tuition waivers (full and partial) also available. *Faculty research:* Biochemistry of exercise, organic and inorganic mechanism studies, inhibition of ice mutation, polymer separation. Total annual research expenditures: $261,191. *Unit head:* Dr. John Wettaw, Interim Chair, 928-523-3008, E-mail: chem@sapphire.ucc.nau.edu. *Application contact:* Information Contact.

Northern Illinois University, Graduate School, College of Liberal Arts and Sciences, Department of Chemistry and Biochemistry, De Kalb, IL 60115-2854. Offers chemistry (MS, PhD). *Faculty:* 16 full-time (1 woman), 3 part-time/adjunct (1 woman). *Students:* 45 full-time (20 women), 6 part-time (2 women); includes 5 minority (2 African Americans, 2 Asian Americans or Pacific Islanders, 1 Hispanic American), 18 international. Average age 27. 69 applicants, 36% accepted, 11 enrolled. In 2003, 3 master's, 5 doctorates awarded. Terminal master's awarded for partial completion of doctoral program. *Degree requirements:* For master's, research seminar, thesis optional; for doctorate, one foreign language, thesis/dissertation, candidacy exam, dissertation defense, research seminar. *Entrance requirements:* For master's, GRE General Test, bachelor's degree in mathematics or science, minimum GPA of 2.75; for doctorate, GRE General Test, bachelor's degree in mathematics or science; minimum undergraduate GPA of 2.75, 3.2 graduate. Additional exam requirements/recommendations for international students: Required—TOEFL (minimum score 550 paper-based; 213 computer-based). *Application deadline:* For fall admission, 6/1 for domestic students, 5/1 for international students; for spring admission, 11/1 for domestic students, 10/1 for international students. Applications are processed on a rolling basis. Application fee: $30. Electronic applications accepted. *Expenses:* Tuition, state resident: full-time $3,968; part-time $165 per credit hour. Tuition, nonresident: full-time $7,936; part-time $330 per credit hour. Required fees: $1,255; $52 per credit hour. *Financial support:* In 2003–04, 6 research assistantships with full tuition reimbursements, 33 teaching assistantships with full tuition reimbursements were awarded. Fellowships with full tuition reimbursements, career-related internships or fieldwork, Federal Work-Study, scholarships/grants, tuition waivers (full), and unspecified assistantships also available. Support available to part-time students. Financial award applicants required to submit FAFSA. *Unit head:* Dr. James Erman, Chair, 815-753-1181, Fax: 815-753-4802. *Application contact:* Dr. Jon Carnahan, Director, Graduate Studies, 815-753-6879.

Northern Michigan University, College of Graduate Studies, College of Arts and Sciences, Department of Chemistry, Marquette, MI 49855-5301. Offers biochemistry (MS); chemistry (MS). Part-time programs available. *Degree requirements:* For master's, thesis. *Entrance requirements:* For master's, GRE General Test, minimum GPA of 3.0.

Northwestern University, The Graduate School, Judd A. and Marjorie Weinberg College of Arts and Sciences, Department of Chemistry, Evanston, IL 60208. Offers PhD. Admissions and degrees offered through The Graduate School. *Degree requirements:* For doctorate, thesis/dissertation. *Entrance requirements:* For doctorate, GRE General Test, GRE Subject Test (chemistry). Additional exam requirements/recommendations for international students: Required—TOEFL, TSE. Electronic applications accepted. *Faculty research:* Inorganic, organic, physical, environmental, materials, and chemistry of life processes.

Oakland University, Graduate Study and Lifelong Learning, College of Arts and Sciences, Department of Chemistry, Rochester, MI 48309-4401. Offers chemistry (MS, PhD); health and environmental chemistry (PhD). *Faculty:* 19 full-time (6 women). *Students:* 6 full-time (2 women), 22 part-time (8 women); includes 3 minority (all Asian Americans or Pacific Islanders), 5 international. Average age 29. 15 applicants, 100% accepted, 9 enrolled. In 2003, 6 master's, 2 doctorates awarded. *Degree requirements:* For master's and doctorate, thesis/dissertation. *Entrance requirements:* For master's, minimum GPA of 3.0 for unconditional admission; for doctorate, GRE Subject Test, minimum GPA of 3.0 for unconditional admission.

Application deadline: For fall admission, 7/15 for domestic students; for winter admission, 12/1 for domestic students; for spring admission, 3/15 for domestic students. Applications are processed on a rolling basis. Application fee: $30. Electronic applications accepted. *Expenses:* Tuition, state resident: full-time $7,032; part-time $293 per credit. Tuition, nonresident: full-time $12,804; part-time $534 per credit. *Financial support:* Federal Work-Study, institutionally sponsored loans, and tuition waivers (full) available. Financial award application deadline: 3/1; financial award applicants required to submit FAFSA. *Faculty research:* C-3 nucleic acid radicals, radiation damage to DNA multidimensional gas chromotograph for toxological analyses, research excellence fund. Total annual research expenditures: $472,159. *Unit head:* Dr. Mark W. Severson, Chair, 248-370-2327, Fax: 248-370-2321, E-mail: severson@oakland.edu. *Application contact:* Dr. Kathleen W. Moore, Coordinator, 248-370-2338, Fax: 248-370-2321, E-mail: kmoore@oakland.edu.

The Ohio State University, Graduate School, College of Mathematical and Physical Sciences, Department of Chemistry, Columbus, OH 43210. Offers MS, PhD. *Faculty:* 39. *Students:* 200 full-time (72 women), 6 part-time (2 women); includes 14 minority (3 African Americans, 4 Asian Americans or Pacific Islanders, 7 Hispanic Americans), 90 international. 683 applicants, 18% accepted. In 2003, 14 master's, 27 doctorates awarded. *Degree requirements:* For master's, thesis optional; for doctorate, thesis/dissertation. *Entrance requirements:* For master's and doctorate, GRE General Test, GRE Subject Test (chemistry). Additional exam requirements/recommendations for international students: Required—TOEFL. *Application deadline:* For fall admission, 8/15 for domestic students. Applications are processed on a rolling basis. Application fee: $40 ($50 for international students). *Expenses:* Tuition, state resident: full-time $7,233. Tuition, nonresident: full-time $18,489. *Financial support:* Fellowships, research assistantships, teaching assistantships, Federal Work-Study and institutionally sponsored loans available. Support available to part-time students. *Unit head:* Dr. Prabir K. Dutta, Chairman, 614-292-4532, Fax: 614-292-1685, E-mail: dutta.2@osu.edu. *Application contact:* Dr. David J. Hart, Director, 614-292-8688, Fax: 614-292-1948, E-mail: hart.10@osu.edu.

Oklahoma State University, Graduate College, College of Arts and Sciences, Department of Chemistry, Stillwater, OK 74078. Offers MS, PhD. *Faculty:* 30 full-time (5 women). *Students:* 14 full-time (4 women), 33 part-time (11 women); includes 5 minority (1 African American, 1 American Indian/Alaska Native, 2 Asian Americans or Pacific Islanders, 1 Hispanic American), 32 international. Average age 30. 15 applicants, 93% accepted. In 2003, 2 master's, 8 doctorates awarded. *Degree requirements:* For master's and doctorate, thesis/dissertation. *Entrance requirements:* For master's, GRE, GMAT recommended, placement exam; for doctorate, GRE recommended, placement exams. Additional exam requirements/recommendations for international students: Required—TOEFL. *Application deadline:* For fall admission, 6/1 for domestic students. Applications are processed on a rolling basis. Application fee: $25 ($50 for international students). Electronic applications accepted. *Expenses:* Tuition, state resident: full-time $3,752; part-time $118 per credit hour. Tuition, nonresident: full-time $10,346; part-time $393 per credit hour. Tuition and fees vary according to course load. *Financial support:* In 2003–04, 15 research assistantships (averaging $15,876 per year), 24 teaching assistantships (averaging $16,969 per year) were awarded. Fellowships, Federal Work-Study and tuition waivers (partial) also available. Support available to part-time students. Financial award application deadline: 3/1. *Faculty research:* Materials science, surface chemistry, and nanoparticles; theoretical physical chemistry; synthetic and medicinal chemistry; bioanalytical chemistry; electromagnetic (UV, VIS, IR, Raman), mass, and x-ray spectroscopes. *Unit head:* Dr. Neil Purdie, Head, 405-744-5920, Fax: 405-744-6007, E-mail: npurdie@okstate.edu.

Old Dominion University, College of Sciences, Program in Chemistry, Norfolk, VA 23529. Offers analytical chemistry (MS); biochemistry (MS); clinical chemistry (MS); environmental chemistry (MS); organic chemistry (MS); physical chemistry (MS). Part-time and evening/weekend programs available. *Faculty:* 15 full-time (4 women). *Students:* 6 full-time (3 women), 9 part-time (5 women); includes 1 minority (Asian American or Pacific Islander), 3 international. Average age 30. 19 applicants, 74% accepted. In 2003, 2 degrees awarded. *Degree requirements:* For master's, thesis, comprehensive exam. *Entrance requirements:* For master's, GRE General Test, minimum GPA of 3.0 in major, 2.5 overall. Additional exam requirements/recommendations for international students: Required—TOEFL. *Application deadline:* For fall admission, 7/1 for domestic students; for spring admission, 11/1 for domestic students. Applications are processed on a rolling basis. Application fee: $30. *Expenses:* Tuition, state resident: part-time $235 per credit hour. Tuition, nonresident: part-time $603 per credit hour. Part-time tuition and fees vary according to campus/location. *Financial support:* In 2003–04, research assistantships with tuition reimbursements (averaging $15,000 per year), teaching assistantships with tuition reimbursements (averaging $15,000 per year) were awarded. Fellowships, career-related internships or fieldwork and scholarships/grants also available. Financial award application deadline: 2/15; financial award applicants required to submit FAFSA. *Faculty research:* Organic and trace metal biogeochemistry, materials chemistry, bioanalytical chemistry, computational chemistry. Total annual research expenditures: $854,968. *Unit head:* Dr. John R. Donat, Graduate Program Director, 757-683-4098, Fax: 757-683-4628, E-mail: chemgpd@odu.edu.

Old Dominion University, Darden College of Education, Programs in Secondary Education, Norfolk, VA 23529. Offers biology (MS Ed); chemistry (MS Ed); English (MS Ed); instructional technology (MS Ed); library science (MS Ed); mathematics (MS Ed); secondary education (MS Ed); social studies (MS Ed). *Accreditation:* NASM; NCATE. Part-time and evening/weekend programs available. Postbaccalaureate distance learning degree programs offered (minimal on-campus study). *Faculty:* 28 full-time (11 women). *Students:* 59 full-time (39 women), 158 part-time (94 women); includes 27 minority (20 African Americans, 2 Asian Americans or Pacific Islanders, 5 Hispanic Americans), 1 international. Average age 36. 44 applicants, 95% accepted. In 2003, 114 degrees awarded. *Degree requirements:* For master's, candidacy exam, thesis optional. *Entrance requirements:* For master's, GRE General Test, or MAT, PRAXIS I for master's with licensure, minimum GPA of 2.8, teaching certificate. *Application deadline:* Applications are processed on a rolling basis. Application fee: $30. Electronic applications accepted. *Expenses:* Tuition, state resident: part-time $235 per credit hour. Tuition, nonresident: part-time $603 per credit hour. Part-time tuition and fees vary according to campus/location. *Financial support:* In 2003–04, 58 students received support, including 2 research assistantships with tuition reimbursements available (averaging $6,777 per year), 3 teaching assistantships with tuition reimbursements available (averaging $5,333 per year); fellowships, career-related internships or fieldwork, Federal Work-Study, institutionally sponsored loans, scholarships/grants, and tuition waivers (partial) also available. Support available to part-time students. Financial award application deadline: 2/15; financial award applicants required to submit FAFSA. *Faculty research:* Mathematics retraining, writing project for teachers, geography teaching, reading. *Unit head:* Dr. Murray Rudisill, Graduate Program Director, 757-683-3300, Fax: 757-683-5862, E-mail: ecisgpd@odu.edu.

Oregon State University, Graduate School, College of Science, Department of Chemistry, Corvallis, OR 97331. Offers analytical chemistry (MS, PhD); chemistry (MA, MAIS); inorganic chemistry (MS, PhD); nuclear and radiation chemistry (MS, PhD); organic chemistry (MS, PhD); physical chemistry (MS, PhD). Part-time programs available. *Faculty:* 30 full-time (5 women). *Students:* 63 full-time (22 women), 1 part-time; includes 5 minority (3 Asian Americans or Pacific Islanders, 2 Hispanic Americans), 29 international. Average age 28. In 2003, 3 master's, 13 doctorates awarded. Terminal master's awarded for partial completion of doctoral program. *Degree requirements:* For master's and doctorate, one foreign language, thesis/dissertation. *Entrance requirements:* For master's and doctorate, minimum GPA of 3.0 in last 90 hours. Additional exam requirements/recommendations for international students: Required—TOEFL. *Application deadline:* For fall admission, 3/1 for domestic students. Applications are processed on a rolling basis. Application fee: $50. *Expenses:* Tuition, state resident: full-time $8,139; part-time $301 per credit. Tuition, nonresident: full-time $14,376; part-time $532 per credit. Required fees: $1,227. *Financial support:* Fellowships, research assistantships, teaching assistantships, institutionally sponsored loans available. Support available to part-time students. Financial award application deadline: 2/1. *Faculty research:* Solid state chemistry, enzyme reaction mechanisms, structure and dynamics of gas molecules, chemiluminescence, nonlinear optical spectroscopy. *Unit head:* Dr. John C. Westall, Chair, 541-737-2591, Fax: 541-737-2062, E-mail: john.westall@orst.edu. *Application contact:* Carolyn Brumley, Graduate Secretary, 541-737-6707, Fax: 541-737-2062, E-mail: carolyn.brumley@orst.edu.

Paper Science and Engineering Program, Graduate Studies and Research, College of Engineering, School of Chemical and Biomolecular Engineering, Graduate Programs, Program in Chemistry, Atlanta, GA 30318-5794. Offers MS, PhD. Part-time programs available. Terminal master's awarded for partial completion of doctoral program. *Degree requirements:* For master's, industrial experience, research project; for doctorate, thesis/dissertation. *Entrance requirements:* For master's and doctorate, GRE, minimum GPA of 3.0.

The Pennsylvania State University University Park Campus, Graduate School, Eberly College of Science, Department of Chemistry, State College, University Park, PA 16802-1503. Offers MS, PhD. *Students:* 251 full-time (92 women), 3 part-time (1 woman); includes 20 minority (6 African Americans, 10 Asian Americans or Pacific Islanders, 4 Hispanic Americans), 55 international. *Entrance requirements:* For master's and doctorate, GRE General Test. Application fee: $45. *Unit head:* Dr. Raymond L. Funk, Graduate Admissions Coordinator, 814-865-2057, E-mail: rlf8@psu.edu. *Application contact:* Dana Coval-Dinant, Graduate Student Recruiting Manager, 814-865-1383, Fax: 814-865-3314, E-mail: dmcb@psu.edu.

See in-depth description on page 135.

Pittsburg State University, Graduate School, College of Arts and Sciences, Department of Chemistry, Pittsburg, KS 66762. Offers MS. *Degree requirements:* For master's, thesis or alternative.

Polytechnic University, Brooklyn Campus, Department of Chemical Engineering, Chemistry and Materials Science, Major in Chemistry, Brooklyn, NY 11201-2990. Offers MS. Part-time and evening/weekend programs available. *Students:* 6 full-time (3 women), 9 part-time (4 women); includes 3 minority (1 African American, 2 Asian Americans or Pacific Islanders), 4 international. Average age 32. 19 applicants, 58% accepted, 7 enrolled. In 2003, 6 degrees awarded. *Degree requirements:* For master's, thesis or alternative. *Entrance requirements:* For master's, GRE General Test, GRE Subject Test. *Application deadline:* Applications are processed on a rolling basis. Application fee: $55. Electronic applications accepted. *Expenses:* Tuition: Full-time $16,416; part-time $855 per credit. Required fees: $320 per term. *Financial support:* Fellowships, research assistantships, teaching assistantships, institutionally sponsored loans available. Support available to part-time students. Financial award applicants required to submit FAFSA. *Faculty research:* Optical rotation of light by plastic films, supramolecular chemistry, unusual stereochemical opportunities, polyaniline copolymers.

Polytechnic University, Brooklyn Campus, Department of Chemical Engineering, Chemistry and Materials Science, Major in Informatics in Chemistry and Biology, Brooklyn, NY 11201-2990. Offers MS. *Students:* 1 applicant, 0% accepted, 0 enrolled. Application fee: $55. *Expenses:* Tuition: Full-time $16,416; part-time $855 per credit. Required fees: $320 per term. *Application contact:* Anthea Jeffrey, Graduate Admissions, 718-260-3200, Fax: 718-260-3624, E-mail: gradinfo@poly.edu.

Polytechnic University, Brooklyn Campus, Department of Chemical Engineering, Chemistry and Materials Science, Major in Materials Chemistry, Brooklyn, NY 11201-2990. Offers PhD. Part-time and evening/weekend programs available. *Students:* 9 full-time (4 women), 3 part-time (1 woman), 10 international. Average age 32. 6 applicants, 33% accepted, 1 enrolled. In 2003, 5 degrees awarded. *Degree requirements:* For doctorate, thesis/dissertation. *Application deadline:* Applications are processed on a rolling basis. Application fee: $55. Electronic applications accepted. *Expenses:* Tuition: Full-time $16,416; part-time $855 per credit. Required fees: $320 per term. *Financial support:* Fellowships, research assistantships, teaching assistantships, institutionally sponsored loans available. Support available to part-time students. Financial award applicants required to submit FAFSA.

Polytechnic University, Long Island Graduate Center, Graduate Programs, Department of Chemical Engineering, Chemistry and Material Science, Major in Chemistry, Melville, NY 11747. Offers MS, PhD. *Students:* Average age 32. *Degree requirements:* For doctorate, thesis/dissertation. Application fee: $55. *Expenses:* Tuition: Full-time $16,416; part-time $855 per credit. Required fees: $320 per term.

Polytechnic University, Westchester Graduate Center, Graduate Programs, Department of Chemical Engineering, Chemistry, and Materials Science, Major in Chemistry, Hawthorne, NY 10532-1507. Offers MS. *Students:* 3 full-time (2 women), 12 part-time (6 women). Average age 33. 4 applicants, 75% accepted, 0 enrolled. In 2003, 4 degrees awarded. *Application deadline:* Applications are processed on a rolling basis. Application fee: $0. Electronic applications accepted. *Expenses:* Tuition: Part-time $855 per credit. Required fees: $320 per term.

Pontifical Catholic University of Puerto Rico, College of Sciences, Department of Chemistry, Ponce, PR 00717-0777. Offers MS. Part-time and evening/weekend programs available. *Faculty:* 3 part-time/adjunct (1 woman). *Students:* 1 (woman) full-time, 17 part-time (8 women); all minorities (all Hispanic Americans) Average age 32. 6 applicants, 100% accepted, 4 enrolled. In 2003, 3 degrees awarded. *Degree requirements:* For master's, thesis. *Entrance requirements:* For master's, GRE General Test, minimum GPA of 3.0, minimum 37 credits in chemistry. *Application deadline:* For fall admission, 4/30 for domestic students. Applications are processed on a rolling basis. Application fee: $25. Electronic applications accepted. *Financial support:* Fellowships, Federal Work-Study and tuition waivers (partial) available. Support available to part-time students. Financial award application deadline: 7/15. *Unit head:* Dr. Gladys Rodriguez, Director, 787-841-2000 Ext. 1537. *Application contact:* Ana O. Bonilla, Director of Admissions, 787-841-2000 Ext. 1000, Fax: 787-840-4295.

Portland State University, Graduate Studies, College of Liberal Arts and Sciences, Department of Chemistry, Portland, OR 97207-0751. Offers MA, MS, PhD. Part-time programs available. *Faculty:* 13 full-time (2 women), 4 part-time/adjunct (3 women). *Students:* 7 full-time (3 women), 6 part-time (3 women); includes 2 minority (1 African American, 1 Asian American or Pacific Islander), 4 international. Average age 32. 7 applicants, 71% accepted, 5 enrolled. In 2003, 1 degree awarded. *Degree requirements:* For master's, one foreign language, thesis; for doctorate, one foreign language, thesis/dissertation, cumulative exams, seminar presentations. *Entrance requirements:* For master's, GRE General Test, GRE Subject Test, minimum GPA of 3.0 in upper-division course work or 2.75 overall, 2 letters of recommendation. Additional exam requirements/recommendations for international students: Required—TOEFL. *Application deadline:* For fall admission, 5/1 for domestic students; for spring admission, 11/1 for domestic students. Applications are processed on a rolling basis. Application fee: $50. *Expenses:* Tuition, state resident: full-time $6,588. Tuition, nonresident: full-time $12,060; part-time $298 per credit. Required fees: $1,041; $19 per credit. $35 per term. *Financial support:* In 2003–04, 2 research assistantships (averaging $7,822 per year), 20 teaching assistantships with tuition reimbursements (averaging $12,302 per year) were awarded. Career-related internships or fieldwork, Federal Work-Study, scholarships/grants, tuition waivers (partial), and unspecified assistantships also available. Support available to part-time students. Financial award application deadline: 3/1; financial award applicants required to submit FAFSA. *Faculty research:* Synthetic inorganic chemistry, atmospheric chemistry, organic photochemistry, enzymology, analytical chemistry. Total annual research expenditures: $451,889. *Unit head:* Dr. David W. McClure, Head, 503-725-3811, Fax: 503-725-3888, E-mail: peytond@pdx.edu. *Application contact:* Su Ikeda, Admission Secretary, 503-725-8756, Fax: 503-725-3888, E-mail: sikeda@pdx.edu.

Prairie View A&M University, Graduate School, College of Arts and Sciences, Department of Chemistry, Prairie View, TX 77446-0519. Offers MS. Part-time and evening/weekend programs available. *Faculty:* 7 full-time (0 women). *Students:* 1 full-time (0 women), 2 part-time (1 woman); all minorities (2 African Americans, 1 Asian American or Pacific Islander). Average

Chemistry

Prairie View A&M University (continued)
age 31. *Degree requirements:* For master's, thesis. *Entrance requirements:* For master's, GRE General Test. *Application deadline:* For fall admission, 4/1 for domestic students; for spring admission, 10/1 for domestic students. Applications are processed on a rolling basis. Application fee: $50. Electronic applications accepted. *Expenses:* Tuition, state resident: part-time $50 per credit hour. Tuition, nonresident: part-time $282 per credit hour. Required fees: $36 per credit hour. $51 per term. *Financial support:* In 2003–04, 8 fellowships with full tuition reimbursements (averaging $12,000 per year), 10 research assistantships (averaging $15,000 per year) were awarded. Career-related internships or fieldwork, Federal Work-Study, institutionally sponsored loans, and tuition waivers (full and partial) also available. Support available to part-time students. Financial award application deadline: 4/1; financial award applicants required to submit FAFSA. *Faculty research:* Material science, environmental characterization (surface phenomena), activation of plasminogens, polymer modifications. Total annual research expenditures: $404,215. *Unit head:* Dr. Remi R. Oki, Head, 936-857-2616, Fax: 936-857-2095, E-mail: remi_oki@pvamu.edu.

Princeton University, Graduate School, Department of Chemistry, Princeton, NJ 08544-1019. Offers chemistry (PhD); industrial chemistry (MS); physics and chemical physics (PhD); polymer sciences and materials (PhD). PhD (polymer sciences and materials) offered in conjunction with the Department of Chemical Engineering. *Faculty:* 28 full-time (3 women), 4 part-time/adjunct (1 woman). *Students:* 134 full-time (47 women); includes 8 minority (2 African Americans, 4 Asian Americans or Pacific Islanders, 2 Hispanic Americans), 65 international. 325 applicants, 23% accepted, 35 enrolled. *Median time to degree:* Doctorate–4.54 years full-time. *Degree requirements:* For doctorate, one foreign language, thesis/dissertation, cumulative and general exams. *Entrance requirements:* For master's, GRE General Test; for doctorate, GRE General Test, GRE Subject Test. Additional exam requirements/recommendations for international students: Required—TOEFL (minimum score 550 paper-based). *Application deadline:* For fall admission, 12/31 for domestic students, 12/1 for international students. Application fee: $80 ($55 for international students). Electronic applications accepted. *Expenses:* Tuition: Full-time $29,910. Required fees: $810. *Financial support:* Fellowships with full tuition reimbursements, research assistantships with full tuition reimbursements, teaching assistantships with full tuition reimbursements, Federal Work-Study and institutionally sponsored loans available. Financial award application deadline: 1/2. *Faculty research:* Chemistry of interfaces, organic synthesis, organometallic chemistry, inorganic reactions, biostructural chemistry. *Unit head:* Prof. Andrew Bocarsly, Director of Graduate Studies, 609-258-3888, Fax: 609-258-6746, E-mail: bocarsly@princeton.edu. *Application contact:* Janice Yip, Director of Graduate Admissions, 609-258-3034, Fax: 609-258-6180, E-mail: gsadmit@princeton.edu.

See in-depth description on page 137.

Purdue University, Graduate School, School of Science, Department of Chemistry, West Lafayette, IN 47907. Offers analytical chemistry (MS, PhD); biochemistry (MS, PhD); chemical education (MS, PhD); inorganic chemistry (MS, PhD); organic chemistry (MS, PhD); physical chemistry (MS, PhD). *Accreditation:* NCATE (one or more programs are accredited). Terminal master's awarded for partial completion of doctoral program. *Degree requirements:* For master's and doctorate, thesis/dissertation. *Entrance requirements:* Additional exam requirements/recommendations for international students: Required—TOEFL. Electronic applications accepted.

Queens College of the City University of New York, Division of Graduate Studies, Mathematics and Natural Sciences Division, Department of Chemistry, Flushing, NY 11367-1597. Offers biochemistry (MA); chemistry (MA). Part-time and evening/weekend programs available. *Faculty:* 16 full-time (2 women). *Students:* 1 (woman) full-time, 8 part-time (5 women). 43 applicants, 44% accepted. In 2003, 7 degrees awarded. *Degree requirements:* For master's, comprehensive exam. *Entrance requirements:* For master's, GRE, previous course work in calculus and physics, minimum GPA of 3.0. Additional exam requirements/recommendations for international students: Required—TOEFL. *Application deadline:* For fall admission, 4/1 for domestic students; for spring admission, 11/1 for domestic students. Applications are processed on a rolling basis. Application fee: $50. *Expenses:* Tuition, state resident: full-time $7,130; part-time $230 per credit. Tuition, nonresident: full-time $11,880; part-time $425 per credit. Required fees: $66; $38 per semester. *Financial support:* Career-related internships or fieldwork, Federal Work-Study, institutionally sponsored loans, tuition waivers (partial), and adjunct lectureships available. Support available to part-time students. Financial award application deadline: 4/1; financial award applicants required to submit FAFSA. *Unit head:* Dr. A. David Baker, Chairperson, 718-997-4100, E-mail: a.davidbaker@qc.edu. *Application contact:* Graduate Adviser, 718-997-4100.

Queen's University at Kingston, School of Graduate Studies and Research, Faculty of Arts and Sciences, Department of Chemistry, Kingston, ON K7L 3N6, Canada. Offers M Sc, PhD. Part-time programs available. *Degree requirements:* For master's, thesis (for some programs); for doctorate, thesis/dissertation, comprehensive exam. *Entrance requirements:* Additional exam requirements/recommendations for international students: Required—TOEFL (minimum score 580 paper-based). *Faculty research:* Medicinal/biological chemistry, materials chemistry, environmental/analytical chemistry, theoretical/computational chemistry.

Rensselaer Polytechnic Institute, Graduate School, School of Science, Department of Chemistry and Chemical Biology, Troy, NY 12180-3590. Offers analytical chemistry (MS, PhD); biochemistry (MS, PhD); inorganic chemistry (MS, PhD); organic chemistry (MS, PhD); physical chemistry (MS, PhD); polymer chemistry (MS, PhD). Part-time and evening/weekend programs available. *Faculty:* 20 full-time (4 women). *Students:* 58 full-time (25 women), 3 part-time (2 women); includes 40 minority (2 African Americans, 37 Asian Americans or Pacific Islanders, 1 Hispanic American), 36 international. Average age 24. 102 applicants, 29% accepted, 19 enrolled. In 2003, 9 master's, 9 doctorates awarded. Terminal master's awarded for partial completion of doctoral program. *Median time to degree:* Of those who began their doctoral program in fall 1995, 100% received their degree in 8 years or less. *Degree requirements:* For master's, thesis (for some programs), registration; for doctorate, thesis/dissertation, comprehensive exam, registration. *Entrance requirements:* For master's, GRE General Test, GRE Subject Test (strongly recommended); for doctorate, GRE General Test, GRE Subject Test (chemistry or biochemistry strongly recommended). Additional exam requirements/recommendations for international students: Required—TOEFL (minimum score 600 paper-based). *Application deadline:* For fall admission, 2/1 for domestic students; for spring admission, 11/15 for domestic students. Applications are processed on a rolling basis. Application fee: $45. Electronic applications accepted. *Expenses:* Tuition: Full-time $27,700; part-time $1,320 per credit. Required fees: $1,470. *Financial support:* In 2003–04, 59 students received support, including 1 fellowship with full tuition reimbursement available (averaging $25,000 per year), 25 research assistantships with full tuition reimbursements available (averaging $18,000 per year), 30 teaching assistantships with full tuition reimbursements available (averaging $18,000 per year); institutionally sponsored loans and tuition waivers (full and partial) also available. Financial award application deadline: 2/1. *Faculty research:* Synthetic polymer and biopolymer chemistry, physical chemistry of polymeric systems, bioanalytical chemistry, synthetic and computational drug design, protein folding and protein design. Total annual research expenditures: $1.9 million. *Unit head:* Dr. Ronald A. Bailey, Acting Chair, 518-276-4856, Fax: 518-276-4887, E-mail: bailer@rpi.edu. *Application contact:* Beth E. McGraw, Department Admissions Assistant, 518-276-6456, Fax: 518-276-4887, E-mail: mcgrae@rpi.edu.

Rensselaer Polytechnic Institute, Graduate School, School of Science, Department of Earth and Environmental Sciences, Troy, NY 12180-3590. Offers environmental chemistry (MS, PhD); geochemistry (MS, PhD); geology (MS, PhD); geophysics (MS, PhD); petrology (MS, PhD). Part-time programs available. *Faculty:* 7 full-time (0 women). *Students:* 15 full-time (7 women); includes 3 minority (all Asian Americans or Pacific Islanders) Average age 24. 35 applicants, 11% accepted. In 2003, 4 master's, 1 doctorate awarded. Terminal master's awarded for partial completion of doctoral program. *Degree requirements:* For master's, thesis (for some programs), comprehensive exam; for doctorate, thesis/dissertation, comprehensive exam. *Entrance requirements:* For master's and doctorate, GRE General Test. Additional exam requirements/recommendations for international students: Required—TOEFL. *Application deadline:* For fall admission, 1/15 for domestic students. Applications are processed on a rolling basis. Application fee: $45. Electronic applications accepted. *Expenses:* Tuition: Full-time $27,700; part-time $1,320 per credit. Required fees: $1,470. *Financial support:* In 2003–04, 9 research assistantships with full tuition reimbursements (averaging $12,000 per year), 5 teaching assistantships with full tuition reimbursements (averaging $12,000 per year) were awarded. Fellowships with full tuition reimbursements, career-related internships or fieldwork, institutionally sponsored loans, and scholarships/grants also available. Financial award application deadline: 2/1; financial award applicants required to submit FAFSA. *Faculty research:* Mantel geochemistry, contaminant geochemistry, seismology, GPS geodesy, remote sensing petrology. Total annual research expenditures: $1.3 million. *Unit head:* Dr. Frank Spear, Chair, 518-276-6474, Fax: 518-276-6680, E-mail: ees@rpi.edu. *Application contact:* Dr. Steven Roecker, Professor, 518-276-6474, Fax: 518-276-6680, E-mail: ees@rpi.edu.

Rice University, Graduate Programs, Wiess School of Natural Sciences, Department of Chemistry, Houston, TX 77251-1892. Offers chemistry (MA); inorganic chemistry (PhD); organic chemistry (PhD); physical chemistry (PhD). *Faculty:* 24 full-time (3 women), 5 part-time/adjunct (0 women). *Students:* 80 full-time (25 women); includes 8 minority (2 African Americans, 1 Asian American or Pacific Islander, 5 Hispanic Americans), 40 international. Average age 24. 259 applicants, 21% accepted, 25 enrolled. In 2003, 1 master's, 14 doctorates awarded. Terminal master's awarded for partial completion of doctoral program. *Median time to degree:* Of those who began their doctoral program in fall 1995, 100% received their degree in 8 years or less. *Degree requirements:* For master's and doctorate, thesis/dissertation. *Entrance requirements:* For master's and doctorate, GRE General Test, minimum GPA of 3.0. Additional exam requirements/recommendations for international students: Required—TOEFL. *Application deadline:* For fall admission, 2/1 for domestic students; for spring admission, 11/1 for domestic students. Applications are processed on a rolling basis. Application fee: $0 ($25 for international students). *Expenses:* Tuition: Full-time $19,700; part-time $1,096 per hour. *Financial support:* In 2003–04, 80 students received support, including 44 fellowships (averaging $19,700 per year), 23 research assistantships (averaging $19,700 per year); Federal Work-Study, scholarships/grants, and tuition waivers (full and partial) also available. *Faculty research:* Nanoscience, biomaterials, nanobioinformatics, fullerene pharmaceuticals. Total annual research expenditures: $75,000. *Unit head:* Kenton H. Whitmire, Chair, 713-348-5650, Fax: 713-348-5155, E-mail: whitmir@rice.edu. *Application contact:* Sofia Medrano, Graduate Recruiting/Administrative Secretary, 713-348-4082, Fax: 713-348-5155, E-mail: gradchem@rice.edu.

Rochester Institute of Technology, Graduate Enrollment Services, College of Science, Department of Chemistry, Rochester, NY 14623-5603. Offers MS. Part-time and evening/weekend programs available. *Students:* 4 full-time (1 woman), 10 part-time (7 women), 8 international. 17 applicants, 65% accepted, 6 enrolled. In 2003, 6 degrees awarded. *Entrance requirements:* For master's, American Chemical Society Exam, GRE, minimum GPA of 3.0. Additional exam requirements/recommendations for international students: Required—TOEFL. *Application deadline:* For fall admission, 3/1 for domestic students. Applications are processed on a rolling basis. Application fee: $50. *Expenses:* Tuition: Full-time $22,965; part-time $644 per hour. Required fees: $174; $29 per quarter. *Financial support:* Teaching assistantships, career-related internships or fieldwork, Federal Work-Study, institutionally sponsored loans, and tuition waivers (full and partial) available. Support available to part-time students. *Faculty research:* Organic polymer chemistry, magnetic resonance and imaging, inorganic coordination polymers, biophysical chemistry, physical polymer chemistry. *Unit head:* Dr. Terence Morrill, Head, 585-475-2497, E-mail: tcmsch@rit.edu.

Rochester Institute of Technology, Graduate Enrollment Services, College of Science, Department of Medical Sciences, Rochester, NY 14623-5603. Offers clinical chemistry (MS). *Students:* 3 full-time (2 women), 4 part-time (2 women), 3 international. 2 applicants, 0% accepted. In 2003, 1 degree awarded. *Entrance requirements:* For master's, minimum GPA of 3.0. *Application deadline:* For fall admission, 3/1 for domestic students. Applications are processed on a rolling basis. Application fee: $50. *Expenses:* Tuition: Full-time $22,965; part-time $644 per hour. Required fees: $174; $29 per quarter. *Financial support:* Teaching assistantships available. *Unit head:* Dr. Richard Doolittle, Head, 585-475-2978, E-mail: rldsbi@rit.edu.

Roosevelt University, Graduate Division, College of Arts and Sciences, School of Science and Mathematics, Program in Biotechnology and Chemical Science, Chicago, IL 60605-1394. Offers MS. Part-time and evening/weekend programs available. *Students:* 8 full-time (7 women), 26 part-time (18 women); includes 9 minority (8 African Americans, 1 Asian American or Pacific Islander), 4 international. Average age 28. 39 applicants, 64% accepted, 12 enrolled. In 2003, 5 degrees awarded. *Median time to degree:* Master's–2.3 years part-time. *Degree requirements:* For master's, thesis optional. *Entrance requirements:* For master's, minimum GPA of 2.7, previous undergraduate course work in science and mathematics. *Application deadline:* For fall admission, 6/1 for domestic students; for spring admission, 11/1 for domestic students. Applications are processed on a rolling basis. Application fee: $25 ($35 for international students). *Expenses:* Tuition: Part-time $624 per semester hour. Required fees: $150 per semester. *Financial support:* In 2003–04, 1 student received support, including 1 teaching assistantship; tuition waivers (partial) also available. Support available to part-time students. Financial award application deadline: 2/15. *Faculty research:* Phase-transfer catalysts, bioinorganic chemistry, long chain dicarboxylic acids, organosilicon compounds, spectroscopic studies. Total annual research expenditures: $1,000. *Application contact:* Joanne Canyon-Heller, Coordinator of Graduate Admission, 312-281-3250, Fax: 312-281-3356, E-mail: applyru@roosevelt.edu.

Royal Military College of Canada, Division of Graduate Studies and Research, Science Division, Department of Chemistry and Chemical Engineering, Kingston, ON K7K 7B4, Canada. Offers chemical engineering (M Eng, MA Sc, PhD); chemistry (M Sc, PhD). *Degree requirements:* For master's, thesis/dissertation, registration; for doctorate, thesis/dissertation, comprehensive exam, registration. Electronic applications accepted.

Rutgers, The State University of New Jersey, Camden, Graduate School, Program in Chemistry, Camden, NJ 08102-1401. Offers MS. Part-time and evening/weekend programs available. *Degree requirements:* For master's, thesis (for some programs). Electronic applications accepted. *Faculty research:* Organic and inorganic synthesis, enzyme biochemistry, trace metal analysis, theoretical and molecular modeling.

Rutgers, The State University of New Jersey, Newark, Graduate School, Program in Chemistry, Newark, NJ 07102. Offers analytical chemistry (MS, PhD); biochemistry (MS, PhD); inorganic chemistry (MS, PhD); organic chemistry (MS, PhD); physical chemistry (MS, PhD). Part-time and evening/weekend programs available. *Faculty:* 22 full-time (5 women). *Students:* 19 full-time (9 women), 35 part-time (12 women); includes 28 minority (3 African Americans, 25 Asian Americans or Pacific Islanders). 107 applicants, 31% accepted, 8 enrolled. In 2003, 4 master's, 6 doctorates awarded. Terminal master's awarded for partial completion of doctoral program. *Degree requirements:* For master's, cumulative exams, thesis optional; for doctorate, thesis/dissertation, exams, research proposal. *Entrance requirements:* For master's and doctorate, GRE General Test, minimum undergraduate B average. Additional exam requirements/recommendations for international students: Required—TOEFL. *Application deadline:* For fall admission, 7/1 for domestic students; for spring admission, 12/1 for domestic students. Applications are processed on a rolling basis. Application fee: $50. Electronic applications accepted. *Expenses:* Tuition, state resident: full-time $10,030. Tuition, nonresident: full-time $14,202. *Financial support:* In 2003–04, 35 students received support, including 6 fellowships with full tuition reimbursements available, 20 teaching assistantships with full tuition reimbursements available (averaging $14,300 per year); Federal Work-Study and institutionally sponsored loans also available. Financial award application deadline: 3/1. *Faculty research:* Medicinal chemistry, natural products, isotope effects, biophysics and biorganic approaches to enzyme mechanisms, organic and organometallic synthesis. *Unit head:* Prof.

W. Philip Huskey, Chairman and Program Director, 973-353-5741, Fax: 973-353-1264, E-mail: huskey@andromeda.rutgers.edu.

Rutgers, The State University of New Jersey, New Brunswick/Piscataway, Graduate School, Program in Chemistry and Chemical Biology, New Brunswick, NJ 08901-1281. Offers analytical chemistry (MS, PhD); biological chemistry (PhD); chemistry education (MST); inorganic chemistry (MS, PhD); organic chemistry (MS, PhD); physical chemistry (MS, PhD). Part-time and evening/weekend programs available. Terminal master's awarded for partial completion of doctoral program. *Degree requirements:* For master's, thesis or alternative, exam, comprehensive exam, registration; for doctorate, thesis/dissertation, cumulative exams, 1 year residency, comprehensive exam, registration. *Entrance requirements:* For master's and doctorate, GRE General Test, GRE Subject Test. Additional exam requirements/recommendations for international students: Required—TOEFL. Electronic applications accepted. *Expenses:* Tuition, state resident: full-time $10,030. Tuition, nonresident: full-time $14,202. *Faculty research:* Biophysical organic/bioorganic, inorganic/bioinorganic, theoretical, and solid-state/surface chemistry.

See in-depth description on page 141.

Rutgers, The State University of New Jersey, New Brunswick/Piscataway, Graduate School, Program in Environmental Sciences, New Brunswick, NJ 08901-1281. Offers air resources (MS, PhD); aquatic biology (MS, PhD); aquatic chemistry (MS, PhD); atmospheric science (MS, PhD); chemistry and physics of aerosol and hydrosol systems (MS, PhD); environmental chemistry (MS, PhD); environmental microbiology (MS, PhD); environmental toxicology (PhD); exposure assessment (PhD); fate and effects of pollutants (MS, PhD); pollution prevention and control (MS, PhD); water and wastewater treatment (MS, PhD); water resources (MS, PhD). *Faculty:* 62 full-time (12 women), 6 part-time/adjunct (1 woman). *Students:* 50 full-time (23 women), 57 part-time (27 women); includes 7 minority (1 African American, 4 Asian Americans or Pacific Islanders, 2 Hispanic Americans), 37 international. Average age 32. 110 applicants, 11% accepted, 8 enrolled. In 2003, 9 master's, 4 doctorates awarded. Terminal master's awarded for partial completion of doctoral program. *Degree requirements:* For master's, thesis or alternative, oral final exam, comprehensive exam; for doctorate, thesis/dissertation, thesis defense, qualifying exam, comprehensive exam. *Entrance requirements:* For master's and doctorate, GRE General Test. Additional exam requirements/recommendations for international students: Required—TOEFL. *Application deadline:* For fall admission, 3/1 for domestic students; for spring admission, 11/1 for domestic students. Applications are processed on a rolling basis. Application fee: $50. Electronic applications accepted. *Expenses:* Tuition, state resident: full-time $10,030. Tuition, nonresident: full-time $14,202. *Financial support:* In 2003–04, 10 fellowships with full tuition reimbursements (averaging $19,000 per year), 34 research assistantships with full tuition reimbursements (averaging $16,400 per year), 3 teaching assistantships with full tuition reimbursements (averaging $14,300 per year) were awarded. Career-related internships or fieldwork and Federal Work-Study also available. Financial award application deadline: 1/15; financial award applicants required to submit FAFSA. *Faculty research:* Atmospheric sciences; biological waste treatment; contaminant fate and transport; exposure assessment; air, soil and water quality. Total annual research expenditures: $5.7 million. *Unit head:* Dr. Barbara Turpin, Director, 732-932-9540, Fax: 732-932-8644, E-mail: env_gradpgm@envsci.rutgers.edu. *Application contact:* Dr. Paul J. Lioy, Graduate Admissions Committee, 732-932-0150, Fax: 732-445-0116, E-mail: plioy@eohsi.rutgers.edu.

Sacred Heart University, Graduate Studies, College of Arts and Sciences, Faculty of Chemistry, Fairfield, CT 06825-1000. Offers MS. Part-time and evening/weekend programs available. *Students:* 1 (woman) full-time, 15 part-time (9 women); includes 6 minority (2 African Americans, 4 Asian Americans or Pacific Islanders), 2 international. Average age 30. 3 applicants, 100% accepted. *Degree requirements:* For master's, thesis optional. *Entrance requirements:* For master's, bachelor's degree in related area, minimum GPA of 2.75. Additional exam requirements/recommendations for international students: Required—TOEFL (minimum score 550 paper-based). *Application deadline:* Applications are processed on a rolling basis. Application fee: $50 ($100 for international students). *Expenses:* Tuition: Part-time $405 per credit. Required fees: $311 per term. *Financial support:* Career-related internships or fieldwork and unspecified assistantships available. Support available to part-time students. Financial award applicants required to submit FAFSA. *Unit head:* Dr. Dhia Habboush, Chair, 203-371-7795, E-mail: gradstudies@sacredheart.edu. *Application contact:* Alexis Haakonsen, Dean of Graduate Admissions, 203-365-7619, Fax: 203-365-4732, E-mail: haakonsena@sacredheart.edu.

St. Francis Xavier University, Graduate Studies, Department of Chemistry, Antigonish, NS B2G 2W5, Canada. Offers M Sc. *Faculty:* 9 full-time (1 woman). *Students:* 2 full-time (both women), 1 part-time. 5 applicants, 40% accepted. *Degree requirements:* For master's, thesis, registration. *Entrance requirements:* For master's, minimum undergraduate B average, undergraduate major in chemistry or related field. Additional exam requirements/recommendations for international students: Required—TOEFL (minimum score 580 paper-based; 236 computer-based). *Application deadline:* For fall admission, 9/1 for domestic students. Applications are processed on a rolling basis. Application fee: $40. Tuition, area resident: Full-time $5,310. International tuition: $9,210 full-time. Full-time tuition and fees vary according to course load and program. *Faculty research:* Photoelectron spectroscopy, synthesis and properties of surfactants, nucleic acid synthesis, transition metal chemistry, colloids. Total annual research expenditures: $200,000. *Unit head:* Dr. Bernard V. Liengme, III, Professor, 902-867-2361, Fax: 902-867-2414, E-mail: bliengme@stfx.ca. *Application contact:* 902-867-2219, Fax: 902-867-2329, E-mail: admit@stfx.ca.

St. John's University, St. John's College of Liberal Arts and Sciences, Department of Chemistry, Jamaica, NY 11439. Offers MS. Part-time and evening/weekend programs available. *Faculty:* 10 full-time (4 women), 19 part-time/adjunct (5 women). *Students:* 2 full-time (1 woman), 13 part-time (2 women); includes 8 minority (4 Asian Americans or Pacific Islanders, 4 Hispanic Americans), 1 international. 16 applicants, 69% accepted, 6 enrolled. In 2003, 4 degrees awarded. *Degree requirements:* For master's, one foreign language, comprehensive exam. *Entrance requirements:* For master's, minimum GPA of 3.0. Additional exam requirements/recommendations for international students: Required—TOEFL (minimum score 500 paper-based). *Application deadline:* Applications are processed on a rolling basis. Application fee: $40. Electronic applications accepted. *Expenses:* Tuition: Full-time $15,840; part-time $8,320 per year. Tuition and fees vary according to course load, degree level, program and student level. *Financial support:* Research assistantships, teaching assistantships, scholarships/grants available. Support available to part-time students. Financial award application deadline: 3/1; financial award applicants required to submit FAFSA. *Faculty research:* Organic chemistry, photochemistry, Lewis-based acid reactions, solution thermodynamics, synthesis and reactivity of heterocyclic systems. *Unit head:* Dr. Victor Cesare, Chairman, 718-990-5692, E-mail: cesarev@stjohns.edu. *Application contact:* Matthew Whelan, Director, Office of Admission, 718-990-2000, Fax: 718-990-2096, E-mail: admissions@stjohns.edu.

Saint Joseph College, Graduate Division, Department of Biology, West Hartford, CT 06117-2700. Offers biology (MS), including general biology, molecular and cellular biology; biology/chemistry (MS). MS biology (including general biology; molecular and cellular biology) offered online only. Part-time and evening/weekend programs available. Postbaccalaureate distance learning degree programs offered (no on-campus study). *Faculty:* 4 full-time (1 woman), 1 (woman) part-time/adjunct. *Students:* 1 (woman) full-time, 38 part-time (29 women); includes 5 minority (3 African Americans, 2 Asian Americans or Pacific Islanders). Average age 33. 19 applicants, 95% accepted, 18 enrolled. In 2003, 3 degrees awarded. *Degree requirements:* For master's, thesis or alternative, comprehensive exam. *Entrance requirements:* For master's, 2 letters of recommendation. *Application deadline:* Applications are processed on a rolling basis. Application fee: $25. Electronic applications accepted. *Expenses:* Tuition: Part-time $540 per credit. Required fees: $50 per course. *Financial support:* In 2003–04, 1 research assistantship with partial tuition reimbursement was awarded; career-related internships or fieldwork, health care benefits, and unspecified assistantships also available. Support available to part-time students. Financial award application deadline: 7/15; financial award applicants required to submit FAFSA. *Faculty research:* Neurology, cardiology, immunology, mircobiology. *Unit head:* Dr. Billye Auclair, Chair, 860-231-5248, E-mail: bauclair@sjc.edu.

Saint Joseph College, Graduate Division, Department of Chemistry, West Hartford, CT 06117-2700. Offers biology/chemistry (MS); chemistry (MS). Part-time and evening/weekend programs available. *Faculty:* 3 full-time (1 woman). *Students:* Average age 33. 2 applicants, 100% accepted, 2 enrolled. In 2003, 3 degrees awarded. *Median time to degree:* Master's–4 years part-time. *Degree requirements:* For master's, thesis optional. *Entrance requirements:* For master's, 2 letters of recommendation. *Application deadline:* Applications are processed on a rolling basis. Application fee: $25. Electronic applications accepted. *Expenses:* Tuition: Part-time $540 per credit. Required fees: $50 per course. *Financial support:* In 2003–04, 1 research assistantship with full tuition reimbursement was awarded; career-related internships or fieldwork, health care benefits, and unspecified assistantships also available. Support available to part-time students. Financial award application deadline: 7/15; financial award applicants required to submit FAFSA. *Faculty research:* Regulation of cancer cells, selective oxidation of organic concept mapping in general chemistry. Total annual research expenditures: $20,000. *Unit head:* Dr. Peter Markow, Chair, 860-231-5240, Fax: 860-233-5695, E-mail: pmarkow@sjc.edu.

Saint Louis University, Graduate School, College of Arts and Sciences and Graduate School, Department of Chemistry, St. Louis, MO 63103-2097. Offers MS, MS(R). Part-time programs available. *Faculty:* 15 full-time (3 women), 4 part-time/adjunct (0 women). *Students:* 12 full-time (7 women), 7 part-time (3 women); includes 1 African American, 2 Asian Americans or Pacific Islanders. Average age 26. 18 applicants, 83% accepted, 13 enrolled. In 2003, 3 degrees awarded. *Degree requirements:* For master's, comprehensive oral exam, thesis for MS(R). *Entrance requirements:* Additional exam requirements/recommendations for international students: Required—TOEFL (minimum score 550 paper-based; 213 computer-based). *Application deadline:* For fall admission, 7/1 for domestic students, 7/1 for international students; for spring admission, 11/1 for domestic students, 11/1 for international students. Applications are processed on a rolling basis. Application fee: $40. *Expenses:* Tuition: Part-time $690 per credit hour. Required fees: $59 per semester. Tuition and fees vary according to program. *Financial support:* In 2003–04, 15 students received support, including 2 research assistantships, 1 teaching assistantship with tuition reimbursement available; fellowships with tuition reimbursements available Financial award application deadline: 6/1; financial award applicants required to submit FAFSA. *Faculty research:* Analytical chemistry, physical chemistry, inorganic chemistry, organic chemistry. Total annual research expenditures: $250,000. *Unit head:* Dr. Steven Buckner, Chairperson, 314-977-2850, Fax: 314-977-2521, E-mail: buckness@slu.edu. *Application contact:* Gary Behrman, Associate Dean of the Graduate School, 314-977-3827, Fax: 314-977-3943, E-mail: behrmang@slu.edu.

Sam Houston State University, College of Arts and Sciences, Department of Chemistry, Huntsville, TX 77341. Offers MS. Part-time programs available. *Students:* 4 full-time (1 woman), 2 part-time (1 woman), 3 international. *Degree requirements:* For master's, thesis (for some programs). *Entrance requirements:* For master's, GRE General Test. Additional exam requirements/recommendations for international students: Required—TOEFL. *Application deadline:* For fall admission, 8/1 for domestic students; for spring admission, 12/1 for domestic students. Applications are processed on a rolling basis. Application fee: $35. *Expenses:* Tuition, state resident: part-time $243 per semester hour. Tuition, nonresident: part-time $479 per semester hour. *Financial support:* Research assistantships, teaching assistantships, Federal Work-Study, institutionally sponsored loans, and tuition waivers (partial) available. Support available to part-time students. Financial award application deadline: 5/31; financial award applicants required to submit FAFSA. *Unit head:* Dr. Rick White, Chair, 936-294-1060, Fax: 936-299-1598. *Application contact:* Dr. Tom Chasteen, Advisor, 936-294-1533, Fax: 936-299-1585.

San Diego State University, Graduate and Research Affairs, College of Sciences, Department of Chemistry, San Diego, CA 92182. Offers chemistry (MA, MS, PhD). *Students:* 8 full-time (4 women), 65 part-time (26 women); includes 14 minority (1 African American, 8 Asian Americans or Pacific Islanders, 5 Hispanic Americans), 21 international. Average age 30. 54 applicants, 67% accepted, 9 enrolled. In 2003, 13 master's, 2 doctorates awarded. Terminal master's awarded for partial completion of doctoral program. *Degree requirements:* For doctorate, thesis/dissertation. *Entrance requirements:* For master's, GRE General Test, bachelor's degree in related field; for doctorate, GRE General Test, GRE Subject Test. Additional exam requirements/recommendations for international students: Required—TOEFL. *Application deadline:* For fall admission, 5/1 for domestic students, 5/1 for international students; for spring admission, 11/1 for domestic students, 10/1 for international students. Applications are processed on a rolling basis. Application fee: $55. Electronic applications accepted. Tuition, nonresident: part-time $282 per unit. Required fees: $1,349; $875 per year. *Financial support:* Fellowships, research assistantships, teaching assistantships available. Financial award applicants required to submit FAFSA. *Faculty research:* Nonlinear, laser, and electrochemistry; surface reaction dynamics; catalysis, synthesis, and organometallics; proteins, enzymology, and gene expression regulation. Total annual research expenditures: $1.3 million. *Unit head:* Carl Carrano, Chair, 619-594-5595, Fax: 619-594-4634. *Application contact:* David Pullman, Graduate Adviser, 619-594-5573, Fax: 619-594-4634, E-mail: pullman@sciences.sdsu.edu.

San Francisco State University, Division of Graduate Studies, College of Science and Engineering, Department of Chemistry and Biochemistry, San Francisco, CA 94132-1722. Offers chemistry (MS), including biochemistry. Part-time programs available. *Faculty:* 14 full-time (3 women), 1 part-time/adjunct (0 women). *Students:* 4 full-time (2 women), 4 part-time (3 women); includes 5 minority (4 Asian Americans or Pacific Islanders, 1 Hispanic American). 47 applicants, 43% accepted, 13 enrolled. In 2003, 8 degrees awarded. *Median time to degree:* Master's–3.5 years full-time, 4.7 years part-time. *Degree requirements:* For master's, thesis, ACS exams in 3 chemical disciplines (including physical chemistry), essay test. *Entrance requirements:* For master's, minimum GPA of 2.5 in last 60 units. Additional exam requirements/recommendations for international students: Required—TOEFL (minimum score 550 paper-based; 213 computer-based). *Application deadline:* For fall admission, 4/2 priority date for domestic students, 5/1 priority date for international students; for spring admission, 9/15 priority date for domestic students, 10/15 priority date for international students. Applications are processed on a rolling basis. Application fee: $55. Electronic applications accepted. *Expenses:* Tuition, state resident: part-time $871 per unit. Tuition, nonresident: part-time $1,093 per unit. *Financial support:* In 2003–04, 10 fellowships (averaging $20,000 per year), 4 research assistantships (averaging $3,600 per year), 11 teaching assistantships (averaging $8,165 per year) were awarded. Federal Work-Study, institutionally sponsored loans, scholarships/grants, and unspecified assistantships also available. Financial award application deadline: 3/1. *Faculty research:* Physical chemistry of macromolecules, physical and synthetic organic chemistry, membrane and enzyme biochemistry, organometallic chemistry. Total annual research expenditures: $750,000. *Unit head:* Dr. James Orenberg, Chair, 415-338-1288, Fax: 415-338-2384, E-mail: orenberg@sfsu.edu. *Application contact:* Dr. James Keeffe, Graduate Coordinator, 415-338-1117, Fax: 415-338-2384, E-mail: keeffe@sfsu.edu.

San Jose State University, Graduate Studies and Research, College of Science, Department of Chemistry, San Jose, CA 95192-0001. Offers MA, MS. Part-time and evening/weekend programs available. *Students:* Average age 32. 23 applicants, 52% accepted, 7 enrolled. In 2003, 7 degrees awarded. *Degree requirements:* For master's, thesis or alternative. *Entrance requirements:* For master's, GRE, minimum B average. *Application deadline:* For fall admission, 6/29 for domestic students; for spring admission, 11/30 for domestic students. Applications are processed on a rolling basis. Application fee: $59. Electronic applications accepted. Tuition, nonresident: part-time $282 per unit. Required fees: $654 per semester. *Financial support:* In 2003–04, 8 teaching assistantships were awarded; career-related internships or fieldwork, Federal Work-Study, and institutionally sponsored loans also available. Support available to part-time students. Financial award application deadline: 6/5; financial award applicants required to submit FAFSA. *Faculty research:* Intercalated compounds, organic/

Chemistry

San Jose State University (continued)
biochemical reaction mechanisms, complexing agents in biochemistry, DNA repair, metabolic inhibitors. *Unit head:* Brad Stone, Interim Chair, 408-924-4938, Fax: 408-924-4945.

The Scripps Research Institute, Kellogg School of Science and Technology, Program in Chemistry and Chemical Biology, La Jolla, CA 92037. Offers chemical biology (PhD); chemistry (PhD). *Faculty:* 20 full-time (0 women). *Students:* 104 full-time (29 women). Average age 22. 298 applicants, 20% accepted, 26 enrolled. In 2003, 11 degrees awarded. *Degree requirements:* For doctorate, thesis/dissertation. *Entrance requirements:* For doctorate, GRE General Test, GRE Subject Test. Additional exam requirements/recommendations for international students: Required—TOEFL. *Application deadline:* For fall admission, 1/1 for domestic students, 1/1 for international students. Application fee: $0. *Expenses:* Tuition: Full-time $5,000. *Financial support:* Institutionally sponsored loans and stipends available. *Faculty research:* Synthetic organic chemistry and natural product synthesis, bio-organic chemistry and molecular design, biocatalysis and protein design, chemical biology. *Unit head:* James R. Williamson, Associate Dean, 858-784-8740. *Application contact:* Marylyn Rinaldi, Administrative Director, 858-784-8469, Fax: 858-784-2802, E-mail: mrinaldi@scripps.edu.

Seton Hall University, College of Arts and Sciences, Department of Chemistry and Biochemistry, South Orange, NJ 07079-2694. Offers analytical chemistry (MS, PhD); biochemistry (MS, PhD); chemistry (MS); inorganic chemistry (MS, PhD); organic chemistry (MS, PhD); physical chemistry (MS, PhD). Part-time and evening/weekend programs available. Terminal master's awarded for partial completion of doctoral program. *Degree requirements:* For master's, formal seminar, thesis optional; for doctorate, thesis/dissertation, annual seminars, comprehensive exam. *Entrance requirements:* For master's, undergraduate major in chemistry or related field with minimum 30 credits in chemistry, including 2 semesters of physical chemistry; for doctorate, oral matriculation exam based on proposed doctoral research, minimum GPA of 3.0 in course distribution requirements, formal seminar. Additional exam requirements/recommendations for international students: Required—TOEFL. *Faculty research:* DNA metal reactions; chromatography; bioinorganic, biophysical, organometallic, polymer chemistry; heterogeneous catalyst.

Announcement: Strong associations with local chemical industry. Program Advisory Committee composed of industrial chemists who aid in program development. Full-time and part-time MS and PhD programs (1-year residency required) with all graduate courses taught in the evenings and on weekends. Research and nonresearch MS tracks, including a minor in business.

Simon Fraser University, Graduate Studies, Faculty of Science, Department of Chemistry, Burnaby, BC V5A 1S6, Canada. Offers chemical physics (M Sc, PhD); chemistry (M Sc, PhD). *Degree requirements:* For master's and doctorate, thesis/dissertation. *Entrance requirements:* For master's, minimum GPA of 3.0; for doctorate, minimum GPA of 3.5. Additional exam requirements/recommendations for international students: Required—TOEFL or IELTS. *Faculty research:* Organic chemistry, nuclear chemistry, physical chemistry, inorganic chemistry, theoretical chemistry.

Smith College, Graduate Studies, Department of Chemistry, Northampton, MA 01063. Offers MAT. Part-time programs available. *Faculty:* 8 full-time (5 women). *Entrance requirements:* For master's, GRE General Test, GRE Subject Test. *Application deadline:* For fall admission, 4/15 for domestic students, 1/15 for international students; for spring admission, 12/1 for domestic students. Application fee: $60. *Expenses:* Tuition: Full-time $27,330; part-time $855 per credit. *Financial support:* Career-related internships or fieldwork and institutionally sponsored loans available. Support available to part-time students. Financial award application deadline: 1/15; financial award applicants required to submit CSS PROFILE or FAFSA. *Unit head:* Robert Linck, Chair, 413-585-3837.

South Dakota School of Mines and Technology, Graduate Division, College of Materials Science and Engineering, Doctoral Program in Materials Engineering and Science, Rapid City, SD 57701-3995. Offers chemical engineering (PhD); chemistry (PhD); civil engineering (PhD); electrical engineering (PhD); mechanical engineering (PhD); metallurgical engineering (PhD); physics (PhD). Part-time programs available. In 2003, 5 degrees awarded. *Degree requirements:* For doctorate, thesis/dissertation. *Entrance requirements:* For doctorate, minimum graduate GPA of 3.0. Additional exam requirements/recommendations for international students: Required—TOEFL, TWE. *Application deadline:* For fall admission, 6/15 for domestic students; for spring admission, 10/15 for domestic students. Applications are processed on a rolling basis. Application fee: $35. Electronic applications accepted. *Expenses:* Tuition, state resident: part-time $109 per credit hour. Tuition, nonresident: part-time $323 per credit hour. Required fees: $100 per credit hour. *Financial support:* In 2003–04, 1 fellowship (averaging $2,700 per year), 9 research assistantships with partial tuition reimbursements (averaging $11,775 per year), 5 teaching assistantships with partial tuition reimbursements (averaging $4,100 per year) were awarded. Federal Work-Study and institutionally sponsored loans also available. Support available to part-time students. Financial award application deadline: 5/15. *Faculty research:* Thermophysical properties of solids, development of multiphase materials and composites, concrete technology, electronic polymer materials. *Unit head:* Dr. Robb Winter, Coordinator, 605-394-1237. *Application contact:* Brenda Brown, Secretary, 800-454-8162 Ext. 2493, Fax: 605-394-5360, E-mail: graduate_admissions@silver.sdsmt.edu.

South Dakota School of Mines and Technology, Graduate Division, College of Materials Science and Engineering, Master's Program in Materials Engineering and Science, Rapid City, SD 57701-3995. Offers chemistry (MS); metallurgical engineering (MS); physics (MS). In 2003, 4 degrees awarded. *Entrance requirements:* Additional exam requirements/recommendations for international students: Required—TOEFL, TWE. *Application deadline:* For fall admission, 6/15 for domestic students; for spring admission, 10/15 for domestic students. Applications are processed on a rolling basis. Application fee: $35. Electronic applications accepted. *Expenses:* Tuition, state resident: part-time $109 per credit hour. Tuition, nonresident: part-time $323 per credit hour. Required fees: $100 per credit hour. *Financial support:* In 2003–04, 3 fellowships (averaging $2,016 per year), 13 research assistantships with partial tuition reimbursements (averaging $11,930 per year), 8 teaching assistantships with partial tuition reimbursements (averaging $10,554 per year) were awarded. Financial award application deadline: 5/15. *Unit head:* Dr. Daniel Heglund, 605-394-1241. *Application contact:* Brenda Brown, Secretary, 800-454-8162 Ext. 2493, Fax: 605-394-5360, E-mail: graduate_admissions@silver.sdsmt.edu.

South Dakota State University, Graduate School, College of Arts and Science and College of Agriculture and Biological Sciences, Department of Chemistry, Brookings, SD 57007. Offers analytical chemistry (MS, PhD); biochemistry (MS, PhD); chemistry (MS, PhD); inorganic chemistry (MS, PhD); organic chemistry (MS, PhD); physical chemistry (MS, PhD). *Degree requirements:* For master's, thesis, oral exam; for doctorate, thesis/dissertation, preliminary oral and written exams, research tool. *Entrance requirements:* For master's, bachelor's degree in chemistry or equivalent. Additional exam requirements/recommendations for international students: Required—TOEFL. *Faculty research:* Environmental chemistry, computational chemistry, organic synthesis and photochemistry, novel material development and characterization.

Southeast Missouri State University, School of Graduate and University Studies, Department of Chemistry, Cape Girardeau, MO 63701-4799. Offers MNS. Part-time and evening/weekend programs available. *Faculty:* 9 full-time (1 woman). *Students:* 2 full-time (1 woman), 8 part-time (5 women). Average age 23. 1 applicant, 0% accepted. *Degree requirements:* For master's, thesis or alternative. *Entrance requirements:* For master's, GRE General Test, minimum undergraduate GPA of 2.5. Additional exam requirements/recommendations for international students: Required—TOEFL (minimum score 550 paper-based; 213 computer-based). *Application deadline:* For fall admission, 8/1 priority date for domestic students, 4/1 priority date for international students; for spring admission, 11/21 priority date for domestic students, 9/1 priority date for international students. Applications are processed on a rolling basis. Application fee: $20 ($100 for international students). Electronic applications accepted. *Expenses:* Tuition, state resident: full-time $4,061; part-time $180 per credit hour. Tuition, nonresident: full-time $7,514; part-time $324 per credit hour. One-time fee: $257. *Financial support:* In 2003–04, 7 students received support, including 8 research assistantships (averaging $6,100 per year) Financial award applicants required to submit FAFSA. *Faculty research:* Ketenes, enhanced microwave, magnetic properties. Total annual research expenditures: $14,915. *Unit head:* Dr. Phillip Crawford, Chairperson, 573-651-2162, Fax: 573-651-2223, E-mail: pcrawford@semo.edu. *Application contact:* Marsha L. Arant, Office of Graduate Studies, 573-651-2192, Fax: 573-651-2001, E-mail: marant@semovm.semo.edu.

Southern Connecticut State University, School of Graduate Studies, School of Arts and Sciences, Department of Chemistry, New Haven, CT 06515-1355. Offers chemistry (MS). Part-time and evening/weekend programs available. *Faculty:* 2 full-time, 3 part-time/adjunct. *Students:* 14 full-time (5 women), 7 part-time; includes 2 minority (1 Asian American or Pacific Islander, 1 Hispanic American). 11 applicants, 45% accepted. In 2003, 2 degrees awarded. *Degree requirements:* For master's, thesis or alternative. *Entrance requirements:* For master's, interview, undergraduate work in chemistry. *Application deadline:* For fall admission, 7/15 for domestic students. Applications are processed on a rolling basis. Application fee: $40. Electronic applications accepted. *Expenses:* Tuition, state resident: full-time $3,298. Tuition, nonresident: full-time $9,190. Full-time tuition and fees vary according to program. *Financial support:* Teaching assistantships available. Financial award application deadline: 4/15; financial award applicants required to submit FAFSA. *Unit head:* Dr. James Barrante, Chairperson, 203-392-6267, Fax: 203-392-6396, E-mail: barrantej1@southernct.edu. *Application contact:* Dr. Robert Snyder, Graduate Coordinator, 203-392-6263, Fax: 203-392-6396, E-mail: snyderr1@southernct.edu.

Southern Illinois University Carbondale, Graduate School, College of Science, Department of Chemistry and Biochemistry, Carbondale, IL 62901-4701. Offers MS, PhD. Part-time programs available. *Faculty:* 18 full-time (1 woman), 2 part-time/adjunct (0 women). *Students:* 35 full-time (15 women), 12 part-time (6 women); includes 2 minority (both African Americans), 33 international. Average age 25. 48 applicants, 42% accepted, 8 enrolled. In 2003, 4 degrees awarded. Terminal master's awarded for partial completion of doctoral program. *Degree requirements:* For master's, one foreign language, thesis; for doctorate, variable foreign language requirement, thesis/dissertation. *Entrance requirements:* For master's, minimum GPA of 2.7; for doctorate, GRE General Test, minimum GPA of 3.25. Additional exam requirements/recommendations for international students: Required—TOEFL. *Application deadline:* Applications are processed on a rolling basis. Application fee: $0. *Expenses:* Tuition, state resident: part-time $478 per hour. Tuition, nonresident: part-time $657 per hour. *Financial support:* In 2003–04, 17 research assistantships with full tuition reimbursements, 23 teaching assistantships with full tuition reimbursements were awarded. Fellowships with full tuition reimbursements, Federal Work-Study, institutionally sponsored loans, and tuition waivers (full) also available. Support available to part-time students. *Faculty research:* Materials, separations, computational chemistry, synthetics. Total annual research expenditures: $1 million. *Unit head:* Lori Vermeuler, Chair, 618-453-6482, Fax: 618-453-6408. *Application contact:* Steve Scheiner, Chair, Graduate Admissions Committee, 618-453-6476, Fax: 618-453-6408, E-mail: scheiner@chem.siu.edu.

Announcement: The SIUC Department of Chemistry and Biochemistry offers opportunities in the following: forensic chemistry; environmental chemistry; design and fabrication of new materials; nanomaterials; biomaterials; smart molecules; biomedical chemistry; computational examinations of environmental, biological, and catalytic chemistries; high-tech instrumentation; new methods for molecular recognition and separations; trace analyses.

See in-depth description on page 143.

Southern Illinois University Edwardsville, Graduate Studies and Research, College of Arts and Sciences, Department of Chemistry, Edwardsville, IL 62026-0001. Offers MS. Part-time programs available. *Degree requirements:* For master's, one foreign language, thesis or alternative, final exam. *Entrance requirements:* Additional exam requirements/recommendations for international students: Required—TOEFL.

Southern Methodist University, Dedman College, Department of Chemistry, Dallas, TX 75275. Offers MS. Part-time programs available. *Faculty:* 10 full-time (3 women). *Students:* 1 (woman) full-time, 1 part-time, (both international). Average age 24. In 2003, 2 degrees awarded. *Degree requirements:* For master's, thesis. *Entrance requirements:* For master's, GRE General Test, bachelor's degree in chemistry, minimum GPA of 3.0. Additional exam requirements/recommendations for international students: Required—TOEFL. *Application deadline:* For fall admission, 4/1 for domestic students; for spring admission, 10/1 for domestic students. Applications are processed on a rolling basis. Application fee: $60. *Expenses:* Tuition: Full-time $11,362; part-time $874 per credit. Required fees: $112 per credit. Tuition and fees vary according to course load and program. *Financial support:* In 2003–04, 4 fellowships with tuition reimbursements (averaging $12,000 per year), 2 teaching assistantships with full tuition reimbursements (averaging $10,000 per year) were awarded. Institutionally sponsored loans, scholarships/grants, tuition waivers (full), and unspecified assistantships also available. Financial award applicants required to submit FAFSA. *Faculty research:* Organic and inorganic synthesis, theoretical chemistry, organometallic chemistry, inorganic polymer chemistry, fundamental quantum chemistry. Total annual research expenditures: $1 million. *Unit head:* Dr. Edward R. Biehl, Chairman, 214-768-1280, Fax: 214-768-4089, E-mail: ebiehl@mail.smu.edu. *Application contact:* Dr. Mark Schell, Graduate Adviser, 214-768-2478, Fax: 214-768-4089, E-mail: mschell@mail.smu.edu.

Southern University and Agricultural and Mechanical College, Graduate School, College of Sciences, Department of Chemistry, Baton Rouge, LA 70813. Offers analytical chemistry (MS); biochemistry (MS); environmental sciences (MS); inorganic chemistry (MS); organic chemistry (MS); physical chemistry (MS). *Degree requirements:* For master's, thesis. *Entrance requirements:* For master's, GMAT or GRE General Test. Additional exam requirements/recommendations for international students: Required—TOEFL. *Faculty research:* Synthesis of macrocyclic ligands, latex accelerators, anticancer drugs, biosensors, absorption isotheums, isolation of specific enzymes from plants.

Southwest Missouri State University, Graduate College, College of Natural and Applied Sciences, Department of Chemistry, Springfield, MO 65804-0094. Offers MS. Part-time programs available. *Faculty:* 13 full-time (1 woman). *Students:* 9 full-time (3 women), 3 part-time (2 women); includes 1 minority (African American), 3 international. Average age 28. 8 applicants, 38% accepted, 3 enrolled. In 2003, 8 degrees awarded. *Degree requirements:* For master's, thesis, comprehensive exam. *Entrance requirements:* For master's, GRE General Test, minimum undergraduate GPA of 3.0. *Application deadline:* For fall admission, 8/5 for domestic students; for spring admission, 12/20 priority date for domestic students. Applications are processed on a rolling basis. Application fee: $30. Electronic applications accepted. *Expenses:* Tuition, state resident: full-time $2,862. Tuition, nonresident: full-time $5,724. *Financial support:* In 2003–04, fellowships with full tuition reimbursements (averaging $27,500 per year), research assistantships with full tuition reimbursements (averaging $8,400 per year), 8 teaching assistantships with full tuition reimbursements (averaging $6,300 per year) were awarded. Federal Work-Study, scholarships/grants, and unspecified assistantships also available. Financial award application deadline: 3/31. *Faculty research:* Chemistry of environmental systems, mechanisms of organic and organometallic reactions, enzymatic activity in lipid and protein reactions, computational chemistry, polymer properties. Total annual research expenditures: $80,000. *Unit head:* Dr. Tamara Jahnke, Head, 417-836-5506, Fax: 417-836-6934, E-mail: tsj118f@smsu.edu.

Stanford University, School of Humanities and Sciences, Department of Chemistry, Stanford, CA 94305-9991. Offers PhD. *Faculty:* 23 full-time (1 woman). *Students:* 141 full-time (48 women), 68 part-time (21 women); includes 23 minority (1 African American, 2 American Indian/Alaska Native, 17 Asian Americans or Pacific Islanders, 3 Hispanic Americans), 83 international. Average age 25. 450 applicants, 29% accepted. In 2003, 33 doctorates awarded.

Degree requirements: For doctorate, thesis/dissertation. *Entrance requirements:* For doctorate, GRE General Test, GRE Subject Test. Additional exam requirements/recommendations for international students: Required—TOEFL. *Application deadline:* For fall admission, 1/1 for domestic students, 1/1 for international students. Application fee: $95. Electronic applications accepted. *Expenses:* Tuition: Full-time $28,563. *Unit head:* Dr. Hans C. Andersen, Chair, 650-723-3507, Fax: 650-725-0259, E-mail: chemchair@stanford.edu.

See in-depth description on page 145.

State University of New York at Binghamton, Graduate School, School of Arts and Sciences, Department of Chemistry, Binghamton, NY 13902-6000. Offers analytical chemistry (PhD); chemistry (MA, MS); inorganic chemistry (PhD); organic chemistry (PhD); physical chemistry (PhD). Part-time programs available. Terminal master's awarded for partial completion of doctoral program. *Degree requirements:* For master's, thesis or alternative, oral exam, seminar presentation; for doctorate, thesis/dissertation, cumulative exams. *Entrance requirements:* For master's and doctorate, GRE General Test, GRE Subject Test. Additional exam requirements/recommendations for international students: Required—TOEFL. Electronic applications accepted.

State University of New York at New Paltz, Graduate School, School of Science and Engineering, Department of Chemistry, New Paltz, NY 12561. Offers MA, MAT, MS Ed. Part-time and evening/weekend programs available. *Faculty:* 5 full-time (1 woman), 1 part-time/adjunct (0 women). *Students:* 1 full-time (0 women), 2 part-time (1 woman); includes 1 minority (Asian American or Pacific Islander), 1 international. In 2003, 1 degree awarded. *Degree requirements:* For master's, thesis. *Entrance requirements:* For master's, GRE General Test, minimum GPA of 3.0. Additional exam requirements/recommendations for international students: Required—TOEFL (minimum score 550 paper-based; 213 computer-based). *Application deadline:* For fall admission, 5/15 priority date for domestic students, 5/15 priority date for international students; for spring admission, 11/15 for domestic students, 11/15 for international students. Applications are processed on a rolling basis. Application fee: $50. *Expenses:* Tuition, state resident: full-time $6,900; part-time $288 per credit hour. Tuition, nonresident: full-time $10,500; part-time $438 per credit hour. Tuition and fees vary according to program. *Financial support:* Federal Work-Study and institutionally sponsored loans available. *Unit head:* Dr. Daniel Freedman, Chair, 845-257-3790. *Application contact:* Dr. Preeti Dhar, Coordinator, 845-257-3797, E-mail: dharp@newpaltz.edu.

State University of New York at Oswego, Graduate Studies, Division of Arts and Sciences, Department of Chemistry, Oswego, NY 13126. Offers MS. Part-time programs available. *Faculty:* 4 full-time. *Students:* 6 full-time (3 women), 1 part-time; includes 1 minority (African American) Average age 25. 8 applicants, 100% accepted. In 2003, 2 degrees awarded. *Degree requirements:* For master's, thesis, comprehensive exam. *Entrance requirements:* For master's, GRE General Test, GRE Subject Test, BA or BS in chemistry. Additional exam requirements/recommendations for international students: Required—TOEFL (minimum score 550 paper-based; 213 computer-based). *Application deadline:* For fall admission, 4/1 for domestic students; for spring admission, 10/1 for domestic students. Applications are processed on a rolling basis. Application fee: $50. *Expenses:* Tuition, state resident: full-time $7,100; part-time $296 per credit. Tuition, nonresident: full-time $10,800; part-time $450 per credit. Required fees: $540. *Financial support:* In 2003–04, 7 students received support, including 7 teaching assistantships with full tuition reimbursements available; career-related internships or fieldwork, Federal Work-Study, institutionally sponsored loans, scholarships/grants, health care benefits, tuition waivers (partial), and unspecified assistantships also available. Support available to part-time students. Financial award application deadline: 4/1; financial award applicants required to submit FAFSA. *Unit head:* Dr. Jeffery Schneider, Chair, 315-312-3048. *Application contact:* Dr. Joseph Leferre, Graduate Coordinator, 315-312-3048.

State University of New York College at Fredonia, Graduate Studies, Department of Chemistry, Fredonia, NY 14063-1136. Offers MS, MS Ed. Part-time and evening/weekend programs available. *Degree requirements:* For master's, thesis optional. *Faculty research:* Gas chromatography, organometallic synthesis, polymer chemistry.

State University of New York College of Environmental Science and Forestry, Faculty of Chemistry, Syracuse, NY 13210-2779. Offers biochemistry (MS, PhD); environmental and forest chemistry (MS, PhD); organic chemistry of natural products (MS, PhD); polymer chemistry (MS, PhD). *Faculty:* 14 full-time (0 women), 1 (woman) part-time/adjunct. *Students:* 27 full-time (13 women), 11 part-time (3 women); includes 1 minority (American Indian/Alaska Native), 17 international. Average age 30. 45 applicants, 71% accepted, 11 enrolled. In 2003, 2 master's, 6 doctorates awarded. *Degree requirements:* For master's, thesis/dissertation, registration; for doctorate, thesis/dissertation, comprehensive exam, registration. *Entrance requirements:* For master's and doctorate, GRE General Test, GRE Subject Test, minimum GPA of 3.0. Additional exam requirements/recommendations for international students: Required—TOEFL (minimum score 550 paper-based; 213 computer-based). *Application deadline:* For fall admission, 2/1 priority date for domestic students, 2/1 priority date for international students; for spring admission, 11/1 priority date for domestic students, 11/1 priority date for international students. Applications are processed on a rolling basis. Application fee: $50. Tuition, area resident: Part-time $288 per credit hour. Tuition, nonresident: part-time $438 per credit hour. Required fees: $300; $5 per credit hour. $18 per semester. One-time fee: $25 full-time. *Financial support:* In 2003–04, 35 students received support, including 8 fellowships with full tuition reimbursements available (averaging $9,446 per year), 15 research assistantships with full tuition reimbursements available (averaging $12,500 per year), 4 teaching assistantships with full tuition reimbursements available (averaging $11,540 per year); Federal Work-Study, institutionally sponsored loans, scholarships/grants, health care benefits, and unspecified assistantships also available. Financial award applicants required to submit FAFSA. *Faculty research:* Polymer chemistry, biochemistry. Total annual research expenditures: $1.4 million. *Unit head:* Dr. John P. Hassett, Chair, 315-470-6827, Fax: 315-470-6856, E-mail: jphasset@syr.edu. *Application contact:* Dr. Dudley J. Raynal, Dean, Instruction and Graduate Studies, 315-470-6599, Fax: 315-470-6978, E-mail: esfgrad@esf.edu.

Stephen F. Austin State University, Graduate School, College of Sciences and Mathematics, Department of Chemistry, Nacogdoches, TX 75962. Offers MS. Part-time programs available. *Faculty:* 10 full-time (5 women), 37 part-time/adjunct (12 women). *Students:* 3 full-time (1 woman), 2 part-time (1 woman). Average age 25. 1 applicant, 100% accepted. In 2003, 2 degrees awarded. *Degree requirements:* For master's, comprehensive exam. *Entrance requirements:* For master's, GRE General Test, minimum GPA of 2.8 in last 60 hours, 2.5 overall. Additional exam requirements/recommendations for international students: Required—TOEFL. *Application deadline:* For fall admission, 8/1 for domestic students; for spring admission, 12/15 for domestic students. Applications are processed on a rolling basis. Application fee: $0 ($50 for international students). *Expenses:* Tuition, state resident: part-time $46 per hour. Tuition, nonresident: part-time $282 per hour. Required fees: $71 per hour. Tuition and fees vary according to reciprocity agreements. *Financial support:* In 2003–04, 2 teaching assistantships (averaging $7,066 per year) were awarded; fellowships, research assistantships, Federal Work-Study, institutionally sponsored loans, health care benefits, and unspecified assistantships also available. Support available to part-time students. Financial award application deadline: 3/1. *Faculty research:* Synthesis and chemistry of ferrate ion, properties of fluoroberyllates, polymer chemistry. *Unit head:* Dr. Michael Janusa, Chair, 936-468-3606, E-mail: janusama@sfasu.edu.

Stevens Institute of Technology, Graduate School, School of Applied Sciences and Liberal Arts, Department of Chemistry and Chemical Biology, Hoboken, NJ 07030. Offers chemistry (MS, PhD, Certificate), including analytical chemistry, chemical biology, chemical physiology (Certificate), instrumental analysis (Certificate), organic chemistry (MS, PhD), physical chemistry (MS, PhD), polymer chemistry. Part-time and evening/weekend programs available. Terminal master's awarded for partial completion of doctoral program. *Degree requirements:* For master's, thesis or alternative; for doctorate, one foreign language, thesis/dissertation; for Certificate, project or thesis. *Entrance requirements:* Additional exam requirements/recommendations for international students: Required—TOEFL. Electronic applications accepted.

Stony Brook University, State University of New York, Graduate School, College of Arts and Sciences, Department of Chemistry, Stony Brook, NY 11794. Offers MAT, MS, PhD. MAT offered through the School of Professional Development and Continuing Studies. *Faculty:* 26 full-time (5 women). *Students:* 136 full-time (51 women), 1 (woman) part-time; includes 6 minority (all Asian Americans or Pacific Islanders), 102 international. Average age 27. 269 applicants, 34% accepted. In 2003, 15 master's, 21 doctorates awarded. Terminal master's awarded for partial completion of doctoral program. *Degree requirements:* For master's, thesis; for doctorate, one foreign language, thesis/dissertation. *Entrance requirements:* For master's and doctorate, GRE General Test. Additional exam requirements/recommendations for international students: Required—TOEFL. *Application deadline:* For fall admission, 1/15 for domestic students. Application fee: $50. *Expenses:* Tuition, state resident: full-time $6,900; part-time $288 per credit hour. Tuition, nonresident: full-time $10,500; part-time $438 per credit hour. Required fees: $22. *Financial support:* In 2003–04, 13 fellowships, 107 research assistantships, 42 teaching assistantships were awarded. Total annual research expenditures: $7.4 million. *Unit head:* Dr. Michael White, Chairman, 631-632-7880, Fax: 631-632-7960. *Application contact:* Dr. Scott Sieburth, Director, 631-632-7851, Fax: 631-632-7960, E-mail: ssieburth@notes.cc.sunysb.edu.

Announcement: Announcing Stony Brook's ACES Project, funded by the Dreyfus Foundation. ACES provides workshops and seminars for graduate and postdoctoral students, focusing on development of the nonlaboratory skills that enable career success. Activities are coordinated with Project WISE, the GAANN Fellowship Program, and the Center for Excellence in Learning and Teaching.

See in-depth description on page 147.

Sul Ross State University, School of Arts and Sciences, Department of Geology and Chemistry, Alpine, TX 79832. Offers MS. Part-time programs available. *Degree requirements:* For master's, thesis optional. *Entrance requirements:* For master's, GRE General Test, minimum GPA of 2.5 in last 60 hours of undergraduate work.

Syracuse University, Graduate School, College of Arts and Sciences, Department of Chemistry, Syracuse, NY 13244-0003. Offers MS, PhD. *Faculty:* 17. *Students:* 64 full-time (30 women), 5 part-time (3 women); includes 5 minority (2 Asian Americans or Pacific Islanders, 3 Hispanic Americans), 30 international. 122 applicants, 41% accepted, 19 enrolled. *Degree requirements:* For master's, one foreign language, thesis (for some programs), comprehensive exam, registration; for doctorate, one foreign language, thesis/dissertation, comprehensive exam, registration. *Entrance requirements:* For master's and doctorate, GRE General Test. *Application deadline:* Applications are processed on a rolling basis. Application fee: $65. Electronic applications accepted. *Expenses:* Tuition: Full-time $13,356; part-time $742 per credit. Required fees: $482. *Financial support:* Fellowships with full tuition reimbursements, research assistantships with full and partial tuition reimbursements, teaching assistantships with full tuition reimbursements, tuition waivers (full) available. *Faculty research:* Synthetic organic chemistry, biophysical spectroscopy, solid state in organic chemistry, biochemistry, organometallic chemistry. *Unit head:* Dr. John Edwin Baldwin, Chair, 315-443-3743, Fax: 315-443-4070, E-mail: jbaldwin@syr.edu.

Temple University, Graduate School, College of Science and Technology, Department of Chemistry, Philadelphia, PA 19122-6096. Offers MA, PhD. Evening/weekend programs available. Terminal master's awarded for partial completion of doctoral program. *Degree requirements:* For master's, thesis (for some programs); for doctorate, thesis/dissertation, teaching experience. *Entrance requirements:* For master's and doctorate, GRE General Test, GRE Subject Test, minimum GPA of 3.0 during previous 2 years, 2.8 overall. Electronic applications accepted. *Faculty research:* Polymers, nonlinear optics, natural products, materials science, enantioselective synthesis.

See in-depth description on page 149.

Tennessee State University, Graduate School, College of Arts and Sciences, Department of Chemistry, Nashville, TN 37209-1561. Offers MS. *Faculty:* 5 full-time (0 women). *Students:* 5 full-time (4 women), 6 part-time (5 women). Average age 28. 13 applicants, 38% accepted. In 2003, 1 degree awarded. *Degree requirements:* For master's, thesis. *Entrance requirements:* For master's, GRE General Test, GRE Subject Test, minimum GPA of 3.0, BS in engineering or science. *Application deadline:* Applications are processed on a rolling basis. Application fee: $15. *Financial support:* In 2003–04, 7 teaching assistantships (averaging $19,501 per year) were awarded; research assistantships, unspecified assistantships also available. Financial award application deadline: 5/1. *Faculty research:* Binding benzol pyrenemetabolites to DNA. *Unit head:* Dr. Carlos L. Lee, Head, 615-963-5004.

Tennessee Technological University, Graduate School, College of Arts and Sciences, Department of Chemistry, Cookeville, TN 38505. Offers MS. Part-time programs available. *Faculty:* 16 full-time (1 woman). *Students:* 7 full-time (3 women), 3 part-time; includes 5 minority (all Asian Americans or Pacific Islanders) Average age 28. 10 applicants, 50% accepted, 1 enrolled. In 2003, 3 degrees awarded. *Degree requirements:* For master's, thesis. *Entrance requirements:* For master's, GRE General Test. Additional exam requirements/recommendations for international students: Required—TOEFL. *Application deadline:* For fall admission, 3/1 for domestic students; for spring admission, 8/1 for domestic students. Application fee: $25 ($30 for international students). *Expenses:* Tuition, state resident: full-time $7,410; part-time $263 per semester hour. Tuition, nonresident: full-time $19,134; part-time $607 per semester hour. *Financial support:* In 2003–04, research assistantships (averaging $8,000 per year), 8 teaching assistantships (averaging $7,500 per year) were awarded. Career-related internships or fieldwork also available. Financial award application deadline: 4/1. *Unit head:* Dr. Scott Northrup, Chairperson, 931-372-3421, Fax: 931-372-3434, E-mail: snorthrup@tntech.edu. *Application contact:* Dr. Francis O. Otuonye, Associate Vice President for Research and Graduate Studies, 931-372-3233, Fax: 931-372-3497, E-mail: fotuonye@tntech.edu.

Texas A&M University, College of Science, Department of Chemistry, College Station, TX 77843. Offers MS, PhD. *Faculty:* 37 full-time (0 women). *Students:* 240 full-time (88 women), 16 part-time (5 women); includes 41 minority (5 African Americans, 2 American Indian/Alaska Native, 13 Asian Americans or Pacific Islanders, 21 Hispanic Americans), 107 international. Average age 24. 468 applicants, 25% accepted. In 2003, 12 master's, 35 doctorates awarded. Terminal master's awarded for partial completion of doctoral program. *Degree requirements:* For master's and doctorate, thesis/dissertation. *Entrance requirements:* For master's and doctorate, GRE General Test. Additional exam requirements/recommendations for international students: Required—TOEFL; Recommended—TSE. *Application deadline:* For fall admission, 3/1 for domestic students. Applications are processed on a rolling basis. Application fee: $75 for international students. Electronic applications accepted. *Expenses:* Tuition, state resident: full-time $3,420. Tuition, nonresident: full-time $9,084. Required fees: $1,861. *Financial support:* In 2003–04, fellowships with full tuition reimbursements (averaging $21,600 per year), research assistantships with full tuition reimbursements (averaging $18,600 per year), teaching assistantships with full tuition reimbursements (averaging $18,600 per year) were awarded. Financial award application deadline: 3/1; financial award applicants required to submit FAFSA. *Faculty research:* Biological chemistry, spectroscopy, structure and bonding, reactions and mechanisms, theoretical chemistry. *Unit head:* Dr. Emile A. Schweikert, Head, 979-845-2011, Fax: 979-845-4719. *Application contact:* Dr. Michael P. Rosynek, Graduate Advisor, 979-845-5345, Fax: 979-854-5211, E-mail: gradmail@mail.chem.tamu.edu.

See in-depth description on page 151.

Texas A&M University–Commerce, Graduate School, College of Arts and Sciences, Department of Chemistry, Commerce, TX 75429-3011. Offers M Ed, MS. Part-time programs available. *Degree requirements:* For master's, thesis (for some programs), comprehensive exam. *Entrance requirements:* For master's, GRE General Test. Electronic applications accepted. *Faculty research:* Analytical organic.

Chemistry

Texas A&M University–Kingsville, College of Graduate Studies, College of Arts and Sciences, Department of Chemistry, Kingsville, TX 78363. Offers MS. Part-time programs available. *Degree requirements:* For master's, thesis or alternative, comprehensive exam. *Entrance requirements:* For master's, GRE General Test, minimum GPA of 3.0. Additional exam requirements/recommendations for international students: Required—TOEFL. *Faculty research:* Organic heterocycles, amino alcohol complexes, rare earth arsine complexes.

Texas Christian University, College of Science and Engineering, Department of Chemistry, Fort Worth, TX 76129-0002. Offers MA, MS, PhD. Part-time and evening/weekend programs available. *Degree requirements:* For master's, one foreign language, thesis optional; for doctorate, one foreign language, thesis/dissertation, cumulative exams. *Entrance requirements:* For master's and doctorate, GRE General Test. Additional exam requirements/recommendations for international students: Required—TOEFL. *Application deadline:* For fall admission, 3/1 for domestic students; for spring admission, 12/1 for domestic students. Applications are processed on a rolling basis. Application fee: $0. *Expenses:* Tuition: Part-time $640 per credit hour. Tuition and fees vary according to program. *Financial support:* Fellowships, teaching assistantships, unspecified assistantships available. Financial award application deadline: 3/1. *Unit head:* Dr. Jeffrey Coffer, Chairperson, 817-257-7195. *Application contact:* Dr. Bonnie Melhart, Associate Dean, College of Science and Engineering, E-mail: b.melhart@tcu.edu.

Texas Southern University, Graduate School, School of Science and Technology, Department of Chemistry, Houston, TX 77004-4584. Offers MS. *Faculty:* 3 full-time (0 women), 1 part-time/adjunct (0 women). *Students:* 5 full-time (2 women), 6 part-time (4 women); includes 7 minority (all African Americans), 4 international. Average age 33. *Degree requirements:* For master's, one foreign language, thesis, comprehensive exam. *Entrance requirements:* For master's, GRE General Test, minimum GPA of 2.5. Additional exam requirements/recommendations for international students: Required—TOEFL. *Application deadline:* For fall admission, 7/15 for domestic students. Applications are processed on a rolling basis. Application fee: $50 ($75 for international students). *Expenses:* Tuition, state resident: full-time $1,656. Tuition, nonresident: full-time $5,940. Required fees: $1,314; $689 per semester. Tuition and fees vary according to course load and degree level. *Financial support:* In 2003–04, 2 research assistantships (averaging $9,000 per year) were awarded; fellowships, teaching assistantships, institutionally sponsored loans also available. Financial award application deadline: 5/1. *Faculty research:* Analytical and physical chemistry, geochemistry, inorganic chemistry, biochemistry, organic chemistry. *Unit head:* Dr. John Sapp, Head, 713-313-7003, Fax: 713-313-7824, E-mail: sapp_jb@tsu.edu.

Texas State University-San Marcos, Graduate School, College of Science, Department of Chemistry and Biochemistry, Program in Chemistry, San Marcos, TX 78666. Offers MA, MS. *Students:* 6 full-time (2 women), 3 part-time; includes 3 minority (all Hispanic Americans), 1 international. Average age 27. 11 applicants, 82% accepted, 6 enrolled. In 2003, 3 degrees awarded. *Degree requirements:* For master's, thesis (for some programs), comprehensive exam. *Entrance requirements:* For master's, GRE General Test, minimum GPA of 2.75 in last 60 hours. Additional exam requirements/recommendations for international students: Required—TOEFL. *Application deadline:* For fall admission, 6/15 for domestic students; for spring admission, 10/15 priority date for domestic students. Applications are processed on a rolling basis. Application fee: $40 ($90 for international students). *Expenses:* Tuition, state resident: full-time $2,484; part-time $138 per semester hour. Tuition, nonresident: full-time $6,732; part-time $374 per semester hour. Required fees: $948; $31 per semester hour. $195 per term. Tuition and fees vary according to course load. *Financial support:* In 2003–04, 6 students received support, including 1 research assistantship (averaging $13,310 per year), 4 teaching assistantships (averaging $10,840 per year); career-related internships or fieldwork, Federal Work-Study, and institutionally sponsored loans also available. Support available to part-time students. Financial award application deadline: 4/1; financial award applicants required to submit FAFSA. *Faculty research:* Metal ions in biological systems, cancer chemotherapy, absorption of pesticides on solid surfaces, polymer chemistry, biochemistry of nucleic acids. *Unit head:* Dr. Michael Blanda, Graduate Advisor, 512-245-3121, E-mail: mb29@txstate.edu. *Application contact:* Dr. J. Michael Willoughby, Dean of Graduate School, 512-245-2581, Fax: 512-245-8365, E-mail: gradcollege@txstate.edu.

Texas Tech University, Graduate School, College of Arts and Sciences, Department of Chemistry and Biochemistry, Lubbock, TX 79409. Offers biotechnology (MS); chemistry (MS, PhD). Part-time programs available. *Faculty:* 26 full-time (2 women), 1 part-time/adjunct (0 women). *Students:* 68 full-time (22 women), 6 part-time (4 women); includes 2 minority (1 American Indian/Alaska Native, 1 Asian American or Pacific Islander), 52 international. Average age 28. 67 applicants, 57% accepted, 13 enrolled. In 2003, 7 master's, 5 doctorates awarded. *Degree requirements:* For master's and doctorate, thesis/dissertation. *Entrance requirements:* For master's and doctorate, GRE General Test. Additional exam requirements/recommendations for international students: Required—TOEFL (minimum score 550 paper-based; 213 computer-based). *Application deadline:* Applications are processed on a rolling basis. Application fee: $50 ($60 for international students). Electronic applications accepted. *Expenses:* Tuition, state resident: full-time $3,312. Tuition, nonresident: full-time $8,976. Required fees: $1,745. Tuition and fees vary according to program. *Financial support:* In 2003–04, 42 students received support, including 30 research assistantships with partial tuition reimbursements available (averaging $14,694 per year), 44 teaching assistantships with partial tuition reimbursements available (averaging $15,204 per year); career-related internships or fieldwork, Federal Work-Study, and institutionally sponsored loans also available. Support available to part-time students. Financial award application deadline: 5/1; financial award applicants required to submit FAFSA. *Faculty research:* Ionic and molecular recognition with synthetic host molecules, ultratrace atmospheric analysis, plant biochemistry and phytochemical signaling, theoretical and computational chemistry, synthesis and applications of ionic liquids. Total annual research expenditures: $3.5 million. *Unit head:* Dr. Richard A. Bartsch, Chair, 806-742-3067, Fax: 806-742-1289, E-mail: chemchair@ttu.edu. *Application contact:* Kathy Jones, Assistant Advisor, 806-742-3282, Fax: 806-742-1289, E-mail: kathy.jones@ttu.edu.

Texas Woman's University, Graduate School, College of Arts and Sciences, Department of Chemistry and Physics, Denton, TX 76201. Offers chemistry (MS); chemistry teaching (MS); science teaching (MS). Part-time programs available. *Students:* 3 full-time (2 women), 1 (woman) part-time; includes 2 minority (1 African American, 1 Asian American or Pacific Islander), 1 international. Average age 33. In 2003, 4 degrees awarded. *Degree requirements:* For master's, thesis, comprehensive exam. *Entrance requirements:* For master's, GRE General Test, bachelors degree in chemistry or equivalent, 2 reference contacts. Additional exam requirements/recommendations for international students: Required—TOEFL (minimum score 550 paper-based; 213 computer-based). *Application deadline:* Applications are processed on a rolling basis. Application fee: $30 ($50 for international students). Electronic applications accepted. *Expenses:* Tuition, state resident: part-time $66 per credit. Tuition, nonresident: part-time $302 per credit. Full-time tuition and fees vary according to reciprocity agreements. *Financial support:* In 2003–04, 4 research assistantships (averaging $10,296 per year), 4 teaching assistantships (averaging $10,296 per year) were awarded. Career-related internships or fieldwork, Federal Work-Study, institutionally sponsored loans, scholarships/grants, traineeships, health care benefits, and unspecified assistantships also available. Support available to part-time students. Financial award application deadline: 3/1; financial award applicants required to submit FAFSA. *Faculty research:* Mechanisms and kinetics of organic reactions, mechanisms of enzyme catalysis, chelation chemistry of macrocyclic ligands. *Unit head:* Dr. Jack Gill, Chair, 940-898-2550, Fax: 940-898-2548. *Application contact:* Holly Kiser, Coordinator of Graduate Admissions, 940-898-3188, Fax: 940-898-3081, E-mail: hkiser@twu.edu.

Trent University, Graduate Studies, Program in Applications of Modeling in the Natural and Social Sciences, Department of Chemistry, Peterborough, ON K9J 7B8, Canada. Offers M Sc. Part-time programs available. *Degree requirements:* For master's, thesis. *Entrance requirements:* For master's, honours degree. *Faculty research:* Synthetic-organic chemistry, mass spectrometry and ion storage.

Tufts University, Graduate School of Arts and Sciences, Department of Chemistry, Medford, MA 02155. Offers analytical chemistry (MS, PhD); bioorganic chemistry (MS, PhD); environmental chemistry (MS, PhD); inorganic chemistry (MS, PhD); organic chemistry (MS, PhD); physical chemistry (MS, PhD). *Faculty:* 13 full-time, 1 part-time/adjunct. *Students:* 56 (24 women); includes 6 minority (1 African American, 4 Asian Americans or Pacific Islanders, 1 Hispanic American) 22 international. 66 applicants, 56% accepted, 17 enrolled. In 2003, 4 master's, 6 doctorates awarded. Terminal master's awarded for partial completion of doctoral program. *Degree requirements:* For master's and doctorate, thesis/dissertation. *Entrance requirements:* For master's and doctorate, GRE General Test, GRE Subject Test. Additional exam requirements/recommendations for international students: Required—TOEFL (minimum score 600 paper-based; 213 computer-based), TSE. *Application deadline:* For fall admission, 2/1 for domestic students, 12/30 for international students; for spring admission, 10/15 for domestic students, 9/15 for international students. Applications are processed on a rolling basis. Application fee: $60. Electronic applications accepted. *Expenses:* Tuition: Full-time $29,949. *Financial support:* Research assistantships with full and partial tuition reimbursements, teaching assistantships with full and partial tuition reimbursements, Federal Work-Study, scholarships/grants, and tuition waivers (partial) available. Financial award application deadline: 2/1; financial award applicants required to submit FAFSA. *Unit head:* Mary Jane Shultz, Chair, 617-627-3477, Fax: 617-627-3443. *Application contact:* Arthur Utz, Information Contact, 617-627-3441, Fax: 617-627-3443.

See in-depth description on page 153.

Tulane University, Graduate School, Department of Chemistry, New Orleans, LA 70118-5669. Offers MA, MS, PhD. *Faculty:* 14 full-time. *Students:* 39 full-time (12 women), 3 part-time (1 woman); includes 4 minority (3 African Americans, 1 Asian American or Pacific Islander), 23 international. 128 applicants, 20% accepted, 13 enrolled. In 2003, 3 master's, 9 doctorates awarded. Terminal master's awarded for partial completion of doctoral program. *Degree requirements:* For master's and doctorate, thesis/dissertation. *Entrance requirements:* For master's, GRE General Test, minimum B average in undergraduate course work; for doctorate, GRE General Test. Additional exam requirements/recommendations for international students: Required—TOEFL; Recommended—TSE. *Application deadline:* For fall admission, 2/1 for domestic students, 2/1 for international students. Application fee: $45. Electronic applications accepted. *Financial support:* Fellowships with full tuition reimbursements, research assistantships with full tuition reimbursements, teaching assistantships with full tuition reimbursements, career-related internships or fieldwork, Federal Work-Study, and institutionally sponsored loans available. Financial award application deadline: 2/1. *Faculty research:* Enzyme mechanisms, organic synthesis, photochemistry, theory of polymer dynamics. Total annual research expenditures: $2.8 million. *Unit head:* Dr. Vaidhyanathan Ramamurthy, Chair, 504-865-5573. *Application contact:* Dr. Russell Schmehl, Director, 504-865-5573, Fax: 504-865-5596.

Tuskegee University, Graduate Programs, College of Agricultural, Environmental and Natural Sciences, Department of Chemistry, Tuskegee, AL 36088. Offers MS. *Faculty:* 6 full-time (1 woman). *Students:* 7 full-time (4 women), 2 part-time (1 woman); includes 7 minority (all African Americans), 1 international. Average age 33. In 2003, 7 degrees awarded. *Degree requirements:* For master's, thesis. *Entrance requirements:* For master's, GRE General Test. *Application deadline:* For fall admission, 7/15 for domestic students. Applications are processed on a rolling basis. Application fee: $25 ($35 for international students). *Expenses:* Tuition: Full-time $11,060; part-time $655 per credit hour. Required fees: $250. Tuition and fees vary according to course load. *Financial support:* Fellowships, teaching assistantships, Federal Work-Study and institutionally sponsored loans available. Support available to part-time students. Financial award application deadline: 4/15. *Unit head:* Dr. Gregory Pritchett, Head, 334-727-8836.

Université de Moncton, Faculty of Science, Department of Chemistry and Biochemistry, Moncton, NB E1A 3E9, Canada. Offers biochemistry (M Sc); chemistry (M Sc). Part-time programs available. *Degree requirements:* For master's, one foreign language, thesis. *Entrance requirements:* For master's, minimum GPA of 3.0. *Faculty research:* Environmental contaminants, natural products synthesis, nutraceutical, organic catalysis, molecular biology of cancer.

Université de Montréal, Faculty of Graduate Studies, Faculty of Arts and Sciences, Department of Chemistry, Montréal, QC H3C 3J7, Canada. Offers M Sc, PhD. *Faculty:* 31 full-time (7 women). *Students:* 170 full-time (56 women), 7 part-time (5 women). 66 applicants, 38% accepted, 23 enrolled. In 2003, 34 master's, 13 doctorates awarded. *Degree requirements:* For master's, thesis; for doctorate, thesis/dissertation, general exam. *Entrance requirements:* For master's, B Sc in chemistry or equivalent; for doctorate, M Sc in chemistry or equivalent. *Application deadline:* For fall and spring admission, 2/1; for winter admission, 11/1 for domestic students. Application fee: $30. Electronic applications accepted. *Expenses:* Tuition, state resident: full-time $834. Tuition, nonresident: full-time $1,253. International tuition: $3,900 full-time. Tuition and fees vary according to program. *Faculty research:* Analytical, inorganic, physical, and organic chemistry. *Unit head:* Robert Prud'homme, Chairman, 514-343-6730, Fax: 514-343-7586. *Application contact:* Andre Beauchamp, Professor, 514-343-6446, Fax: 514-343-7586, E-mail: andre.beauchamp@umontreal.ca.

Université de Sherbrooke, Faculty of Sciences, Department of Chemistry, Sherbrooke, QC J1K 2R1, Canada. Offers M Sc, PhD. *Degree requirements:* For master's and doctorate, thesis/dissertation. *Entrance requirements:* For doctorate, master's degree. *Faculty research:* Organic, electro-, theoretical, and physical chemistry.

Université du Québec à Montréal, Graduate Programs, Program in Chemistry, Montréal, QC H3C 3P8, Canada. Offers M Sc. Part-time programs available. *Degree requirements:* For master's, thesis. *Entrance requirements:* For master's, appropriate bachelor's degree or equivalent and proficiency in French.

Université du Québec à Trois-Rivières, Graduate Programs, Program in Chemistry, Trois-Rivières, QC G9A 5H7, Canada. Offers M Sc. Part-time programs available. *Degree requirements:* For master's, thesis. *Entrance requirements:* For master's, appropriate bachelor's degree, proficiency in French.

Université Laval, Faculty of Sciences and Engineering, Department of Chemistry, Programs in Chemistry, Québec, QC G1K 7P4, Canada. Offers M Sc, PhD. Part-time programs available. Terminal master's awarded for partial completion of doctoral program. *Degree requirements:* For master's, thesis/dissertation; for doctorate, thesis/dissertation, comprehensive exam. *Entrance requirements:* For master's and doctorate, knowledge of French, comprehension of written English. Electronic applications accepted.

University at Albany, State University of New York, College of Arts and Sciences, Department of Chemistry, Albany, NY 12222-0001. Offers MS, PhD. Evening/weekend programs available. *Students:* 33 full-time (12 women), 11 part-time (3 women). Average age 29. 49 applicants, 57% accepted, 15 enrolled. In 2003, 1 master's, 3 doctorates awarded. *Degree requirements:* For master's, one foreign language, thesis, major field exam; for doctorate, 2 foreign languages, thesis/dissertation, cumulative exams, oral proposition. *Entrance requirements:* For doctorate, GRE. Additional exam requirements/recommendations for international students: Required—TOEFL (minimum score 550 paper-based; 213 computer-based). *Application deadline:* For fall admission, 6/1 for domestic students, 6/1 for international students; for spring admission, 11/1 for domestic students, 6/1 for international students. Applications are processed on a rolling basis. Application fee: $50. Electronic applications accepted. *Expenses:* Tuition, state resident: part-time $288 per credit. Tuition, nonresident: part-time $438 per credit. Required fees: $495 per semester. *Financial support:* Research assistantships, teaching assistantships, minority assistantships available. Financial award application deadline: 6/1. *Faculty research:* Synthetic, organic, and inorganic chemistry; polymer chemistry; ESR and NMR spectroscopy; theoretical chemistry; physical biochemistry. *Unit head:* Dr. John Welch, Chair, 518-442-4400.

University at Albany, State University of New York, School of Public Health, Department of Environmental Health and Toxicology, Albany, NY 12222-0001. Offers environmental and occupational health (MS, PhD); environmental chemistry (MS, PhD); toxicology (MS, PhD). *Students:* 23 full-time (13 women), 14 part-time (8 women). Average age 32. 29 applicants, 52% accepted, 11 enrolled. In 2003, 1 master's, 4 doctorates awarded. *Degree requirements:* For master's and doctorate, thesis/dissertation. *Entrance requirements:* For master's and doctorate, GRE General Test, GRE Subject Test. Additional exam requirements/recommendations for international students: Required—TOEFL (minimum score 550 paper-based; 213 computer-based). *Application deadline:* For fall admission, 1/15 for domestic students, 1/15 for international students; for spring admission, 11/1 for domestic students, 11/1 for international students. Applications are processed on a rolling basis. Application fee: $50. Electronic applications accepted. *Expenses:* Tuition, state resident: part-time $288 per credit. Tuition, nonresident: part-time $438 per credit. Required fees: $495 per semester. *Financial support:* Fellowships, research assistantships available. Financial award application deadline: 2/1. *Unit head:* Dr. Laurence Kaminsky, Chair, 518-473-7553.

University at Buffalo, The State University of New York, Graduate School, College of Arts and Sciences, Department of Chemistry, Buffalo, NY 14260. Offers chemistry (MA, PhD); medicinal chemistry (MS, PhD). Part-time programs available. *Faculty:* 33 full-time (3 women), 3 part-time/adjunct (0 women). *Students:* 121 full-time (42 women), 17 part-time (3 women); includes 12 minority (4 African Americans, 1 American Indian/Alaska Native, 2 Asian Americans or Pacific Islanders, 5 Hispanic Americans), 44 international. Average age 24. 296 applicants, 18% accepted. In 2003, 7 master's, 14 doctorates awarded. Terminal master's awarded for partial completion of doctoral program. *Median time to degree:* Of those who began their doctoral program in fall 1995, 100% received their degree in 8 years or less. *Degree requirements:* For master's, thesis or alternative, project; for doctorate, thesis/dissertation. *Entrance requirements:* For master's and doctorate, GRE General Test, GRE Subject Test. Additional exam requirements/recommendations for international students: Required—TOEFL. *Application deadline:* For fall admission, 5/15 for domestic students. Applications are processed on a rolling basis. Application fee: $35. Electronic applications accepted. *Expenses:* Tuition, state resident: full-time $7,110. Tuition, nonresident: full-time $10,920. Tuition and fees vary according to program. *Financial support:* In 2003–04, 10 fellowships with full tuition reimbursements, 63 research assistantships with full tuition reimbursements, 52 teaching assistantships with full tuition reimbursements were awarded. Federal Work-Study, institutionally sponsored loans, and unspecified assistantships also available. Financial award application deadline: 6/15; financial award applicants required to submit FAFSA. *Faculty research:* Synthesis, materials, environmental, analytical bio-organic, protein structure. Total annual research expenditures: $6.6 million. *Unit head:* Dr. Jim D. Atwood, Chairman, 716-645-6800 Ext. 2015, Fax: 716-645-6963, E-mail: chechair@acsu.buffalo.edu. *Application contact:* Dr. Huw M. L. Davies, Director of Graduate Studies, 716-645-6800 Ext. 2030, Fax: 716-645-6963, E-mail: hdavies@acsu.buffalo.edu.

The University of Akron, Graduate School, Buchtel College of Arts and Sciences, Department of Chemistry, Akron, OH 44325-0001. Offers MS, PhD. Part-time and evening/weekend programs available. *Faculty:* 17 full-time (2 women). *Students:* 73 full-time (31 women), 3 part-time (1 woman); includes 10 minority (1 African American, 3 Asian Americans or Pacific Islanders, 6 Hispanic Americans), 43 international. Average age 30. 49 applicants, 47% accepted, 13 enrolled. In 2003, 3 master's, 7 doctorates awarded. Terminal master's awarded for partial completion of doctoral program. *Degree requirements:* For master's, one foreign language, thesis, seminar presentation; for doctorate, 2 foreign languages, thesis/dissertation, cumulative exams. *Entrance requirements:* For master's and doctorate, minimum GPA of 2.75. Additional exam requirements/recommendations for international students: Required—TOEFL (minimum score 550 paper-based; 213 computer-based), Michigan English Language Assessment Battery. *Application deadline:* For fall admission, 3/1 for domestic students. Applications are processed on a rolling basis. Application fee: $40 ($60 for international students). *Expenses:* Tuition, state resident: part-time $277 per credit hour. Tuition, nonresident: part-time $476 per credit hour. *Financial support:* In 2003–04, 7 fellowships with full tuition reimbursements, 21 research assistantships with full tuition reimbursements, 41 teaching assistantships with full tuition reimbursements were awarded. Tuition waivers (full) also available. Support available to part-time students. Total annual research expenditures: $1.5 million. *Unit head:* Dr. Michael Taschner, Acting Chair, 330-972-7372, E-mail: mtaschner@uakron.edu.

The University of Alabama, Graduate School, College of Arts and Sciences, Department of Chemistry, Tuscaloosa, AL 35487. Offers MS, PhD. Postbaccalaureate distance learning degree programs offered (minimal on-campus study). *Faculty:* 18 full-time (1 woman). *Students:* 65 full-time (22 women), 14 part-time (3 women); includes 9 minority (7 African Americans, 1 Asian American or Pacific Islander, 1 Hispanic American), 39 international. Average age 27. 127 applicants, 21% accepted, 14 enrolled. In 2003, 4 master's, 9 doctorates awarded. *Degree requirements:* For master's, thesis (for some programs); for doctorate, thesis/dissertation, exams, research proposal, oral defense. *Entrance requirements:* For master's and doctorate, American Chemical Society Exam, GRE General Test, MAT, minimum GPA of 3.0. *Application deadline:* For fall admission, 1/15 for domestic students. Applications are processed on a rolling basis. Application fee: $25. Electronic applications accepted. *Expenses:* Tuition, state resident: full-time $4,134; part-time $230 per credit hour. Tuition, nonresident: full-time $11,294; part-time $627 per credit hour. Part-time tuition and fees vary according to course load. *Financial support:* In 2003–04, 10 fellowships with full tuition reimbursements (averaging $15,000 per year), 27 research assistantships with full tuition reimbursements (averaging $15,000 per year), 32 teaching assistantships with full tuition reimbursements (averaging $1,500 per year) were awarded. Career-related internships or fieldwork, Federal Work-Study, and scholarships/grants also available. Financial award application deadline: 7/14. *Faculty research:* Synthetic chemistry, environmental chemistry and green manufacturing, materials science and information technology, biological chemistry and biomolecular products. Total annual research expenditures: $3,100. *Unit head:* Dr. Joseph S. Thrasher, Chair, 205-348-8436, Fax: 205-348-9104, E-mail: gradchem@bama.ua.edu.

See in-depth description on page 155.

The University of Alabama at Birmingham, School of Natural Sciences and Mathematics, Department of Chemistry, Birmingham, AL 35294. Offers MS, PhD. *Faculty:* 15 full-time, 6 part-time/adjunct. *Students:* 20 full-time (8 women), 2 part-time; includes 1 minority (Asian American or Pacific Islander), 4 international. 97 applicants, 21% accepted. In 2003, 2 master's, 2 doctorates awarded. *Degree requirements:* For master's and doctorate, thesis/dissertation. *Entrance requirements:* For master's and doctorate, GRE General Test. Additional exam requirements/recommendations for international students: Required—TOEFL. *Application deadline:* Applications are processed on a rolling basis. Application fee: $35 ($60 for international students). *Expenses:* Tuition, state resident: full-time $4,142; part-time $141 per credit hour. Tuition, nonresident: full-time $9,230; part-time $353 per credit hour. Required fees: $4 per credit hour. *Financial support:* In 2003–04, 10 fellowships with full tuition reimbursements (averaging $13,500 per year), 6 research assistantships with full tuition reimbursements (averaging $13,500 per year), 4 teaching assistantships with full tuition reimbursements (averaging $13,500 per year) were awarded. Career-related internships or fieldwork, Federal Work-Study, institutionally sponsored loans, tuition waivers (full and partial), and unspecified assistantships also available. Support available to part-time students. Financial award application deadline: 5/1; financial award applicants required to submit FAFSA. *Faculty research:* General and biochemical synthesis; spectroscopic studies of chemical systems; analysis using chromatography, GC/MS, and designed electrode system. *Unit head:* Dr. David E. Graves, Chair, 205-934-8276, Fax: 205-934-2543.

The University of Alabama in Huntsville, School of Graduate Studies, College of Science, Department of Chemistry, Huntsville, AL 35899. Offers MS. Part-time and evening/weekend programs available. *Faculty:* 8 full-time (1 woman), 1 part-time/adjunct (0 women). *Students:* 9 full-time (4 women), 2 part-time (1 woman); includes 3 minority (2 African Americans, 1 American Indian/Alaska Native), 2 international. Average age 25. 7 applicants, 86% accepted, 6 enrolled. *Degree requirements:* For master's, thesis or alternative, oral and written exams, comprehensive exam, registration. *Entrance requirements:* For master's, GRE General Test, minimum GPA of 3.0. Additional exam requirements/recommendations for international students: Required—TOEFL (minimum score 550 paper-based; 213 computer-based). *Application deadline:* For fall admission, 5/30 priority date for domestic students, 2/30 priority date for international students; for spring admission, 10/10 priority date for domestic students, 7/10 priority date for international students. Applications are processed on a rolling basis. Application fee: $35. *Expenses:* Tuition, state resident: full-time $5,168; part-time $211 per hour. Tuition, nonresident: full-time $10,620; part-time $447 per hour. Tuition and fees vary according to course load. *Financial support:* In 2003–04, 7 students received support, including 1 research assistantship with full and partial tuition reimbursement available (averaging $12,000 per year), 6 teaching assistantships with full and partial tuition reimbursements available (averaging $9,315 per year); fellowships with full and partial tuition reimbursements available, career-related internships or fieldwork, Federal Work-Study, institutionally sponsored loans, scholarships/grants, health care benefits, tuition waivers (full and partial), and unspecified assistantships also available. Support available to part-time students. Financial award application deadline: 4/1; financial award applicants required to submit FAFSA. *Faculty research:* Kinetics and bonding, organic nonlinear optical materials, x-ray crystallography, crystal growth in space, polymers, Raman spectroscopy. Total annual research expenditures: $604,802. *Unit head:* Dr. James Baird, Chair, 256-824-6153, Fax: 256-824-6349, E-mail: jbaird@matsci.uah.edu.

University of Alaska Fairbanks, College of Science, Engineering and Mathematics, Department of Chemistry and Biochemistry, Fairbanks, AK 99775-7520. Offers biochemistry (MS, PhD); chemistry (MA, MS). Part-time programs available. Terminal master's awarded for partial completion of doctoral program. *Degree requirements:* For master's, thesis, seminar, comprehensive exam, registration; for doctorate, thesis/dissertation, comprehensive exam, registration. *Entrance requirements:* For master's, GRE General Test; for doctorate, GRE General Test, GRE Subject Test (biology or chemistry). Additional exam requirements/recommendations for international students: Required—TOEFL. Electronic applications accepted.

University of Alberta, Faculty of Graduate Studies and Research, Department of Chemistry, Edmonton, AB T6G 2E1, Canada. Offers M Sc, PhD. Part-time programs available. *Faculty:* 29 full-time (1 woman), 1 part-time/adjunct (0 women). *Students:* 137 full-time (39 women), 18 part-time (5 women), 37 international. 121 applicants, 69% accepted, 29 enrolled. In 2003, 9 master's, 28 doctorates awarded. Terminal master's awarded for partial completion of doctoral program. *Median time to degree:* Master's–3 years full-time; doctorate–5 years full-time. *Degree requirements:* For master's and doctorate, thesis/dissertation. *Entrance requirements:* For master's and doctorate, minimum GPA of 6.5 on 9 point scale. *Application deadline:* Applications are processed on a rolling basis. *Expenses:* Contact institution. Tuition charges are reported in Canadian dollars. *Financial support:* In 2003–04, 30 fellowships (averaging $21,175 per year), 19 research assistantships (averaging $20,500 per year), 96 teaching assistantships with partial tuition reimbursements (averaging $20,500 per year) were awarded. Scholarships/grants also available. *Faculty research:* Synthetic inorganic and organic chemistry, chemical biology and biochemical analysis, materials and surface chemistry, spectroscopy and instrumentation, computational chemistry. Total annual research expenditures: $10 million Canadian dollars. *Unit head:* Dr. Martin Cowie, Chair, 780-492-3249. *Application contact:* Ilona Baker, Department Office, 780-492-4414, Fax: 780-492-8231, E-mail: grad@chem.ualberta.ca.

The University of Arizona, Graduate College, College of Science, Department of Chemistry, Tucson, AZ 85721. Offers MA, MS, PhD. Part-time programs available. *Faculty:* 26 full-time (6 women). *Students:* Average age 28. 322 applicants, 18% accepted, 41 enrolled. In 2003, 9 master's, 15 doctorates awarded. Terminal master's awarded for partial completion of doctoral program. *Median time to degree:* Of those who began their doctoral program in fall 1995, 40% received their degree in 8 years or less. *Degree requirements:* For master's, thesis (for some programs), registration; for doctorate, thesis/dissertation, comprehensive exam, registration. *Entrance requirements:* For master's and doctorate, American Chemical Society Exam. Additional exam requirements/recommendations for international students: Required—TOEFL (minimum score 550 paper-based; 213 computer-based), SPEAK test or TSE. *Application deadline:* For fall admission, 2/1 priority date for domestic students, 12/1 priority date for international students. Applications are processed on a rolling basis. Application fee: $50. Electronic applications accepted. *Expenses:* Tuition, state resident: part-time $196 per unit. Tuition, nonresident: part-time $326 per unit. *Financial support:* In 2003–04, 74 research assistantships with partial tuition reimbursements (averaging $17,800 per year), 68 teaching assistantships with partial tuition reimbursements (averaging $17,800 per year) were awarded. Institutionally sponsored loans, scholarships/grants, health care benefits, tuition waivers (partial), and unspecified assistantships also available. Financial award applicants required to submit FAFSA. *Faculty research:* Analytical, inorganic, organic, physical chemistry, biological chemistry. Total annual research expenditures: $800,800. *Unit head:* Dr. Mark A. Smith, Head, 520-621-6354, Fax: 520-621-8407, E-mail: chemistry@arizona.edu. *Application contact:* Penny Davis, Information Contact, 520-621-4362, Fax: 520-621-8407, E-mail: chemistry@arizona.edu.

University of Arkansas, Graduate School, J. William Fulbright College of Arts and Sciences, Department of Chemistry and Biochemistry, Fayetteville, AR 72701-1201. Offers chemistry (MS, PhD). *Students:* 56 full-time (21 women), 3 part-time (1 woman); includes 5 minority (2 African Americans, 1 American Indian/Alaska Native, 2 Asian Americans or Pacific Islanders), 17 international. 66 applicants, 39% accepted. In 2003, 1 master's, 6 doctorates awarded. *Degree requirements:* For master's and doctorate, one foreign language, thesis/dissertation. Application fee: $40 ($50 for international students). *Expenses:* Tuition, state resident: full-time $4,032; part-time $224 per credit hour. Tuition, nonresident: full-time $9,540; part-time $530 per credit hour. Tuition and fees vary according to course load and program. *Financial support:* In 2003–04, 22 fellowships, 27 research assistantships, 30 teaching assistantships were awarded. Career-related internships or fieldwork and Federal Work-Study also available. Support available to part-time students. Financial award application deadline: 4/1; financial award applicants required to submit FAFSA. *Unit head:* Dr. Bill Durham, Chair, 479-575-4601, E-mail: dchem@comp.uark.edu.

University of Arkansas at Little Rock, Graduate School, College of Science and Mathematics, Department of Chemistry, Little Rock, AR 72204-1099. Offers MA, MS. Part-time and evening/weekend programs available. *Students:* 6 full-time (3 women), 8 part-time (4 women); includes 1 minority (African American), 4 international. Average age 29. 18 applicants, 72% accepted. In 2003, 2 degrees awarded. *Degree requirements:* For master's, thesis (MS). *Entrance requirements:* For master's, minimum GPA of 2.7. *Application deadline:* Applications are processed on a rolling basis. Application fee: $25 ($30 for international students). Tuition, nonresident: part-time $177 per credit hour. *Financial support:* Research assistantships, teaching assistantships, Federal Work-Study, institutionally sponsored loans, and unspecified assistantships available. *Unit head:* Dr. Robert Steinmeier, Chairperson, 501-569-8823, E-mail: rcsteinmeier@ualr.edu.

The University of British Columbia, Faculty of Graduate Studies, Faculty of Science, Department of Chemistry, Vancouver, BC V6T 1Z1, Canada. Offers M Sc, PhD. *Faculty:* 50 full-time (5 women), 10 part-time/adjunct (1 woman). *Students:* 160 full-time (61 women). Average age 25. 148 applicants, 57% accepted, 45 enrolled. In 2003, 9 master's, 15 doctorates awarded. Terminal master's awarded for partial completion of doctoral program. *Median time to degree:* Of those who began their doctoral program in fall 1995, 100% received their degree in 8 years or less. *Degree requirements:* For master's, thesis/dissertation; for doctorate, thesis/dissertation, comprehensive exam. *Entrance requirements:* For master's and doctorate, GRE General Test, GRE Subject Test. Additional exam requirements/recommendations for international students: Required—TOEFL (minimum score 580 paper-based; 237 computer-based). *Application deadline:* For fall admission, 5/1 for domestic students, 4/1 for international students; for winter admission, 9/1 for domestic students. Applications are processed on a

Chemistry

The University of British Columbia (continued)

rolling basis. Application fee: $90 Canadian dollars ($150 Canadian dollars for international students). Electronic applications accepted. *Financial support:* In 2003–04, 39 students received support, including 22 fellowships with full and partial tuition reimbursements available (averaging $8,000 Canadian dollars per year), 138 research assistantships with full and partial tuition reimbursements available (averaging $12,800 Canadian dollars per year), 155 teaching assistantships with full and partial tuition reimbursements available (averaging $6,500 Canadian dollars per year); institutionally sponsored loans, scholarships/grants, health care benefits, tuition waivers (full and partial), and unspecified assistantships also available. *Faculty research:* Organic, physical, analytical, inorganic, and bio-chemical projects. Total annual research expenditures: $4.2 million Canadian dollars. *Unit head:* Dr. Michael Blades, Acting Head, 604-822-3266, Fax: 604-822-2847, E-mail: head@chem.ubc.ca. *Application contact:* Janis Hanen, Graduate Admissions, 604-822-6102, Fax: 604-822-2847, E-mail: gradsec@chem.ubc.ca.

University of Calgary, Faculty of Graduate Studies, Faculty of Science, Department of Chemistry, Calgary, AB T2N 1N4, Canada. Offers analytical chemistry (M Sc, PhD); applied chemistry (M Sc, PhD); inorganic chemistry (M Sc, PhD); organic chemistry (M Sc, PhD); physical chemistry (M Sc, PhD); polymer chemistry (M Sc, PhD); theoretical chemistry (M Sc, PhD). *Faculty:* 29 full-time (6 women), 1 part-time/adjunct (0 women). *Students:* 74 full-time (29 women). Average age 25. 130 applicants, 20% accepted. In 2003, 12 master's, 6 doctorates awarded. *Degree requirements:* For master's, thesis; for doctorate, thesis/dissertation, candidacy exam. *Entrance requirements:* For master's, minimum GPA of 3.0; for doctorate, honors degree minimum GPA of 3.7, minimum GPA of 3.3. Additional exam requirements/recommendations for international students: Required—TOEFL (minimum score 580 paper-based; 237 computer-based). *Application deadline:* For fall admission, 12/1 for domestic students. Applications are processed on a rolling basis. Application fee: $60. Electronic applications accepted. Tuition, nonresident: full-time $4,765. Tuition and fees vary according to degree level, program and student level. *Financial support:* In 2003–04, research assistantships (averaging $11,000 per year), teaching assistantships (averaging $6,221 per year) were awarded. Fellowships, scholarships/grants also available. Financial award application deadline: 12/1. *Faculty research:* Chemical analysis, chemical dynamics, synthesis theory, polymer, applied chemistry. *Unit head:* Dr. Brian Keay, Head, 403-220-6252, E-mail: gradinfo@chem.ucalgary.ca.

University of California, Berkeley, Graduate Division, College of Chemistry, Department of Chemistry, Berkeley, CA 94720-1500. Offers PhD. *Faculty:* 53 full-time (6 women), 2 part-time/adjunct (1 woman). *Students:* 380 (134 women); includes 65 minority (6 African Americans, 4 American Indian/Alaska Native, 37 Asian Americans or Pacific Islanders, 18 Hispanic Americans) 59 international. 565 applicants, 35% accepted, 87 enrolled. In 2003, 56 degrees awarded. *Degree requirements:* For doctorate, thesis/dissertation, qualifying exam. *Entrance requirements:* For doctorate, GRE General Test, GRE Subject Test, minimum GPA of 3.0. Additional exam requirements/recommendations for international students: Required—TOEFL, TSE. *Application deadline:* For fall admission, 12/15 for domestic students, 12/15 for international students. Applications are processed on a rolling basis. Application fee: $60. Electronic applications accepted. International tuition: $12,491 full-time. Required fees: $5,484. *Financial support:* Fellowships, research assistantships with full tuition reimbursements, teaching assistantships with partial tuition reimbursements, unspecified assistantships available. Financial award application deadline: 12/15. *Faculty research:* Analytical bioinorganic, bio-organic, biophysical environmental, inorganic and organometallic. *Unit head:* Dr. Judith P. Klinman, Chair, 510-643-0573, Fax: 510-642-9675, E-mail: chemgrad@cchem.berkeley.edu. *Application contact:* Student Affairs Officers, 510-642-5882, Fax: 510-642-9675, E-mail: chemgrad@cchem.berkeley.edu.

University of California, Berkeley, Graduate Division, College of Natural Resources, Group in Agricultural and Environmental Chemistry, Berkeley, CA 94720-1500. Offers MS, PhD. *Students:* 3, 2 international. 6 applicants, 17% accepted, 0 enrolled.Terminal master's awarded for partial completion of doctoral program. *Degree requirements:* For master's, exam or thesis; for doctorate, thesis/dissertation, qualifying exam, seminar presentation. *Entrance requirements:* For master's and doctorate, GRE General Test, minimum GPA of 3.0. *Application deadline:* For fall admission, 1/5 for domestic students. Application fee: $60. International tuition: $12,491 full-time. Required fees: $5,484. *Financial support:* Research assistantships, Federal Work-Study, institutionally sponsored loans, and unspecified assistantships available. Financial award application deadline: 1/5. *Unit head:* Dr. Isao Kubo, Chair, 510-642-5167. *Application contact:* Kyle Dukart, Graduate Assistant for Admission, 510-642-5167, Fax: 510-642-4995, E-mail: kdukart@nature.berkeley.edu.

University of California, Davis, Graduate Studies, Graduate Group in Agricultural and Environmental Chemistry, Davis, CA 95616. Offers MS, PhD. *Faculty:* 46 full-time. *Students:* 48 full-time (25 women); includes 5 minority (1 African American, 1 American Indian/Alaska Native, 3 Asian Americans or Pacific Islanders), 25 international. Average age 30. 47 applicants, 79% accepted, 12 enrolled. In 2003, 1 master's, 7 doctorates awarded. *Degree requirements:* For master's and doctorate, thesis/dissertation. *Entrance requirements:* For master's and doctorate, GRE General Test, minimum GPA of 3.0. Additional exam requirements/recommendations for international students: Required—TOEFL (minimum score 550 paper-based; 213 computer-based). *Application deadline:* For fall admission, 1/15 for domestic students, 1/15 for international students. Application fee: $60. Electronic applications accepted. Tuition, nonresident: full-time $12,245. Required fees: $7,062. *Financial support:* In 2003–04, 41 students received support, including 4 fellowships with full and partial tuition reimbursements available (averaging $12,914 per year), 25 research assistantships with full and partial tuition reimbursements available (averaging $13,804 per year), 6 teaching assistantships with partial tuition reimbursements available (averaging $11,787 per year); Federal Work-Study, institutionally sponsored loans, scholarships/grants, tuition waivers (full and partial), and unspecified assistantships also available. Financial award application deadline: 1/15; financial award applicants required to submit FAFSA. *Unit head:* Andrew Clifford, Graduate Group Chair, 530-752-3376, E-mail: ajclifford@ucdavis.edu. *Application contact:* Peggy Royale, Graduate Administrative Assistant, 530-752-1415, Fax: 530-752-4759, E-mail: pbroyale@ucdavis.edu.

University of California, Davis, Graduate Studies, Program in Chemistry, Davis, CA 95616. Offers MS, PhD. *Faculty:* 40 full-time (6 women). *Students:* 176 full-time (69 women); includes 27 minority (3 African Americans, 1 American Indian/Alaska Native, 16 Asian Americans or Pacific Islanders, 7 Hispanic Americans), 65 international. Average age 28. 246 applicants, 45% accepted, 44 enrolled. In 2003, 3 master's, 13 doctorates awarded. *Degree requirements:* For master's and doctorate, thesis/dissertation. *Entrance requirements:* For master's, minimum GPA of 3.0; for doctorate, GRE, minimum GPA of 3.0. Additional exam requirements/recommendations for international students: Required—TOEFL (minimum score 550 paper-based; 213 computer-based). *Application deadline:* For fall admission, 4/1 for domestic students, 3/1 for international students. Applications are processed on a rolling basis. Application fee: $60. Electronic applications accepted. Tuition, nonresident: full-time $12,245. Required fees: $7,062. *Financial support:* In 2003–04, 166 students received support, including 2 fellowships with full and partial tuition reimbursements available (averaging $11,420 per year), 71 research assistantships with full and partial tuition reimbursements available (averaging $12,890 per year), 68 teaching assistantships with partial tuition reimbursements available (averaging $13,644 per year); Federal Work-Study, institutionally sponsored loans, scholarships/grants, and tuition waivers (full and partial) also available. Financial award application deadline: 1/15; financial award applicants required to submit FAFSA. *Faculty research:* Analytical, biological, organic, inorganic, and theoretical chemistry. *Unit head:* William M. Jackson, Chair, 530-752-0504, Fax: 530-752-8995, E-mail: wmjackson@ucdavis.edu. *Application contact:* Carol Barnes, Graduate Program Staff, 530-752-0953, E-mail: cbarnes@ucdavis.edu.

University of California, Irvine, Office of Graduate Studies, School of Physical Sciences, Department of Chemistry, Irvine, CA 92697. Offers chemical and material physics (PhD); chemical and materials physics (MS); chemistry (MS, PhD). *Students:* 175. In 2003, 7 master's, 18 doctorates awarded. *Degree requirements:* For doctorate, thesis/dissertation. *Entrance requirements:* For master's and doctorate, GRE General Test, GRE Subject Test, minimum GPA of 3.0. Additional exam requirements/recommendations for international students: Required—TOEFL (minimum score 550 paper-based; 213 computer-based). *Application deadline:* For fall admission, 1/15 for domestic students; for winter admission, 10/15 for domestic students. Applications are processed on a rolling basis. Application fee: $60. Electronic applications accepted. Tuition, nonresident: full-time $12,245. Required fees: $5,219. Tuition and fees vary according to degree level and program. *Financial support:* Fellowships, research assistantships with full tuition reimbursements, teaching assistantships, institutionally sponsored loans, traineeships, health care benefits, and unspecified assistantships available. Financial award application deadline: 3/1; financial award applicants required to submit FAFSA. *Faculty research:* Analytical, organic, inorganic, physical, and atmospheric chemistry; biogeochemistry and climate; synthetic chemistry. *Unit head:* Dr. Kenneth J. Shea, Chair, 949-824-6018, Fax: 949-824-8571, E-mail: kjshea@uci.edu. *Application contact:* Renee Frigo, Graduate Affairs Officer, 949-824-3082, Fax: 949-824-8571, E-mail: rfrigo@uci.edu.

University of California, Los Angeles, Graduate Division, College of Letters and Science, Department of Chemistry and Biochemistry, Program in Chemistry, Los Angeles, CA 90095. Offers MS, PhD. *Entrance requirements:* For master's, GRE General Test, GRE Subject Test, minimum GPA of 3.0; for doctorate, GRE General Test, GRE Subject Test, minimum undergraduate GPA of 3.0. Electronic applications accepted. Tuition, nonresident: full-time $12,245. Required fees: $6,318.

University of California, Riverside, Graduate Division, Department of Chemistry, Riverside, CA 92521-0102. Offers MS, PhD. *Faculty:* 24 full-time (2 women). *Students:* 76 full-time (23 women), 1 part-time; includes 6 minority (5 Asian Americans or Pacific Islanders, 1 Hispanic American), 36 international. Average age 28. In 2003, 8 master's, 14 doctorates awarded. Terminal master's awarded for partial completion of doctoral program. *Median time to degree:* Master's–1.5 years full-time; doctorate–5.5 years full-time. *Degree requirements:* For master's, comprehensive exams or thesis; for doctorate, thesis/dissertation, qualifying exams, 3 quarters of teaching experience, research proposition. *Entrance requirements:* For master's and doctorate, GRE General Test, minimum GPA of 3.0. Additional exam requirements/recommendations for international students: Required—TOEFL (paper score 550; computer score 213) or TSE (greatly preferred). *Application deadline:* For fall admission, 5/1 for domestic students, 2/1 for international students; for winter admission, 9/1 for domestic students; for spring admission, 12/1 for domestic students. Applications are processed on a rolling basis. Application fee: $60. Electronic applications accepted. Tuition, nonresident: part-time $4,082 per quarter. *Financial support:* In 2003–04, fellowships with full tuition reimbursements (averaging $6,000 per year), research assistantships with full tuition reimbursements (averaging $13,000 per year), 34 teaching assistantships with full tuition reimbursements (averaging $14,000 per year) were awarded. Career-related internships or fieldwork, Federal Work-Study, institutionally sponsored loans, and tuition waivers (full and partial) also available. Financial award application deadline: 2/1; financial award applicants required to submit FAFSA. *Faculty research:* Analytical, inorganic, organic, and physical chemistry; chemical physics. Total annual research expenditures: $4 million. *Unit head:* Prof. Christopher Y. Switzer, Chair, 951-827-3488, Fax: 951-827-4713, E-mail: chemchr@ucr.edu. *Application contact:* Prof. Michael J. Marsella, Graduate Adviser, Recruitment, 800-445-3153, Fax: 951-827-4713, E-mail: gradchem@citurs.ucr.edu.

See in-depth description on page 159.

University of California, San Diego, Graduate Studies and Research, Department of Chemistry and Biochemistry, La Jolla, CA 92093. Offers chemistry (MS, PhD). *Faculty:* 55. *Students:* 240 (100 women); includes 58 minority (2 African Americans, 1 American Indian/Alaska Native, 35 Asian Americans or Pacific Islanders, 20 Hispanic Americans) 32 international. 510 applicants, 28% accepted. In 2003, 44 master's, 21 doctorates awarded. *Degree requirements:* For doctorate, thesis/dissertation. *Entrance requirements:* For doctorate, GRE General Test, GRE Subject Test. *Application deadline:* For fall admission, 1/18 for domestic students. Application fee: $60. Electronic applications accepted. Tuition, nonresident: full-time $12,245. Required fees: $6,959. *Unit head:* Cliff Kubiak, Chair. *Application contact:* Applications Coordinator, 858-534-6871.

See in-depth description on page 161.

University of California, San Francisco, School of Pharmacy and Graduate Division, Chemistry and Chemical Biology Graduate Program, San Francisco, CA 94143. Offers PhD. *Faculty:* 47 full-time (10 women), 1 part-time/adjunct (0 women). *Students:* 55 full-time (22 women); includes 20 minority (2 African Americans, 16 Asian Americans or Pacific Islanders, 2 Hispanic Americans), 2 international. Average age 27. 94 applicants, 16% accepted. In 2003, 5 doctorates awarded, leading to university research/teaching 80%, business/industry 20%. *Median time to degree:* Doctorate–5.5 years full-time. Of those who began their doctoral program in fall 1995, 100% received their degree in 8 years or less. *Degree requirements:* For doctorate, thesis/dissertation. *Entrance requirements:* For doctorate, GRE General Test, GRE Subject Test, minimum GPA of 3.0. Additional exam requirements/recommendations for international students: Required—TOEFL. *Application deadline:* For fall admission, 1/5 for domestic students. Applications are processed on a rolling basis. Application fee: $60. *Financial support:* In 2003–04, 13 fellowships with partial tuition reimbursements (averaging $16,211 per year), 7 research assistantships with full tuition reimbursements (averaging $24,500 per year), 3 teaching assistantships with partial tuition reimbursements (averaging $8,166 per year) were awarded. Institutionally sponsored loans, scholarships/grants, traineeships, and tuition waivers (full) also available. Financial award application deadline: 1/10. *Faculty research:* Biochemistry; macromolecular structure; cellular and molecular pharmacology; physical chemistry and computational biology; synthetic chemistry. *Unit head:* Dr. Charles S. Craik, Director, 415-476-1913, Fax: 415-502-4690. *Application contact:* Christine Olson, Graduate Program Coordinator, 415-476-1914, Fax: 415-514-1546, E-mail: ccb@picasso.ucsf.edu.

See in-depth description on page 163.

University of California, Santa Barbara, Graduate Division, College of Letters and Sciences, Division of Mathematics, Life, and Physical Sciences, Department of Chemistry and Biochemistry, Santa Barbara, CA 93106. Offers MA, MS, PhD. Terminal master's awarded for partial completion of doctoral program. *Degree requirements:* For master's, thesis or alternative; for doctorate, thesis/dissertation. *Entrance requirements:* For master's and doctorate, GRE. Additional exam requirements/recommendations for international students: Required—TOEFL. *Application deadline:* For fall admission, 5/1 for domestic students; for winter admission, 12/1 for domestic students; for spring admission, 1/1 for domestic students. Applications are processed on a rolling basis. Application fee: $60. Electronic applications accepted. *Expenses:* Tuition, state resident: full-time $7,188. Tuition, nonresident: full-time $19,608. *Financial support:* In 2003–04, 10 fellowships with full tuition reimbursements (averaging $12,000 per year), 35 research assistantships with full tuition reimbursements (averaging $17,388 per year), 53 teaching assistantships with full tuition reimbursements (averaging $17,471 per year) were awarded. Career-related internships or fieldwork, Federal Work-Study, institutionally sponsored loans, scholarships/grants, and traineeships also available. Financial award application deadline: 1/15; financial award applicants required to submit FAFSA. *Faculty research:* Organic, biological, inorganic, physical, and materials chemistry. Total annual research expenditures: $7 million. *Unit head:* Dr. Stanley M. Parsons, Chair, 805-893-2056, Fax: 805-893-4120, E-mail: chemchair@chem.ucsb.edu. *Application contact:* Deedrea Anne Edgar, Manager, Student Affairs and External Relations, 805-893-2638, Fax: 805-893-4120, E-mail: edgar@chem.ucsb.edu.

University of California, Santa Cruz, Division of Graduate Studies, Division of Physical and Biological Sciences, Department of Chemistry, Santa Cruz, CA 95064. Offers MS, PhD. *Faculty:* 22 full-time (3 women). *Students:* 80 full-time (38 women); includes 23 minority (2 African Americans, 1 American Indian/Alaska Native, 10 Asian Americans or Pacific Islanders, 10 Hispanic Americans), 11 international. 142 applicants, 41% accepted, 21 enrolled. In 2003,

2 master's, 14 doctorates awarded. *Median time to degree:* Master's–2.75 years full-time; doctorate–5.17 years full-time. *Degree requirements:* For doctorate, one foreign language, thesis/dissertation, qualifying exam. *Entrance requirements:* For master's and doctorate, GRE General Test, GRE Subject Test. *Application deadline:* For fall admission, 1/15 for domestic students. Application fee: $60. Tuition, nonresident: full-time $12,492. *Financial support:* Fellowships, research assistantships, teaching assistantships, Federal Work-Study and institutionally sponsored loans available. Financial award application deadline: 1/15. *Faculty research:* Marine chemistry; biochemistry; inorganic, organic, and physical chemistry. *Unit head:* Dr. Joseph Konopelski, Chair, 831-459-2067. *Application contact:* Evie Alloy, Department Assistant, 831-459-2023, E-mail: gradinfo@chemistry.ucsc.edu.

University of Central Florida, College of Arts and Sciences, Program in Industrial Chemistry, Orlando, FL 32816. Offers MS. Part-time and evening/weekend programs available. *Faculty:* 18 full-time (3 women), 1 part-time/adjunct (0 women). *Students:* 15 full-time (11 women), 41 part-time (17 women); includes 8 minority (1 African American, 4 Asian Americans or Pacific Islanders, 3 Hispanic Americans), 11 international. Average age 33. 63 applicants, 67% accepted, 22 enrolled. In 2003, 10 degrees awarded. *Degree requirements:* For master's, thesis, final exam. *Entrance requirements:* For master's, GRE General Test, minimum GPA of 3.0 in last 60 hours. Additional exam requirements/recommendations for international students: Required—TOEFL. *Application deadline:* For fall admission, 7/15 for domestic students; for spring admission, 12/1 for domestic students. Application fee: $30. Electronic applications accepted. *Expenses:* Tuition, state resident: full-time $4,968; part-time $171 per credit hour. Tuition, nonresident: full-time $18,630; part-time $713 per credit hour. *Financial support:* In 2003–04, 8 fellowships with partial tuition reimbursements (averaging $2,140 per year), 14 research assistantships with partial tuition reimbursements (averaging $5,900 per year), 22 teaching assistantships with partial tuition reimbursements (averaging $7,340 per year) were awarded. Career-related internships or fieldwork, Federal Work-Study, institutionally sponsored loans, tuition waivers (partial), and unspecified assistantships also available. Financial award application deadline: 3/1; financial award applicants required to submit FAFSA. *Faculty research:* Physical and synthetic organic chemistry, lasers, polymers, biochemical action of pesticides, environmental analysis. Total annual research expenditures: $645,000. *Unit head:* Dr. Glenn N. Cunningham, Chair, 407-823-5451, Fax: 407-823-2252, E-mail: gcunning@pegasus.cc.ucf.edu. *Application contact:* Dr. Kevin Belfield, Coordinator, 407-823-1028, Fax: 407-823-2252, E-mail: kbelfiel@mail.ucf.edu.

University of Central Oklahoma, College of Graduate Studies and Research, College of Mathematics and Science, Department of Chemistry, Edmond, OK 73034-5209. Offers MS. Part-time programs available. *Entrance requirements:* For master's, GRE General Test.

University of Chicago, Division of the Physical Sciences, Department of Chemistry, Chicago, IL 60637-1513. Offers PhD. *Faculty:* 24 full-time (2 women). *Students:* 155 full-time (47 women); includes 13 minority (2 African Americans, 7 Asian Americans or Pacific Islanders, 4 Hispanic Americans), 78 international. Average age 24. 327 applicants, 29% accepted, 22 enrolled. In 2003, 14 degrees awarded, leading to university research/teaching 86%, business/industry 7%. *Median time to degree:* Doctorate–6 years full-time. Of those who began their doctoral program in fall 1995, 100% received their degree in 8 years or less. *Degree requirements:* For doctorate, thesis/dissertation, comprehensive exam, registration. *Entrance requirements:* For doctorate, GRE General Test, GRE Subject Test. Additional exam requirements/recommendations for international students: Required—TOEFL (minimum score 600 paper-based; 250 computer-based). *Application deadline:* For fall admission, 1/15 for domestic students, 1/15 for international students. Applications are processed on a rolling basis. Application fee: $55. Electronic applications accepted. *Expenses:* Contact institution. *Financial support:* In 2003–04, 155 students received support, including 28 fellowships with full tuition reimbursements available (averaging $22,192 per year), 92 research assistantships with full tuition reimbursements available (averaging $21,216 per year), 35 teaching assistantships with full tuition reimbursements available (averaging $22,320 per year); institutionally sponsored loans, scholarships/grants, traineeships, health care benefits, and unspecified assistantships also available. Financial award application deadline: 1/15; financial award applicants required to submit FAFSA. *Faculty research:* Organic, inorganic, physical, biological chemistry. Total annual research expenditures: $6.8 million. *Unit head:* Dr. Michael D. Hopkins, Chairman, 773-702-8639, Fax: 773-702-6594, E-mail: chem-chair@uchicago.edu. *Application contact:* Dr. Vera Dragisich, Executive Officer, 773-702-7250, Fax: 773-702-6594, E-mail: v-dragisich@uchicago.edu.

University of Cincinnati, Division of Research and Advanced Studies, McMicken College of Arts and Sciences, Department of Chemistry, Cincinnati, OH 45221. Offers analytical chemistry (MS, PhD); biochemistry (MS, PhD); inorganic chemistry (MS, PhD); organic chemistry (MS, PhD); physical chemistry (MS, PhD); polymer chemistry (MS, PhD); sensors (PhD). Part-time and evening/weekend programs available. Terminal master's awarded for partial completion of doctoral program. *Degree requirements:* For master's, thesis optional; for doctorate, thesis/dissertation, comprehensive exam, registration. *Entrance requirements:* For master's and doctorate, GRE General Test. Additional exam requirements/recommendations for international students: Required—TOEFL (minimum score 580 paper-based; 237 computer-based); Recommended—TSE(minimum score 50). Electronic applications accepted. *Faculty research:* Biomedical chemistry, laser chemistry, surface science, chemical sensors, synthesis.

University of Colorado at Boulder, Graduate School, College of Arts and Sciences, Department of Chemistry and Biochemistry, Boulder, CO 80309. Offers biochemistry (PhD); chemical physics (PhD); chemistry (MS, PhD). *Faculty:* 35 full-time (6 women). *Students:* 116 full-time (53 women), 79 part-time (32 women); includes 9 minority (1 African American, 6 Asian Americans or Pacific Islanders, 2 Hispanic Americans), 16 international. Average age 26. 137 applicants, 39% accepted. In 2003, 2 master's, 23 doctorates awarded. *Degree requirements:* For master's, comprehensive exam or thesis; for doctorate, thesis/dissertation, cumulative exam, comprehensive exam. *Entrance requirements:* For master's, GRE General Test, GRE Subject Test, minimum GPA of 3.0; for doctorate, GRE General Test, GRE Subject Test (chemistry or biochemistry), minimum GPA of 3.0. *Application deadline:* For fall admission, 3/1 for domestic students. Applications are processed on a rolling basis. Application fee: $50 ($60 for international students). *Expenses:* Tuition, state resident: full-time $2,122. Tuition, nonresident: full-time $9,754. Tuition and fees vary according to course load and program. *Financial support:* In 2003–04, 2 fellowships with full tuition reimbursements (averaging $16,832 per year), 67 research assistantships with full tuition reimbursements (averaging $17,438 per year), 60 teaching assistantships with full tuition reimbursements (averaging $16,464 per year) were awarded. Institutionally sponsored loans, traineeships, and tuition waivers (full) also available. Support available to part-time students. Financial award application deadline: 2/28. *Faculty research:* Biochemistry, atmospheric chemistry, analytical chemistry, biophysical chemistry, chemical physics. Total annual research expenditures: $18.4 million. *Unit head:* Veronica Vaida, Chair, 303-492-8605, Fax: 303-492-5894, E-mail: veronica.vaida@colorado.edu. *Application contact:* Graduate Program Assistant, 303-492-8978, Fax: 303-492-5894, E-mail: chem_gradstudents@colorado.edu.

University of Colorado at Denver, Graduate School, College of Liberal Arts and Sciences, Program in Chemistry, Denver, CO 80217-3364. Offers MS. Part-time programs available. *Faculty:* 11 full-time (4 women). *Students:* 5 full-time (1 woman), 11 part-time (5 women); includes 5 minority (2 Asian Americans or Pacific Islanders, 3 Hispanic Americans), 2 international. Average age 26. 7 applicants, 100% accepted, 4 enrolled. In 2003, 9 degrees awarded. *Degree requirements:* For master's, thesis or alternative, registration. *Entrance requirements:* For master's, undergraduate degree in chemistry. *Application deadline:* For fall admission, 6/1 for domestic students; for spring admission, 11/1 priority date for domestic students. Applications are processed on a rolling basis. Application fee: $50 ($60 for international students). Electronic applications accepted. *Expenses:* Tuition, state resident: part-time $255 per credit hour. Tuition, nonresident: part-time $1,025 per credit hour. *Financial support:* Research assistantships, teaching assistantships, Federal Work-Study available. Financial award application deadline: 3/1; financial award applicants required to submit FAFSA. *Faculty research:* Protein electrochemistry, indoor air quality, atmospheric carbonul analysis, chemical education. Total annual research expenditures: $369,828. *Unit head:* Doris Kimbrough, Associate Professor, 303-556-3202, Fax: 303-566-4776, E-mail: doris.kimbrough@cudenver.edu. *Application contact:* Donald Zapien, Associate Professor, 303-556-3203, Fax: 303-556-4776, E-mail: dczapien@carbon.cudenver.edu.

University of Connecticut, Graduate School, College of Liberal Arts and Sciences, Department of Chemistry, Field of Chemistry, Storrs, CT 06269. Offers MS, PhD. *Faculty:* 22 full-time (4 women). *Students:* 101 full-time (43 women), 8 part-time (7 women); includes 5 minority (1 African American, 2 Asian Americans or Pacific Islanders, 2 Hispanic Americans), 63 international. Average age 28. 104 applicants, 41% accepted, 31 enrolled. In 2003, 4 master's, 12 doctorates awarded. Terminal master's awarded for partial completion of doctoral program. *Degree requirements:* For master's, comprehensive exam; for doctorate, thesis/dissertation. *Entrance requirements:* For master's and doctorate, GRE General Test, GRE Subject Test. Additional exam requirements/recommendations for international students: Required—TOEFL (minimum score 550 paper-based; 213 computer-based). *Application deadline:* For fall admission, 2/1 priority date for domestic students, 2/1 priority date for international students; for spring admission, 11/1 for domestic students, 10/1 for international students. Applications are processed on a rolling basis. Application fee: $55. Electronic applications accepted. *Expenses:* Tuition, state resident: part-time $3,860 per semester. Tuition, nonresident: part-time $9,036 per semester. *Financial support:* In 2003–04, 34 research assistantships with full tuition reimbursements, 60 teaching assistantships with full tuition reimbursements were awarded. Fellowships, Federal Work-Study, scholarships/grants, health care benefits, and unspecified assistantships also available. Financial award application deadline: 2/1; financial award applicants required to submit FAFSA. *Application contact:* Emilie Hogrebe, Graduate Program Coordinator, 860-486-3219, Fax: 860-480-2981, E-mail: hogrebe@nucleus.chem.uconn.edu.

University of Connecticut, Graduate School, School of Engineering, Field of Materials Science, Polymer Program, Storrs, CT 06269-3136. Offers chemical engineering (MS, PhD); chemistry (MS, PhD); polymer science (MS, PhD). Part-time programs available. *Faculty:* 14 full-time (1 woman), 6 part-time/adjunct (0 women). *Students:* 55 full-time (10 women), 1 part-time; includes 2 minority (both Asian Americans or Pacific Islanders), 47 international. Average age 27. 154 applicants, 12% accepted, 8 enrolled. In 2003, 1 doctorate awarded, leading to business/industry 100%. Terminal master's awarded for partial completion of doctoral program. *Median time to degree:* Master's–2.75 years full-time; doctorate–4 years full-time. Of those who began their doctoral program in fall 1995, 100% received their degree in 8 years or less. *Degree requirements:* For master's, one foreign language, thesis (for some programs); for doctorate, one foreign language, thesis/dissertation. *Entrance requirements:* For master's, GRE; for doctorate, GRE General Test. Additional exam requirements/recommendations for international students: Required—TOEFL (minimum score 550 paper-based; 213 computer-based). *Application deadline:* For fall admission, 4/1 for domestic students; for spring admission, 11/1 priority date for domestic students. Applications are processed on a rolling basis. Application fee: $55. Electronic applications accepted. *Expenses:* Tuition, state resident: part-time $3,860 per semester. Tuition, nonresident: part-time $9,036 per semester. *Financial support:* In 2003–04, 56 research assistantships with tuition reimbursements (averaging $22,075 per year) were awarded; fellowships with tuition reimbursements, career-related internships or fieldwork, scholarships/grants, health care benefits, and unspecified assistantships also available. Financial award application deadline: 4/1. *Faculty research:* Sensors, photonics, processing morphology, synthesis. Total annual research expenditures: $2.2 million. *Unit head:* Robert A. Weiss, Director, 860-486-4698, Fax: 860-486-4745, E-mail: rweiss@mail.ims.uconn.edu. *Application contact:* Michelle L. Ross, Administrative Assistant, 860-486-4613.

University of Dayton, Graduate School, College of Arts and Sciences, Department of Chemistry, Dayton, OH 45469-1300. Offers MS. Part-time programs available. *Faculty:* 6 full-time (0 women). *Students:* 6 full-time (4 women), 1 part-time, 5 international. Average age 22. 13 applicants, 31% accepted, 2 enrolled. *Degree requirements:* For master's, thesis, registration. *Entrance requirements:* For master's, GRE, ACS standardized exams. Additional exam requirements/recommendations for international students: Required—TOEFL (minimum score 550 paper-based), TWE. *Application deadline:* For winter admission, 3/1 for domestic students. Applications are processed on a rolling basis. Electronic applications accepted. *Expenses:* Tuition: Full-time $6,060; part-time $505 per hour. Required fees: $50; $25 per term. Tuition and fees vary according to degree level, campus/location, program and student's religious affiliation. *Financial support:* In 2003–04, 5 teaching assistantships with full tuition reimbursements (averaging $12,000 per year) were awarded; scholarships/grants, health care benefits, tuition waivers (partial), and unspecified assistantships also available. *Faculty research:* Organic synthesis, medicinal chemistry, enzyme purification, physical organic, materials chemistry and nanotechnology. *Unit head:* Dr. Kevin Church, Director, 937-229-2560, E-mail: kevin.church@notes.udayton.edu.

University of Delaware, College of Arts and Sciences, Department of Chemistry and Biochemistry, Newark, DE 19716. Offers biochemistry (MA, MS, PhD); chemistry (MA, MS, PhD). Part-time programs available. *Faculty:* 34 full-time (6 women), 3 part-time/adjunct (0 women). *Students:* 141 full-time (54 women), 10 part-time (2 women); includes 16 minority (4 African Americans, 9 Asian Americans or Pacific Islanders, 3 Hispanic Americans), 55 international. Average age 27. 182 applicants, 45% accepted, 50 enrolled. In 2003, 6 master's, 14 doctorates awarded. Terminal master's awarded for partial completion of doctoral program. *Degree requirements:* For master's, one foreign language, thesis (for some programs); for doctorate, one foreign language, thesis/dissertation, cumulative exam. *Entrance requirements:* For master's and doctorate, GRE General Test. Additional exam requirements/recommendations for international students: Required—TOEFL, TSE. *Application deadline:* For fall admission, 3/31 for domestic students. Applications are processed on a rolling basis. Application fee: $60. Electronic applications accepted. *Expenses:* Tuition, state resident: full-time $5,890; part-time $327 per credit. Tuition, nonresident: full-time $15,420; part-time $857 per credit. Required fees: $968. *Financial support:* In 2003–04, 89 students received support, including 4 fellowships with full tuition reimbursements available (averaging $20,000 per year), 72 research assistantships with full tuition reimbursements available (averaging $20,000 per year), 50 teaching assistantships with full tuition reimbursements available (averaging $20,000 per year) Financial award application deadline: 3/31. *Faculty research:* Protein studies; mechanism of enzymes; synthesis, electronic structure, and bonding of organic, inorganic and organometallic compounds; spectroscopy including single molecule spectroscopy. Total annual research expenditures: $8.1 million. *Unit head:* Dr. Charles G. Riordan, Chairman, 302-831-1247, Fax: 302-831-6335, E-mail: riordan@udel.edu. *Application contact:* Dr. Eugene G. Mueller, Graduate Coordinator, 302-831-2739, Fax: 302-831-6335, E-mail: emueller@udel.edu.

University of Denver, Graduate Studies, Faculty of Natural Sciences and Mathematics, Department of Chemistry, Denver, CO 80208. Offers MA, MS, PhD. Part-time programs available. *Faculty:* 11 full-time (1 woman), 1 (woman) part-time/adjunct. *Students:* 19 (9 women); includes 1 minority (Hispanic American) 7 international. 31 applicants, 52% accepted. In 2003, 3 master's, 2 doctorates awarded. Terminal master's awarded for partial completion of doctoral program. *Degree requirements:* For master's and doctorate, thesis/dissertation. *Entrance requirements:* For master's and doctorate, GRE General Test. Additional exam requirements/recommendations for international students: Required—TOEFL, TSE. *Application deadline:* Applications are processed on a rolling basis. Application fee: $45. *Expenses:* Tuition: Full-time $24,264. *Financial support:* In 2003–04, 13 students received support, including 3 fellowships with full and partial tuition reimbursements available, 2 research assistantships with full and partial tuition reimbursements available (averaging $16,155 per year), 8 teaching assistantships with full and partial tuition reimbursements available (averaging $10,251 per year); career-related internships or fieldwork, Federal Work-Study, institutionally sponsored loans, and scholarships/grants also available. Support available to part-time students. Financial award application deadline: 3/1; financial award applicants required to submit FAFSA. *Faculty research:* Atmospheric chemistry, magnetic resonance, molecular spectroscopy, laser photolysis,

Chemistry

University of Denver (continued)

biophysical chemistry. Total annual research expenditures: $1.4 million. *Unit head:* Dr. Lawrence Berliner, Chairperson, 303-871-2436. *Application contact:* Dr. Andrei Kutateladze, Graduate Committee, 303-871-2995.

University of Detroit Mercy, College of Engineering and Science, Department of Chemistry and Biochemistry, Detroit, MI 48219-0900. Offers macromolecular chemistry (MS). Evening/weekend programs available. *Degree requirements:* For master's, thesis. *Entrance requirements:* For master's, GRE General Test, minimum GPA of 3.0. *Faculty research:* Polymer and physical chemistry, industrial aspects of chemistry.

University of Florida, College of Medicine and Graduate School, Interdisciplinary Program in Biomedical Sciences, Department of Pathology, Immunology and Laboratory Medicine, Gainesville, FL 32611. Offers clinical chemistry (MS); immunology and molecular pathology (PhD). *Faculty:* 42. Terminal master's awarded for partial completion of doctoral program. *Degree requirements:* For master's and doctorate, thesis/dissertation. *Entrance requirements:* For master's and doctorate, GRE General Test, minimum GPA of 3.0. Additional exam requirements/recommendations for international students: Required—TOEFL. *Application deadline:* For fall admission, 2/15 for domestic students. Application fee: $20. Electronic applications accepted. *Expenses:* Tuition, state resident: part-time $205 per credit hour. Tuition, nonresident: part-time $775 per credit hour. *Financial support:* Fellowships with full tuition reimbursements, research assistantships with full tuition reimbursements, teaching assistantships, institutionally sponsored loans and traineeships available. *Faculty research:* Molecular immunology, autoimmunity and transplantation, tumor biology, oncogenic viruses, human immunodeficiency viruses. *Unit head:* Dr. James M. Crawford, Chairman, 352-392-6840, Fax: 352-392-6249, E-mail: crawford@pathology.ufl.edu. *Application contact:* Dr. Wayne McCormack, Associate Dean of Graduate Education, 352-392-7413, Fax: 352-846-3466, E-mail: mccormac@pathology.ufl.edu.

University of Florida, Graduate School, College of Liberal Arts and Sciences, Department of Chemistry, Gainesville, FL 32611. Offers MS, MST, PhD. *Faculty:* 58. *Students:* 257 full-time (119 women), 8 part-time (2 women); includes 31 minority (11 African Americans, 9 Asian Americans or Pacific Islanders, 11 Hispanic Americans), 128 international. In 2003, 5 master's, 38 doctorates awarded. *Degree requirements:* For master's, thesis; for doctorate, one foreign language, thesis/dissertation. *Entrance requirements:* For master's and doctorate, GRE General Test, minimum GPA of 3.0. Additional exam requirements/recommendations for international students: Required—TOEFL (minimum score 550 paper-based; 213 computer-based). *Application deadline:* For fall admission, 6/1 for domestic students. Applications are processed on a rolling basis. Application fee: $30. Electronic applications accepted. *Expenses:* Tuition, state resident: part-time $205 per credit hour. Tuition, nonresident: part-time $775 per credit hour. *Financial support:* In 2003–04, 180 students received support, including 1 fellowship, 107 research assistantships, 90 teaching assistantships; institutionally sponsored loans and unspecified assistantships also available. *Faculty research:* Organic, analytical, physical, inorganic, and biological chemistry. *Unit head:* Dr. David R. Richardson, Chair, 352-392-5266, Fax: 352-392-8758, E-mail: chair@chem.ufl.edu. *Application contact:* Dr. Ben Smith, Coordinator, 352-392-0256, Fax: 352-392-8758, E-mail: bwsmith@chem.ufl.edu.

University of Georgia, Graduate School, College of Arts and Sciences, Department of Chemistry, Athens, GA 30602. Offers analytical chemistry (MS, PhD); inorganic chemistry (MS, PhD); organic chemistry (MS, PhD); physical chemistry (MS, PhD). *Faculty:* 26 full-time (2 women). *Students:* 130 full-time (43 women). 160 applicants, 29% accepted, 36 enrolled. In 2003, 3 master's, 17 doctorates awarded. Terminal master's awarded for partial completion of doctoral program. *Median time to degree:* Of those who began their doctoral program in fall 1995, 100% received their degree in 8 years or less. *Degree requirements:* For master's, thesis; for doctorate, one foreign language, thesis/dissertation. *Entrance requirements:* For master's and doctorate, GRE General Test. Additional exam requirements/recommendations for international students: Required—TOEFL (minimum score 213 computer-based), TSE(minimum score 50). *Application deadline:* For fall admission, 7/1 for domestic students; for spring admission, 11/15 for domestic students. Application fee: $50. Electronic applications accepted. *Expenses:* Tuition, state resident: part-time $161 per hour. Tuition, nonresident: part-time $690 per hour. One-time fee: $435 part-time. *Financial support:* Fellowships, research assistantships, teaching assistantships, unspecified assistantships available. *Unit head:* Dr. John L. Stickney, Head, 706-542-2726, Fax: 706-542-9454, E-mail: stickney@chem.uga.edu. *Application contact:* Dr. Donald Kurtz, Information Contact, 706-542-2010, Fax: 706-542-9454, E-mail: kurtz@chem.uga.edu.

University of Guelph, Graduate Program Services, College of Physical and Engineering Science, Guelph-Waterloo Centre for Graduate Work in Chemistry and Biochemistry, Guelph, ON N1G 2W1, Canada. Offers biochemistry (M Sc, PhD); chemistry (M Sc, PhD). Part-time programs available. *Faculty:* 59 full-time (8 women). *Students:* 161 full-time (70 women), 4 part-time (2 women). In 2003, 28 master's, 22 doctorates awarded. *Degree requirements:* For master's and doctorate, thesis/dissertation. *Application deadline:* Applications are processed on a rolling basis. Application fee: $75. Tuition and fees charges are reported in Canadian dollars. Tuition, nonresident: full-time $3,440 Canadian dollars. International tuition: $5,432 Canadian dollars full-time. Required fees: $753 Canadian dollars. *Financial support:* Fellowships, research assistantships, teaching assistantships available. *Faculty research:* Inorganic, analytical, biological, physical/theoretical, polymer, and organic chemistry. *Unit head:* Dr. J. F. Honek, Director, 519-888-4567 Ext. 3945, Fax: 519-746-4806, E-mail: gwc@uwaterloo.ca. *Application contact:* A. Wetmore, Administrative Assistant, 519-888-4567 Ext. 3945, Fax: 519-746-4806, E-mail: gwc@uwaterloo.ca.

University of Hawaii at Manoa, Graduate Division, Colleges of Arts and Sciences, College of Natural Sciences, Department of Chemistry, Honolulu, HI 96822. Offers MS, PhD. *Faculty:* 19 full-time (1 woman). *Students:* 34 full-time (10 women); includes 4 minority (all Asian Americans or Pacific Islanders), 12 international. Average age 28. 78 applicants, 44% accepted, 10 enrolled. In 2003, 2 degrees awarded. *Median time to degree:* Master's–5 years full-time. *Degree requirements:* For master's and doctorate, thesis/dissertation. *Entrance requirements:* For master's and doctorate, GRE General Test, GRE Subject Test. *Application deadline:* For fall admission, 5/1 for domestic students, 3/1 for international students; for spring admission, 9/1 for domestic students, 8/1 for international students. Applications are processed on a rolling basis. Application fee: $50. *Expenses:* Tuition, state resident: full-time $4,464; part-time $186 per credit hour. Tuition, nonresident: full-time $10,608; part-time $442 per credit hour. Tuition and fees vary according to program. *Financial support:* In 2003–04, research assistantships (averaging $17,640 per year), teaching assistantships (averaging $14,608 per year) were awarded. Support available to part-time students. *Faculty research:* Marine natural products, biophysical spectroscopy, zeolites, organometallic hydrides, new visual pigments, theory of surfaces. Total annual research expenditures: $2.1 million. *Unit head:* Karl E. Seff, Chair, 808-956-5165, Fax: 808-956-5908, E-mail: kseff@gold.chem.hawaii.edu.

University of Houston, College of Natural Sciences and Mathematics, Department of Chemistry, Houston, TX 77204. Offers MS, PhD. Part-time programs available. *Faculty:* 20 full-time (1 woman), 1 part-time/adjunct (0 women). *Students:* 103 full-time (44 women), 7 part-time (2 women); includes 14 minority (5 African Americans, 4 Asian Americans or Pacific Islanders, 5 Hispanic Americans), 80 international. Average age 28. 34 applicants, 94% accepted, 18 enrolled. In 2003, 6 master's, 14 doctorates awarded. Terminal master's awarded for partial completion of doctoral program. *Degree requirements:* For master's, thesis; for doctorate, thesis/dissertation, oral presentation. *Entrance requirements:* For master's and doctorate, GRE General Test. Additional exam requirements/recommendations for international students: Required—TOEFL, TSE. *Application deadline:* For fall admission, 7/20 for domestic students; for spring admission, 11/20 for domestic students. Applications are processed on a rolling basis. Application fee: $0 ($75 for international students). Electronic applications accepted. *Expenses:* Tuition, state resident: full-time $1,656; part-time $92 per credit hour. Tuition, nonresident: full-time $5,904; part-time $328 per credit hour. Required fees: $1,704. *Financial support:* In 2003–04, 53 research assistantships with full tuition reimbursements (averaging $13,050 per year), 44 teaching assistantships with full tuition reimbursements (averaging $13,050 per year) were awarded. Fellowships, career-related internships or fieldwork, Federal Work-Study, institutionally sponsored loans, scholarships/grants, and tuition waivers (full) also available. Financial award application deadline: 4/1. *Faculty research:* Materials, molecular design, surface science, structural chemistry, synthesis. Total annual research expenditures: $4 million. *Unit head:* Dr. J. Wayne Rabalais, Chairperson, 713-743-3282, Fax: 713-743-2709. *Application contact:* Dr. Thomas Albright, Chair, Graduate Committee, 713-743-3270, Fax: 713-743-2709, E-mail: albright@uh.edu.

See in-depth description on page 165.

University of Houston–Clear Lake, School of Science and Computer Engineering, Program in Chemistry, Houston, TX 77058-1098. Offers MS. Part-time and evening/weekend programs available. *Students:* Average age 34. In 2003, 3 degrees awarded. *Entrance requirements:* For master's, GRE General Test. Additional exam requirements/recommendations for international students: Required—TOEFL (minimum score 550 paper-based; 213 computer-based). *Application deadline:* For fall admission, 8/1 for domestic students, 6/1 for international students; for spring admission, 12/1 for domestic students, 10/1 for international students. Applications are processed on a rolling basis. Application fee: $35 ($75 for international students). *Expenses:* Tuition, state resident: full-time $2,484; part-time $414 per course. Tuition, nonresident: full-time $6,318; part-time $1,053 per course. Required fees: $12 per course. $199 per semester. *Financial support:* Fellowships, research assistantships, teaching assistantships, career-related internships or fieldwork, Federal Work-Study, institutionally sponsored loans, and scholarships/grants available. Support available to part-time students. Financial award application deadline: 5/1; financial award applicants required to submit FAFSA. *Unit head:* Dr. Ramiro Sanchez, Chair, 281-283-3770, Fax: 281-283-3707, E-mail: sanchez@uhcl4.cl.uh.edu. *Application contact:* Dr. Robert Ferebee, Associate Dean, 281-283-3700, Fax: 281-283-3707, E-mail: ferebee@cl.uh.edu.

University of Idaho, College of Graduate Studies, College of Science, Department of Chemistry, Moscow, ID 83844-2282. Offers chemistry (MS, PhD); chemistry education (MAT). *Accreditation:* NCATE (one or more programs are accredited). *Students:* 33 full-time (12 women), 5 part-time (1 woman); includes 3 minority (all Asian Americans or Pacific Islanders), 15 international. Average age 31. *Degree requirements:* For master's, thesis or alternative; for doctorate, one foreign language, thesis/dissertation. *Entrance requirements:* For master's, minimum GPA of 2.8; for doctorate, minimum undergraduate GPA of 2.8, 3.0 graduate. *Application deadline:* For fall admission, 8/1 for domestic students; for spring admission, 12/15 for domestic students. Application fee: $55 ($60 for international students). *Expenses:* Tuition, state resident: full-time $3,348. Tuition, nonresident: full-time $10,740. Required fees: $540. *Financial support:* Fellowships, research assistantships, teaching assistantships available. Financial award application deadline: 2/15. *Unit head:* Dr. Peter R. Griffiths, Chair, 208-885-6552.

See in-depth description on page 167.

University of Illinois at Chicago, College of Pharmacy and Graduate College, Research & Graduate Studies, College of Pharmacy, Chicago, IL 60607-7128. Offers forensic science (MS); medicinal chemistry (MS, PhD); pharmaceutics (MS, PhD); pharmacodynamics (MS, PhD); pharmacognosy (MS, PhD); pharmacy administration (MS, PhD). *Faculty:* 42 full-time (4 women). *Students:* 131 full-time, 20 part-time. Average age 28. 315 applicants, 18% accepted, 28 enrolled. In 2003, 11 master's, 6 doctorates awarded. Terminal master's awarded for partial completion of doctoral program. *Median time to degree:* Of those who began their doctoral program in fall 1995, 70% received their degree in 8 years or less. *Degree requirements:* For master's and doctorate, variable foreign language requirement, thesis/dissertation. *Entrance requirements:* For master's and doctorate, GRE General Test. Additional exam requirements/recommendations for international students: Required—TOEFL. *Application deadline:* For fall admission, 2/1 for domestic students. Application fee: $40 ($50 for international students). *Expenses:* Contact institution. *Financial support:* In 2003–04, 130 students received support; fellowships with full tuition reimbursements available, research assistantships with full tuition reimbursements available, teaching assistantships with full tuition reimbursements available, career-related internships or fieldwork, Federal Work-Study, institutionally sponsored loans, traineeships, tuition waivers (full), and unspecified assistantships available. Financial award application deadline: 3/1; financial award applicants required to submit FAFSA. *Unit head:* Dr. Michael E. Johnson, Associate Dean, Research and Graduate Education, 312-996-0796.

University of Illinois at Chicago, Graduate College, College of Liberal Arts and Sciences, Department of Chemistry, Chicago, IL 60607-7128. Offers MS, PhD. Part-time programs available. *Faculty:* 29 full-time (2 women). *Students:* 144 full-time (50 women), 9 part-time (6 women); includes 19 minority (4 African Americans, 10 Asian Americans or Pacific Islanders, 5 Hispanic Americans), 88 international. Average age 28. 222 applicants, 20% accepted, 31 enrolled. In 2003, 4 master's, 18 doctorates awarded. Terminal master's awarded for partial completion of doctoral program. *Median time to degree:* Of those who began their doctoral program in fall 1995, 48% received their degree in 8 years or less. *Degree requirements:* For master's, thesis or cumulative exam; for doctorate, one foreign language, thesis/dissertation, cumulative exams. *Entrance requirements:* For master's and doctorate, GRE Subject Test, minimum GPA of 4.0 on a 5.0 scale. Additional exam requirements/recommendations for international students: Required—TOEFL. *Application deadline:* For fall admission, 3/15 for domestic students, 2/1 for international students; for spring admission, 10/1 priority date for domestic students. Applications are processed on a rolling basis. Application fee: $40 ($50 for international students). Electronic applications accepted. *Expenses:* Tuition, state resident: part-time $941 per semester. Tuition, nonresident: part-time $2,338 per semester. *Financial support:* In 2003–04, 129 students received support; fellowships with full tuition reimbursements available, research assistantships with full tuition reimbursements available, teaching assistantships with full tuition reimbursements available, Federal Work-Study, institutionally sponsored loans, scholarships/grants, traineeships, tuition waivers (full), and unspecified assistantships available. Financial award application deadline: 3/1; financial award applicants required to submit FAFSA. *Unit head:* Richard Kassner, Director of Graduate Studies, 312-996-5202, E-mail: rkassner@uic.edu. *Application contact:* Patricia Ratajczyk, Graduate Secretary, 312-996-5121.

University of Illinois at Urbana–Champaign, Graduate College, College of Liberal Arts and Sciences, Department of Chemistry, Champaign, IL 61820. Offers MS, PhD. *Faculty:* 38 full-time (4 women), 1 (woman) part-time/adjunct. *Students:* 306 full-time (117 women); includes 15 minority (1 African American, 13 Asian Americans or Pacific Islanders, 1 Hispanic American), 71 international. 323 applicants, 24% accepted, 71 enrolled. In 2003, 11 master's, 44 doctorates awarded. *Degree requirements:* For doctorate, one foreign language, thesis/dissertation. *Entrance requirements:* For master's, GRE General Test; GRE Subject Test, minimum GPA of 3.0. *Application deadline:* For fall admission, 2/15 for domestic students. Applications are processed on a rolling basis. Application fee: $40 ($50 for international students). Electronic applications accepted. *Expenses:* Tuition, state resident: full-time $6,692. Tuition, nonresident: full-time $18,692. *Financial support:* In 2003–04, 26 fellowships, 139 research assistantships, 125 teaching assistantships were awarded. Financial award application deadline: 2/15. *Unit head:* Gregory S. Girolami, Head, 217-333-5071, Fax: 217-244-8068, E-mail: ggirolam@uiuc.edu. *Application contact:* Joyce Beasley, Graduate Student Services Officer, 217-244-4844, Fax: 217-244-8068, E-mail: jhbeasle@uiuc.edu.

The University of Iowa, Graduate College, College of Liberal Arts and Sciences, Department of Chemistry, Iowa City, IA 52242-1316. Offers MS, PhD, JD/PhD. *Faculty:* 27 full-time. *Students:* 56 full-time (26 women), 53 part-time (16 women); includes 8 minority (2 African Americans, 1 American Indian/Alaska Native, 4 Asian Americans or Pacific Islanders, 1 Hispanic American), 58 international. 278 applicants, 12% accepted, 26 enrolled. In 2003, 8 master's, 10 doctorates awarded. *Degree requirements:* For master's, exam, thesis optional; for doctorate, thesis/dissertation, comprehensive exam, registration. *Entrance requirements:* For master's and doctorate, GRE General Test, minimum GPA of 3.0. Additional exam requirements/

recommendations for international students: Required—TOEFL (minimum score 550 paper-based; 213 computer-based). *Application deadline:* For fall admission, 1/15 priority date for domestic students, 1/15 priority date for international students; for spring admission, 10/15 priority date for domestic students, 10/15 priority date for international students. Applications are processed on a rolling basis. Application fee: $50 ($75 for international students). Electronic applications accepted. *Expenses:* Tuition, state resident: full-time $5,038. Tuition, nonresident: full-time $15,072. Tuition and fees vary according to course load and program. *Financial support:* In 2003–04, 2 fellowships, 51 research assistantships, 58 teaching assistantships were awarded. Financial award applicants required to submit FAFSA. *Unit head:* David Wiemer, Chair, 319-335-1350, Fax: 319-335-1270.

University of Kansas, Graduate School, College of Liberal Arts and Sciences, Department of Chemistry, Lawrence, KS 66045. Offers MS, PhD. *Faculty:* 23. *Students:* 65 full-time (24 women), 32 part-time (16 women); includes 7 minority (1 African American, 1 American Indian/Alaska Native, 2 Asian Americans or Pacific Islanders, 3 Hispanic Americans), 22 international. Average age 27. 50 applicants, 56% accepted, 16 enrolled. In 2003, 2 master's, 6 doctorates awarded. *Degree requirements:* For master's, thesis/dissertation; for doctorate, thesis/dissertation, comprehensive exam. *Entrance requirements:* For master's and doctorate, GRE General Test. Additional exam requirements/recommendations for international students: Required—TOEFL, TSE. *Application deadline:* For fall admission, 5/31 for domestic students, 5/31 for international students; for spring admission, 11/15 for domestic students, 10/15 for international students. Applications are processed on a rolling basis. Application fee: $55 ($60 for international students). Electronic applications accepted. *Expenses:* Tuition, state resident: full-time $3,745. Tuition, nonresident: full-time $10,075. Required fees: $574. *Financial support:* In 2003–04, 2 fellowships with full tuition reimbursements (averaging $21,504 per year), 46 research assistantships with full and partial tuition reimbursements (averaging $9,514 per year), 32 teaching assistantships with full and partial tuition reimbursements (averaging $15,479 per year) were awarded. *Faculty research:* Organometallic and inorganic synthetic methodology, home proteins, protein surface interactions, organic chemistry of peptides, supramolecular chemistry. Total annual research expenditures: $4.1 million. *Unit head:* Prof. Craig Lunte, Chair, 785-864-4673, Fax: 785-864-5396, E-mail: clunte@ku.edu. *Application contact:* Prof. Brian B. Laird, Associate Chair for Graduate Studies, 785-864-4632, Fax: 785-864-5396, E-mail: blaird@ku.edu.

University of Kentucky, Graduate School, Graduate School Programs from the College of Arts and Sciences, Program in Chemistry, Lexington, KY 40506-0032. Offers MS, PhD. Part-time programs available. *Faculty:* 30 full-time (3 women). *Students:* 91 full-time (32 women), 26 part-time (6 women); includes 10 minority (4 African Americans, 5 Asian Americans or Pacific Islanders, 1 Hispanic American), 65 international. 255 applicants, 21% accepted, 21 enrolled. In 2003, 7 master's, 8 doctorates awarded. Terminal master's awarded for partial completion of doctoral program. *Degree requirements:* For master's, thesis optional; for doctorate, thesis/dissertation, comprehensive exam. *Entrance requirements:* For master's, GRE General Test, minimum undergraduate GPA of 2.5; for doctorate, GRE General Test, minimum graduate GPA of 3.0. Additional exam requirements/recommendations for international students: Required—TOEFL (minimum score 550 paper-based; 213 computer-based). *Application deadline:* For fall admission, 7/18 for domestic students, 2/1 for international students. Applications are processed on a rolling basis. Application fee: $35 ($45 for international students). *Expenses:* Tuition, state resident: full-time $4,975; part-time $261 per credit hour. Tuition, nonresident: full-time $12,315; part-time $668 per credit hour. *Financial support:* Fellowships, research assistantships, teaching assistantships, career-related internships or fieldwork, Federal Work-Study, and institutionally sponsored loans available. Support available to part-time students. Financial award application deadline: 3/1. *Faculty research:* Analytical, inorganic, organic, and physical chemistry; biological chemistry; nuclear chemistry; radiochemistry; materials chemistry. *Unit head:* Dr. Robert Guthrie, Director of Graduate Studies, 859-257-7068, Fax: 859-323-1069, E-mail: rguthrie@pop.uky.edu. *Application contact:* Dr. Brian Jackson, Associate Dean, 859-257-4905, Fax: 859-323-1928.

The University of Lethbridge, School of Graduate Studies, Lethbridge, AB T1K 3M4, Canada. Offers accounting (MScM); agricultural biotechnology (M Sc); agricultural studies (M Sc, MA); anthropology (MA); archaeology (MA); art (MA); biochemistry (M Sc); biological sciences (M Sc); Canadian studies (MA); chemistry (M Sc); computer science (M Sc); counseling psychology (M Ed); dramatic arts (MA); economics (MA); English (MA); environmental science (M Sc); exercise science (M Sc); finance (MScM); French (MA); French/German (MA); French/Spanish (MA); general education (M Ed); general management (MScM); geography (M Sc, MA); German (MA); health sciences (M Sc, MA); history (MA); human resources/management and labor relations (MScM); information systems (MScM); international management (MScM); kinesiology (M Sc, MA); management (M Sc, MA); marketing (MScM); mathematics (M Sc); music (MA); Native American studies (MA, MScM); neuroscience (M Sc, PhD); nursing (M Sc); philosophy (MA); physics (M Sc); political science (MA); psychology (M Sc, MA); religious studies (MA); sociology (MA); urban and regional studies (MA). Part-time and evening/weekend programs available. *Faculty:* 250. *Students:* 317 (126 women). Average age 39. 35 applicants, 100% accepted, 35 enrolled. In 2003, 40 degrees awarded. *Degree requirements:* For doctorate, thesis/dissertation, comprehensive exam. *Entrance requirements:* For master's, bachelor's degree in related field, minimum GPA of 3.0 (during previous 20 graded semester courses), two years teaching or related experience (M Ed), GMAT for M Sc (management); for doctorate, master's degree, minimum graduate GPA of 3.5. Additional exam requirements/recommendations for international students: Required—TOEFL. Application fee: $60 Canadian dollars. *Expenses:* Tuition, state resident: part-time $475 per course. *Financial support:* Fellowships, research assistantships, teaching assistantships, scholarships/grants, health care benefits, and unspecified assistantships available. *Faculty research:* Movement and brain plasticity, gibberellin physiology, photosynthesis, carbon cycling, molecular properties of main-group ring components. *Unit head:* Dr. Shamsul Alam, Dean, 403-329-2121, Fax: 403-329-2097, E-mail: inquiries@uleth.ca. *Application contact:* Kathy Schrage, Administrative Assistant, Office of the Academic Vice President, 403-329-2121, Fax: 403-329-2097, E-mail: inquiries@uleth.ca.

University of Louisiana at Monroe, Graduate Studies and Research, College of Arts and Sciences, Department of Chemistry, Monroe, LA 71209-0001. Offers MS. *Students:* Average age 29. In 2003, 5 degrees awarded. *Degree requirements:* For master's, one foreign language, thesis. *Entrance requirements:* For master's, GRE General Test, minimum GPA of 3.0 in last 24 hours of chemistry, 2.8 overall. *Application deadline:* For fall admission, 7/1 for domestic students; for spring admission, 11/1 for domestic students. Applications are processed on a rolling basis. Application fee: $15 ($25 for international students). *Expenses:* Tuition, state resident: full-time $2,052. Tuition, nonresident: full-time $8,010. *Financial support:* Research assistantships, teaching assistantships, career-related internships or fieldwork, Federal Work-Study, and unspecified assistantships available. Financial award application deadline: 7/1. *Faculty research:* Organic synthesis, pesticides, equine ovulation, smog analysis, PAH's, VUV photophysics, protein crystallography, evolving factor analysis. *Unit head:* Dr. Harry O'Neil Brotherton, Head, 318-342-1825, Fax: 318-342-1859, E-mail: hbrotherton@ulm.edu.

University of Louisville, Graduate School, College of Arts and Sciences, Department of Chemistry, Louisville, KY 40292-0001. Offers analytical chemistry (MS, PhD); biochemistry (MS, PhD); chemical physics (PhD); inorganic chemistry (MS, PhD); organic chemistry (MS, PhD); physical chemistry (MS, PhD). *Students:* 48 full-time (19 women), 13 part-time (5 women); includes 4 minority (1 African American, 1 Asian American or Pacific Islander, 2 Hispanic Americans), 27 international. Average age 27. In 2003, 7 master's, 1 doctorate awarded. *Degree requirements:* For master's, thesis/dissertation; for doctorate, thesis/dissertation, comprehensive exam. *Entrance requirements:* For master's and doctorate, GRE General Test. Additional exam requirements/recommendations for international students: Required—TOEFL. *Application deadline:* Applications are processed on a rolling basis. Application fee: $50. *Expenses:* Tuition, state resident: full-time $4,842. Tuition, nonresident: full-time $13,338. *Financial support:* In 2003–04, 30 teaching assistantships (averaging $14,000 per year) were awarded. *Unit head:* Dr. George R. Pack, Chair, 502-852-6798, Fax: 502-852-8149, E-mail: george.pack@louisville.edu.

University of Maine, Graduate School, College of Liberal Arts and Sciences, Department of Chemistry, Orono, ME 04469. Offers MS, PhD. *Faculty:* 12 full-time (2 women). *Students:* 23 full-time (9 women), 5 part-time (4 women); includes 2 minority (1 African American, 1 Asian American or Pacific Islander), 14 international. Average age 32. 23 applicants, 43% accepted, 7 enrolled. In 2003, 3 degrees awarded. Terminal master's awarded for partial completion of doctoral program. *Degree requirements:* For master's, thesis; for doctorate, thesis/dissertation, oral exam. *Entrance requirements:* For master's and doctorate, GRE General Test. Additional exam requirements/recommendations for international students: Required—TOEFL. *Application deadline:* For fall admission, 2/1 for domestic students. Applications are processed on a rolling basis. Application fee: $50. Electronic applications accepted. *Expenses:* Tuition, state resident: part-time $235 per credit. Tuition, nonresident: part-time $670 per credit. Tuition and fees vary according to course load. *Financial support:* In 2003–04, 3 research assistantships with tuition reimbursements (averaging $12,300 per year), 15 teaching assistantships with tuition reimbursements (averaging $12,300 per year) were awarded. Tuition waivers (full and partial) also available. Financial award application deadline: 3/1. *Faculty research:* Quantum mechanics, insect chemistry, organic synthesis. *Unit head:* Dr. Barbara J. W. Cole, Chair, 207-581-1169, Fax: 207-581-1191. *Application contact:* Scott G. Delcourt, Associate Dean of the Graduate School, 207-581-3218, Fax: 207-581-3232, E-mail: graduate@maine.edu.

University of Manitoba, Faculty of Graduate Studies, Faculty of Science, Department of Chemistry, Winnipeg, MB R3T 2N2, Canada. Offers M Sc, PhD. *Degree requirements:* For master's, thesis; for doctorate, one foreign language, thesis/dissertation. Tuition charges are reported in Canadian dollars. Tuition, nonresident: full-time $3,878 Canadian dollars.

University of Maryland, Baltimore County, Graduate School, Department of Chemistry and Biochemistry, Program in Chemistry, Baltimore, MD 21250. Offers MS, PhD. Part-time and evening/weekend programs available. *Faculty:* 15 full-time (2 women), 2 part-time/adjunct (0 women). *Students:* 35 full-time (16 women), 12 part-time (3 women); includes 12 minority (6 African Americans, 1 American Indian/Alaska Native, 5 Asian Americans or Pacific Islanders), 15 international. Average age 24. 67 applicants, 19% accepted. In 2003, 5 master's, 6 doctorates awarded. *Degree requirements:* For doctorate, thesis/dissertation, comprehensive exam. *Entrance requirements:* For doctorate, GRE General Test, GRE Subject Test, minimum GPA of 3.0. Additional exam requirements/recommendations for international students: Required—TOEFL. *Application deadline:* For fall admission, 7/1 for domestic students. Applications are processed on a rolling basis. Application fee: $45. *Expenses:* Tuition, state resident: full-time $7,000. Tuition, nonresident: full-time $11,400. Required fees: $1,440. *Financial support:* In 2003–04, fellowships with full tuition reimbursements (averaging $18,000 per year), research assistantships with full tuition reimbursements (averaging $17,000 per year), teaching assistantships with full tuition reimbursements (averaging $17,000 per year) were awarded. Tuition waivers (full) also available. *Faculty research:* Bio-organic chemistry and enzyme catalysis, protein-nucleic acid interactions. Total annual research expenditures: $4.1 million. *Unit head:* Dr. William R. LaCourse, Director, Graduate Program, 410-455-2491, Fax: 410-455-2608, E-mail: chemgrad@umbc.edu. *Application contact:* Patricia Gagne, Graduate Coordinator, 410-455-2491, Fax: 410-455-2608, E-mail: pgagne1@umbc.edu.

See in-depth description on page 169.

University of Maryland, College Park, Graduate Studies and Research, College of Life Sciences, Department of Chemistry and Biochemistry, Chemistry Program, College Park, MD 20742. Offers analytical chemistry (MS, PhD); inorganic chemistry (MS, PhD); organic chemistry (MS, PhD); physical chemistry (MS, PhD). Part-time and evening/weekend programs available. *Students:* 89 full-time (46 women), 4 part-time (2 women); includes 6 minority (2 African Americans, 2 Asian Americans or Pacific Islanders, 2 Hispanic Americans), 39 international. 141 applicants, 19% accepted. In 2003, 16 degrees awarded. Terminal master's awarded for partial completion of doctoral program. *Median time to degree:* Of those who began their doctoral program in fall 1995, 33% received their degree in 8 years or less. *Degree requirements:* For master's, thesis optional; for doctorate, thesis/dissertation, 2 seminar presentations, oral exam. *Entrance requirements:* For master's, GRE General Test, GRE Subject Test (recommended), minimum GPA of 3.1, 3 letters of recommendation; for doctorate, GRE General Test, GRE Subject Test (recommended), minimum GPA of 3.1. *Application deadline:* For fall admission, 5/1 for domestic students, 2/1 for international students; for spring admission, 10/1 for domestic students, 6/1 for international students. Applications are processed on a rolling basis. Application fee: $50. Electronic applications accepted. *Expenses:* Tuition, state resident: part-time $349 per credit hour. Tuition, nonresident: part-time $602 per credit hour. *Financial support:* Fellowships, research assistantships, teaching assistantships with partial tuition reimbursements available. Financial award applicants required to submit FAFSA. *Faculty research:* Environmental chemistry, nuclear chemistry, lunar and environmental analysis, x-ray crystallography. *Application contact:* Trudy Lindsey, Director, Graduate Enrollment Management Services, 301-405-4190, Fax: 301-314-9305, E-mail: tlindsey@gradschool.umd.edu.

University of Massachusetts Amherst, Graduate School, College of Natural Sciences and Mathematics, Department of Chemistry, Amherst, MA 01003. Offers MS, PhD. Part-time programs available. *Faculty:* 25 full-time (3 women). *Students:* 127 full-time (54 women), 7 part-time (3 women); includes 7 minority (1 African American, 2 Asian Americans or Pacific Islanders, 4 Hispanic Americans), 81 international. Average age 29. 318 applicants, 24% accepted, 35 enrolled. In 2003, 12 master's, 16 doctorates awarded. Terminal master's awarded for partial completion of doctoral program. *Degree requirements:* For master's, thesis; for doctorate, one foreign language, thesis/dissertation. *Entrance requirements:* Additional exam requirements/recommendations for international students: Required—TOEFL (minimum score 530 paper-based; 197 computer-based). *Application deadline:* For fall admission, 2/1 priority date for domestic students, 2/1 priority date for international students; for spring admission, 10/1 for domestic students, 10/1 for international students. Applications are processed on a rolling basis. Application fee: $40 ($50 for international students). *Expenses:* Tuition, state resident: full-time $1,320; part-time $110 per credit. Tuition, nonresident: full-time $4,969; part-time $414 per credit. Required fees: $2,626 per term. Tuition and fees vary according to course load. *Financial support:* In 2003–04, fellowships with full tuition reimbursements (averaging $8,596 per year), research assistantships with full tuition reimbursements (averaging $11,442 per year), teaching assistantships with full tuition reimbursements (averaging $10,287 per year) were awarded. Career-related internships or fieldwork, Federal Work-Study, scholarships/grants, traineeships, and unspecified assistantships also available. Support available to part-time students. Financial award application deadline: 2/1. *Unit head:* Dr. Bret Jackson, Director, 413-545-2318, Fax: 413-545-4490, E-mail: jackson@chem.umass.edu.

University of Massachusetts Boston, Office of Graduate Studies and Research, College of Science and Mathematics, Program in Chemistry, Boston, MA 02125-3393. Offers MS. Part-time and evening/weekend programs available. *Students:* 13 full-time (12 women), 8 part-time (3 women); includes 4 minority (1 African American, 3 Asian Americans or Pacific Islanders), 8 international. Average age 32. 15 applicants, 53% accepted, 5 enrolled. In 2003, 5 degrees awarded. *Degree requirements:* For master's, thesis, oral exams, comprehensive exam. *Entrance requirements:* For master's, GRE General Test, GRE Subject Test, minimum GPA of 2.75. *Application deadline:* For fall admission, 3/1 for domestic students; for spring admission, 11/1 for domestic students. Application fee: $25 ($40 for international students). *Expenses:* Tuition, state resident: full-time $4,461. Tuition, nonresident: full-time $9,390. *Financial support:* In 2003–04, 1 research assistantship with full tuition reimbursement (averaging $9,000 per year), 10 teaching assistantships with full tuition reimbursements (averaging $7,000 per year) were awarded. Career-related internships or fieldwork, Federal Work-Study, and unspecified assistantships also available. Support available to part-time students. Financial award application deadline: 3/1; financial award applicants required to submit FAFSA. *Faculty research:* Synthesis and mechanisms of organic nitrogen compounds, application of spin resonance in the study of structure and dynamics, chemical education and teacher training, new synthetic

Chemistry

University of Massachusetts Boston (continued)
reagents, structural study of inorganic solids by infrared and Raman spectroscopy. *Unit head:* Robert Carter, Director, 617-287-6136. *Application contact:* Peggy Roldan, Graduate Admissions Coordinator, 617-287-6400, Fax: 617-287-6236, E-mail: bos.gadm@dpc.umassp.edu.

University of Massachusetts Dartmouth, Graduate School, College of Arts and Sciences, Department of Chemistry, North Dartmouth, MA 02747-2300. Offers MS. Part-time programs available. *Faculty:* 15 full-time (2 women), 3 part-time/adjunct (1 woman). *Students:* 13 full-time (6 women), 8 part-time (3 women); includes 3 minority (all Asian Americans or Pacific Islanders), 11 international. Average age 29. 26 applicants, 77% accepted, 8 enrolled. In 2003, 5 degrees awarded. *Degree requirements:* For master's, thesis or alternative, comprehensive exam (for some programs). *Entrance requirements:* For master's, GRE. Additional exam requirements/recommendations for international students: Required—TOEFL (minimum score 500 paper-based). *Application deadline:* For fall admission, 5/1 for domestic students, 3/1 for international students; for spring admission, 11/1 for domestic students, 9/1 for international students. Application fee: $35 ($55 for international students). Electronic applications accepted. *Expenses:* Tuition, state resident: full-time $2,071; part-time $86 per credit. Tuition, nonresident: full-time $8,099; part-time $337 per credit. Required fees: $248 per credit. One-time fee: $50 full-time. Part-time tuition and fees vary according to course load and program. *Financial support:* In 2003–04, 7 research assistantships with full tuition reimbursements (averaging $12,286 per year), 11 teaching assistantships with full tuition reimbursements (averaging $12,182 per year) were awarded. Federal Work-Study also available. Support available to part-time students. Financial award application deadline: 3/1; financial award applicants required to submit FAFSA. *Faculty research:* Spectrometric analysis, pesticides and DNA, wound-healing, Arabian sea dentrification, oceanic nitrogen fixation. Total annual research expenditures: $1.1 million. *Unit head:* Dr. Timothy Su, Director, 508-999-8238, Fax: 508-999-9167, E-mail: tsu@umassd.edu. *Application contact:* Carol Novo, Graduate Admissions Officer, 508-999-8604, Fax: 508-999-8183, E-mail: graduate@umassd.edu.

University of Massachusetts Lowell, Graduate School, College of Arts and Sciences, Department of Chemistry, Lowell, MA 01854-2881. Offers biochemistry (PhD); chemistry (MS, PhD); environmental studies (PhD); polymer sciences (MS, PhD). Terminal master's awarded for partial completion of doctoral program. *Degree requirements:* For master's, thesis; for doctorate, 2 foreign languages, thesis/dissertation. *Entrance requirements:* For master's and doctorate, GRE General Test. Electronic applications accepted.

The University of Memphis, Graduate School, College of Arts and Sciences, Department of Chemistry, Memphis, TN 38152. Offers MS, PhD. Part-time programs available. *Faculty:* 11 full-time (2 women), 6 part-time/adjunct (2 women). *Students:* 29 full-time (15 women), 10 part-time (6 women); includes 5 minority (4 African Americans, 1 Asian American or Pacific Islander), 18 international. Average age 31. 44 applicants, 27% accepted. In 2003, 4 master's, 2 doctorates awarded. *Degree requirements:* For master's and doctorate, thesis/dissertation, comprehensive exam. *Entrance requirements:* For master's, GRE General Test, 32 undergraduate hours in chemistry; for doctorate, GRE General Test. *Application deadline:* For fall admission, 8/1 for domestic students; for spring admission, 12/1 for domestic students. Applications are processed on a rolling basis. Application fee: $25 ($50 for international students). *Expenses:* Tuition, state resident: full-time $5,142. Tuition, nonresident: full-time $13,296. *Financial support:* In 2003–04, 26 students received support, including 6 research assistantships with full tuition reimbursements available, 17 teaching assistantships with full tuition reimbursements available *Faculty research:* Computational chemistry, molecular spectroscopy, heterocyclic compounds, photochromic materials, nanoscale materials. Total annual research expenditures: $540,000. *Unit head:* Dr. Peter K. Bridson, Chairman, 901-678-4414, Fax: 901-678-3447, E-mail: pbridson@memphis.edu. *Application contact:* Dr. Roger V. Lloyd, Coordinator of Graduate Studies, 901-678-2632, Fax: 901-678-3447, E-mail: rlloyd@memphis.edu.

University of Miami, Graduate School, College of Arts and Sciences, Department of Chemistry, Coral Gables, FL 33124. Offers chemistry (MS); inorganic chemistry (PhD); organic chemistry (PhD); physical chemistry (PhD). *Faculty:* 9 full-time (1 woman). *Students:* 39 full-time (17 women); includes 23 minority (4 African Americans, 15 Asian Americans or Pacific Islanders, 4 Hispanic Americans), 25 international. Average age 25. 104 applicants, 13% accepted, 10 enrolled. In 2003, 2 master's, 1 doctorate awarded. Terminal master's awarded for partial completion of doctoral program. *Degree requirements:* For master's, comprehensive exam; for doctorate, thesis/dissertation, comprehensive exam. *Entrance requirements:* For master's and doctorate, GRE General Test. Additional exam requirements/recommendations for international students: Required—TOEFL (minimum score 550 paper-based; 213 computer-based). *Application deadline:* For fall admission, 1/15 for domestic students, 1/15 for international students. Applications are processed on a rolling basis. Application fee: $50. Electronic applications accepted. *Expenses:* Tuition: Full-time $19,526. *Financial support:* In 2003–04, 39 students received support, including 3 fellowships with full tuition reimbursements available (averaging $20,000 per year), 14 research assistantships with full tuition reimbursements available (averaging $19,000 per year), 21 teaching assistantships with full tuition reimbursements available (averaging $19,000 per year); tuition waivers (full) also available. Financial award application deadline: 5/1; financial award applicants required to submit FAFSA. *Faculty research:* Supramolecular chemistry, electrochemistry, surface chemistry, catalysis, organometalic. *Unit head:* Dr. Cecil M. Criss, Chairman, 305-284-2282, Fax: 305-284-4571. *Application contact:* Eva Johnson, Graduate Secretary, 305-284-6561, Fax: 305-284-4571, E-mail: evaj@miami.edu.

University of Miami, Graduate School, Rosenstiel School of Marine and Atmospheric Science, Division of Marine and Atmospheric Chemistry, Coral Gables, FL 33124. Offers MS, PhD. *Faculty:* 17 full-time (2 women), 13 part-time/adjunct (2 women). *Students:* 11 full-time (4 women), 6 international. Average age 25. 20 applicants, 20% accepted, 1 enrolled. In 2003, 2 master's awarded, leading to continued full-time study 50%, business/industry 50%; 2 doctorates awarded, leading to university research/teaching 50%, government 50%. Terminal master's awarded for partial completion of doctoral program. *Median time to degree:* Master's–3 years full-time; doctorate–5.8 years full-time. *Degree requirements:* For master's and doctorate, thesis/dissertation, comprehensive exam, registration. *Entrance requirements:* For master's and doctorate, GRE General Test. Additional exam requirements/recommendations for international students: Required—TOEFL (minimum score 550 paper-based; 213 computer-based). *Application deadline:* For fall admission, 1/1 priority date for domestic students, 1/1 priority date for international students. Applications are processed on a rolling basis. Application fee: $50. Electronic applications accepted. *Expenses:* Tuition: Full-time $19,526. *Financial support:* In 2003–04, 11 students received support, including 1 fellowship with tuition reimbursement available (averaging $20,124 per year), 9 research assistantships with tuition reimbursements available (averaging $20,124 per year), 1 teaching assistantship with tuition reimbursement available (averaging $20,124 per year); Federal Work-Study, institutionally sponsored loans, scholarships/grants, and unspecified assistantships also available. Financial award application deadline: 3/1; financial award applicants required to submit FAFSA. *Faculty research:* Global change issues, chemistry of marine waters and marine atmosphere. *Unit head:* Dr. Dennis Hansell, Chairperson, 305-361-4922, Fax: 305-361-4689, E-mail: dhansell@rsmas.miami.edu. *Application contact:* Dr. Frank Millero, Associate Dean, 305-361-4155, Fax: 305-361-4771, E-mail: gso@rsmas.miami.edu.

University of Michigan, Horace H. Rackham School of Graduate Studies, College of Literature, Science, and the Arts, Department of Chemistry, Ann Arbor, MI 48109. Offers analytical chemistry (PhD); chemical biology (PhD); inorganic chemistry (PhD); material chemistry (PhD); organic chemistry (PhD); physical chemistry (PhD). *Faculty:* 50 full-time (10 women), 3 part-time/adjunct (0 women). *Students:* 213 full-time (101 women); includes 20 minority (5 African Americans, 1 American Indian/Alaska Native, 9 Asian Americans or Pacific Islanders, 5 Hispanic Americans), 64 international. Average age 26. 310 applicants, 56% accepted, 58 enrolled. In 2003, 27 degrees awarded. *Degree requirements:* For doctorate, thesis/dissertation, oral defense of dissertation, organic cumulative proficiency exams. *Entrance requirements:* For doctorate, GRE General Test, GRE Subject Test (recommended), statement of prior research. Additional exam requirements/recommendations for international students: Required—TOEFL. *Application deadline:* For fall admission, 1/15 priority date for domestic students, 1/15 priority date for international students. Applications are processed on a rolling basis. Application fee: $60 ($75 for international students). Electronic applications accepted. *Expenses:* Tuition, state resident: full-time $7,463. Tuition, nonresident: full-time $13,913. Full-time tuition and fees vary according to course load, degree level and program. *Financial support:* In 2003–04, 10 fellowships with full tuition reimbursements (averaging $20,000 per year), 70 research assistantships with full tuition reimbursements (averaging $19,000 per year), 120 teaching assistantships with full tuition reimbursements (averaging $20,000 per year) were awarded. Financial award applicants required to submit FAFSA. *Faculty research:* Biological catalysis, protein engineering, chemical sensors, de novo metalloprotein design, supramolecular architecture. Total annual research expenditures: $8 million. *Unit head:* Dr. William R. Roush, Chair, 734-763-9681, Fax: 734-647-4847, E-mail: roush@umich.edu. *Application contact:* Linda Deitert, Assistant Director Graduate Studies, 734-764-7278, Fax: 734-647-4865, E-mail: chemadmissions@umich.edu.

University of Minnesota, Duluth, Graduate School, College of Science and Engineering, Department of Chemistry, Duluth, MN 55812-2496. Offers MS. Part-time programs available. *Faculty:* 29 full-time (4 women). *Students:* 24 full-time (6 women); includes 2 minority (1 American Indian/Alaska Native, 1 Asian American or Pacific Islander), 10 international. Average age 24. 13 applicants, 85% accepted, 9 enrolled. In 2003, 8 degrees awarded, leading to continued full-time study 75%, business/industry 25%. *Median time to degree:* Master's–2 years full-time. *Degree requirements:* For master's, thesis (for some programs). *Entrance requirements:* For master's, bachelor's degree in chemistry, minimum GPA of 3.0. Additional exam requirements/recommendations for international students: Required—TOEFL (minimum score 550 paper-based; 213 computer-based). *Application deadline:* For fall admission, 7/15 for domestic students; for spring admission, 11/15 for domestic students. Applications are processed on a rolling basis. Application fee: $55 ($75 for international students). *Expenses:* Tuition, state resident: part-time $614 per credit. Tuition, nonresident: part-time $1,205 per credit. *Financial support:* In 2003–04, 24 students received support, including 1 research assistantship with full tuition reimbursement available (averaging $12,300 per year), 23 teaching assistantships with full tuition reimbursements available (averaging $12,300 per year); Federal Work-Study, institutionally sponsored loans, scholarships/grants, health care benefits, and unspecified assistantships also available. Support available to part-time students. Financial award application deadline: 3/15. *Faculty research:* Physical, inorganic, organic, and analytical chemistry; biochemistry and molecular biology. Total annual research expenditures: $500,000. *Unit head:* Dr. Viktor V. Zhdankin, Director of Graduate Studies, 218-726-6902, Fax: 218-726-7394.

University of Minnesota, Twin Cities Campus, Graduate School, Institute of Technology, Department of Chemistry, Minneapolis, MN 55455-0213. Offers MS, PhD. Part-time programs available. Terminal master's awarded for partial completion of doctoral program. *Degree requirements:* For master's, thesis or alternative; for doctorate, thesis/dissertation, preliminary candidacy exams. *Entrance requirements:* For master's and doctorate, GRE General Test. Additional exam requirements/recommendations for international students: Required—TOEFL. *Expenses:* Tuition, state resident: full-time $3,681; part-time $614 per credit. Tuition, nonresident: full-time $7,231; part-time $1,205 per credit. *Faculty research:* Analytical, biological, inorganic, organic, and physical chemistry.

University of Minnesota, Twin Cities Campus, School of Public Health, Division of Environmental Health Sciences, Area in Environmental Chemistry, Minneapolis, MN 55455-0213. Offers MS, PhD. *Degree requirements:* For doctorate, thesis/dissertation. *Entrance requirements:* For master's and doctorate, GRE General Test. *Application deadline:* For fall admission, 3/1 for domestic students. Applications are processed on a rolling basis. Application fee: $55 ($75 for international students). *Expenses:* Tuition, state resident: full-time $3,681; part-time $614 per credit. Tuition, nonresident: full-time $7,231; part-time $1,205 per credit. *Financial support:* Fellowships, research assistantships available. Financial award application deadline: 3/1. *Application contact:* Kathy Soupir, Major Coordinator, 612-625-0622, Fax: 612-626-4837, E-mail: soupi001@umn.edu.

University of Mississippi, Graduate School, College of Liberal Arts, Department of Chemistry and Biochemistry, Oxford, University, MS 38677. Offers MS, DA, PhD. *Faculty:* 16 full-time (1 woman). *Students:* 28 full-time (10 women), 4 part-time (2 women); includes 3 minority (all African Americans), 17 international. In 2003, 4 master's, 1 doctorate awarded. *Degree requirements:* For master's, thesis; for doctorate, one foreign language, thesis/dissertation. *Entrance requirements:* For master's, GRE General Test, minimum GPA of 3.0; for doctorate, GRE General Test. Additional exam requirements/recommendations for international students: Required—TOEFL. *Application deadline:* For fall admission, 4/1 for domestic students; for spring admission, 10/1 for domestic students. Applications are processed on a rolling basis. Application fee: $25. *Expenses:* Tuition, state resident: part-time $218 per hour. Tuition, nonresident: part-time $273 per hour. *Financial support:* Scholarships/grants available. Financial award application deadline: 3/1; financial award applicants required to submit FAFSA. *Unit head:* Dr. Charles Hussey, Chairman, 662-915-7301, Fax: 662-915-7300, E-mail: chemistry@olemiss.edu.

University of Missouri–Columbia, Graduate School, College of Arts and Sciences, Department of Chemistry, Columbia, MO 65211. Offers analytical chemistry (MS, PhD); inorganic chemistry (MS, PhD); organic chemistry (MS, PhD); physical chemistry (MS, PhD). *Faculty:* 20 full-time (4 women). *Students:* 58 full-time (21 women), 36 part-time (7 women); includes 5 minority (1 African American, 1 American Indian/Alaska Native, 3 Asian Americans or Pacific Islanders), 51 international. In 2003, 7 master's, 7 doctorates awarded. *Degree requirements:* For master's, thesis; for doctorate, one foreign language, thesis/dissertation. *Entrance requirements:* For master's and doctorate, GRE General Test, minimum GPA of 3.0. *Application deadline:* For fall admission, 4/1 for domestic students; for winter admission, 11/1 for domestic students. Applications are processed on a rolling basis. Application fee: $45 ($60 for international students). *Expenses:* Tuition, state resident: full-time $5,205. Tuition, nonresident: full-time $14,058. *Financial support:* Research assistantships, teaching assistantships, institutionally sponsored loans available. *Unit head:* Dr. Silvia S. Jurisson, Director of Graduate Studies, 573-882-2107, E-mail: jurissons@missouri.edu.

University of Missouri–Kansas City, College of Arts and Sciences, Department of Chemistry, Kansas City, MO 64110-2499. Offers analytical chemistry (MS, PhD); inorganic chemistry (MS, PhD); organic chemistry (MS, PhD); physical chemistry (MS, PhD); polymer chemistry (MS, PhD). PhD offered through the School of Graduate Studies. Part-time and evening/weekend programs available. *Faculty:* 11 full-time (1 woman), 1 part-time/adjunct (0 women). *Students:* Average age 30. 56 applicants, 46% accepted. In 2003, 1 master's awarded. *Median time to degree:* Master's–1 year full-time, 1 year part-time; doctorate–5 years full-time. *Degree requirements:* For master's, thesis (for some programs); for doctorate, thesis/dissertation. *Entrance requirements:* For master's, equivalent of American Chemical Society approved bachelor's degree in chemistry; for doctorate, GRE General Test, equivalent of American Chemical Society approved bachelor's degree in chemistry. Additional exam requirements/recommendations for international students: Required—TOEFL (minimum score 580 paper-based; 237 computer-based), TWE. *Application deadline:* For fall and spring admission, 4/15; for winter admission, 10/15 for domestic students. Applications are processed on a rolling basis. Application fee: $25. *Financial support:* In 2003–04, 1 fellowship with partial tuition reimbursement (averaging $18,156 per year), 9 research assistantships with partial tuition reimbursements (averaging $17,632 per year), 16 teaching assistantships with partial tuition reimbursements (averaging $16,416 per year) were awarded. Federal Work-Study, institutionally sponsored loans, and scholarships/grants also available. Support available to part-time students. Financial award application deadline: 2/15. *Faculty research:* Molecular spectroscopy, characterization and synthesis of materials and compounds, computational chemistry, natural products, drug delivery systems and anti-tumor agents. Total annual research expenditures: $551,743. *Unit head:* Dr. Jerry Jean, Chairperson, 816-235-2280, Fax: 816-235-5502, E-mail:

jeany@umkc.edu. *Application contact:* Dr. Kathleen Y. Kilway, Graduate Recruiting Committee, 816-235-2289, Fax: 816-235-5502, E-mail: kilwayk@umkc.edu.

University of Missouri–Rolla, Graduate School, College of Arts and Sciences, Department of Chemistry, Rolla, MO 65409-0910. Offers chemistry (MS, PhD); chemistry education (MST). *Faculty:* 16 full-time (2 women). *Students:* 61 full-time (16 women), 2 part-time (1 woman); includes 4 minority (all African Americans), 47 international. Average age 28. 106 applicants, 56% accepted, 13 enrolled. In 2003, 2 master's, 4 doctorates awarded. Terminal master's awarded for partial completion of doctoral program. *Median time to degree:* Master's–4 years part-time; doctorate–7 years part-time. *Degree requirements:* For doctorate, one foreign language, thesis/dissertation. *Entrance requirements:* For master's and doctorate, minimum GPA of 3.0. *Application deadline:* For fall admission, 7/1 for domestic students. Applications are processed on a rolling basis. Application fee: $50. Electronic applications accepted. *Expenses:* Tuition, state resident: full-time $5,871. Tuition, nonresident: full-time $13,114. Required fees: $820. Tuition and fees vary according to course load. *Financial support:* In 2003–04, 4 fellowships, 25 research assistantships with full and partial tuition reimbursements (averaging $13,191 per year), 32 teaching assistantships with full and partial tuition reimbursements (averaging $13,418 per year) were awarded. Institutionally sponsored loans also available. *Faculty research:* Structure and properties of materials; bioanalytical, environmental, and polymer chemistry. Total annual research expenditures: $2.4 million. *Unit head:* Dr. Ekkehard Sinn, Chairman, 573-341-6702, Fax: 573-341-6033, E-mail: esinn@umr.edu. *Application contact:* Dr. Pericles Stavropaulos, Information Contact, 573-341-7220, E-mail: pericles@umr.edu.

University of Missouri–St. Louis, Graduate School, College of Arts and Sciences, Department of Chemistry, St. Louis, MO 63121-4499. Offers chemistry (MS, PhD), including biochemistry, inorganic chemistry, organic chemistry, physical chemistry. Part-time and evening/weekend programs available. *Faculty:* 16 full-time (3 women). *Students:* 31 full-time (19 women), 20 part-time (9 women); includes 6 minority (5 Asian Americans or Pacific Islanders, 1 Hispanic American), 21 international. In 2003, 8 master's, 5 doctorates awarded. Terminal master's awarded for partial completion of doctoral program. *Degree requirements:* For master's, thesis optional; for doctorate, thesis/dissertation. *Entrance requirements:* For doctorate, GRE General Test, GRE Subject Test. Additional exam requirements/recommendations for international students: Required—TOEFL (minimum score 550 paper-based; 213 computer-based). *Application deadline:* For fall admission, 7/1 for domestic students; for spring admission, 12/7 priority date for domestic students. Applications are processed on a rolling basis. Application fee: $35 ($40 for international students). Electronic applications accepted. *Expenses:* Tuition, state resident: part-time $237 per credit hour. Tuition, nonresident: part-time $639 per credit hour. Required fees: $10 per credit hour. *Financial support:* In 2003–04, 14 research assistantships with full and partial tuition reimbursements (averaging $16,007 per year), 13 teaching assistantships with full and partial tuition reimbursements (averaging $15,408 per year) were awarded. Fellowships with full and partial tuition reimbursements *Faculty research:* Metallaborane chemistry, serum transferrin chemistry, natural products chemistry, organic synthesis. *Unit head:* Dr. F. Christopher Pigge, Director of Graduate Studies, 314-516-5311, Fax: 314-516-5342. *Application contact:* 314-516-5458, Fax: 314-516-5310, E-mail: gradadm@umsl.edu.

The University of Montana–Missoula, Graduate School, College of Arts and Sciences, Department of Chemistry, Missoula, MT 59812-0002. Offers chemistry (MS, PhD), including environmental/analytical chemistry, inorganic chemistry, organic chemistry, physical chemistry; chemistry teaching (MST). *Faculty:* 16 full-time (2 women). *Students:* 26 full-time (5 women), 12 part-time (6 women), 10 international. 25 applicants, 44% accepted, 6 enrolled. In 2003, 2 master's, 4 doctorates awarded. Terminal master's awarded for partial completion of doctoral program. *Degree requirements:* For master's, thesis (for some programs); for doctorate, thesis/dissertation. *Entrance requirements:* For master's and doctorate, GRE General Test. Additional exam requirements/recommendations for international students: Required—TOEFL (minimum score 575 paper-based; 230 computer-based). *Application deadline:* For fall admission, 2/15 for domestic students. Applications are processed on a rolling basis. Application fee: $45. *Expenses:* Tuition, state resident: full-time $1,848; part-time $221 per credit. Tuition, nonresident: full-time $4,880; part-time $333 per credit. Required fees: $2,200. *Financial support:* In 2003–04, 13 research assistantships with tuition reimbursements (averaging $14,000 per year), 12 teaching assistantships with full tuition reimbursements (averaging $14,000 per year) were awarded. Federal Work-Study, scholarships/grants, and unspecified assistantships also available. Financial award application deadline: 3/1; financial award applicants required to submit FAFSA. *Faculty research:* Reaction mechanisms and kinetics, inorganic and organic synthesis, analytical chemistry, natural products. Total annual research expenditures: $789,952. *Unit head:* Dr. Edward Rosenberg, Chair, 406-243-4022, Fax: 406-243-4227.

University of Nebraska–Lincoln, Graduate College, College of Arts and Sciences, Department of Chemistry, Lincoln, NE 68588. Offers analytical chemistry (PhD); chemistry (MS); inorganic chemistry (PhD); organic chemistry (PhD); physical chemistry (PhD). *Degree requirements:* For master's, one foreign language, departmental qualifying exam, thesis optional; for doctorate, one foreign language, thesis/dissertation, departmental qualifying exams, comprehensive exam. *Entrance requirements:* For master's and doctorate, GRE. Additional exam requirements/recommendations for international students: Required—TOEFL (minimum score 550 paper-based; 213 computer-based). Electronic applications accepted. *Faculty research:* Bioorganic and bioinorganic chemistry, biophysical and bioanalytical chemistry, structure-function of DNA and proteins, organometallics, mass spectrometry.

University of Nevada, Las Vegas, Graduate College, College of Science, Department of Chemistry, Las Vegas, NV 89154-9900. Offers MS. Part-time programs available. *Faculty:* 18 full-time (3 women), 8 part-time/adjunct (2 women). *Students:* 9 full-time (5 women), 14 part-time (7 women); includes 1 minority (Asian American or Pacific Islander), 11 international. 14 applicants, 71% accepted, 6 enrolled. In 2003, 9 degrees awarded. *Degree requirements:* For master's, thesis. *Entrance requirements:* For master's, GRE General Test, minimum GPA of 3.0 in last 2 years or 2.75 cumulative. Additional exam requirements/recommendations for international students: Required—TOEFL (minimum score 550 paper-based; 213 computer-based). *Application deadline:* For fall admission, 6/15 for domestic students, 5/1 for international students; for spring admission, 11/15 for domestic students, 10/1 for international students. Application fee: $60 ($75 for international students). *Expenses:* Tuition, state resident: part-time $115 per credit. Tuition, nonresident: part-time $242 per credit. Required fees: $8 per semester. Tuition and fees vary according to course load. *Financial support:* In 2003–04, 12 research assistantships with partial tuition reimbursements (averaging $11,370 per year), 11 teaching assistantships with full and partial tuition reimbursements (averaging $10,000 per year) were awarded. Financial award application deadline: 3/1. *Unit head:* Dr. Spencer Steinberg, Chair, 702-895-3510. *Application contact:* Graduate Coordinator, 702-895-3753, Fax: 702-895-4180, E-mail: gradcollege@ccmail.nevada.edu.

University of Nevada, Reno, Graduate School, College of Science, Department of Chemistry, Reno, NV 89557. Offers MS, PhD. *Faculty:* 15. *Students:* 40 full-time (12 women), 2 part-time; includes 1 minority (Hispanic American), 23 international. Average age 28. In 2003, 2 master's, 6 doctorates awarded. Terminal master's awarded for partial completion of doctoral program. *Degree requirements:* For master's, thesis; for doctorate, one foreign language, thesis/dissertation. *Entrance requirements:* For master's, GRE, minimum GPA of 2.75; for doctorate, GRE, minimum GPA of 3.0. Additional exam requirements/recommendations for international students: Required—TOEFL. *Application deadline:* For fall admission, 3/1 for domestic students; for spring admission, 11/1 for domestic students. Applications are processed on a rolling basis. Application fee: $60 ($95 for international students). *Expenses:* Tuition, state resident: part-time $119 per credit. Tuition, nonresident: part-time $127 per credit. Required fees: $20 per term. Tuition and fees vary according to course load. *Financial support:* In 2003–04, 16 research assistantships, 32 teaching assistantships were awarded. Federal Work-Study and institutionally sponsored loans also available. Financial award application deadline: 3/1. *Unit head:* Dr. John Nelson, Graduate Program Director, 775-784-6588.

University of New Brunswick Fredericton, School of Graduate Studies, Faculty of Science, Department of Chemistry, Fredericton, NB E3B 5A3, Canada. Offers M Sc, PhD. Part-time programs available. *Degree requirements:* For master's and doctorate, thesis/dissertation. *Entrance requirements:* For master's and doctorate, minimum GPA of 3.0. Additional exam requirements/recommendations for international students: Required—TOEFL, TWE. Electronic applications accepted. *Faculty research:* X-ray crystallography, fluorine, electrochemistry, quantum chemical abinitio, spectroscopy, theoretical organic synthesis, NMR, pulp and paper.

University of New Hampshire, Graduate School, College of Engineering and Physical Sciences, Department of Chemistry, Durham, NH 03824. Offers MS, MST, PhD. *Faculty:* 14 full-time. *Students:* 27 full-time (16 women), 23 part-time (7 women); includes 6 minority (4 African Americans, 1 Asian American or Pacific Islander, 1 Hispanic American), 19 international. Average age 26. 37 applicants, 57% accepted, 13 enrolled. In 2003, 5 master's, 3 doctorates awarded. Terminal master's awarded for partial completion of doctoral program. *Degree requirements:* For master's, thesis; for doctorate, one foreign language, thesis/dissertation. *Entrance requirements:* Additional exam requirements/recommendations for international students: Required—TOEFL (minimum score 550 paper-based; 213 computer-based). *Application deadline:* For fall admission, 4/1 for domestic students; for winter admission, 12/1 for domestic students. Applications are processed on a rolling basis. Application fee: $50. Tuition, area resident: Full-time $7,070. *Expenses:* Tuition, state resident: full-time $10,605. Tuition, nonresident: full-time $17,430. Required fees: $15. *Financial support:* In 2003–04, 3 fellowships, 4 research assistantships, 34 teaching assistantships were awarded. Federal Work-Study, scholarships/grants, and tuition waivers (full and partial) also available. Support available to part-time students. Financial award application deadline: 2/15. *Faculty research:* Analytical, physical, organic, and inorganic chemistry. *Unit head:* Dr. Howard Mayne, Chairperson, 603-862-2358. *Application contact:* Cindi Rewer, Coordinator, 603-862-1550, E-mail: chem.dept@unh.edu.

University of New Mexico, Graduate School, College of Arts and Sciences, Department of Chemistry, Albuquerque, NM 87131-2039. Offers MS, PhD. *Faculty:* 21 full-time (5 women), 2 part-time/adjunct (0 women). *Students:* 68 full-time (25 women), 4 part-time; includes 8 minority (1 African American, 2 American Indian/Alaska Native, 1 Asian American or Pacific Islander, 4 Hispanic Americans), 40 international. Average age 29. 36 applicants, 94% accepted, 20 enrolled. In 2003, 7 master's, 10 doctorates awarded. Terminal master's awarded for partial completion of doctoral program. *Degree requirements:* For master's and doctorate, thesis/dissertation, comprehensive exam. *Entrance requirements:* For master's and doctorate, ACS Proficiency Test. Additional exam requirements/recommendations for international students: Required—TOEFL. *Application deadline:* For fall admission, 7/30 for domestic students; for spring admission, 11/30 for domestic students. Application fee: $40. *Expenses:* Tuition, state resident: full-time $1,802; part-time $152 per credit hour. Tuition, nonresident: full-time $6,135; part-time $513 per credit hour. Tuition and fees vary according to program. *Financial support:* In 2003–04, 56 students received support, including fellowships (averaging $4,000 per year), research assistantships (averaging $11,920 per year), teaching assistantships (averaging $13,891 per year); Federal Work-Study and health care benefits also available. Financial award application deadline: 3/1; financial award applicants required to submit FAFSA. *Faculty research:* Analytical, inorganic, organic, and physical chemistry; biological chemistry. Total annual research expenditures: $1.8 million. *Unit head:* Dr. Tom Niemczyk, Chair, 505-277-5319, Fax: 505-277-2609, E-mail: niemczyk@unm.edu. *Application contact:* Michele Penhall, Program Advisor, 505-277-1779, Fax: 505-277-2609, E-mail: chemgrad@unm.edu.

University of New Orleans, Graduate School, College of Sciences, Department of Chemistry, New Orleans, LA 70148. Offers MS, PhD. *Faculty:* 15 full-time (0 women). *Students:* 60 full-time (28 women), 5 part-time (4 women); includes 7 minority (5 African Americans, 1 Asian American or Pacific Islander, 1 Hispanic American), 48 international. Average age 29. 46 applicants, 43% accepted, 9 enrolled. In 2003, 4 master's, 7 doctorates awarded. *Degree requirements:* For master's and doctorate, variable foreign language requirement, thesis/dissertation, departmental qualifying exam. *Entrance requirements:* For master's and doctorate, GRE General Test. Additional exam requirements/recommendations for international students: Required—TOEFL (minimum score 550 paper-based; 213 computer-based). *Application deadline:* For fall admission, 7/1 priority date for domestic students, 6/1 priority date for international students; for spring admission, 11/15 priority date for domestic students, 10/1 priority date for international students. Applications are processed on a rolling basis. Application fee: $20. Electronic applications accepted. *Expenses:* Tuition, state resident: part-time $488 per semester hour. Tuition, nonresident: part-time $1,826 per semester hour. *Financial support:* Application deadline: 5/15; *Faculty research:* Synthesis and reactions of novel compounds, high-temperature kinetics, calculations of molecular electrostatic potentials, structures and reactions of metal complexes. *Unit head:* Dr. Edwin Stevens, Chairperson, 504-280-6856, Fax: 504-280-6860, E-mail: estevens@uno.edu. *Application contact:* Dr. Ronald Evilia, Graduate Coordinator, 504-280-6313, Fax: 504-280-6860, E-mail: revilia@uno.edu.

The University of North Carolina at Chapel Hill, Graduate School, College of Arts and Sciences, Department of Chemistry, Chapel Hill, NC 27599. Offers MA, MS, PhD. *Faculty:* 37 full-time. *Students:* 159 full-time (76 women), 46 part-time (22 women); includes 29 minority (16 African Americans, 9 Asian Americans or Pacific Islanders, 4 Hispanic Americans), 30 international. 571 applicants, 30% accepted, 45 enrolled. In 2003, 11 master's, 40 doctorates awarded. *Degree requirements:* For master's, thesis (for some programs), comprehensive exam; for doctorate, thesis/dissertation, comprehensive exam. *Entrance requirements:* For master's and doctorate, GRE General Test, GRE Subject Test, minimum GPA of 3.0. *Application deadline:* For fall admission, 1/1 for domestic students. Application fee: $60. *Expenses:* Tuition, state resident: full-time $3,163. Tuition, nonresident: full-time $15,161. *Financial support:* In 2003–04, 113 research assistantships, 41 teaching assistantships were awarded. Financial award application deadline: 3/1. *Unit head:* Dr. James Jorgenson, Chairman, 919-962-2172. *Application contact:* Thomas Baer, Director of Graduate Studies, 919-967-4097.

The University of North Carolina at Charlotte, Graduate School, College of Arts and Sciences, Department of Chemistry, Charlotte, NC 28223-0001. Offers MS. Part-time programs available. *Faculty:* 14 full-time (3 women), 4 part-time/adjunct (0 women). *Students:* 1 (woman) full-time, 24 part-time (11 women); includes 5 minority (3 African Americans, 1 Asian American or Pacific Islander, 1 Hispanic American), 6 international. Average age 25. 27 applicants, 70% accepted, 11 enrolled. In 2003, 11 degrees awarded. *Degree requirements:* For master's, thesis. *Entrance requirements:* For master's, GRE General Test or MAT, minimum GPA of 3.0 in undergraduate major, 2.75 overall. Additional exam requirements/recommendations for international students: Required—TOEFL (minimum score 557 paper-based; 220 computer-based). *Application deadline:* For fall admission, 7/1 for domestic students, 5/1 for international students; for spring admission, 11/1 for domestic students, 10/1 for international students. Applications are processed on a rolling basis. Application fee: $35. Electronic applications accepted. *Expenses:* Tuition, state resident: full-time $1,979. Tuition, nonresident: full-time $12,111. Required fees: $1,201. Tuition and fees vary according to course load. *Financial support:* In 2003–04, 5 research assistantships (averaging $8,400 per year), 23 teaching assistantships (averaging $10,272 per year) were awarded. Fellowships, career-related internships or fieldwork, Federal Work-Study, institutionally sponsored loans, scholarships/grants, and unspecified assistantships also available. Support available to part-time students. Financial award application deadline: 4/1; financial award applicants required to submit FAFSA. *Faculty research:* Biophysical organic chemistry and biochemistry; polymers, biomaterials and nanostructures; materials chemistry; synthetic organic and inorganic chemistry; bioanalytical chemistry and mass spectrometry. *Unit head:* Dr. Thomas D. DuBois, Chair, 704-687-4765, Fax: 704-687-3151, E-mail: tddubois@email.uncc.edu. *Application contact:* Kathy B. Giddings, Director of Graduate Admissions, 704-687-3366, Fax: 704-687-3279, E-mail: gradadm@email.uncc.edu.

The University of North Carolina at Greensboro, Graduate School, College of Arts and Sciences, Department of Chemistry, Greensboro, NC 27412-5001. Offers M Ed, MS. *Faculty:* 11 full-time (2 women), 4 part-time/adjunct (0 women). *Students:* 1 full-time (0 women), 15

Chemistry

The University of North Carolina at Greensboro (continued)
part-time (6 women); includes 6 minority (4 African Americans, 1 Asian American or Pacific Islander, 1 Hispanic American), 5 international. 10 applicants, 100% accepted. In 2003, 4 degrees awarded. *Degree requirements:* For master's, one foreign language, thesis. *Entrance requirements:* For master's, GRE General Test. Additional exam requirements/recommendations for international students: Required—TOEFL. *Application deadline:* For fall admission, 6/15 for domestic students; for spring admission, 3/15 priority date for domestic students. Applications are processed on a rolling basis. Application fee: $35. *Expenses:* Tuition, state resident: part-time $1,887 per unit. Tuition, nonresident: part-time $12,862 per unit. *Financial support:* In 2003–04, 5 research assistantships with full tuition reimbursements (averaging $12,199 per year), 5 teaching assistantships with full tuition reimbursements (averaging $11,042 per year) were awarded. Fellowships, career-related internships or fieldwork, scholarships/grants, and traineeships also available. *Faculty research:* Synthesis of novel cyclopentadienes, molybdenum hydroxylase-cata ladder polymers, vinyl silicones. *Unit head:* Dr. Terance Nile, Head, 336-334-5714, Fax: 336-334-5402, E-mail: terry_nile@uncg.edu. *Application contact:* Michelle Harkleroad, Director of Graduate Admissions, 336-334-4886, Fax: 336-334-4424, E-mail: mbharkle@office.uncg.edu.

The University of North Carolina at Wilmington, College of Arts and Sciences, Department of Chemistry, Wilmington, NC 28403-3297. Offers MS. Part-time programs available. *Faculty:* 14 full-time (2 women), 2 part-time/adjunct (0 women). *Students:* 12 full-time (7 women), 27 part-time (18 women); includes 5 minority (2 African Americans, 2 Asian Americans or Pacific Islanders, 1 Hispanic American), 1 international. Average age 29. 13 applicants, 100% accepted, 12 enrolled. In 2003, 11 degrees awarded. *Degree requirements:* For master's, thesis, comprehensive exam. *Entrance requirements:* For master's, GRE General Test, minimum B average in undergraduate major. *Application deadline:* For fall admission, 6/1 for domestic students. Applications are processed on a rolling basis. Application fee: $45. *Expenses:* Tuition, state resident: full-time $2,282. Tuition, nonresident: full-time $11,980. Required fees: $1,659. Tuition and fees vary according to course load. *Financial support:* In 2003–04, 11 teaching assistantships were awarded; career-related internships or fieldwork and Federal Work-Study also available. Support available to part-time students. Financial award application deadline: 3/15. *Unit head:* Charles R. Ward, Chairman, 910-962-3115. *Application contact:* Dr. Robert D. Roer, Dean, Graduate School, 910-962-4117, Fax: 910-962-3787, E-mail: roer@uncw.edu.

University of North Dakota, Graduate School, College of Arts and Sciences, Department of Chemistry, Grand Forks, ND 58202. Offers MS, PhD. *Faculty:* 11 full-time (3 women), 2 part-time/adjunct (1 woman). *Students:* 2 full-time (1 woman), 25 part-time (8 women). 19 applicants, 84% accepted, 8 enrolled. In 2003, 2 master's, 6 doctorates awarded. Terminal master's awarded for partial completion of doctoral program. *Degree requirements:* For master's, thesis/dissertation, final exam; for doctorate, thesis/dissertation, final exam, comprehensive exam. *Entrance requirements:* For master's and doctorate, GRE General Test, GRE Subject Test, minimum GPA of 3.0. Additional exam requirements/recommendations for international students: Required—TOEFL (minimum score 550 paper-based; 213 computer-based). *Application deadline:* For fall admission, 3/1 priority date for domestic students, 2/15 priority date for international students; for spring admission, 10/15 priority date for domestic students, 10/15 priority date for international students. Applications are processed on a rolling basis. Application fee: $35. Electronic applications accepted. *Expenses:* Tuition, state resident: part-time $235 per credit. Tuition, nonresident: part-time $535 per credit. Tuition and fees vary according to course level, course load, program and reciprocity agreements. *Financial support:* In 2003–04, research assistantships with full tuition reimbursements (averaging $8,514 per year), teaching assistantships with full tuition reimbursements (averaging $10,014 per year) were awarded. Fellowships, Federal Work-Study, institutionally sponsored loans, scholarships/grants, and tuition waivers (full and partial) also available. Support available to part-time students. Financial award application deadline: 3/15; financial award applicants required to submit FAFSA. *Faculty research:* Synthetic and structural organometallic chemistry, photochemistry, theoretical chemistry, chromatographic chemistry, x-ray crystallography. *Unit head:* Dr. Harmon B. Abrahamson, Graduate Director, 701-777-4427, Fax: 701-777-2331, E-mail: harmon_abrahamson@und.nodak.edu.

University of Northern Colorado, Graduate School, College of Arts and Sciences, Department of Chemistry, Greeley, CO 80639. Offers chemical education (MA, PhD); chemical research (MA). *Accreditation:* NCATE (one or more programs are accredited). *Faculty:* 7 full-time (1 woman). *Students:* 15 full-time (10 women), 7 part-time (3 women); includes 2 minority (both Asian Americans or Pacific Islanders) Average age 30. 14 applicants, 71% accepted, 7 enrolled. In 2003, 1 degree awarded. *Degree requirements:* For master's, thesis or alternative, comprehensive exam; for doctorate, thesis/dissertation, comprehensive exam. *Entrance requirements:* For doctorate, GRE General Test. *Application deadline:* Applications are processed on a rolling basis. Application fee: $50 ($60 for international students). *Expenses:* Tuition, state resident: full-time $2,980; part-time $166 per semester. Tuition, nonresident: full-time $12,396; part-time $689 per semester. Required fees: $627; $35 per semester. *Financial support:* In 2003–04, 16 students received support, including 6 research assistantships (averaging $14,644 per year), 9 teaching assistantships (averaging $13,836 per year); fellowships, unspecified assistantships also available. Financial award application deadline: 3/1; financial award applicants required to submit FAFSA. *Unit head:* Dr. Richard Hyslop, Chairperson, 970-351-2559.

University of Northern Iowa, Graduate College, College of Natural Sciences, Department of Chemistry, Cedar Falls, IA 50614. Offers MA, MS. Part-time programs available. *Students:* 3 full-time (1 woman), 4 part-time (1 woman), 2 international. 10 applicants, 40% accepted. In 2003, 3 degrees awarded. *Degree requirements:* For master's, thesis or alternative, comprehensive exam (for some programs). *Entrance requirements:* Additional exam requirements/recommendations for international students: Required—TOEFL (minimum score 500 paper-based; 180 computer-based). *Application deadline:* For fall admission, 8/1 for domestic students. Applications are processed on a rolling basis. Application fee: $30 ($50 for international students). Electronic applications accepted. *Expenses:* Tuition, state resident: full-time $2,519. Tuition, nonresident: full-time $6,056. *Financial support:* Career-related internships or fieldwork, Federal Work-Study, scholarships/grants, and tuition waivers (full and partial) available. Support available to part-time students. Financial award application deadline: 2/1. *Unit head:* Dr. Paul Rider, Interim Head, 319-273-2437, Fax: 319-273-7127, E-mail: paul.rider@uni.edu.

University of North Texas, Robert B. Toulouse School of Graduate Studies, College of Arts and Sciences, Department of Chemistry, Denton, TX 76203. Offers MS, PhD. Part-time and evening/weekend programs available. *Faculty:* 18 full-time (5 women). *Students:* 57 full-time (23 women), 20 part-time (9 women); includes 3 minority (1 Asian American or Pacific Islander, 2 Hispanic Americans), 44 international. Average age 27. In 2003, 11 master's, 6 doctorates awarded. Terminal master's awarded for partial completion of doctoral program. *Degree requirements:* For master's, thesis (for some programs), comprehensive exam; for doctorate, one foreign language, thesis/dissertation, comprehensive exam. *Entrance requirements:* For master's and doctorate, GRE General Test. *Application deadline:* For fall admission, 7/15 for domestic students. Application fee: $50 ($75 for international students). Tuition, area resident: Full-time $4,087. Tuition, nonresident: full-time $8,730. Tuition and fees vary according to course load. *Financial support:* Fellowships, research assistantships, teaching assistantships, career-related internships or fieldwork, Federal Work-Study, and institutionally sponsored loans available. Financial award application deadline: 4/1. *Faculty research:* Analytical, inorganic, physical, and organic chemistry and materials. Total annual research expenditures: $2 million. *Unit head:* Dr. Ruthanne Thomas, Chair, 940-565-2713, Fax: 940-565-4318, E-mail: rthomas@unt.edu. *Application contact:* Dr. Thomas R. Cundari, Graduate Adviser, 940-565-3554, Fax: 940-565-4318, E-mail: chem@unt.edu.

University of Notre Dame, Graduate School, College of Science, Department of Chemistry and Biochemistry, Notre Dame, IN 46556. Offers biochemistry (MS, PhD); inorganic chemistry (MS, PhD); organic chemistry (MS, PhD); physical chemistry (MS, PhD). *Faculty:* 30 full-time (3 women). *Students:* 139 full-time (46 women); includes 5 minority (1 African American, 1 American Indian/Alaska Native, 1 Asian American or Pacific Islander, 2 Hispanic Americans), 65 international. 270 applicants, 38% accepted, 44 enrolled. In 2003, 5 master's, 17 doctorates awarded. Terminal master's awarded for partial completion of doctoral program. *Degree requirements:* For master's, thesis, comprehensive exam; for doctorate, thesis/dissertation, qualifying exam. *Entrance requirements:* For master's and doctorate, GRE General Test, GRE Subject Test (strongly recommended). Additional exam requirements/recommendations for international students: Required—TOEFL. *Application deadline:* For fall admission, 2/1 for domestic students. Applications are processed on a rolling basis. Application fee: $50. Electronic applications accepted. *Expenses:* Tuition: Full-time $29,375. *Financial support:* In 2003–04, 139 students received support, including 34 fellowships with full tuition reimbursements available (averaging $20,000 per year), 46 research assistantships with full tuition reimbursements available (averaging $15,500 per year), 51 teaching assistantships with full tuition reimbursements available (averaging $15,500 per year); tuition waivers (full) also available. Financial award application deadline: 2/1. *Faculty research:* Reaction design and mechaninistic studies; reactive intermediates; synthesis, structure and reactivity of organometallic. cluster complexes, and biologically active natural products; bioorganic chemistry; enzymology. Total annual research expenditures: $9.4 million. *Unit head:* Dr. Richard E. Taylor, Director of Graduate Studies, 574-631-7058, Fax: 574-631-6652, E-mail: taylor.61@nd.edu. *Application contact:* Dr. Terrence J. Akai, Director of Graduate Admissions, 574-631-7706, Fax: 574-631-4183, E-mail: gradad@nd.edu.

University of Oklahoma, Graduate College, College of Arts and Sciences, Department of Chemistry and Biochemistry, Norman, OK 73019-0390. Offers MS, PhD. Part-time programs available. *Faculty:* 26 full-time (3 women), 1 part-time/adjunct (0 women). *Students:* 106 full-time (41 women), 7 part-time (1 woman); includes 4 minority (2 African Americans, 1 American Indian/Alaska Native, 1 Asian American or Pacific Islander), 68 international. 64 applicants, 64% accepted, 21 enrolled. In 2003, 5 master's, 6 doctorates awarded. Terminal master's awarded for partial completion of doctoral program. *Degree requirements:* For master's, thesis optional; for doctorate, thesis/dissertation. *Entrance requirements:* For master's, GRE, BS in chemistry; for doctorate, GRE. Additional exam requirements/recommendations for international students: Required—TOEFL (minimum score 550 paper-based; 213 computer-based). *Application deadline:* For fall admission, 4/1 priority date for domestic students, 4/1 priority date for international students; for spring admission, 9/1 priority date for domestic students, 9/1 priority date for international students. Applications are processed on a rolling basis. Application fee: $25 ($75 for international students). *Expenses:* Tuition, state resident: full-time $2,774; part-time $116 per credit hour. Tuition, nonresident: full-time $9,571; part-time $399 per credit hour. Required fees: $953; $33 per credit hour. Full-time tuition and fees vary according to course level, course load and program. *Financial support:* In 2003–04, 12 students received support, including 6 fellowships with full tuition reimbursements available (averaging $5,000 per year), 35 research assistantships with partial tuition reimbursements available (averaging $11,574 per year), 71 teaching assistantships with partial tuition reimbursements available (averaging $12,107 per year); career-related internships or fieldwork, Federal Work-Study, scholarships/grants, traineeships, and tuition waivers (partial) also available. Support available to part-time students. Financial award application deadline: 4/1; financial award applicants required to submit FAFSA. *Faculty research:* Genomics, mechanisms of enzyme action bacterial transport processes, protein and nucleic acid structure and function. Total annual research expenditures: $6.1 million. *Unit head:* Dr. Glenn Dryhurst, Chair, 405-325-4811. *Application contact:* Ariene Crawford, Graduate Recruiting Secretary, 405-325-2946, Fax: 405-325-6111, E-mail: admission@chemdept.chem.ou.edu.

University of Oregon, Graduate School, College of Arts and Sciences, Department of Chemistry, Eugene, OR 97403. Offers biochemistry (MA, MS, PhD); chemistry (MA, MS, PhD). *Faculty:* 34 full-time (7 women), 7 part-time/adjunct (3 women). *Students:* 117 full-time (44 women), 3 part-time (1 woman); includes 8 minority (3 African Americans, 1 American Indian/Alaska Native, 4 Asian Americans or Pacific Islanders), 14 international. 18 applicants, 89% accepted. In 2003, 8 master's, 17 doctorates awarded. Terminal master's awarded for partial completion of doctoral program. *Degree requirements:* For doctorate, thesis/dissertation. *Entrance requirements:* For master's and doctorate, GRE General Test, minimum GPA of 3.0. Additional exam requirements/recommendations for international students: Required—TOEFL. *Application deadline:* For fall admission, 1/10 for domestic students. Applications are processed on a rolling basis. Application fee: $50. *Expenses:* Tuition, state resident: part-time $8,910 per term. Tuition, nonresident: part-time $13,689 per term. *Financial support:* In 2003–04, 54 teaching assistantships were awarded; Federal Work-Study and institutionally sponsored loans also available. Financial award application deadline: 4/15. *Faculty research:* Organic chemistry, organometallic chemistry, inorganic chemistry, physical chemistry, materials science, biochemistry, chemical physics, molecular or cell biology. *Unit head:* Tom Dyke, Head, 541-346-4603. *Application contact:* Lynde Ritzow, Graduate Admissions Coordinator, 541-346-4789, E-mail: lynde@oregon.uoregon.edu.

University of Ottawa, Faculty of Graduate and Postdoctoral Studies, Faculty of Science, Ottawa-Carleton Chemistry Institute, Ottawa, ON K1N 6N5, Canada. Offers M Sc, PhD. *Faculty:* 25 full-time (3 women). *Students:* 72 full-time (35 women), 5 part-time (all women). 61 applicants, 41% accepted, 12 enrolled. In 2003, 14 master's, 6 doctorates awarded. *Degree requirements:* For master's, thesis, seminar; for doctorate, thesis/dissertation, 2 seminars, comprehensive exam. *Entrance requirements:* For master's, honors B Sc degree or equivalent, minimum B average; for doctorate, honors B Sc with minimum B average or M Sc in chemistry with minimum B+ average. *Application deadline:* For fall admission, 3/1 for domestic students. Applications are processed on a rolling basis. Application fee: $60. *Expenses:* Tuition, state resident: full-time $4,467. International tuition: $4,574 full-time. Tuition and fees vary according to program. *Financial support:* Fellowships, research assistantships, teaching assistantships, Federal Work-Study available. Financial award application deadline: 2/15. *Faculty research:* Organic chemistry, physical chemistry, inorganic chemistry, biological chemistry, analytical chemistry. *Unit head:* Dr. Sandro Gambarotta, Director, 613-562-5728 Ext. 5199, Fax: 613-562-5665. *Application contact:* Lise Maisonneuve, Graduate Studies Administrator, 613-562-5800 Ext. 6050, Fax: 613-562-5486, E-mail: lise@science.uottawa.ca.

University of Pennsylvania, School of Arts and Sciences, Graduate Group in Chemistry, Philadelphia, PA 19104. Offers MS, PhD. *Faculty:* 31 full-time (4 women), 10 part-time/adjunct (0 women). *Students:* 186 full-time (72 women), 39 part-time (28 women); includes 13 minority (5 African Americans, 7 Asian Americans or Pacific Islanders, 1 Hispanic American), 91 international. 613 applicants, 17% accepted, 36 enrolled. In 2003, 22 master's, 23 doctorates awarded. *Degree requirements:* For doctorate, thesis/dissertation. *Entrance requirements:* For doctorate, GRE General Test, GRE Subject Test, previous graduate course work in organic, inorganic, and physical chemistry each with a lab, differential and integral calculus, and general physics with a lab. Additional exam requirements/recommendations for international students: Required—TOEFL. *Application deadline:* For fall admission, 12/1 for domestic students. Application fee: $70. Electronic applications accepted. *Expenses:* Tuition: Full-time $28,040; part-time $3,550 per course. Required fees: $1,750; $214 per course. Tuition and fees vary according to degree level, program and student level. *Financial support:* Fellowships, research assistantships, teaching assistantships available. Financial award application deadline: 12/15. *Application contact:* Patricia Rea, Coordinator for Admissions, 215-573-5816, Fax: 215-573-8068, E-mail: gdasadmis@sas.upenn.edu.

University of Pittsburgh, School of Arts and Sciences, Department of Chemistry, Pittsburgh, PA 15260. Offers MS, PhD. Part-time and evening/weekend programs available. *Faculty:* 28 full-time (3 women), 6 part-time/adjunct (2 women). *Students:* 202 full-time (58 women), 10 part-time (3 women); includes 13 minority (2 African Americans, 8 Asian Americans or Pacific Islanders, 3 Hispanic Americans), 103 international. Average age 24. 437 applicants, 34% accepted, 55 enrolled. In 2003, 12 master's, 15 doctorates awarded. Terminal master's awarded for partial completion of doctoral program. *Degree requirements:* For master's and doctorate, thesis/dissertation. *Entrance requirements:* For master's and doctorate, GRE General Test,

GRE Subject Test. Additional exam requirements/recommendations for international students: Required—TOEFL (minimum score 550 paper-based; 213 computer-based). *Application deadline:* For fall admission, 2/1 for domestic students. Applications are processed on a rolling basis. Application fee: $40. Electronic applications accepted. *Expenses:* Tuition, state resident: full-time $11,744; part-time $479 per credit. Tuition, nonresident: full-time $22,910; part-time $941 per credit. Required fees: $560. Tuition and fees vary according to degree level and program. *Financial support:* In 2003–04, 202 students received support, including 4 fellowships with tuition reimbursements available (averaging $16,000 per year), 9 research assistantships with tuition reimbursements available (averaging $17,925 per year), 74 teaching assistantships with tuition reimbursements available (averaging $19,200 per year); Federal Work-Study, scholarships/grants, and health care benefits also available. Financial award application deadline: 2/1. *Faculty research:* Analytical, inorganic, organic, physical, and surface chemistry. Total annual research expenditures: $8.6 million. *Unit head:* Dr. Kenneth D. Jordan, Chairman, 412-624-0415, Fax: 412-624-1162, E-mail: jordan@a.psc.edu. *Application contact:* Fran Nagy, Graduate Program Administrator, 412-624-8501, Fax: 412-624-8611, E-mail: fnagy@pitt.edu.

See in-depth description on page 173.

University of Prince Edward Island, Faculty of Science, Charlottetown, PE C1A 4P3, Canada. Offers biology (M Sc); chemistry (M Sc). *Faculty:* 15 full-time (4 women), 1 part-time/adjunct (0 women). *Students:* 6 full-time (3 women), 1 (woman) part-time. *Degree requirements:* For master's, thesis. *Entrance requirements:* Additional exam requirements/recommendations for international students: Required—TOEFL (minimum score 550 paper-based; 213 computer-based), Canadian Academic English Language Assessment, Michigan English Language Assessment Battery, Canadian Test of English for Scholars and Trainees. *Application deadline:* For fall admission, 12/15 priority date for domestic students, 12/15 priority date for international students. Application fee: $35. Tuition charges are reported in Canadian dollars. Tuition, area resident: Full-time $2,700 Canadian dollars. International tuition: $6,100 Canadian dollars full-time. Part-time tuition and fees vary according to course level, degree level, campus/location, program and student level. *Faculty research:* Ecology and wildlife biology, molecular, genetics and biotechnology, organametallic, bio-organic, supramolecular and synthetic organic chemistry, neurobiology and stoke materials science. *Unit head:* Dr. Roger Gordon, Dean, 902-566-0320, Fax: 902-628-4303. *Application contact:* Dr. Marina Silva, Graduate Studies Coordinator, 902-566-0602, Fax: 902-566-0740, E-mail: msilva@upei.ca.

University of Puerto Rico, Mayagüez Campus, Graduate Studies, College of Arts and Sciences, Department of Chemistry, Mayagüez, PR 00681-9000. Offers MS. *Degree requirements:* For master's, one foreign language, thesis, comprehensive exam. *Faculty research:* Biochemistry, spectroscopy, food chemistry, physical chemistry, electrochemistry.

University of Puerto Rico, Río Piedras, Faculty of Natural Sciences, Department of Chemistry, San Juan, PR 00931. Offers MS, PhD. Part-time and evening/weekend programs available. *Faculty:* 17 full-time (1 woman). *Students:* 104 full-time (61 women), 27 part-time (11 women); includes 127 minority (all Hispanic Americans) 42 applicants, 86% accepted, 36 enrolled. In 2003, 3 master's, 3 doctorates awarded. *Degree requirements:* For master's and doctorate, one foreign language, thesis/dissertation, comprehensive exam. *Entrance requirements:* For master's, GRE General Test, GRE Subject Test, EXADEP, interview, minimum GPA of 3.0, letter of recommendation; for doctorate, GRE General Test, GRE Subject Test, minimum GPA of 3.0, letter of recommendation. Additional exam requirements/recommendations for international students: Required—TOEFL. *Application deadline:* For fall admission, 2/1 for domestic students, 2/1 for international students. Application fee: $17. *Expenses:* Tuition, state resident: part-time $75 per credit. Tuition, nonresident: full-time $1,200; part-time $218 per credit. International tuition: $3,500 full-time. Required fees: $70; $35 per term. *Financial support:* Fellowships, research assistantships, teaching assistantships, Federal Work-Study, institutionally sponsored loans, and tuition waivers (partial) available. Financial award application deadline: 5/31. *Faculty research:* Organometallic synthesis, transition metal chemistry, organic air pollutants. *Unit head:* Dr. Nestor M. Carballeira, Coordinator, 787-764-0000 Ext. 4818, Fax: 787-756-8242.

See in-depth description on page 175.

University of Regina, Faculty of Graduate Studies and Research, Faculty of Science, Department of Chemistry and Biochemistry, Regina, SK S4S 0A2, Canada. Offers analytical chemistry (M Sc, PhD); biochemistry (M Sc, PhD); inorganic chemistry (M Sc, PhD); organic chemistry (M Sc, PhD); physical chemistry (M Sc, PhD). Part-time programs available. *Faculty:* 9 full-time (2 women), 2 part-time/adjunct (1 woman). *Students:* 7 full-time (4 women), 4 part-time (1 woman). 12 applicants. In 2003, 3 degrees awarded. *Degree requirements:* For master's and doctorate, thesis/dissertation, departmental qualifying exam. *Entrance requirements:* For master's and doctorate, GRE. Additional exam requirements/recommendations for international students: Required—TOEFL. *Application deadline:* For fall admission, 1/1 for domestic students; for winter admission, 7/1 for domestic students. Applications are processed on a rolling basis. Application fee: $60. *Expenses:* Tuition, state resident: part-time $130 per credit hour. Tuition and fees vary according to course load and program. *Financial support:* In 2003–04, 4 fellowships, 1 research assistantship, 3 teaching assistantships were awarded. Scholarships/grants also available. Financial award application deadline: 6/15. *Faculty research:* Organic synthesis, organic oxidations, ionic liquids theoretical/computational chemistry, protein biochemistry/biophysics, environmental analytical, photophysical/photochemistry. *Unit head:* Dr. Andrew G. Wee, Head, 306-585-4767, Fax: 306-585-4894, E-mail: chem.chair@uregina.ca. *Application contact:* Teri Dibble, Office Administrator, 306-585-4146, Fax: 306-585-4894, E-mail: teri.dibble@uregina.ca.

University of Rhode Island, Graduate School, College of Arts and Sciences, Department of Chemistry, Kingston, RI 02881. Offers MS, PhD. In 2003, 3 master's, 7 doctorates awarded. *Application deadline:* For fall admission, 4/15 for domestic students. Applications are processed on a rolling basis. Application fee: $35. *Expenses:* Tuition, state resident: full-time $4,338; part-time $281 per credit. Tuition, nonresident: full-time $12,438; part-time $704 per credit. Required fees: $1,840. *Unit head:* Dr. William Euler, Chairperson, 401-874-5090.

University of Rochester, The College, Arts and Sciences, Department of Chemistry, Rochester, NY 14627-0250. Offers MS, PhD. *Faculty:* 20. *Students:* 65 full-time (24 women), 1 (woman) part-time; includes 3 minority (all Hispanic Americans), 28 international. 297 applicants, 21% accepted, 14 enrolled. In 2003, 12 master's, 13 doctorates awarded. Terminal master's awarded for partial completion of doctoral program. *Degree requirements:* For doctorate, thesis/dissertation, qualifying exam. *Entrance requirements:* For master's and doctorate, GRE General Test. Additional exam requirements/recommendations for international students: Required—TOEFL. *Application deadline:* For fall admission, 2/1 for domestic students. Application fee: $25. *Expenses:* Tuition: Part-time $880 per credit hour. Required fees: $522. *Financial support:* Fellowships, research assistantships, teaching assistantships, tuition waivers (full and partial) available. Financial award application deadline: 2/1. *Unit head:* Robert Boeckman, Chair, 585-275-5493. *Application contact:* Stacey Cudzilo, Graduate Program Secretary, 585-275-0635.

University of San Francisco, College of Arts and Sciences, Department of Chemistry, San Francisco, CA 94117-1080. Offers MS. Part-time and evening/weekend programs available. *Faculty:* 5 full-time (1 woman), 1 part-time/adjunct (0 women). *Students:* 12 full-time (8 women), 2 part-time (both women); includes 3 minority (2 Asian Americans or Pacific Islanders, 1 Hispanic American), 10 international. Average age 28. 30 applicants, 73% accepted, 6 enrolled. In 2003, 6 degrees awarded. *Degree requirements:* For master's, thesis. *Entrance requirements:* For master's, GRE General Test, GRE Subject Test, BS in chemistry or related field. *Application deadline:* Applications are processed on a rolling basis. Application fee: $55 ($65 for international students). *Expenses:* Tuition: Full-time $15,840; part-time $880 per unit. Tuition and fees vary according to degree level, campus/location and program. *Financial support:* In 2003–04, 14 students received support; fellowships, research assistantships, teaching assistantships, career-related internships or fieldwork, Federal Work-Study, institutionally sponsored loans, and tuition waivers (partial) available. Support available to part-time students. Financial award application deadline: 3/2; financial award applicants required to submit FAFSA. *Faculty research:* Organic photochemistry, genetics of chromatic adaptation, electron transfer processes in solution, metabolism of protein hormones. Total annual research expenditures: $75,000. *Unit head:* Dr. Kim Summerhays, Chairman, 415-422-6157, Fax: 415-422-5157.

University of Saskatchewan, College of Graduate Studies and Research, College of Arts and Sciences, Department of Chemistry, Saskatoon, SK S7N 5A2, Canada. Offers M Sc, PhD. *Faculty:* 15. *Students:* 46. *Degree requirements:* For master's and doctorate, thesis/dissertation, registration. *Entrance requirements:* Additional exam requirements/recommendations for international students: Required—TOEFL. *Application deadline:* For fall admission, 7/1 for domestic students. Applications are processed on a rolling basis. Application fee: $50. Tuition charges are reported in Canadian dollars. *Expenses:* Tuition, state resident: part-time $483 Canadian dollars per course. *Financial support:* Fellowships, research assistantships, teaching assistantships available. Financial award application deadline: 1/31. *Unit head:* Dr. R. P. Steer, Head, 306-966-4655, Fax: 306-966-4730, E-mail: ron.steer@usask.ca. *Application contact:* Dr. Bill Waltz, Graduate Chair, 306-966-4708, Fax: 306-966-4730, E-mail: waltz@sask.usask.ca.

The University of Scranton, Graduate School, Department of Chemistry, Program in Chemistry, Scranton, PA 18510. Offers MA, MS. Part-time and evening/weekend programs available. *Faculty:* 9 full-time (2 women). *Students:* 2 full-time (0 women), 2 part-time (1 woman), 1 international. Average age 26. 4 applicants, 100% accepted. In 2003, 2 degrees awarded. *Degree requirements:* For master's, thesis (for some programs), capstone experience. *Entrance requirements:* For master's, minimum GPA of 2.75. Additional exam requirements/recommendations for international students: Required—TOEFL. *Application deadline:* Applications are processed on a rolling basis. Application fee: $50. *Expenses:* Tuition: Part-time $590 per credit. Required fees: $25 per term. *Financial support:* Teaching assistantships, career-related internships or fieldwork, Federal Work-Study, and teaching fellowships available. Support available to part-time students. Financial award application deadline: 3/1. *Unit head:* Dr. Christopher A. Baumann, Director, 570-941-6389, Fax: 570-941-7510, E-mail: cab@scranton.edu.

The University of Scranton, Graduate School, Department of Chemistry, Program in Clinical Chemistry, Scranton, PA 18510. Offers MA, MS. Part-time and evening/weekend programs available. *Faculty:* 9 full-time (2 women). *Students:* 3 full-time (2 women), 7 part-time (4 women), 1 international. Average age 24. 4 applicants, 100% accepted. In 2003, 1 degree awarded. *Degree requirements:* For master's, thesis (for some programs), capstone experience. *Entrance requirements:* For master's, minimum GPA of 2.75. Additional exam requirements/recommendations for international students: Required—TOEFL. *Application deadline:* Applications are processed on a rolling basis. Application fee: $50. *Expenses:* Tuition: Part-time $590 per credit. Required fees: $25 per term. *Financial support:* Teaching assistantships, career-related internships or fieldwork, Federal Work-Study, and teaching fellowships available. Support available to part-time students. Financial award application deadline: 3/1. *Unit head:* Dr. Christopher A. Baumann, Director, 570-941-6389, Fax: 570-941-7510, E-mail: cab@scranton.edu.

University of South Carolina, The Graduate School, College of Science and Mathematics, Department of Chemistry and Biochemistry, Columbia, SC 29208. Offers IMA, MAT, MS, PhD. IMA and MAT offered in cooperation with the College of Education. Part-time programs available. *Faculty:* 27 full-time (2 women), 2 part-time/adjunct (both women). *Students:* 101 full-time (44 women), 2 part-time (1 woman); includes 13 minority (8 African Americans, 4 Asian Americans or Pacific Islanders, 1 Hispanic American), 33 international. Average age 26. 401 applicants, 17% accepted, 34 enrolled. In 2003, 5 master's, 7 doctorates awarded. Terminal master's awarded for partial completion of doctoral program. *Median time to degree:* Master's–2.4 years full-time; doctorate–4.5 years full-time. *Degree requirements:* For master's and doctorate, thesis/dissertation, comprehensive exam, registration. *Entrance requirements:* For master's and doctorate, GRE General Test. Additional exam requirements/recommendations for international students: Required—TOEFL. *Application deadline:* For fall admission, 4/15 for domestic students; for spring admission, 10/15 priority date for domestic students. Applications are processed on a rolling basis. Application fee: $40. Electronic applications accepted. *Expenses:* Tuition, state resident: part-time $308 per hour. Tuition, nonresident: part-time $655 per hour. *Financial support:* In 2003–04, 14 fellowships with partial tuition reimbursements (averaging $2,000 per year), 62 research assistantships with partial tuition reimbursements (averaging $19,250 per year), 40 teaching assistantships with partial tuition reimbursements (averaging $19,250 per year) were awarded. Institutionally sponsored loans, tuition waivers (partial), and unspecified assistantships also available. Financial award application deadline: 4/15. *Faculty research:* Spectroscopy, crystallography, organic and organometallic synthesis, analytical chemistry, materials. Total annual research expenditures: $5.7 million. *Unit head:* Dr. Daniel L. Reger, Chair, 803-777-0455, Fax: 803-777-9521, E-mail: reger@mail.chem.sc.edu. *Application contact:* Dr. Thomas Bryson, Chairman, Graduate Admissions, 803-777-2579, Fax: 803-777-9521, E-mail: chemgradoffice@mail.chem.se.edu.

The University of South Dakota, Graduate School, College of Arts and Sciences, Department of Chemistry, Vermillion, SD 57069-2390. Offers MA, MNS. *Degree requirements:* For master's, thesis, comprehensive exam. *Entrance requirements:* For master's, GRE. Additional exam requirements/recommendations for international students: Required—TOEFL (minimum score 550 paper-based; 213 computer-based). *Faculty research:* Electrochemistry, photochemistry, inorganic synthesis, environmental and solid-state chemistry.

University of Southern California, Graduate School, College of Letters, Arts and Sciences, Department of Chemistry, Program in Chemistry, Los Angeles, CA 90089. Offers MA, MS, PhD. *Faculty:* 27 full-time (3 women). *Students:* 120 full-time (44 women); includes 8 minority (1 African American, 5 Asian Americans or Pacific Islanders, 2 Hispanic Americans), 80 international. Average age 27. 800 applicants, 11% accepted, 25 enrolled. In 2003, 3 master's, 16 doctorates awarded. Terminal master's awarded for partial completion of doctoral program. *Degree requirements:* For master's, qualifying exam, thesis optional; for doctorate, thesis/dissertation, qualifying exam. *Entrance requirements:* For master's and doctorate, GRE General Test. *Application deadline:* For fall admission, 3/1 for domestic students. Applications are processed on a rolling basis. Application fee: $0. *Expenses:* Tuition: Full-time $32,784; part-time $949 per unit. Tuition and fees vary according to course load and program. *Financial support:* In 2003–04, 120 students received support, including fellowships with full tuition reimbursements available (averaging $21,333 per year), research assistantships with tuition reimbursements available (averaging $21,333 per year), teaching assistantships with tuition reimbursements available (averaging $21,333 per year); Federal Work-Study, institutionally sponsored loans, scholarships/grants, and health care benefits also available. Financial award application deadline: 3/1. *Faculty research:* Organic chemistry. *Application contact:* Heather Meunier, Information Contact, 213-740-6855, Fax: 213-740-2701, E-mail: rbmartin@usc.edu.

University of Southern Mississippi, Graduate School, College of Science and Technology, Department of Chemistry and Biochemistry, Hattiesburg, MS 39406-0001. Offers analytical chemistry (MS, PhD); biochemistry (MS, PhD); inorganic chemistry (MS, PhD); organic chemistry (MS, PhD); physical chemistry (MS, PhD). *Faculty:* 8 full-time (1 woman). *Students:* 27 full-time (17 women), 1 part-time; includes 14 minority (4 African Americans, 1 American Indian/Alaska Native, 9 Asian Americans or Pacific Islanders). Average age 27. 29 applicants, 45% accepted, 10 enrolled. In 2003, 1 master's, 7 doctorates awarded. *Degree requirements:* For master's and doctorate, thesis/dissertation, comprehensive exam. *Entrance requirements:* For master's, GRE General Test, minimum GPA of 2.75 in last 60 hours; for doctorate, GRE General Test, minimum GPA of 3.5. Additional exam requirements/recommendations for international students: Required—TOEFL. *Application deadline:* For fall admission, 8/6 for domestic students. Applications are processed on a rolling basis. Application fee: $25. *Expenses:*

Chemistry

University of Southern Mississippi (continued)
Tuition, state resident: part-time $1,967 per semester. Tuition, nonresident: part-time $4,376 per semester. *Financial support:* Fellowships, research assistantships with full tuition reimbursements, teaching assistantships with full tuition reimbursements, Federal Work-Study and institutionally sponsored loans available. Support available to part-time students. Financial award application deadline: 3/15. *Faculty research:* Plant biochemistry, photo chemistry, polymer chemistry, x-ray analysis, enzyme chemistry. *Unit head:* Dr. Robert Bateman, Chair, 601-266-4701. *Application contact:* Dr. Gordon Cannon, Information Contact, 601-266-4702.

University of South Florida, College of Graduate Studies, College of Arts and Sciences, Department of Chemistry, Tampa, FL 33620-9951. Offers analytical chemistry (MS, PhD); biochemistry (MS, PhD); inorganic chemistry (MS, PhD); organic chemistry (MS, PhD); physical chemistry (MS, PhD); polymer chemistry (PhD). Part-time programs available. *Faculty:* 26 full-time (8 women), 1 (woman) part-time/adjunct. *Students:* 75 full-time (34 women), 11 part-time (4 women); includes 14 minority (3 African Americans, 3 Asian Americans or Pacific Islanders, 8 Hispanic Americans), 30 international. 75 applicants, 37% accepted, 17 enrolled. In 2003, 3 master's, 6 doctorates awarded. Terminal master's awarded for partial completion of doctoral program. *Degree requirements:* For master's, thesis; for doctorate, 2 foreign languages, thesis/dissertation, colloquium. *Entrance requirements:* For master's and doctorate, GRE General Test, minimum GPA of 3.0 in last 30 hours of chemistry course work, letters of recommendation (3). Additional exam requirements/recommendations for international students: Required—TOEFL (minimum score 550 paper-based; 213 computer-based), TSE(minimum score 50). *Application deadline:* For fall admission, 5/1 priority date for domestic students, 3/1 priority date for international students; for spring admission, 10/1 priority date for domestic students, 8/1 priority date for international students. Applications are processed on a rolling basis. Application fee: $30. Electronic applications accepted. *Financial support:* In 2003–04, 74 students received support, including 3 fellowships with partial tuition reimbursements available (averaging $18,500 per year), 13 research assistantships with partial tuition reimbursements available (averaging $18,500 per year), 58 teaching assistantships with partial tuition reimbursements available (averaging $18,500 per year); career-related internships or fieldwork, institutionally sponsored loans, scholarships/grants, and unspecified assistantships also available. Financial award application deadline: 6/30. *Faculty research:* Synthesis, bio-organic chemistry, bioinorganic chemistry, environmental chemistry, NMR. Total annual research expenditures: $1.6 million. *Unit head:* Michael Zaworotko, Chairperson, 813-974-4129, Fax: 813-974-1731. *Application contact:* Dr. Julie Harmon, Graduate Director, 813-974-3397, Fax: 813-974-3203, E-mail: harmon@chuma1.cas.usf.edu.

The University of Tennessee, Graduate School, College of Arts and Sciences, Department of Chemistry, Knoxville, TN 37996. Offers analytical chemistry (MS, PhD); chemical physics (PhD); environmental chemistry (MS, PhD); inorganic chemistry (MS, PhD); organic chemistry (MS, PhD); physical chemistry (MS, PhD); polymer chemistry (MS, PhD); theoretical chemistry (PhD). Part-time programs available. Terminal master's awarded for partial completion of doctoral program. *Degree requirements:* For master's and doctorate, thesis/dissertation. *Entrance requirements:* For master's and doctorate, GRE General Test, minimum GPA of 2.7. Additional exam requirements/recommendations for international students: Required—TOEFL. Electronic applications accepted.

The University of Texas at Arlington, Graduate School, College of Science, Department of Chemistry and Biochemistry, Arlington, TX 76019. Offers applied chemistry (PhD); chemistry (MS). Part-time programs available. *Faculty:* 8 full-time (0 women). *Students:* 40 full-time (20 women), 4 part-time (1 woman); includes 3 minority (2 African Americans, 1 Asian American or Pacific Islander), 35 international. 32 applicants, 47% accepted, 9 enrolled. In 2003, 5 master's, 4 doctorates awarded. Terminal master's awarded for partial completion of doctoral program. *Median time to degree:* Of those who began their doctoral program in fall 1995, 100% received their degree in 8 years or less. *Degree requirements:* For master's, thesis optional; for doctorate, thesis/dissertation, internship, oral defense of dissertation. *Entrance requirements:* For master's, GRE General Test, minimum GPA of 3.0 in last 60 hours; for doctorate, GRE General Test. *Application deadline:* For fall admission, 6/16 for domestic students. Applications are processed on a rolling basis. Application fee: $35 ($50 for international students). *Expenses:* Tuition, state resident: full-time $3,042. Tuition, nonresident: full-time $8,712. Required fees: $1,269. Tuition and fees vary according to course load. *Financial support:* In 2003–04, 40 students received support, including 4 fellowships (averaging $1,000 per year), 13 research assistantships (averaging $19,000 per year), 27 teaching assistantships (averaging $19,000 per year); career-related internships or fieldwork, Federal Work-Study, institutionally sponsored loans, scholarships/grants, health care benefits, tuition waivers (partial), and unspecified assistantships also available. Financial award application deadline: 6/1; financial award applicants required to submit FAFSA. *Unit head:* Dr. Edward Bellion, Chairman, 817-272-3171, Fax: 817-272-3808. *Application contact:* Dr. Rasika Dias, Graduate Adviser, 817-272-3813, Fax: 817-272-3808, E-mail: dias@uta.edu.

Announcement: The Department of Chemistry and Biochemistry offers a program leading to the PhD in applied chemistry. In addition to the traditional PhD curriculum and dissertation, this program offers a paid industrial internship at a major US corporation and a series of survey courses in various aspects of applied chemistry. Graduates from this program have been 100% successful in obtaining employment after completion of this degree. The program is ideally suited for students interested in a career in the chemical industry or in academics. The department is active in a wide range of modern chemical/biochemical/materials research areas. Visit the department's Web site at http://utachem.uta.edu.

The University of Texas at Austin, Graduate School, College of Natural Sciences, Department of Chemistry and Biochemistry, Austin, TX 78712-1111. Offers analytical chemistry (MA, PhD); biochemistry (MA, PhD); inorganic chemistry (MA, PhD); organic chemistry (MA, PhD); physical chemistry (MA, PhD). *Entrance requirements:* For master's and doctorate, GRE General Test.

The University of Texas at Dallas, School of Natural Sciences and Mathematics, Programs in Chemistry, Richardson, TX 75083-0688. Offers MS, PhD. Part-time and evening/weekend programs available. *Faculty:* 13 full-time (1 woman), 1 part-time/adjunct (0 women). *Students:* 54 full-time (22 women), 3 part-time (all women); includes 14 minority (1 African American, 1 American Indian/Alaska Native, 4 Asian Americans or Pacific Islanders, 8 Hispanic Americans), 27 international. Average age 31. 81 applicants, 42% accepted. In 2003, 8 master's, 2 doctorates awarded. *Degree requirements:* For master's, thesis or internship; for doctorate, research practica. *Entrance requirements:* For master's and doctorate, GRE General Test, minimum GPA of 3.0 in upper-level course work in field. Additional exam requirements/recommendations for international students: Required—TOEFL (minimum score 550 paper-based; 213 computer-based). *Application deadline:* For fall admission, 7/15 for domestic students; for spring admission, 11/15 for domestic students. Applications are processed on a rolling basis. Application fee: $50 ($100 for international students). Electronic applications accepted. *Expenses:* Tuition, state resident: full-time $1,656; part-time $92 per credit. Tuition, nonresident: full-time $5,904; part-time $328 per credit. Required fees: $2,161; $275 per credit. $334 per term. *Financial support:* In 2003–04, 33 research assistantships with tuition reimbursements (averaging $9,296 per year), 18 teaching assistantships with tuition reimbursements (averaging $6,909 per year) were awarded. Fellowships, career-related internships or fieldwork, Federal Work-Study, institutionally sponsored loans, and scholarships/grants also available. Support available to part-time students. Financial award application deadline: 4/30; financial award applicants required to submit FAFSA. *Faculty research:* Organic photochemistry, bioinorganic chemistry, organic solid-state and polymer chemistry, environmental chemistry, scanning probe microscopy. Total annual research expenditures: $4.2 million. *Application contact:* Linda Crane, Graduate Student Adviser, 972-883-2901, Fax: 972-883-2925, E-mail: lcrane@utdallas.edu.

The University of Texas at El Paso, Graduate School, College of Science, Department of Chemistry, El Paso, TX 79968-0001. Offers MS. Part-time and evening/weekend programs available. *Students:* 22 (9 women); includes 5 minority (all Hispanic Americans) 17 international. Average age 34. 10 applicants, 80% accepted. In 2003, 7 degrees awarded. *Degree requirements:* For master's, thesis. *Entrance requirements:* For master's, GRE General Test, minimum GPA of 3.0. Additional exam requirements/recommendations for international students: Required—TOEFL. *Application deadline:* For fall admission, 7/1 for domestic students; for spring admission, 11/1 priority date for domestic students. Applications are processed on a rolling basis. Application fee: $15 ($65 for international students). Electronic applications accepted. *Expenses:* Tuition, state resident: full-time $1,388; part-time $160 per hour. Tuition, nonresident: full-time $3,440; part-time $388 per hour. Tuition and fees vary according to course load, degree level and program. *Financial support:* In 2003–04, 6 fellowships with partial tuition reimbursements, 6 research assistantships with partial tuition reimbursements (averaging $20,250 per year), 11 teaching assistantships with partial tuition reimbursements (averaging $16,200 per year) were awarded. Federal Work-Study, institutionally sponsored loans, scholarships/grants, and tuition waivers (partial) also available. Financial award application deadline: 3/15; financial award applicants required to submit FAFSA. *Unit head:* Dr. Jorge Gardea-Torredey, Chairperson, 915-747-5701, Fax: 915-747-5748, E-mail: jgardea@utep.edu. *Application contact:* Dr. Charles H. Ambler, Dean of the Graduate School, 915-747-5491 Ext. 7886, Fax: 915-747-5788, E-mail: cambler@utep.edu.

The University of Texas at San Antonio, College of Sciences, Department of Chemistry, San Antonio, TX 78249-0617. Offers MS. *Faculty:* 3 full-time (1 woman), 1 part-time/adjunct (0 women). *Students:* 7 full-time (4 women), 6 part-time (2 women); includes 3 minority (1 African American, 1 Asian American or Pacific Islander, 1 Hispanic American), 4 international. Average age 29. 7 applicants, 86% accepted, 4 enrolled. In 2003, 4 degrees awarded. *Degree requirements:* For master's, thesis optional. *Entrance requirements:* For master's, GRE General Test, minimum GPA of 3.0 in all undergraduate chemistry courses, 2 letters of recommendation. Additional exam requirements/recommendations for international students: Required—TOEFL (minimum score 500 paper-based; 173 computer-based). *Application deadline:* For fall admission, 7/1 for domestic students, 4/1 for international students; for spring admission, 11/1 for domestic students, 9/1 for international students. Applications are processed on a rolling basis. Application fee: $40 ($75 for international students). Electronic applications accepted. *Expenses:* Tuition, state resident: part-time $153 per hour. Tuition, nonresident: part-time $625 per hour. Total annual research expenditures: $747,264. *Unit head:* Dr. Judith Walmsley, Chair, 210-458-5469, Fax: 210-458-7428, E-mail: chemistry@utsa.edu.

The University of Texas at Tyler, Graduate Studies, College of Arts and Sciences, Department of Chemistry, Tyler, TX 75799-0001. Offers MSIS. *Expenses:* Tuition, state resident: full-time $4,270. Tuition, nonresident: full-time $12,766. *Faculty research:* Smart coatings in waste remediation. *Unit head:* Dr. Donald L. McClaugherty, Chair/Professor, 903-566-7196, Fax: 903-566-7189. *Application contact:* Carol A. Hodge, Office of Graduate Studies, 903-566-5642, Fax: 903-566-7068, E-mail: chodge@mail.uttyl.edu.

University of the Sciences in Philadelphia, College of Graduate Studies, Program in Chemistry, Biochemistry and Pharmacognosy, Philadelphia, PA 19104-4495. Offers biochemistry (MS, PhD); chemistry (MS, PhD); medicinal chemistry (MS, PhD); pharmacognosy (MS, PhD). Part-time programs available. *Faculty:* 12 full-time (2 women), 3 part-time/adjunct (1 woman). *Students:* 10 full-time (4 women), 5 part-time (3 women); includes 2 minority (both Asian Americans or Pacific Islanders), 11 international. Average age 27. In 2003, 1 master's, 1 doctorate awarded. *Degree requirements:* For master's, thesis/dissertation, qualifying exams; for doctorate, thesis/dissertation, qualifying exams, comprehensive exam. *Entrance requirements:* For master's and doctorate, GRE General Test, GRE Subject Test. Additional exam requirements/recommendations for international students: Required—TOEFL, TWE, TSE. *Application deadline:* Applications are processed on a rolling basis. Application fee: $50. *Expenses:* Tuition: Full-time $19,944; part-time $831 per credit. Required fees: $1,024. *Financial support:* In 2003–04, 13 students received support, including 1 fellowship with full tuition reimbursement available (averaging $19,000 per year), 1 research assistantship with full tuition reimbursement available (averaging $19,000 per year), 12 teaching assistantships with full tuition reimbursements available (averaging $18,500 per year); institutionally sponsored loans, scholarships/grants, and tuition waivers (full) also available. Financial award application deadline: 5/1. *Faculty research:* Organic and medicinal synthesis, mass spectroscopy use in protein analysis, study of analogues of taxol, cholesteryl esters. Total annual research expenditures: $341,700. *Unit head:* Dr. James McKee, Director, 215-596-8847, Fax: 215-596-8543, E-mail: jmckee@usip.edu. *Application contact:* Dr. Rodney J. Wigent, Dean, 215-596-8886, Fax: 215-895-1185, E-mail: graduate@usip.edu.

University of Toledo, Graduate School, College of Arts and Sciences, Department of Chemistry, Toledo, OH 43606-3390. Offers analytical chemistry (MS, PhD); biological chemistry (MS, PhD); inorganic chemistry (MS, PhD); organic chemistry (MS, PhD); physical chemistry (MS, PhD). Part-time programs available. *Students:* 46 full-time (21 women), 9 part-time (4 women); includes 4 minority (3 African Americans, 1 Hispanic American), 31 international. Average age 27. 23 applicants, 87% accepted. In 2003, 3 master's, 5 doctorates awarded. *Degree requirements:* For master's and doctorate, thesis/dissertation. *Entrance requirements:* For master's and doctorate, GRE General Test, GRE Subject Test. Additional exam requirements/recommendations for international students: Required—TOEFL. *Application deadline:* For fall admission, 8/1 for domestic students. Applications are processed on a rolling basis. Application fee: $40. Electronic applications accepted. Tuition, area resident: Part-time $3,817 per semester. *Expenses:* Tuition, state resident: part-time $8,177 per semester. Required fees: $502 per semester. *Financial support:* In 2003–04, 4 research assistantships, 47 teaching assistantships were awarded. Fellowships, Federal Work-Study and institutionally sponsored loans also available. Support available to part-time students. Financial award application deadline: 4/1; financial award applicants required to submit FAFSA. *Faculty research:* Enzymology, materials chemistry, crystallography, theoretical chemistry. *Unit head:* Dr. Alan Pinkerton, Chair, 419-530-2109, Fax: 419-530-4033, E-mail: apinker@uoft02.utoledo.edu.

Announcement: The University of Toledo offers a supportive environment and an outstanding instrumentation base for graduate studies in chemistry. Research groups are typically 4–7 students, which results in close interaction with faculty advisers and students. Research focuses on different areas of biological and materials chemistry and integrates exceptional crystallographic expertise and facilities.

See in-depth description on page 179.

University of Toronto, School of Graduate Studies, Physical Sciences Division, Department of Chemistry, Toronto, ON M5S 1A1, Canada. Offers M Sc, PhD. *Faculty:* 62 full-time (5 women), 1 part-time/adjunct. *Students:* 149 full-time (59 women), 24 international. 207 applicants, 28% accepted. In 2003, 17 master's, 13 doctorates awarded. *Degree requirements:* For master's, thesis; for doctorate, thesis/dissertation, oral exam, thesis defense. *Entrance requirements:* For master's, bachelor's degree in chemistry or a related field; for doctorate, master's degree in chemistry or a related field. Application fee: $90 Canadian dollars. Tuition, nonresident: full-time $4,185. International tuition: $10,739 full-time. *Unit head:* Chair, 416-978-3566, Fax: 416-978-8775, E-mail: chair@chem.utoronto.ca. *Application contact:* Darlene Gorzo, Secretary, 416-978-3605, Fax: 416-978-8775, E-mail: grad@chem.utoronto.ca.

University of Tulsa, Graduate School, College of Engineering and Natural Sciences, Department of Chemistry, Tulsa, OK 74104-3189. Offers MS. *Faculty:* 7 full-time (0 women). *Students:* 12 full-time (7 women), 3 part-time (2 women); includes 2 minority (both Asian Americans or Pacific Islanders), 5 international. Average age 31. 6 applicants, 67% accepted, 3 enrolled. In 2003, 1 degree awarded. *Median time to degree:* Master's–2 years full-time, 3 years part-time. *Degree requirements:* For master's, thesis optional. *Entrance requirements:* For master's, GRE General Test. Additional exam requirements/recommendations for international students: Required—TOEFL. *Application deadline:* Applications are processed on a rolling basis. Application fee: $30. Electronic applications accepted. *Expenses:* Tuition: Full-time $10,584; part-time $588 per credit hour. Required fees: $60; $3 per credit hour. *Financial support:* In 2003–04, 6 research assistantships with full and partial tuition reimbursements (averaging $9,098 per year), 3 teaching assistantships with full tuition reimbursements (averaging $7,310 per year) were awarded. Fellowships, career-related internships or fieldwork, Federal Work-Study, scholarships/grants, tuition waivers (full and partial), and unspecified assistantships also available. Support available to part-time students. Financial award application deadline: 2/1; financial award applicants required to submit FAFSA. *Faculty research:* Nanotechnology, polymer sensors, natural products chemistry, quantum dots. Total annual research expenditures: $1.1 million. *Unit head:* Dr. Dale C. Teeters, Chairperson, 918-631-3147, Fax: 918-631-3404, E-mail: dale-teeters@utulsa.edu. *Application contact:* Information Contact, 918-631-3147, Fax: 918-631-3404, E-mail: grad@utulsa.edu.

University of Utah, Graduate School, College of Science, Department of Chemistry, Salt Lake City, UT 84112-1107. Offers chemical physics (PhD); chemistry (M Phil, MA, MS, PhD); science teacher education (MS). Part-time programs available. Postbaccalaureate distance learning degree programs offered. *Faculty:* 28 full-time (4 women), 1 part-time/adjunct (0 women). *Students:* 132 full-time (53 women), 19 part-time (6 women); includes 11 minority (7 Asian Americans or Pacific Islanders, 4 Hispanic Americans), 60 international. Average age 28. 51 applicants, 84% accepted, 33 enrolled. In 2003, 8 master's, 19 doctorates awarded. *Degree requirements:* For doctorate, thesis/dissertation. *Entrance requirements:* For master's and doctorate, GRE General Test, minimum GPA of 3.0. Additional exam requirements/recommendations for international students: Required—TOEFL, TSE. *Application deadline:* For fall admission, 7/1 for domestic students; for spring admission, 11/1 priority date for domestic students. Applications are processed on a rolling basis. Application fee: $45 ($60 for international students). Electronic applications accepted. Tuition, nonresident: full-time $2,483. International tuition: $8,768 full-time. *Financial support:* In 2003–04, 149 students received support, including 75 research assistantships with tuition reimbursements available (averaging $5,000 per year), 75 teaching assistantships with tuition reimbursements available (averaging $5,000 per year); fellowships with tuition reimbursements available, scholarships/grants also available. Financial award application deadline: 7/1. *Faculty research:* Biological, theoretical, inorganic, organic, and physical-analytical chemistry. *Unit head:* Peter B. Armentrout, Chair, 801-581-7885, Fax: 801-581-8433, E-mail: armentrout@chemistry.utah.edu. *Application contact:* Jo Hoovey, Coordinator, 801-581-4393, Fax: 801-581-5408, E-mail: jhoovey@chem.utah.edu.

University of Vermont, Graduate College, College of Arts and Sciences, Department of Chemistry, Burlington, VT 05405. Offers chemistry (MS, MST, PhD); chemistry education (MAT). *Accreditation:* NCATE (one or more programs are accredited). *Students:* 45 (10 women) 14 international. 72 applicants, 54% accepted, 15 enrolled. In 2003, 2 degrees awarded. *Degree requirements:* For master's, one foreign language, thesis; for doctorate, 2 foreign languages, thesis/dissertation. *Entrance requirements:* For master's and doctorate, GRE General Test. Additional exam requirements/recommendations for international students: Required—TOEFL (minimum score 550 paper-based; 213 computer-based). *Application deadline:* For fall admission, 4/1 for domestic students. Applications are processed on a rolling basis. Application fee: $25. Electronic applications accepted. *Expenses:* Tuition, state resident: part-time $362 per credit hour. Tuition, nonresident: part-time $906 per credit hour. *Financial support:* Fellowships, research assistantships, teaching assistantships available. Financial award application deadline: 3/1. *Unit head:* Dr. D. Matthews, Chairperson, 802-656-2594. *Application contact:* Dr. G. Friestad, Coordinator, 802-656-2594.

University of Victoria, Faculty of Graduate Studies, Faculty of Science, Department of Chemistry, Victoria, BC V8W 2Y2, Canada. Offers M Sc, PhD. *Degree requirements:* For master's and doctorate, thesis/dissertation. *Entrance requirements:* For master's and doctorate, GRE Subject Test. Additional exam requirements/recommendations for international students: Required—TOEFL (minimum score 550 paper-based; 213 computer-based). *Faculty research:* Laser spectroscopy and dynamics; inorganic, organic, and organometallic synthesis; electro and surface chemistry.

University of Virginia, College and Graduate School of Arts and Sciences, Department of Chemistry, Charlottesville, VA 22903. Offers MA, MS, PhD. *Accreditation:* NCATE (one or more programs are accredited). *Faculty:* 27 full-time (4 women), 1 part-time/adjunct (0 women). *Students:* 118 full-time (52 women), 2 part-time; includes 12 minority (7 African Americans, 2 Asian Americans or Pacific Islanders, 3 Hispanic Americans), 19 international. Average age 26. 118 applicants, 63% accepted, 22 enrolled. In 2003, 14 master's, 17 doctorates awarded. *Degree requirements:* For master's and doctorate, thesis/dissertation. *Entrance requirements:* For master's and doctorate, GRE General Test, GRE Subject Test. *Application deadline:* For fall admission, 7/15 for domestic students; for spring admission, 12/1 for domestic students. Applications are processed on a rolling basis. Application fee: $40. Electronic applications accepted. *Expenses:* Tuition, state resident: full-time $6,476. Tuition, nonresident: full-time $18,534. Required fees: $1,380. *Financial support:* Application deadline: 2/1; *Unit head:* Ian Harrison, Chairman, 434-924-3344, Fax: 434-924-3710, E-mail: chem@virginia.edu. *Application contact:* Peter C. Brunjes, Associate Dean for Graduate Programs and Research, 434-924-7184, Fax: 434-924-6737, E-mail: grad-a-s@virginia.edu.

University of Washington, Graduate School, College of Arts and Sciences, Department of Chemistry, Seattle, WA 98195. Offers MS, PhD. Terminal master's awarded for partial completion of doctoral program. *Degree requirements:* For master's, thesis (for some programs); for doctorate, thesis/dissertation. *Entrance requirements:* For master's and doctorate, GRE Subject Test, minimum GPA of 3.0. Additional exam requirements/recommendations for international students: Required—TOEFL, TSE. *Faculty research:* Biopolymers, material science and nanotechnology, organometallic chemistry, analytical chemistry, bioorganic chemistry.

University of Waterloo, Graduate Studies, Faculty of Science, Guelph-Waterloo Centre for Graduate Work in Chemistry and Biochemistry, Waterloo, ON N2L 3G1, Canada. Offers chemistry (M Sc, PhD). Part-time programs available. *Faculty:* 35 full-time (7 women), 22 part-time/adjunct (1 woman). *Students:* 108 full-time (41 women), 6 part-time (5 women). 128 applicants, 20% accepted, 17 enrolled. In 2003, 17 master's, 4 doctorates awarded. *Degree requirements:* For master's, project or thesis; for doctorate, thesis/dissertation. *Entrance requirements:* For master's, GRE, honors degree, minimum B average; for doctorate, GRE, master's degree, minimum B average. Additional exam requirements/recommendations for international students: Required—TOEFL, TWE. *Application deadline:* Applications are processed on a rolling basis. Application fee: $75 Canadian dollars. Electronic applications accepted. Tuition and fees charges are reported in Canadian dollars. *Expenses:* Tuition, state resident: full-time $3,632 Canadian dollars. International tuition: $9,180 Canadian dollars full-time. Required fees: $406 Canadian dollars. *Financial support:* Research assistantships, teaching assistantships available. *Faculty research:* Polymer, physical, inorganic, organic, and theoretical chemistry. *Unit head:* Dr. J. F. Honek, Director, 519-888-4567 Ext. 3945, Fax: 519-746-4806, E-mail: gwc@uwaterloo.ca. *Application contact:* A. Wetmore, Administrative Assistant, 519-888-4567 Ext. 3945, Fax: 519-746-4806, E-mail: gwc@uoguelph.ca.

The University of Western Ontario, Faculty of Graduate Studies, Physical Sciences Division, Department of Chemistry, London, ON N6A 5B8, Canada. Offers M Sc, PhD. *Degree requirements:* For master's and doctorate, thesis/dissertation. *Entrance requirements:* For master's, minimum B+ average, honors B Sc in chemistry; for doctorate, M Sc or equivalent in chemistry. Additional exam requirements/recommendations for international students: Required—TOEFL (paper score 570; computer score 230) or IELTS (paper score 6). *Faculty research:* Materials, inorganic, organic, physical and theoretical chemistry.

University of Windsor, Faculty of Graduate Studies and Research, Faculty of Science, Department of Chemistry and Biochemistry, Windsor, ON N9B 3P4, Canada. Offers biochemistry (M Sc, PhD); chemistry (M Sc, PhD). Part-time programs available. *Faculty:* 17 full-time (1 woman), 10 part-time/adjunct (0 women). *Students:* 58 full-time (23 women), 2 part-time (both women). 110 applicants, 30% accepted. In 2003, 6 master's, 3 doctorates awarded. *Degree requirements:* For master's and doctorate, thesis/dissertation. *Entrance requirements:* For master's, minimum B average. Additional exam requirements/recommendations for international students: Required—TOEFL. *Application deadline:* For fall admission, 7/1 for domestic students. Applications are processed on a rolling basis. Application fee: $55. Tuition charges are reported in Canadian dollars. *Expenses:* Tuition, state resident: full-time $1,704 Canadian dollars. Tuition, nonresident: full-time $2,126 Canadian dollars. International tuition: $2,976 Canadian dollars full-time. *Financial support:* In 2003–04, 30 teaching assistantships (averaging $8,000 per year) were awarded; research assistantships, Federal Work-Study, scholarships/grants, unspecified assistantships, and bursaries also available. Financial award application deadline: 2/15. *Faculty research:* Molecular biology/recombinant DNA techniques (PCR, cloning mutagenesis), No/02 detectors, western immunoblotting and detection, CD/NMR protein/peptide structure determination, confocal/electron microscopes. *Unit head:* Dr. Douglas Stephan, Head, 519-253-3000 Ext. 3537, Fax: 519-973-7098, E-mail: stephan@uwindsor.ca. *Application contact:* Marlene Bezaire, Graduate Secretary, 519-253-3000 Ext. 3520, Fax: 519-971-7098, E-mail: spsgrad@uwindsor.ca.

University of Wisconsin–Madison, Graduate School, College of Engineering, Program in Environmental Chemistry and Technology, Madison, WI 53706-1380. Offers MS, PhD. Part-time programs available. *Faculty:* 12 full-time (2 women). *Students:* 15 full-time (6 women), 1 part-time, 4 international. 95 applicants, 6% accepted, 5 enrolled. In 2003, 1 master's, 1 doctorate awarded. Terminal master's awarded for partial completion of doctoral program. *Median time to degree:* Master's–1 year full-time; doctorate–5.5 years full-time. Of those who began their doctoral program in fall 1995, 100% received their degree in 8 years or less. *Degree requirements:* For master's, thesis or alternative; for doctorate, thesis/dissertation. *Entrance requirements:* For master's and doctorate, GRE General Test. *Application deadline:* For fall admission, 1/1 priority date for domestic students, 1/1 priority date for international students. Application fee: $45. Electronic applications accepted. Tuition, area resident: Full-time $7,593; part-time $476 per credit. Tuition, nonresident: full-time $22,824; part-time $1,430 per credit. Required fees: $292; $38 per credit. Part-time tuition and fees vary according to course load and reciprocity agreements. *Financial support:* In 2003–04, 15 students received support, including 1 fellowship with tuition reimbursement available (averaging $17,000 per year), 14 research assistantships with tuition reimbursements available (averaging $17,000 per year); Federal Work-Study and institutionally sponsored loans also available. Financial award application deadline: 1/1. *Faculty research:* Chemical limnology, chemical remediation, geochemistry, photocatalysis, water quality. Total annual research expenditures: $1 million. *Unit head:* Dr. Marc A. Anderson, Chair, 608-263-3264, E-mail: nanopor@wisc.edu. *Application contact:* Georgia Wagner, Student Services Coordinator, 608-263-3264, Fax: 608-265-2340, E-mail: gwagner@facstaff.wisc.edu.

University of Wisconsin–Madison, Graduate School, College of Letters and Science, Department of Chemistry, Madison, WI 53706-1380. Offers MS, PhD. Part-time programs available. Terminal master's awarded for partial completion of doctoral program. *Degree requirements:* For master's, thesis (for some programs); for doctorate, thesis/dissertation, cumulative exams, research proposal, seminar. *Entrance requirements:* For master's and doctorate, GRE, minimum GPA of 3.0. Additional exam requirements/recommendations for international students: Required—TOEFL. Electronic applications accepted. Tuition, area resident: Full-time $7,593; part-time $476 per credit. Tuition, nonresident: full-time $22,824; part-time $1,430 per credit. Required fees: $292; $38 per credit. Part-time tuition and fees vary according to course load and reciprocity agreements. *Faculty research:* Analytical, inorganic, organic, physical, and macromolecular chemistry.

University of Wisconsin–Milwaukee, Graduate School, College of Letters and Sciences, Department of Chemistry, Milwaukee, WI 53201-0413. Offers MS, PhD. *Faculty:* 17 full-time (1 woman). *Students:* 32 full-time (14 women), 17 part-time (7 women); includes 1 minority (African American), 29 international. 45 applicants, 53% accepted, 10 enrolled. In 2003, 4 degrees awarded. *Degree requirements:* For master's, thesis or alternative; for doctorate, thesis/dissertation. *Application deadline:* For fall admission, 1/1 for domestic students; for spring admission, 9/1 for domestic students. Applications are processed on a rolling basis. Application fee: $45 ($75 for international students). *Expenses:* Tuition, state resident: part-time $634 per credit. Tuition, nonresident: part-time $1,531 per credit. Part-time tuition and fees vary according to course load, campus/location, program and reciprocity agreements. *Financial support:* In 2003–04, 2 fellowships, 8 research assistantships, 39 teaching assistantships were awarded. Career-related internships or fieldwork and unspecified assistantships also available. Support available to part-time students. Financial award application deadline: 4/15. *Unit head:* Mahmun Hossain, Representative, 414-229-5565, Fax: 414-229-5530, E-mail: mahmun@uwm.edu.

University of Wyoming, Graduate School, College of Arts and Sciences, Department of Chemistry, Laramie, WY 82070. Offers MS, PhD. *Faculty:* 12 full-time (1 woman), 1 part-time/adjunct (0 women). *Students:* 28 full-time (7 women), 12 part-time (1 woman); includes 2 minority (1 Asian American or Pacific Islander, 1 Hispanic American), 11 international. Average age 29. 17 applicants, 76% accepted, 9 enrolled. In 2003, 3 master's, 8 doctorates awarded. *Median time to degree:* Master's–2.5 years full-time, 5 years part-time; doctorate–5 years full-time, 5 years part-time. Of those who began their doctoral program in fall 1995, 71% received their degree in 8 years or less. *Degree requirements:* For master's and doctorate, thesis/dissertation. *Entrance requirements:* For master's and doctorate, GRE General Test, minimum GPA of 3.0. Additional exam requirements/recommendations for international students: Required—TOEFL (minimum score 600 paper-based). *Application deadline:* For fall admission, 4/15 priority date for domestic students, 2/28 priority date for international students. Applications are processed on a rolling basis. Application fee: $40. Electronic applications accepted. *Expenses:* Tuition, state resident: part-time $142 per credit hour. Tuition, nonresident: part-time $408 per credit hour. Required fees: $134 per semester. Tuition and fees vary according to course load, campus/location, program and student level. *Financial support:* In 2003–04, 34 research assistantships with full tuition reimbursements (averaging $18,000 per year), 13 teaching assistantships with full tuition reimbursements (averaging $18,000 per year) were awarded. Fellowships, traineeships and tuition waivers (full and partial) also available. Financial award application deadline: 3/1. *Faculty research:* Organic chemistry, inorganic chemistry, analytical chemistry, physical chemistry. Total annual research expenditures: $2.2 million. *Unit head:* Dr. Dean M. Roddick, Head, 307-766-4363, Fax: 307-766-2807, E-mail: chemistry@uwyo.edu. *Application contact:* Jeffrey L. Yarger, Graduate Admissions Coordinator, 307-766-4363, Fax: 307-766-2807, E-mail: chem_grad@uwyo.edu.

Utah State University, School of Graduate Studies, College of Science, Department of Chemistry and Biochemistry, Logan, UT 84322. Offers biochemistry (MS, PhD); chemistry (MS, PhD). Part-time programs available. *Faculty:* 16 full-time (3 women). *Students:* 40 full-time (13 women), 6 part-time (4 women); includes 1 minority (Asian American or Pacific Islander), 24 international. Average age 28. 52 applicants, 33% accepted, 7 enrolled. In 2003, 2 master's, 1 doctorate awarded. Terminal master's awarded for partial completion of doctoral program. *Degree requirements:* For master's and doctorate, thesis/dissertation, oral and written exams. *Entrance requirements:* For master's and doctorate, GRE General Test, minimum GPA of 3.0. Additional exam requirements/recommendations for international students: Required—TOEFL. *Application deadline:* For fall admission, 4/15 priority date for domestic students, 4/15 priority date for international students; for spring admission, 10/15 for domestic students, 10/15 for international students. Applications are processed on a rolling basis. Application fee: $50 ($60 for international students). *Expenses:* Tuition, state resident: part-time $270 per credit hour. Tuition, nonresident: part-time $946 per credit hour. Required fees: $173 per credit hour. *Financial support:* In 2003–04, 29 research assistantships with partial tuition reimbursements (averaging $17,000 per year), 16 teaching assistantships with partial tuition reimbursements (averaging $17,000 per year) were awarded. Fellowships with tuition reimbursements, Federal Work-Study, institutionally sponsored loans, and tuition waivers (partial) also available. Support available to part-time students. Financial award application deadline: 4/15. *Faculty research:* Analytical, inorganic, organic, and physical chemistry; iron in asbestos chemistry and carcinogenicity; dicopper complexes; photothermal spectrometry; metal molecule clusters. Total annual research expenditures: $2.1 million. *Unit head:* Dr. Steve Scheiner, Head, 435-797-7419, Fax: 435-797-3390, E-mail: scheiner@cc.usu.edu. *Application contact:* Dr. Lisa M. Berreau, Admissions Chair, 435-797-1625, Fax: 435-797-3390, E-mail: berreau@cc.usu.edu.

See in-depth description on page 183.

Chemistry

Vanderbilt University, Graduate School, Department of Chemistry, Nashville, TN 37240-1001. Offers analytical chemistry (MAT, MS, PhD); inorganic chemistry (MAT, MS, PhD); organic chemistry (MAT, MS, PhD); physical chemistry (MAT, MS, PhD); theoretical chemistry (MAT, MS, PhD). *Degree requirements:* For master's, thesis or alternative; for doctorate, thesis/dissertation, area, qualifying, and final exams. *Entrance requirements:* For master's and doctorate, GRE General Test, GRE Subject Test (recommended). Additional exam requirements/recommendations for international students: Required—TOEFL. Electronic applications accepted. *Expenses:* Tuition: Part-time $1,155 per semester hour. Required fees: $1,538. *Faculty research:* Chemical synthesis; mechanistic, theoretical, bioorganic, analytical, and spectroscopic chemistry.

See in-depth description on page 185.

Vassar College, Graduate Programs, Poughkeepsie, NY 12604. Offers biology (MA, MS); chemistry (MA, MS). Applicants accepted only if enrolled in undergraduate programs at Vassar College. Part-time programs available. *Degree requirements:* For master's, thesis. *Entrance requirements:* For master's, GRE General Test, bachelor's degree in related field. Application fee: $60. *Expenses:* Tuition: Full-time $29,095; part-time $3,430 per unit. Required fees: $200. *Financial support:* Career-related internships or fieldwork available. *Unit head:* Alexander M. Thompson, Dean of Studies, 914-437-5257, E-mail: thompson@vassar.edu.

Villanova University, Graduate School of Liberal Arts and Sciences, Department of Chemistry, Villanova, PA 19085-1699. Offers MS. Part-time and evening/weekend programs available. *Students:* 8 full-time (4 women), 33 part-time (14 women); includes 3 minority (1 African American, 2 Asian Americans or Pacific Islanders), 6 international. Average age 26. 20 applicants, 55% accepted. In 2003, 4 degrees awarded. *Degree requirements:* For master's, thesis, comprehensive exam. *Entrance requirements:* For master's, GRE General Test, GRE Subject Test, minimum GPA of 3.0. Additional exam requirements/recommendations for international students: Required—TOEFL. *Application deadline:* For fall admission, 8/1 priority date for domestic students, 8/1 priority date for international students; for spring admission, 12/1 for domestic students, 12/1 for international students. Application fee: $40. *Expenses:* Contact institution. *Financial support:* Research assistantships, Federal Work-Study available. Financial award applicants required to submit FAFSA. *Unit head:* Dr. Barry Selinsky, Chair, 610-519-4840.

See in-depth description on page 187.

Virginia Commonwealth University, School of Graduate Studies, College of Humanities and Sciences, Department of Chemistry, Richmond, VA 23284-9005. Offers MS, PhD. Part-time programs available. *Faculty:* 18 full-time (6 women). *Students:* 39 full-time (14 women), 15 part-time (1 woman); includes 13 minority (6 African Americans, 1 American Indian/Alaska Native, 5 Asian Americans or Pacific Islanders, 1 Hispanic American), 13 international. 45 applicants, 62% accepted, 14 enrolled. In 2003, 2 master's, 8 doctorates awarded. Terminal master's awarded for partial completion of doctoral program. *Degree requirements:* For master's, thesis; for doctorate, thesis/dissertation, comprehensive cumulative exams, research proposal. *Entrance requirements:* For master's, GRE General Test, 30 undergraduate credits in chemistry; for doctorate, GRE General Test. *Application deadline:* For fall admission, 3/15 for domestic students; for spring admission, 11/15 for domestic students. Applications are processed on a rolling basis. *Expenses:* Tuition, state resident: full-time $2,889; part-time $321 per credit hour. Tuition, nonresident: full-time $7,952; part-time $884 per credit hour. Required fees: $42 per credit hour. *Financial support:* Fellowships, research assistantships, teaching assistantships, career-related internships or fieldwork and institutionally sponsored loans available. Support available to part-time students. Financial award application deadline: 7/1. *Faculty research:* Physical, organic, inorganic, analytical, and polymer chemistry; chemical physics. *Unit head:* Dr. Fred M. Hawkridge, Chair, 804-828-1298, Fax: 804-828-8599, E-mail: fmhawkri@vcu.edu. *Application contact:* Dr. M. Samy El-Shall, Chair, Graduate Recruiting and Admissions Committee, 804-828-3518, E-mail: mselshal@vcu.edu.

Virginia Polytechnic Institute and State University, Graduate School, College of Science, Department of Chemistry, Blacksburg, VA 24061. Offers MS, PhD. *Faculty:* 35 full-time (7 women). *Students:* 119 full-time (38 women), 9 part-time (3 women); includes 9 minority (6 African Americans, 3 Asian Americans or Pacific Islanders), 64 international. Average age 27. 148 applicants, 32% accepted, 34 enrolled. In 2003, 6 master's, 12 doctorates awarded. *Entrance requirements:* Additional exam requirements/recommendations for international students: Required—TOEFL (minimum score 600 paper-based; 250 computer-based), GRE. *Application deadline:* Applications are processed on a rolling basis. Application fee: $45. Electronic applications accepted. Tuition, area resident: Full-time $6,039; part-time $336 per credit. Tuition, nonresident: full-time $9,708; part-time $539 per credit. Required fees: $905; $130 per credit. *Financial support:* In 2003–04, 3 fellowships with full tuition reimbursements (averaging $5,067 per year), 42 research assistantships with full tuition reimbursements (averaging $18,217 per year), 66 teaching assistantships with full tuition reimbursements (averaging $13,818 per year) were awarded. Career-related internships or fieldwork, Federal Work-Study, scholarships/grants, tuition waivers (partial), and unspecified assistantships also available. Financial award application deadline: 4/1. *Faculty research:* Analytical, inorganic, organic, physical, and polymer chemistry. *Unit head:* Dr. Larry T. Taylor, Head, 540-231-5966, Fax: 540-231-3255, E-mail: ltaylor@vt.edu. *Application contact:* Dr. J. W. Viers, Director of Graduate Studies, 540-231-5742, Fax: 540-231-3255, E-mail: jviers@vt.edu.

Wake Forest University, Graduate School, Department of Chemistry, Winston-Salem, NC 27109. Offers analytical chemistry (MS, PhD); inorganic chemistry (MS, PhD); organic chemistry (MS, PhD); physical chemistry (MS, PhD). Part-time programs available. *Faculty:* 15 full-time (2 women). *Students:* 32 full-time (15 women), 1 part-time; includes 2 minority (both African Americans), 13 international. Average age 28. 34 applicants, 38% accepted, 5 enrolled. In 2003, 4 master's, 2 doctorates awarded. *Degree requirements:* For master's, one foreign language, thesis, comprehensive exam, registration; for doctorate, 2 foreign languages, thesis/dissertation, comprehensive exam, registration. *Entrance requirements:* For master's and doctorate, GRE General Test. Additional exam requirements/recommendations for international students: Required—TOEFL (minimum score 213 computer-based). *Application deadline:* For fall admission, 1/15 for domestic students, 1/15 for international students. Application fee: $25. Electronic applications accepted. *Expenses:* Tuition: Full-time $26,500. *Financial support:* In 2003–04, 32 students received support, including 1 fellowship with full tuition reimbursement available (averaging $19,500 per year), 11 research assistantships with full tuition reimbursements available (averaging $17,500 per year), 17 teaching assistantships with full tuition reimbursements available (averaging $17,500 per year); scholarships/grants and tuition waivers (full and partial) also available. Support available to part-time students. Financial award application deadline: 1/15; financial award applicants required to submit FAFSA. *Unit head:* Dr. Dilip Kondepudi, Director, 336-758-5131, Fax: 336-758-4656, E-mail: dilip@wfu.edu.

Washington State University, Graduate School, College of Sciences, Department of Chemistry, Pullman, WA 99164. Offers analytical chemistry (MS, PhD); biological systems (MS, PhD); inorganic chemistry (MS, PhD); organic chemistry (MS, PhD); physical chemistry (MS, PhD). *Faculty:* 22 full-time (3 women). *Students:* 37 full-time (17 women), 1 part-time; includes 3 minority (2 Asian Americans or Pacific Islanders, 1 Hispanic American), 10 international. Average age 25. 48 applicants, 58% accepted, 12 enrolled. In 2003, 3 master's, 1 doctorate awarded. Terminal master's awarded for partial completion of doctoral program. *Median time to degree:* Master's–2.8 years full-time; doctorate–5 years full-time. *Degree requirements:* For master's, oral exam, teaching experience, thesis optional; for doctorate, thesis/dissertation, oral exam, written exam, comprehensive exam. *Entrance requirements:* For master's and doctorate, GRE General Test, minimum GPA of 3.0, 3 letters of recommendation. *Application deadline:* For fall admission, 3/1 for domestic students; for spring admission, 10/1 priority date for domestic students. Applications are processed on a rolling basis. Application fee: $35. *Expenses:* Tuition, state resident: full-time $6,278; part-time $314 per hour. Tuition, nonresident: full-time $15,514; part-time $765 per hour. Required fees: $444. Full-time tuition and fees vary according to campus/location, program and student level. Part-time tuition and fees vary according to course load. *Financial support:* In 2003–04, 13 research assistantships with full and partial tuition reimbursements (averaging $17,000 per year), 23 teaching assistantships with full and partial tuition reimbursements (averaging $17,000 per year) were awarded. Fellowships, career-related internships or fieldwork, Federal Work-Study, institutionally sponsored loans, scholarships/grants, health care benefits, unspecified assistantships, and summer support also available. Financial award application deadline: 4/1; financial award applicants required to submit FAFSA. *Faculty research:* Environmental chemistry, materials chemistry, radio chemistry, bio-organic, computational chemistry. Total annual research expenditures: $1.9 million. *Unit head:* Dr. Ralph Yount, Chair, 509-335-1516, Fax: 509-335-8867, E-mail: yount@wsu.edu. *Application contact:* Sue B. Clark, Chair, Admissions Committee, 509-335-8866, Fax: 509-335-8867, E-mail: carrie@wsu.edu.

Washington State University Tri-Cities, Graduate Programs, Richland, WA 99352-1671. Offers biology (MS); business and economics (MBA, MTM), including business management (MBA), technology management (MTM); chemical engineering (MS); chemistry (MS); civil engineering (MS); communication (MA); education (Ed M, MA, MIT); electrical engineering and computer science (MS), including computer science, electrical engineering; engineering management (M Eng Mgt); environmental engineering (MS); environmental science (MS); materials engineering (MS); mechanical engineering (MS). Part-time programs available. *Students:* 46 full-time (32 women), 335 part-time (167 women); includes 34 minority (1 African American, 3 American Indian/Alaska Native, 8 Asian Americans or Pacific Islanders, 22 Hispanic Americans), 8 international. *Degree requirements:* For master's, thesis (for some programs), comprehensive exam (for some programs), registration. *Entrance requirements:* For master's, GRE, minimum GPA of 3.0. Additional exam requirements/recommendations for international students: Required—TOEFL (paper score 550; computer score 213) or IELTS (paper score 7). *Application deadline:* Applications are processed on a rolling basis. Application fee: $35. Electronic applications accepted. Tuition, area resident: Full-time $3,139; part-time $314 per credit. Tuition, nonresident: full-time $7,647; part-time $765 per credit. *Financial support:* In 2003–04, 2 research assistantships, 4 teaching assistantships were awarded. Federal Work-Study, health care benefits, and unspecified assistantships also available. *Unit head:* Dr. Larry James, Chancellor, 509-372-7258, Fax: 509-372-7354. *Application contact:* 509-372-7250, Fax: 509-372-7100.

Washington University in St. Louis, Graduate School of Arts and Sciences, Department of Chemistry, St. Louis, MO 63130-4899. Offers MA, PhD. *Students:* 104 full-time (35 women); includes 3 minority (all African Americans), 59 international. 260 applicants, 23% accepted, 27 enrolled. In 2003, 11 master's, 10 doctorates awarded. Terminal master's awarded for partial completion of doctoral program. *Degree requirements:* For master's, thesis optional; for doctorate, thesis/dissertation. *Entrance requirements:* For master's and doctorate, GRE General Test, GRE Subject Test. *Application deadline:* For fall admission, 1/15 for domestic students. Applications are processed on a rolling basis. Application fee: $35. Electronic applications accepted. *Expenses:* Tuition: Full-time $28,300; part-time $1,180 per credit. *Financial support:* Fellowships, research assistantships, teaching assistantships, Federal Work-Study, institutionally sponsored loans, and tuition waivers (full and partial) available. Financial award application deadline: 1/15. *Unit head:* Dr. Joseph J. H. Ackerman, Chairman, 314-935-6550.

Wayne State University, Graduate School, College of Science, Department of Chemistry, Detroit, MI 48202. Offers MA, MS, PhD. *Faculty:* 37. *Students:* 136 full-time (46 women), 14 part-time (8 women); includes 15 minority (4 African Americans, 11 Asian Americans or Pacific Islanders), 101 international. Average age 30. 398 applicants, 21% accepted, 40 enrolled. In 2003, 11 master's, 16 doctorates awarded. *Degree requirements:* For master's, thesis (for some programs); for doctorate, thesis/dissertation. *Entrance requirements:* Additional exam requirements/recommendations for international students: Required—TOEFL (minimum score 550 paper-based; 213 computer-based); Recommended—TWE(minimum score 6). *Application deadline:* For fall admission, 7/1 for domestic students, 6/1 for international students. Applications are processed on a rolling basis. Application fee: $30 ($50 for international students). Electronic applications accepted. *Expenses:* Tuition, state resident: part-time $263 per credit hour. Tuition, nonresident: part-time $580 per credit hour. Required fees: $21 per credit hour. *Financial support:* In 2003–04, 7 fellowships, 52 research assistantships, 75 teaching assistantships were awarded. Financial award application deadline: 7/1. *Faculty research:* Natural products synthesis, molecular biology, molecular mechanics calculations, organometallic chemistry, experimental physical chemistry. Total annual research expenditures: $5.6 million. *Unit head:* James Rigby, Chairperson, 313-577-7784, Fax: 313-577-8822, E-mail: jhr@chem.wayne.edu. *Application contact:* Charles Winter, Graduate Director, 313-577-5224, E-mail: chw@chem.wayne.edu.

Wesleyan University, Graduate Programs, Department of Chemistry, Middletown, CT 06459-0260. Offers biochemistry (MA, PhD); chemical physics (MA, PhD); inorganic chemistry (MA, PhD); organic chemistry (MA, PhD); physical chemistry (MA, PhD); theoretical chemistry (MA, PhD). *Faculty:* 13 full-time (2 women), 2 part-time/adjunct (1 woman). *Students:* 36 full-time (18 women); includes 2 minority (1 African American, 1 Asian American or Pacific Islander), 21 international. In 2003, 2 degrees awarded. Terminal master's awarded for partial completion of doctoral program. *Degree requirements:* For master's and doctorate, one foreign language, thesis/dissertation. *Entrance requirements:* For master's, GRE General Test, GRE Subject Test; for doctorate, GRE Subject Test. *Application deadline:* For fall admission, 3/1 for domestic students. Applications are processed on a rolling basis. Application fee: $0. *Expenses:* Tuition: Full-time $22,338. Required fees: $20. *Financial support:* Fellowships, research assistantships, teaching assistantships, institutionally sponsored loans available. *Unit head:* George Peterson, Chair, 860-685-2508. *Application contact:* Karen Karpa, Information Contact, 860-685-2573, Fax: 860-685-2211, E-mail: kkarpa@wesleyan.edu.

See in-depth description on page 189.

West Chester University of Pennsylvania, Graduate Studies, College of Arts and Sciences, Department of Chemistry, West Chester, PA 19383. Offers chemistry (M Ed, MS); clinical chemistry (MS); physical science (MA). Part-time and evening/weekend programs available. *Students:* 3 full-time (1 woman), 6 part-time (3 women); includes 4 minority (2 African Americans, 2 Asian Americans or Pacific Islanders), 3 international. Average age 35. 16 applicants, 63% accepted. In 2003, 6 degrees awarded. *Degree requirements:* For master's, one foreign language, comprehensive exam. *Entrance requirements:* For master's, GRE General Test (recommended). *Application deadline:* For fall admission, 4/15 for domestic students; for spring admission, 10/15 for domestic students. Applications are processed on a rolling basis. Application fee: $35. *Expenses:* Tuition, state resident: full-time $5,518; part-time $307 per credit. Tuition, nonresident: full-time $8,830; part-time $491 per credit. Required fees: $902; $52 per credit. One-time fee: $35 part-time. *Financial support:* In 2003–04, 3 research assistantships with full tuition reimbursements (averaging $5,000 per year) were awarded Support available to part-time students. Financial award application deadline: 2/15; financial award applicants required to submit FAFSA. *Faculty research:* Solid phase rates into monodisperse polymers and palladium-mediated rates into novel materials. *Unit head:* Dr. James Falcone, Chair, 610-436-2631. *Application contact:* Dr. Naseer Ahmad, Graduate Coordinator, 610-436-2476, E-mail: anaseer@wcupa.edu.

Western Carolina University, Graduate School, College of Arts and Sciences, Department of Chemistry and Physics, Cullowhee, NC 28723. Offers chemistry (MAT, MS); comprehensive education-chemistry (MA Ed). Part-time and evening/weekend programs available. *Faculty:* 13 full-time (2 women). *Students:* 11 full-time (3 women), 4 part-time; includes 2 minority (both Asian Americans or Pacific Islanders), 1 international. 12 applicants, 92% accepted, 6 enrolled. In 2003, 3 degrees awarded. *Degree requirements:* For master's, variable foreign language requirement, thesis, comprehensive exam. *Entrance requirements:* For master's, GRE General Test. Additional exam requirements/recommendations for international students: Required—TOEFL (minimum score 550 paper-based; 213 computer-based). *Application deadline:* For fall admission, 5/1 for domestic students; for spring admission, 10/1 priority date for domestic students. Applications are processed on a rolling basis. Application fee: $40. *Expenses:* Tuition, state resident: full-time $1,426. Tuition, nonresident: full-time $10,787. Required fees: $1,558. *Financial support:* In 2003–04, 11 students received support, including 11 teaching assistantships with full and partial tuition reimbursements available (averaging $7,500 per year); fellowships, research assistantships with full and partial tuition reimbursements available, Federal Work-Study, institutionally sponsored loans, and scholarships/grants also available. Financial award application deadline: 3/15; financial award applicants required to submit FAFSA. *Unit head:* Dr. David Butcher, Head, 828-227-7260, E-mail: butcher@email.wcu.edu. *Application contact:* Josie Bewsey, Assistant to the Dean, 828-227-7398, Fax: 828-227-7480, E-mail: jbewsey@email.wcu.edu.

Western Illinois University, School of Graduate Studies, College of Arts and Sciences, Department of Chemistry, Macomb, IL 61455-1390. Offers MS. Part-time programs available. *Faculty:* 8 full-time (1 woman). *Students:* 15 full-time (10 women), 10 international. Average age 26. 33 applicants, 88% accepted. In 2003, 2 degrees awarded. *Degree requirements:* For master's, thesis or alternative. *Entrance requirements:* Additional exam requirements/recommendations for international students: Required—TOEFL (minimum score 530 paper-based; 197 computer-based). *Application deadline:* Applications are processed on a rolling basis. Application fee: $30. Electronic applications accepted. Tuition, area resident: Part-time $144 per credit hour. Tuition, nonresident: part-time $288 per credit hour. *Financial support:* In 2003–04, 13 students received support, including 13 research assistantships with full tuition reimbursements available (averaging $5,864 per year) Financial award applicants required to submit FAFSA. *Faculty research:* Water quality, blood coagulation, biochemistry, organic chemistry, photoconversion. *Unit head:* Dr. N. Made Gowda, Chairperson, 309-298-1538. *Application contact:* Dr. Barbara Baily, Director of Graduate Studies/Associate Provost, 309-298-1806, Fax: 309-298-2345, E-mail: grad_office@ccmail.wiu.edu.

Western Kentucky University, Graduate Studies, Ogden College of Science, and Engineering, Department of Chemistry, Bowling Green, KY 42101-3576. Offers chemistry (MA Ed, MS). *Accreditation:* NCATE (one or more programs are accredited). *Degree requirements:* For master's, thesis, comprehensive exam. *Entrance requirements:* For master's, GRE General Test, minimum GPA of 2.75. Additional exam requirements/recommendations for international students: Required—TOEFL (minimum score 555 paper-based; 213 computer-based). *Faculty research:* Catatonic surfactants, directed orthometalation reactions, thermal stability and degradation mechanisms, co-firing refused derived fuels, laser fluorescence.

Western Michigan University, Graduate College, College of Arts and Sciences, Department of Chemistry, Kalamazoo, MI 49008-5202. Offers MA, PhD. *Degree requirements:* For master's, thesis, departmental qualifying and oral exams; for doctorate, thesis/dissertation.

Western Washington University, Graduate School, College of Sciences and Technology, Department of Chemistry, Bellingham, WA 98225-5996. Offers MS. Part-time programs available. *Faculty:* 17. *Students:* 8 full-time (4 women). 7 applicants, 71% accepted, 5 enrolled. In 2003, 4 degrees awarded. *Degree requirements:* For master's, thesis (for some programs). *Entrance requirements:* For master's, GRE General Test, minimum GPA of 3.0 in last 60 semester hours or last 90 quarter hours. Additional exam requirements/recommendations for international students: Required—TOEFL. *Application deadline:* For fall admission, 6/1 for domestic students; for winter admission, 10/1 for domestic students; for spring admission, 2/1 for domestic students. Applications are processed on a rolling basis. Application fee: $35. *Expenses:* Tuition, state resident: full-time $5,694; part-time $172 per credit. Tuition, nonresident: full-time $16,221; part-time $523 per credit. *Financial support:* In 2003–04, research assistantships with partial tuition reimbursements (averaging $11,190 per year), 7 teaching assistantships with partial tuition reimbursements (averaging $11,190 per year) were awarded. Career-related internships or fieldwork, Federal Work-Study, institutionally sponsored loans, scholarships/grants, and tuition waivers (partial) also available. Support available to part-time students. Financial award application deadline: 2/15; financial award applicants required to submit FAFSA. *Unit head:* Dr. Mark Wicholas, Chair, 360-650-3071. *Application contact:* Dr. James Vyvyan, Graduate Adviser, 360-650-2883.

West Texas A&M University, College of Agriculture, Nursing, and Natural Sciences, Department of Mathematics, Physical Sciences and Engineering Technology, Program in Chemistry, Canyon, TX 79016-0001. Offers MS. Part-time programs available. *Faculty:* 3 full-time (1 woman), 1 part-time/adjunct (0 women). *Students:* 3 full-time (1 woman), 1 (woman) part-time, 2 international. Average age 34. 4 applicants, 75% accepted, 3 enrolled. In 2003, 2 degrees awarded. *Median time to degree:* Master's–3 years full-time, 6 years part-time. *Degree requirements:* For master's, thesis optional. *Entrance requirements:* For master's, GRE General Test. Additional exam requirements/recommendations for international students: Required—TOEFL (minimum score 550 paper-based). *Application deadline:* Applications are processed on a rolling basis. Application fee: $25 ($75 for international students). Electronic applications accepted. *Expenses:* Tuition, state resident: part-time $56 per credit hour. Tuition, nonresident: part-time $292 per credit hour. Full-time tuition and fees vary according to course level, degree level and program. *Financial support:* In 2003–04, 1 research assistantship (averaging $6,500 per year), teaching assistantships (averaging $6,750 per year) were awarded. Career-related internships or fieldwork, Federal Work-Study, institutionally sponsored loans, scholarships/grants, and tuition waivers (partial) also available. Support available to part-time students. Financial award applicants required to submit FAFSA. *Faculty research:* Biochemistry; inorganic, organic, and physical chemistry; vibrational spectroscopy; magnetic susceptibilities; carbene chemistry. Total annual research expenditures: $137,065. *Application contact:* Dr. Gene Carlisle, Graduate Adviser, 806-651-2282, Fax: 806-651-2544, E-mail: gcarlisle@mail.wtamu.edu.

West Virginia University, Eberly College of Arts and Sciences, Department of Chemistry, Morgantown, WV 26506. Offers analytical chemistry (MS, PhD); inorganic chemistry (MS, PhD); organic chemistry (MS, PhD); physical chemistry (MS, PhD); theoretical chemistry (MS, PhD). Part-time programs available. Postbaccalaureate distance learning degree programs offered (no on-campus study). *Faculty:* 14 full-time (1 woman), 5 part-time/adjunct (3 women). *Students:* 45 full-time (15 women), 3 part-time (2 women); includes 1 minority (Hispanic American), 26 international. Average age 28. 84 applicants, 58% accepted, 11 enrolled. In 2003, 5 master's, 3 doctorates awarded. Terminal master's awarded for partial completion of doctoral program. *Degree requirements:* For master's and doctorate, thesis/dissertation, registration. *Entrance requirements:* For master's, GRE General Test, GRE Subject Test (recommended), minimum GPA of 2.5; for doctorate, GRE General Test, GRE Subject Test (recommended), minimum GPA of 2.75. Additional exam requirements/recommendations for international students: Required—TOEFL. *Application deadline:* For fall admission, 3/1 for domestic students. Applications are processed on a rolling basis. Application fee: $50. Electronic applications accepted. *Expenses:* Tuition, state resident: full-time $4,332. Tuition, nonresident: full-time $12,442. *Financial support:* In 2003–04, fellowships (averaging $2,000 per year), research assistantships with full tuition reimbursements (averaging $13,000 per year), teaching assistantships with full tuition reimbursements (averaging $12,000 per year) were awarded. Tuition waivers (full and partial) also available. Financial award application deadline: 2/1; financial award applicants required to submit FAFSA. *Faculty research:* Analysis of proteins, drug interactions, solids and effluents by advanced separation methods; electro-chemistry, mass spectrometry and atomic spectrometry; development of new synthetic strategies for complex organic molecules; synthesis and structural characterization of metal complexes for polymerization catalysis; nonmagnetic resonance studies of amorphous solids. *Unit head:* Dr. Harry O. Finklea, Chair, 304-293-3435 Ext. 6408, Fax: 304-293-4904, E-mail: harry.finklea@mail.wvu.edu.

Wichita State University, Graduate School, Fairmount College of Liberal Arts and Sciences, Department of Chemistry, Wichita, KS 67260. Offers MS, PhD. *Faculty:* 14 full-time (0 women). *Students:* 17 full-time (7 women), 17 part-time (4 women); includes 1 minority (Hispanic American), 24 international. Average age 29. 14 applicants, 71% accepted. In 2003, 3 master's, 1 doctorate awarded. *Degree requirements:* For master's, variable foreign language requirement, thesis; for doctorate, thesis/dissertation, comprehensive exam. *Entrance requirements:* For master's and doctorate, GRE. Additional exam requirements/recommendations for international students: Required—TOEFL. *Application deadline:* For fall admission, 7/1 for domestic students; for spring admission, 1/1 for domestic students. Applications are processed on a rolling basis. Application fee: $35 ($50 for international students). Electronic applications accepted. *Expenses:* Tuition, state resident: full-time $2,457; part-time $137 per credit hour. Tuition, nonresident: full-time $7,371; part-time $410 per credit hour. Required fees: $364; $20 per credit hour. Tuition and fees vary according to course load. *Financial support:* In 2003–04, research assistantships (averaging $10,588 per year), teaching assistantships with full tuition reimbursements (averaging $10,488 per year) were awarded. Fellowships, career-related internships or fieldwork, Federal Work-Study, institutionally sponsored loans, scholarships/grants, traineeships, and unspecified assistantships also available. Support available to part-time students. Financial award application deadline: 4/1; financial award applicants required to submit FAFSA. *Faculty research:* Biochemistry; analytic, inorganic, organic, and polymer chemistry. *Unit head:* Dr. Dennis Burns, Chair, 316-978-3120, Fax: 316-978-3431, E-mail: dennis.burns@wichita.edu.

Worcester Polytechnic Institute, Graduate Studies and Enrollment, Department of Chemistry and Biochemistry, Worcester, MA 01609-2280. Offers biochemistry (MS, PhD); chemistry (MS, PhD). *Faculty:* 13 full-time (1 woman). *Students:* 18 full-time (8 women), 16 international. 17 applicants, 82% accepted, 4 enrolled. In 2003, 10 master's, 2 doctorates awarded. *Degree requirements:* For master's, thesis/dissertation; for doctorate, thesis/dissertation, comprehensive exam. *Entrance requirements:* For master's and doctorate, GRE General Test. Additional exam requirements/recommendations for international students: Required—TOEFL (minimum score 550 paper-based; 213 computer-based). *Application deadline:* For fall admission, 2/1 for domestic students; for spring admission, 10/15 priority date for domestic students. Applications are processed on a rolling basis. Application fee: $70. Electronic applications accepted. *Expenses:* Tuition: Part-time $897 per credit. *Financial support:* In 2003–04, 14 students received support, including 1 fellowship with full and partial tuition reimbursement available, 5 research assistantships with full tuition reimbursements available, 9 teaching assistantships with full tuition reimbursements available; career-related internships or fieldwork, institutionally sponsored loans, scholarships/grants, health care benefits, and unspecified assistantships also available. Financial award application deadline: 2/15; financial award applicants required to submit FAFSA. *Faculty research:* Plant biochemistry, membrane biophysics, photochemistry, organic synthesis, materials synthesis. Total annual research expenditures: $275,264. *Unit head:* Dr. James P. Dittami, Head, 508-831-5149, Fax: 508-831-5933, E-mail: jdittami@wpi.edu. *Application contact:* Dr. W. Grant McGimpsey, Graduate Coordinator, 508-831-5486, Fax: 508-831-5933, E-mail: wgm@wpi.edu.

Wright State University, School of Graduate Studies, College of Science and Mathematics, Department of Chemistry, Dayton, OH 45435. Offers chemistry (MS); environmental sciences (MS). Part-time and evening/weekend programs available. *Students:* 23 full-time (13 women), 6 part-time (1 woman); includes 3 minority (1 African American, 2 Asian Americans or Pacific Islanders), 8 international. Average age 28. 19 applicants, 84% accepted. In 2003, 8 degrees awarded. *Degree requirements:* For master's, oral defense of thesis, seminar. *Entrance requirements:* Additional exam requirements/recommendations for international students: Required—TOEFL. *Application deadline:* For fall admission, 6/1 for domestic students. Applications are processed on a rolling basis. Application fee: $25. *Expenses:* Tuition, state resident: full-time $8,112; part-time $255 per quarter hour. Tuition, nonresident: full-time $14,127; part-time $442 per quarter hour. International tuition: $14,283 full-time. Tuition and fees vary according to course load, degree level and program. *Financial support:* Fellowships, research assistantships, teaching assistantships, unspecified assistantships available. Support available to part-time students. Financial award applicants required to submit FAFSA. *Faculty research:* Polymer synthesis and characterization, laser kinetics, organic and inorganic synthesis, analytical and environmental chemistry. Total annual research expenditures: $60,000. *Unit head:* Dr. Paul G. Seybold, Chair, 937-775-2855, Fax: 937-775-2717, E-mail: paul.seybold@wright.edu. *Application contact:* Dr. Kenneth Turnbull, Chair, Graduate Studies Committee, 937-775-2671, Fax: 937-775-2717, E-mail: kenneth.turnbull@wright.edu.

Yale University, Graduate School of Arts and Sciences, Department of Chemistry, New Haven, CT 06520. Offers biophysical chemistry (PhD); inorganic chemistry (PhD); organic chemistry (PhD); physical chemistry (PhD). *Degree requirements:* For doctorate, thesis/dissertation. *Entrance requirements:* For doctorate, GRE General Test, GRE Subject Test. Additional exam requirements/recommendations for international students: Required—TOEFL. *Expenses:* Tuition: Full-time $25,600; part-time $6,400 per term.

York University, Faculty of Graduate Studies, Faculty of Pure and Applied Science, Program in Chemistry, Toronto, ON M3J 1P3, Canada. Offers M Sc, PhD. Part-time and evening/weekend programs available. *Degree requirements:* For master's, thesis or alternative; for doctorate, thesis/dissertation. *Entrance requirements:* For master's, GRE (may be required), minimum B average; for doctorate, minimum B average. Electronic applications accepted. Tuition, area resident: Full-time $5,431; part-time $905 per term. Tuition, nonresident: part-time $1,987 per term. International tuition: $11,918 full-time. Required fees: $287. Tuition and fees vary according to program.

Youngstown State University, Graduate School, College of Arts and Sciences, Department of Chemistry, Youngstown, OH 44555-0001. Offers MS. Part-time programs available. *Degree requirements:* For master's, thesis. *Entrance requirements:* For master's, bachelor's degree in chemistry, minimum GPA of 2.7. Additional exam requirements/recommendations for international students: Required—TOEFL. *Expenses:* Tuition, state resident: full-time $4,194; part-time $233 per credit. Tuition, nonresident: full-time $8,352; part-time $464 per credit. Required fees: $42 per credit. Tuition and fees vary according to course load and reciprocity agreements. *Faculty research:* Analysis of antioxidants, chromatography, defects and disorder in crystalline oxides, hydrogen bonding, novel organic and organometallic materials.

Inorganic Chemistry

Boston College, Graduate School of Arts and Sciences, Department of Chemistry, Chestnut Hill, MA 02467-3800. Offers biochemistry (PhD); inorganic chemistry (PhD); organic chemistry (PhD); physical chemistry (PhD); science education (MST). MST is offered through the School of Education for secondary school science teaching. Part-time programs available. *Students:* 95 full-time (31 women); includes 12 minority (2 African Americans, 7 Asian Americans or Pacific Islanders, 3 Hispanic Americans), 22 international. 285 applicants, 24% accepted, 14 enrolled. In 2003, 2 master's, 13 doctorates awarded. *Degree requirements:* For doctorate, thesis/dissertation, qualifying exam. *Entrance requirements:* For doctorate, GRE General Test, GRE Subject Test. Additional exam requirements/recommendations for international students: Required—TOEFL (minimum score 550 paper-based; 213 computer-based). *Application deadline:* For fall admission, 1/2 for domestic students. Application fee: $60. Electronic applications accepted. *Expenses:* Tuition: Part-time $810 per credit. *Financial support:* Fellowships with full tuition reimbursements, research assistantships with full tuition reimbursements, teaching assistantships with full tuition reimbursements, Federal Work-Study available. Support available to part-time students. Financial award application deadline: 3/1; financial award applicants required to submit FAFSA. *Unit head:* Dr. David McFadden, Chairperson, 617-552-3605, E-mail: david.mcfadden@bc.edu. *Application contact:* Dr. John Fourkas, Information Contact, 617-552-3605, Fax: 617-552-0833, E-mail: john.fourkas@bc.edu.

Brandeis University, Graduate School of Arts and Sciences, Department of Chemistry, Waltham, MA 02454-9110. Offers inorganic chemistry (MS, PhD); organic chemistry (MS, PhD); physical chemistry (MS, PhD). *Faculty:* 18 full-time (3 women). *Students:* 39 full-time (20 women), 1 (woman) part-time; includes 2 minority (1 Asian American or Pacific Islander, 1 Hispanic American), 32 international. Average age 25. 114 applicants, 5% accepted. In 2003, 8 master's, 5 doctorates awarded. Terminal master's awarded for partial completion of doctoral program. *Degree requirements:* For master's, 1 year of residency; for doctorate, one foreign language, thesis/dissertation, 3 years of residency, 2 seminars, qualifying exams. *Entrance requirements:* For master's and doctorate, GRE General Test, resumé, letters of recommendation. Additional exam requirements/recommendations for international students: Required—TOEFL (minimum score 600 paper-based; 250 computer-based). *Application deadline:* For fall admission, 1/15 for domestic students. Applications are processed on a rolling basis. Application fee: $60. Electronic applications accepted. *Expenses:* Tuition: Full-time $28,999; part-time $4,867 per course. Required fees: $175. *Financial support:* In 2003–04, 20 fellowships (averaging $20,000 per year), 21 research assistantships (averaging $20,000 per year), 18 teaching assistantships (averaging $20,000 per year) were awarded. Institutionally sponsored loans and scholarships/grants also available. Financial award application deadline: 4/15; financial award applicants required to submit CSS PROFILE or FAFSA. *Faculty research:* Oscillating chemical reactions, molecular recognition systems, protein crystallography, synthesis of natural product spectroscopy and magnetic resonance. Total annual research expenditures: $1,900. *Unit head:* Dr. Thomas C. Pochapsky, Chair, 781-736-2559, Fax: 781-736-2516, E-mail: pochapsky@brandeis.edu. *Application contact:* Charlotte Haygazian, Graduate Admissions Secretary, 781-736-2500, Fax: 781-736-2516, E-mail: chemadm@brandeis.edu.

Brigham Young University, Graduate Studies, College of Physical and Mathematical Sciences, Department of Chemistry and Biochemistry, Provo, UT 84602-1001. Offers analytical chemistry (MS, PhD); biochemistry (MS, PhD); inorganic chemistry (MS, PhD); organic chemistry (MS, PhD); physical chemistry (MS, PhD). *Faculty:* 34 full-time (2 women). *Students:* 90 full-time (56 women); includes 2 minority (1 Asian American or Pacific Islander, 1 Hispanic American), 61 international. Average age 31. 103 applicants, 54% accepted, 23 enrolled. In 2003, 6 master's, 6 doctorates awarded. *Median time to degree:* Master's–2.8 years full-time. Of those who began their doctoral program in fall 1995, 100% received their degree in 8 years or less. *Degree requirements:* For master's, thesis, registration; for doctorate, thesis/dissertation, degree qualifying exam. *Entrance requirements:* For master's, pass 1 (biochemistry), 4 (chemistry) of 5 area exams, GRE General Test, minimum GPA of 3.0 in last 60 hours; for doctorate, pass 1 (biochemistry) or 4 (chemistry) of 5 area exams, GRE General Test, minimum GPA of 3.0 in last 60 hours. Additional exam requirements/recommendations for international students: Required—TOEFL, TWE. *Application deadline:* For fall admission, 2/1 priority date for domestic students, 2/1 priority date for international students. Applications are processed on a rolling basis. Application fee: $50. Electronic applications accepted. *Expenses:* Tuition: Part-time $221 per hour. *Financial support:* In 2003–04, 90 students received support, including 12 fellowships with full tuition reimbursements available (averaging $18,400 per year), 37 research assistantships with full tuition reimbursements available (averaging $18,400 per year), 30 teaching assistantships with full tuition reimbursements available (averaging $18,300 per year); institutionally sponsored loans, scholarships/grants, health care benefits, tuition waivers (full), and unspecified assistantships also available. Financial award application deadline: 2/1. *Faculty research:* Separation science, molecular recognition, organic synthesis and biomedical application, biochemistry and molecular biology, molecular spectroscopy. Total annual research expenditures: $2.7 million. *Unit head:* Dr. Francis R. Nordmeyer, Chair, 801-422-3667, Fax: 801-422-0153, E-mail: fran_nordmeyer@byu.edu. *Application contact:* Dr. Noel L. Owen, Graduate Coordinator, 801-422-2973, Fax: 801-422-0153, E-mail: chemgrad@byu.edu.

See in-depth description on page 97.

California State University, Fullerton, Graduate Studies, College of Natural Science and Mathematics, Department of Chemistry and Biochemistry, Fullerton, CA 92834-9480. Offers analytical chemistry (MS); biochemistry (MS); geochemistry (MS); inorganic chemistry (MS); organic chemistry (MS); physical chemistry (MS). Part-time programs available. *Faculty:* 17 full-time (5 women), 17 part-time/adjunct. *Students:* 21 full-time (9 women), 23 part-time (11 women); includes 19 minority (1 African American, 9 Asian Americans or Pacific Islanders, 9 Hispanic Americans), 8 international. Average age 28. 49 applicants, 61% accepted, 20 enrolled. In 2003, 5 degrees awarded. *Degree requirements:* For master's, thesis, departmental qualifying exam. *Entrance requirements:* For master's, minimum GPA of 2.5 in last 60 units, major in chemistry or related field. Application fee: $55. Tuition, nonresident: part-time $282 per unit. Required fees: $889 per semester. *Financial support:* Teaching assistantships, career-related internships or fieldwork, Federal Work-Study, institutionally sponsored loans, and scholarships/grants available. Support available to part-time students. Financial award application deadline: 3/1. *Unit head:* Dr. Robert Belloli, Chair, 714-278-3621. *Application contact:* Dr. Gregory Williams, Adviser, 714-278-2170.

California State University, Los Angeles, Graduate Studies, College of Natural and Social Sciences, Department of Chemistry and Biochemistry, Los Angeles, CA 90032-8530. Offers analytical chemistry (MS); biochemistry (MS); chemistry (MS); inorganic chemistry (MS); organic chemistry (MS); physical chemistry (MS). Part-time and evening/weekend programs available. *Faculty:* 15 full-time, 12 part-time/adjunct. *Students:* 12 full-time (6 women), 11 part-time (7 women); includes 11 minority (2 African Americans, 5 Asian Americans or Pacific Islanders, 4 Hispanic Americans), 5 international. In 2003, 5 degrees awarded. *Degree requirements:* For master's, one foreign language. *Entrance requirements:* Additional exam requirements/recommendations for international students: Required—TOEFL. *Application deadline:* For fall admission, 6/30 for domestic students; for spring admission, 2/1 for domestic students. Applications are processed on a rolling basis. Application fee: $55. Tuition, nonresident: part-time $188 per unit. Required fees: $2,477. *Financial support:* Federal Work-Study available. Support available to part-time students. Financial award application deadline: 3/1. *Faculty research:* Intercalation of heavy metal, carborane chemistry, conductive polymers and fabrics, titanium reagents, computer modeling and synthesis. *Unit head:* Dr. Wayne Tikkanen, Chair, 323-343-2300.

Case Western Reserve University, School of Graduate Studies, Department of Chemistry, Cleveland, OH 44106. Offers analytical chemistry (MS, PhD); inorganic chemistry (MS, PhD); organic chemistry (MS, PhD); physical chemistry (MS, PhD). Part-time programs available. *Faculty:* 22 full-time (2 women). *Students:* 64 full-time (18 women), 27 part-time (9 women); includes 2 minority (both Asian Americans or Pacific Islanders), 69 international. Average age 27. 483 applicants, 9% accepted, 18 enrolled. In 2003, 5 master's, 13 doctorates awarded. Terminal master's awarded for partial completion of doctoral program. *Degree requirements:* For doctorate, thesis/dissertation. *Entrance requirements:* For master's and doctorate, GRE General Test, GRE Subject Test. Additional exam requirements/recommendations for international students: Required—TOEFL. *Application deadline:* Applications are processed on a rolling basis. Application fee: $50. *Expenses:* Tuition: Full-time $26,900. *Financial support:* In 2003–04, 77 students received support, including 53 research assistantships, 20 teaching assistantships. *Faculty research:* Electrochemistry, synthetic chemistry, chemistry of life process, spectroscopy, kinetics. *Unit head:* Lawrence Sayre, Chairman, 216-368-3622, Fax: 216-368-3006, E-mail: lms3@case.edu. *Application contact:* Zedeara Diaz, Graduate Admissions, 216-368-3621, Fax: 216-368-3006, E-mail: zcd@case.edu.

Clark Atlanta University, School of Arts and Sciences, Department of Chemistry, Atlanta, GA 30314. Offers inorganic chemistry (MS, PhD); organic chemistry (MS, PhD); physical chemistry (MS, PhD); science education (DA). Part-time programs available. *Degree requirements:* For master's, one foreign language, thesis, comprehensive exam; for doctorate, 2 foreign languages, thesis/dissertation, cumulative exam. *Entrance requirements:* For master's, GRE General Test, minimum GPA of 2.5; for doctorate, GRE General Test, GRE Subject Test, minimum graduate GPA of 3.0.

Clarkson University, Graduate School, School of Arts and Sciences, Department of Chemistry, Potsdam, NY 13699. Offers analytical chemistry (MS, PhD); inorganic chemistry (MS, PhD); organic chemistry (MS, PhD); physical chemistry (MS, PhD). *Faculty:* 11 full-time (2 women). *Students:* 31 full-time (12 women); includes 3 minority (2 African Americans, 1 Asian American or Pacific Islander), 14 international. Average age 28. 45 applicants, 67% accepted. In 2003, 4 master's, 1 doctorate awarded. *Median time to degree:* Master's–2.5 years full-time; doctorate–4 years full-time, 6 years part-time. *Degree requirements:* For doctorate, thesis/dissertation, departmental qualifying exam. *Entrance requirements:* For master's, GRE. Additional exam requirements/recommendations for international students: Required—TOEFL. *Application deadline:* For fall admission, 5/15 for domestic students; for spring admission, 10/15 priority date for domestic students. Applications are processed on a rolling basis. Application fee: $25 ($35 for international students). *Expenses:* Tuition: Full-time $19,272; part-time $803 per credit. Tuition and fees vary according to course load. *Financial support:* In 2003–04, 23 students received support, including 2 fellowships (averaging $22,000 per year), 9 research assistantships (averaging $18,000 per year), 12 teaching assistantships (averaging $18,000 per year); scholarships/grants and tuition waivers (partial) also available. *Faculty research:* Particle adhesion phenomena, airborne radon, ceramic materials, materials processing, chemical kinetics. Total annual research expenditures: $1.3 million. *Unit head:* Dr. Phillip A. Christiansen, Division Head, 315-268-6669, Fax: 315-268-6610, E-mail: pac@clarkson.edu. *Application contact:* Donna Brockway, Assistant to Dean/Foreign Student Advisor, 315-268-6447, Fax: 315-268-7994, E-mail: brockway@clarkson.edu.

Cleveland State University, College of Graduate Studies, College of Arts and Sciences, Department of Chemistry, Cleveland, OH 44115. Offers analytical chemistry (MS, PhD); clinical chemistry (MS, PhD); clinical/bioanalytical (PhD); inorganic chemistry (MS); organic chemistry (MS); physical chemistry (MS); structural analysis (MS, PhD). Part-time and evening/weekend programs available. *Faculty:* 16 full-time (1 woman), 3 part-time/adjunct (1 woman). *Students:* 44 full-time (21 women), 23 part-time (9 women); includes 3 minority (1 African American, 1 Asian American or Pacific Islander, 1 Hispanic American), 29 international. Average age 33. 30 applicants, 23% accepted, 2 enrolled. In 2003, 6 master's, 1 doctorate awarded. *Degree requirements:* For master's, thesis (for some programs); for doctorate, thesis/dissertation. *Entrance requirements:* For master's and doctorate, GRE General Test, GRE Subject Test. Additional exam requirements/recommendations for international students: Required—TOEFL (minimum score 525 paper-based; 197 computer-based). *Application deadline:* For fall admission, 1/15 priority date for domestic students, 1/15 priority date for international students. Applications are processed on a rolling basis. Application fee: $30. Electronic applications accepted. Tuition, area resident: Full-time $8,258; part-time $344 per credit hour. Tuition, nonresident: full-time $16,352; part-time $681 per credit hour. *Financial support:* In 2003–04, 37 students received support, including fellowships (averaging $16,000 per year), 19 research assistantships with full tuition reimbursements available (averaging $16,000 per year), 18 teaching assistantships with full tuition reimbursements available (averaging $15,000 per year) Financial award application deadline: 1/15. *Faculty research:* Trace metal analysis in biological systems, application of HPLC/LPCC to clinical systems, synthetic organic and inorganic chemistry, molecular structure determinations, structure-function relationships of factor Va, MALDI-TOF based DNA sequencing, spectroscopic studies of chemical and biochemical phenomena, novel electro-optic tunable filters (AOTFs) to explore biological systems. Total annual research expenditures: $1 million. *Unit head:* Dr. Stan Duraj, Chair, 216-687-2454, Fax: 216-687-9298, E-mail: s.duraj@csuohio.edu. *Application contact:* Richelle P. Emery, Administrative Coordinator, 216-687-2457, Fax: 216-687-9298, E-mail: r.emery@csuohio.edu.

Columbia University, Graduate School of Arts and Sciences, Division of Natural Sciences, Department of Chemistry, New York, NY 10027. Offers chemical physics (M Phil, PhD); inorganic chemistry (M Phil, MS, PhD); organic chemistry (M Phil, MS, PhD). *Faculty:* 17 full-time. *Students:* 115 full-time (35 women). Average age 27. 452 applicants, 20% accepted. In 2003, 13 master's, 20 doctorates awarded. *Degree requirements:* For master's, comp exams (MS); foreign language, teaching experience, oral/written exams (M Phil); for doctorate, one foreign language, thesis/dissertation. *Entrance requirements:* For master's and doctorate, GRE General Test, GRE Subject Test. Additional exam requirements/recommendations for international students: Required—TOEFL. Application fee: $75. *Expenses:* Tuition: Full-time $14,820. *Financial support:* Fellowships, teaching assistantships, Federal Work-Study and institutionally sponsored loans available. Support available to part-time students. Financial award application deadline: 1/5; financial award applicants required to submit FAFSA. *Faculty research:* Biophysics. *Unit head:* Bruce Berne, Chair, 212-854-2186, Fax: 212-932-1289.

Cornell University, Graduate School, Graduate Fields of Arts and Sciences, Field of Chemistry and Chemical Biology, Ithaca, NY 14853-0001. Offers analytical chemistry (PhD); bio-organic chemistry (PhD); biophysical chemistry (PhD); chemical biology (PhD); chemical physics (PhD); inorganic chemistry (PhD); materials chemistry (PhD); organic chemistry (PhD); organometallic chemistry (PhD); physical chemistry (PhD); polymer chemistry (PhD); theoretical chemistry (PhD). *Faculty:* 37 full-time. *Students:* 174 full-time (70 women); includes 22 minority (4 African Americans, 10 Asian Americans or Pacific Islanders, 8 Hispanic Americans), 57 international. 371 applicants, 35% accepted, 42 enrolled. In 2003, 22 doctorates awarded. *Degree requirements:* For doctorate, thesis/dissertation, comprehensive exam. *Entrance requirements:* For doctorate, GRE General Test, GRE Subject Test (chemistry), 3 letters of recommendation. Additional exam requirements/recommendations for international students: Required—TOEFL (minimum score 600 paper-based; 250 computer-based). *Application deadline:* For fall admission, 1/10 for domestic students. Application fee: $60. Electronic applications accepted. *Expenses:* Tuition: Full-time $28,630. One-time fee: $50 full-time. *Financial support:* In 2003–04, 162 students received support, including 28 fellowships with full tuition reimbursements available, 77 research assistantships with full tuition reimbursements available, 57 teaching assistantships with full tuition reimbursements available; institutionally sponsored loans, scholarships/grants, health care benefits, tuition waivers (full and partial), and unspecified assistantships also available. Financial award applicants required to submit FAFSA. *Faculty research:* Analytical, organic, inorganic, physical, materials, chemical biology. *Unit head:* Director of Graduate Studies, 607-255-4139, Fax: 607-255-4137. *Application contact:* Graduate Field Assistant, 607-255-4139, Fax: 607-255-4137, E-mail: chemgrad@cornell.edu.

See in-depth description on page 105.

Florida State University, Graduate Studies, College of Arts and Sciences, Department of Chemistry and Biochemistry, Tallahassee, FL 32306. Offers analytical chemistry (MS, PhD); biochemistry (MS, PhD); chemical physics (MS, PhD); inorganic chemistry (MS, PhD); organic chemistry (MS, PhD); physical chemistry (MS, PhD). Part-time programs available. *Faculty:* 30 full-time (6 women), 4 part-time/adjunct (2 women). *Students:* 142 full-time (46 women); includes 18 minority (9 African Americans, 1 American Indian/Alaska Native, 6 Asian Americans or Pacific Islanders, 2 Hispanic Americans), 51 international. Average age 25. 410 applicants, 15% accepted, 39 enrolled. In 2003, 9 master's, 11 doctorates awarded. Terminal master's awarded for partial completion of doctoral program. *Median time to degree:* Master's–3.5 years full-time; doctorate–5 years full-time. Of those who began their doctoral program in fall 1995, 72% received their degree in 8 years or less. *Degree requirements:* For master's, thesis (for some programs), cumulative and diagnostic exams, comprehensive exam (for some programs); for doctorate, thesis/dissertation, cumulative and diagnostic exams. *Entrance requirements:* For master's and doctorate, GRE General Test, minimum B average in undergraduate course work. Additional exam requirements/recommendations for international students: Required—TOEFL (minimum score 515 paper-based; 213 computer-based). *Application deadline:* For fall admission, 4/15 priority date for domestic students, 4/15 priority date for international students. Applications are processed on a rolling basis. Application fee: $20. Electronic applications accepted. *Expenses:* Tuition, state resident: part-time $196 per credit hour. Tuition, nonresident: part-time $731 per credit hour. Part-time tuition and fees vary according to campus/location. *Financial support:* In 2003–04, 2 fellowships with tuition reimbursements (averaging $15,000 per year), 54 research assistantships with tuition reimbursements (averaging $18,000 per year), 76 teaching assistantships with tuition reimbursements (averaging $18,000 per year) were awarded. Career-related internships or fieldwork, Federal Work-Study, institutionally sponsored loans, and traineeships also available. Financial award application deadline: 2/15; financial award applicants required to submit FAFSA. *Faculty research:* Spectroscopy, computational chemistry, nuclear chemistry, separations, synthesis. *Unit head:* Dr. Naresh Dalal, Chairman, 850-644-3398, Fax: 850-644-8281. *Application contact:* Dr. Oliver Steinbock, Chair, Graduate Admissions Committee, 888-525-9286, Fax: 850-644-8281, E-mail: gradinfo@chem.fsu.edu.

See in-depth description on page 115.

Georgetown University, Graduate School of Arts and Sciences, Department of Chemistry, Washington, DC 20057. Offers analytical chemistry (MS, PhD); biochemistry (MS, PhD); chemical physics (MS, PhD); inorganic chemistry (MS, PhD); organic chemistry (MS, PhD); physical chemistry (MS, PhD); theoretical chemistry (MS, PhD). Terminal master's awarded for partial completion of doctoral program. *Degree requirements:* For master's, thesis (for some programs), qualifying exam; for doctorate, thesis/dissertation, comprehensive exam. *Entrance requirements:* For master's and doctorate, GRE General Test. Additional exam requirements/recommendations for international students: Required—TOEFL.

The George Washington University, Columbian College of Arts and Sciences, Department of Chemistry, Washington, DC 20052. Offers analytical chemistry (MS, PhD); inorganic chemistry (MS, PhD); materials science (MS, PhD); organic chemistry (MS, PhD); physical chemistry (MS, PhD). Part-time and evening/weekend programs available. *Faculty:* 7 full-time (1 woman). *Students:* 16 full-time (6 women), 11 part-time (6 women); includes 4 minority (2 African Americans, 1 Asian American or Pacific Islander, 1 Hispanic American), 11 international. 39 applicants, 95% accepted. In 2003, 3 master's, 2 doctorates awarded. Terminal master's awarded for partial completion of doctoral program. *Degree requirements:* For master's, thesis or alternative, comprehensive exam; for doctorate, thesis/dissertation, general exam. *Entrance requirements:* For master's and doctorate, GRE General Test, interview, minimum GPA of 3.0. Additional exam requirements/recommendations for international students: Required—TOEFL (minimum score 550 paper-based; 213 computer-based). *Application deadline:* For fall admission, 2/1 priority date for domestic students, 2/1 priority date for international students; for spring admission, 10/1 priority date for domestic students, 10/1 priority date for international students. Applications are processed on a rolling basis. Application fee: $60. Electronic applications accepted. *Expenses:* Tuition: Part-time $876 per credit. Required fees: $1 per credit. Tuition and fees vary according to campus/location. *Financial support:* In 2003–04, fellowships with tuition reimbursements (averaging $10,000 per year), teaching assistantships with tuition reimbursements (averaging $5,000 per year) were awarded. Research assistantships, Federal Work-Study also available. Financial award application deadline: 2/1. *Unit head:* Dr. Michael King, Chair, 202-994-6488. *Application contact:* Information Contact, E-mail: gwchem@www.gwu.edu.

Harvard University, Graduate School of Arts and Sciences, Department of Chemistry and Chemical Biology, Cambridge, MA 02138. Offers biochemical chemistry (AM, PhD); inorganic chemistry (AM, PhD); organic chemistry (AM, PhD); physical chemistry (AM, PhD). *Degree requirements:* For doctorate, thesis/dissertation, cumulative exams. *Entrance requirements:* For master's, GRE General Test; for doctorate, GRE General Test, GRE Subject Test. Additional exam requirements/recommendations for international students: Required—TOEFL. *Expenses:* Tuition: Full-time $26,066. Full-time tuition and fees vary according to program and student level.

See in-depth description on page 117.

Howard University, Graduate School of Arts and Sciences, Department of Chemistry, Washington, DC 20059-0002. Offers analytical chemistry (MS, PhD); atmospheric (MS, PhD); biochemistry (MS, PhD); environmental (MS, PhD); inorganic chemistry (MS, PhD); organic chemistry (MS, PhD); physical chemistry (MS, PhD); polymer chemistry (MS, PhD). Part-time programs available. *Degree requirements:* For master's, one foreign language, thesis, teaching experience, comprehensive exam, registration; for doctorate, 2 foreign languages, thesis/dissertation, teaching experience, comprehensive exam, registration. *Entrance requirements:* For master's, GRE General Test, minimum GPA of 2.7; for doctorate, GRE General Test, minimum GPA of 3.0. *Faculty research:* Stratospheric aerosols, liquid crystals, polymer coatings, terrestrial and extraterrestrial atmospheres, amidogen reaction.

Illinois Institute of Technology, Graduate College, College of Science and Letters, Department of Biological, Chemical and Physical Sciences, Chemistry Division, Chicago, IL 60616-3793. Offers analytical chemistry (M Ch, MS, PhD); chemistry (M Chem); inorganic chemistry (MS, PhD); materials and chemical synthesis (M Ch); organic chemistry (MS, PhD); physical chemistry (MS, PhD); polymer chemistry (MS, PhD). Part-time and evening/weekend programs available. Postbaccalaureate distance learning degree programs offered (no on-campus study). *Faculty:* 4 full-time (0 women), 2 part-time/adjunct (0 women). *Students:* 14 full-time (7 women), 32 part-time (18 women); includes 7 minority (1 African American, 4 Asian Americans or Pacific Islanders, 2 Hispanic Americans), 17 international. Average age 32. 94 applicants, 68% accepted, 7 enrolled. In 2003, 14 master's, 2 doctorates awarded. Terminal master's awarded for partial completion of doctoral program. *Degree requirements:* For master's, thesis (for some programs), comprehensive exam; for doctorate, thesis/dissertation, comprehensive exam. *Entrance requirements:* For master's and doctorate, GRE General Test, minimum undergraduate GPA of 3.0. Additional exam requirements/recommendations for international students: Required—TOEFL (minimum score 550 paper-based; 213 computer-based). *Application deadline:* For fall admission, 5/1 for domestic students, 5/1 for international students; for spring admission, 10/15 for domestic students, 10/15 for international students. Applications are processed on a rolling basis. Application fee: $40. Electronic applications accepted. *Expenses:* Tuition: Part-time $628 per credit. Tuition and fees vary according to course load and program. *Financial support:* In 2003–04, 11 students received support, including 1 fellowship with full tuition reimbursement available, 9 research assistantships with full tuition reimbursements available (averaging $15,000 per year), 7 teaching assistantships with full tuition reimbursements available (averaging $15,000 per year); Federal Work-Study, institutionally sponsored loans, scholarships/grants, and tuition waivers (partial) also available. Support available to part-time students. Financial award application deadline: 3/1; financial award applicants required to submit FAFSA. *Faculty research:* Organic and inorganic chemistry, polymers research, physical chemistry, analytical chemistry. *Unit head:* Kenneth Stagliano, Associate Chair, 312-567-3428, Fax: 312-567-3494, E-mail: stagliano@iit.edu. *Application contact:* Kelly A. Cherwin, Director of Graduate Outreach, 312-567-7974, Fax: 312-567-3494, E-mail: inquiry.grad@iit.edu.

Indiana University Bloomington, Graduate School, College of Arts and Sciences, Department of Chemistry, Bloomington, IN 47405. Offers analytical chemistry (PhD); biological chemistry (PhD); chemistry (MAT, MS); inorganic chemistry (PhD); physical chemistry (PhD). PhD offered through the University Graduate School. *Faculty:* 29 full-time (2 women). *Students:* 95 full-time (30 women), 51 part-time (16 women); includes 9 minority (3 African Americans, 4 Asian Americans or Pacific Islanders, 2 Hispanic Americans), 52 international. Average age 26. 309 applicants, 41% accepted. In 2003, 4 master's, 23 doctorates awarded. Terminal master's awarded for partial completion of doctoral program. *Degree requirements:* For master's and doctorate, thesis/dissertation. *Entrance requirements:* For master's and doctorate, GRE General Test, GRE Subject Test. Additional exam requirements/recommendations for international students: Required—TOEFL. *Application deadline:* For fall admission, 1/15 priority date for domestic students, 12/15 priority date for international students; for spring admission, 9/1 priority date for domestic students, 9/1 priority date for international students. Applications are processed on a rolling basis. Application fee: $45 ($55 for international students). *Expenses:* Tuition, state resident: full-time $4,908; part-time $205 per credit. Tuition, nonresident: full-time $14,298; part-time $596 per credit. Required fees: $661. Tuition and fees vary according to campus/location and program. *Financial support:* In 2003–04, 23 fellowships with full tuition reimbursements (averaging $15,091 per year), 57 research assistantships with full tuition reimbursements (averaging $14,844 per year), 78 teaching assistantships with full tuition reimbursements (averaging $15,588 per year) were awarded. Federal Work-Study and institutionally sponsored loans also available. *Faculty research:* Synthesis of complex natural products, organic reaction mechanisms, organic electrochemistry, transitive-metal chemistry, solid-state and surface chemistry. Total annual research expenditures: $7.7 million. *Unit head:* Dr. Gary M. Hieftje, Chairperson, 812-855-6239, Fax: 812-855-8300, E-mail: cemchair@indiana.edu. *Application contact:* Dr. Jack K. Crandall, Chairperson of Admissions, 812-855-2068, Fax: 812-855-8300, E-mail: chemgrad@indiana.edu.

Kansas State University, Graduate School, College of Arts and Sciences, Department of Chemistry, Manhattan, KS 66506. Offers analytical chemistry (MS); chemistry (PhD); inorganic chemistry (MS); organic chemistry (MS); physical chemistry (MS). *Faculty:* 15 full-time (2 women). *Students:* 51 full-time (17 women); includes 1 minority (African American), 33 international. 71 applicants, 20% accepted, 14 enrolled. In 2003, 1 master's, 7 doctorates awarded. Terminal master's awarded for partial completion of doctoral program. *Degree requirements:* For master's and doctorate, thesis/dissertation. *Entrance requirements:* For master's and doctorate, GRE, minimum GPA of 3.0. Additional exam requirements/recommendations for international students: Required—TOEFL. *Application deadline:* For fall admission, 2/1 for domestic students; for spring admission, 10/1 for domestic students. Applications are processed on a rolling basis. Application fee: $0 ($25 for international students). *Expenses:* Tuition, state resident: part-time $155 per credit hour. Tuition, nonresident: part-time $428 per credit hour. Required fees: $11 per credit hour. *Financial support:* In 2003–04, 23 research assistantships (averaging $15,648 per year), 26 teaching assistantships with full tuition reimbursements (averaging $17,890 per year) were awarded. Fellowships, institutionally sponsored loans and scholarships/grants also available. Support available to part-time students. Financial award application deadline: 3/1; financial award applicants required to submit FAFSA. *Faculty research:* Computational, environmental and materials, nanoscale, natural products, theoretical chemistry. Total annual research expenditures: $2.8 million. *Unit head:* Peter M. A. Sherwood, Head, 785-532-6665, Fax: 785-532-6666, E-mail: escachem@ksu.edu. *Application contact:* Robert Hammaker, Director, 785-532-1454, Fax: 785-532-6666, E-mail: rmh3008@ksu.edu.

Kent State University, College of Arts and Sciences, Department of Chemistry, Kent, OH 44242-0001. Offers analytical chemistry (MS, PhD); biochemistry (MS, PhD); chemistry (MA, MS, PhD); inorganic chemistry (MS, PhD); organic chemistry (MS, PhD); physical chemistry (MS, PhD). Terminal master's awarded for partial completion of doctoral program. *Degree requirements:* For master's and doctorate, thesis/dissertation, comprehensive exam, registration. *Entrance requirements:* For master's and doctorate, placement exam, GRE General Test, GRE Subject Test (recommended), minimum GPA of 2.75. Additional exam requirements/recommendations for international students: Required—TOEFL (minimum score 575 paper-based; 230 computer-based). Electronic applications accepted. *Expenses:* Tuition, state resident: part-time $334 per hour. Tuition, nonresident: part-time $627 per hour. *Faculty research:* Biological chemistry, materials chemistry, molecular spectroscopy.

See in-depth description on page 119.

Marquette University, Graduate School, College of Arts and Sciences, Department of Chemistry, Milwaukee, WI 53201-1881. Offers analytical chemistry (MS, PhD); bioanalytical chemistry (MS, PhD); biophysical chemistry (MS, PhD); chemical physics (MS, PhD); inorganic chemistry (MS, PhD); organic chemistry (MS, PhD); physical chemistry (MS, PhD). Part-time programs available. *Faculty:* 19 full-time (2 women), 2 part-time/adjunct (0 women). *Students:* 44 full-time (17 women), 4 part-time (1 woman); includes 1 minority (African American), 36 international. Average age 31. 37 applicants, 32% accepted, 8 enrolled. In 2003, 1 master's, 1 doctorate awarded. Terminal master's awarded for partial completion of doctoral program. *Degree requirements:* For master's, comprehensive exam; for doctorate, thesis/dissertation, cumulative exams. *Entrance requirements:* For master's and doctorate, GRE Subject Test. Additional exam requirements/recommendations for international students: Required—TOEFL. Application fee: $40. *Expenses:* Tuition: Full-time $10,080; part-time $630 per credit. Tuition and fees vary according to program. *Financial support:* In 2003–04, 3 research assistantships, 27 teaching assistantships were awarded. Fellowships, Federal Work-Study, institutionally sponsored loans, scholarships/grants, and tuition waivers (full and partial) also available. Support available to part-time students. Financial award application deadline: 2/15. *Faculty research:* Inorganic complexes, laser Raman spectroscopy, organic synthesis, chemical dynamics, biophysiology. Total annual research expenditures: $586,915. *Unit head:* Dr. Charles Wilkie, Chairman, 414-288-7065, Fax: 414-288-7066. *Application contact:* Dr. Mark Steinmetz, Director of Graduate Studies, 414-288-7374, Fax: 414-288-7066.

Massachusetts Institute of Technology, School of Science, Department of Chemistry, Cambridge, MA 02139-4307. Offers biological chemistry (PhD, Sc D); inorganic chemistry (PhD, Sc D); organic chemistry (PhD, Sc D); physical chemistry (PhD, Sc D). *Faculty:* 31 full-time (6 women). *Students:* 253 full-time (85 women), 7 part-time (5 women); includes 34 minority (8 African Americans, 17 Asian Americans or Pacific Islanders, 9 Hispanic Americans), 81 international. Average age 26. 573 applicants, 25% accepted, 54 enrolled. In 2003, 28 doctorates awarded. *Degree requirements:* For doctorate, thesis/dissertation, comprehensive exam. *Entrance requirements:* For doctorate, GRE General Test. Additional exam requirements/recommendations for international students: Required—TOEFL (minimum score 577 paper-based; 233 computer-based). *Application deadline:* For fall admission, 12/15 for domestic students, 12/15 for international students. Application fee: $70. Electronic applications accepted. *Expenses:* Tuition: Full-time $29,400. Required fees: $200. *Financial support:* In 2003–04, 50 fellowships with tuition reimbursements, 167 research assistantships with tuition reimbursements (averaging $23,760 per year), 59 teaching assistantships with tuition reimbursements (averaging $18,270 per year) were awarded. Career-related internships or fieldwork, Federal Work-Study, institutionally sponsored loans, scholarships/grants, health care benefits, and unspecified assistantships also available. *Faculty research:* Synthetic organic chemistry, enzymatic reaction mechanisms, inorganic and organometallic spectroscopy, high resolution NMR spectroscopy. Total annual research expenditures: $20.7 million. *Unit head:* Prof. Stephen J. Lippard, Head, 617-253-1801, Fax: 617-258-0241. *Application contact:* Susan Brighton, Graduate Administrator, 617-253-1845, Fax: 617-258-0241, E-mail: brighton@mit.edu.

McMaster University, School of Graduate Studies, Faculty of Science, Department of Chemistry, Hamilton, ON L8S 4M2, Canada. Offers analytical chemistry (M Sc, PhD); chemical physics (M Sc, PhD); chemistry (M Sc, PhD); inorganic chemistry (M Sc, PhD); organic chemistry

Inorganic Chemistry

McMaster University (continued)
(M Sc, PhD); physical chemistry (M Sc, PhD); polymer chemistry (M Sc, PhD). Part-time programs available. Terminal master's awarded for partial completion of doctoral program. *Degree requirements:* For master's, thesis/dissertation; for doctorate, thesis/dissertation, comprehensive exam. *Entrance requirements:* For master's, minimum B+ average. Additional exam requirements/recommendations for international students: Required—TOEFL (minimum score 550 paper-based; 213 computer-based).

Miami University, Graduate School, College of Arts and Sciences, Department of Chemistry and Biochemistry, Oxford, OH 45056. Offers analytical chemistry (MS, PhD); biochemistry (MS, PhD); chemical education (MS, PhD); chemistry (MS, PhD); inorganic chemistry (MS, PhD); organic chemistry (MS, PhD); physical chemistry (MS, PhD). Part-time programs available. *Faculty:* 22 full-time (2 women). *Students:* 45 full-time (16 women), 1 part-time; includes 2 minority (both Asian Americans or Pacific Islanders), 21 international. 131 applicants, 98% accepted, 13 enrolled. In 2003, 4 master's, 4 doctorates awarded. *Degree requirements:* For master's, thesis, final exam; for doctorate, thesis/dissertation, final exams, comprehensive exam. *Entrance requirements:* For master's, minimum undergraduate GPA of 3.0 during previous 2 years or 2.75 overall; for doctorate, minimum undergraduate GPA of 2.75, 3.0 graduate. Additional exam requirements/recommendations for international students: Required—TOEFL, TWE. *Application deadline:* For fall admission, 3/1 priority date for domestic students, 3/1 priority date for international students. Applications are processed on a rolling basis. Application fee: $35. Electronic applications accepted. Tuition, area resident: Full-time $9,346. International tuition: $19,924 full-time. Full-time tuition and fees vary according to course level and campus/location. *Financial support:* In 2003–04, 22 fellowships with full tuition reimbursements (averaging $16,813 per year), 3 research assistantships with full tuition reimbursements (averaging $16,813 per year), 17 teaching assistantships with full tuition reimbursements (averaging $18,934 per year) were awarded. Federal Work-Study, tuition waivers (full), and unspecified assistantships also available. Financial award application deadline: 3/1. *Unit head:* Dr. Chris Makaroff, Chair, 513-529-2813. *Application contact:* Dr. Michael Crowder, Director of Graduate Studies, 513-529-2813, Fax: 513-529-5715, E-mail: chemistry@muohio.edu.

Northeastern University, College of Arts and Sciences, Department of Chemistry and Chemical Biology, Boston, MA 02115-5096. Offers analytical chemistry (PhD); chemistry (MS, PhD); inorganic chemistry (PhD); organic chemistry (PhD); physical chemistry (PhD). Part-time and evening/weekend programs available. *Faculty:* 17 full-time (2 women), 3 part-time/adjunct (0 women). *Students:* 46 full-time (23 women), 29 part-time (17 women). Average age 28. 113 applicants, 37% accepted. In 2003, 12 master's, 10 doctorates awarded. Terminal master's awarded for partial completion of doctoral program. *Degree requirements:* For master's, thesis (for some programs); for doctorate, thesis/dissertation, qualifying exam in specialty area. *Entrance requirements:* Additional exam requirements/recommendations for international students: Required—TOEFL. *Application deadline:* For fall admission, 4/15 for domestic students. Applications are processed on a rolling basis. Application fee: $50. Electronic applications accepted. *Expenses:* Tuition: Part-time $790 per credit hour. Tuition and fees vary according to course load and program. *Financial support:* In 2003–04, 27 research assistantships with tuition reimbursements (averaging $16,000 per year) were awarded; fellowships with tuition reimbursements, teaching assistantships with tuition reimbursements, career-related internships or fieldwork, tuition waivers (partial), and unspecified assistantships also available. Financial award application deadline: 4/15; financial award applicants required to submit FAFSA. *Faculty research:* Electron transfer, theoretical chemical physics, analytical biotechnology, mass spectrometry, materials chemistry. Total annual research expenditures: $250,000. *Unit head:* Dr. Graham Jones, Chairman, 617-373-2822, Fax: 617-373-8795, E-mail: chemistry-grad-info@neu.edu. *Application contact:* Dr. Pam Mabrouk, Chair, Graduate Admissions Committee, 617-373-2383, Fax: 617-373-8795, E-mail: chemistry-grad-info@neu.edu.

See in-depth description on page 133.

Oregon State University, Graduate School, College of Science, Department of Chemistry, Corvallis, OR 97331. Offers analytical chemistry (MS, PhD); chemistry (MA, MAIS); inorganic chemistry (MS, PhD); nuclear and radiation chemistry (MS, PhD); organic chemistry (MS, PhD); physical chemistry (MS, PhD). Part-time programs available. *Faculty:* 30 full-time (5 women). *Students:* 63 full-time (22 women), 1 part-time; includes 5 minority (3 Asian Americans or Pacific Islanders, 2 Hispanic Americans), 29 international. Average age 28. In 2003, 3 master's, 13 doctorates awarded. Terminal master's awarded for partial completion of doctoral program. *Degree requirements:* For master's and doctorate, one foreign language, thesis/dissertation. *Entrance requirements:* For master's and doctorate, minimum GPA of 3.0 in last 90 hours. Additional exam requirements/recommendations for international students: Required—TOEFL. *Application deadline:* For fall admission, 3/1 for domestic students. Applications are processed on a rolling basis. Application fee: $50. *Expenses:* Tuition, state resident: full-time $8,139; part-time $301 per credit. Tuition, nonresident: full-time $14,376; part-time $532 per credit. Required fees: $1,227. *Financial support:* Fellowships, research assistantships, teaching assistantships, institutionally sponsored loans available. Support available to part-time students. Financial award application deadline: 2/1. *Faculty research:* Solid state chemistry, enzyme reaction mechanisms, structure and dynamics of gas molecules, chemiluminescence, nonlinear optical spectroscopy. *Unit head:* Dr. John C. Westall, Chair, 541-737-2591, Fax: 541-737-2062, E-mail: john.westall@orst.edu. *Application contact:* Carolyn Brumley, Graduate Secretary, 541-737-6707, Fax: 541-737-2062, E-mail: carolyn.brumley@orst.edu.

Purdue University, Graduate School, School of Science, Department of Chemistry, West Lafayette, IN 47907. Offers analytical chemistry (MS, PhD); biochemistry (MS, PhD); chemical education (MS, PhD); inorganic chemistry (MS, PhD); organic chemistry (MS, PhD); physical chemistry (MS, PhD). *Accreditation:* NCATE (one or more programs are accredited). Terminal master's awarded for partial completion of doctoral program. *Degree requirements:* For master's and doctorate, thesis/dissertation. *Entrance requirements:* Additional exam requirements/recommendations for international students: Required—TOEFL. Electronic applications accepted.

Rensselaer Polytechnic Institute, Graduate School, School of Science, Department of Chemistry and Chemical Biology, Troy, NY 12180-3590. Offers analytical chemistry (MS, PhD); biochemistry (MS, PhD); inorganic chemistry (MS, PhD); organic chemistry (MS, PhD); physical chemistry (MS, PhD); polymer chemistry (MS, PhD). Part-time and evening/weekend programs available. *Faculty:* 20 full-time (4 women). *Students:* 58 full-time (25 women), 3 part-time (2 women); includes 40 minority (2 African Americans, 37 Asian Americans or Pacific Islanders, 1 Hispanic American), 36 international. Average age 24. 102 applicants, 29% accepted, 19 enrolled. In 2003, 9 master's, 9 doctorates awarded. Terminal master's awarded for partial completion of doctoral program. *Median time to degree:* Of those who began their doctoral program in fall 1995, 100% received their degree in 8 years or less. *Degree requirements:* For master's, thesis (for some programs), registration; for doctorate, thesis/dissertation, comprehensive exam, registration. *Entrance requirements:* For master's, GRE General Test, GRE Subject Test (strongly recommended); for doctorate, GRE General Test, GRE Subject Test (chemistry or biochemistry strongly recommended). Additional exam requirements/recommendations for international students: Required—TOEFL (minimum score 600 paper-based). *Application deadline:* For fall admission, 2/1 for domestic students; for spring admission, 11/15 for domestic students. Applications are processed on a rolling basis. Application fee: $45. Electronic applications accepted. *Expenses:* Tuition: Full-time $27,700; part-time $1,320 per credit. Required fees: $1,470. *Financial support:* In 2003–04, 59 students received support, including 1 fellowship with full tuition reimbursement available (averaging $25,000 per year), 25 research assistantships with full tuition reimbursements available (averaging $18,000 per year), 30 teaching assistantships with full tuition reimbursements available (averaging $18,000 per year); institutionally sponsored loans and tuition waivers (full and partial) also available. Financial award application deadline: 2/1. *Faculty research:* Synthetic polymer and biopolymer chemistry, physical chemistry of polymeric systems, bioanalytical chemistry, synthetic and computational drug design, protein folding and protein design. Total annual research expenditures: $1.9 million. *Unit head:* Dr. Ronald A. Bailey, Acting Chair, 518-276-4856, Fax: 518-276-4887, E-mail: bailer@rpi.edu. *Application contact:* Beth E. McGraw, Department Admissions Assistant, 518-276-6456, Fax: 518-276-4887, E-mail: mcgrae@rpi.edu.

Rice University, Graduate Programs, Wiess School of Natural Sciences, Department of Chemistry, Houston, TX 77251-1892. Offers chemistry (MA); inorganic chemistry (PhD); organic chemistry (PhD); physical chemistry (PhD). *Faculty:* 24 full-time (3 women), 5 part-time/adjunct (0 women). *Students:* 80 full-time (25 women); includes 8 minority (2 African Americans, 1 Asian American or Pacific Islander, 5 Hispanic Americans), 40 international. Average age 24. 259 applicants, 21% accepted, 25 enrolled. In 2003, 1 master's, 14 doctorates awarded. Terminal master's awarded for partial completion of doctoral program. *Median time to degree:* Of those who began their doctoral program in fall 1995, 100% received their degree in 8 years or less. *Degree requirements:* For master's and doctorate, thesis/dissertation. *Entrance requirements:* For master's and doctorate, GRE General Test, minimum GPA of 3.0. Additional exam requirements/recommendations for international students: Required—TOEFL. *Application deadline:* For fall admission, 2/1 for domestic students; for spring admission, 11/1 for domestic students. Applications are processed on a rolling basis. Application fee: $0 ($25 for international students). *Expenses:* Tuition: Full-time $19,700; part-time $1,096 per hour. *Financial support:* In 2003–04, 80 students received support, including 44 fellowships (averaging $19,700 per year), 23 research assistantships (averaging $19,700 per year); Federal Work-Study, scholarships/grants, and tuition waivers (full and partial) also available. *Faculty research:* Nanoscience, biomaterials, nanobioinformatics, fullerene pharmaceuticals. Total annual research expenditures: $75,000. *Unit head:* Kenton H. Whitmire, Chair, 713-348-5650, Fax: 713-348-5155, E-mail: whitmir@rice.edu. *Application contact:* Sofia Medrano, Graduate Recruiting/Administrative Secretary, 713-348-4082, Fax: 713-348-5155, E-mail: gradchem@rice.edu.

Rutgers, The State University of New Jersey, Newark, Graduate School, Program in Chemistry, Newark, NJ 07102. Offers analytical chemistry (MS, PhD); biochemistry (MS, PhD); inorganic chemistry (MS, PhD); organic chemistry (MS, PhD); physical chemistry (MS, PhD). Part-time and evening/weekend programs available. *Faculty:* 22 full-time (5 women). *Students:* 19 full-time (9 women), 35 part-time (12 women); includes 28 minority (3 African Americans, 25 Asian Americans or Pacific Islanders). 107 applicants, 31% accepted, 8 enrolled. In 2003, 4 master's, 6 doctorates awarded. Terminal master's awarded for partial completion of doctoral program. *Degree requirements:* For master's, cumulative exams, thesis optional; for doctorate, thesis/dissertation, exams, research proposal. *Entrance requirements:* For master's and doctorate, GRE General Test, minimum undergraduate B average. Additional exam requirements/recommendations for international students: Required—TOEFL. *Application deadline:* For fall admission, 7/1 for domestic students; for spring admission, 12/1 for domestic students. Applications are processed on a rolling basis. Application fee: $50. Electronic applications accepted. *Expenses:* Tuition, state resident: full-time $10,030. Tuition, nonresident: full-time $14,202. *Financial support:* In 2003–04, 35 students received support, including 6 fellowships with full tuition reimbursements available, 20 teaching assistantships with full tuition reimbursements available (averaging $14,300 per year); Federal Work-Study and institutionally sponsored loans also available. Financial award application deadline: 3/1. *Faculty research:* Medicinal chemistry, natural products, isotope effects, biophysics and biorganic approaches to enzyme mechanisms, organic and organometallic synthesis. *Unit head:* Prof. W. Philip Huskey, Chairman and Program Director, 973-353-5741, Fax: 973-353-1264, E-mail: huskey@andromeda.rutgers.edu.

Rutgers, The State University of New Jersey, New Brunswick/Piscataway, Graduate School, Program in Chemistry and Chemical Biology, New Brunswick, NJ 08901-1281. Offers analytical chemistry (MS, PhD); biological chemistry (PhD); chemistry education (MST); inorganic chemistry (MS, PhD); organic chemistry (MS, PhD); physical chemistry (MS, PhD). Part-time and evening/weekend programs available. Terminal master's awarded for partial completion of doctoral program. *Degree requirements:* For master's, thesis or alternative, exam, comprehensive exam, registration; for doctorate, thesis/dissertation, cumulative exams, 1 year residency, comprehensive exam, registration. *Entrance requirements:* For master's and doctorate, GRE General Test, GRE Subject Test. Additional exam requirements/recommendations for international students: Required—TOEFL. Electronic applications accepted. *Expenses:* Tuition, state resident: full-time $10,030. Tuition, nonresident: full-time $14,202. *Faculty research:* Biophysical organic/bioorganic, inorganic/bioinorganic, theoretical, and solid-state/surface chemistry.

See in-depth description on page 141.

Seton Hall University, College of Arts and Sciences, Department of Chemistry and Biochemistry, South Orange, NJ 07079-2694. Offers analytical chemistry (MS, PhD); biochemistry (MS, PhD); chemistry (MS); inorganic chemistry (MS, PhD); organic chemistry (MS, PhD); physical chemistry (MS, PhD). Part-time and evening/weekend programs available. Terminal master's awarded for partial completion of doctoral program. *Degree requirements:* For master's, formal seminar, thesis optional; for doctorate, thesis/dissertation, annual seminars, comprehensive exam. *Entrance requirements:* For master's, undergraduate major in chemistry or related field with minimum 30 credits in chemistry, including 2 semesters of physical chemistry; for doctorate, oral matriculation exam based on proposed doctoral research, minimum GPA of 3.0 in course distribution requirements, formal seminar. Additional exam requirements/recommendations for international students: Required—TOEFL. *Faculty research:* DNA metal reactions; chromatography; bioinorganic, biophysical, organometallic, polymer chemistry; heterogeneous catalyst.

South Dakota State University, Graduate School, College of Arts and Science and College of Agriculture and Biological Sciences, Department of Chemistry, Brookings, SD 57007. Offers analytical chemistry (MS, PhD); biochemistry (MS, PhD); chemistry (MS, PhD); inorganic chemistry (MS, PhD); organic chemistry (MS, PhD); physical chemistry (MS, PhD). *Degree requirements:* For master's, thesis, oral exam; for doctorate, thesis/dissertation, preliminary oral and written exams, research tool. *Entrance requirements:* For master's, bachelor's degree in chemistry or equivalent. Additional exam requirements/recommendations for international students: Required—TOEFL. *Faculty research:* Environmental chemistry, computational chemistry, organic synthesis and photochemistry, novel material development and characterization.

Southern University and Agricultural and Mechanical College, Graduate School, College of Sciences, Department of Chemistry, Baton Rouge, LA 70813. Offers analytical chemistry (MS); biochemistry (MS); environmental sciences (MS); inorganic chemistry (MS); organic chemistry (MS); physical chemistry (MS). *Degree requirements:* For master's, thesis. *Entrance requirements:* For master's, GMAT or GRE General Test. Additional exam requirements/recommendations for international students: Required—TOEFL. *Faculty research:* Synthesis of macrocyclic ligands, latex accelerators, anticancer drugs, biosensors, absorption isotheums, isolation of specific enzymes from plants.

State University of New York at Binghamton, Graduate School, School of Arts and Sciences, Department of Chemistry, Binghamton, NY 13902-6000. Offers analytical chemistry (PhD); chemistry (MA, MS); inorganic chemistry (PhD); organic chemistry (PhD); physical chemistry (PhD). Part-time programs available. Terminal master's awarded for partial completion of doctoral program. *Degree requirements:* For master's, thesis or alternative, oral exam, seminar presentation; for doctorate, thesis/dissertation, cumulative exams. *Entrance requirements:* For master's and doctorate, GRE General Test, GRE Subject Test. Additional exam requirements/recommendations for international students: Required—TOEFL. Electronic applications accepted.

Tufts University, Graduate School of Arts and Sciences, Department of Chemistry, Medford, MA 02155. Offers analytical chemistry (MS, PhD); bioorganic chemistry (MS, PhD); environmental chemistry (MS, PhD); inorganic chemistry (MS, PhD); organic chemistry (MS, PhD); physical chemistry (MS, PhD). *Faculty:* 13 full-time, 1 part-time/adjunct. *Students:* 56 (24 women); includes 6 minority (1 African American, 4 Asian Americans or Pacific Islanders, 1 Hispanic American) 22 international. 66 applicants, 56% accepted, 17 enrolled. In 2003, 4 master's, 6 doctorates awarded. Terminal master's awarded for partial completion of doctoral program. *Degree requirements:* For master's and doctorate, thesis/dissertation. *Entrance requirements:*

For master's and doctorate, GRE General Test, GRE Subject Test. Additional exam requirements/ recommendations for international students: Required—TOEFL (minimum score 600 paper-based; 213 computer-based), TSE. *Application deadline:* For fall admission, 2/1 for domestic students, 12/30 for international students; for spring admission, 10/15 for domestic students, 9/15 for international students. Applications are processed on a rolling basis. Application fee: $60. Electronic applications accepted. *Expenses:* Tuition: Full-time $29,949. *Financial support:* Research assistantships with full and partial tuition reimbursements, teaching assistantships with full and partial tuition reimbursements, Federal Work-Study, scholarships/grants, and tuition waivers (partial) available. Financial award application deadline: 2/1; financial award applicants required to submit FAFSA. *Unit head:* Mary Jane Shultz, Chair, 617-627-3477, Fax: 617-627-3443. *Application contact:* Arthur Utz, Information Contact, 617-627-3441, Fax: 617-627-3443.

See in-depth description on page 153.

University of Calgary, Faculty of Graduate Studies, Faculty of Science, Department of Chemistry, Calgary, AB T2N 1N4, Canada. Offers analytical chemistry (M Sc, PhD); applied chemistry (M Sc, PhD); inorganic chemistry (M Sc, PhD); organic chemistry (M Sc, PhD); physical chemistry (M Sc, PhD); polymer chemistry (M Sc, PhD); theoretical chemistry (M Sc, PhD). *Faculty:* 29 full-time (6 women), 1 part-time/adjunct (0 women). *Students:* 74 full-time (29 women). Average age 25. 130 applicants, 20% accepted. In 2003, 12 master's, 6 doctorates awarded. *Degree requirements:* For master's, thesis; for doctorate, thesis/dissertation, candidacy exam. *Entrance requirements:* For master's, minimum GPA of 3.0; for doctorate, honors degree minimum GPA of 3.7, minimum GPA of 3.3. Additional exam requirements/ recommendations for international students: Required—TOEFL (minimum score 580 paper-based; 237 computer-based). *Application deadline:* For fall admission, 12/1 for domestic students. Applications are processed on a rolling basis. Application fee: $60. Electronic applications accepted. Tuition, nonresident: full-time $4,765. Tuition and fees vary according to degree level, program and student level. *Financial support:* In 2003–04, research assistantships (averaging $11,000 per year), teaching assistantships (averaging $6,221 per year) were awarded. Fellowships, scholarships/grants also available. Financial award application deadline: 12/1. *Faculty research:* Chemical analysis, chemical dynamics, synthesis theory, polymer, applied chemistry. *Unit head:* Dr. Brian Keay, Head, 403-220-6252, E-mail: gradinfo@chem.ucalgary.ca.

University of Cincinnati, Division of Research and Advanced Studies, McMicken College of Arts and Sciences, Department of Chemistry, Cincinnati, OH 45221. Offers analytical chemistry (MS, PhD); biochemistry (MS, PhD); inorganic chemistry (MS, PhD); organic chemistry (MS, PhD); physical chemistry (MS, PhD); polymer chemistry (MS, PhD); sensors (PhD). Part-time and evening/weekend programs available. Terminal master's awarded for partial completion of doctoral program. *Degree requirements:* For master's, thesis optional; for doctorate, thesis/ dissertation, comprehensive exam, registration. *Entrance requirements:* For master's and doctorate, GRE General Test. Additional exam requirements/recommendations for international students: Required—TOEFL (minimum score 580 paper-based; 237 computer-based); Recommended—TSE(minimum score 50). Electronic applications accepted. *Faculty research:* Biomedical chemistry, laser chemistry, surface science, chemical sensors, synthesis.

University of Georgia, Graduate School, College of Arts and Sciences, Department of Chemistry, Athens, GA 30602. Offers analytical chemistry (MS, PhD); inorganic chemistry (MS, PhD); organic chemistry (MS, PhD); physical chemistry (MS, PhD). *Faculty:* 26 full-time (2 women). *Students:* 130 full-time (43 women). 160 applicants, 29% accepted, 36 enrolled. In 2003, 3 master's, 17 doctorates awarded. Terminal master's awarded for partial completion of doctoral program. *Median time to degree:* Of those who began their doctoral program in fall 1995, 100% received their degree in 8 years or less. *Degree requirements:* For master's, thesis; for doctorate, one foreign language, thesis/dissertation. *Entrance requirements:* For master's and doctorate, GRE General Test. Additional exam requirements/recommendations for international students: Required—TOEFL (minimum score 213 computer-based), TSE(minimum score 50). *Application deadline:* For fall admission, 7/1 for domestic students; for spring admission, 11/15 for domestic students. Application fee: $50. Electronic applications accepted. *Expenses:* Tuition, state resident: part-time $161 per hour. Tuition, nonresident: part-time $690 per hour. One-time fee: $435 part-time. *Financial support:* Fellowships, research assistantships, teaching assistantships, unspecified assistantships available. *Unit head:* Dr. John L. Stickney, Head, 706-542-2726, Fax: 706-542-9454, E-mail: stickney@chem.uga.edu. *Application contact:* Dr. Donald Kurtz, Information Contact, 706-542-2010, Fax: 706-542-9454, E-mail: kurtz@chem.uga.edu.

University of Louisville, Graduate School, College of Arts and Sciences, Department of Chemistry, Louisville, KY 40292-0001. Offers analytical chemistry (MS, PhD); biochemistry (MS, PhD); chemical physics (PhD); inorganic chemistry (MS, PhD); organic chemistry (MS, PhD); physical chemistry (MS, PhD). *Students:* 48 full-time (19 women), 13 part-time (5 women); includes 4 minority (1 African American, 1 Asian American or Pacific Islander, 2 Hispanic Americans), 27 international. Average age 27. In 2003, 7 master's, 1 doctorate awarded. *Degree requirements:* For master's, thesis/dissertation; for doctorate, thesis/ dissertation, comprehensive exam. *Entrance requirements:* For master's and doctorate, GRE General Test. Additional exam requirements/recommendations for international students: Required—TOEFL. *Application deadline:* Applications are processed on a rolling basis. Application fee: $50. *Expenses:* Tuition, state resident: full-time $4,842. Tuition, nonresident: full-time $13,338. *Financial support:* In 2003–04, 30 teaching assistantships (averaging $14,000 per year) were awarded. *Unit head:* Dr. George R. Pack, Chair, 502-852-6798, Fax: 502-852-8149, E-mail: george.pack@louisville.edu.

University of Maryland, College Park, Graduate Studies and Research, College of Life Sciences, Department of Chemistry and Biochemistry, Chemistry Program, College Park, MD 20742. Offers analytical chemistry (MS, PhD); inorganic chemistry (MS, PhD); organic chemistry (MS, PhD); physical chemistry (MS, PhD). Part-time and evening/weekend programs available. *Students:* 89 full-time (46 women), 4 part-time (2 women); includes 6 minority (2 African Americans, 2 Asian Americans or Pacific Islanders, 2 Hispanic Americans), 39 international. 141 applicants, 19% accepted. In 2003, 16 degrees awarded. Terminal master's awarded for partial completion of doctoral program. *Median time to degree:* Of those who began their doctoral program in fall 1995, 33% received their degree in 8 years or less. *Degree requirements:* For master's, thesis optional; for doctorate, thesis/dissertation, 2 seminar presentations, oral exam. *Entrance requirements:* For master's, GRE General Test, GRE Subject Test (recommended), minimum GPA of 3.1, 3 letters of recommendation; for doctorate, GRE General Test, GRE Subject Test (recommended), minimum GPA of 3.1. *Application deadline:* For fall admission, 5/1 for domestic students, 2/1 for international students; for spring admission, 10/1 for domestic students, 6/1 for international students. Applications are processed on a rolling basis. Application fee: $50. Electronic applications accepted. *Expenses:* Tuition, state resident: part-time $349 per credit hour. Tuition, nonresident: part-time $602 per credit hour. *Financial support:* Fellowships, research assistantships, teaching assistantships with partial tuition reimbursements available. Financial award applicants required to submit FAFSA. *Faculty research:* Environmental chemistry, nuclear chemistry, lunar and environmental analysis, x-ray crystallography. *Application contact:* Trudy Lindsey, Director, Graduate Enrollment Management Services, 301-405-4190, Fax: 301-314-9305, E-mail: tlindsey@gradschool.umd.edu.

University of Miami, Graduate School, College of Arts and Sciences, Department of Chemistry, Coral Gables, FL 33124. Offers chemistry (MS); inorganic chemistry (PhD); organic chemistry (PhD); physical chemistry (PhD). *Faculty:* 9 full-time (1 woman). *Students:* 39 full-time (17 women); includes 23 minority (4 African Americans, 15 Asian Americans or Pacific Islanders, 4 Hispanic Americans), 25 international. Average age 25. 104 applicants, 13% accepted, 10 enrolled. In 2003, 2 master's, 1 doctorate awarded. Terminal master's awarded for partial completion of doctoral program. *Degree requirements:* For master's, comprehensive exam; for doctorate, thesis/dissertation, comprehensive exam. *Entrance requirements:* For master's and doctorate, GRE General Test. Additional exam requirements/recommendations for international students: Required—TOEFL (minimum score 550 paper-based; 213 computer-based). *Application deadline:* For fall admission, 1/15 for domestic students, 1/15 for international students. Applications are processed on a rolling basis. Application fee: $50. Electronic applications accepted. *Expenses:* Tuition: Full-time $19,526. *Financial support:* In 2003–04, 39 students received support, including 3 fellowships with full tuition reimbursements available (averaging $20,000 per year), 14 research assistantships with full tuition reimbursements available (averaging $19,000 per year), 21 teaching assistantships with full tuition reimbursements available (averaging $19,000 per year); tuition waivers (full) also available. Financial award application deadline: 5/1; financial award applicants required to submit FAFSA. *Faculty research:* Supramolecular chemistry, electrochemistry, surface chemistry, catalysis, organometalic. *Unit head:* Dr. Cecil M. Criss, Chairman, 305-284-2282, Fax: 305-284-4571. *Application contact:* Eva Johnson, Graduate Secretary, 305-284-6561, Fax: 305-284-4571, E-mail: evaj@miami.edu.

University of Michigan, Horace H. Rackham School of Graduate Studies, College of Literature, Science, and the Arts, Department of Chemistry, Ann Arbor, MI 48109. Offers analytical chemistry (PhD); chemical biology (PhD); inorganic chemistry (PhD); material chemistry (PhD); organic chemistry (PhD); physical chemistry (PhD). *Faculty:* 50 full-time (10 women), 3 part-time/adjunct (0 women). *Students:* 213 full-time (101 women); includes 20 minority (5 African Americans, 1 American Indian/Alaska Native, 9 Asian Americans or Pacific Islanders, 5 Hispanic Americans), 64 international. Average age 26. 310 applicants, 56% accepted, 58 enrolled. In 2003, 27 degrees awarded. *Degree requirements:* For doctorate, thesis/dissertation, oral defense of dissertation, organic cumulative proficiency exams. *Entrance requirements:* For doctorate, GRE General Test, GRE Subject Test (recommended), statement of prior research. Additional exam requirements/recommendations for international students: Required—TOEFL. *Application deadline:* For fall admission, 1/15 priority date for domestic students, 1/15 priority date for international students. Applications are processed on a rolling basis. Application fee: $60 ($75 for international students). Electronic applications accepted. *Expenses:* Tuition, state resident: full-time $7,463. Tuition, nonresident: full-time $13,913. Full-time tuition and fees vary according to course load, degree level and program. *Financial support:* In 2003–04, 10 fellowships with full tuition reimbursements (averaging $20,000 per year), 70 research assistantships with full tuition reimbursements (averaging $19,000 per year), 120 teaching assistantships with full tuition reimbursements (averaging $20,000 per year) were awarded. Financial award applicants required to submit FAFSA. *Faculty research:* Biological catalysis, protein engineering, chemical sensors, de novo metalloprotein design, supramolecular architecture. Total annual research expenditures: $8 million. *Unit head:* Dr. William R. Roush, Chair, 734-763-9681, Fax: 734-647-4847, E-mail: roush@umich.edu. *Application contact:* Linda Deitert, Assistant Director Graduate Studies, 734-764-7278, Fax: 734-647-4865, E-mail: chemadmissions@umich.edu.

University of Missouri–Columbia, Graduate School, College of Arts and Sciences, Department of Chemistry, Columbia, MO 65211. Offers analytical chemistry (MS, PhD); inorganic chemistry (MS, PhD); organic chemistry (MS, PhD); physical chemistry (MS, PhD). *Faculty:* 20 full-time (4 women). *Students:* 58 full-time (21 women), 36 part-time (7 women); includes 5 minority (1 African American, 1 American Indian/Alaska Native, 3 Asian Americans or Pacific Islanders), 51 international. In 2003, 7 master's, 7 doctorates awarded. *Degree requirements:* For master's, thesis; for doctorate, one foreign language, thesis/dissertation. *Entrance requirements:* For master's and doctorate, GRE General Test, minimum GPA of 3.0. *Application deadline:* For fall admission, 4/1 for domestic students; for winter admission, 11/1 for domestic students. Applications are processed on a rolling basis. Application fee: $45 ($60 for international students). *Expenses:* Tuition, state resident: full-time $5,205. Tuition, nonresident: full-time $14,058. *Financial support:* Research assistantships, teaching assistantships, institutionally sponsored loans available. *Unit head:* Dr. Silvia S. Jurisson, Director of Graduate Studies, 573-882-2107, E-mail: jurissons@missouri.edu.

University of Missouri–Kansas City, College of Arts and Sciences, Department of Chemistry, Kansas City, MO 64110-2499. Offers analytical chemistry (MS, PhD); inorganic chemistry (MS, PhD); organic chemistry (MS, PhD); physical chemistry (MS, PhD); polymer chemistry (MS, PhD). PhD offered through the School of Graduate Studies. Part-time and evening/weekend programs available. *Faculty:* 11 full-time (1 woman), 1 part-time/adjunct (0 women). *Students:* Average age 30. 56 applicants, 46% accepted. In 2003, 1 master's awarded. *Median time to degree:* Master's–1 year full-time, 1 year part-time; doctorate–5 years full-time. *Degree requirements:* For master's, thesis (for some programs); for doctorate, thesis/dissertation. *Entrance requirements:* For master's, equivalent of American Chemical Society approved bachelor's degree in chemistry; for doctorate, GRE General Test, equivalent of American Chemical Society approved bachelor's degree in chemistry. Additional exam requirements/ recommendations for international students: Required—TOEFL (minimum score 580 paper-based; 237 computer-based), TWE. *Application deadline:* For fall and spring admission, 4/15; for winter admission, 10/15 for domestic students. Applications are processed on a rolling basis. Application fee: $25. *Financial support:* In 2003–04, 1 fellowship with partial tuition reimbursement (averaging $18,156 per year), 9 research assistantships with partial tuition reimbursements (averaging $17,632 per year), 16 teaching assistantships with partial tuition reimbursements (averaging $16,416 per year) were awarded. Federal Work-Study, institutionally sponsored loans, and scholarships/grants also available. Support available to part-time students. Financial award application deadline: 2/15. *Faculty research:* Molecular spectroscopy, characterization and synthesis of materials and compounds, computational chemistry, natural products, drug delivery systems and anti-tumor agents. Total annual research expenditures: $551,743. *Unit head:* Dr. Jerry Jean, Chairperson, 816-235-2280, Fax: 816-235-5502, E-mail: jeany@umkc.edu. *Application contact:* Dr. Kathleen Y. Kilway, Graduate Recruiting Committee, 816-235-2289, Fax: 816-235-5502, E-mail: kilwayk@umkc.edu.

University of Missouri–St. Louis, Graduate School, College of Arts and Sciences, Department of Chemistry, St. Louis, MO 63121-4499. Offers chemistry (MS, PhD), including biochemistry, inorganic chemistry, organic chemistry, physical chemistry. Part-time and evening/weekend programs available. *Faculty:* 16 full-time (3 women). *Students:* 31 full-time (19 women), 20 part-time (9 women); includes 6 minority (5 Asian Americans or Pacific Islanders, 1 Hispanic American), 21 international. In 2003, 8 master's, 5 doctorates awarded. Terminal master's awarded for partial completion of doctoral program. *Degree requirements:* For master's, thesis optional; for doctorate, thesis/dissertation. *Entrance requirements:* For doctorate, GRE General Test, GRE Subject Test. Additional exam requirements/recommendations for international students: Required—TOEFL (minimum score 550 paper-based; 213 computer-based). *Application deadline:* For fall admission, 7/1 for domestic students; for spring admission, 12/7 priority date for domestic students. Applications are processed on a rolling basis. Application fee: $35 ($40 for international students). Electronic applications accepted. *Expenses:* Tuition, state resident: part-time $237 per credit hour. Tuition, nonresident: part-time $639 per credit hour. Required fees: $10 per credit hour. *Financial support:* In 2003–04, 14 research assistantships with full and partial tuition reimbursements (averaging $16,007 per year), 13 teaching assistantships with full and partial tuition reimbursements (averaging $15,408 per year) were awarded. Fellowships with full and partial tuition reimbursements *Faculty research:* Metallaborane chemistry, serum transferrin chemistry, natural products chemistry, organic synthesis. *Unit head:* Dr. F. Christopher Pigge, Director of Graduate Studies, 314-516-5311, Fax: 314-516-5342. *Application contact:* 314-516-5458, Fax: 314-516-5310, E-mail: gradadm@umsl.edu.

The University of Montana–Missoula, Graduate School, College of Arts and Sciences, Department of Chemistry, Missoula, MT 59812-0002. Offers chemistry (MS, PhD), including environmental/analytical chemistry, inorganic chemistry, organic chemistry, physical chemistry; chemistry teaching (MST). *Faculty:* 16 full-time (2 women). *Students:* 26 full-time (5 women), 12 part-time (6 women), 10 international. 25 applicants, 44% accepted, 6 enrolled. In 2003, 2 master's, 4 doctorates awarded. Terminal master's awarded for partial completion of doctoral program. *Degree requirements:* For master's, thesis (for some programs); for doctorate, thesis/dissertation. *Entrance requirements:* For master's and doctorate, GRE General Test. Additional exam requirements/recommendations for international students: Required—TOEFL (minimum score 575 paper-based; 230 computer-based). *Application deadline:* For fall

Inorganic Chemistry

The University of Montana–Missoula (continued)
admission, 2/15 for domestic students. Applications are processed on a rolling basis. Application fee: $45. *Expenses:* Tuition, state resident: full-time $1,848; part-time $221 per credit. Tuition, nonresident: full-time $4,880; part-time $333 per credit. Required fees: $2,200. *Financial support:* In 2003–04, 13 research assistantships with tuition reimbursements (averaging $14,000 per year), 12 teaching assistantships with full tuition reimbursements (averaging $14,000 per year) were awarded. Federal Work-Study, scholarships/grants, and unspecified assistantships also available. Financial award application deadline: 3/1; financial award applicants required to submit FAFSA. *Faculty research:* Reaction mechanisms and kinetics, inorganic and organic synthesis, analytical chemistry, natural products. Total annual research expenditures: $789,952. *Unit head:* Dr. Edward Rosenberg, Chair, 406-243-4022, Fax: 406-243-4227.

University of Nebraska–Lincoln, Graduate College, College of Arts and Sciences, Department of Chemistry, Lincoln, NE 68588. Offers analytical chemistry (PhD); chemistry (MS); inorganic chemistry (PhD); organic chemistry (PhD); physical chemistry (PhD). *Degree requirements:* For master's, one foreign language, departmental qualifying exam, thesis optional; for doctorate, one foreign language, thesis/dissertation, departmental qualifying exams, comprehensive exam. *Entrance requirements:* For master's and doctorate, GRE. Additional exam requirements/recommendations for international students: Required—TOEFL (minimum score 550 paper-based; 213 computer-based). Electronic applications accepted. *Faculty research:* Bioorganic and bioinorganic chemistry, biophysical and bioanalytical chemistry, structure-function of DNA and proteins, organometallics, mass spectrometry.

University of Notre Dame, Graduate School, College of Science, Department of Chemistry and Biochemistry, Notre Dame, IN 46556. Offers biochemistry (MS, PhD); inorganic chemistry (MS, PhD); organic chemistry (MS, PhD); physical chemistry (MS, PhD). *Faculty:* 30 full-time (3 women). *Students:* 139 full-time (46 women); includes 5 minority (1 African American, 1 American Indian/Alaska Native, 1 Asian American or Pacific Islander, 2 Hispanic Americans), 65 international. 270 applicants, 38% accepted, 44 enrolled. In 2003, 5 master's, 17 doctorates awarded. Terminal master's awarded for partial completion of doctoral program. *Degree requirements:* For master's, thesis, comprehensive exam; for doctorate, thesis/dissertation, qualifying exam. *Entrance requirements:* For master's and doctorate, GRE General Test, GRE Subject Test (strongly recommended). Additional exam requirements/recommendations for international students: Required—TOEFL. *Application deadline:* For fall admission, 2/1 for domestic students. Applications are processed on a rolling basis. Application fee: $50. Electronic applications accepted. *Expenses:* Tuition: Full-time $29,375. *Financial support:* In 2003–04, 139 students received support, including 34 fellowships with full tuition reimbursements available (averaging $20,000 per year), 46 research assistantships with full tuition reimbursements available (averaging $15,500 per year), 51 teaching assistantships with full tuition reimbursements available (averaging $15,500 per year); tuition waivers (full) also available. Financial award application deadline: 2/1. *Faculty research:* Reaction design and mechaninistic studies; reactive intermediates; synthesis, structure and reactivity of organometallic. cluster complexes, and biologically active natural products; bioorganic chemistry; enzymology. Total annual research expenditures: $9.4 million. *Unit head:* Dr. Richard E. Taylor, Director of Graduate Studies, 574-631-7058, Fax: 574-631-6652, E-mail: taylor.61@nd.edu. *Application contact:* Dr. Terrence J. Akai, Director of Graduate Admissions, 574-631-7706, Fax: 574-631-4183, E-mail: gradad@nd.edu.

University of Regina, Faculty of Graduate Studies and Research, Faculty of Science, Department of Chemistry and Biochemistry, Regina, SK S4S 0A2, Canada. Offers analytical chemistry (M Sc, PhD); biochemistry (M Sc, PhD); inorganic chemistry (M Sc, PhD); organic chemistry (M Sc, PhD); physical chemistry (M Sc, PhD). Part-time programs available. *Faculty:* 9 full-time (2 women), 2 part-time/adjunct (1 woman). *Students:* 7 full-time (4 women), 4 part-time (1 woman). 12 applicants. In 2003, 3 degrees awarded. *Degree requirements:* For master's and doctorate, thesis/dissertation, departmental qualifying exam. *Entrance requirements:* For master's and doctorate, GRE. Additional exam requirements/recommendations for international students: Required—TOEFL. *Application deadline:* For fall admission, 1/1 for domestic students; for winter admission, 7/1 for domestic students. Applications are processed on a rolling basis. Application fee: $60. *Expenses:* Tuition, state resident: part-time $130 per credit hour. Tuition and fees vary according to course load and program. *Financial support:* In 2003–04, 4 fellowships, 1 research assistantship, 3 teaching assistantships were awarded. Scholarships/grants also available. Financial award application deadline: 6/15. *Faculty research:* Organic synthesis, organic oxidations, ionic liquids theoretical/computational chemistry, protein biochemistry/biophysics, environmental analytical, photophysical/photochemistry. *Unit head:* Dr. Andrew G. Wee, Head, 306-585-4767, Fax: 306-585-4894, E-mail: chem.chair@uregina.ca. *Application contact:* Teri Dibble, Office Administrator, 306-585-4146, Fax: 306-585-4894, E-mail: teri.dibble@uregina.ca.

University of Southern Mississippi, Graduate School, College of Science and Technology, Department of Chemistry and Biochemistry, Hattiesburg, MS 39406-0001. Offers analytical chemistry (MS, PhD); biochemistry (MS, PhD); inorganic chemistry (MS, PhD); organic chemistry (MS, PhD); physical chemistry (MS, PhD). *Faculty:* 8 full-time (1 woman). *Students:* 27 full-time (17 women), 1 part-time; includes 14 minority (4 African Americans, 1 American Indian/Alaska Native, 9 Asian Americans or Pacific Islanders). Average age 27. 29 applicants, 45% accepted, 10 enrolled. In 2003, 1 master's, 7 doctorates awarded. *Degree requirements:* For master's and doctorate, thesis/dissertation, comprehensive exam. *Entrance requirements:* For master's, GRE General Test, minimum GPA of 2.75 in last 60 hours; for doctorate, GRE General Test, minimum GPA of 3.5. Additional exam requirements/recommendations for international students: Required—TOEFL. *Application deadline:* For fall admission, 8/6 for domestic students. Applications are processed on a rolling basis. Application fee: $25. *Expenses:* Tuition, state resident: part-time $1,967 per semester. Tuition, nonresident: part-time $4,376 per semester. *Financial support:* Fellowships, research assistantships with full tuition reimbursements, teaching assistantships with full tuition reimbursements, Federal Work-Study and institutionally sponsored loans available. Support available to part-time students. Financial award application deadline: 3/15. *Faculty research:* Plant biochemistry, photo chemistry, polymer chemistry, x-ray analysis, enzyme chemistry. *Unit head:* Dr. Robert Bateman, Chair, 601-266-4701. *Application contact:* Dr. Gordon Cannon, Information Contact, 601-266-4702.

University of South Florida, College of Graduate Studies, College of Arts and Sciences, Department of Chemistry, Tampa, FL 33620-9951. Offers analytical chemistry (MS, PhD); biochemistry (MS, PhD); inorganic chemistry (MS, PhD); organic chemistry (MS, PhD); physical chemistry (MS, PhD); polymer chemistry (PhD). Part-time programs available. *Faculty:* 26 full-time (8 women), 1 (woman) part-time/adjunct. *Students:* 75 full-time (34 women), 11 part-time (4 women); includes 14 minority (3 African Americans, 3 Asian Americans or Pacific Islanders, 8 Hispanic Americans), 30 international. 75 applicants, 37% accepted, 17 enrolled. In 2003, 3 master's, 6 doctorates awarded. Terminal master's awarded for partial completion of doctoral program. *Degree requirements:* For master's, thesis; for doctorate, 2 foreign languages, thesis/dissertation, colloquium. *Entrance requirements:* For master's and doctorate, GRE General Test, minimum GPA of 3.0 in last 30 hours of chemistry course work, letters of recommendation (3). Additional exam requirements/recommendations for international students: Required—TOEFL (minimum score 550 paper-based; 213 computer-based), TSE(minimum score 50). *Application deadline:* For fall admission, 5/1 priority date for domestic students, 3/1 priority date for international students; for spring admission, 10/1 priority date for domestic students, 8/1 priority date for international students. Applications are processed on a rolling basis. Application fee: $30. Electronic applications accepted. *Financial support:* In 2003–04, 74 students received support, including 3 fellowships with partial tuition reimbursements available (averaging $18,500 per year), 13 research assistantships with partial tuition reimbursements available (averaging $18,500 per year), 58 teaching assistantships with partial tuition reimbursements available (averaging $18,500 per year); career-related internships or fieldwork, institutionally sponsored loans, scholarships/grants, and unspecified assistantships also available. Financial award application deadline: 6/30. *Faculty research:* Synthesis, bio-organic chemistry, bioinorganic chemistry, environmental chemistry, NMR. Total annual research expenditures: $1.6 million. *Unit head:* Michael Zaworotko, Chairperson, 813-974-4129, Fax: 813-974-1731. *Application contact:* Dr. Julie Harmon, Graduate Director, 813-974-3397, Fax: 813-974-3203, E-mail: harmon@chuma1.cas.usf.edu.

The University of Tennessee, Graduate School, College of Arts and Sciences, Department of Chemistry, Knoxville, TN 37996. Offers analytical chemistry (MS, PhD); chemical physics (PhD); environmental chemistry (MS, PhD); inorganic chemistry (MS, PhD); organic chemistry (MS, PhD); physical chemistry (MS, PhD); polymer chemistry (MS, PhD); theoretical chemistry (PhD). Part-time programs available. Terminal master's awarded for partial completion of doctoral program. *Degree requirements:* For master's and doctorate, thesis/dissertation. *Entrance requirements:* For master's and doctorate, GRE General Test, minimum GPA of 2.7. Additional exam requirements/recommendations for international students: Required—TOEFL. Electronic applications accepted.

The University of Texas at Austin, Graduate School, College of Natural Sciences, Department of Chemistry and Biochemistry, Austin, TX 78712-1111. Offers analytical chemistry (MA, PhD); biochemistry (MA, PhD); inorganic chemistry (MA, PhD); organic chemistry (MA, PhD); physical chemistry (MA, PhD). *Entrance requirements:* For master's and doctorate, GRE General Test.

University of Toledo, Graduate School, College of Arts and Sciences, Department of Chemistry, Toledo, OH 43606-3390. Offers analytical chemistry (MS, PhD); biological chemistry (MS, PhD); inorganic chemistry (MS, PhD); organic chemistry (MS, PhD); physical chemistry (MS, PhD). Part-time programs available. *Students:* 46 full-time (21 women), 9 part-time (4 women); includes 4 minority (3 African Americans, 1 Hispanic American), 31 international. Average age 27. 23 applicants, 87% accepted. In 2003, 3 master's, 5 doctorates awarded. *Degree requirements:* For master's and doctorate, thesis/dissertation. *Entrance requirements:* For master's and doctorate, GRE General Test, GRE Subject Test. Additional exam requirements/recommendations for international students: Required—TOEFL. *Application deadline:* For fall admission, 8/1 for domestic students. Applications are processed on a rolling basis. Application fee: $40. Electronic applications accepted. Tuition, area resident: Part-time $3,817 per semester. *Expenses:* Tuition, state resident: part-time $8,177 per semester. Required fees: $502 per semester. *Financial support:* In 2003–04, 4 research assistantships, 47 teaching assistantships were awarded. Fellowships, Federal Work-Study and institutionally sponsored loans also available. Support available to part-time students. Financial award application deadline: 4/1; financial award applicants required to submit FAFSA. *Faculty research:* Enzymology, materials chemistry, crystallography, theoretical chemistry. *Unit head:* Dr. Alan Pinkerton, Chair, 419-530-2109, Fax: 419-530-4033, E-mail: apinker@uoft02.utoledo.edu.

See in-depth description on page 179.

Vanderbilt University, Graduate School, Department of Chemistry, Nashville, TN 37240-1001. Offers analytical chemistry (MAT, MS, PhD); inorganic chemistry (MAT, MS, PhD); organic chemistry (MAT, MS, PhD); physical chemistry (MAT, MS, PhD); theoretical chemistry (MAT, MS, PhD). *Degree requirements:* For master's, thesis or alternative; for doctorate, thesis/dissertation, area, qualifying, and final exams. *Entrance requirements:* For master's and doctorate, GRE General Test, GRE Subject Test (recommended). Additional exam requirements/recommendations for international students: Required—TOEFL. Electronic applications accepted. *Expenses:* Tuition: Part-time $1,155 per semester hour. Required fees: $1,538. *Faculty research:* Chemical synthesis; mechanistic, theoretical, bioorganic, analytical, and spectroscopic chemistry.

See in-depth description on page 185.

Wake Forest University, Graduate School, Department of Chemistry, Winston-Salem, NC 27109. Offers analytical chemistry (MS, PhD); inorganic chemistry (MS, PhD); organic chemistry (MS, PhD); physical chemistry (MS, PhD). Part-time programs available. *Faculty:* 15 full-time (2 women). *Students:* 32 full-time (15 women), 1 part-time; includes 2 minority (both African Americans), 13 international. Average age 28. 34 applicants, 38% accepted, 5 enrolled. In 2003, 4 master's, 2 doctorates awarded. *Degree requirements:* For master's, one foreign language, thesis, comprehensive exam, registration; for doctorate, 2 foreign languages, thesis/dissertation, comprehensive exam, registration. *Entrance requirements:* For master's and doctorate, GRE General Test. Additional exam requirements/recommendations for international students: Required—TOEFL (minimum score 213 computer-based). *Application deadline:* For fall admission, 1/15 for domestic students, 1/15 for international students. Application fee: $25. Electronic applications accepted. *Expenses:* Tuition: Full-time $26,500. *Financial support:* In 2003–04, 32 students received support, including 1 fellowship with full tuition reimbursement available (averaging $19,500 per year), 11 research assistantships with full tuition reimbursements available (averaging $17,500 per year), 17 teaching assistantships with full tuition reimbursements available (averaging $17,500 per year); scholarships/grants and tuition waivers (full and partial) also available. Support available to part-time students. Financial award application deadline: 1/15; financial award applicants required to submit FAFSA. *Unit head:* Dr. Dilip Kondepudi, Director, 336-758-5131, Fax: 336-758-4656, E-mail: dilip@wfu.edu.

Washington State University, Graduate School, College of Sciences, Department of Chemistry, Pullman, WA 99164. Offers analytical chemistry (MS, PhD); biological systems (MS, PhD); inorganic chemistry (MS, PhD); organic chemistry (MS, PhD); physical chemistry (MS, PhD). *Faculty:* 22 full-time (3 women). *Students:* 37 full-time (17 women), 1 part-time; includes 3 minority (2 Asian Americans or Pacific Islanders, 1 Hispanic American), 10 international. Average age 25. 48 applicants, 58% accepted, 12 enrolled. In 2003, 3 master's, 1 doctorate awarded. Terminal master's awarded for partial completion of doctoral program. *Median time to degree:* Master's–2.8 years full-time; doctorate–5 years full-time. *Degree requirements:* For master's, oral exam, teaching experience, thesis optional; for doctorate, thesis/dissertation, oral exam, written exam, comprehensive exam. *Entrance requirements:* For master's and doctorate, GRE General Test, minimum GPA of 3.0, 3 letters of recommendation. *Application deadline:* For fall admission, 3/1 for domestic students; for spring admission, 10/1 priority date for domestic students. Applications are processed on a rolling basis. Application fee: $35. *Expenses:* Tuition, state resident: full-time $6,278; part-time $314 per hour. Tuition, nonresident: full-time $15,514; part-time $765 per hour. Required fees: $444. Full-time tuition and fees vary according to campus/location, program and student level. Part-time tuition and fees vary according to course load. *Financial support:* In 2003–04, 13 research assistantships with full and partial tuition reimbursements (averaging $17,000 per year), 23 teaching assistantships with full and partial tuition reimbursements (averaging $17,000 per year) were awarded. Fellowships, career-related internships or fieldwork, Federal Work-Study, institutionally sponsored loans, scholarships/grants, health care benefits, unspecified assistantships, and summer support also available. Financial award application deadline: 4/1; financial award applicants required to submit FAFSA. *Faculty research:* Environmental chemistry, materials chemistry, radio chemistry, bio-organic, computational chemistry. Total annual research expenditures: $1.9 million. *Unit head:* Dr. Ralph Yount, Chair, 509-335-1516, Fax: 509-335-8867, E-mail: yount@wsu.edu. *Application contact:* Sue B. Clark, Chair, Admissions Committee, 509-335-8866, Fax: 509-335-8867, E-mail: carrie@wsu.edu.

Wesleyan University, Graduate Programs, Department of Chemistry, Middletown, CT 06459-0260. Offers biochemistry (MA, PhD); chemical physics (MA, PhD); inorganic chemistry (MA, PhD); organic chemistry (MA, PhD); physical chemistry (MA, PhD); theoretical chemistry (MA, PhD). *Faculty:* 13 full-time (2 women), 2 part-time/adjunct (1 woman). *Students:* 36 full-time (18 women); includes 2 minority (1 African American, 1 Asian American or Pacific Islander), 21 international. In 2003, 2 degrees awarded. Terminal master's awarded for partial completion of doctoral program. *Degree requirements:* For master's and doctorate, one foreign language, thesis/dissertation. *Entrance requirements:* For master's, GRE General Test, GRE Subject Test; for doctorate, GRE Subject Test. *Application deadline:* For fall admission, 3/1 for domestic students. Applications are processed on a rolling basis. Application fee: $0. *Expenses:* Tuition: Full-time $22,338. Required fees: $20. *Financial support:* Fellowships, research assistantships, teaching assistantships, institutionally sponsored loans available. *Unit head:* George

Peterson, Chair, 860-685-2508. *Application contact:* Karen Karpa, Information Contact, 860-685-2573, Fax: 860-685-2211, E-mail: kkarpa@wesleyan.edu.

See in-depth description on page 189.

West Virginia University, Eberly College of Arts and Sciences, Department of Chemistry, Morgantown, WV 26506. Offers analytical chemistry (MS, PhD); inorganic chemistry (MS, PhD); organic chemistry (MS, PhD); physical chemistry (MS, PhD); theoretical chemistry (MS, PhD). Part-time programs available. Postbaccalaureate distance learning degree programs offered (no on-campus study). *Faculty:* 14 full-time (1 woman), 5 part-time/adjunct (3 women). *Students:* 45 full-time (15 women), 3 part-time (2 women); includes 1 minority (Hispanic American), 26 international. Average age 28. 84 applicants, 58% accepted, 11 enrolled. In 2003, 5 master's, 3 doctorates awarded. Terminal master's awarded for partial completion of doctoral program. *Degree requirements:* For master's and doctorate, thesis/dissertation, registration. *Entrance requirements:* For master's, GRE General Test, GRE Subject Test (recommended), minimum GPA of 2.5; for doctorate, GRE General Test, GRE Subject Test (recommended), minimum GPA of 2.75. Additional exam requirements/recommendations for international students: Required—TOEFL. *Application deadline:* For fall admission, 3/1 for domestic students. Applications are processed on a rolling basis. Application fee: $50. Electronic applications accepted. *Expenses:* Tuition, state resident: full-time $4,332. Tuition, nonresident: full-time $12,442. *Financial support:* In 2003–04, fellowships (averaging $2,000 per year), research assistantships with full tuition reimbursements (averaging $13,000 per year), teaching assistantships with full tuition reimbursements (averaging $12,000 per year) were awarded. Tuition waivers (full and partial) also available. Financial award application deadline: 2/1; financial award applicants required to submit FAFSA. *Faculty research:* Analysis of proteins, drug interactions, solids and effluents by advanced separation methods; electro-chemistry, mass spectrometry and atomic spectrometry; development of new synthetic strategies for complex organic molecules; synthesis and structural characterization of metal complexes for polymerization catalysis; nonmagnetic resonance studies of amorphous solids. *Unit head:* Dr. Harry O. Finklea, Chair, 304-293-3435 Ext. 6408, Fax: 304-293-4904, E-mail: harry.finklea@mail.wvu.edu.

Yale University, Graduate School of Arts and Sciences, Department of Chemistry, New Haven, CT 06520. Offers biophysical chemistry (PhD); inorganic chemistry (PhD); organic chemistry (PhD); physical chemistry (PhD). *Degree requirements:* For doctorate, thesis/dissertation. *Entrance requirements:* For doctorate, GRE General Test, GRE Subject Test. Additional exam requirements/recommendations for international students: Required—TOEFL. *Expenses:* Tuition: Full-time $25,600; part-time $6,400 per term.

Organic Chemistry

Boston College, Graduate School of Arts and Sciences, Department of Chemistry, Chestnut Hill, MA 02467-3800. Offers biochemistry (PhD); inorganic chemistry (PhD); organic chemistry (PhD); physical chemistry (PhD); science education (MST). MST is offered through the School of Education for secondary school science teaching. Part-time programs available. *Students:* 95 full-time (31 women); includes 12 minority (2 African Americans, 7 Asian Americans or Pacific Islanders, 3 Hispanic Americans), 22 international. 285 applicants, 24% accepted, 14 enrolled. In 2003, 2 master's, 13 doctorates awarded. *Degree requirements:* For doctorate, thesis/dissertation, qualifying exam. *Entrance requirements:* For doctorate, GRE General Test, GRE Subject Test. Additional exam requirements/recommendations for international students: Required—TOEFL (minimum score 550 paper-based; 213 computer-based). *Application deadline:* For fall admission, 1/2 for domestic students. Application fee: $60. Electronic applications accepted. *Expenses:* Tuition: Part-time $810 per credit. *Financial support:* Fellowships with full tuition reimbursements, research assistantships with full tuition reimbursements, teaching assistantships with full tuition reimbursements, Federal Work-Study available. Support available to part-time students. Financial award application deadline: 3/1; financial award applicants required to submit FAFSA. *Unit head:* Dr. David McFadden, Chairperson, 617-552-3605, E-mail: david.mcfadden@bc.edu. *Application contact:* Dr. John Fourkas, Information Contact, 617-552-3605, Fax: 617-552-0833, E-mail: john.fourkas@bc.edu.

Brandeis University, Graduate School of Arts and Sciences, Department of Chemistry, Waltham, MA 02454-9110. Offers inorganic chemistry (MS, PhD); organic chemistry (MS, PhD); physical chemistry (MS, PhD). *Faculty:* 18 full-time (3 women). *Students:* 39 full-time (20 women), 1 (woman) part-time; includes 2 minority (1 Asian American or Pacific Islander, 1 Hispanic American), 32 international. Average age 25. 114 applicants, 5% accepted. In 2003, 8 master's, 5 doctorates awarded. Terminal master's awarded for partial completion of doctoral program. *Degree requirements:* For master's, 1 year of residency; for doctorate, one foreign language, thesis/dissertation, 3 years of residency, 2 seminars, qualifying exams. *Entrance requirements:* For master's and doctorate, GRE General Test, resumé, letters of recommendation. Additional exam requirements/recommendations for international students: Required—TOEFL (minimum score 600 paper-based; 250 computer-based). *Application deadline:* For fall admission, 1/15 for domestic students. Applications are processed on a rolling basis. Application fee: $60. Electronic applications accepted. *Expenses:* Tuition: Full-time $28,999; part-time $4,867 per course. Required fees: $175. *Financial support:* In 2003–04, 20 fellowships (averaging $20,000 per year), 21 research assistantships (averaging $20,000 per year), 18 teaching assistantships (averaging $20,000 per year) were awarded. Institutionally sponsored loans and scholarships/grants also available. Financial award application deadline: 4/15; financial award applicants required to submit CSS PROFILE or FAFSA. *Faculty research:* Oscillating chemical reactions, molecular recognition systems, protein crystallography, synthesis of natural product spectroscopy and magnetic resonance. Total annual research expenditures: $1,900. *Unit head:* Dr. Thomas C. Pochapsky, Chair, 781-736-2559, Fax: 781-736-2516, E-mail: pochapsky@brandeis.edu. *Application contact:* Charlotte Haygazian, Graduate Admissions Secretary, 781-736-2500, Fax: 781-736-2516, E-mail: chemadm@brandeis.edu.

Brigham Young University, Graduate Studies, College of Physical and Mathematical Sciences, Department of Chemistry and Biochemistry, Provo, UT 84602-1001. Offers analytical chemistry (MS, PhD); biochemistry (MS, PhD); inorganic chemistry (MS, PhD); organic chemistry (MS, PhD); physical chemistry (MS, PhD). *Faculty:* 34 full-time (2 women). *Students:* 90 full-time (56 women); includes 2 minority (1 Asian American or Pacific Islander, 1 Hispanic American), 61 international. Average age 31. 103 applicants, 54% accepted, 23 enrolled. In 2003, 6 master's, 6 doctorates awarded. *Median time to degree:* Master's–2.8 years full-time. Of those who began their doctoral program in fall 1995, 100% received their degree in 8 years or less. *Degree requirements:* For master's, thesis, registration; for doctorate, thesis/dissertation, degree qualifying exam. *Entrance requirements:* For master's, pass 1 (biochemistry), 4 (chemistry) of 5 area exams, GRE General Test, minimum GPA of 3.0 in last 60 hours; for doctorate, pass 1 (biochemistry) or 4 (chemistry) of 5 area exams, GRE General Test, minimum GPA of 3.0 in last 60 hours. Additional exam requirements/recommendations for international students: Required—TOEFL, TWE. *Application deadline:* For fall admission, 2/1 priority date for domestic students, 2/1 priority date for international students. Applications are processed on a rolling basis. Application fee: $50. Electronic applications accepted. *Expenses:* Tuition: Part-time $221 per hour. *Financial support:* In 2003–04, 90 students received support, including 12 fellowships with full tuition reimbursements available (averaging $18,400 per year), 37 research assistantships with full tuition reimbursements available (averaging $18,400 per year), 30 teaching assistantships with full tuition reimbursements available (averaging $18,300 per year); institutionally sponsored loans, scholarships/grants, health care benefits, tuition waivers (full), and unspecified assistantships also available. Financial award application deadline: 2/1. *Faculty research:* Separation science, molecular recognition, organic synthesis and biomedical application, biochemistry and molecular biology, molecular spectroscopy. Total annual research expenditures: $2.7 million. *Unit head:* Dr. Francis R. Nordmeyer, Chair, 801-422-3667, Fax: 801-422-0153, E-mail: fran_nordmeyer@byu.edu. *Application contact:* Dr. Noel L. Owen, Graduate Coordinator, 801-422-2973, Fax: 801-422-0153, E-mail: chemgrad@byu.edu.

See in-depth description on page 97.

California State University, Fullerton, Graduate Studies, College of Natural Science and Mathematics, Department of Chemistry and Biochemistry, Fullerton, CA 92834-9480. Offers analytical chemistry (MS); biochemistry (MS); geochemistry (MS); inorganic chemistry (MS); organic chemistry (MS); physical chemistry (MS). Part-time programs available. *Faculty:* 17 full-time (5 women), 17 part-time/adjunct. *Students:* 21 full-time (9 women), 23 part-time (11 women); includes 19 minority (1 African American, 9 Asian Americans or Pacific Islanders, 9 Hispanic Americans), 8 international. Average age 28. 49 applicants, 61% accepted, 20 enrolled. In 2003, 5 degrees awarded. *Degree requirements:* For master's, thesis, department qualifying exam. *Entrance requirements:* For master's, minimum GPA of 2.5 in last 60 units, major in chemistry or related field. Application fee: $55. Tuition, nonresident: part-time $282 per unit. Required fees: $889 per semester. *Financial support:* Teaching assistantships, career-related internships or fieldwork, Federal Work-Study, institutionally sponsored loans, and scholarships/grants available. Support available to part-time students. Financial award application deadline: 3/1. *Unit head:* Dr. Robert Belloli, Chair, 714-278-3621. *Application contact:* Dr. Gregory Williams, Adviser, 714-278-2170.

California State University, Los Angeles, Graduate Studies, College of Natural and Social Sciences, Department of Chemistry and Biochemistry, Los Angeles, CA 90032-8530. Offers analytical chemistry (MS); biochemistry (MS); chemistry (MS); inorganic chemistry (MS); organic chemistry (MS); physical chemistry (MS). Part-time and evening/weekend programs available. *Faculty:* 15 full-time, 12 part-time/adjunct. *Students:* 12 full-time (6 women), 11 part-time (7 women); includes 11 minority (2 African Americans, 5 Asian Americans or Pacific Islanders, 4 Hispanic Americans), 5 international. In 2003, 5 degrees awarded. *Degree requirements:* For master's, one foreign language. *Entrance requirements:* Additional exam requirements/recommendations for international students: Required—TOEFL. *Application deadline:* For fall admission, 6/30 for domestic students; for spring admission, 2/1 for domestic students. Applications are processed on a rolling basis. Application fee: $55. Tuition, nonresident: part-time $188 per unit. Required fees: $2,477. *Financial support:* Federal Work-Study available. Support available to part-time students. Financial award application deadline: 3/1. *Faculty research:* Intercalation of heavy metal, carborane chemistry, conductive polymers and fabrics, titanium reagents, computer modeling and synthesis. *Unit head:* Dr. Wayne Tikkanen, Chair, 323-343-2300.

Case Western Reserve University, School of Graduate Studies, Department of Chemistry, Cleveland, OH 44106. Offers analytical chemistry (MS, PhD); inorganic chemistry (MS, PhD); organic chemistry (MS, PhD); physical chemistry (MS, PhD). Part-time programs available. *Faculty:* 22 full-time (2 women). *Students:* 64 full-time (18 women), 27 part-time (9 women); includes 2 minority (both Asian Americans or Pacific Islanders), 69 international. Average age 27. 483 applicants, 9% accepted, 18 enrolled. In 2003, 5 master's, 13 doctorates awarded. Terminal master's awarded for partial completion of doctoral program. *Degree requirements:* For doctorate, thesis/dissertation. *Entrance requirements:* For master's and doctorate, GRE General Test, GRE Subject Test. Additional exam requirements/recommendations for international students: Required—TOEFL. *Application deadline:* Applications are processed on a rolling basis. Application fee: $50. *Expenses:* Tuition: Full-time $26,900. *Financial support:* In 2003–04, 77 students received support, including 53 research assistantships, 20 teaching assistantships. *Faculty research:* Electrochemistry, synthetic chemistry, chemistry of life process, spectroscopy, kinetics. *Unit head:* Lawrence Sayre, Chairman, 216-368-3622, Fax: 216-368-3006, E-mail: lms3@case.edu. *Application contact:* Zedeara Diaz, Graduate Admissions, 216-368-3621, Fax: 216-368-3006, E-mail: zcd@case.edu.

Clark Atlanta University, School of Arts and Sciences, Department of Chemistry, Atlanta, GA 30314. Offers inorganic chemistry (MS, PhD); organic chemistry (MS, PhD); physical chemistry (MS, PhD); science education (DA). Part-time programs available. *Degree requirements:* For master's, one foreign language, thesis, comprehensive exam; for doctorate, 2 foreign languages, thesis/dissertation, cumulative exam. *Entrance requirements:* For master's, GRE General Test, minimum GPA of 2.5; for doctorate, GRE General Test, GRE Subject Test, minimum graduate GPA of 3.0.

Clarkson University, Graduate School, School of Arts and Sciences, Department of Chemistry, Potsdam, NY 13699. Offers analytical chemistry (MS, PhD); inorganic chemistry (MS, PhD); organic chemistry (MS, PhD); physical chemistry (MS, PhD). *Faculty:* 11 full-time (2 women). *Students:* 31 full-time (12 women); includes 3 minority (2 African Americans, 1 Asian American or Pacific Islander), 14 international. Average age 28. 45 applicants, 67% accepted. In 2003, 4 master's, 1 doctorate awarded. *Median time to degree:* Master's–2.5 years full-time; doctorate–4 years full-time, 6 years part-time. *Degree requirements:* For doctorate, thesis/dissertation, departmental qualifying exam. *Entrance requirements:* For master's, GRE. Additional exam requirements/recommendations for international students: Required—TOEFL. *Application deadline:* For fall admission, 5/15 for domestic students; for spring admission, 10/15 priority date for domestic students. Applications are processed on a rolling basis. Application fee: $25 ($35 for international students). *Expenses:* Tuition: Full-time $19,272; part-time $803 per credit. Tuition and fees vary according to course load. *Financial support:* In 2003–04, 23 students received support, including 2 fellowships (averaging $22,000 per year), 9 research assistantships (averaging $18,000 per year), 12 teaching assistantships (averaging $18,000 per year); scholarships/grants and tuition waivers (partial) also available. *Faculty research:* Particle adhesion phenomena, airborne radon, ceramic materials, materials processing, chemical kinetics. Total annual research expenditures: $1.3 million. *Unit head:* Dr. Phillip A. Christiansen, Division Head, 315-268-6669, Fax: 315-268-6610, E-mail: pac@clarkson.edu. *Application contact:* Donna Brockway, Assistant to Dean/Foreign Student Advisor, 315-268-6447, Fax: 315-268-7994, E-mail: brockway@clarkson.edu.

Cleveland State University, College of Graduate Studies, College of Arts and Sciences, Department of Chemistry, Cleveland, OH 44115. Offers analytical chemistry (MS, PhD); clinical chemistry (MS, PhD); clinical/bioanalytical (PhD); inorganic chemistry (MS); organic chemistry (MS); physical chemistry (MS); structural analysis (MS, PhD). Part-time and evening/weekend programs available. *Faculty:* 16 full-time (1 woman), 3 part-time/adjunct (1 woman). *Students:* 44 full-time (21 women), 23 part-time (9 women); includes 3 minority (1 African American, 1 Asian American or Pacific Islander, 1 Hispanic American), 29 international. Average age 33. 30 applicants, 23% accepted, 2 enrolled. In 2003, 6 master's, 1 doctorate awarded. *Degree requirements:* For master's, thesis (for some programs); for doctorate, thesis/dissertation. *Entrance requirements:* For master's and doctorate, GRE General Test, GRE Subject Test. Additional exam requirements/recommendations for international students: Required—TOEFL (minimum score 525 paper-based; 197 computer-based). *Application deadline:* For fall admis-

Organic Chemistry

Cleveland State University (continued)
sion, 1/15 priority date for domestic students, 1/15 priority date for international students. Applications are processed on a rolling basis. Application fee: $30. Electronic applications accepted. Tuition, area resident: Full-time $8,258; part-time $344 per credit hour. Tuition, nonresident: full-time $16,352; part-time $681 per credit hour. *Financial support:* In 2003–04, 37 students received support, including fellowships (averaging $16,000 per year), 19 research assistantships with full tuition reimbursements available (averaging $16,000 per year), 18 teaching assistantships with full tuition reimbursements available (averaging $15,000 per year) Financial award application deadline: 1/15. *Faculty research:* Trace metal analysis in biological systems, application of HPLC/LPCC to clinical systems, synthetic organic and inorganic chemistry, molecular structure determinations, structure-function relationships of factor Va, MALDI-TOF based DNA sequencing, spectroscopic studies of chemical and biochemical phenomena, novel electro-optic tunable filters (AOTFs) to explore biological systems. Total annual research expenditures: $1 million. *Unit head:* Dr. Stan Duraj, Chair, 216-687-2454, Fax: 216-687-9298, E-mail: s.duraj@csuohio.edu. *Application contact:* Richelle P. Emery, Administrative Coordinator, 216-687-2457, Fax: 216-687-9298, E-mail: r.emery@csuohio.edu.

Columbia University, Graduate School of Arts and Sciences, Division of Natural Sciences, Department of Chemistry, New York, NY 10027. Offers chemical physics (M Phil, PhD); inorganic chemistry (M Phil, MS, PhD); organic chemistry (M Phil, MS, PhD). *Faculty:* 17 full-time. *Students:* 115 full-time (35 women). Average age 27. 452 applicants, 20% accepted. In 2003, 13 master's, 20 doctorates awarded. *Degree requirements:* For master's, comp exams (MS); foreign language, teaching experience, oral/written exams (M Phil); for doctorate, one foreign language, thesis/dissertation. *Entrance requirements:* For master's and doctorate, GRE General Test, GRE Subject Test. Additional exam requirements/recommendations for international students: Required—TOEFL. Application fee: $75. *Expenses:* Tuition: Full-time $14,820. *Financial support:* Fellowships, teaching assistantships, Federal Work-Study and institutionally sponsored loans available. Support available to part-time students. Financial award application deadline: 1/5; financial award applicants required to submit FAFSA. *Faculty research:* Biophysics. *Unit head:* Bruce Berne, Chair, 212-854-2186, Fax: 212-932-1289.

Cornell University, Graduate School, Graduate Fields of Arts and Sciences, Field of Chemistry and Chemical Biology, Ithaca, NY 14853-0001. Offers analytical chemistry (PhD); bio-organic chemistry (PhD); biophysical chemistry (PhD); chemical biology (PhD); chemical physics (PhD); inorganic chemistry (PhD); materials chemistry (PhD); organic chemistry (PhD); organometallic chemistry (PhD); physical chemistry (PhD); polymer chemistry (PhD); theoretical chemistry (PhD). *Faculty:* 37 full-time. *Students:* 174 full-time (70 women); includes 22 minority (4 African Americans, 10 Asian Americans or Pacific Islanders, 8 Hispanic Americans), 57 international. 371 applicants, 35% accepted, 42 enrolled. In 2003, 22 doctorates awarded. *Degree requirements:* For doctorate, thesis/dissertation, comprehensive exam. *Entrance requirements:* For doctorate, GRE General Test, GRE Subject Test (chemistry), 3 letters of recommendation. Additional exam requirements/recommendations for international students: Required—TOEFL (minimum score 600 paper-based; 250 computer-based). *Application deadline:* For fall admission, 1/10 for domestic students. Application fee: $60. Electronic applications accepted. *Expenses:* Tuition: Full-time $28,630. One-time fee: $50 full-time. *Financial support:* In 2003–04, 162 students received support, including 28 fellowships with full tuition reimbursements available, 77 research assistantships with full tuition reimbursements available, 57 teaching assistantships with full tuition reimbursements available; institutionally sponsored loans, scholarships/grants, health care benefits, tuition waivers (full and partial), and unspecified assistantships also available. Financial award applicants required to submit FAFSA. *Faculty research:* Analytical, organic, inorganic, physical, materials, chemical biology. *Unit head:* Director of Graduate Studies, 607-255-4139, Fax: 607-255-4137. *Application contact:* Graduate Field Assistant, 607-255-4139, Fax: 607-255-4137, E-mail: chemgrad@cornell.edu.

See in-depth description on page 105.

Florida State University, Graduate Studies, College of Arts and Sciences, Department of Chemistry and Biochemistry, Tallahassee, FL 32306. Offers analytical chemistry (MS, PhD); biochemistry (MS, PhD); chemical physics (MS, PhD); inorganic chemistry (MS, PhD); organic chemistry (MS, PhD); physical chemistry (MS, PhD). Part-time programs available. *Faculty:* 30 full-time (6 women), 4 part-time/adjunct (2 women). *Students:* 142 full-time (46 women); includes 18 minority (9 African Americans, 1 American Indian/Alaska Native, 6 Asian Americans or Pacific Islanders, 2 Hispanic Americans), 51 international. Average age 25. 410 applicants, 15% accepted, 39 enrolled. In 2003, 9 master's, 11 doctorates awarded. Terminal master's awarded for partial completion of doctoral program. *Median time to degree:* Master's–3.5 years full-time; doctorate–5 years full-time. Of those who began their doctoral program in fall 1995, 72% received their degree in 8 years or less. *Degree requirements:* For master's, thesis (for some programs), cumulative and diagnostic exams, comprehensive exam (for some programs); for doctorate, thesis/dissertation, cumulative and diagnostic exams. *Entrance requirements:* For master's and doctorate, GRE General Test, minimum B average in undergraduate course work. Additional exam requirements/recommendations for international students: Required—TOEFL (minimum score 515 paper-based; 213 computer-based). *Application deadline:* For fall admission, 4/15 priority date for domestic students, 4/15 priority date for international students. Applications are processed on a rolling basis. Application fee: $20. Electronic applications accepted. *Expenses:* Tuition, state resident: part-time $196 per credit hour. Tuition, nonresident: part-time $731 per credit hour. Part-time tuition and fees vary according to campus/location. *Financial support:* In 2003–04, 2 fellowships with tuition reimbursements (averaging $15,000 per year), 54 research assistantships with tuition reimbursements (averaging $18,000 per year), 76 teaching assistantships with tuition reimbursements (averaging $18,000 per year) were awarded. Career-related internships or fieldwork, Federal Work-Study, institutionally sponsored loans, and traineeships also available. Financial award application deadline: 2/15; financial award applicants required to submit FAFSA. *Faculty research:* Spectroscopy, computational chemistry, nuclear chemistry, separations, synthesis. *Unit head:* Dr. Naresh Dalal, Chairman, 850-644-3398, Fax: 850-644-8281. *Application contact:* Dr. Oliver Steinbock, Chair, Graduate Admissions Committee, 888-525-9286, Fax: 850-644-8281, E-mail: gradinfo@chem.fsu.edu.

See in-depth description on page 115.

Georgetown University, Graduate School of Arts and Sciences, Department of Chemistry, Washington, DC 20057. Offers analytical chemistry (MS, PhD); biochemistry (MS, PhD); chemical physics (MS, PhD); inorganic chemistry (MS, PhD); organic chemistry (MS, PhD); physical chemistry (MS, PhD); theoretical chemistry (MS, PhD). Terminal master's awarded for partial completion of doctoral program. *Degree requirements:* For master's, thesis (for some programs), qualifying exam; for doctorate, thesis/dissertation, comprehensive exam. *Entrance requirements:* For master's and doctorate, GRE General Test. Additional exam requirements/recommendations for international students: Required—TOEFL.

The George Washington University, Columbian College of Arts and Sciences, Department of Chemistry, Washington, DC 20052. Offers analytical chemistry (MS, PhD); inorganic chemistry (MS, PhD); materials science (MS, PhD); organic chemistry (MS, PhD); physical chemistry (MS, PhD). Part-time and evening/weekend programs available. *Faculty:* 7 full-time (1 woman). *Students:* 16 full-time (6 women), 11 part-time (6 women); includes 4 minority (2 African Americans, 1 Asian American or Pacific Islander, 1 Hispanic American), 11 international. 39 applicants, 95% accepted. In 2003, 3 master's, 2 doctorates awarded. Terminal master's awarded for partial completion of doctoral program. *Degree requirements:* For master's, thesis or alternative, comprehensive exam; for doctorate, thesis/dissertation, general exam. *Entrance requirements:* For master's and doctorate, GRE General Test, interview, minimum GPA of 3.0. Additional exam requirements/recommendations for international students: Required—TOEFL (minimum score 550 paper-based; 213 computer-based). *Application deadline:* For fall admission, 2/1 priority date for domestic students, 2/1 priority date for international students; for spring admission, 10/1 priority date for domestic students, 10/1 priority date for international students. Applications are processed on a rolling basis. Application fee: $60. Electronic applications accepted. *Expenses:* Tuition: Part-time $876 per credit. Required fees: $1 per credit. Tuition and fees vary according to campus/location. *Financial support:* In 2003–04, fellowships with tuition reimbursements (averaging $10,000 per year), teaching assistantships with tuition reimbursements (averaging $5,000 per year) were awarded. Research assistantships, Federal Work-Study also available. Financial award application deadline: 2/1. *Unit head:* Dr. Michael King, Chair, 202-994-6488. *Application contact:* Information Contact, E-mail: gwchem@www.gwu.edu.

Harvard University, Graduate School of Arts and Sciences, Department of Chemistry and Chemical Biology, Cambridge, MA 02138. Offers biochemical chemistry (AM, PhD); inorganic chemistry (AM, PhD); organic chemistry (AM, PhD); physical chemistry (AM, PhD). *Degree requirements:* For doctorate, thesis/dissertation, cumulative exams. *Entrance requirements:* For master's, GRE General Test; for doctorate, GRE General Test, GRE Subject Test. Additional exam requirements/recommendations for international students: Required—TOEFL. *Expenses:* Tuition: Full-time $26,066. Full-time tuition and fees vary according to program and student level.

See in-depth description on page 117.

Howard University, Graduate School of Arts and Sciences, Department of Chemistry, Washington, DC 20059-0002. Offers analytical chemistry (MS, PhD); atmospheric (MS, PhD); biochemistry (MS, PhD); environmental (MS, PhD); inorganic chemistry (MS, PhD); organic chemistry (MS, PhD); physical chemistry (MS, PhD); polymer chemistry (MS, PhD). Part-time programs available. *Degree requirements:* For master's, one foreign language, thesis, teaching experience, comprehensive exam, registration; for doctorate, 2 foreign languages, thesis/dissertation, teaching experience, comprehensive exam, registration. *Entrance requirements:* For master's, GRE General Test, minimum GPA of 2.7; for doctorate, GRE General Test, minimum GPA of 3.0. *Faculty research:* Stratospheric aerosols, liquid crystals, polymer coatings, terrestrial and extraterrestrial atmospheres, amidogen reaction.

Illinois Institute of Technology, Graduate College, College of Science and Letters, Department of Biological, Chemical and Physical Sciences, Chemistry Division, Chicago, IL 60616-3793. Offers analytical chemistry (M Ch, MS, PhD); chemistry (M Chem); inorganic chemistry (MS, PhD); materials and chemical synthesis (M Ch); organic chemistry (MS, PhD); physical chemistry (MS, PhD); polymer chemistry (MS, PhD). Part-time and evening/weekend programs available. Postbaccalaureate distance learning degree programs offered (no on-campus study). *Faculty:* 4 full-time (0 women), 2 part-time/adjunct (0 women). *Students:* 14 full-time (7 women), 32 part-time (18 women); includes 7 minority (1 African American, 4 Asian Americans or Pacific Islanders, 2 Hispanic Americans), 17 international. Average age 32. 94 applicants, 68% accepted, 7 enrolled. In 2003, 14 master's, 2 doctorates awarded. Terminal master's awarded for partial completion of doctoral program. *Degree requirements:* For master's, thesis (for some programs), comprehensive exam; for doctorate, thesis/dissertation, comprehensive exam. *Entrance requirements:* For master's and doctorate, GRE General Test, minimum undergraduate GPA of 3.0. Additional exam requirements/recommendations for international students: Required—TOEFL (minimum score 550 paper-based; 213 computer-based). *Application deadline:* For fall admission, 5/1 for domestic students, 5/1 for international students; for spring admission, 10/15 for domestic students, 10/15 for international students. Applications are processed on a rolling basis. Application fee: $40. Electronic applications accepted. *Expenses:* Tuition: Part-time $628 per credit. Tuition and fees vary according to course load and program. *Financial support:* In 2003–04, 11 students received support, including 1 fellowship with full tuition reimbursement available, 9 research assistantships with full tuition reimbursements available (averaging $15,000 per year), 7 teaching assistantships with full tuition reimbursements available (averaging $15,000 per year); Federal Work-Study, institutionally sponsored loans, scholarships/grants, and tuition waivers (partial) also available. Support available to part-time students. Financial award application deadline: 3/1; financial award applicants required to submit FAFSA. *Faculty research:* Organic and inorganic chemistry, polymers research, physical chemistry, analytical chemistry. *Unit head:* Kenneth Stagliano, Associate Chair, 312-567-3428, Fax: 312-567-3494, E-mail: stagliano@iit.edu. *Application contact:* Kelly A. Cherwin, Director of Graduate Outreach, 312-567-7974, Fax: 312-567-3494, E-mail: inquiry.grad@iit.edu.

Instituto Tecnológico y de Estudios Superiores de Monterrey, Campus Monterrey, Graduate and Research Division, Program in Natural and Social Sciences, Monterrey, , Mexico. Offers biotechnology (MS); chemistry (MS, PhD); communications (MS); education (MA). Part-time programs available. *Degree requirements:* For master's and doctorate, one foreign language, thesis/dissertation. *Entrance requirements:* For master's, PAEG; for doctorate, PAEG, master's degree in related field. Additional exam requirements/recommendations for international students: Required—TOEFL. *Faculty research:* Cultural industries, mineral substances, bioremediation, food processing, CQ in industrial chemical processing.

Kansas State University, Graduate School, College of Arts and Sciences, Department of Chemistry, Manhattan, KS 66506. Offers analytical chemistry (MS); chemistry (PhD); inorganic chemistry (MS); organic chemistry (MS); physical chemistry (MS). *Faculty:* 15 full-time (2 women). *Students:* 51 full-time (17 women); includes 1 minority (African American), 33 international. 71 applicants, 20% accepted, 14 enrolled. In 2003, 1 master's, 7 doctorates awarded. Terminal master's awarded for partial completion of doctoral program. *Degree requirements:* For master's and doctorate, thesis/dissertation. *Entrance requirements:* For master's and doctorate, GRE, minimum GPA of 3.0. Additional exam requirements/recommendations for international students: Required—TOEFL. *Application deadline:* For fall admission, 2/1 for domestic students; for spring admission, 10/1 for domestic students. Applications are processed on a rolling basis. Application fee: $0 ($25 for international students). *Expenses:* Tuition, state resident: part-time $155 per credit hour. Tuition, nonresident: part-time $428 per credit hour. Required fees: $11 per credit hour. *Financial support:* In 2003–04, 23 research assistantships (averaging $15,648 per year), 26 teaching assistantships with full tuition reimbursements (averaging $17,890 per year) were awarded. Fellowships, institutionally sponsored loans and scholarships/grants also available. Support available to part-time students. Financial award application deadline: 3/1; financial award applicants required to submit FAFSA. *Faculty research:* Computational, environmental and materials, nanoscale, natural products, theoretical chemistry. Total annual research expenditures: $2.8 million. *Unit head:* Peter M. A. Sherwood, Head, 785-532-6665, Fax: 785-532-6666, E-mail: escachem@ksu.edu. *Application contact:* Robert Hammaker, Director, 785-532-1454, Fax: 785-532-6666, E-mail: rmh3008@ksu.edu.

Kent State University, College of Arts and Sciences, Department of Chemistry, Kent, OH 44242-0001. Offers analytical chemistry (MS, PhD); biochemistry (MS, PhD); chemistry (MA, MS, PhD); inorganic chemistry (MS, PhD); organic chemistry (MS, PhD); physical chemistry (MS, PhD). Terminal master's awarded for partial completion of doctoral program. *Degree requirements:* For master's and doctorate, thesis/dissertation, comprehensive exam, registration. *Entrance requirements:* For master's and doctorate, placement exam, GRE General Test, GRE Subject Test (recommended), minimum GPA of 2.75. Additional exam requirements/recommendations for international students: Required—TOEFL (minimum score 575 paper-based; 230 computer-based). Electronic applications accepted. *Expenses:* Tuition, state resident: part-time $334 per hour. Tuition, nonresident: part-time $627 per hour. *Faculty research:* Biological chemistry, materials chemistry, molecular spectroscopy.

See in-depth description on page 119.

Marquette University, Graduate School, College of Arts and Sciences, Department of Chemistry, Milwaukee, WI 53201-1881. Offers analytical chemistry (MS, PhD); bioanalytical chemistry (MS, PhD); biophysical chemistry (MS, PhD); chemical physics (MS, PhD); inorganic chemistry (MS, PhD); organic chemistry (MS, PhD); physical chemistry (MS, PhD). Part-time programs available. *Faculty:* 19 full-time (2 women), 2 part-time/adjunct (0 women). *Students:* 44 full-time (17 women), 4 part-time (1 woman); includes 1 minority (African American), 36 international. Average age 31. 37 applicants, 32% accepted, 8 enrolled. In 2003, 1 master's, 1 doctorate awarded. Terminal master's awarded for partial completion of doctoral program. *Degree requirements:* For master's, comprehensive exam; for doctorate, thesis/dissertation, cumulative exams. *Entrance requirements:* For master's and doctorate, GRE Subject Test. Additional exam requirements/recommendations for international students: Required—TOEFL. Application fee: $40. *Expenses:* Tuition: Full-time $10,080; part-time $630 per credit. Tuition and fees vary according to program. *Financial support:* In 2003–04, 3 research assistantships, 27 teaching assistantships were awarded. Fellowships, Federal Work-Study, institutionally sponsored loans, scholarships/grants, and tuition waivers (full and partial) also available. Support available to part-time students. Financial award application deadline: 2/15. *Faculty research:* Inorganic complexes, laser Raman spectroscopy, organic synthesis, chemical dynamics, biophysiology. Total annual research expenditures: $586,915. *Unit head:* Dr. Charles Wilkie, Chairman, 414-288-7065, Fax: 414-288-7066. *Application contact:* Dr. Mark Steinmetz, Director of Graduate Studies, 414-288-7374, Fax: 414-288-7066.

Massachusetts Institute of Technology, School of Engineering, Department of Civil and Environmental Engineering, Cambridge, MA 02139-4307. Offers biological oceanography (PhD, Sc D); chemical oceanography (PhD, Sc D); civil and environmental engineering (M Eng, SM, PhD, Sc D, CE, Env E); civil engineering (PhD, Sc D); coastal engineering (Sc D); construction engineering and management (PhD, Sc D); costal engineering (PhD); environmental biology (PhD, Sc D); environmental chemistry (PhD, Sc D); environmental engineering (PhD, Sc D); environmental fluid mechanics (PhD, Sc D); geotechnical and geoenvironmental engineering (PhD, Sc D); hydrology (PhD, Sc D); information technology (PhD, Sc D); oceanographic engineering (PhD); oceanographic engineering (Sc D); structures and materials (PhD, Sc D); transportation (PhD, Sc D). *Faculty:* 36 full-time (4 women). *Students:* 239 full-time (70 women); includes 17 minority (1 African American, 10 Asian Americans or Pacific Islanders, 6 Hispanic Americans), 147 international. Average age 26. 591 applicants, 37% accepted, 90 enrolled. In 2003, 149 master's, 27 doctorates awarded. *Degree requirements:* For master's and other advanced degree, thesis/dissertation; for doctorate, thesis/dissertation, comprehensive exam. *Entrance requirements:* For master's and doctorate, GRE General Test. Additional exam requirements/recommendations for international students: Required—TOEFL (minimum score 577 paper-based; 233 computer-based). *Application deadline:* For fall admission, 1/2 for domestic students, 1/2 for international students. Application fee: $70. Electronic applications accepted. *Expenses:* Tuition: Full-time $29,400. Required fees: $200. *Financial support:* In 2003–04, 214 students received support, including 42 fellowships with tuition reimbursements available, 112 research assistantships with tuition reimbursements available (averaging $22,740 per year), 29 teaching assistantships with tuition reimbursements available (averaging $17,370 per year); career-related internships or fieldwork, Federal Work-Study, institutionally sponsored loans, scholarships/grants, health care benefits, and unspecified assistantships also available. *Faculty research:* Environmental chemistry and biology, environmental fluid dynamics and hydrodynamics, geoenvironment and geotechnology, surface and groundwater hydrology, materials and structures. Total annual research expenditures: $10.9 million. *Unit head:* Prof. Patrick Jaillet, Head, 617-452-3379, Fax: 617-452-3294, E-mail: jaillet@mit.edu. *Application contact:* Graduate Admissions, 617-253-7101, E-mail: ceed@mit.edu.

Massachusetts Institute of Technology, School of Science, Department of Chemistry, Cambridge, MA 02139-4307. Offers biological chemistry (PhD, Sc D); inorganic chemistry (PhD, Sc D); organic chemistry (PhD, Sc D); physical chemistry (PhD, Sc D). *Faculty:* 31 full-time (6 women). *Students:* 253 full-time (85 women), 7 part-time (5 women); includes 34 minority (8 African Americans, 17 Asian Americans or Pacific Islanders, 9 Hispanic Americans), 81 international. Average age 26. 573 applicants, 25% accepted, 54 enrolled. In 2003, 28 doctorates awarded. *Degree requirements:* For doctorate, thesis/dissertation, comprehensive exam. *Entrance requirements:* For doctorate, GRE General Test. Additional exam requirements/recommendations for international students: Required—TOEFL (minimum score 577 paper-based; 233 computer-based). *Application deadline:* For fall admission, 12/15 for domestic students, 12/15 for international students. Application fee: $70. Electronic applications accepted. *Expenses:* Tuition: Full-time $29,400. Required fees: $200. *Financial support:* In 2003–04, 50 fellowships with tuition reimbursements, 167 research assistantships with tuition reimbursements (averaging $23,760 per year), 59 teaching assistantships with tuition reimbursements (averaging $18,270 per year) were awarded. Career-related internships or fieldwork, Federal Work-Study, institutionally sponsored loans, scholarships/grants, health care benefits, and unspecified assistantships also available. *Faculty research:* Synthetic organic chemistry, enzymatic reaction mechanisms, inorganic and organometallic spectroscopy, high resolution NMR spectroscopy. Total annual research expenditures: $20.7 million. *Unit head:* Prof. Stephen J. Lippard, Head, 617-253-1801, Fax: 617-258-0241. *Application contact:* Susan Brighton, Graduate Administrator, 617-253-1845, Fax: 617-258-0241, E-mail: brighton@mit.edu.

McMaster University, School of Graduate Studies, Faculty of Science, Department of Chemistry, Hamilton, ON L8S 4M2, Canada. Offers analytical chemistry (M Sc, PhD); chemical physics (M Sc, PhD); chemistry (M Sc, PhD); inorganic chemistry (M Sc, PhD); organic chemistry (M Sc, PhD); physical chemistry (M Sc, PhD); polymer chemistry (M Sc, PhD). Part-time programs available. Terminal master's awarded for partial completion of doctoral program. *Degree requirements:* For master's, thesis/dissertation; for doctorate, thesis/dissertation, comprehensive exam. *Entrance requirements:* For master's, minimum B+ average. Additional exam requirements/recommendations for international students: Required—TOEFL (minimum score 550 paper-based; 213 computer-based).

Miami University, Graduate School, College of Arts and Sciences, Department of Chemistry and Biochemistry, Oxford, OH 45056. Offers analytical chemistry (MS, PhD); biochemistry (MS, PhD); chemical education (MS, PhD); chemistry (MS, PhD); inorganic chemistry (MS, PhD); organic chemistry (MS, PhD); physical chemistry (MS, PhD). Part-time programs available. *Faculty:* 22 full-time (2 women). *Students:* 45 full-time (16 women), 1 part-time; includes 2 minority (both Asian Americans or Pacific Islanders), 21 international. 131 applicants, 98% accepted, 13 enrolled. In 2003, 4 master's, 4 doctorates awarded. *Degree requirements:* For master's, thesis, final exam; for doctorate, thesis/dissertation, final exams, comprehensive exam. *Entrance requirements:* For master's, minimum undergraduate GPA of 3.0 during previous 2 years or 2.75 overall; for doctorate, minimum undergraduate GPA of 2.75, 3.0 graduate. Additional exam requirements/recommendations for international students: Required—TOEFL, TWE. *Application deadline:* For fall admission, 3/1 priority date for domestic students, 3/1 priority date for international students. Applications are processed on a rolling basis. Application fee: $35. Electronic applications accepted. Tuition, area resident: Full-time $9,346. International tuition: $19,924 full-time. Full-time tuition and fees vary according to course level and campus/location. *Financial support:* In 2003–04, 22 fellowships with full tuition reimbursements (averaging $16,813 per year), 3 research assistantships with full tuition reimbursements (averaging $16,813 per year), 17 teaching assistantships with full tuition reimbursements (averaging $18,934 per year) were awarded. Federal Work-Study, tuition waivers (full), and unspecified assistantships also available. Financial award application deadline: 3/1. *Unit head:* Dr. Chris Makaroff, Chair, 513-529-2813. *Application contact:* Dr. Michael Crowder, Director of Graduate Studies, 513-529-2813, Fax: 513-529-5715, E-mail: chemistry@muohio.edu.

Northeastern University, College of Arts and Sciences, Department of Chemistry and Chemical Biology, Boston, MA 02115-5096. Offers analytical chemistry (PhD); chemistry (MS, PhD); inorganic chemistry (PhD); organic chemistry (PhD); physical chemistry (PhD). Part-time and evening/weekend programs available. *Faculty:* 17 full-time (2 women), 3 part-time/adjunct (0 women). *Students:* 46 full-time (23 women), 29 part-time (17 women). Average age 28. 113 applicants, 37% accepted. In 2003, 12 master's, 10 doctorates awarded. Terminal master's awarded for partial completion of doctoral program. *Degree requirements:* For master's, thesis (for some programs); for doctorate, thesis/dissertation, qualifying exam in specialty area. *Entrance requirements:* Additional exam requirements/recommendations for international students: Required—TOEFL. *Application deadline:* For fall admission, 4/15 for domestic students. Applications are processed on a rolling basis. Application fee: $50. Electronic applications accepted. *Expenses:* Tuition: Part-time $790 per credit hour. Tuition and fees vary according to course load and program. *Financial support:* In 2003–04, 27 research assistantships with tuition reimbursements (averaging $16,000 per year) were awarded; fellowships with tuition reimbursements, teaching assistantships with tuition reimbursements, career-related internships or fieldwork, tuition waivers (partial), and unspecified assistantships also available. Financial award application deadline: 4/15; financial award applicants required to submit FAFSA. *Faculty research:* Electron transfer, theoretical chemical physics, analytical biotechnology, mass spectrometry, materials chemistry. Total annual research expenditures: $250,000. *Unit head:* Dr. Graham Jones, Chairman, 617-373-2822, Fax: 617-373-8795, E-mail: chemistry-grad-info@neu.edu. *Application contact:* Dr. Pam Mabrouk, Chair, Graduate Admissions Committee, 617-373-2383, Fax: 617-373-8795, E-mail: chemistry-grad-info@neu.edu.

See in-depth description on page 133.

Old Dominion University, College of Sciences, Program in Chemistry, Norfolk, VA 23529. Offers analytical chemistry (MS); biochemistry (MS); clinical chemistry (MS); environmental chemistry (MS); organic chemistry (MS); physical chemistry (MS). Part-time and evening/weekend programs available. *Faculty:* 15 full-time (4 women). *Students:* 6 full-time (3 women), 9 part-time (5 women); includes 1 minority (Asian American or Pacific Islander), 3 international. Average age 30. 19 applicants, 74% accepted. In 2003, 2 degrees awarded. *Degree requirements:* For master's, thesis, comprehensive exam. *Entrance requirements:* For master's, GRE General Test, minimum GPA of 3.0 in major, 2.5 overall. Additional exam requirements/recommendations for international students: Required—TOEFL. *Application deadline:* For fall admission, 7/1 for domestic students; for spring admission, 11/1 for domestic students. Applications are processed on a rolling basis. Application fee: $30. *Expenses:* Tuition, state resident: part-time $235 per credit hour. Tuition, nonresident: part-time $603 per credit hour. Part-time tuition and fees vary according to campus/location. *Financial support:* In 2003–04, research assistantships with tuition reimbursements (averaging $15,000 per year), teaching assistantships with tuition reimbursements (averaging $15,000 per year) were awarded. Fellowships, career-related internships or fieldwork and scholarships/grants also available. Financial award application deadline: 2/15; financial award applicants required to submit FAFSA. *Faculty research:* Organic and trace metal biogeochemistry, materials chemistry, bioanalytical chemistry, computational chemistry. Total annual research expenditures: $854,968. *Unit head:* Dr. John R. Donat, Graduate Program Director, 757-683-4098, Fax: 757-683-4628, E-mail: chemgpd@odu.edu.

Oregon State University, Graduate School, College of Science, Department of Chemistry, Corvallis, OR 97331. Offers analytical chemistry (MS, PhD); chemistry (MA, MAIS); inorganic chemistry (MS, PhD); nuclear and radiation chemistry (MS, PhD); organic chemistry (MS, PhD); physical chemistry (MS, PhD). Part-time programs available. *Faculty:* 30 full-time (5 women). *Students:* 63 full-time (22 women), 1 part-time; includes 5 minority (3 Asian Americans or Pacific Islanders, 2 Hispanic Americans), 29 international. Average age 28. In 2003, 3 master's, 13 doctorates awarded. Terminal master's awarded for partial completion of doctoral program. *Degree requirements:* For master's and doctorate, one foreign language, thesis/dissertation. *Entrance requirements:* For master's and doctorate, minimum GPA of 3.0 in last 90 hours. Additional exam requirements/recommendations for international students: Required—TOEFL. *Application deadline:* For fall admission, 3/1 for domestic students. Applications are processed on a rolling basis. Application fee: $50. *Expenses:* Tuition, state resident: full-time $8,139; part-time $301 per credit. Tuition, nonresident: full-time $14,376; part-time $532 per credit. Required fees: $1,227. *Financial support:* Fellowships, research assistantships, teaching assistantships, institutionally sponsored loans available. Support available to part-time students. Financial award application deadline: 2/1. *Faculty research:* Solid state chemistry, enzyme reaction mechanisms, structure and dynamics of gas molecules, chemiluminescence, nonlinear optical spectroscopy. *Unit head:* Dr. John C. Westall, Chair, 541-737-2591, Fax: 541-737-2062, E-mail: john.westall@orst.edu. *Application contact:* Carolyn Brumley, Graduate Secretary, 541-737-6707, Fax: 541-737-2062, E-mail: carolyn.brumley@orst.edu.

Purdue University, Graduate School, School of Science, Department of Chemistry, West Lafayette, IN 47907. Offers analytical chemistry (MS, PhD); biochemistry (MS, PhD); chemical education (MS, PhD); inorganic chemistry (MS, PhD); organic chemistry (MS, PhD); physical chemistry (MS, PhD). *Accreditation:* NCATE (one or more programs are accredited). Terminal master's awarded for partial completion of doctoral program. *Degree requirements:* For master's and doctorate, thesis/dissertation. *Entrance requirements:* Additional exam requirements/recommendations for international students: Required—TOEFL. Electronic applications accepted.

Rensselaer Polytechnic Institute, Graduate School, School of Science, Department of Chemistry and Chemical Biology, Troy, NY 12180-3590. Offers analytical chemistry (MS, PhD); biochemistry (MS, PhD); inorganic chemistry (MS, PhD); organic chemistry (MS, PhD); physical chemistry (MS, PhD); polymer chemistry (MS, PhD). Part-time and evening/weekend programs available. *Faculty:* 20 full-time (4 women). *Students:* 58 full-time (25 women), 3 part-time (2 women); includes 40 minority (2 African Americans, 37 Asian Americans or Pacific Islanders, 1 Hispanic American), 36 international. Average age 24. 102 applicants, 29% accepted, 19 enrolled. In 2003, 9 master's, 9 doctorates awarded. Terminal master's awarded for partial completion of doctoral program. *Median time to degree:* Of those who began their doctoral program in fall 1995, 100% received their degree in 8 years or less. *Degree requirements:* For master's, thesis (for some programs), registration; for doctorate, thesis/dissertation, comprehensive exam, registration. *Entrance requirements:* For master's, GRE General Test, GRE Subject Test (strongly recommended); for doctorate, GRE General Test, GRE Subject Test (chemistry or biochemistry strongly recommended). Additional exam requirements/recommendations for international students: Required—TOEFL (minimum score 600 paper-based). *Application deadline:* For fall admission, 2/1 for domestic students; for spring admission, 11/15 for domestic students. Applications are processed on a rolling basis. Application fee: $45. Electronic applications accepted. *Expenses:* Tuition: Full-time $27,700; part-time $1,320 per credit. Required fees: $1,470. *Financial support:* In 2003–04, 59 students received support, including 1 fellowship with full tuition reimbursement available (averaging $25,000 per year), 25 research assistantships with full tuition reimbursements available (averaging $18,000 per year), 30 teaching assistantships with full tuition reimbursements available (averaging $18,000 per year); institutionally sponsored loans and tuition waivers (full and partial) also available. Financial award application deadline: 2/1. *Faculty research:* Synthetic polymer and biopolymer chemistry, physical chemistry of polymeric systems, bioanalytical chemistry, synthetic and computational drug design, protein folding and protein design. Total annual research expenditures: $1.9 million. *Unit head:* Dr. Ronald A. Bailey, Acting Chair, 518-276-4856, Fax: 518-276-4887, E-mail: bailer@rpi.edu. *Application contact:* Beth E. McGraw, Department Admissions Assistant, 518-276-6456, Fax: 518-276-4887, E-mail: mcgrae@rpi.edu.

Rice University, Graduate Programs, Wiess School of Natural Sciences, Department of Chemistry, Houston, TX 77251-1892. Offers chemistry (MA); inorganic chemistry (PhD); organic chemistry (PhD); physical chemistry (PhD). *Faculty:* 24 full-time (3 women), 5 part-time/adjunct (0 women). *Students:* 80 full-time (25 women); includes 8 minority (2 African Americans, 1 Asian American or Pacific Islander, 5 Hispanic Americans), 40 international. Average age 24. 259 applicants, 21% accepted, 25 enrolled. In 2003, 1 master's, 14 doctorates awarded. Terminal master's awarded for partial completion of doctoral program. *Median time to degree:* Of those who began their doctoral program in fall 1995, 100% received their degree in 8 years or less. *Degree requirements:* For master's and doctorate, thesis/dissertation. *Entrance requirements:* For master's and doctorate, GRE General Test, minimum GPA of 3.0. Additional exam requirements/recommendations for international students: Required—TOEFL. *Application deadline:* For fall admission, 2/1 for domestic students; for spring admission, 11/1 for domestic students. Applications are processed on a rolling basis. Application fee: $0 ($25 for international students). *Expenses:* Tuition: Full-time $19,700; part-time $1,096 per hour. *Financial support:* In 2003–04, 80 students received support, including 44 fellowships (averaging $19,700 per year), 23 research assistantships (averaging $19,700 per year); Federal Work-Study, scholarships/grants, and tuition waivers (full and partial) also available. *Faculty research:* Nanoscience, biomaterials, nanobioinformatics, fullerene pharmaceuticals. Total annual research

Organic Chemistry

Rice University (continued)

expenditures: $75,000. *Unit head:* Kenton H. Whitmire, Chair, 713-348-5650, Fax: 713-348-5155, E-mail: whitmir@rice.edu. *Application contact:* Sofia Medrano, Graduate Recruiting/Administrative Secretary, 713-348-4082, Fax: 713-348-5155, E-mail: gradchem@rice.edu.

Rutgers, The State University of New Jersey, Newark, Graduate School, Program in Chemistry, Newark, NJ 07102. Offers analytical chemistry (MS, PhD); biochemistry (MS, PhD); inorganic chemistry (MS, PhD); organic chemistry (MS, PhD); physical chemistry (MS, PhD). Part-time and evening/weekend programs available. *Faculty:* 22 full-time (5 women). *Students:* 19 full-time (9 women), 35 part-time (12 women); includes 28 minority (3 African Americans, 25 Asian Americans or Pacific Islanders). 107 applicants, 31% accepted, 8 enrolled. In 2003, 4 master's, 6 doctorates awarded. Terminal master's awarded for partial completion of doctoral program. *Degree requirements:* For master's, cumulative exams, thesis optional; for doctorate, thesis/dissertation, exams, research proposal. *Entrance requirements:* For master's and doctorate, GRE General Test, minimum undergraduate B average. Additional exam requirements/recommendations for international students: Required—TOEFL. *Application deadline:* For fall admission, 7/1 for domestic students; for spring admission, 12/1 for domestic students. Applications are processed on a rolling basis. Application fee: $50. Electronic applications accepted. *Expenses:* Tuition, state resident: full-time $10,030. Tuition, nonresident: full-time $14,202. *Financial support:* In 2003–04, 35 students received support, including 6 fellowships with full tuition reimbursements available, 20 teaching assistantships with full tuition reimbursements available (averaging $14,300 per year); Federal Work-Study and institutionally sponsored loans also available. Financial award application deadline: 3/1. *Faculty research:* Medicinal chemistry, natural products, isotope effects, biophysics and biorganic approaches to enzyme mechanisms, organic and organometallic synthesis. *Unit head:* Prof. W. Philip Huskey, Chairman and Program Director, 973-353-5741, Fax: 973-353-1264, E-mail: huskey@andromeda.rutgers.edu.

Rutgers, The State University of New Jersey, New Brunswick/Piscataway, Graduate School, Program in Chemistry and Chemical Biology, New Brunswick, NJ 08901-1281. Offers analytical chemistry (MS, PhD); biological chemistry (PhD); chemistry education (MST); inorganic chemistry (MS, PhD); organic chemistry (MS, PhD); physical chemistry (MS, PhD). Part-time and evening/weekend programs available. Terminal master's awarded for partial completion of doctoral program. *Degree requirements:* For master's, thesis or alternative, exam, comprehensive exam, registration; for doctorate, thesis/dissertation, cumulative exams, 1 year residency, comprehensive exam, registration. *Entrance requirements:* For master's and doctorate, GRE General Test, GRE Subject Test. Additional exam requirements/recommendations for international students: Required—TOEFL. Electronic applications accepted. *Expenses:* Tuition, state resident: full-time $10,030. Tuition, nonresident: full-time $14,202. *Faculty research:* Biophysical organic/bioorganic, inorganic/bioinorganic, theoretical, and solid-state/surface chemistry.

See in-depth description on page 141.

Seton Hall University, College of Arts and Sciences, Department of Chemistry and Biochemistry, South Orange, NJ 07079-2694. Offers analytical chemistry (MS, PhD); biochemistry (MS, PhD); chemistry (MS); inorganic chemistry (MS, PhD); organic chemistry (MS, PhD); physical chemistry (MS, PhD). Part-time and evening/weekend programs available. Terminal master's awarded for partial completion of doctoral program. *Degree requirements:* For master's, formal seminar, thesis optional; for doctorate, thesis/dissertation, annual seminars, comprehensive exam. *Entrance requirements:* For master's, undergraduate major in chemistry or related field with minimum 30 credits in chemistry, including 2 semesters of physical chemistry; for doctorate, oral matriculation exam based on proposed doctoral research, minimum GPA of 3.0 in course distribution requirements, formal seminar. Additional exam requirements/recommendations for international students: Required—TOEFL. *Faculty research:* DNA metal reactions; chromatography; bioinorganic, biophysical, organometallic, polymer chemistry; heterogeneous catalyst.

South Dakota State University, Graduate School, College of Arts and Science and College of Agriculture and Biological Sciences, Department of Chemistry, Brookings, SD 57007. Offers analytical chemistry (MS, PhD); biochemistry (MS, PhD); chemistry (MS, PhD); inorganic chemistry (MS, PhD); organic chemistry (MS, PhD); physical chemistry (MS, PhD). *Degree requirements:* For master's, thesis, oral exam; for doctorate, thesis/dissertation, preliminary oral and written exams, research tool. *Entrance requirements:* For master's, bachelor's degree in chemistry or equivalent. Additional exam requirements/recommendations for international students: Required—TOEFL. *Faculty research:* Environmental chemistry, computational chemistry, organic synthesis and photochemistry, novel material development and characterization.

Southern University and Agricultural and Mechanical College, Graduate School, College of Sciences, Department of Chemistry, Baton Rouge, LA 70813. Offers analytical chemistry (MS); biochemistry (MS); environmental sciences (MS); inorganic chemistry (MS); organic chemistry (MS); physical chemistry (MS). *Degree requirements:* For master's, thesis. *Entrance requirements:* For master's, GMAT or GRE General Test. Additional exam requirements/recommendations for international students: Required—TOEFL. *Faculty research:* Synthesis of macrocyclic ligands, latex accelerators, anticancer drugs, biosensors, absorption isotheums, isolation of specific enzymes from plants.

State University of New York at Binghamton, Graduate School, School of Arts and Sciences, Department of Chemistry, Binghamton, NY 13902-6000. Offers analytical chemistry (PhD); chemistry (MA, MS); inorganic chemistry (PhD); organic chemistry (PhD); physical chemistry (PhD). Part-time programs available. Terminal master's awarded for partial completion of doctoral program. *Degree requirements:* For master's, thesis or alternative, oral exam, seminar presentation; for doctorate, thesis/dissertation, cumulative exams. *Entrance requirements:* For master's and doctorate, GRE General Test, GRE Subject Test. Additional exam requirements/recommendations for international students: Required—TOEFL. Electronic applications accepted.

State University of New York College of Environmental Science and Forestry, Faculty of Chemistry, Syracuse, NY 13210-2779. Offers biochemistry (MS, PhD); environmental and forest chemistry (MS, PhD); organic chemistry of natural products (MS, PhD); polymer chemistry (MS, PhD). *Faculty:* 14 full-time (0 women), 1 (woman) part-time/adjunct. *Students:* 27 full-time (13 women), 11 part-time (3 women); includes 1 minority (American Indian/Alaska Native), 17 international. Average age 30. 45 applicants, 71% accepted, 11 enrolled. In 2003, 2 master's, 6 doctorates awarded. *Degree requirements:* For master's, thesis/dissertation, registration; for doctorate, thesis/dissertation, comprehensive exam, registration. *Entrance requirements:* For master's and doctorate, GRE General Test, GRE Subject Test, minimum GPA of 3.0. Additional exam requirements/recommendations for international students: Required—TOEFL (minimum score 550 paper-based; 213 computer-based). *Application deadline:* For fall admission, 2/1 priority date for domestic students, 2/1 priority date for international students; for spring admission, 11/1 priority date for domestic students, 11/1 priority date for international students. Applications are processed on a rolling basis. Application fee: $50. Tuition, area resident: Part-time $288 per credit hour. Tuition, nonresident: part-time $438 per credit hour. Required fees: $300; $5 per credit hour. $18 per semester. One-time fee: $25 full-time. *Financial support:* In 2003–04, 35 students received support, including 8 fellowships with full tuition reimbursements available (averaging $9,446 per year), 15 research assistantships with full tuition reimbursements available (averaging $12,500 per year), 4 teaching assistantships with full tuition reimbursements available (averaging $11,540 per year); Federal Work-Study, institutionally sponsored loans, scholarships/grants, health care benefits, and unspecified assistantships also available. Financial award applicants required to submit FAFSA. *Faculty research:* Polymer chemistry, biochemistry. Total annual research expenditures: $1.4 million. *Unit head:* Dr. John P. Hassett, Chair, 315-470-6827, Fax: 315-470-6856, E-mail: jphasset@syr.edu. *Application contact:* Dr. Dudley J. Raynal, Dean, Instruction and Graduate Studies, 315-470-6599, Fax: 315-470-6978, E-mail: esfgrad@esf.edu.

Stevens Institute of Technology, Graduate School, School of Applied Sciences and Liberal Arts, Department of Chemistry and Chemical Biology, Hoboken, NJ 07030. Offers chemistry (MS, PhD, Certificate), including analytical chemistry, chemical biology, chemical physiology (Certificate), instrumental analysis (Certificate), organic chemistry (MS, PhD), physical chemistry (MS, PhD), polymer chemistry. Part-time and evening/weekend programs available. Terminal master's awarded for partial completion of doctoral program. *Degree requirements:* For master's, thesis or alternative; for doctorate, one foreign language, thesis/dissertation; for Certificate, project or thesis. *Entrance requirements:* Additional exam requirements/recommendations for international students: Required—TOEFL. Electronic applications accepted.

Tufts University, Graduate School of Arts and Sciences, Department of Chemistry, Medford, MA 02155. Offers analytical chemistry (MS, PhD); bioorganic chemistry (MS, PhD); environmental chemistry (MS, PhD); inorganic chemistry (MS, PhD); organic chemistry (MS, PhD); physical chemistry (MS, PhD). *Faculty:* 13 full-time, 1 part-time/adjunct. *Students:* 56 (24 women); includes 6 minority (1 African American, 4 Asian Americans or Pacific Islanders, 1 Hispanic American) 22 international. 66 applicants, 56% accepted, 17 enrolled. In 2003, 4 master's, 6 doctorates awarded. Terminal master's awarded for partial completion of doctoral program. *Degree requirements:* For master's and doctorate, thesis/dissertation. *Entrance requirements:* For master's and doctorate, GRE General Test, GRE Subject Test. Additional exam requirements/recommendations for international students: Required—TOEFL (minimum score 600 paper-based; 213 computer-based), TSE. *Application deadline:* For fall admission, 2/1 for domestic students, 12/30 for international students; for spring admission, 10/15 for domestic students, 9/15 for international students. Applications are processed on a rolling basis. Application fee: $60. Electronic applications accepted. *Expenses:* Tuition: Full-time $29,949. *Financial support:* Research assistantships with full and partial tuition reimbursements, teaching assistantships with full and partial tuition reimbursements, Federal Work-Study, scholarships/grants, and tuition waivers (partial) available. Financial award application deadline: 2/1; financial award applicants required to submit FAFSA. *Unit head:* Mary Jane Shultz, Chair, 617-627-3477, Fax: 617-627-3443. *Application contact:* Arthur Utz, Information Contact, 617-627-3441, Fax: 617-627-3443.

See in-depth description on page 153.

University of Calgary, Faculty of Graduate Studies, Faculty of Science, Department of Chemistry, Calgary, AB T2N 1N4, Canada. Offers analytical chemistry (M Sc, PhD); applied chemistry (M Sc, PhD); inorganic chemistry (M Sc, PhD); organic chemistry (M Sc, PhD); physical chemistry (M Sc, PhD); polymer chemistry (M Sc, PhD); theoretical chemistry (M Sc, PhD). *Faculty:* 29 full-time (6 women), 1 part-time/adjunct (0 women). *Students:* 74 full-time (29 women). Average age 25. 130 applicants, 20% accepted. In 2003, 12 master's, 6 doctorates awarded. *Degree requirements:* For master's, thesis; for doctorate, thesis/dissertation, candidacy exam. *Entrance requirements:* For master's, minimum GPA of 3.0; for doctorate, honors degree minimum GPA of 3.7, minimum GPA of 3.3. Additional exam requirements/recommendations for international students: Required—TOEFL (minimum score 580 paper-based; 237 computer-based). *Application deadline:* For fall admission, 12/1 for domestic students. Applications are processed on a rolling basis. Application fee: $60. Electronic applications accepted. Tuition, nonresident: full-time $4,765. Tuition and fees vary according to degree level, program and student level. *Financial support:* In 2003–04, research assistantships (averaging $11,000 per year), teaching assistantships (averaging $6,221 per year) were awarded. Fellowships, scholarships/grants also available. Financial award application deadline: 12/1. *Faculty research:* Chemical analysis, chemical dynamics, synthesis theory, polymer, applied chemistry. *Unit head:* Dr. Brian Keay, Head, 403-220-6252, E-mail: gradinfo@chem.ucalgary.ca.

University of Cincinnati, Division of Research and Advanced Studies, McMicken College of Arts and Sciences, Department of Chemistry, Cincinnati, OH 45221. Offers analytical chemistry (MS, PhD); biochemistry (MS, PhD); inorganic chemistry (MS, PhD); organic chemistry (MS, PhD); physical chemistry (MS, PhD); polymer chemistry (MS, PhD); sensors (PhD). Part-time and evening/weekend programs available. Terminal master's awarded for partial completion of doctoral program. *Degree requirements:* For master's, thesis optional; for doctorate, thesis/dissertation, comprehensive exam, registration. *Entrance requirements:* For master's and doctorate, GRE General Test. Additional exam requirements/recommendations for international students: Required—TOEFL (minimum score 580 paper-based; 237 computer-based); Recommended—TSE(minimum score 50). Electronic applications accepted. *Faculty research:* Biomedical chemistry, laser chemistry, surface science, chemical sensors, synthesis.

University of Georgia, Graduate School, College of Arts and Sciences, Department of Chemistry, Athens, GA 30602. Offers analytical chemistry (MS, PhD); inorganic chemistry (MS, PhD); organic chemistry (MS, PhD); physical chemistry (MS, PhD). *Faculty:* 26 full-time (2 women). *Students:* 130 full-time (43 women). 160 applicants, 29% accepted, 36 enrolled. In 2003, 3 master's, 17 doctorates awarded. Terminal master's awarded for partial completion of doctoral program. *Median time to degree:* Of those who began their doctoral program in fall 1995, 100% received their degree in 8 years or less. *Degree requirements:* For master's, thesis; for doctorate, one foreign language, thesis/dissertation. *Entrance requirements:* For master's and doctorate, GRE General Test. Additional exam requirements/recommendations for international students: Required—TOEFL (minimum score 213 computer-based), TSE(minimum score 50). *Application deadline:* For fall admission, 7/1 for domestic students; for spring admission, 11/15 for domestic students. Application fee: $50. Electronic applications accepted. *Expenses:* Tuition, state resident: part-time $161 per hour. Tuition, nonresident: part-time $690 per hour. One-time fee: $435 part-time. *Financial support:* Fellowships, research assistantships, teaching assistantships, unspecified assistantships available. *Unit head:* Dr. John L. Stickney, Head, 706-542-2726, Fax: 706-542-9454, E-mail: stickney@chem.uga.edu. *Application contact:* Dr. Donald Kurtz, Information Contact, 706-542-2010, Fax: 706-542-9454, E-mail: kurtz@chem.uga.edu.

University of Louisville, Graduate School, College of Arts and Sciences, Department of Chemistry, Louisville, KY 40292-0001. Offers analytical chemistry (MS, PhD); biochemistry (MS, PhD); chemical physics (PhD); inorganic chemistry (MS, PhD); organic chemistry (MS, PhD); physical chemistry (MS, PhD). *Students:* 48 full-time (19 women), 13 part-time (5 women); includes 4 minority (1 African American, 1 Asian American or Pacific Islander, 2 Hispanic Americans), 27 international. Average age 27. In 2003, 7 master's, 1 doctorate awarded. *Degree requirements:* For master's, thesis/dissertation; for doctorate, thesis/dissertation, comprehensive exam. *Entrance requirements:* For master's and doctorate, GRE General Test. Additional exam requirements/recommendations for international students: Required—TOEFL. *Application deadline:* Applications are processed on a rolling basis. Application fee: $50. *Expenses:* Tuition, state resident: full-time $4,842. Tuition, nonresident: full-time $13,338. *Financial support:* In 2003–04, 30 teaching assistantships (averaging $14,000 per year) were awarded. *Unit head:* Dr. George R. Pack, Chair, 502-852-6798, Fax: 502-852-8149, E-mail: george.pack@louisville.edu.

University of Maryland, College Park, Graduate Studies and Research, College of Life Sciences, Department of Chemistry and Biochemistry, Chemistry Program, College Park, MD 20742. Offers analytical chemistry (MS, PhD); inorganic chemistry (MS, PhD); organic chemistry (MS, PhD); physical chemistry (MS, PhD). Part-time and evening/weekend programs available. *Students:* 89 full-time (46 women), 4 part-time (2 women); includes 6 minority (2 African Americans, 2 Asian Americans or Pacific Islanders, 2 Hispanic Americans), 39 international. 141 applicants, 19% accepted. In 2003, 16 degrees awarded. Terminal master's awarded for partial completion of doctoral program. *Median time to degree:* Of those who began their doctoral program in fall 1995, 33% received their degree in 8 years or less. *Degree requirements:* For master's, thesis optional; for doctorate, thesis/dissertation, 2 seminar presentations, oral exam. *Entrance requirements:* For master's, GRE General Test, GRE Subject Test (recommended), minimum GPA of 3.1, 3 letters of recommendation; for doctorate, GRE General Test, GRE Subject Test (recommended), minimum GPA of 3.1. *Application deadline:* For fall admission, 5/1 for domestic students, 2/1 for international students; for spring admission, 10/1 for domestic students, 6/1 for international students. Applications are processed on a rolling basis. Application fee: $50. Electronic applications accepted. *Expenses:* Tuition, state resident:

part-time $349 per credit hour. Tuition, nonresident: part-time $602 per credit hour. *Financial support:* Fellowships, research assistantships, teaching assistantships with partial tuition reimbursements available. Financial award applicants required to submit FAFSA. *Faculty research:* Environmental chemistry, nuclear chemistry, lunar and environmental analysis, x-ray crystallography. *Application contact:* Trudy Lindsey, Director, Graduate Enrollment Management Services, 301-405-4190, Fax: 301-314-9305, E-mail: tlindsey@gradschool.umd.edu.

University of Miami, Graduate School, College of Arts and Sciences, Department of Chemistry, Coral Gables, FL 33124. Offers chemistry (MS); inorganic chemistry (PhD); organic chemistry (PhD); physical chemistry (PhD). *Faculty:* 9 full-time (1 woman). *Students:* 39 full-time (17 women); includes 23 minority (4 African Americans, 15 Asian Americans or Pacific Islanders, 4 Hispanic Americans), 25 international. Average age 25. 104 applicants, 13% accepted, 10 enrolled. In 2003, 2 master's, 1 doctorate awarded. Terminal master's awarded for partial completion of doctoral program. *Degree requirements:* For master's, comprehensive exam; for doctorate, thesis/dissertation, comprehensive exam. *Entrance requirements:* For master's and doctorate, GRE General Test. Additional exam requirements/recommendations for international students: Required—TOEFL (minimum score 550 paper-based; 213 computer-based). *Application deadline:* For fall admission, 1/15 for domestic students, 1/15 for international students. Applications are processed on a rolling basis. Application fee: $50. Electronic applications accepted. *Expenses:* Tuition: Full-time $19,526. *Financial support:* In 2003–04, 39 students received support, including 3 fellowships with full tuition reimbursements available (averaging $20,000 per year), 14 research assistantships with full tuition reimbursements available (averaging $19,000 per year), 21 teaching assistantships with full tuition reimbursements available (averaging $19,000 per year); tuition waivers (full) also available. Financial award application deadline: 5/1; financial award applicants required to submit FAFSA. *Faculty research:* Supramolecular chemistry, electrochemistry, surface chemistry, catalysis, organometalic. *Unit head:* Dr. Cecil M. Criss, Chairman, 305-284-2282, Fax: 305-284-4571. *Application contact:* Eva Johnson, Graduate Secretary, 305-284-6561, Fax: 305-284-4571, E-mail: evaj@miami.edu.

University of Michigan, Horace H. Rackham School of Graduate Studies, College of Literature, Science, and the Arts, Department of Chemistry, Ann Arbor, MI 48109. Offers analytical chemistry (PhD); chemical biology (PhD); inorganic chemistry (PhD); material chemistry (PhD); organic chemistry (PhD); physical chemistry (PhD). *Faculty:* 50 full-time (10 women), 3 part-time/adjunct (0 women). *Students:* 213 full-time (101 women); includes 20 minority (5 African Americans, 1 American Indian/Alaska Native, 9 Asian Americans or Pacific Islanders, 5 Hispanic Americans), 64 international. Average age 26. 310 applicants, 56% accepted, 58 enrolled. In 2003, 27 degrees awarded. *Degree requirements:* For doctorate, thesis/dissertation, oral defense of dissertation, organic cumulative proficiency exams. *Entrance requirements:* For doctorate, GRE General Test, GRE Subject Test (recommended), statement of prior research. Additional exam requirements/recommendations for international students: Required—TOEFL. *Application deadline:* For fall admission, 1/15 priority date for domestic students, 1/15 priority date for international students. Applications are processed on a rolling basis. Application fee: $60 ($75 for international students). Electronic applications accepted. *Expenses:* Tuition, state resident: full-time $7,463. Tuition, nonresident: full-time $13,913. Full-time tuition and fees vary according to course load, degree level and program. *Financial support:* In 2003–04, 10 fellowships with full tuition reimbursements (averaging $20,000 per year), 70 research assistantships with full tuition reimbursements (averaging $19,000 per year), 120 teaching assistantships with full tuition reimbursements (averaging $20,000 per year) were awarded. Financial award applicants required to submit FAFSA. *Faculty research:* Biological catalysis, protein engineering, chemical sensors, de novo metalloprotein design, supramolecular architecture. Total annual research expenditures: $8 million. *Unit head:* Dr. William R. Roush, Chair, 734-763-9681, Fax: 734-647-4847, E-mail: roush@umich.edu. *Application contact:* Linda Deitert, Assistant Director Graduate Studies, 734-764-7278, Fax: 734-647-4865, E-mail: chemadmissions@umich.edu.

University of Missouri–Columbia, Graduate School, College of Arts and Sciences, Department of Chemistry, Columbia, MO 65211. Offers analytical chemistry (MS, PhD); inorganic chemistry (MS, PhD); organic chemistry (MS, PhD); physical chemistry (MS, PhD). *Faculty:* 20 full-time (4 women). *Students:* 58 full-time (21 women), 36 part-time (7 women); includes 5 minority (1 African American, 1 American Indian/Alaska Native, 3 Asian Americans or Pacific Islanders), 51 international. In 2003, 7 master's, 7 doctorates awarded. *Degree requirements:* For master's, thesis; for doctorate, one foreign language, thesis/dissertation. *Entrance requirements:* For master's and doctorate, GRE General Test, minimum GPA of 3.0. *Application deadline:* For fall admission, 4/1 for domestic students; for winter admission, 11/1 for domestic students. Applications are processed on a rolling basis. Application fee: $45 ($60 for international students). *Expenses:* Tuition, state resident: full-time $5,205. Tuition, nonresident: full-time $14,058. *Financial support:* Research assistantships, teaching assistantships, institutionally sponsored loans available. *Unit head:* Dr. Silvia S. Jurisson, Director of Graduate Studies, 573-882-2107, E-mail: jurissons@missouri.edu.

University of Missouri–Kansas City, College of Arts and Sciences, Department of Chemistry, Kansas City, MO 64110-2499. Offers analytical chemistry (MS, PhD); inorganic chemistry (MS, PhD); organic chemistry (MS, PhD); physical chemistry (MS, PhD); polymer chemistry (MS, PhD). PhD offered through the School of Graduate Studies. Part-time and evening/weekend programs available. *Faculty:* 11 full-time (1 woman), 1 part-time/adjunct (0 women). *Students:* Average age 30. 56 applicants, 46% accepted. In 2003, 1 master's awarded. *Median time to degree:* Master's–1 year full-time, 1 year part-time; doctorate–5 years full-time. *Degree requirements:* For master's, thesis (for some programs); for doctorate, thesis/dissertation. *Entrance requirements:* For master's, equivalent of American Chemical Society approved bachelor's degree in chemistry; for doctorate, GRE General Test, equivalent of American Chemical Society approved bachelor's degree in chemistry. Additional exam requirements/recommendations for international students: Required—TOEFL (minimum score 580 paper-based; 237 computer-based), TWE. *Application deadline:* For fall and spring admission, 4/15; for winter admission, 10/15 for domestic students. Applications are processed on a rolling basis. Application fee: $25. *Financial support:* In 2003–04, 1 fellowship with partial tuition reimbursement (averaging $18,156 per year), 9 research assistantships with partial tuition reimbursements (averaging $17,632 per year), 16 teaching assistantships with partial tuition reimbursements (averaging $16,416 per year) were awarded. Federal Work-Study, institutionally sponsored loans, and scholarships/grants also available. Support available to part-time students. Financial award application deadline: 2/15. *Faculty research:* Molecular spectroscopy, characterization and synthesis of materials and compounds, computational chemistry, natural products, drug delivery systems and anti-tumor agents. Total annual research expenditures: $551,743. *Unit head:* Dr. Jerry Jean, Chairperson, 816-235-2280, Fax: 816-235-5502, E-mail: jeany@umkc.edu. *Application contact:* Dr. Kathleen Y. Kilway, Graduate Recruiting Committee, 816-235-2289, Fax: 816-235-5502, E-mail: kilwayk@umkc.edu.

University of Missouri–St. Louis, Graduate School, College of Arts and Sciences, Department of Chemistry, St. Louis, MO 63121-4499. Offers chemistry (MS, PhD), including biochemistry, inorganic chemistry, organic chemistry, physical chemistry. Part-time and evening/weekend programs available. *Faculty:* 16 full-time (3 women). *Students:* 31 full-time (19 women), 20 part-time (9 women); includes 6 minority (5 Asian Americans or Pacific Islanders, 1 Hispanic American), 21 international. In 2003, 8 master's, 5 doctorates awarded. Terminal master's awarded for partial completion of doctoral program. *Degree requirements:* For master's, thesis optional; for doctorate, thesis/dissertation. *Entrance requirements:* For doctorate, GRE General Test, GRE Subject Test. Additional exam requirements/recommendations for international students: Required—TOEFL (minimum score 550 paper-based; 213 computer-based). *Application deadline:* For fall admission, 7/1 for domestic students; for spring admission, 12/7 priority date for domestic students. Applications are processed on a rolling basis. Application fee: $35 ($40 for international students). Electronic applications accepted. *Expenses:* Tuition, state resident: part-time $237 per credit hour. Tuition, nonresident: part-time $639 per credit hour. Required fees: $10 per credit hour. *Financial support:* In 2003–04, 14 research assistantships with full and partial tuition reimbursements (averaging $16,007 per year), 13 teaching assistantships with full and partial tuition reimbursements (averaging $15,408 per year) were awarded. Fellowships with full and partial tuition reimbursements *Faculty research:* Metallaborane chemistry, serum transferrin chemistry, natural products chemistry, organic synthesis. *Unit head:* Dr. F. Christopher Pigge, Director of Graduate Studies, 314-516-5311, Fax: 314-516-5342. *Application contact:* 314-516-5458, Fax: 314-516-5310, E-mail: gradadm@umsl.edu.

The University of Montana–Missoula, Graduate School, College of Arts and Sciences, Department of Chemistry, Missoula, MT 59812-0002. Offers chemistry (MS, PhD), including environmental/analytical chemistry, inorganic chemistry, organic chemistry, physical chemistry; chemistry teaching (MST). *Faculty:* 16 full-time (2 women). *Students:* 26 full-time (5 women), 12 part-time (6 women), 10 international. 25 applicants, 44% accepted, 6 enrolled. In 2003, 2 master's, 4 doctorates awarded. Terminal master's awarded for partial completion of doctoral program. *Degree requirements:* For master's, thesis (for some programs); for doctorate, thesis/dissertation. *Entrance requirements:* For master's and doctorate, GRE General Test. Additional exam requirements/recommendations for international students: Required—TOEFL (minimum score 575 paper-based; 230 computer-based). *Application deadline:* For fall admission, 2/15 for domestic students. Applications are processed on a rolling basis. Application fee: $45. *Expenses:* Tuition, state resident: full-time $1,848; part-time $221 per credit. Tuition, nonresident: full-time $4,880; part-time $333 per credit. Required fees: $2,200. *Financial support:* In 2003–04, 13 research assistantships with tuition reimbursements (averaging $14,000 per year), 12 teaching assistantships with full tuition reimbursements (averaging $14,000 per year) were awarded. Federal Work-Study, scholarships/grants, and unspecified assistantships also available. Financial award application deadline: 3/1; financial award applicants required to submit FAFSA. *Faculty research:* Reaction mechanisms and kinetics, inorganic and organic synthesis, analytical chemistry, natural products. Total annual research expenditures: $789,952. *Unit head:* Dr. Edward Rosenberg, Chair, 406-243-4022, Fax: 406-243-4227.

University of Nebraska–Lincoln, Graduate College, College of Arts and Sciences, Department of Chemistry, Lincoln, NE 68588. Offers analytical chemistry (PhD); chemistry (MS); inorganic chemistry (PhD); organic chemistry (PhD); physical chemistry (PhD). *Degree requirements:* For master's, one foreign language, departmental qualifying exam, thesis optional; for doctorate, one foreign language, thesis/dissertation, departmental qualifying exams, comprehensive exam. *Entrance requirements:* For master's and doctorate, GRE. Additional exam requirements/recommendations for international students: Required—TOEFL (minimum score 550 paper-based; 213 computer-based). Electronic applications accepted. *Faculty research:* Bioorganic and bioinorganic chemistry, biophysical and bioanalytical chemistry, structure-function of DNA and proteins, organometallics, mass spectrometry.

University of Notre Dame, Graduate School, College of Science, Department of Chemistry and Biochemistry, Notre Dame, IN 46556. Offers biochemistry (MS, PhD); inorganic chemistry (MS, PhD); organic chemistry (MS, PhD); physical chemistry (MS, PhD). *Faculty:* 30 full-time (3 women). *Students:* 139 full-time (46 women); includes 5 minority (1 African American, 1 American Indian/Alaska Native, 1 Asian American or Pacific Islander, 2 Hispanic Americans), 65 international. 270 applicants, 38% accepted, 44 enrolled. In 2003, 5 master's, 17 doctorates awarded. Terminal master's awarded for partial completion of doctoral program. *Degree requirements:* For master's, thesis, comprehensive exam; for doctorate, thesis/dissertation, qualifying exam. *Entrance requirements:* For master's and doctorate, GRE General Test, GRE Subject Test (strongly recommended). Additional exam requirements/recommendations for international students: Required—TOEFL. *Application deadline:* For fall admission, 2/1 for domestic students. Applications are processed on a rolling basis. Application fee: $50. Electronic applications accepted. *Expenses:* Tuition: Full-time $29,375. *Financial support:* In 2003–04, 139 students received support, including 34 fellowships with full tuition reimbursements available (averaging $20,000 per year), 46 research assistantships with full tuition reimbursements available (averaging $15,500 per year), 51 teaching assistantships with full tuition reimbursements available (averaging $15,500 per year); tuition waivers (full) also available. Financial award application deadline: 2/1. *Faculty research:* Reaction design and mechaninistic studies; reactive intermediates; synthesis, structure and reactivity of organometallic. cluster complexes, and biologically active natural products; bioorganic chemistry; enzymology. Total annual research expenditures: $9.4 million. *Unit head:* Dr. Richard E. Taylor, Director of Graduate Studies, 574-631-7058, Fax: 574-631-6652, E-mail: taylor.61@nd.edu. *Application contact:* Dr. Terrence J. Akai, Director of Graduate Admissions, 574-631-7706, Fax: 574-631-4183, E-mail: gradad@nd.edu.

University of Regina, Faculty of Graduate Studies and Research, Faculty of Science, Department of Chemistry and Biochemistry, Regina, SK S4S 0A2, Canada. Offers analytical chemistry (M Sc, PhD); biochemistry (M Sc, PhD); inorganic chemistry (M Sc, PhD); organic chemistry (M Sc, PhD); physical chemistry (M Sc, PhD). Part-time programs available. *Faculty:* 9 full-time (2 women), 2 part-time/adjunct (1 woman). *Students:* 7 full-time (4 women), 4 part-time (1 woman). 12 applicants. In 2003, 3 degrees awarded. *Degree requirements:* For master's and doctorate, thesis/dissertation, departmental qualifying exam. *Entrance requirements:* For master's and doctorate, GRE. Additional exam requirements/recommendations for international students: Required—TOEFL. *Application deadline:* For fall admission, 1/1 for domestic students; for winter admission, 7/1 for domestic students. Applications are processed on a rolling basis. Application fee: $60. *Expenses:* Tuition, state resident: part-time $130 per credit hour. Tuition and fees vary according to course load and program. *Financial support:* In 2003–04, 4 fellowships, 1 research assistantship, 3 teaching assistantships were awarded. Scholarships/grants also available. Financial award application deadline: 6/15. *Faculty research:* Organic synthesis, organic oxidations, ionic liquids theoretical/computational chemistry, protein biochemistry/biophysics, environmental analytical, photophysical/photochemistry. *Unit head:* Dr. Andrew G. Wee, Head, 306-585-4767, Fax: 306-585-4894, E-mail: chem.chair@uregina.ca. *Application contact:* Teri Dibble, Office Administrator, 306-585-4146, Fax: 306-585-4894, E-mail: teri.dibble@uregina.ca.

University of Southern Mississippi, Graduate School, College of Science and Technology, Department of Chemistry and Biochemistry, Hattiesburg, MS 39406-0001. Offers analytical chemistry (MS, PhD); biochemistry (MS, PhD); inorganic chemistry (MS, PhD); organic chemistry (MS, PhD); physical chemistry (MS, PhD). *Faculty:* 8 full-time (1 woman). *Students:* 27 full-time (17 women), 1 part-time; includes 14 minority (4 African Americans, 1 American Indian/Alaska Native, 9 Asian Americans or Pacific Islanders). Average age 27. 29 applicants, 45% accepted, 10 enrolled. In 2003, 1 master's, 7 doctorates awarded. *Degree requirements:* For master's and doctorate, thesis/dissertation, comprehensive exam. *Entrance requirements:* For master's, GRE General Test, minimum GPA of 2.75 in last 60 hours; for doctorate, GRE General Test, minimum GPA of 3.5. Additional exam requirements/recommendations for international students: Required—TOEFL. *Application deadline:* For fall admission, 8/6 for domestic students. Applications are processed on a rolling basis. Application fee: $25. *Expenses:* Tuition, state resident: part-time $1,967 per semester. Tuition, nonresident: part-time $4,376 per semester. *Financial support:* Fellowships, research assistantships with full tuition reimbursements, teaching assistantships with full tuition reimbursements, Federal Work-Study and institutionally sponsored loans available. Support available to part-time students. Financial award application deadline: 3/15. *Faculty research:* Plant biochemistry, photo chemistry, polymer chemistry, x-ray analysis, enzyme chemistry. *Unit head:* Dr. Robert Bateman, Chair, 601-266-4701. *Application contact:* Dr. Gordon Cannon, Information Contact, 601-266-4702.

University of South Florida, College of Graduate Studies, College of Arts and Sciences, Department of Chemistry, Tampa, FL 33620-9951. Offers analytical chemistry (MS, PhD); biochemistry (MS, PhD); inorganic chemistry (MS, PhD); organic chemistry (MS, PhD); physical chemistry (MS, PhD); polymer chemistry (PhD). Part-time programs available. *Faculty:* 26 full-time (8 women), 1 (woman) part-time/adjunct. *Students:* 75 full-time (34 women), 11 part-time (4 women); includes 14 minority (3 African Americans, 3 Asian Americans or Pacific Islanders, 8 Hispanic Americans), 30 international. 75 applicants, 37% accepted, 17 enrolled. In 2003, 3 master's, 6 doctorates awarded. Terminal master's awarded for partial completion of doctoral program. *Degree requirements:* For master's, thesis; for doctorate, 2 foreign languages, thesis/dissertation, colloquium. *Entrance requirements:* For master's and doctorate, GRE

Organic Chemistry

University of South Florida (continued)

General Test, minimum GPA of 3.0 in last 30 hours of chemistry course work, letters of recommendation (3). Additional exam requirements/recommendations for international students: Required—TOEFL (minimum score 550 paper-based; 213 computer-based), TSE(minimum score 50). *Application deadline:* For fall admission, 5/1 priority date for domestic students, 3/1 priority date for international students; for spring admission, 10/1 priority date for domestic students, 8/1 priority date for international students. Applications are processed on a rolling basis. Application fee: $30. Electronic applications accepted. *Financial support:* In 2003–04, 74 students received support, including 3 fellowships with partial tuition reimbursements available (averaging $18,500 per year), 13 research assistantships with partial tuition reimbursements available (averaging $18,500 per year), 58 teaching assistantships with partial tuition reimbursements available (averaging $18,500 per year); career-related internships or fieldwork, institutionally sponsored loans, scholarships/grants, and unspecified assistantships also available. Financial award application deadline: 6/30. *Faculty research:* Synthesis, bio-organic chemistry, bioinorganic chemistry, environmental chemistry, NMR. Total annual research expenditures: $1.6 million. *Unit head:* Michael Zaworotko, Chairperson, 813-974-4129, Fax: 813-974-1731. *Application contact:* Dr. Julie Harmon, Graduate Director, 813-974-3397, Fax: 813-974-3203, E-mail: harmon@chuma1.cas.usf.edu.

The University of Tennessee, Graduate School, College of Arts and Sciences, Department of Chemistry, Knoxville, TN 37996. Offers analytical chemistry (MS, PhD); chemical physics (PhD); environmental chemistry (MS, PhD); inorganic chemistry (MS, PhD); organic chemistry (MS, PhD); physical chemistry (MS, PhD); polymer chemistry (MS, PhD); theoretical chemistry (PhD). Part-time programs available. Terminal master's awarded for partial completion of doctoral program. *Degree requirements:* For master's and doctorate, thesis/dissertation. *Entrance requirements:* For master's and doctorate, GRE General Test, minimum GPA of 2.7. Additional exam requirements/recommendations for international students: Required—TOEFL. Electronic applications accepted.

The University of Texas at Austin, Graduate School, College of Natural Sciences, Department of Chemistry and Biochemistry, Austin, TX 78712-1111. Offers analytical chemistry (MA, PhD); biochemistry (MA, PhD); inorganic chemistry (MA, PhD); organic chemistry (MA, PhD); physical chemistry (MA, PhD). *Entrance requirements:* For master's and doctorate, GRE General Test.

University of Toledo, Graduate School, College of Arts and Sciences, Department of Chemistry, Toledo, OH 43606-3390. Offers analytical chemistry (MS, PhD); biological chemistry (MS, PhD); inorganic chemistry (MS, PhD); organic chemistry (MS, PhD); physical chemistry (MS, PhD). Part-time programs available. *Students:* 46 full-time (21 women), 9 part-time (4 women); includes 4 minority (3 African Americans, 1 Hispanic American), 31 international. Average age 27. 23 applicants, 87% accepted. In 2003, 3 master's, 5 doctorates awarded. *Degree requirements:* For master's and doctorate, thesis/dissertation. *Entrance requirements:* For master's and doctorate, GRE General Test, GRE Subject Test. Additional exam requirements/recommendations for international students: Required—TOEFL. *Application deadline:* For fall admission, 8/1 for domestic students. Applications are processed on a rolling basis. Application fee: $40. Electronic applications accepted. Tuition, area resident: Part-time $3,817 per semester. *Expenses:* Tuition, state resident: part-time $8,177 per semester. Required fees: $502 per semester. *Financial support:* In 2003–04, 4 research assistantships, 47 teaching assistantships were awarded. Fellowships, Federal Work-Study and institutionally sponsored loans also available. Support available to part-time students. Financial award application deadline: 4/1; financial award applicants required to submit FAFSA. *Faculty research:* Enzymology, materials chemistry, crystallography, theoretical chemistry. *Unit head:* Dr. Alan Pinkerton, Chair, 419-530-2109, Fax: 419-530-4033, E-mail: apinker@uoft02.utoledo.edu.

See in-depth description on page 179.

Vanderbilt University, Graduate School, Department of Chemistry, Nashville, TN 37240-1001. Offers analytical chemistry (MAT, MS, PhD); inorganic chemistry (MAT, MS, PhD); organic chemistry (MAT, MS, PhD); physical chemistry (MAT, MS, PhD); theoretical chemistry (MAT, MS, PhD). *Degree requirements:* For master's, thesis or alternative; for doctorate, thesis/dissertation, area, qualifying, and final exams. *Entrance requirements:* For master's and doctorate, GRE General Test, GRE Subject Test (recommended). Additional exam requirements/recommendations for international students: Required—TOEFL. Electronic applications accepted. *Expenses:* Tuition: Part-time $1,155 per semester hour. Required fees: $1,538. *Faculty research:* Chemical synthesis; mechanistic, theoretical, bioorganic, analytical, and spectroscopic chemistry.

See in-depth description on page 185.

Wake Forest University, Graduate School, Department of Chemistry, Winston-Salem, NC 27109. Offers analytical chemistry (MS, PhD); inorganic chemistry (MS, PhD); organic chemistry (MS, PhD); physical chemistry (MS, PhD). Part-time programs available. *Faculty:* 15 full-time (2 women). *Students:* 32 full-time (15 women), 1 part-time; includes 2 minority (both African Americans), 13 international. Average age 28. 34 applicants, 38% accepted, 5 enrolled. In 2003, 4 master's, 2 doctorates awarded. *Degree requirements:* For master's, one foreign language, thesis, comprehensive exam, registration; for doctorate, 2 foreign languages, thesis/dissertation, comprehensive exam, registration. *Entrance requirements:* For master's and doctorate, GRE General Test. Additional exam requirements/recommendations for international students: Required—TOEFL (minimum score 213 computer-based). *Application deadline:* For fall admission, 1/15 for domestic students, 1/15 for international students. Application fee: $25. Electronic applications accepted. *Expenses:* Tuition: Full-time $26,500. *Financial support:* In 2003–04, 32 students received support, including 1 fellowship with full tuition reimbursement available (averaging $19,500 per year), 11 research assistantships with full tuition reimbursements available (averaging $17,500 per year), 17 teaching assistantships with full tuition reimbursements available (averaging $17,500 per year); scholarships/grants and tuition waivers (full and partial) also available. Support available to part-time students. Financial award application deadline: 1/15; financial award applicants required to submit FAFSA. *Unit head:* Dr. Dilip Kondepudi, Director, 336-758-5131, Fax: 336-758-4656, E-mail: dilip@wfu.edu.

Washington State University, Graduate School, College of Sciences, Department of Chemistry, Pullman, WA 99164. Offers analytical chemistry (MS, PhD); biological systems (MS, PhD); inorganic chemistry (MS, PhD); organic chemistry (MS, PhD); physical chemistry (MS, PhD). *Faculty:* 22 full-time (3 women). *Students:* 37 full-time (17 women), 1 part-time; includes 3 minority (2 Asian Americans or Pacific Islanders, 1 Hispanic American), 10 international. Average age 25. 48 applicants, 58% accepted, 12 enrolled. In 2003, 3 master's, 1 doctorate awarded. Terminal master's awarded for partial completion of doctoral program. *Median time to degree:* Master's–2.8 years full-time; doctorate–5 years full-time. *Degree requirements:* For master's, oral exam, teaching experience, thesis optional; for doctorate, thesis/dissertation, oral exam, written exam, comprehensive exam. *Entrance requirements:* For master's and doctorate, GRE General Test, minimum GPA of 3.0, 3 letters of recommendation. *Application deadline:* For fall admission, 3/1 for domestic students; for spring admission, 10/1 priority date for domestic students. Applications are processed on a rolling basis. Application fee: $35. *Expenses:* Tuition, state resident: full-time $6,278; part-time $314 per hour. Tuition, nonresident: full-time $15,514; part-time $765 per hour. Required fees: $444. Full-time tuition and fees vary according to campus/location, program and student level. Part-time tuition and fees vary according to course load. *Financial support:* In 2003–04, 13 research assistantships with full and partial tuition reimbursements (averaging $17,000 per year), 23 teaching assistantships with full and partial tuition reimbursements (averaging $17,000 per year) were awarded. Fellowships, career-related internships or fieldwork, Federal Work-Study, institutionally sponsored loans, scholarships/grants, health care benefits, unspecified assistantships, and summer support also available. Financial award application deadline: 4/1; financial award applicants required to submit FAFSA. *Faculty research:* Environmental chemistry, materials chemistry, radio chemistry, bio-organic, computational chemistry. Total annual research expenditures: $1.9 million. *Unit head:* Dr. Ralph Yount, Chair, 509-335-1516, Fax: 509-335-8867, E-mail: yount@wsu.edu. *Application contact:* Sue B. Clark, Chair, Admissions Committee, 509-335-8866, Fax: 509-335-8867, E-mail: carrie@wsu.edu.

Wesleyan University, Graduate Programs, Department of Chemistry, Middletown, CT 06459-0260. Offers biochemistry (MA, PhD); chemical physics (MA, PhD); inorganic chemistry (MA, PhD); organic chemistry (MA, PhD); physical chemistry (MA, PhD); theoretical chemistry (MA, PhD). *Faculty:* 13 full-time (2 women), 2 part-time/adjunct (1 woman). *Students:* 36 full-time (18 women); includes 2 minority (1 African American, 1 Asian American or Pacific Islander), 21 international. In 2003, 2 degrees awarded. Terminal master's awarded for partial completion of doctoral program. *Degree requirements:* For master's and doctorate, one foreign language, thesis/dissertation. *Entrance requirements:* For master's, GRE General Test, GRE Subject Test; for doctorate, GRE Subject Test. *Application deadline:* For fall admission, 3/1 for domestic students. Applications are processed on a rolling basis. Application fee: $0. *Expenses:* Tuition: Full-time $22,338. Required fees: $20. *Financial support:* Fellowships, research assistantships, teaching assistantships, institutionally sponsored loans available. *Unit head:* George Peterson, Chair, 860-685-2508. *Application contact:* Karen Karpa, Information Contact, 860-685-2573, Fax: 860-685-2211, E-mail: kkarpa@wesleyan.edu.

See in-depth description on page 189.

West Virginia University, Eberly College of Arts and Sciences, Department of Chemistry, Morgantown, WV 26506. Offers analytical chemistry (MS, PhD); inorganic chemistry (MS, PhD); organic chemistry (MS, PhD); physical chemistry (MS, PhD); theoretical chemistry (MS, PhD). Part-time programs available. Postbaccalaureate distance learning degree programs offered (no on-campus study). *Faculty:* 14 full-time (1 woman), 5 part-time/adjunct (3 women). *Students:* 45 full-time (15 women), 3 part-time (2 women); includes 1 minority (Hispanic American), 26 international. Average age 28. 84 applicants, 58% accepted, 11 enrolled. In 2003, 5 master's, 3 doctorates awarded. Terminal master's awarded for partial completion of doctoral program. *Degree requirements:* For master's and doctorate, thesis/dissertation, registration. *Entrance requirements:* For master's, GRE General Test, GRE Subject Test (recommended), minimum GPA of 2.5; for doctorate, GRE General Test, GRE Subject Test (recommended), minimum GPA of 2.75. Additional exam requirements/recommendations for international students: Required—TOEFL. *Application deadline:* For fall admission, 3/1 for domestic students. Applications are processed on a rolling basis. Application fee: $50. Electronic applications accepted. *Expenses:* Tuition, state resident: full-time $4,332. Tuition, nonresident: full-time $12,442. *Financial support:* In 2003–04, fellowships (averaging $2,000 per year), research assistantships with full tuition reimbursements (averaging $13,000 per year), teaching assistantships with full tuition reimbursements (averaging $12,000 per year) were awarded. Tuition waivers (full and partial) also available. Financial award application deadline: 2/1; financial award applicants required to submit FAFSA. *Faculty research:* Analysis of proteins, drug interactions, solids and effluents by advanced separation methods; electro-chemistry, mass spectrometry and atomic spectrometry; development of new synthetic strategies for complex organic molecules; synthesis and structural characterization of metal complexes for polymerization catalysis; nonmagnetic resonance studies of amorphous solids. *Unit head:* Dr. Harry O. Finklea, Chair, 304-293-3435 Ext. 6408, Fax: 304-293-4904, E-mail: harry.finklea@mail.wvu.edu.

Yale University, Graduate School of Arts and Sciences, Department of Chemistry, New Haven, CT 06520. Offers biophysical chemistry (PhD); inorganic chemistry (PhD); organic chemistry (PhD); physical chemistry (PhD). *Degree requirements:* For doctorate, thesis/dissertation. *Entrance requirements:* For doctorate, GRE General Test, GRE Subject Test. Additional exam requirements/recommendations for international students: Required—TOEFL. *Expenses:* Tuition: Full-time $25,600; part-time $6,400 per term.

Physical Chemistry

Boston College, Graduate School of Arts and Sciences, Department of Chemistry, Chestnut Hill, MA 02467-3800. Offers biochemistry (PhD); inorganic chemistry (PhD); organic chemistry (PhD); physical chemistry (PhD); science education (MST). MST is offered through the School of Education for secondary school science teaching. Part-time programs available. *Students:* 95 full-time (31 women); includes 12 minority (2 African Americans, 7 Asian Americans or Pacific Islanders, 3 Hispanic Americans), 22 international. 285 applicants, 24% accepted, 14 enrolled. In 2003, 2 master's, 13 doctorates awarded. *Degree requirements:* For doctorate, thesis/dissertation, qualifying exam. *Entrance requirements:* For doctorate, GRE General Test, GRE Subject Test. Additional exam requirements/recommendations for international students: Required—TOEFL (minimum score 550 paper-based; 213 computer-based). *Application deadline:* For fall admission, 1/2 for domestic students. Application fee: $60. Electronic applications accepted. *Expenses:* Tuition: Part-time $810 per credit. *Financial support:* Fellowships with full tuition reimbursements, research assistantships with full tuition reimbursements, teaching assistantships with full tuition reimbursements, Federal Work-Study available. Support available to part-time students. Financial award application deadline: 3/1; financial award applicants required to submit FAFSA. *Unit head:* Dr. David McFadden, Chairperson, 617-552-3605, E-mail: david.mcfadden@bc.edu. *Application contact:* Dr. John Fourkas, Information Contact, 617-552-3605, Fax: 617-552-0833, E-mail: john.fourkas@bc.edu.

Brandeis University, Graduate School of Arts and Sciences, Department of Chemistry, Waltham, MA 02454-9110. Offers inorganic chemistry (MS, PhD); organic chemistry (MS, PhD); physical chemistry (MS, PhD). *Faculty:* 18 full-time (3 women). *Students:* 39 full-time (20 women), 1 (woman) part-time; includes 2 minority (1 Asian American or Pacific Islander, 1 Hispanic American), 32 international. Average age 25. 114 applicants, 5% accepted. In 2003, 8 master's, 5 doctorates awarded. Terminal master's awarded for partial completion of doctoral program. *Degree requirements:* For master's, 1 year of residency; for doctorate, one foreign language, thesis/dissertation, 3 years of residency, 2 seminars, qualifying exams. *Entrance requirements:* For master's and doctorate, GRE General Test, resumé, letters of recommendation. Additional exam requirements/recommendations for international students: Required—TOEFL (minimum score 600 paper-based; 250 computer-based). *Application deadline:* For fall admission, 1/15 for domestic students. Applications are processed on a rolling basis. Application fee: $60. Electronic applications accepted. *Expenses:* Tuition: Full-time $28,999; part-time $4,867 per course. Required fees: $175. *Financial support:* In 2003–04, 20 fellowships (averaging $20,000 per year), 21 research assistantships (averaging $20,000 per year), 18 teaching assistantships (averaging $20,000 per year) were awarded. Institutionally sponsored loans and scholarships/grants also available. Financial award application deadline: 4/15; financial award applicants required to submit CSS PROFILE or FAFSA. *Faculty research:*

Oscillating chemical reactions, molecular recognition systems, protein crystallography, synthesis of natural product spectroscopy and magnetic resonance. Total annual research expenditures: $1,900. *Unit head:* Dr. Thomas C. Pochapsky, Chair, 781-736-2559, Fax: 781-736-2516, E-mail: pochapsky@brandeis.edu. *Application contact:* Charlotte Haygazian, Graduate Admissions Secretary, 781-736-2500, Fax: 781-736-2516, E-mail: chemadm@brandeis.edu.

Brigham Young University, Graduate Studies, College of Physical and Mathematical Sciences, Department of Chemistry and Biochemistry, Provo, UT 84602-1001. Offers analytical chemistry (MS, PhD); biochemistry (MS, PhD); inorganic chemistry (MS, PhD); organic chemistry (MS, PhD); physical chemistry (MS, PhD). *Faculty:* 34 full-time (2 women). *Students:* 90 full-time (56 women); includes 2 minority (1 Asian American or Pacific Islander, 1 Hispanic American), 61 international. Average age 31. 103 applicants, 54% accepted, 23 enrolled. In 2003, 6 master's, 6 doctorates awarded. *Median time to degree:* Master's–2.8 years full-time. Of those who began their doctoral program in fall 1995, 100% received their degree in 8 years or less. *Degree requirements:* For master's, thesis, registration; for doctorate, thesis/dissertation, degree qualifying exam. *Entrance requirements:* For master's, pass 1 (biochemistry), 4 (chemistry) of 5 area exams, GRE General Test, minimum GPA of 3.0 in last 60 hours; for doctorate, pass 1 (biochemistry) or 4 (chemistry) of 5 area exams, GRE General Test, minimum GPA of 3.0 in last 60 hours. Additional exam requirements/recommendations for international students: Required—TOEFL, TWE. *Application deadline:* For fall admission, 2/1 priority date for domestic students, 2/1 priority date for international students. Applications are processed on a rolling basis. Application fee: $50. Electronic applications accepted. *Expenses:* Tuition: Part-time $221 per hour. *Financial support:* In 2003–04, 90 students received support, including 12 fellowships with full tuition reimbursements available (averaging $18,400 per year), 37 research assistantships with full tuition reimbursements available (averaging $18,400 per year), 30 teaching assistantships with full tuition reimbursements available (averaging $18,300 per year); institutionally sponsored loans, scholarships/grants, health care benefits, tuition waivers (full), and unspecified assistantships also available. Financial award application deadline: 2/1. *Faculty research:* Separation science, molecular recognition, organic synthesis and biomedical application, biochemistry and molecular biology, molecular spectroscopy. Total annual research expenditures: $2.7 million. *Unit head:* Dr. Francis R. Nordmeyer, Chair, 801-422-3667, Fax: 801-422-0153, E-mail: fran_nordmeyer@byu.edu. *Application contact:* Dr. Noel L. Owen, Graduate Coordinator, 801-422-2973, Fax: 801-422-0153, E-mail: chemgrad@byu.edu.

See in-depth description on page 97.

California State University, Fullerton, Graduate Studies, College of Natural Science and Mathematics, Department of Chemistry and Biochemistry, Fullerton, CA 92834-9480. Offers analytical chemistry (MS); biochemistry (MS); geochemistry (MS); inorganic chemistry (MS); organic chemistry (MS); physical chemistry (MS). Part-time programs available. *Faculty:* 17 full-time (5 women), 17 part-time/adjunct. *Students:* 21 full-time (9 women), 23 part-time (11 women); includes 19 minority (1 African American, 9 Asian Americans or Pacific Islanders, 9 Hispanic Americans), 8 international. Average age 28. 49 applicants, 61% accepted, 20 enrolled. In 2003, 5 degrees awarded. *Degree requirements:* For master's, thesis, departmental qualifying exam. *Entrance requirements:* For master's, minimum GPA of 2.5 in last 60 units, major in chemistry or related field. Application fee: $55. Tuition, nonresident: part-time $282 per unit. Required fees: $889 per semester. *Financial support:* Teaching assistantships, career-related internships or fieldwork, Federal Work-Study, institutionally sponsored loans, and scholarships/grants available. Support available to part-time students. Financial award application deadline: 3/1. *Unit head:* Dr. Robert Belloli, Chair, 714-278-3621. *Application contact:* Dr. Gregory Williams, Adviser, 714-278-2170.

California State University, Los Angeles, Graduate Studies, College of Natural and Social Sciences, Department of Chemistry and Biochemistry, Los Angeles, CA 90032-8530. Offers analytical chemistry (MS); biochemistry (MS); chemistry (MS); inorganic chemistry (MS); organic chemistry (MS); physical chemistry (MS). Part-time and evening/weekend programs available. *Faculty:* 15 full-time, 12 part-time/adjunct. *Students:* 12 full-time (6 women), 11 part-time (7 women); includes 11 minority (2 African Americans, 5 Asian Americans or Pacific Islanders, 4 Hispanic Americans), 5 international. In 2003, 5 degrees awarded. *Degree requirements:* For master's, one foreign language. *Entrance requirements:* Additional exam requirements/recommendations for international students: Required—TOEFL. *Application deadline:* For fall admission, 6/30 for domestic students; for spring admission, 2/1 for domestic students. Applications are processed on a rolling basis. Application fee: $55. Tuition, nonresident: part-time $188 per unit. Required fees: $2,477. *Financial support:* Federal Work-Study available. Support available to part-time students. Financial award application deadline: 3/1. *Faculty research:* Intercalation of heavy metal, carborane chemistry, conductive polymers and fabrics, titanium reagents, computer modeling and synthesis. *Unit head:* Dr. Wayne Tikkanen, Chair, 323-343-2300.

Case Western Reserve University, School of Graduate Studies, Department of Chemistry, Cleveland, OH 44106. Offers analytical chemistry (MS, PhD); inorganic chemistry (MS, PhD); organic chemistry (MS, PhD); physical chemistry (MS, PhD). Part-time programs available. *Faculty:* 22 full-time (2 women). *Students:* 64 full-time (18 women), 27 part-time (9 women); includes 2 minority (both Asian Americans or Pacific Islanders), 69 international. Average age 27. 483 applicants, 9% accepted, 18 enrolled. In 2003, 5 master's, 13 doctorates awarded. Terminal master's awarded for partial completion of doctoral program. *Degree requirements:* For doctorate, thesis/dissertation. *Entrance requirements:* For master's and doctorate, GRE General Test, GRE Subject Test. Additional exam requirements/recommendations for international students: Required—TOEFL. *Application deadline:* Applications are processed on a rolling basis. Application fee: $50. *Expenses:* Tuition: Full-time $26,900. *Financial support:* In 2003–04, 77 students received support, including 53 research assistantships, 20 teaching assistantships. *Faculty research:* Electrochemistry, synthetic chemistry, chemistry of life process, spectroscopy, kinetics. *Unit head:* Lawrence Sayre, Chairman, 216-368-3622, Fax: 216-368-3006, E-mail: lms3@case.edu. *Application contact:* Zedeara Diaz, Graduate Admissions, 216-368-3621, Fax: 216-368-3006, E-mail: zcd@case.edu.

Clark Atlanta University, School of Arts and Sciences, Department of Chemistry, Atlanta, GA 30314. Offers inorganic chemistry (MS, PhD); organic chemistry (MS, PhD); physical chemistry (MS, PhD); science education (DA). Part-time programs available. *Degree requirements:* For master's, one foreign language, thesis, comprehensive exam; for doctorate, 2 foreign languages, thesis/dissertation, cumulative exam. *Entrance requirements:* For master's, GRE General Test, minimum GPA of 2.5; for doctorate, GRE General Test, GRE Subject Test, minimum graduate GPA of 3.0.

Clarkson University, Graduate School, School of Arts and Sciences, Department of Chemistry, Potsdam, NY 13699. Offers analytical chemistry (MS, PhD); inorganic chemistry (MS, PhD); organic chemistry (MS, PhD); physical chemistry (MS, PhD). *Faculty:* 11 full-time (2 women). *Students:* 31 full-time (12 women); includes 3 minority (2 African Americans, 1 Asian American or Pacific Islander), 14 international. Average age 28. 45 applicants, 67% accepted. In 2003, 4 master's, 1 doctorate awarded. *Median time to degree:* Master's–2.5 years full-time; doctorate–4 years full-time, 6 years part-time. *Degree requirements:* For doctorate, thesis/dissertation, departmental qualifying exam. *Entrance requirements:* For master's, GRE. Additional exam requirements/recommendations for international students: Required—TOEFL. *Application deadline:* For fall admission, 5/15 for domestic students; for spring admission, 10/15 priority date for domestic students. Applications are processed on a rolling basis. Application fee: $25 ($35 for international students). *Expenses:* Tuition: Full-time $19,272; part-time $803 per credit. Tuition and fees vary according to course load. *Financial support:* In 2003–04, 23 students received support, including 2 fellowships (averaging $22,000 per year), 9 research assistantships (averaging $18,000 per year), 12 teaching assistantships (averaging $18,000 per year); scholarships/grants and tuition waivers (partial) also available. *Faculty research:* Particle adhesion phenomena, airborne radon, ceramic materials, materials processing, chemical kinetics. Total annual research expenditures: $1.3 million. *Unit head:* Dr. Phillip A. Christiansen, Division Head, 315-268-6669, Fax: 315-268-6610, E-mail: pac@clarkson.edu. *Application contact:* Donna Brockway, Assistant to Dean/Foreign Student Advisor, 315-268-6447, Fax: 315-268-7994, E-mail: brockway@clarkson.edu.

Cleveland State University, College of Graduate Studies, College of Arts and Sciences, Department of Chemistry, Cleveland, OH 44115. Offers analytical chemistry (MS, PhD); clinical chemistry (MS, PhD); clinical/bioanalytical (PhD); inorganic chemistry (MS); organic chemistry (MS); physical chemistry (MS); structural analysis (MS, PhD). Part-time and evening/weekend programs available. *Faculty:* 16 full-time (1 woman), 3 part-time/adjunct (1 woman). *Students:* 44 full-time (21 women), 23 part-time (9 women); includes 3 minority (1 African American, 1 Asian American or Pacific Islander, 1 Hispanic American), 29 international. Average age 33. 30 applicants, 23% accepted, 2 enrolled. In 2003, 6 master's, 1 doctorate awarded. *Degree requirements:* For master's, thesis (for some programs); for doctorate, thesis/dissertation. *Entrance requirements:* For master's and doctorate, GRE General Test, GRE Subject Test. Additional exam requirements/recommendations for international students: Required—TOEFL (minimum score 525 paper-based; 197 computer-based). *Application deadline:* For fall admission, 1/15 priority date for domestic students, 1/15 priority date for international students. Applications are processed on a rolling basis. Application fee: $30. Electronic applications accepted. Tuition, area resident: Full-time $8,258; part-time $344 per credit hour. Tuition, nonresident: full-time $16,352; part-time $681 per credit hour. *Financial support:* In 2003–04, 37 students received support, including fellowships (averaging $16,000 per year), 19 research assistantships with full tuition reimbursements available (averaging $16,000 per year), 18 teaching assistantships with full tuition reimbursements available (averaging $15,000 per year) Financial award application deadline: 1/15. *Faculty research:* Trace metal analysis in biological systems, application of HPLC/LPCC to clinical systems, synthetic organic and inorganic chemistry, molecular structure determinations, structure-function relationships of factor Va, MALDI-TOF based DNA sequencing, spectroscopic studies of chemical and biochemical phenomena, novel electro-optic tunable filters (AOTFs) to explore biological systems. Total annual research expenditures: $1 million. *Unit head:* Dr. Stan Duraj, Chair, 216-687-2454, Fax: 216-687-9298, E-mail: s.duraj@csuohio.edu. *Application contact:* Richelle P. Emery, Administrative Coordinator, 216-687-2457, Fax: 216-687-9298, E-mail: r.emery@csuohio.edu.

Columbia University, Graduate School of Arts and Sciences, Division of Natural Sciences, Department of Chemistry, Program in Chemical Physics, New York, NY 10027. Offers M Phil, PhD. *Students:* 9 full-time (3 women), 4 international. Average age 26. 21 applicants, 24% accepted. *Entrance requirements:* For master's, GRE General Test, GRE Subject Test. Additional exam requirements/recommendations for international students: Required—TOEFL. Application fee: $75. *Expenses:* Tuition: Full-time $14,820. *Financial support:* Fellowships, teaching assistantships available. Support available to part-time students. Financial award application deadline: 1/5; financial award applicants required to submit FAFSA. *Unit head:* Philip Pechukas, Head, 212-854-2192, Fax: 212-932-1289.

Cornell University, Graduate School, Graduate Fields of Arts and Sciences, Field of Chemistry and Chemical Biology, Ithaca, NY 14853-0001. Offers analytical chemistry (PhD); bio-organic chemistry (PhD); biophysical chemistry (PhD); chemical biology (PhD); chemical physics (PhD); inorganic chemistry (PhD); materials chemistry (PhD); organic chemistry (PhD); organometallic chemistry (PhD); physical chemistry (PhD); polymer chemistry (PhD); theoretical chemistry (PhD). *Faculty:* 37 full-time. *Students:* 174 full-time (70 women); includes 22 minority (4 African Americans, 10 Asian Americans or Pacific Islanders, 8 Hispanic Americans), 57 international. 371 applicants, 35% accepted, 42 enrolled. In 2003, 22 doctorates awarded. *Degree requirements:* For doctorate, thesis/dissertation, comprehensive exam. *Entrance requirements:* For doctorate, GRE General Test, GRE Subject Test (chemistry), 3 letters of recommendation. Additional exam requirements/recommendations for international students: Required—TOEFL (minimum score 600 paper-based; 250 computer-based). *Application deadline:* For fall admission, 1/10 for domestic students. Application fee: $60. Electronic applications accepted. *Expenses:* Tuition: Full-time $28,630. One-time fee: $50 full-time. *Financial support:* In 2003–04, 162 students received support, including 28 fellowships with full tuition reimbursements available, 77 research assistantships with full tuition reimbursements available, 57 teaching assistantships with full tuition reimbursements available; institutionally sponsored loans, scholarships/grants, health care benefits, tuition waivers (full and partial), and unspecified assistantships also available. Financial award applicants required to submit FAFSA. *Faculty research:* Analytical, organic, inorganic, physical, materials, chemical biology. *Unit head:* Director of Graduate Studies, 607-255-4139, Fax: 607-255-4137. *Application contact:* Graduate Field Assistant, 607-255-4139, Fax: 607-255-4137, E-mail: chemgrad@cornell.edu.

See in-depth description on page 105.

Florida State University, Graduate Studies, College of Arts and Sciences, Department of Chemistry and Biochemistry and Department of Physics, Program in Chemical Physics, Tallahassee, FL 32306. Offers MS, PhD. *Faculty:* 17 full-time (0 women). *Degree requirements:* For master's, cumulative and diagnostic exams; for doctorate, thesis/dissertation, cumulative and diagnostic exams. *Entrance requirements:* For master's and doctorate, GRE General Test, minimum B average in undergraduate course work. Additional exam requirements/recommendations for international students: Required—TOEFL (minimum score 515 paper-based; 213 computer-based). *Application deadline:* For fall admission, 4/15 for domestic students. Applications are processed on a rolling basis. Application fee: $20. Electronic applications accepted. *Expenses:* Tuition, state resident: part-time $196 per credit hour. Tuition, nonresident: part-time $731 per credit hour. Part-time tuition and fees vary according to campus/location. *Financial support:* In 2003–04, research assistantships with tuition reimbursements (averaging $18,000 per year), teaching assistantships with tuition reimbursements (averaging $18,000 per year) were awarded. Career-related internships or fieldwork, Federal Work-Study, and institutionally sponsored loans also available. Financial award application deadline: 2/15; financial award applicants required to submit FAFSA. *Faculty research:* Theoretical and experimental research in molecular and solid-state physics and chemistry, statistical mechanics. *Application contact:* Dr. Oliver Steinbock, Chair, Graduate Admissions Committee, 888-525-9286, Fax: 850-644-8281, E-mail: gradinfo@chem.fsu.edu.

See in-depth description on page 115.

Georgetown University, Graduate School of Arts and Sciences, Department of Chemistry, Washington, DC 20057. Offers analytical chemistry (MS, PhD); biochemistry (MS, PhD); chemical physics (MS, PhD); inorganic chemistry (MS, PhD); organic chemistry (MS, PhD); physical chemistry (MS, PhD); theoretical chemistry (MS, PhD). Terminal master's awarded for partial completion of doctoral program. *Degree requirements:* For master's, thesis (for some programs), qualifying exam; for doctorate, thesis/dissertation, comprehensive exam. *Entrance requirements:* For master's and doctorate, GRE General Test. Additional exam requirements/recommendations for international students: Required—TOEFL.

The George Washington University, Columbian College of Arts and Sciences, Department of Chemistry, Washington, DC 20052. Offers analytical chemistry (MS, PhD); inorganic chemistry (MS, PhD); materials science (MS, PhD); organic chemistry (MS, PhD); physical chemistry (MS, PhD). Part-time and evening/weekend programs available. *Faculty:* 7 full-time (1 woman). *Students:* 16 full-time (6 women), 11 part-time (6 women); includes 4 minority (2 African Americans, 1 Asian American or Pacific Islander, 1 Hispanic American), 11 international. 39 applicants, 95% accepted. In 2003, 3 master's, 2 doctorates awarded. Terminal master's awarded for partial completion of doctoral program. *Degree requirements:* For master's, thesis or alternative, comprehensive exam; for doctorate, thesis/dissertation, general exam. *Entrance requirements:* For master's and doctorate, GRE General Test, interview, minimum GPA of 3.0. Additional exam requirements/recommendations for international students: Required—TOEFL (minimum score 550 paper-based; 213 computer-based). *Application deadline:* For fall admission, 2/1 priority date for domestic students, 2/1 priority date for international students; for spring admission, 10/1 priority date for domestic students, 10/1 priority date for international students. Applications are processed on a rolling basis. Application fee: $60. Electronic applica-

Physical Chemistry

The George Washington University (continued)
tions accepted. *Expenses:* Tuition: Part-time $876 per credit. Required fees: $1 per credit. Tuition and fees vary according to campus/location. *Financial support:* In 2003–04, fellowships with tuition reimbursements (averaging $10,000 per year), teaching assistantships with tuition reimbursements (averaging $5,000 per year) were awarded. Research assistantships, Federal Work-Study also available. Financial award application deadline: 2/1. *Unit head:* Dr. Michael King, Chair, 202-994-6488. *Application contact:* Information Contact, E-mail: gwchem@www.gwu.edu.

Harvard University, Graduate School of Arts and Sciences, Committee on Chemical Physics, Cambridge, MA 02138. Offers chemical physics (PhD); chemistry (AM); physics (AM). *Degree requirements:* For doctorate, one foreign language, thesis/dissertation, cumulative exams. *Entrance requirements:* For master's, GRE General Test; for doctorate, GRE General Test, GRE Subject Test. Additional exam requirements/recommendations for international students: Required—TOEFL. *Expenses:* Tuition: Full-time $26,066. Full-time tuition and fees vary according to program and student level.

Harvard University, Graduate School of Arts and Sciences, Department of Chemistry and Chemical Biology, Cambridge, MA 02138. Offers biochemical chemistry (AM, PhD); inorganic chemistry (AM, PhD); organic chemistry (AM, PhD); physical chemistry (AM, PhD). *Degree requirements:* For doctorate, thesis/dissertation, cumulative exams. *Entrance requirements:* For master's, GRE General Test; for doctorate, GRE General Test, GRE Subject Test. Additional exam requirements/recommendations for international students: Required—TOEFL. *Expenses:* Tuition: Full-time $26,066. Full-time tuition and fees vary according to program and student level.

See in-depth description on page 117.

Howard University, Graduate School of Arts and Sciences, Department of Chemistry, Washington, DC 20059-0002. Offers analytical chemistry (MS, PhD); atmospheric (MS, PhD); biochemistry (MS, PhD); environmental (MS, PhD); inorganic chemistry (MS, PhD); organic chemistry (MS, PhD); physical chemistry (MS, PhD); polymer chemistry (MS, PhD). Part-time programs available. *Degree requirements:* For master's, one foreign language, thesis, teaching experience, comprehensive exam, registration; for doctorate, 2 foreign languages, thesis/dissertation, teaching experience, comprehensive exam, registration. *Entrance requirements:* For master's, GRE General Test, minimum GPA of 2.7; for doctorate, GRE General Test, minimum GPA of 3.0. *Faculty research:* Stratospheric aerosols, liquid crystals, polymer coatings, terrestrial and extraterrestrial atmospheres, amidogen reaction.

Illinois Institute of Technology, Graduate College, College of Science and Letters, Department of Biological, Chemical and Physical Sciences, Chemistry Division, Chicago, IL 60616-3793. Offers analytical chemistry (M Ch, MS, PhD); chemistry (M Chem); inorganic chemistry (MS, PhD); materials and chemical synthesis (M Ch); organic chemistry (MS, PhD); physical chemistry (MS, PhD); polymer chemistry (MS, PhD). Part-time and evening/weekend programs available. Postbaccalaureate distance learning degree programs offered (no on-campus study). *Faculty:* 4 full-time (0 women), 2 part-time/adjunct (0 women). *Students:* 14 full-time (7 women), 32 part-time (18 women); includes 7 minority (1 African American, 4 Asian Americans or Pacific Islanders, 2 Hispanic Americans), 17 international. Average age 32. 94 applicants, 68% accepted, 7 enrolled. In 2003, 14 master's, 2 doctorates awarded. Terminal master's awarded for partial completion of doctoral program. *Degree requirements:* For master's, thesis (for some programs), comprehensive exam; for doctorate, thesis/dissertation, comprehensive exam. *Entrance requirements:* For master's and doctorate, GRE General Test, minimum undergraduate GPA of 3.0. Additional exam requirements/recommendations for international students: Required—TOEFL (minimum score 550 paper-based; 213 computer-based). *Application deadline:* For fall admission, 5/1 for domestic students, 5/1 for international students; for spring admission, 10/15 for domestic students, 10/15 for international students. Applications are processed on a rolling basis. Application fee: $40. Electronic applications accepted. *Expenses:* Tuition: Part-time $628 per credit. Tuition and fees vary according to course load and program. *Financial support:* In 2003–04, 11 students received support, including 1 fellowship with full tuition reimbursement available, 9 research assistantships with full tuition reimbursements available (averaging $15,000 per year), 7 teaching assistantships with full tuition reimbursements available (averaging $15,000 per year); Federal Work-Study, institutionally sponsored loans, scholarships/grants, and tuition waivers (partial) also available. Support available to part-time students. Financial award application deadline: 3/1; financial award applicants required to submit FAFSA. *Faculty research:* Organic and inorganic chemistry, polymers research, physical chemistry, analytical chemistry. *Unit head:* Kenneth Stagliano, Associate Chair, 312-567-3428, Fax: 312-567-3494, E-mail: stagliano@iit.edu. *Application contact:* Kelly A. Cherwin, Director of Graduate Outreach, 312-567-7974, Fax: 312-567-3494, E-mail: inquiry.grad@iit.edu.

Indiana University Bloomington, Graduate School, College of Arts and Sciences, Department of Chemistry, Bloomington, IN 47405. Offers analytical chemistry (PhD); biological chemistry (PhD); chemistry (MAT, MS); inorganic chemistry (PhD); physical chemistry (PhD). PhD offered through the University Graduate School. *Faculty:* 29 full-time (2 women). *Students:* 95 full-time (30 women), 51 part-time (16 women); includes 9 minority (3 African Americans, 4 Asian Americans or Pacific Islanders, 2 Hispanic Americans), 52 international. Average age 26. 309 applicants, 41% accepted. In 2003, 4 master's, 23 doctorates awarded. Terminal master's awarded for partial completion of doctoral program. *Degree requirements:* For master's and doctorate, thesis/dissertation. *Entrance requirements:* For master's and doctorate, GRE General Test, GRE Subject Test. Additional exam requirements/recommendations for international students: Required—TOEFL. *Application deadline:* For fall admission, 1/15 priority date for domestic students, 12/15 priority date for international students; for spring admission, 9/1 priority date for domestic students, 9/1 priority date for international students. Applications are processed on a rolling basis. Application fee: $45 ($55 for international students). *Expenses:* Tuition, state resident: full-time $4,908; part-time $205 per credit. Tuition, nonresident: full-time $14,298; part-time $596 per credit. Required fees: $661. Tuition and fees vary according to campus/location and program. *Financial support:* In 2003–04, 23 fellowships with full tuition reimbursements (averaging $15,091 per year), 57 research assistantships with full tuition reimbursements (averaging $14,844 per year), 78 teaching assistantships with full tuition reimbursements (averaging $15,588 per year) were awarded. Federal Work-Study and institutionally sponsored loans also available. *Faculty research:* Synthesis of complex natural products, organic reaction mechanisms, organic electrochemistry, transitive-metal chemistry, solid-state and surface chemistry. Total annual research expenditures: $7.7 million. *Unit head:* Dr. Gary M. Hieftje, Chairperson, 812-855-6239, Fax: 812-855-8300, E-mail: cemchair@indiana.edu. *Application contact:* Dr. Jack K. Crandall, Chairperson of Admissions, 812-855-2068, Fax: 812-855-8300, E-mail: chemgrad@indiana.edu.

Kansas State University, Graduate School, College of Arts and Sciences, Department of Chemistry, Manhattan, KS 66506. Offers analytical chemistry (MS); chemistry (PhD); inorganic chemistry (MS); organic chemistry (MS); physical chemistry (MS). *Faculty:* 15 full-time (2 women). *Students:* 51 full-time (17 women); includes 1 minority (African American), 33 international. 71 applicants, 20% accepted, 14 enrolled. In 2003, 1 master's, 7 doctorates awarded. Terminal master's awarded for partial completion of doctoral program. *Degree requirements:* For master's and doctorate, thesis/dissertation. *Entrance requirements:* For master's and doctorate, GRE, minimum GPA of 3.0. Additional exam requirements/recommendations for international students: Required—TOEFL. *Application deadline:* For fall admission, 2/1 for domestic students; for spring admission, 10/1 for domestic students. Applications are processed on a rolling basis. Application fee: $0 ($25 for international students). *Expenses:* Tuition, state resident: part-time $155 per credit hour. Tuition, nonresident: part-time $428 per credit hour. Required fees: $11 per credit hour. *Financial support:* In 2003–04, 23 research assistantships (averaging $15,648 per year), 26 teaching assistantships with full tuition reimbursements (averaging $17,890 per year) were awarded. Fellowships, institutionally sponsored loans and scholarships/grants also available. Support available to part-time students. Financial award application deadline: 3/1; financial award applicants required to submit FAFSA. *Faculty research:* Computational, environmental and materials, nanoscale, natural products, theoretical chemistry. Total annual research expenditures: $2.8 million. *Unit head:* Peter M. A. Sherwood, Head, 785-532-6665, Fax: 785-532-6666, E-mail: escachem@ksu.edu. *Application contact:* Robert Hammaker, Director, 785-532-1454, Fax: 785-532-6666, E-mail: rmh3008@ksu.edu.

Kent State University, College of Arts and Sciences, Department of Chemistry, Kent, OH 44242-0001. Offers analytical chemistry (MS, PhD); biochemistry (MS, PhD); chemistry (MA, MS, PhD); inorganic chemistry (MS, PhD); organic chemistry (MS, PhD); physical chemistry (MS, PhD). Terminal master's awarded for partial completion of doctoral program. *Degree requirements:* For master's and doctorate, thesis/dissertation, comprehensive exam, registration. *Entrance requirements:* For master's and doctorate, placement exam, GRE General Test, GRE Subject Test (recommended), minimum GPA of 2.75. Additional exam requirements/recommendations for international students: Required—TOEFL (minimum score 575 paper-based; 230 computer-based). Electronic applications accepted. *Expenses:* Tuition, state resident: part-time $334 per hour. Tuition, nonresident: part-time $627 per hour. *Faculty research:* Biological chemistry, materials chemistry, molecular spectroscopy.

See in-depth description on page 119.

Marquette University, Graduate School, College of Arts and Sciences, Department of Chemistry, Milwaukee, WI 53201-1881. Offers analytical chemistry (MS, PhD); bioanalytical chemistry (MS, PhD); biophysical chemistry (MS, PhD); chemical physics (MS, PhD); inorganic chemistry (MS, PhD); organic chemistry (MS, PhD); physical chemistry (MS, PhD). Part-time programs available. *Faculty:* 19 full-time (2 women), 2 part-time/adjunct (0 women). *Students:* 44 full-time (17 women), 4 part-time (1 woman); includes 1 minority (African American), 36 international. Average age 31. 37 applicants, 32% accepted, 8 enrolled. In 2003, 1 master's, 1 doctorate awarded. Terminal master's awarded for partial completion of doctoral program. *Degree requirements:* For master's, comprehensive exam; for doctorate, thesis/dissertation, cumulative exams. *Entrance requirements:* For master's and doctorate, GRE Subject Test. Additional exam requirements/recommendations for international students: Required—TOEFL. Application fee: $40. *Expenses:* Tuition: Full-time $10,080; part-time $630 per credit. Tuition and fees vary according to program. *Financial support:* In 2003–04, 3 research assistantships, 27 teaching assistantships were awarded. Fellowships, Federal Work-Study, institutionally sponsored loans, scholarships/grants, and tuition waivers (full and partial) also available. Support available to part-time students. Financial award application deadline: 2/15. *Faculty research:* Inorganic complexes, laser Raman spectroscopy, organic synthesis, chemical dynamics, biophysiology. Total annual research expenditures: $586,915. *Unit head:* Dr. Charles Wilkie, Chairman, 414-288-7065, Fax: 414-288-7066. *Application contact:* Dr. Mark Steinmetz, Director of Graduate Studies, 414-288-7374, Fax: 414-288-7066.

Massachusetts Institute of Technology, School of Science, Department of Chemistry, Cambridge, MA 02139-4307. Offers biological chemistry (PhD, Sc D); inorganic chemistry (PhD, Sc D); organic chemistry (PhD, Sc D); physical chemistry (PhD, Sc D). *Faculty:* 31 full-time (6 women). *Students:* 253 full-time (85 women), 7 part-time (5 women); includes 34 minority (8 African Americans, 17 Asian Americans or Pacific Islanders, 9 Hispanic Americans), 81 international. Average age 26. 573 applicants, 25% accepted, 54 enrolled. In 2003, 28 doctorates awarded. *Degree requirements:* For doctorate, thesis/dissertation, comprehensive exam. *Entrance requirements:* For doctorate, GRE General Test. Additional exam requirements/recommendations for international students: Required—TOEFL (minimum score 577 paper-based; 233 computer-based). *Application deadline:* For fall admission, 12/15 for domestic students, 12/15 for international students. Application fee: $70. Electronic applications accepted. *Expenses:* Tuition: Full-time $29,400. Required fees: $200. *Financial support:* In 2003–04, 50 fellowships with tuition reimbursements, 167 research assistantships with tuition reimbursements (averaging $23,760 per year), 59 teaching assistantships with tuition reimbursements (averaging $18,270 per year) were awarded. Career-related internships or fieldwork, Federal Work-Study, institutionally sponsored loans, scholarships/grants, health care benefits, and unspecified assistantships also available. *Faculty research:* Synthetic organic chemistry, enzymatic reaction mechanisms, inorganic and organometallic spectroscopy, high resolution NMR spectroscopy. Total annual research expenditures: $20.7 million. *Unit head:* Prof. Stephen J. Lippard, Head, 617-253-1801, Fax: 617-258-0241. *Application contact:* Susan Brighton, Graduate Administrator, 617-253-1845, Fax: 617-258-0241, E-mail: brighton@mit.edu.

McMaster University, School of Graduate Studies, Faculty of Science, Department of Chemistry, Hamilton, ON L8S 4M2, Canada. Offers analytical chemistry (M Sc, PhD); chemical physics (M Sc, PhD); chemistry (M Sc, PhD); inorganic chemistry (M Sc, PhD); organic chemistry (M Sc, PhD); physical chemistry (M Sc, PhD); polymer chemistry (M Sc, PhD). Part-time programs available. Terminal master's awarded for partial completion of doctoral program. *Degree requirements:* For master's, thesis/dissertation; for doctorate, thesis/dissertation, comprehensive exam. *Entrance requirements:* For master's, minimum B+ average. Additional exam requirements/recommendations for international students: Required—TOEFL (minimum score 550 paper-based; 213 computer-based).

Miami University, Graduate School, College of Arts and Sciences, Department of Chemistry and Biochemistry, Oxford, OH 45056. Offers analytical chemistry (MS, PhD); biochemistry (MS, PhD); chemical education (MS, PhD); chemistry (MS, PhD); inorganic chemistry (MS, PhD); organic chemistry (MS, PhD); physical chemistry (MS, PhD). Part-time programs available. *Faculty:* 22 full-time (2 women). *Students:* 45 full-time (16 women), 1 part-time; includes 2 minority (both Asian Americans or Pacific Islanders), 21 international. 131 applicants, 98% accepted, 13 enrolled. In 2003, 4 master's, 4 doctorates awarded. *Degree requirements:* For master's, thesis, final exam; for doctorate, thesis/dissertation, final exams, comprehensive exam. *Entrance requirements:* For master's, minimum undergraduate GPA of 3.0 during previous 2 years or 2.75 overall; for doctorate, minimum undergraduate GPA of 2.75, 3.0 graduate. Additional exam requirements/recommendations for international students: Required—TOEFL, TWE. *Application deadline:* For fall admission, 3/1 priority date for domestic students, 3/1 priority date for international students. Applications are processed on a rolling basis. Application fee: $35. Electronic applications accepted. Tuition, area resident: Full-time $9,346. International tuition: $19,924 full-time. Full-time tuition and fees vary according to course level and campus/location. *Financial support:* In 2003–04, 22 fellowships with full tuition reimbursements (averaging $16,813 per year), 3 research assistantships with full tuition reimbursements (averaging $16,813 per year), 17 teaching assistantships with full tuition reimbursements (averaging $18,934 per year) were awarded. Federal Work-Study, tuition waivers (full), and unspecified assistantships also available. Financial award application deadline: 3/1. *Unit head:* Dr. Chris Makaroff, Chair, 513-529-2813. *Application contact:* Dr. Michael Crowder, Director of Graduate Studies, 513-529-2813, Fax: 513-529-5715, E-mail: chemistry@muohio.edu.

Michigan State University, Graduate School, College of Natural Science, Department of Chemistry, East Lansing, MI 48824. Offers chemical physics (PhD); chemistry (MS, PhD); chemistry-environmental toxicology (PhD); computational chemistry (MS). *Faculty:* 33 full-time (4 women). *Students:* 205 full-time (93 women), 6 part-time (3 women); includes 5 minority (2 African Americans, 1 American Indian/Alaska Native, 2 Hispanic Americans), 132 international. Average age 27. 192 applicants, 50% accepted. In 2003, 13 master's, 18 doctorates awarded. *Degree requirements:* For master's, thesis optional; for doctorate, thesis/dissertation, oral defense of dissertation, comprehensive exam. *Entrance requirements:* For master's, GRE General Test, bachelor's degree in chemistry, coursework in chemistry, physics, and calculus, 3 letters of recommendation; for doctorate, GRE General Test, minimum GPA of 3.0; bachelor's or master's degree in chemistry, coursework in chemistry, physics, and calculus; 3 letters of recommendation. Additional exam requirements/recommendations for international students: Required—TOEFL (minimum score 550 paper-based; 213 computer-based), Michigan State University ELT (85), Michigan ELAB (83). *Application deadline:* For fall admission, 12/23 for domestic students. Application fee: $50. Electronic applications accepted. *Expenses:* Tuition, state resident: part-time $291 per hour. Tuition, nonresident: part-time $589 per hour. *Financial support:* In 2003–04, 34 fellowships with tuition reimbursements (averaging $2,720 per year), 95 research assistantships with tuition reimbursements (averaging $14,460 per year), 118 teaching assistantships (averaging $14,354 per year) were awarded. Financial award applicants required to submit FAFSA. *Faculty research:* Analytical chemistry, inorganic and organic chemistry, nuclear chemistry, physical chemistry, theoretical and computational chemistry. Total annual research expenditures: $8.7 million. *Unit head:* Dr. John L. McCracken, Chairperson, 517-355-9715 Ext. 092, Fax: 517-353-1793, E-mail: chemdept@cem.msu.edu. *Application contact:* Dr. Gregory L. Baker, Director of Admissions, 517-355-9715 Ext. 343, Fax: 517-353-1793, E-mail: gradoff@cem.msu.edu.

Northeastern University, College of Arts and Sciences, Department of Chemistry and Chemical Biology, Boston, MA 02115-5096. Offers analytical chemistry (PhD); chemistry (MS, PhD); inorganic chemistry (PhD); organic chemistry (PhD); physical chemistry (PhD). Part-time and evening/weekend programs available. *Faculty:* 17 full-time (2 women), 3 part-time/adjunct (0 women). *Students:* 46 full-time (23 women), 29 part-time (17 women). Average age 28. 113 applicants, 37% accepted. In 2003, 12 master's, 10 doctorates awarded. Terminal master's awarded for partial completion of doctoral program. *Degree requirements:* For master's, thesis (for some programs); for doctorate, thesis/dissertation, qualifying exam in specialty area. *Entrance requirements:* Additional exam requirements/recommendations for international students: Required—TOEFL. *Application deadline:* For fall admission, 4/15 for domestic students. Applications are processed on a rolling basis. Application fee: $50. Electronic applications accepted. *Expenses:* Tuition: Part-time $790 per credit hour. Tuition and fees vary according to course load and program. *Financial support:* In 2003–04, 27 research assistantships with tuition reimbursements (averaging $16,000 per year) were awarded; fellowships with tuition reimbursements, teaching assistantships with tuition reimbursements, career-related internships or fieldwork, tuition waivers (partial), and unspecified assistantships also available. Financial award application deadline: 4/15; financial award applicants required to submit FAFSA. *Faculty research:* Electron transfer, theoretical chemical physics, analytical biotechnology, mass spectrometry, materials chemistry. Total annual research expenditures: $250,000. *Unit head:* Dr. Graham Jones, Chairman, 617-373-2822, Fax: 617-373-8795, E-mail: chemistry-grad-info@neu.edu. *Application contact:* Dr. Pam Mabrouk, Chair, Graduate Admissions Committee, 617-373-2383, Fax: 617-373-8795, E-mail: chemistry-grad-info@neu.edu.

See in-depth description on page 133.

The Ohio State University, Graduate School, College of Mathematical and Physical Sciences, Program in Chemical Physics, Columbus, OH 43210. Offers MS, PhD. *Faculty:* 34. *Students:* 15 full-time (2 women), 1 part-time, 11 international. 24 applicants, 38% accepted. In 2003, 1 master's, 12 doctorates awarded. *Degree requirements:* For master's, thesis optional; for doctorate, thesis/dissertation. *Entrance requirements:* For master's and doctorate, GRE General Test, GRE Subject Test (chemistry or physics). *Application deadline:* For fall admission, 8/15 for domestic students. Applications are processed on a rolling basis. Application fee: $40 ($50 for international students). *Expenses:* Tuition, state resident: full-time $7,233. Tuition, nonresident: full-time $18,489. *Financial support:* Fellowships, research assistantships, teaching assistantships, Federal Work-Study and institutionally sponsored loans available. Support available to part-time students. *Unit head:* Dr. Terry A. Miller, Director, 614-292-2569, Fax: 614-292-1948, E-mail: miller.104@osu.edu. *Application contact:* Becky Gregory, Program Coordinator, 614-292-2569, Fax: 614-292-1948, E-mail: gregory.10@osu.edu.

Old Dominion University, College of Sciences, Program in Chemistry, Norfolk, VA 23529. Offers analytical chemistry (MS); biochemistry (MS); clinical chemistry (MS); environmental chemistry (MS); organic chemistry (MS); physical chemistry (MS). Part-time and evening/weekend programs available. *Faculty:* 15 full-time (4 women). *Students:* 6 full-time (3 women), 9 part-time (5 women); includes 1 minority (Asian American or Pacific Islander), 3 international. Average age 30. 19 applicants, 74% accepted. In 2003, 2 degrees awarded. *Degree requirements:* For master's, thesis, comprehensive exam. *Entrance requirements:* For master's, GRE General Test, minimum GPA of 3.0 in major, 2.5 overall. Additional exam requirements/recommendations for international students: Required—TOEFL. *Application deadline:* For fall admission, 7/1 for domestic students; for spring admission, 11/1 for domestic students. Applications are processed on a rolling basis. Application fee: $30. *Expenses:* Tuition, state resident: part-time $235 per credit hour. Tuition, nonresident: part-time $603 per credit hour. Part-time tuition and fees vary according to campus/location. *Financial support:* In 2003–04, research assistantships with tuition reimbursements (averaging $15,000 per year), teaching assistantships with tuition reimbursements (averaging $15,000 per year) were awarded. Fellowships, career-related internships or fieldwork and scholarships/grants also available. Financial award application deadline: 2/15; financial award applicants required to submit FAFSA. *Faculty research:* Organic and trace metal biogeochemistry, materials chemistry, bioanalytical chemistry, computational chemistry. Total annual research expenditures: $854,968. *Unit head:* Dr. John R. Donat, Graduate Program Director, 757-683-4098, Fax: 757-683-4628, E-mail: chemgpd@odu.edu.

Oregon State University, Graduate School, College of Science, Department of Chemistry, Corvallis, OR 97331. Offers analytical chemistry (MS, PhD); chemistry (MA, MAIS); inorganic chemistry (MS, PhD); nuclear and radiation chemistry (MS, PhD); organic chemistry (MS, PhD); physical chemistry (MS, PhD). Part-time programs available. *Faculty:* 30 full-time (5 women). *Students:* 63 full-time (22 women), 1 part-time; includes 5 minority (3 Asian Americans or Pacific Islanders, 2 Hispanic Americans), 29 international. Average age 28. In 2003, 3 master's, 13 doctorates awarded. Terminal master's awarded for partial completion of doctoral program. *Degree requirements:* For master's and doctorate, one foreign language, thesis/dissertation. *Entrance requirements:* For master's and doctorate, minimum GPA of 3.0 in last 90 hours. Additional exam requirements/recommendations for international students: Required—TOEFL. *Application deadline:* For fall admission, 3/1 for domestic students. Applications are processed on a rolling basis. Application fee: $50. *Expenses:* Tuition, state resident: full-time $8,139; part-time $301 per credit. Tuition, nonresident: full-time $14,376; part-time $532 per credit. Required fees: $1,227. *Financial support:* Fellowships, research assistantships, teaching assistantships, institutionally sponsored loans available. Support available to part-time students. Financial award application deadline: 2/1. *Faculty research:* Solid state chemistry, enzyme reaction mechanisms, structure and dynamics of gas molecules, chemiluminescence, nonlinear optical spectroscopy. *Unit head:* Dr. John C. Westall, Chair, 541-737-2591, Fax: 541-737-2062, E-mail: john.westall@orst.edu. *Application contact:* Carolyn Brumley, Graduate Secretary, 541-737-6707, Fax: 541-737-2062, E-mail: carolyn.brumley@orst.edu.

Princeton University, Graduate School, Department of Chemistry, Princeton, NJ 08544-1019. Offers chemistry (PhD); industrial chemistry (MS); physics and chemical physics (PhD); polymer sciences and materials (PhD). PhD (polymer sciences and materials) offered in conjunction with the Department of Chemical Engineering. *Faculty:* 28 full-time (3 women), 4 part-time/adjunct (1 woman). *Students:* 134 full-time (47 women); includes 8 minority (2 African Americans, 4 Asian Americans or Pacific Islanders, 2 Hispanic Americans), 65 international. 325 applicants, 23% accepted, 35 enrolled. *Median time to degree:* Doctorate–4.54 years full-time. *Degree requirements:* For doctorate, one foreign language, thesis/dissertation, cumulative and general exams. *Entrance requirements:* For master's, GRE General Test; for doctorate, GRE General Test, GRE Subject Test. Additional exam requirements/recommendations for international students: Required—TOEFL (minimum score 550 paper-based). *Application deadline:* For fall admission, 12/31 for domestic students, 12/1 for international students. Application fee: $80 ($55 for international students). Electronic applications accepted. *Expenses:* Tuition: Full-time $29,910. Required fees: $810. *Financial support:* Fellowships with full tuition reimbursements, research assistantships with full tuition reimbursements, teaching assistantships with full tuition reimbursements, Federal Work-Study and institutionally sponsored loans available. Financial award application deadline: 1/2. *Faculty research:* Chemistry of interfaces, organic synthesis, organometallic chemistry, inorganic reactions, biostructural chemistry. *Unit head:* Prof. Andrew Bocarsly, Director of Graduate Studies, 609-258-3888, Fax: 609-258-6746, E-mail: bocarsly@princeton.edu. *Application contact:* Janice Yip, Director of Graduate Admissions, 609-258-3034, Fax: 609-258-6180, E-mail: gsadmit@princeton.edu.

See in-depth description on page 137.

Princeton University, Graduate School, Department of Physics, Princeton, NJ 08544-1019. Offers applied and computational mathematics (PhD); mathematical physics (PhD); physics (PhD); physics and chemical physics (PhD). *Faculty:* 42 full-time (2 women), 2 part-time/adjunct (0 women). *Students:* 103 full-time (13 women); includes 11 minority (10 Asian Americans or Pacific Islanders, 1 Hispanic American), 48 international. Average age 22. 425 applicants, 12% accepted, 26 enrolled. In 2003, 14 degrees awarded, leading to continued full-time study 86%. *Median time to degree:* Doctorate–5 years full-time. *Degree requirements:* For doctorate, thesis/dissertation, qualifying exam. *Entrance requirements:* For doctorate, GRE General Test, GRE Subject Test. Additional exam requirements/recommendations for international students: Required—TOEFL (minimum score 600 paper-based; 250 computer-based). *Application deadline:* For fall admission, 12/31 for domestic students, 12/1 for international students. Application fee: $80 ($55 for international students). Electronic applications accepted. *Expenses:* Tuition: Full-time $29,910. Required fees: $810. *Financial support:* In 2003–04, 100 students received support, including 40 fellowships with full tuition reimbursements available (averaging $19,360 per year), 30 research assistantships with full tuition reimbursements available (averaging $18,100 per year), 30 teaching assistantships with full tuition reimbursements available (averaging $19,625 per year); Federal Work-Study and institutionally sponsored loans also available. Financial award application deadline: 1/2. Total annual research expenditures: $10.7 million. *Unit head:* Prof. Chiana Nappi, Director of Graduate Studies, 609-258-4322, Fax: 609-258-1549, E-mail: cnappi@princeton.edu. *Application contact:* Janice Yip, Director of Graduate Admissions, 609-258-3034, Fax: 609-258-6180, E-mail: gsadmit@princeton.edu.

Purdue University, Graduate School, School of Science, Department of Chemistry, West Lafayette, IN 47907. Offers analytical chemistry (MS, PhD); biochemistry (MS, PhD); chemical education (MS, PhD); inorganic chemistry (MS, PhD); organic chemistry (MS, PhD); physical chemistry (MS, PhD). *Accreditation:* NCATE (one or more programs are accredited). Terminal master's awarded for partial completion of doctoral program. *Degree requirements:* For master's and doctorate, thesis/dissertation. *Entrance requirements:* Additional exam requirements/recommendations for international students: Required—TOEFL. Electronic applications accepted.

Rensselaer Polytechnic Institute, Graduate School, School of Science, Department of Chemistry and Chemical Biology, Troy, NY 12180-3590. Offers analytical chemistry (MS, PhD); biochemistry (MS, PhD); inorganic chemistry (MS, PhD); organic chemistry (MS, PhD); physical chemistry (MS, PhD); polymer chemistry (MS, PhD). Part-time and evening/weekend programs available. *Faculty:* 20 full-time (4 women). *Students:* 58 full-time (25 women), 3 part-time (2 women); includes 40 minority (2 African Americans, 37 Asian Americans or Pacific Islanders, 1 Hispanic American), 36 international. Average age 24. 102 applicants, 29% accepted, 19 enrolled. In 2003, 9 master's, 9 doctorates awarded. Terminal master's awarded for partial completion of doctoral program. *Median time to degree:* Of those who began their doctoral program in fall 1995, 100% received their degree in 8 years or less. *Degree requirements:* For master's, thesis (for some programs), registration; for doctorate, thesis/dissertation, comprehensive exam, registration. *Entrance requirements:* For master's, GRE General Test, GRE Subject Test (strongly recommended); for doctorate, GRE General Test, GRE Subject Test (chemistry or biochemistry strongly recommended). Additional exam requirements/recommendations for international students: Required—TOEFL (minimum score 600 paper-based). *Application deadline:* For fall admission, 2/1 for domestic students; for spring admission, 11/15 for domestic students. Applications are processed on a rolling basis. Application fee: $45. Electronic applications accepted. *Expenses:* Tuition: Full-time $27,700; part-time $1,320 per credit. Required fees: $1,470. *Financial support:* In 2003–04, 59 students received support, including 1 fellowship with full tuition reimbursement available (averaging $25,000 per year), 25 research assistantships with full tuition reimbursements available (averaging $18,000 per year), 30 teaching assistantships with full tuition reimbursements available (averaging $18,000 per year); institutionally sponsored loans and tuition waivers (full and partial) also available. Financial award application deadline: 2/1. *Faculty research:* Synthetic polymer and biopolymer chemistry, physical chemistry of polymeric systems, bioanalytical chemistry, synthetic and computational drug design, protein folding and protein design. Total annual research expenditures: $1.9 million. *Unit head:* Dr. Ronald A. Bailey, Acting Chair, 518-276-4856, Fax: 518-276-4887, E-mail: bailer@rpi.edu. *Application contact:* Beth E. McGraw, Department Admissions Assistant, 518-276-6456, Fax: 518-276-4887, E-mail: mcgrae@rpi.edu.

Rice University, Graduate Programs, Wiess School of Natural Sciences, Department of Chemistry, Houston, TX 77251-1892. Offers chemistry (MA); inorganic chemistry (PhD); organic chemistry (PhD); physical chemistry (PhD). *Faculty:* 24 full-time (3 women), 5 part-time/adjunct (0 women). *Students:* 80 full-time (25 women); includes 8 minority (2 African Americans, 1 Asian American or Pacific Islander, 5 Hispanic Americans), 40 international. Average age 24. 259 applicants, 21% accepted, 25 enrolled. In 2003, 1 master's, 14 doctorates awarded. Terminal master's awarded for partial completion of doctoral program. *Median time to degree:* Of those who began their doctoral program in fall 1995, 100% received their degree in 8 years or less. *Degree requirements:* For master's and doctorate, thesis/dissertation. *Entrance requirements:* For master's and doctorate, GRE General Test, minimum GPA of 3.0. Additional exam requirements/recommendations for international students: Required—TOEFL. *Application deadline:* For fall admission, 2/1 for domestic students; for spring admission, 11/1 for domestic students. Applications are processed on a rolling basis. Application fee: $0 ($25 for international students). *Expenses:* Tuition: Full-time $19,700; part-time $1,096 per hour. *Financial support:* In 2003–04, 80 students received support, including 44 fellowships (averaging $19,700 per year), 23 research assistantships (averaging $19,700 per year); Federal Work-Study, scholarships/grants, and tuition waivers (full and partial) also available. *Faculty research:* Nanoscience, biomaterials, nanobioinformatics, fullerene pharmaceuticals. Total annual research expenditures: $75,000. *Unit head:* Kenton H. Whitmire, Chair, 713-348-5650, Fax: 713-348-5155, E-mail: whitmir@rice.edu. *Application contact:* Sofia Medrano, Graduate Recruiting/Administrative Secretary, 713-348-4082, Fax: 713-348-5155, E-mail: gradchem@rice.edu.

Rutgers, The State University of New Jersey, Newark, Graduate School, Program in Chemistry, Newark, NJ 07102. Offers analytical chemistry (MS, PhD); biochemistry (MS, PhD); inorganic chemistry (MS, PhD); organic chemistry (MS, PhD); physical chemistry (MS, PhD). Part-time and evening/weekend programs available. *Faculty:* 22 full-time (5 women). *Students:* 19 full-time (9 women), 35 part-time (12 women); includes 28 minority (3 African Americans, 25 Asian Americans or Pacific Islanders). 107 applicants, 31% accepted, 8 enrolled. In 2003, 4 master's, 6 doctorates awarded. Terminal master's awarded for partial completion of doctoral program. *Degree requirements:* For master's, cumulative exams, thesis optional; for doctorate, thesis/dissertation, exams, research proposal. *Entrance requirements:* For master's and doctorate, GRE General Test, minimum undergraduate B average. Additional exam requirements/recommendations for international students: Required—TOEFL. *Application deadline:* For fall admission, 7/1 for domestic students; for spring admission, 12/1 for domestic students. Applications are processed on a rolling basis. Application fee: $50. Electronic applications accepted. *Expenses:* Tuition, state resident: full-time $10,030. Tuition, nonresident: full-time $14,202. *Financial support:* In 2003–04, 35 students received support, including 6 fellowships with full tuition reimbursements available, 20 teaching assistantships with full tuition reimbursements available (averaging $14,300 per year); Federal Work-Study and institutionally sponsored loans also available. Financial award application deadline: 3/1. *Faculty research:* Medicinal chemistry, natural products, isotope effects, biophysics and biorganic approaches to enzyme mechanisms, organic and organometallic synthesis. *Unit head:* Prof. W. Philip Huskey, Chairman and Program Director, 973-353-5741, Fax: 973-353-1264, E-mail: huskey@andromeda.rutgers.edu.

Rutgers, The State University of New Jersey, New Brunswick/Piscataway, Graduate School, Program in Chemistry and Chemical Biology, New Brunswick, NJ 08901-1281. Offers analytical chemistry (MS, PhD); biological chemistry (PhD); chemistry education (MST); inorganic chemistry (MS, PhD); organic chemistry (MS, PhD); physical chemistry (MS, PhD). Part-time and evening/weekend programs available. Terminal master's awarded for partial completion of doctoral program. *Degree requirements:* For master's, thesis or alternative, exam, comprehensive exam, registration; for doctorate, thesis/dissertation, cumulative exams, 1 year residency,

Physical Chemistry

Rutgers, The State University of New Jersey, New Brunswick/Piscataway (continued)
comprehensive exam, registration. *Entrance requirements:* For master's and doctorate, GRE General Test, GRE Subject Test. Additional exam requirements/recommendations for international students: Required—TOEFL. Electronic applications accepted. *Expenses:* Tuition, state resident: full-time $10,030. Tuition, nonresident: full-time $14,202. *Faculty research:* Biophysical organic/bioorganic, inorganic/bioinorganic, theoretical, and solid-state/surface chemistry.

See in-depth description on page 141.

Seton Hall University, College of Arts and Sciences, Department of Chemistry and Biochemistry, South Orange, NJ 07079-2694. Offers analytical chemistry (MS, PhD); biochemistry (MS, PhD); chemistry (MS); inorganic chemistry (MS, PhD); organic chemistry (MS, PhD); physical chemistry (MS, PhD). Part-time and evening/weekend programs available. Terminal master's awarded for partial completion of doctoral program. *Degree requirements:* For master's, formal seminar, thesis optional; for doctorate, thesis/dissertation, annual seminars, comprehensive exam. *Entrance requirements:* For master's, undergraduate major in chemistry or related field with minimum 30 credits in chemistry, including 2 semesters of physical chemistry; for doctorate, oral matriculation exam based on proposed doctoral research, minimum GPA of 3.0 in course distribution requirements, formal seminar. Additional exam requirements/recommendations for international students: Required—TOEFL. *Faculty research:* DNA metal reactions; chromatography; bioinorganic, biophysical, organometallic, polymer chemistry; heterogeneous catalyst.

Simon Fraser University, Graduate Studies, Faculty of Science, Department of Chemistry, Burnaby, BC V5A 1S6, Canada. Offers chemical physics (M Sc, PhD); chemistry (M Sc, PhD). *Degree requirements:* For master's and doctorate, thesis/dissertation. *Entrance requirements:* For master's, minimum GPA of 3.0; for doctorate, minimum GPA of 3.5. Additional exam requirements/recommendations for international students: Required—TOEFL or IELTS. *Faculty research:* Organic chemistry, nuclear chemistry, physical chemistry, inorganic chemistry, theoretical chemistry.

Simon Fraser University, Graduate Studies, Faculty of Science, Department of Physics, Burnaby, BC V5A 1S6, Canada. Offers biophysics (M Sc, PhD); chemical physics (M Sc, PhD); physics (M Sc, PhD). *Degree requirements:* For master's and doctorate, thesis/dissertation. *Entrance requirements:* For master's, minimum GPA of 3.0; for doctorate, minimum GPA of 3.5. Additional exam requirements/recommendations for international students: Required—TOEFL or IELTS. *Faculty research:* Solid-state physics, magnetism, energy research, superconductivity, nuclear physics.

South Dakota State University, Graduate School, College of Arts and Science and College of Agriculture and Biological Sciences, Department of Chemistry, Brookings, SD 57007. Offers analytical chemistry (MS, PhD); biochemistry (MS, PhD); chemistry (MS, PhD); inorganic chemistry (MS, PhD); organic chemistry (MS, PhD); physical chemistry (MS, PhD). *Degree requirements:* For master's, thesis, oral exam; for doctorate, thesis/dissertation, preliminary oral and written exams, research tool. *Entrance requirements:* For master's, bachelor's degree in chemistry or equivalent. Additional exam requirements/recommendations for international students: Required—TOEFL. *Faculty research:* Environmental chemistry, computational chemistry, organic synthesis and photochemistry, novel material development and characterization.

Southern University and Agricultural and Mechanical College, Graduate School, College of Sciences, Department of Chemistry, Baton Rouge, LA 70813. Offers analytical chemistry (MS); biochemistry (MS); environmental sciences (MS); inorganic chemistry (MS); organic chemistry (MS); physical chemistry (MS). *Degree requirements:* For master's, thesis. *Entrance requirements:* For master's, GMAT or GRE General Test. Additional exam requirements/recommendations for international students: Required—TOEFL. *Faculty research:* Synthesis of macrocyclic ligands, latex accelerators, anticancer drugs, biosensors, absorption isotheums, isolation of specific enzymes from plants.

State University of New York at Binghamton, Graduate School, School of Arts and Sciences, Department of Chemistry, Binghamton, NY 13902-6000. Offers analytical chemistry (PhD); chemistry (MA, MS); inorganic chemistry (PhD); organic chemistry (PhD); physical chemistry (PhD). Part-time programs available. Terminal master's awarded for partial completion of doctoral program. *Degree requirements:* For master's, thesis or alternative, oral exam, seminar presentation; for doctorate, thesis/dissertation, cumulative exams. *Entrance requirements:* For master's and doctorate, GRE General Test, GRE Subject Test. Additional exam requirements/recommendations for international students: Required—TOEFL. Electronic applications accepted.

Stevens Institute of Technology, Graduate School, School of Applied Sciences and Liberal Arts, Department of Chemistry and Chemical Biology, Hoboken, NJ 07030. Offers chemistry (MS, PhD, Certificate), including analytical chemistry, chemical biology, chemical physiology (Certificate), instrumental analysis (Certificate), organic chemistry (MS, PhD), physical chemistry (MS, PhD), polymer chemistry. Part-time and evening/weekend programs available. Terminal master's awarded for partial completion of doctoral program. *Degree requirements:* For master's, thesis or alternative; for doctorate, one foreign language, thesis/dissertation; for Certificate, project or thesis. *Entrance requirements:* Additional exam requirements/recommendations for international students: Required—TOEFL. Electronic applications accepted.

Tufts University, Graduate School of Arts and Sciences, Department of Chemistry, Medford, MA 02155. Offers analytical chemistry (MS, PhD); bioorganic chemistry (MS, PhD); environmental chemistry (MS, PhD); inorganic chemistry (MS, PhD); organic chemistry (MS, PhD); physical chemistry (MS, PhD). *Faculty:* 13 full-time, 1 part-time/adjunct. *Students:* 56 (24 women); includes 6 minority (1 African American, 4 Asian Americans or Pacific Islanders, 1 Hispanic American) 22 international. 66 applicants, 56% accepted, 17 enrolled. In 2003, 4 master's, 6 doctorates awarded. Terminal master's awarded for partial completion of doctoral program. *Degree requirements:* For master's and doctorate, thesis/dissertation. *Entrance requirements:* For master's and doctorate, GRE General Test, GRE Subject Test. Additional exam requirements/recommendations for international students: Required—TOEFL (minimum score 600 paper-based; 213 computer-based), TSE. *Application deadline:* For fall admission, 2/1 for domestic students, 12/30 for international students; for spring admission, 10/15 for domestic students, 9/15 for international students. Applications are processed on a rolling basis. Application fee: $60. Electronic applications accepted. *Expenses:* Tuition: Full-time $29,949. *Financial support:* Research assistantships with full and partial tuition reimbursements, teaching assistantships with full and partial tuition reimbursements, Federal Work-Study, scholarships/grants, and tuition waivers (partial) available. Financial award application deadline: 2/1; financial award applicants required to submit FAFSA. *Unit head:* Mary Jane Shultz, Chair, 617-627-3477, Fax: 617-627-3443. *Application contact:* Arthur Utz, Information Contact, 617-627-3441, Fax: 617-627-3443.

See in-depth description on page 153.

University of Calgary, Faculty of Graduate Studies, Faculty of Science, Department of Chemistry, Calgary, AB T2N 1N4, Canada. Offers analytical chemistry (M Sc, PhD); applied chemistry (M Sc, PhD); inorganic chemistry (M Sc, PhD); organic chemistry (M Sc, PhD); physical chemistry (M Sc, PhD); polymer chemistry (M Sc, PhD); theoretical chemistry (M Sc, PhD). *Faculty:* 29 full-time (6 women), 1 part-time/adjunct (0 women). *Students:* 74 full-time (29 women). Average age 25. 130 applicants, 20% accepted. In 2003, 12 master's, 6 doctorates awarded. *Degree requirements:* For master's, thesis; for doctorate, thesis/dissertation, candidacy exam. *Entrance requirements:* For master's, minimum GPA of 3.0; for doctorate, honors degree minimum GPA of 3.7, minimum GPA of 3.3. Additional exam requirements/recommendations for international students: Required—TOEFL (minimum score 580 paper-based; 237 computer-based). *Application deadline:* For fall admission, 12/1 for domestic students. Applications are processed on a rolling basis. Application fee: $60. Electronic applications accepted. Tuition, nonresident: full-time $4,765. Tuition and fees vary according to degree level, program and student level. *Financial support:* In 2003–04, research assistantships (averaging $11,000 per year), teaching assistantships (averaging $6,221 per year) were awarded. Fellowships, scholarships/grants also available. Financial award application deadline: 12/1. *Faculty research:* Chemical analysis, chemical dynamics, synthesis theory, polymer, applied chemistry. *Unit head:* Dr. Brian Keay, Head, 403-220-6252, E-mail: gradinfo@chem.ucalgary.ca.

University of Cincinnati, Division of Research and Advanced Studies, McMicken College of Arts and Sciences, Department of Chemistry, Cincinnati, OH 45221. Offers analytical chemistry (MS, PhD); biochemistry (MS, PhD); inorganic chemistry (MS, PhD); organic chemistry (MS, PhD); physical chemistry (MS, PhD); polymer chemistry (MS, PhD); sensors (PhD). Part-time and evening/weekend programs available. Terminal master's awarded for partial completion of doctoral program. *Degree requirements:* For master's, thesis optional; for doctorate, thesis/dissertation, comprehensive exam, registration. *Entrance requirements:* For master's and doctorate, GRE General Test. Additional exam requirements/recommendations for international students: Required—TOEFL (minimum score 580 paper-based; 237 computer-based); Recommended—TSE(minimum score 50). Electronic applications accepted. *Faculty research:* Biomedical chemistry, laser chemistry, surface science, chemical sensors, synthesis.

University of Colorado at Boulder, Graduate School, College of Arts and Sciences, Department of Chemistry and Biochemistry, Boulder, CO 80309. Offers biochemistry (PhD); chemical physics (PhD); chemistry (MS, PhD). *Faculty:* 35 full-time (6 women). *Students:* 116 full-time (53 women), 79 part-time (32 women); includes 9 minority (1 African American, 6 Asian Americans or Pacific Islanders, 2 Hispanic Americans), 16 international. Average age 26. 137 applicants, 39% accepted. In 2003, 2 master's, 23 doctorates awarded. *Degree requirements:* For master's, comprehensive exam or thesis; for doctorate, thesis/dissertation, cumulative exam, comprehensive exam. *Entrance requirements:* For master's, GRE General Test, GRE Subject Test, minimum GPA of 3.0; for doctorate, GRE General Test, GRE Subject Test (chemistry or biochemistry), minimum GPA of 3.0. *Application deadline:* For fall admission, 3/1 for domestic students. Applications are processed on a rolling basis. Application fee: $50 ($60 for international students). *Expenses:* Tuition, state resident: full-time $2,122. Tuition, nonresident: full-time $9,754. Tuition and fees vary according to course load and program. *Financial support:* In 2003–04, 2 fellowships with full tuition reimbursements (averaging $16,832 per year), 67 research assistantships with full tuition reimbursements (averaging $17,438 per year), 60 teaching assistantships with full tuition reimbursements (averaging $16,464 per year) were awarded. Institutionally sponsored loans, traineeships, and tuition waivers (full) also available. Support available to part-time students. Financial award application deadline: 2/28. *Faculty research:* Biochemistry, atmospheric chemistry, analytical chemistry, biophysical chemistry, chemical physics. Total annual research expenditures: $18.4 million. *Unit head:* Veronica Vaida, Chair, 303-492-8605, Fax: 303-492-5894, E-mail: veronica.vaida@colorado.edu. *Application contact:* Graduate Program Assistant, 303-492-8978, Fax: 303-492-5894, E-mail: chem_gradstudents@colorado.edu.

University of Georgia, Graduate School, College of Arts and Sciences, Department of Chemistry, Athens, GA 30602. Offers analytical chemistry (MS, PhD); inorganic chemistry (MS, PhD); organic chemistry (MS, PhD); physical chemistry (MS, PhD). *Faculty:* 26 full-time (2 women). *Students:* 130 full-time (43 women). 160 applicants, 29% accepted, 36 enrolled. In 2003, 3 master's, 17 doctorates awarded. Terminal master's awarded for partial completion of doctoral program. *Median time to degree:* Of those who began their doctoral program in fall 1995, 100% received their degree in 8 years or less. *Degree requirements:* For master's, thesis; for doctorate, one foreign language, thesis/dissertation. *Entrance requirements:* For master's and doctorate, GRE General Test. Additional exam requirements/recommendations for international students: Required—TOEFL (minimum score 213 computer-based), TSE(minimum score 50). *Application deadline:* For fall admission, 7/1 for domestic students; for spring admission, 11/15 for domestic students. Application fee: $50. Electronic applications accepted. *Expenses:* Tuition, state resident: part-time $161 per hour. Tuition, nonresident: part-time $690 per hour. One-time fee: $435 part-time. *Financial support:* Fellowships, research assistantships, teaching assistantships, unspecified assistantships available. *Unit head:* Dr. John L. Stickney, Head, 706-542-2726, Fax: 706-542-9454, E-mail: stickney@chem.uga.edu. *Application contact:* Dr. Donald Kurtz, Information Contact, 706-542-2010, Fax: 706-542-9454, E-mail: kurtz@chem.uga.edu.

University of Louisville, Graduate School, College of Arts and Sciences, Department of Chemistry, Louisville, KY 40292-0001. Offers analytical chemistry (MS, PhD); biochemistry (MS, PhD); chemical physics (PhD); inorganic chemistry (MS, PhD); organic chemistry (MS, PhD); physical chemistry (MS, PhD). *Students:* 48 full-time (19 women), 13 part-time (5 women); includes 4 minority (1 African American, 1 Asian American or Pacific Islander, 2 Hispanic Americans), 27 international. Average age 27. In 2003, 7 master's, 1 doctorate awarded. *Degree requirements:* For master's, thesis/dissertation; for doctorate, thesis/dissertation, comprehensive exam. *Entrance requirements:* For master's and doctorate, GRE General Test. Additional exam requirements/recommendations for international students: Required—TOEFL. *Application deadline:* Applications are processed on a rolling basis. Application fee: $50. *Expenses:* Tuition, state resident: full-time $4,842. Tuition, nonresident: full-time $13,338. *Financial support:* In 2003–04, 30 teaching assistantships (averaging $14,000 per year) were awarded. *Unit head:* Dr. George R. Pack, Chair, 502-852-6798, Fax: 502-852-8149, E-mail: george.pack@louisville.edu.

University of Maryland, College Park, Graduate Studies and Research, College of Computer, Mathematical and Physical Sciences, Program in Chemical Physics, College Park, MD 20742. Offers MS, PhD. Part-time and evening/weekend programs available. *Students:* 29 full-time (6 women), 4 part-time (2 women); includes 2 minority (1 Asian American or Pacific Islander, 1 Hispanic American), 20 international. 13 applicants, 85% accepted. In 2003, 2 degrees awarded. Terminal master's awarded for partial completion of doctoral program. *Median time to degree:* Of those who began their doctoral program in fall 1995, 57% received their degree in 8 years or less. *Degree requirements:* For master's, paper, qualifying exam, thesis optional; for doctorate, thesis/dissertation, seminars. *Entrance requirements:* For master's, GRE General Test, GRE Subject Test (physics), minimum GPA of 3.3, 3 letters of recommendation; for doctorate, GRE Subject Test, minimum GPA of 3.3. *Application deadline:* For fall admission, 5/1 for domestic students, 2/1 for international students; for spring admission, 10/1 for domestic students, 6/1 for international students. Applications are processed on a rolling basis. Application fee: $50. Electronic applications accepted. *Expenses:* Tuition, state resident: part-time $349 per credit hour. Tuition, nonresident: part-time $602 per credit hour. *Financial support:* Fellowships, research assistantships, teaching assistantships, Federal Work-Study and scholarships/grants available. Financial award applicants required to submit FAFSA. *Faculty research:* Discrete molecules and gases; dynamic phenomena; thermodynamics, statistical mechanical theory and quantum mechanical theory; atmospheric physics; biophysics. *Unit head:* Dr. Michael Coplan, Director, 301-405-4780, Fax: 301-314-9396. *Application contact:* Trudy Lindsey, Director, Graduate Enrollment Management Services, 301-405-4190, Fax: 301-314-9305, E-mail: tlindsey@gradschool.umd.edu.

University of Maryland, College Park, Graduate Studies and Research, College of Life Sciences, Department of Biology, Program in Biophysics, College Park, MD 20742. Offers chemical physics (PhD). Administered by a joint University of Maryland-National Institutes of Health committee. *Entrance requirements:* For doctorate, GRE General Test, GRE Subject Test, 3 letters of recommendation from professional or academic references. *Application deadline:* For fall admission, 5/1 for domestic students, 2/1 for international students; for spring admission, 10/1 for domestic students, 6/1 for international students. Application fee: $50. *Expenses:* Tuition, state resident: part-time $349 per credit hour. Tuition, nonresident: part-time $602 per credit hour. *Financial support:* Fellowships, teaching assistantships, traineeships and specialized fellowships funded by federal agencies, foundations, or the university available. *Application contact:* Dr. Wolfgang Losert, Information Contact, 301-405-0629, E-mail: wlosert@glue.umd.edu.

University of Maryland, College Park, Graduate Studies and Research, College of Life Sciences, Department of Chemistry and Biochemistry, Chemistry Program, College Park, MD 20742. Offers analytical chemistry (MS, PhD); inorganic chemistry (MS, PhD); organic chemistry (MS, PhD); physical chemistry (MS, PhD). Part-time and evening/weekend programs available. *Students:* 89 full-time (46 women), 4 part-time (2 women); includes 6 minority (2 African Americans, 2 Asian Americans or Pacific Islanders, 2 Hispanic Americans), 39 international. 141 applicants, 19% accepted. In 2003, 16 degrees awarded. Terminal master's awarded for partial completion of doctoral program. *Median time to degree:* Of those who began their doctoral program in fall 1995, 33% received their degree in 8 years or less. *Degree requirements:* For master's, thesis optional; for doctorate, thesis/dissertation, 2 seminar presentations, oral exam. *Entrance requirements:* For master's, GRE General Test, GRE Subject Test (recommended), minimum GPA of 3.1, 3 letters of recommendation; for doctorate, GRE General Test, GRE Subject Test (recommended), minimum GPA of 3.1. *Application deadline:* For fall admission, 5/1 for domestic students, 2/1 for international students; for spring admission, 10/1 for domestic students, 6/1 for international students. Applications are processed on a rolling basis. Application fee: $50. Electronic applications accepted. *Expenses:* Tuition, state resident: part-time $349 per credit hour. Tuition, nonresident: part-time $602 per credit hour. *Financial support:* Fellowships, research assistantships, teaching assistantships with partial tuition reimbursements available. Financial award applicants required to submit FAFSA. *Faculty research:* Environmental chemistry, nuclear chemistry, lunar and environmental analysis, x-ray crystallography. *Application contact:* Trudy Lindsey, Director, Graduate Enrollment Management Services, 301-405-4190, Fax: 301-314-9305, E-mail: tlindsey@gradschool.umd.edu.

University of Miami, Graduate School, College of Arts and Sciences, Department of Chemistry, Coral Gables, FL 33124. Offers chemistry (MS); inorganic chemistry (PhD); organic chemistry (PhD); physical chemistry (PhD). *Faculty:* 9 full-time (1 woman). *Students:* 39 full-time (17 women); includes 23 minority (4 African Americans, 15 Asian Americans or Pacific Islanders, 4 Hispanic Americans), 25 international. Average age 25. 104 applicants, 13% accepted, 10 enrolled. In 2003, 2 master's, 1 doctorate awarded. Terminal master's awarded for partial completion of doctoral program. *Degree requirements:* For master's, comprehensive exam; for doctorate, thesis/dissertation, comprehensive exam. *Entrance requirements:* For master's and doctorate, GRE General Test. Additional exam requirements/recommendations for international students: Required—TOEFL (minimum score 550 paper-based; 213 computer-based). *Application deadline:* For fall admission, 1/15 for domestic students, 1/15 for international students. Applications are processed on a rolling basis. Application fee: $50. Electronic applications accepted. *Expenses:* Tuition: Full-time $19,526. *Financial support:* In 2003–04, 39 students received support, including 3 fellowships with full tuition reimbursements available (averaging $20,000 per year), 14 research assistantships with full tuition reimbursements available (averaging $19,000 per year), 21 teaching assistantships with full tuition reimbursements available (averaging $19,000 per year); tuition waivers (full) also available. Financial award application deadline: 5/1; financial award applicants required to submit FAFSA. *Faculty research:* Supramolecular chemistry, electrochemistry, surface chemistry, catalysis, organometalic. *Unit head:* Dr. Cecil M. Criss, Chairman, 305-284-2282, Fax: 305-284-4571. *Application contact:* Eva Johnson, Graduate Secretary, 305-284-6561, Fax: 305-284-4571, E-mail: evaj@miami.edu.

University of Michigan, Horace H. Rackham School of Graduate Studies, College of Literature, Science, and the Arts, Department of Chemistry, Ann Arbor, MI 48109. Offers analytical chemistry (PhD); chemical biology (PhD); inorganic chemistry (PhD); material chemistry (PhD); organic chemistry (PhD); physical chemistry (PhD). *Faculty:* 50 full-time (10 women), 3 part-time/adjunct (0 women). *Students:* 213 full-time (101 women); includes 20 minority (5 African Americans, 1 American Indian/Alaska Native, 9 Asian Americans or Pacific Islanders, 5 Hispanic Americans), 64 international. Average age 26. 310 applicants, 56% accepted, 58 enrolled. In 2003, 27 degrees awarded. *Degree requirements:* For doctorate, thesis/dissertation, oral defense of dissertation, organic cumulative proficiency exams. *Entrance requirements:* For doctorate, GRE General Test, GRE Subject Test (recommended), statement of prior research. Additional exam requirements/recommendations for international students: Required—TOEFL. *Application deadline:* For fall admission, 1/15 priority date for domestic students, 1/15 priority date for international students. Applications are processed on a rolling basis. Application fee: $60 ($75 for international students). Electronic applications accepted. *Expenses:* Tuition, state resident: full-time $7,463. Tuition, nonresident: full-time $13,913. Full-time tuition and fees vary according to course load, degree level and program. *Financial support:* In 2003–04, 10 fellowships with full tuition reimbursements (averaging $20,000 per year), 70 research assistantships with full tuition reimbursements (averaging $19,000 per year), 120 teaching assistantships with full tuition reimbursements (averaging $20,000 per year) were awarded. Financial award applicants required to submit FAFSA. *Faculty research:* Biological catalysis, protein engineering, chemical sensors, de novo metalloprotein design, supramolecular architecture. Total annual research expenditures: $8 million. *Unit head:* Dr. William R. Roush, Chair, 734-763-9681, Fax: 734-647-4847, E-mail: roush@umich.edu. *Application contact:* Linda Deitert, Assistant Director Graduate Studies, 734-764-7278, Fax: 734-647-4865, E-mail: chemadmissions@umich.edu.

University of Missouri–Columbia, Graduate School, College of Arts and Sciences, Department of Chemistry, Columbia, MO 65211. Offers analytical chemistry (MS, PhD); inorganic chemistry (MS, PhD); organic chemistry (MS, PhD); physical chemistry (MS, PhD). *Faculty:* 20 full-time (4 women). *Students:* 58 full-time (21 women), 36 part-time (7 women); includes 5 minority (1 African American, 1 American Indian/Alaska Native, 3 Asian Americans or Pacific Islanders), 51 international. In 2003, 7 master's, 7 doctorates awarded. *Degree requirements:* For master's, thesis; for doctorate, one foreign language, thesis/dissertation. *Entrance requirements:* For master's and doctorate, GRE General Test, minimum GPA of 3.0. *Application deadline:* For fall admission, 4/1 for domestic students; for winter admission, 11/1 for domestic students. Applications are processed on a rolling basis. Application fee: $45 ($60 for international students). *Expenses:* Tuition, state resident: full-time $5,205. Tuition, nonresident: full-time $14,058. *Financial support:* Research assistantships, teaching assistantships, institutionally sponsored loans available. *Unit head:* Dr. Silvia S. Jurisson, Director of Graduate Studies, 573-882-2107, E-mail: jurissons@missouri.edu.

University of Missouri–Kansas City, College of Arts and Sciences, Department of Chemistry, Kansas City, MO 64110-2499. Offers analytical chemistry (MS, PhD); inorganic chemistry (MS, PhD); organic chemistry (MS, PhD); physical chemistry (MS, PhD); polymer chemistry (MS, PhD). PhD offered through the School of Graduate Studies. Part-time and evening/weekend programs available. *Faculty:* 11 full-time (1 woman), 1 part-time/adjunct (0 women). *Students:* Average age 30. 56 applicants, 46% accepted. In 2003, 1 master's awarded. *Median time to degree:* Master's–1 year full-time, 1 year part-time; doctorate–5 years full-time. *Degree requirements:* For master's, thesis (for some programs); for doctorate, thesis/dissertation. *Entrance requirements:* For master's, equivalent of American Chemical Society approved bachelor's degree in chemistry; for doctorate, GRE General Test, equivalent of American Chemical Society approved bachelor's degree in chemistry. Additional exam requirements/recommendations for international students: Required—TOEFL (minimum score 580 paper-based; 237 computer-based), TWE. *Application deadline:* For fall and spring admission, 4/15; for winter admission, 10/15 for domestic students. Applications are processed on a rolling basis. Application fee: $25. *Financial support:* In 2003–04, 1 fellowship with partial tuition reimbursement (averaging $18,156 per year), 9 research assistantships with partial tuition reimbursements (averaging $17,632 per year), 16 teaching assistantships with partial tuition reimbursements (averaging $16,416 per year) were awarded. Federal Work-Study, institutionally sponsored loans, and scholarships/grants also available. Support available to part-time students. Financial award application deadline: 2/15. *Faculty research:* Molecular spectroscopy, characterization and synthesis of materials and compounds, computational chemistry, natural products, drug delivery systems and anti-tumor agents. Total annual research expenditures: $551,743. *Unit head:* Dr. Jerry Jean, Chairperson, 816-235-2280, Fax: 816-235-5502, E-mail: jeany@umkc.edu. *Application contact:* Dr. Kathleen Y. Kilway, Graduate Recruiting Committee, 816-235-2289, Fax: 816-235-5502, E-mail: kilwayk@umkc.edu.

University of Missouri–St. Louis, Graduate School, College of Arts and Sciences, Department of Chemistry, St. Louis, MO 63121-4499. Offers chemistry (MS, PhD), including biochemistry, inorganic chemistry, organic chemistry, physical chemistry. Part-time and evening/weekend programs available. *Faculty:* 16 full-time (3 women). *Students:* 31 full-time (19 women), 20 part-time (9 women); includes 6 minority (5 Asian Americans or Pacific Islanders, 1 Hispanic American), 21 international. In 2003, 8 master's, 5 doctorates awarded. Terminal master's awarded for partial completion of doctoral program. *Degree requirements:* For master's, thesis optional; for doctorate, thesis/dissertation. *Entrance requirements:* For doctorate, GRE General Test, GRE Subject Test. Additional exam requirements/recommendations for international students: Required—TOEFL (minimum score 550 paper-based; 213 computer-based). *Application deadline:* For fall admission, 7/1 for domestic students; for spring admission, 12/7 priority date for domestic students. Applications are processed on a rolling basis. Application fee: $35 ($40 for international students). Electronic applications accepted. *Expenses:* Tuition, state resident: part-time $237 per credit hour. Tuition, nonresident: part-time $639 per credit hour. Required fees: $10 per credit hour. *Financial support:* In 2003–04, 14 research assistantships with full and partial tuition reimbursements (averaging $16,007 per year), 13 teaching assistantships with full and partial tuition reimbursements (averaging $15,408 per year) were awarded. Fellowships with full and partial tuition reimbursements *Faculty research:* Metallaborane chemistry, serum transferrin chemistry, natural products chemistry, organic synthesis. *Unit head:* Dr. F. Christopher Pigge, Director of Graduate Studies, 314-516-5311, Fax: 314-516-5342. *Application contact:* 314-516-5458, Fax: 314-516-5310, E-mail: gradadm@umsl.edu.

The University of Montana–Missoula, Graduate School, College of Arts and Sciences, Department of Chemistry, Missoula, MT 59812-0002. Offers chemistry (MS, PhD), including environmental/analytical chemistry, inorganic chemistry, organic chemistry, physical chemistry; chemistry teaching (MST). *Faculty:* 16 full-time (2 women). *Students:* 26 full-time (5 women), 12 part-time (6 women), 10 international. 25 applicants, 44% accepted, 6 enrolled. In 2003, 2 master's, 4 doctorates awarded. Terminal master's awarded for partial completion of doctoral program. *Degree requirements:* For master's, thesis (for some programs); for doctorate, thesis/dissertation. *Entrance requirements:* For master's and doctorate, GRE General Test. Additional exam requirements/recommendations for international students: Required—TOEFL (minimum score 575 paper-based; 230 computer-based). *Application deadline:* For fall admission, 2/15 for domestic students. Applications are processed on a rolling basis. Application fee: $45. *Expenses:* Tuition, state resident: full-time $1,848; part-time $221 per credit. Tuition, nonresident: full-time $4,880; part-time $333 per credit. Required fees: $2,200. *Financial support:* In 2003–04, 13 research assistantships with tuition reimbursements (averaging $14,000 per year), 12 teaching assistantships with full tuition reimbursements (averaging $14,000 per year) were awarded. Federal Work-Study, scholarships/grants, and unspecified assistantships also available. Financial award application deadline: 3/1; financial award applicants required to submit FAFSA. *Faculty research:* Reaction mechanisms and kinetics, inorganic and organic synthesis, analytical chemistry, natural products. Total annual research expenditures: $789,952. *Unit head:* Dr. Edward Rosenberg, Chair, 406-243-4022, Fax: 406-243-4227.

University of Nebraska–Lincoln, Graduate College, College of Arts and Sciences, Department of Chemistry, Lincoln, NE 68588. Offers analytical chemistry (PhD); chemistry (MS); inorganic chemistry (PhD); organic chemistry (PhD); physical chemistry (PhD). *Degree requirements:* For master's, one foreign language, departmental qualifying exam, thesis optional; for doctorate, one foreign language, thesis/dissertation, departmental qualifying exams, comprehensive exam. *Entrance requirements:* For master's and doctorate, GRE. Additional exam requirements/recommendations for international students: Required—TOEFL (minimum score 550 paper-based; 213 computer-based). Electronic applications accepted. *Faculty research:* Bioorganic and bioinorganic chemistry, biophysical and bioanalytical chemistry, structure-function of DNA and proteins, organometallics, mass spectrometry.

University of Nevada, Reno, Graduate School, College of Science, Department of Chemical Physics, Reno, NV 89557. Offers PhD. *Faculty:* 8. *Students:* 10 full-time (1 woman), 4 international. Average age 32. *Entrance requirements:* For doctorate, GRE, minimum GPA of 3.0. Additional exam requirements/recommendations for international students: Required—TOEFL. *Application deadline:* For fall admission, 3/1 for domestic students; for spring admission, 11/1 for domestic students. Applications are processed on a rolling basis. Application fee: $60 ($95 for international students). *Expenses:* Tuition, state resident: part-time $119 per credit. Tuition, nonresident: part-time $127 per credit. Required fees: $20 per term. Tuition and fees vary according to course load. *Financial support:* Research assistantships, teaching assistantships available. *Unit head:* Dr. Joe Cline, Graduate Program Director, 775-784-4376.

University of Notre Dame, Graduate School, College of Science, Department of Chemistry and Biochemistry, Notre Dame, IN 46556. Offers biochemistry (MS, PhD); inorganic chemistry (MS, PhD); organic chemistry (MS, PhD); physical chemistry (MS, PhD). *Faculty:* 30 full-time (3 women). *Students:* 139 full-time (46 women); includes 5 minority (1 African American, 1 American Indian/Alaska Native, 1 Asian American or Pacific Islander, 2 Hispanic Americans), 65 international. 270 applicants, 38% accepted, 44 enrolled. In 2003, 5 master's, 17 doctorates awarded. Terminal master's awarded for partial completion of doctoral program. *Degree requirements:* For master's, thesis, comprehensive exam; for doctorate, thesis/dissertation, qualifying exam. *Entrance requirements:* For master's and doctorate, GRE General Test, GRE Subject Test (strongly recommended). Additional exam requirements/recommendations for international students: Required—TOEFL. *Application deadline:* For fall admission, 2/1 for domestic students. Applications are processed on a rolling basis. Application fee: $50. Electronic applications accepted. *Expenses:* Tuition: Full-time $29,375. *Financial support:* In 2003–04, 139 students received support, including 34 fellowships with full tuition reimbursements available (averaging $20,000 per year), 46 research assistantships with full tuition reimbursements available (averaging $15,500 per year), 51 teaching assistantships with full tuition reimbursements available (averaging $15,500 per year); tuition waivers (full) also available. Financial award application deadline: 2/1. *Faculty research:* Reaction design and mechaninistic studies; reactive intermediates; synthesis, structure and reactivity of organometallic. cluster complexes, and biologically active natural products; bioorganic chemistry; enzymology. Total annual research expenditures: $9.4 million. *Unit head:* Dr. Richard E. Taylor, Director of Graduate Studies, 574-631-7058, Fax: 574-631-6652, E-mail: taylor.61@nd.edu. *Application contact:* Dr. Terrence J. Akai, Director of Graduate Admissions, 574-631-7706, Fax: 574-631-4183, E-mail: gradad@nd.edu.

University of Puerto Rico, Río Piedras, Faculty of Natural Sciences, Department of Physics, San Juan, PR 00931. Offers applied physics (MS); physics (MS); physics-chemical (PhD). Part-time and evening/weekend programs available. *Faculty:* 15 full-time (1 woman), 2 part-time/adjunct (0 women). *Students:* 21 full-time (10 women), 34 part-time (11 women); includes 53 minority (11 Asian Americans or Pacific Islanders, 42 Hispanic Americans). 20 applicants, 95% accepted, 19 enrolled. In 2003, 3 degrees awarded. *Degree requirements:* For master's and doctorate, one foreign language, thesis/dissertation, comprehensive exam. *Entrance requirements:* For master's, GRE, EXADEP, interview, minimum GPA of 3.0, letter of recommendation; for doctorate, GRE, master's degree, minimum GPA of 3.0, letter of recommendation. Additional exam requirements/recommendations for international students: Required—TOEFL. *Application deadline:* For fall admission, 2/1 for domestic students, 2/1 for international students. Application fee: $17. *Expenses:* Tuition, state resident: part-time $75 per credit. Tuition, nonresident: full-time $1,200; part-time $218 per credit. International tuition: $3,500 full-time. Required fees: $70; $35 per term. *Financial support:* Fellowships, research assistantships, teaching assistantships, Federal Work-Study, institutionally sponsored loans, and tuition waivers (partial) available. Financial award application deadline: 5/31. *Faculty research:* Energy transfer process through Van der Vacqs interactions, study of the photodissociation of ketene. *Unit head:* Luis F. Fonseca, Coordinator of Doctoral Program, 787-764-0000 Ext. 4773, Fax: 787-764-4063.

University of Regina, Faculty of Graduate Studies and Research, Faculty of Science, Department of Chemistry and Biochemistry, Regina, SK S4S 0A2, Canada. Offers analytical chemistry (M Sc, PhD); biochemistry (M Sc, PhD); inorganic chemistry (M Sc, PhD); organic chemistry (M Sc, PhD); physical chemistry (M Sc, PhD). Part-time programs available. *Faculty:* 9

Physical Chemistry

University of Regina (continued)

full-time (2 women), 2 part-time/adjunct (1 woman). *Students:* 7 full-time (4 women), 4 part-time (1 woman). 12 applicants. In 2003, 3 degrees awarded. *Degree requirements:* For master's and doctorate, thesis/dissertation, departmental qualifying exam. *Entrance requirements:* For master's and doctorate, GRE. Additional exam requirements/recommendations for international students: Required—TOEFL. *Application deadline:* For fall admission, 1/1 for domestic students; for winter admission, 7/1 for domestic students. Applications are processed on a rolling basis. Application fee: $60. *Expenses:* Tuition, state resident: part-time $130 per credit hour. Tuition and fees vary according to course load and program. *Financial support:* In 2003–04, 4 fellowships, 1 research assistantship, 3 teaching assistantships were awarded. Scholarships/grants also available. Financial award application deadline: 6/15. *Faculty research:* Organic synthesis, organic oxidations, ionic liquids theoretical/computational chemistry, protein biochemistry/biophysics, environmental analytical, physical/photochemistry. *Unit head:* Dr. Andrew G. Wee, Head, 306-585-4767, Fax: 306-585-4894, E-mail: chem.chair@uregina.ca. *Application contact:* Teri Dibble, Office Administrator, 306-585-4146, Fax: 306-585-4894, E-mail: teri.dibble@uregina.ca.

University of Southern California, Graduate School, College of Letters, Arts and Sciences, Department of Chemistry, Program in Chemical Physics, Los Angeles, CA 90089. Offers PhD. *Faculty:* 27 full-time (3 women). *Students:* Average age 27. *Degree requirements:* For doctorate, thesis/dissertation, qualifying exam. *Entrance requirements:* For doctorate, GRE General Test. *Application deadline:* For fall admission, 3/1 for domestic students. Applications are processed on a rolling basis. Application fee: $0. *Expenses:* Tuition: Full-time $32,784; part-time $949 per unit. Tuition and fees vary according to course load and program. *Financial support:* In 2003–04, fellowships (averaging $21,333 per year), research assistantships with tuition reimbursements (averaging $21,333 per year), teaching assistantships (averaging $21,333 per year) were awarded. Federal Work-Study, institutionally sponsored loans, scholarships/grants, and health care benefits also available. Financial award application deadline: 3/1. *Faculty research:* Inorganic chemistry, polymer chemistry, theoretical chemistry. *Application contact:* Heather Meunier, Graduate Advisor, 213-740-6855, Fax: 213-740-2701, E-mail: meunier@usc.edu.

University of Southern Mississippi, Graduate School, College of Science and Technology, Department of Chemistry and Biochemistry, Hattiesburg, MS 39406-0001. Offers analytical chemistry (MS, PhD); biochemistry (MS, PhD); inorganic chemistry (MS, PhD); organic chemistry (MS, PhD); physical chemistry (MS, PhD). *Faculty:* 8 full-time (1 woman). *Students:* 27 full-time (17 women), 1 part-time; includes 14 minority (4 African Americans, 1 American Indian/Alaska Native, 9 Asian Americans or Pacific Islanders). Average age 27. 29 applicants, 45% accepted, 10 enrolled. In 2003, 1 master's, 7 doctorates awarded. *Degree requirements:* For master's and doctorate, thesis/dissertation, comprehensive exam. *Entrance requirements:* For master's, GRE General Test, minimum GPA of 2.75 in last 60 hours; for doctorate, GRE General Test, minimum GPA of 3.5. Additional exam requirements/recommendations for international students: Required—TOEFL. *Application deadline:* For fall admission, 8/6 for domestic students. Applications are processed on a rolling basis. Application fee: $25. *Expenses:* Tuition, state resident: part-time $1,967 per semester. Tuition, nonresident: part-time $4,376 per semester. *Financial support:* Fellowships, research assistantships with full tuition reimbursements, teaching assistantships with full tuition reimbursements, Federal Work-Study and institutionally sponsored loans available. Support available to part-time students. Financial award application deadline: 3/15. *Faculty research:* Plant biochemistry, photo chemistry, polymer chemistry, x-ray analysis, enzyme chemistry. *Unit head:* Dr. Robert Bateman, Chair, 601-266-4701. *Application contact:* Dr. Gordon Cannon, Information Contact, 601-266-4702.

University of South Florida, College of Graduate Studies, College of Arts and Sciences, Department of Chemistry, Tampa, FL 33620-9951. Offers analytical chemistry (MS, PhD); biochemistry (MS, PhD); inorganic chemistry (MS, PhD); organic chemistry (MS, PhD); physical chemistry (MS, PhD); polymer chemistry (PhD). Part-time programs available. *Faculty:* 26 full-time (8 women), 1 (woman) part-time/adjunct. *Students:* 75 full-time (34 women), 11 part-time (4 women); includes 14 minority (3 African Americans, 3 Asian Americans or Pacific Islanders, 8 Hispanic Americans), 30 international. 75 applicants, 37% accepted, 17 enrolled. In 2003, 3 master's, 6 doctorates awarded. Terminal master's awarded for partial completion of doctoral program. *Degree requirements:* For master's, thesis; for doctorate, 2 foreign languages, thesis/dissertation, colloquium. *Entrance requirements:* For master's and doctorate, GRE General Test, minimum GPA of 3.0 in last 30 hours of chemistry course work, letters of recommendation (3). Additional exam requirements/recommendations for international students: Required—TOEFL (minimum score 550 paper-based; 213 computer-based), TSE(minimum score 50). *Application deadline:* For fall admission, 5/1 priority date for domestic students, 3/1 priority date for international students; for spring admission, 10/1 priority date for domestic students, 8/1 priority date for international students. Applications are processed on a rolling basis. Application fee: $30. Electronic applications accepted. *Financial support:* In 2003–04, 74 students received support, including 3 fellowships with partial tuition reimbursements available (averaging $18,500 per year), 13 research assistantships with partial tuition reimbursements available (averaging $18,500 per year), 58 teaching assistantships with partial tuition reimbursements available (averaging $18,500 per year); career-related internships or fieldwork, institutionally sponsored loans, scholarships/grants, and unspecified assistantships also available. Financial award application deadline: 6/30. *Faculty research:* Synthesis, bio-organic chemistry, bioinorganic chemistry, environmental chemistry, NMR. Total annual research expenditures: $1.6 million. *Unit head:* Michael Zaworotko, Chairperson, 813-974-4129, Fax: 813-974-1731. *Application contact:* Dr. Julie Harmon, Graduate Director, 813-974-3397, Fax: 813-974-3203, E-mail: harmon@chuma1.cas.usf.edu.

The University of Tennessee, Graduate School, College of Arts and Sciences, Department of Chemistry, Knoxville, TN 37996. Offers analytical chemistry (MS, PhD); chemical physics (PhD); environmental chemistry (MS, PhD); inorganic chemistry (MS, PhD); organic chemistry (MS, PhD); physical chemistry (MS, PhD); polymer chemistry (MS, PhD); theoretical chemistry (PhD). Part-time programs available. Terminal master's awarded for partial completion of doctoral program. *Degree requirements:* For master's and doctorate, thesis/dissertation. *Entrance requirements:* For master's and doctorate, GRE General Test, minimum GPA of 2.7. Additional exam requirements/recommendations for international students: Required—TOEFL. Electronic applications accepted.

The University of Texas at Austin, Graduate School, College of Natural Sciences, Department of Chemistry and Biochemistry, Austin, TX 78712-1111. Offers analytical chemistry (MA, PhD); biochemistry (MA, PhD); inorganic chemistry (MA, PhD); organic chemistry (MA, PhD); physical chemistry (MA, PhD). *Entrance requirements:* For master's and doctorate, GRE General Test.

University of Toledo, Graduate School, College of Arts and Sciences, Department of Chemistry, Toledo, OH 43606-3390. Offers analytical chemistry (MS, PhD); biological chemistry (MS, PhD); inorganic chemistry (MS, PhD); organic chemistry (MS, PhD); physical chemistry (MS, PhD). Part-time programs available. *Students:* 46 full-time (21 women), 9 part-time (4 women); includes 4 minority (3 African Americans, 1 Hispanic American), 31 international. Average age 27. 23 applicants, 87% accepted. In 2003, 3 master's, 5 doctorates awarded. *Degree requirements:* For master's and doctorate, thesis/dissertation. *Entrance requirements:* For master's and doctorate, GRE General Test, GRE Subject Test. Additional exam requirements/recommendations for international students: Required—TOEFL. *Application deadline:* For fall admission, 8/1 for domestic students. Applications are processed on a rolling basis. Application fee: $40. Electronic applications accepted. Tuition, area resident: Part-time $3,817 per semester. *Expenses:* Tuition, state resident: part-time $8,177 per semester. Required fees: $502 per semester. *Financial support:* In 2003–04, 4 research assistantships, 47 teaching assistantships were awarded. Fellowships, Federal Work-Study and institutionally sponsored loans also available. Support available to part-time students. Financial award application deadline: 4/1; financial award applicants required to submit FAFSA. *Faculty research:* Enzymology, materials chemistry, crystallography, theoretical chemistry. *Unit head:* Dr. Alan Pinkerton, Chair, 419-530-2109, Fax: 419-530-4033, E-mail: apinker@uoft02.utoledo.edu.

See in-depth description on page 179.

University of Utah, Graduate School, College of Science, Department of Chemistry, Salt Lake City, UT 84112-1107. Offers chemical physics (PhD); chemistry (M Phil, MA, MS, PhD); science teacher education (MS). Part-time programs available. Postbaccalaureate distance learning degree programs offered. *Faculty:* 28 full-time (4 women), 1 part-time/adjunct (0 women). *Students:* 132 full-time (53 women), 19 part-time (6 women); includes 11 minority (7 Asian Americans or Pacific Islanders, 4 Hispanic Americans), 60 international. Average age 28. 51 applicants, 84% accepted, 33 enrolled. In 2003, 8 master's, 19 doctorates awarded. *Degree requirements:* For doctorate, thesis/dissertation. *Entrance requirements:* For master's and doctorate, GRE General Test, minimum GPA of 3.0. Additional exam requirements/recommendations for international students: Required—TOEFL, TSE. *Application deadline:* For fall admission, 7/1 for domestic students; for spring admission, 11/1 priority date for domestic students. Applications are processed on a rolling basis. Application fee: $45 ($60 for international students). Electronic applications accepted. Tuition, nonresident: full-time $2,483. International tuition: $8,768 full-time. *Financial support:* In 2003–04, 149 students received support, including 75 research assistantships with tuition reimbursements available (averaging $5,000 per year), 75 teaching assistantships with tuition reimbursements available (averaging $5,000 per year); fellowships with tuition reimbursements available, scholarships/grants also available. Financial award application deadline: 7/1. *Faculty research:* Biological, theoretical, inorganic, organic, and physical-analytical chemistry. *Unit head:* Peter B. Armentrout, Chair, 801-581-7885, Fax: 801-581-8433, E-mail: armentrout@chemistry.utah.edu. *Application contact:* Jo Hoovey, Coordinator, 801-581-4393, Fax: 801-581-5408, E-mail: jhoovey@chem.utah.edu.

University of Utah, Graduate School, College of Science, Interdepartmental Program in Chemical Physics, Salt Lake City, UT 84112-1107. Offers PhD. *Students:* 1 full-time (0 women). In 2003, 1 degree awarded. Tuition, nonresident: full-time $2,483. International tuition: $8,768 full-time. *Unit head:* Peter J. Stang, Dean, 801-581-6958, Fax: 801-585-3169, E-mail: stang@chemistry.utah.edu. *Application contact:* Information Contact, 801-581-6958, E-mail: office@science.utah.edu.

Vanderbilt University, Graduate School, Department of Chemistry, Nashville, TN 37240-1001. Offers analytical chemistry (MAT, MS, PhD); inorganic chemistry (MAT, MS, PhD); organic chemistry (MAT, MS, PhD); physical chemistry (MAT, MS, PhD); theoretical chemistry (MAT, MS, PhD). *Degree requirements:* For master's, thesis or alternative; for doctorate, thesis/dissertation, area, qualifying, and final exams. *Entrance requirements:* For master's and doctorate, GRE General Test, GRE Subject Test (recommended). Additional exam requirements/recommendations for international students: Required—TOEFL. Electronic applications accepted. *Expenses:* Tuition: Part-time $1,155 per semester hour. Required fees: $1,538. *Faculty research:* Chemical synthesis; mechanistic, theoretical, bioorganic, analytical, and spectroscopic chemistry.

See in-depth description on page 185.

Wake Forest University, Graduate School, Department of Chemistry, Winston-Salem, NC 27109. Offers analytical chemistry (MS, PhD); inorganic chemistry (MS, PhD); organic chemistry (MS, PhD); physical chemistry (MS, PhD). Part-time programs available. *Faculty:* 15 full-time (2 women). *Students:* 32 full-time (15 women), 1 part-time; includes 2 minority (both African Americans), 13 international. Average age 28. 34 applicants, 38% accepted, 5 enrolled. In 2003, 4 master's, 2 doctorates awarded. *Degree requirements:* For master's, one foreign language, thesis, comprehensive exam, registration; for doctorate, 2 foreign languages, thesis/dissertation, comprehensive exam, registration. *Entrance requirements:* For master's and doctorate, GRE General Test. Additional exam requirements/recommendations for international students: Required—TOEFL (minimum score 213 computer-based). *Application deadline:* For fall admission, 1/15 for domestic students, 1/15 for international students. Application fee: $25. Electronic applications accepted. *Expenses:* Tuition: Full-time $26,500. *Financial support:* In 2003–04, 32 students received support, including 1 fellowship with full tuition reimbursement available (averaging $19,500 per year), 11 research assistantships with full tuition reimbursements available (averaging $17,500 per year), 17 teaching assistantships with full tuition reimbursements available (averaging $17,500 per year); scholarships/grants and tuition waivers (full and partial) also available. Support available to part-time students. Financial award application deadline: 1/15; financial award applicants required to submit FAFSA. *Unit head:* Dr. Dilip Kondepudi, Director, 336-758-5131, Fax: 336-758-4656, E-mail: dilip@wfu.edu.

Washington State University, Graduate School, College of Sciences, Department of Chemistry, Pullman, WA 99164. Offers analytical chemistry (MS, PhD); biological systems (MS, PhD); inorganic chemistry (MS, PhD); organic chemistry (MS, PhD); physical chemistry (MS, PhD). *Faculty:* 22 full-time (3 women). *Students:* 37 full-time (17 women), 1 part-time; includes 3 minority (2 Asian Americans or Pacific Islanders, 1 Hispanic American), 10 international. Average age 25. 48 applicants, 58% accepted, 12 enrolled. In 2003, 3 master's, 1 doctorate awarded. Terminal master's awarded for partial completion of doctoral program. *Median time to degree:* Master's–2.8 years full-time; doctorate–5 years full-time. *Degree requirements:* For master's, oral exam, teaching experience, thesis optional; for doctorate, thesis/dissertation, oral exam, written exam, comprehensive exam. *Entrance requirements:* For master's and doctorate, GRE General Test, minimum GPA of 3.0, 3 letters of recommendation. *Application deadline:* For fall admission, 3/1 for domestic students; for spring admission, 10/1 priority date for domestic students. Applications are processed on a rolling basis. Application fee: $35. *Expenses:* Tuition, state resident: full-time $6,278; part-time $314 per hour. Tuition, nonresident: full-time $15,514; part-time $765 per hour. Required fees: $444. Full-time tuition and fees vary according to campus/location, program and student level. Part-time tuition and fees vary according to course load. *Financial support:* In 2003–04, 13 research assistantships with full and partial tuition reimbursements (averaging $17,000 per year), 23 teaching assistantships with full and partial tuition reimbursements (averaging $17,000 per year) were awarded. Fellowships, career-related internships or fieldwork, Federal Work-Study, institutionally sponsored loans, scholarships/grants, health care benefits, unspecified assistantships, and summer support also available. Financial award application deadline: 4/1; financial award applicants required to submit FAFSA. *Faculty research:* Environmental chemistry, materials chemistry, radio chemistry, bio-organic, computational chemistry. Total annual research expenditures: $1.9 million. *Unit head:* Dr. Ralph Yount, Chair, 509-335-1516, Fax: 509-335-8867, E-mail: yount@wsu.edu. *Application contact:* Sue B. Clark, Chair, Admissions Committee, 509-335-8866, Fax: 509-335-8867, E-mail: carrie@wsu.edu.

Wesleyan University, Graduate Programs, Department of Chemistry, Program in Chemical Physics, Middletown, CT 06459-0260. Offers MA, PhD. *Faculty:* 4 full-time (0 women). Terminal master's awarded for partial completion of doctoral program. *Degree requirements:* For master's and doctorate, one foreign language, thesis/dissertation. *Entrance requirements:* For master's, GRE General Test, GRE Subject Test; for doctorate, GRE Subject Test, BA or BS in chemistry or physics. *Application deadline:* For fall admission, 3/1 for domestic students. Applications are processed on a rolling basis. Application fee: $0. *Expenses:* Tuition: Full-time $22,338. Required fees: $20. *Faculty research:* Spectroscopy, photochemistry, reactive collisions, surface physics, quantum theory. *Unit head:* Dr. Johan VareKamp, Chair, 860-685-2248.

See in-depth description on page 189.

West Virginia University, Eberly College of Arts and Sciences, Department of Chemistry, Morgantown, WV 26506. Offers analytical chemistry (MS, PhD); inorganic chemistry (MS, PhD); organic chemistry (MS, PhD); physical chemistry (MS, PhD); theoretical chemistry (MS, PhD). Part-time programs available. Postbaccalaureate distance learning degree programs offered (no on-campus study). *Faculty:* 14 full-time (1 woman), 5 part-time/adjunct (3 women). *Students:* 45 full-time (15 women), 3 part-time (2 women); includes 1 minority (Hispanic American), 26 international. Average age 28. 84 applicants, 58% accepted, 11 enrolled. In 2003, 5 master's, 3 doctorates awarded. Terminal master's awarded for partial completion of doctoral program. *Degree requirements:* For master's and doctorate, thesis/dissertation, registration. *Entrance requirements:* For master's, GRE General Test, GRE Subject Test (recommended), minimum GPA of 2.5; for doctorate, GRE General Test, GRE Subject Test (recommended), minimum GPA of 2.75. Additional exam requirements/recommendations for international students: Required—TOEFL. *Application deadline:* For fall admission, 3/1 for domestic students. Applications are processed on a rolling basis. Application fee: $50. Electronic applications accepted. *Expenses:* Tuition, state resident: full-time $4,332. Tuition, nonresident: full-time $12,442. *Financial support:* In 2003–04, fellowships (averaging $2,000 per year), research assistantships with full tuition reimbursements (averaging $13,000 per year), teaching assistantships with full tuition reimbursements (averaging $12,000 per year) were awarded. Tuition waivers (full and partial) also available. Financial award application deadline: 2/1; financial award applicants required to submit FAFSA. *Faculty research:* Analysis of proteins, drug interactions, solids and effluents by advanced separation methods; electro-chemistry, mass spectrometry and atomic spectrometry; development of new synthetic strategies for complex organic molecules; synthesis and structural characterization of metal complexes for polymerization catalysis; nonmagnetic resonance studies of amorphous solids. *Unit head:* Dr. Harry O. Finklea, Chair, 304-293-3435 Ext. 6408, Fax: 304-293-4904, E-mail: harry.finklea@mail.wvu.edu.

West Virginia University, Eberly College of Arts and Sciences, Department of Physics, Morgantown, WV 26506. Offers applied physics (MS, PhD); astrophysics (MS, PhD); chemical physics (MS, PhD); condensed matter physics (MS, PhD); elementary particle physics (MS, PhD); materials physics (MS, PhD); plasma physics (MS, PhD); solid state physics (MS, PhD); statistical physics (MS, PhD); theoretical physics (MS, PhD). *Faculty:* 17 full-time (3 women), 1 part-time/adjunct (0 women). *Students:* 44 full-time (10 women), 4 part-time (1 woman), 32 international. Average age 28. 60 applicants, 20% accepted. In 2003, 2 master's awarded, leading to continued full-time study 100%; 3 doctorates awarded, leading to university research/teaching 33%, business/industry 33%, government 33%. Terminal master's awarded for partial completion of doctoral program. *Median time to degree:* Master's–2 years full-time; doctorate–5 years full-time. *Degree requirements:* For master's, thesis or alternative, qualifying exam; for doctorate, thesis/dissertation, qualifying exam. *Entrance requirements:* For master's and doctorate, GRE General Test, GRE Subject Test, minimum GPA of 3.0. Additional exam requirements/recommendations for international students: Required—TOEFL. *Application deadline:* For fall admission, 2/15 for domestic students. Applications are processed on a rolling basis. Application fee: $50. *Expenses:* Tuition, state resident: full-time $4,332. Tuition, nonresident: full-time $12,442. *Financial support:* In 2003–04, 30 research assistantships with full and partial tuition reimbursements (averaging $18,000 per year), 10 teaching assistantships with full and partial tuition reimbursements (averaging $16,000 per year) were awarded. Fellowships, Federal Work-Study, institutionally sponsored loans, and tuition waivers (full and partial) also available. Financial award application deadline: 2/1; financial award applicants required to submit FAFSA. *Faculty research:* Experimental and theoretical condensed-matter, plasma, high-energy theory, nonlinear dynamics, space physics. Total annual research expenditures: $3.3 million. *Unit head:* Dr. Earl E. Scime, Chair, 304-293-3422 Ext. 1437, Fax: 304-293-5732, E-mail: escime@wvu.edu.

Yale University, Graduate School of Arts and Sciences, Department of Chemistry, New Haven, CT 06520. Offers biophysical chemistry (PhD); inorganic chemistry (PhD); organic chemistry (PhD); physical chemistry (PhD). *Degree requirements:* For doctorate, thesis/dissertation. *Entrance requirements:* For doctorate, GRE General Test, GRE Subject Test. Additional exam requirements/recommendations for international students: Required—TOEFL. *Expenses:* Tuition: Full-time $25,600; part-time $6,400 per term.

Theoretical Chemistry

Cornell University, Graduate School, Graduate Fields of Arts and Sciences, Field of Chemistry and Chemical Biology, Ithaca, NY 14853-0001. Offers analytical chemistry (PhD); bio-organic chemistry (PhD); biophysical chemistry (PhD); chemical biology (PhD); chemical physics (PhD); inorganic chemistry (PhD); materials chemistry (PhD); organic chemistry (PhD); organometallic chemistry (PhD); physical chemistry (PhD); polymer chemistry (PhD); theoretical chemistry (PhD). *Faculty:* 37 full-time. *Students:* 174 full-time (70 women); includes 22 minority (4 African Americans, 10 Asian Americans or Pacific Islanders, 8 Hispanic Americans), 57 international. 371 applicants, 35% accepted, 42 enrolled. In 2003, 22 doctorates awarded. *Degree requirements:* For doctorate, thesis/dissertation, comprehensive exam. *Entrance requirements:* For doctorate, GRE General Test, GRE Subject Test (chemistry), 3 letters of recommendation. Additional exam requirements/recommendations for international students: Required—TOEFL (minimum score 600 paper-based; 250 computer-based). *Application deadline:* For fall admission, 1/10 for domestic students. Application fee: $60. Electronic applications accepted. *Expenses:* Tuition: Full-time $28,630. One-time fee: $50 full-time. *Financial support:* In 2003–04, 162 students received support, including 28 fellowships with full tuition reimbursements available, 77 research assistantships with full tuition reimbursements available, 57 teaching assistantships with full tuition reimbursements available; institutionally sponsored loans, scholarships/grants, health care benefits, tuition waivers (full and partial), and unspecified assistantships also available. Financial award applicants required to submit FAFSA. *Faculty research:* Analytical, organic, inorganic, physical, materials, chemical biology. *Unit head:* Director of Graduate Studies, 607-255-4139, Fax: 607-255-4137. *Application contact:* Graduate Field Assistant, 607-255-4139, Fax: 607-255-4137, E-mail: chemgrad@cornell.edu.

See in-depth description on page 105.

Georgetown University, Graduate School of Arts and Sciences, Department of Chemistry, Washington, DC 20057. Offers analytical chemistry (MS, PhD); biochemistry (MS, PhD); chemical physics (MS, PhD); inorganic chemistry (MS, PhD); organic chemistry (MS, PhD); physical chemistry (MS, PhD); theoretical chemistry (MS, PhD). Terminal master's awarded for partial completion of doctoral program. *Degree requirements:* For master's, thesis (for some programs), qualifying exam; for doctorate, thesis/dissertation, comprehensive exam. *Entrance requirements:* For master's and doctorate, GRE General Test. Additional exam requirements/recommendations for international students: Required—TOEFL.

University of Calgary, Faculty of Graduate Studies, Faculty of Science, Department of Chemistry, Calgary, AB T2N 1N4, Canada. Offers analytical chemistry (M Sc, PhD); applied chemistry (M Sc, PhD); inorganic chemistry (M Sc, PhD); organic chemistry (M Sc, PhD); physical chemistry (M Sc, PhD); polymer chemistry (M Sc, PhD); theoretical chemistry (M Sc, PhD). *Faculty:* 29 full-time (6 women), 1 part-time/adjunct (0 women). *Students:* 74 full-time (29 women). Average age 25. 130 applicants, 20% accepted. In 2003, 12 master's, 6 doctorates awarded. *Degree requirements:* For master's, thesis; for doctorate, thesis/dissertation, candidacy exam. *Entrance requirements:* For master's, minimum GPA of 3.0; for doctorate, honors degree minimum GPA of 3.7, minimum GPA of 3.3. Additional exam requirements/recommendations for international students: Required—TOEFL (minimum score 580 paper-based; 237 computer-based). *Application deadline:* For fall admission, 12/1 for domestic students. Applications are processed on a rolling basis. Application fee: $60. Electronic applications accepted. Tuition, nonresident: full-time $4,765. Tuition and fees vary according to degree level, program and student level. *Financial support:* In 2003–04, research assistantships (averaging $11,000 per year), teaching assistantships (averaging $6,221 per year) were awarded. Fellowships, scholarships/grants also available. Financial award application deadline: 12/1. *Faculty research:* Chemical analysis, chemical dynamics, synthesis theory, polymer, applied chemistry. *Unit head:* Dr. Brian Keay, Head, 403-220-6252, E-mail: gradinfo@chem.ucalgary.ca.

The University of Tennessee, Graduate School, College of Arts and Sciences, Department of Chemistry, Knoxville, TN 37996. Offers analytical chemistry (MS, PhD); chemical physics (PhD); environmental chemistry (MS, PhD); inorganic chemistry (MS, PhD); organic chemistry (MS, PhD); physical chemistry (MS, PhD); polymer chemistry (MS, PhD); theoretical chemistry (PhD). Part-time programs available. Terminal master's awarded for partial completion of doctoral program. *Degree requirements:* For master's and doctorate, thesis/dissertation. *Entrance requirements:* For master's and doctorate, GRE General Test, minimum GPA of 2.7. Additional exam requirements/recommendations for international students: Required—TOEFL. Electronic applications accepted.

Vanderbilt University, Graduate School, Department of Chemistry, Nashville, TN 37240-1001. Offers analytical chemistry (MAT, MS, PhD); inorganic chemistry (MAT, MS, PhD); organic chemistry (MAT, MS, PhD); physical chemistry (MAT, MS, PhD); theoretical chemistry (MAT, MS, PhD). *Degree requirements:* For master's, thesis or alternative; for doctorate, thesis/dissertation, area, qualifying, and final exams. *Entrance requirements:* For master's and doctorate, GRE General Test, GRE Subject Test (recommended). Additional exam requirements/recommendations for international students: Required—TOEFL. Electronic applications accepted. *Expenses:* Tuition: Part-time $1,155 per semester hour. Required fees: $1,538. *Faculty research:* Chemical synthesis; mechanistic, theoretical, bioorganic, analytical, and spectroscopic chemistry.

See in-depth description on page 185.

Wesleyan University, Graduate Programs, Department of Chemistry, Middletown, CT 06459-0260. Offers biochemistry (MA, PhD); chemical physics (MA, PhD); inorganic chemistry (MA, PhD); organic chemistry (MA, PhD); physical chemistry (MA, PhD); theoretical chemistry (MA, PhD). *Faculty:* 13 full-time (2 women), 2 part-time/adjunct (1 woman). *Students:* 36 full-time (18 women); includes 2 minority (1 African American, 1 Asian American or Pacific Islander), 21 international. In 2003, 2 degrees awarded. Terminal master's awarded for partial completion of doctoral program. *Degree requirements:* For master's and doctorate, one foreign language, thesis/dissertation. *Entrance requirements:* For master's, GRE General Test, GRE Subject Test; for doctorate, GRE Subject Test. *Application deadline:* For fall admission, 3/1 for domestic students. Applications are processed on a rolling basis. Application fee: $0. *Expenses:* Tuition: Full-time $22,338. Required fees: $20. *Financial support:* Fellowships, research assistantships, teaching assistantships, institutionally sponsored loans available. *Unit head:* George Peterson, Chair, 860-685-2508. *Application contact:* Karen Karpa, Information Contact, 860-685-2573, Fax: 860-685-2211, E-mail: kkarpa@wesleyan.edu.

See in-depth description on page 189.

West Virginia University, Eberly College of Arts and Sciences, Department of Chemistry, Morgantown, WV 26506. Offers analytical chemistry (MS, PhD); inorganic chemistry (MS, PhD); organic chemistry (MS, PhD); physical chemistry (MS, PhD); theoretical chemistry (MS, PhD). Part-time programs available. Postbaccalaureate distance learning degree programs offered (no on-campus study). *Faculty:* 14 full-time (1 woman), 5 part-time/adjunct (3 women). *Students:* 45 full-time (15 women), 3 part-time (2 women); includes 1 minority (Hispanic American), 26 international. Average age 28. 84 applicants, 58% accepted, 11 enrolled. In 2003, 5 master's, 3 doctorates awarded. Terminal master's awarded for partial completion of doctoral program. *Degree requirements:* For master's and doctorate, thesis/dissertation, registration. *Entrance requirements:* For master's, GRE General Test, GRE Subject Test (recommended), minimum GPA of 2.5; for doctorate, GRE General Test, GRE Subject Test (recommended), minimum GPA of 2.75. Additional exam requirements/recommendations for international students: Required—TOEFL. *Application deadline:* For fall admission, 3/1 for domestic students. Applications are processed on a rolling basis. Application fee: $50. Electronic applications accepted. *Expenses:* Tuition, state resident: full-time $4,332. Tuition, nonresident: full-time $12,442. *Financial support:* In 2003–04, fellowships (averaging $2,000 per year), research assistantships with full tuition reimbursements (averaging $13,000 per year), teaching assistantships with full tuition reimbursements (averaging $12,000 per year) were awarded. Tuition waivers (full and partial) also available. Financial award application deadline: 2/1; financial award applicants required to submit FAFSA. *Faculty research:* Analysis of proteins, drug interactions, solids and effluents by advanced separation methods; electro-chemistry, mass spectrometry and atomic spectrometry; development of new synthetic strategies for complex organic molecules; synthesis and structural characterization of metal complexes for polymerization catalysis; nonmagnetic resonance studies of amorphous solids. *Unit head:* Dr. Harry O. Finklea, Chair, 304-293-3435 Ext. 6408, Fax: 304-293-4904, E-mail: harry.finklea@mail.wvu.edu.

Cross-Discipline Announcements

Iowa State University of Science and Technology, Graduate College, College of Agriculture and College of Liberal Arts and Sciences, Department of Biochemistry, Biophysics, and Molecular Biology, Ames, IA 50011.

Department offers graduate degree programs in biochemistry; biophysics; genetics; molecular, cellular, and developmental biology; plant physiology; immunobiology; and toxicology. The design of the molecular biology building enhances the opportunities for collaboration among faculty members in the life sciences. Students with degrees in chemistry are strongly encouraged to apply. See the Biochemistry section in Book 3 of this series for a detailed description of the program.

Massachusetts Institute of Technology, School of Engineering, Biological Engineering Division, Cambridge, MA 02139-4307.

Program provides opportunities for study and research at the interface of biology and engineering leading to specialization in bioengineering and applied biosciences. The areas include understanding how biological systems operate, especially when perturbed by genetic, chemical, or materials interventions or subjected to pathogens or toxins, and designing innovative biology-based technologies in diagnostics, therapeutics, materials, and devices for application to human health and diseases, as well as other societal problems and opportunities.

Oklahoma State University, Graduate College, Program in Photonics, Stillwater, OK 74078.

The photonics PhD at Oklahoma State University provides world-class research opportunities in a multidisciplinary program launched jointly by the Departments of Electrical Engineering, Physics, and Chemistry. An NSF IGERT grant supports qualified PhD photonics students with annual stipends of $27,500 as well as complete tuition waivers and cost of education and travel allowances. In addition to this multidisciplinary program, students may also earn a PhD in the traditional discipline of chemistry as they pursue research options in photonics.

University of Michigan, Horace H. Rackham School of Graduate Studies, College of Engineering, Department of Materials Science and Engineering, Ann Arbor, MI 48109.

Interdisciplinary curriculum leads to master's and PhD degrees in materials science and engineering for physics students interested in condensed-matter physics; metals; ceramics; polymers; composites; electronic, magnetic, and optical materials; and other engineering materials. Research assistantships and fellowships available on a competitive basis. See the department's In-Depth Description in the Engineering and Applied Sciences volume of this series.

University of the Pacific, School of Pharmacy and Health Sciences, Pharmaceutical and Chemical Sciences Graduate Program, Stockton, CA 95211-0197.

Pharmaceutical and Chemical Sciences is a joint program between Thomas J. Long School of Pharmacy and Health Sciences and the Department of Chemistry at the University of the Pacific. The program offers PhD, combined Pharm D and PhD, MS and nonthesis MS in the areas of bioanalytical and physical chemistry, drug discovery and chemical synthesis, drug targeting and delivery, cellular pharmacology and toxicology, and translational and clinical research. For additional information, contact Xiaoling Li, PhD, Director of Pharmaceutical and Chemical Sciences Graduate Program.

University of Wisconsin–Madison, Graduate School, Training Program in Biotechnology, Madison, WI 53706-1380.

The University of Wisconsin–Madison offers a predoctoral training program in biotechnology. Trainees receive PhDs in their major field (for example, chemistry) while receiving extensive cross-disciplinary training through the minor degree. Trainees participate in industrial internships and a weekly student seminar series with other program participants. These experiences reinforce the cross-disciplinary nature of the program. Students choose a major and a minor professor from a list of more than 130 faculty members in 40 different departments who do research related to biotechnology. See In-Depth Description in the Bioengineering, Biomedical Engineering, and Biotechnology section of the Engineering and Applied Sciences volume (Book 5) of this series.

BAYLOR UNIVERSITY

Department of Chemistry and Biochemistry

Programs of Study

The Department of Chemistry and Biochemistry offers a program of course work and research leading to the M.S. and Ph.D. degrees. Research interests of the faculty cover all major areas of chemistry, including analytical, inorganic, organic, physical, and biochemistry. A favorable student-faculty ratio makes possible almost daily contact between graduate student and research professor, leading to a productive exchange of ideas. Since the traditional boundaries between the divisions of chemistry are rapidly disappearing, the program stresses breadth in understanding all aspects of chemistry and related disciplines, and cooperation between research groups within the department and between departments is encouraged.

Research Facilities

The Department of Chemistry and Biochemistry has recently relocated to a new $105-million, 500,000 square foot, state-of-the-art building that provides air-conditioned classrooms, modern research laboratories, graduate student offices, and many auxiliary services. The Jesse H. Jones Library subscribes to all major chemical publications, representing more than 300 current subscriptions. Online, desk-top, computer-assisted literature searching is readily available. The presence of a full complement of instrumentation, including a high-field NMR, a new CCD X-ray diffractometer, and a high-resolution mass spectrmeter, enables each graduate research student to acquire hands-on experience with the most modern research equipment available. The Center for Drug Discovery and the Center for Analytical Spectroscopy are housed within the department, while the Center for Molecular Biosciences and the Institute for Biomedical Studies are located in the same building. These bring together students and faculty members with common research interests.

Financial Aid

Research and teaching assistantships are normally available. Teaching assistantships include a full-tuition scholarship up to $17,904 per year, laboratory fees for required courses, and a stipend of up to $18,000 per academic year (2004–05). Various loan plans are also available. Students of Research Professors are supported by research fellowships only. Research fellowships are under the direction of principal investigators of research projects, and final decisions concerning recipients are made by the faculty member. Loan information can be obtained from the Student Loan Officer (Financial Aid Office, Baylor University, One Bear Place #97028, 76798-7028).

Cost of Study

Tuition is $746 per semester hour in 2004–05. Student fees are $56 per semester hour for up to 12 hours, with a flat rate of $745 for 12 hours or more. Payment of student fees entitles the student to use University health-care services and recreational facilities.

Living and Housing Costs

On-campus housing is not provided for graduate students. However, a large number of apartments, many close to campus, offer a wide choice of living accommodations, with prices typically ranging from $425 to $500 per month and up.

Student Group

The total enrollment of Baylor University is about 14,000. There are approximately 45 graduate students in the Department of Chemistry and Biochemistry representing a number of states and several countries. The scientific scope of the department is further enhanced by the presence of postdoctoral research associates from a number of universities in the United States and around the world.

Location

Baylor University is located in Waco, a city of about 105,000 residents in the hill country of central Texas. Nearby Lake Waco and Lake Brazos provide year-round recreational opportunities. The city is only a few hours from such metropolitan centers as Dallas and Houston, the state capitol at Austin, and the historic city of San Antonio.

The University

Baylor University is a private institution affiliated with the Baptist General Convention of Texas. Established in 1845, it is the oldest university in continuous existence in Texas. The 350-acre Waco campus includes the College of Arts and Sciences, the Graduate School, Truett Seminary, and the Schools of Business, Education, Engineering and Computer Science, Law, and Music. The Baylor School of Nursing is located in Dallas. The Academy of Health Sciences is located in San Antonio.

Applying

There is a $40 application fee. Students requesting financial aid should complete their application at least ninety days before the first semester of study. Requirements include a bachelor's degree, a minimum GPA of 3.0 (B) in the major field, a minimum GPA of 2.7 in all undergraduate work, and GRE scores on the General Test and the Advanced Test (chemistry). Most international applicants must submit a score of at least 213 on the TOEFL examination. Students with good GRE scores, but not meeting the minimum GPA, can sometimes be admitted on probation.

Correspondence and Information

For additional information about the graduate program in chemistry and biochemistry, students should contact:

Dr. Carlos E. Manzanares
Director of Graduate Studies
Department of Chemistry and Biochemistry
Baylor University
One Bear Place #97348
Waco, Texas 76798-7348
Telephone: 254-710-4247
Fax: 254-710-2403
E-mail: carlos_manzanares@baylor.edu
World Wide Web: http://www.baylor.edu/Chemistry/

Baylor University

THE FACULTY AND THEIR RESEARCH

Darrin J. Bellert, Assistant Professor of Physical Chemistry; Ph.D., Florida, 1998. Molecular spectroscopy, quantum states of transient negative ions, stability and reactivity of molecular ions, laser photodissociation spectroscopy.

Kenneth W. Busch, Professor of Analytical Chemistry; Ph.D., Florida State, 1971. Chiral analysis, application of multivariate analysis to problems in chemical analysis, near-infrared spectroscopy, design and evaluation of spectroscopic instrumentation for chemical analysis, guest-host chemistry.

Marianna A. Busch, Professor of Analytical and Physical Inorganic Chemistry and Chair of the Department of Chemistry and Biochemistry; Ph.D., Florida State, 1972. Chiral analysis, application of multivariate analysis to problems in chemical analysis, near-infrared spectroscopy, guest-host chemistry, applications of analytical chemistry to problems of environmental interest.

C. Kevin Chambliss, Assistant Professor of Analytical Chemistry; Ph.D., Colorado State, 1998. Microscale separations and analysis, solvent extraction and ion exchange, analytical applications of redox-switchable metal complexts, environmental chemistry.

Charles M. Garner, Associate Professor of Organic Chemistry; Ph.D., Colorado, 1986. Synthesis of new ligands for transition metals, development of reagents/catalysts for asymmetric synthesis, organic gellation agents, physical organic studies, gas chromatography.

Stephen L. Gipson, Professor of Organometallic Chemistry; Ph.D., Caltech, 1986. Electrochemistry of organometallic compounds, electron transfer induced reactions, electrocatalysis.

Jesse W. Jones, Professor of Organic and Medicinal Chemistry; Ph.D., Arizona State, 1963. Synthesis of organic compounds of biological significance.

Robert Kane, Associate Professor of Organic Chemistry; Ph.D., Texas Tech, 1990. Synthesis and study (chemical and biological) of novel molecules, development of anti-fungal nucleoside prodrug constructs, SAR studies of apoptosis-inducing benzamides, synthesis and mechanistic study of photochemical tissue-bonding agents, PARP enzyme inhibition, DNA modification with metal-binding residues.

Kevin K. Klausmeyer, Assistant Professor of Inorganic Chemistry; Ph.D., Texas A&M, 1995. Synthetic organometallic and coordination chemistry, ligand design for metallodendrimer and supramolecular chemistry, metal carbonyl chemistry, X-ray crystallography, some aspects of catalysis and bioinorganic chemistry.

Carlos Manzanares, Professor of Physical Chemistry and Chemical Physics and Director of Graduate Studies; Ph.D., Indiana, 1977. Laser spectroscopy of ionic clusters in molecular beams, molecular-beam characterization by electron impact ionization and time-of-flight mass spectrometry, phase-shift cavity ring down overtone spectroscopy of molecules at low temperatures, laser photoacoustic vibrational overtone spectroscopy of molecules dissolved in cryogenic solvents, ab initio molecular orbital determination of equilibrium geometries and molecular vibrations, FT-IR spectra in cryogenic solutions.

John A. Olson, Associate Professor of Chemical Physics; Ph.D., Florida, 1982, Quantum Theory Project, Florida. Atom diatom and atom surface nonadiabatic reactions.

David E. Pennington, Professor of Inorganic Chemistry; Ph.D., Penn State, 1967. Coordination chemistry, kinetics and mechanism of inorganic reactions, synthesis and characterization of inorganic complexes.

Kevin G. Pinney, Associate Professor of Organic Chemistry; Ph.D., Illinois; 1990. Target-directed synthesis of molecular probes to evaluate protein structure and function; synthesis and biochemical evaluation of anti-mitotic, anti-tumor agents which interact with tubulin; affiinity labeling; radiochemical synthesis.

F. Gordon A. Stone, Robert A. Welch Distinguished Professor of Organometallic Chemistry; Ph.D., Cambridge, 1951. Synthesis, structure, and properties of organometallic compounds.

Mary Lynn Trawick, Associate Professor of Biochemistry; Ph.D., Case Western Reserve, 1974. Purification and properties of gamma-glutamylamine cyclotransferase and application of this enzyme to the analysis of crosslinked proteins, design and synthesis of active-site directed substrates and inhibitors of the enzymes: gamma-glutamylamine cyclotransferase and transglutaminase.

SELECTED REPRESENTATIVE PUBLICATIONS

Bellert, D., D. K. Winn, and W. H. Breckenridge. Spectroscopic Characterization of the first singlet ($^1B_1$) excited sate of $^7Li^{16}O^7Li$. *J. Chem. Phys.* 119:10169, 2003.

Bellert, D., D. K. Winn, and W. H. Breckenridge. Rovibrational energy levels of the LiOLi molecule from dispersed fluorescence and stimulated emission pumping studies. *J. Chem. Phys.* 117:3139, 2002.

Busch, K. W., I. M. Swamidoss, S. O. Fakayode, and **M. A. Busch.** Determination of the enantiomeric composition of guest molecules by chemometric analysis of the UV-visible spectra of cyclodextrin guest-host complexes. *J. Am. Chem. Soc.* 125:1690–1, 2003.

Busch, K. W., D. Rabbe, K. Humphrey, and **M. A. Busch.** Design and evaluation of a near-infrared dispersive spectrometer that uses a He-Ne laser for automatic internal wavelength calibration. *Appl. Spectrosc.* 56:346–9, 2002.

Levitskaia, T. G., P. V. Bonnesen, **C. K. Chambliss**, and B. A. Moyer. Synergistic pseudo-hydroxide ion extraction: Synergism and anion selectivity in sodium extraction using a crown ether and a series of weak lipophilic acids. *Anal. Chem.* 75:405–12, 2003.

Chambliss, C. K., et al. Selective separation of hydroxide from alkaline media by liquid-liquid extraction with weak hydroxy acids. *Environ. Sci. Technol.* 36:1861–7, 2002.

Ghatak, A., J. M. Dorsey, **C. M. Garner**, and **K. G. Pinney**. Synthesis of methoxy and hydroxy containing tetralones: Versatile intermediates for the preparation of biologically relevant molecules. *Tetrahedron Letters,* 44:4145–8, 2003.

Kim, J. and **S. L. Gipson.** Oxidatively induced one-electron reductive elimination of pentafluorophenyl from $[Mo(C_6F_5)(CO)_5]$. *Polyhedron,* 23:1371–4, 2004.

Gipson, S. L., L. A. Bryson, and **K. K. Klausmeyer.** Improved synthesis and X-ray crystal structure of pentafluorophenylcobalt tricarbonyl triphenylphosphine. *Inorg. Chim. Acta* 340:221–4, 2002.

Woods, R. J., J. Zhang, C. R. Green, and **R. R. Kane.** Protein crosslinking by 1,8naphthalimides: Influence of the 4-substituent. *ARKIVOC* XIII:109–18, 2003.

Hua, J., et al. **(K. G. Pinney, C. M. Garner,** and **R. R. Kane).** OXI4503 a novel vascular targeting agent: Effects on bloodflow and antitumor activity in comparison to combretastatin A-4 phosphate. *Anticancer Research,* 23:1433–40, 2003.

Adrian, R. A., M. M. Yaklin, and **K. K. Klausmeyer.** Synthesis and characterization of bi- and trinuclear molybdenum carbonyl compounds obtained by ligand exchange reactions of $[Et_4N]_3[Mo_3(CO)_9(OMe)_3$. *Organometallics,* 23(6):1352–8, 2004.

Klausmeyer, K. K., R. P. Feazell, and J. H. Reibenspies. Two, three, and four coordinate Ag(I) coordination polymers formed by the novel phosphinite, $PPh_2(3\text{-}OCH_2C_5H_4N)$. *Inorg. Chem.* 43:1130–6, 2004.

Manzanares, C. E., et al. Matrix isolation FT-IR, FT-raman spectroscopy, conformational ab initio calculations, and vibrational frequencies of meso and racemic-2,4-pentanediol. *J. Mol. Struct.* 689:183–90, 2004.

Salazar, M. C., et al. **(C. Manzanares).** A DFT test study on the CO...He dimer. *Int. J. Quantum Chem.* 95:177–83, 2003.

Guan, D., et al. **(J. A. Olson).** Charge transfer in gas-surface scattering: The three electronic state system. *Chem. Phys.* 233:35, 1998.

Guan, D., et al. **(J. A. Olson).** A theoretical treatment for the dynamics of near-resonant charge exchange in gas-surface scattering. *Chem. Phys.* 224:243, 1997.

Mullica, D. F., **D. E. Pennington,** J. E. Bradshaw, and E. L. Sappenfield. Crystal structure of a μ_3-oxo-hexakis(μ_2-Carboxylatopyridine*0,0*) triaquatrichromium (III) Perchlorate, $\{[Cr_3O(i\text{-}C_6H_5O_2N)_6(H_2O)_3](ClO_4)_7\cdot 3NaClO4\cdot 3H_2O)\}$. *Inorg. Chim. Acta Lett.* 191:3–6, 1992.

Dorsey, J. M., M. G. Miranda, N. V. Cozzi, and **K. G. Pinney.** Synthesis and biological evaluation of 2-(4-fluorophenoxy)-2-phenyl-ethyl piperazines as serotonin-selective reuptake inhibitors with a potentially improved adverse reaction profile. *Bioorganic Medicinal Chem.* 12(6):1483–91, 2004.

Monk, K. A., R. Siles, **K. G. Pinney**, and **C. M. Garner**. Synthesis of 4-methoxy-3,5-dinitrobenzaldehyde: A correction to supposed *tele* nucleophilic substitution. *Tetrahedron Letters,* 44:3759–61, 2003.

Kautz, J. A., T. D. McGrath, and **F. G. A. Stone.** Nitrosyl-cobalt monocarbollide complexes. *Polyhedron,* 22:109–18, 2003.

Du, S., J. A. Kautz, T. D. McGrath, and **F. G. A. Stone.** Synthesis and structure of the novel eleven-vertex rhenacarborane dianion $[1,1,1\text{-}(CO)_3\text{-}2\text{-}Ph\text{-}closo\text{-}1,2\text{-}ReCB_9H_9]^{2-}$ and its reactivity towards cationic transition-metal fragments. *Organometallics,* 22:2842–50, 2003.

Kautz, J. A., C. Chang, C. Qin, and **M. L. Trawick.** X-ray crystal structure of 2,5-dioxo-4-imidazolidineethanesulfonamide,$C_5H_9N_3O_4S$. *J. Chem. Crystall.* 33:277, 2003.

Trawick, M. L., et al. Evaluation of synthetic analogs of combretastatin A1 and A4 as inhibitors of tubulin assembly. *FASEB J.,* 17:A1314, 2003.

BOWLING GREEN STATE UNIVERSITY

Department of Chemistry
Center for Photochemical Sciences

Program of Study

The M.S. degree in chemistry program offers research opportunities in the traditional areas—biochemistry and organic, inorganic, analytical, and physical chemistry—as they relate to photochemistry. A typical curriculum consists of a combination of course work and research. Students have the option to complete the M.S. degree using either the thesis option or the nonthesis option. The thesis option is recommended for students who intend to pursue careers that involve research or plan to continue on to the Ph.D. program. This plan requires 30 semester hours of graduate credit. The student carries out original research under the supervision of a graduate faculty adviser chosen at the end of the first semester. Work on the research and completion of the written thesis comprise the major activities of the second year. The final oral examination covers both the contents of the thesis and general knowledge of chemistry. The nonthesis option is intended for students who do not intend to work in a research setting. This plan requires 33 semester hours of graduate course work. Students must pass a comprehensive written examination covering the areas of chemistry included in their degree program. Both thesis and nonthesis degree programs require approximately two years of full-time study to complete.

The Center of Photochemical Sciences and the Department of Chemistry have developed a uniquely focused Ph.D. in the photochemical sciences, designed for students with backgrounds in physics, biological sciences, or chemistry. It is an interdisciplinary program developed to prepare students to become research scholars in a chosen, selected area of study. The curriculum consists of a combination of core courses that provide students with a solid foundation in photochemistry and photophysics. Subsequent courses examine fundamentals and applications in areas of chemistry, biological sciences, physics, spectroscopy, and/or photopolymer science. Since the program is interdisciplinary, after completion of the core courses, the student in conjunction with various faculty advisers, plans the remaining course of study . Entering students consult with the graduate coordinator about course selection before passing to their thesis adviser's direction. Students should complete the Ph.D. degree in four to five years of full-time study.

Research Facilities

Chemical research at Bowling Green State University (BGSU) is fully supported by the latest equipment. Support facilities include a machine shop and an electronics shop. Electronics technicians and machinists not only maintain instruments but also design and build custom equipment. The department houses the Ohio Laboratory for Kinetic Spectrometry having major installations for UV-Vis, NIR, IR, IR transient absorption, and visible fluorescence measurement on the femtosecond to millisecond timescales. Other major instrumentation includes 300 and 400 MHz NMR spectrometers, the latter equipped for solution-phase and solid-state studies, a MALDI mass spectrometer, gas chromatography/mass spectrometers, spectrofluorimeters, circular dichroism, an automated peptide synthesizer, stereolithography systems, and a surface profilometer.

Financial Aid

All full-time graduate students in both the M.S. in chemistry and the Ph.D. in photochemical sciences receive tuition scholarships and fee waivers. Students work as teaching assistants in the Department of Chemistry. A limited number of research fellowships are available on a competitive basis at the doctoral level.

Cost of Study

All graduate students receive full tuition scholarships. All students are required to pay a $30 application fee. International students must have health insurance coverage at an annual rate of approximately $600.

Living and Housing Costs

Graduate students generally find reasonably priced housing in the pleasant neighborhoods that are adjacent to the BGSU campus. Financial support is more than adequate to meet the expenses of living in Bowling Green.

Student Group

The total number of graduate students in chemistry is currently about 70 (60 Ph.D. and 10 M.S.). A wide variety of academic, ethnic, and national backgrounds are represented among these students.

Student Outcomes

Graduates with an M.S. in chemistry have either pursued positions in industry, continued their education in a Ph.D. program, or pursued medical school. Graduates with a Ph.D. in photochemical sciences have accepted positions as industrial scientists with Kodak, DuPont, Hewlett-Packard, PPG Industries, Procter and Gamble, and Cycolor, Inc., or with other area high-tech companies. Several graduates have won coveted postdoctoral fellowships from agencies such as the Department of Energy, National Institutes of Health, and Lawrence Berkeley National Laboratory. Others have obtained positions as professors at undergraduate colleges.

Location

Bowling Green is a friendly, vital northwestern Ohio community, rich in history, with a diverse retail and industrial base. The city's early growth was greatly influenced by the prosperous oil boom era of the late 1800s, evident today through downtown Bowling Green's stately architecture. Bowling Green, which is located approximately 20 miles south of Toledo, Ohio, serves as the county seat for Wood County and offers a relaxed hometown atmosphere with interesting attractions.

The University

Beginning as Bowling Green Normal College in 1914, Bowling Green State University's 1,338-acre campus is a pleasant combination of varying architectural styles that reflect the University's growth since 1910. Primarily a residential university, Bowling Green has 18,000 students, with approximately 3,000 people engaged in graduate studies. International students and faculty members from fifty-three other countries add culture and intellectual diversity to the life of the University and the community. The University offers 165 undergraduate degree programs, three master's degrees in sixty-five fields, and doctoral programs in fifteen fields with more than sixty specializations. At the heart of the University's academic community are almost 700 full-time faculty members who are engaged in teaching, research, and public service activities.

Applying

Application forms and information can be requested by e-mailing the Graduate Program Coordinator at ncassid@bgnet.bgsu.edu. To expedite the application process, students are encouraged to apply online at http://www.bgsu.edu/departments/chem/application.html. While applications are accepted throughout the year, applicants are encouraged to apply as early as possible for admission in the fall semester. In addition to the completed application form, college transcripts, three letters of recommendation, and GRE scores should be sent to the Department of Chemistry. International students are also required to submit TOEFL scores.

Correspondence and Information

Graduate Program Coordinator
Department of Chemistry
Bowling Green State University
Bowling Green, Ohio 43403

E-mail: ncassid@bgnet.bgsu.edu
World Wide Web: http://www.bgsu.edu/departments/chem/
http://www.bgsu.edu/departments/photochem

Bowling Green State University

THE FACULTY AND THEIR RESEARCH

Pavel Anzenbacher, Ph.D., Czech Academy of Sciences, 1996. Application of principles and methods of organic photochemistry in design and synthesis of novel photo-activated drugs, development of new methods for light-directed combinatorial synthesis.

George Bullerjahn, Ph.D., Virginia, 1984. Regulation of nutrient-stress-inducible genes in cyanobacteria.

John R. Cable, Ph.D., Cornell, 1986. Supersonic-jet electronic spectroscopy of conformationally flexible molecules and clusters, effect of solvation and hydrogen bonding on structure.

Felix N. Castellano, Ph.D., Johns Hopkins, 1996. Light-harvesting and energy transfer processes in hybrid metal-organic polychromophores, chemical and biochemical luminescence sensors, supramolecular optical devices and materials, biophotonic applications of luminescent inorganic dyes, two-photon light-harvesting chromophores.

Thomas H. Kinstle, Ph.D., Illinois, 1963. Organic synthesis; natural products chemistry, particularly of antitumor compounds from strawberries and green tea; chemistry of small-ring compounds.

Neocles B. Leontis, Ph.D., Yale, 1986. Studies of RNA structure and function and RNA-protein interactions using genetic, biochemical, and physical methods, including high-field spectroscopy.

Douglas C. Neckers, Ph.D., Kansas, 1963. Photopolymers, photopolymerization science, analytical methodology in polymer science, organic photochemical processes, surface photoscience, photoinitiator design, mechanisms of photochemical processes, imaging, stereolithography.

Michael Y. Ogawa, Ph.D., Northwestern, 1987. Mechanisms of long-range electron transfer in biological systems, *de novo* protein design, photodynamic therapy.

Vladimir V. Popik, Ph.D., St. Petersburg State (Russia), 1990. Design and synthesis of photo-activated enediyne anticancer antibiotics, light-directed combinatorial synthesis, development of novel photoresists for deep-UV microlithography.

Michael A. J. Rodgers, Ph.D., Manchester (England), 1964. Excited-state dynamics of metallotetrapyrrole macrocycles, photodynamic and photothermal action in biological systems, energy transfer involving oxygen, electron transfer in proteins and peptides, the design assembly and use of high-technology instrumentation for transient spectroscopy.

William S. Scovell, Ph.D., Minnesota, 1969. Role of HMG-1 protein in the regulation of eukaryotic transcription, defining the interactions with general and regulatory factors, the regulation of the cell cycle, HMG-1 interaction with tumor suppressor gene products.

Deanne L. Snavely, Ph.D., Yale, 1983. Vibrational overtone spectroscopy, photoacoustic spectroscopy, unimolecular reaction kinetics, collisional energy transfer, photopolymerizations, vibrational spectroscopy of polymers.

Bruno Ullrich, Ph.D., Vienna, 1988. Optoelectronic devices (ODs) and thin film preparation by pulsed laser deposition (PLD).

BRIGHAM YOUNG UNIVERSITY

Department of Chemistry and Biochemistry

Programs of Study The Department of Chemistry and Biochemistry at Brigham Young University (BYU) offers courses of study leading to Ph.D. and M.S. degrees in the areas of analytical, inorganic, organic, and physical chemistry and biochemistry. The research experience is the major element of the graduate programs. Most students complete their Ph.D. research in four to five years. Research groups often include cross-disciplinary collaboration with faculty members and students in biology, engineering, and physics as well as with other areas within chemistry and biochemistry. Department faculty members are highly involved in each student's progress and foster a strong tradition of mentoring. All chemistry students must pass proficiency exams demonstrating competence at the undergraduate level in at least four subject areas by the end of their first year; biochemistry students must prove proficiency in biochemistry. An individualized schedule of graduate courses is established for each student based on his or her needs and interests. Most of this course work is taken during the first year, with the remainder completed in the second year. Depending on the area of study chosen by the student, either a form of comprehensive examination or several periodic cumulative examinations are required. Also, all students present annual reviews and a research proposal to their faculty advisory committee. An active seminar schedule provides exposure to recent developments worldwide. Successful defense of a dissertation or thesis completes a student's training.

Research Facilities Research activities occupy more than 50 percent of a 192,000-square-foot building. The University library, where the science collection includes more than 500,000 volumes and about 9,000 journal subscriptions, is located about 150 yards away. In addition to instruments and facilities used by individual research groups, special research facilities used by the entire department include NMR (200, 300, and 500 MHz), mass spectrometry (high-resolution, quadrupole, ion cyclotron resonance, ToF-SIMS, and MALDI), X-ray diffraction (powder and single crystal), spectrophotometry (IR, visible, UV, X-ray, and γ-ray), lasers (YAG, excimer, dye), environmental analysis (PIXE; PIGE; trace gases; X-ray fluorescence; XPS(ESCA); chromatography, including capillary column GC/MS, ion, and supercritical fluid; particle size analyzers; environmental chambers; ICP; and capillary electrophoresis), thermodynamics (calorimeters of all types, including temperature and pressure scanning, titration, flow, heat conduction, power compensation, combustion, and metabolic), and molecular biology (DNA synthesizer and sequencer, phosphorimager, tissue culture facility, recombinant DNA facility, and ultracentrifuges). All computing facilities are fully networked, including computational chemistry and laboratory workstations as well as office personal computers, with convenient connection to supercomputing facilities and the Internet. Fully staffed shops for glassblowing, machining, and electronics also serve research needs.

Financial Aid The department provides full financial assistance to all students through teaching and research assistantships, fellowships, and tuition scholarships. The twelve-month stipend for beginning students for the 2004–05 year is $18,500 (taxable). The amount of the stipend is adjusted annually.

Cost of Study Full tuition scholarships are provided to all graduate students making satisfactory progress. Books average about $200 per semester.

Living and Housing Costs The University Housing Office assists students in locating accommodations for on- and off-campus housing. Monthly rent and utilities range from $220 to $300 for a single student and from $450 to $650 for families. Other expenses range from $150 to $300 for single students and from $250 to $500 for families.

Student Group BYU has about 33,000 full-time students, with about 3,000 full-time graduate students. Students come from various academic and ethnic backgrounds and many geographic areas. The department averages 88 graduate students. Thirty-nine percent are women; currently, 67 percent are international students from eleven countries.

Student Outcomes BYU graduate degrees lead to a wide range of independent careers, with former students serving in academia, government, and industrial positions. About half of recent Ph.D.'s have continued their training in postdoctoral positions at leading research institutions, with the remainder finding employment directly with regional or national firms, in academia, or at government labs.

Location BYU's beautiful 560-acre campus, with all the cultural and sports programs of a major university, is located in Provo, Utah (population 110,500), a semiurban area at the foot of Utah Valley's Wasatch Mountains. Outdoor recreational areas for skiing (snow and water), hiking, and camping are nearby, including nine spectacular national parks, six beautiful national monuments, fourteen major ski resorts, and forty-five diverse state parks. The Utah Symphony, Ballet West, Pioneer Theater Company, and the Utah Jazz basketball team are located in Salt Lake City, 45 miles to the north.

The University Brigham Young University is one of the largest privately owned universities in the United States. Established in 1875 as Brigham Young Academy and sponsored by the Church of Jesus Christ of Latter-day Saints, BYU has a tradition of high standards in moral integrity and academic scholarship. Along with extensive undergraduate programs, BYU offers graduate degrees in a variety of disciplines through fifty-five graduate departments, including the Marriott School of Management and the J. Reuben Clark Law School. The Department of Chemistry and Biochemistry is one of the leading research departments at BYU.

Applying Applicants should apply online at http://www.byu.edu/gradstudies. They must submit transcripts, letters of recommendation, and a $50 application fee. International students must pass the Test of English as a Foreign Language (TOEFL) with a score of 550 or higher, although preference is given to students with scores of 600 or higher. The GRE General Test is required; GRE Subject Tests in chemistry or biochemistry are highly recommended. All application materials should be received by the Office of Graduate Studies no later than February 1 to be considered for admission the following fall. Applicants are not discriminated against on the basis of race, color, national origin, religion, gender, or handicap.

Correspondence and Information

Dr. David V. Dearden
Coordinator, Graduate Admissions
C101 BNSN (Benson Science Building)
Brigham Young University
Provo, Utah 84602
Fax: 801-422-0153
E-mail: chemgrad@byu.edu
World Wide Web: http://www.chem.byu.edu

Brigham Young University

THE FACULTY AND THEIR RESEARCH

Merritt B. Andrus, Associate Professor; Ph.D., Utah, 1991; postdoctoral study at Harvard. Organic chemistry: synthetic organic chemistry that includes asymmetric catalytic methods, natural product synthesis, and combinational libraries.
Matthew C. Asplund, Assistant Professor; Ph.D., Berkeley, 1998; postdoctoral study at Pennsylvania. Physical chemistry: time-resolved infrared spectroscopy, reaction dynamics, biophysical spectroscopy.
David M. Belnap, Assistant Professor; Ph.D. Purdue, 1995; postdoctoral study at National Institutes of Health. Biochemistry: structure, function, assembly, and disassembly of viruses and cellular macromolecules; three-dimensional electron microscopy (cryoelectron microscopy and 3-D image reconstruction).
Juliana Boerio-Goates, Professor; Ph.D., Michigan, 1979; postdoctoral study at Michigan. Physical chemistry: structural and thermodynamic studies of phase transitions in molecular and ionic crystals, thermodynamics of biological materials, energetics of nanomaterials.
Gregory F. Burton, Professor; Ph.D., Virginia Commonwealth, 1989; postdoctoral study at Virgina Commonwealth, 1989–91. Biochemistry: molecular mechanisms of HIV/AIDS pathogenesis focusing on contributions of the follicular dendritic cell reservoir of HIV.
Allen R. Buskirk, Assistant Professor; Ph.D., Harvard, 2004. Biochemistry: directed molecular evolution of proteins and nucleic acids, structure/function of small RNAs in bacteria, protein-protein interactions and allostery in signaling pathways.
Steven L. Castle, Assistant Professor; Ph.D., Scripps Research Institute, 2000. NIH Fellowship, 2000–02, California, Irvine. Organic chemistry: development of new synthetic methods, natural product synthesis.
David V. Dearden, Professor; Ph.D., Caltech, 1989. NRC Fellowship, 1989, U.S. National Institute of Standards and Technology. Analytical/physical chemistry: host-guest molecular recognition in ion-molecule reactions, Fourier transform ion cyclotron resonance mass spectrometry with electrospray ionization.
Delbert J. Eatough, Professor; Ph.D., Brigham Young, 1967. Physical chemistry: environmental atmospheric chemistry of SO_x, NO_x, and organics; environmental analytical techniques; tracers and source apportionment of atmospheric pollutants; indoor atmospheric chemistry.
Paul B. Farnsworth, Professor; Ph.D., Wisconsin, 1981; postdoctoral study at Indiana. Analytical chemistry: fundamental and applied measurements on inductively coupled plasmas, element-specific detectors for chromatography, elemental mass spectrometry.
Steven A. Fleming, Professor; Ph.D., Wisconsin, 1984. NIH Fellowship, 1984–86, Colorado State. Organic chemistry: photochemistry of aromatic compounds, rearrangements of small ring heterocycles, synthesis of natural products and novel compounds, determination of mechanisms of thermal rearrangements and photorearrangements.
Steven R. Goates, Professor; Ph.D., Michigan, 1981; postdoctoral study at Columbia. Analytical chemistry: analysis of complex samples by optical and especially laser-based methods, supersonic jet spectroscopy, spectroscopy of solid-state phenomena, investigation of chromatographic processes.
Steven W. Graves, Associate Professor; Ph.D., Yale, 1978; postdoctoral fellow, Tufts University School of Medicine, 1978–81; clinical chemistry fellow, Washington University School of Medicine, 1981–83. Biochemistry and bioanalytical/clinical chemistry and physiology: mechanisms of hypertensive complications of pregnancy, Na^+ pump regulation in disease, clinical assay development, proteomics of preterm birth and proteomics of preeclampsia.
Lee D. Hansen, Professor; Ph.D., Brigham Young, 1965. NIH Career Development Award, 1969–72. Physical chemistry: calorimetry, thermodynamics of batteries, kinetics of very slow processes, productivity and stress response of green plants and insects from calorespriometric measurements.
Roger G. Harrison, Associate Professor; Ph.D., Utah, 1993; postdoctoral study at Minnesota. Inorganic chemistry: host-guest molecular recognition, catalytic enzyme model complexes, metal-assembled cages, CdSe nanocrystals.
Douglas J. Henderson, Research Professor; Ph.D., Utah, 1961. Physical chemistry: statistical mechanics; intermolecular forces and their effects on the structure of liquids, interfaces, and colloids.
Steven R. Herron, Assistant Research Professor; Ph.D., California, Irvine, 2001. Staff Scientist, 2001–04, California State, Fullerton. Biochemistry: X-ray crystallography and protein structure-function.
John D. Lamb, Eliot A. Butler Professor; Ph.D., Brigham Young, 1978. Program Manager, Separations and Analysis, Office of Basic Energy Sciences, U.S. D.O.E., 1982–84. Inorganic chemistry: macrocyclic ligand chemistry, liquid membrane separations, ion chromatography, calorimetry.
Milton L. Lee, H. Tracy Hall Professor; Ph.D., Indiana, 1975; postdoctoral study at MIT. Analytical chemistry: microcolumn chromatography, capillary column technology, capillary column gas chromatography, capillary column supercritical fluid chromatography, capillary electrophoresis, analytical mass spectrometry, high-resolution chromatography of coal-derived materials.
Matthew R. Linford, Assistant Professor; Ph.D., Stanford, 1996; postdoctoral study at the Max Planck Institute for Surface and Colloid Science. Analytical chemistry: functionalizing and patterning silicon with alkyl monolayers, time-of-flight secondary ion mass spectrometry, chemometrics, ultrathin organic and polymer films.
Francis R. Nordmeyer, Professor; Ph.D., Stanford, 1967. Inorganic chemistry: electron transfer reactions, ion chromatography.
Noel L. Owen, Professor; Ph.D., Cambridge, 1963; postdoctoral study at Harvard. Physical chemistry: FTIR and NMR spectroscopy, structure and confirmation of novel and unstable compounds, bonding between wood and various reagents, molecular structure of wood polymers and other natural products, matrix isolation infrared spectroscopy, NMR studies of medicinally important compounds.
Matt A. Peterson, Associate Professor; Ph.D., Arizona, 1992. NIH Fellowship, 1993–94, Colorado State. Organic chemistry: synthetic methods, nucleosides and nucleotides, enediynes, enzyme inhibitors, development of antiviral and anticancer agents.
Morris J. Robins, J. Rex Goates Professor; Ph.D., Arizona State, 1965. Cancer Research Fellowship, 1965–66, Roswell Park Memorial Institute. Organic chemistry: chemistry of nucleic acid components, nucleoside analogues, and related biomolecules; design of mechanism-based enzyme inhibitors; development of anticancer and antiviral agents.
Paul B. Savage, Associate Professor; Ph.D., Wisconsin, 1993. NIH Fellowship, 1994–95, Ohio State. Organic chemistry: development of new receptors for small molecules, elucidation of the roles of noncovalent interactions in intermolecular association.
Eric T. Sevy, Assistant Professor; Ph.D., Columbia, 1999; postdoctoral study at MIT. Physical chemistry: chemical and molecular dynamics of collisional relaxation, energy transfer processes, and atmospheric and combustion chemistry; high-resolution transient spectroscopy; photolithography.
Randall B. Shirts, Associate Professor; Ph.D., Harvard, 1979; postdoctoral study at Joint Institute for Laboratory Astrophysics and University of Colorado. Physical chemistry: theoretical chemistry, statistical mechanics of nanoscale systems, nonlinear dynamics, semiclassical quantization, laser-molecule interaction, quantum-classical correspondence.
Daniel L. Simmons, Professor; Ph.D., Wisconsin, 1986. NIH and Leukemia Society Fellowships, 1986–89, Harvard. Biochemistry: molecular mechanisms of neoplastic transformation by Rous sarcoma virus, messenger RNA splicing and translation mechanisms, prostaglandins and signal transduction.
Craig D. Thulin, Assistant Professor; Ph.D., Washington (Seattle), 1995; postdoctoral study at Vollum Institute for Advanced Biomedical Research and at Brigham Young. Biochemistry: proteomics and protein chemistry of degenerative diseases and signal transduction pathways.
Heidi R. Vollmer-Snarr, Assistant Professor; D.Phil., Oxford, 2000; NIH Fellowships, 2000–02, Sloan-Ketttering Cancer Center and Columbia. Organic chemistry: synthetic organic, bio-organic and natural products chemistry, applicable to cancer and macular degeneration.
Gerald D. Watt, Professor; Ph.D., Brigham Young, 1968. NIH Fellowship, 1968, Yale. Biochemistry: nitrogenase, ferritins, metalloproteins.
Barry M. Willardson, Associate Professor; Ph.D., Purdue, 1990; postdoctoral study at Los Alamos National Laboratory. Biochemistry: regulation of G-protein-mediated signal transduction by phosducin-like proteins.
Brian F. Woodfield, Associate Professor; Ph.D., Berkeley, 1994; postdoctoral study at Naval Research Laboratory, Material Physics Branch, Washington, D.C. Physical chemistry: solid-state physics and thermodynamic properties of materials at low temperatures; systems of interest include nanomaterials, novel magnetic systems, heavy metals, and other technologically important materials.
Adam T. Woolley, Assistant Professor; Ph.D., Berkeley, 1997; Runyon-Winchell Cancer Research Fund Fellowship, 1998–2000, Harvard. Analytical chemistry: scanning probe microscopy of biomolecules with carbon nanotube tips, self-assembly and nanofabrication from biomolecular templates, microfabrication of miniaturized biochemical analysis systems.
Earl M. Woolley, Professor; Ph.D., Brigham Young, 1969. NRC Canada Fellowship, 1969–70, Lethbridge. Physical chemistry: thermodynamics of reactions in mixed aqueous-organic solvents, intermolecular hydrogen bonding reactions, electrolyte solutions, and of ionic and nonionic reactions in solution including surfactants; calorimetric methods.
S. Scott Zimmerman, Professor; Ph.D., Florida State, 1973. NIH Fellowship, 1973–77, Cornell. Biochemistry: molecular modeling and computational chemistry of biologically important molecules.

SELECTED PUBLICATIONS

Ma, Y., C. Song, J. We, and **M. B. Andrus.** Asymmetric, arylboronic acid addition to enones using novel dicyclophane imidazolium carbene-rhodium catalysts. *Angew. Chem. Int. Ed.* 42:5871–4, 2003.

Andrus, M. B., et al. Total synthesis of (+)-geldanamycin and (-)-ortho-quino-geldanamycin, asymmetric glycolate aldol reactions and biological evaluation. *J. Org. Chem.* 68:8162–9, 2003.

Andrus, M. B., J. Liu, E. L. Meredith, and E. Nartey. Synthesis of resveratrol using a direct decarbonylative heck approach from resorcylic acid. *Tetrahedron Lett.* 44:4819–22, 2003.

Pan, T., et al. **(M. C. Asplund).** Fabrication of calcium fluoride capillary electrophoresis microdevices for on-chip infrared detection. *J. Chromatogr. A* 1027(1–2):231–5, 2004.

Husseini, G. A., et al. **(M. C. Asplund, E. T. Sevy,** and **M. R. Linford).** Photochemical lithography: Creation of patterned, acid chloride functionalized surfaces using UV light and gas-phase oxalyl chloride. *Langmuir* 19(11):4856–8, 2003.

Lua, Y.-Y., et al. **(M. C. Asplund, S. A. Fleming,** and **M. R. Linford).** Amine-reactive monolayers on scribe silicon with controlled levels of functionality: The reaction of scribed silicon with mono- and diepoxides. *Angew. Chem. Int. Ed.* 42:4046–9, 2003.

Asplund, M. C., M. T. Zanni, and R. M. Hochstrasser. Two-dimensional infrared spectroscopy of peptides by phase-controlled femtosecond vibrational photon echoes. *Proc. Natl. Acad. Sci. U.S.A.* 97:8219–24, 2000.

Belnap, D. M., et al. Diversity of core antigen epitopes of hepatitis B virus. *Proc. Natl. Acad. Sci. U.S.A.* 100:10884–9, 2003.

Grünewald, K., et al. **(D. M. Belnap).** Three-dimensional structure of herpes simplex virus from cryo-electron tomography. *Science* 302:1396–8, 2003.

Belnap, D. M., et al. Three-dimensional structure of poliovirus receptor bound to poliovirus. *Proc. Natl. Acad. Sci. U.S.A.* 97:73–8, 2000.

Boerio-Goates, J., R. Stevens, B. Lang, and **B. F. Woodfield.** Heat capacity calorimetry: Detection of low frequency modes in solids and an application to negative thermal expansion materials. *J. Therm. Anal. Calorim.* 69:773–83, 2002.

Boerio-Goates, J., et al. Thermochemistry of adenosine. *J. Chem. Thermodyn.* 33:929–47, 2001.

Burton, G. F., et al. Follicular dendritic cell (FDC) contributions to HIV pathogenesis. *Semin. Immunol.* 14:275–84, 2002.

Estes, J. D., et al. **(G. F. Burton).** Follicular dendritic cell-mediated up-regulation of CXCR4 expression on CD4+T cells and HIV pathogenesis. *J. Immunol.* 169:2313–22, 2002.

Smith, B. A., et al. **(G. F. Burton).** Persistence of infectious human immunodeficiency virus on follicular dendritic cells. *J. Immunol.* 166:690–6, 2001.

Buskirk, A. R., P. D. Kehayova, A. Landrigan, and D. R. Liu. In vivo evolution of an RNA-based transcriptional activator. *Chem. Biol.* 10:533, 2003.

Srikanth, G. S. C., and **S. L. Castle.** Synthesis of β-substituted α-amino acids via Lewis acid promoted radical conjugate additions to α,β-unsaturated α-nitro esters and amides. *Org. Lett.* 6:449–52, 2004.

Castle, S. L., and G. S. C. Srikanth. Catalytic asymmetric synthesis of the central tryptophan residue of celogentin C. *Org. Lett.* 5:3611–4, 2003.

Boger, D. L., et al. **(S. L. Castle).** First and second generation total synthesis of the teicoplanin aglycon. *J. Am. Chem. Soc.* 123:1862–71, 2001.

Zhang, H., et al. **(D. V. Dearden).** Cucurbit[6]uril pseudorotaxanes: Distinctive gas phase dissociation and reactivity. *J. Am. Chem. Soc.* 125:9284–5, 2003.

Anderson, J. D., E. S. Paulsen, and **D. V. Dearden.** Alkali metal binding energies of dibenzo-18-crown-6: Experimental and computational results. *Int. J. Mass Spectrom.* 227:63–76, 2003.

Zhou, L., et al. **(D. V. Dearden** and **M. L. Lee).** Incorporation of a venturi device in electrospray ionization. *Anal. Chem.* 75:5978, 2003.

Liang, Y., J. S. Bradshaw, and **D. V. Dearden.** The thermodynamic basis for enantiodiscrimination: Gas phase measurement of the enthalpy and entropy of chiral amine recognition by dimethyldiketopyridino-18-crown-6. *J. Phys. Chem. A* 106:9665–71, 2002.

Pope, C. A., et al. **(D. J. Eatough).** Ambient particulate air pollution, heart rate variability, and blood markers of inflammation in a panel of elderly subjects. *Environ. Health Perspect.* 112(3):339–45, 2004.

Eatough, D. J., et al. Semi-volatile particulate organic material in southern Africa during SAFARI-2000. *J. Geophys. Res.* 108(D13): 8479–786, 2003.

Long, R. W., et al. **(D. J. Eatough).** The measurement of PM2.5, including semi-volatile components, in the EMPACT program: Results from the Salt Lake City study. *Atmos. Environ.* 37:4407–17, 2003.

Macedone, J. H., A. A. Mills, and **P. B. Farnsworth.** Optical measurements of ion trajectories through the vacuum interface of an inductively coupled plasma mass spectrometer. *Appl. Spectrosc.* 58:463–7, 2004.

Macedone, J. H., D. J. Gammon, and **P. B. Farnsworth.** Factors affecting analyte transport through the sampling orifice of an inductively coupled plasma mass spectrometer. *Spectrochim. Acta* 56B:1687–95, 2001.

Patterson, J. E., B. S. Duersch, and **P. B. Farnsworth.** Optically determined velocity distributions of metastable argon in the second stage of an inductively coupled plasma mass spectrometer. *Spectrochim. Acta* 54B:537–44, 1999.

Fleming, S. A. Alkene + alkene photocycloaddition. In *Synthetic Organic Photochemistry,* chapter 7. 2004.

Carroll, S., and **S. A. Fleming** et al. Asymmetric dihydroxylation of allenes. *Tetrahedron Lett.* 45:3341–3, 2004.

Fleming, S. A., S. C. Ward, C. Mao, and E. E. Parent. Phtocyclization. *Spectrum* 15(3):8–14, 2002.

Goates, S. R., D. A. Schofield, and C. D. Bain. A study of nonionic surfactants at the air-water interface by sum-frequency spectroscopy and ellipsometry. *Langmuir* 15:1400–9, 1999.

Ji, Q., et al. **(S. R. Goates).** New optical design for laser flash photolysis studies in supercritical fluids. *Rev. Sci. Instrum.* 66:222–6, 1995.

Esplin, M. S., M. B. Fausett, D. S. Faux, and **S. W. Graves.** Changes in the isoforms of the sodium pump in the placenta and myometrium of women in labor. *Am. J. Obstet. Gynecol.,* in press.

Carroll, J. S., E. W. Seely, Q.-F. Tao, and **S. W. Graves.** Digitalis-like factor response to the hyperinsulinemia accompanying a euglycemic hyperinsulinemic clamp or oral glucose tolerance test. *Life Sci.* 69:829–37, 2001.

Hansen, L. D. Calorimetric measurement of the kinetics of slow reactions. *Ind. Eng. Chem. Res.* 39(10):3541–9, 2002.

Hansen, L. D., et al. Kinetics of plant growth and metabolism. *Thermochim. Acta* 388:415–25, 2002.

Macfarlane, C., M. A. Adams, and **L. D. Hansen.** Application of an enthalpy balance model of the relation between growth and respiration to temperature acclimatin of *Eucalyptus globulus* seedlings. *Royal Soc.* 269:1499–507, 2002.

Harrison, R. G., et al. Cation control of pore and channel size in cage-based metal-organic porous materials. *Inorg. Chem.* 41:838–43, 2002.

Fox, O. D., et al. **(R. G. Harrison).** Metal-assembled cobalt(II) resorc[4]arene-based cage molecules that reversibly capture organic molecules from water and act as NMR shift reagents. *Inorg. Chem.* 39:783–90, 2000.

Kristof, T., D. Boda, and **D. Henderson.** Phase separation in mixtures of yukawa and charged yukawa particles from Gibbs ensemble Monte Carlo simulations and the mean spherical approximation. *J. Chem. Phys.* 120:2846–50, 2004.

Henderson, D., D. T. Wasan, and A. D. Trokhymchuk. Interaction energy and force between colloidal spheres in a multicomponent solution. *J. Chem. Phys.* 119:11989–97, 2003.

Boda, D., and **D. Henderson.** Computer simulation of the selectivity of a model calcium channel. *J. Phys.: Condens. Matter* 14:9485–8, 2002.

Reinheimer, E. W., et al. **(S. R. Herron).** Crystal structures of diphosphinated group 6 Fischer alkoxy carbenes. *J. Chem. Crystallogr.* 33:503–14, 2003.

Herron, S. R., et al. Characterization and implications of Ca^{2+} binding to pectate lyase C. *J. Biol. Chem.* 278:12271–7, 2003.

Herron, S. R., et al. Structure and function of pectic enzymes: Virulence factors of plant pathogens. *Proc. Natl. Acad. Sci. U.S.A.* 97:8762–9, 2000.

Richens, D. A., et al. **(J. D. Lamb).** Use of mobile phase 18-crown-6 to improve peak resolution between mono- and divalent metal and amine cations in ion chromatography. *J. Chromatogr. A* 1016:155–64, 2003.

Niederhauser, T. L., D. H. Scoville, and **J. D. Lamb.** Surface area determination of a polystyrene-divinylbenzene chromatographic packing material via method based on amphiphile adsorption. *J. Chromatogr. A* 982:49–54, 2002.

Levitskaia, T. G., **J. D. Lamb,** K. L. Fox, and B. A. Moyer. Selective carrier-mediated cesium transport through polymer inclusion membranes by calix[4]arene-crown-6 carriers from complex aqueous mixtures. *Radiochim. Acta.* 90:43–52, 2002.

Xiang, Y., et al. **(M. L. Lee).** Elevated-temperature ultrahigh-pressure liquid chromatography using very small polybutadiene-coated nonporous zirconia particles. *J. Chromatogr. A* 983:83, 2003.

Wang, Q., et al. **(M. L. Lee).** Voltage-controlled separation of proteins by electromobility focusing in a dialysis hollow fiver. *J. Chromatogr. A* 985:455, 2003.

Brigham Young University

Selected Publications (continued)

Wacaser, B. A., et al. **(M. R. Linford).** Chemomechanical surface patterning and functionalization of silicon surfaces using an atomic force microscope. *Appl. Phys. Lett.* 82(5):808–10, 2003.

Niederhauser, T. L., et al. **(M. R. Linford).** Arrays of chemomechanically patterned patches of homogeneous and mixed monolayers of 1-alkenes and alcohols on single silicon surfaces. *Angew. Chem. Int.* 41(13):2353–6, 2002.

Johnson, J. L., et al. **(F. R. Nordmeyer).** Mechanistic interpretation of the dilution effect for *Azotobacter vinelandii* and *Clostridium pasteurianum* nitrogenase catalysis. *Biochim. Biophys. Acta* 1543(1):36–46, 2000.

Johnson, J. L., et al. **(F. R. Nordmeyer).** Analysis of steady state Fe and MoFe protein interactions during nitrogenase catalysis. *Biochim. Biophys. Acta* 1543(1):24–35, 2000.

Evans, P. D., **N. L. Owen,** S. Schmid, and R. D. Webster. Weathering and photostability of benzoylated wood. *Polym. Degrad. Stab.* 76:291–303, 2002.

Moore, A. K., and **N. L. Owen.** Infrared spectroscopic studies of solid wood. *Appl. Spectrosc. Rev.* 36:65–86, 2001.

Gromova, A. S., et al. **(N. L. Owen).** Thalicosides A1–A3, minor cycloartane bisdesmosides from *Thalictrum minus*. *J. Nat. Prod.* 63:911–4, 2000.

Zhao, Z., et al. **(M. A. Peterson).** Bergman cycloaromatization of imidazole-fused enediynes: The remarkable effect of *N*-aryl substitution. *Tetrahedron Lett.* 45:3621–4, 2004.

Peterson, M. A., A. Bowman, and S. Morgan. Efficient preparation of N-benzyl secondary amines via benzylamine-borane mediated reductive amination. *Synthetic Commun.* 32:443–8, 2002.

Kumarasinghe, E. S., **M. A. Peterson,** and **M. J. Robins.** Synthesis of 5,6-bis(alkyny-1-yl)pyrimidines and related nucleosides. *Tetrahedron Lett.* 41:8741–5, 2000.

Janeba, Z., P. Francom, and **M. J. Robins.** Efficient syntheses of 2-chloro-2'-deoxyadenosine (cladribine) from 2'-deoxyguanosine. *J. Org. Chem.* 68:989–92, 2003.

Nowak, I., and **M. J. Robins.** Protection of the amino group of adenosine and guanosine derivatives by elaboration into a 2,5-dimethylpyrrole moiety. *Org. Lett.* 5:3345–8, 2003.

Robins, M. J. Ribonucleotide reductases: Radical chemistry and inhibition at the active site. *Nucleosides Nucleotides Nucl. Acids* 22:519–34, 2003.

Zhou, D., et al. **(P. B. Savage).** Editing of Cd-1-bound lipid antigens by endosomal lipid transfer proteins. *Science* 303:523–7, 2004.

Ning, Y., R. L. Marshall, S. Matheson, and **P. B. Savage.** Synthesis of lipid A derivatives and their interactions with polymyxin B and polymyxin B nonapeptide. *J. Am. Chem. Soc.* 126:2426–35, 2003.

Ding, B., et al. **(P. B. Savage).** Correlation of the antibacterial activities of cationic peptide antibiotics and cationic steroid antibiotics. *J. Med. Chem.* 45:663–9, 2002.

Sevy, E. T., et al. Competition between photochemistry and energy transfer in ultraviolet-excited diazabenzenes: I. Photofragmentation studies of pyrazine at 248 nm and 266 nm. *J. Chem. Phys.* 112:5829–43, 2000.

Sevy, E. T., C. A. Michaels, H. C. Tapalian, and G. W. Flynn. Competition between photochemistry and energy transfer in ultraviolet-excited diazabenzenes: II. Identifying the dominant energy donor for "supercollisions." *J. Chem. Phys.* 112:5844–51, 2000.

Sevy, E. T., S. M. Rubin, Z. Lin, and G. W. Flynn. Translational and rotational excitation of the CO_2 (00^00) vibrationless state in the collisional quenching of highly vibrationally excited 2-methylpyrazine: Kinetics and dynamics of large energy transfers. *J. Chem. Phys.* 113:4912–32, 2000.

Shirts, R. B., and M. R. Shirts. Deviations from the Boltzmann distribution in small microcanonical quantum systems: Two approximate one-particle energy distributions. *J. Chem. Phys.* 117:5564–75, 2002.

Sohlberg, K., and **R. B. Shirts.** The symmetry of approximate Hamiltonians generated in Birkhoff-Gustavson normal form. *Phys. Rev. A* 54:416–22, 1996.

Sohlberg, K., and **R. B. Shirts.** Semiclassical quantization of nonintegrable system: Pushing the Fourier method into the chaotic regime. *J. Chem. Phys.* 101:7763–78, 1994.

Ballif, B. A., et al. **(D. L. Simmons).** Interaction of cyclooxygenases with an apoptosis- and autoimmunity-associated protein. *Proc. Natl. Acad. Sci. U.S.A.* 93:5544–9, 1996.

Lu, X., et al. **(D. L. Simmons).** Nonsteroidal anti-inflammatory drugs cause apoptosis and induce cyclooxygenases in chicken embryo fibroblasts. *Proc. Natl. Acad. Sci. U.S.A.* 92:7961–5, 1995.

Xie, W., et al. **(D. L. Simmons).** Expression of a mitogen-responsive gene encoding prostaglandin synthase is regulated by mRNA splicing. *Proc. Natl. Acad. Sci. U.S.A.* 88:2692–6, 1991.

McLaughlin, J. N., et al. **(C. D. Thulin).** Regulation of cytosolic chaperonin-mediated protein folding by phosducin-like protein. *Proc. Natl. Acad. Sci. U.S.A.* 99:7962–7, 2002.

McLaughlin, J. N., et al. **(C. D. Thulin).** Regulation of angiotensin II–induced G protein signaling by phosducin-like protein. *J. Biol. Chem.* 277:34885–95, 2002.

Thulin, C. D., et al. **(B. M. Willardson).** Modulation of the G-protein regulator phosducin by calcium-calmodulin dependent protein kinase II phosphorylation and 14-3-3 protein binding. *J. Biol. Chem.* 276:23805–15, 2001.

Jockusch, S., et al. **(H. R. Vollmer-Snarr).** Photochemistry of A1E, a retinoid with a conjugated pyridinium moiety: Competition between pericyclic photooxygenation and pericyclization. *J. Am. Chem. Soc.* 126:4646–52, 2004.

Sparrow, J. R., and **H. R. Vollmer-Snarr** et al. A2E-epoxides damage DNA in retinal pigment epithelial cells. Vitamins E and other antioxidants suppress A2E-epoxide formation. *J. Biol. Chem.* 278:18207–13, 2003.

Ben-Shabat, S., et al. **(H. R. Vollmer).** Biosynthetic studies of A2E, a major fluorophore of RPE lipofuscin. *J. Biol. Chem.* 277:7183–90, 2002.

Lindsay, S., et al. **(G. D. Watt).** Kinetic studies of iron deposition in horse spleen ferritin using O2 as oxidant. *Biochem. Biophys. Acta* 1621:57–66, 2003.

Lindsay, S., D. Brosnahan, and **G. D. Watt.** Hydrogen peroxide formation during iron deposition in horse spleen ferritin using O2 as an oxidant. *Biochemistry* 40:3340–7, 2001.

Nyborg, A. C., J. L. Johnson, A. Gunn, and **G. D. Watt.** Evidence for a two-electron transfer using the all-ferrous Fe protein during nitrogenase catalysis. *J. Biol. Chem.* 275:39307–12, 2000.

Lukov, G. L., et al. **(B. M. Willardson).** Role of the isoprenyl pocket of the G protein $\beta\gamma$ subunit complex in the binding of phosducin and phosducin-like protein. *Biochemistry* 43:5651–60, 2004.

McLaughlin, J. N., et al. **(B. M. Willardson).** Regulatory interaction of phosducin-like protein with the cytosolic chaperonin complex. *Proc. Natl. Acad. Sci. U.S.A.* 99:7962–7, 2002.

Crawford, M. K., et al. **(B. F. Woodfield** and **J. Boerio-Goates).** Structure and properties of the integer-spin frustrated antiferromagnet GeNi2O4. *Phys. Rev. B* 68(22):220408/1–4, 2003.

Piccione, P. M., **B. F. Woodfield,** and **J. Boerio-Goates** et al. Entropy of pure molecular sieves. *J. Phys. Chem. B* 105:6025–30, 2001.

Woodfield, B. F., et al. **(J. Boerio-Goates).** Critical phenomena at the antiferromagnetic transition in MnO. *Phys. Rev. B* 60:7335, 1999.

Woodfield, B. F., et al. Superconducting-normal phase transition in $(Ba_{1-x}K_x)BiO_3$, x=0.40, 0.47. *Phys. Rev. Lett.* 83:4622–5, 1999.

Becerril, H. A., R. M. Stoltenberg, C. F. Monson, and **A. T. Woolley.** Ionic surface masking for low background in single- and double-stranded DNA-templated silver and copper nanorods. *J. Mater. Chem.* 14:611–6, 2004.

Kelly, R. T., and **A. T. Woolley.** Thermal bonding of polymeric capillary electrophoresis microdevices in water. *Anal. Chem.* 75:1941–5, 2003.

Xin, H., and **A. T. Woolley.** DNA-templated nanotube localization. *J. Am. Chem. Soc.* 125:8710–1, 2003.

Sorenson, E. C., and **E. M. Woolley.** Thermodynamics of proton dissociation from aqueous bicarbonate: Apparent molar volumes and apparent molar heat capacities of potassium carbonate and potassium bicarbonate at temperatures from 278.15 K to 393.15 K and at the pressure 0.35 MPa. *J. Chem. Thermodyn.* 36(4):289–98, 2004.

Brown, B. R., et al. **(E. M. Woolley).** Apparent molar volumes and apparent molar heat capacities of aqueous nickel(II) nitrate, copper(II) nitrate, and zinc(II) nitrate at temperatures from 278.15 K to 393.15 K at the pressure 0.35 MPa. *J. Chem. Thermodyn.* 36(5):437–46, 2004.

Price, J. L., et al. **(E. M. Woolley).** Thermodynamics of proton dissociations from aqueous **L**-valine and **L**-2-amino-*n*-butanoic acid: Apparent molar volumes and apparent molar heat capacities of the protonated cationic, neutral zwitterionic, and deprotonated anionic species at temperatures from $278.15 \leq T / K \leq 393.15$, at molalities $0.015 \leq m$ / mol kg^{-1} ≤ 0.67, and pressure p = 0/35 MPa. *J. Chem. Thermodyn.* 35(9):1425–67, 2003.

Harris, D. G., J. Shao, B. D. Marrow, and **S. S. Zimmerman.** Molecular modeling of the binding of 5-substituted 2'-deoxyuridine substrates to thymidine kinase of herpes simplex virus type-1. *Nucleosides Nucleotides Nucl. Acids* 23:555–65, 2004.

Harris, D. G., et al. **(S. S. Zimmerman).** Procedure for selecting starting conformations for energy minimization of nucleosides and nucleotides. *Nucleosides Nucleotides Nucl. Acids* 21:803–12, 2002.

Harris, D. G., et al. **(S. S. Zimmerman).** Kinetic and molecular modeling of nucleoside and nucleotide inhibition of malate dehydrogenase. *Nucleosides Nucleotides Nucl. Acids* 21:813–23, 2002.

Carnegie Mellon

CARNEGIE MELLON UNIVERSITY

Mellon College of Science
Department of Chemistry

Programs of Study

The Department of Chemistry offers programs leading to the M.S. and Ph.D. degrees. The majority of students are admitted to the Ph.D. program. Terminal master's programs in polymer science and in colloids, polymers, and surfaces are offered. The graduate program is highly individualized to allow exploration of interdisciplinary interests. Research is carried out in bioorganic, bioinorganic, computational, and theoretical chemistry; materials chemistry; polymer science; magnetochemistry; molecular biophysics; inorganic chemistry; green chemistry; NMR spectroscopy; optical and laser spectroscopy; photochemistry; physical chemistry; organic chemistry; and nuclear chemistry.

The graduate program at Carnegie Mellon emphasizes close interaction with faculty members in small research groups. Students in the Ph.D. program choose a research adviser during the first year and typically complete the course requirements within the first three semesters so that the focus throughout the program is on their thesis research. As part of their development as scientists, students also deliver a formal seminar, defend a research progress report, and develop an original research proposal. To support their overall professional development, students are required to assist in undergraduate teaching for two semesters. Additional opportunities to develop teaching and mentoring skills are available for those interested in future faculty careers. The final step in the program is the Ph.D. dissertation, which includes results of original research and constitutes a scientific contribution that is worthy of publication.

There are excellent opportunities for interdisciplinary programs with the Departments of Biological Sciences, Chemical Engineering, Materials Science, and Physics, along with the Biotechnology Program and the Center for Fluorescence Research in Biomedical Sciences.

Research Facilities

The Department of Chemistry is located in the Mellon Institute Building, a spacious and dramatic eight-story structure located near the main campus of Carnegie Mellon and directly adjacent to the University of Pittsburgh campus. The department has the most modern instrumentation, to which students have hands-on access. This includes the Center for Molecular Analysis, with LC-Q electrospray/ion-trap and MALDI/TOF mass spectrometry and access to high-field NMR (one 500-MHz and two 300-MHz), as well as major laser spectroscopy and chemical synthesis laboratories. Extensive computational facilities are readily available. These include state-of-the-art computers at the Pittsburgh Supercomputing Center, which is housed in the Mellon Institute Building along with the Department of Biological Sciences and the Center for Fluorescence Research in Biomedical Sciences. The library of the Mellon Institute is exceptional.

Financial Aid

All U.S. doctoral degree students are guaranteed financial aid for the first academic year, usually as teaching assistants, with a stipend of $1650 per month and a tuition scholarship. In addition, competitive fellowships are available, which pay an additional $2000–$4000 per year. Research assistantships are also available for succeeding years. International students may be admitted without being granted financial aid.

Cost of Study

Tuition is $28,200 for the 2004–05 academic year.

Living and Housing Costs

Pittsburgh provides an attractive and reasonably priced living environment. On-campus housing is limited, but the Off-Campus Housing Office assists students in finding suitable accommodations. Most graduate students prefer to live in nearby rooms and apartments, which are readily available.

Student Group

Graduate enrollment at Carnegie Mellon totals 4,272 and includes students from all parts of the United States and many other countries. All students in the Department of Chemistry are receiving financial aid. Upon completing the Ph.D., a few students (15 percent) go directly into academic positions, but most continue as postdoctoral fellows (40 percent) or take industrial jobs (45 percent).

Location

Pittsburgh is in a large metropolitan area of 2.3 million people. The city is the headquarters for twelve Fortune 500 corporations, and there is a large concentration of research laboratories in the area. Carnegie Mellon is located in the Oakland neighborhood, one of the cultural and civic centers of Pittsburgh. The campus covers 90 acres and adjoins Schenley Park, the largest city park. The city's cultural and recreational opportunities are truly outstanding.

The University

Carnegie Mellon was first established in 1900 as the Carnegie Technical School through a gift from Andrew Carnegie. In 1912, the name was changed to Carnegie Institute of Technology. The Mellon Institute was founded by A. W. and R. B. Mellon; it carried out both pure research and applied research in cooperation with local industry. In 1967, the two entities merged to form Carnegie-Mellon University. Four colleges—the Carnegie Institute of Technology, the Mellon College of Science, the College of Fine Arts, and the College of Humanities and Social Sciences—offer both undergraduate and graduate programs. The University has assets in excess of $1 billion, a total enrollment of 9,756, and 1,427 faculty members.

Applying

Completed applications and credentials for graduate study in chemistry should be submitted by January 15 for decision by mid-April. However, admission decisions are made on a continuous basis, and applications are considered at any time. In addition to the application form, transcripts from all college-level institutions attended, three letters of recommendation, and an official report of the applicant's scores on the General Test and the Subject Test in chemistry of the Graduate Record Examinations are required. An official report of the score from the Test of English as a Foreign Language (TOEFL) is required for international students. A more detailed description of programs is given online and in the departmental brochure, which will be sent on request.

Correspondence and Information

Committee for Graduate Admissions
Department of Chemistry
Carnegie Mellon University
4400 Fifth Avenue
Pittsburgh, Pennsylvania 15213

Telephone: 412-268-3150
Fax: 412-268-1061
E-mail: vb0g@andrew.cmu.edu
World Wide Web: http://www.chem.cmu.edu

Carnegie Mellon University

THE FACULTY AND THEIR RESEARCH

Catalina Achim, Assistant Professor; Ph.D., Carnegie Mellon, 1998. Synthesis and structural and spectroscopic characterization of coordination compounds; intramolecular and intermolecular electron-transfer properties of mixed-valence complexes; magnetochemistry of clusters; bioinorganic chemistry; investigation of stereochemistry, molecular recognition, and reactivity properties of polynuclear complexes.
Bruce A. Armitage, Associate Professor; Ph.D., Arizona, 1993. Bioorganic and supramolecular chemistry: design and synthesis of functional DNA/RNA analogs, nucleic acid chemistry, photochemistry in supramolecular assemblies of molecules, development of probes for RNA structure and function, sensors for hybridization of nucleic acid probes.
Guy C. Berry, University Professor; Ph.D., Michigan, 1960. Physical chemistry and polymer science, physical chemistry of macromolecules: photon correlation and integrated intensity light scattering, solution properties of flexible and rodlike polymers, rheology of polymers, properties of liquid crystalline polymers.
Mark E. Bier, Associate Research Professor and Director, Center for Molecular Analysis; Ph.D., Purdue, 1988. Bioanalytical mass spectrometry (MS), real-time monitoring of enzyme reactions by electrospray-MS, development of novel ion trap analyzer designs, femtomole level protein identification, educational MS software: http://mass-spec.chem.cmu.edu/VMSL/.
Emile L. Bominaar, Associate Research Professor; Ph.D., Amsterdam (Netherlands), 1986. Theoretical inorganic chemistry and spectroscopy: spin effects on electron transfer in transition-metal compounds and metalloproteins, magnetooptics.
Terrence J. Collins, Thomas Lord Professor; Ph.D., Auckland (New Zealand), 1978. Green chemistry, inorganic chemistry, design of catalysts for activation of hydrogen peroxide, chemistry to eliminate persistent pollutants, bioinorganic chemistry of high-oxidation-state transition metal species, magnetic properties of multinuclear transition metal ions.
Neil M. Donahue, Assistant Professor; Ph.D., MIT, 1991. Kinetics and mechanisms of atmospherically important reactions, especially hydrocarbon oxidation mechanisms; spectroscopy and in-situ measurement of gas-phase free radicals, including FTIR absorption, diode laser absorption, and cavity ringdown spectroscopy; quantum-mechanical and dynamical studies of reactivity; barrier height control in radical-molecule reactions, dynamics, and spectroscopy of highly vibrationally excited intermediates.
Rebecca J. Freeland, Associate Dean and Associate Head; Ph.D., Carnegie Mellon, 1986. Chemical education; graduate education in science; instructional design and assessment of educational software for introductory chemistry; support for faculty, future faculty, and teaching assistants in improving teaching.
Andrew J. Gellman, Thomas Lord Professor and Head, Chemical Engineering; Ph.D., Berkeley, 1985. Surface science and surface chemistry, with particular interest in the areas of heterogeneous catalysis and tribology.
Roberto Gil, Research Scientist and Director of the NMR Facility.
Susan T. Graul, Lecturer; Ph.D., Purdue, 1989. Physical organic chemistry. Gas-phase ion chemistry: reaction mechanisms and dynamics, cluster ions and highly charged ions, photoinduced and collisionally activated dissociation processes, statistical theory and molecular orbital calculations.
Michael P. Hendrich, Associate Professor; Ph.D., Illinois, 1988. Biophysical and bioinorganic chemistry, transition metals associated with fundamental processes of living systems, electronic structure, high-frequency electron paramagnetic resonance, magnetochemistry.
Colin Horwitz, Research Professor; Ph.D., Northwestern, 1986. Inorganic and bioinorganic chemistry: synthesis and characterization of coordination complexes, oxidation chemistry.
Morton Kaplan, Professor; Ph.D., MIT, 1960. Nuclear chemistry, nuclear physics, and chemical physics: nuclear reactions of heavy ions and high-energy projectiles, ultrarelativistic nuclear collisions, recoil properties of radioactive products, Mössbauer resonance, perturbed angular correlations of gamma rays, statistical theory of nuclear reactions and light-particle emission.
Paul J. Karol, Professor; Ph.D., Columbia, 1967. Nuclear chemistry and physical chemistry: high-energy nuclear reactions; chemical separations, especially column chromatography; positronium lifetime quenching.
Hyung J. Kim, Professor and Head; Ph.D., SUNY at Stony Brook, 1988. Theoretical chemistry, equilibrium and nonequilibrium statistical mechanics, chemical reaction dynamics and spectroscopy in condensed phases, molecular dynamics computer simulations and quantum chemistry in solution.
Tomasz Kowalewski, Assistant Professor; Ph.D., Polish Academy of Sciences, 1988. Physical and biophysical chemistry, physical chemistry of macromolecules, nanostructure in soft condensed matter, glass transition, self-assembly, hydrophobic interaction, nanoscale polymer assemblies, protein misfolding, physicochemical aspects of Alzheimer's disease, protein-DNA interactions, nanoscale manipulation of matter and structure-property studies of polymers, scanning probe techniques.
Maria Kurnikova, Assistant Professor; Ph.D., Pittsburgh, 1998. Theoretical chemistry.
Miguel Llinás, Professor; Ph.D., Berkeley, 1971. Molecular biophysics: structural dynamics and functional studies of proteins in solution by NMR spectroscopy, plasminogen and blood coagulation proteins.
Danith Ly, Assistant Professor; Ph.D., Georgia Tech, 1998. Chemical genetics; functional genomics; combinatorial chemistry; characterizing the molecular basis of human embryonic stem cells and other intermediate (adult) stem cells; elucidating the mechanisms of human physiologic processes, pathology, and aging; design and synthesis of artificial transcription factors; application of combinatorial approach to the discovery of drug and novel protein functions.
Krzysztof Matyjaszewski, J. C. Warner Professor; Ph.D., Polish Academy of Sciences, 1976. Polymer organic chemistry: kinetics and thermodynamics of ionic reactions, cationic polymerization, radical polymerization, ring-opening polymerization, living polymers, inorganic and organometallic polymers, electronic materials.
Richard D. McCullough, Professor and Dean; Ph.D., Johns Hopkins, 1988. Organic and materials chemistry: Self-assembly and synthesis of highly conductive organic polymers and oligomers; conjugated polymer sensors, nanoelectronic assembly, and nanowires; synthesis and development of organic-inorganic hybrid magnetic and electronic materials; crystal engineering and self-assembly.
Eckard Münck, Professor; Ph.D., Darmstadt Technical (Germany), 1967. Active sites of metalloproteins, in particular sites containing iron-sulfur clusters or oxo-bridged iron dimers; study of synthetic clusters which mimic structures in proteins; magnetochemistry: Heisenberg and double-exchange; Mössbauer spectroscopy and electron paramagnetic resonance.
Gary D. Patterson, Professor; Ph.D., Stanford, 1972. Chemical physics and polymer science: application of light-scattering spectroscopy to problems of structure and dynamics in amorphous materials, physics and chemistry of liquids and solutions, conformational statistics and molecular dynamics of polymers, nature and dynamics of the glass transition, structure and dynamics of biopolymers, colloid science, complex fluids.
Linda A. Peteanu, Associate Professor; Ph.D., Chicago, 1989. Physical chemistry; biophysical chemistry; laser spectroscopy; application of resonance Raman and Stark effect-based spectroscopies to the study of ultrafast photochemical and biological reactions: proton transfer, electron transfer, charge transfer, and *cis-trans* isomerizations; effect of solvent environment on reactive excited states.
Stuart W. Staley, Professor; Ph.D., Yale, 1964. Physical organic chemistry: synthesis, dynamic NMR studies of electron transfer systems and theoretically interesting molecules, X-ray diffraction and NMR studies of organic crystals, electronic structure calculations of molecular geometries and properties.
Robert F. Stewart, Professor; Ph.D., Caltech, 1962. Physical and theoretical chemistry: X-ray diffraction, high-energy electron-scattering calculations.
Charles H. Van Dyke, Associate Professor; Ph.D., Pennsylvania, 1964. Synthetic inorganic chemistry and chemical education.
Lynn M. Walker, Associate Professor; Ph.D., Delaware, 1995. Rheology of complex fluids, rheo-optics and rheo-SANS of assembled macromolecular solutions, rheo-optics of immiscible polymer blends in complex flows, viscoelasticity and effects on atomization and spraying.
David Yaron, Associate Professor; Ph.D., Harvard, 1990. Theoretical chemistry, electronic structure of conducting polymers and nonlinear optical materials, theoretical description of large-amplitude vibrational motions.

SELECTED PUBLICATIONS

Achim, C. Magnetism. In *Chemistry: Foundations and Applications,* ed. J. Lagowski. Macmillan Reference, in press.

Popescu, D.-L., T. J. Parolin, and **C. Achim.** Metal ion incorporation in PNA duplexes. *J. Am. Chem. Soc.,* 2003.

Zhou, H.-C., et al. **(C. Achim).** High-nuclearity, sulfide-rich, molybdenum-iron-sulfur clusters: Reevaluation and extension. *Inorg. Chem.* 41:3191–201, 2002.

Cadieux, E., et al. **(C. Achim** and **E. Münck).** Biochemical, Mössbauer, and EPR studies of the diiron cluster of phenol hydroxylase from *Pseudomonas* sp. strain CF 600. *Biochemistry* 41:10680–91, 2002.

Wang, M., I. Dilek, and **B. A. Armitage.** Electrostatic contributions to cyanine dye aggregation on peptide nucleic acid templates. *Langmuir* 19:6449–55, 2003.

Berry, G. C. Light scattering, classical: Size and size distribution characterization. In *Encyclopedia of Analytical Chemistry,* vol. 6, pp. 5413–48, ed. R. A. Meyers. New York: John Wiley and Sons, 2002.

Berry, G. C. Polymer rheology: Principles, techniques, and applications. In *Comprehensive Desk Reference of Polymer Characterization and Analysis,* ed. J. R. F. Brady. Washington, D.C.: American Chemical Society, 2002.

Tan, Z., and **G. C. Berry.** Studies on the texture of nematic solutions of rodlike polymers. 3. Rheooptical and rheological behavior in shear. *J. Rheol.* 47:47–104, 2002.

Berry, G. C., and P. M. Cotts. Static and dynamic light scattering. In *Experimental Methods in Polymer Characterization,* eds. J. V. Dawkins and R. S. Stein. New York: John Wiley and Sons, 2000.

Pu, L., A. A. Amoscato, **M. E. Bier,** and J. S. Lazo. Dual G1 and G2 phase inhibition by a novel, selective Cdc25 inhibitor 7-chloro-6-(2-morpholin-4-ylethylamino)-quinoline-5,8-dione. *J. Biol. Chem.* 16: 14586, 2003.

Bier, M. E., C. G. Yang, and J. J. Grabowski. The virtual mass spectrometry laboratory and a polymer analysis case study. *Polym. Mater. Sci. Eng.* 88:70, 2003.

Bier, M. E. The basics of MALDI and ESI mass spectrometers for polymer analysis. *Polym. Mater. Sci. Eng.* 88:17–8, 2003.

Pearce, L. L., B. C. Hill, **E. L. Bominaar,** and J. Peterson. Conformational flexibility at the binuclear pair of pulsed cytochrome c oxidase demonstrated by reversal of cyanide inhibition and different modes of binding the auxiliary substrate nitric oxide. *J. Biol. Chem.* 278:52139–45, 2003.

Ghosh, A., and **T. J. Collins** et al. Controlling acid-induced demetalation of iron peroxide-activating catalysts. *J. Am. Chem. Soc.* 125:12378–9, 2003.

Yano, T., et al. **(T. J. Collins).** Mononuclear–dinuclear helicate interconversion of dibromoN,N'-bis[(S)-1-2-(pyridyl)ethyl]-pyridine-2,6-dicarboxamidatecopper(II) via a deprotonation-protonation process. *Chem. Commun.* 1396–7, 2002.

Collins, T. J. TAML oxidant activators: A new approach to the activation of hydrogen peroxide for environmentally significant problems. *Accounts Chem. Res.* 35:782–90, 2002.

Gupta, S. S., et al. **(T. J. Collins).** Rapid total destruction of chlorophenol pollutants by activated hydrogen peroxide. *Science* 296:326–8, 2002.

Donahue, N. M., and J. S. Clarke. Fitting multiple datasets in kinetics: n-butane + OH → products. *Int. J. Chem. Kinet.,* in press.

Steyert, D. W., et al. **(N. M. Donahue).** Hydrogen and helium pressure broadening of water transitions in the 380–600 cm^{-1} region. *J. Quant. Spectrosc. Radiat. Transfer* 83:183, 2004.

Donahue, N. M. Reaction barriers: Origin and evolution. *Chem. Rev.* 103:4593, 2003.

Steyert, D. W., et al. **(N. M. Donahue).** Pressure broadening coefficients of rotational transitions of water in the 380–600 cm^{-1} range. *J. Quant. Spectrosc. Radiat. Transfer* 72:775, 2002.

Meragelman, T. L., D. S. Pedrosa, and **R. R. Gil.** Diterpenes from *Stevia gilliesii. Biochem. Syst. Ecol.,* in press.

Meragelman, T. L., G. L. Silva, E. Mongelli, and **R. R. Gil.** *-ent-*Pimarane type diterpenes from *Gnaphalium gaudichaudianum. Phytochemistry* 62:569–72, 2003.

Nicotra, V. E., and **R. R. Gil** et al. -15,21-cyclowithanolides from *Jaborosa bergii.* 66:1471–5, 2003.

Golombek, A. P., and **M. P. Hendrich.** Quantitative analysis of dinuclear manganese(II) EPR spectra. *J. Magn. Reson.* 165:33–48, 2003.

Ghosh, A., and **M. P. Hendrich** et al. Understanding the mechanism of H^+-induced demetalation as a design strategy for robust iron(III) peroxide-activating catalysts. *J. Am. Chem. Soc.* 125:12378–9, 2003.

Pierce, B. S., T. E. Elgren, and **M. P. Hendrich.** Mechanistic implications for the formation of the diiron cluster in ribonucleotide reductase provided by quantitative EPR spectroscopy. *J. Am. Chem. Soc.* 125:8748–59, 2003.

Senior, S. Z., et al. **(M. P. Hendrich).** Catecholase activity associated with copper-S100B. *Biochemistry* 42:4392–7, 2003.

Ghosh, A., and **C. P. Horwitz** et al. Understanding the mechanism of H^+-induced demetalation as a design strategy for robust iron(III) peroxide-activating catalysts. *J. Am. Chem. Soc.* 125:12378–9, 2003.

Horwitz, C. P., and A. Ghosh. Method for making macrocyclic tetraamido compounds. *US* 10/371:484, 2003.

Horwitz, C. P., and A. Ghosh. Improved synthesis of macrocyclic tetraamido compounds and new metal insertion process. *US* 10/371:591, 2003.

Glatzel, P., et al. **(C. P. Horwitz** and **T. J. Collins).** Electronic structure of Ni complexes by X-ray resonance Raman spectroscopy (resonant inelastic X-ray scattering). *J. Am. Chem. Soc.* 124:9668–9, 2002.

Adams, J., et al. **(M. Kaplan).** Particle-type dependence of azimuthal anisotropy and nuclear modification of particle production in Au + Au collisions at $\sqrt{s_{NN}}$ = 200 GeV. *Phys. Rev. Lett.,* in press.

Adams, J., et al. **(M. Kaplan).** ρ^0 production and possible modification in Au + Au and p + p collisions at $\sqrt{s_{NN}}$ = 200 GeV. *Phys. Rev. Lett.,* in press.

Adams, J., et al. **(M. Kaplan).** Identified particle distributions in pp and Au + Au collisions at $\sqrt{s_{NN}}$ = 200 GeV. *Phys. Rev. Lett.,* in press.

Adams, J., et al. **(M. Kaplan).** Azimuthal anisotropy at RHIC: The first and fourth harmonics. *Phys. Rev. Lett.,* in press.

Karol, P. The heavy elements. In *Proceedings of the 2nd International Conference on the Periodic Table,* ed. R. B. King. In press.

Nakahara, H., et al. **(P. Karol).** On the discovery of elements 110–118. *J. Pure Appl. Chem.* 75:1601–11, 2003.

Karol, P. The Mendeleev-Seaborg periodic table: Through Z=1138 and beyond. *J. Chem. Educ.* 79:60, 2002.

Holder, D. A., B. A. Johnson, and **P. J. Karol.** A consistent set of oxidation number rules for intelligent computer programming. *J. Chem. Educ.* 79:465, 2002.

Shim, Y. S., J. Duan, M. Y. Choi, and **H. J. Kim.** Solvation in molecular ionic liquids. *J. Chem. Phys.* 119:6411, 2003.

Jeon, J., and **H. J. Kim.** A continuum theory of solvation in polarizable quadrupolar solvents. I. Formulation. *J. Chem. Phys.* 119:8606, 2003.

Jeon, J., and **H. J. Kim.** A continuum theory of solvation in polarizable quadrupolar solvents. II. Solvation free energetics, dynamics and solvatochromism. *J. Chem. Phys.* 119:8626, 2003.

Dorairaj, S. and **H. J. Kim.** Excited-state charge transfer dynamics of DMABN in quadrupolar solvents. *J. Phys. Chem. A* 106:2322, 2002.

Huang, H., **T. Kowalewski,** and K. L. Wooley. Nanodroplets of polyisoprene fluid contained within poly(acrylic acid-co-acrylamide) shells. *J. Polym. Sci., Part A: Polym. Chem.* 41: 1659–68, 2003.

Kowalewski, T., R. D. McCullough, and **K. Matyjaszewski.** Complex nanostructured materials from segmented copolymers prepared by ATRP. *Eur. Phys. J. E: Soft Matter* 10:5–16, 2003.

Carnegie Mellon University

Selected Publications (continued)

Kowalewski, T., K. Matyjaszewski, T. Endo, and H. Nishida. New nanostructured materials from well-defined copolymers synthesized by ATRP. *Mirai Zairyo* 3:12–22, 2003.

Liu, T., et al. **(T. Kowalewski** and **K. Matyjaszewski).** Grafting poly(n-butyl acrylate) from a functionalized carbon black surface by atom transfer radical polymerization. *Langmuir* 19:6342–5, 2003.

Pyun, J., et al. **(T. Kowalewski, G. D. Patterson,** and **K. Matyjaszewski).** Synthesis and characterization of organic/inorganic hybrid nanoparticles: Kinetics of surface-initiated atom transfer radical polymerization and morphology of hybrid nanoparticle ultrathin films. *Macromolecules* 36:5094–104, 2003.

Shilov, I., and **M. Kurnikova.** Energetics and dynamics of a cyclic oligosaccharide molecule in a confined protein pore environment. A molecular dynamics study. *J. Phys. Chem.* 107:71089–201, 2003.

Mamonov, A., R. Coalson, A. Nitzan, and **M. Kurnikova.** The role of the dielectric barrier in narrow biological channels: A novel composite approach to modeling single channel currents. *Biophys. J.* 84:3646–61, 2003.

Graf, P., A. Nitzan, **M. G. Kurnikova,** and R. D. Coalson. A dynamic lattice Monte-Carlo model of ion transport in inhomogeneous dielectric environments: Method and implementation. *J. Phys. Chem.* 104:12324–38, 2000.

Cardenas, A., **M. G. Kurnikova,** and R. D. Coalson. 3D Poisson-Nerst-Planck theory studies of the influence of membrane electrostatics on gramicidin A channel conductance. *Biophys. J.* 79:80–93, 2000.

Briknarová, K., and **M. Llinás.** Proteínas BAG. *Investigación y Ciencia* (Spanish edition of *Scientific American),* in press.

Trexler, M., et al. **(M. Llinás).** Peptide ligands for the FN2 modules of matrix metalloproteinase 2 (MMP-2). *J. Biol. Chem.,* in press.

Örning, L., et al. **(M. Llinás).** A cyclic pentapeptide derived from the second EGF-like domain of factor VII is an inhibitor of tissue factor dependent coagulation and thrombus formation. *Thromb. Haemostasis* 87:13–21, 2002.

Gehrmann, M., et al. **(M. Llinás).** The col-1 module of human matrix metalloproteinase-2 (MMP-2): Structural/functional relatedness between gelatin-binding fibronectin type II modules and lysine-binding kringle domains. *Biol. Chem.* 383:137–48, 2002.

Zhou, P., and **D. Ly.** Embryonic stem cell: A perfect marriage between gene regulation and regenerative medicine. *Curr. Top. Med. Chem.* 3:339, 2003.

Zhou, P., et al. **(D. Ly).** Novel binding and efficient cellular uptake of guanidined-based peptide nucleic acids (G-PNA). *J. Am. Chem. Soc.* 125:6878, 2003.

Simbulan-Rosenthal, C. M., and **D. H. Ly** et al. Misregulation of gene expression in primary fibroblasts lacking poly (ADP-ribose) polymerase. *Proc. Natl. Acad. Sci. U.S.A.* 97:1274, 2000.

Ly, D. H., D. J. Lockhart, P. G. Schultz, and R. A. Lerner. Mitotic misregulation and human aging. *Science* 287:2486, 2000.

Inoue, Y., and **K. Matyjaszewski.** Preparation of polyethylene block copolymers by combination of post-metallocene catalysis of ethylene polymerization and atom transfer polymerization. *J. Polym. Sci., Part A: Polym. Chem.,* in press.

Otazaghine, B., et al. **(K. Matyjaszewski).** Synthesis of telechelic oligomers via ATRP. Part I: Study of styrene. *Macromol. Chem. Phys.,* in press.

Matyjaszewski, K. New polymer materials by atom transfer radical polymerization and other controlled/living radical polymerization systems. *Mol. Cryst. Liq. Cryst. Sci. Technol,* in press.

Matyjaszewski, K. Organic/inorganic hybrid materials prepared by atom transfer radical polymerization. *Nonlinear Opt. Quantum Opt.,* in press.

Jeffries-El, M., G. Sauvé, and **R. D. McCullough.** In-situ end group functionalization of regioregular poly(3-alkylthiophene) using the Grignard metathesis polymerization method. *Adv. Mater.,* in press.

Sheina, E. E., et al. **(R. D. McCullough).** Chain growth mechanism for regioregular nickel-initiated cross-coupling polymerizations. *Macromolecules,* in press.

Zhai, L., and **R. D. McCullough.** Regioregular polythiophene/gold nanoparticle hybrid materials. *J. Mater. Chem.* 14:141–3, 2004.

Stokes, K. K., K. Heuzé, and **R. D. McCullough.** Synthesis and assembly of new phosphonic acid functionalized, regioregular polythiophenes. *Macromolecules* 36:7114–8, 2003.

Sutton, V. R., et al. **(E. Münck).** Superoxide destroys the $[2Fe\text{-}2S]^{2+}$ cluster of FNR from *Escherichia coli. Biochemistry,* in press.

Costas, M., et al. **(E. Münck).** Nonheme $Fe^{IV}O$ and $Fe^{IV}{}_2O_2$ species derived from a common Fe^{III}-OOR intermediate. *J. Am. Chem. Soc.,* in press.

Kaizer, J., et al. **(E. Münck).** Stable nonheme $Fe^{IV}O$ complexes that can oxidize C-H bonds of cyclohexane at room temperature. *J. Am. Chem. Soc.,* in press.

Münck, E., and A. Stubna. Mössbauer spectroscopy in bioinorganic chemistry. In *Comprehensive Coordination Chemistry II,* vol. 2, pp. 279–86, ed. B. Lever. 2003.

Vrajmasu, V. V., **E. Münck,** and **E. L. Bominaar.** Density functional study of electric hyperfine interactions and redoxstructural correlations in cofactor of nitrogenase. Analysis of general trends of ^{57}Fe isomer shift. *Inorg. Chem.* 42:5974–88, 2003.

Cao, R., Z. Gu, **G. D. Patterson,** and **B. A. Armitage.** A recoverable enzymatic microgel based on biomolecular recognition. *J. Am. Chem. Soc.,* in press.

Cao, R., Z. Gu, **G. D. Patterson,** and **B. A. Armitage.** Synthesis and characterization of thermoreversible biopolymer microgels based on hydrogen bonded nucleobase pairing. *J. Am. Chem. Soc.* 125:10250–6, 2003.

Gu, Z., **G. D. Patterson,** R. Cao, and **B. A. Armitage.** Self-assembled supramolecular microgels: Fractal structure and aggregation mechanism. *J. Polym. Sci., Part B: Polym. Phys.* 41:3037–46, 2003.

Wachsmann-Hogiu, S., et al. **(L. A. Peteanu** and **D. J. Yaron).** The effects of structural and micro-environmental disorder on the electronic properties of MEH-PPV and related oligomers. *J. Phys. Chem. B* 107:5133–43, 2003.

Chowdhury, A., et al. **(L. Peteanu** and **D. J. Yaron).** Stark spectroscopy of size-selected helical H-aggregates of a cyanine dye templated by duplex DNA: Effect of exciton coupling on electronic polarizabilites. *J. Phys. Chem. B* 107:3351–62, 2003.

Premvardhan, L. L., and **L. A. Peteanu.** Electronic properties of small model compounds that undergo excited-state intra-molecular proton transfer as measured by electroabsorption spectroscopy. *JPPA* 154:69–80, 2002.

Premvardhan, L. L., et al. **(L. A. Peteanu** and **D. J. Yaron).** Conformational effects on optical charge transfer in the emeraldine base form of polyaniline from electroabsorption measurements and INDO/s calculations. *J. Chem. Phys.* 115:4359–66, 2001.

Staley, S. W., S. A. Vignon, and B. Eliasson. Conformational analysis and kinetics of ring inversion for methylene- and dimethylsilyl-bridged dicyclooctatetraene. *J. Org. Chem.* 66:3871–7, 2001.

Boman, P., B. Eliasson, R. A. Grimm, and **S. W. Staley.** Bond shift and charge transfer dynamics in methylene- and dimethylsilyl-bridged dicyclooctatetraene dianions. *J. Chem. Soc., Perkin Trans.* 2:1130–8, 2001.

Staley, S. W., and J. D. Kehlbeck. Effect of para substituents on the rate of bond shift in arylcyclooctatetraene. *J. Org. Chem.* 66:5572–9, 2001.

Staley, S. W., and J. D. Kehlbeck. Mechanism of a novel exchange process in alkali metal salts of 1,5-dicyclooctatetraenylnaphthalene dianion. *J. Am. Chem. Soc.* 123:8095–100, 2001.

Janesko, B. G., C. J. Gallek, and **D. Yaron.** Using constrained Schroedinger equations to separate resonant and inductive substituent effects: A new methodology for parametrizing simple models in chemistry. *J. Phys. Chem. A,* in press.

Janesko, B. G., and **D. Yaron.** Explicitly correlated divide-and-conquer-type electronic structure calculations based on two-electron reduced density matrices. *J. Chem. Phys.* 119:3, 2003.

Tomlinson, A., and **D. Yaron.** Direct INDO/SCI method for excited state calculations. *J. Comput. Chem.* 24:1782–8, 2003.

CORNELL UNIVERSITY

Field of Chemistry and Chemical Biology

Program of Study

The diverse research specialties of the graduate faculty include both traditional areas and interdisciplinary expertise in biotechnology, chemical communication, polymer science, and molecular engineering. Cornell's graduate program is designed to provide broad training in the fundamentals of chemistry and research methods and to culminate in the award of the doctorate. Several nationally renowned research centers and facilities at Cornell foster inquiry in traditional areas of the discipline and at the interface between chemistry and other physical and biological sciences, engineering, materials science, and mathematics. Graduate students enrolled in the field of chemistry and chemical biology select a major research concentration in one of the following subfields: analytical, bioorganic, biophysical, chemical biology, inorganic, materials, organic, organometallic, physical/chemical physics, polymer, or theoretical. Students also choose a minor concentration from these subfields or a related graduate field, such as materials science or biochemistry. Once major and minor concentrations have been selected, students choose permanent special committees consisting of the research adviser and 2 additional faculty members. First-year graduate students take proficiency examinations in inorganic, organic, and physical chemistry; a level of instruction suited to the student's background and future objectives is then recommended. The number of formal courses required depends on a student's previous preparation, chosen concentration, and the advice of the special committee. Students concentrating in organic chemistry prepare and defend a research proposal. Every student takes an admission-to-candidacy examination within the first two years of study. The Ph.D. is awarded upon completion of an original research project (directed by the chair of the special committee) and successful defense of the thesis.

Research Facilities

Research in the Department of Chemistry and Chemical Biology is supported by several departmental facilities, including the Nuclear Magnetic Resonance Facility, the X-Ray Diffraction Facility, the Mass Spectrometry Facility, and the Glass Shop. Additional facilities at Cornell include the Center for High Energy Synchrotron Studies, the Cornell Nanofabrication Facility, the Center for Theory and Simulation, and the Biotechnology Program in the New York State Center for Advanced Technology as well as specialized facilities associated with the Cornell Center for Materials Research and the Cornell Nanobiotechnology Center.

Financial Aid

Fellowships, scholarships, loans, and teaching and research assistantships are available. Nearly all Ph.D. students have assistantship or fellowship support sufficient to cover tuition, fees, health insurance, and living expenses. Fellowships and scholarships are also offered by state and national government agencies, foundations, and private corporations.

Cost of Study

Tuition and fees for students attending Cornell during the 2003–04 academic year were $28,630. Some increase for 2004–05 is anticipated.

Living and Housing Costs

Living expenses for the academic year are typically $13,365 to $16,869 for single students. Additional expenses may include travel and medical and dental costs. The University maintains married student housing and graduate dormitory accommodations on and near the campus. Privately owned accommodations are available nearby.

Student Group

There are 186 graduate students currently enrolled in the Ph.D. program in the Department of Chemistry and Chemical Biology.

Location

Ithaca, a city of about 30,000 people, is located on Cayuga Lake in the beautiful Finger Lakes region of central New York State. The home of both Ithaca College and Cornell, the city is one of the country's great educational communities, offering cultural advantages that rival those of many large cities. Recreational activities, including hiking, cycling, boating, and skiing, abound. Light industry and technical and consulting firms are active in the area.

The University and The Department

Cornell University, founded in 1865 by Ezra Cornell, is composed of fourteen colleges and schools. Several of these schools and colleges were established under the land-grant college system and are part of the State University of New York; others, are privately endowed. The Department of Chemistry and Chemical Biology occupies more than 300,000 square feet of space in Baker Laboratory and the adjacent S. T. Olin Laboratory.

Applying

Only students who expect to complete a doctoral program (Ph.D.) should apply. Application to the graduate field of chemistry at Cornell is accepted for fall admission only. Early submission of applications is strongly encouraged, with applications being evaluated as early as December 1. Completed applications received before January 10 may also serve as applications for Cornell fellowships. Transcripts of all grades (whether or not a degree has been conferred) and three letters of recommendation are required. Applications must include GRE General Test scores and one GRE Subject Test score in chemistry. International applicants must demonstrate proficiency in English, usually by submitting scores on the TOEFL. Minimum scores of 600 on the paper-based test (250, computer-based test), with at least a score in each of the three categories of 60 on the paper-based test (25, computer-based test), are required for application consideration.

Correspondence and Information

Graduate Coordinator
Field of Chemistry and Chemical Biology
Baker Laboratory
Cornell University
Ithaca, New York 14853-1301

Telephone: 607-255-4139
Fax: 607-255-4137
E-mail: chemgrad@cornell.edu
World Wide Web: http://www.chem.cornell.edu

Cornell University

THE FACULTY AND THEIR RESEARCH

H. D. Abruña, Ph.D., North Carolina. Electrochemistry, chemically modified electrodes, redoxactive dendrimers, biosensor, underpotential deposition of metals, X-ray–based techniques, fuel cells.
B. A. Baird, Ph.D., Cornell. Ligand binding and signal transduction mechanisms of cell membrane receptors involved in immunological responses.
S. H. Bauer, Ph.D. Chicago. Kinetics of very fast gas phase reactions, shock tube pyrolysis, mechanisms of cluster production from supersaturated vapors, oxidation of boron hydrides.
T. P. Begley, Ph.D., Caltech. Bioorganic chemistry, enzymatic reaction mechanisms, DNA photochemistry, prolyl-4-hydroxylase, thiamine biosynthesis.
J. T. Brenna, Ph.D., Cornell. High-precision gas isotope ratio mass spectrometry, interfaces and data processing, ^{13}C and D labeled tracers, mammalian unsaturated fatty acid metabolism.
J. M. Burlitch, Ph.D., MIT. Inorganic chemistry of materials, synthesis, ceramics, nanocomposites, metal-to-ceramic adhesion.
B. K. Carpenter, Ph.D., University College (London). Mechanisms and dynamics of organic reactions, structures and properties of reactive intermediates, combustion reactions, neurochemistry.
R. A. Cerione, Ph.D., Rutgers. Structure and function of small molecular G proteins, cellular signal transduction.
P. J. Chirik, Ph.D., Caltech. Synthetic inorganic and organotransition metal chemistry directed toward small molecule activation and catalysis.
G. W. Coates, Ph.D., Stanford. Stereoselective catalysis, organic and polymer synthesis, reaction mechanisms.
D. B. Collum, Ph.D., Columbia. Organotransition metal and organolithium reaction mechanism, development of organometallic chemistry for organic synthesis.
B. R. Crane, Ph.D., Scripps Research Institute. Biophysical and bioinorganic chemistry, structural principles of redox and photochemistry in biological catalysis and regulation.
H. F. Davis, Ph.D., Berkeley. Chemical reaction dynamics using laser and molecular beam techniques.
F. J. DiSalvo, Ph.D., Stanford. Solid-state chemistry, synthesis and structure, electrical and magnetic properties.
S. E. Ealick, Ph.D., Oklahoma. X-ray crystallography of macromolecules, applications of synchrotron radiation, enzymes of nucleotide metabolism, enzyme mechanism, structure-based drug design.
J. R. Engstrom, Ph.D., Caltech. Surface science, semiconductor surface chemistry, molecular-beam scattering, thin-film deposition, microfluidics.
G. S. Ezra, Ph.D., Oxford. Theoretical chemical physics, intramolecular dynamics, semiclassical mechanics, electron correlation.
R. C. Fay, Ph.D., Illinois. Inorganic stereochemistry, kinetics and mechanism of molecular rearrangements.
J. H. Freed, Ph.D., Columbia. Theoretical and experimental studies of molecular dynamics and structure by magnetic resonance spectroscopy.
B. Ganem, Ph.D., Columbia. Synthetic organic and bioorganic chemistry, methods and reactions for the synthesis of rare natural products and biologically active compounds.
E. P. Giannelis, Ph.D., Michigan State. Materials chemistry, polymer nanocomposites, self-assembling systems.
G. P. Hess, Ph.D., Berkeley. Reaction mechanisms on cell surfaces, transient kinetics and laser-pulse photolysis.
M. A. Hines, Ph.D., Stanford. Fundamental studies of chemical etching, new methods of nanofabrication, properties of nanomechanical systems, scanning tunneling microscopy.
R. Hoffmann, Ph.D., Harvard. Electronic structure of organic, organometallic, and inorganic molecules and extended structures, transition states and reaction intermediates.
P. L. Houston, Ph.D., MIT. Chemical kinetics and reaction dynamics.
S. Lee, Ph.D., Chicago. Materials chemistry, synthesis structure and electronic structure of entended solids.
R. F. Loring, Ph.D., Stanford. Theoretical chemical physics, dynamics in small molecule and polymeric liquids.
J. A. Marohn, Ph.D., Caltech. Scanned-probe microscopy investigations of novel magnetic and electronic materials.
F. W. McLafferty, Ph.D., Cornell. Mass spectrometry, characterization of large biomolecules.
J. E. McMurry, Ph.D., Columbia. Textbook author.
D. T. McQuade, Ph.D., Wisconsin. Design and synthesis of self-assembling small molecules and polymers for application in catalysis, sensing, and biomaterials.
J. Meinwald, Ph.D., Harvard. Organic chemistry; insect chemical ecology; characterization, biosynthesis, and synthesis of natural products.
G. H. Morrison, Ph.D., Princeton. Trace and microanalysis, ion microscopy, ion microprobe, mass spectrometry of solids.
J. T. Njarðarson, Ph.D., Yale. Organic chemistry, development of new synthetic methods, natural product synthesis.
C. K. Ober, Ph.D., Massachusetts. Polymer synthesis, self-assembling materials, microlithography, liquid crystalline polymers.
H. A. Scheraga, Ph.D., Duke. Physical chemical studies of proteins and aqueous solutions.
D. Y. Sogah, Ph.D., UCLA. Supramolecular chemistry, polypeptide and carbohydrate-based polymers, group transfer polymerization; living free-radical polymerization; hyperbranched and helical polymers; organic-inorganic nanocomposites.
D. S. Tan, Ph.D., Harvard. Diversity-oriented organic synthesis of small molecule libraries related to natural products, high-throughput screening for biological probes.
D. A. Usher, Ph.D., Cambridge. Polynucleotide analogs, template reactions, chemical evolution.
B. Widom, Ph.D., Cornell. Statistical mechanics of phase transitions, critical phenomena, and interfaces.
C. F. Wilcox, Ph.D. UCLA. Elucidation of the relationship between molecular structure and energy by theoretical analysis and synthesis of selected novel molecules.
P. T. Wolczanski, Ph.D., Caltech. Synthesis and reactivity of transition metal complexes, materials preparation.
D. B. Zax, Ph.D., Berkeley. Studies of novel synthetic and naturally occurring polymeric materials, structure and dynamical studies in solids.

Analytical Chemistry
H. D. Abruña, J. T. Brenna, R. A. Cerione, J. R. Engstrom, M. A. Hines, J. A. Marohn, F. W. McLafferty, G. H. Morrison, D. B. Zax.

Bioorganic Chemistry
T. P. Begley, G. W. Coates, B. Ganem, F. W. McLafferty, J. E. McMurry, D. T. McQuade, J. Meinwald, D. Y. Sogah, D. S. Tan, D. A. Usher.

Biophysical Chemistry
B. A. Baird, B. R. Crane, S. E. Ealick, J. H. Freed, G. P. Hess, H. A. Scheraga.

Chemical Biology
B. A. Baird, T. P. Begley, R. A. Cerione, B. R. Crane, S. E. Ealick, B. Ganem, D. T. McQuade, J. T. Njarðarson, H. A. Scheraga, D. S. Tan, D. A. Usher.

Inorganic Chemistry
H. D. Abruña, J. M. Burlitch, P. J. Chirik, G. W. Coates, D. B. Collum, B. R. Crane, F. J. DiSalvo, R. C. Fay, R. Hoffmann, S. Lee, P. T. Wolczanski, D. B. Zax.

Materials Chemistry
H. D. Abruña, J. M. Burlitch, G. W. Coates, F. J. DiSalvo, J. R. Engstrom, E. P. Giannelis, M. A. Hines, R. Hoffmann, P. L. Houston, S. Lee, R. F. Loring, J. A. Marohn, D. T. McQuade, C. K. Ober, D. Y. Sogah, P. T. Wolczanski, D. B. Zax.

Organic Chemistry
T. P. Begley, B. K. Carpenter, P. J. Chirik, G. W. Coates, D. B. Collum, B. Ganem, J. E. McMurry, D. T. McQuade, J. Meinwald, J. T. Njarðarson, D. Y. Sogah, D. S. Tan, D. A. Usher, C. F. Wilcox, P. T. Wolczanski.

Organometallic Chemistry
P. J. Chirik, G. W. Coates, D. B. Collum, P. T. Wolczanski.

Physical Chemistry/Chemical Physics
H. D. Abruña, B. A. Baird, S. H. Bauer, H. F. Davis, F. J. DiSalvo, J. R. Engstrom, G. S. Ezra, J. H. Freed, M. A. Hines, R. Hoffmann, P. L. Houston, R. F. Loring, J. A. Marohn, H. A. Scheraga, B. Widom, D. B. Zax.

Polymer Chemistry
P. J. Chirik, G. W. Coates, E. P. Giannelis, R. Hoffmann, R. F. Loring, J. A. Marohn, D. T. McQuade, C. K. Ober, H. A. Scheraga, D. Y. Sogah.

Theoretical Chemistry
G. S. Ezra, J. H. Freed, R. Hoffmann, S. Lee, R. F. Loring, H. A. Scheraga, B. Widom, C. F. Wilcox.

SELECTED PUBLICATIONS

Diaz, D. J., et al. **(H. D. Abruña).** Ordered arrays generated via metal-initiated self-assembly of terpyridine containing dendrimers and bridging ligands. *Langmuir* 15:7351–4, 1999.

Smith, S. P. E., K. F. Ben Dor, and **H. D. Abruña.** Structural effects on the oxidation of COOH by Bismuth modified pt (111) electrodes with (100) monatomic steps. *Langmuir* 15:7325–32, 1999.

Holowka, D., E. D. Sheets, and **B. Baird.** Interactions between FceRI and detergent-resistant membrane domains (rafts) are regulated by the actin cytoskeleton. *J. Cell. Sci.* 113:1009–19, 2000.

Baird, B., E. D. Sheets, and D. Holowka. How does the plasma membrane participate in cellular signaling by receptors for immunoglobulin E? *Biophys. Chem.* 82:109–19, 1999.

Bauer, S. H., Y-X. Zhang, and C. F. Wilcox. Thermochemical and kinetic parameters for H-bonded clusters derived from condensation flux data. *J. Phys. Chem. A* 104:1217, 2000.

Zhang, Y-X., and **S. H. Bauer.** The gas phase pyrolyses of 2-nitropropane and 2-nitropropanol. *J. Phys. Chem. A* 104:1207, 2000.

Begley, T. P., et al. The enzymology of sulfur activation during thiamin and biotin biosynthesis. *Curr. Opin. Chem. Biol.* 3:623–9, 1999.

Begley, T. P. and R. Mehl. Mechanistic studies on the repair of a novel DNA photolesion: The spore photoproduct. *Org. Lett.* 1:1065–6, 1999.

Brenna, J. T., T. N. Corso, H. J. Tobias, and R. J. Caimi. High precision continuous flow isotope ratio mass spectrometry. *Mass Spec. Rev.* 16:227, 1997.

Corso, T. N., and **J. T. Brenna.** High-precision, position-specific isotope analysis. *Proc. Natl. Acad. Sci. U.S.A.* 94(4):1049–53, 1997.

Bender, C. M., **J. M. Burlitch,** D. Barber, and C. Pollock. Synthesis and fluorescence of neodymium-doped barium fluoride nanoparticles. *Chem. Mater.* 12(7):1969–76, 2000.

Jones, S. A., **J. M. Burlitch,** J. C. Duchamp, and T. M. Duncan. Sol-Gel synthesis of protoenstatite and a study of the factors that affect crystallization. *J. Sol-Gel Sci. Tech.* 15:201–9, 1999.

Reyes, M. B., and **B. K. Carpenter.** Mechanism of thermal deazetization of 2,3-diazabicyclo[2.2.1]hept-2-ene, and its reaction dynamics in supercritical fluids. *J. Am. Chem. Soc.* 122:10163, 2000.

Hughes, T. P., and **B. K. Carpenter.** Parallel mechanisms for the cycloaromatization of enyneallenes. *J. Chem. Soc. Perkin Trans.* 2:2291, 1999.

Chirik, P. J., L. M. Henling, and J. E. Bercaw. Synthesis of singly and doubly bridged *ansa*-zirconocene hydrides. Formation of unusual mixed valence trimeric hydride by reaction of H_2 with $\{(Me_2Si)_2(\eta^5\text{-}C_5H_3)_2\}Zr(CH_3)_2$ and generation of a dinitrogen complex by reaction of N_2 with a zirconocene dihydride. *Organometallics* 20:534–44, 2001.

Chirik, P. J., M. W. Day, J. A. Labinger, and J. E. Bercaw. Alkyl rearrangement processes in group IV metallocene chemistry. Identification of internal alkyl complexes during hydrozirconation. *J. Am. Chem. Soc.* 121:10308–17, 1999.

Coates, G. W. Precise control of polyolefin stereochemistry using single-site metal catalysts. *Chem. Rev.* 100:1223, 2000.

Tian, J., and **G. W. Coates.** Development of a diversity-based approach for the discovery of stereoselective polymerization catalysts: Identification of a catalyst for the synthesis of syndiotactic polypropylene. *Angew. Chem. Int. Ed.* 29:3626, 2000.

Crane, B. R., et al. The structure of NO synthase oxygenase dimer with pterin and substrate *Science* 279:2121–5, 1998.

Thompson, A., et al. **(D. B. Collum).** Lithium ephedrate-mediated 1,2-addition of a lithium acetylide to a ketone: Solution structures and relative reactivities of mixed aggregates underlying the high enantioselectivities. *J. Am. Chem. Soc.* 120:2028, 1998.

Remenar, J. F., and **D. B. Collum.** Lithium diisopropylamide-mediated dehydro-bromination: Evidence of competitive monomer- and open dimer-based pathways. *J. Am. Chem. Soc.* 120:4081, 1998.

Strazisar, B., C. Lin, and **H. F. Davis.** Mode specific energy disposal in the 4-atom reaction OH + $D_2 \rightarrow$HOD + D. *Science* 290:958, 2000.

Stauffer, H. U., R. Z. Hinrichs, J. J. Schroden, and **H. F. Davis.** Dynamics of H_2 and C_2H_4 elimination in the Y + C_2H_6 reaction. *J. Phys. Chem.* 104:1107, 2000.

Niewa, R., et al. **(F. J. DiSalvo).** Unusual bonding in ternary nitrides: Preparation, structure and properties of Ce_2MnN_3. *Z. Naturforsh.* 53b:63, 1998.

Gelabert, M. C., et al. **(F. J. DiSalvo).** Structure and properties of $Ba_6Ni_{25}S_{27}$. *Chem.: Eur. J.* 3:1884, 1997.

Campobasso N, Mathews II, T. P. Begley and **S. E. Ealick**. Crystal structure of 4-methyl-5-β-hydroxyethylthiazole kinase from *Bacillus subtilis* at 1.5 Á resolution. *Biochemistry* 39:7868–77, 2000.

Appleby, T. C., C. L. Kinsland, T. P. Begley, and **S. E. Ealick.** The crystal structure and mechanism of orotidine 5'-monophosphate decarboxylase. *Proc. Nat. Acad. Sci. U.S.A.* 97:2005–10, 2000.

Zheng, Y.-J., P. F. Ma, and **J. R. Engstrom.** Etching by atomic hydrogen of Ge overlayers deposited on Si(100). *J. Appl. Phys.* 90:3614, 2001.

Schroeder, T. W., et al. **(J. R. Engstrom).** Selective Si epitaxial growth technique employing atomic hydrogen and substrate temperature modulation. *Appl. Phys. Lett.* 79:2181–3, 2001.

Ezra, G. S. Classical-quantum correspondence and the analysis of highly-excited states: periodic orbits, rational tori and beyond. *Advances in Classical Trajectory Methods,* vol. 3, pp. 35–72, ed. W. L. Hase. Greenwich, Connecticut: JAI Press, 1998.

Ezra, G. S. Classical trajectory studies of intramolecular dynamics: Local mode dynamics, rotation-vibration interaction and the structure of multidimensional phase space. In *Intramolecular Dynamics and Nonlinear Dynamics,* ed. W. L. Hase. Greenwich, Connecticut: JAI Press, 1992.

Fay, R. C. Stereochemistry and molecular rearrangements of some six-, seven-, and eight-coordinate chelates of early transition metals. *Coord. Chem. Rev.* 154:99–124, 1996.

Gau, H.-M., and **R. C. Fay.** NMR studies of inversion and dithiophosphate methyl group exchange in dialkoxybis(O,O'-dimethyl dithiophosphato)titanium(IV) complexes. Evidence for a bond-rupture mechanism. *Inorg. Chem.* 29:4974, 1990.

Freed, J. H., et al. Electron spin resonance in studies of membranes and proteins. *Science,* in press.

Freed, J. H. New technologies in electron spin resonance. *Ann. Rev. Phys. Chem.* Vol. 51, 655–89, 2000.

Huntley, C. F. M., H. B. Wood, and **B. Ganem.** A new synthesis of the glyoxalase I Inhibitor COTC. *Tetrahedron Lett.* 41:2031, 2000.

Zhang, S., D. B. Wilson, **B. Ganem.** Probing the catalytic mechanism of prephenate dehydratase by site-directed mutagenesis of the *Escherichia coli* P-protein dehydratase domain. *Biochemistry* 39:4722–8, 2000.

Vaia, R. H., and **E. P. Giannelis.** Lattice model of polymer melt intercalation in organically-modified layered silicates. *Macromolecules* 30:7990, 1997.

Vaia, R. A., B. B. Sauer, O. K. Tse, and **E. P. Giannelis.** Relaxations of confined chains in polymer nanocomposites: Glass transition properties of poly(ethylene oxide) intercalated in montmorillonite. *J. Poly. Sci. B: Poly. Phys.* 35:59, 1997.

Hess, G. P., et al. Mechanism-based discovery of ligands that prevent inhibition of the nicotinic acetylcholine receptor by cocaine and MK-801. *Proc. Natl. Acad. Sci. U.S.A.* 97:13895, 2000.

Hess, G. P., and C. Grewer. Development and application of caged ligands for neurotransmitter receptors in transient kinetic and neuronal circuit mapping studies. *Methods Enzymol.* 291:443, 1998.

Wind, R. A., and **M. A. Hines.** Macroscopic etch anisotropies and microscopic reaction mechanisms: A micromachined structure for the rapid assay of etchant anisotrophy. *Surf. Sci.* 460:21, 2000.

Huang, Y.-C., J. Flidr, T. A. Newton, and **M. A. Hines.** The effects of dynamic step-step repulsion and autocatalysis on the morphology of etched Si(111) surfaces. *Phys. Rev. Lett.* 80:4462, 1998.

Papoian, G., and **R. Hoffmann.** Hypervalent bonding in one, two, and three dimensions: Extending the Zintl-Klemm concept to nonclassical electron-rich networks. *Angew. Chem.* 39:2408–48, 2000.

Cornell University

Selected Publications (continued)

Konecny, R., and **R. Hoffmann.** Metal fragments and extended arrays on a Si(100)-(2x1) surface: I. Theoretical study of MI_n complexation to Si(100). *J. Am. Chem. Soc.* 121(34) 7918–24, 1999.

Houston, P. L. Snapshots of chemistry: Product imaging of molecular reactions. *Accounts Chem. Res.* 28:453–60, 1995.

Neyer, D. W., X. Luo, I. Burak, and **P. L. Houston.** Photodissociation dynamics of state-selected resonances of HCO X 2A' prepared by stimulated emission pumping. *J. Chem. Phys.* 102:1645–57, 1995.

DiMasi, E., et al. **(S. Lee).** Chemical pressure and charge density waves in rare earth polytellurides. *Phys. Rev. B* 52:404, 1995.

Venkataraman, D., **S. Lee,** J. Zhang, and J. S. Moore. An organic solid with wide channels based on hydrogen bonding between macrocycles. *Nature* 371:591, 1994.

Lee, J. Y., A. R. C. Baljon, D. Y. Sogah, and **R. F. Loring.** Molecular dynamics study of the intercalation of Diblock copolymers into layered silicates. *J. Chem. Phys.* 112:9112, 2000.

Williams, R. B., and **R. F. Loring.** Classical mechanical photon echo of a solvated anharmonic vibration. *J. Chem. Phys.* 113:1932, 2000.

Marohn, J. A., R. Fainchtein, and D. S. Smith. An optimal magnetic tip configuration for magnetic resonance force microscopy of microscale buried features. *Appl. Phys. Lett.* 73(25):3778–80, 1998.

Marohn, J. A., et al. Optical larmor beat detection of high-resolution nuclear magnetic resonance in a semiconductor heterostructure. *Phys. Rev. Lett.* 75:1364–7, 1995.

Horn, D. M., R. A. Zubarev, and **F. W. McLafferty.** Automated *de Novo* sequencing of proteins by tandem high-resolution mass spectrometry. *Proc. Natl. Acad. Sci. U.S.A.* 97:10313–7, 2000.

Horn, D. M., Y. Ge, and **F. W. McLafferty.** Activated ion electron capture dissociation for mass spectral sequencing of larger (42 kDa) proteins. *Anal. Chem.* 72:4778–84, 2000.

Zubarev, R. A., N. L. Kelleher, and **F. W. McLafferty.** Electron capture dissociation of multiply charged protein cations. *J. Am. Chem. Soc.* 120:3265, 1998.

McMurry, J. E. *Organic Chemistry*, 4th ed. Pacific Grove, Calif.: Brooks/Cole, 1996.

McQuade, D. T., A. H. Hegedus, and T. M. Swager. Signal amplification of a turn-on sensor: Harvesting the light captured by a conjugated polymer. *J. Am. Chem. Soc.* 122:12389, 2000.

McQuade, D. T., J. Kim, and T. M. Swager. Two-dimensional conjugated polymer assemblies: Interchain spacing for control of photophysics. *J. Am. Chem. Soc.* 122:5885, 2000.

Eisner, T., et al. **(J. Meinwald).** Firefly "femmes fatales" acquire defensive steroids (Lucibufagins) from their firefly prey. *Proc. Natl. Acad. Sci. U.S.A.* 94:9723, 1997.

Eisner, T., and **J. Meinwald** (eds.). *Chemical Ecology: The Chemistry of Biotic Interaction.* Washington, D.C.: National Academy Press, 1995.

Chandra, S., and **G. H. Morrison.** Imaging ion and molecular transport at subcellular resolution by secondary ion mass spectrometry. *Int. J. Mass Spect. Ion Pro.* 143:161, 1995.

Chandra, S., et al. **(G. H. Morrison).** Imaging of total intracellular calcium and calcium influx and efflux in individual resting and stimulated tumor mast cells using ion microscopy. *J. Biol. Chem.* 269:15186, 1994.

Gaul, C., **J. T. Njarðarson,** and S. J. Danishefsky. The total synthesis of (+)-migrastatin. *J. Am. Chem. Soc.* 125:6042, 2003.

Biswas, K., et al. **(J. T. Njarðarson).** Highly concise routes to epothilones: The total synthesis and evaluation of epothilone 490. *J. Am. Chem. Soc.* 124:9825, 2002.

Xiang, M., et al. **(C. K. Ober).** Surface stability in liquid-crystalline block copolymers with semifluorinated monodendron side groups. *Macromolecules* 33(16):6106–19, 2000.

Muthukumar, M., **C. K. Ober,** and E. L. Thomas. Competing molecular interactions and the formation of ordered structures on different length scales in polymers. *Science* 277:1232–55, 1997.

Lee, J., et al. **(H. A. Scheraga).** Hierarchical energy-based approach to protein-structure prediction: Blind-test evaluation with CASP3 targets. *Intl. J. Quantum Chem.* 71:90, 2000.

Wedemeyer, W. J., et al. **(H. A. Scheraga).** Disulfide bonds and protein folding. *Biochemistry* 39:4207, 2000.

Rathlore, O., M. J. Winningham, and **D. Y. Sogah.** A novel silk-based segmented block copolymer containing GlyAlaGlyAla β-sheets templated by phenoxathiin. *J. Polym. Sci. Part A: Polym. Chem.* 38:352, 2000.

Weimer, M. W., H. Chen, E. P. Giannelis, and **D. Y. Sogah.** Direct synthesis of dispersed nanocomposites by in situ living free radical polymerization using a silicate anchored initiator. *J. Am. Chem. Soc.* 121:1615, 1999.

Tan, D. S., G. B. Dudley, and S. J. Danishefsky. Synthesis of the functionalized tricyclic skeleton of guanacastepene A: A tandem epoxide-opening β-elimination/Knoevenagel cyclization. *Angew. Chem. Int. Ed.* 41:21852188, 2002.

Tan, D. S., et al. Synthesis and preliminary evaluation of a library of polycyclic small molecules for use in chemical genetic assays. *J. Am. Chem. Soc.* 121:9073–87, 1999.

Usher, D. A. Before antisense. *Antisense Nucl. Acid Drug Dev.* 7:445, 1997.

Harris, M., and **D. A. Usher.** A new amide-linked polynucleotide analog. *Origins Life Evol. Biosphere* 26:398, 1996.

Widom, B. What do we know that van der Waals did not know? *Physica A* 263:500, 1999.

Kolomeisky, A. B., and **B. Widom.** Model of the hydrophobic interaction. *Faraday Discuss.* 112:81, 1999.

Wilcox, C. F., and E. N. Farley. Dicyclooctyl[1,2,3,4-def:1'2'3'4'-jkl]-biphenylene: Benzenoid atropism in a highly antiaromatic polycycle. *J. Am. Chem. Soc.* 105:7191, 1983.

Wilcox, C. F. A topological definition of resonance energy. *Croat. Chim. Acta* 47:87, 1975.

Slaughter, L. M., **P. T. Wolczanski,** T. R. Klinckman, and T. R. Cundari. Inter- and intramolecular experimental and calculated equilibrium isotope effects for $(silox)_2({}^tBu_3SiND)TiR$ + RH (silox= ${}^tBu^3Si0$); Inferred kinetic isotope effects for RH/D addition to transient $(silox)_2Ti{=}{}^tBu^3$. *Am. Chem. Soc.* 122:7953–75, 2000.

Tanski, J. M., T. P. Vaid, E. B. Lobhovsky, and **P. T. Wolczanski.** Covalent metal organic networks (CMON): Pyridines induce 2-dimensional oligomerization of $(\mu\text{-}OC_6H_4O)_2Mpy_2$(M=Ti,V,Zr). *Inorg. Chem.* 39:4756–65, 2000.

Liivak, O., and **D. B. Zax.** Multiple simultaneous distance determinations: Applications of rotational echo double resonance NMR to IS_2 spin networks. *J. Chem. Phys.* 113:1088–96, 2000.

Yang, Z., et al. **(D. B. Zax).** Supercontraction and backbone dynamics in spider silk: ^{13}C and ^{2}H NMR studies. *J. Am. Chem. Soc.* 122:9019–25, 2000.

DUQUESNE UNIVERSITY

School of Natural and Environmental Sciences
Department of Chemistry and Biochemistry

Program of Study

The Department of Chemistry and Biochemistry offers a program of graduate study in chemistry and biochemistry leading to the Ph.D. and M.S. degrees.

Graduate students begin laboratory research during their first semester in residence and participate in two semester-long research rotations in the laboratories of two different investigators during their first year. First-year students enroll in several short, intensive courses that emphasize applied research skills. Students typically do not enroll in any other courses during the first year, allowing complete focus upon research during this period. At the end of the first year, students are advanced to Ph.D. candidacy based upon successful completion and defense of their research rotation projects. Academic requirements during the second and subsequent years are determined by the student's dissertation committee and are designed on an individual basis. Candidates for the Ph.D. degree are required to submit and defend an original research proposal in an area unrelated to their dissertation research. The department sponsors a weekly research colloquium series that features speakers from academia, industry, and government.

For the M.S. degree, a minimum of 30 semester hours of combined course and research credits are required.

Research Facilities

The Department of Chemistry and Biochemistry is housed in the Richard King Mellon Hall of Science, an award-winning laboratory designed by Mies van der Rohe. Spectroscopic capability within the department includes multinuclear 500- and 300-MHz NMRs, GC/MS, LC/MS, laser Raman, FT-IR, UV/visible, fluorescence, and atomic absorption spectroscopies. Separations instrumentation includes ultra-high-speed and high-speed centrifuges, gas chromatographs, an ion chromatographic system, capillary electrophoresis, and HPLCs. An electrochemical instrumentation laboratory, a robotics and automation facility, a computer-controlled chemical microwave system, a clean laboratory facility, a single-crystal X-ray diffraction facility, and ICP-MS capabilities are available for research.

Financial Aid

A number of teaching and research assistantships are available for Ph.D students. For 2003–04, annual stipends were $17,500, plus tuition remission. Several prestigious fellowships for graduate studies are offered by the Luce Foundation and Bayer School.

Cost of Study

Tuition and fees in 2004–05 are $711 per credit. Scholarships provide tuition remission for teaching and research assistants as described above.

Living and Housing Costs

Off-campus housing is available within easy walking or commuting distance of the University. Living costs for off-campus housing are very reasonable compared with those in other urban areas of the United States.

Student Group

Duquesne University has a total enrollment of more than 9,500 students in its ten schools. With 176 graduate students and 36 faculty members in the graduate programs in the Bayer School of Natural and Environmental Sciences, the University offers students a highly personalized learning and advisement environment.

Location

Duquesne University is located on a bluff overlooking the city of Pittsburgh. This location offers ready access to the many cultural, social, and entertainment attractions of the city. Within walking distance of the campus are Heinz Hall for the Performing Arts (home of the symphony, opera, ballet, theater, and other musical and cultural institutions), the Mellon Arena (center for indoor sporting events and various exhibitions, concerts, and conventions), Heinz Field and PNC Park (for outdoor sporting events), and Market Square (entertainment and nightlife center). The libraries, museums, art galleries, and music hall of the Carnegie Institute in the Oakland area are easily accessible by public transportation (routes pass immediately adjacent to the campus) or by private automobile. As the third-largest center for corporate headquarters and one of the twenty largest metropolitan areas in the United States, Pittsburgh also offers many professional career opportunities for its residents.

The University

Founded in 1878 by the Fathers and Brothers of the Congregation of the Holy Ghost, Duquesne University has provided the opportunity for an education to students from many backgrounds, without regard to sex, race, creed, color, or national or ethnic origins. In the past twenty-five years, the University has undergone a dramatic physical transformation, from a makeshift physical plant occupying approximately 12 acres to a modern, highly functional educational facility that is located on its own 40-acre hilltop overlooking downtown Pittsburgh.

Applying

Applications for admission to graduate study with financial aid should be submitted no later than February 1 for the academic year beginning in the following September. Applications for admission without financial aid may be made up to one month prior to the beginning of the term in which the student desires to begin graduate work. All applications require official transcripts of previous undergraduate and graduate work and three letters of recommendation from faculty members who are familiar with the applicant's past academic progress. Application forms are available by writing to or calling the office of the Department of Chemistry and Biochemistry.

Correspondence and Information

Graduate Programs
Bayer School of Natural and Environmental Sciences
100 Mellon Hall
Duquesne University
Pittsburgh, Pennsylvania 15282
Telephone: 412-396-4900
Fax: 412-396-4881
E-mail: gradinfo@duq.edu
World Wide Web: http://www.science.duq.edu

Duquesne University

THE FACULTY

Jennifer Aitken, Associate Professor; Ph.D., Michigan State. Solid-state inorganic materials chemistry: elucidation of new crystal structures, synthesis and study of novel solid-state materials with potential use in optical and electronic technologies, crystal growth.
Partha Basu, Assistant Professor; Ph.D., Jadavpur (India), 1991. Inorganic chemistry: synthesis, structure, reactivity, and magnetic interactions of biological and model molecules.
Bruce D. Beaver, Associate Professor; Ph.D., Massachusetts, 1984. Organic chemistry: oxygenation of organic molecules, development of new antioxidants, oxidative degradation of petroleum products, chemistry of wine making.
Charles Dameron, Associate Professor; Ph.D., Texas A&M, 1987. Biochemistry: metals in biology, understanding how metals are chaperoned by proteins and exchanged between proteins.
Jeffrey D. Evanseck, Associate Professor; Ph.D., UCLA, 1990. Theoretical and computational chemistry: quantum and classical simulations coupled with experiment, energy landscapes of biomolecules, novel ionic liquids for catalysis, influence of solvent on organic reaction mechanism, supramolecular complexation for nanotechnology.
Fraser F. Fleming, Associate Professor; Ph.D., British Columbia, 1990. Organic chemistry: application of the chemistry of α,β-unsaturated nitriles to the synthesis of anti-AIDS and anticancer drugs; synthesis of natural products.
Ellen Gawalt, Associate Professor; Ph.D., Princeton. Bioorganic and materials chemistry: chemical modification of metal oxide surfaces used in biomaterials and reaction mechanisms of interfacial reactions.
Mitchell E. Johnson, Assistant Professor; Ph.D., Massachusetts Amherst, 1993. Analytical chemistry: trace analysis of molecular species, fluorescence spectroscopy, high-speed separations, biochemical analysis.
Shahed Khan, Associate Professor; Ph.D., Flinders (Australia), 1977. Physical chemistry: electrochemistry, photoelectrochemistry, solar energy conversion by thin-film organic and inorganic semiconductors, electrocatalytic biosensors, electrosynthesis of conducting polymers, electrochemical surface modification, theory of electron transfer reactions in condensed medium, effect of solvent dynamics on electrochemical electron transfer reactions.
H. M. Kingston, Professor; Ph.D., American, 1978. Analytical and environmental chemistry: microwave chemistry application, environmental methods and instrument development, speciated analysis, ICP-MS clean-room chemistry, chromatography, laboratory automation.
Jeffry D. Madura, Associate Professor and Chair; Ph.D., Purdue, 1985. Theoretical physical chemistry: computational chemistry and biophysics, classical simulations of biomolecules, Poisson-Boltzmann electrostatics coupled to molecular dynamics, simulation of proteins at ice/water interface, simulation of biomolecular diffusion-controlled rate constants, quantum mechanical calculation of small molecules.
David W. Seybert, Professor and Interim Dean; Ph.D., Cornell, 1976. Biochemistry: lipid peroxidation in biomembranes and lipoproteins, antioxidants and inhibition of LDL oxidation, mechanism and regulation of cytochrome P450 catalyzed steroid hydroxylations.
Omar W. Steward, Professor; Ph.D., Penn State, 1957. Inorganic chemistry: synthesis and structural studies of carboxylato metal complexes by X-ray diffraction; magneto-structural studies of transition metal complexes with organosilicon ligands; organosilicon and organogermanium compounds; structure-reactivity studies.
Julian Talbot, Associate Professor; Ph.D., Southampton (England), 1985. Theoretical physical chemistry: statistical mechanics, Monte Carlo and molecular dynamic simulation of classical systems, theory of adsorption kinetics and equilibria, biomolecules at interfaces, gases in porous solids.
Theodore J. Weismann, Adjunct Professor; Ph.D., Duquesne, 1956. Physical chemistry: mass spectrometry, ion optics, free radical reactions, organoboron chemistry, geochemistry, stable isotope MS, petroleum source and characterization.

Richard King Mellon Hall of Science, which houses the Department of Chemistry and Biochemistry.

Research laboratory in Mellon Hall.

A student at work at Duquesne University.

SELECTED PUBLICATIONS

Jayasekera, B., **J. A. Aitken,** M. J. Heeg, and S. L. Brock. Towards an arsenic analog of Hittorf's phosphorus: Mixed pnictogen chains in $Cu_2P_{1.8}As_{1.2}I_2$. *Inorg. Chem.* 42:658–60, 2002.

Aitken, J. A., M. Evain, L. Iordanidis, and M. G. Kanatzidis. $NaCeP_2Se_6$, $Cu_{0.4}Ce_{1.2}P_2Se_6$, $Ce_{1.33}P_2Se_6$ and the incommensurately modulated, $AgCeP_2Se_6$: New selenophosphates featuring the ethane-like $[P_2Se_6]^{4-}$ anion. *Inorg. Chem.* 41:180–91, 2002.

Aitken, J. A., P. Larson, S. D. Mahanti, and M. G. Kanatzidis. Li_2PbGeS_4 and Li_2EuGeS_4: Polar chalcopyrites with a severe tetragonal compression. *Chem. Mater.* 13:4714–21, 2001.

Aitken, J. A., and M. G. Kanatzidis. New information on the Na-Ti-Se ternary system. *Z. Naturforsch. B* 56:49–56, 2001.

Aitken, J. A., and M. G. Kanatzidis. α-$Na_6Pb_3(PS_4)_4$, a noncentrosymmetric thiophosphate with the novel saucer-shaped $[Pb_3(PS_4)_4]^{6-}$ cluster, and its metastable, 3-dimensionally polymerized allotrope β-$Na_6Pb_3(PS_4)_4$. *Inorg. Chem.* 40:2938–9, 2001.

Aitken, J. A., C. Canlas, D. P. Weliky, and M. G. Kanatzidis. $[P_2S_{10}]^{4-}$: A novel polythiophosphate anion containing a tetrasulfide fragment. *Inorg. Chem.* 40:6496–8, 2001.

Basu, P., V. N. Nemykin, and R. Sengar. Synthesis, spectroscopy, and redox chemistry of encapsulated oxo-Mo^V centers: Implications for pyranopterin-containing molybdoenzymes. *Inorg. Chem.,* in press.

Basu, P. Geometric perturbation of electronic structure of discrete molybdenum^V cores and the reduction potential. *CHEMTRACTS: Inorg. Chem.,* in press.

Basu, P., and J. F. Stolz. *Functional Genomics Series,* vol. 3, *Frontiers in Computation Genomics,* eds. M. Y. Galperin and E. V. Koonin. *ChemBioChem,* in press (book review).

Basu, P., et al. Donor atom dependent geometric isomers in mononuclear oxo-molybdenum^V complexes: Implications for coordinated endogenous ligation in molybdoenzymes. *Inorg. Chem.* 42:5999–6007, 2003.

Afkar, E., and **P. Basu** et al. The respiratory arsenate reductase from a haloalkaliphilic bacterium *Bacillus selenitireducens* strain MLS10. *FEMS Microbiol. Lett.* 226:107–12, 2003.

Basu, P., V. N. Nemykin, and R. S. Sengar. Electronic properties of para-substituted thiophenols and disulfides from ^{13}C NMR spectroscopy and ab initio calculations: Relations to the Hammett parameters and atomic charges. *New J. Chem.* 27:1115–23, 2003.

Basu, P., and V. N. Nemykin. Comparative theoretical investigation of the vertical excitation energies and the electronic structure of $[Mo^VOCl_4]^-$: Influence of basis set and geometry. *Inorg. Chem.* 42:4046–56, 2003.

Basu, P., J. F. Stolz, and M. T. Smith. A coordination chemist's view of the active sites of mononuclear molybdenum enzymes. *Curr. Sci.* 84:1412–18, 2003.

Beaver, B., et al. Development of oxygen scavenger additives for future jet fuels. A role for electron-transfer-initiated oxygenation (ETIO) of 1,2,5-trimethylpyrrole? *Energy Fuels* 14:441–7, 2000.

Beaver, B. Motivating students in sophomore organic chemistry by examining Nature's way: Why are vitamins E and C such good antioxidants? *J. Chem. Educ.* 76(8):1108–12, 1999.

Beaver, B., et al. Structural effects on the reactivity of substituted arylphosphines as potential oxygen-scavenging additives for future jet fuels. *Heteroatom Chem.* 9(2):133–8, 1998.

Beaver, B., et al. Model studies directed at the development of new thermal oxidative stability enhancing additives for future jet fuels. *Energy Fuels* 11:396–401, 1997.

Cobine, P., C. E. Jones, and **C. T. Dameron.** Role of zinc(II) in the copper regulated protein CopY. *J. Inorg. Biochem.* 88:192–6, 2002.

Harrison, M. D., C. E. Jones, M. Solioz, and **C. T. Dameron.** Intracellular copper routing: The role of copper chaperones. *Trends Biol. Sci.* 25:29–32, 2000.

Cobine, P., et al. **(C. T. Dameron).** Stoichiometry of the complex formation between copper(I) and the N-terminal domain of the Menkes protein. *Biochemistry* 39:6857–63, 2000.

Harrison, M. D., S. Meier, and **C. T. Dameron.** Characterisation of copper-binding to the second subdomain of the Menkes protein (MNKr2). *Biochim. Biophys. Acta* 1453:254–60, 1999.

Harrison, M. D., and **C. T. Dameron.** Molecular mechanisms of copper metabolism and the role of the Menkes disease protein. *J. Biochem. Mol. Toxicol.* 13:93–106, 1999.

Harrison, M. D., C. E. Jones, and **C. T. Dameron.** Copper chaperones: Function, structure and copper-binding properties. *J. Biol. Inorg. Chem.* 4:145–53, 1999.

Cobine, P., et al. **(C. T. Dameron).** The *Enterococcus hirae* copper chaperone CopZ delivers copper(I) to the CopY repressor. *FEBS Lett.* 445:27–30, 1999.

Pickering, I. J., et al. **(C. T. Dameron).** X-ray absorption spectroscopy of cadmium phytochelatin and model systems. *Biochim. Biophys. Acta* 1429:351–64, 1999.

DeChancie, J., A. Acevedo, and **J. D. Evanseck.** Density functional theory determination of an axial gateway to explain the rate and *endo* selectivity enhancement of Diels-Alder reactions by Bis(oxazoline)-Cu(II). *J. Am. Chem. Soc.,* in press.

Kovacs, J. R., et al. **(J. D. Evanseck).** Fenretinide enhances in vitro differentiation of murine bone marrow progenitors into antigen presenting cells. *Immun. Lett.,* in press.

Loccisano, A. E., et al. **(J. D. Evanseck).** Enhanced sampling by multiple molecular dynamics trajectories: Carbonmonoxy myoglobin 10 micros $A0 \rightarrow A_{1-3}$ transition from ten 400 picosecond simulations. *J. Mol. Graphics Modeling,* in press.

Acevedo, O., and **J. D. Evanseck.** Transition structure models of organic reactions in ionic liquids. In *Ionic Liquids as Green Solvents,* pp. 174–90, eds. R. D. Rogers and K. R. Seddon. ACS Symposium Series (Ionic Liquids), 2003.

Acevedo, O., and **J. D. Evanseck.** The effect of solvent on a Lewis acid catalyzed Diels-Alder reaction using computed an experimental kinetic isotope effects. *Org. Lett.* 649, 2003.

Macias, A. T., J. E. Norton, and **J. D. Evanseck.** Impact of multiple cation-π interactions upon calix[4]arene substrate binding and specificity. *J. Am. Chem. Soc.* 123:2351, 2003.

Fleming, F. F., and B. C. Shook. 1-Oxo-2-cyclohexenyl-2-carbonitrile. *Org. Syn.* 77:254–60, 2001.

Fleming, F. F., Q. Wang, O. W. Steward. Hydroxylated α,β-unsaturated nitriles: Stereoselective synthesis. *J. Org. Chem.* 66:2171–4, 2001.

Fleming, F. F., and P. Iyer. Flood prevention by recirculating condenser cooling water. *J. Chem. Educ.* 78:946, 2001.

Fleming, F. F., and B. C. Shook. α,β-unsaturated nitriles: Preparative MgO elimination. *Tetrahedron Lett.* 41:8847–51, 2000.

Fleming, F. F., Q. Wang, and O. W. Steward. γ-hydroxy unsaturated nitriles: Chelation-controlled conjugate additions. *Org. Lett.* 2:1477–9, 2000.

Fleming, F. F., B. C. Shook, T. Jiang, and O. W. Steward. β-siloxy unsaturated nitriles: Stereoselective cyclizations to *Cis-* and *trans*-decalins. *Org. Lett.* 1:1547–50, 1999.

Fleming, F. F., J. Guo, Q. Wang, and D. Weaver. Unsaturated oxo-nitrile: Stereoselective, chelation-controlled conjugate additions. *J. Org. Chem.* 64:8568–75, 1999.

Fleming, F. F. Nitrile-containing natural products. *Nat. Prod. Rep.* 16:597–606, 1999.

Fleming, F. F., A. Huang, V. Sharief, and Y. Pu. Unsaturated nitriles: Precursors for a domino ozonolysis-aldol synthesis of oxonitriles. *J. Org. Chem.* 64:2830–4, 1999.

Fleming, F. F., and T. Jiang. Unsaturated nitriles: Optimized coupling of the chloroprene Grignard reagent with ω-bromonitriles. *J. Org. Chem.* 62:7890–1, 1997.

Fleming, F. F., Y. Pu, and F. Tercek. Unsaturated nitriles: Conjugate addition-silylation with Grignard reagents. *J. Org. Chem.* 62:4883–5, 1997.

Fleming, F. F., A. Huang, Y. Pu, and V. A. Sharief. α,β-unsaturated nitriles: A domino ozonolysis-aldol synthesis of highly reactive oxonitriles. *J. Org. Chem.* 62:3036–7, 1997.

Fleming, F. F., Z. Hussain, R. E. Norman, and D. Weaver. α,β-unsaturated nitriles: Stereoselective conjugate addition reactions. *J. Org. Chem.* 62:1305–9, 1997.

Gawalt, E. S., et al. Bonding organics to Ti alloys: Facilitating human osteoblast attachment and spreading on surgical implant materials. *Langmuir* 19:200–4, 2003.

Houseman, B. T., **E. S. Gawalt,** and M. Mrksich. Maleimide-functionalized self-assembled monolayers for the preparation of peptide and carbohydrate biochips. *Langmuir* 19:1522–31, 2003.

Schwartz, J., et al. **(E. S. Gawalt).** Cell attachment and spreading on metal implant materials. *Mater. Sci. Eng., C* 23:395–400, 2003,

Gawalt, E. S., et al. Enhanced bonding of organometallics to titanium via a titanium (III) phosphate interface. *Langmuir* 17:6743–5, 2001.

Gawalt, E. S., M. J. Avaltroni, N. Koch, and J. Schwartz. Self-assembly and bonding of alkanephosphonic acids on the native oxide surface of titanium. *Langmuir* 17:5736–8, 2001.

Gawalt, E. S., G. Lu, S. L. Bernasek, and J. Schwartz. Enhanced bonding of alkanephosphonic acids to oxidized titanium using surface-bound alkoxyzirconium complex interfaces. *Langmuir* 15:8929–33, 1999.

Schwartz, J., and **E. S. Gawalt** et al. Organometallic chemistry at the interface with material science. *Polyhedron* 19:505–7, 1999.

VanderKam, S. K., **E. S. Gawalt,** J. Schwartz, and A. B. Bocarsly. Electrochemically active surface zirconium complexes on indium tin oxide. *Langmuir* 15:6598–600, 1999.

Gallaher, D. L., and **M. E. Johnson.** Nonaqueous capillary electrophoresis of fatty acids derivatized with a near-infrared fluorophore. *Anal. Chem.* 72:2080–6, 2000.

Gee, A. J., L. Groen, and **M. E. Johnson.** Ion trap mass spectrometry of trimethylsilylamides following gas chromatography. *J. Mass Spectrom.* 35:305–10, 2000.

Johnson, M. E. Rapid, simple quantitation in thin-layer chromatography using a flatbed scanner. *J. Chem. Educ.* 77:368–72, 2000.

Gallaher, D. L., and **M. E. Johnson.** Development of near-infrared fluorogenic labels for the determination of fatty acids separated by capillary electrophoresis with diode laser-induced fluorescence detection. *Analyst* 124:1541–7, 1999.

Gee, A. J., L. Groen, and **M. E. Johnson.** Determination of fatty acid amides as trimethylsilyl derivatives by gas chromatography with mass spectrometric detection. *J. Chromatogr. A* 849:541–52, 1999.

Feng, L., and **M. E. Johnson.** Selective fluorescence derivatization and capillary electrophoretic separation of amidated amino acids. *J. Chromatogr. A* 832:211–24, 1999.

Johnson, M. E. Fluorescence spectroscopy for environmental analysis.

Duquesne University

Selected Publications (continued)

In *Encyclopedia of Environmental Analysis and Remediation,* pp. 1757–86, ed. R. A. Meyers. New York: Wiley and Sons, 1998.

Akikusa, J., and **S. U. M. Khan.** Photoelectrolysis of water to hydrogen in p-sic/pt and p-sic/n-TiO_2 cells. *Int. J. Hydrogen Energy,* in press.

Shah, J. M., and **S. U. M. Khan.** Detection of glucose by electroreduction at a semiconductor electrode: An implantable non-enzymatic glucose sensor. In *Chemical and Biological Sensors and Analytical Methods II,* vol. 2001–18, pp. 259–71, eds. M. Butler, P. Vanysek, and Y. Yamazoe. Pennington: Electrochem. Soc., 2001.

Sultana, T., and **S. U. M. Khan.** Photoelectrichemical splitting of water on nanocrystalline n-TiO_2 thin film and quantum wire electrodes. In *Quantum Confinement VI: Nanostructured Materials and Devices,* vol. 2001–19, pp. 9–19, eds. M. Cahay et al. Pennington: Electrochemical Society, 2001.

Khan, S. U. M., and J. Akikusa. Photoelectrochemical splitting of water alnanocrystalline n-Fe_2O_3 thin-film electrodes. *J. Phys. Chem.* 103:7186–9, 1999.

Khan, S. U. M., J. C. Worthington, and M. Al-Shehry. Nanocrystalline n-TiO_2 thin films for efficient photoelectrochemical splitting of water. *Electrochemical Society Proceedings on Advanced Luminescent Materials and Quantum Confinement* 99(22):252–60, eds. M. Chuah, S. Bandyopadhyay, et al. Pennington, 1999.

Khan, S. U. M., and J. Akikusa. Stability and photoresponse of nanocrystalline n-TiO_2 and n-TiO_2/Mn_2O_3 thin film electrodes during water-spitting reactions. *J. Electrochem. Soc.* 145:89, 1998.

Khan, S. U. M. Electron transfer reaction in condensed media at electrodes. *Trends Chem. Phys.* 5:45, 1997.

Khan, S. U. M. Quantum mechanical treatments in electrode kinetics. In *Modern Aspects of Electrochemistry,* vol. 31, eds. J. O'M Bockris, B. E. Conway, and R. E. White. New York: Plenum, 1997.

Akikusa, J., and **S. U. M. Khan.** Stability of nanocrystalline n-TiO_2 and n-TiO_2/Mn_2O_3 films during photelectrolysis of water. In the *Chemical Society Proceedings on Quantum Confinement IV: Nanoscale Materials, Devices and Systems.,* vol. 97-11, pp. 65–78, eds. M. Cahay, J. P. Leburton, D. J. Lockwood, and S. Bandypadhyay. Pennington, 1997.

Khan, S. U. M. Quantum aspects of electrochemistry. *R. Soc. Chem. C,* 1996.

Khan, S. U. M., and S. Zhang. Photoresponse of electrochemically and spray pyrolytically deposited CdTe thin film electrodes. *J. Electrochem. Soc.* 142:2539–44, 1995.

Akikusa, J., and **S. U. M. Khan.** Photoresponse and stability of pyrolytically prepared n-TiO2 semiconductor films. In *Nanostructured Materials in Electrochemistry,* ed. P. C. Pearson and G. J. Mayer. Pennington, N.J.: Electrochemistry Society, 1995.

Boylan, H. M., R. D. Cain, and **H. M. Kingston.** A new method to assess mercury emissions: A study of three coal-fired electric generating power stations. *Air Waste Manage. Assoc.* 53:1318–25, 2003.

Bhandari, S., **H. M. Kingston,** and G. M. M. Rahman. Synthesis and characterization of isotopically enriched methylmercury ($CH_3{}^{201}Hg^+$). *Appl. Organometal. Chem.* 17:913–20, 2003.

Gazmuri, R. J., et al. **(H. M. Kingston).** Myocardial protection during ventricular fibrillation by interventions that limit proton-driven sarcolemmal sodium influx, American Heart Association. *J. Lab. Clin. Med.* 137(1):43–55, 2001.

Han, Y., **H. M. Kingston,** R. C. Richter, and C. Pirola. Dual-vessel integrated microwave sample decomposition and digest evaporation for trace element analysis of silicon material by ICP-MS: Design and application. *Anal. Chem.* 73(6):1106–11, 2001.

Richter, R. C., L. Dirk, and **H. M. Kingston.** Microwave enhanced chemistry: Standardizing sample preparation. *Anal. Chem.* 73(1):30A–7A, 2001.

Huo, D., and **H. M. Kingston.** Correction of species transformations in the analysis of Cr(VI) in solid environmental samples using speciated isotope dilution mass spectrometry. *Anal. Chem.* 72(20)5047–54, 2000.

Boylan, H. M., T. A. Ronning, R. L. DeGroot, and **H. M. Kingston.** Field analysis using Method 7473: Minimizing the cost of mercury cleanup. *Environ. Test. Anal.,* 2000.

Link, D. D., and **H. M. Kingston.** Use of microwave-assisted evaporation for the complete recovery of volatile species of inorganic trace analytes. *Anal. Chem.* 72(13):2908–13, 2000.

Richter, R. C., D. D. Link, and **H. M. Kingston.** On demand production of high-purity acids in the analytical laboratory. *Spectroscopy,* 2000.

Kingston, H. M. Method and apparatus for microwave-assisted chemical reactions. U.S. Patent Number 5,883,349, May 1999.

Link, D. D., P. J. Walter, and **H. M. Kingston.** Wastewater standards and extraction chemistry in validation of microwave-assisted EPA Method 3015A. *Environ. Sci. Testing* 33(14), 1999.

Kingston, H. M., D. Huo, and Y. Lu. Accuracy in species analysis: Speciated isotope dilution mass spectrometry (SIDMS) exemplified by the evaluation of chromium species. *Spectrochem. Acta Part B* 53:299–309, 1998.

Huo, D., **H. M. Kingston,** and Y. Lu. Determination and correction of analytical biases and study on chemical mechanisms in the analysis of Cr (VI) in soil samples using EPA protocols. *Environ. Sci. Technol.* 32:3418–23, 1998.

Kingston, H. M., D. D. Link, and P. J. Walter. Development and validation of the new EPA microwave-assisted leach method 3051A. *Environ. Sci. Technol.* 32:3628–32, 1998.

Kingston, H. M., and P. J. Walter. The art and science of microwave sample preparation for trace and ultra-trace elemental analysis. In *Inductively Coupled Plasma Mass Spectrometry: From A to Z,* ed. A. Montaser. New York: Wiley-VCH, 1998.

Chalk, S., **H. M. Kingston,** E. Lorentzen, and P. J. Walter. A review of overview of microwave-assisted sample preparation. In *Microwave Enhanced Chemistry: Fundamentals, Sample Preparation, and Applications.* ACS Professional Reference Book Series, Chap. 2. Washington, D.C.: American Chemical Society, 1997.

Chalk, S., and **H. M. Kingston** et al. Environmental microwave sample preparation: Fundamentals, methods and applications. In *Microwave Enhanced Chemistry: Fundamentals, Sample Preparation, and Applications.* ACS Professional Reference Book Series, Chap. 3. Washington, D.C.: American Chemical Society, 1997.

Spreitzer, G., J. M. Whitling, **J. D. Madura,** and D. Wright. A spatially addressable combinatorial library for the design and synthesis of cysteine containing peptides for the encapsulation of CdS nanoclusters: Analysis of the library diagonal. *Chem. Commun.* 209–210, 2000.

Madura, J. D., K. Baran, and A. Wierzbicki. Molecular recognition and binding of thermal hysteresis proteins to ice. *J. Mol. Recognit.* 13:101–13, 2000.

Espositio, E. X., K. J. Kelly, K. Baran, and **J. D. Madura.** Docking sulfonamides to metalloenzymes. *Mol. Simul.* 24:293–304, 2000.

Espositio, E. X., K. J. Kelly, K. Baran, and **J. D. Madura.** Docking of sulfonamides to carbonic anhydrase II and IV. *J. Mol. Modeling Graphics* 18:283–9, 2000.

Wierzbicki, A., and **J. D. Madura.** Antifreeze proteins: Computational models. In *Computational Molecular Biology,* ed. J. Lesczynski. Elsevier, 1999.

Madura, J. D. Using MOE to visualize molecular orbitals. *J. Mol. Graphics Modeling,* 1999.

Briggs, J. M., R. R. Gabdoulline, **J. D. Madura,** and R. C. Wade. Brownian dynamics. In *Encyclopedia of Computational Chemistry,* vol. 2, pp. 141–54, eds. P. V. R. Schleyer et al. Chichester, UK: John Wiley & Sons, 1998.

Madura, J. D., et al. Physical and structural properties of taurine and taurine analogues. *Amino Acids* 13:131–9, 1997.

Aronson, N. N., C. J. Blanchard, and **J. D. Madura.** Homology modeling of glycosyl hydrolase family 18 enzymes and proteins. *J. Chem. Inf. Comput. Sci.* 37:999–1005, 1997.

Wierzbicki, A., **J. D. Madura,** C. Salmon, and F. Sönnichsen. Modeling studies of sea raven type II antifreeze protein to ice. *J. Chem. Inf. Comput. Sci.* 37:1006–10, 1997.

Madura, J. D., et al. The dynamics and binding of a type III antifreeze protein in water and on ice. *THEOCHEM* 388:65–77,1996.

Owens, J. W., M. B. Perry, and **D. W. Seybert.** Reactions of nitric oxide with cobaltous tetraphenylporphyrin and phthalocyanines. *Inorg. Chim. Acta* 277:1–7, 1998.

Hanlon, M. C., and **D. W. Seybert.** The pH dependence of lipid peroxidation using water-soluble azo initiators. *Free Radical Biol. Med.* 23:712–9, 1997.

Warburton, R. J., and **D. W. Seybert.** Structural and functional characterization of bovine adrenodoxin reductase by limited proteolysis. *Biochim. Biophys. Acta* 1246:39–46, 1995.

Yaukey, T. S., **O. W. Steward,** and S.-C. Chang. Manganese(II) triphenylacetate hydratrate: A manganese(II) complex with a chain structure. *Acta Crystallogr.* C54:1081–3, 1998.

Muto, Y., et al. **(O. W. Steward).** Characterization of dimeric copper(II) trichoroacetate complexes by electron spin resonance, infrared, and electronic reflectance spectra: Correlation of spectral parameters with molecular geometry. *Bull. Chem. Soc. Jpn.* 70:1573, 1997.

Steward, O. W., et al. Structural and magnetic studies of dimeric copper(II) 2,2-diphenylpropanoato and triphenylacetato complexes with oxygen donor ligands: The cage geometry of dimeric α-phenyl substituted copper(II) carboxylates. *Bull. Chem. Soc. Jpn.* 69:34123–7, 1996.

Viot, P., P. R. Tassel, and **J. Talbot.** Nearest-neighbor functions in a one-dimensional generalized ballistic deposition model. *Phys. Rev. E,* in press.

Talbot, J. Analysis of adsorption selectively in a one-dimensional model system. *AIChE J.* 43:2471–8, 1997.

Van Tassel, P. R., **J. Talbot,** G. Tarjus, and P. Viot. A distribution function analysis of the structure of depleted particle configurations. *Phys. Rev. E* 56:1299R, 1997.

Choi, H. S., and **J. Talbot.** Effect of diffusion and convection on the flux of depositing particles near preadsorbed particle. *Korean J. Chem. Eng.* 14:117–24, 1997.

Talbot, J. Molecular thermodynamics of binary mixture adsorption. *J. Chem. Phys.* 196:4696–706, 1997.

Van Tassel, P., **J. Talbot,** G. Tarjus, and P. Viot. The kinetics of irreversible adsorption with particle conformational change. *Phys. Rev. E* 53:785, 1996.

Talbot, J. Time-dependent desorption: A memory function approach. *Adsorption* 2:89, 1996.

FLORIDA INTERNATIONAL UNIVERSITY

Department of Chemistry Graduate Programs

Programs of Study

At the graduate level, the Department of Chemistry offers Master of Science (M.S.) and Doctor of Philosophy (Ph.D.) degrees in chemistry and an interdisciplinary Master of Science in Forensic Science program.

The M.S. in chemistry is a research-intensive degree program that provides flexibility for students with varied interests. The program is designed to significantly advance students' knowledge and skills in the chemical sciences, building from the undergraduate experience and training. The course work requires students to complete a number of traditional courses in analytical, biochemical, inorganic, organic, and/or physical chemistry but includes flexibility to allow students the opportunity to take courses in more specialized topics, such as environmental and forensic chemistry. Students are required to write and defend a thesis. Graduates are well prepared for technical jobs in the chemical industry, teaching, doctoral programs, and professional schools. The degree requires a minimum of 32 credits of course work, at least 9 of which must be in chemistry in at least two of the five major areas of chemistry (analytical, biochemical, inorganic, organic, and physical). Both part-time and full-time study are offered.

The Master of Science in Forensic Science is an interdisciplinary program designed to prepare students for careers in forensic science laboratories. The program is also suitable preparation for doctoral instruction in several disciplines. This is primarily a research program that emphasizes critical thinking through research, presentation, and publication on a student's original problem. The Master of Science in Forensic Science program consists of a minimum of 32 credits, including a thesis based upon the student's original research.

The Ph.D. program is research-intensive and emphasizes critical thinking and original problem solving. While the department's strength is the interdisciplinary nature of faculty members' research, particularly in the areas of environmental and biomedicinal chemistry, research projects in traditional areas of chemistry are also available to the students. The student typically chooses a series of courses focused in one of chemistry subdisciplines. Students are encouraged to take classes relevant to their specific interests and research projects. In addition, students can take courses in disciplines outside their subdisciplines as well as special topics courses. Students are required to pass a series of cumulative exams, write and defend an original proposal, and complete their dissertation. A minimum of 90 credits of course work are required, at least 9 of which must be in at least two of the five major areas of chemistry.

Research Facilities

Research is conducted in the Chemistry and Physics Building. Research facilities include high-field 400-MHz and 600-MHz NMRs, LC/UV/MS, ICP/MS, Pyrolysis/GC/MS, several DEC alpha workstations, Headspace-GC, Headspace-GC/MS, FT-IR, GC/MS, SPME/GC/MS/MS, capillary electrophoresis, supercritical fluid extractors, calorimeters, UV-visible and Raman spectrophotometers, and other specialized instrumentation in individual research groups. The University library maintains an extensive collection of scientific journals, books, monographs, and reference literature and provides rapid automated search capabilities through several retrieval networks, including online searching.

Students in the Department of Chemistry also benefit from several institutes and centers housed at Florida International University (FIU). The Southeast Environmental Research Center (SERC) performs environmentally related research primarily in the southeastern United States and the Caribbean region. The International Forensic Science Institute (IFRI), affiliated with the chemistry department, performs research in the forensic sciences. The Advanced Mass Spectrometry Facility (AMSF), administered by the department, houses state-of-the-art mass spectrometric instrumentation that is used by the department's faculty. The Center for the Study of Matter at Extreme Conditions (CeSMEC) also offers opportunities for research in chemistry. In addition, collaborative research is performed between chemistry faculty members and faculty members in other departments.

Financial Aid

Full-time graduate students who are in good academic standing are eligible for financial support. Teaching and research assistantships are available on a competitive basis. Students may also apply for a waiver of tuition.

Cost of Study

For Florida residents, tuition is $201.51 per credit hour. It is $770.78 for nonresidents.

Living and Housing Costs

Student housing is available in on-campus dormitories and apartments. There is ample off-campus housing available, as well.

Student Group

There are approximately 40 students enrolled in the graduate program in chemistry and 30 in the forensic science master's program. A wide range of academic, ethnic, and national backgrounds are represented.

Location

The main campus, University Park, is located on 342 acres in suburban Miami-Dade County, approximately 10 miles west of downtown Miami. The city of Miami, with its subtropical climate, cultural diversity, and strategic location, provides students with all of the advantages of attending a university in a major urban environment. The greater Miami area is home to a number of nationally recognized cultural and tourist attractions, beautiful beaches, the Florida Everglades, an active night life, and four major professional sports teams.

The University and The Department

Florida International University, a member of the State University System of Florida, was established by the state legislature on June 22, 1965. Classes were first offered on September 19, 1972. The University offers more than 300 degree programs at the undergraduate and graduate levels and has an enrollment of more than 34,000 students.

The Department of Chemistry has 22 faculty members. The department affords access to state-of-the-art instrumentation, its faculty receives outside funding that includes support for graduate and undergraduate research assistants, and the students regularly contribute to research publications in top scientific journals.

Applying

For the M.S. and Ph.D. programs in chemistry, a minimum undergraduate grade point average of 3.0 in chemistry and cognate science and a GRE score of at least 1000 are required except by special permission of the graduate committee. Students whose native language is not English must score 550 or higher (paper-based test) or 213 or higher (computer-based test) on the Test of English as a Foreign Language (TOEFL). Students whose undergraduate degree is not equivalent to the American Chemical Society certified Bachelor of Science degree in chemistry shall make up any deficiencies prior to taking graduate courses in the areas where such deficiencies exist.

To be admitted into the master's degree program in forensic science, a student must hold a bachelor's degree in a relevant discipline from an accredited college or university, have earned a GPA of at least 3.0 during the last two years of the undergraduate program and a minimum combined score of 1000 on the GRE, submit two letters of recommendation describing the student's academic potential, be accepted by a faculty sponsor, and receive approval from the Departmental Graduate Committee.

Correspondence and Information

Chemistry Programs:
Dr. Kevin O'Shea
Graduate Program Director
Department of Chemistry
Florida International University
Miami, Florida 33199
Telephone: 305-348-3968
Fax: 305-348-3772
World Wide Web: http://www.fiu.edu/orgs/chemistry

Forensic Science Program:
Dr. José Almirall
Program Director
Department of Chemistry
Florida International University
Miami, Florida 33199
Telephone: 305-348-3917
Fax: 305-348-3772
World Wide Web: http://www.fiu.edu/orgs/chemistry

Florida International University

THE FACULTY AND THEIR RESEARCH

José R. Almirall, Professor and Director, Forensic Science Graduate Program; Ph.D., Strathclyde (Scotland). Development and application of analytical chemistry tools to enhance the value of scientific evidence in legal disputes, application of novel extraction methodology such as solid-phase microextraction (SPME) for the isolation of ultra-trace quantities of analytes of interest.

David A. Becker, Professor; Ph.D., MIT. Investigation of newly discovered azulenyl nitrones, which are highly efficient free-radical scavengers that provide a new approach to neural disease processes involving free-radical–initiated events, including Parkinson's disease and Alzheimer's disease; synthesis of bioactive natural product analogs; identification of antioxidants produced in adaptation responses of biological systems exposed to solar radiation and hyperoxic atmospheres.

Yong Cai, Assistant Professor; Ph.D., Nankai (China). Environmental and bioanalytical chemistry of trace metals and organometallic compounds, including the development of new analytical techniques for speciation of metals and metalloids, and their fate and transport in the environmental and biological systems.

David Chatfield, Professor; Ph.D., Minnesota. Molecular dynamics simulation of biological macromolecules, particularly proteins; recent and continued application to HIV-1 protease, an enzyme necessary for reproduction of the HIV-1 virus, in order to elucidate the mechanism of catalysis; development of simulation methods incorporating hybrid quantum mechanical and molecular mechanical potentials and their application to the study of enzyme mechanism, especially to HIV-1 protease and to other aspartic proteases.

Kenneth Furton, Associate Dean of Arts and Sciences; Ph.D., Wayne State. Separation science, including SFE, SPME, ELISA, FPLC, HPLC, HPLC/MS, GC, and GC/MSn; clinical chemistry; forensic toxicology; arson analysis; explosive and drug analysis; blood/breath alcohol measurements; sensitivity/selectivity of canines as chemical detectors.

Piero R. Gardinali, Assistant Professor; Ph.D., Texas A&M. Fate and transport of anthropogenic organic compounds in freshwater and coastal environments, LC/MS of polar contaminants, use of pharmaceuticals as tracers for wastewater intrusions, development of analytical techniques for the analysis of trace organic compounds in environmental samples, environmental forensics.

Palmer Graves, General Chemistry Coordinator; Ph.D., Oklahoma. Computers as a tool in teaching chemistry, especially in showing the microscopic view of molecules and reactions through the use of graphics and animation; development of graphics and animation; computers in Web-based teaching; WebCT and other instructional uses of computers.

Rudolf Jaffé, Professor and Associate Director of SERC; Ph.D., Indiana. Analytical/environmental chemistry, organic geochemistry and biogeochemistry.

Jeffrey Joens, Professor; Ph.D., Indiana, 1984. Physical and environmental chemistry; experimental measurement of gas phase absorption spectra of small molecules, with applications to atmospheric chemistry; modeling and analysis of electronic spectra, with emphasis on continuous electronic absorption spectra; thermochemical properties of weakly bound molecular complexes in the gas phase and in solution; analysis of kinetic and thermodynamic data of atmospherically interesting molecules.

Konstantinos Kavallieratos, Assistant Professor; Ph.D., Yale. Molecular recognition and self-assembly: application of supramolecular chemistry principles in anion recognition, organometallic chemistry, catalysis, and toxic metal and metalloid coordination chemistry; novel receptors and extractants for selective separation and sensing of environmentally and biologically important ions and ion pairs.

John T. Landrum, Professor; Ph.D., USC. Hydroxy carotenoids (xanthophylls): their absorption, transport, and metabolism in humans and other animal systems; demonstrating that the carotenoids lutein, zeaxanthin, and meso-zeaxanthin are the principal components of the macular pigment and that the presence of these carotenoids in the retina is correlated to a reduced risk for age-related macular degeneration.

Watson Lees, Associate Professor; Ph.D., Harvard. Organic chemistry and biochemistry: using organic chemistry to study biochemical problems such the folding of disulfide containing proteins and methods of increasing the folding rate.

Fenfei Leng, Assistant Professor; Ph.D., Mississippi Medical Center. Effects of transcription on DNA topology and DNA replication, DNA-protein interactions, DNA topology strongly affects DNA structure, thus dramatically changes the efficiency of gene transcription, DNA replication, and recombination; interactions of small chromosome proteins, such as *E. coli* HU protein and eukaryotic high-mobility group (HMG) proteins, with DNA.

Ramon Lopez de la Vega, Associate Professor; Ph.D., Miami (Florida). Understanding the interplay of kinetics and thermodynamics in inorganic reactions, including metallation and demetallation of macrocycles, ligand substitution reactions, reactions of coordinated ligands, and electron transfer reactions; effects of p and s bonding in reactions of coordinated ligands; enthalpies of metallation of meso substituted octaethylporphyrins.

Alexander Mebel, Assistant Professor; Ph.D., N. S. Kurnakov Institute of General and Inorganic Chemistry (Moscow). Applications of accurate quantum chemical ab initio calculations to solving various chemical problems, including potential energy surfaces for chemical reactions related to combustion, atmospheric, and interstellar chemistry combined with statistical calculations of reaction rate coefficients and product branching ratios; prediction and assignment of absorption and emission spectra based on ab initio calculations of potential energy surfaces for excited electronic states; and quantum chemical modeling of photoabsorption and photoluminescence properties of nanoscale materials.

Kevin O'Shea, Associate Professor and Program Director; Ph.D., UCLA. Mechanistic organic chemistry, particularly as it relates to radical and photochemical processes and their potential application to environmental chemistry; semiconductor photocatalyic-, radiolytic-, and sonolytic-induced oxidation of organic pollutants in aqueous solutions for the implementation and application of oxidation processes for the remediation of harmful organic compounds from groundwater and drinking water.

J. Martin E. Quirke, Professor; Ph.D., Liverpool. Porphyrin and metalloporphyrin chemistry: synthesis, isolation, and characterization of geoporphyrins to determine more precisely the potential of these molecules for oil exploration and the role of the chelated metal ion on metalloporphyrin physical and chemical properties by spectroscopic and calorimetric techniques.

Kathleen Rein, Assistant Professor and Director of the ARCH Program at FIU; Ph.D., Miami (Florida). Isolation and identification of secondary metabolites from marine microalgae, primarily cyanobacteria from both marine and freshwater environments and dinoflagellates from marine environments; biosynthesis of polyketide toxins at the genomic level.

Alberto J. Sabucedo, Lecturer and Director, Forensic Certificate Program; Ph.D., Florida International. Determination of postmortem interval using proteins such as cardiac troponin I, the use of mass spectrometry for the determination of compounds of interest in pharmaceutical and herbal products, illicit drug analysis by mass spectrometry, immunoassay development, immunochemical techniques and protein chemistry.

Stephen A. Winkle, Associate Professor; Ph.D., Berkeley. Unusual DNA structures, such as left-handed DNA, DNA junctions, cruciforms, and carcinogen binding sequences: the effects of such structures on protein-DNA binding, the effects of these structures on protein activities, and the binding of antitumor drugs, carcinogens, and other small ligands to these DNA structures.

Stanislaw Wnuk, Associate Professor and Chemistry Department Chair; Ph.D., Adam Mickiewicz (Poland). Bioorganic chemistry of nucleosides and nucleotides with applications in biochemistry and in anticancer and antiviral medicine, new procedures for radical-mediated desulfonylation reactions.

FLORIDA STATE UNIVERSITY

Department of Chemistry and Biochemistry

Programs of Study

Graduate education in the Department of Chemistry and Biochemistry, leading to the M.S. and Ph.D. degrees, can be pursued in both traditional and contemporary fields. Five areas—biochemistry and analytical, inorganic, organic, and physical chemistry—provide fundamental curricula in their disciplines, and a variety of research-oriented programs are available in each of these traditional areas. In addition, opportunities for chemical research at the interfaces with physics, biology, and materials science are available in research groups participating in the Materials Research and Technology Center, the Institute of Molecular Biophysics, the School of Computational Science and Information Technology (CSIT), and the National High Magnetic Field Laboratory. Interdisciplinary programs leading to advanced degrees in chemical physics and in molecular biophysics are offered in cooperation with the Department of Physics and the Department of Biological Science. A list of chemistry faculty members and their research interests is given on the back of this page.

Ph.D. candidates who perform satisfactorily on entrance examinations may immediately begin advanced course work and research. Although Ph.D. programs of study are structured to meet individual needs and vary among the divisions, most programs incorporate seven to twelve 1-semester courses at the graduate level. Mastery of the material in the area of interest is demonstrated by passing either cumulative examinations or comprehensive examinations, depending on the area of specialization. A thesis or dissertation is required in all but the courses-only option of the master's degree program. The presence of about 40 postdoctoral and visiting faculty researchers, in addition to the low faculty-student ratio, permits a high level of student-scientist interaction.

Research Facilities

Departmental research operations are housed mainly in the interconnected Dittmer Laboratory of Chemistry building and Institute of Molecular Biophysics building. Several adjacent structures serve other departmental teaching functions. Major items of research equipment include a variety of spectrometers and lasers for ultraviolet, visible, infrared, and Raman experiments; an ORD/CD spectrometer; an EPR spectrometer with cryogenic accessories; several high- and medium-resolution mass spectrometers with GC, EI, and CI capabilities; 150-, 200-, 270-, 300-, 400-, and 500-MHz NMR spectrometers; a metal-organic chemical vapor deposition (MOCVD) facility; an automated four-circle X-ray diffractometer with complete in-house solution and refinement capabilities; and a bioanalytical facility containing automated DNA synthesis, peptide synthesis, and protein sequencing equipment. The department has excellently staffed glassworking, machine, electronics, photographic/computer graphics, and woodworking shops in support of the teaching and research programs.

The departmental computing needs are met by a variety of workstations and microcomputers that are linked with the Internet. Several members of the chemistry faculty are members of the of the CSIT school and have access to two Silicon Graphics Power Challenge supercomputers on the Florida State University (FSU) campus as well as to several supercomputers around the world. CSIT maintains two high-performance computer environments—a Connection Machine CM-2 and a large cluster of super-workstations providing more than 8.2 gigaflops of computing power and more than 460 gigabytes of disk storage. The department is a sponsoring academic unit for the National High Magnetic Field Laboratory (NHMFL) and has access to the facilities and instrumentation of the NHMFL.

The University's Strozier Library, which includes the Dirac Science Library, houses 1.2 million volumes and maintains 12,650 active journal subscriptions. The Dirac Science Library is located adjacent to the Dittmer Laboratory of Chemistry.

Financial Aid

In addition to providing teaching and research assistantships, the department offers several special fellowships on a competitive basis. Nearly all graduate students are supported by one of these programs. Twelve-month teaching assistantships with stipends of $18,000 can be augmented by special fellowships ranging up to $3000. Competitive fellowships on the University and College levels are also available.

Cost of Study

Tuition for in-state residents was $2355.24 per semester and for out-of-state residents was $8769.60 per semester in 2003–04. These tuition costs are normally waived for teaching and research assistants, but the number of waivers available each year is determined in part by legislative appropriation. In addition to tuition, nonwaivable fees were $493–$707 per semester and the cost of health insurance was $68 per month.

Living and Housing Costs

Single students sharing a 2-person room in graduate apartment housing paid $350 per month in 2003–04, in addition to utilities and telephone service. The University also operates an apartment complex of 795 units for single and married students. Rents ranged from $320 to $557 per month plus utilities for furnished one- to three-bedroom apartments. Off-campus accommodations began at about $400 per month.

Student Group

The graduate enrollment in the Department of Chemistry and Biochemistry is 137 students. Although students come from all parts of the United States and numerous other countries, many are native to the eastern half of the United States.

Location

Metropolitan Tallahassee has a population of about 300,000 and is recognized for the scenic beauty of its rolling hills, abundant trees and flowers, and seasonal changes. As the capital of Florida, the city is host to many cultural affairs, including symphony, theater, and dance groups. Its location 30 minutes from the Gulf Coast, the area's many lakes, and an average annual temperature of 68°F make the region eminently suitable for a variety of year-round outdoor activities.

The University

Florida State University was founded in 1851 and is one of eleven members of the State University System of Florida. Currently, enrollment is 37,328, including 6,851 graduate students. The University's rapid climb to prominence began with the adoption of an emphasis on graduate studies in 1947. The first doctoral degree was conferred in 1952. In addition to the College of Arts and Sciences, the University is composed of the Colleges of Business, Communication, Education, Engineering, Human Sciences, Law, and Social Sciences and the Schools of Criminology, Library and Information Studies, Music, Social Work, Theatre, and Visual Arts. Several departments, including chemistry, enjoy international recognition.

Applying

Application for admission may be made at any time; however, initial inquiries concerning assistantships, especially fellowships, should be made nine to twelve months prior to the anticipated enrollment date. Later requests are considered as funds are available for the following fall semester. Requests for forms, detailed requirements, and other information should be directed to the address below.

Correspondence and Information

Director of Graduate Admissions
Department of Chemistry and Biochemistry
Florida State University
Tallahassee, Florida 32306-4390

Telephone: 850-644-1897
888-525-9286 (toll-free in the United States)
Fax: 850-644-0465
E-mail: gradinfo@chem.fsu.edu
World Wide Web: http://www.chem.fsu.edu (Department of Chemistry)
http://admissions.fsu.edu (the University)

Florida State University

THE FACULTY AND THEIR RESEARCH

Igor V. Alabugin, Assistant Professor; Ph.D., Moscow State, 1995. Development of new photochemical reactions of medicinal importance, pH-activated anticancer agents, radical cascades in synthesis of conjugated polymers, molecular imprinting and supramolecular control of photochemical reactivity, stereoelectronic effects, improper hydrogen bonding.

Michael Blaber, Associate Professor; Ph.D., California, Irvine, 1990. Protein structure, function, folding, evolution, and engineering; X-ray crystallography and biophysics; serine protease structure and function.

Michael S. Chapman, Professor; Ph.D., UCLA, 1987. Structure-function characterization of enzymes and viruses by X-ray crystallography.

Jerzy Cioslowski, Professor; Ph.D., Georgetown, 1987. Computational quantum chemistry, ab initio electronic structure calculations, development of algorithms for supercomputers.

William T. Cooper, Professor and Director, Terrestrial Waters Institute; Ph.D., Indiana, 1981. Environmental chemistry of organic compounds in surface and ground waters, organic geochemistry of recent sediments, FT-ICR mass spectrometry, solid-state ^{13}C NMR spectroscopy; chromatography and capillary electrophosis.

Timothy A. Cross, Earl Frieden Professor and National High Magnetic Field Lab NMR Program Director; Ph.D., Pennsylvania, 1981. Structural biology and structural genomics of membrane proteins using solid-state nuclear magnetic resonance and a combination of technologies.

Naresh Dalal, Professor and Chairperson; Ph.D., British Columbia, 1971. Materials science, solid-state chemistry, synthesis and characterization of magnetic and ferroelectric compounds, nanochemistry and quantum computation, high field EPR and NMR, scanning probe microscopy, spectroscopic studies of single crystals.

John G. Dorsey, Katherine Blood Hoffman Professor and Editor, *Journal of Chromatography A;* Ph.D., Cincinnati, 1979. Analytical separations, especially liquid chromatography; retention mechanisms; stationary phase design and synthesis; electrochromatography; quantitative structure-retention relationships; theory and technique development.

Ralph C. Dougherty, Professor; Ph.D., Chicago, 1963. Structure of water and aqueous solutions, ion-molecule collisions and reactions, tunneling in chemical reactions, mesoscale (10 km) atmospheric chemical modeling.

Gregory B. Dudley, Assistant Professor; Ph.D., MIT, 2000. Natural products synthesis and application of synthesis to medicinal chemistry research, new strategies and tactics for organic chemistry.

Thomas M. Fischer, Associate Professor; Ph.D., Mainz (Germany), 1992. Dynamic phase behavior of soft matter, experimental and theoretical studies of two-dimensional systems, biomimetic self-organization.

Robert L. Fulton, Professor; Ph.D., Harvard, 1964. Development and application of techniques for the description of the behavior of electrons in molecules and in intermolecular complexes, theories of relaxation phenomena, theories of linear and nonlinear dielectric properties and their relation to molecular motion.

Penny J. Gilmer, Professor; Ph.D., Berkeley, 1972. Biochemistry, chemistry education, science education, scientific research for teachers, collaboration and technology, education of future science teachers.

Kenneth A. Goldsby, Associate Professor; Ph.D., North Carolina at Chapel Hill, 1983. Redox reactions of transition metal complexes, proton-coupled electron transfer, modified electrodes and self-assembled monolayers, electrochemistry and surface-modified electrodes.

Nancy L. Greenbaum, Associate Professor; Ph.D., Pennsylvania, 1984. Structure and function of RNA-RNA, RNA-metal, and RNA-protein interactions studied by multidimensional NMR and other spectroscopic techniques.

Edwin F. Hilinski, Associate Professor; Ph.D., Yale, 1982. Mechanistic studies of photochemical and thermal reactions of organic compounds in solution, time-resolved laser spectroscopy, photoinduced phenomena in solids.

Robert A. Holton, Matthew Suffness Professor; Ph.D., Florida State, 1971. Synthetic organic, organometallic, and bioorganic chemistry; total synthesis of natural products.

Marie E. Krafft, Martin A. Schwartz Professor; Ph.D., Virginia Tech, 1983. Synthetic organic and organometallic chemistry, natural products synthesis.

Susan E. Latturner, Assistant Professor; Ph.D., California, Santa Barbara, 2000. Use of molten salts and metals for the synthesis of new inorganic materials, growth of subvalent clusters in zeolites by ion-exchange and doping, crystallography and electronic properties of inorganic solids.

Hong Li, Assistant Professor; Ph.D., Rochester, 1994. X-ray crystallography, molecular principles of protein and RNA interactions, gene expression and regulation.

Timothy M. Logan, Associate Professor; Ph.D., Chicago, 1991. Structural and biophysical studies of proteins and protein-ligand complexes, glycoprotein structural biology, multidimensional NMR spectroscopy.

A. G. Marshall, Kasha Professor and National High Magnetic Field Laboratory ICR Program Director; Ph.D., Stanford, 1970. Fourier transform ion cyclotron resonance mass spectrometry: instrumentation and technique development; applications to protein structure and posttranslational modifications, biomarkers, mapping of contact interfaces in biomacromolecular assemblies, and petroleomics.

Sanford A. Safron, Professor; Ph.D., Harvard, 1969. He atom-surface scattering experiments; dynamics of crystalline surfaces and interfaces; structure, dynamics, and growth of ultra-thin films.

Jack Saltiel, Professor; Ph.D., Caltech, 1964. Photochemistry of organic molecules, elucidation of the mechanisms of photochemical reactions by chemical and spectroscopic means.

QingXiang Amy Sang, Associate Professor; Ph.D., Georgetown, 1990. Protein chemistry, enzymology, molecular biology, and biochemistry of metalloproteinases; biochemical basis of angiogenesis; molecular carcinogenesis and mechanisms of cancer metastasis.

Joseph B. Schlenoff, Professor and Associate Director, MARTECH Program; Ph.D., Massachusetts Amherst, 1987. Polymer science, ultra-thin films, charged and water-soluble polymers, surface chemistry, polymers in separation.

Oliver Steinbock, Assistant Professor; Ph.D., Göttingen (Germany), 1993. Kinetics, experimental and theoretical studies of nonequilibrium systems, chemical self-organization.

Albert E. Stiegman, Assistant Professor; Ph.D., Columbia, 1984. Synthesis of inorganic and hybrid organic/inorganic materials and nanocomposite structures; optical, dielectric, catalytic, and photochemical processes in solids; spectroscopy and photophysics of reactive metal centers in glasses.

Geoffrey F. Strouse, Associate Professor; Ph.D., North Carolina at Chapel Hill, 1993. Materials science with a principle focus on nanometer-scale materials, including novel synthetic methodology, development of analytical methods (XAFS, mass spectroscopy, magnetism, optical, vibrational), and biomaterial integration.

Kenneth D. Weston, Assistant Professor; Ph.D., California, Santa Barbara, 1998. Single molecule fluorescence spectroscopy techniques and microfluidics are being developed and applied in a complimentary fashion to study a broad range of topics in biology, chemistry, and physics.

HARVARD UNIVERSITY

Department of Chemistry and Chemical Biology

Program of Study

The Department of Chemistry and Chemical Biology offers a program of study that leads to the degree of Doctor of Philosophy in chemistry in the special fields of biological, inorganic, organic, and physical chemistry. An interdepartmental Ph.D. program in chemical physics is also available. Upon entering the program, students formulate a plan of study in consultation with the Graduate Advisory Committee. Students must obtain honor grades in four advanced half courses (five for chemical physics). The course work is usually expected to be completed by the end of the second term of residence. For students studying organic chemistry, written examinations are given on a monthly basis from the time the student starts research until a specified number have been passed. Physical and inorganic chemistry students must present and defend a research proposal in their second year of residence. Although the curriculum for the Ph.D. degree includes the course and cumulative examination requirements, the majority of the graduate student's time and energy is devoted to original investigations in a chosen field of research. Students are expected to join a research group in their second term of residence, but no later than the third. The Ph.D. dissertation is based on independent scholarly research, which, upon conclusion, is defended in an oral examination before a Ph.D. committee. The preparation of a satisfactory thesis normally requires at least four years of full-time research.

Research Facilities

The facilities of the Department of Chemistry and Chemical Biology are housed in five buildings, with the adjacent Science Center providing extensive undergraduate lecture and laboratory areas. An Instrument Center provides a central location for the following research instruments: one Varian 600-MHz NMR; two Varian 500-MHz NMRs; one Bruker 500-MHz NMR; two Varian 400-MHz NMRs; one Bruker 250-MHz NMR; one Varian 300-MHz NMR; one Bruker ESP 300 EPR spectrometer; JEOL-AX505H and JEOL-SX102A mass spectrometers; a Micromass Platform II mass spectrometer equipped with APCI ionization; a Micromass time-of-flight mass spectrometer equipped with electrospray ionization; two PerSeptive Biosystems time-of-flight mass spectrometers for matrix-assisted laser desorption ionization; two Siemens X-ray diffractometers, both with SMART area detection systems; and a Nicolet 7000 Fourier transform infrared spectrometer. Computing in the department is done mostly on workstations in individual research groups, with more than 200 devices linked by a department-wide network. The department, along with the Materials Research Laboratories at Harvard and MIT, operates and manages a Surface Sciences Center.

Financial Aid

The Department of Chemistry and Chemical Biology meets the financial needs of its graduate students through departmental scholarships, departmental fellowships, teaching fellowships, research assistantships, and independent outside fellowships. Financial support is awarded on a twelve-month basis, enabling students to pursue their research throughout the year. Tuition is afforded to all graduate students in good standing for the tenure of the Ph.D. program.

Cost of Study

As stated above, tuition is waived for all Ph.D. students in good standing.

Living and Housing Costs

Dormitory rooms for single students are available, with costs (excluding meals) ranging from $4456 for a single room to $7003 for a two-room suite. Married and single students may apply for apartments managed by Harvard Planning and Real Estate. The monthly costs are studio apartment, $933–$1268; one-bedroom apartment, $1170–$1422; two-bedroom apartment, $1522–$1857; and three-bedroom apartment, $1969–$2434. There are also many privately owned apartments nearby and within commuting distance.

Student Group

The Graduate School of Arts and Sciences (GSAS) has an enrollment of 3,441 graduate students. There are 189 students in the Department of Chemistry and Chemical Biology, 62 of whom are international students.

Student Outcomes

In 2002, 4 percent of the Ph.D. recipients entered positions in academia, and 34 percent accepted permanent positions in industry; 49 percent of the graduates will conduct postdoctoral research before accepting permanent positions in academia or industry, and 12 percent are pursuing other directions.

Location

Cambridge, a city of 101,355, is just minutes away from Boston. It is a scientific and intellectual center, teeming with activities in all areas of creativity and study. The Cambridge/Boston area is a major cultural center, with its many public and university museums, theaters, symphony, and numerous private, special interest, and historical collections and performances. New England abounds in possibilities for recreational pursuits, from camping, hiking, and skiing in the mountains of New Hampshire and Vermont to swimming and sailing on the seashores of Cape Cod and Maine.

The University

Harvard College was established in 1636, and its charter, which still guides the University, was granted in 1650. An early brochure, published in 1643, justified the College's existence: "To advance Learning and perpetuate it to Posterity...." Today, Harvard University, with its network of graduate and professional schools, occupies a noteworthy position in the academic world, and the Department of Chemistry and Chemical Biology offers an educational program in keeping with the University's long-standing record of achievement.

Applying

Applications for admission to study for the Ph.D. degree in chemistry may be obtained from GSAS and are accepted from students who have received a bachelor's degree or equivalent. The application process should begin during the summer or fall of the year preceding desired entrance. Completed application forms and supporting materials should be returned to the GSAS Admissions Office by December 16, though this date may vary slightly from year to year.

Correspondence and Information

Graduate Admissions Office
Department of Chemistry and Chemical Biology
Harvard University
12 Oxford Street
Cambridge, Massachusetts 02138

Telephone: 617-496-3208
E-mail: admissions@chemistry.harvard.edu
World Wide Web: http://www.chem.harvard.edu

Harvard University

THE FACULTY AND THEIR RESEARCH

James G. Anderson, Professor; Ph.D. (physical chemistry), Colorado, 1970. Chemical reactivity of radical-molecule systems, molecular orbital analysis of barrier height control, coupling of chemistry, radiation and climate in the earth system, photochemistry of planetary atmospheres, in situ detection of radicals in troposphere and stratosphere.

David A. Evans, Professor; Ph.D. (organic chemistry), Caltech, 1967. Organic synthesis, organometallic chemistry, asymmetric synthesis.

Cynthia M. Friend, Professor; Ph.D. (physical chemistry), Berkeley, 1981. Physical chemistry of surface phenomena, materials chemistry and catalysis, electron spectroscopies and chemical techniques applied to the understanding of complex surface reactions, relating chemical processes to electronic structure on surfaces.

Roy Gerald Gordon, Professor; Ph.D. (physical chemistry), Harvard, 1964. Intermolecular forces, transport processes and molecular motion, theory of crystal structures and phase transitions, kinetics of crystal growth, solar energy, chemical vapor deposition, synthesis of inorganic precursors to new materials, thin films and their applications to microelectronics and solar cells.

Eric J. Heller, Professor; Ph.D. (chemical physics), Harvard, 1973. Few body quantum mechanics, scattering theory and quantum chaos. Physics of semiconductor devices, ultracold molecular collisions, nonadiabatic I interactions in molecules and gasses.

Richard H. Holm, Professor; Ph.D. (inorganic and bioinorganic chemistry), MIT, 1959. Synthetic, structural, electronic, and reactivity properties of transition-element compounds; structure and function of metallobiomolecules.

Eric N. Jacobsen, Professor; Ph.D. (organic chemistry), Berkeley, 1986. Mechanistic and synthetic organic chemistry. Development of new synthetic methods, with emphasis on asymmetric catalysis. Physical-organic studies of reactivity and recognition phenomena in homogeneous catalysis. Stereoselective synthesis of natural products.

Daniel Kahne, Professor; Ph.D. (organic chemistry), Columbia, 1986. Synthetic organic chemistry and its applications to problems in chemistry and biology.

Charles M. Lieber, Professor; Ph.D. (physical chemistry), Stanford, 1985. Chemistry and physics of materials with an emphasis on nanoscale systems. Rational synthesis of new nanoscale building blocks and nanostructured solids; development of methodologies for hierarchical assembly of nanoscale building blocks into complex and functional systems; investigation of fundamental electronic, optical, and optoelectronic properties of nanoscale materials; design and development of nanoelectronics and nanophotonic systems, with emphasis on electrically-based biological detection, digital and quantum computing, and photonic systems.

David Liu, Associate Professor; Ph.D. (organic chemistry and chemical biology), Berkeley, 1999. Organic chemistry and chemical biology of molecular evolution, nucleic acid-templated organic synthesis, reaction discovery, protein and nucleic acid evolution and engineering, synthetic polymer evolution; generally, effective molarity-based approaches to controlling reactivity and evolution-based approaches to the discovery of functional synthetic and biological molecules.

Gavin MacBeath, Assistant Professor; Ph.D. (organic chemistry and chemical biology), Scripps, 1997. Interdisciplinary, combining proteomics, organic chemistry, and the development of array-based technology to reveal how groups of proteins function as networks inside the cell.

Andrew G. Myers, Professor; Ph.D. (organic chemistry), Harvard, 1985. Synthesis and study of complex organic molecules of importance in biology and human medicine.

Hongkun Park, Professor; Ph.D. (physical chemistry and chemical physics), Stanford, 1996. Physics and chemistry of nanostructured materials; electron transport individual molecules, inorganic clusters, nanowires, and nanotubes; single-molecule optoelectronics; synthesis and characterization of transition-metal-oxide and chalcogenide nanostructures with novel electronic and magnetic properties.

Stuart L. Schreiber, Professor; Ph.D. (organic synthesis), Harvard, 1981. Development and application of diversity-oriented organic synthesis to cell circuitry and genomic medicine.

Matthew D. Shair, Professor; Ph.D. (synthetic chemistry and chemical biology), Columbia, 1995. Synthesis of small molecules that have interesting biological functions and elucidation of their cellular mechanisms; development of organic synthesis.

Eugene I. Shakhnovich, Professor; Ph.D. (physical chemistry), Moscow, 1984. Theoretical biomolecular science including protein folding, theory of molecular evolution, structural bioinformatics, rational drug design, populational genomics, other systems including complex polymers, spin glasses, etc.

Gregory L. Verdine, Professor; Ph.D. (organic chemistry, chemical biology, structural biology), Columbia, 1986. DNA repair; transcriptional control, chemistry for the conversion of peptides to ligands having cellular activity.

Maria-Christina White, Assistant Professor; Ph.D. (organic chemistry), Johns Hopkins, 1998. Discovery of new transition-metal mediated catalytic reactions that address unsolved problems in synthetic methodology. Development of these reactions into practical methods that will find widespread use in organic synthesis.

George M. Whitesides, Professor; Ph.D. (organic chemistry), Caltech, 1964. Physical organic chemistry, materials science, biophysics, complexity, surface science, microfluidics, self-assembly, micro- and nanotechnology, and cell-surface biochemistry.

X. Sunney Xie, Professor; Ph.D. (physical chemistry), California, San Diego, 1990. Biophysical chemistry, single-molecule spectroscopy and dynamics, developments of new approaches for molecular and cellular imaging.

Xiaowei Zhuang, Assistant Professor; Ph.D. (physics), Berkeley, 1996. Biophysical chemistry, single-molecule biophysics, fluorescence microscopy and spectroscopy, microscopic and nanoscopic imaging of biomolecular and cellular systems.

Affiliate Members of the Department of Chemistry and Chemical Biology

Stephen C. Harrison, Higgins Professor of Biochemistry; Ph.D., Harvard, 1968. Chemical biology: macromolecular assembly, virus structure, transcriptional regulation, signal transduction.

David R. Nelson, Mallinckrodt Professor of Physics and Professor of Applied Physics; Ph.D., Cornell, 1975. Statistical mechanics and dynamics in condensed-matter and chemical physics; superfluids and superconductors, polymers, liquid crystals, glasses, and biophysics.

Suzanne Walker, Professor; Ph.D. (organic chemistry), Princeton, 1992. Chemical biology: synthetic organic chemistry applied to the study of biochemical molecules; enzymology; mechanism of action of antibiotics.

KENT STATE UNIVERSITY

Department of Chemistry

Programs of Study The Department of Chemistry offers programs leading to the Master of Science (M.S.) and Doctor of Philosophy (Ph.D.) degrees in the divisions of analytical, inorganic, organic, and physical chemistry and biochemistry. Many faculty members also have research interests in the specialty areas of liquid crystals, materials and spectroscopy, separations, and surface science. A variety of interdisciplinary and collaborative projects are available, in addition to interdisciplinary doctoral programs in chemical physics and molecular and cellular biology.

Graduate students are required to complete a program of core courses in their area of specialization and at least one (for M.S. candidates) or two (for Ph.D. candidates) courses in other areas of chemistry. In addition to these courses, students may choose from a wide variety of electives. The program thus gives students considerable flexibility in curriculum design. At the end of the second year, doctoral candidates must pass a written examination in their field of specialization and present, and subsequently defend, an original research proposal for their dissertation. Students normally complete their doctoral program after four years.

Research Facilities Research laboratories are located primarily in Williams Hall and the adjoining Science Research Laboratory. In addition, facilities in the Liquid Crystal Institute, housed in the Materials Science Building, are available to chemistry students. Williams Hall houses two large lecture halls, classrooms, undergraduate and research laboratories, the research laboratories of the Separation Science Consortium, the Chemistry-Physics Library, chemical stockrooms, and glass and electronics shops. A machine shop, which is jointly operated with the physics department, is located in nearby Smith Hall. Spectrometers include 500-MHz and 300-MHz high-resolution NMR instruments; several FT-IR spectrometers, including a Bruker Equinox system; photon-counting fluorometer; circular dichroism; FPLC, UV/visible spectrometers, and cell culture; an ion-trap GC-MS with MS/MS$^{(m)}$ capability; AA/AE equipment; a EDX-700 energy dispersive X-ray spectrometer, a Bruker Biospin Avance 400 MHz digital NMR spectrometer, and a Shimadzu EDX700 X-ray fluorescence spectrometer. The X-ray facility includes a Siemens D5000 Powder diffractometer and a Bruker AXS CCD instrument for single crystal structural elucidation. Equipment available in specialty areas includes an EMX-A EPR spectrometer system, a microwave spectrometer, an LCQ-Electrospray mass spectrometer with MS/MS$^{(m)}$ capability, a phosphor imager, microcal VP DSC and ITC calorimeters, Bruker Vector 33 FTIR-NIR, Cary Eclipse fluorescence spectrophotometer, Bruker Esquire 300plus MS with Agilent HP1100 HPLC, MALDI-TOF MS and LC-MS, a Cary 5 UV-VIS-NIR spectrophotometer, ThermoFinnigan Polaris Q115W GC-MS, a BAS electrochemical analyzer, various preparative centrifuges, a molecular dynamic Typhoon 8600 imaging system, and PCR and DNA sequencing facilities. Additional equipment available to the Separation Science Consortium includes a 400-MHz high-resolution and solids multinuclear NMR spectrometer, thermal analysis and gas adsorption equipment, and a variety of HPLC and GC instruments. There are a wide range of computer facilities available at Kent State, from microcomputers to supercomputers. Individual research groups in the Department of Chemistry maintain a variety of computer systems, including PCs and workstations. The department has advanced molecular modeling facilities, including Cerius, Felix, Hyperchem, InsightII/Discover, Macromodel, and Spartan packages for modeling surfaces and interfaces, polymers, proteins, and nucleic acids, as well as facilities for performing ab initio calculations of molecular properties and molecular dynamics. University Computer Services maintains a number of microcomputer labs on campus as well as an IBM 4381-R24 mainframe computer that runs the VM/CMS operating system. High-performance computing is available at the Ohio Supercomputer Center, which maintains Cray T94, Cray T3E, IBM SP2, and SGI Origin 2000 supercomputers. The abstracting and indexing service maintains an extensive collection of books in chemistry and physics. There is also online access to a variety of chemical databases, including the Chemical Abstracts Service.

Financial Aid Graduate students are supported through teaching and research assistantships and University fellowships. Students in good academic standing are guaranteed appointments for periods of 4½ years (Ph.D. candidates) or 2½ years (M.S. candidates). Stipends for 2004–05 ranged from $16,000 (M.S.) to $17,000 (Ph.D.) for a twelve-month appointment. A $600 credit is made toward the University's health insurance plan. Renewable merit fellowships providing an additional $2500 per year are available to outstanding applicants.

Cost of Study Graduate tuition and fees for the 2004–05 academic year are $7844, for which a tuition scholarship was provided to students in good academic standing.

Living and Housing Costs Rooms in the graduate hall of residence are $2135 to $2605 per semester; married students' apartments may be rented for $635 to $665 per month (all utilities included). Information concerning off-campus housing may be obtained from the University housing office. Costs vary widely, but apartments typically rent for $500 to $600 per month.

Student Group Graduate students in chemistry currently number about 45. There are approximately 20,000 students enrolled at the main campus of Kent State University; 8,000 additional students attend the seven regional campuses.

Location Kent, a city of about 28,000, is located 35 miles southeast of Cleveland and 12 miles east of Akron in a peaceful suburban setting. Kent offers the cultural advantages of a major metropolitan complex as well as the relaxed pace of semirural living. There are a number of theater and art groups at the University and in the community. Blossom Music Center, the summer home of the Cleveland Orchestra and the site of Kent State's cooperative programs in art, music, and theater, is only 15 miles from the main campus. The Akron and Cleveland art museums are also within easy reach of the campus. There are a wide variety of recreational facilities available on the campus and within the local area, including West Branch State Park and the Cuyahoga Valley National Recreation Area. Opportunities for outdoor activities such as summer sports, ice-skating, swimming, and downhill and cross-country skiing abound.

The University Established in 1910, Kent State University is one of Ohio's largest state universities. The campus contains 820 acres of wooded hillsides plus an airport and an eighteen-hole golf course. There are approximately 100 buildings on the main campus. Bachelor's, master's, and doctoral degrees are offered in more than thirty subject areas. The faculty numbers approximately 800.

Applying Forms for admission to the graduate programs are available on request from the address in the Correspondence and Information section. There is no formal deadline for admission, but graduate assistantships are normally awarded by May for the following fall. Applicants requesting assistantships should apply by March 1.

Correspondence and Information

Graduate Coordinator
Department of Chemistry
Kent State University
Kent, Ohio 44242

Telephone: 330-672-2032
Fax: 330-672-3816
E-mail: chemgc@kent.edu
World Wide Web: http://www.kent.edu/chemistry

Kent State University

THE FACULTY AND THEIR RESEARCH

Nicola E. Brasch, Assistant Professor; Ph.D., Otago (New Zealand), 1994. Bioinorganic and medicinal chemistry; vitamin B_{12} and the B_{12}-dependent enzyme reactions; vanadium chemistry; inorganic drug delivery systems; synthesis, kinetics, and mechanism.
Bansidhar Datta, Assistant Professor; Ph.D., Nebraska–Lincoln, 1989. Biochemistry: mechanism of protein synthesis initiation in mammals; studies of posttranslational modifications, such as glycosylation and phosphorylation of initiation factors, molecular cloning of translational regulatory proteins, and studies of the evolutionary origins of the regulatory/structural domains present in protein synthesis regulator.
Arne Gericke, Assistant Professor; Dr.rer.nat., Hamburg (Germany), 1994. Biophysical chemistry: characterization of lipid-mediated protein functions; infrared spectroscopy, fluorescence, and calorimetric measurements.
Edwin S. Gould, University Professor; Ph.D., UCLA, 1950. Inorganic chemistry: mechanisms of inorganic redox reactions; catalysis of redox reactions by organic species; electron-transfer reactions of flavin-related systems; reactions of cobalt, chromium, vanadium, titanium, europium, uranium, ruthenium, indium, peroxynitrous acid, and trioxodinitrate; reactions of water-soluble radical species.
Roger B. Gregory, Professor; Ph.D., Sheffield (England), 1980. Biochemistry: protein conformational dynamics; the characterization of dynamically distinct substructures in proteins; protein hydration; protein glass transition behavior and its role in protein function, stability, and folding; development and application of high-sensitivity methods for protein characterization, including protein-protein interactions and protein chemical modifications.
Songping D. Huang, Associate Professor; Ph.D., Michigan State, 1993. Inorganic chemistry: molecule-based magnetic and nonlinear optical materials, organic conductors and superconductors, novel microporous and mesoporous materials, synthesis and crystal growth of metal oxides and chalcogenides.
Mietek Jaroniec, Professor; Ph.D., Lublin (Poland), 1976. Physical/analytical/materials chemistry: adsorption and chromatography at the gas/solid and liquid/solid interface; synthesis and modification of adsorbents, catalysts, and chromatographic packings of tailored surface and structural properties; self-assembled organic-inorganic nanomaterials, such as ordered mesoporous silica and other inorganic oxides; ordered mesoporous carbons synthesized via colloidal templating and imprinting processes; characterization of nanoporous materials by using adsorption, thermal analysis, chromatography, and other techniques.
Anatoly K. Khitrin, Associate Professor; Ph.D., Institute of Chemical Physics, Russian Academy of Sciences, 1985. Physical chemistry:NMR techniques, theory of magnetic resonance, material science, quantum computing and microimaging.
Kenneth K. Laali, Professor; Ph.D., Manchester (England), 1977. Organic chemistry, mechanistic organic (organometallic) chemistry, and synthetic applications: generation and NMR studies of persistent carbocations of fused polycyclic aromatics (mechanistic carcinogenesis), superacid chemistry and heterogeneous catalysis, new organic conducting materials (incorporation into polymers and liquid crystals), new fluorinating agents for aromatics and liquid crystals, organophosphorus chemistry, host-guest chemistry.
Paul Sampson, Professor; Ph.D., Birmingham (England), 1983. Synthetic organic chemistry: development of new synthetic methods; synthetic (stereoselective) organofluorine chemistry, with applications to the synthesis of fluorinated liquid crystals and carbohydrate analogs; development of new organometallic synthons as building blocks for organic synthesis; new approaches for the construction of medium-sized and macrocyclic rings, with applications to the synthesis of analogs of the anticancer agent Taxol.
Alexander J. Seed, Associate Professor; Ph.D., Hull (England), 1995. Organic chemistry, design, synthesis, and physical characterization of liquid crystals; ferroelectric, antiferroelectric, and high-twisting power materials for optical applications; new heterocyclic synthetic methodology.
Diane Stroup, Assistant Professor; Ph.D., Ohio State, 1992. Biochemistry: control of mammalian gene expression by regulation of transcriptional and posttranscriptional processes, study of the nuclear hormone receptors and signal transduction events with the molecular biology techniques of tissue culture and molecular cloning.
Yuriy V. Tolmachev, Assistant Professor; Ph.D., Case Western Reserve, 1999. Analytical chemistry: electrochemistry, fuel cells, electrocatalysis, X-ray spectroscopy, microfabrication, nanofabrication.
Chun-che Tsai, Professor; Ph.D., Indiana, 1968. Biochemistry: interaction of drugs with nucleic acids, structure and activity of anticancer drugs, antiviral agents, antibiotic drugs, and interferon inducers, structure and biological function relationships, X-ray diffraction, quantitative structure-activity relationships (QSAR), molecular and drug design.
Michael J. Tubergen, Associate Professor; Ph.D., Chicago, 1991. Physical chemistry: high-resolution microwave spectroscopy for molecular structure determination of hydrogen-bonded complexes and biological molecules.
Robert J. Twieg, Professor; Ph.D., Berkeley, 1976. Organic chemistry: development of organic and polymeric materials with novel electronic and optoelectronic properties, including nonlinear optical chromophores, photorefractive chromophores, transport agents and passive dielectrics, and liquid crystals, with emphasis on applications and durability issues.
Frederick G. Walz, Professor; Ph.D., SUNY Downstate Medical Center, 1966. Biochemistry: site-directed and random-combinatorial mutagenesis and in vitro recombination methods used in studies of ribonuclease T_1; investigation, catalytic perfection, alternate substrate recognition, and catalytic mechanism at the active site and the functional role of enzyme subsites; study of the sexually dimorphic proteome of the rat, using two-dimensional electrophoresis and differential RNA display technologies.
John L. West, Professor, Vice President of Research, and Dean of Graduate Studies; Ph.D., Carnegie Mellon, 1980. Materials science: liquid crystal polymer formulations for display applications, basic studies of liquid crystal alignment.

Kent State University

SELECTED PUBLICATIONS

Hamza, M. S. A., A. G. Cregan, **N. E. Brasch,** and R. van Eldik. Mechanistic insight from activation parameters for the reaction between coenzyme B_{12} and cyanide: Further evidence that heterolytic Co-C bond cleavage is solvent-assisted. *Dalton Trans.* 596, 2003.

Brasch, N. E., A. G. Cregan, and M. L. Vanselow. Studies on the mechanism of the reaction between 5'-deoxyadenosylcobinamide and cyanide. *Dalton Trans.* 1287, 2002.

Suto, R. K., **N. E. Brasch,** O. P. Anderson, and R. G. Finke. Synthesis, characterization, solution stability and X-ray crystal structure of the thiolatocobalamin γ-glutamylcysteinylcobalamin, a dipeptide analog of glutathionylcobalamin: Insights into the enhanced Co-S bond stability of the natural product glutathionylcobalamin. *Inorg. Chem.* 40:2686, 2001.

Cregan, A. G., **N. E. Brasch,** and R. van Eldik. Thermodynamic and kinetic studies on the reaction between the vitamin B_{12} derivative β-(N-methylimidazolyl)cobalamin and N-methylimidazole: Ligand displacement at the α axial site of cobalamins. *Inorg. Chem.* 40:1430, 2001.

Datta R., et al. **(B. Datta).** A glycosylation site, (60)SGTS(63), of p67 is required for its ability to regulate the phosphorylation and activity of eukaryotic initiation factor 2 alpha. *Biochemistry* 42(18):5453–60, 2003.

Datta B., and R. Datta. Mutation at the acidic residue-rich domain of eukaryotic initiation factor 2 (eIF2 alpha)-associated glycoprotein p67 increases the protection of eIF2 alpha phosphorylation during heat shock. *Arch. Biochem. Biophys.* 413(1):116–22, 2003.

Datta R., R. Tammali, and **B. Datta.** Negative regulation of the protection of eIF2 alpha phosphorylation activity by a unique acidic domain present at the N-terminus of p67. *Exp. Cell Res.* 283(2):237–46, 2003.

Datta R., et al. **(B. Datta).** Protection of translation initiation factor eIF2 phosphorylation correlates with eIF2-associated glycoprotein p67 levels and requires the lysine-rich domain I of p67. *Biochimie* 83(10):919–31, 2001.

Wu, F. J., and **A. Gericke**, et al. Domain structure and molecular conformation in annexin V/1,2-dimyristoyl-sn-glycero-3-phosphate/Ca2+ aqueous monolayers: A Brewster angle microscopy/infrared reflection-absorption spectroscopy study. *Biophys. J.* 74:3273–81, 1998.

Gericke, A., C. R. Flach, and R. Mendelsohn. Structure and orientation of lung surfactant SP-C and L. Alpha dipalmitoylphosphatidylcholine in aqueous monolayers. *Biophys. J.* 73:492–9, 1997.

Mendelsohn, R., J. W. Brauner, and **A. Gericke.** External infrared reflection-absorption spectrometry of monolayers at the air/water interface. *Ann. Rev. Phys. Chem.* 46:305–34, 1995.

Yang, Z. and **E. S. Gould.** Electron transfer. 156. Reactions of vanadium(IV) and -(V) with s^2 metal-ion reducing centers. *Dalton Trans.* 3963–7, 2003.

Yang, Z. and **E. S. Gould.** Electron transfer. 155. Reactions of 1,4-benzoquinones with s^2 reducing centers. *Dalton Trans.* 2219–23, 2003.

Babich, O. A., and **E. S. Gould.** Electron transfer. 151. Decomposition of peroxynitrite as catalyzed by copper(II). *Res. Chem. Interm.* 28:575–83, 2002.

Babich, O. A., and **E. S. Gould.** Electron transfer. 146. Aqueous solutions of unipositive cadmium; reactions of $(Cd^1)_2{}^{2+}$ (aq). *Chem. Commun.* 998, 2001.

Swavey, S., V. Manivannan, and **E. S. Gould.** Electron transfer. 147. Reductions with gallium(I). *Inorg. Chem.* 40:1312, 2001.

Gregory, R. B. Protein hydration and glass transitions. In *The Role of Water in Foods,* pp. 55–99, ed. D. Reid. New York: Chapman-Hall, 1997.

Gregory, R. B. Protein hydration and glass transition behavior. In *Protein-Solvent Interactions,* pp. 191–264, ed. R. B. Gregory. New York: Marcel Dekker, Inc., 1995.

Gregory, R. B., M. Gangoda, R. K. Gilpin, and W. Su. Influence of hydration on the conformation of lysozyme studied by solid-state ^{13}C-NMR spectroscopy. *Biopolymers* 33:513–19, 1993.

Vanchura, B. A., et al. **(S. D. Huang)**. Direct synthesis of mesostructured lamellar molybdenum disulfides using a molten neural n-alkylamine as the solvent and template. *J. Am. Chem. Soc.* 124(41): 12090–1, 2002.

Kuehl. C. J., et. al. **(S. D. Huang)**. Self-assembly of nanoscopic coordination cages of D_{3h} symmetry. *Proc. Natl. Acad. Sci. USA* 99(8): 4932–6, 2002.

Kuehl, C. J., **S. D. Huang,** and P. J. Stang. Self-assembly with postmodification: Kinetically stabilized metalla-supramolecular rectangles. *J. Am. Chem. Soc.* 123(39):9634–41, 2001.

Asefa, T., et al. **(M. Jaroniec)**. A novel route to periodic mesoporous aminosilicas, PMAs: Ammonolysis of periodic mesoporous organosilicas. *J. Am. Chem. Soc.* 125: 11662–73, 2003.

Matos, J. R., et al. **(M. Jaroniec)**. Ordered mesoporous silica with large cage-like pores. Structural identification and pore connectivity design by controlling the synthesis temperature and time. *J. Am. Chem. Soc.* 125:821–9, 2003.

Kruk, M., and **M. Jaroniec.** Argon adsorption at 77K as a useful tool for the elucidation of pore connectivity in ordered materials with large cage-like mesopores. *Chem. Mater.* 15:2942–9, 2003.

Li, Z., and **M. Jaroniec.** Synthesis and adsorption properties of colloid-imprinted carbons with surface and volume mesoporosity. *Chem. Mater.* 15:1327–33, 2003.

Khitrin, A. K., V. L. Ermakov, and B. M. Fung. Nuclear magnetic resonance molecular photography. *J. Chem. Phys.* 117:6903–6, 2002.

Khitrin, A. K., and B. M. Fung. NMR simulation of an eight-state quantum system. *Phys. Rev. A* 64:032306/1–4, 2001.

Khitrin, A. K., and B. M. Fung. Indirect NMR detection in solids with multiple cross-polarization periods. *J. Magn. Reson.* 152:185–8, 2001.

Khitrin, A. K., H. Sun, and B. M. Fung. Method of multifrequency excitation for creating pseudopure states for NMR quantum computing. *Phys. Rev. A* 63:020301-1–4, 2001.

Okasaki, T., and **K. K. Laali.** B-silyl-substituted silaadamantyl, silabicyclooctyl, silanorbornyl, and 1-silacyclohexyl cations: A Theoretical (DFT and GIAO-NMR) study. *J. Org. Chem.* 68:1872–7, 2003.

Laali, K. K., et al. Stable ion study of 7.8- and 9,10-dihydrobenzo[a]pyrene (BaP), 6-halo (X=F, Cl, Br)-9,10-dihydro-BaP, 1-methoxy- and 3-methoxy-7,8,9,10-tetrahydrobenzo[a]pyren-7-one, trans-BP-dihydrodiol and its O-benzoylated derivative, combined with a comparative DNA binding study of regioisomeric (1.4,2)pyrenyl CR_2OH. *Organic and Biomolecular Chem.* 1:1509–16, 2003.

Laali, K. K., and T. Okazaki. NMR of persistent carbocations from PAHs. *Annual Report of NMR Spectroscopy.* New York: Academic Press, 47:149–214, 2002.

Laali, K. K., J. F. Koser, **S. D. Huang,** and M. Gangoda. 1-triflato-3,5,7-trimethyl-1,3,5,7-tetrasilaadamantane and 1,3-bistriflato-5,7-dimethyl-1,3,5,7-tetrasilaadamantane: Synthesis, complexation study, and X-ray structure of 1-hydroxy-3,5,7-trimethyl-1,3,5,7-tetrasilaada-manatne. *J. Organomet. Chem.* 658:141–6, 2002.

Novikov, Y. Y., and **P. Sampson.** 1-bromo-1-lithioethene: A practical reagent for the efficient preparation of 2-bromo-1-alken-3-ols. *Organic Lett.* 5:2263–6, 2003.

Kiryanov, A. A., **P. Sampson,** and **A. J. Seed.** Synthesis and

Kent State University

Selected Publications (continued)

mesomorphic properties of 1,1-difluoroalkyl-substituted biphenylthienyl and terphenyl liquid crystals. A comparative study of mesomorphic behavior relative to methylene, alkoxy, and alkanoyl analogs. *J. Mater. Chem.* 11:3068–77, 2001.

Kiryanov, A. A., **P. Sampson,** and **A. J. Seed.** Synthesis of 2-alkoxy-substituted thiophenes, 1,3-thiazoles, and related S-heterocycles via Lawesson's reagent-mediated cyclization under microwave irridiation: Applications for liquid crystal synthesis. *J. Org. Chem.* 66:7925–9, 2001.

Dudones, J. D., and **P. Sampson.** Transannular vs intramolecular insertion reactions of transition metal carbenes: Evaluation of a transannular approach to cyclooctane ring synthesis. *Tetrahedron* 56:9555–67, 2000.

Seed, A. J., K. J. Toyne, and J. W. Goodby. The synthesis, phase transitions, and optical properties of novel tetrathiafulvalene derivatives with extremely high molecular polarizability. *Liq. Cryst.* 28(7):1047–55, 2001.

Kiryanov, A. A., **A. J. Seed,** and **P. Sampson.** Synthesis and stability of 2-(1,1-diflyoroalkyl) thiophenes and related 1,1-diflyoroalkyl benzenes: Fluorinated building blocks for liquid crystal synthesis. *Tetrahedron* 57:5757–67, 2001.

Kiryanov, A. A., **A. J. Seed,** and **P. Sampson.** Ring fluorinated thiophenes: Applications to liquid crystal synthesis. *Tetrahedron Lett.* 42:8797–800, 2001.

Matkin, L. S., et al. **(A. Seed)**. Resonant X-ray scattering at the Se edge in liquid crystal free-standing films and devices. *Appl. Phys. Lett.* 76(14):1863–5, 2000.

Stroup, D., and J. Y. L. Chiang. Hepatocyte nuclear factor 4 (HNF4) and chicken ovalbumin upstream promoter transcription factor II (COUP-TFII) interact to modulate transcription of the rat cholesterol 7α-hydroxylase gene (CYP7A). *J. Lipid Res.* 41:1–11, 2000.

Stroup, D., M. Crestani, and J. Y. L. Chiang. Identification of a bile acid response element in the cholesterol 7α-hydroxylase gene (CYP7A). *Am. J. Physiol.* 273:G508–17, 1997.

Stroup, D., M. Crestani, and J. Y. L. Chiang. Orphan receptors COUP-TFII and retinoid X receptor activate and bind the rat cholesterol 7α-hydroxylase gene (CYP7A). *J. Biol. Chem.* 272:9802–8, 1997.

Bae, I. T., and **Y. V. Tolmachev,** et al. In situ Fe K-edge X-ray absorption spectroscopy of a nytrosyl iron (II) porphyrin adduct adsorbed on high area carbon in aqueous electrolytes. *Inorg. Chem.* 40:3256–8, 2001.

Stefan, I. C., and **Y. V. Tolmachev,** et al. Theoretical analysis of the pulse-clamp method as applied to neural stimulating electrodes. *J. Electrochem. Soc.* 148(3) E73–8, 2001.

Stefan, I. C., **Y. V. Tolmachev,** and D. A. Scherson. Phase sensitive detection in potential modulated in situ absorption and probe beam deflection techniques: Theoretical considerations. *Anal. Chem.* 73:527–32, 2001.

Scherson, D. A., **Y. V. Tolmachev,** and I. C. Stefan. Ultraviolet/visible spectroelectrochemistry. An invited article for *Encyclopedia of Analytical Chemistry: Applications, Theory and Instrumentation,* ed. R. A. Meyer. Chichester, UK: J. Wiley & Sons, 2000.

Durand, P. J., R. Pasari, J. W. Baker, and **C.-c. Tsai.** An efficient algorithm for similarity analysis of molecules. *Internet J. Chem.* 2(17):1–16, 1999.

Lesniewski, M. L., et al. **(C.-c. Tsai).** QSAR studies of antiviral agents using structure-activity maps. *Internet J. Chem.* 2(7):1–59, 1999.

Parakulam, R. R., M. L. Lesniewski, K. J. Taylor-McCabe, and **C.-c. Tsai.** QSAR studies of antiviral agents using molecular similarity analysis and structure-activity maps. *SAR QSAR Environ. Res.* 10:179–206, 1999.

Tubergen, M. J., C. R. Torok, and R. J. Lavrich. Effect of solvent on molecular conformation: Microwave spectra and structures of 2-aminoethanol van der Waals complexes. *J. Chem. Phys.* 119:8397–403, 2003.

Lavrich, R. J., et al. **(M. J. Tubergen)**. Experimental studies of peptide bonds: Identification of the C_7^{eq} conformation of the alanine dipeptide analog N-acetyl-alanine n'-methylamide from torsion-rotation interactions. *J. Chem. Phys.* 118:1253–65, 2003.

Lavrich, R. J., C. R. Torok, and **M. J. Tubergen.** Effect of the bulky side chain on the backbone structure of the amino and derivative valinamide. *J. Phys. Chem. A* 106:8013–8, 2002.

Ostroverkhova, O., M. He, **R. J. Twieg,** and W. E. Moerner. Role of temperature in controlling performance of photorefractive organic glasses. *Chem. Phys. Chem.* 4:732–44, 2003.

Willets, K. A., et al. **(R. J. Twieg)**. Novel fluorophores for single-molecule imaging. *J. Amer. Chem. Soc.* 125:1174–5, 2003.

Adorjan, A., et al. **(R. J. Twieg)**. Light scattering study of a twist grain boundary liquid crystal. *Phys. Rev. Lett.* 90:035503, 2003.

Hayden, L. M., et al. **(R. J. Twieg)**. New materials for optical rectification and electroopic sampling of ultrashort pulses in the terahertz regime. *J. Polym. Sci., Part B: Polym. Phy.* 41:2492–500, 2003.

Bose, A., et. al **(R. J. Twieg and S. D. Huang)**. Strong electronacceptor methylviologen dications confined in a 2-D inorganic host: Synthesis, structural characterization, charge transport and electrochemical properties of $(MV)_{0.25}V_2O_5$. *J. Am. Chem. Soc.* 124(1):4–5, 2002.

Chitester, B. J., and **F. G. Walz Jr.** Kinetic studies of guanine recognition and a phosphate group subsite on ribonuclease T_1 using substitution mutants at Glu46 and Lys41. *Arch. Biochem. Biophys.* 406:73–7, 2002.

Kumar, K., and **F. G. Walz Jr.** Probing functional perfection in substructures of ribonuclease T_1: Double random mutagenesis involving Asn43, Asn44, and Glu46 in the guanine binding loop. *Biochemistry* 40:3748–57, 2001.

Arni, R. K., et al. **(F. G. Walz Jr.).** Three-dimensional structure of ribonuclease T_1 complexed with an isosteric analogue of GpU: Alternate substrate binding modes and catalysis. *Biochemistry* 38:2452–61, 1999.

Reznikov, Y., et al. **(J. L. West).** Ferroelectric nematic suspension. *Appl. Phys. Lett.* 82:1917, 2003.

West, J. L., et al. Drag on particles in a nematic suspension by a moving nematic-isotropic interface. *Phys. Rev. E.* 66:012702, 2002.

Ouskova, E., et al. **(J. L. West).** Photo-orientation of liquid crystals due to light-induced desorption and adsorption of dye molecules on an aligning surface. *Phys. Rev. E.* 64:051709, 2001.

Shiyanovskii, S. V., et al. **(J. L. West).** Tensor and complex anchoring in liquid crystals. *Phys. Rev. E* 62:1477–80, 2000.

LEHIGH UNIVERSITY

College of Arts and Sciences
Department of Chemistry

Programs of Study

The Department of Chemistry offers the Ph.D. degree in chemistry with specialization in the areas of analytical, inorganic, organic, and physical chemistry and biochemistry; the Ph.D. is also offered through interdisciplinary programs in polymer science and engineering and in pharmaceutical chemistry. The Ph.D. program has minimal formal course requirements beyond the M.S. degree, but proficiency in three areas of chemistry must be demonstrated. A doctoral examination (a written examination and an original research proposal) must be passed in the second year. Students then continue performing original research and write and defend a dissertation. The Master of Science degree in chemistry requires 30 hours of course work plus demonstration of proficiency in two areas of chemistry. Interdisciplinary programs leading to an M.S. or M.E. in polymer science and engineering, an M.S. in pharmaceutical chemistry, and an M.S. in clinical chemistry are also available.

Research Facilities

Research facilities are situated in several locations. Most of the facilities are housed in the 90,000-square-foot, seven-story Seeley G. Mudd Building. The top three floors contain modern research laboratories. Many of the laboratories in the Sinclair Laboratory are assigned to chemistry professors who specialize in research involving surface chemistry. Biochemistry research is carried out in the Mudd Building as well as in the Iacocca Building on the Mountaintop Campus.

The department has the instrumentation necessary for all of its areas of specialization. It is superbly equipped for surface analysis, with a very high resolution Scienta ESCA instrument with automated electron diffractometer, high flux rotating anode and spatial resolution capability, and a variety of other surface spectrometers. Three NMR spectrometers are used by students: 360-MHz (with a microimaging accessory), a 500-MHz solution spectrometer, and a 300-MHz solids instrument. A UV-VIS-NIR spectrophotometer is available for diffuse reflectance with vacuum, controlled atmosphere, and variable temperature capabilities. IR facilities include four FT instruments, well equipped for transmission, diffuse reflectance, internal reflectance, and photoacoustic spectroscopy. Numerous chromatographs, spectrometers, centrifuges, electrochemical instruments, a mass spectrometer, and two stopped-flow spectrophotometers are all in active use by graduate students. The department has an open policy in which students use the instruments necessary for their research. The chemistry department has its own electronics and instrumentation maintenance staff.

The Fairchild-Martindale Library has extensive resources to support graduate student classes and research. These include access to Chemical Abstract Service's SciFinder Scholar, INSPEC, Science Citation Index, and materials science databases from Cambridge Scientific Abstracts. In addition, Lehigh has a rich array of reference materials and journal subscriptions, including electronic journals from such publishing programs as Academic Ideal, American Chemical Society, Highwire, Royal Society of Chemistry, Science Direct, Wiley Interscience, and Springer Link. The collection includes more than 11,000 books in chemistry and allied sciences.

The computing environment consists of numerous workstations and microcomputers distributed across campus and an SGI 3800 Origin mainframe computer. The chemistry department houses two computer laboratories; one has five SGI Octane workstations, and the other has eighteen Pentium-based microcomputers.

Financial Aid

Most entering graduate students in chemistry are supported as half-time teaching assistants; the current stipend (2004–05) is equivalent to $18,260 for a twelve-month period. In addition, teaching assistants receive tuition remission for 9 credits per semester and 3 credits during the summer. Students making satisfactory progress are normally supported until the completion of their degree program. Research assistantships are also held by graduate students and typically cover a twelve-month period. Fellowships with stipends comparable to teaching assistants are also available.

Cost of Study

Tuition for the 2004–05 academic year is $950 per credit. Tuition expenses are paid for teaching assistants and research assistants. Graduate students are responsible for a technology fee of $100 per semester.

Living and Housing Costs

Students live in a wide variety of accommodations, and expenses can be reasonable, especially if shared. Lehigh operates a 148-unit garden apartment complex for single and married students located in nearby Saucon Valley. Rent for a one-bedroom, unfurnished apartment is $470 per month. Day care is available nearby, and hourly bus service is provided. Private rental units are also available. Total living expenses average $10,800 per year.

Student Group

In fall 2003, there were 150 students enrolled in the chemistry program, including 35 full-time students and those taking courses through distance education. Students come from many states and several other countries. It is the policy of the University to provide equal opportunity based on merit and without discrimination due to race, color, religion, gender, age, national origin, citizenship status, handicap, or veteran status.

Student Outcomes

Recent graduates have obtained postdoctoral positions at prestigious institutions such as the Universities of Virginia and Rochester, Johns Hopkins, and NASA. Other doctoral graduates obtained employment at Air Products, Merck, J & J, McNeil Consumer Products, Agere, OraSure Technologies, and several pharmaceutical companies. For students seeking careers in teaching, a predoctoral internship at a liberal arts college can be arranged. For graduate students seeking careers in industry, predoctoral industrial research can be arranged.

Location

Bethlehem, Pennsylvania (population 72,000), is located 50 miles north of Philadelphia and 90 miles west of New York City; best access is via Interstate 78, U.S. Route 22, or Lehigh Valley International Airport. Founded in 1741, Bethlehem has a rich cultural heritage in the Moravian tradition. Historical buildings have been well preserved, giving the community a charming Colonial atmosphere. The Lehigh Valley (Allentown, Bethlehem, and Easton) is the chief commercial and industrial center for east-central Pennsylvania.

The University

Lehigh is an independent, nondenominational, coeducational university. Founded in 1865, it has approximately 4,500 undergraduate students within its three major colleges: Arts and Sciences, Engineering and Applied Science, and Business and Economics.There are approximately 1,800 graduate students enrolled in various graduate programs and in the graduate-only College of Education. The 1,500-acre campus includes superb athletic facilities, a health club, and cultural venues, including a $33-million arts center.

Applying

A preliminary application is available for domestic students. The GRE General Test is required for all students; for international students, a minimum TSE score of 55 and a TOEFL computer-based score of 213 are required. There is a $50 fee for the formal application.

Correspondence and Information

Graduate Admissions
Department of Chemistry
Seeley G. Mudd Building
Lehigh University
6 East Packer Avenue
Bethlehem, Pennsylvania 18015-3172
Telephone: 610-758-3471
Fax: 610-758-6536
World Wide Web: http://www.lehigh.edu/~inche/

Ingrid Parson, Ed.D.
Associate Dean of Graduate and Research Programs
College of Arts and Sciences
Lehigh University
9 West Packer Avenue
Bethlehem, Pennsylvania 18015-3174
Telephone: 610-758-4280
Fax: 610-758-6232
World Wide Web: http://www.lehigh.edu/~incas/incas.html

Lehigh University

THE FACULTY AND THEIR RESEARCH

Jack A. Alhadeff, Professor; Ph.D., Oregon, 1972. Biochemistry: purification and characterization of glycosidases, biochemical basis of human diseases involving abnormal glycoprotein metabolism.

Michael J. Behe, Associate Professor; Ph.D., Pennsylvania, 1978. Biochemistry: structure of nucleic acids, specifically oligopurine regions in eukaryotes and the B-Z transition in synthetic polydeoxynucleotides.

Gregory S. Ferguson, Associate Professor; Ph.D., Cornell, 1988. Materials chemistry: chemistry of organic and inorganic surfaces; organometallic chemistry.

Robert A. Flowers II, Professor and Chair; Ph.D., Lehigh, 1989. Chemistry: organometallic reaction mechanisms, lanthanide chemistry, protein folding and renaturation, calorimetry, electrochemical studies of single electron transfer.

Natalie Foster, Associate Professor; Ph.D., Lehigh, 1982. Analytical and organic chemistry: contrast enhancement agents for medical imaging NMR, structural dynamics and molecular associations of biologically significant molecules.

Ned D. Heindel, Howard S. Bunn Professor; Ph.D., Delaware, 1963. Organic and medicinal chemistry: synthesis of potential medicinal agents.

Li Jia, Assistant Professor; Ph.D., Northwestern, 1996. Inorganic, organic, and polymer chemistry; synthesis, characterization, and catalysis of organometallic complexes; organic synthetic methodology; polymer synthesis; polymeric materials.

Kamil Klier, University Professor; Ph.D., Czechoslovak Academy of Sciences, 1961. Physical chemistry: surface science, catalysis, photoelectron spectroscopy.

Tianbo Liu, Assistant Professor; Ph.D., SUNY at Stony Brook, 1999. Physical and materials chemistry.

Linda J. Lowe-Krentz, Associate Professor; Ph.D., Northwestern, 1980. Biochemistry: heparin signaling in the vascular system, receptor structure and function.

Steven L. Regen, Professor; Ph.D., MIT, 1972. Organic chemistry: organic and polymer chemistry, supramolecular assemblies, membrane structure and function, drug design.

James E. Roberts, Associate Professor; Ph.D., Northwestern, 1982. Physical and analytical chemistry: applications of nuclear magnetic resonance to solids, including polymers, one-dimensional conductors, and coal; effects of paramagnetic centers in solid-state NMR.

Keith J. Schray, Professor; Ph.D., Penn State, 1970. Organic chemistry and biochemistry: protein-surface interactions, novel immunoassays.

Gary W. Simmons, Professor; Ph.D., Virginia, 1967. Physical chemistry: surface chemistry, coatings, catalysis, and materials characterization using Auger spectroscopy, Mössbauer spectroscopy, low-energy electron diffraction, and X-ray photoelectron spectroscopy.

Daniel Zeroka, Professor; Ph.D., Pennsylvania, 1966. Physical chemistry: applications of electronic structure methodologies to molecular species; solids and molecular species adsorbed on solid surfaces, with particular emphasis on prediction of spectra (IR, Raman, VCD, NMR).

MICHIGAN TECHNOLOGICAL UNIVERSITY

Department of Chemistry

Programs of Study

The Department of Chemistry offers graduate programs that lead to the Master of Science (M.S.) and Doctor of Philosophy (Ph.D.) degrees in chemistry. The primary focus of the graduate program in chemistry is on the Ph.D. Michigan Technological University (MTU) stresses solid active research involvement, presentation of results at national meetings, publication in refereed journals, and internships in industry. Multidisciplinary research is encouraged and significant opportunities exist to collaborate with researchers in other departments on the University campus.

Students are generally admitted into the department's graduate programs based on an assessment of their ability to succeed as doctoral degree students. A minimum of 30 course and/or research credit hours beyond the M.S. degree (or its equivalent) or a minimum of 60 course and/or research credit hours beyond the bachelor's degree are required. The course work requirements are determined by the department's core-course requirements and by the student's Advisory Committee. All doctoral students commence taking qualifying examinations beginning in the second year of their enrollment.

Research Facilities

Research is conducted in the laboratories within the Department of Chemistry as well as other University facilities in nearby buildings. The Department of Chemistry offers a wide variety of instrumentation. Available for student use are 200 and 400 MHz nuclear magnetic resonance spectrometers, a gas chromatograph/mass spectrometer, a liquid chromatograph/mass spectrometer, and Fourier transform infrared spectrometers. Also available are gas, liquid, and ion chromatographs and UV-visible, atomic absorption, and fluorescence spectrophotometers. Specialized equipment includes a laser Raman spectrometer, a supercritical fluid extraction system, a single crystal Enraf-Nonius CAD4 X-ray diffractometer, a Coulter N4 Plus submicron particle analyzer, and an electrochemical workstation.

The Process Analytical Chemistry Laboratory is equipped with instrumentation designed for the online analysis of process streams, including Fourier transform near-infrared and infrared spectrometers, flow injection analyzers, process gas chromatographs, and an electroanalysis system.

Polymer analyses include gel permeation chromatography (with a light-scattering detector), thermal analysis, and electron microscopy (with atomic force module). Rheometers and a large collection of molders and extruders are also available.

Financial Aid

Financial aid is available to a limited number of qualified full-time students in the form of fellowships, research assistantships, and teaching assistantships. Aid packages include a stipend, tuition, and some student fees. The stipend for M.S. candidates is currently $4415 per semester and for Ph.D. candidates, $5126 per semester. In addition, a health insurance supplement is provided by the University. Funding may be available on a competitive basis for students to travel to professional conferences.

Cost of Study

Tuition for full-time graduate students (resident and nonresident) for the 2004–05 academic year is $3888 per semester; engineering and computer science majors pay $4288 per semester. All students are responsible for a student activity fee of approximately $135 per semester. Health insurance is required for all graduate students; a supplement is subject to financial aid status.

Living and Housing Costs

Michigan Tech residence halls have accommodations for single students; applications may be obtained from the Director of Residential Services. For married students, Michigan Tech has one- and two-bedroom furnished apartments; applications may be obtained from the manager of Daniell Heights Apartments. Because the cost of housing is subject to change, representative costs cannot be stated. There is also off-campus housing available in the surrounding community. Yahoo! lists the overall cost-of-living index for Houghton as 83 (national average is 100). For more information, prospective students should visit the Web site http://list.realestate.yahoo.com/realestate/neighborhood/main.html.

Location

Michigan Tech is located in Houghton on Michigan's scenic Keweenaw Peninsula. The Keweenaw stretches about 70 miles into Lake Superior, and the surrounding area is perfect for any outdoor activity. The campus is a 15-minute walk from downtown Houghton; public transportation is available from Houghton and Hancock. Houghton has been listed as the safest college town in Michigan and was ranked eighth out of 467 nationwide in the report, *Crime at College: Student Guide to Personal Safety*. The Houghton County Memorial Airport (CMX) serves the area with direct flights to Minneapolis and Detroit via Northwest Airlink; Marquette K. I. Sawyer (SAW), an approximate 2-hour drive from Houghton) serves the area via Detroit.

The University

Michigan Tech was founded in 1885 as the Michigan Mining School to serve the nation's first major mining enterprises focused on copper and iron. Several name changes tracked the growth and diversification of the institution, and it was named Michigan Technological University in 1964. Today, the University offers a full range of associate, bachelor's, master's, and doctoral degrees in the sciences, engineering, forestry, business, communication, and technology. MTU has been rated one of the nation's top ten best buys for science and technology by *U.S. News & World Report.*

Applying

The application for admission and an official transcript of previous academic work at the undergraduate and graduate levels must be submitted to the Graduate School. A nonrefundable $40 application fee ($45 for international applications) must accompany the application. Applications should be submitted at least six weeks before the start of the applicant's desired quarter of entrance. Application materials are also available from the Department of Chemistry. Students can also apply online at http://www.admin.mtu.edu/rgs/graduate/apply.html.

Correspondence and Information

Graduate Admissions Committee
Department of Chemistry
Michigan Technological University
1400 Townsend Drive
Houghton, Michigan 49931
World Wide Web: http://chemistry.mtu.edu/index.php

Michigan Technological University

THE FACULTY AND THEIR RESEARCH

Dallas K. Bates, Professor; Ph.D., Idaho, 1974. Organic synthesis, chemistry of pyrroles, novel sulfur chemistry in organic synthesis. (E-mail: dbates@mtu.edu)

Richard E. Brown, Professor; Ph.D., Indiana, 1967. Quantum chemistry, molecular modeling. (E-mail: rebrown@mtu.edu)

Paul Charlesworth, Associate Professor; Ph.D., Keele (England), 1994. Spectroscopy, photochemistry, application of new multimedia technologies to chemical education. (E-mail: pcharles@mtu.edu)

David J. Chesney, Associate Professor; Ph.D., North Dakota State, 1986. Electroanalytical chemistry, supercritical fluid technology, process analytical chemistry. (E-mail: djchesne@mtu.edu)

Bahne C. Cornilsen, Professor; Ph.D., Alfred, College of Ceramics, 1975. Solid-state structure, Raman spectroscopy, nickel hydroxide battery electrode structure. (E-mail: bccornil@mtu.edu)

Shiyue Fang, Assistant Professor; Ph.D., Missouri–St. Louis, 2000. Organic synthesis, interdisciplinary projects in artificial molecular receptors, medicine and nanotechnology. (E-mail: shifang@mtu.edu)

Sarah A. Green, Associate Professor and Department Chair; MIT/Woods Hole Oceanographic Institution, 1992. Photochemistry, environmental chemistry. (E-mail: sgreen@mtu.edu)

Patricia A. Heiden, Associate Professor; Ph.D., Akron, 1994. Synthesis and characterization of polymers, structure/property relationships in polymers and new polymerization methods. (E-mail: paheiden@mtu.edu)

Leslie Leifer, Professor Emeritus; Kansas, 1959. Solution physical chemistry, including structure in liquids and Mossbauer spectroscopy. (E-mail: lleifer@mtu.edu)

Haiying Liu, Assistant Professor; Ph.D., Fudan (China), 1995. Nanosensors (chemical and biosensors) made of self-assembled polymer monolayers and single-wall carbon nanotubes.

Jian Liu, Assistant Professor; Ph.D., Miami (Florida), 1999. Nanoparticle catalysts, luminescent nanosensors, novel photocatalytic (organic/inorganic) nanomaterials.

Marshall Logue, Associate Professor; Ph.D., Ohio State, 1969. Organic synthesis, chemistry of nucleosides and carbohydrates. (E-mail: mwlogue@mtu.edu)

Rudy Luck, Associate Professor; Ph.D., Toronto, 1987. The synthesis of high oxidation state Group VI transition metal oxo and peroxo compounds and studies on their applications as catalysts for epoxidation and allylic alcohol isomerization reactions. (E-mail: rluck@mtu.edu)

Pushpalatha Murthy, Professor; Ph.D., Brown, 1979. Bioorganic chemistry, biochemistry and molecular biology, mechanism of signal transduction, phosphoinositides, inositol phosphates, phytic acid, phytases. (E-mail: ppmurthy@mtu.edu)

Martin Thompson, Assistant Professor; Ph.D., Arizona State, 2000. Chemical genetics, biochemistry, molecular biology and medicinal chemistry, biophysical studies of molecular architecture and recognition events in transcriptional assemblies. (E-mail: mthomps@mtu.edu)

Bela Torok, Assistant Professor; Ph.D., Jozsef Attila (Hungary), 1995. Catalysts for asymmetric synthesis—immobilization of chiral ligands on polymer or inorganic supports.

Eugenijus Urnezius, Assistant Professor; Ph.D., Case Western Reserve, 1999. Organometallic oligomers and polymers and their applications as advanced materials. (E-mail: urnezius@mtu.edu)

John Williams, Professor; Ph.D., Melbourne, 1971. Processing science of composites, crack propagation in glass resins, relaxation properties in polymers. (E-mail: jgwillia@mtu.edu)

SELECTED PUBLICATIONS

Bates, D. K., X. Li, and P. V. Jog. Simple thiazocine-2-acetic acid derivatives via ring-closing metathesis. *J. Org. Chem.* 69:2750–4, 2004.

Ekkati, A. R., and **D. K. Bates.** A convenient synthesis of N-acylpyrroles from primary aromatic amides. *Synthesis* 1959–61, 2003.

Bates, D. K., K. Li, and **R. L. Luck.** 6-methyl-11a 12-dihydro-6H-quino[3,2-b][1,4]benzothiazine: An amidine formed under unusual conditions. *Acta Crystallogr., Sect. E* 59(3):302–3, 2003.

Bates, D. K., and K. Li. Stannous chloride mediated reductive cyclization-rearrangement of nitroarenyl ketones. *J. Org. Chem.* 67:8662, 2002.

Bates, D. K., et al. 2-cyanamidothiazoles from 3-propynylthio-1,2,4-triazoles. *Heterocycles* 51:475–9, 1999.

Bates, D. K., and M. Xia. A sulfoxide-based ring annelation approach to fused, many-membered ring N,S-heterocycles. *J. Org. Chem.* 63:9190–6, 1998.

Jog, P. V., **R. E. Brown,** and **D. K. Bates.** A redox-mediated molecular brake: Dynamic NMR study of 2-[2-(methylthio)phenyl]isoindolin-1-one and S-oxidized counterparts. *J. Org. Chem.* 68:8240–3, 2003.

Volkman, C. J., et al. **(R. E. Brown** and **P. P. N. Murthy).** Conformational flexibility of inositol phosphates: Influence of structural characteristics. *Tetrahedron Lett.* 43:4853–6, 2002.

Brown, R. E., et al. **(R. L. Luck).** Synthesis, 1H NMR, single crystal X-ray determined and ab-initio molecular structural analyses on 1-(isopropylideneaminomethyl)pyrene. *J. Mol. Struct.* 561:93–101, 2001.

Chateauneuf, G. M., **R. E. Brown,** and B. J. Brown. Computational studies of electron-transfer processes in old yellow enzyme. *Int. J. Quantum Chem.* 85:685–92, 2001.

Bauman, A. T., G. M. Chateauneuf, **R. E. Brown,** and **P. P. N. Murthy.** Conformational inversion processes in phytic acid: NMR spectroscopic and molecular modeling studies. *Tetrahedron Lett.* 40:4489–92, 1999.

Charlesworth, P. Review of *The Molecular World, a Series: The Third Dimension*, ed., L. E. Smart. *J. Chem. Educ.* 81:337–8, 2004.

Charlesworth, P., and C. Vician. Leveraging technology for chemical sciences education: An early assessment of WebCT usage in first-year chemistry courses. *J. Chem. Educ.* 80:1333–7, 2003.

Xu, Z., and **B. C. Cornilsen** et al. Quantitative mineral analysis by FTIR spectroscopy. *Internet J. Vibrational Spectroscopy* 5, 2001.

Xu, Z., **B. C. Cornilsen,** and G. Meitzner. Quantitative determination of Ni(II) & Ni(IV) in nickel electrode active mass using X-ray absorption spectroscopy. *Proceedings–Electrochemical Society* 98(15):1–10, 1999.

Srinivasan, V., **B. C. Cornilsen,** and J. W. Weidner. The application of point defect chemistry in characterizing the redox processes in the nickel hydroxide electrode. *Proceedings–Electrochem. Soc.* 98(15): 31–42, 1999.

Cornilsen, B., Z. Xu, and G. Meitzner. Quantitative oxidation state determination of nickel oxyhydroxides by X-ray absorption spectroscopy. *Ceram. Trans.* 92:25–35, 1999.

Cornilsen, B. C. The nonstoichiometric, solid solution structural model for nickel electrode active mass. *Proc.–Electrochem. Soc.* 98-15:23–30, 1999.

Shao-Horn, Y., S. A. Hackney, and **B. C. Cornilsen.** Structural characterization of heat-treated electrolytic manganese dioxide and topotactic transformation of discharge products in the Li-MnO_2 cells. *J. Electrochem. Soc.* 144:3147–53, 1997.

Cornilsen, B., X. Cai, R. Tanbug, and G. Meitzner. Nickel electrode oxidation states, the presence of Ni(IV), and one-electron transfer in oxidized and reduced materials. *Proc.–Electrochem. Soc.* 96(16):88–98, 1997.

Hackney, S. A., **B. C. Cornilsen,** C. R. Walk, and N. Margalit. Microstructural studies of chemically and electrochemically lithiated vanadium pentoxide. *Prog. Batteries Battery Mater.* 16:59–70, 1997.

Wang, X., and **S. A. Green.** Mobilization of copper from mine tailings by dissolved organic matter. *J. Great Lakes Res.* In press.

Cory, R. M., **S. A. Green,** and K. S. Pregitzer. Dissolved organic matter concentration and composition in the forests and streams of Olympic National Park, WA. *Biogeochemistry,* 67:269–88, 2004.

Peterson, M., D. Barber, and **S. A. Green.** Monte-Carlo modeling and measurements of actinic flux levels in Summit, Greenland snowpack. *Atmos. Environ.* 36(15–6):2545–51, 2002.

Qiu, R., and **S. A. Green** et al. Measurements of JNO_3-in snow by nitrate-based actinometry. *Atmos. Environ.* 36(15–16):2563–71, 2002.

Chen, C., et al. **(S. A. Green).** Prognostic modeling studies of the Keweenaw current in Lake Superior. Part I: Formation and evolution. *J. Phys. Oceanogr.* 31:379–95, 2001.

Zhu, J., et al. **(S. A. Green).** Prognostic modeling studies of the Keweenaw current in Lake Superior. Part II: Simulation. *J. Phys. Oceanogr.* 31:396–410, 2001.

Flicker, T. M., and **S. A. Green.** Comparison of gas-phase free radical populations in tobacco smoke and model systems by HPLC. *Environ. Health Perspect.* 109:765–71, 2001.

Honrath, R. E., et al. **(S. A. Green).** Release of NOx from sunlight-irradiated midlatitude snow. *Geophys. Res. Lett.* 27:2237-40, 2000.

Rachtanapun, P., and **P. Heiden.** Thermoplastic polymers as modifiers for urea-formaldehyde (UF) wood adhesives. I. Procedures for the preparation and characterization of thermoplastic-modified UF suspensions. *J. Appl. Polym. Sci.* 87:890–7, 2003.

Rachtanapun, P., and **P. Heiden.** Thermoplastic polymers as modifiers for urea-formaldehyde (UF) wood adhesives. II. Procedures for the preparation and characterization of thermoplastic-modified UF wood composites. *J. Appl. Polym. Sci.* 87:898–907, 2003.

Liu, Y., P. Laks, and **P. Heiden.** Nanoparticles for the controlled release of fungicides in wood: Soil jar studies using G. trabeum and T. versicolor wood decay fungi. *Holzforschung* 57:135–9, 2003.

Liu, Y., P. Laks, and **P. Heiden.** Controlled release of biocides in solid wood. I. Efficacy against brown rot wood decay fungus (Gloeophyllum trabeum). *J. Appl. Polym. Sci.* 86:596–607, 2002.

Liu, Y., P. Laks, and **P. Heiden.** Controlled release of biocides in solid wood. II. Efficacy against Trametes versicolor and Gloeophyllum trabeum wood decay fungi. *J. Appl. Polym. Sci.* 86:608–14, 2002.

Liu, Y., P. Laks, and **P. Heiden.** Controlled release of biocides in solid wood. III. Preparation and characterization of surfactant-free nanoparticles. *J. Appl. Polym. Sci.* 86:615–21, 2002.

Liu, Y., L. Yan, **P. A. Heiden,** and P. Laks. Use of nanoparticles for controlled release of biocides in solid wood. *J. Appl. Polym. Sci.* 79:458–65, 2001.

Gopala, A., J. Xu, H. Wu, and **P. A. Heiden.** Investigation of readily processable thermoplastic-toughened thermosets; part 4. BMIs toughened with hyperbranched polyester. *J. Appl. Polym. Sci.* 71:1809–17, 1999.

Fox, D. M., and **L. Leifer.** Thermodynamic treatment of complex multicomponent electrolyte solutions. *Fluid Phase Equilib.* 213:1–17, 2003.

Maupin, C. L., A. Mondry, **L. Leifer,** and J. P. Riehl. Pressure and temperature dependence of the $^7F_0 \rightarrow {}^5D_0$ excitation spectrum of europium(III) as a probe of the thermodynamics and solvation structure of complexes of europium(III) with polyaminocarboxylate ligands. *J. Phys. Chem. A* 105:3071–6, 2001.

Fox, D. M., and **L. Leifer.** Thermodynamic studies of ternary systems: LiCl–(n-Bu)$_4$NCl–H_2O at 25°C. *J. Phys. Chem.* 104B:1058, 2000.

Leifer, L., and R. J. Wigent. Determination of the contribution of pair, triplet, and higher-order multiplet interactions to the excess free-energy of mixing in mixed electrolyte-solutions. *J. Phys. Chem.* 89:244–5, 1985.

Wigent, R. J., and **L. Leifer.** Determination of osmotic and activity-coefficients in mixed electrolyte systems: Systems containing clathrate-forming salts. *J. Phys. Chem.* 88:4420–6, 1984.

Ramasubramaniam, R., J. Chen, and **H. Liu.** Homogeneous carbon nanotube/polymer composites for electrical applications. *Appl. Phys. Lett.* 83:2928–30, 2003.

Khoshtariya, D. E., et al. **(H. Liu)**. Charge-transfer mechanism for cytochrome c adsorbed on nanometer thick films. Distinguishing frictional control from conformational gating. *J. Am. Chem. Soc.* 125:7704–14, 2003.

Liu, H., H. Yamamoto, J. Wei, and D. H. Waldeck. Control of the electron transfer rate between cytochrome c and gold electrodes by the manipulation of the electrode's hydrogen bonding character. *Langmuir* 19:2378–87, 2003.

Chen, J., and **H. Liu** et al. Noncovalent engineering of carbon nanotube surfaces by rigid, functional conjugated polymers. *J. Am. Chem. Soc.* 124:9034–5, 2002.

Wei, J., and **H. Liu** et al. Electron-transfer dynamics of cytochrome c: A change in the reaction mechanism with distance. *Angew. Chem. Int. Ed.* 41(24):4700–3, 2002.

Wei, J., and **H. Liu** et al. Direct wiring of cytochrome c's heme unit to an electrode: Electrochemical studies. *J. Am. Chem. Soc.* 124(32): 9591–9, 2002.

Michigan Technological University

Selected Publications (continued)

Strimbu, J., **J. Liu,** and A. E. Kaifer. Cyclodextrin-caped palladium nanoparticles as catalysts for the Suzuki reaction. *Langmuir* 19:483–5, 2003.

Liu, J., W. Ong, A. E. Kaifer, and C. Peindor. A "macrocyclic effect" on the formation of capped silver nanoparticles in DMF. *Langmuir* 18:5981, 2002.

Liu, J., et al. Phase transfer of hydrophilic, cyclodextrin-modified gold nanoparticles to chloroform solutions. *J. Am. Chem. Soc.* 123:11148–54, 2001.

Liu, J., et al. Tuning the catalytic activity of cyclodextrin-modified palladium nanoparticles through host-guest binding interactions. *Langmuir* 17:6762–4, 2001.

Alvarez, J., **J. Liu,** E. Roman, and A. E. Kaifer. Water-soluble platinum and palladium nanoparticles modified with thiolated β-cyclodextrin. *Chem. Commun.* 13:1151–2, 2000.

Liu, J., R. Castro, K. A. Abboud, and A. E. Kaifer. Novel ferrocenyl polyene derivatives and their binding to unmodified cyclodextrins. *J. Org. Chem.* 65:6973–7, 2000.

Liu, J., et al. Cyclodextrin-modified gold nanospheres. *Langmuir* 16:3000–2, 2000.

Liu, J., et al. Cyclodextrin-modified gold nanospheres: Host-guest interactions at work to control colloidal properties. *J. Am. Chem. Soc.* 121:4304–5, 1999.

Belair, S. D., C. L. Maupin, **M. W. Logue,** and J. P. Riehl. Analysis of the temperature dependence of the racemization of Eu(III) complexes through measurement of steady-state circularly polarized luminescence. *J. Lumin.* 86:61–6, 2000.

Maupin, C. L., **M. W. Logue, L. Leifer,** and J. P. Riehl. Measurement and analysis of the temperature and pressure dependence of the $^7F_0 \rightarrow {}^5D_0$ excitation spectra of Eu(III) complexes with 4-phenylethynyl-2,6-pyridene-dicarboxylic acid. *J. Alloys Compd.* 300–1:101–6 2000.

Mendenhall, G. D., **R. L. Luck,** R. K. Bohn, and H. J. Castejon. Structure and reactivity of o-phthaladehyde by X-ray, microwave, and molecular orbital calculations. *J. Mol. Struct.* 645(2–3):249–58, 2003.

Fronczek, F. R., **R. L. Luck,** and G. Wang. Packing and compositional disorder with $MoCl_2O_2(OPMePh_2)_2$ and $MoCl_3O(OPMePh_2)_2$ as assessed by single crystal X-ray diffractometry. *Inorg. Chim. Acta* 342C:247–54, 2003.

Carlson, S. J., T.-B. Lu, and **R. L. Luck.** 3D structures constructed by π···π and C-H···π interactions: Synthesis, structures and selected guest molecules binding properties. *Inorg. Chem. Commun.* 6(5):455–8, 2003.

Lu, T.-B., and **R. L. Luck.** Interlocking frameworks. A consequence of enlarging spacers from 4-pyridinecarboxylate to 4-(4-pyridyl)benzoate. *Inorg. Chim. Acta* 351:345–55, 2003.

Lu, T.-B., et al. **(R. L. Luck).** Molecular architecture via coordination and multi-intermolecular interactions: Synthesis, structures and magnetic properties of one-dimensional coordination polymers of macrocyclic nickel(II) complexes with terephthalate and trans-butene dicarboxylate. *Inorg. Chim. Acta* 355:229–41, 2003.

Luck, R. L., K. Li, and **D. K. Bates.** 6-methyl-11a,12-dihydro-6H-quino-[3,2-b][1,4]benzothiazine. An amidine formed under unusual conditions. *Acta Crystallogr. Sect. E: Struct. Reports Online* E59:o302–3, 2003.

Dorsch, J. A., et al. **(P. P. N. Murthy).** Seed phosphorous and inositol phosphate phenotype of barley low phytic acid genotypes. *Phytochemistry* 62:691–706, 2003.

Raboy, V., et al. **(P. P. N. Murthy).** Origin and seed phenotype of maize low phytic acid 1-1 and low phytic acid 2-1. *Plant Physiol.* 124:355–68, 2000.

Loewus, F. A., and **P. P. N. Murthy.** Myo-inositol metabolism in plants. *Plant Sci.* 150:1–19, 2000.

Carstensen, S., et al. **(P. P. N. Murthy).** Biosynthesis and localization of phosphatidyl-scyllo-inositol in barley aleurone cells. *Lipids* 34:67–73, 1999.

Thompson, M., R. A. Haeusler, P. D. Good, and D. R. Engelke. Nucleolar clustering of dispersed tRNA genes. *Science* 302:1399–1401, 2003.

Daniel, D. C., **M. Thompson,** and N. W. Woodbury. DNA-binding interactions and conformational fluctuations of Tc3 transposase DNA binding domain examined with single molecule fluorescence spectroscopy. *Biophys. J.* 82:1654–6, 2002.

Thompson, M., and N. W. Woodbury. Thermodynamics of specific and nonspecific DNA binding by two DNA-binding domains conjugated to fluorescent probes. *Biophys. J.* 81:1793–1804, 2001.

Daniel, D. C., **M. Thompson,** and N. W. Woodbury. Fluorescence intensity fluctuations of individual labeled DNA fragments and a DNA-binding protein in solution at the single molecule level: A comparison of photobleaching, diffusion, and binding dynamics. *J. Phys. Chem. B* 104:1382–90, 2000.

Thompson, M., and N. W. Woodbury. Fluorescent and photochemical properties of a single zinc finger conjugated to a fluorescent DNA-binding probe. *Biochemistry* 39:4327–38, 2000.

Mhadgut Shilpa, C., I. Bucsi, M. Torok, and **B. Torok.** Sonochemical asymmetric hydrogenation of isophorone on proline modified Pd/Al_2O_3 catalysts. *Chem. Commun.* 984–5, 2004.

Torok, B., and G. K. S. Prakash. Synthesis of chiral trifluoromethylated amines by palladium-catalyzed diastereoselective hydrogenation-hydrogenolysis approach (invited paper—special hydrogenation issue). *Adv. Synth. Catal.* 345:165, 2003.

Prakash, G. K. S., P. Yan, **B. Torok,** and G. A. Olah. Superacid catalyzed hydroxyalkylation of aromatics with ethyl trifluoropyruvate: A new synthetic route to Mosher's acid analogs. *Synlett* 527, 2003.

Torok, B., I. Bucsi, G. K. S. Prakash, and G. A. Olah. Deprotection and cleavage of peptides bound to merrified resin by stable dimethyl ether-poly(hydrogen fluoride) (DMEPHF) complex: A new and convenient reagent for peptide chemistry. *Chem. Commun.* 2882–3, 2002.

Rezeli, M., et al. **(B. Torok).** Significant differences in capillary electrophoretic patterns of follicular fluids and sera from women pretreated for in vitro fertilization. *J. Biochem. Biophys. Methods* 53:151–6, 2002.

Bartok, M., **B. Torok,** K. Balazsik, and T. Bartok. Heterogeneous asymmetric reactions. 23. Enantioselective hydrogenation of ethyl pyruvate over cinchonine- and a-isocinchonine-modified platinum catalysts. *Catal. Lett.* 73:127–31, 2001.

Torok, B., K. Balazsik, K. Felfoldi, and M. Bartok. Asymmetric reactions in sonochemistry. *Ultrasonics Sonochemistry* 8:191–200, 2001.

Torok, B., et al. Interactions between solvent molecules and the reduced or unreduced forms of silico-molybdic acid studied by ESR and NMR spectroscopies and molecular modelling. *Inorgan. Chim. Acta* 298:77–83, 2000.

Smith, R. S., S. Shah, **E. Urnezius,** and J. D. Protasiewicz. An unusual equilibrium chlorine atom transfer process and its potential for assessment of steric pressure by bulky aryls. *J. Am. Chem. Soc.* 125:40–1, 2003.

Brennessel, W. W., et al. **(E. Urnezius).** Tris(η^4-naphthalene)- and Tris (1-4η^4-anthracene)tantalate(1-): First homoleptic arene complexes of anionic tantalum. *J. Am. Chem. Soc.* 124:10258–9, 2002.

Smith, R. C., and **E. Urnezius** et al. Syntheses and structural characterizations of the unsymmetrical diphosphene DmpP:PMes* (Dmp = $2,6\text{-}Mes_2C_6H_3$, Mes* = $2,4,6\text{-}^tBu_3C_6H_2$) and the cyclotetraphosphane $[DmpPPPh]_2$. *Inorg. Chem.* 41:5296–9, 2002.

Urnezius, E., et al. A carbon-free sandwich complex $[(P_5)_2Ti]^2$. *Science* 295:832–4, 2002.

Urnezius, E., K.-C. Lam, A. L. Rheingold, and J. D. Protasiewicz. Triphosphane formation from the terminal zirconium phosphinidene complex $[Cp_2Zr{=}PDmp(PMe_3)]$ (Dmp = $2,6\text{-}Mes_2C_6H_3$) and crystal structure of $DmpP(PPh_2)_2$. *J. Organomet. Chem.* 630:193–197, 2001.

Urnezius, E., S. J. Klippenstein, and J. D. Protasiewicz. Sterically promoted zirconium-phosphorus η-bonding: Structural investigations of $[Cp_2Zr(Cl)\{P(H)Dmp\}]$ and $[Cp_2Zr\{P(H)Dmp\}_2]$ (Dmp = $2,6\text{-}Mes_2C_6H_3$). *Inorg. Chim. Acta* 297:181–90, 2000.

Urnezius, E., S. Shah, and J. D. Protasiewicz. Diphosphene and phosphoranylidenephosphine formation from a terminal phosphinidene complex. *Phosphorus, Sulfur Silicon Relat. Elem.* 146:137–9, 1999.

Urnezius, E., and J. D. Protasiewicz. Synthesis and structural characterization of new hindered aryl phosphorus centers (aryl = 2,6-dimesitylphenyl). *Main Group Chem.* 1:369–72, 1996.

Roggermann, M. C., and **J. G. Williams.** Use of an atomic force microscope to measure surface deformations in polymeric systems. *J. Adhes. Sci. Technol.* 16:905–20, 2002.

Li, F., and **J. G. Williams** et al. Studies of the interphase in epoxy-aluminum joints using nano-indentation and atomic force microscopy. *J. Adhes. Sci. Technol.* 16:935–49, 2002.

Williams, J. G. Polymeric materials encyclopedia. *J. Am. Chem. Soc.* 120:6848–9, 1998.

Huang, M. L., and **J. G. Williams.** Mechanisms of solidification of epoxy-amine resins during cure. *Macromolecules* 27:7423–8, 1994.

NEW YORK UNIVERSITY

Department of Chemistry

Programs of Study

The Department of Chemistry at NYU offers programs leading to the degrees of Master of Science (M.S.) and Doctor of Philosophy (Ph.D.) in chemistry. A major focus of the department is in the study of molecules in living systems; faculty members and students in all subdisciplines of chemistry at NYU work on problems relevant to the molecules of life. The department is highly interdisciplinary, including both traditional areas of chemistry and areas involving biophysics, chemical biology, computational chemistry, materials, and nanoscience. The department has a relatively small faculty, which promotes outstanding interactions among students and faculty and staff members. The major requirements for the doctoral degree in chemistry are the successful completion of an original research project and the presentation and defense of the Ph.D. thesis.

A tightly coupled series of requirements and exams has been designed to advance students to Ph.D. candidacy status and to continue to educate them throughout their graduate work. These steps train, challenge, and broaden students in preparation for excellence in research and an independent scientific career. Entering graduate students meet with the Graduate Committee to plan an academic course schedule that best suits each individual's background and career goals. The Ph.D. students are required to take six courses (three per semester) during their first year. During the first year, students also work in different laboratories for one semester each. This research rotation is expected to take roughly half of the student's time, with an oral presentation at the end of each rotation that is attended by other students and members of the lab. The research rotation provides valuable exposure to the diversity of the program and allows the student to gain firsthand experience for choosing a thesis laboratory. Students generally finish the program in approximately five years.

Research Facilities

A new shared instrumentation facility in the chemistry department includes a rotating anode X-ray diffractometer; MALDI-TOF and electrospray mass spectrometers; several GC-MS and LC-MS systems; 300-, 400-, and 500-MHz NMR spectrometers; polarimeter; circular dichroism spectropolarimeter; FT-IR, UV-Vis, and fluorescence spectrophotometers; and phosphorimager. The facility is managed by a full-time staff member who has earned a Ph.D. in NMR spectroscopy. Additional NMR facilities include a 400-MHz wide-bore spectrometer for solids research and several very-high-field NMR instruments located at the nearby New York State Center for Structural Biology.

Other equipment in the department that is available to researchers includes a scanning tunneling microscope with a high-vacuum specimen-coating device, an atomic force microscope, a state-of-the-art laser laboratory for fast time-resolved studies of chemical processes, peptide, DNA and other robotic synthesizers, photoacoustic and photothermal beam deflection spectrometers, microcalorimeters, and a highly automated, high-performance liquid chromatography system (LC-MS) with electrospray mass spectrometry, UV-Vis, and fluorescence detectors. Mass spectrometry facilities are complemented by extensive resources available at the Protein Analysis Facility located at the NYU School of Medicine.

Computing facilities are extensive within research groups, in the department, at the Scientific Visualization Center (located in the Courant Institute of Mathematics), and at the University in general. Bobst Library is one of the largest open-stack research libraries in the nation.

Financial Aid

All students admitted to the Ph.D. program receive financial support in the form of teaching assistantships, research assistantships, or University fellowships. Students usually receive support for the duration of their studies. The basic stipend in 2004–05 for eleven months is $23,000.

Cost of Study

Research and teaching appointments carry a waiver of tuition, which amounts to $23,000 for the 2004–05 academic year, and of registration fees, which are estimated at $1400 per academic year.

Living and Housing Costs

University housing for graduate students is limited. It consists mainly of shared studio apartments and shared suites in residence halls within walking distance of the University. University housing rents in the 2003–04 academic year ranged from $10,250 to $16,040.

Student Group

The Graduate School of Arts and Science has an enrollment of 4,000 graduate students; about 70 are pursuing advanced degrees in chemistry. They represent a wide diversity of ethnic and national groups; more than a third are women. Upon receiving their Ph.D.'s, about 10 percent of recent graduates entered positions in academia, and the others were approximately equally divided between those who accepted industrial employment and those who elected to gain postdoctoral research experience before accepting permanent positions.

Location

Greenwich Village, the home of the University, has long been famous for its contributions to the fine arts, literature, and drama and for its personalized, smaller-scale, European style of living. It is one of the most desirable places to live in the city. New York City is the business, cultural, artistic, and financial center of the nation, and its extraordinary resources enrich both the academic programs and the experience of living at NYU.

The University

New York University, a private university, awarded its first doctorate in chemistry in 1866. Ten years later, the American Chemical Society was founded in the original University building, and the head of the chemistry department, John W. Draper, assumed the presidency.

Applying

Application forms may be obtained by writing to the address below. Students beginning graduate study are accepted only for September admission. Applicants are expected to submit scores on the GRE General Test and the Subject Test in chemistry or a related discipline. Students whose native language is not English must submit a score on the Test of English as a Foreign Language (TOEFL). The application deadline is December 15. Applicants are invited to visit the University but are advised to contact the department beforehand to arrange an appointment.

Correspondence and Information

Director of Graduate Programs
Department of Chemistry
New York University
New York, New York 10003

Telephone: 212-998-8400
Fax: 212-260-7905
E-mail: chem.web@nyu.edu
World Wide Web: http://www.nyu.edu/pages/chemistry/

New York University

THE FACULTY AND THEIR RESEARCH

Paramjit S. Arora, Assistant Professor; Ph.D., California, Irvine, 1999. Bioorganic chemistry, chemical biology, molecular recognition.

Zlatko Bacic, Professor; Ph.D., Utah, 1982. Theoretical chemistry: spectra and dynamics of highly vibrationally excited floppy molecules, dissociation dynamics of rare-gas clusters in collisions with solid surfaces.

Henry C. Brenner, Associate Professor; Ph.D., Chicago, 1972. Physical chemistry: optical and magnetic resonance studies of molecular solids and biological systems, energy transfer and luminescence in condensed phases.

James W. Canary, Professor; Ph.D., UCLA, 1988. Organic, bioorganic, and bioinorganic chemistry; chiral materials; nanoscience; molecular chemistry.

Young-Tae Chang, Assistant Professor; Ph.D., Pohang University of Science and Technology (Korea), 1996. Combinatorial and bioorganic chemistry.

John S. Evans, Associate Professor; Ph.D., Caltech, 1993. Biomolecular materials: solution and solid-state NMR structure and dynamics of biomineralization and structural proteins, computational and molecular modeling of proteins and biomaterials.

Paul J. Gans, Professor; Ph.D., Case Tech, 1959. Theoretical chemistry: determination of conformational and thermodynamic properties of macromolecules by Monte Carlo simulation.

Nicholas E. Geacintov, Professor; Ph.D., Syracuse, 1961. Physical and biophysical chemistry: interaction of polycyclic aromatic carcinogens with nucleic acids, laser studies of fluorescence mechanisms and photoinduced electron transfer.

Alexej Jerschow, Assistant Professor; Ph.D., Linz (Austria). 1997. NMR spectroscopy, imaging, and microscopy; theory and applications in material sciences, biophysics, and quantum computation.

Neville R. Kallenbach, Professor; Ph.D., Yale, 1961. Biophysical chemistry of proteins and nucleic acids: structure, sequence, and site selectivity in DNA-drug interactions, protein folding, model helix and beta sheet structures.

Kent Kirshenbaum, Assistant Professor; Ph.D., California, San Francisco, 1999. Bioorganic and biophysical chemistry: artificial proteins, biomimetic heteropolymers, biomolecular conformational rearrangements.

Edward J. McNelis, Professor; Ph.D., Columbia, 1960. Organic chemistry: oxidation as a route to synthetically useful substances, novel organometallic catalysts.

Johannes P. M. Schelvis, Assistant Professor; Ph.D., Leiden (Netherlands), 1995. Biophysical chemistry: steady-state and time-resolved vibrational and optical spectroscopy of biological systems, structure-function relationship in proteins, and enzyme catalysis.

Tamar Schlick, Professor; Ph.D., NYU, 1987. Molecular mechanics and dynamics, computational and structural biology, nucleic acid structure, nucleic acid and protein interaction.

David I. Schuster, Professor; Ph.D., Caltech, 1961. Synthesis of functionalized fullerenes; supramolecular complexes of fullerenes and carbon nanotubes; photoinduced electron transfer in porphyrin/fullerene hybrids, including dyads, rotaxanes, catenanes, and molecular wires; inhibition of HIV-1 protease by fullerenes.

Nadrian C. Seeman, Professor; Ph.D., Pittsburgh, 1970. Biophysical chemistry: structural DNA nanotechnology, structural chemistry of recombination, catenated and knotted DNA topologies, DNA-based computation, crystallography.

Robert Shapiro, Professor; Ph.D., Harvard, 1959. Organic and bioorganic chemistry: effects of mutagens on the structure and function of nucleic acids.

Mark Tuckerman, Assistant Professor; Ph.D., Columbia, 1993. Theoretical chemistry: ab initio molecular dynamic simulations and statistical mechanics.

Alexander Vologodskii, Research Professor; Ph.D., Moscow Physical Technical Institute, 1975. Statistical mechanical properties of DNA; supercoiling, catenanes, knots; effect of supercoiling on DNA-protein interaction.

Marc A. Walters, Associate Professor; Ph.D., Princeton, 1981. Inorganic chemistry: kinetics and energetics of metal thiolate and selenolate formation, synthesis of complexes for the uptake of many-electron equivalents.

Stephen Wilson, Professor; Ph.D., Rice, 1972. Organic chemistry: total synthesis of natural products, new synthetic methodology, synthesis of enzyme mimics.

John Z. H. Zhang, Professor; Ph.D., Houston, 1987. Theory: study of molecular collision dynamics and chemical reactions in the gas phase and on surfaces.

Yingkai Zhang, Assistant Professor; Ph.D., Duke, 2000. Computational biochemistry and biophysics: multiscale modeling of biological systems, enzyme catalysis and regulation, DNA damage and repair, biomolecular recognition.

New York University

SELECTED PUBLICATIONS

Eisenfuhr, A., et al. **(P. S. Arora).** A ribozyme with 1,4-michaelase activity: Synthesis of the substrate precursors. *Bioorg. Med. Chem.* 11:235–49, 2003.

Arora, P. S., et al. Design of artificial transcriptional activators with rigid poly-L-proline linkers. *J. Am. Chem. Soc.* 124:13067–71, 2002.

Belitsky, J. M., et al. **(P. S. Arora).** Cellular uptake of polyamide-dye conjugates. *Bioorg. Med. Chem.* 10:3313–8, 2002.

Dai, J., and **Z. Bacic** et al. A theoretical study of vibrational mode coupling in H5O+2. *J. Chem. Phys.* 119:6571–80, 2003.

Sarsa, A., **Z. Bacic,** J. W. Moskowitz, and K. E. Schmidt. HF dimer in small helium clusters: Interchange tunneling dynamics in a quantum environment. *Phys. Rev. Lett.* 88:123401, 2002.

Xu, M., **Z. Bacic,** and J. M. Hutson. Clusters containing open-shell molecules: II. Equilibrium structures of ArnOH Van der Waals clusters (X2_, n = 1 to 15). *J. Chem. Phys.* 117:4777–86, 2002.

Dourandin, A., **H. C. Brenner,** and M. Pope. New broad spectrum auto-correlator for ultrashort light pulses based on multiphoton photoemission. *Rev. Sci. Instrum.* 71:1589–94, 2000.

Tringali, A. E., S. K. Kim, and **H. C. Brenner.** ODMR and fluorescence studies of pyrene solubilized in anionic and cationic micelles. *J. Lumin.* 81:85–100, 1999.

Tringali, A. E., and **H. C. Brenner.** Spin-lattice relaxation and ODMR linenarrowing of the photoexcited triplet stat of pyrene in polycrystalline Shpol'skii hosts and glassy matrices. *Chem. Phys.* 226, 1998.

Zhu, L., P. S. Lukeman, **J. W. Canary,** and N. C. Seeman. Nylon-DNA: Single-stranded DNA with a covalently stitched nylon lining. *J. Am. Chem. Soc.* 125:10178–9, 2003.

Barcena, H. S., A. E. Holmes, S. Zahn, and **J. W. Canary.** Inversion of helicity in propeller-shaped molecules derived from s-methyl cysteine and methioninol. *Org. Lett.* 5:709–11, 2003.

Dai, Z., X. Xu, and **J. W. Canary.** Stereochemical control of Zn(II)/Cu(II) selectivity. *Chem. Commun.* 1414–5, 2002.

Mitsopoulos, G., D. P. Walsh, and **Y. T. Chang.** Tagged library approach to chemical genomics and proteomics. *Curr. Opin. Chem. Biol.* 8:26–32, 2004.

Khersonsky, S. M., et al. **(Y. T. Chang).** Facilitated forward chemical genetics using tagged triazine library and zebrafish embryo screening. *J. Am. Chem. Soc.* 125:11804–5, 2003.

Rosania, G. R., et al. **(Y. T. Chang).** Combinatorial approach to organelle-targeted fluorescent library based on the styryl scaffold. *J. Am. Chem. Soc.* 125:1130–1, 2003.

Wustman, B. A., D. E. Morse, and **J. S. Evans.** Structural characterization of the N-terminal mineral binding domains from the molluscan crystal-modulating biomineralization proteins, AP7 and AP24. *Biopolymers,* in press.

Wustman, B. A., J. C. Weaver, D. E. Morse, and **J. S. Evans.** Characterization of a Ca (II)-, mineral-interactive polyelectrolyte sequence from the adhesive elastomeric biomineralization protein, Lustrin A. *Langmuir* 19:9373–81, 2003.

Michenfelder, M., et al. **(J. S. Evans).** Characterization of two molluscan crystal-modulating biomineralization proteins and identification of putative mineral binding domains. *Biopolymers* 70:522–33, 2003.

Gans, P. J. Review of *Statistical Mechanics: Fundamentals and Modern Applications. J. Am. Chem. Soc.* 120:11026, 1998.

Lyu, P. C., **P. J. Gans,** and **N. R. Kallenbach.** Energetic contribution of solvent-exposed ion pairs to alpha-helix structure. *J. Mol. Biol.* 223:343–50, 1992.

Gans, P. J., et al. **(N. R. Kallenbach).** The helix-coil transition in heterogeneous peptides with specific side-chain interactions: Theory and comparison with CD spectral data. *Biopolymers* 31:1605–14, 1991.

Yan, S., et al. **(N. E. Geacintov).** Role of base sequence context in conformational equilibria and nucleotide excision repair of benzo[a]pyrene diol epoxide-adenine adducts. *Biochemistry* 42(8): 2339–54, 2003.

Huang, X., et al. **(N. E. Geacintov).** Effects of base sequence context on translesion synthesis past a bulky (+)-*trans-anti*-B[*a*]P-N^2-dG lesion catalyzed by the Y-family polymerase pol kappa. *Biochemistry* 42(8):2456–66, 2003.

Muheim, R., et al. **(N. E. Geacintov).** Modulation of human nucleotide excision repair by 5-methylcytosines. *Biochemistry* 42(11):3247–54, 2003.

Jerschow, A., and R. Kumar. calculation of coherence pathway selection and cogwheel cycles. *J. Magn. Reson.* 160:59–64, 2003.

Laws, D. D., H.-M. L. Bitter, and **A. Jerschow.** Solid-state NMR methods in chemistry. *Angew. Chem. Int. Ed. Eng.* 41:3096–126, 2002.

Logan, J. W. et al. **(A. Jerschow).** Investigations of low-amplitude radio frequency pulses at and away from rotary resonance conditions for I = 5/2 nuclei. *Solid State Nucl. Magn. Reson.* 22:97–109, 2002.

Shi, Z., C. A. Olson, and **N. R. Kallenbach.** Cation-pi interaction in model alpha-helical peptides. *J. Am. Chem. Soc.* 124:3284–91, 2002.

Shi, Z., B. A. Krantz, **N. R. Kallenbach,** and T. R. Sosnick. Contribution of hydrogen bonding to protein stability estimated from isotope effects. *Biochemistry* 41:2120–9, 2002.

Olson, C. A., Z. Shi, and **N. R. Kallenbach.** Polar interactions with aromatic side chains in alpha-helical peptides: CH...H-bonding and cation-pi interactions. *J. Am. Chem. Soc.* 123:6451–2, 2001.

Wu, C. W., et al. **(K. Kirshenbaum).** Structural and spectroscopic studies of peptoid oligomers with a-chiral aliphatic side chains. *J. Am. Chem. Soc.* 125:13525–30, 2003.

Kwon, I., **K. Kirshenbaum,** and D. A. Tirrell. Breaking the degeneracy of the genetic code. *J. Am. Chem. Soc.* 125:7512–3, 2003.

Kirshenbaum, K., I. S. Carrico, and D. A. Tirrell. Biosynthesis of proteins incorporating a versatile set of phenylalanine analogs. *ChemBioChem* 3:235–7, 2002.

Blandino, M., and **E. McNelis.** Rearrangements of haloalykynol derivatives of glucofuranose. *Org. Lett.* 4:3387–90, 2002.

McNelis, E., and M. Blandino. A method for estimating tetrahedral bond angles. *New J. Chem.* 25:772–4, 2001.

Djuardi, E., and **E. McNelis.** Furo[3,4-b]furan formations from alkynols of xylose. *Tetrahedron Lett.* 40:7193–6, 1999.

Chen, Z., T. W. B. Ost, and **J. P. M. Schelvis.** Phe393 mutants of cytochrome P450 BM3 with modified heme redox potentials have altered heme vinyl and propionate conformations. *Biochemistry* 43:1798–808, 2004.

Schelvis, J. P. M., et al. Resonance Raman and UV-vis spectroscopic characterization of the complex of photolyase with UV-damaged DNA. *J. Phys. Chem. B* 107:12352–62, 2003.

Kapetanaki, S. M., et al. **(J. P. M. Schelvis).** Conformational differences in M. tuberculosis catalase-peroxidase KatG and its S315T mutant revealed by resonance Raman spectroscopy. *Biochemistry* 42:3835–45, 2003.

Radhakrishnan, R., and **T. Schlick.** Orchestration of cooperative events in DNA synthesis and repair mechanism unraveled by transition path sampling of DNA polymerases beta's closing. *Proc. Natl. Acad. Sci. U.S.A.,* in press.

New York University

Selected Publications (continued)

Gan, H. H., et al. **(T. Schlick).** RAG: RNA-As-graphs database—Concepts, analysis, and features. *Bioinformatics,* in press.

Schlick, T. *Molecular Modeling and Simulation: An Interdisciplinary Guide.* New York: Springer-Verlag, 2002.

Li, K., and **D. I. Schuster** et al. Convergent synthesis and photophysics of [60]fullerene/porphyrin-based rotaxanes. *J. Am. Chem. Soc.* 126:3388–9, 2004.

Rosenthal, J., and **D. I. Schuster.** The anomalous reactivity of fluorobenzene in electrophilic aromatic substitution and related phenomena. *J. Chem. Ed.* 80:679–90, 2003.

Guldi, D. M., et al. **(D. I. Schuster).** Synthesis and photophysics of a copper-porphyrin-styrene-C60 hybrid. *J. Phys. Chem. A* 107:3215–21, 2003.

Zhu, Z., **D. I. Schuster,** and **M. E. Tuckerman.** Molecular dynamics study of the connection between flap closing and binding of fullerene-based inhibitors of the HIV-1 protease. *Biochemistry* 42:1326, 2003.

Shen, Z., H. Yan, T. Wang, and **N. C. Seeman.** Paranemic crossover DNA: A generalized Holliday structure with applications in nanotechnology. *J. Am. Chem. Soc.* 126:1666–74, 2004.

Carbone, A., and **N. C. Seeman.** Coding and geometrical shapes in nanostructures: A fractal DNA-assembly. *Nat. Comput.* 2:133–51, 2003.

Seeman, N. C. At the crossroads of chemistry, biology and materials: Structural DNA nanotechnology. *Chem. Biol.* 10:1151–9, 2003.

Wang, L., B. E. Hingerty, **R. Shapiro,** and S. Broyde. Structural and stereoisomer effects of model estrogen quinone-derived adducts: N^6-(2-hydroxyestron-alpha,beta-yl)-2'-deoxyadenosine and N^6-(2-hydroxyestron-alpha,beta-yl)-2'-deoxyguanosine. *Chem. Res. Toxicol.,* in press.

Ding, S., **R. Shapiro, N. E. Geacintov,** and S. Broyde. Conformations of stereoisomeric base adducts to 4-hydroxyequilenin. *Chem. Res. Toxicol.* 16:695–707, 2003.

Shapiro, R. Monomer world. *Origins Life Evol. Biosphere* 33:270, 2003.

Thomas, J. W., R. Iftimie, and **M. E. Tuckerman.** Field theoretic approach to dynamical orbital localization in ab initio molecular dynamics. *Phys. Rev. B,* in press.

Zhu, Z., and **M. E. Tuckerman.** Ab initio molecular dynamics investigation of the concentration dependence of charged defect transport in basic solutions via calculation of the infrared spectrum. *J. Phys. Chem. B* 106:8009, 2002.

Stone, M. D., et al. **(A. Vologodskii).** Chirality sensing by *Escherichia coli* topoisomerase IV and the mechanism of type II topoisomerases. *Proc. Natl. Acad. Sci. U.S.A.* 100:8654–9, 2003.

Klenin, K., J. Langowski, and **A. Vologodskii.** Computational analysis of the chiral action of type II DNA topoisomerases. *J. Mol. Biol.* 320:359–67, 2002.

Vologodskaia, M., and **A. Vologodskii.** Contribution of the intrinsic curvature to measured DNA persistence length. *J. Mol. Biol.* 317:205–13, 2002.

Walters, M. A., et al. Iron (III) nitrilotriacetate and iron (III) iminodiacetate, their X-ray crystallographic structures and chemical properties. *Polyhedron* 22(7):941–6, 2003.

Bokacheva, L., A. D. Kent, and **M. A. Walters.** Micro-Hall magnetometry studies of thermally assisted and pure quantum tunneling in single molecule magnet Mn_{12}-acetate. *Polyhedron* 20:1717–21, 2001.

Rompel, A., et al. **(M. A. Walters).** S K- and Mo L-edge X-ray absorption spectroscopy to determine metal-ligand charge distribution in molybdenum-sulfur compounds. *J. Synchrotron Rad.* 8, 2000.

Schapira, M., et al. **(S. R. Wilson).** Discovery of diverse thyroid hormone receptor antagonists by high-throughput docking. *Proc. Natl. Acad. Sci. U.S.A.* 100(12):7354–9, 2003.

Gharbi, N., et al. **(S. R. Wilson).** Chromatographic separation and identification of a water-soluble dendritic methano[60]fullerene octadeca-acid. *Anal. Chem.* 75(16):4217–22, 2003.

Wilson, S. R., et al. Synthesis and photophysics of a linear non-covalently linked porphyrin–fullerene dyad. *J. Chem. Soc., Chem. Commun.* 226–7, 2003.

Zhang, D. W., Y. Xiang, A. M. Gao, and **J. Z. H. Zhang.** Quantum mechanical map for protein-ligand binding with application to trypsin/benzamidine complex. *J. Chem. Phys.* 120:1145 (communication), 2004.

Zhang, D. W., and **J. Z. H. Zhang.** Molecular fractionation with conjugate caps for full quantum mechanical calculation of protein-molecule interaction energy. *J. Chem. Phys.* 119:3599, 2003.

Xiang, Y., and **J. Z. H. Zhang.** A mixed quantum-classical semirigid vibrating rotor target approach to methane dissociation on Ni surface. *J. Chem. Phys.* 118:8954, 2003.

Zhang, Y., J. Kua, and J. A. McCammon. Influence of structural fluctuation on enzyme reaction energy barriers in combined quantum mechanical/molecular mechanical studies. *J. Phys. Chem. B* 107:4459–63, 2003.

Zhang, Y., J. Kua, and J. A. McCammon. Role of the catalytic triad and oxyanion hole in acetylcholinesterase catalysis: An ab initio QM/MM study. *J. Am. Chem. Soc.* 124:10572–7, 2002.

Kua, J., **Y. Zhang,** and J. A. McCammon. Studying enzyme binding specificity in acetylcholinesterase using a combined molecular dynamics and multiple docking approach. *J. Am. Chem. Soc.* 124:8260–7, 2002.

NORTHEASTERN UNIVERSITY

Department of Chemistry and Chemical Biology
Graduate Programs in Chemistry

Programs of Study

The Department of Chemistry and Chemical Biology offers traditional thesis-based advanced degrees with concentrations in traditional areas of analytical, inorganic, organic, and physical chemistry as well as more interdisciplinary areas, such as nanotechnology and analytical biotechnology. Those students who are unable to pursue their graduate degree full-time or who are employed full-time in industry may opt for the nonthesis M.S. program, for which the program of study is largely course work that can be completed on weekday evenings.

Research Facilities

Faculty members in the Department of Chemistry and Chemical Biology are located in three buildings on the main Northeastern campus in Boston: Hurtig Hall (the main building); Mugar Hall, home of the Barnett Institute of Chemical Analysis; and the Egan Science and Engineering Center. The department is equipped with a wide variety of instrumentation, including two NMR instruments (300 MHz and 500 MHz), several triple-quad mass spectrometers, an ion trap mass spectrometer, several GC-MS instruments, a molecular modeling facility with Silicon Graphics Octane workstations, one Raman spectrometer, several FT-IR systems, a TGA, several DSC instruments, a number of UV-vis spectrometers, a Mössbauer spectrometer, stopped-flow apparatus, a peptide sequencer, a steady-state spectrofluorometer, several electrochemical workstations, HPLC systems, and CE systems.

Research is centered in the major areas of analytical, inorganic, organic, and physical chemistry. Areas of research in analytical chemistry include separation science, with an emphasis on capillary electrophoresis and HPLC applied to biological systems: DNA sequencing, peptide mapping, and protein characterization; combinatorial chemistry and DNA biomarkers; LC- and CZE-mass spectrometry; environmental analysis; spectroscopic and electrochemical studies of metalloproteins; and electrochemistry in supercritical fluids and redox liquids.

Departmental research in inorganic chemistry includes synthesis and characterization of metal catalysts and humic substances, synthesis of organometallic complexes as precursors for advanced materials, and Mössbauer spectrometry applied to solid-state chemistry and biological systems.

Areas of research in organic chemistry include theoretical studies of structure and properties; dynamic NMR; isolation, structural characterization, and synthesis of natural products; anticancer drugs; sequence-specific DNA cleaving and crosslinking agents; enantioselective catalysts; organic nonlinear optical materials and multifunctional polymers; conducting polymers; and low-dielectric-constant polymers and new synthetic methodology for making high-performance polymers.

Departmental research in physical chemistry includes theoretical chemistry, including electron transfer; development of computational methods for identifying enzyme active sites; solid-state chemistry, spectroscopy, and electrochemistry of materials for electrochemical energy conversion and storage; high-field ESR; spin-label studies of polymer and protein dynamics; and synthesis and characterization of structurally engineered materials of nanosized dimensions possessing an array of unique properties.

Financial Aid

Northeastern University awards need-based financial aid to graduate students through the Federal Perkins Loan, Federal Work-Study, and Federal Stafford Student Loan programs and offers a limited number of minority fellowships and Martin Luther King Jr. Scholarships. The graduate schools offer financial assistance through teaching, research, and administrative assistantship awards that include tuition remission and a stipend of approximately $14,100 (departmentally specific). These assistantships require a maximum of 20 hours of work per week and are only available for students studying in the full-time graduate program. There are also a limited number of tuition assistantships that provide partial or full tuition remission and require a maximum of 10 hours of work per week.

Cost of Study

The tuition rate for 2003–04 was $850 per semester hour. There are special tuition charges for theses and dissertations, where applicable. The Student Center fee and health and accident insurance fee required for all full-time students are approximately $1600 per academic year.

Living and Housing Costs

Living expenses both on and off campus are estimated to be between $1200 and $1500 per month. A public transportation system serves the greater Boston area, and there are subway and bus services nearby.

Student Group

For the fall 2003 semester, 71 students were enrolled in the department's graduate programs (46 full-time and 25 part-time).

Student Outcomes

The majority of graduates find employment in various high-technology industries across the United States. Ph.D. graduates are also employed by academic institutions in teaching and research.

Location

Northeastern University is located in the heart of Boston, a city that has played a pioneering role in American education. Within a 25-mile radius of the campus, there are more than fifty degree-granting institutions. Within walking distance of the campus, there are numerous renowned cultural centers, such as the Museum of Fine Arts, Isabella Stewart Gardner Museum, Symphony Hall, Horticultural Hall, and Boston Public Library. Theater in Boston includes everything from pre-Broadway to experimental and college productions. The Boston area is also the site of all home games of the Red Sox, Celtics, Bruins, and Patriots.

The University

Northeastern University is among the nation's largest private universities, with an international reputation as a leader in cooperative education. The cooperative plan of education, initiated by the College of Engineering in 1909 and subsequently adopted by the other colleges of the University, enables students to alternate periods of work and study. Today, Northeastern has eight undergraduate colleges, eight graduate and professional schools, several suburban campuses, and an extensive research division.

Applying

Applications for admission to the full-time M.S. and Ph.D. programs are only accepted for the fall semester each year. Review of all applications begins in early December. Admission with offers of financial support is offered on a rolling basis, so it is best to apply early.

Students applying to the Ph.D. program are expected to have an earned B.A., B.S., or M.S. in chemistry or to have completed the equivalent course work with an overall GPA of 3.0 or better at an accredited college or university.

The application form is available online at http://www.applyweb.com/aw?neuga. Students must have a valid credit card in order to complete the online application. A traditional paper-based application may be requested from the department or by e-mailing Jean Harris, the Graduate Administrator (j.harris@neu.edu). All materials submitted with the application, including transcripts and letters of recommendation, must be originals. Transcripts of all relevant previous undergraduate and graduate course work are required. Letters of recommendation should be completed by someone acquainted with the applicant's academic and personal qualifications. Only those documents required to complete the application package should be sent, as unsolicited documents do not improve the applicant's chances for admission.

Correspondence and Information

Department of Chemistry and Chemical Biology
102 Hurtig Hall
Northeastern University
360 Huntington Avenue
Boston, Massachusetts 02115

Telephone: 617-373-2822
Fax: 617-373-8795
E-mail: n.weston@neu.edu
World Wide Web: http://www.chem.neu.edu

Northeastern University

THE FACULTY AND THEIR RESEARCH

David E. Budil, Associate Professor; Ph.D., Chicago. Electrostatic mapping of protein and polymer surfaces by ESR, molecular dynamics–based simulation of ESR spectra, high-field ESR studies of the photosynthetic reaction center.

Norman Chiu, Assistant Professor; Ph.D., Windsor. Assay development and validation of potential SNP markers for prostate cancer, development of high-throughput methods for mass spectroscopic measurements of DNA adducts and determination of their specific positions in the genomes, separation and detection of diseased prion proteins in biofluids.

Geoffrey Davies, Professor; Ph.D., D.Sc., Birmingham (England). Isolation, purification, properties, and structures of humic acids (HAs), the brown polymers responsible for water retention, metal binding, and solute adsorption in soils and sediments.

David A. Forsyth, Professor; Ph.D., Berkeley. Organic structure and activity through a synergy of experiment and theory, dynamic NMR methods.

Bill C. Giessen, Professor; Sc.D., Göttingen (Germany). Econometric analysis of usage, supply, and pricing patterns of chemicals and materials using pattern recognition and other advanced computer methods.

Thomas R. Gilbert, Associate Professor; Ph.D., MIT. Chemical education, curriculum development in bioanalytical chemistry.

William S. Hancock, Professor; Ph.D., Adelaide (Australia). Disease mechanisms and discovery of potential therapeutic agents by proteomic analysis of biological fluids and tissue samples.

Robert N. Hanson, Professor; Ph.D., Berkeley. Application of contemporary organic chemistry to the design, synthesis, and characterization of biologically active small molecules; synthetic techniques, including the utilization of palladium-catalyzed coupling of organoboranes and stannanes, introduction of isotopes for radio imaging, and solid-phase and solution combinatorial chemistry.

Graham Jones, Professor and Chair; Ph.D., Imperial College (London). Enediyne antitumor antibiotics, enantioselective catalyst design, enantioselective catalyst design, clinical chemistry.

Barry L. Karger, Professor; Ph.D., Cornell. High-performance DNA sequencing and mutational analysis using capillary electrophoresis, proteome analysis using capillary array MALDI/TOF MS, microfabricated devices coupled online to electrospray MS.

Rein U. Kirss, Associate Professor; Ph.D., Wisconsin–Madison. Application of organometallic compounds to organic and materials synthesis with characterization by NMR, electrochemistry, and Mössbauer spectroscopy.

Ira S. Krull, Associate Professor; Ph.D., NYU. Derivatization of phospholipids and proteins for improved separation, detection, and quantitation; HPCE for protein, peptide, and synthetic organic polymer resolutions with improved detection; immunodetection and immunoanalysis in HPLC/HPCE for proteins/peptides (prions).

Philip W. LeQuesne, Professor; Ph.D., Auckland (New Zealand). Chemistry of natural products, development of analogues of natural wound-healing compounds.

P. A. Mabrouk, Professor; Ph.D., MIT. Nonaqueous enzymology, green chemistry, electrochemistry in supercritical fluids and redox liquids, novel methods of synthesizing conducting polymers, chemical education.

Sanjeev Mukerjee, Associate Professor; Ph.D., Texas A&M. Design and testing of novel membranes for PEM fuel cells, electrosynthesis and sensors (such as immunoselective biosensors), materials characterization using synchrotron-based in situ spectroscopic methods.

Mary Jo Ondrechen, Professor; Ph.D., Northwestern. Theoretical and computational chemistry and chemical biology, prediction of the functional roles of gene products (proteins), modeling of enzyme-substrate interactions, rational design of materials, nonlinear optical properties of polymers, modeling for proteomics applications.

William M. Reiff, Professor; Ph.D., Syracuse. The application of Mössbauer spectroscopy to the characterization of the magnetic properties of the organometallic solid state.

Eriks Rozners, Assistant Professor; Ph.D., Riga Technical (Latvia). The chemistry and biochemistry of nucleic acids, with a focus on elucidation of RNA structure and function; synthesis and biophysical exploration of RNA analogs having amides as internucleoside linkages.

Paul Vouros, Professor; Ph.D., MIT. Mass spectrometry and its applications to bioorganic analysis, analysis of DNA adducts through development of techniques for the trace-level detection and characterization of modified nucleosides or nucleotides as a result of the covalent binding of carcinogens with DNA, application of LC-MS and GC-MS to study the metabolic pathways of vitamin D, characterization and sequencing of oligosaccharides by ion trap MS.

Philip M. Warner, Professor; Ph.D., UCLA. Application of modern theoretical methods to the study of organic chemistry and materials, e.g., chemical behavior of enediyne antibiotics and study of the rearrangements of organometallic cyclobutadiene complexes.

PENNSTATE

THE PENNSYLVANIA STATE UNIVERSITY

Eberly College of Science
Department of Chemistry

Programs of Study

An integral part of the research community, graduate students interact frequently with faculty members, a distinguishing feature of the department's program. The Department of Chemistry builds each student's academic career on a solid foundation of interdisciplinary research, an important facet of the chemical sciences. The department offers both an M.S. and a Ph.D. in chemistry, although most students obtain the latter. In the first year, each student selects a faculty adviser who heads a committee that guides the student's research development. Students may choose from a wide range of subject areas, including analytical, biological, inorganic, materials, organic, organometallic, physical, polymer, surface, and theoretical chemistry and chemical physics. Courses in related fields, such as biochemistry, biophysics, computer science, materials science, mathematics, physics, and polymer science, may also be taken. The Ph.D. program requires five graduate-level courses, the first of which combines writing assignments with scientific-writing tutorials to sharpen the student's communication and critical-thinking skills. A second-year writing class focuses these skills on the student's area of individual research. Formal course work, which is tailored to a student's individual needs and special interests, normally takes about twelve to eighteen months to complete, after which students concentrate on research. Students must pass an oral comprehensive exam in which they describe their research progress and defend a brief original research proposal. The Ph.D. program culminates in the oral presentation and defense of a dissertation on the student's research.

The department also offers students opportunities to interact with scientists outside the classroom. The colloquium program attracts highly renowned scientists to the campus to present their latest work, and the annual lecture series brings distinguished visitors to campus from all over the world. The Cooperative Education Program links students directly to industry through on-site research experience in industrial laboratories.

Research Facilities

The Department of Chemistry provides a variety of resources and support services, maintaining a pleasant and modern physical environment. The department office, a physical sciences library, a purchasing office, and several floors of research laboratories are located in Davey Laboratory. Chandlee Laboratory houses five floors of research laboratories and the NMR facilities. The mass spectrometry facilities and a few research laboratories are located in Whitmore Laboratory, along with the undergraduate laboratories, the main stockroom, electronics shops, and the glass-blowing shop. Wartik Laboratory houses the Biotechnology Institute and some of the biochemical research laboratories. In addition, the new Chemistry Building has been completed and will be ready for occupation by summer 2004 (http://www.chem.psu.edu/newchembldg/ncb02.html). The department operates some dedicated research facilities at the Materials Research Institute, which houses major instrumentation for materials research. Each research group has the extensive instrumentation required for modern research in chemistry. Some major instruments, however, are located in facilities that can be shared by all research groups in the department. These include NMR, ESR, and mass spectrometry equipment; X-ray diffraction facilities; computational facilities; biologically related instrumentation; and equipment for time-resolved laser spectroscopy. The NMR and mass spectrometry laboratories have full-time professional operators, but graduate students who frequently use them are encouraged to learn to operate the instruments themselves.

Financial Aid

The department offers many teaching and research assistantships, which usually require 20 hours of work a week. Because teaching is integral to the student's academic experience, teaching assistantships are offered to first- and second-year students. Students can obtain research assistantships after the spring of their first year, which offers them more time to focus on their research. Some fellowships are available, and they provide between $4000 and $12,000 more than the usual stipend. All appointments include a grant-in-aid that covers tuition. Both fellowships and assistantships support virtually all chemistry graduate students.

Cost of Study

Most students accept teaching or research assistantships, which cover the cost of tuition. Full-time tuition for the year 2003–04 was $8350. Medical insurance is available at a minimal cost (http://www.sa.psu.edu/uhs/currentstudents/gafellows.cfm).

Living and Housing Costs

Although most graduate students prefer off-campus housing (http://www.sa.psu.edu/ocl/), with both furnished and unfurnished accommodations available in and near State College (http://www.statecollege.com), the University offers accommodations for both single and married students (http://www.hfs.psu.edu/housing/).

Student Group

Currently, the department has 237 full-time students. Each year, about 40 to 45 new students are admitted.

Student Outcomes

Penn State graduate students are highly successful in attaining employment in major industries and academic laboratories across the United States.

Location

Penn State sits near the tree-lined ridges of the Appalachians in State College, a friendly, modern city in a region with a population of 72,000. The area provides excellent outdoor recreational activities. Pittsburgh, Philadelphia, Baltimore, and Washington, D.C., lie within a reasonable drive (3 to 4 hours). Air, rail, and bus transportation is available.

The Department

Penn State's tradition of excellence in chemistry continues with its current faculty members and students. Recently, 1 faculty member was elected to the National Academy of Sciences and 1 to the American Academy of Arts and Sciences. Graduate students have received such prestigious awards as the Nobel Signature Award of the ACS, the Henkel Award in Colloid and Surface Chemistry, and the Eli Lilly Award for Women Scientists.

Applying

Application requirements include a completed two-page application (which can be downloaded), a personal statement (minimum length, one page), three letters of recommendation, GRE General Test scores, an official undergraduate transcript, and an official graduate transcript, if applicable. The GRE Subject Test in chemistry is recommended but not required. International students must also submit their TOEFL and TSE score reports. No applications are considered for review until all materials have been submitted. Photocopies of the Educational Testing Service exams (GRE, TOEFL, TSE) suffice until the originals are received. The Admissions Committee does not review extra materials, such as publications or curricula vitae, enclosed with applications. U.S. students must apply by March 15 and international students by February 2. All application materials should be submitted to the address listed below.

Correspondence and Information

Dana Coval-Dinant
Graduate Admissions
Department of Chemistry
The Pennsylvania State University
152 Davey Laboratory
University Park, Pennsylvania 16802-6300

Telephone: 814-865-1383
877-688-4234 (toll-free)
Fax: 814-865-3314
E-mail: dmc6@psu.edu
World Wide Web: http://www.chem.psu.edu

The Pennsylvania State University

THE FACULTY AND THEIR RESEARCH

David L. Allara, Professor of Polymer Science and Chemistry; Ph.D., UCLA, 1964. Surface chemistry. Single molecular switches. *Science* 292:2303–7, 2001 (with Donhauser et al.).

Harry R. Allcock, Evan Pugh Professor; Ph.D., London, 1956. Polymer chemistry and materials synthesis. Influence of reaction parameters on the living cationic polymerization of phosphoranimines to polyphosphazenes. *Macromolecules* 34:748–54, 2001 (with Reeves, de Denus, and Crane).

James B. Anderson, Evan Pugh Professor; Ph.D., Princeton, 1963. Quantum chemistry by Monte Carlo methods. Monte Carlo methods in electronic structure for large systems. *Ann. Rev. Phys. Chem.* 51:501–26, 2000 (with Luechow).

Anne M. Andrews, Assistant Professor; Ph.D., American, 1993. Bioanalytical chemistry, with an emphasis on mammalian neurochemistry. Genetic perspectives on the serotonin transporter. *Brain Res. Bull.* 56:487–94, 2001 (with Murphy et al.).

John V. Badding, Associate Professor; Ph.D., Berkeley, 1989. Solid-state and materials chemistry. Pressure tuning in the chemical search for improved thermoelectric materials: NdxCe3-xPt3Sb4. *Chem. Mater.* 12(1):197–201, 2000 (with Meng et al.).

Alan J. Benesi, Lecturer and Director, NMR Facility; Ph.D., Berkeley, 1975. Multinuclear NMR spectroscopy of liquids and solids. Multiple-rotor-cycle QPASS pulse sequences: Separation of quadrupolar spinning sidebands with an application to 139La NMR. *J. Magn. Reson.* 138:320–5, 1999 (with Aurentz, Vogt, and Mueller).

Stephen J. Benkovic, Evan Pugh Professor and Eberly Chair; Ph.D., Cornell, 1963. Chemistry related to biological systems. Combinatorial protein engineering by incremental truncation. *Proc. Natl. Acad. Sci. U.S.A.* 96:3562–7, 1999 (with Ostermeier, Nixon, and Shim).

Philip C. Bevilacqua, Associate Professor; Ph.D., Rochester, 1993. Biological chemistry. Mechanistic considerations for general acid-base catalysis by RNA: Revisiting the mechanism of the hairpin ribozyme. *Biochemistry* 42:2259–65, 2003.

A. Welford Castleman Jr., Evan Pugh Professor of Chemistry and Physics and Eberly Distinguished Chair in Science; Ph.D., Polytechnic of Brooklyn, 1969. Nanoscale science. Clusters: Structure, energetics, and dynamics of intermediate states of matter. *J. Phys. Chem.* 100:12911–44, 1996 (with K. H. Bowen Jr.).

Andrew G. Ewing, Head Professor, Adjunct Professor of Neuroscience and Anatomy, and J. Lloyd Huck Chair in Natural Sciences; Ph.D., Indiana, 1983. Single-cell neurochemistry. Molecule specific imaging of freeze-fractured frozen-hydrated model membrane systems using mass spectrometer. *J. Am. Chem. Soc.* 123:603–10, 2000 (with D. M. Cannon Jr., Pacholski, and Winograd).

Ken S. Feldman, Professor; Ph.D., Stanford, 1984. Total synthesis of natural products. Ellagitannin chemistry: Studies on the stability and reactivity of 2,4-HHDP-containing ellagitannin systems. *J. Org. Chem.* 68:7433–8, 2003 (with Iyer and Liu).

Raymond L. Funk, Professor; Ph.D., Berkeley, 1978. Total synthesis of natural products. Preparation of 2-alkyl- and 2-acylpropenals from 5-(trifluoromethanesulfonyloxy)-4H-1,3 dioxin: A versatile acrolein a-cation synthon. *Tetrahedron* 56:10275, 2000 (with Fearnley and Gregg).

Barbara J. Garrison, Shapiro Professor; Ph.D., Berkeley, 1975. Computer simulations of reactions at surfaces. MD simulations of MALDesorption: Connections to experiment. *Int. J. Mass Spectrom. Ion Processes* 226:85–106, 2003 (with Zhigilei et al.).

Michael T. Green, Assistant Professor; Ph.D., Chicago, 1998. Using a mixture of theory and experiment to investigate the factors that determine enzymatic reactivity. The structure and spin coupling of catalase compound I: A study of non-covalent effects. *J. Am. Chem. Soc.* 123:9218–19, 2001.

Sharon Hammes-Schiffer, Professor; Ph.D., Stanford, 1993. Theoretical and computational investigation of chemically and biologically important processes. Computational studies of the mechanism for proton and hydride transfer in liver alcohol dehydrogenase. *J. Am. Chem. Soc.* 122:4803–12, 2000 (with Agarwal and Webb).

A. Daniel Jones, Senior Scientist and Director, Intercollegiate Mass Spectrometry Center; Ph.D., Penn State, 1984. Bioanalytical chemistry. The carboxyl terminus of the bacteriophage T4 DNA polymerase contacts its sliding clamp at the subunit interface. *J. Biol. Chem.* 274:24485–9, 1999 (with Alley and Soumillion).

Peter C. Jurs, Professor; Ph.D., Washington (Seattle), 1969. Computer applications in chemistry. Prediction of liquid crystal clearing temperatures of organic compounds from molecular structure. *Chem. Mater.* 11:1007–23, 1999 (with Johnson).

Christine D. Keating, Assistant Professor; Ph.D., Penn State, 1997. Cytomimetic chemistry. Aqueous phase separation in giant vesicles. *J. Am. Chem. Soc.* 124:13374–5, 2002 (with Helfrich et al.).

Juliette T. J. Lecomte, Associate Professor; Ph.D., Carnegie-Mellon, 1982. Biophysical chemistry. Binding of ferric heme by the recombinant globin from the cyanobacterium *Synechocystis* sp. PCC 6803. *Biochemistry* 40:6541–52, 2001 (with Scott, Vu, and Falzone).

Thomas E. Mallouk, DuPont Professor of Materials Chemistry; Ph.D., Berkeley, 1983. Application of solid-state materials to interesting problems in chemistry and physics. Layer by layer assembly of rectifying junctions in and on metal nanowires. *J. Phys. Chem. B* 105:8762–9, 2001 (with Kovtyukhova et al.).

Mark Maroncelli, Professor; Ph.D., Berkeley, 1984. Solvation and solvent effects on chemical reactions. Electronic spectral shifts, reorganization energies, and local density augmentation of C153 in supercritical solvents. *Chem. Phys. Lett.* 310:485–94, 1999 (with Biswas and Lewis).

Kenneth M. Merz Jr., Professor; Ph.D., Texas at Austin, 1985. Computer simulations of biologically important molecules. Solvent dynamics and mechanism of proton transfer in human carbonic anhydrase II. *J. Am. Chem. Soc.* 121:2290–302, 1999 (with Toba and Colombo).

Karl T. Mueller, Associate Professor; Ph.D., Berkeley, 1991. New experimental techniques in NMR spectroscopy for the study of solids. Mapping aluminum/phosphorus connectivities in aluminophosphate glasses. *J. Non-Cryst. Solids* 261:115–26, 2000 (with Egan and Wenslow).

Blake R. Peterson, Assistant Professor; Ph.D., UCLA, 1994. Bioorganic, combinatorial, and medicinal chemistry. Sensitive and rapid analysis of protein palmitoylation with a synthetic cell-permeable mimic of Src oncoproteins. *J. Am. Chem. Soc.* 124:2444–5, 2002 (with Creaser).

Ayusman Sen, Professor; Ph.D., Chicago, 1978. Synthetic and mechanistic organotransition metal chemistry. A broad spectrum catalytic system for the deep oxidation of toxic organics in aqueous medium using dioxygen as the oxidant. *J. Am. Chem. Soc.* 121:7485, 1999 (with Pifer et al.).

Erin D. Sheets, Assistant Professor; Ph.D., North Carolina at Chapel Hill, 1997. Development of nanofabricated tools for cell biology. Interactions between FceRI and lipid raft components are regulated by the actin cytoskeleton. *J. Cell Sci.* 113:1009–19, 2000 (with Holowka and Baird).

Steven M. Weinreb, Russell and Mildred Marker Professor of Natural Products Chemistry; Ph.D., Rochester, 1967. Synthesis of natural products. A new enantioselective approach to total synthesis of the securinega alkaloids: Application to (-)-norsecurinine and phyllanthine. *Angew. Chem. Int. Ed.* 39:237, 2000 (with Han et al.).

Paul S. Weiss, Professor; Ph.D., Berkeley, 1986. Surface chemistry and physics. Molecular rulers for scaling down nanostructures. *Science* 291:1019, 2001 (with Hatzor).

Mary Elizabeth Williams, Assistant Professor; Ph.D., North Carolina at Chapel Hill, 1999. Analytical chemistry of hybrid inorganic/organic materials. A DNA molten salt: Electron transfer in hybrid redox polyether melts of nucleic acids. *J. Am. Chem. Soc.* 123:218, 2001 (with Leone et al.).

Nicholas Winograd, Evan Pugh Professor; Ph.D., Case Western Reserve, 1970. Surface chemistry studies with ion beams and femtosecond pulse lasers. The interaction of vapor-deposited Al atoms with CO_2H groups at the surface of a self-assembled alkanethiolate monolayer on gold. *J. Phys. Chem.* 104(14):3267, 2000 (with Fisher et al.).

Xumu Zhang, Professor; Ph.D., Stanford, 1992. Synthetic organic, inorganic, and organometallic chemistry. Rh-catalyzed enzyme cycloisomerization. *J. Am. Chem. Soc.* 122:6490, 2000 (with Cao and Wang).

PRINCETON UNIVERSITY

Department of Chemistry

Programs of Study The Department of Chemistry offers a program of study leading to the degree of Doctor of Philosophy. The graduate program emphasizes research, and students enter a research group by the end of the first semester. Students are required to take six graduate courses in chemistry and allied areas, satisfying at least four of ten areas of distribution, and are expected to participate in the active lecture and seminar programs throughout their graduate careers.

Early in the second year, students take a general examination that consists of an oral defense of a thesis-related subject. Upon satisfactory performance in the general examination, students advance to candidacy for the degree of Doctor of Philosophy in chemistry. The degree is awarded primarily on the basis of a thesis describing original research in one of the areas of chemistry. The normal length of the entire Ph.D. program is five years.

Programs of graduate study in neuroscience, molecular biophysics, and materials are also offered, in cooperation with other science departments at Princeton University.

Research Facilities Research is conducted in Frick Chemical Laboratory and the adjoining Hoyt Laboratory. NMR, IR, ESR, FT-IR, atomic absorption, UV-visible, CD, and vacuum UV spectrometers and departmental computers are available to students. In addition, high-resolution FT-NMR spectrometers and mass spectrometers are run by operators for any research group. There is a wide variety of equipment in individual research groups, including lasers of many kinds, high-resolution spectrographs, molecular-beam instrumentation, a microwave spectrometer, computers, gas chromatographs, and ultrahigh-vacuum systems for surface studies. The department has an electronics shop, a machine shop, a student machine shop, and a glassblower for designing and building equipment. Extensive shop facilities are available on campus, and there is a large supercomputing center.

Financial Aid All admitted students receive tuition plus a maintenance allowance, typically in the form of assistantships in instruction or research. In 2004–05, students earned $18,200 to $21,050 during the academic year for approximately 20 hours per week of work, plus a summer stipend of $4500. First-year graduate students are not required to work; they receive fellowship funds that allow them to concentrate on course work.

Cost of Study See Financial Aid section above.

Living and Housing Costs Rooms at the Graduate College cost from $2894 to $5289 for the 2004–05 academic year of thirty-five weeks. Several meal plans are available, priced from $2813 to $4282. University apartments for married students currently rent for $626 to $1452 per month. Accommodations are also available in the surrounding community.

Student Group The total number of graduate students in chemistry is currently about 130. Postdoctoral students number about 70. A wide variety of academic, ethnic, and national backgrounds are represented among these students.

Location Princeton University and the surrounding community together provide an ideal environment for learning and research. From the point of view of a chemist at the University, the engineering, physics, mathematics, and molecular biology departments, as well as the plasma physics lab on the Forrestal campus, provide valuable associates, supplementary facilities, and sources of special knowledge. Many corporations have located their research laboratories near Princeton, leading to fruitful collaborations, seminars and lecture series, and employment opportunities after graduation.

Because of the nature of the institutions located here, the small community of Princeton has a very high proportion of professional people. To satisfy the needs of this unusual community, the intellectual and cultural activities approach the number and variety ordinarily found only in large cities, but with the advantage that everything is within walking distance. There are many film series, a resident repertory theater, orchestras, ballet, and chamber music and choral groups. Scientific seminars and other symposia bring prominent visitors from every field of endeavor.

Princeton's picturesque and rural countryside provides a pleasant area for work and recreation, yet New York City and Philadelphia are each only about an hour away.

The University Princeton University was founded in 1746 as the College of New Jersey. At its 150th anniversary in 1896, the trustees changed the name to Princeton University. The Graduate School was organized in 1901 and has since won international recognition in mathematics, the natural sciences, philosophy, and the humanities.

Applying Application instructions, including an online application, are available at http://webware.princeton.edu/gso/gao.htm. The application deadlines are December 1 for applicants who currently do not reside in the United States, Canada, or Mexico and December 30 for those who do. All applications must be accompanied by an application fee, which is discounted for online and early applications.

Admission consideration is given to all candidates without regard to race, color, national origin, religion, sex, or handicap.

Correspondence and Information

Shelley Wester
Graduate Administrator
Department of Chemistry
Frick Laboratory
Princeton University
Washington Road
Princeton, New Jersey 08544
Telephone: 609-258-4116
E-mail: wester@princeton.edu
World Wide Web: http://www.princeton.edu/~chemdept

Princeton University

THE FACULTY AND THEIR RESEARCH

Although all major areas of chemistry are represented by the faculty members, the department is small and housed in Frick Chemical Laboratory and the adjoining Hoyt Laboratory so that fruitful collaborations may develop. The following list briefly indicates the areas of interest of each professor.

S. L. Bernasek. Chemical physics of surfaces: basic studies of chemisorption and reaction on well-characterized transition-metal surfaces using electron diffraction and electron spectroscopy, surface reaction dynamics, heterogeneous catalysis, electronic materials.

S. Bernhard. Synthesis and characterization of transition metal complex–based materials for optoelectronics (light-emitting devices, photovoltaics), redox polymers, chiral metal complexes.

A. B. Bocarsly. Inorganic photochemistry, photoelectrochemistry, chemically modified electrodes, electrocatalysis, sensors, applications to solar energy conversion, fuel cells, materials chemistry.

R. Car. Chemical physics and materials science; electronic structure theory and ab initio molecular dynamics; computer modeling and simulation of solids, liquids, disordered systems, and molecular structures; structural phase transitions and chemical reactions.

J. Carey. Biophysical chemistry: protein and nucleic acid structure, function, and interactions; protein folding and stability.

R. Cava. Synthesis, structure, and physical property characterization of new superconductors, magnetic materials, transparent electronic conductors, dielectrics, thermoelectrics, and correlated electron systems.

G. C. Dismukes. Biochemistry and inorganic chemistry, molecular evolution of metalloenzymes, catalysis, photosynthetic water splitting.

J. T. Groves. Organic and inorganic chemistry: synthetic and mechanistic studies of reactions of biological interest, metalloenzymes, siderophores, membrane self-assembly, transition-metal redox catalysis, asymmetric catalysis, and biological oxidations.

M. Hecht. Biochemistry: sequence determinants of protein structure and design of novel proteins, molecular causes of Alzheimer's disease.

M. Jones Jr. Reactions and spin states of carbenes, arynes, twisted p systems, and other reactive intermediates; carborane chemistry.

C. Lee. Organic chemistry: synthetic organic chemistry, organometallic chemistry, bioorganic chemistry, synthetic methodologies, asymmetric catalysis.

K. K. Lehmann. Experimental and theoretical molecular spectroscopy, including spectroscopy in quantum liquids and solids, intramolecular dynamics, and development of spectroscopic tools for trace-species detection, particularly using cavity-enhanced methods.

R. A. Pascal Jr. Aromatic compounds of unusual structure, organic materials chemistry, enzymatic reaction mechanisms and inhibitors.

H. Rabitz. Physical chemistry: atomic and molecular collisions, theory of chemical reactions and chemical kinetics, biodynamics phenomena, heterogeneous phenomena, control of molecular motion.

W. Richter. Magnetic resonance imaging (MRI) and in vivo NMR spectroscopy, investigation of brain function in children and adults during mental tasks, physiological correlates of learning and intelligence, origin and interpretation of the BOLD signal, integration of complementary methodologies (electroencephalography, optical imaging, and NMR spectroscopy), analysis of 4-dimensional imaging data by wavelet methods and independent component analysis (ICA).

C. E. Schutt. Structural biology, crystallography of actin-binding proteins, theories of muscle contraction, structure of viral proteins, structural neurobiology, architectonics.

J. Schwartz. Organometallic chemistry, applications to organic and materials synthesis, surface and interface organometallic chemistry.

G. Scoles. Chemical physics: laser spectroscopy; chemical dynamics and cluster studies with molecular beams; structure, dynamics, and spectroscopic properties of organic overlayers adsorbed on crystal surfaces; nanomaterials and molecular manipulation on surfaces; protein-surface interactions; biosensors.

A. Selloni. Computational physics and chemistry and modeling of materials; structural, electronic, and dynamic properties of semiconductor and oxide surfaces; chemisorption and surface reactions.

M. F. Semmelhack. Organic synthesis and organometallic chemistry: development of synthesis methodology with transition-metal reagents, synthesis of unusual ring systems in natural and unnatural molecules, functional models of the enediyne toxins.

Z. G. Soos. Chemical physics: electronic states of π-molecular crystals and conjugated polymers, paramagnetic and charge-transfer excitons, linear chain crystals, energy transfer, electronic polarization and hopping transport.

E. J. Sorensen. Organic chemistry: chemical synthesis of bioactive natural products and molecular probes for biological research, bioinspired strategies for chemical synthesis, architectural self-constructions and novel methods for synthesis.

T. G. Spiro. Biological structure and dynamics from spectroscopic probes, role of metals in biology, environmental chemistry.

E. I. Stiefel. Bioinorganic chemistry; the metabolism of iron in marine environments; ferritin and bacterioferritin; hydrogenase, nitrogenase, and molybdenum enzymes; synthetic inorganic chemistry for biological models and new technology.

S. Torquato. Statistical mechanics and materials science; theory and computer simulations of disordered heterogeneous materials, liquids, amorphous solids, and biological materials; optimization in materials science; simulations of peptide binding; modeling the growth of tumors.

W. S. Warren. Laser spectroscopy in gaseous and solid phases, coherence effects, multiphoton processes, nuclear magnetic resonance.

Associated Faculty

F. M. Hughson, Department of Molecular Biology. Structural biology of neurotransmitter release, intracellular trafficking, and bacterial quorum sensing.

F. M. M. Morel, Department of Geosciences. Environmental chemistry, metals and metalloproteins in the environment, biogeochemistry.

S. M. Myneni, Department of Geosciences. Environmental chemistry, ion hydration and complexation, interfacial chemistry, X-ray spectroscopy.

Y. Shi, Department of Molecular Biology. Biophysics and structural biology, biochemistry and cancer biology.

J. Stock, Department of Molecular Biology. Receptor-mediated signal transduction, role of protein methylation in degenerative diseases such as Alzheimer's.

Frick Laboratory, Princeton University.

SELECTED PUBLICATIONS

Cai, Y., and **S. L. Bernasek.** Scanning tunneling microscopy of chiral pair self assembled monolayers. In *Encyclopedia of Nanoscience and Nanotechnology,* p. 3305. New York: Marcel Dekker, 2004.

Cai, Y., and **S. L. Bernasek.** Chiral pair monolayer adsorption of iodine-substituted octadecanol molecules on graphite. *J. Am. Chem. Soc.* 125:1655, 2003.

Slinker, J. D., et al. **(S. Bernhard).** Efficient yellow electroluminescence from a single layer of a cyclometalated iridium complex. *J. Am. Chem. Soc.* 126(9):2763–7, 2004.

Slinker, J. D., et al. **(S. Bernhard).** Solid-state electroluminescent devices based on transition metal complexes. *Chem. Commun.* (19):2392–9, 2003.

Barron, J. A., et al. **(S. Bernhard).** Electroluminescence in ruthenium(Ii) dendrimers. *J. Phys. Chem. A* 107(40):8130–3, 2003.

Bernhard, S., J. I. Goldsmith, K. Takada, H. D. Abruna. Iron(Ii) and copper(I) coordination polymers: Electrochromic materials with and without chiroptical properties. *Inorg. Chem.* 42(14):4389–93, 2003.

Barron, J. A., et al. **(S. Bernhard).** Photophysics and redox behavior of chiral transition metal polymers. *Inorg. Chem.* 42(5):1448–55, 2003.

Zhu, S., and **A. B. Bocarsly.** Spin-coated cyanogels: A new approach to the synthesis of nanoscopic metal alloy particles. In *Encyclopedia of Nanoscience and Nanotechnology,* pp. 3667–74. New York: Marcel Dekker, 2004.

Watson, D. F., et al. **(A. B. Bocarsly).** Femtosecond pump-probe spectroscopy of trinuclear transition metal mixed-valence complexes. *J. Phys. Chem. A* 108:3261–7, 2004.

Yang, C., et al. **(A. B. Bocarsly).** A comparison of physical properties and fuel cell performance of nafion and zirconium phosphate/nafion composite membranes. *J. Membrane Sci.* 237:145–61, 2004.

Haataja, M., D. J. Srolovitz, and **A. B. Bocarsly.** Morphological stability during electrodeposition I: Steady states and stability analysis. *J. Electrochem. Soc.* 150(10):C699–707, 2003.

Haataja, M., D. J. Srolovitz, and **A. B. Bocarsly.** Morphological stability during electrodeposition II: Additive effects. *J. Electrochem. Soc.* 150(10):C708–16, 2003.

Deshpande, R. S., et al. **(A. B. Bocarsly).** Morphology and gas adsorption properties of the palladium-cobalt based cyanogels. *Chem. Mat.* 15:4239–46, 2003.

Giannozzi, P., **R. Car,** and **G. Scoles.** Oxygen adsorption on graphite and nanotubes. *J. Chem. Phys.* 118:1003, 2003.

Han, S., et al. **(R. Car).** Interatomic potential for vanadium suitable for radiation damage simulations. *J. Appl. Phys.* 93:3328, 2003.

Zepeda-Ruiz, L. A., et al. **(R. Car).** Molecular dynamics study of the threshold displacement energy in vanadium. *Phys. Rev. B* 67:134114, 2003.

Savage, T., et al. **(R. Car).** Photoinduced oxydation of carbon nanotubes. *J. Phys.: Condens. Matter* 15:5915, 2003.

Sharma, M., Y. D. Wu, and **R. Car.** Ab initio molecular dynamics with maximally localized Wannier functions. *Int. J. Quantum Chem.* 95:821, 2003.

Lawson, C. L., et al. **(J. Carey).** *E. coli* trp repressor forms a domain-swapped array in aqueous alcohol. *Structure* 12:1098–107, 2004.

Szwajkajzer, D., and **J. Carey.** RaPID plots: Affinity and mechanism at a glance. *Biacore J.* 3(1):19, 2003.

McWhirter, A., and **J. Carey.** T-cell receptor recognition of peptide antigen/MHC complexes. *Biacore J.* 3(1):18, 2003.

Cava, R. J., H. W. Zandbergen, and K. Inumaru. The substitutional chemistry of MgB_2. *Physica C* 385:8, 2003.

Yu, A., et al. **(R. J. Cava).** Observation of a low-symmetry crystal structure for superconducting $MgCNi_3$ by Ni K-edge X-ray absorption measurements. *Phys. Rev. B* 67:064509, 2003.

Foo, M. L. et al. **(R. J. Cava).** Chemical instability of the cobalt oxyhydrate superconductor under ambient conditions. *Solid State Commun.* 127:33, 2003.

Mao, Z. Q., et al. **(R. J. Cava).** Experimental determination of superconducting parameters for the intermetallic perovskite superconductor $MgCNi_3$. *Phys. Rev. B* 67:094502, 2003.

Khalifah, P., D. A. Huse, and **R. J. Cava.** Magnetic behavior of $La_7Ru_3O_{18}$. *J. Phys.: Condens. Matter* 15:1, 2003.

Rogado, N., et al. **(R. J. Cava).** β-$Cu_3V_2O_8$: Magnetic ordering in a spin-1/2 Kagome-staircase lattice. *J. Phys.: Condens. Matter* 15:907, 2003.

Baranov, S., et al. **(G. C. Dismukes).** Bicarbonate is a native cofactor for assembly of the manganese cluster of the photosynthetic water oxidizing complex: Kinetics of reconstitution of O_2 evolution by photoactivation. *Biochemistry* 43:2070–9, 2004.

Maneiro, M., et al. **(G. C. Dismukes).** Kinetics of proton-coupled electron transfer in the manganese-oxo "cubane" core complexes containing the $[Mn_4O_4]^{6+}$ and $[Mn_4O_4]^{7+}$ core types. *Proc. Nat. Acad. Sci.* 100(7):3703–12, 2003.

Carrell, T. G., E. Bourles, M. Lin, and **G. C. Dismukes.** Transition from hydrogen atom to hydride abstraction by manganese-oxo cubanes: Contrasting chemistry of $Mn_4O_4(O_2PPh_2)_6$ vs. $[Mn_4O_4(O_2PPh_2)_6]^+$ in the formation of $Mn_4O_3(OH)(O_2PPh_2)_6$. *Inorg. Chem.* 42:2849-58, 2003.

Sanford, M. S., and **J. T. Groves.** Anti-Markovnikov hydrofunctionalization of olefins mediated by rhodium porphyrins. *Angew. Chim.* 116: 598–600, 2004.

Puranik, M. et al. **(J. T. Groves** and **T. G. Spiro).** Dynamics of carbon monoxide binding to CooA. *J. Biol. Chem.* 279:21096–108, 2004.

Phillips-McNaughton, K., and **J. T. Groves.** Zinc-coordination oligomers of phenanthrolinylporphyrins. *Org. Lett.* 5(11):1829–32, 2003.

Naidu, B. V., et al. **(J. T. Groves).** Enhanced peroxynitrite decomposition protects against experimental obliterative bronchiolitis. *Exp. Mol. Pathol.* 75(1):12–7, 2003.

Pacher, P., et al. **(J. T. Groves).** Role of superoxide, NO and peroxynitrite in doxorubicin-induced cardiac dysfunction. *FASEB J.* 17(4):A229, Part 1 Suppl., 2003.

Soriano, F. G., et al. **(J. T. Groves).** Role of peroxynitrite in the pathogenesis of endotoxic and septic shock in rodents. *FASEB J.* 17(5):A1069–70, Part 2 Suppl., 2003.

Wei, Y., and **M. H. Hecht.** Enzyme-like proteins from an unselected library of designed amino acid sequences. *Protein Eng. Design Selection* 17:67-75, 2004.

Wei, Y., et al. **(M. H. Hecht).** Stably folded de novo proteins from a designed combinatorial library. *Protein Sci.* 12:92–102, 2003.

Moffet, D. A., J. Foley, and **M. H. Hecht.** Midpoint reduction potentials and heme binding stoichiometries of de novo proteins from designed combinatorial libraries. *Biophys. Chem.* 105:231–9, 2003.

Wei, Y., et al. **(M. H. Hecht).** Solution structure of a de novo protein from a designed combinatorial library. *Proc. Natl. Acad. Sci. U.S.A.* 100:13270–3, 2003.

Oka, T., D. Ungar, **F. M. Hughson,** and M. Krieger. The COG and COPI complexes interact to control the abundance of GEARs: A subset of golgi integral membrane proteins. *Mol. Biol. Cell* 15:2423–35, 2004.

Ungar, D., and **F. M. Hughson.** SNARE protein structure and function [review]. *Ann. Rev. Cell Devel. Biol.* 19:493–517, 2003.

Kim, H., H. Men, and **C. Lee.** Stereoselective palladium-catalyzed O-glycosylation using glycals. *J. Am. Chem. Soc.* 126:1336–7, 2004.

Tarsa, P. B., P. Rabinowitz, and **K. K. Lehmann.** Evanescent field absorption in a passive optical fiber using continuous wave cavity ring-down spectroscopy. *Chem. Phys. Lett.* 383:297–303, 2004.

Martinez, R. Z., S. Carter, and **K. K. Lehmann.** Spectroscopy of highly excited vibrational states of HCN in its ground electronic state. *J. Chem. Phys.* 120:691–703, 2004.

Çarçabal, P., R. Schmied, **K. K. Lehmann,** and **G. Scoles.** Helium nanodroplet isolation spectroscopy of perylene and its complexes with molecular oxygen. *J. Chem. Phys.* 120:6792–3, 2004.

Lehmann, K. K., and A. Dokter. Evaporative cooling of helium nanodroplets with angular momentum conservation. *Phys. Rev. Lett.* 92:173401, 2004.

Callegari, A., et al. **(K. K. Lehmann** and **G. Scoles).** Intramolecular vibrational relaxation in aromatic molecules II: An experimental and computational study of pyrrole and triazine. *Mol. Phys.* 101:551–68, 2003.

Lehmann, K. K. Microcanonical thermodynamics properties of helium nanodroplets. *J. Chem. Phys.* 119:3336–42, 2003.

Shaked, Y., A. B. Kustka, **F. M. M. Morel,** and Y. Erel. Simultaneous determination of iron reduction and uptake by phytoplankton. *Limnol. Oceanogr.: Methods* 2:137–45, 2004.

Kilway, K. V., et al. **(R. A. Pascal Jr.).** Unexpected conversion of a polycyclic thiophene to a macrocyclic anhydride. *Tetrahedron* 60:2433–8, 2004.

Shen, X. F., D. M. Ho, and **R. A. Pascal Jr.** Synthesis of polyphenylene dendrimers related to "cubic graphite". *J. Am. Chem. Soc.* 126:5798-805, 2004.

Shen, X., D. M. Ho, and **R. A. Pascal Jr.** Synthesis and structure of a polyphenylene macrocycle related to "cubic graphite". *Org. Lett.* 5:369–71, 2003.

Feng, X.-J., and **H. Rabitz.** Optimal identification of biochemical reaction networks. *Biophys. J.* 86:1270–81, 2004.

Alis, O. F., et al. **(H. Rabitz).** On the inversion of quantum mechanical systems: Determining the amount and type of data for a unique solution. *J. Math. Chem.* 35:65–78, 2004.

Turinici, G., V. Ramakrishna, B. Li, and **H. Rabitz.** Optimal discrimination of multiple quantum systems: Controllability analysis. *J. Phys. A* 37:273–82, 2004.

Rabitz, H., M. Hsieh, and C. Rosenthal. Quantum optimally controlled transition landscapes. *Science* 303:998, 2004.

Cheong, B.-S., and **H. Rabitz.** Revealing the roles of Hamiltonian matrix coupling in bound state quantum systems. *J. Chem. Phys.* 120:6874, 2004.

Xu, R., et al. **(H. Rabitz).** Optimal control of quantum non-Markovian dissipation: Reduced Liouville-space theory. *J. Chem. Phys.* 120: 6600, 2004.

Nyåkern-Meazza, M., K. Narayan, **C. E. Schutt,** and U. Lindberg.

Princeton University

Selected Publications (continued)

Tropomyosin and gelsolin cooperate in controlling the microfilament system. *J. Biol. Chem.* 277:28774–9, 2003.

Danahy, M. P., et al. **(J. Schwartz).** Self-assembled monolayers of α,ω-diphosphonic acids on Ti enable complete or spatially controlled surface derivatization. *Langmuir* 20, 2004 (online)

Midwood, K. M., et al. **(J. Schwartz).** Rapid and efficient bonding of biomolecules to the native oxide surface of silicon. *Langmuir* 20, 2004 (online).

Gawalt, E. S., et al. **(J. Schwartz).** Bonding organics to Ti alloys: Facilitating human osteoblast attachment and spreading on surgical implant materials. *Langmuir* 19:200–4, 2003.

Schwartz, J., et al. Cell attachment and spreading on metal implant materials. *Mater. Sci. Eng. C* 23:395–400, 2003.

Schwartz, J., et al. **(S. L. Bernasek).** Controlling the work function of indium tin oxide: Differentiating dipolar from local surface effects. II. *Synth. Met.* 138: 223–7, 2003.

Koch, N., C. Chan, A. Kahn, and **J. Schwartz.** Lack of thermodynamic equilibrium in conjugated organic molecular thin films. *Phys. Rev. B* 67:195330, 2003.

Suo, Z., Y. F. Gao, and **G. Scoles.** Nanoscale domain stability in organic monolayers on metals. *J. Appl. Mech.* 71:24–31, 2004.

Case, M., et al. **(G. Scoles).** Using nanografting to achieve directed assembly of de novo designed metalloproteins on gold. *Nano Lett.* 3(4):425–9, 2003.

Casalis, L., et al. **(G. Scoles).** Hyperthermal molecular beam deposition of highly ordered organic thin films. *Phys. Rev. Lett.* 90(20):206101-1–4, 2003.

Bracco, G., and **G. Scoles.** Study of the interaction potential between a He atom and a SAM of decanethiols *J. Chem. Phys.* 119:6277, 2003.

Schreiber, F., M. G. Gerstenberg, H. Dosch, and **G. Scoles.** Melting point enhancement of a SAM induced by a van der Waals bound capping layer. *Langmuir* 19:10004–6, 2003.

Ruiz, R., et al. **(G. Scoles).** Dynamic scaling, island size distribution and morphology in the aggregation regime of sub-monolayer pentacene films. *Phys. Rev. Lett.* 91:136102, 2003.

De Renzi, V., et al. **(A. Selloni).** Ordered (3x4) high-density phase of methylthiolate on Au(111). *J. Phys. Chem. B* 108:16, 2004.

De Angelis, F., S. Fantacci, and **A. Selloni.** Time-dependent density functional theory study of the absorption spectrum of [Ru(4,4'-COOH-2,2'-bpy)_2(NCS)_2] in water solution: Influence of the pH. *Chem. Phys. Lett.* 389:204, 2004.

Vittadini, A., and **A. Selloni.** Periodic density functional theory studies of vanadia-titania catalysts: Structure and stability of the oxidized monolayer. *J. Phys. Chem. B* 108:7337, 2004.

Tilocca, A., and **A. Selloni.** Structure And reactivity of water layers on defect-free and defective anatase TiO_2(101) surfaces. *J. Phys. Chem. B* 108:4743, 2004.

Di Felice, R., and **A. Selloni.** Adsorption modes of cysteine on Au(111): Thiolate, amino-thiolate, disulfide. *J. Chem. Phys.* 120:4906, 2004 (also in *Virtual J. Biol. Phys. Res.,* 2004).

Wu, X., **A. Selloni,** and S. K. Nayak. First principles study of CO Oxidation on TiO_2(110): The role of surface oxygen vacancies. *J. Chem. Phys.* 120:4512, 2004.

Semmelhack, M. F., and R. J. Hooley. Palladium-catalyzed hydrostannylations of highly hindered acetyolenes in hexane. *Tetrahedron Lett.* 44:5737–9, 2003.

Semmelhack, M. F., L. Wu, **R. A. Pascal Jr.,** and D. M. Ho. Conformational control in activation of an enediyne. *J. Am. Chem. Soc.* 125:10496-7, 2003.

Shiozaki, E. N., L. Gu, N. Yan, and **Y. Shi.** Structure of the BRCT repeats of BRCA1 bound to a BACH1 phosphopeptide: Implications for signaling. *Mol. Cell* 14:405–12, 2004.

Frederick, J. P., et al. **(Y. Shi).** Transforming growth factor β-mediated transcriptional repression of c-myc is dependent on direct binding of Smad3 to a novel repressive Smad binding element. *Mol. Cell. Biol.* 24(6):2546–59, 2004.

Huh, J. R., et al. **(Y. Shi).** Multiple apoptotic caspase cascades are required in non-apoptotic roles for *Drosophila spermatid* individualization. *PLoS Biol.* 2:43–53, 2004.

Soos, Z. G., and E. V. Tsiper. Polarization energies, transport gap and charge transfer states of organic molecular crystals. *Macromol. Symp.* 212:1–12, 2004.

Girlando, A., A. Painelli, S. A. Bewick, and **Z. G. Soos.** Charge fluctuations and electron-phonon coupling in organic charge-transfer salts with neutral-ionic and Peierls transitions. *Synth. Met.* 141:129–38, 2004.

Soos, Z. G., S. A. Bewick, A. Peri, and A. Painelli. Dielectric response of modified Hubbard models with neutral-ionic and Peierls transitions. *J. Chem. Phys.* 120:6712, 2004.

Sin, J. M., and **Z. G. Soos.** Hopping transport in molecularly doped polymers: Positional disorder, donor packing and rate law. *Recent Res. Dev. Chem. Phys.* 3:563–83, 2003.

Massino, M., A. Girlando, and **Z. G. Soos.** Evidence for a soft mode in the temperature induced neutral-ionic transition of TTF-CA. *Chem. Phys. Lett.* 369:428–33, 2003.

Tsiper, E. V., and **Z. G. Soos.** Electronic polarization in pentacene crystals and thin films. *Phys. Rev. B* 68:085301, 2003.

Anderson, E. A., E. J. Alexanian, and **E. J. Sorensen.** A synthesis of the furanosteroidal antibiotic viridian. *Angew. Chem. Int. Ed.* 43:1998–2001, 2004.

Adam, G. C., C. D. Vanderwal, **E. J. Sorensen,** and B. F. Cravatt. (-)-FR182877 is a potent and selective inhibitor of carboxylesterase-1. *Angew. Chem. Int. Ed.* 42:5480–4, 2003.

Vosburg, D. A., S. Weiler, and **E. J. Sorensen.** Concise stereocontrolled routes to fumagillol, fumagillin, and TNP-470. *Chirality* 15:156–66, 2003.

Vanderwal, C. D., D. A. Vosburg, S. Weiler, and **E. J. Sorensen.** An enantioselective synthesis of FR182877 provides a chemical rationalization of its structure and affords multigram quantities of its direct precursor. *J. Am. Chem. Soc.* 125:5393–407, 2003.

Sorensen, E. J. Architectural self-construction in nature and chemical synthesis. *Bioorg. Med. Chem.* 11:3225–8, 2003.

Tamiya, J., and **E. J. Sorensen.** A spontaneous bicyclization facilitates a synthesis of (-)-hispidospermidin. *Tetrahedron* 59:6921–32, 2003.

Jarzecki, A. A., A. D. Anbar, and **T. G. Spiro.** DFT analysis of $Fe(H_2O)_6^{3+}$ and $Fe(H_2O)_6^{2+}$ structure and vibrations: Implications for isotope fractionation. *J. Phys. Chem. A* 108:2726–32, 2004.

Coyle, C. M., et al. **(T. G. Spiro).** Activation mechanism of the CO sensor CooA: Mutational and resonance Raman spectroscopic studies. *J. Biol. Chem.* 278:35384–93, 2003.

Wang, Y., and **T. G. Spiro.** Vibrational and electronic couplings in ultraviolet resonance Raman spectra of cyclic peptides. *Biophys. Chem.* 105:461–70, 2003.

Stiefel, E. I., ed. Dithiolene chemistry: Synthesis, properties, and applications. In *Progress in Inorganic Chemistry,* vol. 52, pp.1&738. John Wiley and Sons, 2004.

Beswick, C., J. M. Schulman, and **E. I. Stiefel.** Structures and structural trends in homoleptic dithiolene complexes. In dithiolene chemistry: synthesis, properties and applications. In *Progress in Inorganic Chemistry,* vol. 52, pp. 55–110. John Wiley and Sons, 2004.

Horvath, I., et al. **(E. I. Stiefel),** eds. *Encyclopedia of Catalysis.* Hoboken, N.J.: John Wiley and Sons, 2003.

Wolanin, P. M., and **J. B. Stock.** Transmembrane signaling and the regulation of histidine kinase activity. In *Histidine Kinases in Signal Transduction,* eds. M. Inouye and R. Dutta, pp. 73–122. New York: Academic Press, 2003.

Webre, D., P. M. Wolanin, and **J. B. Stock.** Bacterial chemotaxis. *Curr. Biol.* 13(2):R47–9, 2003.

Park, S., et al. **(J. B. Stock).** From the cover: Influence of topology on bacterial social interaction. *PNAS* 100:13910–5, 2003.

Wolanin, P. M., D. Webre, and **J. B. Stock.** Mechanism of phosphate activity in the chemotaxis response regulator CheY. *Biochemistry* 42(47):14075–82, 2003.

Donev, A., **S. Torquato,** F. H. Stillinger, and R. Connelly. A linear programming algorithm to test for jamming in hard-sphere packings. *J. Computat. Phys.* 197:139, 2004.

Donev, A., and **S. Torquato.** Energy-efficient actuation in infinite lattice structures. *J. Mech. Phys. Solids* 51:1459, 2003.

Crawford, J., **S. Torquato,** and F. H. Stillinger. Aspects of correlation function realizability. *J. Chem. Phys.* 119:7065, 2003.

Torquato, S., S. Hyun, and A. Donev. Optimal design of manufacturable three-dimensional composites with multifuctional characteristics. *J. Appl. Phys.* 94:5748, 2003.

Hyun, S., A. M. Karlsson, **S. Torquato,** and A. G. Evans. Simulated properties of kagome and tetragonal truss core panels. *Int. J. Sol. Struct.* 40:6989, 2003.

Keusters, D., and **W. S. Warren.** Propagation effects on the peak profile in two-dimensional optical photon echo spectroscopy. *Chem. Phys. Lett.* 383(1–2):21–4, 2004.

Mehendale, M., B. Bosacchi, **W. S. Warren,** and M. O. Scully. Evolutionary pulse shaping in CARS signal enhancement. *Proc. SPIE* 5200:46–55, 2004.

Bosacchi, B., et al. **(W. S. Warren** and **H. Rabitz).** Computational intelligence in bacterial sport detection and identification. *Proc. SPIE* 5200:31–45, 2004.

Cao, H., **W. S. Warren,** A. Dogariu, and L. J. Wang. Reduction of optical intensity noise by means of two-photon absorption. *J. Opt. Soc. B* 20(3):560–3, 2003.

Tian, P., D. Keusters, Y. Suzaki, and **W. S. Warren.** Femtosecond Phase-coherent two-dimensional spectroscopy. *Science* 300:1553–5, 2003.

Keusters, D., and **W. S. Warren.** Effect of pulse propagation on the two-dimensional photon echo spectrum of multi-level systems. *J. Chem. Phys.* 119(8):4478–89, 2003.

RUTGERS, THE STATE UNIVERSITY OF NEW JERSEY, NEW BRUNSWICK/PISCATAWAY

Graduate Program in Chemistry and Chemical Biology

Programs of Study The Graduate Program in Chemistry and Chemical Biology at Rutgers in New Brunswick offers programs leading to the degrees of Master of Science, Master of Science for Teachers, and Doctor of Philosophy.

The principal requirement for the Ph.D. degree is the completion and successful oral defense of a thesis based on original research. A wide variety of research specializations are available in the traditional areas of chemistry—analytical, inorganic, organic, and physical—as well as in related areas and subdisciplines, including biological, bioinorganic, bioorganic, and biophysical chemistry; chemical physics; theoretical chemistry; and solid-state and surface chemistry.

The M.S. degree may be taken with or without a research thesis. The principal requirements are completion of 30 credits of graduate courses, a passing grade on the master's examination, and a master's essay or thesis. When the thesis option is chosen, 6 of the 30 credits may be in research.

Research Facilities The research facilities of the program, located in the Wright and Rieman chemistry laboratories on the Busch campus, include a comprehensive chemistry library and glassworking, electronics, and machine shops. Research instruments of particular note include 600-, 500-, 400-, 300-, and 200-MHz NMR spectrometers with 2-D, 3-D, and solid-state capabilities; ESR spectrometers; single-crystal and powder X-ray diffractometers; multiwire area detectors for macromolecular structure determination; laser flash photolysis systems; a temperature-programmable ORD-CD spectropolarimeter; automated peptide and DNA synthesizers; a SQUID magnetometer; ultrahigh-vacuum surface analysis systems; scanning tunneling and atomic force microscopes; a helium-atom scattering apparatus; molecular beam and supersonic jet apparatuses; GC/quadrupole and ICP mass spectrometers; and extensive laser instrumentation, crystal-growing facilities, and calorimetric equipment. Computing facilities in the Wright-Rieman Laboratories include four multiprocessor servers, more than fifty graphics workstations, a forty-eight-processor cluster of PC-based workstations, a presenter system, video animation equipment, and an assortment of approximately 500 personal computers, X-terminals, and laser and color printers.

Financial Aid Full-time Ph.D. students receive financial assistance in the form of fellowships, research assistantships, teaching assistantships, or a combination of these. Financial assistance for entering students ranges from approximately $19,000 to $22,000 plus tuition remission for a calendar-year appointment. This includes the J. R. L. Morgan fellowships awarded annually to outstanding applicants.

Cost of Study In 2003–04, the full-time tuition (remitted for assistantship and fellowship recipients) was $4476 per semester for New Jersey residents and $6562 per semester for out-of-state residents. There was a fee for full-time students of $539 per semester. All of these fees are subject to change for the next academic year.

Living and Housing Costs A furnished double room in the University residence halls or apartments rented for $5742 to $6602 per person for the 2003–04 calendar year. Married student apartments rented for $735 to $935 per month. Current information may be obtained from the Department of Housing (732-445-2215), which also has information on private housing in the New Brunswick area.

Student Group Total University enrollment is more than 48,000. Graduate and professional enrollment is approximately 13,500, of whom about 8,500 are in the Graduate School. Enrollment of graduate students in chemistry totals 140. Of these, about three fourths are full-time students. Students come from all parts of the United States as well as from other countries. In addition, there are approximately 50 postdoctoral research associates in residence.

Location New Brunswick, with a population of about 49,000, is located in central New Jersey, roughly midway between New York City and Philadelphia. The cultural facilities of these two cities are easily accessible by automobile or regularly scheduled bus and train service. Within a 1½-hour drive of New Brunswick are the recreational areas of the Pocono Mountains of Pennsylvania and the beaches of the New Jersey shore. The University also offers a rich program of cultural, recreational, and social activities.

The University Graduate instruction and research in chemistry and chemical biology are conducted on the University's Busch campus, which has a rural-suburban environment and is a few minutes' drive from downtown New Brunswick. On the same campus, within walking distance, are the Hill Center for the Mathematical Sciences (home of the University's computer center), the Library of Science and Medicine, the physics and biology laboratories, the Waksman Institute of Microbiology, the Robert Wood Johnson Medical School, the Center for Advanced Biotechnology and Medicine, and the College of Engineering. The University provides a free shuttle-bus service between the Busch and New Brunswick campuses.

Applying Applications for assistantships and fellowships should be made at the same time as applications to the Graduate School. All information describing current research programs may be obtained at the program's Web address. Admission consideration is open to all qualified candidates without regard to race, color, national origin, religion, sex, or handicap.

Correspondence and Information
Executive Officer
Graduate Program in Chemistry and Chemical Biology at New Brunswick
Wright-Rieman Laboratories
Rutgers, The State University of New Jersey
610 Taylor Road
Piscataway, New Jersey 08854-8087
Telephone: 732-445-3223
E-mail: gradexec@rutchem.rutgers.edu
World Wide Web: http://rutchem.rutgers.edu

Rutgers, The State University of New Jersey, New Brunswick/Piscataway

THE FACULTY AND THEIR RESEARCH

Stephen Anderson, Associate Professor. Protein engineering, protein folding, molecular recognition, and structural genomics.
Georgia A. Arbuckle-Keil, Professor. Synthesis and properties of conducting polymers, quartz crystal microbalance study of electroactive surfaces, dynamic infrared linear dichroism (DIRLD).
Edward Arnold, Professor. Crystallographic studies of human viruses and viral proteins; molecular design, including drugs and vaccines; polymerase structure.
Jean Baum, Professor. Biophysical chemistry, NMR, protein folding.
Helen M. Berman, Professor and Member of the Board of Governors. Structural biology, structural nucleic acids, bioinformatics, protein nucleic acid interaction.
Robert S. Boikess, Professor. Chemical education.
John G. Brennan, Professor. Molecular and solid-state inorganic chemistry; lanthanide chalcogenides and pnictides; molecular approaches to semiconductor thin films, optical fibers, and nanometer-sized clusters.
Kenneth J. Breslauer, Linus C. Pauling Professor. Characterization of the molecular interactions that control biopolymer structure and stability, drug-binding affinity and specificity, nucleic acid–based diagnostics and therapeutics.
Kieron Burke, Associate Professor. Density functional theory in quantum chemistry and solid-state physics, nanoscience, surface science, proteins, and atomic and molecular structure.
Edward Castner Jr., Associate Professor. Ultrafast molecular dynamics and photoreactions in solution, hydrophilic polymer micelles and hydrogels, room-temperature ionic liquids.
Yves J. Chabal, Professor. Surface and interface chemistry of electronic and photonic materials and nanomaterials; in situ infrared spectroscopy of surface etching, thin-film growth, and solid/biological interfaces.
Kuang-Yu Chen, Professor. Biochemistry and function of polyamines and hypusine, transcription factors and cell senescence, nutrients and selective gene expression, stress and gene expression, molecular mechanism of tumor differentiation.
Martha A. Cotter, Professor and Executive Officer, Graduate Program. Theoretical investigations of liquid crystals and micellar solutions, phase transitions in simple model systems, theory of liquids.
Richard H. Ebright, Professor. Protein-DNA interaction; protein-protein interaction; structure, function, and regulation of transcription initiation complexes; single-molecule microscopy and nanomanipulation.
Eric L. Garfunkel, Professor. Surface chemistry, ultrathin films and interfaces for nanoelectronics, nanomaterials and technology, molecular electronics, organic-inorganic interfaces.
Alan S. Goldman, Professor. Organometallic chemistry: homogeneous catalysis, reactions, and mechanisms; catalytic functionalization of hydrocarbons.
Lionel Goodman, Professor. Laser spectroscopy, particularly involving multiphoton excitation in supersonic jets; theoretical calculation and understanding of internal rotation potential surfaces for key molecules; application to biomolecules.
Martha Greenblatt, Professor. Solid-state inorganic chemistry, low-dimensional transition-metal oxides and chalcogenides, high-T_c superconductors, CMR materials, solid electrolytes and electrodes for fuel cells and sensors.
Gene S. Hall, Associate Professor. Applications of Raman microscopy, ICP-MS, XRF, and FT-IR in biological and environmental samples.
Gregory F. Herzog, Professor. Origin and evolution of meteorites, cosmogenic radioisotopes by accelerator mass spectrometry; stable isotopes by conventional forms of mass spectrometry.
Jane Hinch, Associate Professor. Molecular beam–surface interactions, surface diffractive techniques, scanning tunneling microscopy.
Stephan S. Isied, Professor. Bioinorganic and physical inorganic chemistry, photoinduced electron transfer in proteins, electron mediation by peptides with secondary structures, hydrogen bonding and other molecular recognition sites.
Leslie S. Jimenez, Associate Professor. Synthesis and characterization of analogs of antitumor antibiotics, total synthesis of natural products.
Roger A. Jones, Professor and Chair. Nucleoside and nucleic acid synthesis, including specifically labeled and modified nucleosides to probe ligand-nucleic acid interactions of both DNA and RNA.
Spencer Knapp, Professor. Total synthesis of natural products; design and synthesis of enzyme models and inhibitors and of complex ligands, new synthetic methods.
Joachim Kohn, Professor. Development of structurally new polymers as biomaterials for medical applications, tissue engineering, drug delivery, studies on the interactions of cells with artificial surfaces.
John Krenos, Professor. Chemical physics, energy transfer in hyperthermal collisions and collisions involving electronically excited reactants.
Karsten Krogh-Jespersen, Professor. Computational studies of molecular electronic structure, excited electronic states, solvation effects on photophysical properties, computational inorganic chemistry, catalysis.
Jeehiun Katherine Lee, Assistant Professor. Experimental and theoretical studies of biological and organic reactivity, recognition, and catalysis; DNA duplex stability; mass spectrometry.
Ronald M. Levy, Board of Governors Professor. Biophysical chemistry, chemical physics of liquids, computational biology, protein structure, dynamics and protein folding.
Jing Li, Professor. Inorganic and materials chemistry; synthesis, structure characterization, electronic, optical, and thermal properties of solid-state inorganic materials; coordination polymers, hybrid nanostructures, and nanoporous materials.
Richard D. Ludescher, Professor. Food science: protein structure, dynamics, and function; luminescence spectroscopy; biophysics of amorphous solids.
Theodore E. Madey, State of New Jersey Professor of Surface Science. Structure and reactivity of surfaces and ultrathin films, electron-and photon-induced surface processes.
Gerald S. Manning, Professor. Physics and physical chemistry of polymers, ionic and elastic effects on biopolymer structure and configuration.
Gaetano T. Montelione, Professor. Structure and dynamics of protein-protein and protein–nucleic acid complexes.
Robert A. Moss, Louis P. Hammett Professor. Chemistry of reactive intermediates: carbenes, carbocations, diazirines; laser flash photolysis and fast kinetics.
Wilma K. Olson, Mary I. Bunting Professor. Theoretical and computational studies of nucleic acid conformation, properties, and interactions.
Joseph A. Potenza, Professor. Molecular structure, X-ray diffraction, magnetic resonance.
Laurence S. Romsted, Professor. Theory of micellar effects on reaction rates and equilibria, ion binding at aqueous interfaces, organic reaction mechanisms, antioxidant and dediazoniation chemistries.
Heinz D. Roth, Professor. Electron transfer induced chemistry, physical organic chemistry of reactive intermediates, nuclear spin polarization, electron spin resonance, zeolite-induced chemistry, history of chemistry.
Harvey J. Schugar, Professor. Inorganic and bioinorganic chemistry, modeling of metalloprotein active sites, designing metal complexes for dye-sensitized solar cells, novel polydentate imidazole ligands and proton sponges.
Stanley Stein, Adjunct Professor. Methods development in protein analysis, synthesis of biologically active peptides and oligonucleotides.
David Talaga, Assistant Professor. Protein folding and conformational dynamics, single molecule studies of inorganic and biological polymers, vibrational spectroscopy of inorganic complexes.
John W. Taylor, Associate Professor. Bioactive peptide design and synthesis, multicyclic peptides, peptide conformation, protein engineering, peptide ligand-receptor interactions, peptide-based HIV vaccines.
Kathryn E. Uhrich, Associate Professor. Synthesis and characterization of novel polymers for drug delivery, preparation and analysis of micropatterned polymer surfaces for cell growth.
Ralf Warmuth, Associate Professor. Design and synthesis of conformationally constrained peptides and of ion channels, host-guest chemistry, molecular container chemistry, strained organic molecules and reactive intermediates.
Lawrence J. Williams, Assistant Professor. Molecular design and synthesis; strategies, methods, and applications.

SOUTHERN ILLINOIS UNIVERSITY CARBONDALE

Department of Chemistry and Biochemistry Doctoral Program

Program of Study

The Department of Chemistry and Biochemistry offers a Ph.D. program in chemistry with specializations in analytical chemistry, inorganic chemistry, organic chemistry, physical chemistry, and materials chemistry. The Department also has an interdisciplinary focus in the fields of materials and biological chemistry and employs several faculty members whose research interests overlap in these areas.

The doctoral degree in chemistry is a research degree. To be awarded this degree, the student must, to the satisfaction of the graduate committee, demonstrate the ability to conduct original and independent research within some area of chemistry and must make an original contribution to the science. Candidates must also successfully complete cumulative exams and required graduate course work. In addition, the Ph.D. candidate must write and defend an original research proposal.

Research Facilities

The Department's research activities are supported by a full spectrum of modern chemical instruments and support facilities. Research shops for electronics, machining, fine instruments, and electron and atomic force microscopy provide essential services for many research projects. Major equipment available to the Department includes both Varian VXR 300 and 500 MHz multi-nuclear FT-NMR instruments, FTIR, a Kratos MS80 high-resolution MS/GC-MS/LC-MS, ion-trap, and quadrupole GC-MS. A Varian Mercury 400MHz NMR will soon be added. More routine equipment, such as UV-vis spectrometers, ICP-AES, HPLC, CE, GC, and AA is commonly available. Other major equipment items such Varian Ultramass ICP-MS, Gel Permeation Chromatography, polarized microscopy, ellipsometry, and modern electrochemical instrumentation and materials characterization equipment are associated with specific research groups. A multitude of personal computers connected to a campuswide network, including a twenty-station computer laboratory, are also located within the Department.

Financial Aid

Successful candidates are offered an opening in the Department's graduate program and an assistantship at the current stipend rate for an academic year. Assuming graduate school approval, the assistantship includes a waiver of tuition. Student fees are not considered a part of tuition. Incoming graduate students are usually teaching assistants for the first year, with approximately 6 to 9 contact hours per week as laboratory instructors. Some grading, proctoring, and laboratory preparation may also be assigned. By the end of the first year, graduate students are expected to join a research group and become research assistants. Assuming satisfactory performance, assistantships are renewable.

Fellowships for outstanding students, as well as dedicated fellowships for minority students, are available through the Department and the University.

Cost of Study

In-state graduate tuition is $192 per credit hour in 2004–05. Out-of-state tuition is 2.5 times the in-state tuition rate ($480 per credit hour). Graduate students with at least a 25 percent appointment as a graduate assistant receive a tuition waiver. Fees vary from $356 (1 credit hour) to $707 (12 credit hours).

Living and Housing Costs

For married couples, students with families, and single graduate students, the University had 589 efficiency and one-, two-, and three-bedroom apartments that rent for $396 to $472 per month in 2004–05. Residence halls for single graduate students are also available, as are accessible residence hall rooms and apartments for students with disabilities.

Student Group

The Southern Illinois University Carbondale (SIUC) campus has more than 21,000 students, approximately 4,500 of whom are enrolled in graduate programs. The Department of Chemistry and Biochemistry has a total of approximately 40 graduate students enrolled in the Ph.D. and master's programs.

Student Outcomes

The Department has a distinguished list of alumni making substantial impact at places such as the University of California at Berkeley, the University of Florida, Kansas State, Dupont, Monsanto, Genentech, and Bristol-Meyers Squibb.

Location

SIUC is 350 miles south of Chicago and 100 miles southeast of St. Louis. Nestled in rolling hills bordered by the Ohio and Mississippi Rivers and enhanced by a mild climate, the area has state parks, national forests and wildlife refuges, and large lakes for outdoor recreation. Cultural offerings include theater, opera, concerts, art exhibits, and cinema. Educational facilities for the families of students are excellent.

The University

Southern Illinois University Carbondale is a comprehensive public university with a variety of general and professional education programs. The University offers associate, bachelor's, master's, and doctoral degrees; the J.D. degree; and the M.D. degree. The University is fully accredited by the North Central Association of Colleges and Schools. The Graduate School has an essential role in the development and coordination of graduate instruction and research programs. The Graduate Council has academic responsibility for determining graduate standards, recommending new graduate programs and research centers, and establishing policies to facilitate the research effort.

Applying

Applications for admission may be submitted at any time, and students may start in the fall or, in special cases, in the spring. While there are no specific deadlines in the Department, domestic applications should be completed as early in January as possible for the following fall term if the applicant is interested in nomination for fellowships or scholarships offered outside the Department. International applications have the best opportunity for consideration in the Department if completed applications are on file at least six months in advance. TOEFL and TSE scores are required for international applicants. GRE scores are required for all applicants.

Further information and application packets can be obtained directly from the Department by mail or printed from the Web site. Both addresses are given in the Correspondence and Information section.

Correspondence and Information

Graduate Admissions Chair
c/o Graduate Admissions Secretary
Chemistry-MC 4409
Southern Illinois University Carbondale
Carbondale, Illinois 62901
World Wide Web: http://www.science.siu.edu/chemistry/

Southern Illinois University Carbondale

THE FACULTY AND THEIR RESEARCH

Mark J. Bausch, Associate Professor; Ph.D., Northwestern 1982. Organic chemistry, radical anion basicities, radical acidities, stability of organic cations.

Roger E. Beyler, Professor Emeritus; Ph.D., Illinois, 1949.

Albert L. Caskey, Associate Professor Emeritus; Ph.D., Iowa State 1961.

Bakul Dave, Associate Professor; Ph.D., Houston, 1993. Inorganic/materials chemistry, inorganic and organic nanocomposites, sol-gel based materials, bioinorganic chemistry.

Joe M. Davis, Professor; Ph.D., Utah, 1985. Analytical chemistry, mass transport, separations, statistics, electrokinetic separations.

Daniel J. Dyer, Associate Professor; Ph.D., Colorado, 1996. Organic/materials chemistry, design and synthesis of organic materials and polymers.

Yong Gao, Assistant Professor; Ph.D., Alberta, 1998. Organic/materials/biological chemistry, design and synthesis of nanomaterials for biological applications.

Qingfeng Ge, Assistant Professor; Ph.D., Tianjin University (China), 1991. Theoretical studies of electrocatalytic processes in fuel cells and biological systems.

Boyd Goodson, Assistant Professor; Ph.D., Berkeley, 1999. Physical chemistry, optical/nuclear double resonance spectroscopy.

John C. Guyon, Professor Emeritus; Ph.D., Purdue, 1961.

Herbert I. Hadler, Professor Emeritus; Ph.D., Wisconsin, 1952.

Conrad C. Hinckley, Professor Emeritus; Ph.D., Texas, 1964.

John A. Koropchak, Professor and Vice Chancellor for Research; Ph.D., Georgia, 1980. Analytical chemistry, atomic spectroscopy, metal speciation, separations detection, condensation nucleation light scattering detection, single molecule detection, capillary separations.

Punit Kohli, Assistant Professor; Ph.D., Michigan State, 2000. Organic/materials chemistry, self-assembly of nanotubes and nanoparticles using molecular recognition principles, highly selective biological-tailored nanotube membranes for transport studies.

David F. Koster, Professor Emeritus; Ph.D., Texas A&M, 1965.

Matthew E. McCarroll, Assistant Professor; Ph.D., Idaho, 1998. Analytical chemistry, florescence spectroscopy, chiral and molecular recognition, organized media, stationary-phase development, capillary electrophoresis, development of florescence sensors.

Cal Y. Meyers, Professor Emeritus; Ph.D., Illinois, 1951.

C. David Schmulbach, Professor Emeritus; Ph.D., Illinois, 1958.

Gerard V. Smith, Professor Emeritus; Ph.D., Arkansas, 1959. Organic chemistry, mechanisms of surface reactions, heterogeneous catalytic hydrogenation and exchange, asymmetric catalysis, catalytic oxidation and ozonation, molecular probes for characterization of metal surfaces.

Luke T. Tolley, Assistant Professor; Ph.D., North Carolina, 2001. Analytical chemistry, chromatography, capillary electrophoresis, mass spectrometry, intercellular signaling biomarkers.

Russell F. Trimble, Professor Emeritus; Ph.D., MIT, 1950.

James Tyrrell, Professor and Associate Dean; Ph.D., Glasgow, 1963. Physical chemistry, computational chemistry, transition states, reaction surfaces.

Lori Vermeulen, Associate Professor and Chair; Ph.D., Princeton, 1994. Inorganic/organic/materials chemistry, solid state chemistry, drug delivery, polymers.

Lichang Wang, Assistant Professor; Ph.D., Copenhagen, 1993. Physical/materials chemistry, computational/theoretical, material and catalytic properties of transition metal nanoparticles, hydrogen bonding network in self-assembled monolayers, activities of enzymes in biochemical reactions.

Ling Zang, Assistant Professor; Ph.D., Chinese Academy of Sciences, 1995. Analytical/physical/materials chemistry, nanoscale imaging and spectroscopy, nanostructure assembling and patterning, nanodevices for fluorescence sensing and probing.

STANFORD UNIVERSITY

Department of Chemistry

Program of Study The Department of Chemistry strives for excellence in education and research. Only candidates for the Ph.D. degree are accepted. The department has a relatively small faculty, which promotes outstanding interactions between students and faculty and staff members. The faculty has achieved broad national and international recognition for its outstanding research contributions, and more than a third of its members belong to the National Academy of Sciences. The graduate program is based strongly on research, and students enter a research group by the end of the winter quarter of their first year. Students are also expected to complete a rigorous set of core courses in various areas of chemistry in their first year and to complement these courses later by studying upper-level subjects of their choice. Placement examinations are administered early in the fall quarter of the first year in inorganic, organic, physical, and biophysical chemistry and chemical physics. Students with deficiencies in undergraduate training in these areas are identified and work with the faculty to make them up. No other departmental examinations or orals are required of students progressing toward the Ph.D. degree. Much of the department's instruction is informal and includes diverse and active seminar programs, group meetings, and discussions with visiting scholars and with colleagues in other departments of the University. Stanford Ph.D. recipients are particularly well prepared for advanced scientific and technological study, and chemistry graduates typically accept positions on highly regarded university faculties or enter a wide variety of positions in industry.

Research Facilities The department occupies six buildings with approximately 200,000 square feet of research space. The department has a strong commitment to obtaining and maintaining state-of-the-art instrumentation for analysis and spectroscopy. Equipment available includes 200-, 300-, 400-, 500-, 600- and 800-MHz NMR spectrometers; X-ray crystallography facilities; ultrafast absorption and fluorescence spectroscopy facilities; ultrahigh-resolution laser spectroscopy facilities; ion cyclotron resonance facilities; dynamic light-scattering spectroscopy facilities; tissue culture facilities; electrochemical systems; ultrahigh-vacuum facilities for surface analysis, including ESCA, Auger, EELS, LEED, and UPS; laser-Raman facilities; a superconducting magnetometer; and a GC/MS. The University has fully staffed machine and glass shops available for use by the department.

Extensive computing capabilities are available in all research groups, and these are supplemented by a department computer network and a regional computational facility. The department and library maintain licenses for many of the most popular software packages for the chemical and life sciences.

Additional major instrumentation and expertise are available in the Stanford Nanofabrication Facility, the Stanford Synchrotron Radiation Laboratory, the Stanford University Mass Spectrometry facility, the Stanford Magnetic Resonance Laboratory, and the Laboratory for Advanced Materials.

Financial Aid Financial support of graduate students is provided in the form of teaching assistantships, research assistantships, and fellowships. All graduate students in good standing receive full financial support (tuition and stipend) for the duration of their graduate studies. The stipend for incoming first-year graduate students is $25,185; the amount of the stipend is adjusted annually to allow for inflation. Typical appointments involve teaching assistantships in the first year and research assistantships in subsequent years. Supplements are provided to holders of outside fellowships.

Cost of Study Holders of teaching assistantships or research assistantships pay no academic tuition. In 2004–05, 10-unit tuition is $25,920 for the year (four quarters).

Living and Housing Costs Both University-owned and privately owned housing accommodations are available. Due to the residential nature of the surrounding area, it is not uncommon for several graduate students to share in a house rental. Escondido Village, an apartment development on campus, provides one- to three-bedroom apartments for married students and single parents. Rains Houses and Lyman provide additional apartment residences on campus. The average monthly expenditure for rent is $550 for on-campus housing.

Student Group The total enrollment at Stanford University is 14,444, and there are 7,055 graduate students. The Department of Chemistry has 200 graduate students in its Ph.D. program.

Location Stanford University is located in Palo Alto, a community of 60,000 about 35 miles south of San Francisco. Extensive cultural and recreational opportunities are available at the University and in surrounding areas, as well as in San Francisco. To the west lie the Santa Cruz Mountains and the Pacific Ocean, and to the east, the Sierra Nevada range with its many national parks, hiking and skiing trails, and redwood forests.

The University Stanford is a private university founded in 1885 and ranked in the top few for academic excellence in physical and natural sciences, liberal arts, humanities, and engineering. The campus occupies 8,800 acres of land, of which 5,200 acres are in general academic use. In all disciplines, the University has a primary commitment to excellence in education and research.

Applying Admission to the chemistry department is by competitive application. Applications are available from the World Wide Web and should be filed before January 1 for admission in the fall quarter. All applicants are required to submit GRE scores from the verbal, quantitative, and analytical tests and the Subject Test in chemistry, as well as transcripts and three letters of recommendation. Applicants are notified of admission decisions before March 15. In unusual circumstances, late applications or a deferred enrollment are considered.

Correspondence and Information

Graduate Admissions Committee
Department of Chemistry
Stanford University
Stanford, California 94305-5080

Telephone: 650-723-1525
E-mail: chem.admissions@stanford.edu
World Wide Web: http://www.stanford.edu/dept/chemistry

Stanford University

THE FACULTY AND THEIR RESEARCH

Hans C. Andersen, Professor; Ph.D., MIT, 1966. Physical chemistry: statistical mechanics, theories of the structure and dynamics of liquids, computer simulation methods, glass transition.
Steven G. Boxer, Professor; Ph.D., Chicago, 1976. Physical and biophysical chemistry: structure, function, dynamics, and electrostatics in proteins and membranes; spectroscopy; photosynthesis; GFP; membrane biotechnology; cell-cell interactions.
John I. Brauman, Professor; Ph.D., Berkeley, 1963. Organic and physical chemistry: structure and reactivity of ions in the gas phase, photochemistry and spectroscopy of gas phase ions, electron photodetachment spectroscopy, electron affinities, reaction mechanisms.
Christopher E. D. Chidsey, Associate Professor; Ph.D., Stanford, 1983. Physical chemistry: molecular electronics, nanowire patterning, interfacial electron transfer, monomolecular films on metal and semiconductor surfaces.
James P. Collman, Professor; Ph.D., Illinois, 1958. Inorganic, organic, and organometallic chemistry: synthetic analogues of the active sites in hemoproteins, homogeneous catalysis, multielectron redox catalysts, multiple metal-metal bonds.
Hongjie Dai, Associate Professor; Ph.D., Harvard, 1994. Physical and materials chemistry: condensed-matter physics; materials science; biophysics; synthesis of ordered nanomaterial architectures; electrical, mechanical, electromechanical, and electrochemical characterizations; probing the interactions between biological molecules and nanoscale inorganic materials; molecular electronics.
Carl Djerassi, Professor Emeritus; Ph.D., Wisconsin–Madison, 1945. Organic chemistry: chemistry of steroids, terpenes, and alkaloids with major emphasis on marine sources, application of chiroptical methods—especially circular dichroism and magnetic circular dichroism—to organic and biochemical problems, organic chemical applications of mass spectrometry, use of computer artificial-intelligence techniques in structure elucidation of organic compounds. Author of novels in genre of science-in-fiction and of science-in-theater plays.
Justin Du Bois, Assistant Professor; Ph.D., Caltech, 1997. Organic chemistry: reaction development and transition metal catalysis, natural product synthesis, molecular recognition, ion channel physiology.
Michael D. Fayer, Professor; Ph.D., Berkeley, 1974. Physical chemistry and chemical physics: dynamics in molecular condensed phases; laser spectroscopy; ultrafast nonlinear techniques; infrared and visible studies of dynamics and intermolecular interactions in hydrogen-bonding liquids, supercooled liquids, liquid crystals, supercritical fluids and proteins, and other biological systems.
Keith O. Hodgson; Professor; Ph.D., Berkeley, 1972. Inorganic, biophysical, and structural chemistry: chemistry and structure of metal sites in biomolecules, molecular and crystal structure analysis, protein crystallography, extended X-ray absorption fine-structure spectroscopy.
Wray H. Huestis, Professor; Ph.D., Caltech, 1972. Biophysical chemistry: chemistry of cell-surface receptors, membrane-mediated control mechanisms, biochemical studies of membrane protein complexes in situ, magnetic resonance studies of conformation and function in soluble proteins and protein-lipid complexes, viral fusion mechanisms, drug delivery.
Chaitan Khosla, Professor; Ph.D., Caltech, 1990. Biological chemistry: structure, function, and engineering of multienzyme systems derived from natural product biosynthetic pathways; use of "unnatural" natural products to probe biological and biochemical phenomena.
Jennifer J. Kohler, Assistant Professor; Ph.D., Yale, 2000. Organic chemistry: bioorganic chemistry, chemical biology, glycobiology.
Eric T. Kool, Professor; Ph.D., Columbia, 1988. Organic, biological, and biophysical chemistry: synthetic mimics of nucleic acid structures, mechanistic studies of DNA replication and DNA repair, fluorescence methods for detecting and imaging RNA in cells, combinatorial biosensor discovery, design of new biological pathways.
Harden M. McConnell, Professor Emeritus; Ph.D., Caltech, 1951. Physical chemistry, biophysics, immunology: membrane biophysics with emphasis on immunology and the activity of cholesterol in membranes.
W. E. Moerner, Professor; Ph.D., Cornell, 1982. Physical chemistry: individual molecules in solids, polymers, and proteins probed by far-field and near-field optical spectroscopy; single-molecule biophysics; nanophotonics; quantum optics of single molecules; chemistry of optical materials.
Vijay Pande, Assistant Professor; Ph.D., MIT, 1995. Physical chemistry and biophysics: theoretical models and computer simulations to examine the equilibrium and nonequilibrium statistical mechanics of biological molecules, thermodynamics and kinetics of protein folding, RNA folding, and protein design.
Robert Pecora, Professor; Ph.D., Columbia, 1962. Physical chemistry: statistical mechanics of fluids and macromolecules, molecular motions in fluids, light-scattering spectroscopy of liquids, macromolecules and biological systems.
John Ross, Professor Emeritus; Ph.D., MIT, 1951. Physical chemistry: experimental and theoretical studies of chemical kinetics, chemical instabilities, oscillatory reactions, strategies of determining complex reaction mechanisms, chemical computations, thermodynamics and fluctuations of systems far from equilibrium.
Edward I. Solomon, Professor; Ph.D., Princeton, 1972. Physical, inorganic, and bioinorganic chemistry: inorganic spectroscopy and ligand field, molecular orbital, and density functional theory; active sites; spectral and magnetic studies on bioinorganic systems directed toward understanding the geometric and electronic structural origins of their activity; structure/function correlations; development of new spectroscopic methods in bioinorganic chemistry.
T. Daniel P. Stack, Associate Professor; Ph.D., Harvard, 1988. Inorganic and organic chemistry: bioinspired oxidation catalysis.
Henry Taube, Professor Emeritus; Ph.D., Berkeley, 1940. Inorganic chemistry: mechanisms of inorganic reactions and reactivity of inorganic substances, new aquo ions, dinitrogen as ligand, back-bonding as affecting properties including reactivity of ligands, mixed-valence molecules.
Barry M. Trost, Professor; Ph.D., MIT, 1965. Organic, organometallic, and bioorganic chemistry: new synthetic methods, natural product synthesis and structure determinations, insect chemistry, potentially antiaromatic unsaturated hydrocarbons, chemistry of ylides.
Robert M. Waymouth, Professor; Ph.D., Caltech, 1987. Inorganic, organometallic, and polymer chemistry: mechanistic and synthetic chemistry of the early transition elements, mechanisms of olefin polymerization, design of new polymerization catalysts.
Paul A. Wender, Professor; Ph.D., Yale, 1973. Organic, organometallic, bioorganic, and medicinal chemistry: synthesis of biologically active compounds, synthetic methods, biomacromolecular recognition, computer design, drug mechanisms.
Dmitry V. Yandulov, Assistant Professor; Ph.D., Indiana, 2000. Inorganic chemistry: redox catalysis, bioinorganic modeling, organometallic catalysis, catalytic fluorination.
Richard N. Zare, Professor; Ph.D., Harvard, 1964. Physical and analytical chemistry, chemical physics: application of lasers to chemical problems, molecular structure and molecular reaction dynamics.

Courtesy Faculty

Stacey F. Bent, Associate Professor; Ph.D., Stanford, 1992. Semiconductor processing and surface reactivity, surface functionalization, atomic layer deposition, electronic materials, biological interfaces.
James K. Chen, Assistant Professor; Ph.D., Harvard, 1999. Mechanistic studies of embryonic signaling pathways, modulation of embryonic and oncogenic processes by small molecule probes, chemical approaches to zebrafish development.
Karlene Cimprich, Assistant Professor; Ph.D., Harvard, 1994. Use of chemical and biochemical approaches to understand and control the DNA damage–induced cell cycle checkpoints and signal transduction cascades that allow the cell to detect and respond to DNA damage.
Curtis W. Frank, Professor; Ph.D., Illinois, 1972. Polymer physics: dependence of polymer chain configuration on interactions with its environment.
Daniel Herschlag, Professor; Ph.D., Brandeis, 1988. Biological, bioorganic, and biophysical chemistry: chemical and physical principles of biological catalysis elucidated through study of reactions catalyzed by proteins and RNA and in model systems; RNA folding kinetics and thermodynamics via single molecule fluorescence and other techniques; systems analysis of complex biological processes, including translation initiation and RNA processing elucidated via global microarray analysis.
Robert J. Madix, Professor; Ph.D., Berkeley, 1964. Surface and interface science: relationships between surface composition structure and heterogeneous reactivity of metal and metalloid surfaces, catalysis, organometallic surface chemistry, electrochemistry and corrosion, reaction dynamics.
Thomas J. Wandless, Assistant Professor; Ph.D., Harvard, 1993. Organic and biological chemistry: design and synthesis of molecules that regulate specific biological processes in both cultured cells and in animals.

STONY BROOK UNIVERSITY, STATE UNIVERSITY OF NEW YORK

Department of Chemistry

Program of Study

The Department of Chemistry at Stony Brook offers courses of study leading to the M.S. and Ph.D. degrees. The emphasis of the graduate program is on research. Upon arrival at Stony Brook, each new student meets with a temporary faculty adviser to choose appropriate course work. During the first year, new students get to know the faculty members through courses, departmental activities, and a research seminar in which the faculty members describe their research programs. Students choose a faculty research adviser at the end of the first semester, and many begin their research projects in the second semester.

The faculty members at Stony Brook have diverse backgrounds and research interests, with a significant emphasis on interdisciplinary research. Students have access to research projects in the broad range of chemistry fields, including biological, inorganic, organic, and physical chemistry, as well as studies at the interfaces of chemistry and other disciplines (materials science, physics, molecular biology, pharmacology, earth and space science, computer science, and others). Several faculty members have joint appointments with other University departments or with Brookhaven National Laboratory. Students have the option of pursuing a degree with a concentration in chemical biology or chemical physics, if desired. In addition, nearby Brookhaven National Laboratory and Cold Spring Harbor Laboratory provide many opportunities for collaborative research.

The graduate program is individually tailored to each student, with students finishing in four to six years. Graduates pursue careers both in industry and in academia, including undergraduate and research institutions.

Research Facilities

Graduate students at Stony Brook have access to excellent research facilities. The Chemistry Building is a modern, seven-story, 170,000-square-foot structure designed for research and advanced teaching. Student and faculty offices overlook the densely wooded campus and Long Island Sound.

In-house services include the glass shop, machine shop, and electronics shop, as well as a mass spectrometry facility with GC/MS, FAB, and TOF-MS capabilities. The NMR facility provides equipment for standard analytical characterization as well as sophisticated solution and solid-state experiments. In 2002, a new 400-MHz NMR with robotic auto-sampler was added to the 250-, 300-, 500-, and 600-MHz machines already available.

The Chemistry Library, located in the Chemistry Building, maintains subscriptions to 240 journals, with online access to ninety-two, and provides 24-hour access to databases such as Beilstein Commander, SciFinder, and the Science Citation Index.

Financial Aid

All students in good standing are fully supported as either teaching or research assistants. Twelve-month stipends for 2004–05 are $21,000. Students teach in their first year and then receive research assistantships during the summer. Advanced graduate students receive similar support, more often via research assistantships.

Cost of Study

Tuition is waived for all students in good standing. Students are responsible for fees of approximately $600 per year, as well as subsidized health insurance premiums of approximately $125 per year.

Living and Housing Costs

Housing is available both on and off campus. Rates for graduate apartments on campus range from $400 to $950 per month, depending on the size of the apartment and the number of residents. For students living off campus, the estimate for total living expenses is $17,000 per year.

Student Group

The chemistry graduate program includes 130 students, of whom approximately 40 percent are women. Students in the program come from across the U.S. and a dozen other countries. The department values a diverse student body, united in their excitement about chemistry.

Student Outcomes

Graduates from Stony Brook's Department of Chemistry go on to top industrial and academic positions. Recent graduates have taken research positions at companies such as Merck, Pfizer, and Duracell; postdoctoral positions at research institutions such as Berkeley, Harvard, Oxford, and Sloan-Kettering; and faculty positions at schools such as Manhattan College, the University of North Carolina, and City College, CUNY.

Location

Located near the historic village of Stony Brook, the University lies approximately 60 miles east of Manhattan on the wooded north shore of Long Island, convenient to both New York City's cultural life and Suffolk County's tranquil, recreational countryside and seashores. Long Island offers spectacular beaches, excellent fishing, and some of the East Coast's best wineries.

The University

Stony Brook is a relatively young university, founded only in 1957. In part because of close contacts with Cold Spring Harbor and Brookhaven National Labs, the University has quickly grown to become one of the country's major research universities. Stony Brook has an enrollment of about 20,000 students, including 13,000 undergraduates and 7,000 graduate and professional students. The Department of Chemistry is part of the College of Arts and Science; the University also includes a medical school and colleges of engineering, health sciences, management, and marine sciences.

Applying

The Department of Chemistry uses a rolling admissions system. Most applications are received in December and January for admission in the fall semester. Applications that arrive after February 1 are considered, if possible. Applications for spring admission should arrive by September 1 for full consideration.

Information on downloading an application or applying directly online can be found at http://www.sunysb.edu/chemistry/gradprogram.

Correspondence and Information

For additional information and application forms, students should contact:

Department of Chemistry
Stony Brook University, State University of New York
Stony Brook, New York 11794-3400

Telephone: 631-632-7880
Fax: 631-632-7960
E-mail: chemistry@notes.cc.sunysb.edu
World Wide Web: http://www.sunysb.edu/chemistry

Stony Brook University, State University of New York

THE FACULTY AND THEIR RESEARCH

John M. Alexander, Professor; Ph.D., MIT, 1956. Nuclear chemistry.
Benjamin Chu, Distinguished Professor; Ph.D., Cornell, 1959. Physical chemistry, polymer physics, materials science.
Dale G. Drueckhammer, Associate Professor; Ph.D., Texas A&M, 1987. Bioorganic chemistry.
Frank W. Fowler, Professor; Ph.D., Colorado, 1968. Synthetic chemistry.
Joanna Fowler, Adjunct Professor (Brookhaven National Lab); Ph.D., Colorado, 1967. Biochemical effects of drugs, aging, and selected diseases on the brain.
Nancy S. Goroff, Assistant Professor; Ph.D., UCLA, 1994. Organic molecules and materials.
Clare P. Grey, Professor; D.Phil., Oxford, 1991. Inorganic chemistry, solid-state chemistry and solid-state NMR.
David M. Hanson, Professor; Ph.D., Caltech, 1968. Physical chemistry, soft X-ray photochemistry.
Benjamin S. Hsiao, Professor; Ph.D., Connecticut, 1987. Physical chemistry, polymer physics, materials science.
Francis Johnson, Professor (joint appointment with Department of Pharmacological Sciences, School of Medicine); Ph.D., Glasgow (Scotland), 1954. Organic chemistry, medicinal chemistry.
Philip M. Johnson, Professor; Ph.D., Cornell, 1967. Physical chemistry, molecular spectroscopy and photophysics.
Franco P. Jona, Adjunct Professor, Ph.D., Eidgenössische Technische Hochschule (Zurich), 1949. Surface science.
Robert C. Kerber, Professor; Ph.D., Purdue, 1965. Organic and organometallic chemistry.
Alexei Khokhlov, Adjunct Professor (Moscow State University); Ph.D., 1979, D.Sc., 1983, Moscow. Statistical physics of macromolecules.
Stephen A. Koch, Professor; Ph.D., MIT, 1975. Inorganic chemistry.
Roy A. Lacey, Professor; Ph.D., SUNY at Stony Brook, 1987. Nuclear chemistry.
Joseph W. Lauher, Professor; Ph.D., Northwestern, 1974. Structural chemistry.
Erwin London, Professor (joint appointment with Department of Biochemistry and Cell Biology); Ph.D., Cornell, 1980. Structural biology, membrane protein structure.
Andreas Mayr, Professor; Ph.D., Munich, 1978. Inorganic and organometallic chemistry.
Michelle Millar, Associate Professor; Ph.D., MIT, 1975. Inorganic chemistry.
Marshall D. Newton, Adjunct Professor (Brookhaven National Lab); Ph.D., Harvard, 1966. Theoretical physical chemistry.
Iwao Ojima, Distinguished Professor; Ph.D., Tokyo, 1973. Synthetic, organometallic, and medicinal chemistry.
John B. Parise, Professor (joint appointment with Department of Geosciences); Ph.D., James Cook (Australia), 1981. Inorganic chemistry.
Kathlyn A. Parker, Professor; Ph.D., Stanford, 1971. Organic chemistry.
Fernando Raineri, Adjunct Assistant Professor; Ph.D., Buenos Aires, 1987. Theoretical chemistry.
Daniel Raleigh, Professor; Ph.D., MIT, 1988. Structural biology.
Nicole S. Sampson, Professor; Ph.D., Berkeley, 1990. Biological chemistry.
Trevor J. Sears, Adjunct Professor (Brookhaven National Lab); Ph.D., Southampton (England), 1979. Physical chemistry.
Carlos Simmerling, Assistant Professor; Ph.D., Illinois at Chicago, 1994. Computational structural biology.
George Stell, Distinguished Professor; Ph.D., NYU, 1961. Statistical mechanics.
Peter J. Tonge, Professor; Ph.D., Birmingham (England), 1986. Biological chemistry.
Jin Wang, Assistant Professor; Ph.D., Illinois at Urbana-Champaign, 1991. Physics and chemistry of biomolecules.
Michael White, Professor and Chair (joint appointment with Brookhaven National Lab); Ph.D., Berkeley, 1979. Physical chemistry, dynamics at surfaces.
Arnold Wishnia, Associate Professor; Ph.D., NYU, 1957. Biochemistry.
Stanislaus S. Wong, Assistant Professor (joint appointment with Brookhaven National Lab); Ph.D., Harvard, 1999. Physical chemistry, materials science, biophysics.

TEMPLE UNIVERSITY

College of Science and Technology
Department of Chemistry

Programs of Study

The Department of Chemistry at Temple University has a long tradition of academic excellence and provides a vibrant environment for graduate studies leading to the Ph.D. or M.A. degree. Research areas include organic, inorganic, biological, physical, theoretical, and polymer chemistry. Interdisciplinary research activities include materials science, chemical physics, and environmental chemistry. The graduate program is designed to prepare students for rewarding academic or industrial careers in the chemical sciences. The department size allows individualized attention and mentoring. Faculty members are also associated with the Center for Advanced Photonics Research and the Center for Biotechnology. Research programs are supported by the National Science Foundation, the National Institutes of Health, the Department of Defense, the Department of Energy, the Petroleum Research Fund, and private corporations.

Students in the Ph.D. program take a minimum of 18 semester hours of formal course work, with at least three courses in a specific area of concentration. Six written cumulative examinations must be passed within the first three years of study. Also required are two departmental seminars. A successful dissertation defense of an original research project completes the requirements for the Ph.D. degree. The average time to graduation is 4½ years.

Master's thesis track students must take a total of 12 hours of course work, of which at least 3 are in a specific area. Six credits of research and one semester of seminar are required, along with a thesis defense of an original research project. Master's course work track students must take a total of 21 hours of course work, followed by a comprehensive examination.

Research Facilities

The Department of Chemistry enjoys an excellent breadth of instrumentation, with support staff members, which is available for use by graduate students. Instrumentation includes 300, 400, and 500 MHz NMR spectrometers; an X-ray diffractometer; an epr spectrometer; and UV-VIS, Raman, and IR spectrometers. The department has several advanced computer facilities with support staff members. Cold rooms and a tissue culture facility are available for biochemical and cell biological work. An instrumentation facility houses a phosphorimager, an isothermal calorimeter, a fluorimeter, and a scintillation counter. The Center for Advanced Photonics has state-of-the-art laser equipment for femtosecond studies of chemical reactions. A chemistry storeroom, a glassblowing shop, and an electronics shop are on-site. The Chemistry Library and the Paley Library subscribe to more than 1,400 journal titles (both online and hard copy) and have more than 53,000 bound journals and 33,000 books.

Financial Aid

All students in good academic standing are guaranteed full financial support throughout for the duration of their graduate studies. Financial support is provided by research assistantships or teaching assistantships. The twelve-month stipend for entering predoctoral students is $19,000, which includes a summer research fellowship. University-funded fellowships (Presidential, University, and Future Faculty) are available for highly qualified entering students and provide highly competitive stipends. Graduate student benefits include health, dental, and life insurance. The Philadelphia metropolitan area offers diverse employment opportunities for spouses.

Cost of Study

Full-time graduate students, in good academic standing and supported by a research assistantship or a teaching assistantship, receive full tuition remission. Students are responsible for textbook costs and activity fees.

Living and Housing Costs

The twelve-month stipend of $19,000 can fully meet living expenses, as well as provide opportunities for recreation and entertainment. Both on- and off-campus housing is available for graduate students. Apartments include efficiencies and one- and two-bedroom units, with monthly rents typically ranging from $550 to $700. Campus buses provide free transportation to a number of off-campus housing sites.

Student Group

The chemistry graduate program has about 55 students, most of whom are part-time. Both domestic and international students are in the program. The graduate admissions committee seeks candidates with at least a 3.0 GPA from their undergraduate institution. The graduate admissions committee also seeks students who have demonstrated a strong aptitude and enthusiasm for chemical research. An undergraduate research experience is particularly desirable.

Student Outcomes

Temple graduates are eagerly recruited locally and are successful in their industrial and academic careers. Temple University is in close proximity to many chemical, pharmaceutical, and biotechnological firms. Temple chemistry graduates have found jobs in many high-profile companies, including Bristol-Myers Squibb, Glaxo-SmithKline, Johnson & Johnson, Rohm and Haas, Schering Plough, and Wyeth. Recent graduates also have obtained highly competitive postdoctoral positions at other major Universities throughout the United States.

Location

Philadelphia is a vibrant historical center for science, the arts, and culture. The city provides outstanding environment for professional growth, and other higher educational institutions provide collaborative opportunities. Philadelphia enjoys a four-season climate, with the Atlantic Ocean and the Pocono mountains only short distances away. Philadelphia is affordable and has excellent transportation links to other cities.

The University and The Department

Temple University is one of the three major public universities of the commonwealth of Pennsylvania. Temple is a Carnegie Research Intensive university, based on the renown of its graduate programs. The College of Science and Technology provides a research-intensive environment that supports advanced studies in many areas. Temple University has a vibrant campus, minutes from Center City, with a student population of 34,000. There are many exciting cultural and entertainment diversions both on and off campus.

Applying

Graduate applications can be obtained by contacting the Department of Chemistry at the e-mail address listed below or from the Graduate School Web site at http://www.temple.edu/admissions.html. All applicants are required to take the GRE. The Chemistry Test of the GRE is recommended but not required. The TOEFL exam is required for applicants who received their bachelor's degree outside of the United States. An interview is not required. Completed applications should be submitted by February 15 for the fall semester or by September 15 for the spring semester.

Correspondence and Information

Department of Chemistry
Beury Hall
Temple University
1901 North 13th Street
Philadelphia, Pennsylvania 19122

Telephone: 215-204-1980
Fax: 215-204-1532
E-mail: chemgrad@blue.temple.edu
World Wide Web: http://www.chem.temple.edu

Temple University

THE FACULTY AND THEIR RESEARCH

Eric Borguet, Associate Professor; Ph.D., Pennsylvania. Physical chemistry.
David R. Dalton, Professor; Ph.D., UCLA. Organic chemistry.
Franklin A. Davis, Professor; Ph.D., Syracuse. Organic chemistry.
Jan Feng, Associate Professor; Ph.D., USC. Biochemistry.
Antonio P. Goncalves, Professor; Ph.D., Chicago. Physical chemistry.
Susan A. Jansen-Varnum, Associate Professor; Ph.D., Missouri. Analytical chemistry.
Grant R. Krow, Professor; Ph.D., Princeton. Organic chemistry.
Robert J. Levis, Professor, Acting Chair, and Director, Center for Advanced Photonics Research; Ph.D., Penn State. Physical chemistry.
Spiridoula Matsika, Assistant Professor; Ph.D., Ohio State. Theoretical chemistry.
Allen W. Nicholson, Professor and Acting Dean, College of Science and Technology; Ph.D., Pennsylvania. Biochemistry.
Jerome Schiffer, Associate Professor; Ph.D., Princeton. Physical chemistry.
Scott Sieburth, Professor; Ph.D., Harvard. Organic chemistry.
Frank Spano, Professor; Ph.D., Princeton. Theoretical chemistry.
Robert J. Stanley, Associate Professor; Ph.D., Penn State. Biochemistry.
Daniel R. Strongin, Professor; Ph.D., Berkeley. Physical chemistry.
Donald D. Titus, Associate Professor; Ph.D., Caltech. Inorganic chemistry.
Stephen S. Washburne, Associate Professor; Ph.D., MIT. Organic chemistry.
John R. Williams, Professor; Ph.D., Western Australia. Organic chemistry.
Stephanie L. Wunder, Professor; Ph.D., Massachusetts. Materials science.

TEXAS A&M UNIVERSITY

Department of Chemistry

Programs of Study

The Department of Chemistry offers a Ph.D. degree with programs of study in traditional areas of chemistry as well as in atmospheric, biological, catalytic, environmental, materials and surface science, nuclear, polymer, solid-state, spectroscopy, and theoretical chemistry. A nonthesis M.S. (emphasis in chemical education) degree is also available.

Graduate students pursuing the Ph.D. degree select a research supervisor and formulate a plan of study during their first semester. The majority of a student's time is spent on independent research. Students present and defend a research proposal in their third year. Upon conclusion of their research, a dissertation suitable for publication is defended before their faculty advisory committee. The average time required to complete the Ph.D. degree is four to five years.

Research Facilities

The chemistry complex has 224,000 square feet of new or recently renovated space for teaching and research in four contiguous buildings, with major institutes housed in three other buildings. It maintains professionally staffed laboratories for high-resolution mass spectrometry; solution NMR; solid-state NMR; CCD-equipped, single-crystal, and powder X-ray diffractometers; a SQUID magnetometer; and departmental computing. Departmental instrumentation includes ESCA, SIMS, Auger, and other surface-science instruments; a PerSeptive Biosystems, high-performance MALDI-TOF; two Extrel FTMS 2001 systems; an XPS; and a variety of EPR, ENDOR infrared, Raman, UV-visible, fluorescence, atomic absorption, gamma-ray, and photoelectron spectrometers. Other campus facilities include the Nuclear Science Center (1-MW reactor) and the Cyclotron Institute, which includes a superconducting cyclotron. In addition, there are a number of specialized facilities, including the Center for Biological Nuclear Magnetic Resonance, the Laboratory for Molecular Structure and Bonding, the Center for Chemical Characterization and Analysis, the Laboratory for Biological Mass Spectrometry, the Laboratory for Protein Chemistry, the Laboratory for Molecular Simulation, the Center for Integrated Microchemical Systems, and the Center for Catalysis and Surface Science.

The Evans Library houses 1.6 million volumes and maintains subscriptions to approximately 8,000 scientific and technical journals.

Financial Aid

Graduate students in good standing receive full financial support for the duration of their studies. The 2003–04 stipend for twelve-month research or teaching assistantships is $18,600. All graduate assistants receive the same health-care benefits as faculty and staff members. Additional fellowships are available for outstanding applicants.

Cost of Study

Tuition and all mandatory fees are paid for up to five years of graduate study for domestic students in good standing pursuing Ph.D. degrees.

Living and Housing Costs

The cost of living in the area is low: 93 percent of the national average. University apartments are available; applications for them should be made early. In 2002–03, their costs ranged from $290 to $452 per month. Private apartments and houses for rent are available close to campus, with prices ranging from $350 to $750 per month.

Student Group

Students in the program come from all fifty states and a dozen other countries.

Location

As a university town, College Station has a high proportion of professional people and enjoys many of the advantages of a cosmopolitan center without the disadvantages of a congested urban environment. The crime rate is very low, and students feel safe on campus. There are many film series, a symphony, chamber music, and choral groups. College Station is situated in the middle of a triangle formed by Dallas, Houston, and Austin, and the symphonies, ballets, sporting events, museums, and concerts of these cities are within easy day-trip distance.

Mild, sunny winters make the region eminently suitable for year-round activities, from fishing and hiking in the beautiful piney woods of eastern Texas to boating, bicycling, and camping in the Texas hill country. There are more than 100 state parks within a day's drive of College Station.

The University and The Department

Texas A&M University was founded in 1876 as the state's first public institution of higher education. The University's enrollment includes approximately 44,000 students studying for degrees in ten academic colleges, of whom about 7,500 are in graduate or professional programs. Vigorous research programs in biochemistry, engineering, physics, mathematics, medicine, and veterinary medicine provide chemists with supplementary facilities and intellectual resources.

The Department of Chemistry is among the top ten in the country of those at public universities and is tenth in the nation in spending on chemical research and development. The internationally known faculty members include a National Medal of Science awardee, holders of international medals in a variety of chemistry subdisciplines, and members of both the National Academy of Sciences and Royal Society. The 45 members of the graduate faculty generated approximately 450 publications and more than $14 million in external grant funding in 2002. More than 100 research fellows and visiting scientists and a graduate student body of about 240 support their efforts. Though the department is large, most research groups have 3 to 10 students and thus provide an intensive, personalized learning environment.

Applying

There is no application fee for domestic applicants. Online application forms and a more detailed description of requirements are available at the Web site listed below. Admission decisions are made on a continuous basis beginning in December. Departmental fellowship awards are made in February for the next academic year. Domestic applications for fall admission should arrive by April 1 for preferential consideration. International applications must be received by February 1. Applications and all supporting material should be filed no later than six weeks prior to the opening of the preferred semester of entrance.

Correspondence and Information

Graduate Student Office
Department of Chemistry
Texas A&M University
P.O. Box 30012
College Station, Texas 77842-3012
Telephone: 979-845-5345
800-334-1082 (toll-free)
Fax: 979-845-5211
E-mail: gradmail@mail.chem.tamu.edu
World Wide Web: http://www.chem.tamu.edu

Texas A&M University

THE FACULTY AND THEIR RESEARCH

David Bergbreiter, Professor; Ph.D., MIT, 1974. Organic chemistry.
John Bevan, Professor; Ph.D., London, 1975. Physical chemistry.
Kevin Burgess, Professor; Ph.D., Cambridge, 1983. Organic chemistry.
Abraham Clearfield, Professor; Ph.D., Rutgers, 1954. Inorganic chemistry.
Dwight Conway, Professor; Ph.D., Chicago, 1956. Physical chemistry.
F. Albert Cotton, Distinguished Professor and Doherty-Welch Chair; Ph.D., Harvard, 1955. Inorganic chemistry.
Paul Cremer, Professor; Ph.D., Berkeley, 1996. Surface science.
Richard M. Crooks, Professor; Ph.D., Texas at Austin, 1987. Analytical and materials chemistry.
Donald J. Darensbourg, Professor; Ph.D., Illinois at Urbana-Champaign, 1968. Organometallic chemistry.
Marcetta Y. Darensbourg, Professor; Ph.D., Illinois at Urbana-Champaign, 1967. Organometallic chemistry.
Victoria J. DeRose, Professor; Ph.D., Berkeley, 1990. Biophysical chemistry.
Kim R. Dunbar, Professor; Ph.D., Purdue, 1984. Inorganic chemistry.
John P. Fackler Jr., Distinguished Professor; Ph.D., MIT, 1960. Inorganic chemistry.
Paul F. Fitzpatrick, Professor; Ph.D., Michigan, 1981. Biochemistry.
Francois Gabbai, Associate Professor; Ph.D., Texas at Austin, 1994. Inorganic chemistry.
D. Wayne Goodman, Distinguished Professor and Robert A. Welch Chair; Ph.D., Texas at Austin, 1974. Physical chemistry.
Michael B. Hall, Professor; Ph.D., Wisconsin–Madison, 1971. Inorganic chemistry.
Kenn E. Harding, Professor; Ph.D., Stanford, 1968. Organic chemistry.
John L. Hogg, Professor; Ph.D., Kansas, 1974. Bioorganic chemistry.
Timothy Hughbanks, Professor; Ph.D., Cornell, 1983. Inorganic chemistry.
Arthur Johnson, Professor and Wehner-Welch Chair; Ph.D., Oregon, 1973. Biochemistry.
Jaan Laane, Professor; Ph.D., MIT, 1967. Physical chemistry.
Paul Lindahl, Professor; Ph.D., MIT, 1985. Inorganic chemistry.
Robert R. Lucchese, Professor; Ph.D., Caltech, 1982. Theoretical chemistry.
Jack H. Lunsford, Distinguished Professor Emeritus; Ph.D., Rice, 1962. Physical chemistry.
Ronald D. Macfarlane, Professor; Ph.D., Carnegie Tech, 1959. Bioanalytical chemistry.
Stephen A. Miller, Assistant Professor; Ph.D., Caltech, 1999. Organic chemistry.
Joseph B. Natowitz, Professor; Ph.D., Pittsburgh, 1965. Nuclear chemistry.
Simon North, Associate Professor; Ph.D., Berkeley, 1995. Physical chemistry.
Frank M. Raushel, Professor; Ph.D., Wisconsin–Madison, 1976. Biochemistry.
Daniel Romo, Professor; Ph.D., Colorado State, 1991. Organic chemistry.
Michael P. Rosynek, Professor and Associate Head; Ph.D., Rice, 1972. Physical chemistry.
Marvin W. Rowe, Professor; Ph.D., Arkansas, 1966. Analytical cosmochemistry.
David H. Russell, Professor; Ph.D., Nebraska–Lincoln, 1978. Analytical chemistry.
James C. Sacchettini, Professor; Ph.D., Washington (St. Louis), 1987. Biochemistry.
Raymond E. Schaak, Assistant Professor; Ph.D., Penn State, 2001. Inorganic chemistry.
Emile A. Schweikert, Professor and Head; Ph.D., Paris IV (Sorbonne), 1964. Activation analysis and analytical chemistry.
A. Ian Scott, Distinguished Professor and Robert A. Welch Chair; Ph.D., Glasgow, 1952. Organic chemistry, biochemistry.
Eva Sevick-Muraca, Professor; Ph.D., Carnegie Mellon, 1989. Interfacial science.
Eric E. Simanek, Associate Professor; Ph.D., Harvard, 1996. Organic chemistry.
Daniel A. Singleton, Professor; Ph.D., Minnesota, 1986. Organic chemistry.
Manual P. Soriaga, Professor; Ph.D., Hawaii, 1978. Analytical chemistry.
Gary Sulikowski, Professor; Ph.D., Pennsylvania, 1989. Organic chemistry.
Gyula Vigh, Professor; Ph.D., Veszperm (Hungary), 1975. Analytical chemistry.
Coran Watanabe, Assistant Professor; Ph.D., Johns Hopkins, 1998. Biological chemistry.
Rand L. Watson, Professor; Ph.D., Berkeley, 1966. Nuclear chemistry.
Robert D. Wells, Professor; Ph.D., Pittsburgh, 1964. Biochemistry.
Danny L. Yeager, Professor; Ph.D., Caltech, 1975. Theoretical chemistry.
Sherry J. Yennello, Professor; Ph.D., Indiana, 1990. Nuclear chemistry.

TUFTS UNIVERSITY

Department of Chemistry

Programs of Study

The Department of Chemistry offers graduate programs leading to the degrees of professional Master of Science and Doctor of Philosophy in the fields of analytical, inorganic, organic, and physical chemistry and in the subdisciplinary areas of bioorganic, environmental, and materials science and chemistry-biotechnology. Programs of study may involve collaborations in related science departments or in the Sackler School of Graduate Biomedical Sciences, the Tufts–New England Medical Center, or Tufts Biotechnology Center.

Entering graduate students meet with the Graduate Committee to plan an academic course schedule best suited to the student's background and career goals. New students must complete four graduate courses, one course in each of the four chemistry disciplines (analytical, inorganic, organic, and physical) by the end of the third academic semester. This course of study is to ensure that by the end of the third semester each student has a firm foundation in the fundamentals of chemistry. A research advisory committee, consisting of the thesis adviser and two other faculty members, then directs the student's course and research program.

A Ph.D. candidate must complete a minimum of six formal courses (exclusive of research) and present a departmental seminar. The student must also present an additional independent study topic, successfully defend a research proposal, and complete a dissertation reporting significant research of publishable quality. Additional course work may be required at the discretion of the research adviser.

The professional master's program is very flexible in order to accommodate individual goals. Each student must pass eight graduate-level courses, at least six of which must be formal classroom instruction. Up to half of the courses may be taken outside the Department of Chemistry in related fields. A thesis may or may not be required, depending on the importance of a thesis for the candidate's career plans.

Research Facilities

Research is carried out in the Pearson and Michael laboratories, combined facilities of 66,000 square feet. A wide array of modern instrumentation necessary for cutting-edge research in chemistry is available for general use by graduate students, including FT-NMR, FT-IR, UV-Vis, AA, AES, and fluorescence spectrometers; scanning probe (STM, AFM) and scanning electron microscopes; GC-MS and MALDI-TOF mass spectrometers; analytical and preparative gas and liquid chromotography equipment; pulsed and CW laser systems for analytical and physical measurement; computerized electrochemical instrumentation; UHV surface analysis equipment; a fermentor, incubator, and coldroom; and professionally staffed electronics and machine shops. Complementary instrumentation is available at other Tufts facilities, including the Sackler School of Graduate Biomedical Sciences, the Tufts–New England Medical Center, the Science and Technology Center, and the School of Nutrition. All laboratories, classrooms, and offices are wired for high-speed Internet connections, with access to most online scientific journals.

Financial Aid

To help students whose records indicate scholarly promise, a variety of financial awards and work opportunities are available. All Ph.D. candidates receive twelve months of financial support, which is guaranteed for five years. Students must remain in good academic standing, and make steady progress toward the Ph.D. degree. The 2003–04 twelve-month minimum stipend was $22,000 and was derived from teaching or research assistantships. Graduate students are supported by departmental fellowships during the first summer, enabling them to devote full-time to research. Supplemental fellowship awards are also available for outstanding students. Stipends are reviewed annually.

Cost of Study

All Ph.D. candidates receive tuition scholarships.

Living and Housing Costs

Most graduate students attending Tufts University live off campus in moderately priced apartments in the surrounding metropolitan area. Meal plans are available.

Student Group

At present the total enrollment in all divisions is about 7,000 students, including approximately 2,000 graduate and professional students.

Location

There are a variety of local restaurants and entertainment options close to the Tufts campus. The Boston area offers an excellent environment for the pursuit of academic interests. Due to the high density of world-famous institutions, many distinguished chemists visit the Boston area to present seminars and to confer with colleagues. All graduate students may obtain Boston library consortium privileges, enabling them to use the library facilities of other local universities. Researchers at Tufts have been able to take advantage of various facilities available at other local universities such as MIT and Harvard. The cultural offerings of the Boston area are some of the finest in the world, including the Boston Symphony, the Museum of Fine Arts, the Museum of Science, and the New England Aquarium, as well as innumerable chamber groups, performing groups, and theaters showing first-run and major international films.

The University

Since its designation as Tufts College in 1852, Tufts University has grown to include seven primary divisions: Arts and Sciences; the Fletcher School of Law and Diplomacy; the Schools of Medicine, Dental Medicine, and Veterinary Medicine; the Sackler School of Graduate Biomedical Sciences; and the School of Nutrition.

Applying

Application materials should be submitted directly to the Graduate School Office by February 15 for September enrollment and by October 15 for January enrollment. Applications received after these dates will be considered on a space-available basis. All U.S. applicants must submit their test scores on the General Test of the Graduate Record Examinations (GRE) and are strongly encouraged to take the Subject Test in chemistry. International students must submit scores on both the General Test and Subject Test in chemistry, the results of the Test of English as a Foreign Language (TOEFL), and the Test of Spoken English (TSE). Applicants are urged to take the appropriate tests in October or December. Application forms for admission and support may be obtained directly from the Graduate School of Arts and Sciences or the chemistry department. Applicants are encouraged to visit the University; an appointment can be arranged with the department beforehand. Tufts University is an equal opportunity institution.

Correspondence and Information

Graduate Committee Chair
Department of Chemistry
Tufts University
Medford, Massachusetts 02155
Telephone: 617-627-3441
Fax: 617-627-3443
E-mail: chemgradinfo@tufts.edu
World Wide Web: http://chem.tufts.edu

Tufts University

THE FACULTY AND THEIR RESEARCH

Marc d'Alarcao, Ph.D., Illinois. Synthesis and evaluation of compounds of biological interest, especially inositol-containing carbohydrates and nucleosides.

Robert R. Dewald, Ph.D., Michigan State. Mechanistic studies of metal-ammonia reductions, chemistry of metal metalides and nonaqueous solvents.

Terry E. Haas, Ph.D., MIT. Physical inorganic chemistry; structure and electronic structure and optical, electronic, and transport properties of thin films, solids, and thin-film devices; synthesis and characterization of thin films; X-ray crystallography.

Karl H. Illinger, Ph.D., Princeton. Intermolecular forces and collisional perturbation of molecular spectra; experimental infrared spectroscopy, with applications in environmental chemistry; experimental measurement of absolute infrared intensities and structural correlations of this and other molecular properties employing ab initio quantum-mechanical calculations; infrared radiative properties of atmospheric gases.

Jonathan E. Kenny, Ph.D., Chicago. In situ detection of contaminants in soil and groundwater using laser-induced fluorescence, Raman spectroscopies, and fiber optics; fluorescence fingerprinting of natural waters; multidimensional fluorescence characterization of sediments.

Samuel P. Kounaves, Ph.D., Geneva (Switzerland). Fundamental questions in planetary science using techniques of analytical chemistry and especially electrochemically based sensors; use of in situ autonomous chemical analysis systems to study Martian geochemistry and possible biology, in both the regolith (soil) and polar ice caps, and to investigate the subglacial oceans on Jupiter's moon Europa.

Krishna Kumar, Ph.D., Brown. Organic and bioorganic chemistry, self-assembling and self-organizing systems, peptide and protein design, combinatorial chemistry using dynamic libraries, studies into the origin of exon-intron gene structure of modern-day enzymes.

David H. Lee, Ph.D., Scripps Research Institute. Biomaterials, self-assembly, bionanotechnology.

Albert Robbat Jr., Ph.D., Penn State. Development of analytical methods for hazardous-waste site field investigations—gas, liquid, and supercritical chromatographies and a mobile mass spectrometer; PCBs in marine life, ocean water, and sediment; PAHs in hazardous-waste incinerator and coal combustion emissions; volatile and semivolatile organics in soil, ground, and surface water; electron transfer mechanisms and rate measurements in biological systems.

Elena V. Rybak-Akimova, Ph.D., Kiev (Ukraine). Coordination, supramolecular, and bioinorganic chemistry; synthetic macrocyclic transition metal complexes; molecular tweezers; redox catalysis and enzyme mimics; dioxygen binding and activation; spatiotemporal self-organization (oscillating reactions and pattern formation) in chemical reactions; molecular modeling of macrocyclic supramolecular aggregates.

Mary J. Shultz, Ph.D., MIT. Development of methods for probing liquid, gas/liquid, solid/liquid, or gas/solid interface; probing dynamical processes at high-vapor-pressure interfaces; mechanism of heterogeneous photochemistry of transition metal oxides; heterogeneous processes in atmospheric chemistry, including ozone depletion nanomaterials.

Robert D. Stolow, Ph.D., Illinois. NMR and computational studies of conformational equilibria in solution and in the gas phase; the influence of electrostatic interactions among polar groups upon conformational energies.

Arthur L. Utz, Ph.D., Wisconsin. Dynamics of gas-surface reactions relevant to materials and catalytic chemistry; supersonic molecular beam, laser excitation, and ultrahigh vacuum techniques; laser-induced chemistry at surfaces; mechanisms for heterogeneous catalysis; vibrational and translational energy as synthetic tools in materials chemistry.

David R. Walt, Ph.D., SUNY at Stony Brook. Chemical sensors, microfabrication, genechips, micromaterials, nanomaterials.

THE UNIVERSITY OF ALABAMA

Department of Chemistry

Programs of Study

The Department of Chemistry offers programs of study in the traditional disciplines of analytical, inorganic, organic, physical, and biochemistry. Because chemistry is the central science, exciting research is often found in areas overlapping with other fields of study. Accordingly, the department has applied its strength in synthetic chemistry to a number of interdisciplinary projects. Of special interest are the interdisciplinary research centers on campus where chemistry plays a key role: the Center for Materials Information Technology (MINT), the Center for Green Manufacturing (CGM), and the Coalition for Biomolecular Products (CBP). Chemical research in each of these areas and in the area of fuel-cell development offers students the opportunity to interact with experts in other fields to address important scientific problems that cross disciplines. Further information on these interdisciplinary programs is available through the department and on the department Web site listed in the Correspondence and Information section.

Both the M.S. and Ph.D. programs allow a student to specialize in one of the areas of chemistry and place emphasis on both research and independent study. The programs are tailored to the needs of individual students and take into consideration previous study and research experience. Detailed information on requirements can be found in the current Graduate School Catalog (http://www.ua.edu/academic/colleges/graduate/). For chemistry, these requirements can be summarized as including course work (both formal and research techniques), comprehensive examinations (both written and oral), seminar attendance and presentations (both literature and research), research, and a thesis or dissertation and publications.

Research Facilities

Construction has just been completed on a $56-million interdisciplinary science building, Shelby Hall, which is the new home of the chemistry department. Departmental resources include modern Magnetic Resonance (NMR and EPR), Mass Spectral, X-ray Diffraction, FT/IR, and Laser Raman Facilities and Molecular Modeling Laboratories. Other departmental instruments include several UV-VIS and infrared spectrophotometers, GC-mass spectrometers, gas chromatographs, and high-performance liquid chromatographs. The department maintains and staffs modern glassblowing, electronics, and machine shops for rapid on-site maintenance of laboratory equipment and the creation of custom-designed apparatus. The University also possesses excellent computer (e.g., the Alabama Supercomputer Network) and electron microscope facilities, which are available on a time-sharing basis for chemical research.

Additional facilities for Materials Science and MINT faculty members and students exist in the recently expanded $30-million Bevill Building, including equipment for ion sputtering, ion beam etching, tape coating, transmission electron microscopy, X-ray photoelectron spectroscopy, scanning probe microscopy, and ferromagnetic spectrometry. Construction was completed in 2000 on the $10-million Alabama Institute of Manufacturing Excellence (AIME) Building, offering faculty members and students from the department who participate in the either CGM or the Center for Advanced Vehicle Technology (CAVT) new research space and pilot operations facilities.

Financial Aid

The department supports doctoral students for up to five years during their course of full-time graduate study and research. Support includes generous stipends and tuition and fee waivers in the form of teaching and research assistantships or special fellowships. The annual stipend for 2003–04 was a minimum of $16,500. A number of very attractive, competitive fellowships and other awards, including relocation allowances and first-year add-ons, are also available and make the typical offer much higher than the minimum. Student loans are also available and can be consolidated with any existing undergraduate loans. Qualified applicants, particularly from historically underrepresented groups, are encouraged to apply.

Cost of Study

Virtually every academic cost is met, with the exception of books and graduation fees; however, teaching and research assistantship stipends are subject to both state and federal income taxes. Approximately $100 to $150 per month is deducted for taxes, much of which is refunded upon filing income tax returns.

Living and Housing Costs

The University has a few one- and two-bedroom apartments for graduate students in the price range of $350 to $560 per month, while considerably more possibilities exist in the surrounding private market.

Student Group

The total number of graduate students in chemistry is currently about 85, with an additional 15 to 20 postdoctoral research associates. The vast majority of the students are full-time Ph.D. students. A wide variety of academic, ethnic, and national backgrounds are represented by this group of students. Emphasis will continue to be given to increasing participation by members of minority groups in the graduate program in chemistry.

Location

The University of Alabama is located on a beautiful campus in Tuscaloosa, the hub of a vibrant community of approximately 150,000 inhabitants. The University is well-known for its athletic programs, and it is also blessed with outstanding programs in law, business, and the performing arts. The city has world-class art collections and excellent professional theater companies. Numerous lakes and state parks within a few miles of the campus offer swimming, fishing, sailing, boating, canoeing, camping, and hiking. The large metroplexes of Birmingham and Atlanta are within driving distances (50 and 200 miles, respectively) as are the beautiful emerald Gulf Coast beaches to the south (250 miles) and the Smoky Mountains to the northeast (300 miles).

The University

In 1819, the congress of the United States donated 46,000 acres of land within the state of Alabama for the endowment of a seminary of learning. The General Assembly of Alabama created the board of trustees of the University in 1821, and on April 18, 1831, the University was opened for the admission of students. From the outset, the University offered graduate degrees, the first being an M.A. degree conferred in 1832. Today, the University of Alabama provides a comprehensive program of graduate study that embraces the humanities, the sciences, engineering, education, and several professional areas.

Applying

Application materials may be requested directly from the Department of Chemistry or from the Office of the Graduate School, The University of Alabama, 102 Rose Administration, Box 870118, Tuscaloosa, Alabama 35487-0118. Inquiries from national or international prospects can also be sent via e-mail to the department. A nonrefundable fee of $25 is required with each application, and all letters of recommendation should be sent directly to the department. An electronic application is also available at http://www.ua.edu/academic/colleges/graduate/application/. Prospective applicants should start the application process in the fall and have their applications completed no later than January 15 in order to be considered for the first round of financial aid offers.

Correspondence and Information

Dr. Carolyn Cassady, Director of Graduate Recruiting in Chemistry
Department of Chemistry
The University of Alabama
Tuscaloosa, Alabama 35487

Telephone: 205-348-5955 (collect)
Fax: 205-348-9104
E-mail: gradchem@bama.ua.edu
World Wide Web: http://bama.ua.edu/~chem/

The University of Alabama

THE FACULTY AND THEIR RESEARCH

The Department of Chemistry offers programs of study in the traditional areas of biochemistry and analytical, inorganic, organic, and physical chemistry as well as opportunity for work and training in a number of interdisciplinary areas, including biological, environmental, fuel cell, and materials chemistry. The following list briefly describes the areas of research interests for each research-active faculty member.

Anthony J. Arduengo III, Saxon Professor (organic/inorganic). Reactive intermediates, unusual valence states, fluorine chemistry, main group element chemistry, synthetic methodology, and fuel cells.

Martin G. Bakker, Associate Professor (physical, materials). Synthesis of mesoporous nanostructured materials, electrochemistry, optical data storage, electron paramagnetic resonance spectroscopy.

Wolfgang Bertsch, Associate Professor (analytical). Applications of gas chromatography and mass spectrometry, forensic chemistry, chemometrics, development of sample preparation methods for trace analysis.

Silas C. Blackstock, Professor and Director of Graduate Studies (organic/materials). Patterned organic redox materials as components for molecular magnetics and as new charge transport and charge storage materials, crystal engineering with new types of electron donor-acceptor bonding.

Carolyn J. Cassady, Associate Professor and Director of Graduate Recruiting (analytical). Mass spectrometry of biomolecules, ion/molecule reactions, Fourier transform ion cyclotron resonance, laser desorption time-of-flight.

Michael P. Cava, Professor Emeritus (organic). Heterocyclic chemistry: synthetic approaches to various isoquinoline and indole alkaloids and cyclic systems containing sulfur, selenium, or tellurium.

David A. Dixon, Professor and Robert Ramsay Chair (computational/physical). Application of numerical simulation to chemical problems and methods development in electronic structure theory, including thermochemistry; computational catalysis; environmental chemistry, including actinide chemistry for waste tanks, subsurface, and the atmosphere; hydrogen storage; fluorine and main group chemistry; biochemistry.

Arunava Gupta, MINT Professor (materials/physical). Investigation of nanostructured materials, with emphasis on the controlled fabrication and synthesis of novel structures, manipulating and probing their surface and interface properties, and exploring potential applications.

Michael P. Jennings, Assistant Professor (organic). Total synthesis of biologically active natural products, enantioselective methodology development based on novel chiral ligands, asymmetric catalysis.

Lowell D. Kispert, Research Professor (physical). The role of carotenoids and carotenoid ions in photosynthesis; structure and reaction mechanism of free radicals using Raman, EPR, electrochemistry, and optical techniques.

H. Keith McDowell, Professor and Vice President for Research (physical). Behavior of condensed-phase systems, multistep reaction mechanisms, condensed-phase molecular dynamic computer experiments.

Robert M. Metzger, Professor and Member, Materials Science Program (physical). Molecular electronics: unimolecular rectifiers, organic metals and superconductors, Langmuir-Blodgett films, magnetic nanowires in nanopes of aluminum oxide.

David E. Nikles, Professor (inorganic). Materials science for information storage: organic, inorganic, organometallic, and polymeric materials for optics, electronics, optical data storage, electrophotography, holography, and magnetic recording.

Kevin E. Redding, Associate Professor (biochemistry). Assembly, function, and degradation of integral membrane protein complexes, with an emphasis on photosystem I; biological electron transfer; structure-functional analysis; molecular recognition.

Robin D. Rogers, Professor and Director of Center for Green Manufacturing (inorganic/analytical). Green/sustainable technologies; aqueous biphasic systems, ionic liquids; crystal engineering; radiochemistry.

Kevin H. Shaughnessy, Assistant Professor (organic/inorganic). Applications of organometallic chemistry to organic synthesis, organometallic reaction mechanisms, combinatorial methods for catalyst discovery.

Timothy S. Snowden, Assistant Professor (organic). Synthetic methodology, natural product synthesis.

Shane C. Street, Associate Professor (analytical/physical). Surface science, surface chemistry, and tribology: basic surface studies in ultrahigh vacuum, surface attachment chemistry, structure-property relationships in ultrathin films.

Gregory J. Szulczewski, Associate Professor and Director of Undergraduate Studies (analytical/physical). Surface chemistry; chemical and biological sensors, chemically modified surfaces, photochemistry, and chemical reaction dynamics on surfaces.

Joseph S. Thrasher, Professor and Chair (inorganic/analytical). Novel sulfur-fluorine compounds, industrial fluorine chemistry, fluorous media, fuel-cell technology, new analytical methodologies in fluorine chemistry, computational chemistry.

Russell Timkovich, Professor (biochemistry). Cytochrome structure by NMR, structure and biosynthesis of unusual tetrapyrroles.

John B. Vincent, Professor and Director of Coalition for Biomolecular Products (bioinorganic). Structure, function, and mode of action of metallobiomolecules; synthesis and characterization of biomimetic inorganic complexes; biochemistry of chromium.

Stephen A. Woski, Associate Professor (bioorganic). Synthesis of modified nucleic acids.

Tetrahedral department logo depicting the interplay among research foci in synthetic chemistry and research in areas of biological, environmental, and materials chemistry.

New facility for chemistry: Shelby Hall, an interdisciplinary research science center.

The University of Alabama

SELECTED PUBLICATIONS

Arduengo, A. J., III, et al. Carbene complexes of pnictogen pentafluorides and boron trifluoride. *Monatshe* 131:251, 2000.

Arduengo, A. J., III. Looking for stable carbenes: The difficulty in starting anew. *Acc. Chem. Res.* 32:913–21, 1999.

Arduengo, A. J., III, and R. Schmutzler. C-H insertion reactions of nucleophilic carbenes. *Helv. Chim. Acta* 82:2348–64, 1999.

Arduengo, A. J., III, et al. A tris(trifluoromethyl)antimony adduct of a nucleophilic carbene: Geometric distortions in carbene adducts. *Z. Anorg. Allg. Chem.* 625:1813–7, 1999.

Arduengo, A. J., III, and R. Krafczyk. Auf der Suche nach stabilen Carbenen. *Chem. Unserer Zeit* 32:6–14, 1998.

Campbell, R., **M. G. Bakker,** C. Treiner, and J. Chevelat. Electrodeposition of mesoporous nickel onto foamed metals using surfactant and polymer templates. *Porous Mater.* 11:63, 2004.

Bakker, M. G., D. R. Spears, D. D. Murphy, and G. L. Turner. Whatever happened to shear-flocculation? *Fluids/Part. Sep. J.* 14:155, 2002.

Bakker, M. G., E. L. Granger, and A. I. Smirnov. Studies of cetylpyridinium chloride and cetylpyridinium salicylate in solution and adsorbed on silica surfaces using X-band and W-band electron paramagnetic resonance (EPR) spectroscopy. *Langmuir* 17:2346–56, 2001.

Bakker, M. G., T. Morris, G. L. Turner, and E. Granger. Surfactant aggregates (solloids) adsorbed on silica as stationary chromatographic phases: Structure and properties. *J. Chromatogr. B* 743:65–78, 2000.

Bakker, M. G., G. L. Turner, and C. Treiner. On the nature of the binding sites for cationic surfactants on silica: Studies using electron paramagnetic resonance spectroscopy. *Langmuir* 15:3078–85, 1999.

Bertsch, W. Two-dimensional gas chromatography. Concepts, instrumentation and applications. Part II. Comprehensive two-dimensional gas chromatography. *HRC J. High Res. Chromatogr.* 23:167, 2000.

Bertsch, W., and Q. Ren. Gas chromatography/mass spectrometry (GC/MS). Is it really needed in accelerant analysis? *Fire Arson Invest.* 25:17–23, 1999.

Ren, Q., and **W. Bertsch.** A comprehensive sample preparation scheme for accelerants in suspect arson cases. *J. Forensic Sci.* 44(3):504–12, 1999.

Lytle, C. A., **W. Bertsch,** and M. McKinley. Determination of novolac resin thermal decomposition products by pyrolysis gas chromatography-mass spectrometry. *Anal. Appl. Pyrolysis* 45:121, 1998.

Lytle, C. A., **W. Bertsch,** and M. McKinley. Determination of novolac resin thermal decomposition product from a phenolic resin by pyrolysis gas chromatography/mass spectrometry. *HRC J. High Res. Chromatogr.* 21:128, 1998.

Selby, T. D., K.-Y. Kim, and **S. C. Blackstock.** Patterned redox arrays of poly arylamines I. The synthesis and electrochemistry of a p-phenylenediamine (PD) and arylamino (AA) appended PD arrays. *Chem. Mater.* 14:1685–90, 2002.

Lee, H. B., M. J. Sung, **S. C. Blackstock,** and J. K. Cha. Radical cation-mediated annulation. Stereoselective construction of bicyclo[5.3.0]decan-3-ones by aerobic oxidation of cyclopropylamines. *J. Am. Chem. Soc.* 123:11322–3, 2001.

Chou, P. K., et al. **(S. C. Blackstock).** Reactivity of the gaseous radical cations of trimethylenemethane and 2-isopropylidene-cyclopentane-1,3-diyl. *J. Phys. Chem. A* 104:5530, 2000.

McGee, B. J., L. J. Sherwood, M. J. Greer, and **S. C. Blackstock.** A chiral 2-D donor-acceptor array of a bipyrazine *N*-oxide and tetracyanoethylene. *Org. Lett.* 2:1181–4, 2000.

Clipston, N. L., J. Jai-nhuknan, and **C. J. Cassady.** A comparison of negative and positive ion time-of-flight post-source decay mass spectrometry for peptides containing basic residues. *Int. J. Mass Spectrom.* 222:363, 2003.

Pallante, G. A., and **C. J. Cassady.** Effects of peptide chain length on the gas-phase proton transfer properties of doubly-protonated ions from Bradykinin and its *N*-terminal fragment peptides. *Int. J. Mass Spectrom.* 115:115, 2002.

Ewing, N. P., G. A. Pallante, X. Zhang, and **C. J. Cassady.** Gas-phase basicities for ions from Bradykinin and its des-Arginine analogues. *J. Mass Spectrom.* 36:875–81, 2001.

Ewing, N. P., and **C. J. Cassady.** Dissociation of multiply-charged negative ions for hirudin (54-65), fibrinopeptide B, and insulin A (oxidized). *J. Am. Soc. Mass Spectrom.* 12:105–16, 2001.

Cassady, C. J. Gas-phase ion chemistry of amides, peptides, and proteins. In *The Amide Linkage: Structural Significance in Chemistry, Biochemistry, and Materials Science,* pp. 463–94, eds. A. Greenberg, C. M. Breneman, and J. F. Liebman. London: Wiley Interscience, 2000.

Baldwin, J. W., et al. **(M. P. Cava** and **R. M. Metzger).** Rectification and nonlinear optical properties of a Langmuir-Blodgett monolayer of a pyridinium dye. *J. Phys. Chem. B* 106: 12158, 2002.

Dixon, D. A., et al. Enthalpies of formation of gas phase N_3, N_3^-, N_5^+, and N_5^- from ab initio molecular orbital theory, stability predictions for $N_5^+N_3^-$ and $N_5^+N_5^-$, and experimental evidence for the instability of $N_5^+N_3^-$. *J. Am. Chem. Soc.* 126:834, 2004.

Zhan, C.-G., and **D. A. Dixon.** Hydration of the fluoride anion: Structures and absolute hydration free energy from first-principle selectronic structure calculation. *J. Phys. Chem. A* 108:2020, 2004.

Bylaska, E. J., and **D. A. Dixon** et al. The energetics of the hydrogenolysis, dehydrohalogenation, and hydrolysis of 4,4'-dichlorodiphenyltri-chloroethane from ab initio electronic structure theory. *J. Phys. Chem. A* 108:5883, 2004.

Feller, D., **D. A. Dixon,** and J. S. Francisco. Coupled cluster theory determination of the heats of formation of combustion-related compounds: CO, HCO, CO_2, HCO_2, HOCO, HC(O)OH and HC(O)OOH. *J. Phys. Chem. A* 107:1604, 2003.

Hirata, S., et al. **(D. A. Dixon).** A new, self-contained asymptotic correction scheme to exchange-correlation potentials for time-dependent density functional theory. *J. Phys. Chem. A* 107:10154, 2003.

Anguelouch, A., and **A. Gupta** et al. Properties of epitaxial chromium dioxide films grown by chemical vapor deposition using a liquid precursor. *J. Appl. Phys.* 91:7140, 2002.

Gupta, A., X. W. Li, and G. Xiao. Inverse magnetoresistance in chromium dioxide (CrO_2)-based magnetic tunnel junctions. *Appl. Phys. Lett.* 78:1894, 2001.

Gupta, A., X. W. Li, and G. Xiao. Spin-polarized transport and magnetoresistance in magnetic oxides. *J. Magn. Magn. Mater.* 200: 24, 1999.

Gupta, A. Low-field magnetoresistance induced by grain boundaries in doped manganese perovskites. In *Giant Magnetoresistance and Related Properties of Metal Oxides,* p. 189, eds. C. N. R. Rao and B. Raveau. World Scientific, 1998.

Gupta, A. Thin film synthesis of metastable and artificially structured oxides. *Curr. Opin. Solid State Mater. Sci.* 2:23, 1997.

Jennings, M. P., K. C. Nicolaou, and P. Dagneau. An expedient synthesis of the fused polycyclic skeleton of vannusal A. *Chem. Commun.* 2480, 2002.

Jennings, M. P., and P. V. Ramachandran. Investigation of the factors controlling the regioselectivity of the hydroboration of fluoroolefins. *Chem. Commun.* 386, 2002.

Jennings, M. P., and P. V. Ramachandran. An exceptional hydroboration of substituted fluoroolefins providing tertiary alcohols. *Org. Lett.* 3:3789, 2001.

Jennings, M. P., E. A. Cork, and P. V. Ramachandran. A facile synthesis of perfluoroalkyl vinyl iodides and their palladium mediated cross-coupling reactions. *J. Org. Chem.* 65:8763, 2000.

Jennings, M. P., P. V. Ramachandran, and H. C. Brown. Critical role of catalysts and boranes for controlling the regioselectivity in the rhodium-catalyzed hydroboration of fluoroolefins. *Org. Lett.* 1:1399, 1999.

Konovalova, T. A., **L. D. Kispert,** and **K. Redding.** Photo- and chemically-produced phylloquinone biradicals: EPR and ENDOR study. *J. Photochem. Photobiol. A* 161:255, 2004.

Polyakov,` N. E., et al. **(L. D. Kispert).** Inclusion complexes of carotenoids with cyclodextrins: 1H-NMR, EPR and optical studies. *Free Radical Biol. Med.* 36, 872, 2004.

Gao, Y., et al. **(L. D. Kispert).** Interactions of carotenoids and Cu_2^+ in Cu-MCM-41: Distance-dependent reversible electron transfer. *J. Phys. Chem. B* 107:2459, 2003.

Konovalova, T. A. et al. **(L. D. Kispert).** Characterization of Fe-MCM-41 molecular sieves with incorporated carotenoids by multifrequency electron paramagnetic resonance. *J. Phys. Chem. B* 107:1006, 2003.

Gao, Y., T. A. Konovalova, T. Xu and **L. D. Kispert.** Electron transfer of carotenoids imbedded in MCM-41 and Ti-MCM-41: EPR, ENDOR and UV/Vis studies. *J. Phys. Chem. B* 106:10808, 2002.

Hapiot, P., **L. D. Kispert,** V. V. Konovalov, and J.-M. Saveant. Single two-electron transfers vs. successive one-electron transfers in polyconjugated systems illustrated by the electrochemical oxidation and reduction of carotenoids. *J. Am. Chem. Soc.* 123:6669, 2001.

Gayen, T., and **H. K. McDowell.** Quantum dynamics of electron transfer in a molecular segment with phonon interaction. *J. Chem. Phys.* 112:4310, 2000.

McDowell, H. K. Quantum generalized Langevin equation: Explicit inclusion of nonlinear system dynamics. *J. Chem. Phys.* 112:6971, 2000.

Clogston, A. M., **H. K. McDowell,** P. Tsai, and J. Hanssen. Davydov soliton and polarons in molecular chains: Partial Hamiltonian diagonalization. *Phys. Rev. E* 58:6407, 1998.

Bailey, D., M. Hurley, and **H. K. McDowell.** Dynamics in the spin-boson model by maximum entropy moment imaging. *J. Chem. Phys.* 109:8262, 1998.

McDowell, H. K., and A. M. Clogston. Molecular time scale generalized langevin equation theory and polynomial maximum entropy imaging of spectral densities. *J. Chem. Phys.* 109:8249, 1998.

Metzger, R. M. Unimolecular electrical rectifiers. *Chem. Rev.* 103:3803, 2003.

Adams, D., et al. **(R. M. Metzger).** Charge transfer on the nanoscale. *J. Phys. Chem. B* 10:6668, 2003.

The University of Alabama

Selected Publications (continued)

Metzger, R. M., et al. **(G. Szulczewski).** Large current asymmetries and potential device properties of a Langmuir-Blodgett monolayer of dimethyanilinoazafullerene sandwiched between gold electrodes. *J. Phys. Chem. B* 107:1021, 2003.
Xu, T., and **R. M. Metzger.** Nanoditches fabricated using a carbon nanotube as a contact mask. *Nano Lett.* 2:1061, 2002.
Kang, S. S., Z. Y. Jia, **D. E. Nikles,** and J. W. Harrell. Synthesis, self-assembly, and magnetic properties of [FePt](1-x)Au-x nanoparticles. *IEEE Trans. Magn.* 39:2753, 2003.
Sun, X. C., K. Parvin, J. Ly, and **D. E. Nikles.** Magnetic properties of a mixture of two nanosized Co-S powders produced by hydrothermal reduction. *IEEE Trans. Magn.* 39:2678–80, 2003.
Krishnamurthy, V. V., et al. **(D. E. Nikles).** Shear- and magnetic-field-induced ordering in magnetic nanoparticle dispersion from small-angle neutron scattering. *Phys. Rev. E* 67(1):051406, 2003.
Kang, S. S., **D. E. Nikles,** and J. W. Harrell. Synthesis, chemical ordering, and magnetic properties of self-assembled FePt-Ag nanoparticles. *J. Appl. Phys.* 93:7175, 2003.
Sun, X. C., et al. **(D. E. Nikles).** Synthesis, chemical ordering, and magnetic properties of FePtCu nanoparticle films. *J. Appl. Phys.* 93:7337, 2003.
Petrenko, O., et al. **(K. Redding).** A high-field EPR study of P700+$^{\cdot}$ in wild-type and mutant photosystem I from *Chlamydomonas reinhardtii. Biochemistry,* in press.
Henderson, J. N., J. Y. Zhang, B. W. Evans, and **K. Redding.** Disassembly and degradation of photosystem I in an in vitro system are multievent, metal-dependent processes. *J. Biol. Chem.* 278: 39978, 2003.
Gibasiewicz, K., et al. **(K. Redding).** Excitonic interactions in wild-type and mutant PSI reaction centers. *Biophys. J.* 85:2547, 2003.
Wang, R. L., et al. **(K. Redding).** Mutation induced modulation of hydrogen bonding to P700 studied using FTIR difference spectroscopy. *Biochemistry* 42:9889, 2003.
Gutowski, K. E., et al. **(R. D. Rogers).** Controlling the aqueous miscibility of ionic liquids: Aqueous biphasic systems of water-miscible ionic liquids and water-structuring salts for recycle, metathesis, and separations. *J. Am. Chem. Soc.* 125:6632, 2003.
Holbrey, J. D., et al. **(R. D. Rogers).** Crystal polymorphism in 1-butyl-3-methylimidazolium halides: Supporting ionic liquid formation by inhibition of crystallization. *Chem. Commun.* 1636, 2003.
Holbrey, J. D., M. B. Turner, W. M. Reichert, and **R. D. Rogers.** New ionic liquids containing an appended hydroxyl functionality from the clean, atom-efficient, one-pot reaction of 1-methylimidazole and acid with propylene oxide. *Green Chem.* 5:731, 2003.
Huddleston, J. G., et al. **(R. D. Rogers).** Comparative behavior of poly(ethylene glycol) hydrogels and poly(ethylene glycol) aqueous biphasic systems. *Ind. Eng. Chem. Res.* 42:6088, 2003.
Turner, M. B., et al. **(R. D. Rogers).** Ionic liquid-induced inactivation and unfolding of cellulase from *Trichoderma reesei. Green Chem.* 5:443, 2003.
Klingshirn, M. A., et al. **(R. D. Rogers and K. H. Shaughnessy).** Polar, non-coordinating ionic liquids as solvents for the alternating copolymerization of styrene and CO catalyzed by cationic palladium catalysts. *Chem. Commun.* 1394–5, 2002.
Moore, L. R., and **K. H. Shaughnessy.** Efficient aqueous-phase Heck and Suzuki couplings of aryl bromides using tri(4,6-dimethyl-3-sulfonatophenyl)phosphine trisodium salt (TXPTS). *Org. Lett.* 6:225, 2004.
Western, E. C., et al. **(K. H. Shaughnessy).** Efficient one-step Suzuki arylation of unprotected halonucleosides using water-soluble palladium catalysts. *J. Org. Chem.* 68:6767, 2003.
Shaughnessy, K. H., and R. S. Booth. Sterically demanding, water-soluble alkylphosphines as ligands for high activity Suzuki couplings in aqueous solvents. *Org. Lett.* 3:2757–9, 2001.
Zhong, Z., **T. S. Snowden,** M. Best, and E. V. Anslyn. Rate of enolate formation is not very sensitive to the hydrogen bonding ability of donors to carboxyl oxygen lone pair acceptors: A ramification of the principle of non-perfect synchronization for general-base-catalyzed enolate formation. *J. Am. Chem. Soc.* 126:3488, 2004.
Snowden, T. S., A. P. Bisson, and E. V. Anslyn. Artificial receptors involved in enolization and p*K*a shifts. *Bioorg. Med. Chem.* 9:2467, 2001.
Snowden, T. S., A. P. Bisson, and E. V. Anslyn. A comparison of NH-π versus lone pair hydrogen bonding effects on carbon acid p*K*a shifts. *J. Am. Chem. Soc.* 121:6324, 1999.
Snowden, T. S., and E. V. Anslyn. Anion recognition: Synthetic receptors for anions, application in sensors. *Curr. Opin. Chem. Biol.* 3:740, 1999.
Curry, M., F. Xu, J. Barnard, and **S. C. Street.** Kinetic energy influences on the growth mode of metal overlayers on dendrimer mediated substrates. *J. Vac. Sci. Technol., A* 21:234, 2003.
Xu, F., **S. C. Street,** and J. A. Barnard. Pattern formation in aerosol-deposited dendrimer films. *Langmuir* 19:3066, 2003.
Arrington, D., M. Curry, and **S. C. Street.** Patterned thin films of dendrimers formed using microcontact printing. *Langmuir* 18:7788, 2002.
Morris, T., T. Copeland, and **G. J. Szulczewski.** Synthesis and characterization of gold sulfide nanoparticles. *Langmuir* 18:535–9 2002.
Morris, T., and **G. J. Szulczewski.** A spectroscopic ellipsometry, surface plasmon resonance and X-ray photoelectron spectroscopy study of Hg adsorption on gold surfaces. *Langmuir* 18:2260–4, 2002.
Liu, D., et al. **(G. J. Szulczewski and L. D. Kispert).** A thiol-substituted carotenoid self-assembles on gold surfaces. *J. Phys. Chem. B* 106:2933–6, 2002.
Kim, K.-Y., et al. **(G. J. Szulczewski and S. C. Blackstock).** Patterned redox arrays of poly arylamines II. Growth of thin films and their electrochemical behavior. *Chem. Mater.* 14:1691–4, 2002.
Szulczewski, G. J., et al. **(S. D. Blackstock).** Growth and characterization of poly(arylamine) thin films prepared by vapor deposition. *J. Vac. Sci. Technol.* 18:1875–80, 2000.
Sipyagin, S. M., V. S. Enshov, S. A. Kashtanov, and **J. S. Thrasher.** 1-chloro-2,6-dinitro-4-[(perfluoroalkyl)thio]benzenes in the synthesis of heterocycles. *Chem. Heterocycl. Compd.* 38(11):1375, 2002.
Lu, N., and **J. S. Thrasher.** The direct synthesis of trifluoronitromethane, CF_3NO_2. *J. Fluorine Chem.* 117:181, 2002.
Sipyagin, A. M., C. P. Bateman, Y.-T. Tan, and **J. S. Thrasher.** Preparation of the first *ortho*-substituted pentafluorosulfanylbenzenes. *J. Fluorine Chem.* 112:287, 2001.
Qiao, L., D. Agoumba, A. Waterfeld, and **J. S. Thrasher.** Improvement of polymer electrolyte membranes for polymer electrolyte membrane and direct methanol fuel cell applications. In *Proceedings of the International Symposium on Power Sources for the New Millennium,* vol. 2000–22, pp. 92–102, eds. M. A. Ryan, S. Surampudi, and M. Jain. Pennington, New Jersey: The Electrochemical Society, Inc., 2001.
Buschmann, J., et al. **(J. S. Thrasher).** Crystal and molecular structure of trifluoroacrylnitrile, F_2C=CF-CN, and trifluorovinyl isocyanide, F_2C=CF-NC, by low-temperature X-ray crystallography and ab initio calculations. *Inorg. Chem.* 39:2807–12, 2000.
Timkovich, R. The family of d-type hemes: Tetraphyrroles with unusual substituents. In *The Porphyrin Handbook,* part II, vol. 20 (Biosynthesis), eds. K. Kadish, K. Smith, and R. Guilard. Academic Press, 2002.
Miller, G. T., J. K. Hardman, and **R. Timkovich.** Solution conformation of the Met 61 to His 61 mutant of *Pseudomonas stutzeri* ZoBell ferrocytochrome c-551. *Biophys. J.* 80:2928, 2001.
Miller, G. T., B. Zhang, J. K. Hardman, and **R. Timkovich.** Converting a c-type to a b-type cytochrome: The Met 61 to His 61 mutant of *Pseudomonas* cytochrome c-551. *Biochemistry* 39:9010–7, 2000.
Smith-Somerville, H. E., et al. **(R. Timkovich).** A complex of iron and nucleic acid catabolites is a signal that triggers differentiation in a freshwater protozoan. *Proc. Natl. Acad. Sci. U.S.A.* 97:7325–30, 2000.
Cai, M., and **R. Timkovich.** Solution conformation of ferricytochrome c-551 from *Pseudomonas stutzeri* substrain ZoBell. *Biochem. Biophys. Res. Commun.* 254:675, 1999.
Clodfelder, B. J., R. G. Upchurch, and **J. B. Vincent.** A comparison of the insulin-sensitive transport of chromium in healthy and model diabetic rats. *J. Inorg. Biochem.* 98:522, 2004.
Hepburn, D. D. D., and **J. B. Vincent.** The tissue and subcellular distribution of chromium picolinate with time after entering the bloodstream. *J. Inorg. Biochem.* 94:86, 2003.
Watson, H., J. Hatfield, and **J. B. Vincent.** 1H NMR studies of Cr(III)-imidazole complexes: Can 1H NMR be used as a probe of Cr-guanine DNA adducts. *Inorg. Chim. Acta* 344:265, 2003.
Hepburn, D. D. D., et al. **(J. B. Vincent).** Nutritional supplement chromium picolinate causes sterility and lethal mutations in *Drosophila melanogaster. Proc. Natl. Acad. Sci. U.S.A.* 100:3766, 2003.
Sun, Y., et al. **(J. B. Vincent).** The biomimetic $[Cr_3O(O_2CCH_2CH_3)_6(H_2O)_3]^+$ decreases plasma insulin, cholesterol and triglycerides in healthy and type II diabetic rats but not type I diabetic rats. *J. Biol. Inorg. Chem.* 7:852, 2002.
Speetjens, J. K., R. A. Collins, **J. B. Vincent,** and **S. A. Woski.** The nutritional supplement chromium(III) tris(picolinate) cleaves DNA. *Chem. Res. Toxicol.* 12:483, 1999.
Frey, K. A. and **S. A. Woski.** Fluoroaromatic universal bases in peptide nucleic acids. *Chem. Commun.* 2206, 2002.
Challa, H., M. L. Styers, and **S. A. Woski.** Nitroazole universal bases in peptide nucleic acids. *Org. Lett.* 1:1639–41, 1999.
Wichai, U., and **S. A. Woski.** Disiloxane-protected 2-deoxyribonolactone as an efficient precursor to 1,2-dideoxy-1-β-aryl-D-ribofuranoses. *Org. Lett.* 1:1173–5, 1999.
Challa, H., and **S. A. Woski.** Solution phase synthesis of potential DNA-binding molecules based on the PNA backbone. *Tetrahedron Lett.* 40:419–22, 1999.

UNIVERSITY OF CALIFORNIA, RIVERSIDE

Department of Chemistry

Programs of Study

The Department of Chemistry at the University of California, Riverside (UCR), offers programs leading to the degrees of Master of Science (M.S.) and Doctor of Philosophy (Ph.D.) in chemistry. The department is highly interdisciplinary, including both traditional areas of chemistry (analytical, inorganic, organic, and physical) and areas involving biochemistry, biophysics, bioanalytical chemistry, materials and polymer science, and environmental sciences. The major requirements for the doctoral degree in chemistry are the successful completion of an original research project and the presentation and defense of the Ph.D. thesis. The time to complete a Ph.D. typically ranges from four to five years.

The academic program is developed jointly by the student and the Graduate Advising Committee based on the student's chosen subdiscipline and his or her performance on the orientation exams. For students with a normal B.S.-level preparation, the typical course load consists of a minimum of five one-quarter graduate-level classes to be completed, preferably during the first year. Teaching experience is also considered to be an important part of graduate education. Accordingly, three quarters of service as a half-time teaching assistant or equivalent is required of all students, although this requirement can be reduced or waived when a student has prior experience.

Augmenting the graduate-level classes, a General Colloquium is offered weekly in which nationally recognized scholars present their latest research findings. In addition, each subdiscipline maintains a weekly schedule of seminars presented by visitors, faculty members, and students. Finally, each research group holds informal periodic meetings for the discussion of their own results as well as those of other groups in their field of research.

Research Facilities

Research is conducted in Pierce Hall, which has undergone multimillion-dollar expansion and renovation in recent years. A second chemistry building housing additional research laboratories is slated for occupancy in early 2005. In addition to modern research laboratories, Pierce Hall also houses the Analytical Chemistry Instrumentation Facility (ACIF). The ACIF consists of four components: mass spectrometry, X-ray crystallography, nuclear magnetic resonance (NMR) spectroscopy, and optical spectroscopy. A faculty director oversees the ACIF as a whole, and a support staff of 6 spectroscopists manage and maintain the various facilities. Complete details about the ACIF can be found by following the links from the Web site listed below.

Financial Aid

The Department of Chemistry provides financial support to all full-time domestic and international students making satisfactory progress toward a Ph.D. degree, both during the academic year and during the summer months. This support is typically in the form of fellowships, a graduate student teaching or research assistantship, a waiver of tuition and/or fees, or a combination of the above during the academic year with a research assistantship during the summer. Students who submit a competitive application for admission for graduate study in chemistry automatically are considered for all scholarships and fellowships for which they are eligible, as well as for teaching assistantships. All supported students are covered by health insurance provided by the University. Stipend and fellowship packages currently available range from $18,430 to $24,430 per year and typically include payment of all fees, tuition, and health insurance costs.

Cost of Study

Students from outside California are automatically considered for nonresident tuition grants. If qualified, these students are normally assured grants for a maximum of one academic year. After this period, U.S. citizens and permanent residents normally are eligible to become California residents and are no longer required to pay nonresident tuition. Nonresident tuition fees must also be paid quarterly by those not offered tuition grants. Since fees and tuition levels change periodically, information about their current levels is provided upon request.

Living and Housing Costs

Riverside has some of the least expensive and most varied housing in the University of California system. All of the on-campus housing is heavily subsidized and generally available. Consequently, off-campus rents remain reasonable to stay competitive, and students can easily find apartments for monthly rents of about $300–$750 per person.

Student Group

There are approximately 70 Ph.D. candidates enrolled in the graduate program in chemistry, representing a diversity of academic, ethnic, and national backgrounds.

Student Outcomes

The recent Ph.D.'s from the University of California, Riverside's Department of Chemistry have been very successful at obtaining excellent positions in academia as well as government and industrial laboratories. The following is a representative (not comprehensive) list of employers of some of the department's recent Ph.D. graduates: University of Texas, Pennsylvania State University, University of Arizona, University of Arkansas, W. M. Keck Science Center, Naval Research Laboratory, Argonne National Laboratory, Los Alamos National Laboratory, Lawrence Berkeley National Laboratory, National Institute of Science and Technology, Procter & Gamble Company, Motorola, Beckman Instruments, Perkin Elmer, DuPont, IBM, Exxon, Eli Lilly & Company Pharmaceuticals, SmithKline Beecham Pharmaceuticals, Allergan Pharmaceuticals, Boehringer-Ingelheim, and Rhone-Poulenc.

Location

Riverside is situated in the heart of beautiful Southern California, centrally located between Los Angeles, San Diego, and Palm Springs. Boating and windsurfing facilities, popular ski resorts, Pacific Ocean beaches, and many unique natural wonders such as Joshua Tree National Park, the Salton Sea, the Anza-Borrego and Mojave Deserts, and Mt. San Jacinto are all within a short drive.

The University

The University of California, Riverside is one of ten campuses of the University of California, generally recognized as the preeminent public university system in the world. Located in the Inland Empire of southern California, the 1,200-acre campus lies at the foot of the Box Springs Mountains in Riverside, a city of about 255,000 people. Current total enrollment is 14,429, including 12,836 undergraduates and 1,593 graduate students.

Applying

To be admitted to graduate status, the basic requirement is a bachelor's degree or its equivalent from an accredited institution, with a major appropriate to the proposed graduate program. Applications are considered as received, although it is recommended that applications be received by May 1 for fall admission (ideally, efforts should be made to provide a completed application by February 15). Applicants must complete the online application, which may be accessed by following the links from the UCR Graduate Division Web site (http://www.graddiv.ucr.edu/). The $40 application fee is waived by the department and should not be included with application materials. All students are required to take the GRE (the Chemistry Subject Test is not required). International students whose native language is not English are required to take the Test of English as a Foreign Language (TOEFL). For those international students, preference for admission and fellowships is given to those taking and passing the Test of Spoken English (TSE).

Correspondence and Information

Graduate Advisor, Recruitment
Department of Chemistry
University of California at Riverside
Riverside, California 92521-0403

Telephone: 909-787-3523
Fax: 909-787-4713
E-mail: gradchem@citrus.ucr.edu
World Wide Web: http://www.chem.ucr.edu

University of California, Riverside

THE FACULTY AND THEIR RESEARCH

Dr. Steven Angle (Organic). Development of new synthetic strategies and methodologies that have general utility in the synthesis of complex organic molecules possessing significant and potentially useful biological activity. (E-mail: steven.angle@ucr.edu; Web site: http://www.chem.ucr.edu/faculty/angle/angle.html)

Dr. Roger Atkinson (Atmospheric/Environmental). Kinetics and products of the gas-phase reactions of volatile organic compounds with hydroxyl radicals, nitrate radicals, and ozone. (E-mail: ratkins@ucrac1.ucr.edu; Web site: http://www.chem.ucr.edu/faculty/atkinson/atkinson.html)

Dr. Ludwig Bartels (Physical/Analytical). Visualization and control of fundamental chemical reactions at their intrinsic time and/or length scale using scanning tunneling microscopy (STM) and ultra-fast laser spectroscopy. (E-mail: ludwig.bartels@ucr.edu; Web site: http://www.chem.ucr.edu/faculty/bartels/bartels.html)

Dr. Guy Bertrand (Organic/Inorganic). Main group chemistry from Groups 13 to 16, at the border between organic, organometallic, and inorganic chemistry and some developments in the field of polymers; stabilization of highly reactive species using heavier main group elements. (E-mail: gbertran@mail.ucr.edu; Web site: http://www.chem.ucr.edu/faculty/bertrand/bertrand.html)

Dr. David F. Bocian (Physical/Biological/Materials). Molecular photonic devices and electrically addressable molecular memories; studies of energy-transducing systems, including heme and photosynthetic proteins; synthetic light-harvesting arrays. (E-mail: dbocian@ucrac1.ucr.edu; Web site: http://www.chem.ucr.edu/faculty/bocian/bocian.html)

Dr. Jason Cheng (Analytical/Materials). Development of novel detection technologies for biological and pathogenic agents. (E-mail: quan.cheng@ucr.edu; Web site: http://www.chem.ucr.edu/faculty/cheng/cheng.html)

Dr. Eric L. Chronister (Physical). Ultrafast (~10^{-12} sec.) vibrational and electronic dynamics in molecular solids by the use of coherent nonlinear time-resolved laser spectroscopy; diamond anvil studies. (E-mail: eric.chronister@ucr.edu; Web site: http://bruno.ucr.edu/)

Dr. Pingyun Feng (Inorganic/Materials). Self-assembly and supramolecular templating to prepare novel catalytic, electronic, and optical materials. (E-mail: pingyun.feng@ucr.edu; Web site: http://www.chem.ucr.edu/faculty/feng/feng.html)

Dr. Robert C. Haddon (Organic/Materials). Carbon nanotubes and new electronic materials for transport, magnetism, and superconductivity studies; nanotechnology. (E-mail: robert.haddon@ucr.edu; Web site: http://www.chem.ucr.edu/faculty/haddon/haddon.html)

Dr. T. Keith Hollis (Organic/Inorganic). Application of organometallic chemistry and stereochemistry to the design and development of new catalysts for polymer synthesis and stereoselective organic transformations, applications involving organometallic materials. (E-mail: keith.hollis@ucr.edu; Web site: http://www.chem.ucr.edu/faculty/hollis/hollis.html)

Dr. Werner G. Kuhr (Analytical/Biological). Incorporation of biomolecules onto substrates with nanometer to micron resolution, molecular electronics. (E-mail: werner.kuhr@ucr.edu; Web site: http://www.chem.ucr.edu/groups/kuhr/index.html)

Dr. Sheri J. Lillard (Analytical/Biological). Bioanalytical chemistry of individual cells. (E-mail: sheri.lillard@ucr.edu; Web site: http://www.chem.ucr.edu/faculty/lillard/lillard.html)

Dr. Michael J. Marsella (Organic/Materials). Synthesis of small molecules, oligomers, and polymers designed to function as optical, electronic, and/or biologically relevant molecular devices. (E-mail: michael.marsella@ucr.edu; Web site: http://www.chem.ucr.edu/faculty/marsella/marsella.html)

Dr. Jocelyn Millar (Organic/Entimology). Research focusing on the identification, synthesis, and applications of natural chemicals that insects use for communication, and for identifying the plants that they attack. (E-mail: jocelyn.millar@ucr.edu; Web site: http://www.entomology.ucr.edu/people/millar.html)

Dr. Thomas H. Morton (Organic). Organic reactions in the gas phase, biological receptors, new techniques in mass spectrometry. (E-mail: thomas.morton@ucr.edu; Web site: http://www.chem.ucr.edu/groups/morton/)

Dr. Leonard Mueller (Physical). Development of solid-state and liquid state nuclear magnetic resonance (NMR) as a probe of molecular structure, function, and dynamics with applications in chemistry, physics, and biology. (E-mail: leonard.mueller@ucr.edu; Web site: http://www.chem.ucr.edu/faculty/mueller/mueller.html)

Dr. William Okamura (Organic/Bioorganic). Bioorganic, synthetic, and mechanistic organic chemistry; steroid chemistry and biochemistry; vitamin D and other biologically interesting natural products, pericyclic processes, and molecules of theoretical interest; allenes in organic synthesis; organometallic chemistry.

Dr. Dallas L. Rabenstein (Analytical/Biological). NMR spectroscopy, NMR studies of peptides and carbohydrates, the biological chemistry of sulfur, heparin chemistry and biochemistry. (E-mail: dlrab@mail.ucr.edu; Web site: http://nmr.ucr.edu/)

Dr. Christopher A. Reed (Inorganic/Organic). New superacids, ionic liquids, self-assembling fullerene/porphyrin supramolecular materials, hemoprotein model compounds, novel carbon-based materials, complexes of xenon, carborane anions, and reactive cations across the periodic table. (E-mail: chris.reed@ucr.edu; Web site: http://reedgroup.ucr.edu)

Dr. Gary Scott (Physical/Chemical Physics/Biophysical). Photophysical and photochemical events using conventional and laser spectroscopic techniques to elucidate excited state energetics and kinetics, charge transfer rates and mechanisms, energy migration, nonlinear optical properties, and photochemistry in condensed media. (E-mail: garyscott@ucrac1.ucr.edu; Web site: http://www.chem.ucr.edu/groups/ScottGroup/profes1.htm)

Dr. Christopher Switzer (Organic/Biological). Structure and encoding problems with DNA and RNA. (E-mail: switzer@citrus.ucr.edu; Web site: http://www.chem.ucr.edu/faculty/switzer/switzer.html)

Dr. Yinsheng Wang (Analytical/Biological). Mass spectrometry (MS) in biochemistry, nucleic acid damages induced by reactive oxygen species. (E-mail: yinsheng@citrus.ucr.edu; Web site: http://www.chem.ucr.edu/faculty/wang/wang.html)

Dr. Francisco Zaera (Physical/Environmental). Heterogeneous catalysis, kinetics of surface chemistry, chemical vapor deposition processes. (E-mail: francisco.zaera@ucr.edu; Web site: http://www.chem.ucr.edu/groups/Zaera/lab.html)

Dr. Jingsong Zhang (Physical/Analytical/Environmental). Elementary processes of transient reactive intermediates, with an emphasis on atmospheric and combustion chemistry. (E-mail: jszhang@ucrac1.ucr.edu; Web site: http://www.chem.ucr.edu/faculty/zhang/zhang.html)

Dr. Paul J. Ziemann (Atmospheric/Environmental). Chemistry of submicron atmospheric aerosol particles. (E-mail: pziemann@ucrac1.ucr.edu; Web site: http://www.chem.ucr.edu/faculty/ziemann/ziemann.html)

UNIVERSITY OF CALIFORNIA, SAN DIEGO

Department of Chemistry and Biochemistry

Program of Study

The goal of the program is to prepare students for careers in science as researchers and educators by expanding their knowledge of chemistry while developing their ability for critical analysis, creativity, and independent study. Research opportunities are comprehensive and interdisciplinary, spanning biochemistry; bioinformatics; biophysics; inorganic, organic, physical, analytical, computational, and theoretical chemistry; surface and materials chemistry; and atmospheric and environmental chemistry. During the first year, students take courses, begin their teaching apprenticeships, choose a research adviser, and embark on their thesis research; students whose native language is not English must pass an English proficiency examination. In the second year, there is an oral examination, which includes critical discussion of a recent research article. In the third year, students advance to candidacy for the doctorate by defending the topic, preliminary findings, and future research plans for their dissertation. Subsequent years focus on thesis research and writing the dissertation. Most students graduate during their fifth year.

At the University of California, San Diego (UCSD), chemists and biochemists are part of a thriving community that stretches across the campus and out into research institutions throughout the San Diego area, uniting researchers in substantive interactions and collaborations. Seminars are presented weekly in biochemistry and inorganic, organic, and physical chemistry. Interdisciplinary programs in nonlinear science, materials science, biophysics, bioinformatics, and atmospheric and planetary chemistry also hold regular seminars.

Research Facilities

State-of-the-art facilities include a national laboratory for protein crystal structure determination; high-field nuclear magnetic resonance (NMR) instruments; the Natural Sciences Graphics Laboratory, which provides high-end graphic workstation resources; and laser spectroscopic equipment. Buildings specially designed for chemical research, a computational center, a laboratory fabrication and construction facility, and machine, glass, and electronic shops are part of the high-quality research support system.

The UCSD library collection is one of the largest in the country, with superior computerized reference and research services. Access to the facilities at the Scripps Institute of Oceanography, the San Diego Supercomputer Center, the Salk Institute, the Scripps Research Institute, and a thriving technological park, all within blocks of the campus, make the overall scope of available research facilities among the best in the world.

Financial Aid

All students who remain in good academic standing are provided year-round support packages of a stipend plus fees and tuition. Support comes from a variety of sources, including teaching assistantships, research assistantships, fellowships, and awards. Special fellowships, such as the GAANN, Urey, Cota Robles, and San Diego fellowships, are available to outstanding students. Students are strongly encouraged to apply for outside fellowships, and the department supplements such awards. The twelve-month stipend is adjusted annually and for 2003–04 was $21,500. Emergency short-term as well as long-term loan programs are administered by the UCSD Student Financial Services office.

Cost of Study

Registration fees and tuition (paid by the department) are $6365 and $18,202, respectively, per year. Premiums for a primary health-care program, which covers most major medical expenses and a portion of dental fees, are covered by registration fees. The Student Health Center treats minor illnesses and injuries. Optional health and dental coverage for dependents is at the student's expense.

Living and Housing Costs

The University Housing Service operates more than 1,000 apartments for families, couples, and single graduate students. There are several apartment complexes near the campus at higher rents; rental sharing is a common way to reduce the expense. The Off Campus Student Housing Office, located on campus, maintains extensive current rental and rental-share opportunities.

Student Group

Students are drawn from the top ranks of U.S. and international colleges and universities. There are 3,300 graduate students on the general campus and at the Scripps Institute of Oceanography and 500 in the School of Medicine. Within the department, there are 250 graduate students and 650 undergraduate majors. The graduate student population reflects diversity in culture, gender, and ethnicity.

Student Outcomes

Graduates typically obtain jobs in academia (55 percent) or in the chemical industry (45 percent). Many take postdoctoral research positions in academic institutions or national laboratories that lead to future academic or industrial careers. The departmental Industrial Relations Office assists students with placement in industrial positions and with networking with industry.

Location

The campus sits on 1,200 acres of eucalyptus groves near the Pacific Ocean. Surrounding the campus is La Jolla, a picturesque community of boutiques, bistros, and businesses. Seven miles south of the campus is San Diego, with its world-acclaimed zoo, museums, and theaters. The Laguna Mountains and the Anza-Borrego Desert are within a 2-hour drive east of the campus.

The University

UCSD, a comparatively young university, has already achieved widespread recognition, ranking fifth in federal funding for research and development and in the top ten of all doctoral degree–granting institutions in a study conducted by the National Research Council. Recently, the Institute for Scientific Information ranked UCSD's Department of Chemistry and Biochemistry as third in the nation for "High Impact U.S. Universities, 1994–98." Programs span the arts and humanities, engineering, international studies, and the social, natural, and physical sciences. The intellectual climate is enhanced by a variety of social, educational, professional, political, religious, and recreational opportunities and services.

Applying

Application packets include a completed UCSD application form, a statement of purpose, official transcripts from previous colleges, three letters of recommendation, GRE scores (general and advanced chemistry or biochemistry), and a TOEFL score (for noncitizens only; a minimum score of 550 on the paper-based test or 220 on the computer-based test is required). Research experience should be described. Copies of or references to any publications should be included with the application. Applications received by January 15 receive the highest priority.

Correspondence and Information

Graduate Admissions Coordinator
Department of Chemistry and Biochemistry 0301
University of California, San Diego
9500 Gilman Drive
La Jolla, California 92093-0301
Telephone: 858-534-6870
Fax: 858-534-7687
E-mail: gradinfo@chem.ucsd.edu
World Wide Web: http://www-chem.ucsd.edu/

University of California, San Diego

THE FACULTY AND THEIR RESEARCH

Timothy S. Baker, Ph.D., UCLA. Biochemistry.
Michael D. Burkart, Ph.D., Scripps Research Institute. Biological chemistry, chemo-enzymatic synthesis, natural product biosynthesis. Focus on antibiotic design, synthesis, biosynthesis.
Seth Cohen, Ph.D., Berkeley. Bioinorganic and coordination chemistry; metalloregulatory proteins, zinc proteinase inhibitors, and supramolecular materials proteins); design and synthesis of zinc proteinase inhibitors, synthesis of materials containing coordination clusters as building blocks.
Robert E. Continetti, Ph.D., Berkeley. Dissociation dynamics of transient species, three-body reaction dynamics, novel mass-spectrometric methods.
John E. Crowell, Ph.D., Berkeley. Materials chemistry, surface kinetics of metals/semiconductors, CVD, photo-induced deposition, thin-film spectroscopy.
Edward A. Dennis, Ph.D., Harvard. Biochemistry: phospholipase A2, signal transduction in macrophages, mechanism, prostaglandin regulation, mass spec of lipids and proteins.
Daniel J. Donoghue, Ph.D., MIT. Signal transduction, human cancer, receptor tyrosine kinase, cell cycle, tumor suppressor, oncogenesis.
Gourisankar Ghosh, Ph.D., Yeshiva (Einstein). Biochemistry and biophysics: transcription; signaling; pre-mRNA splicing; mRNA transport; protein/DNA/RNA interactions.
Partho Ghosh, Ph.D., California, San Francisco. Mechanisms of bacterial and protozoan pathogenesis, host response against infectious microbes.
Murray Goodman, Ph.D., Berkeley. Organic, biophysical chemistry: peptide synthesis, peptidomimetics, conformation, molecular modeling, spectroscopy, structure-bioactivities.
David N. Hendrickson, Ph.D., Berkeley. Inorganic chemistry, materials chemistry, single-molecule magnets, dynamics of transition metal complexes.
Alexander Hoffman, Ph.D., Rockefeller. Biochemistry: signaling, transcription, computational network, stress and immune responses, apoptosis, proliferation.
Patricia A. Jennings, Ph.D., Penn State. Biophysical chemistry: protein structure, dynamics and folding, 2-, 3-, and 4-D NMR. equilibrium/kinetic-fluorescence, circular dichroism.
Simpson Joseph, Ph.D., Vermont. Biochemistry and biophysics: ribosome structure, function and dynamics; discovery of novel antibiotics.
Yoshihisa Kobayashi, Ph.D., Tokyo (Japan). Natural product synthesis, new reaction and catalyst, heterocycles synthesis, elucidation of stereostructure.
Elizabeth A. Komives, Ph.D., California, San Francisco. Structure, function, dynamics, and thermodynamics of protein-protein interactions: NMR, mass spectrometry and kinetics.
Clifford P. Kubiak, Chair; Ph.D., Rochester. Inorganic chemistry: electron transfer, organometallic chemistry. Nanoscience: molecular electronics, nanosensors.
Andrew C. Kummel, Ph.D., Stanford. STM/STS of gate oxides on compound semiconductors and adsorbates on organic semiconductor.
Katja Lindenberg, Ph.D., Cornell. Theoretical chemical physics: nonequilibrium statistical mechanics, stochastic processes, nonlinear phenomena, condensed-matter theory.
Douglas Magde, Ph.D., Cornell. Experimental physical chemistry: photochemistry and photobiophysics, pico and femtosecond lasers.
J. Andrew McCammon, Ph.D., Harvard. Statistical mechanics and computational chemistry, with applications to biological systems.
Karsten Meyer, Ph.D., Mulheim (Max-Planck). Inorganic chemistry: bridges coordination chemistry with the fields of organometallic and actinide chemistry.
Mario J. Molina, Ph.D., Berkeley. Atmospheric chemistry; environmental chemistry.
K. C. Nicolaou, Ph.D., University College, London. Total synthesis and chemical biology of natural and designed molecules.
Joseph M. O'Connor, Ph.D., Wisconsin–Madison. Organotransition metal; organic, bioorganometallic, and inorganic chemistry.
Hans Oesterreicher, Ph.D., Vienna. Solid-state science: magnetic information storage, superconductivity.
Stanley Opella, Ph.D., Stanford. NMR structural studies of proteins in membranes and other supramolecular assemblies.
Charles L. Perrin, Ph.D., Harvard. Physical-organic chemistry: stereoelectronic effects, hydrogen bonding, isotope effects, ionic solvation.
Kimberly A. Prather, Ph.D., California, Davis. Environmental, analytical chemistry: gas/particle processes of tropospheric significance; mass spectrometry; laser-based techniques.
Arnold Rheingold, Ph.D., Maryland. Inorganic chemistry: small-molecule crystallography, synthesis of transition metal/p-block clusters.
Michael J. Sailor, Ph.D., Northwestern. Nanomaterials: porous silicon, chemical and biological sensors, biomaterials, electrochemistry.
Barbara A. Sawrey, Ph.D., California, San Diego, and San Diego State. Chemical education: development of computer-based multimedia to assist student learning of complex scientific processes and concepts.
Amitabha Sinha, Ph.D., MIT. Experimental physical chemistry: photochemistry, laser spectroscopy, reaction dynamics of vibrationally excited molecules.
Susan S. Taylor, Ph.D., Johns Hopkins. Protein kinases/signal transduction: structure/function and localization; biophysics; crystallography; NMR, fluorescence/FRET.
Emmanuel A. Theodorakis, Ph.D., Paris XI (South). Synthetic, medicinal, bioorganic, and biological chemistry; methods and strategies in natural products chemistry.
Mark H. Thiemens, Ph.D., Florida State. Atmospheric chemistry: physical chemistry of isotope effects, solar system information.
Yitzhak Tor, Ph.D., Weizmann (Israel). Ligand-nucleic acid interactions, metal-containing materials, new emissive molecules.
William C. Trogler, Ph.D., Caltech. Inorganic chemistry: polymer chemistry, nanotechnology applied to chemical and environmental sensing.
Roger Y. Tsien, Ph.D., Cambridge. Chemical biology; design, synthesis, and application of molecular probes of biological function.
Robert H. Tukey, Ph.D., Iowa. Environmental toxicology: the role of environmental and chemical toxicants on gene expression.
Peter L. van der Geer, Ph.D., Amsterdam. Biochemistry: molecular, biological, and biochemical analysis of signal transduction downstream of normally and malignantly activated protein-tyrosine kinases.
Michael S. VanNieuwenhze, Ph.D., Indiana. Chemical biology, synthetic methods, natural products synthesis, solid-phase synthesis, carbohydrate chemistry.
Wei Wang, Ph.D., California, San Francisco. Inference of gene regulatory networks and determination of protein specificity.
John H. Weare, Ph.D., Johns Hopkins. Physical chemistry: calculations of the dynamics of complex systems, theoretical geochemistry.
John C. Wheeler, Ph.D., Cornell. Physical chemistry: calculations of the dynamics of complex systems, theoretical geochemistry.
Peter Wolynes, Ph.D., Harvard. Theoretical chemical physics, protein folding and function, glasses and stochastic cell biology.
Jerry Yang, Ph.D., Columbia. Bioorganic chemistry: molecular self-assembly, materials chemistry, bionanotechnology.
Huilin Zhou, Ph.D., Stanford. Proteomics, cell biology, biochemistry, biological mass spectrometry to study protein phosphorylation and ubiquitination.

Adjunct Faculty
Kim Baldridge, Ph.D., North Dakota State; Senyon Choe, Ph.D., Berkeley; John E. Johnson, Ph.D., Iowa State; Joseph P. Noel, Ph.D., Ohio State; Leslie E. Orgel, Ph.D., Oxford; Shankar Subramaniam, Ph.D., Indian Institute of Technology (Kanpur).

UNIVERSITY OF CALIFORNIA, SAN FRANCISCO

Chemistry and Chemical Biology Graduate Program

Program of Study The Ph.D. program in chemistry and chemical biology (CCB) provides students with a broad and rigorous background in modern chemistry that includes training in molecular thermodynamics, bioorganic chemistry, computational chemistry, and structural biology. The program is distinctive in its orientation toward the study of molecules in living systems. It is further distinguished by providing integrated training in the sciences related to chemical biology: integrated both with respect to the levels of structure (atomic, molecular, cellular) and with respect to the traditional disciplines of chemistry and biology in the setting of a health science campus. The training objectives for students of the program are met through course work, laboratory rotations, and activities of the program such as journal clubs and research presentations and through thesis research in a specific laboratory.

The CCB curriculum includes a series of core required courses, including molecular thermodynamics, reaction mechanisms, physical organic chemistry, and chemical biology. In addition to these required courses, students must also take two electives. During the first year, students work in three separate laboratories for one quarter each. The rotation is expected to take roughly half of the student's time, with an oral presentation at the end of each rotation that is attended by other students and members of the lab. This provides valuable exposure to the diversity of the program and allows the student to gain firsthand experience for choosing a thesis laboratory. Students generally finish the program in approximately five years.

Research Facilities The faculty has excellent facilities for carrying out research in chemistry and chemical biology. These include a National Bio-organic, Biomedical Mass Spectrometry Laboratory; a National Research Computer Graphics Laboratory; a Nuclear Magnetic Resonance Laboratory for both high-resolution NMR and in vivo spectroscopy and imaging; a high-resolution X-ray crystallography laboratory; and numerous research support laboratories in addition to individual faculty laboratories.

Financial Aid All doctoral candidates receive funding as research assistants, teaching assistants, fellows, or trainees at a standardized level of about $24,500 for 2004–05.

Cost of Study The graduate program covers annual fees for its students ($7089 in 2003–04). Nonresident tuition was an additional $12,245 in 2003–04. Nonresident tuition is paid for the first year for U.S. citizens and permanent residents. After the first year, students are expected to have established California residency.

Living and Housing Costs The University has a limited number of off-campus apartments for students who are married and/or have full-time legal custody of a dependent child. The Campus Housing Office maintains listings of current community-supplied rental information concerning vacant off-campus houses, apartments, rooms, and various types of shared housing.

Student Group Approximately 55 Ph.D. students are enrolled full-time and receive full financial support. A wide range of ethnic, academic, and national backgrounds are represented.

Student Outcomes A need exists for a large number of faculty members qualified in scientific research and teaching, and the need for qualified chemists and chemical biologists in the biotechnology and pharmaceutical industries has never been higher. Such fields as patent law and government also have job openings in this area. There is a strong demand for Ph.D. scientists capable of research and teaching in this cross-disciplinary field of chemistry and chemical biology.

Location The Parnassus Heights campus is located on a hill in a residential area of San Francisco. San Francisco has a diverse collection of ethnic and social traditions, lifestyles, and community groups. An abundance of visual and performing arts events, including opera, symphony, theater, museums, galleries, dance, music, and arts organizations, are available, as are neighborhood street fairs and sporting events.

The Chemistry and Chemical Biology Graduate Program moved into the newly constructed Genentech Hall at the University of California, San Francisco's (UCSF), new Mission Bay campus in January 2003. In addition to Genentech Hall, UCSF is building a campus community center, parking structures, a housing complex for students and staff members, and more than 8 acres of landscaping. By the time the campus is complete, it will have 2 million square feet of space in twenty new buildings.

The University The University of California, San Francisco, one of nine campuses of a statewide university system, is the only UC campus dedicated exclusively to the health sciences. The campus is home to professional schools in dentistry, medicine, nursing, and pharmacy and graduate programs in the biological, biomedical, and behavioral sciences. UCSF encompasses several major sites in San Francisco.

Applying A formal application is required of all persons seeking admission to the CCB program. A baccalaureate degree is required. Other required materials include official transcripts of previous college work with a minimum 3.0 GPA, official GRE General Test scores and a GRE Subject Test score from tests taken within the last five years, a statement of purpose, letters of recommendation, a program application and Graduate Division application, and a $60 fee. Completed forms must be submitted by January 5. Students are admitted for the fall quarter only.

Correspondence and Information

Graduate Program Administrator
Chemistry and Chemical Biology Graduate Program
University of California, San Francisco
600 16th Street, Room 522
San Francisco, California 94143-2280
Telephone: 415-476-1914
Fax: 415-514-1546
E-mail: ccb@picasso.ucsf.edu
World Wide Web: http://www.ucsf.edu/ccb/

University of California, San Francisco

THE FACULTY AND THEIR RESEARCH

Nina Agabian, Professor of Stomatology, Microbiology and Immunology, and Pharmaceutical Chemistry; Ph.D., Yeshiva (Einstein). Microbial pathogenesis.
Dave Agard, Professor of Biochemistry and Biophysics and of Pharmaceutical Chemistry; Ph.D., Caltech. Steroid receptor structure-function, protein folding and centrosome structure.
Patricia Babbitt, Associate Professor of Biopharmaceutical Sciences and of Pharmaceutical Chemistry; Ph.D., California, San Francisco. Protein bioinformatics and protein engineering.
Henry Bourne, Professor of Cellular and Molecular Pharmacology and of Medicine; M.D., Johns Hopkins. Structure and signaling function of trimeric G proteins.
Frances Brodsky, Professor of Biopharmaceutical Sciences and of Pharmaceutical Chemistry; D.Phil., Oxford. Molecular mechanisms of intracellular membrane traffic.
Alma Burlingame, Professor of Pharmaceutical Chemistry; Ph.D., MIT. Protein machines, posttranslational dynamics and mass spectrometry.
Fred Cohen, Professor of Cellular and Molecular Pharmacology, Medicine, Pharmaceutical Chemistry, and Biochemistry and Biophysics; M.D., Stanford. Analysis and prediction of protein structure and protein-ligand interactions.
M. Almira Correia, Professor of Cellular and Molecular Pharmacology, Medicine, Pharmacy, and Pharmaceutical Chemistry; Ph.D., Minnesota. Structure-function relationships and regulation of hepatic hemoproteins.
Charles Craik, Professor of Pharmaceutical Chemistry, Cellular and Molecular Pharmacology, and Biochemistry and Biophysics; Ph.D., Columbia. Chemical biology of proteolysis.
Joe DeRisi, Assistant Professor of Biochemistry and Biophysics; Ph.D., Stanford. DNA microarrays.
Ken Dill, Professor of Pharmaceutical Chemistry and of Biopharmaceutical Sciences; Ph.D., California, San Diego. Statistical mechanics of biomolecules.
Jonathan Ellman, Associate Professor of Chemistry (University of California, Berkeley) and Cellular and Molecular Pharmacology; Ph.D., Harvard. Design, synthesis, and evaluation of small-molecule libraries.
Pamela England, Assistant Professor of Pharmaceutical Chemistry and of Cellular and Molecular Pharmacology; Ph.D., MIT. Chemical neurobiology: ion channel structure-function, synaptic plasticity.
Tom Ferrin, Professor of Pharmaceutical Chemistry; Ph.D., California, San Francisco. Macromolecular structure and function through use of computational algorithms and interactive three-dimensional computer graphics.
Robert Fletterick, Professor of Biochemistry and Biophysics and of Cellular and Molecular Pharmacology; Ph.D., Cornell. Protein structure and function.
Alan Frankel, Professor of Biochemistry and of Cellular and Molecular Pharmacology; Ph.D., Johns Hopkins. RNA-protein recognition.
Bradford Gibson, Professor of Pharmaceutical Chemistry; Ph.D., MIT. Coupling mass spectroscopy to structural biology.
R. Kip Guy, Assistant Professor of Pharmaceutical Chemistry and of Cellular and Molecular Pharmacology; Ph.D., California, San Diego (Scripps). Chemical synthesis and study of biologically active small molecules.
Holly Ingraham, Associate Professor of Physiology, Obstetrics, Gynecology, and Reproductive Sciences; Ph.D., California, San Diego. Gene expression and cellular signaling in reproductive development.
Matthew Jacobson, Assistant Professor of Pharmaceutical Chemistry; Ph.D., MIT. Physical chemistry–based approaches to predictive protein modeling.
Tom James, Professor and Chair of Pharmaceutical Chemistry and Professor of Radiology; Ph.D., Wisconsin. Three-dimensional structure determination by NMR.
David Julius, Professor of Cellular and Molecular Pharmacology; Ph.D., Berkeley. Molecular mechanisms of neurotransmitter action.
Stephen Kahl, Professor of Pharmaceutical Chemistry; Ph.D., Indiana. Synthesis and evaluation of cancer chemotherapeutics.
Irwin Kuntz, Professor of Pharmaceutical Chemistry; Ph.D., Berkeley. Drug design, computational approaches for designing small molecules and proteins.
Wendell Lim, Associate Professor of Cellular and Molecular Pharmacology and of Biochemistry and Biophysics; Ph.D., MIT. Mitosis and cell motility.
Michael Marletta, Professor of Chemistry and Biochemistry and of Molecular Biology (University of California, Berkeley) and Cellular and Molecular Pharmacology; Ph.D., California, San Francisco. Nitric oxide signaling and mechanisms of catalysis.
James McKerrow, Professor of Pathology, Medicine, and Pharmaceutical Chemistry; M.D., SUNY at Stony Brook. Protease structure and biology, protease inhibitor development.
Susan Miller, Associate Professor of Pharmaceutical Chemistry; Ph.D., Berkeley. Enzyme mechanisms and regulation.
Dan Minor, Assistant Professor of Biochemistry and Biophysics and Investigator, Cardiovascular Research Institute; Ph.D., MIT. Molecular structure and mechanism of ion channel action, development of novel molecules for ion channel regulation.
Geeta Narlikar, Assistant Professor of Biochemistry and of Biophysics; Ph.D., Stanford. Mechanisms of chromatin remodeling.
Norman Oppenheimer, Professor of Pharmaceutical Chemistry; Ph.D., California, San Diego. Enzymology and function of dehydrogenases and glycosidases.
Paul Ortiz de Montellano, Professor of Pharmaceutical Chemistry and of Cellular and Molecular Pharmacology; Ph.D., Harvard. Chemical biology of hemeproteins.
Erin O'Shea, Associate Professor of Biochemistry and Biophysics; Ph.D., MIT. Proteomics and quantitative approaches to signaling.
Andrej Sali, Professor of Biopharmaceutical Sciences and of Pharmaceutical Chemistry; Ph.D., London. Structure and function of proteins.
Tom Scanlan, Associate Professor of Pharmaceutical Chemistry and of Cellular and Molecular Pharmacology; Ph.D., Stanford. Chemical ligands that act on intracellular receptors.
Richard Shafer, Professor of Pharmaceutical Chemistry; Ph.D., Harvard. Nucleic acid structure and interactions.
Martin Shetlar, Professor of Pharmaceutical Chemistry; Ph.D., Berkeley. Protein-DNA interactions.
Brian Shoichet, Associate Professor of Cellular and Molecular Pharmacology; Ph.D., California, San Francisco. Structure-based inhibitor discovery.
Kevan Shokat, Professor of Cellular and Molecular Pharmacology; Ph.D., Berkeley. Deciphering cellular protein kinase cascades.
Robert Stroud, Professor of Biochemistry and Biophysics and of Pharmaceutical Chemistry; Ph.D., London. Cellular signaling and molecular mechanisms.
Francis Szoka, Professor of Biopharmaceutical Sciences and of Pharmaceutical Chemistry; Ph.D., SUNY at Buffalo. Gene therapy and macromolecular drug-delivery systems.
Jack Taunton, Assistant Professor of Cellular and Molecular Pharmacology; Ph.D., Harvard. Biochemical mechanisms of regulating the actin cytoskeleton.
Ronald Vale, Professor and Chairman of Cellular and Molecular Pharmacology and Professor of Biochemistry and Biophysics; Ph.D., Stanford. Microtube-based motility.
Christopher Voigt, Assistant Professor of Pharmaceutical Chemistry; Ph.D., Caltech. Design and evolution of complex gene circuits.
Ching Chung Wang, Professor of Pharmaceutical Chemistry; Ph.D., Berkeley. Molecular approaches to combating infectious diseases.
Jonathan Weissman, Associate Professor of Cellular and Molecular Pharmacology and of Biochemistry and Biophysics; Ph.D., MIT. Protein folding in vivo.
Keith Yamamoto, Professor of Cellular and Molecular Pharmacology and of Biochemistry and Biophysics; Ph.D., Princeton. Signaling and regulation by intracellular receptors.

UNIVERSITY OF HOUSTON

Department of Chemistry

Programs of Study

The Department of Chemistry at the University of Houston offers a stimulating graduate program to students pursuing a Master of Science (M.S.) or Doctor of Philosophy (Ph.D.) degree. Strong emphasis is placed on developing a student's ability to initiate and carry out original research projects. The department's teaching and research programs encompass the areas of analytical, biochemical, inorganic, materials, organic, physical, and theoretical chemistry. In addition to these classical areas, active programs in chemical physics, solid-state materials, and bioinorganic chemistry are offered. Interdisciplinary study programs in other fields are also available. Upon entering the program, students are given diagnostic exams in organic, inorganic, and physical chemistry. Students must obtain at least a B average in seven courses. Course work is expected to be completed by the end of the fifth semester in residence. During the fifth semester in residence, all students must present and defend an original research proposal. Although course work is involved in the Ph.D. degree, the majority of the students' efforts are devoted to original investigations in their chosen field of research. Students are expected to join a research group by the end of their first semester in residence. The Ph.D. dissertation is based on independent research that upon completion is defended in an oral examination before a Ph.D. committee. Typically, at least 4½ years of full-time research are required to complete the Ph.D. degree.

Research Facilities

The Department of Chemistry, in conjunction with the Institute for Materials Design, the Materials Research and Science and Engineering Center, and the Texas Center for Superconductivity, offers state-of-the-art instrumentation and facilities. All instrumentation is located on campus and is accessible to graduate students. The instrumentation includes one GE QE-300 NMR, one GE QE-300 NMR with variable temperature and multinuclear capabilities, one JEOL GSX-270 NMR with CP and MAS probes, one AMX-600 NMR with gradients, a JEOL 2000FX transmission electron microscope, a JEOL 2010-F transmission electron microscope, a JEOL 8600 electron microprobe, a PHI D5000 powder diffractometer, two Scintag XDS 2000 powder diffractometers, a Siemens GADDS pole figure system, a Siemens SMART single-crystal diffractometer, a PHI 5700 X-ray photoelectron spectrometer, a PHI 6600 secondary ion mass spectrometer, magnetometers, and a Hall and a four-probe conductivity apparatuses. Computing in the department is done on workstations by individual research groups.

Financial Aid

The Department of Chemistry meets the financial needs of its graduate students through teaching or research assistantships. The stipends vary between $1250 and $1550 per month. All full-time teaching or research assistants in good academic standing (with a GPA above 3.0) are awarded a tuition waiver for up to five years of graduate study.

Cost of Study

Tuition is waived for all Ph.D. students in good standing.

Living and Housing Costs

Graduate students usually live in one of the many apartment complexes situated around campus, or in an apartment in the city of Houston. Typical monthly costs are as follows: for a one-bedroom apartment, $450 to $750; for a two-bedroom apartment, $700 to $1100; and for a three-bedroom apartment, $1000 to $1500.

Student Group

There are 104 students in the Department of Chemistry, 65 of whom are international students.

Location

Houston is the fourth-largest city in the United States, with a population of more than 4 million. The greater Houston area is a major cultural center, with numerous museums, theaters, and a world-class symphony. Professional sports teams include the Astros, who play in the recently constructed Minute Maid Park; Rockets; Comets; and in 2002, the newest NFL expansion team, the Houston Texans. Gulf Coast beaches are just an hour's drive away, and Houston's warm climate allows residents to enjoy outdoor activities throughout the year.

The University

The University of Houston reflects the diversity, challenge, and optimistic spirit that characterize the city of Houston. Part of the public system of higher education in Texas, the University offers a full range of programs to more than 30,000 students from across the United States and around the world.

Applying

Applications for admission to study for the Ph.D. degree in chemistry are accepted from students who have received a bachelor's degree or equivalent. Application forms may be requested online through the chemistry department's Web page listed below.

Correspondence and Information

Dr. Edwin Carrasquillo
Department of Chemistry
University of Houston
4800 Calhoun Boulevard
Houston, Texas 77204-5003
Telephone: 713-743-2701
E-mail: mcarrasquillo@uh.edu
World Wide Web: http://www.chem.uh.edu

University of Houston

THE FACULTY AND THEIR RESEARCH

Rigoberto Advincula, Associate Professor; Ph.D. (polymer chemistry), Florida, 1994. Conjugated polymers, synthesis, organic and polymer ultrathin films, surface analysis, interfacial phenomena.
Thomas A. Albright, Professor; Ph.D. (inorganic, theoretical chemistry), Delaware, 1975. Reaction mechanisms of organometallics, molecular orbital calculations on molecules and solid-state materials.
Steven Baldelli, Assistant Professor; Ph.D. (physical chemistry), Tufts, 1998. Nonlinear optics, vibrational spectroscopy, surface chemistry, electrochemistry, microscopy, batteries/fuel cells, electrodes, polymer surfaces.
John L. Bear, Professor; Ph.D. (inorganic chemistry), Texas Tech, 1960. Synthetic inorganic chemistry; preparation, structure, and reactivity of metal dimers; catalysis, synthesis, and thermochemistry of solid-state materials.
Ivan Bernal, Professor; Ph.D. (inorganic chemistry), Columbia, 1963. Molecular origin of conglomerate crystallization.
Eric R. Bittner, Associate Professor; Ph.D. (physical, theoretical chemistry), Chicago, 1994. Developing novel formal and computational path integration approaches for studying quantum dynamics in the condensed phase and on surfaces.
Chengzhi Cai, Assistant Professor; Ph.D. (organic chemistry), ETH, 1996. Synthesis and properties of polymers, multidisciplinary approach to nanotechnology and advanced materials.
Edwin Carrasquillo, Associate Professor; Ph.D. (physical chemistry), Chicago, 1984. Laser studies of spectroscopy and molecular dynamics at high vibrational energy; spectroscopy and photochemistry of highly excited triplet states.
Dar-chone Chow, Assistant Professor; Ph.D. (biophysics), Berkeley, 1992. Biophysical chemistry, macromolecular crystallography, thermodynamics of protein-protein interactions, biophysics of membrane transport proteins, protein chemistry, protein therapeutic design.
Roman S. Czernuszewicz, Associate Professor; Ph.D. (analytical, bioinorganic chemistry), Marquette, 1981. Vibrational spectroscopy; resonance Raman effect; bioinorganic molecules; metalloporphyrins, Raman spectroelectrochemistry, and surface-enhanced Raman scattering.
Olafs Daugulis, Assistant Professor; Ph.D. (organic chemistry), Wisconsin, 1999. Application of organometallic chemistry to organic synthesis and polymer chemistry, development of new enantio- and diastereoselective transformations.
Don L. Elthon, Professor; Ph.D. (analytical chemistry, geochemistry, materials science), Columbia, 1980. High-temperature, high-pressure phase equilibrium and synthesis; electron/ion beam microanalysis
Xiaolian Gao, Professor; Ph.D. (bioorganic chemistry), Rutgers, 1986. Three-dimensional structures and physical properties of biological molecules in solution, molecular recognition and high-field NMR studies of biologically relevant molecules.
Russell A. Geanangel, Professor; Ph.D. (inorganic chemistry), Ohio State, 1968. Chemical education; use of technology to improve lecture effectiveness; online course tools, including testing/assessment, streaming media, and other measures, to increase retention and success in a diverse student body.
Arnold M. Guloy, Associate Professor; Ph.D. (inorganic chemistry), Iowa State, 1992. Solid-state chemistry, synthesis of novel inorganic solids and high-temperature superconductivity.
P. Shiv Halasyamani, Assistant Professor; Ph.D. (inorganic chemistry), Northwestern, 1996. Solid-state chemistry, synthesis and characterization of new oxide materials, structure-property relationships, nonlinear optical materials.
Tony J. Haymet, Professor; Ph.D. (physical, theoretical chemistry), Chicago, 1981. Statistical mechanics, density functional theory of liquids, understanding phase transitions.
David M. Hoffman, Professor; Ph.D. (inorganic chemistry), Cornell, 1982. Synthesis of inorganic and organometallic compounds, preparation of thin films by chemical vapor deposition.
Allan J. Jacobson, Professor; D. Phil. (inorganic chemistry), Oxford, 1969. Synthesis and structural characterization of mixed metal oxides, ionic and electrical conductivity in solids, synthesis of composite structures.
Karl M. Kadish, Professor; Ph.D. (analytical chemistry), Penn State, 1970. Analytical, bioanalytical, and bioinorganic chemistry; porphyrin chemistry; electrochemistry; redox reactions of dinuclear and metal-metal bonded complexes; Buckyball chemistry.
Jay K. Kochi, Professor; Ph.D. (organic chemistry), Iowa State, 1952. Mechanisms of organic reactions catalyzed by metal complexes, oxidations and reduction mechanisms, photochemistry of organometallic compounds.
Donald J. Kouri, Professor; Ph.D. (theoretical chemistry), Wisconsin, 1965. Quantum theory of atomic and molecular collisions, few body problems, approximate methods of calculating cross sections, theory of reactive scattering, theory of molecule-surface collisions.
T. Randall Lee, Associate Professor; Ph.D. (organic chemistry), Harvard, 1991. Design and synthesis of polymeric material, homogeneous and heterogeneous catalysis, surface and interfacial science.
Mamie W. Moy, Professor; M.S. (chemical education), Houston, 1952. Chemical education.
Scott S. Perry, Associate Professor; Ph.D. (physical chemistry), Texas at Austin, 1991. Atomic force microscopy, molecular-level tribology, surface chemistry of metal oxides and carbides, ultrahigh vacuum surface analysis.
B. Montgomerty Pettitt, Professor; Ph.D. (theoretical chemistry), Houston, 1980. Structure and thermodynamics of fluids and aqueous solutions, theory of molecular fluids and biomolecules in solution.
Wayne J. Rabalais, Professor; Ph.D. (physical chemistry), LSU, 1970. Surface science, chemisorption, ion-surface reactions, photoelectron spectroscopy, ion scattering, ion beam film deposition.
Randolph P. Thummel, Professor; Ph.D. (organic chemistry), California, Santa Barbara, 1971. Synthesis and study of mechanistatistically interesting molecules, small ring-fused aromatic systems, cycloaddition reactions, host-guest chemistry.

UNIVERSITY OF IDAHO

Department of Chemistry

Programs of Study

The Department of Chemistry at the University of Idaho (UI) offers M.S. and Ph.D. degrees in analytical, inorganic, organic, and physical chemistry. Active research areas include synthetic and medicinal chemistry, photochemistry, organometallic chemistry, environmental chemistry, theoretical chemistry, molecular spectroscopy (especially Raman and infrared), fluorine chemistry, supercritical fluids, reaction dynamics, and chemical education. Entering graduate students take qualifying exams in all four areas of chemistry and can earn course credits for passing at the fiftieth percentile or higher. Ph.D. students go on to take a series of cumulative exams in their area of emphasis and are advanced to candidacy upon presentation of a brief research proposal, which forms the basis for the research leading to the Ph.D.

Graduate students in the UI chemistry department enjoy close collaboration and lively discussion with a small group of internationally recognized faculty members plus visiting faculty members and postdoctoral fellows. Every effort is made to support students financially through teaching and research assistantships and to facilitate the timely completion of degree requirements. Students have the choice to work on projects funded by the National Science Foundation, the National Institutes of Health, the Department of Energy, and other agencies. Upon completion of the Ph.D. or M.S. degree in chemistry, UI students go on to pursue careers in industry, government labs, and academia.

Research Facilities

The chemistry department is located in a four-story building recently renovated with support from the National Science Foundation. Further renovations are slated in the near future to enhance graduate and undergraduate education and spectroscopy research. At present, the UI chemistry department houses five Fourier-transform NMR spectrometers, including a 600-MHz, a 500-MHz, and three 300-MHz instruments. Other instrumentation includes a high-resolution GC/MS, a state-of-the-art X-ray diffractometer, three Raman spectrometers, a dozen FT-IR spectrometers, instrumentation for flowing afterglow experiments, several pulsed and continuous wave lasers, and a wide selection of instrumentation for experiments in electronic spectroscopy, light scattering, and electrochemistry. Facilities on campus afford opportunities for performing Auger spectrometry, electron microscopy, and atomic emission spectrometry. Researchers take advantage of excellent, fully networked departmental and campus computing facilities and have access to instrumentation at nearby national laboratories—Pacific Northwest National Labs in Richland, Washington, and Idaho National Engineering and Environmental Lab in Idaho Falls.

Financial Aid

Graduate students are supported by teaching or research assistantships paying roughly $14,800 over ten months, and additional stipends ($1500 minimum) are available for the summer months. Out-of-state tuition is waived for graduate students on teaching or research assistantships, and the department pays for $1000 of registration fees per semester for all teaching assistants. Advisers of students supported on research assistantships typically pay their student fees and health insurance in entirety (about $3000 per semester) from grant funds. Financial aid is also available through the Federal Perkins Loan Program and work-study grants. The Student Financial Aid Office can provide information and applications.

Cost of Study

For 2004–05, full-time graduate fees are $2086 per semester for Idaho residents, with an additional fee of $4010 per semester for nonresidents. Resident students enrolled part-time pay $205 per credit; nonresidents pay an additional $123 per credit for part-time work. Full-time fees are charged for 8 credits or more. Fees are subject to change.

Living and Housing Costs

Graduate student housing is available through the University for $346 to $629 per month for apartments ranging in size from efficiencies to four-bedroom units. Potential graduate students are advised to reserve housing early. Off-campus housing lists are available on the Web at http://www.asui.uidaho.edu.

Student Group

Due to its smaller size, the UI chemistry department attracts students who enjoy individual attention from faculty members and close collaboration with a community of dedicated researchers. There are typically about 40 chemistry graduate students on the campus, all of them full-time students supported by assistantships. Approximately half of these are international students, and one third are women. The UI chemistry department is especially interested in recruiting graduate students from groups that are traditionally underrepresented in chemistry.

Student Outcomes

Graduate studies at the UI chemistry department prepare students for a variety of careers. Some Ph.D. students pursue postdoctoral training upon completion of their graduate studies, while others immediately find permanent employment in academia, national laboratories, and industry. In addition to traditional careers in teaching, industrial research, and chemical manufacturing, graduates have found employment in biotechnology, environmental science, and computer science areas.

Location

Moscow, located in the Idaho panhandle among the rolling hills of the Palouse, is an agricultural and recreational area and is the cultural center of the region. Local music and theater productions have received international acclaim. Skiing and lake and river sports are within easy drives. Spokane is 88 miles north, and Seattle and Portland are each 6 hours west.

The Department

The UI chemistry department has one of the strongest Ph.D.-granting programs in the Northwest and strives to continually upgrade the quality and visibility of the program. Students participate in internationally recognized research projects while benefiting from close interactions with faculty members. Interdisciplinary collaborations with faculty members in other departments and with scientists at nearby national laboratories enhance educational opportunities and access to instrumentation for research.

Applying

Applications for admission are available at http://www.uidaho.edu/cogs or by writing to the address below. Completed applications must include the application fee ($40 for domestic or $60 for international), official copies of all transcripts, three letters of recommendation, and a brief statement of purpose addressing the applicant's interests and experience. International students whose native language is not English must also arrange to send official TOEFL and TSE scores, and graduates from institutions not accredited by the American Chemical Society (ACS) are required to submit GRE General Test scores. Students who wish to apply for a departmental assistantship should consult with the department regarding the process and deadline date, which may be earlier than the application deadline.

Correspondence and Information

Chair, Graduate Admission Committee
Department of Chemistry
University of Idaho
P.O. Box 442343
Moscow, Idaho 83844-2343
Telephone: 208-885-6552
Fax: 208-885-6173
E-mail: chemoff@uidaho.edu
World Wide Web: http://www.chem.uidaho.edu

University of Idaho

THE FACULTY AND THEIR RESEARCH

Analytical Chemistry

Frank Cheng, Assistant Professor; Ph.D., Penn State, 1988. Electrochemical remediation of halocarbons, antioxidant action.
Total dechlorination of DDT by Pd/Mg particles under mild conditions. *Chemosphere* 43:195–8, 2001. With Engelmann and Doyle.

Peter R. Griffiths, Professor; D.Phil., Oxford, 1967. Analytical vibrational spectroscopy; FT-IR, Raman; open-path atmospheric monitoring; surface-enhanced infrared spectroscopy; hyphenated techniques; chemometrics; spectroelectrochemistry.
Surface-enhanced infrared absorption spectroscopy of p-nitrothiophenol on vapor-deposited platinum films. *Appl. Spectrosc.* 56:1275–80, 2002. With Bjerke.

Ray von Wandruszka, Professor; Ph.D., Wyoming, 1977. Chemistry of humic substances, especially their configuration in aqueous solution; the use of humic materials in the decontamination of polluted water; the temperature-induced clouding of nonionic surfactants; stability of micellar and premicellar aggregates in solutions of nonionic and mixed surfactants.
Dynamic light-scattering measurements of particle size development in aqueous humic materials. *Fresenius J. Anal. Chem.* 371:951–4, 2001. With Palmer.

Chien M. Wai, Professor; Ph.D., California, Irvine, 1967. Supercritical fluid extraction, nanomaterials synthesis, and catalysis in supercritical carbon dioxide.
Hydrogenation of olefins in supercritical CO_2 catalyzed by palladium nanoparticles in a water-in-CO_2 microemulsion. *J. Am. Chem. Soc.* 124:4540–1, 2002. With Ohde et al.

Inorganic Chemistry

Thomas E. Bitterwolf, Professor; Ph.D., West Virginia, 1976. Solution of frozen matrix photochemistry directed toward understanding the nature and reactivity of photochemical intermediates of metal carbonyl and nitrosyl compounds, synthesis of homo- and hetero-bimetallic compounds as catalysts for water splitting.
Organic matrix photochemical studies of rhenacarborane nitrosyl complexes. Evidence for linkage isomeric nitrosyl photointermediates. *Organometallics* 21:1856–60, 2002. With Weiss, Scallorn, and Jellis.

Robert L. Kirchmeier, Professor; Ph.D., Idaho, 1975. Inorganic polymers, halogenated cations, new methods for the formation of carbon-fluorine bonds.
Synthesis and characterization of per/polyfluorophenoxy derivatives of octachlorocyclotetraphosphazenes. *J. Fluorine Chem.* 112:307, 2001. With Rule and Selvaraj.

Pamela J. Shapiro, Associate Professor; Ph.D., Caltech, 1991. Synthetic and mechanistic organometallic chemistry; metallocence complexes of the main group and early transition metals; catalysis-directed ligand design, particularly for olefin polymerization catalysis.
Calcium-mediated fulvene couplings: A survey of 6-aryl and 6-alkyl fulvenes for their rac selectivity in the synthesis of ansa-calcocenes. *Organometallics* 21:182–91, 2002. With Sinnema et al.

Jean'ne M. Shreeve, Professor; Ph.D., Washington (Seattle), 1961. Nucleophilic and electrophilic fluorinations and perfluoroalkylations; high-energy compounds; biologically interesting compounds containing fluorine; hypervalent compounds of sulfur and phosphorus; fire extinguishants, poly nitrogen compounds, ionic liquids.
Tetrameric fluorophosphazene, $(NPF_2)_4$, planar or puckered? *J. Am. Chem. Soc.* 123:10299–303, 2001. With Elias et al.

Organic Chemistry

Leszek Czuchajowski, Professor; Ph.D., Krakow Technical (Poland), 1957. Synthesis of phosphorous(V)porphyrins diaxially substituted with nucleobases, nucleotides, amino acids, and peptides; synthesis of porphyrinyl-polynucleosides; studies of their interaction with DNA.
Synthesis and biomedical application of porphyrinyl nucleosides, nucleotides, and oligonucleotides. *Trends Heterocyclic Chem.* 6:57, 1999. With Li.

Gustavo E. Davico, Assistant Professor; Ph.D., Córdoba (Argentina), 1992. Gas-phase ion chemistry; chemistry, structure, and reactivity of singly and multiply charged ions.
Negative-ion photoelectron spectroscopy, gas-phase acidity, and thermochemistry of the peroxyl radicals CH_3OO and CH_3CH_2OO. *J. Am. Chem. Soc.* 123:9585, 2001. With Blanksby et al.

Nicholas R. Natale, Professor; Ph.D., Drexel, 1979. Medicinal chemistry, synthetic methods, heterocyclic and lanthanide chemistry.
Unique structure activity relationship of 4-isoxazolyl-1,4-dihydropyridines. *J. Med. Chem.* 46:87–96, 2003. With Zamponi et al.

Richard V. Williams, Professor; Ph.D., Cambridge, 1978. Physical organic chemistry; molecules of fundamental importance—synthesis, experiment and theory, novel aromatics, pyramidal olefins, and neutral homoaromatics; (homo)aromaticity, pericyclic reactions, and mechanistic investigations; new synthetic methods mediated by silicon and sulfur.
Homoaromaticity. *Chem. Rev.* 101:1185–204, 2001.

Physical Chemistry

W. Daniel Edwards, Associate Professor; Ph.D., Missouri–Rolla, 1976. Computational quantum mechanics, electronic excited state properties, excited state gradients, transition metal spectroscopy, metal-porphyrin complexes, object-oriented programming methods, virtual physical chemistry labs.
Investigation of the solvatochromic electronic transitions of $[Ru(NH_3)_4bipyridine]^{2+}$. *Chem. Phys. Lett.* 312:369–75, 1999. With Streiff and McHale.

T. Rick Fletcher, Associate Professor; Ph.D., California, Davis, 1986. Gas phase reaction dynamics, controlling chemical reactivity using laser excitation, bimolecular and unimolecular reactivity, organic photochemistry, nanochemistry.
The role of translationally excited species in atmospheric reactions. *Phys. Chem. Earth C* 26:487–93, 2001. With Wojcik.

Jeanne L. McHale, Professor; Ph.D, Utah, 1979. Raman and resonance Raman spectroscopy, studies of liquids and intermolecular interactions, spectroscopic studies of intramolecular and interfacial electron transfer, chromophore aggregation, and solvent dynamics.
Thermo-solvatochromism of betaine-30 in CH_3CN. *J. Phys. Chem. A* 105:11110–7, 2001. With Zhao, Burt, and Knorr.

UNIVERSITY OF MARYLAND, BALTIMORE COUNTY

Department of Chemistry and Biochemistry

Programs of Study

The Department of Chemistry and Biochemistry at the University of Maryland, Baltimore County (UMBC), offers programs of graduate study in chemistry and biochemistry leading to the M.S. and the Ph.D. degrees. The department also participates in a biotechnology M.S. program (applied molecular biology) in collaboration with the Department of Biological Sciences, an interdisciplinary Ph.D. program in molecular and cellular biology, an Interface Program that provides cross-disciplinary experience in chemistry and biology, and the Meyerhoff Program in Biomedical Sciences. The department's graduate programs in biochemistry and in molecular and cellular biology benefit from being part of larger intercampus joint programs in those fields, sponsored in conjunction with departments at the medical, dental, and pharmacy schools of the downtown Baltimore campus.

Upon entering the graduate program, both M.S. and Ph.D. students are required to take a set of placement examinations that are designed to test their proficiency at the senior undergraduate level and to indicate any areas of deficiency. Under the guidance of an advisory committee, they next complete a group of courses, constituting a core curriculum, which has been designed to bring them to a minimum level of proficiency in each of the major areas of chemistry. In addition, they are expected to take specialized courses in their field of interest. To fulfill the course requirements normally requires one to two years, depending upon the student's initial level of proficiency as demonstrated by the placement examinations.

To qualify for the degree, M.S. students must pass a comprehensive examination in their major field. Thesis research must be approved by a thesis committee, which also administers an oral examination based on the thesis research. Completing the course requirements, passing the comprehensive and oral examinations, and gaining approval of the thesis constitute fulfillment of the M.S. degree requirements. Candidates for the M.S. also have the option of substituting additional course work for the thesis. Graduate students in the Ph.D. program are expected to pass comprehensive examinations, prepare and defend an acceptable research proposal, present a dissertation based upon original research, and pass an oral defense.

The principal areas of thesis research for both the M.S. and Ph.D. degrees include analytical chemistry; biochemistry; bioinorganic chemistry; enzymology; mass spectrometry; models for enzymic reactions; organic mechanisms; organic synthesis; protein and nucleic acid chemistry; theoretical, physical, bioanalytical, biophysical, and carbohydrate chemistry; and chemistry at the biology interface.

Research Facilities

Extensive facilities are available for cutting-edge research. The specialized research instrumentation available includes calorimetry, chromatography, stopped-flow and temperature-jump kinetics, nanosecond laser flash photolysis and nuclear magnetic resonance spectroscopy (one 200-, one 300-, one 500-, two 600-, and one 800-MHz instruments), electron spin resonance spectroscopy, circular dichroism, X-ray diffraction, infrared spectroscopy, laser fluorescence spectroscopy, atomic absorption, gas chromatography–mass spectrometry, and Fourier transform/Ion cyclotron resonance mass spec, as well as extensive molecular modeling computer facilities. Also located in the department is a Center for Structural Biochemistry, which specializes in the structural analysis of biological molecules (e.g., biopolymers, peptides, glycoproteins). In addition to a laser desorption mass spectrometer and two 500-MHz and 600-MHz NMRs, the center houses one of the few tandem mass spectrometers located in academic institutions worldwide. The Howard Hughes Medical Investigator Suite houses the second 600- and the 800-MHz NMRs, used for high-dimensional studies of HIV proteins, metallobiomolecules, and macromolecular interactions. The main University library contains more than 2,500 volumes of chemistry texts and subscribes to 150 chemistry and biochemistry periodicals. The department reference room also provides access to the principal journals.

Financial Aid

Financial aid packages with twelve-month stipends of $16,500 to $19,500, health insurance, and tuition remission are offered to qualified students. Enhanced stipend fellowships are also available.

Cost of Study

Tuition in 2003–04 was $350 per credit hour for Maryland residents and $570 per credit hour for nonresidents. Fees were $72 per credit hour. New students were charged a one-time orientation fee of $75.

Living and Housing Costs

There are a limited number of on-campus dormitory rooms available for graduate students. Most graduate students are housed in apartments or rooming houses in the nearby communities of Arbutus and Catonsville. A single graduate student can expect living and educational expenses of approximately $14,000 to $16,000 a year.

Student Group

In fall 2002, the department's graduate students included 40 men and 36 women. Approximately 80 percent of the students are receiving some form of financial aid.

Student Outcomes

All of the students plan careers in chemistry and biochemistry in either teaching or research and in associated regulatory and financial areas.

Location

The University has a scenic location on the periphery of the Baltimore metropolitan area. Downtown Baltimore can be reached in 15 minutes by car, while Washington is an hour away. Both Baltimore and Washington have very extensive cultural facilities, including eight major universities, a number of museums and art galleries of international reputation, two major symphony orchestras, and numerous theaters.

The University

UMBC was established in 1966 on a 500-acre campus. The Department of Chemistry and Biochemistry of the University of Maryland Graduate School, Baltimore, is located at the UMBC campus. The University has about 11,700 students drawn primarily from Maryland, although an increasing number have enrolled from other states and countries. The undergraduates are predominantly interested in professional or business careers. Because a high percentage of the students are the first members of their families to attend college, UMBC has a very different atmosphere from that encountered in older institutions and has made a particular effort to attract minority students, who now account for about 36 percent of the undergraduate student body.

Applying

Applications should include an academic transcript, three references, and the results of the General Test of the Graduate Record Examinations.

Correspondence and Information

Graduate Program Director
Department of Chemistry and Biochemistry
University of Maryland, Baltimore County
1000 Hilltop Circle
Baltimore, Maryland 21250

Telephone: 410-455-2491
E-mail: chemgrad@umbc.edu
World Wide Web: http://www.umbc.edu/chem-biochem

University of Maryland, Baltimore County

THE FACULTY AND THEIR RESEARCH

Bradley R. Arnold, Assistant Professor; Ph.D., Utah, 1991; postdoctoral studies at the National Research Council of Canada, Ottawa, and the Center for Photoinduced Charge Transfer, University of Rochester. Physical chemistry, application of time-resolved polarized spectroscopy.

C. Allen Bush, Professor; Ph.D., Berkeley, 1965; postdoctoral studies at Cornell. Biophysical chemistry: conformation and dynamics of carbohydrates, glycoproteins, glycopeptides, and polysaccharides by NMR spectroscopy, computer modeling, and circular dichroism.

Donald Creighton, Professor; Ph.D., UCLA, 1972; postdoctoral studies at the Institute for Cancer Research. Enzyme mechanisms and protein structure, studies on sulfhydryl proteases and glyoxalase enzymes.

Brian M. Cullum, Assistant Professor; Ph.D., South Carolina, 1998; postdoctoral studies at Oak Ridge National Laboratory. Analytical chemistry, development of optical sensors and optical sensing techniques for biomedical and environmental research.

Dan Fabris, Assistant Professor; Ph.D., Padua (Italy), 1989; postdoctoral studies at the National Research Council, Area of Research of Padua (Italy) and the University of Maryland, Baltimore County. Bioanalytical and biomedical applications of mass spectrometry, nucleic acid adducts, and protein–nucleic acid interactions.

James C. Fishbein, Professor; Ph.D., Brandeis, 1985; postdoctoral studies at Toronto. Mechanisms of organic reactions in aqueous solutions; generation and study of reactive intermediates, particularly those involved in nitrosamine and nitrosamide carcinogenesis.

Colin W. Garvie, Assistant Professor; Ph.D., Leeds (England), 1997; postdoctoral studies at Howard Hughes Medical Institute, Johns Hopkins University School of Medicine. Structural studies of the redox regulation of circadian clock proteins, structural studies of the MHCII enhaceosome.

Susan K. Gregurick, Assistant Professor; Ph.D., Maryland, College Park, 1994; postdoctoral studies at Maryland Biotechnology Institute. Development of evolutionary algorithms for use in intricate chemical problems.

Ramachandra S. Hosmane, Professor; Ph.D., South Florida, 1978; postdoctoral studies at Illinois. Organic synthesis; biomedicinal chemistry, with applications in antiviral and anticancer therapy; and biomedical technology, with applications in artificial blood.

Richard L. Karpel, Professor; Ph.D., Brandeis, 1970; postdoctoral studies at Princeton. Interactions of helix destabilizing proteins with nucleic acids and the involvement of such proteins in various aspects of RNA function, metal ion–nucleic acid interactions.

Lisa A. Kelly, Assistant Professor; Ph.D., Bowling Green, 1993; postdoctoral studies at Brookhaven National Laboratory. Photoredox initiated chemical bond cleavage in biological and model systems.

William R. LaCourse, Associate Professor; Ph.D., Northeastern, 1987; postdoctoral studies at Ames Laboratory (USDOE) and Iowa State. Pulsed electrochemical detection techniques for bioanalytical separations.

Joel F. Liebman, Professor; Ph.D., Princeton, 1970; postdoctoral studies at Cambridge and the National Institute of Standards and Technology. Energetics of organic molecules, especially considerations of strain and aromaticity; gaseous ions; noble gas, fluorine, boron, and silicon chemistry; mathematical and quantum chemistry.

Wuyuan Lu, Affiliate Assistant Professor; Ph.D., Purdue, 1994; postdoctoral studies at the Scripps Research Institute and the University of Chicago. Structural and functional relationships of maternin and D-peptides as receptor antagonists and enzyme inhibitors.

Ralph M. Pollack, Professor; Ph.D., Berkeley, 1968; postdoctoral studies at Northwestern. Enzyme reactions, model systems for enzyme mechanisms, organic reaction mechanisms.

Katherine L. Seley, Associate Professor; Ph.D., Auburn, 1996; postdoctoral studies at Auburn. Discovery, design, and synthesis of nucleoside/nucleotide and heterocyclic enzyme inhibitors for use as medicinal agents with chemotherapeutic emphasis in the areas of anticancer, antiviral, antibiotic, and antiparasitic targets.

Paul J. Smith, Assistant Professor; Ph.D., Pittsburgh, 1993; postdoctoral studies at Johns Hopkins. Bioorganic and physical organic chemistry, host-guest chemistry, DNA structure and DNA binding by small molecules.

Michael F. Summers, Professor and Howard Hughes Associate Medical Investigator; Ph.D., Emory, 1984; postdoctoral studies at the Center for Drugs and Biologics, FDA, Bethesda, Maryland. Elucidation of structural, dynamic, and thermodynamic features of metallobiomolecules utilizing advanced two-dimensional and multinuclear NMR methods.

Veronika Szalai, Assistant Professor; Ph.D., Yale, 1988; postdoctoral studies at North Carolina, Chapel Hill. Spectroscopic characterization of biomolecular assemblies containing paramagnetic transition metals or spin labels.

James S. Vincent, Associate Professor; Ph.D., Harvard, 1963; postdoctoral studies at Caltech. Infrared and Raman spectroscopy of phospholipid membrane systems, magnetic spectroscopy of transition-metal complexes.

Dale L. Whalen, Professor; Ph.D., Berkeley, 1965; postdoctoral studies at UCLA. Reactions of carcinogenic polycyclic aromatic hydrocarbon epoxides, organic reaction mechanisms.

University of Maryland, Baltimore County

SELECTED PUBLICATIONS

Arnold, B. R., and A. W. Schill. Rotational dynamics of excited probes: The analysis of experimental data. *Spectrosc. Lett.* 35:229–38, 2002.

Arnold, B. R., A. W. Schill, and P. V. Poliakov. Application of time-resolved linear dichroism spectroscopy: Relaxation of excited hexamethylbenzene/1,2,4,5-tetracyanobenzene charge-transfer complex. *J. Phys. Chem. A* 105:537–43, 2001.

Arnold, B. R., A. C. Euler, A. W. Schill, and P. V. Poliakov. Application of time-resolved linear dichroism spectroscopy: Rapid relaxation of excited charge-transfer complexes. *J. Phys. Chem. A* 105:10404–12, 2001.

Arnold, B. R., A. Euler, K. F. Fields, and R. Zaini. Association constants for 1,2,4,5-tetracyanobenzene and tetracyanoethylene with methyl substituted benzenes. *J. Phys. Org. Chem.* 13:729–34, 2000.

Azurmendi, H. F., M. Martin-Pastor, and **C. A. Bush.** Conformational studies of Lewis X and Lewis A trisaccharides using NMR residual dipolar couplings. *Biopolymers* 63:89–98, 2002.

Azurmendi, H. F., and **C. A. Bush.** Tracking alignment from the moment of inertia tensor (TRAMITE) of biomolecules in neutral dilute liquid crystal solutions. *J. Am. Chem. Soc.* 124:2426–7, 2002.

Azurmendi, H. F., and **C. A. Bush.** Conformational studies of blood group A and blood group B oligosaccharides using NMR residual dipolar couplings. *Carbohydr. Res.* 337:905–15, 2002.

Stroop, C. J. M., **C. A. Bush,** R. L. Marple, and **W. R. LaCourse.** Carbohydrate analysis of bacterial polysaccharides by high-pH anion-exchange chromatography and online polarimetric determination of absolute configuration. *Analyt. Biochem.* 303:176–85, 2002.

Zhang, Q., et al. **(D. J. Creighton** and **D. Fabris).** Alkylation of nucleic acids by the antitumor agent COMC. *Org. Lett.* 4:1459–62, 2002.

Hamilton, D. S., Z. Ding, B. Ganem, and **D. J. Creighton.** Glutathione S-transerase-catalyzed addition of glutathione to COMC: A new hypothesis for antitumor activity. *Org. Lett.* 4:1209–12, 2002.

Hamilton, D. S., and **D. J. Creighton.** Tumor-selective anticancer strategies: Using GSTP1-1 to generate enediol analogue inhibitors of glyoxalase I. In *Chemico-Biological Interactions*, vol. 133, pp. 355–9, Elsevier, 2001.

Creighton, D. J., and D. S. Hamilton. Brief history of glyoxalase I and what we have learned about metal ion-dependent, enzyme-catalyzed isomerizations. *Arch. Biochem. Biophys.* 387:1–10, 2001.

Vo-Dinh, T., J. P. Alarie, **B. M. Cullum,** and G. D. Griffin. Antibody-based nanosensor for measurement in a single cell. *Nat. Biotechnol.* 18:764–7, 2000.

Vo-Dinh, T., and **B. M. Cullum**. Biosensors and biochips for bioanalysis. *Fresenius J. Anal. Chem.* 356:540–51, 2000.

Cullum, B. M., et al. Development of a compact handheld Raman instrument with no moving parts for use in field analysis. *Rev. Sci. Instrum.* 71:1602–7, 2000.

Zhang, Q., et al. **(D. Fabris).** Alkylation of DNA by the antitumor drug COMC. *Org. Lett.* 4:1459–62, 2002.

Cai, M., et al. **(D. Fabris).** Cation-directed self-assembly of lipophilic nucleosides: The cation's central role in the structure and dynamics of a hydrogen-bonded assembly. *Tetrahedron* 58:661–71, 2002.

Hathout, Y., **D. Fabris,** and C. Fenselau. Stoichiometry in zinc ion transfer from metallothionein to a zinc-finger peptide. *Int. J. Mass Spectrom. Ion Processes* 204:1–6, 2001.

Fabris, D. Steady-state kinetics of ricin A-chain reaction with the Sarcin/Ricin loop and with HIV-1 Ψ-RNA hairpins evaluated by electrospray ionization mass spectrometry. *J. Am. Chem. Soc.* 122:8779–80, 2000.

Navamal, M., et al. **(J. C. Fishbein).** Thiolytic chemistry of alternative precursors to the major metabolite of the cancer chemopreventive oltipraz. *J. Org. Chem.,* in press.

Carey, K. A., T. W. Kensler, and **J. C. Fishbein.** Kinetic constraints for the thiolysis of 4-methyl-5-(pyrazine-2-yl)-1, 2-dithiole-3-thione (oltipraz) and related dithiole-3-thiones in aqueous solution. *Chem. Res. Toxicol.* 14:939–45, 2001.

Blans, P., and **J. C. Fishbein.** Predicted exocyclic amino group alkylation of 2'-deoxyadenosine by the isopropyl cation. *Chem. Res. Toxicol.* 13:431–5, 2000.

Mesic', M., J. Peurahlti, P. Blans, and **J. C. Fishbein.** Mechanisms of decomposition of a-hydroxydialkylnitrosamines in aqueous solutions. *Chem. Res. Toxicol.* 13:983–92, 2000.

Garvie, C. W., J. Hagman, and C. Wolberger. Structural studies of Ets-1/Pax5 complex formation on DNA. *Mol. Cell* 8(6):1267–76, 2001.

Garvie, C. W., and C. Wolberger. Recognition of specific DNA sequences. *Mol. Cell* 8:937–46, 2001.

Garvie, C. W., and S. E. V. Phillips. Direct and indirect readout in mutant met repressor-operator complexes. *Struct. Fold Des.* 8(9):905–14, 2000.

Gerber, R. B., B. Brauer, **S. K. Gregurick,** and G. M. Chaban. Calculation of anharmonic vibrational spectroscopy of small biological molecules. *Phys. Chem. Comm.* 5:142, 2002.

Gregurick, S. K., G. M. Chaban, and R. B. Gerber. *Ab initio* and improved empirical potentials for the calculation of the anharmonic vibrational states and intramolecular mode coupling of N-methylacetamide. *J. Phys. Chem.* 106:8696, 2002.

Gregurick, S. K., and S. A. Kafafi. Computation of the electronic and spectroscopic properties of carbohydrates using novel density functional and vibrational self-consistent field methods. *J. Carbohydr. Chem.* 18:867, 1999.

Gregurick, S. K., et al. Anharmonic vibrational self-consistent field calculations as an approach to improving force fields for monosaccharides. *J. Phys. Chem. B* 103:3476, 1998.

Zhang, N., et al. **(R. S. Hosmane).** In vitro inhibition of measles virus replication by novel ring expanded ("fat") nucleoside analogues containing the imidazol[4,5[e][1,3]diazepine ring system. *Bioorg. Med. Chem. Lett.,* 12:3391–4, 2002.

Hosmane, R. Ring-expanded ("fat") nucleosides as broad-spectrum anticancer and antiviral agents. In *Current Topics in Medicinal Chemistry: Recent Developments in Antiviral Nucleosides, Nucleotides, and Oligonucleotides,* vol. 2, pp. 1091–107, ed. R. S. Hosmane, Bentham Science Publishers, 2002.

Borowski, P., et al **(R. S. Hosmane).** Characterization of imidazo[4,5-d]pyridazine nucleosides as modulators of unwinding reaction mediated by West Nile virus NTPase/helicase: Evidence for activity on the level of substrate and/or enzyme. *Antimicrob. Agents Chemother.* 46:1231–9, 2002.

Sood, R. K., et al. **(R. S. Hosmane).** Novel ring-expanded nucleoside analogs exhibit potent and selective inhibition of hepatitis B virus replication in cultured human hepatoblastoma cells. *Antiviral Res.* 53:159–64, 2002.

Karpel, R. L., LAST motifs and SMART domains in gene 32 protein: An unfolding story of autoregulation? *IUBMB Life* 53:161–6, 2002.

Urbaneja, M. A., M. Wu, J. R. Casas-Finet, and **R. L. Karpel.** HIV-1 nucleocapsid protein as a nucleic acid chaperone: Spectroscopic study of its helix-destabilizing properties, structural binding specificity, and annealing activity. *J. Mol. Biol.* 318:749–64, 2002.

Waidner, L. A., et al. **(R. L. Karpel).** Domain effects on the DNA-interactive properties of bacteriophage T4 gene 32 protein. *J. Biol. Chem.* 276:2509–16, 2001.

Wu, M., E. K. Flynn, and **R. L. Karpel.** Details of the nucleic acid binding site of T4 gene 32 protein revealed by proteolysis and DNA T_m depression methods. *J. Mol. Biol.* 286:1107–21, 1999.

Wu, M., M. A. Urbaneja, J. R. Casas-Finet, and **R. L. Karpel.** Nucleic acid helix-destabilizing properties and structural binding specificity of HIV-1 nucleocapsid protein. *Biophys. J.* 76:A27, 1999.

Chandrasekharan, N., and **L. A. Kelly.** A dual fluorescence temperature sensor based on perylene/exciplex interconversion. *J. Am. Chem. Soc.* 123:9898–9, 2001.

Rogers, J. E., B. Abraham, A. Rostkowski, and **L. A. Kelly.** Mechanisms of photoinitiated cleavage of DNA by 1,8-naphthalimide derivatives. *Photochem. Photobiol.* 74:521–31, 2001.

Rogers, J. E., T. P. Le, and **L. A. Kelly.** Nucleotide oxidation mediated by naphthalimide excited states with covalently attached viologen cosensitizers. *Photochem. Photobiol.* 73:223–9, 2001.

Le, T. P., J. E. Rogers, and **L. A. Kelly.** Photoinduced electron transfer in covalently linked 1,8-napthalimide/viologen systems. *J. Phys. Chem. A* 104:6778–85, 2000.

LaCourse, W. R. Column liquid chromatography: Equipment and instrumentation. *Anal. Chem.* 74(12):2813R–32R, 2002.

Hanko, V. P., **W. R. LaCourse,** C. O. Dasenbrock, and J. S. Rohrer.

University of Maryland, Baltimore County

Selected Publications (continued)

Determination of sulfur-containing antibiotics using high-performance liquid chromatography with integrated pulsed amperometric detection. *Drug Dev. Res.* 53:268–80, 2001.

LaCourse, W. R. Electrochemical detectors: Functional group analysis. *Enantiomer,* 2–3, 141–52, 2001.

Kovacevic', B., **J. F. Liebman,** and Z. B. Maksic'. Nibbering's C7H7N: An *ab initio* study of the structure and electronic properties of benzaldimine and its protonated ion. *J. Chem. Soc.* Perkin 2:1544–8, 2002.

Diogo, H. P., et al. **(J. F. Liebman).** The aromaticity of pyraclyene: An experimental and computational study of the energetics of the hydrogenation of acenapthylene and pyracylene. *J. Am. Chem. Soc.* 124:2065–75, 2002.

Balighian, E. D., and **J. F. Liebman.** How anomalous are the anomalous properties of fluorine? Ionization energy and electron affinity revisited. *J. Fluorine Chem.* 116:35–9, 2002.

Roux, M. V., et al. **(J. F. Liebman).** Enthalpy of formation of methyl benzoate: Calorimetry and consequences. *Phys. Chem. Chem. Phys.* 4:3611–3, 2002.

Zeiger, D. N., and **J. F. Liebman.** The strain energy of fluorinated cyclopropanes: Quantum chemical realization of homodesmotic, diagonal and ultradiagonal approaches. *J. Mol. Struct.* 556:83–94, 2000.

Lu, S. M., and **W. Lu** et al. Predicting the reactivity of proteins from their sequence alone: Kazal family of protein inhibitors of serine proteinases. *Proc. Natl. Acad. Sci. U.S.A.* 98:1410–5, 2001.

Bateman, K. S., et al. **(W. Lu).** Contribution of peptide bonds to inhibitor-protease binding: crystal structures of the turkey ovomucoid third domain backbone variants OMTKY3-Pro18i and OMTKY3-Y[COO]-Leu18i in complex with *Streptomyces griseus* proteinase B (SGPB) and the structure of the free inhibitor, OMTKY3-Y[CH2NH2+]-Asp19l. *J. Mol. Biol.* 305:839–49, 2001.

Lu, W-Y., et al. **(W. Lu).** Deciphering the role of the electrostatic interactions involving Gly70 in eglin c by total chemical protein synthesis. *Biochem.* 39:3575–84, 2000.

Thornburg, L. D., Y. R. Goldfeder, T. C. Wilde, and **R. M. Pollack.** Selective catalysis of elementary steps by Asp-99 and Tyr-14 of 3-oxo-delta-5-steroid isomerase. *J. Am. Chem. Soc.* 123:9912–3, 2001.

Hénot, F., and **R. M. Pollack.** Catalytic activity of the D38A mutant of 3-oxo-Δ^5-steroid isomerase: Recruitment of Asp-99 as the base. *Biochem.* 39:3351–9, 2000.

Petrounia, I. P., G. Blotny, and **R. M. Pollack.** Binding of 2-naphthols to D38E mutants of 3-oxo-Δ^5-steroid isomerase: Variation of ligand ionization state with the nature of the electrophilic component. *Biochem.* 39:110–6, 2000.

Pollack, R. M., L. D. Thornburg, Z. R. Wu, and **M. F. Summers.** Mechanistic insights from the three-dimensional structure of 3-oxo-Δ^5-steroid isomerase. *Arch. Biochem. Biophys.* 370:9–15, 1999.

Seley, K. L., et al. Unexpected inhibition of *S*-adenosyl-L-homocysteine hydrolase by a guanosine nucleoside. *Bioorg. Med. Chem.* 13:1985–8, 2003.

Seley, K. L., L. Zhang, A. Hagos, and S. Quirk. Fleximers. Design and synthesis of a new class of novel shape-modified nucleosides. *J. Org. Chem.* 67:3365–73, 2002.

Seley, K. L., L. Zhang, and A. Hagos. Fleximers. Design and synthesis of two novel split nucleosides. *Org. Lett.* 3:3209–10, 2001.

Seley, K. L., et al. Synthesis and antitumor activity of theino-separated tricyclic purines. *J. Med. Chem.* 43:4877–83, 2000.

Chen, T., et al. **(P. J. Smith).** Enzymatic grafting of hexyloxyphenol onto chitosan to alter surface and rheological properties. *Biotechnol. Bioeng.* 70:564–73, 2000.

Hauser, S. L., E. W. Johanson, H. P. Green, and **P. J. Smith.** Aryl phosphate complexation by cationic cyclodextrins. An enthalpic advantage for guanidinium over ammonium and unusual enthalpy-entropy compensation. *Org. Lett.* 2:3575–8, 2000.

Koehler, J., et al. **(P. J. Smith).** Potential approach for fractionating oxygenated aromatic compounds from renewable resources. *Ind. Eng. Chem. Res.* 39:3347–55, 2000.

Kumar, G., P. J. Bristow, **P. J. Smith,** and G. F. Payne. Enzymatic gelation of the natural polymer chitosan. *Polymer* 41:2157–68, 2000.

Shao, L., et al. **(P. J. Smith).** Enzymatic modification of the synthetic polymer polyhydroxystyrene. *Enzyme Microb. Technol.* 25:660–8, 1999.

Amarasinghe, G. K., et al. **(M. F. Summers).** NMR structure of the HIV-1 nucleocapsid protein bound to stem-loop SL2 of the Ψ-RNA packaging signal. Implications for genome recognition. *J. Mol. Biol.* 301:491–511, 2000.

Campos-Olivas, R., J. L. Newman, and **M. F. Summers.** Solution structure and dynamics of the rous sarcoma virus capsid protein and comparison with capsid proteins of other retroviruses. *J. Mol. Biol.* 296:633–49, 2000.

Klein, D. J., et al. **(M. F. Summers).** Structure of the nucleocapsid protein from the mouse mammary tumor virus reveals unusual folding of the C-terminal zinc finger. *Biochem.* 39:1604–12, 2000.

Khorasanizadeh, S., R. Campos-Olivas, C. A. Clark, and **M. F. Summers.** Solution structure of the capsid protein from the human T-cell leukemia virus type 1. *J. Mol. Biol.* 291:491–505, 1999.

Turner, B. G., and **M. F. Summers.** Structural biology of HIV. *J. Mol. Biol.* 285:1–32, 1999.

DeGuzman, R. N., et al. **(M. F. Summers).** Structure of the HIV-1 nucleocapsid protein bound to the SL3 Ψ-RNA recognition element. *Science* 279:384–8, 1998.

Lee, B. M., et al. **(M. F. Summers).** Dynamical behavior of the HIV-1 nucleocapsid protein. *J. Mol. Biol.* 279:633–49, 1998.

Szalai, V. A., M. J. Singer, and H. H. Thorp. Site-specific probing of oxidative reactivity and telomerase function using 7,8-dihydro-8-oxoguanine in telomeric DNA. *J. Am. Chem. Soc.* 124:1625–31, 2002.

Szalai, V. A., J. Jayawickramarajah, and H. H. Thorp. Electrocatalysis of guanine oxidation in poly(ethylene) glycol solutions: The interplay of adsorption and reaction rate. *J. Phys. Chem. B* 106:709–16, 2002.

Szalai, V. A., and H. H. Thorp. Electron transfer in tetrads: Adjacent guanines are not hole traps in G quartets. *J. Am. Chem. Soc.* 122:4524–5, 2000.

Szalai, V. A., and G. W. Brudvig. How plants produce dioxygen. *Am. Scientist* 86:542–51, 1998.

Shenoy, V., J. Rosenblatt, **J. Vincent,** and A. Gaigalas. Measurement of mesh sizes in concentrated rigid and flexible polyelectrolyte solutions by electron spin resonance technique. *Macromolecules* 28:525–30, 1995.

Vincent, J. S., S. D. Revak, C. D. Cochrane, and I. W. Levin. Interactions of model human pulmonary surfactants with a mixed phospholipid bilayer assembly: Raman spectroscopic studies. *Biochem.* 32:8228–38, 1993.

Vincent, J. S., S. D. Revak, C. D. Cochrane, and I. W. Levin. Raman spectroscopic studies of model human pulmonary surfactant systems: Phospholipid interactions with peptide paradigms for the surfactant protein SP-B. *Biochem.* 30:8395–401, 1991.

Vincent, J. S., and I. W. Levin. Raman spectroscopic studies of dimyristoyl-phosphatidic acid and its interactions with ferricytochrome c in cationic binary and ternary lipid-protein complexes. *Biophys. J.* 59:1007–21, 1991.

Doan, L., H. Yagi, D. M. Jerina, and **D. L. Whalen.** Chloride ion-catalyzed conformational inversion of carbocation intermediates in the hydrolysis of a benzo[a]pyrene 7,8-diol 9,10-epoxide. *J. Am. Chem. Soc.,* in press.

Bartas-Yocoubou, J.-M., et al. **(D. L. Whalen).** Aryl epoxide-halohydrin transformations: Stereochemistry of reactions of aryl epoxides with lithium halide-acetic acid reagent. *Tetrahedron Lett.* 43:3781–2, 2002.

Doan, L., et al. **(D. L. Whalen).** New insights on the mechanisms of reaction of benzo[a]pyrene 7,8-diol 9, 10-epoxides. *J. Am. Chem. Soc.* 123:6785–91, 2001.

Kalsi, A., et al. **(D. L. Whalen and D. J. Creighton).** Role of hydrophobic interactions in binding *S*-(*N*-aryl/alkyl-*N*-hydroxycarbamoyl) glutathiones to the active site of the antitumor target enzyme glyoxalase I. *J. Med. Chem.* 43:3981–6, 2000.

UNIVERSITY OF PITTSBURGH

Department of Chemistry

Programs of Study

The department offers programs of study leading to the M.S. and Ph.D. degrees in analytical, biological, inorganic, organic and physical chemistry and in chemical physics. Interdisciplinary research is currently conducted in the areas of surface science, natural product synthesis, biological chemistry, bioanalytical chemistry, combinatorial chemistry, laser spectroscopy, materials science, electrochemistry, nanoscience, organometallic chemistry, and computational and theoretical chemistry. Both advanced degree programs involve original research and course work. Other requirements include a comprehensive examination, a thesis, a seminar, and, for the Ph.D. candidate, a proposal. For the typical Ph.D. candidate, this process takes four to five years. Representative of current research activities in the department in analytical chemistry are techniques in electroanalytical chemistry, in vivo electrochemistry, UV resonance Raman spectroscopy, micro- and nano-separations, sensors and selective extraction, NMR, EPR, mass spectrometry, and vibrational circular dichroism. Fields of research in biological chemistry include structural dynamics of biological systems, design of soluble membrane proteins, neurochemistry, and molecular design and recognition. In inorganic chemistry, studies are being conducted on organotransition metal complexes, redox reactions, complexes of biological interest, transition metal polymers, and optoelectronic materials; in organic chemistry, on reaction mechanisms, ion transport, total synthesis, drug design, natural products synthesis, bioorganic chemistry, synthetic methodology, organometallics, enzyme mechanisms, and physical-organic chemistry. Research areas in physical chemistry include Raman, photoelectron, Auger, NMR, EPR, infrared, and mass spectroscopy; electron-stimulated desorption ion angular distribution (ESDIAD); condensed phase spectroscopy; high-resolution laser spectroscopy; molecular spectroscopy; electron and molecular beam scattering; electronic emission spectroscopy; and catalysis. Theoretical fields of research include electronic structure, reaction mechanisms, electron transfer theory, quantum mechanics, and new material design. Research on computer applications to chemistry is under way in a variety of areas.

Research Facilities

The Department of Chemistry is housed in two buildings, a fifteen-story and a three-story complex, containing a vast array of modern research instruments and in-house machine, electronics, and glassblowing shops. The Chemistry Library is a spacious 6,000-square-foot facility that contains more than 30,000 monographs and bound periodicals and more than 200 maintained journal subscriptions. These and many related journals, as well as search capabilities, are available online for free. Three other chemistry libraries are nearby. In 2002, the Department of Chemistry received a five-year, $9.6-million grant from the National Institute of General Medical Sciences (NIGMS, a subdivision of NIH) to build one of the nation's first Centers for Excellence in Chemical Methods and Library Development. Shared departmental instrumentation includes four 300-MHz NMRs, one 500-MHz NMR, and one 600-MHz NMR with LC-NMR and MAS capabilities; two high-resolution mass spectrometers; an LC/MS, a triple quadrupole MS, and four low-resolution mass spectrometers; a light-scattering instrument; a circular dichroism spectrophotometer; a spectropolarimeter; X-ray systems—single crystal, powder, and fluorescence; a scanning electron microscope; a vibrating sample magnetometer; several FT-IR and UV-VIS spectrophotometers; and computer and workstation clusters.

Financial Aid

Seventy-five teaching assistantships and teaching fellowships are available. The former provides $19,162 in 2004–05 for the three trimesters of the year; the fellowships (awarded to superior students after their first year) carry an annual stipend of $19,935. Most advanced students are supported by research assistantships and fellowships, which pay up to $1661 per month. All teaching assistantships, fellowships, and research assistantships include a full scholarship that covers all tuition, fees, and medical insurance. Special Kaufman Fellowships provide up to an additional $4000 award to truly outstanding incoming Ph.D. candidates. In addition, Bayer Fellowships, Ashe Fellowships, and Sunoco Fellowships provide salary supplements to research or teaching assistantships that range from $2000 to $5000 annually. In some cases, these supplements may be used to begin research in the summer prior to the formal initiation of graduate study.

Cost of Study

All graduate assistants and fellows receive full tuition scholarships. Tuition and fees for full-time study in 2003 were $11,725 per term for out-of-state students and $6142 for state residents.

Living and Housing Costs

Most graduate students prefer private housing, which is available in a wide range of apartments and rooms in areas of Pittsburgh near the campus. The University maintains a housing office to assist students seeking off-campus housing. Living costs compare favorably with other urban areas.

Student Group

The University enrolls about 17,000 students, including about 9,500 graduate and professional school students. Most parts of the United States and many other countries are represented. Almost 200 full-time graduate chemistry students are supported by the various sources listed under Financial Aid. The University is coeducational in all schools and divisions; more than one third of the graduate chemistry students are women. An honorary chemistry society promotes a social program for all faculty members and graduate students in the department.

Location

Deservedly, Pittsburgh is currently ranked "among the most livable cities in the United States" by Rand McNally. It is recognized for its outstanding blend of cultural, educational, and technological resources. Pittsburgh's famous Golden Triangle is enclosed by the Allegheny and Monongahela Rivers, which meet at the Point in downtown Pittsburgh to form the Ohio River. Pittsburgh has enjoyed a dynamic renaissance in the last few years. The city's cultural resources include the Pittsburgh Ballet, Opera Company, Symphony Orchestra, Civic Light Opera, and Public Theatre and the Three Rivers Shakespeare Festival. Many outdoor activities, such as rock climbing, rafting, sailing, skiing, and hunting, are also available within a 50-mile radius.

The University

The University of Pittsburgh, founded in 1787, is the oldest school west of the Allegheny Mountains. Although privately endowed and controlled, the University is state related to permit lower tuition rates for Pennsylvania residents and to provide a steady source of funds for all of its programs. Attracting more than $310 million in sponsored research annually, the University has continued to increase in stature.

Applying

Applications for September admission and assistantships should be made prior to February 1. However, special cases may be considered throughout the year. A background that includes a B.S. degree in chemistry, with courses in mathematics through integral calculus, is preferred. GRE scores, including the chemistry Subject Test, are required for fellowship consideration (see above). For admission, the General Test of the GRE is required, and the chemistry Subject Test is suggested. International applicants must submit TOEFL results and GRE scores.

Correspondence and Information

Graduate Admissions
Department of Chemistry
University of Pittsburgh
Pittsburgh, Pennsylvania 15260

Telephone: 412-624-8501
E-mail: gradadm@pitt.edu
World Wide Web: http://www.chem.pitt.edu

University of Pittsburgh

THE FACULTY AND THEIR RESEARCH

S. Amemiya, Assistant Professor; Ph.D., Tokyo, 1998. Analytical chemistry: electrochemical sensors, scanning electrochemical microscopy, ion and electron transfer at interfaces, liquid-liquid interfaces, biomembranes, molecular recognition, ion channel.

S. A. Asher, Professor; Ph.D., Berkeley, 1977. Analytical and physical chemistry: resonance Raman spectroscopy, biophysical chemistry, material science, protein folding, nanoscale and mesoscale smart materials, heme proteins, photonic crystals.

K. Brummond, Associate Professor; Ph.D., Penn State, 1991. Organic chemistry: organometallic chemistry, synthesis of natural products, solid phase synthesis.

E. Borguet, Assistant Professor; Ph.D., Pennsylvania, 1993. Physical chemistry: surface science, ultrafast interface dynamics, vibrational (SFG) and electronic (SHG) spectroscopy of interfaces, nanotechnology, self-assembly, scanning probe microscopy (STM, AFM), environmental chemistry.

T. M. Chapman, Associate Professor; Ph.D., Polytechnic of Brooklyn, 1965. Organic chemistry: solid-phase synthesis, polyurethane chemistry, polymer surfactants, new polymers of uncommon architecture, polymer surfactants and emulsifiers, dendritic polymers, biocompatible polyurethanes, tissue engineering, controlled drug delivery.

R. D. Coalson, Professor; Ph.D., Harvard, 1984. Physical chemistry: quantum theory of rate processes, optical spectroscopy, computational techniques for quantum dynamics, structure and energetics of macroions in solution; design of optical waveguides and photonic bandgap structures; laser control of condensed-phase electron transfer; theoretical/computational approaches to the transport of ions and polymers through biological (protein) pores.

T. Cohen, Professor Emeritus; Ph.D., USC, 1955. Organic chemistry: new synthetic methods, particularly those involving organometallics, most often organolithiums; synthesis of natural products and ladder polymers using the new synthetic methods; mechanistic studies.

N. J. Cooper, Professor and Dean, School of Arts and Sciences; D.Phil., Oxford, 1976. Inorganic chemistry: synthetic and mechanistic inorganic and organometallic chemistry, transition metal chemistry of carbon dioxide, synthesis of highly reduced complexes containing metals in negative oxidation states, use of highly reduced metal centers to activate arenas and polyaromatic hydrocarbons, synthesis and reactivity of cationic alkylidene complexes of transition metals, organometallic photochemistry.

D. P. Curran, Bayer Professor and Distinguished Service Professor; Ph.D., Rochester, 1979. Organic chemistry: natural products total synthesis and new synthetic methodology, synthesis via free-radical reactions, fluorous chemistry, combinatorial chemistry.

P. Floreancig, Assistant Professor; Ph.D., Stanford, 1997. Organic chemistry: total synthesis of natural products and bioactive analogs, methodology development, electron transfer chemistry.

M. F. Golde, Associate Professor; Ph.D., Cambridge, 1972. Physical chemistry: kinetic and spectroscopic studies of mechanisms of formation and removal of electronically excited atoms and small molecules, ion-electron recombination and similar species.

J. J. Grabowski, Associate Professor; Ph.D., Colorado, 1983. Physical-organic chemistry: reactive intermediates; reaction mechanisms; novel uses of mass spectrometry and photochemistry for organic, analytical, or environmental chemistry; novel uses of the World Wide Web for chemical education.

K. D. Jordan, Professor and Department Chair; Ph.D., MIT, 1974. Physical chemistry: theoretical studies of the electronic structure of molecules, electron-induced chemistry, computer simulations, hydrogen-bonded clusters, chemical reactions at semiconductor and carbon nanotube surfaces, parallel computational methods.

K. Koide, Assistant Professor; Ph.D., California, San Diego, 1997. Organic chemistry and chemical biology: natural product synthesis, combinatorial library synthesis, fluorescence spectroscopy for bioimaging.

T. Y. Meyer, Associate Professor; Ph.D., Iowa, 1991. Inorganic and polymer chemistry: organometallic chemistry, application of transition metal catalysis to polymer synthesis, polymers with functionalized backbones, polymeric materials for biological applications.

A. C. Michael, Associate Professor; Ph.D., Emory, 1987. Analytical chemistry: new microsensor technologies for neurochemical monitoring in the central nervous system; investigations of the chemical aspects of brain disorders such as Parkinson's disease, schizophrenia, and substance abuse; quantitative aspects of in vivo chemical measurements.

S. G. Nelson, Associate Professor; Ph.D., Rochester, 1991. Organic chemistry: natural products total synthesis, new synthetic methods, asymmetric catalysis and organometallic chemistry.

S. Petoud, Assistant Professor, Ph.D., Lausanne, 1997. Design, synthesis, and investigation of luminescent lanthanide complexes and luminescent material for application in biology, biotechnology, medical diagnostics, genomic and proteomic, and flat color display technologies.

D. W. Pratt, Professor; Ph.D., Berkeley, 1967. Physical chemistry: molecular structure and dynamics, as revealed by high-resolution laser and magnetic resonance spectroscopy, in the gas phase and in the condensed phase; optical trapping, nucleation, and imaging using focused laser beams; science education, especially for nonscience students.

S. K. Saxena, Assistant Professor, Ph.D., Cornell, 1997. Analytical, biophysical, and physical chemistry: two-dimensional Fourier transform electron spin resonance, conformational dynamics, self-assembly and global folding patterns in membrane-associated protein complexes.

C. E. Schafmeister, Assistant Professor; Ph.D., San Francisco, 1997. Organic and biological chemistry: molecular building block design, macromolecular design, ligand design, protein-ligand interactions, engineering of soluble membrane proteins.

P. E. Siska, Professor; Ph.D., Harvard, 1970. Physical chemistry: crossed molecular beam and theoretical studies of intermolecular forces and chemical reaction dynamics, scattering and reactions of excited atoms and ions.

D. H. Waldeck, Professor; Ph.D., Chicago, 1983. Analytical and physical chemistry: ultrafast spectroscopy, electrochemistry, homogenous and heterogenous electron transfer, solvation; electron tunneling; bioelectrochemistry; biophysics; nanoscience; molecular electronics.

G. C. Walker, Associate Professor; Ph.D., Minnesota, 1991. Analytical and biophysical chemistry: directed assembly at surfaces, ligand signaling in proteins and DNA, electron transfer, ultrafast spectroscopy, scanning probe microscopy.

H. E. Warriner, Assistant Professor; Ph.D., California, Santa Barbara, 1997. Physical chemistry, biophysics, and materials science; characterization and design of biomembranes and other medically relevant surfactant-based materials, using various optical microscopies and X-ray scattering techniques.

S. G. Weber, Professor; Ph.D., McGill, 1979. Analytical chemistry: microcolumn HPLC and sensitive detection for bioanalysis, sensors and selective extraction, screening and molecular diversity, and electrochemistry.

C. S. Wilcox, Professor; Ph.D., Caltech, 1979. Organic chemistry: drug discovery; precipitons and separation methods for parallel synthesis and combinatorial chemistry; chemical synthesis, ion pair catalysts; molecular recognition; self-assembling materials.

P. Wipf, Professor and Director, Center for Combinatorial Chemistry; Ph.D., Zurich, 1987. Organic chemistry: total synthesis of natural products; organometallic, heterocyclic, and combinatorial chemistry.

J. T. Yates Jr., Mellon Chair Professor and Director, Surface Science Center; Ph.D., MIT, 1960. Surface science: kinetics of surface processes; vibrational spectroscopy of surface species; electronic spectroscopy of surfaces; catalytic and surface chemistry on model clusters, oxides, and single crystals; semiconductor surfaces; scanning tunneling microscopy; nanoscience; photochemistry of surfaces.

UNIVERSITY OF PUERTO RICO, RÍO PIEDRAS

Department of Chemistry

Programs of Study

The Department of Chemistry of the University of Puerto Rico, Río Piedras campus, offers programs of study that lead to the M.S. and Ph.D. degrees. Both degree programs require the presentation and oral defense of a thesis. Students should have knowledge of Spanish and/or English. All students select research advisers and begin research by the end of the first year. Areas of concentration are biochemistry and analytical, inorganic, organic, and physical chemistry. An interdepartmental doctoral program in chemical physics is also offered.

M.S. students normally complete the thesis and the required 21 semester credits in courses during the second year. Students pursuing the Ph.D. degree must pass qualifying examinations in three major areas by the end of the first year, after which they must present two research proposals; one proposal is related to the student research project. Forty-two semester credits in courses and 24 in research are required for the Ph.D. One year as a teaching assistant is required for all students.

Research Facilities

The Facundo Bueso Building houses the Office of the Graduate Program and all the laboratories, classrooms, and services used by the program. Extensive renovation and modernization of the laboratories has been recently completed. Major equipment and instruments necessary for research are available, including lasers, a single photon-counting spectrofluorimeter, two X-ray diffractometers, and FT-NMR, FT-IR, and GC-MS spectrometers. There is a wide variety of equipment in individual research laboratories, including electrochemical analyzers, a quartz-crystal microbalance, UV-Vis spectrophotometers, DSC, HPLC/GC, a fluorometer, and computers. The department has electronics, scientific illustration, machine, and glassblowing shops. Facilities to support research include the Materials Science and Surface Characterization, Biotesting, and Computational Chemistry Centers. Undergraduate chemistry classes and laboratories are held in another building. The Science Library is in a new building of the College of Natural Sciences.

Financial Aid

The research program of the department is supported by funds from the University and from government and industrial grants. Both teaching and research assistantships are available from these sources. Support for students from Latin America may also be obtained from foundations and from the OAS. Support of $1000 to $1200 per month plus remission of tuition and fees is available, depending on the qualifications of the student.

Cost of Study

For 2002–03, tuition and fees for students who were not teaching or research assistants were $75 per credit hour for residents. There is a nonresident fee, which is about $1750 per semester for international students or equal to the nonresident fee charged by the state university in the state where the student resides.

Living and Housing Costs

University housing is very limited, but private apartments and rooms are available in the University area. Housing costs vary from $150 to $300 per month per student.

Student Group

A total of 125 students (local and international) are enrolled in the graduate programs in chemistry, a number that permits careful supervision of each student's progress and needs. Postdoctorals and visiting scientists also participate in the program.

Location

The University is located in a residential suburb of San Juan, the capital and cultural center of Puerto Rico. The numerous historical sites and the carefully restored buildings of Old San Juan give the city a highly individual character. With its perennially pleasant climate, excellent beaches, and convenient transportation to North and South America and all the Caribbean, San Juan is the center of tourism in the Caribbean, and its residents enjoy a wide variety of entertainment and recreational facilities.

The University

The University of Puerto Rico, founded in 1903, is supported by the Commonwealth of Puerto Rico. Río Piedras, the oldest and largest campus, includes the Colleges of Natural Sciences, Social Sciences, Humanities, General Studies, Law, Education, and Business Administration, and a School of Architecture, a graduate School of Planning, and a School of Library Science. The Medical School is located near the Río Piedras campus and the Engineering School is at the Mayagüez campus of the University. Facilities at the 288-acre Río Piedras campus are rapidly being expanded and remodeled. The student body of the Río Piedras campus consists of 22,000 full-time students in eight colleges.

Applying

The application for admission, including scores of the chemistry Subject Test of the Graduate Record Examinations, should be addressed to the Department of Chemistry and returned no later than the first week of February. The application for financial assistance also should be sent to the Department of Chemistry.

Correspondence and Information

Graduate Program Coordinator
Department of Chemistry
University of Puerto Rico, Río Piedras
P.O. Box 23346
San Juan, Puerto Rico 00931-3346
Telephone: 787-764-0000 Ext. 2445, 4818, or 4817
Fax: 787-756-8242
E-mail: ncarball@upracd.upr.clu.edu
World Wide Web: http://web.uprr.pr/chemistry
http://graduados.uprrp.edu

University of Puerto Rico, Río Piedras

THE FACULTY AND THEIR RESEARCH

Rafael Arce, Professor; Ph.D., Wisconsin, 1971. Physical chemistry (photochemistry): photochemistry and photophysics of purine bases and their derivatives, heterogeneous photochemistry of organic pollutants, ESR, laser photolysis, fluorescence.

Carlos R. Cabrera, Professor; Ph.D., Cornell, 1987. Analytical chemistry (electrochemistry): photoelectrochemistry, batteries, electrocatalysis (fuel cells), surface analysis.

Néstor Carballeira, Professor and Graduate Program Coordinator; Ph.D., Würzburg (Germany), 1983. Organic chemistry: organic reaction mechanisms, lipid chemistry and biosynthesis of marine natural products.

Jorge L. Colón, Associate Professor; Ph.D., Texas A&M, 1989. Inorganic and bioinorganic chemistry: electron transfer and ligand binding in heme proteins, photophysics and photochemistry of luminescent molecules in inorganic layered materials and electropolymerized films, photoinduced charge separation.

Fernando A. González, Professor; Ph.D., Cornell, 1989. Biochemistry and molecular biology: signal transduction by nucleotide P2 receptors.

Kai Griebenow, Associate Professor; Ph.D., Max Planck Institute (Mühlheim), 1992. Biochemistry: sustained delivery of proteins, nonaqueous enzymology, protein structure and stability.

Ana R. Guadalupe, Professor; Ph.D., Cornell, 1987. Analytical chemistry (electrochemistry): polymer-modified electrodes, chemical sensors and biosensors, electrocatalysis.

Yasuyuki Ishikawa, Professor; Ph.D., Iowa, 1976. Theoretical chemistry: relativistic effects in atoms and molecules, investigated by relativistic many-body theory; Monte Carlo simulations of quantum many-body systems.

Reginald Morales, Professor; Ph.D., Rutgers, 1976. Biochemistry: phospholipid organization on cell surfaces, phospholipases as probes of membrane structure, structure-function relationships of lipid analogues, phospholipid synthesis and analysis.

José A. Prieto, Professor; Ph.D., Puerto Rico, 1982. Organic chemistry: organic synthesis, synthesis of biologically active compounds, Lewis acid catalysis.

Edwin Quiñones, Professor; Ph.D., Puerto Rico, 1986. Physical chemistry: dynamics of elementary chemical reactions, laser-induced reactions within molecular van der Waals clusters, energy transfer collisions, Doppler spectroscopy, magnetic field effects in small molecules, photochemistry and photophysics in microheterogeneous systems (micelles, microvesicles, cyclodextrins, sol-gels).

Raphael G. Raptis, Associate Professor; Ph.D., Texas A&M, 1988. Inorganic chemistry: synthesis, X-ray crystallography, electrochemistry, spectroelectrochemistry, bioinorganic chemistry, metal clusters, metal-metal bonds, small molecule activation.

José M. Rivera, Assistant Professor; Ph.D., MIT, 2000. Organic chemistry, molecular recognition, supramolecular chemistry, nanotechnology, bioorganic chemistry, organic synthesis.

Abimael D. Rodriguez, Professor; Ph.D., Johns Hopkins, 1983. Organic chemistry: isolation, characterization, and synthesis of marine natural products.

Osvaldo Rosario, Professor; Ph.D., Puerto Rico, 1978. Analytical chemistry: development of methods for the analysis of environmental pollutants, analysis of air pollutants, gas chromatography–mass spectrometry, artifacts during sampling.

Eugene S. Smotkin, Associate Professor; Ph.D., Texas at Austin, 1989. Physical chemistry, electrochemistry, catalysis, high-throughput analytical chemistry.

John A. Soderquist, Professor; Ph.D., Colorado, 1977. Organic chemistry: organometallic reagents in organic synthesis and natural product chemistry, stereochemically defined functional derivatives of main group organometallics, silicon-containing analogues of natural products, metal-metalloid combinations for organic synthesis.

Brad R. Weiner, Professor and Dean; Ph.D., California, Davis, 1986. Physical chemistry: laser studies of molecular reaction dynamics, photochemistry and photophysics with lasers, radical kinetics in gaseous phase, nonlinear processes, molecular energy transfer.

SELECTED PUBLICATIONS

Crespo-Hernández, C., **R. Arce,** and **E. Quiñones.** Magnetic field enhanced photoinization of 6-methypurine. *Chem. Phys. Lett.,* in press.

Fioressi, S., and **R. Arce.** Excited sates and intermediate species of benzo[e] pyrene photolyzed in solution and adsorbed on surfaces. *J. Phys. Chem. B* 107:5968–75, 2003.

Crespo-Hernández, C., and **R. Arce.** Near-threshold photooxidation of dinucleotides containing purines upon 266 nm nanosecond laser exicitation. The effect of base stacking, conformation, and concentration. *J. Phys. Chem. B* 107:1062–70, 2003.

Crespo-Hernández, C., and **R. Arce.** Photoionization of DNA and RNA bases, nucleosides, and nucleotides through a combination of one- and two-photon pathways upon 266 nm nanosecond laser excitation. *Photochem. Photobiol.* 76:259–67, 2002.

Arce, R., et al. Photophysical and photochemical properties of amitriptyline nortriptyline hydrochloride. *J. Photochem. Photobiol., A Chem.* 170:1–13, 2002.

Garcia, C., et al. **(R. Arce).** Photophysical, electrochemical, and theoretical study of protriptyline in several solvents. *J. Phys. Chem. A* 106:9794–801, 2002.

Méndez, E. E., et al. **(R. Arce** and **E. Quiñones).** Mechanism of formation of the MV^+ radical during the UV excitation of methylviologen. *J. Photochem. Photobiol., A Chem.* 142:19–24, 2001.

Blasini, D. R., et al. **(C. R. Cabrera).** Self-assembled (3-mercaptopropyl)trimethoxysilane on iodine coated gold electrodes. *J. Electroanal. Chem.* 540:45–52, 2003.

Brito, R., R. Tremont, and **C. R. Cabrera.** Chemical derivatization of self-assembled 3-mercaptopropionic and 16-mercaptohexadecanoic acids at platinum surfaces with 3-aminopropyltrimethoxusilane: A spectroscopic and electrochemical study. *J. Electroanal. Chem.* 540:53–59, 2003.

Tremont, R., and **C. R. Cabrera.** Pt electrodeposition on copper surfaces modified with 3-mercaptopropyltrimethoxysilane and 1-propanol. *J. Electroanal. Chem.* 558:65–74, 2003.

Fachini, E. R., R. Diaz, E. Casado, and **C. R. Cabrera.** Surface coordination of ruthenim cluster on platinum nanoparticles for methanol oxidation catalysts. *Langmuir* 19:8986–93, 2003.

Tremont, R., and **C. R. Cabrera.** Electrochemical and surface analysis of copper-corrosion protection by 1-propanethiol and propyltrimethoxysilane: A comparison with 3-mercaptopropyltrimethoxysilane. *J. Appl. Electrochem.* 32:783–93, 2002.

Carballeira, N. M., D. Oritz, K. Parang, and S. Sardari. Total synthesis and in vitro antifungal activity of (±)-2-methoxytetradecanoic acid. *Arch. Pharm. Med. Chem.,* in press.

Carballeira, N. M., H. Cruz, E. A. Orellano, and **F. A. González.** The first total synthesis of the marine fatty acid (±)-2-methoxy-13-methyltetradecanoic acid. A cytotoxic fatty acid to leukemia cells. *Chem. Phys. Lipids* 2:149–53, 2003.

Carballeira, N. M., H. Cruz, and G. V. Hillyer. Fatty acids bound to fasciola hepatica 12 kD: Fatty acid binding protein, a candidate vaccine, differ from fatty acids in extracts of adult flukes. *Lipids* 38769–72, 2003.

Carballeira N. M., and C. Miranda. The first total synthesis of the marine fatty acid (±)-9-methoxypentadecanoic acid. A synthetic route towards mid-chain methoxylated fatty acids. *Chem. Phys. Lipids* 12463–7, 2003.

Carballeira, N. M., H. Cruz, and N. L. Ayala. Total synthesis of the 2-methoxy-14-methylpemadecanoic acid and the novel 2-methoxy-14-methylhexadecanoic acid identified in the sponge agelas dispar. *Lipids* 371033–7, 2002.

Carballeira, N. M., J. E. Betancourt, E. A. Orellano, and **F. A. González.** Total synthesis and biological evaluation of (5Z,9Z)-5,9-hexadecadienoic acid, an inhibitor of human topoisomerase I. *J. Nat. Prod.* 65:1715–18, 2002.

Marti, A. A., and **J. L. Colón.** Direct ion exchange of tris(2,2'-bipyridl)ruthenium(ii) into a zirconium phosphate type framework. *Inorg. Chem.* 42:2830–2, 2003.

Langen, R., and **J. L. Colón** et al. Electron tunneling in proteins: Role of the intervening medium. *J. Biol. Inorg. Chem.* 1:221–5, 1996.

Navarro, A. M., et al. **(J. L. Colón).** Control of carbon monoxide–binding states and dynamics in hemoglobin I of *Lucina pectinata* by nearby aromatic residues. *Inorg. Chim. Acta* 243:161–6, 1996.

Casimiro, D. R., et al. **(J. L. Colón).** Electron transfer in ruthenium/zinc porphyrin derivatives of recombinant human myoglobins. Analysis of tunneling pathways in myoglobin and cytochrome c. *J. Am. Chem. Soc.* 115:1485–9, 1993.

Colón, J. L., and C. R. Martin. Luminescence probe studies of ionomers 3. Distribution of decay rate constants for tris(2,2'-bipyridyl)ruthenium(ii) in nafion membranes. *Langmuir* 9:1066–70, 1993.

Xu, J., et al. **(F. A. González).** Prostaglandin E2 production in astrocytesregulation by cytokines, extracellular ATP, and oxidative stress. *Prostaglandins Leukot. Essent. Fatty Acids,* in press.

Gendron, F. P., et al. **(F. A. González).** $P2X_7$ nucleotide receptor activation enhances IFN-γ-induced type II nitric oxide synthase activity in BV-2 microglial cells. *J. Neurochem.* 87:344–52, 2003.

Seye, C. I., et al. **(F. A. González).** The P2Y2 nucleotide receptor mediates UTP-induced vascular cell adhesion molecule-1 expression in coronary artery endothelial cells. *J. Biol. Chem.* 278:24960–5, 2003.

Gendron, F. P., et al. **(F. A. González).** Signal transduction pathways for P2Y2 and P2X7 nucleotide receptors that mediate neuroinflammatory responses in astrocytes and microglial cells. *Biomed. Res.* 1446, 2003.

Gendron, F. P., et al. **(F. A. González).** Mechanisms of $P2X_7$ receptor-mediated ERK1/2 phosphorylation in human astrocytoma cells. *Am. J. Physiol.-Cell Physiol.* 284:C571–81, 2003.

Seye, C.I., et al. **(F. A. González).** Functional $P2Y_2$ nucleotide receptors mediate intimal hyperplasia in collared-rabbit carotid arteries. *Circulation* 106:2720–6, 2002.

Santos, A. M., M. González, Y. Pacheco, and **K. Griebenow.** Comparison of theoretical and experimental data to evaluate substrate diffusional limitations for crown ether- and methyl-b-cyclodextrin-activated serine protease subtilisin Carlsberg in tetrahydrofuran. *Biotechnol. Bioeng.* 84:324–31, 2003.

Eker, F., **K. Griebenow,** and R. Schweitzer-Stenner. Stable conformations of tripeptides in aqueous solution studied by UV circular dichroism spectroscopy. *J. Am. Chem. Soc.* 125:8178–85, 2003.

Huang, Q., W. Al-Azzam, **K. Griebenow,** and R. Schweitzer-Stenner. Heme structural perturbation of PEG-modified horseradish peroxidase c in aromatic organic solvents. *Biophys. J.* 84:3285–98, 2003.

Pérez, C., and **K. Griebenow.** Effect of salts on lysozyme stability at the water-oil interface and upon encapsulation in poly(lactic-*co*-glycolic) acid microspheres. *Biotechnol. Bioeng.* 82:825–32, 2003.

Pérez-Rodríguez, C., N. Montano, K. González, and **K. Griebenow.** Stabilization of chymotrypsin at the CH_2Cl_2/water interface and upon water-in-oil-in-water encapsulation in PLGA microspheres. *J. Controlled Release* 8971–85, 2003.

Feng, M., F. Alejandro, F. González, and **A. Guadalupe.** Electrochemical and spectroscopic studies of the chemical interaction and binding of poly- [Fe (4-vinyl-4'-methyl-2, 2-bipyridine)$_3$]Cl_2 to calf-thymus DNA, in press.

Zhiqin, J., H. Songping, and **A. R. Guadalupe.** Synthesis, X-ray structures, spectroscopic and electrochemical properties of ruthenium (II) complex containing 2,2'- bipyrimidine. *Inorg. Chim. Acta* 305:127–34, 2000.

Guo, Y., and **A. R. Guadalupe.** Chemical-derived Prussian blue sol-gel composite thin films. *Chem. Mater.* 11(1):135–40, 1999.

Ikegami, T., N. Kurita, H. Sekino, and **Y. Ishikawa.** Mechanism of cis-to-trans isomerization of azobenzene. Direct MD study. *J. Phys. Chem. A* 107:4555, 2003.

Vilkas, M. J., and **Y. Ishikawa.** Relativistic multireference many-body perturbation theory calculations on the multiple openshell states in siliconlike Ar and aluminumlike Fe ions. *Phys. Rev. A* 68:12503, 2003.

Vilkas, M. J., and **Y. Ishikawa.** Relativistic multireference many-body perturbation theory calculators on siliconlike argon, iron and krypton ions. *J. Phys. B* 36:4641, 2003.

Ishikawa, Y., M. S. Liao, and **C. Cabrera.** Energetics of H_2O dissociation and CO_{ads} + OH_{ads} reaction on a series of Pt-M mixed-metals clusters: A relativistic density functional study. *Surf. Sci.* 513:98, 2002.

Ishikawa, Y., T. Nakajima, T. Yanai, and K. Hirao. Ab initio-direct MD study of the fragmentation of $F(H_2O)$ complex generated by photodetachment of $F(H_2O)$ anion complex. *Chem. Phys. Lett.* 363:458, 2002.

Kirchstetter, T. W., T. Novakov, **R. Morales,** and **O. Rosario.** Differences in the volatility of organic aerosols in unpolluted tropical and polluted continental atmospheres. *J. Geophys Res. (Atmos.)* 105:26547–54, 2000.

Arbelo, D. O., L. Castro-Rosario, and **J. A. Prieto.** Efficient hydroxyl inversion in polypropionates via cesium carboxylates. *Synthetic Commun.* 33:3211–23, 2003.

University of Puerto Rico, Río Piedras

Selected Publications (continued)

Montes, I., **J. A. Prieto,** and M. García. Using molecular modeling in the organic chemistry course for majors. *Chem. Educator* 7:293–6, 2002.

Arbelo, D. O., and **J. A. Prieto.** A new epoxide-inversion methodology mediated by cesium propionate. *Tetrahedron Lett.* 43:4111–4, 2002.

Arias, L., D. Arbelo, A. Alzérreca, and **J. A. Prieto.** Synthesis of functionalized enamines from lithium alkyl phenyl sulfones and N-carbo-*tert*-butoxy lactams. *J. Heterocyclic Chem.* 38:29–33, 2001.

Cox, O., and **J. A. Prieto** et al. Synthesis and complete 1H and 13C assignments of thiazolo[3,2-quinolinium derivatives. *J. Heterocyclic Chem.* 36:937–42, 1999.

Alzerreca, A., E. Hernandez, E. Magual, and **J. A. Prieto.** Phenylsulfonyl-methylenation of aldonolactones. *J. Heterocyclic Chem.* 36:555–9, 1999.

Lei, Y., V. I. Makarov, C. Conde, and **E. Quiñones.** Laser-initiated processes within (SO2)m(NO)r weakly bound clusters. *Chem. Phys.*, in press.

Makarov, V. I., and **E. Quiñones.** Magnetic field quenching of individual rotational levels of the A1Au, 2v3 state of acetylene. *J. Chem. Phys.* 118:87–92, 2003.

Makarov, V. I., À. R. Cruz, and **E. Quiñones.** Collisional nature of the magnetic-field quenching of the acetylene A^1 *Au* state. *Chem. Phys.* 264:101–10, 2001.

Boca, R., et al. **(R. G. Raptis).** Trinuclear ferromagnetically coupled CuII-pyrazolato complexes as models of particulate methane monooxygenase (pMMO). *Inorg. Chem.* 42:5801, 2003.

Mezei, G., and **R. G. Raptis.** Pyrazole-4-sulphonate networks of alkali and alkaline earh metals. Effects of cation size, charge, H-bonding and aromatic interactions on the three-dimencional supramolecular architecture. *New J. Chem.* 9:1399, 2003.

Yang, G., and **R. G. Raptis.** Synthesis, characterization and crystal structures of two 2-naphthyl substituted pyrazoles. *J. Heterocycl. Chem.* 40:659, 2003.

Yang, G., and **R. G. Raptis.** Supramolecular assembly of trimeric gold(I) pyrazolates through aurophilic attractions. *Inorg. Chem.* 42:261, 2003.

Yang, G., and **R. G. Raptis.** Synthesis, structure, and properties of tetrameric gold(I) 3,5-di-*tert*-butyl-pyrazolate. *Inorg. Chim. Acta* 352:98, 2003.

Rivera, J. M., T. Martín, and J. Rebek Jr. Chiral softballs: Synthesis and molecular recognition properties. *J. Am. Chem. Soc.* 123:5213–20, 2001.

Rivera, J. M., S. L. Craig, T. Martín, and J. Rebek Jr. Chiral guests and their ghosts in reversibly assembled hosts. *Angew. Chem. Int. Ed.* 39:2130–2, 2000.

Rivera, J. M., and J. Rebek Jr. Chiral space in a unimolecular capsule. *J. Am. Chem. Soc.* 122:7811–2, 2000.

Schalley, C. A., and **J. M. Rivera** et al. Structural examination of supramolecular architectures by electrospray ionization mass spectrometry. *Eur. J. Org. Chem.* 1325–31, 1999.

Jimenez, M. S., S. P. Garzon, and **A. D. Rodríguez.** Plakortides M and N bioactive polyketide endoperoxides from the caribbean marine sponge *Plakortis halichondroides. J. Nat. Prod.* 66:655–61, 2003.

Rodríguez, L. I., and **A. D. Rodríguez.** Homopseudopteroxazole: A new antimycobacterial diterpene alkaloid from *Pseudopterogorgia elisabethae* (Bayer). *J. Nat. Prod.* 66:855–7, 2003.

Shi, Y.-P., I. I. Rodríguez, and **A. D. Rodríguez.** Elisapterosins D and E complex polycyclic diterpenes of the rare elisapterane class of natural products from the Caribbean sea whip *Pseudopterogorgia elisabethae* (Bayer). *Tetrahedron Lett.* 44:3249–53, 2003.

Marrero, J., **A. D. Rodríguez,** P. Baran, and **R. G. Raptis.** Isolation and characterization of kallosin A: A novel rearranged pseudopterane diterpenoid from the Caribbean Sea plume *Pseudopterogorgia kallos* (Bielschowsky). *J. Org. Chem.* 68:4977–9, 2003.

Marrero, J., **A. D. Rodríguez,** P. Baran, and **R. G. Raptis.** Isolation and structure of providencin: A highly oxygenated diterpene possessing a unique bicyclo[12.2.0]hexadecanc ring system from the sea plume *Pseudopterogorgia kallos. Org. Lett.* 5:2551–4, 2003.

Colón, I., D. Caro, and **O. Rosario.** Analysis of exogenous compounds in the serum of young Puerto Rican girls with premature thelarche. *Environ. Health Perspect.*, in press.

Reyes, D. R., **O. Rosario,** J. F. Rodríguez, and B. D. Jiménez. Toxic evaluation of organic extracts from airborne particulate matter in Puerto Rico. *Environ. Health Perspect.*, in press.

Mayol, O., et al. **(O. Rosario and R. Morales).** Chemical characterization of submicron, organic aerosols in the tropical trade winds in the Caribbean, using gas chromatograph/mass spectrometry. *Atmos. Environ.* 35:1735–45, 2001.

Rodríguez, J. F., J. L. Rodríguez, J. Santana, and **O. Rosario.** Simultaneous quantitation of intracellular zidovudine and lamivudine-triphosphate in HIV-infected individuals. *Antimicrob. Agents Chemother.* 44:3097, 2000.

Gurau, B., and **E. S. Smotkin.** Methanol crossover in direct methanol fuel cells: A link between power and energy density. *J. Power Sources,* in press.

Liu, R., and **E. S. Smotkin.** Array membrane-electrode assemblies for high-throughput screening of direct methanol fuel-cell catalysts. *J. Electroanal. Chem.,* in press.

Nayar, A., et al. **(E. S. Smotkin).** Laser-activated membrane introduction mass spectrometry for high-throughput evaluation of bulk heterogeneous catalysts. *Anal. Chem.* 74(9):1933–8, 2002.

Viswanathan, R., R. Liu, and **E. S. Smotkin.** In-situ X-ray absorption fuel cell. *Rev. Sci. Instrum.* 73(5):2124–7, 2002.

Lei, H.-W., et al. **(E. S. Smotkin).** Deuterium isotope analysis of methanol oxidation on mixed-metal anode catalysts. *Electrochim. Acta* 47:2913–9, 2002.

Kim, Y.-T., and **E. S. Smotkin.** The effect of plasticizers on transport and electrochemical properties of PEO-based electrolytes for lithium rechargeable batteries. *Solid State Ionics* 149:29–37, 2002.

Sanicharane, S., et al. **(E. S. Smotkin).** In-situ 50°C tandem surface reflective/exhaust-transmission spectroscopy of direct methanol fuel cell-membrane electrode assemblies. *J. Electrochem. Soc.* 149(5): A554–7, 2002.

Viswanathan, R., et al. **(E. S. Smotkin).** In-situ XANES study of carbon-supported Pt-Ru anode electrocatalysts for reformate-air polymer electrolyte fuel cells. *J. Phys. Chem. B* 106(13):3458–65, 2002.

Jones, F., III, et al. **(E. S. Smotkin).** Synthesis and characterization of PtSn/carbon and Pt_3Sn/carbon nanocomposites as methanol electrooxidation catalysts. *J. Nanoscience and Nanotechnology* 2(1):81–7, 2002.

Soderquist, J. A., R. Huertas, and G. Leon-Colon. Aryl and vinyl cyclopropanes through the in-situ generation of B-Cyclopropyl-9-BBN and its suzuki-miyaura coupling. *Tetrahedron Lett.* 41:4251, 2000.

Soderquist, J. A., and J. C. Justo de Pomar. A versatile synthesis of 9-BBN derivatives from organometallic reagents and 9-(Triisopropylsilyl)Thio-9-Borabicyclo[3.3.1]Nonane. *Tetrahedron Lett.* 41:3537, 2000.

Antomattei, A., **J. A. Soderquist,** and S. D. Huang. Hexaisopropyldisilane. *Z. Kristallogr. NCS* 214:43–4, 1999.

Gupta, S., **B. R. Weiner,** and G. Morell. Influence of sulfur incorporation on electron-field emission from chemical vapor–deposited microcrystalline diamond thin films. *J. Vac. Sci. Technol.,* in press.

Gupta, S., **B. R. Weiner,** and G. Morell. Synthesis and characterization of sulfur-incorporated microcrystalline diamond and nanocomposite carbon thin films by hot-filament, chemical vapor deposition. *J. Mater. Res,* in press.

Gupta, S., **B. R. Weiner,** and G. Morell. Ex-situ spectroscopic ellipsometry investigation of sulfur-incorporated, nanocrystalline carbon thin films. *J. Appl. Phys.,* in press.

Gupta, S., et al. **(B. R. Weiner).** Electron field-emission properties of gamma-irradiated microcrystalline diamond and nanocomposite carbon thin films. *J. Appl. Phys.* 92:3311, 2002.

Gupta, S., A. Martínez, **B. R. Weiner,** and G. Morell. Electrical conductivity studies of chemical vapor deposited, sulfur-incorporated nanocomposite carbon thin films. *Appl. Phys. Lett.* 81:283, 2002.

Gupta, S., **B. R. Weiner,** and G. Morell. Electron field-emission properties of microcrystalline and nanocrystalline carbon thin films deposited by S-assisted hot-filament CVD. *Diamond Relat. Mater.* 11:799, 2002.

Gupta, S., **B. R. Weiner,** and G. Morell. Investigations of the electron field-emission properties and microstructure correlation in sulfur-incorporated nanocrystalline carbon thin films. *J. Appl. Phys.* 91:10088, 2002.

Gupta, S., **B. R. Weiner,** and G. Morell. Role of sp^2C cluster on field-emission properties of sulfur-incorporated nanocrystalline carbon thin films grown by chemical vapor deposition. *Appl. Phys. Lett.* 80:1471, 2002.

Gupta, S., **B. R. Weiner,** and G. Morrell. Ex situ spectroscopic ellipsometry investigation of the layered structure of polycrystalline diamond thin films grown by electron cyclotron resonance-assisted chemical vapor deposition. *J. Appl. Phys.* 90:1280, 2001.

UNIVERSITY OF TOLEDO

Department of Chemistry

Programs of Study

The University of Toledo Department of Chemistry offers graduate programs leading to the M.S. and Ph.D. degrees. A wide range of research topics are available for study within the subdisciplines of analytical, biological, inorganic, materials, organic, and physical chemistry. Collaborative interactions with the departments of biology, medicinal and biological chemistry, physics, and chemical engineering, as well as with various industrial partners enhance the research opportunities and interactions for students.

The major purpose of the graduate program is to educate graduate students to participate in the advancing field of chemistry as a professional chemist in industry or academia. This education involves specialized course work, teaching classes as a teaching assistant, attending seminars and scientific meetings, and completing research projects that contribute to the growth of scientific knowledge. The main requirements for the M.S. degree are the satisfactory completion of course work and the research leading to the successful defense of a written thesis. Students typically complete an M.S. degree in two to three years. The Ph.D. program is described in three stages. The first stage involves course work to provide a foundation for chemical research. During the second stage, students undertake research toward their dissertation and take a comprehensive examination for admission to Ph.D. candidacy. The final stage is devoted to research for completion and defense of the dissertation. Ph.D. students also present a literature seminar during this stage. Ph.D. students usually complete these requirements in four to five years.

Research Facilities

The chemistry research facilities are housed in the Bowman-Oddy/Wolfe Hall complex. Wolfe Hall, which opened in 1998 adjacent to the Bowman-Oddy Laboratories, is a 165,000-square-foot research and teaching facility.

The department maintains an extensive array of modern scientific instrumentation for research. This includes the College of Arts and Sciences Instrumentation Center, which houses more than $45 million of instrumentation, and the Ohio Crystallography Consortium, which distinguishes the department as the center of excellence in Ohio for crystallographic research. Single crystal X-ray analysis for both small molecules and biological macromolecules, as well as powders, is routine. In addition to a wide range of specialized equipment found in individual research laboratories, the department has a dedicated NMR laboratory with 200-, 400-, and 600-MHz NMR spectrometers for solution samples and a 200-MHz NMR spectrometer for solids. A separations laboratory includes an LC-MS, three GC-MS, two GCs, and two LC systems for isocratic and gradient capabilities. Hands-on use by students is encouraged and is integrated into graduate course work. Department and college instrumentation specialists are available for training, consultation, and equipment maintenance.

Financial Aid

The 2004–05 assistantship stipends for full-time students are $19,000 for Ph.D. students and $15,000 for M.S. students on twelve-month appointments. Additional merit fellowships from $1000 to $3000 are also available for qualified applicants. Assistantships also include a full waiver of tuition and instructional fees, with a value of approximately $12,500 (in-state) or $25,000 (out-of-state), a subsidy for health insurance, and a subsidy for parking. The total financial package is equivalent to $27,500 to $44,000 per year, depending on the degree program and residence status. Both teaching and research assistantships are available.

Cost of Study

The primary remaining cost of study is the University general fee of $550 per semester and the cost of textbooks. One-time matriculation fees upon entrance to the University and graduation fees upon completion of the program of approximately $100 are also required. Stipends are subject to U.S. Federal and State of Ohio income tax.

Living and Housing Costs

The University of Toledo does not have on-campus graduate student housing. Many apartment complexes, rooms, and houses are available close to the University and connected to campus by a University-operated bus service. An up-to-date housing listing is available at http://www.student-services.utoledo.edu/residencelife/offcampus/. Average monthly rent for a one-bedroom apartment is $350 to $500. Food and entertainment costs are low compared to those in larger cities.

Student Group

The department currently has 55 graduate students, with the goal to increase enrollment to 80 students in the next five years. The typical student group is 50 percent U.S. citizens and 50 percent international students, with half of the international students from countries in Europe. Equal numbers of male and female students are in the program. Two thirds of the students are supported by teaching assistantships and one third are supported by research assistantships from grant-funded research projects. Eighty percent of the students are pursuing the Ph.D. degree. Qualities sought in applicants include intellectual curiosity, strong motivation for learning, and problem-solving ability.

Student Outcomes

Graduates of the chemistry program are very successful obtaining high-profile and rewarding positions in industry and academia. Recent graduates have accepted industrial positions at companies such as Pfizer, Merck, Procter and Gamble, Eli-Lilly, DuPont, and Millenium Pharmaceticals. Graduates have accepted faculty or postdoctoral research positions at numerous colleges and universities throughout the U.S. and the world.

Location

The University's campus is located in the western residential suburbs of Toledo and has the advantage of a suburban parklike setting with the shopping and living conveniences of a large population base. Toledo has an excellent system of metroparks for biking and hiking and is close to the recreational opportunities offered by Lake Erie and the Maumee River. The city is internationally known for the Toledo Mud Hens baseball team, the Toledo Museum of Art, the Toledo Zoo, and the University.

The University and The Department

The University of Toledo is a member of the State University System of Ohio and recognized as one of the nation's major regional universities with an undergraduate and graduate student enrollment of 21,000. The University athletic teams compete in the Mid-American Conference and enjoy a rich tradition of success inside and outside the conference. The Department of Chemistry is considered one of the strongest departments on campus and the top producer of M.S. and Ph.D. students in the sciences. External funding for research averages $100,000 per faculty member per year.

Applying

Applications should be submitted directly to the Graduate Admissions Committee at the address below. An application can be obtained online at the department Web site. A complete application includes the application form, three letters of recommendation, a copy of all previous undergraduate or graduate transcripts, and scores from the aptitude portion of the Graduate Record Examinations (GRE). International students are also required to submit scores from the TOEFL examination. Applications should be completed by March 1 for fall admission and merit fellowship consideration, although later applications are considered depending on the availability of assistantship funds.

Correspondence and Information

Jon R. Kirchhoff, Ph.D.
Chair, Graduate Admissions Committee
Department of Chemistry
Mail Stop 602
University of Toledo
Toledo, Ohio 43606-3390

Telephone: 419-530-2100
Fax: 419-530-4033
E-mail: utchem@uoft02.utoledo.edu
World Wide Web: http://www.chem.utoledo.edu

University of Toledo

THE FACULTY AND THEIR RESEARCH

Bruce A. Averill, Distinguished University Professor; Ph.D., MIT, 1973. Inorganic and Biochemistry: synthetic models for metalloproteins, spectroscopic and mechanistic studies of metalloenzymes.

John Chrysochoos, Professor; Ph.D., British Columbia, 1964. Physical: spectroscopy of lanthanides in solution, single crystals, and glasses; semiconductors; photophysical processes of metalloporhyrins; interfacial electron transfer.

Julian A. Davies, Distinguished University Professor; Ph.D., London, 1979. Inorganic and Organic: synthetic, mechanistic, and structural organometallic and coordination chemistry, including applications in catalysis, materials science, and biology.

Eric W. Findsen, Associate Professor; Ph.D., New Mexico, 1986. Biophysical and Physical: Raman and time-resolved Raman spectroscopy of metalloporphyrins and protein systems.

Max O. Funk, Professor; Ph.D., Duke, 1975. Bioorganic and Biochemistry: investigations of lipoxygenase structure and mechanism of action, enzymology.

Dean M. Giolando, Professor; Ph.D., Illinois, 1987. Inorganic and Organometallic: synthetic, structural analysis, and reactivity studies on compounds containing the main group elements; molecular single-source precursors to solid-state materials.

Xiche Hu, Associate Professor; Ph.D., Wayne State, 1991. Computational and Biophysical: quantum chemical analysis of intermolecular interactions, mechanism of energy transfer in the bacterial photosynthetic membrane, membrane-protein structure prediction, X-ray crystallographic computing.

Xuefei Huang, Assistant Professor; Ph.D., Columbia, 1999. Organic and Bioorganic: synthesis of oligosaccharides, assembly of oligosaccharide libraries, study of carbohydrate-protein interactions and conformational change of proteins.

Richard A. Hudson, Professor; Ph.D., Chicago, 1966. Bioorganic, Biochemistry, and Medicinal Chemistry: design of peptide peptidomimetic and other biological active site–directed monofunctional and bifunctional agents, molecular recognition in proteins, small molecule–protein interactions.

Andrew D. Jorgensen, Associate Professor; Ph.D., Illinois at Chicago, 1976. Physical and Chemical Education: classroom communication in large lecture environments, factors that influence student performance.

Jon R. Kirchhoff, Professor; Ph.D., Purdue, 1985. Analytical: development and applications of microelectrode devices and sensor systems for bioanalysis and capillary electrophoresis detection, redox and spectroscopic properties of metal complexes, spectroelectrochemical methods.

Yun-Ming Lin, Assistant Professor; Ph.D., Notre Dame, 2000. Organic and Chemical Biology: synthetic methodology development, syntheses and mechanistic studies of biologically active small molecules.

Cora Lind, Assistant Professor; Ph.D., Georgia Tech, 2001. Inorganic and Materials: synthesis and characterization of new and improved solids, nonhydrolytic sol-gel chemistry, negative thermal expansion materials, sulfides, phosphides, powder and single crystal X-ray methods, Rietveld method.

Mark R. Mason, Associate Professor; Ph.D., Iowa State, 1991. Inorganic and Organometallic: synthesis, characterization, and reactivity of molecules and materials with catalytic applications; activation of CO by complexes of the group 13 elements; microporous group 13 phosphates and phosphonates; alkylaluminoxane analogues; epoxidation polymerization catalysts; novel phosphine ligands; nitrogen-donor polyindolylmethanes as ligands for electrophilic complexes.

Timothy C. Mueser, Assistant Professor; Ph.D., Nebraska, 1989. Biochemistry and Crystallography: X-ray crystallography and protein chemistry of DNA replication and DNA repair multiprotein complexes.

A. Alan Pinkerton, Professor and Chair; Ph.D., Alberta, 1971. X-ray Crystallography: nonroutine structure determination, charge density analysis, new techniques.

Joseph A. R. Schmidt, Assistant Professor; Ph.D., Berkeley, 2002. Inorganic and Organometallic: design, synthesis, and characterization of homogeneous catalysts for the functionalization of alkenes and alkynes, hydroamination, hydrosilylation, and olefin metathesis reaction chemistry.

Ronald E. Viola, Professor; Ph.D., Penn State, 1976. Biochemistry and Enzymology: mechanistic studies of enzyme catalyzed reactions, mapping of enzyme-active sites, introduction of unnatural amino acids, high-resolution structural studies.

The University of Toledo campus.

Wolfe Hall.

SELECTED PUBLICATIONS

Averill, B. A. Dimetal hydrolases. In *Comprehensive Coordination Chemistry,* 2nd ed., vol. 8, Coordination Chemistry of the Biosphere, eds. L. Que Jr. and W. B. Tolman. In press.

Dikiy, A., E. G. Funhoff, **B. A. Averill,** and S. Ciurli. New insights into the mechanism of purple acid phosphatase through 1H NMR spectrometry. *J. Am. Chem. Soc.* 124:13974–5, 2002.

Funhoff, E. G., et al. **(B. A. Averill).** The highly exposed loop region in mammalian purple acid phosphatases controls the catalytic activity of these enzymes. *Chem. BioChem.* 2:355–63, 2001.

Funhoff, E. G., et al. **(B. A. Averill).** Mutational analysis of the interaction between active site residues and the loop region in mammalian purple acid phosphatases. *Biochemistry* 40:11614–22, 2001.

Ding, X. D., et al. **(B. A. Averill).** Nitric oxide binding to the ferri- and ferroheme states of nitrophorin 1, a reversible NO-binding heme protein from the saliva of the blood-sucking insect *Rhodnius prolixus. J. Am. Chem. Soc.* 121:128–38, 1999.

Merkx, M., M. W. H. Pinkse, and **B. A. Averill.** Evidence for non-bridged coordination of p- nitrophenylphosphate to the dinuclear Fe(III)-M(II) center in bovine spleen purple acid phosphatase during enzymatic turnover. *Biochemistry* 38:9914–25, 1999.

Merkx, M., and **B. A. Averill.** Probing the role of the trivalent metal in phosphate ester hydrolysis: Preparation and characterization of purple acid phosphatases containing M(III)Zn(II) active sites (M(III) = Al, Ga, In, Fe), including the first example of an active aluminum enzyme. *J. Am. Chem. Soc.* 121:6683–9, 1999.

Isarov, A. V., and **J. Chrysochoos.** Photochemical reactivity of ZnTPP induced by nonstoichiometric CdS-nanoparticles in 2-propanol. *Int. J. Photoenergy* 3:17–23, 2001.

Chrysochoos, J., and K. Beyene. Oxidative fluorescence quenching of ZnTPP by Ln^{3+}-ions in several solvents. Role of lanthanide-induced singlet-triplet crossing. *J. Lumin.* 81:209–18, 1999.

Isarov, A. V., and **J. Chrysochoos.** Interfacial electron transfer from nonstoichiometric cadmium sulfide nanoparticles to free and complexed Cu(II) ion in 2-propanol. *Indian Acad. Sci. (Chem. Sci.)* 110:277–91, 1998.

Isarov, A. V., and **J. Chrysochoos.** Optical and photochemical properties of nonstoichiometric cadmium sulfide nanoparticles: Surface modification with Cu(II) ions. *Langmuir* 13:3142–9, 1997.

Bhamro, A., and **J. Chrysochoos.** Photochemistry of ZnTPP-induced by cadmium sulfide nanoparticles in 2-propanol. *J. Photochem. Photobiol. A* 111:187–98, 1997.

Tadd, A., et al. **(J. A. Davies).** Hydroformylation of 1-hexene in supercritical carbon dioxide using a heterogeneous rhodium catalyst. 2. Evaluation of reaction kinetics. *J. Ind. Eng. Chem. Res.,* in press.

Schwert, D., **J. A. Davies,** and N. Richardson. Non-gadolinium-based contrast agents for magnetic resonance imaging. *Top. Curr. Chem.* 201:167–99, 2002.

Steinborn, D., et al. **(J. A. Davies).** On the reactivity of platina-b-diketones–synthesis and characterization of acylplatinum(II) complexes. *Anorg. Allg. Chem.* 626:661–6, 2000.

Richardson, N., **J. A. Davies,** and B. Radüchel. Polyhedron report no. 66: Iron(III)-based contrast agents for magnetic resonance imaging. *Polyhedron* 18:2457–82, 1999.

Brault, P. A., et al. **(M. O. Funk).** Protein micelles from lipoxygenase-3. *Biomacromolecules* 3:649–54, 2002.

Kariapper, M. S. T., W. R. Dunham, and **M. O. Funk.** Iron extraction from soybean lipoxygenase 3 and reconstitution of catalytic activity from the apoenzyme. *Biochem. Biophys. Res. Commun.* 284:563–7, 2001.

Skrzypczak-Jankun, E., et al. **(M. O. Funk).** Three-dimensional structure of a purple lipoxygenase. *J. Am. Chem. Soc.* 123:10814–20, 2001.

Pham, C., et al. **(M. O. Funk).** Structural and thermochemical characterization of lipoxygenase catechol complexes. *Biochemistry* 37:17952–7, 1998.

Skrzypczak-Jankun, E., L. M. Amzel, B. A. Kroa, and **M. O. Funk.** Structure of soybean lipoxygenase L3 and a comparison with the L1 isoenzyme. *Prot. Struct. Funct. Genet.* 29:15–31, 1997.

Giolando, D. M., and **J. R. Kirchhoff** et al. Chemical vapor deposition of alumina on carbon and silicon carbide microfiber substrates for microelectrode development. *Chem. Vap. Deposition* 8:93–8, 2002.

Citeau, H. A. S., and **D. M. Giolando.** Alkyl hex-1-ynyl tellurides: Synthesis and multinuclear NMR (^{125}Te-, ^{13}C- and ^{1}H) studies. *J. Organomet. Chem.* 625:23–31, 2001.

Bozon, J. P., **D. M. Giolando,** and **J. R. Kirchhoff.** Development of metal-based microelectrode sensor platforms by chemical vapor deposition. *Electroanalysis* 13:911–6, 2001.

Friese, J., et al. **(D. M. Giolando).** Trigonal prismatic vs. octahedral coordination geometry (I): Syntheses and structural characterization of hexakis(arylthiolato) zirconate complexes. *Inorg. Chem.* 39:1496–500, 2000.

Witthaut, D., K. Kirschbaum, O. Conrad, and **D. M. Giolando.** Isolation of a catenated organotelluride anion in the sodium borohydride reduction of diphenylditelluride. *Organometallics* 19: 5238–40, 2000.

Mao, L., Y. Wang, and **X. Hu.** π-π stacking interactions in the peridinin-chlorophyll-protein of *Amphidinium carterae. J. Phys. Chem. B* 107:3963–71, 2003.

Wang, Y., and **X. Hu.** A quantum chemistry study of binding carotenoids in the bacterial light-harvesting complexes. *J. Am. Chem. Soc.* 124:8445–51, 2002.

Wang, Y., and **X. Hu.** Quantum chemical study of pi-pi stacking interactions of the bacteriochlorophyll dimer in the photosynthetic reaction center of *rhodobacter sphaeroides. J. Chem. Phys.* 117:1–4, 2002.

Hu, X., et al. Photosynthetic apparatus of purple bacteria. *Q. Rev. Biophys.* 35:1–62, 2002.

Hu, X., A. Damjanovic, T. Ritz, and K. Schulten. Architecture and function of the light-harvesting apparatus of purple bacteria. *Proc. Natl. Acad. Sci. U.S.A.* 95:5935–41, 1998.

Hu, X., and K. Schulten. Model for the light-harvesting complex I (B875) of *Rhodobacter sphaeroides. Biophys. J.* 75:683–94, 1998.

Huang, X., et al. Absolute configurational assignments of secondary amines by CD-sensitive dimeric zinc porphyrin host. *J. Am. Chem. Soc.* 124:10320–35, 2002.

Huang, X., K. L. Witte, D. E. Bergbreiter, and C.-H. Wong. Homogenous enzymatic synthesis using a thermo-responsive water-soluble polymer support. *Adv. Syn. Cat.* 1:675–81, 2001.

Ye, X.-S., **X. Huang,** and C.-H. Wong. Conversion of the carboxy group of sialic acid donors to a protected hydroxymethyl group yields an efficient reagent for the synthesis of the unnatural β-linkage. *Chem. Commun.* 11:974–5, 2001.

Huang, X., Nakanishi, K., and N. Berova. Porphyrins and metalloporphyrins: Versatile circular dichroic reporter groups for structural studies. *Chirality* 12:237–55, 2000.

Huang, X., et al. Zinc porphyrin tweezer in host-guest complexation: Determination of absolute configurations of primary monoamines by circular dichroism. *Chem. Eur. J.* 6:216–24, 2000.

Tsai, C.-Y., **X. Huang,** and C.-H. Wong. Design and synthesis of cyclic sialyl Lewis X mimetics: A remarkable enhancement of inhibition by pre-organizing all essential functional groups. *Tetrahedron Lett.* 41:9499–503, 2000.

Huang, X., et al. Zinc porphyrin tweezer in host-guest complexation: Determination of absolute configurations of diamines, amino acids, and amino alcohols by circular dichroism. *J. Am. Chem. Soc.* 120:6185–6, 1998.

Tillekeratne, L. M. V., et al. **(R. A. Hudson).** Differential inhibitors of polymerase and DNA-strand transfer activities of HIV-1 reverse transcriptase. *Bioorg. Med. Chem. Lett.* 12:525–8, 2002.

Acey, R. A., et al. **(R. A. Hudson).** A butyrlcholinesterase in the early development of brine shrimp *(Artemia salina)* larvae: A target for phthalate ester embryotoxicity. *Biochem. Biophys Res. Commun.* 299:659–62, 2002.

Suleman, A., L. M. V. Tillekeratne, and **R. A. Hudson.** Desilylation of TBDMS ethers of phenols susceptible to polymerization. *Synth. Commun.* 31:3303–8, 2001.

Suleman, A., L. M. V. Tillekeratne, and **R. A. Hudson.** Novel inhibitors of HIV-reverse transcriptase catalyzed DNA strand transfer: Can we alter the fidelity of the enzyme? *Biochem. Biophys. Res. Commun.* 283:896–9, 2001.

Tillekeratne, L. M. V., and **R. A. Hudson.** Reactive quinones: From chemical defense mechanisms in plants to drug design. In *Biologically Active Natural Products: Pharmaceuticals,* p. 109. Boca Raton, Fla.: CRC Press, 2000.

Zhang, Z. P., L. M. V. Tillekeratne, and **R. A. Hudson.** An unusual product in a Doebner-von Miller quinoline synthesis. *Tetrahedron Lett.* 39:5133–4, 1999.

University of Toledo

Selected Publications (continued)

Inoue, T., **J. R. Kirchhoff,** and **R. A. Hudson.** Enhanced measurement stability and selectivity for choline and acetylcholine by capillary electrophoresis with electrochemical detection at a covalently linked enzyme modified electrode. *Anal. Chem.* 74:5321–6, 2002.

Barkhimer, T. V., **J. R. Kirchhoff, R. A. Hudson,** and W. S. Messer Jr. Evaluation of the inhibition of choline uptake in synaptosomes by capillary electrophoresis with electrochemical detection. *Electrophoresis* 23:3699–704, 2002.

Wise, D. D., et al. **(J. R. Kirchhoff** and **R. A. Hudson).** Internal standard method for the measurement of choline and acetylcholine by capillary electrophoresis with electrochemical detection. *J. Chromatogr. B* 775:49–56, 2002.

Inoue, T., and **J. R. Kirchhoff.** Determination of thiols by capillary electrophoresis with amperometric detection at a coenzyme pyrroloquinoline quinone modified electrode. *Anal. Chem.* 74:1349–54, 2002.

Smith, A. R., et al. **(J. R. Kirchhoff** and **R. A. Hudson).** Separation of the enzyme cofactor pyrroloquinoline quinone and three isomeric analogues by capillary electrophoresis with ion-pairing media. *J. Chromatogr. A* 876:193–9, 2000.

Inoue, T., and **J. R. Kirchhoff.** Electrochemical detection of thiols with a coenzyme pyrroloquinoline quinone modified electrode. *Anal. Chem.* 72:5755–60, 2000.

Braun, P. D., et al. **(Y.-M. Lin).** A bifunctional molecule that displays context-dependent cellular activity. *J. Am. Chem. Soc.* 125:7575–80, 2003.

Lin, Y.-M., M. J. Miller, and U. Möllmann. The remarkable hydrophobic effect of a fatty acid side chain on the microbial growth promoting activity of a synthetic siderophore. *BioMetals* 14:153–7, 2001.

Lin, Y.-M., and M. J. Miller. Oxidation of primary amines to oxaziridines using molecular oxygen (O_2) as the ultimate oxidant. *J. Org. Chem.* 66:8282–5, 2001.

Lin, Y.-M., P. Helquist, and M. J. Miller. Synthesis and biological evaluation of a siderophore-virginiamycin conjugate. *Synthesis* 1510–4, 1999.

Lin, Y.-M., and M. J. Miller. Practical synthesis of hydroxamate-derived siderophore components by indirect oxidation method and syntheses of a DIG-siderophore conjugate and a biotin-siderophore conjugate. *J. Org. Chem.* 64:7451–8, 1999.

Stevens, R., et al. **(C. Lind).** Heat capacities, third-law entropies and thermodynamic functions of the negative thermal expansion materials, cubic α-ZrW_2O_8 and cubic $ZrMo_2O_8$, from T = (0 to 400) K. *J. Chem. Thermodyn.* 35(6):919–37, 2003.

Cascado-Rivera, E., et al. **(C. Lind).** Electrocatalytic oxidation of formic acid at an ordered intermetallic ptbi surface. *Chem. Phys. Chem.* 4:193–9, 2003.

Lind, C., and A. P. Wilkinson. Seeding and the nonhydrolytic sol-gel synthesis of ZrW_2O_8 and $ZrMo_2O_8$. *J. Sol-Gel Sci. Technol.* 25:51–6, 2002.

Wilkinson, A. P., and **C. Lind** et al. Preparation, transport properties and structure analysis by resonant X-ray scattering of the type-I clathrate $Cs_8Cd_4Sn_{42}$. *Chem. Mater.* 14:1300–5, 2002.

Lind, C., A. P. Wilkinson, E. A. Payzant, and C. J. Rawn. Kinetics of the cubic to trigonal transformation in $ZrMo_2O_8$ and their dependence on precursor chemistry. *J. Mater. Chem.* 12:990–4, 2002.

Lind, C., et al. New high-pressure form of the negative thermal expansion materials zirconium molybdate and hafnium molybdate. *Chem. Mater.* 13:487–90, 2001.

Mason, M. R., et al. Di- and triindolylmethanes: Molecular structures and spectroscopic characterization of potentially bidentate and tridentate ligands. *J. Chem. Crystallogr.* 33:531–40, 2003.

Mason, M. R. Di- and triindolylmethanes: Versatile ligands for main group and transition elements. *Chemtracts* 16:1–18, 2003.

Hemminger, O., et al. **(M. R. Mason** and **J. A. Davies).** Hydroformylation of 1-hexene in supercritical carbon dioxide using a heterogeneous rhodium catalyst. 3. Evaluation of solvent effects. *Green Chem.* 5:507–12, 2002.

Mason, M. R., R. M. Matthews, A. M. Perkins, and V. Ponomarova. Molecular phosphates and phosphonates of aluminum and gallium: Potential applications in materials synthesis. In *Group 13 Chemistry: Fundamental Research, Materials Science and Catalysis,* ACS symposium series No. 822, pp. 181–94, eds. D. Atwood and P. Shapiro. Washington, D.C.: American Chemical Society, 2002.

Barnard, T. S., and **M. R. Mason.** Synthesis, structure, and coordination chemistry of the bicyclic π-acid phosphatri(3-methylindolyl)methane. *Organometallics* 20:206–14, 2001.

Barnard, T. S., and **M. R. Mason.** Hindered axial-equatorial carbonyl exchange in an $Fe(CO)_4(PR_3)$ complex of a rigid bicyclic phosphine. *Inorg. Chem.* 40:5001–9, 2001.

Mason, M. R., A. M. Perkins, V. Ponomarova, and A. Vij. Acac-promoted rearrangement of an alkylaluminophosphonate tetramer to a decamer. *Organometallics* 20:4833–9, 2001.

Jones, C. E., and **T. C. Mueser** et al. Bacteriophage T4 gene 41 helicase and gene 59 helicase loading protein: A versatile couple with roles in replication and recombination. *Proc. Natl. Acad. Sci. Colloquium* 98:8312–8, 2001.

Mueser, T. C., P. H. Rogers, and A. Arnone. Interface sliding as illustrated by the multiple quaternary structures of liganded hemoglobin. *Biochemistry* 39:15353–64, 2000.

Jones, C. E., **T. C. Mueser,** and N. G. Nossal. Interaction of the bacteriophage T4 gene 59 helicase loading protein and gene 41 helicase with each other, and with fork, flap, and cruciform DNA. *J. Biol. Chem.* 275:27145–54, 2000.

Yang, Z., **T. C. Mueser,** F. Bushman, and C. C. Hyde. Crystal structure of an active two-domain derivative of rous sarcoma virus integrase. *J. Mol. Biol.* 296:535–48, 2000.

Mueser, T. C., C. E. Jones, N. G. Nossal, and C. C. Hyde. Bacteriophage T4 gene 59 helicase assembly protein binds replication fork DNA. The 1.45Å resolution crystal structure reveals a novel alpha helical two-domain fold. *J. Mol. Biol.* 296:597–612, 2000.

Bolotina, N. B., E. A. Zhurova, and **A. A. Pinkerton.** Energetic materials: Variable temperature crystal structure of β-NTO. *J. Appl. Crystallogr.* 36:280–5, 2003.

Zhurova, E. A., A. Martin, and **A. A. Pinkerton.** Chemical bonding in biguanidinium dinitramide and biguanidinium bis-dinitramide from experimental X-ray diffraction data. *J. Am. Chem. Soc.* 124:8741–50, 2002.

Beer, L., et al. **(A. A. Pinkerton).** Resonance stabilized 1,2,3-dithiazolo-1,2,3-dithiazolyls as neutral π-radical conductors. *J. Am. Chem. Soc.* 124:9498–509, 2002.

Hanson, B. L., et al. **(A. A. Pinkerton).** Experiments testing the abatement of radiation damage in D-xylose isomerase crystals with cryogenic helium. *J. Synchr. Rad.* 9:375–81, 2002.

Zhurova, E. A., V. G. Tsirelson, A. I. Stash, and **A. A. Pinkerton.** Characterizing the oxygen-oxygen interaction in the dinitramide anion. *J. Am. Chem. Soc.* 124:4574–5, 2002.

Hardie, M. J., A. Martin, **A. A. Pinkerton,** and E. A. Zhurova. Anisotropic thermal expansion of potassium dinitramide—A variable temperature crystallographic study. *Acta Crystallogr., Sect. B: Struct. Sci.* 57:113–8, 2001.

Chi, X., et al. **(A. A. Pinkerton).** Dimeric phenalenyl-based neutral radical molecular conductors. *J. Am. Chem. Soc.* 123:4041–8, 2001.

Blanco, J., R. A. Moore, and **R. E. Viola.** Capture of an intermediate in the catalytic cycle of L-aspartate-β-semialdehyde dehydrogenase. *Proc. Natl. Acad. Sci. U.S.A.,* in press.

Moore, R. A., C. R. Faehnle, J. LeCoq, and **R. E. Viola.** Purification and preliminary characterization of brain aspartoacylase. *Arch. Biochem. Biophys.* 413:1–8, 2003.

Han, S., R. A. Moore, and **R. E. Viola.** Synthesis and evaluation of alternative substrates for arginase. *Bioorg. Chem.* 30:81–94, 2002.

Moore, R. A., W. A. Bocik, and **R. E. Viola.** Expression and purification of L-aspartate-β-semialdehyde dehydrogenase from infectious microorganisms. *Prot. Express. Purif.* 25:189–94, 2002.

Jude, K. M., et al. **(R. E. Viola).** Crystal structure of F65A/Y131C-methylimidazole carbonic anhydrase V reveals architectural features of an engineered proton shuttle. *Biochemistry* 41:2485–91, 2002.

James, C. L. and **R. E. Viola.** Production and characterization of bifunctional enzymes. Domain swapping to produce new bifunctional enzymes in the aspartate pathway. *Biochemistry* 41:3720–5, 2002.

Viola, R. E. The central enzymes of the aspartate pathway of amino acid biosynthesis. *Acc. Chem. Res.* 34:339–49, 2001.

UTAH STATE UNIVERSITY

Department of Chemistry and Biochemistry

Program of Study

Utah State University offers graduate degree programs leading to the M.S. and Ph.D. in chemistry and biochemistry. Both the M.S. and Ph.D. degree programs require the completion of an original research project and the defense of a thesis (dissertation). The M.S. degree is not a prerequisite for the Ph.D. degree. A diversity of research topics in the department allows incoming students to pursue specific interests and contributes to the enrichment of course work.

Upon completion of interviews with faculty members and/or laboratory rotations, entering students choose an adviser and initiate an appropriate research project to be the basis of the dissertation.

Research Facilities

The department currently occupies two adjoining buildings, Maeser Laboratory and Widtsoe Hall. Widtsoe Hall is a 75,000-square-foot facility that houses state-of-the-art teaching and research laboratories. Construction of a new adjoining building that houses additional teaching facilities was completed in 2001.

Departmental research instrumentation includes a Bruker ARX-400-MHz NMR with broadband multinuclear capabilities, a JEOL GSX-270-MHz NMR, and a Bruker ESP-300 X-band EPR. The Analytical Sciences Laboratory, equipped by a generous donation from the Shimadzu Corporation, contains a GC-MS, a fast-scan UV-VIS spectrophotometer, and a gradient HPLC system with autosampler and UV-VIS and fluorescence detection. Individual research laboratories within the department have additional extensive instrumentation, including small molecule and protein X-ray diffractometers, pulsed laser spectrometers, MALDI time-of-flight mass spectrometers, FTIR and UV-VIS spectrophotometers, stopped-flow kinetics equipment, and a microcalorimeter.

The department has an electronics shop staffed by a full-time professional. A wood/machine shop is housed within the department, as is a storeroom with an extensive inventory of glassware, chemicals, and other supplies for research and teaching.

Financial Aid

All incoming students are supported by teaching assistantships, research assistantships, or fellowships. Assistantships for incoming students include a stipend ($15,700 for 2001–02) and tuition waiver. Highly qualified applicants are considered for the Willard L. Eccles Science Foundation Fellowship, which provides three years of support at $18,000 per year, or for the Presidential Fellowship, which provides $15,000 for one year. Both fellowships may be supplemented with a half-time teaching assistantship position and stipend. The department strongly encourages students with strong academic records to apply for these fellowships. Assistance is provided in obtaining and submitting the appropriate forms.

Cost of Study

Out-of-state tuition for an academic year is $7830. A tuition waiver is included in the support package for all graduate students who have teaching or research assistantships.

Living and Housing Costs

Costs for housing in the immediate vicinity of the University range from $250 to $500 per month, depending on whether a student prefers to live alone or in shared housing.

Student Group

The department's current graduate student population consists of 40 students, 34 of whom are pursuing the Ph.D. and 6 of whom are pursuing the M.S. degree. Women make up 32 percent of the total, and 53 percent are international students.

Location

Utah State University is located in the city of Logan in northern Utah's Cache Valley in the heart of the Rocky Mountains. The local area offers many outdoor activities, including camping, hiking, boating, fishing, and a whole spectrum of winter activities; students can take advantage of the "greatest snow on earth."

The University

Utah State University was founded in 1888 as Utah's land-grant college. The University has an international reputation for research and teaching, is recognized as a Carnegie Foundation Research I institution, and ranks seventh in research expenditures among land-grant universities. The University also offers cultural and athletic programs that feature regional, national, and international participants. With an on-campus enrollment of nearly 20,000, the University population is made up of students from all fifty states and sixty-nine other countries.

Applying

There are no application deadlines; however, submission of application materials by April 15 is strongly encouraged. To be considered for admission to the graduate program, students must submit the following material: official transcripts, three letters of recommendation, and official GRE General Test scores. International students must also include official TOEFL scores. For consideration in the Willard L. Eccles Foundation Science Fellowship competition, applications should be completed by March.

Correspondence and Information

Graduate Admissions Committee Chair
Department of Chemistry and Biochemistry
Utah State University
Logan, Utah 84322-0300
Telephone: 435-797-1618
Fax: 435-797-3390
E-mail: chemgrad@cc.usu.edu
World Wide Web: http://www.chem.usu.edu/faculty/recruiting/index.html

Utah State University

THE FACULTY AND THEIR RESEARCH

Ann E. Aust, Trustee Professor; Ph.D., Michigan State, 1975. Role of iron, glutathione, and nitric oxide in asbestos-induced mutagenesis and carcinogenesis. (Biochemistry)

Steven D. Aust, Professor; Ph.D., Illinois, 1965. Structure-function relationships of fungal enzymes for the metabolism of environmental pollutants and the loading of iron into ferritin by ceruloplasmin. (Biochemistry)

Lisa M. Berreau, Assistant Professor; Ph.D., Iowa State, 1994. Synthetic inorganic and bioinorganic chemistry. (Inorganic Chemistry)

Stephen E. Bialkowski, Professor; Ph.D., Utah, 1978. Applications of novel optical methods for chemical analysis. (Analytical Chemistry)

Alexander I. Boldyrev, Associate Professor; Ph.D./Dr.Sci., Novosibirsk (Russia), 1974. Theory of nonstoichiometric molecules, clusters, and materials; superalkalies; superhalogens; high-spin molecules. (Physical Chemistry)

Robert S. Brown, Associate Professor; Ph.D., Virginia Tech, 1983. Fundamental and applied aspects of mass spectrometry (particularly TOF-MS and FT-MS), application of mass spectrometry to various chemical problems, with particular emphasis on biochemical systems. (Analytical Chemistry)

Cheng-Wei Tom Chang, Assistant Professor; Ph.D., Washington (St. Louis), 1997. Development of novel antibiotics, parallel synthesis of unusual sugars, combinatorial synthesis of polyketide and aminoglycoside antibiotic mimics, combinatorial synthesis of fluoroalkylthiophosphonate as enzyme inhibitors. (Organic Chemistry)

Bradley S. Davidson, Associate Professor; Ph.D., Cornell, 1989. Structural chemistry and synthesis of marine and microbial natural products. (Organic Chemistry)

Scott A. Ensign, Professor; Ph.D., Wisconsin–Madison, 1991. Microbial metabolism of aliphatic hydrocarbons, biochemistry and enzymology of enzymes involved in hydrocarbon metabolism. (Biochemistry)

David Farrelly, Professor; Ph.D., Manchester (England), 1980. Theory of intramolecular energy flow, chaotic dynamics, and diffusion quantum Monte Carlo studies of quantum clusters. (Physical Chemistry)

Alvan C. Hengge, Associate Professor; Ph.D., Cincinnati, 1987. Mechanistic organic and bioorganic chemistry, molecular mechanisms of chemical reactions, particularly the details of enzymatic catalysis. (Organic Chemistry)

Joan M. Hevel, Hansen Assistant Professor; Ph.D., Michigan, 1993. Molecular mechanisms of cellular communication, with emphasis on protein structure and biochemistry. (Biochemistry)

Richard C. Holz, Professor; Ph.D., Penn State, 1989. Hydrolytic chemistry of dinuclear centers, structure-function relationships of metalloproteins. (Inorganic Chemistry)

John L. Hubbard, Associate Professor; Ph.D., Arizona, 1982. Structure/bonding/reactivity relationships in transition metal catalysis. (Inorganic Chemistry)

Tapas Kar, Research Assistant Professor; Ph.D., Indian Institute of Technology (Kharagpur), 1989. Doped fullerenes and nanotubes, functionalized nanotubes, hydrogen and dihydrogen bonds, Li-nano-battery, electronic and optical properties. (Computational Chemistry)

Vernon D. Parker, Professor; Ph.D., Stanford, 1964. Reactive intermediate chemistry, electron transfer reactions. (Organic Chemistry)

Steve Scheiner, Professor and Department Head; Ph.D., Harvard, 1976. Fundamental properties of hydrogen bonds, proton transfer reactions, electronic properties of materials. (Computational Chemistry)

Lance C. Seefeldt, Professor; Ph.D., California, Riverside, 1989. Structure and function studies of metalloproteins, functions of MgATP hydrolysis in electron transfer and substrate reduction in the enzyme nitrogenase. (Biochemistry)

Philip J. Silva, Assistant Professor; Ph.D., California, Riverside, 2000. Chemical analysis of aerosol particles and study of their surface chemistry, development of mass spectrometry methods for analysis of environmental systems.

VANDERBILT UNIVERSITY

Department of Chemistry

Program of Study The Vanderbilt University Department of Chemistry designs a student's individual program of study to enable graduation with their Ph.D. in four years. The department offers research in the traditional areas of chemistry: analytical, inorganic, organic, and physical as well as a growing number of interdisciplinary initiatives including collaborative programs in three major thrust areas: biomedical, materials, and environmental science. Individual research programs range from the study of lipid peroxidation and unique DNA mutagenic adducts to the preparation and characterization of advanced materials using new approaches to nanotechnology such as programmed self-assembly, scanning probe microscopy, and ultrafast laser spectroscopy.

Research Facilities The Department of Chemistry is housed in two buildings in the Stevenson Center complex. State-of-the-art facilities were completed in 1996 and represent a construction project in excess of $30 million. Currently, work is in progress renovating older building space.

Instrumentation housed within the Stevenson Center complex includes a high-field NMR laboratory consisting of 500, 600, and 800 MHz NMR; an analytical NMR laboratory equipped with 300, 400, and 500 MHz NMR spectrometers; a powder X-ray diffraction system; X-ray photoelectron spectrometers; a secondary-ion mass spectrometer; laser microprobe mass spectrometer; UV-Vis, FT-IR, and Raman spectrometers; an electronic circular-dichroism spectrometer; high-resolution continuous wave and ultrafast laser spectrometers; a fluorimeter; an oligonucleotide synthesizer; an atomic-force microscope; polarimeters; a surface area and porosity analyzer; and a high-resolution thermal gravimetric analyzer. Chemistry graduate students also benefit from the availability and proximity of other research facilities on campus through interdisciplinary research initiatives at Vanderbilt. The Center for Mass Spectrometry maintains a wide variety of mass spectrometers for analytical applications. The Vanderbilt Free-Electron Laser Center is a national center for exploring the application of free-electron lasers to scientific problems related to medicine, biology, and material science. Microscopy facilities include transmission electron microscope, scanning electron microscopes, an atomic force/scanning tunneling microscope, confocal microscopes, and a near-field scanning optical microscope.

Financial Aid All applicants are considered for admission with a financial award in the form of either a teaching assistantship, a research assistantship, or special fellowships. In addition, potential graduate student candidates are often very competitive for a number of University, school, and departmental fellowships. For the 2004–05 academic year, these awards include a minimum stipend of $18,500, individual major medical insurance coverage, access to Vanderbilt's student health service, and a full tuition waiver ($29,312 per year) for a benefit package of $49,323.

Cost of Study Costs are covered as stated in the Financial Aid section.

Living and Housing Costs On-campus housing is limited but the community surrounding the Vanderbilt campus and the general Nashville area provide a wide variety of housing options in an equally wide range of prices.

Student Group The graduate program generally includes 95 to 100 full-time students and is roughly 55 percent men.

Student Outcomes Graduates of the Ph.D. program traditionally have opted for postdoctoral positions at Vanderbilt or other academic institutions or national labs. Those not continuing in postdoctoral positions have been recruited for industry or as faculty members in colleges and universities.

Location Nashville is a diverse and growing city of 525,000 with a metropolitan area population of more than 1 million. Situated on a wooded 326-acre residential campus, Vanderbilt University is conveniently located less than 10 minutes from the heart of downtown Nashville, just minutes from major interstate highways, and only 15 minutes from Nashville International Airport.

The University and The Department Founded in 1873, Vanderbilt is primarily known for its medical school and scientific research programs and is traditionally ranked among the top twenty-five research-oriented universities in the United States. The department is currently undergoing a period of aggressive expansion, with several new faculty members joining the department and additional searches currently in progress. With an extensive endowment, Vanderbilt has the resources to sustain this aggressive expansion across the spectrum of modern scientific disciplines. In such a dynamic environment, the opportunities for graduate research in chemistry are constantly growing.

The Vanderbilt University Department of Chemistry is medium sized but has the facilities and research opportunities of a large department. The department interacts extensively with other departments and facilities in the Vanderbilt University Medical Center, including the Vanderbilt Cancer Center, the Center for Molecular Toxicology, the Department of Pharmacology, and numerous interdisciplinary groups, such as the Vanderbilt Institute of Chemical Biology, the Vanderbilt Institute of Nanoscale Science and Engineering, and the Vanderbilt Institute for Integrative Biosystems Research and Education. Members of the basic science departments such as chemistry hold membership in these related fields and vice versa, including medical school faculty members who also hold adjunct appointments in the Department of Chemistry. The collegial atmosphere at Vanderbilt further promotes interactive program projects that enhance progress in science and medicine.

Applying The application deadline for admission to the fall 2005 class is January 15. Vanderbilt has a very aggressive recruiting process that allows for applications to be reviewed as they are completed. Thus, early application is not only encouraged but often results in early admission decisions. Vanderbilt's new online application is simple and allows students to review and edit applications as well as view status. There are no application fees for the online application, which can be accessed at https://graduateapplications.vanderbilt.edu/program_page.asp?PROGRAM_ID=146. Information packets may be requested on the department's Web site.

Correspondence and Information All correspondences and questions should be sent to:

Nancy L. Hanna
Department of Chemistry
Vanderbilt University
7330 Stevenson Center
Nashville, Tennessee 37235

Telephone: 615-322-8695
Fax: 615-343-1234
E-mail: nancy.hanna@vanderbilt.edu
World Wide Web: http://sitemason.vanderbilt.edu/chemistry

Vanderbilt University

THE FACULTY AND THEIR RESEARCH

Richard N. Armstrong, Professor of Chemistry and Biochemistry (Vanderbilt Institute of Chemical Biology, Vanderbilt Center in Molecular Toxicology, and Vanderbilt Center for Structural Biology); Ph.D., Marquette, 1975. Structural and mechanistic chemistry.

Brian O. Bachmann, Assistant Professor (Vanderbilt Institute of Chemical Biology); Ph.D., Johns Hopkins, 2000. Bioorganic/biosynthetic chemistry.

Darryl J. Bornhop, Professor (Vanderbilt Institute of Chemical Biology); Ph.D., Wyoming. Bioanalytical chemistry.

Richard M. Caprioli, Professor of Biochemistry, Chemistry, and Pharmacology (Vanderbilt Institute of Chemical Biology, Vanderbilt Center in Molecular Toxicology, Vanderbilt Center for Structural Biology, and Vanderbilt Brain Institute) and Director, Mass Spectrometry Research Center; Ph.D., Columbia, 1969. Bioanalytical chemistry.

David E. Cliffel, Assistant Professor (Vanderbilt Institute of Nanoscale Science and Engineering and Vanderbilt Institute for Integrative Biosystem Research and Education); Ph.D., Texas at Austin, 1998. Analytical chemistry and electrochemistry.

Timothy P. Hanusa, Associate Professor (Vanderbilt Institute of Nanoscale Science and Engineering); Ph.D., Indiana, 1983. Inorganic chemistry.

Eva Harth, Assistant Professor of Chemistry (Vanderbilt Institute of Nanoscale Science and Engineering); Ph.D., Mainz (Germany), 1998. Polymer research.

Piotr Kaszynski, Associate Professor (Organic Materials Research Group and Vanderbilt Institute of Nanoscale Science and Engineering); Ph.D., Texas at Austin, 1991. Organic chemistry.

Charles M. Lukehart, Professor (Vanderbilt Institute of Nanoscale Science and Engineering); Ph.D., MIT, 1972. Inorganic materials chemistry.

Terry P. Lybrand, Professor (Vanderbilt Institute of Chemical Biology and Vanderbilt Center for Structural Biology); Ph.D., California, San Francisco, 1984. Computational and biophysical chemistry.

Lawrence J. Marnett, Mary Geddes Stahlman Professor of Cancer Research, Professor of Biochemistry, and Professor of Chemistry (Vanderbilt Institute of Chemical Biology, Vanderbilt Center in Molecular Toxicology, and Vanderbilt Center for Structural Biology); Ph.D., Duke, 1973. Organic chemistry, bioorganic chemistry, biochemistry.

Prasad L. Polavarapu, Professor (Vanderbilt Center for Structural Biology); Ph.D., Indian Institute of Technology (Madras), 1977. Physical chemistry.

Ned A. Porter, Stevenson Professor and Chair, Department of Chemistry (Vanderbilt Institute of Chemical Biology and Vanderbilt Center in Molecular Toxicology); Ph.D., Harvard, 1970. Organic chemistry.

Carmelo J. Rizzo, Associate Professor (Vanderbilt Institute of Chemical Biology and Vanderbilt Center in Molecular Toxicology); Ph.D., Pennsylvania, 1990. Organic chemistry.

Sandra J. Rosenthal, Associate Professor (Vanderbilt Institute of Nanoscale Science and Engineering, Vanderbilt Institute of Chemical Biology, and Vanderbilt Brain Institute); Ph.D., Chicago, 1993. Physical and materials chemistry.

Michael P. Stone, Professor (Vanderbilt Institute of Chemical Biology, Vanderbilt Center in Molecular Toxicology, and Vanderbilt Center for Structural Biology); Ph.D., California, Irvine, 1981. Biophysical chemistry.

Gary A. Sulikowski , Professor of Chemistry (Vanderbilt Institute of Chemical Biology); Ph.D., Pennsylvania, 1989. Organic chemistry.

David W. Wright, Assistant Professor (Vanderbilt Institute of Nanoscale Science and Engineering, Vanderbilt Institute of Chemical Biology, and Vanderbilt Institute for Integrative Biosystem Research and Education); Ph.D., MIT, 1994. Bioorganic and biomaterials chemistry.

VILLANOVA UNIVERSITY

College of Liberal Arts and Sciences
Department of Chemistry

Programs of Study

The Department of Chemistry at Villanova offers the Master of Science (M.S.) degree in all traditional areas of chemistry. The degree can be earned full-time or part-time. Part-time students may choose from thesis and nonthesis options. The thesis option requires the successful completion of six courses and a research project culminated by a written thesis. The nonthesis option requires the completion of ten courses and a seminar course based on work experience. All students are required to take three core courses in either analytical, biological, inorganic, organic, or physical chemistry, followed by elective courses. Comprehensive exams are required, and may be taken anytime after the completion of four courses. Thirty-one credits are required for the Master of Science degree.

Research Facilities

In fall 1999, Villanova completed a $35-million expansion renovation to Mendel Science Center, resulting in a state-of-the-art teaching and research facility. The department is well equipped with instrumentation. Two FT-NMR spectrometers (both 300 MHz), including a new Varian Mercury instrument with an MAS probe for solids analysis, are available. Other instrumentation includes an HP GC–mass spectrometer, a Siemens single crystal diffractometer, DSC, TG, ultracentrifugation, and polarimetry. Spectroscopy is performed with several FT-IRs and UV-visible spectrophotometers, CE, and fluorescence. Chromatographs include several GC and LC instruments, along with CE. The Department Computational Chemistry Lab holds an IBM RISC station along with a Linux cluster and a Silicon Graphics O2 workstation.

Financial Aid

Most full-time graduate students in the department hold teaching or research assistantships of $13,525 for nine months plus full tuition remission. Limited research and teaching fellowships are available for summer months.

Cost of Study

The tuition for graduate chemistry at Villanova is $540 per credit hour in 2004–05, with a general fee of $30 per semester.

Living and Housing Costs

Although on-campus housing is not available, ample apartments/rooms are available in the suburban neighborhoods surrounding Villanova. The Office of Residence Life offers assistance by providing rental lists to students. Living expenses for a single student are estimated at $13,000 per year.

Student Group

There are 58 graduate students (16 full-time) and 14 tenure-track faculty members in the department. About 40 percent of the students are women and 20 percent are international.

Student Outcomes

Some graduates are employed by the nine major pharmaceutical firms in the Philadelphia area. Others choose employment at smaller companies, and some continue their studies at Ph.D. programs in chemistry and related areas.

Location

Located in a safe, suburban community 12 miles west of Philadelphia, the picturesque 254-acre campus features sixty buildings. Bryn Mawr and Haverford Colleges are nearby, and major Universities in Philadelphia (Penn, Temple, Drexel, and others) are easily accessible by public transportation. Philadelphia supports many cultural opportunities including theater, opera, symphony concerts, and ballet, as well as professional sports teams of every variety.

The University

Founded in 1842 by the priests and brothers of the Order of St. Augustine, Villanova University is the oldest and largest Catholic university in the Commonwealth of Pennsylvania. The University's commitment to love and service is reflected in the Latin words of its seal, which translate into truth, unity, and love.

Applying

An application form, with full instructions, is available on the Web at http://www.gradartsci.villanova.edu. The application fee is $50. Application deadlines are August 1 (fall), December 1 (spring), and May 1 (summer). Applicants who wish to be considered for assistantships should submit their application by March 1 (fall) and October 1 (spring) for priority evaluation. The GRE General Test is required of all students; the TOEFL is required of international applicants whose native language is not English. The most important criterion for admission is a sincere desire to study chemistry. Applications from second career, older, and other nontraditional chemistry students are encouraged.

Correspondence and Information

Graduate Chairperson
Chemistry Department
Villanova University
800 Lancaster Avenue
Villanova, Pennsylvania 19085-1699
Telephone: 610-519-4840
Fax: 610-519-7167
E-mail: chemistrygrad@villanova.edu
World Wide Web: http://www.chemistry.villanova.edu

Villanova University

THE FACULTY AND THEIR RESEARCH

Temer S. Ahmadi, Ph.D., UCLA. Materials/physical chemistry: synthesis and optical properties of metal-polymer, metal-semiconductor, and luminescent semiconductor nanomaterials.

Joseph W. Bausch, Ph.D., USC. Organic and computational chemistry: synthetic and computational studies of electron-deficient clusters, carborane synthesis, structure prediction.

Carol A. Bessel, Ph.D., SUNY at Buffalo. Inorganic and materials chemistry: carbon nanofibers, electrochemistry, catalysis in supercritical fluids, octahedral ruthenium complexes.

Eduard G. Casillas, Ph.D., Johns Hopkins. Organic chemistry: natural product synthesis, synthesis of antagonists for plant/fungal secondary metabolic pathways, terpene biomimetic synthesis.

Robert M. Giuliano, Ph.D., Virginia. Organic chemistry: carbohydrate chemistry, synthesis of vinyl glycosides and carbohydrate vinyl ethers, branched-chain carbohydrates, nitrosugars.

Amanda M. Grannas, Ph.D., Purdue. Analytical/environmental chemistry: Photochemical degradation of environmental pollutants in surface waters, photo chemistry of organics in snow and ice, redox chemistry of soil and sediments, Arctic climate change.

W. Scott Kassel, Ph.D., Florida. Inorganic chemistry: solid-base catalysis, X-ray diffraction, synthesis of chiral pyrrolidine transition metal complexes as enantioselective catalysts.

Anthony F. Lagalante, Ph.D., Colorado. Analytical/environmental chemistry: environmental/food/agricultural applications of solid phase microextraction (SPME), high-pressure spectroscopy in supercritical fluids used as "green" solvents.

Brian K. Ohta, Ph.D., California, San Diego. Organic chemistry: NMR spectroscopy, intermediate characterization in photosensitized oxidation reactions, hydrogen bond asymmetry.

Joseph B. Rucker, Ph.D., Berkeley. Biochemistry: receptor biochemistry, including receptors involved in HIV entry, chemokine receptors, capsaicin receptors.

Barry S. Selinsky, Ph.D., SUNY at Buffalo. Biochemistry: membrane biophysics, structural analysis of membrane proteins, membrane-active antibiotics, anticoagulants.

John F. Wojcik, Ph.D., Cornell. Physical chemistry: reaction kinetics, calorimetry.

Deanna L. Zubris, Ph.D., Caltech. Inorganic chemistry: synthesis of organometallic complexes as polymerization catalysts, mechanistic studies.

WESLEYAN UNIVERSITY

Department of Chemistry

Program of Study

The Department of Chemistry offers a program of study leading to the Ph.D. degree. Students are awarded this degree upon demonstration of creativity and scholarly achievement. This demands intensive specialization in one field of chemistry as well as broad knowledge of related areas. The department provides coverage of physical, organic, inorganic, bioorganic, and biophysical chemistry.

The first year of graduate study contains much of the required course work, although most students also choose a research adviser and begin a research program at the beginning of the second semester. Students are expected to demonstrate knowledge of five core areas of chemistry, either by taking the appropriate course or by passing a placement examination. In addition, students take advanced courses in their area of specialization. Classes are small (5–10 students) and emphasize interaction and discussion. Student seminar presentations are also emphasized. Election of interdisciplinary programs in chemical physics and molecular biophysics in conjunction with the Departments of Physics and Molecular Biology and Biochemistry, respectively, is also possible. Students are admitted to Ph.D. candidacy, generally in the second year, by demonstrating proficiency in the core course curriculum, passing a specified number of regularly scheduled progress exams, demonstrating an aptitude for original research, and defending a research proposal. The progress and development of a student is monitored throughout by a 3-member faculty advisory committee. The Ph.D. program, culminating in the completion of a Ph.D. thesis, is normally completed within four to five years. Two semesters of teaching in undergraduate courses is required, where the load is, on average, about 5 hours per week during the academic year. This requirement is normally met in the first year.

Research Facilities

The Hall-Atwater Laboratory is equipped with a wide variety of modern instrumentation appropriate to the research interests of the faculty. There are excellent machine and electronics shops and glassblowing facilities. A departmental computer network consisting of several IBM RS/6000, Silicon Graphics, and Linux workstations and an SGI Altix 3000 supercomputer connected to University and national computer networks are available to students. The Science Library, containing an excellent collection of journals, monographs, and reference materials, is located in a building directly adjacent to the Hall-Atwater Laboratory.

Financial Aid

All students receive a twelve-month stipend, which, for 2004–05, is $18,908. In the first year, this stipend derives from a teaching assistantship. In later academic years, students may be supported by research assistantships where funds are available, or by further teaching assistantships.

Cost of Study

Tuition for 2003–04 was $3434 per course credit, but remission of this is granted to all holders of teaching and research assistantships.

Living and Housing Costs

Most graduate students, both single and married, live in houses administered and maintained by the University, with rents ranging between $500 and $750 per month.

Student Group

The student body at Wesleyan is composed of some 2,800 undergraduates and 170 graduate students. Of the latter, most are in the sciences, with 30, divided between men and women, in the Department of Chemistry. Most graduates obtain industrial positions, although some choose academic careers, normally after postdoctoral experience in each case.

Student Outcomes

All Ph.D. graduates in the last two years have gone on to postdoctoral fellowships at major universities such as Harvard, Yale, and California Institute of Technology. Most earlier graduates are now on college faculties or have research positions in the chemical industry.

Location

Middletown is a small city on the west bank of the Connecticut River, 15 miles south of Hartford, the state capital. New Haven is 24 miles to the southwest; New York City and Boston are 2 hours away by automobile. Middletown's population of 50,000 is spread over an area of 43 square miles, much of which is rural. Although Wesleyan is the primary source of cultural activity in Middletown, the city is not a "college town" but serves as a busy commercial center for the region between Hartford and the coast. Water sports, skiing, hiking, and other outdoor activities can be enjoyed in the hills, lakes, and river nearby.

The University

For more than 150 years, Wesleyan University has been identified with the highest aspirations and achievements of private liberal arts higher education. Wesleyan's commitment to the sciences dates from the founding of the University, when natural sciences and modern languages were placed on an equal footing with traditional classical studies. In order to maintain and strengthen this commitment, graduate programs leading to the Ph.D. degree in the sciences were established in the late 1960s. The program in chemistry was designed to be small, distinctive, and personal, emphasizing research, acquisition of a broad knowledge of advanced chemistry, and creative thinking.

Applying

By and large, a rolling admissions policy is in place, although applicants seeking admission in September are advised to submit applications (no application fee) as early as possible in the calendar year. Three letters of recommendation are required, and applicants are required to take the Graduate Record Examinations. Students whose native language is not English should take the TOEFL. Applicants are strongly encouraged to visit the University after arrangements are made with the department.

Correspondence and Information

Ms. Roslyn Brault
Administrative Assistant
Department of Chemistry
Hall-Atwater Laboratories
Wesleyan University
Middletown, Connecticut 06459-0001
Telephone: 860-685-2210
Fax: 860-685-2211
World Wide Web: http://www.wesleyan.edu/chem/

Wesleyan University

THE FACULTY AND THEIR RESEARCH

Anne M. Baranger, Associate Professor; Ph.D., Berkeley, 1993. Bioorganic chemistry: mechanism of RNA folding, molecular origins of RNA–protein complex affinity and specificity.

David L. Beveridge, Professor; Ph.D., Cincinnati, 1965. Theoretical physical chemistry and molecular biophysics: statistical thermodynamics and computer simulation studies of hydrated biological molecules, structure and motions of nucleic acid, environmental effects on conformational stability, organization of water in crystal hydrates.

Philip H. Bolton, Professor; Ph.D., California, San Diego, 1976. Biochemistry and physical chemistry: NMR and modeling studies of duplex DNA; the structure of DNA containing abasic sites and other damaged DNA; studies on aptamer, telomere, and triplet repeat DNA; development of NMR methodology.

Joseph W. Bruno, Professor; Ph.D., Northwestern, 1983. Inorganic and organometallic chemistry: synthetic and mechanistic studies of transition-metal compounds; organometallic photochemistry, metal-mediated reactions of unsaturated organics.

Michael A. Calter, Associate Professor; Ph.D., Harvard, 1993. Synthetic organic chemistry, particularly in the area of asymmetric catalysis.

Michael J. Frisch, Visiting Scholar; Ph.D., Carnegie-Mellon, 1983. Theoretical chemistry: method development and applications to problems of current interest.

Albert J. Fry, Professor; Ph.D., Wisconsin, 1963. Organic chemistry: mechanisms of organic electrode processes, development of synthetically useful organic electrochemical reactions.

Joseph L. Knee, Professor; Ph.D., SUNY at Stony Brook, 1983. Chemical physics: investigation of ultrafast energy redistribution in molecules using picosecond laser techniques, emphasis on isolated molecule processes including unimolecular photodissociation reaction rates.

Stewart E. Novick, Professor; Ph.D., Harvard, 1973. Physical chemistry: pulsed-jet Fabry-Perot Fourier transform microwave spectroscopy, structure and dynamics of weakly bound complexes, high-resolution spectroscopy of radicals important in the interstellar medium.

George A. Petersson, Professor; Ph.D., Caltech, 1970. Theoretical chemistry: development of improved methods for electronic structure calculations, with applications to small molecular systems and chemical reactions.

Rex F. Pratt, Professor; Ph.D., Melbourne (Australia), 1969. Bioorganic chemistry: enzyme mechanisms and inhibitor design, beta-lactam antibiotics and beta-lactamases, protein chemistry.

Wallace C. Pringle, Professor; Ph.D., MIT, 1966. Physical chemistry: spectroscopic studies of internal interactions in small molecules, collision-induced spectra, environmental chemistry.

Irina M. Russo, Professor; Ph.D., Pittsburgh, 1979. Biochemistry and molecular biophysics: structure and dynamics of nucleic acids, allosteric mechanisms in human hemoglobin, nuclear magnetic resonance spectroscopy.

T. David Westmoreland, Associate Professor; Ph.D., North Carolina, 1985. Inorganic and bioinorganic chemistry: electronic structure and mechanism in molybdenum-containing enzymes, EPR spectroscopy of transition-metal complexes, fundamental aspects of atom transfer reactions in solution.

Peter S. Wharton, Professor Emeritus; Ph.D., Yale, 1959. Organic chemistry.

The Hall-Atwater Laboratory, which houses the Department of Chemistry.

SELECTED PUBLICATIONS

Zhao, Y., and **A. M. Baranger.** Design of an adenosine analog that selectively improves the affinity of a mutant U1A protein for RNA. *J. Am. Chem. Soc.* 125:2480, 2003.

Tuite, J. B., J. C. Shields, and **A. M. Baranger.** Substitution of an essential adenine in the U1A-RNA complex with a non-polar isostere. *Nucleic Acids Res.* 30:5269, 2002.

Gayle, A. Y., and **A. M. Baranger.** Inhibition of the U1A-RNA complex by an aminoacridine derivative. *Bioorg. Med. Chem. Lett.* 12:2839, 2002.

Shiels, J. C., et al. **(A. M. Baranger).** Investigation of a conserved stacking interaction in target site recognition by the U1A protein. *Nucleic Acids Res.* 30:550, 2002.

Shiels, J. C., et al. **(A. M. Baranger).** RNA-DNA hybrids containing damaged DNA are substrates for RNase H. *Bioorg. Med. Chem. Lett.* 11:2623, 2001.

Blakaj, D. M., et al. **(A. M. Baranger** and **D. L. Beveridge).** Molecular dynamics and thermodynamics of a protein-RNA complex: Mutation of a conserved aromatic residue modifies stacking interactions and structural adaptation in the U1A-stem loop 2 RNA complex. *J. Am. Chem. Soc.* 123:2548, 2001.

Luchansky, S., et al. **(A. M. Baranger).** Contribution of RNA conformation to the stability of a high-affinity RNA-protein complex. *J. Am. Chem. Soc.* 122:7130, 2000.

Nolan, S. J., et al. **(A. M. Baranger).** Recognition of an essential adenine at a protein-RNA interface: Comparison of the contributions of hydrogen bonds and a stacking interaction. *J. Am. Chem. Soc.* 121:8951, 1999.

Beveridge, D. L., and K. M. Thayer. Measures and analyses of DNA bending. *Biopolymers: Nucleic Acid Sci.,* in press.

Arthanari, H., et al. **(D. L. Beveridge).** Assessment of the molecular dynamics structure of DNA in solution based on calculated and observed NMR NOESY volumes and dihedral angles from scalar coupling constants. *Biopolymers* 68(1):3–15, 2003.

Liu, Y., and **D. L. Beveridge.** Exploratory studies of ab initio protein structure prediction: Multiple copy simulated annealing, AMBER energy functions, and a generalized born/solvent accessibility solvation model. *Proteins* 46(1):128–46, 2002.

Pitici, F., **D. L. Beveridge,** and **A. M. Baranger.** Molecular dynamics simulation studies of induced fit and conformational capture in U1A-RNA binding: Do molecular substates code for specificity? *Biopolymers* 65(6):424–35, 2002.

Thayer, K. M., and **D. L. Beveridge.** Hidden Markov models from molecular dynamics simulations on DNA. *Proc. Natl. Acad. Sci. U.S.A.* 99(13):8642–7, 2002.

Kombo, D. C., et al. **(D. L. Beveridge).** Calculation of the affinity of the λ-repressor-operator complex based on free energy component analysis. *Mol. Simulation* 28:187–211, 2002.

Jayaram, B., et al. **(D. L. Beveridge).** Free-energy component analysis of 40 protein-DNA complexes: A consensus view on the thermodynamics of binding at the molecular level. *J. Comput. Chem.* 23:1, 2002.

McConnell, K. J., and **D. L. Beveridge.** Molecular dynamics simulations of B'-DNA: Sequence effects on A-tract bending and bendability. *J. Mol. Biol.* 314:23, 2001.

Kombo, D. C., et al. **(D. L. Beveridge).** Molecular dynamics simulation reveals sequence-intrinsic and protein-induced geometrical features of the OL1 DNA operator. *Biopolymers* 59:205, 2001.

Liu, Y., and **D. L. Beveridge.** A refined prediction method for gel retardation of DNA oligonucleotides from dinucleotide step parameters: Reconciliation of DNA bending models with crystal structure data. *J. Biomol. Struct. Dyn.* 18:505, 2001.

Arthanari, H., and **P. H. Bolton.** Functional and dysfunctional roles of quadruplex DNA. *Chem. Biol.* 8:221, 2001.

Marathias, V. M., et al. **(P. H. Bolton).** Flexibility and curvature of duplex DNA containing mismatched sites as a function of temperature. *Biochemistry* 39:153, 2000.

Jerkovic, B., and **P. H. Bolton.** The curvature of dA tracts is temperature dependent [in process citation]. *Biochemistry* 39:12121, 2000.

Marathias, V. M., et al. **(P. H. Bolton).** 6-Thioguanine alters the structure and stability of duplex DNA and inhibits quadruplex DNA formation. *Nucleic Acids Res.* 27:2860, 1999.

Smith, A. R., **J. W. Bruno,** and S. D. Pastor. Sterically-congested bisphosphite ligands for the catalytic hydrosilation of ketones. *Phosphorus, Sulfur Silicon Relat. Elem.* 177:479–85, 2002.

Albert, D. F., et al. **(J. W. Bruno).** Supercritical methanol drying as a convenient route to phenolic-furfural aerogels. *J. Non-Cryst. Solids* 296:1, 2001.

Michalczyk, L., et al. **(J. W. Bruno).** Chelating aryloxide ligands in the synthesis of titanium, niobium, and tantalum compounds: Electrochemical studies and styrene polymerization activities. *Organometallics* 20:5547, 2001.

Sarker, N., and **J. W. Bruno.** Thermodynamic studies of hydride transfer for a series of niobium and tantalum compounds. *Organometallics* 20:51, 2001.

Bruno, J. W., and X. J. Li. Use of niobium(III) and niobium(V) compounds in catalytic imine metathesis under mild conditions. *Organometallics* 19:4672, 2000.

Kerr, M. E., et al. **(J. W. Bruno).** Hydride and proton transfer reactions of niobium-bound ligands. Synthetic and thermodynamic studies of ketene, enacyl and vinylketene complexes. *Organometallics* 19:901, 2000.

Sarker, N., and **J. W. Bruno.** Thermodynamic and kinetic studies of hydride transfer for a series of molybdenum and tungsten hydrides. *J. Am. Chem. Soc.* 120:2174, 1999.

Halas, S. M., K. Okyne, and **A. J. Fry.** Anodic oxidation of negatively substituted stilbenes. *Electrochim. Acta* 48:1837, 2003.

Fry, A. J. Strong ion-pairing effects in a room temperature ionic liquid. *J. Electroanal. Chem.* 546:35, 2003.

Kaimakliotis, C., and **A. J. Fry.** Novel desilylation of alpha-dimethylsilyl esters by electrochemically generated superoxide ion. *Tetrahedron Lett.* 44:5859, 2003.

Fry, A. J., and C. Kaimakliotis. Electrochemical oxidation and reduction of alpha-dimethylsilyl esters: A novel silicon gamma-effect. In *Mechanistic and Synthetic Aspects of Organic and Biological Electrochemistry,* pp. 77–80, eds. D. G. Peters, J. Simonet, and H. Tanaka. Pennington, N.J.: The Electrochemical Society, Inc., 2003.

Kaimakliotis, C., and **A. J. Fry.** Anodic oxidation of methyl a-dimethylsilydihydrocinnamate: A novel silicon gamma-aryl effect. *J. Org. Chem.* 68:9893, 2003.

Kaimakliotis, C., H. Arthanari, and **A. J. Fry.** Synthesis, NMR spectroscopy, and conformational analysis of *alpha*-dimethylsilyl esters. *J. Organomet. Chem.* 671:126, 2003.

Taylor, K., K. Miura, F. Akinfaderin, and **A. J. Fry.** Reactions cascade in the anodic oxidation of benzyl silanes in methanol. *J. Electrochem. Soc.* 150:D85, 2003.

Fry, A. J., et al. Pinacol reduction-*cum*-rearrangement. A re-examination of the reduction of aryl alkyl ketones by zinc-aluminum chloride. *Tetrahedron Lett.* 43:4391, 2002.

Fry, A. J., et al. Reduction of diaryl alkenes by hypophosphorous acid-iodine in acetic acid. *Tetrahedron* 58:4411, 2002.

Leonida, M. L., et al. **(A. J. Fry).** Two-enzyme cross-linked crystals for chiral synthesis coupled with electroenzymatic regeneration of the cofactor. *Int. J. Biochromatography* 6:307, 2001.

Gordon, P. E., and **A. J. Fry.** Hypophosphorous acid-iodine: A novel reducing system. II. Reduction of benzhydrols to diaryl methylene derivatives. *Tetrahedron Lett.* 42:831, 2001.

Biscoe, M. R., and **A. J. Fry.** Dual reaction pathways in the magnesium-mediated synthesis of aziridines from benzal halides and imines. *Tetrahedron Lett.* 42:2759, 2001.

Xuan, J. X., and **A. J. Fry.** Fluoride-promoted reactions of unsaturated carbonyl compounds: Dimerization by a non-Baylis-Hillman pathway. *Tetrahedron Lett.* 42:3275, 2001.

Basu, S., and **J. L. Knee.** Conformational analysis and dynamics of 9-propylfluorene and 9-ethylfluorene. *J. Phys. Chem.,* in press.

Pitts, J. D., et al. **(J. L. Knee).** 3-Ethylindole electronic spectroscopy: S_1 and cation torsional potential surfaces. *J. Chem. Phys.* 113:1857, 2000.

Wesleyan University

Selected Publications (continued)

Basu, S., and **J. L. Knee.** Conformational studies of the neutral and cation of several substituted fluorenes. *J. Electron Spectrosc. Relat. Phenom.* 112:209, 2000.

Pitts, J. D., and **J. L. Knee.** Structure and dynamics of 9-ethylfluorene-Ar_n van der Waals complexes. *J. Chem. Phys.* 110:3389, 1998.

Pitts, J. D., et al. **(J. L. Knee).** Conformational energy and dynamics of 9-ethylfluorene. *J. Chem. Phys.* 110:3378, 1998.

Pitts, J. D., and **J. L. Knee.** Electronic spectroscopy and dynamics of the monomer and Ar_n clusters of 9-phenylfluorene. *J. Chem. Phys.* 109:7113, 1998.

Pitts, J. D., and **J. L. Knee.** Dynamics of vibronically excited fluorene-Ar_n (n=4-5) cluster. *J. Chem. Phys.* 108:9632, 1998.

Zhang, X., et al. **(J. L. Knee).** Neutral and cation spectroscopy of fluorene-Ar_n clusters. *J. Chem. Phys.* 107:8239, 1997.

Kang, L., and **S. E. Novick.** The microwave spectrum of cyanophosphine, H_2PCN. *J. Mol. Spectrosc.,* in press.

Lehmann, K. K., **S. E. Novick,** R. W. Field, and A. J. Merer. William A. Klemperer: An appreciation. *J. Mol. Spectrosc.* 222:1, 2003.

Subramanian, R., **S. E. Novick,** and R. K. Bohn. Torsional analysis of 2-butynol. *J. Mol. Spectrosc.* 222:57, 2003.

Kang, L., et al. **(S. E. Novick).** Rotational spectra of argon acetone: A two-top internally rotating complex. *J. Mol. Spectrosc.* 213:122, 2002.

Kang, L., and **S. E. Novick.** Microwave spectra of four new perfluoromethyl polyyne chains, trifluoropentadiyne, CF_3-C≡C-C≡C-H, trifluoroheptatriyne, CF_3-C≡C-C≡C-C≡C-H, tetrafluoropentadiyne, CF_3-C≡C-C≡C-F, and trifluoromethylcyanoacetylene, CF_3-C≡C-C≡N. *J. Phys. Chem. A* 106:3749, 2002.

Lin, W., et al. **(S. E. Novick).** Hyperfine interactions in HSiCl. *J. Phys. Chem. A* 106:7703, 2002.

Chen, W., et al. **(S. E. Novick).** Microwave spectroscopy of the methylpolyynes $CH_3(C{\equiv}C)_6H$ and $CH_3(C{\equiv}C)_7H$. *J. Mol. Spectrosc.* 196:335, 1999.

Munrow, M. R., et al. **(S. E. Novick).** Determination of the structure of the argon cyclobutanone van der Waals complex. *J. Phys. Chem.* 103:2256, 1999.

Chen, W., et al. **(S. E. Novick).** Microwave spectroscopy of the 2,4-pentadiynyl radical: $H_2CCCCCH$. *J. Chem. Phys.* 109:10190, 1998.

Chen, W., et al. **(S. E. Novick).** Microwave spectra of the methylcyanopolynes CH_3 $(C{\equiv}C)_n$ CN(n=2,3,4,5). *J. Mol. Spectrosc.* 192:1, 1998.

Chen, W., et al. **(S. E. Novick).** Laboratory detection of a new carbon radical: H_2CCCCN. *Astrophys. J.* 492:849, 1998.

Nimlos, M. R. et al. **(G. A. Petersson).** Photoelectron spectroscopy of $HCCN^-$ and $HCNC^-$ reveals the quasilinear triplet carbenes, HCCN and HCNC. *J. Chem. Phys.* 117:4323, 2002.

Austin, A. J., et al. **(G. A. Petersson).** An overlap criterion for selection of core orbitals. *Theor. Chem. Acc.* 107:180, 2002.

Petersson, G. A. Complete basis set models for chemical reactivity: From the helium atom to enzyme kinetics. In *Theoretical Thermochemistry,* ed. J. Cioslowski, Kluwer Academic Publishers, 2001.

Montgomery, J. A., Jr., et al. **(G. A. Petersson).** A complete basis set model chemistry. VII. Use of the minimum population localization method. *J. Chem. Phys.* 112:6532, 2000.

Petersson, G. A., and M. J. Frisch. A journey from generalized valence bond theory to the full CI complete basis set limit. *J. Phys. Chem.* 104:2183, 2000.

Petersson, G. A. Perspective on: "The activated complex in chemical reactions" by Henry Eyring [*J. Chem. Phys.* 3:107 (1935)]. *Theo. Chem. Acc.* 103:190, 2000.

Montgomery, J. A., Jr., et al. **(G. A. Petersson).** A complete basis set model chemistry. VI. Use of density functional geometries and frequencies. *J. Chem. Phys.* 110:2822, 1999.

Pratt, R. F. Functional evolution of the β-lactamase active site. *J. Chem. Soc. Perkin Trans. II* 851, 2002.

Kaur, K., et al. **(R. F. Pratt).** Mechanism of inhibition of the class C β-lactamase of *Enterobacter cloacae* P99 by cyclic acyl phosph(on)ates: Rescue by return. *J. Am. Chem. Soc.* 123:10436, 2001.

Morrison, M. J., et al. **(R. F. Pratt).** Inverse acyl phosph(on)ates: Substrates or inhibitors of β-lactam-recognizing enzymes? *Bioorg. Chem.* 29:271, 2001.

Kumar, S., et al. **(R. F. Pratt).** Design, synthesis and evaluation of α-ketoheterocycles as class C β-lactamase inhibitors. *Bioorg. Med. Chem.* 9:2035, 2001.

Bebrone, C., et al. **(R. F. Pratt).** CENTA as a chromogenic substrate for studying β-lactamases. *Antimicrob. Agents Chemother.* 45:1868, 2001.

Adediran, S. A., et al. **(R. F. Pratt).** The synthesis and evaluation of benzofuranones as β-lactamase substrates. *Bioorg. Med. Chem.* 9:1175, 2001.

Kaur, K., and **R. F. Pratt.** Mechanism of reaction of acyl phosph(on)ates with the β-lactamase of *Enterobacter cloacae* P99. *Biochemistry* 40:4610, 2001.

Cabaret, D., et al. **(R. F. Pratt).** Synthesis, hydrolysis, and evaluation of 3-acylamino-3, 4-dihydro-2-oxo-2*H*-1,3-benzoxazinecarboxylic acids and linear azadepsipeptides as potential substrates/inhibitors of β-lactam-recognizing enzymes. *Eur. J. Org. Chem.* 141, 2001.

Curley, K., and **R. F. Pratt.** The oxyanion hole in serine β-lactamase catalysis: Interactions of thiono substrates with the active site. *Bioorg. Chem.* 28:338, 2000.

Anderson, J. W., and **R. F. Pratt.** Dipeptide binding to the extended active site of the *Streptomyces* R61 D-alanyl-D-alanine-peptidase: The path to a specific substrate. *Biochemistry* 39:12200, 2000.

Munrow, M. R., et al. **(W. C. Pringle).** Determination of the structure of the argon cyclobutanone van der Waals complex. *J. Phys. Chem.* 103:2256, 1999.

Pringle, W. C., et al. Collision induced far infrared spectrum of cyclopropane. *Mol. Phys.* 62:669, 1987.

Pringle, W. C., et al. Analysis of collision induced far infrared spectrum of ethylene. *Mol. Phys.* 62:661, 1987.

Jiang, L., and **I. M. Russu.** Internal dynamics in a DNA triple helix probed by ^{1}H-^{13}N NMR spectroscopy. *Biophys. J.,* in press.

Coman, D., and **I. M. Russu.** Site-resolved energetics in DNA triple helices containing GTA and TCG triads. *Biochemistry,* in press.

Mihailescu, M. R., et al. **(I. M. Russu).** Allosteric free energy changes at the α1β2 interface of human hemoglobin probed by proton exchange of Trpβ37. *Proteins Struct. Funct. Genet.* 44:73, 2001.

Mihailescu, M. R., and **I. M. Russu.** A signature of the T→P transition in human hemoglobin. *Proc. Natl. Acad. Sci. U.S.A.* 98:3773, 2001.

Russu, I. M., and C. Fronticelli. Structural design of hemoglobin blood substitute. Invited paper for *Blood Substitutes.* New York: Academic Press, 2001.

Michalczyk, R., and **I. M. Russu.** Rotational dynamics of adenine amino groups in a DNA double helix. *Biophys. J.* 76:2679, 1999.

Michalczyk, R., and **I. M. Russu.** Studies of the dynamics of adenine protons in DNA by ^{15}N-labeling and heteronuclear NMR spectroscopy. In *Proceedings of the 10th Conversation.* SUNY, Albany, NY, 1998.

Shea, T. M., and **T. D. Westmoreland.** Electronic effects on the rates of coupled two-electron/halide self-exchange reactions of substituted ruthenocenes. *Inorg. Chem.* 39:1573, 2000.

Holmer, S. A., et al. **(T. D. Westmoreland).** A new irreversibly inhibited form of xanthine oxidase from ethylisonitrile. *J. Inorg. Biochem.* 66:63, 1997.

Swann, J., and **T. D. Westmoreland.** Density functional calculations of *g* values and molybdenum hyperfine coupling constants for a series of molybdenum(V) oxyhalide anions. *Inorg. Chem.* 36:5348, 1997.

Nipales, N. S., and **T. D. Westmoreland.** Correlation of EPR parameters with electronic structure in the homologous series of low symmetry complexes Tp^*MoOX_2 (Tp^* = tris(3,5-dimethylpyrazol-1-yl)borate; X = F, Cl, Br). *Inorg. Chem.* 36:756, 1997.

Section 3
Geosciences

This section contains a directory of institutions offering graduate work in geosciences, followed by in-depth entries submitted by institutions that chose to prepare detailed program descriptions. Additional information about programs listed in the directory but not augmented by an in-depth entry may be obtained by writing directly to the dean of a graduate school or chair of a department at the address given in the directory.

For programs offering related work, see all other areas in this book. In Book 2, see Geography; in Book 3, see Biological and Biomedical Sciences, Biophysics, and Botany and Plant Biology; in Book 5, see Aerospace/Aeronautical Engineering; Agricultural Engineering; Civil and Environmental Engineering; Energy and Power Engineering (Nuclear Engineering); Engineering and Applied Sciences; Geological, Mineral/Mining, and Petroleum Engineering; and Mechanical Engineering and Mechanics.

CONTENTS

Program Directories

Announcements

In-Depth Descriptions

See also:

Geochemistry

California Institute of Technology, Division of Geological and Planetary Sciences, Pasadena, CA 91125-0001. Offers cosmochemistry (PhD); geobiology (PhD); geochemistry (MS, PhD); geology (MS, PhD); geophysics (MS, PhD); planetary science (MS, PhD). Part-time programs available. *Faculty:* 37 full-time (3 women). *Students:* 61 full-time (29 women); includes 28 minority (1 African American, 26 Asian Americans or Pacific Islanders, 1 Hispanic American). Average age 27. 127 applicants, 20% accepted, 15 enrolled. In 2003, 5 master's, 13 doctorates awarded. *Degree requirements:* For doctorate, thesis/dissertation. *Entrance requirements:* For doctorate, GRE General Test. Additional exam requirements/recommendations for international students: Required—TOEFL. *Application deadline:* For fall admission, 1/15 for domestic students, 1/15 for international students. Application fee: $50. Electronic applications accepted. *Financial support:* In 2003–04, 21 fellowships with full tuition reimbursements (averaging $20,496 per year), 49 research assistantships with full tuition reimbursements (averaging $20,496 per year) were awarded. Teaching assistantships with full tuition reimbursements, institutionally sponsored loans, scholarships/grants, health care benefits, and unspecified assistantships also available. Financial award applicants required to submit FAFSA. *Faculty research:* Astronomy, evolution of anaerobic respiratory processes, structural geology and tectonics, theoretical and numerical seismology, global biogeochemical cycles. Total annual research expenditures: $18.6 million. *Unit head:* Dr. Edward M. Stolper, Chairman, 626-395-6108, Fax: 626-795-6028, E-mail: divgps@gps.caltech.edu. *Application contact:* Dr. George R. Rossman, Academic Officer, 626-395-6125, Fax: 626-568-0935, E-mail: divgps@gps.caltech.edu.

California State University, Fullerton, Graduate Studies, College of Natural Science and Mathematics, Department of Chemistry and Biochemistry, Fullerton, CA 92834-9480. Offers analytical chemistry (MS); biochemistry (MS); geochemistry (MS); inorganic chemistry (MS); organic chemistry (MS); physical chemistry (MS). Part-time programs available. *Faculty:* 17 full-time (5 women), 17 part-time/adjunct. *Students:* 21 full-time (9 women), 23 part-time (11 women); includes 19 minority (1 African American, 9 Asian Americans or Pacific Islanders, 9 Hispanic Americans), 8 international. Average age 28. 49 applicants, 61% accepted, 20 enrolled. In 2003, 5 degrees awarded. *Degree requirements:* For master's, thesis, departmental qualifying exam. *Entrance requirements:* For master's, minimum GPA of 2.5 in last 60 units, major in chemistry or related field. Application fee: $55. Tuition, nonresident: part-time $282 per unit. Required fees: $889 per semester. *Financial support:* Teaching assistantships, career-related internships or fieldwork, Federal Work-Study, institutionally sponsored loans, and scholarships/grants available. Support available to part-time students. Financial award application deadline: 3/1. *Unit head:* Dr. Robert Belloli, Chair, 714-278-3621. *Application contact:* Dr. Gregory Williams, Adviser, 714-278-2170.

Colorado School of Mines, Graduate School, Department of Chemistry and Geochemistry and Department of Geology and Geological Engineering, Program in Geochemistry, Golden, CO 80401-1887. Offers MS, PhD. Part-time programs available. *Students:* 12 full-time (7 women), 6 part-time (3 women), 3 international. 7 applicants, 100% accepted, 2 enrolled. In 2003, 2 degrees awarded. *Degree requirements:* For master's, thesis/dissertation; for doctorate, thesis/dissertation, comprehensive exam. *Entrance requirements:* For master's and doctorate, GRE General Test. Additional exam requirements/recommendations for international students: Required—TOEFL (minimum score 550 paper-based; 213 computer-based). *Application deadline:* For fall admission, 12/1 priority date for domestic students, 12/1 priority date for international students; for spring admission, 5/1 priority date for domestic students, 5/1 priority date for international students. Application fee: $45. Electronic applications accepted. *Expenses:* Tuition, state resident: full-time $5,700; part-time $285 per credit hour. Tuition, nonresident: full-time $19,040; part-time $952 per credit hour. Required fees: $733. *Financial support:* In 2003–04, 3 students received support, including fellowships with full tuition reimbursements available (averaging $12,500 per year), 3 research assistantships with full tuition reimbursements available (averaging $10,000 per year), 2 teaching assistantships with full tuition reimbursements available (averaging $10,000 per year); scholarships/grants and unspecified assistantships also available. *Faculty research:* Geochemical analysis, organic geochemistry, hydrochemical systems, environmental microbiology, process control programming. *Unit head:* G. Mike Reimer, Professor, 303-273-3505, Fax: 303-273-3629, E-mail: mreimer@mines.edu.

Colorado School of Mines, Graduate School, Department of Geology and Geological Engineering, Golden, CO 80401-1887. Offers engineering geology (Diploma); exploration geosciences (Diploma); geochemistry (MS, PhD); geological engineering (ME, MS, PhD, Diploma); geology (MS, PhD); hydrogeology (Diploma). Part-time programs available. *Faculty:* 25 full-time (4 women), 8 part-time/adjunct (4 women). *Students:* 52 full-time (16 women), 34 part-time (13 women); includes 1 minority (American Indian/Alaska Native), 20 international. 89 applicants, 56% accepted, 12 enrolled. In 2003, 19 master's, 4 doctorates, 3 other advanced degrees awarded. *Degree requirements:* For master's, thesis/dissertation; for doctorate, thesis/dissertation, comprehensive exam. *Entrance requirements:* For master's and doctorate, GRE General Test; for Diploma, GRE General Test, minimum GPA of 3.0. Additional exam requirements/recommendations for international students: Required—TOEFL (minimum score 550 paper-based; 213 computer-based). *Application deadline:* For fall admission, 12/1 for domestic students, 12/1 for international students; for spring admission, 5/1 for domestic students, 5/1 for international students. Application fee: $45. Electronic applications accepted. *Expenses:* Tuition, state resident: full-time $5,700; part-time $285 per credit hour. Tuition, nonresident: full-time $19,040; part-time $952 per credit hour. Required fees: $733. *Financial support:* In 2003–04, 23 students received support, including 9 fellowships with full tuition reimbursements available (averaging $12,500 per year), 16 research assistantships with full tuition reimbursements available (averaging $10,000 per year), 9 teaching assistantships with full tuition reimbursements available (averaging $10,000 per year); scholarships/grants and unspecified assistantships also available. Financial award applicants required to submit FAFSA. *Faculty research:* Predictive sediment modeling, petrophysics, aquifer-contaminant flow modeling, water-rock interactions, geotechnical engineering. Total annual research expenditures: $2.1 million. *Unit head:* Dr. Murray W. Hitzman, Head, 303-384-2127, Fax: 303-273-3859, E-mail: mhitzman@mines.edu. *Application contact:* Marilyn Schwinger, Administrative Assistant, 303-273-3800, Fax: 303-273-3859, E-mail: mschwing@mines.edu.

Columbia University, Graduate School of Arts and Sciences, Division of Natural Sciences, Department of Earth and Environmental Sciences, New York, NY 10027. Offers geochemistry (M Phil, MA, PhD); geodetic sciences (M Phil, MA, PhD); geophysics (M Phil, MA, PhD); oceanography (M Phil, MA, PhD). *Faculty:* 21 full-time, 19 part-time/adjunct. *Students:* 78 full-time (31 women), 6 part-time (2 women); includes 4 minority (3 Asian Americans or Pacific Islanders, 1 Hispanic American), 31 international. Average age 32. 115 applicants, 20% accepted. In 2003, 16 master's, 11 doctorates awarded. *Degree requirements:* For master's, thesis or alternative, fieldwork, written exam; for doctorate, one foreign language, thesis/dissertation. *Entrance requirements:* For master's and doctorate, GRE General Test, GRE Subject Test, major in natural or physical science. Additional exam requirements/recommendations for international students: Required—TOEFL. Application fee: $75. *Expenses:* Tuition: Full-time $14,820. *Financial support:* Fellowships, teaching assistantships, Federal Work-Study and institutionally sponsored loans available. Support available to part-time students. Financial award application deadline: 1/5; financial award applicants required to submit FAFSA. *Faculty research:* Structural geology and stratigraphy, petrology, paleontology, rare gas, isotope and aqueous geochemistry. *Unit head:* Dr. William Menke, Chair, 212-864-4525, Fax: 845-365-8163.

Cornell University, Graduate School, Graduate Fields of Engineering, Field of Geological Sciences, Ithaca, NY 14853-0001. Offers economic geology (M Eng, MS, PhD); engineering geology (M Eng, MS, PhD); environmental geophysics (M Eng, MS, PhD); general geology (M Eng, MS, PhD); geobiology (M Eng, MS, PhD); geochemistry and isotope geology (M Eng, MS, PhD); geohydrology (M Eng, MS, PhD); geomorphology (M Eng, MS, PhD); geophysics (M Eng, MS, PhD); geotectonics (M Eng, MS, PhD); marine geology (MS, PhD); mineralogy (M Eng, MS, PhD); paleontology (M Eng, MS, PhD); petroleum geology (M Eng, MS, PhD); petrology (M Eng, MS, PhD); planetary geology (M Eng, MS, PhD); Precambrian geology (M Eng, MS, PhD); Quaternary geology (M Eng, MS, PhD); rock mechanics (M Eng, MS, PhD); sedimentology (M Eng, MS, PhD); seismology (M Eng, MS, PhD); stratigraphy (M Eng, MS, PhD); structural geology (M Eng, MS, PhD). *Faculty:* 31 full-time. *Students:* 27 full-time (12 women); includes 1 minority (Asian American or Pacific Islander), 9 international. 74 applicants, 15% accepted, 7 enrolled. In 2003, 3 master's, 5 doctorates awarded. *Degree requirements:* For master's, thesis (MS); for doctorate, thesis/dissertation, comprehensive exam. *Entrance requirements:* For master's and doctorate, GRE General Test, 3 letters of recommendation. Additional exam requirements/recommendations for international students: Required—TOEFL (minimum score 550 paper-based; 213 computer-based). *Application deadline:* For fall admission, 1/15 for domestic students. Applications are processed on a rolling basis. Application fee: $60. Electronic applications accepted. *Expenses:* Tuition: Full-time $28,630. One-time fee: $50 full-time. *Financial support:* In 2003–04, 21 students received support, including 6 fellowships with full tuition reimbursements available, 8 research assistantships with full tuition reimbursements available, 7 teaching assistantships with full tuition reimbursements available; institutionally sponsored loans, scholarships/grants, health care benefits, tuition waivers (full and partial), and unspecified assistantships also available. Financial award applicants required to submit FAFSA. *Faculty research:* Geophysics, structural geology, petrology, geochemistry, geodynamics. *Unit head:* Director of Graduate Studies, 607-255-3474, Fax: 607-254-4780. *Application contact:* Graduate Field Assistant, 607-255-3474, Fax: 607-254-4780, E-mail: gradprog@geology.cornell.edu.

See in-depth description on page 233.

Georgia Institute of Technology, Graduate Studies and Research, College of Sciences, School of Earth and Atmospheric Sciences, Atlanta, GA 30332-0001. Offers atmospheric chemistry and air pollution (MS, PhD); atmospheric dynamics and climate (MS, PhD); geochemistry (MS, PhD); hydrologic cycle (MS, PhD); ocean sciences (MS, PhD); solid-earth and environmental geophysics (PhD); solid-earth and environmental geophysics (MS). Part-time programs available. *Students:* 80 full-time (40 women); includes 39 minority (5 African Americans, 31 Asian Americans or Pacific Islanders, 3 Hispanic Americans). 143 applicants, 18% accepted, 15 enrolled. In 2003, 14 master's, 6 doctorates awarded. Terminal master's awarded for partial completion of doctoral program. *Median time to degree:* Of those who began their doctoral program in fall 1995, 78% received their degree in 8 years or less. *Degree requirements:* For master's, thesis or alternative; for doctorate, thesis/dissertation, comprehensive exam. *Entrance requirements:* For master's and doctorate, GRE General Test, minimum GPA of 2.7. Additional exam requirements/recommendations for international students: Required—TOEFL (minimum score 550 paper-based; 213 computer-based). *Application deadline:* For fall admission, 1/15 priority date for domestic students, 1/15 priority date for international students; for spring admission, 1/1 for domestic students. Applications are processed on a rolling basis. Application fee: $50. *Expenses:* Tuition, state resident: part-time $1,925 per semester. Tuition, nonresident: part-time $7,700 per semester. Required fees: $434 per semester. Full-time tuition and fees vary according to program. *Financial support:* In 2003–04, 3 fellowships, 52 research assistantships (averaging $20,000 per year), 8 teaching assistantships were awarded. Career-related internships or fieldwork, Federal Work-Study, and institutionally sponsored loans also available. Financial award application deadline: 2/15. *Faculty research:* Geophysics, atmospheric chemistry, atmospheric dynamics, seismology. Total annual research expenditures: $5 million. *Unit head:* Dr. Judith A. Curry, Chair, 404-894-3948, Fax: 404-894-5638. *Application contact:* Derek M. Cunnold, Graduate Coordinator, 404-894-3814, Fax: 404-894-5638, E-mail: cunnold@eas.gatech.edu.

See in-depth description on page 237.

Indiana University Bloomington, Graduate School, College of Arts and Sciences, Department of Geological Sciences, Bloomington, IN 47405. Offers biogeochemistry (MS, PhD); environmental geosciences (MS, PhD); geobiology, stratigraphy, and sedimentology (MS, PhD); geochemistry (MS, PhD); geochemistry, mineralogy, and petrology (MS, PhD); geophysics (MS, PhD); geophysics, tectonics, and structural geology (MS, PhD). PhD offered through the University Graduate School. Part-time programs available. *Faculty:* 14 full-time (1 woman). *Students:* 32 full-time (16 women), 18 part-time (8 women); includes 4 minority (2 African Americans, 2 Asian Americans or Pacific Islanders), 23 international. Average age 29. In 2003, 10 master's, 2 doctorates awarded. Terminal master's awarded for partial completion of doctoral program. *Degree requirements:* For master's, one foreign language, thesis or alternative; for doctorate, thesis/dissertation. *Entrance requirements:* For master's and doctorate, GRE General Test. Additional exam requirements/recommendations for international students: Required—TOEFL. *Application deadline:* For fall admission, 1/15 priority date for domestic students, 12/15 priority date for international students; for spring admission, 9/1 priority date for domestic students, 9/1 priority date for international students. Applications are processed on a rolling basis. Application fee: $45 ($55 for international students). *Expenses:* Tuition, state resident: full-time $4,908; part-time $205 per credit. Tuition, nonresident: full-time $14,298; part-time $596 per credit. Required fees: $661. Tuition and fees vary according to campus/location and program. *Financial support:* In 2003–04, research assistantships with full and partial tuition reimbursements (averaging $11,000 per year); fellowships with tuition reimbursements, teaching assistantships with tuition reimbursements, career-related internships or fieldwork, Federal Work-Study, and institutionally sponsored loans also available. Financial award application deadline: 2/15. *Faculty research:* Geophysics, geochemistry, hydrogeology, igneous and metamorphic petrology and clay minerology. Total annual research expenditures: $289,139. *Unit head:* Dr. Christopher G. Maples, Chairman, 812-855-5582, Fax: 812-855-7899, E-mail: cmaples@indiana.edu. *Application contact:* Mary Iverson, Secretary, Committee for Graduate Studies, 812-855-7214, Fax: 812-855-7899, E-mail: geograd@indiana.edu.

The Johns Hopkins University, Zanvyl Krieger School of Arts and Sciences, The Morton K. Blaustein Department of Earth and Planetary Sciences, Baltimore, MD 21218-2699. Offers geochemistry (MA, PhD); geology (MA, PhD); geophysics (MA, PhD); groundwater (MA, PhD); oceanography (MA, PhD); planetary atmosphere (MA, PhD). *Faculty:* 14 full-time (1 woman), 1 (woman) part-time/adjunct. *Students:* 23 full-time (10 women); includes 2 minority (both Hispanic Americans), 10 international. Average age 25. 48 applicants, 21% accepted, 5 enrolled. In 2003, 5 master's, 3 doctorates awarded. *Median time to degree:* Of those who began their doctoral program in fall 1995, 99% received their degree in 8 years or less. *Degree requirements:* For doctorate, thesis/dissertation, registration. *Entrance requirements:* For master's and doctorate, GRE General Test. Additional exam requirements/recommendations for international students: Required—TOEFL (minimum score 600 paper-based; 250 computer-based). *Application deadline:* For fall admission, 1/15 priority date for domestic students, 1/15 priority date for international students. Application fee: $55. Electronic applications accepted. *Expenses:* Tuition: Full-time $28,730; part-time $1,490 per course. Part-time tuition and fees vary according to course load, campus/location and program. *Financial support:* In 2003–04, 4 fellowships, 13 research assistantships, 7 teaching assistantships were awarded. Federal Work-Study and institutionally sponsored loans also available. Financial award application deadline: 4/15; financial award applicants required to submit FAFSA. Total annual research expenditures: $2.3 million. *Unit head:* Dr. Peter Olson, Chair, 410-516-4659, Fax: 410-516-7933, E-mail: epschair@jhunix.hcf.jhu.edu. *Application contact:* Carol Spangler, Academic Program Assistant, 410-516-7034, Fax: 410-516-7933, E-mail: cspangler@jhu.edu.

Massachusetts Institute of Technology, School of Science, Department of Earth, Atmospheric, and Planetary Sciences, Cambridge, MA 02139-4307. Offers atmospheric chemistry (PhD, Sc D); atmospheric science (SM, PhD, Sc D); climate physics and chemistry (PhD, Sc D); earth and planetary sciences (SM); geochemistry (PhD, Sc D); geology (PhD, Sc D); geophysics (PhD, Sc D); geosystems (SM); oceanography (SM, PhD, Sc D); planetary sciences

(PhD, Sc D). *Faculty:* 37 full-time (3 women). *Students:* 147 full-time (61 women); includes 9 minority (4 Asian Americans or Pacific Islanders, 5 Hispanic Americans), 48 international. Average age 27. 176 applicants, 49% accepted, 31 enrolled. In 2003, 8 master's, 19 doctorates awarded. Terminal master's awarded for partial completion of doctoral program. *Degree requirements:* For master's, thesis/dissertation; for doctorate, thesis/dissertation, comprehensive exam. *Entrance requirements:* For master's, GRE General Test, GRE Subject Test (joint MIT/WHOI program); for doctorate, GRE General Test, GRE Subject Test (chemistry or physics for planetary science program). Additional exam requirements/recommendations for international students: Required—TOEFL (minimum score 577 paper-based; 233 computer-based). *Application deadline:* For fall admission, 1/5 for domestic students, 1/5 for international students; for spring admission, 11/1 for domestic students, 11/1 for international students. Application fee: $70. Electronic applications accepted. *Expenses:* Tuition: Full-time $29,400. Required fees: $200. *Financial support:* In 2003–04, 113 students received support, including 25 fellowships with tuition reimbursements available, 70 research assistantships with tuition reimbursements available (averaging $23,760 per year), 21 teaching assistantships with tuition reimbursements available (averaging $18,270 per year); Federal Work-Study, institutionally sponsored loans, scholarships/grants, health care benefits, and unspecified assistantships also available. *Faculty research:* Evolution of main features of the planetary system; origin, composition, structure, and state of the atmospheres, oceans, surfaces, and interiors of planets; dynamics of planets and satellite motions. Total annual research expenditures: $19.1 million. *Unit head:* Prof. Maria Zuber, 617-253-0149, Fax: 617-253-8298, E-mail: mtz@mit.edu. *Application contact:* Carol Sprague, Administrative Assistant, 617-253-3381, Fax: 617-253-8298, E-mail: eapsinfo@mit.edu.

McMaster University, School of Graduate Studies, Faculty of Science, School of Geography and Geology, Hamilton, ON L8S 4M2, Canada. Offers geochemistry (PhD); geology (M Sc, PhD); human geography (MA, PhD); physical geography (M Sc, PhD). Part-time programs available. Terminal master's awarded for partial completion of doctoral program. *Degree requirements:* For master's, thesis/dissertation; for doctorate, thesis/dissertation, comprehensive exam. *Entrance requirements:* For master's, minimum B+ average. Additional exam requirements/recommendations for international students: Required—TOEFL (minimum score 550 paper-based; 213 computer-based).

Montana Tech of The University of Montana, Graduate School, Geoscience Program, Butte, MT 59701-8997. Offers geochemistry (MS); geological engineering (MS); geology (MS); geophysical engineering (MS); hydrogeological engineering (MS); hydrogeology (MS). Part-time programs available. *Faculty:* 8 full-time (1 woman). *Students:* 15 full-time (5 women), 1 (woman) part-time. 17 applicants, 71% accepted, 9 enrolled. In 2003, 7 degrees awarded. *Degree requirements:* For master's, thesis (for some programs), comprehensive exam (for some programs), registration. *Entrance requirements:* For master's, GRE General Test, minimum GPA of 3.0. Additional exam requirements/recommendations for international students: Required—TOEFL (minimum score 525 paper-based; 195 computer-based). *Application deadline:* For fall admission, 4/1 priority date for domestic students, 3/1 priority date for international students; for spring admission, 10/1 priority date for domestic students, 7/1 priority date for international students. Applications are processed on a rolling basis. Application fee: $30. *Expenses:* Tuition, state resident: full-time $4,741; part-time $233 per credit. Tuition, nonresident: full-time $14,662; part-time $646 per credit. *Financial support:* In 2003–04, 15 students received support, including 10 research assistantships with partial tuition reimbursements available (averaging $4,655 per year), 10 teaching assistantships with partial tuition reimbursements available (averaging $4,800 per year); career-related internships or fieldwork, tuition waivers (full and partial), and unspecified assistantships also available. Financial award application deadline: 4/1; financial award applicants required to submit FAFSA. *Faculty research:* Water resource development, seismic processing, petroleum reservoir characterization, environmental geochemistry, molecular modeling, magmatic and hydrothermal ore deposits. Total annual research expenditures: $623,564. *Unit head:* Dr. Diane Wolfgram, Department Head, 406-496-4353, Fax: 406-496-4260, E-mail: dwolfgram@mtech.edu. *Application contact:* Cindy Dunstan, Administrator, Graduate School, 406-496-4304, Fax: 406-496-4334, E-mail: cdunstan@mtech.edu.

New Mexico Institute of Mining and Technology, Graduate Studies, Department of Earth and Environmental Science, Program in Geology and Geochemistry, Socorro, NM 87801. Offers geochemistry (MS, PhD); geology (MS, PhD). *Students:* 28 full-time (17 women), 3 part-time (all women), 3 international. Average age 29. 35 applicants, 7 enrolled. In 2003, 9 master's, 1 doctorate awarded. *Degree requirements:* For master's, thesis optional; for doctorate, thesis/dissertation. *Entrance requirements:* For master's, GRE General Test; for doctorate, GRE General Test, GRE Subject Test. Additional exam requirements/recommendations for international students: Required—TOEFL (minimum score 540 paper-based; 207 computer-based). *Application deadline:* For fall admission, 3/1 for domestic students; for spring admission, 6/1 for domestic students. Applications are processed on a rolling basis. Application fee: $16 ($30 for international students). Electronic applications accepted. *Expenses:* Tuition, state resident: full-time $2,276; part-time $126 per credit. Tuition, nonresident: full-time $9,170; part-time $509 per credit. Required fees: $924; $27 per credit. $214 per term. Part-time tuition and fees vary according to course load. *Financial support:* In 2003–04, 15 research assistantships (averaging $11,400 per year), 11 teaching assistantships with full and partial tuition reimbursements (averaging $8,366 per year) were awarded. Fellowships, Federal Work-Study, institutionally sponsored loans, and unspecified assistantships also available. Financial award application deadline: 3/1; financial award applicants required to submit CSS PROFILE or FAFSA. *Faculty research:* Care and karst topography, soil/water chemistry and properties, geochemistry of ore deposits. *Unit head:* Dr. Peter Mozley, Coordinator, 505-835-5311, Fax: 505-835-6436, E-mail: mozley@nmt.edu. *Application contact:* Dr. David B. Johnson, Dean of Graduate Studies, 505-835-5513, Fax: 505-835-5476, E-mail: graduate@nmt.edu.

Ohio University, Graduate Studies, College of Arts and Sciences, Department of Geological Sciences, Athens, OH 45701-2979. Offers environmental geochemistry (MS); environmental geology (MS); environmental/hydrology (MS); geology (MS); geology education (MS); geomorphology/surficial processes (MS); geophysics (MS); hydrogeology (MS); sedimentology (MS); structure/tectonics (MS). Part-time programs available. *Faculty:* 10 full-time (3 women), 4 part-time/adjunct (1 woman). *Students:* 13 full-time (4 women), 4 part-time (1 woman); includes 1 minority (Hispanic American), 4 international. Average age 25. 11 applicants, 45% accepted, 4 enrolled. In 2003, 8 degrees awarded. *Median time to degree:* Master's–2.5 years full-time. *Degree requirements:* For master's, thesis, thesis proposal defense. *Entrance requirements:* Additional exam requirements/recommendations for international students: Required—TOEFL (minimum score 550 paper-based; 217 computer-based). *Application deadline:* For fall admission, 2/1 priority date for domestic students, 1/1 priority date for international students. Application fee: $45. *Expenses:* Tuition, state resident: full-time $2,651; part-time $328 per credit. Tuition, nonresident: full-time $5,095; part-time $632 per credit. Tuition and fees vary according to program. *Financial support:* In 2003–04, 16 students received support, including 3 research assistantships with full tuition reimbursements available (averaging $11,000 per year), 13 teaching assistantships with full tuition reimbursements available (averaging $11,000 per year); institutionally sponsored loans, scholarships/grants, tuition waivers (full), and unspecified assistantships also available. Financial award application deadline: 3/15. *Faculty research:* Geoscience education, tectonics, flurial geomorphology, invertebrate paleontology, mine/hydrology. Total annual research expenditures: $506,400. *Unit head:* Dr. Douglas Green, Chair, 740-593-6896, Fax: 740-593-0486, E-mail: green@ohio.edu. *Application contact:* Dr. Dina L. Lopez, Graduate Chair, 740-593-9435, Fax: 740-593-0486, E-mail: lopezd@ohio.edu.

The Pennsylvania State University University Park Campus, Graduate School, College of Earth and Mineral Sciences, Department of Geosciences, Program in Geochemistry, State College, University Park, PA 16802-1503. Offers MS, PhD. *Entrance requirements:* For master's and doctorate, GRE General Test. Additional exam requirements/recommendations for international students: Required—TOEFL. Application fee: $45.

See in-depth description on page 249.

Rensselaer Polytechnic Institute, Graduate School, School of Science, Department of Earth and Environmental Sciences, Troy, NY 12180-3590. Offers environmental chemistry (MS, PhD); geochemistry (MS, PhD); geology (MS, PhD); geophysics (MS, PhD); petrology (MS, PhD). Part-time programs available. *Faculty:* 7 full-time (0 women). *Students:* 15 full-time (7 women); includes 3 minority (all Asian Americans or Pacific Islanders) Average age 24. 35 applicants, 11% accepted. In 2003, 4 master's, 1 doctorate awarded. Terminal master's awarded for partial completion of doctoral program. *Degree requirements:* For master's, thesis (for some programs), comprehensive exam; for doctorate, thesis/dissertation, comprehensive exam. *Entrance requirements:* For master's and doctorate, GRE General Test. Additional exam requirements/recommendations for international students: Required—TOEFL. *Application deadline:* For fall admission, 1/15 for domestic students. Applications are processed on a rolling basis. Application fee: $45. Electronic applications accepted. *Expenses:* Tuition: Full-time $27,700; part-time $1,320 per credit. Required fees: $1,470. *Financial support:* In 2003–04, 9 research assistantships with full tuition reimbursements (averaging $12,000 per year), 5 teaching assistantships with full tuition reimbursements (averaging $12,000 per year) were awarded. Fellowships with full tuition reimbursements, career-related internships or fieldwork, institutionally sponsored loans, and scholarships/grants also available. Financial award application deadline: 2/1; financial award applicants required to submit FAFSA. *Faculty research:* Mantel geochemistry, contaminant geochemistry, seismology, GPS geodesy, remote sensing petrology. Total annual research expenditures: $1.3 million. *Unit head:* Dr. Frank Spear, Chair, 518-276-6474, Fax: 518-276-6680, E-mail: ees@rpi.edu. *Application contact:* Dr. Steven Roecker, Professor, 518-276-6474, Fax: 518-276-6680, E-mail: ees@rpi.edu.

University of California, Los Angeles, Graduate Division, College of Letters and Science, Department of Earth and Space Sciences, Program in Geochemistry, Los Angeles, CA 90095. Offers MS, PhD. *Degree requirements:* For master's, comprehensive exams or thesis; for doctorate, thesis/dissertation, oral and written qualifying exams. *Entrance requirements:* For master's, GRE General Test, minimum GPA of 3.0; for doctorate, GRE General Test, minimum undergraduate GPA of 3.0. Electronic applications accepted. Tuition, nonresident: full-time $12,245. Required fees: $6,318.

University of Hawaii at Manoa, Graduate Division, School of Ocean and Earth Science and Technology, Department of Geology and Geophysics, Honolulu, HI 96822. Offers high-pressure geophysics and geochemistry (MS, PhD); hydrogeology and engineering geology (MS, PhD); marine geology and geophysics (MS, PhD); planetary geosciences and remote sensing (MS, PhD); seismology and solid-earth geophysics (MS, PhD); volcanology, petrology, and geochemistry (MS, PhD). *Faculty:* 73 full-time (13 women), 16 part-time/adjunct (1 woman). *Students:* 57 full-time (19 women); includes 3 minority (1 African American, 2 Asian Americans or Pacific Islanders), 17 international. Average age 29. 116 applicants, 15% accepted, 12 enrolled. Terminal master's awarded for partial completion of doctoral program. *Median time to degree:* Master's–3 years full-time; doctorate–3 years full-time. *Degree requirements:* For master's, thesis/dissertation; for doctorate, thesis/dissertation, comprehensive exam. *Entrance requirements:* For master's and doctorate, GRE General Test, minimum GPA of 3.0. Additional exam requirements/recommendations for international students: Required—TOEFL. *Application deadline:* For fall admission, 1/15 for domestic students, 1/1 for international students; for spring admission, 9/1 for domestic students, 8/15 for international students. Application fee: $50. *Expenses:* Tuition, state resident: full-time $4,464; part-time $186 per credit hour. Tuition, nonresident: full-time $10,608; part-time $442 per credit hour. Tuition and fees vary according to program. *Financial support:* In 2003–04, 44 research assistantships (averaging $19,270 per year), 5 teaching assistantships (averaging $18,198 per year) were awarded. *Unit head:* Dr. Paul Wessel, Chair, 808-956-2582, Fax: 808-956-5512.

University of Illinois at Chicago, Graduate College, College of Liberal Arts and Sciences, Department of Earth and Environmental Sciences, Chicago, IL 60607-7128. Offers crystallography (MS, PhD); environmental geology (MS, PhD); geochemistry (MS, PhD); geology (MS, PhD); geomorphology (MS, PhD); geophysics (MS, PhD); geotechnical engineering and geosciences (PhD); hydrogeology (MS, PhD); low-temperature and organic geochemistry (MS, PhD); mineralogy (MS, PhD); paleoclimatology (MS, PhD); paleontology (MS, PhD); petrology (MS, PhD); quaternary geology (MS, PhD); sedimentology (MS, PhD); water resources (MS, PhD). *Faculty:* 9 full-time (2 women). *Students:* 18 full-time (7 women), 5 part-time (1 woman); includes 3 minority (1 African American, 1 American Indian/Alaska Native, 1 Asian American or Pacific Islander), 11 international. Average age 29. 15 applicants, 27% accepted, 4 enrolled. In 2003, 2 degrees awarded. *Degree requirements:* For master's and doctorate, thesis/dissertation. *Entrance requirements:* For master's and doctorate, GRE General Test, minimum GPA of 3.75 on a 5.0 scale. Additional exam requirements/recommendations for international students: Required—TOEFL. *Application deadline:* For fall admission, 5/15 for domestic students, 2/1 for international students; for spring admission, 11/1 for domestic students, 7/15 for international students. Applications are processed on a rolling basis. Application fee: $40 ($50 for international students). Electronic applications accepted. *Expenses:* Tuition, state resident: part-time $941 per semester. Tuition, nonresident: part-time $2,338 per semester. *Financial support:* In 2003–04, 16 students received support; fellowships with full tuition reimbursements available, research assistantships with full tuition reimbursements available, teaching assistantships with full tuition reimbursements available, Federal Work-Study, scholarships/grants, traineeships, tuition waivers (full), and unspecified assistantships available. Financial award application deadline: 3/1; financial award applicants required to submit FAFSA. *Unit head:* Neil Sturchio, Head, 312-996-3154. *Application contact:* Peter Doran, Director of Graduate Studies, 312-413-7275, E-mail: pdoran@uic.edu.

University of Illinois at Urbana–Champaign, Graduate College, College of Liberal Arts and Sciences, Department of Geology, Champaign, IL 61820. Offers earth sciences (MS, PhD); geochemistry (MS, PhD); geology (MS, PhD); geophysics (MS, PhD). *Faculty:* 14 full-time (3 women). *Students:* 36 full-time (12 women); includes 3 minority (all Asian Americans or Pacific Islanders), 17 international. Average age 26. 72 applicants, 13% accepted, 4 enrolled. In 2003, 1 master's, 3 doctorates awarded. Terminal master's awarded for partial completion of doctoral program. *Degree requirements:* For master's and doctorate, thesis/dissertation. *Entrance requirements:* For master's and doctorate, GRE General Test, minimum GPA of 3.0. Additional exam requirements/recommendations for international students: Required—TOEFL. *Application deadline:* For fall admission, 2/15 for domestic students; for spring admission, 10/15 for domestic students. Applications are processed on a rolling basis. Application fee: $40 ($50 for international students). *Expenses:* Tuition, state resident: full-time $6,692. Tuition, nonresident: full-time $18,692. *Financial support:* In 2003–04, 14 research assistantships, 16 teaching assistantships were awarded. Fellowships, Federal Work-Study and tuition waivers (full and partial) also available. Financial award application deadline: 2/15. *Faculty research:* Hydrogeology, structure/tectonics, mineral science. *Unit head:* Stephen Marshak, Head, 217-333-3542, Fax: 217-244-4996, E-mail: smarshak@uiuc.edu. *Application contact:* Barbara Elmore, Graduate Admissions Secretary, 217-333-3542, Fax: 217-244-4996, E-mail: belmore@uiuc.edu.

University of Michigan, Horace H. Rackham School of Graduate Studies, College of Literature, Science, and the Arts, Department of Geological Sciences, Program in Oceanography: Marine Geology and Geochemistry, Ann Arbor, MI 48109. Offers MS, PhD. *Faculty:* 4 full-time (0 women). *Students:* 6 full-time (all women); includes 3 minority (all Asian Americans or Pacific Islanders) Average age 26. 6 applicants, 0% accepted. In 2003, 2 master's, 2 doctorates awarded. Terminal master's awarded for partial completion of doctoral program. *Median time to degree:* Master's–2.5 years full-time; doctorate–5 years full-time. *Degree requirements:* For master's, thesis; for doctorate, thesis/dissertation, oral defense of dissertation, preliminary exam. *Entrance requirements:* For master's and doctorate, GRE General Test. *Application deadline:* For fall admission, 1/15 for domestic students. Applications are processed on a rolling basis. Application fee: $60 ($75 for international students). Electronic applications accepted. *Expenses:* Tuition, state resident: full-time $7,463. Tuition, nonresident: full-time $13,913. Full-time tuition and fees vary according to course load, degree level and program. *Financial support:* In 2003–04, 1 fellowship with full tuition reimbursement (averaging $12,853 per year), 1 research

Geochemistry

University of Michigan (continued)
assistantship with full tuition reimbursement (averaging $12,853 per year), 2 teaching assistantships with full tuition reimbursements (averaging $12,853 per year) were awarded. Career-related internships or fieldwork, Federal Work-Study, and health care benefits also available. Financial award applicants required to submit FAFSA. *Faculty research:* Paleoceanography, paleolimnology, marine geochemistry, seismic stratigraphy. *Application contact:* Anne Hudon, Student Services Assistant, 734-615-3034, Fax: 734-763-4690, E-mail: ahudon@umich.edu.

University of Missouri–Rolla, Graduate School, School of Materials, Energy, and Earth Resources, Department of Geological Sciences and Engineering, Program in Geology and Geophysics, Rolla, MO 65409-0910. Offers geochemistry (MS, PhD); geology (MS, PhD); geophysics (MS, PhD); groundwater and environmental geology (MS, PhD). Part-time programs available. *Faculty:* 8 full-time (1 woman). *Students:* 26 full-time (10 women), 3 part-time (1 woman); includes 2 minority (1 African American, 1 Hispanic American), 10 international. Average age 31. 26 applicants, 65% accepted, 3 enrolled. In 2003, 13 master's, 4 doctorates awarded. *Median time to degree:* Master's–1.5 years full-time, 5.3 years part-time; doctorate–5 years full-time, 7 years part-time. *Degree requirements:* For master's and doctorate, thesis/dissertation. *Entrance requirements:* For master's, GRE General Test, GRE Subject Test, minimum GPA of 3.0 in last 4 semesters; for doctorate, GRE General Test, GRE Subject Test. Additional exam requirements/recommendations for international students: Required—TOEFL. *Application deadline:* For fall admission, 7/1 for domestic students; for spring admission, 12/1 for domestic students. Applications are processed on a rolling basis. Application fee: $50. Electronic applications accepted. *Expenses:* Tuition, state resident: full-time $5,871. Tuition, nonresident: full-time $13,114. Required fees: $820. Tuition and fees vary according to course load. *Financial support:* In 2003–04, 23 students received support, including 22 fellowships with full tuition reimbursements available (averaging $13,250 per year), 16 research assistantships with partial tuition reimbursements available (averaging $13,250 per year); teaching assistantships with partial tuition reimbursements available, Federal Work-Study and institutionally sponsored loans also available. Support available to part-time students. Financial award application deadline: 3/1; financial award applicants required to submit FAFSA. *Faculty research:* Economic geology, geophysical modeling, seismic wave analysis. Total annual research expenditures: $272,086.

University of Nevada, Reno, Graduate School, College of Science, Mackay School of Earth Sciences and Engineering, Department of Geological Sciences, Reno, NV 89557. Offers geochemistry (MS, PhD); geological engineering (MS, Geol E); geology (MS, PhD); geophysics (MS, PhD). *Faculty:* 37. *Students:* 52 full-time (15 women), 23 part-time (6 women); includes 6 minority (1 American Indian/Alaska Native, 3 Asian Americans or Pacific Islanders, 2 Hispanic Americans), 11 international. Average age 33. In 2003, 8 master's, 2 doctorates awarded. *Degree requirements:* For master's, thesis optional; for doctorate, one foreign language, thesis/dissertation. *Entrance requirements:* For master's, GRE General Test, GRE Subject Test, minimum GPA of 2.75; for doctorate, GRE General Test, GRE Subject Test, minimum GPA of 3.0. Additional exam requirements/recommendations for international students: Required—TOEFL. *Application deadline:* For fall admission, 2/15 for domestic students; for spring admission, 9/15 for domestic students. Applications are processed on a rolling basis. Application fee: $60 ($95 for international students). *Expenses:* Tuition, state resident: part-time $119 per credit. Tuition, nonresident: part-time $127 per credit. Required fees: $20 per term. Tuition and fees vary according to course load. *Financial support:* In 2003–04, 17 research assistantships, 8 teaching assistantships were awarded. Institutionally sponsored loans and tuition waivers (full) also available. Financial award application deadline: 3/1. *Faculty research:* Hydrothermal ore deposits, metamorphic and igneous petrogenesis, sedimentary rock record of earth history, field and petrographic investigation of magnetism, rock fracture mechanics. *Unit head:* Dr. Robert Watters, Graduate Program Director, 775-784-1770.

University of New Hampshire, Graduate School, College of Engineering and Physical Sciences, Department of Earth Sciences, Durham, NH 03824. Offers earth sciences (MS), including geochemical, geology, ocean mapping, oceanography; hydrology (MS). *Faculty:* 29 full-time. *Students:* 18 full-time (7 women), 22 part-time (7 women); includes 3 minority (2 African Americans, 1 American Indian/Alaska Native), 2 international. Average age 31. 49 applicants, 78% accepted, 16 enrolled. In 2003, 9 degrees awarded. *Degree requirements:* For master's, thesis, one foreign language. *Entrance requirements:* For master's, GRE General Test. Additional exam requirements/recommendations for international students: Required—TOEFL (minimum score 550 paper-based; 213 computer-based); Recommended—TSE. *Application deadline:* For fall admission, 4/1 for domestic students; for winter admission, 12/1 for domestic students. Applications are processed on a rolling basis. Application fee: $50. Electronic applications accepted. Tuition, area resident: Full-time $7,070. *Expenses:* Tuition, state resident: full-time $10,605. Tuition, nonresident: full-time $17,430. Required fees: $15. *Financial support:* In 2003–04, 1 fellowship, 7 research assistantships, 9 teaching assistantships were awarded. Career-related internships or fieldwork, Federal Work-Study, scholarships/grants, and tuition waivers (full and partial) also available. Support available to part-time students. Financial award application deadline: 2/15. *Unit head:* Dr. Matt Davis, Chairperson, 603-862-4119, E-mail: earth.sciences@unh.edu. *Application contact:* Linda Wrightsman, Administrative Assistant, 603-862-1720, E-mail: earth.sciences@unh.edu.

University of Victoria, Faculty of Graduate Studies, Faculty of Science, School of Earth and Ocean Sciences, Victoria, BC V8W 2Y2, Canada. Offers geochemistry (M Sc, PhD); geophysics (M Sc, PhD); marine geology and geophysics (M Sc, PhD); ocean acoustics (M Sc, PhD); oceanography (M Sc, PhD); paleobiology (M Sc, PhD); paleoceanography (M Sc, PhD); sedimentology (M Sc, PhD); stratigraphy (M Sc, PhD). Part-time programs available. *Degree requirements:* For master's and doctorate, thesis/dissertation. *Entrance requirements:* Additional exam requirements/recommendations for international students: Required—TOEFL (minimum score 550 paper-based; 213 computer-based). Electronic applications accepted. *Faculty research:* Climate modeling, geology.

Washington University in St. Louis, Graduate School of Arts and Sciences, Department of Earth and Planetary Sciences, St. Louis, MO 63130-4899. Offers earth and planetary sciences (MA); geochemistry (PhD); geology (MA, PhD); geophysics (PhD); planetary sciences (PhD). *Students:* 36 full-time (19 women), 1 (woman) part-time; includes 2 minority (both Asian Americans or Pacific Islanders), 5 international. 69 applicants, 35% accepted, 12 enrolled. In 2003, 9 master's, 2 doctorates awarded. Terminal master's awarded for partial completion of doctoral program. *Degree requirements:* For master's and doctorate, thesis/dissertation. *Entrance requirements:* For master's and doctorate, GRE General Test. *Application deadline:* For fall admission, 1/15 for domestic students. Applications are processed on a rolling basis. Application fee: $35. Electronic applications accepted. *Expenses:* Tuition: Full-time $28,300; part-time $1,180 per credit. *Financial support:* Fellowships, research assistantships, teaching assistantships, Federal Work-Study, institutionally sponsored loans, and tuition waivers (full and partial) available. Financial award application deadline: 1/15. *Unit head:* Dr. Raymond E. Arvidson, Chairman, 314-935-5610.

Woods Hole Oceanographic Institution, MIT/WHOI Joint Program in Oceanography/Applied Ocean Science and Engineering, Woods Hole, MA 02543-1541. Offers applied ocean sciences (PhD); biological oceanography (PhD, Sc D); chemical oceanography (PhD, Sc D); civil and environmental and oceanographic engineering (PhD); electrical and oceanographic engineering (PhD); geochemistry (PhD); geophysics (PhD); marine biology (PhD); marine geochemistry (PhD, Sc D); marine geology (PhD, Sc D); marine geophysics (PhD); mechanical and oceanographic engineering (PhD); ocean engineering (PhD); oceanographic engineering (M Eng, MS, PhD, Sc D, Eng); paleoceanography (PhD); physical oceanography (PhD, Sc D). MS, PhD, and Sc D offered jointly with MIT. *Faculty:* 123 full-time, 8 part-time/adjunct. *Students:* 128 full-time (62 women); includes 8 minority (2 African Americans, 4 Asian Americans or Pacific Islanders, 2 Hispanic Americans), 37 international. Average age 27. 187 applicants, 28% accepted, 32 enrolled. In 2003, 7 master's, 20 doctorates awarded. Terminal master's awarded for partial completion of doctoral program. *Median time to degree:* Master's–2.9 years full-time; doctorate–5.8 years full-time. *Degree requirements:* For master's and Eng, thesis (for some programs); for doctorate, thesis/dissertation. *Entrance requirements:* For master's, GRE General Test; for doctorate, GRE General Test, GRE Subject Test. Additional exam requirements/recommendations for international students: Required—TOEFL. *Application deadline:* For fall admission, 1/15 priority date for domestic students, 1/15 priority date for international students. Application fee: $65. Electronic applications accepted. *Expenses:* Tuition: Full-time $39,200. *Financial support:* In 2003–04, 13 fellowships (averaging $39,200 per year), 69 research assistantships (averaging $39,200 per year) were awarded. Teaching assistantships, scholarships/grants, traineeships, health care benefits, and unspecified assistantships also available. Financial award application deadline: 1/15. *Unit head:* Prof. Paola Rizzoli, Director, 617-253-2451, E-mail: rizzoli@mit.edu. *Application contact:* Ronni Schwartz, Administrator, 617-253-7544, Fax: 617-253-9784, E-mail: mspiggy@mit.edu.

See in-depth description on page 279.

Wright State University, School of Graduate Studies, College of Science and Mathematics, Department of Geological Sciences, Program in Geological Sciences, Dayton, OH 45435. Offers environmental geochemistry (MS); environmental geology (MS); environmental sciences (MS); geological sciences (MS); geophysics (MS); hydrogeology (MS); petroleum geology (MS). Part-time programs available. *Students:* 22 full-time (4 women), 9 part-time (4 women), 2 international. Average age 26. 21 applicants, 100% accepted. In 2003, 15 degrees awarded. *Degree requirements:* For master's, thesis. *Entrance requirements:* Additional exam requirements/recommendations for international students: Required—TOEFL. Application fee: $25. *Expenses:* Tuition, state resident: full-time $8,112; part-time $255 per quarter hour. Tuition, nonresident: full-time $14,127; part-time $442 per quarter hour. International tuition: $14,283 full-time. Tuition and fees vary according to course load, degree level and program. *Financial support:* Fellowships, research assistantships, teaching assistantships, Federal Work-Study and unspecified assistantships available. Support available to part-time students. Financial award application deadline: 3/1; financial award applicants required to submit FAFSA. *Application contact:* Deborah L. Cowles, Assistant to Chair, 937-775-3455, Fax: 937-775-3462, E-mail: deborah.cowles@wright.edu.

Yale University, Graduate School of Arts and Sciences, Department of Geology and Geophysics, New Haven, CT 06520. Offers geochemistry (PhD); geophysics (PhD); meteorology (PhD); mineralogy and crystallography (PhD); oceanography (PhD); paleoecology (PhD); paleontology and stratigraphy (PhD); petrology (PhD); structural geology (PhD). *Degree requirements:* For doctorate, thesis/dissertation. *Entrance requirements:* For doctorate, GRE General Test. Additional exam requirements/recommendations for international students: Required—TOEFL. *Expenses:* Tuition: Full-time $25,600; part-time $6,400 per term.

See in-depth description on page 261.

Geodetic Sciences

Columbia University, Graduate School of Arts and Sciences, Division of Natural Sciences, Department of Earth and Environmental Sciences, New York, NY 10027. Offers geochemistry (M Phil, MA, PhD); geodetic sciences (M Phil, MA, PhD); geophysics (M Phil, MA, PhD); oceanography (M Phil, MA, PhD). *Faculty:* 21 full-time, 19 part-time/adjunct. *Students:* 78 full-time (31 women), 6 part-time (2 women); includes 4 minority (3 Asian Americans or Pacific Islanders, 1 Hispanic American), 31 international. Average age 32. 115 applicants, 20% accepted. In 2003, 16 master's, 11 doctorates awarded. *Degree requirements:* For master's, thesis or alternative, fieldwork, written exam; for doctorate, one foreign language, thesis/dissertation. *Entrance requirements:* For master's and doctorate, GRE General Test, GRE Subject Test, major in natural or physical science. Additional exam requirements/recommendations for international students: Required—TOEFL. Application fee: $75. *Expenses:* Tuition: Full-time $14,820. *Financial support:* Fellowships, teaching assistantships, Federal Work-Study and institutionally sponsored loans available. Support available to part-time students. Financial award application deadline: 1/5; financial award applicants required to submit FAFSA. *Faculty research:* Structural geology and stratigraphy, petrology, paleontology, rare gas, isotope and aqueous geochemistry. *Unit head:* Dr. William Menke, Chair, 212-864-4525, Fax: 845-365-8163.

The Ohio State University, Graduate School, College of Engineering, Program in Geodetic Science and Surveying, Columbus, OH 43210. Offers MS, PhD. *Faculty:* 12. *Students:* 40 full-time (7 women), 7 part-time (1 woman); includes 2 minority (both African Americans), 39 international. 54 applicants, 43% accepted. In 2003, 10 master's, 6 doctorates awarded. *Degree requirements:* For master's, thesis optional; for doctorate, thesis/dissertation. *Application deadline:* For fall admission, 8/15 for domestic students. Applications are processed on a rolling basis. Application fee: $40 ($50 for international students). *Expenses:* Tuition, state resident: full-time $7,233. Tuition, nonresident: full-time $18,489. *Financial support:* Fellowships, research assistantships, teaching assistantships, Federal Work-Study and institutionally sponsored loans available. Support available to part-time students. *Faculty research:* Photogrammetry, cartography, geodesy, land information systems. *Unit head:* Dr. Morton E. O'Kelly, Graduate Studies Committee Chair, 614-292-8744, Fax: 614-292-6213, E-mail: okelly.1@osu.edu. *Application contact:* Irene B. Tesfai, Graduate Program Coordinator, 614-292-2933, Fax: 614-292-3780, E-mail: tesfai.1@osu.edu.

Université Laval, Faculty of Forestry and Geomatics, Department of Geomatics Sciences, Programs in Geomatics Sciences, Québec, QC G1K 7P4, Canada. Offers M Sc, PhD. Terminal master's awarded for partial completion of doctoral program. *Degree requirements:* For master's, thesis (for some programs); for doctorate, thesis/dissertation, comprehensive exam. *Entrance requirements:* For master's and doctorate, knowledge of French and English. Electronic applications accepted.

University of New Brunswick Fredericton, School of Graduate Studies, Faculty of Engineering, Department of Geodesy and Geomatics, Fredericton, NB E3B 5A3, Canada. Offers land information management (Diploma); mapping, charting and geodesy (Diploma); surveying engineering (M Eng, M Sc E, PhD). Part-time programs available. *Degree requirements:* For master's, thesis; for doctorate, thesis/dissertation, qualifying exam. *Entrance requirements:* For master's and doctorate, minimum GPA of 3.0. Additional exam requirements/recommendations for international students: Required—TOEFL, TWE.

Geology

Acadia University, Faculty of Pure and Applied Science, Department of Geology, Wolfville, NS B4P 2R6, Canada. Offers M Sc. *Faculty:* 6 full-time (2 women), 1 part-time/adjunct (0 women). *Students:* 5 full-time (2 women), 1 (woman) part-time. Average age 23. 6 applicants, 83% accepted, 5 enrolled. In 2003, 2 degrees awarded, leading to university research/teaching 50%, business/industry 50%. *Degree requirements:* For master's, thesis. *Entrance requirements:* For master's, bachelor of science in geology or equivalent. *Application deadline:* For fall admission, 2/1 priority date for domestic students, 2/1 priority date for international students. Applications are processed on a rolling basis. Application fee: $50. *Expenses:* Tuition, state resident: full-time $5,611. *Financial support:* In 2003–04, 5 students received support, including 2 teaching assistantships (averaging $8,000 per year); scholarships/grants also available. Financial award application deadline: 2/1. *Faculty research:* Igneous, metamorphic, and Quaternary geology; stratigraphy; remote sensing; micropaleontology. Total annual research expenditures: $196,790. *Unit head:* Dr. Robert Raeside, Head, 902-585-1208, Fax: 902-585-1816, E-mail: geology@acadiau.ca. *Application contact:* Dr. Sandra Barr, Graduate Coordinator, 902-585-1340, Fax: 902-585-1816, E-mail: sandra.barr@acadiau.ca.

Auburn University, Graduate School, College of Sciences and Mathematics, Department of Geology and Geography, Auburn University, AL 36849. Offers MS. Part-time programs available. *Faculty:* 14 full-time (2 women). *Students:* 9 full-time (4 women), 5 part-time (2 women), 2 international. 8 applicants, 75% accepted. In 2003, 5 degrees awarded. *Degree requirements:* For master's, computer language or Geographic Information Systems, field camp. *Entrance requirements:* For master's, GRE General Test. *Application deadline:* For fall admission, 7/7 for domestic students; for spring admission, 11/24 for domestic students. Applications are processed on a rolling basis. Application fee: $25 ($50 for international students). Electronic applications accepted. *Expenses:* Tuition, state resident: part-time $175 per credit hour. Tuition, nonresident: part-time $525 per credit hour. *Financial support:* Research assistantships, teaching assistantships, Federal Work-Study available. Support available to part-time students. Financial award application deadline: 3/15. *Faculty research:* Empirical magma dynamics and melt migration, ore mineralogy, role of terrestrial plant biomass in deposition, metamorphic petrology and isotope geochemistry, reef development, crinoid taphology. *Unit head:* Dr. Robert B. Cook, Head, 334-844-4282. *Application contact:* Dr. John F. Pritchett, Dean of the Graduate School, 334-844-4700, E-mail: hatchlb@mail.auburn.edu.

Announcement: The master's program offers a broad-based curriculum that takes advantage of Auburn's location on the boundary between the Appalachian front and the Gulf Coastal Plain. Low student-faculty ratio results in small class size, close relationships between students and faculty members, and relaxed and informal atmosphere. Research opportunities include hydrology and aqueous and hydrothermal geochemistry; economic geology, petrochemistry, and tectonics of the southern Appalachians; environmental geophysics; coastal-plain stratigraphy/sedimentology; and taphonomy and paleoecology of invertebrate assemblages. Current investigations extend beyond the region to other areas in the US as well as the Bahamas, Scandinavia, and Himalayan foreland basins. For additional information, visit the Web site: http://www.auburn.edu/academic/science_math/geology/docs.

Ball State University, Graduate School, College of Sciences and Humanities, Department of Geology, Muncie, IN 47306-1099. Offers MA, MS. *Faculty:* 7. *Students:* 4 full-time (2 women), 2 part-time (1 woman); includes 1 minority (Asian American or Pacific Islander), 1 international. Average age 39. 6 applicants, 67% accepted, 3 enrolled. In 2003, 1 degree awarded. *Degree requirements:* For master's, thesis (for some programs). *Entrance requirements:* For master's, GRE General Test. Application fee: $25 ($35 for international students). *Expenses:* Tuition, state resident: full-time $5,748. Tuition, nonresident: full-time $14,166. *Financial support:* In 2003–04, 2 research assistantships, 3 teaching assistantships with full tuition reimbursements (averaging $8,374 per year) were awarded. Career-related internships or fieldwork also available. Financial award application deadline: 3/1. *Faculty research:* Environmental geology, geophysics, stratigraphy. *Unit head:* Dr. Alan Samuelson, Chairman, 765-285-8270, Fax: 765-285-8265, E-mail: asamuels@bsu.edu. *Application contact:* Scott Rice-Snow, Director of Graduate Programs, 765-285-8270, Fax: 765-285-8265, E-mail: ricesnow@bsu.edu.

Baylor University, Graduate School, College of Arts and Sciences, Department of Geology, Waco, TX 76798. Offers earth science (MA); geology (MS, PhD). *Faculty:* 12 full-time (1 woman). *Students:* 18 full-time (9 women), 2 part-time (1 woman); includes 2 minority (both Hispanic Americans), 3 international. In 2003, 3 master's, 1 doctorate awarded. *Degree requirements:* For master's and doctorate, thesis/dissertation. *Entrance requirements:* For master's and doctorate, GRE General Test. *Application deadline:* For fall admission, 3/15 for domestic students. Applications are processed on a rolling basis. Application fee: $25. *Expenses:* Tuition: Part-time $698 per hour. *Financial support:* In 2003–04, 18 teaching assistantships were awarded; Federal Work-Study and institutionally sponsored loans also available. *Faculty research:* Petroleum geology, geophysics, engineering geology, hydrogeology. *Unit head:* Dr. Thomas T. Goforth, Graduate Program Director, 254-710-2361, Fax: 254-710-2673, E-mail: thomas_goforth@baylor.edu. *Application contact:* Suzanne Keener, Administrative Assistant, 254-710-3588, Fax: 254-710-3870, E-mail: pauline_johnson@baylor.edu.

Boise State University, Graduate College, College of Arts and Sciences, Department of Geosciences, Program in Geology, Boise, ID 83725-0399. Offers MS. Part-time programs available. *Students:* 10 full-time (5 women), 14 part-time (8 women); includes 1 minority (American Indian/Alaska Native). Average age 36. 6 applicants, 83% accepted. In 2003, 3 degrees awarded. *Degree requirements:* For master's, thesis. *Entrance requirements:* For master's, GRE General Test, BS in related field, minimum GPA of 3.0. *Application deadline:* For fall admission, 7/17 for domestic students; for spring admission, 12/5 priority date for domestic students. Applications are processed on a rolling basis. Application fee: $30. Electronic applications accepted. *Expenses:* Tuition, state resident: full-time $4,668. Tuition, nonresident: full-time $11,388. *Financial support:* In 2003–04, 15 students received support, including 10 research assistantships with full tuition reimbursements available (averaging $11,485 per year); career-related internships or fieldwork, Federal Work-Study, institutionally sponsored loans, and unspecified assistantships also available. Support available to part-time students. Financial award application deadline: 3/1. *Unit head:* Dr. James McNamara, Coordinator, 208-426-1354.

Boston College, Graduate School of Arts and Sciences, Department of Geology and Geophysics, Chestnut Hill, MA 02467-3800. Offers MS, MBA/MS. *Students:* 14 full-time (7 women), 8 part-time (3 women); includes 1 minority (Asian American or Pacific Islander), 4 international. 19 applicants, 79% accepted, 9 enrolled. In 2003, 11 degrees awarded. *Degree requirements:* For master's, thesis. *Entrance requirements:* For master's, GRE General Test, GRE Subject Test. Additional exam requirements/recommendations for international students: Required—TOEFL (minimum score 550 paper-based; 213 computer-based). *Application deadline:* For fall admission, 2/1 for domestic students. Application fee: $60. Electronic applications accepted. *Expenses:* Tuition: Part-time $810 per credit. *Financial support:* Research assistantships, teaching assistantships, Federal Work-Study available. Support available to part-time students. Financial award application deadline: 3/1; financial award applicants required to submit FAFSA. *Faculty research:* Coastal and marine geology, experimental sedimentology, geomagnetism, igneous petrology, paleontology. *Unit head:* Dr. Alan Kafka, Chairperson, 617-552-3650. *Application contact:* Dr. John Ebel, Graduate Program Director, 617-552-3640, E-mail: john.ebel@bc.edu.

Bowling Green State University, Graduate College, College of Arts and Sciences, Department of Geology, Bowling Green, OH 43403. Offers MAT, MS. Part-time programs available. *Faculty:* 13 full-time. *Students:* 18 full-time (7 women), 5 part-time (3 women), 5 international. Average age 27. 21 applicants, 90% accepted, 8 enrolled. In 2003, 9 degrees awarded. *Degree requirements:* For master's, thesis. *Entrance requirements:* For master's, GRE General Test. Additional exam requirements/recommendations for international students: Required—TOEFL. *Application deadline:* For fall admission, 3/1 for domestic students; for spring admission, 11/1 for domestic students. Application fee: $30. Electronic applications accepted. *Expenses:* Tuition, state resident: part-time $436 per hour. Tuition, nonresident: part-time $768 per hour. *Financial support:* In 2003–04, 2 research assistantships with full tuition reimbursements (averaging $9,300 per year), 15 teaching assistantships with full tuition reimbursements (averaging $9,366 per year) were awarded. Career-related internships or fieldwork, institutionally sponsored loans, tuition waivers (full), and unspecified assistantships also available. Financial award applicants required to submit FAFSA. *Faculty research:* Remote sensing, environmental geology, geological information systems, structural geology, geochemistry. *Unit head:* Dr. Charles Onasch, Chair, 419-372-7197. *Application contact:* Dr. Sheila Roberts, Graduate Coordinator, 419-372-0354.

Brigham Young University, Graduate Studies, College of Physical and Mathematical Sciences, Department of Geology, Provo, UT 84602-1001. Offers MS. *Faculty:* 13 full-time (0 women). *Students:* 17 full-time (7 women), 16 part-time (6 women); includes 3 minority (1 African American, 2 Asian Americans or Pacific Islanders). Average age 23. 14 applicants, 57% accepted, 8 enrolled. In 2003, 6 degrees awarded. *Degree requirements:* For master's, thesis. *Entrance requirements:* For master's, GRE General Test, minimum GPA of 3.0 in last 60 hours. Additional exam requirements/recommendations for international students: Required—TOEFL. *Application deadline:* For fall admission, 2/1 priority date for domestic students, 2/1 priority date for international students; for winter admission, 11/15 for domestic students. Applications are processed on a rolling basis. Application fee: $50. *Expenses:* Tuition: Part-time $221 per hour. *Financial support:* In 2003–04, 17 students received support, including 1 research assistantship (averaging $12,000 per year), 7 teaching assistantships (averaging $12,000 per year); fellowships, career-related internships or fieldwork, institutionally sponsored loans, scholarships/grants, and tuition waivers (partial) also available. Financial award application deadline: 2/1. *Faculty research:* Regional tectonics, hydrogeochemistry, crystal chemistry and crystallography, stratigraphy, environmental geophysics. Total annual research expenditures: $88,051. *Unit head:* Dr. Jeffrey D. Keith, Chairman, 801-422-2189, Fax: 801-422-0267, E-mail: jeffrey_keith@byu.edu. *Application contact:* Dr. Bart J. Kowallis, Graduate Coordinator, 801-422-2467, Fax: 801-422-0267, E-mail: bart_kowallis@byu.edu.

Brooklyn College of the City University of New York, Division of Graduate Studies, Department of Geology, Brooklyn, NY 11210-2889. Offers applied geology (MA); geology (MA, PhD). The department offers courses at Brooklyn College that are creditable toward the CUNY doctoral degree (with permission of the executive officer of the doctoral program). Evening/weekend programs available. *Students:* 9 applicants, 67% accepted, 1 enrolled.Terminal master's awarded for partial completion of doctoral program. *Degree requirements:* For master's, qualifying exams. *Entrance requirements:* For master's, GRE or qualifying exam, bachelor's degree in geology or equivalent, fieldwork, 2 letters of recommendation; for doctorate, GRE. Additional exam requirements/recommendations for international students: Required—TOEFL. *Application deadline:* For fall admission, 3/1 for domestic students, 2/1 for international students; for spring admission, 11/1 for domestic students, 10/1 for international students. Applications are processed on a rolling basis. Application fee: $50. *Expenses:* Tuition, state resident: full-time $5,440; part-time $230 per credit. Tuition, nonresident: full-time $10,200; part-time $425 per credit. Required fees: $280; $103 per term. *Financial support:* Fellowships with partial tuition reimbursements, research assistantships with partial tuition reimbursements, teaching assistantships with partial tuition reimbursements, career-related internships or fieldwork, Federal Work-Study, institutionally sponsored loans, scholarships/grants, and tuition waivers (full and partial) available. Support available to part-time students. Financial award application deadline: 5/1; financial award applicants required to submit FAFSA. *Faculty research:* Geochemistry, petrology, tectonophysics, hydrogeology, sedimentary geology, environmental geology. *Unit head:* Dr. Nehru E. Cherukupalli, Chairperson, 718-951-5416, Fax: 718-951-4753, E-mail: nehru@brooklyn.cuny.edu. *Application contact:* Michael Lovaglio, Assistant Director of Graduate Admissions, 718-951-5001, E-mail: adminqry@brooklyn.cuny.edu.

California Institute of Technology, Division of Geological and Planetary Sciences, Pasadena, CA 91125-0001. Offers cosmochemistry (PhD); geobiology (PhD); geochemistry (MS, PhD); geology (MS, PhD); geophysics (MS, PhD); planetary science (MS, PhD). Part-time programs available. *Faculty:* 37 full-time (3 women). *Students:* 61 full-time (29 women); includes 28 minority (1 African American, 26 Asian Americans or Pacific Islanders, 1 Hispanic American). Average age 27. 127 applicants, 20% accepted, 15 enrolled. In 2003, 5 master's, 13 doctorates awarded. *Degree requirements:* For doctorate, thesis/dissertation. *Entrance requirements:* For doctorate, GRE General Test. Additional exam requirements/recommendations for international students: Required—TOEFL. *Application deadline:* For fall admission, 1/15 for domestic students, 1/15 for international students. Application fee: $50. Electronic applications accepted. *Financial support:* In 2003–04, 21 fellowships with full tuition reimbursements (averaging $20,496 per year), 49 research assistantships with full tuition reimbursements (averaging $20,496 per year) were awarded. Teaching assistantships with full tuition reimbursements, institutionally sponsored loans, scholarships/grants, health care benefits, and unspecified assistantships also available. Financial award applicants required to submit FAFSA. *Faculty research:* Astronomy, evolution of anaerobic respiratory processes, structural geology and tectonics, theoretical and numerical seismology, global biogeochemical cycles. Total annual research expenditures: $18.6 million. *Unit head:* Dr. Edward M. Stolper, Chairman, 626-395-6108, Fax: 626-795-6028, E-mail: divgps@gps.caltech.edu. *Application contact:* Dr. George R. Rossman, Academic Officer, 626-395-6125, Fax: 626-568-0935, E-mail: divgps@gps.caltech.edu.

California State University, Bakersfield, Division of Graduate Studies and Research, School of Natural Sciences, Mathematics, and Engineering, Program in Geology, Bakersfield, CA 93311-1099. Offers geology (MS); hydrology (MS). Part-time and evening/weekend programs available. *Degree requirements:* For master's, thesis. *Entrance requirements:* For master's, GRE General Test, BS in geology.

California State University, Chico, Graduate School, College of Natural Sciences, Department of Geological and Environmental Sciences, Chico, CA 95929-0722. Offers environmental science (MS); geosciences (MS), including earth sciences, hydrology/hydrogeology. *Students:* 14 full-time (9 women), 5 part-time (2 women). Average age 32. 7 applicants, 100% accepted, 6 enrolled. In 2003, 3 degrees awarded. *Degree requirements:* For master's, thesis, competency exam. *Entrance requirements:* For master's, GRE General Test. Additional exam requirements/recommendations for international students: Required—TOEFL (minimum score 550 paper-based; 213 computer-based). *Application deadline:* For fall admission, 3/1 for domestic students, 3/1 for international students; for spring admission, 9/15 for domestic students, 9/15 for international students. Applications are processed on a rolling basis. Application fee: $55. Electronic applications accepted. Tuition, nonresident: part-time $282 per semester hour. Required fees: $1,029 per semester. *Financial support:* Fellowships, teaching assistantships available. *Unit head:* Dr. Richard Flory, Chair, 530-898-6369. *Application contact:* Dr. Gregory Taylor, Graduate Coordinator, 530-898-6369.

California State University, Fresno, Division of Graduate Studies, College of Science and Mathematics, Department of Earth and Environmental Sciences, Fresno, CA 93740-8027. Offers geology (MS). Part-time programs available. *Degree requirements:* For master's, thesis. *Entrance requirements:* For master's, GRE General Test, GRE Subject Test, undergraduate geology degree, minimum GPA of 2.7. Additional exam requirements/recommendations for international students: Required—TOEFL. Electronic applications accepted. *Faculty research:* Water drainage, pollution, cartography, creek restoration, nitrate contamination.

California State University, Fullerton, Graduate Studies, College of Natural Science and Mathematics, Department of Geological Sciences, Fullerton, CA 92834-9480. Offers MS. Part-time programs available. *Faculty:* 10 full-time (1 woman), 15 part-time/adjunct. *Students:*

Geology

California State University, Fullerton (continued)
5 full-time (1 woman), 15 part-time (6 women); includes 3 minority (all Hispanic Americans) Average age 32. 15 applicants, 73% accepted, 8 enrolled. *Degree requirements:* For master's, thesis. *Entrance requirements:* For master's, bachelor's degree in geology, minimum GPA of 3.0 in geology courses. Application fee: $55. Tuition, nonresident: part-time $282 per unit. Required fees: $889 per semester. *Unit head:* Dr. John Foster, Chair, 714-278-3882. *Application contact:* Dr. Brady Rhodes, Adviser, 714-278-2942.

California State University, Hayward, Academic Programs and Graduate Studies, College of Science, Department of Geological Sciences, Hayward, CA 94542-3000. Offers geology (MS). Evening/weekend programs available. *Students:* 2 full-time (1 woman), 8 part-time (2 women); includes 1 minority (Asian American or Pacific Islander) 3 applicants, 0% accepted. *Degree requirements:* For master's, thesis. *Entrance requirements:* For master's, GRE, minimum GPA of 2.75 in field, 2.5 overall. Additional exam requirements/recommendations for international students: Required—TOEFL (minimum score 550 paper-based; 213 computer-based). *Application deadline:* For fall admission, 5/31 for domestic students, 2/27 for international students; for winter admission, 9/30 for domestic students. Applications are processed on a rolling basis. Application fee: $55. Electronic applications accepted. Tuition, nonresident: part-time $188 per unit. Required fees: $560 per quarter hour. *Financial support:* Career-related internships or fieldwork, Federal Work-Study, and institutionally sponsored loans available. Support available to part-time students. Financial award application deadline: 3/2. *Unit head:* Dr. Jeffrey Seitz, Interim Chair, 510-885-3486. *Application contact:* Jennifer Cason, Graduate Program Coordinator/Operations Analyst, 510-885-3286, Fax: 510-885-4777, E-mail: jcason@csuhayward.edu.

California State University, Long Beach, Graduate Studies, College of Natural Sciences, Department of Geological Sciences, Long Beach, CA 90840. Offers MS. Part-time programs available. *Faculty:* 8 full-time (3 women), 2 part-time/adjunct (0 women). *Students:* Average age 37. 7 applicants, 57% accepted, 2 enrolled. *Degree requirements:* For master's, thesis. *Entrance requirements:* For master's, GRE General Test. *Application deadline:* For fall admission, 7/1 for domestic students; for spring admission, 12/1 for domestic students. Applications are processed on a rolling basis. Application fee: $55. Electronic applications accepted. Tuition, nonresident: part-time $282 per unit. Required fees: $504 per semester. *Financial support:* Research assistantships, teaching assistantships, Federal Work-Study, institutionally sponsored loans, and scholarships/grants available. Financial award application deadline: 3/2. *Faculty research:* Paleontology, geophysics, structural geology, organic geochemistry, sedimentary geology. *Unit head:* Dr. Stanley C. Finney, Chair, 562-985-4809, Fax: 562-985-8638, E-mail: scfinney@csulb.edu. *Application contact:* Dr. R. Dan Francis, Graduate Coordinator, 562-985-4929, Fax: 562-985-8638, E-mail: rfranics@csulb.edu.

California State University, Los Angeles, Graduate Studies, College of Natural and Social Sciences, Department of Geological Sciences, Los Angeles, CA 90032-8530. Offers MS. Part-time and evening/weekend programs available. *Faculty:* 7 full-time, 3 part-time/adjunct. *Students:* 5 full-time (2 women), 20 part-time (7 women); includes 3 minority (1 Asian American or Pacific Islander, 2 Hispanic Americans), 3 international. In 2003, 5 degrees awarded. *Degree requirements:* For master's, comprehensive exam or thesis. *Entrance requirements:* Additional exam requirements/recommendations for international students: Required—TOEFL. *Application deadline:* For fall admission, 6/30 for domestic students; for spring admission, 2/1 for domestic students. Applications are processed on a rolling basis. Application fee: $55. Tuition, nonresident: part-time $188 per unit. Required fees: $2,477. *Financial support:* Federal Work-Study available. Support available to part-time students. Financial award application deadline: 3/1. *Unit head:* Dr. Pedro Ramirez, Chair, 323-343-2400.

California State University, Northridge, Graduate Studies, College of Science and Mathematics, Department of Geological Sciences, Northridge, CA 91330. Offers MS. Part-time and evening/weekend programs available. *Faculty:* 10 full-time, 6 part-time/adjunct. *Students:* 7 full-time (3 women), 12 part-time (4 women); includes 6 minority (1 African American, 1 Asian American or Pacific Islander, 4 Hispanic Americans), 1 international. Average age 34. 13 applicants, 85% accepted. In 2003, 1 degree awarded. *Degree requirements:* For master's, thesis. *Entrance requirements:* For master's, GRE General Test, minimum GPA of 2.75. Additional exam requirements/recommendations for international students: Required—TOEFL. *Application deadline:* For fall admission, 11/30 for domestic students. Application fee: $55. Required fees: $1,327; $853 per year. *Financial support:* Research assistantships, teaching assistantships, Federal Work-Study available. Financial award application deadline: 3/1. *Faculty research:* Petrology of California Miocene volcanics, sedimentology of California Miocene formations, Eocene gastropods, structure of White/Inyo Mountains, seismology of Californian and Mexican earthquakes. *Unit head:* Dr. George C. Dunne, Chair, 818-677-3541.

Case Western Reserve University, School of Graduate Studies, Department of Geological Sciences, Cleveland, OH 44106. Offers MS, PhD. Part-time programs available. *Faculty:* 6 full-time (0 women). *Students:* 3 full-time (1 woman), 1 part-time; includes 1 minority (African American), 2 international. Average age 27. 16 applicants, 25% accepted, 2 enrolled. In 2003, 1 master's, 1 doctorate awarded. Terminal master's awarded for partial completion of doctoral program. *Degree requirements:* For master's, thesis or alternative; for doctorate, thesis/dissertation. *Entrance requirements:* For master's and doctorate, GRE General Test, GRE Subject Test. Additional exam requirements/recommendations for international students: Required—TOEFL. *Application deadline:* For fall admission, 2/15 for domestic students; for spring admission, 11/15 for domestic students. Applications are processed on a rolling basis. Application fee: $50. *Expenses:* Tuition: Full-time $26,900. *Financial support:* Research assistantships, teaching assistantships, Federal Work-Study and tuition waivers (partial) available. Support available to part-time students. Financial award application deadline: 2/15. *Faculty research:* Geochemistry, hydrology, geochronology, paleoclimates, geomorphology. *Unit head:* Gerald Matisoff, Chairman, 216-368-3677, Fax: 216-368-3691, E-mail: gxm4@case.edu. *Application contact:* Linda Day, Admissions, 216-368-3690, Fax: 216-368-3691, E-mail: lmd3@case.edu.

Central Washington University, Graduate Studies, Research and Continuing Education, College of the Sciences, Department of Geological Sciences, Ellensburg, WA 98926. Offers MS. Part-time programs available. *Faculty:* 9 full-time (4 women). *Students:* 11 full-time (4 women), 1 (woman) part-time; includes 4 minority (2 Asian Americans or Pacific Islanders, 2 Hispanic Americans), 1 international. 14 applicants, 57% accepted, 5 enrolled. In 2003, 6 degrees awarded. *Degree requirements:* For master's, thesis. *Entrance requirements:* For master's, GRE General Test, minimum GPA of 3.0. Additional exam requirements/recommendations for international students: Required—TOEFL (minimum score 550 paper-based; 213 computer-based). *Application deadline:* For fall admission, 4/1 for domestic students; for winter admission, 10/1 for domestic students; for spring admission, 1/1 for domestic students. Applications are processed on a rolling basis. Application fee: $35. *Expenses:* Tuition, state resident: part-time $183 per credit. Tuition, nonresident: part-time $381 per credit. Required fees: $369. *Financial support:* In 2003–04, 4 research assistantships with partial tuition reimbursements (averaging $7,120 per year), 6 teaching assistantships with partial tuition reimbursements (averaging $7,120 per year) were awarded. Career-related internships or fieldwork and Federal Work-Study also available. Financial award application deadline: 3/1; financial award applicants required to submit FAFSA. *Unit head:* Dr. Lisa Ely, Chair, 509-963-2701. *Application contact:* Barbara Sisko, Office Assistant, Graduate Studies, Research and Continuing Education, 509-963-3103, Fax: 509-963-1799, E-mail: masters@cwu.edu.

Cleveland State University, College of Graduate Studies, College of Arts and Sciences, Department of Biological, Geological, and Environmental Sciences, Cleveland, OH 44115. Offers MS, PhD. Part-time programs available. *Faculty:* 19 full-time (5 women), 3 part-time/adjunct (0 women). *Students:* 47 full-time (25 women), 24 part-time (13 women); includes 6 minority (5 African Americans, 1 Asian American or Pacific Islander), 26 international. Average age 31. 71 applicants, 48% accepted, 20 enrolled. In 2003, 5 master's, 5 doctorates awarded, leading to university research/teaching 80%, business/industry 20%. Terminal master's awarded for partial completion of doctoral program. *Median time to degree:* Doctorate–5 years full-time. *Degree requirements:* For master's, thesis (for some programs); for doctorate, thesis/dissertation, comprehensive exam. *Entrance requirements:* For master's and doctorate, GRE General Test, essay on career goals and research interests, two letters of recommendation. Additional exam requirements/recommendations for international students: Required—TOEFL (minimum score 525 paper-based; 197 computer-based); Recommended—TSE. *Application deadline:* For fall admission, 4/1 priority date for domestic students, 4/1 priority date for international students; for spring admission, 12/1 priority date for domestic students. Applications are processed on a rolling basis. Application fee: $30. Electronic applications accepted. Tuition, area resident: Full-time $8,258; part-time $344 per credit hour. Tuition, nonresident: full-time $16,352; part-time $681 per credit hour. *Financial support:* In 2003–04, 36 students received support, including 21 research assistantships with full and partial tuition reimbursements available (averaging $6,134 per year), 21 teaching assistantships with full and partial tuition reimbursements available (averaging $5,810 per year); institutionally sponsored loans and unspecified assistantships also available. *Faculty research:* Molecular and cell biology, immunology, molecular medicine, environmental/science. *Unit head:* Dr. Michael Gates, Chairperson, 216-687-3917, Fax: 216-687-6972, E-mail: m.gates@csuohio.edu. *Application contact:* Dr. Jeffrey Dean, Graduate Program Director, 216-687-2440, Fax: 216-687-6972, E-mail: gpd.bges@csuohio.edu.

Colorado School of Mines, Graduate School, Department of Geology and Geological Engineering, Golden, CO 80401-1887. Offers engineering geology (Diploma); exploration geosciences (Diploma); geochemistry (MS, PhD); geological engineering (ME, MS, PhD, Diploma); geology (MS, PhD); hydrogeology (Diploma). Part-time programs available. *Faculty:* 25 full-time (4 women), 8 part-time/adjunct (4 women). *Students:* 52 full-time (16 women), 34 part-time (13 women); includes 1 minority (American Indian/Alaska Native), 20 international. 89 applicants, 56% accepted, 12 enrolled. In 2003, 19 master's, 4 doctorates, 3 other advanced degrees awarded. *Degree requirements:* For master's, thesis/dissertation; for doctorate, thesis/dissertation, comprehensive exam. *Entrance requirements:* For master's and doctorate, GRE General Test; for Diploma, GRE General Test, minimum GPA of 3.0. Additional exam requirements/recommendations for international students: Required—TOEFL (minimum score 550 paper-based; 213 computer-based). *Application deadline:* For fall admission, 12/1 for domestic students, 12/1 for international students; for spring admission, 5/1 for domestic students, 5/1 for international students. Application fee: $45. Electronic applications accepted. *Expenses:* Tuition, state resident: full-time $5,700; part-time $285 per credit hour. Tuition, nonresident: full-time $19,040; part-time $952 per credit hour. Required fees: $733. *Financial support:* In 2003–04, 23 students received support, including 9 fellowships with full tuition reimbursements available (averaging $12,500 per year), 16 research assistantships with full tuition reimbursements available (averaging $10,000 per year), 9 teaching assistantships with full tuition reimbursements available (averaging $10,000 per year); scholarships/grants and unspecified assistantships also available. Financial award applicants required to submit FAFSA. *Faculty research:* Predictive sediment modeling, petrophysics, aquifer-contaminant flow modeling, water-rock interactions, geotechnical engineering. Total annual research expenditures: $2.1 million. *Unit head:* Dr. Murray W. Hitzman, Head, 303-384-2127, Fax: 303-273-3859, E-mail: mhitzman@mines.edu. *Application contact:* Marilyn Schwinger, Administrative Assistant, 303-273-3800, Fax: 303-273-3859, E-mail: mschwing@mines.edu.

Colorado State University, Graduate School, College of Natural Resources, Department of Geosciences, Fort Collins, CO 80523-0015. Offers earth resources (PhD); geology (MS), including geomorphology, hydrogeology, petrology/geochemistry and economic geology, sedimentology, structural geology. Part-time programs available. *Faculty:* 9 full-time (4 women), 2 part-time/adjunct (0 women). *Students:* 19 full-time (6 women), 17 part-time (7 women); includes 1 minority (American Indian/Alaska Native), 3 international. Average age 31. 56 applicants, 46% accepted, 8 enrolled. In 2003, 6 master's, 2 doctorates awarded. *Degree requirements:* For master's and doctorate, thesis/dissertation, registration. *Entrance requirements:* For master's and doctorate, GRE General Test, minimum GPA of 3.0. Additional exam requirements/recommendations for international students: Required—TOEFL (minimum score 550 paper-based; 213 computer-based). *Application deadline:* For fall admission, 2/1 priority date for domestic students, 2/1 priority date for international students. Applications are processed on a rolling basis. Application fee: $50. Electronic applications accepted. *Expenses:* Tuition, state resident: full-time $4,156. Tuition, nonresident: full-time $14,762. Required fees: $205. Tuition and fees vary according to course load, campus/location, program and reciprocity agreements. *Financial support:* In 2003–04, fellowships (averaging $3,800 per year), research assistantships with partial tuition reimbursements (averaging $14,400 per year), teaching assistantships with full tuition reimbursements (averaging $10,206 per year) were awarded. Career-related internships or fieldwork, Federal Work-Study, institutionally sponsored loans, scholarships/grants, and traineeships also available. Financial award application deadline: 2/15. *Faculty research:* Snow, surface, and groundwater hydrology; fluvial geomorphology; geographic information systems; geochemistry; bedrock geology. Total annual research expenditures: $407,835. *Unit head:* Dr. Judith L. Hannah, Head, 970-491-5662, Fax: 970-491-6307, E-mail: jhannah@cnr.colostate.edu. *Application contact:* Barbara Holtz, Staff Assistant, 970-491-5662, Fax: 970-491-6307, E-mail: barbh@cnr.colostate.edu.

Cornell University, Graduate School, Graduate Fields of Engineering, Field of Geological Sciences, Ithaca, NY 14853-0001. Offers economic geology (M Eng, MS, PhD); engineering geology (M Eng, MS, PhD); environmental geophysics (M Eng, MS, PhD); general geology (M Eng, MS, PhD); geobiology (M Eng, MS, PhD); geochemistry and isotope geology (M Eng, MS, PhD); geohydrology (M Eng, MS, PhD); geomorphology (M Eng, MS, PhD); geophysics (M Eng, MS, PhD); geotectonics (M Eng, MS, PhD); marine geology (MS, PhD); mineralogy (M Eng, MS, PhD); paleontology (M Eng, MS, PhD); petroleum geology (M Eng, MS, PhD); petrology (M Eng, MS, PhD); planetary geology (M Eng, MS, PhD); Precambrian geology (M Eng, MS, PhD); Quaternary geology (M Eng, MS, PhD); rock mechanics (M Eng, MS, PhD); sedimentology (M Eng, MS, PhD); seismology (M Eng, MS, PhD); stratigraphy (M Eng, MS, PhD); structural geology (M Eng, MS, PhD). *Faculty:* 31 full-time. *Students:* 27 full-time (12 women); includes 1 minority (Asian American or Pacific Islander), 9 international. 74 applicants, 15% accepted, 7 enrolled. In 2003, 3 master's, 5 doctorates awarded. *Degree requirements:* For master's, thesis (MS); for doctorate, thesis/dissertation, comprehensive exam. *Entrance requirements:* For master's and doctorate, GRE General Test, 3 letters of recommendation. Additional exam requirements/recommendations for international students: Required—TOEFL (minimum score 550 paper-based; 213 computer-based). *Application deadline:* For fall admission, 1/15 for domestic students. Applications are processed on a rolling basis. Application fee: $60. Electronic applications accepted. *Expenses:* Tuition: Full-time $28,630. One-time fee: $50 full-time. *Financial support:* In 2003–04, 21 students received support, including 6 fellowships with full tuition reimbursements available, 8 research assistantships with full tuition reimbursements available, 7 teaching assistantships with full tuition reimbursements available; institutionally sponsored loans, scholarships/grants, health care benefits, tuition waivers (full and partial), and unspecified assistantships also available. Financial award applicants required to submit FAFSA. *Faculty research:* Geophysics, structural geology, petrology, geochemistry, geodynamics. *Unit head:* Director of Graduate Studies, 607-255-3474, Fax: 607-254-4780. *Application contact:* Graduate Field Assistant, 607-255-3474, Fax: 607-254-4780, E-mail: gradprog@geology.cornell.edu.

See in-depth description on page 233.

Duke University, Graduate School, Department of Biological Anthropology and Anatomy, Durham, NC 27710. Offers cellular and molecular biology (PhD); gross anatomy and physical anthropology (PhD), including comparative morphology of human and non-human primates, primate social behavior, vertebrate paleontology; neuroanatomy (PhD). *Faculty:* 10 full-time. *Students:* 23 full-time (14 women); includes 3 minority (2 African Americans, 1 Hispanic American), 1 international. 43 applicants, 5% accepted, 2 enrolled. In 2003, 4 degrees awarded. *Degree requirements:* For doctorate, one foreign language, thesis/dissertation. *Entrance requirements:* For doctorate, GRE General Test. Additional exam requirements/recommendations for international students: Required—IELT (preferred) or TOEFL. *Application deadline:* For fall admission, 12/31 for domestic students. Application fee: $75. *Expenses:* Tuition: Full-time $23,280; part-time $835 per unit. *Financial support:* Fellowships, teaching assistantships, Federal Work-Study available. Financial award application deadline: 12/31. *Unit head:* Carel Van Schaik, Director of Graduate Studies, 919-684-4124, Fax: 919-684-8034.

Duke University, Graduate School, Department of Earth and Ocean Sciences (Geology), Durham, NC 27708-0586. Offers MS, PhD. Part-time programs available. *Faculty:* 15 full-time. *Students:* 28 full-time (12 women), 4 international. 47 applicants, 28% accepted, 5 enrolled. In 2003, 1 degree awarded. Terminal master's awarded for partial completion of doctoral program. *Degree requirements:* For master's and doctorate, thesis/dissertation. *Entrance requirements:* For master's and doctorate, GRE General Test. Additional exam requirements/recommendations for international students: Required—IELT (preferred) or TOEFL. *Application deadline:* For fall admission, 12/31 for domestic students; for spring admission, 11/1 for domestic students. Application fee: $75. *Expenses:* Tuition: Full-time $23,280; part-time $835 per unit. *Financial support:* Fellowships, research assistantships, teaching assistantships, Federal Work-Study available. Financial award application deadline: 12/31. *Unit head:* Lincoln Pratson, Director of Graduate Studies, 919-684-5847, Fax: 919-684-5833, E-mail: dcgooch@duke.edu.

East Carolina University, Graduate School, Thomas Harriot College of Arts and Sciences, Department of Geology, Greenville, NC 27858-4353. Offers MS. Part-time programs available. *Faculty:* 7 full-time (2 women). *Students:* 8 full-time (5 women), 13 part-time (3 women); includes 1 minority (Hispanic American), 1 international. Average age 27. 11 applicants, 73% accepted. In 2003, 7 degrees awarded. *Degree requirements:* For master's, one foreign language, thesis, comprehensive exam. *Entrance requirements:* For master's, GRE General Test. Additional exam requirements/recommendations for international students: Required—TOEFL. *Application deadline:* For fall admission, 6/1 for domestic students; for spring admission, 10/15 for domestic students. Applications are processed on a rolling basis. Application fee: $50. *Expenses:* Tuition, state resident: full-time $1,991; part-time $249 per hour. Tuition, nonresident: full-time $12,232; part-time $1,529 per hour. Required fees: $1,221; $153 per hour. *Financial support:* Research assistantships with partial tuition reimbursements, teaching assistantships with partial tuition reimbursements available. Support available to part-time students. Financial award application deadline: 6/1. *Unit head:* Dr. Terri Woods, Director of Graduate Studies, 252-328-6360, Fax: 252-328-4391, E-mail: woodst@mail.ecu.edu. *Application contact:* Dr. Paul D. Tschetter, Interim Dean of Graduate School, 252-328-6012, Fax: 252-328-6071, E-mail: gradschool@mail.ecu.edu.

Eastern Kentucky University, The Graduate School, College of Arts and Sciences, Department of Earth Sciences, Richmond, KY 40475-3102. Offers geology (MS, PhD). Part-time programs available. *Faculty:* 8 full-time (2 women). *Students:* 7 full-time (3 women), 5 part-time (2 women), 1 international. 12 applicants, 75% accepted, 4 enrolled. In 2003, 2 degrees awarded. *Degree requirements:* For master's, thesis. *Entrance requirements:* For master's, GRE General Test, minimum GPA of 2.5. Application fee: $0. *Expenses:* Tuition, state resident: full-time $3,550; part-time $197 per credit. Tuition, nonresident: full-time $9,752; part-time $542 per credit. *Financial support:* Research assistantships, teaching assistantships, Federal Work-Study available. Support available to part-time students. *Faculty research:* Hydrogeology, sedimentary geology, geochemistry, environmental geology, tectonics. *Unit head:* Dr. Malcolm P. Frisbee, Chair, 859-622-1273, E-mail: malcolm.frisbee@eku.edu.

Eastern Washington University, Graduate School Studies, College of Science, Mathematics and Technology, Department of Geology, Cheney, WA 99004-2431. Offers MS. *Faculty:* 8 full-time (2 women). *Students:* 1 full-time (0 women). Average age 30. In 2003, 1 degree awarded. *Degree requirements:* For master's, thesis, comprehensive exam. *Entrance requirements:* For master's, minimum GPA of 3.0. *Application deadline:* For fall admission, 4/1 for domestic students; for spring admission, 1/15 for domestic students. Applications are processed on a rolling basis. Application fee: $35. *Expenses:* Tuition, state resident: part-time $385 per credit. Tuition, nonresident: part-time $1,139 per credit. *Financial support:* In 2003–04, 1 teaching assistantship with partial tuition reimbursement (averaging $7,000 per year) was awarded; career-related internships or fieldwork, Federal Work-Study, institutionally sponsored loans, scholarships/grants, health care benefits, tuition waivers (partial), and unspecified assistantships also available. Support available to part-time students. Financial award application deadline: 2/1; financial award applicants required to submit FAFSA. *Unit head:* Dr. Ernest Gilmour, Chair, 509-359-2286, Fax: 509-359-4386.

Florida Atlantic University, Charles E. Schmidt College of Science, Department of Geography and Geology, Program in Geology, Boca Raton, FL 33431-0991. Offers MS. Part-time programs available. *Faculty:* 6 full-time (0 women). *Students:* 8 full-time (6 women), 9 part-time (4 women); includes 5 minority (1 African American, 2 Asian Americans or Pacific Islanders, 2 Hispanic Americans). Average age 33. 7 applicants, 71% accepted, 3 enrolled. In 2003, 5 degrees awarded. *Degree requirements:* For master's, thesis (for some programs). *Entrance requirements:* For master's, GRE General Test, minimum GPA of 3.0. *Application deadline:* For fall admission, 6/1 for domestic students; for spring admission, 10/15 for domestic students. Applications are processed on a rolling basis. Application fee: $30. Electronic applications accepted. *Expenses:* Tuition, state resident: full-time $3,777. Tuition, nonresident: full-time $13,953. *Financial support:* In 2003–04, 2 research assistantships with partial tuition reimbursements (averaging $9,100 per year), 5 teaching assistantships with partial tuition reimbursements (averaging $9,100 per year) were awarded. Federal Work-Study also available. *Faculty research:* Paleontology, beach erosion, stratigraphy, hydrogeology, environmental geology. Total annual research expenditures: $150,000. *Application contact:* Dr. David Warburton, Graduate Coordinator, 561-297-3250, Fax: 561-297-2745, E-mail: warburto@fau.edu.

Florida State University, Graduate Studies, College of Arts and Sciences, Department of Geological Sciences, Tallahassee, FL 32306. Offers MS, PhD. *Faculty:* 13 full-time (3 women). *Students:* 21 full-time (16 women), 4 part-time (2 women), 7 international. Average age 25. *Degree requirements:* For master's and doctorate, thesis/dissertation. *Entrance requirements:* For master's and doctorate, GRE General Test, minimum GPA of 3.0. Additional exam requirements/recommendations for international students: Required—TOEFL. *Application deadline:* For fall admission, 3/1 for domestic students; for spring admission, 11/1 priority date for domestic students. Applications are processed on a rolling basis. Application fee: $20. Electronic applications accepted. *Expenses:* Tuition, state resident: part-time $196 per credit hour. Tuition, nonresident: part-time $731 per credit hour. Part-time tuition and fees vary according to campus/location. *Financial support:* In 2003–04, 12 students received support; fellowships, research assistantships, teaching assistantships, career-related internships or fieldwork and Federal Work-Study available. Financial award application deadline: 2/7; financial award applicants required to submit FAFSA. *Faculty research:* Appalachian and collisional tectonics, surface and groundwater hydrogeology, micropaleontology, isotope and trace element geochemistry, coastal and estuarine studies. Total annual research expenditures: $2.3 million. *Unit head:* Dr. Neil Lundberg, Chairman, 850-644-3743, Fax: 850-644-4214, E-mail: lundberg@gly.fsu.edu. *Application contact:* Tami Karl, Program Assistant, 850-644-5861, Fax: 850-644-4214, E-mail: karl@gly.fsu.edu.

Fort Hays State University, Graduate School, College of Arts and Sciences, Department of Geosciences, Program in Geology, Hays, KS 67601-4099. Offers MS. *Faculty:* 8 full-time (0 women). *Students:* 8 full-time (0 women), 4 part-time (1 woman); includes 1 minority (Asian American or Pacific Islander) Average age 27. 7 applicants, 71% accepted. In 2003, 6 degrees awarded. *Degree requirements:* For master's, thesis, comprehensive exam. *Entrance requirements:* For master's, GRE General Test. Additional exam requirements/recommendations for international students: Required—TOEFL (minimum score 550 paper-based; 213 computer-based). *Application deadline:* For fall admission, 7/1 for domestic students. Applications are processed on a rolling basis. Application fee: $30 ($35 for international students). Electronic applications accepted. *Expenses:* Tuition, state resident: part-time $118 per credit hour. Tuition, nonresident: part-time $317 per credit hour. *Financial support:* In 2003–04, 5 teaching assistantships with tuition reimbursements (averaging $5,000 per year) were awarded; research assistantships, career-related internships or fieldwork and institutionally sponsored loans also available. Support available to part-time students. *Faculty research:* Cretaceous and late Cenozoic stratigraphy, sedimentation, paleontology.

The George Washington University, Columbian College of Arts and Sciences, Department of Earth and Environmental Sciences, Washington, DC 20052. Offers geology (MS, PhD); geosciences (MS, PhD); hominid paleobiology (MS, PhD). Part-time and evening/weekend programs available. *Faculty:* 2 full-time (0 women). *Students:* 3 full-time (2 women), 6 part-time (2 women), 4 international. Average age 32. 5 applicants, 60% accepted. In 2003, 2 master's, 2 doctorates awarded. Terminal master's awarded for partial completion of doctoral program. *Degree requirements:* For master's, thesis or alternative, comprehensive exam; for doctorate, thesis/dissertation, general exam. *Entrance requirements:* For master's, GRE General Test, bachelor's degree in field, interview, minimum GPA of 3.0; for doctorate, GRE General Test, interview, minimum GPA of 3.0. Additional exam requirements/recommendations for international students: Required—TOEFL (minimum score 550 paper-based; 213 computer-based). *Application deadline:* For fall admission, 2/1 priority date for domestic students, 2/1 priority date for international students; for spring admission, 10/1 priority date for domestic students, 10/1 priority date for international students. Application fee: $60. *Expenses:* Tuition: Part-time $876 per credit. Required fees: $1 per credit. Tuition and fees vary according to campus/location. *Financial support:* In 2003–04, fellowships with tuition reimbursements (averaging $10,000 per year), teaching assistantships with tuition reimbursements (averaging $5,000 per year) were awarded. Federal Work-Study also available. Financial award application deadline: 2/1. *Faculty research:* Engineering geology. *Unit head:* Dr. John Lewis, Chair, 202-994-6987. *Application contact:* Information Contact, 202-994-6190, Fax: 202-994-0450.

Georgia State University, College of Arts and Sciences, Department of Geology, Atlanta, GA 30303-3083. Offers geology (MS), including earth science. Part-time and evening/weekend programs available. *Faculty:* 7 full-time (2 women). *Students:* 23; includes 4 minority (2 African Americans, 2 Asian Americans or Pacific Islanders). 25 applicants, 84% accepted. In 2003, 3 degrees awarded. *Median time to degree:* Master's–2 years full-time. *Degree requirements:* For master's, one foreign language, thesis or alternative, comprehensive exam (for some programs), registration. *Entrance requirements:* For master's, GRE General Test, minimum GPA of 2.75. Additional exam requirements/recommendations for international students: Required—TOEFL. *Application deadline:* For fall admission, 7/1 for domestic students, 3/15 for international students; for spring admission, 11/15 for domestic students, 9/15 for international students. Applications are processed on a rolling basis. Application fee: $25. Electronic applications accepted. *Financial support:* In 2003–04, 17 students received support, including research assistantships with tuition reimbursements available (averaging $6,000 per year), teaching assistantships with tuition reimbursements available (averaging $6,000 per year); career-related internships or fieldwork, Federal Work-Study, institutionally sponsored loans, tuition waivers (partial), and unspecified assistantships also available. Support available to part-time students. Financial award application deadline: 7/15; financial award applicants required to submit FAFSA. *Faculty research:* Clay mineralogy, metamorphism, fracture analysis, carbonates, groundwater. Total annual research expenditures: $75,000. *Unit head:* Dr. Timothy LaTour, Chair, 404-651-2272, Fax: 404-651-1376, E-mail: tlatour@gsu.edu. *Application contact:* Dr. W. Crawford Elliott, Director of Graduate Studies, 404-651-2272, Fax: 404-651-1376, E-mail: geowce@langate.gsu.edu.

ICR Graduate School, Graduate Programs, Santee, CA 92071. Offers astro/geophysics (MS); biology (MS); geology (MS); science education (MS). Part-time programs available. *Faculty:* 6 full-time (0 women), 4 part-time/adjunct (1 woman). *Students:* 11 full-time (6 women), 18 part-time (9 women); includes 3 minority (2 African Americans, 1 Asian American or Pacific Islander). Average age 41. In 2003, 4 degrees awarded, leading to university research/teaching 50%, business/industry 50%. *Median time to degree:* Master's–4.6 years full-time. *Degree requirements:* For master's, thesis (for some programs), comprehensive exam (for some programs). *Entrance requirements:* For master's, bachelor's degree in science or science education, minimum GPA of 3.0 (undergraduate). *Application deadline:* Applications are processed on a rolling basis. Application fee: $30. *Expenses:* Tuition: Full-time $1,800; part-time $150 per unit. *Financial support:* In 2003–04, 25 students received support. *Faculty research:* Age of the earth, limits of variation, catastrophe, optimum methods for teaching. Total annual research expenditures: $200,000. *Unit head:* Kenneth B. Cumming, Dean, 619-448-0900, Fax: 619-448-3469. *Application contact:* Dr. Jack Kriege, Registrar, 619-448-0900 Ext. 6016, Fax: 619-448-3469, E-mail: jkriege@icr.org.

Idaho State University, Office of Graduate Studies, College of Arts and Sciences, Department of Geosciences, Pocatello, ID 83209. Offers geology (MS); geophysics/hydrology (MS); geotechnology (Postbaccalaureate Certificate); natural science (MNS). Part-time programs available. Postbaccalaureate distance learning degree programs offered. *Faculty:* 6 full-time (1 woman), 1 part-time/adjunct (0 women). *Students:* 18 full-time (3 women), 17 part-time (7 women), 1 international. Average age 32. In 2003, 6 master's, 3 other advanced degrees awarded. *Degree requirements:* For master's, thesis, comprehensive exam, registration (for some programs); for Postbaccalaureate Certificate, thesis optional. *Entrance requirements:* For master's and Postbaccalaureate Certificate, GRE General Test, 3 letters of recommendation. Additional exam requirements/recommendations for international students: Required—TOEFL (minimum score 550 paper-based; 213 computer-based). *Application deadline:* For fall admission, 7/1 priority date for domestic students, 7/1 priority date for international students; for spring admission, 12/1 priority date for domestic students, 12/1 priority date for international students. Applications are processed on a rolling basis. Application fee: $35. *Expenses:* Tuition, state resident: part-time $205 per credit. Tuition, nonresident: full-time $6,600; part-time $300 per credit. Required fees: $4,108. One-time fee: $35 full-time. *Financial support:* Research assistantships with full and partial tuition reimbursements, teaching assistantships with full and partial tuition reimbursements, career-related internships or fieldwork, Federal Work-Study, institutionally sponsored loans, and tuition waivers (full and partial) available. Financial award application deadline: 1/1. *Faculty research:* Structural geography, stratigraphy, geochemistry, volcanography, geomorphology. Total annual research expenditures: $541,774. *Unit head:* Dr. Scott Hughes, Chairman, 208-282-3365, Fax: 208-282-4414.

Idaho State University, Office of Graduate Studies, Department of Interdisciplinary Studies, Pocatello, ID 83209. Offers biology (MNS); chemistry (MNS); general interdisciplinary (M Ed, MA); geology (MNS); mathematics (MNS); physics (MNS); waste management and environmental science (MS). Part-time programs available. *Students:* 3 full-time, 337 part-time; includes 7 minority (1 African American, 1 Asian American or Pacific Islander, 5 Hispanic Americans). Average age 45. In 2003, 7 degrees awarded. *Degree requirements:* For master's, thesis optional. *Entrance requirements:* For master's, GRE General Test or MAT, minimum GPA of 3.0. Additional exam requirements/recommendations for international students: Required—TOEFL (minimum score 550 paper-based; 213 computer-based). *Application deadline:* For fall admission, 7/1 priority date for domestic students, 7/1 priority date for international students; for spring admission, 12/1 priority date for domestic students, 12/1 priority date for international students. Applications are processed on a rolling basis. Application fee: $35. *Expenses:* Tuition, state resident: part-time $205 per credit. Tuition, nonresident: full-time $6,600; part-time $300 per credit. Required fees: $4,108. One-time fee: $35 full-time. *Financial support:* Research assistantships, teaching assistantships, career-related internships or fieldwork, Federal Work-Study, scholarships/grants, and tuition waivers (full and partial) available. Support available to part-time students. Financial award application deadline: 1/1. Total annual research expenditures: $1.7 million. *Unit head:* Dr. Edwin House, Chief Research Officer/Department Chair, 208-282-2714, Fax: 208-282-4529.

Indiana University Bloomington, Graduate School, College of Arts and Sciences, Department of Geological Sciences, Bloomington, IN 47405. Offers biogeochemistry (MS, PhD); environmental geosciences (MS, PhD); geobiology, stratigraphy, and sedimentology (MS, PhD); geochemistry (MS, PhD); geochemistry, mineralogy, and petrology (MS, PhD); geophysics (MS, PhD); geophysics, tectonics, and structural geology (MS, PhD). PhD offered through the University Graduate School. Part-time programs available. *Faculty:* 14 full-time (1

Geology

Indiana University Bloomington (continued)

woman). *Students:* 32 full-time (16 women), 18 part-time (8 women); includes 4 minority (2 African Americans, 2 Asian Americans or Pacific Islanders), 23 international. Average age 29. In 2003, 10 master's, 2 doctorates awarded. Terminal master's awarded for partial completion of doctoral program. *Degree requirements:* For master's, one foreign language, thesis or alternative; for doctorate, thesis/dissertation. *Entrance requirements:* For master's and doctorate, GRE General Test. Additional exam requirements/recommendations for international students: Required—TOEFL. *Application deadline:* For fall admission, 1/15 priority date for domestic students, 12/15 priority date for international students; for spring admission, 9/1 priority date for domestic students, 9/1 priority date for international students. Applications are processed on a rolling basis. Application fee: $45 ($55 for international students). *Expenses:* Tuition, state resident: full-time $4,908; part-time $205 per credit. Tuition, nonresident: full-time $14,298; part-time $596 per credit. Required fees: $661. Tuition and fees vary according to campus/location and program. *Financial support:* In 2003–04, research assistantships with full and partial tuition reimbursements (averaging $11,000 per year); fellowships with tuition reimbursements, teaching assistantships with tuition reimbursements, career-related internships or fieldwork, Federal Work-Study, and institutionally sponsored loans also available. Financial award application deadline: 2/15. *Faculty research:* Geophysics, geochemistry, hydrogeology, igneous and metamorphic petrology and clay minerology. Total annual research expenditures: $289,139. *Unit head:* Dr. Christopher G. Maples, Chairman, 812-855-5582, Fax: 812-855-7899, E-mail: cmaples@indiana.edu. *Application contact:* Mary Iverson, Secretary, Committee for Graduate Studies, 812-855-7214, Fax: 812-855-7899, E-mail: geograd@indiana.edu.

Indiana University–Purdue University Indianapolis, School of Science, Department of Geology, Indianapolis, IN 46202-3272. Offers MS. Part-time and evening/weekend programs available. *Faculty:* 8 full-time (2 women). *Students:* 3 full-time (all women), 1 international. Average age 26. *Degree requirements:* For master's, thesis (for some programs). *Entrance requirements:* For master's, GRE General Test, minimum GPA of 3.0. Application fee: $45 ($55 for international students). *Expenses:* Tuition, state resident: full-time $4,658; part-time $194 per credit. Tuition, nonresident: full-time $13,444; part-time $560 per credit. Required fees: $571. Tuition and fees vary according to campus/location and program. *Financial support:* In 2003–04, fellowships with full tuition reimbursements (averaging $12,000 per year), research assistantships with full tuition reimbursements (averaging $12,000 per year), teaching assistantships with full tuition reimbursements (averaging $12,000 per year) were awarded. Scholarships/grants also available. Financial award application deadline: 3/1. *Faculty research:* Wetland hydrology, groundwater contamination, soils, sedimentology, sediment chemistry. *Unit head:* Andrew P. Barth, Chair, 317-274-7484, Fax: 317-274-7966, E-mail: ibsz100@iupui.edu. *Application contact:* Lenore P. Tedesco, Associate Professor, 317-274-7484, Fax: 317-274-7966, E-mail: ltedesco@iupui.edu.

Iowa State University of Science and Technology, Graduate College, College of Liberal Arts and Sciences, Department of Geological and Atmospheric Sciences, Ames, IA 50011. Offers earth science (MS, PhD); geology (MS, PhD); meteorology (MS, PhD); water resources (MS, PhD). *Faculty:* 17 full-time. *Students:* 28 full-time (13 women), 7 part-time (2 women); includes 1 minority (African American), 19 international. 24 applicants, 38% accepted, 6 enrolled. In 2003, 12 master's, 1 doctorate awarded. *Median time to degree:* Master's–2.9 years full-time. *Degree requirements:* For master's, thesis (for some programs); for doctorate, thesis/dissertation. *Entrance requirements:* For master's and doctorate, GRE General Test. Additional exam requirements/recommendations for international students: Required—TOEFL (paper score 530; computer score 197) or IELTS (score 6.0). *Application deadline:* For fall admission, 2/15 for domestic students. Applications are processed on a rolling basis. Application fee: $30 ($70 for international students). Electronic applications accepted. Tuition, nonresident: part-time $560 per credit. Required fees: $38 per unit. *Financial support:* In 2003–04, 20 research assistantships with full and partial tuition reimbursements (averaging $15,432 per year), 11 teaching assistantships with full and partial tuition reimbursements (averaging $15,432 per year) were awarded. Fellowships, scholarships/grants, health care benefits, and unspecified assistantships also available. *Unit head:* Dr. Carl E. Jacobson, Chair, 515-294-4477.

The Johns Hopkins University, Zanvyl Krieger School of Arts and Sciences, The Morton K. Blaustein Department of Earth and Planetary Sciences, Program in Geology, Baltimore, MD 21218-2699. Offers MA, PhD. *Faculty:* 10 full-time (2 women). *Students:* 14 full-time (6 women); includes 1 minority (Hispanic American), 5 international. Average age 24. *Degree requirements:* For doctorate, thesis/dissertation, registration. *Entrance requirements:* For master's and doctorate, GRE General Test. *Application deadline:* For fall admission, 1/15 for domestic students. Application fee: $60. Electronic applications accepted. *Expenses:* Tuition: Full-time $28,730; part-time $1,490 per course. Part-time tuition and fees vary according to course load, campus/location and program. *Financial support:* Federal Work-Study and institutionally sponsored loans available. Financial award application deadline: 3/14; financial award applicants required to submit FAFSA. *Application contact:* Carol Spangler, Academic Program Assistant, 410-516-7034, Fax: 410-516-7933, E-mail: cspangler@jhu.edu.

Kansas State University, Graduate School, College of Arts and Sciences, Department of Geology, Manhattan, KS 66506. Offers MS. *Faculty:* 14 full-time (4 women). *Students:* 9 full-time (3 women), 7 part-time (3 women), 4 international. Average age 24. 17 applicants, 88% accepted, 2 enrolled. In 2003, 6 degrees awarded. *Degree requirements:* For master's, thesis. *Entrance requirements:* For master's, GRE General Test, GRE Subject Test. Additional exam requirements/recommendations for international students: Required—TOEFL. *Application deadline:* For fall admission, 3/15 for domestic students; for spring admission, 10/1 for domestic students. Applications are processed on a rolling basis. Application fee: $0 ($25 for international students). Electronic applications accepted. *Expenses:* Tuition, state resident: part-time $155 per credit hour. Tuition, nonresident: part-time $428 per credit hour. Required fees: $11 per credit hour. *Financial support:* In 2003–04, 3 research assistantships (averaging $10,548 per year), 5 teaching assistantships with full tuition reimbursements (averaging $8,676 per year) were awarded. Career-related internships or fieldwork, Federal Work-Study, institutionally sponsored loans, and scholarships/grants also available. Support available to part-time students. Financial award application deadline: 3/1; financial award applicants required to submit FAFSA. *Faculty research:* Seismology/tectonics, volcanology, environmental geochemistry, sedimentology and paleobiology, quarternary geology. Total annual research expenditures: $500,000. *Unit head:* Mary Hubbard, Head, 785-532-2245, Fax: 785-532-5159, E-mail: mhub@ksu.edu. *Application contact:* Charles G. Oviatt, Director, 785-532-2245, Fax: 785-532-5159, E-mail: ioviatt@ksu.edu.

Kent State University, College of Arts and Sciences, Department of Geology, Kent, OH 44242-0001. Offers MS, PhD. *Degree requirements:* For master's, thesis; for doctorate, one foreign language, thesis/dissertation. *Entrance requirements:* For master's, minimum GPA of 2.75; for doctorate, GRE General Test, GRE Subject Test, minimum GPA of 3.0. Additional exam requirements/recommendations for international students: Required—TOEFL (minimum score 575 paper-based; 232 computer-based). Electronic applications accepted. *Expenses:* Tuition, state resident: part-time $334 per hour. Tuition, nonresident: part-time $627 per hour. *Faculty research:* Groundwater, surface water, engineering geology, paleontology, structural geology.

See in-depth description on page 241.

Lakehead University, Graduate Studies, Department of Geology, Thunder Bay, ON P7B 5E1, Canada. Offers M Sc. Part-time and evening/weekend programs available. *Degree requirements:* For master's, thesis, department seminar, oral exam. *Entrance requirements:* For master's, minimum B average, honours bachelors degree in geology. Additional exam requirements/recommendations for international students: Required—TOEFL. *Faculty research:* Rock physics, sedimentology, mineralogy and economic geology, geochemistry, petrology of alkaline rocks.

Laurentian University, School of Graduate Studies and Research, Programme in Geology (Earth Sciences), Sudbury, ON P3E 2C6, Canada. Offers M Sc. Part-time programs available. *Degree requirements:* For master's, thesis. *Entrance requirements:* For master's, honors degree with second class or better. *Faculty research:* Localization and metallogenesis of Ni-Cu-(PGE) sulfide mineralization in the Thompson Nickel Belt, mapping lithology and ore-grade by remote sensing, global reef expansion and collapse, monitoring dissolved organic carbon in lakes using remote sensing, volcanic environments and controls on VMS deposits.

Lehigh University, College of Arts and Sciences, Department of Earth and Environmental Sciences, Bethlehem, PA 18015-3094. Offers MS, PhD. *Faculty:* 14 full-time (2 women). *Students:* 27 full-time (14 women), 2 part-time; includes 3 minority (all Asian Americans or Pacific Islanders) Average age 26. 35 applicants, 40% accepted, 9 enrolled. In 2003, 6 master's, 1 doctorate awarded. Terminal master's awarded for partial completion of doctoral program. *Degree requirements:* For master's, thesis, registration; for doctorate, thesis/dissertation, language at the discretion of the PhD committee, comprehensive exam, registration. *Entrance requirements:* For master's and doctorate, GRE General Test, 2 letters of recommendation. Additional exam requirements/recommendations for international students: Required—TOEFL. *Application deadline:* For fall admission, 1/15 for domestic students; for spring admission, 10/15 priority date for domestic students. Applications are processed on a rolling basis. Application fee: $40. *Expenses:* Tuition: Full-time $16,920; part-time $940 per credit hour. Required fees: $200. Tuition and fees vary according to degree level and program. *Financial support:* In 2003–04, 3 fellowships with full tuition reimbursements (averaging $13,670 per year), 4 research assistantships with full tuition reimbursements (averaging $13,670 per year), 8 teaching assistantships with full tuition reimbursements (averaging $13,670 per year) were awarded. Federal Work-Study, institutionally sponsored loans, and tuition waivers (full and partial) also available. Financial award application deadline: 1/15. *Faculty research:* Tectonics, surficial processes, aquatic ecology. Total annual research expenditures: $1.5 million. *Unit head:* Dr. Anne S. Meltzer, Chairman, 610-758-3660 Ext. 3673, Fax: 610-758-3677, E-mail: asm3@lehigh.edu. *Application contact:* Dr. Frank Jame Pazzaglia, Graduate Coordinator, 610-758-3660 Ext. 3667, Fax: 610-758-3677, E-mail: fjp3@lehigh.edu.

See in-depth description on page 731.

Loma Linda University, Graduate School, Department of Natural Sciences, Department of Geology, Loma Linda, CA 92350. Offers MS. Part-time programs available. *Degree requirements:* For master's, thesis. *Entrance requirements:* For master's, GRE General Test.

Louisiana State University and Agricultural and Mechanical College, Graduate School, College of Basic Sciences, Department of Geology and Geophysics, Baton Rouge, LA 70803. Offers MS, PhD. *Faculty:* 23 full-time (4 women). *Students:* 28 full-time (14 women), 3 part-time (1 woman); includes 5 minority (3 African Americans, 2 Hispanic Americans), 7 international. Average age 29. 33 applicants, 52% accepted, 6 enrolled. In 2003, 6 master's, 1 doctorate awarded. Terminal master's awarded for partial completion of doctoral program. *Degree requirements:* For master's and doctorate, thesis/dissertation. *Entrance requirements:* For master's and doctorate, GRE General Test, minimum GPA of 3.0. Additional exam requirements/recommendations for international students: Required—TOEFL (minimum score 550 paper-based; 213 computer-based). *Application deadline:* For fall admission, 1/25 priority date for domestic students, 5/15 priority date for international students. Applications are processed on a rolling basis. Application fee: $25. Electronic applications accepted. *Expenses:* Tuition, state resident: part-time $337 per hour. Tuition, nonresident: part-time $577 per hour. *Financial support:* In 2003–04, 20 students received support, including 4 fellowships (averaging $16,000 per year), 3 research assistantships with partial tuition reimbursements available (averaging $25,083 per year), 20 teaching assistantships with partial tuition reimbursements available (averaging $16,262 per year); career-related internships or fieldwork, Federal Work-Study, institutionally sponsored loans, and unspecified assistantships also available. Financial award application deadline: 3/15; financial award applicants required to submit FAFSA. *Faculty research:* Geophysics, geochemistry of sediments, isotope geochemistry, igneous and metamorphic petrology, micropaleontology. Total annual research expenditures: $436,889. *Unit head:* Dr. Laurie Anderson, Chair, 225-578-3353, Fax: 225-578-2302, E-mail: landerson@geol.lsu.edu. *Application contact:* Jeffrey Nunn, Graduate Coordinator, 225-578-6657, E-mail: jeff@geol.lsu.edu.

Massachusetts Institute of Technology, School of Science, Department of Earth, Atmospheric, and Planetary Sciences, Cambridge, MA 02139-4307. Offers atmospheric chemistry (PhD, Sc D); atmospheric science (SM, PhD, Sc D); climate physics and chemistry (PhD, Sc D); earth and planetary sciences (SM); geochemistry (PhD, Sc D); geology (PhD, Sc D); geophysics (PhD, Sc D); geosystems (SM); oceanography (SM, PhD, Sc D); planetary sciences (PhD, Sc D). *Faculty:* 37 full-time (3 women). *Students:* 147 full-time (61 women); includes 9 minority (4 Asian Americans or Pacific Islanders, 5 Hispanic Americans), 48 international. Average age 27. 176 applicants, 49% accepted, 31 enrolled. In 2003, 8 master's, 19 doctorates awarded. Terminal master's awarded for partial completion of doctoral program. *Degree requirements:* For master's, thesis/dissertation; for doctorate, thesis/dissertation, comprehensive exam. *Entrance requirements:* For master's, GRE General Test, GRE Subject Test (joint MIT/WHOI program); for doctorate, GRE General Test, GRE Subject Test (chemistry or physics for planetary science program). Additional exam requirements/recommendations for international students: Required—TOEFL (minimum score 577 paper-based; 233 computer-based). *Application deadline:* For fall admission, 1/5 for domestic students, 1/5 for international students; for spring admission, 11/1 for domestic students, 11/1 for international students. Application fee: $70. Electronic applications accepted. *Expenses:* Tuition: Full-time $29,400. Required fees: $200. *Financial support:* In 2003–04, 113 students received support, including 25 fellowships with tuition reimbursements available, 70 research assistantships with tuition reimbursements available (averaging $23,760 per year), 21 teaching assistantships with tuition reimbursements available (averaging $18,270 per year); Federal Work-Study, institutionally sponsored loans, scholarships/grants, health care benefits, and unspecified assistantships also available. *Faculty research:* Evolution of main features of the planetary system; origin, composition, structure, and state of the atmospheres, oceans, surfaces, and interiors of planets; dynamics of planets and satellite motions. Total annual research expenditures: $19.1 million. *Unit head:* Prof. Maria Zuber, 617-253-0149, Fax: 617-253-8298, E-mail: mtz@mit.edu. *Application contact:* Carol Sprague, Administrative Assistant, 617-253-3381, Fax: 617-253-8298, E-mail: eapsinfo@mit.edu.

McMaster University, School of Graduate Studies, Faculty of Science, School of Geography and Geology, Hamilton, ON L8S 4M2, Canada. Offers geochemistry (PhD); geology (M Sc, PhD); human geography (MA, PhD); physical geography (M Sc, PhD). Part-time programs available. Terminal master's awarded for partial completion of doctoral program. *Degree requirements:* For master's, thesis/dissertation; for doctorate, thesis/dissertation, comprehensive exam. *Entrance requirements:* For master's, minimum B+ average. Additional exam requirements/recommendations for international students: Required—TOEFL (minimum score 550 paper-based; 213 computer-based).

Memorial University of Newfoundland, School of Graduate Studies, Department of Earth Sciences, St. John's, NL A1C 5S7, Canada. Offers geology (M Sc, PhD); geophysics (M Sc, PhD). Part-time programs available. *Students:* 43 full-time, 8 part-time. 37 applicants, 24% accepted, 7 enrolled. In 2003, 10 master's, 1 doctorate awarded. *Degree requirements:* For master's, thesis; for doctorate, thesis/dissertation, oral thesis defense, comprehensive exam. *Entrance requirements:* For master's, honors B Sc; for doctorate, M Sc. *Application deadline:* For fall admission, 3/31 for domestic students; for spring admission, 12/31 for domestic students. Applications are processed on a rolling basis. Application fee: $40. Electronic applications accepted. Tuition and fees charges are reported in Canadian dollars. *Expenses:* Tuition, state resident: part-time $733 Canadian dollars per semester. Tuition, nonresident: part-time $953 Canadian dollars per semester. Required fees: $194 Canadian dollars per year. Tuition and fees vary according to degree level and program. *Financial support:* Fellowships, research assistantships, teaching assistantships available. *Faculty research:* Geochemistry, sedimentology, paleoceanography and global change, mineral deposits, petroleum geology, hydrology. *Unit head:* Dr. J. Wright, Head, 709-737-2334, Fax: 709-737-2589, E-mail: jim@waves.esd.mun.ca. *Application contact:* Dr. Ali Aksu, Graduate Officer, 709-737-8385, Fax: 709-737-2589, E-mail: aaksu@sparky2.esd.ucs.mun.ca.

Miami University, Graduate School, College of Arts and Sciences, Department of Geology, Oxford, OH 45056. Offers MA, MS, PhD. Part-time programs available. *Faculty:* 10 full-time (1 woman), 2 part-time/adjunct (0 women). *Students:* 21 full-time (11 women), 9 international. 24 applicants, 83% accepted, 10 enrolled. In 2003, 6 master's, 1 doctorate awarded. *Degree requirements:* For master's, thesis (for some programs), final exam; for doctorate, thesis/dissertation, final exams, comprehensive exam. *Entrance requirements:* For master's, GRE General Test, GRE Subject Test, minimum undergraduate GPA of 3.0 during previous 2 years or 2.75 overall; for doctorate, GRE General Test, GRE Subject Test, minimum GPA of 2.75 (undergraduate) or 3.0 (graduate). Additional exam requirements/recommendations for international students: Required—TOEFL, TWE. *Application deadline:* For fall admission, 3/1 priority date for domestic students, 3/1 priority date for international students. Applications are processed on a rolling basis. Application fee: $35. Electronic applications accepted. Tuition, area resident: Full-time $9,346. International tuition: $19,924 full-time. Full-time tuition and fees vary according to course level and campus/location. *Financial support:* In 2003–04, 14 fellowships with full tuition reimbursements (averaging $12,565 per year), 2 research assistantships with full tuition reimbursements (averaging $12,565 per year), 4 teaching assistantships with full tuition reimbursements (averaging $15,865 per year) were awarded. Federal Work-Study, tuition waivers (full), and unspecified assistantships also available. Financial award application deadline: 3/1. *Unit head:* Dr. William Hart, Chair, 513-529-3216, Fax: 513-529-1542, E-mail: geology@muohio.edu. *Application contact:* Dr. Liz Widom, Director of Graduate Studies, 513-529-3216, Fax: 513-529-1542, E-mail: geology@muohio.edu.

Michigan State University, Graduate School, College of Natural Science, Department of Geological Sciences, East Lansing, MI 48824. Offers environmental geosciences (MS, PhD); environmental geosciences-environmental toxicology (PhD); geological sciences (MS, PhD). Part-time programs available. *Faculty:* 12 full-time (2 women). *Students:* 24 full-time (11 women), 4 part-time (2 women); includes 1 minority (Asian American or Pacific Islander), 3 international. Average age 28. 47 applicants, 62% accepted, 7 enrolled. In 2003, 8 master's, 2 doctorates awarded. *Median time to degree:* Master's–3.1 years full-time; doctorate–3.3 years full-time. *Degree requirements:* For master's and doctorate, thesis/dissertation, registration. *Entrance requirements:* For master's, GRE General Test, minimum GPA of 3.0, geoscience coursework, 3 letters of recommendation; for doctorate, GRE General Test, 3 letters of recommendation. Additional exam requirements/recommendations for international students: Required—TOEFL (minimum score 575 paper-based; 232 computer-based), TSE required only for teaching positions. *Application deadline:* For fall admission, 1/15 priority date for domestic students, 6/1 priority date for international students; for spring admission, 10/15 priority date for domestic students, 11/1 priority date for international students. Applications are processed on a rolling basis. Application fee: $50. Electronic applications accepted. *Expenses:* Tuition, state resident: part-time $291 per hour. Tuition, nonresident: part-time $589 per hour. *Financial support:* In 2003–04, 9 research assistantships with full tuition reimbursements (averaging $11,376 per year), 23 teaching assistantships with full tuition reimbursements (averaging $11,376 per year) were awarded. Fellowships with tuition reimbursements, Federal Work-Study, institutionally sponsored loans, scholarships/grants, health care benefits, and unspecified assistantships also available. Financial award application deadline: 1/15; financial award applicants required to submit CSS PROFILE or FAFSA. *Faculty research:* Water in the environment, biogeochemical cycles, paleobiology and paoleoenvironmental change, crystal dynamics. Total annual research expenditures: $841,206. *Unit head:* Dr. Michael A. Velbel, Chairperson, 517-355-4626, Fax: 517-353-8787, E-mail: geosci@msu.edu.

Michigan Technological University, Graduate School, College of Engineering, Department of Geological and Mining Engineering and Sciences, Program in Geology, Houghton, MI 49931-1295. Offers MS, PhD. Part-time programs available. *Faculty:* 14 full-time (1 woman), 3 part-time/adjunct (1 woman). *Students:* 14 full-time (11 women), 3 part-time; includes 3 minority (all Hispanic Americans), 3 international. Average age 29. 18 applicants, 72% accepted, 3 enrolled. In 2003, 3 master's, 1 doctorate awarded. *Degree requirements:* For master's, comprehensive exam, registration; for doctorate, thesis/dissertation, comprehensive exam, registration. *Entrance requirements:* Additional exam requirements/recommendations for international students: Required—TOEFL. *Application deadline:* For fall admission, 3/15 for domestic students. Applications are processed on a rolling basis. Application fee: $40 ($45 for international students). Electronic applications accepted. Tuition, nonresident: full-time $9,552; part-time $398 per credit. Required fees: $768. *Financial support:* In 2003–04, 10 students received support, including 4 fellowships with tuition reimbursements available (averaging $13,500 per year), 3 research assistantships with full tuition reimbursements available (averaging $8,950 per year), 2 teaching assistantships with full tuition reimbursements available (averaging $8,950 per year); career-related internships or fieldwork, Federal Work-Study, institutionally sponsored loans, scholarships/grants, traineeships, unspecified assistantships, and co-op also available. Support available to part-time students. Financial award application deadline: 2/1; financial award applicants required to submit FAFSA.

Announcement: The Department of Geological and Mining Engineering and Sciences offers 10 graduate programs that allow students to either focus or broaden their studies in geology, geological and mining engineering, and geophysics to explore fundamental and applied issues related to the earth, natural resource development/protection, and natural hazard mitigation—through the Peace Corps.

See in-depth description on page 245.

Montana Tech of The University of Montana, Graduate School, Geoscience Program, Butte, MT 59701-8997. Offers geochemistry (MS); geological engineering (MS); geology (MS); geophysical engineering (MS); hydrogeological engineering (MS); hydrogeology (MS). Part-time programs available. *Faculty:* 8 full-time (1 woman). *Students:* 15 full-time (5 women), 1 (woman) part-time. 17 applicants, 71% accepted, 9 enrolled. In 2003, 7 degrees awarded. *Degree requirements:* For master's, thesis (for some programs), comprehensive exam (for some programs), registration. *Entrance requirements:* For master's, GRE General Test, minimum GPA of 3.0. Additional exam requirements/recommendations for international students: Required—TOEFL (minimum score 525 paper-based; 195 computer-based). *Application deadline:* For fall admission, 4/1 priority date for domestic students, 3/1 priority date for international students; for spring admission, 10/1 priority date for domestic students, 7/1 priority date for international students. Applications are processed on a rolling basis. Application fee: $30. *Expenses:* Tuition, state resident: full-time $4,741; part-time $233 per credit. Tuition, nonresident: full-time $14,662; part-time $646 per credit. *Financial support:* In 2003–04, 15 students received support, including 10 research assistantships with partial tuition reimbursements available (averaging $4,655 per year), 10 teaching assistantships with partial tuition reimbursements available (averaging $4,800 per year); career-related internships or fieldwork, tuition waivers (full and partial), and unspecified assistantships also available. Financial award application deadline: 4/1; financial award applicants required to submit FAFSA. *Faculty research:* Water resource development, seismic processing, petroleum reservoir characterization, environmental geochemistry, molecular modeling, magmatic and hydrothermal ore deposits. Total annual research expenditures: $623,564. *Unit head:* Dr. Diane Wolfgram, Department Head, 406-496-4353, Fax: 406-496-4260, E-mail: dwolfgram@mtech.edu. *Application contact:* Cindy Dunstan, Administrator, Graduate School, 406-496-4304, Fax: 406-496-4334, E-mail: cdunstan@mtech.edu.

New Mexico Institute of Mining and Technology, Graduate Studies, Department of Earth and Environmental Science, Program in Geology and Geochemistry, Socorro, NM 87801. Offers geochemistry (MS, PhD); geology (MS, PhD). *Students:* 28 full-time (17 women), 3 part-time (all women), 3 international. Average age 29. 35 applicants, 7 enrolled. In 2003, 9 master's, 1 doctorate awarded. *Degree requirements:* For master's, thesis optional; for doctorate, thesis/dissertation. *Entrance requirements:* For master's, GRE General Test; for doctorate, GRE General Test, GRE Subject Test. Additional exam requirements/recommendations for international students: Required—TOEFL (minimum score 540 paper-based; 207 computer-based). *Application deadline:* For fall admission, 3/1 for domestic students; for spring admission, 6/1 for domestic students. Applications are processed on a rolling basis. Application fee: $16 ($30 for international students). Electronic applications accepted. *Expenses:* Tuition, state resident: full-time $2,276; part-time $126 per credit. Tuition, nonresident: full-time $9,170; part-time $509 per credit. Required fees: $924; $27 per credit. $214 per term. Part-time tuition and fees vary according to course load. *Financial support:* In 2003–04, 15 research assistantships (averaging $11,400 per year), 11 teaching assistantships with full and partial tuition reimbursements (averaging $8,366 per year) were awarded. Fellowships, Federal Work-Study, institutionally sponsored loans, and unspecified assistantships also available. Financial award application deadline: 3/1; financial award applicants required to submit CSS PROFILE or FAFSA. *Faculty research:* Care and karst topography, soil/water chemistry and properties, geochemistry of ore deposits. *Unit head:* Dr. Peter Mozley, Coordinator, 505-835-5311, Fax: 505-835-6436, E-mail: mozley@nmt.edu. *Application contact:* Dr. David B. Johnson, Dean of Graduate Studies, 505-835-5513, Fax: 505-835-5476, E-mail: graduate@nmt.edu.

New Mexico State University, Graduate School, College of Arts and Sciences, Department of Geological Sciences, Las Cruces, NM 88003-8001. Offers MS. Part-time programs available. *Faculty:* 6 full-time (2 women), 1 part-time/adjunct (0 women). *Students:* 14 full-time (6 women), 7 part-time (2 women); includes 2 minority (1 Asian American or Pacific Islander, 1 Hispanic American), 1 international. Average age 27. 14 applicants, 100% accepted, 5 enrolled. In 2003, 4 degrees awarded. *Degree requirements:* For master's, thesis. *Entrance requirements:* For master's, GRE General Test. *Application deadline:* For fall admission, 7/1 for domestic students; for spring admission, 11/1 for domestic students. Applications are processed on a rolling basis. Application fee: $30 ($50 for international students). Electronic applications accepted. *Expenses:* Tuition, state resident: full-time $2,670; part-time $151 per credit. Tuition, nonresident: full-time $10,596; part-time $481 per credit. Required fees: $954. *Financial support:* In 2003–04, 10 research assistantships, 12 teaching assistantships with partial tuition reimbursements were awarded. Career-related internships or fieldwork, Federal Work-Study, institutionally sponsored loans, scholarships/grants, health care benefits, and unspecified assistantships also available. Support available to part-time students. Financial award application deadline: 2/15. *Faculty research:* Geochemistry, tectonics, sedimentology, stratigraphy, igneous petrology. *Unit head:* Dr. Timothy Lawton, Head, 505-646-2708, Fax: 505-646-1056, E-mail: tlawton@nmsu.edu. *Application contact:* Dr. Katherine A. Giles, Associate Professor, 505-646-2033, Fax: 505-646-1056, E-mail: kgiles@nmsu.edu.

Northern Arizona University, Graduate College, College of Arts and Sciences, Department of Geology, Program in Geology, Flagstaff, AZ 86011. Offers MS. *Students:* 27 full-time (15 women), 15 part-time (6 women). Average age 27. 58 applicants, 19% accepted. In 2003, 12 degrees awarded. *Degree requirements:* For master's, thesis. *Application deadline:* For fall admission, 2/1 for domestic students. Application fee: $45. *Expenses:* Tuition, state resident: full-time $5,103. Tuition, nonresident: full-time $12,623. *Financial support:* In 2003–04, 5 research assistantships, 20 teaching assistantships were awarded. Career-related internships or fieldwork, Federal Work-Study, and tuition waivers (full and partial) also available. Total annual research expenditures: $499,385. *Unit head:* Dr. Paul Umhoeser, Coordinator, 928-523-6464. *Application contact:* Information Contact, E-mail: ms.geology@nau.edu.

Northern Arizona University, Graduate College, College of Arts and Sciences, Program in Quaternary Sciences, Flagstaff, AZ 86011. Offers MS. *Students:* 9 full-time (6 women), 2 part-time; includes 1 minority (Asian American or Pacific Islander) Average age 34. 8 applicants, 63% accepted. In 2003, 3 degrees awarded. *Degree requirements:* For master's, thesis. *Application deadline:* For fall admission, 2/15 for domestic students. Applications are processed on a rolling basis. Application fee: $45. *Expenses:* Tuition, state resident: full-time $5,103. Tuition, nonresident: full-time $12,623. *Financial support:* In 2003–04, 5 research assistantships were awarded; career-related internships or fieldwork, Federal Work-Study, tuition waivers (full and partial), and unspecified assistantships also available. Financial award application deadline: 2/15. *Faculty research:* Sandbar stability in the Grand Canyon; Stone Age site excavation in South Africa; neogene reptile and mammal evolution; mammoths of Hot Springs, South Dakota; Quaternary science of national parks on Colorado Plateau. *Unit head:* Dr. James Mead, Director, 520-523-1717. *Application contact:* Information Contact, E-mail: quaternary.sciences@nau.edu.

Northern Illinois University, Graduate School, College of Liberal Arts and Sciences, Department of Geology and Environmental Geosciences, De Kalb, IL 60115-2854. Offers geology (MS, PhD). Part-time programs available. *Faculty:* 11 full-time (1 woman), 1 (woman) part-time/adjunct. *Students:* 26 full-time (12 women), 10 part-time (3 women); includes 1 minority (Asian American or Pacific Islander), 9 international. Average age 33. 18 applicants, 61% accepted, 6 enrolled. In 2003, 2 degrees awarded. Terminal master's awarded for partial completion of doctoral program. *Degree requirements:* For master's, research seminar, thesis optional; for doctorate, thesis/dissertation, candidacy exam, dissertation defense, internship, research seminar. *Entrance requirements:* For master's, GRE General Test, bachelor's degree in engineering or science, minimum GPA of 2.75; for doctorate, GRE General Test, bachelor's or master's degree in engineering or science, minimum graduate GPA of 3.2. Additional exam requirements/recommendations for international students: Required—TOEFL (minimum score 550 paper-based; 213 computer-based). *Application deadline:* For fall admission, 6/1 for domestic students, 5/1 for international students; for spring admission, 11/1 for domestic students, 10/1 for international students. Applications are processed on a rolling basis. Application fee: $30. Electronic applications accepted. *Expenses:* Tuition, state resident: full-time $3,968; part-time $165 per credit hour. Tuition, nonresident: full-time $7,936; part-time $330 per credit hour. Required fees: $1,255; $52 per credit hour. *Financial support:* In 2003–04, 7 research assistantships with full tuition reimbursements, 17 teaching assistantships with full tuition reimbursements were awarded. Fellowships with full tuition reimbursements, career-related internships or fieldwork, Federal Work-Study, scholarships/grants, tuition waivers (full), and unspecified assistantships also available. Support available to part-time students. Financial award applicants required to submit FAFSA. *Unit head:* Dr. Jonathan Berg, Chair, 815-753-1943, Fax: 815-753-1945. *Application contact:* Dr. James Walker, Director of Graduate Studies, 815-753-7936.

Northwestern University, The Graduate School, Judd A. and Marjorie Weinberg College of Arts and Sciences, Department of Geological Sciences, Evanston, IL 60208. Offers MS, PhD. Admissions and degrees offered through The Graduate School. Part-time programs available. *Degree requirements:* For doctorate, thesis/dissertation. *Entrance requirements:* For master's and doctorate, GRE General Test. Additional exam requirements/recommendations for international students: Required—TOEFL. Electronic applications accepted. *Faculty research:* Tectonophysics, seismology, biogeochemistry, stratigraphy, paleontology.

The Ohio State University, Graduate School, College of Mathematical and Physical Sciences, Department of Geological Sciences, Columbus, OH 43210. Offers MS, PhD. *Faculty:* 44. *Students:* 41 full-time (15 women), 9 part-time (4 women); includes 3 minority (1 Asian American or Pacific Islander, 2 Hispanic Americans), 6 international. 90 applicants, 34% accepted. In 2003, 9 master's, 1 doctorate awarded. *Degree requirements:* For master's, thesis; for doctorate, one foreign language, thesis/dissertation. *Entrance requirements:* For master's and doctorate, GRE General Test. Additional exam requirements/recommendations for international students: Required—TOEFL. *Application deadline:* For fall admission, 8/15 for domestic students. Applications are processed on a rolling basis. Application fee: $40 ($50 for international students). *Expenses:* Tuition, state resident: full-time $7,233. Tuition, nonresident: full-time $18,489. *Financial support:* Fellowships, research assistantships, teaching assistantships, Federal Work-Study and institutionally sponsored loans available. Support available to part-time students. *Unit head:* Dr. E. Scott Bair, Chair, 614-292-0069, Fax: 614-292-7688, E-mail: bair.1@osu.edu. *Application contact:* Dr. David H. Elliot, Graduate Studies Committee Chair, 614-292-5076, Fax: 614-292-7688, E-mail: elliot.1@geology.ohio-state.edu.

Geology

Ohio University, Graduate Studies, College of Arts and Sciences, Department of Geological Sciences, Athens, OH 45701-2979. Offers environmental geochemistry (MS); environmental geology (MS); environmental/hydrology (MS); geology (MS); geology education (MS); geomorphology/surficial processes (MS); geophysics (MS); hydrogeology (MS); sedimentology (MS); structure/tectonics (MS). Part-time programs available. *Faculty:* 10 full-time (3 women), 4 part-time/adjunct (1 woman). *Students:* 13 full-time (4 women), 4 part-time (1 woman); includes 1 minority (Hispanic American), 4 international. Average age 25. 11 applicants, 45% accepted, 4 enrolled. In 2003, 8 degrees awarded. *Median time to degree:* Master's–2.5 years full-time. *Degree requirements:* For master's, thesis, thesis proposal defense. *Entrance requirements:* Additional exam requirements/recommendations for international students: Required—TOEFL (minimum score 550 paper-based; 217 computer-based). *Application deadline:* For fall admission, 2/1 priority date for domestic students, 1/1 priority date for international students. Application fee: $45. *Expenses:* Tuition, state resident: full-time $2,651; part-time $328 per credit. Tuition, nonresident: full-time $5,095; part-time $632 per credit. Tuition and fees vary according to program. *Financial support:* In 2003–04, 16 students received support, including 3 research assistantships with full tuition reimbursements available (averaging $11,000 per year), 13 teaching assistantships with full tuition reimbursements available (averaging $11,000 per year); institutionally sponsored loans, scholarships/grants, tuition waivers (full), and unspecified assistantships also available. Financial award application deadline: 3/15. *Faculty research:* Geoscience education, tectonics, flurial geomorphology, invertebrate paleontology, mine/hydrology. Total annual research expenditures: $506,400. *Unit head:* Dr. Douglas Green, Chair, 740-593-6896, Fax: 740-593-0486, E-mail: green@ohio.edu. *Application contact:* Dr. Dina L. Lopez, Graduate Chair, 740-593-9435, Fax: 740-593-0486, E-mail: lopezd@ohio.edu.

Oklahoma State University, Graduate College, College of Arts and Sciences, School of Geology, Stillwater, OK 74078. Offers MS. *Faculty:* 11 full-time (1 woman). *Students:* 21 full-time (7 women), 11 part-time (3 women); includes 2 minority (1 American Indian/Alaska Native, 1 Hispanic American), 5 international. Average age 31. 15 applicants, 93% accepted. In 2003, 10 degrees awarded. *Degree requirements:* For master's, thesis. *Entrance requirements:* For master's, minimum GPA of 3.0. Additional exam requirements/recommendations for international students: Required—TOEFL. *Application deadline:* For fall admission, 6/1 for domestic students. Applications are processed on a rolling basis. Application fee: $25 ($50 for international students). Electronic applications accepted. *Expenses:* Tuition, state resident: full-time $3,752; part-time $118 per credit hour. Tuition, nonresident: full-time $10,346; part-time $393 per credit hour. Tuition and fees vary according to course load. *Financial support:* In 2003–04, 5 research assistantships (averaging $12,591 per year), 18 teaching assistantships (averaging $9,500 per year) were awarded. Career-related internships or fieldwork, Federal Work-Study, and tuition waivers (partial) also available. Support available to part-time students. Financial award application deadline: 3/1. *Faculty research:* Groundwater hydrology, petroleum geology. *Unit head:* Dr. Ibrahim Cemen, Head, 405-744-6358, E-mail: amm100@okstate.edu.

Oregon State University, Graduate School, College of Science, Department of Geosciences, Program in Geology, Corvallis, OR 97331. Offers MA, MAIS, MS, PhD. Part-time programs available. *Students:* 30 full-time (10 women), 3 part-time; includes 2 minority (1 American Indian/Alaska Native, 1 Hispanic American), 1 international. Average age 28. In 2003, 5 degrees awarded. Terminal master's awarded for partial completion of doctoral program. *Degree requirements:* For master's, variable foreign language requirement, thesis; for doctorate, one foreign language, thesis/dissertation. *Entrance requirements:* For master's and doctorate, GRE General Test, GRE Subject Test, minimum GPA of 3.0 in last 90 hours. Additional exam requirements/recommendations for international students: Required—TOEFL. *Application deadline:* For fall admission, 2/1 for domestic students. Applications are processed on a rolling basis. Application fee: $50. *Expenses:* Tuition, state resident: full-time $8,139; part-time $301 per credit. Tuition, nonresident: full-time $14,376; part-time $532 per credit. Required fees: $1,227. *Financial support:* Fellowships, research assistantships, teaching assistantships, Federal Work-Study and institutionally sponsored loans available. Support available to part-time students. Financial award application deadline: 2/1. *Faculty research:* Hydrogeology, geomorphology, ocean geology, geochemistry, earthquake geology. *Unit head:* Dr. Roger L. Nielsen, Chair, 541-737-1201, Fax: 541-737-1200, E-mail: rnielsen@oce.orst.edu. *Application contact:* Joanne VanGeest, Graduate Admissions Coordinator, 541-737-1204, Fax: 541-737-1200, E-mail: vangeesj@geo.orst.edu.

The Pennsylvania State University University Park Campus, Graduate School, College of Earth and Mineral Sciences, Department of Geosciences, Program in Geology, State College, University Park, PA 16802-1503. Offers MS, PhD. *Entrance requirements:* For master's and doctorate, GRE General Test. Additional exam requirements/recommendations for international students: Required—TOEFL. Application fee: $45.

See in-depth description on page 249.

Portland State University, Graduate Studies, College of Liberal Arts and Sciences, Department of Geology, Portland, OR 97207-0751. Offers geology (MA, MS, PhD); science/geology (MAT, MST). Part-time programs available. *Faculty:* 9 full-time (2 women). *Students:* 15 full-time (4 women), 9 part-time (4 women), 1 international. Average age 30. 14 applicants, 100% accepted, 7 enrolled. In 2003, 6 degrees awarded. *Degree requirements:* For master's, thesis, field comprehensive; for doctorate, thesis/dissertation, 2 years of residency. *Entrance requirements:* For master's, GRE General Test, GRE Subject Test, BA/BS in geology, minimum GPA of 3.0 in upper-division course work or 2.75 overall. Additional exam requirements/recommendations for international students: Required—TOEFL. *Application deadline:* For fall admission, 4/1 for domestic students; for winter admission, 9/1 for domestic students; for spring admission, 11/1 for domestic students. Applications are processed on a rolling basis. Application fee: $50. *Expenses:* Tuition, state resident: full-time $6,588. Tuition, nonresident: full-time $12,060; part-time $298 per credit. Required fees: $1,041; $19 per credit. $35 per term. *Financial support:* In 2003–04, 3 research assistantships with full tuition reimbursements (averaging $10,309 per year), 6 teaching assistantships with full tuition reimbursements (averaging $10,001 per year) were awarded. Career-related internships or fieldwork, Federal Work-Study, scholarships/grants, and unspecified assistantships also available. Support available to part-time students. Financial award application deadline: 3/1; financial award applicants required to submit FAFSA. *Faculty research:* Sediment transport, volcanic environmental geology, coastal and fluvial processes. Total annual research expenditures: $1.1 million. *Unit head:* Dr. Michael L. Cummings, Head, 503-725-3022, Fax: 503-725-3025. *Application contact:* Nancy Eriksson, Office Coordinator, 503-725-3022, Fax: 503-725-3025, E-mail: erikssonn@pdx.edu.

Princeton University, Graduate School, Department of Geosciences, Princeton, NJ 08544-1019. Offers atmospheric and oceanic sciences (PhD); geological and geophysical sciences (PhD). *Faculty:* 29 full-time (2 women), 2 part-time/adjunct (0 women). *Students:* 21 full-time (10 women), 11 international. Average age 24. 51 applicants, 31% accepted, 6 enrolled. In 2003, 6 doctorates awarded, leading to continued full-time study 100%. *Median time to degree:* Doctorate–5.08 years full-time. *Degree requirements:* For doctorate, one foreign language, thesis/dissertation. *Entrance requirements:* For doctorate, GRE General Test. Additional exam requirements/recommendations for international students: Required—TOEFL (minimum score 600 paper-based; 250 computer-based). *Application deadline:* For fall admission, 12/31 for domestic students, 12/1 for international students. Application fee: $80 ($55 for international students). Electronic applications accepted. *Expenses:* Tuition: Full-time $29,910. Required fees: $810. *Financial support:* In 2003–04, 8 fellowships with full tuition reimbursements (averaging $16,500 per year), 12 research assistantships with full tuition reimbursements (averaging $30,570 per year), 11 teaching assistantships with full tuition reimbursements (averaging $22,042 per year) were awarded. Federal Work-Study, institutionally sponsored loans, and summer salary is $7000 also available. Financial award application deadline: 1/2. *Faculty research:* Biogeochemistry, climate science, earth history, regional geology and tectonics, solid–earth geophysics. Total annual research expenditures: $19 million. *Unit head:* Prof. Guust Nolet, Director of Graduate Studies, 609-258-4128, Fax: 609-258-1274, E-mail: nolet@princeton.edu. *Application contact:* Janice Yip, Director of Graduate Admissions, 609-258-3034, Fax: 609-258-6180, E-mail: gsadmit@princeton.edu.

Queens College of the City University of New York, Division of Graduate Studies, Mathematics and Natural Sciences Division, School of Earth and Environmental Science, Flushing, NY 11367-1597. Offers MA. Part-time and evening/weekend programs available. *Faculty:* 11 full-time (3 women). *Students:* 8 applicants, 88% accepted. *Degree requirements:* For master's, thesis, comprehensive exam. *Entrance requirements:* For master's, GRE, previous course work in calculus, physics, and chemistry; minimum GPA of 3.0. Additional exam requirements/recommendations for international students: Required—TOEFL. *Application deadline:* For fall admission, 4/1 for domestic students; for spring admission, 11/1 for domestic students. Applications are processed on a rolling basis. Application fee: $50. *Expenses:* Tuition, state resident: full-time $7,130; part-time $230 per credit. Tuition, nonresident: full-time $11,880; part-time $425 per credit. Required fees: $66; $38 per semester. *Financial support:* Career-related internships or fieldwork, Federal Work-Study, institutionally sponsored loans, tuition waivers (partial), unspecified assistantships, and adjunct lectureships available. Support available to part-time students. Financial award application deadline: 4/1; financial award applicants required to submit FAFSA. *Faculty research:* Sedimentology/stratigraphy, paleontology, field petrology. *Unit head:* Dr. Daniel Habib, Chairperson, 718-997-3300, E-mail: daniel_habib@qc.edu. *Application contact:* Dr. Hannes Brueckner, Graduate Adviser, 718-997-3300, E-mail: hannes_brueckner@qc.edu.

Queen's University at Kingston, School of Graduate Studies and Research, Faculty of Arts and Sciences, Department of Geological Sciences and Geological Engineering, Kingston, ON K7L 3N6, Canada. Offers M Sc, M Sc Eng, PhD. Part-time programs available. *Degree requirements:* For master's, thesis (for some programs); for doctorate, thesis/dissertation, comprehensive exam. *Entrance requirements:* Additional exam requirements/recommendations for international students: Required—TOEFL. *Faculty research:* Geochemistry, sedimentology, geophysics, economic geology, structural geology.

Rensselaer Polytechnic Institute, Graduate School, School of Science, Department of Earth and Environmental Sciences, Program in Geology, Troy, NY 12180-3590. Offers MS, PhD. Part-time programs available. *Faculty:* 7 full-time (0 women). *Students:* 15 full-time (7 women); includes 3 minority (all Asian Americans or Pacific Islanders) Average age 26. 35 applicants, 11% accepted. In 2003, 3 master's, 2 doctorates awarded. Terminal master's awarded for partial completion of doctoral program. *Degree requirements:* For master's, thesis (for some programs), comprehensive exam; for doctorate, thesis/dissertation, comprehensive exam. *Entrance requirements:* For master's and doctorate, GRE General Test. Additional exam requirements/recommendations for international students: Required—TOEFL. *Application deadline:* For fall admission, 1/15 for domestic students. Applications are processed on a rolling basis. Application fee: $45. Electronic applications accepted. *Expenses:* Tuition: Full-time $27,700; part-time $1,320 per credit. Required fees: $1,470. *Financial support:* In 2003–04, 17 research assistantships with full tuition reimbursements (averaging $12,000 per year), 6 teaching assistantships with full tuition reimbursements (averaging $12,000 per year) were awarded. Fellowships with full tuition reimbursements, career-related internships or fieldwork and scholarships/grants also available. Financial award application deadline: 2/1; financial award applicants required to submit FAFSA. *Faculty research:* Geochemistry, petrology, geophysics, environmental geochemistry, planetary geology. *Application contact:* Dr. Steven Roecker, Professor, 518-276-6474, Fax: 518-276-6680, E-mail: ees@rpi.edu.

Rutgers, The State University of New Jersey, Newark, Graduate School, Program in Environmental Geology, Newark, NJ 07102. Offers MS. Part-time and evening/weekend programs available. *Faculty:* 6 full-time (1 woman), 1 part-time/adjunct (0 women). *Students:* 1 (woman) full-time, 7 part-time; includes 7 minority (all Hispanic Americans) 9 applicants, 33% accepted, 2 enrolled. In 2003, 1 degree awarded. *Degree requirements:* For master's, thesis optional. *Entrance requirements:* For master's, GRE General Test, minimum B average. *Application deadline:* For fall admission, 6/1 for domestic students; for spring admission, 12/1 for domestic students. Application fee: $50. Electronic applications accepted. *Expenses:* Tuition, state resident: full-time $10,030. Tuition, nonresident: full-time $14,202. *Faculty research:* Environmental geology, plate tectonics, geoarchaeology, geophysics, mineralogy-petrology. Total annual research expenditures: $124,000. *Unit head:* Dr. Alex Gates, Program Coordinator and Adviser, 973-353-5034, Fax: 973-353-5100, E-mail: agates@andromeda.rutgers.edu.

Rutgers, The State University of New Jersey, New Brunswick/Piscataway, Graduate School, Program in Geological Sciences, New Brunswick, NJ 08901-1281. Offers MS, PhD. Part-time programs available. *Faculty:* 31 full-time (5 women), 3 part-time/adjunct (1 woman). *Students:* 14 full-time (6 women), 16 part-time (8 women); includes 1 minority (African American), 2 international. Average age 31. 42 applicants, 17% accepted, 3 enrolled. In 2003, 1 master's awarded. *Median time to degree:* Master's–2.25 years full-time, 4 years part-time; doctorate–3.5 years full-time, 5 years part-time. *Degree requirements:* For master's, thesis/dissertation; for doctorate, thesis/dissertation, comprehensive exam. *Entrance requirements:* For master's and doctorate, GRE General Test, GRE Subject Test (recommended). *Application deadline:* For fall admission, 5/1 for domestic students; for spring admission, 2/15 for domestic students. Applications are processed on a rolling basis. Application fee: $50. Electronic applications accepted. *Expenses:* Tuition, state resident: full-time $10,030. Tuition, nonresident: full-time $14,202. *Financial support:* In 2003–04, 13 students received support, including 5 fellowships with full tuition reimbursements available (averaging $16,000 per year), 2 research assistantships with full tuition reimbursements available (averaging $15,500 per year), 5 teaching assistantships with full tuition reimbursements available (averaging $15,500 per year); Federal Work-Study and scholarships/grants also available. Financial award application deadline: 3/1; financial award applicants required to submit FAFSA. *Faculty research:* Stratigraphy and basins analysis; volcanology and geochemistry; quaternary studies; structure and geophysics; marine science, biogeochemistry and paleoceanography. Total annual research expenditures: $1 million. *Unit head:* Kenneth G. Miller, Director, 732-445-3622, Fax: 732-445-3374, E-mail: kgm@rci.rutgers.edu.

St. Francis Xavier University, Graduate Studies, Department of Earth Sciences, Antigonish, NS B2G 2W5, Canada. Offers M Sc. *Faculty:* 5 full-time (1 woman). *Students:* 1 full-time (0 women), 3 part-time (all women). *Degree requirements:* For master's, thesis, registration. *Entrance requirements:* Additional exam requirements/recommendations for international students: Required—TOEFL (minimum score 580 paper-based; 236 computer-based). Application fee: $40. Tuition, area resident: Full-time $5,310. International tuition: $9,210 full-time. Full-time tuition and fees vary according to course load and program. *Faculty research:* Environmental earth sciences, global change tectonics, paleoclimatology, crustal fluids. Total annual research expenditures: $300,000. *Unit head:* Dr. Brendan Murphy, Professor, 902-867-2481, Fax: 902-867-5153, E-mail: bmurphy@stfx.ca.

San Diego State University, Graduate and Research Affairs, College of Sciences, Department of Geological Sciences, San Diego, CA 92182. Offers MS. Part-time programs available. *Students:* 16 full-time (5 women), 12 part-time (6 women); includes 2 minority (1 American Indian/Alaska Native, 1 Hispanic American), 1 international. Average age 27. 19 applicants, 63% accepted, 6 enrolled. In 2003, 9 degrees awarded. *Degree requirements:* For master's, thesis. *Entrance requirements:* For master's, GRE General Test, bachelor's degree in related field. Additional exam requirements/recommendations for international students: Required—TOEFL. *Application deadline:* For fall admission, 5/1 for domestic students, 5/1 for international students; for spring admission, 11/1 for domestic students, 10/1 for international students. Applications are processed on a rolling basis. Application fee: $55. Electronic applications accepted. Tuition, nonresident: part-time $282 per unit. Required fees: $1,349; $875 per year. *Financial support:* Fellowships, research assistantships, teaching assistantships available. Financial award applicants required to submit FAFSA. *Faculty research:* Earthquakes, hydrology, meteorological analysis and tomography studies. Total annual research expenditures: $965,830. *Application contact:* Kathryn Thorbjarnarson, Graduate Coordinator, 619-594-1392, Fax: 619-594-4372, E-mail: thorbjarnarson@geology.sdsu.edu.

San Jose State University, Graduate Studies and Research, College of Science, Department of Geology, San Jose, CA 95192-0001. Offers MS. *Students:* 10 full-time (4 women), 18 part-time (11 women); includes 5 minority (3 Asian Americans or Pacific Islanders, 2 Hispanic Americans). Average age 31. 14 applicants, 86% accepted, 10 enrolled. In 2003, 4 degrees awarded. *Degree requirements:* For master's, thesis. *Entrance requirements:* For master's, GRE. *Application deadline:* For fall admission, 6/29 for domestic students; for spring admission, 11/30 for domestic students. Applications are processed on a rolling basis. Application fee: $59. Electronic applications accepted. Tuition, nonresident: part-time $282 per unit. Required fees: $654 per semester. *Financial support:* Teaching assistantships, Federal Work-Study available. Financial award applicants required to submit FAFSA. *Unit head:* John Williams, Chair, 408-924-5050, Fax: 408-924-5053. *Application contact:* Dr. Robert Miller, Graduate Adviser, 408-924-5025.

South Dakota School of Mines and Technology, Graduate Division, Department of Geology and Geological Engineering, Rapid City, SD 57701-3995. Offers geology and geological engineering (MS, PhD); paleontology (MS). Part-time programs available. *Faculty:* 8 full-time (1 woman). *Students:* 13 full-time (4 women), 14 part-time (8 women); includes 1 minority (Hispanic American) Average age 30. In 2003, 10 degrees awarded. *Degree requirements:* For master's and doctorate, thesis/dissertation. *Entrance requirements:* For master's and doctorate, GRE General Test, GRE Subject Test. Additional exam requirements/recommendations for international students: Required—TOEFL, TWE. *Application deadline:* For fall admission, 6/15 for domestic students; for spring admission, 10/15 for domestic students. Applications are processed on a rolling basis. Application fee: $35. Electronic applications accepted. *Expenses:* Tuition, state resident: part-time $109 per credit hour. Tuition, nonresident: part-time $323 per credit hour. Required fees: $100 per credit hour. *Financial support:* In 2003–04, 2 fellowships (averaging $3,000 per year), 6 research assistantships with partial tuition reimbursements (averaging $6,975 per year), 14 teaching assistantships with partial tuition reimbursements were awarded. Federal Work-Study and institutionally sponsored loans also available. Support available to part-time students. Financial award application deadline: 5/15. *Faculty research:* Contaminants in soil, nitrate leaching, environmental changes, fracture formations, greenhouse effect. Total annual research expenditures: $18,865. *Unit head:* Dr. Arden Davis, Dean, 605-394-2461. *Application contact:* Brenda Brown, Secretary, 800-454-8162 Ext. 2493, Fax: 605-394-5360, E-mail: graduate_admissions@silver.sdsmt.edu.

Southern Illinois University Carbondale, Graduate School, College of Science, Department of Geology, Carbondale, IL 62901-4701. Offers environmental resources and policy (PhD); geology (MS, PhD). *Faculty:* 12 full-time (0 women). *Students:* 8 full-time (3 women), 27 part-time (6 women), 6 international. Average age 25. 13 applicants, 69% accepted, 2 enrolled. In 2003, 13 degrees awarded. *Degree requirements:* For master's, thesis; for doctorate, one foreign language, thesis/dissertation. *Entrance requirements:* For master's, GRE, minimum GPA of 2.7; for doctorate, GRE General Test, minimum GPA of 3.25. Additional exam requirements/recommendations for international students: Required—TOEFL. *Application deadline:* For fall admission, 2/15 for domestic students. Applications are processed on a rolling basis. Application fee: $20. *Expenses:* Tuition, state resident: part-time $478 per hour. Tuition, nonresident: part-time $657 per hour. *Financial support:* In 2003–04, 17 students received support; fellowships with full tuition reimbursements available, research assistantships with full tuition reimbursements available, teaching assistantships with full tuition reimbursements available, Federal Work-Study, institutionally sponsored loans, and tuition waivers (full) available. Support available to part-time students. Total annual research expenditures:$720,000. *Unit head:* Steven Esling, Chair, 618-453-3351, Fax: 618-453-7393.

Southern Methodist University, Dedman College, Department of Geological Sciences, Program in Geology, Dallas, TX 75275. Offers MS, PhD. Part-time programs available. *Degree requirements:* For master's and doctorate, thesis/dissertation, qualifying exam. *Entrance requirements:* For master's and doctorate, GRE General Test, minimum GPA of 3.0, letters of recommendation. Additional exam requirements/recommendations for international students: Required—TOEFL; Recommended—TSE. *Expenses:* Tuition: Full-time $11,362; part-time $874 per credit. Required fees: $112 per credit. Tuition and fees vary according to course load and program. *Faculty research:* Geothermal, paleontology, environmental, stable isotope geochemistry.

Southwest Missouri State University, Graduate College, College of Natural and Applied Sciences, Department of Geography, Geology, and Planning, Springfield, MO 65804-0094. Offers earth science (MS Ed); geography (MS Ed); geography, geology and planning (MNAS); natural science (MS Ed); resource planning (MS). Part-time and evening/weekend programs available. *Faculty:* 15 full-time (2 women), 3 part-time/adjunct (0 women). *Students:* 16 full-time (9 women), 19 part-time (9 women); includes 4 minority (2 American Indian/Alaska Native, 1 Asian American or Pacific Islander, 1 Hispanic American), 2 international. Average age 34. 16 applicants, 88% accepted, 11 enrolled. In 2003, 5 degrees awarded. *Degree requirements:* For master's, thesis, comprehensive exam. *Entrance requirements:* For master's, GRE General Test, minimum undergraduate GPA of 3.0. *Application deadline:* For fall admission, 8/5 for domestic students; for spring admission, 12/20 priority date for domestic students. Applications are processed on a rolling basis. Application fee: $30. Electronic applications accepted. *Expenses:* Tuition, state resident: full-time $2,862. Tuition, nonresident: full-time $5,724. *Financial support:* In 2003–04, 6 research assistantships with full tuition reimbursements (averaging $8,400 per year), 9 teaching assistantships with full tuition reimbursements (averaging $6,300 per year) were awarded. Career-related internships or fieldwork, Federal Work-Study, and unspecified assistantships also available. Financial award application deadline: 3/31. *Faculty research:* Water resources, small town planning, recreation and open space planning. *Unit head:* Dr. James Skinner, Head, 417-836-5800, Fax: 417-836-6934. *Application contact:* Dr. Robert T. Pavlowsky, Graduate Adviser, 417-836-5800, Fax: 417-836-6934, E-mail: rtp138f@smsu.edu.

State University of New York at Binghamton, Graduate School, School of Arts and Sciences, Department of Geological Sciences, Binghamton, NY 13902-6000. Offers MA, PhD. Part-time programs available. Terminal master's awarded for partial completion of doctoral program. *Degree requirements:* For master's, thesis or alternative; for doctorate, variable foreign language requirement, thesis/dissertation, departmental qualifying exam. *Entrance requirements:* For master's and doctorate, GRE General Test, GRE Subject Test. Additional exam requirements/recommendations for international students: Required—TOEFL. Electronic applications accepted.

State University of New York at New Paltz, Graduate School, School of Science and Engineering, Department of Geological Sciences, New Paltz, NY 12561. Offers MA, MAT, MS Ed. Part-time and evening/weekend programs available. *Degree requirements:* For master's, thesis, comprehensive exam. *Entrance requirements:* For master's, GRE General Test, minimum GPA of 3.0. Additional exam requirements/recommendations for international students: Required—TOEFL (minimum score 550 paper-based). *Application deadline:* For fall admission, 3/1 priority date for domestic students, 3/1 priority date for international students; for spring admission, 10/1 for domestic students, 10/1 for international students. Applications are processed on a rolling basis. Application fee: $50. *Expenses:* Tuition, state resident: full-time $6,900; part-time $288 per credit hour. Tuition, nonresident: full-time $10,500; part-time $438 per credit hour. Tuition and fees vary according to program. *Financial support:* Federal Work-Study and institutionally sponsored loans available. *Unit head:* Dr. Frederick Vollmer, Chairman, 845-257-3760, E-mail: vollmerf@newpaltz.edu.

Stephen F. Austin State University, Graduate School, College of Sciences and Mathematics, Department of Geology, Nacogdoches, TX 75962. Offers MS, MSNS. *Faculty:* 6 full-time (0 women). *Students:* 8 full-time (4 women), 12 part-time (8 women); includes 4 minority (2 African Americans, 1 Asian American or Pacific Islander, 1 Hispanic American). Average age 23. 14 applicants, 100% accepted. In 2003, 9 degrees awarded. *Degree requirements:* For master's, comprehensive exam. *Entrance requirements:* For master's, GRE General Test, minimum GPA of 2.8 in last 60 hours, 2.5 overall. Additional exam requirements/recommendations for international students: Required—TOEFL. *Application deadline:* For fall admission, 8/1 for domestic students; for spring admission, 12/15 for domestic students. Applications are processed on a rolling basis. Application fee: $0 ($50 for international students). *Expenses:* Tuition, state resident: part-time $46 per hour. Tuition, nonresident: part-time $282 per hour. Required fees: $71 per hour. Tuition and fees vary according to reciprocity agreements. *Financial support:* In 2003–04, 5 teaching assistantships (averaging $7,066 per year) were awarded; Federal Work-Study, health care benefits, and unspecified assistantships also available. Financial award application deadline: 3/1. *Faculty research:* Stratigraphy of Kaibab limestone, Utah; structure of Ouachita Mountains, Arkansas; groundwater chemistry of Carrizo Sand, Texas. *Unit head:* Dr. William Roberts, Chair, 936-468-3701, E-mail: broberts@sfasu.edu. *Application contact:* Dr. R. LaRell Nielson, Director of Graduate Program, 936-468-2248.

Sul Ross State University, School of Arts and Sciences, Department of Geology and Chemistry, Alpine, TX 79832. Offers MS. Part-time programs available. *Degree requirements:* For master's, thesis optional. *Entrance requirements:* For master's, GRE General Test, minimum GPA of 2.5 in last 60 hours of undergraduate work.

Announcement: Program stresses integrated field and laboratory research. The University is situated in an area of diverse and well-exposed geology. Research equipment includes GIS, GPS, XRF, XRD, AA, CL, and NAA. Current faculty research in environmental geology, volcanology, trace-element geochemistry, paleontology, carbonate depositional environments, arid-region hydrogeology, and remote sensing. URL: http://www.sulross.edu/pages/1007.asp

Syracuse University, Graduate School, College of Arts and Sciences, Department of Geology, Syracuse, NY 13244-0003. Offers MA, MS, PhD. Part-time programs available. Postbaccalaureate distance learning degree programs offered. *Faculty:* 9. *Students:* 14 full-time (5 women), 1 (woman) part-time, 3 international. 22 applicants, 27% accepted, 6 enrolled. *Degree requirements:* For master's, thesis (for some programs), research tool; for doctorate, thesis/dissertation, 2 research tools. *Entrance requirements:* For master's and doctorate, GRE General Test, GRE Subject Test. Additional exam requirements/recommendations for international students: Required—TOEFL. Application fee: $65. *Expenses:* Tuition: Full-time $13,356; part-time $742 per credit. Required fees: $482. *Financial support:* Fellowships with full tuition reimbursements, research assistantships with full tuition reimbursements, teaching assistantships with full and partial tuition reimbursements, tuition waivers (partial) available. *Unit head:* Dr. Scott Samson, Chair, 315-443-3762, Fax: 315-443-3363, E-mail: sdsamson@syr.edu. *Application contact:* Information Contact, 315-443-2672.

Temple University, Graduate School, College of Science and Technology, Department of Geology, Philadelphia, PA 19122-6096. Offers MA. *Degree requirements:* For master's, thesis, qualifying exam. *Entrance requirements:* For master's, GRE General Test, minimum GPA of 3.0 during previous 2 years, 2.8 overall. Electronic applications accepted. *Faculty research:* Hydrolic modeling, environmental geochemistry and geophysics, paleosas, cyclic stratigraphy, materials research.

Texas A&M University, College of Geosciences, Department of Geology and Geophysics, College Station, TX 77843. Offers MS, PhD. *Faculty:* 25 full-time (1 woman), 1 part-time/adjunct (0 women). *Students:* 85 full-time (26 women), 21 part-time (8 women); includes 6 minority (1 African American, 1 American Indian/Alaska Native, 2 Asian Americans or Pacific Islanders, 2 Hispanic Americans), 43 international. Average age 31. 57 applicants, 86% accepted, 23 enrolled. In 2003, 28 master's, 6 doctorates awarded. *Degree requirements:* For master's and doctorate, thesis/dissertation. *Entrance requirements:* For master's and doctorate, GRE General Test. Additional exam requirements/recommendations for international students: Required—TOEFL. *Application deadline:* For fall admission, 3/1 priority date for domestic students, 1/15 priority date for international students; for spring admission, 10/1 priority date for domestic students, 8/15 priority date for international students. Applications are processed on a rolling basis. Application fee: $50 ($75 for international students). Electronic applications accepted. *Expenses:* Tuition, state resident: full-time $3,420. Tuition, nonresident: full-time $9,084. Required fees: $1,861. *Financial support:* In 2003–04, 76 students received support, including 20 fellowships with partial tuition reimbursements available (averaging $1,000 per year), 15 research assistantships with partial tuition reimbursements available (averaging $11,925 per year), 50 teaching assistantships with partial tuition reimbursements available (averaging $11,925 per year); Federal Work-Study, institutionally sponsored loans, scholarships/grants, health care benefits, tuition waivers (partial), and unspecified assistantships also available. Financial award application deadline: 3/1; financial award applicants required to submit FAFSA. *Faculty research:* Environmental and engineering geology and geophysics, petroleum geology, tectonophysics, geochemistry. *Unit head:* Dr. Rick Carlson, Head, 979-845-2451, Fax: 979-845-6162. *Application contact:* Robert K. Popp, Graduate Adviser, 979-845-2451, Fax: 979-845-6162, E-mail: popp@geo.tamu.edu.

Texas A&M University–Kingsville, College of Graduate Studies, College of Arts and Sciences, Department of Geosciences, Kingsville, TX 78363. Offers applied geology (MS). Part-time and evening/weekend programs available. *Degree requirements:* For master's, thesis, comprehensive exam. *Entrance requirements:* For master's, GRE General Test, minimum GPA of 3.0. Additional exam requirements/recommendations for international students: Required—TOEFL. *Faculty research:* Stratigraphy and sedimentology of modern coastal sediments, sandstone diagnosis, vertebrate paleontology, structural geology.

Texas Christian University, College of Science and Engineering, Department of Geology, Fort Worth, TX 76129-0002. Offers MS. Part-time and evening/weekend programs available. *Degree requirements:* For master's, thesis, preliminary exam. *Entrance requirements:* For master's, GRE General Test. Additional exam requirements/recommendations for international students: Required—TOEFL. *Application deadline:* For fall admission, 3/1 for domestic students; for spring admission, 12/1 for domestic students. Applications are processed on a rolling basis. Application fee: $0. *Expenses:* Tuition: Part-time $640 per credit hour. Tuition and fees vary according to program. *Financial support:* Teaching assistantships, unspecified assistantships available. Financial award application deadline: 3/1. *Unit head:* Chairperson, 817-257-7270. *Application contact:* Dr. Bonnie Melhart, Associate Dean, College of Science and Engineering, E-mail: b.melhart@tcu.edu.

Tulane University, Graduate School, Department of Earth and Environmental Sciences, New Orleans, LA 70118-5669. Offers geology (MS, PhD); paleontology (PhD). *Faculty:* 9 full-time. *Students:* 24 full-time (8 women), 2 part-time (both women); includes 1 minority (Hispanic American), 5 international. 16 applicants, 50% accepted, 6 enrolled. In 2003, 3 degrees awarded. *Degree requirements:* For master's, one foreign language, thesis or alternative; for doctorate, one foreign language, thesis/dissertation. *Entrance requirements:* For master's, GRE General Test, minimum B average in undergraduate course work; for doctorate, GRE General Test. Additional exam requirements/recommendations for international students: Required—TOEFL; Recommended—TSE. *Application deadline:* For fall admission, 2/1 for domestic students, 2/1 for international students. Application fee: $45. *Financial support:* Research assistantships with full tuition reimbursements, teaching assistantships with full tuition reimbursements, career-related internships or fieldwork, Federal Work-Study, and institutionally sponsored loans available. Financial award application deadline: 2/1. *Faculty research:* Sedimentation, isotopes, biogeochemistry, marine geology, structural geology. *Unit head:* Dr. Stephen Nelson, Chair, 504-865-5198. *Application contact:* Dr. Thomas Bianchi, Graduate Advisor, 504-865-5198.

See in-depth description on page 255.

Université du Québec à Montréal, Graduate Programs, Program in Earth Sciences, Montreal, QC H3C 3P8, Canada. Offers geology-research (M Sc); mineral resources (PhD); non-renewable resources (DESS). Part-time programs available. *Faculty:* 16 full-time (2 women), 16 part-time/adjunct (1 woman). *Students:* 51 full-time (9 women), 15 international. 18 applicants, 56% accepted. In 2003, 7 master's, 4 doctorates awarded. Terminal master's awarded for partial completion of doctoral program. *Median time to degree:* Of those who began their doctoral program in fall 1995, 90% received their degree in 8 years or less. *Degree requirements:*

Geology

Université du Québec à Montréal (continued)

For master's, thesis (for some programs); for doctorate, thesis/dissertation. *Entrance requirements:* For master's, appropriate bachelor's degree or equivalent, proficiency in French. *Application deadline:* Applications are processed on a rolling basis. Application fee: $50. *Financial support:* In 2003–04, fellowships (averaging $5,000 per year), research assistantships (averaging $4,000 per year), teaching assistantships (averaging $1,000 per year) were awarded. Scholarships/grants also available. *Faculty research:* Economic geology, structural geology, geochemistry, Quaternary geology, isotopic geochemistry. *Unit head:* Alfred Jaouich, Director, 514-987-3000 Ext. 3378, Fax: 514-987-7749, E-mail: jaouich.alfred@uqam.ca. *Application contact:* Micheline Lacroix, Admissions Officer, 514-987-3000 Ext. 3370, Fax: 514-987-7749, E-mail: lacroix.micheline@uqam.ca.

Université Laval, Faculty of Sciences and Engineering, Department of Geology and Geological Engineering, Québec, QC G1K 7P4, Canada. Offers earth sciences (M Sc, PhD), including earth sciences, environmental technologies (M Sc); geology (M Sc, PhD). Terminal master's awarded for partial completion of doctoral program. *Degree requirements:* For master's, thesis (for some programs); for doctorate, thesis/dissertation, comprehensive exam. *Entrance requirements:* For master's and doctorate, knowledge of French. Electronic applications accepted. *Faculty research:* Engineering, economics, regional geology.

University at Albany, State University of New York, College of Arts and Sciences, Department of Earth and Atmospheric Sciences, Albany, NY 12222-0001. Offers atmospheric science (MS, PhD); geology (MS, PhD). Evening/weekend programs available. *Students:* 36 full-time (15 women), 8 part-time (3 women). Average age 29. 63 applicants, 41% accepted, 16 enrolled. In 2003, 8 master's, 4 doctorates awarded. *Degree requirements:* For master's, one foreign language, thesis, comprehensive exam; for doctorate, 2 foreign languages, thesis/dissertation, oral exams, comprehensive exam. *Entrance requirements:* For master's and doctorate, GRE General Test. Additional exam requirements/recommendations for international students: Required—TOEFL (minimum score 550 paper-based; 213 computer-based). *Application deadline:* For fall admission, 6/1 for domestic students, 5/1 for international students; for spring admission, 11/1 for domestic students, 11/11 for international students. Applications are processed on a rolling basis. Application fee: $50. Electronic applications accepted. *Expenses:* Tuition, state resident: part-time $288 per credit. Tuition, nonresident: part-time $438 per credit. Required fees: $495 per semester. *Financial support:* Fellowships, research assistantships, teaching assistantships, minority assistantships available. Financial award application deadline: 3/1. *Unit head:* Dr. Vincent Idone, Chair, 518-442-4466.

University at Buffalo, The State University of New York, Graduate School, College of Arts and Sciences, Department of Geology, Buffalo, NY 14260. Offers MA, MS, PhD. Part-time programs available. *Faculty:* 10 full-time (2 women), 4 part-time/adjunct (0 women). *Students:* 41 full-time (18 women), 9 part-time (3 women); includes 2 minority (1 Asian American or Pacific Islander, 1 Hispanic American), 10 international. Average age 30. 58 applicants, 67% accepted, 19 enrolled. In 2003, 12 master's, 1 doctorate awarded. *Degree requirements:* For master's, thesis (for some programs), project, thesis, or exam; for doctorate, thesis/dissertation, dissertation defense. *Entrance requirements:* For master's and doctorate, GRE General Test. Additional exam requirements/recommendations for international students: Required—TOEFL (minimum score 550 paper-based; 213 computer-based); Recommended—TSE. *Application deadline:* For fall admission, 3/1 priority date for domestic students, 3/1 priority date for international students; for spring admission, 10/1 priority date for domestic students, 10/1 priority date for international students. Applications are processed on a rolling basis. Application fee: $35. Electronic applications accepted. *Expenses:* Tuition, state resident: full-time $7,110. Tuition, nonresident: full-time $10,920. Tuition and fees vary according to program. *Financial support:* In 2003–04, 2 fellowships with full tuition reimbursements (averaging $6,000 per year), 8 research assistantships with full tuition reimbursements (averaging $11,000 per year), 14 teaching assistantships with full tuition reimbursements (averaging $9,600 per year) were awarded. Federal Work-Study, scholarships/grants, health care benefits, and unspecified assistantships also available. Financial award applicants required to submit FAFSA. *Faculty research:* Environmental geophysics, hydrogeology, remote sensing, fractured rocks, volcanology. Total annual research expenditures: $1 million. *Unit head:* Dr. Charles E. Mitchell, Professor and Chair, 716-645-6800 Ext. 6100, Fax: 716-645-3999, E-mail: geology@acsu.buffalo.edu. *Application contact:* Dr. Matthew W. Becker, Director of Graduate Studies, 716-645-6800 Ext. 3960, Fax: 716-645-3999, E-mail: mwbecker@geology.buffalo.edu.

The University of Akron, Graduate School, Buchtel College of Arts and Sciences, Department of Geology, Akron, OH 44325-0001. Offers earth science (MS); environmental (MS); geology (MS); geophysics (MS). Part-time programs available. *Faculty:* 11 full-time (3 women). *Students:* 20 full-time (5 women), 2 part-time (1 woman), 6 international. Average age 28. 13 applicants, 69% accepted, 3 enrolled. In 2003, 4 degrees awarded. *Degree requirements:* For master's, thesis, seminar, proficiency exam, comprehensive exam. *Entrance requirements:* For master's, minimum GPA of 2.75. Additional exam requirements/recommendations for international students: Required—TOEFL (minimum score 550 paper-based; 213 computer-based). *Application deadline:* For fall admission, 3/1 for domestic students. Applications are processed on a rolling basis. Application fee: $40 ($60 for international students). *Expenses:* Tuition, state resident: part-time $277 per credit hour. Tuition, nonresident: part-time $476 per credit hour. *Financial support:* In 2003–04, 3 research assistantships with full tuition reimbursements, 13 teaching assistantships with full tuition reimbursements were awarded. Federal Work-Study and tuition waivers (full) also available. *Faculty research:* Broad-range geology, petrology (sedimentary, igneous, metamorphic, and clay), geochemistry, geophysics. Total annual research expenditures: $313,747. *Unit head:* Dr. John Szabo, Chair, 330-972-8039, E-mail: jszabo@uakron.edu. *Application contact:* Dr. David McConnell, Director of Graduate Studies, 330-972-8047, E-mail: mcconnell@uakron.edu.

The University of Alabama, Graduate School, College of Arts and Sciences, Department of Geological Sciences, Tuscaloosa, AL 35487. Offers MS, PhD. *Faculty:* 10 full-time (2 women). *Students:* 30 full-time (5 women), 9 part-time (3 women); includes 3 minority (all Hispanic Americans), 16 international. Average age 27. 28 applicants, 71% accepted, 11 enrolled. In 2003, 5 master's, 3 doctorates awarded. *Degree requirements:* For master's and doctorate, thesis/dissertation. *Entrance requirements:* For master's and doctorate, GRE General Test, minimum GPA of 3.0. Additional exam requirements/recommendations for international students: Required—TOEFL, TSE. *Application deadline:* For fall admission, 3/15 for domestic students; for spring admission, 8/31 priority date for domestic students. Applications are processed on a rolling basis. Application fee: $25. Electronic applications accepted. *Expenses:* Tuition, state resident: full-time $4,134; part-time $230 per credit hour. Tuition, nonresident: full-time $11,294; part-time $627 per credit hour. Part-time tuition and fees vary according to course load. *Financial support:* In 2003–04, 4 fellowships with full tuition reimbursements (averaging $11,000 per year), 14 research assistantships with full tuition reimbursements (averaging $10,269 per year), 13 teaching assistantships with full tuition reimbursements (averaging $10,269 per year) were awarded. Career-related internships or fieldwork, Federal Work-Study, and institutionally sponsored loans also available. Financial award application deadline: 3/15. *Faculty research:* Structure, petrology, stratigraphy, geochemistry, hydrogeology. Total annual research expenditures: $1.5 million. *Unit head:* Dr. Harold H. Stowell, Chairperson, 205-348-5098, Fax: 205-348-0818, E-mail: hstowell@wgs.geo.ua.edu. *Application contact:* Dr. Chunmiao Zheng, Director of Graduate Studies, 205-348-0579, Fax: 205-348-0818, E-mail: czheng@ua.edu.

University of Alaska Fairbanks, College of Science, Engineering and Mathematics, Department of Geology and Geophysics, Fairbanks, AK 99775-7520. Offers geology (MS, PhD); geophysics (MS, PhD); geoscience (MAT). Part-time programs available. Terminal master's awarded for partial completion of doctoral program. *Degree requirements:* For master's and doctorate, thesis/dissertation, comprehensive exam, registration. *Entrance requirements:* For master's and doctorate, GRE General Test, GRE Subject Test. Additional exam requirements/recommendations for international students: Required—TOEFL. Electronic applications accepted. *Faculty research:* Glacial surging, Alaska as geologic fragments, natural zeolites, seismology, volcanology.

University of Arkansas, Graduate School, J. William Fulbright College of Arts and Sciences, Department of Geosciences, Program in Geology, Fayetteville, AR 72701-1201. Offers MS. *Students:* 17 full-time (7 women), 7 part-time (3 women); includes 3 minority (1 African American, 2 American Indian/Alaska Native). 16 applicants, 69% accepted. In 2003, 5 degrees awarded. *Degree requirements:* For master's, thesis. Application fee: $40 ($50 for international students). *Expenses:* Tuition, state resident: full-time $4,032; part-time $224 per credit hour. Tuition, nonresident: full-time $9,540; part-time $530 per credit hour. Tuition and fees vary according to course load and program. *Financial support:* In 2003–04, 2 research assistantships, 12 teaching assistantships were awarded. Career-related internships or fieldwork and Federal Work-Study also available. Support available to part-time students. Financial award application deadline: 4/1; financial award applicants required to submit FAFSA. *Unit head:* Doy Zachry, Chair, 479-575-3355.

The University of British Columbia, Faculty of Graduate Studies, Faculty of Science, Department of Earth and Ocean Sciences, Vancouver, BC V6T 1Z1, Canada. Offers atmospheric science (M Sc, PhD); geological engineering (M Eng, MA Sc, PhD); geological sciences (M Sc, PhD); geophysics (M Sc, MA Sc, PhD); oceanography (M Sc, PhD). *Faculty:* 42 full-time (5 women), 16 part-time/adjunct (0 women). *Students:* 127 full-time (44 women), 1 (woman) part-time. Average age 27. 80 applicants, 41% accepted, 25 enrolled. In 2003, 21 master's, 8 doctorates awarded. *Degree requirements:* For master's, thesis (for some programs); for doctorate, thesis/dissertation, comprehensive exam. *Entrance requirements:* Additional exam requirements/recommendations for international students: Required—TOEFL (minimum score 600 paper-based; 250 computer-based). *Application deadline:* For fall admission, 3/1 for domestic students; for winter admission, 7/1 for domestic students. Applications are processed on a rolling basis. Application fee: $90 Canadian dollars ($150 Canadian dollars for international students). Electronic applications accepted. *Financial support:* In 2003–04, fellowships (averaging $16,000 per year), research assistantships (averaging $13,000 per year), teaching assistantships (averaging $4,500 per year) were awarded. Federal Work-Study, institutionally sponsored loans, scholarships/grants, tuition waivers (full and partial), and unspecified assistantships also available. *Unit head:* Dr. Paul L. Smith, Head, 604-822-6456, Fax: 604-822-6088, E-mail: psmith@cos.ubc.ca. *Application contact:* Alex Allen, Graduate Secretary, 604-822-2713, Fax: 604-822-6088, E-mail: aallen@eos.ubc.ca.

University of Calgary, Faculty of Graduate Studies, Faculty of Science, Department of Geology and Geophysics, Calgary, AB T2N 1N4, Canada. Offers geology (M Sc, PhD); geophysics (M Sc, PhD). Part-time programs available. *Faculty:* 32 full-time (3 women), 16 part-time/adjunct (1 woman). *Students:* 109 full-time (43 women). 106 applicants, 43% accepted, 26 enrolled. In 2003, 15 master's, 5 doctorates awarded. Terminal master's awarded for partial completion of doctoral program. *Degree requirements:* For master's, thesis; for doctorate, thesis/dissertation, candidacy exam. *Entrance requirements:* For master's, B Sc; for doctorate, B Sc (Honors) or M Sc. Additional exam requirements/recommendations for international students: Required—TOEFL. *Application deadline:* For fall admission, 2/1 priority date for domestic students, 2/1 priority date for international students; for winter admission, 9/1 for domestic students. Applications are processed on a rolling basis. Application fee: $60. Electronic applications accepted. Tuition, nonresident: full-time $4,765. Tuition and fees vary according to degree level, program and student level. *Financial support:* In 2003–04, 50 students received support, including 9 fellowships, 15 teaching assistantships; career-related internships or fieldwork, institutionally sponsored loans, and scholarships/grants also available. Financial award application deadline: 2/1. *Faculty research:* Geochemistry, petrology, paleontology, stratigraphy, exploration and solid-earth geophysics. *Unit head:* Larry R. Lines, Head, 403-220-8863, Fax: 403-284-0074, E-mail: lrlines@ucalgary.ca. *Application contact:* Cathy H. Hubbell, Graduate Program Administrator, 403-220-3254, Fax: 403-284-0074, E-mail: geosciencegrad@ucalgary.ca.

University of California, Berkeley, Graduate Division, College of Letters and Science, Department of Earth and Planetary Science, Division of Geology, Berkeley, CA 94720-1500. Offers MA, MS, PhD. *Students:* 42 full-time (16 women); includes 6 minority (2 American Indian/Alaska Native, 3 Asian Americans or Pacific Islanders, 1 Hispanic American), 10 international. 75 applicants, 29% accepted. In 2003, 2 master's, 2 doctorates awarded. Terminal master's awarded for partial completion of doctoral program. *Degree requirements:* For master's, oral exam (MA), thesis (MS); for doctorate, thesis/dissertation, candidacy exams, comprehensive exam. *Entrance requirements:* For master's and doctorate, GRE General Test, minimum GPA of 3.0. Additional exam requirements/recommendations for international students: Required—TOEFL. *Application deadline:* For fall admission, 1/12 for domestic students. Application fee: $60. International tuition: $12,491 full-time. Required fees: $5,484. *Financial support:* Fellowships, research assistantships, teaching assistantships, Federal Work-Study and unspecified assistantships available. Financial award application deadline: 1/12. *Faculty research:* Tectonics, environmental geology, economic geology, mineralogy, geochemistry. *Application contact:* Margie Winn, Graduate Assistant for Admissions, 510-642-5574, Fax: 510-643-6220, E-mail: margie@eps.berkeley.edu.

University of California, Davis, Graduate Studies, Program in Geology, Davis, CA 95616. Offers MS, PhD. *Faculty:* 23. *Students:* 31 full-time (14 women); includes 1 minority (Asian American or Pacific Islander), 4 international. Average age 29. 70 applicants, 36% accepted, 8 enrolled. In 2003, 4 degrees awarded. *Degree requirements:* For master's and doctorate, thesis/dissertation. *Entrance requirements:* For master's and doctorate, GRE General Test, GRE Subject Test, minimum GPA of 3.0. Additional exam requirements/recommendations for international students: Required—TOEFL (minimum score 550 paper-based; 213 computer-based). *Application deadline:* For fall admission, 1/15 for domestic students, 1/15 for international students. Application fee: $60. Electronic applications accepted. Tuition, nonresident: full-time $12,245. Required fees: $7,062. *Financial support:* In 2003–04, 29 students received support, including 1 fellowship with full and partial tuition reimbursement available (averaging $27,500 per year), 12 research assistantships with full and partial tuition reimbursements available (averaging $12,542 per year), 14 teaching assistantships with partial tuition reimbursements available (averaging $13,135 per year); Federal Work-Study, institutionally sponsored loans, and scholarships/grants also available. Financial award application deadline: 1/15; financial award applicants required to submit FAFSA. *Faculty research:* Petrology, paleontology, geophysics, sedimentology, structure/tectonics. *Unit head:* Louise Kellogg, Chair, 530-754-6673, E-mail: kellogg@geology.ucdavis.edu. *Application contact:* Helen Rogers, Administrative Assistant, 530-752-9100, Fax: 530-752-0951, E-mail: rogers@geology.ucdavis.edu.

University of California, Los Angeles, Graduate Division, College of Letters and Science, Department of Earth and Space Sciences, Program in Geology, Los Angeles, CA 90095. Offers MS, PhD. *Degree requirements:* For master's, comprehensive exams or thesis; for doctorate, thesis/dissertation, oral and written qualifying exams. *Entrance requirements:* For master's, GRE General Test, minimum GPA of 3.0; for doctorate, GRE General Test, minimum undergraduate GPA of 3.0. Electronic applications accepted. Tuition, nonresident: full-time $12,245. Required fees: $6,318.

University of California, Riverside, Graduate Division, Department of Earth Sciences, Riverside, CA 92521-0102. Offers geological sciences (MS, PhD). *Faculty:* 13 full-time (1 woman), 5 part-time/adjunct (2 women). *Students:* 27 full-time (6 women), 1 part-time; includes 1 minority (Hispanic American), 7 international. Average age 32. In 2003, 3 master's, 6 doctorates awarded. Terminal master's awarded for partial completion of doctoral program. *Median time to degree:* Master's–3 years full-time; doctorate–7 years full-time. Of those who began their doctoral program in fall 1995, 100% received their degree in 8 years or less. *Degree requirements:* For master's, thesis, final oral exam; for doctorate, thesis/dissertation, qualifying exams, final oral exam. *Entrance requirements:* For master's and doctorate, GRE General Test, minimum GPA of 3.2. Additional exam requirements/recommendations for international students: Required—TOEFL (minimum score 550 paper-based; 213 computer-based); Recommended—TSE. *Application deadline:* For fall admission, 5/1 for domestic students, 2/1 for international students; for winter admission, 9/1 for domestic students; for spring admission, 12/1 for domestic students. Applications are processed on a rolling basis.

Application fee: $60. Electronic applications accepted. Tuition, nonresident: part-time $4,082 per quarter. *Financial support:* In 2003–04, 17 students received support; fellowships with full and partial tuition reimbursements available, research assistantships with full and partial tuition reimbursements available, teaching assistantships with full and partial tuition reimbursements available, career-related internships or fieldwork, Federal Work-Study, institutionally sponsored loans, health care benefits, tuition waivers (full and partial), and unspecified assistantships available. Financial award application deadline: 1/5; financial award applicants required to submit FAFSA. *Faculty research:* Applied and solid earth geophysics, tectonic geomorphology, fluid-rock interaction, paleobiology-ecology, sedimentary-geochemistry. *Unit head:* Dr. Michael O. Woodburne, Chair, 951-827-5028, Fax: 951-827-4324, E-mail: michael.woodburne@ucr.edu. *Application contact:* John Herring, Graduate Program Assistant, 951-827-3435, Fax: 951-827-4324, E-mail: geology@ucr.edu.

Announcement: The geological sciences program offers research opportunities with a strong field-based curriculum in astrobiology, paleobiology, paleoecology and developmental evolution, Neoproterozoic geobiology, sedimentary geochemistry, stable-isotope geochemistry, sequence stratigraphy, quantitative stratigraphy, experimental tectonophysics, heat flow, earthquake physics and modeling, mineral deposits, hydrothermal geochemistry, and groundwater resources and hydrogeology. Deadline for funding: January 5.

University of California, San Diego, Graduate Studies and Research, Scripps Institution of Oceanography, La Jolla, CA 92093. Offers biological oceanography (MS, PhD); geochemistry and marine chemistry (MS, PhD); marine biology (MS, PhD); physical oceanography and geological sciences (MS, PhD). *Faculty:* 88. *Students:* 222 (112 women); includes 22 minority (2 African Americans, 3 American Indian/Alaska Native, 7 Asian Americans or Pacific Islanders, 10 Hispanic Americans) 55 international. 389 applicants, 19% accepted. In 2003, 9 master's, 24 doctorates awarded. *Entrance requirements:* For master's and doctorate, GRE General Test, GRE Subject Test (marine biology). *Application deadline:* For fall admission, 1/6 for domestic students. Application fee: $60. Electronic applications accepted. Tuition, nonresident: full-time $12,245. Required fees: $6,959. *Financial support:* Fellowships, research assistantships available. *Unit head:* Myrl C. Hendershott, Chair. *Application contact:* Graduate Coordinator, 858-534-3206.

University of California, Santa Barbara, Graduate Division, College of Letters and Sciences, Division of Mathematics, Life, and Physical Sciences, Department of Geological Sciences, Santa Barbara, CA 93106. Offers geological sciences (MS, PhD); geophysics (MS). *Faculty:* 25 full-time (4 women). *Students:* 51 full-time (19 women); includes 5 minority (3 Asian Americans or Pacific Islanders, 2 Hispanic Americans), 6 international. Average age 25. 91 applicants, 33% accepted, 14 enrolled. In 2003, 5 master's, 4 doctorates awarded. Terminal master's awarded for partial completion of doctoral program. *Median time to degree:* Master's–2 years full-time; doctorate–5 years full-time. *Degree requirements:* For master's, thesis, thesis or exam, comprehensive exam, registration; for doctorate, thesis/dissertation, comprehensive exam, registration. *Entrance requirements:* For master's and doctorate, GRE General Test. Additional exam requirements/recommendations for international students: Required—TOEFL (minimum score 550 paper-based; 213 computer-based). *Application deadline:* For fall admission, 1/15 for domestic students, 1/15 for international students. Application fee: $60. Electronic applications accepted. *Expenses:* Tuition, state resident: full-time $7,188. Tuition, nonresident: full-time $19,608. *Financial support:* In 2003–04, 45 students received support, including 3 fellowships with full and partial tuition reimbursements available (averaging $7,000 per year), 18 research assistantships with full and partial tuition reimbursements available, 15 teaching assistantships with full and partial tuition reimbursements available; career-related internships or fieldwork, Federal Work-Study, scholarships/grants, traineeships, health care benefits, and tuition waivers (full and partial) also available. Financial award application deadline: 1/1; financial award applicants required to submit FAFSA. *Faculty research:* Structure and tectonics, marine geology, chemical oceanography, geophysics, geobiology and paleobotany. *Unit head:* Dr. James Mattinson, Chair, 805-893-2827, Fax: 805-893-2314. *Application contact:* Susan Leska, Graduate Program Assistant, 805-893-3329, Fax: 805-893-2314, E-mail: leska@geol.ucsb.edu.

University of Chicago, Division of the Physical Sciences, Department of the Geophysical Sciences, Chicago, IL 60637-1513. Offers atmospheric sciences (SM, PhD); earth sciences (SM, PhD); paleobiology (PhD); planetary and space sciences (SM, PhD). *Faculty:* 24 full-time (3 women). *Students:* 29 full-time (13 women); includes 1 minority (Hispanic American), 12 international. Average age 30. 74 applicants, 22% accepted. In 2003, 2 master's, 5 doctorates awarded. Terminal master's awarded for partial completion of doctoral program. *Median time to degree:* Doctorate–6 years full-time. *Entrance requirements:* For master's and doctorate, GRE General Test. Additional exam requirements/recommendations for international students: Required—TOEFL. *Application deadline:* For fall admission, 1/15 for domestic students, 1/15 for international students. Application fee: $55. Electronic applications accepted. *Financial support:* In 2003–04, 29 students received support, including research assistantships with full tuition reimbursements available (averaging $17,196 per year), teaching assistantships with full tuition reimbursements available (averaging $18,096 per year); fellowships, Federal Work-Study, institutionally sponsored loans, scholarships/grants, tuition waivers (partial), and unspecified assistantships also available. Financial award application deadline: 1/15. *Faculty research:* Climatology, evolutionary paleontology, petrology, geochemistry, oceanic sciences. *Unit head:* Dr. David Rowley, Chairman, 773-702-8102, Fax: 773-702-9505. *Application contact:* David J. Leslie, Graduate Student Services Coordinator, 773-702-8180, Fax: 773-702-9505, E-mail: info@geosci.uchicago.edu.

University of Cincinnati, Division of Research and Advanced Studies, McMicken College of Arts and Sciences, Department of Geology, Cincinnati, OH 45221. Offers MS, PhD. Part-time programs available. *Degree requirements:* For master's, thesis/dissertation; for doctorate, thesis/dissertation, comprehensive exam. *Entrance requirements:* For master's and doctorate, GRE General Test, 1 year of course work in physics, chemistry, and calculus. Additional exam requirements/recommendations for international students: Required—TOEFL. Electronic applications accepted. *Faculty research:* Paleobiology, sequence stratigraphy, earth systems history, quaternary, groundwater.

University of Colorado at Boulder, Graduate School, College of Arts and Sciences, Department of Geological Sciences, Boulder, CO 80309. Offers geology (MS, PhD); geophysics (PhD). *Faculty:* 26 full-time (6 women). *Students:* 54 full-time (30 women), 13 part-time (9 women); includes 7 minority (1 Asian American or Pacific Islander, 6 Hispanic Americans), 10 international. Average age 30. 34 applicants, 59% accepted. In 2003, 11 master's, 8 doctorates awarded. Terminal master's awarded for partial completion of doctoral program. *Degree requirements:* For master's and doctorate, thesis/dissertation, comprehensive exam. *Entrance requirements:* For master's and doctorate, GRE General Test, minimum GPA of 2.75. *Application deadline:* For fall admission, 1/15 for domestic students. Application fee: $50 ($60 for international students). *Expenses:* Tuition, state resident: full-time $2,122. Tuition, nonresident: full-time $9,754. Tuition and fees vary according to course load and program. *Financial support:* In 2003–04, 5 fellowships with full tuition reimbursements (averaging $10,636 per year), 14 research assistantships with full tuition reimbursements (averaging $19,327 per year), 14 teaching assistantships with full tuition reimbursements (averaging $15,668 per year) were awarded. Federal Work-Study, institutionally sponsored loans, scholarships/grants, and tuition waivers (full) also available. Financial award application deadline: 1/15. *Faculty research:* Sedimentology, stratigraphy, economic geology of mineral deposits, fossil fuels, hydrogeology and water resources. Total annual research expenditures: $16.3 million. *Unit head:* Charles R. Stern, Chair, 303-492-2330, Fax: 303-492-2606, E-mail: sternc@stripe.colorado.edu. *Application contact:* Graduate Secretary, 303-492-2607, Fax: 303-492-2606, E-mail: geolinfo@colorado.edu.

University of Connecticut, Graduate School, College of Liberal Arts and Sciences, Field of Geology and Geophysics, Storrs, CT 06269. Offers geological sciences (MS, PhD). *Faculty:* 10 full-time (1 woman). *Students:* 18 full-time (10 women), 12 part-time (5 women); includes 1 minority (African American), 2 international. Average age 30. 28 applicants, 43% accepted, 10 enrolled. In 2003, 3 degrees awarded. *Degree requirements:* For doctorate, thesis/dissertation. *Entrance requirements:* For master's and doctorate, GRE General Test. Additional exam requirements/recommendations for international students: Required—TOEFL (minimum score 550 paper-based; 213 computer-based). *Application deadline:* For fall admission, 2/1 priority date for domestic students, 2/1 priority date for international students; for spring admission, 11/1 for domestic students, 10/1 for international students. Applications are processed on a rolling basis. Application fee: $55. Electronic applications accepted. *Expenses:* Tuition, state resident: part-time $3,860 per semester. Tuition, nonresident: part-time $9,036 per semester. *Financial support:* In 2003–04, 4 research assistantships with full tuition reimbursements, 6 teaching assistantships with full tuition reimbursements were awarded. Fellowships, Federal Work-Study, scholarships/grants, health care benefits, and unspecified assistantships also available. Financial award application deadline: 2/1. *Unit head:* Raymond Joesten, Head, 860-486-4434, Fax: 860-486-1383, E-mail: raymond.joesten@uconn.edu. *Application contact:* Timothy Byrne, Chairperson, 860-486-1388, Fax: 860-486-1383, E-mail: tim.byrne@uconn.edu.

University of Delaware, College of Arts and Sciences, Department of Geology, Newark, DE 19716. Offers MS, PhD. Part-time programs available. *Faculty:* 9 full-time (1 woman). *Students:* 20 full-time (9 women), 3 part-time, 4 international. Average age 31. 14 applicants, 64% accepted, 4 enrolled. In 2003, 2 master's, 1 doctorate awarded. *Degree requirements:* For master's and doctorate, thesis/dissertation. *Entrance requirements:* For master's and doctorate, GRE General Test. *Application deadline:* For fall admission, 7/1 for domestic students. Application fee: $60. Electronic applications accepted. *Expenses:* Tuition, state resident: full-time $5,890; part-time $327 per credit. Tuition, nonresident: full-time $15,420; part-time $857 per credit. Required fees: $968. *Financial support:* In 2003–04, 16 students received support, including 1 fellowship with full tuition reimbursement available (averaging $18,000 per year), 7 research assistantships with full tuition reimbursements available (averaging $15,000 per year), 5 teaching assistantships with full tuition reimbursements available (averaging $10,500 per year); Federal Work-Study, institutionally sponsored loans, scholarships/grants, and tuition waivers (full and partial) also available. Financial award application deadline: 3/15; financial award applicants required to submit FAFSA. *Faculty research:* Coastal plain mollusk geochemistry, taxonomy of marsh forams, coastal and marine geology, geomorphology, geophysics. Total annual research expenditures: $190,528. *Unit head:* Dr. James E. Pizzuto, Chair, 302-831-2710, Fax: 302-831-4158, E-mail: pizzuto@udel.edu. *Application contact:* Dr. Susan McGeary, Associate Professor, 302-831-8174, Fax: 302-831-4158, E-mail: smcgeary@udel.edu.

Announcement: With allied faculty in engineering and marine studies, the department emphasizes coastal and marine geology and geophysics, coastal plain geology, geochronology and geochemistry, and fluvial geomorphology and watershed dynamics. Available equipment includes ground-penetrating radar, a high-resolution seismic system, CHIRP sonar, GPS, X-ray diffractometer, chromatographs, research vessels, and a total station.

University of Florida, Graduate School, College of Liberal Arts and Sciences, Department of Geological Sciences, Gainesville, FL 32611. Offers geology (MS, PhD); geology education (MST). *Faculty:* 22. *Students:* 35 full-time (16 women), 14 part-time (8 women); includes 3 minority (1 African American, 2 Hispanic Americans), 8 international. In 2003, 8 master's, 1 doctorate awarded. Terminal master's awarded for partial completion of doctoral program. *Degree requirements:* For master's, thesis (for some programs); for doctorate, one foreign language, thesis/dissertation. *Entrance requirements:* For master's and doctorate, GRE General Test, GRE Subject Test, minimum GPA of 3.0. Additional exam requirements/recommendations for international students: Required—TOEFL (minimum score 550 paper-based; 213 computer-based). *Application deadline:* For fall admission, 6/1 for domestic students; for spring admission, 10/1 priority date for domestic students. Applications are processed on a rolling basis. Application fee: $30. Electronic applications accepted. *Expenses:* Tuition, state resident: part-time $205 per credit hour. Tuition, nonresident: part-time $775 per credit hour. *Financial support:* In 2003–04, 26 students received support, including 2 fellowships with full tuition reimbursements available (averaging $15,000 per year), 6 research assistantships with full tuition reimbursements available (averaging $12,000 per year), 19 teaching assistantships with full tuition reimbursements available (averaging $9,500 per year); career-related internships or fieldwork, Federal Work-Study, institutionally sponsored loans, and scholarships/grants also available. Support available to part-time students. Financial award application deadline: 3/1. *Faculty research:* Paleoclimatology, tectonophysics, petrochemistry, marine geology, geochemistry, hydrology. Total annual research expenditures: $1.5 million. *Unit head:* Dr. Paul Mueller, Chair, 352-392-2231, Fax: 352-392-9294, E-mail: mueller@geology.ufl.edu. *Application contact:* Dr. Michael R. Perfit, Graduate Coordinator, 352-392-2128, Fax: 352-392-9294, E-mail: perfit@geology.ufl.edu.

University of Georgia, Graduate School, College of Arts and Sciences, Department of Geology, Athens, GA 30602. Offers MS, PhD. *Faculty:* 19 full-time (3 women). *Students:* 23 full-time (15 women), 11 part-time (4 women), 5 international. 25 applicants, 48% accepted. In 2003, 7 master's, 5 doctorates awarded. *Degree requirements:* For master's, thesis; for doctorate, one foreign language, thesis/dissertation. *Entrance requirements:* For master's and doctorate, GRE General Test. *Application deadline:* For fall admission, 7/1 for domestic students; for spring admission, 11/15 for domestic students. Application fee: $50. Electronic applications accepted. *Expenses:* Tuition, state resident: part-time $161 per hour. Tuition, nonresident: part-time $690 per hour. One-time fee: $435 part-time. *Financial support:* Fellowships, research assistantships, teaching assistantships, unspecified assistantships available. *Unit head:* Dr. Susan Goldstein, Head, 706-542-2397, Fax: 706-542-2425, E-mail: sgoldst@gly.uga.edu. *Application contact:* Dr. Alberto Patino-Douce, Graduate Coordinator, 706-542-2394, Fax: 706-542-2425, E-mail: alpatino@uga.edu.

University of Hawaii at Manoa, Graduate Division, School of Ocean and Earth Science and Technology, Department of Geology and Geophysics, Honolulu, HI 96822. Offers high-pressure geophysics and geochemistry (MS, PhD); hydrogeology and engineering geology (MS, PhD); marine geology and geophysics (MS, PhD); planetary geosciences and remote sensing (MS, PhD); seismology and solid-earth geophysics (MS, PhD); volcanology, petrology, and geochemistry (MS, PhD). *Faculty:* 73 full-time (13 women), 16 part-time/adjunct (1 woman). *Students:* 57 full-time (19 women); includes 3 minority (1 African American, 2 Asian Americans or Pacific Islanders), 17 international. Average age 29. 116 applicants, 15% accepted, 12 enrolled.Terminal master's awarded for partial completion of doctoral program. *Median time to degree:* Master's–3 years full-time; doctorate–3 years full-time. *Degree requirements:* For master's, thesis/dissertation; for doctorate, thesis/dissertation, comprehensive exam. *Entrance requirements:* For master's and doctorate, GRE General Test, minimum GPA of 3.0. Additional exam requirements/recommendations for international students: Required—TOEFL. *Application deadline:* For fall admission, 1/15 for domestic students, 1/1 for international students; for spring admission, 9/1 for domestic students, 8/15 for international students. Application fee: $50. *Expenses:* Tuition, state resident: full-time $4,464; part-time $186 per credit hour. Tuition, nonresident: full-time $10,608; part-time $442 per credit hour. Tuition and fees vary according to program. *Financial support:* In 2003–04, 44 research assistantships (averaging $19,270 per year), 5 teaching assistantships (averaging $18,198 per year) were awarded. *Unit head:* Dr. Paul Wessel, Chair, 808-956-2582, Fax: 808-956-5512.

University of Houston, College of Natural Sciences and Mathematics, Department of Geosciences, Houston, TX 77204. Offers geology (MS, PhD); geophysics (MS, PhD). Part-time and evening/weekend programs available. *Faculty:* 16 full-time (3 women), 5 part-time/adjunct (1 woman). *Students:* 55 full-time (23 women), 41 part-time (11 women); includes 4 minority (1 African American, 1 American Indian/Alaska Native, 2 Hispanic Americans), 49 international. Average age 33. 64 applicants, 75% accepted, 10 enrolled. In 2003, 11 master's, 2 doctorates awarded. *Degree requirements:* For master's, thesis (for some programs); for doctorate, one foreign language, thesis/dissertation. *Entrance requirements:* For master's and

Geology

University of Houston (continued)
doctorate, GRE General Test. Additional exam requirements/recommendations for international students: Required—TOEFL. *Application deadline:* For fall admission, 9/20 for domestic students; for spring admission, 12/4 for domestic students. Applications are processed on a rolling basis. Application fee: $0 ($75 for international students). *Expenses:* Tuition, state resident: full-time $1,656; part-time $92 per credit hour. Tuition, nonresident: full-time $5,904; part-time $328 per credit hour. Required fees: $1,704. *Financial support:* In 2003–04, 9 fellowships with partial tuition reimbursements (averaging $4,000 per year), 14 research assistantships with partial tuition reimbursements (averaging $12,150 per year), 22 teaching assistantships with partial tuition reimbursements (averaging $12,150 per year) were awarded. Federal Work-Study also available. *Faculty research:* Seismic and solid earth geophysics, tectonics, environmental hydrochemistry, carbonates, micropaleontology, structure and tectonics, petroleum geology. Total annual research expenditures: $1 million. *Unit head:* Dr. John Casey, Chairman, 713-743-3399, Fax: 713-748-7906. *Application contact:* Dr. Charlotte Sullivan, Graduate Adviser, 713-743-3396, Fax: 713-748-7906, E-mail: esulliva@bayou.uh.edu.

University of Idaho, College of Graduate Studies, College of Science, Department of Geological Sciences, Moscow, ID 83844-2282. Offers earth science (MAT); geology (MS, PhD); geophysics (MS); hydrology (MS). *Students:* 29 full-time (11 women), 23 part-time (9 women). Average age 29. *Degree requirements:* For doctorate, one foreign language, thesis/dissertation. *Entrance requirements:* For master's, minimum GPA of 2.8; for doctorate, minimum undergraduate GPA of 2.8, 3.0 graduate. *Application deadline:* For fall admission, 8/1 for domestic students; for spring admission, 12/15 for domestic students. Application fee: $55 ($60 for international students). *Expenses:* Tuition, state resident: full-time $3,348. Tuition, nonresident: full-time $10,740. Required fees: $540. *Financial support:* Fellowships, research assistantships, teaching assistantships available. Financial award application deadline: 2/15. *Unit head:* Dr. Dennis Geist, Head, 208-885-6192.

See in-depth description on page 259.

University of Illinois at Chicago, Graduate College, College of Liberal Arts and Sciences, Department of Earth and Environmental Sciences, Chicago, IL 60607-7128. Offers crystallography (MS, PhD); environmental geology (MS, PhD); geochemistry (MS, PhD); geology (MS, PhD); geomorphology (MS, PhD); geophysics (MS, PhD); geotechnical engineering and geosciences (PhD); hydrogeology (MS, PhD); low-temperature and organic geochemistry (MS, PhD); mineralogy (MS, PhD); paleoclimatology (MS, PhD); paleontology (MS, PhD); petrology (MS, PhD); quaternary geology (MS, PhD); sedimentology (MS, PhD); water resources (MS, PhD). *Faculty:* 9 full-time (2 women). *Students:* 18 full-time (7 women), 5 part-time (1 woman); includes 3 minority (1 African American, 1 American Indian/Alaska Native, 1 Asian American or Pacific Islander), 11 international. Average age 29. 15 applicants, 27% accepted, 4 enrolled. In 2003, 2 degrees awarded. *Degree requirements:* For master's and doctorate, thesis/dissertation. *Entrance requirements:* For master's and doctorate, GRE General Test, minimum GPA of 3.75 on a 5.0 scale. Additional exam requirements/recommendations for international students: Required—TOEFL. *Application deadline:* For fall admission, 5/15 for domestic students, 2/1 for international students; for spring admission, 11/1 for domestic students, 7/15 for international students. Applications are processed on a rolling basis. Application fee: $40 ($50 for international students). Electronic applications accepted. *Expenses:* Tuition, state resident: part-time $941 per semester. Tuition, nonresident: part-time $2,338 per semester. *Financial support:* In 2003–04, 16 students received support; fellowships with full tuition reimbursements available, research assistantships with full tuition reimbursements available, teaching assistantships with full tuition reimbursements available, Federal Work-Study, scholarships/grants, traineeships, tuition waivers (full), and unspecified assistantships available. Financial award application deadline: 3/1; financial award applicants required to submit FAFSA. *Unit head:* Neil Sturchio, Head, 312-996-3154. *Application contact:* Peter Doran, Director of Graduate Studies, 312-413-7275, E-mail: pdoran@uic.edu.

University of Illinois at Urbana–Champaign, Graduate College, College of Liberal Arts and Sciences, Department of Geology, Champaign, IL 61820. Offers earth sciences (MS, PhD); geochemistry (MS, PhD); geology (MS, PhD); geophysics (MS, PhD). *Faculty:* 14 full-time (3 women). *Students:* 36 full-time (12 women); includes 3 minority (all Asian Americans or Pacific Islanders), 17 international. Average age 26. 72 applicants, 13% accepted, 4 enrolled. In 2003, 1 master's, 3 doctorates awarded. Terminal master's awarded for partial completion of doctoral program. *Degree requirements:* For master's and doctorate, thesis/dissertation. *Entrance requirements:* For master's and doctorate, GRE General Test, minimum GPA of 3.0. Additional exam requirements/recommendations for international students: Required—TOEFL. *Application deadline:* For fall admission, 2/15 for domestic students; for spring admission, 10/15 for domestic students. Applications are processed on a rolling basis. Application fee: $40 ($50 for international students). *Expenses:* Tuition, state resident: full-time $6,692. Tuition, nonresident: full-time $18,692. *Financial support:* In 2003–04, 14 research assistantships, 16 teaching assistantships were awarded. Fellowships, Federal Work-Study and tuition waivers (full and partial) also available. Financial award application deadline: 2/15. *Faculty research:* Hydrogeology, structure/tectonics, mineral science. *Unit head:* Stephen Marshak, Head, 217-333-3542, Fax: 217-244-4996, E-mail: smarshak@uiuc.edu. *Application contact:* Barbara Elmore, Graduate Admissions Secretary, 217-333-3542, Fax: 217-244-4996, E-mail: belmore@uiuc.edu.

University of Kansas, Graduate School, College of Liberal Arts and Sciences, Department of Geology, Lawrence, KS 66045. Offers MS, PhD. *Faculty:* 117. *Students:* 37 full-time (15 women), 17 part-time (2 women); includes 1 minority (Hispanic American), 9 international. Average age 29. 67 applicants, 39% accepted, 12 enrolled. In 2003, 7 master's, 3 doctorates awarded. *Median time to degree:* Master's–3 years full-time; doctorate–6 years full-time. *Degree requirements:* For master's, thesis or alternative; for doctorate, thesis/dissertation, comprehensive exam. *Entrance requirements:* For master's and doctorate, GRE General Test. Additional exam requirements/recommendations for international students: Required—TOEFL (minimum score 570 paper-based). *Application deadline:* For fall admission, 2/1 priority date for domestic students, 2/1 priority date for international students; for spring admission, 10/31 priority date for domestic students, 10/31 priority date for international students. Applications are processed on a rolling basis. Application fee: $55 ($60 for international students). Electronic applications accepted. *Expenses:* Tuition, state resident: full-time $3,745. Tuition, nonresident: full-time $10,075. Required fees: $574. *Financial support:* In 2003–04, 1 fellowship with full and partial tuition reimbursement (averaging $13,000 per year), 14 research assistantships with full and partial tuition reimbursements (averaging $11,000 per year), 10 teaching assistantships with full and partial tuition reimbursements (averaging $11,932 per year) were awarded. Financial award application deadline: 2/1. *Faculty research:* Sedimentology, paleontology, tectonics, geophysics, hyrdogeology. Total annual research expenditures: $1.8 million. *Unit head:* W. R. Van Schmus, Chair, 785-864-4974, E-mail: rvschmus@ku.edu. *Application contact:* Yolanda Langdon, Information Contact, 785-864-4974, Fax: 785-864-5276, E-mail: yolanda@ku.edu.

University of Kentucky, Graduate School, Graduate School Programs from the College of Arts and Sciences, Program in Geology, Lexington, KY 40506-0032. Offers MS, PhD. *Faculty:* 21 full-time (2 women). *Students:* 23 full-time (6 women), 4 part-time (1 woman); includes 1 minority (Hispanic American), 4 international. 41 applicants, 20% accepted, 6 enrolled. In 2003, 8 master's, 1 doctorate awarded. *Degree requirements:* For master's and doctorate, thesis/dissertation, comprehensive exam. *Entrance requirements:* For master's, GRE General Test, minimum undergraduate GPA of 2.5; for doctorate, GRE General Test, minimum graduate GPA of 3.0. Additional exam requirements/recommendations for international students: Required—TOEFL (minimum score 550 paper-based; 213 computer-based). *Application deadline:* For fall admission, 2/1 for domestic students, 2/1 for international students; for spring admission, 10/1 for domestic students. Applications are processed on a rolling basis. Application fee: $35 ($45 for international students). *Expenses:* Tuition, state resident: full-time $4,975; part-time $261 per credit hour. Tuition, nonresident: full-time $12,315; part-time $668 per credit hour. *Financial support:* Fellowships, research assistantships, teaching assistantships, Federal Work-Study and institutionally sponsored loans available. Support available to part-time students. *Faculty research:* Structure tectonics, geophysics, stratigraphy, hydrogeology, coal geology. *Unit head:* Dr. Alan Fryar, Director of Graduate Studies, 859-257-4392, Fax: 859-323-1938. *Application contact:* Dr. Brian Jackson, Associate Dean, 859-257-4905, Fax: 859-323-1928.

University of Louisiana at Lafayette, Graduate School, College of Sciences, Department of Geology, Lafayette, LA 70504. Offers MS. Part-time programs available. *Faculty:* 9 full-time (2 women). *Students:* 9 full-time (3 women), 5 part-time (4 women), 2 international. Average age 30. 10 applicants, 60% accepted, 4 enrolled. In 2003, 6 degrees awarded. *Degree requirements:* For master's, thesis, comprehensive exam, registration. *Entrance requirements:* For master's, GRE General Test, minimum GPA of 2.75. Additional exam requirements/recommendations for international students: Required—TOEFL (minimum score 550 paper-based; 213 computer-based). *Application deadline:* For fall admission, 5/15 for domestic students, 5/15 for international students; for spring admission, 10/1 for domestic students, 10/1 for international students. Applications are processed on a rolling basis. Application fee: $20 ($30 for international students). Electronic applications accepted. *Expenses:* Tuition, state resident: full-time $2,786; part-time $85 per credit. Tuition, nonresident: full-time $8,966; part-time $343 per credit. International tuition: $9,102 full-time. *Financial support:* In 2003–04, 2 fellowships with full tuition reimbursements (averaging $14,500 per year), 6 research assistantships with full tuition reimbursements (averaging $6,417 per year) were awarded. Teaching assistantships, Federal Work-Study and tuition waivers (full and partial) also available. Support available to part-time students. Financial award application deadline: 5/1. *Faculty research:* Aquifer contamination, coastal erosion, geochemistry of peat, petroleum geology and geophysics, remote sensing and geographic information systems applications. *Unit head:* Dr. Brian Lock, Head, 337-482-6468, Fax: 337-482-5723, E-mail: bel7415@louisiana.edu. *Application contact:* Dr. Gary Kinsland, Coordinator, 337-482-0693, Fax: 337-482-5723, E-mail: gkinsland@louisiana.edu.

University of Maine, Graduate School, Climate Change Institute, Orono, ME 04469. Offers MS. Part-time programs available. *Faculty:* 13 full-time (2 women). *Students:* 8 full-time (1 woman), 1 (woman) part-time, 1 international. Average age 33. 12 applicants, 83% accepted, 4 enrolled. In 2003, 3 degrees awarded. *Degree requirements:* For master's, thesis. *Entrance requirements:* For master's, GRE General Test. Additional exam requirements/recommendations for international students: Required—TOEFL. *Application deadline:* For fall admission, 2/1 for domestic students. Applications are processed on a rolling basis. Application fee: $50. Electronic applications accepted. *Expenses:* Tuition, state resident: part-time $235 per credit. Tuition, nonresident: part-time $670 per credit. Tuition and fees vary according to course load. *Financial support:* In 2003–04, 6 research assistantships with tuition reimbursements (averaging $14,800 per year) were awarded; tuition waivers (full and partial) also available. Financial award application deadline: 3/1. *Faculty research:* Geology, glacial geology, anthropology, climate. *Unit head:* Dr. Paul Mayewski, Director, 207-581-2190, Fax: 207-581-1203. *Application contact:* Scott G. Delcourt, Associate Dean of the Graduate School, 207-581-3218, Fax: 207-581-3232, E-mail: graduate@maine.edu.

University of Maine, Graduate School, College of Natural Sciences, Forestry, and Agriculture, Department of Earth Sciences, Orono, ME 04469. Offers MS, PhD. Part-time programs available. *Faculty:* 12 full-time. *Students:* 33 full-time (16 women), 12 part-time (5 women), 3 international. Average age 31. 16 applicants, 94% accepted, 7 enrolled. In 2003, 4 master's, 1 doctorate awarded. *Degree requirements:* For master's, thesis; for doctorate, one foreign language, thesis/dissertation. *Entrance requirements:* For master's and doctorate, GRE General Test. Additional exam requirements/recommendations for international students: Required—TOEFL. *Application deadline:* For fall admission, 2/1 for domestic students. Applications are processed on a rolling basis. Application fee: $50. Electronic applications accepted. *Expenses:* Tuition, state resident: part-time $235 per credit. Tuition, nonresident: part-time $670 per credit. Tuition and fees vary according to course load. *Financial support:* In 2003–04, 4 research assistantships with tuition reimbursements (averaging $14,800 per year), 5 teaching assistantships with tuition reimbursements (averaging $9,970 per year) were awarded. Federal Work-Study, institutionally sponsored loans, and tuition waivers (full and partial) also available. Financial award application deadline: 3/1. *Faculty research:* Appalachian bedrock geology, Quaternary studies, marine geology. *Unit head:* Dr. Daniel Belknap, Chair, 207-581-2152, Fax: 207-581-2202. *Application contact:* Scott G. Delcourt, Associate Dean of the Graduate School, 207-581-3218, Fax: 207-581-3232, E-mail: graduate@maine.edu.

University of Manitoba, Faculty of Graduate Studies, Faculty of Science, Department of Geological Sciences, Winnipeg, MB R3T 2N2, Canada. Offers geology (M Sc, PhD); geophysics (M Sc, PhD). *Degree requirements:* For master's and doctorate, thesis/dissertation. *Entrance requirements:* For master's and doctorate, GRE General Test, GRE Subject Test (geology), minimum GPA of 3.0. Additional exam requirements/recommendations for international students: Required—TOEFL. Tuition charges are reported in Canadian dollars. Tuition, nonresident: full-time $3,878 Canadian dollars.

University of Maryland, College Park, Graduate Studies and Research, College of Computer, Mathematical and Physical Sciences, Department of Geology, College Park, MD 20742. Offers MS, PhD. *Faculty:* 23 full-time (5 women), 3 part-time/adjunct (1 woman). *Students:* 26 full-time (15 women); includes 1 minority (African American), 6 international. 49 applicants, 47% accepted. In 2003, 3 master's awarded. *Degree requirements:* For master's, thesis, oral defense; for doctorate, thesis/dissertation. *Entrance requirements:* For master's, GRE General Test, minimum GPA of 3.0, 3 letters of recommendation; for doctorate, GRE General Test. *Application deadline:* For fall admission, 3/15 for domestic students, 2/1 for international students; for spring admission, 10/1 for domestic students, 6/1 for international students. Applications are processed on a rolling basis. Application fee: $50. Electronic applications accepted. *Expenses:* Tuition, state resident: part-time $349 per credit hour. Tuition, nonresident: part-time $602 per credit hour. *Financial support:* In 2003–04, fellowships with full tuition reimbursements (averaging $11,628 per year), research assistantships with tuition reimbursements (averaging $17,253 per year), teaching assistantships with tuition reimbursements (averaging $17,599 per year) were awarded. Federal Work-Study and scholarships/grants also available. Support available to part-time students. Financial award application deadline: 2/15; financial award applicants required to submit FAFSA. *Faculty research:* Metamorphic petrogenesis, phase equilibria, wetland hydrology, glacial geology, origin and evolution of the earth's crust. Total annual research expenditures: $1.5 million. *Unit head:* Dr. Michael Brown, Chairman, 301-405-4065, Fax: 301-314-9661. *Application contact:* Trudy Lindsey, Director, Graduate Enrollment Management Services, 301-405-4190, Fax: 301-314-9305, E-mail: tlindsey@gradschool.umd.edu.

Announcement: MS/PhD degrees are offered in earth interior processes, including mineralogy, petrology, geochemistry, and tectonics, and in earth surface processes, including hydrology, sedimentation, geochemistry, paleoclimatology, global change, and geomorphology. Apply by February 15 for financial aid. For information, contact Graduate Office, Department of Geology, University of Maryland, College Park, MD 20742 (e-mail: grad-sec@geol.umd.edu; WWW: http://www.geol.umd.edu).

The University of Memphis, Graduate School, College of Arts and Sciences, Department of Earth Sciences, Memphis, TN 38152. Offers earth sciences (PhD); geography (MA, MS); geology (MS); geophysics (MS). Part-time programs available. *Faculty:* 23 full-time (3 women), 3 part-time/adjunct (1 woman). *Students:* 34. Average age 29. 13 applicants, 46% accepted. In 2003, 4 master's, 1 doctorate awarded. Terminal master's awarded for partial completion of doctoral program. *Degree requirements:* For master's, thesis, seminar presentation, comprehensive exam; for doctorate, thesis/dissertation. *Entrance requirements:* For master's and doctorate, GRE General Test. Additional exam requirements/recommendations for international students: Required—TOEFL. *Application deadline:* For fall admission, 8/1 for domestic students; for spring admission, 12/1 for domestic students. Applications are processed on a rolling basis.

Application fee: $25 ($50 for international students). Electronic applications accepted. *Expenses:* Tuition, state resident: full-time $5,142. Tuition, nonresident: full-time $13,296. *Financial support:* In 2003–04, 34 students received support, including 2 fellowships with full tuition reimbursements available, 10 research assistantships with full tuition reimbursements available, 11 teaching assistantships with full tuition reimbursements available (averaging $10,000 per year) Financial award application deadline: 1/15. *Faculty research:* Hazards, active tectonics, geophysics, hydrology and water resources, spatial analysis. Total annual research expenditures: $1.8 million. *Unit head:* Dr. Mervin J. Bartholomew, Chair, 901-678-1613, Fax: 901-678-4467, E-mail: jbrthlm1@memphis.edu. *Application contact:* Dr. George Swihart, Coordinator of Graduate Studies, 901-678-2606, Fax: 901-678-2178, E-mail: gswihart@memphis.edu.

University of Miami, Graduate School, Rosenstiel School of Marine and Atmospheric Science, Division of Marine Geology and Geophysics, Coral Gables, FL 33124. Offers MS, PhD. *Faculty:* 13 full-time (3 women), 12 part-time/adjunct (2 women). *Students:* 24 full-time (11 women), 1 part-time, 6 international. Average age 27. 26 applicants, 27% accepted, 6 enrolled. In 2003, 1 master's awarded, leading to continued full-time study 100%; 1 doctorate awarded, leading to government 100%. Terminal master's awarded for partial completion of doctoral program. *Median time to degree:* Master's–3 years full-time; doctorate–6.3 years full-time. *Degree requirements:* For master's and doctorate, thesis/dissertation, comprehensive exam, registration. *Entrance requirements:* For master's and doctorate, GRE General Test. Additional exam requirements/recommendations for international students: Required—TOEFL (minimum score 550 paper-based; 213 computer-based). *Application deadline:* For fall admission, 1/1 priority date for domestic students, 1/1 priority date for international students. Applications are processed on a rolling basis. Application fee: $50. Electronic applications accepted. *Expenses:* Tuition: Full-time $19,526. *Financial support:* In 2003–04, 23 students received support, including 3 fellowships with tuition reimbursements available (averaging $20,124 per year), 15 research assistantships with tuition reimbursements available (averaging $20,124 per year), 5 teaching assistantships with tuition reimbursements available (averaging $20,124 per year); institutionally sponsored loans also available. Financial award application deadline: 3/1; financial award applicants required to submit FAFSA. *Faculty research:* Carbonate sedimentology, low-temperature geochemistry, paleoceanography, geodesy and tectonics. *Unit head:* Dr. Gregor Eberli, Chairperson, 305-361-4678, Fax: 305-361-4632, E-mail: geberli@rsmas.miami.edu. *Application contact:* Dr. Frank Millero, Associate Dean, 305-361-4155, Fax: 305-361-4771, E-mail: gso@rsmas.miami.edu.

University of Michigan, Horace H. Rackham School of Graduate Studies, College of Literature, Science, and the Arts, Department of Geological Sciences, Ann Arbor, MI 48109. Offers geology (MS, PhD); mineralogy (MS, PhD); oceanography: marine geology and geochemistry (MS, PhD). *Faculty:* 27 full-time (5 women), 6 part-time/adjunct (2 women). *Students:* 60 full-time (21 women); includes 3 minority (1 Asian American or Pacific Islander, 2 Hispanic Americans), 20 international. Average age 28. 81 applicants, 30% accepted, 11 enrolled. In 2003, 10 master's, 12 doctorates awarded. Terminal master's awarded for partial completion of doctoral program. *Median time to degree:* Master's–2.2 years full-time; doctorate–5.2 years full-time. *Degree requirements:* For master's, thesis; for doctorate, thesis/dissertation, oral defense of dissertation, preliminary exam. *Entrance requirements:* For master's and doctorate, GRE General Test. *Application deadline:* For fall admission, 1/15 for domestic students. Applications are processed on a rolling basis. Application fee: $60 ($75 for international students). Electronic applications accepted. *Expenses:* Tuition, state resident: full-time $7,463. Tuition, nonresident: full-time $13,913. Full-time tuition and fees vary according to course load, degree level and program. *Financial support:* In 2003–04, 18 fellowships with full tuition reimbursements (averaging $12,853 per year), 23 research assistantships with full tuition reimbursements (averaging $12,853 per year), 17 teaching assistantships with full tuition reimbursements (averaging $12,853 per year) were awarded. Career-related internships or fieldwork, Federal Work-Study, and health care benefits also available. Financial award application deadline: 1/15; financial award applicants required to submit FAFSA. *Faculty research:* Isotope geochemistry, paleoclimatology, mineral physics, tectonics, paleontology. Total annual research expenditures: $2.8 million. *Unit head:* Dr. Joel D. Blum, Chair, 734-764-1435, Fax: 734-763-4690. *Application contact:* Anne Hudon, Student Services Assistant, 734-615-3034, Fax: 734-763-4690, E-mail: ahudon@umich.edu.

University of Minnesota, Duluth, Graduate School, College of Science and Engineering, Department of Geological Sciences, Duluth, MN 55812-2496. Offers MS. Part-time programs available. *Faculty:* 12 full-time (3 women), 2 part-time/adjunct (0 women). *Students:* 10 full-time (5 women), 5 part-time (1 woman). Average age 23. 17 applicants, 47% accepted. In 2003, 3 degrees awarded. *Median time to degree:* Master's–3 years full-time. *Degree requirements:* For master's, thesis, final oral exam. *Entrance requirements:* For master's, GRE General Test, minimum GPA of 3.0. Additional exam requirements/recommendations for international students: Required—TOEFL (minimum score 550 paper-based; 213 computer-based). *Application deadline:* For fall admission, 7/15 for domestic students; for spring admission, 11/15 for domestic students. Applications are processed on a rolling basis. Application fee: $55 ($75 for international students). *Expenses:* Tuition, state resident: part-time $614 per credit. Tuition, nonresident: part-time $1,205 per credit. *Financial support:* In 2003–04, 12 students received support, including 3 research assistantships with full and partial tuition reimbursements available (averaging $11,300 per year), 9 teaching assistantships with full and partial tuition reimbursements available (averaging $11,300 per year); career-related internships or fieldwork, health care benefits, and unspecified assistantships also available. Support available to part-time students. Financial award application deadline: 2/15. *Faculty research:* Surface processes, tectonics, planetary geology, paleoclimate, petrology. Total annual research expenditures: $450,000. *Unit head:* Dr. Penelope Morton, Director of Graduate Studies, 218-726-7962, Fax: 218-726-8275, E-mail: pmorton@d.umn.edu.

Announcement: UMD offers the PhD (in cooperation with UMTC) and MS degrees. UMD is admirably situated for a wide variety of geologic interests, and we have active programs around the globe and on the terrestrial planets. Duluth has an outstanding environment in which to live. TA and RA opportunities are available.

University of Minnesota, Twin Cities Campus, Graduate School, Institute of Technology, Department of Geology and Geophysics, Minneapolis, MN 55455-0213. Offers geology (MS, PhD); geophysics (MS, PhD). Terminal master's awarded for partial completion of doctoral program. *Degree requirements:* For master's, thesis optional; for doctorate, thesis/dissertation. *Entrance requirements:* For master's and doctorate, GRE General Test. Additional exam requirements/recommendations for international students: Required—TOEFL. *Expenses:* Tuition, state resident: full-time $3,681; part-time $614 per credit. Tuition, nonresident: full-time $7,231; part-time $1,205 per credit. *Faculty research:* Hydrogeology, geochemistry, structural geology, sedimentology.

University of Missouri–Columbia, Graduate School, College of Arts and Sciences, Department of Geological Sciences, Columbia, MO 65211. Offers MS, PhD. *Faculty:* 13 full-time (2 women). *Students:* 12 full-time (6 women), 12 part-time (6 women), 5 international. In 2003, 6 master's, 4 doctorates awarded. *Degree requirements:* For master's, thesis; for doctorate, variable foreign language requirement, thesis/dissertation. *Entrance requirements:* For master's and doctorate, GRE General Test, minimum GPA of 3.0. *Application deadline:* For fall admission, 2/15 for domestic students. Applications are processed on a rolling basis. Application fee: $45 ($60 for international students). *Expenses:* Tuition, state resident: full-time $5,205. Tuition, nonresident: full-time $14,058. *Financial support:* Research assistantships, teaching assistantships, institutionally sponsored loans available. *Unit head:* Dr. Kevin Shelton, Director of Graduate Studies, 573-882-6568, E-mail: sheltonk@missouri.edu.

University of Missouri–Kansas City, College of Arts and Sciences, Department of Geosciences, Kansas City, MO 64110-2499. Offers geosciences (PhD); urban environmental geology (MS). PhD offered through the School of Graduate Studies. Part-time programs available. *Faculty:* 10 full-time (2 women). *Students:* 2 full-time (0 women), 6 part-time (2 women); includes 1 minority (African American), 1 international. Average age 33. 5 applicants, 60% accepted. In 2003, 1 degree awarded. *Degree requirements:* For master's and doctorate, thesis/dissertation. *Entrance requirements:* For master's, GRE General Test, minimum GPA of 3.0; for doctorate, qualifying exam. Additional exam requirements/recommendations for international students: Required—TOEFL. *Application deadline:* For fall admission, 3/15 for domestic students. Application fee: $35 ($50 for international students). *Financial support:* In 2003–04, 4 research assistantships with full tuition reimbursements (averaging $12,000 per year), 6 teaching assistantships with full tuition reimbursements (averaging $11,000 per year) were awarded. Federal Work-Study, institutionally sponsored loans, and tuition waivers (full and partial) also available. Support available to part-time students. Financial award application deadline: 3/15. *Faculty research:* Quaternary environments, waste management, black shale geochemistry, history of cartography, neotectonics. Total annual research expenditures:$250,000. *Unit head:* Dr. Raymond M. Coveney, Chair, 816-235-1334, Fax: 816-235-5535, E-mail: coveneyr@umkc.edu. *Application contact:* Dr. James Murowchick, Associate Professor, 816-235-2979, Fax: 816-235-5535, E-mail: murowchickj@umkc.edu.

University of Missouri–Rolla, Graduate School, School of Materials, Energy, and Earth Resources, Department of Geological Sciences and Engineering, Program in Geology and Geophysics, Rolla, MO 65409-0910. Offers geochemistry (MS, PhD); geology (MS, PhD); geophysics (MS, PhD); groundwater and environmental geology (MS, PhD). Part-time programs available. *Faculty:* 8 full-time (1 woman). *Students:* 26 full-time (10 women), 3 part-time (1 woman); includes 2 minority (1 African American, 1 Hispanic American), 10 international. Average age 31. 26 applicants, 65% accepted, 3 enrolled. In 2003, 13 master's, 4 doctorates awarded. *Median time to degree:* Master's–1.5 years full-time, 5.3 years part-time; doctorate–5 years full-time, 7 years part-time. *Degree requirements:* For master's and doctorate, thesis/dissertation. *Entrance requirements:* For master's, GRE General Test, GRE Subject Test, minimum GPA of 3.0 in last 4 semesters; for doctorate, GRE General Test, GRE Subject Test. Additional exam requirements/recommendations for international students: Required—TOEFL. *Application deadline:* For fall admission, 7/1 for domestic students; for spring admission, 12/1 for domestic students. Applications are processed on a rolling basis. Application fee: $50. Electronic applications accepted. *Expenses:* Tuition, state resident: full-time $5,871. Tuition, nonresident: full-time $13,114. Required fees: $820. Tuition and fees vary according to course load. *Financial support:* In 2003–04, 23 students received support, including 22 fellowships with full tuition reimbursements available (averaging $13,250 per year), 16 research assistantships with partial tuition reimbursements available (averaging $13,250 per year); teaching assistantships with partial tuition reimbursements available, Federal Work-Study and institutionally sponsored loans also available. Support available to part-time students. Financial award application deadline: 3/1; financial award applicants required to submit FAFSA. *Faculty research:* Economic geology, geophysical modeling, seismic wave analysis. Total annual research expenditures: $272,086.

The University of Montana–Missoula, Graduate School, College of Arts and Sciences, Department of Geology, Missoula, MT 59812-0002. Offers MS, PhD. *Faculty:* 12 full-time (1 woman), 7 part-time/adjunct (1 woman). *Students:* 31 full-time (12 women), 15 part-time (3 women); includes 1 minority (American Indian/Alaska Native), 2 international. 41 applicants, 63% accepted, 11 enrolled. In 2003, 7 degrees awarded. *Degree requirements:* For doctorate, thesis/dissertation. *Entrance requirements:* For master's and doctorate, GRE General Test. Additional exam requirements/recommendations for international students: Required—TOEFL (minimum score 525 paper-based; 197 computer-based). *Application deadline:* For fall admission, 2/15 for domestic students. Application fee: $45. *Expenses:* Tuition, state resident: full-time $1,848; part-time $221 per credit. Tuition, nonresident: full-time $4,880; part-time $333 per credit. Required fees: $2,200. *Financial support:* In 2003–04, 9 teaching assistantships with full tuition reimbursements (averaging $9,000 per year) were awarded; Federal Work-Study and unspecified assistantships also available. Financial award application deadline: 3/1; financial award applicants required to submit FAFSA. *Faculty research:* Environmental geoscience, regional structure and tectonics, groundwater geology, petrology, mineral deposits. Total annual research expenditures: $533,844. *Unit head:* Dr. Steven D. Sheriff, Chair, 406-243-2341, Fax: 406-243-4028, E-mail: gl_sds@selway.umt.edu. *Application contact:* Dr. Graham Thompson, Graduate Coordinator, 406-243-4953, E-mail: gl_grt@selway.umt.edu.

University of Nevada, Reno, Graduate School, College of Science, Mackay School of Earth Sciences and Engineering, Department of Geological Sciences, Reno, NV 89557. Offers geochemistry (MS, PhD); geological engineering (MS, Geol E); geology (MS, PhD); geophysics (MS, PhD). *Faculty:* 37. *Students:* 52 full-time (15 women), 23 part-time (6 women); includes 6 minority (1 American Indian/Alaska Native, 3 Asian Americans or Pacific Islanders, 2 Hispanic Americans), 11 international. Average age 33. In 2003, 8 master's, 2 doctorates awarded. *Degree requirements:* For master's, thesis optional; for doctorate, one foreign language, thesis/dissertation. *Entrance requirements:* For master's, GRE General Test, GRE Subject Test, minimum GPA of 2.75; for doctorate, GRE General Test, GRE Subject Test, minimum GPA of 3.0. Additional exam requirements/recommendations for international students: Required—TOEFL. *Application deadline:* For fall admission, 2/15 for domestic students; for spring admission, 9/15 for domestic students. Applications are processed on a rolling basis. Application fee: $60 ($95 for international students). *Expenses:* Tuition, state resident: part-time $119 per credit. Tuition, nonresident: part-time $127 per credit. Required fees: $20 per term. Tuition and fees vary according to course load. *Financial support:* In 2003–04, 17 research assistantships, 8 teaching assistantships were awarded. Institutionally sponsored loans and tuition waivers (full) also available. Financial award application deadline: 3/1. *Faculty research:* Hydrothermal ore deposits, metamorphic and igneous petrogenesis, sedimentary rock record of earth history, field and petrographic investigation of magnetism, rock fracture mechanics. *Unit head:* Dr. Robert Watters, Graduate Program Director, 775-784-1770.

University of New Brunswick Fredericton, School of Graduate Studies, Faculty of Science, Department of Geology, Fredericton, NB E3B 5A3, Canada. Offers M Sc, PhD. Part-time programs available. *Degree requirements:* For master's and doctorate, thesis/dissertation. *Entrance requirements:* For master's and doctorate, minimum GPA of 3.0. Additional exam requirements/recommendations for international students: Required—TOEFL, TWE. Electronic applications accepted. *Faculty research:* Hydrogeology, glacial geology, petrology, paleontology, planetary geology.

University of New Hampshire, Graduate School, College of Engineering and Physical Sciences, Department of Earth Sciences, Durham, NH 03824. Offers earth sciences (MS), including geochemical, geology, ocean mapping, oceanography; hydrology (MS). *Faculty:* 29 full-time. *Students:* 18 full-time (7 women), 22 part-time (7 women); includes 3 minority (2 African Americans, 1 American Indian/Alaska Native), 2 international. Average age 31. 49 applicants, 78% accepted, 16 enrolled. In 2003, 9 degrees awarded. *Degree requirements:* For master's, thesis, one foreign language. *Entrance requirements:* For master's, GRE General Test. Additional exam requirements/recommendations for international students: Required—TOEFL (minimum score 550 paper-based; 213 computer-based); Recommended—TSE. *Application deadline:* For fall admission, 4/1 for domestic students; for winter admission, 12/1 for domestic students. Applications are processed on a rolling basis. Application fee: $50. Electronic applications accepted. Tuition, area resident: Full-time $7,070. *Expenses:* Tuition, state resident: full-time $10,605. Tuition, nonresident: full-time $17,430. Required fees: $15. *Financial support:* In 2003–04, 1 fellowship, 7 research assistantships, 9 teaching assistantships were awarded. Career-related internships or fieldwork, Federal Work-Study, scholarships/grants, and tuition waivers (full and partial) also available. Support available to part-time students. Financial award application deadline: 2/15. *Unit head:* Dr. Matt Davis, Chairperson, 603-862-4119, E-mail: earth.sciences@unh.edu. *Application contact:* Linda Wrightsman, Administrative Assistant, 603-862-1720, E-mail: earth.sciences@unh.edu.

University of New Orleans, Graduate School, College of Sciences, Department of Geology and Geophysics, New Orleans, LA 70148. Offers MS. Evening/weekend programs available. *Faculty:* 7 full-time (2 women). *Students:* 18 full-time (12 women), 12 part-time (4 women); includes 5 minority (4 African Americans, 1 Asian American or Pacific Islander), 4 international.

Geology

University of New Orleans (continued)

Average age 30. 16 applicants, 75% accepted, 9 enrolled. In 2003, 7 degrees awarded. *Degree requirements:* For master's, thesis. *Entrance requirements:* For master's, GRE General Test. Additional exam requirements/recommendations for international students: Required—TOEFL (minimum score 550 paper-based; 213 computer-based). *Application deadline:* For fall admission, 7/1 priority date for domestic students, 6/1 priority date for international students; for spring admission, 11/15 priority date for domestic students, 10/1 priority date for international students. Applications are processed on a rolling basis. Application fee: $20. Electronic applications accepted. *Expenses:* Tuition, state resident: part-time $488 per semester hour. Tuition, nonresident: part-time $1,826 per semester hour. *Financial support:* Fellowships, research assistantships, teaching assistantships, career-related internships or fieldwork, Federal Work-Study, and institutionally sponsored loans available. Financial award application deadline: 5/15; financial award applicants required to submit FAFSA. *Faculty research:* Continental margin structure and seismology, burial diagenesis of siliclastic sediments, tectonics at convergent plate margins, continental shelf sediment stability, early diagenesis of carbonates. *Unit head:* Dr. William Busch, Chairperson, 504-280-6793, Fax: 504-280-7396, E-mail: wbusch@uno.edu. *Application contact:* Dr. Christopher Parkinson, Graduate Coordinator, 504-280-6795, Fax: 504-280-7396, E-mail: christopher.parkinson@uno.edu.

The University of North Carolina at Chapel Hill, Graduate School, College of Arts and Sciences, Department of Geological Sciences, Chapel Hill, NC 27599. Offers MS, PhD. *Faculty:* 11 full-time (0 women), 7 part-time/adjunct (1 woman). *Students:* 25 full-time (13 women), 4 international. Average age 29. 30 applicants, 40% accepted, 5 enrolled. In 2003, 3 degrees awarded. *Degree requirements:* For master's, thesis, comprehensive exam; for doctorate, one foreign language, thesis/dissertation, comprehensive exam. *Entrance requirements:* For master's and doctorate, GRE General Test, minimum GPA of 3.0. *Application deadline:* For fall admission, 1/1 for domestic students; for spring admission, 10/15 priority date for domestic students. Application fee: $60. Electronic applications accepted. *Expenses:* Tuition, state resident: full-time $3,163. Tuition, nonresident: full-time $15,161. *Financial support:* In 2003–04, 10 research assistantships with full tuition reimbursements, 15 teaching assistantships with full tuition reimbursements were awarded. Fellowships with full tuition reimbursements, scholarships/grants and summer research assistantships also available. Financial award application deadline: 3/1. *Faculty research:* Paleoceanography, igneous petrology, paleontology, geophysics, structural geology. Total annual research expenditures: $429,464. *Unit head:* Dr. Larry Benninger, Chair, 919-962-0704, Fax: 919-966-4519. *Application contact:* Yvette Thompson, University Administrative Manager, 919-962-0678, Fax: 919-966-4519, E-mail: vette4@email.unc.edu.

The University of North Carolina at Wilmington, College of Arts and Sciences, Department of the Earth Sciences, Wilmington, NC 28403-3297. Offers geology (MS); marine science (MS). *Faculty:* 21 full-time (5 women). *Students:* 14 full-time (11 women), 41 part-time (15 women); includes 3 minority (1 American Indian/Alaska Native, 1 Asian American or Pacific Islander, 1 Hispanic American), 1 international. Average age 35. 42 applicants, 45% accepted, 15 enrolled. In 2003, 14 degrees awarded. *Degree requirements:* For master's, thesis, comprehensive exam. *Entrance requirements:* For master's, GRE General Test, GRE Subject Test, minimum B average in undergraduate major and basic courses for prerequisite to geology. *Application deadline:* For fall admission, 2/15 for domestic students. Applications are processed on a rolling basis. Application fee: $45. *Expenses:* Tuition, state resident: full-time $2,282. Tuition, nonresident: full-time $11,980. Required fees: $1,659. Tuition and fees vary according to course load. *Financial support:* In 2003–04, 9 teaching assistantships were awarded; career-related internships or fieldwork and Federal Work-Study also available. Support available to part-time students. Financial award application deadline: 3/15. *Unit head:* Dr. Richard A. Laws, Chair, 910-962-3736, Fax: 910-962-7077. *Application contact:* Dr. Robert D. Roer, Dean, Graduate School, 910-962-4117, Fax: 910-962-3787, E-mail: roer@uncw.edu.

University of North Dakota, Graduate School, School of Engineering and Mines, Department of Geology, Grand Forks, ND 58202. Offers MA, MS, PhD. *Faculty:* 11 full-time (0 women). *Students:* 2 full-time (both women), 10 part-time (2 women). 9 applicants, 89% accepted, 2 enrolled. In 2003, 2 degrees awarded. *Degree requirements:* For master's, thesis, final exam; for doctorate, one foreign language, thesis/dissertation, final exam, comprehensive exam. *Entrance requirements:* For master's and doctorate, GRE General Test, minimum GPA of 3.0. Additional exam requirements/recommendations for international students: Required—TOEFL (minimum score 550 paper-based; 213 computer-based). *Application deadline:* For fall admission, 3/1 priority date for domestic students, 3/1 priority date for international students; for spring admission, 10/15 priority date for domestic students, 10/15 priority date for international students. Applications are processed on a rolling basis. Application fee: $35. Electronic applications accepted. *Expenses:* Tuition, state resident: part-time $235 per credit. Tuition, nonresident: part-time $535 per credit. Tuition and fees vary according to course level, course load, program and reciprocity agreements. *Financial support:* In 2003–04, 10 students received support, including research assistantships with full tuition reimbursements available (averaging $10,078 per year), teaching assistantships with full tuition reimbursements available (averaging $8,939 per year); fellowships, career-related internships or fieldwork, Federal Work-Study, institutionally sponsored loans, scholarships/grants, and tuition waivers (full and partial) also available. Support available to part-time students. Financial award application deadline: 3/15; financial award applicants required to submit FAFSA. *Faculty research:* Hydrogeology, environmental geology, geological engineering, sedimentology, geomorphology. *Unit head:* Dr. Philip J. Gerla, Director, 701-777-3305, Fax: 701-777-4449, E-mail: phil.gerla@mail.und.nodak.edu.

University of Oklahoma, Graduate College, College of Geosciences, School of Geology and Geophysics, Program in Geology, Norman, OK 73019-0390. Offers MS, PhD. *Students:* 39 full-time (13 women), 11 part-time (3 women); includes 5 minority (3 African Americans, 1 Asian American or Pacific Islander, 1 Hispanic American), 19 international. 42 applicants, 62% accepted, 14 enrolled. In 2003, 11 degrees awarded. *Degree requirements:* For master's, thesis, comprehensive exam; for doctorate, one foreign language, thesis/dissertation, general exam. *Entrance requirements:* For master's, GRE General Test, bachelor's degree in field; for doctorate, GRE General Test. Additional exam requirements/recommendations for international students: Required—TOEFL (minimum score 550 paper-based; 213 computer-based). *Application deadline:* For fall admission, 2/1 priority date for domestic students, 4/1 priority date for international students; for spring admission, 9/1 for domestic students, 9/1 for international students. Applications are processed on a rolling basis. Application fee: $25 ($75 for international students). *Expenses:* Tuition, state resident: full-time $2,774; part-time $116 per credit hour. Tuition, nonresident: full-time $9,571; part-time $399 per credit hour. Required fees: $953; $33 per credit hour. Full-time tuition and fees vary according to course level, course load and program. *Financial support:* In 2003–04, 12 students received support, including 2 fellowships (averaging $1,500 per year); research assistantships with partial tuition reimbursements available, teaching assistantships with partial tuition reimbursements available, career-related internships or fieldwork, scholarships/grants, tuition waivers (partial), and unspecified assistantships also available. Financial award application deadline: 2/1; financial award applicants required to submit FAFSA. *Faculty research:* Stratigraphy/petroleum geology, mineralogy/petrology, structural geology, paleontology and geochemistry. *Application contact:* Donna Mullins, Coordinator, 405-325-3255, Fax: 405-325-3140, E-mail: dsmullins@ou.edu.

University of Oregon, Graduate School, College of Arts and Sciences, Department of Geological Sciences, Eugene, OR 97403. Offers MA, MS, PhD. *Faculty:* 13 full-time (2 women), 4 part-time/adjunct (2 women). *Students:* 30 full-time (17 women), 4 part-time (all women); includes 2 minority (both Hispanic Americans), 4 international. 58 applicants, 31% accepted. In 2003, 6 master's, 11 doctorates awarded. *Degree requirements:* For master's, foreign language (MA). *Entrance requirements:* For master's and doctorate, GRE General Test, GRE Subject Test. *Application deadline:* For fall admission, 2/1 for domestic students. Application fee: $50. *Expenses:* Tuition, state resident: part-time $8,910 per term. Tuition, nonresident: part-time $13,689 per term. *Financial support:* In 2003–04, 22 teaching assistantships were awarded; research assistantships, career-related internships or fieldwork and Federal Work-Study also available. Financial award application deadline: 2/1. *Unit head:* Dana Johnston, Head, 541-346-5588. *Application contact:* Pat Kallunki, Admissions Contact, 541-346-4573.

University of Pennsylvania, School of Arts and Sciences, Graduate Group in Geology, Philadelphia, PA 19104. Offers MS, PhD. Part-time programs available. *Faculty:* 8 full-time (1 woman), 6 part-time/adjunct (0 women). *Students:* 12 full-time (8 women), 2 part-time (both women), 2 international. 44 applicants, 7% accepted, 0 enrolled. In 2003, 4 degrees awarded. *Degree requirements:* For master's and doctorate, one foreign language, thesis/dissertation. *Entrance requirements:* For master's and doctorate, GRE General Test. Additional exam requirements/recommendations for international students: Required—TOEFL. *Application deadline:* For fall admission, 12/1 for domestic students. Application fee: $70. Electronic applications accepted. *Expenses:* Tuition: Full-time $28,040; part-time $3,550 per course. Required fees: $1,750; $214 per course. Tuition and fees vary according to degree level, program and student level. *Financial support:* Fellowships, research assistantships, teaching assistantships, career-related internships or fieldwork and Federal Work-Study available. Financial award application deadline: 12/15. *Faculty research:* Isotope geochemistry, regional tectonics, environmental geology, metamorphic and igneous petrology, paleontology. *Application contact:* Patricia Rea, Coordinator for Admissions, 215-573-5816, Fax: 215-573-8068, E-mail: gdasadmis@sas.upenn.edu.

University of Pittsburgh, School of Arts and Sciences, Department of Geology and Planetary Science, Pittsburgh, PA 15260. Offers geographical information systems (PM Sc); geology and planetary science (MS, PhD). Part-time programs available. *Faculty:* 12 full-time (1 woman), 2 part-time/adjunct (0 women). *Students:* 18 full-time (8 women), 5 part-time (3 women); includes 2 minority (1 Asian American or Pacific Islander, 1 Hispanic American), 1 international. Average age 28. 37 applicants, 24% accepted, 6 enrolled. In 2003, 10 master's, 3 doctorates awarded. *Degree requirements:* For master's, thesis, oral thesis defense; for doctorate, thesis/dissertation, oral dissertation defense. *Entrance requirements:* For master's and doctorate, GRE General Test. Additional exam requirements/recommendations for international students: Required—TOEFL. *Application deadline:* For fall admission, 8/1 priority date for domestic students, 4/30 priority date for international students; for winter admission, 12/1 for domestic students; for spring admission, 4/1 for domestic students. Applications are processed on a rolling basis. Application fee: $40. Electronic applications accepted. *Expenses:* Tuition, state resident: full-time $11,744; part-time $479 per credit. Tuition, nonresident: full-time $22,910; part-time $941 per credit. Required fees: $560. Tuition and fees vary according to degree level and program. *Financial support:* In 2003–04, 17 students received support, including 5 fellowships with tuition reimbursements available (averaging $14,500 per year), 5 research assistantships with tuition reimbursements available (averaging $10,400 per year), 11 teaching assistantships with tuition reimbursements available (averaging $11,752 per year); career-related internships or fieldwork, Federal Work-Study, institutionally sponsored loans, scholarships/grants, and tuition waivers (full and partial) also available. Support available to part-time students. Financial award application deadline: 2/1; financial award applicants required to submit FAFSA. *Faculty research:* Geographical information systems, hydrology, low temperature geochemistry, radiogenic isotopes, volcanology. Total annual research expenditures: $529,714. *Unit head:* Dr. William Harbert, Chair, 412-624-8784, Fax: 412-624-3914, E-mail: harbert@pitt.edu. *Application contact:* Dr. Thomas Anderson, Graduate Adviser, 412-624-9870, Fax: 412-624-3914, E-mail: taco@pitt.edu.

University of Puerto Rico, Mayagüez Campus, Graduate Studies, College of Arts and Sciences, Department of Geology, Mayagüez, PR 00681-9000. Offers MS. Part-time programs available. *Degree requirements:* For master's, thesis, comprehensive exam. *Entrance requirements:* For master's, GRE.

University of Regina, Faculty of Graduate Studies and Research, Faculty of Science, Department of Geology, Regina, SK S4S 0A2, Canada. Offers M Sc. *Faculty:* 7 full-time (2 women). *Students:* 11 full-time (4 women), 7 part-time (3 women). 4 applicants. In 2003, 2 degrees awarded. *Degree requirements:* For master's, thesis. *Entrance requirements:* Additional exam requirements/recommendations for international students: Required—TOEFL. *Application deadline:* Applications are processed on a rolling basis. Application fee: $60. *Expenses:* Tuition, state resident: part-time $130 per credit hour. Tuition and fees vary according to course load and program. *Financial support:* In 2003–04, 4 fellowships, 1 research assistantship, 3 teaching assistantships were awarded. Scholarships/grants also available. Financial award application deadline: 6/15. *Faculty research:* Geochemical, igneous, metamorphic, and structural studies of Canadian shield; Planerozoic carbonate; elastic and evaporite studies; energy. *Unit head:* Dr. B. R. Watters, Head, 306-585-4663, Fax: 306-585-5433, E-mail: brian.watters@uregina.ca.

University of Rochester, The College, Arts and Sciences, Department of Earth and Environmental Sciences, Rochester, NY 14627-0250. Offers geological sciences (MS, PhD). *Faculty:* 7. *Students:* 12 full-time (6 women), 1 part-time, 9 international. 81 applicants, 12% accepted, 6 enrolled. In 2003, 2 master's, 1 doctorate awarded. *Degree requirements:* For doctorate, thesis/dissertation, qualifying exam. *Entrance requirements:* For master's and doctorate, GRE General Test. Additional exam requirements/recommendations for international students: Required—TOEFL. *Application deadline:* For fall admission, 2/1 for domestic students. Application fee: $25. *Expenses:* Tuition: Part-time $880 per credit hour. Required fees: $522. *Financial support:* Fellowships, research assistantships, teaching assistantships, career-related internships or fieldwork and tuition waivers (full and partial) available. Financial award application deadline: 2/1. *Unit head:* John Tarduno, Chair, 585-275-5713. *Application contact:* Kathy Lutz, Graduate Program Secretary, 585-275-5713.

University of Saskatchewan, College of Graduate Studies and Research, College of Arts and Sciences and College of Engineering, Department of Geological Sciences, Saskatoon, SK S7N 5A2, Canada. Offers M Sc, PhD, Diploma. *Faculty:* 15. *Students:* 30. *Degree requirements:* For master's and doctorate, thesis/dissertation, registration. *Entrance requirements:* Additional exam requirements/recommendations for international students: Required—TOEFL. *Application deadline:* For fall admission, 7/1 for domestic students. Applications are processed on a rolling basis. Application fee: $50. Tuition charges are reported in Canadian dollars. *Expenses:* Tuition, state resident: part-time $483 Canadian dollars per course. *Financial support:* Fellowships, research assistantships, teaching assistantships available. Financial award application deadline: 1/31. *Unit head:* Dr. Kevin Ansdell, Head, 306-966-5698, Fax: 306-966-8593, E-mail: kevin.ansdell@usask.ca. *Application contact:* Dr. Yuanming Pan, Graduate Chair, 306-966-5699, Fax: 306-966-8593, E-mail: yuanming.pan@usask.ca.

University of South Carolina, The Graduate School, College of Science and Mathematics, Department of Geological Sciences, Columbia, SC 29208. Offers environmental geoscience (PMS); geological sciences (MS, PhD). Terminal master's awarded for partial completion of doctoral program. *Degree requirements:* For master's, thesis; for doctorate, thesis/dissertation, published paper, comprehensive exam. *Entrance requirements:* For master's and doctorate, GRE General Test. Additional exam requirements/recommendations for international students: Required—TOEFL. Electronic applications accepted. *Expenses:* Tuition, state resident: part-time $308 per hour. Tuition, nonresident: part-time $655 per hour. *Faculty research:* Environmental geology, tectonics, petrology, coastal processes, paleoclimatology.

University of Southern Mississippi, Graduate School, College of Science and Technology, Department of Geology, Hattiesburg, MS 39406-0001. Offers MS. Part-time programs available. *Faculty:* 4 full-time (1 woman). *Students:* 9 full-time (2 women), 1 part-time. Average age 26. 5 applicants, 100% accepted, 4 enrolled. In 2003, 3 degrees awarded. *Degree requirements:* For master's, thesis, comprehensive exam. *Entrance requirements:* For master's, GRE General Test, BS in geology, minimum GPA of 2.75 in last 60 hours. Additional exam requirements/recommendations for international students: Required—TOEFL. *Application deadline:* For fall admission, 8/6 for domestic students. Applications are processed on a rolling basis. Application fee: $25. *Expenses:* Tuition, state resident: part-time $1,967 per semester. Tuition, nonresident: part-time $4,376 per semester. *Financial support:* Fellowships, research assistantships with full tuition reimbursements, teaching assistantships with full tuition reimbursements, career-related internships or fieldwork, Federal Work-Study, and tuition waivers (full) available. Financial award application deadline: 3/15. *Faculty research:* Volcanic rocks and associated minerals, marine stratigraphy and seismology, hydrology, micropaleontology, isotope geology. *Unit head:* Dr. Gail Russell, Chair, 601-266-4526.

University of South Florida, College of Graduate Studies, College of Arts and Sciences, Department of Geology, Tampa, FL 33620-9951. Offers geology (MA, PhD); hydrogeology (MA). Part-time programs available. *Faculty:* 11 full-time (2 women). *Students:* 27 full-time (15 women), 15 part-time (3 women); includes 3 minority (1 African American, 2 Hispanic Americans), 4 international. 32 applicants, 56% accepted, 8 enrolled. *Degree requirements:* For master's, thesis (for some programs); for doctorate, thesis/dissertation. *Entrance requirements:* For master's, GRE General Test, minimum GPA of 3.0 in last 60 hours; for doctorate, GRE General Test. *Application deadline:* For fall admission, 2/15 for domestic students; for spring admission, 10/15 for domestic students. Application fee: $30. Electronic applications accepted. *Financial support:* In 2003–04, 28 students received support, including 3 fellowships with partial tuition reimbursements available (averaging $12,300 per year), 8 research assistantships with partial tuition reimbursements available (averaging $11,034 per year), 17 teaching assistantships with partial tuition reimbursements available (averaging $11,034 per year); institutionally sponsored loans and scholarships/grants also available. Financial award application deadline: 6/30; financial award applicants required to submit FAFSA. *Faculty research:* Coastal geology, environmental geology and hydrogeology, paleontology and geochemistry. Total annual research expenditures: $1 million. *Unit head:* Chuck Connor, Chairperson, 813-974-0325, Fax: 813-974-2654. *Application contact:* Dr. Peter Harries, Graduate Coordinator, 813-974-4974, Fax: 813-974-2654, E-mail: harries@chuma.cas.usf.edu.

The University of Tennessee, Graduate School, College of Arts and Sciences, Department of Geological Sciences, Knoxville, TN 37996. Offers geology (MS, PhD). Part-time programs available. *Degree requirements:* For master's, thesis; for doctorate, one foreign language, thesis/dissertation. *Entrance requirements:* For master's and doctorate, GRE General Test, minimum GPA of 2.7. Additional exam requirements/recommendations for international students: Required—TOEFL. Electronic applications accepted.

The University of Texas at Arlington, Graduate School, College of Science, Department of Geology, Arlington, TX 76019. Offers environmental science (MS, PhD); geology (MS); math: geoscience (PhD). Part-time and evening/weekend programs available. *Faculty:* 4 full-time (0 women), 2 part-time/adjunct (0 women). *Students:* 5 full-time (0 women), 6 part-time (3 women); includes 3 minority (all African Americans), 4 international. 4 applicants, 100% accepted, 4 enrolled. In 2003, 6 degrees awarded. Terminal master's awarded for partial completion of doctoral program. *Median time to degree:* Master's–2 years full-time. *Degree requirements:* For master's, thesis optional; for doctorate, thesis/dissertation, comprehensive exam. *Entrance requirements:* For master's, GRE General Test. *Application deadline:* For fall admission, 6/16 for domestic students. Applications are processed on a rolling basis. Application fee: $35 ($50 for international students). Electronic applications accepted. *Expenses:* Tuition, state resident: full-time $3,042. Tuition, nonresident: full-time $8,712. Required fees: $1,269. Tuition and fees vary according to course load. *Financial support:* In 2003–04, 7 students received support, including 4 fellowships (averaging $1,000 per year), 7 teaching assistantships (averaging $14,700 per year); career-related internships or fieldwork, Federal Work-Study, institutionally sponsored loans, scholarships/grants, health care benefits, and unspecified assistantships also available. Financial award application deadline: 6/1; financial award applicants required to submit FAFSA. *Faculty research:* Hydrology, aqueous geochemistry, biostratigraphy, structural geology, petroleum geology. Total annual research expenditures: $250,000. *Unit head:* Dr. John S. Wickham, Chair, 817-272-2987, Fax: 817-272-2628, E-mail: wickham@uta.edu. *Application contact:* Dr. William L. Balsam, Graduate Adviser, 817-272-2987, Fax: 817-272-2628, E-mail: balsam@uta.edu.

The University of Texas at Austin, Graduate School, College of Natural Sciences, Department of Geological Sciences, Austin, TX 78712-1111. Offers MA, MS, PhD. Part-time programs available. *Degree requirements:* For master's, report (MA), thesis (MS); for doctorate, thesis/dissertation. *Entrance requirements:* For master's and doctorate, GRE General Test. Electronic applications accepted. *Faculty research:* Sedimentary geology, geophysics, hydrogeology, structure/tectonics, vertebrate paleontology.

The University of Texas at El Paso, Graduate School, College of Science, Department of Geological Sciences, El Paso, TX 79968-0001. Offers geological sciences (MS, PhD); geophysics (MS). Part-time and evening/weekend programs available. *Students:* 48 (16 women); includes 8 minority (1 African American, 7 Hispanic Americans) 19 international. Average age 34. 21 applicants, 67% accepted. In 2003, 4 master's, 4 doctorates awarded. *Degree requirements:* For master's, thesis; for doctorate, one foreign language, thesis/dissertation. *Entrance requirements:* For master's, GRE, minimum GPA of 3.0, BS in geology or equivalent; for doctorate, GRE, minimum GPA of 3.0, MS in geology or equivalent. Additional exam requirements/recommendations for international students: Required—TOEFL. *Application deadline:* For fall admission, 7/1 priority date for domestic students, 3/1 priority date for international students; for spring admission, 11/1 priority date for domestic students, 9/1 priority date for international students. Applications are processed on a rolling basis. Application fee: $15 ($65 for international students). Electronic applications accepted. *Expenses:* Tuition, state resident: full-time $1,388; part-time $160 per hour. Tuition, nonresident: full-time $3,440; part-time $388 per hour. Tuition and fees vary according to course load, degree level and program. *Financial support:* In 2003–04, 36 students received support, including research assistantships with partial tuition reimbursements available (averaging $21,812 per year), teaching assistantships with partial tuition reimbursements available (averaging $17,450 per year); fellowships with partial tuition reimbursements available, career-related internships or fieldwork, institutionally sponsored loans, scholarships/grants, and tuition waivers (partial) also available. Support available to part-time students. Financial award application deadline: 3/15; financial award applicants required to submit FAFSA. *Unit head:* Dr. Kate C. Miller, Chairperson, 915-747-5501, Fax: 915-747-5073, E-mail: miller@geo.utep.edu. *Application contact:* Dr. Charles H. Ambler, Dean of the Graduate School, 915-747-5491 Ext. 7886, Fax: 915-747-5788, E-mail: cambler@utep.edu.

The University of Texas at San Antonio, College of Sciences, Department of Earth and Environmental Sciences, San Antonio, TX 78249-0617. Offers environmental science and engineering (PhD); environmental sciences (MS); geology (MS). *Faculty:* 10 full-time (1 woman), 4 part-time/adjunct (2 women). *Students:* 32 full-time (14 women), 62 part-time (27 women); includes 17 minority (1 Asian American or Pacific Islander, 16 Hispanic Americans), 6 international. Average age 33. 41 applicants, 83% accepted, 34 enrolled. In 2003, 14 degrees awarded. *Degree requirements:* For master's, thesis optional; for doctorate, thesis/dissertation, comprehensive exam, registration. *Entrance requirements:* For master's, GRE General Test, minimum GPA of 3.0 in last 60 hours; for doctorate, GRE, resumé, 3 letters of recommendation. Additional exam requirements/recommendations for international students: Required—TOEFL (minimum score 500 paper-based; 173 computer-based). *Application deadline:* For fall admission, 7/1 for domestic students, 4/1 for international students; for spring admission, 11/1 for domestic students, 9/1 for international students. Applications are processed on a rolling basis. Application fee: $40 ($75 for international students). Electronic applications accepted. *Expenses:* Tuition, state resident: part-time $153 per hour. Tuition, nonresident: part-time $625 per hour. *Financial support:* Research assistantships, teaching assistantships available. Total annual research expenditures: $303,352. *Unit head:* Dr. Robert K. Smith, Chair, 210-458-4455.

The University of Texas of the Permian Basin, Office of Graduate Studies, College of Arts and Sciences, Department of Sciences and Mathematics, Program in Geology, Odessa, TX 79762-0001. Offers MS. *Degree requirements:* For master's, thesis or alternative, comprehensive exam, registration. *Entrance requirements:* For master's, GRE General Test. Additional exam requirements/recommendations for international students: Required—TOEFL (minimum score 550 paper-based; 213 computer-based).

University of Toledo, Graduate School, College of Arts and Sciences, Department of Earth, Ecological and Environmental Sciences, Toledo, OH 43606-3390. Offers biology (ecology track) (MS); biology (ecology tract) (PhD); geology (MS), including earth surface processes, general geology; science education (MES). Part-time programs available. *Degree requirements:* For master's, thesis. *Entrance requirements:* For master's, GRE General Test. Additional exam requirements/recommendations for international students: Required—TOEFL. *Application deadline:* For fall admission, 8/1 for domestic students. Applications are processed on a rolling basis. Application fee: $40. Electronic applications accepted. Tuition, area resident: Part-time $3,817 per semester. *Expenses:* Tuition, state resident: part-time $8,177 per semester. Required fees: $502 per semester. *Financial support:* In 2003–04, 6 research assistantships were awarded; teaching assistantships, Federal Work-Study, institutionally sponsored loans, and tuition waivers (full) also available. Support available to part-time students. Financial award application deadline: 4/1; financial award applicants required to submit FAFSA. *Faculty research:* Environmental geochemistry, geophysics, petrology and mineralogy, paleontology, geohydrology. *Unit head:* Dr. Michael Phillips, Chair, 419-530-4572, Fax: 419-530-4421, E-mail: mphilli@geology.utoledo.edu.

University of Toronto, School of Graduate Studies, Physical Sciences Division, Department of Geology, Toronto, ON M5S 1A1, Canada. Offers M Sc, MA Sc, PhD. Part-time programs available. *Faculty:* 38 full-time (3 women), 1 part-time/adjunct. *Students:* 62 full-time (24 women), 8 part-time, 9 international. 36 applicants, 42% accepted. In 2003, 8 master's, 3 doctorates awarded. *Degree requirements:* For master's, thesis (for some programs); for doctorate, thesis/dissertation. *Entrance requirements:* For master's, B Sc or BA Sc, or equivalent; minimum B average; letters of reference; for doctorate, M Sc or equivalent, minimum B+ average, letters of reference. *Application deadline:* For fall admission, 2/2 for domestic students. Application fee: $90 Canadian dollars. Tuition, nonresident: full-time $4,185. International tuition: $10,739 full-time. *Financial support:* Fellowships, research assistantships, teaching assistantships available. *Unit head:* Prof. Steven D. Scott, Chair, 416-978-3022, Fax: 416-978-3938, E-mail: chair@geology.utoronto.ca. *Application contact:* Lynn Slotkin, Secretary, 416-978-3022, Fax: 416-978-3938, E-mail: grad@geology.utoronto.ca.

University of Tulsa, Graduate School, College of Business Administration and College of Engineering and Natural Sciences, Department of Engineering and Technology Management, Tulsa, OK 74104-3189. Offers chemical engineering (METM); computer science (METM); electrical engineering (METM); geological science (METM); mathematics (METM); mechanical engineering (METM); petroleum engineering (METM). Part-time and evening/weekend programs available. *Students:* 1 full-time (0 women), 1 part-time, 1 international. Average age 32. 3 applicants, 100% accepted, 2 enrolled. In 2003, 1 degree awarded. *Entrance requirements:* For master's, GRE General Test or GMAT. Additional exam requirements/recommendations for international students: Required—TOEFL. *Application deadline:* Applications are processed on a rolling basis. Application fee: $30. Electronic applications accepted. *Expenses:* Tuition: Full-time $10,584; part-time $588 per credit hour. Required fees: $60; $3 per credit hour. *Financial support:* In 2003–04, 1 research assistantship with full and partial tuition reimbursement (averaging $6,250 per year) was awarded; fellowships, teaching assistantships, Federal Work-Study, scholarships/grants, tuition waivers (full and partial), and unspecified assistantships also available. Support available to part-time students. Financial award application deadline: 2/1; financial award applicants required to submit FAFSA. *Unit head:* Dr. Rebecca Holland, Director of Graduate Business Studies, 918-631-2242, Fax: 918-631-2142, E-mail: rebecca-holland@utulsa.edu. *Application contact:* Information Contact, E-mail: graduate-business@utulsa.edu.

University of Utah, Graduate School, College of Mines and Earth Sciences, Department of Geology and Geophysics, Salt Lake City, UT 84112-1107. Offers geological engineering (ME, MS, PhD); geology (MS, PhD); geophysics (MS, PhD). *Faculty:* 20 full-time (4 women), 2 part-time/adjunct (0 women). *Students:* 46 full-time (13 women), 19 part-time (5 women); includes 1 minority (Asian American or Pacific Islander), 22 international. Average age 33. 73 applicants, 29% accepted, 10 enrolled. In 2003, 14 master's, 4 doctorates awarded. Terminal master's awarded for partial completion of doctoral program. *Degree requirements:* For master's, thesis, qualifying exam; for doctorate, one foreign language, thesis/dissertation. *Entrance requirements:* For master's and doctorate, GRE General Test, minimum GPA of 3.25. Additional exam requirements/recommendations for international students: Required—TOEFL. *Application deadline:* For fall admission, 1/15 priority date for domestic students, 11/1 priority date for international students. Application fee: $45 ($60 for international students). Tuition, nonresident: full-time $2,483. International tuition: $8,768 full-time. *Financial support:* In 2003–04, 3 students received support, including 4 fellowships with full tuition reimbursements available (averaging $19,240 per year), 22 research assistantships with full tuition reimbursements available (averaging $19,240 per year), 11 teaching assistantships with full tuition reimbursements available (averaging $19,240 per year); institutionally sponsored loans and stipends also available. Financial award application deadline: 2/15; financial award applicants required to submit FAFSA. *Faculty research:* Igneous, metamorphic, and sedimentary petrology; ore deposits; aqueous geochemistry; isotope geochemistry; heat flow. *Unit head:* Dr. Majorie A. Chan, Chair, 801-581-7162, Fax: 801-581-7065, E-mail: gg_chair@mines.utah.edu. *Application contact:* John M. Bartley, Director of Graduate Studies, 801-581-6553, Fax: 801-581-7065, E-mail: jbartley@mines.utah.edu.

University of Vermont, Graduate College, College of Arts and Sciences, Department of Geology, Burlington, VT 05405. Offers geology (MS); geology education (MAT, MST). *Students:* 9 (3 women). 18 applicants, 11% accepted, 2 enrolled. In 2003, 3 degrees awarded. *Degree requirements:* For master's, thesis. *Entrance requirements:* For master's, GRE General Test. Additional exam requirements/recommendations for international students: Required—TOEFL (minimum score 550 paper-based; 213 computer-based). *Application deadline:* For fall admission, 2/15 for domestic students. Applications are processed on a rolling basis. Application fee: $25. Electronic applications accepted. *Expenses:* Tuition, state resident: part-time $362 per credit hour. Tuition, nonresident: part-time $906 per credit hour. *Financial support:* Research assistantships, teaching assistantships available. Financial award application deadline: 3/1. *Faculty research:* Mineralogy, lake sediments, structural geology. *Unit head:* Dr. B. Doolan, Acting Chairperson, 802-656-3396. *Application contact:* Dr. T. Rushmer, Coordinator, 802-656-3396.

University of Victoria, Faculty of Graduate Studies, Faculty of Science, School of Earth and Ocean Sciences, Victoria, BC V8W 2Y2, Canada. Offers geochemistry (M Sc, PhD); geophysics (M Sc, PhD); marine geology and geophysics (M Sc, PhD); ocean acoustics (M Sc, PhD); oceanography (M Sc, PhD); paleobiology (M Sc, PhD); paleoceanography (M Sc, PhD); sedimentology (M Sc, PhD); stratigraphy (M Sc, PhD). Part-time programs available. *Degree requirements:* For master's and doctorate, thesis/dissertation. *Entrance requirements:* Additional exam requirements/recommendations for international students: Required—TOEFL (minimum score 550 paper-based; 213 computer-based). Electronic applications accepted. *Faculty research:* Climate modeling, geology.

University of Washington, Graduate School, College of Arts and Sciences, Department of Earth and Space Sciences, Seattle, WA 98195. Offers geology (MS, PhD); geophysics (MS, PhD). *Students:* 78 full-time (28 women); includes 2 minority (both Hispanic Americans), 9 international. 192 applicants, 16% accepted, 13 enrolled. In 2003, 5 master's, 7 doctorates awarded. *Median time to degree:* Doctorate–6.8 years full-time. Of those who began their doctoral program in fall 1995, 64% received their degree in 8 years or less. *Degree requirements:* For master's, thesis or alternative, departmental qualifying exam, final exam; for doctorate, thesis/dissertation, departmental qualifying exam, general and final exams. *Entrance requirements:* For master's and doctorate, GRE General Test, minimum GPA of 3.0. Additional exam requirements/recommendations for international students: Required—TOEFL (minimum score 580 paper-based). *Application deadline:* For fall admission, 1/15 for domestic students, 11/1 for international students. Application fee: $50. Electronic applications accepted. *Financial support:* In 2003–04, 10 fellowships with full tuition reimbursements, 41 research assistantships with full tuition reimbursements (averaging $12,850 per year), 20 teaching assistantships

Geology

University of Washington (continued)
with full tuition reimbursements (averaging $12,850 per year) were awarded. Financial award application deadline: 1/15. Total annual research expenditures: $9.3 million. *Unit head:* Dr. J. Michael Brown, Chair, 206-543-1190, Fax: 206-543-0489, E-mail: brown@geophys.washington.edu. *Application contact:* Mary Conrad, Director of Academic Services, 206-616-8511, Fax: 206-543-0489, E-mail: advising@ess.washington.edu.

University of Washington, Graduate School, College of Ocean and Fishery Sciences, School of Oceanography, Seattle, WA 98195. Offers biological oceanography (MS, PhD); chemical oceanography (MS, PhD); marine geology and geophysics (MS, PhD); physical oceanography (MS, PhD). Terminal master's awarded for partial completion of doctoral program. *Degree requirements:* For master's, research project; for doctorate, thesis/dissertation. *Entrance requirements:* For master's and doctorate, GRE General Test, minimum GPA of 3.0. Additional exam requirements/recommendations for international students: Required—TOEFL. Electronic applications accepted. *Faculty research:* Global climate change, hydrothermal vent systems, marine microbiology, marine and freshwater biogeochemistry, biological-physical interactions.

The University of Western Ontario, Faculty of Graduate Studies, Physical Sciences Division, Department of Earth Sciences, London, ON N6A 5B8, Canada. Offers geology (M Sc, PhD); geology and environmental science (M Sc, PhD); geophysics (M Sc, PhD); geophysics and environmental science (M Sc, PhD). *Degree requirements:* For master's, thesis, registration; for doctorate, thesis/dissertation, qualifying exam. *Entrance requirements:* For master's, honors in B Sc; for doctorate, M Sc. Additional exam requirements/recommendations for international students: Required—TOEFL. *Faculty research:* Geophysics, geochemistry, paleontology, sedimentology/stratigraphy, glaciology/quaternary.

University of Wisconsin–Madison, Graduate School, College of Letters and Science, Department of Geology and Geophysics, Program in Geology, Madison, WI 53706-1380. Offers MS, PhD. *Degree requirements:* For master's, thesis; for doctorate, one foreign language, thesis/dissertation. *Entrance requirements:* For master's and doctorate, GRE General Test. Tuition, area resident: Full-time $7,593; part-time $476 per credit. Tuition, nonresident: full-time $22,824; part-time $1,430 per credit. Required fees: $292; $38 per credit. Part-time tuition and fees vary according to course load and reciprocity agreements.

University of Wisconsin–Milwaukee, Graduate School, College of Letters and Sciences, Department of Geosciences, Milwaukee, WI 53201-0413. Offers geological sciences (MS, PhD). *Faculty:* 10 full-time (2 women). *Students:* 4 full-time (3 women), 10 part-time (3 women); includes 1 minority (Hispanic American) 7 applicants, 71% accepted, 4 enrolled. In 2003, 3 degrees awarded. *Degree requirements:* For master's, thesis; for doctorate, one foreign language, thesis/dissertation. *Entrance requirements:* For master's and doctorate, GRE General Test. *Application deadline:* For fall admission, 1/1 for domestic students; for spring admission, 9/1 for domestic students. Applications are processed on a rolling basis. Application fee: $45 ($75 for international students). *Expenses:* Tuition, state resident: part-time $634 per credit. Tuition, nonresident: part-time $1,531 per credit. Part-time tuition and fees vary according to course load, campus/location, program and reciprocity agreements. *Financial support:* In 2003–04, 1 fellowship, 8 teaching assistantships were awarded. Research assistantships, career-related internships or fieldwork and unspecified assistantships also available. Support available to part-time students. Financial award application deadline: 4/15. *Unit head:* Douglas Cherauer, Representative, 414-229-4562, Fax: 414-229-5452, E-mail: aquadoc@uwm.edu.

University of Wyoming, Graduate School, College of Arts and Sciences, Department of Geology and Geophysics, Laramie, WY 82070. Offers geology (MS, PhD); geophysics (MS, PhD). Part-time programs available. *Faculty:* 17 full-time (2 women), 3 part-time/adjunct (2 women). *Students:* 36 full-time (11 women), 29 part-time (12 women); includes 3 minority (1 Asian American or Pacific Islander, 2 Hispanic Americans), 10 international. 22 applicants, 95% accepted, 21 enrolled. In 2003, 9 master's, 4 doctorates awarded. *Degree requirements:* For master's and doctorate, variable foreign language requirement, thesis/dissertation. *Entrance requirements:* For master's and doctorate, GRE General Test, minimum GPA of 3.0. *Application deadline:* For fall admission, 1/15 for domestic students. Applications are processed on a rolling basis. Application fee: $40. *Expenses:* Tuition, state resident: part-time $142 per credit hour. Tuition, nonresident: part-time $408 per credit hour. Required fees: $134 per semester. Tuition and fees vary according to course load, campus/location, program and student level. *Financial support:* Fellowships, research assistantships, teaching assistantships, career-related internships or fieldwork, Federal Work-Study, and institutionally sponsored loans available. Financial award application deadline: 3/1. *Faculty research:* Geochemistry and petroleum geology, tectonics and sedimentation, geomorphology and remote sensing, igneous and metamorphic petrology, structure, geohydrology. *Unit head:* Dr. James I. Drever, Head, 307-766-3386. *Application contact:* Sondra S. Cawley, Admissions Coordinator, 307-766-3389, Fax: 307-766-6679, E-mail: acadcoord.geol@uwyo.edu.

Utah State University, School of Graduate Studies, College of Science, Department of Geology, Logan, UT 84322. Offers MS. *Faculty:* 7 full-time (0 women), 2 part-time/adjunct (both women). *Students:* 13 full-time (3 women), 3 part-time. Average age 24. 24 applicants, 38% accepted, 5 enrolled. In 2003, 11 degrees awarded. *Degree requirements:* For master's, thesis. *Entrance requirements:* For master's, GRE General Test, minimum GPA of 3.0. Additional exam requirements/recommendations for international students: Required—TOEFL. *Application deadline:* For fall admission, 2/15 for domestic students; for spring admission, 10/15 for domestic students. Applications are processed on a rolling basis. Application fee: $50 ($60 for international students). *Expenses:* Tuition, state resident: part-time $270 per credit hour. Tuition, nonresident: part-time $946 per credit hour. Required fees: $173 per credit hour. *Financial support:* In 2003–04, 12 students received support, including 1 fellowship with partial tuition reimbursement available (averaging $18,000 per year), 3 research assistantships with partial tuition reimbursements available (averaging $11,500 per year), 9 teaching assistantships with partial tuition reimbursements available (averaging $11,500 per year); career-related internships or fieldwork, Federal Work-Study, and institutionally sponsored loans also available. Financial award application deadline: 2/15. *Faculty research:* Sedimentary geology, structural geology, regional tectonics, hydrogeology petrology. Total annual research expenditures: $400,000. *Unit head:* Dr. John W. Shervais, Head, 435-797-1274, Fax: 435-797-1588, E-mail: geology@cc.usu.edu. *Application contact:* Dr. W. David Liddell, Program Director, 435-797-1261, Fax: 435-797-1588, E-mail: davel@cc.usu.edu.

Vanderbilt University, Graduate School, Department of Geology, Nashville, TN 37240-1001. Offers MS. *Degree requirements:* For master's, thesis or alternative. *Entrance requirements:* For master's, GRE General Test, GRE Subject Test (recommended). Electronic applications accepted. *Expenses:* Tuition: Part-time $1,155 per semester hour. Required fees: $1,538. *Faculty research:* Sedimentology, geochemistry, tectonics, environmental geology, biostratigraphy.

Virginia Polytechnic Institute and State University, Graduate School, College of Science, Department of Geosciences, Blacksburg, VA 24061. Offers geological sciences (MS, PhD); geophysics (MS, PhD). *Faculty:* 20 full-time (4 women), 1 (woman) part-time/adjunct. *Students:* 48 full-time (17 women), 7 part-time (2 women); includes 3 minority (1 American Indian/Alaska Native, 1 Asian American or Pacific Islander, 1 Hispanic American), 13 international. Average age 27. 83 applicants, 29% accepted, 19 enrolled. In 2003, 8 master's, 5 doctorates awarded. *Entrance requirements:* For master's and doctorate, GRE General Test. Additional exam requirements/recommendations for international students: Required—TOEFL (minimum score 550 paper-based; 213 computer-based). *Application deadline:* Applications are processed on a rolling basis. Application fee: $45. Electronic applications accepted. Tuition, area resident: Full-time $6,039; part-time $336 per credit. Tuition, nonresident: full-time $9,708; part-time $539 per credit. Required fees: $905; $130 per credit. *Financial support:* In 2003–04, 2 fellowships with full tuition reimbursements (averaging $6,000 per year), 20 research assistantships with full tuition reimbursements (averaging $12,316 per year), 26 teaching assistantships with full tuition reimbursements (averaging $12,127 per year) were awarded. Career-related internships or fieldwork, Federal Work-Study, scholarships/grants, tuition waivers (full), and unspecified assistantships also available. Financial award application deadline: 4/1. *Faculty research:* Paleontology/geobiology, active tectonics, geomorphology, mineralogy/crystallography, mineral physics. *Unit head:* Dr. Cahit Coruh, Chair, 540-231-6521, Fax: 540-231-3386, E-mail: coruh@vt.edu. *Application contact:* Connie Lowe, Student Program Coordinator, 540-231-8824, Fax: 540-231-3386, E-mail: clowe@vt.edu.

Washington State University, Graduate School, College of Sciences, Department of Geology, Pullman, WA 99164. Offers MS, PhD. *Faculty:* 11 full-time (1 woman), 10 part-time/adjunct (2 women). *Students:* 27 full-time (12 women), 3 part-time (1 woman), 7 international. Average age 26. 39 applicants, 38% accepted, 9 enrolled. In 2003, 7 master's, 1 doctorate awarded. *Degree requirements:* For master's, thesis, oral exam; for doctorate, one foreign language, thesis/dissertation, oral exam, written exam. *Entrance requirements:* For master's and doctorate, GRE General Test, minimum GPA of 3.0. Additional exam requirements/recommendations for international students: Required—TOEFL (minimum score 560 paper-based; 220 computer-based). *Application deadline:* For fall admission, 2/1 priority date for domestic students, 2/1 priority date for international students; for spring admission, 12/1 priority date for domestic students, 7/1 priority date for international students. Applications are processed on a rolling basis. Application fee: $35. Electronic applications accepted. *Expenses:* Tuition, state resident: full-time $6,278; part-time $314 per hour. Tuition, nonresident: full-time $15,514; part-time $765 per hour. Required fees: $444. Full-time tuition and fees vary according to campus/location, program and student level. Part-time tuition and fees vary according to course load. *Financial support:* In 2003–04, 9 research assistantships with full and partial tuition reimbursements (averaging $13,113 per year), 17 teaching assistantships with full and partial tuition reimbursements (averaging $13,113 per year) were awarded. Career-related internships or fieldwork, Federal Work-Study, institutionally sponsored loans, scholarships/grants, and tuition waivers (partial) also available. Financial award application deadline: 2/1; financial award applicants required to submit FAFSA. *Faculty research:* Genesis of ore deposits, geohydrology of the Pacific Northwest, geochemistry and petrology of plateau basalts. Total annual research expenditures: $1.4 million. *Unit head:* Dr. Peter Larson, Chair, 509-335-3009, Fax: 509-335-7816, E-mail: plarson@wsu.edu. *Application contact:* Mary Arndt, Program Coordinator, 509-335-3009, Fax: 509-335-7816, E-mail: arndtm@wsu.edu.

Washington University in St. Louis, Graduate School of Arts and Sciences, Department of Earth and Planetary Sciences, St. Louis, MO 63130-4899. Offers earth and planetary sciences (MA); geochemistry (PhD); geology (MA, PhD); geophysics (PhD); planetary sciences (PhD). *Students:* 36 full-time (19 women), 1 (woman) part-time; includes 2 minority (both Asian Americans or Pacific Islanders), 5 international. 69 applicants, 35% accepted, 12 enrolled. In 2003, 9 master's, 2 doctorates awarded. Terminal master's awarded for partial completion of doctoral program. *Degree requirements:* For master's and doctorate, thesis/dissertation. *Entrance requirements:* For master's and doctorate, GRE General Test. *Application deadline:* For fall admission, 1/15 for domestic students. Applications are processed on a rolling basis. Application fee: $35. Electronic applications accepted. *Expenses:* Tuition: Full-time $28,300; part-time $1,180 per credit. *Financial support:* Fellowships, research assistantships, teaching assistantships, Federal Work-Study, institutionally sponsored loans, and tuition waivers (full and partial) available. Financial award application deadline: 1/15. *Unit head:* Dr. Raymond E. Arvidson, Chairman, 314-935-5610.

Wayne State University, Graduate School, College of Science, Department of Geology, Detroit, MI 48202. Offers MS. *Faculty:* 2. *Students:* 1 full-time (0 women), 1 part-time; includes 1 minority (African American) Average age 35. 2 applicants, 100% accepted, 2 enrolled. In 2003, 1 degree awarded. *Degree requirements:* For master's, thesis. *Entrance requirements:* For master's, GRE General Test. Additional exam requirements/recommendations for international students: Required—TOEFL (minimum score 550 paper-based; 213 computer-based); Recommended—TWE(minimum score 6). *Application deadline:* For fall admission, 7/1 for domestic students, 6/1 for international students. Applications are processed on a rolling basis. Application fee: $30 ($50 for international students). Electronic applications accepted. *Expenses:* Tuition, state resident: part-time $263 per credit hour. Tuition, nonresident: part-time $580 per credit hour. Required fees: $21 per credit hour. *Financial support:* Teaching assistantships available. *Faculty research:* Geologic history of southwestern U.S., heavy metal contamination of soils, role of colloids in the removal of particle reactive radionuclides and contaminants in the Arctic Ocean and Great Lakes Region, environmental radioactivity and geochronology, light stable isotope geochemistry and mineral ore formation. *Unit head:* James Rigby, Chairperson, 313-577-7784, Fax: 313-577-8822, E-mail: jhr@chem.wayne.edu. *Application contact:* Mark Baskaran, Graduate Director, 313-577-3262, E-mail: baskaran@chem.wayne.edu.

West Chester University of Pennsylvania, Graduate Studies, College of Arts and Sciences, Department of Geology and Astronomy, West Chester, PA 19383. Offers physical science (MA). Part-time and evening/weekend programs available. *Students:* 6 full-time (3 women), 6 part-time (2 women). Average age 33. 7 applicants, 86% accepted. In 2003, 4 degrees awarded. *Degree requirements:* For master's, thesis optional. *Entrance requirements:* For master's, GRE General Test, interview. *Application deadline:* For fall admission, 4/15 for domestic students; for spring admission, 10/15 for domestic students. Applications are processed on a rolling basis. Application fee: $35. *Expenses:* Tuition, state resident: full-time $5,518; part-time $307 per credit. Tuition, nonresident: full-time $8,830; part-time $491 per credit. Required fees: $902; $52 per credit. One-time fee: $35 part-time. *Financial support:* In 2003–04, 1 research assistantship with full tuition reimbursement (averaging $5,000 per year) was awarded; unspecified assistantships also available. Support available to part-time students. Financial award application deadline: 2/15; financial award applicants required to submit FAFSA. *Faculty research:* Developing and using a meteorological data station. *Unit head:* Dr. Gil Wiswall, Chair, 610-436-2727. *Application contact:* Dr. Steven Good, Information Contact, 610-436-2203, E-mail: sgood@wcupa.edu.

Western Kentucky University, Graduate Studies, Ogden College of Science, and Engineering, Department of Geography and Geology, Bowling Green, KY 42101-3576. Offers MS. *Degree requirements:* For master's, thesis or alternative, comprehensive exam. *Entrance requirements:* For master's, GRE General Test, minimum GPA of 2.75. Additional exam requirements/recommendations for international students: Required—TOEFL (minimum score 555 paper-based; 213 computer-based). *Faculty research:* Hydroclimatology, electronic data sets, groundwater, sinkhole liquification potential, meteorological analysis.

Western Michigan University, Graduate College, College of Arts and Sciences, Department of Geosciences, Geosciences Department, Kalamazoo, MI 49008-5202. Offers MS, PhD. *Degree requirements:* For master's, oral exam; for doctorate, thesis/dissertation, oral exam. *Entrance requirements:* For master's and doctorate, GRE General Test.

Western Washington University, Graduate School, College of Sciences and Technology, Department of Geology, Bellingham, WA 98225-5996. Offers MS. Part-time programs available. *Faculty:* 12. *Students:* 13 full-time (7 women), 10 part-time (5 women); includes 1 minority (American Indian/Alaska Native). 33 applicants, 70% accepted, 7 enrolled. In 2003, 3 degrees awarded. *Degree requirements:* For master's, thesis. *Entrance requirements:* For master's, GRE General Test, minimum GPA of 3.0 in last 60 semester hours or last 90 quarter hours. Additional exam requirements/recommendations for international students: Required—TOEFL. *Application deadline:* For fall admission, 1/31 for domestic students; for winter admission, 10/1 for domestic students; for spring admission, 2/1 for domestic students. Applications are processed on a rolling basis. Application fee: $35. *Expenses:* Tuition, state resident: full-time $5,694; part-time $172 per credit. Tuition, nonresident: full-time $16,221; part-time $523 per credit. *Financial support:* In 2003–04, 9 teaching assistantships with partial tuition reimbursements (averaging $9,210 per year) were awarded; career-related internships or fieldwork, Federal Work-Study, institutionally sponsored loans, scholarships/grants, and tuition waivers (partial) also available. Support available to part-time students. Financial award application deadline: 2/15; financial award applicants required to submit FAFSA. *Unit head:* Dr. Scott Babcock, Chair, 360-650-3592.

West Virginia University, Eberly College of Arts and Sciences, Department of Geology and Geography, Program in Geology, Morgantown, WV 26506. Offers geomorphology (MS, PhD); geophysics (MS, PhD); hydrogeology (MS); hydrology (PhD); paleontology (MS, PhD); petrology (MS, PhD); stratigraphy (MS, PhD); structure (MS, PhD). Part-time programs available. *Students:* 26 full-time (7 women), 17 part-time (7 women); includes 2 minority (1 American Indian/Alaska Native, 1 Asian American or Pacific Islander), 12 international. Average age 30. 34 applicants, 29% accepted. In 2003, 6 master's, 1 doctorate awarded. Terminal master's awarded for partial completion of doctoral program. *Degree requirements:* For master's, thesis/dissertation; for doctorate, thesis/dissertation, comprehensive exam. *Entrance requirements:* For master's, GRE General Test, GRE Subject Test, minimum GPA of 2.5; for doctorate, GRE General Test, GRE Subject Test, minimum GPA of 3.3. Additional exam requirements/recommendations for international students: Required—TOEFL. *Application deadline:* For fall admission, 2/1 for domestic students; for spring admission, 10/1 for domestic students. Applications are processed on a rolling basis. Application fee: $45. *Expenses:* Tuition, state resident: full-time $4,332. Tuition, nonresident: full-time $12,442. *Financial support:* In 2003–04, 5 research assistantships, 18 teaching assistantships were awarded. Career-related internships or fieldwork, Federal Work-Study, institutionally sponsored loans, and tuition waivers (full and partial) also available. Financial award application deadline: 2/1; financial award applicants required to submit FAFSA. *Unit head:* Dr. Thomas H. Wilson, Associate Chair, 304-293-5603 Ext. 4316, Fax: 304-293-6522. *Application contact:* Dr. Joe Donovan, Associate Professor, 304-293-5603 Ext. 4308, Fax: 304-293-6522, E-mail: joe.donovan@mail.wvu.edu.

Wichita State University, Graduate School, Fairmount College of Liberal Arts and Sciences, Department of Geology, Wichita, KS 67260. Offers MS. Part-time programs available. *Faculty:* 6 full-time (1 woman). *Students:* 3 full-time (2 women), 7 part-time (2 women); includes 1 minority (American Indian/Alaska Native), 2 international. Average age 32. 2 applicants, 50% accepted. In 2003, 1 degree awarded. *Degree requirements:* For master's, thesis. *Entrance requirements:* For master's, GRE General Test. Additional exam requirements/recommendations for international students: Required—TOEFL. *Application deadline:* For fall admission, 7/1 for domestic students; for spring admission, 1/1 for domestic students. Applications are processed on a rolling basis. Application fee: $35 ($50 for international students). Electronic applications accepted. *Expenses:* Tuition, state resident: full-time $2,457; part-time $137 per credit hour. Tuition, nonresident: full-time $7,371; part-time $410 per credit hour. Required fees: $364; $20 per credit hour. Tuition and fees vary according to course load. *Financial support:* In 2003–04, 3 teaching assistantships with full tuition reimbursements (averaging $7,000 per year) were awarded; fellowships, research assistantships, career-related internships or fieldwork, Federal Work-Study, institutionally sponsored loans, scholarships/grants, traineeships, and unspecified assistantships also available. Support available to part-time students. Financial award application deadline: 4/1; financial award applicants required to submit FAFSA. *Faculty research:* Midcontinent and Permian basin stratigraphy studies, recent sediments of Belize and Florida, image analysis of sediments and porosity. *Unit head:* Dr. Collette Burke, Chair, 316-978-3140, E-mail: collette.burke@wichita.edu.

Wright State University, School of Graduate Studies, College of Science and Mathematics, Department of Geological Sciences, Program in Geological Sciences, Dayton, OH 45435. Offers environmental geochemistry (MS); environmental geology (MS); environmental sciences (MS); geological sciences (MS); geophysics (MS); hydrogeology (MS); petroleum geology (MS). Part-time programs available. *Students:* 22 full-time (4 women), 9 part-time (4 women), 2 international. Average age 26. 21 applicants, 100% accepted. In 2003, 15 degrees awarded. *Degree requirements:* For master's, thesis. *Entrance requirements:* Additional exam requirements/recommendations for international students: Required—TOEFL. Application fee: $25. *Expenses:* Tuition, state resident: full-time $8,112; part-time $255 per quarter hour. Tuition, nonresident: full-time $14,127; part-time $442 per quarter hour. International tuition: $14,283 full-time. Tuition and fees vary according to course load, degree level and program. *Financial support:* Fellowships, research assistantships, teaching assistantships, Federal Work-Study and unspecified assistantships available. Support available to part-time students. Financial award application deadline: 3/1; financial award applicants required to submit FAFSA. *Application contact:* Deborah L. Cowles, Assistant to Chair, 937-775-3455, Fax: 937-775-3462, E-mail: deborah.cowles@wright.edu.

Yale University, Graduate School of Arts and Sciences, Department of Geology and Geophysics, New Haven, CT 06520. Offers geochemistry (PhD); geophysics (PhD); meteorology (PhD); mineralogy and crystallography (PhD); oceanography (PhD); paleoecology (PhD); paleontology and stratigraphy (PhD); petrology (PhD); structural geology (PhD). *Degree requirements:* For doctorate, thesis/dissertation. *Entrance requirements:* For doctorate, GRE General Test. Additional exam requirements/recommendations for international students: Required—TOEFL. *Expenses:* Tuition: Full-time $25,600; part-time $6,400 per term.

Announcement: Department offers individualized programs of study leading to the doctorate (6 years). It welcomes applicants interested in earth sciences who have bachelor's or master's degree in biology, chemistry, engineering, mathematics, meteorology, or physics, as well as geology. Program has no required curriculum of credit courses but is designed to encourage development of individual interests under guidance of faculty advisory committee.

See in-depth description on page 261.

Geophysics

Boise State University, Graduate College, College of Arts and Sciences, Department of Geosciences, Master's Program in Geophysics, Boise, ID 83725-0399. Offers MS. Part-time programs available. *Students:* 3 full-time (0 women), 3 part-time (all women). Average age 31. In 2003, 2 degrees awarded. *Degree requirements:* For master's, thesis. *Entrance requirements:* For master's, GRE General Test, minimum GPA of 3.0, BS in related field. Additional exam requirements/recommendations for international students: Required—TOEFL. *Application deadline:* For fall admission, 7/17 for domestic students; for spring admission, 12/5 priority date for domestic students. Applications are processed on a rolling basis. Application fee: $30. Electronic applications accepted. *Expenses:* Tuition, state resident: full-time $4,668. Tuition, nonresident: full-time $11,388. *Financial support:* In 2003–04, research assistantships with full tuition reimbursements (averaging $11,186 per year); career-related internships or fieldwork, Federal Work-Study, institutionally sponsored loans, scholarships/grants, and unspecified assistantships also available. Support available to part-time students. Financial award application deadline: 3/1. *Faculty research:* Shallow seismic profile, seismic hazard, tectonics, hazardous waste disposal. *Unit head:* Dr. Paul R. Michaels, Coordinator, 208-426-1929, Fax: 208-426-4061.

Boise State University, Graduate College, College of Arts and Sciences, Department of Geosciences, Program in Geophysics, Boise, ID 83725-0399. Offers PhD. Part-time programs available. *Students:* 7 full-time (0 women), 3 part-time. *Degree requirements:* For doctorate, thesis/dissertation, comprehensive exam. *Entrance requirements:* For doctorate, GRE General Test. *Application deadline:* For fall admission, 7/17 for domestic students; for spring admission, 12/5 priority date for domestic students. Applications are processed on a rolling basis. Application fee: $30. Electronic applications accepted. *Expenses:* Tuition, state resident: full-time $4,668. Tuition, nonresident: full-time $11,388. *Financial support:* In 2003–04, 5 research assistantships with full tuition reimbursements (averaging $22,036 per year) were awarded; unspecified assistantships also available. *Unit head:* Dr. Paul R. Michaels, Coordinator, 208-426-1929, Fax: 208-426-4061.

Boston College, Graduate School of Arts and Sciences, Department of Geology and Geophysics, Chestnut Hill, MA 02467-3800. Offers MS, MBA/MS. *Students:* 14 full-time (7 women), 8 part-time (3 women); includes 1 minority (Asian American or Pacific Islander), 4 international. 19 applicants, 79% accepted, 9 enrolled. In 2003, 11 degrees awarded. *Degree requirements:* For master's, thesis. *Entrance requirements:* For master's, GRE General Test, GRE Subject Test. Additional exam requirements/recommendations for international students: Required—TOEFL (minimum score 550 paper-based; 213 computer-based). *Application deadline:* For fall admission, 2/1 for domestic students. Application fee: $60. Electronic applications accepted. *Expenses:* Tuition: Part-time $810 per credit. *Financial support:* Research assistantships, teaching assistantships, Federal Work-Study available. Support available to part-time students. Financial award application deadline: 3/1; financial award applicants required to submit FAFSA. *Faculty research:* Coastal and marine geology, experimental sedimentology, geomagnetism, igneous petrology, paleontology. *Unit head:* Dr. Alan Kafka, Chairperson, 617-552-3650. *Application contact:* Dr. John Ebel, Graduate Program Director, 617-552-3640, E-mail: john.ebel@bc.edu.

California Institute of Technology, Division of Geological and Planetary Sciences, Pasadena, CA 91125-0001. Offers cosmochemistry (PhD); geobiology (PhD); geochemistry (MS, PhD); geology (MS, PhD); geophysics (MS, PhD); planetary science (MS, PhD). Part-time programs available. *Faculty:* 37 full-time (3 women). *Students:* 61 full-time (29 women); includes 28 minority (1 African American, 26 Asian Americans or Pacific Islanders, 1 Hispanic American). Average age 27. 127 applicants, 20% accepted, 15 enrolled. In 2003, 5 master's, 13 doctorates awarded. *Degree requirements:* For doctorate, thesis/dissertation. *Entrance requirements:* For doctorate, GRE General Test. Additional exam requirements/recommendations for international students: Required—TOEFL. *Application deadline:* For fall admission, 1/15 for domestic students, 1/15 for international students. Application fee: $50. Electronic applications accepted. *Financial support:* In 2003–04, 21 fellowships with full tuition reimbursements (averaging $20,496 per year), 49 research assistantships with full tuition reimbursements (averaging $20,496 per year) were awarded. Teaching assistantships with full tuition reimbursements, institutionally sponsored loans, scholarships/grants, health care benefits, and unspecified assistantships also available. Financial award applicants required to submit FAFSA. *Faculty research:* Astronomy, evolution of anaerobic respiratory processes, structural geology and tectonics, theoretical and numerical seismology, global biogeochemical cycles. Total annual research expenditures: $18.6 million. *Unit head:* Dr. Edward M. Stolper, Chairman, 626-395-6108, Fax: 626-795-6028, E-mail: divgps@gps.caltech.edu. *Application contact:* Dr. George R. Rossman, Academic Officer, 626-395-6125, Fax: 626-568-0935, E-mail: divgps@gps.caltech.edu.

Colorado School of Mines, Graduate School, Department of Geophysics, Golden, CO 80401-1887. Offers geophysical engineering (ME, MS, PhD); geophysics (MS, PhD, Diploma). Part-time programs available. *Faculty:* 12 full-time (0 women), 3 part-time/adjunct (0 women). *Students:* 45 full-time (16 women), 11 part-time; includes 2 minority (1 African American, 1 American Indian/Alaska Native), 29 international. 59 applicants, 68% accepted, 12 enrolled. In 2003, 4 master's, 4 doctorates awarded. *Degree requirements:* For master's, thesis; for doctorate, one foreign language, thesis/dissertation, oral exams, comprehensive exam. *Entrance requirements:* For master's, doctorate, and Diploma, GRE General Test. Additional exam requirements/recommendations for international students: Required—TOEFL (minimum score 550 paper-based; 213 computer-based). *Application deadline:* For fall admission, 12/1 for domestic students, 12/1 for international students; for spring admission, 5/1 for domestic students, 5/1 for international students. Application fee: $45. Electronic applications accepted. *Expenses:* Tuition, state resident: full-time $5,700; part-time $285 per credit hour. Tuition, nonresident: full-time $19,040; part-time $952 per credit hour. Required fees: $733. *Financial support:* In 2003–04, 8 students received support, including 5 fellowships with full tuition reimbursements available (averaging $12,500 per year), 32 research assistantships with full tuition reimbursements available (averaging $10,000 per year), 6 teaching assistantships with full tuition reimbursements available (averaging $10,000 per year); scholarships/grants and unspecified assistantships also available. Financial award applicants required to submit FAFSA. *Faculty research:* Seismic exploration, gravity and geomagnetic fields, electrical mapping and sounding, bore hole measurements, environmental physics. Total annual research expenditures: $3.6 million. *Unit head:* Dr. Terence K. Young, Head, 303-273-3454, Fax: 303-273-3478, E-mail: tkyoung@mine.edu. *Application contact:* Sara Summers, Program Assistant, 303-273-3935, Fax: 303-273-3478, E-mail: ssummers@mines.edu.

Columbia University, Graduate School of Arts and Sciences, Division of Natural Sciences, Department of Earth and Environmental Sciences, New York, NY 10027. Offers geochemistry (M Phil, MA, PhD); geodetic sciences (M Phil, MA, PhD); geophysics (M Phil, MA, PhD); oceanography (M Phil, MA, PhD). *Faculty:* 21 full-time, 19 part-time/adjunct. *Students:* 78 full-time (31 women), 6 part-time (2 women); includes 4 minority (3 Asian Americans or Pacific Islanders, 1 Hispanic American), 31 international. Average age 32. 115 applicants, 20% accepted. In 2003, 16 master's, 11 doctorates awarded. *Degree requirements:* For master's, thesis or alternative, fieldwork, written exam; for doctorate, one foreign language, thesis/dissertation. *Entrance requirements:* For master's and doctorate, GRE General Test, GRE Subject Test, major in natural or physical science. Additional exam requirements/recommendations for international students: Required—TOEFL. Application fee: $75. *Expenses:* Tuition: Full-time $14,820. *Financial support:* Fellowships, teaching assistantships, Federal Work-Study and institutionally sponsored loans available. Support available to part-time students. Financial award application deadline: 1/5; financial award applicants required to submit FAFSA. *Faculty research:* Structural geology and stratigraphy, petrology, paleontology, rare gas, isotope and aqueous geochemistry. *Unit head:* Dr. William Menke, Chair, 212-864-4525, Fax: 845-365-8163.

Cornell University, Graduate School, Graduate Fields of Engineering, Field of Geological Sciences, Ithaca, NY 14853-0001. Offers economic geology (M Eng, MS, PhD); engineering geology (M Eng, MS, PhD); environmental geophysics (M Eng, MS, PhD); general geology (M Eng, MS, PhD); geobiology (M Eng, MS, PhD); geochemistry and isotope geology (M Eng, MS, PhD); geohydrology (M Eng, MS, PhD); geomorphology (M Eng, MS, PhD); geophysics (M Eng, MS, PhD); geotectonics (M Eng, MS, PhD); marine geology (M Eng, MS, PhD); mineralogy (M Eng, MS, PhD); paleontology (M Eng, MS, PhD); petroleum geology (M Eng, MS, PhD); petrology (M Eng, MS, PhD); planetary geology (M Eng, MS, PhD); Precambrian geology (M Eng, MS, PhD); Quaternary geology (M Eng, MS, PhD); rock mechanics (M Eng, MS, PhD); sedimentology (M Eng, MS, PhD); seismology (M Eng, MS, PhD); stratigraphy (M Eng, MS, PhD); structural geology (M Eng, MS, PhD). *Faculty:* 31 full-time. *Students:* 27 full-time (12 women); includes 1 minority (Asian American or Pacific Islander), 9 international. 74 applicants, 15% accepted, 7 enrolled. In 2003, 3 master's, 5 doctorates awarded. *Degree requirements:* For master's, thesis (MS); for doctorate, thesis/dissertation, comprehensive exam. *Entrance requirements:* For master's and doctorate, GRE General Test, 3 letters of recommendation. Additional exam requirements/recommendations for international students:

Geophysics

Cornell University (continued)

Required—TOEFL (minimum score 550 paper-based; 213 computer-based). *Application deadline:* For fall admission, 1/15 for domestic students. Applications are processed on a rolling basis. Application fee: $60. Electronic applications accepted. *Expenses:* Tuition: Full-time $28,630. One-time fee: $50 full-time. *Financial support:* In 2003–04, 21 students received support, including 6 fellowships with full tuition reimbursements available, 8 research assistantships with full tuition reimbursements available, 7 teaching assistantships with full tuition reimbursements available; institutionally sponsored loans, scholarships/grants, health care benefits, tuition waivers (full and partial), and unspecified assistantships also available. Financial award applicants required to submit FAFSA. *Faculty research:* Geophysics, structural geology, petrology, geochemistry, geodynamics. *Unit head:* Director of Graduate Studies, 607-255-3474, Fax: 607-254-4780. *Application contact:* Graduate Field Assistant, 607-255-3474, Fax: 607-254-4780, E-mail: gradprog@geology.cornell.edu.

See in-depth description on page 233.

Florida State University, Graduate Studies, College of Arts and Sciences, Interdisciplinary Program in Geophysical Fluid Dynamics, Tallahassee, FL 32306. Offers PhD. *Faculty:* 26 full-time (3 women). *Students:* 3 full-time (0 women), 2 international. Average age 30. 6 applicants, 33% accepted, 1 enrolled. *Degree requirements:* For doctorate, thesis/dissertation, departmental qualifying exam. *Entrance requirements:* For doctorate, GRE General Test, GRE Subject Test, minimum GPA of 3.0. Additional exam requirements/recommendations for international students: Required—TOEFL. *Application deadline:* For fall admission, 12/30 for domestic students. Application fee: $20. *Expenses:* Tuition, state resident: part-time $196 per credit hour. Tuition, nonresident: part-time $731 per credit hour. Part-time tuition and fees vary according to campus/location. *Financial support:* In 2003–04, 1 fellowship (averaging $15,000 per year), 2 research assistantships (averaging $17,000 per year) were awarded. Unspecified assistantships also available. Financial award applicants required to submit FAFSA. *Faculty research:* Hurricane dynamics, topography, convection, air-sea interaction, wave-mean flow interaction, numerical models. Total annual research expenditures: $569,000. *Unit head:* Dr. Carol A. Clayson, Director, 850-644-2488, Fax: 850-644-8972, E-mail: clayson@met.fsu.edu.

Georgia Institute of Technology, Graduate Studies and Research, College of Sciences, School of Earth and Atmospheric Sciences, Atlanta, GA 30332-0001. Offers atmospheric chemistry and air pollution (MS, PhD); atmospheric dynamics and climate (MS, PhD); geochemistry (MS, PhD); hydrologic cycle (MS, PhD); ocean sciences (MS, PhD); solid-earth and environmental geophysics (PhD); solid-earth and environmental geophysics (MS). Part-time programs available. *Students:* 80 full-time (40 women); includes 39 minority (5 African Americans, 31 Asian Americans or Pacific Islanders, 3 Hispanic Americans). 143 applicants, 18% accepted, 15 enrolled. In 2003, 14 master's, 6 doctorates awarded. Terminal master's awarded for partial completion of doctoral program. *Median time to degree:* Of those who began their doctoral program in fall 1995, 78% received their degree in 8 years or less. *Degree requirements:* For master's, thesis or alternative; for doctorate, thesis/dissertation, comprehensive exam. *Entrance requirements:* For master's and doctorate, GRE General Test, minimum GPA of 2.7. Additional exam requirements/recommendations for international students: Required—TOEFL (minimum score 550 paper-based; 213 computer-based). *Application deadline:* For fall admission, 1/15 priority date for domestic students, 1/15 priority date for international students; for spring admission, 1/1 for domestic students. Applications are processed on a rolling basis. Application fee: $50. *Expenses:* Tuition, state resident: part-time $1,925 per semester. Tuition, nonresident: part-time $7,700 per semester. Required fees: $434 per semester. Full-time tuition and fees vary according to program. *Financial support:* In 2003–04, 3 fellowships, 52 research assistantships (averaging $20,000 per year), 8 teaching assistantships were awarded. Career-related internships or fieldwork, Federal Work-Study, and institutionally sponsored loans also available. Financial award application deadline: 2/15. *Faculty research:* Geophysics, atmospheric chemistry, atmospheric dynamics, seismology. Total annual research expenditures: $5 million. *Unit head:* Dr. Judith A. Curry, Chair, 404-894-3948, Fax: 404-894-5638. *Application contact:* Derek M. Cunnold, Graduate Coordinator, 404-894-3814, Fax: 404-894-5638, E-mail: cunnold@eas.gatech.edu.

See in-depth description on page 237.

ICR Graduate School, Graduate Programs, Santee, CA 92071. Offers astro/geophysics (MS); biology (MS); geology (MS); science education (MS). Part-time programs available. *Faculty:* 6 full-time (0 women), 4 part-time/adjunct (1 woman). *Students:* 11 full-time (6 women), 18 part-time (9 women); includes 3 minority (2 African Americans, 1 Asian American or Pacific Islander). Average age 41. In 2003, 4 degrees awarded, leading to university research/teaching 50%, business/industry 50%. *Median time to degree:* Master's–4.6 years full-time. *Degree requirements:* For master's, thesis (for some programs), comprehensive exam (for some programs). *Entrance requirements:* For master's, bachelor's degree in science or science education, minimum GPA of 3.0 (undergraduate). *Application deadline:* Applications are processed on a rolling basis. Application fee: $30. *Expenses:* Tuition: Full-time $1,800; part-time $150 per unit. *Financial support:* In 2003–04, 25 students received support. *Faculty research:* Age of the earth, limits of variation, catastrophe, optimum methods for teaching. Total annual research expenditures: $200,000. *Unit head:* Kenneth B. Cumming, Dean, 619-448-0900, Fax: 619-448-3469. *Application contact:* Dr. Jack Kriege, Registrar, 619-448-0900 Ext. 6016, Fax: 619-448-3469, E-mail: jkriege@icr.org.

Idaho State University, Office of Graduate Studies, College of Arts and Sciences, Department of Geosciences, Pocatello, ID 83209. Offers geology (MS); geophysics/hydrology (MS); geotechnology (Postbaccalaureate Certificate); natural science (MNS). Part-time programs available. Postbaccalaureate distance learning degree programs offered. *Faculty:* 6 full-time (1 woman), 1 part-time/adjunct (0 women). *Students:* 18 full-time (3 women), 17 part-time (7 women), 1 international. Average age 32. In 2003, 6 master's, 3 other advanced degrees awarded. *Degree requirements:* For master's, thesis, comprehensive exam, registration (for some programs); for Postbaccalaureate Certificate, thesis optional. *Entrance requirements:* For master's and Postbaccalaureate Certificate, GRE General Test, 3 letters of recommendation. Additional exam requirements/recommendations for international students: Required—TOEFL (minimum score 550 paper-based; 213 computer-based). *Application deadline:* For fall admission, 7/1 priority date for domestic students, 7/1 priority date for international students; for spring admission, 12/1 priority date for domestic students, 12/1 priority date for international students. Applications are processed on a rolling basis. Application fee: $35. *Expenses:* Tuition, state resident: part-time $205 per credit. Tuition, nonresident: full-time $6,600; part-time $300 per credit. Required fees: $4,108. One-time fee: $35 full-time. *Financial support:* Research assistantships with full and partial tuition reimbursements, teaching assistantships with full and partial tuition reimbursements, career-related internships or fieldwork, Federal Work-Study, institutionally sponsored loans, and tuition waivers (full and partial) available. Financial award application deadline: 1/1. *Faculty research:* Structural geography, stratigraphy, geochemistry, volcanography, geomorphology. Total annual research expenditures: $541,774. *Unit head:* Dr. Scott Hughes, Chairman, 208-282-3365, Fax: 208-282-4414.

Indiana University Bloomington, Graduate School, College of Arts and Sciences, Department of Geological Sciences, Bloomington, IN 47405. Offers biogeochemistry (MS, PhD); environmental geosciences (MS, PhD); geobiology, stratigraphy, and sedimentology (MS, PhD); geochemistry (MS, PhD); geochemistry, mineralogy, and petrology (MS, PhD); geophysics (MS, PhD); geophysics, tectonics, and structural geology (MS, PhD). PhD offered through the University Graduate School. Part-time programs available. *Faculty:* 14 full-time (1 woman). *Students:* 32 full-time (16 women), 18 part-time (8 women); includes 4 minority (2 African Americans, 2 Asian Americans or Pacific Islanders), 23 international. Average age 29. In 2003, 10 master's, 2 doctorates awarded. Terminal master's awarded for partial completion of doctoral program. *Degree requirements:* For master's, one foreign language, thesis or alternative; for doctorate, thesis/dissertation. *Entrance requirements:* For master's and doctorate, GRE General Test. Additional exam requirements/recommendations for international students: Required—TOEFL. *Application deadline:* For fall admission, 1/15 priority date for domestic students, 12/15 priority date for international students; for spring admission, 9/1 priority date for domestic students, 9/1 priority date for international students. Applications are processed on a rolling basis. Application fee: $45 ($55 for international students). *Expenses:* Tuition, state resident: full-time $4,908; part-time $205 per credit. Tuition, nonresident: full-time $14,298; part-time $596 per credit. Required fees: $661. Tuition and fees vary according to campus/location and program. *Financial support:* In 2003–04, research assistantships with full and partial tuition reimbursements (averaging $11,000 per year); fellowships with tuition reimbursements, teaching assistantships with tuition reimbursements, career-related internships or fieldwork, Federal Work-Study, and institutionally sponsored loans also available. Financial award application deadline: 2/15. *Faculty research:* Geophysics, geochemistry, hydrogeology, igneous and metamorphic petrology and clay minerology. Total annual research expenditures: $289,139. *Unit head:* Dr. Christopher G. Maples, Chairman, 812-855-5582, Fax: 812-855-7899, E-mail: cmaples@indiana.edu. *Application contact:* Mary Iverson, Secretary, Committee for Graduate Studies, 812-855-7214, Fax: 812-855-7899, E-mail: geograd@indiana.edu.

The Johns Hopkins University, Zanvyl Krieger School of Arts and Sciences, The Morton K. Blaustein Department of Earth and Planetary Sciences, Program in Geophysics, Baltimore, MD 21218-2699. Offers MA, PhD. *Faculty:* 1 full-time (0 women). *Students:* 3 full-time (0 women), 2 international. Average age 24. *Degree requirements:* For doctorate, thesis/dissertation, registration. *Entrance requirements:* For master's and doctorate, GRE General Test. *Application deadline:* For fall admission, 1/15 for domestic students. Application fee: $60. Electronic applications accepted. *Expenses:* Tuition: Full-time $28,730; part-time $1,490 per course. Part-time tuition and fees vary according to course load, campus/location and program. *Financial support:* Application deadline: 3/14; *Application contact:* Carol Spangler, Academic Program Assistant, 410-516-7034, Fax: 410-516-7933, E-mail: cspangler@jhu.edu.

Louisiana State University and Agricultural and Mechanical College, Graduate School, College of Basic Sciences, Department of Geology and Geophysics, Baton Rouge, LA 70803. Offers MS, PhD. *Faculty:* 23 full-time (4 women). *Students:* 28 full-time (14 women), 3 part-time (1 woman); includes 5 minority (3 African Americans, 2 Hispanic Americans), 7 international. Average age 29. 33 applicants, 52% accepted, 6 enrolled. In 2003, 6 master's, 1 doctorate awarded. Terminal master's awarded for partial completion of doctoral program. *Degree requirements:* For master's and doctorate, thesis/dissertation. *Entrance requirements:* For master's and doctorate, GRE General Test, minimum GPA of 3.0. Additional exam requirements/recommendations for international students: Required—TOEFL (minimum score 550 paper-based; 213 computer-based). *Application deadline:* For fall admission, 1/25 priority date for domestic students, 5/15 priority date for international students. Applications are processed on a rolling basis. Application fee: $25. Electronic applications accepted. *Expenses:* Tuition, state resident: part-time $337 per hour. Tuition, nonresident: part-time $577 per hour. *Financial support:* In 2003–04, 20 students received support, including 4 fellowships (averaging $16,000 per year), 3 research assistantships with partial tuition reimbursements available (averaging $25,083 per year), 20 teaching assistantships with partial tuition reimbursements available (averaging $16,262 per year); career-related internships or fieldwork, Federal Work-Study, institutionally sponsored loans, and unspecified assistantships also available. Financial award application deadline: 3/15; financial award applicants required to submit FAFSA. *Faculty research:* Geophysics, geochemistry of sediments, isotope geochemistry, igneous and metamorphic petrology, micropaleontology. Total annual research expenditures: $436,889. *Unit head:* Dr. Laurie Anderson, Chair, 225-578-3353, Fax: 225-578-2302, E-mail: landerson@geol.lsu.edu. *Application contact:* Jeffrey Nunn, Graduate Coordinator, 225-578-6657, E-mail: jeff@geol.lsu.edu.

Massachusetts Institute of Technology, School of Science, Department of Earth, Atmospheric, and Planetary Sciences, Cambridge, MA 02139-4307. Offers atmospheric chemistry (PhD, Sc D); atmospheric science (SM, PhD, Sc D); climate physics and chemistry (PhD, Sc D); earth and planetary sciences (SM); geochemistry (PhD, Sc D); geology (PhD, Sc D); geophysics (PhD, Sc D); geosystems (SM); oceanography (SM, PhD, Sc D); planetary sciences (PhD, Sc D). *Faculty:* 37 full-time (3 women). *Students:* 147 full-time (61 women); includes 9 minority (4 Asian Americans or Pacific Islanders, 5 Hispanic Americans), 48 international. Average age 27. 176 applicants, 49% accepted, 31 enrolled. In 2003, 8 master's, 19 doctorates awarded. Terminal master's awarded for partial completion of doctoral program. *Degree requirements:* For master's, thesis/dissertation; for doctorate, thesis/dissertation, comprehensive exam. *Entrance requirements:* For master's, GRE General Test, GRE Subject Test (joint MIT/WHOI program); for doctorate, GRE General Test, GRE Subject Test (chemistry or physics for planetary science program). Additional exam requirements/recommendations for international students: Required—TOEFL (minimum score 577 paper-based; 233 computer-based). *Application deadline:* For fall admission, 1/5 for domestic students, 1/5 for international students; for spring admission, 11/1 for domestic students, 11/1 for international students. Application fee: $70. Electronic applications accepted. *Expenses:* Tuition: Full-time $29,400. Required fees: $200. *Financial support:* In 2003–04, 113 students received support, including 25 fellowships with tuition reimbursements available, 70 research assistantships with tuition reimbursements available (averaging $23,760 per year), 21 teaching assistantships with tuition reimbursements available (averaging $18,270 per year); Federal Work-Study, institutionally sponsored loans, scholarships/grants, health care benefits, and unspecified assistantships also available. *Faculty research:* Evolution of main features of the planetary system; origin, composition, structure, and state of the atmospheres, oceans, surfaces, and interiors of planets; dynamics of planets and satellite motions. Total annual research expenditures: $19.1 million. *Unit head:* Prof. Maria Zuber, 617-253-0149, Fax: 617-253-8298, E-mail: mtz@mit.edu. *Application contact:* Carol Sprague, Administrative Assistant, 617-253-3381, Fax: 617-253-8298, E-mail: eapsinfo@mit.edu.

Memorial University of Newfoundland, School of Graduate Studies, Department of Earth Sciences, St. John's, NL A1C 5S7, Canada. Offers geology (M Sc, PhD); geophysics (M Sc, PhD). Part-time programs available. *Students:* 43 full-time, 8 part-time. 37 applicants, 24% accepted, 7 enrolled. In 2003, 10 master's, 1 doctorate awarded. *Degree requirements:* For master's, thesis; for doctorate, thesis/dissertation, oral thesis defense, comprehensive exam. *Entrance requirements:* For master's, honors B Sc; for doctorate, M Sc. *Application deadline:* For fall admission, 3/31 for domestic students; for spring admission, 12/31 for domestic students. Applications are processed on a rolling basis. Application fee: $40. Electronic applications accepted. Tuition and fees charges are reported in Canadian dollars. *Expenses:* Tuition, state resident: part-time $733 Canadian dollars per semester. Tuition, nonresident: part-time $953 Canadian dollars per semester. Required fees: $194 Canadian dollars per year. Tuition and fees vary according to degree level and program. *Financial support:* Fellowships, research assistantships, teaching assistantships available. *Faculty research:* Geochemistry, sedimentology, paleoceanography and global change, mineral deposits, petroleum geology, hydrology. *Unit head:* Dr. J. Wright, Head, 709-737-2334, Fax: 709-737-2589, E-mail: jim@waves.esd.mun.ca. *Application contact:* Dr. Ali Aksu, Graduate Officer, 709-737-8385, Fax: 709-737-2589, E-mail: aaksu@sparky2.esd.ucs.mun.ca.

Michigan Technological University, Graduate School, College of Engineering, Department of Geological and Mining Engineering and Sciences, Program in Geophysics, Houghton, MI 49931-1295. Offers MS. Part-time programs available. *Faculty:* 14 full-time (1 woman), 3 part-time/adjunct (1 woman). *Students:* 1 full-time (0 women). Average age 24. In 2003, 2 degrees awarded. *Degree requirements:* For master's, comprehensive exam, registration. *Entrance requirements:* Additional exam requirements/recommendations for international students: Required—TOEFL. *Application deadline:* For fall admission, 3/15 for domestic students. Applications are processed on a rolling basis. Application fee: $40 ($45 for international students). Electronic applications accepted. Tuition, nonresident: full-time $9,552; part-time $398 per credit. Required fees: $768. *Financial support:* In 2003–04, fellowships with full tuition reimbursements (averaging $13,500 per year), research assistantships with full tuition reimbursements (averaging $8,950 per year), teaching assistantships with full tuition reimbursements (averaging $8,950 per year) were awarded. Career-related internships or fieldwork, Federal Work-Study, institutionally sponsored loans, scholarships/grants, traineeships, unspecified assistantships, and co-op also available. Support available to part-time students. Financial award application deadline: 2/1; financial award applicants required to submit FAFSA.

Announcement: The Department of Geological and Mining Engineering and Sciences offers 10 graduate programs that allow students to either focus or broaden their studies in geology, geological and mining engineering, and geophysics to explore fundamental and applied issues related to the earth, natural resource development/protection, and natural hazard mitigation—through the Peace Corps.

See in-depth description on page 243.

New Mexico Institute of Mining and Technology, Graduate Studies, Department of Earth and Environmental Science, Program in Geophysics, Socorro, NM 87801. Offers MS, PhD. *Students:* 13 full-time (3 women), 4 international. Average age 31. 13 applicants, 3 enrolled. In 2003, 2 master's awarded. *Degree requirements:* For master's, thesis optional; for doctorate, thesis/dissertation. *Entrance requirements:* For master's, GRE General Test; for doctorate, GRE General Test, GRE Subject Test. Additional exam requirements/recommendations for international students: Required—TOEFL (minimum score 540 paper-based; 207 computer-based). *Application deadline:* For fall admission, 3/1 for domestic students; for spring admission, 6/1 for domestic students. Applications are processed on a rolling basis. Application fee: $16 ($30 for international students). *Expenses:* Tuition, state resident: full-time $2,276; part-time $126 per credit. Tuition, nonresident: full-time $9,170; part-time $509 per credit. Required fees: $924; $27 per credit. $214 per term. Part-time tuition and fees vary according to course load. *Financial support:* In 2003–04, 9 research assistantships (averaging $12,648 per year), 2 teaching assistantships with full and partial tuition reimbursements (averaging $5,540 per year) were awarded. Fellowships, Federal Work-Study, institutionally sponsored loans, and unspecified assistantships also available. Financial award application deadline: 3/1; financial award applicants required to submit CSS PROFILE or FAFSA. *Faculty research:* Earthquake and volcanic seismology, subduction zone tectonics, network seismology, physical properties of sediments in fault zones. *Unit head:* Dr. Harold J. Tobin, Coordinator, 505-835-5920, Fax: 505-835-6436, E-mail: geos@nmt.edu. *Application contact:* Dr. David B. Johnson, Dean of Graduate Studies, 505-835-5513, Fax: 505-835-5476, E-mail: graduate@nmt.edu.

Ohio University, Graduate Studies, College of Arts and Sciences, Department of Geological Sciences, Athens, OH 45701-2979. Offers environmental geochemistry (MS); environmental geology (MS); environmental/hydrology (MS); geology (MS); geology education (MS); geomorphology/surficial processes (MS); geophysics (MS); hydrogeology (MS); sedimentology (MS); structure/tectonics (MS). Part-time programs available. *Faculty:* 10 full-time (3 women), 4 part-time/adjunct (1 woman). *Students:* 13 full-time (4 women), 4 part-time (1 woman); includes 1 minority (Hispanic American), 4 international. Average age 25. 11 applicants, 45% accepted, 4 enrolled. In 2003, 8 degrees awarded. *Median time to degree:* Master's–2.5 years full-time. *Degree requirements:* For master's, thesis, thesis proposal defense. *Entrance requirements:* Additional exam requirements/recommendations for international students: Required—TOEFL (minimum score 550 paper-based; 217 computer-based). *Application deadline:* For fall admission, 2/1 priority date for domestic students, 1/1 priority date for international students. Application fee: $45. *Expenses:* Tuition, state resident: full-time $2,651; part-time $328 per credit. Tuition, nonresident: full-time $5,095; part-time $632 per credit. Tuition and fees vary according to program. *Financial support:* In 2003–04, 16 students received support, including 3 research assistantships with full tuition reimbursements available (averaging $11,000 per year), 13 teaching assistantships with full tuition reimbursements available (averaging $11,000 per year); institutionally sponsored loans, scholarships/grants, tuition waivers (full), and unspecified assistantships also available. Financial award application deadline: 3/15. *Faculty research:* Geoscience education, tectonics, flurial geomorphology, invertebrate paleontology, mine/hydrology. Total annual research expenditures: $506,400. *Unit head:* Dr. Douglas Green, Chair, 740-593-6896, Fax: 740-593-0486, E-mail: green@ohio.edu. *Application contact:* Dr. Dina L. Lopez, Graduate Chair, 740-593-9435, Fax: 740-593-0486, E-mail: lopezd@ohio.edu.

Oregon State University, Graduate School, College of Oceanic and Atmospheric Sciences, Program in Geophysics, Corvallis, OR 97331. Offers MA, MS, PhD. *Students:* 1 (woman) full-time, 1 international. In 2003, 1 degree awarded. Terminal master's awarded for partial completion of doctoral program. *Degree requirements:* For master's, thesis optional; for doctorate, thesis/dissertation. *Entrance requirements:* For master's and doctorate, GRE General Test, minimum GPA of 3.0 in last 90 hours. Additional exam requirements/recommendations for international students: Required—TOEFL. *Application deadline:* For fall admission, 2/1 for domestic students. Applications are processed on a rolling basis. Application fee: $50. *Expenses:* Tuition, state resident: full-time $8,139; part-time $301 per credit. Tuition, nonresident: full-time $14,376; part-time $532 per credit. Required fees: $1,227. *Financial support:* Fellowships, research assistantships, teaching assistantships, career-related internships or fieldwork, Federal Work-Study, and institutionally sponsored loans available. Support available to part-time students. Financial award application deadline: 2/1. *Faculty research:* Seismic waves; gravitational, geothermal, and electromagnetic fields; rock magnetism; paleomagnetism. *Unit head:* Irma Delson, Assistant Director, Student Services, 541-737-5189, Fax: 541-737-2064, E-mail: student_adviser@oce.orst.edu.

The Pennsylvania State University University Park Campus, Graduate School, College of Earth and Mineral Sciences, Department of Geosciences, Program in Geophysics, State College, University Park, PA 16802-1503. Offers MS, PhD. *Entrance requirements:* For master's and doctorate, GRE General Test. Additional exam requirements/recommendations for international students: Required—TOEFL. Application fee: $45.

See in-depth description on page 249.

Princeton University, Graduate School, Department of Geosciences, Princeton, NJ 08544-1019. Offers atmospheric and oceanic sciences (PhD); geological and geophysical sciences (PhD). *Faculty:* 29 full-time (2 women), 2 part-time/adjunct (0 women). *Students:* 21 full-time (10 women), 11 international. Average age 24. 51 applicants, 31% accepted, 6 enrolled. In 2003, 6 doctorates awarded, leading to continued full-time study 100%. *Median time to degree:* Doctorate–5.08 years full-time. *Degree requirements:* For doctorate, one foreign language, thesis/dissertation. *Entrance requirements:* For doctorate, GRE General Test. Additional exam requirements/recommendations for international students: Required—TOEFL (minimum score 600 paper-based; 250 computer-based). *Application deadline:* For fall admission, 12/31 for domestic students, 12/1 for international students. Application fee: $80 ($55 for international students). Electronic applications accepted. *Expenses:* Tuition: Full-time $29,910. Required fees: $810. *Financial support:* In 2003–04, 8 fellowships with full tuition reimbursements (averaging $16,500 per year), 12 research assistantships with full tuition reimbursements (averaging $30,570 per year), 11 teaching assistantships with full tuition reimbursements (averaging $22,042 per year) were awarded. Federal Work-Study, institutionally sponsored loans, and summer salary is $7000 also available. Financial award application deadline: 1/2. *Faculty research:* Biogeochemistry, climate science, earth history, regional geology and tectonics, solid–earth geophysics. Total annual research expenditures: $19 million. *Unit head:* Prof. Guust Nolet, Director of Graduate Studies, 609-258-4128, Fax: 609-258-1274, E-mail: nolet@princeton.edu. *Application contact:* Janice Yip, Director of Graduate Admissions, 609-258-3034, Fax: 609-258-6180, E-mail: gsadmit@princeton.edu.

Rensselaer Polytechnic Institute, Graduate School, School of Science, Department of Earth and Environmental Sciences, Troy, NY 12180-3590. Offers environmental chemistry (MS, PhD); geochemistry (MS, PhD); geology (MS, PhD); geophysics (MS, PhD); petrology (MS, PhD). Part-time programs available. *Faculty:* 7 full-time (0 women). *Students:* 15 full-time (7 women); includes 3 minority (all Asian Americans or Pacific Islanders) Average age 24. 35 applicants, 11% accepted. In 2003, 4 master's, 1 doctorate awarded. Terminal master's awarded for partial completion of doctoral program. *Degree requirements:* For master's, thesis (for some programs), comprehensive exam; for doctorate, thesis/dissertation, comprehensive exam. *Entrance requirements:* For master's and doctorate, GRE General Test. Additional exam requirements/recommendations for international students: Required—TOEFL. *Application deadline:* For fall admission, 1/15 for domestic students. Applications are processed on a rolling basis. Application fee: $45. Electronic applications accepted. *Expenses:* Tuition: Full-time $27,700; part-time $1,320 per credit. Required fees: $1,470. *Financial support:* In 2003–04, 9 research assistantships with full tuition reimbursements (averaging $12,000 per year), 5 teaching assistantships with full tuition reimbursements (averaging $12,000 per year) were awarded. Fellowships with full tuition reimbursements, career-related internships or fieldwork, institutionally sponsored loans, and scholarships/grants also available. Financial award application deadline: 2/1; financial award applicants required to submit FAFSA. *Faculty research:* Mantel geochemistry, contaminant geochemistry, seismology, GPS geodesy, remote sensing petrology. Total annual research expenditures: $1.3 million. *Unit head:* Dr. Frank Spear, Chair, 518-276-6474, Fax: 518-276-6680, E-mail: ees@rpi.edu. *Application contact:* Dr. Steven Roecker, Professor, 518-276-6474, Fax: 518-276-6680, E-mail: ees@rpi.edu.

Rice University, Graduate Programs, Wiess School of Natural Sciences, Professional Master's Program in Subsurface Geosciences, Houston, TX 77251-1892. Offers geophysics (MS). Part-time programs available. *Degree requirements:* For master's, internship. *Entrance requirements:* For master's, GRE, letters of recommendation (4). Additional exam requirements/recommendations for international students: Required—TOEFL (minimum score 600 paper-based; 250 computer-based). Electronic applications accepted. *Expenses:* Tuition: Full-time $19,700; part-time $1,096 per hour. *Faculty research:* Seismology, geodynamics, wave propogation, bio-geochemistry, remote sensing.

Saint Louis University, Graduate School, College of Arts and Sciences and Graduate School, Department of Earth and Atmospheric Sciences, St. Louis, MO 63103-2097. Offers geophysics (PhD); geoscience (MS, MS(R)); meteorology (M Pr Met, MS(R), PhD). Part-time programs available. *Faculty:* 14 full-time (7 women), 12 part-time/adjunct (6 women). *Students:* 19 full-time (5 women), 6 part-time (1 woman); includes 2 minority (1 African American, 1 Asian American or Pacific Islander), 11 international. Average age 30. 27 applicants, 85% accepted, 7 enrolled. In 2003, 2 master's, 1 doctorate awarded. *Degree requirements:* For master's, comprehensive oral exam, thesis for MS(R); for doctorate, thesis/dissertation, preliminary exams. *Entrance requirements:* For master's and doctorate, GRE General Test. Additional exam requirements/recommendations for international students: Required—TOEFL (minimum score 550 paper-based; 213 computer-based). *Application deadline:* For fall admission, 7/1 for domestic students, 7/1 for international students; for spring admission, 11/1 for domestic students, 11/1 for international students. Applications are processed on a rolling basis. Application fee: $40. *Expenses:* Tuition: Part-time $690 per credit hour. Required fees: $59 per semester. Tuition and fees vary according to program. *Financial support:* In 2003–04, 23 students received support, including 6 research assistantships with tuition reimbursements available, 6 teaching assistantships with tuition reimbursements available; unspecified assistantships also available. Financial award application deadline: 6/1; financial award applicants required to submit FAFSA. *Faculty research:* Seismology and tectonics, earth's core and structure, geochemistry, heavy precipitation convective systems, squall lines and tropical cyclones. *Unit head:* Dr. David Crossley, Acting Chairperson, 314-977-3131, Fax: 314-977-3117, E-mail: crossley@slu.edu. *Application contact:* Gary Behrman, Associate Dean of the Graduate School, 314-977-3827, Fax: 314-977-3943, E-mail: behrmang@slu.edu.

Southern Methodist University, Dedman College, Department of Geological Sciences, Program in Exploration Geophysics, Dallas, TX 75275. Offers MS. Part-time programs available. *Degree requirements:* For master's, qualifying exam, thesis optional. *Entrance requirements:* For master's, GRE General Test, minimum GPA of 3.0, letters of recommendation. Additional exam requirements/recommendations for international students: Required—TOEFL; Recommended—TSE. *Expenses:* Tuition: Full-time $11,362; part-time $874 per credit. Required fees: $112 per credit. Tuition and fees vary according to course load and program. *Faculty research:* Geothermal energy, seismology.

Southern Methodist University, Dedman College, Department of Geological Sciences, Program in Geophysics, Dallas, TX 75275. Offers applied geophysics (MS); geophysics (MS, PhD). Part-time programs available. *Degree requirements:* For master's, thesis (for some programs), qualifying exam; for doctorate, thesis/dissertation, qualifying exam. *Entrance requirements:* For master's and doctorate, GRE General Test, minimum GPA of 3.0, letters of recommendation. Additional exam requirements/recommendations for international students: Required—TOEFL; Recommended—TSE. *Expenses:* Tuition: Full-time $11,362; part-time $874 per credit. Required fees: $112 per credit. Tuition and fees vary according to course load and program. *Faculty research:* Seismology, heat flow, tectonics.

Stanford University, School of Earth Sciences, Department of Geophysics, Stanford, CA 94305-9991. Offers MS, PhD. *Faculty:* 14 full-time (2 women). *Students:* 51 full-time (15 women), 11 part-time (4 women); includes 1 minority (Hispanic American), 34 international. Average age 29. 56 applicants, 39% accepted. In 2003, 6 master's, 9 doctorates awarded. Terminal master's awarded for partial completion of doctoral program. *Degree requirements:* For master's and doctorate, thesis/dissertation. *Entrance requirements:* For master's and doctorate, GRE General Test. Additional exam requirements/recommendations for international students: Required—TOEFL. *Application deadline:* For fall admission, 1/15 for domestic students. Application fee: $65 ($80 for international students). Electronic applications accepted. *Expenses:* Tuition: Full-time $28,563. *Unit head:* Jerry M. Harris, Chair, 650-723-0496, Fax: 650-725-2032, E-mail: harris@pangea.stanford.edu. *Application contact:* Administrative Assistant, 650-723-4746, Fax: 650-725-7344, E-mail: kehoe@stanford.edu.

Texas A&M University, College of Geosciences, Department of Geology and Geophysics, College Station, TX 77843. Offers MS, PhD. *Faculty:* 25 full-time (1 woman), 1 part-time/adjunct (0 women). *Students:* 85 full-time (26 women), 21 part-time (8 women); includes 6 minority (1 African American, 1 American Indian/Alaska Native, 2 Asian Americans or Pacific Islanders, 2 Hispanic Americans), 43 international. Average age 31. 57 applicants, 86% accepted, 23 enrolled. In 2003, 28 master's, 6 doctorates awarded. *Degree requirements:* For master's and doctorate, thesis/dissertation. *Entrance requirements:* For master's and doctorate, GRE General Test. Additional exam requirements/recommendations for international students: Required—TOEFL. *Application deadline:* For fall admission, 3/1 priority date for domestic students, 1/15 priority date for international students; for spring admission, 10/1 priority date for domestic students, 8/15 priority date for international students. Applications are processed on a rolling basis. Application fee: $50 ($75 for international students). Electronic applications accepted. *Expenses:* Tuition, state resident: full-time $3,420. Tuition, nonresident: full-time $9,084. Required fees: $1,861. *Financial support:* In 2003–04, 76 students received support, including 20 fellowships with partial tuition reimbursements available (averaging $1,000 per year), 15 research assistantships with partial tuition reimbursements available (averaging $11,925 per year), 50 teaching assistantships with partial tuition reimbursements available (averaging $11,925 per year); Federal Work-Study, institutionally sponsored loans, scholarships/grants, health care benefits, tuition waivers (partial), and unspecified assistantships also available. Financial award application deadline: 3/1; financial award applicants required to submit FAFSA. *Faculty research:* Environmental and engineering geology and geophysics, petroleum geology, tectonophysics, geochemistry. *Unit head:* Dr. Rick Carlson, Head, 979-845-2451, Fax: 979-845-6162. *Application contact:* Robert K. Popp, Graduate Adviser, 979-845-2451, Fax: 979-845-6162, E-mail: popp@geo.tamu.edu.

The University of Akron, Graduate School, Buchtel College of Arts and Sciences, Department of Geology, Program in Geophysics, Akron, OH 44325-0001. Offers MS. *Students:* 2 full-time (0 women), 1 international. Average age 35. 2 applicants, 50% accepted, 0 enrolled. *Degree requirements:* For master's, thesis, seminar, comprehensive exam. *Entrance requirements:* For master's, minimum GPA of 2.75. Additional exam requirements/recommendations for international students: Required—TOEFL (minimum score 550 paper-based; 213 computer-based), Michigan English Language Assessment Battery. *Application deadline:* For fall admission, 3/1 for domestic students. Applications are processed on a rolling basis. Application fee: $40 ($60 for international students). *Expenses:* Tuition, state

Geophysics

The University of Akron (continued)

resident: part-time $277 per credit hour. Tuition, nonresident: part-time $476 per credit hour. *Unit head:* Dr. David McConnell, Director of Graduate Studies, 330-972-8047, E-mail: mcconnell@uakron.edu.

University of Alaska Fairbanks, College of Science, Engineering and Mathematics, Department of Geology and Geophysics, Fairbanks, AK 99775-7520. Offers geology (MS, PhD); geophysics (MS, PhD); geoscience (MAT). Part-time programs available. Terminal master's awarded for partial completion of doctoral program. *Degree requirements:* For master's and doctorate, thesis/dissertation, comprehensive exam, registration. *Entrance requirements:* For master's and doctorate, GRE General Test, GRE Subject Test. Additional exam requirements/recommendations for international students: Required—TOEFL. Electronic applications accepted. *Faculty research:* Glacial surging, Alaska as geologic fragments, natural zeolites, seismology, volcanology.

University of Alberta, Faculty of Graduate Studies and Research, Department of Physics, Edmonton, AB T6G 2E1, Canada. Offers astrophysics (M Sc, PhD); condensed matter (M Sc, PhD); geophysics (M Sc, PhD); medical physics (M Sc, PhD); subatomic physics (M Sc, PhD). *Faculty:* 36 full-time (3 women), 7 part-time/adjunct (0 women). *Students:* 56 full-time (6 women), 16 part-time (2 women), 25 international. 85 applicants, 35% accepted. In 2003, 7 master's, 10 doctorates awarded. *Degree requirements:* For master's and doctorate, thesis/dissertation. *Entrance requirements:* For master's and doctorate, minimum GPA of 7.0 on a 9.0 scale. Additional exam requirements/recommendations for international students: Required—TOEFL. *Application deadline:* For fall admission, 2/15 for domestic students. Applications are processed on a rolling basis. Tuition charges are reported in Canadian dollars. Tuition, nonresident: full-time $3,921 Canadian dollars. International tuition: $7,113 Canadian dollars full-time. *Financial support:* In 2003–04, 45 students received support, including 6 fellowships with partial tuition reimbursements available, 40 teaching assistantships; research assistantships, career-related internships or fieldwork, institutionally sponsored loans, and scholarships/grants also available. Financial award application deadline: 2/15. *Faculty research:* Cosmology, astroparticle physics, high-intermediate energy, magnetism, superconductivity. Total annual research expenditures: $3.1 million. *Unit head:* Dr. Richard Sydora, Associate Chair, 780-492-1072, E-mail: assoc-chair@phys.ualberta.ca. *Application contact:* Lynn Chandler, Program Advisor, 780-492-1072, Fax: 780-492-0714, E-mail: lynn@phys.ualberta.ca.

The University of British Columbia, Faculty of Graduate Studies, Faculty of Science, Department of Earth and Ocean Sciences, Vancouver, BC V6T 1Z1, Canada. Offers atmospheric science (M Sc, PhD); geological engineering (M Eng, MA Sc, PhD); geological sciences (M Sc, PhD); geophysics (M Sc, MA Sc, PhD); oceanography (M Sc, PhD). *Faculty:* 42 full-time (5 women), 16 part-time/adjunct (0 women). *Students:* 127 full-time (44 women), 1 (woman) part-time. Average age 27. 80 applicants, 41% accepted, 25 enrolled. In 2003, 21 master's, 8 doctorates awarded. *Degree requirements:* For master's, thesis (for some programs); for doctorate, thesis/dissertation, comprehensive exam. *Entrance requirements:* Additional exam requirements/recommendations for international students: Required—TOEFL (minimum score 600 paper-based; 250 computer-based). *Application deadline:* For fall admission, 3/1 for domestic students; for winter admission, 7/1 for domestic students. Applications are processed on a rolling basis. Application fee: $90 Canadian dollars ($150 Canadian dollars for international students). Electronic applications accepted. *Financial support:* In 2003–04, fellowships (averaging $16,000 per year), research assistantships (averaging $13,000 per year), teaching assistantships (averaging $4,500 per year) were awarded. Federal Work-Study, institutionally sponsored loans, scholarships/grants, tuition waivers (full and partial), and unspecified assistantships also available. *Unit head:* Dr. Paul L. Smith, Head, 604-822-6456, Fax: 604-822-6088, E-mail: psmith@cos.ubc.ca. *Application contact:* Alex Allen, Graduate Secretary, 604-822-2713, Fax: 604-822-6088, E-mail: aallen@eos.ubc.ca.

University of Calgary, Faculty of Graduate Studies, Faculty of Science, Department of Geology and Geophysics, Calgary, AB T2N 1N4, Canada. Offers geology (M Sc, PhD); geophysics (M Sc, PhD). Part-time programs available. *Faculty:* 32 full-time (3 women), 16 part-time/adjunct (1 woman). *Students:* 109 full-time (43 women). 106 applicants, 43% accepted, 26 enrolled. In 2003, 15 master's, 5 doctorates awarded. Terminal master's awarded for partial completion of doctoral program. *Degree requirements:* For master's, thesis; for doctorate, thesis/dissertation, candidacy exam. *Entrance requirements:* For master's, B Sc; for doctorate, B Sc (Honors) or M Sc. Additional exam requirements/recommendations for international students: Required—TOEFL. *Application deadline:* For fall admission, 2/1 priority date for domestic students, 2/1 priority date for international students; for winter admission, 9/1 for domestic students. Applications are processed on a rolling basis. Application fee: $60. Electronic applications accepted. Tuition, nonresident: full-time $4,765. Tuition and fees vary according to degree level, program and student level. *Financial support:* In 2003–04, 50 students received support, including 9 fellowships, 15 teaching assistantships; career-related internships or fieldwork, institutionally sponsored loans, and scholarships/grants also available. Financial award application deadline: 2/1. *Faculty research:* Geochemistry, petrology, paleontology, stratigraphy, exploration and solid-earth geophysics. *Unit head:* Larry R. Lines, Head, 403-220-8863, Fax: 403-284-0074, E-mail: lrlines@ucalgary.ca. *Application contact:* Cathy H. Hubbell, Graduate Program Administrator, 403-220-3254, Fax: 403-284-0074, E-mail: geosciencegrad@ucalgary.ca.

University of California, Berkeley, Graduate Division, College of Letters and Science, Department of Earth and Planetary Science, Division of Geophysics, Berkeley, CA 94720-1500. Offers MA, MS, PhD. *Students:* 28 applicants, 43% accepted. In 2003, 1 master's, 3 doctorates awarded. Terminal master's awarded for partial completion of doctoral program. *Degree requirements:* For master's, oral exam; for doctorate, thesis/dissertation, candidacy exams, comprehensive exam. *Entrance requirements:* For master's and doctorate, GRE General Test, minimum GPA of 3.0. *Application deadline:* For fall admission, 1/12 for domestic students; for spring admission, 9/1 for domestic students. Application fee: $60. International tuition: $12,491 full-time. Required fees: $5,484. *Financial support:* Fellowships, research assistantships, teaching assistantships, Federal Work-Study and unspecified assistantships available. Financial award application deadline: 1/12. *Faculty research:* High-pressure geophysics and seismology. *Application contact:* Margie Winn, Graduate Assistant for Admissions, 510-642-5574, Fax: 510-643-6220, E-mail: margie@eps.berkeley.edu.

University of California, Los Angeles, Graduate Division, College of Letters and Science, Department of Earth and Space Sciences, Program in Geophysics and Space Physics, Los Angeles, CA 90095. Offers MS, PhD. *Degree requirements:* For master's, comprehensive exams or thesis; for doctorate, thesis/dissertation, oral and written qualifying exams. *Entrance requirements:* For master's, GRE General Test, minimum GPA of 3.0; for doctorate, GRE General Test, minimum undergraduate GPA of 3.0. Electronic applications accepted. Tuition, nonresident: full-time $12,245. Required fees: $6,318.

University of California, Santa Barbara, Graduate Division, College of Letters and Sciences, Division of Mathematics, Life, and Physical Sciences, Department of Geological Sciences, Santa Barbara, CA 93106. Offers geological sciences (MS, PhD); geophysics (MS). *Faculty:* 25 full-time (4 women). *Students:* 51 full-time (19 women); includes 5 minority (3 Asian Americans or Pacific Islanders, 2 Hispanic Americans), 6 international. Average age 25. 91 applicants, 33% accepted, 14 enrolled. In 2003, 5 master's, 4 doctorates awarded. Terminal master's awarded for partial completion of doctoral program. *Median time to degree:* Master's–2 years full-time; doctorate–5 years full-time. *Degree requirements:* For master's, thesis, thesis or exam, comprehensive exam, registration; for doctorate, thesis/dissertation, comprehensive exam, registration. *Entrance requirements:* For master's and doctorate, GRE General Test. Additional exam requirements/recommendations for international students: Required—TOEFL (minimum score 550 paper-based; 213 computer-based). *Application deadline:* For fall admission, 1/15 for domestic students, 1/15 for international students. Application fee: $60. Electronic applications accepted. *Expenses:* Tuition, state resident: full-time $7,188. Tuition, nonresident: full-time $19,608. *Financial support:* In 2003–04, 45 students received support, including 3 fellowships with full and partial tuition reimbursements available (averaging $7,000 per year), 18 research assistantships with full and partial tuition reimbursements available, 15 teaching assistantships with full and partial tuition reimbursements available; career-related internships or fieldwork, Federal Work-Study, scholarships/grants, traineeships, health care benefits, and tuition waivers (full and partial) also available. Financial award application deadline: 1/1; financial award applicants required to submit FAFSA. *Faculty research:* Structure and tectonics, marine geology, chemical oceanography, geophysics, geobiology and paleobotany. *Unit head:* Dr. James Mattinson, Chair, 805-893-2827, Fax: 805-893-2314. *Application contact:* Susan Leska, Graduate Program Assistant, 805-893-3329, Fax: 805-893-2314, E-mail: leska@geol.ucsb.edu.

University of Chicago, Division of the Physical Sciences, Department of the Geophysical Sciences, Chicago, IL 60637-1513. Offers atmospheric sciences (SM, PhD); earth sciences (SM, PhD); paleobiology (PhD); planetary and space sciences (SM, PhD). *Faculty:* 24 full-time (3 women). *Students:* 29 full-time (13 women); includes 1 minority (Hispanic American), 12 international. Average age 30. 74 applicants, 22% accepted. In 2003, 2 master's, 5 doctorates awarded. Terminal master's awarded for partial completion of doctoral program. *Median time to degree:* Doctorate–6 years full-time. *Entrance requirements:* For master's and doctorate, GRE General Test. Additional exam requirements/recommendations for international students: Required—TOEFL. *Application deadline:* For fall admission, 1/15 for domestic students, 1/15 for international students. Application fee: $55. Electronic applications accepted. *Financial support:* In 2003–04, 29 students received support, including research assistantships with full tuition reimbursements available (averaging $17,196 per year), teaching assistantships with full tuition reimbursements available (averaging $18,096 per year); fellowships, Federal Work-Study, institutionally sponsored loans, scholarships/grants, tuition waivers (partial), and unspecified assistantships also available. Financial award application deadline: 1/15. *Faculty research:* Climatology, evolutionary paleontology, petrology, geochemistry, oceanic sciences. *Unit head:* Dr. David Rowley, Chairman, 773-702-8102, Fax: 773-702-9505. *Application contact:* David J. Leslie, Graduate Student Services Coordinator, 773-702-8180, Fax: 773-702-9505, E-mail: info@geosci.uchicago.edu.

University of Colorado at Boulder, Graduate School, College of Arts and Sciences, Department of Geological Sciences, Boulder, CO 80309. Offers geology (MS, PhD); geophysics (PhD). *Faculty:* 26 full-time (6 women). *Students:* 54 full-time (30 women), 13 part-time (9 women); includes 7 minority (1 Asian American or Pacific Islander, 6 Hispanic Americans), 10 international. Average age 30. 34 applicants, 59% accepted. In 2003, 11 master's, 8 doctorates awarded. Terminal master's awarded for partial completion of doctoral program. *Degree requirements:* For master's and doctorate, thesis/dissertation, comprehensive exam. *Entrance requirements:* For master's and doctorate, GRE General Test, minimum GPA of 2.75. *Application deadline:* For fall admission, 1/15 for domestic students. Application fee: $50 ($60 for international students). *Expenses:* Tuition, state resident: full-time $2,122. Tuition, nonresident: full-time $9,754. Tuition and fees vary according to course load and program. *Financial support:* In 2003–04, 5 fellowships with full tuition reimbursements (averaging $10,636 per year), 14 research assistantships with full tuition reimbursements (averaging $19,327 per year), 14 teaching assistantships with full tuition reimbursements (averaging $15,668 per year) were awarded. Federal Work-Study, institutionally sponsored loans, scholarships/grants, and tuition waivers (full) also available. Financial award application deadline: 1/15. *Faculty research:* Sedimentology, stratigraphy, economic geology of mineral deposits, fossil fuels, hydrogeology and water resources. Total annual research expenditures: $16.3 million. *Unit head:* Charles R. Stern, Chair, 303-492-2330, Fax: 303-492-2606, E-mail: sternc@stripe.colorado.edu. *Application contact:* Graduate Secretary, 303-492-2607, Fax: 303-492-2606, E-mail: geolinfo@colorado.edu.

University of Colorado at Boulder, Graduate School, College of Arts and Sciences, Department of Physics, Boulder, CO 80309. Offers chemical physics (PhD); geophysics (PhD); liquid crystal science and technology (PhD); mathematical physics (PhD); medical physics (PhD); optical sciences and engineering (PhD); physics (MS, PhD). *Faculty:* 43 full-time (3 women). *Students:* 148 full-time (24 women), 42 part-time (8 women); includes 11 minority (2 African Americans, 1 American Indian/Alaska Native, 6 Asian Americans or Pacific Islanders, 2 Hispanic Americans), 56 international. Average age 27. 75 applicants, 65% accepted. In 2003, 1 master's, 20 doctorates awarded. Terminal master's awarded for partial completion of doctoral program. *Degree requirements:* For master's, thesis or alternative, comprehensive exam; for doctorate, thesis/dissertation, comprehensive exam. *Entrance requirements:* For master's and doctorate, GRE General Test, GRE Subject Test, minimum undergraduate GPA of 3.0. Additional exam requirements/recommendations for international students: Required—TOEFL. *Application deadline:* For fall admission, 1/15 for domestic students; for spring admission, 11/1 for domestic students. Applications are processed on a rolling basis. Application fee: $50 ($60 for international students). Electronic applications accepted. *Expenses:* Tuition, state resident: full-time $2,122. Tuition, nonresident: full-time $9,754. Tuition and fees vary according to course load and program. *Financial support:* In 2003–04, 14 fellowships with full tuition reimbursements (averaging $23,854 per year), 34 research assistantships with full tuition reimbursements (averaging $18,725 per year), 25 teaching assistantships with full tuition reimbursements (averaging $15,113 per year) were awarded. Scholarships/grants also available. Financial award application deadline: 1/15. *Faculty research:* Atomic and molecular physics, nuclear physics, condensed matter, elementary particle physics, laser or optical physics. Total annual research expenditures: $19.1 million. *Unit head:* John Cumalat, Chair, 303-492-6952, Fax: 303-492-3352, E-mail: jcumalat@pizero.colorado.edu. *Application contact:* Graduate Program Assistant, 303-492-6954, Fax: 303-492-3352, E-mail: phys@bogart.colorado.edu.

University of Hawaii at Manoa, Graduate Division, School of Ocean and Earth Science and Technology, Department of Geology and Geophysics, Honolulu, HI 96822. Offers high-pressure geophysics and geochemistry (MS, PhD); hydrogeology and engineering geology (MS, PhD); marine geology and geophysics (MS, PhD); planetary geosciences and remote sensing (MS, PhD); seismology and solid-earth geophysics (MS, PhD); volcanology, petrology, and geochemistry (MS, PhD). *Faculty:* 73 full-time (13 women), 16 part-time/adjunct (1 woman). *Students:* 57 full-time (19 women); includes 3 minority (1 African American, 2 Asian Americans or Pacific Islanders), 17 international. Average age 29. 116 applicants, 15% accepted, 12 enrolled. Terminal master's awarded for partial completion of doctoral program. *Median time to degree:* Master's–3 years full-time; doctorate–3 years full-time. *Degree requirements:* For master's, thesis/dissertation; for doctorate, thesis/dissertation, comprehensive exam. *Entrance requirements:* For master's and doctorate, GRE General Test, minimum GPA of 3.0. Additional exam requirements/recommendations for international students: Required—TOEFL. *Application deadline:* For fall admission, 1/15 for domestic students, 1/1 for international students; for spring admission, 9/1 for domestic students, 8/15 for international students. Application fee: $50. *Expenses:* Tuition, state resident: full-time $4,464; part-time $186 per credit hour. Tuition, nonresident: full-time $10,608; part-time $442 per credit hour. Tuition and fees vary according to program. *Financial support:* In 2003–04, 44 research assistantships (averaging $19,270 per year), 5 teaching assistantships (averaging $18,198 per year) were awarded. *Unit head:* Dr. Paul Wessel, Chair, 808-956-2582, Fax: 808-956-5512.

University of Houston, College of Natural Sciences and Mathematics, Department of Geosciences, Houston, TX 77204. Offers geology (MS, PhD); geophysics (MS, PhD). Part-time and evening/weekend programs available. *Faculty:* 16 full-time (3 women), 5 part-time/adjunct (1 woman). *Students:* 55 full-time (23 women), 41 part-time (11 women); includes 4 minority (1 African American, 1 American Indian/Alaska Native, 2 Hispanic Americans), 49 international. Average age 33. 64 applicants, 75% accepted, 10 enrolled. In 2003, 11 master's, 2 doctorates awarded. *Degree requirements:* For master's, thesis (for some programs); for doctorate, one foreign language, thesis/dissertation. *Entrance requirements:* For master's and doctorate, GRE General Test. Additional exam requirements/recommendations for international students: Required—TOEFL. *Application deadline:* For fall admission, 9/20 for domestic students; for spring admission, 12/4 for domestic students. Applications are processed on a rolling basis. Application fee: $0 ($75 for international students). *Expenses:* Tuition, state resident: full-time $1,656; part-time $92 per credit hour. Tuition, nonresident: full-time $5,904;

part-time $328 per credit hour. Required fees: $1,704. *Financial support:* In 2003–04, 9 fellowships with partial tuition reimbursements (averaging $4,000 per year), 14 research assistantships with partial tuition reimbursements (averaging $12,150 per year), 22 teaching assistantships with partial tuition reimbursements (averaging $12,150 per year) were awarded. Federal Work-Study also available. *Faculty research:* Seismic and solid earth geophysics, tectonics, environmental hydrochemistry, carbonates, micropaleontology, structure and tectonics, petroleum geology. Total annual research expenditures: $1 million. *Unit head:* Dr. John Casey, Chairman, 713-743-3399, Fax: 713-748-7906. *Application contact:* Dr. Charlotte Sullivan, Graduate Adviser, 713-743-3396, Fax: 713-748-7906, E-mail: esulliva@bayou.uh.edu.

University of Idaho, College of Graduate Studies, College of Science, Department of Geological Sciences, Program in Geophysics, Moscow, ID 83844-2282. Offers MS. *Entrance requirements:* For master's, minimum GPA of 2.8. *Application deadline:* For fall admission, 8/1 for domestic students; for spring admission, 12/15 for domestic students. Application fee: $55 ($60 for international students). *Expenses:* Tuition, state resident: full-time $3,348. Tuition, nonresident: full-time $10,740. Required fees: $540. *Financial support:* Application deadline: 2/15. *Unit head:* Dr. Dennis Geist, Head, Department of Geological Sciences, 208-885-6192.

University of Illinois at Chicago, Graduate College, College of Liberal Arts and Sciences, Department of Earth and Environmental Sciences, Chicago, IL 60607-7128. Offers crystallography (MS, PhD); environmental geology (MS, PhD); geochemistry (MS, PhD); geology (MS, PhD); geomorphology (MS, PhD); geophysics (MS, PhD); geotechnical engineering and geosciences (PhD); hydrogeology (MS, PhD); low-temperature and organic geochemistry (MS, PhD); mineralogy (MS, PhD); paleoclimatology (MS, PhD); paleontology (MS, PhD); petrology (MS, PhD); quaternary geology (MS, PhD); sedimentology (MS, PhD); water resources (MS, PhD). *Faculty:* 9 full-time (2 women). *Students:* 18 full-time (7 women), 5 part-time (1 woman); includes 3 minority (1 African American, 1 American Indian/Alaska Native, 1 Asian American or Pacific Islander), 11 international. Average age 29. 15 applicants, 27% accepted, 4 enrolled. In 2003, 2 degrees awarded. *Degree requirements:* For master's and doctorate, thesis/dissertation. *Entrance requirements:* For master's and doctorate, GRE General Test, minimum GPA of 3.75 on a 5.0 scale. Additional exam requirements/recommendations for international students: Required—TOEFL. *Application deadline:* For fall admission, 5/15 for domestic students, 2/1 for international students; for spring admission, 11/1 for domestic students, 7/15 for international students. Applications are processed on a rolling basis. Application fee: $40 ($50 for international students). Electronic applications accepted. *Expenses:* Tuition, state resident: part-time $941 per semester. Tuition, nonresident: part-time $2,338 per semester. *Financial support:* In 2003–04, 16 students received support; fellowships with full tuition reimbursements available, research assistantships with full tuition reimbursements available, teaching assistantships with full tuition reimbursements available, Federal Work-Study, scholarships/grants, traineeships, tuition waivers (full), and unspecified assistantships available. Financial award application deadline: 3/1; financial award applicants required to submit FAFSA. *Unit head:* Neil Sturchio, Head, 312-996-3154. *Application contact:* Peter Doran, Director of Graduate Studies, 312-413-7275, E-mail: pdoran@uic.edu.

University of Illinois at Urbana–Champaign, Graduate College, College of Liberal Arts and Sciences, Department of Geology, Champaign, IL 61820. Offers earth sciences (MS, PhD); geochemistry (MS, PhD); geology (MS, PhD); geophysics (MS, PhD). *Faculty:* 14 full-time (3 women). *Students:* 36 full-time (12 women); includes 3 minority (all Asian Americans or Pacific Islanders), 17 international. Average age 26. 72 applicants, 13% accepted, 4 enrolled. In 2003, 1 master's, 3 doctorates awarded. Terminal master's awarded for partial completion of doctoral program. *Degree requirements:* For master's and doctorate, thesis/dissertation. *Entrance requirements:* For master's and doctorate, GRE General Test, minimum GPA of 3.0. Additional exam requirements/recommendations for international students: Required—TOEFL. *Application deadline:* For fall admission, 2/15 for domestic students; for spring admission, 10/15 for domestic students. Applications are processed on a rolling basis. Application fee: $40 ($50 for international students). *Expenses:* Tuition, state resident: full-time $6,692. Tuition, nonresident: full-time $18,692. *Financial support:* In 2003–04, 14 research assistantships, 16 teaching assistantships were awarded. Fellowships, Federal Work-Study and tuition waivers (full and partial) also available. Financial award application deadline: 2/15. *Faculty research:* Hydrogeology, structure/tectonics, mineral science. *Unit head:* Stephen Marshak, Head, 217-333-3542, Fax: 217-244-4996, E-mail: smarshak@uiuc.edu. *Application contact:* Barbara Elmore, Graduate Admissions Secretary, 217-333-3542, Fax: 217-244-4996, E-mail: belmore@uiuc.edu.

University of Manitoba, Faculty of Graduate Studies, Faculty of Science, Department of Geological Sciences, Winnipeg, MB R3T 2N2, Canada. Offers geology (M Sc, PhD); geophysics (M Sc, PhD). *Degree requirements:* For master's and doctorate, thesis/dissertation. *Entrance requirements:* For master's and doctorate, GRE General Test, GRE Subject Test (geology), minimum GPA of 3.0. Additional exam requirements/recommendations for international students: Required—TOEFL. Tuition charges are reported in Canadian dollars. Tuition, nonresident: full-time $3,878 Canadian dollars.

The University of Memphis, Graduate School, College of Arts and Sciences, Department of Earth Sciences, Memphis, TN 38152. Offers earth sciences (PhD); geography (MA, MS); geology (MS); geophysics (MS). Part-time programs available. *Faculty:* 23 full-time (3 women), 3 part-time/adjunct (1 woman). *Students:* 34. Average age 29. 13 applicants, 46% accepted. In 2003, 4 master's, 1 doctorate awarded. Terminal master's awarded for partial completion of doctoral program. *Degree requirements:* For master's, thesis, seminar presentation, comprehensive exam; for doctorate, thesis/dissertation. *Entrance requirements:* For master's and doctorate, GRE General Test. Additional exam requirements/recommendations for international students: Required—TOEFL. *Application deadline:* For fall admission, 8/1 for domestic students; for spring admission, 12/1 for domestic students. Applications are processed on a rolling basis. Application fee: $25 ($50 for international students). Electronic applications accepted. *Expenses:* Tuition, state resident: full-time $5,142. Tuition, nonresident: full-time $13,296. *Financial support:* In 2003–04, 34 students received support, including 2 fellowships with full tuition reimbursements available, 10 research assistantships with full tuition reimbursements available, 11 teaching assistantships with full tuition reimbursements available (averaging $10,000 per year) Financial award application deadline: 1/15. *Faculty research:* Hazards, active tectonics, geophysics, hydrology and water resources, spatial analysis. Total annual research expenditures: $1.8 million. *Unit head:* Dr. Mervin J. Bartholomew, Chair, 901-678-1613, Fax: 901-678-4467, E-mail: jbrthlm1@memphis.edu. *Application contact:* Dr. George Swihart, Coordinator of Graduate Studies, 901-678-2606, Fax: 901-678-2178, E-mail: gswihart@memphis.edu.

University of Miami, Graduate School, Rosenstiel School of Marine and Atmospheric Science, Division of Marine Geology and Geophysics, Coral Gables, FL 33124. Offers MS, PhD. *Faculty:* 13 full-time (3 women), 12 part-time/adjunct (2 women). *Students:* 24 full-time (11 women), 1 part-time, 6 international. Average age 27. 26 applicants, 27% accepted, 6 enrolled. In 2003, 1 master's awarded, leading to continued full-time study 100%; 1 doctorate awarded, leading to government 100%. Terminal master's awarded for partial completion of doctoral program. *Median time to degree:* Master's–3 years full-time; doctorate–6.3 years full-time. *Degree requirements:* For master's and doctorate, thesis/dissertation, comprehensive exam, registration. *Entrance requirements:* For master's and doctorate, GRE General Test. Additional exam requirements/recommendations for international students: Required—TOEFL (minimum score 550 paper-based; 213 computer-based). *Application deadline:* For fall admission, 1/1 priority date for domestic students, 1/1 priority date for international students. Applications are processed on a rolling basis. Application fee: $50. Electronic applications accepted. *Expenses:* Tuition: Full-time $19,526. *Financial support:* In 2003–04, 23 students received support, including 3 fellowships with tuition reimbursements available (averaging $20,124 per year), 15 research assistantships with tuition reimbursements available (averaging $20,124 per year), 5 teaching assistantships with tuition reimbursements available (averaging $20,124 per year); institutionally sponsored loans also available. Financial award application deadline: 3/1; financial award applicants required to submit FAFSA. *Faculty research:* Carbonate sedimentology, low-temperature geochemistry, paleoceanography, geodesy and tectonics. *Unit head:* Dr. Gregor Eberli, Chairperson, 305-361-4678, Fax: 305-361-4632, E-mail: geberli@rsmas.miami.edu. *Application contact:* Dr. Frank Millero, Associate Dean, 305-361-4155, Fax: 305-361-4771, E-mail: gso@rsmas.miami.edu.

University of Minnesota, Twin Cities Campus, Graduate School, Institute of Technology, Department of Geology and Geophysics, Minneapolis, MN 55455-0213. Offers geology (MS, PhD); geophysics (MS, PhD). Terminal master's awarded for partial completion of doctoral program. *Degree requirements:* For master's, thesis optional; for doctorate, thesis/dissertation. *Entrance requirements:* For master's and doctorate, GRE General Test. Additional exam requirements/recommendations for international students: Required—TOEFL. *Expenses:* Tuition, state resident: full-time $3,681; part-time $614 per credit. Tuition, nonresident: full-time $7,231; part-time $1,205 per credit. *Faculty research:* Hydrogeology, geochemistry, structural geology, sedimentology.

University of Missouri–Rolla, Graduate School, School of Materials, Energy, and Earth Resources, Department of Geological Sciences and Engineering, Program in Geology and Geophysics, Rolla, MO 65409-0910. Offers geochemistry (MS, PhD); geology (MS, PhD); geophysics (MS, PhD); groundwater and environmental geology (MS, PhD). Part-time programs available. *Faculty:* 8 full-time (1 woman). *Students:* 26 full-time (10 women), 3 part-time (1 woman); includes 2 minority (1 African American, 1 Hispanic American), 10 international. Average age 31. 26 applicants, 65% accepted, 3 enrolled. In 2003, 13 master's, 4 doctorates awarded. *Median time to degree:* Master's–1.5 years full-time, 5.3 years part-time; doctorate–5 years full-time, 7 years part-time. *Degree requirements:* For master's and doctorate, thesis/dissertation. *Entrance requirements:* For master's, GRE General Test, GRE Subject Test, minimum GPA of 3.0 in last 4 semesters; for doctorate, GRE General Test, GRE Subject Test. Additional exam requirements/recommendations for international students: Required—TOEFL. *Application deadline:* For fall admission, 7/1 for domestic students; for spring admission, 12/1 for domestic students. Applications are processed on a rolling basis. Application fee: $50. Electronic applications accepted. *Expenses:* Tuition, state resident: full-time $5,871. Tuition, nonresident: full-time $13,114. Required fees: $820. Tuition and fees vary according to course load. *Financial support:* In 2003–04, 23 students received support, including 22 fellowships with full tuition reimbursements available (averaging $13,250 per year), 16 research assistantships with partial tuition reimbursements available (averaging $13,250 per year); teaching assistantships with partial tuition reimbursements available, Federal Work-Study and institutionally sponsored loans also available. Support available to part-time students. Financial award application deadline: 3/1; financial award applicants required to submit FAFSA. *Faculty research:* Economic geology, geophysical modeling, seismic wave analysis. Total annual research expenditures: $272,086.

University of Nevada, Reno, Graduate School, College of Science, Mackay School of Earth Sciences and Engineering, Department of Geological Sciences, Reno, NV 89557. Offers geochemistry (MS, PhD); geological engineering (MS, Geol E); geology (MS, PhD); geophysics (MS, PhD). *Faculty:* 37. *Students:* 52 full-time (15 women), 23 part-time (6 women); includes 6 minority (1 American Indian/Alaska Native, 3 Asian Americans or Pacific Islanders, 2 Hispanic Americans), 11 international. Average age 33. In 2003, 8 master's, 2 doctorates awarded. *Degree requirements:* For master's, thesis optional; for doctorate, one foreign language, thesis/dissertation. *Entrance requirements:* For master's, GRE General Test, GRE Subject Test, minimum GPA of 2.75; for doctorate, GRE General Test, GRE Subject Test, minimum GPA of 3.0. Additional exam requirements/recommendations for international students: Required—TOEFL. *Application deadline:* For fall admission, 2/15 for domestic students; for spring admission, 9/15 for domestic students. Applications are processed on a rolling basis. Application fee: $60 ($95 for international students). *Expenses:* Tuition, state resident: part-time $119 per credit. Tuition, nonresident: part-time $127 per credit. Required fees: $20 per term. Tuition and fees vary according to course load. *Financial support:* In 2003–04, 17 research assistantships, 8 teaching assistantships were awarded. Institutionally sponsored loans and tuition waivers (full) also available. Financial award application deadline: 3/1. *Faculty research:* Hydrothermal ore deposits, metamorphic and igneous petrogenesis, sedimentary rock record of earth history, field and petrographic investigation of magnetism, rock fracture mechanics. *Unit head:* Dr. Robert Watters, Graduate Program Director, 775-784-1770.

University of New Orleans, Graduate School, College of Sciences, Department of Geology and Geophysics, New Orleans, LA 70148. Offers MS. Evening/weekend programs available. *Faculty:* 7 full-time (2 women). *Students:* 18 full-time (12 women), 12 part-time (4 women); includes 5 minority (4 African Americans, 1 Asian American or Pacific Islander), 4 international. Average age 30. 16 applicants, 75% accepted, 9 enrolled. In 2003, 7 degrees awarded. *Degree requirements:* For master's, thesis. *Entrance requirements:* For master's, GRE General Test. Additional exam requirements/recommendations for international students: Required—TOEFL (minimum score 550 paper-based; 213 computer-based). *Application deadline:* For fall admission, 7/1 priority date for domestic students, 6/1 priority date for international students; for spring admission, 11/15 priority date for domestic students, 10/1 priority date for international students. Applications are processed on a rolling basis. Application fee: $20. Electronic applications accepted. *Expenses:* Tuition, state resident: part-time $488 per semester hour. Tuition, nonresident: part-time $1,826 per semester hour. *Financial support:* Fellowships, research assistantships, teaching assistantships, career-related internships or fieldwork, Federal Work-Study, and institutionally sponsored loans available. Financial award application deadline: 5/15; financial award applicants required to submit FAFSA. *Faculty research:* Continental margin structure and seismology, burial diagenesis of siliclastic sediments, tectonics at convergent plate margins, continental shelf sediment stability, early diagenesis of carbonates. *Unit head:* Dr. William Busch, Chairperson, 504-280-6793, Fax: 504-280-7396, E-mail: wbusch@uno.edu. *Application contact:* Dr. Christopher Parkinson, Graduate Coordinator, 504-280-6795, Fax: 504-280-7396, E-mail: christopher.parkinson@uno.edu.

University of Oklahoma, Graduate College, College of Geosciences, School of Geology and Geophysics, Program in Geophysics, Norman, OK 73019-0390. Offers MS. *Students:* 14 full-time (4 women), 5 part-time (3 women); includes 1 minority (American Indian/Alaska Native), 12 international. 10 applicants, 70% accepted, 4 enrolled. In 2003, 6 degrees awarded. *Degree requirements:* For master's, thesis, comprehensive exam. *Entrance requirements:* For master's, GRE General Test, bachelor's degree in field. Additional exam requirements/recommendations for international students: Required—TOEFL (minimum score 550 paper-based; 213 computer-based). *Application deadline:* For fall admission, 2/1 priority date for domestic students, 4/1 priority date for international students; for spring admission, 9/1 for domestic students, 9/1 for international students. Applications are processed on a rolling basis. Application fee: $25 ($75 for international students). *Expenses:* Tuition, state resident: full-time $2,774; part-time $116 per credit hour. Tuition, nonresident: full-time $9,571; part-time $399 per credit hour. Required fees: $953; $33 per credit hour. Full-time tuition and fees vary according to course level, course load and program. *Financial support:* In 2003–04, 2 students received support; research assistantships with partial tuition reimbursements available, teaching assistantships with partial tuition reimbursements available, career-related internships or fieldwork, scholarships/grants, tuition waivers (partial), and unspecified assistantships available. Financial award application deadline: 2/1; financial award applicants required to submit FAFSA. *Faculty research:* Exploration geophysics, environmental geophysics, reservoir geophysics, near-surface geophysics. *Application contact:* Donna Mullins, Coordinator, 405-325-3255, Fax: 405-325-3140, E-mail: dsmullins@ou.edu.

The University of Texas at El Paso, Graduate School, College of Science, Department of Geological Sciences, Program in Geophysics, El Paso, TX 79968-0001. Offers MS. Part-time and evening/weekend programs available. *Students:* 9 (3 women); includes 2 minority (both Hispanic Americans) 2 international. Average age 34. 1 applicant, 100% accepted. In 2003, 2 degrees awarded. *Degree requirements:* For master's, thesis. *Entrance requirements:* For master's, GRE, minimum GPA of 3.0, BS in geology or equivalent. Additional exam requirements/recommendations for international students: Required—TOEFL. *Application deadline:* For fall

Geophysics

The University of Texas at El Paso (continued)

admission, 7/1 priority date for domestic students, 3/1 priority date for international students; for spring admission, 11/1 priority date for domestic students, 9/1 priority date for international students. Applications are processed on a rolling basis. Application fee: $15 ($65 for international students). Electronic applications accepted. *Expenses:* Tuition, state resident: full-time $1,388; part-time $160 per hour. Tuition, nonresident: full-time $3,440; part-time $388 per hour. Tuition and fees vary according to course load, degree level and program. *Financial support:* In 2003–04, research assistantships with partial tuition reimbursements (averaging $21,812 per year), teaching assistantships with partial tuition reimbursements (averaging $17,450 per year) were awarded. Fellowships with partial tuition reimbursements, career-related internships or fieldwork, institutionally sponsored loans, scholarships/grants, and tuition waivers (partial) also available. Support available to part-time students. Financial award application deadline: 3/15; financial award applicants required to submit FAFSA. *Unit head:* Dr. Elizabeth Anthony, Graduate Adviser, 915-747-5501, Fax: 915-747-5483, E-mail: eanthony@geo.utep.edu. *Application contact:* Dr. Charles H. Ambler, Dean of the Graduate School, 915-747-5491 Ext. 7886, Fax: 915-747-5788, E-mail: cambler@utep.edu.

University of Utah, Graduate School, College of Mines and Earth Sciences, Department of Geology and Geophysics, Salt Lake City, UT 84112-1107. Offers geological engineering (ME, MS, PhD); geology (MS, PhD); geophysics (MS, PhD). *Faculty:* 20 full-time (4 women), 2 part-time/adjunct (0 women). *Students:* 46 full-time (13 women), 19 part-time (5 women); includes 1 minority (Asian American or Pacific Islander), 22 international. Average age 33. 73 applicants, 29% accepted, 10 enrolled. In 2003, 14 master's, 4 doctorates awarded. Terminal master's awarded for partial completion of doctoral program. *Degree requirements:* For master's, thesis, qualifying exam; for doctorate, one foreign language, thesis/dissertation. *Entrance requirements:* For master's and doctorate, GRE General Test, minimum GPA of 3.25. Additional exam requirements/recommendations for international students: Required—TOEFL. *Application deadline:* For fall admission, 1/15 priority date for domestic students, 11/1 priority date for international students. Application fee: $45 ($60 for international students). Tuition, nonresident: full-time $2,483. International tuition: $8,768 full-time. *Financial support:* In 2003–04, 3 students received support, including 4 fellowships with full tuition reimbursements available (averaging $19,240 per year), 22 research assistantships with full tuition reimbursements available (averaging $19,240 per year), 11 teaching assistantships with full tuition reimbursements available (averaging $19,240 per year); institutionally sponsored loans and stipends also available. Financial award application deadline: 2/15; financial award applicants required to submit FAFSA. *Faculty research:* Igneous, metamorphic, and sedimentary petrology; ore deposits; aqueous geochemistry; isotope geochemistry; heat flow. *Unit head:* Dr. Majorie A. Chan, Chair, 801-581-7162, Fax: 801-581-7065, E-mail: gg_chair@mines.utah.edu. *Application contact:* John M. Bartley, Director of Graduate Studies, 801-581-6553, Fax: 801-581-7065, E-mail: jbartley@mines.utah.edu.

University of Victoria, Faculty of Graduate Studies, Faculty of Science, School of Earth and Ocean Sciences, Victoria, BC V8W 2Y2, Canada. Offers geochemistry (M Sc, PhD); geophysics (M Sc, PhD); marine geology and geophysics (M Sc, PhD); ocean acoustics (M Sc, PhD); oceanography (M Sc, PhD); paleobiology (M Sc, PhD); paleoceanography (M Sc, PhD); sedimentology (M Sc, PhD); stratigraphy (M Sc, PhD). Part-time programs available. *Degree requirements:* For master's and doctorate, thesis/dissertation. *Entrance requirements:* Additional exam requirements/recommendations for international students: Required—TOEFL (minimum score 550 paper-based; 213 computer-based). Electronic applications accepted. *Faculty research:* Climate modeling, geology.

University of Washington, Graduate School, College of Arts and Sciences, Department of Earth and Space Sciences, Seattle, WA 98195. Offers geology (MS, PhD); geophysics (MS, PhD). *Students:* 78 full-time (28 women); includes 2 minority (both Hispanic Americans), 9 international. 192 applicants, 16% accepted, 13 enrolled. In 2003, 5 master's, 7 doctorates awarded. *Median time to degree:* Doctorate–6.8 years full-time. Of those who began their doctoral program in fall 1995, 64% received their degree in 8 years or less. *Degree requirements:* For master's, thesis or alternative, departmental qualifying exam, final exam; for doctorate, thesis/dissertation, departmental qualifying exam, general and final exams. *Entrance requirements:* For master's and doctorate, GRE General Test, minimum GPA of 3.0. Additional exam requirements/recommendations for international students: Required—TOEFL (minimum score 580 paper-based). *Application deadline:* For fall admission, 1/15 for domestic students, 11/1 for international students. Application fee: $50. Electronic applications accepted. *Financial support:* In 2003–04, 10 fellowships with full tuition reimbursements, 41 research assistantships with full tuition reimbursements (averaging $12,850 per year), 20 teaching assistantships with full tuition reimbursements (averaging $12,850 per year) were awarded. Financial award application deadline: 1/15. Total annual research expenditures: $9.3 million. *Unit head:* Dr. J. Michael Brown, Chair, 206-543-1190, Fax: 206-543-0489, E-mail: brown@geophys.washington.edu. *Application contact:* Mary Conrad, Director of Academic Services, 206-616-8511, Fax: 206-543-0489, E-mail: advising@ess.washington.edu.

The University of Western Ontario, Faculty of Graduate Studies, Physical Sciences Division, Department of Earth Sciences, London, ON N6A 5B8, Canada. Offers geology (M Sc, PhD); geology and environmental science (M Sc, PhD); geophysics (M Sc, PhD); geophysics and environmental science (M Sc, PhD). *Degree requirements:* For master's, thesis, registration; for doctorate, thesis/dissertation, qualifying exam. *Entrance requirements:* For master's, honors in B Sc; for doctorate, M Sc. Additional exam requirements/recommendations for international students: Required—TOEFL. *Faculty research:* Geophysics, geochemistry, paleontology, sedimentology/stratigraphy, glaciology/quaternary.

University of Wisconsin–Madison, Graduate School, College of Letters and Science, Department of Geology and Geophysics, Program in Geophysics, Madison, WI 53706-1380. Offers MS, PhD. *Degree requirements:* For master's, thesis; for doctorate, one foreign language, thesis/dissertation. *Entrance requirements:* For master's and doctorate, GRE General Test. Tuition, area resident: Full-time $7,593; part-time $476 per credit. Tuition, nonresident: full-time $22,824; part-time $1,430 per credit. Required fees: $292; $38 per credit. Part-time tuition and fees vary according to course load and reciprocity agreements.

University of Wyoming, Graduate School, College of Arts and Sciences, Department of Geology and Geophysics, Laramie, WY 82070. Offers geology (MS, PhD); geophysics (MS, PhD). Part-time programs available. *Faculty:* 17 full-time (2 women), 3 part-time/adjunct (2 women). *Students:* 36 full-time (11 women), 29 part-time (12 women); includes 3 minority (1 Asian American or Pacific Islander, 2 Hispanic Americans), 10 international. 22 applicants, 95% accepted, 21 enrolled. In 2003, 9 master's, 4 doctorates awarded. *Degree requirements:* For master's and doctorate, variable foreign language requirement, thesis/dissertation. *Entrance requirements:* For master's and doctorate, GRE General Test, minimum GPA of 3.0. *Application deadline:* For fall admission, 1/15 for domestic students. Applications are processed on a rolling basis. Application fee: $40. *Expenses:* Tuition, state resident: part-time $142 per credit hour. Tuition, nonresident: part-time $408 per credit hour. Required fees: $134 per semester. Tuition and fees vary according to course load, campus/location, program and student level. *Financial support:* Fellowships, research assistantships, teaching assistantships, career-related internships or fieldwork, Federal Work-Study, and institutionally sponsored loans available. Financial award application deadline: 3/1. *Faculty research:* Geochemistry and petroleum geology, tectonics and sedimentation, geomorphology and remote sensing, igneous and metamorphic petrology, structure, geohydrology. *Unit head:* Dr. James I. Drever, Head, 307-766-3386. *Application contact:* Sondra S. Cawley, Admissions Coordinator, 307-766-3389, Fax: 307-766-6679, E-mail: acadcoord.geol@uwyo.edu.

Virginia Polytechnic Institute and State University, Graduate School, College of Science, Department of Geosciences, Blacksburg, VA 24061. Offers geological sciences (MS, PhD); geophysics (MS, PhD). *Faculty:* 20 full-time (4 women), 1 (woman) part-time/adjunct. *Students:* 48 full-time (17 women), 7 part-time (2 women); includes 3 minority (1 American Indian/Alaska Native, 1 Asian American or Pacific Islander, 1 Hispanic American), 13 international. Average age 27. 83 applicants, 29% accepted, 19 enrolled. In 2003, 8 master's, 5 doctorates awarded. *Entrance requirements:* For master's and doctorate, GRE General Test. Additional exam requirements/recommendations for international students: Required—TOEFL (minimum score 550 paper-based; 213 computer-based). *Application deadline:* Applications are processed on a rolling basis. Application fee: $45. Electronic applications accepted. Tuition, area resident: Full-time $6,039; part-time $336 per credit. Tuition, nonresident: full-time $9,708; part-time $539 per credit. Required fees: $905; $130 per credit. *Financial support:* In 2003–04, 2 fellowships with full tuition reimbursements (averaging $6,000 per year), 20 research assistantships with full tuition reimbursements (averaging $12,316 per year), 26 teaching assistantships with full tuition reimbursements (averaging $12,127 per year) were awarded. Career-related internships or fieldwork, Federal Work-Study, scholarships/grants, tuition waivers (full), and unspecified assistantships also available. Financial award application deadline: 4/1. *Faculty research:* Paleontology/geobiology, active tectonics, geomorphology, mineralogy/crystallography, mineral physics. *Unit head:* Dr. Cahit Coruh, Chair, 540-231-6521, Fax: 540-231-3386, E-mail: coruh@vt.edu. *Application contact:* Connie Lowe, Student Program Coordinator, 540-231-8824, Fax: 540-231-3386, E-mail: clowe@vt.edu.

Washington University in St. Louis, Graduate School of Arts and Sciences, Department of Earth and Planetary Sciences, St. Louis, MO 63130-4899. Offers earth and planetary sciences (MA); geochemistry (PhD); geology (MA, PhD); geophysics (PhD); planetary sciences (PhD). *Students:* 36 full-time (19 women), 1 (woman) part-time; includes 2 minority (both Asian Americans or Pacific Islanders), 5 international. 69 applicants, 35% accepted, 12 enrolled. In 2003, 9 master's, 2 doctorates awarded. Terminal master's awarded for partial completion of doctoral program. *Degree requirements:* For master's and doctorate, thesis/dissertation. *Entrance requirements:* For master's and doctorate, GRE General Test. *Application deadline:* For fall admission, 1/15 for domestic students. Applications are processed on a rolling basis. Application fee: $35. Electronic applications accepted. *Expenses:* Tuition: Full-time $28,300; part-time $1,180 per credit. *Financial support:* Fellowships, research assistantships, teaching assistantships, Federal Work-Study, institutionally sponsored loans, and tuition waivers (full and partial) available. Financial award application deadline: 1/15. *Unit head:* Dr. Raymond E. Arvidson, Chairman, 314-935-5610.

West Virginia University, Eberly College of Arts and Sciences, Department of Geology and Geography, Program in Geology, Morgantown, WV 26506. Offers geomorphology (MS, PhD); geophysics (MS, PhD); hydrogeology (MS); hydrology (PhD); paleontology (MS, PhD); petrology (MS, PhD); stratigraphy (MS, PhD); structure (MS, PhD). Part-time programs available. *Students:* 26 full-time (7 women), 17 part-time (7 women); includes 2 minority (1 American Indian/Alaska Native, 1 Asian American or Pacific Islander), 12 international. Average age 30. 34 applicants, 29% accepted. In 2003, 6 master's, 1 doctorate awarded. Terminal master's awarded for partial completion of doctoral program. *Degree requirements:* For master's, thesis/dissertation; for doctorate, thesis/dissertation, comprehensive exam. *Entrance requirements:* For master's, GRE General Test, GRE Subject Test, minimum GPA of 2.5; for doctorate, GRE General Test, GRE Subject Test, minimum GPA of 3.3. Additional exam requirements/recommendations for international students: Required—TOEFL. *Application deadline:* For fall admission, 2/1 for domestic students; for spring admission, 10/1 for domestic students. Applications are processed on a rolling basis. Application fee: $45. *Expenses:* Tuition, state resident: full-time $4,332. Tuition, nonresident: full-time $12,442. *Financial support:* In 2003–04, 5 research assistantships, 18 teaching assistantships were awarded. Career-related internships or fieldwork, Federal Work-Study, institutionally sponsored loans, and tuition waivers (full and partial) also available. Financial award application deadline: 2/1; financial award applicants required to submit FAFSA. *Unit head:* Dr. Thomas H. Wilson, Associate Chair, 304-293-5603 Ext. 4316, Fax: 304-293-6522. *Application contact:* Dr. Joe Donovan, Associate Professor, 304-293-5603 Ext. 4308, Fax: 304-293-6522, E-mail: joe.donovan@mail.wvu.edu.

Woods Hole Oceanographic Institution, MIT/WHOI Joint Program in Oceanography/Applied Ocean Science and Engineering, Woods Hole, MA 02543-1541. Offers applied ocean sciences (PhD); biological oceanography (PhD, Sc D); chemical oceanography (PhD, Sc D); civil and environmental and oceanographic engineering (PhD); electrical and oceanographic engineering (PhD); geochemistry (PhD); geophysics (PhD); marine biology (PhD); marine geochemistry (PhD, Sc D); marine geology (PhD, Sc D); marine geophysics (PhD); mechanical and oceanographic engineering (PhD); ocean engineering (PhD); oceanographic engineering (M Eng, MS, PhD, Sc D, Eng); paleoceanography (PhD); physical oceanography (PhD, Sc D). MS, PhD, and Sc D offered jointly with MIT. *Faculty:* 123 full-time, 8 part-time/adjunct. *Students:* 128 full-time (62 women); includes 8 minority (2 African Americans, 4 Asian Americans or Pacific Islanders, 2 Hispanic Americans), 37 international. Average age 27. 187 applicants, 28% accepted, 32 enrolled. In 2003, 7 master's, 20 doctorates awarded. Terminal master's awarded for partial completion of doctoral program. *Median time to degree:* Master's–2.9 years full-time; doctorate–5.8 years full-time. *Degree requirements:* For master's and Eng, thesis (for some programs); for doctorate, thesis/dissertation. *Entrance requirements:* For master's, GRE General Test; for doctorate, GRE General Test, GRE Subject Test. Additional exam requirements/recommendations for international students: Required—TOEFL. *Application deadline:* For fall admission, 1/15 priority date for domestic students, 1/15 priority date for international students. Application fee: $65. Electronic applications accepted. *Expenses:* Tuition: Full-time $39,200. *Financial support:* In 2003–04, 13 fellowships (averaging $39,200 per year), 69 research assistantships (averaging $39,200 per year) were awarded. Teaching assistantships, scholarships/grants, traineeships, health care benefits, and unspecified assistantships also available. Financial award application deadline: 1/15. *Unit head:* Prof. Paola Rizzoli, Director, 617-253-2451, E-mail: rizzoli@mit.edu. *Application contact:* Ronni Schwartz, Administrator, 617-253-7544, Fax: 617-253-9784, E-mail: mspiggy@mit.edu.

See in-depth description on page 279.

Wright State University, School of Graduate Studies, College of Science and Mathematics, Department of Geological Sciences, Program in Geological Sciences, Dayton, OH 45435. Offers environmental geochemistry (MS); environmental geology (MS); environmental sciences (MS); geological sciences (MS); geophysics (MS); hydrogeology (MS); petroleum geology (MS). Part-time programs available. *Students:* 22 full-time (4 women), 9 part-time (4 women), 2 international. Average age 26. 21 applicants, 100% accepted. In 2003, 15 degrees awarded. *Degree requirements:* For master's, thesis. *Entrance requirements:* Additional exam requirements/recommendations for international students: Required—TOEFL. Application fee: $25. *Expenses:* Tuition, state resident: full-time $8,112; part-time $255 per quarter hour. Tuition, nonresident: full-time $14,127; part-time $442 per quarter hour. International tuition: $14,283 full-time. Tuition and fees vary according to course load, degree level and program. *Financial support:* Fellowships, research assistantships, teaching assistantships, Federal Work-Study and unspecified assistantships available. Support available to part-time students. Financial award application deadline: 3/1; financial award applicants required to submit FAFSA. *Application contact:* Deborah L. Cowles, Assistant to Chair, 937-775-3455, Fax: 937-775-3462, E-mail: deborah.cowles@wright.edu.

Yale University, Graduate School of Arts and Sciences, Department of Geology and Geophysics, New Haven, CT 06520. Offers geochemistry (PhD); geophysics (PhD); meteorology (PhD); mineralogy and crystallography (PhD); oceanography (PhD); paleoecology (PhD); paleontology and stratigraphy (PhD); petrology (PhD); structural geology (PhD). *Degree requirements:* For doctorate, thesis/dissertation. *Entrance requirements:* For doctorate, GRE General Test. Additional exam requirements/recommendations for international students: Required—TOEFL. *Expenses:* Tuition: Full-time $25,600; part-time $6,400 per term.

See in-depth description on page 261.

Geosciences

Ball State University, Graduate School, College of Sciences and Humanities, Department of Geography, Muncie, IN 47306-1099. Offers earth sciences (MA). *Faculty:* 11. *Students:* 10 full-time (2 women), 7 part-time (1 woman), 5 international. Average age 29. 15 applicants, 60% accepted, 6 enrolled. In 2003, 1 degree awarded. Application fee: $25 ($35 for international students). *Expenses:* Tuition, state resident: full-time $5,748. Tuition, nonresident: full-time $14,166. *Financial support:* In 2003–04, 5 research assistantships (averaging $8,000 per year), 5 teaching assistantships (averaging $8,000 per year) were awarded. Financial award application deadline: 3/1. *Faculty research:* Remote sensing, tourism and recreation, Latin American urbanization. *Unit head:* Dr. Gopalan Venugopal, Chairman, 765-285-1776.

Baylor University, Graduate School, College of Arts and Sciences, Department of Geology, Waco, TX 76798. Offers earth science (MA); geology (MS, PhD). *Faculty:* 12 full-time (1 woman). *Students:* 18 full-time (9 women), 2 part-time (1 woman); includes 2 minority (both Hispanic Americans), 3 international. In 2003, 3 master's, 1 doctorate awarded. *Degree requirements:* For master's and doctorate, thesis/dissertation. *Entrance requirements:* For master's and doctorate, GRE General Test. *Application deadline:* For fall admission, 3/15 for domestic students. Applications are processed on a rolling basis. Application fee: $25. *Expenses:* Tuition: Part-time $698 per hour. *Financial support:* In 2003–04, 18 teaching assistantships were awarded; Federal Work-Study and institutionally sponsored loans also available. *Faculty research:* Petroleum geology, geophysics, engineering geology, hydrogeology. *Unit head:* Dr. Thomas T. Goforth, Graduate Program Director, 254-710-2361, Fax: 254-710-2673, E-mail: thomas_goforth@baylor.edu. *Application contact:* Suzanne Keener, Administrative Assistant, 254-710-3588, Fax: 254-710-3870, E-mail: pauline_johnson@baylor.edu.

Boise State University, Graduate College, College of Arts and Sciences, Department of Geosciences, Program in Earth Science, Boise, ID 83725-0399. Offers MS. *Accreditation:* NCATE. Part-time programs available. *Students:* Average age 36. In 2003, 2 degrees awarded. *Degree requirements:* For master's, thesis. *Entrance requirements:* For master's, GRE General Test, minimum GPA of 3.0, BS in related field. *Application deadline:* For fall admission, 7/17 for domestic students; for spring admission, 12/5 priority date for domestic students. Applications are processed on a rolling basis. Application fee: $30. Electronic applications accepted. *Expenses:* Tuition, state resident: full-time $4,668. Tuition, nonresident: full-time $11,388. *Financial support:* Career-related internships or fieldwork, Federal Work-Study, institutionally sponsored loans, and unspecified assistantships available. Support available to part-time students. Financial award application deadline: 3/1. *Unit head:* Dr. David Wilkins, Coordinator, 208-426-2290, Fax: 208-426-4061.

Boston University, Graduate School of Arts and Sciences, Department of Earth Sciences, Boston, MA 02215. Offers MA, PhD. *Students:* 22 full-time (14 women), 5 international. Average age 28. 45 applicants, 33% accepted, 8 enrolled. In 2003, 8 master's, 1 doctorate awarded. Terminal master's awarded for partial completion of doctoral program. *Degree requirements:* For master's and doctorate, one foreign language, thesis/dissertation, comprehensive exam, registration. *Entrance requirements:* For master's and doctorate, GRE General Test, 3 letters of recommendation. Additional exam requirements/recommendations for international students: Required—TOEFL (minimum score 550 paper-based; 213 computer-based). *Application deadline:* For fall admission, 7/1 for domestic students, 7/1 for international students; for spring admission, 11/15 for domestic students, 11/15 for international students. Application fee: $60. *Expenses:* Tuition: Full-time $28,512; part-time $891 per credit hour. *Financial support:* In 2003–04, 18 students received support, including 1 fellowship with full tuition reimbursement available (averaging $15,500 per year), 9 research assistantships with tuition reimbursements available (averaging $15,000 per year), 7 teaching assistantships with full tuition reimbursements available (averaging $15,000 per year); Federal Work-Study and unspecified assistantships also available. Support available to part-time students. Financial award application deadline: 1/15; financial award applicants required to submit FAFSA. *Unit head:* Dr. Rick Murray, Chairman, 617-353-6532, Fax: 617-353-3290, E-mail: rickm@bu.edu. *Application contact:* Christopher Burns, Senior Program Coordinator, 617-353-2532, Fax: 617-353-3290, E-mail: cburns@bu.edu.

Brock University, Graduate Studies and Research, Faculty of Mathematics and Science, Department of Earth Sciences, St. Catharines, ON L2S 3A1, Canada. Offers M Sc. Part-time programs available. *Degree requirements:* For master's, thesis. *Entrance requirements:* For master's, honors B Sc in geology. Additional exam requirements/recommendations for international students: Required—TOEFL. *Faculty research:* Quaternary geology, petrology, crustal studies, hydrology, carbonate geochemistry.

Brown University, Graduate School, Department of Geological Sciences, Providence, RI 02912. Offers MA, Sc M, PhD. *Degree requirements:* For doctorate, thesis/dissertation, 1 semester of teaching experience, preliminary exam. *Faculty research:* Geochemistry, mineral kinetics, igneous and metamorphic petrology, tectonophysics including geophysics and structural geology, paleoclimatology, paleoceanography, sedimentation, planetary geology.

California State University, Chico, Graduate School, College of Natural Sciences, Department of Geological and Environmental Sciences, Chico, CA 95929-0722. Offers environmental science (MS); geosciences (MS), including earth sciences, hydrology/hydrogeology. *Students:* 14 full-time (9 women), 5 part-time (2 women). Average age 32. 7 applicants, 100% accepted, 6 enrolled. In 2003, 3 degrees awarded. *Degree requirements:* For master's, thesis, competency exam. *Entrance requirements:* For master's, GRE General Test. Additional exam requirements/recommendations for international students: Required—TOEFL (minimum score 550 paper-based; 213 computer-based). *Application deadline:* For fall admission, 3/1 for domestic students, 3/1 for international students; for spring admission, 9/15 for domestic students, 9/15 for international students. Applications are processed on a rolling basis. Application fee: $55. Electronic applications accepted. Tuition, nonresident: part-time $282 per semester hour. Required fees: $1,029 per semester. *Financial support:* Fellowships, teaching assistantships available. *Unit head:* Dr. Richard Flory, Chair, 530-898-6369. *Application contact:* Dr. Gregory Taylor, Graduate Coordinator, 530-898-6369.

California State University, Chico, Graduate School, College of Natural Sciences, Department of Geological and Environmental Sciences, Program in Geosciences, Option in Earth Sciences, Chico, CA 95929-0722. Offers MS. *Students:* 3 full-time (1 woman), 1 (woman) part-time. Average age 35. 1 applicant, 100% accepted, 1 enrolled. *Degree requirements:* For master's, thesis, oral exam. *Entrance requirements:* For master's, GRE General Test. Additional exam requirements/recommendations for international students: Required—TOEFL (minimum score 550 paper-based; 213 computer-based). *Application deadline:* For fall admission, 3/1 for domestic students, 3/1 for international students; for spring admission, 9/15 for domestic students, 9/15 for international students. Applications are processed on a rolling basis. Application fee: $55. Electronic applications accepted. Tuition, nonresident: part-time $282 per semester hour. Required fees: $1,029 per semester. *Application contact:* Dr. Gregory Taylor, Graduate Coordinator, 530-898-6369.

California University of Pennsylvania, School of Graduate Studies, School of Liberal Arts, Program in Geography and Earth Sciences, California, PA 15419-1394. Offers earth science (MS); geography (M Ed, MA). Part-time and evening/weekend programs available. *Faculty:* 1 full-time (0 women), 3 part-time/adjunct (1 woman). *Students:* 10 (2 women). *Degree requirements:* For master's, thesis optional. *Entrance requirements:* For master's, MAT, minimum GPA of 2.5, teaching certificate (M Ed). Additional exam requirements/recommendations for international students: Required—TOEFL. *Application deadline:* Applications are processed on a rolling basis. Application fee: $25. *Expenses:* Tuition, state resident: full-time $5,518; part-time $307 per credit. Tuition, nonresident: full-time $8,830; part-time $491 per credit. Required fees: $1,000. *Financial support:* Tuition waivers (full) and unspecified assistantships available. *Unit head:* Dr. Chad Kauffman, Coordinator, 724-938-4130, E-mail: moses@cup.edu.

Carleton University, Faculty of Graduate Studies, Faculty of Science, Department of Earth Sciences, Ottawa, ON K1S 5B6, Canada. Offers M Sc, PhD. *Degree requirements:* For master's, thesis/dissertation, seminar; for doctorate, thesis/dissertation, seminar, comprehensive exam. *Entrance requirements:* For master's, honors degree in science; for doctorate, M Sc. Additional exam requirements/recommendations for international students: Required—TOEFL. Application fee: $60 Canadian dollars. *Expenses:* Tuition, state resident: part-time $2,052 per term. Tuition, nonresident: part-time $4,266 per term. Full-time tuition and fees vary according to course load, degree level and program. *Financial support:* Fellowships, research assistantships, teaching assistantships, institutionally sponsored loans, scholarships/grants, and unspecified assistantships available. *Faculty research:* Resource geology, geophysics, basin analysis, lithosphere dynamics. *Unit head:* Claudia Schroeder-Adams, Chair, 613-520-2600 Ext. 1852, Fax: 613-520-4490, E-mail: earth_sciences@carleton.ca. *Application contact:* Shelia Thayer, Graduate Administrator, 613-520-2600 Ext. 8769, Fax: 613-520-2569, E-mail: earth_science@carleton.ca.

Case Western Reserve University, School of Graduate Studies, Department of Geological Sciences, Cleveland, OH 44106. Offers MS, PhD. Part-time programs available. *Faculty:* 6 full-time (0 women). *Students:* 3 full-time (1 woman), 1 part-time; includes 1 minority (African American), 2 international. Average age 27. 16 applicants, 25% accepted, 2 enrolled. In 2003, 1 master's, 1 doctorate awarded. Terminal master's awarded for partial completion of doctoral program. *Degree requirements:* For master's, thesis or alternative; for doctorate, thesis/dissertation. *Entrance requirements:* For master's and doctorate, GRE General Test, GRE Subject Test. Additional exam requirements/recommendations for international students: Required—TOEFL. *Application deadline:* For fall admission, 2/15 for domestic students; for spring admission, 11/15 for domestic students. Applications are processed on a rolling basis. Application fee: $50. *Expenses:* Tuition: Full-time $26,900. *Financial support:* Research assistantships, teaching assistantships, Federal Work-Study and tuition waivers (partial) available. Support available to part-time students. Financial award application deadline: 2/15. *Faculty research:* Geochemistry, hydrology, geochronology, paleoclimates, geomorphology. *Unit head:* Gerald Matisoff, Chairman, 216-368-3677, Fax: 216-368-3691, E-mail: gxm4@case.edu. *Application contact:* Linda Day, Admissions, 216-368-3690, Fax: 216-368-3691, E-mail: lmd3@case.edu.

Central Connecticut State University, School of Graduate Studies, School of Arts and Sciences, Department of Physics and Earth Science, New Britain, CT 06050-4010. Offers earth science (MS); physics (MS). Part-time and evening/weekend programs available. *Faculty:* 12 full-time (4 women), 7 part-time/adjunct (2 women). *Students:* 4 full-time (all women), 31 part-time (22 women); includes 4 minority (1 African American, 1 Asian American or Pacific Islander, 2 Hispanic Americans), 1 international. Average age 33. 23 applicants, 70% accepted, 12 enrolled. In 2003, 3 degrees awarded. *Degree requirements:* For master's, thesis or alternative, comprehensive exam. *Entrance requirements:* For master's, minimum GPA of 2.7. Additional exam requirements/recommendations for international students: Required—TOEFL. *Application deadline:* For fall admission, 8/10 for domestic students; for spring admission, 12/10 for domestic students. Applications are processed on a rolling basis. Application fee: $50. *Expenses:* Tuition, state resident: full-time $3,298. Tuition, nonresident: full-time $9,190. *Financial support:* Federal Work-Study available. Financial award application deadline: 3/15; financial award applicants required to submit FAFSA. *Faculty research:* Elementary/secondary science education, particle and solid states, weather patterns, planetary studies. *Unit head:* Dr. Ali Antar, Chair, 860-832-2930.

City College of the City University of New York, Graduate School, College of Liberal Arts and Science, Division of Science, Department of Earth and Atmospheric Sciences, New York, NY 10031-9198. Offers earth and environmental science (PhD); earth systems science (MA). *Students:* 10 applicants, 70% accepted, 5 enrolled. In 2003, 2 degrees awarded. *Degree requirements:* For master's, thesis, comprehensive exam. *Entrance requirements:* For master's, appropriate bachelor's degree. Additional exam requirements/recommendations for international students: Required—TOEFL. *Application deadline:* For fall admission, 5/1 for domestic students; for spring admission, 11/1 for domestic students. Application fee: $50. *Expenses:* Tuition, state resident: full-time $5,440; part-time $230 per credit. Tuition, nonresident: part-time $425 per credit. Required fees: $63 per semester. *Financial support:* Fellowships, career-related internships or fieldwork available. *Faculty research:* Water resources, high-temperature geochemistry, sedimentary basin analysis, tectonics. *Unit head:* Jeffrey Steiner, Chair, 212-650-6984. *Application contact:* O. Lehn Franke, Adviser, 212-650-6984.

Colorado School of Mines, Graduate School, Department of Geology and Geological Engineering, Golden, CO 80401-1887. Offers engineering geology (Diploma); exploration geosciences (Diploma); geochemistry (MS, PhD); geological engineering (ME, MS, PhD, Diploma); geology (MS, PhD); hydrogeology (Diploma). Part-time programs available. *Faculty:* 25 full-time (4 women), 8 part-time/adjunct (4 women). *Students:* 52 full-time (16 women), 34 part-time (13 women); includes 1 minority (American Indian/Alaska Native), 20 international. 89 applicants, 56% accepted, 12 enrolled. In 2003, 19 master's, 4 doctorates, 3 other advanced degrees awarded. *Degree requirements:* For master's, thesis/dissertation; for doctorate, thesis/dissertation, comprehensive exam. *Entrance requirements:* For master's and doctorate, GRE General Test; for Diploma, GRE General Test, minimum GPA of 3.0. Additional exam requirements/recommendations for international students: Required—TOEFL (minimum score 550 paper-based; 213 computer-based). *Application deadline:* For fall admission, 12/1 for domestic students, 12/1 for international students; for spring admission, 5/1 for domestic students, 5/1 for international students. Application fee: $45. Electronic applications accepted. *Expenses:* Tuition, state resident: full-time $5,700; part-time $285 per credit hour. Tuition, nonresident: full-time $19,040; part-time $952 per credit hour. Required fees: $733. *Financial support:* In 2003–04, 23 students received support, including 9 fellowships with full tuition reimbursements available (averaging $12,500 per year), 16 research assistantships with full tuition reimbursements available (averaging $10,000 per year), 9 teaching assistantships with full tuition reimbursements available (averaging $10,000 per year); scholarships/grants and unspecified assistantships also available. Financial award applicants required to submit FAFSA. *Faculty research:* Predictive sediment modeling, petrophysics, aquifer-contaminant flow modeling, water-rock interactions, geotechnical engineering. Total annual research expenditures: $2.1 million. *Unit head:* Dr. Murray W. Hitzman, Head, 303-384-2127, Fax: 303-273-3859, E-mail: mhitzman@mines.edu. *Application contact:* Marilyn Schwinger, Administrative Assistant, 303-273-3800, Fax: 303-273-3859, E-mail: mschwing@mines.edu.

Colorado State University, Graduate School, College of Natural Resources, Department of Geosciences, Fort Collins, CO 80523-0015. Offers earth resources (PhD); geology (MS), including geomorphology, hydrogeology, petrology/geochemistry and economic geology, sedimentology, structural geology. Part-time programs available. *Faculty:* 9 full-time (4 women), 2 part-time/adjunct (0 women). *Students:* 19 full-time (6 women), 17 part-time (7 women); includes 1 minority (American Indian/Alaska Native), 3 international. Average age 31. 56 applicants, 46% accepted, 8 enrolled. In 2003, 6 master's, 2 doctorates awarded. *Degree requirements:* For master's and doctorate, thesis/dissertation, registration. *Entrance requirements:* For master's and doctorate, GRE General Test, minimum GPA of 3.0. Additional exam requirements/recommendations for international students: Required—TOEFL (minimum score 550 paper-based; 213 computer-based). *Application deadline:* For fall admission, 2/1 priority date for domestic students, 2/1 priority date for international students. Applications are processed on a rolling basis. Application fee: $50. Electronic applications accepted. *Expenses:* Tuition, state resident: full-time $4,156. Tuition, nonresident: full-time $14,762. Required fees: $205. Tuition and fees vary according to course load, campus/location, program and reciprocity agreements. *Financial support:* In 2003–04, fellowships (averaging $3,800 per year), research assistantships with partial tuition reimbursements (averaging $14,400 per year), teaching assistantships with full tuition reimbursements (averaging $10,206 per year) were awarded. Career-related internships or fieldwork, Federal Work-Study, institutionally sponsored loans,

Geosciences

Colorado State University (continued)

scholarships/grants, and traineeships also available. Financial award application deadline: 2/15. *Faculty research:* Snow, surface, and groundwater hydrology; fluvial geomorphology; geographic information systems; geochemistry; bedrock geology. Total annual research expenditures: $407,835. *Unit head:* Dr. Judith L. Hannah, Head, 970-491-5662, Fax: 970-491-6307, E-mail: jhannah@cnr.colostate.edu. *Application contact:* Barbara Holtz, Staff Assistant, 970-491-5662, Fax: 970-491-6307, E-mail: barbh@cnr.colostate.edu.

Columbia University, Graduate School of Arts and Sciences, Division of Natural Sciences, Department of Earth and Environmental Sciences, New York, NY 10027. Offers geochemistry (M Phil, MA, PhD); geodetic sciences (M Phil, MA, PhD); geophysics (M Phil, MA, PhD); oceanography (M Phil, MA, PhD). *Faculty:* 21 full-time, 19 part-time/adjunct. *Students:* 78 full-time (31 women), 6 part-time (2 women); includes 4 minority (3 Asian Americans or Pacific Islanders, 1 Hispanic American), 31 international. Average age 32. 115 applicants, 20% accepted. In 2003, 16 master's, 11 doctorates awarded. *Degree requirements:* For master's, thesis or alternative, fieldwork, written exam; for doctorate, one foreign language, thesis/dissertation. *Entrance requirements:* For master's and doctorate, GRE General Test, GRE Subject Test, major in natural or physical science. Additional exam requirements/recommendations for international students: Required—TOEFL. Application fee: $75. *Expenses:* Tuition: Full-time $14,820. *Financial support:* Fellowships, teaching assistantships, Federal Work-Study and institutionally sponsored loans available. Support available to part-time students. Financial award application deadline: 1/5; financial award applicants required to submit FAFSA. *Faculty research:* Structural geology and stratigraphy, petrology, paleontology, rare gas, isotope and aqueous geochemistry. *Unit head:* Dr. William Menke, Chair, 212-864-4525, Fax: 845-365-8163.

Cornell University, Graduate School, Graduate Fields of Engineering, Field of Geological Sciences, Ithaca, NY 14853-0001. Offers economic geology (M Eng, MS, PhD); engineering geology (M Eng, MS, PhD); environmental geophysics (M Eng, MS, PhD); general geology (M Eng, MS, PhD); geobiology (M Eng, MS, PhD); geochemistry and isotope geology (M Eng, MS, PhD); geohydrology (M Eng, MS, PhD); geomorphology (M Eng, MS, PhD); geophysics (M Eng, MS, PhD); geotectonics (M Eng, MS, PhD); marine geology (MS, PhD); mineralogy (M Eng, MS, PhD); paleontology (M Eng, MS, PhD); petroleum geology (M Eng, MS, PhD); petrology (M Eng, MS, PhD); planetary geology (M Eng, MS, PhD); Precambrian geology (M Eng, MS, PhD); Quaternary geology (M Eng, MS, PhD); rock mechanics (M Eng, MS, PhD); sedimentology (M Eng, MS, PhD); seismology (M Eng, MS, PhD); stratigraphy (M Eng, MS, PhD); structural geology (M Eng, MS, PhD). *Faculty:* 31 full-time. *Students:* 27 full-time (12 women); includes 1 minority (Asian American or Pacific Islander), 9 international. 74 applicants, 15% accepted, 7 enrolled. In 2003, 3 master's, 5 doctorates awarded. *Degree requirements:* For master's, thesis (MS); for doctorate, thesis/dissertation, comprehensive exam. *Entrance requirements:* For master's and doctorate, GRE General Test, 3 letters of recommendation. Additional exam requirements/recommendations for international students: Required—TOEFL (minimum score 550 paper-based; 213 computer-based). *Application deadline:* For fall admission, 1/15 for domestic students. Applications are processed on a rolling basis. Application fee: $60. Electronic applications accepted. *Expenses:* Tuition: Full-time $28,630. One-time fee: $50 full-time. *Financial support:* In 2003–04, 21 students received support, including 6 fellowships with full tuition reimbursements available, 8 research assistantships with full tuition reimbursements available, 7 teaching assistantships with full tuition reimbursements available; institutionally sponsored loans, scholarships/grants, health care benefits, tuition waivers (full and partial), and unspecified assistantships also available. Financial award applicants required to submit FAFSA. *Faculty research:* Geophysics, structural geology, petrology, geochemistry, geodynamics. *Unit head:* Director of Graduate Studies, 607-255-3474, Fax: 607-254-4780. *Application contact:* Graduate Field Assistant, 607-255-3474, Fax: 607-254-4780, E-mail: gradprog@geology.cornell.edu.

See in-depth description on page 233.

Dalhousie University, Faculty of Graduate Studies, College of Arts and Science, Faculty of Science, Department of Earth Sciences, Halifax, NS B3H 4R2, Canada. Offers M Sc, PhD. Part-time programs available. *Degree requirements:* For master's and doctorate, one foreign language, thesis/dissertation. *Entrance requirements:* For doctorate, M Sc. Additional exam requirements/recommendations for international students: Required—TOEFL. *Faculty research:* Marine geology and geophysics, Appalachian and Grenville geology, micropaleontology, geodynamics and structural geology, geochronology.

Dartmouth College, School of Arts and Sciences, Department of Earth Sciences, Hanover, NH 03755. Offers MS, PhD. *Faculty:* 9 full-time (2 women). *Students:* 19 full-time (10 women); includes 1 minority (Asian American or Pacific Islander), 5 international. Average age 27. 65 applicants, 17% accepted, 9 enrolled. In 2003, 7 master's, 5 doctorates awarded. Terminal master's awarded for partial completion of doctoral program. *Degree requirements:* For master's and doctorate, thesis/dissertation. *Entrance requirements:* For master's and doctorate, GRE General Test, GRE Subject Test. Additional exam requirements/recommendations for international students: Required—TOEFL. *Application deadline:* For fall admission, 1/15 for domestic students. Application fee: $15. *Expenses:* Tuition: Full-time $28,965. *Financial support:* In 2003–04, 19 students received support, including fellowships with full tuition reimbursements available (averaging $18,528 per year), research assistantships with full tuition reimbursements available (averaging $18,528 per year); career-related internships or fieldwork, institutionally sponsored loans, scholarships/grants, tuition waivers (full), and unspecified assistantships also available. *Faculty research:* Geochemistry, remote sensing, geophysics, hydrology, economic geology. Total annual research expenditures: $1.1 million. *Unit head:* Dr. Richard Birnie, Chair, 603-646-2373. *Application contact:* Grace Morse, Administrative Assistant, 603-646-2373, Fax: 603-646-3922, E-mail: grace.morse@dartmouth.edu.

Emporia State University, School of Graduate Studies, College of Liberal Arts and Sciences, Department of Physical Sciences, Emporia, KS 66801-5087. Offers chemistry (MS); earth science (MS); physical science (MS); physics (MS). *Faculty:* 18 full-time (2 women), 1 (woman) part-time/adjunct. *Students:* 2 full-time (0 women), 21 part-time (6 women); includes 1 minority (African American), 2 international. 1 applicant, 100% accepted, 1 enrolled. In 2003, 3 degrees awarded. *Degree requirements:* For master's, comprehensive exam or thesis. *Entrance requirements:* For master's, written exam, appropriate undergraduate degree. Additional exam requirements/recommendations for international students: Required—TOEFL. *Application deadline:* For fall admission, 8/15 for domestic students. Applications are processed on a rolling basis. Application fee: $30 ($75 for international students). Electronic applications accepted. *Expenses:* Tuition, state resident: full-time $2,640; part-time $110 per credit hour. Tuition, nonresident: full-time $8,454; part-time $352 per credit hour. Required fees: $576; $35 per credit hour. Tuition and fees vary according to campus/location. *Financial support:* In 2003–04, 3 research assistantships (averaging $6,225 per year), 5 teaching assistantships with full tuition reimbursements (averaging $6,225 per year) were awarded. Federal Work-Study, institutionally sponsored loans, health care benefits, and unspecified assistantships also available. Financial award application deadline: 3/15; financial award applicants required to submit FAFSA. *Faculty research:* Bredigite, larnite, and dicalcium silicates–Marble Canyon. *Unit head:* Dr. DeWayne Backhus, Chair, 620-341-5330, Fax: 620-341-6055, E-mail: backhusd@emporia.edu.

Florida International University, College of Arts and Sciences, Department of Earth Sciences, Miami, FL 33199. Offers MS, PhD. Part-time and evening/weekend programs available. *Faculty:* 12 full-time (2 women). *Students:* 19 full-time (4 women), 6 part-time (3 women); includes 5 minority (1 African American, 4 Hispanic Americans), 8 international. Average age 32. 22 applicants, 41% accepted, 5 enrolled. In 2003, 1 degree awarded. *Degree requirements:* For master's, one foreign language, thesis; for doctorate, thesis/dissertation. *Entrance requirements:* For master's and doctorate, GRE General Test, 3 letters of recommendation. Additional exam requirements/recommendations for international students: Required—TOEFL. *Application deadline:* For fall admission, 4/1 for domestic students; for spring admission, 10/1 for domestic students. Applications are processed on a rolling basis. Application fee: $20. *Expenses:* Tuition, state resident: part-time $202 per credit. Tuition, nonresident: part-time $771 per credit. Required fees: $112 per semester. *Financial support:* Research assistantships, teaching assistantships available. Financial award application deadline: 4/1. *Faculty research:* Determination of dispersivity and hydraulic conductivity in the Biscayne Aquifer. *Unit head:* Dr. Rosemary Hickey-Vargas, Chairperson, 305-348-3572, Fax: 305-348-3877, E-mail: hickey@fiu.edu.

The George Washington University, Columbian College of Arts and Sciences, Department of Earth and Environmental Sciences, Program in Geosciences, Washington, DC 20052. Offers MS, PhD. *Students:* 2 full-time (both women), 1 part-time, 1 international. Average age 33. 8 applicants, 63% accepted. In 2003, 1 degree awarded. *Degree requirements:* For master's, thesis or alternative, comprehensive exam. *Entrance requirements:* For master's and doctorate, GRE General Test, bachelor's degree in field, minimum GPA of 3.0. Additional exam requirements/recommendations for international students: Required—TOEFL (minimum score 550 paper-based; 213 computer-based). *Application deadline:* For fall admission, 2/1 priority date for domestic students, 2/1 priority date for international students; for spring admission, 10/1 priority date for domestic students, 10/1 priority date for international students. Applications are processed on a rolling basis. Application fee: $60. Electronic applications accepted. *Expenses:* Tuition: Part-time $876 per credit. Required fees: $1 per credit. Tuition and fees vary according to campus/location. *Financial support:* In 2003–04, fellowships with full tuition reimbursements (averaging $10,000 per year), teaching assistantships (averaging $5,000 per year) were awarded. Financial award application deadline: 2/1. *Application contact:* Information Contact, 202-994-6190, Fax: 202-994-0450.

Georgia Institute of Technology, Graduate Studies and Research, College of Sciences, School of Earth and Atmospheric Sciences, Atlanta, GA 30332-0001. Offers atmospheric chemistry and air pollution (MS, PhD); atmospheric dynamics and climate (MS, PhD); geochemistry (MS, PhD); hydrologic cycle (MS, PhD); ocean sciences (MS, PhD); solid-earth and environmental geophysics (PhD); solid-earth and environmental geophysics (MS). Part-time programs available. *Students:* 80 full-time (40 women); includes 39 minority (5 African Americans, 31 Asian Americans or Pacific Islanders, 3 Hispanic Americans). 143 applicants, 18% accepted, 15 enrolled. In 2003, 14 master's, 6 doctorates awarded. Terminal master's awarded for partial completion of doctoral program. *Median time to degree:* Of those who began their doctoral program in fall 1995, 78% received their degree in 8 years or less. *Degree requirements:* For master's, thesis or alternative; for doctorate, thesis/dissertation, comprehensive exam. *Entrance requirements:* For master's and doctorate, GRE General Test, minimum GPA of 2.7. Additional exam requirements/recommendations for international students: Required—TOEFL (minimum score 550 paper-based; 213 computer-based). *Application deadline:* For fall admission, 1/15 priority date for domestic students, 1/15 priority date for international students; for spring admission, 1/1 for domestic students. Applications are processed on a rolling basis. Application fee: $50. *Expenses:* Tuition, state resident: part-time $1,925 per semester. Tuition, nonresident: part-time $7,700 per semester. Required fees: $434 per semester. Full-time tuition and fees vary according to program. *Financial support:* In 2003–04, 3 fellowships, 52 research assistantships (averaging $20,000 per year), 8 teaching assistantships were awarded. Career-related internships or fieldwork, Federal Work-Study, and institutionally sponsored loans also available. Financial award application deadline: 2/15. *Faculty research:* Geophysics, atmospheric chemistry, atmospheric dynamics, seismology. Total annual research expenditures: $5 million. *Unit head:* Dr. Judith A. Curry, Chair, 404-894-3948, Fax: 404-894-5638. *Application contact:* Derek M. Cunnold, Graduate Coordinator, 404-894-3814, Fax: 404-894-5638, E-mail: cunnold@eas.gatech.edu.

See in-depth description on page 237.

Georgia State University, College of Arts and Sciences, Department of Geology, Atlanta, GA 30303-3083. Offers geology (MS), including earth science. Part-time and evening/weekend programs available. *Faculty:* 7 full-time (2 women). *Students:* 23; includes 4 minority (2 African Americans, 2 Asian Americans or Pacific Islanders). 25 applicants, 84% accepted. In 2003, 3 degrees awarded. *Median time to degree:* Master's–2 years full-time. *Degree requirements:* For master's, one foreign language, thesis or alternative, comprehensive exam (for some programs), registration. *Entrance requirements:* For master's, GRE General Test, minimum GPA of 2.75. Additional exam requirements/recommendations for international students: Required—TOEFL. *Application deadline:* For fall admission, 7/1 for domestic students, 3/15 for international students; for spring admission, 11/15 for domestic students, 9/15 for international students. Applications are processed on a rolling basis. Application fee: $25. Electronic applications accepted. *Financial support:* In 2003–04, 17 students received support, including research assistantships with tuition reimbursements available (averaging $6,000 per year), teaching assistantships with tuition reimbursements available (averaging $6,000 per year); career-related internships or fieldwork, Federal Work-Study, institutionally sponsored loans, tuition waivers (partial), and unspecified assistantships also available. Support available to part-time students. Financial award application deadline: 7/15; financial award applicants required to submit FAFSA. *Faculty research:* Clay mineralogy, metamorphism, fracture analysis, carbonates, groundwater. Total annual research expenditures: $75,000. *Unit head:* Dr. Timothy LaTour, Chair, 404-651-2272, Fax: 404-651-1376, E-mail: tlatour@gsu.edu. *Application contact:* Dr. W. Crawford Elliott, Director of Graduate Studies, 404-651-2272, Fax: 404-651-1376, E-mail: geowce@langate.gsu.edu.

Graduate School and University Center of the City University of New York, Graduate Studies, Program in Earth and Environmental Sciences, New York, NY 10016-4039. Offers PhD. *Faculty:* 36 full-time (5 women). *Students:* 46 full-time (18 women), 4 part-time (1 woman); includes 10 minority (3 African Americans, 2 Asian Americans or Pacific Islanders, 5 Hispanic Americans), 17 international. Average age 36. 25 applicants, 76% accepted, 11 enrolled. In 2003, 2 degrees awarded. *Degree requirements:* For doctorate, one foreign language, thesis/dissertation, comprehensive exam. *Entrance requirements:* For doctorate, GRE General Test. *Application deadline:* For fall admission, 4/15 for domestic students. Application fee: $50. *Expenses:* Tuition, state resident: part-time $2,435 per semester. Tuition, nonresident: part-time $475 per credit. *Financial support:* In 2003–04, 30 students received support, including 28 fellowships, 2 research assistantships, 1 teaching assistantship; career-related internships or fieldwork, Federal Work-Study, institutionally sponsored loans, and tuition waivers (full and partial) also available. Financial award application deadline: 2/1; financial award applicants required to submit FAFSA. *Unit head:* Dr. Yehuda Klein, Acting Executive Officer, 212-817-8241, Fax: 212-817-1513.

Harvard University, Graduate School of Arts and Sciences, Department of Earth and Planetary Sciences, Cambridge, MA 02138. Offers AM, PhD. *Faculty:* 25 full-time (2 women). *Students:* 50 full-time (25 women); includes 11 minority (8 Asian Americans or Pacific Islanders, 3 Hispanic Americans). 103 applicants, 18% accepted, 11 enrolled. In 2003, 12 master's, 8 doctorates awarded. Terminal master's awarded for partial completion of doctoral program. *Degree requirements:* For master's, registration; for doctorate, thesis/dissertation, comprehensive exam, registration. *Entrance requirements:* For doctorate, GRE General Test. Additional exam requirements/recommendations for international students: Required—TOEFL. *Application deadline:* For fall admission, 1/2 for domestic students. Application fee: $85. Electronic applications accepted. *Expenses:* Tuition: Full-time $26,066. Full-time tuition and fees vary according to program and student level. *Financial support:* In 2003–04, 50 students received support; fellowships with full tuition reimbursements available, research assistantships, teaching assistantships, scholarships/grants and health care benefits available. *Faculty research:* Economic geography, geochemistry, geophysics, mineralogy, crystallography. *Unit head:* Ventatesh Narayanamurti, Dean, 617-495-5829, Fax: 617-495-5264, E-mail: venky@deas.harvard.edu. *Application contact:* Office of Admissions and Financial Aid, 617-495-5315.

See in-depth description on page 239.

Hunter College of the City University of New York, Graduate School, School of Arts and Sciences, Department of Geography, New York, NY 10021-5085. Offers analytical geography

(MA); earth system science (MA); environmental and social issues (MA); geographic information science (Certificate); geographic information systems (MA); teaching earth science (MA). Part-time and evening/weekend programs available. *Faculty:* 11 full-time (5 women), 2 part-time/adjunct (0 women). *Students:* 3 full-time (1 woman), 29 part-time (13 women); includes 5 minority (3 African Americans, 1 Asian American or Pacific Islander, 1 Hispanic American). Average age 35. 12 applicants, 75% accepted. *Degree requirements:* For master's, comprehensive exam or thesis. *Entrance requirements:* For master's, GRE General Test, minimum B average in major, B- overall; 18 credits in geography, 2 letters of recommendation; for Certificate, minimum of B average in major, B- overall. Additional exam requirements/recommendations for international students: Required—TOEFL. *Application deadline:* For fall admission, 4/1 for domestic students; for spring admission, 11/1 for domestic students. Applications are processed on a rolling basis. Application fee: $50. *Expenses:* Tuition, state resident: part-time $230 per credit. Tuition, nonresident: part-time $425 per credit. *Financial support:* In 2003–04, 1 fellowship (averaging $3,000 per year), 2 research assistantships (averaging $10,000 per year), 10 teaching assistantships (averaging $6,000 per year) were awarded. Career-related internships or fieldwork, Federal Work-Study, institutionally sponsored loans, and unspecified assistantships also available. Financial award application deadline: 3/1. *Faculty research:* Urban geography, economic geography, geographic information science, demographic methods, climate change. *Unit head:* Prof. Charles A. Heatwole, Chair, 212-772-5265, Fax: 212-772-5268, E-mail: cah@geo.hunter.cuny.edu. *Application contact:* Prof. Marianna Pavlovskaya, Graduate Adviser, 212-772-5320, Fax: 212-772-5268, E-mail: mpavlov@geo.hunter.cuny.edu.

Hunter College of the City University of New York, Graduate School, School of Education, Programs in Secondary Education, New York, NY 10021-5085. Offers biology education (MA); chemistry education (MA); earth science (MA); English education (MA); French education (MA); Italian education (MA); mathematics education (MA); physics education (MA); social studies education (MA); Spanish education (MA). *Faculty:* 5 full-time (4 women), 4 part-time/adjunct (1 woman). *Students:* 17 full-time (11 women), 134 part-time (83 women); includes 28 minority (10 African Americans, 10 Asian Americans or Pacific Islanders, 8 Hispanic Americans). Average age 36. 201 applicants, 63% accepted. In 2003, 22 degrees awarded. *Degree requirements:* For master's, thesis. *Application deadline:* For fall admission, 4/1 for domestic students, 2/1 for international students; for spring admission, 11/1 for domestic students, 9/1 for international students. Applications are processed on a rolling basis. Application fee: $50. *Expenses:* Tuition, state resident: part-time $230 per credit. Tuition, nonresident: part-time $425 per credit. *Financial support:* Fellowships, tuition waivers (full and partial) available. Support available to part-time students. *Unit head:* Dr. Gess LeBlanc, Coordinator, 212-772-5049, E-mail: gleblanc@hunter.cuny.edu. *Application contact:* William Zlata, Director for Graduate Admissions, 212-772-4482, Fax: 212-650-3336, E-mail: admissions@hunter.cuny.edu.

Idaho State University, Office of Graduate Studies, College of Arts and Sciences, Department of Geosciences, Pocatello, ID 83209. Offers geology (MS); geophysics/hydrology (MS); geotechnology (Postbaccalaureate Certificate); natural science (MNS). Part-time programs available. Postbaccalaureate distance learning degree programs offered. *Faculty:* 6 full-time (1 woman), 1 part-time/adjunct (0 women). *Students:* 18 full-time (3 women), 17 part-time (7 women), 1 international. Average age 32. In 2003, 6 master's, 3 other advanced degrees awarded. *Degree requirements:* For master's, thesis, comprehensive exam, registration (for some programs); for Postbaccalaureate Certificate, thesis optional. *Entrance requirements:* For master's and Postbaccalaureate Certificate, GRE General Test, 3 letters of recommendation. Additional exam requirements/recommendations for international students: Required—TOEFL (minimum score 550 paper-based; 213 computer-based). *Application deadline:* For fall admission, 7/1 priority date for domestic students, 7/1 priority date for international students; for spring admission, 12/1 priority date for domestic students, 12/1 priority date for international students. Applications are processed on a rolling basis. Application fee: $35. *Expenses:* Tuition, state resident: part-time $205 per credit. Tuition, nonresident: full-time $6,600; part-time $300 per credit. Required fees: $4,108. One-time fee: $35 full-time. *Financial support:* Research assistantships with full and partial tuition reimbursements, teaching assistantships with full and partial tuition reimbursements, career-related internships or fieldwork, Federal Work-Study, institutionally sponsored loans, and tuition waivers (full and partial) available. Financial award application deadline: 1/1. *Faculty research:* Structural geography, stratigraphy, geochemistry, volcanography, geomorphology. Total annual research expenditures: $541,774. *Unit head:* Dr. Scott Hughes, Chairman, 208-282-3365, Fax: 208-282-4414.

Indiana State University, School of Graduate Studies, College of Arts and Sciences, Department of Geography, Geology and Anthropology, Terre Haute, IN 47809-1401. Offers earth sciences (MA, MS); economic geography (PhD); geography (MA); geology (MS); physical geography (PhD). *Faculty:* 16 full-time (3 women), 1 part-time/adjunct (0 women). *Students:* 24 full-time (10 women), 18 part-time (7 women); includes 6 minority (1 African American, 1 American Indian/Alaska Native, 3 Asian Americans or Pacific Islanders, 1 Hispanic American), 15 international. In 2003, 12 master's, 3 doctorates awarded. *Degree requirements:* For master's, thesis or alternative; for doctorate, thesis/dissertation, departmental qualifying exam, comprehensive exam. *Entrance requirements:* For doctorate, GRE General Test. *Application deadline:* For fall admission, 7/1 for domestic students; for spring admission, 11/1 priority date for domestic students. Applications are processed on a rolling basis. Application fee: $45. Electronic applications accepted. *Expenses:* Tuition, state resident: full-time $4,356; part-time $242 per credit. Tuition, nonresident: full-time $8,658; part-time $481 per credit. Required fees: $50 per term. *Financial support:* In 2003–04, 9 research assistantships with partial tuition reimbursements (averaging $5,350 per year), 9 teaching assistantships with partial tuition reimbursements (averaging $5,350 per year) were awarded. Tuition waivers (partial) also available. Financial award application deadline: 3/1; financial award applicants required to submit FAFSA. *Unit head:* Dr. Susan Berta, Acting Chairperson, 812-237-2261.

Indiana University Bloomington, Graduate School, College of Arts and Sciences, Department of Geological Sciences, Bloomington, IN 47405. Offers biogeochemistry (MS, PhD); environmental geosciences (MS, PhD); geobiology, stratigraphy, and sedimentology (MS, PhD); geochemistry (MS, PhD); geochemistry, mineralogy, and petrology (MS, PhD); geophysics (MS, PhD); geophysics, tectonics, and structural geology (MS, PhD). PhD offered through the University Graduate School. Part-time programs available. *Faculty:* 14 full-time (1 woman). *Students:* 32 full-time (16 women), 18 part-time (8 women); includes 4 minority (2 African Americans, 2 Asian Americans or Pacific Islanders), 23 international. Average age 29. In 2003, 10 master's, 2 doctorates awarded. Terminal master's awarded for partial completion of doctoral program. *Degree requirements:* For master's, one foreign language, thesis or alternative; for doctorate, thesis/dissertation. *Entrance requirements:* For master's and doctorate, GRE General Test. Additional exam requirements/recommendations for international students: Required—TOEFL. *Application deadline:* For fall admission, 1/15 priority date for domestic students, 12/15 priority date for international students; for spring admission, 9/1 priority date for domestic students, 9/1 priority date for international students. Applications are processed on a rolling basis. Application fee: $45 ($55 for international students). *Expenses:* Tuition, state resident: full-time $4,908; part-time $205 per credit. Tuition, nonresident: full-time $14,298; part-time $596 per credit. Required fees: $661. Tuition and fees vary according to campus/location and program. *Financial support:* In 2003–04, research assistantships with full and partial tuition reimbursements (averaging $11,000 per year); fellowships with tuition reimbursements, teaching assistantships with tuition reimbursements, career-related internships or fieldwork, Federal Work-Study, and institutionally sponsored loans also available. Financial award application deadline: 2/15. *Faculty research:* Geophysics, geochemistry, hydrogeology, igneous and metamorphic petrology and clay minerology. Total annual research expenditures: $289,139. *Unit head:* Dr. Christopher G. Maples, Chairman, 812-855-5582, Fax: 812-855-7899, E-mail: cmaples@indiana.edu. *Application contact:* Mary Iverson, Secretary, Committee for Graduate Studies, 812-855-7214, Fax: 812-855-7899, E-mail: geograd@indiana.edu.

Iowa State University of Science and Technology, Graduate College, College of Liberal Arts and Sciences, Department of Geological and Atmospheric Sciences, Ames, IA 50011. Offers earth science (MS, PhD); geology (MS, PhD); meteorology (MS, PhD); water resources (MS, PhD). *Faculty:* 17 full-time. *Students:* 28 full-time (13 women), 7 part-time (2 women); includes 1 minority (African American), 19 international. 24 applicants, 38% accepted, 6 enrolled. In 2003, 12 master's, 1 doctorate awarded. *Median time to degree:* Master's–2.9 years full-time. *Degree requirements:* For master's, thesis (for some programs); for doctorate, thesis/dissertation. *Entrance requirements:* For master's and doctorate, GRE General Test. Additional exam requirements/recommendations for international students: Required—TOEFL (paper score 530; computer score 197) or IELTS (score 6.0). *Application deadline:* For fall admission, 2/15 for domestic students. Applications are processed on a rolling basis. Application fee: $30 ($70 for international students). Electronic applications accepted. Tuition, nonresident: part-time $560 per credit. Required fees: $38 per unit. *Financial support:* In 2003–04, 20 research assistantships with full and partial tuition reimbursements (averaging $15,432 per year), 11 teaching assistantships with full and partial tuition reimbursements (averaging $15,432 per year) were awarded. Fellowships, scholarships/grants, health care benefits, and unspecified assistantships also available. *Unit head:* Dr. Carl E. Jacobson, Chair, 515-294-4477.

Lehigh University, College of Arts and Sciences, Department of Earth and Environmental Sciences, Bethlehem, PA 18015-3094. Offers MS, PhD. *Faculty:* 14 full-time (2 women). *Students:* 27 full-time (14 women), 2 part-time; includes 3 minority (all Asian Americans or Pacific Islanders) Average age 26. 35 applicants, 40% accepted, 9 enrolled. In 2003, 6 master's, 1 doctorate awarded. Terminal master's awarded for partial completion of doctoral program. *Degree requirements:* For master's, thesis, registration; for doctorate, thesis/dissertation, language at the discretion of the PhD committee, comprehensive exam, registration. *Entrance requirements:* For master's and doctorate, GRE General Test, 2 letters of recommendation. Additional exam requirements/recommendations for international students: Required—TOEFL. *Application deadline:* For fall admission, 1/15 for domestic students; for spring admission, 10/15 priority date for domestic students. Applications are processed on a rolling basis. Application fee: $40. *Expenses:* Tuition: Full-time $16,920; part-time $940 per credit hour. Required fees: $200. Tuition and fees vary according to degree level and program. *Financial support:* In 2003–04, 3 fellowships with full tuition reimbursements (averaging $13,670 per year), 4 research assistantships with full tuition reimbursements (averaging $13,670 per year), 8 teaching assistantships with full tuition reimbursements (averaging $13,670 per year) were awarded. Federal Work-Study, institutionally sponsored loans, and tuition waivers (full and partial) also available. Financial award application deadline: 1/15. *Faculty research:* Tectonics, surficial processes, aquatic ecology. Total annual research expenditures: $1.5 million. *Unit head:* Dr. Anne S. Meltzer, Chairman, 610-758-3660 Ext. 3673, Fax: 610-758-3677, E-mail: asm3@lehigh.edu. *Application contact:* Dr. Frank Jame Pazzaglia, Graduate Coordinator, 610-758-3660 Ext. 3667, Fax: 610-758-3677, E-mail: fjp3@lehigh.edu.

See in-depth description on page 731.

Massachusetts Institute of Technology, School of Science, Department of Earth, Atmospheric, and Planetary Sciences, Cambridge, MA 02139-4307. Offers atmospheric chemistry (PhD, Sc D); atmospheric science (SM, PhD, Sc D); climate physics and chemistry (PhD, Sc D); earth and planetary sciences (SM); geochemistry (PhD, Sc D); geology (PhD, Sc D); geophysics (PhD, Sc D); geosystems (SM); oceanography (SM, PhD, Sc D); planetary sciences (PhD, Sc D). *Faculty:* 37 full-time (3 women). *Students:* 147 full-time (61 women); includes 9 minority (4 Asian Americans or Pacific Islanders, 5 Hispanic Americans), 48 international. Average age 27. 176 applicants, 49% accepted, 31 enrolled. In 2003, 8 master's, 19 doctorates awarded. Terminal master's awarded for partial completion of doctoral program. *Degree requirements:* For master's, thesis/dissertation; for doctorate, thesis/dissertation, comprehensive exam. *Entrance requirements:* For master's, GRE General Test, GRE Subject Test (joint MIT/WHOI program); for doctorate, GRE General Test, GRE Subject Test (chemistry or physics for planetary science program). Additional exam requirements/recommendations for international students: Required—TOEFL (minimum score 577 paper-based; 233 computer-based). *Application deadline:* For fall admission, 1/5 for domestic students, 1/5 for international students; for spring admission, 11/1 for domestic students, 11/1 for international students. Application fee: $70. Electronic applications accepted. *Expenses:* Tuition: Full-time $29,400. Required fees: $200. *Financial support:* In 2003–04, 113 students received support, including 25 fellowships with tuition reimbursements available, 70 research assistantships with tuition reimbursements available (averaging $23,760 per year), 21 teaching assistantships with tuition reimbursements available (averaging $18,270 per year); Federal Work-Study, institutionally sponsored loans, scholarships/grants, health care benefits, and unspecified assistantships also available. *Faculty research:* Evolution of main features of the planetary system; origin, composition, structure, and state of the atmospheres, oceans, surfaces, and interiors of planets; dynamics of planets and satellite motions. Total annual research expenditures: $19.1 million. *Unit head:* Prof. Maria Zuber, 617-253-0149, Fax: 617-253-8298, E-mail: mtz@mit.edu. *Application contact:* Carol Sprague, Administrative Assistant, 617-253-3381, Fax: 617-253-8298, E-mail: eapsinfo@mit.edu.

McGill University, Faculty of Graduate and Postdoctoral Studies, Faculty of Science, Department of Earth and Planetary Sciences, Montréal, QC H3A 2T5, Canada. Offers M Sc, PhD, Diploma. *Faculty:* 12 full-time (3 women). *Students:* 31 full-time. Average age 25. 29 applicants, 45% accepted, 5 enrolled. In 2003, 8 master's, 3 doctorates awarded. *Degree requirements:* For master's and doctorate, thesis/dissertation. *Entrance requirements:* For master's, minimum GPA of 3.0. Additional exam requirements/recommendations for international students: Required—TOEFL. *Application deadline:* For fall admission, 3/1 for domestic students. Applications are processed on a rolling basis. Application fee: $60 Canadian dollars. Tuition, area resident: Full-time $1,668. *Expenses:* Tuition, state resident: full-time $4,173. Tuition, nonresident: full-time $9,468. Required fees: $1,081. *Financial support:* Fellowships, research assistantships, teaching assistantships, institutionally sponsored loans and tuition waivers (partial) available. *Faculty research:* Geochemistry, sedimentary petrology, igneous petrology, theoretical geophysics, economic geology, planetary sciences. *Unit head:* Dr. Alfonso Mucci, Chair, 514-398-4892, Fax: 514-398-4680, E-mail: alm@eps.mcgill.ca. *Application contact:* Dr. Carol Matthews, Graduate Program Coordinator, 514-398-6767, Fax: 514-398-4680, E-mail: carol@eps.mcgill.ca.

McMaster University, School of Graduate Studies, Faculty of Science, School of Geography and Geology, Hamilton, ON L8S 4M2, Canada. Offers geochemistry (PhD); geology (M Sc, PhD); human geography (MA, PhD); physical geography (M Sc, PhD). Part-time programs available. Terminal master's awarded for partial completion of doctoral program. *Degree requirements:* For master's, thesis/dissertation; for doctorate, thesis/dissertation, comprehensive exam. *Entrance requirements:* For master's, minimum B+ average. Additional exam requirements/recommendations for international students: Required—TOEFL (minimum score 550 paper-based; 213 computer-based).

Memorial University of Newfoundland, School of Graduate Studies, Department of Earth Sciences, St. John's, NL A1C 5S7, Canada. Offers geology (M Sc, PhD); geophysics (M Sc, PhD). Part-time programs available. *Students:* 43 full-time, 8 part-time. 37 applicants, 24% accepted, 7 enrolled. In 2003, 10 master's, 1 doctorate awarded. *Degree requirements:* For master's, thesis; for doctorate, thesis/dissertation, oral thesis defense, comprehensive exam. *Entrance requirements:* For master's, honors B Sc; for doctorate, M Sc. *Application deadline:* For fall admission, 3/31 for domestic students; for spring admission, 12/31 for domestic students. Applications are processed on a rolling basis. Application fee: $40. Electronic applications accepted. Tuition and fees charges are reported in Canadian dollars. *Expenses:* Tuition, state resident: part-time $733 Canadian dollars per semester. Tuition, nonresident: part-time $953 Canadian dollars per semester. Required fees: $194 Canadian dollars per year. Tuition and fees vary according to degree level and program. *Financial support:* Fellowships, research assistantships, teaching assistantships available. *Faculty research:* Geochemistry, sedimentology, paleoceanography and global change, mineral deposits, petroleum geology, hydrology. *Unit head:* Dr. J. Wright, Head, 709-737-2334, Fax: 709-737-2589, E-mail: jim@waves.esd.mun.ca. *Application contact:* Dr. Ali Aksu, Graduate Officer, 709-737-8385, Fax: 709-737-2589, E-mail: aaksu@sparky2.esd.ucs.mun.ca.

Geosciences

Michigan State University, Graduate School, College of Natural Science, Department of Geological Sciences, East Lansing, MI 48824. Offers environmental geosciences (MS, PhD); environmental geosciences-environmental toxicology (PhD); geological sciences (MS, PhD). Part-time programs available. *Faculty:* 12 full-time (2 women). *Students:* 24 full-time (11 women), 4 part-time (2 women); includes 1 minority (Asian American or Pacific Islander), 3 international. Average age 28. 47 applicants, 62% accepted, 7 enrolled. In 2003, 8 master's, 2 doctorates awarded. *Median time to degree:* Master's–3.1 years full-time; doctorate–3.3 years full-time. *Degree requirements:* For master's and doctorate, thesis/dissertation, registration. *Entrance requirements:* For master's, GRE General Test, minimum GPA of 3.0, geoscience coursework, 3 letters of recommendation; for doctorate, GRE General Test, 3 letters of recommendation. Additional exam requirements/recommendations for international students: Required—TOEFL (minimum score 575 paper-based; 232 computer-based), TSE required only for teaching positions. *Application deadline:* For fall admission, 1/15 priority date for domestic students, 6/1 priority date for international students; for spring admission, 10/15 priority date for domestic students, 11/1 priority date for international students. Applications are processed on a rolling basis. Application fee: $50. Electronic applications accepted. *Expenses:* Tuition, state resident: part-time $291 per hour. Tuition, nonresident: part-time $589 per hour. *Financial support:* In 2003–04, 9 research assistantships with full tuition reimbursements (averaging $11,376 per year), 23 teaching assistantships with full tuition reimbursements (averaging $11,376 per year) were awarded. Fellowships with tuition reimbursements, Federal Work-Study, institutionally sponsored loans, scholarships/grants, health care benefits, and unspecified assistantships also available. Financial award application deadline: 1/15; financial award applicants required to submit CSS PROFILE or FAFSA. *Faculty research:* Water in the environment, biogeochemical cycles, paleobiology and paleoenvironmental change, crystal dynamics. Total annual research expenditures: $841,206. *Unit head:* Dr. Michael A. Velbel, Chairperson, 517-355-4626, Fax: 517-353-8787, E-mail: geosci@msu.edu.

Mississippi State University, College of Arts and Sciences, Department of Geosciences, Mississippi State, MS 39762. Offers MS. *Faculty:* 17 full-time (2 women), 3 part-time/adjunct (all women). *Students:* 43 full-time (14 women), 321 part-time (193 women); includes 29 minority (13 African Americans, 3 American Indian/Alaska Native, 5 Asian Americans or Pacific Islanders, 8 Hispanic Americans), 6 international. Average age 37. 160 applicants, 94% accepted, 137 enrolled. In 2003, 127 degrees awarded. *Degree requirements:* For master's, thesis (for some programs), comprehensive oral or written exam. *Entrance requirements:* For master's, minimum QPA of 2.75. Additional exam requirements/recommendations for international students: Required—TOEFL. *Application deadline:* For fall admission, 7/1 for domestic students; for spring admission, 11/1 for domestic students. Applications are processed on a rolling basis. Application fee: $25. *Expenses:* Tuition, state resident: full-time $3,874; part-time $215 per hour. Tuition, nonresident: full-time $8,780; part-time $488 per hour. International tuition: $9,105 full-time. Tuition and fees vary according to course load. *Financial support:* In 2003–04, 3 students received support, including 3 research assistantships with full tuition reimbursements available (averaging $8,177 per year), 13 teaching assistantships with full tuition reimbursements available (averaging $7,725 per year); Federal Work-Study, institutionally sponsored loans, tuition waivers (partial), and unspecified assistantships also available. Financial award application deadline: 4/1; financial award applicants required to submit FAFSA. *Faculty research:* Climatology, hydrogeology, sedimentology, meteorology. Total annual research expenditures: $39,695. *Unit head:* Dr. Mark S. Binkley, Head, 662-325-3915, Fax: 662-325-9423, E-mail: binkley@geosci.msstate.edu. *Application contact:* Diane D. Wolfe, Director of Admissions, 662-325-2224, Fax: 662-325-7360, E-mail: admit@admissions.msstate.edu.

Montana State University–Bozeman, College of Graduate Studies, College of Letters and Science, Department of Earth Sciences, Bozeman, MT 59717. Offers earth sciences (MS, PhD); land rehabilitation (interdisciplinary) (MS). Part-time programs available. *Faculty:* 11 full-time (1 woman), 3 part-time/adjunct (0 women). *Students:* 8 full-time (4 women), 24 part-time (10 women). Average age 29. 13 applicants, 85% accepted, 10 enrolled. In 2003, 5 degrees awarded. *Degree requirements:* For master's, thesis (for some programs), comprehensive exam, registration; for doctorate, thesis/dissertation, comprehensive exam, registration. *Entrance requirements:* For master's and doctorate, GRE General Test. Additional exam requirements/recommendations for international students: Required—TOEFL (minimum score 550 paper-based; 213 computer-based). *Application deadline:* For fall admission, 7/15 priority date for domestic students, 5/15 priority date for international students; for spring admission, 12/1 priority date for domestic students. Applications are processed on a rolling basis. Application fee: $50. Electronic applications accepted. *Expenses:* Tuition, state resident: full-time $3,907; part-time $163 per credit. Tuition, nonresident: full-time $12,383; part-time $516 per credit. Required fees: $890; $445 per term. Tuition and fees vary according to course load and program. *Financial support:* In 2003–04, 3 students received support, including 4 research assistantships (averaging $4,471 per year), 13 teaching assistantships with full tuition reimbursements available (averaging $8,787 per year); scholarships/grants and tuition waivers (partial) also available. Financial award application deadline: 3/1; financial award applicants required to submit FAFSA. *Faculty research:* Cultural geography, paleontology, GIS. Total annual research expenditures: $579,446. *Unit head:* Dr. David Lageson, Head, 406-994-3331, Fax: 406-994-6923, E-mail: lageson@montana.edu.

Montana Tech of The University of Montana, Graduate School, Geoscience Program, Butte, MT 59701-8997. Offers geochemistry (MS); geological engineering (MS); geology (MS); geophysical engineering (MS); hydrogeological engineering (MS); hydrogeology (MS). Part-time programs available. *Faculty:* 8 full-time (1 woman). *Students:* 15 full-time (5 women), 1 (woman) part-time. 17 applicants, 71% accepted, 9 enrolled. In 2003, 7 degrees awarded. *Degree requirements:* For master's, thesis (for some programs), comprehensive exam (for some programs), registration. *Entrance requirements:* For master's, GRE General Test, minimum GPA of 3.0. Additional exam requirements/recommendations for international students: Required—TOEFL (minimum score 525 paper-based; 195 computer-based). *Application deadline:* For fall admission, 4/1 priority date for domestic students, 3/1 priority date for international students; for spring admission, 10/1 priority date for domestic students, 7/1 priority date for international students. Applications are processed on a rolling basis. Application fee: $30. *Expenses:* Tuition, state resident: full-time $4,741; part-time $233 per credit. Tuition, nonresident: full-time $14,662; part-time $646 per credit. *Financial support:* In 2003–04, 15 students received support, including 10 research assistantships with partial tuition reimbursements available (averaging $4,655 per year), 10 teaching assistantships with partial tuition reimbursements available (averaging $4,800 per year); career-related internships or fieldwork, tuition waivers (full and partial), and unspecified assistantships also available. Financial award application deadline: 4/1; financial award applicants required to submit FAFSA. *Faculty research:* Water resource development, seismic processing, petroleum reservoir characterization, environmental geochemistry, molecular modeling, magmatic and hydrothermal ore deposits. Total annual research expenditures: $623,564. *Unit head:* Dr. Diane Wolfgram, Department Head, 406-496-4353, Fax: 406-496-4260, E-mail: dwolfgram@mtech.edu. *Application contact:* Cindy Dunstan, Administrator, Graduate School, 406-496-4304, Fax: 406-496-4334, E-mail: cdunstan@mtech.edu.

Montclair State University, The Graduate School, College of Science and Mathematics, Department of Earth and Environmental Studies, Program in Geoscience, Upper Montclair, NJ 07043-1624. Offers geoscience (MS); water resource management (Certificate). Part-time and evening/weekend programs available. *Faculty:* 12 full-time (0 women), 7 part-time/adjunct. *Students:* 1 (woman) full-time, 7 part-time (1 woman), 1 international. 8 applicants, 63% accepted, 3 enrolled. In 2003, 8 degrees awarded. *Degree requirements:* For master's, thesis or alternative, comprehensive exam. *Entrance requirements:* For master's, GRE General Test, 2 letters of recommendation. Additional exam requirements/recommendations for international students: Required—TOEFL (minimum score 550 paper-based; 213 computer-based). *Application deadline:* Applications are processed on a rolling basis. Application fee: $60. *Expenses:* Tuition, state resident: full-time $8,771; part-time $323 per credit. Tuition, nonresident: full-time $10,365; part-time $470 per credit. Required fees: $42 per credit. Tuition and fees vary according to degree level and program. *Financial support:* In 2003–04, research assistantships with full tuition reimbursements (averaging $5,000 per year); Federal Work-Study, scholarships/grants, and unspecified assistantships also available. Support available to part-time students. Financial award application deadline: 3/1; financial award applicants required to submit FAFSA. *Unit head:* Dr. Duke Ophori, Adviser, 973-655-7558, E-mail: ophorid@mail.montclair.edu.

Murray State University, College of Science, Engineering and Technology, Department of Geosciences, Murray, KY 42071-0009. Offers MA, MS. Part-time programs available. *Degree requirements:* For master's, thesis (for some programs). *Entrance requirements:* For master's, GRE General Test. Additional exam requirements/recommendations for international students: Required—TOEFL.

New Mexico Institute of Mining and Technology, Graduate Studies, Department of Earth and Environmental Science, Socorro, NM 87801. Offers geology and geochemistry (MS, PhD), including geochemistry, geology; geophysics (MS, PhD); hydrology (MS, PhD). *Faculty:* 21 full-time (2 women), 29 part-time/adjunct (5 women). *Students:* 68 full-time (32 women), 7 part-time (5 women); includes 2 minority (1 Asian American or Pacific Islander, 1 Hispanic American), 13 international. Average age 29. 76 applicants, 19 enrolled. In 2003, 19 master's, 2 doctorates awarded. *Degree requirements:* For master's, thesis optional; for doctorate, thesis/dissertation. *Entrance requirements:* For master's, GRE General Test; for doctorate, GRE General Test, GRE Subject Test. Additional exam requirements/recommendations for international students: Required—TOEFL. *Application deadline:* For fall admission, 3/1 for domestic students; for spring admission, 6/1 for domestic students. Applications are processed on a rolling basis. Application fee: $16. *Expenses:* Tuition, state resident: full-time $2,276; part-time $126 per credit. Tuition, nonresident: full-time $9,170; part-time $509 per credit. Required fees: $924; $27 per credit. $214 per term. Part-time tuition and fees vary according to course load. *Financial support:* In 2003–04, 1 fellowship (averaging $8,000 per year), 44 research assistantships (averaging $13,000 per year), 18 teaching assistantships with full and partial tuition reimbursements (averaging $7,900 per year) were awarded. Federal Work-Study, institutionally sponsored loans, and unspecified assistantships also available. Financial award application deadline: 3/1; financial award applicants required to submit CSS PROFILE or FAFSA. *Faculty research:* Seismology, geochemistry, caves and karst topography, hydrology, volcanology. *Unit head:* Dr. Andrew Campbell, Coordinator, 505-835-5327, Fax: 505-835-6436, E-mail: geos@nmt.edu. *Application contact:* Dr. David B. Johnson, Dean of Graduate Studies, 505-835-5513, Fax: 505-835-5476, E-mail: graduate@nmt.edu.

North Carolina Central University, Division of Academic Affairs, College of Arts and Sciences, Department of Earth Sciences, Durham, NC 27707-3129. Offers MS. *Faculty:* 1 (woman) full-time. *Students:* 1 full-time (0 women), 6 part-time (1 woman); includes 6 minority (all African Americans) Average age 28. 2 applicants, 100% accepted, 2 enrolled. In 2003, 2 degrees awarded. *Degree requirements:* For master's, one foreign language, comprehensive exam. *Entrance requirements:* For master's, GRE, minimum GPA of 3.0 in major, 2.5 overall. Additional exam requirements/recommendations for international students: Required—TOEFL. *Application deadline:* For fall admission, 8/1 for domestic students. Application fee: $30. *Expenses:* Tuition, state resident: full-time $3,366. Tuition, nonresident: full-time $12,872. *Financial support:* Federal Work-Study, institutionally sponsored loans, and unspecified assistantships available. Support available to part-time students. Financial award application deadline: 5/1. *Unit head:* Dr. Albert P. Barnett, Chairperson, 919-560-5171, Fax: 919-530-7986, E-mail: abarnett@wpo.nccu.edu. *Application contact:* Dr. Mattie Moss, Dean, 919-560-6368, Fax: 919-530-5361, E-mail: mmoss@wpo.nccu.edu.

North Carolina State University, Graduate School, College of Physical and Mathematical Sciences, Department of Marine, Earth, and Atmospheric Sciences, Raleigh, NC 27695. Offers marine, earth, and atmospheric sciences (MS, PhD); meteorology (MS, PhD); oceanography (MS, PhD). *Faculty:* 41 full-time (6 women), 57 part-time/adjunct (4 women). *Students:* 91 full-time (32 women), 16 part-time (3 women); includes 4 minority (2 African Americans, 1 Asian American or Pacific Islander, 1 Hispanic American), 17 international. Average age 30. 106 applicants, 50% accepted. In 2003, 19 master's, 6 doctorates awarded. Terminal master's awarded for partial completion of doctoral program. *Median time to degree:* Master's–2.7 years full-time; doctorate–5 years full-time. Of those who began their doctoral program in fall 1995, 90% received their degree in 8 years or less. *Degree requirements:* For master's, thesis (for some programs), final oral exam; for doctorate, thesis/dissertation, final oral exam, preliminary oral and written exams, comprehensive exam, registration. *Entrance requirements:* For master's, GRE General Test, minimum GPA of 3.0; for doctorate, GRE General Test, GRE Subject Test for disciplines in biological oceanography and geology, minimum GPA of 3.0. Additional exam requirements/recommendations for international students: Required—TOEFL (minimum score 550 paper-based). *Application deadline:* For fall admission, 6/25 for domestic students, 3/1 for international students; for spring admission, 11/25 for domestic students, 7/15 for international students. Applications are processed on a rolling basis. Application fee: $45. Electronic applications accepted. *Expenses:* Tuition, state resident: part-time $396 per hour. Tuition, nonresident: part-time $1,895 per hour. *Financial support:* In 2003–04, 76 students received support, including 1 fellowship with tuition reimbursement available (averaging $10,397 per year), 47 research assistantships with tuition reimbursements available (averaging $5,959 per year), 32 teaching assistantships with tuition reimbursements available (averaging $6,594 per year); institutionally sponsored loans and unspecified assistantships also available. Financial award application deadline: 3/1. *Faculty research:* Boundary layer and air quality meteorology; climate and mesoscale dynamics; biological, chemical, geological, and physical oceanography; hard rock, soft rock, environmental, and paleogeology. Total annual research expenditures: $5.6 million. *Unit head:* Dr. John C. Fountain, Head, 919-515-3717, Fax: 919-515-7802, E-mail: fountain@ncsu.edu. *Application contact:* Dr. Gerald S. Janowitz, Director of Graduate Programs, 919-515-7837, Fax: 919-515-7802, E-mail: janowitz@ncsu.edu.

See in-depth description on page 247.

Northeastern Illinois University, Graduate College, College of Arts and Sciences, Department of Earth Science, Program in Earth Science, Chicago, IL 60625-4699. Offers MS. Part-time and evening/weekend programs available. *Degree requirements:* For master's, oral presentation, thesis optional. *Entrance requirements:* For master's, 15 undergraduate hours in earth science, 8 undergraduate hours in chemistry and physics, minimum GPA of 2.75. *Faculty research:* Coastal engineering, Paleozoic and Precambrian tectonics and volcanology, ravine erosion control, well head protection delineation, genesis and evolution of basaltic magma.

Northern Arizona University, Graduate College, College of Arts and Sciences, Department of Geology, Program in Earth Science, Flagstaff, AZ 86011. Offers MAT, MS. *Students:* 1 full-time (0 women), 1 part-time; includes 1 minority (American Indian/Alaska Native). Average age 28. 1 applicant, 100% accepted. In 2003, 1 degree awarded. *Application deadline:* For fall admission, 3/1 for domestic students; for spring admission, 11/1 for domestic students. Applications are processed on a rolling basis. Application fee: $45. *Expenses:* Tuition, state resident: full-time $5,103. Tuition, nonresident: full-time $12,623. *Financial support:* Career-related internships or fieldwork, Federal Work-Study, and tuition waivers (full and partial) available. *Unit head:* Dr. Paul Morgan, Coordinator, 928-523-7175. *Application contact:* Information Contact, 928-523-4561, Fax: 928-523-9220, E-mail: earth.science@nau.edu.

Northwestern University, The Graduate School, Judd A. and Marjorie Weinberg College of Arts and Sciences, Department of Geological Sciences, Evanston, IL 60208. Offers MS, PhD. Admissions and degrees offered through The Graduate School. Part-time programs available. *Degree requirements:* For doctorate, thesis/dissertation. *Entrance requirements:* For master's and doctorate, GRE General Test. Additional exam requirements/recommendations for international students: Required—TOEFL. Electronic applications accepted. *Faculty research:* Tectonophysics, seismology, biogeochemistry, stratigraphy, paleontology.

Oregon State University, Graduate School, College of Science, Department of Geosciences, Corvallis, OR 97331. Offers geography (MA, MAIS, MS, PhD); geology (MA, MAIS, MS, PhD).

Part-time programs available. *Faculty:* 18 full-time (3 women), 3 part-time/adjunct (2 women). *Students:* 65 full-time (26 women), 9 part-time (1 woman); includes 4 minority (1 American Indian/Alaska Native, 1 Asian American or Pacific Islander, 2 Hispanic Americans), 5 international. Average age 31. In 2003, 16 master's, 3 doctorates awarded. Terminal master's awarded for partial completion of doctoral program. *Degree requirements:* For doctorate, one foreign language, thesis/dissertation. *Entrance requirements:* For master's and doctorate, GRE General Test, GRE Subject Test, minimum GPA of 3.0 in last 90 hours. Additional exam requirements/recommendations for international students: Required—TOEFL. *Application deadline:* For fall admission, 2/1 for domestic students. Applications are processed on a rolling basis. Application fee: $50. *Expenses:* Tuition, state resident: full-time $8,139; part-time $301 per credit. Tuition, nonresident: full-time $14,376; part-time $532 per credit. Required fees: $1,227. *Financial support:* Fellowships, research assistantships, teaching assistantships, career-related internships or fieldwork, Federal Work-Study, and institutionally sponsored loans available. Support available to part-time students. Financial award application deadline: 2/1. *Unit head:* Dr. Roger L. Nielsen, Chair, 541-737-1201, Fax: 541-737-1200, E-mail: rnielsen@oce.orst.edu. *Application contact:* Joanne VanGeest, Graduate Admissions Coordinator, 541-737-1204, Fax: 541-737-1200, E-mail: vangeesj@geo.orst.edu.

The Pennsylvania State University University Park Campus, Graduate School, College of Earth and Mineral Sciences, Department of Geosciences, State College, University Park, PA 16802-1503. Offers geochemistry (MS, PhD); geology (MS, PhD); geophysics (MS, PhD). *Students:* 90 full-time (36 women), 5 part-time (1 woman); includes 2 minority (1 American Indian/Alaska Native, 1 Asian American or Pacific Islander), 30 international. *Entrance requirements:* For master's and doctorate, GRE General Test. Additional exam requirements/recommendations for international students: Required—TOEFL. Application fee: $45. *Unit head:* Dr. Katharine H. Freeman, Professor of Geosciences, 814-863-8177, Fax: 814-863-7823, E-mail: khf4@psu.edu.

See in-depth description on page 249.

Princeton University, Graduate School, Department of Geosciences, Princeton, NJ 08544-1019. Offers atmospheric and oceanic sciences (PhD); geological and geophysical sciences (PhD). *Faculty:* 29 full-time (2 women), 2 part-time/adjunct (0 women). *Students:* 21 full-time (10 women), 11 international. Average age 24. 51 applicants, 31% accepted, 6 enrolled. In 2003, 6 doctorates awarded, leading to continued full-time study 100%. *Median time to degree:* Doctorate–5.08 years full-time. *Degree requirements:* For doctorate, one foreign language, thesis/dissertation. *Entrance requirements:* For doctorate, GRE General Test. Additional exam requirements/recommendations for international students: Required—TOEFL (minimum score 600 paper-based; 250 computer-based). *Application deadline:* For fall admission, 12/31 for domestic students, 12/1 for international students. Application fee: $80 ($55 for international students). Electronic applications accepted. *Expenses:* Tuition: Full-time $29,910. Required fees: $810. *Financial support:* In 2003–04, 8 fellowships with full tuition reimbursements (averaging $16,500 per year), 12 research assistantships with full tuition reimbursements (averaging $30,570 per year), 11 teaching assistantships with full tuition reimbursements (averaging $22,042 per year) were awarded. Federal Work-Study, institutionally sponsored loans, and summer salary is $7000 also available. Financial award application deadline: 1/2. *Faculty research:* Biogeochemistry, climate science, earth history, regional geology and tectonics, solid–earth geophysics. Total annual research expenditures: $19 million. *Unit head:* Prof. Guust Nolet, Director of Graduate Studies, 609-258-4128, Fax: 609-258-1274, E-mail: nolet@princeton.edu. *Application contact:* Janice Yip, Director of Graduate Admissions, 609-258-3034, Fax: 609-258-6180, E-mail: gsadmit@princeton.edu.

Purdue University, Graduate School, School of Science, Department of Earth and Atmospheric Sciences, West Lafayette, IN 47907. Offers MS, PhD. *Degree requirements:* For master's, thesis; for doctorate, one foreign language, thesis/dissertation. *Entrance requirements:* For master's and doctorate, GRE General Test. Additional exam requirements/recommendations for international students: Required—TOEFL. Electronic applications accepted. *Faculty research:* Geology, geophysics, hydrogeology, paleoclimatology, environmental science.

Radford University, Graduate College, College of Arts and Sciences, Department of Geology, Radford, VA 24142. Offers engineering geosciences (MS). Part-time programs available. Postbaccalaureate distance learning degree programs offered (minimal on-campus study). *Degree requirements:* For master's, thesis (for some programs), comprehensive exam. Electronic applications accepted.

Rensselaer Polytechnic Institute, Graduate School, School of Science, Department of Earth and Environmental Sciences, Troy, NY 12180-3590. Offers environmental chemistry (MS, PhD); geochemistry (MS, PhD); geology (MS, PhD); geophysics (MS, PhD); petrology (MS, PhD). Part-time programs available. *Faculty:* 7 full-time (0 women). *Students:* 15 full-time (7 women); includes 3 minority (all Asian Americans or Pacific Islanders) Average age 24. 35 applicants, 11% accepted. In 2003, 4 master's, 1 doctorate awarded. Terminal master's awarded for partial completion of doctoral program. *Degree requirements:* For master's, thesis (for some programs), comprehensive exam; for doctorate, thesis/dissertation, comprehensive exam. *Entrance requirements:* For master's and doctorate, GRE General Test. Additional exam requirements/recommendations for international students: Required—TOEFL. *Application deadline:* For fall admission, 1/15 for domestic students. Applications are processed on a rolling basis. Application fee: $45. Electronic applications accepted. *Expenses:* Tuition: Full-time $27,700; part-time $1,320 per credit. Required fees: $1,470. *Financial support:* In 2003–04, 9 research assistantships with full tuition reimbursements (averaging $12,000 per year), 5 teaching assistantships with full tuition reimbursements (averaging $12,000 per year) were awarded. Fellowships with full tuition reimbursements, career-related internships or fieldwork, institutionally sponsored loans, and scholarships/grants also available. Financial award application deadline: 2/1; financial award applicants required to submit FAFSA. *Faculty research:* Mantel geochemistry, contaminant geochemistry, seismology, GPS geodesy, remote sensing petrology. Total annual research expenditures: $1.3 million. *Unit head:* Dr. Frank Spear, Chair, 518-276-6474, Fax: 518-276-6680, E-mail: ees@rpi.edu. *Application contact:* Dr. Steven Roecker, Professor, 518-276-6474, Fax: 518-276-6680, E-mail: ees@rpi.edu.

Rice University, Graduate Programs, Wiess School of Natural Sciences, Department of Earth Science, Houston, TX 77251-1892. Offers MA, PhD. *Faculty:* 15 full-time (1 woman), 20 part-time/adjunct (0 women). *Students:* 50 full-time (21 women); includes 2 minority (both African Americans), 16 international. Average age 28. 93 applicants, 22% accepted, 13 enrolled. In 2003, 1 degree awarded, leading to business/industry 100%. *Degree requirements:* For master's and doctorate, thesis/dissertation. *Entrance requirements:* For master's and doctorate, GRE General Test, minimum GPA of 3.0. Additional exam requirements/recommendations for international students: Required—TOEFL. *Application deadline:* For fall admission, 2/1 for domestic students, 2/1 for international students; for spring admission, 11/1 for domestic students. Application fee: $35. Electronic applications accepted. *Expenses:* Tuition: Full-time $19,700; part-time $1,096 per hour. *Financial support:* In 2003–04, 41 students received support, including 27 fellowships with full tuition reimbursements available (averaging $14,850 per year), 14 research assistantships with full tuition reimbursements available (averaging $14,850 per year); tuition waivers (full and partial) also available. *Faculty research:* Marine geology/paleocenography; stratigraphy/sedimentology; petrology/geochemistry; seismology/computational geophysics; structure/tectonics. *Unit head:* Dr. Alan Levander, Chairman, 713-348-4652, Fax: 713-348-5214, E-mail: geol@rice.edu. *Application contact:* Sandra Flechsig, Graduate Student Coordinator, 713-348-3326, Fax: 713-348-5214, E-mail: sandraf@rice.edu.

Rice University, Graduate Programs, Wiess School of Natural Sciences, Professional Master's Program in Subsurface Geosciences, Houston, TX 77251-1892. Offers geophysics (MS). Part-time programs available. *Degree requirements:* For master's, internship. *Entrance requirements:* For master's, GRE, letters of recommendation (4). Additional exam requirements/recommendations for international students: Required—TOEFL (minimum score 600 paper-based; 250 computer-based). Electronic applications accepted. *Expenses:* Tuition: Full-time $19,700; part-time $1,096 per hour. *Faculty research:* Seismology, geodynamics, wave propogation, bio-geochemistry, remote sensing.

St. Francis Xavier University, Graduate Studies, Department of Earth Sciences, Antigonish, NS B2G 2W5, Canada. Offers M Sc. *Faculty:* 5 full-time (1 woman). *Students:* 1 full-time (0 women), 3 part-time (all women). *Degree requirements:* For master's, thesis, registration. *Entrance requirements:* Additional exam requirements/recommendations for international students: Required—TOEFL (minimum score 580 paper-based; 236 computer-based). Application fee: $40. Tuition, area resident: Full-time $5,310. International tuition: $9,210 full-time. Full-time tuition and fees vary according to course load and program. *Faculty research:* Environmental earth sciences, global change tectonics, paleoclimatology, crustal fluids. Total annual research expenditures: $300,000. *Unit head:* Dr. Brendan Murphy, Professor, 902-867-2481, Fax: 902-867-5153, E-mail: bmurphy@stfx.ca.

Saint Louis University, Graduate School, College of Arts and Sciences and Graduate School, Department of Earth and Atmospheric Sciences, St. Louis, MO 63103-2097. Offers geophysics (PhD); geoscience (MS, MS(R)); meteorology (M Pr Met, MS(R), PhD). Part-time programs available. *Faculty:* 14 full-time (7 women), 12 part-time/adjunct (6 women). *Students:* 19 full-time (5 women), 6 part-time (1 woman); includes 2 minority (1 African American, 1 Asian American or Pacific Islander), 11 international. Average age 30. 27 applicants, 85% accepted, 7 enrolled. In 2003, 2 master's, 1 doctorate awarded. *Degree requirements:* For master's, comprehensive oral exam, thesis for MS(R); for doctorate, thesis/dissertation, preliminary exams. *Entrance requirements:* For master's and doctorate, GRE General Test. Additional exam requirements/recommendations for international students: Required—TOEFL (minimum score 550 paper-based; 213 computer-based). *Application deadline:* For fall admission, 7/1 for domestic students, 7/1 for international students; for spring admission, 11/1 for domestic students, 11/1 for international students. Applications are processed on a rolling basis. Application fee: $40. *Expenses:* Tuition: Part-time $690 per credit hour. Required fees: $59 per semester. Tuition and fees vary according to program. *Financial support:* In 2003–04, 23 students received support, including 6 research assistantships with tuition reimbursements available, 6 teaching assistantships with tuition reimbursements available; unspecified assistantships also available. Financial award application deadline: 6/1; financial award applicants required to submit FAFSA. *Faculty research:* Seismology and tectonics, earth's core and structure, geochemistry, heavy precipitation convective systems, squall lines and tropical cyclones. *Unit head:* Dr. David Crossley, Acting Chairperson, 314-977-3131, Fax: 314-977-3117, E-mail: crossley@slu.edu. *Application contact:* Gary Behrman, Associate Dean of the Graduate School, 314-977-3827, Fax: 314-977-3943, E-mail: behrmang@slu.edu.

San Francisco State University, Division of Graduate Studies, College of Science and Engineering, Department of Geosciences, San Francisco, CA 94132-1722. Offers applied geosciences (MS). *Entrance requirements:* For master's, minimum GPA of 2.5 in last 60 units. *Application deadline:* For fall admission, 11/30 for domestic students. Applications are processed on a rolling basis. Application fee: $55. *Expenses:* Tuition, state resident: part-time $871 per unit. Tuition, nonresident: part-time $1,093 per unit. *Financial support:* Application deadline:3/1. *Unit head:* Dr. Karen Grove, Chair, 415-338-2061, E-mail: kgrove@sfsu.edu. *Application contact:* Dr. Lisa White, Graduate Coordinator, 415-338-1209, E-mail: lwhite@sfsu.edu.

Simon Fraser University, Graduate Studies, Faculty of Science, Department of Earth Sciences, Burnaby, BC V5A 1S6, Canada. Offers M Sc. Part-time programs available. *Degree requirements:* For master's, thesis. *Entrance requirements:* For master's, minimum GPA of 3.0. Additional exam requirements/recommendations for international students: Required—TOEFL or IELTS. Electronic applications accepted. *Faculty research:* Earth surface processes, environmental geoscience, surficial and Quaternary geology, sedimentology.

Southeast Missouri State University, School of Graduate and University Studies, Department of Geosciences, Cape Girardeau, MO 63701-4799. Offers MNS. *Faculty:* 7 full-time (0 women). *Students:* 3 full-time (0 women), 8 part-time (4 women), 3 international. Average age 30. 1 applicant, 100% accepted. *Degree requirements:* For master's, thesis or alternative. *Entrance requirements:* For master's, GRE General Test, minimum GPA of 2.5. Additional exam requirements/recommendations for international students: Required—TOEFL (minimum score 550 paper-based; 213 computer-based). *Application deadline:* For fall admission, 4/1 priority date for domestic students, 4/1 priority date for international students; for spring admission, 11/1 priority date for domestic students, 9/1 priority date for international students. Applications are processed on a rolling basis. Application fee: $20 ($100 for international students). Electronic applications accepted. *Expenses:* Tuition, state resident: full-time $4,061; part-time $180 per credit hour. Tuition, nonresident: full-time $7,514; part-time $324 per credit hour. One-time fee: $257. *Financial support:* In 2003–04, 8 students received support, including 2 research assistantships (averaging $6,100 per year), 4 teaching assistantships (averaging $6,100 per year) Financial award applicants required to submit FAFSA. *Faculty research:* Rice crop rotation, water quality, soil structure, allostratigraphic. Total annual research expenditures: $8,821. *Unit head:* Dr. David Probst, Chairperson, 573-651-2168. *Application contact:* Marsha L. Arant, Office of Graduate Studies, 573-651-2192, Fax: 573-651-2001, E-mail: marant@semovm.semo.edu.

Southwest Missouri State University, Graduate College, College of Natural and Applied Sciences, Department of Geography, Geology, and Planning, Springfield, MO 65804-0094. Offers earth science (MS Ed); geography (MS Ed); geography, geology and planning (MNAS); natural science (MS Ed); resource planning (MS). Part-time and evening/weekend programs available. *Faculty:* 15 full-time (2 women), 3 part-time/adjunct (0 women). *Students:* 16 full-time (9 women), 19 part-time (9 women); includes 4 minority (2 American Indian/Alaska Native, 1 Asian American or Pacific Islander, 1 Hispanic American), 2 international. Average age 34. 16 applicants, 88% accepted, 11 enrolled. In 2003, 5 degrees awarded. *Degree requirements:* For master's, thesis, comprehensive exam. *Entrance requirements:* For master's, GRE General Test, minimum undergraduate GPA of 3.0. *Application deadline:* For fall admission, 8/5 for domestic students; for spring admission, 12/20 priority date for domestic students. Applications are processed on a rolling basis. Application fee: $30. Electronic applications accepted. *Expenses:* Tuition, state resident: full-time $2,862. Tuition, nonresident: full-time $5,724. *Financial support:* In 2003–04, 6 research assistantships with full tuition reimbursements (averaging $8,400 per year), 9 teaching assistantships with full tuition reimbursements (averaging $6,300 per year) were awarded. Career-related internships or fieldwork, Federal Work-Study, and unspecified assistantships also available. Financial award application deadline: 3/31. *Faculty research:* Water resources, small town planning, recreation and open space planning. *Unit head:* Dr. James Skinner, Head, 417-836-5800, Fax: 417-836-6934. *Application contact:* Dr. Robert T. Pavlowsky, Graduate Adviser, 417-836-5800, Fax: 417-836-6934, E-mail: rtp138f@smsu.edu.

Stanford University, School of Earth Sciences, Department of Geological and Environmental Sciences, Stanford, CA 94305-9991. Offers MS, PhD, Eng. *Faculty:* 22 full-time (4 women). *Students:* 69 full-time (27 women), 31 part-time (11 women); includes 3 minority (1 African American, 2 Asian Americans or Pacific Islanders), 24 international. Average age 28. 102 applicants, 23% accepted. In 2003, 4 master's, 19 doctorates awarded. Terminal master's awarded for partial completion of doctoral program. *Degree requirements:* For masters, doctorate, and Eng, thesis/dissertation. *Entrance requirements:* For master's, doctorate, and Eng, GRE General Test. Additional exam requirements/recommendations for international students: Required—TOEFL. *Application deadline:* For fall admission, 1/15 for domestic students. Application fee: $65 ($80 for international students). Electronic applications accepted. *Expenses:* Tuition: Full-time $28,563. *Unit head:* Jonathan Stebbins, Chair, 650-723-1140, Fax: 650-725-2199, E-mail: stebbins@pangea.stanford.edu. *Application contact:* Graduate Admissions Coordinator, 650-725-0574.

Stanford University, School of Earth Sciences, Earth Systems Program, Stanford, CA 94305-9991. Offers MS. Students admitted at the undergraduate level. *Students:* 9 full-time (4 women), 6 part-time (3 women); includes 4 minority (1 Asian American or Pacific Islander, 3 Hispanic Americans). Average age 23. In 2003, 10 degrees awarded. Application fee: $65 ($80

Geosciences

Stanford University (continued)
for international students). Electronic applications accepted. *Expenses:* Tuition: Full-time $28,563. *Unit head:* Joan Roughgarden, Director, 650-723-3648, Fax: 650-725-0958, E-mail: rough@pangea.stanford.edu.

State University of New York College at Oneonta, Graduate Studies, Department of Earth Sciences, Oneonta, NY 13820-4015. Offers MA. Part-time and evening/weekend programs available. *Students:* 3 full-time (1 woman), 1 part-time. In 2003, 1 degree awarded. *Degree requirements:* For master's, thesis. *Entrance requirements:* For master's, GRE General Test. *Application deadline:* For fall admission, 3/25 for domestic students; for spring admission, 10/1 priority date for domestic students. Applications are processed on a rolling basis. Application fee: $50. *Expenses:* Tuition, state resident: full-time $5,100; part-time $213 per semester hour. Tuition, nonresident: full-time $8,416; part-time $351 per semester hour. Required fees: $666. *Financial support:* Fellowships available. *Unit head:* Dr. Jerome Blechman, Chair, 607-436-3707, E-mail: blechmjb@oneonta.edu.

Stony Brook University, State University of New York, Graduate School, College of Arts and Sciences, Department of Geosciences, Stony Brook, NY 11794. Offers earth and space science (MS, PhD); earth science (MAT). MAT offered through the School of Professional Development and Continuing Studies. *Faculty:* 17 full-time (2 women), 1 part-time/adjunct (0 women). *Students:* 41 full-time (19 women), 7 part-time (4 women); includes 1 minority (Asian American or Pacific Islander), 17 international. 42 applicants, 48% accepted. In 2003, 8 master's, 5 doctorates awarded. Terminal master's awarded for partial completion of doctoral program. *Degree requirements:* For master's, thesis or alternative; for doctorate, thesis/dissertation. *Entrance requirements:* For master's and doctorate, GRE General Test, minimum GPA of 3.0. Additional exam requirements/recommendations for international students: Required—TOEFL. *Application deadline:* For fall admission, 1/15 for domestic students. Application fee: $50. *Expenses:* Tuition, state resident: full-time $6,900; part-time $288 per credit hour. Tuition, nonresident: full-time $10,500; part-time $438 per credit hour. Required fees: $22. *Financial support:* In 2003–04, 6 fellowships, 24 research assistantships, 11 teaching assistantships were awarded. *Faculty research:* Astronomy, theoretical and observational astrophysics, paleontology, petrology, crystallography. Total annual research expenditures: $3.4 million. *Unit head:* Dr. Teng-Fong Wong, Chair, 631-632-8194, Fax: 631-632-6900. *Application contact:* Dr. John Parise, Director, 631-632-8200, Fax: 631-632-8240, E-mail: jparise@notes.cc.sunysb.edu.

Announcement: Many versed in the sciences say that rocks and their formations give clues to the basis of life on Earth and how it evolved. This is a key point of study for the Department of Geosciences, which has the facilities available to both faculty and students to continue to unlock the mysteries of this segment of nature.

See in-depth description on page 253.

Texas A&M University–Commerce, Graduate School, College of Arts and Sciences, Department of Biological and Earth Sciences, Commerce, TX 75429-3011. Offers M Ed, MS. *Degree requirements:* For master's, thesis (for some programs), comprehensive exam. *Entrance requirements:* For master's, GRE General Test. Electronic applications accepted. *Faculty research:* Microbiology, botany, environmental science, birds.

Texas Christian University, College of Science and Engineering, Department of Biology, Program in Environmental Sciences, Fort Worth, TX 76129-0002. Offers earth sciences (MS); ecology (MS). Part-time and evening/weekend programs available. *Degree requirements:* For master's, thesis optional. *Entrance requirements:* For master's, GRE General Test, GRE Subject Test, 1 year of biology and chemistry; 1 semester of calculus, government, and physical geology. Additional exam requirements/recommendations for international students: Required—TOEFL. *Application deadline:* For fall admission, 3/1 for domestic students; for spring admission, 12/1 for domestic students. Applications are processed on a rolling basis. Application fee: $0. *Expenses:* Tuition: Part-time $640 per credit hour. Tuition and fees vary according to program. *Financial support:* Unspecified assistantships available. Financial award application deadline: 3/1. *Unit head:* Dr. Mike Slattery, Director, 817-257-7506. *Application contact:* Dr. Bonnie Melhart, Associate Dean, College of Science and Engineering, E-mail: b.melhart@tcu.edu.

Texas Tech University, Graduate School, College of Arts and Sciences, Department of Geosciences, Lubbock, TX 79409. Offers atmospheric sciences (MS); geoscience (MS, PhD). Part-time programs available. *Faculty:* 14 full-time (2 women). *Students:* 40 full-time (18 women), 9 part-time (2 women); includes 1 minority (African American), 6 international. Average age 29. 40 applicants, 63% accepted, 15 enrolled. In 2003, 12 master's, 3 doctorates awarded. *Degree requirements:* For master's and doctorate, thesis/dissertation. *Entrance requirements:* For master's and doctorate, GRE General Test. Additional exam requirements/recommendations for international students: Required—TOEFL (minimum score 550 paper-based; 213 computer-based). *Application deadline:* Applications are processed on a rolling basis. Application fee: $50 ($60 for international students). Electronic applications accepted. *Expenses:* Tuition, state resident: full-time $3,312. Tuition, nonresident: full-time $8,976. Required fees: $1,745. Tuition and fees vary according to program. *Financial support:* In 2003–04, 24 students received support, including 12 research assistantships with partial tuition reimbursements available (averaging $13,090 per year), 22 teaching assistantships with partial tuition reimbursements available (averaging $14,157 per year); Federal Work-Study and institutionally sponsored loans also available. Support available to part-time students. Financial award application deadline: 5/1; financial award applicants required to submit FAFSA. *Faculty research:* Ophiolites and oceanic lower crust; petroleum geology; tectonics and arc magnetism; aqueous and environmental geochemistry; near-ground high wind phenomenon (hurricanes and severe storms). Total annual research expenditures: $467,442. *Unit head:* Dr. James Barrick, Chairman, 806-742-3102, Fax: 806-742-0100, E-mail: jim.barrick@ttu.edu. *Application contact:* Graduate Adviser, 806-742-3102, Fax: 806-742-0100.

Université du Québec à Chicoutimi, Graduate Programs, Program in Earth Sciences, Chicoutimi, QC G7H 2B1, Canada. Offers M Sc A. Part-time programs available. *Degree requirements:* For master's, thesis. *Entrance requirements:* For master's, appropriate bachelor's degree, proficiency in French.

Université du Québec à Montréal, Graduate Programs, Program in Earth Sciences, Montreal, QC H3C 3P8, Canada. Offers geology-research (M Sc); mineral resources (PhD); non-renewable resources (DESS). Part-time programs available. *Faculty:* 16 full-time (2 women), 16 part-time/adjunct (1 woman). *Students:* 51 full-time (9 women), 15 international. 18 applicants, 56% accepted. In 2003, 7 master's, 4 doctorates awarded. Terminal master's awarded for partial completion of doctoral program. *Median time to degree:* Of those who began their doctoral program in fall 1995, 90% received their degree in 8 years or less. *Degree requirements:* For master's, thesis (for some programs); for doctorate, thesis/dissertation. *Entrance requirements:* For master's, appropriate bachelor's degree or equivalent, proficiency in French. *Application deadline:* Applications are processed on a rolling basis. Application fee: $50. *Financial support:* In 2003–04, fellowships (averaging $5,000 per year), research assistantships (averaging $4,000 per year), teaching assistantships (averaging $1,000 per year) were awarded. Scholarships/grants also available. *Faculty research:* Economic geology, structural geology, geochemistry, Quaternary geology, isotopic geochemistry. *Unit head:* Alfred Jaouich, Director, 514-987-3000 Ext. 3378, Fax: 514-987-7749, E-mail: jaouich.alfred@uqam.ca. *Application contact:* Micheline Lacroix, Admissions Officer, 514-987-3000 Ext. 3370, Fax: 514-987-7749, E-mail: lacroix.micheline@uqam.ca.

Université du Québec, Institut National de la Recherche Scientifique, Graduate Programs, Research Center—Earth and Environment, Ste-Foy, QC G1V 4C7, Canada. Offers earth sciences (M Sc, PhD); earth sciences-environmental technologies (M Sc); water sciences (MA, PhD). Part-time programs available. *Faculty:* 38. *Students:* 155 full-time (67 women), 10 part-time (3 women), 37 international. In 2003, 16 master's, 9 doctorates awarded. *Degree requirements:* For master's, thesis optional; for doctorate, thesis/dissertation. *Entrance requirements:* For master's, appropriate bachelor's degree, proficiency in French; for doctorate, appropriate master's degree, proficiency in French. *Application deadline:* For fall admission, 3/31 for domestic students. Application fee: $30. Tuition, area resident: Full-time $2,639. *Expenses:* Tuition, state resident: full-time $6,155. Tuition, nonresident: full-time $13,889. *Financial support:* Fellowships, research assistantships, teaching assistantships available. *Unit head:* Jean Pierre Villeneuve, Director, 418-654-2575, Fax: 418-654-2615, E-mail: jp_villeneuve@inrs.uquebec.ca. *Application contact:* Michel Barbeau, Registrar, 418-654-2518, Fax: 418-654-3858, E-mail: michel_barbeau@inrs.uquebec.ca.

Université Laval, Faculty of Sciences and Engineering, Department of Geology and Geological Engineering, Programs in Earth Sciences, Québec, QC G1K 7P4, Canada. Offers earth sciences (M Sc, PhD); environmental technologies (M Sc). Offered jointly with INRS-Géressources. Terminal master's awarded for partial completion of doctoral program. *Degree requirements:* For master's, thesis (for some programs); for doctorate, thesis/dissertation, comprehensive exam. *Entrance requirements:* For master's and doctorate, knowledge of French. Electronic applications accepted.

University at Albany, State University of New York, College of Arts and Sciences, Department of Earth and Atmospheric Sciences, Albany, NY 12222-0001. Offers atmospheric science (MS, PhD); geology (MS, PhD). Evening/weekend programs available. *Students:* 36 full-time (15 women), 8 part-time (3 women). Average age 29. 63 applicants, 41% accepted, 16 enrolled. In 2003, 8 master's, 4 doctorates awarded. *Degree requirements:* For master's, one foreign language, thesis, comprehensive exam; for doctorate, 2 foreign languages, thesis/dissertation, oral exams, comprehensive exam. *Entrance requirements:* For master's and doctorate, GRE General Test. Additional exam requirements/recommendations for international students: Required—TOEFL (minimum score 550 paper-based; 213 computer-based). *Application deadline:* For fall admission, 6/1 for domestic students, 5/1 for international students; for spring admission, 11/1 for domestic students, 11/11 for international students. Applications are processed on a rolling basis. Application fee: $50. Electronic applications accepted. *Expenses:* Tuition, state resident: part-time $288 per credit. Tuition, nonresident: part-time $438 per credit. Required fees: $495 per semester. *Financial support:* Fellowships, research assistantships, teaching assistantships, minority assistantships available. Financial award application deadline: 3/1. *Unit head:* Dr. Vincent Idone, Chair, 518-442-4466.

The University of Akron, Graduate School, Buchtel College of Arts and Sciences, Department of Geology, Program in Earth Science, Akron, OH 44325-0001. Offers MS. *Students:* Average age 29. 1 applicant, 0% accepted. In 2003, 2 degrees awarded. *Degree requirements:* For master's, thesis, seminar, comprehensive exam. *Entrance requirements:* For master's, minimum GPA of 2.75. Additional exam requirements/recommendations for international students: Required—TOEFL (minimum score 550 paper-based; 213 computer-based). *Application deadline:* For fall admission, 3/1 for domestic students. Applications are processed on a rolling basis. Application fee: $40 ($60 for international students). *Expenses:* Tuition, state resident: part-time $277 per credit hour. Tuition, nonresident: part-time $476 per credit hour. *Unit head:* Dr. David McConnell, Director of Graduate Studies, 330-972-8047, E-mail: mcconnell@uakron.edu.

University of Alberta, Faculty of Graduate Studies and Research, Department of Earth and Atmospheric Sciences, Edmonton, AB T6G 2E1, Canada. Offers M Sc, MA, PhD. *Faculty:* 38 full-time (4 women), 15 part-time/adjunct (0 women). *Students:* 19 full-time (6 women). Average age 30. 88 applicants, 43% accepted. In 2003, 14 master's, 7 doctorates awarded. *Degree requirements:* For master's and doctorate, thesis/dissertation, residency. *Entrance requirements:* For master's, B Sc degree, GPA of 6.5; for doctorate, M Sc degree. Additional exam requirements/recommendations for international students: Required—TOEFL or Michigan English Language Assessment Battery. *Application deadline:* Applications are processed on a rolling basis. Electronic applications accepted. Tuition charges are reported in Canadian dollars. Tuition, nonresident: full-time $3,921 Canadian dollars. International tuition: $7,113 Canadian dollars full-time. *Financial support:* In 2003–04, 10 fellowships, 15 research assistantships were awarded. Teaching assistantships, scholarships/grants and unspecified assistantships also available. *Faculty research:* Geology, human geography, physical geography, meteorology. Total annual research expenditures: $10 million. *Unit head:* Dr. B. Jones, Chair, 780-492-3329, Fax: 780-492-2030, E-mail: brian.jones@ualberta.ca. *Application contact:* Dr. Martin J. Sharp, Graduate Chair, 403-492-3265, Fax: 403-492-7598, E-mail: martin.sharp@ualberta.ca.

The University of Arizona, Graduate College, College of Science, Department of Geosciences, Tucson, AZ 85721. Offers MS, PhD. Part-time programs available. *Degree requirements:* For master's, thesis or prepublication; for doctorate, one foreign language, thesis/dissertation, comprehensive exam. *Entrance requirements:* For master's and doctorate, GRE General Test. Additional exam requirements/recommendations for international students: Required—TOEFL. *Expenses:* Tuition, state resident: part-time $196 per unit. Tuition, nonresident: part-time $326 per unit. *Faculty research:* Tectonics, geophysics, geochemistry/petrology, economic geology, Quaternary studies, stratigraphy/paleontology.

University of California, Irvine, Office of Graduate Studies, School of Physical Sciences, Department of Earth System Science, Irvine, CA 92697. Offers MS, PhD. *Students:* 23. In 2003, 2 master's, 2 doctorates awarded. *Degree requirements:* For doctorate, thesis/dissertation. *Entrance requirements:* For master's and doctorate, GRE General Test, GRE Subject Test, minimum GPA of 3.0. Additional exam requirements/recommendations for international students: Required—TOEFL (minimum score 550 paper-based; 213 computer-based). *Application deadline:* For fall admission, 1/15 for domestic students; for winter admission, 10/15 for domestic students. Applications are processed on a rolling basis. Application fee: $60. Electronic applications accepted. Tuition, nonresident: full-time $12,245. Required fees: $5,219. Tuition and fees vary according to degree level and program. *Financial support:* Fellowships, research assistantships with full tuition reimbursements, teaching assistantships, career-related internships or fieldwork, institutionally sponsored loans, traineeships, health care benefits, and unspecified assistantships available. Financial award application deadline: 3/1; financial award applicants required to submit FAFSA. *Faculty research:* Atmospheric chemistry, climate change, isotope biogeochemistry, global environmental chemistry. *Unit head:* Eric Saltzman, Chair, 949-824-3936, Fax: 949-824-3256, E-mail: esaltzma@uci.edu. *Application contact:* Kathy Vonk, Department Assistant, 949-824-3876, Fax: 949-824-3256, E-mail: kvonk@uci.edu.

University of California, Los Angeles, Graduate Division, College of Letters and Science, Department of Earth and Space Sciences, Los Angeles, CA 90095. Offers geochemistry (MS, PhD); geology (MS, PhD); geophysics and space physics (MS, PhD). *Degree requirements:* For master's, comprehensive exams or thesis; for doctorate, thesis/dissertation, oral and written qualifying exams. *Entrance requirements:* For master's, GRE General Test, minimum GPA of 3.0; for doctorate, GRE General Test, minimum undergraduate GPA of 3.0. Electronic applications accepted. Tuition, nonresident: full-time $12,245. Required fees: $6,318.

University of California, Santa Cruz, Division of Graduate Studies, Division of Physical and Biological Sciences, Program in Earth Sciences, Santa Cruz, CA 95064. Offers MS, PhD. *Faculty:* 21 full-time (4 women). *Students:* 63 full-time (31 women), 1 (woman) part-time; includes 4 minority (1 Asian American or Pacific Islander, 3 Hispanic Americans), 4 international. 121 applicants, 31% accepted, 22 enrolled. In 2003, 3 master's, 6 doctorates awarded. *Median time to degree:* Master's–2.65 years full-time; doctorate–4.5 years full-time. *Degree requirements:* For master's, thesis; for doctorate, one foreign language, thesis/dissertation, qualifying exam. *Entrance requirements:* For master's and doctorate, GRE General Test, GRE Subject Test. *Application deadline:* For fall admission, 1/15 for domestic students. Application fee: $60. Tuition, nonresident: full-time $12,492. *Financial support:* Fellowships, research assistantships, teaching assistantships, career-related internships or fieldwork, Federal Work-Study, and institutionally sponsored loans available. Financial award application deadline: 1/15. *Faculty research:* Evolution of continental margins and orogenic belts, geologic processes occurring at plate boundaries, deep-sea sediment diagenesis, paleoecology, hydrogeology.

Unit head: Elise Knittle, Chairperson, 831-459-3164. *Application contact:* James M. Moore, Graduate Admissions, Director, 831-459-2301, Fax: 831-459-4843, E-mail: gradadm@ucsc.edu.

University of Chicago, Division of the Physical Sciences, Department of the Geophysical Sciences, Chicago, IL 60637-1513. Offers atmospheric sciences (SM, PhD); earth sciences (SM, PhD); paleobiology (PhD); planetary and space sciences (SM, PhD). *Faculty:* 24 full-time (3 women). *Students:* 29 full-time (13 women); includes 1 minority (Hispanic American), 12 international. Average age 30. 74 applicants, 22% accepted. In 2003, 2 master's, 5 doctorates awarded. Terminal master's awarded for partial completion of doctoral program. *Median time to degree:* Doctorate–6 years full-time. *Entrance requirements:* For master's and doctorate, GRE General Test. Additional exam requirements/recommendations for international students: Required—TOEFL. *Application deadline:* For fall admission, 1/15 for domestic students, 1/15 for international students. Application fee: $55. Electronic applications accepted. *Financial support:* In 2003–04, 29 students received support, including research assistantships with full tuition reimbursements available (averaging $17,196 per year), teaching assistantships with full tuition reimbursements available (averaging $18,096 per year); fellowships, Federal Work-Study, institutionally sponsored loans, scholarships/grants, tuition waivers (partial), and unspecified assistantships also available. Financial award application deadline: 1/15. *Faculty research:* Climatology, evolutionary paleontology, petrology, geochemistry, oceanic sciences. *Unit head:* Dr. David Rowley, Chairman, 773-702-8102, Fax: 773-702-9505. *Application contact:* David J. Leslie, Graduate Student Services Coordinator, 773-702-8180, Fax: 773-702-9505, E-mail: info@geosci.uchicago.edu.

University of Florida, Graduate School, College of Liberal Arts and Sciences, Department of Geological Sciences, Gainesville, FL 32611. Offers geology (MS, PhD); geology education (MST). *Faculty:* 22. *Students:* 35 full-time (16 women), 14 part-time (8 women); includes 3 minority (1 African American, 2 Hispanic Americans), 8 international. In 2003, 8 master's, 1 doctorate awarded. Terminal master's awarded for partial completion of doctoral program. *Degree requirements:* For master's, thesis (for some programs); for doctorate, one foreign language, thesis/dissertation. *Entrance requirements:* For master's and doctorate, GRE General Test, GRE Subject Test, minimum GPA of 3.0. Additional exam requirements/recommendations for international students: Required—TOEFL (minimum score 550 paper-based; 213 computer-based). *Application deadline:* For fall admission, 6/1 for domestic students; for spring admission, 10/1 priority date for domestic students. Applications are processed on a rolling basis. Application fee: $30. Electronic applications accepted. *Expenses:* Tuition, state resident: part-time $205 per credit hour. Tuition, nonresident: part-time $775 per credit hour. *Financial support:* In 2003–04, 26 students received support, including 2 fellowships with full tuition reimbursements available (averaging $15,000 per year), 6 research assistantships with full tuition reimbursements available (averaging $12,000 per year), 19 teaching assistantships with full tuition reimbursements available (averaging $9,500 per year); career-related internships or fieldwork, Federal Work-Study, institutionally sponsored loans, and scholarships/grants also available. Support available to part-time students. Financial award application deadline: 3/1. *Faculty research:* Paleoclimatology, tectonophysics, petrochemistry, marine geology, geochemistry, hydrology. Total annual research expenditures: $1.5 million. *Unit head:* Dr. Paul Mueller, Chair, 352-392-2231, Fax: 352-392-9294, E-mail: mueller@geology.ufl.edu. *Application contact:* Dr. Michael R. Perfit, Graduate Coordinator, 352-392-2128, Fax: 352-392-9294, E-mail: perfit@geology.ufl.edu.

University of Illinois at Chicago, Graduate College, College of Liberal Arts and Sciences, Department of Earth and Environmental Sciences, Chicago, IL 60607-7128. Offers crystallography (MS, PhD); environmental geology (MS, PhD); geochemistry (MS, PhD); geology (MS, PhD); geomorphology (MS, PhD); geophysics (MS, PhD); geotechnical engineering and geosciences (PhD); hydrogeology (MS, PhD); low-temperature and organic geochemistry (MS, PhD); mineralogy (MS, PhD); paleoclimatology (MS, PhD); paleontology (MS, PhD); petrology (MS, PhD); quaternary geology (MS, PhD); sedimentology (MS, PhD); water resources (MS, PhD). *Faculty:* 9 full-time (2 women). *Students:* 18 full-time (7 women), 5 part-time (1 woman); includes 3 minority (1 African American, 1 American Indian/Alaska Native, 1 Asian American or Pacific Islander), 11 international. Average age 29. 15 applicants, 27% accepted, 4 enrolled. In 2003, 2 degrees awarded. *Degree requirements:* For master's and doctorate, thesis/dissertation. *Entrance requirements:* For master's and doctorate, GRE General Test, minimum GPA of 3.75 on a 5.0 scale. Additional exam requirements/recommendations for international students: Required—TOEFL. *Application deadline:* For fall admission, 5/15 for domestic students, 2/1 for international students; for spring admission, 11/1 for domestic students, 7/15 for international students. Applications are processed on a rolling basis. Application fee: $40 ($50 for international students). Electronic applications accepted. *Expenses:* Tuition, state resident: part-time $941 per semester. Tuition, nonresident: part-time $2,338 per semester. *Financial support:* In 2003–04, 16 students received support; fellowships with full tuition reimbursements available, research assistantships with full tuition reimbursements available, teaching assistantships with full tuition reimbursements available, Federal Work-Study, scholarships/grants, traineeships, tuition waivers (full), and unspecified assistantships available. Financial award application deadline: 3/1; financial award applicants required to submit FAFSA. *Unit head:* Neil Sturchio, Head, 312-996-3154. *Application contact:* Peter Doran, Director of Graduate Studies, 312-413-7275, E-mail: pdoran@uic.edu.

University of Illinois at Urbana–Champaign, Graduate College, College of Liberal Arts and Sciences, Department of Geology, Champaign, IL 61820. Offers earth sciences (MS, PhD); geochemistry (MS, PhD); geology (MS, PhD); geophysics (MS, PhD). *Faculty:* 14 full-time (3 women). *Students:* 36 full-time (12 women); includes 3 minority (all Asian Americans or Pacific Islanders), 17 international. Average age 26. 72 applicants, 13% accepted, 4 enrolled. In 2003, 1 master's, 3 doctorates awarded. Terminal master's awarded for partial completion of doctoral program. *Degree requirements:* For master's and doctorate, thesis/dissertation. *Entrance requirements:* For master's and doctorate, GRE General Test, minimum GPA of 3.0. Additional exam requirements/recommendations for international students: Required—TOEFL. *Application deadline:* For fall admission, 2/15 for domestic students; for spring admission, 10/15 for domestic students. Applications are processed on a rolling basis. Application fee: $40 ($50 for international students). *Expenses:* Tuition, state resident: full-time $6,692. Tuition, nonresident: full-time $18,692. *Financial support:* In 2003–04, 14 research assistantships, 16 teaching assistantships were awarded. Fellowships, Federal Work-Study and tuition waivers (full and partial) also available. Financial award application deadline: 2/15. *Faculty research:* Hydrogeology, structure/tectonics, mineral science. *Unit head:* Stephen Marshak, Head, 217-333-3542, Fax: 217-244-4996, E-mail: smarshak@uiuc.edu. *Application contact:* Barbara Elmore, Graduate Admissions Secretary, 217-333-3542, Fax: 217-244-4996, E-mail: belmore@uiuc.edu.

The University of Iowa, Graduate College, College of Liberal Arts and Sciences, Department of Geoscience, Iowa City, IA 52242-1316. Offers MS, PhD. *Faculty:* 16 full-time, 1 part-time/adjunct. *Students:* 15 full-time (5 women), 24 part-time (7 women); includes 3 minority (1 Asian American or Pacific Islander, 2 Hispanic Americans), 7 international. 44 applicants, 43% accepted, 9 enrolled. In 2003, 9 master's, 1 doctorate awarded. *Degree requirements:* For master's, exam, thesis optional; for doctorate, thesis/dissertation, comprehensive exam, registration. *Entrance requirements:* For master's and doctorate, GRE General Test, minimum GPA of 3.0. Additional exam requirements/recommendations for international students: Required—TOEFL (minimum score 550 paper-based; 213 computer-based). *Application deadline:* For fall admission, 2/1 priority date for domestic students, 2/1 priority date for international students; for spring admission, 11/1 priority date for domestic students. Applications are processed on a rolling basis. Application fee: $50 ($75 for international students). Electronic applications accepted. *Expenses:* Tuition, state resident: full-time $5,038. Tuition, nonresident: full-time $15,072. Tuition and fees vary according to course load and program. *Financial support:* In 2003–04, 9 research assistantships, 24 teaching assistantships were awarded. Financial award application deadline: 2/1; financial award applicants required to submit FAFSA. *Unit head:* Ann F. Budd, Chair, 319-335-1820, Fax: 319-335-1821.

University of Louisiana at Monroe, Graduate Studies and Research, College of Arts and Sciences, Department of Geosciences, Monroe, LA 71209-0001. Offers MS. *Faculty:* 2 full-time (0 women). *Students:* 3 full-time (2 women). Average age 35. In 2003, 5 degrees awarded. *Degree requirements:* For master's, thesis. *Entrance requirements:* For master's, GRE General Test, minimum GPA of 2.8 during previous 2 years or 3.0 in 21 hours of geosciences. *Application deadline:* For fall admission, 7/1 for domestic students; for spring admission, 11/1 for domestic students. Applications are processed on a rolling basis. Application fee: $15 ($25 for international students). *Expenses:* Tuition, state resident: full-time $2,052. Tuition, nonresident: full-time $8,010. *Financial support:* Research assistantships, teaching assistantships, Federal Work-Study and unspecified assistantships available. Financial award application deadline:7/1. *Faculty research:* Sedimentology, environmental hydrology, planetary geosciences, micropaleontology. *Unit head:* Dr. Michael Camille, Interim Head, 318-342-1878, Fax: 318-342-1755, E-mail: camille@ulm.edu.

University of Maine, Graduate School, College of Natural Sciences, Forestry, and Agriculture, Department of Earth Sciences, Orono, ME 04469. Offers MS, PhD. Part-time programs available. *Faculty:* 12 full-time. *Students:* 33 full-time (16 women), 12 part-time (5 women), 3 international. Average age 31. 16 applicants, 94% accepted, 7 enrolled. In 2003, 4 master's, 1 doctorate awarded. *Degree requirements:* For master's, thesis; for doctorate, one foreign language, thesis/dissertation. *Entrance requirements:* For master's and doctorate, GRE General Test. Additional exam requirements/recommendations for international students: Required—TOEFL. *Application deadline:* For fall admission, 2/1 for domestic students. Applications are processed on a rolling basis. Application fee: $50. Electronic applications accepted. *Expenses:* Tuition, state resident: part-time $235 per credit. Tuition, nonresident: part-time $670 per credit. Tuition and fees vary according to course load. *Financial support:* In 2003–04, 4 research assistantships with tuition reimbursements (averaging $14,800 per year), 5 teaching assistantships with tuition reimbursements (averaging $9,970 per year) were awarded. Federal Work-Study, institutionally sponsored loans, and tuition waivers (full and partial) also available. Financial award application deadline: 3/1. *Faculty research:* Appalachian bedrock geology, Quaternary studies, marine geology. *Unit head:* Dr. Daniel Belknap, Chair, 207-581-2152, Fax: 207-581-2202. *Application contact:* Scott G. Delcourt, Associate Dean of the Graduate School, 207-581-3218, Fax: 207-581-3232, E-mail: graduate@maine.edu.

University of Massachusetts Amherst, Graduate School, College of Natural Sciences and Mathematics, Department of Geosciences, Program in Geosciences, Amherst, MA 01003. Offers MS, PhD. Postbaccalaureate distance learning degree programs offered. *Students:* 25 full-time (13 women), 24 part-time (11 women), 5 international. Average age 32. 60 applicants, 60% accepted, 12 enrolled. In 2003, 7 master's, 2 doctorates awarded. *Degree requirements:* For doctorate, one foreign language, thesis/dissertation. *Entrance requirements:* For doctorate, GRE General Test. Additional exam requirements/recommendations for international students: Required—TOEFL (minimum score 530 paper-based; 197 computer-based). *Application deadline:* For fall admission, 2/1 for domestic students, 2/1 for international students; for spring admission, 10/1 for domestic students, 10/1 for international students. Applications are processed on a rolling basis. Application fee: $40 ($50 for international students). *Expenses:* Tuition, state resident: full-time $1,320; part-time $110 per credit. Tuition, nonresident: full-time $4,969; part-time $414 per credit. Required fees: $2,626 per term. Tuition and fees vary according to course load. *Financial support:* Fellowships with full tuition reimbursements, research assistantships with full tuition reimbursements, teaching assistantships with full tuition reimbursements, career-related internships or fieldwork, Federal Work-Study, scholarships/grants, traineeships, and unspecified assistantships available. Support available to part-time students. Financial award application deadline: 2/1.

The University of Memphis, Graduate School, College of Arts and Sciences, Department of Earth Sciences, Memphis, TN 38152. Offers earth sciences (PhD); geography (MA, MS); geology (MS); geophysics (MS). Part-time programs available. *Faculty:* 23 full-time (3 women), 3 part-time/adjunct (1 woman). *Students:* 34. Average age 29. 13 applicants, 46% accepted. In 2003, 4 master's, 1 doctorate awarded. Terminal master's awarded for partial completion of doctoral program. *Degree requirements:* For master's, thesis, seminar presentation, comprehensive exam; for doctorate, thesis/dissertation. *Entrance requirements:* For master's and doctorate, GRE General Test. Additional exam requirements/recommendations for international students: Required—TOEFL. *Application deadline:* For fall admission, 8/1 for domestic students; for spring admission, 12/1 for domestic students. Applications are processed on a rolling basis. Application fee: $25 ($50 for international students). Electronic applications accepted. *Expenses:* Tuition, state resident: full-time $5,142. Tuition, nonresident: full-time $13,296. *Financial support:* In 2003–04, 34 students received support, including 2 fellowships with full tuition reimbursements available, 10 research assistantships with full tuition reimbursements available, 11 teaching assistantships with full tuition reimbursements available (averaging $10,000 per year) Financial award application deadline: 1/15. *Faculty research:* Hazards, active tectonics, geophysics, hydrology and water resources, spatial analysis. Total annual research expenditures: $1.8 million. *Unit head:* Dr. Mervin J. Bartholomew, Chair, 901-678-1613, Fax: 901-678-4467, E-mail: jbrthlm1@memphis.edu. *Application contact:* Dr. George Swihart, Coordinator of Graduate Studies, 901-678-2606, Fax: 901-678-2178, E-mail: gswihart@memphis.edu.

University of Missouri–Kansas City, College of Arts and Sciences, Department of Geosciences, Kansas City, MO 64110-2499. Offers geosciences (PhD); urban environmental geology (MS). PhD offered through the School of Graduate Studies. Part-time programs available. *Faculty:* 10 full-time (2 women). *Students:* 2 full-time (0 women), 6 part-time (2 women); includes 1 minority (African American), 1 international. Average age 33. 5 applicants, 60% accepted. In 2003, 1 degree awarded. *Degree requirements:* For master's and doctorate, thesis/dissertation. *Entrance requirements:* For master's, GRE General Test, minimum GPA of 3.0; for doctorate, qualifying exam. Additional exam requirements/recommendations for international students: Required—TOEFL. *Application deadline:* For fall admission, 3/15 for domestic students. Application fee: $35 ($50 for international students). *Financial support:* In 2003–04, 4 research assistantships with full tuition reimbursements (averaging $12,000 per year), 6 teaching assistantships with full tuition reimbursements (averaging $11,000 per year) were awarded. Federal Work-Study, institutionally sponsored loans, and tuition waivers (full and partial) also available. Support available to part-time students. Financial award application deadline: 3/15. *Faculty research:* Quaternary environments, waste management, black shale geochemistry, history of cartography, neotectonics. Total annual research expenditures:$250,000. *Unit head:* Dr. Raymond M. Coveney, Chair, 816-235-1334, Fax: 816-235-5535, E-mail: coveneyr@umkc.edu. *Application contact:* Dr. James Murowchick, Associate Professor, 816-235-2979, Fax: 816-235-5535, E-mail: murowchickj@umkc.edu.

University of Nebraska–Lincoln, Graduate College, College of Arts and Sciences, Department of Geosciences, Lincoln, NE 68588. Offers MS, PhD. *Degree requirements:* For master's, departmental qualifying exam, thesis optional; for doctorate, thesis/dissertation, departmental qualifying exams, comprehensive exam. *Entrance requirements:* For master's and doctorate, GRE General Test. Additional exam requirements/recommendations for international students: Required—TOEFL (minimum score 550 paper-based; 213 computer-based). Electronic applications accepted. *Faculty research:* Hydrogeology, sedimentology, environmental geology, vertebrate paleontology.

University of Nevada, Las Vegas, Graduate College, College of Science, Department of Geoscience, Las Vegas, NV 89154-9900. Offers MS, PhD. Part-time programs available. *Faculty:* 20 full-time (6 women), 7 part-time/adjunct (0 women). *Students:* 27 full-time (11 women), 11 part-time (6 women); includes 2 minority (1 Asian American or Pacific Islander, 1 Hispanic American), 3 international. 30 applicants, 43% accepted, 6 enrolled. In 2003, 4 master's, 2 doctorates awarded. *Degree requirements:* For master's and doctorate, thesis/dissertation, comprehensive exam. *Entrance requirements:* For master's and doctorate, GRE General Test, minimum GPA of 3.0. Additional exam requirements/recommendations for international students: Required—TOEFL (minimum score 550 paper-based; 213 computer-based). *Application deadline:* For fall admission, 4/15 for domestic students, 4/15 for international students; for spring admission, 11/1 for domestic students, 10/1 for international students.

Geosciences

University of Nevada, Las Vegas (continued)

Application fee: $60 ($75 for international students). *Expenses:* Tuition, state resident: part-time $115 per credit. Tuition, nonresident: part-time $242 per credit. Required fees: $8 per semester. Tuition and fees vary according to course load. *Financial support:* In 2003–04, 7 research assistantships with partial tuition reimbursements (averaging $10,000 per year), 22 teaching assistantships with partial tuition reimbursements (averaging $10,000 per year) were awarded. Financial award application deadline: 3/1. *Unit head:* Dr. Rodney Metcalf, Chair, 702-895-3262. *Application contact:* Graduate College Admissions Evaluator, 702-895-3320, Fax: 702-895-4180, E-mail: gradcollege@ccmail.nevada.edu.

University of New Hampshire, Graduate School, College of Engineering and Physical Sciences, Department of Earth Sciences, Durham, NH 03824. Offers earth sciences (MS), including geochemical, geology, ocean mapping, oceanography; hydrology (MS). *Faculty:* 29 full-time. *Students:* 18 full-time (7 women), 22 part-time (7 women); includes 3 minority (2 African Americans, 1 American Indian/Alaska Native), 2 international. Average age 31. 49 applicants, 78% accepted, 16 enrolled. In 2003, 9 degrees awarded. *Degree requirements:* For master's, thesis, one foreign language. *Entrance requirements:* For master's, GRE General Test. Additional exam requirements/recommendations for international students: Required—TOEFL (minimum score 550 paper-based; 213 computer-based); Recommended—TSE. *Application deadline:* For fall admission, 4/1 for domestic students; for winter admission, 12/1 for domestic students. Applications are processed on a rolling basis. Application fee: $50. Electronic applications accepted. Tuition, area resident: Full-time $7,070. *Expenses:* Tuition, state resident: full-time $10,605. Tuition, nonresident: full-time $17,430. Required fees: $15. *Financial support:* In 2003–04, 1 fellowship, 7 research assistantships, 9 teaching assistantships were awarded. Career-related internships or fieldwork, Federal Work-Study, scholarships/grants, and tuition waivers (full and partial) also available. Support available to part-time students. Financial award application deadline: 2/15. *Unit head:* Dr. Matt Davis, Chairperson, 603-862-4119, E-mail: earth.sciences@unh.edu. *Application contact:* Linda Wrightsman, Administrative Assistant, 603-862-1720, E-mail: earth.sciences@unh.edu.

University of New Mexico, Graduate School, College of Arts and Sciences, Department of Earth and Planetary Sciences, Albuquerque, NM 87131-2039. Offers MS, PhD. *Students:* 40 full-time (18 women), 16 part-time (11 women); includes 4 minority (1 Asian American or Pacific Islander, 3 Hispanic Americans), 3 international. Average age 29. 56 applicants, 39% accepted, 15 enrolled. In 2003, 10 master's, 2 doctorates awarded. Terminal master's awarded for partial completion of doctoral program. *Degree requirements:* For master's and doctorate, thesis/dissertation. *Entrance requirements:* For master's, GRE General Test; for doctorate, GRE General Test, GRE Subject Test. *Application deadline:* For fall admission, 1/31 for domestic students; for spring admission, 11/1 priority date for domestic students. Application fee: $40. *Expenses:* Tuition, state resident: full-time $1,802; part-time $152 per credit hour. Tuition, nonresident: full-time $6,135; part-time $513 per credit hour. Tuition and fees vary according to program. *Financial support:* In 2003–04, 2 fellowships (averaging $28,993 per year), 26 research assistantships (averaging $9,903 per year), 24 teaching assistantships (averaging $7,300 per year) were awarded. Scholarships/grants also available. Financial award application deadline: 3/1; financial award applicants required to submit FAFSA. *Faculty research:* Geochemistry, meteoritics, tectonics, igcodynamics, climate and surface processes. Total annual research expenditures: $1.2 million. *Unit head:* Dr. Les D. McFadden, Chair, 505-277-4204, Fax: 505-277-8843, E-mail: lmcfadnm@unm.edu. *Application contact:* Cindy Jaramillo, Administrative Assistant II, 505-277-1635, Fax: 505-277-8843, E-mail: epsdept@unm.edu.

The University of North Carolina at Charlotte, Graduate School, College of Arts and Sciences, Department of Geography and Earth Sciences, Program in Earth Sciences, Charlotte, NC 28223-0001. Offers MS. Part-time and evening/weekend programs available. *Students:* 7 full-time (3 women), 12 part-time (4 women). Average age 32. 10 applicants, 100% accepted, 7 enrolled. In 2003, 1 degree awarded. *Degree requirements:* For master's, thesis optional. *Entrance requirements:* For master's, GRE General Test, minimum GPA of 3.0 in science major. Additional exam requirements/recommendations for international students: Required—TOEFL (minimum score 557 paper-based; 220 computer-based). *Application deadline:* For fall admission, 7/1 for domestic students, 5/1 for international students; for spring admission, 11/1 for domestic students, 10/1 for international students. Applications are processed on a rolling basis. Application fee: $35. Electronic applications accepted. *Expenses:* Tuition, state resident: full-time $1,979. Tuition, nonresident: full-time $12,111. Required fees: $1,201. Tuition and fees vary according to course load. *Financial support:* In 2003–04, 1 research assistantship (averaging $9,919 per year), 1 teaching assistantship (averaging $9,000 per year) were awarded. Financial award application deadline: 4/1; financial award applicants required to submit FAFSA. *Faculty research:* Environmental geology; trace element geochemistry; geomorphology; hydrogeology; mineralogy and petrology. *Unit head:* Dr. John F. Bender, Coordinator, 704-687-4251, Fax: 704-687-3182, E-mail: jfbender@email.uncc.edu. *Application contact:* Kathy B. Giddings, Director of Graduate Admissions, 704-687-3366, Fax: 704-687-3279, E-mail: gradadm@email.uncc.edu.

The University of North Carolina at Wilmington, College of Arts and Sciences, Department of Earth Sciences, Wilmington, NC 28403-3297. Offers geology (MS); marine science (MS). *Faculty:* 21 full-time (5 women). *Students:* 14 full-time (11 women), 41 part-time (15 women); includes 3 minority (1 American Indian/Alaska Native, 1 Asian American or Pacific Islander, 1 Hispanic American), 1 international. Average age 35. 42 applicants, 45% accepted, 15 enrolled. In 2003, 14 degrees awarded. *Degree requirements:* For master's, thesis, comprehensive exam. *Entrance requirements:* For master's, GRE General Test, GRE Subject Test, minimum B average in undergraduate major and basic courses for prerequisite to geology. *Application deadline:* For fall admission, 2/15 for domestic students. Applications are processed on a rolling basis. Application fee: $45. *Expenses:* Tuition, state resident: full-time $2,282. Tuition, nonresident: full-time $11,980. Required fees: $1,659. Tuition and fees vary according to course load. *Financial support:* In 2003–04, 9 teaching assistantships were awarded; career-related internships or fieldwork and Federal Work-Study also available. Support available to part-time students. Financial award application deadline: 3/15. *Unit head:* Dr. Richard A. Laws, Chair, 910-962-3736, Fax: 910-962-7077. *Application contact:* Dr. Robert D. Roer, Dean, Graduate School, 910-962-4117, Fax: 910-962-3787, E-mail: roer@uncw.edu.

University of North Dakota, Graduate School, Program in Earth System Science and Policy, Grand Forks, ND 58202. Offers MEM, MS, PhD. *Faculty:* 9 full-time (3 women). *Entrance requirements:* For master's and doctorate, GRE General Test, minimum GPA of 3.0. Additional exam requirements/recommendations for international students: Required—TOEFL (minimum score 550 paper-based; 213 computer-based). *Application deadline:* For fall admission, 3/1 priority date for domestic students, 3/1 priority date for international students; for spring admission, 10/15 priority date for domestic students, 10/15 priority date for international students. Applications are processed on a rolling basis. Application fee: $35. Electronic applications accepted. *Expenses:* Tuition, state resident: part-time $235 per credit. Tuition, nonresident: part-time $535 per credit. Tuition and fees vary according to course level, course load, program and reciprocity agreements. *Unit head:* Dr. George Seielstad, Graduate Director, 701-777-4755.

University of Northern Colorado, Graduate School, College of Arts and Sciences, Department of Earth Sciences, Greeley, CO 80639. Offers MA. *Faculty:* 3 full-time (0 women). *Students:* 7 full-time (3 women), 4 part-time (3 women). Average age 34. 2 applicants, 50% accepted, 0 enrolled. In 2003, 1 degree awarded. *Degree requirements:* For master's, comprehensive exam. *Application deadline:* Applications are processed on a rolling basis. Application fee: $50 ($60 for international students). *Expenses:* Tuition, state resident: full-time $2,980; part-time $166 per semester. Tuition, nonresident: full-time $12,396; part-time $689 per semester. Required fees: $627; $35 per semester. *Financial support:* In 2003–04, 7 students received support, including 4 research assistantships (averaging $13,293 per year), 4 teaching assistantships (averaging $10,433 per year); fellowships, unspecified assistantships also available. Financial award application deadline: 3/1; financial award applicants required to submit FAFSA. *Unit head:* Dr. William Hoyt, Chairperson, 970-351-2647.

University of Notre Dame, Graduate School, College of Engineering, Department of Civil Engineering and Geological Sciences, Notre Dame, IN 46556. Offers bioengineering (MS Bio E); civil engineering (MSCE); civil engineering and geological sciences (PhD); environmental engineering (MS Env E); geological sciences (MS). *Faculty:* 14 full-time (3 women), 1 part-time/adjunct (0 women). *Students:* 52 full-time (24 women), 2 part-time (1 woman); includes 5 minority (1 African American, 1 Asian American or Pacific Islander, 3 Hispanic Americans), 7 international. 108 applicants, 17% accepted, 9 enrolled. In 2003, 4 master's, 3 doctorates awarded. Terminal master's awarded for partial completion of doctoral program. *Degree requirements:* For master's, comprehensive exam; for doctorate, thesis/dissertation. *Entrance requirements:* For master's and doctorate, GRE General Test. Additional exam requirements/recommendations for international students: Required—TOEFL. *Application deadline:* For fall admission, 2/1 for domestic students; for spring admission, 10/15 for domestic students. Applications are processed on a rolling basis. Application fee: $50. Electronic applications accepted. *Expenses:* Tuition: Full-time $29,375. *Financial support:* In 2003–04, 53 students received support, including 8 fellowships with full tuition reimbursements available (averaging $20,000 per year), 24 research assistantships with full tuition reimbursements available (averaging $14,000 per year), 17 teaching assistantships with full tuition reimbursements available (averaging $13,200 per year); tuition waivers (full) also available. Financial award application deadline: 2/1. *Faculty research:* Environmental modeling, biological-waste treatment, petrology, environmental geology, geochemistry. Total annual research expenditures: $2.7 million. *Unit head:* Dr. Yahya C. Kurama, Director of Graduate Studies, 574-631-8227, Fax: 574-631-9236, E-mail: cegeos@nd.edu. *Application contact:* Dr. Terrence J. Akai, Director of Graduate Admissions, 574-631-7706, Fax: 574-631-4183, E-mail: gradad@nd.edu.

University of Ottawa, Faculty of Graduate and Postdoctoral Studies, Faculty of Science, Ottawa-Carleton Geoscience Centre, Ottawa, ON K1N 6N5, Canada. Offers earth sciences (M Sc, PhD). *Faculty:* 6 full-time (4 women), 2 part-time/adjunct (both women). *Students:* 15 full-time (9 women), 3 part-time (all women). 8 applicants, 100% accepted, 7 enrolled. In 2003, 5 master's, 1 doctorate awarded. *Degree requirements:* For master's, thesis/dissertation, seminar; for doctorate, thesis/dissertation, seminar, comprehensive exam. *Entrance requirements:* For master's, honors B Sc degree or equivalent, minimum B average; for doctorate, honors B Sc with minimum B average or M Sc with minimum B+ average. *Application deadline:* For fall admission, 3/1 for domestic students. Application fee: $60. *Expenses:* Tuition, state resident: full-time $4,467. International tuition: $4,574 full-time. Tuition and fees vary according to program. *Financial support:* Fellowships, research assistantships, teaching assistantships, career-related internships or fieldwork and Federal Work-Study available. Financial award application deadline: 2/15. *Faculty research:* Environmental geoscience, geochemistry/petrology, geomathematics/computing, resource studies, sedimentary systems. *Unit head:* Dr. Robert W. Arnott, Interim Chair, 613-562-5800 Ext. 6854, Fax: 613-562-5192, E-mail: estchair@science.uottawa.ca. *Application contact:* Lise Maisonneuve, Graduate Studies Administrator, 613-562-5800 Ext. 6050, Fax: 613-562-5486, E-mail: lise@science.uottawa.ca.

University of Rhode Island, Graduate School, College of the Environment and Life Sciences, Department of Geosciences, Kingston, RI 02881. Offers MS. *Degree requirements:* For master's, thesis optional. *Application deadline:* For fall admission, 4/15 for domestic students. Applications are processed on a rolling basis. Application fee: $35. *Expenses:* Tuition, state resident: full-time $4,338; part-time $281 per credit. Tuition, nonresident: full-time $12,438; part-time $704 per credit. Required fees: $1,840. *Unit head:* Dr. Daniel Murray, Chairperson, 401-874-2197.

University of Rochester, The College, Arts and Sciences, Department of Earth and Environmental Sciences, Rochester, NY 14627-0250. Offers geological sciences (MS, PhD). *Faculty:* 7. *Students:* 12 full-time (6 women), 1 part-time, 9 international. 81 applicants, 12% accepted, 6 enrolled. In 2003, 2 master's, 1 doctorate awarded. *Degree requirements:* For doctorate, thesis/dissertation, qualifying exam. *Entrance requirements:* For master's and doctorate, GRE General Test. Additional exam requirements/recommendations for international students: Required—TOEFL. *Application deadline:* For fall admission, 2/1 for domestic students. Application fee: $25. *Expenses:* Tuition: Part-time $880 per credit hour. Required fees: $522. *Financial support:* Fellowships, research assistantships, teaching assistantships, career-related internships or fieldwork and tuition waivers (full and partial) available. Financial award application deadline: 2/1. *Unit head:* John Tarduno, Chair, 585-275-5713. *Application contact:* Kathy Lutz, Graduate Program Secretary, 585-275-5713.

University of San Diego, Hahn School of Nursing and Health Sciences, San Diego, CA 92110-2492. Offers adult nurse practitioner (MSN, Post Master's Certificate); case management for vulnerable populations (MSN); family nurse practitioner (MSN, Post Master's Certificate); health care systems (MSN); nursing science (PhD); pediatric nurse practitioner (MSN, Post Master's Certificate). *Accreditation:* AACN. Part-time and evening/weekend programs available. *Faculty:* 11 full-time (9 women), 8 part-time/adjunct (all women). *Students:* 69 full-time (61 women), 94 part-time (87 women); includes 41 minority (10 African Americans, 1 American Indian/Alaska Native, 21 Asian Americans or Pacific Islanders, 9 Hispanic Americans), 6 international. Average age 37. 292 applicants, 63% accepted, 69 enrolled. In 2003, 31 master's, 10 doctorates awarded. *Degree requirements:* For doctorate, thesis/dissertation, administrative residency. *Entrance requirements:* For master's, GRE General Test or MAT, BSN, minimum GPA of 3.0, current California RN licensure; for doctorate, GRE General Test or MAT, minimum GPA of 3.5, MSN, current California RN licensure. Additional exam requirements/recommendations for international students: Required—TOEFL, TWE. *Application deadline:* For fall admission, 5/1 for domestic students; for spring admission, 11/1 priority date for domestic students. Applications are processed on a rolling basis. Application fee: $45. Electronic applications accepted. *Expenses:* Tuition: Full-time $14,850; part-time $825 per unit. Required fees: $126. Full-time tuition and fees vary according to class time, course load, degree level and program. *Financial support:* Institutionally sponsored loans, scholarships/grants, traineeships, tuition waivers (partial), and graduate work program available. Support available to part-time students. Financial award application deadline: 5/1; financial award applicants required to submit FAFSA. *Faculty research:* Health promotion, decision making, psychogeriatric nursing, historical nursing, leadership behavior. *Unit head:* Dr. Sally Hardin, Dean, 619-260-4550, Fax: 619-260-6814. *Application contact:* Stephen Pultz, Director of Admissions, 619-260-4524, Fax: 619-260-4158, E-mail: grads@sandiego.edu.

University of South Carolina, The Graduate School, College of Science and Mathematics, Department of Geological Sciences, Columbia, SC 29208. Offers environmental geoscience (PMS); geological sciences (MS, PhD). Terminal master's awarded for partial completion of doctoral program. *Degree requirements:* For master's, thesis; for doctorate, thesis/dissertation, published paper, comprehensive exam. *Entrance requirements:* For master's and doctorate, GRE General Test. Additional exam requirements/recommendations for international students: Required—TOEFL. Electronic applications accepted. *Expenses:* Tuition, state resident: part-time $308 per hour. Tuition, nonresident: part-time $655 per hour. *Faculty research:* Environmental geology, tectonics, petrology, coastal processes, paleoclimatology.

University of Southern California, Graduate School, College of Letters, Arts and Sciences, Department of Earth Sciences, Los Angeles, CA 90089. Offers MS, PhD. *Students:* 54 full-time (22 women), 1 (woman) part-time; includes 7 minority (1 Asian American or Pacific Islander, 6 Hispanic Americans), 18 international. In 2003, 6 master's, 6 doctorates awarded. *Degree requirements:* For master's and doctorate, thesis/dissertation. *Entrance requirements:* For master's and doctorate, GRE General Test. *Application deadline:* For fall admission, 1/15 for domestic students. Application fee: $65 ($75 for international students). *Expenses:* Tuition: Full-time $32,784; part-time $949 per unit. Tuition and fees vary according to course load and program. *Financial support:* In 2003–04, research assistantships with full tuition reimbursements (averaging $16,000 per year), teaching assistantships with full tuition reimbursements (averaging $16,000 per year) were awarded. Fellowships with full tuition reimbursements,

Federal Work-Study, institutionally sponsored loans, and scholarships/grants also available. Support available to part-time students. Financial award application deadline: 2/15; financial award applicants required to submit FAFSA. *Unit head:* Dr. Thomas Henyey, Chair, 213-740-6106, Fax: 213-740-8801, E-mail: earthsci@usc.edu.

The University of Texas at Arlington, Graduate School, College of Science, Department of Geology, Arlington, TX 76019. Offers environmental science (MS, PhD); geology (MS); math: geoscience (PhD). Part-time and evening/weekend programs available. *Faculty:* 4 full-time (0 women), 2 part-time/adjunct (0 women). *Students:* 5 full-time (0 women), 6 part-time (3 women); includes 3 minority (all African Americans), 4 international. 4 applicants, 100% accepted, 4 enrolled. In 2003, 6 degrees awarded. Terminal master's awarded for partial completion of doctoral program. *Median time to degree:* Master's–2 years full-time. *Degree requirements:* For master's, thesis optional; for doctorate, thesis/dissertation, comprehensive exam. *Entrance requirements:* For master's, GRE General Test. *Application deadline:* For fall admission, 6/16 for domestic students. Applications are processed on a rolling basis. Application fee: $35 ($50 for international students). Electronic applications accepted. *Expenses:* Tuition, state resident: full-time $3,042. Tuition, nonresident: full-time $8,712. Required fees: $1,269. Tuition and fees vary according to course load. *Financial support:* In 2003–04, 7 students received support, including 4 fellowships (averaging $1,000 per year), 7 teaching assistantships (averaging $14,700 per year); career-related internships or fieldwork, Federal Work-Study, institutionally sponsored loans, scholarships/grants, health care benefits, and unspecified assistantships also available. Financial award application deadline: 6/1; financial award applicants required to submit FAFSA. *Faculty research:* Hydrology, aqueous geochemistry, biostratigraphy, structural geology, petroleum geology. Total annual research expenditures: $250,000. *Unit head:* Dr. John S. Wickham, Chair, 817-272-2987, Fax: 817-272-2628, E-mail: wickham@uta.edu. *Application contact:* Dr. William L. Balsam, Graduate Adviser, 817-272-2987, Fax: 817-272-2628, E-mail: balsam@uta.edu.

The University of Texas at Austin, Graduate School, College of Natural Sciences, Department of Geological Sciences, Austin, TX 78712-1111. Offers MA, MS, PhD. Part-time programs available. *Degree requirements:* For master's, report (MA), thesis (MS); for doctorate, thesis/dissertation. *Entrance requirements:* For master's and doctorate, GRE General Test. Electronic applications accepted. *Faculty research:* Sedimentary geology, geophysics, hydrogeology, structure/tectonics, vertebrate paleontology.

The University of Texas at Dallas, School of Natural Sciences and Mathematics, Program in Geosciences, Richardson, TX 75083-0688. Offers MS, PhD. Part-time and evening/weekend programs available. *Faculty:* 12 full-time (0 women). *Students:* 35 full-time (12 women), 19 part-time (3 women); includes 4 minority (2 African Americans, 2 Hispanic Americans), 30 international. Average age 35. 35 applicants, 63% accepted. In 2003, 3 master's, 5 doctorates awarded. *Degree requirements:* For master's, thesis optional; for doctorate, thesis/dissertation. *Entrance requirements:* For master's and doctorate, GRE General Test, minimum GPA of 3.0 in upper-level course work in field. Additional exam requirements/recommendations for international students: Required—TOEFL (minimum score 550 paper-based; 213 computer-based). *Application deadline:* For fall admission, 7/15 for domestic students; for spring admission, 11/15 for domestic students. Applications are processed on a rolling basis. Application fee: $50 ($100 for international students). Electronic applications accepted. *Expenses:* Tuition, state resident: full-time $1,656; part-time $92 per credit. Tuition, nonresident: full-time $5,904; part-time $328 per credit. Required fees: $2,161; $275 per credit. $334 per term. *Financial support:* In 2003–04, 18 research assistantships with tuition reimbursements (averaging $5,746 per year), 12 teaching assistantships with tuition reimbursements (averaging $5,278 per year) were awarded. Fellowships, career-related internships or fieldwork, Federal Work-Study, institutionally sponsored loans, and scholarships/grants also available. Support available to part-time students. Financial award application deadline: 4/30; financial award applicants required to submit FAFSA. *Faculty research:* Hydrology, organic geochemistry, tectonic structures, seismic characteristics, digital geologic mapping. Total annual research expenditures: $1.1 million. *Unit head:* Dr. Robert Stern, Head, 972-883-2401, Fax: 972-883-2537. *Application contact:* Dr. Carlos Aiken, Graduate Adviser, 972-883-2450, Fax: 972-883-2537, E-mail: aiken@utdallas.edu.

University of Toledo, Graduate School, College of Arts and Sciences, Department of Earth, Ecological and Environmental Sciences, Toledo, OH 43606-3390. Offers biology (ecology track) (MS); biology (ecology tract) (PhD); geology (MS), including earth surface processes, general geology; science education (MES). Part-time programs available. *Degree requirements:* For master's, thesis. *Entrance requirements:* For master's, GRE General Test. Additional exam requirements/recommendations for international students: Required—TOEFL. *Application deadline:* For fall admission, 8/1 for domestic students. Applications are processed on a rolling basis. Application fee: $40. Electronic applications accepted. Tuition, area resident: Part-time $3,817 per semester. *Expenses:* Tuition, state resident: part-time $8,177 per semester. Required fees: $502 per semester. *Financial support:* In 2003–04, 6 research assistantships were awarded; teaching assistantships, Federal Work-Study, institutionally sponsored loans, and tuition waivers (full) also available. Support available to part-time students. Financial award application deadline: 4/1; financial award applicants required to submit FAFSA. *Faculty research:* Environmental geochemistry, geophysics, petrology and mineralogy, paleontology, geohydrology. *Unit head:* Dr. Michael Phillips, Chair, 419-530-4572, Fax: 419-530-4421, E-mail: mphilli@geology.utoledo.edu.

University of Tulsa, Graduate School, College of Engineering and Natural Sciences, Department of Geosciences, Tulsa, OK 74104-3189. Offers MS, PhD. Part-time programs available. *Faculty:* 7 full-time (1 woman). *Students:* 16 full-time (7 women), 3 part-time (1 woman), 8 international. Average age 34. 20 applicants, 65% accepted, 6 enrolled. In 2003, 6 master's, 3 doctorates awarded. *Median time to degree:* Master's–2 years full-time, 3 years part-time; doctorate–5 years full-time. *Degree requirements:* For master's, thesis optional; for doctorate, thesis/dissertation, comprehensive exam. *Entrance requirements:* For master's and doctorate, GRE General Test. Additional exam requirements/recommendations for international students: Required—TOEFL. *Application deadline:* Applications are processed on a rolling basis. Application fee: $30. Electronic applications accepted. *Expenses:* Tuition: Full-time $10,584; part-time $588 per credit hour. Required fees: $60; $3 per credit hour. *Financial support:* In 2003–04, 2 fellowships with full and partial tuition reimbursements (averaging $9,900 per year), 6 teaching assistantships with full and partial tuition reimbursements (averaging $9,015 per year) were awarded. Research assistantships with full and partial tuition reimbursements, career-related internships or fieldwork, scholarships/grants, tuition waivers (full and partial), and unspecified assistantships also available. Support available to part-time students. Financial award application deadline: 2/1; financial award applicants required to submit FAFSA. *Faculty research:* Petroleum geology, carbonate and marine geology, exploration geophysics, structural geology. Total annual research expenditures: $51,696. *Unit head:* Dr. Bryan Tapp, Chairperson, 918-631-3018, Fax: 918-631-2091, E-mail: jbt@utulsa.edu.

University of Victoria, Faculty of Graduate Studies, Faculty of Science, School of Earth and Ocean Sciences, Victoria, BC V8W 2Y2, Canada. Offers geochemistry (M Sc, PhD); geophysics (M Sc, PhD); marine geology and geophysics (M Sc, PhD); ocean acoustics (M Sc, PhD); oceanography (M Sc, PhD); paleobiology (M Sc, PhD); paleoceanography (M Sc, PhD); sedimentology (M Sc, PhD); stratigraphy (M Sc, PhD). Part-time programs available. *Degree requirements:* For master's and doctorate, thesis/dissertation. *Entrance requirements:* Additional exam requirements/recommendations for international students: Required—TOEFL (minimum score 550 paper-based; 213 computer-based). Electronic applications accepted. *Faculty research:* Climate modeling, geology.

University of Waterloo, Graduate Studies, Faculty of Science, Department of Earth Sciences, Waterloo, ON N2L 3G1, Canada. Offers M Sc, PhD. Part-time programs available. *Faculty:* 42 full-time (7 women), 32 part-time/adjunct (2 women). *Students:* 79 full-time (37 women), 13 part-time (4 women). 53 applicants, 47% accepted, 21 enrolled. In 2003, 17 master's, 3 doctorates awarded. *Degree requirements:* For master's, research paper or thesis; for doctorate, thesis/dissertation, comprehensive exam, registration. *Entrance requirements:* For master's, GRE, honors degree, minimum B average; for doctorate, GRE, master's degree, minimum B average. Additional exam requirements/recommendations for international students: Required—TOEFL, TWE. *Application deadline:* For fall admission, 8/1 for domestic students. Applications are processed on a rolling basis. Application fee: $75 Canadian dollars. Electronic applications accepted. Tuition and fees charges are reported in Canadian dollars. *Expenses:* Tuition, state resident: full-time $3,632 Canadian dollars. International tuition: $9,180 Canadian dollars full-time. Required fees: $406 Canadian dollars. *Financial support:* Research assistantships, teaching assistantships, career-related internships or fieldwork and institutionally sponsored loans available. *Faculty research:* Environmental geology, soil physics. *Unit head:* Dr. J. F. Barker, Chair, 519-888-4567 Ext. 2103, Fax: 519-746-7484, E-mail: jfbarker@uwaterloo.ca. *Application contact:* S. Fisher, Administrative Graduate Coordinator, 519-888-4567 Ext. 5836, Fax: 519-746-7484, E-mail: sfisher@sciborg.uwaterloo.ca.

The University of Western Ontario, Faculty of Graduate Studies, Physical Sciences Division, Department of Earth Sciences, London, ON N6A 5B8, Canada. Offers geology (M Sc, PhD); geology and environmental science (M Sc, PhD); geophysics (M Sc, PhD); geophysics and environmental science (M Sc, PhD). *Degree requirements:* For master's, thesis, registration; for doctorate, thesis/dissertation, qualifying exam. *Entrance requirements:* For master's, honors in B Sc; for doctorate, M Sc. Additional exam requirements/recommendations for international students: Required—TOEFL. *Faculty research:* Geophysics, geochemistry, paleontology, sedimentology/stratigraphy, glaciology/quaternary.

University of Windsor, Faculty of Graduate Studies and Research, Faculty of Science, Department of Earth Sciences, Windsor, ON N9B 3P4, Canada. Offers M Sc, PhD. Part-time programs available. *Faculty:* 11 full-time (1 woman), 3 part-time/adjunct (0 women). *Students:* 16 full-time (7 women), 2 part-time (1 woman). 24 applicants, 54% accepted. In 2003, 3 degrees awarded. *Degree requirements:* For master's and doctorate, thesis/dissertation. *Entrance requirements:* For master's, minimum B average. Additional exam requirements/recommendations for international students: Required—TOEFL. *Application deadline:* For fall admission, 7/1 for domestic students; for winter admission, 11/1 for domestic students; for spring admission, 3/1 for domestic students. Applications are processed on a rolling basis. Application fee: $55. Tuition charges are reported in Canadian dollars. *Expenses:* Tuition, state resident: full-time $1,704 Canadian dollars. Tuition, nonresident: full-time $2,126 Canadian dollars. International tuition: $2,976 Canadian dollars full-time. *Financial support:* In 2003–04, 7 teaching assistantships (averaging $8,000 per year) were awarded; Federal Work-Study, scholarships/grants, tuition waivers (full and partial), unspecified assistantships, and bursaries also available. Financial award application deadline: 2/15. *Faculty research:* Aqueous geochemistry and hydrothermal processes, igneous petrochemistry, radiogenic isotopes, radiometric age-dating, diagenetic and sedimentary geochemistry. *Unit head:* Dr. Ihsan Al-Aasm, Head, 519-253-3000 Ext. 2494, Fax: 519-971-7081, E-mail: earth@uwindsor.ca. *Application contact:* Applicant Services, 519-253-3000 Ext. 6459, Fax: 519-971-3653, E-mail: gradadmit@uwindsor.ca.

Washington University in St. Louis, Graduate School of Arts and Sciences, Department of Earth and Planetary Sciences, St. Louis, MO 63130-4899. Offers earth and planetary sciences (MA); geochemistry (PhD); geology (MA, PhD); geophysics (PhD); planetary sciences (PhD). *Students:* 36 full-time (19 women), 1 (woman) part-time; includes 2 minority (both Asian Americans or Pacific Islanders), 5 international. 69 applicants, 35% accepted, 12 enrolled. In 2003, 9 master's, 2 doctorates awarded. Terminal master's awarded for partial completion of doctoral program. *Degree requirements:* For master's and doctorate, thesis/dissertation. *Entrance requirements:* For master's and doctorate, GRE General Test. *Application deadline:* For fall admission, 1/15 for domestic students. Applications are processed on a rolling basis. Application fee: $35. Electronic applications accepted. *Expenses:* Tuition: Full-time $28,300; part-time $1,180 per credit. *Financial support:* Fellowships, research assistantships, teaching assistantships, Federal Work-Study, institutionally sponsored loans, and tuition waivers (full and partial) available. Financial award application deadline: 1/15. *Unit head:* Dr. Raymond E. Arvidson, Chairman, 314-935-5610.

Wesleyan University, Graduate Programs, Department of Earth Sciences, Middletown, CT 06459-0260. Offers MA. *Faculty:* 8 full-time (3 women). *Students:* 3 full-time (1 woman). Average age 28. In 2003, 3 degrees awarded. *Degree requirements:* For master's, thesis. *Entrance requirements:* For master's, GRE General Test, GRE Subject Test. *Application deadline:* For fall admission, 3/1 for domestic students. Applications are processed on a rolling basis. Application fee: $0. *Expenses:* Tuition: Full-time $22,338. Required fees: $20. *Financial support:* Teaching assistantships, tuition waivers (partial) available. *Faculty research:* Tectonics, volcanology, stratigraphy, coastal processes, geochemistry. *Unit head:* Dr. Suzanne O'Connell, Chair, 860-685-2262. *Application contact:* Gloria Augeri, Information Contact, 860-685-2320, Fax: 860-685-3651, E-mail: gaugeri@wesleyan.edu.

Western Connecticut State University, Division of Graduate Studies, School of Arts and Sciences, Department of Physics, Astronomy and Meteorology, Danbury, CT 06810-6885. Offers earth and planetary sciences (MA). Part-time and evening/weekend programs available. *Faculty:* 1 full-time (0 women). *Students:* Average age 33. *Degree requirements:* For master's, thesis. *Entrance requirements:* For master's, minimum GPA of 2.5. *Application deadline:* For fall admission, 8/1 for domestic students. Applications are processed on a rolling basis. Application fee: $40. *Expenses:* Tuition, state resident: full-time $3,263. Tuition, nonresident: full-time $6,742. *Financial support:* Fellowships, career-related internships or fieldwork available. Support available to part-time students. Financial award application deadline: 5/1; financial award applicants required to submit FAFSA. *Unit head:* Dr. Alice Chance, Chair, 203-837-8667. *Application contact:* Chris Shankle, Associate Director of Graduate Admissions, 203-837-8244, Fax: 203-837-8338, E-mail: shanklec@wcsu.edu.

Western Michigan University, Graduate College, College of Arts and Sciences, Department of Geosciences, Program in Earth Science, Kalamazoo, MI 49008-5202. Offers MS. *Degree requirements:* For master's, thesis or alternative, oral exam. *Entrance requirements:* For master's, GRE General Test.

Yale University, Graduate School of Arts and Sciences, Department of Geology and Geophysics, New Haven, CT 06520. Offers geochemistry (PhD); geophysics (PhD); meteorology (PhD); mineralogy and crystallography (PhD); oceanography (PhD); paleoecology (PhD); paleontology and stratigraphy (PhD); petrology (PhD); structural geology (PhD). *Degree requirements:* For doctorate, thesis/dissertation. *Entrance requirements:* For doctorate, GRE General Test. Additional exam requirements/recommendations for international students: Required—TOEFL. *Expenses:* Tuition: Full-time $25,600; part-time $6,400 per term.

See in-depth description on page 261.

York University, Faculty of Graduate Studies, Faculty of Pure and Applied Science, Program in Earth and Space Science, Toronto, ON M3J 1P3, Canada. Offers M Sc, PhD. Part-time and evening/weekend programs available. *Degree requirements:* For master's, thesis or alternative; for doctorate, thesis/dissertation. *Entrance requirements:* For master's, minimum B average. Electronic applications accepted. Tuition, area resident: Full-time $5,431; part-time $905 per term. Tuition, nonresident: part-time $1,987 per term. International tuition: $11,918 full-time. Required fees: $287. Tuition and fees vary according to program.

Hydrology

Auburn University, Graduate School, College of Engineering, Department of Civil Engineering, Auburn University, AL 36849. Offers construction engineering and management (MCE, MS, PhD); environmental engineering (MCE, MS, PhD); geotechnical/materials engineering (MCE, MS, PhD); hydraulics/hydrology (MCE, MS, PhD); structural engineering (MCE, MS, PhD); transportation engineering (MCE, MS, PhD). Part-time programs available. *Faculty:* 21 full-time (1 woman). *Students:* 47 full-time (12 women), 24 part-time (4 women); includes 4 minority (3 African Americans, 1 Hispanic American), 20 international. 117 applicants, 60% accepted. In 2003, 17 master's, 1 doctorate awarded. *Degree requirements:* For master's, project (MCE), thesis (MS); for doctorate, thesis/dissertation, comprehensive exam. *Entrance requirements:* For master's and doctorate, GRE General Test. *Application deadline:* For fall admission, 7/7 for domestic students; for spring admission, 11/24 for domestic students. Applications are processed on a rolling basis. Application fee: $25 ($50 for international students). Electronic applications accepted. *Expenses:* Tuition, state resident: part-time $175 per credit hour. Tuition, nonresident: part-time $525 per credit hour. *Financial support:* Fellowships, research assistantships, teaching assistantships, Federal Work-Study available. Support available to part-time students. Financial award application deadline: 3/15. *Unit head:* Dr. J. Michael Stallings, Head, 334-844-4320. *Application contact:* Dr. John F. Pritchett, Dean of the Graduate School, 334-844-4700, E-mail: hatchlb@mail.auburn.edu.

California State University, Bakersfield, Division of Graduate Studies and Research, School of Natural Sciences, Mathematics, and Engineering, Program in Geology, Bakersfield, CA 93311-1099. Offers geology (MS); hydrology (MS). Part-time and evening/weekend programs available. *Degree requirements:* For master's, thesis. *Entrance requirements:* For master's, GRE General Test, BS in geology.

California State University, Chico, Graduate School, College of Natural Sciences, Department of Geological and Environmental Sciences, Program in Geosciences, Chico, CA 95929-0722. Offers earth sciences (MS); hydrology/hydrogeology (MS). *Students:* 4 full-time (2 women), 2 part-time (1 woman). Average age 36. 2 applicants, 100% accepted, 1 enrolled. In 2003, 3 degrees awarded. *Degree requirements:* For master's, thesis, oral exam. *Entrance requirements:* For master's, GRE General Test. Additional exam requirements/recommendations for international students: Required—TOEFL (minimum score 550 paper-based; 213 computer-based). *Application deadline:* For fall admission, 3/1 for domestic students, 3/1 for international students; for spring admission, 9/15 for domestic students, 9/15 for international students. Applications are processed on a rolling basis. Application fee: $55. Electronic applications accepted. Tuition, nonresident: part-time $282 per semester hour. Required fees: $1,029 per semester. *Financial support:* Fellowships available. *Unit head:* Dr. Gregory Taylor, Graduate Coordinator, 530-898-6369.

Clemson University, Graduate School, College of Engineering and Science, Department of Geological Sciences, Program in Hydrogeology, Clemson, SC 29634. Offers MS. *Students:* 18 full-time (9 women), 9 part-time, 3 international. 21 applicants, 62% accepted, 4 enrolled. In 2003, 4 degrees awarded. *Degree requirements:* For master's, thesis optional. *Entrance requirements:* For master's, GRE General Test, minimum GPA of 3.0 during previous 2 years. Additional exam requirements/recommendations for international students: Required—TOEFL. *Application deadline:* For fall admission, 6/1 for domestic students. Application fee: $40. Electronic applications accepted. *Expenses:* Tuition, state resident: full-time $7,432. Tuition, nonresident: full-time $14,732. *Financial support:* Fellowships, research assistantships, teaching assistantships, career-related internships or fieldwork and institutionally sponsored loans available. Support available to part-time students. Financial award application deadline: 6/1; financial award applicants required to submit FAFSA. *Faculty research:* Groundwater, geology, environmental geology, geochemistry, remediation, stratigraphy. Total annual research expenditures: $670,000. *Unit head:* Dr. Jim Castle, Coordinator, 864-656-5015, E-mail: jcastle@clemson.edu.

Colorado School of Mines, Graduate School, Department of Geology and Geological Engineering, Golden, CO 80401-1887. Offers engineering geology (Diploma); exploration geosciences (Diploma); geochemistry (MS, PhD); geological engineering (ME, MS, PhD, Diploma); geology (MS, PhD); hydrogeology (Diploma). Part-time programs available. *Faculty:* 25 full-time (4 women), 8 part-time/adjunct (4 women). *Students:* 52 full-time (16 women), 34 part-time (13 women); includes 1 minority (American Indian/Alaska Native), 20 international. 89 applicants, 56% accepted, 12 enrolled. In 2003, 19 master's, 4 doctorates, 3 other advanced degrees awarded. *Degree requirements:* For master's, thesis/dissertation; for doctorate, thesis/dissertation, comprehensive exam. *Entrance requirements:* For master's and doctorate, GRE General Test; for Diploma, GRE General Test, minimum GPA of 3.0. Additional exam requirements/recommendations for international students: Required—TOEFL (minimum score 550 paper-based; 213 computer-based). *Application deadline:* For fall admission, 12/1 for domestic students, 12/1 for international students; for spring admission, 5/1 for domestic students, 5/1 for international students. Application fee: $45. Electronic applications accepted. *Expenses:* Tuition, state resident: full-time $5,700; part-time $285 per credit hour. Tuition, nonresident: full-time $19,040; part-time $952 per credit hour. Required fees: $733. *Financial support:* In 2003–04, 23 students received support, including 9 fellowships with full tuition reimbursements available (averaging $12,500 per year), 16 research assistantships with full tuition reimbursements available (averaging $10,000 per year), 9 teaching assistantships with full tuition reimbursements available (averaging $10,000 per year); scholarships/grants and unspecified assistantships also available. Financial award applicants required to submit FAFSA. *Faculty research:* Predictive sediment modeling, petrophysics, aquifer-contaminant flow modeling, water-rock interactions, geotechnical engineering. Total annual research expenditures: $2.1 million. *Unit head:* Dr. Murray W. Hitzman, Head, 303-384-2127, Fax: 303-273-3859, E-mail: mhitzman@mines.edu. *Application contact:* Marilyn Schwinger, Administrative Assistant, 303-273-3800, Fax: 303-273-3859, E-mail: mschwing@mines.edu.

Colorado State University, Graduate School, College of Engineering, Department of Civil Engineering, Fort Collins, CO 80523-0015. Offers bioresource and agricultural engineering (MS); bioresource and agriculture engineering (PhD); environmental engineering (MS, PhD); hydraulics and wind engineering (MS, PhD); structural and geotechnical engineering (MS, PhD); water resources planning and management (MS, PhD); water resources, hydrologic and environmental sciences (MS, PhD). Part-time programs available. *Faculty:* 36 full-time (3 women). *Students:* 80 full-time (28 women), 112 part-time (17 women); includes 6 minority (4 Asian Americans or Pacific Islanders, 2 Hispanic Americans), 73 international. Average age 32. 229 applicants, 54% accepted, 46 enrolled. In 2003, 35 master's, 10 doctorates awarded. Terminal master's awarded for partial completion of doctoral program. *Degree requirements:* For master's, thesis or alternative; for doctorate, thesis/dissertation. *Entrance requirements:* For master's and doctorate, GRE General Test, minimum GPA of 3.0. Additional exam requirements/recommendations for international students: Required—TOEFL. *Application deadline:* For fall admission, 3/1 priority date for domestic students, 3/1 priority date for international students; for spring admission, 8/1 priority date for domestic students, 8/1 priority date for international students. Applications are processed on a rolling basis. Application fee: $50. Electronic applications accepted. *Expenses:* Tuition, state resident: full-time $4,156. Tuition, nonresident: full-time $14,762. Required fees: $205. Tuition and fees vary according to course load, campus/location, program and reciprocity agreements. *Financial support:* In 2003–04, 19 fellowships (averaging $1,500 per year), 47 research assistantships (averaging $12,186 per year), 18 teaching assistantships (averaging $12,006 per year) were awarded. Federal Work-Study, institutionally sponsored loans, and traineeships also available. *Faculty research:* Hydraulics, hydrology, water resources, infrastructure, environmental engineering. Total annual research expenditures: $7.8 million. *Unit head:* Sandra Woods, Head, 970-491-5049, Fax: 970-491-7727, E-mail: woods@engr.colostate.edu. *Application contact:* Laurie Howard, Student Adviser, 970-491-5844, Fax: 970-491-7727, E-mail: lhoward@engr.colostate.edu.

Colorado State University, Graduate School, College of Natural Resources, Department of Forest, Rangeland, and Watershed Stewardship, Program in Watershed Science, Fort Collins, CO 80523-0015. Offers MS. Part-time programs available. *Faculty:* 5 full-time (1 woman), 2 part-time/adjunct (1 woman). *Students:* 13 full-time (7 women), 17 part-time (6 women), 1 international. Average age 29. 48 applicants, 44% accepted, 9 enrolled. In 2003, 12 degrees awarded. *Degree requirements:* For master's, thesis, registration. *Entrance requirements:* For master's, GRE General Test, minimum GPA of 3.0. Additional exam requirements/recommendations for international students: Required—TOEFL. *Application deadline:* For fall admission, 2/1 for domestic students. Applications are processed on a rolling basis. Application fee: $50. Electronic applications accepted. *Expenses:* Tuition, state resident: full-time $4,156. Tuition, nonresident: full-time $14,762. Required fees: $205. Tuition and fees vary according to course load, campus/location, program and reciprocity agreements. *Financial support:* In 2003–04, 1 fellowship (averaging $2,500 per year), 10 research assistantships with partial tuition reimbursements (averaging $13,000 per year), 4 teaching assistantships with full tuition reimbursements (averaging $9,720 per year) were awarded. Career-related internships or fieldwork, Federal Work-Study, institutionally sponsored loans, and scholarships/grants also available. Financial award application deadline: 2/15. *Faculty research:* Land use hydrology, water quality, watershed planning and management, snow hydrology, hillslope-wetland hydrology. Total annual research expenditures: $800,000. *Unit head:* Dr. John D. Stednick, Program Leader, 970-491-7248, Fax: 970-491-6307, E-mail: jds@cnr.colostate.edu. *Application contact:* Barbara Holtz, Staff Assistant, 970-491-5662, Fax: 970-491-6307, E-mail: barbh@cnr.colostate.edu.

Colorado State University, Graduate School, College of Natural Resources, Department of Geosciences, Fort Collins, CO 80523-0015. Offers earth resources (PhD); geology (MS), including geomorphology, hydrogeology, petrology/geochemistry and economic geology, sedimentology, structural geology. Part-time programs available. *Faculty:* 9 full-time (4 women), 2 part-time/adjunct (0 women). *Students:* 19 full-time (6 women), 17 part-time (7 women); includes 1 minority (American Indian/Alaska Native), 3 international. Average age 31. 56 applicants, 46% accepted, 8 enrolled. In 2003, 6 master's, 2 doctorates awarded. *Degree requirements:* For master's and doctorate, thesis/dissertation, registration. *Entrance requirements:* For master's and doctorate, GRE General Test, minimum GPA of 3.0. Additional exam requirements/recommendations for international students: Required—TOEFL (minimum score 550 paper-based; 213 computer-based). *Application deadline:* For fall admission, 2/1 priority date for domestic students, 2/1 priority date for international students. Applications are processed on a rolling basis. Application fee: $50. Electronic applications accepted. *Expenses:* Tuition, state resident: full-time $4,156. Tuition, nonresident: full-time $14,762. Required fees: $205. Tuition and fees vary according to course load, campus/location, program and reciprocity agreements. *Financial support:* In 2003–04, fellowships (averaging $3,800 per year), research assistantships with partial tuition reimbursements (averaging $14,400 per year), teaching assistantships with full tuition reimbursements (averaging $10,206 per year) were awarded. Career-related internships or fieldwork, Federal Work-Study, institutionally sponsored loans, scholarships/grants, and traineeships also available. Financial award application deadline: 2/15. *Faculty research:* Snow, surface, and groundwater hydrology; fluvial geomorphology; geographic information systems; geochemistry; bedrock geology. Total annual research expenditures: $407,835. *Unit head:* Dr. Judith L. Hannah, Head, 970-491-5662, Fax: 970-491-6307, E-mail: jhannah@cnr.colostate.edu. *Application contact:* Barbara Holtz, Staff Assistant, 970-491-5662, Fax: 970-491-6307, E-mail: barbh@cnr.colostate.edu.

Cornell University, Graduate School, Graduate Fields of Engineering, Field of Civil and Environmental Engineering, Ithaca, NY 14853-0001. Offers engineering management (M Eng, MS, PhD); environmental engineering (M Eng, MS, PhD); environmental fluid mechanics and hydrology (M Eng, MS, PhD); environmental systems engineering (M Eng, MS, PhD); geotechnical engineering (M Eng, MS, PhD); remote sensing (M Eng, MS, PhD); structural engineering (M Eng, MS, PhD); structural mechanics (M Eng, MS); transportation engineering (MS, PhD); transportation systems engineering (M Eng); water resource systems (M Eng, MS, PhD). *Faculty:* 33 full-time. *Students:* 115 full-time (32 women); includes 9 minority (2 African Americans, 2 Asian Americans or Pacific Islanders, 5 Hispanic Americans), 55 international. 491 applicants, 48% accepted, 64 enrolled. In 2003, 66 master's, 8 doctorates awarded. Terminal master's awarded for partial completion of doctoral program. *Degree requirements:* For master's, thesis (MS); for doctorate, thesis/dissertation, comprehensive exam. *Entrance requirements:* For master's and doctorate, GRE General Test (recommended), 2 letters of recommendation. Additional exam requirements/recommendations for international students: Required—TOEFL (minimum score 600 paper-based; 250 computer-based). *Application deadline:* For fall admission, 1/15 for domestic students; for spring admission, 10/15 for domestic students. Application fee: $60. Electronic applications accepted. *Expenses:* Tuition: Full-time $28,630. One-time fee: $50 full-time. *Financial support:* In 2003–04, 62 students received support, including 23 fellowships with full tuition reimbursements available, 26 research assistantships with full tuition reimbursements available, 13 teaching assistantships with full tuition reimbursements available; institutionally sponsored loans, scholarships/grants, health care benefits, tuition waivers (full and partial), and unspecified assistantships also available. Financial award applicants required to submit FAFSA. *Faculty research:* Environmental engineering, geotechnical engineering remote sensing, environmental fluid mechanics and hydrology, structural engineering. *Unit head:* Director of Graduate Studies, 607-255-7560, Fax: 607-255-9004. *Application contact:* Graduate Field Assistant, 607-255-7560, Fax: 607-255-9004, E-mail: cee_grad@cornell.edu.

Cornell University, Graduate School, Graduate Fields of Engineering, Field of Geological Sciences, Ithaca, NY 14853-0001. Offers economic geology (M Eng, MS, PhD); engineering geology (M Eng, MS, PhD); environmental geophysics (M Eng, MS, PhD); general geology (M Eng, MS, PhD); geobiology (M Eng, MS, PhD); geochemistry and isotope geology (M Eng, MS, PhD); geohydrology (M Eng, MS, PhD); geomorphology (M Eng, MS, PhD); geophysics (M Eng, MS, PhD); geotectonics (M Eng, MS, PhD); marine geology (MS, PhD); mineralogy (M Eng, MS, PhD); paleontology (M Eng, MS, PhD); petroleum geology (M Eng, MS, PhD); petrology (M Eng, MS, PhD); planetary geology (M Eng, MS, PhD); Precambrian geology (M Eng, MS, PhD); Quaternary geology (M Eng, MS, PhD); rock mechanics (M Eng, MS, PhD); sedimentology (M Eng, MS, PhD); seismology (M Eng, MS, PhD); stratigraphy (M Eng, MS, PhD); structural geology (M Eng, MS, PhD). *Faculty:* 31 full-time. *Students:* 27 full-time (12 women); includes 1 minority (Asian American or Pacific Islander), 9 international. 74 applicants, 15% accepted, 7 enrolled. In 2003, 3 master's, 5 doctorates awarded. *Degree requirements:* For master's, thesis (MS); for doctorate, thesis/dissertation, comprehensive exam. *Entrance requirements:* For master's and doctorate, GRE General Test, 3 letters of recommendation. Additional exam requirements/recommendations for international students: Required—TOEFL (minimum score 550 paper-based; 213 computer-based). *Application deadline:* For fall admission, 1/15 for domestic students. Applications are processed on a rolling basis. Application fee: $60. Electronic applications accepted. *Expenses:* Tuition: Full-time $28,630. One-time fee: $50 full-time. *Financial support:* In 2003–04, 21 students received support, including 6 fellowships with full tuition reimbursements available, 8 research assistantships with full tuition reimbursements available, 7 teaching assistantships with full tuition reimbursements available; institutionally sponsored loans, scholarships/grants, health care benefits, tuition waivers (full and partial), and unspecified assistantships also available. Financial award applicants required to submit FAFSA. *Faculty research:* Geophysics, structural geology, petrology, geochemistry, geodynamics. *Unit head:* Director of Graduate Studies, 607-255-3474, Fax: 607-254-4780. *Application contact:* Graduate Field Assistant, 607-255-3474, Fax: 607-254-4780, E-mail: gradprog@geology.cornell.edu.

See in-depth description on page 233.

Georgia Institute of Technology, Graduate Studies and Research, College of Sciences, School of Earth and Atmospheric Sciences, Atlanta, GA 30332-0001. Offers atmospheric chemistry and air pollution (MS, PhD); atmospheric dynamics and climate (MS, PhD); geochemistry (MS, PhD); hydrologic cycle (MS, PhD); ocean sciences (MS, PhD); solid-earth and environmental geophysics (PhD); solid-earth and environmental geophysics (MS). Part-time programs available. *Students:* 80 full-time (40 women); includes 39 minority (5 African Americans, 31 Asian Americans or Pacific Islanders, 3 Hispanic Americans). 143 applicants, 18% accepted, 15 enrolled. In 2003, 14 master's, 6 doctorates awarded. Terminal master's awarded for partial completion of doctoral program. *Median time to degree:* Of those who began their doctoral program in fall 1995, 78% received their degree in 8 years or less. *Degree requirements:* For master's, thesis or alternative; for doctorate, thesis/dissertation, comprehensive exam. *Entrance requirements:* For master's and doctorate, GRE General Test, minimum GPA of 2.7. Additional exam requirements/recommendations for international students: Required—TOEFL (minimum score 550 paper-based; 213 computer-based). *Application deadline:* For fall admission, 1/15 priority date for domestic students, 1/15 priority date for international students; for spring admission, 1/1 for domestic students. Applications are processed on a rolling basis. Application fee: $50. *Expenses:* Tuition, state resident: part-time $1,925 per semester. Tuition, nonresident: part-time $7,700 per semester. Required fees: $434 per semester. Full-time tuition and fees vary according to program. *Financial support:* In 2003–04, 3 fellowships, 52 research assistantships (averaging $20,000 per year), 8 teaching assistantships were awarded. Career-related internships or fieldwork, Federal Work-Study, and institutionally sponsored loans also available. Financial award application deadline: 2/15. *Faculty research:* Geophysics, atmospheric chemistry, atmospheric dynamics, seismology. Total annual research expenditures: $5 million. *Unit head:* Dr. Judith A. Curry, Chair, 404-894-3948, Fax: 404-894-5638. *Application contact:* Derek M. Cunnold, Graduate Coordinator, 404-894-3814, Fax: 404-894-5638, E-mail: cunnold@eas.gatech.edu.

See in-depth description on page 237.

Idaho State University, Office of Graduate Studies, College of Arts and Sciences, Department of Geosciences, Pocatello, ID 83209. Offers geology (MS); geophysics/hydrology (MS); geotechnology (Postbaccalaureate Certificate); natural science (MNS). Part-time programs available. Postbaccalaureate distance learning degree programs offered. *Faculty:* 6 full-time (1 woman), 1 part-time/adjunct (0 women). *Students:* 18 full-time (3 women), 17 part-time (7 women), 1 international. Average age 32. In 2003, 6 master's, 3 other advanced degrees awarded. *Degree requirements:* For master's, thesis, comprehensive exam, registration (for some programs); for Postbaccalaureate Certificate, thesis optional. *Entrance requirements:* For master's and Postbaccalaureate Certificate, GRE General Test, 3 letters of recommendation. Additional exam requirements/recommendations for international students: Required—TOEFL (minimum score 550 paper-based; 213 computer-based). *Application deadline:* For fall admission, 7/1 priority date for domestic students, 7/1 priority date for international students; for spring admission, 12/1 priority date for domestic students, 12/1 priority date for international students. Applications are processed on a rolling basis. Application fee: $35. *Expenses:* Tuition, state resident: part-time $205 per credit. Tuition, nonresident: full-time $6,600; part-time $300 per credit. Required fees: $4,108. One-time fee: $35 full-time. *Financial support:* Research assistantships with full and partial tuition reimbursements, teaching assistantships with full and partial tuition reimbursements, career-related internships or fieldwork, Federal Work-Study, institutionally sponsored loans, and tuition waivers (full and partial) available. Financial award application deadline: 1/1. *Faculty research:* Structural geography, stratigraphy, geochemistry, volcanography, geomorphology. Total annual research expenditures: $541,774. *Unit head:* Dr. Scott Hughes, Chairman, 208-282-3365, Fax: 208-282-4414.

Illinois State University, Graduate School, College of Arts and Sciences, Department of Geography-Geology, Normal, IL 61790-2200. Offers geohydrology (MS). *Faculty:* 11 full-time (2 women). *Students:* 13 full-time (5 women), 2 part-time (both women); includes 1 minority (Hispanic American), 1 international. 5 applicants, 100% accepted. In 2003, 7 degrees awarded. *Entrance requirements:* For master's, GRE General Test. *Application deadline:* Applications are processed on a rolling basis. Application fee: $30. *Expenses:* Tuition, state resident: full-time $3,322; part-time $138 per hour. Tuition, nonresident: full-time $6,922; part-time $288 per hour. Required fees: $974; $41 per hour. *Financial support:* In 2003–04, 6 research assistantships (averaging $8,402 per year), 7 teaching assistantships (averaging $7,887 per year) were awarded. Unspecified assistantships also available. Financial award application deadline: 4/1. *Faculty research:* High-resolution geophysical mapping of the Mahomet and Ticona Valley aquifer systems, improvement of map-use education in Mozambique. Total annual research expenditures: $126,134. *Unit head:* Dr. David Malone, Chairperson.

Massachusetts Institute of Technology, School of Engineering, Department of Civil and Environmental Engineering, Cambridge, MA 02139-4307. Offers biological oceanography (PhD, Sc D); chemical oceanography (PhD, Sc D); civil and environmental engineering (M Eng, SM, PhD, Sc D, CE, Env E); civil engineering (PhD, Sc D); coastal engineering (Sc D); construction engineering and management (PhD, Sc D); costal engineering (PhD); environmental biology (PhD, Sc D); environmental chemistry (PhD, Sc D); environmental engineering (PhD, Sc D); environmental fluid mechanics (PhD, Sc D); geotechnical and geoenvironmental engineering (PhD, Sc D); hydrology (PhD, Sc D); information technology (PhD, Sc D); oceanographic engineering (PhD); oceonographic engineering (Sc D); structures and materials (PhD, Sc D); transportation (PhD, Sc D). *Faculty:* 36 full-time (4 women). *Students:* 239 full-time (70 women); includes 17 minority (1 African American, 10 Asian Americans or Pacific Islanders, 6 Hispanic Americans), 147 international. Average age 26. 591 applicants, 37% accepted, 90 enrolled. In 2003, 149 master's, 27 doctorates awarded. *Degree requirements:* For master's and other advanced degree, thesis/dissertation; for doctorate, thesis/dissertation, comprehensive exam. *Entrance requirements:* For master's and doctorate, GRE General Test. Additional exam requirements/recommendations for international students: Required—TOEFL (minimum score 577 paper-based; 233 computer-based). *Application deadline:* For fall admission, 1/2 for domestic students, 1/2 for international students. Application fee: $70. Electronic applications accepted. *Expenses:* Tuition: Full-time $29,400. Required fees: $200. *Financial support:* In 2003–04, 214 students received support, including 42 fellowships with tuition reimbursements available, 112 research assistantships with tuition reimbursements available (averaging $22,740 per year), 29 teaching assistantships with tuition reimbursements available (averaging $17,370 per year); career-related internships or fieldwork, Federal Work-Study, institutionally sponsored loans, scholarships/grants, health care benefits, and unspecified assistantships also available. *Faculty research:* Environmental chemistry and biology, environmental fluid dynamics and hydrodynamics, geoenvironment and geotechnology, surface and groundwater hydrology, materials and structures. Total annual research expenditures: $10.9 million. *Unit head:* Prof. Patrick Jaillet, Head, 617-452-3379, Fax: 617-452-3294, E-mail: jaillet@mit.edu. *Application contact:* Graduate Admissions, 617-253-7101, E-mail: ceed@mit.edu.

Montana Tech of The University of Montana, Graduate School, Geoscience Program, Butte, MT 59701-8997. Offers geochemistry (MS); geological engineering (MS); geology (MS); geophysical engineering (MS); hydrogeological engineering (MS); hydrogeology (MS). Part-time programs available. *Faculty:* 8 full-time (1 woman). *Students:* 15 full-time (5 women), 1 (woman) part-time. 17 applicants, 71% accepted, 9 enrolled. In 2003, 7 degrees awarded. *Degree requirements:* For master's, thesis (for some programs), comprehensive exam (for some programs), registration. *Entrance requirements:* For master's, GRE General Test, minimum GPA of 3.0. Additional exam requirements/recommendations for international students: Required—TOEFL (minimum score 525 paper-based; 195 computer-based). *Application deadline:* For fall admission, 4/1 priority date for domestic students, 3/1 priority date for international students; for spring admission, 10/1 priority date for domestic students, 7/1 priority date for international students. Applications are processed on a rolling basis. Application fee: $30. *Expenses:* Tuition, state resident: full-time $4,741; part-time $233 per credit. Tuition, nonresident: full-time $14,662; part-time $646 per credit. *Financial support:* In 2003–04, 15 students received support, including 10 research assistantships with partial tuition reimbursements available (averaging $4,655 per year), 10 teaching assistantships with partial tuition reimbursements available (averaging $4,800 per year); career-related internships or fieldwork, tuition waivers (full and partial), and unspecified assistantships also available. Financial award application deadline: 4/1; financial award applicants required to submit FAFSA. *Faculty research:* Water resource development, seismic processing, petroleum reservoir characterization, environmental geochemistry, molecular modeling, magmatic and hydrothermal ore deposits. Total annual research expenditures: $623,564. *Unit head:* Dr. Diane Wolfgram, Department Head, 406-496-4353, Fax: 406-496-4260, E-mail: dwolfgram@mtech.edu. *Application contact:* Cindy Dunstan, Administrator, Graduate School, 406-496-4304, Fax: 406-496-4334, E-mail: cdunstan@mtech.edu.

New Mexico Institute of Mining and Technology, Graduate Studies, Department of Earth and Environmental Science, Program in Hydrology, Socorro, NM 87801. Offers MS, PhD. *Students:* 27 full-time (12 women), 4 part-time (2 women); includes 2 minority (1 Asian American or Pacific Islander, 1 Hispanic American), 6 international. Average age 28. 28 applicants, 9 enrolled. In 2003, 8 master's, 1 doctorate awarded. *Degree requirements:* For master's and doctorate, thesis/dissertation. *Entrance requirements:* For master's, GRE General Test; for doctorate, GRE General Test, GRE Subject Test. Additional exam requirements/recommendations for international students: Required—TOEFL (minimum score 540 paper-based; 207 computer-based). *Application deadline:* For fall admission, 3/1 for domestic students; for spring admission, 6/1 for domestic students. Applications are processed on a rolling basis. Application fee: $16 ($30 for international students). *Expenses:* Tuition, state resident: full-time $2,276; part-time $126 per credit. Tuition, nonresident: full-time $9,170; part-time $509 per credit. Required fees: $924; $27 per credit. $214 per term. Part-time tuition and fees vary according to course load. *Financial support:* In 2003–04, 1 fellowship (averaging $8,000 per year), 20 research assistantships (averaging $14,354 per year), 5 teaching assistantships with full and partial tuition reimbursements (averaging $7,812 per year) were awarded. Federal Work-Study, institutionally sponsored loans, and unspecified assistantships also available. Financial award application deadline: 3/1; financial award applicants required to submit CSS PROFILE or FAFSA. *Faculty research:* Surface and subsurface hydrology, numerical simulation, stochastic hydrology, water quality, modeling. *Unit head:* Dr. Robert Bowman, Coordinator, 505-835-5992, Fax: 505-835-6436, E-mail: geos@mnt.edu. *Application contact:* Dr. David B. Johnson, Dean of Graduate Studies, 505-835-5513, Fax: 505-835-5476, E-mail: graduate@nmt.edu.

Ohio University, Graduate Studies, College of Arts and Sciences, Department of Geological Sciences, Athens, OH 45701-2979. Offers environmental geochemistry (MS); environmental geology (MS); environmental/hydrology (MS); geology (MS); geology education (MS); geomorphology/surficial processes (MS); geophysics (MS); hydrogeology (MS); sedimentology (MS); structure/tectonics (MS). Part-time programs available. *Faculty:* 10 full-time (3 women), 4 part-time/adjunct (1 woman). *Students:* 13 full-time (4 women), 4 part-time (1 woman); includes 1 minority (Hispanic American), 4 international. Average age 25. 11 applicants, 45% accepted, 4 enrolled. In 2003, 8 degrees awarded. *Median time to degree:* Master's–2.5 years full-time. *Degree requirements:* For master's, thesis, thesis proposal defense. *Entrance requirements:* Additional exam requirements/recommendations for international students: Required—TOEFL (minimum score 550 paper-based; 217 computer-based). *Application deadline:* For fall admission, 2/1 priority date for domestic students, 1/1 priority date for international students. Application fee: $45. *Expenses:* Tuition, state resident: full-time $2,651; part-time $328 per credit. Tuition, nonresident: full-time $5,095; part-time $632 per credit. Tuition and fees vary according to program. *Financial support:* In 2003–04, 16 students received support, including 3 research assistantships with full tuition reimbursements available (averaging $11,000 per year), 13 teaching assistantships with full tuition reimbursements available (averaging $11,000 per year); institutionally sponsored loans, scholarships/grants, tuition waivers (full), and unspecified assistantships also available. Financial award application deadline: 3/15. *Faculty research:* Geoscience education, tectonics, flurial geomorphology, invertebrate paleontology, mine/hydrology. Total annual research expenditures: $506,400. *Unit head:* Dr. Douglas Green, Chair, 740-593-6896, Fax: 740-593-0486, E-mail: green@ohio.edu. *Application contact:* Dr. Dina L. Lopez, Graduate Chair, 740-593-9435, Fax: 740-593-0486, E-mail: lopezd@ohio.edu.

State University of New York College of Environmental Science and Forestry, Faculty of Forest and Natural Resources Management, Syracuse, NY 13210-2779. Offers environmental and natural resource policy (MS, PhD); environmental and natural resources policy (MPS); forest management and operations (MF); forestry ecosystems science and applications (MPS, MS, PhD); natural resources management (MPS, MS, PhD); quantitative methods and management in forest science (MPS, MS, PhD); recreation and resource management (MPS, MS, PhD); watershed management and forest hydrology (MPS, MS, PhD). *Faculty:* 28 full-time (5 women). *Students:* 48 full-time (18 women), 26 part-time (10 women); includes 2 minority (1 African American, 1 Hispanic American), 14 international. Average age 32. 47 applicants, 57% accepted, 14 enrolled. In 2003, 35 master's, 5 doctorates awarded. *Degree requirements:* For master's, thesis (for some programs), registration; for doctorate, thesis/dissertation, comprehensive exam, registration. *Entrance requirements:* For master's and doctorate, GRE General Test, minimum GPA of 3.0. Additional exam requirements/recommendations for international students: Required—TOEFL (minimum score 550 paper-based; 213 computer-based). *Application deadline:* For fall admission, 2/1 priority date for domestic students, 2/1 priority date for international students; for spring admission, 11/1 priority date for domestic students, 11/1 priority date for international students. Applications are processed on a rolling basis. Application fee: $50. Tuition, area resident: Part-time $288 per credit hour. Tuition, nonresident: part-time $438 per credit hour. Required fees: $300; $5 per credit hour. $18 per semester. One-time fee: $25 full-time. *Financial support:* In 2003–04, 43 students received support, including 9 fellowships with full and partial tuition reimbursements available (averaging $9,446 per year), 15 research assistantships with full and partial tuition reimbursements available (averaging $10,000 per year), 14 teaching assistantships with full and partial tuition reimbursements available (averaging $9,446 per year); career-related internships or fieldwork, Federal Work-Study, institutionally sponsored loans, scholarships/grants, health care benefits, and unspecified assistantships also available. Financial award applicants required to submit FAFSA. *Faculty research:* Silviculture recreation management, tree improvement, operations management, economics. Total annual research expenditures: $1.9 million. *Unit head:* Dr. Chad P. Dawson, Chair, 315-470-6536, Fax: 315-470-6535, E-mail: cpdawson@esf.edu. *Application contact:* Dr. Dudley J. Raynal, Dean, Instruction and Graduate Studies, 315-470-6599, Fax: 315-470-6978, E-mail: esfgrad@esf.edu.

Texas A&M University, College of Engineering, Department of Civil Engineering, College Station, TX 77843. Offers construction engineering and project management (M Eng, MS, D Eng, PhD); engineering mechanics (M Eng, MS, PhD); environmental engineering (M Eng, MS, D Eng, PhD); geotechnical engineering (M Eng, MS, D Eng, PhD); hydraulic engineering (M Eng, MS, PhD); hydrology (M Eng, MS, PhD); materials engineering (M Eng, MS, D Eng, PhD); ocean engineering (M Eng, MS, D Eng, PhD); public works engineering and management (M Eng, MS, PhD); structural engineering and structural mechanics (M Eng, MS, D Eng, PhD); transportation engineering (M Eng, MS, D Eng, PhD); water resources engineering (M Eng, MS, D Eng, PhD). Part-time programs available. *Faculty:* 33 full-time (2 women), 3 part-time/adjunct (0 women). *Students:* 292 full-time (57 women), 56 part-time (15 women); includes 22 minority (2 African Americans, 7 Asian Americans or Pacific Islanders, 13 Hispanic Americans), 233 international. Average age 29. 488 applicants, 43% accepted, 82 enrolled. In 2003, 65 master's, 25 doctorates awarded. *Degree requirements:* For master's, thesis (MS); for doctorate, dissertation (PhD), internship (D Eng). *Entrance requirements:* For master's and doctorate, GRE General Test. Additional exam requirements/recommendations for international students: Required—TOEFL. *Application deadline:* Applications are processed on a rolling basis. Application fee: $50 ($75 for international students). Electronic applications accepted. *Expenses:* Tuition, state resident: full-time $3,420. Tuition, nonresident: full-time $9,084. Required fees: $1,861. *Financial support:* In 2003–04, 175 students received support, including 15 fellowships (averaging $4,500 per year), 141 research assistantships (averaging $14,000 per year), 38 teaching assistantships (averaging $14,400 per year); career-related internships or fieldwork and institutionally sponsored loans also available. Financial award application deadline: 4/15; financial award applicants required to submit FAFSA. *Unit*

Hydrology

Texas A&M University (continued)

head: Dr. Paul N. Roschke, Interim Head, 979-845-7435, Fax: 979-862-2800, E-mail: ce-grad@tamu.edu. *Application contact:* Dr. Peter B. Keating, Graduate Advisor, 979-845-2498, Fax: 979-862-2800, E-mail: ce-grad@tamu.edu.

Université du Québec, Institut National de la Recherche Scientifique, Graduate Programs, Research Center—Earth and Environment, Ste-Foy, QC G1V 4C7, Canada. Offers earth sciences (M Sc, PhD); earth sciences-environmental technologies (M Sc); water sciences (MA, PhD). Part-time programs available. *Faculty:* 38. *Students:* 155 full-time (67 women), 10 part-time (3 women), 37 international. In 2003, 16 master's, 9 doctorates awarded. *Degree requirements:* For master's, thesis optional; for doctorate, thesis/dissertation. *Entrance requirements:* For master's, appropriate bachelor's degree, proficiency in French; for doctorate, appropriate master's degree, proficiency in French. *Application deadline:* For fall admission, 3/31 for domestic students. Application fee: $30. Tuition, area resident: Full-time $2,639. *Expenses:* Tuition, state resident: full-time $6,155. Tuition, nonresident: full-time $13,889. *Financial support:* Fellowships, research assistantships, teaching assistantships available. *Unit head:* Jean Pierre Villeneuve, Director, 418-654-2575, Fax: 418-654-2615, E-mail: jp_villeneuve@inrs.uquebec.ca. *Application contact:* Michel Barbeau, Registrar, 418-654-2518, Fax: 418-654-3858, E-mail: michel_barbeau@inrs.uquebec.ca.

The University of Arizona, Graduate College, College of Engineering, Department of Hydrology and Water Resources, Tucson, AZ 85721. Offers hydrology (MS, PhD); water resources engineering (M Eng). Part-time programs available. *Faculty:* 30. *Students:* 61 full-time (20 women), 23 part-time (8 women); includes 4 minority (2 American Indian/Alaska Native, 2 Hispanic Americans), 28 international. Average age 32. 58 applicants, 76% accepted, 16 enrolled. In 2003, 19 master's, 8 doctorates awarded. *Median time to degree:* Of those who began their doctoral program in fall 1995, 100% received their degree in 8 years or less. *Degree requirements:* For master's and doctorate, thesis/dissertation. *Entrance requirements:* For master's, GRE General Test, minimum undergraduate GPA of 3.0; for doctorate, GRE General Test, minimum undergraduate GPA of 3.2, 3.4 graduate. Additional exam requirements/recommendations for international students: Required—TOEFL. *Application deadline:* For fall admission, 4/30 for domestic students, 12/1 for international students. Applications are processed on a rolling basis. Application fee: $50. *Expenses:* Tuition, state resident: part-time $196 per unit. Tuition, nonresident: part-time $326 per unit. *Financial support:* In 2003–04, 3 fellowships with partial tuition reimbursements (averaging $15,000 per year), 42 research assistantships with partial tuition reimbursements (averaging $17,074 per year), 5 teaching assistantships with partial tuition reimbursements (averaging $8,537 per year) were awarded. Institutionally sponsored loans, scholarships/grants, health care benefits, and unspecified assistantships also available. Financial award application deadline: 1/31. *Faculty research:* Subsurface and surface hydrology, hydrometeorology/climatology, applied remote sensing, water resource systems, environmental hydrology and water quality. Total annual research expenditures: $7.5 million. *Unit head:* Dr. Victor R. Baker, Head, 520-621-7120, E-mail: baker@hwr.arizona.edu. *Application contact:* Teresa Thompson, Academic Advising Coordinator, 520-621-3131, Fax: 520-621-1422, E-mail: programs@hwr.arizona.edu.

University of California, Davis, Graduate Studies, Graduate Group in Hydrologic Sciences, Davis, CA 95616. Offers MS, PhD. *Faculty:* 48 full-time. *Students:* 32 full-time (12 women); includes 2 minority (both Hispanic Americans), 5 international. Average age 32. 34 applicants, 50% accepted, 10 enrolled. In 2003, 4 degrees awarded. *Degree requirements:* For master's and doctorate, thesis/dissertation. *Entrance requirements:* For master's, GRE General Test, minimum GPA of 3.0; for doctorate, GRE. Additional exam requirements/recommendations for international students: Required—TOEFL (minimum score 550 paper-based; 213 computer-based). *Application deadline:* For fall admission, 4/1 priority date for domestic students, 3/1 priority date for international students. Application fee: $60. Electronic applications accepted. Tuition, nonresident: full-time $12,245. Required fees: $7,062. *Financial support:* In 2003–04, 28 students received support, including 4 fellowships with full and partial tuition reimbursements available (averaging $3,358 per year), 19 research assistantships with full and partial tuition reimbursements available (averaging $11,879 per year), 2 teaching assistantships with partial tuition reimbursements available (averaging $11,773 per year); career-related internships or fieldwork, Federal Work-Study, institutionally sponsored loans, scholarships/grants, and tuition waivers (full and partial) also available. Financial award application deadline: 1/15; financial award applicants required to submit FAFSA. *Faculty research:* Pollutant transport in surface and subsurface waters, subsurface heterogeneity, micrometeorology evaporation, biodegradation. *Unit head:* Dr. Mark Grismer, Chair, 530-752-3243, Fax: 530-752-5262, E-mail: megrismer@ucdavis.edu. *Application contact:* Noeu Leung, Graduate Staff Adviser, 530-752-1669, Fax: 530-752-1552, E-mail: lawradvising@ucdavis.edu.

University of Hawaii at Manoa, Graduate Division, School of Ocean and Earth Science and Technology, Department of Geology and Geophysics, Honolulu, HI 96822. Offers high-pressure geophysics and geochemistry (MS, PhD); hydrogeology and engineering geology (MS, PhD); marine geology and geophysics (MS, PhD); planetary geosciences and remote sensing (MS, PhD); seismology and solid-earth geophysics (MS, PhD); volcanology, petrology, and geochemistry (MS, PhD). *Faculty:* 73 full-time (13 women), 16 part-time/adjunct (1 woman). *Students:* 57 full-time (19 women); includes 3 minority (1 African American, 2 Asian Americans or Pacific Islanders), 17 international. Average age 29. 116 applicants, 15% accepted, 12 enrolled. Terminal master's awarded for partial completion of doctoral program. *Median time to degree:* Master's–3 years full-time; doctorate–3 years full-time. *Degree requirements:* For master's, thesis/dissertation; for doctorate, thesis/dissertation, comprehensive exam. *Entrance requirements:* For master's and doctorate, GRE General Test, minimum GPA of 3.0. Additional exam requirements/recommendations for international students: Required—TOEFL. *Application deadline:* For fall admission, 1/15 for domestic students, 1/1 for international students; for spring admission, 9/1 for domestic students, 8/15 for international students. Application fee: $50. *Expenses:* Tuition, state resident: full-time $4,464; part-time $186 per credit hour. Tuition, nonresident: full-time $10,608; part-time $442 per credit hour. Tuition and fees vary according to program. *Financial support:* In 2003–04, 44 research assistantships (averaging $19,270 per year), 5 teaching assistantships (averaging $18,198 per year) were awarded. *Unit head:* Dr. Paul Wessel, Chair, 808-956-2582, Fax: 808-956-5512.

University of Idaho, College of Graduate Studies, College of Science, Department of Geological Sciences, Program in Hydrology, Moscow, ID 83844-2282. Offers MS. *Entrance requirements:* For master's, minimum GPA of 2.8. *Application deadline:* For fall admission, 8/1 for domestic students; for spring admission, 12/15 for domestic students. Application fee: $55 ($60 for international students). *Expenses:* Tuition, state resident: full-time $3,348. Tuition, nonresident: full-time $10,740. Required fees: $540. *Financial support:* Application deadline: 2/15. *Unit head:* Dr. Dennis Geist, Head, Department of Geological Sciences, 208-885-6192.

University of Illinois at Chicago, Graduate College, College of Liberal Arts and Sciences, Department of Earth and Environmental Sciences, Chicago, IL 60607-7128. Offers crystallography (MS, PhD); environmental geology (MS, PhD); geochemistry (MS, PhD); geology (MS, PhD); geomorphology (MS, PhD); geophysics (MS, PhD); geotechnical engineering and geosciences (PhD); hydrogeology (MS, PhD); low-temperature and organic geochemistry (MS, PhD); mineralogy (MS, PhD); paleoclimatology (MS, PhD); paleontology (MS, PhD); petrology (MS, PhD); quaternary geology (MS, PhD); sedimentology (MS, PhD); water resources (MS, PhD). *Faculty:* 9 full-time (2 women). *Students:* 18 full-time (7 women), 5 part-time (1 woman); includes 3 minority (1 African American, 1 American Indian/Alaska Native, 1 Asian American or Pacific Islander), 11 international. Average age 29. 15 applicants, 27% accepted, 4 enrolled. In 2003, 2 degrees awarded. *Degree requirements:* For master's and doctorate, thesis/dissertation. *Entrance requirements:* For master's and doctorate, GRE General Test, minimum GPA of 3.75 on a 5.0 scale. Additional exam requirements/recommendations for international students: Required—TOEFL. *Application deadline:* For fall admission, 5/15 for domestic students, 2/1 for international students; for spring admission, 11/1 for domestic students, 7/15 for international students. Applications are processed on a rolling basis. Application fee: $40 ($50 for international students). Electronic applications accepted. *Expenses:* Tuition, state resident: part-time $941 per semester. Tuition, nonresident: part-time $2,338 per semester. *Financial support:* In 2003–04, 16 students received support; fellowships with full tuition reimbursements available, research assistantships with full tuition reimbursements available, teaching assistantships with full tuition reimbursements available, Federal Work-Study, scholarships/grants, traineeships, tuition waivers (full), and unspecified assistantships available. Financial award application deadline: 3/1; financial award applicants required to submit FAFSA. *Unit head:* Neil Sturchio, Head, 312-996-3154. *Application contact:* Peter Doran, Director of Graduate Studies, 312-413-7275, E-mail: pdoran@uic.edu.

University of Missouri–Rolla, Graduate School, School of Engineering, Department of Civil, Architectural, and Environmental Engineering, Program in Hydrology and Hydraulic Engineering, Rolla, MO 65409-0910. Offers MS, DE, PhD. *Degree requirements:* For master's, thesis or alternative; for doctorate, thesis/dissertation. *Entrance requirements:* For master's and doctorate, GRE General Test, minimum GPA of 3.0. Additional exam requirements/recommendations for international students: Required—TOEFL. *Application deadline:* For fall admission, 7/1 for domestic students; for spring admission, 12/1 for domestic students. Applications are processed on a rolling basis. Application fee: $50. *Expenses:* Tuition, state resident: full-time $5,871. Tuition, nonresident: full-time $13,114. Required fees: $820. Tuition and fees vary according to course load. *Financial support:* Application deadline: 1/1. *Application contact:* Dr. Rick Stephenson, Graduate Advisor, 573-341-4461, Fax: 573-341-4729, E-mail: stephens@umr.edu.

University of Nevada, Reno, Graduate School, College of Science, Graduate Program in Hydrologic Sciences, Reno, NV 89557. Offers hydrogeology (MS, PhD); hydrology (MS, PhD). Offered through the M. C. Fleischmann College of Agriculture, the College of Engineering, the Mackay School of Mines, and the Desert Research Institute. Part-time programs available. *Faculty:* 37. *Students:* 45 full-time (15 women), 18 part-time (4 women); includes 3 minority (1 African American, 1 American Indian/Alaska Native, 1 Asian American or Pacific Islander), 7 international. Average age 33. In 2003, 17 master's, 1 doctorate awarded. Terminal master's awarded for partial completion of doctoral program. *Degree requirements:* For master's, thesis optional; for doctorate, thesis/dissertation. *Entrance requirements:* For master's and doctorate, GRE General Test, minimum GPA of 3.0. Additional exam requirements/recommendations for international students: Required—TOEFL. *Application deadline:* For fall admission, 1/11 for domestic students; for spring admission, 8/10 for domestic students. Applications are processed on a rolling basis. Application fee: $60 ($95 for international students). *Expenses:* Tuition, state resident: part-time $119 per credit. Tuition, nonresident: part-time $127 per credit. Required fees: $20 per term. Tuition and fees vary according to course load. *Financial support:* In 2003–04, 3 teaching assistantships were awarded; fellowships, research assistantships, career-related internships or fieldwork, institutionally sponsored loans, and tuition waivers (partial) also available. Financial award application deadline: 3/1. *Faculty research:* Groundwater, water resources, surface water, soil science. *Unit head:* Dr. Scott Tyler, Graduate Program Director, 775-784-6250, Fax: 775-784-1983, E-mail: scott@dri.edu.

University of New Brunswick Fredericton, School of Graduate Studies, Faculty of Engineering, Department of Civil Engineering, Fredericton, NB E3B 5A3, Canada. Offers construction engineering and management (M Eng, M Sc E, PhD); environmental engineering (M Eng, M Sc E, PhD); geotechnical engineering (M Eng, M Sc E, PhD); groundwater/hydrology (M Eng, M Sc E, PhD); materials (M Eng, M Sc E, PhD); pavements (M Eng, M Sc E, PhD); structures (M Eng, M Sc E, PhD); transportation (M Eng, M Sc E, PhD). Part-time programs available. *Degree requirements:* For master's, thesis; for doctorate, thesis/dissertation, qualifying exam. *Entrance requirements:* For master's and doctorate, minimum GPA of 3.0. Additional exam requirements/recommendations for international students: Required—TOEFL, TWE. *Faculty research:* Steel and masonry structures, traffic engineering, highway safety, centrifuge modeling, transport and fate of reactive contaminants, durability of marine concrete.

University of New Hampshire, Graduate School, College of Engineering and Physical Sciences, Department of Earth Sciences, Durham, NH 03824. Offers earth sciences (MS), including geochemical, geology, ocean mapping, oceanography; hydrology (MS). *Faculty:* 29 full-time. *Students:* 18 full-time (7 women), 22 part-time (7 women); includes 3 minority (2 African Americans, 1 American Indian/Alaska Native), 2 international. Average age 31. 49 applicants, 78% accepted, 16 enrolled. In 2003, 9 degrees awarded. *Degree requirements:* For master's, thesis, one foreign language. *Entrance requirements:* For master's, GRE General Test. Additional exam requirements/recommendations for international students: Required—TOEFL (minimum score 550 paper-based; 213 computer-based); Recommended—TSE. *Application deadline:* For fall admission, 4/1 for domestic students; for winter admission, 12/1 for domestic students. Applications are processed on a rolling basis. Application fee: $50. Electronic applications accepted. Tuition, area resident: Full-time $7,070. *Expenses:* Tuition, state resident: full-time $10,605. Tuition, nonresident: full-time $17,430. Required fees: $15. *Financial support:* In 2003–04, 1 fellowship, 7 research assistantships, 9 teaching assistantships were awarded. Career-related internships or fieldwork, Federal Work-Study, scholarships/grants, and tuition waivers (full and partial) also available. Support available to part-time students. Financial award application deadline: 2/15. *Unit head:* Dr. Matt Davis, Chairperson, 603-862-4119, E-mail: earth.sciences@unh.edu. *Application contact:* Linda Wrightsman, Administrative Assistant, 603-862-1720, E-mail: earth.sciences@unh.edu.

University of Southern Mississippi, Graduate School, College of Science and Technology, Department of Marine Science, Stennis Space Center, MS 39529. Offers hydrographic science (MS); marine science (MS, PhD). Part-time programs available. *Faculty:* 11 full-time (2 women), 2 part-time/adjunct (0 women). *Students:* 31 full-time (15 women), 14 part-time (2 women), 12 international. Average age 25. 42 applicants, 48% accepted, 18 enrolled. In 2003, 14 master's, 2 doctorates awarded. *Degree requirements:* For master's, thesis, oral qualifying exam (marine science), comprehensive exam; for doctorate, 2 foreign languages, thesis/dissertation, oral qualifying exam, comprehensive exam. *Entrance requirements:* For master's, GRE General Test, minimum GPA of 3.0; for doctorate, GRE General Test, minimum GPA of 3.0 (undergraduate), 3.5 (graduate). Additional exam requirements/recommendations for international students: Required—TOEFL. *Application deadline:* For fall admission, 3/1 for domestic students; for spring admission, 12/13 for domestic students. Applications are processed on a rolling basis. Application fee: $0 ($25 for international students). Electronic applications accepted. *Expenses:* Tuition, state resident: part-time $1,967 per semester. Tuition, nonresident: part-time $4,376 per semester. *Financial support:* In 2003–04, research assistantships with full tuition reimbursements (averaging $16,800 per year), teaching assistantships with full tuition reimbursements (averaging $16,800 per year) were awarded. Federal Work-Study and institutionally sponsored loans also available. Financial award application deadline: 3/15. *Faculty research:* Chemical, biological, physical, and geological marine science; remote sensing; bio-optics; numerical modeling. Total annual research expenditures: $2.6 million. *Unit head:* Dr. Denis A. Wiesenburg, Professor, 228-688-3177, Fax: 228-688-1121. *Application contact:* Dr. Steven E. Lohrenz, Professor, 228-688-1176, Fax: 228-688-1121, E-mail: steven.lohrenz@usm.edu.

University of South Florida, College of Graduate Studies, College of Arts and Sciences, Department of Geology, Tampa, FL 33620-9951. Offers geology (MA, PhD); hydrogeology (MA). Part-time programs available. *Faculty:* 11 full-time (2 women). *Students:* 27 full-time (15 women), 15 part-time (3 women); includes 3 minority (1 African American, 2 Hispanic Americans), 4 international. 32 applicants, 56% accepted, 8 enrolled. *Degree requirements:* For master's, thesis (for some programs); for doctorate, thesis/dissertation. *Entrance requirements:* For master's, GRE General Test, minimum GPA of 3.0 in last 60 hours; for doctorate, GRE General Test. *Application deadline:* For fall admission, 2/15 for domestic students; for spring admission, 10/15 for domestic students. Application fee: $30. Electronic applications accepted. *Financial support:* In 2003–04, 28 students received support, including 3 fellowships with partial tuition reimbursements available (averaging $12,300 per year), 8 research assistantships with partial tuition reimbursements available (averaging $11,034 per year), 17 teaching assistantships with partial tuition reimbursements available (averaging $11,034 per year);

institutionally sponsored loans and scholarships/grants also available. Financial award application deadline: 6/30; financial award applicants required to submit FAFSA. *Faculty research:* Coastal geology, environmental geology and hydrogeology, paleontology and geochemistry. Total annual research expenditures: $1 million. *Unit head:* Chuck Connor, Chairperson, 813-974-0325, Fax: 813-974-2654. *Application contact:* Dr. Peter Harries, Graduate Coordinator, 813-974-4974, Fax: 813-974-2654, E-mail: harries@chuma.cas.usf.edu.

University of Washington, Graduate School, College of Forest Resources, Seattle, WA 98195. Offers forest economics (MS, PhD); forest ecosystem analysis (MS, PhD); forest engineering/forest hydrology (MS, PhD); forest products marketing (MS, PhD); forest soils (MS, PhD); paper science and engineering (MS, PhD); quantitative resource management (MS, PhD); silviculture (MFR); silviculture and forest protection (MS, PhD); social sciences (MS, PhD); urban horticulture (MFR, MS, PhD); wildlife science (MS, PhD). *Degree requirements:* For master's, thesis (for some programs), registration; for doctorate, thesis/dissertation, comprehensive exam (for some programs), registration. *Entrance requirements:* For master's and doctorate, GRE, minimum GPA of 3.0. Additional exam requirements/recommendations for international students: Required—TOEFL. Electronic applications accepted. *Faculty research:* Ecosystem analysis, silviculture and forest protection, paper science and engineering, environmental horticulture and urban forestry, natural resource policy and economics.

West Virginia University, Eberly College of Arts and Sciences, Department of Geology and Geography, Program in Geology, Morgantown, WV 26506. Offers geomorphology (MS, PhD); geophysics (MS, PhD); hydrogeology (MS); hydrology (PhD); paleontology (MS, PhD); petrology (MS, PhD); stratigraphy (MS, PhD); structure (MS, PhD). Part-time programs available. *Students:* 26 full-time (7 women), 17 part-time (7 women); includes 2 minority (1 American Indian/Alaska Native, 1 Asian American or Pacific Islander), 12 international. Average age 30. 34 applicants, 29% accepted. In 2003, 6 master's, 1 doctorate awarded. Terminal master's awarded for partial completion of doctoral program. *Degree requirements:* For master's, thesis/dissertation; for doctorate, thesis/dissertation, comprehensive exam. *Entrance requirements:* For master's, GRE General Test, GRE Subject Test, minimum GPA of 2.5; for doctorate, GRE General Test, GRE Subject Test, minimum GPA of 3.3. Additional exam requirements/recommendations for international students: Required—TOEFL. *Application deadline:* For fall admission, 2/1 for domestic students; for spring admission, 10/1 for domestic students. Applications are processed on a rolling basis. Application fee: $45. *Expenses:* Tuition, state resident: full-time $4,332. Tuition, nonresident: full-time $12,442. *Financial support:* In 2003–04, 5 research assistantships, 18 teaching assistantships were awarded. Career-related internships or fieldwork, Federal Work-Study, institutionally sponsored loans, and tuition waivers (full and partial) also available. Financial award application deadline: 2/1; financial award applicants required to submit FAFSA. *Unit head:* Dr. Thomas H. Wilson, Associate Chair, 304-293-5603 Ext. 4316, Fax: 304-293-6522. *Application contact:* Dr. Joe Donovan, Associate Professor, 304-293-5603 Ext. 4308, Fax: 304-293-6522, E-mail: joe.donovan@mail.wvu.edu.

Wright State University, School of Graduate Studies, College of Science and Mathematics, Department of Geological Sciences, Program in Geological Sciences, Dayton, OH 45435. Offers environmental geochemistry (MS); environmental geology (MS); environmental sciences (MS); geological sciences (MS); geophysics (MS); hydrogeology (MS); petroleum geology (MS). Part-time programs available. *Students:* 22 full-time (4 women), 9 part-time (4 women), 2 international. Average age 26. 21 applicants, 100% accepted. In 2003, 15 degrees awarded. *Degree requirements:* For master's, thesis. *Entrance requirements:* Additional exam requirements/recommendations for international students: Required—TOEFL. Application fee: $25. *Expenses:* Tuition, state resident: full-time $8,112; part-time $255 per quarter hour. Tuition, nonresident: full-time $14,127; part-time $442 per quarter hour. International tuition: $14,283 full-time. Tuition and fees vary according to course load, degree level and program. *Financial support:* Fellowships, research assistantships, teaching assistantships, Federal Work-Study and unspecified assistantships available. Support available to part-time students. Financial award application deadline: 3/1; financial award applicants required to submit FAFSA. *Application contact:* Deborah L. Cowles, Assistant to Chair, 937-775-3455, Fax: 937-775-3462, E-mail: deborah.cowles@wright.edu.

Limnology

Baylor University, Graduate School, College of Arts and Sciences, Department of Biology, Waco, TX 76798. Offers biology (MA, MS, PhD); environmental biology (MS); limnology (MSL). Part-time programs available. *Faculty:* 13 full-time (3 women). *Students:* 18 full-time (10 women), 7 part-time (3 women); includes 1 minority (African American), 2 international. In 2003, 2 degrees awarded. *Degree requirements:* For master's, thesis (for some programs); for doctorate, thesis/dissertation. *Entrance requirements:* For master's and doctorate, GRE General Test. *Application deadline:* For fall admission, 1/31 for domestic students. Applications are processed on a rolling basis. Application fee: $25. *Expenses:* Tuition: Part-time $698 per hour. *Financial support:* Teaching assistantships, career-related internships or fieldwork, Federal Work-Study, institutionally sponsored loans, and tuition waivers (full and partial) available. Support available to part-time students. Financial award application deadline: 2/28. *Faculty research:* Terrestrial ecology, aquatic ecology, genetics. *Unit head:* Dr. Richard E. Duhrkopf, Graduate Program Director, 254-710-2911, Fax: 254-710-2969, E-mail: rick_duhrkopf@baylor.edu. *Application contact:* Sandy Tighe, Administrative Assistant, 254-710-2911, Fax: 254-710-2969, E-mail: sandy_tighe@baylor.edu.

Cornell University, Graduate School, Graduate Fields of Agriculture and Life Sciences, Field of Ecology and Evolutionary Biology, Ithaca, NY 14853-0001. Offers ecology (PhD), including animal ecology, applied ecology, biogeochemistry, community and ecosystem ecology, limnology, oceanography, physiological ecology, plant ecology, population ecology, theoretical ecology, vertebrate zoology; evolutionary biology (PhD), including ecological genetics, paleobiology, population biology, systematics. *Faculty:* 51 full-time. *Students:* 57 full-time (30 women); includes 5 minority (1 African American, 3 Asian Americans or Pacific Islanders, 1 Hispanic American), 9 international. 98 applicants, 8% accepted, 5 enrolled. In 2003, 2 doctorates awarded. *Degree requirements:* For doctorate, thesis/dissertation, 2 semesters of teaching experience, comprehensive exam. *Entrance requirements:* For doctorate, GRE General Test, GRE Subject Test (biology), 2 letters of recommendation. Additional exam requirements/recommendations for international students: Required—TOEFL (minimum score 550 paper-based; 213 computer-based). *Application deadline:* For fall admission, 12/15 for domestic students. Application fee: $60. Electronic applications accepted. *Expenses:* Tuition: Full-time $28,630. One-time fee: $50 full-time. *Financial support:* In 2003–04, 52 students received support, including 17 fellowships with full tuition reimbursements available, 9 research assistantships with full tuition reimbursements available, 26 teaching assistantships with full tuition reimbursements available; institutionally sponsored loans, scholarships/grants, health care benefits, tuition waivers (full and partial), and unspecified assistantships also available. Financial award applicants required to submit FAFSA. *Faculty research:* Population and organismal biology, population and evolutionary genetics, systematics and macroevolution, biochemistry, conservation biology. *Unit head:* Director of Graduate Studies, 607-254-4230. *Application contact:* Graduate Field Assistant, 607-254-4230, E-mail: eeb_grad_req@cornell.edu.

University of Alaska Fairbanks, School of Fisheries and Ocean Sciences, Department of Marine Sciences and Limnology, Fairbanks, AK 99775-7520. Offers marine biology (MS); oceanography (MS, PhD), including biological oceanography (PhD), chemical oceanography (PhD), fisheries (PhD), geological oceanography (PhD), physical oceanography (PhD). Part-time programs available. Terminal master's awarded for partial completion of doctoral program. *Degree requirements:* For master's and doctorate, thesis/dissertation, comprehensive exam, registration. *Entrance requirements:* For master's and doctorate, GRE General Test. Additional exam requirements/recommendations for international students: Required—TOEFL. Electronic applications accepted. *Faculty research:* Seafood science and nutrition, sustainable harvesting, chemical oceanography, marine biology, physical oceanography.

See in-depth description on page 289.

University of Florida, Graduate School, College of Agricultural and Life Sciences, Department of Fisheries and Aquatic Science, Gainesville, FL 32611. Offers MFAS, MS, PhD. *Faculty:* 30. *Students:* 33 full-time (12 women), 21 part-time (9 women); includes 6 minority (3 African Americans, 1 American Indian/Alaska Native, 2 Asian Americans or Pacific Islanders), 2 international. 29 applicants, 31% accepted. In 2003, 8 master's, 1 doctorate awarded. *Degree requirements:* For master's, thesis optional; for doctorate, thesis/dissertation. *Entrance requirements:* For master's and doctorate, GRE General Test, minimum GPA of 3.0. Additional exam requirements/recommendations for international students: Required—TOEFL. *Application deadline:* For fall admission, 6/1 for domestic students. Applications are processed on a rolling basis. Application fee: $20. Electronic applications accepted. *Expenses:* Tuition, state resident: part-time $205 per credit hour. Tuition, nonresident: part-time $775 per credit hour. *Financial support:* In 2003–04, 1 fellowship, 18 research assistantships were awarded. Unspecified assistantships also available. *Unit head:* Dr. Randall Stocker, Interim Chair, 352-392-9613, Fax: 352-392-3672, E-mail: aqplants@ifas.ufl.edu. *Application contact:* Dr. Ed Phlips, Graduate Coordinator, 352-392-9617 Ext. 248, Fax: 352-392-3672, E-mail: phlips@ufl.edu.

University of Wisconsin–Madison, Graduate School, College of Engineering, Program in Limnology and Marine Science, Madison, WI 53706-1380. Offers MS, PhD. *Faculty:* 22 full-time (6 women). *Students:* 14 full-time (5 women); includes 2 minority (both African Americans) 26 applicants, 12% accepted, 3 enrolled. In 2003, 2 degrees awarded, leading to university research/teaching 100%. Terminal master's awarded for partial completion of doctoral program. *Median time to degree:* Doctorate–5.5 years full-time. *Degree requirements:* For master's and doctorate, thesis/dissertation. *Entrance requirements:* For master's and doctorate, GRE General Test. Additional exam requirements/recommendations for international students: Required—TOEFL. *Application deadline:* For fall admission, 1/15 priority date for domestic students, 1/15 priority date for international students. Application fee: $45. Electronic applications accepted. Tuition, area resident: Full-time $7,593; part-time $476 per credit. Tuition, nonresident: full-time $22,824; part-time $1,430 per credit. Required fees: $292; $38 per credit. Part-time tuition and fees vary according to course load and reciprocity agreements. *Financial support:* Fellowships with tuition reimbursements, research assistantships with tuition reimbursements, teaching assistantships with tuition reimbursements, Federal Work-Study and institutionally sponsored loans available. Financial award application deadline: 1/15. *Faculty research:* Lake ecosystems, ecosystem modeling, geochemistry, physiological ecology, chemical limnology. *Unit head:* Dr. Kenneth W. Potter, Chair, 608-262-0400, Fax: 608-265-2340, E-mail: kwpotter@facstaff.wisc.edu. *Application contact:* Georgia Wagner, Student Services Coordinator, 608-263-3264, Fax: 608-265-2340, E-mail: gwagner@facstaff.wisc.edu.

William Paterson University of New Jersey, College of Science and Health, Department of Biology, General Biology Program, Wayne, NJ 07470-8420. Offers general biology (MA); limnology and terrestrial ecology (MA); molecular biology (MA); physiology (MA). Part-time and evening/weekend programs available. *Degree requirements:* For master's, independent study or thesis. *Entrance requirements:* For master's, GRE General Test, minimum GPA of 2.75. Electronic applications accepted.

Mineralogy

Cornell University, Graduate School, Graduate Fields of Engineering, Field of Geological Sciences, Ithaca, NY 14853-0001. Offers economic geology (M Eng, MS, PhD); engineering geology (M Eng, MS, PhD); environmental geophysics (M Eng, MS, PhD); general geology (M Eng, MS, PhD); geobiology (M Eng, MS, PhD); geochemistry and isotope geology (M Eng, MS, PhD); geohydrology (M Eng, MS, PhD); geomorphology (M Eng, MS, PhD); geophysics (M Eng, MS, PhD); geotectonics (M Eng, MS, PhD); marine geology (MS, PhD); mineralogy (M Eng, MS, PhD); paleontology (M Eng, MS, PhD); petroleum geology (M Eng, MS, PhD); petrology (M Eng, MS, PhD); planetary geology (M Eng, MS, PhD); Precambrian geology (M Eng, MS, PhD); Quaternary geology (M Eng, MS, PhD); rock mechanics (M Eng, MS, PhD); sedimentology (M Eng, MS, PhD); seismology (M Eng, MS, PhD); stratigraphy (M Eng, MS, PhD); structural geology (M Eng, MS, PhD). *Faculty:* 31 full-time. *Students:* 27 full-time (12 women); includes 1 minority (Asian American or Pacific Islander), 9 international. 74 applicants, 15% accepted, 7 enrolled. In 2003, 3 master's, 5 doctorates awarded. *Degree requirements:* For master's, thesis (MS); for doctorate, thesis/dissertation, comprehensive exam. *Entrance requirements:* For master's and doctorate, GRE General Test, 3 letters of recommendation. Additional exam requirements/recommendations for international students: Required—TOEFL (minimum score 550 paper-based; 213 computer-based). *Application deadline:* For fall admission, 1/15 for domestic students. Applications are processed on a rolling basis. Application fee: $60. Electronic applications accepted. *Expenses:* Tuition: Full-time $28,630. One-time fee: $50 full-time. *Financial support:* In 2003–04, 21 students received support, including 6 fellowships with full tuition reimbursements available, 8 research assistantships with full tuition reimbursements available, 7 teaching assistantships with full tuition reimbursements available; institutionally sponsored loans, scholarships/grants, health care benefits, tuition waivers (full and partial), and unspecified assistantships also available. Financial award applicants required to submit FAFSA. *Faculty research:* Geophysics, structural geology, petrology, geochemistry, geodynamics. *Unit head:* Director of Graduate Studies, 607-255-

Mineralogy

Cornell University (continued)

3474, Fax: 607-254-4780. *Application contact:* Graduate Field Assistant, 607-255-3474, Fax: 607-254-4780, E-mail: gradprog@geology.cornell.edu.

See in-depth description on page 233.

Indiana University Bloomington, Graduate School, College of Arts and Sciences, Department of Geological Sciences, Bloomington, IN 47405. Offers biogeochemistry (MS, PhD); environmental geosciences (MS, PhD); geobiology, stratigraphy, and sedimentology (MS, PhD); geochemistry (MS, PhD); geochemistry, mineralogy, and petrology (MS, PhD); geophysics (MS, PhD); geophysics, tectonics, and structural geology (MS, PhD). PhD offered through the University Graduate School. Part-time programs available. *Faculty:* 14 full-time (1 woman). *Students:* 32 full-time (16 women), 18 part-time (8 women); includes 4 minority (2 African Americans, 2 Asian Americans or Pacific Islanders), 23 international. Average age 29. In 2003, 10 master's, 2 doctorates awarded. Terminal master's awarded for partial completion of doctoral program. *Degree requirements:* For master's, one foreign language, thesis or alternative; for doctorate, thesis/dissertation. *Entrance requirements:* For master's and doctorate, GRE General Test. Additional exam requirements/recommendations for international students: Required—TOEFL. *Application deadline:* For fall admission, 1/15 priority date for domestic students, 12/15 priority date for international students; for spring admission, 9/1 priority date for domestic students, 9/1 priority date for international students. Applications are processed on a rolling basis. Application fee: $45 ($55 for international students). *Expenses:* Tuition, state resident: full-time $4,908; part-time $205 per credit. Tuition, nonresident: full-time $14,298; part-time $596 per credit. Required fees: $661. Tuition and fees vary according to campus/location and program. *Financial support:* In 2003–04, research assistantships with full and partial tuition reimbursements (averaging $11,000 per year); fellowships with tuition reimbursements, teaching assistantships with tuition reimbursements, career-related internships or fieldwork, Federal Work-Study, and institutionally sponsored loans also available. Financial award application deadline: 2/15. *Faculty research:* Geophysics, geochemistry, hydrogeology, igneous and metamorphic petrology and clay mineralogy. Total annual research expenditures: $289,139. *Unit head:* Dr. Christopher G. Maples, Chairman, 812-855-5582, Fax: 812-855-7899, E-mail: cmaples@indiana.edu. *Application contact:* Mary Iverson, Secretary, Committee for Graduate Studies, 812-855-7214, Fax: 812-855-7899, E-mail: geograd@indiana.edu.

Université du Québec à Chicoutimi, Graduate Programs, Program in Mineral Resources, Chicoutimi, QC G7H 2B1, Canada. Offers PhD. Part-time programs available. *Degree requirements:* For doctorate, thesis/dissertation. *Entrance requirements:* For doctorate, appropriate master's degree, proficiency in French.

Université du Québec à Montréal, Graduate Programs, Program in Earth Sciences, Montreal, QC H3C 3P8, Canada. Offers geology-research (M Sc); mineral resources (PhD); non-renewable resources (DESS). Part-time programs available. *Faculty:* 16 full-time (2 women), 16 part-time/adjunct (1 woman). *Students:* 51 full-time (9 women), 15 international. 18 applicants, 56% accepted. In 2003, 7 master's, 4 doctorates awarded. Terminal master's awarded for partial completion of doctoral program. *Median time to degree:* Of those who began their doctoral program in fall 1995, 90% received their degree in 8 years or less. *Degree requirements:* For master's, thesis (for some programs); for doctorate, thesis/dissertation. *Entrance requirements:* For master's, appropriate bachelor's degree or equivalent, proficiency in French. *Application deadline:* Applications are processed on a rolling basis. Application fee: $50. *Financial support:* In 2003–04, fellowships (averaging $5,000 per year), research assistantships (averaging $4,000 per year), teaching assistantships (averaging $1,000 per year) were awarded. Scholarships/grants also available. *Faculty research:* Economic geology, structural geology, geochemistry, Quaternary geology, isotopic geochemistry. *Unit head:* Alfred Jaouich, Director, 514-987-3000 Ext. 3378, Fax: 514-987-7749, E-mail: jaouich.alfred@uqam.ca. *Application contact:* Micheline Lacroix, Admissions Officer, 514-987-3000 Ext. 3370, Fax: 514-987-7749, E-mail: lacroix.micheline@uqam.ca.

Université du Québec à Montréal, Graduate Programs, Program in Mineral Resources, Montréal, QC H3C 3P8, Canada. Offers PhD. Part-time programs available. *Degree requirements:* For doctorate, thesis/dissertation. *Entrance requirements:* For doctorate, appropriate master's degree or equivalent and proficiency in French.

University of Illinois at Chicago, Graduate College, College of Liberal Arts and Sciences, Department of Earth and Environmental Sciences, Chicago, IL 60607-7128. Offers crystallography (MS, PhD); environmental geology (MS, PhD); geochemistry (MS, PhD); geology (MS, PhD); geomorphology (MS, PhD); geophysics (MS, PhD); geotechnical engineering and geosciences (PhD); hydrogeology (MS, PhD); low-temperature and organic geochemistry (MS, PhD); mineralogy (MS, PhD); paleoclimatology (MS, PhD); paleontology (MS, PhD); petrology (MS, PhD); quaternary geology (MS, PhD); sedimentology (MS, PhD); water resources (MS, PhD). *Faculty:* 9 full-time (2 women). *Students:* 18 full-time (7 women), 5 part-time (1 woman); includes 3 minority (1 African American, 1 American Indian/Alaska Native, 1 Asian American or Pacific Islander), 11 international. Average age 29. 15 applicants, 27% accepted, 4 enrolled. In 2003, 2 degrees awarded. *Degree requirements:* For master's and doctorate, thesis/dissertation. *Entrance requirements:* For master's and doctorate, GRE General Test, minimum GPA of 3.75 on a 5.0 scale. Additional exam requirements/recommendations for international students: Required—TOEFL. *Application deadline:* For fall admission, 5/15 for domestic students, 2/1 for international students; for spring admission, 11/1 for domestic students, 7/15 for international students. Applications are processed on a rolling basis. Application fee: $40 ($50 for international students). Electronic applications accepted. *Expenses:* Tuition, state resident: part-time $941 per semester. Tuition, nonresident: part-time $2,338 per semester. *Financial support:* In 2003–04, 16 students received support; fellowships with full tuition reimbursements available, research assistantships with full tuition reimbursements available, teaching assistantships with full tuition reimbursements available, Federal Work-Study, scholarships/grants, traineeships, tuition waivers (full), and unspecified assistantships available. Financial award application deadline: 3/1; financial award applicants required to submit FAFSA. *Unit head:* Neil Sturchio, Head, 312-996-3154. *Application contact:* Peter Doran, Director of Graduate Studies, 312-413-7275, E-mail: pdoran@uic.edu.

University of Michigan, Horace H. Rackham School of Graduate Studies, College of Literature, Science, and the Arts, Department of Geological Sciences, Ann Arbor, MI 48109. Offers geology (MS, PhD); mineralogy (MS, PhD); oceanography: marine geology and geochemistry (MS, PhD). *Faculty:* 27 full-time (5 women), 6 part-time/adjunct (2 women). *Students:* 60 full-time (21 women); includes 3 minority (1 Asian American or Pacific Islander, 2 Hispanic Americans), 20 international. Average age 28. 81 applicants, 30% accepted, 11 enrolled. In 2003, 10 master's, 12 doctorates awarded. Terminal master's awarded for partial completion of doctoral program. *Median time to degree:* Master's–2.2 years full-time; doctorate–5.2 years full-time. *Degree requirements:* For master's, thesis; for doctorate, thesis/dissertation, oral defense of dissertation, preliminary exam. *Entrance requirements:* For master's and doctorate, GRE General Test. *Application deadline:* For fall admission, 1/15 for domestic students. Applications are processed on a rolling basis. Application fee: $60 ($75 for international students). Electronic applications accepted. *Expenses:* Tuition, state resident: full-time $7,463. Tuition, nonresident: full-time $13,913. Full-time tuition and fees vary according to course load, degree level and program. *Financial support:* In 2003–04, 18 fellowships with full tuition reimbursements (averaging $12,853 per year), 23 research assistantships with full tuition reimbursements (averaging $12,853 per year), 17 teaching assistantships with full tuition reimbursements (averaging $12,853 per year) were awarded. Career-related internships or fieldwork, Federal Work-Study, and health care benefits also available. Financial award application deadline: 1/15; financial award applicants required to submit FAFSA. *Faculty research:* Isotope geochemistry, paleoclimatology, mineral physics, tectonics, paleontology. Total annual research expenditures: $2.8 million. *Unit head:* Dr. Joel D. Blum, Chair, 734-764-1435, Fax: 734-763-4690. *Application contact:* Anne Hudon, Student Services Assistant, 734-615-3034, Fax: 734-763-4690, E-mail: ahudon@umich.edu.

Yale University, Graduate School of Arts and Sciences, Department of Geology and Geophysics, New Haven, CT 06520. Offers geochemistry (PhD); geophysics (PhD); meteorology (PhD); mineralogy and crystallography (PhD); oceanography (PhD); paleoecology (PhD); paleontology and stratigraphy (PhD); petrology (PhD); structural geology (PhD). *Degree requirements:* For doctorate, thesis/dissertation. *Entrance requirements:* For doctorate, GRE General Test. Additional exam requirements/recommendations for international students: Required—TOEFL. *Expenses:* Tuition: Full-time $25,600; part-time $6,400 per term.

See in-depth description on page 261.

Planetary and Space Sciences

Air Force Institute of Technology, Graduate School of Engineering and Management, Department of Operational Sciences, Dayton, OH 45433-7765. Offers logistics management (MS); operations research (MS, PhD); space operations (MS). Part-time programs available. *Degree requirements:* For master's and doctorate, thesis/dissertation. *Entrance requirements:* For doctorate, GRE General Test, minimum GPA of 3.0, must be U.S. citizen. *Faculty research:* Optimization, simulation, combat modeling and analysis, reliability and maintainability, resource scheduling.

California Institute of Technology, Division of Geological and Planetary Sciences, Pasadena, CA 91125-0001. Offers cosmochemistry (PhD); geobiology (PhD); geochemistry (MS, PhD); geology (MS, PhD); geophysics (MS, PhD); planetary science (MS, PhD). Part-time programs available. *Faculty:* 37 full-time (3 women). *Students:* 61 full-time (29 women); includes 28 minority (1 African American, 26 Asian Americans or Pacific Islanders, 1 Hispanic American). Average age 27. 127 applicants, 20% accepted, 15 enrolled. In 2003, 5 master's, 13 doctorates awarded. *Degree requirements:* For doctorate, thesis/dissertation. *Entrance requirements:* For doctorate, GRE General Test. Additional exam requirements/recommendations for international students: Required—TOEFL. *Application deadline:* For fall admission, 1/15 for domestic students, 1/15 for international students. Application fee: $50. Electronic applications accepted. *Financial support:* In 2003–04, 21 fellowships with full tuition reimbursements (averaging $20,496 per year), 49 research assistantships with full tuition reimbursements (averaging $20,496 per year) were awarded. Teaching assistantships with full tuition reimbursements, institutionally sponsored loans, scholarships/grants, health care benefits, and unspecified assistantships also available. Financial award applicants required to submit FAFSA. *Faculty research:* Astronomy, evolution of anaerobic respiratory processes, structural geology and tectonics, theoretical and numerical seismology, global biogeochemical cycles. Total annual research expenditures: $18.6 million. *Unit head:* Dr. Edward M. Stolper, Chairman, 626-395-6108, Fax: 626-795-6028, E-mail: divgps@gps.caltech.edu. *Application contact:* Dr. George R. Rossman, Academic Officer, 626-395-6125, Fax: 626-568-0935, E-mail: divgps@gps.caltech.edu.

Columbia University, Graduate School of Arts and Sciences, Division of Natural Sciences, Program in Atmospheric and Planetary Science, New York, NY 10027. Offers M Phil, PhD. Offered jointly through the Departments of Geological Sciences, Astronomy, and Physics and in cooperation with NASA Goddard Space Flight Center's Institute for Space Studies. *Degree requirements:* For doctorate, variable foreign language requirement, thesis/dissertation. *Entrance requirements:* For doctorate, GRE General Test, GRE Subject Test, previous course work in mathematics and physics. Additional exam requirements/recommendations for international students: Required—TOEFL. Application fee: $75. *Expenses:* Tuition: Full-time $14,820. *Financial support:* Available to part-time students. Application deadline: 1/5; *Faculty research:* Climate, weather prediction.

See in-depth description on page 311.

Cornell University, Graduate School, Graduate Fields of Arts and Sciences, Field of Astronomy and Space Sciences, Ithaca, NY 14853-0001. Offers astronomy (PhD); astrophysics (PhD); general space sciences (PhD); infrared astronomy (PhD); planetary studies (PhD); radio astronomy (PhD); radiophysics (PhD); theoretical astrophysics (PhD). *Faculty:* 28 full-time. *Students:* 31 full-time (11 women), 16 international. 103 applicants, 21% accepted, 6 enrolled. In 2003, 2 doctorates awarded. *Degree requirements:* For doctorate, thesis/dissertation, comprehensive exam. *Entrance requirements:* For doctorate, GRE General Test, GRE Subject Test (physics), 3 letters of recommendation. Additional exam requirements/recommendations for international students: Required—TOEFL (minimum score 600 paper-based; 250 computer-based). *Application deadline:* For fall admission, 1/15 for domestic students. Application fee: $60. Electronic applications accepted. *Expenses:* Tuition: Full-time $28,630. One-time fee: $50 full-time. *Financial support:* In 2003–04, 30 students received support, including 8 fellowships with full tuition reimbursements available, 14 research assistantships with full tuition reimbursements available, 8 teaching assistantships with full tuition reimbursements available; institutionally sponsored loans, scholarships/grants, health care benefits, tuition waivers (full and partial), and unspecified assistantships also available. Financial award applicants required to submit FAFSA. *Faculty research:* Observational astrophysics, planetary sciences, cosmology, instrumentation, gravitational astrophysics. *Unit head:* Director of Graduate Studies, 607-255-4341. *Application contact:* Graduate Field Assistant, 607-255-4341, E-mail: oconnor@astro.cornell.edu.

Florida Institute of Technology, Graduate Programs, College of Science and Liberal Arts, Department of Physics and Space Sciences, Melbourne, FL 32901-6975. Offers physics (MS, PhD); space science (MS, PhD). Part-time programs available. *Faculty:* 12 full-time (0 women). *Students:* 17 full-time (5 women), 7 part-time (3 women), 8 international. Average age 29. 43 applicants, 40% accepted, 11 enrolled. In 2003, 6 master's, 2 doctorates awarded. Terminal master's awarded for partial completion of doctoral program. *Degree requirements:* For master's, thesis optional; for doctorate, thesis/dissertation, publication in referred journal, comprehensive exam, registration. *Entrance requirements:* For master's, GRE General Test, GRE Subject Test, minimum GPA of 3.0, proficiency in a computer language, resumé, letters of recommendation (3), statement of objectives; for doctorate, GRE General Test, GRE Subject Test, minimum GPA of 3.2, resumé, letters of recommendation (3), statement of objectives. Additional exam requirements/recommendations for international students: Required—TOEFL (minimum score 550 paper-based; 213 computer-based). *Application deadline:* Applications are processed on a rolling basis. Application fee: $50. Electronic applications accepted. *Expenses:* Tuition: Part-time $745 per credit. *Financial support:* In 2003–04, 4 research assistantships with full and partial tuition reimbursements (averaging $19,385 per year), 21 teaching assistantships with full and partial tuition reimbursements (averaging $23,401 per year) were awarded. Career-related internships or fieldwork and tuition remissions also available. Financial award application deadline: 3/1; financial award applicants required to submit FAFSA. *Faculty research:* Lasers, semiconductors, magnetism, quantum devices, high energy physics. Total annual research expenditures: $621,446. *Unit head:* Dr. Lazlo A. Baksay, Department Head, 321-674-7367, Fax: 321-674-7482, E-mail: baksay@fit.edu. *Application contact:* Carolyn P. Farrior, Director of Graduate Admissions, 321-674-7118, Fax: 321-723-9468, E-mail: cfarrior@fit.edu.

Harvard University, Graduate School of Arts and Sciences, Department of Earth and Planetary Sciences, Cambridge, MA 02138. Offers AM, PhD. *Faculty:* 25 full-time (2 women). *Students:* 50 full-time (25 women); includes 11 minority (8 Asian Americans or Pacific Islanders, 3 Hispanic Americans). 103 applicants, 18% accepted, 11 enrolled. In 2003, 12 master's, 8 doctorates awarded. Terminal master's awarded for partial completion of doctoral program. *Degree requirements:* For master's, registration; for doctorate, thesis/dissertation, comprehensive exam, registration. *Entrance requirements:* For doctorate, GRE General Test. Additional exam requirements/recommendations for international students: Required—TOEFL. *Application deadline:* For fall admission, 1/2 for domestic students. Application fee: $85. Electronic applications accepted. *Expenses:* Tuition: Full-time $26,066. Full-time tuition and fees vary according to program and student level. *Financial support:* In 2003–04, 50 students received support; fellowships with full tuition reimbursements available, research assistantships, teaching assistantships, scholarships/grants and health care benefits available. *Faculty research:* Economic geography, geochemistry, geophysics, mineralogy, crystallography. *Unit head:* Ventatesh Narayanamurti, Dean, 617-495-5829, Fax: 617-495-5264, E-mail: venky@deas.harvard.edu. *Application contact:* Office of Admissions and Financial Aid, 617-495-5315.

See in-depth description on page 239.

The Johns Hopkins University, Zanvyl Krieger School of Arts and Sciences, The Morton K. Blaustein Department of Earth and Planetary Sciences, Baltimore, MD 21218-2699. Offers geochemistry (MA, PhD); geology (MA, PhD); geophysics (MA, PhD); groundwater (MA, PhD); oceanography (MA, PhD); planetary atmosphere (MA, PhD). *Faculty:* 14 full-time (1 woman), 1 (woman) part-time/adjunct. *Students:* 23 full-time (10 women); includes 2 minority (both Hispanic Americans), 10 international. Average age 25. 48 applicants, 21% accepted, 5 enrolled. In 2003, 5 master's, 3 doctorates awarded. *Median time to degree:* Of those who began their doctoral program in fall 1995, 99% received their degree in 8 years or less. *Degree requirements:* For doctorate, thesis/dissertation, registration. *Entrance requirements:* For master's and doctorate, GRE General Test. Additional exam requirements/recommendations for international students: Required—TOEFL (minimum score 600 paper-based; 250 computer-based). *Application deadline:* For fall admission, 1/15 priority date for domestic students, 1/15 priority date for international students. Application fee: $55. Electronic applications accepted. *Expenses:* Tuition: Full-time $28,730; part-time $1,490 per course. Part-time tuition and fees vary according to course load, campus/location and program. *Financial support:* In 2003–04, 4 fellowships, 13 research assistantships, 7 teaching assistantships were awarded. Federal Work-Study and institutionally sponsored loans also available. Financial award application deadline: 4/15; financial award applicants required to submit FAFSA. Total annual research expenditures: $2.3 million. *Unit head:* Dr. Peter Olson, Chair, 410-516-4659, Fax: 410-516-7933, E-mail: epschair@jhunix.hcf.jhu.edu. *Application contact:* Carol Spangler, Academic Program Assistant, 410-516-7034, Fax: 410-516-7933, E-mail: cspangler@jhu.edu.

Massachusetts Institute of Technology, School of Science, Department of Earth, Atmospheric, and Planetary Sciences, Cambridge, MA 02139-4307. Offers atmospheric chemistry (PhD, Sc D); atmospheric science (SM, PhD, Sc D); climate physics and chemistry (PhD, Sc D); earth and planetary sciences (SM); geochemistry (PhD, Sc D); geology (PhD, Sc D); geophysics (PhD, Sc D); geosystems (SM); oceanography (SM, PhD, Sc D); planetary sciences (PhD, Sc D). *Faculty:* 37 full-time (3 women). *Students:* 147 full-time (61 women); includes 9 minority (4 Asian Americans or Pacific Islanders, 5 Hispanic Americans), 48 international. Average age 27. 176 applicants, 49% accepted, 31 enrolled. In 2003, 8 master's, 19 doctorates awarded. Terminal master's awarded for partial completion of doctoral program. *Degree requirements:* For master's, thesis/dissertation; for doctorate, thesis/dissertation, comprehensive exam. *Entrance requirements:* For master's, GRE General Test, GRE Subject Test (joint MIT/WHOI program); for doctorate, GRE General Test, GRE Subject Test (chemistry or physics for planetary science program). Additional exam requirements/recommendations for international students: Required—TOEFL (minimum score 577 paper-based; 233 computer-based). *Application deadline:* For fall admission, 1/5 for domestic students, 1/5 for international students; for spring admission, 11/1 for domestic students, 11/1 for international students. Application fee: $70. Electronic applications accepted. *Expenses:* Tuition: Full-time $29,400. Required fees: $200. *Financial support:* In 2003–04, 113 students received support, including 25 fellowships with tuition reimbursements available, 70 research assistantships with tuition reimbursements available (averaging $23,760 per year), 21 teaching assistantships with tuition reimbursements available (averaging $18,270 per year); Federal Work-Study, institutionally sponsored loans, scholarships/grants, health care benefits, and unspecified assistantships also available. *Faculty research:* Evolution of main features of the planetary system; origin, composition, structure, and state of the atmospheres, oceans, surfaces, and interiors of planets; dynamics of planets and satellite motions. Total annual research expenditures: $19.1 million. *Unit head:* Prof. Maria Zuber, 617-253-0149, Fax: 617-253-8298, E-mail: mtz@mit.edu. *Application contact:* Carol Sprague, Administrative Assistant, 617-253-3381, Fax: 617-253-8298, E-mail: eapsinfo@mit.edu.

McGill University, Faculty of Graduate and Postdoctoral Studies, Faculty of Science, Department of Earth and Planetary Sciences, Montréal, QC H3A 2T5, Canada. Offers M Sc, PhD, Diploma. *Faculty:* 12 full-time (3 women). *Students:* 31 full-time. Average age 25. 29 applicants, 45% accepted, 5 enrolled. In 2003, 8 master's, 3 doctorates awarded. *Degree requirements:* For master's and doctorate, thesis/dissertation. *Entrance requirements:* For master's, minimum GPA of 3.0. Additional exam requirements/recommendations for international students: Required—TOEFL. *Application deadline:* For fall admission, 3/1 for domestic students. Applications are processed on a rolling basis. Application fee: $60 Canadian dollars. Tuition, area resident: Full-time $1,668. *Expenses:* Tuition, state resident: full-time $4,173. Tuition, nonresident: full-time $9,468. Required fees: $1,081. *Financial support:* Fellowships, research assistantships, teaching assistantships, institutionally sponsored loans and tuition waivers (partial) available. *Faculty research:* Geochemistry, sedimentary petrology, igneous petrology, theoretical geophysics, economic geology, planetary sciences. *Unit head:* Dr. Alfonso Mucci, Chair, 514-398-4892, Fax: 514-398-4680, E-mail: alm@eps.mcgill.ca. *Application contact:* Dr. Carol Matthews, Graduate Program Coordinator, 514-398-6767, Fax: 514-398-4680, E-mail: carol@eps.mcgill.ca.

Stony Brook University, State University of New York, Graduate School, College of Arts and Sciences, Department of Physics and Astronomy, Program in Astronomy, Stony Brook, NY 11794. Offers earth and space sciences (MS, PhD). *Students:* 1 full-time (0 women), 1 international. *Degree requirements:* For master's, thesis or alternative; for doctorate, thesis/dissertation. *Entrance requirements:* For master's and doctorate, GRE General Test, minimum GPA of 3.0. Additional exam requirements/recommendations for international students: Required—TOEFL. *Application deadline:* For fall admission, 1/15 for domestic students. Application fee: $50. *Expenses:* Tuition, state resident: full-time $6,900; part-time $288 per credit hour. Tuition, nonresident: full-time $10,500; part-time $438 per credit hour. Required fees: $22. *Financial support:* Fellowships, research assistantships, teaching assistantships available. Financial award application deadline: 2/1. *Application contact:* Dr. Peter Stephens, Director, 631-632-8279, Fax: 631-632-8176, E-mail: pstephens@ccmail.sunysb.edu.

The University of Arizona, Graduate College, College of Science, Department of Planetary Sciences/Lunar and Planetary Laboratory, Tucson, AZ 85721. Offers MS, PhD. *Faculty:* 34 full-time (11 women). *Students:* 34 full-time (11 women); includes 2 minority (1 Asian American or Pacific Islander, 1 Hispanic American), 5 international. Average age 28. 43 applicants, 35% accepted, 6 enrolled. In 2003, 2 degrees awarded. *Degree requirements:* For master's, thesis (for some programs); for doctorate, one foreign language, thesis/dissertation. *Entrance requirements:* For master's and doctorate, GRE General Test, GRE Subject Test. Additional exam requirements/recommendations for international students: Required—TOEFL. *Application deadline:* For fall admission, 1/15 for domestic students; for spring admission, 8/15 for domestic students. Applications are processed on a rolling basis. Application fee: $50. *Expenses:* Tuition, state resident: part-time $196 per unit. Tuition, nonresident: part-time $326 per unit. *Financial support:* In 2003–04, 6 fellowships (averaging $18,000 per year), 15 research assistantships with full tuition reimbursements (averaging $22,677 per year), 4 teaching assistantships with full tuition reimbursements (averaging $22,677 per year) were awarded. Scholarships/grants and tuition waivers (partial) also available. Financial award application deadline: 2/15. *Faculty research:* Cosmochemistry, planetary geology, astronomy, space physics, planetary physics. *Unit head:* Dr. Michael Drake, Head, 520-621-6962, Fax: 520-621-4933. *Application contact:* Joan Weinberg, Assistant to the Director, 520-621-4128, Fax: 520-621-4933, E-mail: jweinber@w.arizona.edu.

See in-depth description on page 257.

University of California, Los Angeles, Graduate Division, College of Letters and Science, Department of Earth and Space Sciences, Los Angeles, CA 90095. Offers geochemistry (MS, PhD); geology (MS, PhD); geophysics and space physics (MS, PhD). *Degree requirements:* For master's, comprehensive exams or thesis; for doctorate, thesis/dissertation, oral and written qualifying exams. *Entrance requirements:* For master's, GRE General Test, minimum GPA of 3.0; for doctorate, GRE General Test, minimum undergraduate GPA of 3.0. Electronic applications accepted. Tuition, nonresident: full-time $12,245. Required fees: $6,318.

University of Chicago, Division of the Physical Sciences, Department of the Geophysical Sciences, Chicago, IL 60637-1513. Offers atmospheric sciences (SM, PhD); earth sciences (SM, PhD); paleobiology (PhD); planetary and space sciences (SM, PhD). *Faculty:* 24 full-time (3 women). *Students:* 29 full-time (13 women); includes 1 minority (Hispanic American), 12 international. Average age 30. 74 applicants, 22% accepted. In 2003, 2 master's, 5 doctorates awarded. Terminal master's awarded for partial completion of doctoral program. *Median time to degree:* Doctorate–6 years full-time. *Entrance requirements:* For master's and doctorate, GRE General Test. Additional exam requirements/recommendations for international students: Required—TOEFL. *Application deadline:* For fall admission, 1/15 for domestic students, 1/15 for international students. Application fee: $55. Electronic applications accepted. *Financial support:* In 2003–04, 29 students received support, including research assistantships with full tuition reimbursements available (averaging $17,196 per year), teaching assistantships with full tuition reimbursements available (averaging $18,096 per year); fellowships, Federal Work-Study, institutionally sponsored loans, scholarships/grants, tuition waivers (partial), and unspecified assistantships also available. Financial award application deadline: 1/15. *Faculty research:* Climatology, evolutionary paleontology, petrology, geochemistry, oceanic sciences. *Unit head:* Dr. David Rowley, Chairman, 773-702-8102, Fax: 773-702-9505. *Application contact:* David J. Leslie, Graduate Student Services Coordinator, 773-702-8180, Fax: 773-702-9505, E-mail: info@geosci.uchicago.edu.

University of Hawaii at Manoa, Graduate Division, School of Ocean and Earth Science and Technology, Department of Geology and Geophysics, Honolulu, HI 96822. Offers high-pressure geophysics and geochemistry (MS, PhD); hydrogeology and engineering geology (MS, PhD); marine geology and geophysics (MS, PhD); planetary geosciences and remote sensing (MS, PhD); seismology and solid-earth geophysics (MS, PhD); volcanology, petrology, and geochemistry (MS, PhD). *Faculty:* 73 full-time (13 women), 16 part-time/adjunct (1 woman). *Students:* 57 full-time (19 women); includes 3 minority (1 African American, 2 Asian Americans or Pacific Islanders), 17 international. Average age 29. 116 applicants, 15% accepted, 12 enrolled. Terminal master's awarded for partial completion of doctoral program. *Median time to degree:* Master's–3 years full-time; doctorate–3 years full-time. *Degree requirements:* For master's, thesis/dissertation; for doctorate, thesis/dissertation, comprehensive exam. *Entrance requirements:* For master's and doctorate, GRE General Test, minimum GPA of 3.0. Additional exam requirements/recommendations for international students: Required—TOEFL. *Application deadline:* For fall admission, 1/15 for domestic students, 1/1 for international students; for spring admission, 9/1 for domestic students, 8/15 for international students. Application fee: $50. *Expenses:* Tuition, state resident: full-time $4,464; part-time $186 per credit hour. Tuition, nonresident: full-time $10,608; part-time $442 per credit hour. Tuition and fees vary according to program. *Financial support:* In 2003–04, 44 research assistantships (averaging $19,270 per year), 5 teaching assistantships (averaging $18,198 per year) were awarded. *Unit head:* Dr. Paul Wessel, Chair, 808-956-2582, Fax: 808-956-5512.

University of Michigan, Horace H. Rackham School of Graduate Studies, College of Engineering, Department of Atmospheric, Oceanic, and Space Sciences, Ann Arbor, MI 48109. Offers atmospheric and space sciences (PhD); geoscience and remote sensing (PhD); space and planetary physics (PhD); space engineering (M Eng). Part-time programs available. *Faculty:* 44 full-time (4 women), 1 part-time/adjunct (0 women). *Students:* 54 full-time (25 women), 1 part-time; includes 2 minority (1 American Indian/Alaska Native, 1 Asian American or Pacific Islander), 21 international. Average age 27. 58 applicants, 38% accepted, 15 enrolled. In 2003, 13 master's, 3 doctorates awarded. Terminal master's awarded for partial completion of doctoral program. *Degree requirements:* For master's, thesis (for some programs); for doctorate, thesis/dissertation, oral defense of dissertation, preliminary exams. *Entrance requirements:* For master's and doctorate, GRE General Test. Additional exam requirements/recommendations for international students: Required—TOEFL. *Application deadline:* For fall admission, 1/15 for domestic students. Applications are processed on a rolling basis. Application fee: $60 ($75 for international students). Electronic applications accepted. *Expenses:* Tuition, state resident: full-time $7,463. Tuition, nonresident: full-time $13,913. Full-time tuition and fees vary according to course load, degree level and program. *Financial support:* In 2003–04, 9 fellowships with tuition reimbursements (averaging $11,669 per year), 36 research assistantships with tuition reimbursements (averaging $14,288 per year), 2 teaching assistantships with tuition reimbursements (averaging $13,570 per year) were awarded. Career-related internships or fieldwork, Federal Work-Study, and institutionally sponsored loans also available. Support available to part-time students. Financial award application deadline: 3/15; financial award applicants required to submit FAFSA. *Faculty research:* Modeling of atmospheric and aerosol chemistry, radiative transfer, remote sensing, atmospheric dynamics, space weather modeling. Total annual research expenditures: $17.5 million. *Unit head:* Tamas Gombosi, Chair, 734-764-7222, Fax: 734-615-4645, E-mail: tamas@umich.edu. *Application contact:* Margaret Reid, Student Services Associate, 734-936-0482, Fax: 734-763-0437, E-mail: aoss.um@umich.edu.

University of New Mexico, Graduate School, College of Arts and Sciences, Department of Earth and Planetary Sciences, Albuquerque, NM 87131-2039. Offers MS, PhD. *Students:* 40 full-time (18 women), 16 part-time (11 women); includes 4 minority (1 Asian American or Pacific Islander, 3 Hispanic Americans), 3 international. Average age 29. 56 applicants, 39% accepted, 15 enrolled. In 2003, 10 master's, 2 doctorates awarded. Terminal master's awarded for partial completion of doctoral program. *Degree requirements:* For master's and doctorate, thesis/dissertation. *Entrance requirements:* For master's, GRE General Test; for doctorate, GRE General Test, GRE Subject Test. *Application deadline:* For fall admission, 1/31 for domestic students; for spring admission, 11/1 priority date for domestic students. Application fee: $40. *Expenses:* Tuition, state resident: full-time $1,802; part-time $152 per credit hour. Tuition, nonresident: full-time $6,135; part-time $513 per credit hour. Tuition and fees vary according to program. *Financial support:* In 2003–04, 2 fellowships (averaging $28,993 per year), 26 research assistantships (averaging $9,903 per year), 24 teaching assistantships (averaging $7,300 per year) were awarded. Scholarships/grants also available. Financial award application deadline: 3/1; financial award applicants required to submit FAFSA. *Faculty research:* Geochemistry, meteoritics, tectonics, igcodynamics, climate and surface processes. Total annual research expenditures: $1.2 million. *Unit head:* Dr. Les D. McFadden, Chair, 505-277-4204, Fax: 505-277-8843, E-mail: lmcfadnm@unm.edu. *Application contact:* Cindy

Planetary and Space Sciences

University of New Mexico (continued)
Jaramillo, Administrative Assistant II, 505-277-1635, Fax: 505-277-8843, E-mail: epsdept@unm.edu.

University of North Dakota, Graduate School, John D. Odegard School of Aerospace Sciences, Space Studies Program, Grand Forks, ND 58202. Offers MS. Part-time programs available. Postbaccalaureate distance learning degree programs offered (minimal on-campus study). *Faculty:* 9 full-time (0 women). *Students:* 2 full-time (0 women), 111 part-time (32 women). 21 applicants, 100% accepted, 11 enrolled. In 2003, 37 degrees awarded. *Degree requirements:* For master's, thesis or alternative, comprehensive exam. *Entrance requirements:* For master's, minimum GPA of 3.0. Additional exam requirements/recommendations for international students: Required—TOEFL (minimum score 550 paper-based; 213 computer-based). *Application deadline:* For fall admission, 3/1 priority date for domestic students, 3/1 priority date for international students; for spring admission, 10/15 priority date for domestic students, 10/15 priority date for international students. Applications are processed on a rolling basis. Application fee: $35. Electronic applications accepted. *Expenses:* Tuition, state resident: part-time $235 per credit. Tuition, nonresident: part-time $535 per credit. Tuition and fees vary according to course level, course load, program and reciprocity agreements. *Financial support:* In 2003–04, 15 research assistantships with full tuition reimbursements (averaging $7,407 per year) were awarded; fellowships, teaching assistantships, career-related internships or fieldwork, Federal Work-Study, institutionally sponsored loans, scholarships/grants, tuition waivers (full and partial), and unspecified assistantships also available. Support available to part-time students. Financial award application deadline: 3/15; financial award applicants required to submit FAFSA. *Faculty research:* Earth-approaching asteroids, international remote sensing statutes, Mercury fly-by design, origin of meteorites, craters on Venus. *Unit head:* Dr. Eligar Sadeh, Director, 701-777-3462, Fax: 701-777-3711, E-mail: sadeh@aero.und.edu.

University of Pittsburgh, School of Arts and Sciences, Department of Geology and Planetary Science, Pittsburgh, PA 15260. Offers geographical information systems (PM Sc); geology and planetary science (MS, PhD). Part-time programs available. *Faculty:* 12 full-time (1 woman), 2 part-time/adjunct (0 women). *Students:* 18 full-time (8 women), 5 part-time (3 women); includes 2 minority (1 Asian American or Pacific Islander, 1 Hispanic American), 1 international. Average age 28. 37 applicants, 24% accepted, 6 enrolled. In 2003, 10 master's, 3 doctorates awarded. *Degree requirements:* For master's, thesis, oral thesis defense; for doctorate, thesis/dissertation, oral dissertation defense. *Entrance requirements:* For master's and doctorate, GRE General Test. Additional exam requirements/recommendations for international students: Required—TOEFL. *Application deadline:* For fall admission, 8/1 priority date for domestic students, 4/30 priority date for international students; for winter admission, 12/1 for domestic students; for spring admission, 4/1 for domestic students. Applications are processed on a rolling basis. Application fee: $40. Electronic applications accepted. *Expenses:* Tuition, state resident: full-time $11,744; part-time $479 per credit. Tuition, nonresident: full-time $22,910; part-time $941 per credit. Required fees: $560. Tuition and fees vary according to degree level and program. *Financial support:* In 2003–04, 17 students received support, including 5 fellowships with tuition reimbursements available (averaging $14,500 per year), 5 research assistantships with tuition reimbursements available (averaging $10,400 per year), 11 teaching assistantships with tuition reimbursements available (averaging $11,752 per year); career-related internships or fieldwork, Federal Work-Study, institutionally sponsored loans, scholarships/grants, and tuition waivers (full and partial) also available. Support available to part-time students. Financial award application deadline: 2/1; financial award applicants required to submit FAFSA. *Faculty research:* Geographical information systems, hydrology, low temperature geochemistry, radiogenic isotopes, volcanology. Total annual research expenditures: $529,714. *Unit head:* Dr. William Harbert, Chair, 412-624-8784, Fax: 412-624-3914, E-mail: harbert@pitt.edu. *Application contact:* Dr. Thomas Anderson, Graduate Adviser, 412-624-9870, Fax: 412-624-3914, E-mail: taco@pitt.edu.

Washington University in St. Louis, Graduate School of Arts and Sciences, Department of Earth and Planetary Sciences, St. Louis, MO 63130-4899. Offers earth and planetary sciences (MA); geochemistry (PhD); geology (MA, PhD); geophysics (PhD); planetary sciences (PhD). *Students:* 36 full-time (19 women), 1 (woman) part-time; includes 2 minority (both Asian Americans or Pacific Islanders), 5 international. 69 applicants, 35% accepted, 12 enrolled. In 2003, 9 master's, 2 doctorates awarded. Terminal master's awarded for partial completion of doctoral program. *Degree requirements:* For master's and doctorate, thesis/dissertation. *Entrance requirements:* For master's and doctorate, GRE General Test. *Application deadline:* For fall admission, 1/15 for domestic students. Applications are processed on a rolling basis. Application fee: $35. Electronic applications accepted. *Expenses:* Tuition: Full-time $28,300; part-time $1,180 per credit. *Financial support:* Fellowships, research assistantships, teaching assistantships, Federal Work-Study, institutionally sponsored loans, and tuition waivers (full and partial) available. Financial award application deadline: 1/15. *Unit head:* Dr. Raymond E. Arvidson, Chairman, 314-935-5610.

Western Connecticut State University, Division of Graduate Studies, School of Arts and Sciences, Department of Physics, Astronomy and Meteorology, Danbury, CT 06810-6885. Offers earth and planetary sciences (MA). Part-time and evening/weekend programs available. *Faculty:* 1 full-time (0 women). *Students:* Average age 33. *Degree requirements:* For master's, thesis. *Entrance requirements:* For master's, minimum GPA of 2.5. *Application deadline:* For fall admission, 8/1 for domestic students. Applications are processed on a rolling basis. Application fee: $40. *Expenses:* Tuition, state resident: full-time $3,263. Tuition, nonresident: full-time $6,742. *Financial support:* Fellowships, career-related internships or fieldwork available. Support available to part-time students. Financial award application deadline: 5/1; financial award applicants required to submit FAFSA. *Unit head:* Dr. Alice Chance, Chair, 203-837-8667. *Application contact:* Chris Shankle, Associate Director of Graduate Admissions, 203-837-8244, Fax: 203-837-8338, E-mail: shanklec@wcsu.edu.

York University, Faculty of Graduate Studies, Faculty of Pure and Applied Science, Program in Earth and Space Science, Toronto, ON M3J 1P3, Canada. Offers M Sc, PhD. Part-time and evening/weekend programs available. *Degree requirements:* For master's, thesis or alternative; for doctorate, thesis/dissertation. *Entrance requirements:* For master's, minimum B average. Electronic applications accepted. Tuition, area resident: Full-time $5,431; part-time $905 per term. Tuition, nonresident: part-time $1,987 per term. International tuition: $11,918 full-time. Required fees: $287. Tuition and fees vary according to program.

CORNELL UNIVERSITY

Graduate Field of Geological Sciences

Programs of Study

The Graduate Field of Geological Sciences offers programs of study leading to a Master of Science or a Doctor of Philosophy degree in a wide range of geoscience disciplines. A one-year professional master's degree option (Master of Engineering) is also possible in selected areas. The program is highly flexible and allows students to tailor their graduate work to individual interests and career goals. Students take an active role in designing their graduate program, guided by a special committee of faculty members chosen by the student. This committee is usually chaired by the professor who directs the thesis research.

Research and study are often interdisciplinary; the committee may include faculty members in fields other than geological sciences. Cornell has special research strength in regional tectonics (Andes, Himalaya/Tibet, North Africa/Middle East, and Japan), lithospheric geophysics, geofluid flow, geochemistry, remote sensing, and climate change. Areas of concentration include environmental geophysics, general geology, geobiology, geochemistry and isotope geology, geohydrology*, geomorphology, geophysics, geotectonics, mineralogy, paleontology, petroleum geoscience*, petrology, planetary geology, Quaternary geology, rock mechanics, sedimentology, seismology, stratigraphy, structural geology, and marine geology (* also available in the Master of Engineering program). A new option in geoarchaeology, emphasizing geochemical and geophysical methods, is under development.

Six residence units are required for the Ph.D. degree; two residence units are required for the master's. A residence unit equals one semester of satisfactory full-time study. Student progress in the Ph.D. program is evaluated by the committee with a qualifying exam in the first year and an admission to candidacy exam (A-exam) after course work is complete. The Committee judges both the M.S. and the Ph.D. thesis defenses.

Research Facilities

Facilities for geoscience research at Cornell are unusually comprehensive. They include specialized workstation clusters (UNIX and NT) for satellite image analysis, 3-D seismics (processing, modeling, and interpretation), and GIS. In addition, Cornell hosts unique digital libraries of global deep seismic reflection profiles, topographic and geologic data, and satellite imagery. Numerous personal computers and access to Cornell's AC3 cluster supercomputer round out the computational power. Geophysical equipment includes a multichannel seismograph, ground-penetrating radar, a resistivity meter, a magnetometer, and a gravimeter.

Geochemical analysis is facilitated by an X-ray diffraction laboratory, an ICP-MS lab, a nearby nuclear reactor for neutron activation analysis, a high-pressure (diamond anvil) mineralogy lab, electron microprobes, and supporting laboratory facilities, including a clean room, a rock-prep lab, an electronics shop, and wood and metal workshops.

Cornell's nineteen libraries contain more than 6 million volumes, with special and rare collections, and access to hundreds of libraries throughout the country via interlibrary loan.

Financial Aid

Almost all doctoral candidates receive financial aid through fellowships and teaching or research assistantships. Fellowships, awarded by the Graduate School annually on a competitive basis, were $19,500 plus tuition for the nine-month period for 2002–03. Teaching and research assistants receive a stipend of $13,580 and a full tuition fellowship. The application for merit-based aid is part of the application for admission. Summer fellowships are also available. Those applying for need-based aid, such as federal and private loans, must file the FAFSA.

Cost of Study

The 2003–04 academic year tuition was $28,630.

Living and Housing Costs

Estimated living expenses for the twelve-month academic year, including books, housing and dining, personal expenses, and medical insurance for a single graduate student, are between $12,400 and $15,300. Married students should add about $7560 for a spouse. The stipend portion of assistantships is taxable and subject to withholding.

Student Group

The total number of graduate students in 2003 is 34, including 16 women. Twenty-seven percent are international students. One hundred percent receive financial aid. Current students are engaged in a wide range of research, including satellite monitoring of glaciers as a guide to climate change, the deep structure of the Tibet plateau, evolution of the Andes, evolution of the Atlas Mountains of Morocco, lithospheric architecture of the Urals, fluid migration in complex oil structures, acoustic monitoring of oceanic biomass fluctuations, and geochemistry of Himalaya sediments, to mention but a few.

Student Outcomes

Most recent graduates have found subsequent employment in either academic institutions (postdoctoral or faculty positions) or private industry, particularly the oil exploration industry.

Location

Cornell is located in Ithaca in the Finger Lakes region of New York State. The countryside is one of rolling hills traversed by gorges, waterfalls, lakes, and streams. Outdoor recreation includes sailing, windsurfing, swimming, skiing, and hiking; three state parks lie within 10 miles of the city. Ithaca's cuisine, theaters, and exhibits typify the creative vitality of this pluralistic community.

The University

Founded by Ezra Cornell in 1865, Cornell is both the land-grant institution of New York State and a privately endowed university. The student population is more than 19,000. The graduate faculty has more than 1,600 members and includes Nobel laureates, Pulitzer Prize recipients, and members of the National Academy of Sciences. The Department of Geological Sciences is housed in Snee Hall, built in 1984. Beautiful as well as functional, the spacious four-story building includes a large atrium and a variety of modern research facilities.

Applying

Admission applications may be submitted at any time; however, the deadline to be considered for certain forms of financial aid is January 10. The admission application also serves as the application for fellowship, assistantship, or tuition awards. Basic GRE scores are required. All applicants whose native language is not English must meet English proficiency requirements (e.g., a TOEFL score of at least 550 on the paper-based test or 213 on the computer-based test).

Correspondence and Information

Professor Larry D. Brown
Graduate Field of Graduate Studies
Department of Geological Sciences
Snee Hall
Cornell University
Ithaca, New York 14853

Telephone: 607-255-7357
Fax: 607-254-4780
E-mail: gradprog@geology.cornell.edu
World Wide Web: http://www.geo.cornell.edu

Cornell University

THE FACULTY AND THEIR RESEARCH

Richard W. Allmendinger, Professor; Ph.D., Stanford, 1979. Structural geology, tectonics, microscopic and mesoscopic rock fabrics, interpretation of seismic reflection profiles.
Warren Allmon, Adjunct Associate Professor; Ph.D., Harvard, 1988. Paleontology, ecology, paleoecology.
Muawia Barazangi, Professor; Ph.D., Columbia, 1971. Seismology, geophysics, tectonics.
John M. Bird, Professor; Ph.D., Rensselaer, 1962. Geotectonics, plate tectonics, orogeny, economic geology, ophiolites, origin of terrestrial metals, geology of the Appalachians, paleostress indicators.
Larry D. Brown, Professor; Ph.D., Cornell, 1976. Exploration seismology, deep structure of continental crust, recent crustal movements, digital signal processing, computer graphics.
Lawrence M. Cathles, Professor; Ph.D., Princeton, 1971. Economic geology, extractive metallurgy, geophysics, geohydrology.
John L. Cisne, Professor; Ph.D., Chicago, 1973. Paleobiology, paleoceanography, biostratigraphy.
Kerry Cook, Professor; Ph.D., North Carolina State, 1984. Climate dynamics, global and regional climate modeling.
Louis A. Derry, Assistant Professor; Ph.D., Harvard, 1989. Interaction of tectonic, geochemical, and biological processes; geochemistry; isotope geology.
Charles H. Greene, Associate Professor; Ph.D., Washington (Seattle), 1985. Physical oceanography, marine geology, acoustic monitoring of ocean biomass.
David Hysell, Associate Professor; Ph.D., Cornell, 1992. Geophysics, upper-atmosphere physics, radar remote sensing, space plasmas.
Bryan L. Isacks, Professor and Chair; Ph.D., Columbia, 1965. Tectonics, satellite remote sensing, earthquake seismology.
Teresa E. Jordan, Professor; Ph.D., Stanford, 1979. Stratigraphy, continental basin evolution, tectonics.
Robert W. Kay, Professor; Ph.D., Columbia, 1970. Petrology, geochemistry, trace-element and isotope geochemistry applied to the origin of igneous rocks and lower continental crust.
Suzanne Mahlburg Kay, Professor; Ph.D., Brown, 1975. Petrology of convergent margin magmas, relation of tectonics processes to magmatic evolution, silicate mineralogy.
Alexandra Moore, Visiting Associate Professor; Ph.D., Harvard, 1993. Geoscience education, remote sensing, Alpine paleogeography.
William M. White, Professor; Ph.D., Rhode Island, 1977. Isotope and trace-element geochemistry of oceanic igneous rocks and marine sediments, solid-source mass spectrometry, chemical evolution of the mantle and crust.

SELECTED PUBLICATIONS

Beauchamp, W., **R. W. Allmendinger, M. Barazangi,** et al. Inversion tectonics and the evolution of the High Atlas Mountains, Morocco, based on a geological-geophysical transect. *Tectonics* 18:163–84, 1999.

Allmendinger, R. W. Inverse and forward numerical modeling of trishear fault-propagation folds. *Tectonics* 17:640–56, 1998.

Gomez, F., **R. W. Allmendinger, M. Barazangi,** et al. Crustal shortening and vertical strain partitioning in the Middle Atlas Mountains of Morocco. *Tectonics* 17(4):520–33, 1998.

Allmendinger, R. W., T. E. Jordan, **S. M. Kay,** and **B. L. Isacks.** The evolution of the Altiplano-Puna Plateau of the Central Andes. *Ann. Rev. Earth Planetary Sci.* 25:139–174, 1997.

Allmendinger, R. W., and T. Gubbels. Pure and simple shear plateau uplift, Altiplano-Puna, Argentina and Bolivia. *Tectonophysics* 259(1–3):1-13, 1996.

Allmendinger, R. W. Thrust and fold tectonics of the western United States exclusive of the accreted terranes. In *The Cordilleran Orogen: Coterminous U.S.,* pp. 583–607, eds. B. C. Burchfiel, P. Lipman, and M. L. Zoback. Boulder, Colo.: Geological Society of America, 1992.

Allmon, W. D., S. D. Emslie, D. S. Jones, and G. S. Morgan. Late Neogene oceanographic change along Florida's West Coast: Evidence and mechanisms. *J. Geol.* 104:143–62, 1996.

Allmon, W. D. Taxic evolutionary paleoecology and the ecological context of macroevolutionary change. *Evolutionary Ecol.* 8:95–112, 1994.

Allmon, W. D., G. Rosenberg, R. W. Portell, and K. S. Schindler. Diversity of Atlantic coastal plain mollusks since the Pliocene. *Science* 260:1626–8, 1993.

Allmon, W. D. Role of nutrients and temperature in extinction of turritelline gastropods in the northwestern Atlantic and northeastern Pacific. *Palaeogeogr. Palaeoclimatol. Palaeoecol.* 92:41–54, 1992.

Allmon, W. D. Ecology of living turritelline gastropods (Prosobranchia, Turritellidae): Current knowledge and paleontological implications. *Palaios* 3:259–84, 1988.

Mele, G., et al. **(M. Barazangi).** Compressional velocity structure and anisotrophy in the uppermost mantle beneath Italy and surrounding regions. *J. Geophys. Res.* 103(B6):12,529–43, 1998.

Litak, R., **M. Barazangi,** et al. Structure and evolution of the petroliferous euphrates graben system, southeast Syria. *Am. Assoc. Petroleum Geologists Bull.* 82(6):1173–90, 1998.

Sandvol, E., et al. **(M. Barazangi).** Lithospheric seismic velocity discontinuities beneath the Arabian Shield. *Geophys. Res. Lett.* 25(15):2873–3276, 1998.

Sandvol, E., D. Seber, A. Calvert, and **M. Barazangi.** Grid search modeling of receiver functions: Implications for crustal structure in the Middle East and North Africa. *J. Geophys. Res.* 103(B11):26899–917, 1998.

Calvert, A., et al. **(M. Barazangi).** An integrated geophysical investigation of recent seismicity in the Al-Hoceima region of north Morocco. *Bull. Seismological Soc. Am.* 87(3):637–51, 1997.

Mele, G., A. Rovelli, D. Seber, and **M. Barazangi.** Shear wave attenuation in the lithosphere beneath Italy and surrounding regions: Tectonic implications. *J. Geophys. Res.* 102:11,863–75, 1997.

Blythe, A. E., **J. M. Bird,** and G. I. Omar. Deformation history of the central Brooks Range, Alaska; results from fission-track and 40Ar/39Ar analyses. *Tectonics* 15(2):440–55, 1996.

Wirth, K. R., et al. **(J. M. Bird).** Age and evolution of western Brooks Range ophiolites, Alaska; results from 40Ar/39Ar thermochronometry. *Tectonics* 12(2):410–32, 1993.

Harding, D. J., K. R. Wirth, and **J. M. Bird.** Spectral mapping of Alaskan ophiolites using Landsat thematic mapper data. *Remote Sensing Environment* 28:219–32, 1989.

Goodrich, C. A., and **J. M. Bird.** Formation of iron-carbon alloys in basaltic magma at Uivfaq, Disko Island: The role of carbon in mafic magmas. *J. Geol.* 93:475–92, 1985.

Dickey, J. S., Jr., W. A. Bassett, **J. M. Bird,** and M. S. Weathers. Liquid carbon in the lower mantle? *Geology* 11:219–20, 1983.

Alsdorf, D., et al. **(L. D. Brown).** INDEPTH (International Deep Profiling of Tibet and the Himalaya) multichannel seismic reflection data: Description and availability. *J. Geophys. Res.* 103:1126,993–9, 1998.

Alsdorf, D., **L. D. Brown,** et al. Crustal deformation of the Lhasa terrane, Tibet plateau from Project INDEPTH Deep Seismic Reflection Profiles. *Tectonics* 17:501–19, 1998.

Brown, L. D., et al. Bright spots, structure, and magmatism in southern Tibet from INDEPTH seismic reflection profiling. *Science* 274(5293):1688–90, 1996.

Steer, D. N., **L. D. Brown,** J. H. Knapp, and D. J. Baird. Comparison of explosive and vibroseis source energy penetration during COCORP deep seismic reflection profiling in the Williston Basin. *Geophysics* 61:211–21, 1995.

Brown, L. D., and J. E. Oliver. Recent vertical crustal movements from leveling data and their relation to geologic structure in the eastern U.S. *Rev. Geophys. Space Phys.* 14:13–35, 1976.

Revil, A., H. Schwaeger, **L. M. Cathles,** and P. D. Manhardt. Streaming potential in porous media; 2, Theory and application to geothermal systems. *J. Geophys. Res.* 104:920,033–48, 1999.

Hunt, J. M., J. K. Whelan, L. B. Eglinton, and **L. M. Cathles.** Relation of shale porosities, gas generation, and compaction to deep overpressures in the U.S. Gulf coast. *AAPG Memoir* 7087–104, 1998.

Meulbroek, P., **L. M. Cathles,** and J. Whelan. Phase fractionation at South Eugene Island Block 330. *Organic Geochem.* 29:1–3223–39, 1998.

Nunn, J. A., and **L. M. Cathles.** Global basins research network: Advancing the science of fluid flow prediction in sedimentary basins. *AAPG Bull.* 82:101947–8, 1998.

Revil, A., **L. M. Cathles,** et al. Capillary sealing in sedimentary basins: A clear field example. *Geophys. Res. Lett.* 25:3389–92, 1998.

Cathles, L. M., A. H. J. Erendi, and T. Barrie. How long can a hydrothermal system be sustained by a single intrusive event? *Econ. Geology Bull. Soc. Econ. Geologists* 92:7-8766–71, 1997.

Ackerly, S., **J. L. Cisne,** B. L. Railsback, and T. F. Anderson. Punctal density in the Ordovician orthide brachiopod Paucicrura rogata; anatomical and paleoenvironmental variation. *Lethaia* 26(1):17–24, 1993.

Muramoto, J. A., et al. **(J. L. Cisne).** Sulfur, iron and organic carbon fluxes in the Black Sea; sulfur isotopic evidence for origin of sulfur fluxes. *Deep-Sea Res. Part A Oceanogr. Res. Pap. 38* Suppl. 2A:1151–87, 1991.

Gildner, R. F., and **J. L. Cisne.** Quantitative modeling of carbonate stratigraphy and water-depth history using depth-dependent sedimentation function. In *Quantitative Dynamic Stratigraphy,* pp. 417–32, ed. T. A. Cross. Englewood Cliffs, N.J.: Prentice-Hall, 1990.

Railsback, L. B., T. F. Anderson, S. C. Ackerly, and **J. L. Cisne.** Palaeontological and isotope evidence for warm saline deep waters in Ordovician oceans. *Nature* 343:156–9, 1990.

Cisne, J. L. Earthquakes recorded stratigraphically on carbonate platforms. *Nature* 323:320–2, 1986.

Cook, K. H. Generation of the African Easterly Jet and its role in determining West African precipitation. *J. Climate* 12:1165–84, 1999.

Ringler, T. D., and **K. H. Cook.** Understanding the seasonality of orographically forced stationary waves: Interaction between mechanical and thermal forcing. *J. Atmos. Sci.* 56:1154–74, 1999.

Lenters, J. D., and **K. H. Cook.** Summertime precipitation variability in South America: Role of the large-scale circulation. *Mon. Wea. Rev.* 127:409–31, 1999.

Cook, K. H. Large-scale atmospheric dynamics and Sahelian precipitation. *J. Climate* 10:1137–52, 1997.

Nayvelt, L., P. J. Gierasch, and **K. H. Cook.** Modeling and observations of Martian stationary waves. *J. Atmos. Sci.* 8:986–1013, 1997.

Lenters, J. L., and **K. H. Cook.** On the origin of the Bolivian High and related circulation features of the South American climate. *J. Atmos. Sci.* 5:656–77, 1997.

Galy, A., C. France-Lanord, and **L. A. Derry.** The strontium isotopic

Cornell University

Selected Publications (continued)

budget of Himalayan rivers in Nepal and Bangladesh. *Geochim. Cosmochim. Acta* 63:1905–25, 1999.

Chadwick, O. A., **L. A. Derry,** et al. Changing sources of nutrients during four million years of ecosystem development. *Nature* 397:491–7, 1999.

Kennedy, M. J., et al. **(L. A. Derry).** Replacement of weathering with atmospheric sources of base cations during ecosystem development, Hawaiian Islands. *Geology* 26:1015–18, 1998.

France-Lanord, C., and **L. A. Derry.** Organic carbon burial forcing of the carbon cycle from Himalayan erosion. *Nature* 390:65–75, 1997.

Derry, L. A., and C. France-Lanord. Neogene growth of the sedimentary organic carbon reservoir. *Paleoceanography* 11:267–75, 1996.

Derry, L. A., and C. France-Lanord. Neogene Himalayan weathering history and river 87Sr/86Sr: Impact on the marine Sr record. *Earth Planetary Sci. Lett.* 142:59–76, 1996.

Chandy, S. T., and **C. H. Greene.** Estimating the predatory impact of gelatinous zooplankton. *Limnol. Oceanogr.* 40:947–55, 1995.

Genin, A., **C. Greene,** et al. Zooplankton patch dynamics: Daily gap formation over abrupt topography. *Deep-Sea Res.* 41:941–51, 1994.

Greene, C. H., et al. The migration behavior, fine structure, and bioluminescent activity of krill sound-scattering layers. *Limnol. Oceanogr.* 37:650–8, 1992.

Greene, C. H., T. K. Stanton, P. H. Wiebe, and S. McClatchie. Acoustic estimates of Antarctic krill. *Nature* 349:110, 1991.

Greene, C. H., and P. H. Wiebe. Bioacoustical oceanography: New tools for zooplankton and micromekton research in the 1990s. *Oceanography* 3:12–17, 1990.

Hysell, D. L., J. L. Chau, and C. G. Fesen. Effects of large horizontal winds on the equatorial electrojet. *J. Geophys. Res.* 107:1214, 2002.

Hysell, D. L., and E. B. Shume. Electrostatic plasma turbulence in the topside equatorial F region ionosphere. *J. Geophys. Res.* 107:1269, 2002.

Hysell, D. L., and J. L. Chau. Imaging radar observations and nonlocal theory of large-scale waves in the equatorial electrojet. *Ann. Geophys.* 20:1167, 2002.

Hysell, D. L., M. Yamamoto, and S. Fukao. Imaging radar observations and theory of type I and type II quasiperiodic echoes. *J. Geophys. Res.* 107:1360, 2002.

Hysell, D. L., M. Yamamoto, and S. Fukao. Simulations of plasma clouds in the midlatitude E region ionosphere with implications for type I and type II quasiperiodic echoes. *J. Geophys. Res.* 107:1313, 2002.

Smith, L. C., R. R. Forster, **B. L. Isacks,** and D. K. Hall. Seasonal climatic forcings of alpine glaciers revealed with orbital synthetic aperture radar. *J. Glaciol.* 43(145):480–8, 1997.

Whitman, D., **B. L. Isacks,** and **S. M. Kay.** Lithospheric structure and along-strike segmentation of the Central Andean Plateau; seismic Q, magmatism, flexure, topography and tectonics. *Tectonophysics* 259(1–3):29–40, 1996.

Bevis, M., et al. **(B. L. Isacks).** Geodetic observations of very rapid convergence and back-arc extension at the Tonga Arc. *Nature* 374(6519):249–51, 1995.

Masek, J. G., **B. L. Isacks,** T. L. Gubbels, and E. J. Fielding. Erosion and tectonics of margins of continental plateaus. *J. Geophys. Res.* 99:13941–56, 1994.

Isacks, B. L. Uplift of the Central Andean plateau and the bending of the Bolivian Orocline. *J. Geophys. Res.* 93:13841–54, 1988.

Isacks, B. L., J. Oliver, and L. R. Sykes. Seismology and the new global tectonics. *J. Geophys. Res.* 73:5855–99, 1968.

Jordan, T. E., J. H. Reynolds III, and J. P. Erikson. Variability in age of initial shortening and uplift in the Central Andes, 16-33° 30'S. In *Tectonic Uplift and Climate Change,* ed. W. Ruddiman. New York: Plenum, 1997.

Jordan, T. E., R. W. Allmendinger, J. F. Damanti, and R. E. Drake. Chronology of motion in a complete thrust belt: The Precordillera, 30-31°S, Andes Mountains. *J. Geol.* 101:135–56, 1993.

Jordan, T. E., and P. B. Flemings. Large-scale stratigraphic architecture, eustatic variation, and unsteady tectonism: A theoretical evaluation. *J. Geophys. Res.* 96:6681–99, 1991.

Jordan, T. E., and R. N. Alonso. Cenozoic stratigraphy and basin tectonics of the Andes Mountains, 20-28° south latitude. *AAPG Bull.* 71:49–64, 1987.

Jordan, T. E., B. L. Isacks, R. W. Allmendinger, et al. Andean tectonics related to geometry of subducted Nazca plate. *Bull. Geol. Soc. Am.* 94:341–61, 1983.

Yogodzinski, G. M., et al. **(R. W. Kay** and **S. M. Kay).** Magnesian andesite in the western Aleutian Komandorsky region; implications for slab melting and processes in the mantle wedge. *Geol. Soc. Am. Bull.* 107(5):505–19, 1995.

Kay, R. W., and **S. M. Kay.** Delamination and delamination magmatism. *Tectonophysics* 219:177–89, 1993.

Fountain, D. M., R. Arculus, and **R. W. Kay.** *Continental Lower Crust.* New York: Elsevier, 1992.

Kay, R. W., and **S. M. Kay.** Crustal recycling and the Aleutian Arc. *Geochim. Cosmochim. Acta* 52:1351–9, 1988.

Kay, S. M., C. Mpodozis, and B. Coira. Magmatism, tectonism, and mineral deposits of the Central Andes (22°–33°S latitude). In *Geology and Ore Deposits of the Central Andes,* ed. B. Skinner. Society of Economic Geology Special Publication (SEG) No. 7, Ulrich Peterson vol., in press.

Vujuovich, G. I., and **S. M. Kay.** A Laurentian? Grenville-age oceanic arc/backarc terrane in the Pie de Palo Range, Western Sierras Pampeanas, Argentina. In *The Proto-Andean Margin of Gondwana,* pp. 159–80, eds. R. J. Pankhurst and C. W. Rapela. Geological Society Special Publication 142, 1998.

Gorring, M. L., et al. **(S. M. Kay).** Neogene Patagonian plateau lavas; continental magmas associated with ridge collision at the Chile triple junction. *Tectonics* 16(1):1–17, 1997.

Kay, S. M., and J. M. Abbruzzi. Magmatic evidence for Neogene lithospheric evolution of the central Andean "flat-slab" between 30° and 32°S. *Tectonophysics* 259(1–3):15–28, 1996.

Kay, S. M., S. Orrell, and J. M. Abbruzzi. Zircon and whole rock Nd-Pb isotopic evidence for a Grenville age and a Laurentian origin for the basement of the Precordilleran terrane in Argentina. *J. Geol.* 104(6):637–48, 1996.

Kay, S. M., B. Coira, and J. Viramonte. Young mafic back-ark volcanic rocks as guides to lithospheric delamination beneath the Argentine Puna Plateau, Central Andes. *J. Geophys. Res.* 99:24323–39, 1994.

Dunnivant, F. M., et. al. **(A. Moore).** A comprehensive stream study designed for an undergraduate non-majors course in earth science. *J. Geosci. Educ.* 47:158–65, 1999.

Moore, A., and **L. Derry.** Understanding natural systems through simple dynamical systems modeling. *J. Geological Educ.* 43:152–7, 1995.

Keller, R. A., M. R. Fisk, R. A. Duncan, and **W. M. White.** 16 m.y. of hotspot and non-hotspot volcanism on the Patton-Murray seamont platform, Gulf of Alaska. *Geology* 25(6):511–4, 1997.

White, W. M. Crustal recycling: Best friend hides a deep secret. *Nature* 379(6561):117–8, 1996.

White, W. M., A. McBirney, and R. A. Duncan. Petrology and geochemistry of the Galapagos Islands: Portrait of a pathological mantle plume. *J. Geophys. Res.* 98:19533–63, 1993.

White, W. M., and A. W. Hofmann. Sr and Nd isotope geochemistry of oceanic basalts and mantle evolution. *Nature* 296:821–5, 1982.

GEORGIA INSTITUTE OF TECHNOLOGY

School of Earth and Atmospheric Sciences

Programs of Study

The School of Earth and Atmospheric Sciences (EAS) offers graduate programs in the geosciences leading to the degrees of Master of Science (M.S.) and Doctor of Philosophy (Ph.D.) in six areas of specialization: atmospheric chemistry and air pollution, atmospheric dynamics and climate, geochemistry, solid Earth and environmental geophysics, ocean sciences, and hydrologic cycle.

The core curricula in each area of specialization are designed to provide students from diverse academic backgrounds with a common introduction to fundamental chemical and physical principles. More advanced courses are also available to introduce students to current academic and research topics. Doctoral students pursue their thesis research upon successful completion of the comprehensive examination, which consists of a written original research paper or proposal and an oral examination that covers the paper and fundamental principles within the student's area of specialization.

In addition to the required courses in a student's area of specialization, doctoral candidates complete 9 credit hours of study in an academic minor. This can be satisfied in another discipline within the School or in other academic units at Georgia Tech, such as in chemistry and biochemistry, physics, mathematics, public policy, computer sciences, or environmental engineering. EAS students can also participate in a certificate program in geohydrology, which is based on educational criteria of the American Institute of Hydrology and is administered by the School of Civil and Environmental Engineering. To accomplish this, students supplement their graduate program of study with a specified set of engineering and EAS courses. Also, marine science research may be carried out in cooperation with the Skidaway Institute of Oceanography. Students conduct their thesis research at Skidaway after completing course work at Georgia Tech.

Research Facilities

The School is well equipped with a wide variety of computational, laboratory, and field measurement research tools. Computational facilities include a large array of high-performance workstations, personal computers, and data servers that are used to analyze, simulate, and predict different components of the Earth system including global climate, regional air quality, and oceanic hydrothermal systems.

Several chromatographs, spectrophotometers, and various elemental analyzers are available for analytical measurements of chemical constituents in solid, liquid, and gaseous samples. In addition, there are several mass spectrometers equipped for the measurement of isotopic ratios in different types of samples. Interaction of EAS with the Departments of Biology and Civil and Environmental Engineering has resulted in the recent opening of an interdisciplinary instrumental facility to quantify biomolecules and natural substrates involved in geomicrobial processes.

For field studies, equipment includes a reverse osmosis system to separate natural organic matter from aquatic environments; several benthic landers and underwater instruments for in situ measurements in marine and freshwater environments; ground-penetrating radar and electromagnetic conductivity meters to determine the resistivity of soils and sedimentary environments; magnetometers and gravimeters to measure the magnetic properties of the Earth; seismometers, geophones, and seismographs to study earthquakes; and a variety of chemical instruments to collect and analyze the composition of aerosols from airplanes. These instruments are used in research projects that include understanding and quantifying biogeochemical processes in the water column and sediments of rivers, lakes, coastal marine environments, and the open oceans. They are also used in studies aimed at understanding and quantifying the formation and reactivity of aerosols in polluted and pristine environments or to identify past environmental events recorded in ice at the Earth's poles or in deep-sea sediments.

Finally, the School maintains several facilities for environmental monitoring. The geophysics program maintains a seismic network in Georgia to study earthquakes in the region. The atmospheric chemistry program maintains mobile and fixed-site sampling facilities, including state-of-the-art chemical ionization mass spectrometers and laser spectrometers for detection of trace gas species and a variety of meteorological and analytical instruments for detailed studies of chemical processes. Several field stations are also accessible for environmental studies on the Georgia coast, and a research vessel is available for oceanographic research with scientists at the Skidaway Institute of Oceanography.

Financial Aid

Graduate research and teaching assistantships are available to applicants with outstanding records and high research potential. Research and teaching assistants receive a tuition waiver plus a twelve-month stipend of $20,000. President's Fellowships and President's Minority Fellowships are awarded to qualified matriculants on a competitive basis. These fellowships provide stipend supplements of $5500 and are renewable for up to four years. The Institute also participates in a number of fellowship and traineeship programs sponsored by federal agencies. Traineeships associated with specific programs, such as water resources planning and management, are also available through the Environmental Resources Center.

Cost of Study

Nonresident tuition is $8470 per semester in 2004–05 (see above for information regarding tuition waivers for graduate assistants). The 2004–05 matriculation fees for graduate assistants are $455 per semester.

Living and Housing Costs

Room and board costs for individual graduate students are estimated to be $4000 per semester for 2004–05. Contemporary on-campus graduate student housing is available as well as private off-campus housing.

Student Group

There are currently about 70 graduate students in the School, representing a diverse body of academic, ethnic, and national backgrounds. Successful applicants typically have degrees in the physical sciences, biological sciences, or engineering and a keen desire to understand the chemistry and physics of the natural environment.

Location

Georgia Tech is located on a 360-acre campus in the heart of midtown Atlanta, a modern, cosmopolitan city with a variety of cultural, historical, and outdoor attractions. The city benefits from a moderate climate, which permits a broad range of year-round outdoor activities. Additional information on Atlanta can be found on the World Wide Web at http://www.accessatlanta.com.

The Institute

Georgia Tech was founded in 1888 and is a member of the University System of Georgia. The Institute has a tradition of excellence as a center of technological research and education, with a strong focus on interdisciplinary activities. The School of Earth and Atmospheric Sciences is the cornerstone of a new campus building that fosters interdisciplinary research in environmental sciences and technology.

Applying

Application information is available from the Graduate Admissions Committee from the address listed in the Correspondence and Information section. Prospective applicants are also encouraged to directly contact faculty members with whom their interests best coincide. Applicants are required to submit scores from the General Test of the Graduate Record Examinations. Minimum TOEFL scores of 550 (paper-based) or 213 (computer-based) are required of all international applicants whose native language is not English. To ensure full consideration of available fellowships and assistantships, completed applications for the fall term should be received by January 15.

Correspondence and Information

EAS Graduate Admissions Committee
School of Earth and Atmospheric Sciences
Georgia Institute of Technology
Atlanta, Georgia 30332-0340

Telephone: 404-894-3893
Fax: 404-894-5638
E-mail: gradinfo@eas.gatech.edu
World Wide Web: http://www.eas.gatech.edu/

Georgia Institute of Technology

THE FACULTY AND THEIR RESEARCH

Michael H. Bergin, Associate Professor; Ph.D., Carnegie Mellon, 1994. Atmospheric chemistry, atmospheric aerosols, climate impacts.
Robert X. Black, Associate Professor; Ph.D., MIT, 1990. Atmospheric climate dynamics, diagnostic methods, model validation.
William L. Chameides, Regents Professor, Smithgall Chair, and Member of the National Academy of Sciences; Ph.D., Yale, 1974. Atmospheric chemistry, biogeochemical cycles, air pollution.
George Chimonas, Professor; Ph.D., Sussex (England), 1965. Atmospheric dynamics, waves, turbulence, and stability.
Kim M. Cobb, Assistant Professor; Ph.D., California, San Diego (Scripps), 2002. Tropical Pacific climate change (past and present), carbonate geochemistry, multiproxy approaches.
Derek M. Cunnold, Professor; Ph.D., Cornell, 1965. Atmospheric dynamics, remote sensing and modeling of trace gases.
Judith A. Curry, Professor and Chair; Ph.D., Chicago, 1982. Climate, remote sensing, atmospheric modeling, air-sea interactions.
Robert E. Dickinson, Professor, GRA/Georgia Power Chair, and Member of the National Academy of Sciences and the National Academy of Engineering; Ph.D., MIT, 1966. Climate dynamics and modeling, land-atmosphere interactions.
Emanuele DiLorenzo, Assistant Professor; Ph.D., California, San Diego (Scripps), 2003. Ocean and climate dynamics, ocean modeling and data assimilation.
Rong Fu, Associate Professor; Ph.D., Columbia, 1991. Climate, atmospheric hydrological processes, remote sensing.
L. Gregory Huey, Associate Professor; Ph.D., Wisconsin–Madison, 1992. Atmospheric chemistry, chemical kinetics, trace gas measurements.
Ellery Ingall, Associate Professor; Ph.D., 1991. Marine biogeochemistry; carbon, nitrogen, and phosphorus cycling.
Daniel Lizarralde, Assistant Professor; Ph.D., MIT (Woods Hole), 1997. Geophysics, lithospheric evolution, continental margins, marine gas hydrates, seismology.
L. Timothy Long, Professor; Ph.D., Oregon State, 1968. Intraplate seismotectonics, surface wave imaging in environmental geophysics, earthquakes in education.
Robert P. Lowell, Professor; Ph.D., Oregon State, 1972. Marine geophysics, magmatic and hydrothermal processes.
Jean Lynch-Stieglitz, Associate Professor; Ph.D., Columbia, 1995. Paleooceanography, paleoclimatology, stable isotope geochemistry.
Allison Macfarlane, Associate Professor; Ph.D., MIT, 1992. Geosciences, public policy, nuclear waste disposal.
Athanasios Nenes, Assistant Professor; Ph.D., Caltech, 2002. Atmospheric aerosols, clouds, and climate; cloud microphysical processes.
E. Michael Perdue, Professor; Ph.D., Georgia Tech, 1973. Geochemistry and environmental chemistry of humic substances.
Carolyn D. Ruppel, Associate Professor; Ph.D., MIT, 1992. Environmental geophysics, physical hydrology, methane gas hydrates.
Irina M. Sokolik, Professor; Candidate of Science (Ph.D. equivalent), Russian Academy of Sciences, 1989. Radiation, remote sensing, aerosols.
Marc Stieglitz, Associate Professor; Ph.D., Columbia, 1995. Surface hydrology, watershed dynamics, land surface–climate interactions.
Martial Taillefert, Assistant Professor; Ph.D., Northwestern, 1997. Aqueous inorganic geochemistry, chemical oceanography, geomicrobiology, metal cycling in aquatic systems.
David Tan, Associate Professor; Ph.D., Cornell, 1994. Atmospheric chemistry, tropospheric photochemistry and trace gases.
Yuhang Wang, Associate Professor; Ph.D., Harvard, 1997. Atmospheric chemistry, chemical modeling and forecasting.
Rodney J. Weber, Associate Professor; Ph.D., Minnesota, 1995. Atmospheric chemistry, aerosol measurements and formation.
Peter J. Webster, Professor; Ph.D., MIT, 1972. Atmospheric and ocean dynamics, ocean-atmosphere interaction, wave propagation, prediction and decision theory.
Paul H. Wine, Professor; Ph.D., Florida State, 1974. Atmospheric chemistry, photochemical kinetics.

HARVARD UNIVERSITY

Department of Earth and Planetary Sciences

Programs of Study The department offers instruction and opportunities for research in a wide variety of fields within the broad scope of earth and planetary sciences. Requirements for admission are highly flexible, but adequate undergraduate preparation in mathematics, physics, and chemistry is strongly recommended. Students whose undergraduate majors are in science, engineering, or mathematics and who desire a Ph.D. in one of the fields of earth and planetary sciences are encouraged to apply. The master's degree is not a prerequisite for entering the Ph.D. program. Students are not normally admitted to work toward a terminal A.M. degree. The student's Ph.D. research often includes interaction with several faculty members in addition to the primary thesis adviser.

Graduate study leading to the Ph.D. degree is supervised by a faculty advisory committee made up in accordance with each student's aims and interests. Fields of teaching and research include atmospheric chemistry, climatology, dynamic meteorology, economic geology, geochemistry, geophysics, mineralogy, oceanography, paleontology, petrology, sedimentology, seismology, stratigraphy, and structural geology. In addition, courses may be taken in chemistry, physics, engineering, or biology. Under reciprocal arrangements, graduate students at Harvard may take and receive credit for courses given at the Massachusetts Institute of Technology in Cambridge and the Woods Hole Oceanographic Institute.

Research Facilities The department is housed in Hoffman Laboratory, the adjoining Geological Museum, and a building called "the Link" that joins Hoffman Laboratory with the Department of Chemistry. These buildings provide office, classroom, and laboratory space for the faculty, staff, and students. The facilities and equipment include a computing facility based on a network of Sun Workstations with a wide range of peripheral devices such as a massive online storage system for seismological data; a mass spectrometer facility that includes an inductively coupled plasma mass spectrometer with laser ablation capabilities, two stable gas isotope ratio spectrometers, an inductively coupled plasma absorption emission spectrometer, and a thermal ionization mass spectrometer; there is also a state-of-the-art metal-free clean room for sample dissolution; an electron microprobe; a shock-compression laboratory, including a 40 mm single-stage launch system; facilities for geophysical and paleontological fluid dynamics experiments; and associated laboratories for sample preparation and analysis.

Financial Aid All students receive financial support for both tuition and living expenses while studying for advanced degrees. Support comes from Harvard University, independent fellowships, and research and teaching assistantships. The base living expenses stipend is $2100 per month.

Cost of Study The cost of tuition is paid in full by the department. Tuition costs include health insurance and cover the use of facilities and services of the University.

Living and Housing Costs Unmarried students may live at the Graduate Center dormitories at costs that range from $5500 to $8000 for the 2004–05 academic year. These costs include a variety of meal plans. Married students may rent University-owned apartments near the campus.

Student Group The department has from 40 to 50 graduate students and about 20 to 25 undergraduates. The GeoClub, a student organization more than seventy years old, organizes lectures and activities.

Student Outcomes Students who earn graduate degrees from the Department of Earth and Planetary Sciences pursue a range of careers in academia, government, and industry. In addition to teaching, recent graduates have found research positions in planetary magnetism, climatology, atmospheric chemistry, geodynamics, and other areas of earth science. Other graduates are employed in mining, petroleum exploration, and environmental fields.

Location The Cambridge-Boston area is one of the most concentrated centers of educational, intellectual, and cultural activity in the world. At the same time, there is ready access to the scenic and historic New England countryside, which is of diverse and abundant geologic interest. Recreational activities range from the full scope of indoor athletic activities provided by Harvard to sailing and skiing. The great concentration of educational organizations in the area makes the total student population quite large, and the services offered for the benefit of students are correspondingly numerous.

The University Harvard, the oldest institution of higher learning in the United States, offers an educational life covering the entire span of the fields of learning, old and new. Tradition is strong, but innovation and change are characteristic. Graduate students in the Department of Earth and Planetary Sciences mingle with students from other graduate departments, with undergraduates, and with students at the various professional schools.

Applying Completed applications for admission should be submitted no later than January 2. Scores on the GRE General Test are required, but it is not required that a student take a Subject Test. The examination should be taken early in the fall to ensure completion before the admission application deadline.

Correspondence and Information

Professor Jeremy Bloxham, Department Chair
Department of Earth and Planetary Sciences
Harvard University
20 Oxford Street
Cambridge, Massachusetts 02138-2902
Telephone: 617-495-2351
World Wide Web: http://www-eps.harvard.edu/department/studies/grad.html

Harvard University

THE FACULTY AND THEIR RESEARCH

James G. Anderson, Philip S. Weld Professor of Atmospheric Chemistry; Ph.D., Colorado, 1970. Gas-phase kinetics of free radicals, catalytic processes in the atmosphere controlling global change of ozone, high-altitude experiments from balloons and aircraft, development of laser systems for stratospheric and tropospheric studies, development of high-altitude long-duration unmanned aircraft for studies of global change. (telephone: 617-495-5922; e-mail: anderson@huarp.harvard.edu)

Jeremy Bloxham, Harvard Professor, Professor of Geophysics, and Department Chair; Ph.D., Cambridge, 1986. Planetary magnetic fields, dynamo theory, structure and dynamics of the earth's core and lower mantle, inverse theory, mathematical geophysics. (telephone: 617-495-9517; e-mail: bloxham@eps.harvard.edu)

Adam M. Dziewonski, Frank B. Baird Jr. Professor of Science; Ph.D., Polish Academy of Sciences, 1965. Theoretical seismology, internal structure of the earth, seismic tomography, earthquake source mechanisms, geodynamics. (telephone: 617-495-2510; e-mail: dziewons@eps.harvard.edu)

Göran A. Ekström, Professor of Geology and Geophysics; Ph.D., Harvard, 1987. Seismology, forward and inverse problems of seismic source. (telephone: 617-495-8276; e-mail: ekstrom@eps.harvard.edu)

Brian F. Farrell, Robert P. Burden Professor of Meteorology; Ph.D., Harvard, 1981. Explosive development of tropical and midlatitude cyclones, predictability of weather regimes, dynamics of glacial and equable paleoclimates. (telephone: 617-495-2998; e-mail: bff@io.harvard.edu)

Paul F. Hoffman, Sturgis Hooper Professor of Geology; Ph.D., Johns Hopkins, 1970. Global tectonics, evolution of the earth's crust in the Precambrian, sedimentology and stratigraphy. (telephone: 617-496-6380; e-mail: hoffman@eps.harvard.edu)

Heinrich D. Holland, Research Professor of Economic Geology. Chemistry and chemical evolution of the ocean-atmosphere-crust system, chemistry of ore-forming solutions. (telephone: 617-495-5892; e-mail: holland@eps.harvard.edu)

Daniel J. Jacob, Gordon McKay Professor of Atmospheric Chemistry and Environmental Engineering; Ph.D., Caltech, 1985. Air pollution, atmospheric transport, regional and global atmospheric chemistry, biosphere-atmosphere interactions, climate change. (telephone: 617-495-1794; e-mail: djj@io.harvard.edu)

Stein B. Jacobsen, Professor of Geochemistry; Ph.D., Caltech, 1980. Isotope and trace-element geochemistry, chemical evolution of earth's crust-mantle system, isotopic and chemical evolution of seawater. (telephone: 617-495-5233; e-mail: jacobsen@neodymium.harvard.edu)

Andrew H. Knoll, Professor of Biology; Ph.D., Harvard, 1977. Paleontology and sedimentary geology of Precambrian terrains, evolution of vascular plants in geologic time. (telephone 617-495-9306; e-mail: aknoll@oeb.harvard.edu)

Charles H. Langmuir, Professor of Geochemistry; Ph.D., SUNY at Stony Brook, 1980. The solid earth geochemical cycle, petrology, volcanology, ocean ridges, convergent margins, ocean islands, composition and evolution of the earth's mantle. (telephone: 617-384-9948; e-mail: langmuir@eps.harvard.edu)

Charles R. Marshall, Professor of Paleontology; Ph.D., Chicago, 1989. Nature and causes of evolutionary innovation and extinction over geological time scales, using techniques in paleontology, developmental biology, statistics, and molecular and morphological phylogenetics. (telephone: 617-495-2572; e-mail: marshall@eps.harvard.edu)

James J. McCarthy, Alexander Agassiz Professor of Biological Oceanography in the Museum of Comparative Zoology; Ph.D., California, San Diego (Scripps), 1971. Biological oceanography, phytoplankton ecology, nitrogen nutrition of phytoplankton. (telephone: 617-495-2330; e-mail: james_j_mccarthy@harvard.edu)

Michael B. McElroy, Gilbert Butler Professor of Environmental Studies; Ph.D., Queen's at Kingston, 1962. Chemistry of atmosphere and oceans, including interactions with the biosphere; evolution of planetary atmospheres. (telephone: 617-495-4359; e-mail: mbm@io.harvard.edu)

Sujoy Mukhopadhyay, Assistant Professor of Geochemistry; Ph.D., Caltech, 2002. Noble gas geochemistry, record of cosmic dust flux from sediments, production rates of cosmogenic nuclides and application to surface exposure dating, low-temperature thermochronology, chemical evolution of the mantle-crust-atmosphere system. (telephone: 202-478-8459; e-mail: sujoy@dtm.ciw.edu)

Richard J. O'Connell, Professor of Geophysics; Ph.D., Caltech, 1969. Geodynamics: mantle flow, convection, and plate tectonics; models of tectonic processes; elasticity and rheology of rocks and minerals. (telephone: 617-495-2532; e-mail: oconnell@eps.harvard.edu)

Ann Pearson, Assistant Professor of Biogeochemistry; Ph.D., MIT, 2000. Carbon isotope biogeochemistry, compound-specific δ13C and Δ14C analysis of lipids and RNA, global organic carbon cycle, microbial metabolism in anoxic marine systems, sources of carbon to marine sediments. (telephone: 617-384-8392; e-mail: pearson@eps.harvard.edu)

James R. Rice, Gordon McKay Professor of Engineering Sciences and Geophysics; Ph.D., Lehigh, 1963. Crustal stressing and earthquake source processes, fracture theory, solid mechanics, materials science. (telephone: 617-495-3445; e-mail: rice@esag.harvard.edu)

Allan R. Robinson, Gordon McKay Professor of Geophysical Fluid Dynamics; Ph.D., Harvard, 1959. Physical and dynamical oceanography, geophysical fluid dynamics, numerical models of ocean currents and interdisciplinary modeling, design and interpretation of field experiments. (telephone: 617-495-2819; e-mail: robinson@pacific.harvard.edu)

Daniel P. Schrag, Professor of Earth and Planetary Sciences; Ph.D., Berkeley, 1993. Geochemical oceanography, paleoclimatology, stable isotope geochemistry. (telephone: 617-495-7676; e-mail: schrag@eps.harvard.edu)

John H. Shaw, Professor of Structural and Economic Geology; Ph.D., Princeton, 1993. Structure of the earth's crust, active faulting and folding, earthquake hazards assessment, petroleum exploration methods, remote sensing. (telephone: 617-495-8008; e-mail: shaw@eps.harvard.edu)

Sarah T. Stewart-Mukhopadhyay, Assistant Professor of Planetary Science; Ph.D., Caltech, 2002. Experimental and computational study of impact processes; collisional processing and evolution of comets, asteroids, and planetary surfaces; physical properties of planetary materials. (telephone: 202-478-8817; e-mail: sstewart@gl.ciw.edu)

Eli Tziperman, Robert P. Burden Professor of Oceanography and Applied Physics; Ph.D., MIT/Woods Hole Oceanographic Institution, 1987. Physical oceanography; large-scale ocean and climate dynamics, combining ocean data and models. (e-mail: eli@beach.weizmann.ac.il)

Steven C. Wofsy, Abbot Lawrence Rotch Professor of Atmospheric and Environmental Science; Ph.D., Harvard, 1971. Chemistry of the atmosphere on global and regional scales, including stratospheric and tropospheric chemistry. (telephone: 617-495-4566; e-mail: scw@io.harvard.edu)

KENT STATE UNIVERSITY

Department of Geology

Programs of Study The Department of Geology offers two graduate programs, a Master of Science in geology and a Doctor of Philosophy in applied geology. Approximately half the faculty members focus on paleontology, sedimentation, and tectonics. The department's other major focus involves the study of hydrology, geochemistry, and engineering geology. Interdisciplinary research opportunities are available through Kent State University's Water Resources Research Institute (WRRI), which provides access to professors and specialized research laboratories in the Departments of Geology, Biological Sciences, Chemistry, and Geography. At the Ph.D. level, students may focus on five major areas that prepare them to be professional geologists or scholars: hydrogeology and water resources, engineering geology, paleontology, Quaternary studies and climate change, and structural geology, tectonics, and petrology.

Research Facilities In the graduate programs, strong emphasis is placed on research designed not only to advance the understanding of the geological sciences, but also to solve societal problems. Students enrolled in the hydrology and water resource curriculum take advantage of seven specialized labs for research in hydrogeology, hydrology, hydrochemistry, soil mechanics, rock mechanics, geophysics, and computer applications. Facilities in engineering geology include separate labs in soil mechanics, rock mechanics, surface water hydrology, hydrogeology, hydrogeochemistry, geophysics, and computer analysis. Students in paleontology utilize facilities that include well-equipped preparation laboratories for macropaleontological and micropaleontological studies; darkroom, studio, and digital-imaging facilities; and specialized laboratories with scanning electron microscopes, energy dispersive X-ray, X-radiograph, fluorescence microscope and luminoscopy, TIC Coulometer, UV/VIS/NIr spectrophotometer, and several dedicated microscopes with digital-imaging attachments. The Quaternary studies and climate change program features seven specialized labs for research in paleoclimatology, sedimentology, paleolimnology, paleooceanography, hydrology, aqueous geochemistry, and computer applications. The structural geology, tectonics, and petrology program is bolstered by well-equipped laboratories for structural analysis, fission-track dating, elemental analysis (both ICP and graphite-furnace AAS), scanning-electron microscopy, energy-dispersive X-ray spectroscopy, X-ray diffraction analysis, liquid-ion chromatography, paleomagnetic analysis, petrography, computer analysis (HP workstation plus IBM-compatible and Macintosh PCs), rock and thin-section preparation, and mineral separation.

Financial Aid Graduate students receive financial aid in the form of teaching assistantships, research assistantships, federal fellowships, and other types of scholarships. University teaching assistantships currently provide nine-month stipends of $12,000 for M.S.-level students and $15,000 for Ph.D. students, with an exemption from all instructional and out-of-state fees. All first-year graduate assistants are awarded one month of support during their first summer to help them pursue their research. A limited number of summer-session assistantships are available. Research assistantships, fellowships, and scholarships provide twelve-month stipends with a full fee exemption and no service obligation.

Cost of Study For the spring 2004 semester, the graduate tuition per credit was $334 for an Ohio resident and $627 for a nonresident.

Living and Housing Costs Rooms in graduate residence halls are $1475 to $2455 per semester; married students' apartments may be rented for $525 to $550 per month (all utilities included). Information concerning off-campus housing may be obtained from the University Housing Office. Costs vary widely, but apartments typically rent for $450 to $550 per month.

Student Group Each year, the 16 full-time faculty members support about 30 graduate students who pursue a broad range of research interests.

Student Outcomes The University's graduates take positions in the public and private sectors and assume academic posts.

Location Kent, a city of about 28,000, is located 35 miles southeast of Cleveland and 12 miles east of Akron in a peaceful suburban setting. Kent offers the cultural advantages of a major metropolitan complex as well as the relaxed pace of semirural living. There are a number of theater and art groups at the University and in the community. Blossom Music Center, the summer home of the Cleveland Orchestra and the site of Kent State's cooperative programs in art, music, and theater, is only 15 miles from the main campus. The Akron and Cleveland art museums are also within a short distance of the campus. There is a wide variety of recreational facilities available on the campus and within the local area, including West Branch State Park and the Cuyahoga Valley National Recreation Area. Opportunities for outdoor activities such as summer sports, ice skating, swimming, and downhill and cross-country skiing abound.

The University and The Department Since its founding as a teacher-training school in 1910, Kent State has become an engine for economic, cultural, and workforce development in the region and beyond. The University also has earned acclaim for applying new knowledge to address the needs of the communities it serves and society as a whole. The atmosphere within the department is personalized and informal, with major emphasis placed on teaching and research. Close student-faculty relationships are established by participation in various field trips and several annual student-faculty social events. Since 1948, when the Department of Geology awarded its first undergraduate degree, the primary objectives of the department have been to provide students with a strong background in the broad fundamentals of geology and to prepare them for advanced study or for direct employment with industry or government.

Applying The Department of Geology welcomes applicants who possess an undergraduate degree in geology or in an allied field and who wish to pursue advanced studies. To receive full consideration for financial support, applications must be received by February 15 for September admission. Application materials include the online application form for the College of Arts and Sciences, available at http://admissions.rags.kent.edu and submitted to Kent State University's Office of Research and Graduate Studies; the departmental information form, mailed directly to the Department of Geology; scores on the Graduate Record Examinations (required of all Ph.D. applicants), sent directly to the department early in the application process; and a Statement of Goals, which is required by the Geology Graduate Studies Committee with the purpose of informing the committee of the applicant's long-range career goals.

Correspondence and Information

Department of Geology
Kent State University
221 McGilvery Hall
Lincoln and Summitt Streets
Kent, Ohio 44242

Telehone: 330-672-2680
Fax: 330-672-7949
E-mail: geology@kent.edu
World Wide Web: http://dept.kent.edu/geology/index.shtml

Kent State University

THE FACULTY AND THEIR RESEARCH

Ernest H. Carlson, Associate Professor; Ph.D., McGill, 1966. Exploration geochemistry, trace-element dispersion in ground water, soils, and stream sediments.

Rachael G. Craig, Professor; Ph.D., Penn State, 1979. Statistical methods, computer simulation, hydroclimatology, computer modeling of paleoclimates and their effects on regional hydrology and hydrogeology.

Peter S. Dahl, Professor; Ph.D., Indiana, 1977. Metamorphic geology, high-temperature geochemistry, thermobarometry, Precambrian geology of the Wyoming craton.

Yoram Eckstein, Professor; Ph.D., Hebrew, 1977. Hydrogeology, ground water modeling, solute transport, aquifer contamination studies.

Rodney M. Feldmann, Professor; Ph.D., North Dakota, 1967. Invertebrate paleontology, paleobiogeography, stratigraphy.

David B. Hacker, Assistant Professor; Ph.D., Kent State, 1998. Hydrogeology, structural geology, tectonics.

Richard A. Heimlich, Professor; Ph.D., Yale, 1959. Igneous petrology, petrogenesis and geochronology of archean rocks of Wyoming, petrology and emplacement modes of ultramafic rocks.

Daniel K. Holm, Associate Professor; Ph.D., Harvard, 1992. Structural geology, thermochronology, extensional tectonics, tectonics of the Superior craton.

Andrew L. Moore, Assistant Professor; Ph.D., Washington, 1999. Surface water hydrology, coastal processes, sediment transport.

Joseph D. Ortiz, Assistant Professor; Ph.D., Oregon State, 1995. Stable isotope geochemistry, stratigraphy, sedimentology, climatic change, marine micropaleontology, geochemistry and faunal analysis of Foraminifera.

Donald F. Palmer, Professor; Ph.D., Princeton, 1968. Engineering geophysics, water resources, geophysical methods in hydrogeology and engineering geology, magnetic stratigraphy, magnetic susceptibility, paleomagnetism, crustal structure of the eastern mid-continent.

Carrie E. Schweitzer, Assistant Professor; Ph.D., Kent State, 2000. Invertebrate paleontology, paleobiogeography, decapod phylogeny and evolution.

Abdul Shakoor, Professor; Ph.D., Purdue, 1982. Engineering geology, soil and rock mechanics, construction materials, waste management, landfill studies, waste disposal problems, geotechnical site characterization, landslide and subsidence studies.

Alison J. Smith, Professor; Ph.D., Brown, 1991. Limnology, paleolimnology, lacustrine-ground water interactions, lacustrine ostracodes as environmental and climatic indicators, micropaleontology, quaternary and holocene studies, climatic change.

Neil A. Wells, Professor; Ph.D., Michigan, 1984. Geomorphology, clastic sedimentology, sedimentary environments, vertebrates paleontology.

Donna L. Witter, Senior Research Fellow; Ph.D., Oregon State, 1995. Physical oceanography, remote sensing, ocean-atmosphere interactions.

MichiganTech
Michigan's Technological University

MICHIGAN TECHNOLOGICAL UNIVERSITY

College of Engineering
Department of Geological and Mining Engineering and Sciences
Master of Science in Applied Geophysics

Programs of Study The Department of Geological and Mining Engineering and Sciences at Michigan Tech awards the Master of Science (M.S.) in applied geophysics, with concentrations in the areas of geophysics, paleohistory, petroleum, and volcanology. Students can choose either a thesis or report option. The thesis option is typically a two-year program, and the report option is a three-year program. Both require residency every semester except summers or when conducting fieldwork. M.S. students may also pursue a course-and-research curriculum as part of the Peace Corps Master's International Program in the mitigation of natural geologic hazards. Many students go on to pursue the Ph.D. Academic work goes hand-in-hand with the types of research conducted. The department's greatest technical strength is in computational research related to remote sensing (volcanology, limnology) and data analysis and visualization (natural-hazard assessments, subsurface visualization, seismic petrophysics). Field studies are important components in traditional geological research (basin analysis, structural geology, volcanology) as well as in some of the engineering areas (subsurface remediation, groundwater hydrology, mining operations). Some areas focus heavily on laboratory experimentation (subsurface remediation, mineralogy and petrography, geochemistry, rock mechanics). Students work closely with their advisers and their peers. While much of the research is fundamental in nature, strong ties with practical applications exist for mining, hydrogeology, petroleum exploration, and volcanic hazards.

Research Facilities The department utilizes the Remote Sensing Institute (RSI), Seismic Petrophysics: Observation and Theory (SPOT), and Subsurface Visualization Laboratory (SVL). Every graduate student office is equipped with a workstation, with 2 students per office. In addition, Land and Satellite Remote Sensing is equipped with high-end workstations and Seismic Petrophysics is equipped with high-end computers for handling and visualizing large geophysical data sets. There is an Environmental Magnetism Laboratory, a shielded room containing a cryogenic magnetometer, available for student use. There are also specialized laboratories for geochemistry, environmental geochemistry, rock mechanics, sedimentology, rock and thin-section preparation, subsurface remediation and hydrogeology, X-ray diffraction, and remote sensing.

Financial Aid Financial aid is available to a limited number of qualified full-time students in the form of fellowships, research assistantships, and teaching assistantships. Aid packages include a stipend, tuition, and some student fees. The stipend for M.S. candidates is currently $4415 per semester and $5126 per semester for Ph.D. candidates. In addition, a health insurance supplement is provided by the University. Funding may be available on a competitive basis for students to travel to professional conferences.

Cost of Study Tuition for full-time graduate students (resident and nonresident) for the 2004–05 academic year is $3888 per semester ($4288 per semester for engineering and computer science majors). Participants in the Peace Corps Master's International Program and the Master in Applied Science Education Program pay $298 per credit hour. All students are responsible for a student activity fee of approximately $135 per semester. Health insurance is required for all graduate students; a supplement is subject to financial aid approval.

Living and Housing Costs Michigan Tech residence halls have accommodations for single students; applications may be obtained from the Director of Residential Services. For married students, Michigan Tech has one- and two-bedroom furnished apartments; applications may be obtained from the manager of Daniell Heights Apartments. Because the cost of housing is subject to change, representative costs cannot be stated. There is also off-campus housing available in the surrounding community. Yahoo! lists the overall cost-of-living index for Houghton as 83 (the national average is 100). Prospective students should visit the Web site at http://list.realestate.yahoo.com/realestate/neighborhood/main.html for more information.

Student Group Nearly all of the department's students are full-time and in residence. About half are domestic and half are international; traditionally, half are women. Nearly all of the students receive financial aid in the form of a research assistantship, teaching assistantship, or fellowship. The faculty seeks students who are self-motivated, broad-minded, and enthusiastic. Extra emphasis is placed on applicants with strong geological and technical backgrounds and a set of rigorous field experiences. Strong computational skills, or at least a willingness to develop them, are needed.

Student Outcomes Graduates seek employment with government agencies (volcano observatories), public outreach (national parks, the Smithsonian Institution), and petroleum-exploration mining companies. They also work for these agencies and industries in environmental and hydrogeological consulting positions.

Location Michigan Tech is located in Houghton on Michigan's scenic Keweenaw Peninsula. The Keweenaw stretches about 70 miles into Lake Superior, and the surrounding area is perfect for any outdoor activity. The campus is a 15-minute walk from downtown Houghton; public transportation is available from Houghton and Hancock. Houghton has been listed as the safest college town in Michigan and was ranked 8 out of 467 nationwide in the report, "Crime at College: Student Guide to Personal Safety." The Houghton County Memorial Airport (CMX) serves the area with direct flights to Minneapolis and Detroit via Northwest Airlink; Marquette K. I. Sawyer Airport (SAW), about a 2-hour drive from Houghton, serves the area via Detroit.

The University Michigan Tech was founded in 1885 as the Michigan Mining School to serve the nation's first major mining enterprises focused on copper and iron. Several name changes tracked the growth and diversification of the institution, and it was named Michigan Technological University in 1964. Today, the University offers a full range of associate, bachelor's, master's, and doctoral degrees in the sciences, engineering, forestry, business, communication, and technology. Michigan Tech has been rated one of the nation's "Top Ten" best buys for science and technology by *U.S. News & World Report.*

Applying Application materials may be requested from the department via the e-mail address listed in the Correspondence and Information section. Online applications are also accepted through the University's Web site at http://www.mtu.edu/apply/. Completed application materials are reviewed as they are received in the department. Required materials include the application, original transcripts, and three letters of recommendation. A form for the letters can be found at the department's Web site, also listed in the Correspondence and Information section. All applicants must take the GRE General Test, and applicants whose native language is not English must take the TOEFL. Study may begin in August, January, or June.

Correspondence and Information
John S. Gierke, Associate Professor
Department of Geological and Mining Engineering and Sciences
Michigan Technological University
1400 Townsend Drive
Houghton, Michigan 49931-1295

Telephone: 906-487-2535
Fax: 906.487.3371
E-mail: jsgierke@mtu.edu
World Wide Web: http://www.geo.mtu.edu/graduate

Michigan Technological University

THE FACULTY AND THEIR RESEARCH

Suzanne J. Beske-Diehl, Professor of Geophysics; Ph.D., Wyoming, 1977. Paleomagnetism, rock magnetism, sedimentology, geophysics.
Jimmy F. Diehl, Professor of Geophysics; Ph.D., Wyoming, 1977. Applied geophysics, paleomagnetism, tectonics.
Jacqueline E. Huntoon, Professor of Geology; Ph.D., Penn State, 1990. Sedimentology, stratigraphy, tectonics, petroleum geology, basin analysis.
Wayne D. Pennington, Professor of Geophysical Engineering; Ph.D., Wisconsin–Madison, 1979. Petroleum geophysics, well logging, seismology, induced seismicity.
William I. Rose Jr., Professor of Petrology; Ph.D., Dartmouth, 1970. Volcanology, geochemistry, remote sensing, volcano-atmosphere interactions, global change.
Roger Turpening, Research Professor of Geophysical Engineering; Ph.D., Michigan. Geophysics.
James R. Wood Jr., Professor of Geology; Ph.D., Johns Hopkins, 1972. Geochemistry, subsurface visualization, geochemical surveys for petroleum exploration, environmental geology, diagenesis, petroleum geology.
Charles T. Young, Associate Professor of Geophysical Engineering; Ph.D., Wisconsin–Madison, 1977; PE. Exploration geophysics, electrical and electromagnetic geophysics, geophysical signal analysis, ground-penetrating radar, environmental geophysics.

MICHIGAN TECHNOLOGICAL UNIVERSITY

College of Engineering
Department of Geological and Mining Engineering and Sciences
Master of Science and Ph.D. in Geology

Programs of Study

The department offers the Master of Science and Ph.D. in geology degree programs with areas of concentration in geophysics, hydrogeology, limnology, mineralogy and petrography, mining, petroleum, science teacher education, and volcanology. The master's programs feature both a thesis and report option that typically require six semesters of study, including field work or an internship. M.S. students may also pursue a course and research curriculum as part of the Peace Corps Master's International Program in the mitigation of natural geologic hazards. The Ph.D. program typically requires 12 semesters. All programs require residency every semester except summers and other semesters where field work is conducted. Academic work goes hand-in-hand with the various areas of concentration and the types of research conducted. The department's greatest technical strength is in computational research related to data analysis and visualization (natural hazards assessments, subsurface visualization, seismic petrophysics) and modeling (groundwater hydrology, subsurface remediation, rock mechanics). Field studies are important components in many of the research areas. Some areas focus heavily on laboratory experimentation (subsurface remediation, rock mechanics). Students work closely with their advisers and their peers. While much of the research is fundamental in nature, strong ties with practical applications exist for mining, hydrogeology, and petroleum exploration.

Research Facilities

The department utilizes the Remote Sensing Institute (RSI), Seismic Petrophysics: Observation and Theory (SPOT), Subsurface Visualization Laboratory (SVL), Seaman Minerals Museum, Subsurface Remediation Laboratory, and Hydreology Laboratory. As far as computational laboratories are concerned, every graduate student office is equipped with a workstation, with 2 students per office. In addition, seismic petrophysics is equipped with high-end computers for handling and visualizing large geophysical data sets, the Environmental Magnetism Laboratories, a shielded room containing a cryogenic magnetometer, and Mineralogy Laboratories, equipped with an X-ray diffractometer. There are also specialized laboratories for geochemistry, environmental geochemistry, rock mechanics, sedimentology, and rock and thin-section preparation.

Financial Aid

Financial aid is available to a limited number of qualified full-time students in the form of fellowships, research assistantships, and teaching assistantships. Aid packages include a stipend, tuition, and some student fees. The stipend for M.S. candidates is currently $4415 per semester; for Ph.D. candidates, the stipend is $5126 per semester. In addition, a health insurance supplement is provided by the University. Funding may be available on a competitive basis for students to travel to professional conferences.

Cost of Study

Tuition for full-time graduate students (resident and nonresident) for the 2004–05 academic year is $3888 per semester and $4288 per semester for engineering and computer science majors. Participants in the Peace Corps Master's International Program and the Master in Applied Science Education Program pay $298 per credit hour. All students are responsible for a student activity fee of approximately $135 per semester. Health insurance is required for all graduate students; a supplement is subject to financial aid status.

Living and Housing Costs

Michigan Tech residence halls have accommodations for single students; applications may be obtained from the Director of Residential Services. For married students, Michigan Tech has one- and two-bedroom furnished apartments; applications may be obtained from the manager of Daniell Heights Apartments. Because the cost of housing is subject to change, representative costs cannot be stated. There is also off-campus housing available in the surrounding community. Yahoo! lists the overall cost-of-living index for Houghton as 83; the national average is 100. For further information, students may visit http://list.realestate.yahoo.com/realestate/neighborhood/main.html.

Student Group

Nearly all of the students are full-time and in residence. About half of the students are domestic, half are international, and, traditionally, half are female. Nearly all of the students receive financial aid in the form of a research assistantship, teaching assistantship, or fellowship.

Student Outcomes

In addition to academia, doctoral graduates seek employment with government agencies (volcano observatories), public outreach organizations (National Parks, Smithsonian), and petroleum-exploration mining companies. Master's graduates also work for these agencies/industries and in environmental/hydrogeological consulting.

Location

Michigan Tech is located in Houghton on Michigan's scenic Keweenaw Peninsula. The Keweenaw stretches about 70 miles into Lake Superior, and the surrounding area is perfect for any outdoor activity. The campus is a 15-minute walk from downtown Houghton; public transportation is available from Houghton and Hancock. Houghton has been listed as the safest college town in Michigan and was ranked eighth out of 467 nationwide in the report *Crime at College: Student Guide to Personal Safety.* The Houghton County Memorial Airport (CMX) serves the area with direct flights to Minneapolis via Northwest Airlink; Marquette K.I. Sawyer (SAW, about a 2-hour drive from Houghton) serves the area via Detroit.

The University

Michigan Technological University (MTU) was founded in 1885 as the Michigan Mining School to serve the nation's first major mining enterprises focused on copper and iron. Several name changes tracked the growth and diversification of the institution, and it was named Michigan Technological University in 1964. Today, the University offers a full range of associate, bachelor's, master's, and doctoral degrees in the sciences, engineering, forestry, business, communication, and technology. MTU has been rated one of the nation's top ten best buys for science and technology by *U.S. News & World Report.*

Applying

The faculty members seek students who are self-motivated, broad-minded, and enthusiastic. Extra emphasis is placed on applicants with strong geological and technical backgrounds and a set of rigorous field experiences. Strong computational skills, or at least a willingness to develop them, are needed.

Application materials may be requested from the department via e-mail (address listed below); online applications are also accepted through the University Web site at http://www.mtu.edu/apply/. Completed application materials are reviewed as they are received in the department. Required materials include an application, original transcripts, and three letters of recommendation. A form for the letters can be found at the department's Web site (below). All applicants must take the GRE General Test, and applicants whose native language is not English must take the TOEFL. Study may begin in August, January, or June.

Correspondence and Information

John S. Gierke, Associate Professor
Department of Geological and Mining Engineering and Sciences
Michigan Technological University
1400 Townsend Drive
Houghton, Michigan 49931-1295

Telephone: 906-487-2535
Fax: 906-487-3371
E-mail: jsgierke@mtu.edu
World Wide Web: http://www.geo.mtu.edu/graduate

Michigan Technological University

THE FACULTY AND THEIR RESEARCH

Suzanne J. Beske-Diehl, Professor of Geophysics; Ph.D., Wyoming, 1977. Paleomagnetism, rock magnetism, sedimentology, geophysics.
Gregg J. S. Bluth, Associate Professor of Geology; Ph.D., Penn State, 1990. Earth/atmosphere interactions, remote sensing of volcanic emissions, watershed geochemistry.
Theodore J. Bornhorst, Professor of Economic and Engineering Geology; Ph.D., New Mexico, 1979; PG. Economic geology, geochemistry (mineral deposits and environmental), geology of the Lake Superior region, statistical analysis of geoscience data.
Judith Wells Budd, Research Associate Professor of Remote Sensing; Ph.D., Michigan Tech, 1997. Remote sensing of lake water quality.
Jimmy F. Diehl, Professor of Geophysics; Ph.D., Wyoming, 1977. Applied geophysics, paleomagnetism, tectonics.
John S. Gierke, Associate Professor of Geological and Environmental Engineering; Ph.D., Michigan Tech, 1990; PE. Watershed hydrology, subsurface remediation, carbon dioxide sequestration, occurrence of uranium in groundwater.
William J. Gregg, Associate Professor of Geological Engineering; Ph.D. SUNY at Albany, 1979. Structural geology, tectonics, mineral deposits, mining geology, rock slope stability.
Jacqueline E. Huntoon, Professor of Geology; Ph.D., Penn State, 1990. Sedimentology, stratigraphy, tectonics, petroleum geology, basin analysis.
Wayne D. Pennington, Professor of Geophysical Engineering and Department Chair; Ph.D., Wisconsin–Madison, 1979. Petroleum geophysics, well logging, seismology, induced seismicity.
George W. Robinson, Professor of Mineralogy and Curator of Mineral Museum; Ph.D., Queens, 1979. Mineralogy.
William I. Rose Jr., Professor of Petrology; Ph.D., Dartmouth, 1970. Volcanology, geochemistry, remote sensing, volcano/atmosphere interactions, global change.
James. W. Vallance, Research Assistant Professor of Geology; Ph.D., Michigan Tech, 1993. Volcanic debris flows.
Matthew Watson, Research Assistant Professor; Ph.D., Cambridge, 2000. Using satellite data to retrieve information about the gases and particles produced by volcanoes, the importance of volcanic gases during explosive eruptions.
James R. Wood Jr., Professor of Geology; Ph.D., Johns Hopkins, 1972. Geochemistry, subsurface visualization, geochemical surveys for petroleum exploration, environmental geology, diagenesis, petroleum geology.
Albert S. Wylie, Research Assistant Professor of Geology; Ph.D., Michigan Tech, 2000. Sedimentology, subsurface visualization.

NORTH CAROLINA STATE UNIVERSITY

Department of Marine, Earth and Atmospheric Sciences

Programs of Study

The department offers M.S. and Ph.D. degrees with majors in oceanography, meteorology, and geology.

In oceanography, students specialize in biological, chemical, geological, or physical oceanography. In the biological area, research topics are in benthic, plankton, or invertebrate physiological ecology. Research in the chemical area concentrates on the study of organic and inorganic processes in estuarine, coastal, and deep-sea environments. Emphasis in geological oceanography is in sedimentology and micropaleontology. In physical oceanography, research topics include the study of the dynamics of estuarine, shelf-slope, and deep-sea waters.

In meteorology, research topics exist in modeling and parameterizing the planetary atmospheric boundary layer, in physically and theoretically modeling dispersion over complex terrain, in air-sea interaction, in atmospheric chemistry, and in climate dynamics. Other research areas are those of cloud-aerosol interaction, cloud chemistry and acid rain deposition, plant-atmosphere interaction, severe localized storm systems, and mesoscale phenomena and processes related to East Coast fronts and cyclones.

In earth science, research topics are in the areas of hard-rock and soft-rock geology, hydrogeology, tectonics, sedimentary geochemistry, and paleoecology. In hard-rock geology the emphasis is on igneous and metamorphic petrology. Soft-rock studies span both recent and ancient detrital deposits, including economic deposits, with field-based studies of facies relationships and associated depositional environments.

The M.S. degree program requires 30 semester credit hours of course work, a research thesis, and a final oral examination. A nonthesis option is available to students on leave from government or industry. The Ph.D. program requires at least 54 credit hours beyond the M.S. degree, as well as a thesis, preliminary written and oral examinations, and a dissertation defense.

Research Facilities

Jordan Hall, the department's home, is a modern structure dedicated to research in natural resources which has been specially designed to accommodate department research laboratories. Modern facilities currently exist in all program areas. Students have access to the million-volume D. H. Hill Library and the University Computing Center resources, which link the department to local, national, and international networks. The department operates a facility for ocean/atmosphere modeling and visualization; Nextlab, with seventeen networked Sun SPARCstations; and a general computer facility with twelve networked Sun SPARCstations. Other specialized departmental equipment includes a Quorum Communications HRTP satellite receiver, a Finnigan MAT 251 Ratio Mass Spectrometer, a McIDAS workstation, an electron microprobe, an X-ray diffractometer, and an atomic absorption spectrometer. Elsewhere on campus, students have access to electron microscopes, ion microprobes, and a nuclear reactor for neutron activation analyses. The department is a member of the Duke/UNC consortium, which operates the 131-foot R/V *Cape Hatteras,* a vessel used for both educational and research cruises. The department participates in the operation of the Center for Marine Science and Technology, a coastal facility in Morehead City, North Carolina. The department is a member of the University Corporation for Atmospheric Research, which provides access to the computing and observational systems of the National Center for Atmospheric Research.

Financial Aid

A number of teaching and research assistantships are available on a competitive basis. The stipends for 2004–05, for 20 hours of service per week, are $1555 per month on a nine-month basis for teaching assistants and a twelve-month basis for research assistants. Students on assistantships receive paid health insurance and have tuition waived; they are responsible only for in-state fees of $512 per semester.

Cost of Study

Tuition and fees for 2004–05 for a full course load of 9 or more credits are $2035 per semester for in-state students and $8094 per semester for out-of-state students. U.S. citizens may be able to establish North Carolina residence after one year and then be eligible for in-state tuition rates.

Living and Housing Costs

The University has graduate dormitory rooms that cost about $1700 per semester. Married student housing is available at King Village for about $500 per month for a one-bedroom apartment. Off-campus housing is available starting at about $600 per month.

Student Group

University enrollment is approximately 27,200, with an undergraduate enrollment of 18,700, a graduate enrollment of 4,400, and a continuing-education enrollment of 4,100. The department has approximately 225 undergraduate majors and 100 graduate students, with 25 in marine science, 25 in earth science, and 50 in atmospheric science. Presently, 22 of the graduate students are women.

Location

Raleigh, a modern growing city with a population of more than 200,000 in a metropolitan area of more than 1 million, is situated in rolling terrain in the eastern Piedmont near the upper Coastal Plain. Raleigh, the state capital, is one vertex of the Research Triangle area, with Durham and Chapel Hill the other vertices. Numerous colleges and industrial and government laboratories are located in the Triangle area, which each year also attracts some of the world's foremost symphony orchestras and ballet companies. Located within a 3-hour drive of the campus are both the seashore and the mountains, which offer many opportunities for skiing, hiking, swimming, boating, and fishing.

The University

North Carolina State University, the state's land-grant and chief technological institution, recently celebrated its centennial year. A graduate faculty of 1,400 and more than 100 major buildings are located on the 623-acre main campus. The 780-acre Centennial Campus, which has just been acquired adjacent to the main campus, ensures room for future expansion. The University is organized into nine colleges plus the Graduate School. The department is one of six in the College of Physical and Mathematical Sciences.

Applying

For fall admission, the completed application form, transcripts, recommendation forms, GRE scores, and TOEFL scores (for international students) should be received no later than March 1 to ensure full consideration for assistantship support. Applications for summer and spring admission are also considered, but assistantship support is less likely.

Correspondence and Information

Graduate Administrator
Department of Marine, Earth and Atmospheric Sciences
North Carolina State University
Box 8208
Raleigh, North Carolina 27695-8208
Telephone: 919-515-7837
E-mail: janowitz@ncsu.edu
World Wide Web: http://www.meas.ncsu.edu/

North Carolina State University

THE FACULTY AND THEIR RESEARCH

Viney Aneja, Professor; Ph.D., North Carolina State, 1977. Atmospheric chemistry.
S. Pal Arya, Professor; Ph.D., Colorado State, 1968. Micrometeorology, atmospheric turbulence and diffusion, air-sea interaction.
Neal E. Blair, Professor; Ph.D., Stanford, 1980. Chemical oceanography, biogeochemistry, organic geochemistry.
Roscoe R. Braham, Scholar in Residence; Ph.D., Chicago, 1951. Cloud physics, thunderstorms, weather modification.
Victor V. Cavaroc, Emeritus Professor; Ph.D., LSU, 1969. Sedimentary petrology/petrography, lithostratigraphy, coal stratigraphy.
Julia Clark, Assistant Professor; Ph.D., Yale, 2002. Paleoecology, theropod relationships.
Tony F. Clark, Research Professor; Ph.D., North Carolina at Chapel Hill, 1974. Geophysical oceanography.
Cynthia Cudaback, Assistant Professor; Ph.D., Washington (Seattle), 1998. Physical oceanography of coastal and estuarine systems.
Jerry M. Davis, Professor; Ph.D., Ohio State, 1971. Agricultural meteorology, climatology, statistical meteorology, planetary boundary layer.
David J. DeMaster, Professor; Ph.D., Yale, 1979. Marine geochemistry and radio chemistry in the nearshore and deep-sea environments.
David B. Eggleston, Associate Professor; Ph.D., William and Mary, 1991. Marine benthic ecology, epifauna.
Ronald V. Fodor, Professor; Ph.D., New Mexico, 1972. Igneous petrology, volcanoes, meteorites.
John C. Fountain, Professor and Head; Ph.D., California, Santa Barbara, 1975. Geochemistry, contaminant hydrogeology.
David P. Genereux, Associate Professor; Ph.D., MIT, 1991. Hydrogeology.
James Hibbard, Professor; Ph.D., Cornell, 1988. Structural geology.
Thomas S. Hopkins, Emeritus Research Professor; Ph.D., Washington (Seattle), 1971. Physical oceanography.
Gerald S. Janowitz, Professor and Graduate Administrator; Ph.D., Johns Hopkins, 1967. Geophysical fluid mechanics, continental shelf and ocean circulation.
Daniel L. Kamykowski, Professor; Ph.D., California, San Diego, 1973. Effects of physical factors on phytoplankton behavior and physiology, global plant nutrient distributions.
Michael Kaplan, Research Associate Professor; Ph.D., Rutgers, 1972. Modeling and numerical weather prediction.
Michael M. Kimberley, Associate Professor; Ph.D., Princeton, 1974. Sedimentary geochemistry, sedimentary ore deposits, chemistry of natural and polluted water.
Charles E. Knowles, Associate Professor; Ph.D., Texas A&M, 1970. Estuarine and coastal processes, surface gravity wave measurements.
Gary M. Lackmann, Assistant Professor; Ph.D., SUNY at Albany, 1995. Synoptic and mesoscale meteorology.
Elana L. Leithold, Associate Professor; Ph.D., Washington (Seattle), 1987. Nearshore and shelf sedimentation and stratigraphy, sediment transport.
Yuh Lang Lin, Professor; Ph.D., Yale, 1984. Modeling of mesoscale atmospheric dynamics.
Jingpu Liu, Assistant Professor; Ph.D., William and Mary, 2001. Geological oceanography and geomorphology.
Thomas F. Malone, University Distinguished Scholar; Sc.D., MIT, 1946. Meteorology.
John M. Morrison, Professor; Ph.D., Texas A&M, 1977. Descriptive physical oceanography, general ocean circulation, air-sea interaction and climatic problems.
Devdutta Niyogi, Research Assistant Professor; Ph.D., North Carolina State, 2000. Land-atmosphere interactions, hydrometeorology, meteorological instrumentation, terrestrial ecosystem processes, applied climatology.
Leonard J. Pietrafesa, Professor; Ph.D., Washington (Seattle), 1973. Estuarine and continental margin physical processes, seismology.
Sethu S. Raman, Professor; Ph.D., Colorado State, 1972. Air-sea interactions, boundary layer meteorology and air pollution.
Henry G. Reichle Jr., Research Professor; Ph.D., Michigan, 1969. Air pollution detection by satellite.
Allen J. Riordan, Associate Professor; Ph.D., Wisconsin, 1977. Satellite meteorology, Antarctic meteorology.
Dale A. Russell, Emeritus Research Professor; Ph.D., Columbia, 1964. Dinosaurian ecology.
Vin K. Saxena, Professor; Ph.D., Rajasthan, 1969. Cloud physics, acid precipitation, weather modification.
Mary Schweitzer, Assistant Professor; Ph.D., Montana State, 1995. Vertebrate paleontology.
Frederick Semazzi, Professor; Ph.D., Nairobi, 1983. Climate dynamics.
Ping Tung Shaw, Associate Professor; Ph.D., Woods Hole/MIT, 1982. Shelf-slope physical oceanography and Lagrangian analysis.
William J. Showers, Associate Professor; Ph.D., Hawaii, 1982. Stable-isotope geochemistry, paleoceanography, micropaleontology, environmental monitoring, geoarchaeology.
Edward F. Stoddard, Associate Professor; Ph.D., UCLA, 1976. Metamorphic petrology, silicate mineralogy, Piedmont geology.
Carrie Thomas, Visiting Assistant Professor; Ph.D., North Carolina State, 1998. Biogeochemistry, animal-sediment interaction.
Donna L. Wolcott, Associate Professor; Ph.D., Berkeley, 1972. Physiological ecology of terrestrial crabs.
Thomas G. Wolcott, Professor; Ph.D., Berkeley, 1971. Physiological ecology of marine invertebrates, biotelemetry.
Lian Xie, Associate Professor; Ph.D., Miami (Florida), 1992. Air-sea interaction processes.
Yang Zhang, Assistant Professor; Ph.D., Iowa, 1994. Air quality modeling.

Jordan Hall, home of the department.

PENNSYLVANIA STATE UNIVERSITY

Department of Geosciences

Programs of Study

The Department of Geosciences offers M.S. and Ph.D. degree programs. A wide range of faculty interests (see reverse side of page) and exceptional laboratory and other support facilities provide an extensive variety of areas of specialization in which students may choose their course work and research topics. These areas include Earth System Science (an interdepartmental program directed toward a global, multidisciplinary view of the Earth and its variability), Petroleum GeoSystems (a team-based M.S. initiative), the Biogeochemical Research Initiative for Education (BRIE, an NSF-sponsored graduate program in microbial biogeochemistry), and Astrobiology (an interdisciplinary program in the origin and evolution of life in the universe).

Research Facilities

The department maintains a variety of unsurpassed modern facilities and equipment for research, including an extensive computer network. Students have access to laboratories for research on the petrography and petrology of igneous, metamorphic, and sedimentary rocks, including organic sediments; rock preparation and rock mechanics laboratories; high-temperature and high-pressure/high-temperature equipment for dry or hydrothermal experiments; mass spectrometers and ancillary equipment for isotope analysis; a seismic observatory and field equipment for seismic, electrical, magnetic, and gravity surveys; facilities and data for remote sensing of earth resources; laboratories and field facilities for the study of the hydrogeology and geochemistry of natural waters. The department and the Materials Characterization Laboratories are equipped for both classical methods of chemical analysis and modern instrumental methods, such as atomic absorption, emission, and absorption spectroscopy; electron microscopy and scanning transmission electron microscopy; automated X-ray diffractometry; ICP-MS; and ion microprobe and automated electron microprobe analysis. The department has excellent collections of rocks, minerals, and ore samples; and paleontological collections. More than 50,000 volumes related to earth sciences are housed in the library of the College of Earth and Mineral Sciences. A nuclear reactor is available on campus.

Financial Aid

All of the department's on-campus graduate students receive support from assistantships, fellowships, or traineeships. Half-time teaching or research assistantships of $6457.50 per semester, plus full tuition and medical coverage, were available to qualified applicants in 2003–04. One-quarter-time and three-quarter-time assistantships are awarded in special cases. Research assistantships generally involve the study of problems appropriate for thesis research. Financial support for thesis research unsupported by grants is available through a special fund.

Cost of Study

For 2003–04, the self-supporting Pennsylvania resident paid $5005 in tuition per semester; nonresidents paid $9915 per semester.

Living and Housing Costs

The University offers housing to graduate students and their families at several locations across the campus. One- to four-bedroom apartments are available at monthly rates that range from $515 to $905. University meals plans are available at $1380 to $1745 per semester. Privately owned housing can be found within walking distance of the campus.

Student Group

In the department there are approximately 90 graduate students. The student enrollment at the main University Park campus is about 41,500 undergraduate and 6,300 graduate students.

Location

The University Park campus of Pennsylvania State University is in the town of State College—a metropolitan area of about 100,000 people in the center of the commonwealth. Located in a rural and scenic part of the Appalachian Mountains, the area is only 3 to 4 hours away from Washington, D.C., Pittsburgh, and Philadelphia. Varied cultural, educational, and athletic activities are available throughout the year.

The University and The Department

Founded in 1855, Penn State is the land-grant university of Pennsylvania. The University Park campus has 258 major buildings on 4,786 acres, of which 540 acres constitute the beautifully landscaped central campus. The College of Earth and Mineral Sciences, of which the department is a part, has approximately 130 faculty members and 450 graduate students in the earth sciences and closely related fields in the Departments of Geography, Energy and GeoEnvironmental Engineering, Materials Science and Engineering, Meteorology and Energy, and Environmental and Mineral Economics. The College occupies several buildings throughout the campus, with the Department of Geosciences housed primarily in the Deike Building. Facilities for graduate student research are available within the department and in the Materials Characterization Labs, the Energy and Fuels Research Center, the Materials Research Lab, and the Earth System Science Center. The size of the faculty promotes close personal relationships between faculty and students. Each faculty member works with a research group averaging 2–4 students. In cooperation with a faculty adviser and committee, each student designs and pursues a course and research program tailored to his or her individual interests and needs.

Applying

The University offers two 15-week semesters and two 6-week summer sessions beginning approximately September 2, January 13, May 19, and June 30, respectively. Candidates may apply for admission in either fall or spring. Applications must be received by July for admission to the fall semester; if financial support is required, applications must be received by January 15. All correspondence regarding admission and financial aid should be sent to the address given below.

Correspondence and Information

Associate Head for the Geosciences Graduate Program
303 Deike Building
Pennsylvania State University
University Park, Pennsylvania 16802

Telephone: 814-865-7394
Fax: 814-863-7823
E-mail: admissions@geosc.psu.edu
World Wide Web: http://www.geosc.psu.edu

Pennsylvania State University

THE FACULTY AND THEIR RESEARCH

R. B. Alley, Evan Pugh Professor; Ph.D., Wisconsin–Madison, 1987. Glaciology, climate change, ice-sheet stability, ice-core paleoclimatology, glacial erosion.
C. J. Ammon, Associate Professor; Ph.D., Penn State, 1991. Earthquake seismology, continental evolution, inverse theory.
S. Anandakrishnan, Associate Professor; Ph.D., Wisconsin-Madison, 1990. Glaciology, reflection seismology, geophysics.
M. A. Arthur, Professor; Ph.D., Princeton, 1979. Marine geology, stable isotope geochemistry, sedimentary geochemistry, paleoceanography.
E. J. Barron, Distinguished Professor of Geosciences and Dean, College of Earth and Mineral Sciences; Ph.D., Miami (Florida), 1980. Earth system science, paleoclimatology.
T. J. Bralower, Professor and Head of Department; Ph.D., California, San Diego, 1986. Micropaleontology, paleoceanography, marine geology, paleobiology, stratigraphy.
S. L. Brantley, Professor of Geosciences and Director of Environment Institute; Ph.D., Princeton, 1987. Aqueous geochemistry, geochemical kinetics, microbial geomicrobiology.
R. J. Cuffey, Professor of Paleontology; Ph.D., Indiana, 1966. Paleontology, evolution, systematics, paleoecology, bryozoans, reefs.
D. H. Eggler, Professor of Petrology; Ph.D., Colorado, 1967. Experimental mineralogy and petrology of the upper mantle.
T. Engelder, Professor; Ph.D., Texas A&M, 1973. Rock mechanics, structural geology.
D. M. Fisher, Professor; Ph.D., Brown, 1988. Regional tectonics, structural geology.
P. B. Flemings, Professor; Ph.D., Cornell, 1990. Stratigraphy, marine geology, crustal fluid flow, slope stability, petroleum geology.
K. H. Freeman, Professor; Ph.D., Indiana, 1991. Organic geochemistry, isotopic biogeochemistry.
K. P. Furlong, Professor; Ph.D., Utah, 1981. Lithospheric geodynamics, active tectonics, thermal-tectonic evolution of continental crust, fault zone processes, numerical modeling.
T. Furman, Associate Professor and Associate Head of Undergraduate Programs; Ph.D., MIT, 1989. Mantle geochemistry, igneous petrogenesis, volcanology, geoscience education.
P. J. Heaney, Associate Professor; Ph.D., Johns Hopkins, 1989. Mineral and materials sciences, crystallography.
C. H. House, Assistant Professor; Ph.D., UCLA, 1999. Microbial geobiology, astrobiology, genomics, microbial cultivation and biogeochemistry.
J. F. Kasting, Distinguished Professor of Geosciences; Ph.D., Michigan, 1979. Atmospheric evolution, planetary atmospheres, paleoclimates.
K. Keller, Assistant Professor; Ph.D., Princeton, 2000. Oceanography, global carbon cycle, economic analysis of climate policy.
E. Kirby, Assistant Professor of Geosciences; Ph.D., MIT, 2000. Tectonic geomorphology, active tectonics, surface processes and landform evolution.
J. D. Kubicki, Assistant Professor; Ph.D., Yale, 1990. Theoretical geochemistry, environmental geochemistry.
L. R. Kump, Professor; Ph.D., South Florida, 1986. Biogeochemical cycles, low-temperature sedimentary geochemistry, evolution of oceans, atmosphere, and climate.
C. J. Marone, Professor; Ph.D., Columbia, 1988. Experimental geophysics, earthquake physics, rock mechanics, friction constitutive laws, granular mechanics.
R. G. Najjar, Associate Professor; Ph.D., Princeton, 1990. Marine biogeochemistry, air-sea gas exchange, oceans and climate.
A. A. Nyblade, Associate Professor; Ph.D., Michigan, 1992. Applied seismology, tectonics, heat flow, environmental geophysics.
H. Ohmoto, Professor of Geochemistry and Director, Astrobiology Research Center; Ph.D., Princeton, 1969. Astrobiology, stable isotopes, ore deposits.
R. R. Parizek, Professor of Geology and GeoEnvironmental Engineering; Ph.D., Illinois, 1961. Groundwater, glacial, and environmental geology.
M. E. Patzkowsky, Associate Professor; Ph.D., Chicago, 1992. Invertebrate paleontology, stratigraphy, paleoecology, geobiology.
E. B. Richardson, Assistant Professor; Ph.D., MIT, 2002. Earthquake seismology, tectonics.
R. L. Slingerland, Professor; Ph.D., Penn State, 1977. Sedimentology, earth surface processes.
B. Voight, Professor of Geology and Geological Engineering; Ph.D., Columbia, 1964. Volcanology, engineering geology.
P. Wilf, Assistant Professor; Ph.D., Pennsylvania, 1998. Paleobotany, paleoclimatology, effects of past global change on terrestrial ecosystems.

Emeriti

S. S. Alexander, Professor of Geophysics; Ph.D., Caltech, 1963. Seismology, time-series analysis, remote sensing, environmental geophysics.
H. L. Barnes, Distinguished Professor of Geochemistry; Ph.D., Columbia, 1958. Hydrothermal processes, ore deposits, geothermal systems.
C. W. Burnham, Professor of Geochemistry; Ph.D., Caltech, 1955. Experimental petrology, geochemistry of ore deposits.
A. Davis, Professor of Geology; Ph.D., Durham (England), 1965. Organic geology, coal petrology, paleogeology of coal deposits.
P. Deines, Professor of Geochemistry and Associate Head of Graduate Programs; Ph.D., Penn State, 1967. Isotope geochemistry.
D. P. Gold, Professor of Geology; Ph.D., McGill, 1963. Petrology, structural geology, remote sensing, economic geology.
E. K. Graham, Professor of Geophysics; Ph.D., Penn State, 1969. Experimental solid-state geophysics, planetary models.
R. J. Greenfield, Professor of Geophysics; Ph.D., MIT, 1965. Magnetic and electrical fields, seismology.
A. L. Guber, Professor of Geology; Ph.D., Illinois, 1962. Paleozoology, evolution, paleoecology.
B. F. Howell Jr., Professor of Geophysics and Associate Dean of the Graduate School; Ph.D., Caltech, 1949. Seismology, tectonics.
D. M. Kerrick, Professor; Ph.D., Berkeley, 1968. Metamorphic and igneous petrogenesis, fluids in the earth, role of Earth degassing in global geochemical cycles.
P. M. Lavin, Professor of Geophysics; Ph.D., Penn State, 1962. Gravity and magnetic surveying, crustal tectonics.
A. W. Rose, Professor of Geochemistry; Ph.D., Caltech, 1958. Geochemical exploration, ore deposits, environmental geochemistry.
R. F. Schmalz, Professor of Geology; Ph.D., Harvard, 1959. Oceanography, chemistry of sedimentation.
R. Scholten, Professor of Petroleum Geology; Ph.D., Michigan, 1950. Tectonics, Rocky Mountain geology, habitat of oil.
W. Spackman, Professor of Paleobotany; Ph.D., Harvard, 1949. Paleobotany, coal petrology, modern organic sediments.
C. P. Thornton, Professor of Petrology; Ph.D., Yale, 1953. Volcanology, igneous petrology.
A. Traverse, Professor of Palynology; Ph.D., Harvard, 1951. Palynology of Paleozoic-Recent sediments.
W. B. White, Professor of Geochemistry; Ph.D., Penn State, 1962. Chemical hydrogeology, mineral physics, crystal chemistry.
E. G. Williams, Professor of Geology; Ph.D., Penn State, 1957. Carboniferous stratigraphy, sedimentation.
L. A. Wright, Professor of Geology; Ph.D., Caltech, 1951. Industrial minerals, Great Basin geology, tectonics.

The Deike Building, which houses the Department of Geosciences.

Pennsylvania State University

SELECTED PUBLICATIONS

Alley, R. B., et al. Abrupt climate change. *Science* 299: 2005–10, 2003.

Alley, R. B., et al. Stabilizing feedbacks in glacier bed erosion. *Nature* 424(6950):758–60, 2003.

Alley, R. B., and R. A. Bindschalder. The West Antarctic Ice Sheet and sea-level change. In *The West Antarctic Ice Sheet: Behavior and Environment/AGU Antarctic Res. Ser.,* eds. **R. B. Alley** and R. Bindschalder, 77:1–11, 2001.

Alley, R. B. *The Two-Mile Time Machine: Ice Cores, Abrupt Climate Change, and Our Future.* Princeton, NJ: Princeton Press, 2000.

Mokhtar, T., **C. J. Ammon,** and R. B. Herrmann. Seismic wave propagation and the lithosphere structure beneath the Arabian Plate. *Pure Appl. Geophys.* 158:1425–44, 2001.

Maceira, M., **C. J. Ammon,** and R. B. Herrmann. Faulting parameters of the September 25, 1998 Pymatuning, Pennsylvania earthquake. *Seismol. Res. Lett.* 71:714–24, 2000.

Velasco, A. A., **C. J. Ammon,** and S. Beck. Broadband source modeling of the November 8, 1997 Tibet (Mw = 7.5) earthquake and its tectonic implications. *J. Geophys. Res.* 105:28065–80, 2000.

Anandakrishnan, S., D. E. Voigt, **R. B. Alley,** and M. A. King, Ice stream D flow speed is strongly modulated by the tide beneath the Ross Ice Shelf. *Geophys. Res. Lett.* 30(7):13-1–4, 2003.

Anandakrishnan, S. Dilatant till layer near the onset of streaming flow of ice stream C, determined by AVO analysis. *Ann. Glaciol.* 36:283–6, 2003.

Anandakrishnan, S., D. D. Blankenship, **R. B. Alley,** and P. L. Stoffa. Influence of subglacial geology on the position of a West Antarctica ice stream from seismic measurements. *Nature* 394:62–5, 1998.

Anandakrishnan, S., and **R. B. Alley.** Tidal forcing of basal seismicity of ice stream C, West Antarctica seen far inland. *J. Geophys. Res.* 102(B7):15183–15196, 1997.

Pagani, M., **M. A. Arthur,** and **K. H. Freeman.** Variations in Miocene phytoplankton growth rates in the southwest Atlantic: Evidence for changes in ocean circulation. *Paleoceanography* 15:476–86, 2000.

Suits, N. S., and **M. A. Arthur.** Sulfur diagenesis and partitioning in Holocene Peru shelf and upper slope sediments. *Chem. Geol.* 163:219–34, 2000.

Arthur, M. A. Volcanic contributions to the carbon and sulfur geochemical cycles and global change. In *Encyclopedia of Volcanism,* pp. 1045–56, eds. H. Sigurdsson et al. Academic Press, 1999.

Chen, M., D. Pollard, and **E. J. Barron.** Comparison of future climate change over North America simulated by two regional models *J. Geophys. Res.* 108(ACL 3):1–19, 2003.

Pollard, D., and **E. J. Barron.** Causes of model discrepancies in European climate during oxygen isotope stage 3 with insights from the last glacial maximum. *Quaternary Res.* 59:108–13, 2003.

Barron, E. J., and D. Pollard. High-resolution climate simulations of oxygen isotope stage 3 in Europe. *Quaternary Res.* 58:296–309, 2002.

Thomas D. J., **T. J. Bralower,** and C. E. Jones. Neodymium isotopic reconstruction of Late Paleocene-Early Eocene thermohaline circulation. *Earth Planet. Sci. Lett.* 209:309–22, 2003.

Bralower, T. J. Evidence for surface water oligotrophy during the Paleocene-Eocene Thermal Maximum: Nannofossil assemblage data from Ocean Drilling Program Site 690, Maud Rise, Weddell Sea. *Paleoceanography* 17(2):13-1 to 13-13, 2002.

Bralower, T. J., et al. New evidence for abrupt climate change in the Cretaceous and Paleogene: An ocean drilling program expedition to Shatsky Rise, northwest Pacific. *GSA Today* 12(11):4–10, 2002.

Leckie, R. M., **T. J. Bralower,** and R. Cashman. Oceanic anoxic events and plankton evolution: Biotic response to tectonic forcing during the mid-Cretaceous. *Paoleoceanography* 17(4), 2002.

Kalinowski, B. E., L. J. Liermann, S. Givens, and **S. L. Brantley.** Rates of bacteria-promoted solubilization of Fe from minerals: A review of problems and approaches. *Chem. Geol.* 169:357–70, 2002.

Liermann, L. J., B. E. Kalinowski, **S. L. Brantley,** and J. G. Ferry. Role of bacterial siderophores in dissolution of hornblende. *Geochim. Cosmochim. Acta* 64(4):587–602, 2000.

Tang, S., and **R. J. Cuffey.** *Inconobotopora lichenoporoides,* a new genus and species of cystoporate bryozoan from the Silurian of Gotland, and its evolutionary implications. *J. Paleontol.* 72:256–64, 1998.

Cuffey, R. J. Prasopora-bearing event beds in the Coburn Limestone (Bryozoa; Ordovician; Pennsylvania). In *Paleontological Events: Stratigraphic, Ecological, and Evolutionary Implications,* pp. 110–30, eds. C. E. Brett and G. C. Baird. New York: Columbia University Press, 1997.

Ayers, J. C., and **D. H. Eggler.** Partitioning of elements between silicate melt and H_2O-NaCl fluids at 1.5 and 2.0 Gpa pressure: Implications for mantle metasomatism. *Geochim. Cosmochim. Acta* 59:4237–46, 1995.

Eggler, D. H., and J. P. Lorand. Mantle sulfide geobarometry. *Geochim. Cosmochim. Acta* 57:2213–22, 1993.

Scanlin, M. A., and T. Engelder. The basement versus the no-basement hypothesis for folding within the Appalachian Plateau Detachment Sheet. *Am. J. Sci.* 303:519–63, 2003.

Silliphant, L. J., **T. Engelder,** and M. R. Gross. The state of stress in the limb of the Split Mountain Anticline, Utah: Constraints placed by transected joints. *J. Struct. Geol.* 24:155–72, 2002.

Engelder, T., and D. Peacock. Joint development normal to regional compression during flexural-slow folding: The Lilstock buttress anticline, Somerset, England. *J. Struct. Geol.* 23:259–77, 2001.

McConaughy, D. T., and **T. Engelder.** Joint interaction with embedded concretions: Joint loading configurations inferred from propagation paths. *J. Struct. Geol.* 21:1637–52, 1999.

Marshall, J. S., **D. Fisher,** and T. W. Gardner. Central Costa Rica deformed belt: Kinematics of diffuse faulting across the western Panama block. *Tectonics,* in press.

Beam, E., and **D. Fisher.** An estimate of kinematic vorticity from rotated elongate porphyroblasts. *J. Struct. Geol.* 21:1553–60, 1999.

Fisher, D., et al. The effect of subducting seafloor roughness on fore-arc kinematics, Pacific coast, Costa Rica. *Geology* 26:467–70, 1998.

Flemings, P. B., X. Liu, and W. Winters. Critical pressure and multiphase flow in Blake Ridge gas hydrates. *Geology* 31(12):1057–60, 2003.

Flemings, P. B., B. B. Stump, T. Finkbeiner, and M. Zoback. Flow Focusing in overpressured sandstones: Theory, observations, and applications. *Am. J. Sci.* 302:827–55, 2002.

Dugan, B., and **P. B. Flemings.** Overpressure and fluid flow in the New Jersey continental slope: Implications for slope failure and cold seeps. *Science* 289:288–91, 2000.

Dias R. F., **K. H. Freeman,** and S. G. Franks. Gas chromatography-pyrolysis-isotope ratio mass spectrometry: A new method for investigating intramolecular isotopic variation in low molecular weight organic acids. *Org. Geochem.* 33:161–8, 2002.

Freeman, K. H. Isotopic biogeochemistry of marine carbon. In *Stable Isotope Geochemistry,* eds. J. W. Valley and D. R. Cole. *Rev. Mineral. Geochem.* 43:579–605, 2001.

Furlong, K. P., and S. Y. Schwartz. Influence of the Mendocino triple junction on the tectonics of coastal California. *Ann. Rev. Earth Planet. Sci.,* in press.

Malservisi, R., **K. P. Furlong,** and H. Anderson. Dynamic uplift in a transpressional regime; numerical model of the subduction area of Fiordland, New Zealand. *Earth Planet. Sci. Lett.* 206(3–4): 349–64, 2003.

Gans, C. R., **K. P. Furlong,** and R. Malservisi. Fault creep and microseismicity on the Hayward fault, California; Implications for asperity size. *Geophys. Res. Lett.* 30, doi:10.1029/2003GL017904, 2003.

Furlong, K. P., et al. The Mendocino crustal conveyor: Making and breaking the California crust. *Int. Geol. Rev.* 45, 2003.

Furman, T., J. G. Bryce, J. Karson, and A. Iotti. Geochemistry of Quaternary mafic lavas from Turkana, Kenya: Evidence for a common asthenospheric source beneath the East African Rift System. *J. Petrology,* in press.

Furman, T., and H. Gittings. Eocene basalt volcanism in central Virginia: Implications for Cenozoic tectonism. *Southeastern Geology,* in press.

Maguire P. H., et al. **(T. Furman).** Geophysical project in Ethiopia studies continental breakup. *EOS* 84:337–43, 2003.

Bartels K. S., and **T. Furman.** Effect of sonic and ultrasonic frequencies on crystallization of basalt. *Am. Mineral.* 87:217–26, 2002.

Gold, D. P., R. R. Parizek, S. S. Alexander, and E. J. Walters. Development of a strategy for groundwater control and to preserve the Temple-Town of Hierakonpolis: Egyptology at the dawn of the twenty-first century. In *Proceedings of the 8th International Congress of Egyptologists (ICA), Cairo, Egypt, March 2000,* vol. 3, Language Conservation Museology, pp. 196–203, eds. Z. Hawass and L. P. Brock. Cairo: The American University in Cairo Press, 2003.

Heaney, P. J., and **D. M. Fisher.** A new interpretation of the origin of tiger's-eye. *Geology* 31:323–6, 2003.

De, S., **P. J. Heaney,** E. P. Vicenzi, and J. Wang. Chemical heterogeneity in carbonado, an enigmatic polycrystalline diamond. *Earth Planet. Sci. Lett.* 185:315–30, 2001.

Heaney, P. J., and J. E. Post. Evidence for an *I2/a* to *Imab* phase transition in the silica polymorph moganite at ~570 K. *Am. Mineral.* 86:1358–66, 2001.

House, C. H., B. Runnegar, and S. T. Fitz-Gibbon. Geobiological analysis using whole genome-based tree building applied to the bacteri, archaea, and eukarya. *Geobiology* 1:15–26, 2003.

Orphan, V. J., **C. H. House** et al. Multiple archaeal groups mediate methane oxidation in anoxic cold seep sediments. *Proc. Natl. Acad. Sci.* 99:7663–8, 2002.

Pennsylvania State University

Selected Publications (continued)

Orphan, V. J., and **C. H. House** et al. Methane-consuming Archaea revealed by directly coupled isotopic and phylogenetic analysis. *Science* 293:484–7, 2001.

Ono, S., et al. **(J. F. Kasting** and **K. H. Freeman).** Sulfur isotopic constraints on the Archean atmosphere and ocean. *Earth Planet. Sci. Lett.* 213:5–30, 2003.

Pavlov, A. A., and **J. F. Kasting.** Mass-independent fractionation of sulfur isotopes in Archean sediments: Strong evidence for an anoxic Archean atmosphere. *Astrobiology* 2:27–41, 2002.

Kasting, J. F., and J. L. Siefert. Life and the evolution of Earth's atmosphere (Perspective). *Science* 296:1066–8, 2002.

Pavlov, A. A., L. L. Brown, and **J. F. Kasting.** Shielding of NH_3 and O_2 by organic hazes in the Archean atmosphere. *J. Geophys. Res.* 106(23):267–87, 2001.

Pavlov, A. A., **J. F. Kasting,** J. L. Eigenbrode, and **K. H. Freeman.** Hydrocarbon aerosols as a source of low-^{13}C kerogens in Archean sediments. *Geology* 29:1003–6, 2001.

K. Keller, R. Slater, M. Bender, and R. Key. Decadal scale trends in North Pacific nutrient and oxygen concentrations: Biological or physical explanation? *Deep-Sea Res.* 49:345–62, 2002.

N. Gruber, **K. Keller,** and R. Key. What story is told by oceanic tracer concentrations? *Science* 290:455, 2000.

Keller, K., K. Tan, F. M. M. Morel, and D. F. Bradford. Preserving the ocean circulation: Implications for climate policy. *Climatic Change* 47:17–43, 2000.

Kirby, E., K. X. Whipple, W. Tang, and Z. Chen. Distribution of active rock uplift along the eastern margin of the Tibetan Plateau: Inferences from bedrock river profiles: *J. Geophys. Res.* 108:2217, doi: 10,1029/2001JB000861, 2003.

Kirby, E., et al. Late Cenozoic evolution of the eastern margin of the Tibetan Plateau: Inferences from $^{40}Ar/^{39}Ar$ and (U-Th)/He thermochronology. *Tectonics* 21:1–20, 2002.

Kirby, E., and K. X. Whipple. Quantifying differential rock-uplift rates via stream profile analysis. *Geology* 29:415–8, 2001.

Kirby, E., et al. Neotectonics of the Min Shan, China: Implications for mechanisms driving Quaternary deformation along the eastern margin of the Tibetan Plateau. *GSA Bull.* 112:375–93.

Bandura, A. V., and **J. D. Kubicki.** Derivation of force parameters for TiO_2-H_2O systems from ab initio calculations. *J. Phys. Chem. B* 107:11072–81, 2003.

Kubicki, J. D., and **P. J. Heaney.** Modeling interactions of aqueous silica and sorbitol: Complexation, polymerization and association. *Geochim. Cosmochim. Acta* 67:4113–21, 2003.

Kubicki J. D., and S. E. Apitz. Models of natural organic matter and interactions with organic contaminants. *Org. Geochem.* 30:911, 1999.

Kump, L. R., J. F. Kasting, and R. G. Crane. *The Earth System,* second edition. Englewood Cliffs, N.J.: Prentice Hall, 2003.

Richards, P., and **L. R. Kump.** Soil pore-water distributions and the temperature feedback of weathering in the field. *Geochim. Cosmochim. Acta* 67:3803–16, 2003.

Kump, L. R. Reducing uncertainty about carbon dioxide as a climate driver. *Nature* 419:188–90, 2002.

Saffer, D. M., and **C. Marone.** Comparison of smectite and illite frictional properties: Application to the updip limit of the seismogenic zone along subduction megathrusts. *Earth Planet. Sci. Lett.* 215:219–35, 2003.

Frye, K. M., and **C. Marone.** The effect of humidity on granular friction at room temperature. *J. Geophys. Res.* 107(11):2309, doi: 10.1029/2001JB000654, 2002.

Frye, K. M., and **C. Marone.** The effect of particle dimensionality on granular friction in laboratory shear zones. *Geophys. Res. Lett.* 29(19):1916, doi:10.1029/2002GL015709, 2002.

Marone, C. Stressed to the quaking point. *Nature* 419:32, 2002.

Green, H. W., II, and **C. Marone.** Instability of deformation. In *Plastic Deformation of Minerals and Rocks, Reviews in Mineralogy and Geochemistry Series,* vol. 51, eds. S. Karato and H. R. Wenk. Washington, D.C.: Mineralogical Society of America, 2002.

Louanchi, F., and **R. G. Najjar.** A global monthly mean climatology of phosphate, nitrate and silicate in the upper ocean: Spring–summer production and remineralization. *Global Biogeochem. Cycles* 14:957–77, 2000.

Najjar, R. G., and R. F. Keeling. Mean annual cycle of the air-sea oxygen flux: A global view. *Global Biogeochem. Cycles* 14:573–84, 2000.

Najjar, R. G., et al. The potential impacts of climate change on the Mid-Atlantic coastal region. *Climate Res.* 14:219–33, 2000.

Nyblade, A. A., and R. A. Brazier. Precambrian lithospheric controls on the development of the East African rift system. *Geology* 30:755–8, 2002.

Nyblade, A. A., et. al. Seismic evidence for a deep upper mantle thermal anomaly beneath East Africa. *Geology* 28:599–602, 2000.

Nyblade, A. A. Heat flow and the structure of Precambrian lithosphere. *Lithos* 48:81–91, 1999.

Ohmoto, H. Nonredox transformation of magnetic-hematite in hydrothermal systems. *Econ. Geol.* 98:157–61, 2003.

Lasaga, A. C., and **H. Ohmoto.** The oxygen geochemical cycle: Dynamics and stability. *Geochim. Cosmochim. Acta* 66(3):361–81, 2002.

Watanabe, Y., J. E. J. Martini, and **H. Ohmoto.** Geochemical evidence for terrestrial ecosystems 2.6 billion years ago. *Nature* 408:574–8, 2000.

O'Driscoll, M. A., and **R. R. Parizek.** The hydrological catchment area of a chain of Karst wetlands in central Pennsylvania. *Wetlands J.* 23(1):171–9, 2003.

Cordini, M. A., et al. **(R. R. Parizek).** January 1, 2002 to December 31, 2002 Report to the U.S. Congress and Secretary of Energy. Arlington, VA: U.S Nuclear Waste Technical Review Board, 162, 2003.

Olszewski, T. D., and **M. W. Patzkowsky.** Measuring recurrence of marine biotic gradients: A case study from the Pennsylvanian-Permian Midcontinent. *Palaios* 16:444–60, 2001.

Patzkowsky, M. E., and S. M. Holland. Biofacies replacement in a sequence stratigraphic framework: Middle and Upper Ordovician of the Nashville Dome, Tennessee, U.S.A. *Palaios* 14:301–23, 1999.

Richardson, E., and T. H. Jordan. Low-frequency properties of intermediate-focus earthquakes. *Bull. Seism. Soc. Am.* 92:2434–48, 2002.

Richardson, E., and T. H. Jordan. Seismicity in deep gold mines of South Africa: Implications for tectonic earthquakes. *Bull. Seism. Soc. Am.* 92:1766–82, 2002.

Sleep, N. H., **E. Richardson,** and **C. Marone.** Physics of friction and strain rate localization in synthetic fault gouge. *J. Geophys. Res.* 105, 25, 859-28, 878, 2000.

Abbado, D., **R. Slingerland,** and N. D. Smith. The origin of anastomosis on the Columbia River, British Columbia, Canada. Special Publication No. 35, *International Association of Sedimentologists,* in press.

Hartshorn, K., N. Hovius, W. B. Dade, and **R. L. Slingerland.** Climate-driven bedrock incision in an active mountain belt. *Science* 297:2036–8, 2002.

Willett, S. D., **R. Slingerland,** and N. Hovius. Uplift, shortening and steady state topography in active mountain belts. *Am. J. Sci.* 301:455–85, 2001.

Bjerrum, C. J., F. Surlyk, J. H. Callomon, and **R. Slingerland.** Numerical paleoceanographic study of the early Jurrassic transcontinental Laurasian Seaway. *Paleoceanography* 16(4):390–404, 2001.

Clarke, A. B., **B. Voight,** A. Neri, and G. Macedonio. Transient dynamics of vulcanian explosions and column collapse. *Nature* 415: 897-901, G, 2002.

Hidayat, D., et al. **(B. Voight).** Source mechanism of very-long-period signals accompanying dome growth activity at Merapi Volcano, Indonesia. *Geophys. Res. Lett.* 29(23):33-1–4, 2002.

Voight, B., et al. The 26 December (Boxing Day) 1997 Sector collapse and debris avalanche at Soufriere Hills Volcano, Montserrat. In *The Eruption of Soufriere Hills Volcano, Monstserrat, from 1995–1999,* pp. 363–407, eds. T. H. Druitt and B. P. Kokelaav. London: Geological Society, Memoirs 21, 2002.

Voight, B. Structural stability of andesite volcanoes and lava domes. *Phil. Trans. Roy. Soc. Lond. A.* 358:1663–703, 2000.

Wilf, P., et al. High plant diversity in Eocene South America: Evidence from Patagonia. *Science* 300:122–5, 2003.

Wilf, P., K. R. Johnson, and B. T. Huber. Correlated terrestrial and marine evidence for global climate changes before mass extinction at the Cretaceous-Paleogene boundary. *PNAS* 100:599–604, 2003.

Huff, P. M., **P. Wilf,** and E. J. Azumah. Digital future for paleoclimate estimation from fossil leaves? Preliminary results. *Palaios* 18:266–74, 2003.

STONY BROOK UNIVERSITY, STATE UNIVERSITY OF NEW YORK

Department of Geosciences M.A. and Ph.D. in Geosciences M.A.T. in Earth Science

Programs of Study

The department offers programs leading to the Master of Arts in Teaching (M.A.T.), M.S., and Ph.D. degrees in the geosciences. The M.A.T. in earth science is a nonthesis degree for which all requirements can be completed in three semesters. The M.S. degree with a concentration in hydrogeology is a nonthesis M.S., with most courses offered at times appropriate for working professionals. The M.S. degree in geosciences with thesis is typically not a terminal degree. Many students seeking Ph.D. candidacy first earn an M.S. Students become candidates for the Ph.D. in geosciences by completing preparatory work leading to completion of the Ph.D. preliminary examination.

The nonthesis M.S. with a concentration in hydrogeology requires a total of 30 credits. Of these, at least 21 credits must be in the required and approved courses and at least 6 credits must be in approved research. In addition to formal course work, the curriculum for the M.S. with a concentration in hydrogeology includes a minimum of 6 credits of research. The M.S. in geosciences with thesis is typically a nonterminal degree completed by some students before seeking Ph.D. candidacy. All requirements for the M.S. degree must be completed within a period of three years after entry. There are no residence or language requirements.

Research Facilities

The Department of Geosciences occupies the Earth and Science Space (ESS) Building, a modern, well-equipped building that houses extensive experimental and analytical labs, faculty and graduate student offices, numerous computers and workstations, a machine shop, an electronics support group, and the Geosciences Resource Room. The Mineral Physics Institute (MPI), the Consortium for Materials Properties Research (COMPRES), the Center for Environmental Molecular Science (CEMS), the Long Island Groundwater Research Institute (LIGRI), the Marine Sciences Research Center (MSRC), and nearby Brookhaven National Laboratory offer additional support and laboratory facilities for graduate student research. In particular, the National Synchrotron Light Source (NSLS) at Brookhaven, only 20 miles away, offers unparalleled opportunities for faculty members and graduate students to perform unique experiments requiring high-intensity X-rays. COMPRES serves the high-pressure research community through enabling support at national facilities, such as the Brookhaven National Lab, Argon National Lab, and Lawrence Berkeley National Lab. The Center for Environmental Molecular Science, funded by the National Science Foundation, has its main office in the Department of Geosciences and involves several faculty members in geosciences and related departments, as well as scientists at nearby Brookhaven National Laboratory. The center focuses on geochemical aspects of environmental contaminants and includes research, education, and outreach activities.

Financial Aid

Because Stony Brook is committed to attracting high-quality students, the Graduate School provides two competitive fellowships for U.S. citizens and permanent residents. Graduate Council fellowships are for outstanding doctoral candidates studying in any discipline, and the W. Burghardt Turner Fellowships target outstanding African-American, Hispanic-American, and Native American students entering either a doctoral or master's degree program. For doctoral students, both fellowships provide an annual stipend of at least $15,600 for up to five years as well as a full tuition scholarship. For master's students, the Turner Fellowship provides an annual stipend of $10,000 for up to two years, along with a full tuition scholarship. Health insurance subsidies are also provided within a scale depending on the size of the fellow's dependent family. Departments and degree programs award approximately 900 teaching and graduate assistantships and approximately 600 research assistantships on an annual basis. Full assistantships carry a stipend amount that usually ranges from $11,260 to $18,000, depending on the department.

Cost of Study

In 2004–05, full-time tuition was $3450 per semester for state residents and $5225 per semester for nonresidents. Part-time tuition was $287.50 per credit hour for residents and $437.50 per credit hour for nonresidents, plus fees.

Living and Housing Costs

University apartments ranged in cost from approximately $210 per month to approximately $1180 per month, depending on the size of the unit. Off-campus housing options include furnished rooms to rent and houses and/or apartments to share that can be rented for $350 to $550 per month.

Location

Stony Brook's campus is approximately 50 miles east of Manhattan on the north shore of Long Island. The cultural offerings of New York City and Suffolk County's countryside and seashore are conveniently located nearby. Cold Spring Harbor Laboratories and Brookhaven National Laboratories are easily accessible from, and have close relationships with, the University.

The University

The University, established in 1957, achieved national stature within a generation. Founded at Oyster Bay, Long Island, the school moved to its present location in 1962. Stony Brook has grown to encompass more than 110 buildings on 1,100 acres. There are more than 1,568 faculty members, and the annual budget is more than $805 million. The Graduate Student Organization oversees the spending of the student activity fee for graduate student campus events. International students find the additional four-week Summer Institute in American Living very helpful. The Intensive English Center offers classes in English as a second language. The Career Development Office assists with career planning and has information on permanent full-time employment. Disabled Student Services has a Resource Center that offers placement testing, tutoring, vocational assessment, and psychological counseling. The Counseling Center provides individual, group, family, and marital counseling and psychotherapy. Day-care services are provided in four on-campus facilities. The Writing Center offers tutoring in all phases of writing.

Applying

Applicants are judged on the basis of distinguished undergraduate records (and graduate records, if applicable), thorough preparation for advanced study and research in the field of interest, candid appraisals from those familiar with the applicant's academic/professional work, potential for graduate study, and a clearly defined statement of purpose and scholarly interest germane to the program. Applicants are required to have a bachelor's degree in one of the earth and space sciences, biology, chemistry, physics, mathematics, or engineering; a minimum average of B for all undergraduate course work; and a B average for all courses in the sciences. In some cases, students not meeting the degree and GPA requirements are admitted on a provisional basis. Results of the Graduate Record Examinations (GRE) are required. Students should submit admission and financial aid applications by February 1 for the fall semester. Students are admitted for the spring semester only under special circumstances.

Correspondence and Information

William Holt
Department of Geosciences
Stony Brook University, State University of New York
Stony Brook, New York 11794-4433

Telephone: 631-632-8215
Fax: 631-632-8240
E-mail: william.holt@sunysb.edu
World Wide Web: http://pbisotopes.ess.sunysb.edu/geo/

Stony Brook University, State University of New York

THE FACULTY AND THEIR RESEARCH

Robert C. Aller, Distinguished Service Professor; Ph.D., Yale, 1977. Marine geochemistry, early marine diagenesis.
Henry J. Bokuniewicz, Professor; Ph.D., Yale, 1976. Marine geophysics.
Bruce Brownawell, Associate Professor; Ph.D., MIT (Woods Hole), 1986. Biogeochemistry, environmental chemistry, diagenesis.
Jiuhua Chen, Research Assistant Professor; Ph.D., Institute of Materials Structure Science, KEK (Japan), 1994. Mineral physics, mantle petrology, application of synchrotron radiation to earth sciences.
J. Kirk Cochran, Professor; Ph.D., Yale, 1979. Marine geochemistry, use of radionuclides as geochemical tracers, diagenesis of marine sediments.
Daniel M. Davis, Professor; Ph.D., MIT, 1983. Geomechanical modeling of active margins, shallow surface geophysics.
Catherine A. Forster, Associate Professor; Ph.D., Pennsylvania, 1990. Vertebrate paleontology, systematics, functional morphology.
Tibor Gasparik, Research Associate Professor; Ph.D., SUNY at Stony Brook, 1981. Experimental petrology and mineral physics.
Marvin Geller, Professor; Ph.D., MIT, 1969. Atmospheric dynamics, upper atmosphere, climate variability, aeronomy, physical oceanography.
Gilbert N. Hanson, Distinguished Service Professor; Ph.D., Minnesota, 1964. Isotope and trace-element geochemistry, geochronology.
Garman Harbottle, Professor; Ph.D., Columbia, 1949. Nuclear chemistry, archeology.
William Holt, Professor; Ph.D., Arizona, 1989. Tectonophysics, kinematics and dynamics of large-scale deformation of the earth's crust and upper mantle.
David W. Krause, Professor; Ph.D., Michigan, 1982. Vertebrate paleontology; mammalian evolution, including primates.
Baosheng Li, Research Assistant Professor; Ph.D., SUNY at Stony Brook, 1996. Mineral physics, elasticity of minerals, high-pressure research.
Robert C. Liebermann, Distinguished Service Professor; Ph.D., Columbia, 1969. Mineral physics, solid earth geophysics.
Donald H. Lindsley, Distinguished Professor; Ph.D., Johns Hopkins, 1961. Geochemistry, petrology.
Scott M. McLennan, Professor; Ph.D., Australian National, 1981. Geochemistry, planetary science, crustal evolution, sedimentary petrology.
Hanna Nekvasil, Professor; Ph.D., Penn State, 1986. Silicate melt/crystal equilibria, Mars volcanism, thermodynamics of silicate systems.
Maureen O'Leary, Assistant Professor; Ph.D., Johns Hopkins, 1997. Vertebrate paleontology, phylogenetic systematics, mammalian evolution.
John B. Parise, Professor; Ph.D., James Cook (Australia), 1981. Crystal structure-property relations; solid-state synthesis.
Brian L. Phillips, Assistant Professor; Ph.D., Illinois at Urbana-Champaign, 1990. Mineralogy and low temperature geochemistry, structure/reactivity relationships in aqueous fluids and mineral/fluid interfaces.
Troy Rasbury, Assistant Professor; Ph.D., SUNY at Stony Brook, 1998. Sedimentary geology and geochemistry, geochronology.
Richard J. Reeder, Professor; Ph.D., Berkeley, 1980. Geochemistry and mineralogy relating to near-earth's surface processes.
Martin A. A. Schoonen, Professor; Ph.D., Penn State, 1989. Geochemistry of sulfur and sulfides, hydrogeochemistry, catalysis.
Michael T. Vaughan, Research Associate Professor; Ph.D., SUNY at Stony Brook, 1979. Experimental geophysics, crystallography, synchrotron X-ray studies.
Donald J. Weidner, Distinguished Professor; Ph.D., MIT, 1972. Mineral physics and seismology.
Lianxing Wen, Assistant Professor; Ph.D., Caltech, 1998. Seismology, geodynamics, global geophysics.
Teng-fong Wong, Professor; Ph.D., MIT, 1981. Rock deformation and fluid flow, physical properties of geomaterials.

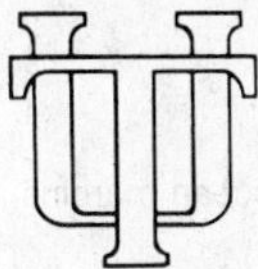

TULANE UNIVERSITY

Department of Earth and Environmental Sciences

Programs of Study The Department of Earth and Environmental Sciences (EES) offers graduate programs leading to the degrees of Master of Science in broad areas of geology and paleontology and Doctor of Philosophy. Two master's degree programs are available: the principal one requires 24 semester hours of graduate course work and successful completion, presentation, and defense of a thesis that reflects individual research accomplishments. A second, nonthesis, program requires 36 semester hours of course work. The Ph.D. program requires 48 semester hours of course work, oral and written examinations, and an original contribution in the form of a written dissertation suitable for publication in a learned journal. Areas of research in EES include sedimentary geochemistry, organic geochemistry, global and biogeochemical cycles, theoretical geochemistry, sedimentary geology, process-oriented sedimentology, isotope geochemistry, global climate change, coastal and marine geology, environmental geology, structural geology, subsurface geology, neotectonics, igneous petrology, volcanology, and paleontology. Special emphasis is given to geology of the Gulf Coast region and Latin America.

Research Facilities The department's research facilities, partially supported by a departmental endowment, include a scanning electron microscope with an energy-dispersive X-ray system, an X-ray fluorescence spectrometer, an electron microprobe, an X-ray diffractometer, a cathodoluminescence microscope, an ICP spectrometer, a wet chemistry laboratory, and a computer laboratory, including a 3-D seismic interpretation laboratory. In addition, single-crystal X-ray diffraction equipment, a transmission electron microscope with an energy-dispersive X-ray system, a high-resolution optical microscope, and other equipment are available in a coordinated instrumentation facility. A variety of field instrumentation is also available for use on the University's 60-foot research vessel, the R/V *Eugenie*.

Financial Aid Graduate teaching and research assistantships are available to all qualified students and provide nine-month stipends, including departmental supplements, that average $17,500. All assistantships and fellowships are accompanied by a tax-free full tuition scholarship. Funding to support research activities during the summer months is available each year.

Cost of Study Full-time tuition for 2003–04 was $14,250 per semester plus a $300 University fee. Tuition on a part-time basis was $1583 per credit hour plus fees.

Living and Housing Costs A limited amount of University housing is available for graduate students. Most graduate students choose to live off campus, where costs vary greatly depending on the type of accommodation selected. A cost-of-living figure of $750 per month is quoted to international graduate students for purposes of entry.

Student Group Tulane currently enrolls 8,750 full-time and 2,320 part-time students. Of these, approximately 800 are registered in the Graduate School. In recent years, graduate students have come to Tulane from more than 380 colleges and universities, from all fifty states, and from thirty-six other countries.

The department seeks to admit 4 to 6 students per year. There are currently 23 students in residence. Graduate students, in coordination with a member of the faculty and with departmental support, organize a program of speakers.

Location Tulane's eleven colleges and schools, with the exception of the medical divisions, are located on 100 acres in a residential area of New Orleans. New Orleans' mild climate, many parks, and proximity to the Gulf Coast provide opportunities for a wide variety of outdoor activities. The city's many art galleries and museums offer regularly scheduled exhibits throughout the year. New Orleans is famous for its French Quarter, Mardi Gras, Creole cuisine, and jazz.

The University and The Department Tulane is a private nonsectarian university offering a wide range of undergraduate, graduate, and professional courses of study for men and women. The University's history dates from 1834, when it was founded as the Medical College of Louisiana. Graduate work was first offered in 1883. In 1884, the University was organized under its present form of administration and renamed for Paul Tulane, a wealthy New Orleans merchant who endowed it generously. Tulane is a member of the American Association of Universities, a group of fifty-six major North American research universities. It is among the top twenty-five private universities in the amount of outside support received for research each year.

The Department of Earth and Environmental Sciences is in the Liberal Arts and Sciences division of the University, which has strong programs in biology, chemistry, mathematics, and physics as well as in earth and environmental sciences. Graduate students in EES are encouraged to enroll in appropriate courses in one or more of these disciplines. Cross-enrollment with the School of Engineering is also available, as are environmental courses offered by the School of Law. EES faculty members play a leadership role in the Tulane Center for River-Ocean Studies (CeROS) which serves as a nexus for multidisciplinary research and education activities related to major world rivers (including the Mississippi) and their role in global change and impact on coastal environments.

Applying For those requesting financial aid, the application deadline is February 1. Students should write to the Dean of the Graduate School for application forms, or they can download the application forms from the Web site http://www.tulane.edu/~gradprog/. The Graduate School will not forward the application to the department for consideration for admission until all of the following documents, plus the $45 application fee, have been received: a completed application form, three completed recommendation forms, official transcripts of all undergraduate and graduate work, and official results of the Graduate Record Examinations General Test, taken within the past five years. International applicants for admission must present satisfactory evidence of competence in English by submitting a score of at least 220 on the TSE (Test of Spoken English) or, if this test is not available, a minimum score of 600 on the TOEFL. Admission is based on academic accomplishments and promise. Admission preference is given to students applying to the Ph.D. program. Tulane is an affirmative action/equal employment opportunity institution.

Correspondence and Information

For application forms and admission:
Dean of the Graduate School
Tulane University
New Orleans, Louisiana 70118
Telephone: 504-865-5100
World Wide Web: http://www.tulane.edu/~gradprog/

For specific information regarding programs:
Director of Graduate Studies
Department of Earth and Environmental Sciences
Tulane University
New Orleans, Louisiana 70118
Telephone: 504-865-5198
E-mail: cdillon@tulane.edu
World Wide Web: http://www.tulane.edu/~eens/

Tulane University

THE FACULTY AND THEIR RESEARCH

Mead A. Allison, Ph.D., SUNY at Stony Brook, 1993. Continental margin sedimentology, high-resolution geophysics of river-ocean margins, marine sediment transport.

Thomas S. Bianchi, Ph.D., Maryland, 1987. Organic geochemistry, organic carbon cycling in coastal and wetland environments, molecular biomarkers as tracers of organic carbon inputs to land-margin ecosystems, chemical biomarkers as paleo-indicators of carbon cycling in past environments.

Nancye H. Dawers, Ph.D., Columbia, 1997. Fault growth and interaction, studies of fault scaling relations, neotectonics, basin analysis and syn-tectonic stratigraphy using 3-D seismic data.

George C. Flowers, Ph.D., Berkeley, 1979. Theoretical geochemistry, sedimentary geochemistry, and environmental geochemistry of estuarine sediments.

Suzanne F. Leclair, Ph.D., SUNY at Binghamton, 2000. Process-oriented sedimentology, bedform development and sediment transport, morphological and sedimentological response of rivers to neotectonism, interactions between depositional systems, paleo-environmental reconstruction.

Franco Marcantonio, Ph.D., Columbia, 1994. Isotope geochemistry, global environmental change.

Brent A. McKee, Ph.D., North Carolina State, 1986. Sedimentary geochemistry, geochemical cycling in river-ocean margins, lakes and anoxic environments, use of radioisotopes as tools to quantify rates of environmental processes.

Stephen A. Nelson, Ph.D., Berkeley, 1979. Igneous petrology: petrologic studies of volcanoes; relationships between volcanism and tectonism, particularly in Mexico; volcanic hazards studies; mechanisms of explosive volcanism; thermodynamic modeling of silicate systems; fluid mechanical processes in magmatic systems.

Ronald L. Parsley, Ph.D., Cincinnati, 1969. Paleontology: paleobiology, paleoecology, and evolution of lower Paleozoic primitive Echinodermata; Paleozoic faunas in general.

Recent Publications

Allison, M. A., S. R. Khan, S. L. Goodbred, and S. A. Kuehl. Stratigraphic evolution of the late Holocene Ganges-Brahmaputra lower delta plain. *Sedimentary Geol.* 155:317–42, 2003.

Allison, M. A., and C. F. Neill. Accumulation rates and stratigraphic character of the modern Atchafalaya River prodelta, Louisiana. *Trans. Gulf Coast Assoc. Geo. Soc.* 52:1031–40, 2002.

Allison, M. A., M. T. Lee, A. S. Ogston, and R. C. Aller. Origin of mudbanks along the northeast coast of South America. *Mar. Geol.* 163:241–56, 2000.

Chen, N., **T. S. Bianchi,** and J.M. Bland. Novel decomposition products of chlorophyll-α in continental shelf (Louisiana shelf) sediments: Formation and transformation of carotenol chlorin esters. *Geochim. Cosmochim. Acta* 67:2027–42, 2003.

Bianchi, T. S., S. Mitra, and **B. McKee.** Sources of terrestrially-derived carbon in the Lower Mississippi River and Louisiana shelf; implications for differential sedimentation and transport at the coastal margin. *Mar. Chem.* 77:211–23, 2002.

Bianchi, T. S., et al. Cyanobacterial blooms in the Baltic Sea: Natural or human-induced? *Limnol. Oceanogr.* 45(3):716–26, 2000.

Mitra, S., **T. S. Bianchi,** L. Guo, and P. H. Santschi. Sources and transport of terrestrially-derived organic matter in the Chesapeake Bay and Middle Atlantic Bight. *Geochim. Cosmochim. Acta* 64:3547–57, 2000.

Dawers, N. H. and J. R. Underhill. The role of fault interaction and linkage in controlling synrift stratigraphic sequences: Late Jurassic, Statfjord East area, northern North Sea. *AAPG Bull.* 84:45–64, 2000.

Dawers, N. H., et al. Controls on Late Jurassic, subtle sand distribution in the Tampen area, northern North Sea. In *Petroleum Geology of NW Europe: Proceedings of the 5th Conference,* Vol. 2, pp. 827–38, eds. A. J. Fleet and S. A. R. Boldy. London: The Geological Society, 1999.

Flowers, G. C. Environmental sedimentology of the Pontchartrain Estuary. *Trans. Gulf Coast Assoc. Geological Soc.* 40:237–50, 1990.

Leclair, S. F. Preservation of cross-strata due to migration of subaqueous dunes: An experimental investigation. *Sedimentology* 49:1157–80, 2002.

Leclair, S. F., and J. S. Bridge. Quantitative interpretation of sedimentary structures formed by river dunes. *J. Sedimentary Res.* 71(5):714–7, 2001.

Marcantonio, F., A. Zimmerman, Y. Xu, and E. Canuel. A record of eastern U.S. atmospheric Pb emissions in Chesapeake Bay sediments: Stable Pb isotopes as a chronological tool. *Mar. Chem.* 77:123–321, 2002.

Marcantonio, F., et al. Sediment focusing in the central equatorial Pacific Ocean. *Paleoceanography* 16:260–7, 2001.

McKee, B. A., et al. **(M. A. Allison** and **T. S. Bianchi).** Transport and transformation of dissolved and particulate materials on continental margins influenced by major rivers: Benthic boundary layer and seabed processes. *Continental Shelf Res.,* in press.

O'Reilly, C. M., et al. **(B. A. McKee).** Climate change decreases aquatic ecosystem productivity of Lake Tanganyika, East Africa. *Nature* 424:766–8, 2003.

McKee, B. A. and M. Baskaran. Sedimentary processes in Gulf of Mexico estuaries: Inputs and dynamics. In *Biogeochemistry of Gulf of Mexico Estuaries,* eds. **T. Bianchi,** J. Pennock, and R. Twilley. New York: John Wiley and Sons, 1998.

McKee, B. A., P. W. Swarzenski, and J. G. Booth. The flux of uranium isotopes from river-dominated shelf sediments. In *Geochemistry of the Earth's Surface,* pp. 85–91, ed. S. H. Bottrell. Leeds: University of Leeds Press, 1996.

Nelson, S. A., E. Gonzalez-Caver, and T. K. Kyser. Constraints on the origin of alkaline and calc-alkaline magmas from the Tuxtla Volcanic Field, Veracruz, Mexico. *Contr. Mineral. Petrol.* 122:191-211, 1995.

Nelson, S. A., and E. Gonzalez-Caver. Geology and K-Ar dating of the Tuxtla volcanic field, Veracruz, Mexico. *Bull. Volcanology.* 55:85–96, 1992.

Verma, S. P., and **S. A. Nelson.** Isotopic and trace-element constraints on the origin and evolution of calc-alkaline and alkaline magmas in the northwestern portion of the Mexican Volcanic Belt. *J. Geophys. Res.* 94:4531–44, 1989.

Parsley, R. L. Community setting and functional morphology of Echinoshpaerites infaustus (Fistuliporita: Echinodermata) from the Ordovician of Bohemia, the Czech Republic. *Vestnik (Bull. Czech Geol. Survey).* 73:252–65, 1998.

Parsley, R. L. The echinoderm classes Stylophora and Homoiostelea: Non-Calcichordata. *Paleontol. Soc. Pap.* 3:225–48, 1997.

Recent Thesis and Dissertation Topics

"Dolomitization and Evolution of the Puerto Rico North Coast Confined Aquifer System," Wilson R. Ramirez Martinez (2000).

"Geology and Petrology of Sierra Las Navajas, Hidalgo Mexico, A Pliocene Peralkaline Rhyolite Volcano in the Mexican Volcanic Belt," Alyson Lighthart (2001).

"Anthropogenic and Natural Controls on Shoreface Evolution Along Galveston Island, Texas," Bethany K. Robb (2003).

"Partitioning of Metals Throughout a Winter Storm-Generated Fluid Mud Event, Atchafalaya Shelf, Louisiana," F. Ryan Clark (2003).

THE UNIVERSITY OF ARIZONA

Department of Planetary Sciences / Lunar and Planetary Laboratory

Program of Study

The graduate program prepares students for careers in solar system research. For this interdisciplinary enterprise, the department maintains faculty expertise in the important areas of planetary science. Through a combination of core courses, minor requirements, and interaction with faculty and research personnel, students are provided with a comprehensive education in modern planetary science. The program is oriented toward granting the Ph.D., although M.S. degrees are now awarded as well.

Upon admission, a student is assigned an adviser in his or her general scientific area. Students advance to Ph.D. candidacy by passing an oral preliminary examination after completing the required major and minor course work. The examination is normally taken two years after matriculation. Students typically complete their dissertations and receive the Ph.D. three to four years later.

Because of the low student-faculty ratio, students receive close supervision and guidance. Dissertation areas include, but are not limited to, observational planetary astronomy; physics of the sun and interplanetary medium; observational, experimental, and theoretical studies of planetary atmospheres, surfaces, and interiors; studies of the interstellar medium and the origin of the solar system; and the geology and chemistry of the surfaces and interiors of solar system bodies.

Research Facilities

The Lunar and Planetary Laboratory (LPL) and the Department of Planetary Sciences function as a single unit to carry out solar system research and education. The department and laboratory are housed in the Gerard P. Kuiper Space Sciences and the Gould-Simpson Buildings on the campus. Neighboring facilities include the Tucson headquarters of the National Optical Astronomy Observatory, the National Radio Astronomy Observatory, Steward Observatory, the Optical Sciences Center, the Flandrau Planetarium, the Department of Geosciences, and the Planetary Sciences Institute.

The facilities of the University observatories are available to all researchers in LPL. These include the multiple-mirror telescope as well as numerous midsize and smaller telescopes. For cosmochemical research, LPL operates a scanning electron microprobe, high-temperature and high-pressure apparatus for rock-melting experiments, a noble gas mass spectrometry laboratory, and a radiochemistry separation facility for neutron activation analysis; these are used for studying meteorites, lunar samples, and terrestrial analogues. Also available in LPL are well-equipped electronics, machine, and photo shops as well as a graphic arts facility.

The Space Imagery Center at the LPL is one of several regional facilities supported by NASA as a repository for spacecraft images and maps of planets and satellites. The Planetary Image Research Laboratory is a modern remote sensing and image processing center for analysis of astronomical and spacecraft data. The Laboratory maintains an extensive computer network; various research groups maintain specialized computer systems for particular applications. University central computing facilities include a variety of systems and network facilities as well as several superminicomputers.

Financial Aid

Most planetary sciences graduate students receive graduate research assistantships for the academic year. These assistantships normally require 20 hours of work per week on a sponsored research project. For the nine-month academic year, such assistantships pay $13,939. For students who pass their preliminary examination and are advanced to Ph.D. candidacy, the pay increases to $15,508. In addition, most students work full-time (40 hours per week) on research projects during the summer term, earning $7169 more.

Cost of Study

For 2003–04, fees for Arizona residents taking 1–6 units were $196 per unit. For 7 or more units, the cost was $1879 per semester. Out-of-state students who do not have a research or teaching assistantship are also charged tuition, but tuition scholarships are frequently available.

Living and Housing Costs

Typical costs for off-campus housing, food, and entertainment for a single graduate student total about $700 to $950 per month. Housing is generally inexpensive and plentiful.

Student Group

In 2003–04, there were 32 graduate students enrolled in the planetary science program. Most came from undergraduate or M.S. programs in chemistry, physics, geology, and astronomy, and some were employed for several years prior to entering graduate school.

Location

Tucson is located in the Sonoran Desert, about 100 kilometers north of the Mexican border. The climate is dry and warm; hiking, mountain climbing, horseback riding, swimming, golf, and tennis are popular year-round activities.

The University

The University is a state-supported institution with an enrollment of approximately 35,700 and ranks in the top twenty research universities. In addition to the planetary sciences program, major research efforts and graduate programs exist in chemistry, engineering, physics, astronomy, optical sciences, and geosciences. LPL interacts closely with these groups.

Applying

Completed application forms, three letters of reference, and GRE scores must be received by January 15 in order to receive full consideration. All applicants are required to submit GRE General Test scores as well as the Subject Test score in a physical science or other relevant area.

Correspondence and Information

Graduate Admissions Secretary
Lunar and Planetary Laboratory
Kuiper Space Sciences Building
The University of Arizona
1629 East University Boulevard
Tucson, Arizona 85721-0092

Telephone: 520-621-6954
E-mail: acad_info@lpl.arizona.edu
World Wide Web: http://www.lpl.arizona.edu/

The University of Arizona

THE FACULTY AND THEIR RESEARCH

Victor R. Baker, Regents Professor; Ph.D., Colorado, 1971. Planetary surfaces, geomorphology.
William V. Boynton, Professor; Ph.D., Carnegie Mellon, 1971. Neutron-activation analysis, cosmochemistry.
Lyle A. Broadfoot, Senior Research Scientist; Ph.D., Saskatchewan, 1963. Planetary atmospheres, ultraviolet spectroscopy.
Robert H. Brown, Professor; Ph.D., Hawaii, 1982. Ground-based, space-based, and theoretical studies of surfaces and satellites in the outer solar system.
Alastair Cameron, Senior Research Scientist Emeritus; Ph.D., Saskatchewan, 1952. Star and planet formation, physics of planets and planetary atmospheres.
Alexander J. Dessler, Senior Research Scientist Emeritus; Ph.D., Duke, 1956. Magnetospheric and space-plasma physics.
Michael J. Drake, Professor, Head, and Director; Ph.D., Oregon, 1972. Lunar samples, meteorites.
Uwe Fink, Professor; Ph.D., Penn State, 1965. Planetary atmospheres, infrared spectroscopy.
Tom Gehrels, Professor; Ph.D., Chicago, 1956. Polarimetry, asteroids, comets.
Joe Giacalone, Assistant Professor; Ph.D., Kansas, 1991. Solar and heliospheric physics, astrophysics.
Richard J. Greenberg, Professor; Ph.D., MIT, 1972. Celestial mechanics, studies of planetary accumulation, satellite and ring dynamics.
Caitlin Griffith, Associate Professor; Ph.D., SUNY at Stony Brook, 1991. Infrared astronomy, evolution of planetary atmospheres, radiative transfer in planetary atmospheres.
Jay Holberg, Senior Research Scientist; Ph.D., Berkeley, 1974. Far-ultraviolet spectra, planetary rings and atmospheres.
Lon L. Hood, Senior Research Scientist; Ph.D., UCLA, 1979. Geophysics, space physics.
William B. Hubbard, Professor; Ph.D., Berkeley, 1967. High-pressure theory, planetary interiors.
Donald M. Hunten, Regents Professor Emeritus; Ph.D., McGill, 1950. Earth and planetary atmospheres, aeronomy.
J. R. Jokipii, Regents Professor; Ph.D., Caltech, 1965. Cosmic rays, solar wind, plasma.
Jozsef Kota, Senior Research Scientist; Ph.D., Budapest (Hungary), 1980. Theoretical space physics, space weather.
David A. Kring, Associate Professor; Ph.D., Harvard, 1989. Cosmochemistry.
Emil R. Kursinski Jr., Associate Professor; Ph.D., Caltech, 1997. Study of climate dynamics using remote sensing techniques, atmospheric physics, weather and climate of Mars.
Harold P. Larson, Professor; Ph.D., Purdue, 1967. Planetary atmospheres, infrared spectroscopy.
Dante Lauretta, Assistant Professor; Ph.D., Washington (St. Louis), 1997. Origin and chemical evolution of the solar system.
Larry A. Lebofsky, Senior Research Scientist; Ph.D., MIT, 1974. Infrared photometry, asteroidal observations.
John S. Lewis, Professor; Ph.D., California, San Diego, 1968. Cosmochemistry.
Ralph D. Lorenz, Assistant Research Scientist; Ph.D., Kent (England), 1994. Planetary climate, aerospace systems.
Jonathan I. Lunine, Professor; Ph.D., Caltech, 1985. Theoretical planetary physics, condensed-matter studies, structure of planets.
Renu Malhotra, Associate Professor; Ph.D., Cornell, 1988. Solar system dynamics.
Alfred McEwen, Associate Professor; Ph.D., Arizona State, 1988. Planetary geology and image processing, multispectral studies of many bodies, volcanism on Io, Calderas in Guatemala, mass movements of Earth and Mars, Copernican craters on the moon, remote sensing.
Robert S. McMillan, Associate Research Scientist; Ph.D., Texas at Austin, 1977. Doppler spectroscopy asteroid-detection survey.
H. Jay Melosh, Professor; Ph.D., Caltech, 1972. Planetary rings.
George H. Rieke, Professor; Ph.D., Harvard, 1969. Infrared astronomy.
Elizabeth Roemer, Professor Emerita; Ph.D., Berkeley, 1955. Comets, minor planets, astrometry.
Bill R. Sandel, Senior Research Scientist; Ph.D., Rice, 1972. Astrophysical plasmas, planetary atmospheres.
Adam Showman, Assistant Professor; Ph.D., Caltech, 1998. Dynamics and evolution of planetary atmospheres.
Peter H. Smith, Senior Research Scientist; M.S., Arizona, 1977. Optical sciences and radiative transfer in planetary atmospheres.
Charles P. Sonett, Regents Professor Emeritus; Ph.D., UCLA, 1954. Planetary physics, solar wind.
Robert G. Strom, Professor Emeritus; M.S., Stanford, 1957. Extraterrestrial geology.
Timothy D. Swindle, Professor; Ph.D., Washington (St. Louis), 1986. Cosmochemistry, noble gas studies of meteorites.
Martin G. Tomasko, Research Professor; Ph.D., Princeton, 1969. Planetary atmospheres, radiative transfer theory.
Elizabeth P. Turtle, Assistant Research Scientist; Ph.D., Arizona, 1998. Modeling and observations of impact craters and tectonic processes.
Roger Yelle, Professor; Ph.D., Wisconsin–Madison, 1984. Atmospheres and icy surfaces in this solar system, atmospheres of extrasolar planets.

Space Sciences Building, which houses the Department of Planetary Sciences and the Lunar and Planetary Laboratory.

UNIVERSITY OF IDAHO

Department of Geological Sciences

Programs of Study

The University of Idaho is situated in north central Idaho, which is an area famous for world-class geology. Students and faculty members of the Department of Geological Sciences have ready access to the Columbia River flood basalts, the Cascades, the Idaho Batholith, the Proterozoic Belt Supergroup, the nearby Coeur d'Alene mining district, and accreted terrane boundaries in Hell's Canyon. The Department also accomplishes field-based research throughout the Cordillera, Italy, the Galapagos, Greenland, Central and South America, Iceland, New Zealand, and the Aleutians. The Department offers M.S. degrees in geology, hydrology, and geophysics and a Ph.D. degree in geology. The thesis is the foundation of graduate education in the Department. Most theses involve both field and laboratory components; however, a nonthesis option in hydrology is offered to those with more than five years of professional experience. The graduate curriculum is flexible to meet the needs of individual students; areas of specialization include hydrogeology, structural geology, geochemistry, volcanology, mineralogy, stratigraphy, igneous petrology, biostratigraphy, geochronology, geomechanics, tectonics, economic geology, and geophysics. Graduates of the Ph.D. program are prepared for research and teaching careers in academia, industry, and government; M.S. graduates find employment in environmental, petroleum, minerals exploration, and educational areas. The normal time for completion of an M.S. degree is two years. The Ph.D. program generally takes four years to complete, although one additional year may be required for students who have not previously obtained an M.S. degree. The University of Idaho is conveniently located close to Washington State University, and a formal collaboration between the two universities permits students to take classes at both campuses.

Research Facilities

The Department is well-equipped for graduate student research. Complete rock preparation and mineral separation facilities are available, as is a wide selection of analytical equipment, including an ICP-AES, ion chromatograph, and a variety of spectrometers. The Department owns and maintains state-of-the-art XRD facilities and an experimental geochemistry laboratory, and SEM and TEM facilities are available on a shared basis with other departments. Geophysical equipment includes seismic, gravity, magnetic, resistivity, and CDM meters, and the North Idaho Seismic Array is operated by and housed in the Department. The Department has twelve dual-frequency GPS instruments and auxiliary tools, including reflectorless laser-mapping equipment. Computer facilities are excellent; graduate student offices have network connections, allowing graduate students convenient access to dozens of institutional computers, workstations, and a departmental HP-UNIX server. The Department is currently developing a geovisualization facility that will provide state-of-the-art computer graphics and geospatial modeling capabilities to support University and external research projects.

Financial Aid

Most graduate students receive stipends for teaching assistantships or research assistantships, and need- or merit-based scholarships are also available. Teaching assistantships are administrated through the Department, and incoming students apply with their departmental application. Students interested in research positions are encouraged to contact the individual faculty administering the awards. Financial aid is also available through the Federal Perkins Loan Program and work-study grants. The Student Financial Aid Office provides information and applications.

Cost of Study

For 2004–05, full-time graduate fees are $2086 per semester for Idaho residents, with an additional fee of $4010 per semester for nonresidents. Resident students enrolled part-time pay $205 per credit; nonresidents pay an additional $123 per credit for part-time work. Full-time fees are charged for 8 credits or more. Fees are subject to change.

Living and Housing Costs

Graduate student housing is available through the University for $346 to $629 per month for apartments ranging in size from efficiencies to four-bedroom units. Potential graduate students are advised to reserve housing early. Off-campus housing lists are available on the Web at http://www.asui.uidaho.edu.

Student Group

Currently, 20 women and 29 men, 2 of whom are international, make up the graduate population. All of the 24 full-time students receive a stipend.

Student Outcomes

M.S. graduates of the past two years are employed in the environmental industry, government, petroleum exploration, minerals exploration, and K–12 and community-college education. Ph.D. graduates are employed in academic teaching/research and postdoctoral research positions and the petroleum industry.

Location

Moscow, located in the Idaho panhandle among the rolling hills of the Palouse, is an agricultural and recreational area and is the cultural center of the region. Local music and theater productions have received international acclaim. Skiing and lake and river sports are within easy drives. Spokane is 88 miles north, and Seattle and Portland are each 6 hours west.

The Department

Students in the Department of Geological Sciences work closely with the faculty members in all aspects of their education. The department emphasizes field-based research and is committed to the application of technologically advanced experimental methods and computational tools to the solution of field-based problems.

Applying

Criteria for admission to the graduate program, roughly in rank of importance, are undergraduate record (GPA), employment and research experience, strength of references, quality of undergraduate program, and scores on the GRE General Test. Applications are due before February 1. Students must submit the following five items: the official Application for Admission to College of Graduate Studies form, complete official undergraduate transcripts, three letters of recommendation, results from the general GRE Test, and the online departmental application form. Students who wish to apply for a departmental assistantship should consult with the department regarding the process and deadline date, which may be earlier than the application deadline.

Correspondence and Information

Dr. Simon Kattenhorn, Director of Graduate Admissions
Department of Geological Sciences
University of Idaho
Moscow, Idaho 83844-3022
Telephone: 208-885-5063
Fax: 208-885-5724
E-mail: simkat@uidaho.edu
World Wide Web: http://geoscience.uidaho.com/

University of Idaho

THE FACULTY AND THEIR RESEARCH

Susan Childers, Assistant Professor; Connecticut, 1997. Geomicrobiology.
Jerry Fairley, Assistant Professor; Berkeley, 2000. Hydrogeology.
Dennis Geist, Professor; Oregon, 1985. Igneous petrology, volcanology.
Mickey Gunter, Professor; Virginia Tech, 1987. Mineralogy.
Peter Isaacson, Professor; Oregon State, 1974. Biostratigraphy.
Gary Johnson, Associate Professor; Idaho, 1991. Hydrogeology.
Simon Kattenhorn, Associate Professor; Stanford, 1998. Geomechanics.
Bill McClelland, Associate Professor; Arizona, 1990. Geochronology, economic geology.
John Oldow, Professor; Northwestern, 1978. Structural geology.
Jim Osiensky, Professor; Idaho, 1983. Hydrogeology.
Ken Sprenke, Professor; Alberta, 1982. Geophysics.
Scott Wood, Professor; Princeton, 1985. Hydrothermal geochemistry.

YALE UNIVERSITY

Department of Geology and Geophysics

Programs of Study

The Department of Geology and Geophysics offers instruction and opportunities for research leading to the Ph.D. degree in a broad range of earth sciences. Fields represented in the department include geochemistry, geophysics, structural geology, tectonics, paleontology, petrology, and oceans and atmosphere. Requirements for admission are flexible, but adequate preparation in the related sciences of physics, chemistry, mathematics, and biology is important for graduate study in geology and geophysics. Those with majors in another science are encouraged to apply. The program includes course work during the first two years, a comprehensive qualifying examination in the area of specialty in the middle of the second year, research on a dissertation topic, and the completion and oral defense of the dissertation. The average time for completion is about six years; at least three full years in residence are required. All entering graduate students are advised by a faculty committee selected by the student and the Director of Graduate Studies. Generally, 8 new students are admitted each year; 33 students are currently enrolled.

Research Facilities

The department is located in the modern Kline Geology Laboratory adjacent to Yale's Peabody Museum of Natural History. This building occupies approximately 100,000 square feet and contains laboratories for research in geophysical fluid dynamics, geophysics, geochemistry, structural geology, and experimental petrology. Laboratories are fully equipped with microscopes, instrumentation, and extensive computer facilities, including a state-of-the-art electron microprobe, mass spectrometers, an X-ray diffractometer, an AA/AE spectrophotometer, and equipment for measurement of mineral surface reaction kinetics. There are numerous personal computers, including Windows, Macs, and UNIX workstations and network connections to parallel-processing computers elsewhere on campus and supercomputers off campus. Also available in the Peabody Museum is one of the world's most important collections of fossil vertebrates, invertebrates, and minerals. The Geology Library is located in the department and contains more than 112,000 volumes and 181,000 maps. The Kline Science Library is nearby.

Financial Aid

All entering students are guaranteed a five-year scholarship that includes a stipend for living expenses (currently $23,000 per year) and tuition. In addition, each student is given a budget of $2000 for travel and scientific conferences in the first two years. After the fifth year, if not sooner, students are typically supported by a research grant or fellowship.

Cost of Study

All students are guaranteed a five-year scholarship, as stated above. Enrollment includes coverage in the University health plan. Spouses and dependents may be enrolled in the health plan for an additional fee.

Living and Housing Costs

Most students live in the attractive residential neighborhood adjacent to the Kline Geology Laboratory. Rooms are available to single students in the Hall of Graduate Studies and Helen Hadley Hall for $4228 to $5022 for the academic year. Additional rooms for single students are available in small residence halls in other nearby locations. The University maintains a number of housing units for married students, ranging from efficiency apartments ($590–$630 per month) to one-, two-, and three-bedroom apartments ($730–$890 per month).

Student Group

Graduate education at Yale is directed toward training the next generation of scholars. The Department of Geology and Geophysics has a diverse Ph.D. program that draws top students from North America and abroad. There are currently 33 full-time graduate students and 17 undergraduate majors. The Dana Club (the graduate student club named after James Dwight Dana) sponsors student activities and social events and consults with the faculty.

Location

The Kline Geology Laboratory is located on Science Hill, which is next to Yale's central campus and close to downtown New Haven. Located on the north shore of Long Island Sound, New Haven is approximately 90 miles from New York City and 150 miles from Boston. Recreational activities include boating, sailing, swimming, fishing, hiking, cycling, and (nearby) skiing. New Haven and Hartford (40 miles away) feature frequent sports events, concerts, theater, ballet, and films.

The University

Yale was founded in 1701 and began offering graduate education in 1847. The Graduate School is one of twelve schools constituting the University. Yale was the first university in North America to award the Ph.D. degree, conferring three in 1861. The University community consists of approximately 5,000 undergraduates, 6,000 students in the various graduate and professional schools, 1,500 faculty members, and hundreds of supporting research staff members. Among the facilities for research and study, beyond those of the department, are the University Library (with more than 6 million volumes), the Beinecke Rare Book and Manuscript Library, the Becton Engineering and Applied Science Center, the Arthur W. Wright Nuclear Structure Laboratory, the Peabody Museum of Natural History, and many other laboratories in various science departments, the School of Medicine, and the School of Forestry and Environmental Studies. Interdepartmental and interdisciplinary study is encouraged throughout the University.

Applying

Inquiries should be made directly to the Department of Geology and Geophysics, Director of Graduate Studies. Applications for admission should be submitted by January 1 to the Office of Admissions, Graduate School, Yale University, Box 208323 Yale Station, New Haven, Connecticut 06520-8323. Scores on the General Test of the Graduate Record Examinations are required, and the examination should be taken before December; applicants are encouraged but not required to submit GRE Subject Test scores. The TOEFL is required for all applicants for whom English is a second language.

Correspondence and Information

Director of Graduate Studies
Department of Geology and Geophysics
Box 208109
Yale University
New Haven, Connecticut 06520-8109
E-mail: dgs@geology.yale.edu
World Wide Web: http://www.geology.yale.edu

Yale University

THE FACULTY AND THEIR RESEARCH

Jay Ague, Professor. Igneous and metamorphic petrology, crustal metamorphism, genesis of granitic batholiths.
David Bercovici, Professor of Geology and Geophysics and Director of Graduate Studies. Mantle convection, geophysical fluid dynamics, lithospheric dynamics and plate tectonics.
Robert Berner, Alan M. Bateman Professor. Earth surface geochemistry cycles.
Ruth Blake, Assistant Professor. Low temperature geochemistry and geomicrobiology.
Mark Brandon, Professor and Director of Graduate Studies. Tectonic evolution of convergent margins, low-temperature deformation, circum-Pacific tectonics.
Derek Briggs, Professor. Paleontology, evolution, taphonomy, biogeochemistry.
Leo Buss, Adjunct Professor and Professor of Biology. Evolutionary biology and paleobiology.
Michael Donoghue, Adjunct Professor and Professor of Ecology and Evolutionary Biology.
David Evans, Assistant Professor. Continental reconstructions; paleomagnetism; long-term evolution of geodynamics, tectonics, climate change, and life.
Alexey Federov. Atmospheric geophysics.
Jacques Gauthier, Professor. Vertebrate paleontology, evolution of reptiles, phylogenetic systematics.
Robert Gordon, Professor of Geophysics and Applied Mechanics. Mechanics of earth materials and surficial processes, utilization of earth resources.
Thomas Graedel, Adjunct Professor and Professor of Forestry and Environmental Studies. Atmospheric chemistry, industrial ecology.
Leo Hickey, Professor and Chairman. Paleobotany, evolution of flowering plants, Cretaceous and Tertiary climates.
Shun-ichiro Karato, Professor of Geology and Geophysics. Mineral and rock physics related to geodynamics, plastic deformation, physical basis for interpretation of seismic tomography.
Jun Korenaga, Assistant Professor. Mantle convection and terrestrial magmatism, thermal and chemical evolution of the Earth, geophysical inverse theory, computational mineral physics.
Mark Pagani, Assistant Professor. Organic geochemistry, paleooceanography, evolution of atmospheric carbon dioxide.
Jeffrey Park, Professor. Global seismology, mantle anisotrophy, geologic time-series analysis.
Peter Reiners, Assistant Professor. Thermochronometry and tectonic/geomorphic applications, mantle petrology and isotope geochemistry.
Danny Rye, Professor. Isotope geochemistry related to ore deposits, metamorphic rocks, and paleoenvironments.
Adolf Seilacher, Adjunct Professor. Latest Precambrian and Paleozoic trace fossils, taphonomy, and morphology.
Steven Sherwood, Assistant Professor. Physical meteorology, climate dynamics.
Brian Skinner, Eugene Higgins Professor. Geochemistry of mineral deposits, sulfide mineralogy.
Ronald B. Smith, Professor and Adjunct Professor of Mechanical Engineering, Director of Undergraduate Studies, and Director of the Center for Earth Observation. Geophysical fluid dynamics, dynamical meteorology, remote sensing.
Karl Turekian, Silliman Professor and Director of the Center for the Study of Global Change. Geochemistry of the earth's surface, oceans, and atmosphere; planetary evolution.
George Veronis, Henry Barnard Davis Professor of Geophysics and Applied Science. Physical oceanography, geophysical fluid dynamics.
Elisabeth S. Vrba, Professor and Adjunct Professor of Biology. Evolutionary paleobiology, vertebrate paleotology, evolution of mammals, phylogenetic systematics, evolutionary theory.
John S. Wettlaufer, Professor. Condensed-matter and materials physics, applied mathematics, geophysical fluid dynamics, ice and climate dynamics, and thermodynamics.

Professors Emeriti
Sydney P. Clark Jr., Sidney J. Weinberg Professor of Geophysics Emeritus. Constitution of the earth's interior, heat flow and the thermal state of the earth.
John H. Ostrom, Professor of Geology and Geophysics Emeritus. Functional morphology; evolution and paleoecology of ancient reptiles, particularly archosaurs.
John Rodgers, Silliman Professor of Geology Emeritus. Structural and regional geology of mountain ranges.

Visiting Research Faculty
Kyoko Matsukage, Assistant Professor. Metamorphic petrology.

Associates
Edward Bolton, Research Scientist. Geophysical fluid dynamics, coupled modeling of geochemical systems.
Laurent Bonneau, Research Associate, Center for Earth Observation.
Deren Dogru, Research Associate. Geochemistry, application of oxygen isotope ratios in P04.
Gerard Olack. Stable Isotope Studies Center.
James Eckert, Research Associate. Petrology.
Roland Geerken, Associate Research Scientist. Remote sensing.
James Greenwood, Associate Research Scientist. Geochemistry, astrobiology, meteoritics.
Zhenting Jiang, Research Associate. Mineral physics.
Stefan Nicolescu, Associate Research Scientist. U-Th/He thermochronology, trace element and isotope geochemistry applied to mineral deposits, silicate mineralogy of skarns, history of science.
Matthew Wells, Associate Research Scientist. Laboratory geophysical fluid dynamics.
Yousheng Xu, Associate Research Scientist. Mineral physics.

Postdoctoral Associates
Idar Barstad. Mountain meteorology, orographic precipitation.
Olivier Bethoux. Paleontology.
Susan Butts. Invertebrate paleontology.
Alexandre Costa. Aerosols and cloud physics.
Jason Evans. Climatology and hydrology.
Jenney Hall. Geochemistry and paleoceanography.
Jeremy Hourigan. Tectonics, geochronology, and thermochronology.
Kyoungwon Kyle Min. Isotope geochemistry.
Yu Nishihara. Experimental mineral physics.
Francis Robinson. Mesoscale modeling, convection, hydrodynamics.
Toru Shimmei. Mineral physics.
Azusa Shito. Seismology.
Stuart Thomson. Tectonics and thermochronology.
Heather Wilson. Arthropod paleobiology.

Postdoctoral Fellows
Scott Bryan. Volcanology, igneous petrology and tectonics.
Nicole Gasparini. Fluvial Geomorphology and tectonic geomorphology.
Xiaoge Huang. Mineral physics.
Ikuo Katayama. Structural geology.
Klaus Meiners. Sea ice ecology.
Stephen Meyers. Paleoclimatology, paleoceanography, biogeochemistry.
Nicolai Pedentchouk.
Henri Samuel, Geodynamicist. Mantle convection, mantle evolution, multidisciplinary approach.

Visiting Fellows
Manuel Hernandez Fernandez. Evolutionary biology, macroecology, mammalian paleoecology.
Aleksandr Surkov. Microbial ecology and biogeochemistry.
Jonathan Tomkin. Geophysics and geomorphology.
Larry Wilen.

Research Affiliates
Elisabeth Berner. Aqueous geochemistry.
John Garver. Tectonics and seismology.
William Graustein. Atmospheric geochemistry.
Dorothy Koch. Atmospheric chemistry, climate modeling.
Robert Knoph.
Neil Ribe. Mantle convection, global geodynamics.
David Seidemann. Geochronometry and environmental studies.
Catherine Skinner. Mineralogist.
Ellen Thomas. Paleoclimatology.

Section 4
Marine Sciences and Oceanography

This section contains a directory of institutions offering graduate work in marine sciences and oceanography, followed by in-depth entries submitted by institutions that chose to prepare detailed program descriptions. Additional information about programs listed in the directory but not augmented by an in-depth entry may be obtained by writing directly to the dean of a graduate school or chair of a department at the address given in the directory.

For programs offering related work, see also in this book Chemistry, Geosciences, Meteorology and Atmospheric Sciences, and Physics. In Book 3, see Biological and Biomedical Sciences; Ecology, Environmental Biology, and Evolutionary Biology; and Marine Biology; and in Book 5, see Civil and Environmental Engineering, Engineering and Applied Sciences, and Ocean Engineering.

CONTENTS

Marine Sciences

California State University, Fresno, Division of Graduate Studies, College of Science and Mathematics, Program in Marine Sciences, Fresno, CA 93740-8027. Offers MS. Part-time programs available. Postbaccalaureate distance learning degree programs offered. *Degree requirements:* For master's, thesis. *Entrance requirements:* For master's, GRE General Test, GRE Subject Test, minimum GPA of 3.0. Additional exam requirements/recommendations for international students: Required—TOEFL. Electronic applications accepted. *Faculty research:* Wetlands ecology, land/water conservation, water irrigation.

California State University, Hayward, Academic Programs and Graduate Studies, College of Science, Department of Biological Sciences, Moss Landing Marine Laboratory, Hayward, CA 94542-3000. Offers MS. *Degree requirements:* For master's, thesis. *Entrance requirements:* For master's, GRE Subject Test, minimum GPA of 3.0 in field, 2.75 overall. Application fee: $55. Tuition, nonresident: part-time $188 per unit. Required fees: $560 per quarter hour. *Financial support:* Application deadline: 3/2. *Unit head:* Director, 832-632-4400. *Application contact:* Jennifer Cason, Graduate Program Coordinator/Operations Analyst, 510-885-3286, Fax: 510-885-4777, E-mail: jcason@csuhayward.edu.

California State University, Monterey Bay, College of Science, Media Arts and Technology, Program in Marine Studies, Seaside, CA 93955-8001. Offers marine science (MS). Program offered in conjunction with Moss Landing Marine Laboratories. Part-time programs available. *Degree requirements:* For master's, thesis, thesis defense. Electronic applications accepted. *Faculty research:* Remote sensing microbiology trace elements; chemistry ecology of birds, mammals, turtles and fish; invasive species; marine phycology.

California State University, Sacramento, Graduate Studies, College of Natural Sciences and Mathematics, Department of Biological Sciences, Sacramento, CA 95819-6048. Offers biological sciences (MA, MS); immunohematology (MS); marine science (MS). Part-time programs available. *Students:* 28 full-time (17 women), 41 part-time (25 women); includes 15 minority (1 African American, 9 Asian Americans or Pacific Islanders, 5 Hispanic Americans), 4 international. *Degree requirements:* For master's, thesis, writing proficiency exam. *Entrance requirements:* For master's, bachelor's degree in biology or equivalent; minimum GPA of 3.0 in biology, 2.75 overall during previous 2 years. Additional exam requirements/recommendations for international students: Required—TOEFL. *Application deadline:* For fall admission, 5/1 for domestic students; for spring admission, 11/1 for domestic students. Application fee: $55. *Expenses:* Tuition, state resident: full-time $2,256. Tuition, nonresident: full-time $10,716. *Financial support:* Research assistantships, teaching assistantships, career-related internships or fieldwork and Federal Work-Study available. Support available to part-time students. Financial award application deadline: 3/1. *Unit head:* Dr. Nick Ewing, Chair, 916-278-6535, Fax: 916-278-6993.

Coastal Carolina University, College of Natural and Applied Science, Program in Coastal Marine and Wetland Studies, Conway, SC 29528-6054. Offers MS. Part-time and evening/weekend programs available. *Faculty:* 1 full-time (0 women), 7 part-time/adjunct (3 women). *Students:* 6 full-time (5 women), 2 part-time (1 woman). Average age 25. *Degree requirements:* For master's, thesis. *Entrance requirements:* For master's, GRE, 2 letters of recommendation. *Application deadline:* For fall admission, 8/15 for domestic students. Applications are processed on a rolling basis. Application fee: $45. Electronic applications accepted. *Expenses:* Tuition, state resident: full-time $5,360; part-time $220 per credit hour. Tuition, nonresident: full-time $13,160; part-time $545 per credit hour. Required fees: $40 per term. *Financial support:* Fellowships, research assistantships available. Support available to part-time students. Financial award application deadline: 4/1; financial award applicants required to submit FAFSA. *Application contact:* Dr. Judy W. Vogt, Vice President, Enrollment Services, 843-349-2037, Fax: 843-349-2127, E-mail: jvogt@coastal.edu.

The College of William and Mary, School of Marine Science/Virginia Institute of Marine Science, Gloucester Point, VA 23062. Offers MS, PhD. *Faculty:* 68 full-time (10 women), 10 part-time/adjunct (0 women). *Students:* 104 full-time (44 women), 8 part-time (4 women); includes 7 minority (1 African American, 4 Asian Americans or Pacific Islanders, 2 Hispanic Americans), 20 international. Average age 27. 150 applicants, 30% accepted, 28 enrolled. In 2003, 21 master's awarded, leading to university research/teaching 38%, continued full-time study19%, business/industry 10%, government 19%; 10 doctorates awarded, leading to university research/teaching 50%, government 10%. *Median time to degree:* Master's–3 years full-time; doctorate–5.33 years full-time. *Degree requirements:* For master's and doctorate, thesis/dissertation, defense, qualifying exam. *Entrance requirements:* For master's, GRE, appropriate bachelor's degree; for doctorate, GRE, appropriate master's degree. Additional exam requirements/recommendations for international students: Required—TOEFL. *Application deadline:* For fall admission, 1/15 for domestic students. Application fee: $50. Electronic applications accepted. *Expenses:* Tuition, state resident: full-time $4,858; part-time $222 per credit hour. Tuition, nonresident: full-time $16,440; part-time $618 per credit hour. Required fees: $2,674. Tuition and fees vary according to program. *Financial support:* In 2003–04, 13 fellowships with full tuition reimbursements (averaging $15,300 per year), 95 research assistantships (averaging $14,900 per year), 6 teaching assistantships (averaging $15,000 per year) were awarded. Career-related internships or fieldwork, Federal Work-Study, and health care benefits also available. Support available to part-time students. Financial award application deadline: 3/15. *Faculty research:* Physical, biological, geological, and chemical oceanography; marine fisheries science; resource management. Total annual research expenditures: $15.9 million. *Unit head:* Dr. L. D. Wright, Dean and Director, 804-684-7105, Fax: 804-684-7097. *Application contact:* Dr. Iris Anderson, Dean of Graduate Studies, 804-684-7105, Fax: 804-684-7188, E-mail: iris@vims.edu.

Cornell University, Graduate School, Graduate Fields of Agriculture and Life Sciences, Field of Natural Resources, Ithaca, NY 14853-0001. Offers aquatic science (MPS, MS, PhD); environmental management (MPS); fishery science (MPS, MS, PhD); forest science (MPS, MS, PhD); resource policy and management (MPS, MS, PhD); wildlife science (MPS, MS, PhD). *Faculty:* 43 full-time. *Students:* 73 full-time (31 women); includes 10 minority (1 African American, 2 American Indian/Alaska Native, 5 Asian Americans or Pacific Islanders, 2 Hispanic Americans), 14 international. 107 applicants, 22% accepted, 18 enrolled. In 2003, 16 master's, 6 doctorates awarded. *Degree requirements:* For master's, thesis (MS), project paper (MPS); for doctorate, thesis/dissertation, comprehensive exam. *Entrance requirements:* For master's and doctorate, GRE General Test, 2 letters of recommendation. Additional exam requirements/recommendations for international students: Required—TOEFL (minimum score 550 paper-based; 213 computer-based). *Application deadline:* ; for spring admission, 10/30 for domestic students. Applications are processed on a rolling basis. Application fee: $60. Electronic applications accepted. *Expenses:* Tuition: Full-time $28,630. One-time fee: $50 full-time. *Financial support:* In 2003–04, 63 students received support, including 11 fellowships with full tuition reimbursements available, 27 research assistantships with full tuition reimbursements available, 25 teaching assistantships with full tuition reimbursements available; institutionally sponsored loans, scholarships/grants, health care benefits, tuition waivers (full and partial), and unspecified assistantships also available. Financial award applicants required to submit FAFSA. *Faculty research:* Ecosystem-level dynamics, systems modeling, conservation biology/management, resource management's human dimensions, biogeochemistry. *Unit head:* Director of Graduate Studies, 607-255-2807, Fax: 607-255-0349. *Application contact:* Graduate Field Assistant, 607-255-2807, Fax: 607-255-0349, E-mail: nrgrad@cornell.edu.

Duke University, Nicholas School of the Environment and Earth Sciences, Durham, NC 27708-0328. Offers coastal environmental management (MEM); environmental health and security (MEM); environmental science and policy (PhD); environmental toxicology, chemistry, and risk assessment (MEM); forest resource management (MF); global environmental change (MEM); resource ecology (MEM); resource economics and policy (MEM); water and air resources (MEM). PhD offered through the Graduate School. *Accreditation:* SAF (one or more programs are accredited). Part-time programs available. Terminal master's awarded for partial completion of doctoral program. *Degree requirements:* For master's, thesis (for some programs); for doctorate, thesis/dissertation. *Entrance requirements:* For master's, GRE General Test, previous course work in biology or ecology, calculus, statistics, and microeconomics; computer familiarity with word processing and data analysis; for doctorate, GRE General Test. Additional exam requirements/recommendations for international students: Required—TOEFL (minimum score 550 paper-based; 213 computer-based). Electronic applications accepted. Expenses: Contact institution. *Faculty research:* Ecosystem management, conservation ecology, earth systems, risk assessment.

Announcement: Two-year professional program provides excellent preparation for careers in coastal environmental management. Core courses emphasize coastal sedimentary and biological processes, ecology, economics, policy, and quantitative analytical methods. Program includes courses on the main Durham campus and at the Duke University Marine Laboratory located at Beaufort, North Carolina. PhD program also available.

See in-depth description on page 787.

Florida Institute of Technology, Graduate Programs, College of Engineering, Department of Marine and Environmental Systems, Program in Oceanography, Melbourne, FL 32901-6975. Offers biological oceanography (MS, PhD); chemical oceanography (MS, PhD); coastal zone management (MS); geological oceanography (MS, PhD); physical oceanography (MS, PhD). Part-time programs available. *Students:* Average age 30.Terminal master's awarded for partial completion of doctoral program. *Degree requirements:* For master's, thesis (for some programs); for doctorate, one foreign language, thesis/dissertation, departmental qualifying exams, comprehensive exam. *Entrance requirements:* For master's, GRE General Test, minimum GPA of 3.0; for doctorate, GRE General Test, minimum GPA of 3.3, resumé. *Application deadline:* Applications are processed on a rolling basis. Electronic applications accepted. *Expenses:* Tuition: Part-time $745 per credit. *Financial support:* Research assistantships with full and partial tuition reimbursements, teaching assistantships with full and partial tuition reimbursements, career-related internships or fieldwork and tuition remissions available. Financial award application deadline: 3/1; financial award applicants required to submit FAFSA. *Faculty research:* Marine geochemistry, ecosystem dynamics, coastal processes, marine pollution, environmental modeling. Total annual research expenditures: $938,395. *Unit head:* Dr. Dean R. Norris, Chair, 321-674-7377, Fax: 321-674-7212, E-mail: norris@fit.edu. *Application contact:* Carolyn P. Farrior, Director of Graduate Admissions, 321-674-7118, Fax: 321-723-9468, E-mail: cfarrior@fit.edu.

See in-depth descriptions on pages 273 and 727.

Memorial University of Newfoundland, School of Graduate Studies, Interdisciplinary Program in Marine Studies, St. John's, NL A1C 5S7, Canada. Offers fisheries resource management (MMS). Part-time programs available. *Students:* 9 full-time, 12 part-time. 9 applicants, 44% accepted, 4 enrolled. In 2003, 2 degrees awarded. *Degree requirements:* For master's, report. Application fee: $40 Canadian dollars. Tuition and fees charges are reported in Canadian dollars. *Expenses:* Tuition, state resident: part-time $733 Canadian dollars per semester. Tuition, nonresident: part-time $953 Canadian dollars per semester. Required fees: $194 Canadian dollars per year. Tuition and fees vary according to degree level and program. *Financial support:* Fellowships, research assistantships, teaching assistantships available. *Faculty research:* Biological, ecological and oceanographic aspects of world fisheries; economics; political science; sociology. *Unit head:* Dr. Peter Fisher, Chair, 709-778-0356, Fax: 709-778-0346, E-mail: pfisher@gill.ifmt.nf.ca.

Murray State University, College of Science, Engineering and Technology, Department of Water Science, Murray, KY 42071-0009. Offers MS. Part-time programs available.

North Carolina State University, Graduate School, College of Physical and Mathematical Sciences, Department of Marine, Earth, and Atmospheric Sciences, Raleigh, NC 27695. Offers marine, earth, and atmospheric sciences (MS, PhD); meteorology (MS, PhD); oceanography (MS, PhD). *Faculty:* 41 full-time (6 women), 57 part-time/adjunct (4 women). *Students:* 91 full-time (32 women), 16 part-time (3 women); includes 4 minority (2 African Americans, 1 Asian American or Pacific Islander, 1 Hispanic American), 17 international. Average age 30. 106 applicants, 50% accepted. In 2003, 19 master's, 6 doctorates awarded. Terminal master's awarded for partial completion of doctoral program. *Median time to degree:* Master's–2.7 years full-time; doctorate–5 years full-time. Of those who began their doctoral program in fall 1995, 90% received their degree in 8 years or less. *Degree requirements:* For master's, thesis (for some programs), final oral exam; for doctorate, thesis/dissertation, final oral exam, preliminary oral and written exams, comprehensive exam, registration. *Entrance requirements:* For master's, GRE General Test, minimum GPA of 3.0; for doctorate, GRE General Test, GRE Subject Test for disciplines in biological oceanography and geology, minimum GPA of 3.0. Additional exam requirements/recommendations for international students: Required—TOEFL (minimum score 550 paper-based). *Application deadline:* For fall admission, 6/25 for domestic students, 3/1 for international students; for spring admission, 11/25 for domestic students, 7/15 for international students. Applications are processed on a rolling basis. Application fee: $45. Electronic applications accepted. *Expenses:* Tuition, state resident: part-time $396 per hour. Tuition, nonresident: part-time $1,895 per hour. *Financial support:* In 2003–04, 76 students received support, including 1 fellowship with tuition reimbursement available (averaging $10,397 per year), 47 research assistantships with tuition reimbursements available (averaging $5,959 per year), 32 teaching assistantships with tuition reimbursements available (averaging $6,594 per year); institutionally sponsored loans and unspecified assistantships also available. Financial award application deadline: 3/1. *Faculty research:* Boundary layer and air quality meteorology; climate and mesoscale dynamics; biological, chemical, geological, and physical oceanography; hard rock, soft rock, environmental, and paleogeology. Total annual research expenditures: $5.6 million. *Unit head:* Dr. John C. Fountain, Head, 919-515-3717, Fax: 919-515-7802, E-mail: fountain@ncsu.edu. *Application contact:* Dr. Gerald S. Janowitz, Director of Graduate Programs, 919-515-7837, Fax: 919-515-7802, E-mail: janowitz@ncsu.edu.

See in-depth description on page 247.

Nova Southeastern University, Oceanographic Center, Program in Coastal-Zone Management, Fort Lauderdale, FL 33314-7796. Offers MS. *Students:* 10 applicants, 80% accepted. In 2003, 6 degrees awarded. *Entrance requirements:* For master's, GRE. Additional exam requirements/recommendations for international students: Required—TOEFL (minimum score 550 paper-based). *Application deadline:* Applications are processed on a rolling basis. Application fee: $50. *Expenses:* Tuition: Full-time $8,715; part-time $484 per credit. Required fees: $75. Full-time tuition and fees vary according to degree level and program. *Application contact:* Dr. Andrew Rogerson, Associate Dean, 954-262-3600, Fax: 954-262-4020, E-mail: arogerso@nsu.nova.edu.

See in-depth description on page 281.

Nova Southeastern University, Oceanographic Center, Program in Marine Environmental Science, Fort Lauderdale, FL 33314-7796. Offers MS. *Students:* 1 (woman) full-time, 16 part-time (9 women). 8 applicants, 63% accepted, 5 enrolled. In 2003, 2 degrees awarded. *Degree requirements:* For master's, thesis. *Entrance requirements:* For master's, GRE. Additional exam requirements/recommendations for international students: Required—TOEFL (minimum score 550 paper-based). *Application deadline:* Applications are processed on a rolling basis. Application fee: $50. *Expenses:* Tuition: Full-time $8,715; part-time $484 per credit. Required fees: $75. Full-time tuition and fees vary according to degree level and program. *Application contact:* Dr. Andrew Rogerson, Associate Dean, 954-262-3600, Fax: 954-262-4020, E-mail: arogerso@nsu.nova.edu.

Oregon State University, Graduate School, College of Oceanic and Atmospheric Sciences, Program in Marine Resource Management, Corvallis, OR 97331. Offers MA, MS. *Students:* 24 full-time (14 women), 3 part-time (2 women), 5 international. Average age 30. In 2003, 8 degrees awarded. *Degree requirements:* For master's, thesis optional. *Entrance requirements:* For master's, GRE General Test, minimum GPA of 3.0 in last 90 hours. Additional exam requirements/recommendations for international students: Required—TOEFL. *Application deadline:* For fall admission, 2/1 for domestic students. Applications are processed on a rolling basis. Application fee: $50. *Expenses:* Tuition, state resident: full-time $8,139; part-time $301 per credit. Tuition, nonresident: full-time $14,376; part-time $532 per credit. Required fees: $1,227. *Financial support:* Fellowships, research assistantships, teaching assistantships, career-related internships or fieldwork, Federal Work-Study, and institutionally sponsored loans available. Support available to part-time students. Financial award application deadline: 2/1. *Faculty research:* Ocean and coastal resources, fisheries resources, marine pollution, marine recreation and tourism. *Unit head:* Dr. Jim W. Good, Director, 541-737-1339, Fax: 541-737-2064, E-mail: good@oce.orst.edu. *Application contact:* Irma Delson, Assistant Director, Student Services, 541-737-5189, Fax: 541-737-2064, E-mail: student_adviser@oce.orst.edu.

San Jose State University, Graduate Studies and Research, College of Science, Program in Marine Science, San Jose, CA 95192-0001. Offers MS. *Students:* 3 full-time (2 women), 12 part-time (7 women). Average age 28. 18 applicants, 39% accepted, 4 enrolled. In 2003, 2 degrees awarded. *Degree requirements:* For master's, thesis, qualifying exam. *Entrance requirements:* For master's, GRE. *Application deadline:* For fall admission, 6/29 for domestic students; for spring admission, 11/30 for domestic students. Applications are processed on a rolling basis. Application fee: $59. Electronic applications accepted. Tuition, nonresident: part-time $282 per unit. Required fees: $654 per semester. *Financial support:* Teaching assistantships, career-related internships or fieldwork available. Support available to part-time students. Financial award applicants required to submit FAFSA. *Faculty research:* Physical oceanography, marine geology, ecology, ichthyology, invertebrate zoology. *Unit head:* Dr. Kenneth Coale, Director, 831-771-4400, Fax: 831-753-2826.

Savannah State University, Program in Marine Science, Savannah, GA 31404. Offers MS.

Stony Brook University, State University of New York, Graduate School, Marine Sciences Research Center, Program in Marine and Atmospheric Sciences, Stony Brook, NY 11794. Offers MS, PhD. Evening/weekend programs available. *Faculty:* 32 full-time (5 women), 1 (woman) part-time/adjunct. *Students:* 107 full-time (60 women), 8 part-time (6 women); includes 9 minority (3 African Americans, 2 Asian Americans or Pacific Islanders, 4 Hispanic Americans), 38 international. Average age 29. 125 applicants, 53% accepted. In 2003, 13 master's, 5 doctorates awarded. *Degree requirements:* For doctorate, one foreign language, thesis/dissertation, comprehensive exam. *Entrance requirements:* For doctorate, GRE General Test, minimum graduate GPA of 3.0. Additional exam requirements/recommendations for international students: Required—TOEFL. *Application deadline:* For fall admission, 1/15 for domestic students. Application fee: $50. *Expenses:* Tuition, state resident: full-time $6,900; part-time $288 per credit hour. Tuition, nonresident: full-time $10,500; part-time $438 per credit hour. Required fees: $22. *Financial support:* In 2003–04, 21 fellowships, 51 research assistantships, 33 teaching assistantships were awarded. Career-related internships or fieldwork also available. Total annual research expenditures: $9.2 million. *Application contact:* Dr. Henry Bokuniewicz, Director, 631-632-8681, Fax: 631-632-8200, E-mail: hbokuniewicz@ccmail.sunysb.edu.

Announcement: Located on Long Island's North Shore, 50 miles from New York City, the Marine Sciences Research Center and the Institute for Terrestrial and Planetary Atmospheres offer close-by opportunities for coastal research along a gradient from urban to pristine, as well as for research in many regions of the globe.

See in-depth description on page 287.

Texas A&M University at Galveston, Department of Marine Sciences, Galveston, TX 77553-1675. Offers marine resources management (MMRM). *Faculty:* 8 full-time (1 woman). *Students:* 14 full-time (8 women), 21 part-time (11 women); includes 4 minority (1 Asian American or Pacific Islander, 3 Hispanic Americans), 1 international. Average age 27. 26 applicants, 50% accepted, 13 enrolled. In 2003, 7 degrees awarded. *Entrance requirements:* For master's, GRE, 1 year of biology, chemistry, and general physics/mathematics, 1 semester of geology, oceanography, and economics. Additional exam requirements/recommendations for international students: Required—TOEFL (minimum score 550 paper-based; 213 computer-based). *Application deadline:* Applications are processed on a rolling basis. Application fee: $50 ($75 for international students). Electronic applications accepted. *Expenses:* Tuition, state resident: full-time $4,140; part-time $92 per hour. Tuition, nonresident: full-time $9,840; part-time $328 per hour. Required fees: $938. Tuition and fees vary according to course load, degree level and program. *Financial support:* In 2003–04, 14 students received support, including 1 research assistantship, 2 teaching assistantships; scholarships/grants, health care benefits, and unspecified assistantships also available. Financial award application deadline: 4/1; financial award applicants required to submit FAFSA. *Faculty research:* Biogeochemistry, physical oceanography, theoretical chemistry, marine policy. Total annual research expenditures: $3.1 million. *Unit head:* Dr. William Seitz, Head, 409-740-4515, Fax: 409-740-4429, E-mail: seitzw@tamug.edu. *Application contact:* Frederick C. Schlemmer, Associate Professor and Graduate Advisor, 409-740-4518, Fax: 409-740-4429, E-mail: schlemme@tamug.edu.

University of Alaska Fairbanks, School of Fisheries and Ocean Sciences, Department of Marine Sciences and Limnology, Fairbanks, AK 99775-7520. Offers marine biology (MS); oceanography (MS, PhD), including biological oceanography (PhD), chemical oceanography (PhD), fisheries (PhD), geological oceanography (PhD), physical oceanography (PhD). Part-time programs available. Terminal master's awarded for partial completion of doctoral program. *Degree requirements:* For master's and doctorate, thesis/dissertation, comprehensive exam, registration. *Entrance requirements:* For master's and doctorate, GRE General Test. Additional exam requirements/recommendations for international students: Required—TOEFL. Electronic applications accepted. *Faculty research:* Seafood science and nutrition, sustainable harvesting, chemical oceanography, marine biology, physical oceanography.

Announcement: The School of Fisheries and Ocean Sciences offers MS and PhD degrees in oceanography, fisheries, and marine biology. Interdisciplinary degrees are offered in seafood science and technology. The School is headquartered in Fairbanks; has coastal facilities at Juneau, Kodiak, Seward, and Kasitsna Bay; and operates the oceanographic vessel *R/V Alpha Helix.*

See in-depth description on page 289.

The University of British Columbia, Faculty of Graduate Studies, Faculty of Science, Department of Earth and Ocean Sciences, Vancouver, BC V6T 1Z1, Canada. Offers atmospheric science (M Sc, PhD); geological engineering (M Eng, MA Sc, PhD); geological sciences (M Sc, PhD); geophysics (M Sc, MA Sc, PhD); oceanography (M Sc, PhD). *Faculty:* 42 full-time (5 women), 16 part-time/adjunct (0 women). *Students:* 127 full-time (44 women), 1 (woman) part-time. Average age 27. 80 applicants, 41% accepted, 25 enrolled. In 2003, 21 master's, 8 doctorates awarded. *Degree requirements:* For master's, thesis (for some programs); for doctorate, thesis/dissertation, comprehensive exam. *Entrance requirements:* Additional exam requirements/recommendations for international students: Required—TOEFL (minimum score 600 paper-based; 250 computer-based). *Application deadline:* For fall admission, 3/1 for domestic students; for winter admission, 7/1 for domestic students. Applications are processed on a rolling basis. Application fee: $90 Canadian dollars ($150 Canadian dollars for international students). Electronic applications accepted. *Financial support:* In 2003–04, fellowships (averaging $16,000 per year), research assistantships (averaging $13,000 per year), teaching assistantships (averaging $4,500 per year) were awarded. Federal Work-Study, institutionally sponsored loans, scholarships/grants, tuition waivers (full and partial), and unspecified assistantships also available. *Unit head:* Dr. Paul L. Smith, Head, 604-822-6456, Fax: 604-822-6088, E-mail: psmith@cos.ubc.ca. *Application contact:* Alex Allen, Graduate Secretary, 604-822-2713, Fax: 604-822-6088, E-mail: aallen@eos.ubc.ca.

University of California, San Diego, Graduate Studies and Research, Scripps Institution of Oceanography, La Jolla, CA 92093. Offers biological oceanography (MS, PhD); geochemistry and marine chemistry (MS, PhD); marine biology (MS, PhD); physical oceanography and geological sciences (MS, PhD). *Faculty:* 88. *Students:* 222 (112 women); includes 22 minority (2 African Americans, 3 American Indian/Alaska Native, 7 Asian Americans or Pacific Islanders, 10 Hispanic Americans) 55 international. 389 applicants, 19% accepted. In 2003, 9 master's, 24 doctorates awarded. *Entrance requirements:* For master's and doctorate, GRE General Test, GRE Subject Test (marine biology). *Application deadline:* For fall admission, 1/6 for domestic students. Application fee: $60. Electronic applications accepted. Tuition, nonresident: full-time $12,245. Required fees: $6,959. *Financial support:* Fellowships, research assistantships available. *Unit head:* Myrl C. Hendershott, Chair. *Application contact:* Graduate Coordinator, 858-534-3206.

University of California, Santa Barbara, Graduate Division, College of Letters and Sciences, Division of Mathematics, Life, and Physical Sciences, Program in Marine Science, Santa Barbara, CA 93106. Offers MS, PhD. *Students:* 46 full-time (29 women); includes 5 minority (1 African American, 1 Asian American or Pacific Islander, 3 Hispanic Americans). 51 applicants, 31% accepted, 13 enrolled. In 2003, 2 doctorates awarded. *Median time to degree:* Master's–2 years full-time; doctorate–6 years full-time. *Degree requirements:* For master's, thesis/dissertation, registration; for doctorate, thesis/dissertation, comprehensive exam, registration. *Entrance requirements:* For master's and doctorate, GRE. Additional exam requirements/recommendations for international students: Required—TOEFL (minimum score 550 paper-based; 213 computer-based). *Application deadline:* For fall admission, 12/15 for domestic students. Application fee: $60. Electronic applications accepted. *Expenses:* Tuition, state resident: full-time $7,188. Tuition, nonresident: full-time $19,608. *Financial support:* In 2003–04, 44 students received support, including 2 fellowships with full tuition reimbursements available (averaging $17,000 per year), 27 research assistantships with full tuition reimbursements available (averaging $15,600 per year), 15 teaching assistantships with full tuition reimbursements available; career-related internships or fieldwork, Federal Work-Study, institutionally sponsored loans, scholarships/grants, traineeships, and tuition waivers (full and partial) also available. Support available to part-time students. Financial award application deadline: 12/15; financial award applicants required to submit FAFSA. *Faculty research:* Ocean carbon cycling, paleo oceanography, physiology of marine organisms, bio-optical oceanography, biological oceanography. Total annual research expenditures: $8 million. *Unit head:* Dr. Alice Alldredge, Chair, 805-893-3997, E-mail: alldredg@lifesci.ucsb.edu. *Application contact:* Melanie Fujii-Abe, Graduate Program Assistant, 805-893-8162, E-mail: abe@lifesci.ucsb.edu.

University of California, Santa Cruz, Division of Graduate Studies, Division of Physical and Biological Sciences, Program in Marine Sciences, Santa Cruz, CA 95064. Offers MS. *Faculty:* 6 full-time. *Students:* 8 full-time (4 women); includes 2 minority (1 Asian American or Pacific Islander, 1 Hispanic American). 39 applicants, 21% accepted, 5 enrolled. In 2003, 5 degrees awarded. *Median time to degree:* Master's–2.33 years full-time. *Degree requirements:* For master's, thesis. *Entrance requirements:* For master's, GRE General Test, GRE Subject Test. *Application deadline:* For fall admission, 1/15 for domestic students. Application fee: $60. Tuition, nonresident: full-time $12,492. *Financial support:* Fellowships, research assistantships, teaching assistantships, career-related internships or fieldwork, Federal Work-Study, and institutionally sponsored loans available. Financial award application deadline: 1/15. *Faculty research:* Oceanography, biology of higher marine vertebrates, ecology of coastal zone, marine geology. *Unit head:* Ken Bruland, Chairperson, 831-459-4736. *Application contact:* James M. Moore, Graduate Admissions, Director, 831-459-2301, Fax: 831-459-4843, E-mail: gradadm@ucsc.edu.

University of California, Santa Cruz, Division of Graduate Studies, Division of Physical and Biological Sciences, Program in Ocean Sciences, Santa Cruz, CA 95064. Offers PhD. *Faculty:* 9 full-time (4 women). *Students:* 28 full-time (23 women); includes 6 minority (1 Asian American or Pacific Islander, 5 Hispanic Americans), 2 international. 42 applicants, 31% accepted, 7 enrolled. In 2003, 1 degree awarded. *Median time to degree:* Doctorate–5.5 years full-time. *Degree requirements:* For doctorate, one foreign language, thesis/dissertation. *Entrance requirements:* For doctorate, GRE General Test, GRE Subject Test. *Application deadline:* For fall admission, 1/1 for domestic students. Application fee: $60. Tuition, nonresident: full-time $12,492. *Unit head:* Ken Bruland, Chairperson, 831-459-4736. *Application contact:* James M. Moore, Graduate Admissions, Director, 831-459-2301, Fax: 831-459-4843, E-mail: gradadm@ucsc.edu.

University of Connecticut, Graduate School, College of Liberal Arts and Sciences, Department of Marine Sciences, Field of Oceanography, Storrs, CT 06269. Offers MS, PhD. *Faculty:* 19 full-time (3 women). *Students:* 23 full-time (12 women), 6 part-time (2 women), 9 international. Average age 33. 54 applicants, 30% accepted, 10 enrolled. In 2003, 3 master's, 1 doctorate awarded. Terminal master's awarded for partial completion of doctoral program. *Degree requirements:* For master's, comprehensive exam; for doctorate, thesis/dissertation. *Entrance requirements:* For master's and doctorate, GRE General Test, GRE Subject Test. Additional exam requirements/recommendations for international students: Required—TOEFL (minimum score 550 paper-based; 213 computer-based). *Application deadline:* For fall admission, 2/1 priority date for domestic students, 2/1 priority date for international students; for spring admission, 11/1 for domestic students, 10/1 for international students. Applications are processed on a rolling basis. Application fee: $55. Electronic applications accepted. *Expenses:* Tuition, state resident: part-time $3,860 per semester. Tuition, nonresident: part-time $9,036 per semester. *Financial support:* In 2003–04, 19 research assistantships with full tuition reimbursements, 4 teaching assistantships with full tuition reimbursements were awarded. Fellowships, Federal Work-Study, scholarships/grants, health care benefits, and unspecified assistantships also available. Financial award application deadline: 2/1; financial award applicants required to submit FAFSA. *Unit head:* Robert B. Whitlatch, Head, 860-445-3467, Fax: 860-405-9153, E-mail: robert.whitlatch@uconn.edu. *Application contact:* Barbara Mahoney, Administrative Assistant, 860-405-9151, Fax: 860-405-9153, E-mail: mscadm03@uconnvm.uconn.edu.

University of Delaware, College of Marine Studies, Newark, DE 19716. Offers marine policy (MS); marine studies (MMP, MS, PhD); oceanography (MS, PhD). *Faculty:* 36 full-time (4 women). *Students:* 101 full-time (50 women), 2 part-time (1 woman); includes 6 minority (2 African Americans, 3 Asian Americans or Pacific Islanders, 1 Hispanic American), 23 international. Average age 29. 141 applicants, 30% accepted, 29 enrolled. In 2003, 17 master's, 12 doctorates awarded. *Degree requirements:* For master's and doctorate, thesis/dissertation. *Entrance requirements:* For master's and doctorate, GRE General Test. Additional exam requirements/recommendations for international students: Required—TOEFL. *Application deadline:* For fall admission, 3/1 for domestic students; for spring admission, 10/1 for domestic students. Applications are processed on a rolling basis. Application fee: $60. Electronic applications accepted. *Expenses:* Tuition, state resident: full-time $5,890; part-time $327 per credit. Tuition, nonresident: full-time $15,420; part-time $857 per credit. Required fees: $968. *Financial support:* In 2003–04, 77 students received support, including 22 fellowships with full tuition reimbursements available (averaging $19,000 per year), 55 research assistantships with full tuition reimbursements available (averaging $19,000 per year), teaching assistantships with full tuition reimbursements available (averaging $19,000 per year); career-related internships or fieldwork, Federal Work-Study, and tuition waivers (full and partial) also available. Financial award application deadline: 3/1. *Faculty research:* Marine biology and biochemistry, oceanography, marine policy, physical ocean science and engineering, ocean engineering. Total annual research expenditures: $10.2 million. *Unit head:* Dr. Carolyn A. Thoroughgood, Dean, 302-831-2841. *Application contact:* Doris Manship, Coordinator, 302-645-4226, E-mail: dmanship@udel.edu.

University of Florida, Graduate School, College of Agricultural and Life Sciences, Department of Fisheries and Aquatic Science, Gainesville, FL 32611. Offers MFAS, MS, PhD.

Marine Sciences

University of Florida (continued)

Faculty: 30. *Students:* 33 full-time (12 women), 21 part-time (9 women); includes 6 minority (3 African Americans, 1 American Indian/Alaska Native, 2 Asian Americans or Pacific Islanders), 2 international. 29 applicants, 31% accepted. In 2003, 8 master's, 1 doctorate awarded. *Degree requirements:* For master's, thesis optional; for doctorate, thesis/dissertation. *Entrance requirements:* For master's and doctorate, GRE General Test, minimum GPA of 3.0. Additional exam requirements/recommendations for international students: Required—TOEFL. *Application deadline:* For fall admission, 6/1 for domestic students. Applications are processed on a rolling basis. Application fee: $20. Electronic applications accepted. *Expenses:* Tuition, state resident: part-time $205 per credit hour. Tuition, nonresident: part-time $775 per credit hour. *Financial support:* In 2003–04, 1 fellowship, 18 research assistantships were awarded. Unspecified assistantships also available. *Unit head:* Dr. Randall Stocker, Interim Chair, 352-392-9613, Fax: 352-392-3672, E-mail: aqplants@ifas.ufl.edu. *Application contact:* Dr. Ed Phlips, Graduate Coordinator, 352-392-9617 Ext. 248, Fax: 352-392-3672, E-mail: phlips@ufl.edu.

University of Georgia, Graduate School, College of Arts and Sciences, Department of Marine Sciences, Athens, GA 30602. Offers MS, PhD. *Faculty:* 18 full-time (5 women). *Students:* 41 full-time (20 women); includes 2 minority (1 Asian American or Pacific Islander, 1 Hispanic American), 9 international. Average age 28. 37 applicants, 32% accepted, 7 enrolled. In 2003, 1 master's, 4 doctorates awarded. *Median time to degree:* Master's–3 years full-time; doctorate–4 years full-time. *Degree requirements:* For master's, thesis; for doctorate, thesis/dissertation, teaching experience, field research experience, comprehensive exam. *Entrance requirements:* For master's and doctorate, GRE General Test. Additional exam requirements/recommendations for international students: Required—TOEFL. *Application deadline:* For fall admission, 2/1 priority date for domestic students, 2/1 priority date for international students; for spring admission, 10/15 priority date for domestic students, 9/1 priority date for international students. Applications are processed on a rolling basis. Application fee: $50. Electronic applications accepted. *Expenses:* Tuition, state resident: part-time $161 per hour. Tuition, nonresident: part-time $690 per hour. One-time fee: $435 part-time. *Financial support:* In 2003–04, 9 fellowships with full tuition reimbursements (averaging $20,000 per year), 21 research assistantships with full tuition reimbursements (averaging $18,000 per year), 11 teaching assistantships with full tuition reimbursements (averaging $18,000 per year) were awarded. *Faculty research:* Microbial ecology, biogeochemistry, polar biology, coastal ecology, coastal circulation. *Unit head:* Dr. James T. Hollibaugh, Director, 706-542-3016, Fax: 706-542-5888, E-mail: aquadoc@uga.edu. *Application contact:* Dr. Mary Ann Moran, Graduate Coordinator, 706-542-6481, Fax: 706-542-5888, E-mail: mmoran@uga.edu.

University of Maine, Graduate School, College of Natural Sciences, Forestry, and Agriculture, School of Marine Sciences, Orono, ME 04469. Offers marine biology (MS, PhD); marine policy (MS); oceanography (MS, PhD). Part-time programs available. *Faculty:* 12. *Students:* 53 full-time (37 women), 15 part-time (6 women); includes 1 minority (Asian American or Pacific Islander), 11 international. Average age 28. 86 applicants, 26% accepted, 11 enrolled. In 2003, 10 master's, 2 doctorates awarded. *Degree requirements:* For master's and doctorate, thesis/dissertation. *Entrance requirements:* For master's and doctorate, GRE General Test. Additional exam requirements/recommendations for international students: Required—TOEFL. *Application deadline:* For fall admission, 2/1 for domestic students. Applications are processed on a rolling basis. Application fee: $50. Electronic applications accepted. *Expenses:* Tuition, state resident: part-time $235 per credit. Tuition, nonresident: part-time $670 per credit. Tuition and fees vary according to course load. *Financial support:* In 2003–04, fellowships with tuition reimbursements (averaging $27,500 per year), research assistantships with tuition reimbursements (averaging $16,500 per year), teaching assistantships with tuition reimbursements (averaging $16,000 per year) were awarded. Career-related internships or fieldwork, Federal Work-Study, and tuition waivers (full and partial) also available. Support available to part-time students. Financial award application deadline: 3/1. *Faculty research:* Coastal processes, microbial ecology, crustacean systematics. *Unit head:* Dr. David Townsend, Director, 207-581-4381, Fax: 207-581-4388. *Application contact:* Scott G. Delcourt, Associate Dean of the Graduate School, 207-581-3218, Fax: 207-581-3232, E-mail: graduate@maine.edu.

University of Maryland, Graduate School, Program in Marine-Estuarine-Environmental Sciences, Baltimore, MD 21201. Offers MS, PhD. An intercampus, interdisciplinary program. Part-time programs available. *Faculty:* 6. *Students:* 1 (woman) full-time, 1 (woman) part-time; includes 1 minority (Hispanic American) 4 applicants, 0% accepted.Terminal master's awarded for partial completion of doctoral program. *Degree requirements:* For master's, thesis; for doctorate, thesis/dissertation, proposal defense, comprehensive exam. *Entrance requirements:* For master's and doctorate, GRE General Test, minimum GPA of 3.0. Additional exam requirements/recommendations for international students: Required—TOEFL. *Application deadline:* For fall admission, 2/1 for domestic students; for spring admission, 9/1 for domestic students. Applications are processed on a rolling basis. Application fee: $50. Electronic applications accepted. *Financial support:* Research assistantships with tuition reimbursements, teaching assistantships with tuition reimbursements, scholarships/grants and unspecified assistantships available. *Unit head:* Dr. Kennedy T. Paynter, Director, 301-405-6938, Fax: 301-314-4139, E-mail: mees@mees.umd.edu.

See in-depth description on page 291.

University of Maryland, Baltimore County, Graduate School, Department of Biological Sciences, Program in Marine-Estuarine-Environmental Sciences, Baltimore, MD 21250. Offers MS, PhD. Part-time programs available. *Faculty:* 12. *Students:* 12 (8 women); includes 1 minority (African American) 2 international. 6 applicants, 50% accepted, 3 enrolled. In 2003, 1 degree awarded. *Degree requirements:* For master's, thesis; for doctorate, thesis/dissertation, proposal defense, comprehensive exam (for some programs). *Entrance requirements:* For master's and doctorate, GRE General Test, minimum GPA of 3.0. Additional exam requirements/recommendations for international students: Required—TOEFL. *Application deadline:* For fall admission, 2/1 for domestic students, 1/1 for international students; for spring admission, 9/1 for domestic students. Applications are processed on a rolling basis. Application fee: $50. Electronic applications accepted. *Expenses:* Tuition, state resident: full-time $7,000. Tuition, nonresident: full-time $11,400. Required fees: $1,440. *Financial support:* In 2003–04, 1 fellowship with tuition reimbursement (averaging $20,000 per year), research assistantships with tuition reimbursements (averaging $19,000 per year), teaching assistantships with tuition reimbursements (averaging $19,000 per year) were awarded. Career-related internships or fieldwork, scholarships/grants, and unspecified assistantships also available. Financial award application deadline: 1/1. *Unit head:* Dr. Kennedy T. Paynter, Director, 301-405-6938, Fax: 301-314-4139, E-mail: mees@mees.umd.edu. *Application contact:* Dr. Thomas Cronin, Graduate Program Director, 410-455-3669, Fax: 410-455-3875, E-mail: biograd@umbc.edu.

University of Maryland, College Park, Graduate Studies and Research, College of Life Sciences, Program in Marine-Estuarine-Environmental Sciences, College Park, MD 20742. Offers MS, PhD. An intercampus, interdisciplinary program. Part-time programs available. *Faculty:* 139. *Students:* 180 (94 women); includes 12 minority (2 African Americans, 1 American Indian/Alaska Native, 3 Asian Americans or Pacific Islanders, 6 Hispanic Americans) 37 international. 176 applicants, 33% accepted, 43 enrolled. In 2003, 18 master's, 17 doctorates awarded. Terminal master's awarded for partial completion of doctoral program. *Degree requirements:* For master's, thesis, oral defense; for doctorate, thesis/dissertation, proposal defense, comprehensive exam. *Entrance requirements:* For master's and doctorate, GRE General Test, minimum GPA of 3.0. Additional exam requirements/recommendations for international students: Required—TOEFL. *Application deadline:* For fall admission, 2/1 for domestic students; for spring admission, 9/1 for domestic students. Applications are processed on a rolling basis. Application fee: $50. Electronic applications accepted. *Expenses:* Tuition, state resident: part-time $349 per credit hour. Tuition, nonresident: part-time $602 per credit hour. *Financial support:* In 2003–04, 9 teaching assistantships with full tuition reimbursements were awarded; fellowships with full tuition reimbursements, research assistantships with full tuition reimbursements, Federal Work-Study, scholarships/grants, traineeships, health care benefits, and unspecified assistantships also available. Financial award application deadline: 1/1; financial award applicants required to submit FAFSA. *Faculty research:* Marine and estuarine organisms, terrestrial and freshwater ecology, remote environmental sensing. *Unit head:* Dr. Kennedy T. Paynter, Director, 301-405-6938, Fax: 301-314-4139, E-mail: mees@mees.umd.edu.

University of Maryland Eastern Shore, Graduate Programs, Program in Marine-Estuarine-Environmental Sciences, Princess Anne, MD 21853-1299. Offers MS, PhD. Part-time programs available. *Faculty:* 13. *Students:* 24 (16 women); includes 13 minority (9 African Americans, 2 Asian Americans or Pacific Islanders, 2 Hispanic Americans) 7 international. 16 applicants, 19% accepted, 2 enrolled. In 2003, 5 master's, 2 doctorates awarded. *Degree requirements:* For master's, thesis; for doctorate, thesis/dissertation, proposal defense, comprehensive exam. *Entrance requirements:* For master's and doctorate, GRE General Test, minimum GPA of 3.0. Additional exam requirements/recommendations for international students: Required—TOEFL. *Application deadline:* For fall admission, 2/1 for domestic students; for spring admission, 9/1 for domestic students. Applications are processed on a rolling basis. Application fee: $30. Electronic applications accepted. *Financial support:* In 2003–04, 30 students received support; fellowships with tuition reimbursements available, research assistantships with tuition reimbursements available, teaching assistantships with tuition reimbursements available, career-related internships or fieldwork, scholarships/grants, and unspecified assistantships available. Support available to part-time students. Financial award application deadline: 1/1. *Unit head:* Dr. Kennedy T. Paynter, Director, 301-405-6938, Fax: 301-314-4139, E-mail: mees@mees.umd.edu.

University of Massachusetts Boston, Office of Graduate Studies and Research, College of Science and Mathematics, Department of Environmental, Coastal and Ocean Sciences, Track in Environmental, Coastal and Ocean Sciences, Boston, MA 02125-3393. Offers PhD. Part-time and evening/weekend programs available. *Students:* 9 full-time (6 women), 14 part-time (6 women), 11 international. Average age 35. 25 applicants, 36% accepted, 4 enrolled. *Degree requirements:* For doctorate, thesis/dissertation, oral exams, comprehensive exam. *Entrance requirements:* For doctorate, GRE General Test, minimum GPA of 2.75. *Application deadline:* For fall admission, 2/1 for domestic students; for spring admission, 10/15 for domestic students. Application fee: $25 ($40 for international students). *Expenses:* Tuition, state resident: full-time $4,461. Tuition, nonresident: full-time $9,390. *Financial support:* In 2003–04, research assistantships with full tuition reimbursements (averaging $8,000 per year), teaching assistantships with full tuition reimbursements (averaging $8,000 per year) were awarded. Career-related internships or fieldwork, Federal Work-Study, and unspecified assistantships also available. Support available to part-time students. Financial award application deadline: 3/1; financial award applicants required to submit FAFSA. *Faculty research:* Conservation genetics, anthropogenic and natural influences on community structures of coral reef factors, geographical variation in mitochondrial DNA, protein chemistry and enzymology pertaining to insect cuticle. *Application contact:* Peggy Roldan, Graduate Admissions Coordinator, 617-287-6400, Fax: 617-287-6236, E-mail: bos.gadm@dpc.umassp.edu.

University of Massachusetts Dartmouth, Graduate School, School of Marine Science and Technology, Program in Marine Science and Technology, North Dartmouth, MA 02747-2300. Offers MS, PhD. *Faculty:* 8 full-time (0 women). *Students:* 8 full-time (3 women), 5 part-time (2 women), 7 international. Average age 29. 19 applicants, 32% accepted, 5 enrolled. *Degree requirements:* For master's, thesis or alternative; for doctorate, thesis/dissertation, comprehensive exam. *Entrance requirements:* For master's and doctorate, GRE, minimum GPA of 3.0. Additional exam requirements/recommendations for international students: Required—TOEFL (minimum score 600 paper-based; 213 computer-based). *Application deadline:* For fall admission, 4/20 priority date for domestic students, 2/20 priority date for international students. Applications are processed on a rolling basis. Application fee: $35 ($55 for international students). Electronic applications accepted. *Expenses:* Tuition, state resident: full-time $2,071; part-time $86 per credit. Tuition, nonresident: full-time $8,099; part-time $337 per credit. Required fees: $248 per credit. One-time fee: $50 full-time. Part-time tuition and fees vary according to course load and program. *Financial support:* In 2003–04, 8 research assistantships with full tuition reimbursements (averaging $16,574 per year) were awarded; unspecified assistantships also available. Financial award application deadline: 3/1; financial award applicants required to submit FAFSA. *Faculty research:* Northeast water quality, oceanography, osmerus mordax, shellfish analysis. Total annual research expenditures: $7.4 million. *Unit head:* Dr. Wendell Brown, Director, 508-910-6395, E-mail: wbrown@umassd.edu. *Application contact:* Carol Novo, Graduate Admissions Officer, 508-999-8604, Fax: 508-999-8183, E-mail: graduate@umassd.edu.

University of Miami, Graduate School, Rosenstiel School of Marine and Atmospheric Science, Division of Applied Marine Physics, Coral Gables, FL 33124. Offers applied marine physics (MS, PhD), including coastal ocean circulation dynamics, ocean acoustics and geoacoustics (PhD), small-scale ocean surface dynamics and air-sea interaction physics (PhD); ocean engineering (MS). Part-time programs available. *Faculty:* 11 full-time (0 women), 14 part-time/adjunct (3 women). *Students:* 16 full-time (1 woman); includes 1 minority (Hispanic American), 11 international. Average age 30. 22 applicants, 41% accepted, 5 enrolled. In 2003, 3 degrees awarded, leading to continued full-time study 67%, government 33%. Terminal master's awarded for partial completion of doctoral program. *Median time to degree:* Master's–5.2 years full-time. *Degree requirements:* For master's and doctorate, thesis/dissertation, comprehensive exam, registration. *Entrance requirements:* For master's and doctorate, GRE General Test. Additional exam requirements/recommendations for international students: Required—TOEFL (minimum score 550 paper-based; 213 computer-based). *Application deadline:* For fall admission, 1/1 priority date for domestic students, 1/1 priority date for international students. Applications are processed on a rolling basis. Application fee: $50. Electronic applications accepted. *Expenses:* Tuition: Full-time $19,526. *Financial support:* In 2003–04, 14 students received support, including 2 fellowships with tuition reimbursements available (averaging $20,124 per year), 11 research assistantships with tuition reimbursements available (averaging $20,124 per year); teaching assistantships with tuition reimbursements available, Federal Work-Study, institutionally sponsored loans, scholarships/grants, and unspecified assistantships also available. Financial award application deadline: 3/1; financial award applicants required to submit FAFSA. Total annual research expenditures: $2.5 million. *Unit head:* Dr. Michael G. Brown, Chair, 305-361-4640, E-mail: mbrown@rsmas.miami.edu. *Application contact:* Dr. Frank Millero, Associate Dean, 305-361-4155, Fax: 305-361-4771, E-mail: gso@rsmas.miami.edu.

University of Miami, Graduate School, Rosenstiel School of Marine and Atmospheric Science, Division of Marine and Atmospheric Chemistry, Coral Gables, FL 33124. Offers MS, PhD. *Faculty:* 17 full-time (2 women), 13 part-time/adjunct (2 women). *Students:* 11 full-time (4 women), 6 international. Average age 25. 20 applicants, 20% accepted, 1 enrolled. In 2003, 2 master's awarded, leading to continued full-time study 50%, business/industry 50%; 2 doctorates awarded, leading to university research/teaching 50%, government 50%. Terminal master's awarded for partial completion of doctoral program. *Median time to degree:* Master's–3 years full-time; doctorate–5.8 years full-time. *Degree requirements:* For master's and doctorate, thesis/dissertation, comprehensive exam, registration. *Entrance requirements:* For master's and doctorate, GRE General Test. Additional exam requirements/recommendations for international students: Required—TOEFL (minimum score 550 paper-based; 213 computer-based). *Application deadline:* For fall admission, 1/1 priority date for domestic students, 1/1 priority date for international students. Applications are processed on a rolling basis. Application fee: $50. Electronic applications accepted. *Expenses:* Tuition: Full-time $19,526. *Financial support:* In 2003–04, 11 students received support, including 1 fellowship with tuition reimbursement available (averaging $20,124 per year), 9 research assistantships with tuition reimbursements available (averaging $20,124 per year), 1 teaching assistantship with tuition reimbursement available (averaging $20,124 per year); Federal Work-Study, institutionally sponsored loans, scholarships/grants, and unspecified assistantships also available. Financial award application deadline: 3/1; financial award applicants required to submit FAFSA. *Faculty research:* Global change issues, chemistry of marine waters and marine atmosphere. *Unit head:* Dr. Dennis Hansell, Chairperson, 305-361-4922, Fax: 305-361-4689, E-mail: dhansell@rsmas.

miami.edu. *Application contact:* Dr. Frank Millero, Associate Dean, 305-361-4155, Fax: 305-361-4771, E-mail: gso@rsmas.miami.edu.

The University of North Carolina at Chapel Hill, Graduate School, College of Arts and Sciences, Department of Marine Sciences, Chapel Hill, NC 27599. Offers MS, PhD. *Faculty:* 24 full-time, 11 part-time/adjunct. *Students:* 28 full-time (18 women). 40 applicants, 28% accepted. In 2003, 1 master's, 1 doctorate awarded. *Degree requirements:* For master's and doctorate, thesis/dissertation, comprehensive exam. *Entrance requirements:* For master's and doctorate, GRE General Test, GRE Subject Test, minimum GPA of 3.0. *Application deadline:* For fall admission, 12/1 for domestic students. Application fee: $60. *Expenses:* Tuition, state resident: full-time $3,163. Tuition, nonresident: full-time $15,161. *Financial support:* In 2003–04, 26 research assistantships, 2 teaching assistantships were awarded. Financial award application deadline: 3/1. *Unit head:* Dr. Francisco E. Werner, Chairman, 919-962-1252, Fax: 919-962-1254.

The University of North Carolina at Chapel Hill, Graduate School, School of Public Health, Department of Environmental Sciences and Engineering, Chapel Hill, NC 27599. Offers air, radiation and industrial hygiene (MPH, MS, MSEE, MSPH, PhD); aquatic and atmospheric sciences (MPH, MS, MSPH, PhD); environmental engineering (MPH, MS, MSEE, MSPH, PhD); environmental health sciences (MPH, MS, MSPH, PhD); environmental management and policy (MPH, MS, MSPH, PhD). *Accreditation:* ABET (one or more programs are accredited). *Faculty:* 34 full-time (5 women), 36 part-time/adjunct. *Students:* 153 full-time (85 women); includes 43 minority (11 African Americans, 30 Asian Americans or Pacific Islanders, 2 Hispanic Americans). Average age 26. 234 applicants, 35% accepted, 40 enrolled. In 2003, 38 master's, 13 doctorates awarded. Terminal master's awarded for partial completion of doctoral program. *Median time to degree:* Master's–2 years full-time; doctorate–4.5 years full-time. *Degree requirements:* For master's, thesis (for some programs), research paper, comprehensive exam; for doctorate, thesis/dissertation, comprehensive exam. *Entrance requirements:* For master's and doctorate, GRE General Test, minimum GPA of 3.0. Additional exam requirements/recommendations for international students: Required—TOEFL. *Application deadline:* For fall admission, 1/1 priority date for domestic students, 1/1 priority date for international students; for spring admission, 9/15 for domestic students. Applications are processed on a rolling basis. Application fee: $60. Electronic applications accepted. *Expenses:* Tuition, state resident: full-time $3,163. Tuition, nonresident: full-time $15,161. *Financial support:* In 2003–04, 120 students received support, including 44 fellowships with tuition reimbursements available (averaging $17,230 per year), 63 research assistantships with tuition reimbursements available (averaging $16,264 per year), 13 teaching assistantships with tuition reimbursements available (averaging $11,120 per year); career-related internships or fieldwork, Federal Work-Study, and traineeships also available. Support available to part-time students. Financial award application deadline: 1/1; financial award applicants required to submit FAFSA. *Faculty research:* Air, radiation and industrial hygiene, aquatic and atmospheric sciences, environmental health sciences, environmental management and policy, water resources engineering. Total annual research expenditures: $7.8 million. *Unit head:* Dr. Casey T. Miller, Chair, 919-966-1024, Fax: 919-966-7911, E-mail: casey_miller@unc.edu. *Application contact:* Jack Whaley, Assistant Registrar, 919-966-3844, Fax: 919-966-7911, E-mail: jack_whaley@unc.edu.

The University of North Carolina at Wilmington, College of Arts and Sciences, Department of Earth Sciences, Wilmington, NC 28403-3297. Offers geology (MS); marine science (MS). *Faculty:* 21 full-time (5 women). *Students:* 14 full-time (11 women), 41 part-time (15 women); includes 3 minority (1 American Indian/Alaska Native, 1 Asian American or Pacific Islander, 1 Hispanic American), 1 international. Average age 35. 42 applicants, 45% accepted, 15 enrolled. In 2003, 14 degrees awarded. *Degree requirements:* For master's, thesis, comprehensive exam. *Entrance requirements:* For master's, GRE General Test, GRE Subject Test, minimum B average in undergraduate major and basic courses for prerequisite to geology. *Application deadline:* For fall admission, 2/15 for domestic students. Applications are processed on a rolling basis. Application fee: $45. *Expenses:* Tuition, state resident: full-time $2,282. Tuition, nonresident: full-time $11,980. Required fees: $1,659. Tuition and fees vary according to course load. *Financial support:* In 2003–04, 9 teaching assistantships were awarded; career-related internships or fieldwork and Federal Work-Study also available. Support available to part-time students. Financial award application deadline: 3/15. *Unit head:* Dr. Richard A. Laws, Chair, 910-962-3736, Fax: 910-962-7077. *Application contact:* Dr. Robert D. Roer, Dean, Graduate School, 910-962-4117, Fax: 910-962-3787, E-mail: roer@uncw.edu.

University of Puerto Rico, Mayagüez Campus, Graduate Studies, College of Arts and Sciences, Department of Marine Sciences, Mayagüez, PR 00681-9000. Offers biological oceanography (MMS, PhD); chemical oceanography (MMS, PhD); geological oceanography (MMS, PhD); physical oceanography (MMS, PhD). *Degree requirements:* For master's, one foreign language, thesis, departmental and comprehensive final exams; for doctorate, one foreign language, thesis/dissertation, qualifying, comprehensive, and final exams. *Faculty research:* Marine botany, ecology, chemistry, and parasitology; fisheries; ichthyology; aquaculture.

See in-depth description on page 293.

University of San Diego, College of Arts and Sciences, Program in Marine and Environmental Studies, San Diego, CA 92110-2492. Offers marine science (MS). Part-time programs available. *Faculty:* 8 full-time (5 women), 1 part-time/adjunct (0 women). *Students:* 9 full-time (5 women), 22 part-time (13 women); includes 2 minority (both Asian Americans or Pacific Islanders), 1 international. Average age 26. 34 applicants, 65% accepted, 8 enrolled. In 2003, 6 degrees awarded. *Degree requirements:* For master's, thesis. *Entrance requirements:* For master's, GRE General Test, minimum GPA of 3.0, undergraduate major in science. Additional exam requirements/recommendations for international students: Required—TOEFL (minimum score 580 paper-based; 237 computer-based), TWE. *Application deadline:* For fall admission, 5/1 for domestic students. Applications are processed on a rolling basis. Application fee: $45. Electronic applications accepted. *Expenses:* Tuition: Full-time $14,850; part-time $825 per unit. Required fees: $126. Full-time tuition and fees vary according to class time, course load, degree level and program. *Financial support:* Career-related internships or fieldwork, Federal Work-Study, institutionally sponsored loans, tuition waivers (partial), and unspecified assistantships available. Support available to part-time students. Financial award application deadline: 5/1; financial award applicants required to submit FAFSA. *Faculty research:* Marine ecology; paleoclimatology; geochemistry; functional morphology; marine zoology of mammals, birds and turtles. *Unit head:* Dr. Hugh I. Ellis, Director, 619-260-4075, Fax: 619-260-6804, E-mail: ellis@sandiego.edu. *Application contact:* Stephen Pultz, Director of Admissions, 619-260-4524, Fax: 619-260-4158, E-mail: grads@sandiego.edu.

University of South Alabama, Graduate School, College of Arts and Sciences, Department of Marine Sciences, Mobile, AL 36688-0002. Offers MS, PhD. *Degree requirements:* For master's, comprehensive exam; for doctorate, one foreign language, thesis/dissertation, research project, comprehensive exam. *Entrance requirements:* For master's, GRE, minimum GPA of 3.0.

University of South Carolina, The Graduate School, College of Science and Mathematics, Marine Science Program, Columbia, SC 29208. Offers MS, PhD. *Faculty:* 36 full-time (5 women), 11 part-time/adjunct (5 women). *Students:* 31 full-time (17 women); includes 8 minority (1 African American, 2 Asian Americans or Pacific Islanders, 5 Hispanic Americans). Average age 28. 37 applicants, 14% accepted. In 2003, 3 master's, 1 doctorate awarded. *Degree requirements:* For master's and doctorate, thesis/dissertation. *Entrance requirements:* For master's and doctorate, GRE General Test. *Application deadline:* For fall admission, 2/1 for domestic students. Applications are processed on a rolling basis. Application fee: $35. Electronic applications accepted. *Expenses:* Tuition, state resident: part-time $308 per hour. Tuition, nonresident: part-time $655 per hour. *Financial support:* In 2003–04, 9 students received support, including 7 fellowships, 9 research assistantships (averaging $11,000 per year), 9 teaching assistantships (averaging $11,000 per year); career-related internships or fieldwork, Federal Work-Study, institutionally sponsored loans, and unspecified assistantships also available. Financial award application deadline: 2/1. *Faculty research:* Biological, chemical, geological, and physical oceanography; policy. *Unit head:* Dr. Björn Kjerfve, Director, 803-777-2572, Fax: 803-777-3955, E-mail: bjorn@msci.sc.edu. *Application contact:* Dr. Timothy J. Shaw, Graduate Studies Director, 803-777-0352, Fax: 803-777-3922, E-mail: shaw@mail.chem.sc.edu.

University of Southern California, Graduate School, College of Letters, Arts and Sciences, Department of Biological Sciences, Program in Marine Environmental Biology, Los Angeles, CA 90089. Offers PhD. *Degree requirements:* For doctorate, thesis/dissertation. *Entrance requirements:* For doctorate, GRE General Test. Additional exam requirements/recommendations for international students: Required—TOEFL. *Expenses:* Tuition: Full-time $32,784; part-time $949 per unit. Tuition and fees vary according to course load and program. *Faculty research:* Microbial ecology, physiology of larval development, biological community structure, Cambrian radiation.

University of Southern Mississippi, Graduate School, College of Science and Technology, Department of Coastal Sciences, Hattiesburg, MS 39406-0001. Offers MS, PhD. Part-time programs available. *Faculty:* 6 full-time (1 woman). *Students:* 18 full-time (11 women), 14 part-time (7 women); includes 1 minority (Asian American or Pacific Islander) Average age 32. 15 applicants, 53% accepted, 6 enrolled. *Degree requirements:* For master's and doctorate, thesis/dissertation, comprehensive exam. *Entrance requirements:* For master's, GRE General Test, minimum GPA of 3.0; for doctorate, GRE General Test, minimum undergraduate GPA of 3.0, graduate 3.5. Additional exam requirements/recommendations for international students: Required—TOEFL. *Application deadline:* For fall admission, 3/1 for domestic students. Applications are processed on a rolling basis. Application fee: $25. Electronic applications accepted. *Expenses:* Tuition, state resident: part-time $1,967 per semester. Tuition, nonresident: part-time $4,376 per semester. *Financial support:* Research assistantships with full tuition reimbursements, teaching assistantships with full tuition reimbursements, Federal Work-Study and institutionally sponsored loans available. Financial award application deadline: 3/15. *Unit head:* Dr. William Hawking, Chair, 228-872-4215.

University of Southern Mississippi, Graduate School, College of Science and Technology, Department of Marine Science, Stennis Space Center, MS 39529. Offers hydrographic science (MS); marine science (MS, PhD). Part-time programs available. *Faculty:* 11 full-time (2 women), 2 part-time/adjunct (0 women). *Students:* 31 full-time (15 women), 14 part-time (2 women), 12 international. Average age 25. 42 applicants, 48% accepted, 18 enrolled. In 2003, 14 master's, 2 doctorates awarded. *Degree requirements:* For master's, thesis, oral qualifying exam (marine science), comprehensive exam; for doctorate, 2 foreign languages, thesis/dissertation, oral qualifying exam, comprehensive exam. *Entrance requirements:* For master's, GRE General Test, minimum GPA of 3.0; for doctorate, GRE General Test, minimum GPA of 3.0 (undergraduate), 3.5 (graduate). Additional exam requirements/recommendations for international students: Required—TOEFL. *Application deadline:* For fall admission, 3/1 for domestic students; for spring admission, 12/13 for domestic students. Applications are processed on a rolling basis. Application fee: $0 ($25 for international students). Electronic applications accepted. *Expenses:* Tuition, state resident: part-time $1,967 per semester. Tuition, nonresident: part-time $4,376 per semester. *Financial support:* In 2003–04, research assistantships with full tuition reimbursements (averaging $16,800 per year), teaching assistantships with full tuition reimbursements (averaging $16,800 per year) were awarded. Federal Work-Study and institutionally sponsored loans also available. Financial award application deadline: 3/15. *Faculty research:* Chemical, biological, physical, and geological marine science; remote sensing; bio-optics; numerical modeling. Total annual research expenditures: $2.6 million. *Unit head:* Dr. Denis A. Wiesenburg, Professor, 228-688-3177, Fax: 228-688-1121. *Application contact:* Dr. Steven E. Lohrenz, Professor, 228-688-1176, Fax: 228-688-1121, E-mail: steven.lohrenz@usm.edu.

University of South Florida, College of Graduate Studies, College of Marine Science, St. Petersburg, FL 33701-5016. Offers MS, PhD. Part-time and evening/weekend programs available. *Faculty:* 82 full-time (15 women). *Students:* 58 full-time (40 women), 61 part-time (34 women); includes 14 minority (7 African Americans, 7 Hispanic Americans), 8 international. Average age 31. 99 applicants, 35% accepted, 29 enrolled. In 2003, 5 master's, 4 doctorates awarded. *Degree requirements:* For master's, thesis; for doctorate, thesis/dissertation, profiency foreign language and relevant skill directly related to area of study. *Entrance requirements:* For master's and doctorate, GRE General Test, minimum GPA of 3.0 in last 60 hours. Additional exam requirements/recommendations for international students: Required—TOEFL. *Application deadline:* For fall admission, 6/1 for domestic students; for spring admission, 11/1 for domestic students. Applications are processed on a rolling basis. Application fee: $30. *Financial support:* Fellowships with partial tuition reimbursements, research assistantships with partial tuition reimbursements, teaching assistantships with partial tuition reimbursements available. *Faculty research:* Trace metal chemistry, water quality, organic and isotopic geochemistry, physical chemistry, nutrient chemistry. Total annual research expenditures: $3.7 million. *Unit head:* Dr. Peter R. Betzer, Dean, 727-553-1130, Fax: 727-553-1189, E-mail: pbetzer@marine.usf.edu. *Application contact:* Dr. Edward VanVleet, Coordinator, 727-553-1165, Fax: 727-553-1189, E-mail: advisor@marine.usf.edu.

See in-depth description on page 295.

The University of Texas at Austin, Graduate School, College of Natural Sciences, Department of Marine Science, Austin, TX 78712-1111. Offers MS, PhD. *Degree requirements:* For master's and doctorate, thesis/dissertation. *Entrance requirements:* For master's and doctorate, GRE General Test. Additional exam requirements/recommendations for international students: Required—TOEFL.

See in-depth description on page 299.

University of Wisconsin–La Crosse, Office of University Graduate Studies, College of Science and Allied Health, Department of Biology, La Crosse, WI 54601-3742. Offers aquatic sciences (MS); biology (MS); cellular and molecular biology (MS); clinical microbiology (MS); microbiology (MS); nurse anesthesia (MS); physiology (MS). *Accreditation:* AANA/CANAEP. Part-time programs available. *Faculty:* 19 full-time (3 women). *Students:* 8 full-time (4 women), 15 part-time (9 women), 1 international. Average age 31. 50 applicants, 30% accepted. In 2003, 14 degrees awarded. *Degree requirements:* For master's, thesis (for some programs), comprehensive exam. *Entrance requirements:* For master's, GRE General Test, minimum GPA of 3.0 during previous 2 years or 2.85 overall. Additional exam requirements/recommendations for international students: Required—TOEFL (minimum score 550 paper-based; 213 computer-based). *Application deadline:* For fall admission, 3/1 for domestic students. Applications are processed on a rolling basis. Application fee: $45. Electronic applications accepted. *Expenses:* Tuition, state resident: part-time $288 per credit. Tuition, nonresident: part-time $878 per credit. Tuition and fees vary according to course load, program and reciprocity agreements. *Financial support:* In 2003–04, 10 students received support, including 4 research assistantships with partial tuition reimbursements available (averaging $12,000 per year), 5 teaching assistantships with partial tuition reimbursements available (averaging $8,000 per year); career-related internships or fieldwork, Federal Work-Study, health care benefits, unspecified assistantships, and grant-funded positions also available. Support available to part-time students. Financial award application deadline: 3/15; financial award applicants required to submit FAFSA. *Faculty research:* Ecology, river studies, aquatic toxicology, aquatic microbiology, molecular biology, physiology. Total annual research expenditures: $700,000. *Unit head:* Dr. Tom Volk, Program Director, 608-785-6972, Fax: 608-785-6959, E-mail: volk.thom@uwlax.edu. *Application contact:* Tim Lewis, Director of Admissions, 608-785-8939, E-mail: lewis.timo@uwlax.edu.

University of Wisconsin–Madison, Graduate School, College of Letters and Science, Department of Atmospheric and Oceanic Sciences, Madison, WI 53706-1380. Offers MS, PhD. Part-time programs available. *Degree requirements:* For master's, thesis (for some programs); for doctorate, thesis/dissertation. *Entrance requirements:* For master's and doctorate, GRE General Test, minimum GPA of 3.0; previous course work in chemistry, mathematics, and phys-

Marine Sciences

University of Wisconsin–Madison (continued)
ics. Electronic applications accepted. Tuition, area resident: Full-time $7,593; part-time $476 per credit. Tuition, nonresident: full-time $22,824; part-time $1,430 per credit. Required fees: $292; $38 per credit. Part-time tuition and fees vary according to course load and reciprocity agreements. *Faculty research:* Satellite meteorology, weather systems, global climate change, numerical modeling, atmosphere-ocean interaction.

Oceanography

Columbia University, Graduate School of Arts and Sciences, Division of Natural Sciences, Department of Earth and Environmental Sciences, New York, NY 10027. Offers geochemistry (M Phil, MA, PhD); geodetic sciences (M Phil, MA, PhD); geophysics (M Phil, MA, PhD); oceanography (M Phil, MA, PhD). *Faculty:* 21 full-time, 19 part-time/adjunct. *Students:* 78 full-time (31 women), 6 part-time (2 women); includes 4 minority (3 Asian Americans or Pacific Islanders, 1 Hispanic American), 31 international. Average age 32. 115 applicants, 20% accepted. In 2003, 16 master's, 11 doctorates awarded. *Degree requirements:* For master's, thesis or alternative, fieldwork, written exam; for doctorate, one foreign language, thesis/dissertation. *Entrance requirements:* For master's and doctorate, GRE General Test, GRE Subject Test, major in natural or physical science. Additional exam requirements/recommendations for international students: Required—TOEFL. Application fee: $75. *Expenses:* Tuition: Full-time $14,820. *Financial support:* Fellowships, teaching assistantships, Federal Work-Study and institutionally sponsored loans available. Support available to part-time students. Financial award application deadline: 1/5; financial award applicants required to submit FAFSA. *Faculty research:* Structural geology and stratigraphy, petrology, paleontology, rare gas, isotope and aqueous geochemistry. *Unit head:* Dr. William Menke, Chair, 212-864-4525, Fax: 845-365-8163.

Cornell University, Graduate School, Graduate Fields of Agriculture and Life Sciences, Field of Ecology and Evolutionary Biology, Ithaca, NY 14853-0001. Offers ecology (PhD), including animal ecology, applied ecology, biogeochemistry, community and ecosystem ecology, limnology, oceanography, physiological ecology, plant ecology, population ecology, theoretical ecology, vertebrate zoology; evolutionary biology (PhD), including ecological genetics, paleobiology, population biology, systematics. *Faculty:* 51 full-time. *Students:* 57 full-time (30 women); includes 5 minority (1 African American, 3 Asian Americans or Pacific Islanders, 1 Hispanic American), 9 international. 98 applicants, 8% accepted, 5 enrolled. In 2003, 2 doctorates awarded. *Degree requirements:* For doctorate, thesis/dissertation, 2 semesters of teaching experience, comprehensive exam. *Entrance requirements:* For doctorate, GRE General Test, GRE Subject Test (biology), 2 letters of recommendation. Additional exam requirements/recommendations for international students: Required—TOEFL (minimum score 550 paper-based; 213 computer-based). *Application deadline:* For fall admission, 12/15 for domestic students. Application fee: $60. Electronic applications accepted. *Expenses:* Tuition: Full-time $28,630. One-time fee: $50 full-time. *Financial support:* In 2003–04, 52 students received support, including 17 fellowships with full tuition reimbursements available, 9 research assistantships with full tuition reimbursements available, 26 teaching assistantships with full tuition reimbursements available; institutionally sponsored loans, scholarships/grants, health care benefits, tuition waivers (full and partial), and unspecified assistantships also available. Financial award applicants required to submit FAFSA. *Faculty research:* Population and organismal biology, population and evolutionary genetics, systematics and macroevolution, biochemistry, conservation biology. *Unit head:* Director of Graduate Studies, 607-254-4230. *Application contact:* Graduate Field Assistant, 607-254-4230, E-mail: eeb_grad_req@cornell.edu.

Dalhousie University, Faculty of Graduate Studies, College of Arts and Science, Faculty of Science, Department of Oceanography, Halifax, NS B3H 4R2, Canada. Offers M Sc, PhD. Part-time programs available. *Degree requirements:* For master's and doctorate, thesis/dissertation. *Entrance requirements:* Additional exam requirements/recommendations for international students: Required—TOEFL. *Faculty research:* Biological and physical oceanography, chemical and geological oceanography, atmospheric sciences.

Florida Institute of Technology, Graduate Programs, College of Engineering, Department of Marine and Environmental Systems, Melbourne, FL 32901-6975. Offers environmental resource management (MS); environmental science (MS, PhD); meteorology (MS); ocean engineering (MS, PhD); oceanography (MS, PhD), including biological oceanography, chemical oceanography, coastal zone management (MS), geological oceanography, physical oceanography. Part-time programs available. *Faculty:* 16 full-time (1 woman), 4 part-time/adjunct (0 women). *Students:* 42 full-time (16 women), 19 part-time (8 women); includes 1 minority (Hispanic American), 25 international. Average age 29. 129 applicants, 55% accepted, 17 enrolled. In 2003, 17 master's, 3 doctorates awarded. Terminal master's awarded for partial completion of doctoral program. *Degree requirements:* For master's, thesis, comprehensive exam, registration; for doctorate, thesis/dissertation, attendance of graduate seminar, internships (oceanography and environmental science), comprehensive exam, registration. *Entrance requirements:* For master's, GRE General Test (environmental science), letters of recommendation(3), minimum GPA of 3.0; for doctorate, GRE General Test (oceanography and environmental science), resumé, letters of recommendation (3), statement of objectives, minimum GPA of 3.2. Additional exam requirements/recommendations for international students: Required—TOEFL (minimum score 550 paper-based; 213 computer-based). *Application deadline:* Applications are processed on a rolling basis. Application fee: $50. Electronic applications accepted. *Expenses:* Tuition: Part-time $745 per credit. *Financial support:* In 2003–04, 35 students received support, including 10 fellowships with full and partial tuition reimbursements available (averaging $5,565 per year), 15 research assistantships with full and partial tuition reimbursements available (averaging $14,657 per year), 10 teaching assistantships with full and partial tuition reimbursements available (averaging $17,533 per year); career-related internships or fieldwork and tuition remissions also available. Financial award application deadline: 3/1; financial award applicants required to submit FAFSA. *Faculty research:* Environmental modeling, coastal processes, exploring marine pollution, marine geophysics, remote sensing . Total annual research expenditures: $1.9 million. *Unit head:* Dr. George Maul, Department Head, 321-674-7453, Fax: 321-674-7212, E-mail: gmaul@fit.edu. *Application contact:* Carolyn P. Farrior, Director of Graduate Admissions, 321-674-7118, Fax: 321-723-9468, E-mail: cfarrior@fit.edu.

See in-depth description on page 727.

Florida State University, Graduate Studies, College of Arts and Sciences, Department of Oceanography, Tallahassee, FL 32306. Offers MS, PhD. *Faculty:* 20 full-time (2 women), 4 part-time/adjunct (0 women). *Students:* 45 full-time (16 women), 20 international. Average age 26. 52 applicants, 17% accepted. In 2003, 3 master's, 5 doctorates awarded. *Degree requirements:* For master's, thesis/dissertation; for doctorate, thesis/dissertation, comprehensive exam. *Entrance requirements:* For master's and doctorate, GRE General Test. Additional exam requirements/recommendations for international students: Required—TOEFL (minimum score 550 paper-based; 213 computer-based). *Application deadline:* For fall admission, 2/1 for domestic students; for spring admission, 7/1 priority date for domestic students. Applications are processed on a rolling basis. Application fee: $20. Electronic applications accepted. *Expenses:* Tuition, state resident: part-time $196 per credit hour. Tuition, nonresident: part-time $731 per credit hour. Part-time tuition and fees vary according to campus/location. *Financial support:* In 2003–04, 36 research assistantships with full tuition reimbursements, 3 teaching assistantships with full tuition reimbursements were awarded. Fellowships with full tuition reimbursements Financial award application deadline: 2/1; financial award applicants required to submit FAFSA. *Faculty research:* Trace metals in seawater, currents and waves, modeling, benthic ecology, marine biogeochemistry. Total annual research expenditures: $3.8 million. *Unit head:* Dr. Nancy Marcus, Chair, 850-644-6700, Fax: 850-644-2581, E-mail: marcus@ocean.fsu.edu. *Application contact:* Michaela Lupiani, Academic Coordinator, 850-644-6700, Fax: 850-644-2581, E-mail: admissions@ocean.fsu.edu.

See in-depth description on page 277.

The Johns Hopkins University, Zanvyl Krieger School of Arts and Sciences, The Morton K. Blaustein Department of Earth and Planetary Sciences, Program in Oceanography, Baltimore, MD 21218-2699. Offers MA, PhD. *Faculty:* 3 full-time (0 women). *Students:* 7 full-time (4 women); includes 1 minority (Hispanic American), 4 international. Average age 25. *Degree requirements:* For doctorate, thesis/dissertation, registration. *Entrance requirements:* For master's and doctorate, GRE General Test. *Application deadline:* For fall admission, 1/15 for domestic students. Application fee: $60. Electronic applications accepted. *Expenses:* Tuition: Full-time $28,730; part-time $1,490 per course. Part-time tuition and fees vary according to course load, campus/location and program. *Financial support:* Federal Work-Study and institutionally sponsored loans available. Financial award application deadline: 3/14; financial award applicants required to submit FAFSA. *Application contact:* Carol Spangler, Academic Program Assistant, 410-516-7034, Fax: 410-516-7933, E-mail: cspangler@jhu.edu.

Louisiana State University and Agricultural and Mechanical College, Graduate School, School of the Coast and Environment, Department of Oceanography and Coastal Sciences, Baton Rouge, LA 70803. Offers MS, PhD. *Faculty:* 28 full-time (2 women), 1 part-time/adjunct (0 women). *Students:* 56 full-time (30 women), 8 part-time (1 woman); includes 2 minority (1 African American, 1 Hispanic American), 16 international. Average age 30. 32 applicants, 31% accepted, 10 enrolled. In 2003, 7 master's, 5 doctorates awarded. *Degree requirements:* For master's, thesis (for some programs); for doctorate, one foreign language, thesis/dissertation. *Entrance requirements:* For master's, GRE General Test, minimum GPA of 3.0; for doctorate, GRE General Test, MA or MS, minimum GPA of 3.0. Additional exam requirements/recommendations for international students: Required—TOEFL (minimum score 550 paper-based; 213 computer-based). *Application deadline:* For fall admission, 1/25 priority date for domestic students, 5/15 priority date for international students. Applications are processed on a rolling basis. Application fee: $25. *Expenses:* Tuition, state resident: part-time $337 per hour. Tuition, nonresident: part-time $577 per hour. *Financial support:* In 2003–04, 17 students received support, including 7 fellowships (averaging $18,071 per year), 42 research assistantships with partial tuition reimbursements available (averaging $17,897 per year), 2 teaching assistantships with partial tuition reimbursements available (averaging $9,875 per year); Federal Work-Study, institutionally sponsored loans, and unspecified assistantships also available. Financial award applicants required to submit FAFSA. *Faculty research:* Management and development of estuarine and coastal areas and resources; physical, chemical, geological, and biological research. Total annual research expenditures: $57,294. *Unit head:* Dr. Lawrence Rouse, Chair, 225-578-2453, Fax: 225-578-6307, E-mail: lrouse@lsu.edu. *Application contact:* Dr. Masamichi Inoue, Graduate Adviser, 225-578-6308, Fax: 225-578-6307, E-mail: coiino@lsu.edu.

Massachusetts Institute of Technology, School of Engineering, Department of Civil and Environmental Engineering, Cambridge, MA 02139-4307. Offers biological oceanography (PhD, Sc D); chemical oceanography (PhD, Sc D); civil and environmental engineering (M Eng, SM, PhD, Sc D, CE, Env E); civil engineering (PhD, Sc D); coastal engineering (Sc D); construction engineering and management (PhD, Sc D); costal engineering (PhD); environmental biology (PhD, Sc D); environmental chemistry (PhD, Sc D); environmental engineering (PhD, Sc D); environmental fluid mechanics (PhD, Sc D); geotechnical and geoenvironmental engineering (PhD, Sc D); hydrology (PhD, Sc D); information technology (PhD, Sc D); oceanographic engineering (PhD); oceonographic engineering (Sc D); structures and materials (PhD, Sc D); transportation (PhD, Sc D). *Faculty:* 36 full-time (4 women). *Students:* 239 full-time (70 women); includes 17 minority (1 African American, 10 Asian Americans or Pacific Islanders, 6 Hispanic Americans), 147 international. Average age 26. 591 applicants, 37% accepted, 90 enrolled. In 2003, 149 master's, 27 doctorates awarded. *Degree requirements:* For master's and other advanced degree, thesis/dissertation; for doctorate, thesis/dissertation, comprehensive exam. *Entrance requirements:* For master's and doctorate, GRE General Test. Additional exam requirements/recommendations for international students: Required—TOEFL (minimum score 577 paper-based; 233 computer-based). *Application deadline:* For fall admission, 1/2 for domestic students, 1/2 for international students. Application fee: $70. Electronic applications accepted. *Expenses:* Tuition: Full-time $29,400. Required fees: $200. *Financial support:* In 2003–04, 214 students received support, including 42 fellowships with tuition reimbursements available, 112 research assistantships with tuition reimbursements available (averaging $22,740 per year), 29 teaching assistantships with tuition reimbursements available (averaging $17,370 per year); career-related internships or fieldwork, Federal Work-Study, institutionally sponsored loans, scholarships/grants, health care benefits, and unspecified assistantships also available. *Faculty research:* Environmental chemistry and biology, environmental fluid dynamics and hydrodynamics, geoenvironment and geotechnology, surface and groundwater hydrology, materials and structures. Total annual research expenditures: $10.9 million. *Unit head:* Prof. Patrick Jaillet, Head, 617-452-3379, Fax: 617-452-3294, E-mail: jaillet@mit.edu. *Application contact:* Graduate Admissions, 617-253-7101, E-mail: ceed@mit.edu.

See in-depth description on page 279.

Massachusetts Institute of Technology, School of Science, Department of Biology, Cambridge, MA 02139-4307. Offers biochemistry (PhD); biological oceanography (PhD); biophysical chemistry and molecular structure (PhD); cell biology (PhD); developmental biology (PhD); genetics/microbiology (PhD); immunology (PhD); neurobiology (PhD). *Faculty:* 50 full-time (12 women). *Students:* 244 full-time (132 women); includes 36 minority (3 African Americans, 1 American Indian/Alaska Native, 25 Asian Americans or Pacific Islanders, 7 Hispanic Americans), 36 international. Average age 26. 643 applicants, 16% accepted, 36 enrolled. In 2003, 21 doctorates awarded. *Degree requirements:* For doctorate, thesis/dissertation, qualifying exam, 2 semesters as a teaching assistant, comprehensive exam. *Entrance requirements:* For doctorate, GRE General Test. Additional exam requirements/recommendations for international students: Required—TOEFL (minimum score 600 paper-based). *Application deadline:* For fall admission, 12/15 for domestic students, 12/15 for international students. Application fee: $70. Electronic applications accepted. *Expenses:* Tuition: Full-time $29,400. Required fees: $200. *Financial support:* In 2003–04, 232 students received support, including 137 fellowships with tuition reimbursements available, 122 research assistantships with tuition reimbursements available (averaging $23,760 per year); teaching assistantships, Federal Work-Study, institutionally sponsored loans, scholarships/grants, traineeships, health care benefits, and unspecified assistantships also available. *Faculty research:* DNA recombination, replication, and repair; transcription and gene regulation; signal transduction; cell cycle; neuronal cell fate. Total annual research expenditures: $167.3 million. *Unit head:* Prof. Robert T. Sauer, Head, 617-253-4701, Fax: 617-253-8699, E-mail: mitbio@mit.edu. *Application contact:*

Betsey Walsh, Assistant, Graduate Program, 617-253-3717, Fax: 617-258-9329, E-mail: gradbio@mit.edu.

Massachusetts Institute of Technology, School of Science, Department of Earth, Atmospheric, and Planetary Sciences, Cambridge, MA 02139-4307. Offers atmospheric chemistry (PhD, Sc D); atmospheric science (SM, PhD, Sc D); climate physics and chemistry (PhD, Sc D); earth and planetary sciences (SM); geochemistry (PhD, Sc D); geology (PhD, Sc D); geophysics (PhD, Sc D); geosystems (SM); oceanography (SM, PhD, Sc D); planetary sciences (PhD, Sc D). *Faculty:* 37 full-time (3 women). *Students:* 147 full-time (61 women); includes 9 minority (4 Asian Americans or Pacific Islanders, 5 Hispanic Americans), 48 international. Average age 27. 176 applicants, 49% accepted, 31 enrolled. In 2003, 8 master's, 19 doctorates awarded. Terminal master's awarded for partial completion of doctoral program. *Degree requirements:* For master's, thesis/dissertation; for doctorate, thesis/dissertation, comprehensive exam. *Entrance requirements:* For master's, GRE General Test, GRE Subject Test (joint MIT/WHOI program); for doctorate, GRE General Test, GRE Subject Test (chemistry or physics for planetary science program). Additional exam requirements/recommendations for international students: Required—TOEFL (minimum score 577 paper-based; 233 computer-based). *Application deadline:* For fall admission, 1/5 for domestic students, 1/5 for international students; for spring admission, 11/1 for domestic students, 11/1 for international students. Application fee: $70. Electronic applications accepted. *Expenses:* Tuition: Full-time $29,400. Required fees: $200. *Financial support:* In 2003–04, 113 students received support, including 25 fellowships with tuition reimbursements available, 70 research assistantships with tuition reimbursements available (averaging $23,760 per year), 21 teaching assistantships with tuition reimbursements available (averaging $18,270 per year); Federal Work-Study, institutionally sponsored loans, scholarships/grants, health care benefits, and unspecified assistantships also available. *Faculty research:* Evolution of main features of the planetary system; origin, composition, structure, and state of the atmospheres, oceans, surfaces, and interiors of planets; dynamics of planets and satellite motions. Total annual research expenditures: $19.1 million. *Unit head:* Prof. Maria Zuber, 617-253-0149, Fax: 617-253-8298, E-mail: mtz@mit.edu. *Application contact:* Carol Sprague, Administrative Assistant, 617-253-3381, Fax: 617-253-8298, E-mail: eapsinfo@mit.edu.

McGill University, Faculty of Graduate and Postdoctoral Studies, Faculty of Science, Department of Atmospheric and Oceanic Sciences, Montréal, QC H3A 2T5, Canada. Offers atmospheric science (M Sc, PhD); physical oceanography (M Sc, PhD). *Faculty:* 11 full-time (1 woman). *Students:* 35 full-time, 2 part-time. Average age 24. 62 applicants, 48% accepted, 12 enrolled. In 2003, 5 master's, 5 doctorates awarded. Terminal master's awarded for partial completion of doctoral program. *Degree requirements:* For master's and doctorate, thesis/dissertation. *Entrance requirements:* For master's, GRE General Test, minimum GPA of 3.2 during last 2 years of full-time study or 3.0 overall; for doctorate, GRE, master's degree in meteorology or related field. Additional exam requirements/recommendations for international students: Required—TOEFL. *Application deadline:* For fall admission, 7/1 for domestic students; for winter admission, 12/1 for domestic students. Applications are processed on a rolling basis. Application fee: $60 Canadian dollars. Tuition, area resident: Full-time $1,668. *Expenses:* Tuition, state resident: full-time $4,173. Tuition, nonresident: full-time $9,468. Required fees: $1,081. *Financial support:* In 2003–04, research assistantships (averaging $16,000 per year), teaching assistantships (averaging $1,000 per year) were awarded. Fellowships, tuition waivers (partial) also available. Financial award application deadline: 7/1. *Faculty research:* Dynamic meteorology and climate dynamics, synoptic meteorology, mesometeorology, radar meteorology, physical oceanography. *Unit head:* Prof. John Gyakum, Chair, 514-398-6076, Fax: 514-398-6115, E-mail: gyakum@zephyr.meteo.mcgill.ca. *Application contact:* Prof. H. G. Leighton, Chair, Graduate Admissions, 514-398-3766, Fax: 514-398-6115, E-mail: gradinfo@zephyr.meteo.mcgill.ca.

Memorial University of Newfoundland, School of Graduate Studies, Department of Physics and Physical Oceanography, St. John's, NL A1C 5S7, Canada. Offers physical oceanography (M Sc, PhD); physics (M Sc, PhD). Part-time programs available. *Students:* 26 full-time. 51 applicants, 22% accepted, 8 enrolled. In 2003, 1 degree awarded. *Degree requirements:* For master's, thesis; for doctorate, thesis/dissertation, oral defense of thesis, comprehensive exam. *Entrance requirements:* For master's, honors B Sc or equivalent; for doctorate, M Sc or equivalent. *Application deadline:* Applications are processed on a rolling basis. Application fee: $40. Electronic applications accepted. Tuition and fees charges are reported in Canadian dollars. *Expenses:* Tuition, state resident: part-time $733 Canadian dollars per semester. Tuition, nonresident: part-time $953 Canadian dollars per semester. Required fees: $194 Canadian dollars per year. Tuition and fees vary according to degree level and program. *Financial support:* Fellowships, research assistantships, teaching assistantships available. *Faculty research:* Experiment and theory in atomic and molecular physics. Total annual research expenditures: $2.1 million. *Unit head:* Dr. John Whitehead, Head, 709-737-8737, Fax: 709-737-8739, E-mail: johnw@physics.mun.ca. *Application contact:* Dr. Jolanta Lagowski, Deputy Head, Graduate Studies, 709-737-2113, Fax: 709-737-8739, E-mail: gradap@physics.mun.ca.

Naval Postgraduate School, Graduate Programs, Department of Oceanography, Monterey, CA 93943. Offers MS, PhD. Program only open to commissioned officers of the United States and friendly nations and selected United States federal civilian employees. Part-time programs available. *Degree requirements:* For master's, thesis; for doctorate, one foreign language, thesis/dissertation.

North Carolina State University, Graduate School, College of Physical and Mathematical Sciences, Department of Marine, Earth, and Atmospheric Sciences, Raleigh, NC 27695. Offers marine, earth, and atmospheric sciences (MS, PhD); meteorology (MS, PhD); oceanography (MS, PhD). *Faculty:* 41 full-time (6 women), 57 part-time/adjunct (4 women). *Students:* 91 full-time (32 women), 16 part-time (3 women); includes 4 minority (2 African Americans, 1 Asian American or Pacific Islander, 1 Hispanic American), 17 international. Average age 30. 106 applicants, 50% accepted. In 2003, 19 master's, 6 doctorates awarded. Terminal master's awarded for partial completion of doctoral program. *Median time to degree:* Master's–2.7 years full-time; doctorate–5 years full-time. Of those who began their doctoral program in fall 1995, 90% received their degree in 8 years or less. *Degree requirements:* For master's, thesis (for some programs), final oral exam; for doctorate, thesis/dissertation, final oral exam, preliminary oral and written exams, comprehensive exam, registration. *Entrance requirements:* For master's, GRE General Test, minimum GPA of 3.0; for doctorate, GRE General Test, GRE Subject Test for disciplines in biological oceanography and geology, minimum GPA of 3.0. Additional exam requirements/recommendations for international students: Required—TOEFL (minimum score 550 paper-based). *Application deadline:* For fall admission, 6/25 for domestic students, 3/1 for international students; for spring admission, 11/25 for domestic students, 7/15 for international students. Applications are processed on a rolling basis. Application fee: $45. Electronic applications accepted. *Expenses:* Tuition, state resident: part-time $396 per hour. Tuition, nonresident: part-time $1,895 per hour. *Financial support:* In 2003–04, 76 students received support, including 1 fellowship with tuition reimbursement available (averaging $10,397 per year), 47 research assistantships with tuition reimbursements available (averaging $5,959 per year), 32 teaching assistantships with tuition reimbursements available (averaging $6,594 per year); institutionally sponsored loans and unspecified assistantships also available. Financial award application deadline: 3/1. *Faculty research:* Boundary layer and air quality meteorology; climate and mesoscale dynamics; biological, chemical, geological, and physical oceanography; hard rock, soft rock, environmental, and paleogeology. Total annual research expenditures: $5.6 million. *Unit head:* Dr. John C. Fountain, Head, 919-515-3717, Fax: 919-515-7802, E-mail: fountain@ncsu.edu. *Application contact:* Dr. Gerald S. Janowitz, Director of Graduate Programs, 919-515-7837; Fax: 919-515-7802, E-mail: janowitz@ncsu.edu.

See in-depth description on page 247.

Nova Southeastern University, Oceanographic Center, Program in Marine Biology and Oceanography, Fort Lauderdale, FL 33314-7796. Offers marine biology (PhD); oceanography (PhD). *Students:* 2 full-time (0 women), 6 part-time (2 women). 4 applicants, 50% accepted, 2 enrolled. In 2003, 1 degree awarded. *Degree requirements:* For doctorate, thesis/dissertation, comprehensive exam. *Entrance requirements:* For doctorate, GRE, master's degree. Application fee: $50. *Expenses:* Tuition: Full-time $8,715; part-time $484 per credit. Required fees: $75. Full-time tuition and fees vary according to degree level and program. *Application contact:* Dr. Andrew Rogerson, Associate Dean, 954-262-3600, Fax: 954-262-4020, E-mail: arogerso@nsu.nova.edu.

See in-depth description on page 281.

Old Dominion University, College of Sciences, Programs in Oceanography, Norfolk, VA 23529. Offers MS, PhD. Part-time programs available. *Faculty:* 20 full-time (3 women), 14 part-time/adjunct (3 women). *Students:* 38 full-time (13 women), 16 part-time (10 women); includes 3 minority (1 African American, 1 Asian American or Pacific Islander, 1 Hispanic American), 18 international. Average age 29. 34 applicants, 62% accepted, 16 enrolled. In 2003, 3 master's, 2 doctorates awarded. Terminal master's awarded for partial completion of doctoral program. *Degree requirements:* For master's, 10 days of ship time, thesis optional; for doctorate, thesis/dissertation, 10 days of ship time, comprehensive exam. *Entrance requirements:* For master's, GRE General Test, minimum GPA of 3.0 in major, 2.7 overall; for doctorate, GRE General Test. Additional exam requirements/recommendations for international students: Required—TOEFL. *Application deadline:* For fall admission, 2/15 for domestic students. Applications are processed on a rolling basis. Application fee: $30. Electronic applications accepted. *Expenses:* Tuition, state resident: part-time $235 per credit hour. Tuition, nonresident: part-time $603 per credit hour. Part-time tuition and fees vary according to campus/location. *Financial support:* In 2003–04, 48 students received support, including 28 research assistantships with tuition reimbursements available (averaging $16,500 per year), 14 teaching assistantships with tuition reimbursements available (averaging $11,000 per year); career-related internships or fieldwork and scholarships/grants also available. Support available to part-time students. Financial award application deadline: 2/15; financial award applicants required to submit FAFSA. *Faculty research:* Biological, chemical, geological and physical oceanography. Total annual research expenditures: $3.6 million. *Unit head:* Dr. David J. Burdige, Graduate Program Director, 757-683-4930, Fax: 757-683-5303, E-mail: oceangpd@odu.edu.

Oregon State University, Graduate School, College of Oceanic and Atmospheric Sciences, Program in Oceanography, Corvallis, OR 97331. Offers MA, MS, PhD. *Students:* 53 full-time (25 women), 1 part-time; includes 2 minority (both Hispanic Americans), 9 international. Average age 30. In 2003, 7 master's, 5 doctorates awarded. Terminal master's awarded for partial completion of doctoral program. *Degree requirements:* For master's, thesis optional; for doctorate, thesis/dissertation. *Entrance requirements:* For master's and doctorate, GRE General Test, minimum GPA of 3.0 in last 90 hours. Additional exam requirements/recommendations for international students: Required—TOEFL. *Application deadline:* For fall admission, 2/1 for domestic students. Applications are processed on a rolling basis. Application fee: $50. *Expenses:* Tuition, state resident: full-time $8,139; part-time $301 per credit. Tuition, nonresident: full-time $14,376; part-time $532 per credit. Required fees: $1,227. *Financial support:* Fellowships, research assistantships, teaching assistantships, career-related internships or fieldwork, Federal Work-Study, and institutionally sponsored loans available. Support available to part-time students. Financial award application deadline: 2/1. *Faculty research:* Biological, chemical, geological, and physical oceanography. *Unit head:* Irma Delson, Assistant Director, Student Services, 541-737-5189, Fax: 541-737-2064, E-mail: student_adviser@oce.orst.edu.

Princeton University, Graduate School, Department of Geosciences, Program in Atmospheric and Oceanic Sciences, Princeton, NJ 08544-1019. Offers PhD. *Students:* 8 full-time (3 women), 7 international. 22 applicants, 32% accepted, 2 enrolled. *Median time to degree:* Doctorate–6.67 years full-time. *Degree requirements:* For doctorate, one foreign language, thesis/dissertation. *Entrance requirements:* For doctorate, GRE General Test, GRE Subject Test. Additional exam requirements/recommendations for international students: Required—TOEFL (minimum score 600 paper-based; 250 computer-based). *Application deadline:* For fall admission, 12/31 for domestic students, 12/1 for international students. Application fee: $80 ($55 for international students). Electronic applications accepted. *Expenses:* Tuition: Full-time $29,910. Required fees: $810. *Financial support:* Fellowships with full tuition reimbursements, research assistantships with full tuition reimbursements, teaching assistantships with full tuition reimbursements, Federal Work-Study and institutionally sponsored loans available. Financial award application deadline: 1/2. *Faculty research:* Climate dynamics, middle atmosphere dynamics and chemistry, oceanic circulation, marine geochemistry, numerical modeling. *Unit head:* Prof. Anand H. Gnadadesikan, Director of Graduate Studies, 609-258-5062, Fax: 609-258-2850, E-mail: ganana@princeton.edu. *Application contact:* Director of Graduate Admissions, 609-258-3034.

Rutgers, The State University of New Jersey, New Brunswick/Piscataway, Graduate School, Program in Oceanography, New Brunswick, NJ 08901-1281. Offers MS, PhD. *Faculty:* 40 full-time (5 women), 1 part-time/adjunct (0 women). *Students:* 26 full-time (12 women), 3 part-time (2 women); includes 1 minority (Hispanic American), 7 international. Average age 27. 42 applicants, 19% accepted, 6 enrolled. In 2003, 2 master's awarded, leading to university research/teaching 100%; 1 doctorate awarded, leading to university research/teaching 100%. Terminal master's awarded for partial completion of doctoral program. *Median time to degree:* Master's–3.17 years full-time; doctorate–7.75 years full-time. Of those who began their doctoral program in fall 1995, 100% received their degree in 8 years or less. *Degree requirements:* For master's, thesis/dissertation; for doctorate, thesis/dissertation, comprehensive exam. *Entrance requirements:* For master's and doctorate, GRE General Test, 1 year of calculus, physics, chemistry. Additional exam requirements/recommendations for international students: Required—TOEFL. *Application deadline:* For fall admission, 2/1 for domestic students; for spring admission, 11/1 for domestic students. Applications are processed on a rolling basis. Application fee: $50. Electronic applications accepted. *Expenses:* Tuition, state resident: full-time $10,030. Tuition, nonresident: full-time $14,202. *Financial support:* In 2003–04, 28 students received support, including 2 fellowships with full tuition reimbursements available (averaging $18,000 per year), 24 research assistantships with full tuition reimbursements available (averaging $16,428 per year), 2 teaching assistantships with full tuition reimbursements available (averaging $14,410 per year); career-related internships or fieldwork, institutionally sponsored loans, health care benefits, and unspecified assistantships also available. Financial award application deadline: 3/1; financial award applicants required to submit FAFSA. *Faculty research:* Coastal observations and modeling, estuarine ecology/fish/benthos, geochemistry, deep sea ecology/hydrothermal vents, molecular biology applications. Total annual research expenditures: $14.7 million. *Unit head:* Dr. Paul Falkowski, Director, 732-932-6555 Ext. 370, Fax: 732-932-4083, E-mail: falko@marine.rutgers.edu. *Application contact:* Gretchen Young, Administrative Assistant, 732-932-6555 Ext. 500, Fax: 732-932-8578, E-mail: gpo@marine.rutgers.edu.

See in-depth description on page 283.

Texas A&M University, College of Geosciences, Department of Oceanography, College Station, TX 77843. Offers MS, PhD. *Faculty:* 22 full-time (3 women), 2 part-time/adjunct (0 women). *Students:* 62 full-time (32 women), 12 part-time (3 women); includes 2 minority (1 Asian American or Pacific Islander, 1 Hispanic American), 26 international. Average age 28. 54 applicants, 50% accepted. In 2003, 8 master's, 7 doctorates awarded. *Degree requirements:* For master's and doctorate, thesis/dissertation. *Entrance requirements:* For master's and doctorate, GRE General Test. Additional exam requirements/recommendations for international students: Required—TOEFL. *Application deadline:* For fall admission, 1/15 for domestic students; for spring admission, 10/1 for domestic students. Applications are processed on a rolling basis. Application fee: $50 ($75 for international students). Electronic applications accepted. *Expenses:* Tuition, state resident: full-time $3,420. Tuition, nonresident: full-time $9,084. Required fees: $1,861. *Financial support:* In 2003–04, 6 fellowships with partial tuition reimbursements (averaging $18,000 per year), 52 research assistantships with partial tuition reimbursements (averaging $18,000 per year), 12 teaching assistantships with partial tuition reimbursements (averaging $18,000 per year) were awarded. Federal Work-Study, scholarships/grants, tuition waivers (partial), and foreign government support also available.

Oceanography

Texas A&M University (continued)
Financial award application deadline: 1/15. *Faculty research:* Ocean circulation, climate studies, coastal and shelf dynamics, marine phytoplankton, stable isotope geochemistry. *Unit head:* Dr. Wilford D. Gardner, Head, 979-845-7211, Fax: 979-845-6331, E-mail: wgardner@ocean.tamu.edu. *Application contact:* Donna Dunlap, Academic Advisor, 979-845-7412, Fax: 979-845-6331.

Université du Québec à Rimouski, Graduate Programs, Program in Oceanography, Rimouski, QC G5L 3A1, Canada. Offers M Sc, PhD. Part-time programs available. *Degree requirements:* For master's and doctorate, thesis/dissertation. *Entrance requirements:* For master's, appropriate bachelor's degree, proficiency in French; for doctorate, appropriate master's degree, proficiency in French.

Université Laval, Faculty of Sciences and Engineering, Program in Oceanography, Québec, QC G1K 7P4, Canada. Offers PhD. *Degree requirements:* For doctorate, thesis/dissertation, comprehensive exam. *Entrance requirements:* For doctorate, knowledge of French, knowledge of English. Additional exam requirements/recommendations for international students: Required—TOEFL. Electronic applications accepted.

University of Alaska Fairbanks, School of Fisheries and Ocean Sciences, Department of Marine Sciences and Limnology, Fairbanks, AK 99775-7520. Offers marine biology (MS); oceanography (MS, PhD), including biological oceanography (PhD), chemical oceanography (PhD), fisheries (PhD), geological oceanography (PhD), physical oceanography (PhD). Part-time programs available. Terminal master's awarded for partial completion of doctoral program. *Degree requirements:* For master's and doctorate, thesis/dissertation, comprehensive exam, registration. *Entrance requirements:* For master's and doctorate, GRE General Test. Additional exam requirements/recommendations for international students: Required—TOEFL. Electronic applications accepted. *Faculty research:* Seafood science and nutrition, sustainable harvesting, chemical oceanography, marine biology, physical oceanography.

See in-depth description on page 289.

The University of British Columbia, Faculty of Graduate Studies, Faculty of Science, Department of Earth and Ocean Sciences, Vancouver, BC V6T 1Z1, Canada. Offers atmospheric science (M Sc, PhD); geological engineering (M Eng, MA Sc, PhD); geological sciences (M Sc, PhD); geophysics (M Sc, MA Sc, PhD); oceanography (M Sc, PhD). *Faculty:* 42 full-time (5 women), 16 part-time/adjunct (0 women). *Students:* 127 full-time (44 women), 1 (woman) part-time. Average age 27. 80 applicants, 41% accepted, 25 enrolled. In 2003, 21 master's, 8 doctorates awarded. *Degree requirements:* For master's, thesis (for some programs); for doctorate, thesis/dissertation, comprehensive exam. *Entrance requirements:* Additional exam requirements/recommendations for international students: Required—TOEFL (minimum score 600 paper-based; 250 computer-based). *Application deadline:* For fall admission, 3/1 for domestic students; for winter admission, 7/1 for domestic students. Applications are processed on a rolling basis. Application fee: $90 Canadian dollars ($150 Canadian dollars for international students). Electronic applications accepted. *Financial support:* In 2003–04, fellowships (averaging $16,000 per year), research assistantships (averaging $13,000 per year), teaching assistantships (averaging $4,500 per year) were awarded. Federal Work-Study, institutionally sponsored loans, scholarships/grants, tuition waivers (full and partial), and unspecified assistantships also available. *Unit head:* Dr. Paul L. Smith, Head, 604-822-6456, Fax: 604-822-6088, E-mail: psmith@cos.ubc.ca. *Application contact:* Alex Allen, Graduate Secretary, 604-822-2713, Fax: 604-822-6088, E-mail: aallen@eos.ubc.ca.

University of California, San Diego, Graduate Studies and Research, Scripps Institution of Oceanography, La Jolla, CA 92093. Offers biological oceanography (MS, PhD); geochemistry and marine chemistry (MS, PhD); marine biology (MS, PhD); physical oceanography and geological sciences (MS, PhD). *Faculty:* 88. *Students:* 222 (112 women); includes 22 minority (2 African Americans, 3 American Indian/Alaska Native, 7 Asian Americans or Pacific Islanders, 10 Hispanic Americans) 55 international. 389 applicants, 19% accepted. In 2003, 9 master's, 24 doctorates awarded. *Entrance requirements:* For master's and doctorate, GRE General Test, GRE Subject Test (marine biology). *Application deadline:* For fall admission, 1/6 for domestic students. Application fee: $60. Electronic applications accepted. Tuition, nonresident: full-time $12,245. Required fees: $6,959. *Financial support:* Fellowships, research assistantships available. *Unit head:* Myrl C. Hendershott, Chair. *Application contact:* Graduate Coordinator, 858-534-3206.

University of Colorado at Boulder, Graduate School, College of Arts and Sciences, Program in Atmospheric and Oceanic Sciences, Boulder, CO 80309. Offers MS, PhD. *Faculty:* 9 full-time (3 women). *Expenses:* Tuition, state resident: full-time $2,122. Tuition, nonresident: full-time $9,754. Tuition and fees vary according to course load and program. *Faculty research:* Large-scale dynamics of the ocean and the atmosphere; air-sea interaction; radiative transfer and remote sensing of the ocean and the atmosphere; sea ice and its role in climate. Total annual research expenditures: $14.1 million. *Unit head:* Brian Toon, Director, 303-492-1534, Fax: 303-492-3524, E-mail: brian.toon@colorado.edu. *Application contact:* Graduate Secretary, 303-492-6633, Fax: 303-492-3524, E-mail: paosasst@colorado.edu.

University of Connecticut, Graduate School, College of Liberal Arts and Sciences, Department of Marine Sciences, Field of Oceanography, Storrs, CT 06269. Offers MS, PhD. *Faculty:* 19 full-time (3 women). *Students:* 23 full-time (12 women), 6 part-time (2 women), 9 international. Average age 33. 54 applicants, 30% accepted, 10 enrolled. In 2003, 3 master's, 1 doctorate awarded. Terminal master's awarded for partial completion of doctoral program. *Degree requirements:* For master's, comprehensive exam; for doctorate, thesis/dissertation. *Entrance requirements:* For master's and doctorate, GRE General Test, GRE Subject Test. Additional exam requirements/recommendations for international students: Required—TOEFL (minimum score 550 paper-based; 213 computer-based). *Application deadline:* For fall admission, 2/1 priority date for domestic students, 2/1 priority date for international students; for spring admission, 11/1 for domestic students, 10/1 for international students. Applications are processed on a rolling basis. Application fee: $55. Electronic applications accepted. *Expenses:* Tuition, state resident: part-time $3,860 per semester. Tuition, nonresident: part-time $9,036 per semester. *Financial support:* In 2003–04, 19 research assistantships with full tuition reimbursements, 4 teaching assistantships with full tuition reimbursements were awarded. Fellowships, Federal Work-Study, scholarships/grants, health care benefits, and unspecified assistantships also available. Financial award application deadline: 2/1; financial award applicants required to submit FAFSA. *Unit head:* Robert B. Whitlatch, Head, 860-445-3467, Fax: 860-405-9153, E-mail: robert.whitlatch@uconn.edu. *Application contact:* Barbara Mahoney, Administrative Assistant, 860-405-9151, Fax: 860-405-9153, E-mail: mscadm03@uconnvm.uconn.edu.

University of Delaware, College of Marine Studies, Newark, DE 19716. Offers marine policy (MS); marine studies (MMP, MS, PhD); oceanography (MS, PhD). *Faculty:* 36 full-time (4 women). *Students:* 101 full-time (50 women), 2 part-time (1 woman); includes 6 minority (2 African Americans, 3 Asian Americans or Pacific Islanders, 1 Hispanic American), 23 international. Average age 29. 141 applicants, 30% accepted, 29 enrolled. In 2003, 17 master's, 12 doctorates awarded. *Degree requirements:* For master's and doctorate, thesis/dissertation. *Entrance requirements:* For master's and doctorate, GRE General Test. Additional exam requirements/recommendations for international students: Required—TOEFL. *Application deadline:* For fall admission, 3/1 for domestic students; for spring admission, 10/1 for domestic students. Applications are processed on a rolling basis. Application fee: $60. Electronic applications accepted. *Expenses:* Tuition, state resident: full-time $5,890; part-time $327 per credit. Tuition, nonresident: full-time $15,420; part-time $857 per credit. Required fees: $968. *Financial support:* In 2003–04, 77 students received support, including 22 fellowships with full tuition reimbursements available (averaging $19,000 per year), 55 research assistantships with full tuition reimbursements available (averaging $19,000 per year); teaching assistantships with full tuition reimbursements available (averaging $19,000 per year); career-related internships or fieldwork, Federal Work-Study, and tuition waivers (full and partial) also available. Financial award application deadline: 3/1. *Faculty research:* Marine biology and biochemistry, oceanography, marine policy, physical ocean science and engineering, ocean engineering. Total annual research expenditures: $10.2 million. *Unit head:* Dr. Carolyn A. Thoroughgood, Dean, 302-831-2841. *Application contact:* Doris Manship, Coordinator, 302-645-4226, E-mail: dmanship@udel.edu.

University of Georgia, Graduate School, College of Arts and Sciences, Department of Marine Sciences, Athens, GA 30602. Offers MS, PhD. *Faculty:* 18 full-time (5 women). *Students:* 41 full-time (20 women); includes 2 minority (1 Asian American or Pacific Islander, 1 Hispanic American), 9 international. Average age 28. 37 applicants, 32% accepted, 7 enrolled. In 2003, 1 master's, 4 doctorates awarded. *Median time to degree:* Master's–3 years full-time; doctorate–4 years full-time. *Degree requirements:* For master's, thesis; for doctorate, thesis/dissertation, teaching experience, field research experience, comprehensive exam. *Entrance requirements:* For master's and doctorate, GRE General Test. Additional exam requirements/recommendations for international students: Required—TOEFL. *Application deadline:* For fall admission, 2/1 priority date for domestic students, 2/1 priority date for international students; for spring admission, 10/15 priority date for domestic students, 9/1 priority date for international students. Applications are processed on a rolling basis. Application fee: $50. Electronic applications accepted. *Expenses:* Tuition, state resident: part-time $161 per hour. Tuition, nonresident: part-time $690 per hour. One-time fee: $435 part-time. *Financial support:* In 2003–04, 9 fellowships with full tuition reimbursements (averaging $20,000 per year), 21 research assistantships with full tuition reimbursements (averaging $18,000 per year), 11 teaching assistantships with full tuition reimbursements (averaging $18,000 per year) were awarded. *Faculty research:* Microbial ecology, biogeochemistry, polar biology, coastal ecology, coastal circulation. *Unit head:* Dr. James T. Hollibaugh, Director, 706-542-3016, Fax: 706-542-5888, E-mail: aquadoc@uga.edu. *Application contact:* Dr. Mary Ann Moran, Graduate Coordinator, 706-542-6481, Fax: 706-542-5888, E-mail: mmoran@uga.edu.

University of Hawaii at Manoa, Graduate Division, School of Ocean and Earth Science and Technology, Department of Oceanography, Honolulu, HI 96822. Offers MS, PhD. Part-time programs available. *Faculty:* 90 full-time (8 women), 8 part-time/adjunct (0 women). *Students:* 54 full-time (23 women), 4 part-time (2 women); includes 4 minority (all Asian Americans or Pacific Islanders), 22 international. Average age 32. 131 applicants. In 2003, 10 master's, 53 doctorates awarded. Terminal master's awarded for partial completion of doctoral program. *Median time to degree:* Master's–3 years full-time; doctorate–8 years full-time. *Degree requirements:* For master's, thesis, field experience; for doctorate, one foreign language, thesis/dissertation, field experience. *Entrance requirements:* For master's and doctorate, GRE. *Application deadline:* For fall admission, 2/1 for domestic students, 1/15 for international students; for spring admission, 9/1 for domestic students, 8/1 for international students. Application fee: $50. *Expenses:* Tuition, state resident: full-time $4,464; part-time $186 per credit hour. Tuition, nonresident: full-time $10,608; part-time $442 per credit hour. Tuition and fees vary according to program. *Financial support:* In 2003–04, 43 research assistantships (averaging $18,394 per year), 11 teaching assistantships (averaging $18,198 per year) were awarded. Fellowships, career-related internships or fieldwork, institutionally sponsored loans, and tuition waivers (full and partial) also available. Financial award applicants required to submit FAFSA. *Faculty research:* Physical oceanography, marine chemistry, biological oceanography, atmospheric chemistry, marine geology. Total annual research expenditures: $6.6 million. *Unit head:* Dr. Edward Laws, Chairperson, 808-956-7633, Fax: 808-956-9225.

University of Maine, Graduate School, College of Natural Sciences, Forestry, and Agriculture, School of Marine Sciences, Program in Oceanography, Orono, ME 04469. Offers MS, PhD. Part-time programs available. *Students:* 11 full-time (8 women), 8 part-time (4 women), 6 international. Average age 29. 22 applicants, 45% accepted, 3 enrolled. In 2003, 3 master's, 2 doctorates awarded. *Degree requirements:* For master's and doctorate, thesis/dissertation. *Entrance requirements:* For master's and doctorate, GRE General Test. Additional exam requirements/recommendations for international students: Required—TOEFL. *Application deadline:* For fall admission, 2/1 for domestic students. Applications are processed on a rolling basis. Application fee: $50. Electronic applications accepted. *Expenses:* Tuition, state resident: part-time $235 per credit. Tuition, nonresident: part-time $670 per credit. Tuition and fees vary according to course load. *Financial support:* Fellowships with tuition reimbursements, research assistantships with tuition reimbursements, teaching assistantships with tuition reimbursements, career-related internships or fieldwork, Federal Work-Study, and tuition waivers (full and partial) available. Support available to part-time students. Financial award application deadline: 3/1. *Faculty research:* Coastal processes, microbial ecology, crustacean systematics. *Unit head:* Dr. Mary Jane Perry, Coordinator, 207-581-3321 Ext. 245. *Application contact:* Scott G. Delcourt, Associate Dean of the Graduate School, 207-581-3218, Fax: 207-581-3232, E-mail: graduate@maine.edu.

University of Miami, Graduate School, Rosenstiel School of Marine and Atmospheric Science, Division of Meteorology and Physical Oceanography, Coral Gables, FL 33124. Offers atmospheric science (MS, PhD); physical oceanography (MS, PhD). *Faculty:* 28 full-time (5 women), 18 part-time/adjunct (3 women). *Students:* 33 full-time (12 women), 1 part-time; includes 2 minority (both Hispanic Americans), 15 international. Average age 27. 61 applicants, 20% accepted, 9 enrolled. In 2003, 6 master's awarded, leading to university research/teaching 33%, continued full-time study33%, business/industry 17%, government 17%; 3 doctorates awarded, leading to university research/teaching 100%. Terminal master's awarded for partial completion of doctoral program. *Median time to degree:* Master's–4 years full-time; doctorate–7.2 years full-time. *Degree requirements:* For master's and doctorate, thesis/dissertation, comprehensive exam, registration. *Entrance requirements:* For master's and doctorate, GRE General Test. Additional exam requirements/recommendations for international students: Required—TOEFL (minimum score 550 paper-based; 213 computer-based). *Application deadline:* For fall admission, 1/1 priority date for domestic students, 1/1 priority date for international students. Applications are processed on a rolling basis. Application fee: $50. Electronic applications accepted. *Expenses:* Tuition: Full-time $19,526. *Financial support:* In 2003–04, 28 students received support, including 4 fellowships with tuition reimbursements available (averaging $20,124 per year), 21 research assistantships with tuition reimbursements available (averaging $20,124 per year), 3 teaching assistantships with tuition reimbursements available (averaging $20,124 per year); institutionally sponsored loans and scholarships/grants also available. Financial award application deadline: 3/1; financial award applicants required to submit FAFSA. *Unit head:* Dr. William Johns, Chairperson, 305-361-4057, E-mail: wjohns@rsmas.miami.edu. *Application contact:* Dr. Frank Millero, Associate Dean, 305-361-4155, Fax: 305-361-4771, E-mail: gso@rsmas.miami.edu.

University of Michigan, Horace H. Rackham School of Graduate Studies, College of Literature, Science, and the Arts, Department of Geological Sciences, Program in Oceanography: Marine Geology and Geochemistry, Ann Arbor, MI 48109. Offers MS, PhD. *Faculty:* 4 full-time (0 women). *Students:* 6 full-time (all women); includes 3 minority (all Asian Americans or Pacific Islanders) Average age 26. 6 applicants, 0% accepted. In 2003, 2 master's, 2 doctorates awarded. Terminal master's awarded for partial completion of doctoral program. *Median time to degree:* Master's–2.5 years full-time; doctorate–5 years full-time. *Degree requirements:* For master's, thesis; for doctorate, thesis/dissertation, oral defense of dissertation, preliminary exam. *Entrance requirements:* For master's and doctorate, GRE General Test. *Application deadline:* For fall admission, 1/15 for domestic students. Applications are processed on a rolling basis. Application fee: $60 ($75 for international students). Electronic applications accepted. *Expenses:* Tuition, state resident: full-time $7,463. Tuition, nonresident: full-time $13,913. Full-time tuition and fees vary according to course load, degree level and program. *Financial support:* In 2003–04, 1 fellowship with full tuition reimbursement (averaging $12,853 per year), 1 research assistantship with full tuition reimbursement (averaging $12,853 per year), 2 teaching assistantships with full tuition reimbursements (averaging $12,853 per year) were awarded. Career-related internships or fieldwork, Federal Work-Study, and health care benefits also available. Financial award applicants required to submit FAFSA. *Faculty research:* Paleoceanography, paleolimnology, marine geochemistry, seismic stratigraphy. *Application contact:* Anne Hudon, Student Services Assistant, 734-615-3034, Fax: 734-763-4690, E-mail: ahudon@umich.edu.

University of New Hampshire, Graduate School, College of Engineering and Physical Sciences, Department of Earth Sciences, Durham, NH 03824. Offers earth sciences (MS), including geochemical, geology, ocean mapping, oceanography; hydrology (MS). *Faculty:* 29 full-time. *Students:* 18 full-time (7 women), 22 part-time (7 women); includes 3 minority (2 African Americans, 1 American Indian/Alaska Native), 2 international. Average age 31. 49 applicants, 78% accepted, 16 enrolled. In 2003, 9 degrees awarded. *Degree requirements:* For master's, thesis, one foreign language. *Entrance requirements:* For master's, GRE General Test. Additional exam requirements/recommendations for international students: Required—TOEFL (minimum score 550 paper-based; 213 computer-based); Recommended—TSE. *Application deadline:* For fall admission, 4/1 for domestic students; for winter admission, 12/1 for domestic students. Applications are processed on a rolling basis. Application fee: $50. Electronic applications accepted. Tuition, area resident: Full-time $7,070. *Expenses:* Tuition, state resident: full-time $10,605. Tuition, nonresident: full-time $17,430. Required fees: $15. *Financial support:* In 2003–04, 1 fellowship, 7 research assistantships, 9 teaching assistantships were awarded. Career-related internships or fieldwork, Federal Work-Study, scholarships/grants, and tuition waivers (full and partial) also available. Support available to part-time students. Financial award application deadline: 2/15. *Unit head:* Dr. Matt Davis, Chairperson, 603-862-4119, E-mail: earth.sciences@unh.edu. *Application contact:* Linda Wrightsman, Administrative Assistant, 603-862-1720, E-mail: earth.sciences@unh.edu.

University of New Hampshire, Graduate School, College of Engineering and Physical Sciences, Department of Ocean Engineering, Durham, NH 03824. Offers ocean engineering (MS, PhD); ocean mapping (MS). *Faculty:* 5 full-time. *Students:* 5 full-time (0 women), 7 part-time (1 woman); includes 2 minority (both Asian Americans or Pacific Islanders), 3 international. Average age 32. 6 applicants, 100% accepted, 3 enrolled. In 2003, 1 degree awarded. *Degree requirements:* For master's, thesis. *Entrance requirements:* Additional exam requirements/recommendations for international students: Required—TOEFL (minimum score 550 paper-based; 213 computer-based); Recommended—TSE. *Application deadline:* For fall admission, 4/1 for domestic students; for winter admission, 12/1 for domestic students. Applications are processed on a rolling basis. Application fee: $50. Electronic applications accepted. Tuition, area resident: Full-time $7,070. *Expenses:* Tuition, state resident: full-time $10,605. Tuition, nonresident: full-time $17,430. Required fees: $15. *Financial support:* In 2003–04, 2 research assistantships were awarded; teaching assistantships, Federal Work-Study, scholarships/grants, and tuition waivers (full and partial) also available. Support available to part-time students. Financial award application deadline: 2/15. *Unit head:* Dr. Kenneth Baldwin, Chairperson, 603-862-1898. *Application contact:* Jennifer Bedsole, Information Contact, 603-862-0672.

University of Puerto Rico, Mayagüez Campus, Graduate Studies, College of Arts and Sciences, Department of Marine Sciences, Mayagüez, PR 00681-9000. Offers biological oceanography (MMS, PhD); chemical oceanography (MMS, PhD); geological oceanography (MMS, PhD); physical oceanography (MMS, PhD). *Degree requirements:* For master's, one foreign language, thesis, departmental and comprehensive final exams; for doctorate, one foreign language, thesis/dissertation, qualifying, comprehensive, and final exams. *Faculty research:* Marine botany, ecology, chemistry, and parasitology; fisheries; ichthyology; aquaculture.

See in-depth description on page 293.

University of Rhode Island, Graduate School, Graduate School of Oceanography, Kingston, RI 02881. Offers MS, PhD. In 2003, 4 master's, 10 doctorates awarded. *Application deadline:* For fall admission, 4/15 for domestic students. Applications are processed on a rolling basis. Application fee: $35. *Expenses:* Tuition, state resident: full-time $4,338; part-time $281 per credit. Tuition, nonresident: full-time $12,438; part-time $704 per credit. Required fees: $1,840. *Unit head:* David Farmer, Dean, 401-874-6222.

University of Southern California, Graduate School, College of Letters, Arts and Sciences, Department of Biological Sciences, Program in Marine Environmental Biology, Los Angeles, CA 90089. Offers PhD. *Degree requirements:* For doctorate, thesis/dissertation. *Entrance requirements:* For doctorate, GRE General Test. Additional exam requirements/recommendations for international students: Required—TOEFL. *Expenses:* Tuition: Full-time $32,784; part-time $949 per unit. Tuition and fees vary according to course load and program. *Faculty research:* Microbial ecology, physiology of larval development, biological community structure, Cambrian radiation.

University of South Florida, College of Graduate Studies, College of Marine Science, St. Petersburg, FL 33701-5016. Offers MS, PhD. Part-time and evening/weekend programs available. *Faculty:* 82 full-time (15 women). *Students:* 58 full-time (40 women), 61 part-time (34 women); includes 14 minority (7 African Americans, 7 Hispanic Americans), 8 international. Average age 31. 99 applicants, 35% accepted, 29 enrolled. In 2003, 5 master's, 4 doctorates awarded. *Degree requirements:* For master's, thesis; for doctorate, thesis/dissertation, proficency foreign language and relevant skill directly related to area of study. *Entrance requirements:* For master's and doctorate, GRE General Test, minimum GPA of 3.0 in last 60 hours. Additional exam requirements/recommendations for international students: Required—TOEFL. *Application deadline:* For fall admission, 6/1 for domestic students; for spring admission, 11/1 for domestic students. Applications are processed on a rolling basis. Application fee: $30. *Financial support:* Fellowships with partial tuition reimbursements, research assistantships with partial tuition reimbursements, teaching assistantships with partial tuition reimbursements available. *Faculty research:* Trace metal chemistry, water quality, organic and isotopic geochemistry, physical chemistry, nutrient chemistry. Total annual research expenditures: $3.7 million. *Unit head:* Dr. Peter R. Betzer, Dean, 727-553-1130, Fax: 727-553-1189, E-mail: pbetzer@marine.usf.edu. *Application contact:* Dr. Edward VanVleet, Coordinator, 727-553-1165, Fax: 727-553-1189, E-mail: advisor@marine.usf.edu.

See in-depth description on page 295.

University of Victoria, Faculty of Graduate Studies, Faculty of Science, School of Earth and Ocean Sciences, Victoria, BC V8W 2Y2, Canada. Offers geochemistry (M Sc, PhD); geophysics (M Sc, PhD); marine geology and geophysics (M Sc, PhD); ocean acoustics (M Sc, PhD); oceanography (M Sc, PhD); paleobiology (M Sc, PhD); paleoceanography (M Sc, PhD); sedimentology (M Sc, PhD); stratigraphy (M Sc, PhD). Part-time programs available. *Degree requirements:* For master's and doctorate, thesis/dissertation. *Entrance requirements:* Additional exam requirements/recommendations for international students: Required—TOEFL (minimum score 550 paper-based; 213 computer-based). Electronic applications accepted. *Faculty research:* Climate modeling, geology.

University of Washington, Graduate School, College of Ocean and Fishery Sciences, School of Oceanography, Programs in Biological Oceanography, Seattle, WA 98195. Offers MS, PhD. Terminal master's awarded for partial completion of doctoral program. *Degree requirements:* For master's, research project; for doctorate, thesis/dissertation. *Entrance requirements:* For master's and doctorate, GRE General Test, minimum GPA of 3.0. Additional exam requirements/recommendations for international students: Required—TOEFL. Electronic applications accepted. *Faculty research:* Immunological techniques, thermophilic and archae-bacteria in hydrothermal systems, remote sensing, astrobiology.

University of Wisconsin–Madison, Graduate School, College of Engineering, Program in Limnology and Marine Science, Madison, WI 53706-1380. Offers MS, PhD. *Faculty:* 22 full-time (6 women). *Students:* 14 full-time (5 women); includes 2 minority (both African Americans) 26 applicants, 12% accepted, 3 enrolled. In 2003, 2 degrees awarded, leading to university research/teaching 100%. Terminal master's awarded for partial completion of doctoral program. *Median time to degree:* Doctorate–5.5 years full-time. *Degree requirements:* For master's and doctorate, thesis/dissertation. *Entrance requirements:* For master's and doctorate, GRE General Test. Additional exam requirements/recommendations for international students: Required—TOEFL. *Application deadline:* For fall admission, 1/15 priority date for domestic students, 1/15 priority date for international students. Application fee: $45. Electronic applications accepted. Tuition, area resident: Full-time $7,593; part-time $476 per credit. Tuition, nonresident: full-time $22,824; part-time $1,430 per credit. Required fees: $292; $38 per credit. Part-time tuition and fees vary according to course load and reciprocity agreements. *Financial support:* Fellowships with tuition reimbursements, research assistantships with tuition reimbursements, teaching assistantships with tuition reimbursements, Federal Work-Study and institutionally sponsored loans available. Financial award application deadline: 1/15. *Faculty research:* Lake ecosystems, ecosystem modeling, geochemistry, physiological ecology, chemical limnology. *Unit head:* Dr. Kenneth W. Potter, Chair, 608-262-0400, Fax: 608-265-2340, E-mail: kwpotter@facstaff.wisc.edu. *Application contact:* Georgia Wagner, Student Services Coordinator, 608-263-3264, Fax: 608-265-2340, E-mail: gwagner@facstaff.wisc.edu.

University of Wisconsin–Madison, Graduate School, College of Letters and Science, Department of Atmospheric and Oceanic Sciences, Madison, WI 53706-1380. Offers MS, PhD. Part-time programs available. *Degree requirements:* For master's, thesis (for some programs); for doctorate, thesis/dissertation. *Entrance requirements:* For master's and doctorate, GRE General Test, minimum GPA of 3.0; previous course work in chemistry, mathematics, and physics. Electronic applications accepted. Tuition, area resident: Full-time $7,593; part-time $476 per credit. Tuition, nonresident: full-time $22,824; part-time $1,430 per credit. Required fees: $292; $38 per credit. Part-time tuition and fees vary according to course load and reciprocity agreements. *Faculty research:* Satellite meteorology, weather systems, global climate change, numerical modeling, atmosphere-ocean interaction.

Woods Hole Oceanographic Institution, MIT/WHOI Joint Program in Oceanography/Applied Ocean Science and Engineering, Woods Hole, MA 02543-1541. Offers applied ocean sciences (PhD); biological oceanography (PhD, Sc D); chemical oceanography (PhD, Sc D); civil and environmental and oceanographic engineering (PhD); electrical and oceanographic engineering (PhD); geochemistry (PhD); geophysics (PhD); marine biology (PhD); marine geochemistry (PhD, Sc D); marine geology (PhD, Sc D); marine geophysics (PhD); mechanical and oceanographic engineering (PhD); ocean engineering (PhD); oceanographic engineering (M Eng, MS, PhD, Sc D, Eng); paleoceanography (PhD); physical oceanography (PhD, Sc D). MS, PhD, and Sc D offered jointly with MIT. *Faculty:* 123 full-time, 8 part-time/adjunct. *Students:* 128 full-time (62 women); includes 8 minority (2 African Americans, 4 Asian Americans or Pacific Islanders, 2 Hispanic Americans), 37 international. Average age 27. 187 applicants, 28% accepted, 32 enrolled. In 2003, 7 master's, 20 doctorates awarded. Terminal master's awarded for partial completion of doctoral program. *Median time to degree:* Master's–2.9 years full-time; doctorate–5.8 years full-time. *Degree requirements:* For master's and Eng, thesis (for some programs); for doctorate, thesis/dissertation. *Entrance requirements:* For master's, GRE General Test; for doctorate, GRE General Test, GRE Subject Test. Additional exam requirements/recommendations for international students: Required—TOEFL. *Application deadline:* For fall admission, 1/15 priority date for domestic students, 1/15 priority date for international students. Application fee: $65. Electronic applications accepted. *Expenses:* Tuition: Full-time $39,200. *Financial support:* In 2003–04, 13 fellowships (averaging $39,200 per year), 69 research assistantships (averaging $39,200 per year) were awarded. Teaching assistantships, scholarships/grants, traineeships, health care benefits, and unspecified assistantships also available. Financial award application deadline: 1/15. *Unit head:* Prof. Paola Rizzoli, Director, 617-253-2451, E-mail: rizzoli@mit.edu. *Application contact:* Ronni Schwartz, Administrator, 617-253-7544, Fax: 617-253-9784, E-mail: mspiggy@mit.edu.

See in-depth description on page 279.

Yale University, Graduate School of Arts and Sciences, Department of Geology and Geophysics, New Haven, CT 06520. Offers geochemistry (PhD); geophysics (PhD); meteorology (PhD); mineralogy and crystallography (PhD); oceanography (PhD); paleoecology (PhD); paleontology and stratigraphy (PhD); petrology (PhD); structural geology (PhD). *Degree requirements:* For doctorate, thesis/dissertation. *Entrance requirements:* For doctorate, GRE General Test. Additional exam requirements/recommendations for international students: Required—TOEFL. *Expenses:* Tuition: Full-time $25,600; part-time $6,400 per term.

See in-depth description on page 261.

Cross-Discipline Announcement

Florida Institute of Technology, Graduate Programs, College of Science and Liberal Arts, Department of Biological Sciences, Melbourne, FL 32901-6975.

MS and PhD in marine biology with research emphases in mollusks, echinoderms, coral reef fishes, and manatees and community studies of lagoonal, mangrove, and reef systems. Applications range from physiological and ecological systematics to biochemical and molecular biological studies in these areas.

Cross-Discipline Announcements

[illegible]

Cross-Discipline Announcement

[illegible]

FLORIDA INSTITUTE OF TECHNOLOGY

Department of Marine and Environmental Systems Programs in Oceanography and Coastal Zone Management

Programs of Study Florida Institute of Technology offers programs of research and study options in the fields of biological, chemical, geological, and physical oceanography and in environmental and marine chemistry that lead to M.S. and Ph.D. degrees in oceanography. An M.S. in oceanography with an option in coastal zone management is also offered. Those students interested in the graduate program in ocean engineering should consult the program description in Book 5 of these guides.

Research Facilities Florida Institute of Technology is conveniently located on the Indian River Lagoon, a major east-central Florida estuarine system recently designated an Estuary of National Significance. Marine and environmental laboratories and field research stations are located on the lagoon and at an oceanfront marine research facility. Marine operations, located just 5 minutes from the campus, house a fleet of small outboard-powered craft and medium-sized work boats. These boats are available to students and faculty members for teaching and research in the freshwater tributaries and the Indian River Lagoon. In addition, the university operates the 60-foot Research Vessel *Delphinus,* which is berthed at Port Canaveral. With its own captain and crew; requisite marine and oceanographic cranes, winches, state-of-the-art sampling equipment, instrumentation, and laboratories, the vessel is the focal point of both marine and estuarine research in the region. The ship can accommodate a scientific team and crew for periods of seven to ten days. The *Delphinus* conducts short research and teaching cruises throughout the year and teaching trips to the Atlantic Ocean each summer.

The Institute's oceanfront marine research facility, the Vero Beach Marine Laboratory, located at Vero Beach just 40 minutes from the campus, provides facilities, including flowing seawater from the Atlantic Ocean, to support research in such areas as aquaculture, biofouling, and corrosion. There is also a permanent research platform, centrally located in the Indian River Lagoon, to support marine research projects. On the campus, the departmental teaching and research facilities include separate laboratories for biological, chemical, physical, geological, and instrumentation investigations. In addition, high-pressure, hydroacoustics, fluid dynamics, and GIS/remote sensing facilities are available in the department. An electron microscope is also available for research work.

About an hour from campus is the Harbor Branch Oceanographic Institution; scientists and engineers there pursue their own research and development activities and interact with the Institute's students and faculty members on projects of mutual interest.

The Biological Oceanography Laboratory is fully equipped for research on plankton, benthos, and fishes of coastal and estuarine ecosystems. Collection gear; analytical equipment, including a flow-through fluorometer; and a controlled environment room are available for student and research use. Areas of research have included toxic algal blooms, seagrass ecology, and artificial and natural reef communities.

The Chemical Oceanography Laboratory is equipped to do both routine and research-level operations on open ocean and coastal lagoonal waters. Major and minor nutrients, heavy-metal contaminants, and biological pollutants can be quantitatively determined. Analytical methods available include gas and liquid chromatography, infrared and visible light spectrophotometry, and atomic absorption spectrometry.

The Physical Oceanography and the Hydrodynamics laboratories support graduate research in ocean waves, coastal processes, circulation, and pollutant transport. In addition, CTD and XBT systems, current meters, tide and wind recorders, salinometers, wave-height gauges, side-scan sonar, and other oceanographic instruments are available for field work. A remote sensing and optics lab provides capabilities for analyzing ocean color data and collecting in situ hydrologic optics data.

The Marine Geology and Geophysics Laboratory is used to study near-shore sedimentation and stratigraphy. The lab equipment includes a state-of-the-art computerized rapid sediment analyzer, a magnetic heavy mineral separator, and computer-assisted sieve systems.

Financial Aid Graduate teaching, research assistantships, and endowed fellowships are available to qualified students. For 2004–05, financial support ranges from approximately $9000 to $16,000, including stipend and tuition, per academic year for approximately half-time duties. Stipend-only assistantships are sometimes awarded for less time commitment. Most coastal zone management students receive support through internship appointments.

Cost of Study In 2004–05, tuition is $780 per graduate semester credit hour.

Living and Housing Costs Room and board on campus cost approximately $2500 per semester in 2004–05. On-campus housing (dormitories and apartments) is available for full-time single and married graduate students, but priority for dormitory rooms is given to undergraduate students. Many apartment complexes and rental houses are available near the campus.

Student Group The College of Engineering has 450 graduate students. Oceanography currently has approximately 25 graduate and 40 undergraduate students.

Student Outcomes Graduates have gone on to careers with such institutions as NOAA, EPA, Florida Water Management Districts, Western Geophysical, Naval Oceanographic Office, Digicon, and with county and state agencies.

Location The campus is located in Melbourne, on Florida's east coast. It is an area, located 4 miles from the Atlantic Ocean beaches, with a year-round subtropical climate. The area's economy is supported by a well-balanced mix of industries in electronics, aviation, light manufacturing, optics, communications, agriculture, and tourism. Many industries support activities at the Kennedy Space Center.

The Institute Florida Institute of Technology is a distinctive, independent university, founded in 1958 by a group of scientists and engineers to fulfill a need for specialized advanced educational opportunities on the Space Coast of Florida. Florida Tech is the only independent technological university in the Southeast. Supported by both industry and the community, Florida Tech is the recipient of many research grants and contracts, a number of which provide financial support for graduate students.

Applying Forms and instructions for applying for admission and assistantships are sent on request. Admission is possible at the beginning of any semester, but admission in the fall semester is recommended. It is advantageous to apply early.

Correspondence and Information

Dr. John G. Windsor Jr., Program Chairman
Oceanography Program
Florida Institute of Technology
Melbourne, Florida 32901-6975
Telephone: 321-674-8096
Fax: 321-674-7212
E-mail: dmes@fit.edu
World Wide Web: http://www.fit.edu/AcadRes/dmes

Graduate Admissions Office
Florida Institute of Technology
Melbourne, Florida 32901-6975
Telephone: 321-674-8027
800-944-4348 (toll-free)
Fax: 321-723-9468
E-mail: grad-admissions@fit.edu
World Wide Web: http://www.fit.edu/grad

Florida Institute of Technology

THE FACULTY AND THEIR RESEARCH

Charles R. Bostater Jr., Associate Professor; Ph.D., Delaware. Remote sensing, hydrologic optics, particle dynamics in estuaries, modeling of toxic substances, physical oceanography of coastal waters, environmental modeling.
Iver W. Duedall, Professor; Ph.D., Dalhousie. Chemical oceanography, physical chemistry of seawater, geochemistry, marine pollution, ocean management.
Lee E. Harris, Associate Professor; Ph.D., Florida Atlantic; PE. Coastal engineering, coastal structures, beach erosion and control, physical oceanography.
Elizabeth A. Irlandi, Assistant Professor; Ph.D., North Carolina. Landscape ecology in aquatic environments, seagrass ecosystems, coastal zone management.
Kevin B. Johnson, Assistant Professor; Ph.D., Oregon. Zooplankton ecology, predator-prey interactions, metamorphosis, larval transport and settlement, larval behavior.
George A. Maul, Professor; Ph.D., Miami (Florida). Physical oceanography, marine meteorology, climate and sea level change, satellite oceanography, earth system science.
Dean R. Norris, Professor Emeritus; Ph.D., Texas A&M. Taxonomy and ecology of marine phytoplankton, particularly dinoflagellates; ecology and life cycles of toxic dinoflagellates.
Geoffrey W. J. Swain, Professor; Ph.D., Southampton. Materials corrosion, biofouling, offshore technology, ship operations.
Eric D. Thosteson, Assistant Professor; Ph.D., Florida; PE. Coastal and nearshore engineering, coastal processes, wave mechanics, sediment transport.
John H. Trefry, Professor; Ph.D., Texas A&M. Trace metal geochemistry and pollution, geochemistry of rivers, global chemical cycles, deep-sea hydrothermal systems.
John G. Windsor, Professor; Ph.D., William and Mary. Trace organic analysis, organic chemistry, sediment-sea interaction, air-sea interaction, mass spectrometry, hazardous/toxic substance research.
Gary Zarillo, Professor; Ph.D., Georgia; PG. Sediment transport and morphodynamics, tidal inlet–barrier dynamics, numerical modeling of inlet hydrodynamics.

Adjunct Faculty
Diane D. Barile, M.S., Florida Tech. Environmental planning, environmental policy.
D. E. DeFreese, Ph.D., Florida Tech. Marine biology.
R. Grant Gilmore, Ph.D., Florida Tech. Bioacoustics, biological oceanography.
M. Dennis Hanisak, Ph.D., Rhode Island. Biological oceanography.
Brian E. LaPointe, Ph.D., South Florida. Riverine and estuarine systems.
Francis J. Merceret, Ph.D., Johns Hopkins. Atmospheric physics, spacecraft meterorology.
Donald T. Resio, Ph.D., Virginia. Ocean waves, inlet dynamics, physical oceanography.
Ned P. Smith, Ph.D., Wisconsin. Physical oceanography, marine observations, marine meteorology.
Robert W. Virnstein, Ph.D., William and Mary. Limnology.
Craig M. Young, Ph.D., Alberta. Benthic ecology.

SELECTED PUBLICATIONS

Bostater, C. Remote sensing methods using aircraft and ships for estimating optimal bands and coefficients related to ecosystem responses. *Int. Soc. Opt. Eng. (SPIE)* 1930:1051–62, 1992.

Bostater, C. Mathematical techniques for spectral discrimination between corals, seagrasses, bottom and water types using high spectral resolution reflectance signatures. In *ISSSR, Spectral Sensing Research,* pp. 526–36, 1992.

Williams, J., F. Doehring, and **I. W. Duedall.** History of Florida hurricanes. *Oceanus,* submitted.

Shieh, C. S., and **I. W. Duedall.** Disposal of wastes at sea in tropical areas. In *Pollution in Tropical Aquatic Systems,* pp. 218–29, eds. D. W. Connell and D. W. Hawker. Boca Raton: CRC Press, 1992.

Shieh, C. S., and **I. W. Duedall.** Cd and Pb in waste-to-energy residues. *Chem. Ecol.* 6:247–58, 1992.

Duedall, I. W., and M. A. Champ. Artificial reefs: Emerging science and technology. *Oceanus* 34:94–101, 1991.

Duedall, I. W. A brief history of ocean disposal. *Oceanus* 33(2):29–38, 1990.

Harris, L. E., Childress, Winder, and Perry. Real-time wave data collection system at Sebastian Inlet, Florida. In *Fifth International Workshop on Wave Hindcasting and Forecasting,* pp. 146–53. Ontario: Environment Canada, 1998.

Smith, J. T., **L. E. Harris,** and J. Tabar. *Preliminary Evaluation of the Vero Beach, FL Prefabricated Submerged Breakwater.* Tallahassee, Fla.: FSBPA, 1998.

Zadikovv, Covello, **L. E. Harris,** and Skornick. Concrete tetrahedrons and sand-filled geotextile containers: New technologies for shoreline stabilization. In *Proceedings of the International Coastal Symposium (ICS98), Journal of Coastal Research,* special issue no. 26, pp. 261–8, 1998.

Harris, L. E. Dredged material used in sand-filled containers for scour and erosion control. In *Dredging 94,* American Society of Civil Engineers (ASCE), 1994.

Chambers, P. A., R. E. DeWreede, **E. A. Irlandi,** and H. Vandermeulen. Management issues in aquatic macrophyte ecology: A Canadian perspective. *Can. J. Botany,* in press.

Irlandi, E. A., B. A. Orlando, and W. G. Ambrose Jr. The effect of habitat patch size on growth and survival of juvenile bay scallops *(Argopecten irradians). J. Exp. Marine Biol. Ecol.* 235:21–43, 1999.

Irlandi, E. A. Seagrass patch size and survivorship of an infaunal bivalve. *Oikos* 78:511–8, 1997.

Irlandi, E. A., S. Macia, and J. Serafy. Salinity reduction from freshwater canal discharge: Effects on mortality and feeding of an urchin *(Lytechinus variegatus)* and a gastropod *(Lithopoma tectum). Bull. Marine Sci.* 61:869–79, 1997.

Irlandi, E. A. The effects of seagrass patch size and energy regime on growth of a suspension-feeding bivalve. *J. Marine Res.* 54:161–85, 1996.

Irlandi, E. A., and M. E. Mehlich. The effect of tissue cropping and disturbance by browsing fishes on growth of two species of suspension-feeding bivalves. *J. Exp. Marine Biol. Ecol.* 197:279–93, 1996.

Smith, D. L., and **K. B. Johnson.** *A Guide to Marine Coastal Plankton and Marine Invertebrate Larvae,* 2nd ed. Dubuque, Iowa: Kendall/Hunt, 2001.

Johnson, K. B., and A. L. Shanks. The importance of prey densities and background plankton in studies of predation on invertebrate larvae. *Mar. Ecol. Prog. Ser.* 158:293–6, 1997.

Maul, G. A., A. M. Davis, and J. W. Simmons. Seawater temperature trends at USA tide gauge sites. *Geophys. Res. Lett.* 28(20):3935–7, 2001.

Pugh, D. T., and **G. A. Maul.** Coastal sea level prediction for climate change. In *Coastal Ocean Prediction,* num. 56, pp. 377–404, ed. C. N. K. Mooers. Washington: American Geophysical Union, Coastal and Estuarine Studies, 1999.

Mooers, C. N. K., and **G. A. Maul.** Intra-Americas sea circulation. In *The Sea,* chap. 7, pp. 183–208, eds. A. R. Robinson and K. H. Brink, 1998.

Maul, G. A. *Small Islands: Marine Science and Sustainable Development.* Washington: American Geophysical Union, Coastal and Estuarine Studies, number 51, 1996.

Maul, G. A. *Climatic Changes in the Intra-Americas Sea.* United Nations Environment Programme. London: Edward Arnold Publishers, 1993.

Maul, G. A., and D. M. Martin. Sea level rise at Key West, Florida, 1846–1992: America's longest instrument record? *Geophys. Res. Lett.* 20(18):1955–59, 1993.

Hanson, D. V., and **G. A. Maul.** Anticyclonic current rings in the eastern tropical Pacific Ocean. *J. Geophys. Res.* 96(C4):6965–79, 1991.

Hanson, K., **G. A. Maul,** and T. R. Karl. Are atmospheric greenhouse effects apparent in the climatic record of the contiguous U.S. (1895–1987)? *Geophys. Res. Lett.* 16(1):49–52, 1989.

Maul, G. A. *Introduction to Satellite Oceanography.* Martinus Nijhoff Publishers, Dordrecht/Boston/Lancaster, 1985.

Swain, G. W. J., J. Griffith, D. Bultman, and H. Vincent. Barnacle adhesion measurements for the field evaluation of candidate anti-fouling surfaces. *Biofouling* 6:105–14, 1992.

Swain, G. W. J., and E. Muller. Oxygen concentration cells and corrosion in a seawater aquarium. *Corrosion* 92(394), 1992.

Swain, G. W. J., and J. Patrick-Maxwell. The effect of biofouling on the performance of Al-Zn-Hg anodes. *Corrosion* 46(3):256–60, 1990.

Swain, G. W. J., and W. Thomason. Cathodic protection and the use of copper anti-fouling systems on fixed offshore steel structures. Presented at Offshore Mechanics and Arctic Engineering 9th International Conference, Houston, February 1990.

Thosteson, E. D., D. M. Hanes, and S. L. Schonfield. Design of a littoral sedimentation processes monitoring system. *J. Oceanic Eng.,* in press.

Hanes, D. M., and **E. D. Thosteson** et al. Field observations of small scale sediment suspension. In *Proceedings of the 26th International Conference on Coastal Engineering.* Copenhagen, Denmark: ASCE, 1998.

Thosteson, E. D., and D. M. Hanes. The time lag between fluid forcing and wave generated sediment suspension. *AGU Fall Meeting,* 1998.

Thosteson, E. D., and D. M. Hanes. A simplified method for determining sediment size and concentration from multiple frequency acoustic backscatter measurements. *J. Acoust. Soc. Am.* 104(2): 820, 1998.

Trefry, J. H., R. P. Trocine, K. L. Naito, and S. Metz. Assessing the potential for enhanced bioaccumulation of heavy metals from produced water discharges to the Gulf of Mexico. In *Produced Water: Environmental Issues and Mitigation Technologies,* pp. 339–54. New York: Plenum Press, 1996.

Trefry, J. H., et al. Transport of particulate organic carbon by the Mississippi River and its fate in the Gulf of Mexico. *Estuaries* 17:839–49, 1994.

Grguric, G., **J. H. Trefry,** and J. J. Keaffaber. Reactions of bromine and chlorine in ozonated artificial seawater systems. *Water Res.* 28:1087–94, 1994.

Trefry, J. H., et al. Trace metals in hydrothermal solutions from Cleft segment on the southern Juan de Fuca Ridge. *J. Geophys. Res.* 99:4925–35, 1994.

Feely, R. A., et al. **(J. H. Trefry).** Composition and sedimentation of hydrothermal plume particles from North Cleft segment, Juan de Fuca Ridge. *J. Geophys. Res.* 99:4985–5006, 1994.

Florida Institute of Technology

Selected Publications (continued)

Frease, R. A., and **J. G. Windsor Jr.** Behavior of selected polycyclic aromatic hydrocarbons associated with a stabilized oil and coal ash reef. *Marine Poll. Bull.* 22:15–19, 1991.

Windsor Jr., J. G. Fate and transport of oil, dispersants, and dispersed oil in the Florida coastal environment. Oil Spill Dispersant Research Program: Technical Advisory Group Workshop, University of Florida, Gainesville, Florida, April 25–26, 1991.

Windsor Jr., J. G., and **L. E. Harris.** SEEAS—Science and Engineering Education At Sea. *MTS '90, Marine Technology Society,* Washington, D.C., September 1990.

Holm, S. E., and **J. G. Windsor Jr.** Exposure assessment of sewage treatment plant effluent by a selected chemical marker method. *Arch. Environ. Contaminat. Toxicol.* 19:674–79, 1990.

Windsor Jr., J. G. Marine Field Projects: An established, unique undergraduate curriculum in ocean science. Presented at the 200th National Meeting of the American Chemical Society, August 26–31, 1990.

Zarillo, G. A., and T. S. Bacchus. Application of seismic profile measurements to sand source studies. In *Handbook of Geophysical Exploration at Sea,* 2nd ed., *Hard Minerals,* pp. 241–58, ed. R. A. Geyer. Boca Raton: CRC Press, 1992.

Zarillo, G. A., and J. Liu. Resolving components of the upper shoreface of a wave-dominated coast using empirical orthogonal functions. *Mar. Geol.* 82:169–86, 1988.

Zarillo, G. A., and M. J. Park. Prediction of sediment transport in a tide-dominated environment using a numerical model. *J. Coastal Res.* 3:429–44, 1987.

FLORIDA STATE UNIVERSITY

Department of Oceanography

Programs of Study A graduate program in oceanography has existed at Florida State University since 1949, first in an interdisciplinary institute and since 1966 in a department within the College of Arts and Sciences. The Department of Oceanography, which offers both the M.S. and Ph.D. degrees in oceanography with specializations in physical, biological, or chemical oceanography, is the center for marine studies at the University. Additional marine and environmental research is conducted by the Departments of Biological Sciences, Chemistry, Geology, Mathematics, Meteorology, Physics, and Statistics, as well as the Geophysical Fluid Dynamics Institute and the Institute of Molecular Biophysics. Both formal and informal cooperative efforts between these science departments and the Department of Oceanography have flourished for years.

The M.S. degree program requires the completion of 33 semester hours of course work and a thesis covering an original research topic. Students pursuing the Ph.D. degree must complete 18 semester hours of formal course work beyond the master's degree course requirements and perform original research leading to a dissertation that makes a contribution to the science of oceanography.

The first year of graduate study is generally concerned with required course work and examinations. A supervisory committee, chosen by the individual student, directs the examinations and supervises the student's progress. Under its direction, the student begins thesis research as soon as possible. There is no foreign language requirement for either the M.S. or the Ph.D.

Research Facilities Oceanography department headquarters, offices, and laboratories are located in the Oceanography-Statistics Building in the science area of the campus. Some of the laboratories currently in operation are for water quality analysis, organic geochemistry, trace-element analysis, radiochemistry, microbial ecology, phytoplankton ecology, numerical modeling, and fluid dynamics. The department also has the benefit of a fully equipped machine shop and a current-meter facility with state-of-the-art instruments. The Florida State University Marine Laboratory on the Gulf of Mexico is located at Turkey Point near Carrabelle, about 45 miles southwest of Tallahassee. The R/V *Bellows,* a 65-foot research vessel, is shared by FSU and other campuses of the State University System of Florida.

Departmental facilities are augmented by those in other FSU departments and institutes, such as the Van de Graaff accelerator in the physics department, the Antarctic Marine Geology Research Facility and Core Library in the geology department, the Geophysical Fluid Dynamics Institute laboratories, the Electron Microscopy Laboratory in the biological sciences department, the Statistical Consulting Center in the statistics department, and the IBM RS/6000 SP supercomputer in the School of Computational Science and Information Technology.

The research activities of the faculty members are heavily supported by federal funding, and these programs involve fieldwork, often at sea, all over the world. Faculty members and students have worked aboard a great many of the major research vessels of the U.S. fleet; because this kind of active collaboration works so well, it has not seemed necessary for the University to have its own major research vessel.

Financial Aid Fellowships and teaching and research assistantships are available on a competitive basis. University fellowships pay $15,000 per academic year. Research and teaching assistantships range from $15,550 to $17,490 for the year, including summer. In addition, out-of-state tuition waivers are available for assistantship and fellowship recipients. Currently, most of the full-time students in the department receive financial assistance.

Cost of Study Tuition for 2003–04 was $196.27 per credit hour for Florida residents; out-of-state students paid $730.80 per credit hour. The normal course load is 9 to 12 credit hours per semester for research and teaching assistants receiving tuition waivers.

Living and Housing Costs A double room for single students in the graduate dormitories on campus costs about $300 per month (including utilities and local telephone). Married student housing at Alumni Village costs $278 to $485 per month. There are many off-campus apartment complexes in Tallahassee, with rents beginning at about $275 per month.

Student Group The department currently has 49 full-time graduate students enrolled in the program (17 M.S., 32 Ph.D.). The students come from all areas of the country, with the greatest number representing the Northeast, South, and Midwest. Fifteen of the students are women. During the last five years, twenty-seven M.S. and twenty-three Ph.D. degrees were awarded in oceanography. Graduates have taken positions in federal and state agencies, universities, and private companies.

Location Florida State University is located in Tallahassee, the state capital. Although it is among the nation's fastest-growing cities, Tallahassee has managed to preserve its natural beauty. The northern Florida location has a landscape and climate that are substantially different from those of southern Florida. Heavy forest covers much of the area, with the giant live oak being the chief tree of the clay hills. Five large lakes and the nearby Gulf of Mexico offer numerous recreational opportunities. Life in Tallahassee has been described as a combination of the ambience of traditional southern living with the bustle of a modern capital city.

The University Florida State University is a public coeducational institution founded in 1851. Current enrollment is more than 35,000. The University has great diversity in its cultural offerings and is rich in traditions. It has outstanding science departments and excellent schools and departments in law, music, theater, and religion.

Applying Applications should be submitted as early as possible in the academic year prior to anticipated enrollment. The deadline for applications for fall semester enrollment is in February. Each prospective candidate must have a bachelor's degree, with a major pertinent to the student's chosen specialty area in oceanography. Minimum undergraduate preparation must include one year of calculus, chemistry, and physics. A minimum undergraduate GPA of 3.0 and a minimum GRE General Test score of 1100 (combined verbal and quantitative scores) are required. The average undergraduate GPA and the average GRE score of currently enrolled students are 3.45 and 1230 (verbal and quantitative), respectively.

Correspondence and Information

Academic Coordinator
Department of Oceanography
Florida State University
Tallahassee, Florida 32306-4320

Telephone: 850-644-6700
Fax: 850-644-2581
E-mail: admissions@ocean.fsu.edu
World Wide Web: http://ocean.fsu.edu/

Florida State University

THE FACULTY AND THEIR RESEARCH

William C. Burnett, Professor of Oceanography; Ph.D., Hawaii. Uranium-series isotopes and geochemistry of authigenic minerals of the seafloor, elemental composition of suspended material from estuaries and the deep ocean, environmental studies.

Jeffrey P. Chanton, Professor of Oceanography; Ph.D., North Carolina at Chapel Hill. Major element cycling, light stable isotopes, methane production and transport, coastal biogeochemical processes.

Allan J. Clarke, Professor of Oceanography; Ph.D., Cambridge. Climate dynamics, coastal oceanography, equatorial dynamics, tides. Fellow, American Meteorological Society.

William K. Dewar, Professor of Oceanography; Ph.D., MIT. Gulf Stream ring dynamics, general circulation theory, intermediate- and large-scale interaction, mixed layer processes.

Thorsten Dittmar, Professor of Oceanography; Ph.D., Bremen, (West Germany). Marine biogeochemistry, molecular tracer techniques, major element cycling in coastal zones (mangroves) and polar oceans (Arctic Ocean, Antarctica).

Phillip Froelich, Francis Epps Professor of Oceanography; Ph.D., Rhode Island. Marine geochemistry, paleoceanography, paleoclimatology, global biogeochemical dynamics.

Markus H. Huettel, Professor of Oceanography; Ph.D., Kiel (Germany). Benthic ecology, biogeochemistry, transport mechanisms in sediments, effect of boundary layer flows on benthic processes.

Richard L. Iverson, Professor of Oceanography; Ph.D., Oregon State. Physiology and ecology of marine phytoplankton.

Joel E. Kostka, Associate Professor of Oceanography; Ph.D., Delaware. Microbial ecology and biogeochemistry, carbon and nutrient cycling in coastal marine environments, bacteria-mineral interactions.

Ruby E. Krishnamurti, Professor of Oceanography; Ph.D., UCLA. Ocean circulation, atmospheric convection, bioconvection, stability and transition to turbulence. Fellow, American Meteorological Society.

William M. Landing, Professor of Oceanography; Ph.D., California, Santa Cruz. Biogeochemistry of trace elements in the oceans, with emphasis on the effects of biological and inorganic processes on dissolved/particulate fractionation.

Nancy H. Marcus, Professor and Chair, Department of Oceanography; Ph.D., Yale. Population biology and genetics of marine zooplankton dormancy, photoperiodism, biological rhythms. Fellow, AAAS.

Doron Nof, Professor of Oceanography; Ph.D., Wisconsin–Madison. Fluid motions in the ocean, dynamics of equatorial outflows and formation of eddies, geostrophic adjustment in sea straits and estuaries, generation of oceanfronts. Fellow, American Meteorological Society.

Douglas P. Nowacek, Professor of Oceanography; Ph.D., MIT. Behavioral ecology and bioacoustics of marine mammals, including foraging behavior, response of marine mammals to anthropogenic noise, controlled exposure experiments or playbacks, and tagging.

James J. O'Brien, Professor of Oceanography; Ph.D., Texas A&M. Modeling of coastal upwelling and equatorial circulation, upper oceanfronts, climate scale fluctuations. Fellow, American Meteorological Society; Recipient, Sverdrup Gold Medal in Air-Sea Interactions.

Louis St. Laurent, Assistant Professor of Oceanography; Ph.D., MIT. Small-scale mixing processes and turbulence and double diffusion; buoyancy forcing and secondary circulation; internal waves and internal tides; flow over rough topography.

Kevin G. Speer, Professor of Oceanography; Ph.D., MIT. Deep-ocean circulation, observations and dynamics; water-mass formation; thermohaline flow; hydrothermal sources and circulation.

Melvin E. Stern, Professor of Oceanography; Ph.D., MIT. Theory of ocean circulation, salt fingers. Fellow, American Geophysical Union; Member, National Academy of Sciences.

David Thistle, Professor of Oceanography; Ph.D., California, San Diego (Scripps). Ecology of sediment communities, meiofauna ecology, deep-sea biology, crustacean systematics. Fellow, AAAS.

Georges L. Weatherly, Professor of Oceanography; Ph.D., Nova. Deep-ocean circulation and near-bottom currents.

Professors Emeritus

Ya Hsueh, Professor of Oceanography; Ph.D., Johns Hopkins. Variabilities in sea level, coastal currents, water density in continental shelf waters.

Wilton Sturges III, Professor of Oceanography; Ph.D., Johns Hopkins. Ocean currents.

John W. Winchester, Professor of Oceanography; Ph.D., MIT. Atmospheric chemistry, trace-element and aerosol-particle analysis.

AFFILIATED FACULTY

These faculty members are important in the academic program of students in the Department of Oceanography. This list includes faculty members from other departments who interact regularly with the department's faculty members and students.

Lawrence G. Abele, Professor of Biological Sciences and Provost; Ph.D., Miami (Florida). Ecology, community biology, systematics of decapod crustaceans.

David Balkwill, Professor of Medical Sciences; Ph.D., Penn State. Environmental microbiology.

Steven L. Blumsack, Associate Professor of Mathematics; Ph.D., MIT. Theory of rotating fluids.

William F. Herrnkind, Professor of Biological Sciences; Ph.D., Miami (Florida). Behavior and migration of marine animals.

Louis N. Howard, Professor of Mathematics; Ph.D., Princeton. Theory of rotating and stratified flows, hydrodynamic stability, bifurcation theory, geophysical fluid dynamics, chemical waves, biological oscillations. Member, National Academy of Sciences.

Christopher Hunter, Professor of Mathematics; Ph.D., Cambridge. Dynamics of fluids and stellar systems.

Charles L. Jordan, Professor of Meteorology; Ph.D., Chicago. Synoptic meteorology.

Michael Kasha, Professor of Chemistry, Institute of Molecular Biophysics; Ph.D., Berkeley. Molecular electronic spectroscopy, molecular quantum mechanics. Member, National Academy of Sciences.

Robley J. Light, Professor of Chemistry; Ph.D., Duke. Biosynthesis, metabolism, and structure of lipids and related compounds.

Robert J. Livingston, Professor of Biological Sciences; Ph.D., Miami (Florida). Estuarine ecology, aquatic pollution biology.

John K. Osmond, Professor of Geology; Ph.D., Wisconsin–Madison. Uranium-series isotopes.

Paul C. Ragland, Professor of Geology; Ph.D., Rice. Petrology, geochemistry.

William F. Tanner, Professor of Geology; Ph.D., Oklahoma. Fluid dynamics, paleoceanography, sedimentology, structural geology.

Thomas J. Vickers, Professor of Chemistry; Ph.D., Florida. Spectroscopic techniques for chemical analysis of trace elements relating to human health.

Sherwood W. Wise, Professor of Geology; Ph.D., Illinois. Micropaleontology, marine geology, diagenesis of pelagic sediments, biomineralization.

MASSACHUSETTS INSTITUTE OF TECHNOLOGY / WOODS HOLE OCEANOGRAPHIC INSTITUTION

Joint Program in Oceanography / Applied Ocean Science and Engineering

Program of Study
The Massachusetts Institute of Technology (MIT) and the Woods Hole Oceanographic Institution (WHOI) offer joint doctoral and professional degrees in oceanography and in applied ocean science and engineering. The Joint Program leads to a single degree awarded by both institutions. Graduate study in oceanography encompasses virtually all of the basic sciences as they apply to the marine environment: physics, chemistry, geochemistry, geology, geophysics, and biology. Oceanographic engineering allows for concentration in the major engineering fields of civil, mechanical, electrical, and ocean engineering. The graduate programs are administered by joint MIT/WHOI committees drawn from the faculty and staff of both institutions. The Joint Program involves several departments at MIT: Earth, Atmospheric, and Planetary Sciences and Biology in the School of Science; and Civil and Environmental Engineering, Electrical Engineering and Computer Science, Mechanical Engineering, and Ocean Engineering in the School of Engineering. WHOI departments are Physical Oceanography, Biology, Marine Chemistry and Geochemistry, Geology and Geophysics, and Applied Ocean Physics and Engineering. Upon admission, students register in the appropriate MIT department and at WHOI simultaneously and are assigned academic advisers at each institution. The usual steps to a doctoral degree are entering the program the summer preceding the first academic year and working in a laboratory at WHOI, following an individually designed program in preparation for a general (qualifying) examination to be taken before the third year, submitting a dissertation of significant original theoretical or experimental research, and conducting a public oral defense of the thesis. The guideline for time to achieve the doctoral degree is about five years from the bachelor's degree. Students entering with a master's degree in the field may need less time. Each student is expected to become familiar with the principal areas of oceanography in addition to demonstrating a thorough knowledge of at least one major field. Subjects, seminars, and opportunities for research participation are offered at both MIT and WHOI. Courses and seminars are supplemented by cross-registration privileges with Harvard, Brown, and the Boston University Marine Program. Students also have the opportunity to participate in oceanographic cruises during graduate study.

Research Facilities
A broad spectrum of equipment and facilities are available. The wide-ranging deep-sea research vessels at WHOI include *Oceanus, Atlantis,* and *Knorr*. In addition, the deep-diving submersible *ALVIN,* which is carried on *Atlantis,* is operated by WHOI, as are several smaller coastal vessels. Both MIT and WHOI utilize the latest developments in computer technology, from personal computers to large multiuser access systems. Videoconferencing between MIT and WHOI provides interactive transmission for classes, and a high-speed data link for research is provided. Broad-based engineering design and support shop facilities (machining, electronics) are available at both MIT and WHOI. There are more than twelve libraries at MIT containing more than 2 million volumes. Cooperative arrangements with other libraries in the Boston area provide students with access to substantial research collections. WHOI library facilities are shared with the Marine Biological Laboratory and are supplemented by collections of the Northeast Fisheries Center and the U.S. Geological Survey, all located in Woods Hole.

Financial Aid
Research assistantships are available to most entering graduate students in the Joint Program and are usually awarded on a full-year basis. Such awards, as well as a few special fellowships, cover full tuition and provide a stipend adjusted periodically to current living expenses. For the 2004–05 academic year, the stipend is approximately $1980 per month.

Cost of Study
Because tuition and stipend are usually paid for students in good standing, the main costs to the student are for medical insurance, books, and supplies.

Living and Housing Costs
Place of residence is determined by the student's selected program of study and research interests. Graduate students traditionally live off campus at both MIT and WHOI, although there is some graduate housing at both campuses. Housing and living costs tend to be expensive in both the Cambridge and Woods Hole areas, although reasonable housing is available. Estimated twelve-month living costs for 2004–05 are $24,735 for a single graduate student and $26,985 for a married student.

Student Group
There are 130 graduate students registered in the Joint Program. They are divided among the five disciplines as follows: physical oceanography (22), marine geology and geophysics (22), biological oceanography (38), chemical oceanography (18), and applied ocean science and engineering (30).

Student Outcomes
Graduates of the program are employed in a various number of areas. Fifty-four percent are employed in academic/universities, 11 percent are in civilian government, 15 percent are employed in the private sector, 9 percent are in the military service, and 11 percent are employed in a variety of other areas. Recent graduates are employed by Lamont Doherty Earth Observatory, Monterey Bay Aquarium Research Institute, George Mason University, USGS, Oregon State University, Shell, Exxon, University of Hawaii, University of Chicago, Harvard University, Computer Motion, and Mote Marine Lab.

Location
MIT's 146-acre campus extends more than a mile along the Cambridge side of the Charles River, overlooking downtown Boston. Metropolitan Boston offers diverse recreational and cultural opportunities. New England beaches and mountains are within easy reach. WHOI is in the village of Woods Hole on Cape Cod, about 80 miles southeast of Boston.

The University and The Institution
MIT is an independent, coeducational, privately endowed university. It is broadly organized into five academic schools: Architecture and Planning, Engineering, Humanities and Social Sciences, Management, and Science. Within these schools there are twenty-two academic departments. Total enrollment is approximately 9,800 divided almost evenly between undergraduate and graduate students. The MIT faculty numbers approximately 1,000 with a total teaching staff of 1,940. WHOI is one of the largest independent, unaffiliated oceanographic institutions and research fleet operators in the world. There is a staff of approximately 900 scientists, engineers, technicians, research vessel crews, and support personnel organized into five research and academic departments, two centers, and four ocean institutes.

Applying
Application for admission to the Joint Program is made on the MIT graduate school application forms. Complete application files, including college transcripts, three letters of recommendation, test scores, and the application fee should be filed no later than January 15 for admission beginning in June or September. The General Test and one Subject Test of the GRE are required. The TOEFL is required of all international students whose schooling has not been predominantly in English.

Admission is offered on a competitive basis to those who appear most likely to benefit from the Joint Program. Notification of admission decisions are sent out in early April.

Correspondence and Information
Academic Programs Office
Woods Hole Oceanographic Institution MS #31
360 Wood Hole Road, Clark 223
Woods Hole, Massachusetts 02543-1546
Telephone: 508-289-2219
World Wide Web: http://web.mit.edu/mit-whoi/www

MIT/WHOI Joint Program Office
Room 54-911
Massachusetts Institute of Technology
77 Massachusetts Avenue
Cambridge, Massachusetts 02139
Telephone: 617-253-7544
World Wide Web: http://web.mit.edu/mit-whoi/www

Massachusetts Institute of Technology / Woods Hole Oceanographic Institution

THE DEPARTMENTS AND THEIR RESEARCH

Oceanography and applied ocean science and engineering are fields that naturally lead to interdisciplinary research. In the following departmental program sections, brief descriptions of the research areas covered by the faculty are given. It is quite common for students to pursue research problems that cross the disciplinary lines of the given departments.

BIOLOGICAL OCEANOGRAPHY

Patrick Jaillet, Ph.D., Head, Civil and Environmental Engineering Department, MIT.
Robert T. Sauer, Ph.D., Head, Biology Department, MIT.
John J. Stegeman, Ph.D., Chair, Biology Department, WHOI.

Phytoplankton and zooplankton ecology; regulation of primary and secondary production; population biology; natural history and biology of oceanic fishes; comparative physiology; biochemical toxicology in marine species; biochemical and physiological adaptations; toxic algae and red tides; theoretical and experimental population ecology; estuarine and salt marsh ecology; ecology of deep and coastal benthos; microbial ecology and biochemistry; development and reproductive biology of marine invertebrates; larval dispersal mechanisms; behavior of marine mammals; symbiotic relationships; biogeochemistry of aquatic systems; biodegradation of aquatic contaminants; cell biology; molecular biology and evolution; synthesis, shape, and structure of macromolecules; cellular and molecular immunology; gene expression.

CHEMICAL OCEANOGRAPHY

Patrick Jaillet, Ph.D., Head, Civil and Environmental Engineering Department, MIT.
Maria Zuber, Ph.D., Head, Department of Earth, Atmospheric, and Planetary Sciences, MIT.
Ken O. Buesseler, Ph.D., Chair, Marine Chemistry and Geochemistry Department, WHOI.

Water columns (open and coastal oceans, estuaries, rivers): organic and inorganic cycles of particulate and dissolved carbon, oxygen, nitrogen, phosphorous, sulfur, and trace metals (redox transformations, rare earths); stable and radioisotopic tracers; noble gases; air-sea exchange; remote sensing and modeling; environmental quality; oil and gas geochemistry; colloids and particle-reactive tracers; weathering.
Sedimentary geochemistry: major and minor elements, radionuclides and their paleoceanographic applications, diagenesis and preservation of organic matter, modeling.
Seawater-basalt interactions: major and trace elements, stable isotopes, solid phases and hydrothermal solutions, laboratory experiments, modeling.

MARINE GEOLOGY AND GEOPHYSICS

Maria Zuber, Ph.D., Head, Department of Earth, Atmospheric, and Planetary Sciences, MIT.
Susan E. Humphris, Ph.D., Chair, Geology and Geophysics Department, WHOI.

Micropaleontological biostratigraphy, planktonic and benthonic foraminifera, paleoceanography, paleobiogeography, benthic boundary-layer processes, paleocirculation and paleoecology, igneous petrology and volcanic processes, crustal structure and tectonics, marine magnetic anomalies, heat flow of the ocean floor, upper mantle petrology, seismic stratigraphy, fractionation processes of stable isotopes and stable isotope stratigraphy, metamorphosis of high-strain zones, gravity, observational and theoretical reflection and refraction seismology, earthquake seismology, relative and absolute plate motions, coastal processes, marine sedimentation.

OCEANOGRAPHIC ENGINEERING

Patrick Jaillet, Ph.D., Head, Civil and Environmental Engineering Department, MIT.
John V. Guttag, Ph.D., Head, Electrical Engineering and Computer Sciences Department, MIT.
Rohan Abeyaratne, Ph.D., Head, Mechanical Engineering Department, MIT.
Henrik Schmidt, Ph.D., Head (Acting), Ocean Engineering Department, MIT.
W. Rockwell Geyer, Ph.D., Chairman, Applied Ocean Physics and Engineering Department, WHOI.

Optical instrumentation, laser velocimetry; volcanic, tectonic, and hydrothermal processes; deep submergence systems (imaging, control, robotics); underwater acoustics (acoustic tomography, scattering, remote sensing, Arctic acoustics, bottom acoustics propagation through the ocean interior and sediments, array design); buoy and mooring engineering; ocean instrumentation; signal processing theory; fluid dynamics, sediment transport, nearshore processes, bottom boundary layer and mixed layer dynamics; turbulence, wave prediction, numerical modeling; seismic profiling; data acquisition and communication systems, microprocessor-based instrumentation; fiber optics; sonar systems; marsh ecology; ship design; offshore structures; material science; groundwater flow.

PHYSICAL OCEANOGRAPHY

Ronald G. Prinn, Ph.D., Head, Department of Earth, Atmospheric, and Planetary Sciences, MIT.
Nelson Hogg, Ph.D., Chair, Physical Oceanography Department, WHOI.

General circulation: distribution of tracer fields, models of idealized gyres, abyssal circulation, heat transport.
Air-sea interaction: water mass transportation, upper ocean response to atmospheric forcing, equatorial ocean circulation.
Shelf dynamics: coastal upwelling and fronts, coastal-trapped waves, deep ocean-shelf exchange.
Mesoscale processes: Gulf Stream Rings, oceanic fronts, barotropic and baroclinic instability, eddy-mean interactions.
Small-scale processes: double diffusion, intrusion, internal waves, convection.

NOVA SOUTHEASTERN UNIVERSITY

Oceanographic Center
Programs in Marine Biology, Coastal Zone Management, Marine Environmental Sciences, and Oceanography

Programs of Study

The Oceanographic Center through the Institute of Marine and Coastal Studies offers the M.S. degree in marine biology, coastal zone management, and marine environmental sciences; the joint M.S. degree in marine biology/coastal zone management/marine environmental sciences; and the Ph.D. degree in oceanography and marine biology. The M.S. and Ph.D. programs contain a common core of five marine courses: concepts in physical oceanography, ecosystems, geology, chemistry, and biostatistics. Specialty and tutorial courses in each program provide depth. The Oceanographic Center operates on a quarter-term system with twelve-week courses.

Classes for the M.S. programs meet one evening per week in a 3-hour session. Capstone Review and Thesis tracks are offered. The Capstone Review Track requires a minimum of 45 credits, which includes thirteen 3-credit courses and a 6-credit paper. The paper is usually an extended literature review of an approved subject, which the student defends before the Advisory Committee. The Thesis Track requires a minimum of 39 credits, including ten 3-credit courses and at least 9 credits of master's thesis research. The number of research credits depends upon the time needed to complete the thesis research, typically a minimum of three terms. The thesis is formally defended before the committee. All students admitted to the program are placed in the Capstone Review Track. To enter the Thesis Track, students must have approval of the major professor and complete an approved thesis proposal.

The joint M.S. degree in marine biology/coastal zone management/marine environmental science requires a minimum of 51 to 54 credits, depending upon the student's track—Capstone Review or thesis research.

The Ph.D. program consists of upper-level course work and original research on a selected topic of importance in the ocean sciences. Requirements include general core courses as well as tutorial studies with the major professor. The Ph.D. degree requires a minimum of 90 credits beyond the baccalaureate; at least 48 credits must consist of dissertation research and at least 42 credits must consist of upper-level course work, usually tutorial studies with the major professor. The student must successfully complete the Ph.D. comprehensive examination and defend the dissertation before Oceanographic Center faculty members. Students are expected to complete the Ph.D. program in nine years or less, a minimum of three years of which must be in residence.

The Oceanographic Center also offers a graduate certificate in coastal studies. This is a distance learning program. Enrollment in the certificate program is designed for those who do not wish to enroll in the graduate program of study at this time. The flexible format of the certificate program makes it ideal for working professionals and college graduates in a variety of fields related to the coastal zone. Distance courses bring the learning to the student, whether online, by CD-ROM, or through written materials. The graduate certificate in coastal studies is awarded upon successful completion of four of the Oceanographic Center's graduate distance learning courses. Successful completion of the graduate certificate program awards the equivalent of 12 graduate credits.

Research Facilities

The center is composed of three main buildings, several modulars, and two houseboats. The two-story houseboat contains a student center and ten student offices. The second houseboat is used as visiting scientist housing. The main buildings contain a conference room, a classroom, a warehouse bay staging area, an electron microscopy laboratory, a darkroom, a machine shop, a carpentry shop, an electronics laboratory, a computer center with ready room, a wetlab/classroom, a coral workshop, a filtered seawater facility, eight working biology laboratories, and twenty-four additional offices.

The William Springer Richardson Library contains 2,700 books as well as 80 active and 33 inactive periodicals. Audiovisual equipment is available as well as computer-assisted CD-ROM and Internet database searches. A general library facility is maintained on the main campus in Davie.

The computer center operates a multinode OpenVMS cluster consisting of DEC AXP workstations, with high-resolution color monitors, DAT tape drives, and CD-ROM readers. Also available are two networked HP 4SiMX PostScript printers, a networked Tektronix Phaser 550 color laser printer, a color flatbed scanner, and imaging hardware and software. The center also operates a LAN consisting of approximately forty PCs for faculty and staff member and student use that is connected to the Internet via a T-1 link.

Financial Aid

There is limited financial aid available in the form of undergraduate laboratory teaching assistantships and graduate research assistantships. The Office of Student Financial Aid helps students finance tuition, fees, books, and other costs, drawing on a variety of public and private aid programs. For more information, students should call 800-541-6682 Ext. 7411.

Cost of Study

In 2003–04, tuition costs are $525 per credit hour for students enrolled in the M.S. programs and $3607 per term for students enrolled in the Ph.D. program.

Living and Housing Costs

All full-time students are eligible for main-campus housing, which is located 12 miles due west of the Oceanographic Center. Furnished one- and two-bedroom apartments are available. For more information, students should call 800-541-6682 Ext. 7052. Numerous apartments, condominiums, and other rental housing are available in Hollywood, Dania Beach, and Ft. Lauderdale.

Student Group

There are 145 students enrolled in the M.S. programs and 5 students enrolled in the Ph.D. program.

Student Outcomes

M.S. graduates find positions in city, county, and state governments or private industry, including consulting companies. Graduates also go on for further education and enter Ph.D. programs.

Location

The Center is located in Dania Beach, Florida, just south of Ft. Lauderdale, on a 10-acre site on the ocean side of Port Everglades and is easily accessible from I-95 and the Ft. Lauderdale airport. The Center has a 1-acre boat basin, and its location affords immediate access to the Gulf Stream and the open sea, the Florida Straits, and the Bahama Banks.

The University

Nova Southeastern University was chartered by the State of Florida in 1964 and currently, with nearly 19,000 students, is the largest independent university in Florida. The main campus is situated on 227 acres in Davie, Florida, near Ft. Lauderdale.

Applying

When applying, students must submit an application form, application fee, transcripts from other schools attended, GRE scores, and letters of recommendation. Applicants interested in the M.S. program in marine biology should hold a bachelor's degree in biology, oceanography, or a closely related field, including science education. Due to the discipline's diversity, applicants with any undergraduate major will be considered for admission into the M.S. program in coastal zone management or marine environmental science. However, a science major is most useful, and a science background is essential.

Correspondence and Information

Nova Southeastern University
Oceanographic Center
Institute of Marine and Coastal Studies
8000 North Ocean Drive
Dania Beach, Florida 33004
Telephone: 954-262-3600
Fax: 954-262-4020
E-mail: imcs@nova.edu
World Wide Web: http://www.nova.edu/ocean/

Nova Southeastern University

THE FACULTY AND THEIR RESEARCH

The Oceanographic Center pursues studies and investigations in biological oceanography and observational and theoretical oceanography. Research interests include: modeling of large-scale ocean circulation, coastal dynamics, ocean-atmosphere coupling, surface gravity waves, biological oceanography, chemical oceanography, coral reef assessment, Pleistocene and Holocene sea level changes, benthic ecology, marine biodiversity, calcification of invertebrates, marine fisheries, molecular ecology and evolution, wetlands ecology, aquaculture, and nutrient dynamics. Regions of interest include not only Florida's coastal waters and the continental shelf/slope waters of the southeastern United States, but also the waters of the Caribbean Sea, the Gulf of Mexico, and the Antarctic, Atlantic, Indian, and Pacific oceans.

Professors
Richard E. Dodge: Coral reefs and reef-building corals, effects of pollution and past climatic changes.
Charles Messing: Systematics of crinoids and macroinvertebrate communities.
Andrew Rogerson: Ecology of eukaryotic microbes (the protists) in the cycling of carbon and nutrients in coastal waters, particularly the amoeboid protozoa.
Richard Spieler: Fish chronobiology, artificial reefs, and habitat assessment.
James Thomas: Marine biodiversity, invertebrate systematics.

Associate Professors
Patricia Blackwelder: Calcification and distribution of marine microfauna, a historical record of the past.
Curtis Burney: Dissolved nutrients and marine microbes, especially bacteria.
Veljko Dragojlovic: Isolation, characterization, and synthesis of natural products.
Edward Keith: Structure, function, and evolution of milk and tear proteins; physiological ecology of terrestrial and marine mammals; molecular phylogenetics and evolution of marine mammals.
Mahmood Shivji: Conservation biology, biodiversity, evolution, molecular ecology, and population biology.
Alexander Soloviev: Measurement and modeling of near-surface turbulence and air/sea exchange.

Assistant Professors
Joshua Feingold: Coral reef ecology.
Sean Keenan: Physical oceanography.
Alexander Yankovsky: Wind- and buoyancy-driven currents on the continental shelf and slope, their mesoscale variability, and adjustment to realistic shelf topography.

Adjunct Professors
Brion Blackwelder: Coastal law.
Jane Dougan: Environmental sustainability, life on a water planet.
Mark Farber: Biostatistics.
Nancy Gassman: Marine biology, coastal zone management, and marine environmental sciences internships.
David Gilliam: Coral reef assessment.
Richard Grosso: Coastal law.
Philip Light: Conservation biology.
Donald McCorquodale: Microbiology, marine chemistry.
Stacy Myers: GIS and remote sensing, coastal zone management.
Keith Ronald: Marine mammals.
Scott Schatz: Microbiology.
Steffen Schmidt: Coastal policy, international integrated coastal zone management.
Marianne Walch: Coral reef ecology.

The Oceanographic Center.

RUTGERS, THE STATE UNIVERSITY OF NEW JERSEY, NEW BRUNSWICK/PISCATAWAY

Institute of Marine and Coastal Sciences
Graduate Program in Oceanography

Programs of Study

Oceanography is the discipline encompassing all aspects of the scientific study of the oceans, including their physical, biological, chemical, and geological properties. The basic goals of oceanography are to obtain a systematic description of the oceans and a quantitative understanding sufficient for prediction of their behavior. The Graduate Program in Oceanography is centered in the Institute of Marine and Coastal Sciences, which serves as a focus of interdisciplinary studies and research in estuarine, coastal, and open-ocean environments. A broad range of research opportunities are available, including real-time studies in the coastal ocean using advanced underwater instrumentation, biological and geological processes at deep-sea hydrothermal vents, remote sensing and ocean modeling, advanced underwater optics, fish behavior, biodiversity, marine molecular biology, coastal geomorphology, organism-sediment interactions, cycling of organic and inorganic materials in the ocean, and watershed ecosystems.

Candidates with a baccalaureate degree may apply for either the Doctor of Philosophy (Ph.D.) or Master of Science (M.S.) degree program. The Ph.D. degree requires the completion of 72 credit hours of course work and research beyond the baccalaureate degree and the writing and defense of a dissertation resulting from the candidate's independent, original research in oceanography. The M.S. degree requires the completion of 30 credit hours of course work and research beyond the baccalaureate degree and the writing and defense of a thesis. All students are required to complete a program of core courses in oceanography; additional courses are chosen by students in consultation with their major professors and program committees. Ph.D. students must pass a written and oral qualifying examination upon completion of their course work.

Research Facilities

The Institute of Marine and Coastal Sciences is housed in a state-of-the-art research building that includes seawater, molecular biology, analytical chemistry, remote sensing, and ocean modeling laboratories. Major equipment includes seawater annular and racetrack flumes; a satellite receiving station; a network of small (PCs), medium (UNIX-based workstations), and large (multiprocessor and Beowulf-type) computer platforms; plasma mass spectrometry; and electron microscopes. The Rutgers University Marine Field Station, located at the northern entrance to Great Bay, is the site of a large tract of pristine marsh and a major estuary that retains most of its natural characteristics. Great Bay connects with adjoining bays and has direct access to the Atlantic Ocean. An extensive program of long-term oceanographic and ecosystems research is underway at the station. The Haskin Shellfish Research Laboratory, located on Delaware Bay, includes molecular genetics, cytogenetics, microbiology, histopathology, shell structure, shellfish physiology, and pathophysiology laboratories.

Financial Aid

Graduate assistantships are available from sponsored research grants and contracts awarded to the faculty. In addition, a limited number of state-supported teaching assistantships and fellowships are available each year. All assistantships and fellowships include a stipend (from $15,000 to $16,555 per year) and full tuition remission. Virtually all full-time students who are accepted receive financial aid.

Cost of Study

Tuition for 2003–04, for a full course load of 12 or more credits, was $4476 per semester for New Jersey residents and $6562.20 for out-of-state residents.

Living and Housing Costs

Graduate students traditionally live off campus. University housing is also available in dormitory/apartment-style accommodations that range from $4700 to $5200 per academic year. A variety of meal plans that average $3070 per academic year are also available.

Student Group

Currently, there are 25 full-time students in the program, 11 women and 14 men. Twenty are pursuing the Ph.D. degree. Due to the highly interdisciplinary nature of much of the research conducted at the Institute, students share a unique rapport with each other and faculty members.

Student Outcomes

The graduate program was established in 1994 and has granted fifteen Ph.D. degrees and twelve M.S. degrees; several M.S. students continued their studies toward a Ph.D. at Rutgers.

Location

The Institute of Marine and Coastal Sciences is located on Rutgers University's Cook Campus in New Brunswick, New Jersey. A wealth of cultural and recreational opportunities are nearby. Several accomplished repertory companies are housed in New Brunswick and nearby Princeton. The major metropolitan areas of New York City and Philadelphia are only short (less than 1 hour) train rides away. The world-famous New Jersey shore, with its beaches, swimming, and fishing, is readily accessible.

The University and The Institute

Rutgers, The State University of New Jersey, traces its origins back to 1766 when it was chartered as Queen's College, the eighth institution of higher learning founded in the colonies. Today, more than 50,000 students are enrolled on campuses in New Brunswick, Camden, and Newark. The Institute of Marine and Coastal Sciences was established in 1989 to develop research programs in marine and coastal sciences and to provide a center for the education of marine scientists.

Applying

Applicants to the program are expected to have an undergraduate degree in either mathematics, science, or engineering. Scores on the GRE General Test are required. International students must show proficiency in English. Application deadlines are February 1 for admission the following fall semester and November 1 for admission the following spring semester. Early submission is encouraged, especially for students seeking financial aid. Applicants are strongly encouraged to contact faculty members with complementary interests before and during the application process.

Correspondence and Information

Graduate Program in Oceanography
Institute of Marine and Coastal Sciences
Rutgers, The State University of New Jersey
71 Dudley Road
New Brunswick, New Jersey 08901-8521
Telephone: 732-932-6555 Ext. 500
Fax: 732-932-8578
E-mail: gpo@imcs.rutgers.edu
World Wide Web: http://marine.rutgers.edu/gpo/GradProg.html

Rutgers, The State University of New Jersey, New Brunswick/Piscataway

THE FACULTY AND THEIR RESEARCH

Kenneth W. Able, Professor; Ph.D., William and Mary. Life history, ecology, and behavior of fishes.
James W. Ammerman, Associate Research Professor; Ph.D., California, San Diego (Scripps). Aquatic (especially marine and estuarine) microbial ecology and biochemistry.
Gail M. Ashley, Professor; Ph.D., British Columbia. Sedimentology, geomorphology, environmental ecology, modern processes.
David Bushek, Assistant Professor; Ph.D., Rutgers. Shellfish ecology in estuarine ecosystems, ecological aspects of microparasites on shellfish.
Robert J. Chant, Assistant Professor; Ph.D., SUNY at Stony Brook. Observations and numerical modeling of estuarine and coastal processes.
Colomban de Vargas, Assistant Professor; Ph.D., Geneva (Switzerland). Molecular ecology and evolution of unicellular organisms in the ocean.
Richard H. Dunk, Adjunct Professor; Ph.D., Rutgers. Meteorology, air-sea interactions, sea breezes.
Paul G. Falkowski, Professor; Ph.D., British Columbia. Biological oceanography: photosynthesis and biogeochemical cycles, application of molecular and biophysical techniques to the marine environment.
Jennifer A. Francis, Associate Research Professor; Ph.D., Washington (Seattle). Satellite remote sensing of polar regions, air/ice/ocean transfer, Arctic climate and polar meteorology.
Scott M. Glenn, Professor; Sc.D., MIT/Woods Hole Oceanographic Institution. Physical oceanography, satellite remote sensing.
J. Frederick Grassle, Professor; Ph.D., Duke. Marine ecology, oceanography.
Judith P. Grassle, Professor; Ph.D., Duke. Population genetics, marine benthic ecology.
Ximing Guo, Associate Professor; Ph.D., Washington (Seattle). Shellfish genetics and genomics, cytogenetics, shellfish breeding, aquaculture.
Dale B. Haidvogel, Professor; Ph.D., MIT/Woods Hole Oceanographic Institution. Physical oceanography, numerical ocean circulation modeling.
Michael J. Kennish, Assistant Research Professor; Ph.D., Rutgers. Marine geology, estuarine and marine ecology, marine pollution.
Lee J. Kerkhof, Associate Professor; Ph.D., California, San Diego (Scripps). Marine microbiology–molecular biology, microbial population dynamics.
Uwe Kils, Associate Professor; Ph.D., Kiel (Germany). Behavior and microdistribution of juvenile fish, in situ optics.
Julia C. Levin, Assistant Research Professor; Ph.D., Columbia. Ocean modeling, computational fluid dynamics, numerical analysis.
Richard A. Lutz, Professor; Ph.D., Maine. Marine ecology and paleoecology, shellfish ecology, biology of deep-sea hydrothermal vents.
George R. McGhee, Professor; Ph.D., Rochester. Marine paleoecology, evolutionary theory, mass extinction.
James R. Miller, Professor; Ph.D., Maryland. Air-sea interactions, remote sensing, climate modeling, earth system science.
Kenneth G. Miller Sr., Professor; Ph.D., MIT/Woods Hole Oceanographic Institution. Cenozoic stratigraphy and paleoceanography; integrated biostratigraphy, isotope stratigraphy, magnetostratigraphy, and seismic stratigraphy.
Michael R. Muller, Associate Professor; Ph.D., Brown. Fluid mechanics, internal gravity waves and thermals.
Karl F. Nordstrom, Professor; Ph.D., Rutgers. Geomorphology, sedimentology.
Richard K. Olsson, Professor Emeritus of Geological Sciences; Ph.D., Princeton. Micropaleontology, stratigraphy, paleoecology, paleobathymetry of Cretaceous and Cenozoic formations.
Eric N. Powell, Professor; Ph.D., North Carolina. Shellfish biology/modeling, carbonate preservation, reproductive biology, fisheries management.
Norbert P. Psuty, Professor Emeritus; Ph.D., LSU. Coastal geomorphology, shoreline erosion, coastal zone management.
John A. Quinlan, Assistant Professor; Ph.D., North Carolina at Chapel Hill. Fisheries oceanography, management, biophysical interactions, modeling.
John R. Reinfelder, Assistant Professor; Ph.D., SUNY at Stony Brook. Trace element biogeochemistry, phytoplankton physiology and marine primary production, marine carbon cycle.
Alan Robock, Professor; Ph.D., MIT. Climatological data analysis, climate modeling, impacts of climate change, soil moisture, remote sensing.
Peter A. Rona, Professor; Ph.D., Yale. Seafloor hydrothermal system, ocean ridge processes, geology of Atlantic continental margins, genesis of seafloor mineral and energy resources.
Yair Rosenthal, Assistant Professor; Ph.D., MIT/Woods Hole Oceanographic Institution. Quaternary paleoceanography, trace metal and isotope biogeochemistry, estuarine and coastal geochemistry.
Oscar M. E. Schofield, Associate Professor; Ph.D., California, Santa Barbara. Marine phytoplankton ecology, biooptics, effects of UV radiation on phytoplankton.
Sybil P. Seitzinger, Visiting Professor; Ph.D., Rhode Island. Nutrient dynamics in marine, freshwater, and terrestrial ecosystems.
Robert E. Sheridan, Professor, Ph.D.; Columbia. Geology and geophysics of the Atlantic continental margin.
Robert M. Sherrell, Associate Professor; Ph.D., MIT/Woods Hole Oceanographic Institution. Trace metals in the oceanic water column, environmental chemistry.
Elisabeth L. Sikes, Associate Research Professor; Ph.D., MIT/Woods Hole Oceanographic Institution. Paleoceanography, marine organic geochemistry.
Peter Smouse, Professor; Ph.D., North Carolina State. Genetics and ecology.
Gary L. Taghon, Associate Professor; Ph.D., Washington (Seattle). Marine benthic ecology.
Christopher G. Uchrin, Professor; Ph.D., Michigan. Mathematical modeling of contaminant transport in surface and ground waters.
Dana E. Veron, Assistant Professor; Ph.D., California, San Diego (Scripps). Cloud-aerosol-radiation interactions, climate modeling, remote sensing.
Costantino Vetriani, Assistant Professor; Ph.D., Rome (Italy). Deep-sea microbiology, thermophiles, microbial adaptations to extreme environments.
Michael P. Weinstein, Visiting Professor; Ph.D., Florida State. Coastal ecology, habitat utilization (nekton) secondary production, restoration ecology, ecological engineering.
John L. Wilkin, Assistant Professor; Ph.D., MIT/Woods Hole Oceanographic Institution. Physical oceanography, coastal dynamics, coupled physical/biological modeling.

Rutgers, The State University of New Jersey, New Brunswick/Piscataway

SELECTED PUBLICATIONS

Able, K. W. Measures of juvenile fish habitat quality: Examples from a national estuarine research reserve. In *Fish Habitat: Essential Fish Habitat and Rehabilitation,* pp. 134–47, ed. L. R. Benaka. American Fisheries Society Symp. 22, Bethesda, Maryland, 1999.

Able, K. W., and M. P. Fahay. *The First Year in the Life of Estuarine Fishes in the Middle Atlantic Bight.* New Brunswick, New Jersey: Rutgers University Press, 1998.

Ammerman, J. W., R. R. Hood, D. A. Case, and J. B. Cotner. Phosphorus deficiency in the Atlantic: An emerging paradigm in oceanography. *EOS (Trans., Am. Geophys. Union)* 84:165, 170, 2003.

Ammerman, J. W. Phosphorus cycling in aquatic environments: Role of bacteria. In *The Encyclopedia of Environmental Microbiology,* vol. 5, pp. 2448–53, ed. G. Bitton. John Wiley & Sons, Inc., 2002.

Ashley, G. M., and N. D. Smith. Marine sedimentation at a subpolar calving ice margin, Antarctic, Peninsula. *Geo. Soc. Am. Bull.* 112(5):657–67, 2000.

Smith, N. D., and **G. M. Ashley.** A study of brash ice in the proximal marine zone of a sub-polar tidewater glacier. *Mar. Geol.* 133:75–87, 1996.

Ford, S. E., M. M. Chintala, and **D. Bushek.** Comparison of in vitro cultured and wild-type *Perkinsus marinus* I. Pathogen virulence. *Dis. Aquat. Org.* 51:187–201, 2002.

Dame, R., and **D. Bushek** et al. Ecosystem response to bivalve density reduction: Management implications. *Aquat. Ecol.* 36:51–65, 2002.

Chant, R. J. Secondary flows in a region of flow curvature: Relationship with tidal forcing and river discharge. *J. Geophys. Res.* 10.1029/2001JC001082, 2002.

Chant, R. J., and A. Stoner. Particle trapping in a stratified flood-dominated estuary. *J. Mar. Res.* 59:29–51, 2001.

de Vargas, C., A. Garcia-Saez, L. K. Medlin, and H. Thierstein. Super-species in the calcareous plankton. In *Coccolithophores: From Molecular Processes to Global Impact,* eds. H. R. Thierstein and J. R. Young. New York: Springer-Verlag, in press.

de Vargas, C., et al. Molecular evidence of cryptic speciation in planktonic foraminifera and their relation to oceanic provinces. *Proc. Natl. Acad. Sci.* 96:2864–8, 1999.

Ratcliff, M., R. Petersen, **R. Dunk,** and J. DeToro. Comparison of wind tunnel and ISDM model simulations of sea breeze fumigations. *Annual AWMA Meeting,* Atlanta, Georgia, 1996.

Peterson, R., B. Cochran, and **R. Dunk.** Wind tunnel determined building heights for modeling combustion turbines with ISC. *74th AMS Meeting, 8th Conference on the Applications of Air Pollution Meteorology,* Nashville, Tennessee, 1994.

Falkowski, P. G. The ocean's invisible forest. *Sci. Am.* 287:38–45, 2002.

Falkowski, P. G., and J. Raven. *Aquatic Photosynthesis,* p. 375. Oxford: Blackwell, 1997.

Francis, J. A. Validation of reanalysis upper-level winds in the Arctic with independent rawinsonde data. *Geophys. Res. Lett.* 29:1315, 2002.

Groves, D. G., and **J. A. Francis.** The moisture budget of the Arctic atmosphere from TOVS satellite data. *J. Geophys. Res.* 107(D19): 4391, 2002.

Glenn, S. M., T. D. Dickey, B. Parker, and W. Boicourt. Long-term, real-time coastal ocean observation networks. *Oceanography* 13:24–34, 2000.

Glenn, S. M., W. Boicourt, B. Parker, and T. D. Dickey. Operational observation networks for ports, a large estuary and an open shelf. *Oceanography* 132:12–23, 2000.

Snelgrove, P. V. R., et al. (**J. F. Grassle** and **J. P. Grassle).** The role of colonization in establishing patterns of community composition and diversity in shallow-water sedimentary communities. *J. Mar. Res.* 59:813–30, 2001.

Grassle, J. F. The Ocean Biogeographic Information System (OBIS): An on-line, worldwide atlas for accessing, modeling, and mapping marine biological data in a multidimensional context. *Oceanography* 13(3):5–7, 2000.

Snelgrove, P. V. R., et al. (**J. F. Grassle** and **J. P. Grassle).** In situ habitat selection by settling larvae of marine soft-sediment invertebrates. *Limnol. Oceanogr.* 44(5):1341–7, 1999.

Weissberger, E. J., and **J. P. Grassle.** Settlement, first-year growth, and mortality of surfclams *Spisula solidissima. Est. Cstl. Shelf Sci.* 56:669–84, 2003.

Yu, Z., and **X. Guo.** Genetic linkage map of the eastern oyster *Crassostrea virginica* Gmelin. *Biol. Bull.* 204:327–38, 2003.

Guo, X., et al. Genetic determinants of protandric sex in Crassostrea oyster. *Evolution* 52:394–402, 1998.

Hermann, A. J., and **D. B. Haidvogel** et al. A coupled global/regional circulation model for ecosystem studies in the coastal Gulf of Alaska. *Prog. Oceanogr.* 53:335–67, 2002.

Haidvogel, D. B., and A. Beckmann. *Numerical Ocean Circulation Modeling,* p. 318. London: Imperial College Press, 1999.

Estuarine Research, Monitoring, and Resource Protection, ed. **M. J. Kennish.** Boca Raton, Florida: CRC Press, 2003.

Kennish, M. J. Environmental threats and environmental future of estuaries. *Environ. Conserv.* 29:78–107, 2002.

Paerl, H., et al. **(L. Kerkhof)**. Characterizing man-made and natural modifications of microbial diversity and activity in coastal ecosystems. *Antonie van Leeuwenhoek* 81:487–507, 2002.

Perez-Jimenez, J., L. Young, and **L. Kerkhof.** Dissimilatory sulfite reductase genes from novel anaerobic bacteria capable of PAH degradation. *FEMS Microb. Ecol.* 35:145–50, 2001.

Rademacher, K., and **U. Kils.** Predator/prey dynamics of fifteen-spined stickleback (Spinachia spinachia) and the mysid (Neomysis integer). *Arch. Fish. Mar. Res.* 43:171–81, 1996.

Thetmeyer, H., and **U. Kils.** To see and not to be seen: The visibility of predator and prey with respect to feeding behavior. *Mar. Ecol. Prog. Ser.* 126:1–8, 1995.

Levin, J., M. Iskandarani, and D. Haidvogel. A nonconforming spectral element ocean model. *Int. J. Numer. Methods Fluids* 34(6):495–525, 2000.

Levin, J., M. Iskandarani, and D. Haidvogel. A spectral filtering procedure for eddy-resolving simulations with a spectral element ocean model. *J. Comput. Phys.* 13(1):130–54, 1997.

Lutz, R. A. Dawn in the deep. *Natl. Geograph.* 203(2):92–103, 2003.

Lutz, R. A., T. A. Shank, and R. Evans. Life after death in the deep-sea. *Am. Scientist* 89:422–31, 2001.

McGhee, G. R., Jr. *Theoretical Morphology.* New York: Columbia University Press, 1999.

McGhee, G. R., Jr. *The Late Devonian Mass Extinction.* New York: Columbia University Press, 1996.

Miller, J. R., and G. L. Russell. Projected impact of climate change on the energy budget of the Arctic Ocean by a global climate model. *J. Climate* 15(21):3028–42, 2002.

Miller, J. R., G. L. Russell, and G. Caliri. Continental scale river flow in climate models. *J. Climate* 7:914–28, 1994.

Miller, K. G., et al. A chronology of Late Cretaceous sequences and sea-level history: Glacioeustasy during the Greenhouse World. *Geology* 31(7):585–8, 2003.

Miller, K. G. The role of ODP in understanding the causes and effects of global sea-level change, accomplishments and opportunities of the ODP. *JOIDES J.* 28(1):23–8, 2002.

Nordstrom, K. F., N. L. Jackson, J. R. Allen, and D. J. Sherman. Longshore sediment transport rates on a microtidal estuarine beach. *J. Waterway, Port, Coastal, Ocean Eng.* 129:1–4, 2003.

Rutgers, The State University of New Jersey, New Brunswick/Piscataway

Selected Publications (continued)

Nordstrom, K. F. *Beaches and Dunes of Developed Coasts.* Cambridge: Cambridge University Press, 2000.

Olsson, R. K., and **K. G. Miller** et al. Sequence stratigraphy and sea-level change across the Cretaceous-Tertiary boundary on the New Jersey passive margin. *Geo. Soc. Am. Spec. Paper* 336:97–108, 2002.

Powell, E. N., A. J. Bonner, B. Muller, and E. A. Bochenek. Vessel time allocation in the US *Illex illecebrosus* fishery. *Fish. Res.* 61:35–55, 2003.

Powell, E. N., G. M. Staff, R. J. Stanton Jr., and W. R. Callender. Application of trophic transfer efficiency and age structure in the trophic analysis of fossil assemblages. *Lethaia* 34(2):97–118, 2001.

Coastal Dunes: Ecology and Conservation, Ecological Studies 171, eds. M. L. Martinez and **N. P. Psuty.** Berlin: Springer-Verlag, 2004.

Psuty, N. P., and D. D. Ofiara. *Coastal Hazard Management: Lessons and Future Directions from New Jersey.* New Brunswick, New Jersey: Rutgers University Press, 2002.

Werner, F. E., et al. **(J. A. Quinlan).** Larval trophodynamics, turbulence and drift on Georges Bank: A sensitivity analysis of cod and haddock. *Scientia Marina* 65(1):99–115, 2001.

Quinlan, J. A., B. O. Blanton, T. J. Miller, and F. E. Werner. From spawning grounds to the estuary: Using linked individual-based and hydrodynamic models to interpret patterns and processes in the oceanic phase of Atlantic menhaden life history. *Fish. Oceanogr.* 8(2):224–46, 1999.

Fan, C.-W., and **J. R. Reinfelder.** Phenanthrene accumulation kinetics in marine diatoms. *Environ. Sci. Technol.* 37:3405–12, 2003.

Chang, S. I., and **J. R. Reinfelder.** Relative importance of dissolved versus trophic bioaccumulation of copper in marine copepods. *Mar. Ecol. Prog. Ser.* 231:179–86, 2002.

Robock, A. Volcanic eruptions and climate. *Rev. Geophys.* 38:191–219, 2000.

Robock, A., et al. The global soil moisture data bank. *Bull. Am. Met. Soc.* 81:1281–99, 2000.

Rona, P. A. Resources of the sea floor. *Science* 299:673–4, 2003.

Rona, P. A., K. G. Bemis, D. Silver, and C. D. Jones. Acoustic imaging, visualization, and quantification of buoyant hydrothermal plumes in the ocean *Mar. Geophys. Res.* 23:147–68, 2002b.

Rosenthal, Y., D. W. Oppo, and B. K. Linsley. The amplitude and phasing of climate change during the last deglaciation in the Sulu Sea, western equatorial Pacific. *Geophys. Res. Lett.* 30(8):1428 doi:10.1029/2002GL016612, 2003.

Lear, C. H., **Y. Rosenthal,** and J. D. Wright. The closing of a seaway: Ocean water masses and global climate change. *Earth Planet. Sci. Lett.* 210:425–36, 2003.

Schofield, O., et al. Development of regional coastal ocean observatories and the potential benefits to marine sanctuaries. *Mar. Technol. Soc.* 37:54–67, 2003.

Schofield, O., et al. Linking regional coastal observatories to provide the foundation for a national ocean observation network. *J. Oceanic Eng.* 27(2):146–54, 2002.

Seitzinger, S. P., et al. Global patterns of dissolved inorganic and particulate nitrogen inputs to coastal systems: Recent conditions and future projections. *Estuaries* 25(4b):640–55, 2002.

Seitzinger, S. P., R. W. Sanders, and R. V. Styles. Bioavailability of DON from natural and anthropogenic sources to estuarine plankton. *Limnol. Oceanogr.* 47(2):353–66, 2002.

Cullen, J. T., et al. **(R. M. Sherrell).** Effect of iron limitation on the cadmium to phosphorus ratio of natural phytoplankton assemblages from the Southern Ocean. *Limnol. Oceanogr.* 48:1079–87, 2003.

Sherrell, R. M., M. P. Field, and G. Ravizza. Uptake and fractionation of rare earth elements on hydrothermal plume particles at 9 45N, East Pacific Rise. *Geochim. Cosmochim. Acta* 63:1709–22, 1999.

Sikes, E. L., W. R. Howard, H. L. Neil, and J. K. Volkman. Glacial-interglacial sea surface temperature changes across the subtropical front east of New Zealand based on alkenone unsaturation ratios and foraminiferal assemblages. *Paleoceaongraphy* 17(2): 10.1029/2001PA000640, 2002.

Sikes, E. L., C. R. Samson, T. P. Guilderson, and W. R. Howard. Old radiocarbon ages in the southwest Pacific at 11,900 years ago and the last glaciation. *Nature* 405:555–9, 2000.

Smouse, P. E., R. J. Dyer, R. D. Westfall, and V. L. Sork. Two-generation analysis of pollen flow across a landscape. I. Male gamete heterogeneity among females. *Evolution* 55:260–71, 2001.

Smouse, P. E., T. R. Meagher, and C. J. Kobak. Parentage analysis in *Chamaelirium luteum* (L.): Why do some males have disproportionate reproductive contributions? *J. Evol. Biol.* 12:1056–68, 1999.

Rockne, K. J, et al. **(G. L. Taghon).** Distributed sequestration and release of PAHs in weathered sediment: The role of sediment structure and organic carbon properties. *Environ. Sci. Technol.* 36:2636–44, 2002.

Linton, D. L., and **G. L. Taghon.** Feeding, growth, and fecundity of *Abarenicola pacifica* in relation to sediment organic concentration. *J. Exp. Mar. Biol. Ecol.* 2254:85–107, 2000.

Park, S. S., Y. Na, and **C. G. Uchrin.** An Oxygen Equivalent Model for water quality dynamics in a macrophyte dominated river. *Ecol. Modell.* 168:1–12, 2003.

Park, S. S., J. W. Park, **C. G. Uchrin,** and M. A. Cheney. A Micelle Inhibition Model for the availability of PAHs in aquatic systems. *Environ. Toxicol. Chem.* 21:2737–41, 2002.

Feingold, G., W. L. Eberhard, **D. E. Veron,** and M. Previdi. First measurement of the Twomey indirect effect using ground-based remote sensors. *Geophys. Res. Lett.* 30(6):1287, doi:10.1029/2002GL016633, 2003.

Veron, D. E., K. Goris, and R. C. J. Somerville. Radiative transfer through broken cloud fields: Observations and model validation. *J. Climate* 15(20):2921–33, 2002.

Vetriani, C., et al. *Thermovibrio ammonificans* sp. nov., a thermophilic, chemolithotrophic, nitrate ammonifying bacterium from deep-sea hydrothermal vents. *Int. J. Syst. Evol. Microbiol.* 54:175–81, 2004.

Vetriani, C. Origin of Archaea. In *Encyclopedia of Biodiversity,* pp. 219–30, ed. S. Levin. Academic Press, 2001.

Beck, M. W., et al. **(M. P. Weinstein).** The role of nearshore ecosystems as fish and shellfish nurseries. *Issues Ecol.* 11:1–12, 2003.

Litvin, S. Y., and **M. P. Weinstein.** Life history strategies of estuarine nekton: The role of marsh macrophytes, microphytobenthos and phytoplankton in the trophic spectrum. *Estuaries* 26(2B):553–653, 2003.

Wilkin, J. L., M. M. Bowen, and W. J. Emery. Mapping mesoscale currents by optimal interpolation of satellite radiometer and altimeter data. *Ocean Dynamics* 52:95–103, 2002.

Griffin, D., and **J. L. Wilkin** et al. Ocean currents and the larval phase of Australian western rock lobster, *Panulirus cygnus. Mar. Freshwater Res.* 52:1187–200, 2001.

STONY BROOK UNIVERSITY, STATE UNIVERSITY OF NEW YORK

Marine Sciences Research Center and the Institute for Terrestrial and Planetary Atmospheres

Program of Study

The Marine Sciences Research Center (MSRC) and the Institute for Terrestrial and Planetary Atmospheres (ITPA) offer an M.S. degree in Marine and Atmospheric Sciences, with specializations in marine sciences and atmospheric sciences. MSRC and ITPA are top-rated research centers that maintain a collegial, cooperative atmosphere among students and faculty members. The M.S. degree program includes the writing of an original research thesis, which many students consider to be the most important part of their training, and which sets them apart from graduates of nonthesis M.S. programs.

A typical program of study begins with a coordinated set of core courses covering fundamental principles of marine sciences or atmospheric sciences. At the same time, students are encouraged to join an ongoing research activity to help identify an area of specialization. Approximately five years are required to complete the Ph.D. Oceanographic research and teaching in marine sciences focuses on the collaborative, interdisciplinary study of oceanographic processes, combining biological, chemical, geological, and physical approaches to examine a wide range of issues, including biogeochemical cycling, fate and effects of contaminants, coastal environmental health, habitat destruction, and living marine resources. An important focus of the Center is regional coastal problems, such as coastal habitat alteration, diseases of marine animals, harmful algal blooms, and effects of contaminants on biota. Equally important are studies of diverse problems throughout the world; faculty members at MSRC are currently carrying out research in the Caribbean Sea, the Mediterranean Sea, Papua New Guinea, Bangladesh, and the Canadian Arctic, among other locations. A wide variety of approaches are employed, including shipboard sampling, remote sensing, field and laboratory experiments, laboratory analyses, and computer modeling and simulation. More information about marine research at MSRC can be found on the Web at http://msrc.sunysb.edu.

The Institute for Terrestrial and Planetary Atmospheres teaches students how to apply their knowledge of mathematics, physics, and chemistry to increase understanding of the atmospheres of Earth and other planets. Completion of the degree program requires a thorough understanding of the principles of atmospheric science coupled with the ability to apply that knowledge to significant problems. Research is conducted at various temporal and spatial scales, from the daily evolution of the atmospheric state—weather—to longer-scale climate variabilities, including those associated with El Niño and global warming. Comprehensive data sets from satellites, field experiments, laboratory measurements, and meteorological observations are analyzed in the context of global three-dimensional weather and climate models and simplified conceptual models. A key goal is to achieve better understanding of the physical bases of numerical weather forecasting and climate prediction, including the size and timing of future greenhouse warming. More information on the research program can be found at http://atmos.msrc.sunysb.edu.

Research Facilities

Facilities at the Marine Sciences Research Center are modern and comprehensive and support a wide range of oceanographic research. Major shared-use facilities include the R/V *Seawolf,* a 24-meter research ship; a running seawater laboratory; a multibeam echosounder for detailed seabed mapping; a laser ablation/inductively coupled plasma/mass spectrometer (LA-ICP-MS); a liquid chromatograph/time of flight/mass spectrometer (LC/TF/MS); and an analytical facility for CHN and nutrient analyses. A "clean" laboratory and environmental incubators are also available. Individual research laboratories contain facilities for a wide range of biological, chemical, physical, and geological research, including molecular biology, marine geochemistry, and naturally occurring radioisotopes. A marine disease and pathology laboratory is available, as are a large number of computers.

The Institute for Terrestrial and Planetary Atmospheres' computer facilities include several high-end multiple-processor Alpha UNIX stations, plus a large network of PC, UNIX, Linux, and Macintosh computers; printers; graphics terminals; and hard-copy plotters. The Institute maintains a comprehensive system to display real-time weather data, satellite measurements, and numerical model products. It has a state-of-the-art weather laboratory and a remote-sensing laboratory for students to use. The spectroscopy laboratory has infrared (grating) spectrometers, low-temperature absorption cells, a tunable diode laser spectrometer, and a Fourier-transform spectrometer. A stable-isotope mass spectrometer is maintained in the atmospheric isotope laboratory. Students have access to millimeter-wavelength remote-sensing equipment, developed at Stony Brook, and to data from NASA missions.

Financial Aid

Assistantships and fellowships provide academic-year stipends ranging from $11,655 to $21,000 for 2004–05, depending on status.

Cost of Study

Tuition for the 2004–05 academic year is $6900 for residents of New York State and $10,500 for nonresidents. Miscellaneous fees, such as insurance and activity fees, total approximately $300. Tuition waivers are available.

Living and Housing Costs

In 2003–04, living costs ranged from $600 to $1000 per month for single students living on campus. Off-campus rentals are also available and are preferred by most students.

Student Group

Approximately 95 students are engaged in research in marine science, and about 25 graduate students are in atmospheric sciences.

Location

Stony Brook is located about 50 miles east of Manhattan on the wooded North Shore of Long Island. It is convenient to New York City's cultural life and Suffolk County's recreational countryside and seashores. Long Island's hundreds of miles of magnificent coastline attract many swimming, boating, and fishing enthusiasts from around the world.

The University

Established forty years ago as New York's comprehensive state university center for Long Island and metropolitan New York, Stony Brook offers excellent programs in a broad spectrum of academic subjects. The University conducts major research and public service projects. Over the past decade, externally funded support for Stony Brook's research programs has grown faster than that of any other university in the United States and now exceeds $125 million per year. The University's internationally renowned faculty members teach courses from the undergraduate to the doctoral level to more than 22,000 students. More than 100 undergraduate and graduate departmental and interdisciplinary majors are offered. Extensive resources and expert support services help foster intellectual and personal growth.

Applying

Students applying for graduate study in marine sciences should have a B.S. degree in a science, including biology, chemistry, geology, or physics. Students applying for atmospheric sciences should have a B.S. degree in a science such as physics, chemistry, mathematics, engineering, or atmospheric science. For additional information about admission and financial aid, applicants may write for information about research opportunities to a graduate program faculty member whose research is of primary interest to them. Applications for September admission should be received by January 15 to ensure consideration for the widest range of support opportunities.

Students may request an application online at http://www.msrc.sunysb.edu/pages/gradapp.html and apply online at http://www.grad.sunysb.edu/applying/applying.htm.

Correspondence and Information

Nancy Glover
Marine Sciences Research Center
Stony Brook University, State University of New York
Stony Brook, New York 11794-5000
Telephone: 631-632-8681
Fax: 631-632-8820
E-mail: nglover@notes.cc.sunysb.edu

Gina Gartin
Institute for Terrestrial and Planetary Atmospheres
Stony Brook University, State University of New York
Stony Brook, New York 11794-5000
Telephone: 631-632-8009
Fax: 631-632.6251
E-mail: ggartin@notes.cc.sunysb.edu

Stony Brook University, State University of New York

THE FACULTY AND THEIR RESEARCH

MARINE SCIENCES

Bassem Allam, Assistant Professor; Ph.D., Western Brittany (France), 1998. Pathology and immunology of marine bivalves.
Josephine Y. Aller, Associate Professor; Ph.D., USC, 1975. Marine benthic ecology, invertebrate zoology, marine microbiology, biogeochemistry.
Robert C. Aller, Distinguished Professor; Ph.D., Yale, 1977. Marine geochemistry, marine animal-sediment relations.
Robert A. Armstrong, Associate Professor; Ph.D., Minnesota, 1975. Mathematical modeling in marine ecology and biogeochemistry.
Henry J. Bokuniewicz, Professor; Ph.D., Yale, 1976. Nearshore transport processes, coastal groundwater hydrology, coastal sedimentation, marine geophysics.
Malcolm J. Bowman, Professor; Ph.D., Saskatchewan, 1970. Coastal ocean and estuarine dynamics.
Bruce J. Brownawell, Associate Professor; Ph.D., MIT (Woods Hole), 1986. Biogeochemistry of organic pollutants in seawater and groundwater.
Robert M. Cerrato, Associate Professor; Ph.D., Yale, 1980. Benthic ecology, population and community dynamics.
J. Kirk Cochran, Professor; Ph.D., Yale, 1979. Marine geochemistry, use of radionuclides as geochemical tracers, diagenesis of marine sediments.
Jackie Collier, Assistant Professor; Ph.D., Stanford, 1994. Phytoplankton ecology, physiology, and molecular genetics.
David O. Conover, Professor and Dean, Marine Sciences Research Center; Ph.D., Massachusetts, 1982. Ecology of fish, fisheries biology.
Alistair Dove, Assistant Research Professor; Ph.D., Queensland (Australia), 1999. Pathology, taxonomy, life cycles/ecology.
Nicholas S. Fisher, Professor; Ph.D., SUNY at Stony Brook, 1974. Marine phytoplankton physiology and ecology, biogeochemistry of metals, marine pollution.
Roger D. Flood, Professor; Ph.D., MIT (Woods Hole), 1978. Marine geology, sediment dynamics, continental margin sedimentation.
Steven L. Goodbred Jr., Assistant Professor; Ph.D., William and Mary, 1999. Coastal marine sedimentology, Quaternary development of continental margins, salt-marsh processes.
Paul F. Kemp, Associate Research Professor; Ph.D., Oregon State, 1985. Growth and activity of marine microbes, benthic-pelagic interactions, molecular ecology of marine bacteria.
Cindy Lee, Distinguished Professor; Ph.D., California, San Diego (Scripps), 1975. Ocean carbon cycle, marine geochemistry of organic compounds, nitrogen-cycle biochemistry, biomineralization.
Darcy J. Lonsdale, Associate Professor; Ph.D., Maryland, 1979. Ecology and physiology of marine zooplankton, food web dynamics of estuarine plankton, impacts of harmful algal blooms.
Glenn R. Lopez, Professor; Ph.D., SUNY at Stony Brook, 1976. Marine benthic ecology, animal-sediment interactions, contaminant uptake.
Kamazima M. M. Lwiza, Associate Professor; Ph.D., Wales, 1990. Structure and dynamics of shelf seas, remote-sensing oceanography.
Anne E. McElroy, Associate Professor; Ph.D., MIT (Woods Hole), 1985. Toxicology of aquatic organisms, contaminant bioaccumulation, estrogenicity of organic contaminants.
Frank J. Roethel, Lecturer; Ph.D., SUNY at Stony Brook, 1982. Environmental chemistry, municipal solid-waste management impacts.
Sergio A. Sañudo-Wilhelmy, Associate Professor; Ph.D., California, Santa Cruz, 1993. Geochemical cycles of trace elements, marine pollution.
Mary I. Scranton, Professor; Ph.D., MIT (Woods Hole), 1977. Marine geochemistry, biological-chemical interactions in seawater.
R. Lawrence Swanson, Adjunct Professor; Ph.D., Oregon State, 1971. Recycling and reuse of waste materials, waste management.
Gordon T. Taylor, Associate Professor; Ph.D., USC, 1983. Marine microbiology; interests in microbial ecology, plankton trophodynamics, and marine biofouling.
Dong-Ping Wang, Professor; Ph.D., Miami (Florida), 1975. Coastal ocean dynamics.
Robert E. Wilson, Associate Professor; Ph.D., Johns Hopkins, 1974. Estuarine and coastal ocean dynamics.
Peter M. J. Woodhead, Adjunct Professor; B.Sc.Hon., Durham (England), 1953. Behavior and physiology of fish, coral reef ecology, ocean energy conversion systems.

ATMOSPHERIC SCIENCES

Robert D. Cess, Distinguished Professor Emeritus; Ph.D., Pittsburgh, 1959. Radiative transfer and climate modeling, greenhouse effect, intercomparison of global climate models.
Edmund K. M. Chang, Associate Professor; Ph.D., Princeton, 1993. Atmospheric dynamics and diagnoses, climate dynamics, synoptic meteorology.
Brian A. Colle, Assistant Professor; Ph.D., Washington (Seattle), 1997. Synaptic meteorology, weather forecasting, mesoscale modeling.
Robert L. de Zafra, Professor Emeritus (Department of Physics, with joint appointment in Marine Sciences Research Center); Ph.D., Maryland, 1958. Monitoring and detection of trace gases in the terrestrial stratosphere, changes in the ozone layer, remote-sensing instrumentation.
Marvin A. Geller, Professor; Ph.D., MIT, 1969. Atmospheric dynamics, stratosphere dynamics and transport, climate dynamics.
Sultan Hameed, Professor; Ph.D., Manchester (England), 1968. Analysis of climate change using observational data and climate models, interannual variations in climate, climate predictability.
John E. Mak, Associate Professor; Ph.D., California, San Diego (Scripps), 1992. Isotopic analysis of atmospheric gases.
Prasad Varanasi, Professor; Ph.D., California, San Diego (Scripps), 1967. Infrared spectroscopic measurements in support of NASA's space missions, atmospheric remote sensing, greenhouse effect and climate research, molecular physics at low temperatures.
Minghua Zhang, Professor and Director of ITPA; Ph.D., Academia Sinica (China), 1987. Atmospheric dynamics and climate modeling.

UNIVERSITY OF ALASKA FAIRBANKS

School of Fisheries and Ocean Sciences
Graduate Program in Marine Sciences and Limnology
Fisheries Program

Programs of Study The School of Fisheries and Ocean Sciences (SFOS) offers the M.S. degree in biological, chemical, fisheries, geological, and physical oceanography; fisheries; and marine biology. It offers the Ph.D. degree in oceanography, fisheries, and marine biology. Students can also pursue an interdisciplinary M.S. or Ph.D. degree in seafood science and technology. Oceanography and marine biology require at least one year of residence at the Fairbanks campus, but research may be conducted at any of the SFOS coastal facilities. Student research areas include the biology and ecology of benthos, plankton, fish, seabirds, and marine mammals; marine pollution; paleooceanography; and global climate change and its effects on ocean productivity. Fisheries degrees can be earned by students in residence at either the Fairbanks or Juneau campus; student research ranges across Alaska and its adjacent seas and includes biology, genetics, ecology, quantitative stock assessment, and harvest management. Seafood science and technology is offered through the Fishery Industrial Technology Center (FITC) in Kodiak, where research improves harvesting, preservation, processing, and packaging of seafoods.

The oceanography, marine biology, and fisheries M.S. degrees require a minimum of 30 credits. At least 24 credits, including thesis credits, must be at the graduate level. A comprehensive examination and a defense of the thesis are required of all master's students. An M.S. degree is not required to earn the Ph.D. in oceanography or marine biology, and there are no fixed course requirements, although the student is expected to complete course work equivalent at least to that required for the M.S. degree. An M.S. degree is required for admission to the Ph.D. program in fisheries. The Ph.D. in oceanography, fisheries, or marine biology is awarded for proven ability and scholarly attainment, and each candidate's program is planned with the graduate advisory committee. At least three full years of study beyond the baccalaureate degree and 18 credits of dissertation research are required. All Ph.D. candidates must pass a written qualifying examination. Marine biology and oceanography Ph.D. students must also pass an oral qualifying exam. A dissertation is required of all candidates.

Research Facilities Oceanographic research is the focus of the Institute of Marine Science, which has its major laboratory facilities in Fairbanks. Its coastal facilities include the Seward Marine Center, home port of the National Science Foundation research vessel, *Alpha Helix,* and the Kasitsna Bay Laboratory, near spectacular intertidal and subtidal communities. Students also have access to the Alaska SeaLife Center in Seward. The Juneau Center is adjacent to the Auke Bay National Marine Fisheries Laboratory, which shares its library and other facilities. The FITC at Kodiak houses research in seafood science and sustainable harvest technology. SFOS research capabilities include stable isotope mass spectrometry, flow cytometry, automated nutrient analysis, DNA sequencing, microsatellite, and DNA-RFLP facilities and freshwater and marine culture facilities.

Financial Aid Graduate research and teaching assistantships are available to qualified students. Stipends start at about $13,000 for M.S. candidates and $15,000 for Ph.D. candidates; tuition is waived for students with research or teaching assistantships.

Cost of Study Tuition is determined by the level of the course and residency status. For 2003–04, graduate students who are Alaskan residents paid $202 per credit and nonresidents paid $393 per credit; enrollment in at least 9 credits is required for full-time graduate students.

Living and Housing Costs On the Fairbanks campus, residence hall charges range from $1255 per semester for a double room in a dormitory to $1670 per semester for a single room in the graduate student dormitory. A meal ticket ranges from $1220 to $1400 per semester. A limited number of apartments are available for married students. Off-campus housing is available nearby.

For students attending UAF at FITC or the Juneau Center, the semester rental rates are approximately $1500 for a one- or two-bedroom apartment (FITC) or a single-occupancy bedroom in a four-bedroom apartment (Juneau). There is family housing available.

Student Group The Fisheries Program currently has 35 M.S. and 15 Ph.D. students attending at Juneau and 14 M.S. and 1 Ph.D. student on the Fairbanks campus. In addition, there are 19 M.S. and 8 Ph.D. students in marine biology and 18 M.S. students and 16 Ph.D. students in oceanography on the Fairbanks campus. More than half of the students are women, and 10 percent are from other countries.

Location The University of Alaska Fairbanks is 4 miles from downtown Fairbanks on 2,250 acres. It has an enrollment of 7,680 undergraduate and 750 graduate students. The Fairbanks area, with a population of about 75,000 people, is only 130 miles from the Arctic Circle, making the University the northernmost institution of higher education in North America.

The Juneau Center is adjacent to the NOAA Fisheries Auke Bay Laboratory. Juneau, with a population of 30,000, is the state capital and headquarters for several public agencies responsible for fisheries management and conservation. Accessible only by air or sea, it is surrounded by the Tongass National Forest.

The University and The School The University of Alaska Fairbanks is a land-, space-, and sea-grant University and the home of internationally recognized research institutes. The School of Fisheries and Ocean Sciences was created in 1987 to combine the fisheries and marine programs of the University of Alaska system. It was recently selected by the University of Alaska Fairbanks for development as a "Program of Distinction." It consists of the Fisheries Program, the Fisheries Division, the Fishery Industrial Technology Center, the Graduate Program in Marine Sciences and Limnology, the Institute of Marine Science, the Global Undersea Research Unit, the Alaska Sea Grant College Program, and the Marine Advisory Program. There are about 60 faculty members within SFOS, and students enjoy a low student-to-faculty ratio.

Applying An official transcript from each college or university attended is required, with at least three letters of recommendation. A $50 fee must accompany the application. The Graduate Record Examination General Test score is required, with a subject test recommended. A statement of academic goals should be sent along with the other application materials. Applications are accepted continuously throughout the year, although there is a March 1 deadline to have the best chance of receiving a research assistantship.

Correspondence and Information

Academic Programs Office
School of Fisheries and Ocean Sciences
University of Alaska Fairbanks
P.O. Box 757220
Fairbanks, Alaska 99775-7220

Telephone: 907-474-7289
Fax: 907-474-7204
E-mail: fysfos@uaf.edu
World Wide Web: http://www.sfos.uaf.edu

University of Alaska Fairbanks

THE FACULTY AND THEIR RESEARCH

Milo Adkison, Assistant Professor; Ph.D. (population dynamics and biometry). Fisheries biology and management, with emphasis on Pacific salmon.
Vera Alexander, Professor and Dean, School of Fisheries and Ocean Sciences; Ph.D. (biological oceanography). Arctic limnology; biological oceanography, with emphasis on nitrogen cycles and primary productivity.
Russell D. Andrews, Assistant Research Professor; Ph.D. (marine biology). Physiology, behavior, and ecology of seabirds, marine mammals, and sea turtles, using biotelemetry devices .
Shannon Atkinson, Professor and Science Director, Alaska SeaLife Center; Ph.D. (marine mammals). Reproductive and growth physiology of marine wildlife species, environmental endocrinology.
Bodil Bluhm, Research Assistant Professor; Ph.D. (marine invertebrates). Benthic ecology, age determination and population dynamics.
Loren Buck, Assistant Professor; Ph.D. (marine ecology). Sustainable harvesting, physiological ecology, energy metabolism.
Don K. Button, Professor; Ph.D. (biological oceanography). Kinetics and molecular biology of nutrient incorporation by microorganisms.
Michael A. Castellini, Professor and Director, Institute of Marine Science; Ph.D. (marine mammals). Biology of diving, comparative biochemistry, physiology, and behavior of diving vertebrates, especially marine mammals.
Kenneth Coyle, Research Associate; Ph.D. (biological oceanography). Zooplankton and fish acoustics, zooplankton ecology.
Charles A. Crapo, Professor; Ph.D. (seafood technology). Seafood quality, preservation, and processing.
Paula Cullenburg, Associate Professor; M.S. (fisheries). Coastal community development specialist.
Alexandra deOliveira, Assistant Professor; Ph.D. (seafood chemistry). Marine lipid chemistry and seafood quality.
Ginny L. Eckert, Assistant Professor; Ph.D. (marine ecology). Biology of marine invertebrates.
Robert M. Fagen, Associate Professor; Ph.D. (population dynamics and biometry). Data analysis for fisheries and resource management.
Bruce P. Finney, Professor; Ph.D. (geological oceanography). Paleoceanography, paleoclimatology, geochemistry.
Quentin Fong, Assistant Professor; Ph.D. (seafood marketing). Business development and fishery economics.
Robert Foy, Assistant Professor; Ph.D. (fisheries oceanography). Fish energetics, aquatic ecology.
Anthony J. Gharrett, Professor; Ph.D. (genetics and aquaculture). Molecular, population, and quantitative genetics.
Rolf R. Gradinger, Assistant Professor; Ph.D. (biological oceanography). Phytoplankton and their productivity in polar waters.
Gordon Haas, Assistant Professor; Ph.D. (fisheries ecology). Ichthyology, herpetology, fisheries, evolutionary ecology.
Susan M. Henrichs, Professor, Dean of the Graduate School, and Vice Provost of Instructional Affairs; Ph.D. (chemical oceanography). Organic matter decomposition in the marine environment.
Raymond C. Highsmith, Professor and Director of GURU; Ph.D. (marine invertebrates). Community ecology, population biology, reproduction and behavior of marine invertebrates.
Susan Hills, Research Assistant Professor; Ph.D. (marine mammals). Marine ecosystem management.
Nicola Hillgruber, Assistant Professor; Ph.D. (fisheries). Marine fish biology, early life history of marine fishes.
Brian H. Himelbloom, Associate Professor; Ph.D. (seafood science and technology). Microbiology of fish processing, seafood safety and spoilage, microbial physiology, enzymology.
Charles Hocutt, Professor and Associate Dean of the School of Fisheries and Ocean Sciences; Ph.D. (fisheries ecology). Ocean and freshwater ecology of fishes.
Tuula Hollmen, Assistant Research Professor; Ph.D. Physiology and health of sea ducks, including methodologies to evaluate body condition, immune function, and disease/contaminant effects on birds.
Russell Hopcroft, Assistant Professor; Ph.D. (biological oceanograhy). Plankton ecology, trophodynamics, metazoan zooplankton.
Nicholas Hughes, Assistant Professor; Ph.D. (fisheries ecology). Ecology of freshwater fishes, behavior of salmonids.
Katrin Iken, Assistant Professor; Ph.D. (marine invertebrates). Chemical ecology of marine invertebrates and algae.
Stephen Jewett, Research Professor and Diving Officer; Ph.D. (marine invertebrates). Benthic ecology, trophic interactions.
Mark A. Johnson, Associate Professor; Ph.D. (physical oceanography). Coastal and high-latitude physical oceanography.
Brendan Kelly, Assistant Professor of Fisheries; Ph.D. (marine mammals). Ecology and behavior of marine vertebrates.
John J. Kelley, Professor; Ph.D. (marine acoustics and chemical oceanography). Sea ice, air-sea-gas transfer, marine acoustics, atmospheric chemistry.
Brenda Konar, Research Assistant Professor; Ph.D. (marine invertebrates). Subtidal, intertidal, and benthic ecology, phycology.
Zygmunt Kowalik, Professor; Ph.D. (physical oceanography). Numerical modeling of tides, storm surges, and tsunamis.
Gordon Kruse, President's Professor of Fisheries; Ph.D. (fisheries). Fish stock assessment modeling, population dynamics.
F. Joseph Margraf, Professor and Unit Leader, Alaska Cooperative Fish and Wildlife Research Unit; Ph.D. (fisheries ecology). Population and community ecology, trophic interaction, bioenergetics of freshwater and estuarine fishes.
C. Peter McRoy, Professor; Ph.D. (biological oceanography). Pelagic and benthic ecosystem studies in extreme environments.
Jo-Ann E. Mellish, Research Assistant Professor; Ph.D. (marine mammals). Pinniped physiology.
David L. Musgrave, Associate Professor; Ph.D. (physical oceanography). North Pacific and coastal ocean observing systems.
A. Sathy Naidu, Professor; Ph.D. (geological oceanography). Marine sedimentation processes emphasizing arctic and subarctic waters.
Brenda L. Norcross, Professor; Ph.D. (fisheries oceanography). Larval fish transport, larval and juvenile fishes.
F. Gerald Plumley, Professor and Head, Graduate Program in Marine Sciences and Limnology; Ph.D. (biological oceanography). Algal responses to the environment.
Terrance J. Quinn II, Professor; Ph.D. (population dynamics and biometry). Fish population dynamics and molecular biology, modeling, and forecasting.
Raymond L. RaLonde, Professor; M.S. (aquaculture). Development of shellfish hatchery and nursery culture technology, expansion of shellfish farming.
Jennifer R. Reynolds, Assistant Professor and Science Director, West Coast and Polar Regions Undersea Research Center (NOAA/NURP); Ph.D. (geological oceanography). Formation of the ocean crust at midocean ridges, submarine volcanism.
Subramaniam Sathivel, Assistant Professor; Ph.D. (seafood science and technology). Seafood processing and engineering.
Thomas C. Shirley, Professor; Ph.D. (fisheries ecology). Invertebrate ecology with emphasis on crabs, meiofauna.
Scott T. Smiley, Associate Professor and Director, Fishery Industrial Technology Center; Ph.D. (seafood science and technology). Development of standards for surimi, commercial pinbone-removing machine, effects of fish gear on bottom fauna.
William W. Smoker, Professor and Director, Fisheries Division; Ph.D. (aquaculture). Biology of Pacific salmon with applications to salmon fisheries enhancement and salmon conservation biology.
Alan M. Springer, Research Associate Professor; Ph.D. (biological oceanography). Pelagic, food webs, and sea bird ecology.
Michael S. Stekoll; Professor; Ph.D. (biochemistry). Biology, ecology, pollution, restoration of marine benthic communities
Dean Stockwell, Research Assistant Professor; Ph.D. (biological oceanography). Phytoplankton ecology, harmful algal blooms.
Sherry L. Tamone, Assistant Professor; Ph.D. Crustacean physiology and biochemistry.
Thomas J. Weingartner, Associate Professor; Ph.D. (physical oceanography). Arctic Ocean processes.
Terry Whitledge, Professor; Ph.D. (biological and chemical oceanography). Chemical oceanography, nutrient.
Kathleen M. Wynne, Research Associate Professor; M.S. (marine mammals). Marine mammal population assessment.

UNIVERSITY OF MARYLAND

Graduate Program in Marine-Estuarine-Environmental Sciences

Program of Study The specific objective of the all-University Graduate Program in Marine-Estuarine-Environmental Sciences (MEES) is the training of qualified graduate students, working toward the M.S. or Ph.D. degree, who have research interests in fields of study that involve interactions between biological systems and physical or chemical systems in the marine, estuarine, or terrestrial environments. The program comprises six Areas of Specialization (AOS): Oceanography, Environmental Chemistry (and toxicology), Ecology, Environmental Molecular Biology/ Biotechnology, Fisheries Science, and Environmental Science (including management, policy, and economics). Students work with their Advisory Committee to develop a customized course of study based on research interests and previous experience.

All students must demonstrate competence in statistics. Each student is required to complete a thesis or dissertation reporting the results of an original investigation. The research problem is selected and pursued under the guidance of the student's adviser and advisory committee.

Research Facilities Students may conduct their research either in the laboratories and facilities of the College Park (UMCP), Baltimore (UMB), Baltimore County (UMBC), or Eastern Shore (UMES) campuses or in one of the laboratories of the University of Maryland Center for Environmental Science (UMCES): Chesapeake Biological Laboratory (CBL) at Solomons, Maryland; the Horn Point Laboratory (HPL) in Cambridge, Maryland; and the Appalachian Laboratory (AL) in Frostburg, Maryland; or at the Center of Marine Biotechnology (COMB). CBL and HPL are located on the Chesapeake Bay. They include excellent facilities for the culture of estuarine organisms. The laboratories are provided with running salt water, which may be heated or cooled and may be filtered. Berthed at CBL are the University's research vessels, which range from the 65-foot *Aquarius* to a variety of smaller vessels for various specialized uses. At HPL there are extensive marshes, intertidal areas, oyster reefs, tidal creeks, and rock jetties. AL, located in the mountains of western Maryland, specializes in terrestrial and freshwater ecology.

Specialized laboratory facilities for environmental research are located on the campuses. These facilities provide space for microbiology, biotechnology, water chemistry, and cellular, molecular, and organismal biology, as well as specialized facilities for the rearing and maintenance of both terrestrial and aquatic organisms of all kinds. There are extensive facilities for remote sensing of the environment. Extensive field sites for environmental research are available through the University's agricultural programs and through cooperation with many other organizations in the state.

Financial Aid University fellowships, research assistantships and traineeships, and teaching assistantships are available. In general, aid provides for full living and educational expenses. Some partial assistance may also be available. Research support from federal, state, and private sources often provides opportunities for additional student support through either research assistantships or part-time employment on research projects.

Cost of Study In 2003–04, tuition for graduate students was $349 for Maryland residents and $602 for nonresidents for each credit hour. In addition, stipulated fees were $238 for up to 8 credits and $380 for 9 or more credits per semester for each student. However, financial aid typically covers most of these expenses.

Living and Housing Costs Commercial housing is plentiful in the area around the campuses. For students who are working at HPL or CBL, limited dormitory-type housing is available on site. Minimum living expenses for a year's study at College Park or in the Baltimore area are about $12,000, exclusive of tuition and fees. Costs are lower at the UMES campus.

Student Group About 230 students are enrolled in the program. They come from a variety of academic backgrounds. There are a number of international students. About 50 percent of the students are in the doctoral program, and 50 percent are working toward the M.S. Some of the master's students expect to continue toward the doctorate. While most of the students are biologists, some come with undergraduate majors in chemistry, biochemistry, geology, economics, political science, or engineering. The program encourages and accommodates such diversity in its students.

Location The MEES program is offered on campuses of the University at College Park, Baltimore, Baltimore County, and Eastern Shore and at the UMCES laboratories and COMB. Students normally enroll on the campus where their adviser is located. Of particular relevance for the MEES program is the University's location near Chesapeake Bay, one of the world's most important estuarine systems, which in many aspects serves as the program's principal laboratory resource.

The University The University of Maryland is the state's land-grant and sea-grant university. It has comprehensive programs at both the undergraduate and graduate levels on the campuses at College Park, Baltimore County, and Eastern Shore. Programs in the health sciences and the professions are located in Baltimore. There are approximately 8,400 graduate students at College Park, 800 at Baltimore, 300 at Baltimore County, and 75 at Eastern Shore.

Applying Applications for admission in the fall semester must be filed by February 1; however, to be considered for financial support, it is better to apply by December 1. Some students will be admitted for the semester starting in January, for which the deadline is September 1. Applicants must submit an official application to the University of Maryland Graduate School, along with official transcripts of all previous collegiate work, three letters of recommendation, and scores on the General Test (aptitude) of the Graduate Record Examinations. It is particularly important that a student articulate clearly in the application a statement of goals and objectives pertaining to their future work in the field. Because of the interdisciplinary and interdepartmental nature of the program, only students for whom a specific adviser is identified in advance can be admitted. Prior communication with individual members of the faculty is encouraged.

Correspondence and Information
Graduate Program in Marine-Estuarine-Environmental Sciences
0105 Cole
University of Maryland
College Park, Maryland 20742
Telephone: 301-405-6938
Fax: 301-314-4139
E-mail: mees@mees.umd.edu
World Wide Web: http://www.mees.umd.edu

University of Maryland

THE FACULTY AND THEIR RESEARCH

Baltimore Campus. Da-Wei Gong: molecular and cell biology of energy metabolism. Raymond T. Jones: pathophysiology of elasmobranch and teleost fishes. Robert K. Nauman: spirochetes and their relationship with marine mollusks. Henry N. Williams: ecology of the bacterial predator, *Bdellovibrio,* in the Chesapeake Bay.

Baltimore County Campus. Brian P. Bradley: zooplankton physiology and genetics. C. Allen Bush: environmental molecular biology, molecular structure determination. Thomas W. Cronin: vision in marine animals. Erle C. Ellis: landscape ecology, biogeochemistry, sustainable resource management. Raymond M. Hoff: pathways and fates of toxic organic and elemental chemicals in the environment. Upal Ghosh: experimental investigation, design, and modeling of physiochemical and biological processes that affect water quality. Jin Ping (Jack) Gwo: theoretical and computational aspects of subsurface, multispecies solute and microbial transport. Andrew J. Miller: surface-water hydrology and fluvial geomorphology, effects of human activities on watershed hydrology and river channels. Robert R. Provine: fish and waterfowl behavioral ecology. Brian E. Reed: sorption of organics/inorganics, surface chemistry, water and wastewater treatment, soil and site remediation. Youngsinn Sohn: applications of GIS and digital image analysis for addressing environmental problems, monitoring, and mapping. Philip G. Sokolove: endogenous rhythms and neuroendocrinology. Christopher Swan: benthic evolution and ecology, community ecology, limnology, systems, biostatistics. Carl Weber: benthic ecology, systems ecology. Claire Welty: fundamental understanding of transport processes in aquifiers, mathematical modeling of groundwater flow.

College Park Campus. Lowell W. Adams: wildlife biology, ecology, and management. J. Scott Angle: application of organic wastes to soil, aflatoxin ecology. Andrew H. Baldwin: wetland ecology, plant community ecology of coastal marshes and mangroves. Jennifer Becker: microbial communities that biodegrade xenobiotics, bioremediation of contaminated groundwater systems, anaerobic biological treatment processes for waste streams. Amy Brown: toxicology, epidemiology, effects of pesticides on human health. Kaye L. Brubaker: physical hydrology, numerical modeling, stream and estuary water-quality modeling. James Carton: physical oceanography, ocean modeling, atmosphere/ocean interactions. Mary C. Christman: biostatistics, spatial modeling, spatial and environmental statistics. Allen P. Davis: environmental chemistry as related to water/wastewater treatment. James Dietz: mammalian ecology and conservation. E. Kudjo Dzantor: use of plants for cleaning up environmental pollution, use of biological processes in combination with chemical/physical processes to address disposal of pesticides. Irwin Forseth: plant ecology and physiology. Oliver J. Hao: waste management and environmental engineering. Matthew P. Hare: population and conservation genetics of marine organisms, invasion biology, phylogeography. Robert L. Hill: soil runoff, nonpoint source pollution in soil systems. David W. Inouye: terrestrial ecology, especially plant-animal interactions. Andrew S. Kane: environmental pathology, toxicology, and husbandry of aquatic and marine organisms, with emphasis on Chesapeake Bay fauna and captive fish species. Patrick Kangas: modeling and measuring of whole ecosystems with emphasis on management and ecology. Michael S. Kearney: pollen analytical investigations of tidal marsh sediments. William O. Lamp: crop protection from arthropods through integration of crop management practices with arthropod/plant interactions, development of non-pesticide management tactics. Marla McIntosh: sludge utilization in woodlands, genetic diversity of food crops. Bahram Momem: applied statistics. Judd O. Nelson: environmental toxicology of pesticides. Mary Ann Ottinger: effect of toxic substances on avian reproduction. Margaret Palmer: stream and estuarine ecology and hydrodynamics. Michael Paolisso: applied anthropology, environment and pollution, international and rural development. Kennedy T. Paynter Jr.: physiology and biochemistry of estuarine organisms, oyster reef restoration. Karen Prestegaard: watershed and wetland hydrology. Marjorie Reaka-Kudla: zoogeography, symbiosis, and behavior of marine crustaceans. Estelle Russek-Cohen: statistical problems in wildlife management, biomonitoring and sampling. Paul D. Schreuders: cryobiology/cryopreservation, biofilm function in nitrification processes. Miranda Schreurs: comparative environmental and energy politics in northeast Asia and Europe. Kenneth P. Sebens: community ecology of subtidal benthos, coral reef ecology. Adel Shirmohammadi: impact of agricultural pest management practices on water quality. Eugene B. Small: estuarine and marine protozoology. Joseph H. Soares Jr.: waterfowl nutrition, calcification, vitamin and mineral metabolism. Daniel E. Terlizzi: plant aquaculture, phycology. David Tilley: ecological engineering, industrial ecology, ecological decision making for sustainable development. Alba Torrents: organic pollutants, soil/water interface. Ray R. Weil: disturbed-land revegetation, land application of organic wastes. Ronald M. Weiner: environmental bacteriology. Richard Weismiller: agriculture and natural resources, remote sensing. L. Curry Woods: aquaculture, larviculture.

Eastern Shore Campus. Eugene L. Bass: algal toxins, acclimatization of animals to environmental variables. Dixie Bounds: wildlife ecology and management, natural resources. Carolyn B. Brooks: microbial insecticides: symbiotic nitrogen fixation. Robert B. Dadson: soybean breeding, insect resistance, biological nitrogen fixation. Joseph Dodoo: coal technology, kinetic studies of coal pyrolysis. Gian C. Gupta: environmental chemistry, soil science, water and wastewater recycling. Youssef Hafez: nutrition, effects of processing on bioavailability of peptides. Thomas Handwerker: small-scale alternative crops. Jeannine M. Harter-Dennis: roasters chicken nutrition, reduction of fat. George E. Heath: food safety and drug residues, pharmokinetics. Steven G. Hughes: fish physiology, nutrition, feeding behavior, and ecology. Jagmohan Joshi: plant breeding and genetics. Gerald E. Kananen: analytical instrumentation, environmental pollutants. Eric P. May: responses of fish to injurious agents, markers of population health. Joseph Okoh: carbon reaction chemistry. Douglas E. Ruby: population ecology and behavior of reptiles. Jeurel Singleton: aquatic and terrestrial invertebrate community ecology and population dynamics; population dynamics of phyto- and zooplankton communities in reservoirs, lakes, and fish rearing facilities. Yan Waguespeck: spectroscopic studies of temperature- and gas pressure–induced chemical changes.

Appalachian Laboratory. Mark S. Castro: atmosphere-biosphere interactions. Katharina Engelhardt: effects of species richness on wetland ecosystem functioning and services, community and ecosystem ecology. Keith N. Eshleman: watershed and wetlands hydrology and hydrobiogeochemistry. Robert H. Gardner: landscape ecology, ecosystem modeling. J. Edward Gates: behavioral ecology of vertebrates, habitat analysis and evaluation. Robert H. Hilderbrand: ecology and conservation biology of running waters, watershed and stream habitat restoration, linking landscapes and populations, dynamic modeling of watersheds. John L. Hoogland: vertebrate behavioral ecology, evolutionary biology of mammals. Kenneth R. McKaye: evolution, behavior, and community ecology of fishes. Raymond P. Morgan: pollution ecology, fisheries genetics. Louis Pitelka: plant ecology, including population biology and ecosystem dynamics. Steven Seagle: ecosystem and landscape simulation modeling. Cathlyn D. Stylinski: environmental science education and scientific inquiry in precollege classrooms. Philip A. Townsend: landscape ecology and biogeography; remote sensing for vegetation characterization and analysis.

Chesapeake Biological Laboratory. Robert Anderson: biochemical toxicology, effects of stress on marine invertebrate immunology. Joel Baker: behavior of organic contaminants in marine/estuarine systems. Walter R. Boynton: nutrient cycling in estuarine systems, food-web studies. H. Rodger Harvey: sources and fates of organic compounds in aquatic environments. Edward D. Houde: fishery science, population dynamics, ecology of the larval stage. Roberta L. Marinelli: benthic ecology, animal-sediment interaction, benthic larval recruitment, modeling benthic processes. Steven Martell: fisheries stock assessment, fishery management regimes, stock dynamics and species interactions. Robert P. Mason: environmental chemistry, trace metals. Joseph A. Mihursky: population and community dynamics, temperature effects on estuarine organisms. Thomas J. Miller: fish ecology, population dynamics. Carys L. Mitchelmore: molecular, biochemical, and cellular responses of aquatic organisms to inorganic and organic pollutants. Kennedy T. Paynter Jr.: physiology and biochemistry of estuarine organisms, oyster reef restoration. Christopher L. Rowe: physiological, population and community responses to sublethal levels of pollutants. David H. Secor: fisheries ecology, demographics, migration. Ronald L. Siefert: aqueous chemistry and photochemistry of metals in natural environments, aerosol dynamics. Marcelino Suzuki: marine microbial ecology, application of molecular approaches to the study of aquatic microbes. Kenneth Tenore: bioenergetics of detritus-based food chains, nutrition of marine invertebrates. Robert E. Ulanowicz: estuarine food-chain dynamics, hydrological-biological modeling. David A. Wright: comparative physiology of marine and estuarine animals, inorganic pollutants.

Horn Point Laboratory. William Boicourt: physical oceanography, continental shelf and estuarine circulation. Shenn-yu Chao: physical oceanography, continental shelf and slope circulation, western boundary currents. Louis A. Codispoti: chemical oceanography, oceanic nitrogen cycle. Victoria J. Coles: observation and modeling of seasonal to climate-scale variability in ocean circulation. Jeffrey C. Cornwell: nutrient, metal, and sulfur cycling in estuaries and wetlands. Byron C. Crump: microbial ecology, bacterial and Achaeal diversity, organic matter and nutrient cycling. William C. Dennison: coastal ecosystem ecology, ecophysiology of marine plants. Thomas R. Fisher Jr.: nitrogen cycles in Atlantic coastal plain estuaries, nutrient cycling in tropical lakes. Patricia M. Glibert: phytoplankton and microplankton ecology, nitrogen cycling, photosynthesis. Lawrence W. Harding: biological oceanography, phytoplankton physiology and ecology. Raleigh R. Hood: phytoplankton production and light response, modeling of primary production. Todd M. Kana: phytoplankton physiology. W. Michael Kemp: systems ecology, watershed nutrient budgets, submerged aquatic vegetation. Victor S. Kennedy: ecology and dynamics of benthic communities, particularly bivalves. Evamaria W. Koch: ecology of submerged aquatic vegetation and coastal seagrass ecosystems. Andrew Lazur: food and baitfish culture, integration of aquaculture with agriculture for nutrient reduction. Ming Li: geophysical fluid dynamics, ocean mixing processes, numerical modeling, biological/physical interactions, marine pollution. Thomas Malone: phytoplankton ecology and nutrient cycling. Donald W. Meritt: oyster aquaculture and restoration. Laura Murray: wetlands, seagrass ecology. Roger I. E. Newell: physiological and behavioral adaptations of invertebrates, especially bivalve mollusks. Judith O'Neil: cyanobacteria ecophysiology, plankton trophodynamics. Michael R. Roman: zooplankton ecology, plankton food-chain energetics, detrital food chains. Lawrence P. Sanford: physical oceanography, geophysical boundary layers, turbulence and mixing processes. J. Court Stevenson: marsh ecology, nutrient loading in coastal watersheds. Diane Stoecker: role of heterotrophic and mixotrophic protists in food webs. William Van Heukelem: behavior of crab and oyster larvae as related to dispersal.

Center of Marine Biotechnology. Hafiz Ahmed: biological roles of galectins in early embryo development and immune function, structure-function studies of galectins. Robert M. Belas Jr.: sensory transduction and genetic regulation of gram-negative bacteria. Feng Chen: bacterio- and phyto-plankton production, biomass and growth in aquatic environments; ecological interaction among marine viruses, bacteria, and phytoplankton; phylogenetic relationship and co-evolution among marine microorganisms. Shiladitya DasSarma: halophilic archael genomes; structure, function, and evolution of genomes. Shao-Jun (Jim) Du: cellular and molecular mechanisms controlling differentiation of muscle and nerve cells during embryogenesis. John D. Hansen: genetic organization of the rainbow trout MHC and its inducibility during viral infection. Russell T. Hill: natural products from marine microorganisms; actinomycete molecular biology and ecology, use in bioremediation. Anwarul Huq: isolation, identification, and characterization of enteric bacterial agents using conventional, immunological, and genetic methods. Rosemary Jagus: developmental regulation of gene expression in sea urchin embryos. Allen Place: biochemical adaptations in marine organisms. Frank T. Robb: genetics of thermophilic marine bacteria. Harold J. Schreier: adaptation of microorganisms to extreme environments, biochemistry and molecular biology of Archaea. Kevin R. Sowers: molecular genetics and adaptation of anaerobic archaebacteria. John M. Trant: reproductive physiology, molecular endocrinology. Gerardo Vasta: cellular nonself recognition and cell-cell interactions. Yonathan Zohar: physiology and endocrinology of fish reproduction.

UNIVERSITY OF PUERTO RICO, MAYAGÜEZ CAMPUS

Department of Marine Sciences

Programs of Study

The Department of Marine Sciences is a graduate department offering instruction leading to the degrees of Master of Science (M.S.) and Doctor of Philosophy (Ph.D.) in marine sciences. The primary aim of the department is to train marine scientists for careers in teaching, research, and management of marine resources. Students specialize in biological, chemical, geological, or physical oceanography; fisheries biology; or aquaculture or through core courses and electives. Much of the teaching and research is carried out at the marine station, 22 miles south of Mayagüez, but students are able to elect courses in other departments and to use facilities of the computer center and the Research Development Center.

A minimum of 36 semester hours of credit in approved graduate courses is required for the M.S. degree; 72 for the Ph.D. Courses in the Department of Marine Sciences are taught in English and Spanish. Because Puerto Rico has a Spanish culture and the University is bilingual, candidates are expected to gain a functional knowledge of Spanish as well as English before finishing their degree. Further requirements for the M.S. are residence of at least one academic year, passing a departmental examination, completing a satisfactory thesis, and passing a comprehensive final examination. For the Ph.D. degree, residence of at least two years, passing a qualifying examination, subsequently passing a comprehensive examination, completing a satisfactory thesis, and passing a final examination in defense of the thesis are required. Prospective students can visit the Web page at http://cima.uprm.edu.

Research Facilities

Modern teaching and sophisticated research facilities are available both on campus and at the field station. A department library specializing in marine science publications is located at the main campus. The field station is on 18-acre Magueyes Island within a protected embayment off La Parguera, 22 miles from Mayagüez. In addition to classroom and laboratory facilities, the marine station has indoor and outdoor aquaria and tanks with running seawater and three museums containing reference collections of fish, invertebrates, and algae. Boats include the 127-foot R/V *Chapman,* a 51-foot Thompson trawler, a 35-foot diesel Downeast, and a number of small open boats. Research facilities for warm-water aquaculture include some 8 acres of earthen ponds, two hatcheries and numerous concrete tanks, plastic pools, and aquarium facilities with running water available for controlled environmental studies.

Financial Aid

Some graduate students receive tuition waivers and stipends for their work as teaching or research assistants. Student support is also available through research grants awarded to faculty members and through the University of Puerto Rico, Mayagüez (UPRM), Financial Aid Office.

Cost of Study

Residents carrying a full program (9 to 12 credits) paid $75 per credit hour in 2001–02. General fees of approximately $75 per semester are added to these costs. Resident status may be established in one year. Nonresidents, including aliens, pay $3500 per year, except for students from U.S. institutions having reciprocal tuition-reduction agreements with Puerto Rico (a list is available on request).

Living and Housing Costs

Apartments and houses can be found in Mayagüez, San Germán, Lajas, and La Parguera for roughly $200 to $450 per month. Single rooms may be obtained for less. Single students in the department frequently share apartments.

Student Group

Total enrollment at the Mayagüez campus of the University of Puerto Rico is about 13,000. The department's enrollment is 80 to 120 graduate students.

Location

Mayagüez, the third-largest city in Puerto Rico, has a population of 150,000. It is a seaport on the west coast of the island. The economy of the city centers largely on shipping, commercial fishing, light industry, and the University. San Germán and Lajas, where many University people live, are 10 and 18 miles south of Mayagüez, respectively. The main campus of Inter-American University is located in San Germán. An increasing number of concerts, art exhibits, and other cultural activities are arranged in Mayagüez, Lajas, and San Germán, although San Juan, a 3-hour drive from Mayagüez, remains the island center for music (for example, the yearly Casals Festival), drama, art, as well as other activities sponsored by various civic entities and the Institute of Puerto Rican Culture. Many of these events are held at the Center for Fine Arts. In addition, repertory theaters are becoming very popular in the metropolitan area.

The University and The Department

The University of Puerto Rico, Mayagüez (http://www.uprm.edu), had its beginning in 1911 as the College of Agriculture, an extension of the University in Río Piedras. In 1912 the name was changed to the College of Agriculture and Mechanic Arts. Following a general reform of the University in 1942, the college became a regular campus of the University under a vice-chancellor and, in 1966, an autonomous campus with its own chancellor. The marine sciences program of the University of Puerto Rico is in Mayagüez. It began in 1954 with the establishment of the Institute of Marine Biology. A master's degree program in marine biology was initiated in 1963. In 1968 the institute became the Department of Marine Sciences, a graduate department, with its own academic staff. The doctoral program began in 1972. Research remains an important function of the department.

Applying

Application forms are available from the Graduate School and at http://grad.uprm.edu. An undergraduate science degree is required. The applicant should have had at least basic courses in biology, chemistry, physics, geology, and mathematics through calculus. An engineering degree may be acceptable in some circumstances. Applications should be submitted before February 15 for the fall semester and before September 15 for the spring semester. A late fee is applied to applications received after the set deadlines.

Correspondence and Information

Director, Graduate School
Box 9020
University of Puerto Rico
Mayagüez, Puerto Rico 00681-9020
World Wide Web: http://grad.uprm.edu

Director, Department of Marine Sciences
Box 9013
University of Puerto Rico
Mayagüez, Puerto Rico 00681-9013
E-mail: director@cima.uprm.edu
World Wide Web: http://cima.uprm.edu

University of Puerto Rico, Mayagüez Campus

THE FACULTY AND THEIR RESEARCH

Dallas E. Alston, Professor; Ph.D. (invertebrate aquaculture), Auburn. Culture of invertebrate organisms.
Nilda E. Aponte, Professor and Director of the Department; Ph.D. (marine botany), Puerto Rico, Mayagüez. Taxonomy, morphology, and life history of marine algae.
Richard S. Appeldoorn, Professor; Ph.D. (fisheries biology), Rhode Island. Fisheries biology.
Roy Armstrong, Associate Professor; Ph.D. (biooptical oceanography), Puerto Rico, Mayagüez. Remote sensing, water optics.
David L. Ballantine, Professor; Ph.D. (marine botany), Puerto Rico, Mayagüez. Taxonomy and ecology of marine algae.
Jorge E. Corredor, Professor; Ph.D. (chemical oceanography), Miami (Florida). Chemical oceanography, pollution.
Dannie A. Hensley, Professor; Ph.D. (ichthyology), South Florida. Systematics and ecology of fishes.
Aurelio Mercado Irizarry, Professor; M.S. (physical oceanography), Miami (Florida). Geophysical fluid dynamics.
John Kubaryk, Professor and Associate Director of the Department; Ph.D. (seafood technology), Auburn. Seafood technology, aquatic nutrition, water quality.
José M. López-Díaz, Associate Professor; Ph.D. (environmental chemistry), Texas at Dallas. Water pollution control.
Ricardo Cortés Maldonado, Professor; M.S. (aquaculture), Puerto Rico, Mayagüez. Aquaculture.
Ernesto Otero Morales, Auxiliary Investigator; Ph.D. (microbial ecology), Georgia. Microbial utilization of organic matter, microbial diversity and ecological application of stable isotopes.
Julio Morell, Associate Investigator; M.S. (chemical oceanography), Puerto Rico, Mayagüez. Biogeochemistry and environmental chemistry.
Jack Morelock, Professor; Ph.D. (geological oceanography), Texas A&M. Sediments, beach and littoral studies, reef sediments and marine terraces, geophysical surveys.
Govind S. Nadathur, Professor; Ph.D. (molecular microbiology), Baroda (India). Genetics and biotechnology of marine organisms.
Jorge R. García Sais, Associate Investigator; Ph.D. (biological oceanography), Rhode Island. Zooplankton ecology.
Nikolaos V. Schizas, Associate Professor; Ph.D. (invertebrate zoology), South Carolina. Molecular intertebrate zoology.
Thomas R. Tosteson, Professor; Ph.D. (physiology), Pennsylvania. Marine physiology and pharmacology.
Ernesto Weil, Associate Professor; Ph.D. (zoology), Texas at Austin. Coral systematics, ecology and evolution, coral reef ecology.
Ernest H. Williams, Professor; Ph.D. (parasitology), Auburn. Systematics and culture of parasites of fishes.
Robin G. Williams, Associate Professor; Ph.D. (physical oceanography), California, San Diego (Scripps). Atmospheric sciences and oceanography.
Amos Winter, Professor; Ph.D. (paleoceanography), Hebrew (Jerusalem). Paleoceanography.
Paul Yoshioka, Professor; Ph.D. (marine ecology), California, San Diego. Marine ecology.
Baqar R. Zaidi, Investigator; Ph.D. (marine microbiology and physiology), Puerto Rico, Mayagüez. Marine physiology, bioremediation.

Field station at Magueyes Island, La Parguera, Puerto Rico.

UNIVERSITY OF SOUTH FLORIDA

College of Marine Science

Programs of Study
The College of Marine Science on the St. Petersburg Campus of the University of South Florida offers M.S. and Ph.D. degrees with specializations in biological, chemical, geological, and physical oceanography. Students are strongly encouraged to take interdisciplinary programs encompassing two or more of the four basic disciplines.

Both M.S. and Ph.D. candidates are required to complete a core course program covering the four basic oceanographic disciplines. Requirements for the M.S. degree include 32 credit hours of course and research work and defense of a thesis that makes an original contribution to oceanography. Ph.D. candidates must successfully complete a written and oral comprehensive examination. After completing 90 credit hours of course and research work, they must defend a dissertation that represents a publishable contribution to marine science. Students are encouraged to participate in oceanographic research cruises during the course of their enrollment.

As part of a variety of national and international programs supported by the National Science Foundation and other federal agencies, over the past five years the department's students and faculty have conducted research in the Pacific, Atlantic, Indian, and Antarctic Oceans; the Gulf of Mexico; and the Mediterranean, Norwegian, Arabian, and Bering Seas.

Research Facilities
The College of Marine Science is located at Bayboro Harbor in St. Petersburg. The harbor has immediate access to Tampa Bay and can accommodate any ship in the fleet of U.S. oceanographic vessels. Bayboro Harbor is home port to the R/V *Suncoaster* (110 feet) and the R/V *Bellows* (71 feet), the principal vessels operated by the Florida Institute of Oceanography (FIO) for the entire state university system. FIO is located within the original building (82,000 square feet) of the College of Marine Science. The College's newest building, opened in 1994, is the 50,000-square-foot Knight Oceanographic Research Center. Renovation of the College's original building is ongoing and has added 10,000 square feet of laboratory and office space to accommodate the College's Center for Ocean Technology. The College's research facilities are adjacent to the Florida Marine Research Institute, the research arm of the Florida Fish and Wildlife Conservation Commission. In 1988, the St. Petersburg Campus became the site of the Center for Coastal Geology of the United States Geological Survey.

The College's specialized laboratories include those for trace-metal analysis, physical chemistry, water quality, organic and isotope geochemistry, optical oceanography, satellite imagery and numerical modeling, sedimentology, micropaleontology, physiology, benthic ecology, microbiology, ichthyology, planktology, paleoceanography, and geophysics. Major items of equipment include an ISI (DS-130) scanning electron microscope; a Hewlett Packard 4500 inductively coupled plasma mass spectrometer; a Hitachi H-7100 transmission electron microscope; two Finnigan MAT DeltaPlus XL stable isotope ratio mass spectrometers with Kiel III carbonate, high- and low-temperature elemental analyzers, and gas chromatograph peripheral devices; high-resolution gas chromatographs; a combined gas chromatograph–mass spectrometer; flame and graphite furnace atomic absorption spectrometers; multichannel autoanalyzer systems; UV-visible scanning spectrophotometers; an EG&G uniboom high-resolution continuous seismic reflection profiling system; an EG&G side-scan sonar system; a Polytec Laser Vibrometer; an ABI model 7700 sequence detection system; a Simrad EM 3000 multibeam bathymetric mapper; X-ray diffraction systems; and a Mössbauer spectroscopy system. The College has its own marine science library collection on the St. Petersburg Campus as well as access to the University's Tampa Campus facilities.

Financial Aid
Approximately fifteen state-supported assistantships are available each year for beginning students. In addition, approximately ten fellowships are available from endowments. After their first year, students can obtain support by pursuing research on grant-supported projects. Assistantships pay in the range of $16,000 to $18,000 for twelve months. A number of out-of-state tuition waivers are available for first-year students.

Cost of Study
For 2003–04, tuition was $197.93 per semester hour for state residents and $767.20 per semester hour for nonresident students. Out-of-state students who are American citizens may establish Florida residency after one year if certain criteria are met.

Living and Housing Costs
There are no on-campus accommodations in St. Petersburg, but students easily find apartments or houses near the campus. The rents range between $350 and $650 per month, and single students often share rental expenses. The average total living expenses for students are currently about $700 per month.

Student Group
For the 2003–04 academic year, there were more than 120 graduate students enrolled in the marine science program. More than half are working toward a Ph.D. degree. Fifty-eight students are in biological oceanography, 18 are in chemical oceanography, 32 are in geological oceanography, and 13 are in physical oceanography. Most program graduates have obtained positions in their field or have gone on to other universities for their Ph.D.'s.

Location
The College is situated just a few blocks from downtown St. Petersburg and the Bayfront Center Arena-Theater (where major performing groups entertain), museums (including the Salvador Dali Museum), Florida Power Park (where major-league spring training games are held), Albert Whitted Airport (a general aviation airport servicing the USF Flying Club), numerous restaurants, department stores, shops, the St. Petersburg Yacht Club, and marinas. The Gulf Coast beaches are within a 20-minute drive of the campus. Because the marine environment is extremely important in this area—both from a commercial and a leisure-activity point of view—the College receives considerable attention and support from the community.

The University and The College
The University of South Florida was founded in 1956. The first major state university in America to be planned and built entirely in this century, it is the second-largest public university in Florida. The Department of Marine Science, established in 1967, became the College of Marine Science in summer 2000. It is the only College located entirely on the St. Petersburg Campus. The main campus in Tampa, with its wealth of supportive and cultural activities, is just 35 miles away via Interstate Highway 275.

Applying
Applications should be submitted by May 1 for the fall semester and October 1 for the spring semester. (The deadlines for international applicants are January 2 for the fall semester and July 1 for the spring semester.) The financial aid deadlines are February 15 and October 1 for fall and spring, respectively. Minimum requirements for admission are an undergraduate major in biology, chemistry, engineering, geology, math, or physics; an upper-level GPA of 3.0; and a GRE General Test (verbal and quantitative sections) score of 1100. Applicants are also expected to have successfully completed 1 year of calculus.

Correspondence and Information
Edward S. Van Vleet, Director of Academic Affairs
Nadina Piehl, Assistant Director/Coordinator
College of Marine Science
University of South Florida
140 7th Avenue, South
St. Petersburg, Florida 33701
Telephone: 727-553-1130
World Wide Web: http://www.marine.usf.edu

University of South Florida

THE FACULTY AND THEIR RESEARCH

Peter R. Betzer, Professor and Acting Dean; Ph.D., Rhode Island, 1971. Chemical oceanography, chemical tracers, pollutant transfer, particle fluxes, role of organisms in modifying chemistry of seawater.
Norman J. Blake, Professor; Ph.D., Rhode Island, 1972. Ecology and physiology of marine invertebrates, inshore environmental ecology and pollution, reproductive physiology of mollusks and crustaceans.
Robert H. Byrne, Professor; Ph.D., Rhode Island, 1974. Chemical oceanography, physical chemistry of seawater, ionic interactions, marine surface chemistry, oceanic CO_2 system chemistry.
Kendall L. Carder, Professor; Ph.D., Oregon State, 1970. Physical oceanography, ocean optics, suspended-particle dynamics, instrument development, ocean remote sensing.
Paula G. Coble, Associate Professor; Ph.D., MIT (Woods Hole Joint Program), 1990. Chemical oceanography, marine organic geochemistry, fluorescence and remote sensing of dissolved organic matter in seawater.
Kendra Daly, Assistant Professor; Ph.D., Tennessee, 1995. Biological oceanography, marine plankton dynamics, influence of physical forcing on biological variability, role of marine biota in biogeochemical cycles.
Larry J. Doyle, Professor; Ph.D., USC, 1973. Marine geology, sedimentology, sedimentary processes of the continental margins.
Kent A. Fanning, Professor; Ph.D., Rhode Island, 1973. Chemical oceanography, pore-water geochemistry, nutrients in the ocean, marine radiochemistry.
Benjamin P. Flower, Assistant Professor; Ph.D., California, Santa Barbara, 1993. Paleoceanography, paleoclimatology, isotope geochemistry.
Boris Galperin, Associate Professor; Ph.D., Technion (Israel), 1982. Physical oceanography, boundary layers, turbulence, renormalization group theory, numerical modeling of oceanic circulation.
Pamela Hallock-Muller, Professor; Ph.D., Hawaii, 1977. Micropaleontology, paleoceanography, carbonate sedimentology, coral reef ecology.
Albert C. Hine, Professor; Ph.D., South Carolina, 1975. Carbonate sedimentology, coastal sedimentary processes, geological oceanography, sequence stratigraphy.
David J. Hollander, Associate Professor; Ph.D., Swiss Federal Institute of Technology, 1989. Isotopic biogeochemistry, molecular organic geochemistry, carbon cycling in modern lakes and oceans, paleolimnology/paleoceanography, chemical sedimentology.
Thomas L. Hopkins, Professor; Ph.D., Florida State, 1964. Biological oceanography, marine plankton and micronekton ecology, oceanic food webs.
Peter A. Howd, Assistant Professor; Ph.D., Oregon State, 1991. Beach and inner-shelf processes, beach morphodynamics, wave-driven processes on coral reefs.
Mark E. Luther, Associate Professor; Ph.D., North Carolina at Chapel Hill, 1982. Physical oceanography, numerical modeling of ocean circulation, equatorial dynamics, air-sea interaction, climate variability, estuarine circulation.
David A. Mann, Assistant Professor; Ph.D., MIT (Woods Hole Joint Program), 1995. Biological oceanography, ichthyology, marine mammals, sensory physiology, bioacoustics.
Gary T. Mitchum, Associate Professor; Ph.D., Florida State, 1984. Physical oceanography, ocean's role in climate variability, physical factors influencing biological variability.
Frank E. Müller-Karger, Associate Professor; Ph.D., Maryland, 1988. Marine, estuarine, and environmental science; biological oceanography; remote sensing; nutrient cycles.
David F. Naar, Assistant Professor; Ph.D., California, San Diego (Scripps), 1990. Marine geophysics, plate tectonics, marine tectonics, midocean ridge processes, physical modeling using molten wax.
John H. Paul, Professor; Ph.D., Miami (Florida), 1980. Marine microbiology, genetics, viral genomics, and microbial gene expression.
Terrence M. Quinn, Associate Professor; Ph.D., Brown, 1989. Paleoclimatology, paleoceanography, carbonate geology, isotope geochemistry.
Joan B. Rose, Associate Professor; Ph.D., Arizona, 1985. Water pollution microbiology, risk assessment, coastal water quality, parasites and viruses.
Sarah F. Tebbens, Assistant Professor; Ph.D., Columbia, 1994. Marine geophysics, aeromagnetics, plate boundary processes, triple junction evolution, natural hazard assessment.
Joseph J. Torres, Professor; Ph.D., California, Santa Barbara, 1980. Biological oceanography, deep-sea biology, bioenergetics of pelagic animals, comparative physiology.
Edward S. Van Vleet, Professor; Ph.D., Rhode Island, 1978. Chemical oceanography, organic geochemistry, molecular biomarkers, hydrocarbon pollution.
Gabriel A. Vargo, Associate Professor; Ph.D., Rhode Island, 1976. Biological oceanography; phytoplankton ecology, physiology, and nutrient dynamics.
John J. Walsh, Distinguished Professor; Ph.D., Miami (Florida), 1969. Continental shelf ecosystems, systems analysis of marine food webs, global carbon and nitrogen cycles.
Robert W. Weisberg, Professor; Ph.D., Rhode Island, 1975. Physical oceanography, equatorial, estuarine, and continental shelf circulation and air-sea interaction studies using in situ measurements and numerical models.

Adjunct Faculty

Thomas G. Bailey, Assistant Professor; Ph.D., California, Santa Barbara, 1984. Physiology and ecology of deep-sea fishes and invertebrates.
Theresa M. Bert, Assistant Professor; Ph.D., Yale, 1985. Evolution, systematics, population biology, physiology, genetics of fish and shellfish.
Greg R. Brooks, Assistant Professor; Ph.D., South Florida, 1986. Sediments and sedimentary processes in coastal and offshore environments.
Roy E. Crabtree, Assistant Professor; Ph.D., William and Mary, 1984. Ecology, physiology, and early life history of gamefish; ichthyology.
Robert B. Halley (U.S. Geological Survey), Professor; Ph.D., SUNY at Stony Brook, 1974. Carbonate sedimentation, chemistry and diagenesis, stratigraphy, coastal sedimentation, coral reefs, paleoclimate records and climate variability.
Gary W. Litman, Professor; Ph.D., Minnesota, 1972. Molecular genetics, evolution, immunology, developmental regulation.
R. Edmond Matheson, Assistant Professor; Ph.D., Texas A&M, 1983. Ecology and population biology of estuarine fish, ichthyology.
Anne Meylan, Assistant Professor; Ph.D., Florida, 1984. Ecology, migrations, and evolution of marine turtles; biology of demosponges.
Robert G. Muller, Assistant Professor; Ph.D., Hawaii, 1976. Fisheries biology, population dynamics, modeling of exploited populations, fisheries statistics.
Esther C. Peters, Assistant Professor; Ph.D., Rhode Island, 1985. Comparative histopathology, coral biology, invertebrate oncology.
John E. Reynolds III, Associate Professor; Ph.D., Miami (Florida), 1980. Marine mammals: population dynamics, management, and functional anatomy.
Gary E. Rodrick, Associate Professor; Ph.D., Oklahoma, 1971. Medical malacology, comparative physiology and immunology of invertebrates, biochemistry of mitochondrial enzymes and nucleic acids, parasite metabolism.
Asbury H. Sallenger Jr. (U.S. Geological Survey), Professor; Ph.D., Virginia, 1975. Nearshore sedimentary and wave processes, coastal erosion, sediment transport.
Eugene A. Shinn (U.S. Geological Survey), Professor; H.C., Kensington, 1987. Carbonate diagenesis, tidal flat deposition, reef development, coral reef ecology and geology.
Karen A. Steidinger, Ph.D., South Florida, 1979. Dinoflagellates, red tides, ultrastructure of unicells, cytology.
Yves Tardy, Distinguished Professor; Ph.D., Louis Pasteur (Strasbourg), 1969. Geochemical thermodynamics, mineral-solution equilibria, global chemical cycles, weathering and erosion.

University of South Florida

SELECTED PUBLICATIONS

Shinn, E. A., et al. **(P. Betzer).** African dust and the demise of Caribbean coral reefs. *Geophys. Res. Lett.* 27(19):3029–32, 2000.

Schijf, J., and **R. H. Byrne.** Determination of stability constants for the mono- and difluoro-complexes of Y and the REE, using a cation-exchange resin and ICP-MS. *Polyhedron* 18:2839–44, 1999.

Short, R. T., et al. **(R. H. Byrne).** Development of an underwater mass-spectrometry system for *in-situ* chemical analysis. *Meas. Sci. Technol.* 10:1195–1201, 1999.

Yao, W., and **R. H. Byrne.** Determination of trace chromium (VI) and molybdenum (VI) in natural and bottled mineral waters using long pathlength absorbance spectroscopy (LPAS). *Talanta* 48:277–82, 1999.

Byrne, R. H., S. McElligott, R. A. Feely, and F. J. Millero. The role of pH_T measurements in marine CO_2-system investigations. *Deep-Sea Res. I* 46:1985–97, 1999.

Byrne, R. H., and S. H. Laurie. Influence of pressure on chemical equilibria in aqueous systems—with particular reference to seawater. *Pure Appl. Chem.* 71:871–90, 1999.

Hu, C., **K. L. Carder,** and **F. E. Müller-Karger.** Atmospheric correction of SeaWiFS imagery over turbid coastal waters: A practical method. *Remote Sensing Environ.,* in press.

Carder, K. L., F. R. Chen, Z. P. Lee, and S. K. Hawes. Semianalytic moderate-resolution imaging spectrometer algorithms for chlorophyll *a* and adsorption with bio-optical domains based on nitrate-depletion temperatures. *J. Geophys. Res.* 104(C3):5403–21, 1999.

Lee, Z., and **K. L. Carder** et al. Hyperspectral remote sensing for shallow waters: 2. Deriving bottom depths and water properties by optimization. *Appl. Opt.* 38(18):3831–43, 1999.

Zhang, M., et al. **(K. Carder** and **F. E. Müller-Karger).** Noise reduction and atmospheric correction for coastal applications of landsat thematic mapper imagery. *Remote Sensing Environ.* 70:167–80, 1999.

Walker, S. H., **P. G. Coble,** and F. L. Larkin. Ocean sciences education for the 21st century. *Oceanography* 13:32–9, 2000.

Boehme, J. E., and **P. G. Coble.** Characterization of colored dissolved organic matter using high-energy laser fragmentation. *Environ. Sci. Technol.* 34:3283–90, 2000.

Del Castillo, C. E., F. Gilbes, **P. G. Coble,** and **F. E. Müller-Karger.** On dispersal of riverine colored dissolved organic matter over the west Florida shelf. *Limnol. Oceanogr.* 45:1425–32, 2000.

Coble, P. G., C. E. Del Castillo, and B. Avril. Distribution and optical properties of CDOM in the Arabian Sea during the 1995 summer monsoon. *Deep-Sea Res.* 45:2195–223, 1998.

Coble, P. G., Characterization of marine and terrestrial DOM in seawater rising excitation-emission matrix spectroscopy. *Mar. Chem.* 51:325–46, 1996.

Daly, K. L., et al. Hydrography, nutrients, and carbon pools in the Pacific sector of the Southern Ocean: Implications for carbon flux. *J. Geophys. Res.,* in press.

Daly, K. L., et al. Non-Redfield carbon and nitrogen cycling in the Arctic: Effects of ecosystem structure and function. *J. Geophys. Res.* 104(C2):3185–99, 1999.

Daly, K. L. Physioecology of juvenile Antarctic krill *(Euphausia superba)* during spring in ice-covered seas. In *Antarctic Sea Ice: Biological Processes,* eds. M. Lizotte and K. Arrigo. AGU Antarctic Research Series 73:183–198, 1998.

Daly, K. L. Flux of particulate matter through copepods in the Northeast Water Polynya. *J. Marine Sys.* 10:319–42, 1997.

Masserini, R. T., Jr., and **K. A. Fanning.** A sensor package for the simultaneous determination of nanomolar concentrations of nitrite, nitrate, and ammonia in seawater by fluorescence detection. *Mar. Chem.* 68:323–33, 2000.

Flower, B. P., et al. North Atlantic intermediate- to deep-water circulation and chemical stratification during the past 1 m.y. *Paleoceanography* 15:388–403, 2000.

Paul, H., J. C. Zachos, **B. P. Flower,** and A. Tripati. Orbitally induced climate and geochemical variability across the Oligocene/Miocene boundary. *Paleoceanography* 15:471–85, 2000.

Flower, B. P. Warming without high CO_2? *Nature* 399:313–4, 2000.

Flower, B. P. Cenozoic deep-sea temperatures and polar glaciation: The oxygen isotope record. In *Geological Records of Global and Planetary Changes,* pp. 27–42, eds. P. J. Barrett and G. Orombelli. Terra Antarctica Reports 3, 1999.

Hallock, P. Coral reefs, carbonate sedimentation, nutrients, and global change. In *The History and Sedimentology of Ancient Reef Ecosystems,* pp. 387–427, ed. G. D. Stanley. Kluwer Academic/Plenum Publishers, 2001.

McField, M. D., **P. Hallock,** and W. Jaap. Multivariate analysis of reef community structure in the Belize Barrier Reef complex. *Bull. Mar. Sci.* 69(2):745–58, 2001.

Toler, S. K., **P. Hallock,** and J. Schijf. Mg/Ca ratios in stressed *Amphistegina gibbosa* from the Florida Keys. *Mar. Micropaleontol.* 43:199–206, 2001.

Hallock, P. Larger foraminifers as indicators of coral-reef vitality. In *Environmental Micropaleontology,* pp. 121–50, ed. R. Martin. Plenum Press Topics in Geobiology, 2000.

Duncan, D. S., **A. C. Hine,** A. W. Droxler. Tectonic controls on carbonate sequence formation in an active strike-slip setting: Serranilla Basin, northern Nicaraguan Rise, western Caribbean Sea. *Mar. Geol.* 160:355–82, 1999.

Hine, A. C., D. A. Feary, and M. J. Malone. Research in Great Australian Bight yields exciting early results. *EOS* 80:521, 525–6, 1999.

Goodbred, S. L., E. E. Wright, and **A. C. Hine.** A record of sea-level change and storm-surge deposition in the late Holocene stratigraphy of a Florida salt-marsh shoreline. *J. Sedimentary Res.* 68:240–52, 1998.

Hollander, D. J., and M. A. Smith. Microbially mediated carbon cycling as a control on the $\delta^{13}C$ of sedimentary carbon in eutrophic Lake Mendota (USA): New models for interpreting isotopic excursions in the sedimentary record. *Geochim. Cosmochim. Acta,* in press.

Van Mooy, B., et al. **(D. Hollander).** Evidence for tight coupling between active bacteria and particulate organic carbon during seasonal stratification of Lake Michigan. *Limnol. Oceanogr.,* in press.

Murphy, A. E., B. B. Sageman, and **D. J. Hollander.** Eutrophication by decoupling of the marine biogeochemical cycles of C, N, and P: A mechanism for the Late Devonian mass extinction. *Geology* 28:427–30, 2000.

Werne, J. P, **D. J. Hollander,** T. W. Lyons, and L. C. Peterson. Climate-induced variations in productivity and planktonic ecosystem structure from the Younger Dryas to Holocene in the Cariaco Basin, Venezuela. *Paleoceanography* 15(1):19–29, 2000.

Rich, J., **D. J. Hollander,** and E. G. Birchfield. The role of regional oceanic bioproductivity in atmospheric pCO_2 changes. *Global Biogeochem. Cycles* 13(2):531–53, 1999.

Johnson, Z., and **P. A. Howd.** Marine photosynthetic performance forcing and periodicity for the Bermuda Atlantic Time Series, 1989–1995. *Deep Sea Res. I.,* in press.

Sallenger, A., **P. A. Howd** et al. Scaling winter storm impacts on Assateague Island, Maryland, Virginia. *Proceedings, Coastal Sediments '99* 3:1814–25, 1999.

Haines, J., **P. A. Howd,** and K. Hanson. Cross-shore transport and profile evolution at Duck, North Carolina. *Proceedings, Coastal Sediments '99* 2:1050–64, 1999.

Welch, J., R. Forward, and **P. A. Howd.** Behavioral responses of blue crab *(Callinectes sapidus)* postlarvae to turbulence: Implications for selective tidal stream transport. *Mar. Ecol. Prog. Ser.* 179:135–43, 1999.

Luther, M. E. Interannual variability in the Somali Current, 1954–1976. *Nonlinear Analysis: Real World Appl.* 35:59–83, 1999.

Haines, M. A., R. A. Fine, **M. E. Luther,** and Z. Ji. Particle trajectories in an Indian Ocean model and sensitivity to seasonal forcing. *J. Phys. Oceanogr.* 29:584–98, 1999.

Bartolacci, D. M., and **M. E. Luther.** Patterns of co-variability between physical and biological parameters in the Arabian Sea, 1933–1964. *Deep-Sea Res.* 46, 1999.

Mann, D. A., et al. Ultrasound detection by clupeiform fishes. *J. Acoust. Soc. Am.* 109:3048–54, 2001.

Mann, D. A., and P. S. Lobel. Acoustic behavior of the damselfish *Dascyllus albisella:* Behavior and geographic variation. *Environ. Biol. Fish.* 51:421–8, 1998.

Mann, D. A., Z. Lu, and A. N. Popper. A clupeid fish can detect ultrasound. *Nature* 389:341, 1997.

Nerem, R., and **G. T. Mitchum.** Observations of sea level change from satellite altimetry. In *Sea Level Rise: History and Consequences,* ed. B. Douglas. Academic Press, 2000.

University of South Florida

Selected Publications (continued)

Mitchum, G. T. An improved calibration of satellite altimetric heights using tide gauge sea levels. *Mar. Geod.* 23:145–66, 2000.

Mitchum, G. T., and S. Chiswell. Coherence of internal tide variations along the Hawaiian Ridge. *J. Geophys. Res.* 105:28653–62, 2000.

Nerem, R., et al. **(G. T. Mitchum).** Variations in global mean sea level associated with the 1997–98 ENSO event. *Geophys. Res. Lett.* 26:3005–9, 1999.

Melo, N., and **F. E. Müller-Karger** et al. Near-surface time-space distribution of phytoplankton in the western Caribbean Sea as determined by satellite observations. *J. Geophys. Res.,* in press.

Müller-Karger, F. E., and C. Fuentes-Yaco. Characteristics of wind-generated rings in the eastern tropical Pacific Ocean. *J. Geophys. Res.* 105(C1):1271–84, 2000.

Thunell, R., et al. **(F. Müller-Karger).** Organic carbon flux in an anoxic water column: Sediment trap results from the Cariaco Basin. *Limnol. Oceanogr.* 45:300–8, 2000.

Thunell, R., et al. **(F. Müller-Karger).** Increased marine sediment suspension and fluxes following an earthquake. *Nature* 398:233–6, 1999.

Bird, R. T., **D. F. Naar** et al. New models for the origin and tectonic development of the Juan Fernandez Microplate. *J. Geophys. Res.* 103:7049–67, 1998.

Rappaport, Y., **D. F. Naar** et al. Two types of seamounts surrounding Easter Island: Their statistics and distribution. *J. Geophys. Res.* 102:24713–28, 1997.

Kruse, S. E., Z. J. Liu, and **D. F. Naar.** Effective elastic thickness of the lithosphere along the Easter Seamount Chain. *J. Geophys. Res.* 102:27305–17, 1997.

McDaniel, L., L. Houchin, S. Williamson, and **J. H. Paul.** Lysogeny in natural populations of marine Synechococcus. *Nature* 214:496, 2002.

Paul, J. H., A. Alfreider, and B. Wawrik. Micro and macrodiversity in rbcL sequences in ambient phytoplankton populations from the Southeastern Gulf of Mexico. *Mar. Ecol. Prog. Ser.* 198:9–17, 2002.

Paul, J. H. Marine microbiology. In *Methods in Microbiology Series,* vol. 30., 666 pp. Academic Press, 2001.

Griffin, D. W., et al. **(J. H. Paul and J. B. Rose).** Detection of viral pathogens by reverse transcriptase PCR and of microbial indicators by standard methods in the canals of the Florida Keys. *Appl. Environ. Microbiol.* 65(9):4118–25, 1999.

Paul, J. H., et al. Evidence for a clade-specific temporal and spatial separation in ribulose bisphosphate carboxylase gene expression in phytoplankton populations off Cape Hatteras and Bermuda. *Limnol. Oceanogr.* 44:12–23, 1999.

Quinn, T. M., and D. S. Sampson. A multi-proxy approach to reconstructing sea-surface conditions using coral skeleton geochemistry. *Paleoceanography,* in press.

Getty, S. R., Y. Asmeron, **T. M. Quinn,** and A. F. Budd. Uranium-lead dating of Pleistocene corals, and coral extinction rates in the Caribbean basin. *Geology,* in press.

Correge, T., and **T. M. Quinn** et al. Little Ice Age sea-surface temperature variability in the southwest tropical Pacific. *Geophys. Res. Lett.* 28(18)3477–80, 2001.

Quinn, T. M., and G. S. Mountain. Shallow-water science and ocean drilling: Challenges for the new millennium. *EOS Trans. Am. Geophys. Union* 81(35):397–404, 2000.

Crowley, T. J., **T. M. Quinn,** and W. T. Hyde. Validation of coral temperature calibrations. *Paleoceanography* 14(5):605–15, 1999.

Quinn, T. M., et al. A multicentury stable isotope record from a New Caledonia coral: Interannual and decadal SST variability in the southwest Pacific since 1657. *Paleoceanography* 13(4):412–26, 1998.

Rose, J. B., and D. J. Grimes. Reevaluation of microbial water quality: Powerful new tools for detection and risk assessment. American Academy of Microbiology, Washington, D.C., 2001.

Lipp, E. K., N. Schmidt, M. E. Luther, and **J. B. Rose.** Determining the effects of El Niño–southern oscillation events on coastal water quality. *Estuaries* 24(4):491–7, 2001.

Lipp, E. K., et al. **(J. B. Rose).** The effects of seasonal variability and weather on microbial fecal pollution and enteric pathogens in a subtropical estuary. *Estuaries* 24:266–76, 2001.

Rose, J. B., et al. Climate variability and change in the United States: Potential impacts on water- and foodborne diseases caused by microbiologic agents. *Environ. Health Perspect.* 109(S2):211–21, 2001.

Bird, R., **S. F. Tebbens, D. F. Naar,** and M. C. Kleinrock. Evidence for and implications of stepwise triple junction migration. *Geology* 27:911–4, 1999.

Wetzel, D. L., and **E. S. Van Vleet.** Petroleum hydrocarbons in the sediments of Venice, Italy, 1995 and 1998. *Mar. Pollut. Bull.,* in press.

Ames, A. L., and **E. S. Van Vleet.** Lipids in the zygomatic process of the squamosal bone of the Florida manatee, *Trichechus manatus latirostris. Comp. Biochem. Physiol.,* in press.

Hagen, W., G. Kattner, A. Terbruggen, and **E. S. Van Vleet.** Lipid metabolism of the Antarctic krill *Euphausia superba* and its ecological implications. *Mar. Biol.* 139:95–104, 2001.

Nasci, C., et al. **(E. S. Van Vleet).** Clam transplantation and stress-related biomarkers as useful tools for assessing water quality in coastal environments. *Mar. Pollut. Bull.* 39:255–60, 1999.

Burghart, S. E., T. L. Hopkins, **G. A. Vargo,** and **J. J. Torres.** Effects of a rapidly receding ice edge on the abundance, age structure and feeding of three dominant calanoid copepods in the Weddell Sea, Antarctica. *Polar Biol.* 22:279–88, 1999.

Steidinger, K. A., **G. A. Vargo,** P. A. Tester, and C. R. Tomas. Bloom dynamics and physiology of *Gymnodinium breve,* with emphasis on the Gulf of Mexico. In *Physiological Ecology of Harmful Algal Blooms,* Ecological Sciences, vol. 41, pp. 133–154, eds. D. M. Anderson, A. D. Cembella, and G. M. Hallegraeff. Springer, New York: NATO ASI Series, 1998.

Wanninkhof, R., et al. **(G. A. Vargo).** Gas exchange, dispersion, and biological productivity on the west Florida Shelf: Results from a Lagrangian tracer study. *Geophys. Res. Lett.* 24:1767–70, 1997.

Morrison, G., et al. **(G. A. Vargo).** Estimated nitrogen fluxes and nitrogen-chlorophyll relationships in Tampa Bay. In *Proceedings, Tampa Bay Area Scientific Information Symposium 3,* Oct. 21–23, 1996, pp. 249–68, ed. S. Treat; Clearwater, Florida, 1985–1994, p. 396, 1997.

Walsh, J. J., et al. **(F. E. Müller-Karger** and **K. A. Fanning).** Simulation of carbon/nitrogen cycling during spring upwelling in the Cariaco Basin. *J. Geophys. Res.* 104:7807–25, 2000.

He, R., and **R. H. Weisberg.** West Florida shelf circulation and temperature budget for the 1999 spring transition. *Cont. Shelf Res.* 22:719–48, 2002.

Weisberg, R. H. An observer's view of the equatorial ocean currents. *Oceanography* 14:27–33, 2001.

Weisberg, R. H., Z. Li, and **F. E. Müller-Karger.** West Florida shelf response to local wind forcing: April 1998. *J. Geophys. Res.* 106:31239–62, 2001.

Weisberg, R. H., B. Black, and Z. Li. An upwelling case study on Florida's west coast. *J. Geophys. Res.* 104:7807–25, 2000.

Weisberg, R. H., and L. Qiao. Equatorial upwelling in the central Pacific estimated from moored velocity profilers. *J. Phys. Oceanogr.* 30:105–24, 2000.

THE UNIVERSITY OF TEXAS AT AUSTIN

Department of Marine Science

Programs of Study

The Department of Marine Science offers research opportunities and course work leading to the M.S. and Ph.D. degrees in marine science. Graduate students usually begin their academic program with course work on the Austin campus and move to the University of Texas Marine Science Institute at Port Aransas for specialized advanced courses and thesis or dissertation research. Core courses are required in several subdisciplines, including marine ecosystem dynamics, marine biogeochemistry, and adaptations to the marine environment. Areas of research available in Port Aransas include physiology and ecology of marine organisms, biological oceanography, geochemistry, marine environmental quality, coastal processes, and mariculture.

Research Facilities

The Marine Science Institute at Port Aransas is located near Corpus Christi and provides opportunities to study living organisms in the laboratory and under field conditions. A wide variety of environments are readily accessible, such as the pass connecting Corpus Christi Bay with the Gulf of Mexico, the continental shelf, and many bays and estuaries, including brackish estuaries and the hypersaline Laguna Madre. There are outside open and covered seawater tanks, a pier lab with running seawater, a reference collection of most of the plants and animals of the area, and controlled-environment chambers. Vessels include the *R/V Longhorn*, a 105-foot research vessel with navigation and laboratory capabilities for most research projects; the *R/V Katy*, a 54-foot boat with dredge and trawl equipment for collection of specimens; and several smaller boats. A remote terminal is linked with the computation center in Austin. Laboratories are equipped to study animal physiology, toxicology, bacterial and algal physiology, bacterial and algal ecology, fish ecology, marine phycology, mariculture, sea grass ecology and physiology, and geochemistry. Research is under way in benthic ecology, biological oceanography, fish behavior, invertebrate biology, phytoplankton ecology, and taxonomy of marine organisms. The Institute also provides teaching facilities in Port Aransas, including upper-division and graduate course offerings during the summer. Facilities are available on the Austin campus for research in marine sedimentology and in marine mineral deposits, including genesis, exploration, and recovery.

Financial Aid

Research and teaching assistantships are available through graduate advisers or the department chairman. E. J. Lund Fellowships and Scholarships for research at the Marine Science Institute are awarded annually.

Cost of Study

In 2004–05, tuition and required fees for Texas residents and any students holding an assistantship are approximately $2550 per semester for 9 credit hours. Nonresident tuition and required fees for 9 credit hours total $4750 per semester.

Living and Housing Costs

In Port Aransas, furnished University apartments are available for students at approximately $300–$400 per month plus utilities. Non-University housing off campus costs approximately $600–$800 per month. For the Department of Marine Science's Summer Program, dormitory and dining facilities are also available to registered students.

In Austin, University dormitories and apartments, furnished and unfurnished, are available. Rooms and apartments are conveniently situated near the campus. There is also a shuttle bus service.

Student Group

The enrollment of the University of Texas at Austin is more than 50,000, including approximately 12,000 graduate students. The College of Natural Sciences has about 1,500 graduate students. An average of 25 graduate students reside at the Marine Science Institute in Port Aransas.

Location

Austin is the state capital, with a population of approximately 550,000. Cultural events sponsored by the University are abundant, and there are many recreational facilities available. Port Aransas is a small coastal town approximately 200 miles south of Austin, where the Gulf of Mexico and surrounding bays and estuaries provide excellent boating, fishing, and swimming.

The University

The University of Texas at Austin was founded in 1883 and is part of the University of Texas System. The Department of Marine Science is in the College of Natural Sciences.

Applying

Prospective students must apply to both the Director of Admissions of the Graduate School and the Graduate Studies Committee of the Department of Marine Science in order to be considered for admission to the department. Application forms may be obtained from the Graduate School and from the department office. Only admission applications completed by January 1 can be considered for fellowship or teaching assistantship awards.

Correspondence and Information

Graduate Adviser
Marine Science Institute
The University of Texas at Austin
750 Channel View Drive
Port Aransas, Texas 78373-5015
Telephone: 361-749-6721
E-mail: gradinfo@utmsi.utexas.edu
World Wide Web: http://www.utmsi.utexas.edu

Chairman
Department of Marine Science
The University of Texas at Austin
750 Channel View Drive
Port Aransas, Texas 78373-5015
Telephone: 361-749-6721

The University of Texas at Austin

THE FACULTY AND THEIR RESEARCH

Jay A. Brandes, Assistant Professor, Port Aransas; Ph.D., Washington (Seattle), 1996. Biogeochemical cycles of C, H, N, O, and S in present-day and prebiotic oceans.

Edward J. Buskey, Professor, Port Aransas; Ph.D., Rhode Island, 1983. Marine plankton ecology, sensory perception and behavior of marine organisms, bioluminescence of marine organisms, role of planktonic grazers in harmful algal bloom dynamics.

Kenneth H. Dunton, Professor, Port Aransas; Ph.D., Alaska Fairbanks, 1985. Physiological ecology and productivity of benthic algal, seagrass, coral reef, and marsh ecosystems; nutrient and carbon cycling; ecosystem response to nutrient loading; food web structure; coral reef ecology; linkages between pelegic and benthic communities; application of GIS to landscape and climate change control.

Henrietta N. Edmonds, Assistant Professor, Port Aranas; Ph.D., MIT and Woods Hole Oceanographic, 1997. Marine geochemistry; natural and anthropogenic isotopes as tracers of ocean circulation and biogeochemical processes; submarine hydrothermal systems.

Lee A. Fuiman, Professor, Port Aransas (also Professor in the School of Biological Sciences-Integrative Biology); Ph.D., Michigan, 1983. Marine vertebrate ecology, with emphasis on behavior and development; use of sensory and locomotor systems in predator-prey interactions; sublethal effects of contaminants on behavior of fish larvae.

Wayne S. Gardner, Professor, Port Aransas; Ph.D., Wisconsin, 1971. Nitrogen dynamics in water column and sediments, nutrient-organism interactions in coastal ecosystems.

G. Joan Holt, Professor, Port Aransas; Ph.D., Texas A&M, 1976. Larval fish feeding dynamics and nutrition, transport and recruitment, reef fishes, RNA-DNA ratio, condition indices, osmoregulation.

Izhar A. Khan, Assistant Professor, Port Aransas, Ph.D., Banaras Hindu (India), 1990. Neuroendocrine control of reproduction in marine fishes, induced spawning of important aquaculture species, hormonal control of puberty in fishes, mechanisms of neuroendocrine toxicity of environmental chemicals.

Paul A. Montagna, Professor, Port Aransas; Ph.D., South Carolina, 1983. Benthic ecology, especially invertebrate community structure, population genetics, and trophic dynamics; environmental science, modeling, and biostatistics.

B. Scott Nunez, Assistant Professor, Port Aransas; Ph.D., LSU, 1996. Fish molecular endocrinology, synthesis and effects of steroids, effects of stress in fish, molecular physiology of sharks and stingrays.

Tamara K. Pease, Assistant Professor, Port Aransas, Ph.D., North Carolina at Chapel Hill, 2000. Geochemistry of organic compounds, sources and processes which control the distributions of organic matter in marine and estuarine environments, organic matter and microbial interactions.

Peter Thomas, Professor, Port Aransas (also Professor in the School of Biological Sciences-Integrative Biology); Ph.D., Leicester (England), 1977. Environmental and neuroendocrine control of reproduction, molecular mechanisms of steroid hormone action, cloning and characterization of steroid nuclear and membrane receptors, gonadal and gamete physiology, applications of endocrinology in fish culture, environmental and reproductive toxicology of marine fishes, especially mechanisms of endocrine disruption and molecular biomarkers of reproductive impairment in fish populations.

Tracy A. Villareal, Associate Professor, Port Aransas; Ph.D., Rhode Island, 1989. Marine phytoplankton, autecology of harmful algal species, biological oceanography.

SELECTED PUBLICATIONS

Haberer, J. L., and **J. A. Brandes.** A high sensitivity, low volume HPLC based method to determine soluble reactive phosphate (SRP) in freshwater and saltwater. *Mar. Chem.* 82:185–96, 2003.

Sigman, D. M., et. al. **(J. A. Brandes).** Distinguishing between water column and sedimentary denitrification in the Santa Barbara Basin using the nitrogen isotopes of nitrate. *Geochem. Geophys. Geosys.* 4(5)1040:10.1029/2002GC000384, 2003.

Brandes, J. A., and A. H. Devol. A marine fixed nitrogen isotopic budget: Implications for holocene nitrogen cycling. *Global Biogeochem. Cycles* 16(4)1120:10.1029/2001GB 001856, 2002.

Brandes, J. A., et al. Isotopic composition of nitrate in the central Arabian Sea and eastern tropical North Pacific: A tracer for mixing and nitrogen cycles. *Limnol. Oceanogr.* 43(7):1680–9, 1999.

Brandes, J. A., et al. Abiotic nitrogen reduction in the early Earth. *Nature* 395:365–7, 1998.

Buskey, E. J. Behavioral adaptations of the cubozoan medusae *Tripedalia cystophora* for feeding on copepod swarms. *Mar. Biol.* 142:225–32, 2003.

Buskey, E. J., H. DeYoe, F. Jochem, and **T. Villareal**. Effects of mesazooplankton removal on trophic structure during a bloom of the Texas "brown tide": a mesocosm study. *J. Plank. Res.* 25:215–28, 2003.

Bersano, J. B. F., **E. J. Buskey,** and **T. A. Villareal.** Viability of the Texas brown tide alga, *Aureoumbra lagunensis*, in fecal pellets of the copepod *Acartia tonsa*. *J. Plankton Biol.* 49(2):88–92, 2002.

Buskey, E. J., P. H. Lenz, and D. K. Hartline. Escape behavior of planktonic copepods to hydrodynamic disturbance: High speed video analysis. *Mar. Ecol. Prog. Ser.* 235:135–46, 2002.

Buskey, E. J., H. Liu, C. Collumb, and J. Bersano. The decline and recovery of a persistent brown tide algal bloom in the Laguna Madre (Texas, USA). *Estuarine* 24:337–46, 2001.

Buskey, E. J. The role of vision in the aggregative behavior of the mysid *Mysidium columbiae. Mar. Biol.* 137:257–65, 2000.

Alexander, H. D., and **K. H. Dunton.** Freshwater inundation effects on emergent vegetation of a hypersaline salt marsh. *Estuaries* 25:1426–35, 2002.

Dunton, K. H. Del ^{15}N and del ^{13}C measurements of Antarctic peninsular fauna: Trophic relationships and assimilation of benthic seaweeds. *Am. Zool.* 41(1):99–112, 2001.

Dunton, K. H., and S. V. Schonberg. The benthic faunal assemblage of the Boulder Patch kelp community. In *The Natural History of an Arctic Oil Field,* pp. 338–59, eds. J. C. Truett and S. R. Johnson. Academic Press, 2000.

Lee, K-S., and **K. H. Dunton.** Inorganic nitrogen acquisition in the seagrass *Thalassia testudinum*: Development of a whole-plant nitrogen budget. *Liminol. Oceanogr.* 44(5):1204–15, 1999.

Herzka, S. Z., and **K. H. Dunton.** Light and carbon balance in the seagrass *Thalassia testudinum:* Evaluation of current production models. *Mar. Biol.* 132:711–21, 1998.

Edmonds, H. N., et al. Discovery of abundant hydrothermal venting on the ultraslow-spreading Gakkel ridge in the Arctic Ocean. *Nature* 421:252–6, 2003.

Michael, P. J., et al. **(H. N. Edmonds)**. Magmatic and amagmatic seafloor generation at the ultraslow-spreading Gallel ridge, Arctic Ocean. *Nature* 423:956–61, 2003.

Moran, S. B., et al. **(H. N. Edmonds)**. Does $^{234}Th/^{238}U$ disequilibrium provide an accurate record of the export flux of particulate organic carbon from the upper ocean? *Limnol. Oceanogr.* 48:1018–29, 2003.

Shen. C.-C., et al. **(H. N. Edmonds).** Measurement of attogram quantities of ^{231}Pa in dissolved and particulate fractions of seawater by isotope dilution mass spectroscopy. *Anal. Chem.* 75:1075–9, 2003.

Edmonds, H. N., et al. Distribution and behavior of anthropogenic ^{129}I in water masses ventilating the North Atlantic Ocean. *J. Geophys. Res.* 106:6881–94, 2001.

Fuiman, L. A., and J. H. Cowan Jr. Behavior and recruitment success in fish larvae: repeatability and covariation of survival skills. *Ecology* 84:53–67, 2003.

McCarthy, I. D., **L. A. Fuiman,** and M. C. Alvarez. Aroclor 1254 affects growth and survival skills of Atlantic croaker (*Micropogonias undulatus*) larvae. *Mar. Ecol. Prog. Ser.* 252:295–301, 2003.

Rose, K. A., et al. **(L. A. Furiman** and **P. Thomas).** Using nested models and laboratory data for predicting population effects of contaminants on fish: A step toward a bottom-up approach for establishing causality in field studies. *Hum. Ecol. Risk Assess.* 9:231–57, 2003.

Smith, M. E., and **L. A. Fuiman.** Causes of growth depensation in red drum, *Sciaenops ocellatus,* larvae. *Environ. Biol. Fishes* 66:49–60, 2003.

Fuiman, L. A., R. W. Davis, and T. M. Williams. Behavior of midwater fishes under the Antarctic ice: Observations by a predator. *Mar. Biol.* 140:815–22, 2002.

An, S., and **W. S. Gardner.** Dissimilatory nitrate reduction to ammonium (DNRA) as a nitrogen link, versus denitrification as a sink in a shallow estuary (Laguna Madre/Baffin Bay, Texas). *Mar. Ecol. Prog. Ser.* 237:41–50, 2002.

An, S., **W. S. Gardner,** and T. Kana. Simultaneous measurement of denitrification and nitrogen fixation using isotope pairing with membrane inlet mass spectrometry analysis. *Appl. Environ. Microbiol.* 67:1171–8, 2001.

Gardner, W. S., et al. Nitrogen dynamics in sandy freshwater sediments (Saginaw Bay, Lake Huron). *J. Great Lakes Res.* 27:84–97, 2001.

Gardner, W. S., et al. Effects of natural light on nitrogen dynamics in diverse aquatic environments. *Verh. Internat. Limnol.* 27:1–10, 1999.

Gardner, W. S., et al. Nitrogen cycling rates and light effects in tropical Lake Maracaibo, Venezuela. *Limnol. Oceanogr.* 43(8):1814–25, 1998.

Holt, G. J. Research on culturing the early life history stages of marine ornamental species. In *Marine Ornamental Species: Collection, Culture and Conservation,* pp. 252–4, eds. J. C. Cato and C. L. Brown. Iowa State Press, 2003.

Applebaum, S. L., and **G. J. Holt.** The digestive protease, chymotrypsin, as an indicator of nutritional condition in larval red drum (*Sciaenops ocellatus*). *Mar. Biol.* 142:1159–67, 2003.

Holt, G. J. Ecophysiology, growth, and development of larvae and juveniles for aquaculture. *Fish. Sci.* 68(1):867–71, 2002.

Holt, G. J. Human impacts. In *Concepts in Fisheries Science: The Unique Contribution of Early Life Stages,* pp. 222–42, eds. **L. A. Fuiman** and R. G. Werner. Ames, Iowa: Iowa State University Press, A Blackwell Science Company, 2002.

Holt, G. J., and S. A. Holt. Effects of variable salinity on reproduction and early life stages of spotted seatrout. In *Biology of Spotted Seatrout,* pp. 135–45, ed. S. A. Bartone. Boca Raton, Florida: CRC Marine Biology Series, CRC Press, 2002.

Mathews, S., **I. A. Khan,** and **P. Thomas.** Effects of maturation-inducing steroid on LH secretion and the GnRH system at different stages of the reproductive cycle in Atlantic croaker. *Gen. Comp. Endocrinol.* 126:287–97, 2002.

The University of Texas at Austin

Selected Publications (continued)

Khan, I. A., and **P. Thomas.** Disruption of neuroendocrine control of luteinizing hormone secretion in Atlantic croaker by Aroclor 1254 involves inhibition of hypothalamic tryptophan hydroxylase activity. *Biol. Reprod.* 64:955-64, 2001.

Khan, I. A., and **P. Thomas.** GABA exerts stimulatory and inhibitory influences on gonadtropin II secretion in the Atlantic croaker *(Micropogonias undulatus)*. *Neuroendocrinology* 69:261–8, 1999.

Khan, I. A., et al. Gonadal stage-dependent effects of gonadal steroids on gonadotropin II secretion in the Atlantic croaker *(Micropogonias undulatus)*. *Biol. Reprod.* 61:834–41, 1999.

Khan, I. A., and **P. Thomas.** Ovarian cycles, teleost fish. In *Encyclopedia of Reproduction,* vol. 3, pp. 552–64, eds. E. Knobil and J. D. Neil. San Diego: Academic Press, 1998.

Montagna, P. A., R. D. Kalke, and C. Ritter. Effect of restored freshwater inflow on macrofauna and meiofauna in upper Rincon Bayou, Texas, USA. *Estuaries* 25:1436–47, 2002.

Montagna, P. A., S. C. Jarvis, and M. C. Kennicutt II. Distinguishing between contaminant and reef effects on meiofauna near offshore hydrocarbon platforms in the Gulf of Mexico. *Can. J. Fish Aquat. Sci.* 59:1584–92, 2002.

Ritter, M. C., and **P. A. Montagna.** Seasonal hypoxia and models of benthic response in a Texas bay. *Estuaries* 22:7–20, 1999.

Montagna, P. A., and J. Li. Modeling contaminant effects on deposit feeding nematodes near Gulf of Mexico production platforms. *Ecol. Model.* 98:151–62, 1997.

Montagna, P. A., and D. E. Harper Jr. Benthic infaunal long-term response to offshore production platforms. *Can. J. Fish. Aquatic Sci.* 53:2567–88, 1996.

Nunez, B. S., and W. V. Vedeckis. Characterization of promoter 1B of the human glucocorticocoid receptor. *Mol. Cell. Endocrinol.* 189:191–9, 2002.

Nunez, B. S., and W. V. Vedeckis. Monitoring nuclear receptor function. In *Receptors: Structure and Function,* pp. 233–56, eds. S. C. Stanford and R. W. Horton. Oxford: Oxford University Press, 2001.

Nikkila, H., et al. **(B. S. Nunez).** Sequence similarities between a novel putative G-protein coupled receptor and Na^{+}/Ca^{++} exchangers define a novel cation binding domain. *Mol. Endocrinol.* 14:1351–64, 2000.

Nunez, B. S., and J. M. Trant. Regulation of interrenal steroidogenesis in the Atlantic stingray *(Dasyatis sabina)*. *J. Exp. Zool.* 284:517–25, 1999.

Nunez, B. S., and J. M. Trant. Molecular biology and enzymology of elasmobranch 3β-hydroxysteroid dehydrogenase. *Fish Physiol. Biochem.* 19(4):293–304, 1998.

Wakeham, S. G., **T. K. Pease,** and R. Benner. Hydroxy fatty acids in marine dissolved organic matter as indicators of bacterial membrane material. *Org. Geochem.,* 34:857–68, 2003.

Hee, C., **T. K. Pease,** M. J. Alpern, and C. S. Martens. DOC production and consumption in anoxic marine sediments: A pulsed-tracer experiment. *Limnol. Oceanogr.* 46:1908–20, 2002.

Pease, T. K., et al. Simulated degradation of glyceryl ethers by hydrous and flash pyrolysis. *Org. Geochem.* 29:979–88, 1998.

King, L. L., **T. K. Pease,** and S. G. Wakeham. Archaea in Black Sea water column particulate matter and sediments—evidence from ether lipid derivatives. *Org. Geochem.* 28:677–88, 1998.

Zhu, Y., et al. **(P. Thomas).** Cloning, expression, and characterization of a membrane progestin receptor and evidence it is an intermediary in meiotic maturation of fish oocytes. *Proc. Ntl. Acad. Sci. USA* 100:2231–6, 2003.

Zhu. U., J. Bond, and **P. Thomas.** Identification, classification, and partial characterization of genes in humans and other vertebrates homologous to a fish membrane progestin receptor. *Proc. Ntl. Acad. Sci. USA* 100:2237–42, 2003.

Thomas, P., Y. Zhu, and M. Pace. Progestin membrane receptors involved in the meiotic maturation of teleost oocytes: A review with some new findings. *Steroids* 67:511–17, 2002.

Larsson, D. G. J., T. S. Sperry, and **P. Thomas.** Regulation of androgen receptors in Atlantic croaker brains by testosterone and estradiol. *Gen. Comp. Endocrinol.* 128:224–30, 2002.

Wainwright, S. E., M. A. Mora, J. L. Sericano, and **P. Thomas.** Chlorinated hydrocarbons and biomarkers of exposure in wading birds and fish of the Lower Rio Grande Valley, Texas. *Arch. Toxicol.* 255:201–14, 2001.

Villareal, T. A., and E. J. Carpenter. Buoyancy regulation and the potential for vertical migration in the oceanic cyanobacterium *Trichodesmium*. *Microb. Ecol.* 45:1–10, 2003.

Villareal, T. A., and S. Morton. Use of cell specific PAM-fluorometry to characterize host shading in the epiphytic dinoflagellate Gambierdiscus toxicus. *Mar. Ecol.* 23:1–14, 2002.

Loret, P., et al. **(T. A. Villareal).** No difference found in ribosomal DNA sequences from physiologically diverse clones of Karenia brevis *(Dinophyceae)* from the Gulf of Mexico. *Plankton Res.* 24(7):735–9, 2002.

Liu, H., E. A. Laws, **T. A. Villareal,** and **E. J. Buskey.** Nutrient-limited growth of Aureoumbra lagunensis *(Pelagophyceae)*, with implications of its capability to outgrow other phytoplankton species in phosphate-limited environments. *J. Phycol.* 37:500–8, 2001.

Section 5
Meteorology and Atmospheric Sciences

This section contains a directory of institutions offering graduate work in meteorology and atmospheric sciences, followed by in-depth entries submitted by institutions that chose to prepare detailed program descriptions. Additional information about programs listed in the directory but not augmented by an in-depth entry may be obtained by writing directly to the dean of a graduate school or chair of a department at the address given in the directory.

For programs offering related work, see also in this book Astronomy and Astrophysics, Geosciences, Marine Sciences and Oceanography, and Physics. In Book 3, see Biological and Biomedical Sciences and Biophysics; and in Book 5, see Aerospace/Aeronautical Engineering, Civil and Environmental Engineering, Engineering and Applied Sciences, and Mechanical Engineering and Mechanics.

CONTENTS

Program Directories

Announcement

In-Depth Descriptions

See also:

Atmospheric Sciences

City College of the City University of New York, Graduate School, College of Liberal Arts and Science, Division of Science, Department of Earth and Atmospheric Sciences, New York, NY 10031-9198. Offers earth and environmental science (PhD); earth systems science (MA). *Students:* 10 applicants, 70% accepted, 5 enrolled. In 2003, 2 degrees awarded. *Degree requirements:* For master's, thesis, comprehensive exam. *Entrance requirements:* For master's, appropriate bachelor's degree. Additional exam requirements/recommendations for international students: Required—TOEFL. *Application deadline:* For fall admission, 5/1 for domestic students; for spring admission, 11/1 for domestic students. Application fee: $50. *Expenses:* Tuition, state resident: full-time $5,440; part-time $230 per credit. Tuition, nonresident: part-time $425 per credit. Required fees: $63 per semester. *Financial support:* Fellowships, career-related internships or fieldwork available. *Faculty research:* Water resources, high-temperature geochemistry, sedimentary basin analysis, tectonics. *Unit head:* Jeffrey Steiner, Chair, 212-650-6984. *Application contact:* O. Lehn Franke, Adviser, 212-650-6984.

Clemson University, Graduate School, College of Engineering and Science, Department of Physics and Astronomy, Program in Physics, Clemson, SC 29634. Offers astronomy and astrophysics (MS, PhD); atmospheric physics (MS, PhD); biophysics (MS, PhD). Part-time programs available. *Students:* 40 full-time (11 women), 5 part-time; includes 1 minority (African American), 19 international. 59 applicants, 53% accepted, 8 enrolled. In 2003, 7 master's, 5 doctorates awarded. Terminal master's awarded for partial completion of doctoral program. *Degree requirements:* For master's, thesis or alternative; for doctorate, thesis/dissertation. *Entrance requirements:* For master's and doctorate, GRE General Test. Additional exam requirements/recommendations for international students: Required—TOEFL. *Application deadline:* For fall admission, 2/15 for domestic students. Applications are processed on a rolling basis. Application fee: $40. *Expenses:* Tuition, state resident: full-time $7,432. Tuition, nonresident: full-time $14,732. *Financial support:* Fellowships, research assistantships, teaching assistantships available. Financial award application deadline: 6/1; financial award applicants required to submit FAFSA. *Faculty research:* Radiation physics, solid-state physics, nuclear physics, radar and lidar studies of atmosphere. *Unit head:* Dr. Brad Myer, Head, 864-656-5320. *Application contact:* Dr. Miguel Larsen, Coordinator, 864-656-5309, Fax: 864-656-0805, E-mail: milarsen@clemson.edu.

Colorado State University, Graduate School, College of Engineering, Department of Atmospheric Science, Fort Collins, CO 80523-0015. Offers M Eng, MS, PhD. Part-time programs available. *Faculty:* 16 full-time (1 woman). *Students:* 70 full-time (23 women), 20 part-time (7 women); includes 6 minority (1 African American, 1 American Indian/Alaska Native, 2 Asian Americans or Pacific Islanders, 2 Hispanic Americans), 14 international. Average age 28. 149 applicants, 20% accepted, 17 enrolled. In 2003, 15 master's, 12 doctorates awarded. *Degree requirements:* For master's, thesis or alternative; for doctorate, thesis/dissertation, qualifying exam. *Entrance requirements:* For master's and doctorate, GRE General Test, minimum GPA of 3.0. Additional exam requirements/recommendations for international students: Required—TOEFL (minimum score 550 paper-based; 213 computer-based). *Application deadline:* For fall admission, 2/1 priority date for domestic students, 2/1 priority date for international students; for spring admission, 9/15 priority date for domestic students, 9/15 priority date for international students. Applications are processed on a rolling basis. Application fee: $50. Electronic applications accepted. *Expenses:* Tuition, state resident: full-time $4,156. Tuition, nonresident: full-time $14,762. Required fees: $205. Tuition and fees vary according to course load, campus/location, program and reciprocity agreements. *Financial support:* In 2003–04, 12 fellowships (averaging $2,583 per year), 67 research assistantships with full tuition reimbursements (averaging $18,585 per year), 7 teaching assistantships (averaging $4,203 per year) were awarded. Traineeships also available. Financial award application deadline: 4/15. *Faculty research:* Global circulation and climate, atmospheric chemistry, radiation and remote sensing, marine meteorology, mesoscale meteorology. Total annual research expenditures: $10.1 million. *Unit head:* Dr. Steven A. Rutledge, Head, 970-491-8360, Fax: 970-491-8449, E-mail: rutledge@atmos.colostate.edu. *Application contact:* Dr. Jeffrey L. Collett, Student Counselor, 970-491-8360, Fax: 970-491-8449, E-mail: collett@lamar.colostate.edu.

Columbia University, Graduate School of Arts and Sciences, Division of Natural Sciences, Program in Atmospheric and Planetary Science, New York, NY 10027. Offers M Phil, PhD. Offered jointly through the Departments of Geological Sciences, Astronomy, and Physics and in cooperation with NASA Goddard Space Flight Center's Institute for Space Studies. *Degree requirements:* For doctorate, variable foreign language requirement, thesis/dissertation. *Entrance requirements:* For doctorate, GRE General Test, GRE Subject Test, previous course work in mathematics and physics. Additional exam requirements/recommendations for international students: Required—TOEFL. Application fee: $75. *Expenses:* Tuition: Full-time $14,820. *Financial support:* Available to part-time students. Application deadline: 1/5; *Faculty research:* Climate, weather prediction.

See in-depth description on page 311.

Cornell University, Graduate School, Graduate Fields of Agriculture and Life Sciences, Department of Soil and Crop Sciences, Ithaca, NY 14853. Offers agronomy (MPS, MS, PhD); atmospheric sciences (MPS, MS, PhD); environmental information science (MPS, MS, PhD); environmental management (MPS); field crop science (MPS, MS, PhD); soil science (MPS, MS, PhD). Terminal master's awarded for partial completion of doctoral program. *Degree requirements:* For master's, thesis (MS), project paper (MPS); for doctorate, thesis/dissertation. *Entrance requirements:* For master's and doctorate, GRE General Test. Additional exam requirements/recommendations for international students: Required—TOEFL. Electronic applications accepted. Expenses: Contact institution. One-time fee: $50 full-time. *Faculty research:* Environmental modeling, soil chemistry and physics, international agriculture, weather and climate, crop physiology.

Cornell University, Graduate School, Graduate Fields of Agriculture and Life Sciences, Field of Atmospheric Science, Ithaca, NY 14853-0001. Offers MS, PhD. *Faculty:* 13 full-time. *Students:* 9 full-time (2 women), 6 international. 30 applicants, 7% accepted, 2 enrolled. In 2003, 2 master's, 2 doctorates awarded. *Degree requirements:* For master's, thesis/dissertation; for doctorate, thesis/dissertation, comprehensive exam. *Entrance requirements:* For master's and doctorate, GRE General Test, 2 letters of recommendation. Additional exam requirements/recommendations for international students: Required—TOEFL (minimum score 550 paper-based; 213 computer-based). *Application deadline:* For fall admission, 2/1 for domestic students; for spring admission, 8/1 priority date for domestic students. Application fee: $60. Electronic applications accepted. *Expenses:* Tuition: Full-time $28,630. One-time fee: $50 full-time. *Financial support:* In 2003–04, 9 students received support, including 1 fellowship with full tuition reimbursement available, 8 research assistantships with full tuition reimbursements available; teaching assistantships with full tuition reimbursements available, institutionally sponsored loans, traineeships, health care benefits, tuition waivers (full and partial), and unspecified assistantships also available. Financial award applicants required to submit FAFSA. *Faculty research:* Applied climatology, climate dynamics, statistical meteorology/climatology, synoptic meteorology, upper atmospheric science. *Unit head:* Director of Graduate Studies, 607-255-3034, Fax: 607-255-2106, E-mail: atmscigradfield@cornell.edu. *Application contact:* Graduate Field Assistant, 607-255-3034, Fax: 607-255-2106, E-mail: atmscigradfield@cornell.edu.

Creighton University, Graduate School, College of Arts and Sciences, Program in Atmospheric Sciences, Omaha, NE 68178-0001. Offers MS. *Degree requirements:* For master's, thesis. *Entrance requirements:* For master's, GRE General Test. Additional exam requirements/recommendations for international students: Required—TOEFL.

Georgia Institute of Technology, Graduate Studies and Research, College of Sciences, School of Earth and Atmospheric Sciences, Atlanta, GA 30332-0001. Offers atmospheric chemistry and air pollution (MS, PhD); atmospheric dynamics and climate (MS, PhD); geochemistry (MS, PhD); hydrologic cycle (MS, PhD); ocean sciences (MS, PhD); solid-earth and environmental geophysics (PhD); solid-earth and environmental geophysics (MS). Part-time programs available. *Students:* 80 full-time (40 women); includes 39 minority (5 African Americans, 31 Asian Americans or Pacific Islanders, 3 Hispanic Americans). 143 applicants, 18% accepted, 15 enrolled. In 2003, 14 master's, 6 doctorates awarded. Terminal master's awarded for partial completion of doctoral program. *Median time to degree:* Of those who began their doctoral program in fall 1995, 78% received their degree in 8 years or less. *Degree requirements:* For master's, thesis or alternative; for doctorate, thesis/dissertation, comprehensive exam. *Entrance requirements:* For master's and doctorate, GRE General Test, minimum GPA of 2.7. Additional exam requirements/recommendations for international students: Required—TOEFL (minimum score 550 paper-based; 213 computer-based). *Application deadline:* For fall admission, 1/15 priority date for domestic students, 1/15 priority date for international students; for spring admission, 1/1 for domestic students. Applications are processed on a rolling basis. Application fee: $50. *Expenses:* Tuition, state resident: part-time $1,925 per semester. Tuition, nonresident: part-time $7,700 per semester. Required fees: $434 per semester. Full-time tuition and fees vary according to program. *Financial support:* In 2003–04, 3 fellowships, 52 research assistantships (averaging $20,000 per year), 8 teaching assistantships were awarded. Career-related internships or fieldwork, Federal Work-Study, and institutionally sponsored loans also available. Financial award application deadline: 2/15. *Faculty research:* Geophysics, atmospheric chemistry, atmospheric dynamics, seismology. Total annual research expenditures: $5 million. *Unit head:* Dr. Judith A. Curry, Chair, 404-894-3948, Fax: 404-894-5638. *Application contact:* Derek M. Cunnold, Graduate Coordinator, 404-894-3814, Fax: 404-894-5638, E-mail: cunnold@eas.gatech.edu.

See in-depth description on page 237.

Howard University, Graduate School of Arts and Sciences, Department of Chemistry, Washington, DC 20059-0002. Offers analytical chemistry (MS, PhD); atmospheric (MS, PhD); biochemistry (MS, PhD); environmental (MS, PhD); inorganic chemistry (MS, PhD); organic chemistry (MS, PhD); physical chemistry (MS, PhD); polymer chemistry (MS, PhD). Part-time programs available. *Degree requirements:* For master's, one foreign language, thesis, teaching experience, comprehensive exam, registration; for doctorate, 2 foreign languages, thesis/dissertation, teaching experience, comprehensive exam, registration. *Entrance requirements:* For master's, GRE General Test, minimum GPA of 2.7; for doctorate, GRE General Test, minimum GPA of 3.0. *Faculty research:* Stratospheric aerosols, liquid crystals, polymer coatings, terrestrial and extraterrestrial atmospheres, amidogen reaction.

Howard University, Graduate School of Arts and Sciences and School of Engineering and Computer Science, Program in Atmospheric Sciences, Washington, DC 20059-0002. Offers MS, PhD. Part-time programs available. *Faculty:* 7 full-time (1 woman). *Students:* 15 full-time (8 women); includes 13 minority (11 African Americans, 2 Hispanic Americans), 2 international. Average age 25. 20 applicants, 20% accepted, 4 enrolled. In 2003, 2 degrees awarded. Terminal master's awarded for partial completion of doctoral program. *Degree requirements:* For master's, thesis, comprehensive exam; for doctorate, one foreign language, thesis/dissertation, comprehensive exam. *Entrance requirements:* For master's, GRE General Test, minimum GPA of 3.0; for doctorate, GRE General Test, minimum GPA of 3.2. Additional exam requirements/recommendations for international students: Required—TOEFL (minimum score 550 paper-based; 213 computer-based). *Application deadline:* For fall admission, 4/1 for domestic students; for spring admission, 11/1 for domestic students. Applications are processed on a rolling basis. Application fee: $45. *Financial support:* In 2003–04, 5 fellowships with full tuition reimbursements (averaging $15,000 per year), research assistantships with full tuition reimbursements (averaging $16,000 per year) were awarded. Career-related internships or fieldwork, scholarships/grants, tuition waivers (partial), and unspecified assistantships also available. Financial award application deadline: 4/1. *Faculty research:* Atmospheric chemistry, climate, ionospheric physics, gravity waves, aerosols, extraterrestrial atmospheres, turbulence. Total annual research expenditures: $550,000. *Unit head:* Dr. Vernon R. Morris, Director, 202-806-5450, Fax: 202-806-4430, E-mail: vmorris@howard.edu. *Application contact:* Dr. Everette Joseph, Director, 202-806-6256, Fax: 202-806-5830, E-mail: ejoseph@howard.edu.

Massachusetts Institute of Technology, School of Science, Department of Earth, Atmospheric, and Planetary Sciences, Cambridge, MA 02139-4307. Offers atmospheric chemistry (PhD, Sc D); atmospheric science (SM, PhD, Sc D); climate physics and chemistry (PhD, Sc D); earth and planetary sciences (SM); geochemistry (PhD, Sc D); geology (PhD, Sc D); geophysics (PhD, Sc D); geosystems (SM); oceanography (SM, PhD, Sc D); planetary sciences (PhD, Sc D). *Faculty:* 37 full-time (3 women). *Students:* 147 full-time (61 women); includes 9 minority (4 Asian Americans or Pacific Islanders, 5 Hispanic Americans), 48 international. Average age 27. 176 applicants, 49% accepted, 31 enrolled. In 2003, 8 master's, 19 doctorates awarded. Terminal master's awarded for partial completion of doctoral program. *Degree requirements:* For master's, thesis/dissertation; for doctorate, thesis/dissertation, comprehensive exam. *Entrance requirements:* For master's, GRE General Test, GRE Subject Test (joint MIT/WHOI program); for doctorate, GRE General Test, GRE Subject Test (chemistry or physics for planetary science program). Additional exam requirements/recommendations for international students: Required—TOEFL (minimum score 577 paper-based; 233 computer-based). *Application deadline:* For fall admission, 1/5 for domestic students, 1/5 for international students; for spring admission, 11/1 for domestic students, 11/1 for international students. Application fee: $70. Electronic applications accepted. *Expenses:* Tuition: Full-time $29,400. Required fees: $200. *Financial support:* In 2003–04, 113 students received support, including 25 fellowships with tuition reimbursements available, 70 research assistantships with tuition reimbursements available (averaging $23,760 per year), 21 teaching assistantships with tuition reimbursements available (averaging $18,270 per year); Federal Work-Study, institutionally sponsored loans, scholarships/grants, health care benefits, and unspecified assistantships also available. *Faculty research:* Evolution of main features of the planetary system; origin, composition, structure, and state of the atmospheres, oceans, surfaces, and interiors of planets; dynamics of planets and satellite motions. Total annual research expenditures: $19.1 million. *Unit head:* Prof. Maria Zuber, 617-253-0149, Fax: 617-253-8298, E-mail: mtz@mit.edu. *Application contact:* Carol Sprague, Administrative Assistant, 617-253-3381, Fax: 617-253-8298, E-mail: eapsinfo@mit.edu.

McGill University, Faculty of Graduate and Postdoctoral Studies, Faculty of Science, Department of Atmospheric and Oceanic Sciences, Montréal, QC H3A 2T5, Canada. Offers atmospheric science (M Sc, PhD); physical oceanography (M Sc, PhD). *Faculty:* 11 full-time (1 woman). *Students:* 35 full-time, 2 part-time. Average age 24. 62 applicants, 48% accepted, 12 enrolled. In 2003, 5 master's, 5 doctorates awarded. Terminal master's awarded for partial completion of doctoral program. *Degree requirements:* For master's and doctorate, thesis/dissertation. *Entrance requirements:* For master's, GRE General Test, minimum GPA of 3.2 during last 2 years of full-time study or 3.0 overall; for doctorate, GRE, master's degree in meteorology or related field. Additional exam requirements/recommendations for international students: Required—TOEFL. *Application deadline:* For fall admission, 7/1 for domestic students; for winter admission, 12/1 for domestic students. Applications are processed on a rolling basis. Application fee: $60 Canadian dollars. Tuition, area resident: Full-time $1,668. *Expenses:* Tuition, state resident: full-time $4,173. Tuition, nonresident: full-time $9,468. Required fees: $1,081. *Financial support:* In 2003–04, research assistantships (averaging $16,000 per year), teaching assistantships (averaging $1,000 per year) were awarded. Fellowships, tuition waivers (partial) also available. Financial award application deadline: 7/1. *Faculty research:* Dynamic meteorology and climate dynamics, synoptic meteorology, mesometeorology, radar meteorology, physical oceanography. *Unit head:* Prof. John Gyakum, Chair, 514-398-6076, Fax: 514-398-6115, E-mail: gyakum@zephyr.meteo.mcgill.ca. *Application contact:* Prof. H. G. Leighton, Chair, Graduate Admissions, 514-398-3766, Fax: 514-398-6115, E-mail: gradinfo@zephyr.meteo.mcgill.ca.

New Mexico Institute of Mining and Technology, Graduate Studies, Department of Physics, Socorro, NM 87801. Offers astrophysics (MS, PhD); atmospheric physics (MS, PhD);

instrumentation (MS); mathematical physics (PhD). *Faculty:* 14 full-time (2 women), 19 part-time/adjunct (2 women). *Students:* 19 full-time (5 women), 2 part-time (1 woman); includes 2 minority (1 Asian American or Pacific Islander, 1 Hispanic American), 3 international. Average age 28. 21 applicants, 5 enrolled. In 2003, 1 master's, 3 doctorates awarded. *Degree requirements:* For master's, thesis optional; for doctorate, thesis/dissertation. *Entrance requirements:* For master's, GRE General Test; for doctorate, GRE General Test, GRE Subject Test. Additional exam requirements/recommendations for international students: Required—TOEFL (minimum score 540 paper-based; 207 computer-based). *Application deadline:* For fall admission, 3/1 for domestic students; for spring admission, 6/1 for domestic students. Applications are processed on a rolling basis. Application fee: $16 ($30 for international students). *Expenses:* Tuition, state resident: full-time $2,276; part-time $126 per credit. Tuition, nonresident: full-time $9,170; part-time $509 per credit. Required fees: $924; $27 per credit. $214 per term. Part-time tuition and fees vary according to course load. *Financial support:* In 2003–04, 10 research assistantships (averaging $14,242 per year), 10 teaching assistantships with full and partial tuition reimbursements (averaging $9,600 per year) were awarded. Fellowships, Federal Work-Study, institutionally sponsored loans, and unspecified assistantships also available. Financial award application deadline: 3/1; financial award applicants required to submit CSS PROFILE or FAFSA. *Faculty research:* Cloud physics, stellar and extragalactic processes. *Unit head:* Dr. Kenneth Minschwaner, Chairman, 505-835-5226, Fax: 505-835-5707, E-mail: krm@kestrel.nmt.edu. *Application contact:* Dr. David B. Johnson, Dean of Graduate Studies, 505-835-5513, Fax: 505-835-5476, E-mail: graduate@nmt.edu.

North Carolina State University, Graduate School, College of Physical and Mathematical Sciences, Department of Marine, Earth, and Atmospheric Sciences, Raleigh, NC 27695. Offers marine, earth, and atmospheric sciences (MS, PhD); meteorology (MS, PhD); oceanography (MS, PhD). *Faculty:* 41 full-time (6 women), 57 part-time/adjunct (4 women). *Students:* 91 full-time (32 women), 16 part-time (3 women); includes 4 minority (2 African Americans, 1 Asian American or Pacific Islander, 1 Hispanic American), 17 international. Average age 30. 106 applicants, 50% accepted. In 2003, 19 master's, 6 doctorates awarded. Terminal master's awarded for partial completion of doctoral program. *Median time to degree:* Master's–2.7 years full-time; doctorate–5 years full-time. Of those who began their doctoral program in fall 1995, 90% received their degree in 8 years or less. *Degree requirements:* For master's, thesis (for some programs), final oral exam; for doctorate, thesis/dissertation, final oral exam, preliminary oral and written exams, comprehensive exam, registration. *Entrance requirements:* For master's, GRE General Test, minimum GPA of 3.0; for doctorate, GRE General Test, GRE Subject Test for disciplines in biological oceanography and geology, minimum GPA of 3.0. Additional exam requirements/recommendations for international students: Required—TOEFL (minimum score 550 paper-based). *Application deadline:* For fall admission, 6/25 for domestic students, 3/1 for international students; for spring admission, 11/25 for domestic students, 7/15 for international students. Applications are processed on a rolling basis. Application fee: $45. Electronic applications accepted. *Expenses:* Tuition, state resident: part-time $396 per hour. Tuition, nonresident: part-time $1,895 per hour. *Financial support:* In 2003–04, 76 students received support, including 1 fellowship with tuition reimbursement available (averaging $10,397 per year), 47 research assistantships with tuition reimbursements available (averaging $5,959 per year), 32 teaching assistantships with tuition reimbursements available (averaging $6,594 per year); institutionally sponsored loans and unspecified assistantships also available. Financial award application deadline: 3/1. *Faculty research:* Boundary layer and air quality meteorology; climate and mesoscale dynamics; biological, chemical, geological, and physical oceanography; hard rock, soft rock, environmental, and paleogeology. Total annual research expenditures: $5.6 million. *Unit head:* Dr. John C. Fountain, Head, 919-515-3717, Fax: 919-515-7802, E-mail: fountain@ncsu.edu. *Application contact:* Dr. Gerald S. Janowitz, Director of Graduate Programs, 919-515-7837, Fax: 919-515-7802, E-mail: janowitz@ncsu.edu.

See in-depth description on page 247.

The Ohio State University, Graduate School, College of Social and Behavioral Sciences, Department of Geography, Program in Atmospheric Sciences, Columbus, OH 43210. Offers MS, PhD. *Faculty:* 11. *Students:* 9 full-time (4 women), 4 part-time (1 woman), 2 international. 33 applicants, 30% accepted. In 2003, 4 master's, 2 doctorates awarded. *Degree requirements:* For master's and doctorate, thesis/dissertation. *Entrance requirements:* For master's and doctorate, GRE General Test, minimum GPA of 3.0. Additional exam requirements/recommendations for international students: Required—TOEFL. *Application deadline:* For fall admission, 8/15 for domestic students. Applications are processed on a rolling basis. Application fee: $40 ($50 for international students). *Expenses:* Tuition, state resident: full-time $7,233. Tuition, nonresident: full-time $18,489. *Financial support:* Fellowships, research assistantships, teaching assistantships, Federal Work-Study and institutionally sponsored loans available. Support available to part-time students. *Faculty research:* Climatology, aeronomy, solar-terrestrial physics, air environment. *Unit head:* Dr. Jay S. Hobgood, Director, 614-292-3999, Fax: 614-292-6213, E-mail: hobgood.1@osu.edu. *Application contact:* Dr. Edward J. Behrman, Graduate Studies Committee Chair, 614-292-9485, E-mail: behrman.1@osu.edu.

Oregon State University, Graduate School, College of Oceanic and Atmospheric Sciences, Program in Atmospheric Sciences, Corvallis, OR 97331. Offers MA, MS, PhD. *Students:* 7 full-time (2 women), 1 part-time, 3 international. Average age 37. In 2003, 3 degrees awarded. Terminal master's awarded for partial completion of doctoral program. *Degree requirements:* For master's, variable foreign language requirement, thesis, qualifying exams; for doctorate, thesis/dissertation, qualifying exams. *Entrance requirements:* For master's and doctorate, GRE General Test, minimum GPA of 3.0 in last 90 hours. Additional exam requirements/recommendations for international students: Required—TOEFL. *Application deadline:* For fall admission, 2/1 for domestic students. Applications are processed on a rolling basis. Application fee: $50. *Expenses:* Tuition, state resident: full-time $8,139; part-time $301 per credit. Tuition, nonresident: full-time $14,376; part-time $532 per credit. Required fees: $1,227. *Financial support:* Fellowships, research assistantships, teaching assistantships, career-related internships or fieldwork, Federal Work-Study, and institutionally sponsored loans available. Support available to part-time students. Financial award application deadline: 2/1. *Faculty research:* Planetary atmospheres, boundary layer dynamics, climate, statistical meteorology, satellite meteorology, atmospheric chemistry. *Unit head:* Dr. Mike Unsworth, Director, 541-737-5428, Fax: 541-737-2540, E-mail: unswortm@oce.orst.edu. *Application contact:* Irma Delson, Assistant Director, Student Services, 541-737-5189, Fax: 541-737-2064, E-mail: student_adviser@oce.orst.edu.

Princeton University, Graduate School, Department of Geosciences, Program in Atmospheric and Oceanic Sciences, Princeton, NJ 08544-1019. Offers PhD. *Students:* 8 full-time (3 women), 7 international. 22 applicants, 32% accepted, 2 enrolled. *Median time to degree:* Doctorate–6.67 years full-time. *Degree requirements:* For doctorate, one foreign language, thesis/dissertation. *Entrance requirements:* For doctorate, GRE General Test, GRE Subject Test. Additional exam requirements/recommendations for international students: Required—TOEFL (minimum score 600 paper-based; 250 computer-based). *Application deadline:* For fall admission, 12/31 for domestic students, 12/1 for international students. Application fee: $80 ($55 for international students). Electronic applications accepted. *Expenses:* Tuition: Full-time $29,910. Required fees: $810. *Financial support:* Fellowships with full tuition reimbursements, research assistantships with full tuition reimbursements, teaching assistantships with full tuition reimbursements, Federal Work-Study and institutionally sponsored loans available. Financial award application deadline: 1/2. *Faculty research:* Climate dynamics, middle atmosphere dynamics and chemistry, oceanic circulation, marine geochemistry, numerical modeling. *Unit head:* Prof. Anand H. Gnadadesikan, Director of Graduate Studies, 609-258-5062, Fax: 609-258-2850, E-mail: ganana@princeton.edu. *Application contact:* Director of Graduate Admissions, 609-258-3034.

Purdue University, Graduate School, School of Science, Department of Earth and Atmospheric Sciences, West Lafayette, IN 47907. Offers MS, PhD. *Degree requirements:* For master's, thesis; for doctorate, one foreign language, thesis/dissertation. *Entrance requirements:* For master's and doctorate, GRE General Test. Additional exam requirements/recommendations for international students: Required—TOEFL. Electronic applications accepted. *Faculty research:* Geology, geophysics, hydrogeology, paleoclimatology, environmental science.

Rutgers, The State University of New Jersey, New Brunswick/Piscataway, Graduate School, Program in Environmental Sciences, New Brunswick, NJ 08901-1281. Offers air resources (MS, PhD); aquatic biology (MS, PhD); aquatic chemistry (MS, PhD); atmospheric science (MS, PhD); chemistry and physics of aerosol and hydrosol systems (MS, PhD); environmental chemistry (MS, PhD); environmental microbiology (MS, PhD); environmental toxicology (PhD); exposure assessment (PhD); fate and effects of pollutants (MS, PhD); pollution prevention and control (MS, PhD); water and wastewater treatment (MS, PhD); water resources (MS, PhD). *Faculty:* 62 full-time (12 women), 6 part-time/adjunct (1 woman). *Students:* 50 full-time (23 women), 57 part-time (27 women); includes 7 minority (1 African American, 4 Asian Americans or Pacific Islanders, 2 Hispanic Americans), 37 international. Average age 32. 110 applicants, 11% accepted, 8 enrolled. In 2003, 9 master's, 4 doctorates awarded. Terminal master's awarded for partial completion of doctoral program. *Degree requirements:* For master's, thesis or alternative, oral final exam, comprehensive exam; for doctorate, thesis/dissertation, thesis defense, qualifying exam, comprehensive exam. *Entrance requirements:* For master's and doctorate, GRE General Test. Additional exam requirements/recommendations for international students: Required—TOEFL. *Application deadline:* For fall admission, 3/1 for domestic students; for spring admission, 11/1 for domestic students. Applications are processed on a rolling basis. Application fee: $50. Electronic applications accepted. *Expenses:* Tuition, state resident: full-time $10,030. Tuition, nonresident: full-time $14,202. *Financial support:* In 2003–04, 10 fellowships with full tuition reimbursements (averaging $19,000 per year), 34 research assistantships with full tuition reimbursements (averaging $16,400 per year), 3 teaching assistantships with full tuition reimbursements (averaging $14,300 per year) were awarded. Career-related internships or fieldwork and Federal Work-Study also available. Financial award application deadline: 1/15; financial award applicants required to submit FAFSA. *Faculty research:* Atmospheric sciences; biological waste treatment; contaminant fate and transport; exposure assessment; air, soil and water quality. Total annual research expenditures: $5.7 million. *Unit head:* Dr. Barbara Turpin, Director, 732-932-9540, Fax: 732-932-8644, E-mail: env_gradpgm@envsci.rutgers.edu. *Application contact:* Dr. Paul J. Lioy, Graduate Admissions Committee, 732-932-0150, Fax: 732-445-0116, E-mail: plioy@eohsi.rutgers.edu.

South Dakota School of Mines and Technology, Graduate Division, Department of Atmospheric Sciences, Rapid City, SD 57701-3995. Offers MS, PhD. Part-time programs available. *Faculty:* 7 part-time/adjunct (0 women). *Students:* 11 full-time (3 women), 4 part-time (1 woman). In 2003, 2 master's, 2 doctorates awarded. *Degree requirements:* For master's and doctorate, thesis/dissertation. *Entrance requirements:* Additional exam requirements/recommendations for international students: Required—TOEFL, TWE. *Application deadline:* For fall admission, 6/15 for domestic students; for spring admission, 10/15 for domestic students. Applications are processed on a rolling basis. Application fee: $35. Electronic applications accepted. *Expenses:* Tuition, state resident: part-time $109 per credit hour. Tuition, nonresident: part-time $323 per credit hour. Required fees: $100 per credit hour. *Financial support:* In 2003–04, 2 fellowships (averaging $1,000 per year), 1 research assistantship with partial tuition reimbursement (averaging $15,300 per year) were awarded. Teaching assistantships with partial tuition reimbursements, Federal Work-Study and institutionally sponsored loans also available. Support available to part-time students. Financial award application deadline: 5/15. *Faculty research:* Hailstorm observations and numerical modeling, microbursts and lightning, radiative transfer, remote sensing. Total annual research expenditures: $1.3 million. *Unit head:* Dr. Andrew Detwiler, Chair, 605-394-2291. *Application contact:* Brenda Brown, Secretary, 800-454-8162 Ext. 2493, Fax: 605-394-5360, E-mail: graduate_admissions@silver.sdsmt.edu.

South Dakota School of Mines and Technology, Graduate Division, Joint PhD Program in Atmospheric, Environmental, and Water Resources, Rapid City, SD 57701-3995. Offers PhD. *Students:* 3 full-time (1 woman), 9 part-time (2 women); includes 1 minority (American Indian/Alaska Native), 3 international. In 2003, 2 degrees awarded. *Degree requirements:* For doctorate, thesis/dissertation. *Entrance requirements:* For doctorate, GRE General Test, GRE Subject Test. Additional exam requirements/recommendations for international students: Required—TOEFL, TWE. *Application deadline:* For fall admission, 6/15 for domestic students; for spring admission, 10/15 for domestic students. Applications are processed on a rolling basis. Application fee: $35. Electronic applications accepted. *Expenses:* Tuition, state resident: part-time $109 per credit hour. Tuition, nonresident: part-time $323 per credit hour. Required fees: $100 per credit hour. *Financial support:* In 2003–04, 5 research assistantships with partial tuition reimbursements (averaging $23,500 per year) were awarded; teaching assistantships with partial tuition reimbursements *Unit head:* Dr. Andrew Detwiler, Chair, 605-394-2291. *Application contact:* Brenda Brown, Secretary, 800-454-8162 Ext. 2493, Fax: 605-394-5360, E-mail: graduate_admissions@silver.sdsmt.edu.

See in-depth description on page 313.

South Dakota State University, Graduate School, College of Engineering, Joint PhD Program in Atmospheric, Environmental, and Water Resources, Brookings, SD 57007. Offers PhD. Postbaccalaureate distance learning degree programs offered (minimal on-campus study). *Degree requirements:* For doctorate, thesis/dissertation, preliminary oral and written exams. *Entrance requirements:* Additional exam requirements/recommendations for international students: Required—TOEFL (minimum score 525 paper-based). *Expenses:* Contact institution.

See in-depth description on page 313.

Stony Brook University, State University of New York, Graduate School, Institute for Terrestrial and Planetary Atmospheres, Stony Brook, NY 11794. Offers PhD. *Application deadline:* For fall admission, 3/1 for domestic students. Application fee: $50. *Expenses:* Tuition, state resident: full-time $6,900; part-time $288 per credit hour. Tuition, nonresident: full-time $10,500; part-time $438 per credit hour. Required fees: $22. *Financial support:* Fellowships available. *Unit head:* Minghua Zhang, Director, 631-632-8318.

See in-depth description on page 317.

Stony Brook University, State University of New York, Graduate School, Marine Sciences Research Center, Program in Marine and Atmospheric Sciences, Stony Brook, NY 11794. Offers MS, PhD. Evening/weekend programs available. *Faculty:* 32 full-time (5 women), 1 (woman) part-time/adjunct. *Students:* 107 full-time (60 women), 8 part-time (6 women); includes 9 minority (3 African Americans, 2 Asian Americans or Pacific Islanders, 4 Hispanic Americans), 38 international. Average age 29. 125 applicants, 53% accepted. In 2003, 13 master's, 5 doctorates awarded. *Degree requirements:* For doctorate, one foreign language, thesis/dissertation, comprehensive exam. *Entrance requirements:* For doctorate, GRE General Test, minimum graduate GPA of 3.0. Additional exam requirements/recommendations for international students: Required—TOEFL. *Application deadline:* For fall admission, 1/15 for domestic students. Application fee: $50. *Expenses:* Tuition, state resident: full-time $6,900; part-time $288 per credit hour. Tuition, nonresident: full-time $10,500; part-time $438 per credit hour. Required fees: $22. *Financial support:* In 2003–04, 21 fellowships, 51 research assistantships, 33 teaching assistantships were awarded. Career-related internships or fieldwork also available. Total annual research expenditures: $9.2 million. *Application contact:* Dr. Henry Bokuniewicz, Director, 631-632-8681, Fax: 631-632-8200, E-mail: hbokuniewicz@ccmail.sunysb.edu.

See in-depth description on page 287.

Texas Tech University, Graduate School, College of Arts and Sciences, Department of Geosciences, Lubbock, TX 79409. Offers atmospheric sciences (MS); geoscience (MS, PhD). Part-time programs available. *Faculty:* 14 full-time (2 women). *Students:* 40 full-time (18 women), 9 part-time (2 women); includes 1 minority (African American), 6 international. Average age 29. 40 applicants, 63% accepted, 15 enrolled. In 2003, 12 master's, 3 doctor-

Atmospheric Sciences

Texas Tech University (continued)

ates awarded. *Degree requirements:* For master's and doctorate, thesis/dissertation. *Entrance requirements:* For master's and doctorate, GRE General Test. Additional exam requirements/recommendations for international students: Required—TOEFL (minimum score 550 paper-based; 213 computer-based). *Application deadline:* Applications are processed on a rolling basis. Application fee: $50 ($60 for international students). Electronic applications accepted. *Expenses:* Tuition, state resident: full-time $3,312. Tuition, nonresident: full-time $8,976. Required fees: $1,745. Tuition and fees vary according to program. *Financial support:* In 2003–04, 24 students received support, including 12 research assistantships with partial tuition reimbursements available (averaging $13,090 per year), 22 teaching assistantships with partial tuition reimbursements available (averaging $14,157 per year); Federal Work-Study and institutionally sponsored loans also available. Support available to part-time students. Financial award application deadline: 5/1; financial award applicants required to submit FAFSA. *Faculty research:* Ophiolites and oceanic lower crust; petroleum geology; tectonics and arc magnetism; aqueous and environmental geochemistry; near-ground high wind phenomenon (hurricanes and severe storms). Total annual research expenditures: $467,442. *Unit head:* Dr. James Barrick, Chairman, 806-742-3102, Fax: 806-742-0100, E-mail: jim.barrick@ttu.edu. *Application contact:* Graduate Adviser, 806-742-3102, Fax: 806-742-0100.

Université du Québec à Montréal, Graduate Programs, Programs in Atmospheric Sciences and Meteorology, Montréal, QC H3C 3P8, Canada. Offers atmospheric sciences (M Sc); meteorology (PhD, Diploma). Part-time programs available. *Degree requirements:* For master's, thesis. *Entrance requirements:* For master's and Diploma, appropriate bachelor's degree or equivalent and proficiency in French; for doctorate, appropriate master's degree or equivalent and proficiency in French.

University at Albany, State University of New York, College of Arts and Sciences, Department of Earth and Atmospheric Sciences, Albany, NY 12222-0001. Offers atmospheric science (MS, PhD); geology (MS, PhD). Evening/weekend programs available. *Students:* 36 full-time (15 women), 8 part-time (3 women). Average age 29. 63 applicants, 41% accepted, 16 enrolled. In 2003, 8 master's, 4 doctorates awarded. *Degree requirements:* For master's, one foreign language, thesis, comprehensive exam; for doctorate, 2 foreign languages, thesis/dissertation, oral exams, comprehensive exam. *Entrance requirements:* For master's and doctorate, GRE General Test. Additional exam requirements/recommendations for international students: Required—TOEFL (minimum score 550 paper-based; 213 computer-based). *Application deadline:* For fall admission, 6/1 for domestic students, 5/1 for international students; for spring admission, 11/1 for domestic students, 11/11 for international students. Applications are processed on a rolling basis. Application fee: $50. Electronic applications accepted. *Expenses:* Tuition, state resident: part-time $288 per credit. Tuition, nonresident: part-time $438 per credit. Required fees: $495 per semester. *Financial support:* Fellowships, research assistantships, teaching assistantships, minority assistantships available. Financial award application deadline: 3/1. *Unit head:* Dr. Vincent Idone, Chair, 518-442-4466.

The University of Alabama in Huntsville, School of Graduate Studies, College of Science, Department of Atmospheric and Environmental Science, Huntsville, AL 35899. Offers MS, PhD. Part-time and evening/weekend programs available. *Faculty:* 6 full-time (0 women), 7 part-time/adjunct (1 woman). *Students:* 30 full-time (13 women), 5 part-time (4 women); includes 2 minority (1 African American, 1 Hispanic American), 13 international. Average age 27. 23 applicants, 91% accepted, 10 enrolled. In 2003, 3 master's, 2 doctorates awarded. *Degree requirements:* For master's, thesis or alternative, oral and written exams, comprehensive exam, registration; for doctorate, thesis/dissertation, oral and written exams, comprehensive exam, registration. *Entrance requirements:* For master's and doctorate, GRE General Test, minimum GPA of 3.0. Additional exam requirements/recommendations for international students: Required—TOEFL (minimum score 550 paper-based; 213 computer-based). *Application deadline:* For fall admission, 5/30 priority date for domestic students, 2/30 priority date for international students; for spring admission, 10/10 priority date for domestic students, 7/10 priority date for international students. Applications are processed on a rolling basis. Application fee: $35. *Expenses:* Tuition, state resident: full-time $5,168; part-time $211 per hour. Tuition, nonresident: full-time $10,620; part-time $447 per hour. Tuition and fees vary according to course load. *Financial support:* In 2003–04, 27 students received support, including 26 research assistantships with full and partial tuition reimbursements available (averaging $12,473 per year), 1 teaching assistantship with full and partial tuition reimbursement available (averaging $12,600 per year); fellowships with full and partial tuition reimbursements available, career-related internships or fieldwork, Federal Work-Study, institutionally sponsored loans, scholarships/grants, health care benefits, tuition waivers (full and partial), and unspecified assistantships also available. Support available to part-time students. Financial award application deadline: 4/1; financial award applicants required to submit FAFSA. Total annual research expenditures: $648,082. *Unit head:* Dr. Ronald Welch, Chair, 256-961-7754, Fax: 256-961-7755, E-mail: ron.welch@atmos.uah.edu.

University of Alaska Fairbanks, College of Science, Engineering and Mathematics, Department of Physics, Fairbanks, AK 99775-7520. Offers atmospheric science (MS, PhD); physics (MS, PhD); space physics (MS, PhD). Part-time programs available. Terminal master's awarded for partial completion of doctoral program. *Degree requirements:* For master's, thesis or alternative, comprehensive exam, registration; for doctorate, one foreign language, thesis/dissertation, comprehensive exam, registration. *Entrance requirements:* For master's and doctorate, GRE General Test, GRE Subject Test. Additional exam requirements/recommendations for international students: Required—TOEFL. Electronic applications accepted. *Faculty research:* Atmospheric and ionospheric radar studies, space plasma theory, magnetospheric dynamics, space weather and auroral studies, turbulence and complex systems.

University of Alaska Fairbanks, College of Science, Engineering and Mathematics, Program in Atmospheric Science, Fairbanks, AK 99775-7520. Offers MS, PhD. Part-time programs available. Terminal master's awarded for partial completion of doctoral program. *Degree requirements:* For master's, thesis or alternative, comprehensive exam, registration; for doctorate, thesis/dissertation, comprehensive exam, registration. *Entrance requirements:* For master's, GRE General Test. Additional exam requirements/recommendations for international students: Required—TOEFL. Electronic applications accepted. *Faculty research:* Sea ice, climate modeling, atmospheric chemistry, global change, cloud and aerosol physics.

The University of Arizona, Graduate College, College of Science, Department of Atmospheric Sciences, Tucson, AZ 85721. Offers MS, PhD. *Faculty:* 9 full-time (1 woman). *Students:* 18 full-time (10 women), 3 part-time (2 women); includes 4 minority (2 African Americans, 2 Asian Americans or Pacific Islanders), 7 international. Average age 30. 29 applicants, 14% accepted, 4 enrolled. In 2003, 2 master's awarded, leading to continued full-time study 50%, government 50%; 2 doctorates awarded, leading to university research/teaching 50%, government 50%. *Median time to degree:* Master's–2 years full-time; doctorate–3 years full-time. Of those who began their doctoral program in fall 1995, 100% received their degree in 8 years or less. *Degree requirements:* For master's, thesis or alternative, registration; for doctorate, thesis/dissertation, comprehensive exam, registration. *Entrance requirements:* For master's and doctorate, GRE General Test. Additional exam requirements/recommendations for international students: Required—TOEFL. *Application deadline:* For fall admission, 4/15 priority date for domestic students, 12/1 priority date for international students. Applications are processed on a rolling basis. Application fee: $50. Electronic applications accepted. *Expenses:* Tuition, state resident: part-time $196 per unit. Tuition, nonresident: part-time $326 per unit. *Financial support:* In 2003–04, 5 fellowships with full and partial tuition reimbursements (averaging $2,000 per year), 8 research assistantships with full and partial tuition reimbursements (averaging $20,763 per year), 7 teaching assistantships with full and partial tuition reimbursements (averaging $20,763 per year) were awarded. Scholarships/grants, health care benefits, and tuition waivers (full) also available. *Faculty research:* Climate dynamics, radiative transfer and remote sensing, atmospheric chemistry, atmosphere dynamics, atmospheric electricity. Total annual research expenditures: $1.6 million. *Unit head:* Dr. Steven L. Mullen, Head, 520-621-6842. *Application contact:* Brian A. Auvine, Coordinator, 520-621-6841, Fax: 520-621-6833, E-mail: baa@atmo.arizona.edu.

The University of British Columbia, Faculty of Graduate Studies, Faculty of Science, Department of Earth and Ocean Sciences, Vancouver, BC V6T 1Z1, Canada. Offers atmospheric science (M Sc, PhD); geological engineering (M Eng, MA Sc, PhD); geological sciences (M Sc, PhD); geophysics (M Sc, MA Sc, PhD); oceanography (M Sc, PhD). *Faculty:* 42 full-time (5 women), 16 part-time/adjunct (0 women). *Students:* 127 full-time (44 women), 1 (woman) part-time. Average age 27. 80 applicants, 41% accepted, 25 enrolled. In 2003, 21 master's, 8 doctorates awarded. *Degree requirements:* For master's, thesis (for some programs); for doctorate, thesis/dissertation, comprehensive exam. *Entrance requirements:* Additional exam requirements/recommendations for international students: Required—TOEFL (minimum score 600 paper-based; 250 computer-based). *Application deadline:* For fall admission, 3/1 for domestic students; for winter admission, 7/1 for domestic students. Applications are processed on a rolling basis. Application fee: $90 Canadian dollars ($150 Canadian dollars for international students). Electronic applications accepted. *Financial support:* In 2003–04, fellowships (averaging $16,000 per year), research assistantships (averaging $13,000 per year), teaching assistantships (averaging $4,500 per year) were awarded. Federal Work-Study, institutionally sponsored loans, scholarships/grants, tuition waivers (full and partial), and unspecified assistantships also available. *Unit head:* Dr. Paul L. Smith, Head, 604-822-6456, Fax: 604-822-6088, E-mail: psmith@cos.ubc.ca. *Application contact:* Alex Allen, Graduate Secretary, 604-822-2713, Fax: 604-822-6088, E-mail: aallen@eos.ubc.ca.

University of California, Davis, Graduate Studies, Graduate Group in Atmospheric Sciences, Davis, CA 95616. Offers MS, PhD. *Faculty:* 23 full-time. *Students:* 17 full-time (5 women); includes 2 minority (1 American Indian/Alaska Native, 1 Hispanic American), 6 international. Average age 28. 27 applicants, 63% accepted, 6 enrolled. In 2003, 1 master's, 2 doctorates awarded. *Degree requirements:* For master's, comprehensive exam or thesis; for doctorate, thesis/dissertation, 3 part qualifying exam. *Entrance requirements:* For master's and doctorate, GRE General Test, minimum GPA of 3.0. Additional exam requirements/recommendations for international students: Required—TOEFL (minimum score 550 paper-based; 213 computer-based). *Application deadline:* For fall admission, 1/15 for domestic students, 1/15 for international students. Application fee: $60. Electronic applications accepted. Tuition, nonresident: full-time $12,245. Required fees: $7,062. *Financial support:* In 2003–04, 15 students received support, including 1 fellowship with full and partial tuition reimbursement available (averaging $1,543 per year), 8 research assistantships with full and partial tuition reimbursements available (averaging $11,096 per year), 3 teaching assistantships with partial tuition reimbursements available (averaging $9,430 per year); career-related internships or fieldwork, Federal Work-Study, institutionally sponsored loans, scholarships/grants, and tuition waivers (full and partial) also available. Financial award application deadline: 1/15; financial award applicants required to submit FAFSA. *Faculty research:* Air quality, biometeorology, climate dynamics, boundary layer large-scale dynamics. Total annual research expenditures: $1.2 million. *Unit head:* Bryan Weare, Graduate Chair, 530-752-3445, E-mail: bcweare@ucdavis.edu. *Application contact:* Noeu Leung, Graduate Staff Adviser, 530-752-1669, Fax: 530-752-1552, E-mail: lawradvising@ucdavis.edu.

University of California, Los Angeles, Graduate Division, College of Letters and Science, Department of Atmospheric Sciences, Los Angeles, CA 90095. Offers MS, PhD. *Students:* 45 (20 women); includes 4 minority (3 Asian Americans or Pacific Islanders, 1 Hispanic American) 20 international. 63 applicants, 81% accepted, 11 enrolled. In 2003, 4 master's, 3 doctorates awarded. *Degree requirements:* For master's, comprehensive exam or thesis; for doctorate, thesis/dissertation, oral and written qualifying exams. *Entrance requirements:* For master's, GRE General Test, minimum GPA of 3.0; for doctorate, GRE General Test, minimum undergraduate GPA of 3.0. *Application deadline:* For fall admission, 12/15 for domestic students. Application fee: $60. Electronic applications accepted. Tuition, nonresident: full-time $12,245. Required fees: $6,318. *Financial support:* In 2003–04, 25 fellowships, 28 research assistantships, 5 teaching assistantships were awarded. Federal Work-Study, institutionally sponsored loans, scholarships/grants, and tuition waivers (full and partial) also available. Financial award application deadline: 3/1. *Unit head:* Dr. Kuo-Nan Liou, Chair, 310-825-5039. *Application contact:* Departmental Office, 310-825-1217, E-mail: lori@atmos.ucla.edu.

University of Chicago, Division of the Physical Sciences, Department of the Geophysical Sciences, Chicago, IL 60637-1513. Offers atmospheric sciences (SM, PhD); earth sciences (SM, PhD); paleobiology (PhD); planetary and space sciences (SM, PhD). *Faculty:* 24 full-time (3 women). *Students:* 29 full-time (13 women); includes 1 minority (Hispanic American), 12 international. Average age 30. 74 applicants, 22% accepted. In 2003, 2 master's, 5 doctorates awarded. Terminal master's awarded for partial completion of doctoral program. *Median time to degree:* Doctorate–6 years full-time. *Entrance requirements:* For master's and doctorate, GRE General Test. Additional exam requirements/recommendations for international students: Required—TOEFL. *Application deadline:* For fall admission, 1/15 for domestic students, 1/15 for international students. Application fee: $55. Electronic applications accepted. *Financial support:* In 2003–04, 29 students received support, including research assistantships with full tuition reimbursements available (averaging $17,196 per year), teaching assistantships with full tuition reimbursements available (averaging $18,096 per year); fellowships, Federal Work-Study, institutionally sponsored loans, scholarships/grants, tuition waivers (partial), and unspecified assistantships also available. Financial award application deadline: 1/15. *Faculty research:* Climatology, evolutionary paleontology, petrology, geochemistry, oceanic sciences. *Unit head:* Dr. David Rowley, Chairman, 773-702-8102, Fax: 773-702-9505. *Application contact:* David J. Leslie, Graduate Student Services Coordinator, 773-702-8180, Fax: 773-702-9505, E-mail: info@geosci.uchicago.edu.

University of Colorado at Boulder, Graduate School, College of Arts and Sciences, Department of Astrophysical and Planetary Sciences, Boulder, CO 80309. Offers astrophysical and geophysical fluid dynamics (MS, PhD); astrophysics (MS, PhD); plasma physics (MS, PhD). *Faculty:* 17 full-time (1 woman). *Students:* 70 full-time (22 women), 21 part-time (8 women); includes 6 minority (3 Asian Americans or Pacific Islanders, 3 Hispanic Americans), 9 international. Average age 28. 103 applicants, 50% accepted. In 2003, 7 master's, 12 doctorates awarded. Terminal master's awarded for partial completion of doctoral program. *Degree requirements:* For master's, thesis or alternative, comprehensive exam; for doctorate, one foreign language, thesis/dissertation. *Entrance requirements:* For master's and doctorate, GRE General Test, GRE Subject Test. *Application deadline:* For fall admission, 3/1 for domestic students. Applications are processed on a rolling basis. Application fee: $50 ($60 for international students). *Expenses:* Tuition, state resident: full-time $2,122. Tuition, nonresident: full-time $9,754. Tuition and fees vary according to course load and program. *Financial support:* In 2003–04, 6 fellowships (averaging $17,509 per year), 23 research assistantships (averaging $15,762 per year), 20 teaching assistantships (averaging $17,065 per year) were awarded. Tuition waivers (full) also available. Support available to part-time students. Financial award application deadline: 2/1. *Faculty research:* Stellar and extragalactic astrophysics cosmology, space astronomy, planetary science. Total annual research expenditures: $30.6 million. *Unit head:* J. Michael Shull, Chair, 303-492-8915, Fax: 303-492-3822, E-mail: mshull@casa.colorado.edu. *Application contact:* Graduate Program Assistant, 303-492-8914, Fax: 303-492-3822, E-mail: admin@aps.colorado.edu.

University of Colorado at Boulder, Graduate School, College of Arts and Sciences, Program in Atmospheric and Oceanic Sciences, Boulder, CO 80309. Offers MS, PhD. *Faculty:* 9 full-time (3 women). *Expenses:* Tuition, state resident: full-time $2,122. Tuition, nonresident: full-time $9,754. Tuition and fees vary according to course load and program. *Faculty research:* Large-scale dynamics of the ocean and the atmosphere; air-sea interaction; radiative transfer and remote sensing of the ocean and the atmosphere; sea ice and its role in climate. Total annual research expenditures: $14.1 million. *Unit head:* Brian Toon, Director, 303-492-1534, Fax: 303-492-3524, E-mail: brian.toon@colorado.edu. *Application contact:* Graduate Secretary, 303-492-6633, Fax: 303-492-3524, E-mail: paosasst@colorado.edu.

University of Delaware, College of Arts and Sciences, Department of Geography, Program in Climatology, Newark, DE 19716. Offers PhD. *Faculty:* 12 full-time (3 women). *Students:* 8 full-time (5 women); includes 1 minority (African American), 1 international. Average age 26. 5 applicants, 0% accepted, 60 enrolled. In 2003, 3 degrees awarded. *Degree requirements:* For doctorate, thesis/dissertation. *Entrance requirements:* For doctorate, GRE General Test. Additional exam requirements/recommendations for international students: Required—TOEFL. *Application deadline:* For fall admission, 2/1 for domestic students, 2/1 for international students. Application fee: $50. Electronic applications accepted. *Expenses:* Tuition, state resident: full-time $5,890; part-time $327 per credit. Tuition, nonresident: full-time $15,420; part-time $857 per credit. Required fees: $968. *Financial support:* In 2003–04, 6 students received support, including 3 fellowships with full tuition reimbursements available (averaging $12,900 per year), 1 research assistantship with full tuition reimbursement available (averaging $12,900 per year), 2 teaching assistantships with full tuition reimbursements available (averaging $12,900 per year) Financial award application deadline: 2/1. *Faculty research:* Physical and applied climatology, synoptic climatology, glaciology, hydroclimatology, cryospheric studies. Total annual research expenditures: $750,000. *Application contact:* Janice Spry, Assistant to the Chair, 302-831-8998, Fax: 302-831-6654, E-mail: jspry@udel.edu.

University of Guelph, Graduate Program Services, Ontario Agricultural College, Department of Land Resource Science, Guelph, ON N1G 2W1, Canada. Offers atmospheric science (M Sc, PhD); environmental and agricultural earth sciences (M Sc, PhD); land resources management (M Sc, PhD); soil science (M Sc, PhD). Part-time programs available. *Faculty:* 19 full-time (5 women), 3 part-time/adjunct (0 women). *Students:* 47 full-time (24 women), 3 part-time; includes 1 African American, 6 Asian Americans or Pacific Islanders, 2 Hispanic Americans, 2 international. Average age 28. 24 applicants, 46% accepted. In 2003, 9 master's, 4 doctorates awarded. *Degree requirements:* For master's and doctorate, thesis/dissertation. *Entrance requirements:* For master's, minimum B- average during previous 2 years; for doctorate, minimum B average during previous 2 years. Additional exam requirements/recommendations for international students: Required—TOEFL (minimum score 550 paper-based; 213 computer-based). *Application deadline:* For fall admission, 7/1 priority date for domestic students, 5/1 priority date for international students; for winter admission, 10/1 for domestic students; for spring admission, 3/1 for domestic students. Applications are processed on a rolling basis. Application fee: $75 Canadian dollars. Electronic applications accepted. Tuition and fees charges are reported in Canadian dollars. Tuition, nonresident: full-time $3,440 Canadian dollars. International tuition: $5,432 Canadian dollars full-time. Required fees: $753 Canadian dollars. *Financial support:* In 2003–04, 30 students received support, including 40 research assistantships (averaging $16,500 Canadian dollars per year), 15 teaching assistantships (averaging $3,800 Canadian dollars per year); fellowships, scholarships/grants also available. *Faculty research:* Soil science, environmental earth science, land resource management. Total annual research expenditures: $2.1 million Canadian dollars. *Unit head:* Dr. S. Hilts, Chairman, 519-824-4120 Ext. 52447, Fax: 519-824-5730, E-mail: shilts@uoguelph.ca. *Application contact:* Dr. T. J. Gillespie, Graduate Coordinator, 519-824-4120 Ext. 54276, Fax: 519-824-5730, E-mail: tgillesp@lrs.uoguelph.ca.

University of Illinois at Urbana–Champaign, Graduate College, College of Liberal Arts and Sciences, Department of Atmospheric Science, Champaign, IL 61820. Offers MS, PhD. *Faculty:* 9 full-time (0 women). *Students:* 41 full-time (15 women); includes 1 minority (Hispanic American), 22 international. 87 applicants, 13% accepted, 10 enrolled. In 2003, 5 degrees awarded. *Degree requirements:* For master's and doctorate, thesis/dissertation. *Entrance requirements:* For master's and doctorate, GRE General Test, minimum GPA of 3.0. *Application deadline:* For fall admission, 2/15 for domestic students. Applications are processed on a rolling basis. Application fee: $40 ($50 for international students). Electronic applications accepted. *Expenses:* Tuition, state resident: full-time $6,692. Tuition, nonresident: full-time $18,692. *Financial support:* In 2003–04, 1 fellowship, 29 research assistantships, 6 teaching assistantships were awarded. Tuition waivers (full and partial) also available. Financial award application deadline: 2/15. *Unit head:* Donald Wuebbles, Head, 217-244-1568, Fax: 217-244-4393. *Application contact:* Karen Garrelts, Office Administrator, 217-333-4752, Fax: 217-244-4393, E-mail: astro@astro.uiuc.edu.

University of Maryland, Baltimore County, Graduate School, Department of Physics, Baltimore, MD 21250. Offers applied physics (MS, PhD), including optics, solid state physics; atmospheric physics (MS, PhD). Part-time programs available. Terminal master's awarded for partial completion of doctoral program. *Degree requirements:* For master's, thesis optional; for doctorate, thesis/dissertation. *Entrance requirements:* For master's and doctorate, GRE General Test, GRE Subject Test, minimum GPA of 3.0. Additional exam requirements/recommendations for international students: Required—TOEFL. Electronic applications accepted. *Expenses:* Tuition, state resident: full-time $7,000. Tuition, nonresident: full-time $11,400. Required fees: $1,440. *Faculty research:* Optics, solid state physics, astrophysics, atmospheric physics.

University of Miami, Graduate School, Rosenstiel School of Marine and Atmospheric Science, Division of Meteorology and Physical Oceanography, Coral Gables, FL 33124. Offers atmospheric science (MS, PhD); physical oceanography (MS, PhD). *Faculty:* 28 full-time (5 women), 18 part-time/adjunct (3 women). *Students:* 33 full-time (12 women), 1 part-time; includes 2 minority (both Hispanic Americans), 15 international. Average age 27. 61 applicants, 20% accepted, 9 enrolled. In 2003, 6 master's awarded, leading to university research/teaching 33%, continued full-time study33%, business/industry 17%, government 17%; 3 doctorates awarded, leading to university research/teaching 100%. Terminal master's awarded for partial completion of doctoral program. *Median time to degree:* Master's–4 years full-time; doctorate–7.2 years full-time. *Degree requirements:* For master's and doctorate, thesis/dissertation, comprehensive exam, registration. *Entrance requirements:* For master's and doctorate, GRE General Test. Additional exam requirements/recommendations for international students: Required—TOEFL (minimum score 550 paper-based; 213 computer-based). *Application deadline:* For fall admission, 1/1 priority date for domestic students, 1/1 priority date for international students. Applications are processed on a rolling basis. Application fee: $50. Electronic applications accepted. *Expenses:* Tuition: Full-time $19,526. *Financial support:* In 2003–04, 28 students received support, including 4 fellowships with tuition reimbursements available (averaging $20,124 per year), 21 research assistantships with tuition reimbursements available (averaging $20,124 per year), 3 teaching assistantships with tuition reimbursements available (averaging $20,124 per year); institutionally sponsored loans and scholarships/grants also available. Financial award application deadline: 3/1; financial award applicants required to submit FAFSA. *Unit head:* Dr. William Johns, Chairperson, 305-361-4057, E-mail: wjohns@rsmas.miami.edu. *Application contact:* Dr. Frank Millero, Associate Dean, 305-361-4155, Fax: 305-361-4771, E-mail: gso@rsmas.miami.edu.

University of Michigan, Horace H. Rackham School of Graduate Studies, College of Engineering, Department of Atmospheric, Oceanic, and Space Sciences, Ann Arbor, MI 48109. Offers atmospheric and space sciences (PhD); geoscience and remote sensing (PhD); space and planetary physics (PhD); space engineering (M Eng). Part-time programs available. *Faculty:* 44 full-time (4 women), 1 part-time/adjunct (0 women). *Students:* 54 full-time (25 women), 1 part-time; includes 2 minority (1 American Indian/Alaska Native, 1 Asian American or Pacific Islander), 21 international. Average age 27. 58 applicants, 38% accepted, 15 enrolled. In 2003, 13 master's, 3 doctorates awarded. Terminal master's awarded for partial completion of doctoral program. *Degree requirements:* For master's, thesis (for some programs); for doctorate, thesis/dissertation, oral defense of dissertation, preliminary exams. *Entrance requirements:* For master's and doctorate, GRE General Test. Additional exam requirements/recommendations for international students: Required—TOEFL. *Application deadline:* For fall admission, 1/15 for domestic students. Applications are processed on a rolling basis. Application fee: $60 ($75 for international students). Electronic applications accepted. *Expenses:* Tuition, state resident: full-time $7,463. Tuition, nonresident: full-time $13,913. Full-time tuition and fees vary according to course load, degree level and program. *Financial support:* In 2003–04, 9 fellowships with tuition reimbursements (averaging $11,669 per year), 36 research assistantships with tuition reimbursements (averaging $14,288 per year), 2 teaching assistantships with tuition reimbursements (averaging $13,570 per year) were awarded. Career-related internships or fieldwork, Federal Work-Study, and institutionally sponsored loans also available. Support available to part-time students. Financial award application deadline: 3/15; financial award applicants required to submit FAFSA. *Faculty research:* Modeling of atmospheric and aerosol chemistry, radiative transfer, remote sensing, atmospheric dynamics, space weather modeling. Total annual research expenditures: $17.5 million. *Unit head:* Tamas Gombosi, Chair, 734-764-7222, Fax: 734-615-4645, E-mail: tamas@umich.edu. *Application contact:* Margaret Reid, Student Services Associate, 734-936-0482, Fax: 734-763-0437, E-mail: aoss.um@umich.edu.

University of Missouri–Columbia, Graduate School, School of Natural Resources, Department of Soil, Environmental, and Atmospheric Sciences, Columbia, MO 65211. Offers atmospheric science (MS); soil science (PhD); spo scoemce (MS); stmospheric science (PhD). *Faculty:* 7 full-time (0 women). *Students:* 12 full-time (3 women), 15 part-time (6 women); includes 1 minority (Asian American or Pacific Islander), 13 international. In 2003, 1 master's, 1 doctorate awarded. *Degree requirements:* For doctorate, thesis/dissertation. *Entrance requirements:* For master's and doctorate, GRE General Test, minimum GPA of 3.0. *Application deadline:* Applications are processed on a rolling basis. Application fee: $45 ($60 for international students). *Expenses:* Tuition, state resident: full-time $5,205. Tuition, nonresident: full-time $14,058. *Financial support:* Fellowships, research assistantships, teaching assistantships, institutionally sponsored loans and scholarships/grants available. *Unit head:* Dr. Anthony Lupo, Director of Graduate Studies, 573-884-1638.

University of Nevada, Reno, Graduate School, College of Science, Interdisciplinary Program in Atmospheric Sciences, Reno, NV 89557. Offers MS, PhD. *Faculty:* 35. *Students:* 20 full-time (7 women), 1 part-time; includes 2 minority (1 African American, 1 Asian American or Pacific Islander), 8 international. Average age 31. In 2003, 6 master's, 3 doctorates awarded. *Entrance requirements:* For master's, GRE (recommended), minimum GPA of 2.75; for doctorate, GRE (recommended), minimum GPA of 3.0. Additional exam requirements/recommendations for international students: Required—TOEFL. *Application deadline:* For fall admission, 3/1 for domestic students; for spring admission, 11/1 for domestic students. Application fee: $60 ($95 for international students). *Expenses:* Tuition, state resident: part-time $119 per credit. Tuition, nonresident: part-time $127 per credit. Required fees: $20 per term. Tuition and fees vary according to course load. *Financial support:* Fellowships, research assistantships, teaching assistantships available. *Unit head:* Dr. Melanie Wetzel, Director, 775-674-7024, Fax: 775-677-3157.

University of New Hampshire, Climate Change Research Center., Durham, NH 03824.

The University of North Carolina at Chapel Hill, Graduate School, School of Public Health, Department of Environmental Sciences and Engineering, Chapel Hill, NC 27599. Offers air, radiation and industrial hygiene (MPH, MS, MSEE, MSPH, PhD); aquatic and atmospheric sciences (MPH, MS, MSPH, PhD); environmental engineering (MPH, MS, MSEE, MSPH, PhD); environmental health sciences (MPH, MS, MSPH, PhD); environmental management and policy (MPH, MS, MSPH, PhD). *Accreditation:* ABET (one or more programs are accredited). *Faculty:* 34 full-time (5 women), 36 part-time/adjunct. *Students:* 153 full-time (85 women); includes 43 minority (11 African Americans, 30 Asian Americans or Pacific Islanders, 2 Hispanic Americans). Average age 26. 234 applicants, 35% accepted, 40 enrolled. In 2003, 38 master's, 13 doctorates awarded. Terminal master's awarded for partial completion of doctoral program. *Median time to degree:* Master's–2 years full-time; doctorate–4.5 years full-time. *Degree requirements:* For master's, thesis (for some programs), research paper, comprehensive exam; for doctorate, thesis/dissertation, comprehensive exam. *Entrance requirements:* For master's and doctorate, GRE General Test, minimum GPA of 3.0. Additional exam requirements/recommendations for international students: Required—TOEFL. *Application deadline:* For fall admission, 1/1 priority date for domestic students, 1/1 priority date for international students; for spring admission, 9/15 for domestic students. Applications are processed on a rolling basis. Application fee: $60. Electronic applications accepted. *Expenses:* Tuition, state resident: full-time $3,163. Tuition, nonresident: full-time $15,161. *Financial support:* In 2003–04, 120 students received support, including 44 fellowships with tuition reimbursements available (averaging $17,230 per year), 63 research assistantships with tuition reimbursements available (averaging $16,264 per year), 13 teaching assistantships with tuition reimbursements available (averaging $11,120 per year); career-related internships or fieldwork, Federal Work-Study, and traineeships also available. Support available to part-time students. Financial award application deadline: 1/1; financial award applicants required to submit FAFSA. *Faculty research:* Air, radiation and industrial hygiene, aquatic and atmospheric sciences, environmental health sciences, environmental management and policy, water resources engineering. Total annual research expenditures: $7.8 million. *Unit head:* , Dr. Casey T. Miller, Chair, 919-966-1024, Fax: 919-966-7911, E-mail: casey_miller@unc.edu. *Application contact:* Jack Whaley, Assistant Registrar, 919-966-3844, Fax: 919-966-7911, E-mail: jack_whaley@unc.edu.

University of North Dakota, Graduate School, John D. Odegard School of Aerospace Sciences, Department of Atmospheric Sciences, Grand Forks, ND 58202. Offers MS. *Faculty:* 7 full-time (0 women), 1 part-time/adjunct (0 women). *Students:* 4 full-time (1 woman), 10 part-time (2 women). 11 applicants, 91% accepted, 4 enrolled. In 2003, 2 degrees awarded. *Degree requirements:* For master's, thesis or alternative, comprehensive exam. *Entrance requirements:* For master's, GRE General Test, minimum GPA of 3.0. Additional exam requirements/recommendations for international students: Required—TOEFL (minimum score 550 paper-based; 213 computer-based). *Application deadline:* For fall admission, 3/1 priority date for domestic students, 3/1 priority date for international students; for spring admission, 10/15 priority date for domestic students, 10/15 priority date for international students. Applications are processed on a rolling basis. Application fee: $35. Electronic applications accepted. *Expenses:* Tuition, state resident: part-time $235 per credit. Tuition, nonresident: part-time $535 per credit. Tuition and fees vary according to course level, course load, program and reciprocity agreements. *Financial support:* In 2003–04, 5 students received support, including 2 research assistantships with full tuition reimbursements available (averaging $9,455 per year), 2 teaching assistantships with full tuition reimbursements available (averaging $9,455 per year); Federal Work-Study, institutionally sponsored loans, scholarships/grants, and tuition waivers (full and partial) also available. Support available to part-time students. Financial award application deadline: 3/15; financial award applicants required to submit FAFSA. *Unit head:* Dr. Leon F. Osborne, Director, 701-777-2184, Fax: 701-777-5032.

University of Washington, Graduate School, College of Arts and Sciences, Department of Atmospheric Sciences, Seattle, WA 98195. Offers MS, PhD. *Degree requirements:* For master's, thesis; for doctorate, thesis/dissertation, qualifying exam. *Entrance requirements:* For master's and doctorate, GRE General Test, minimum GPA of 3.0. Additional exam requirements/recommendations for international students: Required—TOEFL. *Faculty research:* Climate change, synoptic and mesoscale meteorology, atmospheric chemistry, cloud physics, dynamics of the atmosphere.

University of Wisconsin–Madison, Graduate School, College of Letters and Science, Department of Atmospheric and Oceanic Sciences, Madison, WI 53706-1380. Offers MS, PhD. Part-time programs available. *Degree requirements:* For master's, thesis (for some programs); for doctorate, thesis/dissertation. *Entrance requirements:* For master's and doctorate, GRE General Test, minimum GPA of 3.0; previous course work in chemistry, mathematics, and physics. Electronic applications accepted. Tuition, area resident: Full-time $7,593; part-time $476 per credit. Tuition, nonresident: full-time $22,824; part-time $1,430 per credit. Required fees: $292; $38 per credit. Part-time tuition and fees vary according to course load and reciprocity agreements. *Faculty research:* Satellite meteorology, weather systems, global climate change, numerical modeling, atmosphere-ocean interaction.

University of Wyoming, Graduate School, College of Engineering, Department of Atmospheric Science, Laramie, WY 82070. Offers MS, PhD. *Faculty:* 8 full-time (0 women). *Students:* 14 full-time (7 women), 5 part-time, 9 international. Average age 26. 14 applicants, 100% accepted, 7 enrolled. In 2003, 5 master's, 1 doctorate awarded. Terminal master's awarded for partial completion of doctoral program. *Median time to degree:* Master's–2.6 years full-time; doctorate–

Atmospheric Sciences

University of Wyoming (continued)

2.2 years full-time. *Degree requirements:* For master's and doctorate, thesis/dissertation. *Entrance requirements:* For master's and doctorate, GRE General Test, minimum GPA of 3.0. Additional exam requirements/recommendations for international students: Required—TOEFL. *Application deadline:* For fall admission, 4/15 priority date for domestic students, 4/15 priority date for international students. Applications are processed on a rolling basis. Application fee: $40. Electronic applications accepted. *Expenses:* Tuition, state resident: part-time $142 per credit hour. Tuition, nonresident: part-time $408 per credit hour. Required fees: $134 per semester. Tuition and fees vary according to course load, campus/location, program and student level. *Financial support:* In 2003–04, 14 research assistantships with full tuition reimbursements (averaging $17,114 per year) were awarded; career-related internships or fieldwork, Federal Work-Study, and institutionally sponsored loans also available. Support available to part-time students. Financial award application deadline: 3/1. *Faculty research:* Cloud and precipitation processes, mesoscale dynamics, weather modification, winter storms, aircraft instrumentation. Total annual research expenditures: $2.7 million. *Unit head:* Dr. Alfred R. Rodi, Head, 307-766-4945, Fax: 307-766-2635, E-mail: rodi@uwyo.edu. *Application contact:* Susan R. Allen, Graduate Coordinator, 307-766-5352, Fax: 307-766-2635, E-mail: sallen@uwyo.edu.

Meteorology

Columbia University, Graduate School of Arts and Sciences, Program in Climate and Society, New York, NY 10027. Offers MA. Application fee: $75. *Expenses:* Tuition: Full-time $14,820. *Unit head:* Mark A. Cane, Chair, 845-365-8344, Fax: 845-365-8736, E-mail: mcane@ideo.columbia.edu.

Florida Institute of Technology, Graduate Programs, College of Engineering, Department of Marine and Environmental Systems, Melbourne, FL 32901-6975. Offers environmental resource management (MS); environmental science (MS, PhD); meteorology (MS); ocean engineering (MS, PhD); oceanography (MS, PhD), including biological oceanography, chemical oceanography, coastal zone management (MS), geological oceanography, physical oceanography. Part-time programs available. *Faculty:* 16 full-time (1 woman), 4 part-time/adjunct (0 women). *Students:* 42 full-time (16 women), 19 part-time (8 women); includes 1 minority (Hispanic American), 25 international. Average age 29. 129 applicants, 55% accepted, 17 enrolled. In 2003, 17 master's, 3 doctorates awarded. Terminal master's awarded for partial completion of doctoral program. *Degree requirements:* For master's, thesis, comprehensive exam, registration; for doctorate, thesis/dissertation, attendance of graduate seminar, internships (oceanography and environmental science), comprehensive exam, registration. *Entrance requirements:* For master's, GRE General Test (environmental science), letters of recommendation(3), minimum GPA of 3.0; for doctorate, GRE General Test (oceanography and environmental science), resumé, letters of recommendation (3), statement of objectives, minimum GPA of 3.2. Additional exam requirements/recommendations for international students: Required—TOEFL (minimum score 550 paper-based; 213 computer-based). *Application deadline:* Applications are processed on a rolling basis. Application fee: $50. Electronic applications accepted. *Expenses:* Tuition: Part-time $745 per credit. *Financial support:* In 2003–04, 35 students received support, including 10 fellowships with full and partial tuition reimbursements available (averaging $5,565 per year), 15 research assistantships with full and partial tuition reimbursements available (averaging $14,657 per year), 10 teaching assistantships with full and partial tuition reimbursements available (averaging $17,533 per year); career-related internships or fieldwork and tuition remissions also available. Financial award application deadline: 3/1; financial award applicants required to submit FAFSA. *Faculty research:* Environmental modeling, coastal processes, exploring marine pollution, marine geophysics, remote sensing . Total annual research expenditures: $1.9 million. *Unit head:* Dr. George Maul, Department Head, 321-674-7453, Fax: 321-674-7212, E-mail: gmaul@fit.edu. *Application contact:* Carolyn P. Farrior, Director of Graduate Admissions, 321-674-7118, Fax: 321-723-9468, E-mail: cfarrior@fit.edu.

See in-depth description on page 727.

Florida State University, Graduate Studies, College of Arts and Sciences, Department of Meteorology, Tallahassee, FL 32306. Offers MS, PhD. *Faculty:* 19 full-time (3 women). *Students:* 54 full-time (17 women), 5 part-time (3 women); includes 12 minority (1 African American, 10 Asian Americans or Pacific Islanders, 1 Hispanic American). Average age 27. 80 applicants, 58% accepted. In 2003, 10 master's, 3 doctorates awarded. Terminal master's awarded for partial completion of doctoral program. *Degree requirements:* For master's, thesis optional; for doctorate, thesis/dissertation, comprehensive exam. *Entrance requirements:* For master's and doctorate, GRE General Test, minimum GPA of 3.0. Additional exam requirements/recommendations for international students: Required—TOEFL (minimum score 550 paper-based; 213 computer-based). *Application deadline:* For fall admission, 2/15 priority date for domestic students, 2/1 priority date for international students; for spring admission, 11/1 for domestic students, 6/30 for international students. Applications are processed on a rolling basis. Application fee: $20. *Expenses:* Tuition, state resident: part-time $196 per credit hour. Tuition, nonresident: part-time $731 per credit hour. Part-time tuition and fees vary according to campus/location. *Financial support:* In 2003–04, 51 students received support, including 2 fellowships with partial tuition reimbursements available (averaging $15,000 per year), 40 research assistantships with partial tuition reimbursements available (averaging $17,000 per year), 9 teaching assistantships with partial tuition reimbursements available (averaging $17,000 per year); career-related internships or fieldwork, scholarships/grants, and unspecified assistantships also available. *Faculty research:* Physical, dynamic, and synoptic meteorology; climatology. Total annual research expenditures: $5.3 million. *Unit head:* Dr. Robert G. Ellingson, Chairman, 850-644-6205, Fax: 850-644-9642, E-mail: bobe@met.fsu.edu. *Application contact:* Angie Waller, Academic Coordinator, 850-644-8582, Fax: 850-644-9642, E-mail: awaller@met.fsu.edu.

Iowa State University of Science and Technology, Graduate College, College of Liberal Arts and Sciences, Department of Geological and Atmospheric Sciences, Ames, IA 50011. Offers earth science (MS, PhD); geology (MS, PhD); meteorology (MS, PhD); water resources (MS, PhD). *Faculty:* 17 full-time. *Students:* 28 full-time (13 women), 7 part-time (2 women); includes 1 minority (African American), 19 international. 24 applicants, 38% accepted, 6 enrolled. In 2003, 12 master's, 1 doctorate awarded. *Median time to degree:* Master's–2.9 years full-time. *Degree requirements:* For master's, thesis (for some programs); for doctorate, thesis/dissertation. *Entrance requirements:* For master's and doctorate, GRE General Test. Additional exam requirements/recommendations for international students: Required—TOEFL (paper score 530; computer score 197) or IELTS (score 6.0). *Application deadline:* For fall admission, 2/15 for domestic students. Applications are processed on a rolling basis. Application fee: $30 ($70 for international students). Electronic applications accepted. Tuition, nonresident: part-time $560 per credit. Required fees: $38 per unit. *Financial support:* In 2003–04, 20 research assistantships with full and partial tuition reimbursements (averaging $15,432 per year), 11 teaching assistantships with full and partial tuition reimbursements (averaging $15,432 per year) were awarded. Fellowships, scholarships/grants, health care benefits, and unspecified assistantships also available. *Unit head:* Dr. Carl E. Jacobson, Chair, 515-294-4477.

McGill University, Faculty of Graduate and Postdoctoral Studies, Faculty of Agricultural and Environmental Sciences, Department of Natural Resource Sciences, Montréal, QC H3A 2T5, Canada. Offers agrometeorology (M Sc, PhD); entomology (M Sc, PhD); forest science (M Sc, PhD); microbiology (M Sc, PhD); neotropical environment (M Sc, PhD); soil science (M Sc, PhD); wildlife biology (M Sc, PhD). *Faculty:* 18 full-time (1 woman). *Students:* 69 full-time, 2 part-time. 51 applicants, 37% accepted, 15 enrolled. In 2003, 12 master's, 4 doctorates awarded. *Degree requirements:* For master's and doctorate, thesis/dissertation. *Entrance requirements:* For master's, minimum GPA of 3.0; for doctorate, M Sc, minimum GPA of 3.0. Additional exam requirements/recommendations for international students: Required—TOEFL (paper score 550; computer score 213) or IELTS (paper score 6). *Application deadline:* For fall admission, 6/1 for domestic students, 3/1 for international students; for winter admission, 10/15 for domestic students; for spring admission, 2/15 for domestic students. Applications are processed on a rolling basis. Application fee: $60 Canadian dollars. Electronic applications accepted. Tuition, area resident: Full-time $1,668. *Expenses:* Tuition, state resident: full-time $4,173. Tuition, nonresident: full-time $9,468. Required fees: $1,081. *Financial support:* In 2003–04, 2 fellowships with partial tuition reimbursements (averaging $8,000 per year), 34 teaching assistantships were awarded. Institutionally sponsored loans also available. *Faculty research:* Toxicology, reproductive physiology, parasites, wildlife management, genetics. *Unit head:* Dr. Benoit Côté, Chair, 514-398-7952, Fax: 514-398-7990, E-mail: coteb@nrs.mcgill.ca. *Application contact:* Marie Kubecki, Graduate Student Coordinator, 514-398-7991, Fax: 514-398-7990, E-mail: kubecki@nrs.mcgill.ca.

Naval Postgraduate School, Graduate Programs, Department of Meteorology, Monterey, CA 93943. Offers MS, PhD. Program only open to commissioned officers of the United States and friendly nations and selected United States federal civilian employees. Part-time programs available. *Degree requirements:* For master's, thesis; for doctorate, one foreign language, thesis/dissertation.

North Carolina State University, Graduate School, College of Physical and Mathematical Sciences, Department of Marine, Earth, and Atmospheric Sciences, Raleigh, NC 27695. Offers marine, earth, and atmospheric sciences (MS, PhD); meteorology (MS, PhD); oceanography (MS, PhD). *Faculty:* 41 full-time (6 women), 57 part-time/adjunct (4 women). *Students:* 91 full-time (32 women), 16 part-time (3 women); includes 4 minority (2 African Americans, 1 Asian American or Pacific Islander, 1 Hispanic American), 17 international. Average age 30. 106 applicants, 50% accepted. In 2003, 19 master's, 6 doctorates awarded. Terminal master's awarded for partial completion of doctoral program. *Median time to degree:* Master's–2.7 years full-time; doctorate–5 years full-time. Of those who began their doctoral program in fall 1995, 90% received their degree in 8 years or less. *Degree requirements:* For master's, thesis (for some programs), final oral exam; for doctorate, thesis/dissertation, final oral exam, preliminary oral and written exams, comprehensive exam, registration. *Entrance requirements:* For master's, GRE General Test, minimum GPA of 3.0; for doctorate, GRE General Test, GRE Subject Test for disciplines in biological oceanography and geology, minimum GPA of 3.0. Additional exam requirements/recommendations for international students: Required—TOEFL (minimum score 550 paper-based). *Application deadline:* For fall admission, 6/25 for domestic students, 3/1 for international students; for spring admission, 11/25 for domestic students, 7/15 for international students. Applications are processed on a rolling basis. Application fee: $45. Electronic applications accepted. *Expenses:* Tuition, state resident: part-time $396 per hour. Tuition, nonresident: part-time $1,895 per hour. *Financial support:* In 2003–04, 76 students received support, including 1 fellowship with tuition reimbursement available (averaging $10,397 per year), 47 research assistantships with tuition reimbursements available (averaging $5,959 per year), 32 teaching assistantships with tuition reimbursements available (averaging $6,594 per year); institutionally sponsored loans and unspecified assistantships also available. Financial award application deadline: 3/1. *Faculty research:* Boundary layer and air quality meteorology; climate and mesoscale dynamics; biological, chemical, geological, and physical oceanography; hard rock, soft rock, environmental, and paleogeology. Total annual research expenditures: $5.6 million. *Unit head:* Dr. John C. Fountain, Head, 919-515-3717, Fax: 919-515-7802, E-mail: fountain@ncsu.edu. *Application contact:* Dr. Gerald S. Janowitz, Director of Graduate Programs, 919-515-7837, Fax: 919-515-7802, E-mail: janowitz@ncsu.edu.

See in-depth description on page 247.

The Pennsylvania State University University Park Campus, Graduate School, College of Earth and Mineral Sciences, Department of Meteorology, State College, University Park, PA 16802-1503. Offers MS, PhD. *Students:* 61 full-time (14 women), 2 part-time (1 woman); includes 3 minority (2 African Americans, 1 Asian American or Pacific Islander), 14 international. *Entrance requirements:* For master's and doctorate, GRE General Test. Application fee: $45. *Unit head:* Dr. William H. Brune, Head, 814-865-3286, Fax: 814-865-3663, E-mail: whb2@psu.edu. *Application contact:* Dr. Johannes Verlinde, Graduate Officer, 814-865-0478, E-mail: verlind@essc.psu.edu.

Saint Louis University, Graduate School, College of Arts and Sciences and Graduate School, Department of Earth and Atmospheric Sciences, St. Louis, MO 63103-2097. Offers geophysics (PhD); geoscience (MS, MS(R)); meteorology (M Pr Met, MS(R), PhD). Part-time programs available. *Faculty:* 14 full-time (7 women), 12 part-time/adjunct (6 women). *Students:* 19 full-time (5 women), 6 part-time (1 woman); includes 2 minority (1 African American, 1 Asian American or Pacific Islander), 11 international. Average age 30. 27 applicants, 85% accepted, 7 enrolled. In 2003, 2 master's, 1 doctorate awarded. *Degree requirements:* For master's, comprehensive oral exam, thesis for MS(R); for doctorate, thesis/dissertation, preliminary exams. *Entrance requirements:* For master's and doctorate, GRE General Test. Additional exam requirements/recommendations for international students: Required—TOEFL (minimum score 550 paper-based; 213 computer-based). *Application deadline:* For fall admission, 7/1 for domestic students, 7/1 for international students; for spring admission, 11/1 for domestic students, 11/1 for international students. Applications are processed on a rolling basis. Application fee: $40. *Expenses:* Tuition: Part-time $690 per credit hour. Required fees: $59 per semester. Tuition and fees vary according to program. *Financial support:* In 2003–04, 23 students received support, including 6 research assistantships with tuition reimbursements available, 6 teaching assistantships with tuition reimbursements available; unspecified assistantships also available. Financial award application deadline: 6/1; financial award applicants required to submit FAFSA. *Faculty research:* Seismology and tectonics, earth's core and structure, geochemistry, heavy precipitation convective systems, squall lines and tropical cyclones. *Unit head:* Dr. David Crossley, Acting Chairperson, 314-977-3131, Fax: 314-977-3117, E-mail: crossley@slu.edu. *Application contact:* Gary Behrman, Associate Dean of the Graduate School, 314-977-3827, Fax: 314-977-3943, E-mail: behrmang@slu.edu.

San Jose State University, Graduate Studies and Research, College of Science, Department of Meteorology, San Jose, CA 95192-0001. Offers MS. *Students:* 5 full-time (1 woman), 6 part-time (2 women); includes 3 minority (1 African American, 2 Asian Americans or Pacific Islanders). Average age 32. 12 applicants, 58% accepted, 3 enrolled. In 2003, 3 degrees awarded. *Degree requirements:* For master's, thesis or alternative. *Entrance requirements:* For master's, GRE. *Application deadline:* For fall admission, 6/29 for domestic students; for spring admission, 11/30 for domestic students. Applications are processed on a rolling basis. Application fee: $59. Electronic applications accepted. Tuition, nonresident: part-time $282 per unit.

Required fees: $654 per semester. *Financial support:* Applicants required to submit FAFSA. *Unit head:* Jindra Goodman, Chair, 408-924-5200, Fax: 408-924-5191.

Texas A&M University, College of Geosciences, Department of Atmospheric Sciences, College Station, TX 77843. Offers MS, PhD. *Faculty:* 5 full-time (0 women), 1 part-time/adjunct (0 women). *Students:* 55 full-time (17 women), 7 part-time (1 woman); includes 12 minority (1 African American, 11 Asian Americans or Pacific Islanders), 21 international. Average age 28. *Degree requirements:* For master's and doctorate, thesis/dissertation. *Entrance requirements:* For master's and doctorate, GRE General Test. Additional exam requirements/recommendations for international students: Required—TOEFL. *Application deadline:* For fall admission, 3/1 for domestic students; for spring admission, 10/1 for domestic students. Applications are processed on a rolling basis. Application fee: $50 ($75 for international students). Electronic applications accepted. *Expenses:* Tuition, state resident: full-time $3,420. Tuition, nonresident: full-time $9,084. Required fees: $1,861. *Financial support:* In 2003–04, 2 students received support, including fellowships (averaging $16,500 per year), research assistantships with tuition reimbursements available (averaging $15,000 per year), teaching assistantships (averaging $15,000 per year); career-related internships or fieldwork, institutionally sponsored loans, scholarships/grants, and tuition waivers (partial) also available. Financial award application deadline: 3/1; financial award applicants required to submit FAFSA. *Faculty research:* Radar- and satellite-rainfall relationships, mesoscale dynamics and numerical modeling, climatology. *Unit head:* Dr. Richard Orville, Head, 979-845-7671, Fax: 979-862-4466. *Application contact:* Patricia Price, Academic Advisor, 979-845-7688, Fax: 979-862-4466, E-mail: pprice@ariel.net.tamu.edu.

Université du Québec à Montréal, Graduate Programs, Programs in Atmospheric Sciences and Meteorology, Montréal, QC H3C 3P8, Canada. Offers atmospheric sciences (M Sc); meteorology (PhD, Diploma). Part-time programs available. *Degree requirements:* For master's, thesis. *Entrance requirements:* For master's and Diploma, appropriate bachelor's degree or equivalent and proficiency in French; for doctorate, appropriate master's degree or equivalent and proficiency in French.

University of Hawaii at Manoa, Graduate Division, School of Ocean and Earth Science and Technology, Department of Meteorology, Honolulu, HI 96822. Offers MS, PhD. Part-time programs available. *Faculty:* 17 full-time (1 woman), 8 part-time/adjunct (1 woman). *Students:* 42 full-time (13 women), 4 part-time (2 women); includes 2 minority (1 Asian American or Pacific Islander, 1 Hispanic American), 26 international. Average age 31. 39 applicants, 54% accepted, 9 enrolled. In 2003, 9 master's, 17 doctorates awarded. *Median time to degree:* Master's–3 years full-time; doctorate–5 years full-time. *Degree requirements:* For master's and doctorate, thesis/dissertation. *Entrance requirements:* For master's and doctorate, GRE General Test. *Application deadline:* For fall admission, 3/1 for domestic students, 1/15 for international students; for spring admission, 9/1 for domestic students, 8/1 for international students. Application fee: $50. *Expenses:* Tuition, state resident: full-time $4,464; part-time $186 per credit hour. Tuition, nonresident: full-time $10,608; part-time $442 per credit hour. Tuition and fees vary according to program. *Financial support:* In 2003–04, 34 research assistantships (averaging $17,301 per year), 3 teaching assistantships (averaging $16,176 per year) were awarded. Fellowships, Federal Work-Study and tuition waivers (full) also available. *Faculty research:* Tropical cyclones, air-sea interactions, mesoscale meteorology, intraseasonal oscillations, tropical climate. Total annual research expenditures: $1.2 million. *Unit head:* Dr. Thomas A. Schroeder, Chairperson, 808-956-7476, Fax: 808-956-2877, E-mail: tas@soest.hawaii.edu.

University of Maryland, College Park, Graduate Studies and Research, College of Computer, Mathematical and Physical Sciences, Department of Meteorology, College Park, MD 20742. Offers MS, PhD. Part-time and evening/weekend programs available. Postbaccalaureate distance learning degree programs offered. *Faculty:* 38 full-time (10 women), 3 part-time/adjunct (1 woman). *Students:* 43 full-time (22 women), 15 part-time (3 women); includes 6 minority (3 Asian Americans or Pacific Islanders, 3 Hispanic Americans), 30 international. 82 applicants, 23% accepted. In 2003, 9 master's, 5 doctorates awarded. Terminal master's awarded for partial completion of doctoral program. *Median time to degree:* Of those who began their doctoral program in fall 1995, 25% received their degree in 8 years or less. *Degree requirements:* For master's, scholarly paper, written and oral exams; for doctorate, thesis/dissertation, exam. *Entrance requirements:* For master's, GRE General Test, math background and scientific computer language experience, 3 letter of recommendation; for doctorate, GRE General Test. *Application deadline:* For fall admission, 5/1 for domestic students, 2/1 for international students; for spring admission, 10/1 for domestic students, 6/1 for international students. Applications are processed on a rolling basis. Application fee: $50. Electronic applications accepted. *Expenses:* Tuition, state resident: part-time $349 per credit hour. Tuition, nonresident: part-time $602 per credit hour. *Financial support:* In 2003–04, 2 fellowships with full tuition reimbursements (averaging $9,491 per year), 26 research assistantships with tuition reimbursements (averaging $19,122 per year), 5 teaching assistantships with tuition reimbursements (averaging $19,479 per year) were awarded. Federal Work-Study and scholarships/grants also available. Support available to part-time students. Financial award applicants required to submit FAFSA. *Faculty research:* Weather, atmospheric chemistry, air pollution, global change, radiation. Total annual research expenditures: $4.3 million. *Unit head:* Dr. Russ Dickerson, Chairman, 301-405-5364, Fax: 301-314-9482. *Application contact:* Trudy Lindsey, Director, Graduate Enrollment Management Services, 301-405-4190, Fax: 301-314-9305, E-mail: tlindsey@gradschool.umd.edu.

University of Miami, Graduate School, Rosenstiel School of Marine and Atmospheric Science, Division of Meteorology and Physical Oceanography, Coral Gables, FL 33124. Offers atmospheric science (MS, PhD); physical oceanography (MS, PhD). *Faculty:* 28 full-time (5 women), 18 part-time/adjunct (3 women). *Students:* 33 full-time (12 women), 1 part-time; includes 2 minority (both Hispanic Americans), 15 international. Average age 27. 61 applicants, 20% accepted, 9 enrolled. In 2003, 6 master's awarded, leading to university research/teaching 33%, continued full-time study33%, business/industry 17%, government 17%; 3 doctorates awarded, leading to university research/teaching 100%. Terminal master's awarded for partial completion of doctoral program. *Median time to degree:* Master's–4 years full-time; doctorate–7.2 years full-time. *Degree requirements:* For master's and doctorate, thesis/dissertation, comprehensive exam, registration. *Entrance requirements:* For master's and doctorate, GRE General Test. Additional exam requirements/recommendations for international students: Required—TOEFL (minimum score 550 paper-based; 213 computer-based). *Application deadline:* For fall admission, 1/1 priority date for domestic students, 1/1 priority date for international students. Applications are processed on a rolling basis. Application fee: $50. Electronic applications accepted. *Expenses:* Tuition: Full-time $19,526. *Financial support:* In 2003–04, 28 students received support, including 4 fellowships with tuition reimbursements available (averaging $20,124 per year), 21 research assistantships with tuition reimbursements available (averaging $20,124 per year), 3 teaching assistantships with tuition reimbursements available (averaging $20,124 per year); institutionally sponsored loans and scholarships/grants also available. Financial award application deadline: 3/1; financial award applicants required to submit FAFSA. *Unit head:* Dr. William Johns, Chairperson, 305-361-4057, E-mail: wjohns@rsmas.miami.edu. *Application contact:* Dr. Frank Millero, Associate Dean, 305-361-4155, Fax: 305-361-4771, E-mail: gso@rsmas.miami.edu.

Announcement: The Division is engaged in education and research in the physical processes governing the motion and composition of the ocean and atmosphere through observational, diagnostic, modeling, and theoretical explorations. Research apprenticeships are integral to the Division's education program. Students receive tuition waivers and financial aid as research assistantships or fellowships.

University of Oklahoma, Graduate College, College of Geosciences, School of Meteorology, Norman, OK 73019-0390. Offers MS Metr, PhD. Part-time programs available. *Faculty:* 34 full-time (2 women), 3 part-time/adjunct (0 women). *Students:* 61 full-time (17 women), 20 part-time (4 women); includes 2 minority (1 Asian American or Pacific Islander, 1 Hispanic American), 15 international. 59 applicants, 27% accepted, 12 enrolled. In 2003, 18 master's, 7 doctorates awarded. *Degree requirements:* For master's, thesis or alternative, comprehensive exam; for doctorate, one foreign language, thesis/dissertation, departmental qualifying exam. *Entrance requirements:* For master's, GRE, bachelor's degree in related area; for doctorate, GRE. Additional exam requirements/recommendations for international students: Required—TOEFL (minimum score 600 paper-based). *Application deadline:* For fall admission, 2/1 priority date for domestic students, 4/1 priority date for international students; for spring admission, 11/1 for domestic students, 9/1 for international students. Applications are processed on a rolling basis. Application fee: $25 ($75 for international students). *Expenses:* Tuition, state resident: full-time $2,774; part-time $116 per credit hour. Tuition, nonresident: full-time $9,571; part-time $399 per credit hour. Required fees: $953; $33 per credit hour. Full-time tuition and fees vary according to course level, course load and program. *Financial support:* In 2003–04, 8 students received support, including 6 fellowships with full tuition reimbursements available (averaging $5,000 per year), 60 research assistantships (averaging $13,398 per year), 11 teaching assistantships with partial tuition reimbursements available (averaging $13,405 per year); career-related internships or fieldwork, Federal Work-Study, institutionally sponsored loans, scholarships/grants, health care benefits, tuition waivers (partial), and unspecified assistantships also available. Financial award application deadline: 2/1; financial award applicants required to submit FAFSA. *Faculty research:* Radar meteorology, synoptic and dynamic meteorology, mesoscale meteorology, numerical weather prediction, regional and global climate. Total annual research expenditures: $1.4 million. *Unit head:* Dr. Frederick H. Carr, Director, 405-325-6561, Fax: 405-325-7689, E-mail: fcarr@ou.edu. *Application contact:* Celia Jones, Coordinator, Academic Student Services, 405-325-6571, Fax: 405-325-7689, E-mail: cjones@ou.edu.

University of Utah, Graduate School, College of Mines and Earth Sciences, Department of Meteorology, Salt Lake City, UT 84112-1107. Offers MS, PhD. Part-time programs available. *Faculty:* 7 full-time (0 women). *Students:* 18 full-time (5 women), 4 part-time (2 women), 7 international. Average age 30. 37 applicants, 27% accepted, 5 enrolled. In 2003, 4 master's, 1 doctorate awarded. Terminal master's awarded for partial completion of doctoral program. *Degree requirements:* For master's, thesis optional; for doctorate, thesis/dissertation. *Entrance requirements:* For master's and doctorate, GRE General Test, minimum GPA of 3.0, 3 letters of reference. Additional exam requirements/recommendations for international students: Required—TOEFL. *Application deadline:* For fall admission, 12/31 priority date for domestic students, 12/31 priority date for international students. Applications are processed on a rolling basis. Application fee: $45 ($60 for international students). Electronic applications accepted. Tuition, nonresident: full-time $2,483. International tuition: $8,768 full-time. *Financial support:* In 2003–04, 13 students received support, including 2 fellowships (averaging $18,000 per year), 14 research assistantships with full tuition reimbursements available (averaging $36,600 per year); teaching assistantships with full tuition reimbursements available, unspecified assistantships also available. Financial award application deadline: 2/15; financial award applicants required to submit FAFSA. *Faculty research:* Global and regional climates, weather in the Intermountain West, boundary layer meteorology and air quality, clouds and radiation, remote sensing and satellite meteorology. Total annual research expenditures: $2.2 million. *Unit head:* Dr. Edward J. Zipser, Chair, 801-585-9482, Fax: 801-585-3681, E-mail: ezipser@met.utah.edu. *Application contact:* Kathy Roberts, Executive Secretary, 801-581-6136, Fax: 801-585-3681, E-mail: kroberts@met.utah.edu.

Utah State University, School of Graduate Studies, College of Agriculture, Department of Plants, Soils, and Biometeorology, Logan, UT 84322. Offers biometeorology (MS, PhD); ecology (MS, PhD); plant science (MS, PhD); soil science (MS, PhD). Part-time programs available. *Faculty:* 31 full-time (4 women), 13 part-time/adjunct (0 women). *Students:* 29 full-time (9 women), 5 part-time; includes 1 minority (African American), 6 international. Average age 26. 18 applicants, 50% accepted, 2 enrolled. In 2003, 10 master's, 4 doctorates awarded. Terminal master's awarded for partial completion of doctoral program. *Median time to degree:* Of those who began their doctoral program in fall 1995, 100% received their degree in 8 years or less. *Degree requirements:* For master's and doctorate, thesis/dissertation. *Entrance requirements:* For master's, GRE General Test, BS in plant, soil, atmospheric science, or related field, minimum GPA of 3.0; for doctorate, GRE General Test, minimum GPA of 3.0. Additional exam requirements/recommendations for international students: Required—TOEFL. *Application deadline:* For fall admission, 6/15 priority date for domestic students, 3/15 priority date for international students; for spring admission, 10/15 for domestic students, 9/15 for international students. Applications are processed on a rolling basis. Application fee: $50 ($60 for international students). *Expenses:* Tuition, state resident: part-time $270 per credit hour. Tuition, nonresident: part-time $946 per credit hour. Required fees: $173 per credit hour. *Financial support:* In 2003–04, 23 research assistantships with partial tuition reimbursements (averaging $15,000 per year) were awarded; Federal Work-Study, institutionally sponsored loans, and tuition waivers (full) also available. Support available to part-time students. Financial award application deadline: 3/1. *Faculty research:* Biotechnology and genomics, plant physiology and biology, nutrient and water efficient landscapes, physical-chemical-biological proceses in soil, environmental biophysics and climate. Total annual research expenditures: $4.5 million. *Unit head:* Dr. Larry A. Rupp, Head, 435-797-2099, Fax: 435-797-3376, E-mail: larryr@ext.usu.edu. *Application contact:* Dr. Janis L. Boettinger, Graduate Program Coordinator, 435-797-4026, Fax: 435-797-3376, E-mail: janis.boettinger@usu.edu.

Yale University, Graduate School of Arts and Sciences, Department of Geology and Geophysics, New Haven, CT 06520. Offers geochemistry (PhD); geophysics (PhD); meteorology (PhD); mineralogy and crystallography (PhD); oceanography (PhD); paleoecology (PhD); paleontology and stratigraphy (PhD); petrology (PhD); structural geology (PhD). *Degree requirements:* For doctorate, thesis/dissertation. *Entrance requirements:* For doctorate, GRE General Test. Additional exam requirements/recommendations for international students: Required—TOEFL. *Expenses:* Tuition: Full-time $25,600; part-time $6,400 per term.

See in-depth description on page 261.

COLUMBIA UNIVERSITY / NASA GODDARD SPACE FLIGHT CENTER'S INSTITUTE FOR SPACE STUDIES

Atmospheric and Planetary Science Program

Program of Study

The Departments of Earth and Environmental Sciences and Applied Physics and Applied Mathematics jointly offer a graduate program in atmospheric and planetary science leading to the Ph.D. degree. Four to six years are generally required to complete the Ph.D., including the earning of M.A. and M.Phil. degrees. Applicants should have a strong background in physics and mathematics, including advanced undergraduate courses in mechanics, electromagnetism, advanced calculus, and differential equations.

The program is conducted in cooperation with the NASA Goddard Space Flight Center's Institute for Space Studies, which is adjacent to Columbia University. Members of the Institute hold adjunct faculty appointments, offer courses, and supervise the research of graduate students in the program. The Institute holds colloquia and scientific conferences in which the University community participates. Opportunities for visiting scientists to conduct research at the Institute are provided by postdoctoral research programs administered by the National Academy of Sciences–National Research Council and Columbia and supported by NASA.

Research at the Institute focuses on broad studies of natural and anthropogenic global changes. Areas of study include global climate, earth observations, biogeochemical cycles, planetary atmosphere, and related interdisciplinary studies. The global climate involves basic research on climatic variations and climate processes, including the development of global numerical models to study the climate effects of increasing carbon dioxide and other trace gases, aerosols, solar variability, and changing surface conditions. The earth observations program entails research in the retrieval of cloud, aerosol, and surface radiative properties from global satellite radiance data to further understanding of their effects on climate. Biogeochemical cycles research utilizes three-dimensional models to study in the distribution of trace gases in the troposphere and stratosphere and to examine the role of the biosphere in the global carbon cycle. The planetary atmospheres program includes comparative modeling of radiative transfer and dynamics applied to Venus, Titan, Mars, and the Jovian planets; participation in spacecraft experiments; and analysis of ground-based observations. Interdisciplinary research includes studies of turbulence and solar system formation, and the evolution of solar-type stars.

Research Facilities

The Institute operates a modern general-purpose scientific computing facility consisting of a Compaq ES45 with 32 processors operating on Tru 64 UNIX; one each of 4-, 8-, and 96-processor SGI Origin 2000 servers; one 8-processor SGI Power Challenge development server; eighty workstations, including sixty IBM RS/6000 and twenty SGI IRIX; and PCs, Macs, and peripheral equipment. Spyglass, AVS, IDL, NCAR graphics, and in-house software permit interactive processing, display, and analysis of satellite imagery and other digital data. The Institute is the Global Processing Center for the International Satellite Cloud Climatology Project, which uses satellite observations to create a multidecadal record of cloud and surface variations. Institute personnel frequently collaborate with scientists at the Goddard Space Flight Center in Greenbelt, Maryland. Close research ties also exist with the Lamont-Doherty Earth Observatory of Columbia University, especially in the areas of geochemistry, oceanography, and paleoclimate studies. All facilities, including the Institute's library containing approximately 17,000 volumes, are made available to students in the program.

Financial Aid

Research assistantships are available to most students in the program. Graduate assistantships in 2004–05 carry a twelve-month stipend of $2000 per month and include a tuition waiver and payment of fees.

Cost of Study

Tuition and fees for 2004–05 are estimated at $35,035. As noted above, tuition and fees are paid for graduate students holding research assistantships.

Living and Housing Costs

Limited on-campus housing is available for single and married graduate students on 350-day contracts. Rates range from $6900 for a double room to $10,800 for a single room. Studios, suites, and one-bedroom apartments range from $8640 to $15,300. Most students live off campus, many of them in apartments owned and operated by the University within a few blocks of the campus.

Student Group

Of the 18,500 students at Columbia, 3,500 are students in the Graduate School of Arts and Sciences. Currently, there are 9 Columbia students at the Institute for Space Studies, all of whom are Ph.D. candidates in the Atmospheric and Planetary Science Program. There are also 21 University research appointments at the Institute.

Location

Columbia University is located in the Morningside Heights section of Manhattan in New York City. New York's climate is moderate, with average maximum and minimum temperatures of 85 and 69 degrees in July and 40 and 28 in January. New York is one of the top cultural centers in the United States and, as such, provides unrivaled opportunities for attending concerts, operas, and plays and for visiting world-renowned art, scientific, and historical museums. Student discount tickets for many musical and dramatic performances are available in the Graduate Student Lounge. A comprehensive network of public transportation alleviates the need for keeping an automobile in the city. The superb beaches of Long Island, including the Fire Island National Seashore, are within easy driving distance, as are the numerous ski slopes, state parks, and other mountain recreational areas of upstate New York and southern New England.

The University

Columbia University, founded in 1754 by royal charter of King George II of England, is a member of the Ivy League. It is the oldest institution of higher learning in New York State and the fifth-oldest in the United States. It consists of sixteen separate schools and colleges with more than 1,700 full-time faculty members.

Applying

To enter the program, an application must be submitted to one of the participating departments. Completed forms should be received by January 15 from students applying for September admission.

Correspondence and Information

Dr. Anthony D. Del Genio
Atmospheric and Planetary Science Program
Armstrong Hall—GISS
Columbia University
2880 Broadway
New York, New York 10025
Telephone: 212-678-5588
E-mail: adelgenio@giss.nasa.gov

Columbia University/NASA Goddard Space Flight Center's Institute for Space Studies

THE INSTITUTE STAFF AND THEIR RESEARCH

Michael Allison, Ph.D., Rice, 1982. Planetary atmospheric dynamics, remote sensing meteorology of Mars, Jupiter, and the outer planets.
Vittorio M. Canuto, Ph.D., Turin (Italy), 1960. Theory of fully developed turbulence, analytical models for large-scale turbulence and their applications to geophysics and astrophysics.
Barbara E. Carlson, Ph.D., SUNY at Stony Brook, 1984. Radiative transfer in planetary atmospheres, remote sensing and cloud modeling of Earth and Jovian planets.
Mark A. Chandler, Ph.D., Columbia, 1992. Paleoclimate reconstruction and modeling, role of oceans in climate change.
Anthony D. Del Genio, Ph.D., UCLA, 1978. Dynamics of planetary atmospheres, parameterization of clouds and cumulus convection, climate change, general circulation.
Leonard M. Druyan, Ph.D., NYU, 1971. Tropical climate, African climate, Sahel drought, regional climate remodeling.
Timothy M. Hall, Ph.D., Cornell, 1991. Atmosphere and ocean transport processes, atmospheric chemistry, ocean carbon, modeling and interpretation of observations.
James E. Hansen, Head of the Institute for Space Studies; Ph.D., Iowa, 1967. Remote sensing of Earth and planetary atmospheres, global modeling of climate processes and climate sensitivity.
Nancy Y. Kiang, Ph.D., Berkeley, 2002. Interaction between terrestrial ecosystems and the atmosphere, biogeochemistry, plant ecophysiology, micrometeorology, photosynthesis, mathematical modeling, extensions to astrobiology.
Andrew A. Lacis, Ph.D., Iowa, 1970. Radiative transfer, climate modeling, remote sensing of Earth and planetary atmospheres.
Ron L. Miller, Ph.D., MIT, 1990. Tropical climate, coupled ocean-atmosphere dynamics, interannual and decadal variability.
Michael I. Mishchenko, Ph.D., Ukrainian Academy of Sciences, 1987. Radiative transfer, electromagnetic scattering, remote sensing of Earth and planetary atmospheres.
Jan Perlwitz, Ph.D., Hamburg, 1997. Soil dust aerosol modeling, effect of tropospheric aerosols on Earth's past, present, and future climate.
Dorothy M. Peteet, Ph.D., NYU, 1983. Paleoclimatology, palynology, ecology, botany.
David H. Rind, Ph.D., Columbia, 1976. Atmospheric and climate dynamics, stratospheric modeling and remote sensing.
Cynthia Rosenzweig, Ph.D., Massachusetts at Amherst, 1991. Parameterization of ground hydrology and biosphere, impacts of climate change on agriculture.
William B. Rossow, Ph.D., Cornell, 1976. Planetary atmospheres and climate, cloud physics and climatology, general circulation.
Gary L. Russell, Ph.D., Columbia, 1976. Numerical methods, general circulation modeling.
Gavin A. Schmidt, Ph.D., London, 1994. Physical oceanography, paleoclimate, coupled atmosphere-ocean general circulation models.
Drew T. Shindell, Ph.D., SUNY at Stony Brook, 1995. Atmospheric chemistry and climate change.
Richard B. Stothers, Ph.D., Harvard, 1964. Astronomy, climatology, geophysics, solar physics, history of science.
Larry D. Travis, Associate Chief of the Institute for Space Studies; Ph.D., Penn State, 1971. Remote sensing of Earth and planetary atmospheres, radiative transfer, numerical modeling.

The Institute hosts conferences and workshops that bring scientists together to discuss relevant dynamics, radiation, and chemistry issues. Conferences and workshops on satellite cloud data analysis, long-term climate monitoring, and tropospheric aerosols have been held recently.

Fossil pollen and spores obtained by coring swamp sediments are used by Institute scientists to document ancient climate changes.

Graduate students can use a variety of workstations to process and analyze visible and infrared data from earth-orbiting satellites and to conduct and view the results of global climate model simulations.

SOUTH DAKOTA SCHOOL OF MINES AND TECHNOLOGY/ SOUTH DAKOTA STATE UNIVERSITY

Joint Program in Atmospheric, Environmental, and Water Resources

Program of Study

This joint program provides Ph.D. education and degrees in the three fields of atmospheric, environmental, and water resources (AEWR). The primary departments and disciplines involved in the programs are atmospheric sciences, civil and environmental engineering (CEE), geology and geological engineering, mining engineering, mathematics and computer science, and chemical engineering and chemistry at South Dakota School of Mines and Technology (SDSM&T); and CEE, agricultural engineering, chemistry, agriculture, biology, water resources, and hydrology at South Dakota State University (SDSU). Degree candidates are expected to complete an approved program of study that integrates course work from among these disciplines to provide both breadth and a focus for their research areas. A modern audio/video telecommunications network is used to provide instruction from one university to the other. A minimum total of 90 semester course credit hours beyond the bachelor's degree are required in each AEWR student's program of study. Course credits range from 45 to 60 credit hours, and dissertation research credits range from 30 to 45 credit hours. Entering students with an appropriate Master of Science degree are allowed to apply a maximum of 24 semester credit hours of prior course work to the Ph.D. requirement. If applicable to the specific dissertation project, a maximum of 6 hours of prior research credits may be applied to the Ph.D. requirement. The program includes qualifying and comprehensive examinations and a dissertation that represents the culmination of between one and two academic years of full-time research. The residence requirement is two consecutive semesters.

Research Facilities

At SDSM&T, the library has 217,500 volumes and more than 800 periodicals, subscribes to several electronic full-text publication databases, and is also a selective depository of U.S. government documents. The Institute of Atmospheric Sciences is extensively involved in field research. It operates a specially instrumented, armored aircraft to collect storm data and maintains instrumented towers and tethered balloons for chemical sampling and radiometric observations. The campus has modern analytical laboratories for trace gas, water, and solid earth material analysis. There is active collaboration in remote sensing research with the EROS Data Center in Sioux Falls. In addition, state-of-the-art computing facilities and scientific software packages are maintained within the Institute, with access to supercomputing facilities off-campus via the Internet-2. The civil and environmental engineering and geology and geological engineering departments collaborate with local, state, and federal agencies in a variety of laboratory and field studies utilizing state-of-the-art facilities and equipment. At SDSU, the Briggs Library collections contain more than 575,000 bound volumes, 300,000 government publications, and 500,000 items in microfilm, microfiche, or microcards in addition to newspapers, maps, and pamphlet materials. More than 3,100 periodical titles are received currently, with 9,000 available electronically. Open 98 hours per week, the library contains seating for more than 1,000 readers. A computerized system links Briggs with other major academic and research libraries nationwide. Both schools have excellent facilities for GIS/remote sensing work. Faculty members and graduate students from both universities also participate in the relatively new Joint Center for Biocomplexity Studies in the Northern Great Plains.

Financial Aid

Information about aid for U.S. students is available upon request from the Financial Aid Office at each institution. Teaching and research assistantships are available. These awards range from about $8000 to $12,000 for nine months and from $11,000 to $18,000 for twelve months.

Cost of Study

Graduate tuition in 2004–05 is $109.40 per semester hour for state residents and $322.45 for nonresidents. Students on an assistantship pay one third the resident tuition rate. In addition, students are assessed course fees of approximately $108 per credit hour. Other fees are a guarantee deposit, parking, late registration, and health insurance, as applicable.

Living and Housing Costs

At SDSM&T, assistance in finding off-campus rooms and apartments is available from the Director of Housing. Off-campus rooms range in cost from $100 to $150 per week. Apartments rent for a minimum of $300 per month. On-campus board is payable by the meal or is available through various plans that range from $546 to $967 per semester. When available to graduate students, dormitory rooms cost $812 per semester for double occupancy or $1083 for a single room. At SDSU, assistance in finding on-campus housing (i.e., family housing, residence halls, or residence apartments) is available from the Office of Residential Life. For 2003–04, family apartments ranged in cost from $350 to $400 per month. Assistance in finding off-campus housing is available in the Off-Campus Housing Office. Students may purchase a discounted food program or meals may be purchased on a walk-in basis.

Student Group

Total enrollment (primarily science and engineering) at SDSM&T is approximately 2,500 students, with about 350 students registered in graduate programs. Of all students, 66 percent are from outside South Dakota, and 24 percent are women. Total enrollment at SDSU is more than 8,000 students, making SDSU the state's largest university, with eight colleges and a fully accredited graduate school. There are about 850 students registered in graduate degree programs. Of all graduate students, 19 percent are from outside South Dakota, and 50 percent are women.

Location

Rapid City, home of SDSM&T, has a population of about 60,000 residents. Described as the gateway to the Black Hills, it is located a short distance from the Mount Rushmore Memorial and the White River Badlands. SDSU is located on the eastern edge of South Dakota in Brookings, a city of 18,000 residents. McCrory Gardens, the State Agricultural Heritage Museum, and the South Dakota Art Museum are located on the SDSU campus. The Brookings Art Festival, held every summer, draws thousands of people from across the United States. Climatic conditions in both locations are favorable in winter and summer for a variety of recreational activities—skiing, hunting, fishing, hiking, biking, and camping—with easy access to many area lakes, streams, and rivers.

The School and The University

In 1885, the territorial legislature established the Dakota School of Mines in Rapid City, where it served the frontier communities of the Black Hills as a mining college and prospectors' analytical laboratory. Since 1900, however, the educational emphasis at SDSM&T has shifted to include a broad spectrum of engineering and scientific disciplines. About sixty graduate degrees are awarded annually. SDSM&T is accredited by the North Central Association of Colleges and Schools. An act of the Territorial Legislature, approved in 1881, provided that an "Agricultural College for the Territory of Dakota be established at Brookings." As a land-grant university, South Dakota State University subscribes to the land-grant philosophy of education, research, and extension as its threefold mission. The main campus includes more than 109 major buildings on 282 acres. More than 200 majors, minors, and options are available, with more than 1,600 different course offerings. Students may join any of the more than 170 organizations and clubs at SDSU. Career and academic planning, counseling, health services, and legal aid are available to all students.

Applying

Applications from U.S. residents should normally be received at SDSM&T sixty days before the beginning of the semester; at SDSU, thirty days prior. International students should apply 150 days prior to their expected date of matriculation at SDSM&T. For SDSU, international students residing outside of the U.S. should apply five months prior to matriculation; students in the United States, three months prior. All applicants are required to submit GRE General Test and Subject Test scores. A minimum TOEFL score of 520 (paper-based test) or 190 (computer-based test) is required (560/220 for admission without additional English tutoring) of applicants from non-English-speaking countries.

Correspondence and Information

AEWR Program Coordinator
Graduate Education and Research Office
South Dakota School of Mines and Technology
501 East Saint Joseph Street
Rapid City, South Dakota 57701-3995
E-mail: graduate.admissions@sdsmt.edu
World Wide Web: http://www.sdsmt.edu/admin/gesp/

AEWR Program Coordinator
College of Engineering
South Dakota State University
P.O. Box 2219
Brookings, South Dakota 57007

South Dakota School of Mines and Technology / South Dakota State University

DEPARTMENTS AND RESEARCH AREAS

SOUTH DAKOTA SCHOOL OF MINES AND TECHNOLOGY

Institute of Atmospheric Sciences
Director: P. R. Zimmerman, Ph.D., Colorado State. Telephone: 605-394-2291.
Trace gas biogeochemistry, troposphere chemistry, airborne measurements, atmospheric electricity, cloud physics, hailstorms, nucleation processes, mesoscale meteorology, numerical cloud modeling, radar meteorology, radiative transfer, land use and change, weather modification, climate change, hydrology.

Department of Atmospheric Sciences
Department Chair: P. R. Zimmerman, Ph.D., Colorado State. Telephone: 605-394-2291.
Research areas are listed under the Institute of Atmospheric Sciences above.

Department of Chemical Engineering
Department Chair: Robb M. Winter, Ph.D., Utah. Telephone: 605-394-2421.
Trace chemical analysis, supercritical fluid extraction, Fourier-transform infrared spectroscopy, solid phase microextraction technology, chromatography detectors, static and dynamic infrared emission, HPLC, NMR, molecular modeling, biomass conversions, mining wastes characterization, hazardous waste incineration pollutants, environmental and forensic chemistries, combustion chemistry and syntheses, natural products, synthetic plant growth regulators, organophosphorous chemistry, polymers and polymer/composites, kinetics and mechanisms of inorganic reactions, bioinorganic chemistry, supermolecular assemblies, nanotechnology, process control.

Department of Civil and Environmental Engineering
Department Chair: Scott J. Kenner, Ph.D., Florida. Telephone: 605-394-2439.
Advanced materials, environmental engineering, geotechnical engineering, hazardous-waste treatment and remediation, soil mechanics and hydraulics, structural engineering, water and wastewater treatment, water resources, water-quality engineering.

Department of Geology and Geological Engineering
Department Chair: Arden D. Davis, Ph.D., South Dakota Mines and Tech. Telephone: 605-394-2461.
Bioremediation, Black Hills geology, economic geology, engineering geophysics, geochemistry, geographic information systems, geohydrology, gold deposits, groundwater, igneous and metamorphic petrology, mineralogy, ore-forming systems, pegmatite petrogenesis, remote sensing, sedimentology, stratigraphy, surficial processes, tectonics, vertebrate paleontology.

Graduate Education and Research Office
Dean: S. O. Farwell, Ph.D., Montana State. Telephone: 605-394-2493.
Analytical atmospheric chemistry; atmospheric chemistry; air pollution; instrumentation for airborne sampling and measurements; calibration techniques and intercomparison experiments; biogeochemistry of S, N, and C compounds; climate change; remote sensing; land use and change; atmospheric water; statistics and sampling strategy; experimental design.

SOUTH DAKOTA STATE UNIVERSITY

Department of Agricultural Engineering
Department Head: R. Alcock, Ph.D., Reading (England). Telephone: 605-688-5141.
Machine vision, biomaterials processing, soil and water engineering, irrigation and drainage, climatology, groundwater in agriculture, structures and machine design.

Department of Civil and Environmental Engineering
Department Head: D. A. Rollag, Ph.D., Purdue. Telephone: 605-688-5427.
Structural engineering; transportation; engineering; geotechnical and geoenvironmental engineering; water resources; hydrology; hydraulics; environmental engineering; engineering mechanics; water quality; solid, hazardous, and industrial waste; water and wastewater treatment plant design; land application of wastes.

Department of Plant Science
Department Head: F. A. Cholick, Ph.D., Colorado State. Telephone: 605-688-5125.
Soil chemistry, water management, crop-water relationships, water quality, soil physics, weed science, entomology, nutrient movement in the subsurface, best management practices.

Department of Biology/Microbiology
Department Head: C. R. McMullen, Ph.D., South Dakota State. Telephone: 605-688-6141.
Ecology, environmental stress, aquatics, environmental management, industrial microbiology, wetlands.

Department of Chemistry
Department Head: L. I. Peterson, Ph.D., Yale. Telephone: 605-688-4526.
Biochemistry, physical chemistry, organic chemistry, analytical chemistry, environmental chemistry, plant biochemistry, geochemistry.

Department of Wildlife and Fisheries
Department Head: C. G. Scalet, Ph.D., Oklahoma. Telephone: 605-688-4777.
Limnology, ecology and management, aquatic ecology, wetland ecology and management, aquaculture.

Northern Great Plains Water Resources Research Center
Director: V. R. Schaefer, Ph.D., Virginia Tech. Telephone: 605-688-6252.
Artificial recharge of groundwater, numerical modeling, solid and hazardous landfill design, till hydrology, drinking water, wastewater, wetland groundwater modeling, watershed management, expert systems, statistical hydrology, animal waste lagoons.

South Dakota School of Mines and Technology / South Dakota State University

SELECTED PUBLICATIONS

Capehart, W. J., and T. N. Carlson. Decoupling of surface and near-surface soil water content: A remote sensing perspective. *Water Resour. Res.* 33:1383–95, 1997.

Davis, A. D., C. J. Webb, and T. V. Durkin. A watershed approach to evaluating impacts of abandoned mines in the Bear Butte Creek basin of the Black Hills. *Mining Eng.* 51(9):49–56, 1997.

Davis, A. D., and **C. J. Webb.** Ground-water flow simulations and geochemical modeling of arsenic transport in the Madison aquifer of the Black Hills. In *SME Pre-Print 97-81.* Littleton, Colo.: Society for Mining, Metallurgy, and Exploration, Inc., 1997.

Davis, A. D., C. J. Webb, and C. J. Paterson. Comprehensive inventory of abandoned mines in the Black Hills of South Dakota. *Mining Eng.* 50(7):84–6, 1997.

Davis, A. D., and P. H. Rahn. Karstic gypsum problems at wastewater stabilization sites in the Black Hills of South Dakota. *Carbonates Evaporites* 12(1):73–80, 1997.

Rahn, P. H., and **A. D. Davis.** An educational and research well field. *J. Geosci. Educ.* 44:506–17, 1996.

Davis, A. D., A. Heriba, and **C. J. Webb.** Prediction of nitrate concentrations in effluent from spent ore. *Mining Eng.* 48(2):79–83, 1996.

Davis, A. D., and G. A. Zabolotney. Ground-water flow simulations for the determination of post-mining recharge rates at the Belle Ayr Mine. *Mining Eng.* 48(11):80–3, 1996.

Rahn, P. H., and **A. D. Davis.** Gypsum foundation problems in the Black Hills area, South Dakota. *Environ. Eng. Geosci.* 2(2):213–23, 1996.

Rahn, P. H., **A. D. Davis, C. J. Webb,** and A. D. Nichols. Water quality impacts from mining in the Black Hills, South Dakota, USA. *Environ. Geol.* 27(1):38–53, 1996.

Rahn, P. H., and **A. D. Davis.** Engineering geology of the central and northern Black Hills. Road Log. Field Trip 7. In *Guidebook to the Geology of the Black Hills, South Dakota, Bulletin No. 19,* pp. 38–50, eds. C. J. Paterson and J. G. Kirchner. Rapid City, S. Dak.: South Dakota School of Mines and Technology, 1996.

Detwiler, A. G., and H. Norment. The M-meter: A simple airborne hydrometer measurement instrument. *J. Atmos. Oceanic Technol.* 16:960–9, 1999.

Rogerson, A., and **A. G. Detwiler.** Abundance of airborne heterotrophic protists in ground level air of South Dakota. *Atmos. Res.* 51:35–44, 1999.

Mo, Q., R. E. Feind, F. J. Kopp, and **A. G. Detwiler.** Improved electric field measurements with the T-28 armored research aircraft. *J. Geophys. Res.* 104(24):485–97, 1999.

Ramachandran, R., et al. **(A. G. Detwiler, J. H. Helsdon,** and **P. L. Smith).** Precipitation development and electrification in Florida thunderstorm cells during CaPE. *J. Geophys. Res.* 101(D1):1599–619, 1996.

Farwell, S. O., J. R. Burdge, and D. L. MacTaggart. Realistic detection limits from confidence bands. *J. Chem. Educ.,* in press.

Farwell, S. O., et al. A continuous monitor-sulfur chemiluminescence detector (CM-SCD) system for the measurement of total gaseous sulfur species in air. *Atmos. Environ.,* in press.

Farwell, S. O., et al. Generation and evaluation of test gas mixtures for the Gaseous Sulfur Intercomparison Experiment (GASIE). *J. Geophys. Res.* 102(D13):16237, 1997.

Farwell, S. O. *Modern Gas Chromatographic Instrumentation in Analytical Instrumentation Handbook,* 2nd ed., pp. 1205–85. New York: Marcel Dekker, Inc., 1997.

Farwell, S. O., et al. Results of the Gas-Phase Sulfur Intercomparison Experiment (GASIE): Overview of experimental setup, results, and general conclusions. *J. Geophys. Res.* 102(D13):16219, 1997.

Farwell, S. O., et al. Airborne measurements of total sulfur gases during NASA GTE/CITE 3. *J. Geophys. Res.* 100:7223, 1995.

Farwell, S. O., et al. A modified microcomputer-controlled proportioning valve instrument for programmable dilution of gases. *Instrum. Sci. Technol.* 23:277, 1995.

Farwell, S. O., J. R. Burdge, Z. Cei, and J. Papillon. A novel focusing injection technique for chemiluminescent detection of volatile sulfur compounds separated by GC. *J. High Resolut. Chromatogr.* 17:1, 1994.

French, J. R., **J. H. Helsdon, A. G. Detwiler,** and **P. L. Smith.** Microphysical and electrical evolution of a Florida thunderstorm. Part 1: Observations. *J. Geophys. Res.* 101:18961–77, 1996.

Cooper, K. A., et al. **(M. R. Hjelmfelt).** Numerical simulation of transitions in boundary layer convective structures in a lake-effect snow event. *Mon. Weather Rev.* 128, in press.

Kristovich, D. A. R., et al. **(M. R. Hjelmfelt).** Transitions in boundary layer meso-gamma convective structures: An observational case study. *Mon. Weather Rev.* 127:2895–909, 1999.

Kilmowski, B. A., et al. **(M. R. Hjelmfelt** and **L. R. Johnson).** Hailstorm damage observed from the GOES-B satellite: The 05-06 July Butte-Meade Storm. *Mon. Weather Rev.* 126:352–5, 1997.

Nair, U. S., **M. R. Hjelmfelt,** and R. A. Pielke. Numerical simulation of the June 9–10, 1972 Black Hills storm using CSU RAMS. *Mon. Weather Rev.* 125:1753–66, 1997.

Farley, R. D., D. L. Hjermstad, and **H. D. Orville.** Numerical simulation of cloud seeding effects during a four-day storm period. *J. Appl. Meteorol.,* in press.

Orville, H. D., C. Wang, and F. J. Kopp. A simplified concept for hygroscopic seeding. *J. Weather Modif.* 30:7–21, 1998.

Orville, H. D. History of research in cloud dynamics and microphysics. In *Historical Essays on Meteorology 1919–1995,* pp. 225–59, ed. J. R. Fleming. Boston: American Meteorological Society, 1996.

Orville, H. D. A review of cloud modeling in weather modification. *Bull. Am. Meteorol. Soc.* 77:1535–55, 1996.

Tanaka, K. L., D. A. Senske, **M. Price,** and R. L. Kirk. Physiography, geomorphic/geologic mapping, and stratigraphy of Venus. In *Venus II–Geology, Geophysics, Atmosphere, and Solar Wind Environment,* eds. R. J. Phillips et al. Tucson, Ariz.: University of Arizona Press, 1997.

Herrick, R., and **M. Price.** It's a dry heat: The geology of Venus from Magellan. Set of 40 slides. Houston, Tex.: Lunar and Planetary Institute, 1997.

Price, M., G. Watson, J. Suppe, and C. Brankman. Dating volcanism and rifting on Venus using impact crater densities. *J. Geophys. Res.* 101(E2):4657–71, 1996.

Price, M., and J. Suppe. Constraints on the resurfacing history of Venus from the hypsometry and distribution of tectonism, volcanism, and impact craters. *Earth Moon Planets* 71:99–145, 1995.

Price, M., and J. Suppe. Mean age of rifting and volcanism on Venus deduced from impact crater densities. *Nature* 372:756–9, 1994.

Smith, P. L., D. J. Musil, **A. G. Detwiler,** and R. Ramachandran. Observations of mixed-phase precipitation within a CaPE thunderstorm. *J. Appl. Meteorol.* 38:145–55, 1999.

Vierling, L. A., and C. A. Wessman. Photosynthetically active radiation heterogeneity within a central African monodominant rain forest canopy. *Agric. Forest Meteorol.,* in press.

South Dakota School of Mines and Technology/South Dakota State University

Selected Publications (continued)

Guenther, A., et al. **(L. A. Vierling).** Isoprene emission estimates and uncertainties for the Central African EXPRESSO study domain. *J. Geophys. Res. (Atmos.)* 104(D23):30, 625–30, 639, 1999.

Guenther, A., et al. **(L. A. Vierling** and **P. Zimmerman).** Biogenic hydrocarbon emissions and landcover/climate change in a subtropical savanna. *Phys. Chem. Earth* 24(6):659–67, 1999.

Vierling, L. A. Palynological evidence for late and postglacial environmental change in central Colorado. *Quaternary Res.* 49:222–32, 1998.

Vierling, L. A., D. W. Deering, and T. F. Eck. Differences in arctic tundra vegetation type and phenology as seen using bidirectional radiometry in the early growing season. *Remote Sens. Environ.* 60(1):71–82, 1997.

Eck, T. F., D. W. Deering, and **L. A. Vierling**. Estimation of total albedo from spectral hemispheric reflectance for arctic tundra. *Int. J. Remote Sens.* 18(17):3535–49, 1997.

Delmas, R. A., et al. **(P. Zimmerman).** Experiment for regional sources and sinks of oxidants (EXPRESSO): An overview. *J. Geophys. Res. (Atmos.)* 104(D23):30, 609–30, 1999.

Isebrands, J. G., et al. **(P. Zimmerman).** Volatile organic compound emission rates from mixed deciduous and coniferous forests in northern Wisconsin, USA. *Atmos. Environ.* 33:2527–36, 1999.

Greenberg, J. P., et al. **(P. Zimmerman).** Tethered balloon measurements of biogenic VOCs in the atmospheric boundary layer. *Atmos. Environ.* 33:855–67, 1998.

Helmig, D., J. Greenberg, A. Guenther, and **P. Zimmerman.** Volatile organic compounds and isoprene oxidation products at a temperate deciduous forest site. *J. Geophys. Res.* 103:22, 397–414, 1998.

Helmig, D., et al. **(P. Zimmerman).** Biogenic volatile organic compound emissions (BVOCs). I. Identifications from three continental sites in the U.S. *Chemosphere* 38:2163–87, 1998.

Helmig, D., et al. **(P. Zimmerman).** Biogenic volatile organic compound emissions (BVOCs). II. Landscape flux potentials from three continental sites in the U.S. *Chemosphere* 38:2189–204, 1998.

Klinger, L. F., et al. **(P. Zimmerman).** Patterns in volatile organic compound emissions along a savanna-rainforest gradient in central Africa. *J. Geophys. Res.* 103:1143–54, 1998.

Serca, D., et al. **(P. Zimmerman).** Methyl bromide deposition to soils. *Atmos. Environ.* 32:1581–6, 1998.

Harley, P., A. Guenther, and **P. Zimmerman.** Environmental controls over isoprene emission in deciduous oak canopies. *Tree Phys.* 17:705–14, 1997.

Singh, G. P., and **P. Zimmerman.** A new method for estimation of methane from ruminant using sulphur hexafluoride tracer technique. *Pashudhan* 12(7):50488/87. Bengalore, India: Brindavan Printers and Publishers (P) Ltd., 1997.

STONY BROOK UNIVERSITY, STATE UNIVERSITY OF NEW YORK

Marine Sciences Research Center and the Institute for Terrestrial and Planetary Atmospheres

Programs of Study

The Marine Sciences Research Center (MSRC) and the Institute for Terrestrial and Planetary Atmospheres (ITPA) offer a Ph.D. degree in Marine and Atmospheric Sciences, with specializations in marine sciences and atmospheric sciences. MSRC and ITPA are top-rated research centers that maintain a collegial, cooperative atmosphere among students and faculty members.

A typical program of study begins with a coordinated set of core courses covering fundamental principles of marine sciences or atmospheric sciences. At the same time, students are encouraged to join an ongoing research activity to help identify an area of specialization. Approximately five years are required to complete the Ph.D.

Oceanographic research and teaching in marine sciences focus on collaborative, interdisciplinary study of oceanographic processes, combining biological, chemical, geological, and physical oceanographic approaches, to examine a wide range of issues, including biogeochemical cycling, fate and effects of contaminants, coastal environmental health, habitat destruction, and living marine resources. An important focus of the Center is regional coastal problems, such as coastal habitat alteration, diseases of marine animals, harmful algal blooms, and effects of contaminants on biota. Equally important are studies of diverse problems throughout the world; faculty members at MSRC are currently carrying out research in the Caribbean Sea, the Mediterranean Sea, Papua New Guinea, Bangladesh, and the Canadian Arctic, among others. A wide variety of approaches are employed, including shipboard sampling, remote sensing, field and laboratory experiments, laboratory analyses, and computer modeling and simulation. More information can be found at http://msrc.sunysb.edu.

The Institute for Terrestrial and Planetary Atmospheres teaches students how to apply their knowledge of mathematics, physics, and chemistry to increase understanding of the atmospheres of Earth and other planets. Completion of the degree program requires a thorough understanding of principles of atmospheric science, coupled with the ability to apply that knowledge to significant problems. Research is conducted at various temporal and spatial scales, from the daily evolution of the atmospheric state—weather—to longer-scale climate variabilities, including those associated with El Niño and global warming. Comprehensive data sets from satellites, field experiments, laboratory measurements, and meteorological observations are analyzed in the context of global three-dimensional weather and climate models and simplified conceptual models. A key goal is to achieve better understanding of the physical bases of numerical weather forecasting and climate prediction, including the size and timing of future greenhouse warming. More information can be found at http://atmos.msrc.sunysb.edu.

Research Facilities

Facilities at the Marine Sciences Research Center are modern and comprehensive and support a wide range of oceanographic research. Major shared-use facilities include the *R/V Seawolf,* a 24-meter research ship; a running seawater laboratory; a multibeam echosounder for detailed seabed mapping; a laser ablation/inductively coupled plasma/mass spectrometer (LA-ICP-MS); a liquid chromatograph/time of flight/mass spectrometer (LC/TF/MS); and an analytical facility for CHN and nutrient analyses. A "clean" laboratory and environmental incubators are also available. Individual research laboratories contain facilities for a wide range of biological, chemical, physical, and geological research, including molecular biology, marine geochemistry, and naturally occurring radioisotopes. A marine disease and pathology laboratory is available, as are a large number of computers.

The Institute for Terrestrial and Planetary Atmospheres' computer facilities include several high-end multiple processor alpha UNIX stations, plus a large network of PC/UNIX/LINUX/Mac computers, printers, graphics terminals, and hard-copy plotters. The Institute maintains a comprehensive system to display real-time weather data, satellite measurements, and numerical model products. It has a state-of-the-art weather laboratory and remote sensing laboratory. The spectroscopy laboratories have infrared (grating) spectrometers, low-temperature absorption cells, a tunable diode laser spectrometer, and a high-resolution Fourier-transform spectrometer. A stable isotope mass spectrometer is maintained in the atmospheric isotope laboratory. Students have access to millimeter-wavelength remote-sensing equipment, developed at Stony Brook, and to data from NASA missions.

Financial Aid

Assistantships and fellowships provide academic-year stipends ranging from $11,655 to $21,000 for 2004–05, depending on status.

Cost of Study

Tuition for 2004–05 is $6900 for residents of New York State and $10,500 for nonresidents. Miscellaneous fees, such as insurance and activity fees, total about $300. Tuition scholarships are available.

Living and Housing Costs

In 2003–04, living costs ranged from $600 to $1000 per month for single students living on campus. Off-campus rentals, preferred by most students, are also available.

Student Group

Approximately 95 students are engaged in research in marine sciences, and about 25 graduate students are in atmospheric sciences.

Location

Stony Brook is located about 50 miles east of Manhattan on the wooded North Shore of Long Island, convenient to New York City's cultural life and Suffolk County's recreational countryside and seashores. Long Island's hundreds of miles of magnificent coastline attract many swimming, boating, and fishing enthusiasts from around the world.

The University

Established forty years ago as New York's comprehensive State University Center for Long Island and metropolitan New York, Stony Brook offers excellent programs in a broad spectrum of academic subjects. The University conducts major research and public service projects. Over the past decade, externally funded support for Stony Brook's research programs has grown faster than that of any other university in the United States and now exceeds $125 million per year. The University's renowned faculty members teach courses from the undergraduate to the doctoral level to more than 22,000 students. More than 100 undergraduate and graduate departmental and interdisciplinary majors are offered.

Applying

Students applying for graduate study in marine sciences should have a B.S. in biology, chemistry, geology, or physics. Students applying for atmospheric sciences should have a B.S. in physics, chemistry, mathematics, engineering, or atmospheric science. Applicants may write for information about research opportunities to a graduate program faculty member whose research is of primary interest to them. Applications for September admission should be received by January 15 to ensure consideration for the widest range of support opportunities. Students may request an online application at http://www.msrc.sunysb.edu/pages/gradapp.html and apply online at http://www.grad.sunysb.edu/applying/applying.htm.

Correspondence and Information

Nancy Glover
Marine Sciences Research Center
Stony Brook University, State University of New York
Stony Brook, New York 11794-5000
Telephone: 631-632-8681
Fax: 631-632-8820
E-mail: nglover@notes.cc.sunysb.edu

Gina Gartin
Institute for Terrestrial and Planetary Atmospheres
Stony Brook University, State University of New York
Stony Brook, New York 11794-5000
Telephone: 631-632-8009
Fax: 631-632-6251
E-mail: ggartin@notes.cc.sunysb.edu

Stony Brook University, State University of New York

THE FACULTY AND THEIR RESEARCH

MARINE SCIENCES

Bassem Allam, Assistant Professor; Ph.D., Western Brittany (France), 1998. Pathology and immunology of marine bivalves.
Josephine Y. Aller, Associate Professor; Ph.D., USC, 1975. Marine benthic ecology, invertebrate zoology, marine microbiology, biogeochemistry.
Robert C. Aller, Distinguished Professor; Ph.D., Yale, 1977. Marine geochemistry, marine animal-sediment relations.
Robert A. Armstrong, Associate Professor; Ph.D., Minnesota, 1975. Mathematical modeling in marine ecology and biogeochemistry.
Henry J. Bokuniewicz, Professor; Ph.D., Yale, 1976. Nearshore transport processes, coastal groundwater hydrology, coastal sedimentation, marine geophysics.
Malcolm J. Bowman, Professor; Ph.D., Saskatchewan, 1970. Coastal ocean and estuarine dynamics.
Bruce J. Brownawell, Associate Professor; Ph.D., MIT (Woods Hole), 1986. Biogeochemistry of organic pollutants in seawater and groundwater.
Robert M. Cerrato, Associate Professor; Ph.D., Yale, 1980. Benthic ecology, population and community dynamics.
J. Kirk Cochran, Professor; Ph.D., Yale, 1979. Marine geochemistry, use of radionuclides as geochemical tracers; diagenesis of marine sediments.
Jackie Collier, Assistant Professor; Ph.D., Stanford, 1994. Phytoplankton ecology, physiology, and molecular genetics.
David O. Conover, Professor and Dean, MSRC; Ph.D., Massachusetts, 1982. Ecology of fish, fisheries biology.
Alistair Dove, Adjunct Assistant Professor; Ph.D., Queensland (Australia), 1999. Pathology, taxonomy, life cycles/ecology.
Nicholas S. Fisher, Professor; Ph.D., SUNY at Stony Brook, 1974. Marine phytoplankton physiology and ecology, biogeochemistry of metals, marine pollution.
Roger D. Flood, Professor; Ph.D., MIT (Woods Hole), 1978. Marine geology, sediment dynamics, continental margin sedimentation.
Steven L. Goodbred Jr., Assistant Professor; Ph.D., William and Mary, 1999. Coastal marine sedimentology, quaternary development of continental margins, salt-marsh processes.
Paul F. Kemp, Adjunct Associate Professor; Ph.D., Oregon State, 1985. Growth and activity of marine microbes, benthic-pelagic interactions, molecular ecology of marine bacteria.
Cindy Lee, Distinguished Professor; Ph.D., California, San Diego (Scripps), 1975. Ocean carbon cycle, marine geochemistry of organic compounds, nitrogen-cycle biochemistry, biomineralization.
Darcy J. Lonsdale, Associate Professor; Ph.D., Maryland, 1979. Ecology and physiology of marine zooplankton, food web dynamics of estuarine plankton, impacts of harmful algal blooms.
Glenn R. Lopez, Professor; Ph.D., SUNY at Stony Brook, 1976. Marine benthic ecology, animal-sediment interactions, contaminant uptake.
Kamazima M.M. Lwiza, Associate Professor; Ph.D., Wales, 1990. Structure and dynamics of shelf-seas and remote sensing oceanography.
Anne E. McElroy, Associate Professor; Ph.D., MIT (Woods Hole), 1985. Toxicology of aquatic organisms, contaminant bioaccumulation, estrogenicity of organic contaminants.
Frank J. Roethel, Lecturer; Ph.D., SUNY at Stony Brook, 1982. Environmental chemistry, municipal solid waste management impacts.
Sergio A. Sañudo-Wilhelmy, Associate Professor; Ph.D., California, Santa Cruz, 1993. Geochemical cycles of trace elements, marine pollution.
Mary I. Scranton, Professor; Ph.D., MIT (Woods Hole), 1977. Marine geochemistry, biological-chemical interactions in seawater.
R. Lawrence Swanson, Adjunct Professor; Ph.D., Oregon State, 1971. Recycling and reuse of waste materials, waste management.
Gordon T. Taylor, Associate Professor; Ph.D., Southern California, 1983. Marine microbiology; interests in microbial ecology, plankton trophodynamics, and marine biofouling.
Dong-Ping Wang, Professor; Ph.D., Miami, 1975. Coastal ocean dynamics.
Robert E. Wilson, Associate Professor; Ph.D., Johns Hopkins, 1974. Estuarine and coastal ocean dynamics.
Peter M.J. Woodhead, Adjunct Professor; B.Sc.Hon. 1 Cl., Durham (England), 1953. Behavior and physiology of fish, coral reef ecology, ocean energy conversion systems.

ATMOSPHERIC SCIENCES

Robert D. Cess, Distinguished Professor Emeritus; Ph.D., Pittsburgh, 1959. Radiative transfer and climate modeling, greenhouse effect, intercomparison of global climate models.
Edmund K.M. Chang, Associate Professor; Ph.D., Princeton, 1993. Atmospheric dynamics and diagnoses, climate dynamics, synoptic meteorology.
Brian A. Colle, Assistant Professor; Ph.D., Washington (Seattle), 1997. Synaptic meteorology, weather forecasting, mesoscale modeling.
Robert L. de Zafra, Professor Emeritus (Department of Physics with joint appointment in Marine Sciences Research Center); Ph.D., Maryland, 1958. Monitoring and detection of trace gases in the terrestrial stratosphere, changes in the ozone layer, remote-sensing instrumentation.
Marvin A. Geller, Professor; Ph.D., MIT, 1969. Atmospheric dynamics, stratosphere dynamics and transport, climate dynamics.
Sultan Hameed, Professor; Ph.D., Manchester (England), 1968. Analysis of climate change using observational data and climate models, interannual variations in climate, climate predictability.
John E. Mak, Associate Professor; Ph.D., California, San Diego (Scripps), 1992. Isotopic analysis of atmospheric gases.
Prasad Varanasi, Professor; Ph.D., California, San Diego (Scripps), 1967. Infrared spectroscopic measurements in support of NASA's space missions, atmospheric remote sensing, greenhouse effect and climate research, molecular physics at low temperatures.
Minghua Zhang, Professor and Director, ITPA; Ph.D., Academia Sinica (China), 1987. Atmospheric dynamics and climate modeling.

Section 6
Physics

This section contains a directory of institutions offering graduate work in physics, followed by in-depth entries submitted by institutions that chose to prepare detailed program descriptions. Additional information about programs listed in the directory but not augmented by an in-depth entry may be obtained by writing directly to the dean of a graduate school or chair of a department at the address given in the directory.

For programs offering related work, see all other areas in this book. In Book 3, see Biological and Biomedical Sciences and Biophysics; in Book 5, see Aerospace/Aeronautical Engineering, Electrical and Computer Engineering, Energy and Power Engineering (Nuclear Engineering), Engineering and Applied Sciences, Engineering Physics, Materials Sciences and Engineering, and Mechanical Engineering and Mechanics; and in Book 6, see Allied Health and Optometry and Vision Sciences.

CONTENTS

Program Directories

Announcements

Cross-Discipline Announcements

In-Depth Descriptions

Acoustics

The Catholic University of America, School of Engineering, Department of Mechanical Engineering, Washington, DC 20064. Offers design (D Engr, PhD); design and robotics (MME, D Engr, PhD); fluid mechanics and thermal science (MME, D Engr, PhD); mechanical design (MME); ocean and structural acoustics (MME, MS Engr, PhD). Part-time and evening/weekend programs available. *Students:* 3 full-time (1 woman), 7 part-time (1 woman), 2 international. Average age 33. 27 applicants, 41% accepted, 1 enrolled. In 2003, 4 master's, 4 doctorates awarded. *Degree requirements:* For master's, thesis or alternative; for doctorate, thesis/dissertation, oral exams, comprehensive exam. *Entrance requirements:* For master's and doctorate, 2 letters of recommendation. Additional exam requirements/recommendations for international students: Required—TOEFL (minimum score 550 paper-based; 213 computer-based). *Application deadline:* For fall admission, 2/1 for domestic students; for spring admission, 11/15 priority date for domestic students. Applications are processed on a rolling basis. Application fee: $55. Electronic applications accepted. *Expenses:* Contact institution. *Financial support:* Research assistantships, teaching assistantships, career-related internships or fieldwork, Federal Work-Study, institutionally sponsored loans, and tuition waivers (full and partial) available. Support available to part-time students. Financial award application deadline: 2/1; financial award applicants required to submit FAFSA. *Faculty research:* Automated engineering. *Unit head:* Dr. J. Steven Brown, Chair, 202-319-5170, Fax: 202-319-5173, E-mail: brownjs@cua.edu.

Naval Postgraduate School, Graduate Programs, Program in Engineering Acoustics, Monterey, CA 93943. Offers MS, D Eng, PhD. Program only open to commissioned officers of the United States and friendly nations and selected United States federal civilian employees. Part-time programs available. *Degree requirements:* For master's, thesis; for doctorate, one foreign language, thesis/dissertation.

The Pennsylvania State University University Park Campus, Graduate School, Intercollege Graduate Programs and College of Engineering, Intercollege Graduate Program in Acoustics, State College, University Park, PA 16802-1503. Offers M Eng, MS, PhD. Postbaccalaureate distance learning degree programs offered (minimal on-campus study). *Students:* 49 full-time (11 women), 9 part-time (1 woman); includes 5 minority (2 Asian Americans or Pacific Islanders, 3 Hispanic Americans), 11 international. *Degree requirements:* For doctorate, thesis/dissertation. *Entrance requirements:* For master's and doctorate, GRE General Test. Application fee: $45. *Expenses:* Tuition, state resident: full-time $10,010; part-time $417 per credit. Tuition, nonresident: full-time $19,830; part-time $826 per credit. Full-time tuition and fees vary according to course level, course load, campus/location and program. *Unit head:* Dr. Anthony Atchley, Chair, 814-865-6364, Fax: 814-865-3119, E-mail: atchley@psu.edu.

Rensselaer Polytechnic Institute, Graduate School, School of Architecture, Program in Building Sciences, Troy, NY 12180-3590. Offers building science (MS), including acoustics, workplace design. *Faculty:* 9 full-time (1 woman), 2 part-time/adjunct (0 women). *Students:* 11 full-time (6 women). 42 applicants, 38% accepted, 10 enrolled. In 2003, 10 degrees awarded. *Degree requirements:* For master's, thesis, registration. *Entrance requirements:* For master's, GRE General Test, portfolio (except acoustics). Additional exam requirements/recommendations for international students: Required—TOEFL. *Application deadline:* For fall admission, 1/15 priority date for domestic students, 1/15 priority date for international students. Applications are processed on a rolling basis. Application fee: $45. Electronic applications accepted. *Expenses:* Tuition: Full-time $27,700; part-time $1,320 per credit. Required fees: $1,470. *Financial support:* In 2003–04, 10 students received support, including 1 fellowship with full tuition reimbursement available (averaging $10,000 per year), 9 research assistantships with full tuition reimbursements available (averaging $12,000 per year); teaching assistantships with full tuition reimbursements available Financial award application deadline: 2/15. *Faculty research:* Digital simulation and theory, architectural acoustics, lighting performance, building conservation, emerging technologies. Total annual research expenditures: $110,000. *Application contact:* Kim Newson, Admissions Coordinator, 518-276-6466, Fax: 518-276-3034, E-mail: iverskz@rpi.edu.

Applied Physics

Air Force Institute of Technology, Graduate School of Engineering and Management, Department of Engineering Physics, Dayton, OH 45433-7765. Offers applied physics (MS, PhD); electro-optics (MS, PhD); materials science (PhD); nuclear engineering (MS, PhD); space physics (MS). *Accreditation:* ABET (one or more programs are accredited). Part-time programs available. *Degree requirements:* For master's and doctorate, thesis/dissertation. *Entrance requirements:* For master's and doctorate, GRE General Test, minimum GPA of 3.0, U.S. citizenship. *Faculty research:* High-energy lasers, space physics, nuclear weapon effects, semiconductor physics.

Alabama Agricultural and Mechanical University, School of Graduate Studies, School of Arts and Sciences, Department of Natural and Physical Sciences, Huntsville, AL 35811. Offers biology (MS); physics (MS, PhD), including applied physics (PhD), materials science (PhD), optics (PhD), physics (MS). Part-time and evening/weekend programs available. *Faculty:* 17. *Students:* 37 full-time (25 women), 36 part-time (14 women); includes 67 minority (55 African Americans, 1 American Indian/Alaska Native, 10 Asian Americans or Pacific Islanders, 1 Hispanic American). In 2003, 3 master's, 1 doctorate awarded. *Degree requirements:* For doctorate, thesis/dissertation. *Entrance requirements:* For master's and doctorate, GRE General Test. *Application deadline:* For fall admission, 5/1 for domestic students. Applications are processed on a rolling basis. Application fee: $25. Electronic applications accepted. *Expenses:* Tuition, state resident: full-time $3,250; part-time $370 per credit hour. Tuition, nonresident: full-time $6,490; part-time $740 per credit hour. *Financial support:* In 2003–04, 1 fellowship with tuition reimbursement (averaging $18,000 per year), 5 research assistantships with tuition reimbursements (averaging $10,000 per year), 1 teaching assistantship with tuition reimbursement (averaging $10,000 per year) were awarded. Career-related internships or fieldwork and Federal Work-Study also available. Financial award application deadline: 4/1. Total annual research expenditures: $1.5 million. *Unit head:* Dr. R. V. Lal, Chair, 256-372-8148.

Appalachian State University, Cratis D. Williams Graduate School, College of Arts and Sciences, Department of Physics and Astronomy, Boone, NC 28608. Offers applied physics (MS). *Faculty:* 7 full-time (0 women). *Students:* 7 full-time (3 women), 1 part-time; includes 2 minority (1 African American, 1 Asian American or Pacific Islander). 5 applicants, 100% accepted, 4 enrolled. In 2003, 8 degrees awarded. *Degree requirements:* For master's, thesis optional. *Entrance requirements:* For master's, GRE General Test. Additional exam requirements/recommendations for international students: Required—TOEFL (minimum score 570 paper-based; 230 computer-based). *Application deadline:* For fall admission, 7/1 for domestic students, 1/1 for international students; for spring admission, 11/1 for domestic students, 6/1 for international students. Applications are processed on a rolling basis. Application fee: $35. *Expenses:* Tuition, state resident: full-time $1,668; part-time $208 per credit. Tuition, nonresident: full-time $11,176; part-time $1,397 per credit. Required fees: $1,361; $196 per term. *Financial support:* In 2003–04, 6 students received support, including 1 fellowship (averaging $1,000 per year), 6 research assistantships with tuition reimbursements available (averaging $8,500 per year), 1 teaching assistantship with tuition reimbursement available (averaging $8,000 per year); career-related internships or fieldwork, Federal Work-Study, scholarships/grants, and unspecified assistantships also available. Support available to part-time students. Financial award application deadline: 7/1; financial award applicants required to submit FAFSA. *Faculty research:* Raman spectroscopy, applied electrostatics, scanning tunneling microscope/atomic force microscope (STM/AFM), stellar spectroscopy and photometry, surface physics, remote sensing. Total annual research expenditures: $132,812. *Unit head:* Dr. Anthony Calamai, Chairperson, 828-262-3090, E-mail: calamai@appstate.edu. *Application contact:* Dr. Sid Clements, Director, 828-262-2447, E-mail: clementsjs@appstate.edu.

Brooklyn College of the City University of New York, Division of Graduate Studies, Department of Physics, Brooklyn, NY 11210-2889. Offers applied physics (MA); physics (MA, PhD). The department is a full participant in the PhD program; it offers a complete sequence of courses that are creditable toward the CUNY doctoral degree, and a wide range of research opportunities in fulfillment of the doctoral dissertation requirements for that degree. Part-time programs available. *Students:* 1 (woman) full-time; minority (Asian American or Pacific Islander) 8 applicants, 38% accepted, 1 enrolled.Terminal master's awarded for partial completion of doctoral program. *Degree requirements:* For master's, comprehensive exam. *Entrance requirements:* For master's, GRE, 2 letters of recommendation; for doctorate, GRE. Additional exam requirements/recommendations for international students: Required—TOEFL. *Application deadline:* For fall admission, 3/1 for domestic students, 2/1 for international students; for spring admission, 11/1 for domestic students, 10/1 for international students. Application fee: $50. *Expenses:* Tuition, state resident: full-time $5,440; part-time $230 per credit. Tuition, nonresident: full-time $10,200; part-time $425 per credit. Required fees: $280; $103 per term. *Financial support:* Fellowships, research assistantships, teaching assistantships, Federal Work-Study, institutionally sponsored loans, scholarships/grants, and tuition waivers (full and partial) available. Support available to part-time students. Financial award application deadline: 5/1; financial award applicants required to submit FAFSA. *Unit head:* Dr. Peter Lesser, Chairperson, 718-951-5418, Fax: 718-951-4407, E-mail: cshakin@brooklyn.cuny.edu. *Application contact:* Michael Lovaglio, Assistant Director of Graduate Admissions, 718-951-5001, E-mail: adminqry@brooklyn.cuny.edu.

California Institute of Technology, Division of Engineering and Applied Science, Option in Applied Physics, Pasadena, CA 91125-0001. Offers MS, PhD. *Faculty:* 10 full-time (0 women), 1 part-time/adjunct (0 women). *Students:* 84 full-time (14 women); includes 12 minority (9 Asian Americans or Pacific Islanders, 3 Hispanic Americans), 39 international. 118 applicants, 17% accepted, 9 enrolled. In 2003, 16 master's, 4 doctorates awarded. *Degree requirements:* For doctorate, thesis/dissertation. *Application deadline:* For fall admission, 1/15 for domestic students. Application fee: $0. Electronic applications accepted. *Financial support:* In 2003–04, 18 research assistantships were awarded. *Faculty research:* Solid-state electronics, quantum electronics, plasmas, linear and nonlinear laser optics, electromagnetic theory. *Unit head:* Dr. Kerry Vahala, Representative, 626-395-2144.

Christopher Newport University, Graduate Studies, Department of Physics, Computer Science, and Engineering, Newport News, VA 23606-2998. Offers applied physics and computer science (MS). Part-time and evening/weekend programs available. *Faculty:* 15 full-time (2 women). *Students:* 4 full-time (0 women), 33 part-time (5 women); includes 6 minority (3 African Americans, 1 American Indian/Alaska Native, 2 Asian Americans or Pacific Islanders), 1 international. Average age 36. 6 applicants, 100% accepted. In 2003, 5 degrees awarded. *Degree requirements:* For master's, thesis or alternative, comprehensive exam. *Entrance requirements:* For master's, GRE General Test, minimum GPA of 3.0. *Application deadline:* For fall admission, 5/1 for domestic students; for spring admission, 11/1 for domestic students. Applications are processed on a rolling basis. Application fee: $40. Electronic applications accepted. *Expenses:* Tuition, state resident: part-time $139 per credit hour. Tuition, nonresident: part-time $448 per credit hour. Required fees: $74 per credit hour. *Financial support:* In 2003–04, 5 fellowships with full tuition reimbursements (averaging $3,300 per year), 1 research assistantship with full and partial tuition reimbursement (averaging $2,000 per year) were awarded. Career-related internships or fieldwork and Federal Work-Study also available. Support available to part-time students. Financial award application deadline: 3/1; financial award applicants required to submit FAFSA. *Faculty research:* Advanced programming methodologies, experimental nuclear physics, computer architecture, semiconductor nanophysics, laser and optical fiber sensors. *Unit head:* Dr. David Hibler, Coordinator, 757-594-7360, Fax: 757-594-7919, E-mail: dhibler@pcs.cnu.edu. *Application contact:* Susan R. Chittenden, Graduate Admissions, 757-594-7359, Fax: 757-594-7333, E-mail: gradstdy@cnu.edu.

Colorado School of Mines, Graduate School, Department of Physics, Golden, CO 80401-1887. Offers applied physics (PhD); physics (MS). Part-time programs available. *Faculty:* 16 full-time (2 women), 3 part-time/adjunct (1 woman). *Students:* 23 full-time (7 women), 8 part-time (3 women); includes 3 minority (2 Asian Americans or Pacific Islanders, 1 Hispanic American), 8 international. 29 applicants, 55% accepted, 7 enrolled. In 2003, 3 degrees awarded. *Degree requirements:* For master's, thesis/dissertation; for doctorate, thesis/dissertation, comprehensive exam. *Entrance requirements:* For master's and doctorate, GRE General Test, GRE Subject Test. Additional exam requirements/recommendations for international students: Required—TOEFL (minimum score 550 paper-based; 213 computer-based). *Application deadline:* For fall admission, 12/1 priority date for domestic students, 12/1 priority date for international students; for spring admission, 5/1 priority date for domestic students, 5/1 priority date for international students. Application fee: $45. Electronic applications accepted. *Expenses:* Tuition, state resident: full-time $5,700; part-time $285 per credit hour. Tuition, nonresident: full-time $19,040; part-time $952 per credit hour. Required fees: $733. *Financial support:* In 2003–04, 13 students received support, including fellowships with full tuition reimbursements available (averaging $12,500 per year), 14 research assistantships with full tuition reimbursements available (averaging $10,000 per year), 9 teaching assistantships with full tuition reimbursements available (averaging $10,000 per year); scholarships/grants and unspecified assistantships also available. Financial award applicants required to submit FAFSA. *Faculty research:* Light scattering, low-energy nuclear physics, high fusion plasma diagnostics, laser operations, mathematical physics. Total annual research expenditures: $6.6 million. *Unit head:* Dr. James A. McNeil, Head, 303-273-3844, Fax: 303-273-3919, E-mail: jamcneil@mine.edu. *Application contact:* Jeff Squier, Professor, 303-384-2385, Fax: 303-273-3919, E-mail: jsquier@mines.edu.

Columbia University, Fu Foundation School of Engineering and Applied Science, Department of Applied Physics and Applied Mathematics, New York, NY 10027. Offers applied physics (MS, PhD), including applied mathematics (PhD), optical physics (PhD), plasma physics (PhD), solid state physics (PhD); applied physics and applied mathematics (Eng Sc D); materials science and engineering (MS, Eng Sc D, PhD); medical physics (MS); minerals engineering and materials science (Eng Sc D, PhD, Engr). Part-time programs available. *Faculty:* 29 full-time (3 women), 11 part-time/adjunct (1 woman). *Students:* 82 full-time (25 women), 27 part-time (13 women); includes 14 minority (5 African Americans, 8 Asian Americans or Pacific Islanders, 1 Hispanic American), 51 international. 371 applicants, 17% accepted, 41 enrolled. In 2003, 36 master's, 9 doctorates awarded. Terminal master's awarded for partial completion of doctoral program. *Degree requirements:* For doctorate, thesis/dissertation, qualifying exam. *Entrance requirements:* For master's and doctorate, GRE General Test, GRE Subject Test (strongly recommended). Additional exam requirements/recommendations for international students: Required—TOEFL. *Application deadline:* For fall admission, 12/15 priority date for domestic students, 12/15 priority date for international students; for spring admission, 10/1 priority date for domestic students, 10/1 priority date for international students. Application fee: $55. Electronic applications accepted. *Expenses:* Tuition: Full-time $14,820. *Financial support:* In 2003–04, 62 students received support, including 4 fellowships with full tuition reimbursements available, 40 research assistantships with full tuition reimbursements available (averaging $22,725 per year), 14 teaching assistantships with full tuition reimbursements available (averaging $22,725 per year); Federal Work-Study and unspecified assistantships also available. Financial award application deadline: 12/15; financial award applicants required to submit FAFSA. *Faculty research:* Plasma physics, applied mathematics, solid-state and optical physics, atmospheric, oceanic and earth physics, materials science and engineering. Total annual research expenditures: $7.9 million. *Unit head:* Dr. Michael E. Mauel, Chairman, 212-854-4457, E-mail: seasinfo.apam@columbia.edu. *Application contact:* Marlene Arbo, Department Administrator, 212-854-4458, Fax: 212-854-8257, E-mail: seasinfo.apam@columbia.edu.

See in-depth description on page 357.

Cornell University, Graduate School, Graduate Fields of Engineering, Field of Applied Physics, Ithaca, NY 14853-0001. Offers applied physics (PhD); engineering physics (M Eng). *Faculty:* 46 full-time. *Students:* 85 full-time (20 women); includes 12 minority (1 American Indian/Alaska Native, 10 Asian Americans or Pacific Islanders, 1 Hispanic American), 28 international. 123 applicants, 37% accepted, 27 enrolled. In 2003, 21 master's, 4 doctorates awarded. *Degree requirements:* For doctorate, thesis/dissertation, written exams, comprehensive exam. *Entrance requirements:* For master's, GRE General Test, 3 letters of recommendation; for doctorate, GRE General Test, GRE Subject Test (physics), GRE writing assessment, 3 letters of recommendation. Additional exam requirements/recommendations for international students: Required—TOEFL (minimum score 600 paper-based; 250 computer-based). *Application deadline:* For fall admission, 1/15 for domestic students. Application fee: $60. Electronic applications accepted. *Expenses:* Tuition: Full-time $28,630. One-time fee: $50 full-time. *Financial support:* In 2003–04, 79 students received support, including 12 fellowships with full tuition reimbursements available, 56 research assistantships with full tuition reimbursements available, 11 teaching assistantships with full tuition reimbursements available; institutionally sponsored loans, scholarships/grants, health care benefits, tuition waivers (full and partial), and unspecified assistantships also available. *Faculty research:* Quantum and nonlinear optics, plasma physics, solid state physics, condensed matter physics and nanotechnology, electron and x-ray spectroscopy. *Unit head:* Graduate Faculty Representative, 607-255-0638. *Application contact:* Graduate Field Assistant, 607-255-0638, E-mail: aep_info@cornell.edu.

DePaul University, College of Liberal Arts and Sciences, Department of Physics, Chicago, IL 60604-2287. Offers applied physics (MS). Part-time and evening/weekend programs available. *Faculty:* 7 full-time (1 woman), 3 part-time/adjunct (0 women). *Students:* 4 full-time (1 woman), 3 part-time; includes 3 minority (1 African American, 1 Asian American or Pacific Islander, 1 Hispanic American), 1 international. Average age 23. 12 applicants, 42% accepted. In 2003, 4 degrees awarded. *Degree requirements:* For master's, thesis, oral exams. *Entrance requirements:* For master's, minimum GPA of 2.7. *Application deadline:* For fall admission, 6/15 for domestic students; for spring admission, 9/1 for domestic students. Applications are processed on a rolling basis. Application fee: $25. *Expenses:* Tuition: Part-time $395 per hour. *Financial support:* In 2003–04, teaching assistantships with full tuition reimbursements (averaging $6,000 per year); tuition waivers (partial) also available. *Faculty research:* Optics, solid-state physics, comology, atomic physics, nuclear physics. Total annual research expenditures: $54,000. *Unit head:* Dr. Christopher G. Goedde, Chairman, 773-325-7330, Fax: 773-325-7334, E-mail: egoedde@condor.depaul.edu. *Application contact:* Dr. Ross A. Hyman, Departmental Office, 773-325-7330, Fax: 773-325-7334.

George Mason University, College of Arts and Sciences, Department of Physics, Fairfax, VA 22030. Offers applied and engineering physics (MS). *Faculty:* 19 full-time (6 women), 11 part-time/adjunct (2 women). *Students:* Average age 30. 18 applicants, 61% accepted, 7 enrolled. In 2003, 4 degrees awarded. *Degree requirements:* For master's, thesis optional. *Entrance requirements:* For master's, minimum GPA of 2.75 in last 60 hours. *Application deadline:* For fall admission, 5/1 for domestic students; for spring admission, 11/1 for domestic students. Application fee: $60. Electronic applications accepted. *Expenses:* Tuition, state resident: full-time $4,398. Tuition, nonresident: full-time $14,952. Required fees: $1,482. *Financial support:* Research assistantships, teaching assistantships available. Support available to part-time students. Financial award application deadline: 3/1; financial award applicants required to submit FAFSA. *Unit head:* Dr. Maria Dworzecka, Chairman, 703-993-1280, Fax: 703-993-1269, E-mail: mdworzecka@gmu.edu. *Application contact:* Dr. Paul So, Information Contact, 703-993-1280, E-mail: physics@gmu.edu.

Harvard University, Graduate School of Arts and Sciences, Department of Physics, Cambridge, MA 02138. Offers experimental physics (AM, PhD); medical engineering/medical physics (PhD, Sc D), including applied physics (PhD), engineering sciences (PhD), medical engineering/medical physics (Sc D), physics (PhD); theoretical physics (AM, PhD). *Students:* 174. *Degree requirements:* For doctorate, thesis/dissertation, final exams, laboratory experience. *Entrance requirements:* For master's, GRE General Test; for doctorate, GRE General Test, GRE Subject Test. Additional exam requirements/recommendations for international students: Required—TOEFL. *Application deadline:* For fall admission, 12/14 for domestic students. Application fee: $60. *Expenses:* Tuition: Full-time $26,066. Full-time tuition and fees vary according to program and student level. *Financial support:* Fellowships, research assistantships, teaching assistantships, career-related internships or fieldwork, Federal Work-Study, and institutionally sponsored loans available. Financial award application deadline: 12/30. *Faculty research:* Particle physics, condensed matter physics, atomic physics. *Unit head:* Prof. John Huth, Chair, 617-495-8144, E-mail: huth@physics.harvard.edu. *Application contact:* Office of Admissions and Financial Aid, 617-495-5315.

See in-depth description on page 365.

Harvard University, Graduate School of Arts and Sciences, Division of Engineering and Applied Sciences, Cambridge, MA 02138. Offers applied mathematics (ME, SM, PhD); applied physics (ME, SM, PhD); computer science (ME, SM, PhD); computing technology (PhD); engineering science (ME); engineering sciences (SM, PhD). Part-time programs available. *Faculty:* 65 full-time (4 women), 10 part-time/adjunct (1 woman). *Students:* 230 full-time (55 women), 9 part-time; includes 27 minority (4 African Americans, 3 American Indian/Alaska Native, 16 Asian Americans or Pacific Islanders, 4 Hispanic Americans), 87 international. 1,112 applicants, 9% accepted. In 2003, 63 master's, 18 doctorates awarded, leading to university research/teaching 50%. Terminal master's awarded for partial completion of doctoral program. *Median time to degree:* Master's–1 year full-time, 1.5 years part-time; doctorate–6 years full-time. Of those who began their doctoral program in fall 1995, 94% received their degree in 8 years or less. *Degree requirements:* For master's, registration; for doctorate, thesis/dissertation, comprehensive exam, registration. *Entrance requirements:* For master's and doctorate, GRE General Test, GRE Subject Test (recommended), 3 letters of recommendation. Additional exam requirements/recommendations for international students: Required—TOEFL (minimum score 550 paper-based; 213 computer-based). *Application deadline:* For fall admission, 12/15 for domestic students; for winter admission, 1/2 for domestic students. Application fee: $85. Electronic applications accepted. *Expenses:* Tuition: Full-time $26,066. Full-time tuition and fees vary according to program and student level. *Financial support:* In 2003–04, 191 students received support, including 52 fellowships with full tuition reimbursements available (averaging $18,450 per year), 137 research assistantships (averaging $29,716 per year), 106 teaching assistantships (averaging $4,938 per year); Federal Work-Study and institutionally sponsored loans also available. *Faculty research:* Applied mathematics, applied physics, computer science & electrical engineering, environmental engineering, mechanical and biomedical engineering. *Unit head:* Ventatesh Narayanamurti, Dean, 617-495-5829, Fax: 617-495-5264, E-mail: venky@deas.harvard.edu. *Application contact:* Office of Admissions and Financial Aid, 617-495-5315, E-mail: admissions@deas.harvard.edu.

Iowa State University of Science and Technology, Graduate College, College of Liberal Arts and Sciences, Department of Physics and Astronomy, Ames, IA 50011. Offers applied physics (MS, PhD); astrophysics (MS, PhD); condensed matter physics (MS, PhD); high energy physics (MS, PhD); nuclear physics (MS, PhD); physics (MS, PhD). Part-time programs available. *Faculty:* 45 full-time, 4 part-time/adjunct. *Students:* 83 full-time (12 women), 5 part-time; includes 1 minority (Hispanic American), 66 international. 174 applicants, 59% accepted, 31 enrolled. In 2003, 3 master's, 4 doctorates awarded. Terminal master's awarded for partial completion of doctoral program. *Median time to degree:* Master's–2.9 years full-time; doctorate–7.1 years full-time. *Degree requirements:* For master's, thesis (for some programs); for doctorate, thesis/dissertation. *Entrance requirements:* For master's and doctorate, GRE General Test, GRE Subject Test (physics). Additional exam requirements/recommendations for international students: Required—TOEFL (paper score 550; computer score 213) or IELTS (score 6.5). *Application deadline:* For fall admission, 2/15 priority date for domestic students, 2/15 priority date for international students; for spring admission, 10/15 for domestic students, 10/15 for international students. Applications are processed on a rolling basis. Application fee: $30 ($70 for international students). Electronic applications accepted. Tuition, nonresident: part-time $560 per credit. Required fees: $38 per unit. *Financial support:* In 2003–04, 38 research assistantships with full tuition reimbursements (averaging $17,400 per year), 42 teaching assistantships with full tuition reimbursements (averaging $17,400 per year) were awarded. Fellowships, Federal Work-Study, institutionally sponsored loans, scholarships/grants, health care benefits, and unspecified assistantships also available. Support available to part-time students. Financial award application deadline: 2/15. *Faculty research:* Condensed-matter physics, including superconductivity and new materials; high-energy and nuclear physics; astronomy and astrophysics; atmospheric and environmental physics. Total annual research expenditures: $8.8 million. *Unit head:* Dr. Eli Rosenberg, Chair, 515-294-5441, Fax: 515-294-6027, E-mail: phys_astro@iastate.edu. *Application contact:* Dr. Steven Kawaler, Director of Graduate Education, 515-294-9728, E-mail: phys_astro@iastate.edu.

The Johns Hopkins University, G. W. C. Whiting School of Engineering, Part-Time Programs in Engineering and Applied Science, Department of Applied Physics, Baltimore, MD 21218-2699. Offers MS. Part-time and evening/weekend programs available. *Faculty:* 7 part-time/adjunct (1 woman). In 2003, 17 degrees awarded. *Application deadline:* Applications are processed on a rolling basis. Application fee: $70. Electronic applications accepted. *Expenses:* Tuition: Full-time $28,730; part-time $1,490 per course. Part-time tuition and fees vary according to course load, campus/location and program. *Application contact:* Bonnie Duggins, Assistant Director of Admissions, 410-540-2960, Fax: 410-579-8049, E-mail: bonnie@jhu.edu.

Laurentian University, School of Graduate Studies and Research, Programme in Physics and Astronomy, Sudbury, ON P3E 2C6, Canada. Offers M Sc. Part-time programs available. *Degree requirements:* For master's, thesis or alternative. *Entrance requirements:* For master's, honors degree with second class or better. *Faculty research:* Solar neutrino physics and astrophysics, applied acoustics and ultrasonics, powder science and technology, solid state physics, theoretical physics.

New Jersey Institute of Technology, Office of Graduate Studies, College of Science and Liberal Arts, Department of Physics, Program in Applied Physics, Newark, NJ 07102. Offers MS, PhD. Part-time and evening/weekend programs available. *Students:* 28 full-time (5 women), 9 part-time (2 women); includes 6 minority (4 Asian Americans or Pacific Islanders, 2 Hispanic Americans), 22 international. Average age 32. 43 applicants, 72% accepted, 8 enrolled. In 2003, 4 degrees awarded. Terminal master's awarded for partial completion of doctoral program. *Degree requirements:* For master's, thesis; for doctorate, thesis/dissertation, residency. *Entrance requirements:* For master's, GRE General Test; for doctorate, GRE General Test, minimum graduate GPA of 3.5. *Application deadline:* For fall admission, 6/5 for domestic students; for spring admission, 10/15 for domestic students. Applications are processed on a rolling basis. Application fee: $50. Electronic applications accepted. *Expenses:* Tuition, state resident: full-time $9,620; part-time $520 per credit. Tuition, nonresident: full-time $13,542; part-time $715 per credit. Tuition and fees vary according to course load. *Financial support:* Fellowships with full and partial tuition reimbursements, research assistantships with full and partial tuition reimbursements, teaching assistantships with full and partial tuition reimbursements, career-related internships or fieldwork, Federal Work-Study, institutionally sponsored loans, and unspecified assistantships available. Financial award application deadline: 3/15. *Application contact:* Kathryn Kelly, Director of Admissions, 973-596-3300, Fax: 973-596-3461, E-mail: admissions@njit.edu.

Northern Arizona University, Graduate College, College of Arts and Sciences, Department of Physics and Astronomy, Flagstaff, AZ 86011. Offers applied physics (MS); physical science (MAT). Part-time programs available. *Students:* 10 full-time (1 woman), 2 part-time (1 woman); includes 2 minority (both Asian Americans or Pacific Islanders) Average age 37. 7 applicants, 86% accepted. In 2003, 2 degrees awarded. *Degree requirements:* For master's, thesis optional. *Entrance requirements:* For master's, GRE. *Application deadline:* For fall admission, 3/15 for domestic students. Applications are processed on a rolling basis. Application fee: $45. *Expenses:* Tuition, state resident: full-time $5,103. Tuition, nonresident: full-time $12,623. *Financial support:* In 2003–04, 1 research assistantship was awarded; Federal Work-Study also available. *Unit head:* Dr. Tim Porter, Chair, 928-523-2661. *Application contact:* Dr. Dan MacIsaac, Graduate Coordinator, 928-523-5921, E-mail: astro@nau.edu.

Pittsburg State University, Graduate School, College of Arts and Sciences, Department of Physics, Pittsburg, KS 66762. Offers applied physics (MS); physics (MS); professional physics (MS). *Degree requirements:* For master's, thesis or alternative.

Princeton University, Graduate School, Department of Mechanical and Aerospace Engineering, Princeton, NJ 08544. Offers applied physics (M Eng, MSE, PhD); computational methods (M Eng, MSE); dynamics and control systems (M Eng, MSE, PhD); energy and environmental policy (M Eng, MSE, PhD); energy conversion, propulsion, and combustion (M Eng, MSE, PhD); flight science and technology (M Eng, MSE, PhD); fluid mechanics (M Eng, MSE, PhD). Part-time programs available. *Faculty:* 21 full-time (2 women), 2 part-time/adjunct (0 women). *Students:* 76 full-time (13 women); includes 5 minority (1 African American, 1 Asian American or Pacific Islander, 3 Hispanic Americans), 43 international. Average age 24. 315 applicants, 17% accepted, 17 enrolled. In 2003, 7 master's, 8 doctorates awarded. Terminal master's awarded for partial completion of doctoral program. *Median time to degree:* Master's–2.4 years full-time; doctorate–5.75 years full-time. *Degree requirements:* For master's, thesis/dissertation; for doctorate, thesis/dissertation, comprehensive exam. *Entrance requirements:* For master's and doctorate, GRE General Test. Additional exam requirements/recommendations for international students: Required—TOEFL (minimum score 600 paper-based; 250 computer-based). *Application deadline:* For fall admission, 12/31 for domestic students, 12/1 for international students. Application fee: $80 ($55 for international students). Electronic applications accepted. *Expenses:* Tuition: Full-time $29,910. Required fees: $810. *Financial support:* In 2003–04, 12 fellowships with full tuition reimbursements (averaging $8,800 per year), 36 research assistantships with full tuition reimbursements (averaging $27,461 per year), 9 teaching assistantships with full tuition reimbursements (averaging $21,641 per year) were awarded. Federal Work-Study and institutionally sponsored loans also available. Financial award application deadline: 1/2. Total annual research expenditures: $6.2 million. *Unit head:* Prof. Luigi Martinelli, Director of Graduate Studies, 609-258-6652, Fax: 609-258-1918, E-mail: gigi@princeton.edu. *Application contact:* Janice Yip, Director of Graduate Admissions, 609-258-3034, Fax: 609-258-6180, E-mail: gsadmit@princeton.edu.

Rensselaer Polytechnic Institute, Graduate School, School of Science, Department of Physics, Applied Physics and Astronomy, Troy, NY 12180-3590. Offers physics (MS, PhD). *Faculty:*

Applied Physics

Rensselaer Polytechnic Institute (continued)

23 full-time (3 women), 2 part-time/adjunct (0 women). *Students:* 45 full-time (9 women); includes 22 minority (all Asian Americans or Pacific Islanders), 39 international. Average age 28. 101 applicants, 12% accepted. In 2003, 10 master's, 13 doctorates awarded. *Degree requirements:* For doctorate, thesis/dissertation. *Entrance requirements:* For master's and doctorate, GRE General Test, GRE Subject Test. Additional exam requirements/recommendations for international students: Required—TOEFL (minimum score 600 paper-based; 250 computer-based). *Application deadline:* For fall admission, 1/15 for domestic students; for spring admission, 10/1 priority date for domestic students. Applications are processed on a rolling basis. Application fee: $45. Electronic applications accepted. *Expenses:* Tuition: Full-time $27,700; part-time $1,320 per credit. Required fees: $1,470. *Financial support:* In 2003–04, 2 fellowships with tuition reimbursements (averaging $25,000 per year), 19 research assistantships with tuition reimbursements (averaging $18,700 per year), 22 teaching assistantships with tuition reimbursements (averaging $19,000 per year) were awarded. Career-related internships or fieldwork and institutionally sponsored loans also available. Financial award application deadline: 2/1. *Faculty research:* Astrophysics, condensed matter, nuclear physics, optics, physics education. Total annual research expenditures: $3.6 million. *Unit head:* Dr. G. C. Wang, Chair, 518-276-8387, Fax: 518-276-6680, E-mail: wangg@rpi.edu. *Application contact:* Dr. Toh-Ming Lu, Chair, Graduate Recruitment Committee, 518-276-8391, Fax: 518-276-6680, E-mail: mcquade@rpi.edu.

Rice University, Rice Quantum Institute, Houston, TX 77251-1892. Offers MS, PhD. *Faculty:* 57 full-time (6 women). *Students:* 33 full-time (8 women); includes 12 minority (1 African American, 11 Asian Americans or Pacific Islanders), 9 international. Average age 24. 89 applicants, 24% accepted, 8 enrolled. In 2003, 2 master's, 1 doctorate awarded. *Median time to degree:* Master's–2 years full-time; doctorate–5.5 years full-time. *Degree requirements:* For master's and doctorate, thesis/dissertation. *Entrance requirements:* For master's and doctorate, GRE General Test, GRE Subject Test (physics), minimum GPA of 3.0. Additional exam requirements/recommendations for international students: Required—TOEFL (minimum score 600 paper-based; 250 computer-based). *Application deadline:* For fall admission, 2/1 for domestic students, 2/1 for international students. Application fee: $35. Electronic applications accepted. *Expenses:* Tuition: Full-time $19,700; part-time $1,096 per hour. *Financial support:* Fellowships, research assistantships available. *Faculty research:* Nanotechnology, solid state materials, atomic physics, thin films. *Unit head:* Dr. Peter Nordlander, Executive Director, 713-348-5103, Fax: 713-348-5401, E-mail: quantum@rice.edu. *Application contact:* Yvonne Creed, Executive Assistant, 713-348-6356, Fax: 713-348-5401, E-mail: ycreed@rice.edu.

Rutgers, The State University of New Jersey, Newark, Graduate School, Program in Applied Physics, Newark, NJ 07102. Offers MS, PhD. *Faculty:* 6 full-time (1 woman). *Students:* 2 full-time (1 woman), 3 part-time (1 woman); includes 2 minority (both American Indian/Alaska Native). 17 applicants, 0% accepted. In 2003, 1 degree awarded. *Entrance requirements:* For master's and doctorate, GRE. Additional exam requirements/recommendations for international students: Required—TOEFL. *Application deadline:* For fall admission, 7/1 for domestic students; for spring admission, 12/1 for domestic students. Application fee: $50. *Expenses:* Tuition, state resident: full-time $10,030. Tuition, nonresident: full-time $14,202. *Financial support:* In 2003–04, 3 teaching assistantships with full tuition reimbursements (averaging $14,300 per year) were awarded *Unit head:* Zhen Wu, Program Coordinator, 973-353-1311, E-mail: zwu@andromeda.rutgers.edu. *Application contact:* Elizabeth Wheeler, Administrative Assistant, 201-973-1312, E-mail: ewheeler@andromeda.rutgers.edu.

Stanford University, School of Humanities and Sciences, Department of Applied Physics, Stanford, CA 94305-9991. Offers MS, PhD. *Faculty:* 11 full-time (1 woman). *Students:* 94 full-time (21 women), 36 part-time (7 women); includes 21 minority (2 African Americans, 1 American Indian/Alaska Native, 14 Asian Americans or Pacific Islanders, 4 Hispanic Americans), 63 international. Average age 26. 104 applicants, 31% accepted. In 2003, 9 master's, 7 doctorates awarded. Terminal master's awarded for partial completion of doctoral program. *Degree requirements:* For doctorate, thesis/dissertation. *Entrance requirements:* For master's and doctorate, GRE General Test, GRE Subject Test. Additional exam requirements/recommendations for international students: Required—TOEFL. *Application deadline:* For fall admission, 1/1 for domestic students. Application fee: $65 ($80 for international students). Electronic applications accepted. *Expenses:* Tuition: Full-time $28,563. *Unit head:* Robert Byer, Chair, 650-723-0226, Fax: 650-723-2666, E-mail: byer@stanford.edu. *Application contact:* Graduate Admissions Coordinator, 650-723-4028.

State University of New York at Binghamton, Graduate School, School of Arts and Sciences, Department of Physics, Applied Physics, and Astronomy, Binghamton, NY 13902-6000. Offers applied physics (MS); physics (MA, MS). *Degree requirements:* For master's, thesis or alternative. *Entrance requirements:* For master's, GRE General Test, GRE Subject Test. Additional exam requirements/recommendations for international students: Required—TOEFL. Electronic applications accepted.

Texas A&M University, College of Science, Department of Physics, College Station, TX 77843. Offers applied physics (PhD); physics (MS, PhD). *Faculty:* 36 full-time (1 woman). *Students:* 122 full-time (9 women), 7 part-time (1 woman); includes 5 minority (1 African American, 1 Asian American or Pacific Islander, 3 Hispanic Americans), 95 international. Terminal master's awarded for partial completion of doctoral program. *Degree requirements:* For master's, thesis (for some programs), registration; for doctorate, thesis/dissertation, registration. *Entrance requirements:* For master's and doctorate, GRE General Test, GRE Subject Test. Additional exam requirements/recommendations for international students: Required—TOEFL. *Application deadline:* For fall admission, 3/1 for domestic students; for spring admission, 8/1 for domestic students. Application fee: $50 ($75 for international students). Electronic applications accepted. *Expenses:* Tuition, state resident: full-time $3,420. Tuition, nonresident: full-time $9,084. Required fees: $1,861. *Financial support:* In 2003–04, research assistantships (averaging $16,200 per year), teaching assistantships (averaging $16,200 per year) were awarded. Financial award application deadline: 3/1; financial award applicants required to submit FAFSA. *Faculty research:* Condensed-matter, atomic/molecular, high-energy, and nuclear physics, quantum optics. *Unit head:* Dr. Edward S. Fry, Head, 979-845-7717, Fax: 979-845-2590, E-mail: fry@physics.tamu.edu. *Application contact:* Dr. George W. Kattawar, Professor, 979-845-1180, Fax: 979-845-2590, E-mail: kattawar@physics.tamu.edu.

Texas Tech University, Graduate School, College of Arts and Sciences, Department of Physics, Lubbock, TX 79409. Offers applied physics (MS, PhD); physics (MS, PhD). Part-time programs available. *Faculty:* 19 full-time (3 women). *Students:* 34 full-time (2 women), 6 part-time; includes 2 minority (both Hispanic Americans), 19 international. Average age 30. 33 applicants, 70% accepted, 12 enrolled. In 2003, 7 master's, 4 doctorates awarded. *Degree requirements:* For master's and doctorate, variable foreign language requirement, thesis/dissertation. *Entrance requirements:* For master's and doctorate, GRE General Test. Additional exam requirements/recommendations for international students: Required—TOEFL (minimum score 550 paper-based; 213 computer-based). *Application deadline:* Applications are processed on a rolling basis. Application fee: $50 ($60 for international students). Electronic applications accepted. *Expenses:* Tuition, state resident: full-time $3,312. Tuition, nonresident: full-time $8,976. Required fees: $1,745. Tuition and fees vary according to program. *Financial support:* In 2003–04, 21 students received support, including 16 research assistantships with partial tuition reimbursements available (averaging $14,693 per year), 19 teaching assistantships with partial tuition reimbursements available (averaging $15,457 per year); career-related internships or fieldwork, Federal Work-Study, and institutionally sponsored loans also available. Support available to part-time students. Financial award application deadline: 5/1; financial award applicants required to submit FAFSA. *Faculty research:* Molecular spectroscopy of biological membranes, thin films and semiconductor characterization, muon spin rotation defect, characterization of semiconductors, nanotechnology of magnetic materials, theory of impurities and complexes in semiconductors. Total annual research expenditures: $177,229. *Unit head:* Dr. Lynn L. Hatfield, Chair, 806-742-3767, Fax: 806-742-1182, E-mail: lynnhatfield@ttu.edu. *Application contact:* Dr. Wallace L. Glab, Graduate Recruiter, 806-742-3767, Fax: 806-742-1182, E-mail: wallace.glab@ttu.edu.

The University of Arizona, Graduate College, College of Science, Department of Physics, Applied and Industrial Physics, Professional Program, Tucson, AZ 85721. Offers MS. Part-time programs available. *Degree requirements:* For master's, thesis or alternative, internship, colloquium, business courses. *Entrance requirements:* For master's, GRE General Test, 3 letters of recommendation. *Expenses:* Tuition, state resident: part-time $196 per unit. Tuition, nonresident: part-time $326 per unit. *Faculty research:* Nanotechnology, optics, medical imaging, high energy physics, biophysics.

University of Arkansas, Graduate School, J. William Fulbright College of Arts and Sciences, Department of Physics, Program in Applied Physics, Fayetteville, AR 72701-1201. Offers MS. *Students:* 1 full-time (0 women), 1 international. 1 applicant, 100% accepted. *Degree requirements:* For master's, thesis. Application fee: $40 ($50 for international students). *Expenses:* Tuition, state resident: full-time $4,032; part-time $224 per credit hour. Tuition, nonresident: full-time $9,540; part-time $530 per credit hour. Tuition and fees vary according to course load and program. *Financial support:* Applicants required to submit FAFSA. *Unit head:* Dr. Paul Thibado, Head, 479-575-2506.

University of California, San Diego, Graduate Studies and Research, Department of Electrical and Computer Engineering, La Jolla, CA 92093. Offers applied ocean science (MS, PhD); applied physics (MS, PhD); communication theory and systems (MS, PhD); computer engineering (MS, PhD); electrical engineering (M Eng); electronic circuits and systems (MS, PhD); intelligent systems, robotics and control (MS, PhD); photonics (MS, PhD); signal and image processing (MS, PhD). MS only offered to students who have been admitted to the PhD program. *Faculty:* 73. *Students:* 415 (62 women); includes 98 minority (2 African Americans, 1 American Indian/Alaska Native, 89 Asian Americans or Pacific Islanders, 6 Hispanic Americans) 183 international. 2,053 applicants, 12% accepted. In 2003, 58 master's, 31 doctorates awarded. *Entrance requirements:* For master's and doctorate, GRE General Test. *Application deadline:* For fall admission, 1/12 for domestic students. Application fee: $60. Electronic applications accepted. Tuition, nonresident: full-time $12,245. Required fees: $6,959. *Unit head:* Paul Yu, Chair. *Application contact:* Graduate Coordinator, 858-534-6606.

University of Central Oklahoma, College of Graduate Studies and Research, College of Mathematics and Science, Department of Industrial and Applied Physics, Edmond, OK 73034-5209. Offers MS. Part-time programs available. *Degree requirements:* For master's, thesis optional. *Entrance requirements:* For master's, 24 hours of course work in physics. *Faculty research:* Acoustics, solid-state physics/optical properties, molecular dynamics, nuclear physics, crystallography.

University of Maryland, Baltimore County, Graduate School, Department of Physics, Baltimore, MD 21250. Offers applied physics (MS, PhD), including optics, solid state physics; atmospheric physics (MS, PhD). Part-time programs available. Terminal master's awarded for partial completion of doctoral program. *Degree requirements:* For master's, thesis optional; for doctorate, thesis/dissertation. *Entrance requirements:* For master's and doctorate, GRE General Test, GRE Subject Test, minimum GPA of 3.0. Additional exam requirements/recommendations for international students: Required—TOEFL. Electronic applications accepted. *Expenses:* Tuition, state resident: full-time $7,000. Tuition, nonresident: full-time $11,400. Required fees: $1,440. *Faculty research:* Optics, solid state physics, astrophysics, atmospheric physics.

University of Massachusetts Boston, Office of Graduate Studies and Research, College of Science and Mathematics, Program in Applied Physics, Boston, MA 02125-3393. Offers MS. Part-time and evening/weekend programs available. *Students:* 2 full-time (1 woman), 10 part-time (2 women); includes 1 minority (Hispanic American), 6 international. Average age 29. 12 applicants, 42% accepted, 2 enrolled. In 2003, 5 degrees awarded. *Degree requirements:* For master's, thesis optional. *Entrance requirements:* For master's, minimum GPA of 2.75. *Application deadline:* For fall admission, 3/1 for domestic students; for spring admission, 11/1 for domestic students. Application fee: $25 ($40 for international students). *Expenses:* Tuition, state resident: full-time $4,461. Tuition, nonresident: full-time $9,390. *Financial support:* In 2003–04, research assistantships with full tuition reimbursements (averaging $4,000 per year), 10 teaching assistantships with full tuition reimbursements (averaging $4,000 per year) were awarded. Career-related internships or fieldwork, Federal Work-Study, and unspecified assistantships also available. Support available to part-time students. Financial award application deadline: 3/1; financial award applicants required to submit FAFSA. *Faculty research:* Experimental laser research, nonlinear optics, experimental and theoretical solid state physics, semiconductor devices, opto-electronics. *Unit head:* Dr. Steven Arnason, Director, 617-287-6050. *Application contact:* Peggy Roldan, Graduate Admissions Coordinator, 617-287-6400, Fax: 617-287-6236, E-mail: bos.gadm@dpc.umassp.edu.

University of Massachusetts Lowell, Graduate School, College of Arts and Sciences, Department of Physics and Applied Physics, Program in Applied Physics, Lowell, MA 01854-2881. Offers applied mechanics (PhD); applied physics (MS, PhD), including optical sciences (MS). Terminal master's awarded for partial completion of doctoral program. *Degree requirements:* For master's, thesis; for doctorate, 2 foreign languages, thesis/dissertation. *Entrance requirements:* For master's and doctorate, GRE General Test.

University of Michigan, Horace H. Rackham School of Graduate Studies, College of Engineering and College of Literature, Science, and the Arts, Interdepartmental Program in Applied Physics, Ann Arbor, MI 48109. Offers PhD. *Faculty:* 75 full-time (6 women), 1 part-time/adjunct (0 women). *Students:* 62 full-time (17 women); includes 25 minority (10 African Americans, 12 Asian Americans or Pacific Islanders, 3 Hispanic Americans). Average age 23. 110 applicants, 7% accepted. In 2003, 6 degrees awarded. *Degree requirements:* For doctorate, oral defense of dissertation, preliminary and qualifying exams. *Entrance requirements:* For doctorate, GRE General Test. Additional exam requirements/recommendations for international students: Required—TOEFL. *Application deadline:* For fall admission, 1/15 for domestic students. Applications are processed on a rolling basis. Application fee: $60 ($75 for international students). Electronic applications accepted. *Expenses:* Tuition, state resident: full-time $7,463. Tuition, nonresident: full-time $13,913. Full-time tuition and fees vary according to course load, degree level and program. *Financial support:* In 2003–04, 8 fellowships with full tuition reimbursements were awarded; research assistantships with full tuition reimbursements, teaching assistantships with full tuition reimbursements, traineeships also available. Financial award application deadline: 1/15; financial award applicants required to submit FAFSA. *Faculty research:* Optical sciences, materials research, quantum structures, medical imaging, environment and science policy. Total annual research expenditures: $1.1 million. *Unit head:* Bradford Orr, Director, 734-936-0653, Fax: 734-764-2193. *Application contact:* Cynthia L. D'Agostino, Administrative Assistant, 734-936-0653, Fax: 734-764-2193, E-mail: ap.phys@umich.edu.

University of Missouri–St. Louis, Graduate School, College of Arts and Sciences, Department of Physics and Astronomy, St. Louis, MO 63121-4499. Offers applied physics (MS); astrophysics (MS); physics (PhD). Part-time and evening/weekend programs available. *Faculty:* 14 full-time (0 women). *Students:* 9 full-time (2 women), 10 part-time (3 women); includes 1 minority (Asian American or Pacific Islander), 5 international. Average age 25. In 2003, 3 master's, 1 doctorate awarded. Terminal master's awarded for partial completion of doctoral program. *Degree requirements:* For master's, thesis optional; for doctorate, thesis/dissertation. *Entrance requirements:* For master's and doctorate, GRE General Test. Additional exam requirements/recommendations for international students: Required—TOEFL (minimum score 550 paper-based; 213 computer-based). *Application deadline:* For fall admission, 4/1 for domestic students; for spring admission, 12/1 priority date for domestic students. Applications are processed on a rolling basis. Application fee: $35 ($40 for international students). Electronic applications accepted. *Expenses:* Tuition, state resident: part-time $237 per credit hour. Tuition, nonresident: part-time $639 per credit hour. Required fees: $10 per credit hour. *Financial* *support:* In 2003–04, 1 research assistantship with full and partial tuition reimbursement (averaging $6,750 per year), 9 teaching assistantships with full and partial tuition reimbursements (averaging $12,978 per year) were awarded. Fellowships with full tuition reimbursements, career-related internships or fieldwork also available. *Faculty research:* Biophysics, atomic physics, nonlinear dynamics, materials science. *Unit head:* Dr. Ricardo Flores, Director of Graduate Studies, 314-516-5931, Fax: 314-516-6152, E-mail: graduate@newton.umsl.edu. *Application contact:* 314-516-5458, Fax: 314-516-5310, E-mail: gradadm@umsl.edu.

The University of North Carolina at Charlotte, Graduate School, College of Arts and Sciences, Department of Physics and Optical Science, Charlotte, NC 28223-0001. Offers applied physics (MS); optical science and engineering (MS, PhD). *Faculty:* 11 full-time (1 woman), 9 part-time/adjunct (0 women). *Students:* 9 full-time (2 women), 18 part-time (2 women); includes 2 minority (1 African American, 1 Asian American or Pacific Islander), 15 international. Average age 29. 18 applicants, 83% accepted, 8 enrolled. In 2003, 2 degrees awarded. *Degree requirements:* For master's, thesis optional. *Entrance requirements:* For master's, GRE General Test, minimum GPA of 3.0 during previous 2 years, 2.75 overall. Additional exam requirements/recommendations for international students: Required—TOEFL (minimum score 557 paper-based; 220 computer-based). *Application deadline:* For fall admission, 7/15 for domestic students, 5/1 for international students; for spring admission, 11/15 for domestic students, 10/1 for international students. Applications are processed on a rolling basis. Application fee: $35. Electronic applications accepted. *Expenses:* Tuition, state resident: full-time $1,979. Tuition, nonresident: full-time $12,111. Required fees: $1,201. Tuition and fees vary according to course load. *Financial support:* In 2003–04, 3 fellowships (averaging $2,667 per year), 14 research assistantships (averaging $6,500 per year), 21 teaching assistantships (averaging $7,005 per year) were awarded. Career-related internships or fieldwork, Federal Work-Study, institutionally sponsored loans, scholarships/grants, and unspecified assistantships also available. Support available to part-time students. Financial award application deadline: 4/1; financial award applicants required to submit FAFSA. *Faculty research:* Optics, lasers, microscopy, fibers, astrophysics. *Unit head:* Dr. Faramarz Farahi, Chair, 704-687-2537, Fax: 704-687-3160, E-mail: ffarahi@uncc.edu. *Application contact:* Kathy B. Giddings, Director of Graduate Admissions, 704-687-3366, Fax: 704-687-3279, E-mail: gradadm@email.uncc.edu.

University of Puerto Rico, Río Piedras, Faculty of Natural Sciences, Department of Physics, San Juan, PR 00931. Offers applied physics (MS); physics (MS); physics-chemical (PhD). Part-time and evening/weekend programs available. *Faculty:* 15 full-time (1 woman), 2 part-time/adjunct (0 women). *Students:* 21 full-time (10 women), 34 part-time (11 women); includes 53 minority (11 Asian Americans or Pacific Islanders, 42 Hispanic Americans). 20 applicants, 95% accepted, 19 enrolled. In 2003, 3 degrees awarded. *Degree requirements:* For master's and doctorate, one foreign language, thesis/dissertation, comprehensive exam. *Entrance requirements:* For master's, GRE, EXADEP, interview, minimum GPA of 3.0, letter of recommendation; for doctorate, GRE, master's degree, minimum GPA of 3.0, letter of recommendation. Additional exam requirements/recommendations for international students: Required—TOEFL. *Application deadline:* For fall admission, 2/1 for domestic students, 2/1 for international students. Application fee: $17. *Expenses:* Tuition, state resident: part-time $75 per credit. Tuition, nonresident: full-time $1,200; part-time $218 per credit. International tuition: $3,500 full-time. Required fees: $70; $35 per term. *Financial support:* Fellowships, research assistantships, teaching assistantships, Federal Work-Study, institutionally sponsored loans, and tuition waivers (partial) available. Financial award application deadline: 5/31. *Faculty research:* Energy transfer process through Van der Vacqs interactions, study of the photodissociation of ketene. *Unit head:* Luis F. Fonseca, Coordinator of Doctoral Program, 787-764-0000 Ext. 4773, Fax: 787-764-4063.

University of Washington, Graduate School, College of Arts and Sciences, Department of Physics, Seattle, WA 98195. Offers MS, PhD. Part-time and evening/weekend programs available. Terminal master's awarded for partial completion of doctoral program. *Degree requirements:* For doctorate, thesis/dissertation. *Entrance requirements:* For master's, GRE; for doctorate, GRE General Test, GRE Subject Test. Additional exam requirements/recommendations for international students: Required—TOEFL. Electronic applications accepted. *Faculty research:* Astro-, atomic, condensed-matter, nuclear, and particle physics; physics education.

Virginia Commonwealth University, School of Graduate Studies, College of Humanities and Sciences, Department of Physics, Richmond, VA 23284-9005. Offers applied physics (MS); physics (MS). Part-time programs available. *Faculty:* 7 full-time (3 women). *Students:* 5 full-time (1 woman). 9 applicants, 78% accepted, 2 enrolled. In 2003, 5 degrees awarded. *Degree requirements:* For master's, thesis optional. *Entrance requirements:* For master's, GRE. *Application deadline:* For fall admission, 8/1 for domestic students; for spring admission, 12/1 for domestic students. Applications are processed on a rolling basis. Application fee: $30. *Expenses:* Tuition, state resident: full-time $2,889; part-time $321 per credit hour. Tuition, nonresident: full-time $7,952; part-time $884 per credit hour. Required fees: $42 per credit hour. *Financial support:* Fellowships, teaching assistantships, Federal Work-Study, institutionally sponsored loans, and tuition waivers (full and partial) available. Support available to part-time students. *Faculty research:* Condensed-matter theory and experimentation, electronic instrumentation, relativity. *Unit head:* Dr. Robert H. Gowdy, Chair, 804-828-1821, Fax: 804-828-7073, E-mail: rhgowdy@vcu.edu. *Application contact:* Dr. Alison Baski, Graduate Program Director, 804-828-8295, Fax: 804-828-7073, E-mail: aabaski@vcu.edu.

Virginia Polytechnic Institute and State University, Graduate School, College of Science, Department of Physics, Blacksburg, VA 24061. Offers applied physics (MS, PhD); physics (MS, PhD). *Faculty:* 21 full-time (2 women). *Students:* 44 full-time (9 women), 2 part-time; includes 4 minority (2 African Americans, 2 Asian Americans or Pacific Islanders), 18 international. Average age 27. 53 applicants, 57% accepted, 17 enrolled. In 2003, 9 master's, 7 doctorates awarded. *Entrance requirements:* For master's and doctorate, GRE Subject Test. Additional exam requirements/recommendations for international students: Required—TOEFL (minimum score 550 paper-based; 213 computer-based). *Application deadline:* Applications are processed on a rolling basis. Application fee: $45. Electronic applications accepted. Tuition, area resident: Full-time $6,039; part-time $336 per credit. Tuition, nonresident: full-time $9,708; part-time $539 per credit. Required fees: $905; $130 per credit. *Financial support:* In 2003–04, 3 fellowships with full tuition reimbursements (averaging $6,000 per year), 9 research assistantships with full tuition reimbursements (averaging $16,231 per year), 18 teaching assistantships with full tuition reimbursements (averaging $13,223 per year) were awarded. Career-related internships or fieldwork, Federal Work-Study, scholarships/grants, and unspecified assistantships also available. Financial award application deadline: 4/1. *Faculty research:* Condensed matter, particle physics, theoretical and experimental astrophysics, biophysics, mathematical physics. *Unit head:* Dr. John R. Ficenec, Head, 540-231-6544, Fax: 540-231-7511, E-mail: jficenec@vt.edu. *Application contact:* Christa C. Thomas, Graduate Program Coordinator, 540-231-8728, Fax: 540-231-7511, E-mail: chris.thomas@vt.edu.

West Virginia University, Eberly College of Arts and Sciences, Department of Physics, Morgantown, WV 26506. Offers applied physics (MS, PhD); astrophysics (MS, PhD); chemical physics (MS, PhD); condensed matter physics (MS, PhD); elementary particle physics (MS, PhD); materials physics (MS, PhD); plasma physics (MS, PhD); solid state physics (MS, PhD); statistical physics (MS, PhD); theoretical physics (MS, PhD). *Faculty:* 17 full-time (3 women), 1 part-time/adjunct (0 women). *Students:* 44 full-time (10 women), 4 part-time (1 woman), 32 international. Average age 28. 60 applicants, 20% accepted. In 2003, 2 master's awarded, leading to continued full-time study 100%; 3 doctorates awarded, leading to university research/teaching 33%, business/industry 33%, government 33%. Terminal master's awarded for partial completion of doctoral program. *Median time to degree:* Master's–2 years full-time; doctorate–5 years full-time. *Degree requirements:* For master's, thesis or alternative, qualifying exam; for doctorate, thesis/dissertation, qualifying exam. *Entrance requirements:* For master's and doctorate, GRE General Test, GRE Subject Test, minimum GPA of 3.0. Additional exam requirements/recommendations for international students: Required—TOEFL. *Application deadline:* For fall admission, 2/15 for domestic students. Applications are processed on a rolling basis. Application fee: $50. *Expenses:* Tuition, state resident: full-time $4,332. Tuition, nonresident: full-time $12,442. *Financial support:* In 2003–04, 30 research assistantships with full and partial tuition reimbursements (averaging $18,000 per year), 10 teaching assistantships with full and partial tuition reimbursements (averaging $16,000 per year) were awarded. Fellowships, Federal Work-Study, institutionally sponsored loans, and tuition waivers (full and partial) also available. Financial award application deadline: 2/1; financial award applicants required to submit FAFSA. *Faculty research:* Experimental and theoretical condensed-matter, plasma, high-energy theory, nonlinear dynamics, space physics. Total annual research expenditures: $3.3 million. *Unit head:* Dr. Earl E. Scime, Chair, 304-293-3422 Ext. 1437, Fax: 304-293-5732, E-mail: escime@wvu.edu.

Yale University, Graduate School of Arts and Sciences, Programs in Engineering and Applied Science, Department of Applied Physics, New Haven, CT 06520. Offers MS, PhD. Terminal master's awarded for partial completion of doctoral program. *Degree requirements:* For doctorate, thesis/dissertation, area exam. *Entrance requirements:* For master's and doctorate, GRE General Test. Additional exam requirements/recommendations for international students: Required—TOEFL. *Expenses:* Tuition: Full-time $25,600; part-time $6,400 per term.

Condensed Matter Physics

Cleveland State University, College of Graduate Studies, College of Arts and Sciences, Department of Physics, Cleveland, OH 44115. Offers applied optics (MS); condensed matter physics (MS); medical physics (MS). Part-time and evening/weekend programs available. *Faculty:* 5 full-time (1 woman), 4 part-time/adjunct (0 women). *Students:* Average age 30. 7 applicants, 100% accepted, 5 enrolled. In 2003, 4 degrees awarded, leading to business/industry 4%. *Median time to degree:* Master's–2 years full-time. *Degree requirements:* For master's, exit project. *Entrance requirements:* For master's, undergraduate degree in engineering or physics, chemistry or mathematics. Additional exam requirements/recommendations for international students: Required—TOEFL (minimum score 525 paper-based; 197 computer-based), GRE. *Application deadline:* For fall admission, 7/15 priority date for domestic students, 7/15 priority date for international students. Applications are processed on a rolling basis. Application fee: $30. Electronic applications accepted. Tuition, area resident: Full-time $8,258; part-time $344 per credit hour. Tuition, nonresident: full-time $16,352; part-time $681 per credit hour. *Financial support:* In 2003–04, 1 research assistantship with full and partial tuition reimbursement (averaging $5,666 per year) was awarded; fellowships with tuition reimbursements, teaching assistantships, tuition waivers (full) also available. *Faculty research:* Statistical mechanics of phase transitions, low-temperature and solid-state physics, superconductivity, theoretical light scattering, medical physics. Total annual research expenditures: $350,000. *Unit head:* Dr. Miron Kaufman, Chairperson, 216-687-2436, Fax: 216-523-7268, E-mail: m.kaufman@csuohio.edu. *Application contact:* Dr. James A. Lock, Director, 216-687-2425, Fax: 216-523-7268, E-mail: j.lock@csuohio.edu.

Iowa State University of Science and Technology, Graduate College, College of Liberal Arts and Sciences, Department of Physics and Astronomy, Ames, IA 50011. Offers applied physics (MS, PhD); astrophysics (MS, PhD); condensed matter physics (MS, PhD); high energy physics (MS, PhD); nuclear physics (MS, PhD); physics (MS, PhD). Part-time programs available. *Faculty:* 45 full-time, 4 part-time/adjunct. *Students:* 83 full-time (12 women), 5 part-time; includes 1 minority (Hispanic American), 66 international. 174 applicants, 59% accepted, 31 enrolled. In 2003, 3 master's, 4 doctorates awarded. Terminal master's awarded for partial completion of doctoral program. *Median time to degree:* Master's–2.9 years full-time; doctorate–7.1 years full-time. *Degree requirements:* For master's, thesis (for some programs); for doctorate, thesis/dissertation. *Entrance requirements:* For master's and doctorate, GRE General Test, GRE Subject Test (physics). Additional exam requirements/recommendations for international students: Required—TOEFL (paper score 550; computer score 213) or IELTS (score 6.5). *Application deadline:* For fall admission, 2/15 priority date for domestic students, 2/15 priority date for international students; for spring admission, 10/15 for domestic students, 10/15 for international students. Applications are processed on a rolling basis. Application fee: $30 ($70 for international students). Electronic applications accepted. Tuition, nonresident: part-time $560 per credit. Required fees: $38 per unit. *Financial support:* In 2003–04, 38 research assistantships with full tuition reimbursements (averaging $17,400 per year), 42 teaching assistantships with full tuition reimbursements (averaging $17,400 per year) were awarded. Fellowships, Federal Work-Study, institutionally sponsored loans, scholarships/grants, health care benefits, and unspecified assistantships also available. Support available to part-time students. Financial award application deadline: 2/15. *Faculty research:* Condensed-matter physics, including superconductivity and new materials; high-energy and nuclear physics; astronomy and astrophysics; atmospheric and environmental physics. Total annual research expenditures: $8.8 million. *Unit head:* Dr. Eli Rosenberg, Chair, 515-294-5441, Fax: 515-294-6027, E-mail: phys_astro@iastate.edu. *Application contact:* Dr. Steven Kawaler, Director of Graduate Education, 515-294-9728, E-mail: phys_astro@iastate.edu.

Rutgers, The State University of New Jersey, New Brunswick/Piscataway, Graduate School, Program in Physics and Astronomy, New Brunswick, NJ 08901-1281. Offers astronomy (MS, PhD); biophysics (PhD); condensed matter physics (MS, PhD); elementary particle physics (MS, PhD); intermediate energy nuclear physics (MS); nuclear physics (MS, PhD); physics (MST); surface science (PhD); theoretical physics (MS, PhD). Part-time programs available. *Faculty:* 67 full-time (5 women). *Students:* 90 full-time (13 women), 18 part-time (3 women); includes 5 minority (2 African Americans, 3 Asian Americans or Pacific Islanders), 67 international. Average age 28. 269 applicants, 16% accepted, 21 enrolled. In 2003, 5 master's, 16 doctorates awarded. Terminal master's awarded for partial completion of doctoral program. *Median time to degree:* Master's–2 years full-time; doctorate–6 years full-time. *Degree requirements:* For master's, thesis or alternative, comprehensive exam; for doctorate, thesis/dissertation, comprehensive exam. *Entrance requirements:* For master's and doctorate, GRE General Test, GRE Subject Test. Additional exam requirements/recommendations for international students: Required—TOEFL, TSE. *Application deadline:* For fall admission, 1/2 priority date for domestic students, 1/2 priority date for international students; for spring admission, 11/1 for domestic students, 11/1 for international students. Applications are processed on a rolling basis. Application fee: $50. Electronic applications accepted. *Expenses:* Tuition, state resident: full-time $10,030. Tuition, nonresident: full-time $14,202. *Financial support:* In 2003–04, 19 fellowships with full tuition reimbursements (averaging $18,000 per year), 50 research assistantships with full tuition reimbursements (averaging $15,300 per year), 8 teaching assistantships with full tuition reimbursements (averaging $15,300 per year) were awarded. Health care benefits and unspecified assistantships also available. Financial award application deadline: 1/2; financial award applicants required to submit FAFSA. *Faculty research:* Astronomy, high energy, condensed matter, surface, nuclear physics. Total annual research expenditures:

Condensed Matter Physics

Rutgers, The State University of New Jersey, New Brunswick/Piscataway (continued)

$7.8 million. *Unit head:* Dr. Ted Williams, Director, 732-445-2516, Fax: 732-445-4343, E-mail: williams@physics.rutgers.edu. *Application contact:* Kathy DiMeo, Administrative Assistant, 732-445-2502, Fax: 732-445-4343, E-mail: graduate@physics.rutgers.edu.

See in-depth description on page 401.

University of Alberta, Faculty of Graduate Studies and Research, Department of Physics, Edmonton, AB T6G 2E1, Canada. Offers astrophysics (M Sc, PhD); condensed matter (M Sc, PhD); geophysics (M Sc, PhD); medical physics (M Sc, PhD); subatomic physics (M Sc, PhD). *Faculty:* 36 full-time (3 women), 7 part-time/adjunct (0 women). *Students:* 56 full-time (6 women), 16 part-time (2 women), 25 international. 85 applicants, 35% accepted. In 2003, 7 master's, 10 doctorates awarded. *Degree requirements:* For master's and doctorate, thesis/dissertation. *Entrance requirements:* For master's and doctorate, minimum GPA of 7.0 on a 9.0 scale. Additional exam requirements/recommendations for international students: Required—TOEFL. *Application deadline:* For fall admission, 2/15 for domestic students. Applications are processed on a rolling basis. Tuition charges are reported in Canadian dollars. Tuition, nonresident: full-time $3,921 Canadian dollars. International tuition: $7,113 Canadian dollars full-time. *Financial support:* In 2003–04, 45 students received support, including 6 fellowships with partial tuition reimbursements available, 40 teaching assistantships; research assistantships, career-related internships or fieldwork, institutionally sponsored loans, and scholarships/grants also available. Financial award application deadline: 2/15. *Faculty research:* Cosmology, astroparticle physics, high-intermediate energy, magnetism, superconductivity. Total annual research expenditures: $3.1 million. *Unit head:* Dr. Richard Sydora, Associate Chair, 780-492-1072, E-mail: assoc-chair@phys.ualberta.ca. *Application contact:* Lynn Chandler, Program Advisor, 780-492-1072, Fax: 780-492-0714, E-mail: lynn@phys.ualberta.ca.

University of Victoria, Faculty of Graduate Studies, Faculty of Science, Department of Physics and Astronomy, Victoria, BC V8W 2Y2, Canada. Offers astronomy and astrophysics (M Sc, PhD); condensed matter physics (M Sc, PhD); medical physics (M Sc, PhD); nuclear and particle studies (M Sc, PhD); ocean physics (M Sc, PhD); theoretical physics (M Sc, PhD). *Degree requirements:* For master's, thesis/dissertation, registration; for doctorate, thesis/dissertation, comprehensive exam, registration. *Entrance requirements:* Additional exam requirements/recommendations for international students: Required—TOEFL (minimum score 575 paper-based; 213 computer-based). *Faculty research:* Old stellar populations; observational cosmology and large scale structure; cp violation; atlas.

West Virginia University, Eberly College of Arts and Sciences, Department of Physics, Morgantown, WV 26506. Offers applied physics (MS, PhD); astrophysics (MS, PhD); chemical physics (MS, PhD); condensed matter physics (MS, PhD); elementary particle physics (MS, PhD); materials physics (MS, PhD); plasma physics (MS, PhD); solid state physics (MS, PhD); statistical physics (MS, PhD); theoretical physics (MS, PhD). *Faculty:* 17 full-time (3 women), 1 part-time/adjunct (0 women). *Students:* 44 full-time (10 women), 4 part-time (1 woman), 32 international. Average age 28. 60 applicants, 20% accepted. In 2003, 2 master's awarded, leading to continued full-time study 100%; 3 doctorates awarded, leading to university research/teaching 33%, business/industry 33%, government 33%. Terminal master's awarded for partial completion of doctoral program. *Median time to degree:* Master's–2 years full-time; doctorate–5 years full-time. *Degree requirements:* For master's, thesis or alternative, qualifying exam; for doctorate, thesis/dissertation, qualifying exam. *Entrance requirements:* For master's and doctorate, GRE General Test, GRE Subject Test, minimum GPA of 3.0. Additional exam requirements/recommendations for international students: Required—TOEFL. *Application deadline:* For fall admission, 2/15 for domestic students. Applications are processed on a rolling basis. Application fee: $50. *Expenses:* Tuition, state resident: full-time $4,332. Tuition, nonresident: full-time $12,442. *Financial support:* In 2003–04, 30 research assistantships with full and partial tuition reimbursements (averaging $18,000 per year), 10 teaching assistantships with full and partial tuition reimbursements (averaging $16,000 per year) were awarded. Fellowships, Federal Work-Study, institutionally sponsored loans, and tuition waivers (full and partial) also available. Financial award application deadline: 2/1; financial award applicants required to submit FAFSA. *Faculty research:* Experimental and theoretical condensed-matter, plasma, high-energy theory, nonlinear dynamics, space physics. Total annual research expenditures: $3.3 million. *Unit head:* Dr. Earl E. Scime, Chair, 304-293-3422 Ext. 1437, Fax: 304-293-5732, E-mail: escime@wvu.edu.

Mathematical Physics

New Mexico Institute of Mining and Technology, Graduate Studies, Department of Physics, Socorro, NM 87801. Offers astrophysics (MS, PhD); atmospheric physics (MS, PhD); instrumentation (MS); mathematical physics (PhD). *Faculty:* 14 full-time (2 women), 19 part-time/adjunct (2 women). *Students:* 19 full-time (5 women), 2 part-time (1 woman); includes 2 minority (1 Asian American or Pacific Islander, 1 Hispanic American), 3 international. Average age 28. 21 applicants, 5 enrolled. In 2003, 1 master's, 3 doctorates awarded. *Degree requirements:* For master's, thesis optional; for doctorate, thesis/dissertation. *Entrance requirements:* For master's, GRE General Test; for doctorate, GRE General Test, GRE Subject Test. Additional exam requirements/recommendations for international students: Required—TOEFL (minimum score 540 paper-based; 207 computer-based). *Application deadline:* For fall admission, 3/1 for domestic students; for spring admission, 6/1 for domestic students. Applications are processed on a rolling basis. Application fee: $16 ($30 for international students). *Expenses:* Tuition, state resident: full-time $2,276; part-time $126 per credit. Tuition, nonresident: full-time $9,170; part-time $509 per credit. Required fees: $924; $27 per credit. $214 per term. Part-time tuition and fees vary according to course load. *Financial support:* In 2003–04, 10 research assistantships (averaging $14,242 per year), 10 teaching assistantships with full and partial tuition reimbursements (averaging $9,600 per year) were awarded. Fellowships, Federal Work-Study, institutionally sponsored loans, and unspecified assistantships also available. Financial award application deadline: 3/1; financial award applicants required to submit CSS PROFILE or FAFSA. *Faculty research:* Cloud physics, stellar and extragalactic processes. *Unit head:* Dr. Kenneth Minschwaner, Chairman, 505-835-5226, Fax: 505-835-5707, E-mail: krm@kestrel.nmt.edu. *Application contact:* Dr. David B. Johnson, Dean of Graduate Studies, 505-835-5513, Fax: 505-835-5476, E-mail: graduate@nmt.edu.

Princeton University, Graduate School, Department of Mathematics, Princeton, NJ 08544-1019. Offers applied and computational mathematics (PhD); mathematical physics (PhD); mathematics (PhD). *Faculty:* 47 full-time (5 women), 9 part-time/adjunct (1 woman). *Students:* 58 full-time (12 women); includes 6 minority (1 African American, 5 Asian Americans or Pacific Islanders), 36 international. 202 applicants, 14% accepted, 14 enrolled. *Median time to degree:* Doctorate–4.64 years full-time. *Degree requirements:* For doctorate, 2 foreign languages, thesis/dissertation. *Entrance requirements:* For doctorate, GRE General Test, GRE Subject Test. Additional exam requirements/recommendations for international students: Required—TOEFL (minimum score 600 paper-based; 250 computer-based). *Application deadline:* For fall admission, 12/31 for domestic students, 12/1 for international students. Application fee: $80 ($55 for international students). Electronic applications accepted. *Expenses:* Tuition: Full-time $29,910. Required fees: $810. *Financial support:* Fellowships with full tuition reimbursements, research assistantships with full tuition reimbursements, teaching assistantships with full tuition reimbursements, Federal Work-Study and institutionally sponsored loans available. Financial award application deadline: 1/2. *Unit head:* Prof. Sergiu Klainerman, Director of Graduate Studies, 609-258-4188, Fax: 609-258-1367, E-mail: seri@princeton.edu. *Application contact:* Janice Yip, Director of Graduate Admissions, 609-258-3034, Fax: 609-258-6180, E-mail: gsadmit@princeton.edu.

Princeton University, Graduate School, Department of Physics, Princeton, NJ 08544-1019. Offers applied and computational mathematics (PhD); mathematical physics (PhD); physics (PhD); physics and chemical physics (PhD). *Faculty:* 42 full-time (2 women), 2 part-time/adjunct (0 women). *Students:* 103 full-time (13 women); includes 11 minority (10 Asian Americans or Pacific Islanders, 1 Hispanic American), 48 international. Average age 22. 425 applicants, 12% accepted, 26 enrolled. In 2003, 14 degrees awarded, leading to continued full-time study 86%. *Median time to degree:* Doctorate–5 years full-time. *Degree requirements:* For doctorate, thesis/dissertation, qualifying exam. *Entrance requirements:* For doctorate, GRE General Test, GRE Subject Test. Additional exam requirements/recommendations for international students: Required—TOEFL (minimum score 600 paper-based; 250 computer-based). *Application deadline:* For fall admission, 12/31 for domestic students, 12/1 for international students. Application fee: $80 ($55 for international students). Electronic applications accepted. *Expenses:* Tuition: Full-time $29,910. Required fees: $810. *Financial support:* In 2003–04, 100 students received support, including 40 fellowships with full tuition reimbursements available (averaging $19,360 per year), 30 research assistantships with full tuition reimbursements available (averaging $18,100 per year), 30 teaching assistantships with full tuition reimbursements available (averaging $19,625 per year); Federal Work-Study and institutionally sponsored loans also available. Financial award application deadline: 1/2. Total annual research expenditures: $10.7 million. *Unit head:* Prof. Chiana Nappi, Director of Graduate Studies, 609-258-4322, Fax: 609-258-1549, E-mail: cnappi@princeton.edu. *Application contact:* Janice Yip, Director of Graduate Admissions, 609-258-3034, Fax: 609-258-6180, E-mail: gsadmit@princeton.edu.

University of Alberta, Faculty of Graduate Studies and Research, Department of Mathematical and Statistical Sciences, Edmonton, AB T6G 2E1, Canada. Offers applied mathematics (M Sc, PhD); biostatistics (M Sc); mathematical finance (M Sc, PhD); mathematical physics (M Sc, PhD); mathematics (M Sc, PhD); statistics (M Sc, PhD, Postgraduate Diploma). Part-time programs available. *Faculty:* 48 full-time (4 women). *Students:* 112 full-time (41 women), 5 part-time. Average age 24. 776 applicants, 5% accepted, 34 enrolled. In 2003, 12 master's, 10 doctorates awarded. Terminal master's awarded for partial completion of doctoral program. *Median time to degree:* Master's–2 years full-time; doctorate–5 years full-time. Of those who began their doctoral program in fall 1995, 100% received their degree in 8 years or less. *Degree requirements:* For master's, thesis (for some programs); for doctorate, thesis/dissertation, comprehensive exam. *Entrance requirements:* Additional exam requirements/recommendations for international students: Required—TOEFL (minimum score 580 paper-based; 237 computer-based). *Application deadline:* For fall admission, 3/1 for domestic students, 2/1 for international students. Applications are processed on a rolling basis. Application fee: $0. Electronic applications accepted. Tuition charges are reported in Canadian dollars. Tuition, nonresident: full-time $3,921 Canadian dollars. International tuition: $7,113 Canadian dollars full-time. *Financial support:* In 2003–04, 51 research assistantships, 88 teaching assistantships with full and partial tuition reimbursements were awarded. Scholarships/grants also available. Financial award application deadline: 5/1. *Faculty research:* Classical and functional analysis, algebra, differential equations, geometry. *Unit head:* Dr. Anthony To-Ming Lau, Chair, 403-492-5799, E-mail: tlau@math.ualberta.ca. *Application contact:* Dr. Yau Shu Wong, Associate Chair, Graduate Studies, 403-492-5799, Fax: 403-492-6828, E-mail: gradstudies@math.ualberta.ca.

University of Colorado at Boulder, Graduate School, College of Arts and Sciences, Department of Physics, Boulder, CO 80309. Offers chemical physics (PhD); geophysics (PhD); liquid crystal science and technology (PhD); mathematical physics (PhD); medical physics (PhD); optical sciences and engineering (PhD); physics (MS, PhD). *Faculty:* 43 full-time (3 women). *Students:* 148 full-time (24 women), 42 part-time (8 women); includes 11 minority (2 African Americans, 1 American Indian/Alaska Native, 6 Asian Americans or Pacific Islanders, 2 Hispanic Americans), 56 international. Average age 27. 75 applicants, 65% accepted. In 2003, 1 master's, 20 doctorates awarded. Terminal master's awarded for partial completion of doctoral program. *Degree requirements:* For master's, thesis or alternative, comprehensive exam; for doctorate, thesis/dissertation, comprehensive exam. *Entrance requirements:* For master's and doctorate, GRE General Test, GRE Subject Test, minimum undergraduate GPA of 3.0. Additional exam requirements/recommendations for international students: Required—TOEFL. *Application deadline:* For fall admission, 1/15 for domestic students; for spring admission, 11/1 for domestic students. Applications are processed on a rolling basis. Application fee: $50 ($60 for international students). Electronic applications accepted. *Expenses:* Tuition, state resident: full-time $2,122. Tuition, nonresident: full-time $9,754. Tuition and fees vary according to course load and program. *Financial support:* In 2003–04, 14 fellowships with full tuition reimbursements (averaging $23,854 per year), 34 research assistantships with full tuition reimbursements (averaging $18,725 per year), 25 teaching assistantships with full tuition reimbursements (averaging $15,113 per year) were awarded. Scholarships/grants also available. Financial award application deadline: 1/15. *Faculty research:* Atomic and molecular physics, nuclear physics, condensed matter, elementary particle physics, laser or optical physics. Total annual research expenditures: $19.1 million. *Unit head:* John Cumalat, Chair, 303-492-6952, Fax: 303-492-3352, E-mail: jcumalat@pizero.colorado.edu. *Application contact:* Graduate Program Assistant, 303-492-6954, Fax: 303-492-3352, E-mail: phys@bogart.colorado.edu.

Virginia Polytechnic Institute and State University, Graduate School, College of Science, Department of Mathematics, Blacksburg, VA 24061. Offers applied mathematics (MS, PhD); mathematical physics (MS, PhD); pure mathematics (MS, PhD). *Faculty:* 66 full-time (18 women), 1 (woman) part-time/adjunct. *Students:* 65 full-time (22 women), 50 part-time (35 women); includes 13 minority (5 African Americans, 3 Asian Americans or Pacific Islanders, 5 Hispanic Americans), 17 international. Average age 31. 152 applicants, 47% accepted, 51 enrolled. In 2003, 24 master's, 2 doctorates awarded. *Entrance requirements:* For master's and doctorate, GRE. Additional exam requirements/recommendations for international students: Required—TOEFL (minimum score 550 paper-based; 213 computer-based). *Application deadline:* Applications are processed on a rolling basis. Application fee: $45. Electronic applications accepted. Tuition, area resident: Full-time $6,039; part-time $336 per credit. Tuition, nonresident: full-time $9,708; part-time $539 per credit. Required fees: $905; $130 per credit. *Financial support:* In 2003–04, 3 fellowships with full tuition reimbursements (averaging $4,000 per year), 6 research assistantships with full tuition reimbursements (averaging $14,752 per year), 36 teaching assistantships with full tuition reimbursements (averaging $12,858 per year) were awarded. Career-related internships or fieldwork, Federal Work-Study, scholarships/grants, and unspecified assistantships also available. *Faculty research:* Differential equations, operator theory, numerical analysis, algebra, control theory. *Unit head:* Dr. John Rossi, Head, 540-231-6536, Fax: 540-231-5960, E-mail: rossi@math.vt.edu. *Application contact:* Hannah Swiger, Information Contact, 540-231-6537, Fax: 540-231-5960, E-mail: hsswiger@math.vt.edu.

Optical Sciences

Air Force Institute of Technology, Graduate School of Engineering and Management, Department of Electrical and Computer Engineering, Dayton, OH 45433-7765. Offers computer engineering (MS, PhD); computer systems/science (MS); electrical engineering (MS, PhD); electro-optics (MS, PhD). *Accreditation:* ABET (one or more programs are accredited). Part-time programs available. *Degree requirements:* For master's and doctorate, thesis/dissertation. *Entrance requirements:* For master's and doctorate, GRE General Test, minimum GPA of 3.0, U.S. citizenship. *Faculty research:* Remote sensing, information survivability, microelectronics, computer networks, artificial intelligence.

Air Force Institute of Technology, Graduate School of Engineering and Management, Department of Engineering Physics, Dayton, OH 45433-7765. Offers applied physics (MS, PhD); electro-optics (MS, PhD); materials science (PhD); nuclear engineering (MS, PhD); space physics (MS). *Accreditation:* ABET (one or more programs are accredited). Part-time programs available. *Degree requirements:* For master's and doctorate, thesis/dissertation. *Entrance requirements:* For master's and doctorate, GRE General Test, minimum GPA of 3.0, U.S. citizenship. *Faculty research:* High-energy lasers, space physics, nuclear weapon effects, semiconductor physics.

Alabama Agricultural and Mechanical University, School of Graduate Studies, School of Arts and Sciences, Department of Natural and Physical Sciences, Huntsville, AL 35811. Offers biology (MS); physics (MS, PhD), including applied physics (PhD), materials science (PhD), optics (PhD), physics (MS). Part-time and evening/weekend programs available. *Faculty:* 17. *Students:* 37 full-time (25 women), 36 part-time (14 women); includes 67 minority (55 African Americans, 1 American Indian/Alaska Native, 10 Asian Americans or Pacific Islanders, 1 Hispanic American). In 2003, 3 master's, 1 doctorate awarded. *Degree requirements:* For doctorate, thesis/dissertation. *Entrance requirements:* For master's and doctorate, GRE General Test. *Application deadline:* For fall admission, 5/1 for domestic students. Applications are processed on a rolling basis. Application fee: $25. Electronic applications accepted. *Expenses:* Tuition, state resident: full-time $3,250; part-time $370 per credit hour. Tuition, nonresident: full-time $6,490; part-time $740 per credit hour. *Financial support:* In 2003–04, 1 fellowship with tuition reimbursement (averaging $18,000 per year), 5 research assistantships with tuition reimbursements (averaging $10,000 per year), 1 teaching assistantship with tuition reimbursement (averaging $10,000 per year) were awarded. Career-related internships or fieldwork and Federal Work-Study also available. Financial award application deadline: 4/1. Total annual research expenditures: $1.5 million. *Unit head:* Dr. R. V. Lal, Chair, 256-372-8148.

Cleveland State University, College of Graduate Studies, College of Arts and Sciences, Department of Physics, Cleveland, OH 44115. Offers applied optics (MS); condensed matter physics (MS); medical physics (MS). Part-time and evening/weekend programs available. *Faculty:* 5 full-time (1 woman), 4 part-time/adjunct (0 women). *Students:* Average age 30. 7 applicants, 100% accepted, 5 enrolled. In 2003, 4 degrees awarded, leading to business/industry 4%. *Median time to degree:* Master's–2 years full-time. *Degree requirements:* For master's, exit project. *Entrance requirements:* For master's, undergraduate degree in engineering or physics, chemistry or mathematics. Additional exam requirements/recommendations for international students: Required—TOEFL (minimum score 525 paper-based; 197 computer-based), GRE. *Application deadline:* For fall admission, 7/15 priority date for domestic students, 7/15 priority date for international students. Applications are processed on a rolling basis. Application fee: $30. Electronic applications accepted. Tuition, area resident: Full-time $8,258; part-time $344 per credit hour. Tuition, nonresident: full-time $16,352; part-time $681 per credit hour. *Financial support:* In 2003–04, 1 research assistantship with full and partial tuition reimbursement (averaging $5,666 per year) was awarded; fellowships with tuition reimbursements, teaching assistantships, tuition waivers (full) also available. *Faculty research:* Statistical mechanics of phase transitions, low-temperature and solid-state physics, superconductivity, theoretical light scattering, medical physics. Total annual research expenditures: $350,000. *Unit head:* Dr. Miron Kaufman, Chairperson, 216-687-2436, Fax: 216-523-7268, E-mail: m.kaufman@csuohio.edu. *Application contact:* Dr. James A. Lock, Director, 216-687-2425, Fax: 216-523-7268, E-mail: j.lock@csuohio.edu.

Columbia University, Fu Foundation School of Engineering and Applied Science, Department of Applied Physics and Applied Mathematics, New York, NY 10027. Offers applied physics (MS, PhD), including applied mathematics (PhD), optical physics (PhD), plasma physics (PhD), solid state physics (PhD); applied physics and applied mathematics (Eng Sc D); materials science and engineering (MS, Eng Sc D, PhD); medical physics (MS); minerals engineering and materials science (Eng Sc D, PhD, Engr). Part-time programs available. *Faculty:* 29 full-time (3 women), 11 part-time/adjunct (1 woman). *Students:* 82 full-time (25 women), 27 part-time (13 women); includes 14 minority (5 African Americans, 8 Asian Americans or Pacific Islanders, 1 Hispanic American), 51 international. 371 applicants, 17% accepted, 41 enrolled. In 2003, 36 master's, 9 doctorates awarded. Terminal master's awarded for partial completion of doctoral program. *Degree requirements:* For doctorate, thesis/dissertation, qualifying exam. *Entrance requirements:* For master's and doctorate, GRE General Test, GRE Subject Test (strongly recommended). Additional exam requirements/recommendations for international students: Required—TOEFL. *Application deadline:* For fall admission, 12/15 priority date for domestic students, 12/15 priority date for international students; for spring admission, 10/1 priority date for domestic students, 10/1 priority date for international students. Application fee: $55. Electronic applications accepted. *Expenses:* Tuition: Full-time $14,820. *Financial support:* In 2003–04, 62 students received support, including 4 fellowships with full tuition reimbursements available, 40 research assistantships with full tuition reimbursements available (averaging $22,725 per year), 14 teaching assistantships with full tuition reimbursements available (averaging $22,725 per year); Federal Work-Study and unspecified assistantships also available. Financial award application deadline: 12/15; financial award applicants required to submit FAFSA. *Faculty research:* Plasma physics, applied mathematics, solid-state and optical physics, atmospheric, oceanic and earth physics, materials science and engineering. Total annual research expenditures: $7.9 million. *Unit head:* Dr. Michael E. Mauel, Chairman, 212-854-4457, E-mail: seasinfo.apam@columbia.edu. *Application contact:* Marlene Arbo, Department Administrator, 212-854-4458, Fax: 212-854-8257, E-mail: seasinfo.apam@columbia.edu.

See in-depth description on page 357.

École Polytechnique de Montréal, Graduate Programs, Department of Engineering Physics, Montréal, QC H3C 3A7, Canada. Offers optical engineering (M Eng, M Sc A, PhD); solid-state physics and engineering (M Eng, M Sc A, PhD). Part-time programs available. *Degree requirements:* For master's and doctorate, one foreign language, thesis/dissertation. *Entrance requirements:* For master's, minimum GPA of 2.75; for doctorate, minimum GPA of 3.0. *Faculty research:* Optics, thin-film physics, laser spectroscopy, plasmas, photonic devices.

Indiana University Bloomington, School of Optometry and Graduate School, Graduate Program in Visual Sciences and Physiological Optics, Bloomington, IN 47405. Offers MS, PhD. PhD offered through the University Graduate School. *Students:* 10 full-time (7 women), 6 part-time (5 women), 13 international. Average age 31.Terminal master's awarded for partial completion of doctoral program. *Degree requirements:* For master's and doctorate, thesis/dissertation. *Entrance requirements:* For master's and doctorate, GRE. Additional exam requirements/recommendations for international students: Required—TOEFL. *Application deadline:* For fall admission, 2/15 priority date for domestic students, 1/1 priority date for international students. Application fee: $45 ($55 for international students). *Expenses:* Tuition, state resident: full-time $4,908; part-time $205 per credit. Tuition, nonresident: full-time $14,298; part-time $596 per credit. Required fees: $661. Tuition and fees vary according to campus/location and program. *Financial support:* In 2003–04, 7 fellowships with full tuition reimbursements (averaging $16,000 per year), 3 research assistantships with full tuition reimbursements (averaging $3,000 per year), 2 teaching assistantships with full tuition reimbursements (averaging $6,800 per year) were awarded. Scholarships/grants and tuition waivers (full) also available. Financial award application deadline: 3/1; financial award applicants required to submit FAFSA. *Faculty research:* Corneal physiology, contact lenses, adaptive optics, dry eye, low vision, refractive anomalies. Total annual research expenditures: $361,764. *Unit head:* P. Sarita Soni, Associate Dean, 812-855-4475, Fax: 812-855-7045, E-mail: sonip@indiana.edu. *Application contact:* Jacqueline S. Olson, Director of Student Affairs, 812-855-1917, Fax: 812-855-4389, E-mail: iubopt@indiana.edu.

Norfolk State University, School of Graduate Studies, School of Science and Technology, Program in Optical Engineering, Norfolk, VA 23504. Offers MS. *Expenses:* Tuition, state resident: full-time $4,998; part-time $244 per credit. Tuition, nonresident: full-time $13,170; part-time $698 per credit. *Unit head:* Dr. C. Washington, Head.

The Ohio State University, College of Optometry and Graduate School, Program in Vision Science, Columbus, OH 43210. Offers MS, PhD, OD/MS. *Faculty:* 19 full-time (6 women), 3 part-time/adjunct (0 women). *Students:* 36 full-time (17 women). In 2003, 9 master's, 2 doctorates awarded. *Degree requirements:* For master's and doctorate, thesis/dissertation. *Entrance requirements:* For master's and doctorate, GRE General Test. *Application deadline:* Applications are processed on a rolling basis. Application fee: $40 ($50 for international students). Electronic applications accepted. *Expenses:* Tuition, state resident: full-time $7,233. Tuition, nonresident: full-time $18,489. *Financial support:* In 2003–04, fellowships with tuition reimbursements (averaging $42,000 per year), research assistantships with full tuition reimbursements (averaging $12,000 per year), teaching assistantships with full tuition reimbursements (averaging $22,000 per year) were awarded. Federal Work-Study, scholarships/grants, traineeships, and unspecified assistantships also available. Financial award application deadline: 2/1; financial award applicants required to submit FAFSA. *Faculty research:* Ocular development, myopia, cornea, refractive error, quality of life, tears. Total annual research expenditures: $9 million. *Application contact:* Dr. Ronald Jones, Graduate Chair, 614-292-3246, Fax: 614-292-7493, E-mail: grad@optometry.osu.edu.

Rochester Institute of Technology, Graduate Enrollment Services, College of Science, Center for Imaging Science, Rochester, NY 14623-5603. Offers MS, PhD. *Students:* 52 full-time (18 women), 41 part-time (4 women); includes 3 minority (1 Asian American or Pacific Islander, 2 Hispanic Americans), 36 international. 65 applicants, 78% accepted, 32 enrolled. In 2003, 15 master's, 6 doctorates awarded. *Degree requirements:* For master's, thesis. *Entrance requirements:* For master's, minimum GPA of 3.0. Additional exam requirements/recommendations for international students: Required—TOEFL. *Application deadline:* For fall admission, 3/1 for domestic students. Applications are processed on a rolling basis. Application fee: $50. Electronic applications accepted. *Expenses:* Tuition: Full-time $22,965; part-time $644 per hour. Required fees: $174; $29 per quarter. *Financial support:* Research assistantships, teaching assistantships available. *Unit head:* Dr. Ronald Jodoin, Interim Director, 585-475-6220, E-mail: jodoin@cis.rit.edu.

Rose-Hulman Institute of Technology, Faculty of Engineering and Applied Sciences, Department of Physics and Optical Engineering, Terre Haute, IN 47803-3999. Offers optical engineering (MS). Part-time programs available. *Faculty:* 14 full-time (2 women), 3 part-time/adjunct (0 women). *Students:* 4 full-time (1 woman), 2 part-time; includes 1 minority (Asian American or Pacific Islander), 3 international. Average age 25. 7 applicants, 14% accepted, 1 enrolled. In 2003, 5 degrees awarded. *Degree requirements:* For master's, thesis. *Entrance requirements:* For master's, GRE, minimum GPA of 3.0. Additional exam requirements/recommendations for international students: Required—TOEFL (minimum score 550 paper-based; 210 computer-based). *Application deadline:* For fall admission, 2/1 for domestic students. Applications are processed on a rolling basis. Application fee: $0. *Expenses:* Tuition: Full-time $24,255; part-time $696 per credit hour. *Financial support:* In 2003–04, 4 students received support; fellowships with full and partial tuition reimbursements available, research assistantships with full and partial tuition reimbursements available, teaching assistantships, institutionally sponsored loans, scholarships/grants, and tuition waivers (full and partial) available. Financial award application deadline: 2/1. *Faculty research:* Optical instrument design and prototypes, photorefractive phenomena, speckle techniques, holography, fiber-optic sensors. Total annual research expenditures: $2.2 million. *Unit head:* Dr. Charles Joenathan, Chairman, 812-877-8494, Fax: 812-877-8023, E-mail: charles.joenathan@rose-hulman.edu. *Application contact:* Dr. Daniel J. Moore, Associate Dean of the Faculty, 812-877-8110, Fax: 812-877-8061, E-mail: daniel.j.moore@rose-hulman.edu.

The University of Alabama in Huntsville, School of Graduate Studies, Interdisciplinary Program in Optical Science and Engineering, Huntsville, AL 35899. Offers PhD. Part-time programs available. *Students:* 23 full-time (9 women), 7 part-time; includes 2 minority (1 African American, 1 Asian American or Pacific Islander), 16 international. Average age 30. 14 applicants, 57% accepted, 5 enrolled. *Degree requirements:* For doctorate, thesis/dissertation, written and oral exams, comprehensive exam, registration. *Entrance requirements:* For doctorate, GRE General Test, combined score of 1600 preferred, minimum GPA of 3.0, BS in physical science or engineering. Additional exam requirements/recommendations for international students: Required—TOEFL (minimum score 550 paper-based; 213 computer-based). *Application deadline:* For fall admission, 5/30 priority date for domestic students, 2/30 priority date for international students; for spring admission, 10/10 priority date for domestic students, 7/10 priority date for international students. Applications are processed on a rolling basis. Application fee: $35. *Expenses:* Tuition, state resident: full-time $5,168; part-time $211 per hour. Tuition, nonresident: full-time $10,620; part-time $447 per hour. Tuition and fees vary according to course load. *Financial support:* In 2003–04, 21 students received support, including 14 research assistantships with full and partial tuition reimbursements available (averaging $11,395 per year), 7 teaching assistantships with full and partial tuition reimbursements available (averaging $9,064 per year); fellowships with full and partial tuition reimbursements available, career-related internships or fieldwork, Federal Work-Study, institutionally sponsored loans, scholarships/grants, health care benefits, tuition waivers (full and partial), and unspecified assistantships also available. Support available to part-time students. Financial award application deadline: 4/1; financial award applicants required to submit FAFSA. *Faculty research:* Laser technology, holography, optical communications, medical image processing, computer design. *Unit head:* Dr. Joe Geary, Director, 256-824-2528, Fax: 256-824-6803, E-mail: gearyj@uah.edu.

The University of Arizona, Optical Sciences Center, Tucson, AZ 85721. Offers MS, PhD. Part-time programs available. *Degree requirements:* For master's, thesis (for some programs), exam; for doctorate, thesis/dissertation, oral and written exams. *Entrance requirements:* For master's and doctorate, GRE General Test, GRE Subject Test. Additional exam requirements/recommendations for international students: Required—TOEFL. *Expenses:* Tuition, state resident: part-time $196 per unit. Tuition, nonresident: part-time $326 per unit. *Faculty research:* Medical optics, medical imaging, optical data storage, optical bistability, nonlinear optical effects.

University of Central Florida, School of Optics, Orlando, FL 32816. Offers applied optics (Certificate); lasers (Certificate); optical communication (Certificate); optics (MS, PhD). Part-time and evening/weekend programs available. *Faculty:* 20 full-time (2 women). *Students:* 75 full-time (10 women), 40 part-time (5 women); includes 5 minority (1 African American, 3 Asian Americans or Pacific Islanders, 1 Hispanic American), 73 international. Average age 28. 180 applicants, 51% accepted, 22 enrolled. In 2003, 19 master's, 6 doctorates awarded. *Degree requirements:* For master's, thesis or alternative; for doctorate, thesis/dissertation, departmental qualifying exam, candidacy exam. *Entrance requirements:* For master's, GRE General Test, minimum GPA of 3.0 in last 60 hours; for doctorate, GRE General Test, minimum GPA of 3.5 in last 60 hours. Additional exam requirements/recommendations for international students: Required—TOEFL. *Application deadline:* For fall admission, 2/1 for domestic students; for

Optical Sciences

University of Central Florida (continued)
spring admission, 12/1 for domestic students. Application fee: $30. Electronic applications accepted. *Expenses:* Tuition, state resident: full-time $4,968; part-time $171 per credit hour. Tuition, nonresident: full-time $18,630; part-time $713 per credit hour. *Financial support:* In 2003–04, 45 fellowships with partial tuition reimbursements (averaging $4,700 per year), 109 research assistantships with partial tuition reimbursements (averaging $13,700 per year) were awarded. Teaching assistantships with partial tuition reimbursements, career-related internships or fieldwork, Federal Work-Study, institutionally sponsored loans, tuition waivers (partial), and unspecified assistantships also available. Financial award application deadline: 3/1; financial award applicants required to submit FAFSA. *Unit head:* Dr. Eric W. Van Stryland, Director, 407-823-6814, E-mail: cwvs@mail.creol.ucf.edu. *Application contact:* Dr. David J. Hagan, Coordinator, 407-823-6817, E-mail: dhagan@creol.ucf.edu.

University of Colorado at Boulder, Graduate School, College of Arts and Sciences, Department of Physics, Boulder, CO 80309. Offers chemical physics (PhD); geophysics (PhD); liquid crystal science and technology (PhD); mathematical physics (PhD); medical physics (PhD); optical sciences and engineering (PhD); physics (MS, PhD). *Faculty:* 43 full-time (3 women). *Students:* 148 full-time (24 women), 42 part-time (8 women); includes 11 minority (2 African Americans, 1 American Indian/Alaska Native, 6 Asian Americans or Pacific Islanders, 2 Hispanic Americans), 56 international. Average age 27. 75 applicants, 65% accepted. In 2003, 1 master's, 20 doctorates awarded. Terminal master's awarded for partial completion of doctoral program. *Degree requirements:* For master's, thesis or alternative, comprehensive exam; for doctorate, thesis/dissertation, comprehensive exam. *Entrance requirements:* For master's and doctorate, GRE General Test, GRE Subject Test, minimum undergraduate GPA of 3.0. Additional exam requirements/recommendations for international students: Required—TOEFL. *Application deadline:* For fall admission, 1/15 for domestic students; for spring admission, 11/1 for domestic students. Applications are processed on a rolling basis. Application fee: $50 ($60 for international students). Electronic applications accepted. *Expenses:* Tuition, state resident: full-time $2,122. Tuition, nonresident: full-time $9,754. Tuition and fees vary according to course load and program. *Financial support:* In 2003–04, 14 fellowships with full tuition reimbursements (averaging $23,854 per year), 34 research assistantships with full tuition reimbursements (averaging $18,725 per year), 25 teaching assistantships with full tuition reimbursements (averaging $15,113 per year) were awarded. Scholarships/grants also available. Financial award application deadline: 1/15. *Faculty research:* Atomic and molecular physics, nuclear physics, condensed matter, elementary particle physics, laser or optical physics. Total annual research expenditures: $19.1 million. *Unit head:* John Cumalat, Chair, 303-492-6952, Fax: 303-492-3352, E-mail: jcumalat@pizero.colorado.edu. *Application contact:* Graduate Program Assistant, 303-492-6954, Fax: 303-492-3352, E-mail: phys@bogart.colorado.edu.

University of Dayton, Graduate School, School of Engineering, Program in Electro-Optics, Dayton, OH 45469-1300. Offers MSEO, PhD. Part-time and evening/weekend programs available. *Faculty:* 4 full-time (0 women), 14 part-time/adjunct (0 women). *Students:* 29 full-time (7 women), 8 part-time (3 women); includes 3 minority (2 African Americans, 1 Hispanic American), 15 international. Average age 24. In 2003, 3 master's, 1 doctorate awarded. *Degree requirements:* For master's, thesis optional; for doctorate, thesis/dissertation, departmental qualifying exam. *Entrance requirements:* Additional exam requirements/recommendations for international students: Required—TOEFL. *Application deadline:* For fall admission, 8/1 for domestic students. Applications are processed on a rolling basis. Electronic applications accepted. *Expenses:* Tuition: Full-time $6,060; part-time $505 per hour. Required fees: $50; $25 per term. Tuition and fees vary according to degree level, campus/location, program and student's religious affiliation. *Financial support:* In 2003–04, 22 students received support, including 19 research assistantships with full tuition reimbursements available (averaging $13,500 per year), 3 teaching assistantships with full tuition reimbursements available (averaging $13,500 per year); fellowships, institutionally sponsored loans also available. Financial award application deadline: 2/1. *Faculty research:* Fiber optics, optical materials, computational optics, holography, laser diagnostics. Total annual research expenditures: $485,840. *Unit head:* Dr. Joseph W. Haus, Director, 937-229-2797, Fax: 937-229-2097, E-mail: jhaus@notes.udayton.edu. *Application contact:* Dr. Donald L. Moon, Associate Dean, 937-229-2241, Fax: 937-229-2471, E-mail: dmoon@notes.udayton.edu.

University of Maryland, Baltimore County, Graduate School, Department of Physics, Baltimore, MD 21250. Offers applied physics (MS, PhD), including optics, solid state physics; atmospheric physics (MS, PhD). Part-time programs available. Terminal master's awarded for partial completion of doctoral program. *Degree requirements:* For master's, thesis optional; for doctorate, thesis/dissertation. *Entrance requirements:* For master's and doctorate, GRE General Test, GRE Subject Test, minimum GPA of 3.0. Additional exam requirements/recommendations for international students: Required—TOEFL. Electronic applications accepted. *Expenses:* Tuition, state resident: full-time $7,000. Tuition, nonresident: full-time $11,400. Required fees: $1,440. *Faculty research:* Optics, solid state physics, astrophysics, atmospheric physics.

University of Massachusetts Lowell, Graduate School, College of Arts and Sciences, Department of Physics and Applied Physics, Program in Applied Physics, Lowell, MA 01854-2881. Offers applied mechanics (PhD); applied physics (MS, PhD), including optical sciences (MS). Terminal master's awarded for partial completion of doctoral program. *Degree requirements:* For master's, thesis; for doctorate, 2 foreign languages, thesis/dissertation. *Entrance requirements:* For master's and doctorate, GRE General Test.

University of New Mexico, Graduate School, College of Arts and Sciences, Department of Physics and Astronomy, Albuquerque, NM 87131-2039. Offers optical sciences (PhD); physics (MS, PhD). Part-time programs available. *Faculty:* 44. *Students:* 78 full-time (15 women), 22 part-time (6 women); includes 6 minority (1 African American, 3 Asian Americans or Pacific Islanders, 2 Hispanic Americans), 35 international. Average age 27. 67 applicants, 61% accepted, 20 enrolled. In 2003, 12 master's, 11 doctorates awarded. Terminal master's awarded for partial completion of doctoral program. *Degree requirements:* For master's, thesis optional; for doctorate, thesis/dissertation, comprehensive exam. *Entrance requirements:* Additional exam requirements/recommendations for international students: Required—TOEFL or Michigan English Language Assessment Battery. *Application deadline:* For fall admission, 2/1 for domestic students; for spring admission, 10/1 for domestic students. Application fee: $40. *Expenses:* Tuition, state resident: full-time $1,802; part-time $152 per credit hour. Tuition, nonresident: full-time $6,135; part-time $513 per credit hour. Tuition and fees vary according to program. *Financial support:* In 2003–04, 50 research assistantships with full and partial tuition reimbursements (averaging $10,943 per year), 31 teaching assistantships with full and partial tuition reimbursements (averaging $8,058 per year) were awarded. Fellowships with full tuition reimbursements, career-related internships or fieldwork, scholarships/grants, health care benefits, and unspecified assistantships also available. Financial award application deadline: 3/1; financial award applicants required to submit FAFSA. *Faculty research:* High-energy and particle physics, optical and laser sciences, condensed matter, nuclear and particle physics, surface physics. Total annual research expenditures: $4.6 million. *Unit head:* Dr. Bernd Bassalleck, Chair, 505-277-1517, Fax: 505-277-1520, E-mail: bassek@unm.edu. *Application contact:* Mary De Witt, Program Advisement Coordinator, 505-277-1514, Fax: 505-277-1520, E-mail: mdewitt@unm.edu.

University of New Mexico, Graduate School, School of Engineering, Department of Electrical and Computer Engineering, Albuquerque, NM 87131-2039. Offers electrical engineering (MS); engineering (PhD); optical sciences (PhD). MEME offered through the Manufacturing Engineering Program. Part-time and evening/weekend programs available. *Faculty:* 32 full-time (3 women), 18 part-time/adjunct (1 woman). *Students:* 189 full-time (45 women), 69 part-time (10 women); includes 40 minority (2 African Americans, 3 American Indian/Alaska Native, 13 Asian Americans or Pacific Islanders, 22 Hispanic Americans), 136 international. Average age 31. 299 applicants, 29% accepted, 46 enrolled. In 2003, 50 master's, 11 doctorates awarded. *Degree requirements:* For master's, thesis (for some programs); for doctorate, thesis/dissertation. *Entrance requirements:* For master's, GRE General Test, minimum GPA of 3.0; for doctorate, GRE General Test, minimum GPA of 3.5. *Application deadline:* For fall admission, 7/30 for domestic students; for spring admission, 11/30 for domestic students. Application fee: $40. *Expenses:* Tuition, state resident: full-time $1,802; part-time $152 per credit hour. Tuition, nonresident: full-time $6,135; part-time $513 per credit hour. Tuition and fees vary according to program. *Financial support:* In 2003–04, 1 fellowship (averaging $4,000 per year), 114 research assistantships (averaging $9,625 per year), 1 teaching assistantship (averaging $5,400 per year) were awarded. Scholarships/grants, health care benefits, and unspecified assistantships also available. Financial award application deadline: 3/1; financial award applicants required to submit FAFSA. *Faculty research:* Applied electromagnetics, high performance computing, wireless communications, optoelectronics, control systems. Total annual research expenditures: $2.4 million. *Unit head:* Dr. Christos Christodoulou, Chair, 505-277-2436, Fax: 505-277-1439, E-mail: christos@eece.unm.edu. *Application contact:* Maryellen Missik, Graduate Coordinator, 505-277-2600, Fax: 505-277-1439, E-mail: maryellen@eece.unm.edu.

The University of North Carolina at Charlotte, Graduate School, College of Arts and Sciences, Department of Physics and Optical Science, Program in Optical Science and Engineering, Charlotte, NC 28223-0001. Offers MS, PhD. Part-time programs available. *Students:* 8 full-time (1 woman), 13 part-time (2 women); includes 2 minority (1 African American, 1 Asian American or Pacific Islander), 13 international. Average age 29. 16 applicants, 81% accepted, 8 enrolled. *Degree requirements:* For master's and doctorate, thesis/dissertation. *Entrance requirements:* For master's, GRE, minimum GPA of 3.0; for doctorate, GRE, minimum GPA of 3.2 in major, 3.0 overall. Additional exam requirements/recommendations for international students: Required—TOEFL (minimum score 557 paper-based; 220 computer-based). *Application deadline:* For fall admission, 7/15 for domestic students, 5/1 for international students; for spring admission, 11/15 for domestic students, 10/1 for international students. Applications are processed on a rolling basis. Application fee: $35. Electronic applications accepted. *Expenses:* Tuition, state resident: full-time $1,979. Tuition, nonresident: full-time $12,111. Required fees: $1,201. Tuition and fees vary according to course load. *Financial support:* In 2003–04, 3 fellowships (averaging $2,667 per year), 11 research assistantships (averaging $5,163 per year), 13 teaching assistantships (averaging $7,614 per year) were awarded. Career-related internships or fieldwork, Federal Work-Study, institutionally sponsored loans, scholarships/grants, and unspecified assistantships also available. Support available to part-time students. Financial award application deadline: 4/1; financial award applicants required to submit FAFSA. *Unit head:* Dr. Robert K. Tyson, Graduate Coordinator, 704-687-3399, Fax: 704-687-3160, E-mail: rtyson@email.uncc.edu. *Application contact:* Kathy B. Giddings, Director of Graduate Admissions, 704-687-3366, Fax: 704-687-3279, E-mail: gradadm@email.uncc.edu.

University of Rochester, The College, School of Engineering and Applied Sciences, Institute of Optics, Rochester, NY 14627-0250. Offers MS, PhD. *Faculty:* 16. *Students:* 89 full-time (23 women), 5 part-time; includes 6 minority (2 African Americans, 4 Hispanic Americans), 22 international. 357 applicants, 9% accepted, 23 enrolled. In 2003, 10 master's, 9 doctorates awarded. Terminal master's awarded for partial completion of doctoral program. *Degree requirements:* For master's, comprehensive exam; for doctorate, thesis/dissertation, preliminary and qualifying exams. *Entrance requirements:* For master's and doctorate, GRE. Additional exam requirements/recommendations for international students: Required—TOEFL. *Application deadline:* For fall admission, 2/1 for domestic students. Application fee: $25. *Expenses:* Tuition: Part-time $880 per credit hour. Required fees: $522. *Financial support:* Fellowships, research assistantships, teaching assistantships, tuition waivers (full and partial) available. Financial award application deadline: 2/1. *Unit head:* Wayne Knox, Director, 585-273-5520. *Application contact:* Joan Christian, Graduate Program Secretary, 585-275-7764.

Photonics

Boston University, College of Engineering, Department of Electrical and Computer Engineering, Boston, MA 02215. Offers computer engineering (PhD); computer systems engineering (MS); electrical engineering (MS, PhD); photonics (MS); systems engineering (PhD). Part-time programs available. *Faculty:* 58 full-time (4 women), 7 part-time/adjunct (0 women). *Students:* 165 full-time (42 women), 27 part-time (3 women); includes 21 minority (8 African Americans, 9 Asian Americans or Pacific Islanders, 4 Hispanic Americans), 85 international. 811 applicants, 22% accepted, 71 enrolled. In 2003, 36 master's, 7 doctorates awarded. Terminal master's awarded for partial completion of doctoral program. *Degree requirements:* For master's, thesis optional; for doctorate, thesis/dissertation, comprehensive exam, registration. *Entrance requirements:* For master's and doctorate, GRE General Test. Additional exam requirements/recommendations for international students: Required—TOEFL (minimum score 550 paper-based; 213 computer-based). *Application deadline:* For fall admission, 4/1 for domestic students, 4/1 for international students; for spring admission, 10/1 for domestic students, 10/1 for international students. Applications are processed on a rolling basis. Application fee: $60. Electronic applications accepted. *Expenses:* Tuition: Full-time $28,512; part-time $891 per credit hour. *Financial support:* In 2003–04, 129 students received support, including 3 fellowships with full tuition reimbursements available (averaging $22,500 per year), 64 research assistantships with full tuition reimbursements available (averaging $15,750 per year), 22 teaching assistantships with full tuition reimbursements available (averaging $15,000 per year); career-related internships or fieldwork, Federal Work-Study, institutionally sponsored loans, scholarships/grants, traineeships, and health care benefits also available. Financial award application deadline: 1/15; financial award applicants required to submit FAFSA. *Faculty research:* Computer networks, computer reliability, photonics, signal and image processing, solid state materials, subsurface imaging. Total annual research expenditures: $12.6 million. *Unit head:* Dr. Bahaa Saleh, Chairman, 617-353-7176, Fax: 617-353-6440. *Application contact:* Cheryl Kelley, Director of Graduate Programs, 617-353-9760, Fax: 617-353-0259, E-mail: enggrad@bu.edu.

Lehigh University, College of Arts and Sciences, Department of Physics, Bethlehem, PA 18015-3094. Offers photonics (MS); physics (MS, PhD). Part-time programs available. *Faculty:* 18 full-time (0 women), 1 part-time/adjunct (0 women). *Students:* 41 full-time (11 women), 3 part-time; includes 18 minority (5 African Americans, 11 Asian Americans or Pacific Islanders, 2 Hispanic Americans), 19 international. 65 applicants, 12% accepted, 6 enrolled. In 2003, 3 master's, 5 doctorates awarded. Terminal master's awarded for partial completion of doctoral program. *Median time to degree:* Master's–1.5 years full-time; doctorate–5 years full-time. *Degree requirements:* For master's, research project; for doctorate, thesis/dissertation, exam. *Entrance requirements:* For doctorate, GRE General Test. Additional exam requirements/recommendations for international students: Required—TOEFL (minimum score 600 paper-based; 235 computer-based); Recommended—TSE. *Application deadline:* For fall admission, 7/15 for domestic students; for spring admission, 1/15 priority date for domestic students. Applications are processed on a rolling basis. Application fee: $50. Electronic applications accepted. *Expenses:* Tuition: Full-time $16,920; part-time $940 per credit hour. Required fees: $200. Tuition and fees vary according to degree level and program. *Financial support:* In 2003–04, 6 fellowships with tuition reimbursements (averaging $15,480 per year), 8 research assistantships with tuition reimbursements (averaging $15,480 per year), 14 teaching assistantships with tuition reimbursements (averaging $15,480 per year) were awarded. Federal Work-Study and institutionally sponsored loans also available. Financial award application deadline: 1/15. *Faculty research:* Condensed matter physics; atomic, molecular and optical physics; plasma physics; complex fluids; computational physics. Total annual research expenditures: $2.3 million. *Unit head:* Dr. Michael J. Stavola, Chair, 610-758-3903, Fax: 610-758-5730, E-mail: mjsa@lehigh.edu. *Application contact:* Dr. A. Peet Hickman, Graduate Admissions Officer, 610-758-3917, Fax: 610-758-5730, E-mail: aph2@lehigh.edu.

See in-depth description on page 379.

Lehigh University, P.C. Rossin College of Engineering and Applied Science, Department of Electrical and Computer Engineering, Bethlehem, PA 18015-3094. Offers computer engineering (MS, PhD); electrical engineering (M Eng, MS, PhD); photonics (MS). Part-time programs available. *Faculty:* 25 full-time (3 women), 3 part-time/adjunct (0 women). *Students:* 70 full-time (14 women), 20 part-time (2 women); includes 8 minority (7 Asian Americans or Pacific Islanders, 1 Hispanic American), 57 international. Average age 25. 261 applicants, 63% accepted, 26 enrolled. In 2003, 21 master's, 4 doctorates awarded. *Degree requirements:* For master's, oral presentation of thesis, thesis optional; for doctorate, thesis/dissertation, qualifying, general, and oral exams. *Entrance requirements:* For master's, GRE General Test, minimum GPA of 3.0; for doctorate, GRE General Test, MS, minimum GPA of 3.25. Additional exam requirements/recommendations for international students: Required—TOEFL (minimum score 550 paper-based; 213 computer-based). *Application deadline:* For fall admission, 4/1 for domestic students; for spring admission, 11/1 for domestic students. Applications are processed on a rolling basis. Application fee: $50. Electronic applications accepted. *Expenses:* Tuition: Full-time $16,920; part-time $940 per credit hour. Required fees: $200. Tuition and fees vary according to degree level and program. *Financial support:* In 2003–04, 7 fellowships with full tuition reimbursements (averaging $17,400 per year), 28 research assistantships with full and partial tuition reimbursements (averaging $17,400 per year), 9 teaching assistantships with full tuition reimbursements (averaging $17,700 per year) were awarded. Financial award application deadline: 1/15. *Faculty research:* Computer architecture, digital design software systems, computer vision, nanotechnology, signal processing and communication. Total annual research expenditures: $1.9 million. *Unit head:* Dr. Donald Bolle, Chairman, 610-758-4069, Fax: 610-758-6279, E-mail: dmb4@lehigh.edu. *Application contact:* Brianne Clapp, Graduate Coordinator, 610-758-4072, Fax: 610-758-6279, E-mail: brc3@lehigh.edu.

Lehigh University, P.C. Rossin College of Engineering and Applied Science, Department of Materials Science and Engineering, Bethlehem, PA 18015-3094. Offers materials science and engineering (M Eng, MS, PhD); photonics (MS). Part-time programs available. *Faculty:* 14 full-time (1 woman), 1 part-time/adjunct (0 women). *Students:* 40 full-time (5 women), 5 part-time (1 woman); includes 2 minority (both African Americans), 11 international. 141 applicants, 6% accepted, 6 enrolled. In 2003, 9 master's, 7 doctorates awarded. *Degree requirements:* For master's and doctorate, thesis/dissertation. *Entrance requirements:* For master's and doctorate, GRE General Test, minimum GPA of 3.0. Additional exam requirements/recommendations for international students: Required—TOEFL. *Application deadline:* For fall admission, 2/15 for domestic students; for spring admission, 10/1 priority date for domestic students. Applications are processed on a rolling basis. Application fee: $50. *Expenses:* Tuition: Full-time $16,920; part-time $940 per credit hour. Required fees: $200. Tuition and fees vary according to degree level and program. *Financial support:* In 2003–04, 6 fellowships with full and partial tuition reimbursements (averaging $18,700 per year), 31 research assistantships with full tuition reimbursements (averaging $18,400 per year), 10 teaching assistantships with full tuition reimbursements (averaging $17,700 per year) were awarded. Financial award application deadline: 1/15. *Faculty research:* Metals, ceramics, crystals, polymers, fatigue crack propagation. Total annual research expenditures: $4.9 million. *Unit head:* Dr. G. Slade Cargill, Chairperson, 610-758-4207, Fax: 610-758-4244, E-mail: gsc3@lehigh.edu. *Application contact:* Maxine C. Mattie, Graduate Administrative Coordinator, 610-758-4222, Fax: 610-758-4244, E-mail: mcm1@lehigh.edu.

Oklahoma State University, Graduate College, College of Arts and Sciences, Department of Physics, Stillwater, OK 74078. Offers photonics (MS, PhD); physics (MS, PhD). *Faculty:* 27 full-time (4 women), 1 (woman) part-time/adjunct. *Students:* 14 full-time (4 women), 23 part-time (3 women), 24 international. Average age 28. 26 applicants, 88% accepted. In 2003, 1 degree awarded. *Degree requirements:* For master's, thesis or report; for doctorate, thesis/dissertation, oral defense of dissertation, preliminary exam, qualifying exam. *Entrance requirements:* Additional exam requirements/recommendations for international students: Required—TOEFL. *Application deadline:* For fall admission, 3/15 for domestic students. Applications are processed on a rolling basis. Application fee: $25 ($50 for international students). Electronic applications accepted. *Expenses:* Tuition, state resident: full-time $3,752; part-time $118 per credit hour. Tuition, nonresident: full-time $10,346; part-time $393 per credit hour. Tuition and fees vary according to course load. *Financial support:* In 2003–04, 24 research assistantships (averaging $16,516 per year), 26 teaching assistantships with partial tuition reimbursements (averaging $14,806 per year) were awarded. Federal Work-Study, traineeships, tuition waivers (partial), and unspecified assistantships also available. Support available to part-time students. Financial award application deadline: 3/1. *Faculty research:* Lasers and photonics, non-linear optical materials, turbulence, structure and function of biological membranes, particle theory. *Unit head:* Dr. John Mintmire, Head, 405-744-5796. *Application contact:* Dr. Paul A. Westhaus, Graduate Coordinator, 405-744-5815, E-mail: physpaw@okstate.edu.

Oklahoma State University, Graduate College, Program in Photonics, Stillwater, OK 74078. Offers biophotonics (MS, PhD). *Degree requirements:* For master's, thesis or report; for doctorate, thesis/dissertation. *Entrance requirements:* For master's, Baccalaureate Degree in physics, chemistry, electrical engineering, or a related field. *Application deadline:* For fall admission, 3/15 for domestic students. Applications are processed on a rolling basis. Application fee: $25 ($50 for international students). Electronic applications accepted. *Expenses:* Tuition, state resident: full-time $3,752; part-time $118 per credit hour. Tuition, nonresident: full-time $10,346; part-time $393 per credit hour. Tuition and fees vary according to course load. *Financial support:* Traineeships available. Financial award application deadline: 3/15. *Faculty research:* Nanostructure quantum well semiconductor growth, characterizations for UV-blue photonics applications, interaction of light with biological materials at the tissue, cellular and molecular levels. *Unit head:* Dr. Paul A. Westhaus, Graduate Coordinator, 405-744-5815, E-mail: physpaw@okstate.edu. *Application contact:* Information Contact, 405-744-5815, Fax: 405-744-6406, E-mail: physpaw@okstate.edu.

Announcement: Photonics at Oklahoma State University provides world-class research opportunities in multidisciplinary MS/PhD programs launched by the Departments of Electrical Engineering, Physics, and Chemistry. An NSF IGERT grant supports qualified PhD photonics students with annual stipends of $27,500 as well as complete tuition waivers and cost of education and travel allowances.

See in-depth description on page 395.

Princeton University, Center for Photonic and Optoelectronic Materials (POEM)., Princeton, NJ 08544-1019.

University of Arkansas, Graduate School, Interdisciplinary Program in Microelectronics and Photonics, Fayetteville, AR 72701-1201. Offers MS, PhD. *Students:* 27 full-time (8 women), 21 part-time (2 women); includes 10 minority (7 African Americans, 1 Asian American or Pacific Islander, 2 Hispanic Americans), 23 international. 31 applicants, 61% accepted. In 2003, 7 master's, 2 doctorates awarded. *Degree requirements:* For doctorate, thesis/dissertation. Application fee: $40 ($50 for international students). *Expenses:* Tuition, state resident: full-time $4,032; part-time $224 per credit hour. Tuition, nonresident: full-time $9,540; part-time $530 per credit hour. Tuition and fees vary according to course load and program. *Financial support:* In 2003–04, 7 fellowships, 14 research assistantships were awarded. Financial award application deadline: 4/1; financial award applicants required to submit FAFSA. *Unit head:* , Dr. Ken Vickers, Head, 479-575-2875.

University of California, San Diego, Graduate Studies and Research, Department of Electrical and Computer Engineering, La Jolla, CA 92093. Offers applied ocean science (MS, PhD); applied physics (MS, PhD); communication theory and systems (MS, PhD); computer engineering (MS, PhD); electrical engineering (M Eng); electronic circuits and systems (MS, PhD); intelligent systems, robotics and control (MS, PhD); photonics (MS, PhD); signal and image processing (MS, PhD). MS only offered to students who have been admitted to the PhD program. *Faculty:* 73. *Students:* 415 (62 women); includes 98 minority (2 African Americans, 1 American Indian/Alaska Native, 89 Asian Americans or Pacific Islanders, 6 Hispanic Americans) 183 international. 2,053 applicants, 12% accepted. In 2003, 58 master's, 31 doctorates awarded. *Entrance requirements:* For master's and doctorate, GRE General Test. *Application deadline:* For fall admission, 1/12 for domestic students. Application fee: $60. Electronic applications accepted. Tuition, nonresident: full-time $12,245. Required fees: $6,959. *Unit head:* Paul Yu, Chair. *Application contact:* Graduate Coordinator, 858-534-6606.

Physics

Alabama Agricultural and Mechanical University, School of Graduate Studies, School of Arts and Sciences, Department of Natural and Physical Sciences, Huntsville, AL 35811. Offers biology (MS); physics (MS, PhD), including applied physics (PhD), materials science (PhD), optics (PhD), physics (MS). Part-time and evening/weekend programs available. *Faculty:* 17. *Students:* 37 full-time (25 women), 36 part-time (14 women); includes 67 minority (55 African Americans, 1 American Indian/Alaska Native, 10 Asian Americans or Pacific Islanders, 1 Hispanic American). In 2003, 3 master's, 1 doctorate awarded. *Degree requirements:* For doctorate, thesis/dissertation. *Entrance requirements:* For master's and doctorate, GRE General Test. *Application deadline:* For fall admission, 5/1 for domestic students. Applications are processed on a rolling basis. Application fee: $25. Electronic applications accepted. *Expenses:* Tuition, state resident: full-time $3,250; part-time $370 per credit hour. Tuition, nonresident: full-time $6,490; part-time $740 per credit hour. *Financial support:* In 2003–04, 1 fellowship with tuition reimbursement (averaging $18,000 per year), 5 research assistantships with tuition reimbursements (averaging $10,000 per year), 1 teaching assistantship with tuition reimbursement (averaging $10,000 per year) were awarded. Career-related internships or fieldwork and Federal Work-Study also available. Financial award application deadline: 4/1. Total annual research expenditures: $1.5 million. *Unit head:* Dr. R. V. Lal, Chair, 256-372-8148.

American University, College of Arts and Sciences, Department of Computer Science, Audio Technology, and Physics, Program in Physics, Washington, DC 20016-8001. Offers Certificate. Part-time and evening/weekend programs available. *Application deadline:* For fall admission, 2/1 for domestic students; for spring admission, 10/1 for domestic students. Applications are processed on a rolling basis. Application fee: $50. *Expenses:* Tuition: Full-time $15,786; part-time $877 per credit hour. Required fees: $300. Tuition and fees vary according to course load and program. *Financial support:* Fellowships with full tuition reimbursements, teaching assistantships, career-related internships or fieldwork, Federal Work-Study, institutionally sponsored loans, and unspecified assistantships available. Financial award application deadline: 2/1. *Faculty research:* Artificial intelligence, database systems, software engineering, expert systems.

Arizona State University, Graduate College, College of Liberal Arts and Sciences, Department of Physics and Astronomy, Tempe, AZ 85287. Offers MNS, MS, PhD. *Degree requirements:* For master's, thesis, oral and written exams; for doctorate, thesis/dissertation. *Entrance requirements:* For master's and doctorate, GRE. *Expenses:* Tuition, state resident: full-time $3,708; part-time $194 per credit hour. Tuition, nonresident: full-time $12,228; part-time $510 per credit hour. Required fees: $87; $22 per semester. Part-time tuition and fees vary according to program. *Faculty research:* Electromagnetic interaction of hadrons, investigation of tripartition fission, and beta activity of various elements formed in fission processes; phase transitions in solids.

Auburn University, Graduate School, College of Sciences and Mathematics, Department of Physics, Auburn University, AL 36849. Offers MS, PhD. Part-time programs available. *Faculty:* 18 full-time (1 woman). *Students:* 18 full-time (1 woman), 5 part-time; includes 2 minority (1 African American, 1 Asian American or Pacific Islander), 11 international. 22 applicants, 86% accepted. In 2003, 4 master's, 3 doctorates awarded. *Degree requirements:* For doctorate, thesis/dissertation, oral and written exams. *Entrance requirements:* For master's and doctorate, GRE General Test. *Application deadline:* For fall admission, 7/7 for domestic students; for spring admission, 11/24 for domestic students. Applications are processed on a rolling basis. Application fee: $25 ($50 for international students). Electronic applications accepted. *Expenses:* Tuition, state resident: part-time $175 per credit hour. Tuition, nonresident: part-time $525 per credit hour. *Financial support:* Research assistantships, teaching assistantships, career-related internships or fieldwork and Federal Work-Study available. Support available to part-time students. Financial award application deadline: 3/15. *Faculty research:* Atomic/radiative physics, plasma physics, condensed matter physics, space physics, nonlinear dynamics. *Unit head:* Dr. Joe D. Perez, Head, 334-844-4264. *Application contact:* Dr. John F. Pritchett, Dean of the Graduate School, 334-844-4700, E-mail: hatchlb@mail.auburn.edu.

See in-depth description on page 351.

Ball State University, Graduate School, College of Sciences and Humanities, Department of Physics and Astronomy, Program in Physics, Muncie, IN 47306-1099. Offers MA, MS. *Faculty:* 14. *Students:* 8 full-time (1 woman), 7 part-time, 3 international. Average age 26. 8 applicants, 75% accepted, 5 enrolled. In 2003, 3 degrees awarded. *Entrance requirements:* For master's, GRE General Test. Application fee: $25 ($35 for international students). *Expenses:* Tuition, state resident: full-time $5,748. Tuition, nonresident: full-time $14,166. *Financial support:* Teaching assistantships with full tuition reimbursements available. Financial award application deadline: 3/1. *Faculty research:* Solar energy, particle physics, atomic spectroscopy.

Baylor University, Graduate School, College of Arts and Sciences, Department of Physics, Waco, TX 76798. Offers MA, MS, PhD. *Students:* 21 full-time (2 women), 10 international. In 2003, 3 master's, 1 doctorate awarded. *Degree requirements:* For master's, thesis or alterna-

Physics

Baylor University (continued)

tive; for doctorate, one foreign language, thesis/dissertation. *Entrance requirements:* For master's and doctorate, GRE General Test. *Application deadline:* Applications are processed on a rolling basis. Application fee: $25. *Expenses:* Tuition: Part-time $698 per hour. *Financial support:* Fellowships, teaching assistantships, Federal Work-Study and institutionally sponsored loans available. *Unit head:* Dr. Dwight Russell, Graduate Program Director, 254-710-2511, Fax: 254-710-3878, E-mail: dwight_russell@baylor.edu. *Application contact:* Suzanne Keener, Administrative Assistant, 254-710-3588, Fax: 254-710-3870, E-mail: pauline_johnson@baylor.edu.

Boston College, Graduate School of Arts and Sciences, Department of Physics, Chestnut Hill, MA 02467-3800. Offers MS, PhD. *Students:* 11 full-time (2 women), 28 part-time (3 women), 31 international. 195 applicants, 8% accepted, 10 enrolled. In 2003, 4 master's, 3 doctorates awarded. Terminal master's awarded for partial completion of doctoral program. *Degree requirements:* For master's, thesis (for some programs); for doctorate, thesis/dissertation. *Entrance requirements:* For master's and doctorate, GRE General Test, GRE Subject Test. Additional exam requirements/recommendations for international students: Required—TOEFL (minimum score 550 paper-based; 213 computer-based). *Application deadline:* For fall admission, 2/1 for domestic students. Application fee: $60. Electronic applications accepted. *Expenses:* Tuition: Part-time $810 per credit. *Financial support:* Fellowships, research assistantships, teaching assistantships, Federal Work-Study and scholarships/grants available. Support available to part-time students. Financial award application deadline: 3/1; financial award applicants required to submit FAFSA. *Faculty research:* Atmospheric/space physics, astrophysics, atomic and molecular physics, fusion and plasmas, solid-state physics. *Unit head:* Dr. Kevin Bedell, Chairperson, 617-552-3576, E-mail: kevin.bedell@bc.edu. *Application contact:* Dr. Rein Uritam, Graduate Program Director, 617-552-3576, E-mail: rein.uritam@bc.edu.

Boston University, Graduate School of Arts and Sciences, Department of Physics, Boston, MA 02215. Offers MA, PhD. *Students:* 102 full-time (13 women); includes 3 minority (1 African American, 2 Asian Americans or Pacific Islanders), 67 international. Average age 28. 265 applicants, 29% accepted, 26 enrolled. In 2003, 7 master's, 5 doctorates awarded. Terminal master's awarded for partial completion of doctoral program. *Degree requirements:* For master's, one foreign language, thesis or alternative, comprehensive exam, registration; for doctorate, one foreign language, thesis/dissertation, comprehensive exam, registration. *Entrance requirements:* For master's and doctorate, GRE General Test, GRE Subject Test. Additional exam requirements/recommendations for international students: Required—TOEFL (minimum score 600 paper-based; 250 computer-based). *Application deadline:* For fall admission, 1/15 for domestic students, 1/15 for international students; for spring admission, 11/1 for domestic students, 11/1 for international students. Application fee: $60. *Expenses:* Tuition: Full-time $28,512; part-time $891 per credit hour. *Financial support:* In 2003–04, 2 fellowships with full tuition reimbursements (averaging $15,500 per year), 65 research assistantships (averaging $15,000 per year), 31 teaching assistantships with full tuition reimbursements (averaging $15,000 per year) were awarded. Federal Work-Study and scholarships/grants also available. Support available to part-time students. Financial award application deadline: 1/15; financial award applicants required to submit FAFSA. *Unit head:* Dr. Sidney Redner, Acting Chairman, 617-353-2618, Fax: 617-353-9393, E-mail: sulak@bu.edu. *Application contact:* Mirtha M. Cabello, Administrative Coordinator, 617-353-2623, Fax: 617-353-9393, E-mail: cabello@bu.edu.

See in-depth description on page 353.

Bowling Green State University, Graduate College, College of Arts and Sciences, Department of Physics and Astronomy, Bowling Green, OH 43403. Offers physics (MAT, MS); physics and astronomy (MAT). *Faculty:* 8 full-time. *Students:* 8 full-time (1 woman), 12 part-time (9 women), 6 international. Average age 32. 21 applicants, 62% accepted, 4 enrolled. In 2003, 5 degrees awarded. *Degree requirements:* For master's, thesis or alternative. *Entrance requirements:* For master's, GRE General Test. Additional exam requirements/recommendations for international students: Required—TOEFL. Application fee: $30. Electronic applications accepted. *Expenses:* Tuition, state resident: part-time $436 per hour. Tuition, nonresident: part-time $768 per hour. *Financial support:* In 2003–04, 7 teaching assistantships with full tuition reimbursements (averaging $10,242 per year) were awarded; research assistantships with full tuition reimbursements, career-related internships or fieldwork, institutionally sponsored loans, and unspecified assistantships also available. Financial award applicants required to submit FAFSA. *Faculty research:* Computational physics, solid-state physics, materials science, theoretical physics. *Unit head:* Dr. John Laird, Chair, 419-372-7244. *Application contact:* Dr. Lewis Fulcher, Graduate Coordinator, 419-372-2635.

Brandeis University, Graduate School of Arts and Sciences, Department of Physics, Waltham, MA 02454-9110. Offers MS, PhD. Part-time programs available. *Faculty:* 12 full-time (1 woman). *Students:* 31 full-time (8 women), 1 part-time; includes 10 minority (all Asian Americans or Pacific Islanders), 11 international. Average age 23. 108 applicants, 15% accepted, 8 enrolled. In 2003, 1 master's awarded, leading to continued full-time study 100%; 3 doctorates awarded, leading to university research/teaching 33%, business/industry 67%. Terminal master's awarded for partial completion of doctoral program. *Median time to degree:* Doctorate–7.5 years full-time. *Degree requirements:* For master's, qualifying exam, 1 year in residence, 6 semester courses numbered above 160; for doctorate, thesis/dissertation, advanced exam, 9 semester courses above 160. *Entrance requirements:* For doctorate, GRE General Test, GRE Subject Test, resumé, 2 letters of recommendation (3rd suggested). Additional exam requirements/recommendations for international students: Required—TOEFL (minimum score 600 paper-based; 250 computer-based). *Application deadline:* For fall admission, 1/15 for domestic students. Application fee: $60. Electronic applications accepted. *Expenses:* Tuition: Full-time $28,999; part-time $4,867 per course. Required fees: $175. *Financial support:* In 2003–04, 17 students received support, including 17 fellowships with full tuition reimbursements available (averaging $19,800 per year), 14 research assistantships with full tuition reimbursements available (averaging $19,500 per year); scholarships/grants and tuition waivers (full) also available. Financial award application deadline: 1/15; financial award applicants required to submit CSS PROFILE or FAFSA. *Faculty research:* Theoretical physics, experimental physics, astrophysics, computational neuroscience, condensed matter, high energy physics. Total annual research expenditures: $2.2 million. *Unit head:* Dr. Robert B. Meyer, Chair, 781-736-2870, Fax: 781-736-2915, E-mail: meyer@brandeis.edu. *Application contact:* Chairman, Graduate Admissions Committee, 781-736-2800, Fax: 781-736-2915, E-mail: physics1@brandeis.edu.

Brigham Young University, Graduate Studies, College of Physical and Mathematical Sciences, Department of Physics and Astronomy, Provo, UT 84602-1001. Offers physics (MS, PhD); physics and astronomy (PhD). Part-time programs available. *Faculty:* 31 full-time (0 women). *Students:* 24 full-time (11 women), 12 part-time (3 women); includes 5 minority (4 Asian Americans or Pacific Islanders, 1 Hispanic American). Average age 28. 19 applicants, 37% accepted, 7 enrolled. In 2003, 11 master's, 1 doctorate awarded. Terminal master's awarded for partial completion of doctoral program. *Median time to degree:* Master's–2.3 years full-time; doctorate–7.25 years full-time. Of those who began their doctoral program in fall 1995, 100% received their degree in 8 years or less. *Degree requirements:* For master's, thesis/dissertation, registration; for doctorate, thesis/dissertation, comprehensive exam, registration. *Entrance requirements:* For master's and doctorate, GRE Subject Test (physics), minimum GPA of 3.0 in last 60 hours. Additional exam requirements/recommendations for international students: Required—TOEFL (minimum score 550 paper-based; 213 computer-based). *Application deadline:* For fall admission, 1/15 priority date for domestic students, 1/15 priority date for international students. Application fee: $50. Electronic applications accepted. *Expenses:* Tuition: Part-time $221 per hour. *Financial support:* In 2003–04, 2 fellowships with full tuition reimbursements (averaging $15,000 per year), 8 research assistantships with full tuition reimbursements (averaging $15,000 per year), 18 teaching assistantships with full tuition reimbursements (averaging $15,000 per year) were awarded. Career-related internships or fieldwork, institutionally sponsored loans, and tuition waivers (partial) also available. Support available to part-time students. Financial award application deadline: 1/15. *Faculty research:* Acoustics; astrophysics; atomic, molecular, and optical physics; plasma; theoretical and mathematical physics. Total annual research expenditures: $807,360. *Unit head:* Dr. Scott D. Sommerfeldt, Graduate Coordinator, 801-422-2205, Fax: 801-422-0553, E-mail: scott_sommerfeldt@byu.edu. *Application contact:* Dr. Ross L. Spencer, Graduate Coordinator, 801-422-2341, Fax: 801-422-0553, E-mail: graduatep_physics@byu.edu.

Brock University, Graduate Studies and Research, Faculty of Mathematics and Science, Department of Physics, St. Catharines, ON L2S 3A1, Canada. Offers M Sc. Part-time programs available. *Degree requirements:* For master's, thesis. *Entrance requirements:* For master's, honors B Sc in physics. Additional exam requirements/recommendations for international students: Required—TOEFL. *Faculty research:* Tunneling spectroscopy of superconductors; structure, stability, and transport structure of quasi crystals; NMR spectroscopy.

Brooklyn College of the City University of New York, Division of Graduate Studies, Department of Physics, Brooklyn, NY 11210-2889. Offers applied physics (MA); physics (MA, PhD). The department is a full participant in the PhD program; it offers a complete sequence of courses that are creditable toward the CUNY doctoral degree, and a wide range of research opportunities in fulfillment of the doctoral dissertation requirements for that degree. Part-time programs available. *Students:* 1 (woman) full-time; minority (Asian American or Pacific Islander) 8 applicants, 38% accepted, 1 enrolled.Terminal master's awarded for partial completion of doctoral program. *Degree requirements:* For master's, comprehensive exam. *Entrance requirements:* For master's, GRE, 2 letters of recommendation; for doctorate, GRE. Additional exam requirements/recommendations for international students: Required—TOEFL. *Application deadline:* For fall admission, 3/1 for domestic students, 2/1 for international students; for spring admission, 11/1 for domestic students, 10/1 for international students. Application fee: $50. *Expenses:* Tuition, state resident: full-time $5,440; part-time $230 per credit. Tuition, nonresident: full-time $10,200; part-time $425 per credit. Required fees: $280; $103 per term. *Financial support:* Fellowships, research assistantships, teaching assistantships, Federal Work-Study, institutionally sponsored loans, scholarships/grants, and tuition waivers (full and partial) available. Support available to part-time students. Financial award application deadline: 5/1; financial award applicants required to submit FAFSA. *Unit head:* Dr. Peter Lesser, Chairperson, 718-951-5418, Fax: 718-951-4407, E-mail: cshakin@brooklyn.cuny.edu. *Application contact:* Michael Lovaglio, Assistant Director of Graduate Admissions, 718-951-5001, E-mail: adminqry@brooklyn.cuny.edu.

Brown University, Graduate School, Department of Physics, Providence, RI 02912. Offers Sc M, PhD. *Degree requirements:* For doctorate, thesis/dissertation, qualifying and oral exams.

Bryn Mawr College, Graduate School of Arts and Sciences, Department of Physics, Bryn Mawr, PA 19010-2899. Offers MA, PhD. In 2003, 1 master's, 1 doctorate awarded. *Degree requirements:* For master's and doctorate, one foreign language, thesis/dissertation. *Entrance requirements:* For master's and doctorate, GRE General Test, GRE Subject Test. Additional exam requirements/recommendations for international students: Required—TOEFL (minimum score 600 paper-based; 250 computer-based). *Application deadline:* For fall admission, 1/15 for domestic students, 1/15 for international students. Application fee: $30. *Expenses:* Tuition: Full-time $24,540; part-time $4,150 per unit. One-time fee: $60 part-time. *Financial support:* In 2003–04, 3 teaching assistantships with partial tuition reimbursements were awarded; research assistantships with full tuition reimbursements, Federal Work-Study, scholarships/grants, tuition waivers (partial), and tuition awards also available. Support available to part-time students. Financial award application deadline: 1/15. *Unit head:* Dr. Liz McCormack, Chair, 610-526-5358. *Application contact:* Graduate School of Arts and Sciences, 610-526-5072.

California Institute of Technology, Division of Physics, Mathematics and Astronomy, Department of Physics, Pasadena, CA 91125-0001. Offers PhD. *Degree requirements:* For doctorate, thesis/dissertation, candidacy and final exams. *Entrance requirements:* For doctorate, GRE General Test, GRE Subject Test. Additional exam requirements/recommendations for international students: Required—TOEFL. *Faculty research:* High-energy physics, nuclear physics, condensed-matter physics, theoretical physics and astrophysics, gravity physics.

California State University, Fresno, Division of Graduate Studies, College of Science and Mathematics, Department of Physics, Fresno, CA 93740-8027. Offers MS. Part-time programs available. *Degree requirements:* For master's, thesis or alternative. *Entrance requirements:* For master's, GRE General Test, minimum GPA of 2.5. Additional exam requirements/recommendations for international students: Required—TOEFL. Electronic applications accepted. *Faculty research:* Energy, astronomy, silicon vertex detector, neuroimaging.

California State University, Fullerton, Graduate Studies, College of Natural Science and Mathematics, Department of Physics, Fullerton, CA 92834-9480. Offers MA. *Faculty:* 9 full-time (2 women), 14 part-time/adjunct. *Students:* 7 full-time (2 women), 15 part-time (2 women); includes 10 minority (1 African American, 2 Asian Americans or Pacific Islanders, 7 Hispanic Americans), 2 international. Average age 30. 17 applicants, 82% accepted, 7 enrolled. In 2003, 4 degrees awarded. Application fee: $55. Tuition, nonresident: part-time $282 per unit. Required fees: $889 per semester. *Financial support:* Scholarships/grants available. Financial award application deadline: 3/1. *Unit head:* Dr. Roger Nanes, Chair, 714-278-3366.

California State University, Long Beach, Graduate Studies, College of Natural Sciences, Department of Physics and Astronomy, Long Beach, CA 90840. Offers metals physics (MS); physics (MS). Part-time programs available. *Faculty:* 13 full-time (1 woman). *Students:* 7 full-time (2 women), 14 part-time (3 women); includes 8 minority (1 African American, 5 Asian Americans or Pacific Islanders, 2 Hispanic Americans), 1 international. Average age 31. 21 applicants, 52% accepted, 8 enrolled. In 2003, 2 degrees awarded. *Degree requirements:* For master's, comprehensive exam or thesis. *Application deadline:* For fall admission, 7/1 for domestic students; for spring admission, 12/1 for domestic students. Applications are processed on a rolling basis. Application fee: $55. Electronic applications accepted. Tuition, nonresident: part-time $282 per unit. Required fees: $504 per semester. *Financial support:* Federal Work-Study, institutionally sponsored loans, and scholarships/grants available. Financial award application deadline: 3/2. *Faculty research:* Musical acoustics, modern optics, neutrino physics, quantum gravity, atomic physics. *Unit head:* Dr. Alfred Leung, Chair, 562-985-4924, Fax: 562-985-7924, E-mail: aleung@csulb.edu. *Application contact:* Information Contact, 562-985-4924, Fax: 562-985-7924.

California State University, Los Angeles, Graduate Studies, College of Natural and Social Sciences, Department of Physics and Astronomy, Los Angeles, CA 90032-8530. Offers physics (MS). Part-time and evening/weekend programs available. *Faculty:* 11 full-time, 8 part-time/adjunct. *Students:* 4 full-time (0 women), 7 part-time (1 woman); includes 2 minority (1 African American, 1 Asian American or Pacific Islander), 4 international. In 2003, 1 degree awarded. *Degree requirements:* For master's, comprehensive exam or thesis. *Entrance requirements:* Additional exam requirements/recommendations for international students: Required—TOEFL. *Application deadline:* For fall admission, 6/30 for domestic students; for spring admission, 2/1 for domestic students. Applications are processed on a rolling basis. Application fee: $55. Tuition, nonresident: part-time $188 per unit. Required fees: $2,477. *Financial support:* Federal Work-Study available. Support available to part-time students. Financial award application deadline: 3/1. *Faculty research:* Intermediate energy, nuclear physics, condensed-matter physics, biophysics. *Unit head:* Dr. William Taylor, Chair, 323-343-2100.

California State University, Northridge, Graduate Studies, College of Science and Mathematics, Department of Physics and Astronomy, Northridge, CA 91330. Offers physics (MS). Part-time and evening/weekend programs available. *Faculty:* 14 full-time, 11 part-time/adjunct. *Students:* 11 full-time (3 women), 15 part-time (4 women); includes 6 minority (1 African American, 3 Asian Americans or Pacific Islanders, 2 Hispanic Americans), 4 international. Average age 32. 18 applicants, 83% accepted, 11 enrolled. In 2003, 4 degrees awarded. *Degree requirements:* For master's, thesis optional. *Entrance requirements:* For master's, GRE General Test or minimum GPA of 3.0. Additional exam requirements/recommendations for international students: Required—TOEFL. *Application deadline:* For fall admission, 11/30 for domestic students. Application fee: $55. Required fees: $1,327; $853 per year. *Financial support:* Teaching assistantships available. Financial award application deadline: 3/1. *Unit head:* Dr. Julio R. Blanca, Chair, 818-677-2775.

Carleton University, Faculty of Graduate Studies, Faculty of Science, Department of Physics, Ottawa, ON K1S 5B6, Canada. Offers M Sc, PhD. *Degree requirements:* For master's, seminar, thesis optional; for doctorate, thesis/dissertation, seminar, comprehensive exam. *Entrance requirements:* For master's, honors degree in science; for doctorate, M Sc. Additional exam requirements/recommendations for international students: Required—TOEFL. *Application deadline:* Applications are processed on a rolling basis. Application fee: $60 Canadian dollars. *Expenses:* Tuition, state resident: part-time $2,052 per term. Tuition, nonresident: part-time $4,266 per term. Full-time tuition and fees vary according to course load, degree level and program. *Financial support:* Fellowships, research assistantships, teaching assistantships, institutionally sponsored loans, scholarships/grants, and unspecified assistantships available. *Faculty research:* Experimental and theoretical elementary particle physics, medical physics. *Unit head:* Patricia Kalyniak, Chair, 613-520-2600 Ext. 4376, Fax: 613-520-4061, E-mail: physics@carleton.ca. *Application contact:* Gerald Oakham, Associate Chair, Graduate Studies, 613-520-2600 Ext. 7539, Fax: 613-520-4061, E-mail: grad_supervisor@physics.carleton.ca.

Carnegie Mellon University, Mellon College of Science, Department of Physics, Pittsburgh, PA 15213-3891. Offers PhD. *Degree requirements:* For doctorate, thesis/dissertation, qualifying exam. *Entrance requirements:* For doctorate, GRE General Test, GRE Subject Test. Additional exam requirements/recommendations for international students: Required—TOEFL. Electronic applications accepted. *Expenses:* Tuition: Full-time $28,200; part-time $392 per unit. Required fees: $220. *Faculty research:* Astrophysics, condensed matter physics, biological physics, medium energy and nuclear physics, high-energy physics.

Case Western Reserve University, School of Graduate Studies, Department of Physics, Cleveland, OH 44106. Offers MS, PhD. Part-time programs available. *Faculty:* 25 full-time (1 woman). *Students:* 50 full-time (12 women), 8 part-time (3 women); includes 1 African American, 3 Asian Americans or Pacific Islanders, 27 international. Average age 29. 403 applicants, 10% accepted, 17 enrolled. In 2003, 13 master's, 4 doctorates awarded. Terminal master's awarded for partial completion of doctoral program. *Degree requirements:* For master's, exam; for doctorate, thesis/dissertation, qualifying exam, topical exam. *Entrance requirements:* Additional exam requirements/recommendations for international students: Required—TOEFL. *Application deadline:* For fall admission, 2/1 for domestic students. Applications are processed on a rolling basis. Application fee: $50. *Expenses:* Tuition: Full-time $26,900. *Financial support:* In 2003–04, 32 students received support, including 21 research assistantships, 11 teaching assistantships. Financial award application deadline: 2/1. *Faculty research:* Condensed-matter physics, imaging physics, nonlinear optics, high-energy physics, cosmology and astrophysics. *Unit head:* Lawrence M. Krauss, Chairman, 216-368-4001, E-mail: lmk9@po.cwru.edu. *Application contact:* Patricia Bacevice, Admissions, 216-368-4000, Fax: 216-368-4671, E-mail: pab6@case.edu.

The Catholic University of America, School of Arts and Sciences, Department of Physics, Washington, DC 20064. Offers MS, PhD. Part-time programs available. *Faculty:* 9 full-time (1 woman). *Students:* 17 full-time (2 women), 17 part-time (1 woman); includes 2 minority (1 African American, 1 Hispanic American), 11 international. Average age 33. 26 applicants, 77% accepted, 7 enrolled. In 2003, 3 master's, 1 doctorate awarded. Terminal master's awarded for partial completion of doctoral program. *Degree requirements:* For master's, thesis or alternative, comprehensive exam; for doctorate, thesis/dissertation, comprehensive exam. *Entrance requirements:* For master's and doctorate, GRE General Test, 3 letters of recommendation. Additional exam requirements/recommendations for international students: Required—TOEFL (minimum score 580 paper-based; 237 computer-based). *Application deadline:* For fall admission, 2/1 for domestic students; for spring admission, 11/5 priority date for domestic students. Applications are processed on a rolling basis. Application fee: $55. Electronic applications accepted. *Expenses:* Tuition: Full-time $23,600; part-time $895 per credit hour. Required fees: $1,040; $270 per term. One-time fee: $175 part-time. Part-time tuition and fees vary according to campus/location and program. *Financial support:* Fellowships, research assistantships, teaching assistantships, career-related internships or fieldwork, Federal Work-Study, institutionally sponsored loans, scholarships/grants, and tuition waivers (full and partial) available. Support available to part-time students. Financial award application deadline: 2/1; financial award applicants required to submit FAFSA. *Faculty research:* Condensed-matter physics, intermediate-energy physics, astrophysics, biophysics. *Unit head:* Dr. Charles Montrose, Chair, 202-319-5347, Fax: 202-319-4448, E-mail: montrose@cua.edu. *Application contact:* Gail Hershey, Assistant to the Chair, 202-319-5315, Fax: 202-319-4448, E-mail: hershey@cua.edu.

The Catholic University of America, School of Arts and Sciences, Department of Politics, Washington, DC 20064. Offers American government (MA, PhD); congressional studies (MA); international affairs (MA); international political economics (MA); political theory (MA, PhD); world politics (MA, PhD). Part-time programs available. *Faculty:* 13 full-time (2 women), 10 part-time/adjunct (0 women). *Students:* 28 full-time (16 women), 76 part-time (22 women); includes 12 minority (5 African Americans, 1 American Indian/Alaska Native, 2 Asian Americans or Pacific Islanders, 4 Hispanic Americans), 12 international. Average age 32. 109 applicants, 72% accepted, 24 enrolled. In 2003, 21 master's, 7 doctorates awarded. *Degree requirements:* For master's, one foreign language, thesis or alternative, comprehensive exam; for doctorate, 2 foreign languages, thesis/dissertation, comprehensive exam. *Entrance requirements:* For master's and doctorate, GRE General Test, 3 letters of recommendation, minimum GPA of 3.0. Additional exam requirements/recommendations for international students: Required—TOEFL (minimum score 580 paper-based; 237 computer-based). *Application deadline:* For fall admission, 2/1 for domestic students; for spring admission, 11/15 priority date for domestic students. Applications are processed on a rolling basis. Application fee: $55. Electronic applications accepted. *Expenses:* Tuition: Full-time $23,600; part-time $895 per credit hour. Required fees: $1,040; $270 per term. One-time fee: $175 part-time. Part-time tuition and fees vary according to campus/location and program. *Financial support:* Teaching assistantships, career-related internships or fieldwork, Federal Work-Study, institutionally sponsored loans, and tuition waivers (full and partial) available. Support available to part-time students. Financial award application deadline: 2/1; financial award applicants required to submit FAFSA. *Faculty research:* Political philosophy, American political institutions and processes, political economy, national security. *Unit head:* Dr. Mark Rozell, Chair, 202-319-5128, Fax: 202-319-6289, E-mail: rozell@cua.edu.

Central Connecticut State University, School of Graduate Studies, School of Arts and Sciences, Department of Physics and Earth Science, New Britain, CT 06050-4010. Offers earth science (MS); physics (MS). Part-time and evening/weekend programs available. *Faculty:* 12 full-time (4 women), 7 part-time/adjunct (2 women). *Students:* 4 full-time (all women), 31 part-time (22 women); includes 4 minority (1 African American, 1 Asian American or Pacific Islander, 2 Hispanic Americans), 1 international. Average age 33. 23 applicants, 70% accepted, 12 enrolled. In 2003, 3 degrees awarded. *Degree requirements:* For master's, thesis or alternative, comprehensive exam. *Entrance requirements:* For master's, minimum GPA of 2.7. Additional exam requirements/recommendations for international students: Required—TOEFL. *Application deadline:* For fall admission, 8/10 for domestic students; for spring admission, 12/10 for domestic students. Applications are processed on a rolling basis. Application fee: $50. *Expenses:* Tuition, state resident: full-time $3,298. Tuition, nonresident: full-time $9,190. *Financial support:* Federal Work-Study available. Financial award application deadline: 3/15; financial award applicants required to submit FAFSA. *Faculty research:* Elementary/secondary science education, particle and solid states, weather patterns, planetary studies. *Unit head:* Dr. Ali Antar, Chair, 860-832-2930.

Central Michigan University, College of Graduate Studies, College of Science and Technology, Department of Physics, Mount Pleasant, MI 48859. Offers MS. *Faculty:* 14 full-time (0 women). *Students:* 3 full-time (0 women), 10 part-time (3 women). Average age 28. In 2003, 1 degree awarded. *Degree requirements:* For master's, thesis or alternative. *Entrance requirements:* For master's, GRE, bachelor's degree in physics, minimum GPA of 2.6. Additional exam requirements/recommendations for international students: Required—TOEFL. *Application deadline:* Applications are processed on a rolling basis. Application fee: $35 ($45 for international students). *Expenses:* Tuition, state resident: part-time $200 per credit hour. Tuition, nonresident: part-time $397 per credit hour. *Financial support:* In 2003–04, 6 research assistantships with tuition reimbursements, 5 teaching assistantships with tuition reimbursements were awarded. Fellowships with tuition reimbursements, career-related internships or fieldwork and Federal Work-Study also available. Financial award application deadline: 3/7. *Faculty research:* Polymer physics, laser spectroscopy, observational astronomy, nuclear physics, thin films. *Unit head:* Dr. Stanley Hirschi, Chairperson, 989-774-3321, Fax: 989-774-2697, E-mail: stanley.hirschi@cmich.edu.

Christopher Newport University, Graduate Studies, Department of Teacher Preparation, Newport News, VA 23606-2998. Offers art (PK-12) (MAT); biology (6-12) (MAT); computer science (6-12) (MAT); elementary (PK-6) (MAT); English (6-12) (MAT); French (PK-12) (MAT); history (6-12) (MAT); history and social science (MAT); mathematics (6-12) (MAT); music (PK-12) (MAT), including choral, instrumental; physics (6-12) (MAT); Spanish (PK-12) (MAT); theater (PK-12) (MAT). Part-time and evening/weekend programs available. *Faculty:* 25 full-time (13 women). *Students:* 1 (woman) full-time, 25 part-time (23 women); includes 5 minority (4 African Americans, 1 American Indian/Alaska Native). Average age 39. 9 applicants, 100% accepted. In 2003, 15 degrees awarded. *Degree requirements:* For master's, thesis or alternative, comprehensive exam. *Entrance requirements:* For master's, PRAXIS I, minimum GPA of 3.0. *Application deadline:* For fall admission, 5/1 for domestic students; for spring admission, 11/1 for domestic students. Applications are processed on a rolling basis. Application fee: $40. Electronic applications accepted. *Expenses:* Tuition, state resident: part-time $139 per credit hour. Tuition, nonresident: part-time $448 per credit hour. Required fees: $74 per credit hour. *Financial support:* In 2003–04, 2 research assistantships with full and partial tuition reimbursements (averaging $2,000 per year) were awarded; career-related internships or fieldwork and Federal Work-Study also available. Support available to part-time students. Financial award application deadline: 3/1; financial award applicants required to submit FAFSA. *Faculty research:* Early literacy development, instructional innovations, professional teaching standards, multicultural issues, aesthetic education. *Unit head:* Dr. Marsha Sprague, Coordinator, 757-594-7388, Fax: 757-594-7304, E-mail: msprague@cnu.edu. *Application contact:* Susan R. Chittenden, Graduate Admissions, 757-594-7359, Fax: 757-594-7333, E-mail: gradstdy@cnu.edu.

City College of the City University of New York, Graduate School, College of Liberal Arts and Science, Division of Science, Department of Physics, New York, NY 10031-9198. Offers MA, PhD. *Students:* 2 full-time (1 woman), 2 part-time; includes 3 minority (1 Asian American or Pacific Islander, 2 Hispanic Americans), 1 international. 8 applicants, 88% accepted, 1 enrolled. In 2003, 3 degrees awarded. Terminal master's awarded for partial completion of doctoral program. *Degree requirements:* For master's, comprehensive exam; for doctorate, thesis/dissertation. *Entrance requirements:* For doctorate, GRE. Additional exam requirements/recommendations for international students: Required—TOEFL. *Application deadline:* For fall admission, 5/1 for domestic students; for spring admission, 11/1 for domestic students. Application fee: $50. *Expenses:* Tuition, state resident: full-time $5,440; part-time $230 per credit. Tuition, nonresident: part-time $425 per credit. Required fees: $63 per semester. *Financial support:* Fellowships available. *Unit head:* Dr. Victor Chung, Chair, 212-650-6832.

See in-depth description on page 355.

Clark Atlanta University, School of Arts and Sciences, Department of Physics, Atlanta, GA 30314. Offers MS. Part-time programs available. *Degree requirements:* For master's, one foreign language, thesis. *Entrance requirements:* For master's, GRE General Test, minimum GPA of 2.5. *Faculty research:* Fusion energy, investigations of nonlinear differential equations, difference schemes, collisions in dense plasma.

Clarkson University, Graduate School, School of Arts and Sciences, Department of Physics, Potsdam, NY 13699. Offers MS, PhD. Part-time programs available. *Faculty:* 7 full-time (0 women). *Students:* 13 full-time (0 women), 10 international. Average age 27. 33 applicants, 33% accepted. In 2003, 2 master's, 4 doctorates awarded. *Median time to degree:* Master's–2.5 years full-time; doctorate–3.5 years full-time. *Degree requirements:* For doctorate, thesis/dissertation, departmental qualifying exam. *Entrance requirements:* For master's, GRE. Additional exam requirements/recommendations for international students: Required—TOEFL. *Application deadline:* For fall admission, 5/15 for domestic students; for spring admission, 10/15 priority date for domestic students. Applications are processed on a rolling basis. Application fee: $25 ($35 for international students). *Expenses:* Tuition: Full-time $19,272; part-time $803 per credit. Tuition and fees vary according to course load. *Financial support:* In 2003–04, 10 students received support, including 4 research assistantships (averaging $18,000 per year), 9 teaching assistantships (averaging $18,000 per year); fellowships, scholarships/grants and tuition waivers (partial) also available. *Faculty research:* Computer simulation, stochastic processes, adhesion mechanisms, metals and alloys, thin film. Total annual research expenditures: $623,348. *Unit head:* Dr. Phillip A. Christiansen, Division Head, 315-268-6669, Fax: 315-268-2308, E-mail: tony.collins@clarkson.edu. *Application contact:* Donna Brockway, Assistant to Dean/Foreign Student Advisor, 315-268-6447, Fax: 315-268-7994, E-mail: brockway@clarkson.edu.

Clark University, Graduate School, Department of Physics, Worcester, MA 01610-1477. Offers MA, PhD. Part-time programs available. *Faculty:* 7 full-time (0 women), 1 part-time/adjunct (0 women). *Students:* 13 full-time (6 women), 1 (woman) part-time, 10 international. Average age 27. 46 applicants, 24% accepted, 5 enrolled. In 2003, 1 degree awarded. Terminal master's awarded for partial completion of doctoral program. *Degree requirements:* For master's, thesis or alternative; for doctorate, one foreign language, thesis/dissertation. *Entrance requirements:* Additional exam requirements/recommendations for international students: Required—TOEFL. *Application deadline:* For fall admission, 3/1 for domestic students. Application fee: $40. *Expenses:* Tuition: Full-time $26,700. *Financial support:* In 2003–04, fellowships with full and partial tuition reimbursements (averaging $16,500 per year), 8 research assistantships with full tuition reimbursements (averaging $16,500 per year), 6 teaching assistantships with full tuition reimbursements (averaging $16,500 per year) were awarded. Federal Work-Study and tuition waivers (full and partial) also available. Financial award application deadline: 4/1. *Faculty research:* Statistical and thermal physics, magnetic properties of materials, computer simulation. Total annual research expenditures: $96,000. *Unit head:* Dr. S. Leslie Blatt, Chair, 508-793-7169. *Application contact:* Sujata Davis, Department Secretary, 508-793-7169, Fax: 508-793-8861, E-mail: sdavis1@clarku.edu.

Clemson University, Graduate School, College of Engineering and Science, Department of Physics and Astronomy, Program in Physics, Clemson, SC 29634. Offers astronomy and astrophysics (MS, PhD); atmospheric physics (MS, PhD); biophysics (MS, PhD). Part-time programs available. *Students:* 40 full-time (11 women), 5 part-time; includes 1 minority (African American), 19 international. 59 applicants, 53% accepted, 8 enrolled. In 2003, 7 master's, 5 doctorates awarded. Terminal master's awarded for partial completion of doctoral program. *Degree requirements:* For master's, thesis or alternative; for doctorate, thesis/dissertation. *Entrance requirements:* For master's and doctorate, GRE General Test. Additional exam requirements/recommendations for international students: Required—TOEFL. *Application deadline:* For fall admission, 2/15 for domestic students. Applications are processed on a rolling basis. Application fee: $40. *Expenses:* Tuition, state resident: full-time $7,432. Tuition, nonresident: full-time $14,732. *Financial support:* Fellowships, research assistantships, teaching assistantships available. Financial award application deadline: 6/1; financial award applicants required to submit FAFSA. *Faculty research:* Radiation physics, solid-state physics, nuclear physics, radar and lidar studies of atmosphere. *Unit head:* Dr. Brad Myer, Head, 864-656-

Physics

Clemson University (continued)
5320. *Application contact:* Dr. Miguel Larsen, Coordinator, 864-656-5309, Fax: 864-656-0805, E-mail: milarsen@clemson.edu.

Cleveland State University, College of Graduate Studies, College of Arts and Sciences, Department of Physics, Cleveland, OH 44115. Offers applied optics (MS); condensed matter physics (MS); medical physics (MS). Part-time and evening/weekend programs available. *Faculty:* 5 full-time (1 woman), 4 part-time/adjunct (0 women). *Students:* Average age 30. 7 applicants, 100% accepted, 5 enrolled. In 2003, 4 degrees awarded, leading to business/industry 4%. *Median time to degree:* Master's–2 years full-time. *Degree requirements:* For master's, exit project. *Entrance requirements:* For master's, undergraduate degree in engineering or physics, chemistry or mathematics. Additional exam requirements/recommendations for international students: Required—TOEFL (minimum score 525 paper-based; 197 computer-based), GRE. *Application deadline:* For fall admission, 7/15 priority date for domestic students, 7/15 priority date for international students. Applications are processed on a rolling basis. Application fee: $30. Electronic applications accepted. Tuition, area resident: Full-time $8,258; part-time $344 per credit hour. Tuition, nonresident: full-time $16,352; part-time $681 per credit hour. *Financial support:* In 2003–04, 1 research assistantship with full and partial tuition reimbursement (averaging $5,666 per year) was awarded; fellowships with tuition reimbursements, teaching assistantships, tuition waivers (full) also available. *Faculty research:* Statistical mechanics of phase transitions, low-temperature and solid-state physics, superconductivity, theoretical light scattering, medical physics. Total annual research expenditures: $350,000. *Unit head:* Dr. Miron Kaufman, Chairperson, 216-687-2436, Fax: 216-523-7268, E-mail: m.kaufman@csuohio.edu. *Application contact:* Dr. James A. Lock, Director, 216-687-2425, Fax: 216-523-7268, E-mail: j.lock@csuohio.edu.

The College of William and Mary, Faculty of Arts and Sciences, Department of Physics, Williamsburg, VA 23187-8795. Offers MA, MS, PhD. *Faculty:* 26 full-time (2 women), 1 part-time/adjunct (0 women). *Students:* 50 full-time (13 women), 2 part-time; includes 4 minority (2 African Americans, 2 Asian Americans or Pacific Islanders), 15 international. Average age 26. 19 applicants, 53% accepted, 10 enrolled. In 2003, 9 master's, 7 doctorates awarded. Terminal master's awarded for partial completion of doctoral program. *Degree requirements:* For master's, comprehensive exam; for doctorate, thesis/dissertation, final exams, comprehensive exam. *Entrance requirements:* For master's and doctorate, GRE General Test, GRE Subject Test, minimum GPA of 2.5. Additional exam requirements/recommendations for international students: Required—TOEFL. *Application deadline:* For fall admission, 1/15 priority date for domestic students, 2/1 priority date for international students. Applications are processed on a rolling basis. Application fee: $30. *Expenses:* Tuition, state resident: full-time $4,858; part-time $222 per credit hour. Tuition, nonresident: full-time $16,440; part-time $618 per credit hour. Required fees: $2,674. Tuition and fees vary according to program. *Financial support:* In 2003–04, 48 students received support, including 32 research assistantships with full tuition reimbursements available (averaging $13,300 per year), 16 teaching assistantships with full tuition reimbursements available (averaging $13,300 per year); career-related internships or fieldwork also available. *Faculty research:* Nuclear/particle, condensed-matter, atomic, and plasma physics; accelerator physics; molecular/optical physics; computational/nonlinear physics. Total annual research expenditures: $3.1 million. *Unit head:* Dr. William Cooke, Chair, 757-221-3500, Fax: 757-221-3540, E-mail: cooke@physics.wm.edu. *Application contact:* Dr. Marc Sher, Chair of Admissions, 757-221-3538, Fax: 757-221-3540, E-mail: grad@physics.wm.edu.

Colorado School of Mines, Graduate School, Department of Physics, Golden, CO 80401-1887. Offers applied physics (PhD); physics (MS). Part-time programs available. *Faculty:* 16 full-time (2 women), 3 part-time/adjunct (1 woman). *Students:* 23 full-time (7 women), 8 part-time (3 women); includes 3 minority (2 Asian Americans or Pacific Islanders, 1 Hispanic American), 8 international. 29 applicants, 55% accepted, 7 enrolled. In 2003, 3 degrees awarded. *Degree requirements:* For master's, thesis/dissertation; for doctorate, thesis/dissertation, comprehensive exam. *Entrance requirements:* For master's and doctorate, GRE General Test, GRE Subject Test. Additional exam requirements/recommendations for international students: Required—TOEFL (minimum score 550 paper-based; 213 computer-based). *Application deadline:* For fall admission, 12/1 priority date for domestic students, 12/1 priority date for international students; for spring admission, 5/1 priority date for domestic students, 5/1 priority date for international students. Application fee: $45. Electronic applications accepted. *Expenses:* Tuition, state resident: full-time $5,700; part-time $285 per credit hour. Tuition, nonresident: full-time $19,040; part-time $952 per credit hour. Required fees: $733. *Financial support:* In 2003–04, 13 students received support, including fellowships with full tuition reimbursements available (averaging $12,500 per year), 14 research assistantships with full tuition reimbursements available (averaging $10,000 per year), 9 teaching assistantships with full tuition reimbursements available (averaging $10,000 per year); scholarships/grants and unspecified assistantships also available. Financial award applicants required to submit FAFSA. *Faculty research:* Light scattering, low-energy nuclear physics, high fusion plasma diagnostics, laser operations, mathematical physics. Total annual research expenditures: $6.6 million. *Unit head:* Dr. James A. McNeil, Head, 303-273-3844, Fax: 303-273-3919, E-mail: jamcneil@mine.edu. *Application contact:* Jeff Squier, Professor, 303-384-2385, Fax: 303-273-3919, E-mail: jsquier@mines.edu.

Colorado State University, Graduate School, College of Natural Sciences, Department of Physics, Fort Collins, CO 80523-0015. Offers MS, PhD. Part-time programs available. *Faculty:* 20 full-time (1 woman), 5 part-time/adjunct (1 woman). *Students:* 21 full-time (3 women), 32 part-time (9 women); includes 2 minority (both African Americans), 19 international. Average age 29. 141 applicants, 20% accepted, 10 enrolled. In 2003, 8 master's, 7 doctorates awarded. Terminal master's awarded for partial completion of doctoral program. *Degree requirements:* For master's, thesis (for some programs); for doctorate, thesis/dissertation. *Entrance requirements:* For master's and doctorate, GRE General Test or physics subject test, minimum GPA of 3.0. Additional exam requirements/recommendations for international students: Required—TOEFL. *Application deadline:* For fall admission, 2/15 priority date for domestic students, 2/15 priority date for international students. Applications are processed on a rolling basis. Application fee: $50. Electronic applications accepted. *Expenses:* Tuition, state resident: full-time $4,156. Tuition, nonresident: full-time $14,762. Required fees: $205. Tuition and fees vary according to course load, campus/location, program and reciprocity agreements. *Financial support:* In 2003–04, 4 fellowships (averaging $900 per year), 14 research assistantships with full tuition reimbursements (averaging $12,800 per year), 25 teaching assistantships with full tuition reimbursements (averaging $12,600 per year) were awarded. Career-related internships or fieldwork, Federal Work-Study, and traineeships also available. *Faculty research:* Experimental condensed-matter physics, laser spectroscopy, optics, theoretical condensed-matter physics, particle physics. Total annual research expenditures: $2.4 million. *Unit head:* David A. Krueger, Chair, 970-491-6206, Fax: 970-491-7947, E-mail: krueger@lamar.colostate.edu. *Application contact:* Sandy Demlow, Secretary, Graduate Admissions Committee, 970-491-6207, Fax: 970-491-7947, E-mail: demlow@lamar.colostate.edu.

Columbia University, Graduate School of Arts and Sciences, Division of Natural Sciences, Department of Physics, New York, NY 10027. Offers philosophical foundations of physics (MA); physics (M Phil, PhD). *Faculty:* 23 full-time, 5 part-time/adjunct. *Students:* 90 full-time (10 women), 1 (woman) part-time. Average age 27. 199 applicants, 28% accepted. In 2003, 4 master's, 11 doctorates awarded. *Degree requirements:* For doctorate, thesis/dissertation. *Entrance requirements:* For master's and doctorate, GRE General Test, GRE Subject Test, 3 years of course work in physics. Additional exam requirements/recommendations for international students: Required—TOEFL. Application fee: $75. *Expenses:* Tuition: Full-time $14,820. *Financial support:* Fellowships, teaching assistantships, Federal Work-Study and institutionally sponsored loans available. Support available to part-time students. Financial award application deadline: 1/5; financial award applicants required to submit FAFSA. *Faculty research:* Theoretical physics; astrophysics; low-, medium-, and high-energy physics. *Unit head:* Erick Weinberg, Chair, 212-854-5870, Fax: 212-854-3379.

Cornell University, Graduate School, Graduate Fields of Arts and Sciences, Field of Physics, Ithaca, NY 14853-0001. Offers experimental physics (MS, PhD); physics (MS, PhD); theoretical physics (MS, PhD). *Faculty:* 52 full-time. *Students:* 193 full-time (41 women); includes 13 minority (1 African American, 9 Asian Americans or Pacific Islanders, 3 Hispanic Americans), 70 international. 464 applicants, 21% accepted, 41 enrolled. In 2003, 17 master's, 14 doctorates awarded. *Degree requirements:* For doctorate, thesis/dissertation, comprehensive exam. *Entrance requirements:* For doctorate, GRE General Test, GRE Subject Test (physics), supplementary application, 3 letters of recommendation. Additional exam requirements/recommendations for international students: Required—TOEFL (minimum score 550 paper-based; 213 computer-based). *Application deadline:* For fall admission, 1/3 for domestic students. Application fee: $60. Electronic applications accepted. *Expenses:* Tuition: Full-time $28,630. One-time fee: $50 full-time. *Financial support:* In 2003–04, 187 students received support, including 36 fellowships with full tuition reimbursements available, 88 research assistantships with full tuition reimbursements available, 63 teaching assistantships with full tuition reimbursements available; institutionally sponsored loans, scholarships/grants, health care benefits, tuition waivers (full and partial), and unspecified assistantships also available. Financial award applicants required to submit FAFSA. *Faculty research:* Experimental condensed matter physics, theoretical condensed matter physics, experimental high energy particle physics, theoretical particle physics and field theory, theoretical astrophysics. *Unit head:* Director of Graduate Studies, 607-255-7561. *Application contact:* Graduate Field Assistant, 607-255-7561, E-mail: physics-grad-adm@cornell.edu.

Creighton University, Graduate School, College of Arts and Sciences, Program in Physics, Omaha, NE 68178-0001. Offers MS. *Degree requirements:* For master's, one foreign language, thesis or alternative. *Entrance requirements:* For master's, GRE General Test, GRE Subject Test. Additional exam requirements/recommendations for international students: Required—TOEFL.

Dalhousie University, Faculty of Graduate Studies, College of Arts and Science, Faculty of Science, Department of Physics, Halifax, NS B3H 4R2, Canada. Offers M Sc, PhD. *Degree requirements:* For master's and doctorate, thesis/dissertation. *Entrance requirements:* Additional exam requirements/recommendations for international students: Required—TOEFL. *Faculty research:* Applied, experimental, and solid-state physics.

Dartmouth College, School of Arts and Sciences, Department of Physics and Astronomy, Hanover, NH 03755. Offers MS, PhD. *Faculty:* 11 full-time (3 women). *Students:* 32 full-time (11 women); includes 1 minority (African American), 13 international. Average age 25. 251 applicants, 14% accepted, 13 enrolled. In 2003, 2 master's, 5 doctorates awarded. Terminal master's awarded for partial completion of doctoral program. *Degree requirements:* For master's and doctorate, thesis/dissertation. *Entrance requirements:* For master's and doctorate, GRE General Test, GRE Subject Test. Additional exam requirements/recommendations for international students: Required—TOEFL. *Application deadline:* For fall admission, 2/1 for domestic students. Application fee: $15. *Expenses:* Tuition: Full-time $28,965. *Financial support:* In 2003–04, 32 students received support, including fellowships with full tuition reimbursements available (averaging $18,528 per year), research assistantships with full tuition reimbursements available (averaging $18,528 per year); institutionally sponsored loans, scholarships/grants, and tuition waivers (full) also available. *Faculty research:* Matter physics, plasma and beam physics, space physics, astronomy, cosmology. Total annual research expenditures: $2.4 million. *Unit head:* Mary K. Hudson, Chair, 603-646-0350, Fax: 603-646-1446, E-mail: mary.k.hudson@dartmouth.edu. *Application contact:* Jean Blandin, Administrative Assistant, 603-646-2854, Fax: 603-646-1446, E-mail: jean.blandin@dartmouth.edu.

Delaware State University, Graduate Programs, Department of Physics, Dover, DE 19901-2277. Offers physics (MS); physics teaching (MS). Part-time and evening/weekend programs available. *Entrance requirements:* For master's, minimum GPA of 3.0 in major, 2.75 overall. Electronic applications accepted. *Faculty research:* Thermal properties of solids, nuclear physics, radiation damage in solids.

DePaul University, College of Liberal Arts and Sciences, Department of Physics, Chicago, IL 60604-2287. Offers applied physics (MS). Part-time and evening/weekend programs available. *Faculty:* 7 full-time (1 woman), 3 part-time/adjunct (0 women). *Students:* 4 full-time (1 woman), 3 part-time; includes 3 minority (1 African American, 1 Asian American or Pacific Islander, 1 Hispanic American), 1 international. Average age 23. 12 applicants, 42% accepted. In 2003, 4 degrees awarded. *Degree requirements:* For master's, thesis, oral exams. *Entrance requirements:* For master's, minimum GPA of 2.7. *Application deadline:* For fall admission, 6/15 for domestic students; for spring admission, 9/1 for domestic students. Applications are processed on a rolling basis. Application fee: $25. *Expenses:* Tuition: Part-time $395 per hour. *Financial support:* In 2003–04, teaching assistantships with full tuition reimbursements (averaging $6,000 per year); tuition waivers (partial) also available. *Faculty research:* Optics, solid-state physics, comology, atomic physics, nuclear physics. Total annual research expenditures: $54,000. *Unit head:* Dr. Christopher G. Goedde, Chairman, 773-325-7330, Fax: 773-325-7334, E-mail: egoedde@condor.depaul.edu. *Application contact:* Dr. Ross A. Hyman, Departmental Office, 773-325-7330, Fax: 773-325-7334.

Drexel University, College of Arts and Sciences, Physics Program, Philadelphia, PA 19104-2875. Offers MS, PhD. Terminal master's awarded for partial completion of doctoral program. *Degree requirements:* For doctorate, thesis/dissertation. *Entrance requirements:* For master's and doctorate, GRE. Additional exam requirements/recommendations for international students: Required—TOEFL. Electronic applications accepted. *Faculty research:* Nuclear structure, mesoscale meteorology, numerical astrophysics, numerical weather prediction, earth energy radiation budget.

Duke University, Graduate School, Department of Physics, Durham, NC 27708-0586. Offers PhD. Part-time programs available. *Faculty:* 37 full-time. *Students:* 69 full-time (13 women); includes 4 minority (2 Asian Americans or Pacific Islanders, 2 Hispanic Americans), 37 international. 200 applicants, 22% accepted, 11 enrolled. In 2003, 9 doctorates awarded. *Degree requirements:* For doctorate, thesis/dissertation. *Entrance requirements:* For doctorate, GRE General Test, GRE Subject Test. Additional exam requirements/recommendations for international students: Required—IELT (preferred) or TOEFL. *Application deadline:* For fall admission, 12/31 for domestic students. Application fee: $75. *Expenses:* Tuition: Full-time $23,280; part-time $835 per unit. *Financial support:* Fellowships, research assistantships, teaching assistantships, Federal Work-Study available. Financial award application deadline: 12/31. *Unit head:* Dr. Henry Weller, Director of Graduate Studies, 919-660-2502, Fax: 919-660-2525, E-mail: donna@phy.duke.edu.

East Carolina University, Graduate School, Thomas Harriot College of Arts and Sciences, Department of Physics, Greenville, NC 27858-4353. Offers applied and biomedical physics (MS); medical physics (MS); physics (PhD). Part-time programs available. *Faculty:* 12 full-time (0 women). *Students:* 16 full-time (4 women), 13 part-time (2 women); includes 3 minority (1 American Indian/Alaska Native, 1 Asian American or Pacific Islander, 1 Hispanic American), 10 international. Average age 31. 24 applicants, 67% accepted. In 2003, 2 master's, 1 doctorate awarded. *Degree requirements:* For master's, one foreign language, comprehensive exam. *Entrance requirements:* For master's, GRE General Test. Additional exam requirements/recommendations for international students: Required—TOEFL. *Application deadline:* Applications are processed on a rolling basis. Application fee: $50. *Expenses:* Tuition, state resident: full-time $1,991; part-time $249 per hour. Tuition, nonresident: full-time $12,232; part-time $1,529 per hour. Required fees: $1,221; $153 per hour. *Financial support:* Research assistantships with partial tuition reimbursements, teaching assistantships with partial tuition reimbursements, Federal Work-Study available. Support available to part-time students. Financial award application deadline: 6/1. *Unit head:* Dr. Larry Toburen, Director of Graduate Studies, 252-328-6739, Fax: 252-328-6314, E-mail: toburenl@mail.ecu.edu. *Application contact:* Dr. Paul D. Tschetter, Interim Dean of Graduate School, 252-328-6012, Fax: 252-328-6071, E-mail: gradschool@mail.ecu.edu.

Announcement: The graduate program in the Department of Physics offers PhD degrees in biomedical physics and MS degrees in physics with options in applied physics and medical physics to satisfy the career goals of most physics students. This program draws on faculty members in ECU's physical and medical science departments to meet the need for highly trained scientists who can integrate knowledge of the physical sciences with biomedical research. More information at http://www.ecu.edu/physics/grad.htm or e-mail physics@mail.ecu.edu.

Eastern Michigan University, Graduate School, College of Arts and Sciences, Department of Physics and Astronomy, Program in Physics, Ypsilanti, MI 48197. Offers MS. *Degree requirements:* For master's, thesis (for some programs). *Entrance requirements:* Additional exam requirements/recommendations for international students: Required—TOEFL. *Application deadline:* For fall admission, 5/15 for domestic students; for spring admission, 3/15 for domestic students. Applications are processed on a rolling basis. Application fee: $30. *Expenses:* Tuition, state resident: full-time $4,324. Tuition, nonresident: full-time $8,769. Required fees: $496. Tuition and fees vary according to course level. *Financial support:* Fellowships, teaching assistantships available. Support available to part-time students. Financial award application deadline: 3/15; financial award applicants required to submit FAFSA. *Unit head:* Dr. James Sheerin, Coordinator, 734-487-4144.

Emory University, Graduate School of Arts and Sciences, Department of Physics, Atlanta, GA 30322-1100. Offers physics (PhD), including biophysics, radiological physics, solid-state physics. *Faculty:* 16 full-time (1 woman), 3 part-time/adjunct (0 women). *Students:* 12 full-time (3 women); includes 1 minority (African American), 6 international. Average age 24. 43 applicants, 19% accepted, 4 enrolled. *Degree requirements:* For doctorate, thesis/dissertation, comprehensive exam, registration. *Entrance requirements:* For doctorate, GRE General Test, minimum GPA of 3.0. Additional exam requirements/recommendations for international students: Required—TOEFL. *Application deadline:* For fall admission, 1/20 for domestic students. Application fee: $50. Electronic applications accepted. *Expenses:* Tuition: Part-time $1,115 per hour. Required fees: $5 per hour. $125 per term. *Financial support:* In 2003–04, 12 students received support, including 4 fellowships (averaging $20,000 per year); institutionally sponsored loans, scholarships/grants, health care benefits, and tuition waivers (full) also available. Financial award application deadline: 1/20; financial award applicants required to submit FAFSA. *Faculty research:* Theory of semiconductors and superlattices, experimental laser optics and submillimeter spectroscopy theory, neural networks and stereoscopic vision, experimental studies of the structure and function of metalloproteins. Total annual research expenditures: $1.4 million. *Unit head:* Dr. Raymond DuVarney, Chair, 404-727-4296, Fax: 404-727-0873, E-mail: phsrcd@physics.emory.edu. *Application contact:* Dr. Kurt Warncke, Director of Graduate Studies, 404-727-2975, Fax: 404-727-0873, E-mail: kwarncke@physics.emory.edu.

Emporia State University, School of Graduate Studies, College of Liberal Arts and Sciences, Department of Physical Sciences, Emporia, KS 66801-5087. Offers chemistry (MS); earth science (MS); physical science (MS); physics (MS). *Faculty:* 18 full-time (2 women), 1 (woman) part-time/adjunct. *Students:* 2 full-time (0 women), 21 part-time (6 women); includes 1 minority (African American), 2 international. 1 applicant, 100% accepted, 1 enrolled. In 2003, 3 degrees awarded. *Degree requirements:* For master's, comprehensive exam or thesis. *Entrance requirements:* For master's, written exam, appropriate undergraduate degree. Additional exam requirements/recommendations for international students: Required—TOEFL. *Application deadline:* For fall admission, 8/15 for domestic students. Applications are processed on a rolling basis. Application fee: $30 ($75 for international students). Electronic applications accepted. *Expenses:* Tuition, state resident: full-time $2,640; part-time $110 per credit hour. Tuition, nonresident: full-time $8,454; part-time $352 per credit hour. Required fees: $576; $35 per credit hour. Tuition and fees vary according to campus/location. *Financial support:* In 2003–04, 3 research assistantships (averaging $6,225 per year), 5 teaching assistantships with full tuition reimbursements (averaging $6,225 per year) were awarded. Federal Work-Study, institutionally sponsored loans, health care benefits, and unspecified assistantships also available. Financial award application deadline: 3/15; financial award applicants required to submit FAFSA. *Faculty research:* Bredigite, larnite, and dicalcium silicates–Marble Canyon. *Unit head:* Dr. DeWayne Backhus, Chair, 620-341-5330, Fax: 620-341-6055, E-mail: backhusd@emporia.edu.

Fisk University, Graduate Programs, Department of Physics, Nashville, TN 37208-3051. Offers MA. *Degree requirements:* For master's, thesis. *Entrance requirements:* For master's, GRE General Test, GRE Subject Test, minimum GPA of 3.0. *Faculty research:* Molecular physics, astrophysics, surface physics, nanobase materials, optical processing.

Florida Agricultural and Mechanical University, Division of Graduate Studies, Research, and Continuing Education, College of Arts and Sciences, Department of Physics, Tallahassee, FL 32307-3200. Offers MS, PhD. *Faculty:* 18 full-time (2 women). *Students:* 14 full-time (9 women), 5 part-time (3 women); includes 17 minority (all African Americans) In 2003, 2 degrees awarded. *Degree requirements:* For master's, thesis optional; for doctorate, thesis/dissertation, comprehensive exam. *Entrance requirements:* For master's, GRE General Test, minimum GPA of 3.0; for doctorate, GRE General Test, minimum GPA of 3.0, letters of recommendation (2). Additional exam requirements/recommendations for international students: Required—TOEFL (minimum score 550 paper-based). *Application deadline:* For fall admission, 5/18 for domestic students, 12/18 for international students; for spring admission, 11/12 for domestic students, 5/12 for international students. Application fee: $20. *Expenses:* Tuition, state resident: part-time $192 per credit. Tuition, nonresident: part-time $727 per credit. Tuition and fees vary according to course load. *Faculty research:* Plasma physics, quantum mechanics, condensed matter physics, astrophysics, laser ablation. *Unit head:* Dr. Mogus Mochena, Chairperson, 850-599-3470, Fax: 850-599-3577.

Florida Atlantic University, Charles E. Schmidt College of Science, Department of Physics, Boca Raton, FL 33431-0991. Offers MS, MST, PhD. Part-time programs available. *Faculty:* 7 full-time (1 woman), 2 part-time/adjunct (0 women). *Students:* 22 full-time (6 women), 6 part-time (2 women); includes 5 minority (2 African Americans, 1 Asian American or Pacific Islander, 2 Hispanic Americans), 13 international. Average age 34. 15 applicants, 47% accepted, 4 enrolled. In 2003, 3 master's, 7 doctorates awarded. *Median time to degree:* Of those who began their doctoral program in fall 1995, 90% received their degree in 8 years or less. *Degree requirements:* For master's, thesis (for some programs); for doctorate, thesis/dissertation. *Entrance requirements:* For master's, GRE General Test, minimum GPA of 3.0; for doctorate, GRE General Test. Additional exam requirements/recommendations for international students: Required—TOEFL (minimum score 500 paper-based; 173 computer-based). *Application deadline:* For fall admission, 7/1 for domestic students, 2/15 for international students; for spring admission, 11/1 for domestic students, 8/15 for international students. Applications are processed on a rolling basis. Application fee: $30. *Expenses:* Tuition, state resident: full-time $3,777. Tuition, nonresident: full-time $13,953. *Financial support:* In 2003–04, 3 research assistantships with tuition reimbursements (averaging $17,372 per year), 18 teaching assistantships with tuition reimbursements (averaging $17,372 per year) were awarded. Fellowships, Federal Work-Study and unspecified assistantships also available. *Faculty research:* Astrophysics, spectroscopy, mathematical physics, theory of metals, superconductivity. Total annual research expenditures: $123,700. *Unit head:* Dr. Fernando Medina, Graduate Coordinator, 561-297-3382, Fax: 561-297-2662, E-mail: medina@fau.edu.

Florida Institute of Technology, Graduate Programs, College of Science and Liberal Arts, Department of Physics and Space Sciences, Melbourne, FL 32901-6975. Offers physics (MS, PhD); space science (MS, PhD). Part-time programs available. *Faculty:* 12 full-time (0 women). *Students:* 17 full-time (5 women), 7 part-time (3 women), 8 international. Average age 29. 43 applicants, 40% accepted, 11 enrolled. In 2003, 6 master's, 2 doctorates awarded. Terminal master's awarded for partial completion of doctoral program. *Degree requirements:* For master's, thesis optional; for doctorate, thesis/dissertation, publication in referred journal, comprehensive exam, registration. *Entrance requirements:* For master's, GRE General Test, GRE Subject Test, minimum GPA of 3.0, proficiency in a computer language, resumé, letters of recommendation (3), statement of objectives; for doctorate, GRE General Test, GRE Subject Test, minimum GPA of 3.2, resumé, letters of recommendation (3), statement of objectives. Additional exam requirements/recommendations for international students: Required—TOEFL (minimum score 550 paper-based; 213 computer-based). *Application deadline:* Applications are processed on a rolling basis. Application fee: $50. Electronic applications accepted. *Expenses:* Tuition: Part-time $745 per credit. *Financial support:* In 2003–04, 4 research assistantships with full and partial tuition reimbursements (averaging $19,385 per year), 21 teaching assistantships with full and partial tuition reimbursements (averaging $23,401 per year) were awarded. Career-related internships or fieldwork and tuition remissions also available. Financial award application deadline: 3/1; financial award applicants required to submit FAFSA. *Faculty research:* Lasers, semiconductors, magnetism, quantum devices, high energy physics. Total annual research expenditures: $621,446. *Unit head:* Dr. Lazlo A. Baksay, Department Head, 321-674-7367, Fax: 321-674-7482, E-mail: baksay@fit.edu. *Application contact:* Carolyn P. Farrior, Director of Graduate Admissions, 321-674-7118, Fax: 321-723-9468, E-mail: cfarrior@fit.edu.

Florida International University, College of Arts and Sciences, Department of Physics, Miami, FL 33199. Offers MS, PhD. Part-time and evening/weekend programs available. *Faculty:* 21 full-time (2 women). *Students:* 22 full-time (7 women), 4 part-time; includes 8 minority (1 Asian American or Pacific Islander, 7 Hispanic Americans), 12 international. Average age 30. 14 applicants, 50% accepted, 3 enrolled. In 2003, 2 degrees awarded. *Degree requirements:* For master's and doctorate, one foreign language, thesis/dissertation. *Entrance requirements:* For master's and doctorate, GRE General Test. Additional exam requirements/recommendations for international students: Required—TOEFL. *Application deadline:* For fall admission, 4/1 for domestic students; for spring admission, 10/1 for domestic students. Applications are processed on a rolling basis. Application fee: $20. *Expenses:* Tuition, state resident: part-time $202 per credit. Tuition, nonresident: part-time $771 per credit. Required fees: $112 per semester. *Financial support:* Application deadline: 4/1. *Faculty research:* Molecular collision processes (molecular beams), biophysical optics. *Unit head:* Dr. Stephan L. Mintz, Chairperson, 305-348-2605, Fax: 305-348-3053, E-mail: mintz@fiu.edu.

Florida State University, Graduate Studies, College of Arts and Sciences, Department of Physics, Tallahassee, FL 32306. Offers MS, PhD. *Faculty:* 40 full-time (3 women). *Students:* 113 full-time (18 women); includes 51 minority (44 Asian Americans or Pacific Islanders, 7 Hispanic Americans). Average age 28. 355 applicants, 8% accepted, 26 enrolled. In 2003, 4 master's, 10 doctorates awarded. *Median time to degree:* Master's–2.5 years full-time; doctorate–4 years full-time. Of those who began their doctoral program in fall 1995, 42% received their degree in 8 years or less. *Degree requirements:* For doctorate, thesis/dissertation. *Entrance requirements:* For master's and doctorate, GRE General Test, minimum GPA of 3.0. Additional exam requirements/recommendations for international students: Required—TOEFL (minimum score 550 paper-based; 213 computer-based). *Application deadline:* For fall admission, 2/15 for domestic students, 1/15 for international students. Applications are processed on a rolling basis. Application fee: $20. Electronic applications accepted. *Expenses:* Tuition, state resident: part-time $196 per credit hour. Tuition, nonresident: part-time $731 per credit hour. Part-time tuition and fees vary according to campus/location. *Financial support:* In 2003–04, 113 students received support, including 87 research assistantships with full tuition reimbursements available (averaging $17,000 per year), 26 teaching assistantships with full tuition reimbursements available (averaging $17,000 per year); career-related internships or fieldwork and Federal Work-Study also available. Financial award application deadline: 2/15; financial award applicants required to submit FAFSA. *Faculty research:* High energy physics, computational physics, biophysics, condensed matter physics, nuclear physics. Total annual research expenditures: $4 million. *Unit head:* Dr. David H. Van Winkle, Chairman, 850-644-2867, Fax: 850-644-2338, E-mail: rip@phy.fsu.edu. *Application contact:* Sherry Ann Tointigh, Program Assistant, 850-644-4473, Fax: 850-644-8630, E-mail: graduate@phy.fsu.edu.

Announcement: Extensive research opportunities exist in theoretical and experimental physics in the areas of atomic, condensed-matter, high-energy, and nuclear physics. This research makes use of extensive computers and instrumentation at the National High-Magnetic Field Laboratory at FSU. Each full-time graduate student has an assistantship.

See in-depth description on page 361.

George Mason University, College of Arts and Sciences, Department of Physics, Fairfax, VA 22030. Offers applied and engineering physics (MS). *Faculty:* 19 full-time (6 women), 11 part-time/adjunct (2 women). *Students:* Average age 30. 18 applicants, 61% accepted, 7 enrolled. In 2003, 4 degrees awarded. *Degree requirements:* For master's, thesis optional. *Entrance requirements:* For master's, minimum GPA of 2.75 in last 60 hours. *Application deadline:* For fall admission, 5/1 for domestic students; for spring admission, 11/1 for domestic students. Application fee: $60. Electronic applications accepted. *Expenses:* Tuition, state resident: full-time $4,398. Tuition, nonresident: full-time $14,952. Required fees: $1,482. *Financial support:* Research assistantships, teaching assistantships available. Support available to part-time students. Financial award application deadline: 3/1; financial award applicants required to submit FAFSA. *Unit head:* Dr. Maria Dworzecka, Chairman, 703-993-1280, Fax: 703-993-1269, E-mail: mdworzecka@gmu.edu. *Application contact:* Dr. Paul So, Information Contact, 703-993-1280, E-mail: physics@gmu.edu.

The George Washington University, Columbian College of Arts and Sciences, Department of Physics, Washington, DC 20052. Offers MA, PhD. Part-time and evening/weekend programs available. *Faculty:* 9 full-time (0 women). *Students:* 11 full-time (0 women), 8 part-time; includes 1 minority (Hispanic American), 14 international. Average age 31. 11 applicants, 73% accepted, 4 enrolled. In 2003, 1 master's, 2 doctorates awarded. *Degree requirements:* For doctorate, thesis/dissertation, general exam. *Entrance requirements:* For master's and doctorate, GRE General Test, minimum GPA of 3.0. Additional exam requirements/recommendations for international students: Required—TOEFL (minimum score 550 paper-based; 213 computer-based). *Application deadline:* For fall admission, 2/1 priority date for domestic students, 2/1 priority date for international students; for spring admission, 4/1 priority date for domestic students, 4/1 priority date for international students. Applications are processed on a rolling basis. Application fee: $60. Electronic applications accepted. *Expenses:* Tuition: Part-time $876 per credit. Required fees: $1 per credit. Tuition and fees vary according to campus/location. *Financial support:* In 2003–04, 7 fellowships with full tuition reimbursements (averaging $10,000 per year), 8 teaching assistantships with tuition reimbursements (averaging $5,000 per year) were awarded. Research assistantships, Federal Work-Study also available. Financial award application deadline: 2/1. *Unit head:* Dr. William Parke, Chair, 202-994-6275. *Application contact:* Dr. Mark Reeves, Director, 202-994-6279, Fax: 202-994-3001, E-mail: reevesme@gwu.edu.

Georgia Institute of Technology, Graduate Studies and Research, College of Sciences, School of Physics, Atlanta, GA 30332-0001. Offers MS, PhD. Part-time programs available. *Faculty:* 31 full-time (2 women). *Students:* 122 full-time (21 women); includes 76 minority (6 African Americans, 65 Asian Americans or Pacific Islanders, 5 Hispanic Americans). Average age 24. 360 applicants, 27% accepted, 45 enrolled. In 2003, 1 master's, 6 doctorates awarded. Terminal master's awarded for partial completion of doctoral program. *Degree requirements:* For doctorate, thesis/dissertation, comprehensive exam. *Entrance requirements:* For master's, GRE General Test, GRE Subject Test, minimum GPA of 3.0; for doctorate, GRE General Test, GRE Subject Test, minimum GPA of 3.4. Additional exam requirements/recommendations for international students: Required—TOEFL. *Application deadline:* For fall admission, 1/31 priority date for domestic students, 1/31 priority date for international students. Applications are processed on a rolling basis. Application fee: $50. Electronic applications accepted. *Expenses:* Tuition, state resident: part-time $1,925 per semester. Tuition, nonresident: part-time $7,700 per semester. Required fees: $434 per semester. Full-time tuition and fees vary according to program. *Financial support:* In 2003–04, 45 teaching assistantships with full tuition reimbursements (averaging $17,000 per year) were awarded; unspecified assistantships also available.

Physics

Georgia Institute of Technology (continued)

Financial award application deadline: 1/31. *Faculty research:* Atomic and molecular physics, chemical physics, condensed matter, optics, nonlinear physics and chaos. Total annual research expenditures: $6 million. *Unit head:* Dr. Ronald F. Fox, Chair, 404-894-5200, E-mail: ron.fox@physics.gatech.edu. *Application contact:* Dr. James R. Sowell, Graduate Recruiter, 404-385-1294, Fax: 404-894-9958, E-mail: grad.recruiter@physics.gatech.edu.

See in-depth description on page 363.

Georgia State University, College of Arts and Sciences, Department of Physics and Astronomy, Program in Physics, Atlanta, GA 30303-3083. Offers MS, PhD. Part-time and evening/weekend programs available. Terminal master's awarded for partial completion of doctoral program. *Degree requirements:* For master's, one foreign language, thesis or alternative, exam; for doctorate, 2 foreign languages, thesis/dissertation, exam. *Entrance requirements:* For master's and doctorate, GRE General Test. Additional exam requirements/recommendations for international students: Required—TOEFL. Electronic applications accepted. *Faculty research:* Biophysics; nuclear, condensed-matter, and atomic physics; astrophysics.

Graduate School and University Center of the City University of New York, Graduate Studies, Program in Physics, New York, NY 10016-4039. Offers PhD. *Faculty:* 105 full-time (3 women). *Students:* 68 full-time (13 women), 2 part-time; includes 4 minority (1 African American, 1 American Indian/Alaska Native, 1 Asian American or Pacific Islander, 1 Hispanic American), 51 international. Average age 29. 82 applicants, 46% accepted, 18 enrolled. In 2003, 6 degrees awarded. *Degree requirements:* For doctorate, thesis/dissertation. *Entrance requirements:* For doctorate, GRE General Test. *Application deadline:* For fall admission, 4/15 for domestic students. Application fee: $50. *Expenses:* Tuition, state resident: part-time $2,435 per semester. Tuition, nonresident: part-time $475 per credit. *Financial support:* In 2003–04, 52 students received support, including 51 fellowships, 1 teaching assistantship; research assistantships, career-related internships or fieldwork, Federal Work-Study, institutionally sponsored loans, and tuition waivers (full and partial) also available. Financial award application deadline: 2/1; financial award applicants required to submit FAFSA. *Faculty research:* Condensed-matter, particle, nuclear, and atomic physics. *Unit head:* Dr. Sultan Catto, Executive Officer, 212-817-8650, Fax: 212-817-1531, E-mail: scatto@gc.cuny.edu.

Hampton University, Graduate College, Department of Physics, Hampton, VA 23668. Offers MS, PhD. Part-time and evening/weekend programs available. Terminal master's awarded for partial completion of doctoral program. *Degree requirements:* For master's, thesis optional; for doctorate, thesis/dissertation, oral defense, qualifying exam. *Entrance requirements:* For master's, GRE General Test; for doctorate, minimum GPA of 3.0 or master's degree in physics or related field. *Faculty research:* Laser optics, remote sensing.

Harvard University, Graduate School of Arts and Sciences, Committee on Chemical Physics, Cambridge, MA 02138. Offers chemical physics (PhD); chemistry (AM); physics (AM). *Degree requirements:* For doctorate, one foreign language, thesis/dissertation, cumulative exams. *Entrance requirements:* For master's, GRE General Test; for doctorate, GRE General Test, GRE Subject Test. Additional exam requirements/recommendations for international students: Required—TOEFL. *Expenses:* Tuition: Full-time $26,066. Full-time tuition and fees vary according to program and student level.

Harvard University, Graduate School of Arts and Sciences, Department of Physics, Cambridge, MA 02138. Offers experimental physics (AM, PhD); medical engineering/medical physics (PhD, Sc D), including applied physics (PhD), engineering sciences (PhD), medical engineering/medical physics (Sc D), physics (PhD); theoretical physics (AM, PhD). *Students:* 174. *Degree requirements:* For doctorate, thesis/dissertation, final exams, laboratory experience. *Entrance requirements:* For master's, GRE General Test; for doctorate, GRE General Test, GRE Subject Test. Additional exam requirements/recommendations for international students: Required—TOEFL. *Application deadline:* For fall admission, 12/14 for domestic students. Application fee: $60. *Expenses:* Tuition: Full-time $26,066. Full-time tuition and fees vary according to program and student level. *Financial support:* Fellowships, research assistantships, teaching assistantships, career-related internships or fieldwork, Federal Work-Study, and institutionally sponsored loans available. Financial award application deadline: 12/30. *Faculty research:* Particle physics, condensed matter physics, atomic physics. *Unit head:* Prof. John Huth, Chair, 617-495-8144, E-mail: huth@physics.harvard.edu. *Application contact:* Office of Admissions and Financial Aid, 617-495-5315.

See in-depth description on page 365.

Howard University, Graduate School of Arts and Sciences, Department of Physics and Astronomy, Washington, DC 20059-0002. Offers physics (MS, PhD). *Faculty:* 17 full-time (1 woman). *Students:* 16 full-time (5 women), 2 part-time; includes 11 minority (all African Americans), 7 international. Average age 25. 10 applicants, 20% accepted, 2 enrolled. *Degree requirements:* For master's, thesis (for some programs), comprehensive exam (for some programs); for doctorate, thesis/dissertation, departmental qualifying exam, final comprehensive exam, comprehensive exam. *Entrance requirements:* For master's, GRE General Test, bachelor's degree in physics or related field, minimum GPA of 3.0; for doctorate, GRE General Test, bachelor's or master's degree in physics or related field, minimum GPA of 3.0. Additional exam requirements/recommendations for international students: Required—TOEFL (minimum score 550 paper-based; 213 computer-based). *Application deadline:* For fall admission, 4/1 for domestic students; for spring admission, 11/1 for domestic students. Applications are processed on a rolling basis. Application fee: $45. *Financial support:* In 2003–04, 8 students received support, including fellowships with tuition reimbursements available (averaging $15,000 per year), 12 research assistantships with tuition reimbursements available (averaging $15,000 per year), 8 teaching assistantships with tuition reimbursements available (averaging $13,000 per year); career-related internships or fieldwork, Federal Work-Study, institutionally sponsored loans, scholarships/grants, traineeships, tuition waivers (partial), and unspecified assistantships also available. Support available to part-time students. Financial award application deadline: 4/1. *Faculty research:* Atmospheric physics, spectroscopy and optical physics, high energy physics, condensed matter. Total annual research expenditures: $5.5 million. *Unit head:* Dr. Demetrius D. Venable, Chairman, 202-806-6245, Fax: 202-806-5830, E-mail: dvenable@howard.edu. *Application contact:* Dr. Tristan Hubsch, Director of Graduate Studies, 202-806-6267, Fax: 202-806-5830, E-mail: thubsch@howard.edu.

Hunter College of the City University of New York, Graduate School, School of Arts and Sciences, Department of Physics, New York, NY 10021-5085. Offers MA, PhD. Part-time programs available. *Faculty:* 3 full-time (0 women). *Students:* 3 full-time (0 women), 7 part-time (2 women); includes 2 minority (1 African American, 1 Hispanic American). Average age 29. 5 applicants, 60% accepted. In 2003, 2 degrees awarded. Terminal master's awarded for partial completion of doctoral program. *Degree requirements:* For master's, comprehensive exam or thesis. *Entrance requirements:* For master's, minimum 36 credits in mathematics and physics. Additional exam requirements/recommendations for international students: Required—TOEFL. *Application deadline:* For fall admission, 4/1 for domestic students, 2/1 for international students; for spring admission, 11/1 for domestic students, 9/1 for international students. Application fee: $50. *Expenses:* Tuition, state resident: part-time $230 per credit. Tuition, nonresident: part-time $425 per credit. *Financial support:* In 2003–04, research assistantships (averaging $20,000 per year), teaching assistantships (averaging $9,000 per year) were awarded. Scholarships/grants also available. *Faculty research:* Experimental and theoretical quantum optics, experimental and theoretical condensed matter, mathematical physics. *Unit head:* Godfrey Gumbs, Chairperson, 212-650-3935, Fax: 212-772-5390, E-mail: ggumbs@hunter.cuny.edu. *Application contact:* William Zlata, Director for Graduate Admissions, 212-772-4482, Fax: 212-650-3336, E-mail: admissions@hunter.cuny.edu.

Idaho State University, Office of Graduate Studies, College of Arts and Sciences, Department of Physics, Pocatello, ID 83209. Offers natural science (MNS); physics (MS). Part-time programs available. *Faculty:* 8 full-time (1 woman), 1 part-time/adjunct (0 women). *Students:* 19 full-time (3 women), 10 part-time (2 women); includes 1 minority (Hispanic American), 7 international. Average age 31. In 2003, 2 degrees awarded. *Degree requirements:* For master's, thesis (for some programs), comprehensive exam, registration (for some programs). *Entrance requirements:* For master's, GRE General Test, 3 letters of recommendation, BS or BA in physics. Additional exam requirements/recommendations for international students: Required—TOEFL (minimum score 550 paper-based; 213 computer-based). *Application deadline:* For fall admission, 7/1 priority date for domestic students, 7/1 priority date for international students; for spring admission, 12/1 priority date for domestic students, 12/1 priority date for international students. Applications are processed on a rolling basis. Application fee: $35. *Expenses:* Tuition, state resident: part-time $205 per credit. Tuition, nonresident: full-time $6,600; part-time $300 per credit. Required fees: $4,108. One-time fee: $35 full-time. *Financial support:* Research assistantships with full and partial tuition reimbursements, teaching assistantships with full and partial tuition reimbursements, career-related internships or fieldwork, Federal Work-Study, and tuition waivers (full) available. Support available to part-time students. Financial award application deadline: 1/1. *Faculty research:* Ion beam applications, low-energy nuclear physics, relativity and cosmology, observational astronomy. Total annual research expenditures: $677,657. *Unit head:* Douglas Wells, Chair, 208-282-2350, Fax: 208-282-4649.

See in-depth description on page 367.

Idaho State University, Office of Graduate Studies, Department of Interdisciplinary Studies, Pocatello, ID 83209. Offers biology (MNS); chemistry (MNS); general interdisciplinary (M Ed, MA); geology (MNS); mathematics (MNS); physics (MNS); waste management and environmental science (MS). Part-time programs available. *Students:* 3 full-time, 337 part-time; includes 7 minority (1 African American, 1 Asian American or Pacific Islander, 5 Hispanic Americans). Average age 45. In 2003, 7 degrees awarded. *Degree requirements:* For master's, thesis optional. *Entrance requirements:* For master's, GRE General Test or MAT, minimum GPA of 3.0. Additional exam requirements/recommendations for international students: Required—TOEFL (minimum score 550 paper-based; 213 computer-based). *Application deadline:* For fall admission, 7/1 priority date for domestic students, 7/1 priority date for international students; for spring admission, 12/1 priority date for domestic students, 12/1 priority date for international students. Applications are processed on a rolling basis. Application fee: $35. *Expenses:* Tuition, state resident: part-time $205 per credit. Tuition, nonresident: full-time $6,600; part-time $300 per credit. Required fees: $4,108. One-time fee: $35 full-time. *Financial support:* Research assistantships, teaching assistantships, career-related internships or fieldwork, Federal Work-Study, scholarships/grants, and tuition waivers (full and partial) available. Support available to part-time students. Financial award application deadline: 1/1. Total annual research expenditures: $1.7 million. *Unit head:* Dr. Edwin House, Chief Research Officer/Department Chair, 208-282-2714, Fax: 208-282-4529.

Illinois Institute of Technology, Graduate College, College of Science and Letters, Department of Biological, Chemical and Physical Sciences, Physics Division, Chicago, IL 60616-3793. Offers health physics (MHP); physics (MS, PhD). Part-time programs available. Postbaccalaureate distance learning degree programs offered. *Faculty:* 2 full-time (0 women), 3 part-time/adjunct (0 women). *Students:* 12 full-time (2 women), 24 part-time (5 women); includes 8 minority (1 American Indian/Alaska Native, 5 Asian Americans or Pacific Islanders, 2 Hispanic Americans), 15 international. Average age 33. 99 applicants, 56% accepted, 12 enrolled. In 2003, 5 master's, 4 doctorates awarded. Terminal master's awarded for partial completion of doctoral program. *Degree requirements:* For master's, thesis (for some programs), comprehensive exam; for doctorate, thesis/dissertation, comprehensive exam. *Entrance requirements:* For master's and doctorate, GRE General Test, minimum undergraduate GPA of 3.0. Additional exam requirements/recommendations for international students: Required—TOEFL (minimum score 550 paper-based; 213 computer-based). *Application deadline:* For fall admission, 5/1 for domestic students, 5/1 for international students; for spring admission, 10/15 for domestic students, 10/15 for international students. Applications are processed on a rolling basis. Application fee: $40. Electronic applications accepted. *Expenses:* Tuition: Part-time $628 per credit. Tuition and fees vary according to course load and program. *Financial support:* In 2003–04, 11 students received support, including 6 research assistantships with full tuition reimbursements available (averaging $15,000 per year), 9 teaching assistantships with full tuition reimbursements available (averaging $15,000 per year); fellowships, Federal Work-Study, institutionally sponsored loans, scholarships/grants, and unspecified assistantships also available. Support available to part-time students. Financial award application deadline: 3/1; financial award applicants required to submit FAFSA. *Faculty research:* Biophysics, condensed matter physics, high energy physics, surface physics, theoretical physics. *Unit head:* Dr. Howard Rubin, Associate Chair, 312-567-3395, Fax: 312-567-3494, E-mail: rubin@iit.edu. *Application contact:* Kelly A. Cherwin, Director of Graduate Outreach, 312-567-7974, Fax: 312-567-3494, E-mail: inquiry.grad@iit.edu.

Indiana University Bloomington, Graduate School, College of Arts and Sciences, Department of Physics, Bloomington, IN 47405. Offers MAT, MS, PhD. PhD offered through the University Graduate School. Part-time programs available. *Faculty:* 35 full-time (3 women). *Students:* 67 full-time (18 women), 27 part-time (4 women); includes 5 minority (2 African Americans, 1 Asian American or Pacific Islander, 2 Hispanic Americans), 54 international. Average age 27. In 2003, 7 master's, 8 doctorates awarded. Terminal master's awarded for partial completion of doctoral program. *Degree requirements:* For master's, qualifying exam; for doctorate, thesis/dissertation, qualifying exam. *Entrance requirements:* For master's and doctorate, GRE General Test, GRE Subject Test (physics). Additional exam requirements/recommendations for international students: Required—TOEFL. *Application deadline:* For fall admission, 1/15 priority date for domestic students, 12/15 priority date for international students; for spring admission, 9/1 for domestic students, 9/1 for international students. Application fee: $45 ($55 for international students). *Expenses:* Tuition, state resident: full-time $4,908; part-time $205 per credit. Tuition, nonresident: full-time $14,298; part-time $596 per credit. Required fees: $661. Tuition and fees vary according to campus/location and program. *Financial support:* In 2003–04, research assistantships with partial tuition reimbursements (averaging $16,464 per year), teaching assistantships with partial tuition reimbursements (averaging $11,280 per year) were awarded. Career-related internships or fieldwork also available. Financial award application deadline: 2/1. *Unit head:* Dr. V. Alan Kostelecký, Chair, 812-855-1247, Fax: 812-855-5533. *Application contact:* June Dizer, Student Affairs Administrator, 812-855-3973, E-mail: gradphys@indiana.edu.

Announcement: Theoretical and experimental nuclear, particle, condensed matter, accelerator, astrophysics, biophysics, biocomplexity, and chemical physics. IUCF electron-cooled storage ring; nuclear theory center, supercomputers. Low-temperature clean room, cryostats, photolithograph, STM, UHV analysis, 14T magnet, X-ray diffraction, squid magnetometer, and microwave facilities. Experiments at national and international laboratories. Financial support available.

See in-depth description on page 369.

Indiana University of Pennsylvania, Graduate School and Research, College of Natural Sciences and Mathematics, Department of Physics, Program in Physics, Indiana, PA 15705-1087. Offers MA, MS. Part-time programs available. *Faculty:* 7 full-time (1 woman). *Students:* 5 full-time (1 woman), 3 part-time (1 woman); includes 1 minority (Asian American or Pacific Islander), 2 international. Average age 27. 14 applicants, 71% accepted. In 2003, 4 degrees awarded. *Degree requirements:* For master's, thesis (for some programs), comprehensive exam (for some programs). *Application deadline:* For fall admission, 7/1 for domestic students; for spring admission, 11/1 for domestic students. Applications are processed on a rolling basis. Application fee: $30. *Expenses:* Tuition, state resident: full-time $5,518; part-time $307 per credit. Tuition, nonresident: full-time $8,830; part-time $491 per credit. Required fees: $31 per credit. $111 per semester. Tuition and fees vary according to degree level. *Financial support:* In 2003–04, 5 research assistantships with full and partial tuition reimbursements (averaging $5,660 per year) were awarded; Federal Work-Study also available. Support available to part-time students. Financial award application deadline: 3/15; financial award applicants required to submit FAFSA. *Unit head:* Dr. Muhammad Numan, Graduate Coordinator, 724-357-2318, E-mail: mznuman@iup.edu.

Indiana University–Purdue University Indianapolis, School of Science, Department of Physics, Indianapolis, IN 46202-2896. Offers MS, PhD. Part-time programs available. *Faculty:* 4 full-time (0 women). *Students:* 8 full-time (3 women), 5 part-time (1 woman); includes 2 minority (1 African American, 1 Asian American or Pacific Islander), 4 international. Average age 35. In 2003, 1 degree awarded. Terminal master's awarded for partial completion of doctoral program. *Degree requirements:* For master's, thesis optional; for doctorate, thesis/dissertation. *Entrance requirements:* Additional exam requirements/recommendations for international students: Required—TOEFL. *Application deadline:* For fall admission, 3/1 for domestic students. Applications are processed on a rolling basis. Application fee: $45 ($55 for international students). *Expenses:* Tuition, state resident: full-time $4,658; part-time $194 per credit. Tuition, nonresident: full-time $13,444; part-time $560 per credit. Required fees: $571. Tuition and fees vary according to campus/location and program. *Financial support:* In 2003–04, 1 fellowship with full tuition reimbursement (averaging $12,000 per year), 2 research assistantships with full tuition reimbursements (averaging $12,000 per year), 3 teaching assistantships with full tuition reimbursements (averaging $12,000 per year) were awarded. Federal Work-Study, institutionally sponsored loans, and tuition waivers (full and partial) also available. Support available to part-time students. Financial award application deadline: 3/1. *Faculty research:* Magnetic resonance, photosynthesis, optical physics, biophysics, physics of materials. *Unit head:* Guantam Vemuri, Chair, 317-274-0002, E-mail: gnamuri@iupui.edu. *Application contact:* Z. Ou, Chair, Graduate Committee, 317-274-2125, Fax: 317-274-2393, E-mail: zou@iupui.edu.

Iowa State University of Science and Technology, Graduate College, College of Liberal Arts and Sciences, Department of Physics and Astronomy, Ames, IA 50011. Offers applied physics (MS, PhD); astrophysics (MS, PhD); condensed matter physics (MS, PhD); high energy physics (MS, PhD); nuclear physics (MS, PhD); physics (MS, PhD). Part-time programs available. *Faculty:* 45 full-time, 4 part-time/adjunct. *Students:* 83 full-time (12 women), 5 part-time; includes 1 minority (Hispanic American), 66 international. 174 applicants, 59% accepted, 31 enrolled. In 2003, 3 master's, 4 doctorates awarded. Terminal master's awarded for partial completion of doctoral program. *Median time to degree:* Master's–2.9 years full-time; doctorate–7.1 years full-time. *Degree requirements:* For master's, thesis (for some programs); for doctorate, thesis/dissertation. *Entrance requirements:* For master's and doctorate, GRE General Test, GRE Subject Test (physics). Additional exam requirements/recommendations for international students: Required—TOEFL (paper score 550; computer score 213) or IELTS (score 6.5). *Application deadline:* For fall admission, 2/15 priority date for domestic students, 2/15 priority date for international students; for spring admission, 10/15 for domestic students, 10/15 for international students. Applications are processed on a rolling basis. Application fee: $30 ($70 for international students). Electronic applications accepted. Tuition, nonresident: part-time $560 per credit. Required fees: $38 per unit. *Financial support:* In 2003–04, 38 research assistantships with full tuition reimbursements (averaging $17,400 per year), 42 teaching assistantships with full tuition reimbursements (averaging $17,400 per year) were awarded. Fellowships, Federal Work-Study, institutionally sponsored loans, scholarships/grants, health care benefits, and unspecified assistantships also available. Support available to part-time students. Financial award application deadline: 2/15. *Faculty research:* Condensed-matter physics, including superconductivity and new materials; high-energy and nuclear physics; astronomy and astrophysics; atmospheric and environmental physics. Total annual research expenditures: $8.8 million. *Unit head:* Dr. Eli Rosenberg, Chair, 515-294-5441, Fax: 515-294-6027, E-mail: phys_astro@iastate.edu. *Application contact:* Dr. Steven Kawaler, Director of Graduate Education, 515-294-9728, E-mail: phys_astro@iastate.edu.

John Carroll University, Graduate School, Department of Physics, University Heights, OH 44118-4581. Offers MS. Part-time programs available. *Faculty:* 4 full-time (1 woman), 1 part-time/adjunct (0 women). *Students:* 5 full-time (1 woman), 2 part-time; includes 1 minority (African American) Average age 29. 1 applicant, 100% accepted, 1 enrolled. *Median time to degree:* Master's–2 years full-time, 5 years part-time. *Degree requirements:* For master's, essay or thesis. *Entrance requirements:* For master's, bachelor's degree in electrical engineering or physics. *Application deadline:* For fall admission, 8/15 for domestic students; for spring admission, 1/8 for domestic students. Applications are processed on a rolling basis. Application fee: $25 ($35 for international students). *Expenses:* Tuition: Part-time $600 per semester hour. Tuition and fees vary according to program. *Financial support:* In 2003–04, 5 students received support, including teaching assistantships with full tuition reimbursements available (averaging $9,700 per year); tuition waivers (full) and unspecified assistantships also available. *Faculty research:* Fiber optics, ultrasonics, atomic force microscopy, computational materials science, transport properties. *Unit head:* Dr. Anthony Roy Day, Chairperson, 216-397-4613, E-mail: physics@jcu.edu.

The Johns Hopkins University, Zanvyl Krieger School of Arts and Sciences, Henry A. Rowland Department of Physics and Astronomy, Baltimore, MD 21218-2699. Offers astronomy (PhD); physics (PhD). *Faculty:* 32 full-time (3 women), 1 part-time/adjunct (0 women). *Students:* 104 full-time (26 women); includes 5 minority (1 African American, 1 American Indian/Alaska Native, 2 Asian Americans or Pacific Islanders, 1 Hispanic American), 49 international. Average age 25. 384 applicants, 26% accepted, 32 enrolled. In 2003, 16 doctorates awarded. *Median time to degree:* Doctorate–6.5 years full-time. Of those who began their doctoral program in fall 1995, 75% received their degree in 8 years or less. *Degree requirements:* For doctorate, thesis/dissertation, comprehensive exam, registration. *Entrance requirements:* For doctorate, GRE General Test, GRE Subject Test. Additional exam requirements/recommendations for international students: Required—TOEFL (minimum score 600 paper-based; 250 computer-based). *Application deadline:* For fall admission, 1/15 priority date for domestic students, 1/15 priority date for international students. Application fee: $55. Electronic applications accepted. *Expenses:* Tuition: Full-time $28,730; part-time $1,490 per course. Part-time tuition and fees vary according to course load, campus/location and program. *Financial support:* In 2003–04, 17 fellowships (averaging $2,500 per year), 63 research assistantships with full tuition reimbursements (averaging $19,333 per year), 40 teaching assistantships with full tuition reimbursements (averaging $14,500 per year) were awarded. Career-related internships or fieldwork, Federal Work-Study, institutionally sponsored loans, and tuition waivers (full and partial) also available. Financial award application deadline: 4/15; financial award applicants required to submit FAFSA. *Faculty research:* High-energy physics, condensed-matter astrophysics, particle and experimental physics, physics theory. Total annual research expenditures: $27 million. *Unit head:* Dr. Jonathan A. Bagger, Chair, 410-516-7346, Fax: 410-516-7239, E-mail: bagger@jhu.edu. *Application contact:* Carmelita D. King, Academic Affairs Administrator, 410-516-7344, Fax: 410-516-7239, E-mail: jazzy@pha.jhu.edu.

See in-depth description on page 373.

Kansas State University, Graduate School, College of Arts and Sciences, Department of Physics, Manhattan, KS 66506. Offers MS, PhD. *Faculty:* 33 full-time (3 women). *Students:* 57 full-time (13 women), 43 international. 87 applicants, 41% accepted, 8 enrolled. In 2003, 2 master's, 5 doctorates awarded. Terminal master's awarded for partial completion of doctoral program. *Degree requirements:* For master's, thesis; for doctorate, one foreign language, thesis/dissertation, preliminary exams. *Entrance requirements:* For master's and doctorate, GRE Subject Test. Additional exam requirements/recommendations for international students: Required—TOEFL. *Application deadline:* For fall admission, 2/1 for domestic students; for spring admission, 10/1 for domestic students. Applications are processed on a rolling basis. Application fee: $0 ($25 for international students). Electronic applications accepted. *Expenses:* Tuition, state resident: part-time $155 per credit hour. Tuition, nonresident: part-time $428 per credit hour. Required fees: $11 per credit hour. *Financial support:* In 2003–04, 43 research assistantships (averaging $11,295 per year), 12 teaching assistantships with full tuition reimbursements (averaging $10,818 per year) were awarded. Fellowships, career-related internships or fieldwork, Federal Work-Study, institutionally sponsored loans, and scholarships/grants also available. Support available to part-time students. Financial award application deadline: 3/1; financial award applicants required to submit FAFSA. *Faculty research:* Physics education, atomic physics, condensed matter physics, high energy physics, cosmology. Total annual research expenditures: $5.5 million. *Unit head:* Dean Zollman, Head, 785-532-1619, Fax: 785-532-6806, E-mail: dzollman@phys.ksu.edu. *Application contact:* Brett Esry, Director, 785-532-1630, Fax: 785-532-6808, E-mail: esry@phys.ksu.edu.

Kent State University, College of Arts and Sciences, Chemical Physics Interdisciplinary Program, Kent, OH 44242-0001. Offers MS, PhD. Offered in cooperation with the Departments of Chemistry, Mathematics and Computer Science, and Physics and the Liquid Crystal Institute. Terminal master's awarded for partial completion of doctoral program. *Degree requirements:* For master's, thesis; for doctorate, thesis/dissertation, candidacy exam. *Entrance requirements:* For master's and doctorate, GRE. Additional exam requirements/recommendations for international students: Required—TOEFL (minimum score 525 paper-based; 197 computer-based). Electronic applications accepted. *Expenses:* Tuition, state resident: part-time $334 per hour. Tuition, nonresident: part-time $627 per hour.

See in-depth description on page 377.

Kent State University, College of Arts and Sciences, Department of Physics, Kent, OH 44242-0001. Offers MA, MS, PhD. Terminal master's awarded for partial completion of doctoral program. *Degree requirements:* For master's, thesis/dissertation, registration; for doctorate, thesis/dissertation, comprehensive exam, registration. *Entrance requirements:* For master's and doctorate, GRE, minimum GPA of 3.0. Additional exam requirements/recommendations for international students: Required—TOEFL. Electronic applications accepted. *Expenses:* Tuition, state resident: part-time $334 per hour. Tuition, nonresident: part-time $627 per hour. *Faculty research:* Correlated electron materials physics, liquid crystals, complex fluids, computational biophysics, QCD-Hadranphysics.

See in-depth description on page 375.

Lakehead University, Graduate Studies, Department of Physics, Thunder Bay, ON P7B 5E1, Canada. Offers M Sc. *Degree requirements:* For master's, thesis or alternative. *Entrance requirements:* For master's, minimum B average. Additional exam requirements/recommendations for international students: Required—TOEFL. *Faculty research:* Absorbed water, radiation reaction, superlattices and quantum well structures, polaron interactions.

Lehigh University, College of Arts and Sciences, Department of Physics, Bethlehem, PA 18015-3094. Offers photonics (MS); physics (MS, PhD). Part-time programs available. *Faculty:* 18 full-time (0 women), 1 part-time/adjunct (0 women). *Students:* 41 full-time (11 women), 3 part-time; includes 18 minority (5 African Americans, 11 Asian Americans or Pacific Islanders, 2 Hispanic Americans), 19 international. 65 applicants, 12% accepted, 6 enrolled. In 2003, 3 master's, 5 doctorates awarded. Terminal master's awarded for partial completion of doctoral program. *Median time to degree:* Master's–1.5 years full-time; doctorate–5 years full-time. *Degree requirements:* For master's, research project; for doctorate, thesis/dissertation, exam. *Entrance requirements:* For doctorate, GRE General Test. Additional exam requirements/recommendations for international students: Required—TOEFL (minimum score 600 paper-based; 235 computer-based); Recommended—TSE. *Application deadline:* For fall admission, 7/15 for domestic students; for spring admission, 1/15 priority date for domestic students. Applications are processed on a rolling basis. Application fee: $50. Electronic applications accepted. *Expenses:* Tuition: Full-time $16,920; part-time $940 per credit hour. Required fees: $200. Tuition and fees vary according to degree level and program. *Financial support:* In 2003–04, 6 fellowships with tuition reimbursements (averaging $15,480 per year), 8 research assistantships with tuition reimbursements (averaging $15,480 per year), 14 teaching assistantships with tuition reimbursements (averaging $15,480 per year) were awarded. Federal Work-Study and institutionally sponsored loans also available. Financial award application deadline: 1/15. *Faculty research:* Condensed matter physics; atomic, molecular and optical physics; plasma physics; complex fluids; computational physics. Total annual research expenditures: $2.3 million. *Unit head:* Dr. Michael J. Stavola, Chair, 610-758-3903, Fax: 610-758-5730, E-mail: mjsa@lehigh.edu. *Application contact:* Dr. A. Peet Hickman, Graduate Admissions Officer, 610-758-3917, Fax: 610-758-5730, E-mail: aph2@lehigh.edu.

See in-depth description on page 379.

Louisiana State University and Agricultural and Mechanical College, Graduate School, College of Basic Sciences, Department of Physics and Astronomy, Baton Rouge, LA 70803. Offers astronomy (PhD); astrophysics (PhD); physics (MS, PhD). *Faculty:* 36 full-time (2 women), 3 part-time/adjunct (0 women). *Students:* 58 full-time (13 women), 1 (woman) part-time; includes 3 minority (2 Asian Americans or Pacific Islanders, 1 Hispanic American), 33 international. Average age 28. 69 applicants, 32% accepted, 13 enrolled. In 2003, 7 master's, 10 doctorates awarded. Terminal master's awarded for partial completion of doctoral program. *Degree requirements:* For master's, thesis or alternative; for doctorate, thesis/dissertation. *Entrance requirements:* For master's and doctorate, GRE General Test, minimum GPA of 3.0. Additional exam requirements/recommendations for international students: Required—TOEFL (minimum score 550 paper-based; 213 computer-based). *Application deadline:* For fall admission, 1/25 priority date for domestic students, 5/15 priority date for international students. Applications are processed on a rolling basis. Application fee: $25. Electronic applications accepted. *Expenses:* Tuition, state resident: part-time $337 per hour. Tuition, nonresident: part-time $577 per hour. *Financial support:* In 2003–04, 15 students received support, including 5 fellowships (averaging $18,000 per year), 28 research assistantships with partial tuition reimbursements available (averaging $18,041 per year), 23 teaching assistantships with partial tuition reimbursements available (averaging $19,196 per year); institutionally sponsored loans and unspecified assistantships also available. Financial award application deadline: 3/15; financial award applicants required to submit FAFSA. *Faculty research:* Experimental and theoretical atomic, nuclear, particle, cosmic-ray, low-temperature, and condensed-matter physics. Total annual research expenditures: $4.9 million. *Unit head:* Dr. Roger McNeil, Chair, 225-578-2261, Fax: 225-578-5855, E-mail: mcneil@phys.lsu.edu. *Application contact:* Dr. James Matthews, Graduate Adviser, 225-578-8598, Fax: 225-578-5855, E-mail: jmatth5@lsu.edu.

Louisiana Tech University, Graduate School, College of Engineering and Science, Department of Physics, Ruston, LA 71272. Offers applied computational analysis and modeling (PhD); physics (MS). Part-time programs available. *Degree requirements:* For master's, thesis or alternative; for doctorate, thesis/dissertation. *Entrance requirements:* For master's, GRE General Test, minimum GPA of 3.0 in last 60 hours. Additional exam requirements/recommendations for international students: Required—TOEFL. *Expenses:* Tuition, state resident: full-time $3,120. Tuition, nonresident: full-time $9,120. Tuition and fees vary according to course load. *Faculty research:* Experimental high energy physics, laser/optics, computational physics, quantum gravity.

Marshall University, Academic Affairs Division, Graduate College, College of Science, Department of Physical Science and Physics, Huntington, WV 25755. Offers physical science (MS). *Faculty:* 5 full-time (0 women), 1 part-time/adjunct (0 women). *Students:* 17 full-time (3 women), 4 part-time (1 woman); includes 2 minority (1 Asian American or Pacific Islander, 1 Hispanic American), 1 international. Average age 29. In 2003, 4 degrees awarded. *Degree requirements:* For master's, thesis optional. *Entrance requirements:* For master's, GRE General Test. Tuition, area resident: Part-time $1,730 per semester. *Expenses:* Tuition, state resident: part-time $3,295 per semester. Tuition, nonresident: part-time $5,003 per semester. *Unit head:* Dr. Nicola Orsini, Chairperson, 304-696-6738, E-mail: orsini@marshall.edu. *Application contact:* Information Contact, 304-746-1900, Fax: 304-746-1902, E-mail: services@marshall.edu.

Massachusetts Institute of Technology, School of Science, Department of Physics, Cambridge, MA 02139-4307. Offers SM, PhD. *Faculty:* 68 full-time (6 women). *Students:* 250 full-time (30 women), 1 part-time; includes 17 minority (2 African Americans, 15 Asian Americans or Pacific Islanders), 114 international. Average age 26. 707 applicants, 18% accepted, 42

Physics

Massachusetts Institute of Technology (continued)
enrolled. In 2003, 6 master's, 31 doctorates awarded. *Degree requirements:* For master's, thesis/dissertation; for doctorate, thesis/dissertation, comprehensive exam. *Entrance requirements:* For master's and doctorate, GRE General Test, GRE Subject Test in physics. Additional exam requirements/recommendations for international students: Required—TOEFL. *Application deadline:* For fall admission, 1/1 for domestic students, 1/1 for international students; for spring admission, 11/1 for domestic students, 11/1 for international students. Application fee: $70. Electronic applications accepted. *Expenses:* Tuition: Full-time $29,400. Required fees: $200. *Financial support:* In 2003–04, 38 fellowships with tuition reimbursements, 181 research assistantships with tuition reimbursements (averaging $23,760 per year), 34 teaching assistantships with tuition reimbursements (averaging $18,270 per year) were awarded. Career-related internships or fieldwork, Federal Work-Study, institutionally sponsored loans, scholarships/grants, health care benefits, and unspecified assistantships also available. *Faculty research:* Particle/QCD physics, condensed matter physics, atomic physics, astro physics, string theory. Total annual research expenditures: $47.6 million. *Unit head:* Prof. Marc A. Kastner, Head, 617-253-4801, Fax: 617-253-8554. *Application contact:* Department of Physics, 617-253-4841, E-mail: physics@mit.edu.

McGill University, Faculty of Graduate and Postdoctoral Studies, Faculty of Science, Department of Physics, Montréal, QC H3A 2T5, Canada. Offers M Sc, PhD. *Faculty:* 28 full-time (2 women). *Students:* 107 full-time, 1 part-time. Average age 25. 162 applicants, 32% accepted, 35 enrolled. In 2003, 7 master's, 9 doctorates awarded. Terminal master's awarded for partial completion of doctoral program. *Degree requirements:* For master's and doctorate, thesis/dissertation. *Entrance requirements:* For master's and doctorate, minimum GPA of 3.30. Additional exam requirements/recommendations for international students: Required—TOEFL. *Application deadline:* For fall admission, 2/1 for domestic students; for winter admission, 8/1 for domestic students. Applications are processed on a rolling basis. Application fee: $60 Canadian dollars. Tuition, area resident: Full-time $1,668. *Expenses:* Tuition, state resident: full-time $4,173. Tuition, nonresident: full-time $9,468. Required fees: $1,081. *Financial support:* In 2003–04, teaching assistantships (averaging $3,300 per year); fellowships, research assistantships, tuition waivers (partial) and bursaries also available. Financial award application deadline: 2/1. *Faculty research:* High-energy, condensed-matter, and nuclear physics; biophysics; mathphysics; geophysics/atmospheric physics; astrophysics. *Unit head:* Prof. Charles Gale, Graduate Program Director, 514-398-6495, Fax: 514-398-8434, E-mail: gale@physics.mcgill.ca. *Application contact:* Paula Domingues, Student Affairs Assistant, 514-398-6485, Fax: 514-398-8434, E-mail: paula.domingues@mcgill.ca.

McMaster University, School of Graduate Studies, Faculty of Science, Department of Physics and Astronomy, Hamilton, ON L8S 4M2, Canada. Offers astrophysics (PhD); medical physics and applied radiation sciences (M Sc, PhD), including health and radiation physics (M Sc), medical physics; physics (PhD). Part-time programs available. *Degree requirements:* For master's, thesis or alternative; for doctorate, thesis/dissertation, comprehensive exam. *Entrance requirements:* For master's and doctorate, minimum B+ average. Additional exam requirements/recommendations for international students: Required—TOEFL (minimum score 550 paper-based; 213 computer-based). *Faculty research:* Condensed matter, astrophysics, nuclear, medical, nonlinear dynamics.

Memorial University of Newfoundland, School of Graduate Studies, Department of Physics and Physical Oceanography, St. John's, NL A1C 5S7, Canada. Offers physical oceanography (M Sc, PhD); physics (M Sc, PhD). Part-time programs available. *Students:* 26 full-time. 51 applicants, 22% accepted, 8 enrolled. In 2003, 1 degree awarded. *Degree requirements:* For master's, thesis; for doctorate, thesis/dissertation, oral defense of thesis, comprehensive exam. *Entrance requirements:* For master's, honors B Sc or equivalent; for doctorate, M Sc or equivalent. *Application deadline:* Applications are processed on a rolling basis. Application fee: $40. Electronic applications accepted. Tuition and fees charges are reported in Canadian dollars. *Expenses:* Tuition, state resident: part-time $733 Canadian dollars per semester. Tuition, nonresident: part-time $953 Canadian dollars per semester. Required fees: $194 Canadian dollars per year. Tuition and fees vary according to degree level and program. *Financial support:* Fellowships, research assistantships, teaching assistantships available. *Faculty research:* Experiment and theory in atomic and molecular physics. Total annual research expenditures: $2.1 million. *Unit head:* Dr. John Whitehead, Head, 709-737-8737, Fax: 709-737-8739, E-mail: johnw@physics.mun.ca. *Application contact:* Dr. Jolanta Lagowski, Deputy Head, Graduate Studies, 709-737-2113, Fax: 709-737-8739, E-mail: gradap@physics.mun.ca.

Miami University, Graduate School, College of Arts and Sciences, Department of Physics, Oxford, OH 45056. Offers MS. Part-time programs available. *Faculty:* 14 full-time (2 women), 1 part-time/adjunct (0 women). *Students:* 13 full-time (3 women), 1 part-time; includes 1 minority (Hispanic American), 6 international. 32 applicants, 84% accepted, 9 enrolled. In 2003, 7 degrees awarded. *Degree requirements:* For master's, final exam. *Entrance requirements:* For master's, minimum undergraduate GPA of 3.0 during previous 2 years or 2.75 overall. Additional exam requirements/recommendations for international students: Required—TOEFL, TWE. *Application deadline:* For fall admission, 3/1 priority date for domestic students, 3/1 priority date for international students. Applications are processed on a rolling basis. Application fee: $35. Electronic applications accepted. Tuition, area resident: Full-time $9,346. International tuition: $19,924 full-time. Full-time tuition and fees vary according to course level and campus/location. *Financial support:* In 2003–04, 16 fellowships with full tuition reimbursements (averaging $12,452 per year), 1 research assistantship (averaging $12,452 per year) were awarded. Teaching assistantships, Federal Work-Study, tuition waivers (full), and unspecified assistantships also available. Financial award application deadline: 3/1. *Unit head:* Dr. Michael Pechan, Acting Chair, 513-529-5625, Fax: 513-529-5629, E-mail: physics@muohio.edu. *Application contact:* Dr. Steve Alexander, Director of Graduate Studies, E-mail: physics@muohio.edu.

Michigan State University, Graduate School, College of Natural Science, Department of Physics and Astronomy, East Lansing, MI 48824. Offers astrophysics and astronomy (MS, PhD); physics (MS, PhD). *Faculty:* 52 full-time (2 women). *Students:* 128 full-time (21 women), 5 part-time; includes 5 minority (1 American Indian/Alaska Native, 3 Asian Americans or Pacific Islanders, 1 Hispanic American), 72 international. Average age 28. 291 applicants, 6% accepted. In 2003, 27 master's, 13 doctorates awarded. *Degree requirements:* For master's, qualifying exam, thesis optional; for doctorate, thesis/dissertation, qualifying exam, comprehensive exam. *Entrance requirements:* For master's and doctorate, minimum GPA of 3.0 in science/math courses, course work equivalent to a major in physics or astronomy, 3 letters of recommendation. Additional exam requirements/recommendations for international students: Required—TOEFL (minimum score 550 paper-based; 213 computer-based), Michigan State University ELT (85), Michigan ELAB (83). *Application deadline:* For fall admission, 1/15 for domestic students; for spring admission, 9/30 for domestic students. Application fee: $50. Electronic applications accepted. *Expenses:* Tuition, state resident: part-time $291 per hour. Tuition, nonresident: part-time $589 per hour. *Financial support:* In 2003–04, 14 fellowships with tuition reimbursements (averaging $7,077 per year), 18 research assistantships with tuition reimbursements (averaging $13,681 per year), 39 teaching assistantships with tuition reimbursements (averaging $12,741 per year) were awarded. Financial award applicants required to submit FAFSA. *Faculty research:* Nuclear and accelerator physics, high-energy physics, condensed-matter physics, astrophysics and astronomy, biophysics. Total annual research expenditures: $4.8 million. *Unit head:* Dr. Wolfgang Bauer, Chairperson, 517-355-9200 Ext. 2015, Fax: 517-355-4500. *Application contact:* Dr. S. D. Mahanti, Director of Graduate Studies, 517-355-9200 Ext. 2303, Fax: 517-355-4500, E-mail: mahanti@pa.msu.edu.

See in-depth description on page 381.

Michigan Technological University, Graduate School, College of Sciences and Arts, Department of Physics, Houghton, MI 49931-1295. Offers engineering physics (PhD); physics (MS, PhD). Part-time programs available. *Faculty:* 17 full-time (1 woman). *Students:* 33 full-time (5 women), 1 part-time, 27 international. Average age 28. 51 applicants, 37% accepted, 7 enrolled. In 2003, 1 master's, 2 doctorates awarded. *Degree requirements:* For master's, comprehensive exam, registration; for doctorate, thesis/dissertation, comprehensive exam, registration. *Entrance requirements:* Additional exam requirements/recommendations for international students: Required—TOEFL. *Application deadline:* For fall admission, 3/15 for domestic students. Applications are processed on a rolling basis. Application fee: $40 ($45 for international students). Electronic applications accepted. Tuition, nonresident: full-time $9,552; part-time $398 per credit. Required fees: $768. *Financial support:* In 2003–04, 23 students received support, including 1 fellowship with full tuition reimbursement available (averaging $13,500 per year), 10 research assistantships with full tuition reimbursements available (averaging $8,950 per year), 12 teaching assistantships with full tuition reimbursements available (averaging $8,950 per year); career-related internships or fieldwork, Federal Work-Study, institutionally sponsored loans, scholarships/grants, traineeships, unspecified assistantships, and co-op also available. Support available to part-time students. Financial award application deadline: 3/1; financial award applicants required to submit FAFSA. *Faculty research:* Computational quantum/statistical physics, atmospheric physics, astrophysics, nano-material/laser physics, biophysics. Total annual research expenditures: $1.3 million. *Unit head:* Dr. Ravindra Pandey, Chair, 906-487-2831, Fax: 906-487-2933, E-mail: pandey@mtu.edu. *Application contact:* Elizabeth A. Pollins, Coordinator, 906-487-2086, Fax: 906-487-2933, E-mail: epollins@mtu.edu.

Announcement: Michigan Technological University offers MS and PhD degrees in physics. Research areas include biomolecular modeling, condensed matter and materials physics, atomic and molecular physics, astrophysics, and atmospheric physics. Teaching and research assistantships and fellowships are available. For more information, contact Department of Physics, Michigan Technological University, 1400 Townsend Drive, Houghton, MI 49931-1295 or visit http://www.phy.mtu.edu/engphysics.html.

See in-depth description on page 383.

Minnesota State University Mankato, College of Graduate Studies, College of Science, Engineering and Technology, Department of Physics and Astronomy, Mankato, MN 56001. Offers MS, MT. *Faculty:* 7 full-time (1 woman). *Students:* 4 full-time (3 women), 3 part-time (1 woman). Average age 34. In 2003, 1 degree awarded. *Degree requirements:* For master's, one foreign language, thesis or alternative, comprehensive exam. *Entrance requirements:* For master's, minimum GPA of 3.0 during previous 2 years. *Application deadline:* For fall admission, 7/9 for domestic students; for spring admission, 11/27 for domestic students. Applications are processed on a rolling basis. Application fee: $40. *Expenses:* Tuition, state resident: part-time $226 per credit hour. Tuition, nonresident: part-time $339 per credit hour. Tuition and fees vary according to reciprocity agreements. *Financial support:* Research assistantships, teaching assistantships with full tuition reimbursements, Federal Work-Study and unspecified assistantships available. Support available to part-time students. Financial award application deadline: 3/15; financial award applicants required to submit FAFSA. *Unit head:* Dr. Sandford Schuster, Chairperson, 507-389-5743. *Application contact:* Joni Roberts, Admissions Coordinator, 507-389-5244, Fax: 507-389-5974, E-mail: grad@mankato.msus.edu.

Mississippi State University, College of Arts and Sciences, Department of Physics and Astronomy, Mississippi State, MS 39762. Offers engineering physics (PhD); physics (MS). Part-time programs available. *Faculty:* 16 full-time (1 woman), 5 part-time/adjunct (1 woman). *Students:* 12 full-time (3 women), 3 part-time; includes 2 minority (both African Americans), 9 international. Average age 29. 10 applicants, 70% accepted, 5 enrolled. In 2003, 3 degrees awarded. *Degree requirements:* For master's and doctorate, thesis/dissertation, comprehensive oral or written exam. *Entrance requirements:* Additional exam requirements/recommendations for international students: Required—TOEFL, TSE. *Application deadline:* For fall admission, 7/1 for domestic students; for spring admission, 11/1 priority date for domestic students. Applications are processed on a rolling basis. Application fee: $25 for international students. Electronic applications accepted. *Expenses:* Tuition, state resident: full-time $3,874; part-time $215 per hour. Tuition, nonresident: full-time $8,780; part-time $488 per hour. International tuition: $9,105 full-time. Tuition and fees vary according to course load. *Financial support:* In 2003–04, 3 research assistantships with full tuition reimbursements (averaging $13,064 per year), 7 teaching assistantships with full tuition reimbursements (averaging $8,838 per year) were awarded. Federal Work-Study, institutionally sponsored loans, and unspecified assistantships also available. Financial award application deadline: 3/15; financial award applicants required to submit FAFSA. *Faculty research:* Atomic/molecular spectroscopy, theoretical optics, gamma-ray astronomy, experimental nuclear physics, computational physics. Total annual research expenditures: $965,602. *Unit head:* Dr. Mark A. Novotny, Head, 662-325-2806, Fax: 662-325-8898, E-mail: man40@ra.msstate.edu. *Application contact:* Diane D. Wolfe, Director of Admissions, 662-325-2224, Fax: 662-325-7360, E-mail: admit@admissions.msstate.edu.

Montana State University–Bozeman, College of Graduate Studies, College of Letters and Science, Department of Physics, Bozeman, MT 59717. Offers MS, PhD. Part-time programs available. *Faculty:* 15 full-time (2 women), 4 part-time/adjunct (1 woman). *Students:* 39 full-time (9 women), 6 part-time (2 women), 12 international. Average age 29. 51 applicants, 41% accepted, 13 enrolled. In 2003, 6 master's, 4 doctorates awarded. *Degree requirements:* For master's, thesis (for some programs), comprehensive exam, registration; for doctorate, thesis/dissertation, comprehensive exam, registration. *Entrance requirements:* For master's and doctorate, GRE General Test. Additional exam requirements/recommendations for international students: Required—TOEFL (minimum score 550 paper-based; 213 computer-based). *Application deadline:* For fall admission, 7/15 priority date for domestic students, 5/15 priority date for international students; for spring admission, 12/1 priority date for domestic students, 10/1 priority date for international students. Applications are processed on a rolling basis. Application fee: $50. Electronic applications accepted. *Expenses:* Tuition, state resident: full-time $3,907; part-time $163 per credit. Tuition, nonresident: full-time $12,383; part-time $516 per credit. Required fees: $890; $445 per term. Tuition and fees vary according to course load and program. *Financial support:* In 2003–04, 43 students received support, including 4 fellowships with full and partial tuition reimbursements available (averaging $16,666 per year), 27 research assistantships with full and partial tuition reimbursements available (averaging $16,666 per year), 12 teaching assistantships with full and partial tuition reimbursements available (averaging $16,666 per year) Financial award application deadline: 3/1; financial award applicants required to submit FAFSA. *Faculty research:* Astrophysics, relativity and cosmology, condensed matter, materials and surface science. optics. Total annual research expenditures: $7.9 million. *Unit head:* Dr. William Hiscock, Head, 406-994-3614, Fax: 406-994-4452, E-mail: hiscock@physics.montana.edu.

Morgan State University, School of Graduate Studies, School of Computer, Mathematical, and Natural Sciences, Department of Biology, Interdisciplinary Program in Science, Baltimore, MD 21251. Offers science (MS), including biology, chemistry, physics. *Students:* 14; includes 11 minority (all African Americans), 3 international. In 2003, 2 degrees awarded. *Degree requirements:* For master's, thesis, comprehensive exam. *Entrance requirements:* For master's, GRE, minimum GPA of 2.5. Additional exam requirements/recommendations for international students: Required—TOEFL (minimum score 550 paper-based; 213 computer-based). *Application deadline:* For fall admission, 2/1 for domestic students; for spring admission, 10/1 for domestic students. Applications are processed on a rolling basis. Application fee: $0. *Expenses:* Tuition, state resident: part-time $215 per credit hour. Tuition, nonresident: part-time $409 per credit hour. Required fees: $48 per credit hour. *Application contact:* Dr. James E. Waller, Admissions and Programs Officer, 443-885-3185, Fax: 443-885-8226, E-mail: jwaller@moac.morgan.edu.

Naval Postgraduate School, Graduate Programs, Department of Physics, Monterey, CA 93943. Offers MS, PhD. Program only open to commissioned officers of the United States and friendly nations and selected United States federal civilian employees. Part-time programs available. *Degree requirements:* For master's, thesis; for doctorate, one foreign language, thesis/dissertation.

New Mexico Institute of Mining and Technology, Graduate Studies, Department of Physics, Socorro, NM 87801. Offers astrophysics (MS, PhD); atmospheric physics (MS, PhD); instrumentation (MS); mathematical physics (PhD). *Faculty:* 14 full-time (2 women), 19 part-time/adjunct (2 women). *Students:* 19 full-time (5 women), 2 part-time (1 woman); includes 2 minority (1 Asian American or Pacific Islander, 1 Hispanic American), 3 international. Average age 28. 21 applicants, 5 enrolled. In 2003, 1 master's, 3 doctorates awarded. *Degree requirements:* For master's, thesis optional; for doctorate, thesis/dissertation. *Entrance requirements:* For master's, GRE General Test; for doctorate, GRE General Test, GRE Subject Test. Additional exam requirements/recommendations for international students: Required—TOEFL (minimum score 540 paper-based; 207 computer-based). *Application deadline:* For fall admission, 3/1 for domestic students; for spring admission, 6/1 for domestic students. Applications are processed on a rolling basis. Application fee: $16 ($30 for international students). *Expenses:* Tuition, state resident: full-time $2,276; part-time $126 per credit. Tuition, nonresident: full-time $9,170; part-time $509 per credit. Required fees: $924; $27 per credit. $214 per term. Part-time tuition and fees vary according to course load. *Financial support:* In 2003–04, 10 research assistantships (averaging $14,242 per year), 10 teaching assistantships with full and partial tuition reimbursements (averaging $9,600 per year) were awarded. Fellowships, Federal Work-Study, institutionally sponsored loans, and unspecified assistantships also available. Financial award application deadline: 3/1; financial award applicants required to submit CSS PROFILE or FAFSA. *Faculty research:* Cloud physics, stellar and extragalactic processes. *Unit head:* Dr. Kenneth Minschwaner, Chairman, 505-835-5226, Fax: 505-835-5707, E-mail: krm@kestrel.nmt.edu. *Application contact:* Dr. David B. Johnson, Dean of Graduate Studies, 505-835-5513, Fax: 505-835-5476, E-mail: graduate@nmt.edu.

New Mexico State University, Graduate School, College of Arts and Sciences, Department of Physics, Las Cruces, NM 88003-8001. Offers MS, PhD. Part-time programs available. *Faculty:* 9 full-time (0 women), 9 part-time/adjunct (1 woman). *Students:* 34 full-time (3 women), 3 part-time; includes 5 minority (1 Asian American or Pacific Islander, 4 Hispanic Americans), 21 international. Average age 30. 32 applicants, 78% accepted, 7 enrolled. In 2003, 2 master's, 10 doctorates awarded. Terminal master's awarded for partial completion of doctoral program. *Median time to degree:* Of those who began their doctoral program in fall 1995, 100% received their degree in 8 years or less. *Degree requirements:* For master's, thesis optional; for doctorate, thesis/dissertation, comprehensive exam. *Entrance requirements:* For master's and doctorate, GRE General Test, GRE Subject Test. Additional exam requirements/recommendations for international students: Required—TOEFL. *Application deadline:* For fall admission, 3/1 priority date for domestic students, 3/1 priority date for international students; for spring admission, 10/1 priority date for domestic students, 10/1 priority date for international students. Applications are processed on a rolling basis. Application fee: $30 ($50 for international students). Electronic applications accepted. *Expenses:* Tuition, state resident: full-time $2,670; part-time $151 per credit. Tuition, nonresident: full-time $10,596; part-time $481 per credit. Required fees: $954. *Financial support:* In 2003–04, 13 research assistantships, 18 teaching assistantships were awarded. Financial award application deadline: 3/15. *Faculty research:* Nuclear and particle physics, optics, materials science, geophysics, physics education, atmospheric physics. *Unit head:* Dr. Gary S. Kyle, Head, 505-646-3831, Fax: 505-646-1934, E-mail: kyle@nmsu.edu. *Application contact:* Dr. Matthias Burkhardt, Information Contact, 505-646-1928, Fax: 505-646-1934, E-mail: physics@nmsu.edu.

New York University, Graduate School of Arts and Science, Department of Physics, New York, NY 10012-1019. Offers MS, PhD. Part-time programs available. *Faculty:* 25 full-time (1 woman), 5 part-time/adjunct. *Students:* 46 full-time (5 women), 2 part-time; includes 1 minority (Hispanic American), 39 international. Average age 27. 224 applicants, 12% accepted. In 2003, 2 master's, 6 doctorates awarded. Terminal master's awarded for partial completion of doctoral program. *Degree requirements:* For master's, thesis (for some programs); for doctorate, one foreign language, thesis/dissertation, research seminar, teaching experience. *Entrance requirements:* For master's, GRE General Test, GRE Subject Test, bachelor's degree in physics; for doctorate, GRE General Test, GRE Subject Test. Additional exam requirements/recommendations for international students: Required—TOEFL. *Application deadline:* For fall admission, 1/4 for domestic students. Application fee: $75. *Expenses:* Tuition: Full-time $22,056; part-time $919 per credit. Required fees: $1,664; $49 per credit. Tuition and fees vary according to course load and program. *Financial support:* Fellowships with tuition reimbursements, research assistantships with tuition reimbursements, teaching assistantships with tuition reimbursements, Federal Work-Study and institutionally sponsored loans available. Financial award application deadline: 1/4; financial award applicants required to submit FAFSA. *Faculty research:* Atomic physics, elementary particles and fields, astrophysics, condensed-matter physics, neuromagnetism. *Unit head:* Allen Mincer, Chairman, 212-998-7700, Fax: 212-995-4016, E-mail: dgsphys@nyu.edu. *Application contact:* Len Rosenberg, Director of Graduate Studies, 212-998-7700, Fax: 212-995-4016, E-mail: dgsphys@nyu.edu.

North Carolina State University, Graduate School, College of Physical and Mathematical Sciences, Department of Physics, Raleigh, NC 27695. Offers MS, PhD. Part-time programs available. *Faculty:* 47 full-time (7 women), 18 part-time/adjunct (2 women). *Students:* 92 full-time (10 women), 6 part-time (1 woman); includes 12 minority (10 African Americans, 1 American Indian/Alaska Native, 1 Asian American or Pacific Islander), 29 international. Average age 30. 76 applicants, 53% accepted. In 2003, 10 master's, 10 doctorates awarded. Terminal master's awarded for partial completion of doctoral program. *Degree requirements:* For master's, thesis (for some programs); for doctorate, thesis/dissertation. *Entrance requirements:* For master's and doctorate, GRE General Test, GRE Subject Test. *Application deadline:* For fall admission, 6/25 for domestic students, 3/1 for international students; for spring admission, 11/25 for domestic students, 7/15 for international students. Applications are processed on a rolling basis. Application fee: $45. *Expenses:* Tuition, state resident: part-time $396 per hour. Tuition, nonresident: part-time $1,895 per hour. *Financial support:* In 2003–04, 4 fellowships with tuition reimbursements (averaging $8,295 per year), 44 research assistantships with tuition reimbursements (averaging $6,905 per year), 42 teaching assistantships with tuition reimbursements (averaging $7,039 per year) were awarded. Institutionally sponsored loans also available. Financial award application deadline: 3/1. *Faculty research:* Astrophysics, optics, physics education, biophysics, geophysics. Total annual research expenditures: $5.6 million. *Unit head:* Dr. Christopher Gould, Head, 919-515-2522, Fax: 919-515-6538, E-mail: chris_gould@ncsu.edu. *Application contact:* Dr. Michael A. Paesler, Director of Graduate Programs, 919-515-8706, Fax: 919-515-3099, E-mail: paesler@ncsu.edu.

North Dakota State University, The Graduate School, College of Science and Mathematics, Department of Physics, Fargo, ND 58105. Offers MS, PhD. Part-time programs available. *Faculty:* 7 full-time (0 women), 4 part-time/adjunct (0 women). *Students:* 5 full-time (0 women); includes 4 minority (all Asian Americans or Pacific Islanders) Average age 25. 11 applicants, 0% accepted.Terminal master's awarded for partial completion of doctoral program. *Degree requirements:* For master's and doctorate, thesis/dissertation. *Entrance requirements:* Additional exam requirements/recommendations for international students: Required—TOEFL. *Application deadline:* For fall admission, 3/1 for domestic students. Applications are processed on a rolling basis. Application fee: $35 ($50 for international students). Tuition, nonresident: full-time $4,071. Required fees: $493. *Financial support:* In 2003–04, 3 students received support, including 2 research assistantships with tuition reimbursements available (averaging $16,000 per year), teaching assistantships with tuition reimbursements available (averaging $12,000 per year); career-related internships or fieldwork, scholarships/grants, and unspecified assistantships also available. Support available to part-time students. Financial award application deadline: 4/15; financial award applicants required to submit FAFSA. *Faculty research:* Biophysics; condensed matter; surface physics; general relativity, gravitation, and space physics; nonlinear physics, atmospheric physics. Total annual research expenditures: $122,730. *Unit head:* Dr. Charles Sawicki, Chair, 701-231-8968. *Application contact:* Dr. Alexander Wagner, Graduate Advisory Committee Chair, 701-231-9582, Fax: 701-231-7088, E-mail: alexander.wagner@ndsu.nodak.edu.

Northeastern University, College of Arts and Sciences, Department of Physics, Boston, MA 02115-5096. Offers MS, PhD. Part-time programs available. *Faculty:* 28 full-time (1 woman), 6 part-time/adjunct (2 women). *Students:* 64 full-time (11 women), 2 part-time (1 woman). Average age 30. 32 applicants, 97% accepted. In 2003, 4 master's, 5 doctorates awarded. Terminal master's awarded for partial completion of doctoral program. *Degree requirements:* For master's, thesis optional; for doctorate, thesis/dissertation. *Entrance requirements:* Additional exam requirements/recommendations for international students: Required—TOEFL. *Application deadline:* For fall admission, 4/15 for domestic students. Application fee: $50. *Expenses:* Tuition: Part-time $790 per credit hour. Tuition and fees vary according to course load and program. *Financial support:* In 2003–04, 32 teaching assistantships with tuition reimbursements (averaging $15,190 per year) were awarded; research assistantships with tuition reimbursements, Federal Work-Study, tuition waivers (full and partial), and unspecified assistantships also available. Financial award application deadline: 2/15; financial award applicants required to submit FAFSA. *Faculty research:* High-energy theory and experimentation, astrophysics, biophysics, condensed-matter theory and experimentation. *Unit head:* Dr. Jorge Jose, Chairman, 617-373-2902, Fax: 617-373-2943, E-mail: gradphysics@neu.edu. *Application contact:* Sara Simeone, Administrative Secretary, 617-373-4240, Fax: 617-373-2943, E-mail: gradphysics@neu.edu.

See in-depth description on page 387.

Northern Illinois University, Graduate School, College of Liberal Arts and Sciences, Department of Physics, De Kalb, IL 60115-2854. Offers MS, PhD. Part-time programs available. *Faculty:* 18 full-time (3 women), 3 part-time/adjunct (0 women). *Students:* 28 full-time (8 women), 22 part-time (4 women); includes 5 minority (3 African Americans, 2 Asian Americans or Pacific Islanders), 19 international. Average age 31. 30 applicants, 70% accepted, 17 enrolled. In 2003, 6 degrees awarded. Terminal master's awarded for partial completion of doctoral program. *Degree requirements:* For master's, thesis or alternative, research seminar, comprehensive exam; for doctorate, thesis/dissertation, candidacy exam, dissertation defense, research seminar. *Entrance requirements:* For master's, GRE General Test, minimum GPA of 2.75; for doctorate, GRE General Test, GRE Subject Test (physics), bachelor's degree in physics or related field, minimum GPA of 3.2 (graduate), 2.75 (undergraduate). Additional exam requirements/recommendations for international students: Required—TOEFL (minimum score 550 paper-based; 213 computer-based). *Application deadline:* For fall admission, 6/1 for domestic students, 5/1 for international students; for spring admission, 11/1 for domestic students, 10/1 for international students. Applications are processed on a rolling basis. Application fee: $30. Electronic applications accepted. *Expenses:* Tuition, state resident: full-time $3,968; part-time $165 per credit hour. Tuition, nonresident: full-time $7,936; part-time $330 per credit hour. Required fees: $1,255; $52 per credit hour. *Financial support:* In 2003–04, 18 research assistantships with full tuition reimbursements, 21 teaching assistantships with full tuition reimbursements were awarded. Fellowships with full tuition reimbursements, career-related internships or fieldwork, Federal Work-Study, scholarships/grants, and unspecified assistantships also available. Support available to part-time students. Financial award applicants required to submit FAFSA. *Unit head:* Dr. Susan Mini, Chair, 815-753-6470, Fax: 815-753-8565. *Application contact:* Dr. David Hedin, Director of Graduate Studies, 815-753-6483, E-mail: dhedin@niu.edu.

Northwestern University, The Graduate School, Judd A. and Marjorie Weinberg College of Arts and Sciences, Department of Physics and Astronomy, Evanston, IL 60208. Offers astrophysics (PhD); physics (MS, PhD). Admissions and degrees offered through The Graduate School. Terminal master's awarded for partial completion of doctoral program. *Degree requirements:* For doctorate, thesis/dissertation, qualifying exam. *Entrance requirements:* For doctorate, GRE General Test, GRE Subject Test. Additional exam requirements/recommendations for international students: Required—TOEFL. *Faculty research:* Nuclear and particle physics, condensed-matter physics, nonlinear physics, astrophysics.

Oakland University, Graduate Study and Lifelong Learning, College of Arts and Sciences, Department of Physics, Rochester, MI 48309-4401. Offers medical physics (PhD); physics (MS). *Faculty:* 10 full-time (1 woman). *Students:* 12 full-time (4 women), 2 part-time, 4 international. Average age 29. 9 applicants, 78% accepted. In 2003, 1 degree awarded. *Degree requirements:* For doctorate, thesis/dissertation. *Entrance requirements:* For master's, minimum GPA of 3.0 for unconditional admission; for doctorate, GRE Subject Test, GRE General Test, minimum GPA of 3.0 for unconditional admission. Additional exam requirements/recommendations for international students: Required—TOEFL (minimum score 550 paper-based; 213 computer-based). *Application deadline:* For fall admission, 7/15 priority date for domestic students, 5/1 priority date for international students; for winter admission, 12/1 for domestic students; for spring admission, 3/15 for domestic students. Applications are processed on a rolling basis. Application fee: $30. Electronic applications accepted. *Expenses:* Contact institution. *Financial support:* Fellowships, career-related internships or fieldwork, Federal Work-Study, institutionally sponsored loans, and tuition waivers (full) available. Financial award application deadline: 3/1; financial award applicants required to submit FAFSA. *Faculty research:* High pressure Raman studies of modified forms of carbon nanotubes, microscopic MRI T2 anistrapy in articular cartilage, giant magnetoelectric effects, studies in singularities. Total annual research expenditures: $491,507. *Unit head:* Dr. Andrei N. Slavin, Interim Chair, 248-370-3416, Fax: 248-370-3401, E-mail: slavin@oakland.edu.

The Ohio State University, Graduate School, College of Mathematical and Physical Sciences, Department of Physics, Columbus, OH 43210. Offers MS, PhD. *Faculty:* 61. *Students:* 130 full-time (20 women), 8 part-time; includes 6 minority (2 African Americans, 1 Asian American or Pacific Islander, 3 Hispanic Americans), 67 international. 548 applicants, 18% accepted. In 2003, 16 master's, 16 doctorates awarded. *Degree requirements:* For master's, thesis optional; for doctorate, thesis/dissertation. *Entrance requirements:* For master's and doctorate, GRE General Test, GRE Subject Test. *Application deadline:* For fall admission, 8/15 for domestic students. Applications are processed on a rolling basis. Application fee: $40 ($50 for international students). *Expenses:* Tuition, state resident: full-time $7,233. Tuition, nonresident: full-time $18,489. *Financial support:* Fellowships, research assistantships, teaching assistantships, Federal Work-Study and institutionally sponsored loans available. Support available to part-time students. *Unit head:* Dr. William F. Saam, Chair, 614-292-1772, Fax: 614-292-7557, E-mail: saam.1@osu.edu. *Application contact:* Dr. Thomas J. Humanic, Graduate Studies Committee Chair, 614-292-4775, Fax: 614-292-7557, E-mail: humanic@mps.ohio-state.edu.

Ohio University, Graduate Studies, College of Arts and Sciences, Department of Physics and Astronomy, Athens, OH 45701-2979. Offers physics (MS, PhD). *Students:* 72 full-time (16 women), 61 international. Average age 27. 166 applicants, 31% accepted, 19 enrolled. In 2003, 12 master's, 5 doctorates awarded. Terminal master's awarded for partial completion of doctoral program. *Degree requirements:* For master's, thesis or alternative; for doctorate, thesis/dissertation, comprehensive exam. *Entrance requirements:* Additional exam requirements/recommendations for international students: Required—TOEFL (minimum score 600 paper-based; 250 computer-based). *Application deadline:* For fall admission, 4/1 priority date for domestic students, 4/1 priority date for international students. Applications are processed on a rolling basis. Application fee: $30. *Expenses:* Tuition, state resident: full-time $2,651; part-time $328 per credit. Tuition, nonresident: full-time $5,095; part-time $632 per credit. Tuition and fees vary according to program. *Financial support:* In 2003–04, 67 students received support, including 2 fellowships with full tuition reimbursements available, 30 research assistantships with full tuition reimbursements available (averaging $19,000 per year), 40 teaching assistantships with full tuition reimbursements available (averaging $15,600 per year); Federal Work-Study and institutionally sponsored loans also available. Financial award application deadline: 4/1. *Faculty research:* Nuclear physics, condensed-matter physics, nonlinear systems, acoustics, astrophysics. Total annual research expenditures: $3 million. *Unit head:* Dr. Louis E. Wright, Chair, 740-593-1713, Fax: 740-593-0433, E-mail: wright@ohiou.edu. *Application contact:* Dr. Arthur Smith, Graduate Admissions Chair, 740-593-0336, Fax: 740-593-0433, E-mail: gradapp@phy.ohiou.edu.

See in-depth description on page 391.

Oklahoma State University, Graduate College, College of Arts and Sciences, Department of Physics, Stillwater, OK 74078. Offers photonics (MS, PhD); physics (MS, PhD). *Faculty:* 27

Physics

Oklahoma State University (continued)
full-time (4 women), 1 (woman) part-time/adjunct. *Students:* 14 full-time (4 women), 23 part-time (3 women), 24 international. Average age 28. 26 applicants, 88% accepted. In 2003, 1 degree awarded. *Degree requirements:* For master's, thesis or report; for doctorate, thesis/dissertation, oral defense of dissertation, preliminary exam, qualifying exam. *Entrance requirements:* Additional exam requirements/recommendations for international students: Required—TOEFL. *Application deadline:* For fall admission, 3/15 for domestic students. Applications are processed on a rolling basis. Application fee: $25 ($50 for international students). Electronic applications accepted. *Expenses:* Tuition, state resident: full-time $3,752; part-time $118 per credit hour. Tuition, nonresident: full-time $10,346; part-time $393 per credit hour. Tuition and fees vary according to course load. *Financial support:* In 2003–04, 24 research assistantships (averaging $16,516 per year), 26 teaching assistantships with partial tuition reimbursements (averaging $14,806 per year) were awarded. Federal Work-Study, traineeships, tuition waivers (partial), and unspecified assistantships also available. Support available to part-time students. Financial award application deadline: 3/1. *Faculty research:* Lasers and photonics, non-linear optical materials, turbulence, structure and function of biological membranes, particle theory. *Unit head:* Dr. John Mintmire, Head, 405-744-5796. *Application contact:* Dr. Paul A. Westhaus, Graduate Coordinator, 405-744-5815, E-mail: physpaw@okstate.edu.

Old Dominion University, College of Sciences, Program in Physics, Norfolk, VA 23529. Offers MS, PhD. *Faculty:* 18 full-time (2 women). *Students:* 30 full-time (9 women), 4 part-time, 23 international. Average age 30. 19 applicants, 68% accepted. In 2003, 3 master's, 6 doctorates awarded. Terminal master's awarded for partial completion of doctoral program. *Median time to degree:* Of those who began their doctoral program in fall 1995, 100% received their degree in 8 years or less. *Degree requirements:* For master's, thesis optional; for doctorate, thesis/dissertation, comprehensive exam. *Entrance requirements:* For master's, BS in physics or related field, minimum GPA of 3.0 in major; for doctorate, GRE General Test, minimum GPA of 3.0. Additional exam requirements/recommendations for international students: Required—TOEFL. *Application deadline:* For fall admission, 7/1 for domestic students, 7/1 for international students. Applications are processed on a rolling basis. Application fee: $30 ($40 for international students). Electronic applications accepted. *Expenses:* Tuition, state resident: part-time $235 per credit hour. Tuition, nonresident: part-time $603 per credit hour. Part-time tuition and fees vary according to campus/location. *Financial support:* In 2003–04, 4 research assistantships with full tuition reimbursements (averaging $19,500 per year), 8 teaching assistantships with full tuition reimbursements (averaging $19,500 per year) were awarded. Fellowships, career-related internships or fieldwork, scholarships/grants, and tuition waivers (partial) also available. Support available to part-time students. Financial award application deadline: 2/15; financial award applicants required to submit FAFSA. *Faculty research:* Atomic physics, condensed-matter physics, plasma physics, ultra-cold physics, nuclear and particle physics. Total annual research expenditures: $1.2 million. *Unit head:* Dr. Larry Weinstein, Graduate Program Director, 757-683-5803, Fax: 757-683-3038, E-mail: physgpd@odu.edu.

Oregon State University, Graduate School, College of Science, Department of Physics, Corvallis, OR 97331. Offers MA, MS, PhD. Part-time programs available. *Faculty:* 11 full-time (2 women). *Students:* 31 full-time (6 women), 2 part-time; includes 1 minority (Asian American or Pacific Islander), 8 international. Average age 30. In 2003, 2 master's, 7 doctorates awarded. Terminal master's awarded for partial completion of doctoral program. *Degree requirements:* For master's, qualifying exam, thesis optional; for doctorate, thesis/dissertation, qualifying exam. *Entrance requirements:* For master's and doctorate, minimum GPA of 3.0 in last 90 hours. Additional exam requirements/recommendations for international students: Required—TOEFL. *Application deadline:* For fall admission, 3/1 for domestic students. Application fee: $50. *Expenses:* Tuition, state resident: full-time $8,139; part-time $301 per credit. Tuition, nonresident: full-time $14,376; part-time $532 per credit. Required fees: $1,227. *Financial support:* Fellowships, research assistantships, teaching assistantships, Federal Work-Study and institutionally sponsored loans available. Support available to part-time students. Financial award application deadline: 2/1. *Unit head:* Dr. Henri J.F. Jansen, Chair, 541-737-1668, Fax: 541-737-1683, E-mail: chair@physics.orst.edu.

Announcement: Solid-state research: transparent conductors, defects in semiconductors, magnetic anisotropy theory, magnetic semiconductors, superlattices. Nuclear/particle research: nucleon structure, exotic nuclear matter, superstring theory. Optics research: nonlinear optics, surface physics, laser cooling and trapping, atomic interferometry, terahert, spectroscopy. Computational physics. Teaching apprentice program for future college teachers. PhysTEC site.

Paper Science and Engineering Program, Graduate Studies and Research, College of Engineering, School of Chemical and Biomolecular Engineering, Graduate Programs, Program in Physics/Mathematics, Atlanta, GA 30318-5794. Offers MS, PhD. Part-time programs available. Terminal master's awarded for partial completion of doctoral program. *Degree requirements:* For master's, industrial experience, research project; for doctorate, thesis/dissertation. *Entrance requirements:* For master's and doctorate, GRE, minimum GPA of 3.0.

The Pennsylvania State University University Park Campus, Graduate School, Eberly College of Science, Department of Physics, State College, University Park, PA 16802-1503. Offers M Ed, MS, D Ed, PhD. *Students:* 119 full-time (15 women); includes 9 minority (4 African Americans, 5 Hispanic Americans), 63 international. *Entrance requirements:* For master's and doctorate, GRE General Test. Application fee: $45. *Unit head:* Dr. Jayanth R. Banavar, Head, 814-863-1089, Fax: 814-865-0978, E-mail: jrb16@psu.edu.

See in-depth description on page 397.

Pittsburg State University, Graduate School, College of Arts and Sciences, Department of Physics, Pittsburg, KS 66762. Offers applied physics (MS); physics (MS); professional physics (MS). *Degree requirements:* For master's, thesis or alternative.

Polytechnic University, Brooklyn Campus, Program in Physics, Brooklyn, NY 11201-2990. Offers MS, PhD. Part-time and evening/weekend programs available. *Students:* Average age 32. *Degree requirements:* For doctorate, thesis/dissertation. *Entrance requirements:* For master's, BA in physics; for doctorate, departmental qualifying exam, BS in physics. *Application deadline:* Applications are processed on a rolling basis. Application fee: $55. Electronic applications accepted. *Expenses:* Tuition: Full-time $16,416; part-time $855 per credit. Required fees: $320 per term. *Financial support:* Fellowships, research assistantships, teaching assistantships, institutionally sponsored loans available. Support available to part-time students. Financial award applicants required to submit FAFSA. *Faculty research:* Combining microdroplets, UHV cryogenic scanning, tunneling, surface spectroscopy of a single aerosol particle. Total annual research expenditures: $294,623. *Unit head:* Dr. Edward Wolf, Head, 718-260-3629, E-mail: ewolf@poly.edu.

Portland State University, Graduate Studies, College of Liberal Arts and Sciences, Department of Physics, Portland, OR 97207-0751. Offers MA, MS, PhD. Part-time programs available. *Faculty:* 9 full-time (1 woman), 3 part-time/adjunct (2 women). *Students:* 10 full-time (2 women), 2 part-time; includes 3 minority (all Hispanic Americans), 3 international. Average age 28. 13 applicants, 92% accepted, 8 enrolled. In 2003, 9 degrees awarded. *Degree requirements:* For master's, variable foreign language requirement, thesis, oral exam; for doctorate, thesis/dissertation. *Entrance requirements:* For master's, GRE General Test, minimum GPA of 3.0 in upper-division course work or 2.75 overall, 2 letters of recommendation. Additional exam requirements/recommendations for international students: Required—TOEFL. *Application deadline:* For fall admission, 4/1 for domestic students; for winter admission, 9/1 for domestic students; for spring admission, 11/1 for domestic students. Applications are processed on a rolling basis. Application fee: $50. *Expenses:* Tuition, state resident: full-time $6,588. Tuition, nonresident: full-time $12,060; part-time $298 per credit. Required fees: $1,041; $19 per credit. $35 per term. *Financial support:* In 2003–04, 1 research assistantship with full tuition reimbursement (averaging $14,400 per year), 15 teaching assistantships with full tuition reimbursements (averaging $11,500 per year) were awarded. Career-related internships or fieldwork, Federal Work-Study, and unspecified assistantships also available. Support available to part-time students. Financial award application deadline: 3/1; financial award applicants required to submit FAFSA. *Faculty research:* Statistical physics, membrane biophysics, low-temperature physics, electron microscopy, atmospheric physics. Total annual research expenditures: $1 million. *Unit head:* Dr. Eric Bodegom, Head, 503-725-3812, Fax: 503-725-3888, E-mail: bodegome@pdx.edu. *Application contact:* Peter Leung, Coordinator, 503-725-3812, Fax: 503-725-3888, E-mail: leungp@pdx.edu.

Princeton University, Graduate School, Department of Physics, Princeton, NJ 08544-1019. Offers applied and computational mathematics (PhD); mathematical physics (PhD); physics (PhD); physics and chemical physics (PhD). *Faculty:* 42 full-time (2 women), 2 part-time/adjunct (0 women). *Students:* 103 full-time (13 women); includes 11 minority (10 Asian Americans or Pacific Islanders, 1 Hispanic American), 48 international. Average age 22. 425 applicants, 12% accepted, 26 enrolled. In 2003, 14 degrees awarded, leading to continued full-time study 86%. *Median time to degree:* Doctorate–5 years full-time. *Degree requirements:* For doctorate, thesis/dissertation, qualifying exam. *Entrance requirements:* For doctorate, GRE General Test, GRE Subject Test. Additional exam requirements/recommendations for international students: Required—TOEFL (minimum score 600 paper-based; 250 computer-based). *Application deadline:* For fall admission, 12/31 for domestic students, 12/1 for international students. Application fee: $80 ($55 for international students). Electronic applications accepted. *Expenses:* Tuition: Full-time $29,910. Required fees: $810. *Financial support:* In 2003–04, 100 students received support, including 40 fellowships with full tuition reimbursements available (averaging $19,360 per year), 30 research assistantships with full tuition reimbursements available (averaging $18,100 per year), 30 teaching assistantships with full tuition reimbursements available (averaging $19,625 per year); Federal Work-Study and institutionally sponsored loans also available. Financial award application deadline: 1/2. Total annual research expenditures: $10.7 million. *Unit head:* Prof. Chiana Nappi, Director of Graduate Studies, 609-258-4322, Fax: 609-258-1549, E-mail: cnappi@princeton.edu. *Application contact:* Janice Yip, Director of Graduate Admissions, 609-258-3034, Fax: 609-258-6180, E-mail: gsadmit@princeton.edu.

Purdue University, Graduate School, School of Science, Department of Physics, West Lafayette, IN 47907. Offers MS, PhD. Part-time programs available. Terminal master's awarded for partial completion of doctoral program. *Degree requirements:* For master's, qualifying exam; for doctorate, thesis/dissertation, qualifying exam. *Entrance requirements:* For master's and doctorate, GRE General Test, GRE Subject Test. Additional exam requirements/recommendations for international students: Required—TOEFL. Electronic applications accepted. *Faculty research:* Solid-state, elementary particle, and nuclear physics; biological physics; acoustics; astrophysics.

Queens College of the City University of New York, Division of Graduate Studies, Mathematics and Natural Sciences Division, Department of Physics, Flushing, NY 11367-1597. Offers MA. Part-time and evening/weekend programs available. *Faculty:* 9 full-time (1 woman). *Students:* 8 applicants, 63% accepted. *Degree requirements:* For master's, comprehensive exam. *Entrance requirements:* For master's, previous course work in calculus, minimum GPA of 3.0. Additional exam requirements/recommendations for international students: Required—TOEFL. *Application deadline:* For fall admission, 4/1 for domestic students; for spring admission, 11/1 for domestic students. Applications are processed on a rolling basis. Application fee: $40. *Expenses:* Tuition, state resident: full-time $7,130; part-time $230 per credit. Tuition, nonresident: full-time $11,880; part-time $425 per credit. Required fees: $66; $38 per semester. *Financial support:* Career-related internships or fieldwork, Federal Work-Study, institutionally sponsored loans, and tuition waivers (partial) available. Support available to part-time students. Financial award application deadline: 4/1; financial award applicants required to submit FAFSA. *Faculty research:* Solid-state physics, low temperature physics, elementary particles and fields. *Unit head:* Dr. Alexander Lisyansky, Chairperson, 718-997-3350, E-mail: alexander_lisyansky@qc.edu. *Application contact:* Dr. J. Marion Dickey, Graduate Adviser, 718-997-3350.

Queen's University at Kingston, School of Graduate Studies and Research, Faculty of Arts and Sciences, Department of Physics, Kingston, ON K7L 3N6, Canada. Offers M Sc, M Sc Eng, PhD. Part-time programs available. *Degree requirements:* For master's, thesis/dissertation; for doctorate, thesis/dissertation, comprehensive exam. *Entrance requirements:* For master's, first or upper second class honours in Physics; for doctorate, M Sc or M Sc Eng. Additional exam requirements/recommendations for international students: Required—TOEFL (minimum score 550 paper-based; 213 computer-based). *Faculty research:* Theoretical physics, astronomy and astrophysics, subatomic, condensed matter, applied and engineering.

Rensselaer Polytechnic Institute, Graduate School, School of Science, Department of Physics, Applied Physics and Astronomy, Troy, NY 12180-3590. Offers physics (MS, PhD). *Faculty:* 23 full-time (3 women), 2 part-time/adjunct (0 women). *Students:* 45 full-time (9 women); includes 22 minority (all Asian Americans or Pacific Islanders), 39 international. Average age 28. 101 applicants, 12% accepted. In 2003, 10 master's, 13 doctorates awarded. *Degree requirements:* For doctorate, thesis/dissertation. *Entrance requirements:* For master's and doctorate, GRE General Test, GRE Subject Test. Additional exam requirements/recommendations for international students: Required—TOEFL (minimum score 600 paper-based; 250 computer-based). *Application deadline:* For fall admission, 1/15 for domestic students; for spring admission, 10/1 priority date for domestic students. Applications are processed on a rolling basis. Application fee: $45. Electronic applications accepted. *Expenses:* Tuition: Full-time $27,700; part-time $1,320 per credit. Required fees: $1,470. *Financial support:* In 2003–04, 2 fellowships with tuition reimbursements (averaging $25,000 per year), 19 research assistantships with tuition reimbursements (averaging $18,700 per year), 22 teaching assistantships with tuition reimbursements (averaging $19,000 per year) were awarded. Career-related internships or fieldwork and institutionally sponsored loans also available. Financial award application deadline: 2/1. *Faculty research:* Astrophysics, condensed matter, nuclear physics, optics, physics education. Total annual research expenditures: $3.6 million. *Unit head:* Dr. G. C. Wang, Chair, 518-276-8387, Fax: 518-276-6680, E-mail: wangg@rpi.edu. *Application contact:* Dr. Toh-Ming Lu, Chair, Graduate Recruitment Committee, 518-276-8391, Fax: 518-276-6680, E-mail: mcquade@rpi.edu.

Rice University, Graduate Programs, Wiess School of Natural Sciences, Department of Physics and Astronomy, Houston, TX 77251-1892. Offers physics (MA); physics and astronomy (MS, PhD). *Faculty:* 46 full-time (3 women). *Students:* 90 full-time (12 women), 2 part-time (1 woman); includes 11 minority (1 African American, 3 Asian Americans or Pacific Islanders, 7 Hispanic Americans), 46 international. Average age 28. 169 applicants, 36% accepted, 24 enrolled. In 2003, 7 master's awarded, leading to continued full-time study 71%; 10 doctorates awarded. *Median time to degree:* Doctorate–7 years full-time. Of those who began their doctoral program in fall 1995, 50% received their degree in 8 years or less. *Degree requirements:* For master's and doctorate, thesis/dissertation. *Entrance requirements:* For master's and doctorate, GRE General Test, GRE Subject Test (physics), minimum GPA of 3.0. Additional exam requirements/recommendations for international students: Required—TOEFL (minimum score 600 paper-based; 250 computer-based). *Application deadline:* For fall admission, 2/1 for domestic students, 2/1 for international students. Applications are processed on a rolling basis. Application fee: $35. Electronic applications accepted. *Expenses:* Tuition: Full-time $19,700; part-time $1,096 per hour. *Financial support:* In 2003–04, 24 fellowships with full tuition reimbursements (averaging $21,000 per year), 68 research assistantships with full tuition reimbursements (averaging $21,000 per year) were awarded. Tuition waivers (full and partial) also available. *Faculty research:* Atomic, solid-state, and molecular physics; biophysics; medium- and high-energy physics, magnetospheric physics, planetary atmospheres, astrophysics. Total annual research expenditures: $6.6 million. *Unit head:* Dr. F. Barry Dunning, Acting Chairman, 713-348-3544, Fax: 713-348-4510, E-mail: fbd@rice.edu. *Application contact:* Bridgitt G. Ayers, Graduate Program Director, 713-348-6348, Fax: 713-348-4150, E-mail: physgrad@rice.edu.

Rice University, Graduate Programs, Wiess School of Natural Sciences, Professional Master's Program in Nanoscale Physics, Houston, TX 77251-1892. Offers MS. *Degree requirements:*

For master's, internship. *Entrance requirements:* For master's, GRE General Test, bachelor's in physics and related field, letters of recommendation (4). Additional exam requirements/recommendations for international students: Required—TOEFL. Electronic applications accepted. *Expenses:* Tuition: Full-time $19,700; part-time $1,096 per hour. *Faculty research:* Atomic, molecular, and applied physics, surface and condensed matter physics.

Royal Military College of Canada, Division of Graduate Studies and Research, Science Division, Department of Physics, Kingston, ON K7K 7B4, Canada. Offers M Sc. *Degree requirements:* For master's, thesis, registration. Electronic applications accepted.

Rutgers, The State University of New Jersey, New Brunswick/Piscataway, Graduate School, Program in Physics and Astronomy, New Brunswick, NJ 08901-1281. Offers astronomy (MS, PhD); biophysics (PhD); condensed matter physics (MS, PhD); elementary particle physics (MS, PhD); intermediate energy nuclear physics (MS); nuclear physics (MS, PhD); physics (MST); surface science (PhD); theoretical physics (MS, PhD). Part-time programs available. *Faculty:* 67 full-time (5 women). *Students:* 90 full-time (13 women), 18 part-time (3 women); includes 5 minority (2 African Americans, 3 Asian Americans or Pacific Islanders), 67 international. Average age 28. 269 applicants, 16% accepted, 21 enrolled. In 2003, 5 master's, 16 doctorates awarded. Terminal master's awarded for partial completion of doctoral program. *Median time to degree:* Master's–2 years full-time; doctorate–6 years full-time. *Degree requirements:* For master's, thesis or alternative, comprehensive exam; for doctorate, thesis/dissertation, comprehensive exam. *Entrance requirements:* For master's and doctorate, GRE General Test, GRE Subject Test. Additional exam requirements/recommendations for international students: Required—TOEFL, TSE. *Application deadline:* For fall admission, 1/2 priority date for domestic students, 1/2 priority date for international students; for spring admission, 11/1 for domestic students, 11/1 for international students. Applications are processed on a rolling basis. Application fee: $50. Electronic applications accepted. *Expenses:* Tuition, state resident: full-time $10,030. Tuition, nonresident: full-time $14,202. *Financial support:* In 2003–04, 19 fellowships with full tuition reimbursements (averaging $18,000 per year), 50 research assistantships with full tuition reimbursements (averaging $15,300 per year), 8 teaching assistantships with full tuition reimbursements (averaging $15,300 per year) were awarded. Health care benefits and unspecified assistantships also available. Financial award application deadline: 1/2; financial award applicants required to submit FAFSA. *Faculty research:* Astronomy, high energy, condensed matter, surface, nuclear physics. Total annual research expenditures: $7.8 million. *Unit head:* Dr. Ted Williams, Director, 732-445-2516, Fax: 732-445-4343, E-mail: williams@physics.rutgers.edu. *Application contact:* Kathy DiMeo, Administrative Assistant, 732-445-2502, Fax: 732-445-4343, E-mail: graduate@physics.rutgers.edu.

See in-depth description on page 401.

St. Francis Xavier University, Graduate Studies, Department of Physics, Antigonish, NS B2G 2W5, Canada. Offers M Sc. *Faculty:* 6 full-time (0 women), 2 part-time/adjunct (0 women). *Degree requirements:* For master's, thesis, registration. *Entrance requirements:* For master's, minimum B average in undergraduate course work, honors degree in physics or related area. Additional exam requirements/recommendations for international students: Required—TOEFL (minimum score 580 paper-based; 236 computer-based). *Application deadline:* For fall admission, 9/1 for domestic students. Applications are processed on a rolling basis. Application fee: $40. Tuition, area resident: Full-time $5,310. International tuition: $9,210 full-time. Full-time tuition and fees vary according to course load and program. *Faculty research:* Atomic and molecular spectroscopy, quantum theory, many body theory, mathematical physics, phase transitions. Total annual research expenditures: $600,000. *Unit head:* Dr. Douglas L. Hunter, Chair, 902-867-2104, Fax: 902-867-2414, E-mail: dhunter@stfx.ca. *Application contact:* 902-867-2219, Fax: 902-867-2329, E-mail: admit@stfx.ca.

Sam Houston State University, College of Arts and Sciences, Department of Physics, Huntsville, TX 77341. Offers MS. In 2003, 1 degree awarded. *Degree requirements:* For master's, thesis. *Entrance requirements:* For master's, GRE General Test. Additional exam requirements/recommendations for international students: Required—TOEFL. *Application deadline:* For fall admission, 8/1 for domestic students; for spring admission, 12/1 for domestic students. Applications are processed on a rolling basis. Application fee: $35. *Expenses:* Tuition, state resident: part-time $243 per semester hour. Tuition, nonresident: part-time $479 per semester hour. *Financial support:* Research assistantships, teaching assistantships, institutionally sponsored loans available. Financial award application deadline: 5/31; financial award applicants required to submit FAFSA. *Unit head:* Dr. Rex Isham, Chair, 936-294-1606, Fax: 936-294-1585. *Application contact:* Anita Shipman, Advisor, 936-294-3962.

San Diego State University, Graduate and Research Affairs, College of Sciences, Department of Physics, Program in Physics, San Diego, CA 92182. Offers MA, MS. Part-time programs available. *Students:* 4 full-time (0 women), 18 part-time (2 women); includes 5 minority (1 Asian American or Pacific Islander, 4 Hispanic Americans), 1 international. 13 applicants, 69% accepted, 5 enrolled. In 2003, 1 degree awarded. *Degree requirements:* For master's, thesis, oral exam. *Entrance requirements:* For master's, GRE General Test. Additional exam requirements/recommendations for international students: Required—TOEFL. *Application deadline:* For fall admission, 5/1 for domestic students, 5/1 for international students; for spring admission, 11/1 for domestic students, 10/1 for international students. Applications are processed on a rolling basis. Application fee: $55. Electronic applications accepted. Tuition, nonresident: part-time $282 per unit. Required fees: $1,349; $875 per year. *Financial support:* Career-related internships or fieldwork available. Financial award applicants required to submit FAFSA. *Unit head:* Milton Torikachvili, Graduate Advisor, 619-594-6274, Fax: 619-594-5485, E-mail: milton@sciences.sdsu.edu.

San Francisco State University, Division of Graduate Studies, College of Science and Engineering, Department of Physics and Astronomy, San Francisco, CA 94132-1722. Offers physics (MS). Part-time programs available. *Faculty:* 10 full-time (4 women), 6 part-time/adjunct (0 women). *Students:* 52 full-time (12 women), 10 part-time (4 women). 19 applicants, 74% accepted, 12 enrolled. In 2003, 11 degrees awarded. *Median time to degree:* Master's–2 years full-time, 3 years part-time. *Degree requirements:* For master's, thesis, registration. *Entrance requirements:* For master's, minimum GPA of 2.5 in last 60 units. Additional exam requirements/recommendations for international students: Required—TOEFL (minimum score 550 paper-based; 213 computer-based). *Application deadline:* For fall admission, 5/1 for domestic students, 4/2 for international students; for spring admission, 11/15 for domestic students. Applications are processed on a rolling basis. Application fee: $55. Electronic applications accepted. *Expenses:* Tuition, state resident: part-time $871 per unit. Tuition, nonresident: part-time $1,093 per unit. *Financial support:* In 2003–04, 35 students received support, including research assistantships (averaging $10,000 per year), teaching assistantships with partial tuition reimbursements available (averaging $8,500 per year); career-related internships or fieldwork, Federal Work-Study, institutionally sponsored loans, and tuition waivers (partial) also available. Financial award application deadline: 3/1. *Faculty research:* Quark search, thin-films, dark matter detection, search for planetary systems, low temperature. Total annual research expenditures: $500,000. *Unit head:* Dr. James Lockhart, Chair, 415-338-1659, E-mail: lockhart@stars.sfsu.edu. *Application contact:* Dr. Susan Lea, Graduate Coordinator, 415-338-1691, E-mail: lea@stars.sfsu.edu.

San Jose State University, Graduate Studies and Research, College of Science, Department of Physics, San Jose, CA 95192-0001. Offers computational physics (MS); physics (MS). Part-time and evening/weekend programs available. *Students:* 10 full-time (3 women), 20 part-time (5 women); includes 8 minority (1 African American, 7 Asian Americans or Pacific Islanders). Average age 35. 20 applicants, 85% accepted, 9 enrolled. In 2003, 4 degrees awarded. *Degree requirements:* For master's, thesis optional. *Entrance requirements:* For master's, GRE. *Application deadline:* For fall admission, 6/29 for domestic students; for spring admission, 11/30 for domestic students. Applications are processed on a rolling basis. Application fee: $59. Electronic applications accepted. Tuition, nonresident: part-time $282 per unit. Required fees: $654 per semester. *Financial support:* In 2003–04, 7 teaching assistantships were awarded; career-related internships or fieldwork, Federal Work-Study, and institutionally sponsored loans also available. Support available to part-time students. Financial award application deadline: 3/1; financial award applicants required to submit FAFSA. *Faculty research:* Astrophysics, atmospheric physics, elementary particles, dislocation theory, general relativity. *Unit head:* John Gruber, Chair, 408-924-5210, Fax: 408-924-2917. *Application contact:* Dr. Karamjeet Arya, Graduate Adviser, 408-924-5267.

Simon Fraser University, Graduate Studies, Faculty of Science, Department of Physics, Burnaby, BC V5A 1S6, Canada. Offers biophysics (M Sc, PhD); chemical physics (M Sc, PhD); physics (M Sc, PhD). *Degree requirements:* For master's and doctorate, thesis/dissertation. *Entrance requirements:* For master's, minimum GPA of 3.0; for doctorate, minimum GPA of 3.5. Additional exam requirements/recommendations for international students: Required—TOEFL or IELTS. *Faculty research:* Solid-state physics, magnetism, energy research, superconductivity, nuclear physics.

South Dakota School of Mines and Technology, Graduate Division, College of Materials Science and Engineering, Doctoral Program in Materials Engineering and Science, Rapid City, SD 57701-3995. Offers chemical engineering (PhD); chemistry (PhD); civil engineering (PhD); electrical engineering (PhD); mechanical engineering (PhD); metallurgical engineering (PhD); physics (PhD). Part-time programs available. In 2003, 5 degrees awarded. *Degree requirements:* For doctorate, thesis/dissertation. *Entrance requirements:* For doctorate, minimum graduate GPA of 3.0. Additional exam requirements/recommendations for international students: Required—TOEFL, TWE. *Application deadline:* For fall admission, 6/15 for domestic students; for spring admission, 10/15 for domestic students. Applications are processed on a rolling basis. Application fee: $35. Electronic applications accepted. *Expenses:* Tuition, state resident: part-time $109 per credit hour. Tuition, nonresident: part-time $323 per credit hour. Required fees: $100 per credit hour. *Financial support:* In 2003–04, 1 fellowship (averaging $2,700 per year), 9 research assistantships with partial tuition reimbursements (averaging $11,775 per year), 5 teaching assistantships with partial tuition reimbursements (averaging $4,100 per year) were awarded. Federal Work-Study and institutionally sponsored loans also available. Support available to part-time students. Financial award application deadline: 5/15. *Faculty research:* Thermophysical properties of solids, development of multiphase materials and composites, concrete technology, electronic polymer materials. *Unit head:* Dr. Robb Winter, Coordinator, 605-394-1237. *Application contact:* Brenda Brown, Secretary, 800-454-8162 Ext. 2493, Fax: 605-394-5360, E-mail: graduate_admissions@silver.sdsmt.edu.

South Dakota School of Mines and Technology, Graduate Division, College of Materials Science and Engineering, Master's Program in Materials Engineering and Science, Rapid City, SD 57701-3995. Offers chemistry (MS); metallurgical engineering (MS); physics (MS). In 2003, 4 degrees awarded. *Entrance requirements:* Additional exam requirements/recommendations for international students: Required—TOEFL, TWE. *Application deadline:* For fall admission, 6/15 for domestic students; for spring admission, 10/15 for domestic students. Applications are processed on a rolling basis. Application fee: $35. Electronic applications accepted. *Expenses:* Tuition, state resident: part-time $109 per credit hour. Tuition, nonresident: part-time $323 per credit hour. Required fees: $100 per credit hour. *Financial support:* In 2003–04, 3 fellowships (averaging $2,016 per year), 13 research assistantships with partial tuition reimbursements (averaging $11,930 per year), 8 teaching assistantships with partial tuition reimbursements (averaging $10,554 per year) were awarded. Financial award application deadline: 5/15. *Unit head:* Dr. Daniel Heglund, 605-394-1241. *Application contact:* Brenda Brown, Secretary, 800-454-8162 Ext. 2493, Fax: 605-394-5360, E-mail: graduate_admissions@silver.sdsmt.edu.

South Dakota State University, Graduate School, College of Engineering, Department of Physics, Brookings, SD 57007. Offers MS. *Degree requirements:* For master's, thesis, oral exam. *Entrance requirements:* Additional exam requirements/recommendations for international students: Required—TOEFL. *Faculty research:* Materials science, astrophysics, remote sensing and atmospheric corrections, theoretical and computational physics, applied physics.

Southern Illinois University Carbondale, Graduate School, College of Science, Department of Physics, Carbondale, IL 62901-4701. Offers MS. *Faculty:* 9 full-time (0 women). *Students:* 10 full-time (1 woman), 1 part-time; includes 1 minority (Asian American or Pacific Islander), 6 international. 22 applicants, 23% accepted, 1 enrolled. In 2003, 7 degrees awarded. *Degree requirements:* For master's, one foreign language, thesis. *Entrance requirements:* For master's, minimum GPA of 2.7. Additional exam requirements/recommendations for international students: Required—TOEFL. *Application deadline:* Applications are processed on a rolling basis. Application fee: $20. *Expenses:* Tuition, state resident: part-time $478 per hour. Tuition, nonresident: part-time $657 per hour. *Financial support:* In 2003–04, 1 fellowship with full tuition reimbursement, 9 teaching assistantships with full tuition reimbursements were awarded. Research assistantships with full tuition reimbursements, career-related internships or fieldwork, Federal Work-Study, institutionally sponsored loans, and tuition waivers (full) also available. Support available to part-time students. Financial award application deadline: 2/15. *Faculty research:* Atomic, molecular, nuclear, and mathematical physics; statistical mechanics; solid-state and low-temperature physics; rheology; material science. Total annual research expenditures: $773,352. *Unit head:* Dr. Aldo Migone, Chairperson, 618-453-1054. *Application contact:* Graduate Admissions Committee, 618-453-2643.

Southern Illinois University Edwardsville, Graduate Studies and Research, College of Arts and Sciences, Department of Physics, Edwardsville, IL 62026-0001. Offers MS. Part-time programs available. *Degree requirements:* For master's, thesis or alternative, final exam. *Entrance requirements:* Additional exam requirements/recommendations for international students: Required—TOEFL.

Southern Methodist University, Dedman College, Department of Physics, Dallas, TX 75275. Offers MS, PhD. Part-time and evening/weekend programs available. *Faculty:* 9 full-time (0 women). *Students:* 6 full-time (2 women), 1 part-time, 4 international. Average age 29. In 2003, 1 degree awarded. Terminal master's awarded for partial completion of doctoral program. *Median time to degree:* Of those who began their doctoral program in fall 1995, 100% received their degree in 8 years or less. *Degree requirements:* For master's, oral exam, thesis optional; for doctorate, thesis/dissertation, written exam. *Entrance requirements:* For master's, GRE General Test, minimum GPA of 3.0; for doctorate, GRE General Test, GRE Subject Test (physics), minimum GPA of 3.0. Additional exam requirements/recommendations for international students: Required—TOEFL. *Application deadline:* For fall admission, 2/1 for domestic students. Application fee: $60. Electronic applications accepted. *Expenses:* Tuition: Full-time $11,362; part-time $874 per credit. Required fees: $112 per credit. Tuition and fees vary according to course load and program. *Financial support:* In 2003–04, 2 research assistantships with full tuition reimbursements (averaging $17,040 per year), 5 teaching assistantships with full tuition reimbursements (averaging $15,600 per year) were awarded. Health care benefits and tuition waivers (partial) also available. Financial award application deadline: 2/1; financial award applicants required to submit FAFSA. *Faculty research:* Particle physics, cosmology, astrophysics, mathematics physics, computational physics. Total annual research expenditures: $1 million. *Unit head:* Fredrick Olness, Head, 214-768-2500, Fax: 214-768-4095, E-mail: olness@natl.physics.smu.edu. *Application contact:* Dr. Ryszard Stroynowski, Director of Graduate Recruitment, 214-768-4076, Fax: 214-768-4095.

Southern University and Agricultural and Mechanical College, Graduate School, College of Sciences, Department of Physics, Baton Rouge, LA 70813. Offers MS. *Degree requirements:* For master's, thesis. *Entrance requirements:* For master's, GMAT or GRE General Test. Additional exam requirements/recommendations for international students: Required—TOEFL. *Faculty research:* Piezoelectric materials and devices, predictive ab-instio calculations, high energy physics, surface growth studies, semiconductor and intermetallics.

Stanford University, School of Humanities and Sciences, Department of Physics, Stanford, CA 94305-9991. Offers PhD. *Faculty:* 27 full-time (3 women). *Students:* 120 full-time (18 women), 35 part-time (6 women); includes 14 minority (1 African American, 11 Asian Americans or Pacific Islanders, 2 Hispanic Americans), 68 international. Average age 26. 377 applicants,

Physics

Stanford University (continued)
17% accepted. In 2003, 18 doctorates awarded. *Degree requirements:* For doctorate, thesis/dissertation, oral exam, qualifying exam. *Entrance requirements:* For doctorate, GRE General Test, GRE Subject Test. Additional exam requirements/recommendations for international students: Required—TOEFL. *Application deadline:* For fall admission, 1/5 for domestic students. Application fee: $65 ($80 for international students). Electronic applications accepted. *Expenses:* Tuition: Full-time $28,563. *Unit head:* Steve Chu, Chair, 650-723-3571, Fax: 650-723-9173, E-mail: schu@stanford.edu. *Application contact:* Graduate Administrator, 650-723-0830, Fax: 650-723-1821.

State University of New York at Binghamton, Graduate School, School of Arts and Sciences, Department of Physics, Applied Physics, and Astronomy, Binghamton, NY 13902-6000. Offers applied physics (MS); physics (MA, MS). *Degree requirements:* For master's, thesis or alternative. *Entrance requirements:* For master's, GRE General Test, GRE Subject Test. Additional exam requirements/recommendations for international students: Required—TOEFL. Electronic applications accepted.

Stephen F. Austin State University, Graduate School, College of Sciences and Mathematics, Department of Physics and Astronomy, Nacogdoches, TX 75962. Offers physics (MS). Part-time programs available. *Faculty:* 7 full-time (0 women), 1 part-time/adjunct (0 women). *Students:* 5 full-time (0 women), 1 part-time; includes 1 minority (Hispanic American), 1 international. Average age 30. 3 applicants, 100% accepted. In 2003, 2 degrees awarded. *Degree requirements:* For master's, comprehensive exam. *Entrance requirements:* For master's, GRE General Test, minimum GPA of 2.8 in last 60 hours, 2.5 overall. Additional exam requirements/recommendations for international students: Required—TOEFL. *Application deadline:* For fall admission, 8/1 for domestic students; for spring admission, 12/15 for domestic students. Applications are processed on a rolling basis. Application fee: $0 ($50 for international students). *Expenses:* Tuition, state resident: part-time $46 per hour. Tuition, nonresident: part-time $282 per hour. Required fees: $71 per hour. Tuition and fees vary according to reciprocity agreements. *Financial support:* In 2003–04, 4 teaching assistantships (averaging $7,066 per year) were awarded; Federal Work-Study, institutionally sponsored loans, health care benefits, and unspecified assistantships also available. Financial award application deadline: 3/1. *Faculty research:* Low-temperature physics, x-ray spectroscopy and metallic glasses, infrared spectroscopy. *Unit head:* Dr. Harry D. Downing, Chair, 936-468-3001.

Stevens Institute of Technology, Graduate School, School of Applied Sciences and Liberal Arts, Department of Physics and Engineering Physics, Hoboken, NJ 07030. Offers applied optics (Certificate); engineering physics (M Eng), including engineering optics, engineering physics; physics (MS, PhD); surface physics (Certificate). Part-time and evening/weekend programs available. Terminal master's awarded for partial completion of doctoral program. *Degree requirements:* For master's, thesis optional; for doctorate, thesis/dissertation. *Entrance requirements:* For master's and doctorate, GRE. Additional exam requirements/recommendations for international students: Required—TOEFL. Electronic applications accepted. *Faculty research:* Laser spectroscopy, physical kinetics, semiconductor-device physics, condensed-matter theory.

Stony Brook University, State University of New York, Graduate School, College of Arts and Sciences, Department of Physics and Astronomy, Program in Physics, Stony Brook, NY 11794. Offers MA, MAT, MS, PhD. *Students:* 170 full-time (28 women), 1 part-time; includes 8 minority (1 African American, 6 Asian Americans or Pacific Islanders, 1 Hispanic American), 109 international. *Degree requirements:* For doctorate, one foreign language, thesis/dissertation. *Entrance requirements:* For master's and doctorate, GRE General Test. Additional exam requirements/recommendations for international students: Required—TOEFL. *Application deadline:* For fall admission, 1/15 for domestic students. Application fee: $50. *Expenses:* Tuition, state resident: full-time $6,900; part-time $288 per credit hour. Tuition, nonresident: full-time $10,500; part-time $438 per credit hour. Required fees: $22. *Financial support:* Fellowships, research assistantships, teaching assistantships available. Financial award application deadline: 2/1. *Application contact:* Dr. Peter Stephens, Director, 631-632-8279, Fax: 631-632-8176, E-mail: pstephens@ccmail.sunysb.edu.

Announcement: Graduate students in the department engage in a broad range of experimental, observational, and theoretical research activities both on campus and at major facilities, including the nearby Brookhaven National Laboratory. Students work with leaders in their fields and enjoy personal attention in the development of their education.

See in-depth description on page 405.

Syracuse University, Graduate School, College of Arts and Sciences, Department of Physics, Syracuse, NY 13244-0003. Offers MS, PhD. Part-time programs available. *Faculty:* 23. *Students:* 44 full-time (15 women), 6 part-time (2 women); includes 3 minority (1 African American, 1 Asian American or Pacific Islander, 1 Hispanic American), 39 international. 203 applicants, 12% accepted, 11 enrolled.Terminal master's awarded for partial completion of doctoral program. *Degree requirements:* For master's, thesis or alternative; for doctorate, thesis/dissertation. *Entrance requirements:* For master's and doctorate, GRE General Test, GRE Subject Test. Additional exam requirements/recommendations for international students: Required—TOEFL. *Application deadline:* Applications are processed on a rolling basis. Application fee: $65. *Expenses:* Tuition: Full-time $13,356; part-time $742 per credit. Required fees: $482. *Financial support:* Fellowships with full tuition reimbursements, research assistantships with full and partial tuition reimbursements, teaching assistantships with full and partial tuition reimbursements, tuition waivers (partial) available. *Unit head:* Dr. Edward Lipson, Chair, 315-443-9107, Fax: 315-443-9103, E-mail: edlipson@syr.edu. *Application contact:* Joseph Schecter, Graduate Program Director, 315-443-5968, E-mail: jmschech@syr.edu.

Temple University, Graduate School, College of Science and Technology, Department of Physics, Philadelphia, PA 19122-6096. Offers MA, PhD. Terminal master's awarded for partial completion of doctoral program. *Degree requirements:* For master's, thesis or alternative, comprehensive exam; for doctorate, thesis/dissertation, 2 comprehensive exams. *Entrance requirements:* For master's and doctorate, minimum GPA of 3.0 during previous 2 years, 2.8 overall. Electronic applications accepted. *Faculty research:* Laser-based molecular spectroscopy, elementary particle physics, statistical mechanics, solid-state physics.

See in-depth description on page 407.

Texas A&M International University, Division of Graduate Studies, College of Arts and Sciences, Department of Math and Physical Science, Laredo, TX 78041-1900. Offers MAIS. *Students:* 1 (woman) full-time, 4 part-time (2 women); all Hispanic Americans *Application deadline:* For fall admission, 7/15 for domestic students; for spring admission, 11/12 for domestic students. Applications are processed on a rolling basis. Application fee: $0. *Expenses:* Tuition, state resident: part-time $158 per hour. Tuition, nonresident: part-time $394 per hour. *Financial support:* Application deadline: 11/1. *Unit head:* Dr. Juan H. Hinojosa, Dean, 956-326-2440, Fax: 956-326-2439, E-mail: jhhinojosa@tamiu.edu. *Application contact:* Veronica Gonzalez, Director of Enrollment Management and School Relations, 956-326-2270, Fax: 956-326-2269, E-mail: enroll@tamiu.edu.

Texas A&M University, College of Science, Department of Physics, College Station, TX 77843. Offers applied physics (PhD); physics (MS, PhD). *Faculty:* 36 full-time (1 woman). *Students:* 122 full-time (9 women), 7 part-time (1 woman); includes 5 minority (1 African American, 1 Asian American or Pacific Islander, 3 Hispanic Americans), 95 international. Terminal master's awarded for partial completion of doctoral program. *Degree requirements:* For master's, thesis (for some programs), registration; for doctorate, thesis/dissertation, registration. *Entrance requirements:* For master's and doctorate, GRE General Test, GRE Subject Test. Additional exam requirements/recommendations for international students: Required—TOEFL. *Application deadline:* For fall admission, 3/1 for domestic students; for spring admission, 8/1 for domestic students. Application fee: $50 ($75 for international students). Electronic applications accepted. *Expenses:* Tuition, state resident: full-time $3,420. Tuition, nonresident: full-time $9,084. Required fees: $1,861. *Financial support:* In 2003–04, research assistantships (averaging $16,200 per year), teaching assistantships (averaging $16,200 per year) were awarded. Financial award application deadline: 3/1; financial award applicants required to submit FAFSA. *Faculty research:* Condensed-matter, atomic/molecular, high-energy, and nuclear physics, quantum optics. *Unit head:* Dr. Edward S. Fry, Head, 979-845-7717, Fax: 979-845-2590, E-mail: fry@physics.tamu.edu. *Application contact:* Dr. George W. Kattawar, Professor, 979-845-1180, Fax: 979-845-2590, E-mail: kattawar@physics.tamu.edu.

Texas A&M University–Commerce, Graduate School, College of Arts and Sciences, Department of Physics, Commerce, TX 75429-3011. Offers M Ed, MS. Part-time programs available. *Degree requirements:* For master's, thesis (for some programs), comprehensive exam. *Entrance requirements:* For master's, GRE General Test. Electronic applications accepted.

Texas Christian University, College of Science and Engineering, Department of Physics and Astronomy, Fort Worth, TX 76129-0002. Offers physics (PhD), including astrophysics, business, physics. Part-time and evening/weekend programs available. *Degree requirements:* For doctorate, thesis/dissertation, qualifying exams. *Entrance requirements:* For doctorate, GRE General Test. Additional exam requirements/recommendations for international students: Required—TOEFL. *Application deadline:* For fall admission, 3/1 for domestic students; for spring admission, 12/1 for domestic students. Applications are processed on a rolling basis. Application fee: $0. *Expenses:* Tuition: Part-time $640 per credit hour. Tuition and fees vary according to program. *Financial support:* Fellowships, teaching assistantships available. Financial award application deadline: 3/1. *Unit head:* Dr. C. Magnus Rittby, Chairperson, 817-257-7375, E-mail: m.rittby@tcu.edu. *Application contact:* Dr. Bonnie Melhart, Associate Dean, College of Science and Engineering, E-mail: b.melhart@tcu.edu.

Texas State University-San Marcos, Graduate School, College of Science, Department of Physics, San Marcos, TX 78666. Offers MS. Part-time programs available. *Faculty:* 4 full-time (1 woman). *Students:* 10 full-time (4 women), 10 part-time (3 women); includes 5 minority (1 African American, 4 Hispanic Americans), 1 international. Average age 29. 11 applicants, 100% accepted, 8 enrolled. In 2003, 1 degree awarded. *Degree requirements:* For master's, thesis (for some programs), comprehensive exam. *Entrance requirements:* For master's, GRE General Test, minimum GPA of 2.75 in last 60 hours. Additional exam requirements/recommendations for international students: Required—TOEFL. *Application deadline:* For fall admission, 6/15 for domestic students; for spring admission, 10/15 priority date for domestic students. Applications are processed on a rolling basis. Application fee: $40 ($90 for international students). *Expenses:* Tuition, state resident: full-time $2,484; part-time $138 per semester hour. Tuition, nonresident: full-time $6,732; part-time $374 per semester hour. Required fees: $948; $31 per semester hour. $195 per term. Tuition and fees vary according to course load. *Financial support:* In 2003–04, 10 students received support, including 5 research assistantships (averaging $10,930 per year), 7 teaching assistantships (averaging $10,300 per year); career-related internships or fieldwork, Federal Work-Study, and institutionally sponsored loans also available. Support available to part-time students. Financial award application deadline: 4/1; financial award applicants required to submit FAFSA. *Faculty research:* High-temperature superconductors, historical astronomy, general relativity. *Unit head:* Dr. James R. Crawford, Chair, 512-245-2131, Fax: 512-245-8233, E-mail: jc03@txstate.edu.

Texas Tech University, Graduate School, College of Arts and Sciences, Department of Physics, Lubbock, TX 79409. Offers applied physics (MS, PhD); physics (MS, PhD). Part-time programs available. *Faculty:* 19 full-time (3 women). *Students:* 34 full-time (2 women), 6 part-time; includes 2 minority (both Hispanic Americans), 19 international. Average age 30. 33 applicants, 70% accepted, 12 enrolled. In 2003, 7 master's, 4 doctorates awarded. *Degree requirements:* For master's and doctorate, variable foreign language requirement, thesis/dissertation. *Entrance requirements:* For master's and doctorate, GRE General Test. Additional exam requirements/recommendations for international students: Required—TOEFL (minimum score 550 paper-based; 213 computer-based). *Application deadline:* Applications are processed on a rolling basis. Application fee: $50 ($60 for international students). Electronic applications accepted. *Expenses:* Tuition, state resident: full-time $3,312. Tuition, nonresident: full-time $8,976. Required fees: $1,745. Tuition and fees vary according to program. *Financial support:* In 2003–04, 21 students received support, including 16 research assistantships with partial tuition reimbursements available (averaging $14,693 per year), 19 teaching assistantships with partial tuition reimbursements available (averaging $15,457 per year); career-related internships or fieldwork, Federal Work-Study, and institutionally sponsored loans also available. Support available to part-time students. Financial award application deadline: 5/1; financial award applicants required to submit FAFSA. *Faculty research:* Molecular spectroscopy of biological membranes, thin films and semiconductor characterization, muon spin rotation defect, characterization of semiconductors, nanotechnology of magnetic materials, theory of impurities and complexes in semiconductors. Total annual research expenditures: $177,229. *Unit head:* Dr. Lynn L. Hatfield, Chair, 806-742-3767, Fax: 806-742-1182, E-mail: lynnhatfield@ttu.edu. *Application contact:* Dr. Wallace L. Glab, Graduate Recruiter, 806-742-3767, Fax: 806-742-1182, E-mail: wallace.glab@ttu.edu.

Trent University, Graduate Studies, Program in Applications of Modeling in the Natural and Social Sciences, Department of Physics, Peterborough, ON K9J 7B8, Canada. Offers M Sc. Part-time programs available. *Degree requirements:* For master's, thesis. *Entrance requirements:* For master's, honours degree. *Faculty research:* Radiation physics, chemical physics.

Tufts University, Graduate School of Arts and Sciences, Department of Physics and Astronomy, Medford, MA 02155. Offers physics (MS, PhD). *Faculty:* 14 full-time, 3 part-time/adjunct. *Students:* 32 (8 women); includes 1 minority (Hispanic American) 18 international. 90 applicants, 11% accepted, 6 enrolled. In 2003, 8 master's, 2 doctorates awarded. Terminal master's awarded for partial completion of doctoral program. *Degree requirements:* For master's, thesis optional; for doctorate, thesis/dissertation. *Entrance requirements:* For master's and doctorate, GRE General Test. Additional exam requirements/recommendations for international students: Required—TOEFL (minimum score 550 paper-based; 213 computer-based). *Application deadline:* For fall admission, 2/15 for domestic students, 12/30 for international students; for spring admission, 10/15 for domestic students, 9/15 for international students. Applications are processed on a rolling basis. Application fee: $60. Electronic applications accepted. *Expenses:* Tuition: Full-time $29,949. *Financial support:* Research assistantships with full and partial tuition reimbursements, teaching assistantships with full and partial tuition reimbursements, Federal Work-Study, scholarships/grants, and tuition waivers (partial) available. Financial award application deadline: 2/15; financial award applicants required to submit FAFSA. *Unit head:* Bill Oliver, Chair, 617-627-3029. *Application contact:* Dr. Krzysztof Sliwa, Information Contact, 617-627-3029.

Tulane University, Graduate School, Department of Physics, New Orleans, LA 70118-5669. Offers MS, PhD. *Faculty:* 11 full-time. *Students:* 21 full-time (3 women), 1 part-time; includes 2 minority (1 African American, 1 American Indian/Alaska Native), 8 international. 52 applicants, 8% accepted, 4 enrolled. In 2003, 2 master's, 5 doctorates awarded. *Degree requirements:* For master's, thesis or alternative; for doctorate, thesis/dissertation. *Entrance requirements:* For master's, GRE General Test, minimum B average in undergraduate course work; for doctorate, GRE General Test. Additional exam requirements/recommendations for international students: Required—TOEFL; Recommended—TSE. *Application deadline:* For fall admission, 2/1 for domestic students, 2/1 for international students. Application fee: $45. *Financial support:* Fellowships, research assistantships with full tuition reimbursements, teaching assistantships with full tuition reimbursements, career-related internships or fieldwork, Federal Work-Study, and institutionally sponsored loans available. Financial award application deadline: 2/1. *Faculty research:* Surface physics, condensed-matter experiment, condensed-matter theory, nuclear theory, polymers. Total annual research expenditures: $700,000. *Unit head:* Dr. James McGuire, Chair, 504-865-5520, Fax: 504-862-8702. *Application contact:* Dr. Arthur Hancock, Graduate Adviser, 504-865-5520.

Université de Moncton, Faculty of Science, Department of Physics and Astronomy, Moncton, NB E1A 3E9, Canada. Offers M Sc. *Degree requirements:* For master's, thesis. *Entrance* *requirements:* For master's, proficiency in French. Electronic applications accepted. *Faculty research:* Thin films, optical properties, solar selective surfaces, microgravity and photonic materials.

Université de Montréal, Faculty of Graduate Studies, Faculty of Arts and Sciences, Department of Physics, Montréal, QC H3C 3J7, Canada. Offers M Sc, PhD. *Faculty:* 35 full-time (2 women), 9 part-time/adjunct (0 women). *Students:* 106 full-time (28 women). 28 applicants, 29% accepted, 8 enrolled. In 2003, 15 master's, 8 doctorates awarded. *Degree requirements:* For doctorate, thesis/dissertation, general exam. *Application deadline:* For fall and spring admission, 2/1; for winter admission, 11/1 for domestic students. Electronic applications accepted. *Expenses:* Tuition, state resident: full-time $834. Tuition, nonresident: full-time $1,253. International tuition: $3,900 full-time. Tuition and fees vary according to program. *Financial support:* Fellowships, research assistantships, teaching assistantships available. *Faculty research:* Astronomy; biophysics; solid-state, plasma, and nuclear physics. Total annual research expenditures: $5.8 million. *Unit head:* Laurent Lewis, Chairman, 514-343-6669, Fax: 514-343-2071. *Application contact:* Louise La Fortune, Student Files Management Technician, 514-343-6667, Fax: 514-343-2071.

Université de Sherbrooke, Faculty of Sciences, Department of Physics, Sherbrooke, QC J1K 2R1, Canada. Offers M Sc, PhD. *Degree requirements:* For master's and doctorate, thesis/dissertation. *Entrance requirements:* For doctorate, master's degree. *Faculty research:* Solid-state physics.

Université Laval, Faculty of Sciences and Engineering, Department of Physics, Physical Engineering, and Optics, Programs in Physics, Québec, QC G1K 7P4, Canada. Offers M Sc, PhD. Terminal master's awarded for partial completion of doctoral program. *Degree requirements:* For master's, thesis/dissertation; for doctorate, thesis/dissertation, comprehensive exam. *Entrance requirements:* For master's and doctorate, knowledge of French, comprehension of written English. Electronic applications accepted.

University at Albany, State University of New York, College of Arts and Sciences, Department of Physics, Albany, NY 12222-0001. Offers MS, PhD. Evening/weekend programs available. *Students:* 53 full-time (6 women), 15 part-time (1 woman). Average age 29. 44 applicants, 41% accepted, 10 enrolled. In 2003, 17 master's, 5 doctorates awarded. *Degree requirements:* For master's, one foreign language; for doctorate, one foreign language, thesis/dissertation. *Entrance requirements:* Additional exam requirements/recommendations for international students: Required—TOEFL (minimum score 550 paper-based; 213 computer-based). *Application deadline:* For fall admission, 8/1 for domestic students, 5/1 for international students. Applications are processed on a rolling basis. Application fee: $50. Electronic applications accepted. *Expenses:* Tuition, state resident: part-time $288 per credit. Tuition, nonresident: part-time $438 per credit. Required fees: $495 per semester. *Financial support:* Fellowships, research assistantships, teaching assistantships, minority assistantships available. Financial award application deadline: 6/15. *Faculty research:* Condensed-matter physics, high-energy physics, applied physics, electronic materials, theoretical particle physics. *Unit head:* Mohammed Sajjad Alam, Chair, 518-442-4500.

University at Buffalo, The State University of New York, Graduate School, College of Arts and Sciences, Department of Physics, Buffalo, NY 14260. Offers MS, PhD. Part-time programs available. *Faculty:* 20 full-time (2 women), 2 part-time/adjunct (0 women). *Students:* 73 full-time (12 women), 5 part-time (1 woman); includes 2 minority (1 Asian American or Pacific Islander, 1 Hispanic American), 58 international. Average age 29. 213 applicants, 23% accepted, 20 enrolled. In 2003, 5 master's, 5 doctorates awarded. Terminal master's awarded for partial completion of doctoral program. *Median time to degree:* Of those who began their doctoral program in fall 1995, 33% received their degree in 8 years or less. *Degree requirements:* For master's, thesis, qualifying exam; for doctorate, thesis/dissertation, qualifying exams. *Entrance requirements:* For master's and doctorate, GRE Subject Test, letters of recommendation. Additional exam requirements/recommendations for international students: Required—TOEFL (minimum score 550 paper-based; 213 computer-based). *Application deadline:* For fall admission, 2/1 priority date for domestic students, 2/1 priority date for international students; for spring admission, 10/1 priority date for domestic students, 10/1 priority date for international students. Applications are processed on a rolling basis. Application fee: $35. Electronic applications accepted. *Expenses:* Tuition, state resident: full-time $7,110. Tuition, nonresident: full-time $10,920. Tuition and fees vary according to program. *Financial support:* In 2003–04, 58 students received support, including 6 fellowships with full tuition reimbursements available (averaging $19,850 per year), 26 research assistantships with full tuition reimbursements available (averaging $16,700 per year), 34 teaching assistantships with full tuition reimbursements available (averaging $11,435 per year); Federal Work-Study, institutionally sponsored loans, and unspecified assistantships also available. Financial award application deadline: 3/1; financial award applicants required to submit FAFSA. *Faculty research:* Condensed-matter physics (experimental and theoretical), high energy and particle physics (experimental and theoretical), computational physics, medical physics, materials physics. Total annual research expenditures: $1.9 million. *Unit head:* Dr. Richard J. Gonsalves, Chairman, 716-645-2017 Ext. 191, Fax: 716-645-2507, E-mail: phygons@buffalo.edu. *Application contact:* Dr. Athos C. Petrou, Director of Graduate Studies, 716-645-2017 Ext. 30, Fax: 716-645-2507, E-mail: petrou@buffalo.edu.

The University of Akron, Graduate School, Buchtel College of Arts and Sciences, Department of Physics, Akron, OH 44325-0001. Offers MS. Part-time and evening/weekend programs available. *Faculty:* 9 full-time (1 woman). *Students:* 9 full-time (2 women), 5 international. Average age 30. 10 applicants, 40% accepted, 2 enrolled. In 2003, 3 degrees awarded. *Degree requirements:* For master's, thesis or written exam or formal report, thesis optional. *Entrance requirements:* For master's, minimum GPA of 2.75. Additional exam requirements/recommendations for international students: Required—TOEFL (minimum score 550 paper-based; 213 computer-based), Michigan English Language Assessment Battery. *Application deadline:* For fall admission, 8/15 for domestic students. Applications are processed on a rolling basis. Application fee: $40 ($60 for international students). *Expenses:* Tuition, state resident: part-time $277 per credit hour. Tuition, nonresident: part-time $476 per credit hour. *Financial support:* In 2003–04, 1 research assistantship with full tuition reimbursement, 12 teaching assistantships with full tuition reimbursements were awarded. Tuition waivers (full) also available. *Faculty research:* Polymer physics, statistical physics, NMR, electron tunneling, solid-state physics. Total annual research expenditures: $273,323. *Unit head:* Dr. Robert Mallik, Chair, 330-972-7145, E-mail: rmallik@uakron.edu. *Application contact:* Dr. Jutta Luettmer-Strathman, Head, 330-972-8029, E-mail: jutta@uakron.edu.

The University of Alabama, Graduate School, College of Arts and Sciences, Department of Physics and Astronomy, Tuscaloosa, AL 35487. Offers physics (MS, PhD). *Faculty:* 20 full-time (0 women), 2 part-time/adjunct (1 woman). *Students:* 38 full-time (7 women), 7 part-time; includes 3 minority (1 African American, 1 Asian American or Pacific Islander, 1 Hispanic American), 30 international. Average age 29. 63 applicants, 27% accepted, 5 enrolled. In 2003, 5 master's, 2 doctorates awarded. Terminal master's awarded for partial completion of doctoral program. *Degree requirements:* For master's, oral exam, thesis optional; for doctorate, thesis/dissertation, oral and written exams. *Entrance requirements:* For master's and doctorate, GRE General Test or GRE Subject Test, minimum GPA of 3.0. Additional exam requirements/recommendations for international students: Required—TOEFL. *Application deadline:* For fall admission, 7/6 for domestic students; for spring admission, 11/22 for domestic students. Applications are processed on a rolling basis. Application fee: $25. Electronic applications accepted. *Expenses:* Tuition, state resident: full-time $4,134; part-time $230 per credit hour. Tuition, nonresident: full-time $11,294; part-time $627 per credit hour. Part-time tuition and fees vary according to course load. *Financial support:* In 2003–04, 28 students received support, including 3 fellowships with full tuition reimbursements available (averaging $14,000 per year), 18 research assistantships with full tuition reimbursements available (averaging $11,000 per year), 19 teaching assistantships with full tuition reimbursements available (averaging $11,000 per year); career-related internships or fieldwork and institutionally sponsored loans also available. Financial award application deadline: 4/1. *Faculty research:* Condensed-matter, high-energy physics; optics; molecular spectroscopy; astrophysics. Total annual research expenditures: $1.3 million. *Unit head:* Dr. Stanley T. Jones, Chair, 205-348-5050, Fax: 205-348-5051, E-mail: stjones@bama.ua.edu.

The University of Alabama at Birmingham, School of Natural Sciences and Mathematics, Department of Physics, Birmingham, AL 35294. Offers MS, PhD. *Students:* 23 full-time (4 women), 1 part-time; includes 1 minority (Hispanic American), 11 international. 57 applicants, 39% accepted. In 2003, 4 master's, 5 doctorates awarded. Terminal master's awarded for partial completion of doctoral program. *Degree requirements:* For master's, thesis optional; for doctorate, thesis/dissertation. *Entrance requirements:* For master's and doctorate, GRE General Test, minimum GPA of 3.0. Additional exam requirements/recommendations for international students: Required—TOEFL. *Application deadline:* Applications are processed on a rolling basis. Application fee: $35 ($60 for international students). Electronic applications accepted. *Expenses:* Tuition, state resident: full-time $4,142; part-time $141 per credit hour. Tuition, nonresident: full-time $9,230; part-time $353 per credit hour. Required fees: $4 per credit hour. *Financial support:* In 2003–04, 9 fellowships with full tuition reimbursements (averaging $16,898 per year), 4 research assistantships (averaging $15,170 per year), 8 teaching assistantships with full tuition reimbursements (averaging $12,825 per year) were awarded. Career-related internships or fieldwork, Federal Work-Study, institutionally sponsored loans, scholarships/grants, traineeships, and unspecified assistantships also available. Support available to part-time students. Financial award application deadline: 4/15; financial award applicants required to submit FAFSA. *Faculty research:* Laser physics, space physics, optics, biophysics, material physics. *Unit head:* Dr. David L. Shealy, Chair, 205-934-4736, Fax: 205-934-8042.

The University of Alabama in Huntsville, School of Graduate Studies, College of Science, Department of Physics, Huntsville, AL 35899. Offers MS, PhD. Part-time and evening/weekend programs available. *Faculty:* 11 full-time (0 women), 1 part-time/adjunct (0 women). *Students:* 34 full-time (8 women), 16 part-time (2 women); includes 2 minority (1 American Indian/Alaska Native, 1 Hispanic American), 17 international. Average age 29. 39 applicants, 92% accepted, 23 enrolled. In 2003, 4 master's, 3 doctorates awarded. *Degree requirements:* For master's, thesis or alternative, oral and written exams, comprehensive exam, registration; for doctorate, thesis/dissertation, oral and written exams, comprehensive exam, registration. *Entrance requirements:* For master's and doctorate, GRE General Test, minimum GPA of 3.0. Additional exam requirements/recommendations for international students: Required—TOEFL (minimum score 550 paper-based; 213 computer-based). *Application deadline:* For fall admission, 5/30 priority date for domestic students, 2/30 priority date for international students; for spring admission, 10/10 priority date for domestic students, 7/10 priority date for international students. Applications are processed on a rolling basis. Application fee: $35. *Expenses:* Tuition, state resident: full-time $5,168; part-time $211 per hour. Tuition, nonresident: full-time $10,620; part-time $447 per hour. Tuition and fees vary according to course load. *Financial support:* In 2003–04, 30 students received support, including 21 research assistantships with full and partial tuition reimbursements available (averaging $9,798 per year), 9 teaching assistantships with full and partial tuition reimbursements available (averaging $9,800 per year); fellowships with full and partial tuition reimbursements available, career-related internships or fieldwork, Federal Work-Study, institutionally sponsored loans, scholarships/grants, health care benefits, tuition waivers (full and partial), and unspecified assistantships also available. Support available to part-time students. Financial award application deadline: 4/1; financial award applicants required to submit FAFSA. *Faculty research:* Space sciences, solid state/materials, optics/quantum electronics, astrophysics, crystal growth. Total annual research expenditures: $1.1 million. *Unit head:* Dr. Lloyd Hillman, Chair, 256-824-2482, Fax: 256-824-6873, E-mail: hillmanl@email.uah.edu.

University of Alaska Fairbanks, College of Science, Engineering and Mathematics, Department of Physics, Fairbanks, AK 99775-7520. Offers atmospheric science (MS, PhD); physics (MS, PhD); space physics (MS, PhD). Part-time programs available. Terminal master's awarded for partial completion of doctoral program. *Degree requirements:* For master's, thesis or alternative, comprehensive exam, registration; for doctorate, one foreign language, thesis/dissertation, comprehensive exam, registration. *Entrance requirements:* For master's and doctorate, GRE General Test, GRE Subject Test. Additional exam requirements/recommendations for international students: Required—TOEFL. Electronic applications accepted. *Faculty research:* Atmospheric and ionospheric radar studies, space plasma theory, magnetospheric dynamics, space weather and auroral studies, turbulence and complex systems.

University of Alberta, Faculty of Graduate Studies and Research, Department of Physics, Edmonton, AB T6G 2E1, Canada. Offers astrophysics (M Sc, PhD); condensed matter (M Sc, PhD); geophysics (M Sc, PhD); medical physics (M Sc, PhD); subatomic physics (M Sc, PhD). *Faculty:* 36 full-time (3 women), 7 part-time/adjunct (0 women). *Students:* 56 full-time (6 women), 16 part-time (2 women), 25 international. 85 applicants, 35% accepted. In 2003, 7 master's, 10 doctorates awarded. *Degree requirements:* For master's and doctorate, thesis/dissertation. *Entrance requirements:* For master's and doctorate, minimum GPA of 7.0 on a 9.0 scale. Additional exam requirements/recommendations for international students: Required—TOEFL. *Application deadline:* For fall admission, 2/15 for domestic students. Applications are processed on a rolling basis. Tuition charges are reported in Canadian dollars. Tuition, nonresident: full-time $3,921 Canadian dollars. International tuition: $7,113 Canadian dollars full-time. *Financial support:* In 2003–04, 45 students received support, including 6 fellowships with partial tuition reimbursements available, 40 teaching assistantships; research assistantships, career-related internships or fieldwork, institutionally sponsored loans, and scholarships/grants also available. Financial award application deadline: 2/15. *Faculty research:* Cosmology, astroparticle physics, high-intermediate energy, magnetism, superconductivity. Total annual research expenditures: $3.1 million. *Unit head:* Dr. Richard Sydora, Associate Chair, 780-492-1072, E-mail: assoc-chair@phys.ualberta.ca. *Application contact:* Lynn Chandler, Program Advisor, 780-492-1072, Fax: 780-492-0714, E-mail: lynn@phys.ualberta.ca.

The University of Arizona, Graduate College, College of Science, Department of Physics, Tucson, AZ 85721. Offers M Ed, MS, PhD. Part-time programs available. Terminal master's awarded for partial completion of doctoral program. *Degree requirements:* For master's, thesis optional; for doctorate, thesis/dissertation, comprehensive exam. *Entrance requirements:* For master's and doctorate, GRE General Test, GRE Subject Test, minimum GPA of 3.0. Additional exam requirements/recommendations for international students: Required—TOEFL; Recommended—TSE. *Expenses:* Tuition, state resident: part-time $196 per unit. Tuition, nonresident: part-time $326 per unit. *Faculty research:* Astrophysics; high-energy, condensed-matter, atomic and molecular physics; optics.

University of Arkansas, Graduate School, J. William Fulbright College of Arts and Sciences, Department of Physics, Fayetteville, AR 72701-1201. Offers applied physics (MS); physics (MS, PhD); physics education (MA). *Students:* 38 full-time (5 women), 7 part-time (3 women); includes 3 minority (2 Asian Americans or Pacific Islanders, 1 Hispanic American), 21 international. 47 applicants, 32% accepted. In 2003, 7 master's, 1 doctorate awarded. *Degree requirements:* For master's and doctorate, thesis/dissertation. Application fee: $40 ($50 for international students). *Expenses:* Tuition, state resident: full-time $4,032; part-time $224 per credit hour. Tuition, nonresident: full-time $9,540; part-time $530 per credit hour. Tuition and fees vary according to course load and program. *Financial support:* In 2003–04, 5 fellowships, 11 research assistantships, 23 teaching assistantships were awarded. Career-related internships or fieldwork and Federal Work-Study also available. Support available to part-time students. Financial award application deadline: 4/1; financial award applicants required to submit FAFSA. *Unit head:* Dr. William F. Oliver, Chair, 479-575-6571, E-mail: woliver@uark.edu. *Application contact:* Raj Gupta, Graduate Coordinator, 479-575-5933, E-mail: rgupta@uark.edu.

The University of British Columbia, Faculty of Graduate Studies, Faculty of Science, Department of Physics and Astronomy, Vancouver, BC V6T 1Z1, Canada. Offers engineering physics (MA Sc); physics (M Sc, PhD). *Degree requirements:* For master's, thesis/dissertation;

Physics

The University of British Columbia (continued)

for doctorate, thesis/dissertation, comprehensive exam. *Entrance requirements:* For master's, GRE General Test, honors degree; for doctorate, GRE General Test, master's degree. Additional exam requirements/recommendations for international students: Required—TOEFL. *Faculty research:* Applied physics, astrophysics, condensed matter, plasma physics, subatomic physics, astronomy.

University of Calgary, Faculty of Graduate Studies, Faculty of Science, Department of Physics and Astronomy, Calgary, AB T2N 1N4, Canada. Offers M Sc, PhD. Part-time programs available. *Faculty:* 22 full-time (1 woman), 12 part-time/adjunct (0 women). *Students:* 39 full-time (8 women), 3 part-time (2 women). Average age 28. 50 applicants, 46% accepted, 13 enrolled. In 2003, 4 master's, 1 doctorate awarded. *Degree requirements:* For master's, thesis; for doctorate, thesis/dissertation, oral candidacy exam, written qualifying exam. *Entrance requirements:* For master's and doctorate, GRE General Test, GRE Subject Test. Additional exam requirements/recommendations for international students: Required—TOEFL (minimum score 550 paper-based; 213 computer-based). *Application deadline:* For fall admission, 3/1 for domestic students, 3/1 for international students; for winter admission, 7/1 for domestic students. Applications are processed on a rolling basis. Application fee: $60. Electronic applications accepted. Tuition, nonresident: full-time $4,765. Tuition and fees vary according to degree level, program and student level. *Financial support:* Fellowships with full and partial tuition reimbursements, research assistantships, teaching assistantships, institutionally sponsored loans available. Financial award application deadline: 2/1. *Faculty research:* Astronomy and astrophysics, mass spectrometry, atmospheric physics, space physics, medical physics. Total annual research expenditures: $4.6 million. *Unit head:* Dr. R. B. Hicks, Head, 403-220-5385, Fax: 403-289-3331, E-mail: hicks@ucalgary.ca. *Application contact:* Dr. R. I. Thompson, Chairman, Graduate Affairs, 403-220-5407, Fax: 403-289-3331, E-mail: gradinfo@ucalgary.ca.

University of California, Berkeley, Graduate Division, College of Letters and Science, Department of Physics, Berkeley, CA 94720-1500. Offers PhD. *Faculty:* 48 full-time (4 women), 11 part-time/adjunct. *Students:* 232 (29 women); includes 34 minority (5 African Americans, 1 American Indian/Alaska Native, 17 Asian Americans or Pacific Islanders, 11 Hispanic Americans) 55 international. Average age 25. 778 applicants, 14% accepted, 38 enrolled. In 2003, 28 degrees awarded. *Degree requirements:* For doctorate, thesis/dissertation, qualifying exam. *Entrance requirements:* For doctorate, GRE General Test, GRE Subject Test, minimum GPA of 3.0. Additional exam requirements/recommendations for international students: Required—TOEFL (minimum score 570 paper-based; 230 computer-based); Recommended—TSE(minimum score 50). *Application deadline:* For fall admission, 1/5 for domestic students, 1/5 for international students. Application fee: $60. International tuition: $12,491 full-time. Required fees: $5,484. *Financial support:* In 2003–04, fellowships with full tuition reimbursements (averaging $18,000 per year), research assistantships with full tuition reimbursements (averaging $20,203 per year), teaching assistantships with full tuition reimbursements (averaging $7,072 per year) were awarded. Institutionally sponsored loans, health care benefits, and unspecified assistantships also available. Financial award application deadline: 1/5; financial award applicants required to submit FAFSA. *Faculty research:* Astrophysics (experimental and theoretical), condensed matter physics (experimental and theoretical), particle physics (experimental and theoretical), atomic/molecular/botical physics, biophysics and complex systems. Total annual research expenditures: $4.6 million. *Unit head:* Dr. Christopher F. McKee, Chair, 510-642-3316, Fax: 510-643-8497, E-mail: chair@physics.berkeley.edu. *Application contact:* Donna K. Sakima, Student Affairs Officer, 510-642-0596, Fax: 510-643-8497, E-mail: sakima@physics.berkeley.edu.

University of California, Davis, Graduate Studies, Program in Physics, Davis, CA 95616. Offers MS, PhD. *Faculty:* 33 full-time (3 women), 12 part-time/adjunct (3 women). *Students:* 103 full-time (18 women); includes 14 minority (2 African Americans, 10 Asian Americans or Pacific Islanders, 2 Hispanic Americans), 22 international. Average age 30. 128 applicants, 47% accepted, 27 enrolled. In 2003, 1 master's, 3 doctorates awarded. Terminal master's awarded for partial completion of doctoral program. *Degree requirements:* For master's, thesis optional; for doctorate, thesis/dissertation. *Entrance requirements:* For master's and doctorate, GRE General Test, GRE Subject Test, minimum GPA of 3.0. Additional exam requirements/recommendations for international students: Required—TOEFL (minimum score 550 paper-based; 213 computer-based). *Application deadline:* For fall admission, 4/1 for domestic students, 3/1 for international students. Application fee: $60. Electronic applications accepted. Tuition, nonresident: full-time $12,245. Required fees: $7,062. *Financial support:* In 2003–04, 94 students received support, including fellowships with full and partial tuition reimbursements available (averaging $5,394 per year), 34 research assistantships with full and partial tuition reimbursements available (averaging $12,964 per year), 40 teaching assistantships with partial tuition reimbursements available (averaging $14,309 per year); Federal Work-Study, institutionally sponsored loans, scholarships/grants, and tuition waivers (full and partial) also available. Financial award application deadline: 1/15; financial award applicants required to submit FAFSA. *Faculty research:* Astrophysics, condensed-matter physics, nuclear physics, particle physics, quantum optics. *Unit head:* Shirley Chiang, Chair, 530-752-8538, E-mail: chiang@physics.ucdavis.edu. *Application contact:* Robyn Tornay, Administrative Assistant, 530-752-4086, E-mail: tornay@physics.ucdavis.edu.

University of California, Irvine, Office of Graduate Studies, School of Physical Sciences, Department of Physics and Astronomy, Irvine, CA 92697. Offers physics (MS, PhD). *Students:* 76. In 2003, 3 master's, 4 doctorates awarded. Terminal master's awarded for partial completion of doctoral program. *Degree requirements:* For doctorate, thesis/dissertation. *Entrance requirements:* For master's and doctorate, GRE General Test, GRE Subject Test, minimum GPA of 3.0. Additional exam requirements/recommendations for international students: Required—TOEFL (minimum score 550 paper-based; 213 computer-based). *Application deadline:* For fall admission, 1/15 for domestic students; for winter admission, 10/15 for domestic students. Applications are processed on a rolling basis. Application fee: $60. Electronic applications accepted. Tuition, nonresident: full-time $12,245. Required fees: $5,219. Tuition and fees vary according to degree level and program. *Financial support:* In 2003–04, fellowships with full tuition reimbursements (averaging $7,500 per year), research assistantships with full tuition reimbursements (averaging $18,300 per year), teaching assistantships with partial tuition reimbursements (averaging $13,595 per year) were awarded. Institutionally sponsored loans, traineeships, health care benefits, and unspecified assistantships also available. Financial award application deadline: 3/1; financial award applicants required to submit FAFSA. *Faculty research:* Condensed-matter physics, plasma physics, astrophysics, particle physics, chemical and materials physics. *Unit head:* Dr. Andrew Lankford, Chair, 949-824-2632, Fax: 949-824-2174, E-mail: ajlankfo@uci.edu. *Application contact:* Julie Aird, Graduate Student Affairs Officer, 949-824-5438, Fax: 949-824-2174, E-mail: jaird@uci.edu.

University of California, Los Angeles, Graduate Division, College of Letters and Science, Department of Physics and Astronomy, Program in Physics, Los Angeles, CA 90095. Offers physics (MS, PhD); physics education (MAT). MAT admits only applicants whose objective is PhD. *Degree requirements:* For master's, comprehensive exam or thesis; for doctorate, thesis/dissertation, oral and written qualifying exams. *Entrance requirements:* For master's, GRE General Test, GRE Subject Test (physics), minimum GPA of 3.0; for doctorate, GRE General Test, GRE Subject Test (physics), minimum undergraduate GPA of 3.0. Electronic applications accepted. Tuition, nonresident: full-time $12,245. Required fees: $6,318.

Announcement: Strong, broad research and graduate student programs in both experimental and theoretical physics: condensed matter, low temperature, plasma, astrophysics, biophysics, high energy, intermediate energy, nuclear physics. Approximately 60 faculty members, 110 graduate students; 20 PhDs per year. Strong research funding. Financial support for essentially all graduate students. Near ocean in attractive West Los Angeles. http://www.physics.ucla.edu.

University of California, Riverside, Graduate Division, Department of Physics, Riverside, CA 92521-0102. Offers MS, PhD. Part-time programs available. *Faculty:* 23 full-time (2 women), 8 part-time/adjunct (1 woman). *Students:* 53 full-time (10 women); includes 9 minority (1 African American, 3 Asian Americans or Pacific Islanders, 5 Hispanic Americans), 27 international. Average age 29. In 2003, 9 master's, 8 doctorates awarded. Terminal master's awarded for partial completion of doctoral program. *Median time to degree:* Master's–2 years full-time; doctorate–6 years full-time. *Degree requirements:* For master's, comprehensive exams or thesis; for doctorate, thesis/dissertation, qualifying exams. *Entrance requirements:* For master's and doctorate, GRE General Test, minimum GPA of 3.2. Additional exam requirements/recommendations for international students: Required—TOEFL (minimum score 550 paper-based; 213 computer-based); Recommended—TSE. *Application deadline:* For fall admission, 5/1 for domestic students, 2/1 for international students; for winter admission, 9/1 for domestic students; for spring admission, 12/1 for domestic students. Applications are processed on a rolling basis. Application fee: $60. Electronic applications accepted. Tuition, nonresident: part-time $4,082 per quarter. *Financial support:* In 2003–04, fellowships (averaging $12,000 per year); research assistantships, teaching assistantships, career-related internships or fieldwork, Federal Work-Study, institutionally sponsored loans, scholarships/grants, health care benefits, and unspecified assistantships also available. Financial award application deadline: 1/5; financial award applicants required to submit FAFSA. *Faculty research:* Laser physics and surface science, elementary particle and heavy ion physics, plasma physics, optical physics, astrophysics. *Application contact:* Pat Brooks, Student Affairs Officer, 951-827-5332, Fax: 951-827-4529, E-mail: gophysics@ucr.edu.

University of California, San Diego, Graduate Studies and Research, Department of Physics, La Jolla, CA 92093. Offers biophysics (MS, PhD); physics (MS, PhD); physics/materials physics (MS). *Faculty:* 51. *Students:* 128 (16 women); includes 13 minority (6 Asian Americans or Pacific Islanders, 7 Hispanic Americans) 37 international. 607 applicants, 22% accepted. In 2003, 16 master's, 15 doctorates awarded. *Degree requirements:* For doctorate, thesis/dissertation. *Entrance requirements:* For master's and doctorate, GRE General Test, GRE Subject Test. Additional exam requirements/recommendations for international students: Required—TOEFL. *Application deadline:* For fall admission, 1/16 for domestic students. Application fee: $60. Electronic applications accepted. Tuition, nonresident: full-time $12,245. Required fees: $6,959. *Unit head:* John Goodkind, Chair, 858-534-6857, E-mail: jgookind@ucsd.edu. *Application contact:* Debra Bomar, Graduate Coordinator, 858-534-3293, E-mail: dbomar@physics.ucsd.edu.

University of California, Santa Barbara, Graduate Division, College of Letters and Sciences, Division of Mathematics, Life, and Physical Sciences, Department of Physics, Santa Barbara, CA 93106. Offers PhD. *Degree requirements:* For doctorate, thesis/dissertation. *Entrance requirements:* For doctorate, GRE General Test, GRE Subject Test. Additional exam requirements/recommendations for international students: Required—TOEFL. *Application deadline:* For fall admission, 3/15 for domestic students. Application fee: $60. *Expenses:* Tuition, state resident: full-time $7,188. Tuition, nonresident: full-time $19,608. *Financial support:* Fellowships, research assistantships, teaching assistantships, career-related internships or fieldwork, Federal Work-Study, institutionally sponsored loans, and tuition waivers (full and partial) available. Financial award application deadline: 1/15; financial award applicants required to submit FAFSA. *Unit head:* James Allen, Chair, 805-893-4888. *Application contact:* Shilo Creek, Graduate Program Assistant, 805-893-4646, E-mail: shilo@physics. ucsb.edu.

University of California, Santa Cruz, Division of Graduate Studies, Division of Physical and Biological Sciences, Program in Physics, Santa Cruz, CA 95064. Offers MS, PhD. *Faculty:* 19 full-time (1 woman). *Students:* 61 full-time (18 women); includes 9 minority (1 African American, 5 Asian Americans or Pacific Islanders, 3 Hispanic Americans), 5 international. 151 applicants, 31% accepted, 12 enrolled. In 2003, 4 master's, 6 doctorates awarded. *Median time to degree:* Master's–2.2 years full-time; doctorate–5.87 years full-time. *Degree requirements:* For master's, thesis; for doctorate, one foreign language, thesis/dissertation, qualifying exam. *Entrance requirements:* For master's and doctorate, GRE General Test, GRE Subject Test. *Application deadline:* For fall admission, 1/15 for domestic students. Application fee: $60. Tuition, nonresident: full-time $12,492. *Financial support:* Fellowships, research assistantships, teaching assistantships, career-related internships or fieldwork, Federal Work-Study, and institutionally sponsored loans available. Financial award application deadline: 1/15. *Faculty research:* Theoretical and experimental high-energy physics, theoretical and experimental solid-state physics, critical phenomena, theoretical fluid dynamics, experimental biophysics. *Unit head:* Dr. David Dorfan, Chair, 831-459-2327. *Application contact:* James M. Moore, Graduate Admissions, Director, 831-459-2301, Fax: 831-459-4843, E-mail: gradadm@ucsc.edu.

University of Central Florida, College of Arts and Sciences, Department of Physics, Orlando, FL 32816. Offers MS, PhD. Part-time and evening/weekend programs available. *Faculty:* 20 full-time (4 women), 4 part-time/adjunct (2 women). *Students:* 29 full-time (5 women), 21 part-time (4 women); includes 8 minority (7 African Americans, 1 Asian American or Pacific Islander), 14 international. Average age 30. 56 applicants, 48% accepted, 17 enrolled. In 2003, 7 master's, 5 doctorates awarded. *Degree requirements:* For master's, thesis or alternative; for doctorate, thesis/dissertation, candidacy and qualifying exams. *Entrance requirements:* For master's, GRE General Test, minimum GPA of 3.0 in last 60 hours; for doctorate, GRE General Test, GRE Subject Test, minimum GPA of 3.0 in last 60 hours or master's qualifying exam. Additional exam requirements/recommendations for international students: Required—TOEFL. *Application deadline:* For fall admission, 2/15 for domestic students. Application fee: $30. Electronic applications accepted. *Expenses:* Tuition, state resident: full-time $4,968; part-time $171 per credit hour. Tuition, nonresident: full-time $18,630; part-time $713 per credit hour. *Financial support:* In 2003–04, 9 fellowships with partial tuition reimbursements (averaging $6,144 per year), 22 research assistantships with partial tuition reimbursements (averaging $10,844 per year), 28 teaching assistantships with partial tuition reimbursements (averaging $8,120 per year) were awarded. Career-related internships or fieldwork, Federal Work-Study, institutionally sponsored loans, tuition waivers (partial), and unspecified assistantships also available. Financial award application deadline: 3/1; financial award applicants required to submit FAFSA. *Faculty research:* Atomic-molecular physics, condensed-matter physics, biophysics of proteins, laser physics. *Unit head:* Dr. Ralph A. Llewellyn, Interim Chair, 407-823-2790, E-mail: ral@pysics.ucf.edu. *Application contact:* Dr. Robert Peale, Coordinator, 407-823-5208, Fax: 407-823-5112, E-mail: rep@physics.ucf.edu.

University of Chicago, Division of the Physical Sciences, Department of Physics, Chicago, IL 60637-1513. Offers PhD. *Faculty:* 32 full-time (3 women), 5 part-time/adjunct (0 women). *Students:* 128 full-time (13 women); includes 8 minority (7 Asian Americans or Pacific Islanders, 1 Hispanic American), 73 international. Average age 25. In 2003, 18 degrees awarded. Terminal master's awarded for partial completion of doctoral program. *Median time to degree:* Of those who began their doctoral program in fall 1995, 72% received their degree in 8 years or less. *Degree requirements:* For doctorate, thesis/dissertation, candidacy exam. *Entrance requirements:* For doctorate, GRE General Test, GRE Subject Test, BS or equivalent. Additional exam requirements/recommendations for international students: Required—TOEFL (minimum score 600 paper-based; 250 computer-based). *Application deadline:* For fall admission, 12/28 for domestic students, 12/28 for international students. Applications are processed on a rolling basis. Application fee: $55. *Financial support:* In 2003–04, 24 fellowships with full tuition reimbursements (averaging $18,000 per year), 72 research assistantships with full tuition reimbursements (averaging $19,800 per year), 32 teaching assistantships with full tuition reimbursements (averaging $14,850 per year) were awarded. Institutionally sponsored loans, tuition waivers (partial), and unspecified assistantships also available. Financial award application deadline: 12/28. *Faculty research:* Astrophysics, particle physics, condensed-matter physics, statistical physics, relativity. Total annual research expenditures: $20.3 million. *Unit head:* Robert Wald, Chair, 773-702-7006, Fax: 773-702-2045. *Application contact:* Nobuko B. McNeill, Assistant to the Chairman for Graduate Affairs, 773-702-7007, Fax: 773-702-2045, E-mail: n-mcneill@uchicago.edu.

University of Chicago, Division of the Physical Sciences, Program in the Physical Sciences, Chicago, IL 60637-1513. Offers MS. Part-time programs available. *Students:* 3 full-time (1 woman), 2 part-time. Average age 24. 5 applicants, 60% accepted. *Degree requirements:* For master's, thesis. *Entrance requirements:* For master's, GRE. Additional exam requirements/recommendations for international students: Required—TOEFL. *Application deadline:* For fall admission, 2/28 for domestic students. Applications are processed on a rolling basis. Application fee: $55. *Financial support:* In 2003–04, 4 students received support; fellowships with partial tuition reimbursements available, research assistantships, teaching assistantships available. Financial award application deadline: 2/28; financial award applicants required to submit FAFSA. *Unit head:* Robert Wald, Chair, 773-702-7006, Fax: 773-702-2045. *Application contact:* Richard Hefley, Dean of Students, 773-702-8789.

University of Cincinnati, Division of Research and Advanced Studies, McMicken College of Arts and Sciences, Department of Physics, Cincinnati, OH 45221. Offers MS, PhD. Terminal master's awarded for partial completion of doctoral program. *Degree requirements:* For master's, thesis optional; for doctorate, thesis/dissertation. *Entrance requirements:* For master's and doctorate, GRE General Test, GRE Subject Test. Additional exam requirements/recommendations for international students: Required—TOEFL (minimum score 540 paper-based; 207 computer-based). Electronic applications accepted. *Faculty research:* Condensed matter physics, elementary particle physics, high energy physics, astronomy and astrophysics, astrophysics and relativity.

University of Colorado at Boulder, Graduate School, College of Arts and Sciences, Department of Physics, Boulder, CO 80309. Offers chemical physics (PhD); geophysics (PhD); liquid crystal science and technology (PhD); mathematical physics (PhD); medical physics (PhD); optical sciences and engineering (PhD); physics (MS, PhD). *Faculty:* 43 full-time (3 women). *Students:* 148 full-time (24 women), 42 part-time (8 women); includes 11 minority (2 African Americans, 1 American Indian/Alaska Native, 6 Asian Americans or Pacific Islanders, 2 Hispanic Americans), 56 international. Average age 27. 75 applicants, 65% accepted. In 2003, 1 master's, 20 doctorates awarded. Terminal master's awarded for partial completion of doctoral program. *Degree requirements:* For master's, thesis or alternative, comprehensive exam; for doctorate, thesis/dissertation, comprehensive exam. *Entrance requirements:* For master's and doctorate, GRE General Test, GRE Subject Test, minimum undergraduate GPA of 3.0. Additional exam requirements/recommendations for international students: Required—TOEFL. *Application deadline:* For fall admission, 1/15 for domestic students; for spring admission, 11/1 for domestic students. Applications are processed on a rolling basis. Application fee: $50 ($60 for international students). Electronic applications accepted. *Expenses:* Tuition, state resident: full-time $2,122. Tuition, nonresident: full-time $9,754. Tuition and fees vary according to course load and program. *Financial support:* In 2003–04, 14 fellowships with full tuition reimbursements (averaging $23,854 per year), 34 research assistantships with full tuition reimbursements (averaging $18,725 per year), 25 teaching assistantships with full tuition reimbursements (averaging $15,113 per year) were awarded. Scholarships/grants also available. Financial award application deadline: 1/15. *Faculty research:* Atomic and molecular physics, nuclear physics, condensed matter, elementary particle physics, laser or optical physics. Total annual research expenditures: $19.1 million. *Unit head:* John Cumalat, Chair, 303-492-6952, Fax: 303-492-3352, E-mail: jcumalat@pizero.colorado.edu. *Application contact:* Graduate Program Assistant, 303-492-6954, Fax: 303-492-3352, E-mail: phys@bogart.colorado.edu.

University of Connecticut, Graduate School, College of Liberal Arts and Sciences, Department of Physics, Field of Physics, Storrs, CT 06269. Offers MS, PhD. *Faculty:* 41 full-time (2 women). *Students:* 61 full-time (11 women), 5 part-time; includes 1 minority (Asian American or Pacific Islander), 46 international. Average age 29. 98 applicants, 23% accepted, 23 enrolled. In 2003, 11 master's, 3 doctorates awarded. Terminal master's awarded for partial completion of doctoral program. *Degree requirements:* For master's, comprehensive exam; for doctorate, thesis/dissertation. *Entrance requirements:* For master's and doctorate, GRE General Test, GRE Subject Test. Additional exam requirements/recommendations for international students: Required—TOEFL (minimum score 550 paper-based; 213 computer-based). *Application deadline:* For fall admission, 2/1 priority date for domestic students, 2/1 priority date for international students; for spring admission, 11/1 for domestic students, 10/1 for international students. Applications are processed on a rolling basis. Application fee: $55. Electronic applications accepted. *Expenses:* Tuition, state resident: part-time $3,860 per semester. Tuition, nonresident: part-time $9,036 per semester. *Financial support:* In 2003–04, 29 research assistantships with full tuition reimbursements, 31 teaching assistantships with full tuition reimbursements were awarded. Fellowships, Federal Work-Study, scholarships/grants, health care benefits, and unspecified assistantships also available. Financial award application deadline: 2/1; financial award applicants required to submit FAFSA. *Unit head:* Gerald Dunne, Chairperson, 860-486-4978, E-mail: gerald.dunne@uconn.edu. *Application contact:* Lorraine Smurra, Administrative Assistant, 860-486-0449, Fax: 860-486-3346, E-mail: physadm@uconnvm.uconn.edu.

See in-depth description on page 409.

University of Dayton, Graduate School, College of Arts and Sciences, Department of Physics, Dayton, OH 45469-1300. Offers MS. *Expenses:* Tuition: Full-time $6,060; part-time $505 per hour. Required fees: $50; $25 per term. Tuition and fees vary according to degree level, campus/location, program and student's religious affiliation. *Unit head:* Dr. Mike O'Hara, Chair, 937-229-2136.

University of Delaware, College of Arts and Sciences, Joint Graduate Program of Department of Physics and Astronomy and Bartol Research Institute, Newark, DE 19716. Offers physics (MA, MS, PhD). Part-time programs available. *Faculty:* 21 full-time (2 women), 3 part-time/adjunct (1 woman). *Students:* 70 full-time (15 women), 2 part-time; includes 3 minority (2 African Americans, 1 Asian American or Pacific Islander), 55 international. Average age 26. 134 applicants, 34% accepted, 24 enrolled. In 2003, 4 master's, 5 doctorates awarded. Terminal master's awarded for partial completion of doctoral program. *Degree requirements:* For master's and doctorate, thesis/dissertation. *Entrance requirements:* For master's and doctorate, GRE General Test, GRE Subject Test. *Application deadline:* For fall admission, 7/1 for domestic students. Application fee: $60. Electronic applications accepted. *Expenses:* Tuition, state resident: full-time $5,890; part-time $327 per credit. Tuition, nonresident: full-time $15,420; part-time $857 per credit. Required fees: $968. *Financial support:* In 2003–04, 70 students received support, including 2 fellowships with full tuition reimbursements available (averaging $11,000 per year), 27 research assistantships with full tuition reimbursements available (averaging $18,000 per year), 25 teaching assistantships with full tuition reimbursements available (averaging $18,000 per year); career-related internships or fieldwork, Federal Work-Study, institutionally sponsored loans, and corporate sponsorships also available. Financial award application deadline: 3/1. *Faculty research:* Magnetoresistance and magnetic materials, ultrafast optical phenomena, superfluidity, elementary particle physics, stellar atmospheres and interiors. Total annual research expenditures: $2.6 million. *Unit head:* Dr. George Hadjipanayis, Chair, 302-831-3361. *Application contact:* Dr. John Xiao, Information Contact, 302-831-1995, E-mail: grad.physics@udel.edu.

University of Denver, Graduate Studies, Faculty of Natural Sciences and Mathematics, Department of Physics and Astronomy, Denver, CO 80208. Offers MS, PhD. Part-time programs available. *Faculty:* 7 full-time (0 women), 3 part-time/adjunct (1 woman). *Students:* 8 (4 women) 2 international. 21 applicants, 62% accepted. In 2003, 2 degrees awarded. Terminal master's awarded for partial completion of doctoral program. *Degree requirements:* For master's, thesis optional; for doctorate, thesis/dissertation. *Entrance requirements:* For master's and doctorate, GRE General Test, minimum GPA of 3.0. Additional exam requirements/recommendations for international students: Required—TOEFL, TSE. *Application deadline:* Applications are processed on a rolling basis. Application fee: $45. *Expenses:* Tuition: Full-time $24,264. *Financial support:* In 2003–04, 3 students received support, including 3 research assistantships with full and partial tuition reimbursements available (averaging $12,285 per year), 3 teaching assistantships with full and partial tuition reimbursements available (averaging $12,096 per year); career-related internships or fieldwork, Federal Work-Study, institutionally sponsored loans, and scholarships/grants also available. Support available to part-time students. Financial award application deadline: 3/1; financial award applicants required to submit FAFSA. *Faculty research:* Atomic and molecular beams and collisions, infrared astronomy, acoustic emission from stressed solids. Total annual research expenditures: $2.3 million. *Unit head:* Dr. Herschel Neumann, Chair, 303-871-3544. *Application contact:* Information Contact, 303-871-2238.

University of Florida, Graduate School, College of Liberal Arts and Sciences, Department of Physics, Gainesville, FL 32611. Offers physics (MS, PhD); physics education (MST). *Accreditation:* NCATE (one or more programs are accredited). *Faculty:* 62. *Students:* 127 full-time (20 women), 2 part-time; includes 3 minority (1 African American, 1 Asian American or Pacific Islander, 1 Hispanic American), 89 international. In 2003, 14 master's, 3 doctorates awarded. *Degree requirements:* For master's, variable foreign language requirement, thesis (for some programs); for doctorate, one foreign language, thesis/dissertation. *Entrance requirements:* For master's and doctorate, GRE General Test, minimum GPA of 3.0. Additional exam requirements/recommendations for international students: Required—TOEFL (minimum score 550 paper-based; 213 computer-based). *Application deadline:* For fall admission, 6/1 for domestic students. Applications are processed on a rolling basis. Application fee: $30. Electronic applications accepted. *Expenses:* Tuition, state resident: part-time $205 per credit hour. Tuition, nonresident: part-time $775 per credit hour. *Financial support:* In 2003–04, 9 fellowships with tuition reimbursements (averaging $20,000 per year), 48 research assistantships with tuition reimbursements (averaging $18,000 per year), 41 teaching assistantships with tuition reimbursements (averaging $18,000 per year) were awarded. Unspecified assistantships also available. *Faculty research:* Astrophysics, condensed-matter physics, elementary particle physics, statistical mechanics, quantum theory. *Unit head:* Dr. Alan Dorsey, Chair, 352-392-0521, Fax: 352-392-0524, E-mail: chair@phys.ufl.edu. *Application contact:* Dr. Mark W. Meisel, Coordinator, 352-392-0521, Fax: 352-392-0524, E-mail: meisel@phys.ufl.edu.

University of Georgia, Graduate School, College of Arts and Sciences, Department of Physics and Astronomy, Athens, GA 30602. Offers physics (MS, PhD). *Faculty:* 21 full-time (0 women). *Students:* 28 full-time (5 women), 2 part-time (1 woman); includes 3 minority (1 African American, 1 American Indian/Alaska Native, 1 Asian American or Pacific Islander), 18 international. 74 applicants, 19% accepted. In 2003, 4 master's, 2 doctorates awarded. *Degree requirements:* For master's, thesis; for doctorate, one foreign language, thesis/dissertation. *Entrance requirements:* For master's and doctorate, GRE General Test. *Application deadline:* For fall admission, 7/1 for domestic students; for spring admission, 11/15 for domestic students. Application fee: $50. Electronic applications accepted. *Expenses:* Tuition, state resident: part-time $161 per hour. Tuition, nonresident: part-time $690 per hour. One-time fee: $435 part-time. *Financial support:* Fellowships, research assistantships, teaching assistantships, unspecified assistantships available. *Unit head:* Dr. Heinz-Bernd Schüttler, Head, 706-542-2485, Fax: 706-542-2492, E-mail: hbs@physast.uga.edu. *Application contact:* Dr. F. Todd Baker, Graduate Coordinator, 706-542-0979, Fax: 706-542-2492, E-mail: tbaker@physast.uga.edu.

University of Guelph, Graduate Program Services, College of Physical and Engineering Science, Guelph-Waterloo Physics Institute, Guelph, ON N1G 2W1, Canada. Offers M Sc, PhD. Part-time programs available. *Faculty:* 42 full-time (6 women), 45 part-time/adjunct (4 women). *Students:* 87 full-time (11 women), 4 part-time. 70 applicants, 54% accepted, 21 enrolled. In 2003, 7 master's, 3 doctorates awarded. *Median time to degree:* Master's–3 years full-time. *Degree requirements:* For master's, thesis or alternative, project or thesis; for doctorate, thesis/dissertation, comprehensive exam, registration. *Entrance requirements:* For master's, GRE Subject Test, minimum B average for honors degree; for doctorate, GRE Subject Test, minimum B average. Additional exam requirements/recommendations for international students: Required—TOEFL (minimum score 550 paper-based; 213 computer-based), TWE(minimum score 4). *Application deadline:* For fall admission, 7/1 priority date for domestic students, 1/31 priority date for international students; for winter admission, 11/1 for domestic students; for spring admission, 3/1 for domestic students. Applications are processed on a rolling basis. Application fee: $75. Tuition and fees charges are reported in Canadian dollars. Tuition, nonresident: full-time $3,440 Canadian dollars. International tuition: $5,432 Canadian dollars full-time. Required fees: $753 Canadian dollars. *Financial support:* In 2003–04, research assistantships (averaging $11,481 per year), teaching assistantships (averaging $9,212 per year) were awarded. Fellowships, career-related internships or fieldwork, scholarships/grants, and unspecified assistantships also available. *Faculty research:* Condensed matter and material physics, quantum computing, astrophysics and gravitation, industrial and applied physics, subatomic physics. Total annual research expenditures: $4 million. *Unit head:* Dr. D. E. Sullivan, Director, 519-824-4120 Ext. 2263, Fax: 519-836-9967, E-mail: gwp@physics.uoguelph.ca. *Application contact:* M. M. O'Neill, Administrative Assistant, 519-824-4120 Ext. 52263, Fax: 519-836-9967, E-mail: gwp@physics.uoguelph.ca.

University of Hawaii at Manoa, Graduate Division, Colleges of Arts and Sciences, College of Natural Sciences, Department of Physics and Astronomy, Honolulu, HI 96822. Offers MS, PhD. *Faculty:* 66 full-time (4 women), 4 part-time/adjunct (1 woman). *Students:* 57 full-time (19 women), 3 part-time; includes 5 minority (1 African American, 3 Asian Americans or Pacific Islanders, 1 Hispanic American), 21 international. 156 applicants, 29% accepted, 17 enrolled. *Median time to degree:* Master's–4 years full-time; doctorate–7 years full-time. *Degree requirements:* For master's, qualifying exam or thesis; for doctorate, thesis/dissertation, oral comprehensive and qualifying exams. *Entrance requirements:* For master's and doctorate, GRE General Test, GRE Subject Test. *Application deadline:* For fall admission, 1/15 for domestic students, 1/15 for international students. Application fee: $50. *Expenses:* Tuition, state resident: full-time $4,464; part-time $186 per credit hour. Tuition, nonresident: full-time $10,608; part-time $442 per credit hour. Tuition and fees vary according to program. *Financial support:* In 2003–04, 37 research assistantships (averaging $18,849 per year), 16 teaching assistantships (averaging $15,222 per year) were awarded. *Unit head:* Dr. Michael Peters, Chairperson, 808-956-7087, Fax: 808-956-7107. *Application contact:* Dr. Gareth Wynn-Williams, Graduate Chair, 808-956-8807, Fax: 808-956-9580, E-mail: wynnwill@ifa.hawaii.edu.

University of Houston, College of Natural Sciences and Mathematics, Department of Physics, Houston, TX 77204. Offers MS, PhD. Part-time programs available. *Faculty:* 20 full-time (0 women), 4 part-time/adjunct (0 women). *Students:* 80 full-time (17 women), 4 part-time; includes 6 minority (1 African American, 3 Asian Americans or Pacific Islanders, 2 Hispanic Americans), 63 international. Average age 30. 19 applicants, 89% accepted, 9 enrolled. In 2003, 13 master's, 4 doctorates awarded. Terminal master's awarded for partial completion of doctoral program. *Degree requirements:* For doctorate, thesis/dissertation. *Entrance requirements:* For master's and doctorate, GRE General Test. Additional exam requirements/recommendations for international students: Required—TOEFL. *Application deadline:* For fall admission, 7/20 for domestic students; for spring admission, 11/20 for domestic students. Applications are processed on a rolling basis. Application fee: $0 ($75 for international students). *Expenses:* Tuition, state resident: full-time $1,656; part-time $92 per credit hour. Tuition, nonresident: full-time $5,904; part-time $328 per credit hour. Required fees: $1,704. *Financial support:* In 2003–04, 41 research assistantships (averaging $14,400 per year), 30 teaching assistantships (averaging $14,400 per year) were awarded. *Faculty research:* Condensed-matter, particle physics, high-temperature superconductivity, material/space physics, chaos. Total annual research expenditures: $1.5 million. *Unit head:* Dr. Lawrence Pinsky, Chairman, 713-743-3552. *Application contact:* Advising Assistant, 713-743-3550, Fax: 713-743-3589.

University of Idaho, College of Graduate Studies, College of Science, Department of Physics, Moscow, ID 83844-2282. Offers physics (MS, PhD); physics education (MAT). *Accreditation:* NCATE (one or more programs are accredited). *Students:* 19 full-time (2 women), 15 international. Average age 28. *Degree requirements:* For master's and doctorate, thesis/dissertation. *Entrance requirements:* For master's, GRE, minimum GPA of 2.8; for doctorate, GRE, minimum undergraduate GPA of 2.8, 3.0 graduate. *Application deadline:* For fall admission, 8/1 for domestic students; for spring admission, 12/15 for domestic students. Application fee: $55 ($60 for international students). *Expenses:* Tuition, state resident: full-time $3,348. Tuition, nonresident: full-time $10,740. Required fees: $540. *Financial support:* Research

Physics

University of Idaho (continued)
assistantships, teaching assistantships available. Financial award application deadline: 2/15. *Unit head:* Dr. Rex Gandy, Chair, 208-885-6380.

See in-depth description on page 411.

University of Illinois at Chicago, Graduate College, College of Liberal Arts and Sciences, Department of Physics, Chicago, IL 60607-7128. Offers MS, PhD. *Faculty:* 26 full-time (2 women), 3 part-time/adjunct (0 women). *Students:* 32 full-time (7 women), 19 part-time (3 women); includes 2 minority (1 African American, 1 Asian American or Pacific Islander), 34 international. Average age 29. 81 applicants, 21% accepted, 9 enrolled. In 2003, 8 master's, 10 doctorates awarded. Terminal master's awarded for partial completion of doctoral program. *Median time to degree:* Of those who began their doctoral program in fall 1995, 42% received their degree in 8 years or less. *Degree requirements:* For doctorate, thesis/dissertation. *Entrance requirements:* For master's and doctorate, GRE General Test, minimum GPA of 4.0 on a 5.0 scale. Additional exam requirements/recommendations for international students: Required—TOEFL. *Application deadline:* For fall admission, 5/15 for domestic students; for spring admission, 11/1 for domestic students. Applications are processed on a rolling basis. Application fee: $40 ($50 for international students). Electronic applications accepted. *Expenses:* Tuition, state resident: part-time $941 per semester. Tuition, nonresident: part-time $2,338 per semester. *Financial support:* In 2003–04, 42 students received support; fellowships with full tuition reimbursements available, research assistantships with full tuition reimbursements available, teaching assistantships with full tuition reimbursements available, Federal Work-Study, scholarships/grants, traineeships, tuition waivers (full), and unspecified assistantships available. Financial award application deadline: 3/1; financial award applicants required to submit FAFSA. *Faculty research:* High-energy, laser, and solid-state physics. *Unit head:* Christoph Grein, Director of Graduate Studies, 312-996-6753, E-mail: grein@uic.edu. *Application contact:* Inder Batra, Head, 312-413-2798.

University of Illinois at Urbana–Champaign, Graduate College, College of Engineering, Department of Physics, Champaign, IL 61820. Offers MS, PhD. *Faculty:* 59 full-time (4 women), 10 part-time/adjunct (3 women). *Students:* 271 full-time (36 women); includes 19 minority (15 Asian Americans or Pacific Islanders, 4 Hispanic Americans), 104 international. 458 applicants, 15% accepted, 57 enrolled. In 2003, 35 master's, 20 doctorates awarded. *Degree requirements:* For doctorate, thesis/dissertation, departmental qualifying exam. *Entrance requirements:* For master's, GRE, minimum GPA of 3.0. *Application deadline:* For fall admission, 1/15 for domestic students; for spring admission, 10/15 for domestic students. Applications are processed on a rolling basis. Application fee: $40 ($50 for international students). Electronic applications accepted. *Expenses:* Tuition, state resident: full-time $6,692. Tuition, nonresident: full-time $18,692. *Financial support:* In 2003–04, 21 fellowships, 149 research assistantships, 86 teaching assistantships were awarded. Financial award application deadline: 2/15. *Unit head:* Secretary, 217-333-3645, Fax: 217-333-9819. *Application contact:* Secretary, 217-333-3645, Fax: 217-333-9819.

The University of Iowa, Graduate College, College of Liberal Arts and Sciences, Department of Physics and Astronomy, Program in Physics, Iowa City, IA 52242-1316. Offers MS, PhD. *Students:* 28 full-time (7 women), 34 part-time (3 women); includes 1 minority (Hispanic American), 39 international. 158 applicants, 24% accepted, 10 enrolled. In 2003, 1 master's, 2 doctorates awarded. *Degree requirements:* For master's, exam, thesis optional; for doctorate, thesis/dissertation, comprehensive exam, registration. *Entrance requirements:* For master's and doctorate, GRE General Test, GRE Subject Test, minimum GPA of 3.0. Additional exam requirements/recommendations for international students: Required—TOEFL (minimum score 550 paper-based; 213 computer-based). *Application deadline:* For fall admission, 2/1 priority date for domestic students, 2/1 priority date for international students. Applications are processed on a rolling basis. Application fee: $50 ($75 for international students). Electronic applications accepted. *Expenses:* Tuition, state resident: full-time $5,038. Tuition, nonresident: full-time $15,072. Tuition and fees vary according to course load and program. *Financial support:* In 2003–04, 1 fellowship, 32 research assistantships, 22 teaching assistantships were awarded. Financial award applicants required to submit FAFSA. *Unit head:* Thomas Boggess, Chair, Department of Physics and Astronomy, 319-335-1688, Fax: 319-335-1753.

University of Kansas, Graduate School, College of Liberal Arts and Sciences, Department of Physics and Astronomy, Lawrence, KS 66045. Offers computational physics and astronomy (MS); physics (MS, PhD). *Faculty:* 30. *Students:* 35 full-time (11 women), 7 part-time (3 women); includes 2 minority (1 Asian American or Pacific Islander, 1 Hispanic American), 20 international. Average age 29. 69 applicants, 39% accepted, 8 enrolled. In 2003, 3 master's, 6 doctorates awarded. *Median time to degree:* Master's–3 years full-time; doctorate–5.5 years full-time. *Degree requirements:* For master's, thesis (for some programs); for doctorate, thesis/dissertation, comprehensive exam. *Entrance requirements:* Additional exam requirements/recommendations for international students: Required—TOEFL; Recommended—TSE. *Application deadline:* For fall admission, 3/1 priority date for domestic students, 3/1 priority date for international students; for spring admission, 10/1 priority date for domestic students, 10/1 priority date for international students. Applications are processed on a rolling basis. Application fee: $55 ($60 for international students). Electronic applications accepted. *Expenses:* Tuition, state resident: full-time $3,745. Tuition, nonresident: full-time $10,075. Required fees: $574. *Financial support:* In 2003–04, 27 research assistantships with full and partial tuition reimbursements (averaging $12,097 per year), 21 teaching assistantships with full and partial tuition reimbursements (averaging $12,864 per year) were awarded. Financial award application deadline: 3/1. *Faculty research:* Condensed-matter, cosmology, elementary particles, nuclear physics, space physics. Total annual research expenditures: $3.1 million. *Unit head:* Dr. Stephen J. Sanders, Chair, 785-864-4626, Fax: 785-864-5262. *Application contact:* Patricia Marvin, Graduate Admission Specialist, 785-864-4626, Fax: 785-864-5262, E-mail: physics@ku.edu.

See in-depth description on page 413.

University of Kentucky, Graduate School, Graduate School Programs from the College of Arts and Sciences, Program in Physics and Astronomy, Lexington, KY 40506-0032. Offers MS, PhD. *Faculty:* 32 full-time (2 women). *Students:* 53 full-time (14 women), 16 part-time (4 women); includes 1 minority (Asian American or Pacific Islander), 53 international. 104 applicants, 48% accepted, 20 enrolled. In 2003, 3 master's, 3 doctorates awarded. *Degree requirements:* For master's, thesis optional; for doctorate, thesis/dissertation, comprehensive exam. *Entrance requirements:* For master's, GRE General Test, minimum undergraduate GPA of 2.5; for doctorate, GRE General Test, minimum graduate GPA of 3.0. Additional exam requirements/recommendations for international students: Required—TOEFL (minimum score 550 paper-based; 213 computer-based). *Application deadline:* For fall admission, 7/18 for domestic students, 2/1 for international students. Applications are processed on a rolling basis. Application fee: $35 ($45 for international students). *Expenses:* Tuition, state resident: full-time $4,975; part-time $261 per credit hour. Tuition, nonresident: full-time $12,315; part-time $668 per credit hour. *Financial support:* Fellowships, research assistantships, teaching assistantships, Federal Work-Study, institutionally sponsored loans, and unspecified assistantships available. Support available to part-time students. *Faculty research:* Astrophysics, active galactic nuclei, interstellar masses, and radio astronomy; atomic physics, Rydbert atoms, and electron scattering; TOF spectroscopy, hyperon interactions and muons; solid-state, STM, charge-density waves, fulleneues, and 1-dimensional systems; particle theory, lattice gauge theory, quark, and skyrmion models. Total annual research expenditures: $3.1 million. *Unit head:* Dr. Thomas Troland, Director of Graduate Studies, 859-257-8620, Fax: 859-323-2846, E-mail: troland@asta.pa.uky.edu. *Application contact:* Dr. Brian Jackson, Associate Dean, 859-257-4905, Fax: 859-323-1928.

The University of Lethbridge, School of Graduate Studies, Lethbridge, AB T1K 3M4, Canada. Offers accounting (MScM); agricultural biotechnology (M Sc); agricultural studies (M Sc, MA); anthropology (MA); archaeology (MA); art (MA); biochemistry (M Sc); biological sciences (M Sc); Canadian studies (MA); chemistry (M Sc); computer science (M Sc); counseling psychology (M Ed); dramatic arts (MA); economics (MA); English (MA); environmental science (M Sc); exercise science (M Sc); finance (MScM); French (MA); French/German (MA); French/Spanish (MA); general education (M Ed); general management (MScM); geography (M Sc, MA); German (MA); health sciences (M Sc, MA); history (MA); human resources/management and labor relations (MScM); information systems (MScM); international management (MScM); kinesiology (M Sc, MA); management (M Sc, MA); marketing (MScM); mathematics (M Sc); music (MA); Native American studies (MA, MScM); neuroscience (M Sc, PhD); nursing (M Sc); philosophy (MA); physics (M Sc); political science (MA); psychology (M Sc, MA); religious studies (MA); sociology (MA); urban and regional studies (MA). Part-time and evening/weekend programs available. *Faculty:* 250. *Students:* 317 (126 women). Average age 39. 35 applicants, 100% accepted, 35 enrolled. In 2003, 40 degrees awarded. *Degree requirements:* For doctorate, thesis/dissertation, comprehensive exam. *Entrance requirements:* For master's, bachelor's degree in related field, minimum GPA of 3.0 (during previous 20 graded semester courses), two years teaching or related experience (M Ed), GMAT for M Sc (management); for doctorate, master's degree, minimum graduate GPA of 3.5. Additional exam requirements/recommendations for international students: Required—TOEFL. Application fee: $60 Canadian dollars. *Expenses:* Tuition, state resident: part-time $475 per course. *Financial support:* Fellowships, research assistantships, teaching assistantships, scholarships/grants, health care benefits, and unspecified assistantships available. *Faculty research:* Movement and brain plasticity, gibberellin physiology, photosynthesis, carbon cycling, molecular properties of main-group ring components. *Unit head:* Dr. Shamsul Alam, Dean, 403-329-2121, Fax: 403-329-2097, E-mail: inquiries@uleth.ca. *Application contact:* Kathy Schrage, Administrative Assistant, Office of the Academic Vice President, 403-329-2121, Fax: 403-329-2097, E-mail: inquiries@uleth.ca.

University of Louisiana at Lafayette, Graduate School, College of Sciences, Department of Physics, Lafayette, LA 70504. Offers MS. Part-time programs available. *Faculty:* 8 full-time (1 woman). *Students:* 9 full-time (1 woman), 3 international. 9 applicants, 78% accepted, 6 enrolled. In 2003, 4 degrees awarded. *Degree requirements:* For master's, thesis, registration. *Entrance requirements:* For master's, GRE General Test, minimum GPA of 2.75. Additional exam requirements/recommendations for international students: Required—TOEFL (minimum score 550 paper-based; 213 computer-based). *Application deadline:* For fall admission, 5/15 for domestic students, 5/15 for international students; for spring admission, 10/1 for domestic students, 10/1 for international students. Applications are processed on a rolling basis. Application fee: $20 ($30 for international students). Electronic applications accepted. *Expenses:* Tuition, state resident: full-time $2,786; part-time $85 per credit. Tuition, nonresident: full-time $8,966; part-time $343 per credit. International tuition: $9,102 full-time. *Financial support:* In 2003–04, 1 fellowship with full tuition reimbursement (averaging $14,500 per year), 3 research assistantships with full tuition reimbursements (averaging $10,000 per year) were awarded. Federal Work-Study also available. Financial award application deadline: 5/1. *Faculty research:* Environmental physics, geophysics, astrophysics, acoustics, atomic physics. *Unit head:* Dr. John Meriwether, Head, 337-482-6691, Fax: 337-482-6699, E-mail: meriwether@louisiana.edu. *Application contact:* Dr. Daniel Whitmire, Graduate Coordinator, 337-482-6185, Fax: 337-482-6699, E-mail: whitmire@louisiana.edu.

University of Louisville, Graduate School, College of Arts and Sciences, Department of Physics, Louisville, KY 40292-0001. Offers MS. *Students:* 13 full-time (1 woman), 3 part-time (2 women); includes 1 minority (Hispanic American), 7 international. Average age 30. In 2003, 8 degrees awarded. *Degree requirements:* For master's, thesis. *Entrance requirements:* For master's, GRE General Test. *Application deadline:* Applications are processed on a rolling basis. Application fee: $50. *Expenses:* Tuition, state resident: full-time $4,842. Tuition, nonresident: full-time $13,338. *Financial support:* In 2003–04, 14 teaching assistantships with tuition reimbursements (averaging $12,500 per year) were awarded *Unit head:* Dr. Joseph S. Chalmers, Chair, 502-852-6787, Fax: 502-852-0742, E-mail: chalmers@louisville.edu.

University of Maine, Graduate School, College of Liberal Arts and Sciences, Department of Physics and Astronomy, Orono, ME 04469. Offers engineering physics (M Eng); physics (MS, PhD). *Faculty:* 17 full-time (1 woman), 1 part-time/adjunct (0 women). *Students:* 25 full-time (5 women), 5 part-time; includes 1 minority (African American), 4 international. Average age 29. 31 applicants, 65% accepted, 12 enrolled. In 2003, 1 master's, 3 doctorates awarded. Terminal master's awarded for partial completion of doctoral program. *Degree requirements:* For doctorate, thesis/dissertation. *Entrance requirements:* For master's, GRE General Test, GRE Subject Test; for doctorate, GRE General Test. Additional exam requirements/recommendations for international students: Required—TOEFL. *Application deadline:* For fall admission, 2/1 for domestic students. Applications are processed on a rolling basis. Application fee: $50. Electronic applications accepted. *Expenses:* Tuition, state resident: part-time $235 per credit. Tuition, nonresident: part-time $670 per credit. Tuition and fees vary according to course load. *Financial support:* In 2003–04, 3 research assistantships with tuition reimbursements (averaging $17,000 per year), 15 teaching assistantships with tuition reimbursements (averaging $12,000 per year) were awarded. Fellowships with tuition reimbursements, tuition waivers (full and partial) also available. Financial award application deadline: 3/1. *Faculty research:* Solid-state physics, fluids, biophysics, plasma physics, surface physics. *Unit head:* Dr. David Batuski, Chair, 207-581-1039, Fax: 207-581-3410. *Application contact:* Scott G. Delcourt, Associate Dean of the Graduate School, 207-581-3218, Fax: 207-581-3232, E-mail: graduate@maine.edu.

University of Manitoba, Faculty of Graduate Studies, Faculty of Science, Department of Physics, Winnipeg, MB R3T 2N2, Canada. Offers M Sc, PhD. *Degree requirements:* For master's, thesis; for doctorate, one foreign language, thesis/dissertation. Tuition charges are reported in Canadian dollars. Tuition, nonresident: full-time $3,878 Canadian dollars.

University of Maryland, Baltimore County, Graduate School, Department of Physics, Baltimore, MD 21250. Offers applied physics (MS, PhD), including optics, solid state physics; atmospheric physics (MS, PhD). Part-time programs available. Terminal master's awarded for partial completion of doctoral program. *Degree requirements:* For master's, thesis optional; for doctorate, thesis/dissertation. *Entrance requirements:* For master's and doctorate, GRE General Test, GRE Subject Test, minimum GPA of 3.0. Additional exam requirements/recommendations for international students: Required—TOEFL. Electronic applications accepted. *Expenses:* Tuition, state resident: full-time $7,000. Tuition, nonresident: full-time $11,400. Required fees: $1,440. *Faculty research:* Optics, solid state physics, astrophysics, atmospheric physics.

University of Maryland, College Park, Graduate Studies and Research, College of Computer, Mathematical and Physical Sciences, Department of Physics, College Park, MD 20742. Offers MS, PhD. Part-time and evening/weekend programs available. *Faculty:* 141 full-time (12 women), 19 part-time/adjunct (2 women). *Students:* 229 full-time (32 women), 11 part-time (3 women); includes 13 minority (3 African Americans, 1 American Indian/Alaska Native, 7 Asian Americans or Pacific Islanders, 2 Hispanic Americans), 104 international. 530 applicants, 23% accepted. In 2003, 12 master's, 21 doctorates awarded. Terminal master's awarded for partial completion of doctoral program. *Median time to degree:* Of those who began their doctoral program in fall 1995, 39% received their degree in 8 years or less. *Degree requirements:* For master's, thesis optional; for doctorate, thesis/dissertation. *Entrance requirements:* For master's, GRE General Test, Advanced Physics Test, minimum GPA of 3.0; for doctorate, GRE General Test, Advanced Physics Test. *Application deadline:* For fall admission, 2/15 for domestic students, 2/1 for international students; for spring admission, 10/1 for domestic students, 6/1 for international students. Applications are processed on a rolling basis. Application fee: $50. Electronic applications accepted. *Expenses:* Tuition, state resident: part-time $349 per credit hour. Tuition, nonresident: part-time $602 per credit hour. *Financial support:* In 2003–04, 35 fellowships with full tuition reimbursements (averaging $13,140 per year), 112 research assistantships with tuition reimbursements (averaging $18,418 per year), 56 teaching assistantships with tuition reimbursements (averaging $13,645 per year) were awarded. Federal Work-Study and scholarships/grants also available. Support available to part-time students. Financial award applicants required to submit FAFSA. *Faculty research:* Astrometeorology, superconductivity, particle astrophysics, plasma physics, elementary particle theory. Total annual research expenditures: $16.9 million. *Unit head:* Dr. Jordan A. Goodman, Chair, 301-405-5946, Fax: 301-405-0327. *Application contact:* Linda O'Hara, Administrative Assistant, 301-405-5982.

Announcement: UM Physics, one of the nation's leading recipients of research grants, has more than 30 research programs and institutes, including the nation's #1 ranked nonlinear dynamics/chaos program. Others include condensed matter, particle astrophysics, and centers in superconductivity, plasma, and materials science. Contact Linda O'Hara, 301-405-5982; lohara@physics.umd.edu; www.physics.umd.edu.

See in-depth description on page 415.

University of Massachusetts Amherst, Graduate School, College of Natural Sciences and Mathematics, Department of Physics, Amherst, MA 01003. Offers MS, PhD. Part-time programs available. *Faculty:* 39 full-time (1 woman). *Students:* 76 full-time (14 women); includes 3 minority (1 African American, 2 Hispanic Americans), 46 international. Average age 28. 133 applicants, 47% accepted, 20 enrolled. In 2003, 10 master's, 5 doctorates awarded. Terminal master's awarded for partial completion of doctoral program. *Degree requirements:* For doctorate, thesis/dissertation. *Entrance requirements:* For master's and doctorate, GRE General Test, GRE Subject Test. Additional exam requirements/recommendations for international students: Required—TOEFL (minimum score 530 paper-based; 197 computer-based). *Application deadline:* For fall admission, 2/1 priority date for domestic students, 2/1 priority date for international students; for spring admission, 10/1 for domestic students. Applications are processed on a rolling basis. Application fee: $40 ($50 for international students). *Expenses:* Tuition, state resident: full-time $1,320; part-time $110 per credit. Tuition, nonresident: full-time $4,969; part-time $414 per credit. Required fees: $2,626 per term. Tuition and fees vary according to course load. *Financial support:* In 2003–04, fellowships with full tuition reimbursements (averaging $1,206 per year), research assistantships with full tuition reimbursements (averaging $12,226 per year), teaching assistantships with full tuition reimbursements (averaging $10,416 per year) were awarded. Career-related internships or fieldwork, Federal Work-Study, scholarships/grants, traineeships, and unspecified assistantships also available. Support available to part-time students. Financial award application deadline: 2/1. *Unit head:* Dr. Jonathan Machta, Director, 413-545-2545, Fax: 413-545-0648, E-mail: machta@physics.umass.edu. *Application contact:* Dr. Donald Candela, Chair, Admissions Committee, 413-545-2407, E-mail: candela@phast.umass.edu.

University of Massachusetts Dartmouth, Graduate School, College of Engineering, Department of Physics, North Dartmouth, MA 02747-2300. Offers MS. Part-time programs available. *Faculty:* 13 full-time (2 women), 2 part-time/adjunct (0 women). *Students:* 8 full-time (3 women), 2 part-time (1 woman), 4 international. Average age 28. 8 applicants, 100% accepted, 5 enrolled. In 2003, 7 degrees awarded. *Degree requirements:* For master's, thesis or alternative. *Entrance requirements:* For master's, GRE General Test. Additional exam requirements/recommendations for international students: Required—TOEFL (minimum score 500 paper-based). *Application deadline:* For fall admission, 4/20 priority date for domestic students, 2/20 priority date for international students; for spring admission, 11/15 priority date for domestic students, 9/15 priority date for international students. Applications are processed on a rolling basis. Application fee: $35 ($55 for international students). Electronic applications accepted. *Expenses:* Tuition, state resident: full-time $2,071; part-time $86 per credit. Tuition, nonresident: full-time $8,099; part-time $337 per credit. Required fees: $248 per credit. One-time fee: $50 full-time. Part-time tuition and fees vary according to course load and program. *Financial support:* In 2003–04, 1 research assistantship with full tuition reimbursement (averaging $14,500 per year), 7 teaching assistantships with full tuition reimbursements (averaging $10,000 per year) were awarded. Federal Work-Study and unspecified assistantships also available. Support available to part-time students. Financial award application deadline: 3/1; financial award applicants required to submit FAFSA. *Faculty research:* Real-time physics dissemination, four-dimensional symmetry principle, physical and biological variability of Northeast Massachusetts coast, light atoms and molecules interaction with photons, property fluxes in the North Atlantic. Total annual research expenditures: $208,000. *Unit head:* Dr. J.P. Hsu, Director, 508-999-8363, Fax: 508-999-9115, E-mail: jhsu@umassd.edu. *Application contact:* Carol Novo, Graduate Admissions Officer, 508-999-8604, Fax: 508-999-8183, E-mail: graduate@umassd.edu.

University of Massachusetts Lowell, Graduate School, College of Arts and Sciences, Department of Physics and Applied Physics, Program in Physics, Lowell, MA 01854-2881. Offers MS, PhD. *Degree requirements:* For master's, thesis; for doctorate, 2 foreign languages, thesis/dissertation. *Entrance requirements:* For master's and doctorate, GRE General Test.

The University of Memphis, Graduate School, College of Arts and Sciences, Department of Physics, Memphis, TN 38152. Offers MS. Part-time programs available. *Students:* Average age 28. *Degree requirements:* For master's, thesis or alternative, comprehensive exam. *Entrance requirements:* For master's, GRE General Test or MAT, 20 undergraduate hours in physics. *Application deadline:* For fall admission, 8/1 for domestic students; for spring admission, 12/1 for domestic students. Applications are processed on a rolling basis. Application fee: $25 ($50 for international students). Electronic applications accepted. *Expenses:* Tuition, state resident: full-time $5,142. Tuition, nonresident: full-time $13,296. *Financial support:* In 2003–04, research assistantships (averaging $7,000 per year), teaching assistantships (averaging $5,150 per year) were awarded. Federal Work-Study and institutionally sponsored loans also available. Financial award application deadline: 5/1; financial award applicants required to submit CSS PROFILE. *Faculty research:* Solid-state physics, materials science, biophysics, astrophysics, physics education. Total annual research expenditures: $405,913. *Unit head:* Dr. M. Shah Jahan, Chairman, 901-678-2620, Fax: 901-678-4733, E-mail: mjahan@memphis.edu. *Application contact:* Dr. Narahari Achar, Coordinator of Graduate Studies, 901-678-3119, Fax: 901-678-4733, E-mail: nachar@memphis.edu.

University of Miami, Graduate School, College of Arts and Sciences, Department of Physics, Coral Gables, FL 33124. Offers MS, DA, PhD. *Faculty:* 16 full-time (0 women). *Students:* 19 full-time (7 women); includes 2 minority (1 African American, 1 Hispanic American), 16 international. Average age 25. 250 applicants, 2% accepted. In 2003, 3 master's, 2 doctorates awarded. Terminal master's awarded for partial completion of doctoral program. *Degree requirements:* For doctorate, thesis/dissertation. *Entrance requirements:* For master's and doctorate, GRE General Test, GRE Subject Test. Additional exam requirements/recommendations for international students: Required—TOEFL. *Application deadline:* For fall admission, 3/1 for domestic students. Applications are processed on a rolling basis. Application fee: $50. *Expenses:* Tuition: Full-time $19,526. *Financial support:* In 2003–04, 17 students received support, including 1 fellowship, 4 research assistantships, 15 teaching assistantships awarded. Financial award applicants required to submit FAFSA. *Faculty research:* High-energy theory, marine and atmospheric optics, plasma physics, solid-state physics. Total annual research expenditures: $1.5 million. *Unit head:* Dr. George Alexandrakis, Chairman, 305-284-2323 Ext. 9, Fax: 305-284-4222. *Application contact:* Dr. Josef Ashkenazi, Chairman, Graduate Recruitment Committee, 305-284-2323 Ext. 3, Fax: 305-284-4222.

See in-depth description on page 419.

University of Michigan, Horace H. Rackham School of Graduate Studies, College of Literature, Science, and the Arts, Department of Physics, Ann Arbor, MI 48109. Offers MS, PhD. *Faculty:* 61 full-time (4 women). *Students:* 130 full-time (32 women); includes 10 minority (3 African Americans, 3 Asian Americans or Pacific Islanders, 4 Hispanic Americans), 64 international. Average age 29. 445 applicants, 20% accepted, 24 enrolled. In 2003, 11 master's, 11 doctorates awarded. Terminal master's awarded for partial completion of doctoral program. *Degree requirements:* For doctorate, oral defense of dissertation, preliminary exam. *Entrance requirements:* For master's and doctorate, GRE General Test. Additional exam requirements/recommendations for international students: Required—TOEFL (minimum score 560 paper-based; 220 computer-based). *Application deadline:* For fall admission, 1/15 for domestic students, 12/8 for international students. Application fee: $60 ($75 for international students). Electronic applications accepted. *Expenses:* Tuition, state resident: full-time $7,463. Tuition, nonresident: full-time $13,913. Full-time tuition and fees vary according to course load, degree level and program. *Financial support:* In 2003–04, 6 fellowships with full tuition reimbursements (averaging $21,000 per year), 65 research assistantships with full tuition reimbursements (averaging $20,355 per year), 42 teaching assistantships with full tuition reimbursements (averaging $20,355 per year) were awarded. *Faculty research:* Elementary particle, solid-state, atomic, and molecular physics (theoretical and experimental). Total annual research expenditures: $14.9 million. *Unit head:* Dr. Myron Campbell, Chair, 734-764-4437. *Application contact:* Kimberly A. Smith, Graduate Coordinator, 734-936-0658, Fax: 734-763-9694, E-mail: physics.inquiries@umich.edu.

See in-depth description on page 423.

University of Minnesota, Duluth, Graduate School, College of Science and Engineering, Department of Physics, Duluth, MN 55812-2496. Offers MS. Part-time programs available. *Faculty:* 8 full-time (1 woman). *Students:* 6 full-time (1 woman), 1 international. Average age 27. 10 applicants, 40% accepted. In 2003, 1 degree awarded, leading to university research/teaching 100%. *Median time to degree:* Master's–2 years full-time. *Degree requirements:* For master's, thesis (for some programs). *Entrance requirements:* For master's, minimum GPA of 3.0. Additional exam requirements/recommendations for international students: Required—TOEFL (minimum score 550 paper-based; 213 computer-based). *Application deadline:* For fall admission, 7/15 for domestic students; for spring admission, 11/15 for domestic students. Applications are processed on a rolling basis. Application fee: $55 ($75 for international students). *Expenses:* Tuition, state resident: part-time $614 per credit. Tuition, nonresident: part-time $1,205 per credit. *Financial support:* In 2003–04, 3 students received support, including 3 teaching assistantships with full tuition reimbursements available (averaging $11,154 per year); Federal Work-Study, institutionally sponsored loans, scholarships/grants, and health care benefits also available. Support available to part-time students. Financial award application deadline: 3/15. *Faculty research:* Computational physics, solid-state physics, physical oceanography, high energy neutrinos. Total annual research expenditures: $70,000. *Unit head:* Dr. Elise A. Ralph, Director of Graduate Studies, 218-726-7627, Fax: 218-726-6942, E-mail: eralph@d.umn.edu.

Announcement: MS in physics: concentrations in condensed matter, particle physics, and physical limnology. Thesis projects provide experience in computational physics, instrumentation, optics, and data analysis. Current research areas include neutrinos, quark models, scanned probe microscopy, photoreflectance, remote sensing and environmental optics, dynamics of large and mesoscale circulation, turbulence, and mixing dynamics.

University of Minnesota, Twin Cities Campus, Graduate School, Institute of Technology, School of Physics and Astronomy, Department of Physics, Minneapolis, MN 55455-0213. Offers MS, PhD. Part-time programs available. *Degree requirements:* For master's and doctorate, thesis/dissertation. *Entrance requirements:* For master's and doctorate, GRE General Test, GRE Subject Test. *Expenses:* Tuition, state resident: full-time $3,681; part-time $614 per credit. Tuition, nonresident: full-time $7,231; part-time $1,205 per credit. *Faculty research:* Condensed matter, elementary particle, space, nuclear and atomic physics.

University of Mississippi, Graduate School, College of Liberal Arts, Department of Physics and Astronomy, Oxford, University, MS 38677. Offers physics (MA, MS, PhD). *Faculty:* 12 full-time (0 women). *Students:* 15 full-time (3 women), 2 part-time (1 woman). In 2003, 1 degree awarded. *Degree requirements:* For master's, thesis (for some programs); for doctorate, thesis/dissertation. *Entrance requirements:* For master's, GRE General Test, minimum GPA of 3.0; for doctorate, GRE General Test. Additional exam requirements/recommendations for international students: Required—TOEFL. *Application deadline:* For fall admission, 4/1 for domestic students; for spring admission, 10/1 for domestic students. Applications are processed on a rolling basis. Application fee: $25. *Expenses:* Tuition, state resident: part-time $218 per hour. Tuition, nonresident: part-time $273 per hour. *Financial support:* Scholarships/grants available. Financial award application deadline: 3/1; financial award applicants required to submit FAFSA. *Unit head:* Thomas C. Marshall, Chairman, 662-915-5325, Fax: 662-915-5045, E-mail: physics@phy.olemiss.edu.

University of Missouri–Columbia, Graduate School, College of Arts and Sciences, Department of Physics and Astronomy, Columbia, MO 65211. Offers MS, PhD. *Faculty:* 23 full-time (4 women). *Students:* 27 full-time (5 women), 6 part-time (1 woman), 21 international. In 2003, 1 master's, 5 doctorates awarded. Terminal master's awarded for partial completion of doctoral program. *Degree requirements:* For doctorate, one foreign language, thesis/dissertation. *Entrance requirements:* For master's and doctorate, GRE General Test, minimum GPA of 3.0. *Application deadline:* For fall admission, 4/15 for domestic students. Applications are processed on a rolling basis. Application fee: $45 ($60 for international students). *Expenses:* Tuition, state resident: full-time $5,205. Tuition, nonresident: full-time $14,058. *Financial support:* Research assistantships, teaching assistantships, institutionally sponsored loans available. *Unit head:* Dr. H. R. Chandrasekhar, Director of Graduate Studies, 573-882-6086, E-mail: chandra@missouri.edu.

University of Missouri–Kansas City, College of Arts and Sciences, Department of Physics, Kansas City, MO 64110-2499. Offers MS, PhD. PhD offered through the School of Graduate Studies. Part-time and evening/weekend programs available. *Faculty:* 11 full-time (1 woman), 3 part-time/adjunct (0 women). *Students:* 4 full-time (1 woman), 7 part-time (2 women), 6 international. Average age 32. In 2003, 1 degree awarded. Terminal master's awarded for partial completion of doctoral program. *Degree requirements:* For master's, thesis optional; for doctorate, thesis/dissertation, comprehensive exam. *Entrance requirements:* For doctorate, GRE General Test. Additional exam requirements/recommendations for international students: Required—TOEFL. *Application deadline:* For fall admission, 6/1 for domestic students; for spring admission, 11/1 for domestic students. Applications are processed on a rolling basis. Application fee: $35 ($50 for international students). *Financial support:* In 2003–04, research assistantships with full and partial tuition reimbursements (averaging $11,000 per year), teaching assistantships with full and partial tuition reimbursements (averaging $11,000 per year) were awarded. Federal Work-Study, institutionally sponsored loans, and tuition waivers (full and partial) also available. Support available to part-time students. Financial award application deadline: 4/1. *Faculty research:* Surface physics, material science, statistical mechanics, computational physics, relativity and quantum theory. Total annual research expenditures: $550,000. *Unit head:* Dr. David M. Wieliczka, Chairperson, 816-235-2504, E-mail: wieliczkad@umkc.edu. *Application contact:* Da Ming Zhu, Principal Graduate Adviser, 816-235-5326, Fax: 816-235-5221, E-mail: zhud@umkc.edu.

University of Missouri–Rolla, Graduate School, College of Arts and Sciences, Department of Physics, Rolla, MO 65409-0910. Offers MS, PhD. *Students:* 23 full-time (5 women), 7 part-time (2 women); includes 3 minority (1 African American, 2 Asian Americans or Pacific Islanders), 13 international. Average age 30. 49 applicants, 61% accepted, 10 enrolled. In 2003, 4 master's, 2 doctorates awarded. *Median time to degree:* Doctorate–5 years part-time. *Expenses:* Tuition, state resident: full-time $5,871. Tuition, nonresident: full-time $13,114. Required fees: $820. Tuition and fees vary according to course load. Total annual research expenditures: $817,668. *Unit head:* Dr. Don Madison, Chairman.

University of Missouri–St. Louis, Graduate School, College of Arts and Sciences, Department of Physics and Astronomy, St. Louis, MO 63121-4499. Offers applied physics (MS); astrophysics (MS); physics (PhD). Part-time and evening/weekend programs available. *Faculty:* 14 full-time (0 women). *Students:* 9 full-time (2 women), 10 part-time (3 women); includes 1 minority (Asian American or Pacific Islander), 5 international. Average age 25. In 2003, 3 master's, 1 doctorate awarded. Terminal master's awarded for partial completion of doctoral program. *Degree requirements:* For master's, thesis optional; for doctorate, thesis/dissertation. *Entrance requirements:* For master's and doctorate, GRE General Test. Additional exam requirements/recommendations for international students: Required—TOEFL (minimum score 550 paper-based; 213 computer-based). *Application deadline:* For fall admission, 4/1 for domestic students; for spring admission, 12/1 priority date for domestic students. Applications

Physics

University of Missouri–St. Louis (continued)

are processed on a rolling basis. Application fee: $35 ($40 for international students). Electronic applications accepted. *Expenses:* Tuition, state resident: part-time $237 per credit hour. Tuition, nonresident: part-time $639 per credit hour. Required fees: $10 per credit hour. *Financial support:* In 2003–04, 1 research assistantship with full and partial tuition reimbursement (averaging $6,750 per year), 9 teaching assistantships with full and partial tuition reimbursements (averaging $12,978 per year) were awarded. Fellowships with full tuition reimbursements, career-related internships or fieldwork also available. *Faculty research:* Biophysics, atomic physics, nonlinear dynamics, materials science. *Unit head:* Dr. Ricardo Flores, Director of Graduate Studies, 314-516-5931, Fax: 314-516-6152, E-mail: graduate@newton.umsl.edu. *Application contact:* 314-516-5458, Fax: 314-516-5310, E-mail: gradadm@umsl.edu.

University of Nebraska–Lincoln, Graduate College, College of Arts and Sciences, Department of Physics and Astronomy, Lincoln, NE 68588. Offers astronomy (MS, PhD); physics (MS, PhD). *Degree requirements:* For master's, thesis optional; for doctorate, thesis/dissertation, comprehensive exam. *Entrance requirements:* For master's and doctorate, GRE General Test. Additional exam requirements/recommendations for international students: Required—TOEFL (minimum score 550 paper-based; 213 computer-based). Electronic applications accepted. *Faculty research:* Electromagnetics of solids and thin films, photoionization, ion collisions with atoms, molecules and surfaces, nanostructures.

University of Nevada, Las Vegas, Graduate College, College of Science, Department of Physics, Las Vegas, NV 89154-9900. Offers MS, PhD. Part-time programs available. *Faculty:* 16 full-time (3 women), 3 part-time/adjunct (0 women). *Students:* 9 full-time (1 woman), 6 part-time; includes 1 minority (Asian American or Pacific Islander), 6 international. 16 applicants, 56% accepted, 5 enrolled. In 2003, 2 master's, 1 doctorate awarded. *Degree requirements:* For master's, thesis, oral exam; for doctorate, thesis/dissertation, comprehensive exam. *Entrance requirements:* For master's, GRE General Test, GRE Subject Test, minimum GPA of 3.0 during previous 2 years, 2.75 overall; for doctorate, GRE General Test, GRE Subject Test, minimum GPA of 3.25 during previous 2 years, 3.0 overall. Additional exam requirements/recommendations for international students: Required—TOEFL (minimum score 550 paper-based; 213 computer-based). *Application deadline:* For fall admission, 6/15 for domestic students, 5/1 for international students; for spring admission, 11/15 for domestic students, 10/1 for international students. Application fee: $60 ($75 for international students). *Expenses:* Tuition, state resident: part-time $115 per credit. Tuition, nonresident: part-time $242 per credit. Required fees: $8 per semester. Tuition and fees vary according to course load. *Financial support:* In 2003–04, 14 teaching assistantships with partial tuition reimbursements (averaging $11,000 per year) were awarded; research assistantships with partial tuition reimbursements, unspecified assistantships also available. Financial award application deadline: 3/1. *Faculty research:* Laser (atomic, molecular, and optical) physics, astronomy/astrophysics, condensed-matter physics. *Unit head:* Dr. James Selser, Chair, 702-895-3084. *Application contact:* Graduate College Admissions Evaluator, 702-895-3320, Fax: 702-895-4180, E-mail: gradcollege@ccmail.nevada.edu.

University of Nevada, Reno, Graduate School, College of Science, Department of Physics, Reno, NV 89557. Offers MS, PhD. *Faculty:* 16. *Students:* 32 full-time (12 women), 1 part-time; includes 2 minority (1 Asian American or Pacific Islander, 1 Hispanic American), 21 international. Average age 30. In 2003, 2 master's, 4 doctorates awarded. Terminal master's awarded for partial completion of doctoral program. *Degree requirements:* For master's, thesis optional; for doctorate, thesis/dissertation. *Entrance requirements:* For master's, GRE General Test, minimum GPA of 2.75; for doctorate, GRE General Test, minimum GPA of 3.0. Additional exam requirements/recommendations for international students: Required—TOEFL. *Application deadline:* For fall admission, 3/1 for domestic students; for spring admission, 11/1 for domestic students. Applications are processed on a rolling basis. Application fee: $0 ($95 for international students). *Expenses:* Tuition, state resident: part-time $119 per credit. Tuition, nonresident: part-time $127 per credit. Required fees: $20 per term. Tuition and fees vary according to course load. *Financial support:* In 2003–04, 21 research assistantships, 9 teaching assistantships were awarded. Federal Work-Study and institutionally sponsored loans also available. Financial award application deadline: 3/1. *Faculty research:* Atomic and molecular physics. *Unit head:* Dr. Katherine McCall, Graduate Program Director, 775-784-6792.

University of New Brunswick Fredericton, School of Graduate Studies, Faculty of Science, Department of Physics, Fredericton, NB E3B 5A3, Canada. Offers M Sc, PhD. Part-time programs available. *Degree requirements:* For master's and doctorate, thesis/dissertation. *Entrance requirements:* For master's and doctorate, minimum GPA of 3.0. Additional exam requirements/recommendations for international students: Required—TOEFL, TWE.

University of New Hampshire, Graduate School, College of Engineering and Physical Sciences, Department of Physics, Durham, NH 03824. Offers MS, PhD. *Faculty:* 29 full-time. *Students:* 17 full-time (4 women), 20 part-time (1 woman), 20 international. Average age 27. 26 applicants, 92% accepted, 11 enrolled. In 2003, 1 master's, 2 doctorates awarded. Terminal master's awarded for partial completion of doctoral program. *Degree requirements:* For master's, thesis or alternative; for doctorate, thesis/dissertation. *Entrance requirements:* For master's and doctorate, GRE General Test. Additional exam requirements/recommendations for international students: Required—TOEFL (minimum score 550 paper-based; 213 computer-based); Recommended—TSE. *Application deadline:* For fall admission, 4/1 for domestic students; for winter admission, 12/1 for domestic students. Applications are processed on a rolling basis. Application fee: $50. Electronic applications accepted. Tuition, area resident: Full-time $7,070. *Expenses:* Tuition, state resident: full-time $10,605. Tuition, nonresident: full-time $17,430. Required fees: $15. *Financial support:* In 2003–04, 3 fellowships, 18 research assistantships, 12 teaching assistantships were awarded. Federal Work-Study, scholarships/grants, and tuition waivers (full and partial) also available. Support available to part-time students. Financial award application deadline: 2/15. *Faculty research:* Astrophysics and space physics, nuclear physics, atomic and molecular physics, nonlinear dynamical systems. *Unit head:* Dr. Dawn Meredith, Chairperson, 603-862-1960. *Application contact:* Katie Makem, Graduate Coordinator, 603-862-5096, E-mail: physics.grad.info@unh.edu.

University of New Mexico, Graduate School, College of Arts and Sciences, Department of Physics and Astronomy, Albuquerque, NM 87131-2039. Offers optical sciences (PhD); physics (MS, PhD). Part-time programs available. *Faculty:* 44. *Students:* 78 full-time (15 women), 22 part-time (6 women); includes 6 minority (1 African American, 3 Asian Americans or Pacific Islanders, 2 Hispanic Americans), 35 international. Average age 27. 67 applicants, 61% accepted, 20 enrolled. In 2003, 12 master's, 11 doctorates awarded. Terminal master's awarded for partial completion of doctoral program. *Degree requirements:* For master's, thesis optional; for doctorate, thesis/dissertation, comprehensive exam. *Entrance requirements:* Additional exam requirements/recommendations for international students: Required—TOEFL or Michigan English Language Assessment Battery. *Application deadline:* For fall admission, 2/1 for domestic students; for spring admission, 10/1 for domestic students. Application fee: $40. *Expenses:* Tuition, state resident: full-time $1,802; part-time $152 per credit hour. Tuition, nonresident: full-time $6,135; part-time $513 per credit hour. Tuition and fees vary according to program. *Financial support:* In 2003–04, 50 research assistantships with full and partial tuition reimbursements (averaging $10,943 per year), 31 teaching assistantships with full and partial tuition reimbursements (averaging $8,058 per year) were awarded. Fellowships with full tuition reimbursements, career-related internships or fieldwork, scholarships/grants, health care benefits, and unspecified assistantships also available. Financial award application deadline: 3/1; financial award applicants required to submit FAFSA. *Faculty research:* High-energy and particle physics, optical and laser sciences, condensed matter, nuclear and particle physics, surface physics. Total annual research expenditures: $4.6 million. *Unit head:* Dr. Bernd Bassalleck, Chair, 505-277-1517, Fax: 505-277-1520, E-mail: bassek@unm.edu. *Application contact:* Mary De Witt, Program Advisement Coordinator, 505-277-1514, Fax: 505-277-1520, E-mail: mdewitt@unm.edu.

University of New Orleans, Graduate School, College of Sciences, Department of Physics, New Orleans, LA 70148. Offers MS, PhD. Part-time and evening/weekend programs available. *Faculty:* 5 full-time (1 woman), 1 part-time/adjunct (0 women). *Students:* 13 full-time (2 women), 5 part-time (1 woman); includes 2 minority (both African Americans), 3 international. Average age 29. 21 applicants, 48% accepted, 8 enrolled. In 2003, 8 degrees awarded. *Degree requirements:* For master's, thesis (for some programs). *Entrance requirements:* For master's, GRE General Test. Additional exam requirements/recommendations for international students: Required—TOEFL (minimum score 550 paper-based; 213 computer-based). *Application deadline:* For fall admission, 7/1 priority date for domestic students, 6/1 priority date for international students; for spring admission, 11/15 priority date for domestic students, 10/1 priority date for international students. Applications are processed on a rolling basis. Application fee: $20. Electronic applications accepted. *Expenses:* Tuition, state resident: part-time $488 per semester hour. Tuition, nonresident: part-time $1,826 per semester hour. *Financial support:* Research assistantships, teaching assistantships, career-related internships or fieldwork available. Financial award application deadline: 5/15; financial award applicants required to submit FAFSA. *Faculty research:* Underwater acoustics, applied electromagnetics, experimental atomic beams, digital signal processing, astrophysics. *Unit head:* Dr. Greg Seab, Chairperson, 504-280-1062, Fax: 504-280-6048, E-mail: cseab@uno.edu. *Application contact:* Dr. Ashok Puri, Graduate Coordinator, 504-280-6682, Fax: 504-280-6048, E-mail: apuri@uno.edu.

The University of North Carolina at Chapel Hill, Graduate School, College of Arts and Sciences, Department of Physics and Astronomy, Chapel Hill, NC 27599. Offers physics (MS, PhD). *Faculty:* 31 full-time (3 women), 7 part-time/adjunct (1 woman). *Students:* 65 full-time (21 women). Average age 26. 200 applicants, 21% accepted, 19 enrolled. In 2003, 8 master's, 6 doctorates awarded. Terminal master's awarded for partial completion of doctoral program. *Median time to degree:* Master's–3 years full-time; doctorate–6 years full-time. *Degree requirements:* For master's, comprehensive exam, registration; for doctorate, thesis/dissertation, comprehensive exam, registration. *Entrance requirements:* For master's and doctorate, GRE General Test, minimum GPA of 3.0. *Application deadline:* For fall admission, 1/1 for domestic students. Application fee: $60. Electronic applications accepted. *Expenses:* Tuition, state resident: full-time $3,163. Tuition, nonresident: full-time $15,161. *Financial support:* In 2003–04, 2 fellowships with full tuition reimbursements (averaging $14,000 per year), 31 research assistantships with full tuition reimbursements (averaging $18,600 per year), 38 teaching assistantships with full tuition reimbursements (averaging $13,950 per year) were awarded. Federal Work-Study, scholarships/grants, health care benefits, and unspecified assistantships also available. Financial award application deadline: 3/1. *Faculty research:* Observational astronomy, fullerenes, polarized beams, nanotubes, nucleosynthesis in stars and supernovae, superstring theory, ballistic transport in semiconductors, gravitation. Total annual research expenditures: $5.5 million. *Unit head:* Dr. Bruce W. Carney, Chairman, 919-962-2079, Fax: 919-962-8205, E-mail: bruce@physics.unc.edu. *Application contact:* Prof. Thomas B. Clegg, Director of Graduate Admissions, 919-843-8168, Fax: 919-962-0480, E-mail: clegg@physics.unc.edu.

University of North Dakota, Graduate School, College of Arts and Sciences, Department of Physics, Grand Forks, ND 58202. Offers MS, PhD. *Faculty:* 9 full-time (0 women), 2 part-time/adjunct (1 woman). *Students:* 4 full-time (0 women), 9 part-time (4 women). 23 applicants, 83% accepted, 5 enrolled. *Degree requirements:* For master's, thesis/dissertation, final exam; for doctorate, thesis/dissertation, final exam, comprehensive exam. *Entrance requirements:* For master's, minimum GPA of 3.0; for doctorate, minimum GPA of 3.5. Additional exam requirements/recommendations for international students: Required—TOEFL (minimum score 550 paper-based; 213 computer-based). *Application deadline:* For fall admission, 3/1 priority date for domestic students, 3/1 priority date for international students; for spring admission, 10/15 priority date for domestic students, 10/15 priority date for international students. Applications are processed on a rolling basis. Application fee: $35. Electronic applications accepted. *Expenses:* Tuition, state resident: part-time $235 per credit. Tuition, nonresident: part-time $535 per credit. Tuition and fees vary according to course level, course load, program and reciprocity agreements. *Financial support:* In 2003–04, 7 students received support, including research assistantships with full tuition reimbursements available (averaging $8,134 per year), teaching assistantships with full tuition reimbursements available (averaging $10,762 per year); fellowships, Federal Work-Study, institutionally sponsored loans, scholarships/grants, and tuition waivers (full and partial) also available. Support available to part-time students. Financial award application deadline: 3/15; financial award applicants required to submit FAFSA. *Faculty research:* Solid state physics, atomic and molecular physics, astrophysics, health physics. *Unit head:* Dr. Tar-Pin Chen, Chairperson, 701-777-3529, Fax: 701-777-3523, E-mail: tar.pin.chen@und.nodak.edu.

University of North Texas, Robert B. Toulouse School of Graduate Studies, College of Arts and Sciences, Department of Physics, Denton, TX 76203. Offers MA, MS, PhD. *Faculty:* 22 full-time (3 women). *Students:* 98 full-time (28 women), 26 part-time (9 women); includes 6 minority (1 African American, 2 Asian Americans or Pacific Islanders, 3 Hispanic Americans), 70 international. Average age 26. In 2003, 7 master's, 5 doctorates awarded. Terminal master's awarded for partial completion of doctoral program. *Degree requirements:* For master's, thesis or problems; for doctorate, one foreign language, thesis/dissertation, comprehensive exam. *Entrance requirements:* For master's and doctorate, GRE General Test. Additional exam requirements/recommendations for international students: Recommended—TOEFL (minimum score 550 paper-based; 213 computer-based). *Application deadline:* For fall admission, 7/15 for domestic students. Applications are processed on a rolling basis. Application fee: $50 ($75 for international students). Electronic applications accepted. Tuition, area resident: Full-time $4,087. Tuition, nonresident: full-time $8,730. Tuition and fees vary according to course load. *Financial support:* Fellowships, research assistantships, teaching assistantships available. *Faculty research:* Accelerator physics, chaos. *Unit head:* Dr. Samuel E. Matteson, Chair, 940-565-2626, Fax: 940-565-2515, E-mail: matteson@unt.edu. *Application contact:* Dr. Duncan Weathers, Graduate Adviser, 940-565-2626, Fax: 940-565-2515, E-mail: weathers@unt.edu.

University of Notre Dame, Graduate School, College of Science, Department of Physics, Notre Dame, IN 46556. Offers PhD. *Faculty:* 41 full-time (5 women), 5 part-time/adjunct (1 woman). *Students:* 85 full-time (18 women), 1 part-time; includes 2 minority (both Hispanic Americans), 42 international. 133 applicants, 47% accepted. In 2003, 8 doctorates awarded. *Degree requirements:* For doctorate, thesis/dissertation. *Entrance requirements:* For doctorate, GRE General Test, GRE Subject Test. Additional exam requirements/recommendations for international students: Required—TOEFL. *Application deadline:* For fall admission, 2/1 for domestic students; for spring admission, 10/15 for domestic students. Applications are processed on a rolling basis. Application fee: $25. Electronic applications accepted. *Expenses:* Tuition: Full-time $29,375. *Financial support:* In 2003–04, 85 students received support, including 7 fellowships with full tuition reimbursements available (averaging $20,000 per year), 27 research assistantships with full tuition reimbursements available (averaging $14,700 per year), 42 teaching assistantships with full tuition reimbursements available (averaging $14,700 per year); tuition waivers (full) also available. Financial award application deadline: 2/1. *Faculty research:* High energy, nuclear, atomic, condensed-matter physics; astrophysics; biophysics. Total annual research expenditures: $6.8 million. *Unit head:* Dr. Ani Aprahamian, Director of Graduate Studies, 574-631-6387, Fax: 574-631-5952. *Application contact:* Dr. Terrence J. Akai, Director of Graduate Admissions, 574-631-7706, Fax: 574-631-4183, E-mail: gradad@nd.edu.

See in-depth description on page 425.

University of Oklahoma, Graduate College, College of Arts and Sciences, Department of Physics and Astronomy, Norman, OK 73019-0390. Offers astrophysics (MS, PhD); physics (MS, PhD). Part-time programs available. *Faculty:* 29 full-time (4 women), 1 part-time/adjunct (0 women). *Students:* 50 full-time (15 women), 3 part-time (1 woman); includes 6 minority (2 African Americans, 3 American Indian/Alaska Native, 1 Asian American or Pacific Islander), 27 international. Average age 26. 28 applicants, 100% accepted, 9 enrolled. In 2003, 4 master's, 5 doctorates awarded. Terminal master's awarded for partial completion of doctoral program. *Degree requirements:* For master's, thesis or alternative, departmental qualifying exam; for doctorate, thesis/dissertation, comprehensive, departmental qualifying, oral, and written exams. *Entrance requirements:* For master's and doctorate, GRE General Test, GRE Subject Test, previous course work in physics. Additional exam requirements/recommendations for international students: Required—TOEFL (minimum score 600 paper-based; 250 computer-based). *Application deadline:* For fall admission, 3/1 for domestic students. Application fee: $25 ($75 for international students). *Expenses:* Tuition, state resident: full-time $2,774; part-time $116 per credit hour. Tuition, nonresident: full-time $9,571; part-time $399 per credit hour. Required fees: $953; $33 per credit hour. Full-time tuition and fees vary according to course level, course load and program. *Financial support:* In 2003–04, 10 students received support, including 3 fellowships with full tuition reimbursements available (averaging $4,333 per year), 26 research assistantships with partial tuition reimbursements available (averaging $13,733 per year), 29 teaching assistantships with partial tuition reimbursements available (averaging $12,533 per year); Federal Work-Study, scholarships/grants, health care benefits, tuition waivers (full), and unspecified assistantships also available. Financial award application deadline: 3/1; financial award applicants required to submit FAFSA. *Faculty research:* Atomic, molecular, and chemical physics; high energy, solid state and applied physics, astrophysics. Total annual research expenditures: $3.9 million. *Unit head:* Dr. Ryan Doezema, Chair, 405-325-3961, Fax: 405-325-7557, E-mail: rdoezema@ou.edu. *Application contact:* Sonya Brindle, Curriculum Advisor, 405-325-3961 Ext. 36127, Fax: 405-325-7557, E-mail: brindle@mail.ou.edu.

University of Oregon, Graduate School, College of Arts and Sciences, Department of Physics, Eugene, OR 97403. Offers MA, MS, PhD. *Faculty:* 36 full-time (2 women), 11 part-time/adjunct (3 women). *Students:* 88 full-time (16 women), 1 part-time; includes 6 minority (5 Asian Americans or Pacific Islanders, 1 Hispanic American), 25 international. 55 applicants, 49% accepted. In 2003, 10 master's, 14 doctorates awarded. Terminal master's awarded for partial completion of doctoral program. *Degree requirements:* For doctorate, thesis/dissertation. *Entrance requirements:* For master's and doctorate, GRE General Test, GRE Subject Test, minimum GPA of 3.0. Additional exam requirements/recommendations for international students: Required—TOEFL. *Application deadline:* For fall admission, 3/15 for domestic students. Applications are processed on a rolling basis. Application fee: $50. *Expenses:* Tuition, state resident: part-time $8,910 per term. Tuition, nonresident: part-time $13,689 per term. *Financial support:* In 2003–04, 56 teaching assistantships were awarded; Federal Work-Study, institutionally sponsored loans, and traineeships also available. Financial award application deadline: 2/15. *Faculty research:* Solid-state and chemical physics, optical physics, elementary particle physics, astrophysics, atomic and molecular physics. *Unit head:* Dr. Dietrich Belitz, Head, 541-346-5826. *Application contact:* Jani Calavan, Admissions Contact, 541-346-4751, Fax: 541-346-4787, E-mail: jcalavan@uoregon.edu.

University of Ottawa, Faculty of Graduate and Postdoctoral Studies, Faculty of Science, Ottawa-Carleton Institute for Physics, Ottawa, ON K1N 6N5, Canada. Offers M Sc, PhD. *Faculty:* 30 full-time (2 women). *Students:* 37 full-time (7 women), 9 part-time (2 women). 42 applicants, 38% accepted, 12 enrolled. In 2003, 7 master's, 3 doctorates awarded. *Degree requirements:* For master's, thesis or alternative; for doctorate, thesis/dissertation, seminar, comprehensive exam. *Entrance requirements:* For master's, honors B Sc degree or equivalent, minimum B average; for doctorate, M Sc with minimum B+ average. *Application deadline:* For fall admission, 3/1 for domestic students. Application fee: $60. *Expenses:* Tuition, state resident: full-time $4,467. International tuition: $4,574 full-time. Tuition and fees vary according to program. *Financial support:* Fellowships, research assistantships, teaching assistantships, Federal Work-Study available. Financial award application deadline: 2/15. *Faculty research:* Condensed matter physics and statistical physics (CMS), subatomic physics (SAP), medical physics (Med), health physics, atomic physics (AP). *Unit head:* Dr. André Longtin, Chair, 613-562-5757, Fax: 613-562-5190. *Application contact:* Lise Maisonneuve, Graduate Studies Administrator, 613-562-5800 Ext. 6050, Fax: 613-562-5486, E-mail: lise@science.uottawa.ca.

University of Pennsylvania, School of Arts and Sciences, Graduate Group in Physics and Astronomy, Philadelphia, PA 19104. Offers medical physics (MS); physics (PhD). Part-time programs available. *Faculty:* 43 full-time (4 women), 28 part-time/adjunct (3 women). *Students:* 89 full-time (17 women), 4 part-time (1 woman); includes 3 minority (1 Asian American or Pacific Islander, 2 Hispanic Americans), 41 international. 465 applicants, 9% accepted, 13 enrolled. In 2003, 29 master's, 6 doctorates awarded. *Degree requirements:* For doctorate, thesis/dissertation, oral, preliminary, and final exams. *Entrance requirements:* For doctorate, GRE General Test, GRE Subject Test (recommended). Additional exam requirements/recommendations for international students: Required—TOEFL; Recommended—TSE. *Application deadline:* For fall admission, 12/1 for domestic students. Application fee: $70. Electronic applications accepted. *Expenses:* Tuition: Full-time $28,040; part-time $3,550 per course. Required fees: $1,750; $214 per course. Tuition and fees vary according to degree level, program and student level. *Financial support:* Fellowships, research assistantships, teaching assistantships, institutionally sponsored loans available. Financial award application deadline: 12/15. *Faculty research:* Astrophysics, condensed matter experiment, condensed matter theory, particle experiment, particle theory. Total annual research expenditures: $7.3 million. *Application contact:* Patricia Rea, Coordinator for Admissions, 215-573-5816, Fax: 215-573-8068, E-mail: gdasadmis@sas.upenn.edu.

University of Pittsburgh, School of Arts and Sciences, Department of Physics and Astronomy, Pittsburgh, PA 15260. Offers physics (MS, PhD). *Faculty:* 42 full-time (4 women), 1 (woman) part-time/adjunct. *Students:* 84 full-time (13 women), 2 part-time; includes 5 minority (2 African Americans, 3 Asian Americans or Pacific Islanders), 59 international. Average age 20. 222 applicants, 29% accepted, 23 enrolled. In 2003, 3 master's awarded, leading to continued full-time study 100%; 8 doctorates awarded. Terminal master's awarded for partial completion of doctoral program. *Median time to degree:* Of those who began their doctoral program in fall 1995, 100% received their degree in 8 years or less. *Degree requirements:* For master's, thesis optional; for doctorate, thesis/dissertation, teaching present seminar. *Entrance requirements:* For master's and doctorate, GRE General Test, GRE Subject Test, minimum QPA of 3.0. Additional exam requirements/recommendations for international students: Required—TOEFL (minimum score 550 paper-based; 213 computer-based), IELT. *Application deadline:* For fall admission, 1/31 priority date for domestic students, 1/13 priority date for international students. Applications are processed on a rolling basis. Application fee: $0 ($40 for international students). Electronic applications accepted. *Expenses:* Tuition, state resident: full-time $11,744; part-time $479 per credit. Tuition, nonresident: full-time $22,910; part-time $941 per credit. Required fees: $560. Tuition and fees vary according to degree level and program. *Financial support:* In 2003–04, 5 fellowships with full tuition reimbursements (averaging $14,000 per year), 42 research assistantships with full tuition reimbursements (averaging $12,775 per year), 32 teaching assistantships with full tuition reimbursements (averaging $12,775 per year) were awarded. Scholarships/grants, health care benefits, and unspecified assistantships also available. Financial award application deadline: 1/31; financial award applicants required to submit FAFSA. *Faculty research:* Astrophysics, cosmology, condensed-matter physics, atomic physics, intermediate energy and elementary particle physics. Total annual research expenditures: $5 million. *Unit head:* Dr. David Jasnow, Chairman, 412-624-6381, Fax: 412-624-9163, E-mail: dmj@pitt.edu. *Application contact:* Dr. David Turnshek, Admissions, 412-624-9000, Fax: 412-624-9163, E-mail: turnshek@pitt.edu.

See in-depth description on page 429.

University of Puerto Rico, Mayagüez Campus, Graduate Studies, College of Arts and Sciences, Department of Physics, Mayagüez, PR 00681-9000. Offers MS. Part-time programs available. *Degree requirements:* For master's, thesis, comprehensive exam. *Faculty research:* Atomic and molecular physics, nuclear physics, nonlinear thermostatics, fluid dynamics, molecular spectroscopy.

University of Puerto Rico, Río Piedras, Faculty of Natural Sciences, Department of Physics, San Juan, PR 00931. Offers applied physics (MS); physics (MS); physics-chemical (PhD). Part-time and evening/weekend programs available. *Faculty:* 15 full-time (1 woman), 2 part-time/adjunct (0 women). *Students:* 21 full-time (10 women), 34 part-time (11 women); includes 53 minority (11 Asian Americans or Pacific Islanders, 42 Hispanic Americans). 20 applicants, 95% accepted, 19 enrolled. In 2003, 3 degrees awarded. *Degree requirements:* For master's and doctorate, one foreign language, thesis/dissertation, comprehensive exam. *Entrance requirements:* For master's, GRE, EXADEP, interview, minimum GPA of 3.0, letter of recommendation; for doctorate, GRE, master's degree, minimum GPA of 3.0, letter of recommendation. Additional exam requirements/recommendations for international students: Required—TOEFL. *Application deadline:* For fall admission, 2/1 for domestic students, 2/1 for international students. Application fee: $17. *Expenses:* Tuition, state resident: part-time $75 per credit. Tuition, nonresident: full-time $1,200; part-time $218 per credit. International tuition: $3,500 full-time. Required fees: $70; $35 per term. *Financial support:* Fellowships, research assistantships, teaching assistantships, Federal Work-Study, institutionally sponsored loans, and tuition waivers (partial) available. Financial award application deadline: 5/31. *Faculty research:* Energy transfer process through Van der Vacqs interactions, study of the photodissociation of ketene. *Unit head:* Luis F. Fonseca, Coordinator of Doctoral Program, 787-764-0000 Ext. 4773, Fax: 787-764-4063.

University of Regina, Faculty of Graduate Studies and Research, Faculty of Science, Department of Physics, Regina, SK S4S 0A2, Canada. Offers M Sc, PhD. *Faculty:* 9 full-time (0 women), 2 part-time/adjunct (0 women). *Students:* 6 full-time (2 women), 3 part-time. 6 applicants. In 2003, 2 degrees awarded. Terminal master's awarded for partial completion of doctoral program. *Degree requirements:* For master's and doctorate, thesis/dissertation. *Entrance requirements:* For master's, GRE recommended for foreign applicants, honors degree in physics or engineering physics; for doctorate, GRE recommended for foreign applicants, M Sc or equivalent. Additional exam requirements/recommendations for international students: Required—TOEFL. *Application deadline:* For fall admission, 5/15 for domestic students; for winter admission, 8/15 for domestic students. Applications are processed on a rolling basis. Application fee: $60. *Expenses:* Tuition, state resident: part-time $130 per credit hour. Tuition and fees vary according to course load and program. *Financial support:* In 2003–04, 2 fellowships, 3 teaching assistantships were awarded. Research assistantships, career-related internships or fieldwork and scholarships/grants also available. Financial award application deadline: 6/15. *Faculty research:* Experimental and theoretical subatomic physics. Total annual research expenditures: $2.1 million. *Unit head:* Dr. G. J. Lolos, Head, 306-585-4149, Fax: 306-585-5659, E-mail: gjlolos@meena.cc.uregina.ca. *Application contact:* Dr. B. Dutta, Graduate Coordinator, 306-585-5384, Fax: 306-585-5659, E-mail: duttabh@uregina.ca.

University of Rhode Island, Graduate School, College of Arts and Sciences, Department of Physics, Kingston, RI 02881. Offers MS, PhD. In 2003, 1 master's, 6 doctorates awarded. *Application deadline:* For fall admission, 4/15 for domestic students. Applications are processed on a rolling basis. Application fee: $35. *Expenses:* Tuition, state resident: full-time $4,338; part-time $281 per credit. Tuition, nonresident: full-time $12,438; part-time $704 per credit. Required fees: $1,840. *Unit head:* Jan Northby, Chair, 401-874-2074.

University of Rochester, The College, Arts and Sciences, Department of Physics and Astronomy, Rochester, NY 14627-0250. Offers physics (MA, MS, PhD); physics and astronomy (PhD). Part-time programs available. *Faculty:* 28. *Students:* 134 full-time (23 women); includes 7 minority (2 African Americans, 2 Asian Americans or Pacific Islanders, 3 Hispanic Americans), 70 international. 487 applicants, 15% accepted, 33 enrolled. In 2003, 11 master's, 8 doctorates awarded. Terminal master's awarded for partial completion of doctoral program. *Degree requirements:* For master's, thesis (for some programs), comprehensive exam; for doctorate, thesis/dissertation, qualifying exam, comprehensive exam. *Entrance requirements:* For master's and doctorate, GRE General Test. Additional exam requirements/recommendations for international students: Required—TOEFL. *Application deadline:* For fall admission, 2/1 for domestic students. Application fee: $25. *Expenses:* Tuition: Part-time $880 per credit hour. Required fees: $522. *Financial support:* Fellowships, research assistantships, teaching assistantships, tuition waivers (full and partial) available. Financial award application deadline: 2/1. *Unit head:* Arie Bodek, Chair, 585-275-4351. *Application contact:* Barbara Warren, Graduate Program Secretary, 585-275-4351.

See in-depth description on page 431.

University of Saskatchewan, College of Graduate Studies and Research, College of Arts and Sciences, Department of Physics and Engineering Physics, Saskatoon, SK S7N 5A2, Canada. Offers M Sc, PhD. *Faculty:* 16. *Students:* 25. *Degree requirements:* For master's and doctorate, thesis/dissertation, registration. *Entrance requirements:* Additional exam requirements/recommendations for international students: Required—TOEFL. *Application deadline:* For fall admission, 7/1 for domestic students. Applications are processed on a rolling basis. Application fee: $50. Tuition charges are reported in Canadian dollars. *Expenses:* Tuition, state resident: part-time $483 Canadian dollars per course. *Financial support:* Fellowships, research assistantships, teaching assistantships available. Financial award application deadline: 1/31. *Unit head:* Dr. Rob Pywell, Head, 306-966-6404, Fax: 306-966-6400, E-mail: rob.pywell@usask.ca. *Application contact:* Dr. Andrei Smolyakov, Graduate Chair, 306-966-6432, Fax: 306-966-6400, E-mail: andrei.smolyakov@usask.ca.

University of South Carolina, The Graduate School, College of Science and Mathematics, Department of Physics and Astronomy, Columbia, SC 29208. Offers IMA, MAT, MS, PMS, PhD. IMA and MAT offered in cooperation with the College of Education. Part-time programs available. *Faculty:* 24 full-time (2 women), 1 part-time/adjunct (0 women). *Students:* 46 full-time (8 women); includes 4 minority (all African Americans), 26 international. Average age 28. 52 applicants, 73% accepted, 18 enrolled. In 2003, 6 master's awarded, leading to continued full-time study 50%, business/industry 50%; 1 doctorate awarded, leading to university research/teaching 100%. Terminal master's awarded for partial completion of doctoral program. *Median time to degree:* Master's–2.5 years full-time; doctorate–2 years full-time. *Degree requirements:* For master's, thesis, comprehensive exam, registration; for doctorate, one foreign language, thesis/dissertation, comprehensive exam, registration. *Entrance requirements:* For master's and doctorate, GRE General Test, GRE Subject Test. Additional exam requirements/recommendations for international students: Required—TOEFL (minimum score 570 paper-based; 230 computer-based). *Application deadline:* For fall admission, 8/1 priority date for domestic students, 8/1 priority date for international students. Applications are processed on a rolling basis. Application fee: $40. Electronic applications accepted. *Expenses:* Tuition, state resident: part-time $308 per hour. Tuition, nonresident: part-time $655 per hour. *Financial support:* In 2003–04, 41 students received support, including 4 fellowships with full tuition reimbursements available (averaging $20,727 per year), 13 research assistantships (averaging $19,000 per year), 24 teaching assistantships (averaging $16,000 per year); Federal Work-Study and unspecified assistantships also available. Support available to part-time students. *Faculty research:* Condensed matter, intermediate-energy nuclear physics, foundations of quantum mechanics, astronomy/astrophysics. Total annual research expenditures: $2.5 million. *Unit head:* Dr. Fred Myhrer, Chair, 803-777-4121, Fax: 803-777-3065, E-mail: myhrer@sc.edu. *Application contact:* Dr. Chaden Djalali, Director of Graduate Studies, 803-777-8104, Fax: 803-777-3065, E-mail: djalali@sc.edu.

See in-depth description on page 433.

University of Southern California, Graduate School, College of Letters, Arts and Sciences, Department of Physics and Astronomy, Los Angeles, CA 90089. Offers physics (MA, MS, PhD). Part-time programs available. *Students:* 57 full-time (8 women), 5 part-time (1 woman), 48 international. In 2003, 3 master's, 3 doctorates awarded. Terminal master's awarded for partial completion of doctoral program. *Degree requirements:* For master's, thesis (for some programs); for doctorate, thesis/dissertation. *Entrance requirements:* For master's and doctorate, GRE General Test, GRE Subject Test. *Application deadline:* For fall admission, 1/15 for domestic students; for spring admission, 11/1 for domestic students. Application fee: $65 ($75 for international students). *Expenses:* Tuition: Full-time $32,784; part-time $949 per unit. Tuition and fees vary according to course load and program. *Financial support:* In 2003–04, 52

Physics

University of Southern California (continued)

students received support, including research assistantships with tuition reimbursements available (averaging $16,000 per year), teaching assistantships with tuition reimbursements available (averaging $16,000 per year); fellowships, career-related internships or fieldwork, Federal Work-Study, and institutionally sponsored loans also available. Financial award application deadline: 2/15; financial award applicants required to submit FAFSA. *Faculty research:* Space physics, laser physics, high-energy particle theory, condensed matter physics, atomic and molecular physics. *Unit head:* Dr. N. Eugene Bickers, Chairman, 213-740-0848, Fax: 213-740-8094, E-mail: physdept@usc.edu. *Application contact:* Dr. Stephen Haas, Associate Professor, 213-740-0848.

University of Southern Mississippi, Graduate School, College of Science and Technology, Department of Physics and Astronomy, Hattiesburg, MS 39406-0001. Offers MS. *Faculty:* 2 full-time (0 women). *Students:* 2 full-time (both women); includes 1 minority (Asian American or Pacific Islander) Average age 27. 6 applicants, 67% accepted, 4 enrolled. In 2003, 1 degree awarded. *Degree requirements:* For master's, thesis, comprehensive exam. *Entrance requirements:* For master's, GRE General Test, minimum GPA of 2.75 in last 60 hours. Additional exam requirements/recommendations for international students: Required—TOEFL. *Application deadline:* For fall admission, 8/6 for domestic students. Applications are processed on a rolling basis. Application fee: $25. *Expenses:* Tuition, state resident: part-time $1,967 per semester. Tuition, nonresident: part-time $4,376 per semester. *Financial support:* Teaching assistantships with full tuition reimbursements, Federal Work-Study available. Financial award application deadline: 3/15. *Faculty research:* Polymers, atomic physics, fluid mechanics, liquid crystals, refractory materials. *Unit head:* Dr. Joe B. Whitehead, Chair, 601-266-4934, Fax: 601-266-5149.

University of South Florida, College of Graduate Studies, College of Arts and Sciences, Department of Physics, Tampa, FL 33620-9951. Offers MA, PhD. Part-time programs available. *Faculty:* 16 full-time (1 woman). *Students:* 36 full-time (9 women), 5 part-time (1 woman); includes 1 minority (African American), 16 international. 38 applicants, 39% accepted, 10 enrolled. In 2003, 4 degrees awarded. *Degree requirements:* For master's, thesis optional; for doctorate, 2 foreign languages, thesis/dissertation. *Entrance requirements:* For master's, GRE General Test, minimum GPA of 3.0 in last 60 hours; for doctorate, GRE General Test, minimum graduate GPA of 3.2. *Application deadline:* For fall admission, 6/1 for domestic students; for spring admission, 10/1 for domestic students. Applications are processed on a rolling basis. Application fee: $30. Electronic applications accepted. *Financial support:* In 2003–04, 23 students received support, including 3 fellowships (averaging $4,000 per year), 15 research assistantships with full tuition reimbursements available (averaging $17,526 per year), 20 teaching assistantships with full tuition reimbursements available (averaging $17,475 per year); career-related internships or fieldwork, scholarships/grants, and unspecified assistantships also available. Financial award application deadline: 6/30. *Faculty research:* Laser, medical, and solid-state physics. Total annual research expenditures: $721,571. *Unit head:* Dr. Pritish Mukherjee, Chairperson, 813-974-2871, Fax: 813-974-5813.

The University of Tennessee, Graduate School, College of Arts and Sciences, Department of Physics and Astronomy, Knoxville, TN 37996. Offers physics (MS, PhD). Part-time programs available. *Degree requirements:* For master's, thesis or alternative; for doctorate, thesis/dissertation. *Entrance requirements:* For master's and doctorate, minimum GPA of 2.7. Additional exam requirements/recommendations for international students: Required—TOEFL. Electronic applications accepted.

The University of Tennessee Space Institute, Graduate Programs, Program in Physics, Tullahoma, TN 37388-9700. Offers MS, PhD. *Faculty:* 5 full-time (0 women). *Students:* 5 full-time (1 woman), 4 part-time (1 woman), 3 international. 5 applicants, 100% accepted. In 2003, 2 master's, 1 doctorate awarded. *Degree requirements:* For master's, thesis (for some programs); for doctorate, one foreign language, thesis/dissertation. *Entrance requirements:* For master's and doctorate, GRE General Test, GRE Subject Test. *Application deadline:* Applications are processed on a rolling basis. Application fee: $35. *Expenses:* Tuition, state resident: full-time $5,828; part-time $243 per semester hour. Tuition, nonresident: full-time $17,612; part-time $735 per semester hour. Required fees: $10 per semester hour. Tuition and fees vary according to course load. *Financial support:* Fellowships with full and partial tuition reimbursements, research assistantships with full tuition reimbursements, career-related internships or fieldwork, Federal Work-Study, tuition waivers (full and partial), and unspecified assistantships available. Financial award applicants required to submit FAFSA. *Unit head:* Dr. Horace Crater, Degree Program Chairman, 931-393-7469, Fax: 931-393-7444, E-mail: hcrater@utsi.edu. *Application contact:* Dr. Alfonso Pujol, Assistant Vice President and Dean for Student Affairs, 931-393-7432, Fax: 931-393-7346, E-mail: apujol@utsi.edu.

The University of Texas at Arlington, Graduate School, College of Science, Department of Physics, Arlington, TX 76019. Offers physics (MS); physics and applied physics (PhD). Part-time programs available. *Faculty:* 5 full-time (0 women). *Students:* 28 full-time (8 women), 4 part-time (1 woman), 21 international. 9 applicants, 67% accepted, 3 enrolled. In 2003, 7 master's, 4 doctorates awarded. Terminal master's awarded for partial completion of doctoral program. *Median time to degree:* Of those who began their doctoral program in fall 1995, 95% received their degree in 8 years or less. *Degree requirements:* For master's, thesis optional; for doctorate, thesis/dissertation, internship or substitute, comprehensive exam. *Entrance requirements:* For master's, GRE General Test, minimum GPA of 3.0 in last 60 hours of coursework; for doctorate, GRE General Test, minimum GPA of 3.0 in last 60 hours of coursework, 30 hours graduate work in physics. Additional exam requirements/recommendations for international students: Required—TOEFL. *Application deadline:* For fall admission, 6/16 for domestic students. Applications are processed on a rolling basis. Application fee: $35 ($50 for international students). *Expenses:* Tuition, state resident: full-time $3,042. Tuition, nonresident: full-time $8,712. Required fees: $1,269. Tuition and fees vary according to course load. *Financial support:* In 2003–04, 25 students received support, including 4 fellowships (averaging $1,000 per year), research assistantships (averaging $18,000 per year), 11 teaching assistantships (averaging $18,000 per year); career-related internships or fieldwork, Federal Work-Study, institutionally sponsored loans, scholarships/grants, health care benefits, tuition waivers (full and partial), and unspecified assistantships also available. Support available to part-time students. Financial award application deadline: 6/1; financial award applicants required to submit FAFSA. *Faculty research:* Particle physics, astrophysics, condensed matter theory and experiment. Total annual research expenditures: $1.5 million. *Unit head:* Dr. John L. Fry, Chair, 817-272-2266, Fax: 817-272-3637, E-mail: fry@uta.edu. *Application contact:* Dr. Ciming Zhang, Graduate Advisor, 817-272-2266, Fax: 817-272-3637, E-mail: zhang@uta.edu.

The University of Texas at Austin, Graduate School, College of Natural Sciences, Department of Physics, Austin, TX 78712-1111. Offers MA, MS, PhD. *Degree requirements:* For master's and doctorate, thesis/dissertation, registration. *Entrance requirements:* For master's and doctorate, GRE General Test, GRE Subject Test (physics). Electronic applications accepted.

See in-depth description on page 435.

The University of Texas at Dallas, School of Natural Sciences and Mathematics, Program in Physics, Richardson, TX 75083-0688. Offers applied physics (MS); physics (PhD). Part-time and evening/weekend programs available. *Faculty:* 14 full-time (0 women). *Students:* 40 full-time (9 women), 24 part-time (1 woman); includes 8 minority (3 African Americans, 2 Asian Americans or Pacific Islanders, 3 Hispanic Americans), 16 international. Average age 34. 82 applicants, 40% accepted. In 2003, 7 master's, 3 doctorates awarded. *Degree requirements:* For master's, industrial internship, thesis optional; for doctorate, thesis/dissertation, publishable paper. *Entrance requirements:* For master's and doctorate, GRE General Test, minimum GPA of 3.0 in upper-level coursework in field. Additional exam requirements/recommendations for international students: Required—TOEFL (minimum score 550 paper-based; 213 computer-based). *Application deadline:* For fall admission, 7/15 for domestic students; for spring admission, 11/15 for domestic students. Applications are processed on a rolling basis. Application fee: $50 ($100 for international students). Electronic applications accepted. *Expenses:* Tuition, state resident: full-time $1,656; part-time $92 per credit. Tuition, nonresident: full-time $5,904; part-time $328 per credit. Required fees: $2,161; $275 per credit. $334 per term. *Financial support:* In 2003–04, 1 fellowship, 20 research assistantships with tuition reimbursements (averaging $7,112 per year), 15 teaching assistantships with tuition reimbursements (averaging $5,625 per year) were awarded. Career-related internships or fieldwork, Federal Work-Study, institutionally sponsored loans, scholarships/grants, and unspecified assistantships also available. Support available to part-time students. Financial award application deadline: 4/30; financial award applicants required to submit FAFSA. *Faculty research:* Atomic, molecular, atmospheric, chemical, solid-state, and space physics; optics and quantum electronics; relativity and astrophysics; high-energy particles. Total annual research expenditures: $3.2 million. *Unit head:* Dr. Roderick A. Heelis, Department Head, 972-883-2822, Fax: 972-883-2848, E-mail: heelis@utdallas.edu. *Application contact:* Margorie Renfrow, Information Contact, 972-883-2884, Fax: 972-883-2848, E-mail: margie@utdallas.edu.

The University of Texas at El Paso, Graduate School, College of Science, Department of Physics, El Paso, TX 79968-0001. Offers MS. Part-time and evening/weekend programs available. *Students:* 27 (3 women); includes 7 minority (all Hispanic Americans) 16 international. Average age 34. 7 applicants, 71% accepted. In 2003, 1 degree awarded. *Degree requirements:* For master's, thesis. *Entrance requirements:* For master's, GRE General Test, minimum GPA of 3.0. Additional exam requirements/recommendations for international students: Required—TOEFL. *Application deadline:* For fall admission, 7/1 priority date for domestic students, 3/1 priority date for international students; for spring admission, 11/1 priority date for domestic students, 9/1 priority date for international students. Applications are processed on a rolling basis. Application fee: $15 ($65 for international students). Electronic applications accepted. *Expenses:* Tuition, state resident: full-time $1,388; part-time $160 per hour. Tuition, nonresident: full-time $3,440; part-time $388 per hour. Tuition and fees vary according to course load, degree level and program. *Financial support:* In 2003–04, research assistantships with partial tuition reimbursements (averaging $20,250 per year), teaching assistantships (averaging $16,200 per year) were awarded. Federal Work-Study, institutionally sponsored loans, scholarships/grants, and tuition waivers (partial) also available. Financial award application deadline: 3/15; financial award applicants required to submit FAFSA. *Unit head:* Dr. Ramon E. Lopez, Chairperson, 915-747-5715, Fax: 915-747-5636, E-mail: relopez@miners.utep.edu. *Application contact:* Dr. Charles H. Ambler, Dean of the Graduate School, 915-747-5491 Ext. 7886, Fax: 915-747-5788, E-mail: cambler@utep.edu.

University of Toledo, Graduate School, College of Arts and Sciences, Department of Physics and Astronomy, Toledo, OH 43606-3390. Offers physics (MES, MS, PhD). *Faculty:* 23. *Students:* 40 full-time (6 women), 7 part-time, 31 international. Average age 29. 46 applicants, 30% accepted. In 2003, 9 master's, 4 doctorates awarded. *Degree requirements:* For master's, thesis; for doctorate, thesis/dissertation, departmental qualifying exam. *Entrance requirements:* For master's and doctorate, GRE General Test, GRE Subject Test. Additional exam requirements/recommendations for international students: Required—TOEFL. *Application deadline:* For fall admission, 5/31 for domestic students. Applications are processed on a rolling basis. Application fee: $40. Electronic applications accepted. Tuition, area resident: Part-time $3,817 per semester. *Expenses:* Tuition, state resident: part-time $8,177 per semester. Required fees: $502 per semester. *Financial support:* In 2003–04, 3 research assistantships, 30 teaching assistantships were awarded. Federal Work-Study, institutionally sponsored loans, and tuition waivers (full) also available. Support available to part-time students. Financial award application deadline: 4/1; financial award applicants required to submit FAFSA. *Faculty research:* Atomic physics, solid-state physics, materials science, astrophysics. *Unit head:* Dr. Philip James, Chair, 419-530-4906, Fax: 419-530-2723, E-mail: pbj@physics.utoledo.edu. *Application contact:* Cheryl Colwell, Information Contact, 419-530-2241, Fax: 419-530-2723, E-mail: ccolwell@physics.utoledo.edu.

Announcement: The University of Toledo Department of Physics and Astronomy offers MS, MSE, and PhD degrees in physics with specializations in astronomy and astrophysics, atomic and molecular physics, biophysics, condensed-matter physics and materials science, medical physics, and photonics.

See in-depth description on page 437.

University of Toronto, School of Graduate Studies, Physical Sciences Division, Department of Physics, Toronto, ON M5S 1A1, Canada. Offers M Sc, PhD. *Faculty:* 55 full-time (1 woman), 1 part-time/adjunct. *Students:* 116 full-time (31 women), 3 part-time, 18 international. 86 applicants, 57% accepted. In 2003, 22 master's, 17 doctorates awarded. *Degree requirements:* For master's, thesis optional; for doctorate, thesis/dissertation. *Entrance requirements:* For master's, minimum B+ average in an honors physics program or equivalent, 2 letters of reference; for doctorate, M Sc degree in physics or a related field, 2 letters of reference. *Application deadline:* For fall admission, 2/28 for domestic students. Application fee: $90 Canadian dollars. Tuition, nonresident: full-time $4,185. International tuition: $10,739 full-time. *Unit head:* Michael Luke, Chair, 416-978-2945, Fax: 416-978-1547, E-mail: chair@physics.utoronto.ca. *Application contact:* Secretary, 416-978-2945, Fax: 416-978-1547, E-mail: marianne@physics.utoronto.ca.

University of Utah, Graduate School, College of Science, Department of Physics, Salt Lake City, UT 84112-1107. Offers chemical physics (PhD); physics (MA, MS, PhD). Part-time programs available. *Faculty:* 21 full-time (1 woman). *Students:* 79 full-time (14 women), 15 part-time (2 women); includes 1 minority (Hispanic American), 54 international. Average age 31. In 2003, 10 master's, 10 doctorates awarded. Terminal master's awarded for partial completion of doctoral program. *Degree requirements:* For master's, thesis or alternative, teaching experience; for doctorate, thesis/dissertation, departmental qualifying exam. *Entrance requirements:* For master's and doctorate, GRE General Test, GRE Subject Test, minimum GPA of 3.0. Additional exam requirements/recommendations for international students: Required—TOEFL. *Application deadline:* For fall admission, 2/1 for domestic students. Applications are processed on a rolling basis. Application fee: $45 ($60 for international students). Electronic applications accepted. Tuition, nonresident: full-time $2,483. International tuition: $8,768 full-time. *Financial support:* In 2003–04, 22 research assistantships with full and partial tuition reimbursements (averaging $13,800 per year), 31 teaching assistantships with full and partial tuition reimbursements (averaging $13,800 per year) were awarded. Fellowships, Federal Work-Study, institutionally sponsored loans, and scholarships/grants also available. Financial award application deadline: 2/15; financial award applicants required to submit FAFSA. *Faculty research:* High-energy, cosmic-ray, astrophysics, medical physics, condensed matter, relativity applied physics. Total annual research expenditures: $5 million. *Unit head:* Dr. Zeev Valy Vardeny, Chair, 801-581-6901, Fax: 801-581-4801, E-mail: val@physics.utah.edu. *Application contact:* Heidi Frank, Director of Graduate Studies, 801-581-5697, Fax: 801-581-4801, E-mail: heidi@physics.utah.edu.

University of Utah, Graduate School, College of Science, Interdepartmental Program in Chemical Physics, Salt Lake City, UT 84112-1107. Offers PhD. *Students:* 1 full-time (0 women). In 2003, 1 degree awarded. Tuition, nonresident: full-time $2,483. International tuition: $8,768 full-time. *Unit head:* Peter J. Stang, Dean, 801-581-6958, Fax: 801-585-3169, E-mail: stang@chemistry.utah.edu. *Application contact:* Information Contact, 801-581-6958, E-mail: office@science.utah.edu.

University of Vermont, Graduate College, College of Arts and Sciences, Department of Physics, Burlington, VT 05405. Offers physical sciences (MST); physics (MAT, MS). *Students:* 4 (2 women) 1 international. 6 applicants, 0% accepted, 0 enrolled. In 2003, 3 degrees awarded. *Entrance requirements:* For master's, GRE General Test. Additional exam requirements/recommendations for international students: Required—TOEFL. *Application deadline:* For fall admission, 4/1 for domestic students. Applications are processed on a rolling basis. Application fee: $25. *Expenses:* Tuition, state resident: part-time $362 per credit hour. Tuition, nonresident: part-time $906 per credit hour. *Financial support:* Fellowships, research assistantships, teaching assistantships available. Financial award application deadline: 3/1. *Unit head:* Dr. J. Wu, Chairperson, 802-656-2644. *Application contact:* K. Spartalian, Coordinator, 802-656-2644.

University of Victoria, Faculty of Graduate Studies, Faculty of Science, Department of Physics and Astronomy, Victoria, BC V8W 2Y2, Canada. Offers astronomy and astrophysics (M Sc, PhD); condensed matter physics (M Sc, PhD); medical physics (M Sc, PhD); nuclear and particle studies (M Sc, PhD); ocean physics (M Sc, PhD); theoretical physics (M Sc, PhD). *Degree requirements:* For master's, thesis/dissertation, registration; for doctorate, thesis/dissertation, comprehensive exam, registration. *Entrance requirements:* Additional exam requirements/recommendations for international students: Required—TOEFL (minimum score 575 paper-based; 213 computer-based). *Faculty research:* Old stellar populations; observational cosmology and large scale structure; cp violation; atlas.

University of Virginia, College and Graduate School of Arts and Sciences, Department of Physics, Charlottesville, VA 22903. Offers physics (MA, MS, PhD); physics education (MA). *Faculty:* 31 full-time (2 women), 1 part-time/adjunct (0 women). *Students:* 81 full-time (13 women); includes 2 minority (both Asian Americans or Pacific Islanders), 38 international. Average age 26. 148 applicants, 19% accepted, 10 enrolled. In 2003, 11 master's, 9 doctorates awarded. *Degree requirements:* For master's and doctorate, thesis/dissertation. *Entrance requirements:* For master's and doctorate, GRE General Test, GRE Subject Test. *Application deadline:* For fall admission, 7/15 for domestic students; for spring admission, 12/1 for domestic students. Applications are processed on a rolling basis. Application fee: $40. Electronic applications accepted. *Expenses:* Tuition, state resident: full-time $6,476. Tuition, nonresident: full-time $18,534. Required fees: $1,380. *Financial support:* Application deadline: 3/15; *Unit head:* Thomas F. Gallagher, Chairman, 434-924-3781, Fax: 434-924-4576, E-mail: info@physics.virginia.edu. *Application contact:* Peter C. Brunjes, Associate Dean for Graduate Programs and Research, 434-924-7184, Fax: 434-924-6737, E-mail: grad-a-s@virginia.edu.

University of Washington, Graduate School, College of Arts and Sciences, Department of Physics, Seattle, WA 98195. Offers MS, PhD. Part-time and evening/weekend programs available. Terminal master's awarded for partial completion of doctoral program. *Degree requirements:* For doctorate, thesis/dissertation. *Entrance requirements:* For master's, GRE; for doctorate, GRE General Test, GRE Subject Test. Additional exam requirements/recommendations for international students: Required—TOEFL. Electronic applications accepted. *Faculty research:* Astro-, atomic, condensed-matter, nuclear, and particle physics; physics education.

University of Waterloo, Graduate Studies, Faculty of Science, Guelph-Waterloo Physics Institute, Waterloo, ON N2L 3G1, Canada. Offers M Sc, PhD. Part-time programs available. *Faculty:* 35 full-time (3 women), 32 part-time/adjunct (1 woman). *Students:* 52 full-time (8 women), 6 part-time (2 women). 54 applicants, 39% accepted, 12 enrolled. In 2003, 7 master's, 3 doctorates awarded. *Degree requirements:* For master's, project or thesis; for doctorate, thesis/dissertation, registration. *Entrance requirements:* For master's, GRE Subject Test, honors degree, minimum B average; for doctorate, GRE Subject Test, master's degree, minimum B average. Additional exam requirements/recommendations for international students: Required—TOEFL, TWE. *Application deadline:* For fall admission, 7/1 for domestic students; for winter admission, 11/1 for domestic students; for spring admission, 3/1 for domestic students. Applications are processed on a rolling basis. Application fee: $75 Canadian dollars. Electronic applications accepted. Tuition and fees charges are reported in Canadian dollars. *Expenses:* Tuition, state resident: full-time $3,632 Canadian dollars. International tuition: $9,180 Canadian dollars full-time. Required fees: $406 Canadian dollars. *Financial support:* Research assistantships, teaching assistantships, career-related internships or fieldwork, scholarships/grants, and unspecified assistantships available. *Faculty research:* Condensed-matter and materials physics; industrial and applied physics; subatomic physics; astrophysics and gravitation; atomic, molecular, and optical physics. *Unit head:* Dr. Robert Mann, Director, 519-888-4567 Ext. 6285, Fax: 519-746-8115, E-mail: gwp@scimail.uwaterloo.ca. *Application contact:* M. M. O'Neill, Administrative Assistant, 519-888-4567 Ext. 6874, Fax: 519-746-8115, E-mail: gwp@scimail.uwaterloo.ca.

The University of Western Ontario, Faculty of Graduate Studies, Physical Sciences Division, Department of Applied Mathematics, London, ON N6A 5B8, Canada. Offers applied mathematics (M Sc, PhD); theoretical physics (PhD). *Degree requirements:* For master's, thesis or alternative; for doctorate, thesis/dissertation, comprehensive exam. *Entrance requirements:* For master's and doctorate, minimum B average. *Faculty research:* Fluid dynamics, mathematical and computational methods, theoretical physics.

The University of Western Ontario, Faculty of Graduate Studies, Physical Sciences Division, Department of Physics and Astronomy, Program in Physics, London, ON N6A 5B8, Canada. Offers M Sc, PhD. Terminal master's awarded for partial completion of doctoral program. *Degree requirements:* For master's, thesis/dissertation; for doctorate, thesis/dissertation, comprehensive exam. *Entrance requirements:* For master's, GRE Physics Test, honors B Sc degree, minimum B average (Canadian), A- (international); for doctorate, minimum B average (Canadian), A- (international). Additional exam requirements/recommendations for international students: Required—TOEFL (minimum score 580 paper-based; 237 computer-based). *Faculty research:* Condensed-matter and surface science, space and atmospheric physics, atomic and molecular physics, medical physics, theoretical physics.

University of Windsor, Faculty of Graduate Studies and Research, Faculty of Science, Department of Physics, Windsor, ON N9B 3P4, Canada. Offers M Sc, PhD. Part-time programs available. *Faculty:* 9 full-time (1 woman), 2 part-time/adjunct (0 women). *Students:* 21 full-time (2 women). 34 applicants, 29% accepted. In 2003, 2 master's, 3 doctorates awarded. *Degree requirements:* For master's, thesis (for some programs); for doctorate, thesis/dissertation. *Entrance requirements:* For master's, GRE, minimum B average; for doctorate, GRE General Test, master's degree. Additional exam requirements/recommendations for international students: Required—TOEFL. *Application deadline:* For fall admission, 7/1 for domestic students; for winter admission, 11/1 for domestic students; for spring admission, 3/1 for domestic students. Applications are processed on a rolling basis. Application fee: $55. Tuition charges are reported in Canadian dollars. *Expenses:* Tuition, state resident: full-time $1,704 Canadian dollars. Tuition, nonresident: full-time $2,126 Canadian dollars. International tuition: $2,976 Canadian dollars full-time. *Financial support:* In 2003–04, 10 teaching assistantships (averaging $8,000 per year) were awarded; research assistantships, Federal Work-Study, scholarships/grants, tuition waivers (full and partial), unspecified assistantships, and bursaries also available. Financial award application deadline: 2/15. *Faculty research:* Electrodynamics, plasma physics, atomic structure/particles, spectroscopy, quantum mechanics. *Unit head:* Dr. Gordon W. Drake, Head, 519-253-3000 Ext. 2647, Fax: 519-973-7075, E-mail: gdrake@uwindsor.ca. *Application contact:* Marlene Bezaire, Graduate Secretary, 519-253-3000 Ext. 3520, Fax: 519-971-7098, E-mail: spsgrad@uwindsor.ca.

University of Wisconsin–Madison, Graduate School, College of Letters and Science, Department of Physics, Madison, WI 53706-1380. Offers MA, MS, PhD. Terminal master's awarded for partial completion of doctoral program. *Degree requirements:* For master's, thesis (for some programs), qualifying exam, thesis (MS); for doctorate, thesis/dissertation, preliminary and qualifying exams. *Entrance requirements:* For master's and doctorate, GRE, minimum of 3.0. Additional exam requirements/recommendations for international students: Required—TOEFL. Electronic applications accepted. Tuition, area resident: Full-time $7,593; part-time $476 per credit. Tuition, nonresident: full-time $22,824; part-time $1,430 per credit. Required fees: $292; $38 per credit. Part-time tuition and fees vary according to course load and reciprocity agreements. *Faculty research:* Atomic, physics, condensed matter, astrophysics, particles and fields.

University of Wisconsin–Milwaukee, Graduate School, College of Letters and Sciences, Department of Physics, Milwaukee, WI 53201-0413. Offers MS, PhD. *Faculty:* 19 full-time (2 women). *Students:* 20 full-time (2 women), 9 part-time (1 woman), 20 international. 35 applicants, 60% accepted, 10 enrolled. In 2003, 5 master's, 2 doctorates awarded. *Degree requirements:* For master's, thesis or alternative; for doctorate, one foreign language, thesis/dissertation. *Entrance requirements:* For master's and doctorate, GRE General Test. *Application deadline:* For fall admission, 1/1 for domestic students; for spring admission, 9/1 for domestic students. Applications are processed on a rolling basis. Application fee: $45 ($75 for international students). *Expenses:* Tuition, state resident: part-time $634 per credit. Tuition, nonresident: part-time $1,531 per credit. Part-time tuition and fees vary according to course load, campus/location, program and reciprocity agreements. *Financial support:* In 2003–04, 4 fellowships, 8 research assistantships, 16 teaching assistantships were awarded. Career-related internships or fieldwork and unspecified assistantships also available. Support available to part-time students. Financial award application deadline: 4/15. *Unit head:* Richard Sorbello, Representative, 414-229-6266, Fax: 414-229-4474, E-mail: sorbello@uwm.edu.

University of Wisconsin–Oshkosh, The School of Graduate Studies, College of Letters and Science, Department of Physics and Astronomy, Oshkosh, WI 54901. Offers physics (MS), including instrumentation, physics education, professional. Part-time programs available. *Faculty:* 7 full-time (1 woman). *Students:* Average age 27. 2 applicants, 100% accepted. *Degree requirements:* For master's, thesis, registration. *Entrance requirements:* For master's, minimum GPA of 2.75, BS in physics or related field. Additional exam requirements/recommendations for international students: Required—TOEFL (minimum score 550 paper-based; 213 computer-based). *Application deadline:* Applications are processed on a rolling basis. Application fee: $45. Electronic applications accepted. *Expenses:* Tuition, state resident: full-time $5,335; part-time $298 per credit. Tuition, nonresident: full-time $15,945; part-time $887 per credit. Tuition and fees vary according to program and reciprocity agreements. *Financial support:* Fellowships, research assistantships with partial tuition reimbursements, institutionally sponsored loans, scholarships/grants, tuition waivers (partial), and unspecified assistantships available. Financial award application deadline: 3/15; financial award applicants required to submit FAFSA. *Faculty research:* Digital signal processing, stellar atmospheres and abundances, phase transitions, thin-film magnetism. *Unit head:* Dr. Dennis Rioux, Coordinator, 920-424-4433. *Application contact:* Dr. Dennis Rioux, Program Coordinator, 920-424-4429, E-mail: rioux@uwosh.edu.

Utah State University, School of Graduate Studies, College of Science, Department of Physics, Logan, UT 84322. Offers MS, PhD. Part-time programs available. *Faculty:* 26 full-time (1 woman), 16 part-time/adjunct (1 woman). *Students:* 23 full-time (1 woman), 4 part-time (1 woman); includes 1 minority (Hispanic American), 8 international. Average age 34. 17 applicants, 53% accepted, 4 enrolled. In 2003, 1 master's, 3 doctorates awarded. Terminal master's awarded for partial completion of doctoral program. *Degree requirements:* For master's, thesis/dissertation; for doctorate, thesis/dissertation, comprehensive exam. *Entrance requirements:* For master's and doctorate, GRE General Test, minimum GPA of 3.0. Additional exam requirements/recommendations for international students: Required—TOEFL. *Application deadline:* For fall admission, 6/15 for domestic students; for spring admission, 10/15 for domestic students. Applications are processed on a rolling basis. Application fee: $50 ($60 for international students). *Expenses:* Tuition, state resident: part-time $270 per credit hour. Tuition, nonresident: part-time $946 per credit hour. Required fees: $173 per credit hour. *Financial support:* In 2003–04, 10 students received support, including 3 fellowships with partial tuition reimbursements available (averaging $12,000 per year), 7 research assistantships with partial tuition reimbursements available (averaging $14,000 per year), 10 teaching assistantships with partial tuition reimbursements available (averaging $10,500 per year); Federal Work-Study and institutionally sponsored loans also available. Support available to part-time students. Financial award application deadline: 3/1. *Faculty research:* Upper-atmosphere physics, relativity, gravitational magnetism, particle physics, nanotechnology. Total annual research expenditures: $1.6 million. *Unit head:* Dr. W. John Raitt, Head, 435-797-2848, Fax: 435-797-2492, E-mail: physics@cc.usu.edu. *Application contact:* Dr. David Peak, Assistant Head, 435-797-2884, Fax: 435-797-2492, E-mail: physics@cc.usu.edu.

Vanderbilt University, Graduate School, Department of Physics and Astronomy, Nashville, TN 37240-1001. Offers astronomy (MS); physics (MA, MAT, MS, PhD). *Degree requirements:* For master's, thesis; for doctorate, thesis/dissertation, final and qualifying exams. *Entrance requirements:* For master's, GRE General Test; for doctorate, GRE General Test, GRE Subject Test. Electronic applications accepted. *Expenses:* Tuition: Part-time $1,155 per semester hour. Required fees: $1,538. *Faculty research:* Experimental and theoretical physics, free electron laser, living-state physics, heavy-ion physics, nuclear structure.

Virginia Commonwealth University, School of Graduate Studies, College of Humanities and Sciences, Department of Physics, Richmond, VA 23284-9005. Offers applied physics (MS); physics (MS). Part-time programs available. *Faculty:* 7 full-time (3 women). *Students:* 5 full-time (1 woman). 9 applicants, 78% accepted, 2 enrolled. In 2003, 5 degrees awarded. *Degree requirements:* For master's, thesis optional. *Entrance requirements:* For master's, GRE. *Application deadline:* For fall admission, 8/1 for domestic students; for spring admission, 12/1 for domestic students. Applications are processed on a rolling basis. Application fee: $30. *Expenses:* Tuition, state resident: full-time $2,889; part-time $321 per credit hour. Tuition, nonresident: full-time $7,952; part-time $884 per credit hour. Required fees: $42 per credit hour. *Financial support:* Fellowships, teaching assistantships, Federal Work-Study, institutionally sponsored loans, and tuition waivers (full and partial) available. Support available to part-time students. *Faculty research:* Condensed-matter theory and experimentation, electronic instrumentation, relativity. *Unit head:* Dr. Robert H. Gowdy, Chair, 804-828-1821, Fax: 804-828-7073, E-mail: rhgowdy@vcu.edu. *Application contact:* Dr. Alison Baski, Graduate Program Director, 804-828-8295, Fax: 804-828-7073, E-mail: aabaski@vcu.edu.

Virginia Polytechnic Institute and State University, Graduate School, College of Science, Department of Physics, Blacksburg, VA 24061. Offers applied physics (MS, PhD); physics (MS, PhD). *Faculty:* 21 full-time (2 women). *Students:* 44 full-time (9 women), 2 part-time; includes 4 minority (2 African Americans, 2 Asian Americans or Pacific Islanders), 18 international. Average age 27. 53 applicants, 57% accepted, 17 enrolled. In 2003, 9 master's, 7 doctorates awarded. *Entrance requirements:* For master's and doctorate, GRE Subject Test. Additional exam requirements/recommendations for international students: Required—TOEFL (minimum score 550 paper-based; 213 computer-based). *Application deadline:* Applications are processed on a rolling basis. Application fee: $45. Electronic applications accepted. Tuition, area resident: Full-time $6,039; part-time $336 per credit. Tuition, nonresident: full-time $9,708; part-time $539 per credit. Required fees: $905; $130 per credit. *Financial support:* In 2003–04, 3 fellowships with full tuition reimbursements (averaging $6,000 per year), 9 research assistantships with full tuition reimbursements (averaging $16,231 per year), 18 teaching assistantships with full tuition reimbursements (averaging $13,223 per year) were awarded. Career-related internships or fieldwork, Federal Work-Study, scholarships/grants, and unspecified assistantships also available. Financial award application deadline: 4/1. *Faculty research:* Condensed matter, particle physics, theoretical and experimental astrophysics, biophysics, mathematical physics. *Unit head:* Dr. John R. Ficenec, Head, 540-231-6544, Fax: 540-231-7511, E-mail: jficenec@vt.edu. *Application contact:* Christa C. Thomas, Graduate Program Coordinator, 540-231-8728, Fax: 540-231-7511, E-mail: chris.thomas@vt.edu.

Virginia State University, School of Graduate Studies, Research, and Outreach, School of Engineering, Science and Technology, Department of Chemistry and Physics, Petersburg, VA 23806-0001. Offers physics (MS). *Degree requirements:* For master's, one foreign language, thesis. *Entrance requirements:* For master's, GRE General Test.

Wake Forest University, Graduate School, Department of Physics, Winston-Salem, NC 27109. Offers MS, PhD. Part-time programs available. *Faculty:* 16 full-time (2 women), 3 part-time/adjunct (0 women). *Students:* 23 full-time (9 women), 1 part-time; includes 2 minority (1 African American, 1 Hispanic American), 10 international. Average age 25. 22 applicants, 32% accepted, 7 enrolled. In 2003, 4 degrees awarded. *Degree requirements:* For master's, one foreign language, thesis, comprehensive exam, registration; for doctorate, 2 foreign languages, thesis/dissertation, comprehensive exam, registration. *Entrance requirements:* For master's and doctorate, GRE General Test. Additional exam requirements/recommendations

Physics

Wake Forest University (continued)
for international students: Required—TOEFL (minimum score 213 computer-based). *Application deadline:* For fall admission, 1/15 for domestic students, 1/15 for international students. Application fee: $25. Electronic applications accepted. *Expenses:* Tuition: Full-time $26,500. *Financial support:* In 2003–04, 24 students received support, including 1 fellowship with full tuition reimbursement available (averaging $17,500 per year), 10 research assistantships with full tuition reimbursements available (averaging $14,500 per year), 11 teaching assistantships with full tuition reimbursements available (averaging $14,500 per year); scholarships/grants and tuition waivers (full and partial) also available. Support available to part-time students. Financial award application deadline: 1/15; financial award applicants required to submit FAFSA. *Unit head:* Dr. Keith Bonin, Director, 336-758-4962.

See in-depth description on page 441.

Washington State University, Graduate School, College of Sciences, Department of Physics, Pullman, WA 99164. Offers MS, PhD. *Faculty:* 19 full-time (2 women), 2 part-time/adjunct (1 woman). *Students:* 43 full-time (9 women), 1 part-time, 24 international. Average age 30. 56 applicants, 48% accepted, 16 enrolled. In 2003, 3 master's, 5 doctorates awarded. Terminal master's awarded for partial completion of doctoral program. *Degree requirements:* For master's, oral exam; for doctorate, thesis/dissertation, oral exam, written exam. *Entrance requirements:* For master's and doctorate, GRE General Test, GRE Subject Test, minimum GPA of 3.0. Additional exam requirements/recommendations for international students: Required—TOEFL. *Application deadline:* For fall admission, 3/1 priority date for domestic students, 3/1 priority date for international students; for spring admission, 7/1 priority date for domestic students, 7/1 priority date for international students. Applications are processed on a rolling basis. Application fee: $35. *Expenses:* Tuition, state resident: full-time $6,278; part-time $314 per hour. Tuition, nonresident: full-time $15,514; part-time $765 per hour. Required fees: $444. Full-time tuition and fees vary according to campus/location, program and student level. Part-time tuition and fees vary according to course load. *Financial support:* In 2003–04, 18 research assistantships with full and partial tuition reimbursements (averaging $17,322 per year), 19 teaching assistantships with full and partial tuition reimbursements (averaging $17,322 per year) were awarded. Fellowships, Federal Work-Study and institutionally sponsored loans also available. Financial award application deadline: 3/1; financial award applicants required to submit FAFSA. *Faculty research:* Linear and nonlinear acoustics and optics, shock wave dynamics, solid-state physics, surface physics, high-pressure and semi conductor physics. Total annual research expenditures: $2.2 million. *Unit head:* Dr. Steve Tomsovic, Chair, 509-335-9532, E-mail: physics@wsu.edu. *Application contact:* Sabreen Yamini Dodson, Graduate Coordinator, 509-335-9532, Fax: 509-335-7816, E-mail: sabreen@wsu.edu.

Washington University in St. Louis, Graduate School of Arts and Sciences, Department of Physics, St. Louis, MO 63130-4899. Offers MA, PhD. *Students:* 78 full-time (19 women), 1 part-time; includes 3 minority (2 Asian Americans or Pacific Islanders, 1 Hispanic American), 38 international. 185 applicants, 28% accepted, 20 enrolled. In 2003, 8 master's, 5 doctorates awarded. Terminal master's awarded for partial completion of doctoral program. *Degree requirements:* For master's, thesis or alternative; for doctorate, thesis/dissertation. *Entrance requirements:* For master's and doctorate, GRE General Test. *Application deadline:* For fall admission, 1/15 for domestic students. Applications are processed on a rolling basis. Application fee: $35. Electronic applications accepted. *Expenses:* Tuition: Full-time $28,300; part-time $1,180 per credit. *Financial support:* Fellowships, research assistantships, teaching assistantships, Federal Work-Study, institutionally sponsored loans, and tuition waivers (full and partial) available. Support available to part-time students. Financial award application deadline: 1/15. *Unit head:* Dr. John M Clark, Chairperson, 314-935-6250.

See in-depth description on page 445.

Wayne State University, Graduate School, College of Science, Department of Physics and Astronomy, Detroit, MI 48202. Offers physics (MA, MS, PhD). *Faculty:* 26. *Students:* 36 full-time (7 women), 4 part-time (2 women), 26 international. Average age 29. 37 applicants, 78% accepted, 13 enrolled. In 2003, 2 master's, 5 doctorates awarded. *Degree requirements:* For doctorate, thesis/dissertation. *Entrance requirements:* Additional exam requirements/recommendations for international students: Required—TOEFL (minimum score 550 paper-based; 213 computer-based); Recommended—TWE(minimum score 6). *Application deadline:* For fall admission, 7/1 for domestic students, 6/1 for international students. Applications are processed on a rolling basis. Application fee: $30 ($50 for international students). Electronic applications accepted. *Expenses:* Tuition, state resident: part-time $263 per credit hour. Tuition, nonresident: part-time $580 per credit hour. Required fees: $21 per credit hour. *Financial support:* In 2003–04, 1 fellowship, 11 research assistantships, 16 teaching assistantships were awarded. Federal Work-Study also available. Financial award application deadline: 7/1. *Faculty research:* High energy particle physics, relativistic heavy ion physics, theoretical physics, positron and atomic physics, condensed matter and nano-scale physics. Total annual research expenditures: $4.6 million. *Unit head:* Juei-Teng Chen, Interim Chairperson, 313-577-2721, Fax: 313-577-3932, E-mail: aa2458@wayne.edu. *Application contact:* Paul Keyes, Graduate Director, 313-577-2606, E-mail: keyes@physics.wayne.edu.

Wesleyan University, Graduate Programs, Department of Physics, Middletown, CT 06459-0260. Offers MA, PhD. *Faculty:* 9 full-time (1 woman). *Students:* 16 full-time (7 women); includes 1 minority (Hispanic American), 8 international. Average age 25. In 2003, 2 degrees awarded. Terminal master's awarded for partial completion of doctoral program. *Degree requirements:* For master's and doctorate, thesis/dissertation. *Entrance requirements:* For master's, GRE General Test, GRE Subject Test; for doctorate, GRE Subject Test. *Application deadline:* For fall admission, 3/1 for domestic students. Applications are processed on a rolling basis. Application fee: $0. *Expenses:* Tuition: Full-time $22,338. Required fees: $20. *Financial support:* Teaching assistantships, institutionally sponsored loans and tuition waivers (full) available. *Faculty research:* Low-temperature physics, magnetic resonance, atomic collisions, laser spectroscopy, surface physics. *Unit head:* Dr. Fred Ellis, Chairman, 860-685-2046. *Application contact:* Anna Milardo, Information Contact, 860-685-2030, Fax: 860-685-2031, E-mail: amilardo@wesleyan.edu.

See in-depth description on page 447.

Western Illinois University, School of Graduate Studies, College of Arts and Sciences, Department of Physics, Macomb, IL 61455-1390. Offers MS. Part-time programs available. *Faculty:* 6 full-time (0 women). *Students:* 12 full-time (3 women), 8 international. Average age 30. 20 applicants, 70% accepted. In 2003, 4 degrees awarded. *Degree requirements:* For master's, thesis or alternative. *Entrance requirements:* Additional exam requirements/recommendations for international students: Required—TOEFL (minimum score 500 paper-based; 173 computer-based). *Application deadline:* Applications are processed on a rolling basis. Application fee: $30. Electronic applications accepted. Tuition, area resident: Part-time $144 per credit hour. Tuition, nonresident: part-time $288 per credit hour. *Financial support:* In 2003–04, 11 students received support, including 11 research assistantships with full tuition reimbursements available (averaging $5,864 per year) Financial award applicants required to submit FAFSA. *Faculty research:* Optimized hybrid collector, secondary physics instrumentation laboratory, high-energy physics, metaphysics. *Unit head:* Dr. Harold Hart, Chairperson, 309-298-1596. *Application contact:* Dr. Barbara Baily, Director of Graduate Studies/Associate Provost, 309-298-1806, Fax: 309-298-2345, E-mail: grad-office@wiu.edu.

Western Michigan University, Graduate College, College of Arts and Sciences, Department of Physics, Kalamazoo, MI 49008-5202. Offers MA, PhD. *Degree requirements:* For master's, thesis; for doctorate, thesis/dissertation, oral exam. *Entrance requirements:* For doctorate, GRE General Test.

West Virginia University, Eberly College of Arts and Sciences, Department of Physics, Morgantown, WV 26506. Offers applied physics (MS, PhD); astrophysics (MS, PhD); chemical physics (MS, PhD); condensed matter physics (MS, PhD); elementary particle physics (MS, PhD); materials physics (MS, PhD); plasma physics (MS, PhD); solid state physics (MS, PhD); statistical physics (MS, PhD); theoretical physics (MS, PhD). *Faculty:* 17 full-time (3 women), 1 part-time/adjunct (0 women). *Students:* 44 full-time (10 women), 4 part-time (1 woman), 32 international. Average age 28. 60 applicants, 20% accepted. In 2003, 2 master's awarded, leading to continued full-time study 100%; 3 doctorates awarded, leading to university research/teaching 33%, business/industry 33%, government 33%. Terminal master's awarded for partial completion of doctoral program. *Median time to degree:* Master's–2 years full-time; doctorate–5 years full-time. *Degree requirements:* For master's, thesis or alternative, qualifying exam; for doctorate, thesis/dissertation, qualifying exam. *Entrance requirements:* For master's and doctorate, GRE General Test, GRE Subject Test, minimum GPA of 3.0. Additional exam requirements/recommendations for international students: Required—TOEFL. *Application deadline:* For fall admission, 2/15 for domestic students. Applications are processed on a rolling basis. Application fee: $50. *Expenses:* Tuition, state resident: full-time $4,332. Tuition, nonresident: full-time $12,442. *Financial support:* In 2003–04, 30 research assistantships with full and partial tuition reimbursements (averaging $18,000 per year), 10 teaching assistantships with full and partial tuition reimbursements (averaging $16,000 per year) were awarded. Fellowships, Federal Work-Study, institutionally sponsored loans, and tuition waivers (full and partial) also available. Financial award application deadline: 2/1; financial award applicants required to submit FAFSA. *Faculty research:* Experimental and theoretical condensed-matter, plasma, high-energy theory, nonlinear dynamics, space physics. Total annual research expenditures: $3.3 million. *Unit head:* Dr. Earl E. Scime, Chair, 304-293-3422 Ext. 1437, Fax: 304-293-5732, E-mail: escime@wvu.edu.

Wichita State University, Graduate School, Fairmount College of Liberal Arts and Sciences, Department of Physics, Wichita, KS 67260. Offers MS. Part-time programs available. *Faculty:* 7 full-time (1 woman). *Students:* 5 full-time (1 woman), 8 part-time (1 woman), 5 international. Average age 33. 1 applicant, 0% accepted. In 2003, 5 degrees awarded. *Degree requirements:* For master's, qualifying exam, thesis optional. *Entrance requirements:* For master's, GRE. Additional exam requirements/recommendations for international students: Required—TOEFL. *Application deadline:* For fall admission, 7/1 for domestic students; for spring admission, 1/1 for domestic students. Applications are processed on a rolling basis. Application fee: $35 ($50 for international students). Electronic applications accepted. *Expenses:* Tuition, state resident: full-time $2,457; part-time $137 per credit hour. Tuition, nonresident: full-time $7,371; part-time $410 per credit hour. Required fees: $364; $20 per credit hour. Tuition and fees vary according to course load. *Financial support:* In 2003–04, 3 research assistantships (averaging $7,864 per year), 4 teaching assistantships with full tuition reimbursements (averaging $8,030 per year) were awarded. Fellowships, Federal Work-Study, institutionally sponsored loans, scholarships/grants, traineeships, and unspecified assistantships also available. Support available to part-time students. Financial award application deadline: 4/1; financial award applicants required to submit FAFSA. *Faculty research:* Condensed matter experiment and theory, low-mass stellar atmospheres. *Unit head:* Dr. Elizabeth Behreman, Chair, 316-978-5224, E-mail: elizabeth.behreman@wichita.edu.

Worcester Polytechnic Institute, Graduate Studies and Enrollment, Department of Physics, Worcester, MA 01609-2280. Offers MS, PhD. *Faculty:* 15 full-time (2 women). *Students:* 10 full-time (2 women); includes 1 minority (African American), 6 international. 17 applicants, 12% accepted, 2 enrolled. In 2003, 4 degrees awarded. *Degree requirements:* For master's, thesis/dissertation; for doctorate, thesis/dissertation, comprehensive exam. *Entrance requirements:* Additional exam requirements/recommendations for international students: Required—TOEFL (minimum score 550 paper-based; 213 computer-based). *Application deadline:* For fall admission, 2/1 for domestic students; for spring admission, 10/15 priority date for domestic students. Applications are processed on a rolling basis. Application fee: $70. Electronic applications accepted. *Expenses:* Tuition: Part-time $897 per credit. *Financial support:* In 2003–04, 10 students received support, including 4 research assistantships, 7 teaching assistantships with full tuition reimbursements available; fellowships with full tuition reimbursements available, career-related internships or fieldwork, institutionally sponsored loans, scholarships/grants, health care benefits, and unspecified assistantships also available. Financial award application deadline: 2/15; financial award applicants required to submit FAFSA. *Faculty research:* Chemical and biochemical physics, materials research, classical and quantum optics, relativity, solid state physics. Total annual research expenditures: $323,114. *Unit head:* Dr. Thomas Keil, Head, 508-831-5419, Fax: 508-831-5886, E-mail: thkeil@wpi.edu. *Application contact:* Dr. Germano S. Iannacchione, Graduate Coordinator, 508-831-5631, Fax: 508-831-5886, E-mail: gsiannac@wpi.edu.

Wright State University, School of Graduate Studies, College of Science and Mathematics, Department of Physics, Program in Physics, Dayton, OH 45435. Offers medical physics (MS); physics (MS). Part-time and evening/weekend programs available. *Students:* 4 full-time (0 women), 2 part-time; includes 1 minority (African American) Average age 34. 3 applicants, 100% accepted. *Degree requirements:* For master's, thesis. *Entrance requirements:* Additional exam requirements/recommendations for international students: Required—TOEFL. *Application deadline:* For fall admission, 3/1 for domestic students. Applications are processed on a rolling basis. Application fee: $25. *Expenses:* Tuition, state resident: full-time $8,112; part-time $255 per quarter hour. Tuition, nonresident: full-time $14,127; part-time $442 per quarter hour. International tuition: $14,283 full-time. Tuition and fees vary according to course load, degree level and program. *Financial support:* Fellowships, research assistantships, teaching assistantships, Federal Work-Study, institutionally sponsored loans, and tuition waivers (full and partial) available. Support available to part-time students. Financial award application deadline: 3/1; financial award applicants required to submit FAFSA. *Faculty research:* Solid-state physics, optics, geophysics. *Unit head:* Dr. Gust Bambakidis, Chair, Department of Physics, 937-775-2954, Fax: 937-775-2571, E-mail: gust.bambakidis@wright.edu.

Yale University, Graduate School of Arts and Sciences, Department of Physics, New Haven, CT 06520. Offers PhD. *Degree requirements:* For doctorate, thesis/dissertation. *Entrance requirements:* For doctorate, GRE General Test, GRE Subject Test. *Expenses:* Tuition: Full-time $25,600; part-time $6,400 per term.

See in-depth description on page 449.

York University, Faculty of Graduate Studies, Faculty of Pure and Applied Science, Program in Physics and Astronomy, Toronto, ON M3J 1P3, Canada. Offers M Sc, PhD. Part-time and evening/weekend programs available. *Degree requirements:* For master's, thesis or alternative; for doctorate, thesis/dissertation. *Entrance requirements:* For master's, minimum B+ average. Electronic applications accepted. Tuition, area resident: Full-time $5,431; part-time $905 per term. Tuition, nonresident: part-time $1,987 per term. International tuition: $11,918 full-time. Required fees: $287. Tuition and fees vary according to program.

Plasma Physics

Columbia University, Fu Foundation School of Engineering and Applied Science, Department of Applied Physics and Applied Mathematics, New York, NY 10027. Offers applied physics (MS, PhD), including applied mathematics (PhD), optical physics (PhD), plasma physics (PhD), solid state physics (PhD); applied physics and applied mathematics (Eng Sc D); materials science and engineering (MS, Eng Sc D, PhD); medical physics (MS); minerals engineering and materials science (Eng Sc D, PhD, Engr). Part-time programs available. *Faculty:* 29 full-time (3 women), 11 part-time/adjunct (1 woman). *Students:* 82 full-time (25 women), 27 part-time (13 women); includes 14 minority (5 African Americans, 8 Asian Americans or Pacific Islanders, 1 Hispanic American), 51 international. 371 applicants, 17% accepted, 41 enrolled. In 2003, 36 master's, 9 doctorates awarded. Terminal master's awarded for partial completion of doctoral program. *Degree requirements:* For doctorate, thesis/dissertation, qualifying exam. *Entrance requirements:* For master's and doctorate, GRE General Test, GRE Subject Test (strongly recommended). Additional exam requirements/recommendations for international students: Required—TOEFL. *Application deadline:* For fall admission, 12/15 priority date for domestic students, 12/15 priority date for international students; for spring admission, 10/1 priority date for domestic students, 10/1 priority date for international students. Application fee: $55. Electronic applications accepted. *Expenses:* Tuition: Full-time $14,820. *Financial support:* In 2003–04, 62 students received support, including 4 fellowships with full tuition reimbursements available, 40 research assistantships with full tuition reimbursements available (averaging $22,725 per year), 14 teaching assistantships with full tuition reimbursements available (averaging $22,725 per year); Federal Work-Study and unspecified assistantships also available. Financial award application deadline: 12/15; financial award applicants required to submit FAFSA. *Faculty research:* Plasma physics, applied mathematics, solid-state and optical physics, atmospheric, oceanic and earth physics, materials science and engineering. Total annual research expenditures: $7.9 million. *Unit head:* Dr. Michael E. Mauel, Chairman, 212-854-4457, E-mail: seasinfo.apam@columbia.edu. *Application contact:* Marlene Arbo, Department Administrator, 212-854-4458, Fax: 212-854-8257, E-mail: seasinfo.apam@columbia.edu.

See in-depth description on page 357.

Massachusetts Institute of Technology, School of Engineering, Department of Aeronautics and Astronautics, Cambridge, MA 02139-4307. Offers aeroacoustics (PhD, Sc D); aerodynamics (PhD, Sc D); aeroelasticity (PhD, Sc D); aeronautics and astronautics (M Eng, SM, EAA); aerospace systems (PhD, Sc D); air craft propulsion (PhD, Sc D); astrodynamics (PhD, Sc D); biomedical engineering (PhD, Sc D); computational fluid dynamics (PhD, Sc D); computer systems (PhD, Sc D); dynamics energy conversion (PhD, Sc D); estimation and control (PhD, Sc D); flight transportation (PhD, Sc D); fluid mechanics (PhD, Sc D); gas turbine structures (PhD, Sc D); gas turbines (PhD, Sc D); humans and automation (PhD, Sc D); instrumentation (PhD, Sc D); materials engineering (PhD, Sc D); navigation and control systems (PhD, Sc D); physics of fluids (PhD, Sc D); plasma physics (PhD, Sc D); space propulsion (PhD, Sc D); structural dynamics (PhD, Sc D); structures technology (PhD, Sc D); vehicle design (PhD, Sc D). *Faculty:* 36 full-time (6 women), 2 part-time/adjunct (0 women). *Students:* 245 full-time (59 women); includes 27 minority (5 African Americans, 2 American Indian/Alaska Native, 14 Asian Americans or Pacific Islanders, 6 Hispanic Americans), 108 international. Average age 25. 314 applicants, 40% accepted, 78 enrolled. In 2003, 64 master's, 11 doctorates awarded. *Degree requirements:* For master's, thesis; for doctorate, thesis/dissertation, written and oral qualifying exam, comprehensive exam. *Entrance requirements:* For master's and doctorate, GRE General Test. Additional exam requirements/recommendations for international students: Required—TOEFL (minimum score 600 paper-based; 250 computer-based). *Application deadline:* For fall admission, 12/15 for domestic students, 12/15 for international students; for spring admission, 10/1 for domestic students, 10/1 for international students. Application fee: $70. Electronic applications accepted. *Expenses:* Tuition: Full-time $29,400. Required fees: $200. *Financial support:* In 2003–04, 42 fellowships with tuition reimbursements, 177 research assistantships with tuition reimbursements (averaging $22,740 per year), 9 teaching assistantships with tuition reimbursements (averaging $17,370 per year) were awarded. Federal Work-Study, institutionally sponsored loans, scholarships/grants, health care benefits, and unspecified assistantships also available. *Faculty research:* Fluid mechanics and propulsion, aerospace systems engineering, aerospace information engineering, controls and estimation, humans and automation, structures and materials. Total annual research expenditures: $26.4 million. *Unit head:* Prof. Wesley L. Harris, Head, 617-253-0911, E-mail: weslhar@mit.edu. *Application contact:* Marie Stuppard, Coordinator, Academic Programs, 617-253-2279, Fax: 617-258-7566, E-mail: mas@mit.edu.

Princeton University, Graduate School, Department of Astrophysical Sciences, Program in Plasma Physics, Princeton, NJ 08544-1019. Offers PhD. *Students:* 25 full-time (3 women). 38 applicants, 29% accepted, 5 enrolled. *Degree requirements:* For doctorate, thesis/dissertation. *Entrance requirements:* For doctorate, GRE General Test, GRE Subject Test. Additional exam requirements/recommendations for international students: Required—TOEFL (minimum score 600 paper-based; 250 computer-based). *Application deadline:* For fall admission, 12/31 for domestic students, 12/1 for international students. Application fee: $80 ($55 for international students). *Expenses:* Tuition: Full-time $29,910. Required fees: $810. *Financial support:* In 2003–04, 8 fellowships (averaging $15,469 per year), 16 research assistantships (averaging $28,335 per year), 1 teaching assistantship (averaging $9,504 per year) were awarded. Federal Work-Study and institutionally sponsored loans also available. Financial award application deadline: 1/4. *Faculty research:* Magnetic fusion energy research, plasma physics, x-ray laser studies. Total annual research expenditures: $77.9 million. *Unit head:* Nathaniel Fisch, Director of Graduate Studies, 609-125-2643, Fax: 609-125-2662, E-mail: fisch@princeton.edu. *Application contact:* Janice Yip, Director of Graduate Admissions, 609-258-3034, Fax: 609-258-6180, E-mail: gsadmit@princeton.edu.

University of Colorado at Boulder, Graduate School, College of Arts and Sciences, Department of Astrophysical and Planetary Sciences, Boulder, CO 80309. Offers astrophysical and geophysical fluid dynamics (MS, PhD); astrophysics (MS, PhD); plasma physics (MS, PhD). *Faculty:* 17 full-time (1 woman). *Students:* 70 full-time (22 women), 21 part-time (8 women); includes 6 minority (3 Asian Americans or Pacific Islanders, 3 Hispanic Americans), 9 international. Average age 28. 103 applicants, 50% accepted. In 2003, 7 master's, 12 doctorates awarded. Terminal master's awarded for partial completion of doctoral program. *Degree requirements:* For master's, thesis or alternative, comprehensive exam; for doctorate, one foreign language, thesis/dissertation. *Entrance requirements:* For master's and doctorate, GRE General Test, GRE Subject Test. *Application deadline:* For fall admission, 3/1 for domestic students. Applications are processed on a rolling basis. Application fee: $50 ($60 for international students). *Expenses:* Tuition, state resident: full-time $2,122. Tuition, nonresident: full-time $9,754. Tuition and fees vary according to course load and program. *Financial support:* In 2003–04, 6 fellowships (averaging $17,509 per year), 23 research assistantships (averaging $15,762 per year), 20 teaching assistantships (averaging $17,065 per year) were awarded. Tuition waivers (full) also available. Support available to part-time students. Financial award application deadline: 2/1. *Faculty research:* Stellar and extragalactic astrophysics cosmology, space astronomy, planetary science. Total annual research expenditures: $30.6 million. *Unit head:* J. Michael Shull, Chair, 303-492-8915, Fax: 303-492-3822, E-mail: mshull@casa.colorado.edu. *Application contact:* Graduate Program Assistant, 303-492-8914, Fax: 303-492-3822, E-mail: admin@aps.colorado.edu.

West Virginia University, Eberly College of Arts and Sciences, Department of Physics, Morgantown, WV 26506. Offers applied physics (MS, PhD); astrophysics (MS, PhD); chemical physics (MS, PhD); condensed matter physics (MS, PhD); elementary particle physics (MS, PhD); materials physics (MS, PhD); plasma physics (MS, PhD); solid state physics (MS, PhD); statistical physics (MS, PhD); theoretical physics (MS, PhD). *Faculty:* 17 full-time (3 women), 1 part-time/adjunct (0 women). *Students:* 44 full-time (10 women), 4 part-time (1 woman), 32 international. Average age 28. 60 applicants, 20% accepted. In 2003, 2 master's awarded, leading to continued full-time study 100%; 3 doctorates awarded, leading to university research/teaching 33%, business/industry 33%, government 33%. Terminal master's awarded for partial completion of doctoral program. *Median time to degree:* Master's–2 years full-time; doctorate–5 years full-time. *Degree requirements:* For master's, thesis or alternative, qualifying exam; for doctorate, thesis/dissertation, qualifying exam. *Entrance requirements:* For master's and doctorate, GRE General Test, GRE Subject Test, minimum GPA of 3.0. Additional exam requirements/recommendations for international students: Required—TOEFL. *Application deadline:* For fall admission, 2/15 for domestic students. Applications are processed on a rolling basis. Application fee: $50. *Expenses:* Tuition, state resident: full-time $4,332. Tuition, nonresident: full-time $12,442. *Financial support:* In 2003–04, 30 research assistantships with full and partial tuition reimbursements (averaging $18,000 per year), 10 teaching assistantships with full and partial tuition reimbursements (averaging $16,000 per year) were awarded. Fellowships, Federal Work-Study, institutionally sponsored loans, and tuition waivers (full and partial) also available. Financial award application deadline: 2/1; financial award applicants required to submit FAFSA. *Faculty research:* Experimental and theoretical condensed-matter, plasma, high-energy theory, nonlinear dynamics, space physics. Total annual research expenditures: $3.3 million. *Unit head:* Dr. Earl E. Scime, Chair, 304-293-3422 Ext. 1437, Fax: 304-293-5732, E-mail: escime@wvu.edu.

Theoretical Physics

Cornell University, Graduate School, Graduate Fields of Arts and Sciences, Field of Physics, Ithaca, NY 14853-0001. Offers experimental physics (MS, PhD); physics (MS, PhD); theoretical physics (MS, PhD). *Faculty:* 52 full-time. *Students:* 193 full-time (41 women); includes 13 minority (1 African American, 9 Asian Americans or Pacific Islanders, 3 Hispanic Americans), 70 international. 464 applicants, 21% accepted, 41 enrolled. In 2003, 17 master's, 14 doctorates awarded. *Degree requirements:* For doctorate, thesis/dissertation, comprehensive exam. *Entrance requirements:* For doctorate, GRE General Test, GRE Subject Test (physics), supplementary application, 3 letters of recommendation. Additional exam requirements/recommendations for international students: Required—TOEFL (minimum score 550 paper-based; 213 computer-based). *Application deadline:* For fall admission, 1/3 for domestic students. Application fee: $60. Electronic applications accepted. *Expenses:* Tuition: Full-time $28,630. One-time fee: $50 full-time. *Financial support:* In 2003–04, 187 students received support, including 36 fellowships with full tuition reimbursements available, 88 research assistantships with full tuition reimbursements available, 63 teaching assistantships with full tuition reimbursements available; institutionally sponsored loans, scholarships/grants, health care benefits, tuition waivers (full and partial), and unspecified assistantships also available. Financial award applicants required to submit FAFSA. *Faculty research:* Experimental condensed matter physics, theoretical condensed matter physics, experimental high energy particle physics, theoretical particle physics and field theory, theoretical astrophysics. *Unit head:* Director of Graduate Studies, 607-255-7561. *Application contact:* Graduate Field Assistant, 607-255-7561, E-mail: physics-grad-adm@cornell.edu.

Harvard University, Graduate School of Arts and Sciences, Department of Physics, Cambridge, MA 02138. Offers experimental physics (AM, PhD); medical engineering/medical physics (PhD, Sc D), including applied physics (PhD), engineering sciences (PhD), medical engineering/medical physics (Sc D), physics (PhD); theoretical physics (AM, PhD). *Students:* 174. *Degree requirements:* For doctorate, thesis/dissertation, final exams, laboratory experience. *Entrance requirements:* For master's, GRE General Test; for doctorate, GRE General Test, GRE Subject Test. Additional exam requirements/recommendations for international students: Required—TOEFL. *Application deadline:* For fall admission, 12/14 for domestic students. Application fee: $60. *Expenses:* Tuition: Full-time $26,066. Full-time tuition and fees vary according to program and student level. *Financial support:* Fellowships, research assistantships, teaching assistantships, career-related internships or fieldwork, Federal Work-Study, and institutionally sponsored loans available. Financial award application deadline: 12/30. *Faculty research:* Particle physics, condensed matter physics, atomic physics. *Unit head:* Prof. John Huth, Chair, 617-495-8144, E-mail: huth@physics.harvard.edu. *Application contact:* Office of Admissions and Financial Aid, 617-495-5315.

See in-depth description on page 365.

Rutgers, The State University of New Jersey, New Brunswick/Piscataway, Graduate School, Program in Physics and Astronomy, New Brunswick, NJ 08901-1281. Offers astronomy (MS, PhD); biophysics (PhD); condensed matter physics (MS, PhD); elementary particle physics (MS, PhD); intermediate energy nuclear physics (MS); nuclear physics (MS, PhD); physics (MST); surface science (PhD); theoretical physics (MS, PhD). Part-time programs available. *Faculty:* 67 full-time (5 women). *Students:* 90 full-time (13 women), 18 part-time (3 women); includes 5 minority (2 African Americans, 3 Asian Americans or Pacific Islanders), 67 international. Average age 28. 269 applicants, 16% accepted, 21 enrolled. In 2003, 5 master's, 16 doctorates awarded. Terminal master's awarded for partial completion of doctoral program. *Median time to degree:* Master's–2 years full-time; doctorate–6 years full-time. *Degree requirements:* For master's, thesis or alternative, comprehensive exam; for doctorate, thesis/dissertation, comprehensive exam. *Entrance requirements:* For master's and doctorate, GRE General Test, GRE Subject Test. Additional exam requirements/recommendations for international students: Required—TOEFL, TSE. *Application deadline:* For fall admission, 1/2 priority date for domestic students, 1/2 priority date for international students; for spring admission, 11/1 for domestic students, 11/1 for international students. Applications are processed on a rolling basis. Application fee: $50. Electronic applications accepted. *Expenses:* Tuition, state resident: full-time $10,030. Tuition, nonresident: full-time $14,202. *Financial support:* In 2003–04, 19 fellowships with full tuition reimbursements (averaging $18,000 per year), 50 research assistantships with full tuition reimbursements (averaging $15,300 per year), 8 teaching assistantships with full tuition reimbursements (averaging $15,300 per year) were awarded. Health care benefits and unspecified assistantships also available. Financial award application deadline: 1/2; financial award applicants required to submit FAFSA. *Faculty research:* Astronomy, high energy, condensed matter, surface, nuclear physics. Total annual research expenditures: $7.8 million. *Unit head:* Dr. Ted Williams, Director, 732-445-2516, Fax: 732-445-4343, E-mail: williams@physics.rutgers.edu. *Application contact:* Kathy DiMeo, Administrative Assistant, 732-445-2502, Fax: 732-445-4343, E-mail: graduate@physics.rutgers.edu.

See in-depth description on page 401.

Theoretical Physics

St. John's University, St. John's College of Liberal Arts and Sciences, Institute of Asian Studies, Jamaica, NY 11439. Offers Asian and African cultural studies (Adv C); Asian studies (Adv C); Chinese studies (MA, Adv C); East Asian culture studies (Adv C); East Asian studies (MA). Part-time and evening/weekend programs available. *Faculty:* 7 part-time/adjunct (5 women). *Students:* 10 full-time (2 women), 4 part-time (3 women); includes 5 minority (3 Asian Americans or Pacific Islanders, 2 Hispanic Americans), 8 international. 18 applicants, 83% accepted, 2 enrolled. In 2003, 2 degrees awarded. *Degree requirements:* For master's, one foreign language, comprehensive exam. *Entrance requirements:* For master's, 18 hours in the field, minimum GPA of 3.0. Additional exam requirements/recommendations for international students: Required—TOEFL (minimum score 500 paper-based). *Application deadline:* Applications are processed on a rolling basis. Application fee: $40. Electronic applications accepted. *Expenses:* Tuition: Full-time $15,840; part-time $8,320 per year. Tuition and fees vary according to course load, degree level, program and student level. *Financial support:* Research assistantships, scholarships/grants available. Support available to part-time students. Financial award application deadline: 3/1; financial award applicants required to submit FAFSA. *Faculty research:* East Asian philosophy and religion, Chinese language and literature, Japanese language, modern Japan, Chinese art and history. *Unit head:* Dr. Abraham Ho, Director, 718-990-6582. *Application contact:* Matthew Whelan, Director, Office of Admission, 718-990-2000, Fax: 718-990-2096, E-mail: admissions@stjohns.edu.

University of Victoria, Faculty of Graduate Studies, Faculty of Science, Department of Physics and Astronomy, Victoria, BC V8W 2Y2, Canada. Offers astronomy and astrophysics (M Sc, PhD); condensed matter physics (M Sc, PhD); medical physics (M Sc, PhD); nuclear and particle studies (M Sc, PhD); ocean physics (M Sc, PhD); theoretical physics (M Sc, PhD). *Degree requirements:* For master's, thesis/dissertation, registration; for doctorate, thesis/dissertation, comprehensive exam, registration. *Entrance requirements:* Additional exam requirements/recommendations for international students: Required—TOEFL (minimum score 575 paper-based; 213 computer-based). *Faculty research:* Old stellar populations; observational cosmology and large scale structure; cp violation; atlas.

West Virginia University, Eberly College of Arts and Sciences, Department of Physics, Morgantown, WV 26506. Offers applied physics (MS, PhD); astrophysics (MS, PhD); chemical physics (MS, PhD); condensed matter physics (MS, PhD); elementary particle physics (MS, PhD); materials physics (MS, PhD); plasma physics (MS, PhD); solid state physics (MS, PhD); statistical physics (MS, PhD); theoretical physics (MS, PhD). *Faculty:* 17 full-time (3 women), 1 part-time/adjunct (0 women). *Students:* 44 full-time (10 women), 4 part-time (1 woman), 32 international. Average age 28. 60 applicants, 20% accepted. In 2003, 2 master's awarded, leading to continued full-time study 100%; 3 doctorates awarded, leading to university research/teaching 33%, business/industry 33%, government 33%. Terminal master's awarded for partial completion of doctoral program. *Median time to degree:* Master's–2 years full-time; doctorate–5 years full-time. *Degree requirements:* For master's, thesis or alternative, qualifying exam; for doctorate, thesis/dissertation, qualifying exam. *Entrance requirements:* For master's and doctorate, GRE General Test, GRE Subject Test, minimum GPA of 3.0. Additional exam requirements/recommendations for international students: Required—TOEFL. *Application deadline:* For fall admission, 2/15 for domestic students. Applications are processed on a rolling basis. Application fee: $50. *Expenses:* Tuition, state resident: full-time $4,332. Tuition, nonresident: full-time $12,442. *Financial support:* In 2003–04, 30 research assistantships with full and partial tuition reimbursements (averaging $18,000 per year), 10 teaching assistantships with full and partial tuition reimbursements (averaging $16,000 per year) were awarded. Fellowships, Federal Work-Study, institutionally sponsored loans, and tuition waivers (full and partial) also available. Financial award application deadline: 2/1; financial award applicants required to submit FAFSA. *Faculty research:* Experimental and theoretical condensed-matter, plasma, high-energy theory, nonlinear dynamics, space physics. Total annual research expenditures: $3.3 million. *Unit head:* Dr. Earl E. Scime, Chair, 304-293-3422 Ext. 1437, Fax: 304-293-5732, E-mail: escime@wvu.edu.

Cross-Discipline Announcements

Dartmouth College, Thayer School of Engineering, Hanover, NH 03755.

Thayer School offers MS and PhD programs in applied sciences. The interdisciplinary character of the institution, modern laboratories, computing facilities, and active collaborations with other departments provide unique opportunities for study and research in space plasma physics, nonlinear optics, electromagnetism, molecular materials, image and signal processing, fluid mechanics, and oceanography. See In-Depth Description in Book 5, Section 1, of this series.

Oklahoma State University, Graduate College, Program in Photonics, Stillwater, OK 74078.

The photonics PhD at Oklahoma State University provides world-class research opportunities in a multidisciplinary program launched jointly by the Departments of Electrical Engineering, Physics, and Chemistry. An NSF IGERT grant supports qualified PhD photonics students with annual stipends of $27,500 as well as complete tuition waivers and cost of education and travel allowances. In addition to this multidisciplinary program, students may also earn a PhD in the traditional discipline of physics as they pursue research options in photonics.

University of Michigan, Horace H. Rackham School of Graduate Studies, College of Engineering, Department of Nuclear Engineering and Radiological Sciences, Ann Arbor, MI 48109.

NERS offers master's and doctoral programs in nuclear engineering and radiological sciences and in nuclear science, as well as a joint degree in scientific computing. Programs of study: fission systems and radiation transport; materials; plasmas and fusion; radiation measurements and imaging; and radiation safety, environmental sciences, and medical physics, including medical applications and radiation protection. Students with degrees in engineering, computer sciences, or the physical sciences are encouraged to apply.

University of Michigan, Horace H. Rackham School of Graduate Studies, College of Engineering, Department of Materials Science and Engineering, Ann Arbor, MI 48109.

Interdisciplinary curriculum leads to master's and PhD degrees in materials science and engineering for chemistry students interested in solid-state chemistry, metals, ceramics, polymers, composites, electronic materials, and other engineering materials. Research assistantships and fellowships available on a competitive basis. See the department's In-Depth Description in the Engineering and Applied Sciences volume of this series.

AUBURN UNIVERSITY

Department of Physics

Program of Study

The Auburn University Department of Physics offers the Ph.D. degree in physics to students who complete at least 60 semester hours (30 hours of graded course work in graduate-level physics), pass a written and oral general doctoral examination, and successfully defend a research dissertation. The Ph.D. degree program takes approximately five years to complete. The student's research is in one of the areas in which the department has active research groups: plasma physics, especially magnetically confined plasmas with applications to the development of fusion energy; condensed-matter physics, especially semiconductors for microelectronic applications; atomic and molecular physics; dusty plasmas; and space physics, especially in the Earth's magnetosphere with applications to space weather.

An M.S. degree with a thesis or nonthesis option is also offered. With the nonthesis option, 30 hours (21 hours of graduate-level physics) are required as is an acceptable grade on a written examination. Students who elect the thesis option take similar courses but do a thesis instead of a written examination. The nonthesis M.S. option takes about two years to complete, and the thesis option takes about three years.

Research Facilities

The Department of Physics offices and research laboratories are housed in the Allison Lab (37,000 square feet) and the Leach Science Center (46,000 square feet). Major research equipment includes the Accelerator Lab with a new 2-megavolt Tandem Ion Accelerator; the Compact Toroidal Hybrid, a magnetic fusion device; the Scanning Tunneling Electron Microscope Lab; a Molecular Beam Epitaxy facility; the Epitaxial Growth Laboratory; the Surface Science Laboratory; Laboratories for Plasma Physics; and a 96-processor Beowulf Cluster for parallel processing. Physics faculty members and students also collaborate with scientists in the Space Research Institute and the College of Engineering, expanding the facilities available for developing new knowledge.

Auburn's libraries, ranked third among more than 300 of the nation's top colleges and universities according to a poll taken by the the *Princeton Review* for its guide to the best universities, are also available to students.

Financial Aid

Students admitted to graduate study in physics are offered teaching assistantships, with an annual stipend of $18,000 and full tuition remission. Students pay only a $200 registration fee per semester. As students progress toward their degrees, they usually become research assistants with similar monetary remuneration.

Auburn physics graduate students also often compete successfully for special fellowships from various government agencies.

Cost of Study

Tuition is covered for all teaching and research assistants. Only a $200 registration fee per semester is required.

Living and Housing Costs

Official estimates of living expenses are less than $14,000 per year. Actual costs can be lower.

Student Group

Main campus enrollment is more than 21,500, with approximately 1,200 full-time faculty members. The Department of Physics has 23 full-time faculty members, between 30 and 40 undergraduate physics majors, and 30 to 40 graduate students. Physics faculty members and students, both men and women, come from all areas of the United States as well as from Africa, Asia, Europe, and South America.

Student Outcomes

Students who finish with a Ph.D. go on to jobs in academia, postdoctoral research, teaching, government research labs, and industrial research. Students who finish with an M.S. go on to jobs teaching in junior colleges or doing research at government and industrial labs or continue their education.

Location

Auburn, a city of 45,000 people, is beautiful, convenient, and friendly and offers easy living. It is located 125 miles southwest of Atlanta and 60 miles east of Montgomery, the state capitol. Auburn is surrounded by farms and woodlands. The name comes from the line, "Sweet Auburn, loveliest village of the Plain," in Oliver Goldsmith's poem *The Deserted Village.*

The University and The Department

Large enough to provide an enriched educational and cultural environment for students from more than thirty countries around the world, Auburn retains the charm and civility of the New South. Yet, the bright lights of Atlanta are only about 2 hours away by car.

The Department of Physics, with its 1:2 faculty-student ratio, provides a nurturing environment in which the student is treated as an individual and also has the opportunity to experience the joy of discovery in world-class research groups.

Applying

To apply for graduate admission and financial assistance, students should go to the department's Web site (listed below) and click on Graduate Program and then Apply on Line - Physics Assistantship Application. After completing the online form, students should send their transcripts, GRE scores, and letters of recommendation directly to the department. No application fee is required if application is made in this manner.

Correspondence and Information

To submit application materials:

Physics Department
Graduate Admissions
206 Allison Lab
Auburn University, Alabama 36849

For information and other correspondence:

Professor J. D. Perez
Head, Department of Physics
206 Allison Lab
Auburn University, Alabama 36849
E-mail: perez@physics.auburn.edu
Telephone: 334-844-4264
Fax: 334-844-4613
World Wide Web: http://www.physics.auburn.edu/

Auburn University

THE FACULTY AND THEIR RESEARCH

Robert F. Boivin, Assistant Professor; Ph.D., Quebec. Experimental plasma physics and propulsion.
Michael J. Bozack, Associate Professor; Ph.D., Oregon. Experimental surface science and semiconductor physics.
An-Ban Chen, Professor, Ph.D.; William and Mary. Theoretical condensed-matter physics.
Eugene J. Clothiaux, Professor; Ph.D., New Mexico State. Spectroscopy.
Jianjun Dong, Assistant Professor; Ph.D., Ohio. Theoretical condensed-matter physics and computational physics.
Albert T. Fromhold, Professor; Ph.D., Cornell. Condensed-matter physics.
Junichiro Fukai, Associate Professor; Ph.D., Tennessee. Fundamentals of electricity and magnetism.
James D. Hanson, Professor; Ph.D., Maryland. Theoretical plasma physics and fusion science.
Satoshi Hinata, Professor; Ph.D., Illinois. Theoretical space physics and solar physics.
Stephen F. Knowlton, Professor; Ph.D., MIT. Experimental plasma physics and fusion science.
Allen L. Landers, Assistant Professor; Ph.D., Kansas State. Experimental atomic physics.
Yu Lin, Associate Professor; Ph.D., Alaska. Theoretical space physics and magnetospheric physics.
Eugene Oks, Professor; Ph.D., Moscow Physical Technical Institute. Theoretical atomic and molecular physics and econophysics.
Minseo Park, Assistant Professor; Ph.D., North Carolina. Experimental condensed-matter physics.
Joseph D. Perez, Professor and Department Head; Ph.D., Maryland. Theoretical space (magnetospheric) and plasma physics.
Michael S. Pindzola, Professor; Ph.D., Virginia. Theoretical atomic and molecular physics and computational physics.
Francis J. Robicheaux, Associate Professor; Ph.D., Chicago. Theoretical atomic and molecular physics.
Marllin L. Simon, Associate Professor; Ph.D., Missouri. Physics education.
D. Gary Swanson, Professor; Ph.D., Caltech. Theoretical plasma physics.
Edward Thomas Jr., Associate Professor; Ph.D., Auburn. Experimental plasma physics and dusty plasmas.
Chin-Che Tin, Associate Professor; Ph.D., Alberta. Experimental condensed-matter physics and epitaxial growth.
Jean-Marie P. Wersinger, Associate Professor; Ph.D., Lausanne. Remote sensing and theoretical plasma physics.
John R. Williams, Professor; Ph.D., North Carolina State. Experimental condensed-matter physics, semiconductors, and low-energy accelerator applications.

BOSTON UNIVERSITY

Department of Physics

Programs of Study

The Department of Physics offers programs leading to the Ph.D. and M.A. degrees in physics. Through research opportunities in experimental high-energy and medium-energy physics, particle astrophysics, theoretical particle physics and cosmology, molecular biophysics, experimental biophysics and condensed-matter physics, and theoretical condensed-matter, polymer, and statistical physics.

The M.A. degree requires the completion of eight semester courses, passed with a grade of B– or better; evidence of having successfully completed undergraduate courses in a modern language or passing the departmental language exam; and achieving a passing grade on the departmental comprehensive exam or the completion of a master's thesis. Each student must satisfy a residency requirement of a minimum of two consecutive semesters of full-time graduate study at Boston University.

The Ph.D. requires the completion of eight semester courses beyond the M.A. degree, passed with a grade of B– or better; passing of the departmental language exam; an honors grade on the departmental comprehensive exam; passing of an oral exam; and the completion of a dissertation and a dissertation defense. The dissertation must exhibit an original contribution to the field. Each student must satisfy a residency requirement of a minimum of two consecutive semesters of full-time graduate study at Boston University. The time it takes to obtain a Ph.D. degree is approximately 5½ years, although students have obtained their degree in as short a time as four years and as long as eight.

Research Facilities

The Department of Physics is part of Boston University's $250-million Science and Engineering Complex, centrally located on the main Charles River Campus. Condensed-matter physics facilities include electronic and mechanical nanostructure fabrication and measurement, metastable-helium-atom probes of surface spin order and dynamics, photoemission and soft X-ray fluorescence probes of electronic structure in novel materials, X-ray diffractometery, and the optics and transport of electrons at high fields and low temperatures. Biophysics/polymer labs include dynamical light scattering, Raman and Brillouin scattering, and infrared and far-infrared absorption spectroscopy as well as modern facilities for genetically manipulating biomolecules. Physicists at the Photonics Center develop and use near-field scanning optical and infrared microscopy and spectroscopy, entangled photons for quantum information processing and entangled photon microscopy, and a full complement of molecular beam epitaxy and device processing facilities, the latter primarily with InGaAl-nitride wide-band-gap semiconductor materials and devices. The high-energy physics labs include facilities for the design, production, and testing of key components of various particle detectors. Collaborations include the D0 experiment at Fermilab; the ATLAS and CMS experiments at CERN; the muon g-2 experiment at Brookhaven; the Mulan experiment at PSI, Switzerland; the MACRO experiment at Gran Sasso, Italy; the SuperKamiokande experiment in Kamioka, Japan; and the K2K experiment at KEK. For computation, workstations are networked to two major departmental SGI servers as well as computer clusters provided by the University for general student use. In addition, students have access to the University's high-end computational resources, which include an SGI/Cray Origin 2000 supercomputer with 192 processors (75 Gflops), an IBM RS6000 SP with 64 processors (96 Gflops), and advanced visualization facilities.

Financial Aid

Through a combination of teaching fellowships, research assistantships, and University fellowships, the department provides stipends and full tuition scholarships for essentially all students. The standard stipend for teaching fellows and research assistants is expected to be $22,500 per calendar year.

Cost of Study

Tuition and fees are provided for as described above. Books and supplies cost an additional $400.

Living and Housing Costs

There is limited graduate student housing available on the Boston University campus at $8978 per year for room and board. However, students generally rent apartments in the Boston area. The cost of apartments varies widely, depending on the area.

Student Group

Currently, the department has 104 graduate students engaged in work toward the Ph.D. and M.A. degrees, and it prides itself on the close contact maintained between students and faculty members.

Student Outcomes

Recent Ph.D. recipients from the Department of Physics have been awarded the Wigner Fellowship at Oak Ridge, National Research Council Postdoctoral Fellowships, and the IBM Supercomputer Research Award, among others. Other graduates have gone on to permanent positions at Bell Laboratories, LANL, NEC Corporation, NASA, NIST, and to tenured faculty positions at major universities.

Location

Boston University is located in Boston, Massachusetts, which is a major metropolitan center of cultural, scholarly, scientific, and technological activity. Besides Boston University, there are many major academic institutions in the area. Seminars and colloquia are announced in a Boston Area Physics Calendar.

The University and The Department

Boston University is a private urban university with a faculty of 3,492 members and a student population of 28,512. The University consists of fifteen schools and colleges. The Department of Physics is part of the College of Arts and Sciences and the Graduate School. The department has a young and active faculty of 35 full-time members and has experienced significant growth in recent years. Among the recent additions to the faculty is Nobel laureate Sheldon Glashow.

Applying

The application deadlines are January 15 for fall admission and November 1 for spring admission. Application information and forms are available online at http://physics.bu.edu/grad.html. For admission to the graduate programs, a bachelor's degree in physics or astronomy is required. Scores on the General Test and Subject Test in physics of the GRE are required. The acceptable score for admission is dependent on the applicant's overall record; there is no specified minimum. Students from non-English-speaking countries are required to demonstrate proficiency in English by earning a minimum acceptable score of 280 on the computer-based Test of English as a Foreign Language (TOEFL).

Correspondence and Information

Chair, Graduate Admissions Committee
Department of Physics
Boston University
590 Commonwealth Avenue
Boston, Massachusetts 02215

Telephone: 617-353-2623
E-mail: dept@physics.bu.edu
World Wide Web: http://physics.bu.edu/

Boston University

THE FACULTY AND THEIR RESEARCH

Professors

Steven Paul Ahlen, Ph.D., Berkeley, 1976. Experimental astrophysics, heavy-ion physics, monopole and quark searches.
Rama Bansil, Ph.D., Rochester, 1974. Biophysics, polymers.
Edward C. Booth, Emeritus; Ph.D., Johns Hopkins, 1955. Intermediate-energy particle physics.
Kenneth Brecher, joint appointment with the Department of Astronomy; Ph.D., MIT, 1969. Theoretical astrophysics, relativity, cosmology.
David Campbell, joint appointment with the College of Engineering; Ph.D., Cambridge, 1970. Theoretical physics and applied mathematics.
Antonio H. Castro Neto, Ph.D., Illinois, 1994. Condensed-matter physics.
Bernard Chasan, Emeritus; Ph.D., Cornell, 1961. Biophysics.
Andrew G. Cohen, Ph.D., Harvard, 1986. Elementary particle physics.
Robert S. Cohen, Emeritus; Ph.D., Yale, 1948. Philosophical and historical foundations of physics.
Ernesto Corinaldesi, Emeritus; Ph.D., Manchester (England), 1951. Quantum mechanics.
Charles Delisi, joint appointment with the College of Engineering; Ph.D., NYU, 1969. Biological physicist.
Alvaro DeRújula, joint appointment with CERN; Ph.D., Madrid, 1968. Theoretical particle physics, phenomenology.
Dean S. Edmonds Jr., Emeritus; Ph.D., MIT, 1958. Electronics and instrumentation.
Maged El-Batanouny, Ph.D., California, Davis, 1978. Surface physics, solitons.
Evan Evans, joint appointment with the College of Engineering; Ph.D., California, San Diego 1970. Condensed-matter theory.
Wolfgang Franzen, Emeritus; Ph.D., Pennsylvania, 1949. Atomic physics, surface physics.
Sheldon Glashow, Distinguished Physicist and Research Scholar (Harvard); Ph.D., Harvard, 1958. Theoretical particle physics.
Bennett B. Goldberg, Ph.D., Brown, 1987. Condensed-matter physics.
William S. Hellman, Emeritus; Ph.D., Syracuse, 1961. Elementary particle theory.
Arthur Jaffe, joint appointment with Mathematics; Ph.D., Princeton, 1966. Mathematical physicist.
Edward Kearns, Ph.D., Harvard, 1990. Particle astrophysics.
William Klein, Ph.D., Temple, 1972. Condensed-matter theory.
Dirk Kriemer, joint appointment with Mathematics; Ph.D., Mainz, 1992. High-energy physics.
Frank Krienen, Emeritus Professor of Engineering and Applied Physics; I.R., Amsterdam, 1947. Experimental particle and accelerator physics, muon g-2.
Kenneth D. Lane, Ph.D., Johns Hopkins, 1970. Theoretical high-energy physics.
Karl Ludwig, Ph.D., Stanford, 1986. Experimental condensed-matter physics.
James Miller, Ph.D., Carnegie Mellon, 1974. Intermediate- and high-energy experimental physics, muon g-2, CP violation.
Theodore Moustakas, joint appointment with the College of Engineering; Ph.D., Columbia, 1974. Synthetic novel materials.
So-Young Pi, Ph.D., SUNY at Stony Brook, 1974. Field theory, theoretical elementary particle physics.
Claudio Rebbi, Ph.D., Turin (Italy), 1967. Theoretical physics, lattice quantum chromodynamics, computational physics.
Sidney Redner, Ph.D., MIT, 1977. Statistical physics, condensed-matter theory.
B. Lee Roberts, Ph.D., William and Mary, 1974. Intermediate- and high-energy experimental physics, muon g-2, CP violation.
James Rohlf, Ph.D., Caltech, 1980. Experimental particle physics, hadron collider physics.
Kenneth Rothschild, Ph.D., MIT, 1973. Biophysics, molecular electronics, physics of vision.
Anders Sandvik, Ph.D., California, Santa Barbara, 1993. Condensed-matter computational physics.
Alexander Sergienko, joint appointment with the College of Engineering; Ph.D., Moscow State, 1987. Electrical and computer engineering.
Abner Shimony, Emeritus; Ph.D. (philosophy), Yale, 1953; Ph.D. (physics), Princeton, 1962. Philosophical and historical foundations of physics, theoretical quantum mechanics.
William J. Skocpol, Ph.D., Harvard, 1974. Experimental condensed-matter physics.
Kevin E. Smith, Ph.D., Yale, 1988. Experimental condensed-matter physics.
John Stachel, Emeritus, Curator of Einstein papers in the United States; Ph.D., Stevens, 1952. General relativity, foundations of relativistic space-time theories.
H. Eugene Stanley, Ph.D., Harvard, 1967. Phase transitions, scaling, polymer physics, fractals and chaos.
James L. Stone, Ph.D., Michigan, 1976. Experimental particle physics and astrophysics, neutrinos, proton decay, monopole studies.
Lawrence R. Sulak, Ph.D., Princeton, 1970. Experimental particle physics, proton decay, monopoles, muon g-2, neutrinos.
Malvin Teich, joint appointment with the College of Engineering; Ph.D., Cornell, 1966. Theoretical/experimental condensed-matter physics.
Charles R. Willis, Emeritus; Ph.D., Syracuse, 1957. Theory of interaction of radiation with matter, statistical physics.
J. Scott Whitaker, Ph.D., Berkeley, 1976. Experimental colliding-beam physics, supersymmetric particle searches.
George O. Zimmerman, Emeritus; Ph.D., Yale, 1963. Low-temperature physics, magnetism.

Associate Professors

John Butler, Ph.D., Stanford, 1986. Experimental high-energy physics.
Robert Carey, Ph.D., Harvard, 1989. Experimental high-energy physics.
Claudio Chamon, Ph.D., MIT, 1996. Condensed matter theory.
Shyamsunder Erramilli, Ph.D., Illinois, 1986. Biophysics.

Assistant Professors

Andrew G. Duffy, Ph.D., Queen's at Kingston, 1995.
Ulrich Heintz, Ph.D., SUNY at Stony Brook, 1991. High-energy physics.
Pritiraj Mohanty, Ph.D., Maryland, 1998. Condensed-matter experimentation.
Meenakshi Narain, Ph.D., SUNY at Stony Brook.
Martin Schmaltz, Ph.D., California, San Diego, 1995. High-energy physics.

Research Faculty and Staff

Mi Kyuny Hong, Ph.D., Illinois, 1988. Experimental biophysics.
James Shank, Ph.D., Berkeley, 1988. High-energy physics.
Christopher Walter, Ph.D., Caltech, 1996. High-energy physics.

CITY COLLEGE OF THE CITY UNIVERSITY OF NEW YORK

Department of Physics

Programs of Study

The Department of Physics offers students the opportunity for study and research leading to the degrees of Doctor of Philosophy (Ph.D) and Master of Arts (M.A.).

Students in the Ph.D. program usually take a year of graduate courses before the first qualifying examination, although some advanced students take the examination after half a year of course work or even upon entering the program. The examination tests classical mechanics and electromagnetism, quantum theory, and general undergraduate physics. Students entering the biophysics subspecialty are allowed to substitute a biophysics examination for classical mechanics. Sixty credits of course work are normally required for the Ph.D. degree program; advanced students with an M.A. degree can usually transfer 30 credits of previous graduate work. In addition, arrangements are always made so that advanced students meet course requirements by working at their appropriate level in connection with their anticipated thesis research. After passing the qualifying examination, students choose faculty mentors for their thesis research. When student and mentor feel confident of the area of thesis research, the student takes an oral second examination before an appropriately chosen thesis committee. During this examination, the student describes the proposed research and demonstrates familiarity with the physics in the area of research. When students complete their original research, they defend a written thesis before their thesis committee at a final thesis defense.

Students in the M.A. program normally take the qualifying examination after 1 or 1½ years, when they have completed the necessary course work. Students who pass the qualifying examination are often admitted to the Ph.D. program. Students who do not pass the qualifying examination but show satisfactory performance at the master's level are awarded a master's degree when they have completed 30 credits of course work. The M.A. program normally requires 1½ years to complete.

Research Facilities

The physics department is housed on three floors (about 70,000 square feet) of the thirteen-story Marshak Science Building, which also houses the other CCNY science departments. FT-IR, X-ray diffraction, UV-visible spectrometers, ultrafast laser instrumentation in picosecond and femtosecond regimes, and departmental computers are available to students. In addition, high-resolution FT-NMR spectrometers and mass spectrometers are run by operators for any research group. A wide variety of equipment is used by individual research groups, including lasers of many kinds, molecular beam instrumentation, a microwave spectrometer, computers, ultrahigh-vacuum systems for surface studies, two He3-He4 dilution refrigerators, a SQUID-based magnetometer, e-beam evaporators, crystal growing equipment, Raman spectrometers, ultrafast time-resolving instrumentation, and atomic beam systems. The department has an electronics shop, a machine shop, a student machine shop, and a glassblower available for designing and building equipment. The Institute for Ultrafast Spectroscopy and Lasers has eight laboratories in the Science Building and the Engineering Building. The New York State Center for Advanced Technology in Ultrafast Photonic Materials and Applications focuses on photonics research with commercial applications.

Financial Aid

Students accepted into the Ph.D. program are normally offered financial support by the Department of Physics. The support is in the form of fellowships and/or research assistantships, for a total stipend of $16,000 (taxable) per year, plus tuition. The exact amount depends on the student's progress in the program, tuition costs, and need. Some New York State residents are also eligible for other stipends or awards. More advanced students are generally awarded research assistantships.

Cost of Study

Tuition for fall 2003 was $5700 for an entering student ($2435 for New York residents), $3390 for an intermediate-level student ($1520 for New York residents), and $1210 for an advanced student ($605 for New York residents).

Living and Housing Costs

There is no on-campus housing available at City College. Graduate student housing is available for some students and is run by the City University of New York in midtown Manhattan. Many students live in rooms and apartments throughout New York City, paying $550–$750 per person per month.

Student Group

The total number of graduate students in the physics department is currently about 35. There are about 15 postdoctoral assistants. A wide variety of academic, ethnic, and national backgrounds are represented among these students.

Location

The City College is located in an urban setting in the upper part of Manhattan. The College is part of the City University of New York, which includes eighteen campuses—among them Brooklyn, Hunter, and Queens colleges. Physics research at these other branches of the City University complements that at City College. The College is near many other institutions in the New York metropolitan area, including Columbia University, Rockefeller University, and Polytechnic University of New York, and has cooperative arrangements with Brookhaven National Laboratory on Long Island. A number of world-famous industrial research laboratories are near New York City, including AT&T Bell Laboratories, IBM's Thomas J. Watson Laboratory, RCA's David Sarnoff Laboratory, and the Exxon Research Center.

New York City is a major cultural, artistic, communications, medical, and scientific center with numerous resources and opportunities. The city is also a focus of international travel, and visiting scientists often come to City College as part of their itinerary in the United States.

The College

The City College of the City University of New York is the lineal descendant of the Free Academy of New York City, founded in 1847. City College is the oldest and best-known component of the City University of New York.

Applying

Information and application forms can be obtained from the Department of Physics at the address below. An application fee of $40 must accompany the application, with the exception of international students with financial difficulties, for whom the fee can be deferred until registration.

Correspondence and Information

Chairman
Graduate Admissions Committee
Department of Physics
City College of the City University of New York
New York, New York 10031

Fax: 212-650-6940
E-mail: physdept@sci.ccny.cuny.edu
World Wide Web: http://www.sci.ccny.cuny.edu/physics/

City College of the City University of New York

THE FACULTY AND THEIR RESEARCH

Adolf A. Abrahamson, Professor; Ph.D., NYU. Atomic and nuclear structure, properties of superheavy elements.

Robert R. Alfano, Distinguished Professor; Ph.D., NYU. Ultrafast picosecond and femtosecond laser spectroscopy applied to physical and biological systems: nonlinear optics, optical imaging, medical applications of photonics, laser development.

Joseph L. Birman, Distinguished Professor; Ph.D., Columbia. Theoretical physics—condensed matter theory; symmetry and symmetry breaking and restoration; optical response of matter, including nonlinear response and response of strongly correlated electronic systems (quantum Hall systems); microscopic theory of high-Tc superconductors; many-body theory, including use of quantum deformed algebras.

Timothy Boyer, Professor; Ph.D., Harvard. Connections between classical and quantum theories: zero-point radiation, stochastic electrodynamics, van der Waals forces, classical electromagnetism.

Ngee-Pong Chang, Professor; Ph.D., Columbia. Unification and dynamical symmetry breaking: origin of mass and chirality, quark-gluon plasma and handedness of the early universe, neutrino mass oscillations.

Victor Chung, Professor; Ph.D., Berkeley. Administration, physics instruction.

Herman Z. Cummins, Distinguished Professor; Ph.D., Columbia. Light-scattering studies of liquids and solids: phase transitions and critical phenomena, crystal-growth kinetics, pattern formation in nonequilibrium crystal growth, biological problems, liquid-glass transition.

Harold Falk, Professor; Ph.D., Washington (Seattle). Statistical mechanics, especially exact results for spin-systems: discrete-time, nonlinear, and stochastic models.

Swapan K. Gayen, Associate Professor; Ph.D., Connecticut. Optical biomedical imaging, tunable solid-state lasers, spectroscopy of impurity ions in solids, ultrafast laser spectroscopy, near-field scanning optical spectroscopy.

Joel Gersten, Professor and Acting Dean; Ph.D., Columbia. Solid-state theory: interactions involving small solid-state particles or solid-state surfaces, sonoluminescence.

Daniel M. Greenberger, Professor; Ph.D., Illinois. Fundamental problems in quantum mechanics: the neutron interferometer, coherence in and interpretation of quantum theory, relativistic considerations.

Marilyn Gunner, Associate Professor; Ph.D., Pennsylvania. Experimental and theoretical biophysics: proteins in electron and proton transfer reactions, time-resolved spectroscopic measurements in photosynthesis.

Michio Kaku, Professor; Ph.D., Berkeley. Superstring theory, supersymmetry, supergravity, string field theory, quantum gravity, quantum chromodynamics.

Joel Koplik, Professor; Ph.D., Berkeley. Molecular dynamics of microscopic fluid flow: transport in disordered systems, superfluid vortex dynamics, pattern selection in nonequilibrium growth processes.

Michael S. Lubell, Professor and Chair; Ph.D., Yale. Photon-atom interactions, synchrotron radiation studies, polarized electron physics, two-electron systems, science and technology policy.

Herman Makse, Assistant Professor; Ph.D., Boston University. Condensed-matter physics, granular materials, nonlinear elasticity, Edwards thermodynamics and jamming, discrete element modeling, interface roughening, porous media, dynamics of urban populations.

Carlos A. Meriles, Assistant Professor; Ph.D., Córdoba (Argentina). Nobel magnetic resonance methods and instruments, hyperpolarization and ultrasensitive detection, optical NMR, low/zero field spectroscopy and imaging, applications to semiconductors and spintronics.

Vangal N. Muthukumar, Associate Professor; Ph.D., Indian Institute of Mathematical Sciences, Madras. Theoretical condensed matter, superconductivity, magnetism, transport phenomena, oxides and the physics of strong correlation.

V. Parameswaran Nair, Professor; Ph.D., Syracuse. Mathematical and topological aspects of quantum field theory: skyrmions, quantum breaking of classical symmetries, conformal field theory, black holes, quantum chromodynamics, interaction of anyons.

Vladimir Petricevic, Associate Professor; Ph.D., CUNY. Growth of solid-state laser materials, laser development, photonics, spectroscopy of ions in solids, ultrafast phenomena.

Alexios Polchronakos, Professor; Ph.D., Caltech. Quantum field theory, mathematical physics.

Myriam P. Sarachik, Distinguished Professor; Ph.D., Columbia. Low-temperature studies of metal-insulator transitions, Anderson localization, disordered systems, strongly correlated systems; mesoscopic tunneling of magnetization, molecular magnets.

David Schmeltzer, Associate Professor; D.Sc., Technion (Israel). Many-body physics of strongly correlated fermions: Fermi and non-Fermi liquids, Luttinger liquids, fractional quantum Hall effect, renormalization group, bosonization; metal-insulator transition, persistent currents; high-Tc superconductivity.

Mark Shattuck, Assistant Professor; Ph.D., Duke. Soft condensed matter, granular media, pattern formation, nonlinear dynamics.

David I. Shelupsky, Associate Professor; Ph.D., Princeton. General relativity and quantum gravity, abstract harmonic analysis.

Frederick W. Smith, Professor; Ph.D., Brown. Deposition and characterization of semiconducting and dielectric thin films; modeling of local atomic bonding in amorphous films; chemical vapor deposition of diamond.

Richard N. Steinberg, Associate Professor; Ph.D., Yale. Physics education research.

Jiufeng, J. Tu, Assistant Professor; Ph.D., Cornell. Optical studies of correlated systems and nanosystems, infrared and Raman studies of superconductors and nanosystems.

Sergey A. Vitkalov, Assistant Professor; Ph.D., Russian Academy of Sciences. Experimental condensed-matter physics, dynamical properties of low-dimensional quantum systems.

Professors Emeriti

Michael E. Arons, Joseph Aschner, Alvin Bachman, Arthur Bierman, Robert Callender, Erich Erlbach, Paul Harris, Hiram Hart, Martin Kramer, Robert M. Lea, S. J. Lindenbaum, Harry Lustig, William Miller, Marvin Mittleman, Leonard Roellig, Harry Soodak, Harold L. Stolov, Peter Tea, Martin Tiersten, Chi Yuan.

COLUMBIA UNIVERSITY

Department of Applied Physics and Applied Mathematics

Programs of Study

The Department of Applied Physics and Applied Mathematics offers graduate study leading to the degrees of Master of Science (M.S), Doctor of Engineering Science (Eng.Sc.D.), and Doctor of Philosophy (Ph.D.).

The following fields of research (topics of emphasis in parentheses) are available for doctoral study: theoretical and experimental plasma physics (fusion and space plasmas), applied mathematics (analysis of partial differential equations, large-scale scientific computing, nonlinear dynamics, geophysical/geological fluid dynamics, and biomathematics), solid-state physics (semiconductor, surface, and low-dimensional physics), optical and laser physics (free-electron lasers and laser interactions with matter), nuclear science (medical applications), earth science (atmosphere, ocean, and climate science and geophysics), and materials science and engineering (thin films; nanomaterials; electronic, optical, and magnetic materials). Successful completion of 30 points (semester hours) or more of approved graduate course work beyond the master's degree is required for the doctoral degree. Candidates must pass written and oral qualifying exams and successfully defend an approved dissertation based on original research. For the M.S. degree, candidates must successfully complete a minimum of 30 points of credit of approved graduate course work at Columbia. A 35-point M.S. degree with a concentration in medical physics is offered in collaboration with faculty members from the College of Physicians and Surgeons. It prepares students for careers in medical physics and provides preparation for the ABMP certification exam.

Research Facilities

Research equipment in the Plasma Physics Laboratory includes a toroidal high-beta tokamak for basic and applied research, a steady-state plasma experiment using a linear magnetic mirror, a large laboratory collisionless terrella used to investigate space plasma physics. A laser for Wakefield experimentation is available for research at Brookhaven National Laboratory, and an rf linac accelerator test facility is available at Yale. The plasma physics group is jointly constructing a new plasma confinement experiment, LDX, with MIT, incorporating a levitated superconducting ring. The plasma physics group is also actively involved in the NSTX experiment at the Princeton Plasma Physics Laboratory and on the DIII-D Tokamak at General Atomics in San Diego. A stellarator is under construction at Columbia to study nonneutral and antimatter plasmas. Research equipment in the solid-state physics and quantum electronics laboratories includes extensive laser and spectroscopy facilities, a microfabrication laboratory, ultra high-vacuum surface preparation and analysis chambers, direct laser writing stations, a molecular beam epitaxy machine, picosecond and femtosecond lasers, and diamond anvil cells. Research is also conducted in the shared characterization laboratories and clean room operated by the NSF Materials Research Science and Engineering Center and the NSF Nanoscale Science and Engineering Center. Materials science and engineering facilities include transmission and scanning electron microscopes; scanning, tunneling, and atomic force microscopes; X-ray diffractometer; ellipsometer; X-ray photoelectron spectrometer; and laser processing equipment. Magnetic electrical measurement equipment is also available.

There are research opportunities in medical physics at the Columbia–Presbyterian Medical Center, as well as at other medical institutes, employing state-of-the-art medical diagnostic imaging and treatment equipment.

The applied mathematics division is closely linked with the Lamont Doherty Earth Observatory (LDEO), with 5 faculty members sharing appointments in the Department of Earth and Environmental Sciences, and with the NASA Goddard Institute for Space Studies (GISS). There are also close ties with Columbia's Center for Computational Biology and Biomathematics (C2B2); and Columbia's Center for Computational Learning Systems (CLASS).

The department maintains an extensive network of workstations and desktop computers. The research of the plasma physics group is supported by a dedicated data acquisition/data analysis system. Computational researchers have local access to Columbia's 128-processor Linux cluster (soon to be 256 processors); to the Columbia-Brookhaven QCDOC computer, which is scheduled to expand to 10 Tflop/s; and to IBM SP and Cray X-1 systems at the National Center for Atmospheric Research and the Lawrence Berkeley and Oak Ridge National Laboratories, in the 3 Tflop/s to 10 Tflop/s performance range.

Financial Aid

Financial support is awarded on a competitive basis in the form of assistantships that provide a stipend, a tuition allowance, and medical fees. For 2004–05, the stipend for teaching assistants is $18,000 for nine months; for research assistants, the stipend is $24,000 for twelve months.

Cost of Study

For 2004–05, full-time tuition for the academic year is $30,532; for part-time study, the cost is $1008 per credit. In addition to medical fees (approximately $1600), annual fees are approximately $250.

Living and Housing Costs

The cost of on-campus, single-student housing (dormitories, suites, and apartments) ranges from $2900 to $4000 per term; married student accommodations range from $900 to $1350 per month. For the single student, a minimum of $17,000 should be allowed for board, room, and personal expenses for the academic year.

Student Group

Approximately 20,000 students attend the fifteen schools and colleges of Columbia University; more than half are graduate students. On average, the department has 100 graduate and 70 undergraduate students. The student population has a diverse and international character. Admission is highly competitive; in 2003–04, 17 percent of the application pool of 368 was admitted.

Student Outcomes

Recent Ph.D. recipients have found employment as postdoctoral research scientists at universities in the United States and abroad and as staff members in advanced technology industries and at national laboratories such as NRL. Some have secured college-level faculty positions. Most M.S. graduates continue studying for the doctorate; a few go on to medical school. M.S. graduates from the program in medical physics have secured positions in hospital departments of radiology and nuclear medicine or have entered doctoral programs.

Location

The 32-acre campus is situated in Morningside Heights on the upper west side of Manhattan. This location, 15 minutes from the heart of New York City, allows Columbia to be an integral part of the city while maintaining the character of a unique neighborhood. Cultural, recreational, and athletic opportunities abound at city museums, libraries, concert halls, theaters, restaurants, stadiums, parks, and beaches.

The University and The Department

With extensive resources and an outstanding faculty, Columbia University has played an eminent role in American education since its founding in 1754. The Department of Applied Physics and Applied Mathematics, a department at the forefront of interdisciplinary research and teaching, was established in 1978 as part of the Graduate School of Arts and Sciences and the Fu Foundation School of Engineering and Applied Sciences. The Graduate Program in Materials Science and Engineering joined the department in fall 2000.

Applying

For fall admission, applications should be submitted as follows: December 15 for doctoral, doctoral-track, and all financial aid applicants; applications for Master of Science, part-time, and nondegree candidates are reviewed on a rolling basis. Scores from the GRE General Test are required; GRE Subject Test scores are strongly urged. TOEFL scores are required for students from non-English-speaking countries.

Correspondence and Information

Chairman, Graduate Admissions Committee
200 S. W. Mudd Building, MC 4701
Columbia University
New York, New York 10027
Telephone: 212-854-4457
E-mail: seasinfo.apam@columbia.edu
World Wide Web: http://www.apam.columbia.edu

Columbia University

THE FACULTY AND THEIR RESEARCH

In the Department of Applied Physics and Applied Mathematics, theoretical and experimental research is conducted by 30 full-time faculty members, 11 adjunct professors, and 42 research scientists. Areas of research include applied mathematics, atmospheric/space physics, surface physics, computational and geophysical fluid dynamics, condensed-matter physics, electromagnetism, free-electron lasers, materials science, medical physics, nuclear science, oceanography, optical physics, plasma physics, and fusion.

William Bailey, Assistant Professor; Ph.D., Stanford, 1999. Nanoscale magnetic films and heterostructures, materials issues in spin-polarized transport, materials engineering of magnetic dynamics.

Guillaume Bal, Associate Professor; Ph.D., Paris, 1997. Applied mathematics, wave propagation in random media and applications to time reversal, inverse problems with applications to medical imaging and earth science.

Allen H. Boozer, Professor; Ph.D., Cornell, 1970. Plasma theory, theory of magnetic confinement for fusion energy, nonlinear dynamics.

Mark A. Cane, Professor (joint with Earth and Environmental Sciences); Ph.D., MIT, 1975. Climate dynamics, physical oceanography, geophysical fluid dynamics, computational fluid dynamics.

Siu-Wai Chan, Professor; Sc.D., MIT, 1985. Nanoparticles, electronic ceramics, grain boundaries and interfaces, oxide thin films.

C. K. Chu, Professor Emeritus; Ph.D., NYU (Courant), 1959. Applied mathematics, large-scale scientific computing, fluid dynamics.

Morton B. Friedman, Professor (joint with Civil Engineering); D.Sc., NYU, 1948. Applied mathematics and mechanics, numerical analysis, parallel computing.

Irving P. Herman, Professor; Ph.D., MIT, 1977. Nanocrystals, laser diagnostics of thin-film processing, optical spectroscopy of nanostructured materials, physics of solids at high pressure, plasma processing of materials.

James Im, Professor; Ph.D., MIT, 1985. Laser-induced crystallization of thin films, phase transformations and nucleation in condensed systems.

David E. Keyes, Professor; Ph.D., Harvard, 1984. Applied and computational mathematics for PDEs, computational science, parallel numerical algorithms, parallel performance analysis, PDE-constrained optimization.

Thomas C. Marshall, Professor; Ph.D., Illinois, 1960. Accelerator concepts, relativistic beams and radiation, free-electron lasers.

Michael E. Mauel, Professor; Sc.D., MIT, 1983. Plasma physics, waves and instabilities, fusion and equilibrium control; space physics; plasma processing.

Gerald A. Navratil, Professor; Ph.D., Wisconsin–Madison, 1976. Plasma physics, plasma diagnostics, fusion reactor design.

Gertrude Neumark, Professor; Ph.D., Columbia, 1979. Materials science and physics of semiconductors, with emphasis on optical and electrical properties of wide bandgap semiconductors and their light-emitting devices.

Stephen O'Brien, Assistant Professor; Ph.D., Oxford, 1998. Inorganic materials science, synthesis of novel nanocrystals, molecule-based nanoscale design.

Richard M. Osgood, Professor (joint with Electrical Engineering); Ph.D., MIT, 1973. Lasers, quantum electronics, two-dimensional physics, integrated optics, nanofabrication.

Thomas S. Pedersen, Assistant Professor; Ph.D., MIT, 2000. Plasma physics, magnetic confinement, plasma turbulence, non-neutral plasmas, positron-electron plasmas, antimatter plasmas.

Aron Pinczuk, Professor; Ph.D., Pennsylvania, 1969. Spectroscopy of semiconductors and insulators; quantum structures and interfaces; electrons in systems of reduced dimensions.

Lorenzo M. Polvani, Professor; Ph.D., MIT, 1988. Atmospheric, oceanic, and planetary science; geophysical fluid dynamics; computational fluid mechanics.

Malvin A. Ruderman, Professor (joint with Physics); Ph.D., Caltech, 1947. Theoretical astrophysics, neutron stars, pulsars, early universe, cosmic gamma rays.

Christopher H. Scholz, Professor (joint with Earth and Environmental Sciences); Ph.D., MIT, 1967. Experimental and theoretical rock mechanics, especially friction, fracture, and hydraulic transport properties; nonlinear systems; mechanics of earthquakes and faulting.

Amiya K. Sen, Professor (joint with Electrical Engineering); Ph.D., Columbia, 1963. Plasma physics, fluctuations and anomalous transport in plasmas, control of plasma instabilities.

Adam Sobel, Associate Professor; Ph.D., MIT, 1998. Atmospheric science, geophysical fluid dynamics, tropical meteorology, climate dynamics.

Marc Spiegelman, Associate Professor; Ph.D., Cambridge, 1989. Coupled fluid/solid mechanics, reactive fluid flow, solid earth and magma dynamics, scientific computation/modeling.

Horst Stormer, Professor; Ph.D., Stuttgart, 1977. Semiconductors, electronic transport, lower-dimensional physics.

Wen I. Wang, Professor (joint with Electrical Engineering); Ph.D., Cornell, 1981. Heterostructure devices and physics, materials properties, molecular beam epitaxy.

Michael I. Weinstein, Professor; Ph.D., NYU (Courant), 1982. Nonlinear partial differential equations and analysis; applied mathematics; waves in nonlinear, inhomogeneous, and random media; dynamical systems; homogenization; multiscale phenomena; applications to nonlinear optics; communications; fluid dynamics; mathematical physics.

Chris H. Wiggins, Assistant Professor; Ph.D., Princeton, 1998. Applied mathematics, mathematical biology, biopolymer dynamics, soft condensed matter, genetic networks and network inference, machine learning.

Cheng Shie Wuu, Professor (joint with Radiation Oncology); Ph.D., Kansas, 1985. Microdosimetry, biophysical modeling, dosimetry of brachytherapy, gel dosimetry, medical physics.

The Schapiro Center for Engineering and Physical Science Research; to the right, the Seeley W. Mudd Building, home of the Fu Foundation School of Engineering and Applied Science.

Faculty, research staff, and students of the Plasma Physics Laboratory in front of the Tokamak, HBT-EP.

Low Memorial Library and grounds.

SELECTED PUBLICATIONS

Reidy, S., L. Cheng, and **W. E. Bailey.** Dopants for independent control of precessional frequency and damping in $Ni_{81}Fe_{19}$(50 nm). *Appl. Phys. Lett.* 82(8):1254–6, 2003.

Bailey, W. E., et al. Control of magnetization dynamics in $Ni_{81}Fe_{19}$ thin films through the use of rare-earth dopants. *IEEE Trans.* 37(4):1749–55, 2001.

Bailey, W. E., et al. Electronic scattering from Co/Cu interfaces: In-situ measurement and comparison with theory. *Phys. Rev. B* 61(2):1330–6, 2000.

Bailey, W. E., et al. Direct measurement of surface scattering in GMR spin valves. *Appl. Phys.* 85(10), 1999.

Bal, G., and L. Ryzhik. Time reversal and refocusing in random media. *SIAM J. Appl. Math.* 63(5):1475–98, 2003.

Bal, G. Transport through diffusive and non-diffusive regions, embedded objects, and clear layers. *SIAM J. Appl. Math.* 62(5):1677–97, 2002.

Bal, G., G. Papanicolaou and L. Ryzhik. Radiative transport limit for the random Schroedinger equation. *Nonlinearity* 15:513–29, 2002.

Bal, G. Inverse problems for homogeneous transport equations. Parts I and II. *Inverse Problems* 16:997–1028, 2000.

Williams, J. D., and **A. H. Boozer.** Delta-f method to calculate plasma transport and rotation damping. *Phys. Plasmas* 10:103–11, 2003.

Boozer, A. H. Reconnection and the ideal evolution of magnetic fields. *Phys. Rev. Lett.* 88:215005, 2002.

Hudson, S. R., et al. **(A. H. Boozer).** Eliminating islands in high-pressure free-boundary stellarator magnetohydrodynamic equilibrium solutions. *Phys. Rev. Lett.* 89:275003, 2000.

Cane, M. A., and P. Molnar. Closing of the Indonesian Seaway as a precursor to east African aridification around 3–4 million years ago. *Nature,* 411:157–62, 2001.

Israeli, M., N. Naik, and **M. A. Cane.** An unconditionally stable scheme for the shallow water equations. *Mon. Wea. Rev.* 128:810–23, 1999.

Clement, A., R. Seager, and **M. A. Cane.** Orbital controls on tropical climate. *Paleoceanography* 14:441–56, 1999.

Cane, M. A., et al. Twentieth-century sea surface temperature trends. *Science* 275:957–60, 1997.

Tian, C., and **S.-W. Chan.** Electrical conductivities of $(CeO_2)_{1-x}(Y_2O_3)_x$ thin films. *J. Am. Ceram. Soc.* 85(9):2222–9, 2002.

Perebeinos, V., **S.-W. Chan,** and F. Zhang. Madelung-model prediction for the lattice constant scaling with the size of ionic nanocrystals of CeO_2 and $BaTiO_3$. *Solid State Commun.* 123(6–7): 295–7, 2002.

Jin, Q., and **S.-W. Chan.** Grain boundary faceting in ybco bicrystal thin films on $SrTiO_3$ substrates. *J. Mater. Res.* 17:323–35, 2002.

Zhang, F., and **S.-W. Chan** et al. **(I. P. Herman).** Cerium oxide nanoparticles: Size-selective formation and structure analysis. *Appl. Phys. Lett.* 80:127, 2002.

Chefter, J. G., **C. K. Chu,** and E. E. Keyes. Domain decomposition for shallow water equations. In *Contemporary Mathematics, Proceedings of the 7th International Conference on Domain Decomposition Methods in Science and Engineering,* October 1993.

Yin, F. L., I. Y. Fung, and **C. K. Chu.** Equilibrium response of ocean deep-water circulation to variations in Ekman pumping and deep-water sources. *J. Phys. Oceanogr.* 22:1129, 1992.

Chaiken, J., **C. K. Chu,** M. Tabor, and Q. M. Tan. Lagrangian turbulence in Stokes flow. *Phys. Fluids* 30:687, 1987.

Chu, C. K., L. W. Xiang, and Y. Baransky. Solitary waves generated by boundary motion. *Comm. Pure Appl. Math.* 36:495, 1983.

Chen, J., B. E. Carlson, and **A. D. Del Genio.** Evidence for strengthening of the tropical general circulation in the 1990s. *Science* 295:838, 2002.

Del Genio, A. D., and W. Kovari. Climatic properties of tropical precipitating convection under varying environmental conditions. *J. Climate* 15:2597, 2002.

Yao, M.-S., and **A. D. Del Genio.** Effects of cloud parameterization on the simulation of climate changes in the GISS GCM. Part II: Sea surface temperature and cloud feedbacks. *J. Climate* 15:2491, 2002.

Del Genio, A. D., and A. B. Wolf. The temperature dependence of the liquid water path of low clouds in the Southern Great Plains. *J. Climate* 13:3465–86, 2000.

Islam, M. A., and **I. P. Herman.** Electrodeposition of patterned CdSe nanocrystal films using thermally charged nanocrystals. *Appl. Phys. Lett.* 80:3823, 2002.

Kim, B., et al. **(I. P. Herman).** Organic ligand and solvent kinetics during the self assembly of CdSe nanocrystal arrays using infrared attenuated total reflection. *Appl. Phys. Lett.* 76:3715–7, 2000.

Choe, J. Y., et al. **(I. P. Herman).** Transient plasma-induced emission analysis of laser-desorbed species during Cl_2 plasma etching of Si. *J. Vac. Sci. Technol. A* 18:2669–79, 2000.

Herman, I. P. *Optical Diagnostics for Thin Film Processing.* San Diego, California: Academic Press, 1996.

Im, J. S., et al. Controlled super-lateral growth of Si films for microstructural manipulation and optimization. *Phys. Status Solidi* 166:603, 1998.

Crowder, M. A., et al. **(J. S. Im).** Low-temperature single-crystal Si TFTs fabricated on Si films processed via sequential lateral solidification. *IEEE Electron Device Lett.* 19:306, 1998.

Im, J. S., V. V. Gupta, and M. A. Crowder. On determining the relevance of athermal nucleation in rapidly quenched liquids. *Appl. Phys. Lett.* 72:662, 1998.

Gupta, V. V., H. J. Song, and **J. S. Im.** Numerical analysis of excimer-laser induced melting and solidification of thin Si films. *Appl. Phys. Lett.* 71:99, 1997.

Knoll, D. A., and **D. E. Keyes.** Jacobian-free Newton-Krylov methods: A survey of approaches and application. *J. Comp. Phys.* 193:357, 2004.

Keyes, D. E. (ed.) A science-based case for large-scale simulation. *U. S. DOE Office of Science, www.pnl.gov/scales,* 2003.

Coffey, T. S., et al. **(D. E. Keyes).** Pseudo-transient continuation and differential-algebraic equations. *SIAM J. Sci. Comp.* 25:553–69, 2003.

Keyes, D. E. Domain decomposition methods in the mainstream of computational science. *Proceedings of the 14th International Conference on Domain Decomposition Methods, UNAM Press, Mexico City,* 79–93, 2003.

Marshall, T. C., et al. Wake fields excited in a micron-scale dielectric rectangular structure by a train of femtosecond bunches. *Advanced Accelerator Concepts Tenth Workshop in AIP Conference Proceedings* (eds. C. E. Clayton and P. Muggli) 647:361, 2002.

Schlhelkunov, S. V., et al. **(T. C. Marshall).** Status report on the lacara experiment. *Advanced Accelerator Concepts Tenth Workshop in AIP Conference Proceedings* (eds. C. E. Clayton and P. Muggli) 647:349, 2002.

Marshall, T. C., C. Wang, and J. L. Hirshfield. Femtosecond planar electron beam source for micron-scale dielectric wake field accelerators. *Phys. Rev. Special Top. Accel. Beams* 4:121301, 2001.

Yoder, R. B., **T. C. Marshall,** and J. L. Hirshfield. Energy-gain measurements from a microwave inverse free-electron-laser accelerator. *Phys. Rev. Lett.* 86:1765, 2001.

Kesner, J., et al. **(M. E. Mauel).** Helium-catalyzed D-D fusion in a levitated dipole. *Nucl. Fusion* 44:193–203, 2004.

Maslovsky, D., B. Levitt, and **M. E. Mauel.** Observation of nonlinear frequency-sweeping suppression with rf diffusion. *Phys. Rev. Lett.* 90:185001, 2003.

Levitt, B., D. Maslovsky, and **M. E. Mauel.** Measurement of the global structure of interchange modes driven by energetic electrons trapped in a magnetic dipole. *Phys. Plasmas* 9:2507–17, 2002.

Kesner, J., et al. **(M. E. Mauel).** Dipole equilibrium and stability. *Nucl. Fusion* 41:301–8, 2001.

Cates, C., et al. **(M. E. Mauel** and **G. A. Navratil).** Suppression of resistive wall instabilities with distributed, independently controlled, active feedback coils. *Phys. Plasmas* 7:3133–6, 2000.

Garofalo, A. M., et al. **(G. A. Navratil).** Sustained rotational stabilization of DIII-D plasmas above the no-wall beta limit. *Phys. Plasmas* 9:1997, 2002.

Bialek, James, et al. **(G. A. Navratil).** Modeling of active control of external MHD instabilities. *Phys. Plasmas* 8:2170, 2001.

Navratil, G. A., et al. **(M. E. Mauel).** Active control of 2/1 magnetic islands in a tokamak. *Phys. Plasmas* 5:1855, 1998.

Lazarus, E. A., and **G. A. Navratil** et al. Higher fusion power gain with profile control in DIII-D tokamak plasmas. *Nucl. Fusion* 37:7, 1997.

Gu, Y., et al. **(G. F. Neumark).** Determination of size and composition of optically active CdZnSe/ZnBeSe quantum dots. *Appl. Phys. Lett.* 83:3779, 2003.

Kuskovsky, I., **G. F. Neumark,** V. N. Bondarer, and P. V. Pikhitsa. Decay dynamics in disordered systems: Application to heavily doped semiconductors. *Phys. Rev. Lett.* 80:2413, 1998.

Neumark, G. F. Defects In wide bandgap II-VI crystals. *Mat. Sci. Eng. Rep.* R,21:1. Amsterdam: Elsevier, 1997.

Neumark, G. F. Wide bandgap light-emitting device materials and doping problems. *Mat. Lett.* 30:131, 1997 (published as materials update).

Levine, Z., et al. **(I. C. Noyan).** Imaging material components of an integrated circuit interconnect. *J. Appl. Phys.* 95:405, 2004.

Murray, C. E., and **I. C. Noyan,** et al. Mapping of strain fields about thin-film structures using X-ray microdiffraction. *Appl. Phys. Lett.* 83:4163, 2003.

Kaldor, S. K., and **I. C. Noyan.** Differentiating between elastically bent rectangular beams and plates. *Appl. Phys. Lett.* 80:2284, 2002.

Columbia University

Selected Publications (continued)

Wang, P.-C., et al. **(I. C. Noyan).** Real-time X-ray microbeam characterization of electromigration effects in Al(Cu) wires. *Appl. Phys. Lett.* 78:2712, 2001.

Turro, N. J., et al. **(S. O'Brien).** Spectroscopic probe of the surface of iron oxide nanocrystals. *Nanoletters* 2(4):325–32, 2002.

O'Brien, S., et al. Synthesis and characterization of nanocrystals of barium titanate, towards a generalized synthesis of oxide nanoparticles. *J. Am. Chem. Soc.,* 2001.

O'Brien, S., et al. Time-resolved in situ X-ray powder diffraction study of the formation of mesoporous silicates. *Chem. Mat.* 11:1822–32, 1999.

Ahmad, R. U., et al. **(R. M. Osgood Jr.).** Ultra-compact corner-mirrors and t-branches in silicon-on-insulator. *Photon. Tech. Lett.* 14:65–7, 2002.

Radojevic, A. M., **R. M. Osgood Jr.,** N. A. Roy, and H. Bakhru. Prepatterned optical circuits in thin ion-sliced single-crystal films of $LiNbO_3$. *Photon. Tech. Lett.* 14:322–4, 2002.

Shen, X. J., et al. **(R. M. Osgood Jr.).** Momentum-resolved excited-electron lifetimes on stepped Cu (775). *Chem. Phys. Lett.* 351:1–8, 2001.

Luo, Y., et al. **(R. M. Osgood Jr.).** Low-temperature, chemically driven atomic layer epitaxy: In situ monitored growth of CdS/ZnSe100. *Appl. Phys. Lett.* 71:3799, 1997.

Pedersen, T. S., et al. Prospects for the creation of positron-electron plasmas in a nonneutral stellarator. *J. Phys. B* 36:1029, 2003.

Pedersen, T. S. Numerical investigation of two-dimensional pure electron plasma equilibria on magnetic surfaces. *Phys. Plasmas* 10:334, 2003.

Pedersen, T. S., and **A. H. Boozer.** Confinement of nonneutral plasmas on magnetic surfaces. *Phys. Rev. Lett.* 88:205002, 2002.

Pedersen, T. S., et al. Radial impurity transport in the H-Mode transport barrier region in Alcator C-Mod. *Nucl. Fusion* 40:1795, 2000.

He, R., and **A. Pinczuk** et al. Resonant Raman scattering in nanoscale pentacene films. *Appl. Phys. Lett.* 84:7, 2004.

Hirjibejedin, C. F., and **A. Pinczuk** et al. Crossover and coexistence of quasiparticle excitations in the fractional quantum Hall regime at nu>⅓. *Phys. Rev. Lett.* 91:186802, 2003.

Dujovne, I., and **A. Pinczuk** et al. Evidence of Landau levels and interactions in low-lying excitations of composite fermions at $1/3 \leq \upsilon \leq 2/5$ *Phys. Rev. Lett.* 90:036803, 2003.

Kang, M., et al. **(A. Pinczuk).** Observation of multiple magnetorotons in the fractional quantum Hall effect. *Phys. Rev. Lett.* 86:2637, 2001.

Pellegrini, V., et al. **(A. Pinczuk).** Evidence of soft-mode quantum phase transitions in electron double layers. *Science* 181:799, 1998.

Polvani, L. M., and P. J. Kushner. Tropospheric response to stratospheric perturbations in a relatively simple general circulation model. *Geophys. Res. Lett.* 29, 2002.

Rivier, L., R. Loft, and **L. M. Polvani.** An efficient spectral dynamical core for distributed memory computers, *Mon. Weather Rev.* 130:1384–96, 2002.

Polvani, L. M., and R. Saravanan. The three-dimensional structure of breaking Rossby waves in the polar wintertime stratosphere. *J. Atmos. Sci.* 57:3663–85, 2000.

Polvani, L. M., et al. Simple dynamical models of Neptune's Great Dark Spot. *Science* 249:1393–8, 1990.

Cho, J. Y.-K., and **L. M. Polvani.** The morphogenesis of bands and zonal winds with the atmospheres of the giant outer plants. *Science* 273:335–7, 1996.

Ruderman, M., L. Tao, and W. Kluzniak. A central engine for cosmic gamma-ray burst sources. *Astrophys. J.* 542:243, 2000.

Ruderman, M., K. Chen, and T. Zhu. Millisecond pulsar alignment: PSR 0437–47. *Astrophys. J.* 493:397, 1998.

Ruderman, M., K. Chen, and T. Zhu. Neutron star magnetic field evolution, crust movement and glitches. *Astrophys. J.* 492:267, 1998.

Ruderman, M., F. Wang, J. Halpern, and T. Zhu. Models for X-ray emission from isolated pulsars. *Astrophys. J.* 498:373, 1998.

Spyropoulos, C., **C. H. Scholz,** and B. E. Shaw. Transition regimes for growing crack populations. *Phys. Rev. E* 65:056105, 2002.

Shaw, B. E., and **C. H. Scholz.** Slip-length scaling for earthquakes: Observations and theory and implications for earthquake physics. *Geophys. Res. Lett.* 28:2995–8, 2001.

Scholz, C. H. Evidence of a strong San Andreas fault. *Geology* 28:163–6, 2000.

Spyropoulos, C., W. J. Griffith, **C. H. Scholz,** and B. E. Shaw. Experimental evidence for different strain regimes of crack populations in a clay model. *Geophys. Res. Lett.* 26:1081–4, 1999.

Bose, T., and **A. K. Sen.** A basic experiment on isotope scaling of transport. *Phys. Plasmas,* 2001.

Sen, A. K., et al. A hybrid ion temperature gradient and Kelvin-Helmholtz instability. *Phys. Plasmas,* 2001.

Chiu, J. S., and **A. K. Sen.** Experimental determination of attractor dimension of $E \times B$ turbulence. *Phys. Plasmas* 1:4492, 2000.

Sen, A. K., and J. C. Chiu. Control and diagnostic uses of feedback. *Phys. Plasmas,* 2000.

Sobel, A. H., and H. Gildor. A simple model of SST hot spots. *J. Climate* 16:3978–92, 2003.

Sobel, A. H., J. Nilsson, and L. M. Polvani. The weak temperature gradient approximation and balanced tropical moisture waves. *J. Atmos. Sci.* 58:3650–65, 2001.

Sobel, A. H., and C. S. Bretherton. Modeling tropical precipitation in a single-column. *J. Climate* 13:4378–92, 2000.

Sobel, A. H., and R. A. Plumb. Quantitative diagnostics of mixing in a shallow-water model of the stratosphere. *J. Atmos. Sci.* 56:2811–29, 1999.

Spiegelman M., and P. B. Kelemen. Extreme chemical variability as a consequence of channelized melt transport. *Geochem. Geophys. Geosyst.,* in press.

Spiegelman M., P. B. Kelemen, and E. Aharonov. Causes and consequences of flow organization during melt transport. *J. Geophys. Res.* 106:2061–77, 2001.

Spiegelman, M., and J. Reynolds. Combined theoretical and observational evidence for convergent melt flow beneath the {EPR}. *Nature* 402:282–5, 1999.

Spiegelman, M. Flow in deformable porous media: Parts I and II. *J. Fluid Mech.* 247:17–63, 1993.

Pan, W., et al. **(H. L. Stormer).** Fractional quantum Hall effect of composite fermions. *Phys. Rev. Lett.* 90:16801, 2003.

Zhu, J., et al. **(H. L. Stormer).** Spin susceptibility of an ultra-low density, two-dimensional electron gas system. *Phys. Rev. Lett.* 90:056805, 2003.

Syed, S., et al. **(H. L. Stormer).** Large splitting of the cyclotron-resonance line in AlGaN/GaN heterostructures. *Phys. Rev. B* 67:241304, 2003.

De Picciotto, R., et al **(H. L. Stormer).** Four-terminal resistance of a ballistic quantum wire. *Nature* 411:51, 2001.

Kang, W., et al. **(H. L. Stormer).** Tunneling between the edges of two lateral quantum Hall systems. *Nature* 403:59, 2000.

Stormer, H. L. The fractional quantum Hall effect. *Rev. Mod. Phys.* 71:875, 1999.

Katz, J., Y. Zhang, and **W. I. Wang.** Normal incidence intervalence subband absorption in GaSb quantum well enhanced by coupling to InAs conduction band. *Appl. Phys. Lett.* 62:609–11, 1993.

Katz, J., Y. Zhang, and **W. I. Wang.** Normal incidence infrared absorption in AlAs/AlGaAs x-valley multiquantum wells. *Appl. Phys. Lett.* 61:1697–9, 1992.

Li, X., K. F. Longenbach, Y. Wang, and **W. I. Wang.** High breakdown voltage AlSbAs/InAs n-channel field effect transistors. *IEEE Electron Dev. Lett.* 13:192–4, 1992.

Golowich, S., and **M. I. Weinstein.** Homogenization expansion for resonances of microstructured photonic waveguides. *J. Opt. Soc. Am. B: Opt. Phys.* 20(4):633–47, 2003.

Goodman, R. H., R. E. Slusher, and **M. I. Weinstein.** Stopping light on a defect. *J. Opt. Soc. B: Opt. Phys.* 19(7):1635–52, 2002.

Soffer, A., and **M. I. Weinstein.** Resonances, radiation damping and instability of Hamiltonian nonlinear waves. *Inventiones Mathematicae* 136:9–74, 1999.

Weinstein, M. I. Lyapunov stability of ground states of nonlinear dispersive evolution equations. *Comm. Pure Appl. Math.* 39:51–68, 1985.

Wiggins, C. H. Biopolymer mechanics: Stability, dynamics, and statistics. *Math. Methods Appl. Sci.,* in press. (Special themed issue: Biofluiddynamics—In Memory of Sir James Lighthill.)

Belmonte, A., et al **(C. H. Wiggins).** Patterns and self-knotting of a driven hanging chain. *Phys. Rev. Lett.* 87:114301, 2001.

Goldstein, R. E., T. R. Powers, and **C. H. Wiggins.** The viscous nonlinear dynamics of twist and writhe. Phys. Rev. Lett. 80:5232, 1998.

Wiggins, C. H., et al. Trapping and wiggling: Elastohydrodynamics of driven microfilaments. *Biophys. J.* 74:1043, 1998.

Wuu, C. S., et al. Dosimetry study of Re-188 liquid balloon for intravascular brachytherapy using polymer gel dosimeters and laser-beam optical CT scanner. *Med. Phys.* 30(2):132–7, 2003.

Wuu, C. S., et al. Dosimetric and volumetric criteria for selecting a source activity and/or a source type (I-125 or Pd-103) in the presence of irregular seed placement in permanent prostate implants. *Int. J. Radiat. Oncol. Biol. Phys.* 47:815–20, 2000.

Wuu, C. S., et al. Microdosimetric evaluation of relative biological effectiveness for Pd-103, I-125, Am-241 and Ir-192 brachytherapy sources. *Int. J. Radiat. Oncol. Biol. Phys.* 36:689–97, 1996.

Wuu, C. S., and M. Zaider. A mathematical description of sublethal damage repair and interaction for continuous low-dose rate irradiation. *Radiat. Protection Dosimetry* 52:211–5, 1994.

FLORIDA STATE UNIVERSITY

Department of Physics

Programs of Study

The Department of Physics at Florida State University (FSU) offers programs of study that lead to the M.S. and Ph.D. degrees. The department has approximately 40 teaching faculty members, including Nobel Laureate Professor Robert Schrieffer, and another 40 Ph.D. physicists engaged in a variety of research programs. The graduate program has approximately 90 students and almost all hold research or teaching assistantships. The programs of study include experimental and theoretical atomic, condensed-matter, high-energy, materials science, and nuclear physics. Two University institutes have major physics research components—the Material Science and Technology Center (MARTECH) for condensed-matter physics and the National High Magnetic Field Laboratory (NHMFL) for research on materials using very high magnetic fields.

The department offers both course work only and thesis-type M.S. degrees. Five-year B.S./M.S. programs in computational physics and physics education have been introduced. All students are required to pass a proficiency examination before the middle of their second year. Students studying for the Ph.D. degree are also required to pass a comprehensive examination on electrodynamics and quantum, classical, and statistical mechanics. Within six months of passing the comprehensive examination, students should pass an oral examination on the subject of the student's prospective research. The only formal course requirement is to take three advanced topics courses and a course in field theory.

Research Facilities

The department occupies three adjacent buildings: an eight-story Physics Research Building, a Nuclear Research Building, and an undergraduate physics classroom and laboratory building. The experimental facilities include a 9.5-MV Super FN Tandem Van de Graaff accelerator with superconducting post accelerator; a large gamma detection array; 3- and 4-MeV Van de Graaffs; a detector development laboratory for high-energy particle detectors; facilities for ion implantation; liquid helium temperature research facilities; UHV facilities (including surface characterization, molecular beam epitaxy, and surface analysis by He atom scattering); facilities for high- and low-temperature superconductivity, small-angle and standard X-ray diffractometry, scanning electron and tunneling microscopy, image analysis, quasi-elastic light scattering, polarized electron energy loss spectroscopy, thick- and thin-film preparation, and high magnetic field studies; and the National High Magnetic Field Laboratory. In addition to using in-house facilities, those engaged in ongoing experiments use accelerator and other research equipment at Fermilab, Brookhaven, Los Alamos, MIT-Bates, TJNAF, Oak Ridge, and CERN. The Department of Physics and the University have extensive computational facilities that are networked throughout the world through T1 and T3 lines. Within the department there are several clusters of state-of-the-art computer workstations comprising more than 100 individual units. More information on individual faculty research can be found on the department's Web site, which is listed in the Correspondence and Information section.

Financial Aid

The department offers teaching and research assistantships and fellowships. The fellowships include several that are designed to help develop promising young minority physicists. The assistantship stipend is $17,000 for twelve months, with a workload equivalent to 6 contact hours in an elementary laboratory. In general, summer assistantships are provided for all students. Students are teaching assistants during the first academic year but most are supported by research assistantships during and after their first summer.

Cost of Study

All tuition and fees for Florida residents were covered by the department in 2003–04. The additional charge for out-of-state tuition is normally waived for assistants and fellows.

Living and Housing Costs

Apartments and houses are readily available in Tallahassee. A typical one-bedroom unfurnished apartment within walking distance of the physics building rents for $450 per month. The University has married student housing with rents that in 2003–04 ranged from $289 to $320 per month for a one-bedroom apartment to $390 to $460 per month for a two or three-bedroom apartment. National surveys show that the cost of living in Tallahassee is 10 to 15 percent lower than that in most areas of the United States.

Student Group

Florida State University is a comprehensive university with a total of 30,519 students, of whom 5,903 are graduate or professional students. The physics department has about 115 graduate students. Students entering with a B.S. degree in physics typically attain the Ph.D. within 5½ years.

Location

Tallahassee is the capital city of the state of Florida. Its population is about 185,000. Many employment opportunities exist for students' spouses in Tallahassee. Students can live in relatively rural surroundings and still be only 20 minutes from the University. Extensive sports facilities and active city leagues exist in the city. Graduate students' fees cover membership in a state-of-the-art, on-campus recreation center. Because of the mild winter climate, people in this region tend to be outdoor oriented. The Gulf of Mexico is about 30 miles from campus.

The University and The Department

The presentations of the Schools of Fine Arts and Music provide cultural opportunities that are usually available only in much larger cities. The University Symphony, the Flying High Circus, and other theater and music groups give students the opportunity to participate in many activities in addition to their physics studies. FSU has active programs in intercollegiate and intramural sports.

Recent major additions in the FSU Science Center have been an interdisciplinary Materials Sciences and Technology Center and the National High Magnetic Field Laboratory. The NHMFL houses the world's highest field D.C. magnets, making FSU one of the principal centers for magnetic research. In addition to the teaching faculty at the Department of Physics, there are 8 research faculty members at the NHMFL.

Applying

Assistantship decisions are based on a student's transcript, GRE General Test scores, and three letters of reference. The deadline for completed applications to be on file with the physics department is January 15 for international students and February 15 for U.S. citizens. Application forms can be printed from the department's Web site.

Correspondence and Information

Professor Simon Capstick
Graduate Physics Program
Department of Physics
Florida State University
Tallahassee, Florida 32306-4350

Telephone: 850-644-4473
Fax: 850-644-8630
E-mail: graduate@hep.fsu.edu
World Wide Web: http://www.physics.fsu.edu

Florida State University

THE FACULTY AND THEIR RESEARCH

Todd Adams, Assistant Professor; Ph.D., Notre Dame, 1997. Experimental high-energy physics, particle physics, supersymmetry.
Howard Baer, Professor; Ph.D., Wisconsin–Madison, 1984. Theoretical physics: elementary particle physics.
Bernd Berg, Professor; Ph.D., Berlin, 1977. Theoretical physics: statistical mechanics, lattice gauge theory, quantum measurement process, computational physics.
Susan K. Blessing, Associate Professor; Ph.D., Indiana, 1989. Experimental physics: elementary particle physics.
Gregory S. Boebinger, Professor and Director, National High Magnetic Field Laboratory; Ph.D., Massachusetts, 1986. High magnetic fields.
Nicholas Bonesteel, Associate Professor; Ph.D., Cornell, 1991. Theoretical physics: condensed-matter physics, many-body theory, magnetism, quantum Hall effect.
James S. Brooks, Professor; Ph.D., Oregon, 1973. Experimental physics: low temperature, high–magnetic field condensed matter, organic conductor, quantum fluid physics.
Jianming Cao, Assistant Professor; Ph.D., Rochester, 1996. Experimental condensed-matter physics, ultrafast dynamics probed by lasers.
Simon C. Capstick, Associate Professor; Ph.D., Toronto, 1986. Theoretical physics: theoretical nuclear and particle physics, computational physics.
Paul Cottle, Professor; Ph.D., Yale, 1986. Experimental physics: heavy-ion nuclear physics, teacher preparation.
Jack Crow, Professor; Ph.D., Rochester, 1967. Experimental physics: correlated electron systems, high-T_c superconductors and heavy fermions.
Lawrence C. Dennis, Professor; Ph.D., Virginia, 1979. Experimental physics: intermediate-energy, electron-scattering, and computational physics.
Vladimir Dobrosavljivic, Associate Professor; Ph.D, Brown, 1988. Theoretical condensed-matter physics, disordered systems and glasses, metal-insulator transitions.
Dennis Duke, Professor; Ph.D., Iowa State, 1974. Theoretical physics: elementary particle physics, computational physics.
Paul M. Eugenio, Assistant Professor; Ph.D., Massachusetts Amherst, 1998. Experimental nuclear/particle physics, search for new mesons.
Yuri Gershstein, Assistant Professor; Ph.D., Moscow, 1996. Experimental elementary particle physics.
Vasken Hagopian, Professor; Ph.D., Pennsylvania, 1963. Experimental physics: elementary particle physics.
Kirby Kemper, Professor; Ph.D., Indiana, 1968. Experimental physics: polarization studies of nuclear reactions, radioactive-beam physics.
David M. Lind, Associate Professor; Ph.D., Rice, 1986. Experimental physics: surfaces, thin films, magnetic properties of solids, magnetic and oxide superlattices.
Efstratios Manousakis, Professor; Ph.D., Illinois at Urbana-Champaign, 1985. Theoretical physics: condensed-matter physics, many-body theory, superfluidity, superconductivity.
H. K. Ng, Associate Professor; Ph.D., McMaster, 1984. Experimental condensed-matter physics: far-infrared spectroscopy, superconductivity, highly correlated electron systems, spectroscopy in high-magnetic fields.
Joseph F. Owens, Professor; Ph.D., Tufts, 1973. Theoretical physics: elementary particle theory.
Jorge Piekarewicz, Associate Professor; Ph.D., Pennsylvania, 1985. Theoretical physics, interface between nuclear and particle theory.
Hans S. Plendl, Professor Emeritus; Ph.D., Yale, 1958. Experimental physics: medium-energy nuclear and particle physics.
Harrison B. Prosper, Professor; Ph.D., Manchester (England), 1980. Experimental physics: particle physics, computational physics.
Laura Reina, Assistant Professor; Ph.D., Trieste, 1992. Theoretical physics: elementary particle physics.
Per Arne Rikvold, Professor; Ph.D., Temple, 1983. Theoretical physics: condensed-matter physics, surface and interface science, computational physics.
Mark A. Riley, Professor; Ph.D., Liverpool, 1985. Experimental physics: nuclear structure physics.
Grigory Rogachev; Ph.D., Kurchatov Institute (Moscow), 1999. Experimental nuclear physics: nuclear structure.
Pedro Schlottmann, Professor; Ph.D., Munich Technical, 1973. Theoretical physics: condensed-matter physics, heavy fermions, magnetism, correlated electrons in one dimension.
Robert Schrieffer, Professor; Ph.D., Illinois, 1957. Theoretical physics: condensed matter, many-body theory, superconductivity, magnetism.
Shahid A. Shaheen, Associate Professor; Ph.D., Ruhr-Bochum, 1985. Experimental physics: permanent magnets, superconductivity, magnetism, materials science.
Samuel L. Tabor, Professor; Ph.D., Stanford, 1972. Experimental physics: high-spin states in nuclei.
David Van Winkle, Professor and Chairman of the Department; Ph.D., Colorado, 1984. Experimental physics: liquid crystals, colloids, macromolecules, teacher preparation.
Alexander Volya, Assistant Professor; Ph.D., Michigan State, 2000. Theoretical nuclear physics, nuclear structure models.
Stephan von Molnár, Professor; Ph.D., California, Riverside, 1965. Experimental physics: correlation effects in electronic systems, magnetic semiconductors, magnetic nanostructures.
Horst Wahl, Professor; Ph.D., Vienna, 1969. Experimental physics: particle physics.
Ingo Wiedenhöver, Assistant Professor; Ph.D., Cologne (Germany), 1995. Nuclear experimental physics, complete gamma spectroscopy of 127 xe.
Peng Xiong, Assistant Professor; Ph.D., Brown, 1994. Experimental physics, mesoscopic physics, quantum-phase transitions in low-dimensional systems, electron tunneling into complex solids.
Kun Yang, Assistant Professor; Ph.D., Indiana, 1994. Theoretical physics: condensed matter, computational physics.

RESEARCH ACTIVITIES

Theoretical

Condensed Matter. Many-body theory of magnetism, magnetic properties of solids, heavy fermions, high-temperature superconductivity, quantum Hall effect, metal-insulator transitions, adsorption, phase transitions, numerical simulations, quantum information theory.
Elementary Particles and Fields. Strong and electroweak interaction phenomenology in high-energy particle physics, lattice gauge theory, numerical simulations, computational quantum gravity.
Nuclear Theory. Quark models of hadrons and hadronic matter, electroproduction and photoproduction studies of hadronic systems, nuclear structure and studies of nuclear matter at extreme densities.

Experimental

Atomic and Molecular Physics. Electron scattering by atoms and molecules, infrared studies of gases of planetary atmospheres, radiation effects, studies of He-like ions.
Condensed-Matter Physics/Materials Science. Liquid crystals, magnetic nanostructures, modulated structures, surface physics, electron and optical spectroscopy, magnetic properties of solids, highly correlated electron systems.
Elementary Particles and Fields. Collider physics, strong and electroweak interactions in high-energy particle physics, detector development and simulation.
Nuclear Physics. Reactions using polarized alkali beams, studies of fragmentation, fusion, fission, properties of nuclear systems at high angular momentum and extreme shapes, electroproduction and photoproduction of hypernuclei and hyperons, nuclear octupole excitations, relativistic heavy-ion reactions, fast radioactive beams.
Surface Physics. He-surface scattering, clusters, electron spectroscopies.
K–12 Education. Techniques for in-service and science teacher preparation.

GEORGIA INSTITUTE OF TECHNOLOGY

School of Physics

Programs of Study

The primary aim of the graduate program in physics is to train innovative and productive scientists with a thorough knowledge of basic physics and the ability to effectively approach original research problems in academia and industry. Major areas of research include condensed-matter and materials physics; atomic, molecular, and chemical physics; optical physics; nonlinear dynamics, chaos, and statistical physics; computational physics; and physics of nanoscopic systems.

The Ph.D. program consists of formal course work and original research leading to a doctoral thesis. A student becomes a candidate for the Ph.D. degree after passing a comprehensive exam, usually at the beginning of the second year. A review course is offered each summer to assist students in their preparation. A typical Ph.D. program consists of course work in the first year, a combination of classes and research in the second, and mainly research thereafter. The median time to earn a Ph.D. is 5½ years.

The M.S. degree in physics is acquired by completing a two-semester sequence of lecture-style courses. In addition, students are required to include a research component through either special problems courses or a written master's thesis that replaces one third of the course work.

Research Facilities

The Howey Physics Building offers ample space and modern facilities for experimental and theoretical research. Equipment for condensed-matter research includes a scanning probe microscope; nanotube and fullerene generator; high-power excimer laser; tunable solid-state laser (IR to UV); ultra-low-temperature nanoparticle source; high-resolution mass spectrometer; molecular beam apparatus; ultra-high-vacuum, high-resolution, low-energy electron diffractometer; X-ray diffraction beam line (at the Advanced Photon Source); dilution refrigerator; cryoevaporator; cryogenic scanning tunneling microscope; ballistic electron emission microscope; and a field ion microscope. Atomic, molecular, and chemical physics equipment includes atom-trapping apparatus, chemical laser systems, spectroscopes, and a time-of-flight mass spectrometer. The optical physics instruments are amplified and unamplified Ti:Sapphire femtosecond laser systems, laser-related diagnostic equipment, and a phase-shifting interferometer. The nonlinear dynamics/chaos group has a high-speed image acquisition system, and the Center for Computational Materials Science in the School of Physics has an IBM RS/6000 supercomputer. Students have access to the Oak Ridge Nuclear Laboratories in Tennessee. The support facilities include a fine machine shop and an electronics fabrication/repair facility staffed by expert personnel.

Financial Aid

Ph.D. students typically receive a tuition waiver and financial support through teaching assistantships, research assistantships, or fellowships. No support is available for students enrolled in the M.S. programs.

Exceptional domestic students are eligible for a Presidential Fellowship. This award carries an extra stipend (currently $5500 per year for four years) in addition to the standard assistantship stipend. There are no extra duties. Applicants with a high GPA are urged to apply early to ensure consideration for the fellowships. The School of Physics makes the nomination; no further action is required by the applicant.

Cost of Study

As a state school, Georgia Tech is considerably less expensive than other private universities with comparable reputations. Each year, both *Money* magazine and *U.S. News & World Report* consistently rate Georgia Tech as one of the nation's best academic values. For 2003–04, graduate tuition fees for Georgia residents (and those with an assistantship) are approximately $450 per semester for full-time students.

Living and Housing Costs

A limited number of Institute-owned apartments are available for students. A large number of private apartments are also available near the campus. For information, students should visit http://www.housing.gatech.edu.

Student Group

An energetic and dedicated faculty provides stimulating programs of graduate study in a department of medium size. About 30 faculty members, several research scientists, and 130 graduate students form a research community where the informal exchange of ideas and close student-faculty interactions are encouraged. Georgia Tech has an enrollment of 17,000, of whom about 5,000 are graduate students.

Location

Georgia Tech is a self-contained campus near the center of Atlanta, one of the most vibrant cities in the United States. With a population of 3 million, Atlanta serves as the regional melting pot for a wide range of recreational, cultural, intellectual, and social resources, including theaters, art galleries, orchestras, and historic venues. Many Fortune 500 businesses are headquartered in Atlanta. The city is home to several professional sports teams.

The Institute

From its beginnings more than a century ago, the Georgia Institute of Technology has established a tradition of excellence in technological research and education. Georgia Tech is one of the world's premier technology-oriented universities, with a superb faculty of world-class teachers, researchers, and consultants. In addition, Georgia Tech is the South's largest industrial and engineering research agency.

Applying

Inquiries regarding information or admission to the physics graduate program should be directed to the School of Physics at the address below.

Correspondence and Information

Graduate Programs Recruiter
School of Physics
Georgia Institute of Technology
Atlanta, Georgia 30332-0430
E-mail: grad.recruiter@physics.gatech.edu
World Wide Web: http://www.physics.gatech.edu

Georgia Institute of Technology

THE FACULTY AND THEIR RESEARCH

Regent's Professors

M. Raymond Flannery, Ph.D., Queen's (Belfast), 1964. Theoretical atomic and molecular collisions.
Ronald F. Fox, Ph.D., Rockefeller, 1969. Stochastic processes, nonlinear phenomena, biophysics.
Uzi Landman, Ph.D., Israel Institute of Technology, 1969. Materials science, computational physics.
Turgay Uzer, Ph.D., Harvard, 1979. Nonlinear dynamics in atomic and molecular physics.

Professors

Jean Bellissard, Ph.D., Marseille, 1974. Mathematical physics.
Helmut Biritz, Ph.D., Vienna, 1962. Particles and fields.
Michael Chapman, Ph.D., MIT, 1995. Experimental atomic physics, quantum optics.
Mei-Yin Chou, Ph.D., Berkeley, 1986. Quantum theory of materials.
Predrag Cvitanovic, Ph.D., Cornell, 1973. Nonlinear dynamics of complex systems.
Walter A. de Heer, Ph.D., Berkeley, 1984. Experimental condensed-matter physics.
Ahmet Erbil, Ph.D., MIT, 1983. Physics of advanced materials.
James L. Gole, Ph.D., Rice, 1971. High-temperature chemical physics and material science.
T. A. Brian Kennedy, Ph.D., Queen's (Belfast), 1986. Theoretical quantum optics.
Donald C. O'Shea, Ph.D., Johns Hopkins, 1968. Optics and optical engineering.
Rick Trebino, Ph.D., Stanford, 1983. Experimental optics.
Robert L. Whetten, Ph.D., Cornell, 1984. Nanocrystal research.
Kurt Wiesenfeld, Ph.D., Berkeley, 1985. Theoretical nonlinear dynamics.
John L. Wood, Ph.D., Clark, 1971. Nuclear structure.
Li You, Ph.D., Colorado, 1993. Physics of light-matter interactions.
Andrew Zangwill, Ph.D., Pennsylvania, 1981. Epitaxial phenomena.

Associate Professors

Edward H. Conrad, Ph.D., Wisconsin, 1983. Surface physics.
Phillip First, Ph.D., Illinois, 1988. Experimental physics at the atomic scale.
Carlos Sa de Melo, Ph.D., Stanford, 1991. Theoretical condensed-matter physics, theoretical biophysics.
Michael Schatz, Ph.D., Texas at Austin, 1991. Experimental nonlinear dynamics of pattern formation.

Assistant Professors

Dragomir Davidovich, Ph.D., Johns Hopkins, 1996. Mesoscopics, low-temperature physics.
Roman Grigoriev, Ph.D., Caltech, 1998. Nonlinear dynamics of complex systems.
Alex Kuzmich, Ph.D., Rochester, 1999. Experimental atomic physics, quantum optics.
Alexei Marchenkov, Ph.D., Leiden, 1997. Experimental mesoscopics, low-temperature physics.
Michael Pustilnik, Ph.D., Bar Ilan, 1997. Condensed-matter theory.
Chandra Raman, Ph.D., Michigan, 1997. Experimental atomic physics, Bose-Einstein condensation.
Elisa Riedo, Ph.D., Milan, 2000. Condensed-matter experimental.

Adjunct Professor

Thomas Orlando, Ph.D., SUNY at Stony Brook, 1988. Nonthermal surface processes and reactions at supercooled liquid interfaces (School of Chemistry and Biochemistry, Georgia Tech).

Academic Professionals

Martin Jarrio, Ph.D., Georgia Tech, 1996. Nuclear structure.
Eric Murray, Ph.D., Cornell, 1992. Materials science.
James Sowell, Ph.D., Michigan, 1986. Astronomy.

Professors Emeriti

Tino Ahrens, Ph.D., Washington (St. Louis), 1952. Particles and fields.
David Finkelstein, Ph.D., MIT, 1953. Quantum topology.
Ian R. Gatland, Ph.D., Imperial College (London), 1960. Computational physics.
Don S. Harmer, Ph.D., UCLA, 1956. Nuclear physics.
Eugene T. Patronis, Ph.D., Georgia Tech, 1961. Acoustics.
Edward W. Thomas, Ph.D., London, 1964. Atomic collisions in solids.
Henry S. Valk, Ph.D., Washington (St. Louis), 1957. Few-body physics.
R. A. Young, Ph.D., Polytechnic of Brooklyn, 1959. Crystal physics.

HARVARD UNIVERSITY

Department of Physics

Program of Study

The Department of Physics offers a program of graduate study leading to the Ph.D. degree in physics. The primary areas of experimental and theoretical research in the physics department are particle physics, atomic and molecular physics, quantum optics, physics of solids and fluids, quantum field theory, statistical mechanics, and mathematical and string theory. The department is closely linked with the Division of Engineering and Applied Sciences, which has an extensive program in theoretical and experimental studies of the properties of crystalline and disordered solids. The Division of Engineering and Applied Sciences also offers nonlinear optics and light scattering, earth and planetary physics, computer science, and applied mathematics.

The first year and a half of graduate study is normally spent on lecture courses. In the second year, students are expected to pass an oral examination on a subject of their choice and choose a field and adviser for their Ph.D. work. The requirements for the Ph.D. degree are demonstration of competence (usually through a year course in each field) in four fields of physics, satisfactory performance on a preliminary oral examination, and a Ph.D. dissertation based on independent scholarly research, which, upon conclusion, is defended in an oral examination before a Ph.D. committee. With normal preparation, students can usually complete the requirements for the Ph.D. degree in four to six years. The research interests of the faculty members in the physics department are listed on the reverse of this page.

A limited number of openings for postdoctoral research, with or without a stipend, are available each year to qualified applicants without regard to race, color, sex, or creed. Inquiries should be addressed to individual professors, under whose sponsorship these appointments are made.

Research Facilities

The facilities of the Department of Physics are concentrated in several buildings. Lyman Laboratory and Jefferson Laboratory form the center of departmental activity. These two buildings contain facilities for atomic physics experiments with fast atomic beams, apparatus for trapping and studying individual electrons and ions, equipment for producing nuclear and atomic polarization, superconducting magnets, lasers, dilution refrigerators for attaining very low temperatures, equipment for high-pressure studies, and equipment for optical and ultrasonic measurements. Additional facilities for the study of solid-state physics, laser physics, and materials science are located in Gordon McKay Laboratory. These include high-resolution electron microscopes, low-temperature facilities, a clean room for fabricating submicrometer structures, an MeV heavy-ion accelerator, high-resolution X-ray facilities, and materials preparation and characterization equipment. Studies of condensed-matter systems using synchrotron radiation are carried out at Brookhaven National Laboratory. Current projects in particle physics are being carried out at the Fermi National Accelerator Laboratory; at the European Center for Nuclear Research (CERN) in Geneva, Switzerland; and at the Stanford Linear Accelerator Center (SLAC). Apparatus for these projects is built and data from these experiments are analyzed in part at the High Energy Physics Laboratory at Harvard.

Financial Aid

The Department of Physics has generally provided full tuition and fees for all graduate students who are not supported in full by outside scholarships. Living stipends are provided via scholarships, teaching fellowships, and research assistantships. Summer support is also included and is available in the form of either a teaching fellowship or a research assistantship. Physics graduate students also receive financial support to encourage attendance at professional conferences.

Cost of Study

Tuition and fees are provided for all graduate students as described above.

Living and Housing Costs

There are a wide variety of dormitory rooms for single students, with costs that range in 2004–05 from $4456 (for a small single room) up to $7003 (for a two-room suite) per academic year. These figures do not include meals.

Married students and single graduate students may apply for apartments in graduate student housing or other University-owned apartments. The monthly costs for 2004–05 range from $877 to $1550 for a one-room studio apartment, $1108 to $1564 for a one-bedroom apartment, $1415 to $2050 for a two-bedroom apartment, and $1833 and up for a three-bedroom apartment. There are also many privately owned accommodations nearby and within commuting distance.

Student Group

The Graduate School of Arts and Sciences has an enrollment of 3,383. About 174 men and women are pursuing Ph.D. research in the physics laboratories with physics department faculty members. Students come from all parts of the United States, and about one third are from other countries.

Location

Cambridge, Massachusetts, is a city of 101,355, adjacent to Boston and its cultural benefits, yet suburban in nature. All of New England is within driving distance—the mountains of New Hampshire and Vermont with camping and skiing, the beaches and woodlands of Maine, and the seashore and seaports of Massachusetts, as well as the great array of colleges and universities spread across all six states. Cambridge itself is a scientific and intellectual center teeming with activity in all areas of creativity and study.

The University

Harvard College was established in 1636, and its charter, which still guides the University, was granted in 1650. Today, Harvard University, with its network of graduate schools, occupies a noteworthy position in the academic world, and the Department of Physics offers an educational program in keeping with the University's long-standing record of achievement.

Applying

Men and women who are completing a bachelor's degree or the equivalent should write to the Admissions Office of the Graduate School of Arts and Sciences for application material and to the Department of Physics for additional information on the program. Completed application forms and all supporting material should be returned to the Admissions Office by December 13. Application may also be made online at the Web address listed below.

Correspondence and Information

Information on the program:
Office of the Chair
Department of Physics
Jefferson Physical Laboratory, Room 370
Harvard University
17 Oxford Street
Cambridge, Massachusetts 02138
World Wide Web: http://www.physics.harvard.edu

Application forms for admission:
Admissions Office
Graduate School of Arts and Sciences
Harvard University
8 Garden Street, 2nd Floor
Cambridge, Massachusetts 02138
World Wide Web: http://www.gsas.harvard.edu

Harvard University

THE FACULTY AND THEIR RESEARCH

Howard C. Berg, Ph.D., Professor of Molecular and Cellular Biology and Professor of Physics. Motile behavior of bacteria.
George Brandenburg, Ph.D., Senior Research Fellow and Director of the High Energy Physics Laboratory. Experimental high-energy physics.
Sidney R. Coleman, Ph.D., Donner Professor of Science. Quantum field theory, relativity.
Eugene Demler, Ph.D., Assistant Professor of Physics. Theoretical condensed-matter physics.
John Doyle, Ph.D., Professor of Physics. Experimental atomic, molecular, and elementary particle physics.
Gary Feldman, Ph.D., Frank B. Baird Jr. Professor of Science. Experimental high-energy physics.
Daniel S. Fisher, Ph.D., Professor of Physics and Professor of Applied Physics. Statistical physics, condensed-matter theory.
Andrew Foland, Ph.D., Assistant Professor of Physics. Experimental high-energy physics.
Melissa Franklin, Ph.D., Professor of Physics. Experimental high-energy physics.
Gerald Gabrielse, Ph.D., Professor of Physics. Experimental atomic, optical, plasma, and elementary particle physics.
Peter L. Galison, Ph.D., Mallinckrodt Professor of the History of Science and of Physics (joint appointment with the Department of History of Science). History and philosophy of physics.
Howard Georgi, Ph.D., Mallinckrodt Professor of Physics. Field theory, elementary particle physics.
Roy J. Glauber, Ph.D., Mallinckrodt Professor of Physics. Elementary particle theory, high-energy nuclear physics, quantum optics, statistical mechanics.
Jene A. Golovchenko, Ph.D., Gordon McKay Professor of Applied Physics and Professor of Physics (joint appointment with the Division of Engineering and Applied Sciences). Solid-state and atomic physics.
Bertrand I. Halperin, Ph.D., Hollis Professor of Mathematicks and Natural Philosophy. Condensed-matter theory, statistical theory.
Lene Vestergaard Hau, Ph.D., Gordon McKay Professor of Applied Physics and Professor of Physics (joint appointment with the Division of Engineering and Applied Sciences). Experimental atomic physics, Bose-Einstein condensation, nonlinear optics.
Eric J. Heller, Ph.D., Professor of Chemistry and Physics. Theoretical atomic, molecular, and optical physics.
Jennifer Hoffman, Ph.D., Assistant Professor of Physics. Experimental condensed-matter physics.
Paul Horowitz, Ph.D., Professor of Physics and Professor of Electrical Engineering. Experimental astrophysics, search for extraterrestrial intelligence.
John Huth, Ph.D., Professor of Physics and Chairman. Experimental high-energy physics.
Arthur M. Jaffe, Ph.D., Landon T. Clay Professor of Mathematics and Theoretical Science (joint appointment with the Department of Mathematics). Mathematical physics.
Efthimios Kaxiras, Ph.D., Gordon McKay Professor of Applied Physics and Professor of Physics. Theoretical and computational condensed-matter physics.
Mikhail Lukin, Ph.D., Assistant Professor of Physics. Quantum optics.
Charles M. Marcus, Ph.D., Professor of Physics. Experimental condensed-matter physics, mesoscopic systems, nanofabrication.
Paul C. Martin, Ph.D., John H. Van Vleck Professor of Pure and Applied Physics (joint appointment with the Division of Engineering and Applied Sciences). Statistical physics, condensed-matter theory.
Eric Mazur, Ph.D., Harvard College Professor, Gordon McKay Professor of Applied Physics and Professor of Physics (joint appointment with the Division of Engineering and Applied Sciences). Optical condensed-matter physics.
Shiraz Minwalla, Ph.D., Assistant Professor of Physics. String theory, quantum field theory, quantum gravity.
Masahiro Morii, Ph.D., Assistant Professor of Physics. Experimental high-energy physics.
Venkatesh Narayanamurti, Ph.D., Gordon McKay Professor of Engineering and Applied Sciences, Dean of the Division of Engineering and Applied Sciences, and Professor of Physics (joint appointment with the Division of Engineering and Applied Sciences). Experimental condensed matter: Ballistic transport in semiconductors, nanostructures, and tunneling microscopy.
David R. Nelson, Ph.D., Mallinckrodt Professor of Physics and Professor of Applied Physics. Statistical physics, condensed-matter theory.
David W. Norcross, Ph.D., Director of the Physics Laboratories.
Peter S. Pershan, Ph.D., Frank B. Baird Jr. Professor of Science (joint appointment with the Division of Engineering and Applied Sciences). Experimental condensed-matter physics, synchrotron radiation studies of properties of matter at interfaces and surfaces.
Mara Prentiss, Ph.D., Professor of Physics. Experimental atomic physics, optical devices, optical tweezers, biophysics.
Lisa Randall, Ph.D., Professor of Physics. Field theory, the standard model and beyond.
Aravinthan D. T. Samuel, Ph.D., Assistant Professor of Physics. Biophysics, neurobiology, and animal behavior.
Irwin I. Shapiro, Ph.D., Timken University Professor (joint appointment with the Department of Astronomy). Radar and radio astronomy, experimental relativity.
Isaac F. Silvera, Ph.D., Thomas D. Cabot Professor of the Natural Sciences. Low-temperature physics of quantum fluids and solids, ultrahigh-pressure physics.
Andrew Strominger, Ph.D., Professor of Physics. String theory, field theory and general relativity.
Christopher Stubbs, Ph.D., Professor of Physics and of Astronomy. Observational cosmology and experimental gravitation.
Michael Tinkham, Ph.D., Rumford Professor of Physics and Gordon McKay Professor of Applied Physics (joint appointment with the Division of Engineering and Applied Sciences). Superconductivity, mesoscopic physics.
Cumrun Vafa, Ph.D., Professor of Physics. Elementary particle theory and string theory.
David A. Weitz, Ph.D., Gordon McKay Professor of Applied Physics and Professor of Physics (joint appointment with the Division of Engineering and Applied Sciences). Experimental soft condensed-matter physics.
Robert M. Westervelt, Ph.D., Gordon McKay Professor of Applied Physics and Professor of Physics (joint appointment with the Division of Engineering and Applied Sciences). Experimental condensed-matter physics, mesoscopic physics.
Tai T. Wu, Ph.D., Gordon McKay Professor of Applied Physics and Professor of Physics (joint appointment with the Division of Engineering and Applied Sciences). Theoretical elementary particle physics, electromagnetic theory, statistical mechanics.
Matias Zaldarriaga, Ph.D., Associate Professor of Astronomy and of Physics (joint appointment with the Department of Astronomy). Theoretical astrophysics, cosmology.
Xiaowei Zhuang, Ph.D., Assistant Professor of Chemistry and Chemical Biology and of Physics. Biophysics single-molecule fluorescence and force spectroscopy, biomolecular and cellular imaging.

Professors Emeriti

Nicolaas Bloembergen, Ph.D., Gerhard Gade University Professor, Emeritus. Nonlinear optics.
Henry Ehrenreich, Ph.D., Clowes Research Professor of Science. Theoretical condensed-matter physics.
Sheldon L. Glashow, Ph.D., Higgins Professor of Physics, Emeritus. Theoretical elementary particle physics.
Gerald Holton, Ph.D., Mallinckrodt Professor of Physics and Professor of the History of Science, Emeritus. Experimental physics, history of nineteenth- and twentieth-century physics.
William Paul, Ph.D., Mallinckrodt Research Professor of Applied Physics and Research Professor of Physics. Experimental condensed-matter physics, amorphous semiconductors.
Robert V. Pound, D.Sc., Mallinckrodt Professor of Physics, Emeritus. Experimental physics.
Norman F. Ramsey, Ph.D., Higgins Professor of Physics, Emeritus. Experimental physics, tests of time-reversal symmetry.
Richard Wilson, D.Phil., Mallinckrodt Research Professor of Physics. Experimental nuclear physics, elementary particle physics, energy-related environmental and medical physics.

IDAHO STATE UNIVERSITY

Department of Physics

Program of Study

The Doctor of Philosophy degree in engineering and applied science is offered jointly by the College of Engineering and the Department of Physics at Idaho State University (ISU). Research areas emphasized are radiation science, accelerator applications, applied nuclear physics, and health physics. All applicants must meet ISU Graduate School admission requirements for doctoral programs. In addition, applicants must have attained a master's degree in engineering, physics, or a closely related field. To attain a degree in this program, a student must demonstrate scholarly achievement and an ability in independent investigation. The program normally requires three years of full-time study beyond the master's degree, including research and preparation of the dissertation.

Master of Science degrees are offered in physics, health physics, and natural science. The Master of Science degree in physics is a thesis program that requires 30 credits, 15 of which are required 600-level courses. The Master of Science (health physics emphasis) is a thesis program that prepares students for radiation protection careers leading to upper technical and management levels. This program requires 30 credits, 15 of which must be at the 600 course level. The Master of Natural Science degree is a nonthesis option available for those planning a teaching career in primary or secondary education. The program requires a minimum of 30 credits, 22 of which must be in residence. A final oral examination is required.

Research Facilities

Research is conducted in the Particle Beam Laboratory (PBL), the Idaho Accelerator Center (IAC), the Environmental Monitoring Laboratory (EML), and the Environmental Assessment Laboratory (EAL) with emphases on experimental low-energy nuclear physics, health physics, accelerator-produced radiation effects, and ion beam analysis of materials. The laboratories house a 400-keV Van de Graaff with two beam lines, a 2-MeV Van de Graaff with four beam lines, a second 2-MeV Van de Graaff with four beam lines, and six electron linacs with energies from 4 to 30 MeV. The 30-MeV high-current traveling wave electron LINAC has a pulse width adjustable from a few microseconds down to 12 picoseconds. Lab space is expected to double in fall 2003 with completion of two additions to the Idaho Accelerator Center. The 9-MeV, 10-kA pulsed power spiral line accelerator is scheduled to be installed in the 2004 academic year. Also available for recommissioning are a 4-MeV Van de Graff, a 1-8-MeV tandem, 2-MeV RFQ (q/m = 2), and a 500-KeV Febetron. The EML consists of a complete wet lab with two fume hoods, tritium enrichment capabilities to achieve MDC of 10 to 15 pCi/L, 3 ICB-controlled gamma spectrometry systems that include two 23 percent relative efficiency p-type high-purity germanium detectors and one extended-range 50 percent relative efficiency n-type beryllium windowed high-purity germanium detector, one Wallac 14145 low-background liquid scintillation counter, and one 5-inch automatic low-background gas proportional counter. The EAL provides a Beckman LS5000TA liquid scintillation counter, Canberra 2404 proportional counter, and fout high-purity intrinsic germanium detectors along with an SEM. There are collaborative research projects with Sandia National Laboratory (Albuquerque); Idaho National Environmental and Engineering Laboratory; Los Alamos; CEBAF; TUNL; DFEL; the state of Idaho; Positron Systems, Inc.; and Stoller, Inc.

Financial Aid

Graduate assistantships in 2001–02 carried stipends of approximately $10,000 per academic year, plus waiver of fees and tuition. Summer support of $3000 to $4000 is generally available. Research assistantships of up to $18,000 are also available. A University work-study program allows eligible students to work up to 20 hours per week, and student loans are available. Spouses of students may obtain local or campus employment. Assistance for graduate research has been received from a variety of sources, including the National Science Foundation, the Department of Energy, the Idaho State Board of Education, Bechtel BWXT Idaho, the Stoller Corporation, and NSF EpSCOR. Most full-time graduate students receive financial aid.

Cost of Study

In 2002–03, registration costs were $2159 per semester for residents of Idaho and $5279 for nonresidents. Tuition and fees for students on teaching or research assistantships are usually waived. Books cost between $200 and $300 per semester.

Living and Housing Costs

Room and board for single students living on campus cost approximately $3000 per year. Apartments for married students rent for approximately $460 per month (including utilities).

Student Group

The University's total enrollment is approximately 13,000 students. The 1,600 graduate students come from almost every state in the U.S. and from many other countries.

Location

Pocatello (population 52,000) is situated at the edge of the Snake River plain in southeastern Idaho. There are mountains on three sides of town. The climate is pleasant, with an average winter temperature of 28 degrees and summer temperatures seldom exceeding 95 degrees. The climate is dry (annual precipitation of about 12 inches), with many days of sunshine. Because of the town's 4,500-foot elevation and latitude, winters are relatively long but not severe in the Portneuf Valley, where Pocatello is located. ISU, the region's premier nuclear research institution, is located within easy driving distance of world-class skiing (Sun Valley, Jackson Hole, Salt Lake City), several national parks, monuments, and wilderness areas and some of the country's best hunting, fishing, kayaking, white-water rafting, climbing, and backpacking.

The University

Idaho State University is composed of the Colleges of Education, Business, Pharmacy, Arts and Sciences, Engineering, and Health-Related Professions. The history of the institution goes back to 1901, but a full four-year curriculum was not begun until 1947. Master's degree programs were initiated in 1958 and those leading to the Ph.D. in 1969. The University is accredited by the Northwest Association of Colleges and Schools. Graduate classes are small enough to permit the faculty members to give students individual attention. Semesters run from late August to mid-December and from mid-January to mid-May. Summer sessions run from mid-May to early August.

Applying

Application forms for admission to graduate study may be downloaded from the Web site (listed below) or obtained from the graduate admissions office or by writing to the Department of Physics. Applications are accepted at any time, but applications for assistantships must be submitted by March 1. GRE General Test scores must be submitted as part of the applications for admission and for financial support.

Correspondence and Information

Department of Physics
Box 8106
Idaho State University
Pocatello, Idaho 83209
Telephone: 208-282-2350
Fax: 208-282-4649
E-mail: office@physics.isu.edu
World Wide Web: http://www.physics.isu.edu

Idaho State University

THE FACULTY AND THEIR RESEARCH

Wendland Beezhold, Research Professor (Physics); Ph.D., Washington (Seattle), 1969. Semiconductor physics, radiation physics, electron and particle beam accelerators, nanotechnologies, and modeling and simulation of radiation response of electronics and materials.
Richard R. Brey, Associate Professor (Health Physics); Ph.D., Purdue, 1994.
Khalid Choufanni, Visiting Associate Professor (Physics), Ph.D., Catholic University, 1995. Exotic X-ray sources, electron beam monitoring, X-ray sources and application to medical and industrial field, X-ray FEL, laser-Compton, laser plasma and crystal accelerators.
Thomas F. Gesell, Professor (Physics); Ph.D., Tennessee, 1971. Environmental radiation and radionuclides.
Martin H. Hackworth, Senior Lecturer–Lab Supervisor (Physics); M.S., Eastern Kentucky, 1992. Acoustics and meteorology.
J. Frank Harmon, Professor (Physics); Ph.D., Wyoming, 1969. Director of Idaho Accelerator Center, which is studying the use of nuclear physics in a wide range of applied activities.
Alan W. Hunt, Research Assistant Professor (Physics); Ph.D., Harvard, 2000. Wide band-gap, semiconductors, positron production, isometric nuclei production.
Kara J. Keeter, Associate Professor (Physics); Ph.D., Duke, 1990. Experimental low- and medium-energy nuclear physics and astrophysics: photonuclear reactions, few-body systems and neutrinoless double beta decay, investigating theories ranging from QCD and CPT to massive neutrinos.
John M. Knox, Professor (Ion Beam Analysis); Ph.D., Wyoming, 1981. Ion beam analysis of materials: RBS, PIXE, NRA, ERD; proton microbeam analysis; neutron elastic recoil detection of hydrogen isotopes.
Ernest B. Nieschmidt, Visiting Associate Professor (Physics); M.S., San Diego State, 1961. Nuclear physics, detectors, laser isotope separation, sonoluminiscense.
Steven L. Shropshire, Associate Professor (Physics); Ph.D., Washington State, 1991. Teacher training, physics education, defects and diffusion in solids, nuclear spectroscopies applied to materials science.
Eddie Tatar, Assistant Professor (Experimental Physics); Ph.D., Notre Dame, 2000. Quantum interference phenomena in particle physics and optics, study of exotic mesons, partial wave analysis techniques, lie groups and representation theory, supersymmetry, weak interactions and neutrino physics.
Douglas P. Wells, Associate Professor (Experimental Nuclear Physics); Ph.D., Illinois, 1990. Applied accelerator physics, photonuclear physics, health physics.

Postdoctoral Fellows

Mohamed Reda (Nuclear Engineering), Ph.D., Alexandria (Egypt), 1988. Monte Carlo simulation, interaction of charged particles with solids, sputtering phenomena, inelastic effects in low-temperature plasma, design and operation of control systems for electric networks.
Farida Selim (Physics), Ph.D., Alexandria (Egypt) and Harvard, 1999. Atomic physics, positron physics.
Jagoda Mary Urban-Klaehn (Physics), Ph.D., Texas Christian, 1998. Application of physical methods (X-ray, gamma rays, positron annihilation spectroscopy, accelerator techniques, scanning electron microscopy, and other spectroscopic techniques) to the investigation of the internal physical structure of materials.

Professors Emeriti

Barry R. Parker, Ph.D., Utah State, 1968.
Joseph E. Price, Ph.D., Rice, 1959.
Stanley H. Vegors, Ph.D., Illinois, 1955.

INDIANA UNIVERSITY BLOOMINGTON

Department of Physics

Programs of Study

Physics research at Indiana University (IU) is conducted in the subfields of nuclear physics, accelerator physics, biophysics, particle physics, condensed-matter physics, physics education, astrophysics, and theoretical physics. M.S., M.A.T., and PH.D. degrees are offered. A Ph.D. program in biophysics has been established with the addition of several new faculty members. Some areas of specialization in biophysics include neuroscience, experimental and theoretical models of development, networks, pattern formation, and cell signaling. An interdisciplinary scientific computing minor and an M.S. in beam physics and technology are offered.

M.S. candidates must complete 30 credit hours of graduate work (including a minimum of 20 hours in physics) and either pass a written comprehensive exam or, for some programs, complete a thesis. The M.A.T. requires 20 hours in physics and an additional 16 hours in mathematics, astronomy, chemistry, and education.

To obtain the Ph.D., the candidate must demonstrate an ability to do research by carrying out an investigation and presenting a publishable thesis. The requirements for the Ph.D. include a minimum of 90 hours of graduate credit that consists of course work, supervised reading, and research. A qualifying exam is required no later than one year after arrival; two attempts at the exam are allowed. The great majority of students at IU pass the qualifying exam and are soon involved in thesis research. The final oral exam is conducted by the candidate's doctoral committee and consists of questions on the major and minor fields of work as well as on the thesis.

Research Facilities

The Indiana University Cyclotron Facility/Nuclear Theory Center is a national facility for nuclear, condensed-matter, and medical physics research. It consists of a cyclotron and a low-energy neutron source and extensive support facilities. Other experiments in nuclear, particle and accelerator physics, and astrophysics are conducted at Fermilab, Thomas Jefferson Lab, Brookhaven, NIST, Los Alamos, Argonne, CERN, and CIDA. Local facilities include high-bay assembly areas, machine shops, electronic design facilities, a large open-bore superconducting magnet for balloon studies, a high-vacuum sputtering system, X-ray diffractometers, ultrahigh-vacuum surface analysis systems, a scanning tunneling microscope, a class 1000 clean room with photolithographic equipment, a 14-Tesla superconducting magnet with pumped ^{3}He and dilution refrigerator inserts, and several standard cryostats for transport measurements from DC to 20 GHz. Computing facilities include numerous workstations and Linux clusters, a 600-CPU IBM SP, a 64-CPU Sun E 10000, an AVIDD cluster, and a data visualization cave.

Financial Aid

Teaching assistantships carried stipends of at least $14,000 for the ten-month 2003–04 academic year. Research assistantship stipends averaged $20,000 for twelve months. Students are eligible for a number of University fellowships, which pay $20,000 per year for five years. Teaching and research positions are also available that pay at least $2150 for the two summer months. Over the last ten years, 98 percent of the students who finished the Ph.D. received full financial support throughout their graduate careers.

Cost of Study

In 2003–04, fees per credit hour for in-state graduate students were $204.50; for out-of-state graduate students, $595.75. Teaching and research assistants ordinarily paid only a fee of $560.36 per semester.

Living and Housing Costs

Indiana University's Residential Programs and Services (RPS) Office offers a variety of housing and meal plans, which include many options, from single dormitory rooms to four-bedroom apartments. Rates may include room, utilities (including local telephone service), cable TV, and Ethernet connections. For detailed information, including rates, students may visit the RPS Web site at http://www.rps.indiana.edu.

Student Group

Indiana University is a large institution, with 38,589 students enrolled at the Bloomington campus, including 7,808 graduate and professional school students. In fall 2003, there were 96 graduate students in physics, almost all of whom received full financial support.

Student Outcomes

IU physics Ph.D. graduates are currently employed by national laboratories such as FNAL, BNL, SLAC, LANL, and LBNL; by universities such as Duke, Ohio, Rice, Penn State, Purdue, and Towson; and by companies such as Lucent, Intel, Microsoft, and Battelle. Recent postdoctoral students have obtained positions at Argonne, Lawrence Berkeley Lab, Northwestern University, MIT, Princeton University, NIST, the University of Maryland, and the National High Magnetic Field Lab.

Location

Bloomington is located in the picturesque hills of southern Indiana, 50 miles south of Indianapolis, the state capital. It is close to five state parks, two state forests, and the state's largest lake. It has consistently been chosen in national rankings as having a high quality of life.

The University

Indiana University is the oldest state university west of the Allegheny Mountains. It was founded in 1820 and has been a pioneer in higher education in the Midwest. It is widely recognized for the beauty of its campus and for the diversity and high quality of its graduate programs in the arts, humanities, and sciences. The campus provides numerous facilities for all types of sports. The School of Music presents concerts and opera. Lectures, dramatic and musical productions, ballet, drama, and concerts are presented by the Auditorium and the University Theatre.

Applying

The deadline for assistantship and fellowship applications for the fall semester is January 15. For further information, students should write to one of the addresses or call one of the numbers given below. Applications can be submitted over the World Wide Web at http://www.gradapp.indiana.edu.

Correspondence and Information

Chairperson
Department of Physics
Indiana University
Bloomington, Indiana 47405-4201
Telephone: 812-855-1247

Graduate Admissions Committee
Department of Physics
Indiana University
Bloomington, Indiana 47405-4201
Telephone: 812-855-3973
E-mail: gradphys@indiana.edu
World Wide Web: http://physics.indiana.edu

Indiana University Bloomington

THE FACULTY AND THEIR RESEARCH

Professors Emeriti
Ethan D. Alyea, Ph.D., Caltech, 1962. Astrophysics (experimental).
Robert D. Bent, Ph.D., Rice, 1954. Experimental nuclear physics: nuclear structure, reactions, astrophysics.
Ray R. Crittenden, Ph.D., Wisconsin, 1960. Elementary particle physics (experimental).
Charles Goodman, Ph.D., Rochester, 1959. Nuclear physics (experimental).
Richard R. Hake, Ph.D., Illinois, 1955. Condensed-matter and low-temperature physics.
Archibald W. Hendry, Ph.D., Glasgow, 1962. Theoretical physics: elementary particles.
Andrew A. Lenard, Ph.D., Iowa, 1953. Theoretical physics, mathematical physics.
Don B. Lichtenberg, Ph.D., Illinois, 1955. Elementary particle physics (theory).
Malcolm Macfarlane, Ph.D., Rochester, 1959. Nuclear theory.
Hugh J. Martin, Ph.D., Caltech, 1956. Elementary particle physics (experimental).
Daniel W. Miller, Ph.D., Wisconsin, 1951. Nuclear physics (experimental): nuclear reactions.
Roger G. Newton, Distinguished Professor Emeritus; Ph.D., Harvard, 1953. Theoretical and mathematical physics: scattering theory.
Robert E. Pollock, Distinguished Professor; Ph.D., Princeton, 1963. Nuclear physics: nuclear reactions, cyclotron design.
Peter Schwandt, Ph.D., Wisconsin, 1967. Nuclear physics (experimental).
James C. Swihart, Ph.D., Purdue, 1955. Condensed-matter theory.
John G. Wills, Ph.D., Washington (Seattle), 1963. Theoretical nuclear physics: intermediate energy.

Professors
Andrew D. Bacher, Ph.D., Caltech, 1967. Intermediate-energy nuclear physics (experimental).
David V. Baxter, Ph.D., Caltech, 1984. Condensed-matter physics (experimental).
Bennet B. Brabson, Ph.D., MIT, 1966. Elementary particle physics (experimental).
John M. Cameron, Ph.D., UCLA, 1967. Nuclear physics (experimental).
John L. Challifour, Ph.D., Cambridge, 1963. Theoretical physics, mathematical physics.
Rob deRuyter, Ph.D., Groningen (Netherlands), 1986. Biophysics and soft condensed-matter physics (experimental).
Alex R. Dzierba, Ph.D., Notre Dame, 1969. Elementary particle physics (experimental).
James A. Glazier, Ph.D., Chicago, 1989. Biophysics and soft condensed-matter physics (experimental).
Steven A. Gottlieb, Ph.D., Princeton, 1978. Theoretical physics.
G. C. Fox, Ph.D., Cambridge, 1967. Computational physics.
Richard M. Heinz, Ph.D., Michigan, 1964. Astrophysics (experimental).
Charles J. Horowitz, Ph.D., Stanford, 1981. Nuclear theory.
Larry L. Kesmodel, Ph.D., Texas, 1974. Condensed-matter physics (experimental).
V. Alan Kostelecký, Ph.D., Yale, 1982. Theoretical physics.
S. Y. Lee, Ph.D., SUNY at Stony Brook, 1972. Accelerator physics.
J. Timothy Londergan, D.Phil., Oxford, 1969. Theoretical physics, nuclear theory.
Hans Otto Meyer, Ph.D., Basel, 1970. Nuclear physics (experimental).
James A. Musser, Ph.D., Berkeley, 1984. Astrophysics (experimental).
Hermann Nann, Ph.D., Frankfurt, 1967. Intermediate-energy nuclear physics (experimental).
Harold Ogren, Ph.D., Cornell, 1970. Elementary particle physics (experimental).
Catherine Olmer, Ph.D., Yale, 1976. Intermediate-energy nuclear physics (experimental).
William L. Schaich, Ph.D., Cornell, 1970. Condensed-matter theory.
Brian D. Serot, Ph.D., Stanford, 1979. Nuclear theory.
Kumble R. Subbaswamy, Ph.D., Indiana, 1976. Condensed-matter theory.
Richard J. Vankooten, Ph.D., Stanford, 1990. Elementary particle physics (experimental).
Steven E. Vigdor, Ph.D., Wisconsin, 1973. Nuclear physics (experimental).
George E. Walker, Ph.D., Case Tech, 1966. Nuclear theory.
Scott W. Wissink, Ph.D., Stanford, 1986. Nuclear physics (experimental).
Andrej Zieminski, Ph.D., Warsaw, 1971. Elementary particle physics (experimental).

Associate Professors
Michael S. Berger, Ph.D., Berkeley, 1991. Elementary particle physics (theory).
John P. Carini, Ph.D., Chicago, 1988. Condensed-matter physics (experimental).
William M. Snow, Ph.D., Harvard, 1990. Nuclear physics (experimental).
Adam P. Szczepaniak, Ph.D., Washington (Seattle), 1990. Theoretical physics.

Assistant Professors
John Beggs, Ph.D., Yale, 1998. Biophysics and soft condensed-matter physics (experimental).
Mark D. Messier, Ph.D., Boston University, 1999. High-energy astrophysics (experimental).
Sima Setayeshgar, Ph.D., MIT, 1998. Biophysics and soft condensed-matter physics (theoretical).
Rex Tayloe, Ph.D., Illinois, 1995. Nuclear physics (experimental).
Jon Urheim, Ph.D., Pennsylvania, 1990. Astrophysics (experimental).

Indiana University Bloomington

SELECTED PUBLICATIONS

Stephenson, E. J., et al. **(A. D. Bacher** and **H. Nann).** Observation of the charge symmetry breaking d + d → ^{4}He + π^0 reaction near threshold. *Phys. Rev. Lett.* 91:142302, 2003.

Fujita, H., et al. **(A. D. Bacher).** Realization of matching conditions for high-resolution spectrometers. *Nucl. Instrum. Methods Phys. Res., Sect. A* 484, 2002.

Allgower, C. E., et al. **(A. D. Bacher** and **S. W. Wissink).** Spin transfer in *pp* elastic scattering at 198 MeV: Implications for the π *NN* coupling constant. *Phys. Rev. Lett.* 83:4498, 1999.

Baxter, D. V. LENS: A university-based pulsed neutron source for research and education. *International Collaboration on Advanced Neutron Sources (ICANS-XVI) Conference Proceedings,* Germany, 2003.

Baxter, D. V. Anisotropic magnetoresistance in $Ga_{1-x}Mn_xAs$. *Phys. Rev. B* 65:212407, 2002.

Helgren, E., et al. **(D. V. Baxter** and **J. P. Carini).** Measurements of the complex conductivity of Nb_xSi_{1-x} allows on the insulating side of the metal-insulator transition. *Phys. Rev. Lett.* 87:116602, 2001.

Kalke, M., and **D. V. Baxter.** Kinetic Monte Carlo simulations of chemical vapor deposition: Non-monotonic variation of surface roughness with growth temperature. *Surf. Sci.* 477:96, 2001.

Beggs, J. M., and D. Plenz. Neuronal avalanches in neocortical circuits. *J. Neurosci.* 23(35):11167, 2003.

Beggs, J. M. A statistical theory of long-term potentiation and depression. *Neural Computation* 13(1):87, 2001.

Beggs, J. M., J. R. Moyer, J. P. McGann, and T. H. Brown. Prolonged synaptic integration in perirhinal cortical neurons. *J. Neurophysiol.* 83:3294, 2000.

Beggs, J. M., and E. W. Kairiss. Intrinsic electrophysiology and morphology of neurons in rat perirhinal cortex. *Brain Res.* 665:18, 1994.

Bent, R., L. Orr, and R. Baker, eds. *Energy: Science, Policy, and the Pursuit of Sustainability.* Washington: Island Press, 2002.

Berger, M. S. Superfield realizations of Lorentz and CPT violation. *Phys. Rev. D* 68:115005, 2003.

Berger, M. S., and **V. A. Kostelecký.** Supersymmetry and Lorentz violation. *Phys. Rev. D* 65:091701, 2002.

Berger, M. S., and K. Siyeon. Leptogenesis and low-energy observables. *Phys. Rev. D* 65:053019, 2002.

Berger, M. S. Higgs sector radiative corrections and s-channel production. *Phys. Rev. Lett.* 87:131801, 2001.

Lewis, R. M., and **J. P. Carini.** Frequency scaling of microwave conductivity in the integer quantum Hall effect minima. *Phys. Rev. B* 64:073310, 2001.

Lee, H.-L., et al. **(J. P. Carini** and **D. V. Baxter).** Quantum-critical conductivity scaling for a metal-insulator transition. *Science* 287:633, 2000.

Lee, H.-L., et al. **(J. P. Carini** and **D. V. Baxter).** Temperature-frequency scaling in niobium-silicon near the metal-insulator transition. *Phys. Rev. Lett.* 78:4261–4, 1998.

Carini, J. P., and **J. T. Londergan** et al. Bound states in waveguides and bent quantum wires, I: Applications to waveguide systems. *Phys. Rev. B* 55:9842, 1997.

Challifour, J. L., and J. P. Clancy. A path space formula for gauss vectors in chern-simons quantum electrodynamics. *J. Math. Phys.* 40:5318, 1999.

Fairhall, A. L., et al. **(R. R. de Ruyter).** Efficiency and ambiguity in an adaptive neural code. *Nature* 412:787, 2001.

Lewen, G. D., et al. **(R. R. de Ruyter).** Neural coding of naturalistic motion stimuli. *Network: Computation in Neural Syst.* 12:317, 2001.

de Ruyter, R. R., and W. Bialek. Timing and counting precision in the blowfly visual system. In *Methods in Neural Networks IV,* eds. J. van Hemmen, J. D. Cowan, and E. Domany. Heidelberg and New York: Springer-Verlag, 2001.

Rieke, D., et al. **(R. R. de Ruyter).** *Spikes: Exploring the Neural Code.* Cambridge, Mass.: Bradford Book–MIT Press, 1997.

Dzierba, A. R. The science of confinement and the glueX project at Jefferson Lab. *Int. J. Mod. Phys. A* 18:397, 2003.

Dzierba, A. R., et al. A study of the $\eta\pi^0$ spectrum and search for a $J^{PC} = 1^{-+}$ exotic meson. *Phys. Rev. D* 67:094015, 2003.

Denisov, S., et al. **(A. Dzierba** and **R. Heinz).** Characteristics of the TOF counter for GlueX experiment. *Nucl. Instrum. Methods Phys. Res., Sect. A* 494, 2002.

Fox, G. C. Planning a new generation of multiparticle phase shift analyses in peripheral reactions. In *Proc. Jefferson Lab. Workshop Gluonic Excitations,* 2003.

Fox, G. C., and D. Walker. *e-Science Gap Analysis.* June 2003 (available online).

Berman, F., **G. C. Fox,** and A. J. G. Hey, eds. *Grid Computing: Making the Global Infrastructure a Reality.* Chicester, England: John Wiley & Sons, 2003.

Dongarra, J., et al. **(G. C. Fox),** eds. *The Sourcebook of Parallel Computing.* Morgan Kaufmann, 2002.

Chaturvedi, R., et al. **(J. A. Glazier).** Multi-model simulations of chicken limb morphogenesis. In *Computational Science—ICCS 2003, Proceedings Part III,* LNCS vol. 2659, eds. P. M. A. Sloot, et al. New York: Springer-Verlag, 2003.

Beysens, D. A., G. Forgacs, and **J. A. Glazier.** Cell sorting is analogous to phase ordering in fluids. *Proc. Natl. Acad. Sci. U.S.A.* 97:9467, 2000.

Rieu, J. P., et al. **(J. A. Glazier).** Diffusion and deformations of single hydra cells in cellular aggregates. *Biophys. J.* 79:1903, 2000.

Glazier, J. A., et al. Hysteresis and avalanches in two-dimensional foam rheology simulations. *Phys. Rev. E* 59:5819, 1999.

Carlos, J., et al. **(J. A. Glazier).** Quantitative comparison between differential adhesion models and cell sorting in the presence and absence of fluctuations. *Phys. Rev. Lett.* 75:2244, 1995.

DeTar, C., and **S. Gottlieb.** Lattice quantum chromodynamics comes of age. *Phys. Today* 45, 2004.

Davies, C. T. H., et al. **(S. Gottlieb).** High-precision lattice QCD confronts experiment. *Phys. Rev. Lett.* 92:0022001, 2004.

Gottlieb, S. Lattice results with three quark flavours. Invited talk presented at Strangeness in Quark Matter, SWM 2003. *J. Phys. G* 30:S421, 2004.

Gottlieb, S. Results on improved KS dynamical configurations: Spectrum, decay constants, etc. In *Proc. 21st Intl. Symp. Lattice Field Theory,* 2003.

Ambrosio, M., et al. **(R. Heinz** and **J. Musser).** Search for cosmic ray sources using muons detected by the MACRO experiment. *Astropart. Phys.* 18:615, 2003.

Ambrosio, M., et al. **(R. Heinz** and **J. Musser).** Search for diffuse neutrino flux from astrophysical sources with MACRO. *Astropart. Phys.* 19:1, 2003.

Ambrosio, M., et al. **(R. Heinz** and **J. Musser).** Measurement of the residual energy of muons in the Gran Sasso laboratories. *Astropart. Phys.* 19:313, 2003.

Ambrosio, M., et al. **(R. Heinz** and **J. Musser).** Moon and sun shadowing effect in the MACRO detector. *Astropart. Phys.* 20:145, 2003.

Ambrosio, M., et al. **(R. Heinz** and **J. Musser).** Search for the sidereal and solar diurnal modulations in the total MACRO data set. *Phys. Rev. D* 67:042002, 2003.

Ambrosio, M., et al. **(R. Heinz** and **J. Musser).** Atmospheric neutrino oscillations from upward through-going muon multiple scattering in MACRO. *Phys. Lett. B* 566:35, 2003.

Ambrosio, M., et al. **(R. Heinz** and **J. Musser).** Callibrations of CR39 and makrofol nuclear track detectors and search for exotic particles. *Nucl. Phys. B — Proc. Supl.* 125:217, 2003.

Horowitz, C. J., et al. Realistic neutrino opacities for supernova simulations with correlations and weak magnetism. *Phys. Rev. C* 68:025803, 2003.

Carriere, J., et al. **(C. J. Horowitz).** Low mass neutron stars and the equation state of dense matter. *Astrophys. J.* 593:463, 2003.

Horowitz, C. J., et al. Supernova observation via neutrino-nucleus elastic scattering in the CLEAN detector. *Phys. Rev. D* 68:203005, 2003.

Horowitz, C. J., and **B. D. Serot.** Self-consistent Hartree description of finite nuclei in a relativistic quantum field theory. *Nucl. Phys. A* 368:503, 1981.

Wild, S., and **L. L. Kesmodel.** HREELS investigation of plasma-modified polystyrene surfaces. *J. Vac. Sci. Technol. A* 19:856, 2001.

Jungwirthova, I., and **L. L. Kesmodel.** Thermal evolution of acetylene overlayers on Pd(111). *J. Phys. Chem. B* 105:674, 2001.

Kesmodel, L. L. Recent studies of insulating polymers with high-resolution electron energy loss spectroscopy. *J. Electron. Spectrosc. Relat. Phenom.* 121:75, 2001.

Wild, S., **L. L. Kesmodel,** and G. Apai. High-resolution electron energy loss spectroscopy of polystyrene surfaces. *J. Phys. Chem. B* 104:3179, 2000.

Kostelecký, V. A., R. Bluhm, C. Lane, and N. Russell. Clock-comparison tests of Lorentz and CPT symmetry in space. *Phys. Rev. Lett.,* 2002.

Kostelecký, V. A., et al. Limit on Lorentz and CPT violation of the neutron using a two-species noble-gas maser. *Phys. Rev. Lett.* 85:5038, 2000.

Kostelecký, V. A., and D. Colladay. Lorentz-violating extension of the standard model. *Phys. Rev. D* 58:116002, 1998.

Kostelecký, V. A. Sensitivity of CPT tests with neutral mesons. *Phys. Rev. Lett.* 80:1818, 1998.

Kostelecký, V. A., L. Hall, and S. Raby. New flavor violations in supergravity models. *Nucl. Phys. B* 267:415, 1986.

Cousineau, C., et al. **(S. Y. Lee).** Envelope and particles instabilities of space charge dominated beams in synchrotrons. *Phys. Rev. Special Top.: Accelerators Beams* 6:034205, 2003.

Hahn, H., et al. **(S. Y. Lee).** The RHIC design overview. *Nucl. Instrum. Methods Phys. Res., Sect. A* 499:245, 2003.

Ranjbar, V., et al. **(S. Y. Lee).** Observation of higher order snake resonances in polarized proton acceleration in RHIC. *Phys. Rev. Lett.* 91:034801, 2003.

Chou, P., et al. **(S. Y. Lee).** Effect of the RF cavity-cooling-water temperature on electron beams with RF voltage modulation. *Phys. Rev. Special Top.: Accelerators Beams* 6:052803, 2003.

Londergan, J. T., et al. Charge symmetry violating contributions to neutrino reactions. *Phys. Lett. B* 558:132, 2003.

Londergan, J. T., et al. Charge symmetry violating contributions to determination of the Weinberg angle in neutrino reactions. *Phys. Rev. D* 67:111901, 2003.

Boros, C., **J. T. Londergan,** and A. W. Thomas. Spin and flavor dependent structure and production of lambda baryons. *Nucl. Phys. A* 680:66c, 2001.

Yoo, J., et al. **(M. D. Messier).** A search for periodic modulations of the solar neutrino flux in Super-Kamiokande I. *Phys. Rev. D* 68:092002, 2003.

Fukuda, Y., et al. **(M. D. Messier).** The Super-Kamiokande detector. *Nucl. Instrum. Methods Phys. Res., Sect. A* 501:418, 2003.

Indiana University Bloomington

Selected Publications (continued)

Gando, Y., et al. **(M. D. Messier).** Search for anto-nu(e) from the sun at Super-Kamiokande I. *Phys. Rev. Lett.* 90:171302, 2003.

Adamson, P., et al. **(M. D. Messier** and **J. Musser).** (The MINOS Collaboration). The Minos scintillator calorimeter system. *IEEE Trans. Nucl. Sci.* 49:861, 2002.

Morozov, V. S., et al. **(H. O. Meyer** and **P. Schwandt).** First spin flipping of a stored spin-1 polarized beam. *Phys. Rev. Lett.* 91:214801, 2003.

von Przewoski, B., et al. **(H. O. Meyer** and **P. Schwandt).** Vector- and tensor polarization lifetimes for a stored deuteron beam. *Phys. Rev. E* 68:046501, 2003.

Meyer, H. O. Polarization experiments with storage rings. *Phys. Scr.* T104:19, 2003.

von Przewoski, B., et al. **(H. O. Meyer, R. Pollock,** and **P. Schwandt).** Spin exchange in polarized deuterium. *Phys. Rev. A* 68:042705, 2003.

Abdel-Samad, S., et al. **(H. Nann).** Isospin symmetry breaking and scaling observed in pion production in p + d reactions. *Phys. Lett. B* 553:31, 2003.

Penttila, S. I., et al. **(H. Nann).** A measurement of the parity-violating gamma-ray asymmetry in the neutron-proton capture. In *Proc. 11th Intl. Symp. Capture Gamma-Ray Spectroscopy Related Top.,* p. 604. Singapore: World Scientific, 2003.

Abdel-Samad, S., et al. **(H. Nann).** Study of $p + d \to {}^3A + \pi$ reactions in the Δ-resonance region. *Eur. Phys. J. A* 17:879, 2003.

Stephenson, E. J., et al. **(H. Nann).** Observation of the charge symmetry breaking $d + d \to {}^4\text{He} + \pi^0$ reaction near threshold. *Phys. Rev. Lett.* 91:142302, 2003.

Newton, R. What is a state in quantum mechanics? *Am. J. Phys.* 72(3):348–50, 2004.

Newton, R. *Galileo's Pendulum: From the Rhythm of Time to the Making of Matter.* Harvard University Press, 2004.

Newton, R. *Quantum Physics: A Text for Graduate Students.* New York: Springer-Verlag, 2002.

Newton, R. *Thinking About Physics.* Princeton University Press, 2000.

Akesson, T., et al. **(H. O. Ogren).** An X-ray scanner for wire chambers. *Nucl. Instrum. Methods Phys. Res., Sect. A* 507:622, 2003.

Akesson, T., et al. **(H. O. Ogren).** Aging studies for the ATLAS transition radiation tracker (TRT). *Nucl. Instrum. Methods Phys. Res., Sect. A* 515:166, 2003.

Akesson, T., et al. **(H. O. Ogren).** Tracking performance of the transition radiation tracker prototype for the ATLAS experiment. *Nucl. Instrum. Methods Phys. Res., Sect. A* 485:298, 2002.

Akesson, T., et al. **(H. O. Ogren).** Particle identification using the time-over-threshold method in the ATLAS transition radiation tracker. *Nucl. Instrum. Methods Phys. Res., Sect. A* 474:172, 2001.

Schider, G., et al. **(W. L. Schaich).** Plasmon dispersion relation of Au and Ag nanowires. *Phys. Rev. B* 68:155247, 2003.

Schider, G., et al. **(W. L. Schaich).** Optical resonances in periodic surface arrays of metallic patches. *Appl. Opt.* 42:5714, 2003.

Schaich, W. L. Electromagnetic velocity fields near a conducting slab. *Phys. Rev. E* 64:046605, 2001.

Schaich, W. L. Surface response of a conductor: Static and dynamic, electric and magnetic. *Am. J. Phys.* 69:1267, 2001.

Furnstahl, R. E., et al. **(B. D. Serot).** A chiral effective lagrangian for nuclei. *Nucl. Phys. A* 615:441–82, 1998.

Serot, B. D., and J. D. Walecka. Recent progress in quantum hadrodynamics. *Int. J. Mod. Phys. E* 6:515–631, 1997.

Müller, H., and **B. D Serot.** Phase transitions in warm, asymmetric nuclear. *Phys. Rev. C* 52:2072, 1995.

Serot, B. D., and J. D. Walecka. The relativistic nuclear many-body problem. *Adv. Nucl. Phys.* 16:1, 1986.

Setayeshgar, S., and A. J. Bernoff. Scroll waves in the presence of slowly varying anisotropy with application to the heart. *Phys. Rev. Lett.* 88:028101, 2002.

Setayeshgar, S., and M. C. Cross. Numerical bifurcation diagram for the two-dimensional boundary-fed CDIMA system. *Phys. Rev. E* 59:4258, 1999.

Setayeshgar, S., and M. C. Cross. Turing instability in a boundary-fed system. *Phys. Rev. E* 58:4485, 1998.

Chowdhuri, Z., et al. **(W. M. Snow).** A cryogenic neutron radiometer for absolute neutron fluence measurement. *Rev. Sci. Inst.* 74:4280, 2003.

Dewey, M. S., et al. **(W. M. Snow).** Measurement of the neutron lifetime using a proton trap. *Phys. Rev. Lett.* 91:152301, 2003.

Chen, W., et al. **(W. M. Snow).** Polarized 3He analyzers for neutron reflectometry. *Physica B* 335:196, 2003.

Black, T., et al. **(W. M. Snow).** Precision neutron interferometric measurement of the n-D coherent neutron scattering length and consequences for the nuclear three-body force. *Phys. Rev. Lett.* 90:192502, 2003.

Schoen, K., et al. **(W. M. Snow).** Precision neutron interferometric measurements and updated evalutations of the n-p and n-d coherent neutron scattering lengths. *Phys. Rev. C* 67: 044005, 2003.

Menon, M., and **K. R. Subbaswamy.** Covalent bonding between fullerenes. In *Fullerene Polymers and Fullerene Polymer Composites,* p. 229, eds. P. C. Eklund and A. M. Rao. Berlin: Springer, 1999.

Menon, M., E. Richter, and **K. R. Subbaswamy.** Fused fullerenes and 'gearoids': Proposed new forms of carbon. *Phys. Rev. B* 57:4063, 1998.

Richter, E., and **K. R. Subbaswamy.** Theory of size-dependent resonance Raman scattering from single-walled carbon nanotubes. *Phys. Rev. Lett.* 79:2738, 1997.

Menon, M., E. Richter, and **K. R. Subbaswamy.** Structure and vibrational properties of silicon clathrates in a generalized tight-binding molecular dynamics scheme. *Phys. Rev. B* 56:12290, 1997.

Szczepaniak, A. P. Confinement and exotic meson spectroscopy at 12-GEV JLab. *Braz. J. Phys.* 33:174, 2003.

Szczepaniak, A. P. Description of the D^*_s (2320) resonance as the Dπ atom. *Phys. Lett. B* 567:23, 2003.

Szczepaniak, A. P., and E. S. Swanson. The low lying glueball spectrum. *Phys. Lett. B* 577:61, 2003.

Brisudova, M. M., et al. **(A. P. Szczepaniak).** Nonlinear Regge trajectories and glueballs. *Phys. Rev. D* 67:094016, 2003.

Glazek, S. D., and **A. P. Szczepaniak.** Special relativity constraints on the effective constituent theory of hybrids. *Phys. Rev. D* 67:034019, 2003.

Szczepaniak, A. P., M. Swat, **A. R. Dzierba,** and S. Teige. On the nature of the π_1 ((1400) exotic meson. *Phys. Rev. Lett.* 91:092002, 2003.

Szczepaniak, A. P., M. Swat, **A. R. Dzierba,** and S. Teige. A study of the ηπ and η'π spectra and interpretation of a possible exotic $J^{PC} = 1^{-+}$ meson. *Phys. Rev. Lett.* 91:902002, 2003.

Gardestig, A., **A. P. Szczepaniak,** and **J. T. Londergan.** Separation of hard and soft physics in deeply virtual compton scattering. *Phys. Rev. D* 68:034005, 2003.

Pichowsky, M. A., **A. P. Szczepaniak,** and **J. T. Londergan.** Relativistic unitary description of final state interactions. *Phys. Rev. D* 64:036009, 2001.

von Przewoski, B., **R. Tayloe,** and J. Whitmore. A new life for Indiana's cyclotron. *CERN Courier* 43N5:13, 2003.

Auerbach, L. B., et al. **(R. Tayloe).** Measurements of charged current reactions of muon neutrinos on ^{12}C. *Phys. Rev. C* 66:015501, 2002.

Bassalleck, B., et al. **(R. Tayloe).** Measurement of spin transfer observables in anti-proton proton → anti-lambda at 1.637-GeV/c. *Phys. Rev. Lett.* 89:212302, 2002.

Auerbach, L. B., et al. **(R. Tayloe).** Measurement of electron-neutrino electron elastic scattering. *Phys. Rev. D* 63:112001, 2001.

Besson, D., et al. **(J. Urheim).** Observation of a narrow resonance of mass 2.46 GeV/c^2 and confirmation of the D_{sJ} (2317) state. *Phys. Rev. D* 68:032002, 2003.

Asner, D., et al. **(J. Urheim).** Hadronic structure in the decay $T^- \to \upsilon_\tau {}^-\pi^0 \pi^0$ and the sign of the tau neutrino helicity. *Phys. Rev. D* 61:012002, 2000.

Anderson, S., et al. **(J. Urheim).** Hadronic structure in the decay $T^- \to {}^-\pi^0 \pi^0 \upsilon_\tau$. *Phys. Rev. D* 61:112002, 2000.

Abazov, V. M., et al. **(R. Vankooten** and **A. Zieminski).** Observation of diffractively produced *W* and *Z* bosons in *pp-bar* collisions at $\sqrt{s}$ = 1.8 TeV. *Phys. Lett. B* 574:169, 2003.

Abazov, V. M., et al. **(R. Vankooten** and **A. Zieminski).** Search for large extra dimensions in the monojet + missing E_T channel at D0. *Phys. Rev. Lett.* 90:251802, 2003.

Abazov, V. M., et al. **(R. Vankooten** and **A. Zieminski).** Multiple jet production at low transverse energies in *pp-bar* collisions at $\sqrt{s}$ = 1.8 TeV. *Phys. Rev. D* 67:052001, 2003.

Abazov, V. M., et al. **(R. Vankooten** and **A. Zieminski).** *tt-bar* production cross-section in *pp-bar* collisions at $\sqrt{s}$ = 1.8 TeV. *Phys. Rev. D* 67:012004, 2003.

Abazov, V. M., et al. **(R. Vankooten** and **A. Zieminski).** Search for the production of single leptons through R-parity violation in $p(\bar{p})$ collisions at $\sqrt{s}$ = 1.8 TeV. *Phys. Rev. Lett.* 89:261801, 2002.

Abazov, V. M., et al. **(R. Vankooten** and **A. Zieminski).** Search for R-parity violating supersymmetry in two-muon and four-jet topologies. *Phys. Rev. Lett.* 89:171801, 2002.

Abazov, V. M., et al. **(R. Vankooten** and **A. Zieminski).** Direct measurement of the W boson decay width. *Phys. Rev. D* 66:032008, 2002.

Abazov, V. M., et al. **(R. Vankooten** and **A. Zieminski).** Improved W boson mass measurement with the DO detector. *Phys. Rev. D* 66:012001, 2002.

Beddo, M., et al. **(S. E. Vigdor).** The STAR barrel electromagnetic calorimeter. *Nucl. Instrum. Methods Phys. Res., Sect. A* 499:740, 2003.

Ackermann, K. H., et al. **(S. E. Vigdor** and **S. W. Wissink).** (STAR Collaboration). STAR detector overview. *Nucl. Instrum. Methods Phys. Res., Sect. A* 499:624, 2003.

Adler, C., et al. **(S. E. Vigdor** and **S. W. Wissink).** (STAR Collaboration). Azimuthal anisotropy and correlations in the hard scattering regime at RHIC. *Phys. Rev. Lett.* 90:032301, 2003.

Adams, J., et al. **(S. E. Vigdor** and **S. W. Wissink).** (STAR Collaboration). Strange anti-particle to particle ratios at mid-rapidity in $\sqrt{SNN}$ = 130 GeV Au + Au collisions. *Phys. Lett. B* 567:167, 2003.

Allgower, C. E., et al. **(S. E. Vigdor** and **S. W. Wissink).** (STAR Collaboration). The STAR endcap electromagnetic calorimeter. *Nucl. Instrum. Methods Phys. Res., Sect. A* 499:740, 2003.

Adler, C., et al. **(S. E. Vigdor** and **S. W. Wissink).** Disappearance of back-to-back high-$p_\perp$ hadron correlations in central Au + Au collisions at $\sqrt{SNN}$ = 200 GeV. *Phys. Rev. Lett.* 90:082302, 2003.

Wissink, S. W. (for STAR Collaboration). Extracting $\Delta G(x)$ from the $p+p \to \gamma$ + jet + X reaction with the STAR detector at RHIC. In *Proc. 14th Intl. Spin Phys. Symp.,* p. 447. Osaka, Japan: Spin 2000, 2001.

THE JOHNS HOPKINS UNIVERSITY

Henry A. Rowland Department of Physics and Astronomy

Program of Study The department offers a broad program for graduate and postdoctoral study in physics and astronomy in which intermediate, advanced, and specialized courses are offered. These courses and student research, begun as soon as possible, form the basis of the Ph.D. program. Considerable flexibility is available in each student's program, which is shaped to individual needs by recommendation from faculty and staff advisers. Students may choose to specialize in either physics or astrophysics, with a full curriculum of graduate courses available in both areas. In addition to required courses, candidates take written and oral preliminary examinations. Written examinations, covering intermediate-level material, must be passed by the end of the third semester. These exams are followed by an intermediate-level oral examination in the second year. A comprehensive oral examination is taken at the beginning of full-time research (usually in the third year). After completion of the student's research, an oral defense of the thesis is required. During residence, some teaching is usually required. Only those students who expect to complete the Ph.D. are admitted.

Research Facilities The high-energy-physics group has facilities for constructing the electronics and detectors needed in experiments and also has independent computing capabilities that allow full analyses of data. Nuclear physics equipment includes facilities for relativistic heavy-ion collision studies. Facilities for condensed matter physics include systems for molecular beam epitaxy, He^3-He^4 dilution refrigeration, high-rate sputtering, ultrahigh-vacuum thin-film deposition, automatic X-ray diffraction, scanning electron microscopy, X-ray fluorescence, LEED/Auger spectroscopy, SQUID and vibrating-sample magnetometry, ferromagnetic resonance, magnetooptics, neutron scattering, four-circle X-ray diffractometry, optical and electron-beam lithography, and dielectric susceptibility. For atomic, molecular, and plasma physics, facilities include high-resolution and very sensitive spectrometers for measurements of infrared to ultraviolet wavelengths, a high-precision X-ray spectrometer, extensive spectroscopic facilities, and lasers. The astrophysics group maintains a calibration and test facility for testing instrumentation for rocket and space flights. Computer facilities in the department include a large number of Sun, DEC, SGI, HP, and Intel-based workstations. These machines support a wide range of functions, including data reduction, image processing, and simulation of physical processes. All are networked to universities, national laboratories, and supercomputer facilities throughout the world, and Hopkins is part of Internet2 and VBNS. The Johns Hopkins University is the home of the Space Telescope Science Institute, is a partner in the Sloan Digital Sky Survey, and owns a share of the ARC 3.5 meter optical/infrared telescope. The University and its partners manage a space astronomy mission (FUSE) that was launched in June 1999. The Materials Research Science and Engineering Center (MRSEC) at Hopkins is one of twenty-four centers funded by the National Science Foundation to confront major challenges in the field of materials research. Facilities at the following laboratories and observatories are also frequently used: Brookhaven National Laboratory, Stanford Linear Accelerator Center, Fermi National Accelerator Laboratory, CERN, the University's own Applied Physics Laboratory, National Institute of Standards and Technology, Lawrence Berkeley Laboratory, Francis Bitter National Magnet Laboratory, Lawrence Livermore National Laboratory, the White Sands Missile Range, Kitt Peak National Observatory, Cerro Tololo Interamerican Observatory, the Very Large Array of the National Radio Astronomy Observatory, the Las Campanas Observatory, NASA's Goddard Space Flight Center and Space Telescope Science Institute, Anglo-Australian Observatory, Gemini Observatories, Chandra and XMM-Neutron X-ray Observatories, Argonne National Laboratory, NIST Center for Neutron Research, ISIS Facility, and Rutherford Appleton Laboratory.

Financial Aid Various tuition fellowships are usually awarded to all full-time Ph.D. candidates. Nonservice University fellowships and teaching assistantships offer a minimum of $14,700 (plus full tuition remission) for the nine-month academic year in 2004–05. Summer research assistantships may be available at approximately $4700. Holders of teaching assistantships must assist in teaching general physics and introductory courses. This experience is useful for students interested in a college teaching career. In addition to teaching assistantships, research assistantships that pay $1633 per month (plus full tuition remission) are also available for graduate students. These assistantships are awarded on the basis of experience, merit, and academic performance. (These awards are not usually given to first-year students unless they have special experience.)

Cost of Study Tuition is $30,140 for the 2004–05 academic year; however, full tuition support is given to all Ph.D. candidates as part of the financial package, which also includes either a full teaching or research assistantship. A one-time matriculation fee of $500 is required at registration.

Living and Housing Costs The University owns apartment buildings adjacent to the campus. In 2002–03, rates for unfurnished and furnished rooms and apartments varied from $350 to $800 per month. A campus housing office assists students in finding rooms and apartments in the surrounding residential area.

Student Group The University's Homewood Campus (the Schools of Arts and Sciences and of Engineering) had 4,112 undergraduates and 1,439 graduate students in 2002–03. There were 89 graduate students in physics and astronomy; all received financial support of some kind. Admission to graduate study in the department is highly competitive. An average of 20 new students are admitted each year; the majority enroll directly from college.

Location Located in the northern section of Baltimore, the University is adjacent to one of the finest residential areas of the city, while most of the cultural activities of the large metropolitan area are but minutes away.

The University The concept of graduate study came into being in America with the founding of the Johns Hopkins University in 1876. From the beginning, the hallmark of the University has been one of creative scholarship.

Applying Requirements for admission after completion of the bachelor's or master's degree are transcripts of previous academic work, letters of recommendation, and GRE scores, including the General Test and the Subject Test in physics. International students whose native language is not English must submit their scores on the Test of English as a Foreign Language (TOEFL). Students are admitted only in September. Applications and all supporting materials must be received by January 15. The application fee is $60, but it is temporarily waived for students with either financial need or foreign exchange problems. Application materials may be obtained on the World Wide Web at the address listed below.

Correspondence and Information

Graduate Admissions
The Henry A. Rowland Department of Physics and Astronomy
Bloomberg Center
The Johns Hopkins University
3400 North Charles Street
Baltimore, Maryland 21218-2686
Telephone: 410-516-7344
Fax: 410-516-7239
E-mail: admissions@pha.jhu.edu
World Wide Web: http://www.pha.jhu.edu

The Johns Hopkins University

THE FACULTY AND THEIR RESEARCH

Ronald J. Allen, Adjunct Professor; Ph.D., MIT, 1967. Spiral structure of galaxies, interstellar medium, radio and optical imaging.
Jonathan A. Bagger, Krieger Eisenhower Professor and Chair; Ph.D., Princeton, 1983. Theoretical high-energy physics.
Bruce A. Barnett, Professor; Ph.D., Maryland, 1970. High-energy physics.
Steven Beckwith, Professor and Director, Space Telescope Science Institute; Ph.D., Caltech, 1978. Infrared astronomy.
William P. Blair, Research Professor; Ph.D., Michigan, 1981. Astrophysics, shockwaves, spectroscopy of plasmas.
Barry J. Blumenfeld, Professor; Ph.D., Columbia, 1974. High-energy physics, neutrino physics.
Collin Broholm, Professor; Ph.D., Copenhagen, 1988. Experimental condensed-matter physics.
Chia-Ling Chien, Jacob L. Hain Professor; Ph.D., Carnegie Mellon, 1972. Condensed-matter physics, artificially structured solids.
Chih-Yung Chien, Professor; Ph.D., Yale, 1966. High-energy physics.
Mark Dickinson, Adjunct Assistant Professor (Space Telescope Science Institute); Ph.D., Berkeley, 1994. Optical, infrared, and X-ray observational astronomy.
Gabor Domokos, Professor; Ph.D., Dubna (Russia), 1963. Theoretical high-energy physics, astroparticle physics.
Adam Falk, Professor and Vice Dean, Krieger School of Arts and Sciences; Ph.D., Harvard, 1991. Theoretical high-energy physics.
Gordon Feldman, Professor Emeritus; Ph.D., Birmingham (England), 1953. Quantum field theory, theory of elementary particles.
Paul D. Feldman, Professor; Ph.D., Columbia, 1964. Astrophysics, spectroscopy, space physics, planetary and cometary atmospheres.
Henry Ferguson, Adjunct Associate Professor (Space Telescope Science Institute); Ph.D., Johns Hopkins, 1990. Observational cosmology, galaxy evolution, dwarf galaxies, space astronomy instrumentation, calibration.
Michael Finkenthal, Research Professor, Principal Research Scientist; Ph.D., Hebrew (Jerusalem), 1977. Plasma physics.
Holland Ford, Professor; Ph.D., Wisconsin, 1970. Stellar dynamics, evolution of galaxies, active galactic nuclei, astronomical instrumentation.
Thomas Fulton, Professor Emeritus; Ph.D., Harvard, 1954. Quantum electrodynamics, atomic theory, high-energy particle physics.
Riccardo Giacconi, Research Professor; Ph.D., Milan, 1954. Astrophysics.
Karl Glazebrook, Associate Professor; Ph.D., Edinburgh, 1992. Astronomy, astrophysics, galaxy evolution and formation.
Michael G. Hauser, Adjunct Professor; Ph.D., Caltech, 1967. Astrophysics, cosmology, especially infrared background radiation.
Timothy Heckman, Professor and Director, Center for Astrophysical Sciences; Ph.D., Washington (Seattle), 1978. Astrophysics, active galaxies and quasars.
Richard C. Henry, Professor and Director, Maryland Space Grant Consortium; Ph.D., Princeton, 1967. Astronomy, astrophysics.
Brian R. Judd, Gerhard H. Dieke Professor Emeritus; D.Phil., Oxford, 1955. Theoretical atomic and molecular physics, group theory, solid-state theory.
David Kaplan, Assistant Professor; Ph.D., Washington (Seattle), 1999. Theoretical high-energy physics.
Chung W. Kim, Professor Emeritus; Ph.D., Indiana, 1963. Nuclear theory, elementary particle theory, cosmology.
Susan Kövesi-Domokos, Professor; Ph.D., Budapest, 1963. Theoretical high-energy physics, astroparticle physics.
Gerard A. Kriss, Adjunct Associate Professor; Ph.D., MIT, 1982. Astrophysics, observation of galactic nuclei.
Julian H. Krolik, Professor; Ph.D., Berkeley, 1977. Theoretical astrophysics.
Yung Keun Lee, Professor; Ph.D., Columbia, 1961. Nuclear physics.
Robert Leheny, Assistant Professor; Ph.D., Chicago, 1997. Experimental condensed-matter physics.
Mario Livio, Adjunct Professor; Ph.D., Tel-Aviv, 1978. Theoretical astrophysics, accretion onto white dwarfs, neutron stars and black holes, novae and supernovae.
Markus Luty, Adjunct Assistant Professor; Ph.D., Chicago, 1991. Elementary particle theory.
Petar Maksimovic, Assistant Professor; Ph.D., MIT, 1997. Experimental high-energy physics.
Bruce Margon, Adjunct Professor; Ph.D., Berkeley, 1973. High-energy astrophysics, space astronomy.
Nina Markovic, Assistant Professor; Ph.D., Minnesota, 1998. Experimental condensed-matter physics.
H. Warren Moos, Gerhard H. Dieke Professor; Ph.D., Michigan, 1962. Astrophysics, plasma physics.
Jack Morava, Professor (Mathematics); Ph.D., Rice, 1967. Conformal field theory, topological gravity.
David A. Neufeld, Professor and Director, Theoretical Interdisciplinary Physics and Astrophysics Center; Ph.D., Harvard, 1987. Theoretical astrophysics, interstellar medium, astrophysical masers.
Colin A. Norman, Professor; D.Phil., Oxford, 1973. Theoretical astrophysics.
Aihud Pevsner, Jacob L. Hain Professor Emeritus; Ph.D., Columbia, 1954. High-energy physics.
Daniel H. Reich, Professor; Ph.D., Chicago, 1988. Experimental condensed-matter physics.
Adam Reiss, Adjunct Assistant Professor (Space Telescope Science Institute); Ph.D., Harvard, 1996. Astrophysics.
Mark O. Robbins, Professor; Ph.D., Berkeley, 1983. Theoretical condensed-matter physics.
Ethan Schreier, Adjunct Professor; Ph.D., MIT, 1970. Astrophysics, active galaxies and jets.
Darrell F. Strobel, Professor (Earth and Planetary Sciences); Ph.D., Harvard, 1969. Planetary atmospheres and astrophysics.
Raman Sundrum, Professor; Ph.D., Yale, 1990. Higher dimensional theories, supersymmetric theories, and physics beyond the standard model.
Alexander S. Szalay, Alumni Centennial Professor; Ph.D., Eötvös Loránd (Budapest), 1975. Theoretical astrophysics, galaxy formation.
Oleg Tchernyshyov, Assistant Professor; Ph.D., Columbia, 1998. Theoretical condensed-matter physics, geometrically frustrated magnets.
Zlatko Tesanovic, Professor; Ph.D., Minnesota, 1985. Theoretical condensed-matter physics.
Roeland van der Marel, Adjunct Associate Professor (Space Telescope Science Institute); Ph.D., Leiden (Netherlands), 1994. Black holes, cluster of galaxies, dark halos, galaxy structure and dynamics.
Ethan Vishniac, Professor; Ph.D., Harvard, 1980. Theoretical astrophysics.
J. C. Walker, Professor Emeritus; Ph.D., Princeton, 1961. Condensed-matter physics, thin films and surfaces, nuclear physics.
Kimberly Weaver, Adjunct Assistant Professor; Ph.D., Maryland, 1993. High-energy astrophysics.
Robert Williams, Adjunct Professor; Ph.D., Wisconsin–Madison, 1965. Astronomy and astrophysics, novae, space science.
Rosemary F. G. Wyse, Professor; Ph.D., Cambridge, 1982. Astrophysics: galaxy formation and evolution.

RESEARCH ACTIVITIES

Astrophysics. Observational programs include the use of ground-based optical and radio telescopes, analysis of archival data from previous space experiments, new research with existing satellites and sounding rockets, and space experiments. There is extensive laboratory work on detectors and instrument development for ultraviolet and optical astronomy. Research is concentrated in the following areas of astrophysics: cosmology, active galactic nuclei and quasars, galaxies and galaxy dynamics, stellar populations, the interstellar medium, comets and planetary atmospheres, and diffuse ultraviolet background studies.

Atomic Physics. Research in this area includes theoretical work on the electronic structure of atoms and molecules.

Condensed-Matter Physics. Research programs involve studies of very thin magnetic films; interfaces and surfaces; amorphous materials; conducting, superconducting, and magnetic properties of artificially structured materials; nanocrystals of metals and alloys; low-dimensional quantum magnets; highly correlated electron systems; high-T_c superconductors; complex fluids; glass-forming systems; and nonequilibrium phenomena. Techniques involve SQUID magnetometry, X-ray diffraction, atomic force and magnetic force microscopy, neutron scattering, various cryogenic techniques, DC and AC conductivity, LEED and Auger spectroscopies, ferromagnetic resonance, and vibrating-sample magnetometry and dielectric susceptibility.

High-Energy Physics. Current programs involve the study of strong, electromagnetic, and weak interactions. Experiments currently in progress are being performed at the Tevatron $p\bar{p}$ collider at Fermilab, at LEP and SPS, in CERN in Switzerland, and an experiment CMS at LHC in CERN. Data analysis is in progress at these facilities and at the Homewood Campus. Facilities for the construction and testing of particle detectors and associated electronics are available.

Plasma Spectroscopy. Extreme ultraviolet and soft X-ray diagnostic instrumentation is used to study high-temperature plasma devices used in controlled thermonuclear research.

Relativistic Heavy-Ion and Medium-Energy Nuclear Physics. The heavy-ion physics program includes the study of quark gluon plasma at the RHIC collider with the STAR and the BRAMS detectors at the Brookhaven National Laboratory.

Theoretical Physics. Areas of current research include particle physics, condensed-matter physics, molecular and atomic structure, quantum optics, and astrophysics. The particle theory group currently conducts research in supersymmetric theories, heavy quark theory, and astroparticle physics. The condensed-matter theory group studies superconductivity, quantum Hall effect, magnetism, quantum critical phenomena, and various forms of nonequilibrium and growth phenomena. Members of the theory group specializing in different areas maintain close contact with each other and with the experimental groups.

KENT STATE UNIVERSITY

Department of Physics

Programs of Study The Department of Physics offers a diverse program of graduate study and research leading to the Master of Arts, Master of Science, and Doctor of Philosophy degrees. Areas of concentration include experimental, theoretical, and computational research into the physics of condensed matter, with emphases on novel electron systems, high-T_c superconductors, liquid crystal physics, and display applications, and high-energy nuclear physics, with emphasis on the quark-gluon structure of hadrons and hot hadronic matter produced in heavy-ion collisions. Theoretical research opportunities also provide training in quantum field theory and chromodynamics, statistical physics, and theoretical research in computational biophysics. The department maintains collaborations with the Departments of Biology, Chemistry, Chemical Physics, and Computer Science, offering students interdisciplinary opportunities.

A student typically takes core courses during the first year of study. The M.A. and M.S. degrees require 32 semester credit hours. The M.S. degree requires a thesis. The Ph.D. degree requires courses, seminars, and dissertation research. Doctoral students normally pass the candidacy examination in their second year. Over the past ten years, the average time to the completion of the Ph.D. degree has been 5.7 years—about nine months shorter than the national average for physics.

Research Facilities The Department of Physics has extensive and modern facilities for condensed-matter research, including nonlinear optics, electrooptics, tunneling and atomic force microscopy, nuclear magnetic resonance, high-resolution synchrotron X-ray scattering, light scattering, microcalorimetry, millikelvin refrigeration, SQUID magnetometry, magnetoresistance and Hall effect measurement. The experimental nuclear physics group has an extensive collection of the state-of-the-art apparatus. Of special note are the large-volume, ultrafast neutron detectors and neutron polarimeters developed by Kent faculty members and students. Researchers receive specialized support from a machine shop and an electronics shop; have access to a class 100 clean room, a materials synthesis facility, and an X-ray diffraction sector at the Advanced Photon Source of Argonne National Laboratory as well as the KSU Planetarium and KSU/NASA Observatory. The Center for Nuclear Research has the mission to support, enhance, and promote academic activities in nuclear physics. The Liquid Crystal Institute (LCI) at Kent State University is a strong (and international) academic and technology center for liquid crystal research and is a major source of physics Ph.D.'s employed in the liquid crystal and flat-panel display industry worldwide.

Financial Aid In 2004–05, graduate appointments for the calendar year carry a stipend of $14,250 (over nine months), a full tuition scholarship, and partial health insurance coverage. It is possible to enter the program at midyear.

Cost of Study All appointees receive a full tuition scholarship covering their cost of study. The 2003–04 annual tuition was $9324 (or $334 per credit hour) for in-state residents pursuing full-time study and $17,514 (or $627 per credit hour) for out-of-state and international students.

Living and Housing Costs The cost of living in Kent is low, well below the national average. Both on-campus and off-campus living accommodations are available. Rooms are available for single graduate students in dormitories. Current costs per month are $488 for a single, $459 for a double, and $599 for a 2-person suite. Furnished one- and two-bedroom apartments for married students are available in the attractive University-owned Allerton Apartments. Current costs per month are $600 for a one-bedroom and $630 for a two-bedroom apartment. Reasonably priced rental housing also can be easily found. The Campus Bus Service provides free transportation on campus and to the surrounding area.

Student Group Of the approximately 24,200 students on the Kent campus, about 5,000 are graduate students. The physics department has about 50 graduate students from more than twelve countries. Kent State University emphasizes diversity, successfully attracting students from traditionally underrepresented groups, including minorities and women.

Student Outcomes Students find rewarding positions in academic, government, and industrial institutions. Kent physics graduates enter initial employment in permanent positions at a higher rate than national norms. The alumni currently include 4 chairs of physics departments, professors, presidents and vice presidents of companies, managers, directors, researchers at national laboratories, and consultants.

Location Kent is a beautiful city of approximately 30,000 residents, located in northeastern Ohio, within a 50-minute drive of the metropolitan areas of Cleveland, Akron-Canton, and Youngstown. Its geographic location offers excellent job opportunities for students and their spouses. Downtown Cleveland is home to the Cleveland Symphony Orchestra, major-league sports (Cleveland Indians, Browns, Cavaliers, Crunch), and world-class museums (Museum of Art, Museum of Natural History, Rock and Roll Hall of Fame and Museum). Visitors to Akron enjoy the Akron Art Museum, the National Inventors Hall of Fame, and the Akron Aeros baseball team. Canton, located south of Kent, has attractions such as the Pro Football Hall of Fame and the U.S. First Ladies exhibit in the McKinley Museum. The nearby Cuyahoga Valley National Recreation Area provides excellent recreational opportunities for every season. Blossom Music Center, the Cleveland Orchestra, and the Porthouse Theatre are among many excellent cultural opportunities in the area.

The University and The Department Kent State University offers degree programs ranging from undergraduate degrees in creative and performing arts to graduate degrees in the sciences. Kent State holds the highest-level ranking by the Carnegie Research Foundation as a Doctoral/Research University–Extensive. A modern research library provides access to all Ohio libraries through OhioLink. It houses more than 2 million volumes in its collection to support scholars and researchers.

The physics department has offices, classrooms, and laboratories in Smith Hall and the adjacent Science Research Building. There are 20 regular faculty members, who receive the highest per capita funding in the state of Ohio—about $1.4 million per year in research support from federal and state agencies and the private sector.

Applying Graduate study may be initiated during any term, including summer. Application forms for admission and financial assistance may be obtained by writing to the Department of Physics. Additional information and Web-based application forms are available at the address listed below.

Correspondence and Information

Dr. Gerassimos G. Petratos, Chair
Department of Physics
Kent State University
Kent, Ohio 44242-0001
Telephone: 330-672-2246
Fax: 330-672-2959
E-mail: gradprogram@physics.kent.edu
World Wide Web: http://phys.kent.edu

Kent State University

THE FACULTY AND THEIR RESEARCH

David W. Allender, Professor; Ph.D., Illinois, 1975. Theoretical physics of condensed matter, liquid crystals, and superconductivity.
Carmen C. Almasan, Associate Professor; Ph.D., South Carolina, 1989. Experimental condensed-matter physics, superconductivity, correlated electron systems, magnetism, low-temperature physics.
Bryon D. Anderson, Professor; Ph.D., Case Western Reserve, 1972. Experimental nuclear physics, nuclear force, nucleon structure.
Brett D. Ellman, Associate Professor; Ph.D., Chicago, 1992. Superconductivity, organic semiconductor, conduction mechanics in insulators and semiconductors, phonon physics, disordered magnets.
George Fai, Professor and Director of the Center for Nuclear Research; Ph.D., Eötvös Loránd (Budapest), 1974. Theoretical nuclear physics, relativistic nuclear collisions.
Daniele Finotello, Professor and Associate Dean, Research and Graduate Studies; Ph.D., SUNY at Buffalo, 1985. Low-temperature and liquid crystal physics, superconductivity.
James T. Gleeson, Associate Professor; Ph.D., Kent State, 1991. Nonequilibrium dynamics and pattern formation.
A. Mina T. Katramatou, Assistant Professor; Ph.D., American, 1988. Nuclear particle physics.
Declan Keane, Professor; Ph.D., University College (Dublin), 1981. Relativistic nuclear collisions.
Satyendra Kumar, Professor; Ph.D., Illinois at Urbana-Champaign, 1981. Liquid crystal structure, phase transition, electrooptical effects, complex fluids, biophysics, nanostructured materials, carbon nanotube composites.
Michael A. Lee, Professor; Ph.D., Northwestern, 1977. Condensed-matter theory, biophysics, computational physics.
D. Mark Manley, Professor; Ph.D., Wyoming, 1981. Experimental medium-energy nuclear physics.
Elizabeth K. Mann, Associate Professor; Ph.D., Paris VI (Curie), 1992. Experimental soft-matter physics, complex fluids.
Spyridon Margetis, Associate Professor; Ph.D., Frankfurt, 1990. Experimental high-energy nuclear physics.
Gerassimos Petratos, Professor and Chair; Ph.D., American, 1988. Experimental nuclear/particle physics.
John J. Portman, Assistant Professor; Ph.D., Illinois at Urbana-Champaign, 2000. Theoretical biological physics.
Khandker F. Quader, Professor; Ph.D., SUNY at Stony Brook, 1983. Theoretical condensed-matter physics, superconductivity, strongly correlated systems, low-temperature physics.
Almut Schroeder, Assistant Professor; Ph.D., Karlsruhe, 1991. Experimental condensed-matter physics, strongly correlated electron physics, quantum phase transitions.
Samuel N. Sprunt Jr., Associate Professor; Ph.D., MIT, 1989. Experimental liquid crystal physics, phase transitions, quasi-elastic light scattering, confocal microscopy.
Peter C. Tandy, Professor; Ph.D., Flinders (Australia), 1973. Theoretical nuclear physics, nonperturbative QCD, hadron physics.
John W. Watson, Professor; Ph.D., Maryland, 1970. Experimental medium-energy nuclear physics.

FACULTY IN RELATED DISCIPLINES

James Blank, Professor, Biological Sciences and Director of the School of Biomedical Sciences; Ph.D., Indiana, 1982. Male reproductive physiology, physiological ecology and neuroendocrinology, behavioral neuroendocrinology.
Philip J. Bos, Professor and Associate Director, Liquid Crystal Institute, Chemical Physics Interdisciplinary Program; Ph.D., Kent State, 1978. Liquid crystal applications.
Paul Farrell, Professor, Computer Science; Ph.D., Dublin, 1983. Numerical computation and analysis.
Arne Gericke, Assistant Professor, Biophysical Chemistry; Dr.rer.nat., Hamburg (Germany), 1994. Lipid-mediated protein functions/lytropic liquid crystals.
Robert T. Heath, Professor, Biological Sciences and Director of the Water Resources Research Institute; Ph.D., USC, 1968. Biochemical limnology, phosphorus dynamics in aquatic ecosystems, planktonic biochemistry, physiological ecology.
Jack R. Kelly, Professor, Chemical Physics Interdisciplinary Program; Ph.D., Clarkson, 1979. Electrooptic and dielectric properties of liquid crystals.
Oleg Lavrentovich, Professor and Interim Director, Liquid Crystal Institute, Chemical Physics Interdisciplinary Program; Ph.D., 1984, D.Sc., 1990, Ukrainian Academy of Sciences. Defects in liquid crystals, electrooptics of smectic liquid crystals, physics of liquid crystalline dispersions.
Peter Palffy-Muhoray, Professor and Associate Director, Liquid Crystal Institute, Chemical Physics Interdisciplinary Program; Ph.D., British Columbia, 1977. Nonlinear optics, pattern formation in liquid crystals.
Arden Ruttan, Professor, Computer Science; Ph.D., Kent State, 1977. Numerical computation and analysis.

ACTIVE RESEARCH TOPICS

Correlated Electron Physics

Theoretical investigation of fluctuation phenomena and mechanisms of superconductivity.
Thermodynamic properties.
Study of systems displaying strong electronic correlations, e.g., unconventional superconductivity and magnetism, Bose-Einstein condensation, colossal magnetoresistance, non-Fermi liquid states, quantum phase transitions, quantum fluids, physics of novel semiconductors, and role of disorder and dimensionality.
Experimental studies utilize low-temperature and high-field electron/phonon transport, thermodynamic, neutron scattering, and magnetic techniques.
Theoretical studies employ techniques of many-particle quantum statistical mechanics, e.g., diagrammatic crossing-symmetric and functional integral methods, quantum transport equation, Fermi liquid theory, homotopic topology and elements of critical phenomena.
Examples of systems studied are high-T_c cuprate, heavy fermion, and magnetic superconductors, manganites, rare-earth magnets, organic crystalline and liquid crystalline semiconductors.

Soft Condensed-Matter Physics and Applications

Nonlinear optics of ordered fluids.
Pattern formation in liquid crystals.
Phase transitions in liquid crystals in bulk and under confinement.
High-precision heat capacity measurements of phase transitions in lyotropic liquid crystals and nonionic surfactant solutions.
Surface effects on liquid crystals.
High-resolution synchrotron X-ray diffraction and small-angle neutron scattering studies of structure and critical phenomena in complex fluids; thermotropic, polymer, and lyotropic liquid crystals; nanostructured systems; and carbon nanotube composites.
Neutron scattering from condensed matter.
Liquid crystal display physics; ferroelectric liquid crystal displays, optical beam modulating, and steering devices.
High-definition systems: theoretical and experimental research in the use of liquid crystals in high-resolution display devices, including high-definition television.
Dynamics, thermodynamics, and microrheology in Langmuir films.

Computational Physics

Quantum Monte Carlo and many-body physics, large-scale biological simulations, parallel scientific algorithms.

Nuclear Physics

Experimental and theoretical investigation of the nuclear matter equation of state.
Signals of the quark-gluon phase in relativistic nuclear collisions.
Extended field-theory model studies of nucleons, mesons, and nuclear systems in terms of elementary (quark) degrees of freedom.
Measurements to probe the charge and magnetic structure of the neutron.
Nuclear structure studies with electron scattering and charge-exchange reactions.
Spin structure of the nucleons from polarized deep inelastic electron scattering.
Electromagnetic form-factors of deuterium and helium.
Studies of nucleon resonances with electromagnetic and hadronic probes.
Few-nucleon reaction studies.
Spin-transfer studies in nuclear reactions.
Nonperturbative QCD for hadron structure and interactions.

KENT STATE UNIVERSITY

Chemical Physics Interdisciplinary Program at the Liquid Crystal Institute

Program of Study

The Chemical Physics Interdisciplinary Program (CPIP) offers graduate courses and research leading to the Master of Science and Doctor of Philosophy degrees in chemical physics. The program concentrates on basic and applied sciences of liquid crystals, complex fluids, and related materials, with concentrations in optoelectronics, physical properties of liquid crystals, liquid-crystal synthesis and molecular design, lyotropic liquid crystals and membranes, and general chemical physics.

The courses are taught by faculty members of CPIP and the Departments of Chemistry, Physics, and Mathematics. The M.S. degree requires 32 semester hours of courses and a thesis. The Ph.D. degree requires 90 semester hours of courses, seminars, and research beyond the bachelor's degree or 60 semester hours beyond the master's degree. Doctoral students are required to pass the candidacy examination before the start of their second year.

Research Facilities

The program is housed in the Liquid Crystal Institute at Kent State University. The institute is a strong academic center of liquid-crystal and soft condensed-matter research and is the only institute of its kind in the United States. In 1991, the National Science Foundation established the Science and Technology Center on Advanced Liquid Crystalline Optical Materials (ALCOM), with the Liquid Crystal Institute as its hub. CPIP students have access to the expertise and research equipment of ALCOM and the Liquid Crystal Institute. Facilities for condensed-matter research include state-of-the-art equipment for NMR, microcalorimetry, optical, scanning-tunneling, atomic-force, and scanning-electron microscopy; image analysis; high-resolution X-ray and light scattering; dielectric, magnetic, surface, and optical studies; and nonlinear optics. The Institute houses clean rooms for display device prototyping, as well as laser facilities and materials synthesis and characterization laboratories.

Financial Aid

In 2003–04, graduate appointments carried a stipend of $17,880 plus a full tuition scholarship. A limited number of fellowships from sponsoring industries are also available.

Cost of Study

The 2003–04 annual full-time tuition was $8075 for in-state residents and $15,210 for out-of-state residents.

Living and Housing Costs

Rooms are available for single graduate students in campus dormitories; current costs per month are $390 for single rooms, $358 for double rooms, and $468 for a deluxe single accommodation. Furnished apartments for married students in the University-owned Allerton Apartments currently cost $575 per month for one bedroom and $600 per month for two bedrooms. A variety of reasonably priced rental housing can be found in the Kent area. The Campus Bus Service provides a transportation network for the Kent campus and links the campus with shopping centers and residential neighborhoods in nearby communities; this service is free to all Kent students.

Student Group

Kent State is Ohio's second-largest university, with more than 33,000 students on eight campuses. The University is third in the number of doctoral graduates and doctoral programs. The Chemical Physics Interdisciplinary Program, now in its eighth year, has 30 graduate students who represent seven countries. Approximately 20 out of a total of 50 graduate students from physics are also involved in liquid crystal–related research.

Student Outcomes

More than 100 Ph.D. degrees have been awarded by Kent State University in the field of liquid crystals. Graduates are employed in industry (Allied Signal, Phillips, Xerox, 3M, Tektronix, Westinghouse, and Samsung) and at universities (Calgary, Stanford, Southern Mississippi, Brown, Calabria, and others). Current employment prospects are excellent for graduates of the program, both in the rapidly growing flat panel display industry and in the soft condensed-matter materials/optics areas.

Location

Kent is a beautiful city of approximately 30,000 residents, located in northeastern Ohio within a 60-minute drive from the metropolitan areas of Cleveland, Akron-Canton, and Youngstown. Its geographic location offers excellent job opportunities for students. Downtown Cleveland is home to the Cleveland Symphony Orchestra, major league sports (Cleveland Browns, Indians, Cavaliers, and Barons), and world-class museums (Museum of Art, Museum of Natural History, Rock and Roll Hall of Fame and Museum). Visitors to Akron enjoy the Akron Art Museum, the National Inventors Hall of Fame, and the Akron Aeros baseball team. Canton, located south of Kent, has attractions such as the Pro Football Hall of Fame and the First Ladies exhibit in the McKinley Museum. The nearby Cuyahoga Valley National Recreation Area provides excellent recreational opportunities for every season. Blossom Music Center, the Cleveland Orchestra, and the Porthouse Theatre are among many cultural opportunities in the area.

The University and The Program

The Chemical Physics Interdisciplinary Program is housed in a new modern building for the Liquid Crystal Institute.

The Chemical Physics Interdisciplinary Program has 12 faculty members, with 6 having appointments in CPIP and 6 having joint appointments in chemistry, physics, and mathematics and computer science. Research funding per year to CPIP faculty members is in excess of $2.5 million from federal and state agencies, which also provide research assistantship support.

Applying

Application forms for admission and financial assistance may be obtained by writing to the Chemical Physics Interdisciplinary Program. Completed applications should be received before January 31 for fall admission. Due to strong competition for limited enrollment, early application is encouraged.

Correspondence and Information

L. C. Chien, Graduate Coordinator
Chemical Physics Interdisciplinary Program
Liquid Crystal Institute
Kent State University
Kent, Ohio 44242
Telephone: 330-672-4844
Fax: 330-672-2796
E-mail: lfagan@kent.edu
World Wide Web: http://www.lci.kent.edu/cpip.html

Kent State University

THE FACULTY AND THEIR RESEARCH

David A. Allender, Professor (physics); Ph.D., Illinois, 1975. Theoretical physics of condensed matter, superconductivity theory, liquid crystals and membrane models.
Philip J. Bos, Professor; Ph.D., Kent State, 1979. Electrooptics, liquid-crystal displays, beam-steering devices.
L. C. Chien, Professor; Ph.D., Southern Mississippi, 1988. Display materials, polymeric liquid crystals, polymer-stabilized liquid crystals.
J. William Doane, Emeritus Professor; Ph.D., Missouri, 1965. Nuclear magnetic resonance of liquid crystals.
E. C. Gartland, Professor (mathematics and computer science); Ph.D., Purdue, 1980. Numerical modeling and computation of liquid-crystal systems.
Jack R. Kelly, Professor; Ph.D., Clarkson, 1979. Electrooptic and dielectric properties of liquid crystals.
Satyendra Kumar, Professor (physics); Ph.D., Illinois at Urbana-Champaign, 1981. Liquid-crystal structure and phase transitions, liquid-crystal electrooptic effects.
Oleg D. Lavrentovich, Professor; Ph.D., 1984, D.Sc., 1990, Ukrainian Academy of Sciences. Defects in liquid crystals, electrooptics of liquid crystals.
Peter Palffy-Muhoray, Professor; Ph.D., British Columbia, 1977. Nonlinear optics, pattern formation in liquid crystals.
John L. West, Professor (chemistry); Ph.D., Carnegie Mellon, 1980. Display materials, liquid crystal surface alignment, polymer wall formation.
Deng-Ke Yang, Associate Professor; Ph.D., Hawaii, 1989. Electrooptics, polymer-stabilized liquid crystals.

ACTIVE RESEARCH TOPICS

Beam-steering devices.
Confocal microscopy of liquid crystals.
Defect structure and dynamics.
Design and synthesis of liquid crystalline materials having new structures and effects.
Dynamic light scattering and photon localization.
Ferroelectric displays.
Ferroelectric liquid-crystal displays.
Finite-element methods in free-energy minimization.
High-resolution X-ray and small-angle neutron scattering from complex fluids.
Liquid crystals as biological defectors.
Liquid crystals in porous media.
Modeling reaction-diffusion systems.
Modeling structural properties and transitions.
Modeling the optical response of nematic displays.
Nanostructured liquid crystalline systems.
Nematodynamics and the effects of shear.
NMR of confined liquid crystals.
Optical field–induced instabilities.
Optical information storage.
Pattern formation in liquid crystals.
Phase separation dynamics in polymer–liquid-crystal systems.
Phase transitions in confined liquid crystals.
Photonic application of liquid crystals.
Surface analysis and treatment.
Surface-anchoring measurements.
Switching phenomena in polymer-stabilized materials.
Location:

LEHIGH UNIVERSITY

College of Arts and Sciences
Department of Physics

Programs of Study

The department offers a program of course work and research leading to the M.S. and Ph.D. degrees in physics. The active research areas of the department include atomic and molecular physics, condensed matter physics, nonlinear optics and photonics, biophysics, complex fluids and polymers, plasma physics, and statistical physics. Experimental, theoretical, and computational projects are underway in most areas. Active collaborations also exist with research programs in other departments and interdisciplinary centers at Lehigh, particularly electrical engineering, materials science and engineering, and the Centers for Optical Technologies (COT), Advanced Materials and Nontechnologies (CAMN), and the Sherman Fairfield Center for Microelectronics.

The department's graduate program is designed mainly to lead to a Ph.D. degree. Most students who enter with a bachelor's degree earn a master's degree after three semesters and one summer. Some of these students have structured their master's program with some specialization so that they are prepared for employment when they complete the program, but others treat the master's program as just part of the core program for the Ph.D. program. The student must do either a research project (Physics 491) or a master's thesis for the master's degree. The master's program requires 30 credit hours of course work, including the 3 credits of a research project or 6 credits on master's thesis research.

The Ph.D. program includes a set of core courses, including some at the advanced graduate level that provide the broad background in physics that is essential, specialized courses relevant to the research area of the student, and the research for the Ph.D. dissertation. Most students take five to six years to complete the Ph.D., which includes an M.S.

Research Facilities

Research in the physics department is carried out in the Sherman Fairchild Center for the Physical Sciences, which consists of two connected buildings containing a wide variety of laboratory and computer facilities, as well as offices, classrooms, and lecture halls. Major equipment includes a 3-MeV Van de Graaff accelerator; three electron spin resonance laboratories; ultraviolet, visible, and infrared spectrophotometers; liquid nitrogen, hydrogen, and helium cryogenic equipment; optical tweezers and confocal microscopes; many specialty lasers (gas, dye, and solid state); a 20J pulsed laser facility; crystal-growing facilities; a fiber drawing tower; a mass spectrometer, large interferometers, a Raman spectrometer, an electron microscope, and a high-density plasma source; optical multichannel analyzers; streak cameras; and digital signal processors. A well-equipped machine shop employs two skilled machinists. This facility can handle such tasks as precision machine work, vacuum, and welding jobs of moderate size. In addition, the department employs 2 experienced electronics technicians for in-house servicing of electronics instrumentation.

Lehigh University provides high-quality computer resources to support research. The University is completely networked through a digital PBX system that provides access to hundreds of microcomputers and workstations on campus as well as connections to the Internet. The University library system houses more than 1,000,000 volumes and also offers catalog access, searching, and other library services through the computer network.

Lehigh University is a charter member of the Internet2 project. A high-performance connection (155 megabits per second) to the Mid-Atlantic Gigapop in Philadelphia for Internet2 (MAGPI) allows members of the campus community to participate in research and educational activities with other Internet2 schools and with corporations and research sites on the various interconnected national and international high-speed networks.

Financial Aid

Teaching assistantships are normally available for graduate students. For 2004–05, the stipend for beginning teaching assistants is $17,800 for twelve months. Tuition is remitted for the standard course load, which is up to 9 hours of course work per semester. In addition, summer support may be available during the summer prior to beginning graduate study. University-endowed fellowships are available to outstanding candidates and the stipend depends on the award. Research assistantships are available for advanced students and typically furnish a twelve-month stipend.

Cost of Study

Tuition for 2004–05 is $950 per credit hour for teaching and research assistants, however nearly all assistantships include full tuition credit.

Living and Housing Costs

Graduate students live in a wide variety of accommodations, ranging from apartments within walking distance of campus to modern garden apartments a few miles away. Expenses can be reasonable, especially if accommodations are shared. The University operates a 148-unit, five-building garden apartment complex for married and graduate students, located on the Saucon Valley campus. The monthly cost for an efficiency apartment is $440, for a one-bedroom apartment is $510, and for a two-bedroom apartment is $545 to $575 with electricity. Free bus service to the main campus is provided hourly.

Student Group

The department has approximately 40 graduate students and 11 are women. All full-time graduate students currently receive financial aid from Lehigh. Fifty percent of graduate students are U.S. citizens.

Student Outcomes

Recent physics graduates are employed in academic and industrial positions. The academic positions include post-doctoral positions, but several have found tenure-track assistant professorships at institutions that include the following: Drew University, Rowan College, and the United States Naval Academy. In addition, schools in Pennsylvania include Moravian College, Lebanon Valley College, King's College, and Kutztown University. Industrial positions include NIST, Lucent Technology, Texas Instruments, and Brookhaven National Laboratory.

Location

Lehigh is located in Bethlehem, Pennsylvania. The immediate vicinity is urban, but the greater Lehigh Valley area includes many scenic, rural areas. Bethlehem is 50 miles north of Philadelphia and 75 miles southwest of New York City. The University is located near several major highways and the Lehigh Valley International Airport.

The University

The University offers a wide variety of resources for the personal and professional development of its diverse student body. Organizations exist for theater, music, volunteer and community service, intramural athletics, religious activities, and various hobbies.

The Department of Physics is part of the College of Arts and Sciences, which is one of four Colleges at Lehigh University. Physics graduate students may participate in all University sponsored activities.

Applying

For admission to the graduate programs, a bachelor's degree in physics or a related field is required with a minimum undergraduate grade point average of 3.0. Scores from the GRE are required. The minimum acceptable score suggested for admission is Verbal, 550 and Quantitative, 650, for a total of 1,200. The GRE Advanced scores are also required. The minimum acceptable score suggested for admission is 600. Students from non-English speaking countries are required to demonstrate proficiency in English via the TOEFL exam and the University SPEAK test for teaching assistants. Applicants are normally expected to have TOEFL scores of at least 600 on the paper-based test or 250 on the new, computer-based test. The deadline for applications for fall admission and financial aid is March 15.

Correspondence and Information

For more information, students may contact:

Graduate Admissions Officer
Department of Physics
16 Memorial Drive East
Lehigh University
Bethlehem, Pennsylvania 18015

Telephone: 610-758-3930
Fax: 610-758-5730
E-mail: physics@lehigh.edu
World Wide Web: www.physics.lehigh.edu

Lehigh University

THE FACULTY AND THEIR RESEARCH

Ivan Biaggio, Associate Professor, Ph.D., ETH Zurich (Switzerland), 1993, Nonlinear optics, four-wave mixing, self-assembled supramolecular films for guided-wave applications, charge transport in polar crystals and organic semiconductors.

Garold Borse, Professor, Ph.D., Virginia, 1966. Nuclear theory, investigation of anomalous properties of spherical-vibrational nuclei using the techniques of boson expansion.

Gary G. DeLeo, Professor, Ph.D., Connecticut, 1979. Theoretical astrophysics, theoretical solid state physics.

Volkmar Dierolf, Associate Professor, Ph.D., Utah, 1992. Solid state physics and integrated optics, optical spectroscopy and microscopy of insulating and semiconducting materials.

Robert T. Folk, Professor, Ph.D., Lehigh, 1958. Theory of very light nuclei, elastic properties of solids.

W. Beall Fowler, Professor Emeritus, Ph.D., Rochester, 1963. Theoretical solid state physics, calculations of electronic properties of defects in insulators and semiconductors using molecular orbital theory, theory of defects near oxide-semiconductor interfaces.

James D. Gunton, Professor, Ph.D., Stanford, 1967. Theoretical statistical physics, kinetics of first-order phase transitions and the development of order from disorder, pattern formation in nonlinear nonequilibrium systems.

A. Peet Hickman, Professor, Ph.D., Rice, 1973. Theoretical atomic and molecular physics. Quantum mechanical calculations of atom-atom collisions important in the atmosphere.

John P. Huennekens, Professor, Ph.D., Colorado, 1982. Experimental atomic and molecular physics, studies of collisional processes in atomic vapors including excitation transfer, energy pooling, velocity-changing collisions, and line broadening.

Alvin S. Kanofsky, Professor, Ph.D., Pennsylvania, 1966. High-energy experimental physics.

Yong W. Kim, Professor, Ph.D., Michigan, 1968. Experimental statistical physics (nonlinear dynamics of intrinsic fluctuations, transport properties) and atomic physics (nonideality effects in dense laser-produced plasmas).

Arnold H. Kritz, Professor, Ph.D., Yale, 1961. Theoretical and computational plasma physics, studies of heating and transport effects of magnetically confined toroidal plasmas, research is closely related to experiments at major fusion laboratories.

Jerome Licini, Associate Professor, Ph.D., M.I.T., 1987. Experimental solid state physics, quantum behavior of electrons in ultra-small silicon and gallium arsenide transistors, micromagnetics for biophysics applications.

George E. McCluskey, Jr., Professor, Ph.D., Pennsylvania, 1965. Binary stars, space astronomy.

H. Daniel Ou-Yang, Professor, Ph.D., UCLA, 1985. Experimental studies of complex fluids such as polymer solutions, colloidal suspensions, and cellular biophysics.

Russell A. Shaffer, Associate Professor, Ph.D., Johns Hopkins, 1962. Elementary particle theory.

Michael Stavola, Professor and Chair, Ph.D., Rochester, 1980. Experimental solid state physics, vibrational spectroscopy and uniaxial stress techniques used to study point defects in semiconductors.

Jean Toulouse, Professor, Ph.D., Columbia, 1981. Experimental solid state physics, structural and ferroelectric phase transitions is disordered or partially ordered crystals, structure and dynamic effects of glasses, nonlinear fiber optics.

George D. Watkins, Professor Emeritus, Ph.D., Harvard, 1952. Experimental solid state physics, studies of point defects in elemental and compound semiconductors, magnetic resonance and optical spectroscopy in solids.

MICHIGAN STATE UNIVERSITY

Department of Physics and Astronomy

Programs of Study

M.S. and Ph.D. degrees are offered with specializations in accelerator physics, biomolecular physics, beam physics, chemical physics, condensed-matter physics, elementary particle theory, experimental particle physics, low-temperature physics, many-body theory, nuclear physics, and observational and theoretical astrophysics. The semester system is followed. The ratio of faculty members to graduate students is about 1:2, and formal class sizes range from 5 to 40.

Research Facilities

Research facilities include two superconducting cyclotrons, K500 and K1200, each injected by ECR ion sources and associated apparatus, including the modern A1200 fragment separator that allows efficient production and in-flight separation of rare isotopes; the recently completed high-resolution S800 superconducting magnetic spectrograph; a large 92-inch scattering chamber; a recoil mass separator; 4-pi neutron and charged-particle detectors; a high-energy gamma ray detector array; neutron and charged-particle detector hodoscopes; a number of data acquisition and analysis computers; X-ray apparatus for study of structure on atomic and mesoscopic length scales; extensive photo and electron-beam lithographic facilities, housed in a clean room and including an atomic force microscope, field-emission SEM, and a micro-Raman spectrometer, for device fabrication with 50-nm resolution; cryogenic facilities, including one helium-3 refrigerator and four helium-3/helium-4 dilution refrigerators; five (5T, 6T, 9T, 9T, and 14T) superconducting magnets; two automated SQUID magnetometers; an electron spin resonance laboratory; an ultrahigh-vacuum four-gun sputtering system; and an electron photo emission spectrometer.

Studies of advanced and nanostructured materials are carried out using world-leading national user facilities and X-ray synchrotron sources in Chicago, New Mexico, New York, and the United Kingdom. Students get privileged access to the third-generation X-ray synchrotron source at Argonne Laboratory in Chicago through Michigan State University (MSU) membership of a collaboration; a high-energy physics laboratory, which is a state-of-the-art electronics design facility where detectors for experiments are developed, tested, and constructed; and numerous minicomputers and microcomputers in all research areas.

Important off-campus facilities in the high-energy area include the accelerator at Fermilab in Batavia, Illinois, and CERN in Geneva, Switzerland, where experiments are currently being carried out by MSU faculty members and students. The experimental high-energy group makes use of well-equipped high-energy physics laboratories in which state-of-the-art detectors are being constructed for use at the CDF and Dzero experiments at Fermilab and the ATLAS experiment at the Large Hadron Collider at CERN. The departmental electronics shops, using up-to-date design facilities where the fast-trigger system for the DZero experiment was designed, are now occupied with upgrade efforts in DZero as well as with designs of portions of the fast trigger for ATLAS.

Faculty members and students are involved with the STAR Collaboration at the Relativistic Heavy Ion Collider at Brookhaven National Laboratory, where there is an ongoing search for the quark-gluan plasma in high-energy Au+Au collisions. A major portion of the STAR Colorimeter is being designed and constructed at MSU before being transported and installed at Brookhaven.

MSU is a partner and has at least forty nights per year of guaranteed observing time on the SOAR 4m telescope, which is located in Chile at one of the world's best astronomical sites. This superb new facility is equipped with a wide range of optical and infrared cameras and spectrographs, including some developed at MSU. Astronomy faculty members also use a wide range of national ground-based and space telescopes at X-ray through infrared wavelengths. In addition, MSU is a member of the Joint Institute for Nuclear Astrophysics (JINA).

The Biomedical and Physical Science (BPS) Library has up-to-date collections of books and journals. Current research programs are described in materials available from the department.

Financial Aid

Half-time graduate assistantship stipends began at $16,200 for the 2003–04 calendar year. Assistants spend up to 20 hours a week on their duties. In-class contact hours for teaching assistants range from 6 to 8 hours for recitation and laboratory classes. The normal course load for assistants is 6 to 9 credit hours. The duties of research assistants are commonly in the general area in which the Ph.D. thesis is written. Fellowships and scholarships are available.

Cost of Study

Tuition for 2003–04 was $291 per credit hour for Michigan residents. Teaching and research assistants pay in-state rates and receive a full tuition waiver. Out-of-state tuition was $589.25 per credit hour.

Living and Housing Costs

Single rooms in Owen Hall, the graduate residence center, rented for $2410 per semester for 2003–04. This cost included credit toward one meal per day (approximately $280 per month). Food may be obtained from several campus cafeterias and local restaurants. The University owns and operates more than 2,000 one- and two-bedroom apartments to help meet the housing needs of married students. These rent for $498 and $594 per month, respectively, and include all utilities, essential furniture, and a private telephone. Privately owned off-campus rooms and apartments are also available.

Student Group

The on-campus enrollment at Michigan State University for the 2003 fall semester was 44,937, including 8,349 graduate and professional students. There were 130 physics graduate students and 19 postdoctoral research associates.

Location

East Lansing is a residential city adjacent to the Michigan State University campus and close to Lansing, the state capital. Many opportunities for cultural and social development are offered by the University and neighboring civic groups. Examples include the Wharton Center for the Performing Arts, the Kresge Art Center, the University Museum, and the lecture-concert, World Travel, and foreign film series.

The University and The Department

Michigan State University, one of the oldest land-grant colleges, was founded in 1855 for the purpose of furthering the interests of agriculture and the mechanic arts. From this modest beginning it has grown to become one of America's largest universities, with many educational innovations to its credit. Through its fourteen colleges and more than 100 departments, it offers 200 different programs leading to undergraduate and graduate degrees.

Applying

Application forms may be obtained by e-mailing the Graduate Secretary at simmons@pa.msu.edu or writing to the address listed below. Applications for admission and supporting documents should be received at least one month prior to the first enrollment together with a $50 application fee. Applicants should request that registrars of colleges previously attended send transcripts directly to the department office listed below. Applications for a graduate assistantship, fellowship, or scholarship should reach the office no later than six months prior to the first anticipated enrollment. Acceptance of graduate students is decided by a departmental committee maintained for this purpose.

Correspondence and Information

Professor S. D. Mahanti, Associate Chairperson, Graduate Program
1312 Biomedical and Physical Sciences Building
Department of Physics and Astronomy
Michigan State University
East Lansing, Michigan 48824-2320
Telephone: 517-355-9200 Ext. 2032
E-mail: mahanti@pa.msu.edu
World Wide Web: http://www.pa.msu.edu/

Michigan State University

THE FACULTY

Physics
Maris A. Abolins, Professor; Ph.D., California, San Diego, 1965.
Sam M. Austin, Professor Emeritus; Ph.D., Wisconsin–Madison, 1960.
Jack Bass, Professor; Ph.D., Illinois, 1964.
Wolfgang Bauer, Professor and Chairperson; Ph.D., Giessen (Germany), 1987.
Walter Benenson, University Distinguished Professor; Ph.D., Wisconsin–Madison, 1962.
Martin Berz, Professor; Ph.D., Giessen (Germany), 1986.
Simon Billinge, Professor; Ph.D., Pennsylvania, 1992.
Norman Birge, Professor; Ph.D., Chicago, 1986.
Henry G. Blosser, Professor Emeritus; Ph.D., Virginia, 1954.
Georg Bollen, Professor; Ph.D., Kaiserslautern (Germany), 1989.
Jerzy Borysowicz, Professor Emeritus; Ph.D., Institute for Nuclear Research (Warsaw), 1965.
Raymond L. Brock, Professor; Ph.D., Carnegie Mellon, 1980.
Carl M. Bromberg, Professor; Ph.D., Rochester, 1974.
B. Alex Brown, Professor; Ph.D., SUNY at Stony Brook, 1974.
Edward H. Carlson, Professor Emeritus; Ph.D., Johns Hopkins, 1959.
Sekhar Chivukula, Professor; Ph.D., Harvard, 1987.
Pawel Danielewicz, Professor; Ph.D., Warsaw, 1981.
Phillip M. Duxbury, Professor; Ph.D., New South Wales (Australia), 1983.
Mark Dykman, Professor; Ph.D., Kiev, 1973.
Michael Feig, Assistant Professor; Ph.D., Houston, 1999.
Aaron Galonsky, Professor Emeritus; Ph.D., Wisconsin–Madison, 1954.
C. Konrad Gelbke, University Distinguished Professor and Director, National Superconducting Cyclotron Laboratory; Ph.D., Heidelberg (Germany), 1972.
Thomas Glasmacher, Professor; Ph.D., Florida State, 1992.
Brage Golding, Professor and Director, Center for Sensor Materials; Ph.D., MIT, 1966.
Morton M. Gordon, Professor Emeritus; Ph.D., Washington (St. Louis), 1950.
Gregers Hansen, Hannah Professor; Ph.D., Copenhagen, 1965.
Michael J. Harrison, Professor; Ph.D., Chicago, 1960.
William M. Hartmann, Professor; D.Phil., Oxford, 1965.
Jack Hetherington, Professor Emeritus; Ph.D., Illinois, 1962.
Joey W. Huston, Professor; Ph.D., Rochester, 1982.
Thomas Kaplan, Professor Emeritus; Ph.D., Pennsylvania, 1954.
Edwin Kashy, University Distinguished Professor; Ph.D., Rice, 1959.
Gabor Kemeny, Professor Emeritus; Ph.D., NYU, 1962.
Julius S. Kovacs, Professor Emeritus; Ph.D., Indiana, 1955.
James T. Linnemann, Professor; Ph.D., Cornell, 1978.
William G. Lynch, Professor; Ph.D., Washington (Seattle), 1980.
S. D. Mahanti, Professor and Associate Chairperson, Graduate Program; Ph.D., California, Riverside, 1968.
Hugh McManus, Professor Emeritus; Ph.D., Birmingham (England), 1947.
Filomena Nunes, Assistant Professor; Ph.D., Surrey (England), 1995.
Paul M. Parker, Professor Emeritus; Ph.D., Ohio State, 1958.
Carlo Piermarocchi, Assistant Professor; Ph.D., Lausanne Federal Polytechnic, 1998.
Gerald L. Pollack, Professor; Ph.D., Caltech, 1962.
Bernard G. Pope, Professor; Ph.D., Columbia, 1971.
Scott Pratt, Assistant Professor; Ph.D., Minnesota, 1985.
William Pratt, Professor; Ph.D., Minnesota, 1967.
Jon Pumplin, Professor; Ph.D., Michigan, 1968.
Wayne Repko, Professor; Ph.D., Wayne State, 1967.
Hendrik Schatz, Assistant Professor; Ph.D., Heidelberg (Germany), 1997.
Carl Schmidt, Associate Professor; Ph.D., Harvard, 1990.
Peter A. Schroeder, Professor Emeritus; Ph.D., Bristol (England), 1955.
Bradley Sherrill, Professor; Ph.D., Michigan State, 1985.
Peter S. Signell, Professor Emeritus; Ph.D., Rochester, 1958.
Elizabeth H. Simmons, Professor and Director of Lyman Briggs School; Ph.D., Harvard, 1990.
Krzysztof Starosta, Assistant Professor; Ph.D., Warsaw, 1996.
Daniel R. Stump, Professor and Associate Chairperson, Undergraduate Program; Ph.D., MIT, 1976.
Stuart Tessmer, Assistant Professor; Ph.D., Illinois, 1992.
Michael Thoennessen, Professor and Associate Director, National Superconducting Cyclotron Laboratory; Ph.D., SUNY at Stony Brook, 1988.
Michael F. Thorpe, Professor Emeritus; D.Phil., Oxford, 1968.
Kirsten Tollefson, Assistant Professor; Ph.D., Rochester, 1997.
David Tomanek, Professor; Ph.D., Berlin, 1983.
Wu-ki Tung, Professor; Ph.D., Yale, 1966.
William J. Wedermeyer, Assistant Professor; Ph.D., Cornell, 1988.
Hendrik J. Weerts, Professor; Ph.D., Aachen (Germany), 1981.
Gary D. Westfall, Professor; Ph.D., Texas at Austin, 1975.
Richard York, Professor; Ph.D., Iowa, 1976.
Chien-Peng Yuan, Associate Professor; Ph.D., Michigan, 1988.
Remco Zegers, Visiting Assistant Professor; Ph.D., Gronigen (Netherlands), 1999.
Vladimir Zelevinsky, Professor; Ph.D., Budker Institute of Nuclear Physics, 1974.

Astronomy
Jack Baldwin, Professor; Ph.D., California, Santa Cruz, 1974.
Timothy C. Beers, Professor; Ph.D., Harvard, 1983.
Eugene Capriotti, Professor and Associate Chairperson; Ph.D., Wisconsin, 1962.
Megan E. Donahue, Associate Professor; Ph.D., Colorado, 1990.
Albert P. Linnell, Professor Emeritus; Ph.D., Harvard, 1958.
Edwin D. Loh, Associate Professor; Ph.D., Princeton, 1977.
Susan M. Simkin, Professor Emerita; Ph.D., Wisconsin–Madison, 1967.
Horace Smith, Professor; Ph.D., Yale, 1980.
Robert F. Stein, Professor; Ph.D., Columbia, 1966.
G. Mark Voit, Associate Professor; Ph.D., Colorado, 1990.
Stephen E. Zepf, Associate Professor; Ph.D., Johns Hopkins, 1992.

MICHIGAN TECHNOLOGICAL UNIVERSITY

Department of Physics

Programs of Study

The Department of Physics graduate program is primarily a doctoral program leading to the Doctor of Philosophy (Ph.D.) degrees in physics as well as in engineering physics. The Master of Science (M.S.) degree in physics is also available. Major research areas in the department include experimental and computational atomic and molecular physics, theoretical and experimental atmospheric physics, experimental and computational materials physics, photonics, and solid-state physics, biomolecular modeling, astrophysics, cosmic ray physics, remote sensing, and statistical physics. Michigan Technological University (MTU) stresses a solid foundation, research involvement, presentation of results at national meetings, publication in refereed journals, and internships in industry. Multidisciplinary research is encouraged, and significant opportunities exist to collaborate with researchers in geological engineering and science, materials science and engineering, electrical and computer engineering, chemistry, mathematics, and computer science.

Students are generally admitted into the department's graduate programs based on an assessment of their ability to succeed as doctoral degree students. A minimum of 30 course and/or research credit hours beyond the M.S. degree (or its equivalent) or a minimum of 60 course and/or research credit hours beyond the bachelor's degree are required. The course work requirements are determined by the department's core course requirements and by the student's Advisory Committee. Students accepted into the Ph.D. program must pass a written qualifying examination. After passing the qualifying examination, the preliminary examination is administered by the student's Advisory Committee to review the student's proposed plan of research. The final oral examination may be scheduled anytime after completion of the dissertation.

Research Facilities

Research is conducted in the Fisher Hall physics laboratories as well as other University facilities in nearby buildings. University facilities routinely used by physics faculty members and graduate students include scanning and transmission electron microscope facilities, X-ray diffraction facilities, atomic force microscopes, and materials processing and characterization facilities in the Institute for Materials Processing. The physics department has numerous faculty laboratories, including the hyperspectral imaging, high-field NMR, dislocation physics, computational atomic physics, auger observatory instrumentation, and laser spectroscopy laboratories. Each faculty member and graduate student has immediate access to a variety of high-performance workstations and has access to local and distributed high-performance parallel computation facilities through the Center for Experimental Computation, which is jointly operated by the physics, math, and computer science departments. The department has a student machine shop and machine shop, and with a professional support staff.

Financial Aid

Financial aid is available to a limited number of qualified full-time students in the form of fellowships, research assistantships, and teaching assistantships. Aid packages include a stipend, tuition, and some student fees. The stipend for M.S. candidates is currently $4415 per semester and for Ph.D. candidates, $5126 per semester. In addition, a health insurance supplement is provided by the University. Funding may be available on a competitive basis for students to travel to professional conferences.

Cost of Study

Tuition for full-time graduate students (resident and nonresident) for the 2004–05 academic year is $3888 per semester; engineering and computer science majors pay $4288 per semester. All students are responsible for a student activity fee of approximately $135 per semester. Health insurance is required for all graduate students; the supplement is subject to financial aid status.

Living and Housing Costs

Michigan Tech residence halls have accommodations for single students; applications may be obtained from the Director of Residential Services. For married students, Michigan Tech has one- and two-bedroom furnished apartments; applications may be obtained from the manager of Daniell Heights Apartments. Because the cost of housing is subject to change, representative costs cannot be stated. There is also off-campus housing available in the surrounding community. *Yahoo! Internet Life* lists the overall cost-of-living index for Houghton as 83 (national average is 100). For more information, prospective students should visit http://list.realestate.yahoo.com/realestate/neighborhood/main.html.

Student Group

The number of physics graduate students in the department is typically between 30 and 35. A wide variety of academic, ethnic, and national backgrounds are represented. Four to eight graduate degrees are awarded by the department each year. An active undergraduate program in physics of about 40 students, 17 faculty members, and numerous research faculty members and postdoctoral researchers brings the total membership in the Department of Physics to approximately 100 scientists and support staff members.

Student Outcomes

The graduate program prepares students for careers in academia, the national laboratories, or industry. Recent graduates have found employment at IBM (San Jose), Ford (Dearborn), Argonne National Laboratory, the University of Colorado at Boulder, Integraph, and Chrysler.

Location

Michigan Tech is located in Houghton on Michigan's scenic Keweenaw Peninsula. The Keweenaw stretches about 70 miles into Lake Superior, and the surrounding area is perfect for any outdoor activity. The campus is a 15-minute walk from downtown Houghton; public transportation is available from Houghton and Hancock. Houghton has been listed as the safest college town in Michigan and was ranked eighth out of 467 nationwide in the report, "Crime at College: Student Guide to Personal Safety." The Houghton County Memorial Airport (CMX) serves the area with direct flights to Minneapolis via Northwest Airlink; Marquette K. I. Sawyer International Airport (SAW), approximately a 2-hour drive from Houghton, serves the area with direct flights to Detroit.

The University

Michigan Tech was founded in 1885 as the Michigan Mining School to serve the nation's first major mining enterprises focused on copper and iron. Several name changes tracked the growth and diversification of the institution, and it was named Michigan Technological University in 1964. Today, the University offers a full range of associate, bachelor's, master's, and doctoral degrees in the sciences, engineering, forestry, business, communication, and technology. MTU has been rated one of the nation's "Top Ten" best buys for science and technology by *U.S. News & World Report*.

Applying

Application packets are available from the Department of Physics or students may visit the Web at http://www.phy.mtu.edu/physicsgradprog.html for downloadable or online applications. Completed applications should be sent to the Graduate School, along with the nonrefundable application fee. Official transcripts should be sent to the Graduate School from all colleges or universities previously attended. All students are required to take the GRE General Test and have official scores sent to the Graduate School. International students must also submit TOEFL scores. Three letters of recommendation may be sent to the Department of Physics.

Correspondence and Information

Graduate Studies Chair
Department of Physics
Michigan Technological University
1400 Townsend Drive
Houghton, Michigan 49931-1295
E-mail: physics@mtu.edu
World Wide Web: http://www.phy.mtu.edu/

Michigan Technological University

THE FACULTY AND THEIR RESEARCH

Gary P. Agin, Associate Professor; Ph.D., Kansas State, 1968. Low-energy nuclear physics. (e-mail: gagin@mtu.edu)
Donald R. Beck, Professor; Ph.D., Lehigh, 1968. Theoretical atomic physics, properties of transition metal and rare earth atoms and ions, discovery of new negative ions, including correlation and relativistic effects. (e-mail: donald@mtu.edu)
Aleksandra Borysow, Associate Professor; Ph.D., Texas at Austin, 1985. Molecular physics; development of classical and quantum mechanical computational techniques to quantitatively describe collision-induced absorption and light scattering by dense nonpolar gases such as hydrogen, nitrogen, carbon dioxide, and methane, particularly for planetary and stellar atmosphere studies. (e-mail: aborysow@mtu.edu)
Jacek Borysow, Associate Professor; Ph.D., Texas at Austin, 1986. Atomic, molecular, and laser physics; ionization, dissociation, and collisional energy transfer; plasma diagnostics and laser development. (e-mail: jborysow@mtu.edu)
Will H. Cantrell II, Assistant Professor; Ph.D., Alaska Fairbanks, 1999. Physics and chemistry of aerosols and clouds, with an emphasis on heterogeneous nucleation of ice and the interaction of thin films with solid substrates. (e-mail: cantrell@mtu.edu)
Donald A. Daavettila, Professor Emeritus; M.S., Michigan Tech, 1958. Radiation safety. (e-mail: daavetti@mtu.edu)
Brian E. Fick, Associate Professor; Ph.D., Virginia Tech, 1985. Experimental astroparticle physics, investigations into the nature and origin of extremely high energy cosmic rays using the Pierre Auger Cosmic Ray Observatory. (e-mail: fick@mtu.edu)
Ulrich Hansmann, Professor; Ph.D., Berlin, 1990. Biomolecular modeling, complex systems, global optimization problems. (e-mail: hansmann@mtu.edu)
John A. Jaszczak, Associate Professor and Adjunct Curator, Seaman Mineral Museum; Ph.D., Ohio State, 1989. Simulations of materials, Monte Carlo simulations of dynamics and etching of silicon surfaces with intersecting dislocations, molecular dynamics studies of structure-property correlations in metallic superlattices and amorphous alloys. (e-mail: jaszczak@mtu.edu)
Alexander B. Kostinski, Professor; Ph.D., Illinois at Chicago, 1984. Atmospheric physics, statistical physics, fluid mechanics, optics, radar signal processing. (e-mail: kostinsk@mtu.edu)
Miguel Levy, Associate Professor; Ph.D., CUNY, 1988. Experimental surface physics, spanning the boundary of physics and metallurgical and materials engineering.
Robert H. Mount, Professor Emeritus; B.Sc., Ohio State, 1952. General physics pedagogy.
Edward Nadgorny, Presidential Professor; Ph.D., 1963, D.Sc., 1971, St. Petersburg (Russia). Dislocation physics, dislocation dynamics in semiconductors and intermetallics, fundamental processes for nanoscale engineering involving dislocations (dislocation engineering). (e-mail: nadgorny@mtu.edu)
Robert Nemiroff, Professor; Ph.D., Pennsylvania, 1987. Gravitational lensing, gamma ray burst data analysis. (e-mail: nemiroff@mtu.edu)
David Nitz, Associate Professor; Ph.D., Rochester, 1978. High-energy particle astrophysics, origin of highest energy cosmic rays, Pierre Auger Observatory. (e-mail: dfnitz@mtu.edu)
Ravindra Pandey, Professor and Department Chair; Ph.D., Manitoba, 1988. Materials modeling, semiconductors and oxides, nanoclusters and surfaces. (e-mail: pandey@mtu.edu)
Ranjit Pati, Assistant Professor; Ph.D., SUNY at Albany, 1998. Condensed-matter theory and materials science, computational modeling of nanoelectronic devices, electron transport theory, theoretical modeling of molecular self-assembly, surface physics, optical and magnetic properties of nanoscale materials, spectroscopic (NQR) properties of molecular and solid-state systems. (e-mail: patir@mtu.edu)
Warren F. Perger, Associate Professor; Ph.D., Colorado State, 1986. Quantum electronics, use of atomic physics theory to calculate electroweak parameters of the Standard Model, the calculation of relativistic continuum orbitals with application to atomic many-body theory, scattering. (e-mail: wfp@mtu.edu)
Max Seel, Professor and Dean of the College of Sciences and Arts; Ph.D., Erlangen, 1978. Quantum chemistry, computational biophysics.
Raymond Shaw, Associate Professor; Ph.D., Penn State, 1998. Physics of atmospheric clouds: particle nucleation and growth, particle-turbulence interactions. (e-mail: rashaw@mtu.edu)
Bryan H. Suits, Professor; Ph.D., Illinois, 1981. NMR of materials, inorganic nanometer-sized particles, and nanophase materials made from those particles; NMR and NQR imaging for materials exhibiting quadrupolar broadened resonances; development of NMR theory for slowly rotating solids containing quadrupole nuclei; materials detection using magnetic resonance. (e-mail: suits@mtu.edu)
Robert S. Weidman, Associate Professor; Ph.D., Illinois, 1980. Physics education. (e-mail: weidman@mtu.edu)
Yoke Khin Yap, Assistant Professor; Ph.D., Osaka, 1999. Materials physics and laser physics, search of new nonlinear optical crystals for laser frequency conversion, rational synthesis of thin films and nanostructures of carbon and nitrides by in situ ion bombardment, intensive plasma and catalysts. (e-mail: ykyap@mtu.edu)

Associated Faculty

P. E. Doak, Professor Emeritus, University of Southampton (England); senior editor, *Journal of Sound and Vibration.* Fluid dynamics and acoustics.
U. G. Jorgensen, Adjunct Professor; Copenhagen University Observatory, Niels Bohr Institute. Astrophysics.
J. M. Vail, Adjunct Professor; Department of Physics, University of Manitoba. Solid-state theory.
Michael Wertheim, Professor Emeritus; Ph.D., Yale, 1957. Theory of liquids. (e-mail: wertheim@mtu.edu)

Michigan Technological University

SELECTED PUBLICATIONS

Beck, D. R. Magnetic quadrople lifetimes for np^5 (n+1)s J=2 states of rare gases. *Phys. Rev. A* 66:034502, 2002.

O'Malley, S. M., **D. R. Beck,** and D. P. Oros. Oscillator strengths, Lande g-values, and hyperfine structure for $3d^4$ J=0 $\rightarrow$ $3d^34$ J=1 transitions in Fe V. *Phys. Rev. A* 63:032501, 2001.

Norquist, P. L., and **D. R. Beck.** Ab initio lifetimes, Lande g-values and hyperfine structure for Ta II states. *J. Phys. B* 34:2107, 2001.

O'Malley, S. M., and **D. R. Beck.** Electron affinities and E1 f-values for 15 bound states of Ce- formed by 6p and 5d attachment. *Phys. Rev. A* 61:34501, 2000.

Beck, D. R. Energy differences and magnetic dipole decay rates for the W52+ and Bi61+ members of the nearly Z independent (3d3/2) 3 3d5/2 J=3-J=2 transition. *Phys. Rev. A* 60:3304, 1999.

Brodbeck, C., J.-P. Bouanich, N. van Thanh, and **A. Borysow.** The binary collision-induced second overtone band of gaseous hydrogen: Modelling and laboratory measurements. *Planet. Space Sci.,* in press.

Fu, Y., C. Zheng, and **A. Borysow.** Quantum mechanical computations of collision induced absorption in the second overtone band of hydrogen. *J. Quant. Spectrosc. Radiat. Transfer* 67:303–21, 2000.

Borysow, A., U. G. Jorgensen, and Y. Fu. High temperature (1000—{7000~K}) collision induced absorption of H_2-H_2 pairs computed from the first principles, with application to cool and dense stellar atmosphere. *J. Quant. Spectrosc. Radiat. Transfer,* 2000.

Borysow, A., J. Borysow, and Y. Fu. Semiempirical model of collision induced infrared absorption spectra of H_2-H_2 complexes in the second overtone band of hydrogen temperatures from 50 to {500 K}. *Icarus* 145:601–8, 2000.

Jorgensen, U. G., D. Hammer, **A. Borysow,** and J. Falkesgaard. The atmospheres of cool, helium-rich white dwarfs. *Astron. Astrophys.,* 2000.

Borysow, A., and U. G. Jorgensen. Collision induced absorption in dwarfs and cool white dwarfs. In *Proc. Astron. Soc. Pacific: From Giant Planets to Cool Stars,* eds. C. Griffith and M. Marley. Astronomical Society of the Pacific, 2000.

Borysow, A., and **J. Borysow.** Collision-induced absorption spectra of H_2-H_2 pairs in the second overtone (3-0) hydrogen band at temperatures from 50 to 500 K: new semi-empirical model. *Bull. AAS* 31: 1157, 1999.

Brodbeck, C., et al. **(A. Borysow).** Collision-induced absorption by H_2 pairs in the second overtone band at 298 and 77.5 K. *J. Chem. Phys.* 110:4750, 1999.

Cantrell, W., C. McCrory, and G. Ewing. Nucleated deliquescence of salt. *J. Chem. Phys.,* in press.

Cantrell, W., et al. Closure between aerosol particles and cloud condensation nuclei at Kaashidhoo Climate Observatory. *J. Geophys. Res.* 106:28711–8, 2001.

Cantrell, W., and G. Ewing. Thin film water on muscovite mica. *J. Phys. Chem. B* 105:5435–9, 2001.

Watson, A. A., et al. **(B. E. Fick).** Properties and performance of the prototype instrument for the Pierre Auger Observatory (Auger Collaboration): Nuclear instruments and methods. *Phys. Rev. A* 523(1-2):50–95, 2004.

Abu-Zayyad, T., et al. **(B. E. Fick).** Measurement of the cosmic ray energy spectrum and composition from 10^{17} to $18^{18.3}$ eV using hybrid fluorescence technique. *Astrophys. J.* 557:689–9, 2001.

Abu-Zayyad, T., et al. **(B. E. Fick).** A measurement of the average longitudinal development profile of cosmic ray air showers between 10^{17} eV and 10^{18} eV. *Astropart. Phys.* 16:1, 2001.

Abu-Zayyad, T., et al. **(B. E. Fick).** A multicomponent measurement of the cosmic ray composition between 10^{17} eV and 10^{18} eV. *Phys. Rev. Lett.* 84:4276, 2000.

Song, C., et al. **(B. E. Fick).** Energy estimation of UHE cosmic rays using the atmospheric fluorescence technique. *Astropart. Phys.* 14:7, 2000.

Glasmacher, M. A. K., et al. **(B. E. Fick).** The cosmic ray composition between 10^{14} and 10^{16} eV. *Astropart. Phys.* 12:1, 1999.

Hansmann, U. H. E., and L. Wille. Global optimization by energy landscape paving. *Phys. Rev. Lett.* 88:068105, 2002.

Eisenmenger, F., **U. H. E. Hansmann,** S. Hayryan, and C.-K. Hu. [SMMP]: A modern package for simulation of proteins. *Comp. Phys. Comm.* 138:192–212, 2001.

Hansmann, U. H. E., and Y. Okamoto. Multicanonical and other generalized-ensemble algorithms in protein folding. In *Encyclopedia of Optimization,* vol. IV, pp. 392–401, eds. C. A. Floudas and P. M. Pardalos. Norwell: Kluwer Academic, 2001.

Hansmann, U. H. E., and J. N. Onuchic. Thermodynamics and kinetics of folding of small peptide. *J. Chem. Phys.* 115:1601–6, 2001.

Alves, N. A., and **U. H. E. Hansmann.** Glass transition temperature and fractal dimension of protein free energy landscapes. *Int. J. Mod. Phys. C.* 11:301, 2000.

Alves, N. A., and **U. H. E. Hansmann.** Partition function zeros and finite size scaling of helix-coil transitions in a polypeptide. *Phys. Rev. Lett.* 84:1836, 2000.

Kemp, J. P., **U. H. E. Hansmann,** and Z. Y. Chen. Is there a universality of the helix-coil transition in protein models? *Eur. Phys. J. B* 15:371, 2000.

Hansmann, U. H. E. Thermodynamics of protein folding: The generalized-ensemble approach. In *Optimization in Computational Chemistry and Molecular Biology,* eds. C. A. Floudas and P. M. Pardalos. Norwell: Kluwer Academic, 2000.

Hansmann, U. H. E. Protein folding simulations in a deformed energy landscape. *Eur. Phys. J. B* 12:607, 1999.

Hansmann, U. H. E., and Y. Okamoto. New Monte Carlo algorithms for protein folding. *Curr. Opin. Struct. Biol.* 9:177–84, 1999.

Hansmann, U. H. E., and Y. Okamoto. Effects of side-chain charges on a-helix stability in C-peptide of ribonuclease A studied by multicanonical algorithm. *J. Phys. Chem. B* 103:1595–604, 1999.

Gao, D., and **J. A. Jaszczak.** Monte Carlo simulations of surface phase transitions in a modulated layered structure. *Phys. Rev. B* 67:155420, 2003.

Rakovan, J., and **J. A. Jaszczak.** Multiple length scale growth spirals on metamorphic graphite {001} surfaces studied by atomic force microscopy. *Am. Mineral.* 87:17–24, 2002.

Kvasnitsa, V. N., V. G. Yatsenko, and **J. A. Jaszczak.** Disclinations in unusual graphite crystals from anorthosites of Ukraine. *Can. Mineral.* 37(4):951–60, 1999.

Woodraska, D. L., and **J. A. Jaszczak.** Roughening and preroughening of diamond-cubic {111} surfaces. *Phys. Rev. Lett.* 78:256–61, 1997.

Jameson, A. R., and **A. B. Kostinski.** What is a raindrop size distribution? *Bull. Am. Meteorol. Soc.* 1169–78, 2001.

Jameson, A. R., and **A. B. Kostinski.** Reconsideration of the physical and empirical origins of Z-R relations in radar meteorology. *Q. J. R. Meteorol. Soc.* 127:517–38, 2001.

Kostinski, A. B. On the extinction of radiation by a homogeneous but spatially correlated random medium. *J. Opt. Soc. Am. A* 18:1929–33, 2001.

Kostinski, A. B., and **R. A. Shaw.** Scale-dependent droplet clustering in turbulent clouds. *J. Fluid Mech.* 434:389–98, 2001.

Kostinski, A. B., and A. R. Jameson. On the spatial distribution of cloud particles. *J. Atmos. Sci.* 57(7):901–15, 2000.

Jameson, A. R., and **A. B. Kostinski.** The effect of stochastic cloud structure on the icing process. *J. Atmos. Sci.* 57(17):2883–91, 2000.

Jameson, A. R., and **A. B. Kostinski.** Fluctuation properties of precipitation. Part VI: Observations of hyperfine clustering and drop size distribution structures in three-dimensional rain. *J. Atmos. Sci.* 57(3):373–88, 2000.

Kostinski, A. B., and A. Koivunen. On the condition number of Gaussian sample covariance matrices. *IEEE Trans. Geosci. Remote Sensing* 38(1):329–32, 2000.

Jameson, A. R., and **A. B. Kostinski.** Fluctuation properties of precipitation. Part V: On the distribution of rain rates: Theory and observations in clustered rain. *J. Atmos. Sci.* 56(22):3920–32, 1999.

Ramadan, T., **M. Levy,** and R. M. Osgood Jr. Electro-optic modulation in crystal-ion-sliced z-cut LiNbO3 thin films. *Appl. Phys. Lett.* 76:1407, 2000.

Michigan Technological University

Selected Publications (continued)

Fujita, J., and **M. Levy** et al. Integrated optical isolator based on Mach-Zehnder interferometer. *Appl. Phys. Lett.* 76:2158, 2000.

Izuhara, T., **M. Levy,** and R. M. Osgood Jr. Direct water bonding and transfer of 10-μm-thick magnetic garnet films onto semiconductor surfaces. *Appl. Phys. Lett.* 76:1261, 2000.

Liu, R., et al. **(M. Levy).** Dielectric and pyroelectric properties of crystal ion sliced (CIS) $LiNbO_3$ thin films. *Ferroelectrics,* 1999.

Radojevic, A. M., and **M. Levy** et al. Large etch selectivity enhancement in the epitaxial liftoff of single crystal LiNbO3 films. *Appl. Phys. Lett.* 74:3197, 1999.

Radojevic, A. M., **M. Levy,** H. Kwak, and R. M. Osgood Jr. Strong nonlinear optical response in epitaxial liftoff single-crystal $LiNbO_3$ films. *Appl. Phys. Lett.* 75:2888, 1999.

Fujita, J., and **M. Levy** et al. Observation of optical isolation based on nonreciprocal phase shift in a Mach-Zehender interferometer. *Appl. Phys. Lett.* 75:998, 1999.

Nadgorny, E. M., C. Zhou, J. Drelich, and R. Zahn. MTU laser-based direct-write techniques: Recent development and nanoparticles patterning results. In *MRS Symp. Proc., Rapid Prototyping Technol.,* eds. A. S. Holmes, A. Pique, and D. B. Dimos, pp. 758:LL4.4.1–.6, 2003.

Drelich, J., and **E. M. Nadgorny** et al. Patterning of gold and polystyrene nanoparticles into mesostructures using a laser-based particle deposition. In *MME Soc. Proc., Littleton, Colo., Functional Fillers Nanoscale Mater.,* eds. J. J. Kellar, M. A. Herpfer, and B. M. Moudgil, pp. 85–94, 2003.

Hiratani, M., and **E. M. Nadgorny.** Combined model of dislocation motion with thermally activated and drag-dependent stages. *Acta Mater.* 49(20):4337–46, 2001.

Nemiroff, R. J., G. F. Marani, J. P. Norris, and J. T. Bonnell. Limits on the cosmological abundance of supermassive compact objects from a millilensing search in gamma-ray burst data. *Phys. Rev. Lett.* 86:580, 2001.

Che, H., Y. Yang, and **R. J. Nemiroff.** Source destiny evolution of gamma-ray bursts. *Astrophys. J.* 516(2):559–62, 1999.

Marani, G. F., et al. **(R. J. Nemiroff).** Gravitationally lensed gamma-ray bursts as probes of dark compact objects. *Astrophys. J.* 512:L13–6, 1999.

Nemiroff, R. J., and J. T. Bonnell. The nature of the universe debate in 1998. *Publications Astron. Soc. Pacific* 111(757):285–7, 1999.

Nemiroff, R. J., and J. B. Rafert. Toward a continuous record of the sky. *Publications Astron. Soc. Pacific* 111(761):886–97, 1999.

Zimmer, G. A., W. E. Pereira, **R. J. Nemiroff,** and J. B. Rafert. A passive sky variability monitor for under $1500. *BAAS, 194th Meeting of the AAS* 70(9):194, 1999.

Nitz, D., et al. Evidence for changing of cosmic ray composition between 10^{17}eV and 10^{18}eV from multi-component measurements. *Phys. Rev. Let.* 84:4276, 2000.

Nitz, D., et al. The cosmic ray energy spectrum with CASA-MIA. *Astropart. Phys.* 10:291, 1999.

Nitz, D., et al. The cosmic ray composition with CASA-MIA. *Astropart. Phys.* 12:1, 1999.

Rerat, M., W.-D. Cheng, and **R. Pandey.** First principles calculations of nonlinear optical susceptibility of inorganic materials. *J. Phys.: Condens. Matter* 13:343, 2001.

Blanco, M. A., J. M. Reico, A. Costales, and **R. Pandey.** Transition path for the B3 → B1 phase transformation in semiconductors. *Phys. Rev. B* 62:R10599, 2000.

Cheng, W.-D., K. Xiang, **R. Pandey,** and U. C. Pernisz. Calculations of linear and nonlinear optical properties H-silsesquioxanes. *J. Phys. Chem.* B104:6737, 2000.

Costales, A., et al. **(R. Pandey).** First principles study of polyatomic clusters of AlN, GaN, and InN. 2. Chemical bonding. *J. Phys. Chem.* B104:4361, 2000.

Jiang, H., et al. **(R. Pandey).** Theoretical study of native and rare-earth defect complexes in β-PbF_2. *Phys. Rev. B* 62:803, 2000.

Pandey, R., M. Ohmer, J. M. Recio, and A. Costales. Modeling of the properties of dopants in the NLO semiconductor $CdGeAs_2$. In *MRS Symp. Proc. Ser.,* eds. M. O. Manasreh, B. J. H. Stadler, I. Ferguson, and Y.-H. Zhang, p. 607, 2000.

Pandey, R., B. K. Rao, P. Jena, and J. Newsam. Unique magnetic signature of transition metal atoms supported by benzene. *Chem. Phys. Lett.* 321:142, 2000.

Pandey, R., M. Rerat, C. Darrigan, and M. Causa. A theoretical study of stability, electronic and optical properties of GeC and SnC. *J. Appl. Phys.* 88:6462, 2000.

Pati, R., and S. P. Karna. Current switching by conformational change in a π-σ-π molecular wire. *Phys. Rev. B* 69:1554191–4, 2004.

Pati, R., L. Senapati, P. M. Ajayan, and S. K. Nayak. First principles calculations of spin-polarized electron transport in a molecular wire: Molecular spin valve. *Phys. Rev. B (R)* 68:1004071–4, 2003.

Pati, R., et al. Oscillatory spin-polarized conductance in carbon atom wires. *Phys. Rev. B* 68:0144121–5, 2003.

Pati, R., Y. Zhang, S. K. Nayak, and P. M. Ajayan. Effect of H20 adsorption on electron transport in a carbon nanotube. *Appl. Phys. Lett.* 81:2638–40, 2002.

Pati, R., and S. P. Karna. Length dependence of intramolecular electron transfer in σ-bonded rigid molecular rods: An ab initio molecular orbital study. *Chem. Phys. Lett.* 351:302–10, 2002.

Shaw, R. A. Particle-turbulence interactions in atmospheric clouds. *Annu. Rev. Fluid Mech.* 35:183–227, 2003.

Shaw, R. A., A. B. Kostinski, and D. Lanterman. Super-exponential extinction of radiation in a negatively-correlated random medium. *J. Quant. Spectrosc. Radiat. Transfer* 75:13–20, 2002.

Shaw, R. A. Supersaturation intermittency in turbulent clouds. *J. Atmos. Sci.* 57:3452–6, 2000.

Shaw, R. A., D. Lamb, and A. M. Moyle. An electrodynamic levitation system for studying single particles under upper-tropospheric conditions. *J. Atmos. Oceanic Technol.* 17:940–8, 2000.

Shaw, R. A., and D. Lamb. Experimental determination of the thermal accommodation and condensation coefficients of water. *J. Chem. Phys.* 111:10659–63, 1999.

Garroway, A. N., et al. **(B. H. Suits).** Remote sensing by nuclear quadrupole resonance (NQR). *IEEE Trans. Geosci. Remote Sensing* 39:1108, 2001.

Miller, J. B., **B. H. Suits,** and A. N. Garroway, Circularly polarized RF magnetic fields for spin-1 NQR. *J. Magn. Reson.* 151:228–34, 2001.

Suits, B. H. Basic physics of xylophone and marimba bars. *Am. J. Phys.* 69:743, 2001.

Trout, B. L., **B. H. Suits,** R. J. Gorte, and D. White. Molecular motions of hydrogen bonded CH_3CN in CHA: Comparison of first-principle molecular dynamics simulations with results from ^{1}H, ^{2}H, and ^{13}C NMR. *J. Phys. Chem.* B104:11734, 2000.

Miller, J. B., **B. H. Suits,** A. N. Garroway, and M. A. Hepp. Interplay among recovery time, signal, and noise: Series- and parallel-tuned circuits are not always the same. *Concepts Magn. Reson.* 12:125, 2000.

Suits, B. H., J. Şepa, R. J. Gorte, and D. White. Molecular motion of hydrogen-bonded CH_3CN in H-MFI: A ^{1}H, ^{2}H, and ^{13}C multinuclear NMR study. *J. Phys. Chem. B.* 104:5124, 2000.

Swaminathan, S. V., and **B. H. Suits.** Reconstructing powder NQR images with real gradient coils. *J. Magn. Reson.* 138:123, 1999.

Hirao, T., et al. **(Y. K. Yap).** Formation of vertically aligned carbon nanotubes by dual-RF-plasma chemical vapor deposition. *Jpn. J. Appl. Phys.* 40:L631, 2001.

Sasaki, T., et al. **(Y. K. Yap).** Recent development of nonlinear optical borate crystals: Key materials for generation of visible and UV light. *Mater. Sci. Eng.* R30:1, 2000.

Yap, Y. K., et al. Influence of negative dc bias voltage on structural transformation of carbon nitride at 600°C. *Appl. Phys. Lett.* 73:915, 1998.

NORTHEASTERN UNIVERSITY

Department of Physics

Programs of Study The department offers a full-time program leading to the Ph.D. and full-time and part-time evening programs leading to the M.S. or M.A.T. Requirements for the Ph.D. include 44 semester hours of course work, a written qualifying examination, a thesis describing the results of independent research, and a final oral examination. Students may pursue basic research in elementary particle physics, condensed-matter physics, and molecular biophysics or in interdisciplinary areas such as materials science, surface sciences, chemical physics, biophysics, and applied engineering physics. They also may carry out cooperative research at technologically advanced industrial, governmental, and national and international laboratories and at medical research institutions in the Boston area. Requirements for the M.S. and M.A.T. are 32 semester hours of credit, up to 8 of which may be transfer credit, if approved. There is no language requirement for any of the three degrees.

Research Facilities The department is housed in the Dana Research Center, with optics and condensed matter labs in the new Egan Research Center. There are ample modern research laboratories, department and student machine shops, an electronics shop, conference and seminar rooms, and faculty and graduate student offices. The Egan Center provides a direct interface with materials researchers in chemistry and engineering and includes extensive meeting space in the Technology Transfer Center. In 1999, the department received a $1.2-million NSF grant to establish the Advanced Scientific Computing Center (ASCC) in the Dana Research Center. The ASCC houses three clusters of computational/visualization workstations connected to an Alpha multiprocessor server. The High Energy Group has its own facilities with an Alpha cluster, an NT cluster, several Linux machines, and links to computer facilities at Fermilab and the Organisation Europeene pour la Recherche Nucleaire (CERN). The Condensed Matter Theory Group carries out large-scale simulations with Cray and Connection Machine supercomputers as well as locally on Alphas. In addition to the research they do at campus facilities, faculty members and graduate students also work at research centers located in the United States and Europe. High-energy physics experiments are underway at Fermilab in Batavia, Illinois, and at CERN, Geneva, Switzerland. High-magnetic-field experiments are in progress at the National High-Field Magnet Laboratory in Tallahassee, Florida, and Los Alamos National Laboratory, New Mexico. Several groups use the synchrotron facilities at Brookhaven National Laboratory, Long Island, New York, and Argonne National Laboratory, Argonne, Illinois, and many faculty members have flourishing collaborations with scientists in Europe, Asia, and South America.

Financial Aid Northeastern awards financial aid through the Federal Perkins Loan, Federal Work-Study, and Federal Stafford Student Loan Programs; through Graduate Assistantships in Areas of National Need (GAANN) fellowships; and through minority fellowships, including G. E. Fellowships and Martin Luther King, Jr. Scholarships. The Graduate School offers teaching and research assistantships that include tuition remission and a stipend (currently $14,750 for two semesters) and require 20 hours of work per week. Tuition assistantships provide tuition remission and require 10 hours of work per week. The department's newly established Lawrence Award Program honors students with Excellence in Teaching Awards, Academic Excellence Awards, and a Speaker's Prize.

Cost of Study Tuition for the 2003–04 academic year was $790 per semester hour. Books and supplies cost about $850 per year. Tuition charges are made for Ph.D. thesis and continuation. Other charges include the Student Center fee and health and accident insurance fee, which are required of all full-time students.

Living and Housing Costs For 2003–04, semester on-campus room rates for a single bedroom within an apartment ranged from $2830 to $3320. Single apartments ranged from $4360 to $4550. A shared bedroom in an apartment ranged from $2260 to $2640. On-campus housing for graduate students is limited and granted on a space-available basis. An off-campus referral service is available through Housing Services (telephone: 617-373-4872 or 617-373-2814; e-mail: nucommuter@neu.edu). While there were several board options available, graduate students typically paid $1825 per semester for ten meals per week. A public transportation system serves the greater Boston area, and there are subway and bus services convenient to the University.

Student Group In fall 2003, 19,568 students were enrolled at the University, representing a wide variety of academic, professional, geographic, and cultural backgrounds. The department enrolled 67 full-time students, of whom 97 percent received some form of financial support. A small number of students were enrolled in the part-time, evening M.S. program. The department awards roughly six Ph.D. degrees and eight M.S. degrees per year. Most graduates have continued to pursue research careers, either in academic institutions as postdoctoral fellows or in industrial, medical, or government laboratories.

Location Boston, Massachusetts, offers a rich cultural and intellectual history and is the premiere educational center of the country with more than thirty-five colleges in the city region. Cultural offerings, including several world-class museums, a bevy of art galleries, and the Boston Symphony, are diverse, and the city is home to people of every race, ethnicity, political persuasion, and religion. Boston also offers world-class restaurants, a range of outdoor activities, and is steeped in New England tradition.

The University and The Department Founded in 1898, Northeastern University is a privately endowed, nonsectarian institution of higher learning. Located in heart of Boston, Massachusetts, Northeastern is a world leader in cooperative education and recognized for its expert faculty and first-rate academic and research facilities. It offers a variety of curricula through seven undergraduate colleges, nine graduate and professional schools, two part-time undergraduate divisions, a number of continuing education programs, an extensive research division, and several institutes. The department offers opportunities for students to work on a wide range of groundbreaking research programs with an internationally recognized faculty whose goal is to provide an effective education to students with varied backgrounds.

Applying Although there is no absolute deadline for applying, completed applications should be received by February 15 to secure priority consideration for September acceptance, especially if financial assistance is sought. Scores on the GRE General Test and Physics Subject Test are required. The latter is given considerable weight in the admissions and assistantship awarding process. For international students, a TOEFL or IELTS score is required for admission.

Correspondence and Information

Graduate Coordinator (Admissions)
Department of Physics
Northeastern University
Boston, Massachusetts 02115

Telephone: 617-373-2902
Fax: 617-373-2943
E-mail: gradphysics@neu.edu
World Wide Web: http://www.physics.neu.edu

Northeastern University

THE FACULTY AND THEIR RESEARCH

Professors

Jorge V. José, Chairperson; D.Sc., National of Mexico, 1976. Condensed-matter theory.

Ronald Aaron, Ph.D., Pennsylvania, 1961. Medical physics.

Petros Argyres (Emeritus), Ph.D., Berkeley, 1954. Condensed-matter theory.

Arun Bansil, Ph.D., Harvard, 1974. Condensed-matter theory.

Paul M. Champion, Ph.D., Illinois at Urbana-Champaign, 1975. Biological and medical physics.

Alan H. Cromer (Emeritus), Ph.D., Cornell, 1960. Education.

William L. Faissler (Emeritus), Ph.D., Harvard, 1967. High-energy experimental physics.

David A. Garelick, Ph.D., MIT, 1963. Medical physics.

Michael J. Glaubman (Emeritus), Ph.D., Illinois, 1953. High-energy experimental physics.

Haim Goldberg, Ph.D., MIT, 1963. Particle theory.

Donald Heiman, Ph.D., California, Irvine, 1975. Condensed-matter experimental physics.

Alain Karma, Ph.D., California, Santa Barbara, 1986. Condensed-matter theory.

Sergy Kravchenko, Ph.D., Institute of Solid State Physics (Chernogolovka), 1988. Condensed-matter experimental physics.

Robert P. Lowndes, Ph.D., London, 1966. Condensed-matter experimental physics.

Bertram J. Malenka (Emeritus), Ph.D., Harvard, 1951. Particle theory.

Robert S. Markiewicz, Ph.D., Berkeley, 1975. Condensed-matter experimental physics.

Pran Nath, Ph.D., Stanford, 1964. Particle theory.

Clive H. Perry, Ph.D., London, 1960. Condensed-matter experimental physics.

Stephen Reucroft, Ph.D., Liverpool, 1969. High-energy experimental physics.

Eugene J. Saletan (Emeritus), Ph.D., Princeton, 1962. High-energy experimental physics.

Carl A. Shiffman (Emeritus), D.Phil., Oxford, 1956. Medical physics.

Jeffrey B. Sokoloff, Graduate Coordinator; Ph.D., MIT, 1967. Condensed-matter theory.

Srinivas Sridhar, Ph.D., Caltech, 1983. Condensed-matter experimental physics.

Yogendra N. Srivastava, Ph.D., Indiana, 1964. Particle theory.

Tomasz Taylor, Ph.D., Warsaw, 1981. Particle theory.

Michael T. Vaughn, Ph.D., Purdue, 1960. Particle theory.

Eberhard von Goeler (Emeritus), Ph.D., Illinois, 1961. High-energy experimental physics.

Allan Widom, Ph.D., Cornell, 1967. Condensed-matter theory.

Fa-Yueh Wu, Ph.D., Washington (St. Louis), 1963. Condensed-matter theory.

Associate Professors

George Alverson, Ph.D., Illinois at Urbana-Champaign, 1979. High-energy experimental physics.

Nathan Israeloff, Ph.D., Illinois at Urbana-Champaign, 1990. Condensed-matter experimental physics.

J. Timothy Sage, Ph.D., Illinois at Urbana-Champaign, 1986. Molecular biophysics.

John D. Swain, Ph.D., Toronto, 1990. High-energy experimental physics.

Darien Wood, Ph.D., Berkeley, 1987. High-energy experimental physics.

Assistant Professors

Emanuela Barberis, Ph.D., California, Santa Cruz, 1996. High-energy experimental physics.

Armen Stepanyants, Ph.D., Rhode Island, 1999. Condensed-matter theory.

Mark C. Williams, Ph.D., Minnesota, 1998. Molecular biophysics.

Research Associates

Luis Anchordoqui, Ph.D., National University of La Plata (Argentina),1998: high-energy physics. Bernardo Barbiellini, Ph.D., Geneva, 1991: condensed-matter theory. Christopher Daly, Ph.D., Northeastern, 1996: condensed-matter physics. Georgi Georgiev, Ph.D., Tufts, 2002: molecular biophysics. Gavin Hesketh, Ph.D., Manchester (England), 2003: high-energy experimental physics. Scott Hill, Ph.D., Chicago, 2002: complex systems (CIRCS). Stanislaw Kaprzyk, Ph.D., Academy of Metallurgy (Krakow), 1981: condensed-matter theory. Cristian Kusko, Ph.D., Northeastern, 2003: condensed-matter theory. Matti Lindroos, Ph.D., Tampere Tech (Finland), 1979: condensed-matter theory. Wentao Lu, Ph.D., Northeastern, 2001: condensed-matter theory. Micah McCauley, Ph.D., Colorado State, 2001: laser physics, biophysics. Jorge H. Moromisato, Ph.D., Northeastern, 1971: high-energy experimental physics. Pantanjali V. Parimi, Ph.D., Hyderabad (India), 1998: condensed-matter physics. Thomas Paul, Ph.D., Johns Hopkins, 1994: high-energy experimental physics. Seppo Sahrakorpi, Ph.D., Tampere Tech (Finland), 2001: condensed-matter theory. Yohannes Shiferaw, Ph.D., Pittsburgh, 2001: condensed-matter theory. Dennis Shpakov, Ph.D., SUNY at Stony Brook, 2000: high-energy experimental physics. Xiong Ye, Ph.D., Northeastern, 2003: biological physics. Anchi Yu, Ph.D., Beijing, 1999: physical chemistry and laser spectroscopy.

Adjunct Professors

George Tze Yung Chen, Ph.D., Brown, 1972: biomedical physics. Graham Farmelo, Ph.D., Liverpool, 1977: high-energy experimental physics. Howard Fenker, Ph.D., Vanderbilt, 1978: high-energy experimental physics. Wolfhard Kern, Ph.D., Bonn (Germany), 1958: high-energy experimental physics and education. Peter Mijnarends, Ph.D., Delft (the Netherlands), 1969: condensed-matter theory. C. Robert Morgan, Ph.D., MIT, 1969: condensed-matter theory. Fabio Sauli, Ph.D., Trieste (Italy), 1963: high-energy experimental physics.

RESEARCH ACTIVITIES

Experimental Biological and Medical Physics. The group probes the structure and function of macromolecules, metalloproteins, and protein complexes. Specific research areas include electron transport, macromolecular structure, enzyme catalysis, and ligand binding and protein dynamics, using quasi-elastic scattering; transient absorption spectroscopy; Raman, FTIR, and fluorescence spectroscopy; femtosecond coherence spectroscopy; nuclear resonance vibrational spectroscopy; single-molecule-force spectroscopy using optical tweezers; measurements of human balance; and novel imaging technologies.

Experimental Condensed-Matter Physics. Research activities focus on high-temperature superconductors (HTSC), semiconductors, and magnetic materials. HTSC research includes fundamental studies of order parameter symmetry and vortex dynamics; flux-lattice melting; Josephson-junction arrays; low-field HTSC magnets; linear and nonlinear electrodynamics of HTSCs; electromagnetic response of HTSCs at far infrared, microwave, and radio frequencies; growth and characterization of new HTSC ceramics and single crystals; and factors limiting critical currents. Research on semiconductors includes correlated electron and quantum Hall effects, 2-D metal-insulator transition and electron solid; magnetooptical spectroscopy of nanostructures and quantum layers and molecular-beam epitaxy (MBE) crystal growth. Other areas under investigation are electromagnetic and quantum chaos; left-handed metamaterials; Raman, FT-IR, mesoscopic systems, noise, scanning probe microscopy, and nanoscale properties of materials.

Experimental High-Energy Physics. The group is working on three major collider experiments: the L3 detector at LEP at CERN (the European Laboratory for Particle Physics in Geneva, Switzerland), the DZero experiment at Fermi National Laboratory outside Chicago, and the CMS experiment now under construction at CERN. These are all frontier experiments probing the electroweak and strong interactions at the highest energy scales, and represent a phased program of research keeping the group at the cutting edge of the experimental investigation of the structure of matter and the forces by which it interacts.

Particle Physics. The group has begun an active program in particle astrophysics and is involved in the construction of the Pierre Auger Cosmic Ray Observatory in Argentina, which aims to elucidate the origin and nature of the highest energy cosmic rays, and a related outreach program called SCROD, which will put cosmic ray detectors in schools throughout the world. The group has a strong history of doing not just straight experimental particle physics but also the related phenomenology, and keeping an eye out for creative spin-offs of its research with applications in other fields.

Theoretical Condensed-Matter Physics. Research topics include transport theory, quantum chaos, Fermi liquid theory, charge density waves, and dense dipolar suspensions; and theory of Josephson junctions, catalytic properties of alloys, transport in nanostructures, structural phase transitions in DNA, nanotribology (atomic-level friction), electronic structure of disordered materials, magnetism, ferrites, Fermiology of HTSCs, Van Hove scenario and stripes in HTSCs, exact and rigorous results in statistical mechanics, localization and percolation in order-disorder phase transitions, positron annihilation and photoemission spectroscopy, and nonlinear dynamics and pattern formation.

Theoretical Elementary Particle Physics. Fundamental research includes the study of unified models based on supersymmetry and superstrings; unified gauge theories in the TeV range and precision calculations within and beyond the Standard Model; particle physics in the early universe; proton stability and neutrino masses; electroweak anomaly in the observed asymmetry of the baryon number, gravitational theory and quantum gravity, Kaluza-Klein theories and large-radius compactification, and computer simulations of topological structures in field theory; finite temperature effects in quantum chromodynamics; numerical simulations of pregalactic structure formation; quasar absorption line systems; and observational and theoretical analysis of X-ray galaxy clusters.

Northeastern University

SELECTED PUBLICATIONS

Rutkove, S. B., **R. Aaron,** and **C. A. Shiffman.** Localized bioimpedance analysis in the evaluation of neuromuscular disease. *Muscle Nerve* 25:390, 2002.

Aaron, R., and **C. A. Shiffman.** Localized muscle impedance measurements. In *Skeletal Muscle: Pathology, Diagnosis and Management of Disease,* chap. 45, eds. V. R. Preedy and V. J. Peters. London: Greenwich Medical Media, 2002.

Aaron, R., and **C. A. Shiffman.** Using localized impedance measurements to study muscle changes resulting from injury and disease. *Ann. N.Y. Acad. Sci.* 904:171, 2000.

Alverson, G., et al. Iguana architecture, framework and toolkit for interactive graphics. In *2003 Conference for Computing in High-Energy Nuclear Physics (CHEP-03) EconfC0303241:MOLT008,* e-Print Archive:cs.se/0306042, 2003.

Alverson, G., et al. The IGUANA Interactive Graphics Toolkit with examples from CMS and DØ. In *Proceedings of CHEP 2001,* ed. H. Chen. Beijing, China, 2001.

Alverson, G. (The HEPVis 2001 Group). Summary of the HEPVis '01 workshop. In *CHEP 2001.* Beijing, China, 2001.

Alverson, G., et al. Coherent and non-invasive open analysis architecture and framework with applications in CMS. In *Proceedings of CHEP 2001,* ed. H. S. Chen. Beijing, China, 2001.

Alverson, G., I. Gaponenko, and L. Taylor. The CMS IGUANA (Interactive Graphical User Analysis) Project. In *CHEP 2000.* Padova, Italy, 2000.

Bansil, A., et al. Angle-resolved photoemission spectra, electronic structure and spin-dependent scattering in Ni_{1-x}Fe_x permalloys. *Phys. Rev. B* 65:075106, 2002.

Bansil, A., et al. Electron momentum density in Cu_{0.9}A1_{0.1}. *Appl. Phys. A,* 2002.

Bansil, A., M. Lindroos, and S. Sahrakorpi. Matrix element effects in angle-resolved photoemission from Bi2212: Energy and polarization dependencies, final state spectrum, spectral signatures of specific transitions and related issues. *Phys. Rev. B* 65:054514, 2002.

Bansil, A., and B. Barbiellini. Electron momentum density and Compton profile in disordered alloys. *J. Phys. Chem. Solids* 62:2191, 2001.

Bansil, A., and B. Barbiellini. Electron momentum distribution in A1 and A1_{0.97}Li_{0.3}. *J. Phys. Chem. Solids* 62:2223, 2001.

Barberis, E., S. Reucroft, and **D. Wood** et al. (D-Zero Collaboration). Observation of diffractively produced W and Z bosons in antiproton-proton collisions at s** (1/2) = 1800-Gev. *Phys. Lett. B* 574:169–79, 2003.

Barberis, E., S. Reucroft, and **D. Wood** et al. (D-Zero Collaboration). Search for large extra dimensions in the monojet E(T) channel at D0. *Phys. Rev. Lett.* 90:251802, 2003.

Barberis, E., S. Reucroft, and **D. Wood** et al. (D-Zero Collaboration). Top anti-top production cross-section in proton-antiproton collisions at s** (1/2) = 1.8-Tev. *Phys. Rev. D* 67:012004, 2003.

Barberis, E., S. Reucroft, and **D. Wood** et al. (D-zero Collaboration). Subjet multiplicity of gluon and quark jets reconstructed with the K(T) algorithm in P anti-P collisions. *Phys. Rev. D* 65:052008, 2002.

Barberis, E., S. Reucroft, and **D. Wood** et al. (D-zero Collaboration). The inclusive jet cross-section in P anti-P collisions at S**(1/2) = 1.8-Tev using the K(T) algorithm. *Phys. Lett. B* 525:211, 2002.

Rosca, F., et al. **(P. M. Champion).** Investigations of heme protein absorption lineshapes, vibrational relaxation, and resonance Raman scattering on ultrafast timescales. *J. Phys. Chem.* 107:8156, 2003.

S. Berezhna, **P. M. Champion,** and H. Wohlrab. Resonance Raman investigations of cytochrome c conformational change upon interaction with the membranes of intact and Ca2+ exposed mitochrondria. *Biochemistry* 42:6149, 2003.

Unno, M., et al. **(P. M. Champion).** Effects of complex formation of cytochrome P450 with putidaredoxin: Evidence for protein-specific interactions involving the proximal thiolate ligand. *J. Biol. Chem.* 277:2547, 2002.

Rosca, F., et al. **(P. M. Champion).** Investigations of anharmonic low-frequency oscillations in heme proteins. *J. Phys. Chem. A* 106:3540, 2002.

Ye, X., A. Demidov, and **P. M. Champion.** Measurements of the photodissociation quantum yields of MbNO and MbO2 and the vibrational relaxation of the six-coordinate heme species. *J. Am. Chem. Soc.* 124:5914, 2002.

Garelick, D. A., A. Widom, M. Harris, and R. Koleva. Posture sway and the transition rate for a fall. *Physica A* 293:605, 2001.

Garelick, D. A. (Co-Leader), et al. Balance evaluation with an ultrasonic measuring system. In *Proceedings of the January 1994 Meeting jointly sponsored by the Association of Academic Physiatrists and the American Academy of Physical Medicine and Rehabilitation,* 1994.

Anchordoqui, L., and **H. Goldberg.** Black hold chromosphere at the LHC. *Phys. Rev. D* 67:064010, 2003.

Anchordoqui, L., **H. Goldberg,** and D. F. Torres. Anisotropy at the end of the cosmic ray spectrum? *Phys. Rev. D* 67:123006, 2003.

Anchordoqui, L., and **H. Goldberg.** Time variation of the fine structure constant driven by quintessence. *Phys. Rev. D* 68:083513, 2003.

Anchordoqui, L., J. L. Feng, **H. Goldberg,** and A. D. Shapere. Updated limits on TeV-scale gravity from absence of neutrino cosmic ray showers mediated by black holes. *Phys. Rev. D* 68:104025, 2003.

Heiman, D., and **C. H. Perry.** Magneto-optics. In *Characterization of Reduced Dimensional Semiconductor Microstructures,* ed. F. H. Pollak. In series *Optoelectronic Properties of Semiconductor Quantum Wells and Superlattices.* Gordon and Breach Publishers, 2002.

Heiman, D., and **C. H. Perry.** Magneto-optics of semiconductors. In *High Magnetic Fields: Science and Technology; Theory and Experimentation,* vol. 2, pp. 47–72, eds. F. Herlach and N. Miura. World Scientific, 2003.

Heiman, D., and **C. H. Perry.** Magneto-optics of semiconductors. In *Physics of High Magnetic Fields and their Applications,* eds. F. Herlach and N. Miura. World Scientific, 2002.

Okamura, H., et al. **(D. Heiman).** Inhibited recombination of charged magnetoexcitons. *Phys. Rev. B Rapid Commun.* 58:R15985, 1998.

Okamura, H., et al. **(D. Heiman).** Inhibited recombination of negatively-charged excitons in GaAs quantum wells at high magnetic fields. *Physica B* 470:256–8, 1998.

Israeloff, N. E., and T. S. Grigera. Numerical study of aging in coupled two-level systems. *Philos. Mag. B* 82:313, 2001.

Vidal, R. E., and **N. E. Israeloff.** Direct observation of molecular cooperativity near the glass transition. *Nature* 408:659, 2000.

Grigera, T. S., and **N. E. Israeloff.** Observation of fluctuation dissipation violations in a structural glass. *Phys. Rev. Lett.* 83:5038, 1999.

Walther, L. E., et al. **(N. E. Israeloff).** Atomic force measurement of low frequency dielectric noise. *Appl. Phys. Lett.* 72:3223, 1998.

Gongora-T, A., **J. V. José,** and S. Schaffner. Classical solutions of an electron in magnetized wedge billiards. *Phys. Rev. E* 66:047201, 2002.

José, J. V., and M. V. José. Thermodynamic distributions of heterogeneous receptor populations. In *Drug Receptor Thermodynamics: Introduction and Applications,* p. 593, ed. R. Raffa. Chichester, Sussex, England: J. Wiley and Sons, Ltd., 2001.

Tiesinga, P. H. E., et al. **(J. V. José).** Computational model of carbachol-induced delta, theta, and gamma oscillations in the hippocampus. *Hippocampus* 11:25, 2001.

Gibbons, F., et al. **(J. V. José).** A dynamical model of kinesin-microtubule motility assays. *Biophys. J.* 80:2515, 2001.

José, J. V., and E. Saletan. *Classical Mechanics: A Contemporary Approach.* Cambridge University Press, 1998. Third edition, 2002.

Echebarria, B., and **A. Karma.** Instability and spatiotemporal dynamics of alternans in paced cardiac tissue. *Phys. Rev. Lett.* 88:208101, 2002.

Karma, A., H. Levine, and D. Kessler. Phase-field model of mode-III dynamic fracture. *Phys. Rev. Lett.* 87:045501, 2001.

Karma, A. Phase-field formulation for quantitative modeling of alloy solidification. *Phys. Rev. Lett.* 87:115701, 2001.

Erlebacher, J., et al. **(A. Karma).** Evolution of nanoporosity in dealloying. *Nature* 410:450, 2001.

Plapp, M., and **A. Karma.** Multiscale random-walk algorithm for simulating interfacial pattern formation. *Phys. Rev. Lett.* 84:1740, 2000.

Karma, A. New paradigm for drug therapies of cardiac fibrillation. *Proc. Natl. Acad. Sci. U.S.A.* 97:5687, 2000.

Kravchenko, S. V., and M. P. Sarachik. Metal-insulator transition in two-dimensional electron systems. *Rep. Prog. Phys.* 67:1, 2004.

Rahimi, M., et al. **(S. V. Kravchenko).** Coherent back-scattering near the two-dimensional metal-insulator transition. *Phys. Rev. Lett.* 91:116402, 2003.

Shashkin, A. A., et al. **(S. V. Kravchenko).** Spin-independent origin of the strongly enhanced effective mass in a dilute 2D electron system. *Phys. Rev. Lett.* 91:046403, 2003.

Abrahams, E., **S. V. Kravchenko,** and M. P. Sarachik. Metallic behavior and related phenomena in two dimensions. *Rev. Mod. Phys.* 73:251, 2001.

Shashkin, A. A., **S. V. Kravchenko,** V. T. Dolgopolov, and T. M. Klapwijk. Indication of the ferromagnetic instability in a dilute two-dimensional electron system. *Phys. Rev. Lett.* 87:086801, 2001.

Kusko, C., and **R. S. Markiewicz.** White-Scalapino-like stripes in the mean-field Hubbard model. *Phys. Rev. B* 65:041102, 2002.

Markiewicz, R. S., and C. Kusko. Phase separation models for cuprate stripe arrays. *Phys. Rev. B* 65:064520, 2002.

Markiewicz, R. S., and C. Kusko. Flux phase as a dynamic Jahn-Teller phase: Berryonic matter in the cuprates? *Phys. Rev. B* 66:024506, 2002.

Northeastern University

Selected Publications (continued)

Kusko, C., **R. S. Markiewicz,** M. Lindroos, and **A. Bansil.** Fermi surface evolution and collapse of the Mott pseudogap in Nd2-x CexCuO4 delta. *Phys. Rev. B* 66:140513, 2002.
Markiewicz, R. S., et al. Cluster spin glass distribution functions in La2-xSrxCuO4. *Phys. Rev. B* 054409-1, 2001.
Kusko, C., et al. **(R. S. Markiewicz** and **S. Sridhar).** Anomalous microwave conductivity due to collective transport in the pseupseudogap state of cuprate superconductors. *Phys. Rev. B.,* 2001.
Kusko, C., and **R. S. Markiewicz.** Remnant Fermi surfaces in photoemission. *Phys. Rev. Lett.* 84:963, 2000.
Markiewicz, R. S., and **M. T. Vaughn.** Stripe disordering transition. In *University of Miami Conference on High Temperature Superconductivity,* Miami, Florida, January 7–13, 1999.
Markiewicz, R. S., C. Kusko, and **M. T. Vaughn.** SO(6)-generalized pseudogap model of the cuprates. In *University of Miami Conference on High Temperature Superconductivity,* Miami, Florida, January 7–13, 1999.
Markiewicz, R. S., and **M. T. Vaughn.** Higher symmetries in condensed matter physics. In *Particles, Strings and Cosmology—PASCOS98,* ed. **P. Nath.** Singapore: World Scientific, 1999.
Nath, P., and R. Syed. Coupling the supersymmetric 210 vector multiplet to matter in SO(10). *Nucl. Phys. B* 676:64–98, 2004.
Nath, P., and T. Ibrahim. Decays of Higgs to b anti-b, tau anti-tau and c anti-c as signatures of supersymmetry and CP phases. *Phys. Rev. D* 68:015008, 2003.
Nath, P., and P. Frampton. MSUGRA celebrates its 20th year. *CERN Cour.* 43N7:27–8, 2003.
Nath, P., and T. Ibrahim. Supersymmetric QCD and supersymmetric electroweak loop corrections to b, t, and tau masses including the effects of CP phases. *Phys. Rev. D* 67:095003, 2003.
Nath, P., and U. Chattopadhyay. WMAP Constraints, SUSY dark matter and implications for the direct detection of SUSY. *Phys. Rev. D* 68:035005, 2003.
Kim, Y., K.-S. Lee, and **C. H. Perry.** Optically detected heavy- and light-hold anti-crossing in GaAs quantum wells under pulsed magnetic fields. *Appl. Phys. Lett.* 84:738, 2004.
Russell, K. J., et al. **(C. H. Perry).** Room temperature electro-optic up conversion via internal photoemission. *Appl. Phys. Lett.* 82:2960, 2003.
Appelbaum, I., et al. **(C. H. Perry).** Ballistic electron emission luminescence. *Appl. Phys. Lett.* 82:4498, 2003.
Kim, Y., and **C. H. Perry** et al. Electron-hole separation studies of the v=1 quantum Hall state in modulation-doped GaAs/AlGaAs single heterojunctions in high magnetic fields. *Phys. Rev. B* 64:195302, 2001.
Reucroft, S., and **J. Swain** et al. (L3 Collaboration). Inclusive Pi0 And K0(S) production in two photon collisions at LEP. *Phys. Lett. B* 524:44–54, 2002.
Reucroft, S., and **J. Swain** et al. (L3 Collaboration). Search for R parity violating decays of supersymmetric particles in E+ E- collisions at LEP. *Phys. Lett. B* 524:65–80, 2002.
Reucroft, S., and **J. Swain** et al. (L3 Collaboration). Study of the W+ W- gamma process and limits on anomalous quartic gauge boson couplings at LEP. *Phys. Lett. B* 527:29–38, 2002.
Reucroft, S., and **J. Swain** et al. (L3 Collaboration). F(1)(1285) formation in two photon collisions at LEP. *Phys. Lett. B* 526:269–77, 2002.
Reucroft, S., and **J. Swain.** *An Introduction to Science,* 2nd ed. McGraw-Hill/Primis, 2000.
Rai, B. K., et al. **(J. T. Sage).** Direct determination of the complete set of iron normal modes in a porphyrin-imidazole model for carbonmonoxy-heme proteins: [Fe(TPP)(CO)(1-MeIm)]. *J. Am. Chem. Soc.* 125:6927–36, 2003.
Budarz, T. E., et al. **(J. T. Sage).** Determination of the complete set of iron normal modes in the heme model compound Fe III (OEP) Cl from nuclear resonance vibrational spectroscopic data. *J. Phys. Chem. B* 107:11170–7, 2003.
Rai, B. K., et al. **(J. T. Sage).** Iron normal mode dynamics in a porphyrin-imidazole model for deoxyheme proteins. *Phys. Rev. E* 66:051904, 2002.
Parimi, P. V., et al. **(J. B. Sokoloff** and **S. Sridhar).** Negative refraction and left-handed electromagnetism in microwave photonic crystals. *Phys. Rev. Lett.,* in press.
Daly, C., J. Zhang, and **J. B. Sokoloff.** Dry friction due to absorbed molecules. *Phys. Rev. Lett.* 90:246101, 2003.
Daly, C., J. Zhang, and **J. B. Sokoloff.** Friction in the zero sliding velocity limit. *Phys. Rev. E* 68:0661, 2003.
Sokoloff, J. B. Explaining the virtual universal occurrence of static friction. *Phys. Rev. B* 65:115415, 2002.
Sokoloff, J. B. Static friction between elastic solids due to random asperities. *Phys. Rev. Lett.* 86:3312, 2001.
Parimi, P. V., W. T. Lu, P. Vodo, and **S. Sridhar.** Imaging by flat lens using negative refraction. *Nature* 426:404, 2003.
Bishop, A. R., S. R. Shenoy, and **S. Sridhar.** Intrinsic multiscale structure and dynamics in novel electronic oxides. *World Scientific,* 2003.
Lu, W. T., **S. Sridhar,** and M. Zworski. Fractal Weyl laws for chaotic open systems. *Phys. Rev. Lett.* 91:154101, 2003.
Rao, D. M., et al. **(S. Sridhar).** Isospectrality in chaotic billiards. *Phys. Rev. E* 68:26208, 2003.
Grau, A., R. Godbole, G. Pancheri, and **Y. N. Srivastava.** The role of soft gluon radiation in the fall and rise of total cross sections. *Nucl. Phys. B Proc. Suppl.* 126, 2003.
Grau, A., S. Pacetti, G. Pancheri, and **Y. N. Srivastava.** Bloch-Nordsieck resummation for QCD processes. *Nucl. Phys. B. Proc. Suppl.* 126, 2003.
Sivasubramanian, S., **Y. N. Srivastava,** G. Vitiello, and **A. Widom.** Quantum dissipation induced noncommutative geometry. *Phys. Lett. A* 311:97, 2003.
Srivastava, Y. N., and **A. Widom.** Dirac analysis of the muon (g-2) measurements and non-commutative geometry of quantum beams. *J. Phys.* 53:1628, 2003.
Stepanyants, A., G. Tamás, and D. B. Chklovskii. Class-specific features of neuronal wiring. *Neuron* 43:251–9, 2004.
Chklovskii, D. B., and **A. Stepanyants.** Power-law for axon diameters at branch point. *BMC Neurosci.* 4:18, 2003.
Stepanyants, A., P. R. Hof, and D. B. Chklovskii. Geometry and structural plasticity of synaptic connectivity. *Neuron* 34:275–88, 2002.
Stepanyants, A. Diffusion and localization of surface gravity waves over irregular bathymetry. *Phys. Rev. E* 63(3):031202, 2001
Swain, J. Anomalous electroweak couplings of the tau and tau neutrino. In *Proceedings of the Sixth International Workshop on Tau LEPton Physics (TAU2000),* Victoria, B.C., Canada, September 18–21, 2000. *Nucl. Phys. Proc. Suppl.* 98:351, 2001.
Taylor, T. R., and P. Khorsand. Renormalization of boundary fermions and world-volume potentials on D-branes. *Nucl. Phys. B* 611:239, 2001.
Taylor, T. R., and A. Fotopoulos. Remarks on two-loop free energy in N=4 supersymmetric Yang-Mills theory at finite temperature. *Phys. Rev. D* 59:61701, 1999.
Taylor, T. R., et al. Duality in superstring compactifications with magnetic field backgrounds. *Nucl. Phys. B* 511:611, 1998.
Taylor, T. R., I. Antoniadis, and B. Pioline. Calculable e{-1/lambda} effects. *Nucl. Phys. B* 512:61, 1998.
Vaughn, M. T., and **R. S. Markiewicz.** Classification of the Van Hove scenario as an SO(8) spectrum generating algebra. *Phys. Rev. B Rapid Commun.* 57:14052–5, 1998.
Sivasubramanian, S., **A. Widom,** and **Y. Srivastava.** Equivalent circuit and simulations for the Landau-Khalatnikov model of ferroelectric hysteresis. *IEEE (UFFC)* 50:950, 2003.
Sivasubramanian, S., **A. Widom,** and **Y. N. Srivastava.** Microscopic basis of thermal superradiance. *J. Phys.: Condens. Matter* 15:1109, 2003.
Pant, K., R. L. Karpel, I. Rouzina, and **M. C. Williams.** Mechanical measurement of single molecule binding rates: Kinetics of DNA helix-destabilization by T4 gene 32 protein. *J. Mol. Biol.* 336:851–70, 2004.
Pant, K., R. L. Karpel, and **M. C. Williams.** Kinetic regulation of single DNA molecule denaturation by T4 gene 32 protein structural domains. *J. Mol. Biol.* 327:571–8, 2003.
Williams, M. C., R. J. Gorelick, and K. Musier-Forsyth. Specific zinc finger architecture required for HIV-1 nucleocapsid protein's nucleic acid chaperone function. *Proc. Natl. Acad. Sci. U.S.A.* 99:8614–9, 2002.
Williams, M. C. Optical tweezers: Measuring piconewton forces, in single molecule techniques. In *Biophysics Textbook Online,* editor-in-chief L. DeFelice, ed. Petra Schwille. Bethesda, Md.: Biophysical Society, 2002.
Williams, M. C., and I. Rouzina. Force spectroscopy of single DNA and RNA molecules. *Curr. Opin. Struct. Biol.* 12:330–6, 2002.
Wu, F. Y., and H. Kunz. The odd eight-vertex model. *J. Stat. Phys.,* in press.
Tzeng, W. J., and **F. Y. Wu.** Dimers on a simple-quartic net with a vacancy. *J. Stat. Phys.* 110:671–89, 2003.
Lee, D. H., and **F. Y. Wu.** Duality relation for frustrated spin models. *Phys. Rev. E* 67:026111, 2003.
Lieb, E. H., and **F. Y. Wu.** The one-dimensional Hubbard model: A reminiscence. *Physica A* 321:1–27, 2003.
Wu, F. Y. Dimers and spanning trees: Some recent results. *Int. J. Mod. Phys. B* 16:1951–61, 2002.
King, C., and **F. Y. Wu.** New correlation relations for the planar Potts model. *J. Stat. Phys.* 107:919–40, 2002.
Wu, F. Y., C. King, and W. T. Lu. On the rooted Tutte polynomial. *Ann. Inst. Fourier, Grenoble* 49:101–12, 1999.
Lu, W. T., and **F. Y. Wu.** Partition function zeroes of a self-dual Ising model. *Physica A* 258:157–70, 1998.
Wu, F. Y. The exact solution of a class of three-dimensional lattice statistical model. In *Proc. 7th Asia Pacific Phys. Conf.,* pp. 20–8, ed. H. Chem. Beijing: Science Press, 1998.
Lu, W. T., and **F. Y. Wu.** On the duality relation for correlation functions of the Potts model. *J. Phys. A* 31:2823, 1998.

OHIO UNIVERSITY

Department of Physics and Astronomy

Programs of Study

The Department of Physics and Astronomy offers graduate study and research programs leading to the Master of Arts, Master of Science, and Doctor of Philosophy degrees. The program of study emphasizes individual needs and interests in addition to essential general requirements of the discipline. Major areas of current research are experimental and theoretical nuclear and intermediate-energy physics, experimental condensed-matter and surface physics, theoretical condensed-matter and statistical physics, nonlinear systems and chaos, biophysics, acoustics, atomic physics, mathematical and computational physics, biological physics, geophysics, astronomy and astrophysics.

A student typically takes core courses (mechanics, math, quantum, electrodynamics) during the first year in preparation for the comprehensive exam that is given at the end of the summer following the first year. Students can usually retake the exam during the winter break of the second year if necessary. The courses in the second year cover more advanced topics. Master's degrees require completion of 45 graduate credits in physics and have both thesis and nonthesis options. Applied master's degrees (e.g., computational physics) are under development. The Ph.D. requirements include passing the comprehensive exam and writing and orally defending the dissertation.

Research Facilities

The physics department occupies two wings of Clippinger Laboratories, a modern, well-equipped research building; the Edwards Accelerator Building, which contains Ohio University's 4.5-MV high-intensity tandem accelerator; and the Surface Science Research Laboratory, which is isolated from mechanical and electrical disturbances. Specialized facilities for measuring structural, thermal, transport, optical, and magnetic properties of condensed matter are available. In addition to research computers in laboratories, students have access to a Beowulf cluster and the Ohio Supercomputer Center, where massively parallel systems (e.g. a CRAY SVI, a SGIB Origin 2000, and an Itanium Cluster) are located.

Financial Aid

Financial aid is available in the form of teaching assistantships (TAs) and research assistantships (RAs). All cover the full cost of tuition plus a stipend from which a quarterly fee of $430 must be paid by the student. Current stipend levels for TAs are $19,000 per year. The stipend levels for RAs are set by the research grant holders but are at or above the level of the TA stipends. TAs require approximately 15 hours per week of laboratory and/or teaching duties. Merit stipends of $20,000 per year are available for outstanding applicants. Special assistantships through the Condensed Matter and Surface Science (CMSS) program are also available.

Cost of Study

Tuition and fees are $2165 per quarter for Ohio residents and $4610 per quarter for out-of-state students. Tuition and fees for part-time students are prorated.

Living and Housing Costs

On-campus rooms for single students are $1265 per quarter, while married student apartments cost from $578 to $707 per month. A number of off-campus apartments and rooms are available at various costs.

Student Group

About 19,800 students study on the main campus of the University, and about 2,700 of these are graduate students. The graduate student enrollment in the physics department ranges from 60 to 70.

Location

Athens is a city of about 25,000, situated in the rolling Appalachian foothills of southeastern Ohio. The surrounding landscape consists of wooded hills rising about the Hocking River valley, and the area offers many outdoor recreational opportunities. Eight state parks lie within easy driving distance of the campus and are popular spots for relaxation. The outstanding intellectual and cultural activities sponsored by this diverse university community are pleasantly blended in Athens with a lively tradition of music and crafts.

The University and The Department

Ohio University, founded in 1804 and the oldest institution of higher education in the Northwest Territory, is a comprehensive university with a wide range of graduate and undergraduate programs. The Ph.D. program in physics began in 1959, and more than 220 doctoral degrees have been awarded. Currently, the department has 33 regular faculty members, and additional part-time faculty and postdoctoral fellows. Sponsored research in the department amounts to approximately $3.2 million per year and comes from NSF, DOE, DOD, ONR, BMDO, NASA, and the state of Ohio. Further information can be found at the department's home page listed below.

Applying

Information on application procedures and downloadable forms can be found at http://www.ohiou.edu/graduate/apps.htm. These materials can also be obtained by writing to the Department of Physics and Astronomy at the address listed below.

Correspondence and Information

Graduate Admissions Chair
Department of Physics and Astronomy
Ohio University
Athens, Ohio 45701
Telephone: 740-593-1718
World Wide Web: http://www.phy.ohiou.edu

Ohio University

THE FACULTY AND THEIR RESEARCH

Professors

David A. Drabold, Ph.D., Washington (St. Louis), 1989. Theoretical condensed matter, computational methodology for electronic structure, theory of topologically disordered materials.

Charlotte Elster, Dr.rer.nat, Bonn, 1986. Nuclear and intermediate-energy theory.

Steven M. Grimes, Ph.D., Wisconsin–Madison, 1968. Nuclear physics.

Kenneth H. Hicks, Ph.D., Colorado, 1984; Director, Institute for Nuclear and Particle Physics. Nuclear and intermediate-energy physics.

David C. Ingram, Ph.D., Salford (England), 1980. Atomic collisions in solids, thin films, deposition and analysis.

Martin E. Kordesch, Ph.D., Case Western Reserve, 1984. Surface physics.

Jaccobo Rapaport, Distinguished Professor Emeritus, Ph.D., MIT, 1963. Nuclear physics.

Roger W. Rollins, Ph.D., Cornell, 1967. Solid-state physics, superconductivity, chaotic systems.

Folden B. Stumpf, Professor Emeritus, Ph.D., IIT, 1956. Accoustics, ultrasonics.

Sergio E. Ulloa, Ph.D., SUNY at Buffalo, 1984. Theoretical condensed-matter physics.

Louis E. Wright, Ph.D., Duke, 1966; Chair of the Department. Nuclear theory, electrodynamics, intermediate-energy theory.

Associate Professors

Charles E. Brient, Ph.D., Texas at Austin, 1963. Nuclear physics, surface physics.

Daniel S. Carman, Ph.D., Indiana, 1995. Experimental nuclear and particle physics.

Alexander O. Govorov, Ph.D., Novosibirsk, 1991. Theoretical condensed-matter physics, nanoscience.

Peter Jung, Ph.D., Ulm (Germany), 1985. Nonequilibrium statistical physics, nonlinear stochastic processes, pattern formation.

Brian R. McNamara, Ph.D., Virginia, 1991. Astrophysics, galaxy clusters, and X-ray astronomy.

Allena K. Opper, Ph.D., Indiana Bloomington, 1991. Intermediate-energy physics.

Daniel Phillips, Ph.D., Flinders (Australia), 1995. Theoretical nuclear and particle physics.

Joseph C. Shields, Ph.D., Berkeley, 1991. Astrophysics, interstellar medium, active galactic nuclei.

Thomas S. Statler, Ph.D., Princeton, 1986. Astrophysics, galactic structure and dynamics.

Larry A. Wilen, Ph.D., Princeton, 1986. Experimental acoustics, condensed-matter physics, surface melting.

Assistant Professors

Markus Böttcher, Ph.D., Bonn, 1997. High-energy astrophysics.

Ido Braslovsky, Ph.D., Israel Institute of Technology, 1998. Biophysics.

Carl R. Brune, Ph.D., Caltech, 1994. Experimental nuclear astrophysics.

Horacio E. Castillo, Ph.D., Illinois, 1998. Theoretical condensed-matter physics.

Jean Heremans, Ph.D., Princeton, 1994. Experimental condensed-matter and surface physics.

Saw-Wai Hla, Ph.D., Ljubljana, 1997. Experimental condensed-matter and surface physics, nanoscience.

Mark Lucas, Ph.D., Illinois, 1994. Experimental nuclear physics.

Michael G. Moore, Ph.D., Arizona, 1999. Atomic physics and atom optics.

Alexander Neiman, Ph.D., Saratov State (Russia), 1991. Biophysics, nonlinear dynamics, stochastic processes.

Arthur Smith, Ph.D., Texas at Austin, 1995. Experimental condensed-matter and surface physics.

Victoria Soghomonian, Ph.D., Syracuse, 1995. Experimental chemical physics.

David F. J. Tees, Ph.D., McGill, 1996. Experimental biophysics, nanoscience.

THEORETICAL RESEARCH ACTIVITIES

Astrophysics. Galactic structure, stellar dynamics, and galaxy formation, with emphasis on elliptical galaxies, numerical-studies of disk galaxies, ionization structure of and emission from HII regions, modeling of broad-line emission from active galactic nuclei.

Condensed Matter and Statistical Physics. Collective electronic excitations, semiconductor superlattices, quantum Hall effect, electronic ballistic transport, phase transitions and critical phenomena, resonance and relaxation in magnetic systems, optical properties, transport theory, electronic states in novel semiconductor nanostructures and heterojunctions, ab initio density functional studies of amorphous and glassy systems, semiclassical and ab initio modeling of growth, and development of efficient algorithms for electronic structure calculations, novel methods for exploring configuration space for complex systems.

Mathematical and Computational Physics. Analytical studies and numerical simulations of nonlinear classical and quantum systems and studies of deterministic chaos; quantum simulations, ab initio calculations, and visualization of many-body and few-body systems in condensed-matter and nuclear physics; numerical methods and algorithmic development for high-performance vector and parallel computers; software development for application of computers in classroom teaching; analytical and algorithmic studies in differential and integral equations, probability theory, and series expansions.

Nuclear and Intermediate Energy Physics. Major areas of concentration include investigation of the atomic nucleus by both electromagnetic and strong interaction probes; the description of the strong force and nuclear structure in terms of effective hadronic field theories; baryonic, mesonic, and electromagnetic interactions in the constituent quark model. For the study of strongly interacting systems the emphasis is placed on investigating reactions with nuclei up to A=4, in which exact calculations can be carried out based on the Faddeev-Yakubovsky equations. Specific topics include relativistic electron theory, elastic and inelastic electron and nucleon scattering from nuclei, virtual photon spectra, few-nucleon systems, meson production in two nucleon collisions at intermediate energies, pion and kaon photoproduction and electroproduction from nucleons and nuclei, quasielastic nucleon knockout, relativistic effects in nuclear physics, Coulomb distortion effects, and associated mathematical problems.

EXPERIMENTAL RESEARCH ACTIVITIES

Acoustics. Precision measurements of the properties of thermoacoustic "stack" elements. Novel techniques are used to characterize the properties of stacks of unusual geometry. Nonlinear effects as well as the effect of gas mixtures are explored. The results are applied to the development of lumped element themoacoustic primemovers and refrigerators.

Astrophysics. Spectroscopic observations of stellar motions and stellar populations in elliptical galaxies and evidence for dark matter, ionized gas in galaxies, X-ray studies of galaxy clusters, nuclear physics applied to astrophysics.

Biological Physics. Stochastic modeling of neuronal dynamics in the context of stochastic resonance; modeling of glial processes and cortical calcium waves. In collaboration with Cog-netix/Viatech and the Children's Medical Center in Cincinnati, statistical properties of calcium waves in healthy brain are compared with those of tissue from epileptic foci and glioma. Experimental determination of the response of single cell adhesion molecules to applied forces.

Condensed Matter and Surface Science. Current projects include the fabrication of crystalline and amorphous wide bandgap semiconductor alloys and their characterization via novel electron microscopes and MeV ion-beam techniques; molecular beam epitaxial growth of novel electronic materials, including wide band gap and transition metal nitrides; ultrahigh vacuum scanning tunneling microscopy investigations of semiconductor surfaces; synthesis of nanophase materials from simple precursors and their characterization via X-ray diffraction and nuclear magnetic resonance techniques; experimental transport studies of low-dimensional, nanoscopic, and mesoscopic structures and devices in high-magnetic fields and at lower temperatures; transport phenomena in high-mobility III-V semiconductor heterostructures; and narrow-gap semiconductors (InSb, InAs) for magnetic sensor devices. There are also several projects on hyperthermal beam growth, chemical vapor deposition of thin films, their characterization and fabrication of devices based on wide bandgap semiconductors such as GaN and AlN.

Geophysics. Current studies concern interfacial melting of ice at grain boundaries. Optical techniques are employed to measure the thickness of the melted layer as a function of temperature, mismatch between adjacent grains, and impurity concentration.

Nonlinear Dynamics and Chaos. Nonlinear systems exhibiting deterministic chaos are studied using both experimental and computational methods. Present studies include methods of controlling chaos and techniques of nonlinear analysis of time-series data including the estimation of Lyapunov exponents, noise reduction, forecasting, and control. Some of these techniques are applied to experiments on nonlinear electrical circuits and metal passivation in an electrochemical cell operating in a highly nonlinear regime where spontaneous oscillations and chaos are observed. Numerical and experimental studies include the development of adaptive learning techniques applied to the control of chaotic systems and investigations of spatiotemporal waves in convectively unstable open-flow systems.

Nuclear and Intermediate Energy Physics. Contemporary research in nuclear physics necessarily involves heavy use of specialized accelerator facilities around the world, and collaborations with scientists from many other institutions. Ohio University nuclear physicists play central roles in the study of fundamental symmetries in nuclear reactions (tests of charge symmetry breaking at TRIUMF in Canada), the two- and three-nucleon interaction (np and nd measurements at Los Alamos), weak interactions and spin degrees of freedom (via the charge-exchange reaction at Indiana University Cyclotron Facility), exotic nuclei-far from the line of beta stability (at GANIL and Hahn-Meitner Institute in Europe), and pion photoproduction (at the Laser-Electron Gamma Source (LEGS) at Brookhaven National Laboratory). At higher energy, interests include electronuclear phenomena tests of QCD sum rules (at LEGS) and electroproduction of strange mesons (at the new Thomas Jefferson National Accelerator Facility in Virginia). The high-intensity pulsed beam capability of the Ohio University Tandem Van de Graaff accelerator, with its unique beam swinger magnet and long flight path, is used for high-precision measurements of various nuclear cross-sections and projects in medical physics, materials science, nuclear astrophysics, instrument development, and other projects in applied nuclear physics. The entire research program is supported by the Ohio University Institute for Nuclear and Particle Physics.

Ohio University

SELECTED PUBLICATIONS

Böttcher M., et al. Coordinated multiwavelength observations of BL Lacertae in 2000. *Astrophys. J.* 596:847, 2003.

Böttcher M., R. Mukherjee, and A. Reimer. Predictions of the high-energy emission from BL Lac objects: The case of W Comae. *Astrophys. J.* 581:143, 2002.

Brune, C. R., et al. Proton-deuteron elasctic scattering at low energies. *Phys. Rev. C* 63:044013–21, 2001.

Brune, C. R., W. H. Geist, R. W. Kavanagh, and K. D. Veal. Sub-coulomb alpha transfers on ^{12}C and the $^{12}C(\alpha,\gamma)^{16}O$ S factor. *Phys. Rev. Lett.* 83:4025–8, 1999.

DeVita, R. et al. **(D. S. Carman, K. Hicks, A. Opper,** and **M. Lucas)** (CLAS Collaboration). First measurement of the double spin asymmetry in ep→é pit η in the resonance region. *Phys. Rev. Lett.* 88:082001, 2002.

Joo, K., et al. (**D. S. Carman, K. Hicks, A. Opper,** and **M. Lucas)** (CLAS Collaboration). Q-squared dependence of quadrupole strength in the gamma + p→p+piϕ transition. *Phys. Rev. Lett.* 88:12001, 2002.

Castillo, H. E., C. Chamon, L. F. Cugliandolo, and M. P. Kennett. Heterogeneous aging in spin glasses. *Phys. Rev. Lett.* 88(23): 237201, 2002.

Goldbart P. M., **H. E. Castillo,** and A. Zippelius. Randomly crosslinked macromolecular systems: Vulcanization transition to and properties of the amorphous solid state. *Adv. Phys.* 45(5):393–468, 1996.

Dong, J., and **D. A. Drabold.** Atomistic structure of band tail states in amorphous silicon. *Phys. Rev. Lett.* 80:1928, 1998.

Taraskin, S. N., **D. A. Drabold,** and S. R. Elliott. Spatial decay of the single-particle density matrix in insulators: analytic results in two and three dimensions. *Phys. Rev. Lett.* 88:196405, 2002.

Fachruddin, I., **C. Elster,** and W. Glöckle. The Nd break-up process in leading order in a three-dimensional approach. *Phys. Rev. C* 68:054003, 2003.

Liu, H., **C. Elster,** and W. Glöckle. Model study of three-body forces in the three-body bound state. *Few-Body Syst.* 33:241, 2003.

Govorov A. O., and **J. J. Heremans.** Hydrodynamic effects in interacting Fermi electron jets. *Phys. Rev. Lett.* 92:26803, 2004.

Govorov, A. O., et al. Self-induced acoustic transparency in semiconductor quantum films. *Phys. Rev. Lett.* 87:226803, 2001.

Rotter, M., et al. **(A. O. Govorov).** Charge conveyance and nonlinear acoustoelectric phenomena for intense surface acoustic waves on a semiconductor quantum well. *Phys. Rev. Lett.* 82:2171–4, 1999.

Howard, W. B., **S. M. Grimes,** et al. **(C. E. Brient).** Measurement of the thick target $^{9}Be(p,n)$ neutron energy spectra. *Nucl. Sci. Eng.* 138:145, 2001.

Al-Quraishi, S. I., **S. M. Grimes,** T. N. Massey, and D. A. Resler. Are the level densities for r- and rp- process nuclei different from nearby nuclei in the valley of stability? *Phys. Rev. C* 63:065803, 2001.

Chen, H., and **J. J. Heremans** et al. Ballistic transport in InSb/InAlSb antidot lattices. *Appl. Phys. Lett.,* 2004.

Hartzell B., et al. **(J. J. Heremans** and **V. Soghomonian).** Current-voltage characteristics of diversely disulfide terminated lambda-deoxyribonucleic acid molecules. *J. Appl. Phys.* 94(4):2764–6, 2003.

Hartzell B., et al. **(J. J. Heremans** and **V. Soghomonian).** Comparative current-voltage characteristics of nicked and repaired lambda-DNA. *Appl. Phys. Lett.* 82(26):4800–2, 2003.

DeMeyer, G., et al. **(K. H. Hicks).** Alpha-cluster correlations in the 16O(e,e'alpha)12C reaction. *Phys. Lett. B* 513:258–64, 2001.

Hicks, K. H., M. Mestayer, and G. Niculescu. Hyperon production experiments from CLAS. *Proc. 11th International Conference on Hyperons in Nuclei,* pp. 32–43, Hampton University Press, 2001.

Hla, S.-W., and K.-H. Rieder, STM control of chemical reactions: Single molecule synthesis. *Ann. Rev. Phys. Chem.* 54:307–30, 2003.

Hla, S.-W., K.-F. Braun, and K.-H. Rieder. Single-atom manipulation mechanisms during a quantum corral construction. *Phys. Rev. B* 67:201402(R), 2003.

Kang, Y., and **D. C. Ingram.** Properties of amorphous GaNx prepared by ion beam assisted deposition at room temperature. *J. Appl. Phys.* 93:3954, 2003.

Haider, M. B., et al. **(D. C. Ingram** and **A. R. Smith).** Ga/N flux ratio influence on Mn incorporation, surface morphology, and lattice polarity during radio frequency molecular beam epitaxy of (Ga,Mn)N. *J. Appl. Phys.* 93:5274, 2003.

Shuai, J. W., and **P. Jung.** Optimal ion channel clustering for intracellular calcium signaling. *PNAS* 100:506–10, 2003.

Nadkarni, S., and **P. Jung.** Spontaneous oscillations of dressed neurons: A new mechanism for epilepsy? *Phys. Rev. Lett.* 91(26):268101, 2003.

Perjeru, F., X. Bai, and **M. E. Kordesch.** Electronic characterization of n-ScN/p(+) Si heterojunctions. *Appl. Phys. Lett.* 80:995–7, 2002.

Perjeru, F., R. L. Woodin, and **M. E. Kordesch.** Influence of annealing temperature upon deep levels in 6H SiC. *Physica B* 308:695–7, 2001.

Blanpied, G., et al. **(M. Lucas).** The N → Δ transition from simultaneous measurements of $p(\gamma,\pi^{+})$ and $p(\gamma,\gamma)$. *Phys. Rev. Lett.* 79:4337, 1997.

Feldman, G., et al. **(M. Lucas).** Compton scattering, meson-exchange, and the polarizabilities of bound nucleons. *Phys. Rev. C: Nucl. Phys.* 54:2124, 1996.

McNamara, B. R., et al. Chandra X-ray observations of the Hydra A Cluster: An interaction between the radio source and the X ray–emitting gas. *Astrophys. J.,* 534(L):135, 2000.

Harris, D. E., et al. **(B. R. McNamara).** Chandra X ray detection of the radio hot spots of 3C 295. *Astrophys. J.* 530(L):81, 2000.

Moore, M. G., and P. Meystre. Atomic four-wave mixing: Fermioins versus bosons. *Phys. Rev. Lett.* 86:4199, 2001.

Moore, M. G., and P. Meystre. Theory of superradiant scattering of laser light from Bose-Einstein condensates. *Phys. Rev. Lett.* 83:5202, 1999.

Neiman, A., and D. F. Russell. Stochastic biperiodic oscillations in the electroreceptors of paddlefish. *Phys. Rev. Lett.* 86(15):3443–6, 2001.

Neiman A., et al. Synchronization of the noisy electrosensitive cells in the paddlefish. *Phys. Rev. Lett.* 82(3):660–3, 1999.

Opper, A. K., et al. Measurements of the spin observables D_{NN}, P and A_y in inelastic proton scattering from ^{12}C at 200 MeV. *Phys. Rev. C* 63:034614, 2001.

Opper, A. K., et al. Charge symmetry breaking in the reaction np → $d\pi^{0}$. *Nucl. Phys.* A663:505–8, 2000.

Pascalutsa, V., an **D. R. Phillips.** Effective theory of the delta(1232) in Compton scattering off the nucleon. *Phys. Rev. C* 67:055202, 2003.

Phillips, D. R. Building light nuclei from neutrons, protons, and pions, 14th Summer School on Understanding the Structure of Hadrons (HADRONS 01), Prague, Czech Republic, 9–13 July 2001. *Czech. J. Phys.* 52:B49, 2002.

Ohio University

Selected Publications (continued)

Rhode, M. A., **R. W. Rollins,** and H. D. Dewald. On a simple recursive control algorithm automated and applied to an electrochemical experiment. *Chaos* 7:653–63, 1997.

Rhode, M. A., et al. **(R. W. Rollins).** Automated adaptive recursive control of unstable orbits in high-dimensional chaotic systems. *Phys. Rev. E* 54:4880–7, 1996.

Constantin, A., et al. **(J. C. Shields).** Emission-line properties of z^4 quasars. *Astrophys. J.* 565:50, 2002.

Shields, J. C., et al. Evidence for a black hole and accretion disk in the LINER NGC 4203. *Astrophys. J.,* 534(L):27, 2000.

Yang, H., **A. R. Smith,** M. Prikhodko, and W. R. L. Lambrecht. Atomic-scale spin-polarized scanning tunneling microscopy applied to Mn3N2 (010). *Phys. Rev. Lett.* 89:226101, 2002.

Smith, A. R., et al. Reconstructions of the GaN(000-1) surface. *Phys. Rev. Lett.* 79:3934, 1997.

Statler, T. S., E. Emsellem, R. F. Peletier, and R. Bacon. Long-lived triaxiality in the dynamically old elliptical galaxy NGC 4365: Limits on chaos and black hole mass. *Mon. Not. R. Astron. Soc.,* in press.

Salow, R. M., and **T. S. Statler.** Self-gravitating eccentric disk models for the double nucleus of M31. *Astrophys. J.,* in press.

Tees, D. F. J., J. T. Woodward, and D. A. Hammer. Reliability theory for recepton-ligand bond dissociation. *J. Chem. Phys.* 114:7483–96, 2001.

Tees, D. F. J., R. E. Waugh, and D. A. Hammer. A microcantilever device to assess the effect of force on the lifetime of selectin-carbohydrate bonds. *Biophys. J.* 80:668–82, 2001.

Destefani, C. F., **S. E. Ulloa,** and G. E. Marques. Spin-orbit coupling and intrinsic spin mixing in quantum dots. *Phys. Rev. B* 69:125302, 2004.

Weichselbaum, A., and **S. E. Ulloa.** Potential landscapes and induced charges near metallic islands in three dimensions. *Phys. Rev. E* 68:056707, 2003.

Petculescu, G., and **L. A. Wilen.** Thermoacoustics in a single pore with an applied temperature gradient. *J. Acoust. Soc. Am.* 106:688, 1999.

Wilen, L. A., and J. G. Dash. Frost heave dynamics at a single crystal interface. *Phys. Rev. Lett.* 74:5076, 1995.

Caia, G. L., V. Pascalutsa, and **L. E. Wright.** Solving potential scattering equations without partial wave decomposition. *Phys. Rev. C* 69:034003, 2004.

Kim, K. S., and **L. E. Wright.** Constraints on medium modifications of nucleon form factors from quasielastic scattering. *Phys. Rev. C* 68:027601, 2003.

OKLAHOMA STATE UNIVERSITY

Photonics M.S. and Ph.D. Programs

Programs of Study

The Departments of Physics, Electrical and Computer Engineering, and Chemistry at Oklahoma State University (OSU) offer multidisciplinary programs leading to the M.S. and Ph.D. degrees in photonics. A specialization in biophotonics is also available for each of these programs.

The M.S. degree in photonics requires 24 semester credit hours of courses selected by the student and his or her adviser, along with 6 credit hours of research. The course work is flexible but typically focuses on optics, optical material science, electromagnetism, quantum mechanics, solid-state physics, and devices. Students choosing a specialization in biophotonics may substitute courses in biology and/or veterinary medicine. The majority of courses are taken in the "home department" of the student's chosen research adviser. A nonthesis M.S. option requires a total of 32 semester credit hours, including a 2-semester-credit-hour report. The M.S. thesis and report must be defended before the student's advisory committee.

The Ph.D. in photonics requires 60 semester credit hours beyond the M.S. degree (90 beyond the B.S. degree). Upon entering the photonics Ph.D. program, a student forms a Preliminary Advisory Committee (PAC) to guide him or her through the initial stage of the program, which includes a laboratory course in advanced optics and one course from each of the three departments. During these first two years, the PAC also administers a preliminary exam, the successful completion of which allows the student to form a Research Advisory Committee to guide him or her through the candidacy stage of the program. During this period, in addition to carrying out a research program, the student must complete at least six additional courses, with at least one course selected from each of the three departments. Courses in biology and/or veterinary medicine may be substituted for the biophotonics option. A menu of the courses may be found by accessing the OSU Photonics Web site. The photonics program is completed by the candidate's defense of a dissertation before the Research Advisory Committee.

Research Facilities

Faculty research interests range from developing fiber-optics materials and the use of terahertz radiation in telecommunication technologies and molecular sensing, to MOCVD tailoring of electrical and optical properties of semiconducting lasers and devices, to using lasers to study protein dynamics in photoreceptors. Detailed research descriptions of the faculty may be found by visiting the OSU Photonics Web site. Many of the faculty members in the photonics program have strong ties to the Center for Sensors and Sensor Technologies, located on the Oklahoma State University campus in Stillwater. The Physics Department has a number of research groups investigating carbon nanotubes, gold nonowires, and molecular sensors. The research laboratories of the photonics faculty are located in the new Advanced Research and Technology Center, the Noble Research Center, and the newly renovated Physical Sciences Building. Research facilities include general and specialized laser systems; a crystal growth laboratory; an MBE growth and characterization laboratory; a Class 100 clean room for semiconductor device preparation, including two MOCVD chambers and optical, X-ray, and electronic characterization facilities; femtosecond spectroscopy systems, including photon correlation and multiple photon excitation systems, streak camera, boxcar integrators, Brillouin and Raman scattering laboratories, and standard cryogenic equipment.

Financial Aid

The photonics program supports up to 15 NSF-IGERT Fellows (U.S. citizens and permanent residents only). The current annual IGERT stipend is $27,500 (approximately $2300 per month). In addition, all tuition is covered by the fellowship, and an educational expenses allowance may be used for books and supplies as well as travel to professional meetings. If the applicant is offered an IGERT Fellowship, he or she is invited to OSU to look over the program with all expenses paid by the IGERT. The University pays the health insurance premiums for the fellows. IGERT Fellows may have their stipend supplemented by also accepting a research assistantship (RA). More information regarding the NSF-IGERT Fellowships can be obtained at the program's Web site (http://ee.okstate.edu/IGERT); by contacting Dmitry Migunov, OSU NSF-IGERT Administrator (telephone: 405-744-9244 or e-mail: migunov@okstate.edu); or by contacting Dr. Paul Westhaus (information listed below). Incoming photonics students may apply for a teaching assistantship (TA) in their home department. Generally, each department sets aside two or three TAs for photonics students each year. The teaching assistantships provide monthly stipends, which vary among departments (averaging $1300) and also include the waiver of nonresident tuition. U.S. citizens and permanent residents usually have all or part of their remaining resident tuition waived as well. The University pays health insurance policy premiums for all TAs and RAs. The initial nine-month TA appointment (August 16 through May 15) is usually extended to eleven months with the addition of summer assistantships. Photonics students typically choose a research adviser during their second semester, and many are then offered a research assistantship. Thus, all photonics graduate students are supported by half-time (20 hours per week) assistantships as TAs or RAs for eleven or twelve months of each calendar year.

Cost of Study

For fall 2004, the resident tuition in the Graduate Division was $130 per credit hour. Nonresident tuition was $445 per credit hour. Additional semester fees amounted to $50.

Living and Housing Costs

Living costs in Stillwater are relatively modest. Newly constructed two- and four-bedroom on-campus apartments and off-campus housing is plentiful. More details are available at http://www.reslife.okstate.edu/housing03.htm.

Student Group

The photonics graduate students have a home department in physics, electrical engineering, or chemistry. Each of these departments also maintains vibrant graduate and undergraduate programs in their respective disciplines.

Location

Oklahoma State University at Stillwater is located in a medium-size college town of 35,000 residents and about 22,000 students. There are a number of high-tech electronic/photonics entrepreneurial companies in Stillwater. The town has many parks and lakes that are easily accessible. Stillwater is within an hour's drive of the larger-city attractions of Tulsa and Oklahoma City.

The University

Oklahoma State University was founded in 1890 as a land-grant institution, Oklahoma A&M College. Continuing its land-grant mission as it became Oklahoma State University in 1957, it is one of the Big XII comprehensive universities with 22,000 students, of whom 6,000 are graduate students. The University offers myriad cultural and entertainment attractions, including an excellent music school and theater department. The University's teams compete in Bix XII Conference sports.

Applying

All application materials may be obtained from Dr. Paul Westhaus, Graduate Coordinator (Physics/Photonics) and returned to him by way of the Department of Physics. Priority applications should be received by February 15. If a student is offered a teaching assistantship, the student's credentials are forwarded to the Graduate College. Applications should include a statement of purpose for pursing the degree in photonics, transcripts of all previous academic work (unofficial transcripts suffice for the application process), and three letters of reference. The GRE is not required, but all relevant scores to support the application are useful. International students must provide evidence of a TOEFL score of at least 600.

Correspondence and Information

Dr. Paul Westhaus
Graduate Selection Committee
Department of Physics
Oklahoma State University
Stillwater, Oklahoma 74078

Telephone: 405-744-5796
Fax: 405-744-6811
E-mail: physpaw@okstate.edu
World Wide Web: http://www.ee.okstate.edu/photonics

Oklahoma State University

THE FACULTY AND THEIR RESEARCH

Chemistry

Allen Apblett, Associate Professor; Ph.D. Calgary, 1989. Industrial, materials, and environmental chemistry; catalysis; metallo-organic chemistry applied to development of new chemical processes, protective coatings, advanced materials, and refining of metals.

Nicholas F. Materer, Associate Professor; Ph.D., California, Berkeley, 1996. Interfacial chemistry and physics relevant to semiconductor devices, micro-mechanical machines, catalysis and sensors.

Electrical and Computer Engineering

Alan Cheville, Associate Professor; Ph.D., Rice, 1994. Terahertz radiation phenomena; application of free-space terahertz radiation to time-resolved gas analyses, combustion technologies, and impulse ranging. (e-mail: kridnix@okstate.edu)

Daniel Grischkowsky, Bellmon Professor of Optoelectronics; Ph.D., Columbia, 1968. Ultrafast optoelectronics, THz photonics. (e-mail: grischd@okstate.edu)

Jerzy Krasinski, Professor; Ph.D., Warsaw, 1973. Laser spectroscopy and applications, nonlinear optics. (e-mail: krasins@okstate.edu)

Weili Zhang, Associate Professor; Ph.D., Tianjin (China), 1993. Ultrafast lasers and phenomena, THz optoelectronics, semiconductor physics, time-resolved spectroscopy.

Physics

Bruce Ackerson, Regents Professor; Ph.D., Colorado, 1976. Light scattering, colloid, and particle suspension phenomena. (e-mail: bjack@okstate.edu)

Girish Agarwal, Professor and Nobel Chair; Ph.D., Rochester, 1969. Optical and laser physics, nonequilibrium statistical mechanics.

Donna K. Bandy, Professor; Ph.D., Drexel, 1984. Theoretical laser physics, nonlinear behavior, chaos, optical bistabilities. (e-mail: bandy@okstate.edu)

Thomas C. Collins, Professor; Ph.D., Florida, 1967. Electronic and phonon structure, high Tc superconductivity in ceramic materials. (e-mail: collins@okstate.edu)

Bret Flanders, Assistant Professor; Ph.D., Chicago, 1999. Lung surfactants, electrical and optical properties of nanomaterials (e-mail: flandeb@okstate.edu)

H. James Harmon, Professor; Ph.D., Purdue, 1974. Biophysics, spectroscopic studies of kinetics, chemical and biological sensors, photocatalytic destruction of chemical and energetic agents. (e-mail: jharmon@okstate.edu)

Robert J. Hauenstein, Associate Professor; Ph.D., Caltech, 1987. Semiconductor physics, epitaxial growth and characterization, heterostructural materials and devices. (e-mail: rjh@okstate.edu)

Stephen S. W. S. McKeever, Regents Professor; Ph.D., North Wales, 1975. Experimental solid state, optically stimulated luminescence, radiation dosimetry, semiconductors. (e-mail: u1759aa@okstate.edu)

John Mintmire, Professor and Head; Ph.D, Florida, 1980. Density functions theory, nanoscale materials. (e-mail: mintmir@okstate.edu)

Albert T. Rosenberger, Associate Professor; Ph.D., Illinois, 1979. Experimental and theoretical quantum and nonlinear optics, coherent resonant effects, instabilities and nonlinear dynamics. (e-mail: atr@okstate.edu)

Gil Summy, Assistant Professor; Ph.D., Griffith (Australia), 1995. Bose Einstein Condensation (BEC). (e-mail: summy@okstate.edu)

Penger Tong, Professor; Ph.D., Pittsburgh, 1988. Experimental soft-matter physics, nonlinear or nonequilibrium dynamics, turbulence. (e-mail: ptong@okstate.edu)

Paul A. Westhaus, Professor; Ph.D. Washington (St. Louis), 1966. Intermolecular forces, density functional theory. (e-mail: physpaw@okstate.edu)

James P. Wicksted, Professor; Ph.D., CUNY, 1983. Experimental solid-state physics, nonlinear optical studies, Brillouin and Raman scattering, rare-earth doped glasses, carbon nanotubes, semiconductors, biophysics. (e-mail: jpw519@okstate.edu)

Timothy Wilson, Professor; Ph.D., Florida, 1966. Theoretical solid state, electronic structure of point defects. (e-mail: tpraf@okstate.edu)

Aihua Xie, Associate Professor; Ph.D., Carnegie Mellon, 1987. Biological physics of proteins: biological signal transduction, energy flow in proteins, studies of structural, dynamic, and energetic basis for the functional mechanisms of proteins. (e-mail: xaihua@okstate.edu)

Xincheng Xie, Professor; Ph.D., Maryland, 1988. Theoretical solid state, fractional quantum Hall effect, superconductivity, transport properties of semiconductors. (e-mail: xie@solid.phy.okstate.edu)

Eduardo Yukihara, Assistant Professor; Ph.D., San Paulo (Brazil), 2001. Radiation dosimetry, photo- and thermo-luminescence.

THE PENNSYLVANIA STATE UNIVERSITY

Department of Physics

Programs of Study

The department is committed to offering an outstanding graduate education in a broad range of fields in experimental and theoretical physics, including condensed-matter physics, elementary particle physics, materials physics, atomic and molecular physics, optics, particle astrophysics, and gravitational physics. The department has 48 faculty members and 100 graduate students. Nearly all of the faculty members have externally funded research, and one third of the faculty was hired in the last five years. The department is thus very dynamic in research. There are a weekly colloquium series and several series of special lectures from distinguished physicists, in addition to approximately three to five specialized weekly physics seminars.

The graduate program is aimed primarily at the attainment of a Ph.D. degree in physics. An M.S. program is also offered. Upon arrival, each graduate student is appointed a mentoring committee to provide personalized guidance during graduate school. The first year of study covers basic courses in graduate physics. Arriving students with advanced backgrounds can obtain course exemptions, thus effectively becoming second-year students. During the second year, after passing the candidacy exam, students take advanced courses in their area of specialization, form a thesis committee, and choose a research adviser. Completion of all the Ph.D. requirements is typically accomplished in a total of five years. The M.S. degree is typically conferred after one year of research beyond the first-year graduate course work through the submission of a thesis.

Research Facilities

The department occupies two buildings on campus. Extensive state-of-the-art equipment is available for research, including thin-film preparation by sputtering and molecular-beam epitaxy; photoelectron spectrometers; numerous pulsed and continuous lasers; a variety of cryostats operating between 77K and 5mK; atomic-scale microscopes, including scanning tunneling microscopes (STM), field ion microscopes (FIM), and a field emission microscope (FEM); a low-energy electron diffraction apparatus (LEED); and in situ ultrahigh-vacuum ellipsometry. Condensed-matter experiments are also conducted at national facilities such as Argonne National Laboratory (outside Chicago), the National Institute for Science and Technology (NIST) in Maryland, and Brookhaven National Laboratory on Long Island. Experimental high-energy physics research is carried out at various laboratories, including Brookhaven and DESY (Hamburg, Germany). A convenient, excellent Physical Sciences Library is available in the same building as the physics department. A complete mathematics library is across the street from the physics department. The department has several networked UNIX workstations and various other computer facilities, including Beowulf Linux clusters, immersive virtual reality scientific visualization systems, and specially designed rooms for computer-based physics instruction. An SP2 parallel supercomputer is available at the University.

Financial Aid

The department offers incoming students teaching assistantships with full coverage of tuition. The nine-month stipend for the assistantships was approximately $13,900 in 2003–04. Additional summer support of $2000 to $3000 is usually available. Graduate assistants average a total income of $16,905 for twelve months from the assistantship stipend, summer wages, and possible departmental awards. Students from their second year on are commonly supported by the research grants of their advisers through research assistantships. The graduate school and the Eberly College of Science provide a few research fellowships and several supplemental fellowships for qualified students.

Cost of Study

Tuition in 2003–04 was $417 per credit for Pennsylvania residents and $826 per credit for nonresidents, with a mandatory $160 information technology fee and a $45 activity fee. For 2003, tuition for a normal two-semester load was $19,830 (nonresidents).

Living and Housing Costs

There is limited graduate student housing on campus. Rentals in State College for a one-bedroom apartment range from $530 to $650 per month. Health-care coverage is offered at a rate of $200 per year to graduate assistants.

Student Group

The department typically hosts about 100 graduate students with a variety of ethnic backgrounds and nationalities. The vast majority of students are on teaching or research assistantships. About 50 percent of the students are from the United States.

Location

The University Park campus of Penn State is home to approximately 41,800 students, including approximately 35,000 undergraduates, 6,800 graduate students, and more than 2,900 faculty members. It is located in the municipality of State College, nestled amid the picturesque valleys and wooded mountains of central Pennsylvania. State College has an airport with twenty-three flights a day. The town is within 3½ hours' driving distance of Pittsburgh, Philadelphia, and Washington, D.C. New York City is 4½ hours away. In 1988, *Psychology Today* chose State College as the least stressful place to live in the United States.

The University

Penn State, founded in 1855, is Pennsylvania's land-grant university and has twenty-four campuses throughout the state. Penn State has more than 565,600 living alumni. One in every 122 Americans and one in every 8 Pennsylvanians are graduates of Penn State. The University hosts a legendary football team, and its home turf, Beaver Stadium (capacity 106,537), is the second-largest university stadium in the United States.

Applying

The formal deadline for applications for the fall is April 15, but applications are reviewed beginning in late January until all assistantships are offered. GRE (especially Subject Test in physics) scores are strongly preferred. The TOEFL score is mandatory for students from non-English-speaking countries. Applications sent directly to the physics department do not initially require an application fee.

Correspondence and Information

Chair, Graduate Admissions
104 Davey Laboratory
The Pennsylvania State University
University Park, Pennsylvania 16802

Telephone: 814-863-0118
800-876-5348 (toll-free within the United States)
Fax: 814-865-0978
E-mail: graduate-admissions@phys.psu.edu
World Wide Web: http://www.phys.psu.edu

The Pennsylvania State University

THE FACULTY AND THEIR RESEARCH

R. Albert, Assistant Professor; Ph.D., Notre Dame, 2001. Statistical mechanics, network theory, systems biology.
J. Anderson, Professor; Ph.D., Princeton, 1963. Quantum chemistry by Monte Carlo methods.
A. Ashtekar, Eberly Professor and Director of Center for Gravitational Physics and Geometry; Ph.D., Chicago, 1974. General relativity, quantum gravity and quantum field theory.
J. R. Banavar, Distinguished Professor and Department Head; Ph.D., Pittsburgh, 1978. Condensed-matter theory.
B. Brügmann, Associate Professor; Ph.D., Syracuse, 1993. Gravitational physics.
A. W. Castleman Jr., Evan Pugh Professor of Chemistry and Physics; Ph.D., Polytechnic, 1969. Atomic, molecular, and optical physics; condensed-matter physics.
M. H. W. Chan, Evan Pugh Professor and Director of Center for Collective Phenomena in Restricted Geometries; Ph.D., Cornell, 1974. Low-temperature physics.
M. W. Cole, Distinguished Professor; Ph.D., Chicago, 1970. Chemical physics and condensed-matter theory.
J. Collins, Professor; Ph.D., Cambridge, 1974. Perturbative quantum chromodynamics.
S. Coutu, Associate Professor; Ph.D., Caltech, 1993. High-energy cosmic-ray positrons and antiprotons as a possible signal for annihilating dark matter particles; the highest-energy cosmic rays.
D. Cowen, Associate Professor; Ph.D., Wisconsin–Madison, 1990. Astrophysics, particles and fields.
V. H. Crespi, Professor; Ph.D., Berkeley, 1994. Theory of superconducting, transport, electronic, and structural/mechanical properties of novel materials.
R. D. Diehl, Professor; Ph.D., Washington (Seattle), 1982. Surface structure and phase transitions.
P. Eklund, Professor; Ph.D., Purdue, 1974. Fundamental properties and applications of new materials, spectroscopy and thermal/electrical transport.
K. A. Fichthorn, Professor; Ph.D., Michigan, 1989. Condensed-matter simulation and theory.
L. S. Finn, Professor and Director of Center for Gravitational Wave Physics; Ph.D., Caltech, 1987. Detection of gravitational waves, gravitational wave astronomy, relativistic astrophysics, numerical relativity.
N. Freed, Professor and Associate Dean of Eberly College of Science; Ph.D., Case Western Reserve, 1964.
K. E. Gibble, Associate Professor; Ph.D., Colorado at Boulder, 1990. Atomic, molecular, and optical physics.
M. Gunaydin, Professor; Ph.D., Yale, 1973. Superstrings and supergravity.
S. F. Heppelmann, Professor; Ph.D., Minnesota, 1981. Experimental high-energy physics.
J. Jain, Erwin W. Mueller Professor of Physics; Ph.D., SUNY at Stony Brook, 1984. Condensed-matter theory and the composite Fermion description of the fractional quantum Hall effect.
D. Jin, Assistant Professor; Ph.D., California, San Diego, 1999. Theory of biological neural networks and computational models of neurobiological functions.
P. Laguna, Professor; Ph.D., Texas at Austin, 1987. Numerical relativity, astronomy.
D. Larson, Professor and Verne M. Williaman Dean of Eberly College of Science; Ph.D., Harvard, 1971. Atomic, molecular, and optical physics.
Q. Li, Professor; Ph.D., Peking, 1989. Superconducting and magnetic thin films and artificial structures.
Y. Liu, Associate Professor; Ph.D., Minnesota, 1991. Superconductivity and related phenomena in disordered mesoscopic systems and perovskite compounds.
G. D. Mahan, Distinguished Professor; Ph.D., Berkeley, 1964. Theoretical condensed-matter physics: many-body theory, transport, semiconductor devices.
J. D. Maynard, Distinguished Professor; Ph.D., Princeton, 1974. Quantum and acoustic wave phenomena.
P. Mészáros, Distinguished Professor of Astronomy and Astrophysics and Physics; Ph.D., Berkeley, 1972. Astrophysics, gravitational physics.
A. Mizel, Assistant Professor; Ph.D., Berkeley, 1999. Condensed-matter theory.
K. O'Hara, Assistant Professor and Downsbrough Professor; Ph.D., Duke, 2000. Experimental atomic, molecular, and optical physics; condensed-matter physics.
B. Owen, Assistant Professor; Ph.D., Caltech, 1998. Astrophysics, gravitational physics.
R. Penrose, Pentz Professor; Ph.D., Cambridge, 1957. General relativity.
A. Perez, Assistant Professor; Ph.D., Pittsburgh, 2000. Quantum gravity, spin foam models.
R. W. Robinett, Professor; Ph.D., Minnesota, 1981. Collider physics.
N. Samarth, Professor and Director of Center for Materials Physics; Ph.D., Purdue, 1986. Spin transport and coherence in mesoscopic and nanostructured magnetic systems.
P. E. Schiffer, Professor; Ph.D., Stanford, 1993. Condensed-matter experiments.
D. Shoemaker, Assistant Professor; Ph.D., Texas at Austin, 1999. Numerical relativity and gravitational wave physics.
J. Sofo, Associate Professor and Research Associate and Director of Materials Simulation Center; Ph.D., Instituto Balseiro (Argentina), 1991. Materials simulation.
P. E. Sokol, Professor; Ph.D., Ohio State, 1981. Neutron scattering and phase transitions.
M. Strikman, Professor; Ph.D., St. Petersburg Nuclear Physics Institute, 1978. High-energy probes of hadron and nuclear structure.
D. S. Weiss, Associate Professor, Ph.D., Stanford, 1993. Optical lattices.
P. Weiss, Professor; Ph.D., Berkeley, 1986. Surface chemistry and physics.
J. J. Whitmore, Professor; Ph.D., Illinois, 1970. Experimental high-energy physics.
R. F. Willis, Professor; Ph.D., Cambridge, 1967. Electronic states of atomic layers.
X. Xi, Professor; Ph.D., Peking, 1987. Materials physics of electronic and photonic thin films.
J. Ye, Assistant Professor; Ph.D., Yale, 1993. Theoretical condensed-matter theory, strongly correlated electron systems.

The Pennsylvania State University

SELECTED PUBLICATIONS

Leuchow, A., and **J. B. Anderson.** Monte Carlo methods in electronic structure for large systems. *Annu. Rev. Phys. Chem.* 51:501–26, 2000.

Anderson, J. B. Predicting rare events in molecular dynamics. *Adv. Phys. Chem.* 91:381–431, 1995.

Diedrich, D. L., and **J. B. Anderson.** An accurate Monte Carlo calculation of the barrier height for the reaction of $H+H_2 \rightarrow H_2+H$. *Science* 258:786, 1992.

Ashtekar, A., S. Fairhurst, and J. Willis. *Quantum Gravity, Shadow States and Quantum Mechanics, Classical and Quantum Gravity,* in press.

Ashtekar, A. Quantum geometry and gravity: Recent advances in the Proceedings of the 16th Tri-annual International Conference on General Relativity and Gravitation. *World Sci.,* 2002.

Ashtekar, A., and B. Krishman. Dynamical horizons: Energy, angular momentum, fluxes and balance laws. *Phys. Rev. Lett.* 89:261101, 2002.

Banavar, J. R., O. Gonzolez, J. H. Maddocks, and A. Maritan. Self-interactions of strands and sheets. *J. Stat. Phys.* 110:35–50, 2003.

Banavar, J. R., and A. Maritan. Colloquium: Geometrical approach to protein folding: A tube picture. *Rev. Mod. Phys.* 75:23–4, 2003.

Banavar, J. R., J. Damuth, A. Maritan, and A. Rinaldo. Supply-demand balance and metabolic scaling. *Proc. Natl. Acad. Sci.* 99:10506–9, 2002.

Alcubierre, M., et al. **(B. Brügmann).** 3D grazing collision of two black holes. *Phys. Rev. Lett.* 87:271103, 2001.

Baker, J. and **B. Brügmann** et al. Plunge waveforms from inspiralling binary black holes. *Phys. Rev. Lett.* 87:121103, 2001.

Brügmann, B. Programmieren lernen fur teens mit C. *Addison-Wesley,* 2001.

Kooi, S. E., and **A. W. Castleman Jr.** Delayed ionization in transition metal-carbon clusters: Further evidence for the role of thermionic emission. *J. Chem. Phys.* 108:8864–9, 1998.

Castleman, A. W., Jr., and K. H. Bowen Jr. Clusters: Structure, energetics, and dynamics of intermediate states of matter. *J. Phys. Chem.* 100:12911–44, 1996.

Snyder, E. M., S. A. Buzza, and **A. W. Castleman Jr.** Intense field-matter interactions: Multiple ionization clusters. *Phys. Rev. Lett.* 77:3347–9, 1996.

Csathy, G. A., E. Kim, and **M. H. W. Chan.** Condensation of ^3He and re-entrant superfluidity in submonolayer ^3He - ^4He mixture films on H_2. *Phys. Rev. Lett.* 88:045301, 2002.

Garcia, R., and *M. H. W. Chan.* Critical Casimir effect near the tricritical point. *Phys. Rev. Lett.* 88:086101, 2002.

Csathy, G. A., and **M. H. W. Chan.** Effect of ^3He submonolayer superfuidity. Phys. Rev. Lett. 87:045301, 2001.

Calbi, M. M., and **M. W. Cole.** Dimensional crossover and quantum effects of gases adsorbed on nanotube bundles. *Phys. Rev. B* 66:115413, 2002.

Kostov, M. K., **M. W. Cole,** and **G. D. Mahan.** Variational approach to the Coulomb problem on a cylinder. *Phys. Rev. B* 67:075407, 2002.

Narehood, D. G., et al. **(M. W. Cole** and **P. E. Sokol).** Deep inelastic neutron scattering of H_2 in single walled carbon nanotubes. *Phys. Rev. Lett.* 65:233401, 2002.

Calbi, M. M., et al. **(M. W. Cole).** Condensed phases of gases inside nanotube bundles. *Rev. Mod. Phys.* 73:857–65, 2001.

Ancilotto, F., S. Curtarolo, F. Tiogo, and **M. W. Cole.** Evidence concerning drying behavior and Ne at the Cs surface. *Phys. Rev. Lett.* 87:206103–6, 2001.

Collins, J. C. Leading-twist single-transverse-spin asymmentries: Dresll-Yan and deep-inelastic scattering. *Phys. Lett. B* 536:43–8, 2002.

Collins, J. C. Monte-Carlo event generatirs at NLO. *Phys. Rev. D* 65:094016, 2002.

Ahrens, J., et al. **(D. Cowen).** Search for neutrino-induced cascades with the AMANDA detector. *Phys. Rev. D* 67:012003, 2003.

Ahrens, J., et al. **(D. Cowen).** Limits to the muon flux from WIMP annihilation in the center of the Earth with the AMANDA detector. *Phys. Rev. D* 66:032006, 2002.

Ahren, J., et al. **(D. Cowen).** Observation of high energy atomspheric neutrinos with the anatarctic neuon and neutrino detector array. *Phys. Rev. D* 66:012005, 2002.

Beach, A. S., et al. **(S. Coutu).** Measurement of the cosmic-ray antiproton-to-proton abundance ratio between 4 and 50 GeV. *Phys. Rev. Lett.* 87:271101, 2001.

DuVernios, M. A., et al. **(S. Coutu).** Cosmic-ray electrons and positrons from 1-100 GeV: Measurements with HEAT and their interpretation. *Astophys. J.* 559:296–303, 2001.

Coutu, S., et al. Energy spectra, altitude profiles and charge ratios of atmospheric muons. *Phys. Rev. D* 62:032001, 2000.

Crespi, V. H., and P. Zhang. Theory of B^2) and BeB^2 nanotubes: New semiconductors and metals in one dimension. *Phys. Rev. Lett.* 89, 2002.

Han, J. E., and **V. H. Crespi.** Abrupt topological transitions in the hysteresis curves of ferromagnetic metalattices. *Phys. Rev. Lett.* 89:197203, 2002.

Zhang, P., and **V. H. Crespi** et al. Computational design of direct bandgap semiconductors that lattice match silicon. *Nature* 69:409, 2001.

Mayer, A., N. M. Miskovsky, and **P. H. Cutler.** Photostimulated field emission from semiconducting (10,0) and metallic (5,5) carbon nanotubes. *Phys. Rev. B* 65:195416-1–6, 2002.

Cutler, P. H., N. M. Miskovsky, N. Kumar, and M. S. Chung. New results on microelectric cooling using the inverse Nottingham effect. *Cold Cathode Proceedings of the Electrochemical Society* 2000–28: 98–114, 2001.

Mayer, A., N. Miskovsky, and **P. H. Cutler.** Three-dimensional calculation of field electron energy distribution from open hydrogen-saturated and capped metallic (5,5) carbon nanotubes. *Appl. Phys. Lett.* 79:3338–40, 2001.

McGrath, R., J. Ledieu, E. J. Cox, and **R. D. Diehl.** Quasicrystal surfaces: Structure and potential as templates. *J. Phys.: Condens. Matter* 14:R119, 2002.

Caragiu, M., T. Seyller, and **R. D. Diehl.** Dynamical LEED study and Pd(111)-($\sqrt{3}$ x $\sqrt{3}$)R30°-Xe. *Phys. Rev. B* 66:195411, 2002.

Diehl, R. D., and R. McGrath. Alkali metals on metals. In *Physics of Covered Solid Surfaces,* vol. III/42A, pp. 131–77. Landolt-Boernstein, 2001.

Finn, S. L., S. D. Mohanty, and J. D. Romano. Detecting an association between gamma ray and gravitational wave bursts. *Phys. Rev. D* 60:121101, 1999.

Finn, S. L. Issues in gravitational wave data analysis. In *Second Edoardo Amaldi Conference on Gravitational Waves,* vol. 4, pp. 180–91, eds. E. Coccia, G. Veneziano, and G. Pizzella. Edoardo Amaldi Foundation Series, Singapore: World Scientific, 1998.

Finn, S. L. A numerical approach to binary black hole coalescence. In *Proceedings of the 14th International Conference on General Relativity and Gravitation,* pp. 147–66, eds. M. Francavigli, G. Longhi, L. Lusanna, and E. Sorace. Singapore: World Scientific, 1997.

Gunaydin, M., S. Fernando, and O. Pavlyk. Spectra of PP-wave limits of M/superstring theory on AdS_pxS^q spaces. *J. High Energy Phys.* 10:007, 2002.

Gunaydin, M., R. Corrado, N. P. Warner, and M. Zagermann. Orbifolds and flows from gauged supergravity. *Phys. Rev. D* 65:125024, 2002.

Gunaydin, M., J. R. Ellis, and M. Zagermann. Options for gauge groups in five dimensional supergravity. *J. High Energy Phys.* 11:024, 2001.

Scarola, V. W., K. Park, and **J. K. Jain.** Cooper instability of composite Fermions: Pairing from purely repulsive interaction. *Nature,* in press.

Park, J., and **J. K. Jain.** Spontaneous magnetization of composite Fermions. *Phys. Rev. Lett.* 83:5543–6, 1999.

Jain, J. K. Composite Fermion approach for the fractional quantum Hall effect. *Phys. Rev. Lett.* 63:199–202, 1989.

MacLaren, Z., L. Wang, H. S. Wang, and **Q. Li.** Stain induced crystal structure change in ultrathin films of $Pr_{0.67}Sr_{0.33}MnO_{3-x}$. *Appl. Phys. Lett.* 80:1405, 2002.

Li. Q., and H. S. Wang. Anomalous domain wall magnetoresistance

The Pennsylvania State University

Selected Publications (continued)

in ultrathin manganite films near M-I Transition Boundary. *J. Superconductivity Incorporating Novel Magnetism* 14:231, 2001.

Liu, Y., et al. Destruction of the global phase coherence in ultrathin, doubly connected superconducting cylinders. *Science* 294:2332, 2001.

Khalifah, P., et al. **(Y. Liu).** Non-Fermi-liquid behavior in $La_4Ru_6O_{19}$. *Nature* 411:669–671, 2001.

Mao, Z. Q., et al. **(Y. Liu).** Observation of Andreev surface bound state in the 3-K phase region of Sr_2RuO_4. *Phys. Rev. Lett.* 87:037003, 2001.

Mahan, G. D. Oscillations of a thin hollow cylinder: Carbon nanotubes. *Phys. Rev. B* 65:235402, 2002.

Scarola, V. W., and **G. D. Mahan.** Phonon drag effect in single-walled carbon nanotubes. *Phys. Rev. B* 66:205405, 2002.

Jin H. S., et al. **(J. D. Maynard** and **Q. Li).** Measurements of elastic constants in thin films of colassal magnetoresistance material. *Phys. Rev. Lett.* 90:036103, 2003.

Maynard, J. D. Acoustical analogs of condensed matter problems. *Rev. Mod. Phys.* 73:401–17, 2001.

Maynard, J. D. Resonant ultrasound spectroscopy. *Phys. Today* 49:26–31, 1996.

Kobayashi, S., and **P. Mészáros.** Polarized graviational waves from gamma-ray bursts. *Astrophys. J. Lett.,* in press.

Dai, Z. G., et al. **(P. Mészáros).** GeV emission from TeV blazers and intergalactic magnetic fields. *Astrophys. J. Lett.* 580:L7, 2002.

Mészáros, P., and E. Waxman. TeV neutrinos from successful and choked gamma-ray bursts. *Phys. Rev. Lett.* 87:171102, 2001.

Mizel, A., M. W. Mitchell, and M. L. Cohen. Energy barrier to decoherence. *Phys. Rev. A Rapid Commun.* 63:40302, 2001.

Mizel, A., and D. A. Lidar. Exchange interaction between three and four coupled quantum dots: Theory and applications to quantum computing. http://xxx.lanl.gov/abs/cond-mat/0302018.

Mizel, A. Quantum vortex tunneling: Microscopic theory and application to d-wave superconductors. http://xxx.lanl.gov/abs/cond-mat/0107530.

Owen, B. J., and L. Lindblom. Gravitational radiation from the r-mode instability. *Classical Quantum Gravity* 19:1247–53, 2002.

Lindblom, L., and **B. J. Owen.** Effect of hyperon bulk viscosity on neutron-star r-modes. *Phys. Rev. D* 65:063006, 2002.

Tagoshi, H., A. Ohashi, and **B. J. Owen.** Gravitational field and equations of motion of spinning compact binaries to 2.5 post-Newtonian order. *Phys. Rev. D* 63:044006, 2001.

Redwing, R. D., et al. Observation of strong to Josephson coupled transition in 10° low angle [001] tilt YBa2Cu3Ox bicrystal junctions. *Appl. Phys. Lett.* 75:3171, 1999.

Heinig, N. F., **R. D. Redwing,** J. E. Nordman, and D. C. Larbalestier. The strong to weak coupling transition in low misorientation angle thin film Yba2Cu307-x bicrystals. *Phys. Rev. B* 60:1409, 1999.

Hinaus, B. M., M. S. Rzchowski, **R. D. Redwing,** and J. E. Nordman. Flux penetration in bicrystal substrate thin-film YBCO Josephson junctions. *Appl. Phys. Lett.* 70:571, 1997.

Robinett, R. W., and **S. Heppelmann.** Quantum wave packet revivals in circular billiards. *Phys. Rev. A* 65:062103–10, 2002.

Doncheski, M. A., **R. W. Robinett,** and D. C. Tussey. Quantum mechanical analysis of the equilateral triangle billiard: Periodic orbit theory and wave packet revivals. *Ann. Phys.* 299:208–27, 2002.

Catalonglu, E., and **R. W. Robinett.** Testing the development of student conceptual and visualization skills in quantum mechanics through the undergraduate career. *Am. J. Phys.* 70:238–51, 2002.

Potashnik,. S. J., et al. **(N. Samarth** and **P. Schiffer).** Effects of annealing time of defect-controlled ferromagnetism in $Ga_{1-x}Mn_xAs$. *Appl. Phys. Lett.* 79:1495–7, 2001.

Ray, O., et al. **(N. Samarth).** Exciton spin polarization in magnetic semiconductor quantum wires. *Appl. Phys. Lett.* 76:1167–9, 2000.

Malajovich, I., et al. **(N. Samarth).** Coherent spin transport across a semiconductor heterointerface. *Phys. Rev. Lett.* 84:1015–8, 2000.

Smorchkova, I. P., **N. Samarth,** J. M. Kikkawa, and D. D. Awschalom. Spin transport and localization in a magnetic two-dimensional electron gas. *Phys. Rev. Lett.* 78:3571–4, 1997.

Tegzes, P., T. Vicsek, and **P. Schiffer.** Avalanche dynamics in wet granular materials. *Phys. Rev. Lett.* 90:094301-1–4, 2002.

Snyder, J., J. S. Slusky, R. J. Cava, and **P. Schiffer.** How spin ice freezes. *Nature* 413:48–51, 2001.

Silva, D. E., **P. E. Sokol,** and S. N. Ehrlich. Mobility transition of solid rare gases in confined environments. *Phys. Rev. Lett.* 88:155701, 2002.

Dimeo, R. M., and **P. E. Sokol** et al. Localized collective excitations in superfluid helium in vycor. *Phys. Rev. Lett.* 81:5860, 1998.

Strikman, M., and D. Treleani. Measuring double parton distributions in nucleons at proton nucleus colliders. *Phys. Rev. Lett.* 88:0318021, 2002.

Frankfurt, L., V. Guzey, M. McDermott, and **M. Strikman.** Revealing the black body regime of small x DIS through final state signals. *Phys. Rev. Lett.* 87:192301, 2001.

Pobylitsa, P. V., V. Polyadov, and **M. Strikman.** Soft pion theorems for hard near threshold pion production. *Phys. Rev. Lett.* 87:022001, 2001.

Olshanii, M., and **D. S. Weiss.** Producing Bose condensates using optical lattices. *Phys. Rev. Lett.* 89:090401-1, 2002.

Han, D. J., et al. **(D. S. Weiss).** 3D Raman sideband cooling at high density. *Phys. Rev. Lett.* 85:724, 2000.

Wolf, S., S. J. Oliver, and **D. S. Weiss.** Suppression of recoil heating by an optical lattice. *Phys. Rev. Lett.* 85:4249, 2000.

Checkanov, S., et al. **(J. Whitmore).** ZEUS next-to-leading-order QCD analysis of data on deep inelastic scattering, ZEUS collaboration. *Phys. Rev. D* 67:012007, 2003.

Checkanov, S., et al. **(J. Whitmore).** Measurement of high-Q_2 charged current cross sections in e^-p deep inelastic scattering at HERA, ZEUS collaboration. *Phys. Lett. B* 539:197, 2002.

Checkanov, S., et al. **(J. Whitmore).** Exclusive photoproduction of J/Ψ mesons at HERA, ZEUS collaboration. *Eur. Phys. J.* C24:345, 2002.

Zeng, X., et al. **(X. X. Xi** and **Q. Li).** In situ epitaxial MgB_2 thin films for superconducting electronics. *Nat. Mat.* 1:35, 2002.

Tenne, D. A., et al. **(X. X. Xi).** Soft phonon modes in $Ba_{0.5}Sr_{0.5}TiO_3$ thin films studied by Raman spectoscopy. *Appl. Phys. Lett.* 79:3836, 2001.

Sirenko, A. A., et al. **(X. X. Xi).** Soft-mode hardening in $SrTiO_3$ thin films. *Nature* 404:373, 2000.

Ye, J. Thermally generated vorticies, guage invariance and electron spectral function in the pseudo-gap regime. *Phys. Rev. Lett.* 87:227003, 2001.

Ye, J. On Emery-Kivelson line and universality of Wilson ratio of spin anisotropic Kondo model. *Phys. Rev. Lett.* 79:3224, 1996.

Ye, J. Abelian Bosonization approach to quantum impurity problems. *Phys. Rev. Lett.* 79:1385, 1996.

RUTGERS, THE STATE UNIVERSITY OF NEW JERSEY, NEW BRUNSWICK/PISCATAWAY

Department of Physics and Astronomy

Programs of Study

The Department of Physics and Astronomy offers programs leading to the Ph.D., M.S., M.S.T. (Master of Science for Teachers), and M.Phil. (Master of Philosophy) degrees in physics and astronomy. The program for the Ph.D. degree involves an appropriate combination of research and course work, including several required courses. Most students should expect to obtain the Ph.D. degree in about five years. The qualifying examinations, including both written and oral sections, are normally taken at the beginning of the second year. No foreign languages are required. The M.S. requires a minimum of 30 credit hours, of which 6 can be devoted to research. In addition to passing an oral examination, the candidate must present either a critical essay or a thesis on some research problem. Two years are normally required to complete the M.S. program. While almost all of the currently enrolled graduate students are in the Ph.D. program, the master's programs provide attractive and useful alternatives to students who wish to complete their advanced education more quickly.

Research Facilities

The department has more than 60 faculty members. This includes new faculty members in experimental high-energy and condensed-matter physics and astronomy, expansion of programs in theoretical condensed-matter and high-energy physics and experimental surface and nuclear physics, and new opportunities in biological physics. The department is housed in a modern, fully equipped research laboratory with networks of Sun Workstations and PCs that provide easy computer access for all students and faculty members. The astrophysics group is focused on galactic dynamics and cosmology; observation facilities include the Southern African Large Telescope and a Fabry-Perot interferometer at the U.S. National Observatory in Chile. Condensed-matter theory faculty members study strongly correlated electron systems and electronic properties of materials. The multidisciplinary Laboratory for Surface Modification includes 6 physics faculty members and members of the chemistry, materials science, and engineering departments. The research in low-temperature physics is supported by three dilution refrigerators to study the properties of liquid ^{3}He and two-dimensional electron systems. New research initiatives in experimental condensed matter probe the properties of new materials using a variety of spectroscopic probes and transport studies. High-energy theory research includes phenomenological studies and abstract approaches such as string theory and conformal field theories. High-energy experimentalists do research with the CDF detector at Fermilab, SLD at SLAC, and CMS for future LHC at CERN. They have been involved in the discovery of the top quark, rare decay modes of neutral K mesons, and the properties of the Z0 vector boson. Nuclear physics research in both theory and experiment span a broad range of questions, from few-body systems to the limits of angular momentum and stability. Experiments are carried out at Berkeley, Argonne, and Oak Ridge national labs; Yale and Michigan State Universities; TJNAF in Virginia; and MAMI at Mainz, Germany.

Financial Aid

Virtually all students receive financial support from the department. First-year students are generally awarded teaching assistantships with stipends of at least $15,300 for the academic year, a waiver of tuition, and comprehensive health insurance. More advanced students frequently have research assistantships, with a stipend of at least $17,555 for the calendar year and a waiver of tuition. Outstanding applicants may be eligible for fellowships of at least $19,000 for the calendar year. Summer jobs for teaching and research assistants are available, and research assistants and fellows may supplement their income with limited teaching assignments.

Cost of Study

The tuition for 2003–04 was $8952 per year for New Jersey residents and $13,124 per year for nonresidents and is waived for students with assistantships or internships. In 2003–04, fees were $1076 per year.

Living and Housing Costs

Assistantships provide modest but adequate support for students. For 2003–04, the cost of rooms in University housing for single students ranged from $4274 per academic year in a dormitory to $4658 to $5282 in a University apartment shared with 3 other students. The cost of University apartments for married students for 2003–04 ranged from $619 to $935 per month.

Student Group

About 110 full-time graduate students are currently enrolled in the department; almost all of these are supported by assistantships or fellowships. Students come from a number of countries as well as from all parts of the United States.

Location

The department is located in Rutgers' Science Center in Piscataway, a pleasant suburban community about 10 minutes from urban New Brunswick in central New Jersey. Rutgers is about 35 miles from New York City, 40 miles from the New Jersey ocean beaches, and 16 miles from Princeton. Academic life in New Brunswick is enriched by lecture series, films, and, in particular, an extensive program of high-quality musical events. Athletic fields, a student center, and a recreation center are within easy walking distance.

The University and The Department

Rutgers was founded in 1766 and is now the State University of New Jersey. There are more than 50,000 students on six campuses. About 33,300 of these students, including about 4,500 graduate students, are in New Brunswick and Piscataway. The Department of Physics and Astronomy has grown significantly in recent years, with new faculty members in condensed-matter theory, high-energy theory, experimental condensed-matter and surface science, and astronomy. The department currently receives research support from outside sources in excess of $6 million per year.

Applying

All necessary forms for admission to the Graduate School and for appointment as an assistant or fellow may be obtained by writing to the address below. Applications are accepted until about May 1; applicants for financial aid are expected to apply before January 2. The GRE General Test and the Subject Test in physics are required. The Test of English as a Foreign Language (TOEFL) or IELTS is required of students whose native language is not English.

Correspondence and Information

Dr. Theodore Williams, Graduate Program Director
Department of Physics and Astronomy
Rutgers University
136 Freylinghuysen Road
Piscataway, New Jersey 08854-8019
Telephone: 732-445-2502
Fax: 732-445-4343
E-mail: graduate@physics.rutgers.edu
World Wide Web: http://www.physics.rutgers.edu/

Rutgers, The State University of New Jersey, New Brunswick/Piscataway

THE FACULTY AND THEIR RESEARCH

Professors

Elihu Abrahams, Bernard Serin Professor of Physics and Astronomy; Ph.D., Berkeley, 1952. Theoretical condensed-matter physics.
Eva Y. Andrei, Ph.D., Rutgers, 1980. Experimental condensed-matter physics.
Natan Andrei, Ph.D., Princeton, 1979. Theoretical elementary particle/condensed-matter physics.
Thomas Banks, Ph.D., MIT, 1973. Theoretical elementary particle physics.
Robert Bartynski, Ph.D., Pennsylvania, 1986. Experimental condensed-matter physics.
John B. Bronzan, Ph.D., Princeton, 1963. Theoretical elementary particle physics.
Herman Y. Carr, Ph.D., Harvard, 1953. Experimental condensed-matter physics.
Yves Chabal, Ph.D., Cornell, 1980. Interface physics of electronic, photonic, and biomaterials.
Premala Chandra, Ph.D., California, Santa Barbara, 1988. Condensed-matter theory.
Sang-Wook Cheong, Ph.D. UCLA, 1989. Experimental condensed-matter physics and material science.
Jolie A. Cizewski, Ph.D., SUNY at Stony Brook, 1978. Experimental nuclear physics.
Piers Coleman, Ph.D., Princeton, 1984. Theoretical condensed-matter physics.
Mark Croft, Ph.D., Rochester, 1977. Experimental condensed-matter physics.
Thomas Devlin, Ph.D., Berkeley, 1961. Experimental elementary particle physics.
Michael Douglas, Ph.D., Caltech, 1988. Theoretical particle physics.
Daniel Friedan, Ph.D., Berkeley, 1980. Theoretical elementary particle physics.
Eric Garfunkel, Ph.D., Berkeley, 1983. Experimental surface science.
Charles Glashausser, Ph.D., Princeton, 1966. Experimental nuclear physics.
Gerald Goldin, Ph.D., Princeton, 1969. Mathematical physics.
Sheldon Goldstein, Ph.D., Yeshiva, 1974. Statistical mechanics, foundations of quantum mechanics.
Torgny Gustafsson, D.Sc., Chalmers (Sweden), 1973. Experimental condensed-matter physics, experimental surface physics.
David Harrington, Ph.D., Carnegie Tech, 1961. Theoretical nuclear physics.
George K. Horton, Ph.D., Birmingham (England), 1949. Theoretical condensed-matter physics.
Mohan S. Kalelkar, Undergraduate Coordinator and Associate Chair; Ph.D., Columbia, 1975. Experimental elementary particle physics.
Willem M. Kloet, Ph.D., Utrecht (Netherlands), 1973. Theoretical nuclear physics.
Haruo Kojima, Ph.D., UCLA, 1972. Experimental condensed-matter physics.
Noémie B. Koller, Ph.D., Columbia, 1958. Experimental nuclear physics.
B. Gabriel Kotliar, Ph.D., Princeton, 1983. Theoretical condensed-matter physics.
David C. Langreth, Ph.D., Illinois, 1964. Theoretical condensed-matter physics.
Paul L. Leath, Chair of the Department; Ph.D., Missouri–Columbia, 1966. Theoretical condensed-matter physics.
Joel Lebowitz, George William Hill Professor of Mathematics and Physics; Ph.D., Syracuse, 1956. Theoretical statistical mechanics, math physics.
Ronald M. Levy, Ph.D., Harvard, 1976. Biological physics theory and simulation.
Peter Lindenfeld, Emeritus; Ph.D., Columbia, 1954. Experimental condensed-matter physics.
Claud Lovelace, B.S., Cape Town (South Africa), 1954. Theoretical elementary particle physics.
Theodore Madey, Director, Surface Modification and Interface Dynamics Lab; Ph.D., Notre Dame, 1963. Experimental surface science physics, experimental condensed-matter physics.
Aram Mekjian, Ph.D., Maryland, 1968. Theoretical nuclear physics.
David R. Merritt, Ph.D., Princeton, 1982. Theoretical astrophysics.
Gregory Moore, Ph.D., Harvard, 1985. Theoretical particle physics.
Daniel E. Murnick, Ph.D., MIT, 1966. Experimental nuclear and atomic physics.
Herbert Neuberger, Ph.D., Tel Aviv, 1979. Theoretical elementary particle physics.
Wilma K. Olson, Mary I. Bunting Professor; Ph.D., Stanford, 1971. Biological physics theory and simulation.
Richard J. Plano, Ph.D., Chicago, 1956. Experimental elementary particle physics.
Karin Rabe, Ph.D., MIT, 1987. Theoretical condensed-matter physics, theoretical surface physics.
Ronald Ransome, Ph.D., Texas at Austin, 1981. Experimental nuclear physics.
Andrei E. Ruckenstein, Ph.D., Cornell, 1984. Theoretical condensed-matter physics and biophysics.
Joseph Sak, Ph.D., Institute of Solid-State Physics (Czechoslovakia), 1968. Theoretical condensed-matter physics.
Stephen R. Schnetzer, Ph.D., Berkeley, 1981. Experimental elementary particle physics.
Jeremy Sellwood, Ph.D., Manchester (England), 1977. Theoretical astrophysics.
Joel Shapiro, Ph.D., Cornell, 1967. Theoretical elementary particle physics.
Earl D. Shaw, Ph.D., Berkeley, 1969. Experimental laser physics.
Boris I. Shraiman, Ph.D., Harvard, 1983. Theoretical physics.
Gordon Thomson, Ph.D., Harvard, 1972. Experimental elementary particle physics.
Alan Van Heuvelen, Ph.D., Colorado, 1964. Physics education.
David Vanderbilt, Ph.D., MIT, 1981. Theoretical condensed-matter physics, theoretical surface physics.
Russell E. Walstedt, Ph.D., Berkeley, 1961. Experimental condensed-matter physics.
Terence Watts, Ph.D., Yale, 1963. Experimental elementary particle physics.
Theodore B. Williams, Associate Chair and Graduate Program Director; Ph.D., Caltech, 1974. Experimental astrophysics.
Larry Zamick, Ph.D., MIT, 1961. Theoretical nuclear physics.
Alexander Zamolodchikov, Ph.D., Institute of Theoretical and Experimental Physics (Moscow), 1978. Theoretical particle physics.
Harold S. Zapolsky, Ph.D., Cornell, 1962. Theoretical astrophysics.

Associate Professors

John Conway, Ph.D., Chicago, 1987. Experimental elementary particle physics.
Michael E. Gershenson, Ph.D., Institute of Radio Engineering and Electronics (Moscow), 1982. Experimental condensed-matter physics.
Ronald Gilman, Ph.D., Pennsylvania, 1985. Experimental nuclear physics.
B. Jane Hinch, Ph.D., Cambridge, 1987. Surface studies using atomic and molecular scattering.
John Hughes, Ph.D., UCLA, 1984. Observational astronomy.
Lev Ioffe, Ph.D., Landau Institute for Theoretical Physics (Russia), 1985. Theoretical condensed-matter physics.
Charles L. Joseph, Ph.D., Colorado, 1985. Observational astronomy and detector development.
Terry A. Matilsky, Ph.D., Princeton, 1971. Experimental astrophysics.
Carlton Pryor, Ph.D., Harvard, 1982. Experimental astrophysics.
Anirvan Sengupta, Ph.D., Bombay, 1994. Biological physics.
Sunil Somalwar, Ph.D., Chicago, 1988. Experimental elementary particle physics.
Frank M. Zimmermann, Ph.D., Cornell, 1995. Experimental surface science physics.

Assistant Professors

Kieron Burke, Ph.D., California, Santa Barbara, 1989. Theoretical condensed-matter physics.
Patrick Coté, Ph.D., McMaster, 1994. Observational astronomy and astrophysics.
Duiliu-Emanuel Diaconescu, Ph.D., Rutgers, 1998. Theoretical high-energy physics.
Eugenia Etkina, Ph.D., Moscow State Pedagogical, 1997. Physics education.
Laura Ferrarese, Ph.D., Johns Hopkins, 1996. Observational astronomy and astrophysics.
Valery Kiryukhin, Ph.D., Princeton, 1997. Experimental condensed-matter physics.
Arthur Kosowsky, Ph.D., Chicago, 1994. Theoretical astrophysics.
Amitabh Lath, Ph.D., MIT, 1994. Experimental elementary particle physics.
Sergei Lukyanov, Ph.D., Landau Institute of Theoretical Physics (Russia), 1989. Theoretical high-energy physics.
Steven Worm, Ph.D., Texas, 1995. Experimental high-energy physics.

Rutgers, The State University of New Jersey, New Brunswick/Piscataway

SELECTED PUBLICATIONS

Tanasković, D., V. Dobrosavljević, **E. Abrahams,** and **G. Kotliar.** Disorder screening in strongly correlated systems. *Phys. Rev. Lett.* 91:066603, 2003.

Xiao, Z. L., **E. Y. Andrei,** P. Shuk, and M. Greenblatt. Depinning of a metastable disordered vortex lattice. *Phys. Rev. Lett.* 86(11):2431–4, 2001.

Rosch, A., and **N. Andrei.** Conductivity of a clean one-dimensional wire. *Phys. Rev. Lett.* 85:1092–5, 2000.

Banks, T., M. Dine, and **M. Douglas.** Time-varying and particle physics. *Phys. Rev. Lett.* 88:131301, 2002.

Hopkinson, J., and **P. Coleman.** Frustration induced heavy fermion metal. *Phys. Rev. Lett.* 89:267201, 2002.

Ernst, R., et al. **(N. Benczer-Koller** and **L. Zamick).** Stringent tests of shell model calculations in fp shell nuclei 46,48Ti and 50,52Cr from measurements of g factors and B(E2) values. *Phys. Rev. Lett.* 84:416–9, 2000.

Souchkov, A. B., et al. **(S.-W. Cheong).** Exchange interaction effects on the optical properties of LuMnO. *Phys. Rev. Lett.* 91:027203, 2003.

Sharma, P. A., et al. **(S.-W. Cheong).** Percolative superconductivity in Mg. *Phys. Rev. Lett.* 89:167003, 2002.

Seweryniak, D., and **J. A. Cizewski** et al. Rotational bands in the proton emitter 141Ho. *Phys. Rev. Lett.* 86:1458, 2001.

Coleman, P., C. Hooley, and O. Parcollet. Is the quantum dot at large bias a weak-coupling problem? *Phys. Rev. Lett.* 86(18):4088–91, 2001.

Ferrarese, L., and **D. Merritt.** A fundamental relation between supermassive black holes and their host galaxies. *Astrophys. J.* 539:L9–12, 2000.

Pudalov, V. M., et al. **(M. E. Gershenson** and **H. Kojima).** Interaction effects in conductivity of Si inversion layers at intermediate temperatures. *Phys. Rev. Lett.* 91:126403, 2003.

Volmer, J., and **R. Gilman** et al. Measurement of the charged pion electromagnetic form factor. *Phys. Rev. Lett.* 86:1713–6, 2001.

Rakowski, C., P. Ghavamian, and **J. P. Hughes.** The physics of supernova remnant blast waves. II. Electron-ion equilibration in DEM L71 in the large magellanic cloud. *Astron. J.* 590:846–57, 2003.

Hughes, J. P., C. E. Rakowski, D. N. Burrows, and P. O. Slane. Nucleosynthesis and mixing in Cassiopeia A. *Astrophys. J. Lett.* 528:L109–13, 2000.

Douçot, B., M. V. Feigel'man, and **L. B. Ioffe.** Topological order in the insulating Josephson junction array. *Phys. Rev. Lett.* 90:107003, 2003.

Abe, K., **M. Kalelkar,** and **R. Plano** et al. First symmetry tests in polarized Z0 decays to *bg*. *Phys. Rev. Lett.* 86:962–6, 2001.

Walstedt, R. E., **H. Kojima,** N. Butch, and N. Bernhoeft. Cu nuclear relaxation in the quantum critical point system CeCu. *Phys. Rev. Lett.* 90:067601, 2003.

Kotliar, G., S. Murthy, and M. J. Rozenberg. Compressibility divergence and the finite temperature Mott transition. *Phys. Rev. Lett.* 89:046401, 2002.

Acosta, D., and **A. Lath** et al. Diffractive dijet production at =630 and 1800 GeV at the Fermilab Tevatron. *Phys. Rev. Lett.* 88:151802, 2002.

Alavi-Harati et al. **(A. Lath, S. Schnetzer, S. V. Somalwar,** and **G. B. Thomson).** Search for the decay *KL 0e+e–*. *Phys. Rev. Lett.* 86:397–401, 2001.

Mekjian, A. Z. Model for studying branching processes, multiplicity distributions, and non-Poissonian fluctuations in heavy-ion collisions. *Phys. Rev. Lett.* 86:220–3, 2001.

Merritt, D. R., M. Milosavljević, L. Verde, and R. Jimenez. Dark matter spikes and annihilation radiation from the galactic center. *Phys. Rev. Lett.* 88:191301, 2002.

Gerssen, J., et al. **(C. Pryor).** Hubble space telescope evidence for an intermediate-mass black hole in the globular cluster M15, II. Kinematic analysis and dynamical modeling. *Astron. J.* 124:3270–88, 2002.

Souza, I., J. Iniguez, and **D. Vanderbilt.** First principles approach to insulators in finite electric fields. *Phys. Rev. Lett.* 89:117602, 2002.

He, L., and **D. Vanderbilt.** Exponential decay properties of Wannier functions and related quantities. *Phys. Rev. Lett.* 86(23):5341–4, 2001.

Affolder, T., et al. **(T. Watts, J. Conway,** and **A. Lath).** Study of B0 J/K(*)0 +- decays with the collider detector at Fermilab. *Phys. Rev. Lett.* 88:071801, 2002.

STONY BROOK UNIVERSITY, STATE UNIVERSITY OF NEW YORK

Department of Physics and Astronomy

Programs of Study The department offers four graduate degrees. Students in the Ph.D. program gain a solid background in the breadth of physics and astronomy and demonstrate their ability to carry out research and overcome new challenges in a specific area of interest. A Master of Arts in Teaching (M.A.T.) provides students who have a B.A. degree in a physical science or engineering with the preparation needed for New York State certification as a secondary school teacher. This program addresses the widely known shortage of well-trained high school physics teachers. A Master of Science (M.S.) program in instrumentation prepares students with undergraduate degrees in physical science, mathematics, or engineering to enter modern technological enterprises such as research labs, industries, and hospitals as professional physicists with expertise in instrumentation. The program offers both course work and an original instrumentation project in one of the department's cutting-edge research labs. The department does not recruit candidates seeking only the Master of Arts (M.A.) in physics degree. However, many students who come to Stony Brook on limited-time exchange programs enroll in the M.A. program. The M.A. may also be awarded to students originally enrolled in the Ph.D. program, either en route to the Ph.D. or as a terminal degree.

Research Facilities The department is involved in a wide range of activities in an array of laboratories. Accelerator and beam physics is concerned with the development of novel accelerator concepts, free-electron lasers, and instrumentation. This work is carried out at nearby Brookhaven National Laboratory and includes Stony Brook adjunct faculty members and graduate students.

The astronomy faculty members are interested in many areas of astronomy and astrophysics: extragalactic astronomy and cosmology, including studies of the Hubble Deep Field, which contains the most distant galaxies ever seen; radio and millimeter-wave studies of molecular clouds and galaxies and the stratosphere; nuclear astrophysics, including studies of supernovae, neutron stars, the equation of state, and merging neutron star binaries; star formation and properties of low-mass (cool) stars observed with IR, optical, and X-radiation; and studies of supergiants and space interferometry. In atmospheric physics, molecular spectroscopy is applied to the study of stratospheric trace gases that regulate the chemical equilibrium of ozone, radiative heating and cooling of the atmosphere, and other physical processes. The work is carried out in collaboration with NASA scientists and with other faculty members in Stony Brook's Institute for Terrestrial and Planetary Atmospheres.

The condensed matter–experimental and device physics group studies fundamental phenomena such as phase transitions and electronic and magnetic properties of materials and does applied research on devices based on superconductor and semiconductor structures, rapid single flux quantum (RSFQ) logic, single-electron tunneling (SET), and powder diffraction. The condensed matter–theory group is interested in the theory of superconductors. The group has played a major role in the theory of the fractional quantum Hall effect and in the development of the ideas of single-electron and single flux quantum device physics. The particle physics–experimental group studies fundamental forces and the constituents of matter at the D0 experiment at the 2-TeV Fermilab proton-antiproton collider and at the ATLAS experiment at the 14-TeV CERN collider. Rare K decays are investigated in the KOPIO experiment in Brookhaven Lab, and neutrino oscillations and proton decay are studied at the SuperKamiokande and K2K experiments in Japan. The C. N. Yang Institute for Theoretical Physics is dedicated to research in fundamental theory, such as the standard model of elementary particles, string theory, supersymmetry, and statistical mechanics. The nuclear and heavy-ion physics–experimental group operates a superconducting linear accelerator for nuclear physics research on campus (including the recently reported trapping of francium atoms) and is engaged in the PHENIX experiment in Brookhaven. Phenix is one of the two experiments on the Relativistic Heavy Ion Collider (RHIC) at Brookhaven. RHIC collides high-energy heavy ions to create matter at extremely large density. The nuclear physics–theory group is working on the theory of hadronic matter (including conditions such as those that are produced at the RHIC) and nuclear astrophysics (such as the theory of supernovae and gamma ray bursters). The atomic, molecular, and optical physics group includes a broad range of activities, including laser spectroscopy and cooling to micro-Kelvin temperatures, interactive control of molecular dynamics, and quantum chaos. The X-ray optics and microscopy group studies X-ray optics and microscopy of biological and materials science applications.

Financial Aid New assistantships and fellowships provide stipends at a minimum of $18,000 for the calendar year starting in September 2004. All assistants and fellows receive full tuition scholarships. The department offers financial support in the form of teaching assistantships or fellowships to essentially every member of the entering class, and all applicants are considered for such support. Awards are renewable as long as good academic standing is maintained. Support from research grants is available for all full-time students in the doctoral program.

Cost of Study In 2003–04, full-time tuition was $6900 per academic year for state residents and $10,500 per academic year for nonresidents. All assistants and fellows receive full tuition scholarships. Part-time tuition was $213 per credit hour for residents and $351 per credit hour for nonresidents. Additional charges included an activity fee of $20.50 and a comprehensive fee of $287.50 per semester.

Living and Housing Costs University apartments range in cost from approximately $300 per month to approximately $1300 per month, depending on the size of the unit. Off-campus housing options include furnished rooms to rent and houses and/or apartments to share that can be rented for $350 to $1500 per month.

Student Group Stony Brook's current enrollment is 20,921 students. Graduate students number 7,563 and come from all states in the nation, as well as from some seventy-five countries. International students, both graduate and undergraduate, represent about 10 percent of the total student body. There are about 180 graduate students in the department.

Student Outcomes Students often go on to traditional research positions at universities and national laboratories as well as to industrial labs and to other careers, including medical physics and analysis in technological and financial settings. In addition, many graduates fill positions in high school or higher education, while others contribute to research programs in laboratories in the public, private, and educational sectors.

Location Stony Brook's campus is approximately 50 miles east of Manhattan on the north shore of Long Island. The cultural offerings of New York City and Suffolk County's countryside and seashore are conveniently located nearby. Cold Spring Harbor Laboratories and Brookhaven National Laboratories are easily accessible and have close relationships with the University.

The University The University, established in 1957, achieved national stature within a generation. Founded at Oyster Bay, Long Island, the school moved to its present location in 1962. Stony Brook has grown to encompass more than 110 buildings on 1,100 acres. There are more than 1,500 faculty members, and the annual budget is more than $800 million. The Graduate Student Organization oversees the spending of the student activity fee for graduate student campus events. International students find the additional four-week Summer Institute in American Living very helpful. The Intensive English Center offers classes in English as a second language. The Career Development Office assists with career planning and has information on permanent full-time employment. Disabled Student Services has a Resource Center that offers placement testing, tutoring, vocational assessment, and psychological counseling. The Counseling Center provides individual, group, family, and marital counseling and psychotherapy. Day-care services are provided in four on-campus facilities. The Writing Center offers tutoring in all phases of writing.

Applying Information is available at http://graduate.physics.sunysb.edu. This Web page is updated more frequently than any of the printed or PDF documents related to the graduate program. Online application is encouraged. For information related to applications, students should contact Diane Siegel at diane.siegel@sunysb.edu. For specific questions about the department's academic graduate program, students should contact Professor Laszlo Mihaly, Graduate Program Director, at graduate.physics@sunysb.edu.

Correspondence and Information

Paul Grannis, Chairman
Pam Burris, Assistant to the Chair
Department of Physics and Astronomy
Stony Brook University, State University of New York
Stony Brook, New York 11794-3800
Telephone: 631-632-8100
Fax: 631-632-8176
E-mail: pam.burris@sunysb.edu
World Wide Web: http://www.physics.sunysb.edu/Physics

Stony Brook University, State University of New York

THE FACULTY AND THEIR RESEARCH

Accelerator and Beam Physics

Ilan Ben-Zvi, Adjunct Professor and Head of the Brookhaven National Laboratory Accelerator Test Facility; Ph.D., Weizmann Institute (Israel), 1970. Nuclear physics.
Vladimir Litvinenko, Adjunct Professor; Ph.D., Institute of Nuclear Physics (Russia), 1989. Accelerator physics and free-electron lasers.
Steve Peggs, Adjunct Professor; Ph.D., Cornell, 1981. Accelerator physics.

Astronomy

Aaron Evans, Assistant Professor; Ph.D., Hawaii, 1996. Extragalactic astronomy.
Kenneth Lanzetta, Associate Professor; Ph.D., Pittsburgh, 1988. Extragalactic astronomy.
James Lattimer, Professor; Ph.D., Texas at Austin, 1976. Astrophysics.
Deane Peterson, Associate Professor; Ph.D., Harvard, 1968. Stellar and galactic astronomy.
Michal Simon, Professor; Ph.D., Cornell, 1967. Star formation.
Philip Solomon, Distinguished Professor; Ph.D., Wisconsin, 1964. Millimeter-wave astronomy.
F. Douglas Swesty, Research Assistant Professor and Computer System Manager; Ph.D., SUNY at Stony Brook, 1993.
Frederick Walter, Professor; Ph.D., Berkeley, 1981. Astronomy and astrophysics.
Ralph Wijers, Adjunct Professor; Ph.D., Amsterdam, 1991. High-energy astrophysics.
Amos Yahil, Professor; Ph.D., Caltech, 1970. Astrophysics.

Atmospheric Physics

Robert L. de Zafra, Research Professor; Ph.D., Maryland College Park, 1958. Stratospheric dynamics, development of instrumentation for remote measurement of stratospheric trace gases.
Marvin A. Geller, Adjunct Professor and Professor of Atmospheric Sciences; Ph.D., MIT, 1969. Atmospheric dynamics.

Atomic, Molecular, and Optical Physics and Quantum Electronics

Thomas Bergeman, Research Professor; Ph.D., Harvard, 1971.
Louis DiMauro, Adjunct Professor; Ph.D., Connecticut, 1980. Chemical physics.
Peter M. Koch, Professor and Associate Dean for the College of Arts and Sciences; Ph.D., Yale, 1974. Experimental atomic physics, nonlinear dynamical systems.
John H. Marburger, Professor (on leave), Science Adviser to the President, and Director, Office of Science and Technology Policy; Ph.D., Stanford, 1966. Theoretical nonlinear optics.
Harold J. Metcalf, Distinguished Teaching Professor; Ph.D., Brown, 1967. Atomic physics, level crossing techniques.
Luis A. Orozco, Adjunct Professor; Ph.D., Texas at Austin, 1987. Experimental atomic physics, quantum optics.
Thomas Weinacht, Assistant Professor; Ph.D., Michigan, 2000.

Condensed Matter–Experimental and Device Physics

Peter Abbamonte, Adjunct Professor; Ph.D., Illinois, 1999. Experimental condensed-matter physics.
Steven Dierker, Adjunct Professor; Ph.D., Illinois at Urbana-Champaign, 1983.
Vladimir J. Goldman, Professor; Ph.D., Maryland College Park, 1985. Experimental solid-state physics.
Michael Gurvitch, Professor; Ph.D., SUNY at Stony Brook, 1978. Experimental solid-state physics.
Chi-chang Kao, Adjunct Professor; Ph.D., Cornell, 1988. Condensed-matter physics.
Konstantin K. Likharev, Distinguished Professor; Ph.D., Moscow State, 1969. Solid-state physics and electronics.
James Lukens, Professor; Ph.D., California, San Diego, 1968. Experimental solid-state physics.
Emilio E. Mendez, Professor; Ph.D., MIT, 1979. Experimental solid-state physics.
Laszlo Mihaly, Professor and Director of Graduate Studies for the Department of Physics and Astronomy; Ph.D., Eötvös Lorand (Budapest), 1977. Experimental solid-state physics.
Vasili Semenov, Research Associate Professor; Ph.D., Moscow State, 1975.
Peter W. Stephens, Professor; Ph.D., MIT, 1978. Experimental solid-state physics.
Sergey Tolpygo, Adjunct Associate Professor; Ph.D., Academy of Sciences (Moscow), 1984. Mesoscopic physics.

Condensed Matter–Theory

Alexandre Abanov, Assistant Professor; Ph.D., Chicago, 1997. Interference effects in strongly correlated electronic systems.
Philip B. Allen, Professor; Ph.D., Berkeley, 1969. Theoretical solid-state physics.
Dmitri V. Averin, Professor; Ph.D., Moscow State, 1987. Solid-state physics.
Konstantin K. Likharev, Distinguished Professor; Ph.D., Moscow State, 1969. Solid-state physics and electronics.
Alexei Tsvelik, Adjunct Professor; Ph.D., Kurchatov Institute of Atomic Energy (Moscow), 1980.

C. N. Yang Institute for Theoretical Physics

Gerald E. Brown, Distinguished Professor; Ph.D., Yale, 1950; D.Sc., Birmingham, 1957. Theoretical nuclear physics.
Michael Creutz, Adjunct Professor (Brookhaven National Laboratory); Ph.D., Stanford, 1970. Physics.
Sally Dawson, Adjunct Professor; Ph.D., Harvard, 1981. Theoretical physics, collider phenomenology.
Alfred Goldhaber, Professor; Ph.D., Princeton, 1964. Theoretical physics, nuclear theory, particle physics.
Maria Concepcion Gonzalez-Garcia, Assistant Professor; Ph.D., Valencia, 1991.
Vladimir Korepin, Professor; Ph.D., Leningrad, 1977. Mathematical physics, statistical mechanics, condensed matter, exactly solvable models, quantum computing.
Barry McCoy, Distinguished Professor; Ph.D., Harvard, 1967. Statistical mechanics.
Martin Rocek, Professor; Ph.D., Harvard, 1979. Theoretical physics, supersymmetry.
Robert Shrock, Professor; Ph.D., Princeton, 1975. Particle physics, field theory, statistical mechanics.
Warren Siegel, Professor; Ph.D., Berkeley, 1977. Theoretical physics, strings.
Jack Smith, Professor and Deputy Director of the C. N. Yang Institute for Theoretical Physics; Ph.D., Edinburgh, 1963. Elementary particle physics.
George Sterman, Professor and Director of the C. N. Yang Institute for Theoretical Physics; Ph.D., Maryland College Park, 1974. Theoretical physics, elementary particles.
Peter van Nieuwenhuizen, Distinguished Professor; Ph.D., Utrecht, 1971. Theoretical physics.
William Weisberger, Professor; Ph.D., MIT, 1964. Theoretical physics.
Chen Ning Yang, Albert Einstein Professor Emeritus; D.Sc., Princeton; Ph.D., Chicago, 1948. Theoretical physics, field theory, statistical mechanics, particle physics.

High-Energy Physics–Experimental

Roderich Engelmann, Professor; Ph.D., Heidelberg, 1966. Experimental elementary particle physics.
Guido Finocchiaro, Professor Emeritus; Ph.D., Catania, 1957. Experimental particle physics.
Paul D. Grannis, Distinguished Professor and Chairman of the Department of Physics and Astronomy; Ph.D., Berkeley, 1965. Experimental high-energy physics, elementary particle reactions.
John Hobbs, Associate Professor; Ph.D., Chicago, 1991.
Chang Kee Jung, Professor; Ph.D., Indiana, 1986. Experimental high-energy physics.
Juliet Lee-Franzini, Adjunct Professor; Ph.D., Columbia, 1960. Experimental high-energy physics.
Michael Marx, Professor; Ph.D., MIT, 1974. Experimental high-energy physics.
Robert L. McCarthy, Professor; Ph.D., Berkeley, 1971. Experimental elementary particle physics.
Clark McGrew, Assistant Professor; Ph.D., California, Irvine, 1994. Physics.
Michael Rijssenbeek, Professor; Ph.D., Amsterdam, 1979. Experimental high-energy physics.
R. Dean Schamberger, Senior Scientist; Ph.D., SUNY at Stony Brook, 1977. Experimental high-energy physics.
Chiaki Yanagisawa, Research Professor; Ph.D., Tokyo, 1981. Experimental high-energy physics.

Nuclear and Heavy-Ion Physics–Experimental

Ralf Averbeck, Research Assistant Professor; Dr.rer.nat., Justus-Liebig (Germany), 1996.
Abhay Deshpande, Assistant Professor; Ph.D., Yale, 1995. Relativistic heavy-ion physics.
Axel Drees, Associate Professor; Dr.rer.nat., Ruprecht-Karls (Heidelberg), 1989.
Thomas Hemmick, Professor; Ph.D., Rochester, 1989. Experimental relativistic heavy-ion physics.
Barbara Jacak, Professor; Ph.D., Michigan State, 1984. Experimental relativistic heavy-ion physics.
Linwood L. Lee Jr., Professor Emeritus; Ph.D., Yale, 1955. Experimental nuclear structure.
Robert L. McGrath, Professor (on leave), Provost and Executive Vice President for Academic Affairs, and Vice President for Brookhaven Affairs; Ph.D., Iowa, 1965. Heavy-ion reaction studies from low to relativistic energies.
Peter Paul, Distinguished Service Professor (on leave) and Deputy Director of Brookhaven National Laboratory; Ph.D., Freiburg, 1959. Experimental nuclear physics.
Norbert Pietralla, Assistant Professor; Ph.D., Cologne (Germany), 1996. Experimental nuclear physics.
Gene D. Sprouse, Professor and Director of the Nuclear Structure Laboratory; Ph.D., Stanford, 1968. Neutral atom trapping and laser spectroscopy of radioactive atoms, development of radioactive beams.

Nuclear Physics–Theory

Gerald E. Brown, Distinguished Professor; Ph.D., Yale, 1950; D.Sc., Birmingham, 1957. Theoretical nuclear physics.
Thomas T. S. Kuo, Professor; Ph.D., Pittsburgh, 1964. Nuclear theory.
Madappa Prakash, Research Professor; Ph.D., Bombay, 1979. Nuclear theory.
Ralf Rapp, Adjunct Professor; Ph.D., Bonn, 1996. Nuclear theory.
Thomas Schaefer, Associate Professor; Ph.D., Regensburg, 1992.
Edward Shuryak, Distinguished Professor; Ph.D., Novosibirsk Institute of Nuclear Physics, 1974. Theoretical nuclear physics.
Jacobus Verbaarschot, Professor; Ph.D., Utrecht, 1982. Statistical theory of spectra.
Ismail Zahed, Professor; Ph.D., MIT, 1983. Theoretical nuclear physics.

Optics–X-ray Optics and Microscopy

Chris Jacobsen, Professor and Director of the Undergraduate Program for the Department of Physics and Astronomy; Ph.D., SUNY at Stony Brook, 1988. X-ray physics.
Janos Kirz, Distinguished Professor; Ph.D., Berkeley, 1963. High-energy physics.

Other Research Areas

Arnold Feingold, Professor Emeritus.
Miriam A. Forman, Adjunct Professor; Ph.D., SUNY at Stony Brook, 1972. Cosmic rays in interplanetary space, space physics.
Erlend H. Graf, Associate Professor; Ph.D., Cornell, 1967. Experimental low-temperature physics.
Peter B. Kahn, Professor Emeritus; Ph.D., Northwestern, 1960. Theoretical physics, nonlinear dynamics.
Richard Mould, Professor Emeritus; Ph.D., Yale, 1957.
Clifford Swartz, Professor Emeritus; Ph.D., Rochester, 1951. Particle physics.

TEMPLE UNIVERSITY

of the Commonwealth System of Higher Education

Department of Physics

Programs of Study

The department offers the M.A. and Ph.D. degrees. The M.A. program requires 24 semester hours of credit. Normally, required courses for the M.A. degree encompass 18 hours; the other 6 semester hours are used for thesis research or for additional courses. The student must also pass the M.A. comprehensive examination in physics. No specific number of graduate credits is required for the Ph.D. degree, but an approved program of graduate courses must be satisfactorily completed. A dissertation and dissertation examination are required. An M.A. degree is not necessary for the Ph.D. degree. The Ph.D. qualifying examination in physics is taken after completion of one year of graduate study. There is a one-year residence requirement for the Ph.D. degree. Students whose native language is not English must pass an examination in spoken and written English. There is no other language requirement for either the M.A. or the Ph.D. degree. Each full-time graduate student is given a desk in one of several student offices. Lecturers from other institutions describe their research activities at a weekly colloquium, and informal discussions with members of the faculty are frequent.

Research Facilities

The department is housed in Barton Hall, which has "smart" lecture theaters, offices, classrooms, and laboratories. The Physics Department Library contains frequently used journals and books; several thousand additional volumes are located in the Paley Library across the street from Barton Hall. A student shop and a materials preparation facility are available. The University computer facilities are based on a UNIX-cluster-composed Digital Equipment Corporation Alphas, including a high-performance numerical compute-server. The departmental computer facilities include a local area network (LAN) of six Silicon Graphics IRIS Indigo R4000 workstations, five Windows NT workstations, and eight host LAN of Linux workstations. The departmental local area networks are connected to a fiber-optic campus backbone through which all University mainframe computer facilities can be reached. High-speed access to the Internet is readily available from all departmental computers. Electronic information retrieval is provided by the Temple University library's Scholars Information System, which subscribes to a wide range of online databases. The research laboratories are conducting a variety of studies on optical holeburning and multiple quantum well structures; laser-based molecular spectroscopy; low-temperature properties of alloys and intermetallics, including valence fluctuations and heavy fermion behavior; high temperature superconductivity; Mössbauer spectroscopy; neutrino oscillation; nucleon structure; dark matter detection; and electrorheology and magnetorheology. The department also uses outside facilities, including the Los Alamos Meson Physics Facility, the Brookhaven National Laboratory, the Stanford Linear Accelerator Center, the Thomas Jefferson National Accelerator Facility, and the National High Magnetic Laboratory. Theoretical work is being conducted in such areas as elementary particles and their interactions, statistical mechanics, biophysics, general relativity, and condensed-matter theory.

Financial Aid

Aid is available to qualified full-time students in the form of assistantships and fellowships funded by the University and various extramural agencies. All forms of financial aid include a stipend plus tuition. The specific type of aid offered to a particular student depends on the student's qualifications and program of study. Summer support for qualified students is also normally available. Current stipends are $13,768 for the academic year. For students with grant-supported research assistantships, the stipend is much higher.

Cost of Study

The annual tuition for full-time graduate study in 2003–04 was $430 per credit hour for residents of Pennsylvania and $626 per credit hour for nonresidents. Minimal fees are charged for various services, such as microfilming theses.

Living and Housing Costs

Room and board costs for students living on campus were approximately $7318 per year in 2003–04. University-sponsored apartments, both furnished and unfurnished, are also available on the edge of the campus.

Student Group

The department has 29 full-time graduate students; nearly all are supported by assistantships or fellowships.

Location

Philadelphia is the fifth-largest city in the country, with a metropolitan population of more than 2 million. The city has a world-renowned symphony orchestra, a ballet company, two professional opera companies, and a chamber music society. Besides attracting touring plays, Philadelphia has a professional repertory theater and many amateur troupes. All sports and forms of recreation are easily accessible. The city is world famous for its historic sites and parks and for the eighteenth-century charm that is carefully maintained in the oldest section. The climate is temperate, with an average winter temperature of 33 degrees and an average summer temperature of 75 degrees.

The University

The development of Temple University has been in line with the ideal of "educational opportunity for the able and deserving student of limited means." With a rich heritage of social purpose, Temple seeks to provide the opportunity for high-quality education without regard to a student's race, creed, or station in life. Affiliation with the Commonwealth System of Higher Education undergirds Temple's character as a public institution.

Applying

All application material, both for admission and for financial awards, should be received by early March for admission in the fall semester. Notification regarding admission and the awarding of an assistantship is made as soon as the application has been screened.

Correspondence and Information

For program information and all applications:
Graduate Chairman
Department of Physics 009-00
Barton Hall
Temple University
Philadelphia, Pennsylvania 19122-6052
Telephone: 215-204-7736
Fax: 215-204-5652
E-mail: physics@temple.edu
World Wide Web: http://www.temple.edu/physics

For general information on graduate programs:
Dean
Graduate School
Temple University
Philadelphia, Pennsylvania 19122

Temple University

THE FACULTY AND THEIR RESEARCH

Condensed-Matter Physics

Z. Hasan, Professor; Ph.D., Australian National, 1979. Optical and magneto-optical properties of solids.
C. L. Lin, Associate Professor; Ph.D., Temple, 1985. Heavy fermions, crystal fields, valence fluctuations, the Kondo effect, high-temperature superconductivity.
T. Mihalisin, Professor; Ph.D., Rochester, 1967. Crystal fields, valence fluctuations and the Kondo effect in magnetic systems.
P. Riseborough, Professor; Ph.D., Imperial College, London, 1977. Theoretical condensed-matter physics and statistical mechanics.
R. Tao, Professor; Ph.D., Columbia, 1982. Electrorheological and magnetorheological fluids, self-aggregation of superconducting particles.
R. Tahir-Kheli, Professor; D.Phil., Oxford, 1962. Theory of magnetism, randomly disordered systems.
T. Yuen, Associate Professor; Ph.D., Temple, 1990. Experimental condensed-matter physics, Mössbauer spectroscopy.

Educational Development Physics

L. Dubeck, Professor; Ph.D., Rutgers, 1965. Development, publication, and testing of precollege science materials.
Z. Dziembowski, Associate Professor; Ph.D., Warsaw, 1975. In-service elementary and secondary teacher training, inquiry-based instruction.
J. Karra, Associate Professor; Ph.D., Rutgers, 1964. Teaching physicist.
R. B. Weinberg, Professor Emeritus; Ph.D., Columbia, 1963. Teaching physicist.

Elementary Particle Physics and Cosmology

L. B. Auerbach, Professor; Ph.D., Berkeley, 1962. Experimental particle physics; investigations of the properties of fundamental particles at Los Alamos Meson Physics Facility, Brookhaven National Laboratory, and CERN.
Z. Dziembowski, Associate Professor; Ph.D., Warsaw, 1975. Theoretical particle physics.
J. Franklin, Professor Emeritus; Ph.D., Illinois, 1956. Theoretical particle physics; quark and parton theory, S-matrix theory.
C. J. Martoff, Professor; Ph.D., Berkeley, 1980. Experimental particle physics: investigation of weak interactions and dynamics of nuclei and particles, development of particle detectors for the study of "dark matter" using superconductivity.
Z.-E. Meziani, Professor; Ph.D., Paris, 1984. Experimental high-energy nuclear physics: investigation of the flavor and spin structure of the nucleon at the Stanford Linear Accelerator Center, search for transition region between nucleon-meson to quark-gluon description of few-body nuclear systems at the Continuous Electron Beam Accelerator Facility.
D. E. Neville, Professor; Ph.D., Chicago, 1962. Theoretical particle physics; symmetries and quark models, quantum gravity.

Optics

Z. Hasan, Professor; Ph.D., Australian National, 1979. Laser materials, laser spectroscopy of solids.
M. Lyyra, Professor; Ph.D., Stockholm, 1984. Laser spectroscopy.
R. Tao, Professor; Ph.D., Columbia, 1982. Photonic crystals, nonlinear optics.

Relativity

P. Havas, Professor Emeritus; Ph.D., Columbia, 1944. Special and general relativity, elementary particle physics, mathematical physics.

Statistical Physics

T. Burkhardt, Professor; Ph.D., Stanford, 1967. Statistical mechanics and many-body theory.
D. Forster, Professor; Ph.D., Harvard, 1969. Statistical mechanics and many-body theory.
E. Gawlinski, Associate Professor and Chairman; Ph.D., Boston University, 1983. Statistical mechanics and computational physics.
S. Y. Larsen, Professor Emeritus; Ph.D., Columbia, 1962. Quantum statistical physics, few-body problem, hyperspherical harmonics, molecular physics, chemical reactions.

Theoretical Atomic Physics

R. L. Intemann, Professor; Ph.D., Stevens, 1964. Atomic physics, inner-shell processes.

Barton Hall, the physics building.

The Elementary Particle Physics Laboratory.

UNIVERSITY OF CONNECTICUT

Department of Physics

Programs of Study

The Department of Physics offers programs of study and research leading to both the M.S. and Ph.D. degrees in atomic and molecular physics (experimental and theoretical), condensed-matter physics (experimental and theoretical), elementary particle and field theory, theory of general relativity and cosmology, nuclear physics (experimental and theoretical), and quantum optics and lasers (experimental and theoretical). The master's degree may be earned under either of two plans. One requires at least 15 credits and a thesis. The second plan, appropriate for those intending to pursue a Ph.D., requires 24 credits of course work but no thesis. Ordinarily, 24 credits of course work beyond the master's degree are included in the doctoral plan of study. Students continuing toward the Ph.D. must pass a general examination. The doctoral dissertation, written under the immediate and continuous supervision of an advisory committee, is expected to represent a significant contribution to the field of physics.

Admission to the graduate programs is limited and selective. Ordinarily, students who do not qualify for assistantships are not admitted. The master's degree generally requires one to two years to complete. The Ph.D. degree represents the equivalent of at least an additional two years of full-time study and research.

Research Facilities

The Department of Physics is located in the Edward Gant Science Complex, which also houses the Institute of Materials Science, the Department of Mathematics, and the University's Computer Center. The department provides well-equipped research facilities for theoretical and experimental atomic, molecular, and optical physics; condensed-matter physics; nuclear physics; and theoretical particle physics, astrophysics, and general relativity. The adjacent Institute of Materials Science provides additional research facilities for theoretical and experimental condensed-matter physics. The University's Computer Center maintains extensive computing facilities and high-speed digital communication links. The Department of Physics provides a computer research network consisting of advanced-function workstations and a variety of software for visualization, numerical analysis, program development, and symbolic processing.

Faculty members from the Department of Physics have developed joint research programs with Brookhaven National Laboratory, the Thomas Jefferson National Accelerator Facility, the Lawrence Livermore National Laboratory, Oak Ridge National Laboratory, the National Institute for Science and Technology, and many other American and international universities and research institutions.

Financial Aid

For the 2004–05 academic year, the nine-month graduate assistantship stipend ranges from $17,220 for entering students to $20,145 for those who have passed the general examinations. In addition, health insurance and tuition waivers (but not a waiver of fees) are provided to those holding assistantships. Assistantships are awarded competitively, and fellowship support is available for exceptionally well qualified candidates. Summer support is also available.

Cost of Study

In 2004–05, the cost per semester for a full-time graduate student is $3239 (tuition) plus $601 (fees) for Connecticut residents and $8415 (tuition) plus $601 (fees) for out-of-state students. The tuition portion is waived for those holding assistantships.

Living and Housing Costs

A limited amount of space is available in a graduate dormitory. The cost is $2087 per semester for 2004–05 (not including meals). In addition, rental units are available off campus. A description of local apartments is available on the World Wide Web at http://www.drl.uconn.edu.

Student Group

There are 80 full-time graduate students, almost all of whom are enrolled in the doctoral program. Nearly all the students have financial support, teaching or research assistantships, or fellowships. The atmosphere in the department is friendly and informal; students conducting thesis research can expect to work individually and closely with their faculty advisers.

Location

The University of Connecticut is located in the scenic New England community of Storrs, 25 miles northeast of Hartford, near Interstate 84. Boston (90 miles), New York (130 miles), and the Rhode Island beaches are all within easy driving distance. Hiking, cross-country skiing, canoeing, and fishing may be enjoyed within a 10-minute drive from campus. Many students ski in Vermont and New Hampshire during the winter. The University hosts a number of cultural and social events during the academic year.

The University and The Department

The University is a state-supported institution with an enrollment of approximately 17,200 undergraduate and 5,500 graduate students. It is the flagship institution in the state's system of higher education and has strong research programs in many areas. The physics faculty currently numbers 44 members, of whom 36 are from the Storrs campus and 8 are from other institutions. In addition to the core curriculum, the department provides a variety of courses and seminar series in several specialized areas. There is also a weekly colloquium series.

Applying

Prospective students are encouraged to apply in January for the following fall semester. While applications are considered at any time, early application optimizes the probability of receiving financial aid. International applications must include a TOEFL score for those whose native language is not English. All applicants must submit GRE General Test scores, and the Subject Test in physics is recommended, though optional. There is a $55 application fee when applying online; the fee is $75 for paper applications. Prospective students should consult the *Graduate Education and Research in Physics at the University of Connecticut* brochure, which can be obtained from the department. The brochure is also available at the department's Web site listed in the Correspondence and Information section.

Correspondence and Information

Professor William C. Stwalley, Head
Department of Physics, U-3046
University of Connecticut
2152 Hillside Road
Storrs, Connecticut 06269-3046

Telephone: 860-486-4924
Fax: 860-486-3346
E-mail: gradphysics@uconn.edu
World Wide Web: http://www.phys.uconn.edu

University of Connecticut

THE FACULTY AND THEIR RESEARCH

William C. Stwalley, Professor and Head; Ph.D., Harvard. Experimental atomic and molecular interactions, laser spectroscopy and dynamics of atoms and molecules, ultracold atoms and molecules.

Philip E. Best, Professor; Ph.D., Western Australia. Experimental condensed-matter physics: X-ray and electron spectrometry, surface physics.

Thomas Blum, Assistant Professor; Ph.D., Arizona. Theoretical high-energy physics, lattice gauge theory, quantum chromodynamics (QCD), electro-weak physics.

Joseph I. Budnick, Professor; Ph.D., Rutgers. Experimental condensed-matter physics: nuclear magnetic resonance, superconductivity, X-ray studies using synchrotron radiation.

Vernon F. Cormier, Professor of Geology and Geophysics; Ph.D., Columbia. Wave propagation in deep earth structures.

Robin Côté, Associate Professor; Ph.D., MIT. Theoretical atomic and molecular physics, ultracold collisions, Bose-Einstein condensation.

Andrey V. Dobrynin, Assistant Professor; Ph.D., Moscow Institute of Physics and Technology. Theoretical polymer physics; self-assembling polymers, polymer/nanoparticle mixtures.

Gerald V. Dunne, Professor; Ph.D., Imperial College (London). Theoretical high-energy physics: particle theory, quantum field theory.

Niloy K. Dutta, Professor; Ph.D., Cornell. Experimental condensed matter and optical physics, semiconductor laser technology, quantum wires, fiber optic transmission systems.

Edward E. Eyler, Professor; Ph.D., Harvard. Experimental atomic, molecular, and optical physics; precision laser spectroscopy.

Gayanath W. Fernando, Associate Professor; Ph.D., Cornell. Condensed-matter theory: electronic structure calculations.

George N. Gibson, Associate Professor; Ph.D., Illinois at Chicago. High-intensity short-pulse laser physics.

Phillip L. Gould, Professor; Ph.D., MIT. Experimental quantum optics: laser cooling and trapping of atoms.

Douglas S. Hamilton, Professor; Ph.D., Wisconsin–Madison. Experimental condensed-matter physics: laser spectroscopy.

William A. Hines, Professor; Ph.D., Berkeley. Experimental condensed-matter physics: nuclear magnetic resonance, magnetic susceptibility of metals and alloys.

Muhammad M. Islam, Professor; Ph.D., Imperial College (London). Theoretical high-energy physics: scattering, nucleon substructure.

Juha Javanainen, Professor; Ph.D., Helsinki Tech. Theoretical quantum optics, interaction of light with atoms.

Richard T. Jones, Associate Professor; Ph.D., Virginia Tech. Experimental nuclear physics: meson spectroscopy, low-energy QCD.

Kyungseon Joo, Assistant Professor; Ph.D., MIT. Experimental nuclear physics: electromagnetic excitation of nucleon resonances.

Lawrence A. Kappers, Professor; Ph.D., Missouri. Experimental condensed-matter physics: optical properties, color centers, radiation damage.

Birgit Kaufmann, Assistant Professor; Ph.D., Bonn (Germany). Condensed-matter theory, nonequilibrium statistical mechanics.

Quentin C. Kessel, Professor; Ph.D., Connecticut. Experimental atomic and molecular physics: ionization, X rays, and Auger electrons.

Alexander Kovner, Associate Professor; Ph.D., Tel-Aviv. Theoretical particle physics: strongly coupled gauge theories.

David P. Madacsi, Professor; Ph.D., Connecticut. Condensed-matter physics: paramagnetic resonance, computer modeling of lattice defects. (Avery Point Campus)

Ronald L. Mallett, Professor; Ph.D., Penn State. Theory of general relativity and cosmology.

Philip D. Mannheim, Professor; Ph.D., Weizmann (Israel). Elementary particle theory, field theory, general relativity, cosmology and astrophysics.

H. Harvey Michels, Research Professor; Ph.D., Delaware. Theoretical atomic and molecular physics.

Douglas M. Pease, Professor; Ph.D., Connecticut. Experimental condensed-matter physics: X-ray studies of alloys.

Cynthia W. Peterson, Professor; Ph.D., Cornell. Experimental condensed-matter physics.

Edward Pollack, Professor; Ph.D., NYU. Experimental atomic physics: atomic and molecular beams, atom-molecule collisions.

George H. Rawitscher, Professor; Ph.D., Stanford. Theoretical nuclear physics: nuclear reactions, electron-nucleus scattering.

Chandrasekhar Roychoudhari, Research Professor; Ph.D., Rochester. Experimental optical physics and semiconductor laser technology.

Jeffrey S. Schweitzer, Research Professor; Ph.D., Purdue. Experimental nuclear physics, nuclear astrophysics, solar physics.

Boris Sinkovic, Associate Professor; Ph.D., Hawaii. Experimental condensed-matter physics: spin-polarized photoemission, magnetic properties of films, surfaces, and nanostructures.

Winthrop W. Smith, Professor; Ph.D., MIT. Atomic and molecular physics: ion-atom collisions, XUV and laser spectroscopy.

Marcel Utz, Assistant Professor; Dr.Sc. (Techn.), ETH Zurich (Switzerland). Experimental polymer physics, NMR studies and computer modeling of plastic deformation.

Barrett O. Wells, Associate Professor; Ph.D., Stanford. Experimental condensed-matter physics: neutron scattering, photoemission, superconductivity.

Suzanne F. Yelin, Assistant Professor; Ph.D., Ludwig-Maximilians (Munich). Theoretical quantum optics and condensed-matter physics, spin physics in semiconductors, quantum coherence and quantum information.

Associated and Adjunct Faculty

John T. Bahns, Adjunct Associate Professor; Ph.D., Iowa. Experimental atomic, molecular, and optical physics. Research scientist, Northern Illinois University.

Stephen C. Bates, Adjunct Professor; Sc.D., MIT. Experimental condensed-matter physics. President, Thoughtventions Unlimited LLC.

Robert R. Birge, Schwenk Professor of Chemistry; Ph.D., Wesleyan. Biomolecular electronics, biomolecular spectroscopy.

Steven A. Boggs, Research Professor of Materials Science; Ph.D., Toronto. High-voltage dielectrics.

Edward S.-T. Chang, Adjunct Professor; Ph.D., California, Riverside. Theoretical atomic and molecular physics. Professor of Physics, University of Massachusetts.

Edward F. Deveney, Adjunct Assistant Professor; Ph.D., Connecticut. Experimental atomic and nuclear physics. Assistant Professor, Bridgewater State College.

David B. Fenner, Adjunct Associate Professor; Ph.D., Washington. Vice President and Director of Research, Epion, Corp.

Salvador M. Fernandez, Adjunct Professor; Ph.D., Connecticut. Medical physics. President, Ciencia, Inc.

A. Marjatta Lyyra, Adjunct Professor; Ph.D., Stockholm. Experimental atomic, molecular, and optical physics. Professor of Physics, Temple University.

Peter B. Mumola, Adjunct Professor; Ph.D., Texas. Vice President of the Optics Division, Zygo Corp.

Michael J. Ramsey-Musolf, Associate Professor; Ph.D., Princeton. Theoretical nuclear physics, electroweak interactions in nuclei, low energy QCD.

Henry Wang, Adjunct Associate Professor; Ph.D., Iowa. Experimental atomic, molecular, and optical physics. Research Associate II, Aerospace Corp.

Charles W. Wolgemuth, Assistant Professor of Physiology, UConn Health Center; Ph.D., Arizona. Physics of cellular motility, morphology, growth, and pattern formation.

Yide Zhang, Research Professor; Ph.D., Lanzhou (China). Experimental condensed-matter physics. Research Scientist, Infomat Corp.

Teaching assistants teach in modern laboratories using innovative methods.

A graduate student working on his dissertation with a postdoctoral fellow.

UNIVERSITY OF IDAHO

Department of Physics

Programs of Study

The department offers the M.S. (thesis and nonthesis) and Ph.D. degrees in physics. Areas of concentration are nuclear, condensed matter, plasma, atomic, and molecular physics; astrophysics; and physics education. The intellectual aim of the program is to train independent thinkers who are capable of identifying and solving research problems.

The M.S. degree is typically completed in two years. The Ph.D. degree typically requires two years of course work followed by a written qualifying examination and three years of research, culminating in the oral defense of the dissertation.

The department's research emphasizes theoretical and experimental topics in the areas of concentration. In the condensed matter area there is a growing and active interest in nanophysics. In all areas of research the graduate students work closely with faculty members, who pride themselves on close interaction with their graduate students.

Research Facilities

The University of Idaho (UI) Department of Physics has state-of-the-art laboratories with UV lasers, visible lasers, high-field magnets, high-performance computers, ultrahigh vacuum chambers, plasma devices, and advanced microscopes.

Financial Aid

Teaching and research assistants are paid approximately $1500 per month. These stipends are for twelve months. The department provides full tuition remission for both in-state and out-of-state students who are teaching and research assistants. Financial aid is also available through the Federal Perkins Loan Program and work-study grants. The Student Financial Aid Office can provide information and applications.

Cost of Study

For 2004–05, full-time graduate fees are $2086 per semester for Idaho residents, with an additional fee of $4010 per semester for nonresidents. Resident students enrolled part-time pay $205 per credit; nonresidents pay an additional $123 per credit for part-time work. There is no additional fee charged for nonresident credits for credits during the summer session. Full-time fees are charged for 8 credits or more. Fees are subject to change.

Living and Housing Costs

Graduate student housing is available through the University for $462 to $684 per month for apartments ranging in size from efficiencies to four-bedroom units. Potential graduate students are advised to reserve housing early. Off-campus housing lists are available on the Web at http://www.asui.udaho.edu.

Student Group

Graduate students in the department are an internationally diverse group. All students receive financial assistance, either through fellowships or assistantships, and all attend UI full-time.

Student Outcomes

University of Idaho's graduates successfully pursue careers in academia, industry, and national laboratories and are involved in entrepreneurial activities. Graduates include physics professors as well as research scientists in national laboratories. Graduates also work in such companies as Intel, Micron, and Hewlett-Packard.

Location

Moscow, located in the Idaho panhandle among the rolling hills of the Palouse, is an agricultural and recreational area and the cultural center of the region. Local music and theater productions have received international acclaim. Skiing and lake and river sports are within and easy drive. Spokane is 88 miles north, and Seattle and Portland are each 6 hours west.

The University

The University of Idaho was created in 1889, a year before Idaho became a state. UI is a publicly supported, comprehensive land-grant institution with principal responsibility in Idaho for performing research and granting the Ph.D. degree. More than 750 faculty members participate in teaching and research. In addition to the accreditation of individual programs, the University is accredited by the Northwest Association of Schools and Colleges.

Applying

Information regarding program offerings, deadlines, and requirements as well as general University information and the online application for admission can be accessed on the University's Web site. Requests by mail should be forwarded to the Graduate Admissions Office with an indication of the department or program of interest. All application materials should be forwarded to the Graduate Admissions Office. Official transcripts from every college and university attended should also be sent directly from the institution to the Graduate Admissions Office. Students who wish to apply for a departmental assistantship should consult with the department regarding the process and the deadline date, which may be earlier than the application deadline date.

Correspondence and Information

Ms. Luanne Semler
Department of Physics
University of Idaho
Moscow, Idaho 83844
Telephone: 208-885-6380
Fax: 208-885-4055
E-mail: luannes@uidaho.edu
World Wide Web: http://www.phys.uidaho.edu

University of Idaho

THE FACULTY AND THEIR RESEARCH

Atomic and Molecular Physics
Bernhard J. Stumpf, Associate Professor. Experimental atomic physics.

Condensed Matter Physics
Leah Bergman, Assistant Professor. Experimental condensed matter.
Chris Berven, Assistant Professor. Experimental nanophysics.
David N. McIlroy, Associate Professor. Experimental condensed matter.
You Qiang, Assistant Professor. Experimental nanophysics.
Wei-Jiang Yeh, Professor. Experimental condensed matter.

Nuclear Physics
Ruprecht Machleidt, Professor. Theoretical nuclear physics.
Francesca Sammarruca, Associate Professor. Theoretical nuclear physics.

Physics Education
George Patsakos, Associate Professor. Physics education.

UNIVERSITY OF KANSAS

Department of Physics and Astronomy

Programs of Study

The Department of Physics and Astronomy offers programs of study leading to the Ph.D. in physics and the M.S. in physics and computational physics and astronomy.

The master's degree in physics requires 30 hours of advanced courses (up to 6 of which may be transferred from another accredited university) and at least 2 hours of master's research with satisfactory progress. A minimum average of B is required, as is a general examination in physics. The various master's programs differ in their detailed requirements.

The Ph.D. program begins with formal course work (which typically extends through two years for a well-prepared student) and, after admission to candidacy, is followed by Ph.D. research. The required courses include those needed for the M.S. in physics, so it is possible to obtain the M.S. on the way to the Ph.D. degree. Course work should average better than a B. There is no language requirement, but a demonstrated skill in computer programming related to the student's field of study is required. A written preliminary exam and a comprehensive exam are required for admission to candidacy. Following the comprehensive exam, the student may choose a research project from the broad spectrum of experimental and theoretical research areas represented within the department. These include high-energy particle physics, astrophysics and cosmology, biophysics, astrobiology, space physics, plasma physics, solid-state and condensed-matter physics, nonlinear dynamics, and nuclear physics. After carrying out the research project under the guidance of a faculty member, the student must submit a dissertation showing the results of original research and must defend it in a final oral examination. A minimum of three full academic years of residency is required; the actual time taken to complete the Ph.D. varies considerably.

Research Facilities

Extensive computing facilities exist both in the department and at the University. A large collection of books and journals is contained in the adjacent student shop. Condensed-matter physics facilities include an advanced materials research lab, a quantum electronics lab, and a semiconductor laser optics lab. These labs are well equipped with thin–film deposition systems, a new scanning electron microscope, a unique UHV multiprobe scanning microscopy system, an X-ray diffractometer, SQUID magnetometers, a 6-mK dilution refrigerator, microwave synthesizers and a vector network analyzer, a Nd:YAG laser, and an optical parametric oscillator. A clean room with photo- and electron-beam lithography as well as wafer processing tools is also available for micro- and nanofabrication of solid state devices and circuits. The high-energy physics and nuclear physics groups utilize experimental facilities at various universities and national laboratories as part of collaborative experiments. The Kansas Institute of Theoretical and Computational Science sponsors interdisciplinary research among the Departments of Physics and Anatomy, Mathematics, and Chemistry. The Astrobiology Working Group collaborates with the Biodiversity Research Institute, the Department of Geology, and the Department of Ecology and Evolutionary Biology.

Financial Aid

The principal form of financial aid is the graduate teaching assistantship; most first-year graduate students in the department have this type of support. A half-time teaching assistantship, which is the usual appointment, carries a nine-month stipend of $13,000 plus a 100 percent tuition fee waiver. Summer support is also available. Beginning graduate students may also be considered for graduate school fellowships in a University-wide competition. A few research assistantships are available for qualified first-year students, although the tendency is to award such assistantships to more advanced students.

Cost of Study

Full-time students with private support or with fellowships from sources outside the University paid tuition of $135 per credit hour for graduate-level courses in 2002–03 if they were Kansas residents and $389 per credit hour if they were nonresidents. Typical enrollments range from about 9 to 12 credit hours per semester during the first year. University fees are set by the Board of Regents and are subject to change at any time.

Living and Housing Costs

Room and board are available in University dormitories; the starting cost for the 2003–04 academic year was $4642. There are a limited number of one- and two-bedroom University apartments for married students and their families; the rent for 2003–04 was $268–$520 per month plus utilities. Many rooms and apartments, both furnished and unfurnished, are available off campus.

Student Group

The University of Kansas has an enrollment of approximately 26,000 students, including about 6,000 graduate students. The department enrolls approximately 45 graduate students drawn from throughout the United States and abroad. Most of these students are supported as either teaching assistants or research assistants.

Location

The University's main campus occupies 1,000 acres on and around Mount Oread in the city of Lawrence, a growing community of 75,000 located among the forested, rolling hills of eastern Kansas. Near Lawrence are four lake resort areas for boating, fishing, and swimming. Metropolitan Kansas City lies about 40 miles east of Lawrence via interstate highway and offers a variety of cultural and recreational activities.

The University

The University of Kansas is a state-supported school founded in 1866. Long known for its commitment to academic excellence, the University considers research an important part of the educational process. In addition to the College of Liberal Arts and Sciences and the Graduate School, the University houses a number of professional schools and programs, which include Engineering, Medicine, Law, Business, Journalism, and many others.

Applying

Completed applications should be received by March 1, for those requesting graduate teaching assistantships for the fall semester; applications are accepted until all the positions are filled, but preference is given to those received by the priority date. Applications for admissions that do not require assistantships should be completed by July 1.

Correspondence and Information

For application forms and admission:

Graduate Admissions Officer
Department of Physics and Astronomy
1251 Wescoe Hall Drive, Room 1082
University of Kansas
Lawrence, Kansas 66045-7582

Telephone: 785-864-4626
E-mail: physics@ku.edu
World Wide Web: http://www.physics.ku.edu

University of Kansas

THE FACULTY AND THEIR RESEARCH

Raymond G. Ammar, Professor; Ph.D., Chicago, 1959. Experimental high-energy physics.
Barbara J. Anthony-Twarog, Professor; Ph.D., Yale, 1981. Observational astronomy, stellar evolution in open star clusters, CCD and photoelectric photometry, globular clusters.
Thomas P. Armstrong, Professor Emeritus; Ph.D., Iowa, 1966. Space physics, plasma physics.
Scott R. Baird, Adjunct Professor; Ph.D., Washington (Seattle), 1979. Stellar spectroscopy, variable stars.
Philip S. Baringer, Professor; Ph.D., Indiana, 1985. Experimental high-energy physics.
Alice L. Bean, Professor; Ph.D., Carnegie Mellon, 1987. Experimental high-energy physics.
Robert C. Bearse, Professor Emeritus; Ph.D., Rice, 1964. Experimental nuclear physics, nuclear safeguards, materials control and accounting, computer database applications.
David Z. Besson, Professor; Ph.D., Rutgers, 1986. Experimental high-energy physics.
Wai-Yim Ching, Adjunct Professor; Ph.D., LSU, 1974. Solid-state physics, electronic structures.
Thomas E. Cravens, Professor; Ph.D., Harvard, 1975. Space physics, plasma physics.
Jack W. Culvahouse, Professor Emeritus; Ph.D., Harvard, 1957. Experimental condensed-matter physics, magnetic properties of solids, computer simulations of transport in solids.
John P. Davidson, Professor Emeritus; Ph.D., Washington (St. Louis), 1952. Theoretical nuclear structure physics, atomic physics, astrophysics.
Robin E. P. Davis, Professor and Associate Chairman; D.Phil., Oxford, 1962. Experimental high-energy physics.
Gisela Dreschhoff, Courtesy Associate Professor; Dr.Sc., Braunschweig Technical (Germany), 1972. Geophysics, energy storage in solids.
Joe R. Eagleman, Professor Emeritus; Ph.D., Missouri, 1963. Atmospheric science.
Jacob Enoch, Associate Professor Emeritus; Ph.D., Wisconsin, 1956. Theoretical physics.
Hume A. Feldman, Associate Professor; Ph.D., SUNY at Stony Brook, 1989. Astrophysics and cosmology.
Christopher J. Fischer, Assistant Professor; Ph.D., Michigan, 2000. Biophysics.
Robert J. Friauf, Professor Emeritus; Ph.D., Chicago, 1953. Experimental condensed-matter physics, diffusion and color centers, molecular dynamics and Monte Carlo simulations.
Paul Goldhammer, Professor Emeritus; Ph.D., Washington (St. Louis), 1956. Theoretical physics, nuclear structure physics, atomic physics.
Siyuan Han, Professor; Ph.D., Iowa State, 1986. Experimental condensed-matter physics.
Ralph W. Krone, Professor Emeritus; Ph.D., Johns Hopkins, 1949. Experimental nuclear physics.
Nowhan Kwak, Professor; Ph.D., Tufts, 1962. Experimental high-energy physics.
Danny Marfatia, Assistant Professor; Ph.D., Wisconsin, 2001. Particle astrophysics.
Carl D. McElwee, Courtesy Professor; Ph.D., Kansas, 1970. Geophysics, magnetic properties of solids.
Douglas W. McKay, Professor; Ph.D., Northwestern, 1968. Theoretical elementary particle physics and particle astrophysics.
Mikhail V. Medvedev, Assistant Professor; Ph.D., California, San Diego, 1996. Astrobiology, theoretical astrophysics, space physics and plasma physics.
Adrian L. Melott, Professor; Ph.D., Texas, 1981. Astrobiology, astrophysics and cosmology.
Herman J. Munczek, Professor Emeritus; Ph.D., Buenos Aires, 1958. Theoretical elementary particle physics.
Michael J. Murray, Assistant Professor; Ph.D., Pittsburgh, 1989. Experimental nuclear physics.
Jeffrey S. Olafsen, Assistant Professor; Ph.D., Duke, 1994. Experimental physics, nonlinear dynamics and granular media.
Linda J. Olafsen, Assistant Professor; Ph.D., Duke, 1997. Experimental condensed-matter physics, semiconductor physics.
Francis W. Prosser, Professor Emeritus; Ph.D., Kansas, 1955. Experimental nuclear physics.
John P. Ralston, Professor; Ph.D., Oregon, 1980. Theoretical elementary particle physics and particle astrophysics.
Stephen J. Sanders, Professor and Department Chairman; Ph.D., Yale, 1977. Experimental nuclear physics.
Richard C. Sapp, Professor Emeritus; Ph.D., Ohio State, 1955. Experimental solid-state physics.
Sergei F. Shandarin, Professor; Ph.D., Moscow Physical Technical Institute, 1971. Astrophysics and cosmology, large-scale structure, nonlinear dynamics, computational physics.
Stephen J. Shawl, Professor; Ph.D., Texas, 1972. Observational astronomy, stellar astronomy, polarization, globular clusters.
Jicong Shi, Associate Professor; Ph.D., Houston, 1991. Theoretical physics, nonlinear dynamics, beam dynamics, accelerator physics.
Don W. Steeples, Courtesy Professor; Ph.D., Stanford, 1975. Geophysics.
Robert Stump, Professor Emeritus; Ph.D., Illinois, 1950. Experimental high-energy physics.
Bruce A. Twarog, Professor; Ph.D., Yale, 1980. Observational astronomy, stellar nucleosynthesis, chemical evolution of galaxies, stellar photometry.
Graham W. Wilson, Assistant Professor; Ph.D., Lancaster, 1989. Experimental high-energy physics.
Gordon G. Wiseman; Professor Emeritus; Ph.D., Kansas, 1950. Experimental solid-state physics.
Kai-Wai Wong, Professor Emeritus; Ph.D., Northwestern, 1962. Many-body theory, superconductivity, liquid helium.
Judy Z. Wu, Professor; Ph.D., Houston, 1993. Experimental condensed-matter physics, low-temperature physics.

UNIVERSITY OF MARYLAND, COLLEGE PARK

Department of Physics

Programs of Study With an exceptional breadth of research programs and numerous outstanding faculty members, the University of Maryland's Department of Physics explores both theoretical and experimental physics.

The department offers a Doctor of Philosophy (Ph.D.) program and a Master of Science (M.S.) program both with and without a thesis. Typically, doctoral candidates pass a written qualifying examination and complete core course work in their first year and pass the Graduate Laboratory in their second year. In their third and fourth years, candidates complete advanced course work (including courses outside their fields of specialization), seminars, and dissertation research before presenting and defending their dissertations.

Students pursuing a master's degree without a thesis complete 30 credits of course work, present a scholarly paper for review by faculty members, and must pass a comprehensive examination. Students pursuing a master's degree with a thesis complete 30 credits of course work and research before taking an oral examination defending their thesis.

The department comprises more than thirty research groups and centers, including Atomic, Molecular, and Optical Physics; Chaos and Non-Linear Dynamics (currently ranked number one in the country); Charged Particles Beam Research, Chemical Physics; Dynamical Systems and Accelerator Theory; Condensed Matter (Theory and Experiment); the East West Space Science Center; Gravitation (Theory and Experiment); Elementary Particle and Quantum Field Theory; High Energy Physics; the Institute for Advanced Computer Studies; the Institute for Physical Science and Technology; the Institute for Research in Electronics and Applied Physics; Materials Research Science and Engineering Center; Mathematical Physics; Nuclear Physics; Particle Astrophysics; the Center for Particle and String Theory; Physics Education; Plasma Physics (Theory and Experiment); Space Physics; the Center for Superconductivity Research; Quantum Electronics and Relativity; and Quarks, Hadrons, and Nuclear Theory.

Research Facilities The University of Maryland Department of Physics has world-renowned, state-of-the-art facilities, including instrumentation for fabricating nanostructures with characterization down to the atomic scale, ultrahigh-sensitivity electrical and magnetic properties measurement, ion beam research with high-brightness ion beam sources, advanced accelerator applications using charged particle beams, high-power microwave generation, and plasma spectroscopy and diagnostics.

The department possesses a variety of microscopes—a low-energy electron, holographic laser tweezer array, optical, tunneling, microwave, magnetic force, electrostatic force, atomic force, photoemission electron, and SQUID (superconducting quantum interference device) systems—for extensive research in a variety of fields. Through key collaborations, Maryland students, faculty members, and researchers also have access to the facilities of government agencies, private laboratories, and peer institutions. The department has also developed the largest collection of physics lecture demonstrations in the United States and one of the best in the world with two revolving stage auditoriums and 1,500 demonstrations. It also boasts world-class shop facilities including Mechanical Development, Electronic Development, and Engineering and Design.

Financial Aid Appointments as teaching assistants (compensation taxable) are normally available to all entering students. In addition to tuition remission, students received a $14,302 stipend for the 2003–04 academic year (20 hours per week) and a $3698 (also taxable) summer stipend for a total calendar year stipend of $18,000. Fellowships, research assistantships, and student loans are available.

Cost of Study Students in good standing are fully supported for their entire graduate careers, and the majority of entering students are also awarded full tuition remission.

Living and Housing Costs Housing is available within walking distance to campus. One-bedroom apartments in the area currently rent for $600 to $1000 per month, and efficiency/studios are generally $500 to $800 per month. Trained off-campus housing peer advisers are available for consultation or any questions that students may have (telephone: 301-314-3645).

Student Group The department's 200 physics graduate students represent a diversity in gender and national, ethnic, and academic backgrounds.

Location Nine miles from downtown Washington, D.C., and 30 miles from Baltimore and Annapolis, the department is surrounded by the nation's foremost physics associations, a growing corridor of private industry, and some of the world's best government laboratories, including NASA Goddard Space Flight Center, the National Institutes of Health, the Naval Research Laboratory, and the National Institute of Standards and Technology. These neighbors provide students with unparalleled opportunities for work, study, and collaboration.

The University Established in 1859, the University of Maryland is a large, diverse research university of national stature, highly regarded for its broad base of excellence in both teaching and research. According to *U.S. News & World Report,* the department's doctoral program is ranked fourth among physics departments at public universities and thirteenth overall nationwide.

Applying Applications are available from the Graduate Entrance Committee, Department of Physics, University of Maryland, College Park, Maryland 20742-4111 or online at http://www.inform.umd.edu/grad. A nonrefundable fee of $50 for U.S. residents and international students must accompany each application. The application deadline for all applicants is February 1. Spring applications are not accepted. Admission consideration is open to all qualified candidates without regard to race, color, national origin, religion, sex, or handicap.

Correspondence and Information

Linda O'Hara
Department of Physics Graduate Secretary
1120 Physics Building
University of Maryland
College Park, Maryland 20742
Telephone: 301-405-5982
Fax: 301-405-4061
E-mail: lohara@physics.umd.edu
World Wide Web: http://www.physics.umd.edu

University of Maryland, College Park

THE FACULTY AND THEIR RESEARCH

Professors

Carroll O. Alley Jr., Ph.D., Princeton, 1962: atomic physics, quantum electronics–quantum mechanics, relativistic gravity. J. Robert Anderson, Ph.D., Iowa State, 1963: experimental condensed-matter physics, diluted semiconductors, electronic structures of metals and semimetals. Steven Anlage, Ph.D., Caltech, 1988: superconductivity–electromagnetic properties, proximity effect, near-field microwave microscopy, experimental chaos. Thomas Antonsen, Ph.D., Cornell, 1977: plasma physics. Andrew R. Baden, Ph.D., Berkeley, 1986: experimental high-energy physics, data acquisition, high-performance computing, data analysis. Manoj K. Banerjee, Ph.D., Calcutta, 1956: nuclear chemistry, Baryon structure, Baryon-Meson interactions. Elizabeth J. Beise, Ph.D., MIT, 1988: experimental nuclear physics–intermediate energy, electron scattering, polarization, few-nucleon and subnucleon systems. Satindar M. Bhagat, Ph.D., Delhi, 1956: experimental condensed-matter physics, magnetic resonance, exotic magnetic phases, high-temperature superconductors. Derek A. Boyd, Ph.D., Stevens, 1973: plasma diagnostics, far-infrared spectroscopy, microwave optics. Dieter R. Brill, Ph.D., Princeton, 1959: general relativity and gravitation. Chia-Cheh Chang, Ph.D., USC, 1968: experimental nuclear physics–intermediate energy. Nicholas S. Chant, D.Phil., Oxford, 1966: experimental nuclear physics, electron physics. Hsing-Hen Chen, Ph.D., Columbia, 1973: plasma physics, nonlinear dynamical systems. Thomas D. Cohen, Ph.D., Pennsylvania, 1984: nuclear theory, soliton models, chiral symmetry, low-energy models for QCD. Sankar Das Sarma, Distinguished University Professor; Ph.D., Brown, 1979: theoretical condensed matter, many-body theory, semiconductor nanostructures, nonequilibrium statistical mechanics. J. Robert Dorfman, Ph.D., Johns Hopkins, 1961: statistical and thermal physics, dynamical systems. James F. Drake, Ph.D., UCLA, 1975: plasma physics, magnetic reconnection, tokamak transport. Dennis Drew, Ph.D., Cornell, 1967: experimental condensed matter, statistical and thermal physics, semiconductor heterostructures, infrared properties of superconductors. Theodore L. Einstein, Ph.D., Pennsylvania, 1973: condensed-matter theory, surface physics, statistical and thermal physics. Michael E. Fisher, Distinguished University Professor and University System of Maryland Regents Professor; Ph.D., King's College (London), 1957: statistical physics, condensed-matter theory, theoretical chemistry, phase transitions and critical phenomena. S. James Gates, John S. Toll Professor of Physics; Ph.D., MIT, 1977: elementary particles–supersymmetry, supergravity, and superstrings. Arnold J. Glick, Ph.D., Maryland, 1961: condensed-matter theory, statistical and thermal physics. George Gloeckler, Distinguished University Professor; Ph.D., Chicago, 1965: space physics, heliospheric physics. Jordan A. Goodman, Department Chair; Ph.D., Maryland, 1978: particle astrophysics. Oscar W. Greenberg, Ph.D., Princeton, 1956: elementary particles and field theory. Richard L. Greene, Ph.D., Stanford, 1967: experimental condensed matter. James J. Griffin, Ph.D., Princeton, 1956: nuclear theory, nuclear heavy ion physics. Nicholas J. Hadley, Ph.D., Berkeley, 1983: high-energy physics. Douglas C. Hamilton, Ph.D., Chicago, 1977: experimental space physics, magnetospheric physics, solar wind, particle acceleration and transport. Adil B. Hassam, Ph.D., Princeton, 1978: plasma physics of the sun, thermonuclear fusion. Wendell Hill, Ph.D., Stanford, 1980: plasma physics of the sun, thermonuclear fusion. Bei-Lok Hu, Ph.D., Princeton, 1972: general relativity, gravitation and cosmology, quantum field theory. Theodore A. Jacobson, Ph.D., Texas at Austin, 1983: gravitation theory, quantum gravity, black hole thermodynamics. Abolhassan Jawahery, Ph.D., Tufts, 1981: high-energy physics with accelerators. Xiangdong Ji, Ph.D., Drexel, 1987: theoretical nuclear physics, quantum chromodynamics, quark and gluon structure of hadrons. James J. Kelly, Ph.D., MIT, 1981: experimental nuclear physics. Young Suh Kim, Ph.D., Princeton, 1961: elementary particles, group theory. Theodore Kirkpatrick, Ph.D., Rockefeller, 1981: theoretical statistical mechanics, condensed matter. Victor Korenman, Assistant Provost; Ph.D., Harvard, 1966: theoretical condensed-matter physics. Donald N. Langenberg, Chancellor, University of Maryland System; Ph.D., Berkeley, 1959: condensed-matter physics. Chuan Sheng Liu, Ph.D., Berkeley, 1968: plasma physics, fusion and space science. Christopher J. Lobb, Ph.D., Harvard, 1980: experimental superconductivity, superconducting devices, mesoscopic systems. Glenn M. Mason, Ph.D., Chicago, 1971: space plasma physics, cosmic rays, heliospheric physics. Howard Milchberg, Ph.D., Princeton, 1985: atomic, molecular, and optical physics. Charles W. Misner, Ph.D., Princeton, 1957: general relativity, physics education. Rabindra N. Mohapatra, Ph.D., Rochester, 1969: elementary particles, quantum field theory, cosmology. Gottlieb Oehrlein, Ph.D., SUNY at Albany, 1981. Novel materials, low-temperature plasma science. Luis Orozco, Ph.D., Texas at Austin, 1987: experimental AMO physics, quantum optics, precision measurements and fundamental interactions. Edward Ott, Distinguished University Professor; Ph.D., Polytechnic of Brooklyn, 1967: chaotic dynamics, plasmas. Ho Jung Paik, Ph.D., Stanford, 1974: experimental general relativity, gravitational waves, precision tests of laws of gravity. Dennis Papadopoulos, Ph.D., Maryland, 1968: space plasma physics, lightning, photoconducting plasmas. Robert L. Park, Ph.D., Brown, 1964: experimental condensed-matter physics, surface physics, science policy. Jogesh C. Pati, Ph.D., Maryland, 1960: theoretical particle physics–grand unification, supersymmetry, superstrings, particle cosmology. William D. Phillips, Distinguished University Professor and Nobel Laureate; Ph.D., MIT, 1976: AMO physics, laser trapping and cooling. Raymond J. Phaneuf, Ph.D., Wisconsin–Madison, 1985: materials research. Ramamoorthy Ramesh (joint with Materials and Nuclear Engineering), Ph.D., Berkeley, 1987: superconductivity–metal oxide thin films, nanofabrications technologies, information storage, technology transfer. Edward F. Redish, Ph.D., MIT, 1968: physics education research. Philip G. Roos, Ph.D., MIT, 1964: experimental nuclear physics–electroweak interactions, hadron-induced reactions. Steven Rolston, Ph.D., SUNY at Stony Brook. AMO physics, laser spectroscopy of isotopes. Rajarshi Roy, Ph.D., Rochester, 1981: nonlinear dynamics, laser physics, optical fibers, coherence and stochastic processes. Roald Z. Sagdeev, , Ph.D., Institute of Physical Problems, Moscow, 1960; D.S., USSR Academy of Sciences, 1962: plasma physics, controlled fusion, space physics, arms control, science policy, global security and environment. Andris Skuja, Ph.D., Berkeley, 1972: experimental particle physics. Stephen J. Wallace, Ph.D., Washington (Seattle), 1971: scattering theory, nucleon-nucleon interactions, relativistic bound states, electron scattering. Richard Webb, Distinguished University Professor and Alford Ward Chaired Professor of Semiconductor Physics; Ph.D., California, San Diego, 1973: experimental condensed-matter physics, mesoscopic physics. John Weeks, Ph.D., Chicago, 1969: materials research. Frederick C. Wellstood, Ph.D., Berkeley, 1988: superconductivity–high-T_c (YBCO), superconducting quantum interference devices, magnetic microscopy, Coulomb blockade electrometers. Ellen D. Williams, Distinguished University Fellow; Ph.D., Caltech, 1982: condensed-matter physics, surface science, scanning tunneling microscopy, statistical mechanics of surfaces. James A. Yorke, Ph.D., Maryland, 1966. Chaos and nonlinear dynamics.

Associate Professors

Richard F. Ellis, Ph.D., Princeton, 1970: experimental plasma physics, plasma waves and instabilities, microwave and far-infrared diagnostics. Sarah C. Eno, Ph.D., Rochester, 1990: experimental high-energy physics. David Hammer (joint with Department of Curriculum and Instruction, Science Teaching Center), Ph.D., Berkeley, 1991: physics education—learning and teaching. Daniel P. Lathrop, Ph.D., Texas at Austin, 1991: nonlinear dynamics and chaos, turbulence, fluid dynamics. Markus A. Luty, Ph.D., Chicago, 1991: particle theory: nonperturbative QCD, dynamical symmetry breaking, nonperturbative supersymmetry, particle cosmology. Douglas A. Roberts, Ph.D., UCLA, 1994: experimental high-energy physics with accelerators. Gregory W. Sullivan, Ph.D., Illinois, 1990: electroweak physics, standard model, top quark search. Victor M. Yakovenko, Ph.D., Landau Institute for Theoretical Physics (Moscow), 1987: condensed-matter theory, organic and high-T_c superconductors, quantum Hall effect, high magnetic fields.

Assistant Professors

Melanie Becker, Ph.D., Rheinische Friedrich-Wilhelms-Universität (Germany), 1994: elementary particle theory, string and M-theory, black hole physics, mirror symmetry, D-branes. William Dorland, Ph.D., Princeton, 1993: computational plasma physics. Michael Fuhrer, Ph.D., Berkeley, 1998: electronic properties of carbon nanotubes and other nanostructures. Wolfgang Losert, Ph.D., CUNY, City College, 1998: nonlinear dynamics, pattern formation.

Research Faculty

Andrei Belitsky, Ph.D., Bogoliubov, Lab of Theoretical Physics (Russia): theoretical quarks, hadrons, and nuclei. Eric Blaufuss, Ph.D., LSU, 2000: particle astrophysics. Oleksandr Bondarchuk, Ph.D., Kiev Shevchenko (Ukraine), 1995: materials research science and engineering. Herbert Breuer, Ph.D., Heidelberg (Germany), 1976: experimental nuclear physics. Mihir Desai, Birmingham, Ph.D., 1995: space physics. Victor Galitsky, Ph.D., Moscow Engineering Physics Institute, 2000: condensed-matter theory. Stephanie Getty, Ph.D., Florida, 2001: experimental condensed matter. Robert Gluckstern, Ph.D., MIT, 2000: dynamical systems. Tullio Grassi, Padova (Italy), 2000: high-energy physics. Matthew Hill, Ph.D., Maryland, 2001: space physics. Fred M. Ipavich, Ph.D., Maryland, 1972: space physics. Alexei Kaminski, Ph.D., Minnesota, 2001: condensed-matter theory. Hung-Chih Kan, Ph.D., Maryland, 1986: condensed matter. Richard G. Kellogg, Ph.D., Yale, 1975: high-energy physics. Eam Khor, Ph.D, Monash (Australia), 1971: condensed-matter theory. Byong Kim, Ph.D., Rensselaer, 1996: condensed matter. Annamaria Kiss, Ph.D., Aix-Marseilles II, 2000: string and particle theory. Axel Krause, Ph.D., Hamburg (Germany), 2000: elementary particles. Suichi Kunori, Tohoku, 1981: high-energy physics. Laura Lising, Ph.D., Berkeley, 1999: physics education. Baoting Liu, Ph.D., Academia Sinica Beijing, 1999: superconductivity. John, Matthews, Ph.D., Maryland, 2002: superconductivity. Martin Moody, Ph.D., Virginia, 1980: gravitation experiment. Satishchandra Ogale, Ph.D., Poona (India), 1980: superconductivity. John Paquette, Ph.D., Maryland, 1992: space physics. Jeong-Young Park, Ph.D., Seoul National, 1999: experimental condensed matter. Kwon Park, Ph.D., SUNY at Stony Brook, 2000: condensed-matter theory. Donald Priour, Ph.D., Princeton, 2000: condensed-matter theory. Wilfried Rabaud, Ph.D., Grenoble (France): experimental condensed matter. Danilo Romero, Ph.D., Maryland, 1989: experimental condensed matter. Albert Roura, Ph.D., Barcelona, 2002: gravitation theory. Vito Scarola, Ph.D., Penn State, 2002: condensed-matter theory. Jochen Schieck, Ph.D., Heidelberg, 1999: high-energy physics. Don Schmadel, Ph.D., Maryland, 2002: experimental condensed matter. Rajeshwar P. Sharma, Ph.D., Bombay, 1964: superconductivity. Edward Shaya, Ph.D., Hawaii, 1984: astrometrology. Sanjay Shinde, Ph.D., Poona (India), 1999: superconductivity. Kazutomu Shiokawa, Ph.D., Maryland, 1997: gravitation theory. Andrew Smith, Ph.D., California, Irvine, 1996: particle astrophysics. Andrei Stanishevsky, Ph.D., Belarus Academy of Sciences: materials research science. T. Venky Venkatesan, Ph.D., CUNY, Brooklyn, 1977: superconductivity. Igor Zutic, Ph.D., Minnesota, Twin Cities, 1998: condensed-matter theory.

University of Maryland, College Park

SELECTED PUBLICATIONS

Alley, C. O., D. Leiter, Y. Mizobuchi, and H. Yilmaz. Energy crisis in astrophysics: Black holes vs. N-body metrics. *Los Alamos E-Print Archive* astro-ph/9906458, 1999.

Anderson, J. R., et al. Concentration dependence of the exchange interaction in Pb(1-x)Eu(x)Te. *Phys. Rev. B* 55:4400, 1997.

Booth, J. C., et al. **(S. M. Anlage).** Large dynamical fluctuations in the microwave conductivity of YBa_2Cu_3O_{7-delta}. *Phys. Rev. Lett.* 77:4438, 1996.

Baden, A. R. Jets and kinematics in hadronic collisions. *Int. J. Mod. Phys. A* 13:1817–45, 1998.

Banerjee, M. K., and J. Milana. Baryon mass splitting in chiral perturbation theory. *Phys. Rev. D: Part. Fields* 54:6451, 1995.

Spayde, D. T., et al. **(E. J. Beise** and **H. Breuer).** Parity violation in elastic electron-proton scattering and the proton's strange magnetic form factor. *Phys. Rev. Lett.* 84, 2000.

Abbott, D., et al. **(E. J. Beise, N. S. Chant,** and **P. G. Roos).** A precise measurement of the deuteron elastic structure function $A(Q^2)$. *Phys. Rev. Lett.* 82:1379, 1999.

Meekins, D. G., **E. J. Beise,** and **N. S. Chant.** Coherent pi^0 photoproduction on the deuteron up to 4 GeV. *Phys. Rev. C* 60:052201, 1999.

Lofland, S. E., et al. **(S. M. Bhagat** and **R. Ramesh).** Magnetic imaging of perovskite thin films by ferromagnetic resonance microscopy—$La_{0.7}Sr_{0.3}MnO_3$. *Appl. Phys. Lett.* V75(12):1947–8, 1999.

Celata, C. M., and **D. A. Boyd**. Cyclotron radiation as a diagnostic tool for tokamak plasmas. *Nucl. Fusion* 17:735, 1977.

Naples, D., et al. **(H. Breuer** and **C. C. Chang).** A dependence of photoproduced dijets. *Phys. Rev. Lett.* 72:2341, 1994.

Brill, D., G. Horowitz, D. Kastor, and J. Traschen. Testing cosmic censorship with black hole collisions. *Phys. Rev. D* 49:840, 1994.

Chen, H. H., and J. E. Lin. Integrability of higher dimensional nonlinear Hamiltonian systems. *J. Math. Phys.,* 1998.

Cohen, T. D., R. J. Furnstahl, and D. K. Griegel. Quark and gluon condensates in nuclear matter. *Phys. Rev. C: Nucl. Phys.* 45:1881, 1992.

Das Sarma, S., and D. W. Wang. Many-body renormalization of semiconductor quantum wire excitons: Absorption, gain, binding, and unbinding. *Phys. Rev. Lett.* 84:2010, 2000.

Dorfman, J. R. *An Introduction to Chaos in Nonequilibrium Statistical Mechanics.* Cambridge: Cambridge University Press, 1999.

Jenko, F. and **W. Dorland.** Prediction of significant tokamak turbulence at electron gyroradius scales. *Phys. Rev. Lett.* 89:225001, 2002.

Drake, J. F., et al. Formation of electron holes and particle energization during magnetic reconnection. *Science* 299:873, 2003.

M. Grayson, et al. **(H. D. Drew).** Spectral measurement of the Hall angle response in normal state cuprate superconductors. *Phys. Rev. Lett.* 89:037003, 2002.

Einstein, T. L. Interactions between adsorbate particles. In *Physical Structure of Solid Surfaces,* ed. W. N. Unertl. Amsterdam: Elsevier, 1996.

Austin, M. E., **R. F. Ellis,** R. A. James, and T. C. Luce. Electron temperature measurements from optically gray third harmonic electron cyclotron emission in the DIII-D tokamak. *Phys. Plasmas* 3:10, 3725, 1996.

Carena, M., et al. **(S. Eno).** Searches for supersymmetric particles at the tevatron collider. *Rev. Mod. Phys.* 71:937–81, 1999.

Luijten, E., **M. E. Fisher,** and A. Z. Panagiotopoulos. Universality class of criticality in the restricted primitive model electrolyte. *Phys. Rev. Lett.* 88:185701:1–4, 2002.

Gates Jr., S. J., and O. Lebedev. Searching for supersymmetry in hadrons. *Phys. Lett. B* 477:216, 2000.

Glick, A., L. E. Henrickson, G. W. Bryant, and D. F. Barbe. Nonequilibrium green's function theory of transport in interacting quantum dots. *Phys. Rev. B* 50:4482, 1994.

Geiss, J., et al. **(G. Gloeckler** and **F. M. Ipavich).** The southern high speed stream: Results from SWICS/Ulysses. *Science,* May 1995.

Gluckstern, R. L., and B. Zotter. Analysis of shielding charged particle beams by thin conductors. *Phys. Rev. ST Accel. Beams* 4:024402, 2001.

Fukuda, Y., et al. **(J. A. Goodman).** Evidence for oscillation of atmospheric neutrinos. (Super-Kamiokande Collaboration.) *Phys. Rev. Lett.* 81:1562–7, 1998.

Greenberg, O. W. CPT violation implies violation of Lorentz invariance. *Phys. Rev. Lett.* 89:231602, 2002.

Parkin, S. S. P., et al. **(R. L. Greene).** Superconductivity in a new family of organic conductors. *Phys. Rev. Lett.* 50:270, 1983.

Griffin, J. J. The statistical model of intermediate structure. *Phys. Rev. Lett.* 17:478, 1966.

Abachi, S., and **N. J. Hadley.** Observation of the top quark. *Phys. Rev. Lett.* 74:2632, 1995.

Hamilton, D. C., G. Gloeckler, S. M. Krimigis and L. J. Lanzerotti. Composition of nonthermal ions in the Jovian magnetosphere. *J. Geophys. Res.* 86:8301, 1981.

Hammer, D. Student resources for learning introductory physics. *Am. J. Phys. Phys. Educ. Res. Suppl.* 68(S1):S52–9, 2000.

Hassam, A. B. Reconnection of stressed magnetic fields. *Astrophys. J.* 399:159, 1992.

Hu, B. L. Stochastic gravity. *Int. J. Theor. Phys.* 38:2987, 1999.

Jacobson, T. Trans-Planckian redshifts and the substance of the space-time river. *Prog. Theor. Phys. Suppl.* 136:1, 1999.

Abbiendi, G., et al. (OPAL Collaboration with **A. Jawahery).** Measurement of the W mass and width in e+e- collisions at 183 GeV. *Phys. Lett. B* 453:138, 1999.

Ji, X. Gauge-invariant decomposition of nucleon spin and its spin-off. *Phys. Rev. Lett.* 78:610, 1997.

Kelly, J. J. Nucleon knockout by intermediate energy electrons. *Adv. Nucl. Phys.* 23:75, 1996.

Kim, Y. S. Observable gauge transformation in the parton picture. *Phys. Rev. Lett.* 63:348–51, 1989.

Belitz, D., and **T. R. Kirkpatrick**. The Anderson-Mott Transition. *Rev. Mod. Phys.* 66:261–380, 1994.

Zeff, B. W., J. Fineberg, and **D. P. Lathrop**. The dynamics of finite-time singularities: Curvature collapse and jet eruption on a fluid surface. *Nature* 403:401, 2000.

Liu, C. S., R. Z. Sagdeev, and M. N. Rosenbluth. The radial electric field dynamics in the neoclassical plasmas. *Phys. Plasmas* 4:12, 1997.

Giudice, G. F., **M. A. Luty,** H. Murayama, and R. Rattazzi. Gaugino mass without singlets. *J. High Energy Phys.* 9812:027, 1998.

Mason, G. M., J. E. Mazur, and J. R. Dwyer. 3He enhancements in large solar energetic particle events. *Astrophys. J. Lett.* 525:L133–6, 1999.

University of Maryland, College Park

Selected Publications (continued)

Misner, C. W., K. S. Thorne, and J. A. Wheeler. *Gravitation.* San Francisco: W. H. Freeman and Co., 1973.

Mohapatra, R. N., and G. Senjanovic. Spontaneous parity violation and neutrino masses. *Phys. Rev. Lett.* 44:912, 1980.

Hendrey, M., **E. Ott,** and **T. M. Antonsen Jr.** Effect of inhomogeneity on spiral wave dynamics. *Phys. Rev. Lett.* 82:859, 1999.

Ott, E., C. Grebogi, and **J. A. Yorke.** Controlling chaos. *Phys. Rev. Lett.* 64:1196, 1990.

Paik, H. J. Superconducting accelerometers, gravitational-wave transducers, and gravity gradiometers. In *SQUID Sensors: Fundamentals, Fabrication and Applications,* ed. H. Weinstock, pp. 569–98. Dordrecht: Kluwer, 1996.

Papadopoulos, K., et al. The physics of substorms as revealed by the ISTP. *Phys. Chem. Earth* 24:1–3, 189–202, 1999.

Park, R. *Voodoo Science: The Road from Foolishness to Fraud.* New York: Oxford University Press, 2000.

Pati, J. C., and A. Salam. Lepton number as the fourth color. *Phys. Rev. D* 10:275, 1974.

Redish, E. F., J. M. Saul, and R. N. Steinberg. Student expectations in introductory physics. *Am. J. Phys.* 66:212, 1998.

CLEO Collaboration et al. **(D. Roberts).** First observation of the decay $\tau^- \rightarrow K^{*-}\eta\nu_\tau$. *Phys. Rev. Lett.* 82:281, 1999. hep-ex/9809012.

Roos, P. G., and **N. S. Chant.** Photopion production from polarized nuclear targets. *Phys. Rev. C* 52:2591, 1995.

VanWiggeren, G. D., and **R. Roy.** Communication with chaotic lasers. *Science* 279:1198, 1998.

Mukhin, L., L. Marochnic, and **R. Sagdeev.** Estimates of mass and angular momentum in the Oort cloud. *Science* 242:547–50, 1988.

Sharma, R. P., and **S. B. Ogale** et al. **(T. Venkatesan).** Phase transition in the incoherent lattice fluctuations in optimally and underdoped YBCO. *Nature* 404:736, 2000.

Sharma, R. P., and **S. B. Ogale** et al. **(T. Venkatesan).** Phase transitions in the incoherent lattice fluctuations in $YBa_2Cu_3O_{7-\delta}$. *Lett. Nature* 404:736–9, 2000.

Akrawy, M. Z., **A. Skuja,** and the OPAL Collaboration. Measurement of the Z-zero mass and width with the OPAL detector at LEP. *Phys. Lett. B* 231:530, 1989.

Super-Kamiokande Collaboration and **G. Sullivan.** Measurement of the solar neutrino energy spectrum using neutrino-electron scattering. *Phys. Rev. Lett.* 82:2430, 1999.

Strachan, D. R., et al. **(T. Venkatesan** and **C. J. Lobb).** Do superconductors have zero resistance in a magnetic field? *Phys. Rev. Lett.* 87:067007, 2001.

Wallace, S. J., and N. Devine. Instant two-body equation in Breit frame. *Phys. Rev. C: Nucl. Phys.* 51:3222, 1995.

Mohanty, P., E. M. Q. Jariwala, and **R. A. Webb.** Intrinsic decoherence in mesoscopic systems. *Phys. Rev. Lett.* 78:3366, 1997.

Mathai, A., et al. **(F. C. Wellstood).** Experimental proof of a time-reversal-invariant order parameter with a Π shift in $YBa_2Cu_3O_{7-\delta}$, *Phys. Rev. Lett.* 74:4523, 1995.

Dougherty, D. B., et al. **(E. D. Williams** and **S. Das Sarma).** Experimental persistence probability for fluctuating steps. *Phys. Rev. Lett.* 89:36144–7, 2002.

Kwon, H.-J., and **V. M. Yakovenko.** Spontaneous formation of a pi soliton in a superconducting wire with an odd number of electrons. *Phys. Rev. Lett.* 89:017002, 2002.

UNIVERSITY OF MIAMI

Department of Physics

Programs of Study The Department of Physics offers programs leading to the M.S. and Ph.D. degrees, and both thesis and nonthesis M.S. tracks are available. Usually a Ph.D. student devotes most of the first year to basic courses and takes the qualifying exam in the first January following arrival. Students should become involved with a research project by the second year and, after passing the qualifying exam, must present the beginnings of a research project to a committee within six months. This presentation normally turns into a dissertation, but the student is not bound to it and can switch to another project or even another area of research later.

Experimental research in the Department of Physics is in the areas of nonlinear phenomena and chaos, optics, optical oceanography, plasmas, and solid-state physics. Theoretical research is in elementary particles, environmental optics, plasmas, nonlinear phenomena and chaos, and solid-state physics. In addition to the research projects, the activities of research groups include seminars where both visitors and the department faculty members and graduate students present results of their research.

Research Facilities The physics building includes 20,000 square feet of research laboratories and workshops. Major experimental instrumentation includes lasers, a radiometric calibration facility, CCD camera systems for measurements of radiance distribution and the point spread function under water, a very-high-resolution spectroradiometer, instruments for measuring spectral attenuation and scattering under water, an optical and a microwave spectrum analyzer, a UHV pumping station, vibration isolated optical tables, high-speed data acquisition systems, RF power sources, high-resolution video data systems, a transmission resonance spectrometer, cryogenic probes (0.05–330 K), a SQUID magnetometer, a 12-tesla superconducting magnet, thin films deposition systems (evaporator and pulsed excimer laser), high-temperature furnaces, polishing and cutting instruments, a Philips MRD thin-film X-ray diffractometer, and an adiabatic demagnetization refrigerator.

Computing services are provided by the University Computing Center and by the physics department and include a number of VAX, DEC, and IBM computers in addition to numerous IBM PCs and Macintosh computers scattered in the various PC labs in the dorms and the computer center. Research groups utilize many VAX and DEC workstations, including Alpha AXP Digital DECstations, and have access to supercomputers.

Financial Aid Financial support is available in several forms. Research assistantships (RAs) and teaching assistantships (TAs) include a stipend of $18,000 per year (additional stipend for summer teaching may be available) plus tuition for 9 credits per semester. Fellowships, with no teaching duties, include a stipend of $17,000 per year plus tuition for 9 credits per semester. For some teaching and/or research duties, the support is upgraded to the level of TA support. Summer research fellowships are available on a competitive basis.

Cost of Study In 2003–04, the tuition for one semester of full-time graduate study (9 credits) was $9763. An additional $221 per semester covered student activity and athletics fees.

Living and Housing Costs The cost of a single room in the dormitories is $6538 per year (an additional $1684 for meals) per person per semester. Typical rents for off-campus apartments are $700–$800 per month for one bedroom and $800–$1000 per month for two bedrooms. A typical rent for a room in a house off campus is $400–$500 per month, and the cost of living is generally lower than in the urban areas of the northern and western United States.

Student Group In fall 2003, 25 graduate students were enrolled in the department. All of them received financial aid in the form of a TA, an RA, a fellowship, or external support (exchange students). The majority of the students are international.

Student Outcomes Recent Ph.D. graduates have chosen a variety of work environments. Students have gone on to postdoctoral positions at schools such as the University of Chicago and Brown, government positions in agencies such as NASA and NOAA, and industrial positions with corporations such as the Coulter Corporation.

Location The department is housed in the James L. Knight Physics Building on the Coral Gables campus. This campus occupies 260 beautifully landscaped acres in a predominantly residential area. Coral Gables is an affluent suburb of metropolitan Miami, which is the largest urban area in Florida. Downtown Miami is readily accessible by Metrorail train, which has a stop next to the campus. Miami is a center of Latin culture and is the commercial gateway to Latin America. It offers all the amenities of a large and prosperous city, as well as an excellent oceanside climate of warm winters and moderate summers.

The University The University of Miami was founded in 1925 and is accredited by the Southern Association of Colleges and Schools. Individual programs are accredited by a total of twelve professional agencies. The University of Miami is the largest private university in the Southeast and has a full-time enrollment of more than 14,000, including more than 3,000 graduate students and 2,000 law and medical students. Two colleges and ten schools are located on the main campus in Coral Gables. The University's medical school, the fourth largest in the United States, is situated in Miami's civic center, and the Rosentiel School of Marine and Atmospheric Science is located on Virginia Key. Funded research activities total more than $100 million per year.

Applying Consideration is given to applicants who have a B.S. degree in physics with a minimum undergraduate GPA of 3.0 (B). The GRE is required. Applicants from non-English-speaking countries must demonstrate proficiency in English via the TOEFL, and the minimum acceptable score for admission is 550.

The application deadline for the fall semester is February 1, and application for financial aid is made at the time of application for admission. Forms should be requested from the address below.

Correspondence and Information

Professor Josef Ashkenazi
Chairman of the Graduate Recruitment Committee
Department of Physics
University of Miami
P.O. Box 248046
Coral Gables, Florida 33124

Telephone: 305-284-2323/3
Fax: 305-284-4222
E-mail: ashkenazi@phyvax.ir.miami.edu

University of Miami

THE FACULTY AND THEIR RESEARCH

George C. Alexandrakis, Professor and Chairman of the Department; Ph.D., Princeton, 1968. Solid-state experiment, transmission resonance, magneto-acoustic propagation in ferromagnetic metals.
Orlando Alvarez, Professor; Ph.D., Harvard, 1979. Theory of elementary particles.
Josef Ashkenazi, Associate Professor; Ph.D., Hebrew (Jerusalem), 1975. Solid-state theory, first-principles band structure methods, many-body physics, high-temperature superconductors.
Stewart E. Barnes, Professor; Ph.D., UCLA, 1972. Solid-state theory, many-body theory, superconductivity and magnetism.
Joshua L. Cohn, Professor; Ph.D., Michigan, 1989. Condensed matter, experiment, materials physics, electronic and lattice transport.
Thomas L. Curtright, Professor; Ph.D., Caltech, 1977. Theory of elementary particles.
Massimiliano Galeazzi, Assistant Professor; Ph.D., Genoa, 1999. X-ray astrophysics, study of the interstellar/intergalactic medium and X-ray sources, development of X-ray detectors.
Howard R. Gordon, Professor; Ph.D., Penn State, 1965. Optical oceanography, light scattering, radiative transfer, remote sensing.
Joshua O. Gundersen, Assistant Professor; Ph.D., California, Santa Barbara, 1995. Experimental cosmology and astrophysics.
Joseph G. Hirschberg, Professor Emeritus; Ph.D., Wisconsin, 1952. Physical optics, Fabry-Perot interferometry, plasma spectroscopy.
Manuel A. Huerta, Professor; Ph.D., Miami (Florida), 1970. Statistical mechanics, plasma physics, numerical simulations in MHD.
Luca Mezincescu, Professor; Ph.D., Bucharest, 1978. Theory of elementary particles.
James C. Nearing, Associate Professor and Associate Chairman of the Department; Ph.D., Columbia, 1965. Theoretical physics, bifurcation theory in fully nonlinear plasma systems.
Rafael I. Nepomechie, Professor; Ph.D., Chicago, 1982. Theory of elementary particles.
William B. Pardo, Associate Professor; Ph.D., Northwestern, 1957. Experimental physics, plasma physics, nonlinear dynamics.
Arnold Perlmutter, Professor Emeritus; Ph.D., NYU, 1955. Nuclear and particle physics.
Carolyne M. Van Vliet, Adjunct Professor and Professor Emerita, University of Montréal; Ph.D., Free University, Amsterdam, 1956. Equilibrium and nonequilibrium statistical mechanics, stochastic processes, quantum transport in solids.
Kenneth J. Voss, Professor; Ph.D., Texas A&M, 1984. Hydrologic optics, light scattering, atmospheric optics.
Fulin Zuo, Associate Professor; Ph.D., Ohio State, 1988. Condensed matter, experiment.

RESEARCH ACTIVITIES

Experimental Cosmology and Astrophysics. Studies of the cosmic microwave and infrared background, studies of the interstellar/intergalactic medium and X-ray sources, instrumentation for low-noise RF and mm-wave detectors and telescopes, development of high-resolution cryogenic microcalorimeters and bolometers. (Galeazzi, Gundersen)

Experimental and Theoretical Nonlinear Dynamics. Study of instabilities and chaotic oscillations in systems exhibiting complex dynamical behavior; dripping faucets, electronic circuits, lasers, athletes, inert-gas plasmas at low fractional ionization, phase synchronization and communication with chaos. (Pardo) More information is available through http://ndl.physics.miami.edu.

Experimental Ocean Optics. Light scattering and absorption by marine particulates; instrumentation for measurement of optical properties of ocean water and of the atmosphere. (Voss)

Experimental Solid State Physics. Ferromagnetic transmission resonance in metals, spin relaxation, exchange energy, phonon excitation and propagation, nonlinear phenomena. (Alexandrakis)
Transport and magnetic properties of materials at low temperatures; transition metal oxides; high-temperature and organic superconductors and reduced dimensional systems (e.g., layered systems and thin films); electrical and thermal conduction, thermoelectric effects; vortex dynamics, critical currents, quantum tunneling. (Cohn, Zuo)

Theoretical Elementary Particles Physics. Quantum field theory, supergravity, superstrings. (Alvarez, Curtright, Mezincescu, Nepomechie)

Theoretical Environmental Optics. Radiative transfer, remote determination of ocean chlorophyll concentrations. (Gordon)

Theoretical Plasma Physics. Numerical simulations in plasmas and other systems. (Huerta, Nearing)

Theoretical Solid State Physics. Electronic structure of solids, many-body physics, high-temperature superconductivity, magnetism. (Ashkenazi, Barnes)
Linear and nonlinear quantum transport, reduced-dimensionality systems. (Van Vliet)
More information is available through http://www.miami.edu/physics/.

The James L. Knight Physics Building.

SELECTED PUBLICATIONS

Zuo, F., et al. **(G. C. Alexandrakis).** Anomalous magnetization in single-crystal κ-[bis(ethylenedithiotetrathiafulvalene)]$_2$Cu[N(CN)$_2$]Br superconductors. *Phys. Rev. B* 52:R13126, 1995.

Rittenmyer, K. M., **G. C. Alexandrakis,** and P. S. Dubbelday. Detection of fluid velocity and hydroacoustic particle velocity using a temperature autostabilized nonlinear dielectric element (Tandel). *J. Acoust. Soc. Am.* 84:2002, 1988.

Alexandrakis, G. C., and G. Dewar. Electromagnetic generation of 9.4 GHz phonons in Fe and Ni. *J. Appl. Phys.* 55:2467, 1984.

Abeles, J. H., T. R. Carver, and **G. C. Alexandrakis.** Microwave transmission measurement of the critical exponent beta in iron and iron-silicon. *J. Appl. Phys.* 53:8116, 1982.

Alexandrakis, G. C., R. A. B. Devine, and J. H. Abeles. High frequency sound as a probe of exchange energy in nickel. *J. Appl. Phys.* 53:2095, 1982.

Alexandrakis, G. C. Determination of the molecular size and the Avogadro number: A student experiment. *Am. J. Phys.* 46:810, 1978.

Alvarez, O., I. M. Singer, and P. Windey. The supersymmetric σ-model and the geometry of the Weyl-Kac character formula. *Nucl. Phys. B* 373:647, 1992.

Alvarez, O., T. P. Killingback, M. Mangano, and P. Windey. The Dirac-Ramond operator in string theory and loop space index theorems. *Nucl. Phys. Proc. Suppl.* B1A:189, 1987.

Alvarez, O., T. P. Killingback, M. Mangano, and P. Windey. String theory and loop space index theorems. *Comm. Math. Phys.* 111:1, 1987.

Alvarez, O., I. M. Singer, and B. Zumino. Gravitational anomalies and the family's index theorem. *Comm. Math. Phys.* 96:409, 1984.

Alvarez, O. Theory of strings with boundaries: Fluctuations, topology and quantum geometry. *Nucl. Phys. B* 216:125, 1983.

Ashkenazi, J. Stripelike inhomogeneities, carriers, and BCS-BEC crossover in the high-T_c cuprates. In *New Trends in Superconductivity,* pp. 51–60, eds. J. F. Annett and S. Kruchinin. Kluwer Academic Publishers, 2002.

Ashkenazi, J. Stripe fluctuations, carriers, spectroscopies, transport, and BCS-BEC crossover in the high-T_c cuprates. *J. Phys. Chem. Solids* 63:2277–85, 2002.

Ashkenazi, J. Stripes, carriers, and high-T_c in the cuprates. In *High-Temperature Superconductivity*, pp. 12–21, eds. **S. E. Barnes, J. Ashkenazi, J. L. Cohn,** and **F. Zuo.** AIP Conference Proceedings 483, 1999.

Ashkenazi, J. A realistic microscopic theory for the high-T_c cuprates. *J. Supercond.* 7:719–36, 1994.

Ashkenazi, J., and C. G. Kuper. Charge-fluctuation excitations as mechanisms for high-T_c. In *Studies of High-Temperature Superconductors,* vol. III, pp. 1–49, ed. A. V. Narlikar. New York: Nova Science Publishers, Inc., 1989.

Vacaru, D., and **S. E. Barnes.** A new auxiliary particle method for the Hubbard, t-J and Heisenberg models. *J. Phys.: Condens. Matter* 6:719, 1994.

Nagashpur, M., and **S. E. Barnes.** Nonuniversality in the Kondo effect. *Phys. Rev. Lett.* 69:3824, 1992.

Barnes, S. E. Spinon-holon statistics, and broken statistical symmetry for the t-J and Hubbard models in 2D. In *High Temperature Superconductivity: Physical Properties, Microscopic Theory, and Mechanisms; Proceedings of the University of Miami Workshop on Electronic Structure and Mechanisms of High-Temperature Superconductivity, held January 3–9, 1991, in Coral Gables, Florida,* pp. 95–105, eds. **J. Ashkenazi, S. E. Barnes, F. Zuo,** G. C. Vezzoli, and B. M. Klein. New York: Plenum Press, 1992.

Barnes, S. E. Theory of the Jahn-Teller-Kondo effect. *Phys. Rev.* 37:3671, 1988.

Barnes, S. E. Theory of electron paramagnetic resonance of ions in metals. *Adv. Physics* 30:801–938, 1981.

Cohn, J. L., and J. J. Neumeier. Heat conduction and magnetic phase behavior in electron-doped $Ca_{1-x}La_xMnO_3$ ($0 \leq x \leq 0.2$). *Phys. Rev. B* 66:1004041, 2002.

Maier, R., **J. L. Cohn,** J. J. Neumeier, and L. A. Bendersky. Ferroelectricity and ferrimagnetism in iron-doped $BaTiO_3$. *Appl. Phys. Lett.* 78:2536–8, 2001.

Neumeier, J. J., and **J. L. Cohn.** Possible signatures of magnetic phase segregation in electron-doped antiferromagnetic CaMnO3. *Phys. Rev. B* 61:14319–22, 2000.

Cohn, J. L. Electrical and thermal transport in perovskite manganites. *J. Supercond.* 13:291–304, 2000.

Cohn, J. L., et al. Glass-like heat conduction in high-mobility semiconductors. *Phys. Rev. Lett.* 82:779–82, 1999.

Curtright, T. L., T. Uetmatsu, and C. K. Zachos. Generating all Wigner functions. *J. Math. Phys.* 42, 2001.

Curtright, T. L., D. Fairlie, and C. K. Zachos. Integrable symplectic trilinear interaction terms for matrix membranes. *Phys. Lett. B* 405:37–44, 1997.

Curtright, T. L., and C. K. Zachos. Canonical non-Abelian dual transformations in supersymmetric field theories. *Phys Rev D* 52:R572–6, 1995.

Curtright, T. L., and C. K. Zachos. Deforming maps for quantum algebras. *Phys. Lett. B* 243:237–44, 1990.

Curtright, T. L. Extrinsic geometry of superimmersions. In *Perspectives in String Theory,* pp. 437–80, eds. P. Di Vechia and J. L. Petersen. World Scientific, 1988.

Curtright, T. L., and C. K. Zachos. Geometry, topology, and supersymmetry in nonlinear models. *Phys. Rev. Lett.* 53:1799–801, 1984.

Curtright, T. L., and C. B. Thorn. Conformally invariant quantization of the Liouville theory. *Phys. Rev. Lett.* 48:1309–13, 1982.

Galeazzi, M., and D. McCammon. A microcalorimeter and bolometer model. *J. Appl. Phys.* 93:4856, 2003.

McCammon, D., et al. **(M. Galeazzi).** A high-spectral resolution observation of the soft X-ray diffuse background with thermal detectors. *Astrophys. J.* 576:188, 2002.

Galeazzi, M., et al. Limits on the existence of heavy neutrinos in the range 50–1000 eV from the study of the ^{187}Re beta decay. *Phys. Rev. Lett.* 86:1978, 2001.

Galeazzi, M., et al. The end-point energy and half life of the ^{187}Re beta decay. *Phys. Rev. C* 63:014302, 2001.

Gatti, F., et al. **(M. Galeazzi).** Detection of environmental fine structure in the low-energy beta-decay spectrum of ^{187}Re. *Nature* 397:137, 1999.

Gordon, H. R., et al. Retrieval of coccolithophore calcite concentration from SeaWiFS imagery. *Geophys. Res. Lett.* 28:1587–90, 2001.

Moulin, C., and **H. R. Gordon** et al. Atmospheric correction of ocean color imagery through thick layers of Saharan dust. *Geophys. Res. Lett.* 28:5–8, 2001.

Boynton, G. C., and **H. R. Gordon.** Irradiance inversion algorithm for estimating the absorption and backscattering coefficients of natural waters: Raman scattering effects. *Appl. Opt.* 39:3012–22, 2000.

Gordon, H. R., and G. C. Boynton. A radiance-irradiance inversion algorithm for estimating the absorption and backscattering coefficients of natural water: Homogenous waters. *Appl. Opt.* 36:2636–41, 1997.

Gordon, H. R., et al. Phytoplankton pigment concentrations in the Middle Atlantic bight: Comparison of ship determinations and coastal zone color scanner measurements. *Appl. Opt.* 22:20–36, 1983.

Gordon, H. R., D. K. Clark, J. L. Mueller, and W. A. Hovis. Phytoplankton pigments derived from the Nimbus-7 CZCS: Initial comparisons with surface measurements. *Science* 210:63–6, 1980.

Hedman, M. M., et al. **(J. O. Gundersen).** A limit on the polarized anisotropy of the cosmic microwave background at subdegree angular scales. *Astrophys. J.* 548:L114, 2001.

Devlin, M. J., et al. **(J. O. Gundersen).** BLAST–A balloon-borne aperture submillimeter telescope. In *Proceedings of the Conference on Deep Millimeter Surveys: Implications for Galaxy Formation and Evolution,* 2000.

Gundersen, J. O., et al. A long lifetime balloon-borne cryostat and magnetic refrigerator. *Adv. Cryog. Eng.* 45B:1639, 1999.

University of Miami

Selected Publications (continued)

Gundersen, J. O., et al. Degree scale anisotropy in the cosmic microwave background: SP94 results. *Astrophys. J.* 443:L57, 1995.

Gundersen, J. O., et al. A degree scale anisotropy measurement of the cosmic background radiation near Gamma Ursa Minoris. *Astrophys. J.* 413:L1, 1993.

Hirschberg, J. G., and T. N. Veziroglu. Tidal energy for inexpensive power. CD *Proceedings, 13th World Hydrogen Energy Conference,* Beijing, China, June 11–15, 2000.

Hirschberg, J. G., and E. Kohen. A new spectral method for fluorescence excitation. In *Applications of Optical Engineering to the Study of Cellular Pathology,* pp. 91–7, eds. E. Kohen and **J. G. Hirschberg.** Research Signpost Scientific Information Guild. Recent Developments in Optical Engineering, Trivandrum, Kerala, India. 1999.

Skinner, C. H., et al. **(J. G. Hirschberg).** Contact microscopy with a soft X-ray laser. *J. Microsc.* 159(1):51–60, 1990.

Hirschberg, J. G. A long range microscope phase condensing system. *Appl. Opt.* 29:1409–10, 1990.

Thio, Y. C., **M. A. Huerta,** and G. C. Boynton. The projectile-wall interface in rail launchers. *IEEE Trans. Magnetics* 29:1213–8, 1993.

Thio, Y. C., **M. A. Huerta,** and **J. C. Nearing.** On some techniques to achieve ablation free operation of electromagnetic rail launchers. *IEEE Trans. Magnetics* 29, 1993.

Castillo, J. L., and **M. A. Huerta.** Effect of resistivity on the Rayleigh-Taylor instability in an accelerated plasma. *Phys. Rev. E* 48:3849–66, 1993.

Boynton, G. C., **M. A. Huerta,** and Y. C. Thio. 2-D MHD numerical simulations of EML plasma armatures with ablation. *IEEE Trans. Magnetics* 29:751–6, 1993.

Huerta, M. A., and **J. C. Nearing.** Conformal mapping calculation of the railgun skin inductance. *IEEE Trans. Magnetics* 27:112–5, 1991.

Huerta, M. A. Steady detonation waves with losses. *Phys. Fluids* 28:2735–43, 1985.

Huerta, M. A., and J. Magnan. Spatial structures in plasmas with metastable states as bifurcation phenomena. *Phys. Rev. A* 26:539–55, 1982.

Grisaru, M. T., **L. Mezincescu,** and **R. I. Nepomechie.** Direct calculation of boundary S matrix for open Heisenberg chain. *J. Phys. A* 28:1027–45, 1995.

de Vega, H. J., **L. Mezincescu,** and **R. I. Nepomechie.** Scalar kinks. *Intl. J. Mod. Phys. B* 8:3473–85, 1994.

Mezincescu, L., and **R. I. Nepomechie.** Analytical Bethe ansatz for quantum-algebra-invariant spin chains. *Nucl. Phys. B* 372:597–621, 1992.

Mezincescu, L., and **R. I. Nepomechie.** Integrability of open spin chains with quantum algebra symmetry. *Int. J. Mod. Phys.* A6:5231–48, 1991 (Addendum—A7:5657–9, 1992).

Mezincescu, L., and M. Henneaux. A σ model interpretation of Green-Schwarz covariant superstrings. *Phys. Lett.* 152B:340–2, 1985.

Jones, D. R. T., and **L. Mezincescu.** The chiral anomaly and a class of two-loop finite supersymmetric theories. *Phys. Lett.* 138B:293–5, 1984.

Mezincescu, L. On the superfield approach for 0(2) supersymmetry. Preprint JINR Dubna P2-12572 (in Russian), pp. 1–19, 1979.

Nearing, J. C., and **M. A. Huerta.** Skin and heating effects of railgun currents. *IEEE Trans. Magnetics* 25:381–6, 1989.

Nepomechie, R. I. Solving the open XXZ spin chain with nondiagonal boundary terms at roots of unity. *Nucl. Phys. B* 622:615–32, 2002.

Nepomechie, R. I. The boundary supersymmetric sine-Gordon model revisited. *Phys. Lett. B* 509:183–8, 2001.

Nepomechie, R. I. Magnetic monopoles from antisymmetric tensor gauge fields. *Phys. Rev. D* 31:1921–4, 1985.

Pardo, W. B., et al. Pacing a chaotic plasma with a music signal. *Phys. Lett. A* 284:259, 2001.

Rosa, E., Jr., and **W. B. Pardo** et al. Phase synchronization of chaos in a plasma discharge tube. *Int. J. Bifurcation Chaos* 10:2551, 2000.

Ticos, C. M., et al. **(W. B. Pardo).** Experimental real-time phase synchronization of a paced chaotic plasma discharge. *Phys. Rev. Lett.* 85:2929, 2000.

Monti, M., and **W. B. Pardo** et al. Color map of Lyapunov exponents of invariant sets. *Int. J. Bifurcation Chaos* 9:1459, 1999.

Walkenstein, J. A., **W. B. Pardo,** M. Monti, and E. Rosa Jr. Chaotic moving striations in inert gas plasmas. *Phys. Lett. A* 261:183, 1999.

Perlmutter, A., et al. Spin analyzing power in p-p elastic scattering at 28 GeV/c. *Phys. Rev. Lett.* 50:802–6, 1983.

Perlmutter, A., et al. Spin-spin forces in 6 GeV/c neutron-proton elastic scattering. *Phys. Rev. Lett.* 43:983–6, 1979.

Friedmann, M., D. Kessler, A. Levy, and **A. Perlmutter.** The coulomb field in $\Sigma\pi$ production by slow K-mesons in complex nuclei. *Nuovo Cimento* 35:355–76, 1965.

Cox, J., and **A. Perlmutter.** A method for the determination of the S matrix for scattering by a tensor potential. *Nuovo Cimento* 37:76–87, 1965.

Van Vliet, C. M. Electronic noise due to multiple trap levels in homogenous solids and in space-charge layers. *J. Appl. Phys.,* 2003.

Van Vliet, C. M., and A. Barrios. Quantum electron transport beyond linear response. *Physica* A315:493–536, 2002.

Van Vliet, C. M. Random walk and 1/f noise. *Physica* A303:421–6, 2002.

Guillon, S., P. Vasilopoulos, and **C. M. Van Vliet.** Magnetoconductance of parabolically confined quasi-onedimensional channels. *J. Phys. C: Condens. Matter* 14:803–14, 2002.

Van Vliet, C. M. Quantum transport in solids. *Advances in Mathematical Sciences, CRM Proceedings and Lecture Notes,* vol. 11, pp. 21–48, ed. L. Vinet. Providence, Rhode Island: American Mathematical Society, 1997.

Zhang, H., **K. J. Voss,** R. P. Reid, and E. Louchard. Bidirectional reflectance measurements of sediments in the vicinity of Lee Stocking Island, Bahamas. *Limnol. Oceanogr.* 48:380–9, 2003.

Voss, K. J., et al. **(H. R. Gordon).** Lidar measurements during aerosols. *J. Geophys. Res.* 106:20821–32, 2001.

Voss, K. J., A. Chapin, M. Monti, and H. Zhang. An instrument to measure the bidirectional reflectance distribution function (BRDF) of surfaces. *Appl. Opt.* 39:6197–206, 2000.

Ritter, J. M., and **K. J. Voss.** A new instrument to measure the solar aureole from an unstable platform. *J. Atmos. Ocean. Tech.* 17:1040–7, 2000.

Voss, K. J., and Y. Liu. Polarized radiance distribution measurements of skylight: I. system description and characterization. *Appl. Opt.* 36:6083–94, 1997.

Su, X., and **F. Zuo** et al. Anisotropic magnetoresistance in the organic superconductor β"-$(ET)_2SF_5CH_2CF_2SO_3$. *Phys. Rev. B* 59:4376, 1999.

Zuo, F., X. Su, and W. K. Wu. Magnetic properties of the pre-martensitic transition in Ni_2MnGa alloys. *Phys. Rev. B* 58:11127, 1998.

Su, X., and **F. Zuo** et al. Structural disorder and its effect on the superconducting transition temperature in organic superconductor k-$(BEDT\text{-}TTF)_2Cu[N(CN)_2]Br$. *Phys. Rev. B* 57:R14056, 1998.

Zuo, F., J. Schlueter, and J. W. Williams. Mixed state magnetoresistance in organic superconductors k-$(ET)_2Cu[N(CN)_2]Br$. *Phys. Rev. B* 54:11973, 1996.

Zuo, F., et al. Josephson decoupling in single crystal $Nd_{1.85}Ce_{0.15}CuO_{4-y}$ superconductors. *Phys. Rev. Lett.* 72:1746–9, 1994.

UNIVERSITY OF MICHIGAN

Department of Physics

Program of Study

The department offers a program leading to the Doctor of Philosophy in physics. The department offers research opportunities in theoretical and experimental fields, including atomic physics, astrophysics, biophysics, optical physics, condensed-matter physics, elementary particle physics, and nuclear physics. The requirements for the Ph.D. are as follows. Students must pass, with a grade of B or better, nine prescribed graduate physics courses (500 level) or show equivalent competence, 4 credits of cognate courses, one advanced graduate physics course (600 level) on a special topic, and a 4-credit course of supervised nonthesis research. Students must also pass a two-part written qualifying examination on advanced undergraduate material no later than the beginning of their third year. Ph.D. students are expected to attain candidacy by the end of their fifth term. Completion of the degree involves writing a thesis based on independent research done under the supervision of a faculty adviser and passing a final oral exam.

Research Facilities

Physics research is focused at the Randall Laboratory/West Hall complex, which includes a 65,000-square-foot laboratory addition. The physics laboratories house state-of-the-art space and facilities that support the department's research activities. Individual investigators use tools such as atomic scale and positron microscopes, lasers of all sorts (CW, pulsed, Q-switched, mode-locked, ultrafast, frequency-stabilized, ion, dye, solid-state, and diode), dilution refrigerators and cryogenic equipment, laser tweezers, and a Mössbauer spectrometer for the study of active sites in protein. Nuclear and high-energy physics groups use campus laboratories to build and test apparatus used at accelerator facilities around the world. Apparatus for beams of radioactive nuclei, for polarized beams and targets, and for detector facilities used in fixed target and colliding beam experiments are among those developed on the University of Michigan campus. Collaborations in the medical sciences take place at the University Hospital and Medical School. The School of Engineering on the University's North Campus is the site of the Center for Ultrafast Optical Sciences, an NSF science and technology center exploring ultrafast and high-intensity laser science. Department computer facilities are state-of-the-art, based on a professionally managed, distributed network with powerful workstations and high-speed network connections among department and University computers and to the Internet. Department shop facilities include a well-equipped student shop, a large instrument shop with computerized numerically controlled milling machines, and an electronics shop with custom VLSI circuit design facilities. Other University shop facilities complete the technical support necessary for state-of-the-art research. The University of Michigan libraries house one of the country's largest science libraries and employ modern computerized catalogs, databases, and information retrieval.

Financial Aid

The University's Regents' Fellowships paid a stipend of $22,200, plus full tuition and fees, in 2003–04. Several other merit-based scholarships are available through the department, to both incoming and advanced students. Graduate student instructorships cover a period of eight months and paid a stipend of $13,570 plus tuition in 2003–04; teaching loads usually consist of two to four 2-hour elementary lab sections per week. GSIs are represented by a union. Graduate research assistantship stipends were $20,355 for twelve months in 2003–04. Summer RA appointments are available for most students. A very small number of spring GSI appointments are also available. Students who have at least a one-quarter-time appointment (half a normal appointment) as an RA or GSI are eligible to participate in the University's group health insurance plan.

Cost of Study

For 2003–04, tuition was $6005 per term for full-time in-state residents and $13,570 per term for full-time out-of-state students; candidates paid $4127 per term. Tuition is waived for students with one-quarter-time or more teaching or research assistantships. Most fees are included in the tuition; fees not included total about $95 each semester. Books and supplies cost approximately $400 per term.

Living and Housing Costs

Living costs, including room and board, transportation, and personal needs, are estimated at $7600 per academic year for a single student with no dependents.

Student Group

The University of Michigan has approximately 39,000 students, of whom 11,147 are graduate students. The Department of Physics has approximately 125 graduate students.

Location

The University is in Ann Arbor, 40 miles west of Detroit in the Huron River Valley, in a beautiful, tree-lined town that combines the charm of a small city with the sophistication of cities many times its size. Regarded as a cultural center of the Midwest, it offers numerous opportunities for recreation and enjoyment.

The University and The Department

The University of Michigan, founded in 1817, is one of the nation's oldest public institutions of higher education. Consistently ranked among the great universities in the world, Michigan has a strong tradition of leadership in the development of the modern American research university—a tradition sustained by the wide-ranging interests and activities of its faculty members and students. Exceptional facilities and programs, both academic and nonacademic, are available. The Department of Physics has played a leading role in the development of modern physics, with accomplishments ranging from the discovery of spin, the invention of the racetrack synchrotron, and the bubble chamber to the birth of nonlinear optics, the detection of neutrinos from supernova 1987A, and evidence of the top quark.

Applying

Applications for admission in the fall term are due by January 15 of the preceding spring; international students must submit applications by December 8. The GRE General Test is required, and the GRE Subject Test in physics is recommended. For further information on admission requirements, students should write to the address given below.

Correspondence and Information

Professor James Wells, Associate Chair for Graduate Studies
2464 Randall Laboratory of Physics
University of Michigan
Ann Arbor, Michigan 48109-1120
Telephone: 734-936-0658
World Wide Web: http://www.physics.lsa.umich.edu/

University of Michigan

THE FACULTY AND THEIR RESEARCH

Fred C. Adams, Professor; Ph.D., Berkeley, 1988. Theoretical astrophysics.
Carl W. Akerlof, Professor; Ph.D., Cornell, 1967. Experimental high-energy physics, astrophysics, cosmic rays.
Ratindranath Akhoury, Professor; Ph.D., SUNY at Stony Brook, 1980. Theoretical high-energy physics.
James W. Allen, Professor; Ph.D., Stanford, 1968. Experimental condensed-matter physics.
Dante E. Amidei, Professor; Ph.D., Berkeley, 1984. Experimental high-energy physics.
Meigan C. Aronson, Professor; Ph.D., Illinois at Urbana-Champaign, 1988. Experimental condensed-matter physics.
Daniel Axelrod, Professor; Ph.D., Berkeley, 1974. Experimental biophysics.
Frederick D. Becchetti Jr., Professor; Ph.D., Minnesota, 1969. Experimental nuclear physics.
Paul Berman, Professor; Ph.D., Yale, 1969. Theoretical atomic, molecular, and optical physics.
Michael Bretz, Professor; Ph.D., Washington (Seattle), 1971. Experimental low-temperature physics, condensed-matter physics.
Philip H. Bucksbaum, Otto Laporte Professor of Physics and Associate Director, NSF Center for Ultrafast Optical Science; Ph.D., Berkeley, 1980. Experimental atomic and optical physics.
Myron Campbell, Professor; Ph.D., Yale, 1982. Experimental high-energy physics, elementary particles.
J. Wehrley Chapman, Professor; Ph.D., Duke, 1966. Experimental high-energy physics.
Timothy E. Chupp, Professor; Ph.D., Washington (Seattle), 1983. Experimental atomic physics.
Roy Clarke, Professor and Director, Applied Physics Program; Ph.D., Queen Mary College (London), 1973. Experimental condensed-matter physics.
C. Tristram Coffin, Emeritus Professor; Ph.D., Washington (Seattle), 1956. Biophysics.
H. Richard Crane, Emeritus Professor; Ph.D., Caltech, 1934. Nuclear physics, precision measurements, biophysics.
Steven Dierker, Professor; Ph.D., Illinois at Urbana-Champaign, 1983. Experimental condensed-matter physics.
Luming Duan, Assistant Professor; Ph.D., University of Science and Technology (China), 1994. Quantum information.
Michael Duff, Professor; Ph.D., Imperial College (London), 1972. Theoretical high-energy physics.
Martin B. Einhorn, Professor; Ph.D., Princeton, 1968. Theoretical high-energy physics, elementary particles.
August Evrard, Associate Professor; Ph.D., SUNY at Stony Brook, 1980. Theoretical astrophysics.
George W. Ford, Emeritus Professor; Ph.D., Michigan, 1954. Theoretical physics.
Katherine Freese, Professor; Ph.D., Chicago, 1984. Theoretical astrophysics.
David Gerdes, Associate Professor; Ph.D., Chicago, 1992. High-energy physics.
David W. Gidley, Professor; Ph.D., Michigan, 1979. Experimental physics, atomic physics.
Walter S. Gray, Emeritus Professor; Ph.D., Colorado, 1964. Experimental nuclear physics.
Wayne E. Hazen, Emeritus Professor; Ph.D., California, 1941. Cosmic rays, nuclear physics, elementary particles.
Karl T. Hecht, Emeritus Professor; Ph.D., Michigan, 1955. Theoretical nuclear physics.
Dennis J. Hegyi, Emeritus Professor; Ph.D., Princeton, 1968. Experimental physics, astrophysics.
Alfred Z. Hendel, Emeritus Professor; Ph.D., Paris, 1955. Cosmic rays, elementary particles.
Joachim W. Jänecke, Emeritus Professor; Dr.rer.nat., Heidelberg, 1955. Experimental nuclear physics.
Lawrence W. Jones, Professor; Ph.D., Berkeley, 1952. Experimental high-energy physics, elementary particles.
Gordon L. Kane, Professor; Ph.D., Illinois, 1963. Theoretical physics, elementary particles.
Ernst Katz, Emeritus Professor; Ph.D., Utrecht (Netherlands), 1941. Solid-state physics.
Samuel Krimm, Emeritus Professor; Ph.D., Princeton, 1950. Experimental biophysics.
Alan D. Krisch, Professor; Ph.D., Cornell, 1964. Experimental high-energy physics, elementary particles.
Jean P. Krisch, Professor; Ph.D., Cornell, 1965. Theoretical physics, elementary particles, physics teaching.
Cagliyan Kurdak, Assistant Professor; Ph.D., Princeton, 1995. Condensed-matter physics.
Finn Larsen, Assistant Professor; Ph.D., Princeton, 1996. Theoretical high-energy physics.
Robert R. Lewis, Emeritus Professor; Ph.D., Michigan, 1954. Theoretical low-energy physics.
James T. Liu, Assistant Professor; Ph.D., Princeton, 1991. Theoretical high-energy physics.
Michael J. Longo, Professor; Ph.D., Berkeley, 1961. Experimental high-energy physics, instrumentation.
Wolfgang B. Lorenzon, Associate Professor; Ph.D., Basel (Switzerland), 1988. Experimental high-energy physics.
Timothy McKay, Associate Professor; Ph.D., Chicago, 1992. Astrophysics.
Jens-Christian D. Meiners, Assistant Professor; Ph.D., Constance (Germany), 1997. Experimental biophysics.
Roberto D. Merlin, Professor; Dr.rer.nat., Stuttgart, 1978. Experimental condensed-matter physics, applied physics.
Donald I. Meyer, Emeritus Professor; Ph.D., Washington (Seattle), 1953. Astrophysics, experimental high-energy physics.
Christopher Monroe, Professor; Ph.D., Colorado at Boulder, 1992. Experimental atomic, molecular, and optical physics.
Samuel Moukouri, Assistant Professor; Ph.D., Paris, 1993. Condensed-matter theory.
Homer A. Neal, Professor, Vice President Emeritus for Research, and Director, Project ATLAS; Ph.D., Michigan, 1966. Experimental high-energy physics.
Mark Newman, Assistant Professor; D.Phil., Oxford, 1988. Statistical physics theory.
Franco Nori, Associate Professor; Ph.D., Illinois at Urbana-Champaign, 1987. Condensed-matter theory.
Bradford G. Orr, Professor; Ph.D., Minnesota, 1985. Experimental condensed-matter physics, applied physics.
Oliver E. Overseth, Emeritus Professor; Ph.D., Brown, 1958. Experimental high-energy physics, elementary particles.
William C. Parkinson, Emeritus Professor; Ph.D., Michigan, 1948. Nuclear physics, biophysics.
Jian-Ming Qian, Associate Professor; Ph.D., MIT, 1991. Experimental high-energy physics.
Georg Raithel, Associate Professor; Ph.D., Munich, 1990. Experimental atomic, molecular, and optical physics.
Steven Rand, Associate Professor; Ph.D., Toronto, 1978. Optical physics, applied physics.
David Reis, Assistant Professor; Ph.D., Rochester, 1999. Experimental condensed-matter physics.
John Keith Riles, Professor; Ph.D., Stanford, 1989. Experimental high-energy physics.
Byron P. Roe, Professor; Ph.D., Cornell, 1959. Experimental high-energy physics, elementary particles.
Marc H. Ross, Emeritus Professor; Ph.D., Wisconsin, 1952. Energy resources, theoretical physics.
Leonard M. Sander, Professor; Ph.D., Berkeley, 1968. Theoretical physics, condensed matter.
T. Michael Sanders, Professor Emeritus; Ph.D., Columbia, 1954. Experimental physics, low temperatures, condensed matter.
Richard H. Sands, Emeritus Professor; Ph.D., Washington (St. Louis), 1954. Biophysics.
Robert S. Savit, Professor; Ph.D., Stanford, 1973. Theoretical condensed-matter physics, elementary particles.
Daniel Sinclair, Emeritus Professor; Ph.D., Glasgow, 1957. Experimental high-energy physics, particle astrophysics.
Duncan G. Steel, Professor; Ph.D., Michigan, 1976. Experimental atomic and optical physics.
Gregory Tarlé, Professor; Ph.D., Berkeley, 1978. Experimental astrophysics, nuclear physics.
Rudolf P. Thun, Professor; Ph.D., SUNY at Stony Brook, 1980. Experimental high-energy physics, elementary particles.
Alexei Tkachenko, Assistant Professor; Ph.D., Bar-Ilan, 1998. Theoretical condensed matter and complex systems.
Yukio Tomozawa, Professor; Ph.D., Tokyo, 1961. Theoretical high-energy physics, astrophysics.
Ctirad Uher, Professor and Chair; Ph.D., New South Wales, 1975. Experimental condensed-matter physics, applied physics.
John C. van der Velde, Emeritus Professor; Ph.D., Michigan, 1958. Experimental high-energy physics, astrophysics.
Martinus J. G. Veltman, MacArthur Professor Emeritus of Theoretical Physics; Ph.D., Utrecht (Netherlands), 1963. Elementary particles.
John F. Ward, Professor Emeritus; D.Phil., Oxford, 1961. Experimental atomic and optical physics.
James Wells, Assistant Professor; Ph.D., Michigan, 1995. Elementary particle physics.
Gabriel Weinreich, Emeritus Professor; Ph.D., Columbia, 1954. Experimental physics, atomic physics, musical acoustics.
David N. Williams, Emeritus Professor; Ph.D., Berkeley, 1964. Theoretical physics, elementary particles.
Alfred C. T. Wu, Emeritus Professor; Ph.D., Maryland, 1960. Theoretical physics.
Y. P. Edward Yao, Professor; Ph.D., Harvard, 1964. Theoretical high-energy physics, elementary particles.
Leopoldo Pando Zayas, Assistant Professor; Ph.D., Moscow State, 1998. High-energy theory.
Bing Zhou, Professor; Ph.D., MIT, 1987. High-energy physics.
Michal Zochowski, Assistant Professor; Ph.D., Warsaw, 1995. Biophysics, complex systems, neuroscience.
Jens C. Zorn, Professor; Ph.D., Yale, 1961. Experimental physics, atomic physics.

UNIVERSITY OF NOTRE DAME

Department of Physics

Programs of Study The Department of Physics graduate program is primarily a doctoral program leading to a Doctor of Philosophy (Ph.D.) degree, and the department ordinarily does not accept students who intend to complete only a master's degree. Major areas of research include astronomy, astrophysics, atomic physics, biophysics, condensed-matter physics, cosmology, general relativity, high-energy elementary particle physics, nuclear physics, radiation physics, and statistical physics. Interdisciplinary programs are available in radiation physics, biophysics, and chemical physics. Requirements for the Ph.D. include 36 course credit hours, seminars, and research. Students are expected to become actively involved in research during the first year and take a first-year qualifying exam. Both oral and written candidacy examinations are normally completed early in the third year. The candidate must demonstrate the ability to perform research and must show a broad understanding of physics. A thesis is required and must be approved by and defended orally before the student's doctoral committee.

Research Facilities The department has excellent research facilities on and off campus. Astronomy/astrophysics research facilities include twenty nights a year at the 1.8-meter Vatican Advanced Technology Telescope (VATT) and ten nights a year at the soon-to-be-completed 2x 8.5-meter Large Binocular Telescope (LBT). Current research is also conducted using a variety of telescopes, including the Hubble Space Telescope (HST), the Keck Telescope, the NASA Infrared Telescope (IRTF), and the Steward and Cerro-Telolo Observatories. An air-shower array located next to the campus is used to study high- (30-300GeV) and ultrahigh-energy (greater than 100TeV) cosmic rays, utilizing position-sensitive proportional wire detectors for precision angle measurements and particle identification. Facilities for accelerator-based atomic physics research include the Atomic Physics Accelerator Lab (APAL) at Notre Dame, which includes a 200 kV heavy-ion accelerator and various vacuum ultraviolet and visible monochromators, high-resolution position-sensitive photon detectors, and Doppler-free laser excitation chambers as well as other tabletop laser excitation systems. Precision measurements in atomic Cs, necessary for interpretation of parity nonconservation experiments, are carried out using Ti-sapphire, dye, and diode laser. Experiments on highly charged ions are also carried out at Argonne National Laboratory (ANL) and at GSI-Darmstadt, Germany. X-ray–atom interactions are also studied at national synchrotron radiation facilities. In biophysics, a 300-Mhz magnetic resonance imager (MRI) is available. The MRI has a vertical superwide bore 7 Tesla magnet with exchangeable probes (up to 64 mm in diameter) and gradient sets (up to 100 Gauss/cm) for imaging microscopy and biological applications. The facility is equipped for in vivo study of small animals. Condensed-matter physics facilities are available for molecular-beam epitaxy (MBE) of semiconductor films, superlattices, and microstructures and for bulk crystal growth, including a traveling solvent floating zone furnace; low-temperature electron tunneling; microwave, optical, and infrared photoresponse studies of superconductors; resonance studies in ferromagnetic and paramagnetic materials; surface physics; X-ray and fluorescence characterization of solids; low-temperature thermodynamic studies; and optical and far-infrared studies of semiconductors. XAFS and X-ray–scattering experiments are also carried out at the ANL, and neutron diffraction studies are performed at the National Institute of Standards and Technology (NIST). High-energy elementary particle physics research is carried out at the Tevatron Collider at Fermi National Accelerator Laboratory (FNAL), Brookhaven National Laboratory (BNL), Stanford Linear Accelerator (SLAC), and the Large Hadron Collider at the CERN Laboratory in Geneva, Switzerland. On-campus facilities are used for the development of new particle detection systems, including scintillating fiber tracking and tile-fiber calorimeter detectors, and for detector development and instruction for the QuarkNet education and outreach project. Facilities for research in nuclear physics include 1-MV, 4-MV, and 10-MV Van de Graaff accelerators; a multidetector array for gamma-ray spectroscopy; and a dual superconducting solenoid system for radioactive beam studies. Nuclear physics programs are also under way at ANL, the National Superconducting Cyclotron Laboratory (NCSL) at Michigan State University, Oak Ridge National Laboratory, and Los Alamos National Laboratory, as well as several laboratories abroad. Computing facilities include the University's supercomputers plus departmental computer clusters. Wireless connections are available in all offices, laboratories, residences, and other campus locations. The department has an extensive research library and state-of-the-art machine shop.

Financial Aid Graduate teaching assistantships are normally available to all Ph.D. students and for 2004–05 include a minimum nine-month stipend of $14,500, plus payment of tuition and fees. In 2004–05, most incoming graduate assistants are supported at a level of $15,000 for nine months. Higher stipends are available for exceptionally well-qualified applicants. Summer support is normally provided, though not guaranteed, from federal and external research funding. Research fellowships are available on a competitive basis. Advanced students often receive support as research assistants.

Cost of Study Graduate tuition for 2004–05 is $28,970; summer tuition and fees are $328. Payment of tuition and fees is provided in addition to the student stipends.

Living and Housing Costs Accommodations for single students are available on campus at a cost of $3702 to $4462 for nine months. Accommodations for married students are available near the campus for $431 to $527 (utilities extra) per month. Privately owned rooms and apartments are also for rent near the campus.

Student Group There are 90 graduate students in the Department of Physics. In 2003–04, the University had an enrollment of 11,415 students, of whom 3,104 were graduate students.

Student Outcomes The department has current employment data on most former graduate students. Of 46 students who completed their degrees from 1999 to 2003, 15 percent have accepted academic or research faculty positions; 30 percent are employed by industry in physics and 7 percent by industry in computing; 48 percent now hold postdoctoral positions.

Location The University is located in South Bend, a city at the northernmost edge of Indiana a few miles from Michigan. Chicago is about 90 miles west, Lake Michigan is about 35 miles northwest, and Indianapolis is about 140 miles south. The population of South Bend is roughly 100,000, but the city merges with surrounding communities to form a greater Michiana (Michigan and Indiana) area that is home to more than 250,000 people. The city's name derives from the bend in the St. Joseph River, which winds through the city and provides various forms of recreation, including a nationally recognized white-water site. South Bend is home to the College Football Hall of Fame; the Studebaker Museum; the South Bend Regional Museum of Art; several theaters, including the historic Morris Performing Arts Center; the South Bend Symphony Orchestra; Broadway Theater League; and the Silver Hawks minor league baseball team.

The University The University of Notre Dame, founded in 1842, is a private, independent coeducational school. The 1,250-acre campus offers a spacious setting, with lakes and wooded areas. The intellectual, cultural, and athletic traditions at Notre Dame, coupled with the beauty of the campus, contribute to the University's fine reputation. The University offers a variety of cultural and recreational activities, including plays, concerts, and lecture series. The Rolfs Sports Recreation Center provides indoor space for a wide variety of health and recreation activities; tennis and ice-skating can be enjoyed year-round. The students and faculty members represent a rich diversity of religious, racial, and ethnic backgrounds.

Applying Applications are invited from qualified students without regard to sex, race, religion, or national or ethnic origin. Both the General Test and the Subject Test in physics of the GRE and three letters of recommendation are required. Complete applications should be submitted by February 1. A detailed departmental brochure and application information are available by writing to the department or by visiting the department's Web site.

Correspondence and Information

Chair, Admissions Committee, Department of Physics
225 Nieuwland Science Hall
University of Notre Dame
Notre Dame, Indiana 46556-5670
Telephone: 574-631-6386
E-mail: physics@nd.edu
World Wide Web: http://www.science.nd.edu/physics/index.htm

University of Notre Dame

THE FACULTY AND THEIR RESEARCH

Ani Aprahamian, Ph.D., Clark, 1986. Experimental nuclear physics: gamma-ray spectroscopy, nuclear masses, lifetimes, astrophysics.
Gerald B. Arnold, Ph.D., UCLA, 1977. Theoretical solid-state physics: magnetism, high-temperature superconductivity.
Dinshaw Balsara, Ph.D., Illinois at Urbana-Champaign, 1990. Theoretical and computational astrophysics.
Albert-László Barabási, Ph.D., Boston University, 1994. Theoretical physics, statistical mechanics, nonlinear systems, networks, biophysics.
H. Gordon Berry, Ph.D., Wisconsin, 1967. Experimental atomic physics.
Ikaros I. Bigi, Ph.D., Munich, 1976. Theoretical high-energy physics.
Howard A. Blackstead, Ph.D., Rice, 1967. Experimental physics: solid-state physics, magnetism and acoustics.
Bruce A. Bunker, Ph.D., Washington (Seattle), 1980. Experimental physics: X-ray, UV, and electron spectroscopy of condensed-matter and biological/environmental systems.
Neal M. Cason, Ph.D., Wisconsin, 1964. Experimental physics: high-energy elementary particle physics, particle spectroscopy.
Philippe A. Collon, Ph.D., Vienna, 1999. Experimental nuclear physics: new techniques, AMS.
Malgorzata Dobrowolska-Furdyna, Director of Undergraduate Studies; Ph.D., Polish Academy of Sciences, 1979. Experimental solid-state physics.
Morten R. Eskildsen, Ph.D., Copenhagen, 1998. Experimental condensed matter.
Stefan G. Frauendorf, Ph.D., Dresden Technical (Germany), 1971. Theoretical nuclear physics, atomic physics, mesoscopic systems.
Jacek K. Furdyna, Marquez University Professor; Ph.D., Northwestern, 1960. Experimental solid-state physics: man-made materials.
Umesh Garg, Ph.D., SUNY at Stony Brook, 1978. Experimental nuclear physics: nuclear structure, giant resonances, gamma-ray spectroscopy, high-spin states.
Peter Garnavich, Ph.D., Washington (Seattle), 1991. Astrophysics, observational cosmology.
Anna Goussiou, Ph.D., Wisconsin–Madison, 1995. Experimental high-energy elementary particle physics.
Michael D. Hildreth, Ph.D., Stanford, 1995. Experimental high-energy elementary particle physics.
Anthony Hyder, Ph.D., Air Force Tech, 1971. Experimental nuclear physics.
Boldizsar Jankó, Ph.D., Cornell, 1996. Theoretical condensed-matter physics.
Colin Jessop, Ph.D., Harvard, 1994. Experimental high-energy elementary particle physics.
Walter R. Johnson, Freimann Professor of Physics; Ph.D., Michigan, 1957. Theoretical physics: quantum electrodynamics, atomic physics.
Gerald L. Jones, Ph.D., Kansas, 1961. Theoretical physics: statistical mechanics.
James J. Kolata, Ph.D., Michigan State, 1969. Experimental physics: nuclear structure, heavy-ion reactions, radioactive beam physics.
Christopher F. Kolda, Ph.D., Michigan, 1995. Theoretical high-energy physics.
A. Eugene Livingston, Ph.D., Alberta, 1974. Experimental physics: atomic physics, spectroscopy of highly ionized atoms.
John M. LoSecco, Ph.D., Harvard, 1976. Experimental and theoretical physics: high-energy elementary particle physics.
Grant J. Mathews, Ph.D., Maryland, 1977. Theoretical astrophysics/cosmology, general relativity.
Kathie E. Newman, Director of Graduate Studies; Ph.D., Washington (Seattle), 1981. Theoretical physics: statistical mechanics, semiconductors.
Terrence W. Rettig, Ph.D., Indiana, 1976. Observational astronomy: comets, solar system formation, and T Tauri stars.
Randal C. Ruchti, Ph.D., Michigan State, 1973. Experimental physics: high-energy elementary particle physics.
Steven T. Ruggiero, Ph.D., Stanford, 1981. Experimental physics: condensed-matter and low-temperature physics, superconductivity.
Jonathan R. Sapirstein, Ph.D., Stanford, 1979. Theoretical physics: quantum electrodynamics.
Carol E. Tanner, Ph.D., Berkeley, 1985. Experimental physics: atomic physics.
Mitchell R. Wayne, Associate Dean of Science; Ph.D., UCLA, 1985. Experimental high-energy elementary particle physics.
Michael Wiescher, Ph.D., Münster (Germany), 1980. Experimental nuclear physics: nuclear astrophysics.

RESEARCH ACTIVITIES

Theoretical

Astrophysics/Cosmology: inflationary cosmology, primordial nucleosynthesis, cosmic microwave background, galaxy formation and evolution, large-scale structure, neutrino physics, dark matter, stellar evolution and nucleosynthesis, neutron star binaries, gravity waves, gamma-ray bursts, supernovae. (Balsara, Kolda, Mathews, Wiescher, 1 adjunct professor, 1 research professor, 3 postdoctoral fellows)
Atomic Physics: quantum electrodynamics, weak interactions, atomic many-body theory, photoionization and photoexcitation. (Johnson, Sapirstein, 1 adjunct professor, 1 postdoctoral fellow)
Biophysics: bioinformatics, cellular networks, modeling, morphogenesis. (Barabási, Jones)
Condensed Matter: many-body problem, high-temperature superconductivity, superconductivity and magnetism on the nanoscale, tunneling phenomena, metal-metal interfaces, inhomogeneous and layered superconductors, electronic structure of clusters and mesoscopic systems, hopping transport, studies of ordering in semiconductors, magnetic semiconductors. (Arnold, Barabási, Frauendorf, Jankó, Newman, 1 postdoctoral fellow)
Elementary Particle Physics: formal properties of quantum field theories, supersymmetry, grand unification, spontaneous breaking symmetry, phenomenology of strong and weak processes, rare decays, CP violation, supergravity, extra dimensions, and new particles. (Bigi, Kolda, 1 adjunct associate professor, 1 postdoctoral fellow)
General Relativity: black holes in a magnetic field, charged black holes, neutron stars, numerical relativity, gravity waves. (Mathews)
Nuclear Physics: many-body problem, nuclear reactions, few-body problem, boson expansions, structure of nuclei with momentum, high angular momentum, and exotic proton and neutron numbers. (Frauendorf, Hyder, Mathews, 1 research assistant professor)
Statistical Mechanics: phase transitions, critical phenomena in fluids, networks. (Barabási, Jones, Newman)

Experimental

Astrophysics/Astronomy: air shower array measurements of ultrahigh-energy cosmic rays, spectra and images of comets, stellar nuclear reaction rates, high redshift supernovae, cosmological parameters. (Garnavich, LoSecco, Rettig, Wiescher, 1 adjunct professor, 1 visiting research assistant professor, 1 postdoctoral fellow)
Atomic Physics: atomic structure, parity violation, tests of fundamental symmetries, excitation mechanisms, and radiative decays in neutral and ionized atoms; precision lifetimes. (Berry, Livingston, Tanner, 1 postdoctoral fellow)
Biological Physics and Molecular Environmental Science: structure and function in metalloproteins, metals in biological and geo-environmental systems. (Bunker)
Chemical Physics: carbon nanostructures, molecular recognition and biomimetic motifs, layered nanostructures, metallotexaphyrin.
Condensed-Matter Physics: low-temperature physics, superconducting microwave absorption, metal and semiconductor superlattices, magnetism, granular materials, magnetic resonance, magnetoelastic effects, high-temperature superconductivity, optical and far-infrared spectroscopy of semiconductors, crystal growth and MBE of semiconductors, magnetostatic effects, layered superconductors, single-electron tunneling, optical and infrared photoresponse, X-ray absorption spectroscopy and X-ray scattering, condensed-matter systems. (Blackstead, Bunker, Dobrowolska-Furdyna, Eskildsen, Furdyna, Ruggiero, 1 adjunct assistant professor, 1 visiting research associate professor, 1 visiting research assistant professor, 1 visiting professor, 1 guest professor, 3 postdoctoral fellows)
High-Energy Elementary Particle Physics: Fermilab D0 experiment (study of the top quark, bottom quark, W boson, and physics beyond the standard model), BaBar experiment at SLAC (CP violation in the b-quark system), CMS at CERN (search for the Higgs boson). (Cason, Goussiou, Hildreth, Jessop, LoSecco, Ruchti, Wayne, 1 research professor, 1 professional specialist, 1 postdoctoral fellow, 1 guest assistant professor, 2 research assistant professors, 1 adjunct assistant professor, 1 adjunct assistant research professor)
Nuclear Physics: nuclear structure, reaction energies, electromagnetic transitions, gamma-ray spectroscopy, high-spin states, polarized particles, giant resonances, heavy-ion reactions, radioactive beam studies, nuclear astrophysics. (Aprahamian, Collon, Garg, Kolata, Wiescher, 2 research professors, 1 visiting professor, 3 adjunct professors, 1 professional specialist, 1 research assistant professor, 2 assistant professional specialists, 1 research associate, 1 postdoctoral fellow)
Radiation Physics: low energy electrons in condensed media; determination of product yields in the radiolysis of water, aqueous solutions, liquid hydrocarbons, and liquefied rare gases; diffusion-kinetic modeling of transient species produced by ionizing radiation.

SELECTED PUBLICATIONS

Aprahamian, A. From ripples to tidal waves: Low lying vibrational motion in nuclei. *Nucl. Phys. A* 731:291–8, 2004.

Goldberg, V. Z., et al. **(A. Aprahamian).** The lowest levels in ^{15}F and shell model potential for drip line nuclei. *Phys. Rev. C* 69:031302, 2004.

Sun, Y., **A. Aprahamian,** J.-Y. Zhang, and C.-T. Lee. Nature of excited O^+ states in deformed nuclei. *Phys. Rev. C* 68:061301, 2003.

Arnold, G. B., and R. A. Klemm. Theory of coherent c-axis Josephson tunneling between layered superconductors. *Phys. Rev. B* 62:661–70, 2000.

Klemm, R. A., and **G. B. Arnold.** Coherent versus incoherent c-axis Josephson tunneling beyond layered superconductors. *Phys. Rev. B* 58:14203–6, 1998.

Balsara, D. Divergence-free adaptive mesh refinement for magnetohydrodynamics. *J. Comput. Phys.* 174:(2)614–48, 2001.

Balsara, D., R. Benjamin, and D. Cox. The evolution of adiabatic supernova remnants in a turbulent magnetized medium. *Astrophys. J.* 563:800–5, 2001.

Barabási, A.-L., and E. Bonabeau. Scale-free networks. *Sci. Am.* 288(5):60, 2003.

Barabási, A.-L. *Linked: The New Science of Networks.* Cambridge: Perseus Publishing, 2002.

Ravasz, E., and **A.-L. Barabási** et al. Hierarchical organization of modularity in metabolic networks. *Science* 297:1551–5, 2002.

Lin, B., et al. **(H. G. Berry and A. E. Livingston).** $1s2s2p^23s^6P$—$1s2p^33s^6S^o$ transitions in O IV. *Phys. Rev. A* 67:062507–15, 2003.

Savukov, I. M., and **H. G. Berry.** Laser gas-discharge absorption measurements of the ratio of two transition rates in argon. *Phys. Archives* 0208024, *Phys. Rev. A* 67:032505, 2003.

Vasilyev, A. A., I. M. Savukov, M. S. Safronova, and **H. G. Berry.** Measurement of the 6s-7p transition probabilities in atomic cesium and a revised value for the weak charge Q_w. *Phys. Rev. A* 66:020101, 2002.

Benson, D., **I. I. Bigi,** T. Mannel, and N. Uraltsev. Imprecated, yet impeccable: On the theoretical evaluation of $\Gamma(B \rightarrow X_c \ell \upsilon)$. *Nucl. Phys. B* 665:367, 2003.

Bigi, I. I., and N. Uraltsev. A vademecum on quark-hadron duality. *Int. J. Mod. Phys. A* 16: 5201, 2001.

Bigi, I. I., and A. I. Sanda. *CP Violation.* Cambridge University Press, 1999.

Blackstead, H. A., et al. Magnetically ordered Cu and Ru in $Ba_2GdRu_{1-u}Cu_uO_6$ and in $Sr_2YRu_{1-u}Cu_uO_6$. *Phys. Rev. B* 63(21): 214412, 1–11, 2001.

Boyanov, M. I., and **B. A. Bunker** et al. Mechanism of Pb adsorption to fatty acid Langmuir monolayers studied by XAFS spectroscopy. *J. Phys. Chem. B* 107:9780–8, 2003.

Shibata, T., **B. A. Bunker,** and J. Mitchell. Local distortion of MnO_6 clusters in the metallic phase of $La_{1-x}Sr_xMnO_3$. *Phys. Rev. B* 68:024103, 2003.

Shibata, T., and **B. A. Bunker** et al. Size dependent spontaneous alloying of Au-Ag nanoparticles. *J. Am. Chem. Soc.* 124:11989–96, 2002.

Kemner, K. M., et al. **(B. A. Bunker, J. K. Furdyna, and K. E. Newman).** Atomic rearrangement of interfaces in ZnTe/CdSe super-lattices. *Phys. Rev. B* 50:4327, 1994.

Chung, S. U., and **N. Cason** et al. Exotic and $q\bar{q}$ resonances in the $\pi^+\pi^-\pi^-$ system produced in π^-p collisions at 18 GeV. *Phys. Rev. D* 65:072001, 1–16, 2002.

Ivanov, I. E., and **N. M. Cason** et al. Observation of exotic meson production in the reaction $\pi^-p \rightarrow \eta'\pi^-p$ at 18 GeV/c. *Phys. Rev. Lett.* 86:3977–80, 2001.

Manak, J. J., and **N. Cason** et al. Partial-wave analysis of the $\eta\pi^+\pi^-$ system produced in the reaction $\pi^-p \rightarrow \eta\pi^+\pi^-p$ at 18 GeV/c. *Phys. Rev. D* 62:012003, 1–8, 2000.

Wojtowicz, T., et al. **(M. Dobrowolska and J. K. Furdyna).** InMnSb— a narrow gap ferromagnetic semiconductor. *Appl. Phys. Lett.* 82:4310, 2003.

Lee, S., et al. **(M. Dobrowolska and J. K. Furdyna).** Coupling between magnetic-nonmagnetic semiconductor quantum dots in double-layer geometry. *Appl. Phys. Lett.* 83:2865, 2003.

Eskildsen, M. R., et al. Vortex imaging in magnesium diboride with H ⊥ c. *Phys. Rev. B* 68:100508(R), 2003.

Cubitt, R., and **M. R. Eskildsen** et al. Effects of two-band superconductivity on the flux-line lattice in magnesium diboride. *Phys. Rev. Lett.* 91:047002, 2003.

Eskildsen, M. R., et al. Vortex imaging in the p band of magnesium diboride. *Phys. Rev. Lett.* 89:187003, 2002.

Simons, A. J., and **S. Frauendorf** et al. Evidence for a new type of shears mechanism in ^{106}Cd. *Phys. Rev. Lett.* 91:162501, 2003.

Frauendorf, S. Spontaneous symmetry breaking in rotating nuclei. *Rev. Mod. Phys.* 680:463, 2001 .

Näher, U., and **S. Frauendorf** et al. Fission of metal clusters. *Phys. Rep.* 285:245, 1997.

Kudelski, A., et al. **(J. K. Furdyna and M. Dobrowolska).** Excitonic luminescence from non-symmetric heterovalent AlAs/GaAs/ZnSe quantum wells. *Appl. Phys. Lett.* 82:1854, 2003.

Bao, J., A. V. Bragas, **J. K. Furdyna,** and R. Merlin. Optically induced multispin entanglement in a semiconductor quantum wells. *Nature Mater.* 2:175–9, 2003.

Furdyna, J. K., and **M. Dobrowolska.** Coherent superposition of electric- and magnetic-dipole spin-flip transitions in zinc-blende semiconductors. *J. Superconductivity* 16:647–59, 2003.

Welp, U., et al. **(J. K. Furdyna).** Magnetic domain structure and magnetic anisotropy in $Ga_{1-x}Mn_xAs$. *Phys. Rev. Lett.* 90:167206, 2003.

Garg, U. The isoscalar giant dipole resonance: A status report. *Nucl. Phys. A* 731:3, 2004.

Zhu, S., and **U. Garg** et al. A composite chiral pair of rotational bands in the odd-A nucleus ^{135}Nd. *Phys. Rev. Lett.* 91:132501, 2003.

Zhu, S., and **U. Garg** et al. Investigation of antimagnetic rotation in ^{100}Pd. *Phys. Rev. C* 64:041302(R), 2001.

Garnavich, P. M., et al. Discovery of the low-redshift optical afterglow of GRB 011121 and its progenitor supernova SN 2001ke. *Astrophys. J.* 582:924, 2003.

Ichiki, K., et al. **(P. M. Garnavich and G. J. Mathews).** Disappearing dark matter in brane world cosmology: New limits on noncompact extra dimensions. *Phys. Rev. D* 68:083518, 2003.

Garnavich, P. M., A. Loeb, and K. Stanek. Resolving gamma-ray burst 000301C with a gravitational microlens. *Astophys. J. Lett.* 544:11, 2000.

Garnavich, P. M., et al. Constraints on cosmological models from HST observations of high-z supernovae. *Astrophys. J. Lett.* 493:93, 1998.

Goussiou, A., et al. Results of the Tevatron Higgs sensitivity study. CDF and D0 collaborations. *FERMILAB-Pub-03/320-E,* 2003.

Carena, M., and **A. Goussiou** et al. Report of the Tevatron Higgs Working Group. Tevatron Run II SUSY/Higgs Workshop. *FERMILAB-Conf-00/279-T, SCIPP 00/37,* hep-ph/0010338, 2000.

Abazov, V. M., et al. **(M. Hildreth, R. Ruchti, and M. Wayne).** Subject multiplicity of gluon and quark jets reconstructed using the kT algorithm in $p\bar{p}$ collisions. D0 collaboration. *Phys. Rev. D* 65:052008, 2002.

Blondel, A., and **M. D. Hildreth** et al. Evaluation of the LEP center-of-mass energy above the W Pair Production Threshold. (LEP Energy Working Group), CERN-EP-98-191, Dec. 1998. *Eur. Phys. J. C* 11:573, 1999.

Abbiendi, G., and **M. D. Hildreth** et al. Measurement of the W mass and width in e+ e- collisions at 183 GeV. (OPAL collaboration). *Phys. Lett. B* 453:138, 1999.

Berciu, M., and **B. Jankó.** Zeeman-splitting induced bound states in diluted magnetic semiconductors. *Phys. Rev. Lett.* 90(24):246804, 2003.

Zarand, G., and **B. Jankó.** $Ga_{1-x}Mn_xAs$: A frustrated ferromagnet. *Phys. Rev. Lett.* 89:047201, 2002.

University of Notre Dame

Selected Publications (continued)

Lee, C. S., **B. Jankó**, I. Derényi, and **A.-L. Barabási.** Ratchet effect in vortex dynamics: Reducing vortex densities in superconductors. *Nature* 400:337–40, 1999.

Jessop, C., et al. Search for the exclusive radiative decays $B \rightarrow \rho\gamma$ and $B \rightarrow \omega\gamma$. BaBar collaboration, hep-ex 0207076. *Phys. Rev. Lett.* 92:11180, 2004.

Jessop, C., et al. Measurement of CP violating asymmetries in B0 decays to CP Eigenstates. BaBar collaboration. *Phys. Rev. Lett.* 86:2515, 2001.

Jessop, C., et al. Evidence for top quark production in proton-antiproton collisions. CDF collaboration. *Phys. Rev. Lett.* 73:225, 1994.

Johnson, W. R., V. A. Dzuba, U. I. Safronova, and M. S. Safronova. Finite-field evaluation of the Lennard-Jones atom-wall interaction constant C_3 for alkali-metal atoms. *Phys. Rev. A* 69:022508, 1–6, 2004.

Savukov, I. M., and **W. R. Johnson** et al. Energies, transition rates, and electric dipole moment enhancement factors for Ce IV and Pr V. *Phys. Rev. A* 67:042504, 1–5, 2003.

Hemmers, O., and **W. R. Johnson** et al. Dramatic nondipole effects in low-energy photoionization: Experimental and theoretical study of Xe 5s. *Phys. Rev. Lett.* 91:53002, 1–4, 2003.

Zajac, M., **G. L. Jones,** and J. A. Glazier. Simulating convergent extension by way of anisotropic differential adhesion. *J. Theor. Biol.* 222(2):247, 2003

Zajac, M., **G. L. Jones,** and J. A. Glazier. Model of covergent extension in animal morphogenesis. *Phys. Rev. Lett.* 85:2022, 2000.

Jones, G. L. Symmetries and conservation laws of differential equations. *Il Nouvo Cimento* 112B:1053–9, 1997.

Rogachev, G. V., et al. **(J. J. Kolata).** T=5/2 states in ^{9}Li: Isobaric analog states of ^{9}He. *Phys. Rev. C* 67:041603(R), 2003.

Voytas, P. A., and **J. J. Kolata** et al. Direct measurement of the L/K ratio in ^{7}Be electron capture. *Phys. Rev. Lett.* 88(1):012501, 2002.

Rogachev, G. V., and **J. J. Kolata** et al. Proton elastic scattering from ^{7}Be at low energies. *Phys. Rev. C* 64:061601(R), 2001.

Babu, K., and **C. F. Kolda.** Higgs-mediated $\tau \rightarrow 3\mu$ in the supersymmetric seesaw model. *Phys. Rev. Lett.* 89:241802, 2002.

Arkani-Hamed, N., L. Hall, **C. F. Kolda,** and H. Murayama. A new perspective on cosmic coincidence problems. *Phys. Rev. Lett.* 85:4434 2000.

Babu, K., and **C. F. Kolda.** Higgs-mediated $B^o \rightarrow \mu^+\mu^-$ in minimal supersymmetry. *Phys. Rev. Lett.* 84:228, 2000.

Feili, D., et al. **(A. E. Livingston).** Access to two-photon QED contributions via 2s $^{2}S_{1/2}$-2p $^{2}P_{1/2}$ transitions in heavy Li-like ions. *Physics Scripta T* 92:300–2, 2001.

Wolf, A., and **A. E. Livingston** et al. Spectroscopy using stimulated electron-ion recombination. *Hyperfine Interact.* 127:203–10, 2000.

Glancy, S., **J. M. LoSecco,** H. M. Vasconcelos, and **C. E. Tanner.** Imperfect detectors in linear optical quantum computers. *Phys. Rev. A* 65:062317-1, 2002.

Aubert, B., and **J. M. LoSecco** et al. Observation of CP violation in the B^0 meson system, hep-ex/0107013. *Phys. Rev. Lett.* 87:091801, 2001.

Bionta, R. M., and **J. M. LoSecco** et al. Observation of a neutrino burst in coincidence with Supernova 1987A in the large Magellanic cloud. *Phys. Rev. Lett.* 58:1494, 1987.

Ashenfelter, T., **G. J. Mathews,** and K. A. Olive. Chemical evolution of Mg isotopes versus the time variation of the fine structure constant. *Phys. Rev. Lett.* 92:041102, 2004.

Iwamoto, N., et al. **(G. J. Mathews).** Flash-driven convective mixing in low-mass, metal-deficient asymptotic giant branch stars: A new paradigm for lithium enrichment and a possible s-process. *Astrophys. J.* 602:377, 2004.

Vandeworp, E. M., and **K. E. Newman.** Coherent alloy separation: Differences in canonical and grand canonical ensembles. *Phys. Rev. B* 55:14222–9, 1997.

Cohen, R. J., and **K. E. Newman.** Commensurate and incommensurate phases of epitaxial semiconductor antiferromagnets with "built-in" strain. *Phys. Rev. B* 46:14282, 1992.

Brittain, S., T. Simon, C. Kulesa, and **T. Rettig.** Interstellar H_3^+ line absorption toward LkHα101. *Astrophys. J.* 606:911, 2004.

Brittain, S., and **T. Rettig** et al. CO emission from disks around AB aurigae and HD141569: Implications for disk structure and planet formation timescales. *Astrophys. J.* 588, 2003.

Brittain, S., and **T. Rettig.** Detection of CO and H_3^+ from the pre-planetary disk around the Herbig AeBe star HD141569. *Nature* 418:57–9, 2002.

Abazov, V. M., and **R. C. Ruchti** et al. Search for studies of large extra dimensions in the monojet +missing E_T channel with the DØ detector. *Phys. Rev. Lett.* 90, 2003.

Ruchti, R. Studies of the response of the prototype CMS hadron calorimeter, including magnetic field effects to pion, electron, and muon beams. *Nucl. Instrum. Methods Phys. Res., Sect. A* 457:75, 2001.

Abachi, S., and **R. C. Ruchti** et al. Observation of the top quark. (D0 collaboration.) *Phys. Rev. Lett.* 74(14):2632–7, 1995.

Clark, A. M., et al. **(S. T. Ruggiero).** Practical tunneling refrigerator. *Appl. Phys. Lett.* 84:625–7, 2004.

Ruggiero, S. T., T. B. Ekkens, and **G. B. Arnold.** Periodic tunnel-current oscillations in metal droplets. *J. Appl. Phys.* 94:3660–2, 2003.

Ruggiero, S. T., et al. Magnetooptic effects in spin-injection devices. *Appl. Phys. Lett.* 82:4599–601, 2003.

Ruggiero, S. T., and D. A. Rudman, eds. *Superconducting Devices.* New York: Academic, 1990.

Sapirstein, J., and K. T. Cheng. Calculation of radiative corrections to hyperfine splittings in the neutral alkalis. *Phys. Rev. A* 67:022512, 2003.

Adkins, G. S., R. N. Fell, and **J. Sapirstein.** Order $m\alpha^8$ contribution to the orthopositronium decay rate. *Ann. Phys.* 295:136, 2002.

Sapirstein, J. Parity violation. In *Relativistic Electronic Structure Theory: Part I, Fundamentals,* ed. P. Schwerdtfeger. Amsterdam: Elsevier Science, 2002.

Bize, S., et al. **(C. E. Tanner).** Testing the stability of fundamental constants with the 199Hg+ single ion optical clock. *Phys. Rev. Lett.* 90:150802-1–4, 2003.

Gerginov, V., A. Derevianko, and **C. E. Tanner.** Observation of the nuclear magnetic octupole moment of 133Cs. *Phys. Rev. Lett.* 91:072501-1–4, 2003.

Wayne, M., et al. Performance of a large scale scintillating fiber tracker using VLPC readout. *IEEE Trans. Nucl. Sci.* 43:1146–52, 1996.

Baumbaugh, B., and **M. Wayne** et al. Performance of multiclad scintillating and clear waveguide fibers read out with visible light photon counters. *Nucl. Instrum. Methods Phys. Res., Sect. A* 345:271, 1994.

Woosley, S. E., and **M. Wiescher** et al. Models for Type I X-ray bursts with improved nuclear physics. *Astrophys. J. Suppl. Ser.* 151:75–102, 2004.

Dababneh, S., et al. **(M. Wiescher).** Stellar He burning of ^{18}O: A measurement of low-energy resonances and their astrophysical implications. *Phys. Rev. C* 68:025801, 2003.

Beard, M. and **M. Wiescher.** The fate of matter on accreting neutron stars. *Rev. Mexicana de Fisica* 49(4):139–44, 2003.

UNIVERSITY OF PITTSBURGH

Department of Physics and Astronomy

Programs of Study

The graduate programs in the Department of Physics and Astronomy are designed primarily for students who wish to obtain the Ph.D. degree, although the M.S. degree is also offered. The Ph.D. program provides high-quality training for students without needlessly emphasizing formal requirements. Upon arrival, each graduate student is appointed a faculty adviser to provide personalized guidance through the core curriculum. A set of basic courses is to be taken by all graduate students unless the equivalent material has been demonstrably mastered in other ways. These basic courses include dynamical systems, quantum mechanics, electromagnetic theory, and statistical physics. More advanced and special topics courses are offered in a range of areas, including, but not limited to, high energy and particle physics, condensed matter, statistical and solid-state physics, astrophysics, astronomy, and relativity.

Students have a wide variety of programs from which to choose a thesis topic. University faculty members have active research programs in atomic physics, astronomy, astrophysics and cosmology employing ground- and space-based telescopes, particle astrophysics, condensed-matter and solid-state physics, high- and intermediate-energy elementary particle physics, chemical physics, and biological physics.

Under the department program in applied physics, students can arrange to do multidisciplinary thesis research that involves faculty members from other departments of the University in, for example, biophysics, geophysics, radiation physics, materials science, surface science, laser physics, or magnetic resonance imaging.

Research Facilities

The department's facilities include the physics library, an electronics shop, a glassblowing shop, a professionally staffed machine shop, and extensive departmental and University computer resources. Departmental students have easy access to the facilities and expertise available at the Pittsburgh Supercomputing Center (PSC). Other facilities include the Allegheny Observatory (for positional astronomy). Experiments in particle physics are carried out at such national and international facilities as Brookhaven National Laboratory in New York; Fermi National Laboratory in Chicago; CERN in Switzerland; and Thomas Jefferson Accelerator Facility in Virginia. Similarly, programs are conducted at national and international observatories, such as at Kitt Peak and Mount Hopkins, Arizona; at Cerro Tololo, Las Campanas, and La Silla in Chile; at Apache Point in New Mexico for collection of Sloan Digital Sky Survey data; at Mauna Kea in Hawaii; and on the Hubble Space Telescope, the Chandra X-ray Observatory, and other space observatories.

Financial Aid

Financial aid is normally provided through teaching assistantships during the first year and through research assistantships thereafter. The department has several fellowships established for entering graduate students. They are awarded on a competitive basis, with all qualified applicants automatically entered into a pool. Some University fellowships are also available and are awarded in a University-wide competition. Students are generally supported throughout their entire graduate career, provided good academic standing is maintained. Teaching and research assistantship appointments carried a stipend of $6387.50 per term in 2003–04, plus a tuition scholarship, bringing the annual stipend to $19,162.50 for students supported throughout the year. Research assistantship appointments may be held in connection with most of the department's research programs.

Cost of Study

For full-time students who are not Pennsylvania residents, tuition and fees per term in 2003–04 were $11,725. Part-time students paid $941 per credit plus fees. Full-time Pennsylvania residents paid $6142 per term, including fees, and part-time Pennsylvania residents paid $479 per credit plus fees.

Living and Housing Costs

Most University of Pittsburgh students live in rooms or apartments in the Oakland area. The typical cost of rooms or apartments ranges from $340 to $550 per month for housing. Meals range from $300 to $400 per month.

Student Group

The department's graduate student body in 2003–04 consisted of 84 students; 80 students received financial support. These figures are typical of the department's graduate enrollment.

Student Outcomes

Many Ph.D. graduates accept postdoctoral positions at major research universities, often leading to teaching and research positions at outstanding universities in the United States and around the world. Other recent graduates have entered research careers in the private sector. One recent graduate received the American Physical Society's Nicholas Metropolis Award for Outstanding Doctoral Thesis Work in Computational Physics.

Location

Pittsburgh is situated in a hilly and wooded region of western Pennsylvania where the Allegheny and Monongahela Rivers join to form the Ohio. The region has a natural beauty. The terrain of western Pennsylvania and nearby West Virginia is excellent for outdoor activities, including cycling, hiking, downhill and cross-country skiing, white-water rafting and kayaking, rock climbing, hunting, and fishing. The University is located about 3 miles east of downtown Pittsburgh in the city's cultural center. Adjacent to the campus are Carnegie Mellon University and the Carnegie, comprising the Museum of Art, the Museum of Natural History, the Carnegie Library, and the Carnegie Music Hall. Schenley Park adjoins the campus; it has picnic areas, playing fields, jogging trails, and an excellent botanical conservatory. The Pittsburgh area has several professional sports teams; for detailed information, students should visit http://www.phyast.pitt.edu/Resources/PITT_INFO.htm.

The Department

The department has long been active in research and has trained more than 500 recipients of the Ph.D. degree. Close cooperation exists between this department and the physics department of Carnegie Mellon University; all seminars, colloquia, and courses are shared. The graduate students of both institutions benefit from belonging to one of the largest communities of active physicists in the country. Furthermore, basic research, conducted at the University of Pittsburgh Medical Center and the School of Medicine, provides additional opportunities for research with multidisciplinary perspectives.

Applying

Students who wish to apply for admission or financial aid should take the GRE, including the Subject Test in physics. Applicants should request that the registrars of their undergraduate and graduate schools send transcripts of their records to the department. Three letters of recommendation are required for admission with aid. Unless English is the applicant's native language, the TOEFL is required. The application deadline is January 31. Late applications are accepted on the basis of space availability.

Correspondence and Information

Professor David Turnshek
Admissions Committee
Department of Physics and Astronomy
University of Pittsburgh
Pittsburgh, Pennsylvania 15260

Telephone: 412-624-9066
E-mail (graduate secretary): lmh@pitt.edu
World Wide Web: http://www.phyast.pitt.edu/

University of Pittsburgh

THE FACULTY AND THEIR RESEARCH

Elizabeth U. Baranger, Professor and Vice Provost for Graduate Studies; Ph.D., Cornell. Theoretical nuclear physics.
Joseph Boudreau, Associate Professor; Ph.D., Wisconsin. Experimental particle physics.
Daniel Boyanovsky, Professor; Ph.D., California, Santa Barbara. Condensed-matter physics, particle astrophysics.
Wolfgang J. Choyke, Research Professor; Ph.D., Ohio State. Solid-state physics, defect states in semiconductors, large bandgap spectroscopy.
Russell Clark, Lecturer/Lab Supervisor; Ph.D., LSU.
Rob Coalson, Professor; Ph.D., Harvard. Chemical physics.
Andrew Connolly, Assistant Professor; Ph.D., Imperial College (London). Astrophysics, extragalactic astronomy, observational cosmology.
Robert P. Devaty, Associate Professor; Ph.D., Cornell. Experimental solid-state physics.
H. E. Anthony Duncan, Professor; Ph.D., MIT. Theoretical high-energy physics.
Steven A. Dytman, Professor; Ph.D., Carnegie Mellon. Experimental intermediate-energy physics.
George D. Gatewood, Professor; Ph.D., Pittsburgh. Astronomy, astrometry, search for planetary systems orbiting neighboring stars.
Yadin Y. Goldschmidt, Professor; Ph.D., Hebrew (Jerusalem). Condensed-matter theory, statistical mechanics.
D. John Hillier, Associate Professor; Ph.D., Australian National. Theoretical and observational astrophysics, computational physics.
David M. Jasnow, Professor and Department Chair; Ph.D., Illinois. Theory of phase transitions, statistical mechanics.
Rainer Johnsen, Professor and Graduate Director; Ph.D., Kiel (Germany). Experimental atomic and plasma physics.
Peter F. M. Koehler, Professor; Ph.D., Rochester. Experimental high-energy physics.
Jeremy Levy, Associate Professor; Ph.D., California, Santa Barbara. Experimental condensed matter.
Irving J. Lowe, Professor; Ph.D., Washington (St. Louis). Experimental solid-state physics, nuclear magnetic resonance, nuclear magnetic resonance imaging.
James V. Maher, Professor and Provost; Ph.D., Yale. Experimental solid-state physics, critical phenomena, physics of fluids.
James Mueller, Associate Professor; Ph.D., Cornell. Experimental intermediate-energy particle physics.
Donna Naples, Assistant Professor; Ph.D., Maryland. Experimental high-energy physics.
Vittorio Paolone, Associate Professor; Ph.D., California, Davis. Experimental high-energy physics.
Hrvoje Petek, Professor; Ph.D., Berkeley. Experimental condensed matter.
Sandhya Rao, Research Assistant Professor; Ph.D., Pittsburgh. Astrophysics, extragalactic astronomy, observational cosmology.
Ralph Z. Roskies, Professor; Ph.D., Princeton. Theoretical high-energy physics, use of computer in theoretical physics.
Vladimir Savinov, Assistant Professor; Ph.D., Minnesota. Experimental intermediate-energy physics.
Regina E. Schulte-Ladbeck, Associate Professor; Ph.D., Heidelberg. Astrophysics.
Paul F. Shepard, Professor; Ph.D., Princeton. Experimental high-energy physics.
Ravi K. Sheth, Assistant Professor; Ph.D., Cambridge. Astrophysics theory, statistics, and cosmology.
Chandralekha Singh, Senior Lecturer; Ph.D., California, Santa Barbara. Physics education research, polymer physics.
David Snoke, Associate Professor; Ph.D., Illinois at Urbana-Champaign. Solid-state experimental.
G. Alec Stewart, Associate Professor and Dean, University Honors College; Ph.D., Washington (Seattle). Experimental solid-state physics.
Eric Swanson, Assistant Professor; Ph.D., Toronto. Experimental intermediate-energy physics.
Frank Tabakin, Professor; Ph.D., MIT. Theoretical nuclear physics.
Julia A. Thompson, Professor; Ph.D., Yale. Experimental high-energy physics, optical instrumentation.
David A. Turnshek, Professor; Ph.D., Arizona. Astrophysics, extragalactic astronomy, observational cosmology.
Xiao-Lun Wu, Associate Professor; Ph.D., Cornell. Experimental condensed matter, biophysics.
John T. Yates, Professor; Ph.D., MIT. Physical chemistry.

EMERITUS FACULTY

James E. Bayfield, Professor; Ph.D., Yale. Experimental atomic physics and quantum optics.
Manfred A. Biondi, Professor; Ph.D., MIT. Experimental atomic physics and aeronomy.
Wilfred W. Cleland, Professor; Ph.D., Yale. Experimental high-energy physics.
Bernard L. Cohen, Professor; Ph.D., Carnegie Mellon. Energy and environment.
Richard M. Drisko, Professor; Ph.D., Carnegie Mellon. Theoretical nuclear physics.
Eugene Engels Jr., Professor; Ph.D., Princeton. Experimental high-energy physics.
Myron P. Garfunkel, Professor; Ph.D., Rutgers. Experimental low-temperature physics, superconductivity.
Edward Gerjuoy, Professor; Ph.D., Berkeley. Theoretical atomic physics.
Walter I. Goldburg, Professor; Ph.D., Duke. Experimental solid-state physics, phase transitions, light scattering, turbulence.
Cyril Hazard, Professor; Ph.D., Manchester. Astrophysics, extragalactic astronomy, observational cosmology.
Allen I. Janis, Professor; Ph.D., Syracuse. General relativity, philosophy of science.
Ezra T. Newman, Professor; Ph.D., Syracuse. General relativity, twistor theory.
Richard H. Pratt, Professor; Ph.D., Chicago. Theoretical atomic and low-energy particle physics, bremsstrahlung, hot plasma processes, photon scattering.
Juerg X. Saladin, Professor; Ph.D., Swiss Federal Institute of Technology. Experimental nuclear physics.
C. Martin Vincent, Professor; Ph.D., Witwatersrand (South Africa). Theoretical intermediate-energy physics.
Raymond S. Willey, Professor; Ph.D., Stanford. Theoretical high-energy physics.
Jeffrey Winicour, Research Professor; Ph.D., Syracuse. General relativity.
Edward C. Zipf, Professor; Ph.D., Johns Hopkins. Experimental atomic and atmospheric physics.

Allen Hall, home to the department.

Collider detector at Fermilab.

M51, the Whirlpool Galaxy, a spiral galaxy in the constellation of Canes Venatici.

UNIVERSITY OF ROCHESTER

Department of Physics and Astronomy

Programs of Study

The department offers programs of study leading to the Ph.D. degree in physics or physics and astronomy. Students normally earn the M.A. or M.S. degree in physics en route to the Ph.D. The M.A. is awarded after the completion of 30 semester hours of course work and a comprehensive examination; the M.S. degree in physics requires a thesis in addition to the course work. Students are not usually admitted to work toward a master's degree unless they intend to obtain a Ph.D. (exceptions include students in the 3-2 programs in physics and medical physics).

Most candidates for the Ph.D. degree take two years of course work and a written preliminary examination during their second year. Requirements for the Ph.D. include demonstrating competence in quantum mechanics, mathematical methods, electromagnetic theory, and statistical physics, as well as in an advanced area of specialization. A doctoral thesis, based on a significant piece of original research, and a final oral thesis defense are required of all Ph.D. candidates. A typical program of study takes five or six years to complete. A minor is not required, although students are encouraged to broaden their understanding of other subfields of physics or astronomy beyond the area of their thesis research. There is no foreign language requirement.

The department provides opportunities for research in observational astronomy, theoretical and laboratory astrophysics, biological and medical physics, and experimental and theoretical areas of condensed-matter physics, chemical physics, cross-disciplinary physics, elementary particle physics, nuclear physics, plasma physics, quantum optics, and atomic, molecular, and optical physics.

Research Facilities

The infrared astronomy group has extensive programs in the development of advanced detector arrays, electronics, and instrumentation for astronomy. The results are in use on several ground-based observatories in Arizona and Hawaii and in space on the NASA Spitzer Space Telescope. The high energy densities that can be produced by the Omega laser at the Laboratory for Laser Energetics offer unique opportunities for the laboratory study of matter under conditions ordinarily associated with high-energy astrophysical phenomena such as supernova blasts. The atomic molecular and optical physics group offers extensive facilities, including a broad range of ultraviolet, visible, and infrared lasers; ultra-high-stability CW dye, solid-state, and diode laser systems; ultrafast lasers (femtosecond); and an ultra-high-power (psec, chirped-pulse, regeneratively amplified) pulsed solid-state laser system. The group's capabilities include sophisticated photon-counting, laser cooling and trapping, atomic beam, and laser physics experimentation. For research in condensed matter, the department offers a unique magnetooptical spectroscopy lab and an advanced surface science research lab that is equipped with X-ray, ultraviolet, and inverse photoemission spectroscopy; scanning-tunneling, atomic-force, and near-field microscopy; low-energy electron and photoelectron diffraction facilities; and advanced thin-film deposition systems. In its low-temperature lab, there is a helium dilution refrigerator and a superconducting magnet for measurements of correlated and mesoscopic systems. Research in high-energy and nuclear physics includes a project to develop state-of-the-art sensitive detectors for application in high-energy and nuclear physics, which are designed and tested on campus and then assembled and operated at international and national laboratories, including CERN (CMS), Fermilab (Dzero, CDF, NuTeV, and MINERvA), Brookhaven (PHOBOS/RHIC), the Stanford Linear Accelerator Center, Jefferson Laboratory, Lawrence Berkeley Laboratory, Argonne, KEK/JPARC (Japan), and Wilson Lab at Ithaca, New York. The Physics-Optics-Astronomy Library, within the physics building, provides ready access to more than 225 journals. The facilities of the University's Laboratory for Laser Energetics, the Institute of Optics, and the Center for Optoelectronics and Imaging are also available for collaborative efforts.

Financial Aid

In 2004–05, graduate teaching and research assistantships, which require 16 hours of work per week during the academic year, carry stipends of $15,300 for nine months. Additional support is available for participation in summer research. A graduate assistant who also takes part in full-time summer research receives a total of $19,890 for the calendar year. A few special University and departmental fellowships provide stipends of up to $21,890 for the calendar year. In addition, the Department of Education GAANN, Robert E. Marshak Fellowships, Provost Fellowships, and Sproul Fellowships for academic excellence are available to supplement teaching or research assistantships for outstanding international students.

Cost of Study

For students with fewer than 90 credit hours of accumulated graduate course work, tuition for the 2004–05 academic year is $28,160. Tuition for more advanced students is $1412 per academic year. (Currently, all graduate students in the department receive special awards to cover tuition.) All full-time graduate students are charged a health service fee of $880 per year. The cost of books and supplies is about $600 per year.

Living and Housing Costs

The cost of living in Rochester is among the lowest for metropolitan areas. Supermarkets with moderate prices are located near the University, or meals can be obtained on campus. University-operated housing for either single or married graduate students is available within easy walking distance of the campus. Free shuttle-bus service is available within the University complex. Additional privately owned rooms and apartments are available in the residential areas near the University.

Student Group

There are approximately 135 graduate students in physics and astronomy; about 17 percent are women, and about 27 percent of the students are married. All full-time students receive some form of financial aid. Admission to graduate study is highly competitive, with only about 20 new students admitted each year; about 50 percent have undergraduate degrees from institutions outside the United States.

Location

With approximately 735,500 inhabitants, the Rochester metropolitan area is the third largest in the state. A city with its economy based on high-technology industries, it is located on the southern shore of Lake Ontario. Niagara Falls, the scenic Finger Lakes district, and the rugged Adirondack Mountains are all within a few hours' drive. The Rochester Philharmonic Orchestra and the Rochester Americans ice-hockey team provide two examples of the range of experiences available. Rochester is readily accessible both by air and by car.

The University and The Department

The University of Rochester is a private institution with 4,610 undergraduates, 3,587 graduate students, and 1,410 faculty members. The Department of Physics and Astronomy, one of the largest and strongest departments within the University, has a reputation for excellence in graduate education and research spanning more than fifty years. Many faculty members of the department have been awarded major fellowships and prizes in recognition of their research accomplishments.

Applying

Catalogs and application information can be obtained from the department's Web site. Students are admitted only in September, and completed applications should be received by January 1 in order for applicants to be considered for financial aid. Applicants should take the GRE General Test and physics Subject Test in time for scores to arrive by January 1. TOEFL scores are required of international students whose native language is not English.

Correspondence and Information

Graduate Student Counselor
Department of Physics and Astronomy
University of Rochester
Rochester, New York 14627
Telephone: 585-275-4356
World Wide Web: http://www.pas.rochester.edu

University of Rochester

THE FACULTY AND THEIR RESEARCH

G. P. Agrawal, Professor; Ph.D., Indian Institute of Technology (New Delhi), 1974. Fiber optics, lasers, optical communications.

R. Betti, Professor; Ph.D., MIT, 1992. Theoretical plasma physics, nuclear and mechanical engineering, computational and plasma physics.

N. P. Bigelow, Lee A. DuBridge Professor; Ph.D., Cornell, 1989. Experimental and theoretical quantum optics and quantum physics, studies of BEC and laser-cooled and trapped atoms.

E. G. Blackman, Associate Professor; Ph.D., Harvard, 1995. Theoretical astrophysics, astrophysical plasmas and magnetic fields, accretion and ejection phenomena, relativistic and high-energy astrophysics.

A. Bodek, Professor and Chair; Ph.D., MIT, 1972. Experimental elementary particle physics, proton-antiproton collisions, QCD and structure functions, neutrino physics, electron scattering, tile-fiber calorimetric detectors.

R. W. Boyd, M. Parker Givens Professor; Ph.D., Berkeley, 1977. Nonlinear optics.

T. G. Castner, Professor Emeritus; Ph.D., Illinois, 1958. Experimental condensed-matter physics, metal insulator transition.

D. Cline, Professor; Ph.D., Manchester (England), 1963. Extreme states of nuclei pairing and shape correlations in nuclei.

E. Conwell, Professor; Ph.D., Chicago, 1948. Theoretical chemical physics, condensed-matter physics, biological physics.

A. Das, Professor; Ph.D., SUNY at Stony Brook, 1977. Theoretical particle physics, finite temperature field theory, integrable systems, phenomenology, noncommutative field theory and string/M theory.

R. Demina, Associate Professor; Ph.D., Northeastern, 1994. Experimental particle physics, proton-antiproton collisions, top and electroweak physics.

D. H. Douglass, Professor; Ph.D., MIT, 1959. Experimental condensed-matter physics, climate change and pollution.

J. H. Eberly, Andrew Carnegie Professor; Ph.D., Stanford, 1962. Theoretical quantum optics, quantum entanglement, cavity QED, atoms in strong laser fields, dark-state optical control theory.

T. Ferbel, Professor; Ph.D., Yale, 1963. Experimental elementary particle physics, studies of the top quark in hadronic collisions.

W. J. Forrest, Professor and Director, C. E. Kenneth Mees Observatory; Ph.D., California, San Diego, 1974. Observational infrared astronomy, infrared array detectors.

T. H. Foster, Professor; Ph.D., Rochester, 1990. Biological and medical physics.

A. Frank, Associate Professor; Ph.D., Washington (Seattle), 1992. Theoretical astrophysics, numerical hydrodynamics and magnetohydrodynamics.

H. W. Fulbright, Professor Emeritus; Ph.D., Washington (St. Louis), 1944. Experimental nuclear physics, radio astronomy of the top quark, phenomenology of strong interactions.

Y. Gao, Professor; Ph.D., Purdue, 1986. Experimental condensed-matter physics, surface physics.

H. E. Gove, Professor Emeritus; Ph.D., MIT, 1950. Experimental nuclear physics, heavy ions, accelerator mass spectrometry.

C. R. Hagen, Professor; Ph.D., MIT, 1962. Theoretical elementary particle physics; quantum field theory, particularly 2+1 dimensional theories.

H. L. Helfer, Professor Emeritus; Ph.D., Chicago, 1953. Theoretical astrophysics, dense plasma equations of state, production and acceleration of cosmic-ray particles.

J. Howell, Assistant Professor; Ph.D., Penn State, 2000. Experimental quantum optics and quantum physics, quantum cryptography and quantum computation.

R. S. Knox, Professor Emeritus; Ph.D., Rochester, 1958. Theoretical biological physics and condensed-matter physics, energy-balance models of climate.

D. S. Koltun, Professor; Ph.D., Princeton, 1961. Theoretical nuclear physics, meson interactions with nuclei, many-body theory, electron scattering.

S. L. Manly, Mercer Brugler Professor; Ph.D., Columbia, 1989. Experimental relativistic heavy-ion physics, experimental elementary particle physics.

R. L. McCrory, Professor and Director of the Laboratory for Laser Energetics; Ph.D., MIT, 1973. Nuclear and mechanical engineering, computational hydrodynamics.

K. S. McFarland, Associate Professor; Ph.D., Chicago, 1994. Experimental elementary particle physics: properties of top quarks, neutrino physics, electroweak unification.

A. C. Melissinos, Professor; Ph.D., MIT, 1958. Experimental particle physics, high-intensity laser-particle interactions, free-electron lasers, searches for relic gravitational radiation.

D. D. Meyerhofer, Professor; Ph.D., Princeton, 1987. Experimental plasma and laser physics, high-energy-density physics and inertial confinement fusion, high-intensity laser-matter interaction experiments, quantum optics.

S. Okubo, Professor Emeritus; Ph.D., Rochester, 1958. Theoretical particle physics and mathematical physics, Lie and nonassociative algebras.

L. Orr, Associate Professor; Ph.D., Chicago, 1991. Theoretical elementary particle physics, phenomenology, quantum chromodynamics and electroweak physics.

J. L. Pipher, Professor Emeritus; Ph.D., Cornell, 1971. Observational and experimental astronomy; development of infrared detector arrays for ground-based and space astronomy, including the successful Spitzer Space Telescope, which was launched in August 2003; infrared observations from the ground and from space of young star forming regions, active and starburst galaxies, brown dwarfs, and planetary nebulae.

A. Quillen, Assistant Professor; Ph.D., Caltech, 1993. Experimental astrophysics, observational infrared astronomy, galactic structure and dynamics, active galactic nuclei, dynamics of planetary and protoplanetary systems.

S. G. Rajeev, Professor; Ph.D., Syracuse, 1984. Theoretical particle physics, nonperturbative quantum field theory applied to strong interactions.

L. Rothberg, Professor; Ph.D., Harvard, 1983. Experimental chemical physics, organic electronics and biomolecular sensing.

M. P. Savedoff, Professor Emeritus; Ph.D., Princeton, 1957. Theoretical astrophysics, stellar interiors, interstellar matter, high-energy astrophysics.

Y. Shapir, Professor; Ph.D., Tel-Aviv, 1981. Theoretical condensed-matter physics, statistical mechanics, critical phenomena in ordered and disordered systems, fractal growth.

A. Simon, Professor; Ph.D., Rochester, 1950. Theoretical plasma physics, controlled thermonuclear fusion.

P. F. Slattery, Professor; Ph.D., Yale, 1967. Experimental elementary particle physics, investigation of QCD via direct photon production, top quark studies and searches for new phenomena using high-energy colliders.

J. P. Spoonhower, Associate Professor; Ph.D., Cornell, 1977. Experimental condensed-matter/optical physics, defects and impurities in solids, novel spectroscopy.

R. L. Sproull, Professor Emeritus; Ph.D., Cornell, 1943. Experimental condensed-matter physics.

C. R. Stroud Jr., Professor; Ph.D., Washington (St. Louis), 1969. Quantum optics, short-pulse excitation of atoms and molecules, quantum information.

S. L. Teitel, Professor; Ph.D., Cornell, 1981. Statistical and condensed-matter physics.

J. H. Thomas, Professor; Ph.D., Purdue, 1966. Theoretical astrophysics, astrophysical fluid dynamics and magnetohydrodynamics, solar physics.

E. H. Thorndike, Professor; Ph.D., Harvard, 1960. Experimental elementary particle physics, weak decays of bottom and charm quarks.

P. L. Tipton, Professor; Ph.D., Rochester, 1987. Experimental elementary particle physics, production and decay of top and b quarks in proton-antiproton collisions at 1.8 TeV.

H. M. Van Horn, Professor; Ph.D., Cornell, 1965. Theoretical astrophysics, degenerate stars.

D. M. Watson, Professor; Ph.D., Berkeley, 1983. Experimental astrophysics, star formation, galactic structure.

E. Wolf, Wilson Professor; Ph.D., Bristol (England), 1948. Statistical optics, theory of partial coherence, inverse scattering, diffraction tomography.

F. L. H. Wolfs, Professor; Ph.D., Chicago, 1987. Experimental nuclear physics, relativistic heavy-ion physics.

W. Wu, Assistant Professor; Ph.D., Chicago, 1992. Experimental condensed-matter physics, disordered condensed-matter systems, superconducting films.

J. Zhong, Associate Professor; Ph.D., Brown, 1988. Biological and medical physics, advanced medical imaging, novel MRI techniques, physiological properties, biological tissues.

RECENT FACULTY PUBLICATIONS

Agarwal, G. S., and **R. W. Boyd.** Influence on damping on the vanishing of the electro-optic effect in chiral isotropic media. *Phys. Rev. A* 67:043821, 2003.

Bhattacharya, M., C. Haimberger, and **N. P. Bigelow.** Forbidden transitions in a MOT. *Phys. Rev. Lett.* 91:213004, 2003.

Kastner, J. H., et al. **(E. G. Blackman** and **A. Frank).** A compact X-ray source and possible X-ray jets within the planetary nebula Menzel 3. *Astrophys. J.* 591L:37, 2003.

Bodek, A., K. S. McFarland, and **P. Tipton** (CDF Collaboration). Momentum distribution of charged particles in jets in dijet events in p anti-p collisions at s** (1/2) = 1.8-TeV and comparisons to perturbative QCD predictions. *Phys. Rev. D* 68:012003, 2003.

Hua, H., et al. **(D. Cline).** The sudden onset of the band crossing for the aligned Iig9/2 orbitals: A possible transition of a triaxial shape from prolate to oblate? *Phys. Lett. B* 562:201, 2003.

Constandache, A., **A. Das,** and Z. Popowicz. Generalized Benney lattice and the heavenly equation. *Czechoslovak J. Phys.* 52:1021, 2003.

Abasov, V. M., et al. **(R. Demina** and **T. Ferbel).** tt bar production cross section in pbarp collisions at sqrt(s) = 1.8 TeV. *Phys. Rev. D* 67:012004, 2003.

Eberly, J. H., K. W. Chan, and C. K. Law. Spontaneous-noise entanglement and photon wave functions. *Chaos Solitons Fractals* 16:399, 2003.

Forrest, W. J., J. L. Pipher, and A. Moore. Next generation space telescope NIR InSb array development. *SPIE* 4850:847, 2003.

Furlan, E., **W. J. Forrest,** and **D. M. Watson** et al. Near-infrared adaptive optics observations of the T Tauri multi-star system. *Astrophys. J. Lett.* 596:L87, 2003.

Sahai, R., et al. **(A. Frank** and **E. G. Blackman).** X-ray emission from the pre-planetary nebula He3-1475. *Appl. Phys. Lett.* 599:L87, 2003.

Yan, L., N. J. Watkins, C. W. Tang, and **Y. Gao.** Fermi level pinning in Cs doped CuPc. *Synth. Met.* 137:1037, 2003.

Lamas-Linares, A., W. T. M. Irvine, **J. C. Howell,** and D. Bouwmeester. Generalized Bell inequalities with parametric down-conversion. *Quantum Information Computation* 3:471, 2003.

Knox, R. S. Dipole and oscillator strengths of chromophores in solution. *Photochem. Photobiol.* 77:497, 2003.

Back, B. B., et al. **(S. L. Manly** and **F. L. H. Wolfs).** Ratios of charged antiparticles to particles near mid-rapidity in Au+Au collisions at sqrt(s_{NN})=200 GeV. *Phys. Rev. C* 67:021901R, 2003.

Melissinos, A. C., and J. Napolitano. *Experiments in Modern Physics,* 2nd ed. Academic/Elsevier, 2003.

Sangster, T. C., et al. **(D. D. Meyerhofer).** Direct-drive cryogenic target implosion performance on OMEGA. *Phys. Plasmas* 10:1937, 2003.

Kao, C., G. Lovelace, and **L. H. Orr.** Detecting a Higgs pseudoscalar with a Z boson at the LHC. *Phys. Lett. B* 567:259, 2003.

Quillen, A. C. Chaos caused by resonance overlap in the solar neighborhood—Spiral structure t the Bar's outer Lindblad resonance. *Astron. J.* 125:785, 2003.

Levent, A., **S. G. Rajeev,** F. Yaman, and **G. P. Agrawal.** Nonlinear theory of polarization-mode dispersion for fiber solitons. *Phys. Rev. Lett.* 90:13902, 2003.

De, S., **Y. Shapir,** and E. H. Chimowitz. Diffusion in random structures in the critical region. *Mol. Simulation* 29:167, 2003.

Olsson, P., and **S. Teitel.** In search of the vortex loop blowout transition for a type-II superconductor in a finite magnetic field. *Phys. Rev. B* 67:144514, 2003.

Briere, R. A., et al. **(E. H. Thorndike)** (CLEO Collaboration). Branching fractions of τ leptons to three charged hadrons. *Phys. Rev. Lett.* 90:181802, 2003.

Van Horn, H. M., J. H. Thomas, A. Frank, and **E. G. Blackman.** Fuel-supply-limited stellar relaxation oscillations: Application to multiple rings around AGB strs and planetary nebulae, *Astrophys. J.* 585:983, 2003.

Li, Y., C. Mecca, and **E. Wolf.** Optimum depth of the information pit on the data surface of a compact disk. *J. Mod. Phys.* 50:199, 2003.

Wu, W., and E. Bielejec. Hysteresis, fluctuations and correlations in the electron glass. *Proc. SPIE Int. Soc. Opt. Eng.* 52112:114, 2003.

Kwok, W. E., and **J. Zhong** et al. A four-element phased array coil for high resolution and parallel MR imaging of the knee. *Magn. Reson. Imaging* 21:961, 2003.

UNIVERSITY OF SOUTH CAROLINA

Department of Physics and Astronomy

Programs of Study

The department offers comprehensive experimental research programs in intermediate-energy nuclear physics; elementary particle physics; observational astronomy; and condensed-matter physics, including high-temperature superconductivity and magnetic properties of materials and chemical physics. There is a broad effort in theoretical research, with programs in the foundations of quantum theory, nuclear theory, quantum gravity, general relativity, cosmology, astrophysics, and critical phenomena.

In addition to the M.S. and Ph.D. in physics, the Master of Arts in Teaching (M.A.T.) in physics and natural science is offered.

The intermediate-energy nuclear physics group performs experiments at Brookhaven National Laboratory and the Thomas Jefferson National Accelerator Facility. These experiments use high-flux electromagnetic probes to study the properties of the hadronic force and the structure of protons and neutrons. A major effort in double beta decay and the search for cosmic dark matter has installations in the United States, the Commonwealth of Independent States, and Spain. The high-energy physics group participates in experiments at Fermilab and at CERN on the detection of neutrinos and neutrino oscillations and at the Stanford Linear Accelerator Center (SLAC) on CP violation in B meson decays. The theoretical effort in the foundations of quantum theory is a cooperative venture with Tel-Aviv University, and one of its faculty members holds a joint appointment. The observational astronomy research studies optical, infrared, and radio sources. This research uses satellite telescopes and the Very Large Array radio telescope in New Mexico.

The remainder of the experimental programs are carried out on campus. They include the investigation of phase transitions, computational physics, electron-spin resonance, superconductivity, magnetism, ferroelectrics, thermal properties, ultrahigh-current phenomena, and coherent transport. The condensed-matter group is actively participating in the nanoscale research initiative. Particular directions include novel magnetic and superconducting nanostructures, nanoelectronics, spintronics, quantum computing, and precise measurements of electromagnetic and quantum properties of matter in confined geometries. In condensed-matter theory, there are programs in superconductivity, critical phenomena, and computational physics.

The program in the foundations of quantum theory is coupled with the theoretical efforts in quantum optics and atomic physics. The main thrust uses very simple models to investigate problems of renormalization, dissipation, and relaxation of a physical system coupled to a larger reservoir; potential effects in quantum phenomena; quantum optics; and the development of better techniques in perturbative calculations.

Research Facilities

An eight-story science complex houses an electronics shop, a machine shop, an electron microscopy center, classrooms, and laboratories. The research equipment includes a novel electron-resonance spectrometer, a large-bore Teslatron (16-T), SQUID susceptometers, and a variety of instrumentation for sensitive high-resolution experiments. Sample fabrication facilities, such as photo and electron lithography facilities, ultrahigh-vacuum and electrodeposition systems for thin films, and furnaces for material preparation, are also available. The high-energy and intermediate-energy nuclear physics programs are carried out at national and international laboratories, as described above. Both programs have state-of-the-art computer facilities on campus to analyze the data taken during experiments, to model complex detector systems, and to calculate theoretical models for planning future experiments.

Financial Aid

Graduate teaching assistantships are available that require 20 hours of work per week and carry a minimum stipend of $16,000 per calendar year. All full-time graduate students receive full graduate assistantships. Additional teaching and research assistantships are available during the summer. Many applicants qualify for Dean's fellowships and/or participate in summer research, which increases the annual stipend up to $21,000.

Cost of Study

In 2001–02, tuition for graduate students who are South Carolina residents was $220 per semester hour; tuition was $481 per semester hour for nonresidents. This rate was reduced to $789 per semester with teaching assistantships for the fall and spring semesters and $207 per semester with teaching assistantships in the summer.

Living and Housing Costs

Apartments were available for graduate students at rents ranging from $457 to $718 per month during 2001–02.

Student Group

There are approximately 27,000 students, including about 8,000 graduate students, at the University. The graduate student body in the physics department numbers between 30 and 40. These students come from many states and countries.

Location

The Columbia metropolitan area, with a population of 472,800, is situated in the center of South Carolina. The climate is moderate, with an average annual temperature of 64°F. Recreational opportunities include camping, swimming, golf, and tennis. Sesquicentennial State Park and ten other state parks are within a 75-mile radius of the city, and Lake Murray, with more than 500 miles of shoreline, is only a few miles northwest of the city.

The University and The Department

The University of South Carolina was founded in 1801 and is located in the center of Columbia, the state capital. The University offers graduate degrees in most of the departments of the Colleges of Liberal Arts and Science and Mathematics and in the Colleges of Business Administration, Education, Engineering, Journalism, Pharmacy, and Public Health. The University's School of Medicine offers the degree of Doctor of Medicine. In addition, graduate professional degrees are offered in accountancy, audiology, business administration, criminal justice, engineering, fine arts, international business studies, librarianship, media arts, music, music education, social work, and speech pathology. The course offerings represent strong traditional curricula at both the undergraduate and graduate levels, with additional courses in the above research areas. The Department of Physics and Astronomy offers a variety of service courses (lower-level courses open to students not majoring in physics), which have total enrollments of more than 2,000 students from other departments and colleges on campus.

Applying

Application forms should be obtained from the Graduate School. Completed applications should be submitted directly to the Dean of the Graduate School.

Correspondence and Information

Director of Graduate Admissions
Department of Physics and Astronomy
University of South Carolina
Columbia, South Carolina 29208

Telephone: 803-777-8104
World Wide Web: http://www.physics.sc.edu

University of South Carolina

THE FACULTY AND THEIR RESEARCH

Yakir Aharonov, Professor (joint appointment with Tel-Aviv University); Ph.D., Bristol (England). Theoretical physics.
Chi-Kwan Au, Professor; Ph.D., Columbia. Theoretical physics.
Frank T. Avignone III, Professor; Ph.D., Georgia Tech. Nuclear and elementary particle physics.
Gary S. Blanpied, Professor; Ph.D., Texas at Austin. Nuclear physics.
Richard J. Creswick, Professor; Ph.D., Berkeley. Theoretical condensed-matter physics.
Timir Datta, Professor; Ph.D., Tulane. Solid-state physics.
Chaden Djalali, Professor; Ph.D., Paris XI. Nuclear physics.
Ralf W. Gothe, Associate Professor; Ph.D., Mainz. Nuclear physics.
Vladimir Gudkov, Associate Professor; Ph.D., Leningrad Nuclear Physics Institute. Theoretical nuclear physics.
Joseph E. Johnson, Associate Professor; Ph.D., SUNY at Stony Brook. Theoretical physics.
James M. Knight, Professor; Ph.D., Maryland. Theoretical physics.
Kuniharu Kubodera, Professor; Ph.D., Tokyo. Theoretical nuclear physics.
Varsha P. Kulkarni, Assistant Professor; Ph.D., Chicago. Astronomy and astrophysics.
Milind Kunchur, Associate Professor; Ph.D., Rutgers. Condensed-matter physics.
Christina K. Lacey, Assistant Professor; Ph.D., New Mexico. Astronomy and astrophysics.
Pawel O. Mazur, Professor; Ph.D., Jagiellonian (Krakow). Theoretical physics.
Sanjib R. Mishra, Professor; Ph.D., Columbia. High-energy physics.
Fred Myhrer, Professor and Chair; Ph.D., Rochester. Theoretical nuclear physics.
Barry M. Preedom, Professor; Ph.D., Tennessee. Nuclear physics.
Ruslan Prozorov, Assistant Professor; Ph.D., Bar-Ilan. Condensed-matter physics.
Milind V. Purohit, Professor; Ph.D., Caltech. High-energy physics.
Carl Rosenfeld, Professor; Ph.D., Caltech. High-energy physics.
David J. Tedeschi, Associate Professor; Ph.D., Rensselaer. Nuclear physics.
Jeffrey R. Wilson, Associate Professor; Ph.D., Purdue. High-energy physics.

A lecture on the foundations of quantum theory.

Detectors used in nuclear physics experiments at the LEGS facility at Brookhaven National Laboratory.

Surface scattering of ions experiment.

UNIVERSITY OF TEXAS AT AUSTIN

Department of Physics

Programs of Study

The Department of Physics offers programs leading to the Master of Arts, Master of Science in Applied Physics, and Doctor of Philosophy degrees. Requirements for the M.S. and M.A. degrees include 30 semester hours, with a minimum of 6 hours in a supporting subject or subjects outside the major program, and a thesis.

The Master of Science in Applied Physics requires graduate courses in experimental physics, electromagnetic theory, and quantum mechanics. In addition, supporting work must be in engineering, chemistry, or geology.

For the Ph.D., students must satisfy core course requirements in classical, statistical, and quantum mechanics and electromagnetic theory; show evidence of exposure to modern methods of experimental physics; and pass an oral qualifying examination. Further course work and a dissertation, followed by a final oral examination, is required. For general information and additional requirements, students should consult the Graduate School Catalog.

The Department of Physics has active research groups in nine main areas of current physics research: atomic, molecular, and optical physics; classical physics; condensed-matter physics; nonlinear dynamics; nuclear physics; plasma physics; relativity and cosmology; statistical mechanics and thermodynamics; and elementary particle physics. In most of these fields, both experimental and theoretical work is in progress.

Research Facilities

The Department of Physics occupies an area of more than 190,000 square feet in Robert Lee Moore (RLM) Hall. The building is shared with mathematics and astronomy, and has complete facilities for state-of-the-art laboratories along with the Physics Mathematcs Astronomy Library. Resources for research computing are available in the graduate computer lab and the Texas Advanced Computing Center.

Financial Aid

Graduate students in the Department of Physics have several possible sources of financial support. Some are employed directly by the department as teaching assistants or graduate assistants, some as research assistants for individual faculty members, and others as physicists for local research organizations. In addition, a limited number of University and federal fellowships are available for students with superior records. The stipends for these positions are comparable to those of other major universities and, where applicable, also include a tuition scholarship for the out-of-state portion of the tuition. Application should be made in the early fall, if at all possible.

Cost of Study

For 2003–04, tuition and required fees for 9 semester hours (a typical course load for graduate students) were $4052 for Texas residents and $8340 for nonresidents and international students. These rates are subject to change.

Living and Housing Costs

University-owned housing is available for both unmarried and married students. During the 2003–04 academic year, room and meal costs for single graduate students were $6184 for a double room and $8325 for a single room. Tax on meals is not included. There are a limited number of single rooms. The University Apartments offer housing accommodations that ranged in cost from $440 to $651 per month in 2003–04. Rates are subject to change. Private housing, including co-ops, apartments, duplexes, and houses, is also available. There is currently a waiting list for University housing.

Student Group

The University of Texas had an enrollment in 2003–04 of 25,474 men and 25,952 women. The majority of students are Texas residents, but students from all other states and more than 100 countries and U.S. possessions are also in attendance. The University is one of the nation's leading sources of doctors, dentists, scientists, and teachers.

Location

Austin is located in central Texas. It is the state capital and has a population of 656,562 in the Austin city limits and 1.2 million in the metropolitan area. The principal employers are the University, federal and state government agencies, and industrial research laboratories. Austin is a city of many parks and recreational facilities, located in an area of rolling hills and lakes. The climate is moderate, with mild winters and warm-to-hot summers.

The University and The Department

The University of Texas is a state-supported institution. In 2003–04, its enrollment was 51,426 at its Austin campus, with 11,297 in its Graduate School and 1,835 faculty members above the rank of instructor. The Department of Physics currently consists of 56 faculty members, 52 nonteaching research personnel, 269 graduate students, and 241 undergraduates majoring in physics. In addition to offering the basic graduate courses, the department has courses and seminars in each area of specialization, as well as frequent colloquia featuring distinguished scientists from other institutions.

Applying

Correspondence concerning admission to the Graduate School should be directed to the Office of Graduate and International Admissions. The Graduate School requires that applicants have a bachelor's degree or the equivalent. Also required for admission is the GRE (Graduate Record Examinations) and the Subject Test in physics. The Test of English as a Foreign Language (TOEFL) with a minimum score of 550 is required for all international students. Applications should be returned by January 15 for fall and summer admission and October 1 for spring admission.

Correspondence and Information

Graduate Coordinator
Department of Physics
University of Texas at Austin
Austin, Texas 78712-1081

Telephone: 512-471-1664
E-mail: carol@physics.utexas.edu
World Wide Web: http://www.ph.utexas.edu/graduate.html

University of Texas at Austin

THE FACULTY AND THEIR RESEARCH

Atomic and Molecular Physics

R. D. Bengtson, Professor; Ph.D., Maryland, 1968. Atomic transition probabilities, Stark broadening.
T. Ditmire, Associate Professor; Ph.D., California, Davis, 1995. Intense ultrafast laser interactions.
M. C. Downer, Professor; Ph.D., Harvard, 1983. Condensed-matter physics, atomic physics, femtosecond spectroscopy.
M. Fink, Professor; Ph.D., Karlsruhe (Germany), 1966. Electron diffraction.
L. W. Frommhold, Professor; Dr.Habil., Hamburg (Germany), 1964. Atomic and molecular physics, gas discharge.
D. Heinzen, Professor; Ph.D., MIT, 1988. Ion trapping, photon-ion interactions.
J. W. Keto, Professor; Ph.D., Michigan, 1968. Reactions and radiative processes of excited atoms and molecules.
F. A. Matsen, Professor Emeritus; Ph.D., Princeton, 1940. Quantum mechanics, groups, linear algebra.
C. F. Moore, Professor; Ph.D., Florida State, 1964. High-energy electron collision.
M. Raizen, Professor; Ph.D., Texas at Austin, 1989. Quantum optics, photon-ion interactions.
C. W. Scherr, Professor Emeritus; Ph.D., Chicago, 1954. Theoretical quantum-mechanical studies of high accuracy on simple systems.
G. O. Sitz, Professor; Ph.D., Stanford, 1987. Scattering of molecules from surfaces.

Classical Physics

A. M. Gleeson, Professor; Ph.D., Pennsylvania, 1966. Field theory, underwater acoustics.
T. A. Griffy, Professor Emeritus; Ph.D., Rice, 1961. Wave propagation, underwater acoustics.
H. L. Swinney, Professor; Ph.D., Johns Hopkins, 1968. Light-scattering studies of hydrodynamic and thermal instabilities.

Condensed-Matter Physics

P. R. Antoniewicz, Professor; Ph.D., Purdue, 1965. Theoretical solid-state physics.
A. L. de Lozanne, Professor; Ph.D., Stanford, 1982. Low-temperature vacuum tunneling microscopy.
F. W. de Wette, Professor Emeritus; Ph.D., Utrecht (Netherlands), 1959. Theoretical solid-state physics, surface dynamics.
M. C. Downer, Professor; Ph.D., Harvard, 1983. Condensed-matter physics, atomic physics, femtosecond spectroscopy.
J. L. Erskine, Professor; Ph.D., Washington (Seattle), 1973. Experimental studies of surface and surface adsorbate phenomena.
E. L. Florin, Assistant Professor; Ph.D., Munich Technical, 1990. Experimentalist, nonlinear dynamics.
J. D. Gavenda, Professor Emeritus; Ph.D., Brown, 1959. Properties of conduction electrons in metals.
L. Kleinman, Professor; Ph.D., Berkeley, 1960. Theoretical studies of thin-metal films.
A. H. MacDonald, Professor; Ph.D., Toronto, 1978. Condensed matter theory with emphasis on electron-electron interactions.
M. P. Marder, Professor; Ph.D., California, Santa Barbara, 1986. Pattern formation, material science.
J. T. Markert, Professor; Ph.D., Cornell, 1987. Study of physical properties of bulk material, particularly high T_c ceramics.
W. D. McCormick, Professor Emeritus; Ph.D., Duke, 1959. Experimental low-temperature and solid-state physics, phase transitions.
Q. Niu, Professor; Ph.D., Washington (Seattle), 1985. Field theory of condensed-matter physics, theory of superconductivity.
A. W. Nolle, Professor Emeritus; Ph.D., MIT, 1947. Magnetic resonance relaxation, spectroscopy, luminescence.
C. K. Shih, Professor; Ph.D., Stanford, 1988. Study of surface properties of microelectronic materials.
J. B. Swift, Professor; Ph.D., Illinois at Urbana-Champaign, 1968. Many-body theory, phase transitions.
H. L. Swinney, Professor; Ph.D., Johns Hopkins, 1968. Light-scattering studies of hydrodynamic and thermal instabilities.
J. C. Thompson, Professor Emeritus; Ph.D., Rice, 1956. Transport in liquid metals, amorphous semiconductors, metal-to-nonmetal transition.
M. Tsoi, Assistant Professor; Ph.D., Konstanz (Germany), 1998. Condensed-matter experiment, nanostructures, spintronics.
Z. Yao, Assistant Professor; Ph.D., Harvard, 1997. Nanostructures and mesoscopic physics.

Elementary Particle Physics

A. Böhm, Professor; Ph.D., Marburg (Germany), 1966. Particle phenomena—algebraic and group-theoretic methods.
C. B. Chiu, Professor; Ph.D., Berkeley, 1965. Strong interaction physics.
D. Dicus, Professor; Ph.D., UCLA, 1968. Field theory of weak interactions.
J. Distler, Professor; Ph.D., Harvard, 1987. High-energy theory, mathematical physics, string theory.
W. Fischler, Professor; Ph.D., Brussels, 1976. Invisible axion, supersymmetry.
V. Kaplunovsky, Professor; Ph.D., Tel-Aviv, 1983. Phenomenology of string theory.
Y. Ne'eman, Professor Emeritus; Ph.D., Imperial College (London), 1961. Symmetries in elementary particle physics.
E. C. G. Sudarshan, Professor; Ph.D., Rochester, 1958. Theoretical particle physics.
S. Weinberg, Professor; Ph.D., Princeton, 1957. Theory of strong and weak particle interaction.

High-Energy Physics

J. Klein, Assistant Professor; Ph.D., Princeton, 1994. The solar neutrino problem, particle astrophysics.
S. Kopp, Assistant Professor; Ph.D., Chicago, 1994. CP violation, weak decays of heavy quarks, neutrino oscillations.
K. Lang, Professor; Ph.D., Rochester, 1985. Experimental study of rare decay of the K-meson.
J. L. Ritchie, Professor; Ph.D., Rochester, 1983. Experimental study of rare decay of the K-meson.
R. F. Schwitters, Professor and Chairman; Ph.D., MIT, 1971. Experimental high-energy physics—detector development and B-physics studies.

Nuclear Physics

W. R. Coker, Professor; Ph.D., Georgia, 1966. Mechanisms of nuclear reactions, three-body final-state problem.
G. W. Hoffmann, Professor; Ph.D., UCLA, 1971. Experimental nuclear physics.
E. V. Ivash, Professor (retired); Ph.D., Michigan, 1952. Theoretical nuclear physics, particularly direct reactions, quantum mechanics.
C. F. Moore, Professor; Ph.D., Florida State, 1964. Experimental nuclear physics.
P. J. Riley, Professor; Ph.D., Alberta, 1962. Nuclear reactions and nuclear structure physics.
T. Udagawa, Professor; Ph.D., Tokyo University of Education, 1962. Theoretical nuclear structure.
S. A. A. Zaidi, Associate Professor (retired); Ph.D., Heidelberg (Germany), 1964. Experimental and theoretical nuclear physics.

Plasma Physics

R. D. Bengtson, Professor; Ph.D., Maryland, 1968. Plasma spectroscopy, experimental plasma physics.
H. Berk, Professor; Ph.D., Princeton, 1964. Theoretical plasma physics, computer simulation of plasmas.
W. E. Drummond, Professor; Ph.D., Stanford, 1958. Theoretical plasma physics.
R. Fitzpatrick, Associate Professor; Ph.D., Sussex, 1988. Magnetic reconnection and gross plasma instabilities in fusion.
K. W. Gentle, Professor; Ph.D., MIT, 1966. Nonlinear plasma processes.
R. D. Hazeltine, Professor; Ph.D., Michigan, 1968. Theoretical plasma physics.
C. W. Horton Jr., Professor; Ph.D., California, San Diego, 1967. Theoretical plasma physics.
P. J. Morrison, Professor; Ph.D., California, San Diego, 1979. Plasma physics.
M. E. Oakes, Professor; Ph.D., Florida State, 1964. Wave propagation in plasmas with emphasis on resonances.
G. Shvets, Assistant Professor; Ph.D., MIT, 1995. Theory and simulations: laser-plasma interactions, plasma-based accelerators, photonics, nanoplasmonics; experiment: phonon-assisted nanolithography, compact surface-wave accelerators.

Relativity, Cosmology, and Quantum Field Theory

B. S. DeWitt, Professor Emeritus; Ph.D., Harvard, 1950. Quantum field theory.
C. DeWitt-Morette, Professor Emeritus; Ph.D., Paris, 1947. Mathematical physics, relativity theory.
W. Fischler, Professor; Ph.D., Brussels, 1976. Cosmology, gravity.
R. A. Matzner, Professor; Ph.D., Maryland, 1967. General cosmology, gravitational radiation.
S. Paban, Assistant Professor; Ph.D., Barcelona (Spain), 1988. Quantum mechanics, particle phenomenology, string theory.
L. C. Shepley, Associate Professor (retired); Ph.D., Princeton, 1965. Cosmology, interaction of matter with gravitation.
S. Weinberg, Professor; Ph.D., Princeton, 1957. Cosmology, astrophysics.

Statistical Mechanics and Thermodynamics

L. E. Reichl, Professor; Ph.D., Denver, 1969. Strong-coupling, nonequilibrium, and quantum statistical mechanics.
W. C. Schieve, Professor; Ph.D., Lehigh, 1959. Nonequilibrium statistical mechanics.
J. S. Turner, Associate Professor; Ph.D., Indiana, 1969. Self-organization in physics, chemistry, and biology.

UNIVERSITY OF TOLEDO

Department of Physics and Astronomy

Programs of Study

The University of Toledo (UT) Department of Physics and Astronomy offers M.S., M.S.E., and Ph.D. degrees in physics with specializations in astronomy and astrophysics, atomic and molecular physics, biophysics, condensed-matter physics and materials science, medical physics, and photonics. The M.S. in physics is a professional master's degree, preparing students for responsible positions in industrial and academic/government research support. It has flexible course requirements, requires a thesis, and usually requires two years of full-time study to complete. A joint M.S. program with the Department of Electrical Engineering and Computer Science is also available. The Ph.D. has a number of required courses and takes five to seven years to complete. Requirements include residence for at least two consecutive semesters, successful completion of a qualifying and a comprehensive examination, completion of a thesis, and successful defense of the thesis.

A major graduate research focus is in experimental and theoretical studies of thin films, especially photovoltaics, magnetic nanostructures, and surface growth. A second major focus is in astronomy/astrophysics, with studies of stellar atmospheres and envelopes, interstellar matter, and climate on Mars. The atomic and molecular physics focus includes studies of quantum-condensed phases, Rydberg state lifetimes, and accelerator-based optical spectroscopy. The medical and biological physics includes accelerator-based research in radiation oncology and DNA bonding and structure. The plasma physics focus is on the self-consistent kinetic description of low-pressure discharges, especially under external electric and magnetic field influence. The photonics research focuses on the design of optical integrated circuits and waveguides. The department has a collective strength and focus on advanced computational methods in treating astrophysical, atomic, plasma, and materials problems.

Research collaboration on-campus includes chemists and chemical, electrical, and mechanical engineers. Department faculty members serve as the core of UT's Center for Photovoltaic Electricity and Hydrogen recently established by a major state of Ohio grant with matching support from several industrial collaborators.

Research Facilities

Thin-film materials laboratories include high- and ultrahigh-vacuum deposition systems using glow-discharge and hot-wire deposition, sputtering, MBE, and incorporate in situ spectroscopic ellipsometry. Other materials and device characterization include the magnetooptical Kerr effect, Raman, photoluminescence, AFM/STM, SEM/EDS, quantum efficiency, and current voltage under solar simulation. Ritter Observatory houses a 1-meter reflecting telescope instrumented for stellar spectroscopy. Much UT astronomy research is done on collaborative access telescopes, satellites, and Mars orbiters. Atomic physics research is done with 300-keV heavy-ion and 80-keV negative-ion accelerators. Lasers are also used for thin-film scribing and thin-film index-of-refraction measurements. Computing facilities include two cluster computing systems and UNIX workstations. Supercomputer access is provided through the Ohio Supercomputing Center.

Financial Aid

Assistantship stipends for the twelve-month period beginning August 2004 totaled $19,000. Scholarships/stipend enhancements and fellowships are available for exceptionally qualified students. Students who advance in the program are eligible for research assistantships, some of which pay higher stipends. Assistants spend about 20 hours per week on their duties.

Cost of Study

Graduate assistants do not pay tuition. They contribute $1221 per year to University-provided medical insurance and pay a general fee of $574 each semester. Stipends are subject to U.S. federal (about 15 percent) and Ohio state (much lower) income tax.

Living and Housing Costs

Major apartment complexes, smaller apartment buildings, houses, rooms, and duplexes are all listed on the University housing Web site (http://www.student-services.utoledo.edu/off-campus-housing/). For example, complexes within 1 mile of campus or served by campus shuttle buses offer one-bedroom apartments for $350 to $400 per month. Food and entertainment costs are low compared with those in larger cities.

Student Group

As of the fall semester of 2004, the department included 50 graduate students, of whom 8 were women, 30 were international students, and 41 had research or teaching assistantships. Of those who did not have assistantships, 1 had a fellowship and the rest were part-time students. Most were pursuing the Ph.D. degree. Qualities sought in applicants include intellectual curiosity, strong motivation for advanced study, and physical and mathematical reasoning ability.

Student Outcomes

Examples of professional situations of recent graduates include postdoctoral fellowships at Vanderbilt, LSU, Johns Hopkins, and Malin Space Science Systems and a staff research scientist position at Arizona. Several recent photonics and materials science graduates are employed in Silicon Valley and other industrial jobs.

Location

The University's attractive campus is located in an urban, residential setting, near good shopping and excellent housing. The city's principal cultural attraction is the Toledo Museum of Art, which is served by University shuttle buses. Toledo has upper-division minor-league baseball and ice hockey teams. Major recreational areas on Lake Erie are within an hour's drive.

The University and The Department

As a member of the State of Ohio System, the University of Toledo is recognized as one of the nation's major regional universities. The Department of Physics and Astronomy is recognized as one of its flagship departments. The department has strong research collaborations with the Department of Chemistry and the College of Engineering through interdisciplinary research in materials science.

Applying

Applications should be submitted to the Graduate School, UH 3240, University of Toledo, Toledo, Ohio 43606-3390, or online at http://www.utoledo.edu/grad-school/application.html. The aptitude section of the Graduate Record Examinations is required of international students and of domestic students whose GPA is less than 2.7 on a 4-point scale. Applications for assistantships should be completed six months before intended first enrollment, although later applications can sometimes be accepted.

Correspondence and Information

Nancy D. Morrison
Associate Professor of Astronomy and
Chairman, Graduate Admissions Committee
Department of Physics and Astronomy
Mail Stop 113
University of Toledo
Toledo, Ohio 43606
Telephone: 419-530-2659
Fax: 419-530-5167 (Ritter Astrophysical Research Center)
E-mail: office@physics.utoledo.edu
World Wide Web: http://www.physics.utoledo.edu

University of Toledo

THE FACULTY AND THEIR RESEARCH

Astronomy

Lawrence Anderson-Huang, Professor; Ph.D., Berkeley, 1977. Stellar atmospheres.
Jon Bjorkman, Assistant Professor; Ph.D, Wisconsin, 1992. Theory of stellar envelopes and winds.
Karen Bjorkman, Professor; Ph.D., Colorado, 1989. Circumstellar matter/stellar winds.
Bernard Bopp, Professor; Ph.D., Texas, 1973. Stellar surface phenomena, science education.
Steven Federman, Professor; Ph.D., NYU, 1979. Interstellar chemistry.
Philip James, Distinguished University Professor; Ph.D., Wisconsin, 1966. Martian climate and weather.
Nancy Morrison, Associate Professor; Ph.D., Hawaii, 1975. Stellar spectroscopy: massive stars.
Adolf Witt, Distinguished University Professor; Ph.D., Chicago, 1967. Interstellar dust.

Physics

Jacques Amar, Assistant Professor; Ph.D., Temple, 1985. Condensed matter/materials science.
Brian Bagley, Professor; Ph.D., Harvard, 1968. Optics/materials science.
Randy Bohn, Emeritus Professor; Ph.D., Ohio State, 1969. Solid-state physics.
Song Cheng, Associate Professor; Ph.D., Kansas State, 1991. Atomic physics.
Robert Collins, Professor and NEG Endowed Chair in Silicate and Materials Science; Ph.D., Harvard, 1982. Condensed matter/materials science.
Alvin Compaan, Professor and Chair; Ph.D., Chicago, 1971. Condensed-matter physics/materials science.
Larry Curtis, Distinguished University Professor; Ph.D., Michigan, 1963. Atomic spectroscopy.
Robert Deck, Emeritus Professor; Ph.D., Notre Dame, 1961. Nonlinear optics.
Xunming Deng, Professor; Ph.D., Chicago, 1990. Materials science/photovoltaics.
David Ellis, Professor; Ph.D., Cornell, 1964. Theoretical atomic physics.
Bo Gao, Associate Professor; Ph.D., Nebraska–Lincoln, 1989. Theoretical physics.
Victor Karpov, Professor; Ph.D., Polytechnic (Russia), 1979. Condensed-matter physics/materials science.
Sanjay V. Khare, Assistant Professor; Ph.D., Maryland, 1996. Theoretical condensed matter/materials science.
Thomas Kvale, Professor; Ph.D., Missouri–Rolla, 1984. Experimental atomic physics.
Scott Lee, Professor; Ph.D., Cincinnati, 1983. Biological physics and high-pressure physics.
R. Ale Lukaszew, Assistant Professor; Ph.D., Wayne State, 1996. Condensed matter/materials science.
Richard Schectman, Emeritus Professor; Ph.D., Cornell, 1962. Atomic physics.
Constantine Theodosiou, Professor; Ph.D., Chicago, 1977. Atomic and plasma physics.

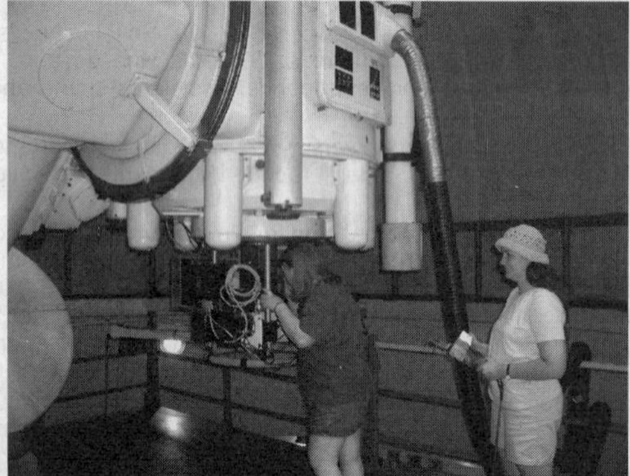

Graduate students at the base of the Ritter Observatory telescope preparing for a night of observations.

Graduate student working on one of the two ion accelerators used for research in the department.

Multiple UHV chamber system for plasma-enhanced CVD and sputter deposition of triple-junction, amorphous silicon solar cells.

University of Toledo

SELECTED PUBLICATIONS

Yu, J., **J. G. Amar,** and A. Bogicevic. First principles calculations of steering forces in epitaxial growth. *Phys. Rev. B* 69:113406, 2004.

Yu, J., and **J. G. Amar.** Short-range attraction, surface currents, and mound formation in metal (111) epitaxial growth. *Phys. Rev. B* 69:04526, 2004.

Amar, J. G., and M. N. Popescu. Asymptotic capture number and island-size distributions for one-dimensional irreversible submonolayer growth. *Phys. Rev. B* 69:033401, 2004.

Deck, R. T., A. L. Sala, Y. Sikorski, and **B. G. Bagley.** Loss in a rectangular optical waveguide induced by the crossover of a second waveguide. *Opt. Laser Technol.* 34:351–6, 2002.

Mirkov, M. G., **B. G. Bagley,** and R. T. Deck. Design of multichannel optical splitter without bends. *Fiber Integr. Opt.* 20:241–55, 2001.

Sala, A. L., R. T. Deck, and **B. G. Bagley.** Use of depressed index cladding layers to tailor the chromatic dispersion and birefringence of planar geometry waveguides. *IEEE Photonics Technol. Lett.* 12:305–7, 2000.

Walker, C., et al. **(J. E. Bjorkman).** The structure of brown dwarf circumstellar disks. *Mon. Not. R. Astron. Soc.* 351:607, 2004.

Carciofi, A. C., **J. E. Bjorkman,** and A. M. Magalhaes. Effects of grain size on the spectral energy distribution of dusty circumstellar envelopes. *Astrophys. J.* 604:238, 2004.

Whitney, B. A., K. Wood, **J. E. Bjorkman,** and M. Cohen. 2-D radiative transfer in protostellar envelopes: II. An evolutionary sequence. *Astrophys. J.* 598:1079, 2003.

Pogodin, M. A., et al. **(K. S. Bjorkman** and **N. D. Morrison).** A new phase of activity of the Herbig Be star HD 200775 in 2001: Evidence for binarity. *Astron. Astrophys.* 417:715–23, 2004.

Miroshnichenko, A. S., et al. **(K. S. Bjorkman,** and **N. D. Morrison).** Spectroscopy of the growing circumstellar disk in the δ Scorpii Be binary. *Astron. Astrophys.* 408:305–11, 2003.

Wisniewski, J. P., **K. S. Bjorkman,** and A. M. Magalhaes. Evolution of the inner circumstellar envelope of V838 monocerotis. *Astrophys. J. Lett.* 598:L43, 2003.

Bjorkman, K. S., A. S. Miroshnichenko, D. McDavid, and T. M. Pogrosheva. A study of Pi Aquarii during a quasi-normal star phase: Refined fundamental parameters and evidence for binarity. *Astrophys. J.* 573:812, 2002.

Collins, R. W. Ellipsometry. In *The Optics Encyclopedia,* vol. 1, pp. 609–70, eds. T. G. Brown, et al. Weinheim, Germany: Wiley-VCH Verlag, 2004.

Collins, R. W., et al. Evolution of microstructure and phase in amorphous protocrystalline, and microcrystalline silicon studied by real time spectroscopic ellipsometry. *Sol. Energy Mater. Sol. Cells* 78:143–80, 2003.

Chen, C., I. An, and **R. W. Collins.** Multichannel Mueller matrix ellipsometry for simultaneous real-time measurement of bulk isotropic and surface anisotropic complex dielectric functions of semiconductors. *Phys. Rev. Lett.* 90:217402, 2003.

Roussillon, Y., et al. **(A. D. Compaan** and **V. G. Karpov).** Blocking thin film nonuniformities: Photovoltaic self-healing. *Appl. Phys. Lett.* 84:616, 2004.

Compaan, A. D., et al. 14% sputtered thin-film solar cells based on CdTe. *Phys. Status Solidi B* 241:779–82, 2004.

Liu, X., **A. D. Compaan,** N. Leyarovska, and J. Terry. Cu K-edge EXAFS in CdTe before and after treatment with $CdCl_2$. *Mater. Res. Soc. Symp. Proc.* 763:139–44, 2003.

Curtis, L. J., and I. Martinson. Atomic structure. In *Electrostatic Accelerators,* chap. 14, ed. R. Hellborg. Springer-Verlag, in press.

Curtis, L. J., and **D. G. Ellis.** Use of the Einstein-Brillouin-Keller action quantization. *Am. J. Phys.* 72, 2004.

Curtis, L. J. *Atomic Structure and Lifetimes: A Conceptual Approach.* Cambridge University Press, 2003.

Curtis, L. J., R. Matulioniene, **D. G. Ellis,** and C. Froese Fischer. A predictive data-based exposition of $5s5p^{1,3}P_1$ lifetimes in the Cd isoelectronic sequence. *Phys. Rev. A* 62:52513, 2000.

Deng, X., and E. Schiff. Amorphous silicon based solar cells. In *The Handbook of Photovoltaic Science and Engineering,* eds. A. Luque and S. Hegedus. John Wiley & Sons, Ltd., 2003.

Povolny, H., and **X. Deng.** High rate deposition of amorphous silicon films using HWCVD with coil-shaped filament. *Thin Solid Films* 430:125, 2003.

Miller, E. L., R. E. Rocheleau, and **X. Deng.** Design considerations for a hybrid amorphous silicon photoelectrochemical multijunction cell for hydrogen production. *Int. J. Hydrogen Energy* 28:615–23, 2003.

Ellis, D. G. Interaction of correlated-variable with configuration-state basis functions. *American Physical Society, The Division of Atomic, Molecular, and Optical Physics Meeting,* Williamsburg, Virginia, 29 May–1 June, 2002.

Ellis, D. G. Electron correlations in multiconfiguration atomic wavefunctions. *Phys. Rev. A* 53:3986, 1996.

Federman, S. R., et al. The interstellar rubidium isotope ratio toward ρ Ophiuchi A. *Astrophys. J. Lett.* 603:L105, 2004.

Sheffer, Y. et al. **(S. R. Federman).** Ultraviolet detection of interstellar $^{12}C^{17}O$ and the CO isotopomeric ratios toward X Per. *Astrophys. J. Lett.* 574:L171, 2002.

Federman, S. R., et al. **(S. Cheng).** Oscillator strengths for B-X, C-X, and E-X transitions in carbon monoxide. *Astrophys. J. Suppl.* 134:133, 2001.

Pan, K., et al. **(S. R. Federman).** Density variations over sub-parsec scales in diffuse molecular gas. *Astrophys. J. Lett.* 558:L105, 2001.

Gao, B. Universal properties of Bose systems with van der Waals interaction. *J. Phys. B: At., Mol. Opt. Phys.* 37:L227, 2004.

Fu, H., Y. Wang, and **B. Gao.** Beyond Fermi pseudopotential: A modified GP equation. *Phys. Rev. A* 67:053612, 2003.

Gao, B. Effective potentials for atom-atom interaction at low temperatures. *J. Phys. B: At., Mol. Opt. Phys.* 36:211, 2003.

Benson, J., et al. **(P. B. James).** A study of seasonal and short period variation of water ice clouds in the Tharsis and Valles Marineris regions of Mars with Mars Global Surveyor. *Icarus* 165:34–52, 2003.

James, P. B., and B. A. Cantor. Atmospheric monitoring of Mars by the Mars Orbiter camera on Mars Global Surveyor. *Adv. Space Res.* 29:121–9, 2002.

Bonev, B. P., **P. B. James, J. E. Bjorkman,** and M.J. Wolff. Regression of the mountains of Mitchel Polar Ice after the onset of a global dust storm on Mars. *Geophys. Res. Lett.* 29:2017, 2002.

Karpov, V. G., A. D. Compaan, and D. Shvydka. Random diode arrays and mesoscale physics of large-area semiconductor devices. *Phys. Rev. B* 69:045325, 2004.

Shvydka, D., **V. G. Karpov,** and **A. D. Compaan.** Low light divergence in photovoltaic parameter fluctuations. *Appl. Phys. Lett.* 82:2157, 2003.

Karpov, V. G. Critical disorder and phase transition in random diode arrays. *Phys. Rev. Lett.* 91:226806, 2003.

Kodambaka, S., and **S. V. Khare** et al. Dislocation-driven surface dynamics on solids. *Nature* 429:49, 2004.

University of Toledo

Selected Publications (continued)

Ghosh, A. W., and **S. V. Khare.** Breaking of general rotational symmetries by multi-dimensional classical ratchets. *Phys. Rev. E* 67:56110, 2003.

Khare, S. V., R .V. Kulkarni, D. Stroud, and J. W. Wilkins. Energetics and bias-dependent scanning tunneling microscopy images of Si ad-dimers on Ge(001). *Phys. Rev. B* 60:4458, 1999.

Covington, A. M., D. Calabrese, J. S. Thompson, and **T. J. Kvale.** Measurement of the electron affinity of lanthanum. *J. Phys. B* 31:L855, 1998.

Kvale, T. J., et al. Single electron detachment cross sections for 5- to 50-keV H- ions incident on helium, neon, and argon atoms. *Phys. Rev. A* 51:1351, 1995.

Reineck, I., et al. **(S. A. Lee).** A Raman study of the hydration of wet-spun films of Li-hyaluronate. *J. Biomol. Struc. Dyn.* 21:153–7, 2003.

Pinnick, D. A., and **S. A. Lee.** High pressure Raman scattering study of the Al mode of $CuInS_2$. *J. Raman Spectrosc.* 34:142–4, 2003.

Marlowe, R. L., A. Szabo, **S. A. Lee,** and A. Rupprecht. Experimental studies on the nature of bonding of DNA-bipyridl-(ethylenediamine) platinum (II) and DNA-netropsin complexes in solution and oriented wet-spun films. *J. Biomol. Struc. Dyn.* 19:681–90, 2002.

Lukaszew, R. A., et al. Surface morphology structure and magnetic anisotropy in epitaxial Ni Films. *J. Alloys Compd.* 369(1–2):213–6, 2004.

Lukaszew, R. A., Z. Zhang, D. Pearson, and A. Zambano. Epitaxial Ni films, E-beam nano-patterning and BMR. *J. Magn. Magn. Mater.* 272–6:1864, 2004.

Lukaszew, R. A., Z. Zhang, V. Stoica, and R. Clarke. *AIP Conf. Proc.* 696:629, 2003.

Wisniewski, J. P., et al. **(N. D. Morrison** and **K. S. Bjorkman).** Spectroscopic and spectropolarimetric observations of V838 monocerotis. *Astrophys. J.* 588:486–93, 2003.

Kaganovich, I. D., O. V. Polomarov, and **C. E. Theodosiou.** Landau damping and anomalous skin effect in low-pressure gas discharges: Self consistent treatment of collisionless heating. *Phys. Plasmas* 11(5):2399–410, 2004.

Sosov, Y., and **C. E. Theodosiou.** Determination of electric field-dependent effective secondary emission coefficients for He/Xe ions on brass. *J. Appl. Phys.* 95(8):4385–8, 2004.

Sosov Y., and **C. E. Theodosiou.** A well known boundary value problem requires unusual eigenfunctions. *Am. J. Phys.* 72(2):185–9, 2004.

Vijh, U. P., **A. N. Witt,** and K. D. Gordon. Discovery of blue luminescence in the red rectangle: Possible fluorescence from neutral polycyclic aromatic hydrocarbon molecules. *Astrophys. J.* 606:L65, 2004.

Witt, A. N., G. C. Clayton, and B. T. Draine, eds. *ASP Conference Series: Astrophysics of Dust. Proceedings of the ASP Conference,* vol. 309. San Francisco: ASP, 2004.

Vijh, U. P., **A. N. Witt,** and K. D. Gordon. The dust in Lyman break galaxies. *Astrophys. J.* 587:533, 2002.

WAKE FOREST UNIVERSITY

Department of Physics

Programs of Study

The Department of Physics offers graduate programs of study leading to the M.S. and Ph.D. degrees in the fields of condensed matter; biological physics; gravitation; field theory; cosmology; atomic, molecular, and optical physics; particle physics; and physics related to medicine. Study in these fields satisfies the needs of students with differing career plans. A low student-faculty ratio allows close contact with the faculty.

The entering graduate student is expected to have a sound knowledge of undergraduate mechanics, electromagnetism, thermodynamics, and atomic physics. Provision is made for the beginning graduate student to make up deficiencies in these areas.

For the M.S. degree, a student completes 24 hours of course work, submits a thesis based on his or her completed research, and passes an oral examination based on the thesis. Students normally complete the requirements for the M.S. degree in two years.

The principal requirement of the Ph.D. degree is the solution of an important physics problem at the frontier of current knowledge. Students are encouraged to choose a faculty adviser and to begin research during or after the first year of course work. The course requirements for the Ph.D. are determined by the student's graduate committee and are tailored to meet the needs of the individual student while providing a broad, well-balanced background. Ph.D. students are required to pass a general examination and to defend their dissertation, based on research, in an oral examination.

Research Facilities

The Department of Physics is located in the Olin Physical Laboratory, a building near the center of the campus. The building has excellent space for teaching, research, and study. Research instrumentation includes a femtosecond Ti:sapphire laser system with regenerative amplifier, a subpicosecond amplified dye laser and streak, an excimer laser, chambers for pulsed-laser deposition and planar magnetron sputtering, and an ultrahigh-vacuum surface analysis system, two nanomanipulators (modified Topometrix AFMs; nM-AFM), an inverted optical microscope, a computer-controlled spectrometer, low-temperature facilities for studies to 4K, and X-ray and laser equipment for sample irradiation. Two high-powered Nd:YAG lasers, an Ar+ laser, a pulsed-dye laser, two research class microscopes, a molecular beam apparatus, microwave absorption in biosystems, and magnetic resonance imaging facilities are located at the medical school. Excellent computer facilities include a ninety-eight-node Linux cluster connected with a high-speed network and access to national supercomputing resources. The entire campus has wireless Internet accessibiltity.

The Center for Nanotechnology is a world-class equipment infrastructure for nanosciences. Experimental capabilities within the center include high-resolution microscopy (low temperature, ultrahigh-vacuum tunneling microscopy, near-field microscopy and spectroscopy, vacuum and in situ AFM, scanning electron microscopy, and high-resolution transmission electron microscopy), transport (LHe cryostat with multiple probes, noise spectral analysis, thermopower, and electrical and thermal transport capabilities), optics (Raman spectroscopy, Z-scan and nonlinear transmission, pulse-probe, photoluminescence and electroluminescence, AM1.5g standard for photovoltaic testing, and coloration test beds), and device fabrication (glove box prototyping, evaporators, spinners, synthesis capabilities, and device testing, including time-of-flight techniques). To learn more, prospective students should visit http://www.wfu.edu/nanotech.

Financial Aid

Most students admitted to graduate study in physics receive financial assistance. In 2003–04, teaching assistantships were $16,000 per year, plus a full tuition scholarship ($23,310). Research assistantships were $17,000 per year, plus a full tuition scholarship. In addition, one or two Dean's Fellowships ($17,000 for ten months plus tuition) may be offered to exceptional students. During the fall and spring semesters, teaching assistants are expected to work approximately 12 hours per week in introductory laboratory classes or grading undergraduate problem sets.

Cost of Study

The 2004–05 tuition of $23,310 is remitted for all scholarship and assistantship recipients.

Living and Housing Costs

Apartments near the campus, where most graduate students live, rent from about $350 to $500 per month.

Student Group

The total number of graduate students in physics is currently 26. Twelve have teaching assistantships, and the others have either research assistantships or scholarships.

Location

Winston-Salem is a city in northwestern North Carolina with a population of about 200,000. It is located about 200 miles from the ocean, 70 miles from the Blue Ridge Mountains, and 300 miles from Atlanta and Washington, D.C.

The University

Wake Forest University has a rich tradition going back to its founding as a college in 1834. Currently, its enrollment consists of 4,050 undergraduates and 2,350 graduate and professional (law, medicine, and business) students. The main campus is a wooded 300-acre site on the northwest edge of Winston-Salem surrounded by many scenic walking and jogging paths, grassy picnic areas, and a beautiful public garden.

Applying

Men and women who are completing a bachelor's degree or its equivalent are invited to obtain additional information and application materials by writing to the physics department at the address given below. GRE General Test scores, transcripts, and three letters of recommendation are required. Submission of scores on the GRE Subject Test in Physics is recommended but not required. Students may be admitted in the fall or spring semester. The deadline for fall application is January 15, but late applicants will be considered if positions are still available. The deadline for spring application is November 1.

Correspondence and Information

Graduate Program Director
Department of Physics
Wake Forest University
P.O. Box 7507
Winston-Salem, North Carolina 27109

Telephone: 336-758-5337
E-mail: gradphy@wfu.edu
World Wide Web: http://www.wfu.edu/physics/Graduate-studies.html

Wake Forest University

THE FACULTY AND THEIR RESEARCH

Paul R. Anderson, Ph.D., California, Santa Barbara. General relativity and quantum field theory in curved space.
Keith D. Bonin, Ph.D., Maryland. Laser-particle interactions, nanomotors and nanostructures, molecular motors in biophysics.
J. D. Bourland, Ph.D., North Carolina at Chapel Hill. Radiation oncology.
Eric D. Carlson, Ph.D., Harvard. Particle physics and particle astrophysics.
David Carroll, Ph.D., Wesleyan. Nanostructures and nanotechnology.
Greg Cook, Ph.D., North Carolina at Chapel Hill. General relativity, numerical relativity, black-hole coalescence.
Jacquelyn Fetrow, Ph.D., Penn State. Computational methods in genomic sequencing, protein structure and function.
Martin Guthold, Ph.D., Oregon. Biophysics and nanotechnology, scanning probe microscopy.
Natalie A. W. Holzwarth, Ph.D., Chicago. First-principles computer modeling of electronic and structural properties of materials, surfaces, and defects in crystals.
William C. Kerr, Ph.D., Cornell. Statistical physics, nonlinearity, solitons, and chaos, with applications to structural phase transitions in solids.
Daniel B. Kim-Shapiro, Ph.D., Berkeley. Biological physics, dynamic monitoring of macromolecular structure, kinetics and mechanism of sickle cell hemoglobin depolymerization.
Jed Macosko, Ph.D., Berkeley. Biophysics of molecular motors and biopolymers.
G. Eric Matthews Jr., Ph.D., North Carolina at Chapel Hill. Point defects in solids and high-temperature superconductors, first-principles structure calculations.
Fred Salsbury, Ph.D., Berkeley. Theoretical and computational biophysics, density functionality theory.
Peter Santago, Adjunct Associate Professor; Ph.D., North Carolina State. Medical physics, magnetic resonance imaging, tomography.
K. Burak Ucer, Ph.D., Rochester. Multiphoton microscopy and imaging, defect dynamics in oxide materials, photoluminescence dynamics of ZnO, sickle cell hemoglobin photolysis dynamics.
Richard T. Williams, Ph.D., Princeton. Ultrafast spectroscopy of solids and surfaces, laser processing of materials, scanning probe microscopy.

Olin Physical Laboratory.

Wake Forest University

SELECTED PUBLICATIONS

Anderson, P. R., and B. L. Hu. Radiation reaction in Schwarzschild spacetime: Retarded Green's Function via Hadamard-WKB expansion. *Phys. Rev. D* 69:064039, 2004.

Groves, P., **P. R. Anderson,** and **E. D. Carlson.** Method to compute the stress-energy tensor for the massless spin-½ field in a general static spherically symmetric spacetime. *Phys. Rev. D* 66:124017, 2002.

Hill, D., M. Plaza, **K. D. Bonin,** and G. Holzwarth. Vesicle transport in PC12 neurites: Forces and saltatory motion. *Eur. Biophys. J.* 33, 2004.

Bonin, K. D., and W. Happer. Atomic spectroscopy. In *The Optics Encyclopedia: Basic Foundations and Practical Applications,* pp. 187–233, eds. T. G. Brown, et al. New York: Wiley-VCH, 2003.

Bonin, K. D., B. Kourmanov, and T. G. Walker. Light torque nanocontrol, nanomotors and nanorockers. *Opt. Express* 10:984–9, 2002.

Holzwarth, G., **K. Bonin,** and D. B. Hill. Forces required of kinesin during processive transport through cytoplasm. *Biophys. J.* 82:1784–90, 2002.

Hinson, W. H., and **J. D. Bourland.** Spectral reconstruction of high energy photon beams for kernel based dose calculations. *Med. Phys.* 29:1789–96, 2002.

Ekstrand, K. E., and **J. D. Bourland.** A film technique for the determination of output factors and end effect times for the Leksell gamma knife. *Phys. Med. Biol.* 46:703–6, 2001.

Carlson, E. D., et al. **(P. R. Anderson).** Stress-energy tensor for massless spin-1/2 in static black hole spacetimes. *Phys. Rev. Lett.* 91:051301, 2003.

Xu, J., M. Xiao, R. Czerw, and **D. L. Carroll.** Optical limiting and enhanced optical nonlinearity in boron-doped carbon nanotubes. *Chem. Phys. Lett.* 389:247–50, 2004.

Czerw, R., J. Liu, and **D. L. Carroll.** Electronic effects in scanning tunneling microscopy of metal-filled multiwalled carbon nanotubes. *New J. Phys.* 6:31, 2004.

Chen, S., et al. **(D. L. Carroll).** Monopod, bipod, and tetrapod gold nanocrystals. *J. Am. Chem. Soc.* ja038927, 2003.

Yang, P., **D. L. Carroll,** and J. Ballato. AC conduction mechanism of $SrBi_2Ta_2O_9$ thin films below room temperature. *J. Mater. Sci. Lett.* 22(1):5–7, 2003.

Chakrapani, N., et al. **(D. L. Carroll).** Adsorption of acetone on carbon nanotubes. *J. Phys. Chem. B* 107(35):9308–11, 2003.

Choi, Y.-M., et al. **(D. L. Carroll).** Nonlinear behavior in the thermopower of doped carbon nanotubes due to strong localized states. *Nano Lett.* 3(6):839–42, 2003.

DiMaio, J., et al. **(D. L. Carroll).** Transparent silica glasses containing single walled carbon nanotubes. *Inf. Sci.* 149(1–3):69–73, 2003.

Hill, T. A., and **D. L. Carroll** et al. Atomic force microscopy studies on the dewetting of perfluorinated ionomer thin films. *J. Polym. Sci., Part B: Polym. Phys.* 41(2):149–58, 2003.

Hannam, M. D., C. E. Evans, **G. B. Cook,** and T. W. Baumgarte. Can a combination of the conformal thin-sandwich and puncture methods yield binary black hole solutions in quasiequilibrium? *Phys. Rev. D* 68:064003, 2003.

Harald, P., P. Pfeiffer, **G. B. Cook,** and S. A. Teukolsky. Comparing initial-data sets for binary black holes. *Phys. Rev. D* 66:024047, 2002.

Cook, G. B. Corotating and irrotational binary black holes in quasicircular orbit. *Phys. Rev. D* 65:084003, 2002.

Baxter, S. M., et al. **(J. S. Fetrow).** Synergistic computational and experimental proteomics approaches for more accurate detection of active serine hydrolases in yeast. *Mol. Cell. Proteomics* 3(3):209–25, 2004.

Cammer, S. A., et al. **(J. S. Fetrow).** Structure-based active site profiles for genome analysis and sub-family classification. *J. Mol. Biol.* 334(3):387–401, 2003.

Herrgard, S., et al. **(J. S. Fetrow).** Prediction of deleterious nsSNPs using a library of structure-based function descriptors. *Proteins: Struct. Funct. Genet.* 53(4):806–16, 2003.

Zhou, H., et al. **(J. S. Fetrow).** ^{1}H, ^{13}C, and ^{15}N resonance assignments and secondary structure for the human protein tyrosine phosphatase, PRL-2. *J. Biomol. NMR* 27(4):397–8, 2003.

Baxter, S., S. Knutson, and **J. Fetrow.** The importance of structure-based function annotation to drug discovery. In *Protein Structure: Determination, Analysis and Applications for Drug Discovery,* ed. D. Chasman. New York: Dekker Publishing, 2003.

Fetrow, J., A. Giammona, A. Kolinski, and J. Skolnick. The protein folding problem: A biophysical enigma. *Curr. Pharm. Biotechnol.* 3(4):329–47, 2002.

Betz, S., S. Baxter, and **J. Fetrow.** Function first: A powerful approach to post-genomic drug discovery. *Drug Discovery Today* 7(16):865–71, 2002.

Taylor, R. M. II, et al. **(M. Guthold).** Visualization and natural control systems for microscopy. In *Visualization Handbook,* eds. C. Johnson and C. Hansen. Academic Press, 2003.

Rivetti, C., and **M. Guthold.** Single DNA molecule analysis of transcription complexes. *Methods Enzymol.* 371:34–50, 2003.

Dwyer, C., and **M. Guthold** et al. DNA-functionalized single-walled carbon nanotubes. *Nanotechnology* 13:601–4, 2002.

Tang, P., and **N. A. W. Holzwarth.** Electronic structures of $FePO_4$, $LiFePO_4$, and related materials. *Phys. Rev. B* 68:165107, 2003.

Abraham, Y. B., **N. A. W. Holzwarth, R. T. Williams,** and **G. E. Matthews.** Electronic structure of oxygen-related defects in $PbWO_4$ and $CaMoO_4$ crystals. *Phys. Rev. B* 64:245109 (1–10), 2001.

Holzwarth, N. A. W., A. R. Tackett, and **G. E. Matthews.** A projector augmented wave (PAW) code for electronic structure calculations, Part I: *Atompaw* for generating atom-centered functions. *Comput. Phys. Commun.* 135(3):329–47, 2001.

Tackett, A. R., **N. A. W. Holzwarth,** and **G. E. Matthews.** A projector augmented wave (PAW) code for electronic structure calculations, Part II: *Pwpaw* for periodic solids in a plane-wave basis. *Comput. Phys. Commun.* 135(3):348–76, 2001.

Kerr, W. C., G. Lei, and S. N. Kerr. Reusable C++ code for an electron-phonon simulation. In *OOPSLA '02 Companion: Conference on Object-Oriented Programming, Systems, Languages, and Applications,* pp. 74–5, 2002.

Graham, A. J., and **W. C. Kerr.** Solution of Kramers' problem for a moderately to heavily damped elastic string. *Phys. Rev. E* 65:016106-1–016106-4, 2001.

Kim-Shapiro, D. B. Hemoglobin-nitric oxide cooperativity: Is NO the third respiratory ligand? *Free Radical Biol. Med.* 36:402–12, 2004.

Cosby, K., et al. **(D. B. Kim-Shapiro).** Nitrite reduction to nitric oxide by deoxyhemoglobin vasodilates the human circulation. *Nat. Med.* 9:1498–505, 2003.

Xu, X., et al. **(D. B. Kim-Shapiro).** Measurements of nitric oxide on the heme iron and β-93 thiol of human hemoglobin during cycles of oxygenation and deoxygenation. *Proc. Natl. Acad. Sci. U.S.A.* 100:11303–8, 2003.

Wake Forest University

Selected Publications (continued)

Huang, J., et al. **(D. B. Kim-Shapiro).** Hydroxyurea analogs as kinetic and mechanistic probes of the nitric oxide producing reactions of hydroxyurea and oxyhemoglobin. *J. Med. Chem.* 46:3748–53, 2003.

Lockamy, V. L., et al. **(D. B. Kim-Shapiro).** Urease enhances the formation of iron nitrosyl hemogolobin in the presence of hydroxyurea. *Biochim. Biophys. Acta* 1622:109–16, 2003.

Huang, Z., et al. **(D. B. Kim-Shapiro).** Kinetics of increased deformability of deoxygenated sickle cells upon oxygenation. *Biophys. J.* 85, 2003.

Xu, X., et al. **(D. B. Kim-Shapiro).** Effects of iron nitrosylation on sickle cell hemoglobin solubility. *J. Biol. Chem.* 277:36787–92, 2002.

Kim-Shapiro, D. B., et al. **(K. B. Ucer** and **R. T. Williams).** Kinetics of nitric oxide binding to r-state hemoglobin. *Biophys. Biochem. Res. Commun.* 292:812–8, 2002.

Poirier, M. A., et al. **(J. C. Macosko).** Huntingtin spheroids and protofibrils as precursors in polyglutamine fibrilization. *J. Biol. Chem.* 277(43):41032–7, 2002.

Leikina, E., et al. **(J. C. Macosko).** The 1-127 HA2 construct of influenza virus hemagglutinin induces cell-cell hemifusion. *Biochemistry* 28(40):8378–86, 2001.

Lee, M. S., M. Feig, **F. R. Salsbury,** and C. L. Brooks. New analytic approximation to the standard molecular volume definition and its application to generalized born calculations. *J. Comput. Chem.* 24:1348, 2003.

Salsbury, F. R., W. G. Han, L. Noodleman, and C. L. Brooks. Temperature-dependent behavior of protein-chromophore interactions: A theoretical study of a blue fluorescent antibody. *Chemphyschem* 4, 2003.

Lee, M. S., **F. R. Salsbury,** and C. L. Brooks. New and novel generalized born methods. *J. Chem. Phys.* 116(24):10606–14, 2002.

Fan, L., **P. Santago,** W. Riley, and D. M. Herrington. An adaptive template matching method and its application to the boundary detection of brachial artery ultrasound scans. *Ultrasound Bio.* 27(3):399–408, 2001.

Xiong, G., et al. **(K. B. Ucer** and **R. T. Williams).** Luminescence and stimulated emission in zinc oxide nanoparticles, films, and crystals. *Radiat. Eff. Defects Solids* 158:83–8, 2003.

Wilkinson, J., G. Xiong, and **K. B. Ucer.** Lifetime and oscillator strength of excitonic luminescence in zinc oxide. Nonlinear Opt. 29:529, 2002.

Xiong, G., J. Wilkinson, S. Tuzeman, and **K. B. Ucer.** Toward a new ultraviolet diode laser: Luminescence and p-n junctions in ZnO films. *SPIE Proc.* 4644:256, 2002.

Xiong, G., et al. **(K. B. Ucer** and **R. T. Williams).** Control of p- and n-type conductivity in sputter deposition of undoped ZnO. *Appl. Phys. Lett.* 80:1195, 2002.

Qui, Y., et al. **(K. B. Ucer** and **R. T. Williams).** Transient absorption of polarons in $KNbO_3$. *Nucl. Instrum. Methods Phys. Res. Sect. B* 191:98–101, 2002.

Grigorjeva, L., et al. **(R. T. Williams).** Experimental and theoretical studies of polaron optical properties in $KNbO_3$ perovskite. *Solid State Commun.* 129:691–6, 2004.

Khudobenko, A. I., et al. **(R. T. Williams** and **K. B. Ucer).** Laser deposition of ZnO thin films on silicon and sapphire substrates. *Quant. Electron.* 33:975–80, 2003.

Tuzemen, S., et al. **(R. T. Williams).** Convertibility of conductivity type in reactively sputtered ZnO thin films. *Phys. Status Solidi A* 195:165, 2003.

WASHINGTON UNIVERSITY IN ST. LOUIS

Department of Physics

Programs of Study

The Department of Physics at Washington University offers programs leading to the Ph.D. and M.A. degrees. A minimum of 72 hours is required for the Ph.D., including 36 hours in classroom courses. Candidates must also pass a general qualifying examination and an oral defense of the dissertation research. For the M.A., requirements include 30 hours (at least 24 in classroom courses) and a thesis or final examination. Interdisciplinary studies are facilitated by the McDonnell Center for the Space Sciences, a University-wide center that involves the faculties of the Departments of Physics, Earth and Planetary Sciences, Chemistry, and Engineering.

Research Facilities

The Department of Physics maintains extensive research laboratories in its two buildings, Crow Hall and Compton Hall. The McDonnell Center for the Space Sciences has recently installed the NANOSIMS, a first-of-its-kind ion microprobe with greatly enhanced resolution, and has design, fabrication, and testing facilities for experimental astrophysics research. Experimental condensed matter, materials physics, and biophysics laboratories have equipment for electron microscopy, X-ray diffraction, calorimetry, atomic force microscopy, magnetic resonance imaging, and ultrasonic imaging. The Center for Scientific Parallel Computing has recently acquired an Altix 3000 with 128 Itanium 2 nodes. The department has several Beowulf clusters, and maintains an extensive, heterogeneous network.

Financial Aid

The department awards a number of teaching and research assistantships. For the 2004–05 academic year, nine-month stipends are $16,500 plus tuition remission. Fellowships and scholarships range from $22,000 to $28,000 for twelve months plus tuition remission. Stipends of up to $5500 are available for summer support.

Cost of Study

The cost of graduate study at Washington University is comparable to that at other institutions of its type and caliber. For the 2004–05 academic year, tuition for full-time students is $14,850 per semester. Physics department teaching and research assistants receive tuition remission in addition to a stipend.

Living and Housing Costs

Moderately priced rental units may be obtained near the University at average monthly rates of $450 to $850 for one to three bedrooms.

Student Group

Almost half of the approximately 12,765 students at the University are graduate and professional school students. The faculty has 2,721 full-time members. The department has 68 graduate students, 13 of whom are women.

Student Outcomes

Most recent graduates have gone on to postdoctoral research positions at distinguished institutions and laboratories such as Brookhaven National Laboratory, the University of Chicago, the California Institute of Technology, and the Naval Research Laboratory. Former students who completed their postdoctoral research include an assistant professor at Brown University; a staff scientist at MEMC Corporation in St. Peters, Missouri; and a staff scientist at Los Alamos National Laboratory.

Location

The community surrounding the University is both residential and commercial. Entertainment is varied: music lovers can enjoy the St. Louis Symphony, the St. Louis Philharmonic, and many jazz, blues, rock, and dance clubs; theatergoers can attend performances of several repertory groups and musicals at the summer Municipal Opera. Forest Park, which is within walking distance of the campus, contains a golf course, bicycle and running paths, horseback-riding facilities, a fine zoo, the St. Louis Science Center, and the St. Louis Art Museum.

The University

Washington University in St. Louis was founded in 1853 as a private, coeducational institution. In 1904, the University moved to its present 168-acre hilltop campus bordering on the 1,430 acres of Forest Park. Undergraduate programs are offered in arts and science, engineering, business, and fine arts, and graduate programs are offered in all major fields of human inquiry. Twenty Nobel Prize recipients have done all or part of their distinguished work at Washington University. Since 1976, Washington University has placed first in the William Lowell Putnam Mathematical Competition four times and among the top ten all but two times. Graduates often receive such prestigious graduate study awards as Fulbright, Marshall, Beinecke, and Truman scholarships and Mellon, Putnam, National Science Foundation, and NASA graduate fellowships.

Applying

To ensure consideration of a student for admission in September, a completed application, transcript, financial statement, Graduate Record Examinations (GRE) scores, and three letters of recommendation must be received by January 15. Applications are considered at other times as well. Applicants should have had courses in calculus and physics and should have specialized in physics or a related subject in physical science, engineering, or mathematics.

Correspondence and Information

Graduate Admissions
Department of Physics
Washington University in St. Louis
One Brookings Drive
St. Louis, Missouri 63130-4899
Telephone: 314-935-6250
E-mail: gradinfo@wuphys.wustl.edu
World Wide Web: http://www.physics.wustl.edu/

Washington University in St. Louis

THE FACULTY AND THEIR RESEARCH

Professors
Carl M. Bender, Ph.D., Harvard, 1969. Theoretical physics, mathematical physics, particle physics.
Claude W. Bernard, Ph.D., Harvard, 1976. Theoretical physics, mathematical physics, particle physics.
Thomas Bernatowicz, Ph.D., Washington (St. Louis), 1980. Mass spectrometry, transmission electron microscopy.
Anders E. Carlsson, Ph.D., Harvard, 1981. Condensed-matter theory, biophysics.
John W. Clark, Wayman Crow Professor and Department Chair; Ph.D., Washington (St. Louis), 1959. Theoretical physics and astrophysics, many-body theory, biophysics.
Mark S. Conradi, Ph.D., Washington (St. Louis), 1977. Experimental magnetic resonance: lung imaging and solid-state systems.
Ramanath Cowsik, Ph.D., Bombay, 1968. Theoretical astrophysics.
Willem H. Dickhoff, Ph.D., Free University (Amsterdam), 1981. Theoretical physics, many-body theory.
Peter A. Fedders, Emeritus; Ph.D., Harvard, 1965. Solid-state theory.
Michael W. Friedlander, Ph.D., Bristol, 1955. Cosmic rays, astrophysics.
Patrick C. Gibbons, Ph.D., Harvard, 1971. Experimental solid-state physics, electron microscopy, materials science.
Charles M. Hohenberg, Ph.D., Berkeley, 1968. Experimental space science, rare-gas mass spectroscopy.
Martin H. Israel, Ph.D., Caltech, 1968. Cosmic ray astrophysics.
Jonathan I. Katz, Ph.D., Cornell, 1973. Theoretical astrophysics.
Kenneth F. Kelton, Ph.D., Harvard, 1983. Experimental solid-state physics and materials science.
Joseph Klarmann, Emeritus; Ph.D., Rochester, 1958. Cosmic ray astrophysics.
Kazimierz Luszczynski, Emeritus; Ph.D., London, 1959. Solid-state and low-temperature physics, magnetic resonance.
James G. Miller, Hill Professor; Ph.D., Washington (St. Louis), 1969. Ultrasonics, biomedical physics, elastic properties of inhomogeneous media.
Richard E. Norberg, Ph.D., Illinois, 1951. Solid-state and low-temperature physics, magnetic resonance.
Michael C. Ogilvie, Ph.D., Brown, 1980. Theoretical physics, mathematical physics, particle physics.
Peter R. Phillips, Emeritus; Ph.D., Stanford, 1961. General relativity and cosmology.
John H. Scandrett, Emeritus; Ph.D., Wisconsin, 1963. Biomedical physics and computer applications.
James S. Schilling, Ph.D., Wisconsin, 1969. Solid-state and high-pressure physics.
J. Ely Shrauner, Emeritus; Ph.D., Chicago, 1963. Theoretical physics, elementary particle theory, high-energy physics, applied physics.
Stuart A. Solin, Ph.D., Purdue, 1969. Experimental solid-state and materials physics.
Wai-Mo Suen, Ph.D., Caltech, 1985. Theoretical astrophysics, general relativity, cosmology.
Ronald K. Sundfors, Emeritus; Ph.D., Cornell, 1963. Nuclear acoustic resonance, ultrasonics.
Clifford M. Will, Ph.D., Caltech, 1971. Theoretical astrophysics, general relativity.

Associate Professor
James H. Buckley, Ph.D., Chicago, 1994. High-energy astrophysics.

Joint Professors
Shankar Sastry, Ph.D., Toronto, 1974. Materials science and metallurgy, alloys and intermetallic compounds. (Department of Mechanical Engineering)
Lee G. Sobotka, Ph.D., Berkeley, 1982. Nuclear physics, heavy ion reactions. (Department of Chemistry)

Assistant Professors
Mark G. Alford, Ph.D., Harvard, 1990. Quantum field theory and particle physics.
Ramki Kalyanaraman, Ph.D., North Carolina State, 1998. Experimental materials science and solid-state physics.
Henric Krawczynski, Ph.D., Hamburg (Germany), 1997. Astrophysics.
Ralf Wessel, Ph.D., Cambridge, 1992. Experimental biophysics, neuroscience.

Professors (Courtesy)
Donald P. Ames, Ph.D., Wisconsin–Madison, 1949. Materials research, magnetic resonance.
Charles H. Anderson, Ph.D., Harvard, 1962. Biophysics.
Vijai V. Dixit, Ph.D., Purdue, 1972. Theoretical physics.
Elliot L. Elson, Ph.D., Stanford, 1966. Molecular biophysics.
Robert Falster, Ph.D., Stanford, 1983. Experimental materials science, semiconductors.
Solomon L. Linder, Ph.D., Washington (St. Louis), 1955. Electrooptics.
Jeffrey E. Mandula, Ph.D., Harvard, 1966. Theoretical physics, particle physics, mathematical physics.
Manfred L. Ristig, Ph.D., Köln (Germany), 1966. Nuclear theory.
Dmitriy Yablonsky, Ph.D., Ukraine, 1973. Radiation physics.

Associate Professors (Courtesy)
Thomas E. Conturo, M.D./Ph.D., Vanderbilt, 1989. Biophysics, magnetic resonance imaging.
Philip B. Fraundorf, Ph.D., Washington (St. Louis), 1980. Space physics, solid-state physics.
Sandor J. Kovacs, M.D., Miami (Florida), 1979; Ph.D., Caltech, 1977. Cardiology, astrophysics.
Samuel A. Wickline, M.D., Hawaii, 1980. Cardiology.

Assistant Professors (Courtesy)
Gregory L. Comer, Ph.D., North Carolina, 1990. General relativity.
David A. Feinberg, Ph.D., Berkeley, 1982; M.D., Miami (Florida), 1988. Magnetic resonance.
Mary M. Leopold, Ph.D., Washington (St. Louis), 1985. Semiconductor physics.
Craig W. Lincoln, Ph.D., Washington (St. Louis). Astrophysics, general relativity.
Ian Redmount, Ph.D., Caltech, 1984. General relativity.

Research Professors
Robert W. Binns, Ph.D., Colorado State, 1969. Astrophysics, medical and health physics.
Ernst Zinner, Ph.D., Washington (St. Louis), 1972. Experimental space science, extraterrestrial materials.

Research Associate Professor
Daniel J. Leopold, Ph.D., Washington (St. Louis), 1983. Chemical physics.

Research Assistant Professor
Mark R. Holland, Ph.D., Washington (St. Louis), 1989. Ultrasonics, medical physics, biomedical ultrasound.

WESLEYAN UNIVERSITY

Department of Physics

Program of Study

The Department of Physics offers a program of study leading to the Ph.D. degree in physics within the context of a small liberal arts university. Students interested in pursuing physics at the graduate level need not go exclusively to a large university to learn physics and to do high-quality independent research. Wesleyan University has a track record of more than thirty-five years of producing Ph.D. physicists who have gone on to productive professional careers. The Department of Physics offers a small, focused Ph.D. program that can be tailored to the individual and is designed to allow graduate students early involvement in research with a faculty member. It is an environment that is flexible and personal rather than large and impersonal. There are 9 faculty members (6 experimental and 3 theoretical), 3 postdoctoral fellows, and 12 to 15 graduate students in the department.

The department has several research areas. In the area of condensed-matter physics there is active work in quantum fluids, dealing with state-of-the-art applications of quantum mechanics; two-dimensional physics, focused on the quantum mechanics of phase transitions and surfaces; and a new laboratory with a new faculty member whose field is in nanostructure physics. In the area of atomic, molecular, and optical physics there is active work on highly excited Rydberg atoms in strong fields testing quantum/classical correspondence and investigating chaos; molecular collisions of rapidly rotating molecules investigating collisional dynamics in this unusual regime; and molecular photonics, addressing the behavior of fragmenting molecules and the generation and time evolution of laser-prepared plasmas. In the area of theory, there is work on nonlinear dynamics focused on classical and quantum chaos; nanostructure science; computational neuroscience; and manifestations of chaos and complexity in physical systems.

The physics department is closely linked to the chemistry department through a joint program in chemical physics that has several related research areas, including molecular biophysics, laser-energized molecular systems, molecular beam spectroscopy, computational quantum mechanics, and collision-induced spectroscopy. Interdisciplinary study in chemical physics and molecular biophysics is possible.

Classes are small and emphasize interaction and discussion, with student seminar presentations playing an important role. Course work is spread out over a few years, which allows the student to become involved in research with faculty members during their first semester on campus. Normally, a student has one or two research rotations to different faculty labs in order to better appreciate the opportunities for their Ph.D. work. In the second year, students are expected to pass a written exam covering four major areas of physics: classical mechanics, quantum mechanics, electromagnetism, and thermal and statistical physics. Also in the second year, a student associates with an adviser for their Ph.D. work. The requirements for the Ph.D. degree are demonstration of competence in the four fields on the written exam, satisfactory performance on an oral exam on their intended Ph.D. work (usually taken by the end of the second year), and a Ph.D. dissertation based on independent research, which, upon conclusion, is defended in an oral examination. Students are expected to complete the requirements for the Ph.D. degree in five to six years. The research interests of individual faculty members in the department are listed on the reverse of this page.

Research Facilities

The physics research laboratories are equipped with a wide array of modern instrumentation appropriate to the research activities of the faculty. These include several lasers, both continuous and pulsed, for energizing atoms and molecules; a particle accelerator for preparing fast beams; a thermal beam apparatus; a cryostat and dilution refrigerator for reaching very low temperatures; and an NMR magnet. There are excellent machine and electronics shops. A departmental 50-node Beowulf cluster computer plus several computer work stations are available to students. The Science Library, containing an excellent collection of journals, monographs, and reference materials, is located in the same building as the physics department.

Financial Aid

All admitted students receive a twelve-month University stipend; for 2004–05, the stipend is $19,664. Some students may also be supported on individual faculty research grants.

Cost of Study

Tuition and fees are waived for all graduate students.

Living and Housing Costs

Most graduate students, both single and married, live in nearby houses administered and maintained by the University with rents (which include utilities) ranging from $450 to $700 per month. For married students, there is a monthly dependent allowance available of $109 each for spouse and children.

Student Group

The Wesleyan student body is composed of 2,800 undergraduates and 170 graduate students. Most of the graduate students are in the sciences, and of the 12 to 15 students in the Department of Physics—who come from all corners of the globe—more than one third are women.

Student Outcomes

Graduates obtain both industrial positions and faculty academic positions, with several entering the medical physics profession. The department's four most recent Ph.D.'s are now at IBM, Microsoft, the University of Wisconsin, and the University of Illinois.

Location

Middletown is a small city that was settled 350 years ago on the west bank of the Connecticut River, 15 miles south of Hartford, the state capital. New Haven is 24 miles to the southwest; New York City and Boston are about 2 hours away by automobile. Middletown's population of 50,000 is spread over an area of 43 square miles, much of which is rural. Although Wesleyan is a primary source of cultural activity in Middletown, the city is not a "college town," but serves as a busy commercial center for the region between Hartford and the coast. Water sports, skiing, hiking, and other outdoor activities can be enjoyed in the hills, lakes, and river nearby. Ocean beaches are a short drive away and the mountains of Vermont and Hew Hampshire a within a few hours' drive.

The University

For more than 170 years, Wesleyan University has been identified with the highest aspirations and achievements of private liberal arts higher education. Wesleyan's commitment to the sciences dates from the founding of the University. The Ph.D. degree programs were established in the 1960s. The science programs were designed to be small, distinctive, and personal and emphasize independent research, acquisition of broad scientific knowledge, and creative thinking.

Applying

Men and women who have completed their bachelor's degree or the equivalent and who seek a small intimate environment in which to pursue a Ph.D. degree in physics are encouraged to apply. Applications are available on the Internet at the department home page (address is listed below). A rolling admissions policy is in place, although applicants seeking admission for September are advised to submit applications as early as possible in the calendar year. There is no application fee. Three letters of recommendation are required, and applicants are required to take the General Test of the Graduate Record Examinations. Students whose native language is not English should take the TOEFL. Applicants are strongly encouraged to visit the department.

Correspondence and Information

Chairman
Graduate Admissions Committee
Department of Physics
Wesleyan University
Middletown, Connecticut 06459
World Wide Web: http://www.wesleyan.edu/physics

Wesleyan University

THE FACULTY AND THEIR RESEARCH

Reinhold Blümel, Associate Professor; Ph.D., Munich, 1983. Nonlinear dynamics, chaos, theoretical atomic physics.
Fred Ellis, Professor; Ph.D., Massachusetts, 1983. Low-temperature physics, quantum fluids.
Lutz Hüwel, Professor; Ph.D., Göttingen, 1980. Atomic and molecular physics, photophysics, plasmas.
Rick Jensen, Charlotte Ayres Professor; Ph.D., Princeton, 1981. Nonlinear dynamics, chaos, theoretical atomic physics, computational neuroscience.
Tom Morgan, Foss Professor; Ph.D., Berkeley, 1971. Atomic and molecular physics, Rydberg states in strong fields.
Rollie Rollefson, Professor; Ph.D., Cornell, 1970. Condensed matter physics, surface physics, 2-D systems.
Francis Starr, Assistant Professor; Ph.D., Boston University, 1999. Computational soft condensed matter physics, polymeric materials, liquid, glasses.
Brian Stewart, Associate Professor; Ph.D., MIT, 1987. Atomic and molecular physics, molecular collisions.
Greg Voth, Assistant Professor; Ph.D., Cornell, 2000. Soft condensed-matter physics, turbulent and granular flow.

RESEARCH ACTIVITIES

Atomic, Molecular, and Optical (Hüwel, Morgan, Stewart). These laboratories utilize lasers, particle-beam machines, and alkali atom heat pipe ovens to investigate the spectroscopic and collisional properties of atomic and molecular systems. Photoabsorption studies of highly excited Rydberg states in strong electric fields investigate the structure and dynamics of semiclassical states and bridge the gap between quantum and classical physics. In an electric field, all Rydberg atoms (except hydrogen) exhibit chaotic properties and serve as a testing ground for quantum chaos. Photoabsorption experiments also study molecular photofragmentation and ionization, in which a perfectly stable diatomic molecule can disintegrate into three particles, sometimes without any excess kinetic energy. These events are currently investigated in molecular sodium. Photoabsorption also serves to prepare highly excited rotational states of molecules for collision studies to determine the dynamics under these unusual circumstances. Other work includes laser-induced optical breakdown of gases, with the twin goal of studying the spatial and temporal evolution of the recombining plasma and the broadening of atomic and ionic emission lines.

Condensed-Matter Physics (Ellis, Rollefson, Voth). A question of fundamental concern for condensed-matter physics is how the nature and properties of matter change as one goes from three to two dimensions. Studies involve phase transition in two dimensions, with potential impact on practical problems such as catalysis and lubrication. Other studies address phenomena at low temperatures, where the microscopic dynamic properties of any material become dominated by quantum mechanics. Superfluid helium films are studied with "third sound" waves, and quantized vortices are investigated. The creation and destruction of superfluid flow probes the relationship between the underlying classical and quantum mechanisms responsible. Work in the areas of soft condensed-matter physics and nonlinear dynamics seeks to understand the dynamics of particle motion in granular and fluid flows. High-resolution imaging systems are used to explore mixing and transport processes in these systems.

Theoretical and Computational Physics (Blümel, Jensen, Starr). Activity centers on ideas associated with nonlinear dynamics, complexity, and chaos. These phenomena exhibit properties that are responsible for the behavior of a wide class of physical systems, such as atoms and molecules in strong fields, the electronic properties of nanostructures, the dynamics of supercooled liquids, and trapped atomic and molecular ions. All of these systems are studied using modern computational techniques and approaches. Other topics of study include crystallized electron beams, functional genomics, polymeric nanocomposites, vitrification, and neural networks as well as others.

YALE UNIVERSITY

Graduate School of Arts and Sciences
Department of Physics

Program of Study

The Department of Physics offers a program of study leading to the Ph.D. degree. To complete the course requirements for the degree, students are expected to take a set of nine term courses. Students normally take three courses during each of their first three semesters. In addition, all students are required to be proficient and familiar with mathematical methods of physics (such as those necessary to master the material covered in the five core courses) and to be proficient and familiar with advanced laboratory techniques. These requirements can be met either by having had sufficiently advanced prior course work or by taking a course offered by the department. All students also attend a seminar during their first term in order to be introduced to the various research efforts and opportunities at Yale. Those who pass their courses with satisfactory grades and who pass the qualifying exam are admitted to doctoral candidacy for the Ph.D. Dissertation research then becomes the primary activity.

The qualifying exam, normally taken at the beginning of the third semester (although it can be taken earlier), is devoted to graduate-level physics, with special attention to material at the level of courses taken during the first two semesters.

Formal association with a dissertation adviser normally begins in the fourth semester after the qualifying examination has been passed. An adviser from a department other than physics can be chosen in consultation with the Director of Graduate Studies, provided that the dissertation topic is deemed suitable for a physics Ph.D.

Approximately eighteen months after passing the qualifying exam, but no later than the end of the fourth year, students take an oral exam centering on a recently published research paper in the field (but not on the topic) of their dissertation research. The final examination is an oral defense of the dissertation. The average time needed to complete all of the Ph.D. requirements has been six years.

Research Facilities

The physics department occupies the Sloane Physics Laboratory, part of the J. W. Gibbs Laboratories, and the Wright Nuclear Structure Laboratory. Research on condensed-matter physics is also done in the Becton Laboratory. Sloane has newly constructed laboratories for research in atomic, molecular, optical, and condensed-matter physics. The theoretical physicists are located in Sloane. The Wright Laboratory contains an Extended Stretch Transuranium (ESTU) 20-megavolt tandem electrostatic accelerator, the most powerful of its kind in the world. The Wright and Gibbs Laboratories house design facilities used in supporting high-energy experiments at Brookhaven National Laboratories, Fermilab, and the Stanford Linear Accelerator Center. Experiments are also done at European accelerators and observations taken at South American astronomical observatories. In addition to the centralized University computer system, each research group has its own appropriate computing facilities. There are four libraries of major pertinence to physics—Kline Science, Astronomy, Mathematics, and Engineering and Applied Science. Research areas in the Department of Physics include atomic physics, nuclear physics, particle physics, astrophysics, cosmology, condensed-matter physics, quantum information physics, applied physics, and other areas in collaboration with the faculties of engineering and applied science, chemistry, mathematics, geology and geophysics, and astronomy.

Financial Aid

Virtually all entering graduate students in the Department of Physics are offered financial aid for the first three terms in the form of a Yale University Fellowship. This is a combination of stipend, teaching fellowship, tuition, and payment for an Assistantship in Research for the summer following the first year. After the third or fourth semester, when a student has begun dissertation research, full financial support is provided by the student's thesis adviser in the form of an Assistantship in Research. The total support for 2004–05 is $23,500 for twelve months plus full tuition and health and hospitalization coverage. There are also teaching fellowships available to advanced students.

Cost of Study

After four years, tuition (currently $26,800 per annum) is replaced by an annual continuing registration fee of $536. Purchase of course texts is an additional expense.

Living and Housing Costs

The rents of dormitory rooms for the 2004–05 academic year range from $3280 for a single room to $5178 for a deluxe single room. Three-bedroom suites, which include a study, are also available. Board plans are offered. The cost for an apartment ranges from $640 to $920 per month. The lease period for graduate housing apartments is usually July 1 through June 30. Off-campus housing in the vicinity of the physics department is plentiful.

Student Group

The total number of students for 2004–05 is 95, all of whom attend full-time. Of these, about 52 percent are international students, and about 24 percent are women. Students with a strong basic undergraduate physics education, together with some research experience, are prime candidates for admission. Advanced commitment to a particular field is not required.

Location

Yale is located in the center of the city of New Haven (population about 125,000; metropolitan area about 400,000). The city offers an unusually wide variety of activities—especially in theater, music, film, fine arts, sports, and international dining. Frequent rail service to New York City and Boston takes less than 2 hours and about 3 hours, respectively.

The University

Chartered in 1701 as the Collegiate School, Yale was named for Elihu Yale, a London merchant who made a modest donation to help the fledgling school. A medical school was added in 1810. The Department of Philosophy and the Arts was organized in 1847, awarding the first three Ph.D. degrees in the United States in 1861 and becoming the Graduate School in 1892. Women were admitted early in the century to the graduate and professional schools and to Yale College as undergraduates in 1969.

Applying

Application forms are available from the Admissions Office, Yale Graduate School, P.O. Box 208323, New Haven, Connecticut 06520-8323 (telephone: 203-432-2770; e-mail: graduate.admissions@yale.edu). Candidates submitting completed applications and supporting materials before January 3, 2005, will be considered for admission in fall 2005. Applications must be accompanied by an application fee of $85. Students are required to take the GRE General Test as well as the GRE Subject Test in physics. Those whose native language is not English must also take the TOEFL; the TSE is recommended. Admission consideration is open to all qualified candidates without regard to race, color, national origin, religion, sex, sexual preference, or handicap.

Correspondence and Information

Director of Graduate Studies
Department of Physics
Yale University
P.O. Box 208120
New Haven, Connecticut 06520-8120
Telephone: 203-432-3607
Fax: 203-432-6175
E-mail: graduatephysics@yale.edu
World Wide Web: http://www.yale.edu/physics

Yale University

THE FACULTY AND THEIR RESEARCH

Robert K. Adair, Professor Emeritus and Senior Research Scientist; Ph.D., Wisconsin, 1951. Elementary particle physics.
Charles H. Ahn, Associate Professor (joint with Applied Physics); Ph.D, Stanford, 1996. Condensed-matter physics.
Yoram Alhassid, Professor; Ph.D., Hebrew (Jerusalem), 1979. Nuclear theory.
Thomas Appelquist, Professor; Ph.D., Cornell, 1968. Particle theory.
Charles Bailyn, Professor (joint with Astronomy); Ph.D., Harvard, 1987. High-energy astrophysics.
Charles Baltay, Professor; Ph.D., Yale, 1963. Elementary particle physics.
Sean E. Barrett, Professor; Ph.D., Illinois, 1992. Condensed-matter physics.
D. Allan Bromley, Professor; Ph.D., Rochester, 1952. Nuclear physics.
Helen L. Caines, Assistant Professor; Ph.D., Birmingham (England), 1996. Experimental nuclear physics.
Richard Casten, Professor; Ph.D., Yale, 1967. Nuclear physics.
Richard K. Chang, Professor (joint with Applied Physics); Ph.D., Harvard, 1965. Condensed-matter and laser physics.
Paolo Coppi, Professor (joint with Astronomy); Ph.D., Caltech, 1990. High-energy astrophysics.
David P. DeMille, Associate Professor; Ph.D., Berkeley, 1994. Atomic physics.
Michel Devoret, Professor (joint with Applied Physics); Ph.D., D'Orsay (France), 1982. Applied physics.
Satish Dhawan, Senior Research Scientist; Ph.D., Tsukuba (Japan), 1984. Elementary particle physics.
Richard Easther, Assistant Professor; Ph.D., Canterbury, 1994. Particle theory and cosmology.
Bonnie Fleming, Assistant Professor; Ph.D., Columbia, 2001. High-energy physics.
Paul A. Fleury, Professor (joint with Engineering and Applied Physics); Ph.D., MIT, 1965. Applied physics.
Moshe Gai, Adjunct Professor; Ph.D., SUNY at Stony Brook, 1980. Nuclear physics.
Colin Gay, Associate Professor; Ph.D., Toronto, 1991. Elementary particle physics.
Steven M. Girvin, Professor (joint with Applied Physics); Ph.D., Princeton, 1977. Theoretical condensed-matter physics.
Robert D. Grober, Professor (joint with Applied Physics); Ph.D., Maryland, 1991. Condensed-matter physics.
Martin Gutzwiller, Adjunct Professor; Ph.D., Kansas, 1953. Condensed-matter theory.
Jack Harris, Assistant Professor; Ph.D., California, Santa Barbara, 2000. Atomic physics.
John Harris, Professor; Ph.D., SUNY at Stony Brook, 1978. Relativistic heavy-ion physics.
Andreas Heinz, Assistant Professor; Ph.D., GSI Darmstadt (Germany), 1998. Nuclear physics.
Victor E. Henrich, Professor (joint with Applied Physics); Ph.D., Michigan, 1967. Condensed-matter physics.
Jay L. Hirshfield, Adjunct Professor; Ph.D., MIT, 1960. Beam physics.
Francesco Iachello, Professor (joint with Chemistry); Ph.D., MIT, 1969. Nuclear theory.
Stephen Irons, Lecturer; Ph.D., California, Davis, 1996. Condensed-matter physics.
Sohrab Ismail-Beigi, Assistant Professor (joint with Applied Physics); Ph.D., MIT, 2002. Condensed-matter physics.
Henry Kasha, Lecturer; D.Sc., Technion (Israel), 1960. Elementary particle physics.
Martin J. Klein, Professor; Ph.D., MIT, 1948. History of nineteenth- and twentieth-century physics.
Samuel W. MacDowell, Senior Research Scientist; Ph.D., Birmingham (England), 1958. Particle theory.
Richard D. Majka, Senior Research Scientist; Ph.D., Yale, 1974. Elementary particle physics.
William J. Marciano, Adjunct Professor; Ph.D., NYU, 1957. Particle theory.
Daniel McKinsey, Assistant Professor; Ph.D., Harvard, 2002. Atomic physics.
Simon Mochrie, Professor (joint with Applied Physics); Ph.D., MIT, 1985. Condensed matter.
Vincent E. Moncrief, Professor (joint with Mathematics); Ph.D., Maryland, 1972. Gravitation and cosmology.
Priyamvada Natarajan, Assistant Professor (joint with Astronomy); Ph.D., Cambridge, 1998. Astrophysics.
Homer A. Neal Jr., Assistant Professor; Ph.D., Stanford, 1995. Experimental elementary particle physics.
Corey O'Hern, Assistant Professor (joint with Medical Engineering); Ph.D., Pennsylvania, 1999. Mechanical engineering.
Peter D. M. Parker, Professor; Ph.D., Caltech, 1963. Experimental nuclear physics and nuclear astrophysics.
Daniel E. Prober, Professor (joint with Applied Physics); Ph.D., Harvard, 1975. Condensed-matter physics.
Nicholas Read, Professor (joint with Applied Physics); Ph.D., London, 1986. Condensed-matter theory.
Subir Sachdev, Professor (joint with Applied Physics); Ph.D., Harvard, 1985. Condensed-matter theory.
Jack Sandweiss, Professor; Ph.D., Berkeley, 1957. Elementary particle physics.
Michael P. Schmidt, Professor; Ph.D., Yale, 1979. Elementary particle physics.
Robert J. Schoelkopf, Professor (joint with Applied Physics); Ph.D., Caltech, 1995. Experimental condensed-matter physics.
Ramamurti Shankar, Professor (joint with Applied Physics); Ph.D., Berkeley, 1974. Condensed-matter theory and statistical physics.
Witold Skiba, Assistant Professor; Ph.D., MIT, 1997. Particle theory.
Charles M. Sommerfield, Professor; Ph.D., Harvard, 1957. Particle theory.
A. Douglas Stone, Professor (joint with Applied Physics); Ph.D., MIT, 1983. Condensed-matter theory.
Andrew Szymkowiak, Senior Research Scientist; Ph.D., Maryland, 1984. Astrophysics.
John C. Tully, Professor (joint with Chemistry); Ph.D., Chicago, 1968. Theoretical chemical physics.
C. Megan Urry, Professor; Ph.D. Johns Hopkins, 1984. Astrophysics.
John Wettlaufer, Professor (joint with Geophysics); Ph.D., Washington (Seattle), 1991. Geophysics.
Robert G. Wheeler, Professor Emeritus (joint with Applied Physics); Ph.D., Yale, 1955. Condensed-matter physics.
N. Victor Zamfir, Senior Research Scientist; Ph.D., Institute of Physics, Bucharest, 1984. Nuclear physics.
Michael E. Zeller, Professor; Ph.D., UCLA, 1968. Elementary particle physics.

ACADEMIC AND PROFESSIONAL PROGRAMS IN MATHEMATICS

Section 7
Mathematical Sciences

This section contains a directory of institutions offering graduate work in mathematical sciences, followed by in-depth entries submitted by institutions that chose to prepare detailed program descriptions. Additional information about programs listed in the directory but not augmented by an in-depth entry may be obtained by writing directly to the dean of a graduate school or chair of a department at the address given in the directory.

For programs offering work in related fields, see all other areas in this book. In Book 2, see Economics and Psychology and Counseling; in Book 3, see Biological and Biomedical Sciences; Biophysics; Genetics, Developmental Biology, and Reproductive Biology; and Pharmacology and Toxicology; in Book 5, see Bioengineering, Biomedical Engineering, and Biotechnology; Chemical Engineering (Biochemical Engineering); Computer Science and Information Technology; Electrical and Computer Engineering; Engineering and Applied Sciences; and Industrial Engineering; and in Book 6, see Business Administration and Management, Library and Information Studies, and Public Health.

CONTENTS

Program Directories

Announcements

Cross-Discipline Announcements

In-Depth Descriptions

See also:

Applied Mathematics

Acadia University, Faculty of Pure and Applied Science, Department of Mathematics and Statistics, Wolfville, NS B4P 2R6, Canada. Offers applied mathematics and statistics (M Sc). *Faculty:* 12 full-time (1 woman). *Degree requirements:* For master's, thesis, 4-8 month industry internship. *Entrance requirements:* For master's, honors, degree in mathematics or statistics or equivalent. Additional exam requirements/recommendations for international students: Required—TOEFL (minimum score 550 paper-based). *Application deadline:* For fall admission, 2/1 priority date for domestic students, 2/1 priority date for international students. Applications are processed on a rolling basis. Application fee: $50. *Expenses:* Tuition, state resident: full-time $5,611. *Financial support:* Career-related internships or fieldwork and unspecified assistantships available. *Faculty research:* Geophysical fluid dynamics, machine scheduling problems, control theory, stochastic optimization, survival analysis. *Unit head:* Tom Archibald, Acting Head, 902-585-1382, Fax: 902-585-1074, E-mail: tom.archibald@acadiau.ca. *Application contact:* Dr. Richard H. Karsten, Professor, 902-585-1608, Fax: 902-585-1074, E-mail: richard.karsten@acadiau.ca.

Air Force Institute of Technology, Graduate School of Engineering and Management, Department of Mathematics and Statistics, Dayton, OH 45433-7765. Offers applied mathematics (MS, PhD). Part-time programs available. *Degree requirements:* For master's and doctorate, thesis/dissertation. *Entrance requirements:* For master's, GRE General Test, minimum GPA of 3.0, must be U.S. citizen or permanent U.S. resident; for doctorate, GRE General Test, minimum GPA of 3.5, must be U.S. citizen or permanent U.S. resident. *Faculty research:* Electromagnetics, groundwater modeling, nonlinear diffusion, goodness of fit, finite element analysis.

Arizona State University, Graduate College, College of Liberal Arts and Sciences, Department of Mathematics, Tempe, AZ 85287. Offers applied mathematics (MA, PhD); mathematics (MA, MNS, PhD); statistics (MA, PhD). *Degree requirements:* For master's, thesis or alternative; for doctorate, one foreign language, thesis/dissertation. *Entrance requirements:* For master's and doctorate, GRE General Test. *Expenses:* Tuition, state resident: full-time $3,708; part-time $194 per credit hour. Tuition, nonresident: full-time $12,228; part-time $510 per credit hour. Required fees: $87; $22 per semester. Part-time tuition and fees vary according to program. *Faculty research:* Mathematical biology, ordinary and partial differential equations, calculus of variations.

Auburn University, Graduate School, College of Sciences and Mathematics, Department of Discrete and Statistical Sciences, Auburn University, AL 36849. Offers M Prob S, MAM, MS, PhD. *Faculty:* 12 full-time (0 women). *Students:* 13 full-time (9 women), 12 part-time (6 women); includes 4 minority (3 African Americans, 1 Hispanic American), 3 international. 20 applicants, 50% accepted. In 2003, 5 master's, 2 doctorates awarded. *Degree requirements:* For doctorate, thesis/dissertation. *Entrance requirements:* For master's and doctorate, GRE General Test. *Application deadline:* For fall admission, 7/7 for domestic students; for spring admission, 11/24 for domestic students. Applications are processed on a rolling basis. Application fee: $25 ($50 for international students). Electronic applications accepted. *Expenses:* Tuition, state resident: part-time $175 per credit hour. Tuition, nonresident: part-time $525 per credit hour. *Financial support:* Fellowships, teaching assistantships available. Financial award application deadline: 3/15. *Faculty research:* Discrete mathematics, applied probability, differential equations, cryptography. *Unit head:* Dr. Kevin T. Phelps, Head, 334-844-5111, Fax: 334-844-3611, E-mail: phelpkt@mail.auburn.edu.

Brown University, Graduate School, Division of Applied Mathematics, Providence, RI 02912. Offers Sc M, PhD. *Degree requirements:* For master's, thesis or alternative; for doctorate, one foreign language, thesis/dissertation, oral exam. *Entrance requirements:* For master's and doctorate, GRE General Test.

See in-depth description on page 525.

California Institute of Technology, Division of Engineering and Applied Science, Option in Applied and Computational Mathematics, Pasadena, CA 91125-0001. Offers MS, PhD. *Faculty:* 6 full-time (0 women), 3 part-time/adjunct (0 women). *Students:* 41 full-time (5 women); includes 9 minority (1 African American, 8 Asian Americans or Pacific Islanders), 15 international. 82 applicants, 10% accepted, 6 enrolled. In 2003, 6 degrees awarded. *Degree requirements:* For doctorate, thesis/dissertation. *Entrance requirements:* For doctorate, GRE Subject Test. *Application deadline:* For fall admission, 1/15 for domestic students. Application fee: $0. Electronic applications accepted. *Financial support:* In 2003–04, 5 research assistantships were awarded. *Faculty research:* Theoretical and computational fluid mechanics, numerical analysis, ordinary and partial differential equations, linear and nonlinear wave propagation, perturbation and asymptotic methods. *Unit head:* Dr. Yizhao Thomas Hou, Executive Officer, 626-395-4546, E-mail: hou@ama.caltech.edu.

California State Polytechnic University, Pomona, Academic Affairs, College of Science, Program in Mathematics, Pomona, CA 91768-2557. Offers applied mathematics (MS); pure mathematics (MS). Part-time programs available. *Students:* 24 full-time (12 women), 24 part-time (8 women); includes 21 minority (2 African Americans, 13 Asian Americans or Pacific Islanders, 6 Hispanic Americans), 3 international. Average age 29. 35 applicants, 80% accepted, 15 enrolled. In 2003, 5 degrees awarded. *Degree requirements:* For master's, thesis or alternative. *Entrance requirements:* For master's, GRE General Test. *Application deadline:* For fall admission, 5/1 for domestic students; for winter admission, 10/15 for domestic students; for spring admission, 1/20 for domestic students. Applications are processed on a rolling basis. Application fee: $55. Electronic applications accepted. Tuition, nonresident: full-time $6,016; part-time $188 per unit. Required fees: $2,256. *Financial support:* Career-related internships or fieldwork, Federal Work-Study, and institutionally sponsored loans available. Support available to part-time students. Financial award application deadline: 3/2; financial award applicants required to submit FAFSA. *Unit head:* Dr. Alan C. Krinik, Graduate Coordinator, 909-869-3479, E-mail: ackrinik@csupomona.edu.

California State University, Fullerton, Graduate Studies, College of Natural Science and Mathematics, Department of Mathematics, Fullerton, CA 92834-9480. Offers applied mathematics (MA); mathematics (MA); mathematics for secondary school teachers (MA). Part-time programs available. *Faculty:* 33 full-time (8 women), 71 part-time/adjunct. *Students:* 8 full-time (3 women), 70 part-time (34 women); includes 40 minority (3 African Americans, 26 Asian Americans or Pacific Islanders, 11 Hispanic Americans). Average age 32. 64 applicants, 86% accepted, 44 enrolled. In 2003, 19 degrees awarded. *Degree requirements:* For master's, comprehensive exam or project. *Entrance requirements:* For master's, minimum GPA of 2.5 in last 60 units, major in mathematics or related field. Application fee: $55. Tuition, nonresident: part-time $282 per unit. Required fees: $889 per semester. *Financial support:* Research assistantships, teaching assistantships, career-related internships or fieldwork, Federal Work-Study, institutionally sponsored loans, and scholarships/grants available. Support available to part-time students. Financial award application deadline: 3/1. *Unit head:* Dr. James Friel, Chair, 714-278-3631.

California State University, Long Beach, Graduate Studies, College of Engineering, Department of Civil Engineering and Construction Engineering Management, Long Beach, CA 90840. Offers civil engineering (MSCE, CE); engineering (MSE); engineering and industrial applied mathematics (PhD); waste engineering and management (Graduate Certificate). Part-time programs available. *Faculty:* 12 full-time (1 woman), 8 part-time/adjunct (0 women). *Students:* 18 full-time (4 women), 54 part-time (10 women); includes 35 minority (1 African American, 1 American Indian/Alaska Native, 25 Asian Americans or Pacific Islanders, 8 Hispanic Americans), 5 international. Average age 31. 51 applicants, 69% accepted, 18 enrolled. In 2003, 14 degrees awarded. *Degree requirements:* For master's, comprehensive exam or thesis. *Entrance requirements:* Additional exam requirements/recommendations for international students: Required—TOEFL. *Application deadline:* For fall admission, 7/1 for domestic students; for spring admission, 12/1 for domestic students. Application fee: $55. Electronic applications accepted. Tuition, nonresident: part-time $282 per unit. Required fees: $504 per semester. *Financial support:* Career-related internships or fieldwork, Federal Work-Study, institutionally sponsored loans, scholarships/grants, and unspecified assistantships available. Financial award application deadline: 3/2. *Faculty research:* Soils, hydraulics, seismic structures, composite metals, computer-aided manufacturing. *Unit head:* Dr. Joseph Plecnik, Chair, 562-985-4406, Fax: 562-985-2380, E-mail: plecnik@csulb.edu. *Application contact:* Dr. Gene Chu, Graduate Adviser, 562-985-5768, Fax: 562-985-2380, E-mail: chu@csulb.edu.

California State University, Long Beach, Graduate Studies, College of Engineering, Department of Mechanical and Aerospace Engineering, Long Beach, CA 90840. Offers aerospace engineering (MSAE); engineering and industrial applied mathematics (PhD); interdisciplinary engineering (MSE); management engineering (MSE); mechanical engineering (MSME). Part-time programs available. *Faculty:* 18 full-time (1 woman), 14 part-time/adjunct (2 women). *Students:* 27 full-time (3 women), 53 part-time (7 women); includes 41 minority (29 Asian Americans or Pacific Islanders, 12 Hispanic Americans), 5 international. Average age 31. 65 applicants, 65% accepted, 18 enrolled. In 2003, 21 degrees awarded. *Entrance requirements:* Additional exam requirements/recommendations for international students: Required—TOEFL. *Application deadline:* For fall admission, 7/1 for domestic students; for spring admission, 12/1 for domestic students. Application fee: $55. Electronic applications accepted. Tuition, nonresident: part-time $282 per unit. Required fees: $504 per semester. *Financial support:* Career-related internships or fieldwork, Federal Work-Study, institutionally sponsored loans, scholarships/grants, and unspecified assistantships available. Financial award application deadline: 3/2. *Faculty research:* Unsteady turbulent flows, solar energy, energy conversion, CAD/CAM, computer-assisted instruction. *Unit head:* Dr. Hamid Hefazi, Chairman, 562-985-4407, Fax: 562-985-4408, E-mail: hefazi@csulb.edu. *Application contact:* Dr. Hamid Rahai, Graduate Coordinator, 562-985-5132, Fax: 562-985-4408, E-mail: rahai@engr.csulb.edu.

California State University, Long Beach, Graduate Studies, College of Natural Sciences, Department of Mathematics, Long Beach, CA 90840. Offers applied mathematics (MA); mathematics (MA). Part-time programs available. *Faculty:* 20 full-time (1 woman). *Students:* 21 full-time (6 women), 43 part-time (16 women); includes 34 minority (3 African Americans, 19 Asian Americans or Pacific Islanders, 12 Hispanic Americans), 2 international. Average age 33. 46 applicants, 54% accepted, 15 enrolled. In 2003, 8 degrees awarded. *Degree requirements:* For master's, comprehensive exam or thesis. *Application deadline:* For fall admission, 7/1 for domestic students; for spring admission, 12/1 for domestic students. Applications are processed on a rolling basis. Application fee: $55. Electronic applications accepted. Tuition, nonresident: part-time $282 per unit. Required fees: $504 per semester. *Financial support:* Teaching assistantships, Federal Work-Study, institutionally sponsored loans, scholarships/grants, and traineeships available. Financial award application deadline: 3/2. *Faculty research:* Algebra, functional analysis, partial differential equations, operator theory, numerical analysis. *Unit head:* Dr. Arthur Wayman, Chair, 562-985-4721, Fax: 562-985-8227, E-mail: away@csulb.edu. *Application contact:* Dr. Ngo N.P. Viet, Graduate Coordinator, 562-985-5610, Fax: 562-985-8227, E-mail: viet@csulb.edu.

California State University, Los Angeles, Graduate Studies, College of Natural and Social Sciences, Department of Mathematics, Los Angeles, CA 90032-8530. Offers mathematics (MS), including applied mathematics, mathematics. Part-time and evening/weekend programs available. *Faculty:* 22 full-time, 43 part-time/adjunct. *Students:* 31 full-time (10 women), 41 part-time (13 women); includes 47 minority (3 African Americans, 26 Asian Americans or Pacific Islanders, 18 Hispanic Americans), 9 international. In 2003, 2 degrees awarded. *Degree requirements:* For master's, comprehensive exam or thesis. *Entrance requirements:* For master's, previous course work in mathematics. Additional exam requirements/recommendations for international students: Required—TOEFL. *Application deadline:* For fall admission, 6/30 for domestic students; for spring admission, 2/1 for domestic students. Applications are processed on a rolling basis. Application fee: $55. Tuition, nonresident: part-time $188 per unit. Required fees: $2,477. *Financial support:* Teaching assistantships, Federal Work-Study available. Support available to part-time students. Financial award application deadline: 3/1. *Faculty research:* Group theory, functional analysis, convexity theory, ordered geometry. *Unit head:* Dr. P. K. Subramanian, Chair, 323-343-2150.

Case Western Reserve University, School of Graduate Studies, Department of Mathematics, Cleveland, OH 44106. Offers applied mathematics (MS, PhD); mathematics (MS, PhD). Part-time programs available. *Faculty:* 14 full-time (1 woman). *Students:* 9 full-time (2 women), 1 part-time, 5 international. Average age 25. 77 applicants, 3% accepted, 1 enrolled. In 2003, 1 degree awarded. Terminal master's awarded for partial completion of doctoral program. *Degree requirements:* For master's, thesis (applied mathematics); for doctorate, one foreign language, thesis/dissertation. *Entrance requirements:* For master's and doctorate, GRE General Test. Additional exam requirements/recommendations for international students: Required—TOEFL. *Application deadline:* For fall admission, 6/25 for domestic students; for spring admission, 11/12 for domestic students. Applications are processed on a rolling basis. Application fee: $50. *Expenses:* Tuition: Full-time $26,900. *Financial support:* In 2003–04, 7 students received support, including 5 teaching assistantships. Financial award application deadline: 4/15. *Faculty research:* Probability theory, differential equations and control theory, differential geometry and topology, Lie groups, functional and harmonic analysis. Total annual research expenditures: $268,000. *Unit head:* Dr. James G. Alexander, Chair, 216-368-2882, Fax: 216-368-5163, E-mail: jcal0@case.edu. *Application contact:* Gaythresa Lewis, Admissions, 216-368-5014, Fax: 216-368-5163, E-mail: gxl34@case.edu.

Central Missouri State University, School of Graduate Studies, College of Arts and Sciences, Department of Mathematics and Computer Science, Warrensburg, MO 64093. Offers applied mathematics (MS); mathematics (MS); mathematics education (MSE), including elementary mathematics, secondary mathematics. *Accreditation:* NCATE (one or more programs are accredited). Part-time programs available. *Faculty:* 12 full-time (4 women), 1 part-time/adjunct (0 women). *Students:* 3 full-time (2 women), 7 part-time (2 women); includes 1 minority (Hispanic American), 1 international. Average age 27. 3 applicants, 67% accepted. In 2003, 5 degrees awarded. *Degree requirements:* For master's, thesis (MS); comprehensive exam or thesis (MSE). *Entrance requirements:* For master's, GRE General Test (MSE), bachelor's degree in mathematics, minimum GPA of 3.0 (MS); minimum GPA of 2.75, teaching certificate (MSE). Additional exam requirements/recommendations for international students: Required—TOEFL (minimum score 500 paper-based; 173 computer-based). *Application deadline:* For fall admission, 6/1 priority date for domestic students, 5/1 priority date for international students; for spring admission, 10/1 priority date for domestic students, 10/1 priority date for international students. Applications are processed on a rolling basis. Application fee: $25 ($50 for international students). *Expenses:* Tuition, state resident: part-time $198 per credit hour. Tuition, nonresident: part-time $396 per credit hour. Required fees: $12 per credit hour. *Financial support:* In 2003–04, 4 teaching assistantships (averaging $8,670 per year) were awarded; Federal Work-Study, scholarships/grants, unspecified assistantships, and administrative assistantships also available. Support available to part-time students. Financial award application deadline: 3/1; financial award applicants required to submit FAFSA. *Faculty research:* Graph theory, topology, applied statistics, risk theory, mathematics education. *Unit head:* Dr. Edward W. Davenport, Chair, 660-543-4931, Fax: 660-543-8006, E-mail: davenport@cmsu1.cmsu.edu.

Claremont Graduate University, Graduate Programs, School of Mathematical Sciences, Claremont, CA 91711-6160. Offers computational science (PhD); engineering mathematics (PhD); financial engineering (MS); operations research and statistics (MA, MS); physical applied mathematics (MA, MS); pure mathematics (MA, MS, PhD); scientific computing (MA, MS); systems and control theory (MA, MS). Part-time programs available. *Faculty:* 2 full-time (0 women), 3 part-time/adjunct (0 women). *Students:* 41 full-time (8 women), 11 part-time (3 women). Average age 36. In 2003, 9 master's, 4 doctorates awarded. Terminal master's awarded for partial completion of doctoral program. *Degree requirements:* For doctorate, 2 foreign languages, thesis/dissertation. *Entrance requirements:* For master's and doctorate, GRE General Test. *Application deadline:* For fall admission, 2/15 for domestic students. Applications are processed on a rolling basis. Electronic applications accepted. *Expenses:* Tuition: Full-time $25,250; part-time $1,099 per semester. *Financial support:* Fellowships, research assistantships, career-related internships or fieldwork, Federal Work-Study, institutionally sponsored loans, and tuition waivers (full and partial) available. Support available to part-time students. Financial award application deadline: 2/15; financial award applicants required to submit FAFSA. *Unit head:* John Angus, Chair, 909-621-8080, Fax: 909-607-8261, E-mail: john.angus@cgu.edu. *Application contact:* Mary Solberg, Administrative Assistant, 909-621-8080, Fax: 909-607-8261, E-mail: math@cgu.edu.

Clark Atlanta University, School of Arts and Sciences, Department of Mathematical Sciences, Atlanta, GA 30314. Offers applied mathematics (MS); computer science (MS). Part-time programs available. *Degree requirements:* For master's, one foreign language, thesis. *Entrance requirements:* For master's, GRE General Test, minimum GPA of 2.5. *Faculty research:* Numerical methods for operator equations, Ada language development.

Clemson University, Graduate School, College of Engineering and Science, Department of Mathematical Sciences, Clemson, SC 29634. Offers applied and pure mathematics (MS, PhD); computational mathematics (MS, PhD); management science (PhD); operations research (MS, PhD); statistics (MS, PhD). Part-time programs available. *Students:* 73 full-time (25 women), 5 part-time (1 woman); includes 3 minority (2 African Americans, 1 Asian American or Pacific Islander), 33 international. Average age 29. 116 applicants, 74% accepted, 31 enrolled. In 2003, 25 master's, 5 doctorates awarded. *Degree requirements:* For master's, final project, thesis optional; for doctorate, thesis/dissertation, qualifying exams. *Entrance requirements:* For master's and doctorate, GRE General Test. Additional exam requirements/recommendations for international students: Required—TOEFL. *Application deadline:* For fall admission, 6/1 for domestic students. Application fee: $40. *Expenses:* Tuition, state resident: full-time $7,432. Tuition, nonresident: full-time $14,732. *Financial support:* Fellowships, research assistantships, teaching assistantships available. Financial award application deadline: 4/15; financial award applicants required to submit FAFSA. *Faculty research:* Applied and computational analysis, discrete mathematics, mathematical programming statistics. *Unit head:* Dr. Perino Dearing, Interim Dean, 864-656-5240, Fax: 864-656-5230, E-mail: pmdrn@clemson.edu. *Application contact:* Dr. Douglas Shier, Graduate Coordinator, 864-656-1100, Fax: 864-656-5230, E-mail: shierd@clemson.edu.

Cleveland State University, College of Graduate Studies, College of Arts and Sciences, Department of Mathematics, Cleveland, OH 44115. Offers applied mathematics (MS); mathematics (MA). Part-time programs available. *Faculty:* 15 full-time (5 women). *Students:* 3 full-time (1 woman), 16 part-time (3 women); includes 4 minority (1 African American, 3 Asian Americans or Pacific Islanders), 1 international. Average age 32. 18 applicants, 67% accepted, 3 enrolled. In 2003, 6 degrees awarded. *Degree requirements:* For master's, exit project. *Entrance requirements:* For master's, GRE. Additional exam requirements/recommendations for international students: Required—TOEFL (minimum score 515 paper-based; 197 computer-based). *Application deadline:* For fall admission, 6/15 for domestic students. Applications are processed on a rolling basis. Application fee: $30. Tuition, area resident: Full-time $8,258; part-time $344 per credit hour. Tuition, nonresident: full-time $16,352; part-time $681 per credit hour. *Financial support:* In 2003–04, 6 students received support, including 1 teaching assistantship with full and partial tuition reimbursement available (averaging $5,000 per year); Federal Work-Study, institutionally sponsored loans, and tuition waivers (full and partial) also available. Financial award application deadline: 3/15. *Unit head:* Dr. Sherwood D. Silliman, Chairperson, 216-687-4681, Fax: 216-523-7340, E-mail: silliman@csuohio.edu. *Application contact:* Dr. John F. Oprea, Director, 216-687-4702, Fax: 216-523-7340, E-mail: oprea@csuohio.edu.

Columbia University, Fu Foundation School of Engineering and Applied Science, Department of Applied Physics and Applied Mathematics, New York, NY 10027. Offers applied physics (MS, PhD), including applied mathematics (PhD), optical physics (PhD), plasma physics (PhD), solid state physics (PhD); applied physics and applied mathematics (Eng Sc D); materials science and engineering (MS, Eng Sc D, PhD); medical physics (MS); minerals engineering and materials science (Eng Sc D, PhD, Engr). Part-time programs available. *Faculty:* 29 full-time (3 women), 11 part-time/adjunct (1 woman). *Students:* 82 full-time (25 women), 27 part-time (13 women); includes 14 minority (5 African Americans, 8 Asian Americans or Pacific Islanders, 1 Hispanic American), 51 international. 371 applicants, 17% accepted, 41 enrolled. In 2003, 36 master's, 9 doctorates awarded. Terminal master's awarded for partial completion of doctoral program. *Degree requirements:* For doctorate, thesis/dissertation, qualifying exam. *Entrance requirements:* For master's and doctorate, GRE General Test, GRE Subject Test (strongly recommended). Additional exam requirements/recommendations for international students: Required—TOEFL. *Application deadline:* For fall admission, 12/15 priority date for domestic students, 12/15 priority date for international students; for spring admission, 10/1 priority date for domestic students, 10/1 priority date for international students. Application fee: $55. Electronic applications accepted. *Expenses:* Tuition: Full-time $14,820. *Financial support:* In 2003–04, 62 students received support, including 4 fellowships with full tuition reimbursements available, 40 research assistantships with full tuition reimbursements available (averaging $22,725 per year), 14 teaching assistantships with full tuition reimbursements available (averaging $22,725 per year); Federal Work-Study and unspecified assistantships also available. Financial award application deadline: 12/15; financial award applicants required to submit FAFSA. *Faculty research:* Plasma physics, applied mathematics, solid-state and optical physics, atmospheric, oceanic and earth physics, materials science and engineering. Total annual research expenditures: $7.9 million. *Unit head:* Dr. Michael E. Mauel, Chairman, 212-854-4457, E-mail: seasinfo.apam@columbia.edu. *Application contact:* Marlene Arbo, Department Administrator, 212-854-4458, Fax: 212-854-8257, E-mail: seasinfo.apam@columbia.edu.

See in-depth description on page 357.

Cornell University, Graduate School, Graduate Fields of Arts and Sciences, Center for Applied Mathematics, Ithaca, NY 14853-0001. Offers PhD. *Faculty:* 83 full-time. *Students:* 34 full-time (14 women); includes 13 minority (2 African Americans, 4 Asian Americans or Pacific Islanders, 7 Hispanic Americans), 10 international. 138 applicants, 7% accepted, 6 enrolled. In 2003, 8 doctorates awarded. *Degree requirements:* For doctorate, one foreign language, thesis/dissertation, comprehensive exam. *Entrance requirements:* For doctorate, GRE General Test, GRE Subject Test (mathematics)(recommended), 3 letters of recommendation. Additional exam requirements/recommendations for international students: Required—TOEFL (minimum score 550 paper-based; 213 computer-based). *Application deadline:* For fall admission, 1/15 for domestic students. Application fee: $60. Electronic applications accepted. *Expenses:* Tuition: Full-time $28,630. One-time fee: $50 full-time. *Financial support:* In 2003–04, 33 students received support, including 15 fellowships with full tuition reimbursements available, 5 research assistantships with full tuition reimbursements available, 13 teaching assistantships with full tuition reimbursements available; institutionally sponsored loans, scholarships/grants, health care benefits, tuition waivers (full and partial), and unspecified assistantships also available. Financial award applicants required to submit FAFSA. *Faculty research:* Nonlinear systems and PDE's, numerical methods, signal and image processing, mathematical biology, discrete mathematics and optimization. *Unit head:* Director of Graduate Studies, 607-255-4756, Fax: 607-255-9860. *Application contact:* Graduate Field Assistant, 607-255-4756, Fax: 607-255-9860, E-mail: appliedmath@cornell.edu.

Announcement: The Center for Applied Mathematics is an interdepartmental program with more than 80 faculty members. Students may pursue PhD studies over a broad range of the mathematical sciences and are admitted to the field from a variety of educational backgrounds with strong mathematical components. Students are normally awarded fellowships or teaching or research assistantships.

Cornell University, Graduate School, Graduate Fields of Engineering, Field of Chemical Engineering, Ithaca, NY 14853-0001. Offers advanced materials processing (M Eng, MS, PhD); applied mathematics and computational methods (M Eng, MS, PhD); biochemical engineering (M Eng, MS, PhD); chemical reaction engineering (M Eng, MS, PhD); classical and statistical thermodynamics (M Eng, MS, PhD); fluid dynamics, rheology and biorheology (M Eng, MS, PhD); heat and mass transfer (M Eng, MS, PhD); kinetics and catalysis (M Eng, MS, PhD); polymers (M Eng, MS, PhD); surface science (M Eng, MS, PhD). *Faculty:* 23 full-time. *Students:* 92 full-time (22 women); includes 13 minority (11 Asian Americans or Pacific Islanders, 2 Hispanic Americans), 43 international. 321 applicants, 29% accepted, 36 enrolled. In 2003, 17 master's, 8 doctorates awarded. *Degree requirements:* For master's, thesis (MS); for doctorate, thesis/dissertation, comprehensive exam. *Entrance requirements:* For master's and doctorate, GRE General Test, pre-application, 2 letters of recommendation. Additional exam requirements/recommendations for international students: Required—TOEFL (minimum score 580 paper-based; 237 computer-based). *Application deadline:* For fall admission, 1/15 for domestic students. Application fee: $60. Electronic applications accepted. *Expenses:* Tuition: Full-time $28,630. One-time fee: $50 full-time. *Financial support:* In 2003–04, 72 students received support, including 19 fellowships with full tuition reimbursements available, 43 research assistantships with full tuition reimbursements available, 10 teaching assistantships with full tuition reimbursements available; institutionally sponsored loans, scholarships/grants, health care benefits, tuition waivers (full and partial), and unspecified assistantships also available. Financial award applicants required to submit FAFSA. *Faculty research:* Biochemical, biomedical and metabolic engineering; fluid and polymer dynamics; surface science and chemical kinetics; electronics materials; microchemical systems and nanotechnology. *Unit head:* Director of Graduate Studies, 607-255-4550. *Application contact:* Graduate Field Assistant, 607-255-4550, E-mail: dgs@cheme.cornell.edu.

Cornell University, Graduate School, Graduate Fields of Engineering, Field of Operations Research and Industrial Engineering, Ithaca, NY 14853-0001. Offers applied probability and statistics (PhD); manufacturing systems engineering (PhD); mathematical programming (PhD); operations research and industrial engineering (M Eng). *Faculty:* 31 full-time. *Students:* 110 full-time (32 women); includes 22 minority (1 African American, 18 Asian Americans or Pacific Islanders, 3 Hispanic Americans), 62 international. 493 applicants, 40% accepted, 67 enrolled. In 2003, 96 master's, 5 doctorates awarded. *Degree requirements:* For doctorate, thesis/dissertation, comprehensive exam. *Entrance requirements:* For master's and doctorate, GRE General Test, 3 letters of recommendation. Additional exam requirements/recommendations for international students: Required—TOEFL (minimum score 600 paper-based; 250 computer-based). *Application deadline:* For fall admission, 1/15 for domestic students. Application fee: $60. Electronic applications accepted. *Expenses:* Tuition: Full-time $28,630. One-time fee: $50 full-time. *Financial support:* In 2003–04, 41 students received support, including 5 fellowships with full tuition reimbursements available, 6 research assistantships with full tuition reimbursements available, 30 teaching assistantships with full tuition reimbursements available; institutionally sponsored loans, scholarships/grants, health care benefits, tuition waivers (full and partial), and unspecified assistantships also available. Financial award applicants required to submit FAFSA. *Faculty research:* Mathematical programming and combinatorial optimization, statistics, stochastic processes, mathematical finance, simulation, manufacturing, and e-commerce. *Unit head:* Director of Graduate Studies, 607-255-9128, Fax: 607-255-9129. *Application contact:* Graduate Field Assistant, 607-255-9128, Fax: 607-255-9129, E-mail: orphd@cornell.edu.

Dalhousie University, Faculty of Graduate Studies, DalTech, Faculty of Engineering, Department of Engineering Mathematics, Halifax, NS B3H 4R2, Canada. Offers M Sc, PhD. *Degree requirements:* For master's and doctorate, thesis/dissertation. *Entrance requirements:* Additional exam requirements/recommendations for international students: Required—TOEFL. *Faculty research:* Piecewise regression and robust statistics, random field theory, dynamical systems, wave loads on offshore structures, digital signal processing.

East Carolina University, Graduate School, Thomas Harriot College of Arts and Sciences, Department of Mathematics, Greenville, NC 27858-4353. Offers applied mathematics (MA); mathematics (MA). Part-time and evening/weekend programs available. *Faculty:* 15 full-time (4 women). *Students:* 2 full-time (1 woman), 4 part-time (3 women), 1 international. Average age 30. 4 applicants, 100% accepted. In 2003, 3 degrees awarded. *Degree requirements:* For master's, comprehensive exam. *Entrance requirements:* For master's, GRE General Test, MAT. Additional exam requirements/recommendations for international students: Required—TOEFL. *Application deadline:* For fall admission, 6/1 for domestic students; for spring admission, 10/15 for domestic students. Applications are processed on a rolling basis. Application fee: $50. *Expenses:* Tuition, state resident: full-time $1,991; part-time $249 per hour. Tuition, nonresident: full-time $12,232; part-time $1,529 per hour. Required fees: $1,221; $153 per hour. *Financial support:* Research assistantships with partial tuition reimbursements, teaching assistantships with partial tuition reimbursements available. Financial award application deadline: 6/1. *Unit head:* Dr. John Daughtry, Director of Graduate Studies, 252-328-6415, Fax: 252-328-6414, E-mail: daughtryj@mail.ecu.edu. *Application contact:* Dr. Paul D. Tschetter, Interim Dean of Graduate School, 252-328-6012, Fax: 252-328-6071, E-mail: gradschool@mail.ecu.edu.

École Polytechnique de Montréal, Graduate Programs, Department of Mathematics, Montréal, QC H3C 3A7, Canada. Offers mathematical method in CA engineering (M Eng, M Sc A, PhD); operational research (M Eng, M Sc A, PhD). Part-time programs available. *Degree requirements:* For master's and doctorate, one foreign language, thesis/dissertation. *Entrance requirements:* For master's, minimum GPA of 2.75; for doctorate, minimum GPA of 3.0. *Faculty research:* Statistics and probability, fractal analysis, optimization.

Florida Atlantic University, Charles E. Schmidt College of Science, Department of Mathematical Science, Boca Raton, FL 33431-0991. Offers applied mathematics and statistics (MS); mathematics (MS, MST, PhD). Part-time programs available. *Faculty:* 25 full-time (2 women), 3 part-time/adjunct (0 women). *Students:* 31 full-time (11 women), 18 part-time (12 women); includes 12 minority (4 African Americans, 8 Hispanic Americans), 18 international. Average age 32. 36 applicants, 67% accepted, 16 enrolled. In 2003, 6 master's, 1 doctorate awarded. Terminal master's awarded for partial completion of doctoral program. *Degree requirements:* For master's, thesis (for some programs), comprehensive exam (for some programs), registration; for doctorate, thesis/dissertation, comprehensive exam, registration. *Entrance requirements:* For master's and doctorate, GRE General Test, minimum GPA of 3.0. Additional exam requirements/recommendations for international students: Required—TOEFL (minimum score 500 paper-based; 173 computer-based). *Application deadline:* For fall admission, 6/1 priority date for domestic students, 2/15 priority date for international students; for spring admission, 10/20 priority date for domestic students, 8/15 priority date for international students. Applications are processed on a rolling basis. Application fee: $30. Electronic applications accepted. *Expenses:* Tuition, state resident: full-time $3,777. Tuition, nonresident: full-time $13,953. *Financial support:* In 2003–04, fellowships with partial tuition reimbursements (averaging $20,000 per year), 20 teaching assistantships with partial tuition reimbursements (averaging $20,000 per year) were awarded. Federal Work-Study also available. Financial award application deadline: 4/1. *Faculty research:* Cryptography, statistics, algebra, analysis, combinatorics. Total annual research expenditures: $550,000. *Unit head:* Dr. Yoram Sagher, Chair, 561-297-3341, Fax: 561-297-2436, E-mail: sagher@fau.edu. *Application contact:* Dr. Heinrich Niederhausen, Graduate Director, 561-297-3237, Fax: 561-297-2436, E-mail: grad@math.fau.edu.

Florida Institute of Technology, Graduate Programs, College of Science and Liberal Arts, Department of Mathematical Sciences, Melbourne, FL 32901-6975. Offers applied mathematics (MS, PhD); operations research (MS, PhD). Part-time and evening/weekend programs available. *Faculty:* 11 full-time (2 women). *Students:* 19 full-time (4 women), 8 part-time (2 women); includes 4 minority (2 African Americans, 1 Asian American or Pacific Islander, 1 Hispanic American), 15 international. Average age 30. 55 applicants, 69% accepted, 15 enrolled. In 2003, 6 master's, 7 doctorates awarded. Terminal master's awarded for partial completion of

Applied Mathematics

Florida Institute of Technology (continued)

doctoral program. *Degree requirements:* For master's and doctorate, thesis/dissertation, comprehensive exam, registration. *Entrance requirements:* For master's, minimum GPA of 3.0; for doctorate, minimum GPA of 3.2, resumé, letters of recommendation (3), statement of objectives. Additional exam requirements/recommendations for international students: Required—TOEFL (minimum score 550 paper-based; 213 computer-based). *Application deadline:* Applications are processed on a rolling basis. Application fee: $50. Electronic applications accepted. *Expenses:* Tuition: Part-time $745 per credit. *Financial support:* In 2003–04, 19 students received support, including 1 research assistantship with full and partial tuition reimbursement available (averaging $8,640 per year), 18 teaching assistantships with full and partial tuition reimbursements available (averaging $21,535 per year); career-related internships or fieldwork and tuition remissions also available. Financial award application deadline: 3/1; financial award applicants required to submit FAFSA. *Faculty research:* Real analysis, ODE, PDE, numerical analysis, statistics, data analysis, combinatorics, artificial intelligence, simulation. Total annual research expenditures: $44,008. *Unit head:* Dr. V. Lakshmikantham, Department Head, 321-674-7412, Fax: 321-674-7412, E-mail: lakshmik@fit.edu. *Application contact:* Carolyn P. Farrior, Director of Graduate Admissions, 321-674-7118, Fax: 321-723-9468, E-mail: cfarrior@fit.edu.

Florida State University, Graduate Studies, College of Arts and Sciences, Department of Mathematics, Tallahassee, FL 32306. Offers applied mathematics (MA, MS, PhD); financial mathematics (PhD); mathematical sciences (MA, MS); pure mathematics (MA, MS, PhD). Part-time programs available. *Faculty:* 35 full-time (3 women), 8 part-time/adjunct (4 women). *Students:* 110 full-time (36 women), 7 part-time (3 women); includes 54 minority (4 African Americans, 45 Asian Americans or Pacific Islanders, 5 Hispanic Americans), 4 international. Average age 26. 250 applicants, 60% accepted, 50 enrolled. In 2003, 18 master's, 3 doctorates awarded. Terminal master's awarded for partial completion of doctoral program. *Degree requirements:* For master's, thesis optional; for doctorate, thesis/dissertation. *Entrance requirements:* For master's and doctorate, GRE General Test, minimum GPA of 3.0. *Application deadline:* For fall admission, 2/1 priority date for domestic students, 1/1 priority date for international students; for winter admission, 7/1 for domestic students. Applications are processed on a rolling basis. Application fee: $20. Electronic applications accepted. *Expenses:* Tuition, state resident: part-time $196 per credit hour. Tuition, nonresident: part-time $731 per credit hour. Part-time tuition and fees vary according to campus/location. *Financial support:* In 2003–04, 2 fellowships with full tuition reimbursements (averaging $15,000 per year), 10 research assistantships with full tuition reimbursements, 78 teaching assistantships with full tuition reimbursements (averaging $15,000 per year) were awarded. Institutionally sponsored loans also available. Financial award application deadline: 3/1. *Unit head:* Dr. Dewitt Sumners, Chairperson, 850-644-4406, Fax: 850-644-4053, E-mail: sumners@math.fsu.edu. *Application contact:* Dr. Sam Huckaba, Director of Graduate Studies, 850-644-1479, Fax: 850-644-4053, E-mail: huckaba@math.fsu.edu.

The George Washington University, Columbian College of Arts and Sciences, Department of Mathematics, Washington, DC 20052. Offers applied mathematics (MA, MS); pure mathematics (MA, PhD). Part-time and evening/weekend programs available. *Faculty:* 8 full-time (2 women). *Students:* 14 full-time (7 women), 6 part-time (2 women); includes 1 minority (Hispanic American), 7 international. Average age 31. 33 applicants, 76% accepted. In 2003, 4 degrees awarded. Terminal master's awarded for partial completion of doctoral program. *Degree requirements:* For master's, comprehensive exam; for doctorate, one foreign language, thesis/dissertation, general exam. *Entrance requirements:* For master's and doctorate, GRE General Test, minimum GPA of 3.0, interview. Additional exam requirements/recommendations for international students: Required—TOEFL (minimum score 550 paper-based; 213 computer-based). *Application deadline:* For fall admission, 2/1 priority date for domestic students, 2/1 priority date for international students; for spring admission, 10/1 priority date for domestic students, 10/1 priority date for international students. Applications are processed on a rolling basis. Application fee: $60. Electronic applications accepted. *Expenses:* Tuition: Part-time $876 per credit. Required fees: $1 per credit. Tuition and fees vary according to campus/location. *Financial support:* In 2003–04, fellowships with full tuition reimbursements (averaging $10,000 per year), teaching assistantships with tuition reimbursements (averaging $5,000 per year) were awarded. Federal Work-Study also available. Financial award application deadline: 2/1. *Unit head:* Dr. Daniel Ullman, Chair, 202-994-6235.

Georgia Institute of Technology, Graduate Studies and Research, College of Sciences, School of Mathematics, Atlanta, GA 30332-0001. Offers algorithms, combinatorics, and optimization (PhD); applied mathematics (MS); bioinformatics (PhD); mathematics (PhD); quantitative and computational finance (MS); statistics (MS Stat). *Faculty:* 50 full-time (3 women). *Students:* 59 full-time (17 women), 8 part-time (2 women); includes 3 minority (2 African Americans, 1 Hispanic American), 32 international. Average age 25. In 2003, 20 master's, 7 doctorates awarded, leading to university research/teaching 55%, business/industry 30%, government 15%. Terminal master's awarded for partial completion of doctoral program. *Degree requirements:* For master's, thesis or alternative; for doctorate, one foreign language, thesis/dissertation. *Entrance requirements:* For master's, GRE General Test, minimum GPA of 3.0; for doctorate, GRE General Test, GRE Subject Test, minimum GPA of 3.0. Additional exam requirements/recommendations for international students: Required—TOEFL. *Application deadline:* For fall admission, 3/1 priority date for domestic students, 3/1 priority date for international students; for spring admission, 10/1 priority date for domestic students, 10/1 priority date for international students. Applications are processed on a rolling basis. Application fee: $50. Electronic applications accepted. *Expenses:* Tuition, state resident: part-time $1,925 per semester. Tuition, nonresident: part-time $7,700 per semester. Required fees: $434 per semester. Full-time tuition and fees vary according to program. *Financial support:* In 2003–04, 7 fellowships with tuition reimbursements, 20 research assistantships with tuition reimbursements, 40 teaching assistantships with tuition reimbursements were awarded. Career-related internships or fieldwork, Federal Work-Study, institutionally sponsored loans, tuition waivers (partial), and supplements also available. Financial award application deadline: 2/1. *Faculty research:* Dynamical systems, discrete mathematics, probability and statistics, mathematical physics. Total annual research expenditures: $1.1 million. *Unit head:* Dr. William Thomas Trotter, Chair, 404-894-2700. *Application contact:* Dr. Evans Harrell, Graduate Coordinator, 404-894-9203, Fax: 404-894-4409, E-mail: grad.coordinator@math.gatech.edu.

Hampton University, Graduate College, Program in Applied Mathematics, Hampton, VA 23668. Offers MS. *Degree requirements:* For master's, thesis optional. *Entrance requirements:* For master's, GRE General Test.

Harvard University, Graduate School of Arts and Sciences, Division of Engineering and Applied Sciences, Cambridge, MA 02138. Offers applied mathematics (ME, SM, PhD); applied physics (ME, SM, PhD); computer science (ME, SM, PhD); computing technology (PhD); engineering science (ME); engineering sciences (SM, PhD). Part-time programs available. *Faculty:* 65 full-time (4 women), 10 part-time/adjunct (1 woman). *Students:* 230 full-time (55 women), 9 part-time; includes 27 minority (4 African Americans, 3 American Indian/Alaska Native, 16 Asian Americans or Pacific Islanders, 4 Hispanic Americans), 87 international. 1,112 applicants, 9% accepted. In 2003, 63 master's, 18 doctorates awarded, leading to university research/teaching 50%. Terminal master's awarded for partial completion of doctoral program. *Median time to degree:* Master's–1 year full-time, 1.5 years part-time; doctorate–6 years full-time. Of those who began their doctoral program in fall 1995, 94% received their degree in 8 years or less. *Degree requirements:* For master's, registration; for doctorate, thesis/dissertation, comprehensive exam, registration. *Entrance requirements:* For master's and doctorate, GRE General Test, GRE Subject Test (recommended), 3 letters of recommendation. Additional exam requirements/recommendations for international students: Required—TOEFL (minimum score 550 paper-based; 213 computer-based). *Application deadline:* For fall admission, 12/15 for domestic students; for winter admission, 1/2 for domestic students. Application fee: $85. Electronic applications accepted. *Expenses:* Tuition: Full-time $26,066. Full-time tuition and fees vary according to program and student level. *Financial support:* In 2003–04, 191 students received support, including 52 fellowships with full tuition reimbursements available (averaging $18,450 per year), 137 research assistantships (averaging $29,716 per year), 106 teaching assistantships (averaging $4,938 per year); Federal Work-Study and institutionally sponsored loans also available. *Faculty research:* Applied mathematics, applied physics, computer science & electrical engineering, environmental engineering, mechanical and biomedical engineering. *Unit head:* Ventatesh Narayanamurti, Dean, 617-495-5829, Fax: 617-495-5264, E-mail: venky@deas.harvard.edu. *Application contact:* Office of Admissions and Financial Aid, 617-495-5315, E-mail: admissions@deas.harvard.edu.

Hofstra University, College of Liberal Arts and Sciences, Division of Natural Sciences, Mathematics, Engineering, and Computer Science, Department of Mathematics, Hempstead, NY 11549. Offers applied mathematics (MS); mathematics (MA). Part-time and evening/weekend programs available. *Faculty:* 4 full-time (1 woman). *Students:* 5 full-time (4 women), 10 part-time (3 women); includes 1 minority (Asian American or Pacific Islander), 1 international. Average age 28. 15 applicants, 60% accepted, 8 enrolled. In 2003, 2 degrees awarded. *Entrance requirements:* For master's, bachelor's degree in related field. Additional exam requirements/recommendations for international students: Required—TOEFL (minimum score 550 paper-based; 213 computer-based). *Application deadline:* Applications are processed on a rolling basis. Application fee: $60. Electronic applications accepted. *Expenses:* Tuition: Full-time $10,800; part-time $600 per credit. Required fees: $910; $155 per semester. Tuition and fees vary according to course load and program. *Financial support:* In 2003–04, 8 students received support; research assistantships with partial tuition reimbursements available, tuition waivers (partial) available. Financial award applicants required to submit FAFSA. *Faculty research:* Dynamical systems, algebraic topology, set theory, number theory, mathematical biology. Total annual research expenditures: $200,000. *Unit head:* Dr. Maryisa T. Weiss, Chairperson, 516-463-5580, Fax: 516-463-6596, E-mail: matmtw@hofstra.edu. *Application contact:* Dr. Tina Montgomery-Sneed, Dean of Graduate Admissions, 516-463-4876, Fax: 516-463-4664, E-mail: gradstudent@hofstra.edu.

Howard University, Graduate School of Arts and Sciences, Department of Mathematics, Washington, DC 20059-0002. Offers applied mathematics (MS, PhD); mathematics (MS, PhD). Part-time programs available. *Faculty:* 29. *Students:* 19 full-time (8 women), 8 part-time (1 woman); includes 18 minority (all African Americans), 8 international. Average age 29. In 2003, 2 master's, 1 doctorate awarded. Terminal master's awarded for partial completion of doctoral program. *Degree requirements:* For master's, thesis or alternative, qualifying exam, comprehensive exam; for doctorate, 2 foreign languages, thesis/dissertation, qualifying exams, comprehensive exam. *Entrance requirements:* For master's, GRE General Test, minimum GPA of 3.0; for doctorate, GRE General Test. Additional exam requirements/recommendations for international students: Required—TOEFL. *Application deadline:* For fall admission, 2/15 for domestic students; for spring admission, 11/1 for domestic students. Application fee: $45. *Financial support:* In 2003–04, fellowships with full tuition reimbursements (averaging $16,000 per year), 2 research assistantships with full tuition reimbursements (averaging $15,000 per year), 5 teaching assistantships with full tuition reimbursements (averaging $13,000 per year) were awarded. Institutionally sponsored loans and scholarships/grants also available. Financial award application deadline: 4/1. Total annual research expenditures: $95,000. *Unit head:* Dr. Louis W. Shapiro, Interim Chairman, 202-806-6830. *Application contact:* Dr. Neil Hindman, Information Contact, 202-806-5927, Fax: 202-806-6831, E-mail: nhindman@howard.edu.

Hunter College of the City University of New York, Graduate School, School of Arts and Sciences, Department of Mathematics and Statistics, New York, NY 10021-5085. Offers applied mathematics (MA); mathematics for secondary education (MA); pure mathematics (MA). Part-time and evening/weekend programs available. *Faculty:* 7 full-time (2 women). *Students:* 4 full-time (all women), 39 part-time (22 women); includes 9 minority (2 African Americans, 6 Asian Americans or Pacific Islanders, 1 Hispanic American). Average age 34. 12 applicants, 75% accepted. In 2003, 14 degrees awarded. *Degree requirements:* For master's, one foreign language, thesis (for some programs), comprehensive exam. *Entrance requirements:* For master's, GRE General Test, 24 credits in mathematics, minimum B average. Additional exam requirements/recommendations for international students: Required—TOEFL. *Application deadline:* For fall admission, 4/1 for domestic students, 2/1 for international students; for spring admission, 11/1 for domestic students, 9/1 for international students. Application fee: $50. *Expenses:* Tuition, state resident: part-time $230 per credit. Tuition, nonresident: part-time $425 per credit. *Financial support:* Institutionally sponsored loans and tuition waivers (partial) available. Support available to part-time students. *Faculty research:* Data analysis, dynamical systems, computer graphics, topology, statistical decision theory. *Unit head:* Ada Peluso, Chairperson, 212-772-5300, Fax: 212-772-4858, E-mail: peluso@math.hunter.cuny.edu. *Application contact:* William Zlata, Director for Graduate Admissions, 212-772-4482, Fax: 212-650-3336, E-mail: admissions@hunter.cuny.edu.

Illinois Institute of Technology, Graduate College, College of Science and Letters, Department of Applied Mathematics, Chicago, IL 60616-3793. Offers applied mathematics (MS, PhD); financial mathematics (MS). *Faculty:* 14 full-time (1 woman), 6 part-time/adjunct (1 woman). *Students:* 8 full-time (2 women), 3 part-time (1 woman); includes 4 minority (1 African American, 1 Asian American or Pacific Islander, 2 Hispanic Americans), 4 international. Average age 32. 43 applicants, 33% accepted, 2 enrolled. In 2003, 1 degree awarded. Terminal master's awarded for partial completion of doctoral program. *Degree requirements:* For master's, comprehensive exam; for doctorate, thesis/dissertation, comprehensive exam. *Entrance requirements:* For master's, GRE General Test (combined score of 1100), minimum undergraduate GPA of 3.0; for doctorate, GRE General Test (combined score of 1150), minimum undergraduate GPA of 3.5. Additional exam requirements/recommendations for international students: Required—TOEFL (minimum score 550 paper-based; 213 computer-based). *Application deadline:* For fall admission, 5/1 for domestic students, 5/1 for international students; for spring admission, 10/15 for domestic students, 10/15 for international students. Application fee: $40. *Expenses:* Tuition: Part-time $628 per credit. Tuition and fees vary according to course load and program. *Financial support:* In 2003–04, 10 students received support, including 1 fellowship with full tuition reimbursement available (averaging $16,000 per year), 2 research assistantships with full tuition reimbursements available (averaging $13,000 per year), 7 teaching assistantships with full tuition reimbursements available (averaging $13,000 per year); tuition waivers (partial) and unspecified assistantships also available. Financial award application deadline: 3/1. Total annual research expenditures: $120,488. *Unit head:* Dr. Edwin F. Cherwin, Chairman, 312-567-8981, Fax: 312-567-3135. *Application contact:* Kelly A. Cherwin, Director of Graduate Outreach, 312-567-7974, Fax: 312-567-3494, E-mail: inquiry.grad@iit.edu.

Indiana University Bloomington, Graduate School, College of Arts and Sciences, Department of Mathematics, Bloomington, IN 47405. Offers applied mathematics–numerical analysis (MA, PhD); mathematics education (MAT); probability-statistics (MA, PhD). PhD offered through the University Graduate School. *Faculty:* 36 full-time (1 woman). *Students:* 102 full-time (33 women), 31 part-time (7 women); includes 5 minority (all Asian Americans or Pacific Islanders), 76 international. Average age 27. In 2003, 14 master's, 13 doctorates awarded. Terminal master's awarded for partial completion of doctoral program. *Degree requirements:* For doctorate, one foreign language, thesis/dissertation. *Entrance requirements:* For master's and doctorate, GRE General Test, GRE Subject Test. Additional exam requirements/recommendations for international students: Required—TOEFL. *Application deadline:* For fall admission, 1/15 priority date for domestic students, 12/15 priority date for international students; for spring admission, 9/1 priority date for domestic students, 9/1 priority date for international students. Applications are processed on a rolling basis. Application fee: $45 ($55 for international students). Electronic applications accepted. *Expenses:* Tuition, state resident: full-time $4,908; part-time $205 per credit. Tuition, nonresident: full-time $14,298; part-time $596 per credit. Required fees: $661. Tuition and fees vary according to campus/location and program. *Financial support:* In 2003–04, 8 fellowships with full tuition reimbursements (averaging $15,000 per year), 101 teaching assistantships with full tuition reimbursements (averaging $12,200 per year) were awarded. Research assistantships, Federal Work-Study also available. Support available to part-time students. Financial award application deadline: 2/1. *Faculty research:* Topology, geometry, algebra. *Unit head:* Daniel Maki, Chair, 812-855-2200, Fax: 812-855-0046, E-mail:

maki@indiana.edu. *Application contact:* Misty Cummings, Graduate Secretary, 812-855-2645, Fax: 812-855-0046, E-mail: gradmath@indiana.edu.

Indiana University of Pennsylvania, Graduate School and Research, College of Natural Sciences and Mathematics, Department of Mathematics, Program in Applied Mathematics, Indiana, PA 15705-1087. Offers MS. *Faculty:* 15 full-time (3 women). *Students:* 9 full-time (1 woman), 4 part-time (2 women), 2 international. Average age 25. 17 applicants, 88% accepted. In 2003, 3 degrees awarded. *Degree requirements:* For master's, thesis optional. *Entrance requirements:* For master's, 2 letters of recommendation. Additional exam requirements/recommendations for international students: Required—TOEFL. *Application deadline:* For fall admission, 7/1 for domestic students; for spring admission, 11/1 for domestic students. Applications are processed on a rolling basis. Application fee: $30. *Expenses:* Tuition, state resident: full-time $5,518; part-time $307 per credit. Tuition, nonresident: full-time $8,830; part-time $491 per credit. Required fees: $31 per credit. $111 per semester. Tuition and fees vary according to degree level. *Financial support:* In 2003–04, 8 research assistantships with full and partial tuition reimbursements (averaging $5,660 per year) were awarded; Federal Work-Study also available. Support available to part-time students. Financial award application deadline: 3/15; financial award applicants required to submit FAFSA. *Unit head:* Dr. Frederick Morgan, Graduate Coordinator, 724-357-4765, E-mail: fwmorgan@iup.edu.

Indiana University–Purdue University Fort Wayne, School of Arts and Sciences, Department of Mathematical Sciences, Fort Wayne, IN 46805-1499. Offers applied mathematics (MS); mathematics (MS); operations research (MS). Part-time and evening/weekend programs available. *Faculty:* 6 full-time (2 women). *Students:* 2 full-time (0 women), 11 part-time (6 women); includes 1 minority (Asian American or Pacific Islander) Average age 33. 10 applicants, 90% accepted, 2 enrolled. In 2003, 6 degrees awarded. *Entrance requirements:* For master's, minimum GPA of 3.0, major or minor in mathematics. *Application deadline:* For fall admission, 7/1 for domestic students; for spring admission, 12/1 for domestic students. Applications are processed on a rolling basis. Application fee: $30. *Expenses:* Tuition, state resident: full-time $3,443; part-time $191 per credit hour. Tuition, nonresident: full-time $7,760; part-time $431 per credit hour. Required fees: $344; $19 per credit hour. *Financial support:* In 2003–04, 8 teaching assistantships with partial tuition reimbursements (averaging $7,350 per year) were awarded; Federal Work-Study, scholarships/grants, and unspecified assistantships also available. Support available to part-time students. Financial award application deadline: 3/1; financial award applicants required to submit FAFSA. *Faculty research:* Graph theory, biostatistics, statistical design, mathematics education, partial differential equations. *Unit head:* Dr. David A. Legg, Chair, 260-481-6821, Fax: 260-481-6880, E-mail: legg@ipfw.edu. *Application contact:* Dr. W. Douglas Weakley, Director of Graduate Studies, 260-481-6821, Fax: 260-481-6880, E-mail: weakley@ipfw.edu.

Indiana University–Purdue University Indianapolis, School of Science, Department of Mathematical Sciences, Indianapolis, IN 46202-3216. Offers applied mathematics (MS, PhD); applied statistics (MS); mathematics (MS, PhD). Part-time programs available. *Faculty:* 10 full-time (0 women), 1 part-time/adjunct (0 women). *Students:* 20 full-time (10 women), 40 part-time (19 women); includes 4 minority (all Asian Americans or Pacific Islanders), 20 international. Average age 32. In 2003, 13 degrees awarded. Terminal master's awarded for partial completion of doctoral program. *Degree requirements:* For master's, thesis optional; for doctorate, one foreign language, thesis/dissertation. *Entrance requirements:* For doctorate, GRE. Additional exam requirements/recommendations for international students: Required—TOEFL. *Application deadline:* For fall admission, 2/1 for domestic students. Application fee: $45 ($55 for international students). *Expenses:* Tuition, state resident: full-time $4,658; part-time $194 per credit. Tuition, nonresident: full-time $13,444; part-time $560 per credit. Required fees: $571. Tuition and fees vary according to campus/location and program. *Financial support:* In 2003–04, 14 students received support, including 2 research assistantships with tuition reimbursements available (averaging $11,000 per year), 10 teaching assistantships with tuition reimbursements available (averaging $11,000 per year); fellowships with tuition reimbursements available, career-related internships or fieldwork, Federal Work-Study, and tuition waivers (full and partial) also available. Financial award application deadline: 3/1. *Faculty research:* Mathematical physics, analysis, operator theory, functional analysis, integrated systems. *Unit head:* Benzion Boukai, Chair, 317-274-6918, Fax: 317-274-3460, E-mail: bboukai@math.iupui.edu. *Application contact:* Joan Morand, Student Services Specialist, 317-274-4127, Fax: 317-274-3460.

Indiana University South Bend, College of Liberal Arts and Sciences, Program in Applied Mathematics and Computer Science, South Bend, IN 46634-7111. Offers MS. *Students:* 5 full-time (1 woman), 11 part-time (5 women), 8 international. Average age 29. *Expenses:* Tuition, state resident: part-time $159 per credit hour. Tuition, nonresident: full-time $3,811; part-time $387 per credit hour. International tuition: $9,287 full-time. Tuition and fees vary according to campus/location and program. *Unit head:* Dr. James Wolfer, Graduate Director, 574-237-6521, Fax: 574-237-4335, E-mail: amcs@iusb.edu.

Inter American University of Puerto Rico, San Germán Campus, Graduate Studies Center, Graduate Program in Applied Mathematics, San Germán, PR 00683-5008. Offers MA. *Faculty:* 2 full-time (0 women). *Degree requirements:* For master's, comprehensive exam. *Entrance requirements:* For master's, EXADEP or GRE General Test, minimum GPA of 3.0. *Application deadline:* For fall admission, 4/30 for domestic students; for spring admission, 11/15 for domestic students. Application fee: $31. *Expenses:* Tuition: Part-time $170 per credit. *Application contact:* Dr. Alvaro Lecompte, Graduate Coordinator, 787-264-1912 Ext. 7358, Fax: 787-892-7510, E-mail: alecompte@sg.inter.edu.

Iowa State University of Science and Technology, Graduate College, College of Liberal Arts and Sciences, Department of Mathematics, Ames, IA 50011. Offers applied mathematics (MS, PhD); mathematics (MS, PhD); school mathematics (MSM). *Faculty:* 45 full-time. *Students:* 48 full-time (13 women), 14 part-time (4 women); includes 1 minority (Asian American or Pacific Islander), 29 international. 72 applicants, 44% accepted, 14 enrolled. In 2003, 17 master's, 2 doctorates awarded. *Median time to degree:* Master's–3 years full-time; doctorate–5.3 years full-time. *Degree requirements:* For master's, thesis or alternative; for doctorate, thesis/dissertation. *Entrance requirements:* For master's and doctorate, GRE General Test. Additional exam requirements/recommendations for international students: Required—TOEFL (paper score 550; computer score 213) or IELTS (score 6.5). *Application deadline:* For fall admission, 2/1 priority date for domestic students, 2/1 priority date for international students. Application fee: $30 ($70 for international students). Electronic applications accepted. Tuition, nonresident: part-time $560 per credit. Required fees: $38 per unit. *Financial support:* In 2003–04, 6 research assistantships with full and partial tuition reimbursements (averaging $15,996 per year), 48 teaching assistantships with full and partial tuition reimbursements (averaging $18,756 per year) were awarded. Fellowships, scholarships/grants, health care benefits, and unspecified assistantships also available. *Unit head:* Dr. Justin R. Peters, Chair, 515-294-1752, Fax: 515-294-5454, E-mail: gradmath@iastate.edu. *Application contact:* Dr. Jonathan Smith, Director of Graduate Education, 515-294-8172, E-mail: gradmath@iastate.edu.

The Johns Hopkins University, G. W. C. Whiting School of Engineering, Department of Mathematical Sciences, Baltimore, MD 21218-2699. Offers discrete mathematics (MA, MSE, PhD); operations research/optimization/decision science (MA, MSE, PhD); statistics/probability/stochastic processes (MA, MSE, PhD). Terminal master's awarded for partial completion of doctoral program. *Degree requirements:* For master's, thesis (for some programs); for doctorate, thesis/dissertation, oral exam. *Entrance requirements:* For master's and doctorate, GRE General Test, GRE Subject Test. Additional exam requirements/recommendations for international students: Required—TOEFL. Electronic applications accepted. *Expenses:* Tuition: Full-time $28,730; part-time $1,490 per course. Part-time tuition and fees vary according to course load, campus/location and program. *Faculty research:* Discrete mathematics, probability, statistics, optimization and operations research, matrix and numerical analysis.

The Johns Hopkins University, G. W. C. Whiting School of Engineering, Part-Time Programs in Engineering and Applied Science, Department of Applied Mathematics and Statistics, Baltimore, MD 21218-2699. Offers applied and computational mathematics (MS). Part-time and evening/weekend programs available. *Faculty:* 13 full-time (0 women). *Students:* 30 full-time (13 women), 2 part-time (1 woman); includes 1 minority (African American), 23 international. Average age 29. 165 applicants, 45% accepted, 14 enrolled. In 2003, 10 degrees awarded. *Degree requirements:* For master's, comprehensive exam (for some programs). *Entrance requirements:* For master's, GRE General Test. Additional exam requirements/recommendations for international students: Required—TOEFL. *Application deadline:* For fall admission, 1/15 for domestic students. Applications are processed on a rolling basis. Electronic applications accepted. *Expenses:* Tuition: Full-time $28,730; part-time $1,490 per course. Part-time tuition and fees vary according to course load, campus/location and program. *Financial support:* In 2003–04, 23 students received support, including 3 fellowships (averaging $22,500 per year), 6 research assistantships (averaging $15,000 per year), 14 teaching assistantships (averaging $15,000 per year); tuition waivers (partial) also available. Financial award application deadline: 1/15; financial award applicants required to submit FAFSA. Total annual research expenditures: $606,210. *Unit head:* Dr. Daniel Q. Naiman, Chair, 410-516-7203, Fax: 410-516-7459, E-mail: daniel.naiman@jhu.edu. *Application contact:* Kristin Bechtel, Graduate Coordinator, 410-516-7198, Fax: 410-579-8049, E-mail: bechtel@ams.jhu.

Kent State University, College of Arts and Sciences, Department of Mathematical Sciences, Kent, OH 44242-0001. Offers applied mathematics (MA, PhD); pure mathematics (MA, MS, PhD). Part-time programs available. *Degree requirements:* For master's, thesis optional; for doctorate, one foreign language, thesis/dissertation. Electronic applications accepted. *Expenses:* Tuition, state resident: part-time $334 per hour. Tuition, nonresident: part-time $627 per hour. *Faculty research:* Approximation theory, measure theory, ring theory, functional analysis, complex analysis.

See in-depth description on page 545.

Lehigh University, College of Arts and Sciences, Department of Mathematics and Department of Mechanical Engineering and Mechanics, Division of Applied Mathematics, Bethlehem, PA 18015-3094. Offers MS, PhD. *Degree requirements:* For master's, comprehensive exam; for doctorate, one foreign language, thesis/dissertation, qualifying exams, comprehensive exam. *Entrance requirements:* For master's and doctorate, minimum GPA of 3.0. Additional exam requirements/recommendations for international students: Required—TOEFL. *Application deadline:* For fall admission, 7/15 for domestic students; for spring admission, 12/1 for domestic students. Applications are processed on a rolling basis. Application fee: $40. *Expenses:* Tuition: Full-time $16,920; part-time $940 per credit hour. Required fees: $200. Tuition and fees vary according to degree level and program. *Financial support:* Fellowships, research assistantships, teaching assistantships, tuition waivers (full) available. Financial award application deadline: 1/15. *Faculty research:* Probability, statistics, differential equations, computational methods, mechanics. *Application contact:* Dr. Garth Isaak, Graduate Coordinator, 610-758-3734, Fax: 610-758-3767, E-mail: mathgrad@lehigh.edu.

Lehigh University, P.C. Rossin College of Engineering and Applied Science, Department of Mechanical Engineering and Mechanics, Bethlehem, PA 18015-3094. Offers applied mathematics (MS, PhD); mechanical engineering (M Eng, MS, PhD); mechanics (M Eng, MS, PhD). Part-time programs available. *Faculty:* 29 full-time (0 women). *Students:* 60 full-time (5 women), 5 part-time; includes 2 minority (1 African American, 1 Asian American or Pacific Islander), 34 international. 611 applicants, 31% accepted, 20 enrolled. In 2003, 19 master's, 9 doctorates awarded. Terminal master's awarded for partial completion of doctoral program. *Degree requirements:* For master's and doctorate, thesis/dissertation. *Entrance requirements:* Additional exam requirements/recommendations for international students: Required—TOEFL (minimum score 550 paper-based; 213 computer-based). *Application deadline:* For fall admission, 7/15 for domestic students; for spring admission, 12/1 for domestic students. Applications are processed on a rolling basis. Application fee: $50. *Expenses:* Tuition: Full-time $16,920; part-time $940 per credit hour. Required fees: $200. Tuition and fees vary according to degree level and program. *Financial support:* In 2003–04, 10 fellowships with full and partial tuition reimbursements (averaging $6,750 per year), 28 research assistantships with full and partial tuition reimbursements (averaging $13,500 per year), 7 teaching assistantships with full and partial tuition reimbursements (averaging $13,275 per year) were awarded. Financial award application deadline: 1/15. *Faculty research:* Thermofluids, dynamic systems, CAD/CAM. Total annual research expenditures: $4.6 million. *Unit head:* Dr. Herman F. Nied, Chairman, 610-758-4102, Fax: 610-758-6224, E-mail: hfn2@lehigh.edu. *Application contact:* Donna Reiss, Graduate Coordinator, 610-758-4139, Fax: 610-758-6224, E-mail: dmr1@lehigh.edu.

Long Island University, C.W. Post Campus, College of Liberal Arts and Sciences, Department of Mathematics, Brookville, NY 11548-1300. Offers applied mathematics (MS); mathematics education (MS); mathematics for secondary school teachers (MS). Part-time and evening/weekend programs available. *Faculty:* 14 full-time (3 women). *Students:* 26 full-time (14 women), 35 part-time (26 women); includes 5 minority (1 African American, 2 Asian Americans or Pacific Islanders, 2 Hispanic Americans). Average age 25. 32 applicants, 81% accepted, 13 enrolled. In 2003, 21 degrees awarded. *Degree requirements:* For master's, thesis or alternative, oral presentation. *Entrance requirements:* Additional exam requirements/recommendations for international students: Required—TOEFL. *Application deadline:* Applications are processed on a rolling basis. Application fee: $30. Electronic applications accepted. *Expenses:* Tuition: Part-time $658 per credit. Tuition and fees vary according to course load, degree level and program. *Financial support:* In 2003–04, 10 students received support. Career-related internships or fieldwork, Federal Work-Study, institutionally sponsored loans, tuition waivers (full and partial), and unspecified assistantships available. Support available to part-time students. Financial award application deadline: 5/15; financial award applicants required to submit CSS PROFILE or FAFSA. *Faculty research:* Differential geometry, topological groups, general topology, number theory, analysis and statistics, numerical analysis. *Unit head:* Dr. Neo Cleopa, Chair, 516-299-2448, Fax: 516-299-4049, E-mail: ncleopa@liu.edu. *Application contact:* Dr. Shahla Ahdout, Graduate Adviser, 516-299-2043, Fax: 516-299-4049, E-mail: sahdout@liu.edu.

Michigan State University, Graduate School, College of Natural Science, Department of Mathematics, East Lansing, MI 48824. Offers applied mathematics (MS, PhD); industrial mathematics (MS); mathematics (MAT, MS, PhD); mathematics education (PhD). *Faculty:* 58 full-time (11 women). *Students:* 124 full-time (41 women), 10 part-time (4 women); includes 7 minority (2 African Americans, 3 Asian Americans or Pacific Islanders, 2 Hispanic Americans), 86 international. Average age 29. 185 applicants, 17% accepted. In 2003, 24 master's, 8 doctorates awarded. *Degree requirements:* For master's, certifying exam, thesis optional; for doctorate, one foreign language, thesis/dissertation, qualifying exam, seminar presentations, comprehensive exam. *Entrance requirements:* For master's, GRE General Test, bachelor's degree in mathematics, physics, or engineering, mathematics course work beyond calculus, 3 letters of recommendation; for doctorate, GRE General Test, minimum GPA of 3.0, MS in mathematics or equivalent, 3 letters of recommendation. Additional exam requirements/recommendations for international students: Required—TOEFL (minimum score 550 paper-based; 213 computer-based), Michigan State University ELT (85), Michigan ELAB (83). *Application deadline:* For fall admission, 2/1 for domestic students. Application fee: $50. Electronic applications accepted. *Expenses:* Tuition, state resident: part-time $291 per hour. Tuition, nonresident: part-time $589 per hour. *Financial support:* In 2003–04, 17 fellowships with tuition reimbursements (averaging $3,321 per year), 31 research assistantships with tuition reimbursements (averaging $13,512 per year), 87 teaching assistantships with tuition reimbursements (averaging $12,854 per year) were awarded. Financial award applicants required to submit FAFSA. *Faculty research:* Applied and industrial mathematics, analysis, geometry and topology, logic, combinatories and graph theory. Total annual research expenditures: $2.3 million. *Unit head:* Dr. Peter W. Bates, Chairperson, 517-353-9680, Fax: 517-432-1562, E-mail: bates@math.msu.edu. *Application contact:* Zhengfang Zhou, Graduate Director, 517-353-4650, Fax: 517-432-1562, E-mail: grad@mth.msu.edu.

Applied Mathematics

Montclair State University, The Graduate School, College of Science and Mathematics, Department of Computer Science, Upper Montclair, NJ 07043-1624. Offers applied mathematics (MS); applied statistics (MS); informatics (MS); object oriented computing (Certificate). Part-time and evening/weekend programs available. *Faculty:* 14 full-time (1 woman), 10 part-time/adjunct. *Students:* 18 full-time (4 women), 35 part-time (6 women); includes 8 minority (2 African Americans, 5 Asian Americans or Pacific Islanders, 1 Hispanic American), 18 international. 60 applicants, 33% accepted, 9 enrolled. In 2003, 51 degrees awarded. *Degree requirements:* For master's, comprehensive exam. *Entrance requirements:* For master's, GRE General Test, minimum GPA of 2.67, 15 undergraduate math credits, bachelors degree in computer science, math, science or engineering, 2 letters of recommendation. Additional exam requirements/recommendations for international students: Required—TOEFL (minimum score 550 paper-based; 213 computer-based). *Application deadline:* Applications are processed on a rolling basis. Application fee: $60. Electronic applications accepted. *Expenses:* Tuition, state resident: full-time $8,771; part-time $323 per credit. Tuition, nonresident: full-time $10,365; part-time $470 per credit. Required fees: $42 per credit. Tuition and fees vary according to degree level and program. *Financial support:* In 2003–04, 4 research assistantships with full tuition reimbursements (averaging $5,000 per year) were awarded; Federal Work-Study, scholarships/grants, and unspecified assistantships also available. Support available to part-time students. Financial award application deadline: 3/1; financial award applicants required to submit FAFSA. *Unit head:* Dr. Dorothy Deremer, Chairperson, 973-655-4166. *Application contact:* Dr. James Benham, Adviser, 973-655-3746, E-mail: benham@pegasus.montclair.edu.

Montclair State University, The Graduate School, College of Science and Mathematics, Department of Mathematics, Upper Montclair, NJ 07043-1624. Offers mathematics (MS), including computer science, mathematics education, pure and applied mathematics, statistics. Part-time and evening/weekend programs available. *Faculty:* 31 full-time (12 women), 20 part-time/adjunct. *Students:* 12 full-time (7 women), 46 part-time (28 women); includes 6 minority (4 African Americans, 2 Asian Americans or Pacific Islanders), 3 international. 40 applicants, 73% accepted, 19 enrolled. In 2003, 50 degrees awarded. *Degree requirements:* For master's, comprehensive exam. *Entrance requirements:* For master's, GRE General Test, minimum GPA of 2.67, 2 letters of recommendation. Additional exam requirements/recommendations for international students: Required—TOEFL (minimum score 550 paper-based; 213 computer-based). *Application deadline:* Applications are processed on a rolling basis. Application fee: $60. *Expenses:* Tuition, state resident: full-time $8,771; part-time $323 per credit. Tuition, nonresident: full-time $10,365; part-time $470 per credit. Required fees: $42 per credit. Tuition and fees vary according to degree level and program. *Financial support:* In 2003–04, 9 research assistantships with full tuition reimbursements (averaging $5,000 per year) were awarded; Federal Work-Study, scholarships/grants, and unspecified assistantships also available. Support available to part-time students. Financial award application deadline: 3/1; financial award applicants required to submit FAFSA. *Unit head:* Dr. Helen Roberts, Chairperson, 973-655-5132. *Application contact:* Dr. Ted Williamson, Advisor, 973-655-5146, E-mail: williamsont@mail.montclair.edu.

Montclair State University, The Graduate School, College of Science and Mathematics, Department of Mathematics, Programs in Mathematics, Concentration in Pure and Applied Mathematics, Upper Montclair, NJ 07043-1624. Offers MS. Part-time and evening/weekend programs available. *Faculty:* 31 full-time (12 women), 20 part-time/adjunct. *Students:* 5 full-time (3 women), 6 part-time (2 women); includes 1 minority (Asian American or Pacific Islander), 1 international. 9 applicants, 78% accepted, 5 enrolled. In 2003, 11 degrees awarded. *Degree requirements:* For master's, comprehensive exam. *Entrance requirements:* For master's, GRE General Test, minimum GPA of 2.67, 2 letters of recommendation. Additional exam requirements/recommendations for international students: Required—TOEFL (minimum score 550 paper-based; 213 computer-based). *Application deadline:* Applications are processed on a rolling basis. Application fee: $60. Electronic applications accepted. *Expenses:* Tuition, state resident: full-time $8,771; part-time $323 per credit. Tuition, nonresident: full-time $10,365; part-time $470 per credit. Required fees: $42 per credit. Tuition and fees vary according to degree level and program. *Financial support:* In 2003–04, research assistantships with full tuition reimbursements (averaging $5,000 per year); Federal Work-Study, scholarships/grants, and unspecified assistantships also available. Support available to part-time students. Financial award application deadline: 3/1; financial award applicants required to submit FAFSA. *Application contact:* Dr. Ted Williamson, Advisor, 973-655-5146, E-mail: williamsont@mail.montclair.edu.

New Jersey Institute of Technology, Office of Graduate Studies, College of Science and Liberal Arts, Department of Mathematical Sciences, Program in Applied Mathematics, Newark, NJ 07102. Offers MS. Part-time and evening/weekend programs available. *Students:* 6 full-time (2 women), 5 part-time (2 women); includes 7 minority (2 African Americans, 3 Asian Americans or Pacific Islanders, 2 Hispanic Americans), 1 international. Average age 26. 31 applicants, 65% accepted, 6 enrolled. In 2003, 1 degree awarded. *Entrance requirements:* For master's, GRE General Test. *Application deadline:* For fall admission, 6/5 for domestic students; for spring admission, 10/15 for domestic students. Applications are processed on a rolling basis. Application fee: $50. Electronic applications accepted. *Expenses:* Tuition, state resident: full-time $9,620; part-time $520 per credit. Tuition, nonresident: full-time $13,542; part-time $715 per credit. Tuition and fees vary according to course load. *Financial support:* Fellowships with full and partial tuition reimbursements, research assistantships with full and partial tuition reimbursements, teaching assistantships with full and partial tuition reimbursements, career-related internships or fieldwork, Federal Work-Study, institutionally sponsored loans, and unspecified assistantships available. Financial award application deadline: 3/15. *Application contact:* Kathryn Kelly, Director of Admissions, 973-596-3300, Fax: 973-596-3461, E-mail: admissions@njit.edu.

New Mexico Institute of Mining and Technology, Graduate Studies, Department of Mathematics, Socorro, NM 87801. Offers applied math (PhD); mathematics (MS); operations research (MS). *Faculty:* 11 full-time (0 women), 2 part-time/adjunct (1 woman). *Students:* 9 full-time (4 women), 3 part-time; includes 2 minority (both Hispanic Americans), 5 international. Average age 26. 18 applicants, 6 enrolled. In 2003, 3 degrees awarded. *Degree requirements:* For master's, thesis optional; for doctorate, thesis/dissertation. *Entrance requirements:* For master's, GRE General Test. Additional exam requirements/recommendations for international students: Required—TOEFL (minimum score 540 paper-based; 207 computer-based). *Application deadline:* For fall admission, 3/1 for domestic students; for spring admission, 6/1 for domestic students. Applications are processed on a rolling basis. Application fee: $16 ($30 for international students). *Expenses:* Tuition, state resident: full-time $2,276; part-time $126 per credit. Tuition, nonresident: full-time $9,170; part-time $509 per credit. Required fees: $924; $27 per credit. $214 per term. Part-time tuition and fees vary according to course load. *Financial support:* In 2003–04, 8 teaching assistantships with full and partial tuition reimbursements (averaging $10,888 per year) were awarded; fellowships, research assistantships, Federal Work-Study and institutionally sponsored loans also available. Financial award application deadline: 3/1; financial award applicants required to submit CSS PROFILE or FAFSA. *Faculty research:* Applied mathematics, differential equations, industrial mathematics, numerical analysis, stochastic processes. *Unit head:* Brian Borchers, Chairman, 505-835-5393, Fax: 505-835-5813, E-mail: borchers@nmt.edu. *Application contact:* Dr. David B. Johnson, Dean of Graduate Studies, 505-835-5513, Fax: 505-835-5476, E-mail: graduate@nmt.edu.

Nicholls State University, Graduate Studies, College of Arts and Sciences, Department of Mathematics, Thibodaux, LA 70310. Offers applied mathematics (MS). Part-time and evening/weekend programs available. *Faculty:* 5 full-time (0 women). *Students:* 15 full-time (7 women), 1 (woman) part-time; includes 2 minority (both Asian Americans or Pacific Islanders) Average age 23. 7 applicants, 100% accepted, 7 enrolled. In 2003, 4 degrees awarded. *Median time to degree:* Master's–2 years full-time. *Degree requirements:* For master's, comprehensive exam. *Entrance requirements:* For master's, GRE General Test. *Application deadline:* For fall admission, 6/17 for domestic students; for spring admission, 11/15 priority date for domestic students. Applications are processed on a rolling basis. Application fee: $20 ($30 for international students). Electronic applications accepted. Tuition, area resident: Part-time $341 per course. *Expenses:* Tuition, state resident: full-time $2,681. Tuition, nonresident: full-time $8,129. International tuition: $8,249 full-time. Tuition and fees vary according to course load. *Financial support:* In 2003–04, 12 students received support, including teaching assistantships with full tuition reimbursements available (averaging $10,000 per year); Federal Work-Study, scholarships/grants, and unspecified assistantships also available. Support available to part-time students. Financial award application deadline: 6/17. *Faculty research:* Operations research, statistics, numerical analysis, algebra. *Unit head:* Dr. Donald M. Bardwell, Head, 985-448-4380, E-mail: math-dmb@nicholls.edu.

North Carolina State University, Graduate School, College of Physical and Mathematical Sciences, Department of Mathematics, Program in Applied Mathematics, Raleigh, NC 27695. Offers MS, PhD. *Faculty:* 66 full-time (8 women), 20 part-time/adjunct (1 woman). *Students:* 38 full-time (17 women), 4 part-time (2 women); includes 8 minority (4 African Americans, 4 Asian Americans or Pacific Islanders), 6 international. Average age 28. 70 applicants, 31% accepted. In 2003, 7 master's, 11 doctorates awarded. *Degree requirements:* For master's, thesis (for some programs). *Entrance requirements:* For master's, GRE, GRE Subject Test. *Application deadline:* For fall admission, 6/25 for domestic students, 3/1 for international students; for spring admission, 11/25 for domestic students, 7/15 for international students. *Expenses:* Tuition, state resident: part-time $396 per hour. Tuition, nonresident: part-time $1,895 per hour. *Financial support:* In 2003–04, 2 fellowships with tuition reimbursements (averaging $7,487 per year), 15 research assistantships with tuition reimbursements (averaging $7,700 per year), 19 teaching assistantships with tuition reimbursements (averaging $6,725 per year) were awarded. *Unit head:* Dr. Stephen L. Campbell, Director of Graduate Programs, 919-515-3300, Fax: 919-515-3798, E-mail: s_campbell@ncsu.edu.

North Dakota State University, The Graduate School, College of Science and Mathematics, Department of Mathematics, Fargo, ND 58105. Offers applied mathematics (MS, PhD); mathematics (MS, PhD). *Faculty:* 14 full-time (1 woman). *Students:* 21 full-time (7 women), 3 part-time (1 woman), 13 international. Average age 30. 18 applicants, 56% accepted. In 2003, 3 master's awarded. *Median time to degree:* Master's–3.5 years full-time; doctorate–7 years full-time. *Degree requirements:* For master's, thesis, comprehensive exam, registration; for doctorate, one foreign language, thesis/dissertation, comprehensive exam, registration. *Entrance requirements:* For master's and doctorate, GRE General Test. Additional exam requirements/recommendations for international students: Required—TOEFL. *Application deadline:* For fall admission, 3/15 for domestic students. Applications are processed on a rolling basis. Application fee: $35 ($50 for international students). Tuition, nonresident: full-time $4,071. Required fees: $493. *Financial support:* In 2003–04, 16 students received support, including 1 fellowship with tuition reimbursement available, 1 research assistantship with tuition reimbursement available, 16 teaching assistantships with tuition reimbursements available; Federal Work-Study, institutionally sponsored loans, and tuition waivers (full) also available. Support available to part-time students. Financial award application deadline: 3/31. *Faculty research:* Differential equations, discrete mathematics, number theory, ergodic theory, algebra. Total annual research expenditures: $37,284. *Unit head:* Dr. Warren Shreve, Chair, 701-231-7707, Fax: 701-231-7598.

Northwestern University, The Graduate School, Interdepartmental Degree Programs, Program in Mathematical Methods in Social Science, Evanston, IL 60208. Offers MS.

Northwestern University, McCormick School of Engineering and Applied Science, Program in Applied Mathematics, Evanston, IL 60208. Offers MS, PhD. Admissions and degrees offered through The Graduate School. Part-time programs available. Terminal master's awarded for partial completion of doctoral program. *Degree requirements:* For master's, thesis or alternative, comprehensive exam, registration; for doctorate, thesis/dissertation, comprehensive exam, registration. *Entrance requirements:* For master's and doctorate, GRE. Additional exam requirements/recommendations for international students: Required—TOEFL. Electronic applications accepted. *Faculty research:* Combustion, interfacial phenomena, nonlinear optics, dynamical systems, scientific computation.

See in-depth description on page 565.

Oakland University, Graduate Study and Lifelong Learning, College of Arts and Sciences, Department of Mathematical Sciences, Program in Industrial Applied Mathematics, Rochester, MI 48309-4401. Offers MS. Part-time and evening/weekend programs available. *Students:* Average age 35. 1 applicant, 100% accepted. *Entrance requirements:* For master's, minimum GPA of 3.0 for unconditional admission. Additional exam requirements/recommendations for international students: Required—TOEFL (minimum score 550 paper-based; 213 computer-based). *Application deadline:* For fall admission, 7/15 priority date for domestic students, 5/1 priority date for international students; for winter admission, 12/1 for domestic students; for spring admission, 3/15 for domestic students. Applications are processed on a rolling basis. Application fee: $30. Electronic applications accepted. *Expenses:* Contact institution. *Financial support:* Federal Work-Study, institutionally sponsored loans, and tuition waivers (full) available. Financial award application deadline: 3/1; financial award applicants required to submit FAFSA. *Unit head:* Dr. Meir Shillor, Coordinator, Graduate Programs, 248-370-3439, Fax: 248-370-4184, E-mail: shillor@oakland.edu.

Oklahoma State University, Graduate College, College of Arts and Sciences, Department of Mathematics, Stillwater, OK 74078. Offers applied mathematics (MS); mathematics (MS, Ed D, PhD). *Faculty:* 36 full-time (6 women), 9 part-time/adjunct (5 women). *Students:* 14 full-time (6 women), 25 part-time (6 women), 13 international. Average age 30. 44 applicants, 68% accepted. In 2003, 8 degrees awarded. *Degree requirements:* For doctorate, one foreign language, thesis/dissertation. *Entrance requirements:* For master's, GRE. Additional exam requirements/recommendations for international students: Required—TOEFL. *Application deadline:* For fall admission, 6/1 for domestic students. Applications are processed on a rolling basis. Application fee: $25 ($50 for international students). Electronic applications accepted. *Expenses:* Tuition, state resident: full-time $3,752; part-time $118 per credit hour. Tuition, nonresident: full-time $10,346; part-time $393 per credit hour. Tuition and fees vary according to course load. *Financial support:* In 2003–04, 1 research assistantship (averaging $18,000 per year), 37 teaching assistantships (averaging $15,906 per year) were awarded. Career-related internships or fieldwork, Federal Work-Study, and tuition waivers (partial) also available. Support available to part-time students. Financial award application deadline: 3/1. *Unit head:* Dr. Alan Adolphson, Head, 405-744-5688, Fax: 405-744-8275.

See in-depth description on page 569.

The Pennsylvania State University University Park Campus, Graduate School, Eberly College of Science, Department of Mathematics, State College, University Park, PA 16802-1503. Offers mathematics (M Ed, MA, D Ed, PhD), including applied mathematics (MA, PhD). *Students:* 94 full-time (22 women), 2 part-time (1 woman); includes 4 minority (1 African American, 3 Asian Americans or Pacific Islanders), 44 international. *Entrance requirements:* For master's and doctorate, GRE General Test. Application fee: $45. *Unit head:* Dr. Nigel D. Higson, Head, 814-865-7527, Fax: 814-865-3735, E-mail: higson@psu.edu. *Application contact:* Information Contact, E-mail: gradstudies@math.psu.edu.

See in-depth description on page 573.

Princeton University, Graduate School, Department of Chemical Engineering, Princeton, NJ 08544-1019. Offers applied and computational mathematics (PhD); chemical engineering (M Eng, MSE, PhD); plasma science and technology (MSE, PhD); polymer sciences and materials (MSE, PhD). *Faculty:* 17 full-time (2 women), 1 part-time/adjunct (0 women). *Students:* 64 full-time (20 women); includes 8 minority (2 African Americans, 1 American Indian/Alaska Native, 5 Asian Americans or Pacific Islanders), 18 international. Average age 23. 205 applicants, 26% accepted, 18 enrolled. In 2003, 4 master's, 15 doctorates awarded. Terminal master's awarded for partial completion of doctoral program. *Median time to degree:* Master's–2 years full-time; doctorate–5.6 years full-time. Of those who began their doctoral program in fall 1995, 99% received their degree in 8 years or less. *Degree requirements:* For master's, thesis; for doctorate, thesis/dissertation, general exam. *Entrance requirements:* For master's and doctorate, GRE General Test. Additional exam requirements/recommendations for international students: Required—TOEFL (minimum score 600 paper-based; 250 computer-based). *Application deadline:* For fall admission, 12/31 for domestic students, 12/1 for international students. Application fee: $80 ($55 for international students). Electronic applications accepted. *Expenses:* Tuition: Full-time $29,910. Required fees: $810. *Financial support:* In 2003–04, 16 students received support, including 29 fellowships with full tuition reimbursements available (averaging $20,636 per year), 21 research assistantships with full tuition reimbursements available (averaging $18,600 per year), 11 teaching assistantships with full tuition reimbursements available (averaging $20,450 per year) *Faculty research:* Applied and computational mathematics; bioengineering; fluid mechanics and transport phenomena; materials synthesis, processing, structure and properties; process engineering and science. Total annual research expenditures: $6.4 million. *Unit head:* Prof. A. Panagiotopoulos, Director of Graduate Studies, 609-258-4591, Fax: 609-258-0211, E-mail: azp@princeton.edu. *Application contact:* Janice Yip, Director of Graduate Admissions, 609-258-3034, Fax: 609-258-6180, E-mail: gsadmit@princeton.edu.

Princeton University, Graduate School, Department of Mathematics, Princeton, NJ 08544-1019. Offers applied and computational mathematics (PhD); mathematical physics (PhD); mathematics (PhD). *Faculty:* 47 full-time (5 women), 9 part-time/adjunct (1 woman). *Students:* 58 full-time (12 women); includes 6 minority (1 African American, 5 Asian Americans or Pacific Islanders), 36 international. 202 applicants, 14% accepted, 14 enrolled. *Median time to degree:* Doctorate–4.64 years full-time. *Degree requirements:* For doctorate, 2 foreign languages, thesis/dissertation. *Entrance requirements:* For doctorate, GRE General Test, GRE Subject Test. Additional exam requirements/recommendations for international students: Required—TOEFL (minimum score 600 paper-based; 250 computer-based). *Application deadline:* For fall admission, 12/31 for domestic students, 12/1 for international students. Application fee: $80 ($55 for international students). Electronic applications accepted. *Expenses:* Tuition: Full-time $29,910. Required fees: $810. *Financial support:* Fellowships with full tuition reimbursements, research assistantships with full tuition reimbursements, teaching assistantships with full tuition reimbursements, Federal Work-Study and institutionally sponsored loans available. Financial award application deadline: 1/2. *Unit head:* Prof. Sergiu Klainerman, Director of Graduate Studies, 609-258-4188, Fax: 609-258-1367, E-mail: seri@princeton.edu. *Application contact:* Janice Yip, Director of Graduate Admissions, 609-258-3034, Fax: 609-258-6180, E-mail: gsadmit@princeton.edu.

Princeton University, Graduate School, Department of Physics, Princeton, NJ 08544-1019. Offers applied and computational mathematics (PhD); mathematical physics (PhD); physics (PhD); physics and chemical physics (PhD). *Faculty:* 42 full-time (2 women), 2 part-time/adjunct (0 women). *Students:* 103 full-time (13 women); includes 11 minority (10 Asian Americans or Pacific Islanders, 1 Hispanic American), 48 international. Average age 22. 425 applicants, 12% accepted, 26 enrolled. In 2003, 14 degrees awarded, leading to continued full-time study 86%. *Median time to degree:* Doctorate–5 years full-time. *Degree requirements:* For doctorate, thesis/dissertation, qualifying exam. *Entrance requirements:* For doctorate, GRE General Test, GRE Subject Test. Additional exam requirements/recommendations for international students: Required—TOEFL (minimum score 600 paper-based; 250 computer-based). *Application deadline:* For fall admission, 12/31 for domestic students, 12/1 for international students. Application fee: $80 ($55 for international students). Electronic applications accepted. *Expenses:* Tuition: Full-time $29,910. Required fees: $810. *Financial support:* In 2003–04, 100 students received support, including 40 fellowships with full tuition reimbursements available (averaging $19,360 per year), 30 research assistantships with full tuition reimbursements available (averaging $18,100 per year), 30 teaching assistantships with full tuition reimbursements available (averaging $19,625 per year); Federal Work-Study and institutionally sponsored loans also available. Financial award application deadline: 1/2. Total annual research expenditures: $10.7 million. *Unit head:* Prof. Chiana Nappi, Director of Graduate Studies, 609-258-4322, Fax: 609-258-1549, E-mail: cnappi@princeton.edu. *Application contact:* Janice Yip, Director of Graduate Admissions, 609-258-3034, Fax: 609-258-6180, E-mail: gsadmit@princeton.edu.

Princeton University, Graduate School, Program in Applied and Computational Mathematics, Princeton, NJ 08544-1019. Offers PhD. *Students:* 19 full-time (5 women), 11 international. 76 applicants, 12% accepted, 5 enrolled. In 2003, 4 degrees awarded, leading to university research/teaching 25%, continued full-time study 50%. *Median time to degree:* Doctorate–4.28 years full-time. *Degree requirements:* For doctorate, thesis/dissertation. *Entrance requirements:* For doctorate, GRE General Test, GRE Subject Test. Additional exam requirements/recommendations for international students: Required—TOEFL (minimum score 600 paper-based; 250 computer-based). *Application deadline:* For fall admission, 12/31 for domestic students, 12/1 for international students. Application fee: $80 ($55 for international students). Electronic applications accepted. *Expenses:* Tuition: Full-time $29,910. Required fees: $810. *Financial support:* In 2003–04, 8 fellowships with full tuition reimbursements (averaging $19,218 per year), 3 research assistantships with full tuition reimbursements (averaging $31,467 per year), 3 teaching assistantships with full tuition reimbursements (averaging $19,000 per year) were awarded. Federal Work-Study and institutionally sponsored loans also available. Financial award application deadline: 1/2. Total annual research expenditures: $1.1 million. *Unit head:* Prof. Paul Seymour, Director of Graduate Studies, 609-258-4685, Fax: 609-258-1735, E-mail: pds@princeton.edu. *Application contact:* Janice Yip, Director of Graduate Admissions, 609-258-3034, Fax: 609-258-6180, E-mail: gsadmit@princeton.edu.

Announcement: The program in applied and computational mathematics at Princeton is an interdisciplinary PhD program offering a select group of highly qualified students the opportunity to obtain a thorough knowledge of branches of mathematics indispensable for science and engineering applications, including numerical analysis and other computational methods. Before being admitted to a third year of study, students must sustain the general examination. The general examination is designed as a sequence of interviews with assigned professors that begins in the first year and covers 3 areas of applied mathematics. The generals culminate in a seminar on a research topic, usually delivered toward the end of the fourth semester. The doctoral dissertation may consist of a mathematical contribution to some field of science or engineering or the development or analysis of mathematical or computational methods useful for, inspired by, or relevant to science or engineering. Satisfactory completion of the requirements leads to the PhD degree in applied and computational mathematics. For more information, visit http://www.pacm.princeton.edu.

Rensselaer Polytechnic Institute, Graduate School, School of Science, Department of Mathematical Sciences, Program in Applied Mathematics, Troy, NY 12180-3590. Offers MS. Part-time programs available. *Faculty:* 24 full-time (3 women). *Students:* 18 full-time (3 women), 3 part-time (1 woman); includes 3 minority (1 African American, 2 Hispanic Americans), 5 international. Average age 22. 27 applicants, 81% accepted, 8 enrolled. In 2003, 5 degrees awarded, leading to university research/teaching 33%, continued full-time study27%, business/industry 40%. *Median time to degree:* Master's–2 years full-time. *Degree requirements:* For master's, registration. *Entrance requirements:* For master's, GRE General Test. Additional exam requirements/recommendations for international students: Required—TOEFL. *Application deadline:* For fall admission, 1/15 for domestic students. Applications are processed on a rolling basis. Application fee: $45. Electronic applications accepted. *Expenses:* Tuition: Full-time $27,700; part-time $1,320 per credit. Required fees: $1,470. *Financial support:* In 2003–04, 6 students received support, including 1 research assistantship, 5 teaching assistantships; fellowships, career-related internships or fieldwork and institutionally sponsored loans also available. Financial award application deadline: 2/1. *Faculty research:* Mathematical modeling, differential equations, applications of mathematics in science and engineering, operations research, analysis. Total annual research expenditures: $3.2 million. *Application contact:* Dawnmarie Robens, Graduate Student Coordinator, 518-276-6414, Fax: 518-276-4824, E-mail: robensd@rpi.edu.

Rice University, Graduate Programs, George R. Brown School of Engineering, Department of Computational and Applied Mathematics, Houston, TX 77251-1892. Offers MA, MCAM, MCSE, PhD. *Faculty:* 9 full-time (1 woman). *Students:* 34 full-time (13 women); includes 13 minority (6 African Americans, 3 Asian Americans or Pacific Islanders, 4 Hispanic Americans), 10 international. Average age 28. 110 applicants, 16% accepted, 6 enrolled. In 2003, 8 master's awarded, leading to continued full-time study 50%, business/industry 50%; 5 doctorates awarded, leading to university research/teaching 20%, business/industry 20%, government 60%. *Median time to degree:* Master's–2 years full-time; doctorate–5 years full-time. Of those who began their doctoral program in fall 1995, 100% received their degree in 8 years or less. *Degree requirements:* For master's, thesis (for some programs), comprehensive exam (for some programs), registration; for doctorate, thesis/dissertation, comprehensive exam, registration. *Entrance requirements:* For master's and doctorate, GRE General Test, minimum GPA of 3.0. Additional exam requirements/recommendations for international students: Required—TOEFL (minimum score 600 paper-based; 250 computer-based). *Application deadline:* For fall admission, 2/1 priority date for domestic students, 2/1 priority date for international students; for spring admission, 11/1 for domestic students, 11/1 for international students. Applications are processed on a rolling basis. Application fee: $35. Electronic applications accepted. *Expenses:* Tuition: Full-time $19,700; part-time $1,096 per hour. *Financial support:* In 2003–04, 16 fellowships with full tuition reimbursements (averaging $22,666 per year), 11 research assistantships with full tuition reimbursements (averaging $18,660 per year), 4 teaching assistantships with full tuition reimbursements (averaging $7,500 per year) were awarded. *Faculty research:* Inverse problems, partial differential equations, computer algorithms, computational modeling, optimization theory. Total annual research expenditures: $2.3 million. *Unit head:* Dr. William W. Symes, Chairman, 713-348-4805, Fax: 713-348-5318, E-mail: symes@caam.rice.edu. *Application contact:* Daria A. Lawrence, Graduate Secretary, 713-348-4657, Fax: 713-348-5318, E-mail: gradapps@caam.rice.edu.

Rochester Institute of Technology, Graduate Enrollment Services, College of Science, Department of Mathematics and Statistics, Rochester, NY 14623-5603. Offers industrial and applied mathematics (MS). *Students:* 7 full-time (3 women), 2 part-time (1 woman); includes 1 minority (Asian American or Pacific Islander), 2 international. 11 applicants, 100% accepted, 5 enrolled. In 2003, 14 degrees awarded. *Entrance requirements:* For master's, minimum GPA of 3.0. *Application deadline:* For fall admission, 3/1 for domestic students. Applications are processed on a rolling basis. Application fee: $50. *Expenses:* Tuition: Full-time $22,965; part-time $644 per hour. Required fees: $174; $29 per quarter. *Unit head:* Sophia Maggelakis, Head, 585-475-2498, E-mail: sxmsma@rit.edu.

Rutgers, The State University of New Jersey, New Brunswick/Piscataway, Graduate School, Program in Mathematics, New Brunswick, NJ 08901-1281. Offers applied mathematics (MS, PhD); mathematics (MS, PhD). Part-time programs available. *Faculty:* 113 full-time (12 women). *Students:* 65 full-time (15 women), 10 part-time; includes 8 minority (1 African American, 3 Asian Americans or Pacific Islanders, 4 Hispanic Americans), 30 international. Average age 28. 271 applicants, 10% accepted, 16 enrolled. In 2003, 1 master's awarded, leading to business/industry 100%, 7 doctorates. *Median time to degree:* Master's–3 years full-time; doctorate–5 years full-time. Of those who began their doctoral program in fall 1995, 88% received their degree in 8 years or less. *Degree requirements:* For doctorate, one foreign language, thesis/dissertation, comprehensive exam. *Entrance requirements:* For master's and doctorate, GRE General Test, GRE Subject Test. Additional exam requirements/recommendations for international students: Required—TOEFL. *Application deadline:* For fall admission, 2/1 for domestic students; for spring admission, 11/1 for domestic students. Application fee: $50. *Expenses:* Tuition, state resident: full-time $10,030. Tuition, nonresident: full-time $14,202. *Financial support:* In 2003–04, 49 students received support, including 6 fellowships with full tuition reimbursements available (averaging $16,000 per year), 9 research assistantships with full tuition reimbursements available (averaging $13,700 per year), 34 teaching assistantships with full tuition reimbursements available (averaging $13,800 per year); tuition waivers (full) also available. Financial award application deadline: 2/1; financial award applicants required to submit FAFSA. *Faculty research:* Logic and set theory, number theory, mathematical physics, control theory, partial differential equations. *Unit head:* Prof. Charles A. Weibel, Director, 732-445-3864, Fax: 732-445-5530, E-mail: grad-director@math.rutgers.edu. *Application contact:* Carla I. Ortiz, Graduate Secretary, 732-445-3864, Fax: 732-445-5530, E-mail: ortizc@math.rutgers.edu.

St. John's University, St. John's College of Liberal Arts and Sciences, Department of Mathematics and Computer Science, Jamaica, NY 11439. Offers algebra (MA); analysis (MA); applied mathematics (MA); computer science (MA); geometry-topology (MA); logic and foundations (MA); probability and statistics (MA). Part-time and evening/weekend programs available. *Faculty:* 20 full-time (2 women), 18 part-time/adjunct (8 women). *Students:* 4 full-time (3 women), 3 part-time (1 woman); includes 2 minority (1 African American, 1 Hispanic American). 16 applicants, 63% accepted, 5 enrolled. In 2003, 4 degrees awarded. *Degree requirements:* For master's, thesis optional. *Entrance requirements:* For master's, minimum GPA of 3.0. Additional exam requirements/recommendations for international students: Required—TOEFL (minimum score 500 paper-based). *Application deadline:* Applications are processed on a rolling basis. Application fee: $40. Electronic applications accepted. *Expenses:* Tuition: Full-time $15,840; part-time $8,320 per year. Tuition and fees vary according to course load, degree level, program and student level. *Financial support:* Research assistantships, scholarships/grants available. Support available to part-time students. Financial award application deadline: 3/1; financial award applicants required to submit FAFSA. *Faculty research:* Development of a computerized metabolic map. *Unit head:* Dr. Charles Traina, Chair, 718-990-6166, E-mail: trainac@stjohns.edu. *Application contact:* Matthew Whelan, Director, Office of Admission, 718-990-2000, Fax: 718-990-2096, E-mail: admissions@stjohns.edu.

San Diego State University, Graduate and Research Affairs, College of Sciences, Department of Mathematical Sciences, Program in Applied Mathematics, San Diego, CA 92182. Offers MS. Part-time programs available. *Students:* 5 full-time (3 women), 13 part-time (1 woman); includes 5 minority (4 Asian Americans or Pacific Islanders, 1 Hispanic American), 4 international. Average age 29. 12 applicants, 75% accepted, 2 enrolled. In 2003, 5 degrees awarded. *Degree requirements:* For master's, comprehensive exam. *Entrance requirements:* For master's, GRE General Test. Additional exam requirements/recommendations for international students: Required—TOEFL. *Application deadline:* For fall admission, 5/1 for domestic students, 5/1 for international students; for spring admission, 11/1 for domestic students, 11/1 for international students. Applications are processed on a rolling basis. Application fee: $55. Electronic applications accepted. Tuition, nonresident: part-time $282 per unit. Required fees: $1,349; $875 per year. *Financial support:* Applicants required to submit FAFSA. *Faculty research:* Modeling, computational fluid dynamics, biomathematics, thermodynamics. *Unit head:* Peter Salamon, Graduate Advisor, 619-594-7204, Fax: 619-594-6746, E-mail: salamon@math.sdsu.edu.

Santa Clara University, School of Engineering, Department of Applied Mathematics, Santa Clara, CA 95053. Offers MSAM. Part-time and evening/weekend programs available. *Students:* Average age 34. 5 applicants, 100% accepted. In 2003, 3 degrees awarded. *Degree requirements:* For master's, thesis or alternative. *Entrance requirements:* For master's, GRE General Test, minimum GPA of 2.75. Additional exam requirements/recommendations for international students: Required—TOEFL. *Application deadline:* For fall admission, 6/1 for domestic students; for spring admission, 1/1 for domestic students. Applications are processed on a rolling basis. Application fee: $45 ($55 for international students). Electronic applications accepted. *Expenses:* Tuition: Part-time $618 per unit. *Financial support:* Fellowships, research assistantships, teaching assistantships, Federal Work-Study, institutionally sponsored loans, and scholarships/grants available. Support available to part-time students. Financial award application deadline: 3/1; financial award applicants required to submit FAFSA. *Unit head:* Dr. George Fegan, Chair, 408-554-4061. *Application contact:* Tina Samms, Assistant Director of Graduate Admissions, 408-554-4313, Fax: 408-554-5474, E-mail: engr-grad@scu.edu.

Simon Fraser University, Graduate Studies, Faculty of Science, Department of Mathematics, Burnaby, BC V5A 1S6, Canada. Offers applied mathematics (M Sc, PhD); pure mathematics

Applied Mathematics

Simon Fraser University (continued)
(M Sc, PhD); statistics and actuarial science (M Sc, PhD). *Degree requirements:* For master's and doctorate, thesis/dissertation. *Entrance requirements:* For master's, GRE Subject Test, minimum GPA of 3.0; for doctorate, GRE Subject Test, minimum GPA of 3.5. Additional exam requirements/recommendations for international students: Required—TWE or IELTS. *Faculty research:* Semi-groups, number theory, optimization, combinations.

Southern Methodist University, Dedman College, Department of Mathematics, Dallas, TX 75275. Offers computational and applied mathematics (MS, PhD). *Faculty:* 20 full-time (3 women). *Students:* 12 full-time (3 women), 5 part-time (3 women); includes 4 minority (1 African American, 3 Asian Americans or Pacific Islanders), 11 international. Average age 30. In 2003, 7 master's, 2 doctorates awarded. *Degree requirements:* For doctorate, thesis/dissertation, oral and written exams. *Entrance requirements:* For master's and doctorate, GRE General Test, minimum GPA of 3.0, 18 undergraduate hours in mathematics beyond first and second year calculus. Additional exam requirements/recommendations for international students: Required—TOEFL. *Application deadline:* For fall admission, 6/30 for domestic students; for winter admission, 11/30 for domestic students. Applications are processed on a rolling basis. Application fee: $60. Electronic applications accepted. *Expenses:* Tuition: Full-time $11,362; part-time $874 per credit. Required fees: $112 per credit. Tuition and fees vary according to course load and program. *Financial support:* In 2003–04, 7 teaching assistantships with full tuition reimbursements (averaging $14,000 per year) were awarded; career-related internships or fieldwork, scholarships/grants, and tuition waivers (partial) also available. Support available to part-time students. Financial award applicants required to submit FAFSA. *Faculty research:* Numerical analysis, scientific computation, fluid dynamics, software development, differential equations. Total annual research expenditures: $195,000. *Unit head:* Dr. Douglas Reinelt, Chairman, 214-768-2506, Fax: 214-768-2355, E-mail: mathchair@mail.smu.edu. *Application contact:* Dr. Zhangxin Chen, Director of Graduate Studies, 214-768-4338, E-mail: math@mail.smu.edu.

Stevens Institute of Technology, Graduate School, School of Applied Sciences and Liberal Arts, Department of Mathematical Sciences, Program in Applied Mathematics, Hoboken, NJ 07030. Offers MS, PhD. *Degree requirements:* For master's, thesis optional; for doctorate, one foreign language, thesis/dissertation. *Entrance requirements:* For master's and doctorate, GRE. Additional exam requirements/recommendations for international students: Required—TOEFL. Electronic applications accepted.

Stony Brook University, State University of New York, Graduate School, College of Engineering and Applied Sciences, Department of Applied Mathematics and Statistics, Stony Brook, NY 11794. Offers MS, PhD. *Faculty:* 21 full-time (3 women), 1 part-time/adjunct (0 women). *Students:* 135 full-time (67 women), 19 part-time (5 women); includes 25 minority (5 African Americans, 15 Asian Americans or Pacific Islanders, 5 Hispanic Americans), 88 international. 219 applicants, 30% accepted. In 2003, 35 master's, 14 doctorates awarded. *Degree requirements:* For master's, thesis or alternative; for doctorate, one foreign language, thesis/dissertation, comprehensive exam. *Entrance requirements:* For master's and doctorate, GRE General Test. Additional exam requirements/recommendations for international students: Required—TOEFL. *Application deadline:* For fall admission, 1/15 for domestic students. Application fee: $50. *Expenses:* Tuition, state resident: full-time $6,900; part-time $288 per credit hour. Tuition, nonresident: full-time $10,500; part-time $438 per credit hour. Required fees: $22. *Financial support:* In 2003–04, 12 fellowships, 35 research assistantships, 31 teaching assistantships were awarded. *Faculty research:* Biostatistics, combinatorial analysis, differential equations, modeling. Total annual research expenditures: $3 million. *Unit head:* Dr. J. Glimm, Chairman, 631-632-8360. *Application contact:* Dr. Woo Jong Kim, Director, 631-632-8360, Fax: 631-632-8490, E-mail: wjkim@ccmail.sunysb.edu.

Announcement: The department offers programs leading to the master's and PhD degrees, covering areas in computational applied mathematics, operations research, and statistics. Its faculty comprises 21 departmental and 22 affiliated members, among whom are 2 National Academy of Sciences members and recipients of prestigious awards. The research focus is on applied, interdisciplinary problems.

See in-depth description on page 585.

Temple University, Graduate School, College of Science and Technology, Department of Mathematics, Philadelphia, PA 19122-6096. Offers applied and computational mathematics (MA, PhD); pure mathematics (MA, PhD). Part-time and evening/weekend programs available. Terminal master's awarded for partial completion of doctoral program. *Degree requirements:* For master's, written exam, thesis optional; for doctorate, 2 foreign languages, thesis/dissertation, oral and written exams. *Entrance requirements:* For master's and doctorate, GRE General Test, GRE Subject Test, minimum GPA of 3.0 during previous 2 years, 2.8 overall. *Faculty research:* Differential geometry, numerical analysis.

Texas State University-San Marcos, Graduate School, College of Science, Department of Mathematics, Program in Industrial Mathematics, San Marcos, TX 78666. Offers MS. *Expenses:* Tuition, state resident: full-time $2,484; part-time $138 per semester hour. Tuition, nonresident: full-time $6,732; part-time $374 per semester hour. Required fees: $948; $31 per semester hour. $195 per term. Tuition and fees vary according to course load. *Unit head:* Dr. Maria Acosta, Graduate Adviser, 512-245-2497, E-mail: ma05@txstate.edu.

Towson University, Graduate School, Program in Applied and Industrial Mathematics, Towson, MD 21252-0001. Offers MS. Part-time and evening/weekend programs available. *Faculty:* 5 full-time (1 woman). *Students:* 18. 9 applicants. In 2003, 1 degree awarded. *Median time to degree:* Master's–2 years full-time, 4 years part-time. *Degree requirements:* For master's, internships. *Entrance requirements:* Additional exam requirements/recommendations for international students: Required—TOEFL (minimum score 500 paper-based). *Application deadline:* Applications are processed on a rolling basis. Application fee: $40. Electronic applications accepted. *Expenses:* Tuition, state resident: part-time $244 per unit. Tuition, nonresident: part-time $510 per unit. Required fees: $61 per unit. *Financial support:* In 2003–04, 3 students received support; teaching assistantships with full tuition reimbursements available, unspecified assistantships available. Financial award application deadline: 4/1; financial award applicants required to submit FAFSA. *Faculty research:* Partial differential equations, numerical computations, statisitics, probability, game theory. *Unit head:* Dr. Mostafa Aminzadeh, Director, 410-704-2978, Fax: 410-704-4149, E-mail: maminzadeh@towson.edu. *Application contact:* 410-704-2501, Fax: 410-704-4675, E-mail: grads@towson.edu.

Tulane University, Graduate School, Department of Mathematics, New Orleans, LA 70118-5669. Offers applied mathematics (MS); mathematics (MS, PhD); statistics (MS). *Faculty:* 24 full-time. *Students:* 29 full-time (15 women), 1 part-time; includes 7 minority (2 African Americans, 2 Asian Americans or Pacific Islanders, 3 Hispanic Americans), 8 international. 68 applicants, 26% accepted, 9 enrolled. In 2003, 5 master's, 2 doctorates awarded. *Degree requirements:* For master's, thesis (for some programs); for doctorate, thesis/dissertation. *Entrance requirements:* For master's, GRE General Test, minimum B average in undergraduate course work; for doctorate, GRE General Test. Additional exam requirements/recommendations for international students: Required—TOEFL; Recommended—TSE. *Application deadline:* For fall admission, 2/1 for domestic students, 2/1 for international students. Application fee: $45. *Financial support:* Fellowships with full tuition reimbursements, research assistantships with full tuition reimbursements, teaching assistantships with full tuition reimbursements, career-related internships or fieldwork, Federal Work-Study, and institutionally sponsored loans available. Financial award application deadline: 2/1. *Unit head:* Dr. Morris Kalka, Chair, 504-865-5727. *Application contact:* Dr. Ricardo Cortez, Graduate Adviser, 504-865-5727.

The University of Akron, Graduate School, Buchtel College of Arts and Sciences, Department of Theoretical and Applied Mathematics, Program in Applied Mathematics, Akron, OH 44325-0001. Offers MS. *Students:* 9 full-time (2 women), 3 part-time; includes 2 minority (1 African American, 1 Asian American or Pacific Islander), 4 international. Average age 30. 8 applicants, 100% accepted, 3 enrolled. In 2003, 2 degrees awarded. *Degree requirements:* For master's, seminar and comprehensive exam or thesis, thesis optional. *Entrance requirements:* For master's, minimum GPA of 2.75. Additional exam requirements/recommendations for international students: Required—TOEFL (minimum score 550 paper-based; 213 computer-based), Michigan English Language Assessment Battery. *Application deadline:* For fall admission, 3/1 for domestic students. Applications are processed on a rolling basis. Application fee: $40 ($60 for international students). *Expenses:* Tuition, state resident: part-time $277 per credit hour. Tuition, nonresident: part-time $476 per credit hour. *Financial support:* Application deadline: 3/1. *Unit head:* Dr. Gerald Young, Coordinator, 330-972-5731, E-mail: gwyoung@uakron.edu.

The University of Akron, Graduate School, College of Engineering, Program in Engineering-Applied Mathematics, Akron, OH 44325-0001. Offers PhD. *Students:* 8 full-time (0 women), 1 part-time, 5 international. Average age 31. 2 applicants, 50% accepted, 0 enrolled. In 2003, 19 degrees awarded. *Degree requirements:* For doctorate, one foreign language, thesis/dissertation, candidacy exam, qualifying exam. *Entrance requirements:* For doctorate, GRE. Additional exam requirements/recommendations for international students: Required—TOEFL (minimum score 550 paper-based; 213 computer-based), Michigan English Language Assessment Battery. *Application deadline:* Applications are processed on a rolling basis. Application fee: $40 ($60 for international students). *Expenses:* Tuition, state resident: part-time $277 per credit hour. Tuition, nonresident: part-time $476 per credit hour. *Financial support:* In 2003–04, 2 teaching assistantships were awarded. Financial award application deadline: 3/1. *Unit head:* Dr. Subramaniya Hariharan, Head, 330-972-6580.

The University of Alabama, Graduate School, College of Arts and Sciences, Department of Mathematics, Tuscaloosa, AL 35487. Offers applied mathematics (PhD); mathematics (MA); pure mathematics (PhD). *Faculty:* 26 full-time (1 woman). *Students:* 28 full-time (13 women), 6 part-time (1 woman); includes 9 minority (all African Americans), 19 international. Average age 30. 32 applicants, 25% accepted, 6 enrolled. In 2003, 3 master's, 4 doctorates awarded. Terminal master's awarded for partial completion of doctoral program. *Degree requirements:* For master's, thesis or alternative; for doctorate, one foreign language, thesis/dissertation, teaching experience. *Entrance requirements:* For master's and doctorate, GRE General Test, minimum GPA of 3.0. Additional exam requirements/recommendations for international students: Required—TOEFL. *Application deadline:* For fall admission, 7/1 for domestic students. Applications are processed on a rolling basis. Application fee: $25. Electronic applications accepted. *Expenses:* Tuition, state resident: full-time $4,134; part-time $230 per credit hour. Tuition, nonresident: full-time $11,294; part-time $627 per credit hour. Part-time tuition and fees vary according to course load. *Financial support:* In 2003–04, 3 fellowships with full tuition reimbursements (averaging $14,834 per year), 21 teaching assistantships with full tuition reimbursements (averaging $10,209 per year) were awarded. Research assistantships with full tuition reimbursements, Federal Work-Study and institutionally sponsored loans also available. Support available to part-time students. Financial award application deadline: 7/1. *Faculty research:* Analysis, topology, algebra, fluid mechanics and system control theory, optimization, stochastic processes. *Unit head:* Dr. Zhijian Wu, Chair, 205-348-5080, Fax: 205-348-7067, E-mail: zwu@gp.as.ua.edu. *Application contact:* Dr. Tan Yu Lee, Director, Graduate Programs in Mathematics, 205-348-5155, Fax: 205-348-7067, E-mail: tlee@gp.as.ua.edu.

The University of Alabama at Birmingham, School of Natural Sciences and Mathematics, Department of Mathematics, Birmingham, AL 35294. Offers applied mathematics (PhD); mathematics (MS). *Students:* 22 full-time (10 women), 6 part-time (4 women); includes 3 minority (all African Americans), 14 international. 58 applicants, 64% accepted. In 2003, 5 degrees awarded. Terminal master's awarded for partial completion of doctoral program. *Degree requirements:* For master's, thesis optional; for doctorate, one foreign language, thesis/dissertation, comprehensive exam. *Entrance requirements:* For master's and doctorate, GRE General Test. *Application deadline:* Applications are processed on a rolling basis. Application fee: $35 ($60 for international students). Electronic applications accepted. *Expenses:* Tuition, state resident: full-time $4,142; part-time $141 per credit hour. Tuition, nonresident: full-time $9,230; part-time $353 per credit hour. Required fees: $4 per credit hour. *Financial support:* In 2003–04, 18 teaching assistantships with tuition reimbursements (averaging $14,000 per year) were awarded; fellowships, research assistantships, career-related internships or fieldwork, Federal Work-Study, institutionally sponsored loans, tuition waivers (full and partial), and unspecified assistantships also available. Support available to part-time students. Financial award application deadline: 3/31; financial award applicants required to submit FAFSA. *Faculty research:* Differential equations, topology, mathematical physics, dynamic systems. *Unit head:* Dr. Rudi Weikard, Chair, 205-934-2154, Fax: 205-934-9025, E-mail: weikard@uab.edu.

The University of Alabama in Huntsville, School of Graduate Studies, College of Science, Department of Mathematical Sciences, Huntsville, AL 35899. Offers applied mathematics (PhD); mathematics (MA, MS). Part-time and evening/weekend programs available. *Faculty:* 13 full-time (1 woman), 2 part-time/adjunct (0 women). *Students:* 14 full-time (7 women), 10 part-time (4 women); includes 1 minority (Asian American or Pacific Islander), 3 international. Average age 33. 25 applicants, 84% accepted, 14 enrolled. In 2003, 4 degrees awarded. *Degree requirements:* For master's, thesis or alternative, oral and written exams, comprehensive exam, registration; for doctorate, one foreign language, thesis/dissertation, oral and written exams, comprehensive exam, registration. *Entrance requirements:* For master's and doctorate, GRE General Test, minimum GPA of 3.0. Additional exam requirements/recommendations for international students: Required—TOEFL (minimum score 550 paper-based; 213 computer-based). *Application deadline:* For fall admission, 5/30 priority date for domestic students, 2/30 priority date for international students; for spring admission, 10/10 priority date for domestic students, 7/10 priority date for international students. Applications are processed on a rolling basis. Application fee: $35. *Expenses:* Tuition, state resident: full-time $5,168; part-time $211 per hour. Tuition, nonresident: full-time $10,620; part-time $447 per hour. Tuition and fees vary according to course load. *Financial support:* In 2003–04, 17 students received support, including 1 research assistantship with full and partial tuition reimbursement available (averaging $4,766 per year), 15 teaching assistantships with full and partial tuition reimbursements available (averaging $7,753 per year); fellowships with full and partial tuition reimbursements available, career-related internships or fieldwork, Federal Work-Study, institutionally sponsored loans, scholarships/grants, health care benefits, tuition waivers (full and partial), and unspecified assistantships also available. Support available to part-time students. Financial award application deadline: 4/1; financial award applicants required to submit FAFSA. *Faculty research:* Statistical modeling, stochastic processes, numerical analysis, combinatorics, fracture mechanics. Total annual research expenditures: $232,708. *Unit head:* Dr. Kyle Siegrist, Chair, 256-824-6470, Fax: 256-824-6173, E-mail: chair@math.uah.edu.

University of Alberta, Faculty of Graduate Studies and Research, Department of Mathematical and Statistical Sciences, Edmonton, AB T6G 2E1, Canada. Offers applied mathematics (M Sc, PhD); biostatistics (M Sc); mathematical finance (M Sc, PhD); mathematical physics (M Sc, PhD); mathematics (M Sc, PhD); statistics (M Sc, PhD, Postgraduate Diploma). Part-time programs available. *Faculty:* 48 full-time (4 women). *Students:* 112 full-time (41 women), 5 part-time. Average age 24. 776 applicants, 5% accepted, 34 enrolled. In 2003, 12 master's, 10 doctorates awarded. Terminal master's awarded for partial completion of doctoral program. *Median time to degree:* Master's–2 years full-time; doctorate–5 years full-time. Of those who began their doctoral program in fall 1995, 100% received their degree in 8 years or less. *Degree requirements:* For master's, thesis (for some programs); for doctorate, thesis/dissertation, comprehensive exam. *Entrance requirements:* Additional exam requirements/recommendations for international students: Required—TOEFL (minimum score 580 paper-based; 237 computer-based). *Application deadline:* For fall admission, 3/1 for domestic students, 2/1 for international students. Applications are processed on a rolling basis. Application fee: $0. Electronic applications accepted. Tuition charges are reported in Canadian dollars. Tuition, nonresident: full-time $3,921 Canadian dollars. International tuition: $7,113 Canadian dollars full-time. *Financial support:* In 2003–04, 51 research assistantships, 88 teaching assistantships with full and partial tuition reimbursements were awarded. Scholarships/grants also available. Financial award application deadline: 5/1. *Faculty research:* Classical and functional analysis, algebra, differential equations, geometry. *Unit head:* Dr. Anthony To-Ming Lau, Chair, 403-492-5799, E-mail: tlau@math.ualberta.ca. *Application contact:* Dr. Yau Shu Wong, Associate Chair, Graduate Studies, 403-492-5799, Fax: 403-492-6828, E-mail: gradstudies@math.ualberta.ca.

The University of Arizona, Graduate College, Graduate Interdisciplinary Programs, Graduate Interdisciplinary Program in Applied Mathematics, Tucson, AZ 85721. Offers applied mathematics (MS, PhD); mathematical sciences (PMS). *Faculty:* 34. *Students:* 44 full-time (15 women), 3 part-time (1 woman); includes 6 minority (2 Asian Americans or Pacific Islanders, 4 Hispanic Americans), 15 international. Average age 26. 72 applicants, 28% accepted, 10 enrolled. In 2003, 2 master's awarded, leading to university research/teaching 50%, business/industry 50%; 4 doctorates awarded, leading to university research/teaching 25%, continued full-time study 50%, business/industry 25%. Terminal master's awarded for partial completion of doctoral program. *Median time to degree:* Master's–2 years full-time; doctorate–6 years full-time. Of those who began their doctoral program in fall 1995, 100% received their degree in 8 years or less. *Degree requirements:* For master's, thesis (for some programs), registration; for doctorate, one foreign language, thesis/dissertation, comprehensive exam, registration. *Entrance requirements:* For master's and doctorate, GRE. Additional exam requirements/recommendations for international students: Required—TOEFL (minimum score 575 paper-based; 230 computer-based), TSE(minimum score 45). *Application deadline:* For fall admission, 1/30 priority date for domestic students, 2/15 priority date for international students. Applications are processed on a rolling basis. Application fee: $50. *Expenses:* Tuition, state resident: part-time $196 per unit. Tuition, nonresident: part-time $326 per unit. *Financial support:* In 2003–04, 42 students received support, including 4 fellowships with full tuition reimbursements available (averaging $27,500 per year), 21 research assistantships with full tuition reimbursements available (averaging $15,400 per year), 17 teaching assistantships with full tuition reimbursements available (averaging $15,400 per year); institutionally sponsored loans, scholarships/grants, health care benefits, tuition waivers (full), and unspecified assistantships also available. Financial award application deadline: 3/1. *Faculty research:* Dynamical systems and chaos, partial differential equations, pattern formation, fluid dynamics and turbulence, scientific computation, mathematical physics, mathematical biology, medical imaging, applied probability and stochastic processes. *Unit head:* Dr. Michael Tabor, Head, 520-621-4664, Fax: 520-626-5048, E-mail: tabor@math.arizona.edu. *Application contact:* Linda Silverman, Graduate Coordinator, 520-621-2016, Fax: 520-626-5048, E-mail: applmath@u.arizona.edu.

See in-depth description on page 587.

University of Arkansas at Little Rock, Graduate School, College of Science and Mathematics, Department of Mathematics and Statistics, Little Rock, AR 72204-1099. Offers applied mathematics (MS), including applied analysis, mathematical statistics. Part-time and evening/weekend programs available. *Students:* 2 full-time (1 woman), 7 part-time (5 women); includes 2 minority (both African Americans), 3 international. Average age 28. 7 applicants, 86% accepted. In 2003, 4 degrees awarded. *Degree requirements:* For master's, comprehensive exam. *Entrance requirements:* For master's, GRE General Test, GRE Subject Test, minimum GPA of 2.7, previous course work in advanced mathematics. *Application deadline:* For fall admission, 8/1 for domestic students; for spring admission, 11/1 for domestic students. Application fee: $25 ($30 for international students). Tuition, nonresident: part-time $177 per credit hour. *Financial support:* Research assistantships, teaching assistantships, Federal Work-Study, institutionally sponsored loans, and unspecified assistantships available. Support available to part-time students. Financial award application deadline: 8/1. *Unit head:* Dr. Timothy McMillan, Chairperson, 501-569-8100. *Application contact:* Dr. Alan M. Johnson, Coordinator, 501-569-8100.

The University of British Columbia, Faculty of Graduate Studies, Institute of Applied Mathematics, Vancouver, BC V6T 1Z1, Canada. Offers M Sc, PhD. *Degree requirements:* For master's, thesis (for some programs); for doctorate, thesis/dissertation, comprehensive exam. *Entrance requirements:* For doctorate, master's degree. Additional exam requirements/recommendations for international students: Required—TOEFL. *Faculty research:* Applied analysis, optimization, mathematical biology, numerical analysis, fluid mechanics.

University of California, Berkeley, Graduate Division, College of Letters and Science, Department of Mathematics, Program in Applied Mathematics, Berkeley, CA 94720-1500. Offers PhD. *Degree requirements:* For doctorate, 2 foreign languages, thesis/dissertation, qualifying exam. *Entrance requirements:* For doctorate, GRE General Test, GRE Subject Test, minimum GPA of 3.0. *Application deadline:* For fall admission, 2/15 for domestic students. Application fee: $60. International tuition: $12,491 full-time. Required fees: $5,484. *Financial support:* Fellowships, research assistantships, teaching assistantships, unspecified assistantships available. Financial award application deadline: 12/15. *Application contact:* Graduate Assistant for Admission, 510-642-0665, Fax: 510-642-8204, E-mail: brown@math.berkeley.edu.

University of California, Davis, Graduate Studies, Graduate Group in Applied Mathematics, Davis, CA 95616. Offers MS, PhD. *Faculty:* 68 full-time. *Students:* 35 full-time (10 women); includes 5 minority (4 Asian Americans or Pacific Islanders, 1 Hispanic American), 14 international. Average age 27. 56 applicants, 32% accepted, 6 enrolled. In 2003, 2 degrees awarded. Terminal master's awarded for partial completion of doctoral program. *Degree requirements:* For master's, thesis; for doctorate, one foreign language, thesis/dissertation. *Entrance requirements:* For master's, GRE General Test, GRE Subject Test, minimum GPA of 3.0; for doctorate, GRE General Test, GRE Subject Test, master's degree, minimum GPA of 3.0. Additional exam requirements/recommendations for international students: Required—TOEFL (minimum score 550 paper-based; 213 computer-based). *Application deadline:* For fall admission, 1/15 for domestic students. Application fee: $60. Electronic applications accepted. Tuition, nonresident: full-time $12,245. Required fees: $7,062. *Financial support:* In 2003–04, 34 students received support, including 6 fellowships with full and partial tuition reimbursements available (averaging $12,000 per year), 8 research assistantships with full and partial tuition reimbursements available (averaging $11,431 per year), 17 teaching assistantships with partial tuition reimbursements available (averaging $13,848 per year); Federal Work-Study, institutionally sponsored loans, scholarships/grants, traineeships, and tuition waivers (full and partial) also available. Financial award application deadline: 1/15; financial award applicants required to submit FAFSA. *Faculty research:* Mathematical biology, control and optimization, atmospheric sciences, theoretical chemistry, mathematical physics. *Unit head:* Bruno Nachtergaele, Graduate Group Chair, 530-752-8061, E-mail: bxn@math.ucdavis.edu. *Application contact:* Celia Davis, Administrative Assistant, 530-752-8131, Fax: 530-752-6635, E-mail: davis@math.ucdavis.edu.

University of California, San Diego, Graduate Studies and Research, Department of Mathematics, La Jolla, CA 92093. Offers applied mathematics (MA); mathematics (MA, PhD); statistics (MS). *Faculty:* 63. *Students:* 91 (25 women); includes 11 minority (2 African Americans, 6 Asian Americans or Pacific Islanders, 3 Hispanic Americans) 14 international. 294 applicants, 27% accepted. In 2003, 20 master's, 10 doctorates awarded. *Degree requirements:* For doctorate, thesis/dissertation. *Entrance requirements:* For master's and doctorate, GRE General Test, GRE Subject Test. Application fee: $60. Electronic applications accepted. Tuition, nonresident: full-time $12,245. Required fees: $6,959. *Unit head:* James Bunch, Chair, E-mail: jbunch@ucsd.edu. *Application contact:* Lois Stewart, Graduate Coordinator, 858-534-6887, E-mail: lstewart@ucsd.edu.

University of California, Santa Barbara, Graduate Division, College of Letters and Sciences, Division of Mathematics, Life, and Physical Sciences, Department of Mathematics, Program in Applied Mathematics, Santa Barbara, CA 93106. Offers MA. *Students:* Average age 26. *Degree requirements:* For master's, thesis or alternative, comprehensive exam (for some programs), registration. *Entrance requirements:* For master's, GRE General Test, GRE Subject Test. Additional exam requirements/recommendations for international students: Required—TOEFL (minimum score 550 paper-based; 213 computer-based); Recommended—TSE. *Application deadline:* For fall admission, 1/1 for domestic students, 1/1 for international students. Application fee: $60. Electronic applications accepted. *Expenses:* Tuition, state resident: full-time $7,188. Tuition, nonresident: full-time $19,608. *Financial support:* Teaching assistantships with partial tuition reimbursements, Federal Work-Study, institutionally sponsored loans, and health care benefits available. Financial award application deadline: 1/1; financial award applicants required to submit FAFSA. *Faculty research:* PDE's, numerical analysis. *Application contact:* Medina Teel, Staff Graduate Adviser, 805-893-8192, Fax: 805-893-2385, E-mail: teel@math.ucsb.edu.

University of California, Santa Cruz, Division of Graduate Studies, Division of Physical and Biological Sciences, Department of Mathematics, Santa Cruz, CA 95064. Offers applied mathematics (MA, PhD); mathematics (MA, PhD). *Faculty:* 15 full-time (2 women). *Students:* 32 full-time (7 women); includes 3 minority (2 Asian Americans or Pacific Islanders, 1 Hispanic American), 6 international. 59 applicants, 0% accepted. In 2003, 4 master's, 1 doctorate awarded. *Median time to degree:* Master's–2.17 years full-time; doctorate–5.75 years full-time. *Degree requirements:* For doctorate, one foreign language, thesis/dissertation, qualifying exam. *Entrance requirements:* For doctorate, GRE General Test, GRE Subject Test. *Application deadline:* For fall admission, 2/1 for domestic students. Application fee: $60. Tuition, nonresident: full-time $12,492. *Financial support:* Fellowships, research assistantships, teaching assistantships, Federal Work-Study and institutionally sponsored loans available. Financial award application deadline: 2/1. *Unit head:* Dr. Tony Tromba, Chair, 831-459-2215, E-mail: gem@cats.ucsc.edu. *Application contact:* James M. Moore, Graduate Admissions, Director, 831-459-2301, Fax: 831-459-4843, E-mail: gradadm@ucsc.edu.

University of Central Oklahoma, College of Graduate Studies and Research, College of Mathematics and Science, Department of Mathematics and Statistics, Edmond, OK 73034-5209. Offers applied mathematical sciences (MS), including computer science, mathematics, mathematics/computer science teaching, statistics. *Accreditation:* NCATE. Part-time programs available. *Degree requirements:* For master's, thesis. *Faculty research:* Curvature, FAA, math education.

University of Chicago, Division of the Physical Sciences, Department of Mathematics, Program in Applied Mathematics, Chicago, IL 60637-1513. Offers SM, PhD. *Degree requirements:* For master's, one foreign language; for doctorate, one foreign language, thesis/dissertation, 2 qualifying exams. *Entrance requirements:* For master's and doctorate, GRE General Test, GRE Subject Test. Additional exam requirements/recommendations for international students: Required—TOEFL (minimum score 600 paper-based; 250 computer-based). *Application deadline:* For fall admission, 1/5 for domestic students. Application fee: $55. Electronic applications accepted. *Financial support:* Fellowships, research assistantships, teaching assistantships available. Financial award application deadline: 1/5. *Faculty research:* Applied analysis, dynamical systems, theoretical biology, math-physics. *Unit head:* Norman R. Lebovitz, Head, 773-702-7329. *Application contact:* Laurie Wail, Graduate Studies Assistant, 773-702-7358, Fax: 773-702-9787, E-mail: lwail@math.uchicago.edu.

University of Cincinnati, Division of Research and Advanced Studies, McMicken College of Arts and Sciences, Department of Mathematical Sciences, Cincinnati, OH 45221. Offers applied mathematics (MS, PhD); mathematics education (MAT); pure mathematics (MS, PhD); statistics (MS, PhD). *Accreditation:* NCATE (one or more programs are accredited). Part-time programs available. Terminal master's awarded for partial completion of doctoral program. *Degree requirements:* For master's, thesis or alternative, comprehensive exam; for doctorate, one foreign language, thesis/dissertation, comprehensive exam. *Entrance requirements:* For master's, GRE, teacher certification (MAT); for doctorate, GRE. Additional exam requirements/recommendations for international students: Required—TOEFL. Electronic applications accepted. *Faculty research:* Algebra, analysis, differential equations, numerical analysis, statistics.

University of Colorado at Boulder, Graduate School, College of Arts and Sciences, Department of Applied Mathematics, Boulder, CO 80309. Offers MS, PhD. Part-time programs available. *Faculty:* 13 full-time (2 women). *Students:* 63 full-time (16 women), 11 part-time (3 women); includes 9 minority (3 Asian Americans or Pacific Islanders, 6 Hispanic Americans), 16 international. Average age 28. 85 applicants, 58% accepted. In 2003, 16 master's, 6 doctorates awarded. Terminal master's awarded for partial completion of doctoral program. *Degree requirements:* For master's, thesis or alternative, comprehensive exam; for doctorate, one foreign language, thesis/dissertation, comprehensive exam. *Entrance requirements:* For master's and doctorate, GRE General Test. Additional exam requirements/recommendations for international students: Required—TOEFL. *Application deadline:* For fall admission, 3/1 for domestic students. Applications are processed on a rolling basis. Application fee: $50 ($60 for international students). *Expenses:* Tuition, state resident: full-time $2,122. Tuition, nonresident: full-time $9,754. Tuition and fees vary according to course load and program. *Financial support:* In 2003–04, 17 fellowships (averaging $13,971 per year), 4 research assistantships (averaging $17,786 per year), 29 teaching assistantships (averaging $13,936 per year) were awarded. Scholarships/grants and traineeships also available. Support available to part-time students. Financial award application deadline: 2/15. *Faculty research:* Non-linear phenomena, computational mathematics, physical applied mathematics, statistics. Total annual research expenditures: $2.1 million. *Unit head:* Harvey Segur, Chair, 303-492-0592, Fax: 303-492-4066, E-mail: harvey.segur@colorado.edu. *Application contact:* Graduate Program Assistant, 303-492-4668, Fax: 303-492-4066, E-mail: appm_app@colorado.edu.

University of Colorado at Colorado Springs, Graduate School, College of Engineering and Applied Science, Department of Mathematics, Colorado Springs, CO 80918. Offers applied mathematics (MS). Part-time and evening/weekend programs available. *Faculty:* 5 full-time (0 women), 1 part-time/adjunct (0 women). *Students:* 11 full-time (5 women), 3 part-time (1 woman); includes 3 minority (1 Asian American or Pacific Islander, 2 Hispanic Americans). Average age 30. In 2003, 4 degrees awarded. *Degree requirements:* For master's, thesis. *Entrance requirements:* For master's, GRE General Test, minimum GPA of 3.0. Additional exam requirements/recommendations for international students: Required—TOEFL. *Application deadline:* For fall admission, 6/15 for domestic students. Application fee: $60 ($75 for international students). *Expenses:* Tuition, state resident: full-time $3,745; part-time $226 per semester hour. Tuition, nonresident: full-time $13,602; part-time $804 per semester hour. Required fees: $19 per semester hour. $135 per semester. One-time fee: $40 full-time. Tuition and fees vary according to course load and program. *Financial support:* Teaching assistantships available. *Faculty research:* Abelian groups and noncommutative rings, hormone analysis and computer vision, probability and mathematical physics, stochastic dynamics, probability models. Total annual research expenditures: $33,777. *Unit head:* Robert Carlson, Chair, 719-262-3561, Fax: 719-262-3605, E-mail: carlson@math.uccs.edu. *Application contact:* Joan Stephens, Director of Graduate Studies, 719-262-3311, Fax: 719-262-3605, E-mail: mathinfo@math.uccs.edu.

University of Colorado at Denver, Graduate School, College of Liberal Arts and Sciences, Program in Applied Mathematics, Denver, CO 80217-3364. Offers MS, PhD. Part-time and evening/weekend programs available. *Students:* 19 full-time (7 women), 39 part-time (16 women); includes 10 minority (6 Asian Americans or Pacific Islanders, 4 Hispanic Americans), 5 international. Average age 26. 42 applicants, 79% accepted, 19 enrolled. In 2003, 11 master's, 4 doctorates awarded. *Degree requirements:* For master's, thesis or alternative; for doctorate, thesis/dissertation, comprehensive exam. *Entrance requirements:* For master's, GRE, 30 hours in mathematics, 24 hours of upper division mathematics; for doctorate, GRE, 24 hours of upper division mathematics. Additional exam requirements/recommendations for international students: Required—TOEFL. *Application deadline:* For fall admission, 6/1 for domestic students; for spring admission, 11/1 for domestic students. Applications are processed on a rolling basis. Application fee: $50 ($60 for international students). Electronic applications accepted. *Expenses:* Tuition, state resident: part-time $255 per credit hour. Tuition, nonresident: part-time $1,025 per credit hour. *Financial support:* In 2003–04, 2 fellowships with partial tuition reimbursements (averaging $12,000 per year), 4 research assistantships with full tuition reimbursements, 15 teaching assistantships with full tuition reimbursements (averaging $12,000 per year) were awarded. Federal Work-Study also available. Financial award application deadline: 3/1; financial award applicants required to submit FAFSA. *Faculty research:* Computational mathematics, computational biology, discrete mathematics and geometry prob-

Applied Mathematics

University of Colorado at Denver (continued)
ability and statistics, optimization. Total annual research expenditures: $390,522. *Unit head:* Prof. Mike Jacobson, Chair, 303-556-6270, Fax: 303-556-8550, E-mail: msj@math.cudenver.edu. *Application contact:* Prof. Bill Briggs, Coordinator, 303-556-2341, Fax: 303-556-8550, E-mail: wbriggs@math.cudenver.edu.

University of Connecticut, Graduate School, College of Liberal Arts and Sciences, Department of Mathematics, Field of Applied Financial Mathematics, Storrs, CT 06269. Offers MS. *Faculty:* 8 full-time (0 women). *Students:* 2 full-time (0 women), 3 part-time (1 woman), 3 international. Average age 36. 9 applicants, 67% accepted, 5 enrolled. *Degree requirements:* For master's, comprehensive exam. *Entrance requirements:* Additional exam requirements/recommendations for international students: Required—TOEFL (minimum score 550 paper-based; 213 computer-based). *Application deadline:* For fall admission, 2/1 priority date for domestic students, 2/1 priority date for international students; for spring admission, 11/1 for domestic students, 10/1 for international students. Applications are processed on a rolling basis. Application fee: $55. Electronic applications accepted. *Expenses:* Tuition, state resident: part-time $3,860 per semester. Tuition, nonresident: part-time $9,036 per semester. *Financial support:* Federal Work-Study and scholarships/grants available. Financial award application deadline: 2/1; financial award applicants required to submit FAFSA. *Unit head:* James Bridgeman, Chairperson, 860-486-8382, Fax: 860-486-4283, E-mail: james.bridgeman@uconn.edu. *Application contact:* Sharon McDermott, Administrative Assistant, 860-486-6452, Fax: 860-486-4283, E-mail: gradadm@math.uconn.edu.

University of Connecticut, Graduate School, College of Liberal Arts and Sciences, Department of Mathematics, Field of Mathematics, Storrs, CT 06269. Offers actuarial science (MS, PhD); applied mathematics (MS); financial mathematics (MS); mathematics (MS); mathematics and computer science (MS). *Faculty:* 32 full-time (4 women). *Students:* 68 full-time (27 women), 39 part-time (19 women); includes 5 minority (1 African American, 4 Asian Americans or Pacific Islanders), 62 international. Average age 29. 235 applicants, 53% accepted, 50 enrolled. In 2003, 37 master's, 5 doctorates awarded. Terminal master's awarded for partial completion of doctoral program. *Degree requirements:* For master's, comprehensive exam; for doctorate, thesis/dissertation. *Entrance requirements:* For master's and doctorate, GRE General Test. Additional exam requirements/recommendations for international students: Required—TOEFL (minimum score 550 paper-based; 213 computer-based). *Application deadline:* For fall admission, 2/1 priority date for domestic students, 2/1 priority date for international students; for spring admission, 11/1 for domestic students, 10/1 for international students. Applications are processed on a rolling basis. Application fee: $55. Electronic applications accepted. *Expenses:* Tuition, state resident: part-time $3,860 per semester. Tuition, nonresident: part-time $9,036 per semester. *Financial support:* In 2003–04, 7 research assistantships with full tuition reimbursements, 51 teaching assistantships with full tuition reimbursements were awarded. Fellowships, Federal Work-Study, scholarships/grants, health care benefits, and unspecified assistantships also available. Financial award application deadline: 2/1; financial award applicants required to submit FAFSA. *Unit head:* Eugene Spiegel, Chairperson, 860-486-3844, Fax: 860-486-4283, E-mail: eugene.spiegel@uconn.edu. *Application contact:* Sharon McDermott, Administrative Assistant, 860-486-6452, Fax: 860-486-4283, E-mail: gradadm@math.uconn.edu.

University of Dayton, Graduate School, College of Arts and Sciences, Department of Mathematics, Dayton, OH 45469-1300. Offers applied mathematics (MS). Part-time and evening/weekend programs available. *Faculty:* 8 full-time (2 women). *Students:* 5 full-time (0 women), 1 part-time; includes 1 minority (African American), 3 international. Average age 25. 7 applicants, 86% accepted, 4 enrolled. In 2003, 5 degrees awarded. *Entrance requirements:* For master's, minimum undergraduate GPA of 2.8. Additional exam requirements/recommendations for international students: Required—TOEFL (minimum score 550 paper-based; 219 computer-based). *Application deadline:* For fall admission, 3/1 for domestic students. Application fee: $30. Electronic applications accepted. *Expenses:* Tuition: Full-time $6,060; part-time $505 per hour. Required fees: $50; $25 per term. Tuition and fees vary according to degree level, campus/location, program and student's religious affiliation. *Financial support:* In 2003–04, 5 students received support, including 5 teaching assistantships with full tuition reimbursements available (averaging $10,290 per year) *Faculty research:* Differential equations, integral equations, general topology, measure theory, graph theory. *Unit head:* Dr. Paul W. Eloe, Chair, 937-229-2016, Fax: 937-229-2566, E-mail: paul.eloe@notes.udayton.edu. *Application contact:* Dr. Muhammad N. Islam, Graduate Director, 937-229-2109, Fax: 937-229-2566, E-mail: muhammad.islam@notes.udayton.edu.

University of Delaware, College of Arts and Sciences, Department of Mathematical Sciences, Newark, DE 19716. Offers applied mathematics (MS, PhD); mathematics (MS, PhD). Part-time programs available. *Faculty:* 40 full-time (5 women). *Students:* 42 full-time (17 women), 1 part-time; includes 1 minority (Asian American or Pacific Islander), 26 international. Average age 25. 146 applicants, 17% accepted, 16 enrolled. In 2003, 7 master's, 3 doctorates awarded. Terminal master's awarded for partial completion of doctoral program. *Degree requirements:* For master's, thesis (for some programs); for doctorate, one foreign language, thesis/dissertation, qualifying exam. *Entrance requirements:* For master's and doctorate, GRE General Test. Additional exam requirements/recommendations for international students: Required—TOEFL. *Application deadline:* For fall admission, 3/1 for domestic students; for spring admission, 12/15 priority date for domestic students. Applications are processed on a rolling basis. Application fee: $60. Electronic applications accepted. *Expenses:* Tuition, state resident: full-time $5,890; part-time $327 per credit. Tuition, nonresident: full-time $15,420; part-time $857 per credit. Required fees: $968. *Financial support:* In 2003–04, 4 fellowships with tuition reimbursements (averaging $15,000 per year), 3 research assistantships with tuition reimbursements (averaging $13,000 per year), 27 teaching assistantships with tuition reimbursements (averaging $12,240 per year) were awarded. Career-related internships or fieldwork, institutionally sponsored loans, scholarships/grants, and tuition waivers (full and partial) also available. Financial award application deadline: 3/1. *Faculty research:* Scattering theory, inverse problems, fluid dynamics, numerical analysis, combinatorics. Total annual research expenditures:$600,000. *Unit head:* Dr. Philip Broadbridge, Chair, 302-831-2652, E-mail: pbroad@math.udel.edu. *Application contact:* Dr. Robert Gilbert, Graduate Chair, 302-831-2315, Fax: 302-831-4511, E-mail: gilbert@math.udel.edu.

See in-depth description on page 593.

University of Denver, Graduate Studies, Faculty of Natural Sciences and Mathematics, Department of Mathematics, Denver, CO 80208. Offers applied mathematics (MA, MS); computer science (MS). Part-time programs available. *Faculty:* 18 full-time (7 women), 1 (woman) part-time/adjunct. *Students:* 6 (5 women) 1 international. 7 applicants, 86% accepted. In 2003, 2 degrees awarded. Terminal master's awarded for partial completion of doctoral program. *Degree requirements:* For master's, computer language, foreign language, or laboratory experience, one foreign language. *Entrance requirements:* For master's, GRE General Test. Additional exam requirements/recommendations for international students: Required—TOEFL. *Application deadline:* Applications are processed on a rolling basis. Application fee: $45. *Expenses:* Tuition: Full-time $24,264. *Financial support:* In 2003–04, 21 students received support, including 5 fellowships with full and partial tuition reimbursements available, 2 research assistantships with full and partial tuition reimbursements available (averaging $9,081 per year), 14 teaching assistantships with full and partial tuition reimbursements available (averaging $9,972 per year); career-related internships or fieldwork, Federal Work-Study, institutionally sponsored loans, and scholarships/grants also available. Support available to part-time students. Financial award application deadline: 3/1; financial award applicants required to submit FAFSA. *Faculty research:* Real-time software, convex bodies, multidimensional data, parallel computer clusters. Total annual research expenditures: $163,312. *Unit head:* Dr. Scott Leutenegger, Chairperson, 303-871-2821. *Application contact:* Roy James Rosa, Graduate Secretary, 303-871-3017.

University of Florida, Graduate School, College of Liberal Arts and Sciences, Department of Mathematics, Gainesville, FL 32611. Offers applied mathematics (MS, PhD); mathematics (MA, MS, PhD); mathematics teaching (MAT, MST). *Accreditation:* NCATE (one or more programs are accredited). Part-time programs available. *Faculty:* 58. *Students:* 75 full-time (21 women), 3 part-time; includes 4 minority (1 Asian American or Pacific Islander, 3 Hispanic Americans), 47 international. In 2003, 11 master's, 2 doctorates awarded. Terminal master's awarded for partial completion of doctoral program. *Degree requirements:* For master's, thesis optional; for doctorate, one foreign language, thesis/dissertation. *Entrance requirements:* For master's and doctorate, GRE General Test, minimum GPA of 3.0. Additional exam requirements/recommendations for international students: Required—TOEFL (minimum score 550 paper-based; 213 computer-based). *Application deadline:* For fall admission, 6/1 for domestic students. Applications are processed on a rolling basis. Application fee: $30. Electronic applications accepted. *Expenses:* Tuition, state resident: part-time $205 per credit hour. Tuition, nonresident: part-time $775 per credit hour. *Financial support:* In 2003–04, 65 students received support, including 3 fellowships, 2 research assistantships, 61 teaching assistantships; career-related internships or fieldwork and unspecified assistantships also available. Financial award application deadline: 3/1. *Faculty research:* Combinatorics and number theory, group theory, probability theory, logic, differential geometry and mathematical physics. *Unit head:* Dr. Krishnaswani Alladi, Chairman, 352-392-0281 Ext. 236, Fax: 352-392-8357, E-mail: alladi@math.ufl.edu. *Application contact:* Dr. Paul Robinson, Coordinator, 352-392-0281 Ext. 273, Fax: 352-392-8357, E-mail: robinson@math.ufl.edu.

University of Georgia, Graduate School, College of Arts and Sciences, Department of Mathematics, Athens, GA 30602. Offers applied mathematical science (MAMS); mathematics (MA, PhD). *Faculty:* 42 full-time (3 women). *Students:* 45 full-time (11 women), 2 part-time; includes 3 minority (1 African American, 1 Asian American or Pacific Islander, 1 Hispanic American), 23 international. 97 applicants, 16% accepted. In 2003, 2 master's, 4 doctorates awarded. *Degree requirements:* For master's, one foreign language, thesis (for some programs); for doctorate, 2 foreign languages, thesis/dissertation. *Entrance requirements:* For master's and doctorate, GRE General Test. *Application deadline:* For fall admission, 7/1 for domestic students; for spring admission, 11/15 for domestic students. Application fee: $50. Electronic applications accepted. *Expenses:* Tuition, state resident: part-time $161 per hour. Tuition, nonresident: part-time $690 per hour. One-time fee: $435 part-time. *Financial support:* Fellowships, research assistantships, teaching assistantships, unspecified assistantships available. *Unit head:* Dr. Dan Kannan, Head, 706-542-2643, Fax: 706-542-2573, E-mail: kannan@math.uga.edu. *Application contact:* Dr. Joe Fu, Graduate Coordinator, 706-542-2562, Fax: 706-542-5907, E-mail: fu@math.uga.edu.

University of Guelph, Graduate Program Services, College of Physical and Engineering Science, Department of Mathematics and Statistics, Guelph, ON N1G 2W1, Canada. Offers applied mathematics (PhD); applied statistics (PhD); mathematics and statistics (M Sc). Part-time programs available. *Faculty:* 26 full-time (5 women), 5 part-time/adjunct (1 woman). *Students:* 46 full-time, 2 part-time, 10 international. Average age 22. 96 applicants, 30% accepted, 22 enrolled. In 2003, 15 master's, 6 doctorates awarded. *Median time to degree:* Of those who began their doctoral program in fall 1995, 88% received their degree in 8 years or less. *Degree requirements:* For master's, thesis (for some programs); for doctorate, thesis/dissertation. *Entrance requirements:* For master's, minimum B- average during previous 2 years; for doctorate, minimum B average. Additional exam requirements/recommendations for international students: Required—TOEFL (minimum score 550 paper-based; 210 computer-based). *Application deadline:* For fall admission, 3/1 for domestic students, 2/1 for international students. Application fee: $75. Tuition and fees charges are reported in Canadian dollars. Tuition, nonresident: full-time $3,440 Canadian dollars. International tuition: $5,432 Canadian dollars full-time. Required fees: $753 Canadian dollars. *Financial support:* In 2003–04, 20 students received support, including 29 research assistantships (averaging $2,200 per year), 32 teaching assistantships (averaging $11,000 per year); fellowships, scholarships/grants also available. *Faculty research:* Dynamical systems, mathematical biology, numerical analysis, linear and nonlinear models, reliability and bioassay. Total annual research expenditures: $315,000. *Unit head:* Dr. O. Brian Allen, Chair, 519-824-4120 Ext. 56556, Fax: 519-837-0221, E-mail: chair@uoguelph.ca. *Application contact:* Susan McCormick, Graduate Administrative Assistant, 519-824-4120 Ext. 56553, Fax: 519-837-0221, E-mail: smccormi@uoguelph.ca.

University of Houston, College of Natural Sciences and Mathematics, Department of Mathematics, Houston, TX 77204. Offers applied mathematics (MSAM); mathematics (MSM, PhD). Part-time and evening/weekend programs available. *Faculty:* 23 full-time (2 women), 2 part-time/adjunct (0 women). *Students:* 79 full-time (30 women), 34 part-time (15 women); includes 20 minority (2 African Americans, 11 Asian Americans or Pacific Islanders, 7 Hispanic Americans), 46 international. Average age 29. 61 applicants, 87% accepted, 27 enrolled. In 2003, 15 master's, 7 doctorates awarded. *Degree requirements:* For master's, thesis optional; for doctorate, thesis/dissertation. *Entrance requirements:* For master's, GRE General Test, minimum GPA of 3.0 in last 60 hours, bachelor's degree in mathematics or related area; for doctorate, GRE General Test, MS in mathematics or equivalent, minimum GPA of 3.0 in last 60 hours. Additional exam requirements/recommendations for international students: Required—TOEFL. *Application deadline:* For fall admission, 7/3 for domestic students; for spring admission, 12/4 for domestic students. Applications are processed on a rolling basis. Application fee: $0 ($75 for international students). *Expenses:* Tuition, state resident: full-time $1,656; part-time $92 per credit hour. Tuition, nonresident: full-time $5,904; part-time $328 per credit hour. Required fees: $1,704. *Financial support:* In 2003–04, 41 students received support, including 13 research assistantships with tuition reimbursements available (averaging $12,000 per year), 41 teaching assistantships (averaging $12,000 per year); fellowships with tuition reimbursements available, institutionally sponsored loans, tuition waivers (partial), and teaching fellowships also available. Support available to part-time students. Financial award application deadline: 3/15. *Faculty research:* Applied mathematics, modern analysis, computational science, geometry, dynamical systems. Total annual research expenditures: $310,295. *Unit head:* Dr. William E. Fitzgibbon, Chair, 713-743-3465, Fax: 713-743-3505, E-mail: fitz@math.uh.edu. *Application contact:* Pamela K. Draughn, Graduate Adviser, 713-743-3517, Fax: 713-743-3505, E-mail: pamela@math.uh.edu.

University of Illinois at Chicago, Graduate College, College of Liberal Arts and Sciences, Department of Mathematics, Statistics, and Computer Science, Chicago, IL 60607-7128. Offers applied mathematics (MS, DA, PhD); computer science (MS, DA, PhD); math and information science for the industry (MS); probability and statistics (MS, DA, PhD); pure mathematics (MS, DA, PhD); teaching of mathematics (MST). Part-time programs available. *Faculty:* 69 full-time (4 women). *Students:* 145 full-time (61 women), 62 part-time (34 women); includes 41 minority (13 African Americans, 21 Asian Americans or Pacific Islanders, 7 Hispanic Americans), 86 international. Average age 32. 285 applicants, 30% accepted, 36 enrolled. In 2003, 38 master's, 14 doctorates awarded. *Median time to degree:* Of those who began their doctoral program in fall 1995, 50% received their degree in 8 years or less. *Degree requirements:* For master's, comprehensive exam; for doctorate, one foreign language, thesis/dissertation. *Entrance requirements:* For master's and doctorate, GRE General Test, minimum GPA of 3.75 on a 5.0 scale. Additional exam requirements/recommendations for international students: Required—TOEFL. *Application deadline:* For fall admission, 1/9 for domestic students, 1/9 for international students; for spring admission, 10/1 for domestic students. Applications are processed on a rolling basis. Application fee: $40 ($50 for international students). Electronic applications accepted. *Expenses:* Tuition, state resident: part-time $941 per semester. Tuition, nonresident: part-time $2,338 per semester. *Financial support:* In 2003–04, 118 students received support; fellowships with full tuition reimbursements available, research assistantships with full tuition reimbursements available, teaching assistantships with full tuition reimbursements available, Federal Work-Study, scholarships/grants, traineeships, tuition waivers (full), and unspecified assistantships available. Financial award application deadline: 3/1; financial award applicants required to submit FAFSA. *Unit head:* Jerry Bona, Head, 312-996-3044. *Application contact:* Charles Knessl, Director of Graduate Studies, 312-996-3041, E-mail: knessl@uic.edu.

See in-depth description on page 599.

University of Illinois at Urbana–Champaign, Graduate College, College of Liberal Arts and Sciences, Department of Mathematics, Champaign, IL 61820. Offers applied mathematics (MS); mathematics (MS, PhD); teaching of mathematics (MS). *Faculty:* 73 full-time (6 women), 7 part-time/adjunct (3 women). *Students:* 201 full-time (55 women); includes 15 minority (2 African Americans, 10 Asian Americans or Pacific Islanders, 3 Hispanic Americans), 122 international. 388 applicants, 13% accepted, 37 enrolled. In 2003, 42 master's, 23 doctorates awarded. *Degree requirements:* For doctorate, 2 foreign languages, thesis/dissertation. *Entrance requirements:* For master's, GRE, minimum GPA of 3.0. *Application deadline:* For fall admission, 1/15 for domestic students. Applications are processed on a rolling basis. Application fee: $40 ($50 for international students). Electronic applications accepted. *Expenses:* Tuition, state resident: full-time $6,692. Tuition, nonresident: full-time $18,692. *Financial support:* In 2003–04, 26 fellowships, 24 research assistantships, 113 teaching assistantships were awarded. Tuition waivers (full and partial) also available. Financial award application deadline: 2/15. *Unit head:* Joseph Rosenblatt, Chair, 217-333-3352, Fax: 217-333-9576, E-mail: jrsnbltt@math.uiuc.edu. *Application contact:* Lori Dick, Staff Secretary, 217-244-0539, Fax: 217-333-9576, E-mail: ldick@math.uiuc.edu.

The University of Iowa, Graduate College, Program in Applied Mathematical and Computational Sciences, Iowa City, IA 52242-1316. Offers PhD. *Students:* 12 full-time (5 women), 16 part-time (6 women); includes 8 minority (3 African Americans, 5 Hispanic Americans), 16 international. 41 applicants, 34% accepted, 4 enrolled. In 2003, 5 degrees awarded. *Degree requirements:* For doctorate, thesis/dissertation, comprehensive exam, registration. *Entrance requirements:* For doctorate, GRE General Test, minimum GPA of 3.0. Additional exam requirements/recommendations for international students: Required—TOEFL (minimum score 600 paper-based; 250 computer-based). *Application deadline:* For fall admission, 1/15 for domestic students, 1/15 for international students; for spring admission, 10/1 priority date for domestic students. Application fee: $50 ($75 for international students). Electronic applications accepted. *Expenses:* Tuition, state resident: full-time $5,038. Tuition, nonresident: full-time $15,072. Tuition and fees vary according to course load and program. *Financial support:* In 2003–04, 6 fellowships, 3 research assistantships, 21 teaching assistantships were awarded. Financial award applicants required to submit FAFSA. *Unit head:* Herbert W. Hethcote, Chair, 319-335-0790.

University of Kansas, Graduate School, College of Liberal Arts and Sciences, Department of Mathematics, Lawrence, KS 66045. Offers applied mathematics and statistics (MA, PhD); mathematics (MA, PhD). *Faculty:* 41. *Students:* 55 full-time (21 women), 12 part-time (5 women); includes 4 minority (1 American Indian/Alaska Native, 2 Asian Americans or Pacific Islanders, 1 Hispanic American), 29 international. Average age 29. 57 applicants, 49% accepted, 16 enrolled. In 2003, 10 master's, 4 doctorates awarded. Terminal master's awarded for partial completion of doctoral program. *Median time to degree:* Master's–2.5 years full-time; doctorate–5.5 years full-time. *Degree requirements:* For master's, thesis or alternative; for doctorate, 2 foreign languages, thesis/dissertation, comprehensive exam. *Entrance requirements:* For master's and doctorate, GRE. Additional exam requirements/recommendations for international students: Required—TOEFL. *Application deadline:* For fall admission, 3/1 priority date for domestic students, 3/1 priority date for international students. Applications are processed on a rolling basis. Application fee: $55 ($60 for international students). Electronic applications accepted. *Expenses:* Tuition, state resident: full-time $3,745. Tuition, nonresident: full-time $10,075. Required fees: $574. *Financial support:* In 2003–04, 2 research assistantships with full and partial tuition reimbursements (averaging $14,180 per year), 44 teaching assistantships with full and partial tuition reimbursements (averaging $14,845 per year) were awarded. Fellowships, institutionally sponsored loans also available. Support available to part-time students. Financial award application deadline: 2/1. *Faculty research:* Commutative algebra/algebraic geometry; stochastic adaptive control/stochastic processes analysis/harmonic analysis/PDES; numerical analysis/dynamical systems; topology/set theory. Total annual research expenditures: $801,000. *Unit head:* Jack Porter, Chair, 785-864-3651, Fax: 785-864-5255, E-mail: porter@math.ukans.edu. *Application contact:* David Lerner, Graduate Director, 785-864-3651, E-mail: lerner@ukans.edu.

University of Louisville, Graduate School, College of Arts and Sciences, Department of Mathematics, Louisville, KY 40292-0001. Offers applied and industrial mathematics (PhD); mathematics (MA). Evening/weekend programs available. *Students:* 28 full-time (10 women), 14 part-time (4 women); includes 2 minority (1 African American, 1 Asian American or Pacific Islander), 10 international. Average age 30. In 2003, 4 degrees awarded. *Degree requirements:* For master's, thesis optional; for doctorate, thesis/dissertation, internship, project, comprehensive exam. *Entrance requirements:* For master's and doctorate, GRE General Test. *Application deadline:* Applications are processed on a rolling basis. Application fee: $50. *Expenses:* Tuition, state resident: full-time $4,842. Tuition, nonresident: full-time $13,338. *Financial support:* In 2003–04, 25 teaching assistantships with full tuition reimbursements (averaging $12,500 per year) were awarded *Unit head:* Dr. Kevin Clancey, Chair, 502-852-5974, Fax: 802-852-7132, E-mail: kfclan01@louisville.edu. *Application contact:* Dr. Lee M. Larson, Graduate Studies Director, 502-852-6826, Fax: 502-852-7132, E-mail: llarson@louisville.edu.

University of Maryland, Baltimore County, Graduate School, Department of Mathematics and Statistics, Program in Applied Mathematics, Baltimore, MD 21250. Offers MS, PhD. Part-time and evening/weekend programs available. *Faculty:* 18 full-time (2 women). *Students:* 23 full-time (8 women), 16 part-time (7 women); includes 2 minority (both Asian Americans or Pacific Islanders), 15 international. Average age 23. 24 applicants, 50% accepted, 4 enrolled. In 2003, 2 master's awarded, leading to continued full-time study 50%, business/industry 50%; 1 doctorate awarded, leading to university research/teaching 100%. Terminal master's awarded for partial completion of doctoral program. *Median time to degree:* Master's–2 years full-time, 4 years part-time; doctorate–4 years full-time, 6 years part-time. Of those who began their doctoral program in fall 1995, 80% received their degree in 8 years or less. *Degree requirements:* For master's, thesis (for some programs), comprehensive exam (for some programs), registration; for doctorate, thesis/dissertation, comprehensive exam, registration. *Entrance requirements:* For master's and doctorate, GRE General Test, minimum GPA of 3.0. Additional exam requirements/recommendations for international students: Required—TOEFL. *Application deadline:* For fall admission, 2/15 priority date for domestic students, 1/1 priority date for international students; for spring admission, 10/15 priority date for domestic students, 9/15 priority date for international students. Applications are processed on a rolling basis. Application fee: $50. Electronic applications accepted. *Expenses:* Tuition, state resident: full-time $7,000. Tuition, nonresident: full-time $11,400. Required fees: $1,440. *Financial support:* In 2003–04, 22 students received support, including 4 research assistantships with full tuition reimbursements available (averaging $15,000 per year), 19 teaching assistantships with full tuition reimbursements available (averaging $15,000 per year); career-related internships or fieldwork, scholarships/grants, health care benefits, and unspecified assistantships also available. Support available to part-time students. Financial award application deadline: 2/15. *Faculty research:* Numerical analysis and scientific computation, optimization theory and algorithms, differential equations and mathematical modeling, mathematical biology and bioinformatics. Total annual research expenditures: $796,000. *Application contact:* Dr. Rouben Rostamian, Director of Graduate Programs, 410-455-2412, Fax: 410-455-1066, E-mail: rostamian@umbc.edu.

University of Maryland, College Park, Graduate Studies and Research, College of Computer, Mathematical and Physical Sciences, Department of Mathematics, Applied Mathematics Program, College Park, MD 20742. Offers MS, PhD. Part-time and evening/weekend programs available. *Students:* 81 full-time (21 women), 25 part-time (6 women); includes 18 minority (9 African Americans, 7 Asian Americans or Pacific Islanders, 2 Hispanic Americans), 45 international. 145 applicants, 37% accepted.Terminal master's awarded for partial completion of doctoral program. *Degree requirements:* For master's, seminar, scholarly paper, thesis optional; for doctorate, thesis/dissertation, exams, seminars, comprehensive exam. *Entrance requirements:* For master's, GRE General Test, GRE Subject Test, minimum GPA of 3.0, 3 letters of recommendation; for doctorate, GRE General Test, GRE Subject Test, minimum GPA of 3.0. *Application deadline:* For fall admission, 5/1 for domestic students, 2/1 for international students; for spring admission, 10/1 for domestic students, 6/1 for international students. Applications are processed on a rolling basis. Application fee: $50. Electronic applications accepted. *Expenses:* Tuition, state resident: part-time $349 per credit hour. Tuition, nonresident: part-time $602 per credit hour. *Financial support:* Fellowships, teaching assistantships available. Financial award applicants required to submit FAFSA. *Unit head:* Dr. David Levermore, Director, 301-405-5127, Fax: 301-314-8027. *Application contact:* Trudy Lindsey, Director, Graduate Enrollment Management Services, 301-405-4190, Fax: 301-314-9305, E-mail: tlindsey@gradschool.umd.edu.

University of Massachusetts Amherst, Graduate School, College of Natural Sciences and Mathematics, Department of Mathematics and Statistics, Program in Applied Mathematics, Amherst, MA 01003. Offers MS. *Students:* 11 full-time (5 women); includes 1 minority (Asian American or Pacific Islander), 5 international. Average age 25. 29 applicants, 31% accepted, 5 enrolled. In 2003, 1 degree awarded. *Entrance requirements:* Additional exam requirements/recommendations for international students: Required—TOEFL (minimum score 530 paper-based; 197 computer-based). *Application deadline:* For fall admission, 2/1 priority date for domestic students, 2/1 priority date for international students. Applications are processed on a rolling basis. Application fee: $40 ($50 for international students). *Expenses:* Tuition, state resident: full-time $1,320; part-time $110 per credit. Tuition, nonresident: full-time $4,969; part-time $414 per credit. Required fees: $2,626 per term. Tuition and fees vary according to course load. *Financial support:* Fellowships with full tuition reimbursements, research assistantships with full tuition reimbursements, teaching assistantships with full tuition reimbursements, career-related internships or fieldwork, Federal Work-Study, scholarships/grants, traineeships, and unspecified assistantships available. Support available to part-time students. Financial award application deadline: 2/1. *Unit head:* Dr. Eduardo Cattani, Director, 413-545-2282, Fax: 413-545-1801, E-mail: cattani@math.umass.edu.

University of Massachusetts Lowell, Graduate School, College of Arts and Sciences, Department of Mathematics, Lowell, MA 01854-2881. Offers applied mathematics (MS); computational mathematics (PhD); mathematics (MS). Part-time programs available. *Entrance requirements:* For master's, GRE General Test.

The University of Memphis, Graduate School, College of Arts and Sciences, Department of Mathematical Sciences, Memphis, TN 38152-3420. Offers applied mathematics (MS); applied statistics (PhD); bioinformatics (MS); computer science (PhD); computer sciences (MS); mathematics (MS, PhD); statistics (MS, PhD). Part-time programs available. *Faculty:* 24 full-time (5 women), 3 part-time/adjunct (0 women). *Students:* 106 full-time (40 women), 42 part-time (15 women); includes 8 minority (5 African Americans, 3 Asian Americans or Pacific Islanders), 108 international. Average age 30. 139 applicants, 37% accepted. In 2003, 31 master's, 8 doctorates awarded. Terminal master's awarded for partial completion of doctoral program. *Median time to degree:* Master's–2 years full-time, 4 years part-time; doctorate–2 years full-time, 4 years part-time. *Degree requirements:* For master's, comprehensive exam; for doctorate, one foreign language, thesis/dissertation, oral exams. *Entrance requirements:* For master's and doctorate, GRE General Test, minimum GPA of 2.5. Additional exam requirements/recommendations for international students: Required—TOEFL (minimum score 550 paper-based; 210 computer-based), WES evaluation of transcript. *Application deadline:* For fall admission, 8/1 for domestic students, 5/1 for international students; for spring admission, 12/1 for domestic students, 9/1 for international students. Applications are processed on a rolling basis. Application fee: $25 ($50 for international students). Electronic applications accepted. *Expenses:* Tuition, state resident: full-time $5,142. Tuition, nonresident: full-time $13,296. *Financial support:* In 2003–04, 58 students received support, including fellowships with full tuition reimbursements available (averaging $17,500 per year), 9 research assistantships with full tuition reimbursements available (averaging $9,000 per year), 30 teaching assistantships with full tuition reimbursements available (averaging $9,000 per year); career-related internships or fieldwork, Federal Work-Study, scholarships/grants, unspecified assistantships, and minority scholarships also available. Financial award application deadline: 2/2. *Faculty research:* Combinatorics, ergodic theory, graph theory, Ramsey theory, applied statistics. Total annual research expenditures: $1.5 million. *Unit head:* Dr. James E. Jamison, Chairman, 901-678-2482, Fax: 901-678-2480, E-mail: jjamison@memphis.edu. *Application contact:* Coordinator of Graduate Studies, 901-678-2482, Fax: 901-678-2480, E-mail: dfwilson@memphis.edu.

University of Michigan–Dearborn, College of Arts, Sciences, and Letters, Program in Applied and Computational Mathematics, Dearborn, MI 48128-1491. Offers MS. Part-time and evening/weekend programs available. *Faculty:* 2 full-time (0 women), 8 part-time/adjunct (3 women). *Students:* 2 full-time (1 woman), 10 part-time (6 women), 2 international. Average age 31. 5 applicants, 100% accepted, 3 enrolled. In 2003, 3 degrees awarded. *Median time to degree:* Master's–2 years part-time. *Degree requirements:* For master's, thesis or alternative. *Entrance requirements:* For master's, 3 letters of recommendation, minimum GPA of 3.0, 2 years of math. *Application deadline:* For fall admission, 8/1 for domestic students; for winter admission, 12/1 for domestic students; for spring admission, 4/1 for domestic students. Applications are processed on a rolling basis. Application fee: $60 ($75 for international students). Electronic applications accepted. *Expenses:* Tuition, state resident: part-time $357 per credit hour. Tuition, nonresident: part-time $820 per credit hour. Required fees: $107. *Financial support:* Federal Work-Study and scholarships/grants available. Support available to part-time students. Financial award application deadline: 4/1; financial award applicants required to submit FAFSA. *Faculty research:* Partial differential equations, statistics, discrete optimization, approximation theory. *Unit head:* Dr. Frank Massey, Director, 313-593-5198, E-mail: fmassey@umd.umich.edu. *Application contact:* Carol Ligienza, Administrative Assistant, 313-593-1183, Fax: 313-593-5552, E-mail: cligienz@umd.umich.edu.

University of Minnesota, Duluth, Graduate School, College of Science and Engineering, Department of Mathematics and Statistics, Duluth, MN 55812-2496. Offers applied and computational mathematics (MS). Part-time programs available. *Faculty:* 16 full-time (3 women). *Students:* 25 full-time (11 women), 13 international. Average age 24. 25 applicants, 80% accepted, 11 enrolled. In 2003, 9 degrees awarded, leading to university research/teaching 20%, continued full-time study60%, business/industry 20%. *Median time to degree:* Master's–2 years full-time, 6 years part-time. *Degree requirements:* For master's, thesis or alternative. *Entrance requirements:* For master's, GRE General Test, minimum GPA of 3.0. Additional exam requirements/recommendations for international students: Required—TOEFL (minimum score 550 paper-based; 213 computer-based); Recommended—TWE, TSE. *Application deadline:* For fall admission, 3/1 priority date for domestic students, 3/1 priority date for international students; for spring admission, 11/15 for domestic students, 9/1 for international students. Applications are processed on a rolling basis. Application fee: $55 ($75 for international students). *Expenses:* Tuition, state resident: part-time $614 per credit. Tuition, nonresident: part-time $1,205 per credit. *Financial support:* In 2003–04, 6 research assistantships with full tuition reimbursements (averaging $11,154 per year), 20 teaching assistantships with full tuition reimbursements (averaging $11,154 per year) were awarded. Fellowships, scholarships/grants, health care benefits, unspecified assistantships, and summer fellowships also available. Financial award application deadline: 3/1. *Faculty research:* Discrete mathematics, diagnostic markers, combinatorics, biostatistics, mathematical modeling and scientific computation. Total annual research expenditures: $137,193. *Unit head:* Dr. Zhuangyi Liu, Director of Graduate Studies, 218-726-7179, Fax: 218-726-8399, E-mail: zliu@d.umn.edu.

Announcement: The program prepares graduates for jobs in industry, government, and teaching, as well as for subsequent PhD studies. Computational facilities are excellent. Faculty research includes graph theory, combinatorics, number theory, scientific computation, dynamical systems, control theory, numerical methods, statistics, biostatistics, and probability.

University of Missouri–Columbia, Graduate School, College of Arts and Sciences, Department of Mathematics, Program in Applied Mathematics, Columbia, MO 65211. Offers MS. *Students:* 10 full-time (4 women); includes 1 minority (African American), 3 international. In

Applied Mathematics

University of Missouri–Columbia (continued)
2003, 11 degrees awarded. *Degree requirements:* For master's, thesis. *Entrance requirements:* For master's, GRE General Test, minimum GPA of 3.0. *Application deadline:* Applications are processed on a rolling basis. Application fee: $45 ($60 for international students). *Expenses:* Tuition, state resident: full-time $5,205. Tuition, nonresident: full-time $14,058. *Financial support:* Fellowships, research assistantships, teaching assistantships, institutionally sponsored loans available. *Unit head:* Dr. Yuri Latushkin, Director of Graduate Studies, Department of Mathematics, 573-882-8275, E-mail: yuri@math.missouri.edu.

University of Missouri–Rolla, Graduate School, College of Arts and Sciences, Department of Mathematics and Statistics, Program in Applied Mathematics, Rolla, MO 65409-0910. Offers MS. *Students:* 8 full-time (4 women), 3 part-time (1 woman); includes 2 minority (1 African American, 1 Asian American or Pacific Islander), 3 international. Average age 30. 13 applicants, 46% accepted, 3 enrolled. In 2003, 12 degrees awarded. *Median time to degree:* Master's–3 years full-time. *Degree requirements:* For master's, thesis or alternative. *Entrance requirements:* For master's, GRE General Test, GRE Subject Test. *Application deadline:* For fall admission, 7/1 for domestic students. Applications are processed on a rolling basis. Application fee: $50. Electronic applications accepted. *Expenses:* Tuition, state resident: full-time $5,871. Tuition, nonresident: full-time $13,114. Required fees: $820. Tuition and fees vary according to course load. *Financial support:* In 2003–04, 12 teaching assistantships with partial tuition reimbursements (averaging $12,985 per year) were awarded; fellowships, research assistantships, institutionally sponsored loans also available. *Faculty research:* Analysis, differential equations, statistics, topological dynamics. *Application contact:* Dr. V. A. Samaranayake, Director of Graduate Studies, 573-341-4658, Fax: 573-341-4741, E-mail: vsam@umr.edu.

University of Missouri–St. Louis, Graduate School, College of Arts and Sciences, Department of Mathematical Sciences, St. Louis, MO 63121-4499. Offers applied mathematics (MA, PhD); computer science (MS); telecommunications science (Certificate). Part-time and evening/weekend programs available. *Faculty:* 15 full-time (0 women). *Students:* 36 full-time (13 women), 75 part-time (29 women); includes 20 minority (1 African American, 1 American Indian/Alaska Native, 18 Asian Americans or Pacific Islanders), 35 international. In 2003, 43 degrees awarded. *Degree requirements:* For master's, thesis optional; for doctorate, thesis/dissertation. *Entrance requirements:* For master's, GRE if no BS in computer science; for doctorate, GRE General Test. Additional exam requirements/recommendations for international students: Required—TOEFL (minimum score 550 paper-based; 213 computer-based). *Application deadline:* For fall admission, 5/1 for domestic students; for spring admission, 12/1 for domestic students. Applications are processed on a rolling basis. Application fee: $35 ($40 for international students). Electronic applications accepted. *Expenses:* Tuition, state resident: part-time $237 per credit hour. Tuition, nonresident: part-time $639 per credit hour. Required fees: $10 per credit hour. *Financial support:* In 2003–04, 9 teaching assistantships with full and partial tuition reimbursements (averaging $13,500 per year) were awarded; fellowships with full tuition reimbursements, research assistantships with full tuition reimbursements *Faculty research:* Applied mathematics, statistics, algebra, analysis, computer science. *Unit head:* Dr. Haiyun Cai, Director of Graduate Studies, 314-516-5741, Fax: 314-516-5400, E-mail: caih@msx.umsl.edu. *Application contact:* 314-516-5458, Fax: 314-516-5310, E-mail: gradadm@umsl.edu.

University of Nevada, Las Vegas, Graduate College, College of Science, Department of Mathematical Sciences, Las Vegas, NV 89154-9900. Offers applied mathematics (MS); applied statistics (MS); pure mathematics (MS). Part-time programs available. *Faculty:* 28 full-time (6 women). *Students:* 28 full-time (9 women), 21 part-time (9 women); includes 12 minority (1 African American, 7 Asian Americans or Pacific Islanders, 4 Hispanic Americans), 16 international. 35 applicants, 69% accepted, 16 enrolled. In 2003, 8 degrees awarded. *Degree requirements:* For master's, thesis (for some programs), oral exam, comprehensive exam (for some programs). *Entrance requirements:* For master's, minimum GPA of 3.0 during previous 2 years, 2.75 overall. Additional exam requirements/recommendations for international students: Required—TOEFL (minimum score 550 paper-based; 213 computer-based). *Application deadline:* For fall admission, 6/15 for domestic students, 5/1 for international students; for spring admission, 11/15 for domestic students, 10/1 for international students. Application fee: $60 ($75 for international students). *Expenses:* Tuition, state resident: part-time $115 per credit. Tuition, nonresident: part-time $242 per credit. Required fees: $8 per semester. Tuition and fees vary according to course load. *Financial support:* In 2003–04, 36 teaching assistantships with partial tuition reimbursements (averaging $10,000 per year) were awarded. Financial award application deadline: 3/1. *Unit head:* Dr. Dieudonne Phanord, Head, 702-895-3567. *Application contact:* Graduate College Admissions Evaluator, 702-895-3320, Fax: 702-895-4180, E-mail: gradcollege@ccmail.nevada.edu.

University of New Hampshire, Graduate School, College of Engineering and Physical Sciences, Department of Mathematics and Statistics, Durham, NH 03824. Offers applied mathematics (MS); mathematics (MS, MST, PhD); mathematics education (PhD); statistics (MS). *Faculty:* 26 full-time. *Students:* 18 full-time (6 women), 30 part-time (12 women); includes 2 minority (1 African American, 1 Hispanic American), 17 international. Average age 28. 39 applicants, 79% accepted, 11 enrolled. In 2003, 16 master's, 1 doctorate awarded. Terminal master's awarded for partial completion of doctoral program. *Degree requirements:* For doctorate, 2 foreign languages, thesis/dissertation. *Entrance requirements:* Additional exam requirements/recommendations for international students: Required—TOEFL (minimum score 550 paper-based; 213 computer-based); Recommended—TSE. *Application deadline:* For fall admission, 4/1 for domestic students; for winter admission, 12/1 for domestic students. Applications are processed on a rolling basis. Application fee: $50. Electronic applications accepted. Tuition, area resident: Full-time $7,070. *Expenses:* Tuition, state resident: full-time $10,605. Tuition, nonresident: full-time $17,430. Required fees: $15. *Financial support:* In 2003–04, 1 fellowship, 27 teaching assistantships were awarded. Research assistantships, Federal Work-Study, scholarships/grants, and tuition waivers (full and partial) also available. Support available to part-time students. Financial award application deadline: 2/15. *Faculty research:* Operator theory, complex analysis, algebra, nonlinear dynamics, statistics. *Unit head:* Dr. Eric Grinberg, Chairperson, 603-862-2320. *Application contact:* Jan Jankawski, Graduate Coordinator, 603-862-2688, E-mail: janj@cisunix.unh.edu.

The University of North Carolina at Charlotte, Graduate School, College of Arts and Sciences, Department of Mathematics, Program in Applied Math, Charlotte, NC 28223-0001. Offers MS, PhD. *Students:* 25 full-time (5 women), 10 part-time (2 women); includes 4 minority (3 African Americans, 1 Asian American or Pacific Islander), 22 international. Average age 33. 6 applicants, 100% accepted, 5 enrolled. In 2003, 1 degree awarded. *Degree requirements:* For doctorate, thesis/dissertation. *Entrance requirements:* For doctorate, GRE General Test. Additional exam requirements/recommendations for international students: Required—TOEFL (minimum score 557 paper-based; 220 computer-based). *Application deadline:* For fall admission, 7/15 for domestic students, 5/1 for international students; for spring admission, 11/15 for domestic students, 10/1 for international students. Application fee: $35. Electronic applications accepted. *Expenses:* Tuition, state resident: full-time $1,979. Tuition, nonresident: full-time $12,111. Required fees: $1,201. Tuition and fees vary according to course load. *Financial support:* In 2003–04, 3 teaching assistantships (averaging $14,413 per year) were awarded; fellowships, research assistantships, career-related internships or fieldwork, Federal Work-Study, institutionally sponsored loans, scholarships/grants, and unspecified assistantships also available. Support available to part-time students. Financial award application deadline: 4/1; financial award applicants required to submit FAFSA. *Unit head:* Dr. Joel D. Avrin, Director, 704-687-4929, Fax: 704-687-0415, E-mail: jdavrin@email.uncc.edu. *Application contact:* Kathy B. Giddings, Director of Graduate Admissions, 704-687-3366, Fax: 704-687-3279, E-mail: gradadm@email.uncc.edu.

University of Notre Dame, Graduate School, College of Science, Department of Mathematics, Notre Dame, IN 46556. Offers algebra (PhD); algebraic geometry (PhD); applied mathematics (MSAM); complex analysis (PhD); differential geometry (PhD); logic (PhD); partial differential equations (PhD); topology (PhD). *Faculty:* 45 full-time (5 women). *Students:* 40 full-time (14 women). 153 applicants, 12% accepted, 6 enrolled. In 2003, 2 master's, 4 doctorates awarded. Terminal master's awarded for partial completion of doctoral program. *Degree requirements:* For doctorate, one foreign language, thesis/dissertation, qualifying exam. *Entrance requirements:* For master's and doctorate, GRE General Test, GRE Subject Test. Additional exam requirements/recommendations for international students: Required—TOEFL. *Application deadline:* For fall admission, 2/1 for domestic students. Applications are processed on a rolling basis. Application fee: $50. Electronic applications accepted. *Expenses:* Tuition: Full-time $29,375. *Financial support:* In 2003–04, 37 students received support, including 4 fellowships with full tuition reimbursements available (averaging $20,000 per year), 4 research assistantships with full tuition reimbursements available (averaging $12,000 per year), 29 teaching assistantships with full tuition reimbursements available (averaging $17,500 per year); tuition waivers (full) also available. Financial award application deadline: 2/1. *Faculty research:* Algebra, analysis, geometry/topology, logic, applied math. Total annual research expenditures: $1.5 million. *Unit head:* Dr. Julia Knight, Director of Graduate Studies, 574-631-7484, E-mail: mathgrad@nd.edu. *Application contact:* Dr. Terrence J. Akai, Director of Graduate Admissions, 574-631-7706, Fax: 574-631-4183, E-mail: gradad@nd.edu.

See in-depth description on page 607.

University of Pittsburgh, School of Arts and Sciences, Department of Mathematics, Pittsburgh, PA 15260. Offers applied mathematics (MA, MS); financial mathematics (PMS); mathematics (MA, MS, PhD). Part-time programs available. *Faculty:* 35 full-time (5 women), 13 part-time/adjunct (5 women). *Students:* 66 full-time (27 women), 10 part-time (3 women); includes 4 minority (3 African Americans, 1 Asian American or Pacific Islander), 30 international. 167 applicants, 42% accepted, 23 enrolled. In 2003, 8 master's, 5 doctorates awarded, leading to university research/teaching 100%. Terminal master's awarded for partial completion of doctoral program. *Median time to degree:* Doctorate–6 years full-time, 9.5 years part-time. *Degree requirements:* For master's, thesis (for some programs), comprehensive exam; for doctorate, thesis/dissertation, preliminary exams, comprehensive exam. *Entrance requirements:* For master's and doctorate, GRE General Test, GRE Subject Test (recommended), minimum GPA of 3.0. Additional exam requirements/recommendations for international students: Required—TOEFL (minimum score 550 paper-based; 213 computer-based). *Application deadline:* For fall admission, 1/15 priority date for domestic students, 1/15 priority date for international students; for spring admission, 9/1 for domestic students, 9/1 for international students. Applications are processed on a rolling basis. Application fee: $40. Electronic applications accepted. *Expenses:* Tuition, state resident: full-time $11,744; part-time $479 per credit. Tuition, nonresident: full-time $22,910; part-time $941 per credit. Required fees: $560. Tuition and fees vary according to degree level and program. *Financial support:* In 2003–04, 61 students received support, including 6 fellowships with full and partial tuition reimbursements available (averaging $14,700 per year), 6 research assistantships with full and partial tuition reimbursements available (averaging $12,400 per year), 48 teaching assistantships with full and partial tuition reimbursements available (averaging $12,775 per year); Federal Work-Study, institutionally sponsored loans, scholarships/grants, tuition waivers (partial), and unspecified assistantships also available. Financial award application deadline: 1/15. *Faculty research:* Computational math, mathbiology, math finance, algebra, analysis. Total annual research expenditures: $700,000. *Unit head:* John Chadam, Chairman, 412-624-8361, Fax: 412-624-8397, E-mail: chadam@pitt.edu. *Application contact:* Molly Williams, Administrator, 412-624-1175, Fax: 412-624-8397, E-mail: mollyw@pitt.edu.

University of Puerto Rico, Mayagüez Campus, Graduate Studies, College of Arts and Sciences, Department of Mathematics, Mayagüez, PR 00681-9000. Offers applied mathematics (MS); computational sciences (MS); pure mathematics (MS); statistics (MS). Part-time programs available. *Degree requirements:* For master's, one foreign language, comprehensive exam. *Faculty research:* Automata theory, linear algebra, logic.

University of Rhode Island, Graduate School, College of Business Administration, Kingston, RI 02881. Offers accounting (MS); applied mathematics (PhD); finance (MBA); international business (MBA); international sports management (MBA); management (MBA); management science (MBA), including management information systems, manufacturing; marketing (MBA). *Accreditation:* AACSB. In 2003, 86 master's, 1 doctorate awarded. *Entrance requirements:* For master's and doctorate, GMAT. Additional exam requirements/recommendations for international students: Required—TOEFL. *Application deadline:* For fall admission, 4/15 for domestic students. Applications are processed on a rolling basis. Application fee: $35. *Expenses:* Tuition, state resident: full-time $4,338; part-time $281 per credit. Tuition, nonresident: full-time $12,438; part-time $704 per credit. Required fees: $1,840. *Financial support:* Unspecified assistantships available. *Unit head:* Dr. Edward Mazze, Dean, 401-874-2337. *Application contact:* Dr. Laura Beauvais, Director of Graduate Programs, 401-874-2377.

University of Southern California, Graduate School, College of Letters, Arts and Sciences, Department of Mathematics, Program in Applied Mathematics, Los Angeles, CA 90089. Offers MA, MS, PhD. *Students:* 40 full-time (14 women), 8 part-time (1 woman); includes 2 minority (both Hispanic Americans), 39 international. In 2003, 14 master's, 3 doctorates awarded. *Degree requirements:* For master's, thesis (for some programs); for doctorate, 2 foreign languages, thesis/dissertation. *Entrance requirements:* For master's and doctorate, GRE General Test. *Application deadline:* For fall admission, 12/15 for domestic students; for spring admission, 11/1 priority date for domestic students. Applications are processed on a rolling basis. Application fee: $65 ($75 for international students). *Expenses:* Tuition: Full-time $32,784; part-time $949 per unit. Tuition and fees vary according to course load and program. *Financial support:* In 2003–04, research assistantships with tuition reimbursements (averaging $16,000 per year), teaching assistantships with tuition reimbursements (averaging $16,000 per year) were awarded. Fellowships with tuition reimbursements, career-related internships or fieldwork, Federal Work-Study, institutionally sponsored loans, and scholarships/grants also available. Support available to part-time students. Financial award application deadline: 2/15; financial award applicants required to submit FAFSA.

University of South Florida, College of Graduate Studies, College of Arts and Sciences, Department of Mathematics, Tampa, FL 33620-9951. Offers applied mathematics (PhD); mathematics (MA, PhD). Part-time and evening/weekend programs available. *Faculty:* 34 full-time (2 women). *Students:* 55 full-time (23 women), 17 part-time (8 women); includes 10 minority (1 African American, 6 Asian Americans or Pacific Islanders, 3 Hispanic Americans), 32 international. 78 applicants, 38% accepted, 21 enrolled. In 2003, 2 degrees awarded. Terminal master's awarded for partial completion of doctoral program. *Degree requirements:* For master's, one foreign language, thesis optional; for doctorate, 2 foreign languages, thesis/dissertation. *Entrance requirements:* For master's, GRE General Test, minimum GPA of 3.0 in mathematics course work (undergraduate), 3.5 (graduate); for doctorate, GRE General Test. *Application deadline:* For fall admission, 6/1 for domestic students; for spring admission, 10/15 for domestic students. Application fee: $30. Electronic applications accepted. *Financial support:* In 2003–04, 48 students received support, including 34 teaching assistantships with full tuition reimbursements available (averaging $12,290 per year); unspecified assistantships also available. Financial award application deadline: 3/1. *Faculty research:* Approximation theory, differential equations, discrete mathematics, functional analysis topology. Total annual research expenditures: $129,212. *Unit head:* Marcus McWaters, Chairperson, 813-974-9530, Fax: 813-974-2700, E-mail: marcus@chuma.cas.usf.edu. *Application contact:* James Tremmel, Graduate Program Assistant, 813-974-5329, Fax: 813-974-2700, E-mail: ga@math.usf.edu.

The University of Tennessee, Graduate School, College of Arts and Sciences, Department of Mathematics, Knoxville, TN 37996. Offers applied mathematics (MS); mathematical ecology (PhD); mathematics (M Math, MS, PhD). Part-time programs available. *Degree requirements:* For master's, thesis or alternative; for doctorate, one foreign language, thesis/dissertation. *Entrance requirements:* For master's and doctorate, minimum GPA of 2.7. Additional exam requirements/recommendations for international students: Required—TOEFL. Electronic applications accepted.

The University of Tennessee Space Institute, Graduate Programs, Program in Applied Mathematics, Tullahoma, TN 37388-9700. Offers MS. Part-time programs available. *Faculty:* 2 full-time (0 women), 1 part-time/adjunct (0 women). *Students:* 1 full-time (0 women), 1 (woman) part-time, 1 international. 1 applicant, 0% accepted. *Degree requirements:* For master's, thesis (for some programs). *Entrance requirements:* Additional exam requirements/recommendations for international students: Required—TOEFL (minimum score 550 paper-based; 213 computer-based). *Application deadline:* Applications are processed on a rolling basis. Application fee: $35. *Expenses:* Tuition, state resident: full-time $5,828; part-time $243 per semester hour. Tuition, nonresident: full-time $17,612; part-time $735 per semester hour. Required fees: $10 per semester hour. Tuition and fees vary according to course load. *Financial support:* Fellowships with full and partial tuition reimbursements, research assistantships with full tuition reimbursements, career-related internships or fieldwork, Federal Work-Study, tuition waivers (partial), and unspecified assistantships available. Financial award applicants required to submit FAFSA. *Unit head:* Dr. Ken Kimble, Degree Program Chairman, 931-393-7484, Fax: 931-393-7542, E-mail: kkimble@utsi.edu. *Application contact:* Dr. Alfonso Pujol, Assistant Vice President and Dean for Student Affairs, 931-393-7432, Fax: 931-393-7346, E-mail: apujol@utsi.edu.

The University of Texas at Austin, Graduate School, Program in Computational and Applied Mathematics, Austin, TX 78712-1111. Offers MA, PhD. Terminal master's awarded for partial completion of doctoral program. *Degree requirements:* For master's, thesis optional; for doctorate, thesis/dissertation, 3 area qualifying exams. Electronic applications accepted.

The University of Texas at Dallas, School of Natural Sciences and Mathematics, Programs in Mathematical Sciences, Richardson, TX 75083-0688. Offers applied mathematics (MS, PhD); engineering mathematics (MS); mathematical science (MS); statistics (MS, PhD). Part-time and evening/weekend programs available. *Faculty:* 10 full-time (1 woman), 2 part-time/adjunct (0 women). *Students:* 37 full-time (13 women), 19 part-time (8 women); includes 14 minority (5 African Americans, 7 Asian Americans or Pacific Islanders, 2 Hispanic Americans), 20 international. Average age 33. 118 applicants, 58% accepted. In 2003, 13 master's, 3 doctorates awarded. *Degree requirements:* For master's, thesis optional; for doctorate, thesis/dissertation. *Entrance requirements:* For master's, GRE General Test, minimum GPA of 3.0 in upper-level course work in field; for doctorate, GRE General Test, minimum GPA of 3.5 in upper-level course work in field. Additional exam requirements/recommendations for international students: Required—TOEFL (minimum score 550 paper-based; 213 computer-based). *Application deadline:* For fall admission, 7/15 for domestic students; for spring admission, 11/15 for domestic students. Applications are processed on a rolling basis. Application fee: $50 ($100 for international students). Electronic applications accepted. *Expenses:* Tuition, state resident: full-time $1,656; part-time $92 per credit. Tuition, nonresident: full-time $5,904; part-time $328 per credit. Required fees: $2,161; $275 per credit. $334 per term. *Financial support:* In 2003–04, 1 research assistantship (averaging $6,975 per year), 29 teaching assistantships with tuition reimbursements (averaging $5,625 per year) were awarded. Fellowships, career-related internships or fieldwork, Federal Work-Study, institutionally sponsored loans, and scholarships/grants also available. Support available to part-time students. Financial award application deadline: 4/30; financial award applicants required to submit FAFSA. *Faculty research:* Statistical methods, control theory, mathematical modeling and analyses of biological and physical systems. Total annual research expenditures: $151,159. *Unit head:* Dr. M. Ali Hooshyar, Head, 972-883-2171, Fax: 972-883-6622, E-mail: utdmath@utdallas.edu. *Application contact:* Joan Gladwell, Information Contact, 972-883-6432, Fax: 972-883-6622, E-mail: gladwell@utdallas.edu.

See in-depth description on page 613.

The University of Texas at San Antonio, College of Sciences, Department of Applied Mathematics, San Antonio, TX 78249-0617. Offers mathematics (MS), including mathematics education. Part-time and evening/weekend programs available. *Faculty:* 10 full-time (2 women). *Students:* 25 full-time (6 women), 42 part-time (21 women); includes 31 minority (3 African Americans, 5 Asian Americans or Pacific Islanders, 23 Hispanic Americans), 8 international. Average age 33. 37 applicants, 100% accepted, 28 enrolled. In 2003, 6 degrees awarded. *Degree requirements:* For master's, thesis optional. *Entrance requirements:* For master's, GRE General Test, minimum GPA of 3.0 in last 60 hours. Additional exam requirements/recommendations for international students: Required—TOEFL (minimum score 500 paper-based; 173 computer-based). *Application deadline:* For fall admission, 7/1 for domestic students, 4/1 for international students; for spring admission, 11/1 for domestic students, 9/1 for international students. Applications are processed on a rolling basis. Application fee: $40 ($75 for international students). Electronic applications accepted. *Expenses:* Tuition, state resident: part-time $153 per hour. Tuition, nonresident: part-time $625 per hour. *Financial support:* Research assistantships, teaching assistantships available. Total annual research expenditures: $177,065. *Unit head:* Dr. Lucio Tavernini, Interim Chair, 210-458-4451, Fax: 210-458-4439, E-mail: ltavernini@utsa.edu.

University of Toledo, Graduate School, College of Arts and Sciences, Department of Mathematics, Toledo, OH 43606-3390. Offers applied mathematics (MS); mathematics (MA, PhD); statistics (MS). Part-time programs available. *Students:* 32 full-time (12 women), 11 part-time (3 women), 32 international. Average age 29. 74 applicants, 53% accepted. In 2003, 19 master's, 1 doctorate awarded. *Degree requirements:* For doctorate, 2 foreign languages, thesis/dissertation. *Entrance requirements:* For master's and doctorate, GRE General Test, GRE Subject Test. *Application deadline:* For fall admission, 8/1 for domestic students. Application fee: $40. Electronic applications accepted. Tuition, area resident: Part-time $3,817 per semester. *Expenses:* Tuition, state resident: part-time $8,177 per semester. Required fees: $502 per semester. *Financial support:* In 2003–04, 6 research assistantships, 27 teaching assistantships were awarded. Federal Work-Study and institutionally sponsored loans also available. Support available to part-time students. Financial award application deadline: 4/1; financial award applicants required to submit FAFSA. *Faculty research:* Topology. *Unit head:* Dr. Geoffrey Martin, Chair, 419-530-2569, Fax: 419-530-4720. *Application contact:* Dr. Robert Ochs, Advising Coordinator, 419-530-2069, Fax: 419-530-4720, E-mail: rochs@math.utoledo.edu.

See in-depth description on page 617.

University of Victoria, Faculty of Graduate Studies, Faculty of Science, Department of Mathematics and Statistics, Victoria, BC V8W 2Y2, Canada. Offers applied mathematics (M Sc, MA, PhD); pure mathematics (M Sc, MA, PhD); statistics (M Sc, MA). Part-time programs available. *Degree requirements:* For doctorate, one foreign language, thesis/dissertation, 3 qualifying exams. *Entrance requirements:* Additional exam requirements/recommendations for international students: Required—TOEFL. *Faculty research:* Functional analysis and operator theory, applied ordinary and partial differential equations, discrete mathematics and graph theory.

University of Washington, Graduate School, College of Arts and Sciences, Department of Applied Mathematics, Seattle, WA 98195. Offers MS, PhD. Terminal master's awarded for partial completion of doctoral program. *Degree requirements:* For master's, thesis optional; for doctorate, thesis/dissertation. *Entrance requirements:* For master's and doctorate, GRE, minimum GPA of 3.0. Additional exam requirements/recommendations for international students: Required—TOEFL. Electronic applications accepted. *Faculty research:* Mathematical modeling for physical, biological, social, and engineering sciences; development of mathematical methods for analysis, including perturbation, asymptotic, transform, vocational, and numerical methods.

University of Waterloo, Graduate Studies, Faculty of Mathematics, Department of Applied Mathematics, Waterloo, ON N2L 3G1, Canada. Offers M Math, PhD. Part-time programs available. *Faculty:* 20 full-time (4 women), 22 part-time/adjunct (1 woman). *Students:* 28 full-time (7 women). 73 applicants, 22% accepted, 6 enrolled. In 2003, 1 master's, 3 doctorates awarded. *Degree requirements:* For master's, research paper or thesis; for doctorate, thesis/dissertation. *Entrance requirements:* For master's, honors degree in field, minimum B+ average; for doctorate, master's degree, minimum B+ average. Additional exam requirements/recommendations for international students: Required—TOEFL (minimum score 600 paper-based; 250 computer-based), TWE(minimum score 4). *Application deadline:* For fall admission, 3/1 for domestic students. Applications are processed on a rolling basis. Application fee: $75 Canadian dollars. Electronic applications accepted. Tuition and fees charges are reported in Canadian dollars. *Expenses:* Tuition, state resident: full-time $3,632 Canadian dollars. International tuition: $9,180 Canadian dollars full-time. Required fees: $406 Canadian dollars. *Financial support:* Research assistantships, teaching assistantships available. *Faculty research:* Differential equations, quantum theory, statistical mechanics, fluid mechanics, relativity, control theory. *Unit head:* Dr. S. P. Lipshitz, Associate Chair, 519-888-4567 Ext. 6246, Fax: 519-746-4319, E-mail: spl@audiolab.uwaterloo.ca. *Application contact:* Helen A. Warren, Graduate Secretary, 519-888-4567 Ext. 3170, Fax: 519-746-4319, E-mail: amgrad@math.uwaterloo.ca.

The University of Western Ontario, Faculty of Graduate Studies, Physical Sciences Division, Department of Applied Mathematics, London, ON N6A 5B8, Canada. Offers applied mathematics (M Sc, PhD); theoretical physics (PhD). *Degree requirements:* For master's, thesis or alternative; for doctorate, thesis/dissertation, comprehensive exam. *Entrance requirements:* For master's and doctorate, minimum B average. *Faculty research:* Fluid dynamics, mathematical and computational methods, theoretical physics.

Utah State University, School of Graduate Studies, College of Science, Department of Mathematics and Statistics, Logan, UT 84322. Offers industrial mathematics (MS); mathematical sciences (PhD); mathematics (M Math, MS); statistics (MS). Part-time programs available. *Faculty:* 30 full-time (5 women). *Students:* 30 full-time (12 women), 6 part-time, 24 international. Average age 29. 68 applicants, 19% accepted, 8 enrolled. In 2003, 9 degrees awarded. Terminal master's awarded for partial completion of doctoral program. *Degree requirements:* For master's, qualifying exam, thesis optional; for doctorate, one foreign language, thesis/dissertation, comprehensive exam. *Entrance requirements:* For master's and doctorate, GRE General Test, minimum GPA of 3.0. Additional exam requirements/recommendations for international students: Required—TOEFL. *Application deadline:* For fall admission, 6/15 for domestic students; for spring admission, 10/15 for domestic students. Applications are processed on a rolling basis. Application fee: $50 ($60 for international students). *Expenses:* Tuition, state resident: part-time $270 per credit hour. Tuition, nonresident: part-time $946 per credit hour. Required fees: $173 per credit hour. *Financial support:* In 2003–04, 1 fellowship with partial tuition reimbursement (averaging $12,000 per year), 17 teaching assistantships with partial tuition reimbursements (averaging $14,500 per year) were awarded. Research assistantships with partial tuition reimbursements Support available to part-time students. Financial award application deadline: 4/1. *Faculty research:* Differential equations, computational mathematics, dynamical systems, probability and statistics, pure mathematics. *Unit head:* Dr. Russell C. Thompson, Head, 435-797-2810, Fax: 435-797-1822, E-mail: thompson@math.usu.edu. *Application contact:* Dr. Joseph Koebbe, Graduate Chairman, 435-797-2825, Fax: 435-797-1822, E-mail: koebbe@math.usu.edu.

Virginia Commonwealth University, School of Graduate Studies, College of Humanities and Sciences, Department of Mathematical Sciences, Program in Applied Mathematics, Richmond, VA 23284-9005. Offers MS. *Students:* 2 full-time (0 women), 2 part-time (1 woman); includes 1 minority (Asian American or Pacific Islander), 1 international. 5 applicants, 40% accepted, 2 enrolled. *Entrance requirements:* For master's, GRE General Test, GRE Subject Test. Additional exam requirements/recommendations for international students: Required—TOEFL. *Application deadline:* For fall admission, 7/1 for domestic students; for spring admission, 11/15 for domestic students. Applications are processed on a rolling basis. Application fee: $30. *Expenses:* Tuition, state resident: full-time $2,889; part-time $321 per credit hour. Tuition, nonresident: full-time $7,952; part-time $884 per credit hour. Required fees: $42 per credit hour. *Application contact:* Dr. James A. Wood, Information Contact, 804-828-1301, E-mail: jawood@vcu.edu.

Virginia Polytechnic Institute and State University, Graduate School, College of Science, Department of Mathematics, Blacksburg, VA 24061. Offers applied mathematics (MS, PhD); mathematical physics (MS, PhD); pure mathematics (MS, PhD). *Faculty:* 66 full-time (18 women), 1 part-time/adjunct. *Students:* 65 full-time (22 women), 50 part-time (35 women); includes 13 minority (5 African Americans, 3 Asian Americans or Pacific Islanders, 5 Hispanic Americans), 17 international. Average age 31. 152 applicants, 47% accepted, 51 enrolled. In 2003, 24 master's, 2 doctorates awarded. *Entrance requirements:* For master's and doctorate, GRE. Additional exam requirements/recommendations for international students: Required—TOEFL (minimum score 550 paper-based; 213 computer-based). *Application deadline:* Applications are processed on a rolling basis. Application fee: $45. Electronic applications accepted. Tuition, area resident: Full-time $6,039; part-time $336 per credit. Tuition, nonresident: full-time $9,708; part-time $539 per credit. Required fees: $905; $130 per credit. *Financial support:* In 2003–04, 3 fellowships with full tuition reimbursements (averaging $4,000 per year), 6 research assistantships with full tuition reimbursements (averaging $14,752 per year), 36 teaching assistantships with full tuition reimbursements (averaging $12,858 per year) were awarded. Career-related internships or fieldwork, Federal Work-Study, scholarships/grants, and unspecified assistantships also available. *Faculty research:* Differential equations, operator theory, numerical analysis, algebra, control theory. *Unit head:* Dr. John Rossi, Head, 540-231-6536, Fax: 540-231-5960, E-mail: rossi@math.vt.edu. *Application contact:* Hannah Swiger, Information Contact, 540-231-6537, Fax: 540-231-5960, E-mail: hsswiger@math.vt.edu.

Wayne State University, Graduate School, College of Science, Department of Mathematics, Program in Applied Mathematics, Detroit, MI 48202. Offers MA, PhD. *Students:* 4 full-time (2 women), 2 part-time; includes 2 minority (1 African American, 1 Hispanic American), 1 international. 4 applicants, 50% accepted, 0 enrolled. In 2003, 2 degrees awarded. *Degree requirements:* For doctorate, thesis/dissertation. *Entrance requirements:* Additional exam requirements/recommendations for international students: Required—TOEFL (minimum score 550 paper-based; 213 computer-based); Recommended—TWE(minimum score 6). *Application deadline:* For fall admission, 7/1 for domestic students, 6/1 for international students. Applications are processed on a rolling basis. Application fee: $30 ($50 for international students). Electronic applications accepted. *Expenses:* Tuition, state resident: part-time $263 per credit hour. Tuition, nonresident: part-time $580 per credit hour. Required fees: $21 per credit hour. *Application contact:* Dr. Tze-Chien Sun, Graduate Director, 313-577-8840, Fax: 313-577-7596, E-mail: tsun@wayne.edu.

Western Michigan University, Graduate College, College of Arts and Sciences, Department of Mathematics, Program in Applied Mathematics, Kalamazoo, MI 49008-5202. Offers MS.

West Virginia University, Eberly College of Arts and Sciences, Department of Mathematics, Morgantown, WV 26506. Offers applied mathematics (MS, PhD); discrete mathematics (PhD); interdisciplinary mathematics (MS); mathematics for secondary education (MS); pure mathematics (MS). Part-time programs available. *Faculty:* 28 full-time (1 woman), 11 part-time/adjunct (3 women). *Students:* 33 full-time (15 women), 8 part-time (2 women); includes 3 minority (1 African American, 2 Asian Americans or Pacific Islanders), 23 international. Average age 29. 30 applicants, 100% accepted, 16 enrolled. In 2003, 5 master's awarded, leading to continued full-time study 80%, business/industry 20%; 6 doctorates awarded, leading to university research/teaching 100%. Terminal master's awarded for partial completion of doctoral program. *Median time to degree:* Master's–2 years full-time; doctorate–4 years full-time. *Degree requirements:* For master's, thesis optional; for doctorate, one foreign language, thesis/dissertation, comprehensive exam. *Entrance requirements:* For master's, minimum GPA of 2.5; for doctorate, master's degree in mathematics. Additional exam requirements/recommendations for international students: Required—TOEFL (paper score 550; computer score 213) or IELTS (paper score 6). *Application deadline:* For fall admission, 2/15 priority date for domestic students, 2/15 priority date for international students. Applications are processed on a rolling basis. Application fee: $50. *Expenses:* Tuition, state resident: full-time $4,332. Tuition, nonresident: full-time $12,442. *Financial support:* In 2003–04, 25 students received support,

Applied Mathematics

West Virginia University (continued)

including 6 research assistantships with full tuition reimbursements available (averaging $1,000 per year), 18 teaching assistantships with full tuition reimbursements available (averaging $9,500 per year); Federal Work-Study, institutionally sponsored loans, and tuition waivers (full and partial) also available. Financial award application deadline: 2/15; financial award applicants required to submit FAFSA. *Faculty research:* Combinatorics and graph theory, topology, differential equations, applied and computational mathematics. Total annual research expenditures: $80,423. *Unit head:* Dr. Sherman Riemenschneider, Chair, 304-293-2011 Ext. 2322, Fax: 304-293-3982, E-mail: sherm.riemenschneider@mail.wvu.edu. *Application contact:* Dr. Harvey R. Diamond, Director of Graduate Studies, 304-293-2011 Ext. 2347, Fax: 304-293-3982, E-mail: gradprog@math.wvu.edu.

Wichita State University, Graduate School, Fairmount College of Liberal Arts and Sciences, Department of Mathematics and Statistics, Wichita, KS 67260. Offers applied mathematics (PhD); mathematics (MS); statistics (MS). Part-time programs available. *Faculty:* 22 full-time (0 women). *Students:* 17 full-time (5 women), 9 part-time (4 women); includes 1 minority (Hispanic American), 12 international. Average age 33. 20 applicants, 70% accepted. In 2003, 3 master's, 2 doctorates awarded. *Degree requirements:* For master's, thesis optional; for doctorate, thesis/dissertation. *Entrance requirements:* For master's, GRE; for doctorate, GRE Subject Test. Additional exam requirements/recommendations for international students: Required—TOEFL. *Application deadline:* For fall admission, 7/1 for domestic students; for spring admission, 1/1 for domestic students. Applications are processed on a rolling basis. Application fee: $35 ($50 for international students). Electronic applications accepted. *Expenses:* Tuition, state resident: full-time $2,457; part-time $137 per credit hour. Tuition, nonresident: full-time $7,371; part-time $410 per credit hour. Required fees: $364; $20 per credit hour. Tuition and fees vary according to course load. *Financial support:* In 2003–04, 1 research assistantship (averaging $14,000 per year), 15 teaching assistantships with full tuition reimbursements (averaging $11,027 per year) were awarded. Fellowships, Federal Work-Study, institutionally sponsored loans, scholarships/grants, traineeships, and unspecified assistantships also available. Support available to part-time students. Financial award application deadline: 4/1; financial award applicants required to submit FAFSA. *Faculty research:* Partial differential equations, combinatorics, ring theory, minimal surfaces, several complex variables. *Unit head:* Dr. Buma Fridman, Chair, 316-978-3160, Fax: 316-978-3748, E-mail: buma.fridman@wichita.edu.

Worcester Polytechnic Institute, Graduate Studies and Enrollment, Department of Mathematical Science, Worcester, MA 01609-2280. Offers applied mathematics (MS); applied statistics (MS); financial mathematics (MS); industrial mathematics (MS); mathematical science (PhD, Certificate); mathematics (MME). Part-time and evening/weekend programs available. *Faculty:* 28 full-time (2 women), 1 (woman) part-time/adjunct. *Students:* 26 full-time (13 women), 27 part-time (12 women); includes 2 minority (1 African American, 1 Asian American or Pacific Islander), 17 international. 71 applicants, 93% accepted, 19 enrolled. In 2003, 18 degrees awarded. *Degree requirements:* For master's, thesis optional; for doctorate, thesis/dissertation, comprehensive exam. *Entrance requirements:* Additional exam requirements/recommendations for international students: Required—TOEFL (minimum score 550 paper-based; 213 computer-based). *Application deadline:* For fall admission, 2/1 for domestic students; for spring admission, 10/15 priority date for domestic students. Applications are processed on a rolling basis. Application fee: $70. Electronic applications accepted. *Expenses:* Tuition: Part-time $897 per credit. *Financial support:* In 2003–04, 10 students received support, including 6 fellowships with full tuition reimbursements available, 9 research assistantships, 10 teaching assistantships with full tuition reimbursements available; career-related internships or fieldwork, institutionally sponsored loans, scholarships/grants, health care benefits, and unspecified assistantships also available. Financial award application deadline: 2/15; financial award applicants required to submit FAFSA. *Faculty research:* Applied mathematical modeling and analysis, computational mathematics, discrete mathematics, applied and computational statistics, industrial and financial mathematics. Total annual research expenditures: $592,514. *Unit head:* Dr. Bogdan Vernesca, Head, 508-831-5316, Fax: 508-831-5824. *Application contact:* Dr. Joseph Petruccelli, Graduate Coordinator, 508-831-5362, Fax: 508-831-5824, E-mail: jdp@wpi.edu.

See in-depth description on page 631.

Wright State University, School of Graduate Studies, College of Science and Mathematics, Department of Mathematics and Statistics, Program in Applied Mathematics, Dayton, OH 45435. Offers MS. *Students:* 2 full-time (0 women), (both international). Average age 32. 5 applicants, 100% accepted. In 2003, 1 degree awarded. *Degree requirements:* For master's, comprehensive exam. *Entrance requirements:* For master's, bachelor's degree in mathematics or related field. Additional exam requirements/recommendations for international students: Required—TOEFL. *Application deadline:* Applications are processed on a rolling basis. Application fee: $25. *Expenses:* Tuition, state resident: full-time $8,112; part-time $255 per quarter hour. Tuition, nonresident: full-time $14,127; part-time $442 per quarter hour. International tuition: $14,283 full-time. Tuition and fees vary according to course load, degree level and program. *Financial support:* Fellowships, research assistantships, teaching assistantships, tuition waivers (full and partial) available. Support available to part-time students. Financial award application deadline: 2/15; financial award applicants required to submit FAFSA. *Faculty research:* Control theory, ordinary differential equations, partial differential equations, numerical analysis, mathematical modeling. *Unit head:* Dr. Lop-Fat Ho, Director, 937-775-2078, Fax: 937-778-3068, E-mail: lop-fat.ho@wright.edu.

Yale University, Graduate School of Arts and Sciences, Program in Applied Mathematics, New Haven, CT 06520. Offers M Phil, MS, PhD. *Entrance requirements:* For doctorate, GRE General Test. *Expenses:* Tuition: Full-time $25,600; part-time $6,400 per term.

York University, Faculty of Graduate Studies, Faculty of Arts, Program in Mathematics and Statistics, Toronto, ON M3J 1P3, Canada. Offers industrial and applied mathematics (M Sc); mathematics and statistics (MA, PhD). Part-time programs available. *Degree requirements:* For master's, thesis optional; for doctorate, one foreign language, thesis/dissertation, comprehensive exam. *Entrance requirements:* For master's, minimum B average; for doctorate, minimum B+ average. Electronic applications accepted. Tuition, area resident: Full-time $5,431; part-time $905 per term. Tuition, nonresident: part-time $1,987 per term. International tuition: $11,918 full-time. Required fees: $287. Tuition and fees vary according to program.

Biometrics

Cornell University, Graduate School, Graduate Fields of Agriculture and Life Sciences, Field of Biometry, Ithaca, NY 14853-0001. Offers MS, PhD. *Faculty:* 13 full-time. *Students:* 11 full-time (7 women); includes 4 minority (all Hispanic Americans), 7 international. 22 applicants, 14% accepted, 1 enrolled. In 2003, 3 master's, 2 doctorates awarded. Terminal master's awarded for partial completion of doctoral program. *Degree requirements:* For master's, thesis/dissertation; for doctorate, thesis/dissertation, comprehensive exam. *Entrance requirements:* For master's and doctorate, GRE General Test, 2 letters of recommendation. Additional exam requirements/recommendations for international students: Required—TOEFL (minimum score 550 paper-based; 213 computer-based). *Application deadline:* For fall admission, 1/15 for domestic students. Application fee: $60. Electronic applications accepted. *Expenses:* Tuition: Full-time $28,630. One-time fee: $50 full-time. *Financial support:* In 2003–04, 11 students received support, including 4 fellowships with full tuition reimbursements available, 1 research assistantship with full tuition reimbursement available, 6 teaching assistantships with full tuition reimbursements available; institutionally sponsored loans, scholarships/grants, health care benefits, tuition waivers (full and partial), and unspecified assistantships also available. Financial award applicants required to submit FAFSA. *Faculty research:* Environmental, agricultural, and biological statistics; biomathematics; modern nonparametric statistics; statistical genetics; computational statistics. *Unit head:* Director of Graduate Studies, 607-255-8066. *Application contact:* Graduate Field Assistant, 607-255-8066, E-mail: bscb@cornell.edu.

Cornell University, Graduate School, Graduate Fields of Industrial and Labor Relations, Field of Statistics, Ithaca, NY 14853-0001. Offers applied statistics (MPS); biometry (MS, PhD); decision theory (MS, PhD); economic and social statistics (MS, PhD); engineering statistics (MS, PhD); experimental design (MS, PhD); mathematical statistics (MS, PhD); probability (MS, PhD); sampling (MS, PhD); statistical computing (MS, PhD); stochastic processes (MS, PhD). *Faculty:* 23 full-time. *Students:* 37 full-time (17 women); includes 6 minority (5 Asian Americans or Pacific Islanders, 1 Hispanic American), 22 international. 265 applicants, 19% accepted, 16 enrolled. In 2003, 20 master's, 2 doctorates awarded. Terminal master's awarded for partial completion of doctoral program. *Median time to degree:* Master's–1 year full-time. Of those who began their doctoral program in fall 1995, 100% received their degree in 8 years or less. *Degree requirements:* For master's, project (MPS), thesis (MS); for doctorate, one foreign language, thesis/dissertation. *Entrance requirements:* For master's, GRE General Test (MS), 2 letters of recommendation (MS and MPS); for doctorate, GRE General Test, 2 letters of recommendation. Additional exam requirements/recommendations for international students: Required—TOEFL (minimum score 550 paper-based; 213 computer-based). *Application deadline:* For fall admission, 1/15 for domestic students. Applications are processed on a rolling basis. Application fee: $60. Electronic applications accepted. *Expenses:* Tuition: Full-time $28,630. One-time fee: $50 full-time. *Financial support:* In 2003–04, 18 students received support, including 4 fellowships with full tuition reimbursements available, 1 research assistantship with full tuition reimbursement available, 13 teaching assistantships with full tuition reimbursements available; institutionally sponsored loans, scholarships/grants, tuition waivers (full and partial), and unspecified assistantships also available. Financial award applicants required to submit FAFSA. *Faculty research:* Bayesian analysis, survival analysis, nonparametric statistics, stochastic processes, mathematical statistics. *Unit head:* Director of Graduate Studies, 607-255-8066. *Application contact:* Graduate Field Assistant, 607-255-8066, E-mail: csc@cornell.edu.

Louisiana State University Health Sciences Center, School of Graduate Studies in New Orleans, Department of Biometry, New Orleans, LA 70112-2223. Offers MPH, MS. Part-time programs available. *Degree requirements:* For master's, thesis, comprehensive exam. *Entrance requirements:* For master's, GRE General Test. Additional exam requirements/recommendations for international students: Required—TOEFL. *Faculty research:* Longitudinal data, repeated measures, missing data, generalized estimating equations, multivariate methods.

Medical University of South Carolina, College of Graduate Studies, Program in Biometry and Epidemiology, Charleston, SC 29425-0002. Offers biometrics (MBS, PhD); biostatistics (MBS, PhD); clinical research (MCR); epidemiology (MCR, PhD). *Faculty:* 26 full-time (9 women). *Students:* 38 full-time (24 women); includes 5 minority (1 African American, 4 Asian Americans or Pacific Islanders), 5 international. Average age 28. 176 applicants, 44% accepted, 49 enrolled. In 2003, 4 master's, 4 doctorates awarded. Terminal master's awarded for partial completion of doctoral program. *Degree requirements:* For master's, thesis, research seminar; for doctorate, thesis/dissertation, teaching and research seminar, oral and written exams. *Entrance requirements:* For master's, GRE General Test; for doctorate, GRE General Test, interview. Additional exam requirements/recommendations for international students: Required—TOEFL (minimum score 600 paper-based; 250 computer-based). *Application deadline:* For fall admission, 1/15 priority date for domestic students, 1/15 priority date for international students. Application fee: $65. Electronic applications accepted. *Expenses:* Tuition, state resident: full-time $7,234; part-time $402 per semester hour. Tuition, nonresident: full-time $15,140; part-time $841 per semester hour. Required fees: $91 per term. Tuition and fees vary according to degree level, program and student level. *Financial support:* In 2003–04, 8 students received support, including fellowships with partial tuition reimbursements available (averaging $21,000 per year); Federal Work-Study and scholarships/grants also available. Support available to part-time students. Financial award application deadline: 3/15; financial award applicants required to submit FAFSA. *Faculty research:* Health disparities, central nervous system injuries, radiation exposure, analysis of clinical trial data, biomedical information. Total annual research expenditures: $6 million. *Unit head:* Dr. Barbara Tilley, Chair, 873-876-1327, Fax: 873-792-6950, E-mail: tilleyb@musc.edu. *Application contact:* Dr. Lana A. Cook, Assistant Dean for Admissions, 843-792-3391, Fax: 843-792-6590, E-mail: cookla@musc.edu.

Mount Sinai School of Medicine of New York University, Graduate School of Biological Sciences, Department of Biomathematical Sciences, New York, NY 10029-6504. Offers PhD, MD/PhD. *Degree requirements:* For doctorate, thesis/dissertation. *Entrance requirements:* For doctorate, GRE General Test, GRE Subject Test. Additional exam requirements/recommendations for international students: Required—TOEFL.

North Carolina State University, Graduate School, College of Physical and Mathematical Sciences, Department of Statistics, Raleigh, NC 27695. Offers biomathematics (M Biomath, MS, PhD), including biomathematics, ecology (PhD); statistics (M Stat, MS, PhD). Part-time programs available. *Students:* 155 full-time (89 women), 13 part-time (8 women); includes 15 minority (6 African Americans, 7 Asian Americans or Pacific Islanders, 2 Hispanic Americans), 93 international. Average age 29. 327 applicants, 23% accepted. In 2003, 46 master's, 19 doctorates awarded. *Degree requirements:* For master's, thesis (for some programs), final oral exam, comprehensive exam; for doctorate, thesis/dissertation, final oral and written exams, written and oral preliminary exams. *Entrance requirements:* For master's and doctorate, GRE General Test. Additional exam requirements/recommendations for international students: Required—TOEFL. *Application deadline:* For fall admission, 6/25 for domestic students, 3/1 for international students; for spring admission, 11/25 for domestic students, 7/15 for international students. Applications are processed on a rolling basis. Application fee: $55 ($65 for international students). *Expenses:* Tuition, state resident: part-time $396 per hour. Tuition, nonresident: part-time $1,895 per hour. *Financial support:* In 2003–04, 2 fellowships with tuition reimbursements (averaging $5,552 per year), 60 research assistantships with tuition reimbursements (averaging $7,078 per year), 55 teaching assistantships with tuition reimbursements (averaging $6,581 per year) were awarded. Career-related internships or fieldwork, health care benefits, and tuition waivers (full) also available. Financial award application deadline: 3/1. *Faculty research:* Biostatistics; time series; spatial, inference, environmental, industrial, genetics applications; nonlinear models; DOE. Total annual research expenditures: $1.5 million. *Unit head:* Dr. Sastry G. Pantula, Head, 919-515-1949, Fax: 919-515-7591, E-mail: head@stat.ncsu.edu. *Application contact:* Dr. William Swallow, Director of Graduate Programs, 919-515-1916, Fax: 919-515-7591, E-mail: stat_dgp@stat.ncsu.edu.

North Carolina State University, Graduate School, College of Physical and Mathematical Sciences, Department of Statistics, Program in Biomathematics, Raleigh, NC 27695. Offers biomathematics (M Biomath, MS, PhD); ecology (PhD). Part-time programs available. *Faculty:* 25 full-time (5 women), 6 part-time/adjunct (0 women). *Students:* 17 full-time (6 women), 2 part-time (1 woman); includes 1 minority (Asian American or Pacific Islander), 9 international. Average age 31. 23 applicants, 9% accepted. In 2003, 3 master's, 2 doctorates awarded. Terminal master's awarded for partial completion of doctoral program. *Degree requirements:* For master's, thesis (for some programs); for doctorate, thesis/dissertation. *Entrance requirements:* For master's and doctorate, GRE General Test. Additional exam requirements/recommendations for international students: Required—TOEFL. *Application deadline:* For fall admission, 6/25 for domestic students, 3/1 for international students; for spring admission, 11/25 for domestic students, 7/15 for international students. Application fee: $45. *Expenses:* Tuition, state resident: part-time $396 per hour. Tuition, nonresident: part-time $1,895 per hour. *Financial support:* In 2003–04, 8 research assistantships with tuition reimbursements (averaging $6,650 per year), 6 teaching assistantships with tuition reimbursements (averaging $6,679 per year) were awarded. Fellowships with tuition reimbursements, career-related internships or fieldwork also available. Financial award application deadline: 3/1. *Faculty research:* Theory and methods of biological modeling, theoretical biology (genetics), applied biology (wildlife). *Unit head:* Dr. Charles E. Smith, Director of Graduate Programs, 919-515-1907, Fax: 919-515-1909, E-mail: bmasmith@stat.ncsu.edu. *Application contact:* Peggy Morris, Graduate Secretary, 919-515-1912, Fax: 919-515-7909, E-mail: bma_dgp-assistan@stat.ncsu.edu.

Oregon State University, Graduate School, College of Science, Department of Statistics, Corvallis, OR 97331. Offers applied statistics (MA, MS, PhD); biometry (MA, MS, PhD); environmental statistics (MA, MS, PhD); mathematical statistics (MA, MS, PhD); operations research (MA, MAIS, MS); statistics (MA, MS, PhD). Part-time programs available. *Faculty:* 11 full-time (4 women), 1 part-time/adjunct (0 women). *Students:* 29 full-time (16 women), 9 part-time (3 women); includes 6 minority (4 Asian Americans or Pacific Islanders, 2 Hispanic Americans), 13 international. Average age 30. In 2003, 8 degrees awarded. *Degree requirements:* For master's, consulting experience; for doctorate, thesis/dissertation, consulting experience. *Entrance requirements:* For master's and doctorate, minimum GPA of 3.0 in last 90 hours. Additional exam requirements/recommendations for international students: Required—TOEFL. *Application deadline:* For fall admission, 2/15 for domestic students. Applications are processed on a rolling basis. Application fee: $50. *Expenses:* Tuition, state resident: full-time $8,139; part-time $301 per credit. Tuition, nonresident: full-time $14,376; part-time $532 per credit. Required fees: $1,227. *Financial support:* In 2003–04, 8 research assistantships, 19 teaching assistantships were awarded. Federal Work-Study and institutionally sponsored loans also available. Financial award application deadline: 2/15. *Faculty research:* Analysis of enumerative data, nonparametric statistics, asymptotics, experimental design, generalized regression models, linear model theory, reliability theory, survival analysis, wildlife and general survey methodology. *Unit head:* Dr. Robert T. Smythe, Chair, 541-737-3480, Fax: 541-737-3489, E-mail: symthe@stat.orst.edu. *Application contact:* Dr. Daniel W. Schafer, Director of Graduate Studies, 541-737-3366, Fax: 541-737-3489, E-mail: statoff@stat.orst.edu.

San Diego State University, Graduate and Research Affairs, College of Sciences, Department of Biological Sciences, Program in Biostatistics and Biometry, San Diego, CA 92182. Offers PhD. Program offered jointly with the University of California, Davis. *Degree requirements:* For doctorate, thesis/dissertation. *Entrance requirements:* For doctorate, GRE General Test, GRE Subject Test. *Application deadline:* For fall admission, 5/1 for domestic students; for spring admission, 11/1 for domestic students, 10/1 for international students. Applications are processed on a rolling basis. Application fee: $55. Electronic applications accepted. Tuition, nonresident: part-time $282 per unit. Required fees: $1,349; $875 per year. *Financial support:* Research assistantships, teaching assistantships, career-related internships or fieldwork, scholarships/grants, and unspecified assistantships available. *Unit head:* K. J. Lui, Graduate Advisor, 619-594-7239, Fax: 619-594-6746, E-mail: kil@rohan.sdsu.edu.

University at Albany, State University of New York, School of Public Health, Department of Biometry and Statistics, Albany, NY 12222-0001. Offers MS, PhD. *Students:* 20 full-time (10 women), 21 part-time (10 women). Average age 31. 41 applicants, 39% accepted, 11 enrolled. In 2003, 17 degrees awarded. *Degree requirements:* For doctorate, thesis/dissertation. *Entrance requirements:* For master's and doctorate, GRE General Test. Additional exam requirements/recommendations for international students: Required—TOEFL (minimum score 550 paper-based; 213 computer-based). *Application deadline:* For fall admission, 6/30 for domestic students, 5/1 for international students; for spring admission, 11/1 for domestic students, 11/1 for international students. Applications are processed on a rolling basis. Application fee: $50. Electronic applications accepted. *Expenses:* Tuition, state resident: part-time $288 per credit. Tuition, nonresident: part-time $438 per credit. Required fees: $495 per semester. *Financial support:* Application deadline: 4/1. *Unit head:* Dr. David Strogatz, Chair, 518-402-0400.

The University of Alabama at Birmingham, School of Public Health, Department of Biostatistics, Birmingham, AL 35294. Offers biomathematics (MS, PhD); biostatistics (MS, PhD). *Students:* 13 full-time (3 women), 2 part-time (1 woman); includes 3 minority (all African Americans), 6 international. 88 applicants, 35% accepted. In 2003, 3 master's, 1 doctorate awarded. *Degree requirements:* For master's, variable foreign language requirement, thesis, fieldwork, research project; for doctorate, variable foreign language requirement, thesis/dissertation, comprehensive exam. *Entrance requirements:* For master's, GRE General Test or MAT, minimum GPA of 3.0; for doctorate, GRE General Test or MAT, MPH or MSPH, minimum GPA of 3.0, interview. *Application deadline:* Applications are processed on a rolling basis. Application fee: $35 ($60 for international students). Electronic applications accepted. *Expenses:* Contact institution. *Financial support:* Fellowships, career-related internships or fieldwork available. *Unit head:* Dr. George Howard, Chair, 205-934-4905, Fax: 205-975-2540, E-mail: ghoward@uab.edu. *Application contact:* Nancy O. Pinson, Coordinator of Student Admissions, 205-934-4993, Fax: 205-975-5484.

University of California, Los Angeles, School of Medicine and Graduate Division, Graduate Programs in Medicine, Department of Biomathematics, Los Angeles, CA 90095. Offers biomathematics (MS, PhD); clinical research (MS). *Degree requirements:* For master's, comprehensive exam or thesis; for doctorate, thesis/dissertation, oral and written qualifying exams. *Entrance requirements:* For master's and doctorate, GRE General Test, GRE Subject Test. Tuition, nonresident: full-time $12,245. Required fees: $6,318.

See in-depth description on page 589.

University of Colorado Health Sciences Center, Graduate School, Programs in Biological Sciences, Program in Biometrics, Denver, CO 80262. Offers analytic health sciences (PhD); biometrics (MS). In 2003, 1 master's, 3 doctorates awarded. *Degree requirements:* For master's and doctorate, thesis/dissertation. *Entrance requirements:* For master's and doctorate, GRE General Test, minimum GPA of 3.0, 2 semesters of calculus. Additional exam requirements/recommendations for international students: Required—TOEFL. *Application deadline:* For fall admission, 3/1 for domestic students. Application fee: $50. *Expenses:* Tuition, state resident: part-time $201 per credit hour. Tuition, nonresident: part-time $440 per credit hour. *Financial support:* Application deadline: 3/1. *Unit head:* Dr. Richard H. Jones, Director, 303-315-6860. *Application contact:* Kendra Burghardt, Information Contact, 303-315-7605.

University of Nebraska–Lincoln, Graduate College, College of Agricultural Sciences and Natural Resources, Department of Biometry, Lincoln, NE 68588. Offers MS. *Degree requirements:* For master's, thesis optional. *Entrance requirements:* For master's, GRE General Test. Additional exam requirements/recommendations for international students: Required—TOEFL (minimum score 550 paper-based; 213 computer-based). Electronic applications accepted. *Faculty research:* Design of experiments, linear models, spatial variability, statistical modeling and inference, sampling.

University of Southern California, Keck School of Medicine and Graduate School, Graduate Programs in Medicine, Department of Preventive Medicine, Master of Public Health Program, Los Angeles, CA 90089. Offers biometry/epidemiology (MPH); health communication (MPH); health promotion (MPH); preventive nutrition (MPH). *Accreditation:* CEPH. Part-time programs available. *Faculty:* 22 full-time (11 women), 10 part-time/adjunct (8 women). *Students:* 84 full-time (71 women), 16 part-time (14 women); includes 59 minority (4 African Americans, 1 American Indian/Alaska Native, 33 Asian Americans or Pacific Islanders, 21 Hispanic Americans), 10 international. Average age 24. 150 applicants, 76% accepted, 59 enrolled. In 2003, 30 degrees awarded. *Degree requirements:* For master's, practicum, final report, oral presentation. *Entrance requirements:* For master's, GRE General Test, minimum GPA of 3.0. Additional exam requirements/recommendations for international students: Required—TOEFL (minimum score 600 paper-based; 250 computer-based). *Application deadline:* For fall admission, 3/1 priority date for domestic students, 3/1 priority date for international students; for spring admission, 11/15 for domestic students, 11/15 for international students. Application fee: $65 ($75 for international students). Electronic applications accepted. *Expenses:* Tuition: Full-time $32,784; part-time $949 per unit. Tuition and fees vary according to course load and program. *Financial support:* In 2003–04, 81 students received support, including 12 research assistantships with full tuition reimbursements available (averaging $24,398 per year), 11 teaching assistantships with full tuition reimbursements available (averaging $24,398 per year); institutionally sponsored loans, scholarships/grants, and staff tuition remission also available. Support available to part-time students. Financial award application deadline: 2/1; financial award applicants required to submit CSS PROFILE or FAFSA. *Faculty research:* Substance abuse prevention, cancer and heart disease prevention, mass media and health communication research, health promotion, treatment compliance. Total annual research expenditures: $12 million. *Unit head:* Dr. Thomas W. Valente, Director, 626-457-6678, Fax: 626-457-6699, E-mail: tvalente@usc.edu. *Application contact:* Nemesia P. Lockhart, Program Specialist, 626-457-6676, Fax: 626-457-6699, E-mail: lockhart@usc.edu.

The University of Texas Health Science Center at Houston, Graduate School of Biomedical Sciences, Program in Biomathematics and Biostatistics, Houston, TX 77225-0036. Offers MS, PhD, MD/PhD. *Faculty:* 29 full-time (6 women). *Students:* 1 full-time (0 women), 1 international. Average age 26. 8 applicants, 38% accepted, 0 enrolled. Terminal master's awarded for partial completion of doctoral program. *Degree requirements:* For master's and doctorate, thesis/dissertation. *Entrance requirements:* For master's and doctorate, GRE General Test. Additional exam requirements/recommendations for international students: Required—TOEFL, TWE. *Application deadline:* For fall admission, 1/15 for domestic students; for spring admission, 11/1 for domestic students. Applications are processed on a rolling basis. Application fee: $10. Electronic applications accepted. *Expenses:* Tuition, state resident: full-time $3,312; part-time $92 per hour. Tuition, nonresident: full-time $11,808; part-time $328 per hour. *Financial support:* Fellowships with full tuition reimbursements, research assistantships with full tuition reimbursements, institutionally sponsored loans available. Financial award application deadline: 1/15. *Faculty research:* Statistical and mathematical modeling, development of new models for design and analysis of research studies, formulation of mathematical models of biological systems. *Unit head:* Dr. Gary L. Rosner, Coordinator, 713-794-1798, Fax: 713-745-4940, E-mail: glrosner@mdanderson.org. *Application contact:* Dr. Victoria P. Knutson, Assistant Dean of Admissions, 713-500-9860, Fax: 713-500-9877, E-mail: victoria.p.knutson@uth.tmc.edu.

See in-depth description on page 615.

University of Wisconsin–Madison, Graduate School, College of Agricultural and Life Sciences, Biometry Program, Madison, WI 53706-1380. Offers MS. Application fee: $38. Tuition, area resident: Full-time $7,593; part-time $476 per credit. Tuition, nonresident: full-time $22,824; part-time $1,430 per credit. Required fees: $292; $38 per credit. Part-time tuition and fees vary according to course load and reciprocity agreements. *Unit head:* Murray Clayton, Chair, 608-262-1009.

Biostatistics

Arizona State University, Graduate College, College of Liberal Arts and Sciences, Department of Biology, Program in Computational, Statistical, and Mathematical Biology, Tempe, AZ 85287. Offers MS, PhD. *Entrance requirements:* Additional exam requirements/recommendations for international students: Required—TOEFL (minimum score 600 paper-based); Recommended—TSE. *Expenses:* Tuition, state resident: full-time $3,708; part-time $194 per credit hour. Tuition, nonresident: full-time $12,228; part-time $510 per credit hour. Required fees: $87; $22 per semester. Part-time tuition and fees vary according to program.

Boston University, Graduate School of Arts and Sciences, Program in Biostatistics, Boston, MA 02215. Offers MA, PhD. *Students:* 25 full-time (18 women), 41 part-time (26 women); includes 10 minority (1 African American, 9 Asian Americans or Pacific Islanders), 24 international. Average age 33. 112 applicants, 38% accepted, 15 enrolled. In 2003, 4 degrees awarded. Terminal master's awarded for partial completion of doctoral program. *Degree requirements:* For master's, one foreign language, comprehensive exam, registration; for doctorate, one foreign language, thesis/dissertation, comprehensive exam, registration. *Entrance requirements:* For master's and doctorate, GRE General Test, 2 letters of recommendation. Additional exam requirements/recommendations for international students: Required—TOEFL (minimum score 550 paper-based; 213 computer-based). *Application deadline:* For fall admission, 5/1 for domestic students, 5/1 for international students; for spring admission, 10/15 for domestic students, 10/15 for international students. Application fee: $60. *Expenses:* Tuition: Full-time $28,512; part-time $891 per credit hour. *Financial support:* In 2003–04, 14 students received support, including 14 research assistantships with full tuition reimbursements available (averaging $15,000 per year); fellowships, teaching assistantships Support available to part-time students. Financial award application deadline: 1/15; financial award applicants required to submit FAFSA. *Unit head:* Ralph D'Agostino, Director, 617-353-2767, Fax: 617-638-4458, E-mail: ralph@bu.edu. *Application contact:* Sharon Milewits, Administrative Assistant, 617-638-5172, Fax: 617-638-4458, E-mail: sharonm@bu.edu.

Boston University, School of Public Health, Biostatistics Department, Boston, MA 02215. Offers MA, MPH, PhD. Application fee: $60. *Expenses:* Tuition: Full-time $28,512; part-time $891 per credit hour. *Unit head:* L. Adrienne Cupples, Chairman, 617-638-5176, Fax: 617-638-4458, E-mail: adrienne@bu.edu. *Application contact:* LePhan Quan, Assistant Director of Admissions, 617-638-4640, Fax: 617-638-5299, E-mail: sphadmis@bu.edu.

Brown University, Graduate School, Division of Biology and Medicine, Department of Community Health, Providence, RI 02912. Offers health services research (MS, PhD); public health (MPH); statistical science (MS, PhD), including biostatistics, epidemiology. *Accreditation:* CEPH. *Faculty:* 32 full-time (16 women). *Students:* Average age 24. 29 applicants, 0% accepted. *Degree requirements:* For doctorate, thesis/dissertation, preliminary exam. *Entrance requirements:* For master's and doctorate, GRE General Test. *Application deadline:* For fall admission, 1/2 for domestic students. Applications are processed on a rolling basis. Application fee: $60. *Financial support:* Fellowships, research assistantships available. Financial award application

Biostatistics

Brown University (continued)
deadline: 1/2. *Unit head:* Dr. Joseph Hogan, Director, 401-863-9183, Fax: 401-863-9182, E-mail: joseph_hogan@brown.edu.

Brown University, Graduate School, Division of Biology and Medicine, Department of Community Health, Center for Statistical Science, Program in Biostatistics, Providence, RI 02912. Offers MS, PhD, MD/PhD. *Degree requirements:* For doctorate, thesis/dissertation, preliminary exam. *Entrance requirements:* For master's and doctorate, GRE General Test. *Application deadline:* For fall admission, 1/2 for domestic students. Applications are processed on a rolling basis. Application fee: $60. *Financial support:* Application deadline: 1/2. *Application contact:* Debra Papa, Administrative Assistant, Fax: 401-863-3492, E-mail: debra_papa@brown.edu.

Case Western Reserve University, School of Medicine and School of Graduate Studies, Graduate Programs in Medicine, Department of Epidemiology and Biostatistics, Program in Biostatistics, Cleveland, OH 44106. Offers MS, PhD. Part-time programs available. *Students:* Average age 31.Terminal master's awarded for partial completion of doctoral program. *Degree requirements:* For master's, exam/practicum; for doctorate, thesis/dissertation. *Entrance requirements:* For master's and doctorate, GRE General Test. Additional exam requirements/recommendations for international students: Required—TOEFL. *Application deadline:* For fall admission, 2/1 for domestic students. Applications are processed on a rolling basis. Application fee: $25. *Expenses:* Tuition: Full-time $26,900. *Financial support:* In 2003–04, fellowships with full tuition reimbursements (averaging $29,166 per year), research assistantships with full and partial tuition reimbursements (averaging $10,400 per year), teaching assistantships with full and partial tuition reimbursements (averaging $10,800 per year) were awarded. Career-related internships or fieldwork and tuition waivers (partial) also available. Support available to part-time students. Financial award application deadline: 2/1. *Faculty research:* Survey sampling and statistical computing, generalized linear models, statistical modeling, models in breast cancer survival. *Application contact:* Sherye A. Sirrel, Graduate Secretary, 216-368-5957, Fax: 216-368-3970, E-mail: srr4@po.cwru.edu.

Columbia University, Joseph L. Mailman School of Public Health, Division of Biostatistics, New York, NY 10032. Offers MPH, MS, Dr PH, PhD. PhD offered in cooperation with the Graduate School of Arts and Sciences. Part-time programs available. *Degree requirements:* For doctorate, thesis/dissertation. *Entrance requirements:* For master's, GRE General Test; for doctorate, GRE General Test, MPH or equivalent (Dr PH). Electronic applications accepted. *Expenses:* Tuition: Full-time $14,820. *Faculty research:* Application of statistics in public policy, medical experiments, and legal processing; clinical trial results; statistical methods in epidemiology.

Drexel University, School of Biomedical Engineering, Science and Health Systems, Philadelphia, PA 19104-2875. Offers biomedical engineering (MS, PhD); biomedical science (MS, PhD); biostatistics (MS); clinical/rehabilitation engineering (MS). *Degree requirements:* For doctorate, thesis/dissertation, 1 year of residency, qualifying exam. *Entrance requirements:* For master's, minimum GPA of 3.0; for doctorate, minimum GPA of 3.0, MS. Additional exam requirements/recommendations for international students: Required—TOEFL. Electronic applications accepted. *Faculty research:* Cardiovascular dynamics, diagnostic and therapeutic ultrasound.

Emory University, Graduate School of Arts and Sciences, Department of Biostatistics, Atlanta, GA 30322-1100. Offers biostatistics (MPH, MSPH, PhD); public health informatics (MSPH). *Faculty:* 22 full-time (8 women), 14 part-time/adjunct (5 women). *Students:* 24 full-time (17 women); includes 6 minority (2 African Americans, 4 Asian Americans or Pacific Islanders), 8 international. Average age 26. 101 applicants, 10% accepted, 5 enrolled. In 2003, 4 degrees awarded, leading to university research/teaching 50%, business/industry 25%, government 25%. *Median time to degree:* Doctorate–5 years full-time. Of those who began their doctoral program in fall 1995, 100% received their degree in 8 years or less. *Degree requirements:* For doctorate, thesis/dissertation, comprehensive exam, registration. *Entrance requirements:* For doctorate, GRE General Test. Additional exam requirements/recommendations for international students: Required—TOEFL. *Application deadline:* For fall admission, 1/10 priority date for domestic students, 1/10 priority date for international students. Application fee: $50. Electronic applications accepted. *Expenses:* Tuition: Part-time $1,115 per hour. Required fees: $5 per hour. $125 per term. *Financial support:* In 2003–04, 5 fellowships with full tuition reimbursements (averaging $18,000 per year) were awarded; career-related internships or fieldwork and scholarships/grants also available. Financial award application deadline: 1/20. *Faculty research:* Vaccine efficacy, clinical trials, spatial statistics, statistical genetics, neuroimaging. Total annual research expenditures: $28 million. *Unit head:* Dr. Michael H. Kutner, Chair, 404-712-9708, Fax: 404-727-1370, E-mail: mkutner@sph.emory.edu. *Application contact:* Dr. John J. Hanfelt, Director of Graduate Studies, 404-727-2876, Fax: 404-727-1370, E-mail: jhanfel@sph.emory.edu.

See in-depth description on page 537.

Emory University, The Rollins School of Public Health, Department of Biostatistics, Atlanta, GA 30322-1100. Offers MPH, MSPH, PhD. Part-time programs available. *Students:* 4 full-time (3 women), 4 part-time (3 women). Average age 26. In 2003, 1 degree awarded. *Degree requirements:* For master's, thesis (for some programs), practicum. *Entrance requirements:* For master's, GRE General Test. Additional exam requirements/recommendations for international students: Required—TOEFL (minimum score 550 paper-based; 213 computer-based). *Application deadline:* For fall admission, 1/15 priority date for domestic students, 1/1 priority date for international students. Application fee: $60. Electronic applications accepted. *Expenses:* Tuition: Part-time $1,115 per hour. Required fees: $5 per hour. $125 per term. *Financial support:* Application deadline: 1/15. *Unit head:* Dr. Michael H. Kutner, Chair, 404-712-9708, Fax: 404-727-1370, E-mail: mkutner@sph.emory.edu. *Application contact:* Marsha Daly, Assistant Director of Academic Programs, 404-727-3968, E-mail: mdaly@sph.emory.edu.

See in-depth description on page 537.

Georgetown University, Graduate School of Arts and Sciences, Programs in Biomedical Sciences, Division of Biostatistics and Epidemiology, Washington, DC 20057. Offers MS. *Entrance requirements:* For master's, GRE General Test. Additional exam requirements/recommendations for international students: Required—TOEFL. *Faculty research:* Occupation epidemiology, cancer.

The George Washington University, Columbian College of Arts and Sciences, Department of Statistics, Program in Biostatistics, Washington, DC 20052. Offers MS, PhD. *Students:* 5 full-time (3 women), 16 part-time (10 women); includes 2 minority (both Asian Americans or Pacific Islanders), 6 international. Average age 34. 31 applicants, 68% accepted. In 2003, 1 master's, 1 doctorate awarded. *Degree requirements:* For master's, comprehensive exam; for doctorate, thesis/dissertation, general exam. *Entrance requirements:* For master's and doctorate, GRE General Test, minimum GPA of 3.0. Additional exam requirements/recommendations for international students: Required—TOEFL (minimum score 550 paper-based; 213 computer-based). *Application deadline:* For fall admission, 2/1 priority date for domestic students, 2/1 priority date for international students; for spring admission, 10/1 priority date for domestic students, 10/1 priority date for international students. Applications are processed on a rolling basis. Application fee: $60. Electronic applications accepted. *Expenses:* Tuition: Part-time $876 per credit. Required fees: $1 per credit. Tuition and fees vary according to campus/location. *Financial support:* In 2003–04, fellowships with full tuition reimbursements (averaging $10,000 per year), teaching assistantships (averaging $5,000 per year) were awarded. Financial award application deadline: 2/1. *Unit head:* Dr. John Lachin, Director and Adviser, 202-994-9296.

The George Washington University, School of Public Health and Health Services, Department of Epidemiology and Biostatistics, Washington, DC 20052. Offers biostatistics (MPH); epidemiology (MPH); health information systems (MPH); microbiology and emerging infectious diseases (MSPH). *Accreditation:* CEPH. *Students:* 44 full-time (34 women), 66 part-time (49 women); includes 49 minority (22 African Americans, 19 Asian Americans or Pacific Islanders, 8 Hispanic Americans), 4 international. Average age 28. 123 applicants, 79% accepted. In 2003, 26 degrees awarded. *Degree requirements:* For master's, case study or special project. *Entrance requirements:* For master's, GMAT, GRE General Test, or MCAT. Additional exam requirements/recommendations for international students: Required—TOEFL. *Application deadline:* For fall admission, 5/15 for domestic students; for winter admission, 11/15 for domestic students; for spring admission, 4/1 for domestic students. Applications are processed on a rolling basis. Application fee: $60. *Expenses:* Tuition: Part-time $876 per credit. Required fees: $1 per credit. Tuition and fees vary according to campus/location. *Unit head:* Dr. Dante Verme, Chair, 202-994-7895, Fax: 202-994-0082, E-mail: sphdav@gwumc.edu. *Application contact:* Jane Smith, Director of Admissions, 202-994-2160, Fax: 202-994-1860, E-mail: sphhsinfo@gwumc.edu.

Harvard University, School of Public Health, Department of Biostatistics, Boston, MA 02115-6096. Offers SM, SD. Part-time programs available. *Degree requirements:* For doctorate, thesis/dissertation, oral and written qualifying exams. *Entrance requirements:* For master's and doctorate, GRE, prior training in mathematics and/or statistics. Additional exam requirements/recommendations for international students: Required—TOEFL (minimum score 560 paper-based; 220 computer-based). Electronic applications accepted. *Expenses:* Tuition: Full-time $26,066. Full-time tuition and fees vary according to program and student level. *Faculty research:* Statistical genetics, clinical trials, cancer and AIDS research, environmental and mental health.

Iowa State University of Science and Technology, Graduate College, Interdisciplinary Programs, Bioinformatics and Computational Biology Program, Ames, IA 50011-3260. Offers MS, PhD. *Students:* 50 full-time (14 women), 2 part-time; includes 3 minority (all African Americans), 25 international. 276 applicants, 7% accepted, 7 enrolled. In 2003, 5 master's, 4 doctorates awarded. *Degree requirements:* For doctorate, thesis/dissertation. *Entrance requirements:* For doctorate, GRE General Test. Additional exam requirements/recommendations for international students: Required—TOEFL or IELTS. *Application deadline:* For fall admission, 2/1 priority date for domestic students, 2/1 priority date for international students. Application fee: $30 ($70 for international students). Electronic applications accepted. Tuition, nonresident: part-time $560 per credit. Required fees: $38 per unit. *Financial support:* In 2003–04, 14 fellowships with full tuition reimbursements (averaging $23,250 per year), 35 research assistantships with full and partial tuition reimbursements (averaging $18,240 per year) were awarded. Scholarships/grants, traineeships, health care benefits, and unspecified assistantships also available. *Faculty research:* Functional and structural genomics, genome evolution, macromolecular structure and function, mathematical biology and biological statistics, metabolic and developmental networks. *Unit head:* Dr. Vasant Honavar, Chair, Supervising Committee, 515-294-5122, Fax: 515-294-6790, E-mail: bcb@cs.iastate.edu. *Application contact:* Tori Frjelich, Program Assistant, 888-569-8509, Fax: 515-294-6790, E-mail: bcb@iastate.edu.

The Johns Hopkins University, Bloomberg School of Public Health, Department of Biostatistics, Baltimore, MD 21205-2179. Offers bioinformatics (MHS); biostatistics (MHS, Sc M, PhD). Part-time programs available. *Faculty:* 25 full-time (7 women), 12 part-time/adjunct (2 women). *Students:* 39 full-time (24 women), 18 part-time (7 women); includes 8 minority (all Asian Americans or Pacific Islanders), 33 international. Average age 29. 230 applicants, 35% accepted, 19 enrolled. In 2003, 11 master's, 2 doctorates awarded, leading to university research/teaching 100%. *Median time to degree:* Master's–2 years full-time; doctorate–4.5 years full-time. Of those who began their doctoral program in fall 1995, 100% received their degree in 8 years or less. *Degree requirements:* For master's, thesis (for some programs), written exam, field placement, comprehensive exam (for some programs), registration; for doctorate, thesis/dissertation, 1 year full-time residency, oral and written exams, comprehensive exam, registration. *Entrance requirements:* For master's, GRE General Test, prior coursework in calculus and matrix algegra; for doctorate, GRE General Test, prior coursework in calculus and matrix algebra. Additional exam requirements/recommendations for international students: Required—TOEFL. *Application deadline:* For fall admission, 2/1 priority date for domestic students, 2/1 priority date for international students. Applications are processed on a rolling basis. Application fee: $75. Electronic applications accepted. *Expenses:* Tuition: Full-time $28,730; part-time $1,490 per course. Part-time tuition and fees vary according to course load, campus/location and program. *Financial support:* In 2003–04, 32 students received support, including 26 research assistantships with tuition reimbursements available (averaging $22,000 per year); fellowships, teaching assistantships, Federal Work-Study, institutionally sponsored loans, scholarships/grants, traineeships, health care benefits, tuition waivers (partial), and stipends also available. Financial award application deadline: 4/15; financial award applicants required to submit FAFSA. *Faculty research:* Statistical genetics, bioinformatics, statistical computing, statistical methods, environmental statistics. *Unit head:* Dr. Scott Zeger, Chair, 410-955-3067, Fax: 410-955-0958, E-mail: szeger@jhsph.edu. *Application contact:* Mary Joy Argo, Academic Administrator, 410-614-4454, Fax: 410-955-0958, E-mail: margo@jhsph.edu.

Loma Linda University, School of Public Health, Programs in Biostatistics, Loma Linda, CA 92350. Offers MPH, MSPH. *Entrance requirements:* Additional exam requirements/recommendations for international students: Required—Michigan English Language Assessment Battery or TOEFL.

McGill University, Faculty of Graduate and Postdoctoral Studies, Faculty of Medicine, Department of Epidemiology and Biostatistics and Occupational Health, Montréal, QC H3A 2T5, Canada. Offers community health (M Sc); environmental health (M Sc); epidemiology (M Sc); epidemiology and biostatistics (PhD, Diploma); health care evaluation (M Sc); medical statistics (M Sc); occupational health (M Sc). *Accreditation:* CEPH (one or more programs are accredited). *Degree requirements:* For master's, thesis optional; for doctorate, thesis/dissertation. *Entrance requirements:* For master's, GRE, minimum GPA of 3.0; for doctorate, GRE. Tuition, area resident: Full-time $1,668. *Expenses:* Tuition, state resident: full-time $4,173. Tuition, nonresident: full-time $9,468. Required fees: $1,081. *Faculty research:* Chronic and infectious disease epidemiology, health services research, pharmacoepidemiology.

Medical College of Wisconsin, Graduate School of Biomedical Sciences, Division of Biostatistics, Milwaukee, WI 53226-0509. Offers PhD. Part-time programs available. *Degree requirements:* For doctorate, thesis/dissertation, comprehensive exam, registration. *Entrance requirements:* For doctorate, GRE General Test. Additional exam requirements/recommendations for international students: Required—TOEFL. Electronic applications accepted. *Faculty research:* Survival analysis, spatial statistics, time series, genetic statistics, Bayesian statistics.

See in-depth description on page 549.

Medical University of South Carolina, College of Graduate Studies, Program in Biometry and Epidemiology, Charleston, SC 29425-0002. Offers biometrics (MBS, PhD); biostatistics (MBS, PhD); clinical research (MCR); epidemiology (MCR, PhD). *Faculty:* 26 full-time (9 women). *Students:* 38 full-time (24 women); includes 5 minority (1 African American, 4 Asian Americans or Pacific Islanders), 5 international. Average age 28. 176 applicants, 44% accepted, 49 enrolled. In 2003, 4 master's, 4 doctorates awarded. Terminal master's awarded for partial completion of doctoral program. *Degree requirements:* For master's, thesis, research seminar; for doctorate, thesis/dissertation, teaching and research seminar, oral and written exams. *Entrance requirements:* For master's, GRE General Test; for doctorate, GRE General Test, interview. Additional exam requirements/recommendations for international students: Required—TOEFL (minimum score 600 paper-based; 250 computer-based). *Application deadline:* For fall admission, 1/15 priority date for domestic students, 1/15 priority date for international students. Application fee: $65. Electronic applications accepted. *Expenses:* Tuition, state resident: full-time $7,234; part-time $402 per semester hour. Tuition, nonresident: full-time $15,140; part-time $841 per semester hour. Required fees: $91 per term. Tuition and fees vary according to degree level, program and student level. *Financial support:* In 2003–04, 8 students received support, including fellowships with partial tuition reimbursements available (averaging $21,000 per year); Federal Work-Study and scholarships/grants also available. Support available to part-time students. Financial award application deadline: 3/15; financial award applicants required to submit FAFSA. *Faculty research:* Health disparities, central nervous system injuries, radiation exposure, analysis of clinical trial data, biomedical information. Total annual research expenditures: $6 million. *Unit head:* Dr. Barbara Tilley, Chair, 873-876-1327, Fax: 873-792-6950, E-mail: tilleyb@musc.edu. *Application contact:* Dr. Lana A. Cook, Assistant Dean for Admissions, 843-792-3391, Fax: 843-792-6590, E-mail: cookla@musc.edu.

Mount Sinai School of Medicine of New York University, Graduate School of Biological Sciences, Biophysics, Structural Biology and Biomathematics (BSBB) Training Area, New York, NY 10029-6504. Offers PhD, MD/PhD. *Degree requirements:* For doctorate, thesis/dissertation. *Entrance requirements:* For doctorate, GRE General Test, GRE Subject Test, MCAT. Additional exam requirements/recommendations for international students: Required—TOEFL.

New York Medical College, School of Public Health, Program in Biostatistics, Valhalla, NY 10595-1691. Offers MPH, MS. Part-time and evening/weekend programs available. In 2003, 4 degrees awarded. *Degree requirements:* For master's, thesis, registration. *Entrance requirements:* For master's, minimum undergraduate GPA of 3.0. Additional exam requirements/recommendations for international students: Required—TOEFL (minimum score 600 paper-based; 250 computer-based). *Application deadline:* For fall admission, 8/1 priority date for domestic students, 5/15 priority date for international students; for spring admission, 12/1 priority date for domestic students, 10/15 priority date for international students. Applications are processed on a rolling basis. Application fee: $35 ($60 for international students). Electronic applications accepted. *Financial support:* Career-related internships or fieldwork, Federal Work-Study, and institutionally sponsored loans available. Financial award application deadline: 6/15; financial award applicants required to submit FAFSA. *Unit head:* Dr. Quihu Shi, Director, 914-594-4804, Fax: 914-594-4292, E-mail: quihu_shi@nymc.edu. *Application contact:* Marian F. McGowan, Information Contact, 914-594-4510, Fax: 914-594-4292, E-mail: sph_admissions@nymc.edu.

The Ohio State University, Graduate School, College of Mathematical and Physical Sciences, Department of Statistics, Program in Biostatistics, Columbus, OH 43210. Offers PhD. *Faculty:* 14. *Students:* 12 full-time (9 women), 3 part-time (2 women), 11 international. 67 applicants, 19% accepted. In 2003, 13 degrees awarded. *Degree requirements:* For doctorate, thesis/dissertation. *Entrance requirements:* For doctorate, GRE General Test. Additional exam requirements/recommendations for international students: Required—TOEFL. *Application deadline:* For fall admission, 8/15 for domestic students. Applications are processed on a rolling basis. Application fee: $40 ($50 for international students). *Expenses:* Tuition, state resident: full-time $7,233. Tuition, nonresident: full-time $18,489. *Financial support:* Fellowships, research assistantships, teaching assistantships, Federal Work-Study and institutionally sponsored loans available. Support available to part-time students. *Application contact:* Dr. Elizabeth A. Stasny, Graduate Studies Committee Chair, 614-292-0784, Fax: 614-292-2096, E-mail: stasny.1@osu.edu.

Oregon Health & Science University, School of Medicine, Department of Public Health and Preventive Medicine, Portland, OR 97239-3098. Offers epidemiology and biostatistics (MPH). *Accreditation:* CEPH. Part-time programs available. *Degree requirements:* For master's, thesis, fieldwork/internship. *Entrance requirements:* For master's, GRE General Test, previous undergraduate course work in statistics. Additional exam requirements/recommendations for international students: Required—TOEFL. *Faculty research:* Health services, health care access, health policy, environmental and occupational health.

Rice University, Graduate Programs, George R. Brown School of Engineering, Department of Statistics, Houston, TX 77251-1892. Offers biostatistics (PhD); computational finance (PhD); statistics (M Stat, MA, PhD). *Faculty:* 9 full-time (2 women), 17 part-time/adjunct (1 woman). *Students:* 44 full-time (17 women), 1 (woman) part-time; includes 12 minority (5 African Americans, 2 Asian Americans or Pacific Islanders, 5 Hispanic Americans), 12 international. Average age 28. 130 applicants, 10% accepted, 9 enrolled. In 2003, 4 master's, 1 doctorate awarded. Terminal master's awarded for partial completion of doctoral program. *Median time to degree:* Of those who began their doctoral program in fall 1995, 90% received their degree in 8 years or less. *Degree requirements:* For master's, thesis/dissertation; for doctorate, thesis/dissertation, comprehensive exam. *Entrance requirements:* For master's and doctorate, GRE General Test, GRE Subject Test, minimum GPA of 3.0. Additional exam requirements/recommendations for international students: Required—TOEFL (minimum score 630 paper-based; 250 computer-based). *Application deadline:* For fall admission, 2/1 priority date for domestic students, 2/1 priority date for international students; for spring admission, 11/1 for domestic students, 11/1 for international students. Applications are processed on a rolling basis. Application fee: $35. Electronic applications accepted. *Expenses:* Tuition: Full-time $19,700; part-time $1,096 per hour. *Financial support:* In 2003–04, 15 fellowships with tuition reimbursements (averaging $20,000 per year), 15 research assistantships with tuition reimbursements (averaging $20,000 per year), 5 teaching assistantships with tuition reimbursements (averaging $20,000 per year) were awarded. Career-related internships or fieldwork, institutionally sponsored loans, scholarships/grants, traineeships, health care benefits, tuition waivers (full), and unspecified assistantships also available. Financial award application deadline: 1/15. *Faculty research:* Statistical genetics, non parametric function estimation, computational statistics and visualization, stochastic processes. Total annual research expenditures: $800,000. *Unit head:* Dr. Katherine B. Ensor, Chair, 713-527-6032, Fax: 713-348-5476, E-mail: kathy@rice.edu. *Application contact:* Leticia Gonzales, Recruiting Assistant, 713-348-6032, Fax: 713-348-5476, E-mail: lgonzale@rice.edu.

Rutgers, The State University of New Jersey, New Brunswick/Piscataway, Graduate School, Program in Statistics, New Brunswick, NJ 08901-1281. Offers quality and productivity management (MS); statistics (MS, PhD), including biostatistics (PhD), data mining (PhD). Part-time programs available. *Faculty:* 20 full-time (2 women). *Students:* 56 full-time (35 women), 90 part-time (56 women); includes 39 minority (36 Asian Americans or Pacific Islanders, 3 Hispanic Americans), 62 international. Average age 30. 253 applicants, 11% accepted, 18 enrolled. In 2003, 22 master's, 3 doctorates awarded. Terminal master's awarded for partial completion of doctoral program. *Degree requirements:* For master's, essay, exam, non-thesis essay paper; for doctorate, one foreign language, thesis/dissertation, qualifying oral and written exams. *Entrance requirements:* For master's, GRE General Test; for doctorate, GRE General Test, GRE Subject Test (recommended). Additional exam requirements/recommendations for international students: Required—TOEFL (minimum score 550 paper-based; 213 computer-based). *Application deadline:* For fall admission, 5/1 for domestic students; for spring admission, 12/1 priority date for domestic students. Applications are processed on a rolling basis. Application fee: $50. Electronic applications accepted. *Expenses:* Tuition, state resident: full-time $10,030. Tuition, nonresident: full-time $14,202. *Financial support:* In 2003–04, 16 students received support, including 4 fellowships with full tuition reimbursements available (averaging $16,000 per year), research assistantships with full tuition reimbursements available (averaging $14,500 per year), 11 teaching assistantships with full tuition reimbursements available (averaging $14,300 per year); career-related internships or fieldwork, Federal Work-Study, institutionally sponsored loans, scholarships/grants, health care benefits, unspecified assistantships, and grant/tuition remission also available. Financial award application deadline: 3/1; financial award applicants required to submit FAFSA. *Faculty research:* Probability, decision theory, linear models, multivariate statistics, statistical computing. *Unit head:* Dr. Cuh-Hui Zhang, Director, 732-445-2693, Fax: 732-445-3428, E-mail: czhang@stat.rutgers.edu. *Application contact:* Angela T. Klein, Department Secretary, 732-445-2693, Fax: 732-445-3428, E-mail: aklein@stat.rutgers.edu.

Saint Louis University, Graduate School, School of Public Health and Graduate School, Department of Community Health, St. Louis, MO 63103-2097. Offers behavioral science in health education (MPH); biostatistics (MPH); biostatistics and epidemiology (MPH); environmental and occupational health (MPH); environmental health and epidemiology (MPH); epidemiology (MPH). *Accreditation:* CEPH. Part-time programs available. *Faculty:* 29 full-time (13 women), 10 part-time/adjunct (4 women). *Students:* 85 full-time (62 women), 54 part-time (38 women); includes 38 minority (24 African Americans, 9 Asian Americans or Pacific Islanders, 5 Hispanic Americans), 14 international. Average age 32. 151 applicants, 70% accepted, 52 enrolled. In 2003, 63 degrees awarded. *Degree requirements:* For master's, comprehensive exam. *Entrance requirements:* For master's, GRE General Test. Additional exam requirements/recommendations for international students: Required—TOEFL (minimum score 550 paper-based; 213 computer-based). *Application deadline:* For fall admission, 7/1 for domestic students, 5/1 for international students; for spring admission, 11/1 for domestic students. Applications are processed on a rolling basis. Application fee: $40. *Expenses:* Tuition: Part-time $690 per credit hour. Required fees: $59 per semester. Tuition and fees vary according to program. *Financial support:* In 2003–04, 65 students received support, including 20 research assistantships; unspecified assistantships also available. Financial award application deadline: 6/1; financial award applicants required to submit FAFSA. *Faculty research:* Health communication, prevention research, obesity prevention, bioterrorism, community intervention. Total annual research expenditures: $9.7 million. *Unit head:* Dr. Ross C. Brownson, Chairperson, 314-977-8110, E-mail: brownson@slu.edu. *Application contact:* Gary Behrman, Associate Dean of the Graduate School, 314-977-3827, Fax: 314-977-3943, E-mail: behrmang@slu.edu.

San Diego State University, Graduate and Research Affairs, College of Health and Human Services, Graduate School of Public Health, San Diego, CA 92182. Offers environmental health (MPH); epidemiology (MPH, PhD), including biostatistics (MPH); health behavior (PhD); health promotion (MPH); health services administration (MPH); industrial hygiene (MS); toxicology (MS). *Accreditation:* ABET (one or more programs are accredited); ACEHSA (one or more programs are accredited); CEPH (one or more programs are accredited). Part-time programs available. *Faculty:* 29 full-time (13 women), 78 part-time/adjunct (34 women). *Students:* 263 full-time (181 women), 84 part-time (58 women); includes 121 minority (8 African Americans, 7 American Indian/Alaska Native, 68 Asian Americans or Pacific Islanders, 38 Hispanic Americans), 24 international. 406 applicants, 63% accepted, 115 enrolled. In 2003, 85 master's, 7 doctorates awarded. *Degree requirements:* For master's, thesis (for some programs), comprehensive exam (for some programs); for doctorate, thesis/dissertation. *Entrance requirements:* For master's, GMAT (health services administration (MPH) only), GRE General Test; for doctorate, GRE General Test. Additional exam requirements/recommendations for international students: Required—TOEFL. *Application deadline:* For fall admission, 5/1 for domestic students, 5/1 for international students; for spring admission, 11/1 for domestic students, 10/1 for international students. Applications are processed on a rolling basis. Application fee: $55. Tuition, nonresident: part-time $282 per unit. Required fees: $1,349; $875 per year. *Financial support:* Research assistantships, teaching assistantships, career-related internships or fieldwork, Federal Work-Study, and traineeships available. Financial award applicants required to submit FAFSA. *Faculty research:* Evaluation of tobacco, AIDS prevalence and prevention, mammography, infant death project, Alzheimer's in elderly Chinese. *Unit head:* Dr. Kenneth Bart, Director, 619-594-6317. *Application contact:* Brenda Fass-Holmes, Coordinator, Admissions and Student Affairs, 619-594-6317, E-mail: brenda.fass-holmes@sdsu.edu.

San Diego State University, Graduate and Research Affairs, College of Sciences, Department of Biological Sciences, Program in Biostatistics and Biometry, San Diego, CA 92182. Offers PhD. Program offered jointly with the University of California, Davis. *Degree requirements:* For doctorate, thesis/dissertation. *Entrance requirements:* For doctorate, GRE General Test, GRE Subject Test. *Application deadline:* For fall admission, 5/1 for domestic students; for spring admission, 11/1 for domestic students, 10/1 for international students. Applications are processed on a rolling basis. Application fee: $55. Electronic applications accepted. Tuition, nonresident: part-time $282 per unit. Required fees: $1,349; $875 per year. *Financial support:* Research assistantships, teaching assistantships, career-related internships or fieldwork, scholarships/grants, and unspecified assistantships available. *Unit head:* K. J. Lui, Graduate Advisor, 619-594-7239, Fax: 619-594-6746, E-mail: kil@rohan.sdsu.edu.

Tufts University, Sackler School of Graduate Biomedical Sciences, Division of Clinical Care Research, Medford, MA 02155. Offers MS, PhD. Part-time programs available. *Faculty:* 18 full-time (6 women), 1 part-time/adjunct (0 women). *Students:* 20 full-time (9 women), 12 part-time (4 women); includes 4 minority (all Asian Americans or Pacific Islanders), 3 international. Average age 35. 17 applicants, 71% accepted, 12 enrolled. In 2003, 7 degrees awarded. Terminal master's awarded for partial completion of doctoral program. *Degree requirements:* For master's and doctorate, thesis/dissertation. *Entrance requirements:* For master's and doctorate, MD or PhD, strong clinical research background. Additional exam requirements/recommendations for international students: Required—TOEFL. *Application deadline:* For fall admission, 1/15 priority date for domestic students, 1/15 priority date for international students. Applications are processed on a rolling basis. Application fee: $60. Electronic applications accepted. *Expenses:* Tuition: Full-time $29,949. *Financial support:* In 2003–04, 32 fellowships with full tuition reimbursements (averaging $44,000 per year) were awarded. Financial award application deadline: 1/15. *Faculty research:* Clinical study design, mathematical modeling, meta analysis, epidemiologic research, coronary heart disease. *Unit head:* Dr. Harry P. Selker, Program Director, 617-636-5009, Fax: 617-636-8023, E-mail: hselker@lifespan.org. *Application contact:* 617-636-6767, Fax: 617-636-0375, E-mail: sackler-school@tufts.edu.

Tulane University, School of Public Health and Tropical Medicine, Department of Biostatistics, New Orleans, LA 70118-5669. Offers MS, MSPH, PhD, Sc D. MS and PhD offered through the Graduate School. Part-time programs available. *Faculty:* 7 full-time (4 women). *Students:* 44 full-time (21 women), 6 part-time (2 women); includes 3 minority (1 African American, 2 Asian Americans or Pacific Islanders), 14 international. Average age 35. In 2003, 19 degrees awarded. *Degree requirements:* For doctorate, thesis/dissertation, comprehensive exam. *Entrance requirements:* For master's and doctorate, GRE General Test. Additional exam requirements/recommendations for international students: Required—TOEFL. *Application deadline:* For fall admission, 4/15 priority date for domestic students, 4/15 priority date for international students; for spring admission, 10/15 priority date for domestic students, 10/15 priority date for international students. Applications are processed on a rolling basis. Application fee: $40. Electronic applications accepted. *Financial support:* In 2003–04, 2 students received support, including 1 research assistantship with partial tuition reimbursement available, 1 teaching assistantship with partial tuition reimbursement available; Federal Work-Study, scholarships/grants, traineeships, and tuition waivers (partial) also available. Financial award application deadline: 4/15. *Faculty research:* Clinical trials, measurement, longitudinal analyses. *Unit head:* Dr. Janet Hughes, Chairman, 504-587-7334, Fax: 504-584-1706, E-mail: hughes@tulane.edu. *Application contact:* Susan Gautier, Program Coordinator, 504-588-1706, E-mail: sgautier@tulane.edu.

University at Buffalo, The State University of New York, Graduate School, School of Public Health and Health Professions, Department of Biostatistics, Buffalo, NY 14260. Offers MA, PhD. *Faculty:* 5 full-time (1 woman). *Students:* 1 full-time (0 women), 1 part-time, 1 international. *Degree requirements:* For master's, final oral exam, practical data, analysis experience, thesis optional; for doctorate, thesis/dissertation, final oral exam. *Entrance requirements:* For master's, 3 semesters of calculus. Additional exam requirements/recommendations for international students: Required—TOEFL (minimum score 550 paper-based; 213 computer-based). *Application deadline:* For fall admission, 2/1 priority date for domestic students, 2/1 priority date for international students. Application fee: $35. Electronic applications accepted. *Expenses:* Tuition, state resident: full-time $7,110. Tuition, nonresident: full-time $10,920. Tuition and fees vary according to program. *Financial support:* In 2003–04, research assistantships with full tuition reimbursements (averaging $15,000 per year), teaching assistantships with full tuition reimbursements (averaging $15,000 per year) were awarded. Tuition waivers (partial) also available. *Faculty research:* Biostatistics, longitudinal data analysis, nonparametrics, statistical genetics, categorical data analysis. *Unit head:* Dr. Alan D. Hutson, Chair and Associate Professor, 716-829-2594, Fax: 716-829-2200, E-mail: ahutson@buffalo.edu. *Application contact:* Dr.

Biostatistics

University at Buffalo, The State University of New York (continued)
Randolph L. Carter, Associate Chair and Professor, 716-829-2884, Fax: 716-829-2200, E-mail: rcarter@buffalo.edu.

The University of Alabama at Birmingham, School of Public Health, Department of Biostatistics, Birmingham, AL 35294. Offers biomathematics (MS, PhD); biostatistics (MS, PhD). *Students:* 13 full-time (3 women), 2 part-time (1 woman); includes 3 minority (all African Americans), 6 international. 88 applicants, 35% accepted. In 2003, 3 master's, 1 doctorate awarded. *Degree requirements:* For master's, variable foreign language requirement, thesis, fieldwork, research project; for doctorate, variable foreign language requirement, thesis/dissertation, comprehensive exam. *Entrance requirements:* For master's, GRE General Test or MAT, minimum GPA of 3.0; for doctorate, GRE General Test or MAT, MPH or MSPH, minimum GPA of 3.0, interview. *Application deadline:* Applications are processed on a rolling basis. Application fee: $35 ($60 for international students). Electronic applications accepted. *Expenses:* Contact institution. *Financial support:* Fellowships, career-related internships or fieldwork available. *Unit head:* Dr. George Howard, Chair, 205-934-4905, Fax: 205-975-2540, E-mail: ghoward@uab.edu. *Application contact:* Nancy O. Pinson, Coordinator of Student Admissions, 205-934-4993, Fax: 205-975-5484.

University of Alberta, Faculty of Graduate Studies and Research, Department of Mathematical and Statistical Sciences, Edmonton, AB T6G 2E1, Canada. Offers applied mathematics (M Sc, PhD); biostatistics (M Sc); mathematical finance (M Sc, PhD); mathematical physics (M Sc, PhD); mathematics (M Sc, PhD); statistics (M Sc, PhD, Postgraduate Diploma). Part-time programs available. *Faculty:* 48 full-time (4 women). *Students:* 112 full-time (41 women), 5 part-time. Average age 24. 776 applicants, 5% accepted, 34 enrolled. In 2003, 12 master's, 10 doctorates awarded. Terminal master's awarded for partial completion of doctoral program. *Median time to degree:* Master's–2 years full-time; doctorate–5 years full-time. Of those who began their doctoral program in fall 1995, 100% received their degree in 8 years or less. *Degree requirements:* For master's, thesis (for some programs); for doctorate, thesis/dissertation, comprehensive exam. *Entrance requirements:* Additional exam requirements/recommendations for international students: Required—TOEFL (minimum score 580 paper-based; 237 computer-based). *Application deadline:* For fall admission, 3/1 for domestic students, 2/1 for international students. Applications are processed on a rolling basis. Application fee: $0. Electronic applications accepted. Tuition charges are reported in Canadian dollars. Tuition, nonresident: full-time $3,921 Canadian dollars. International tuition: $7,113 Canadian dollars full-time. *Financial support:* In 2003–04, 51 research assistantships, 88 teaching assistantships with full and partial tuition reimbursements were awarded. Scholarships/grants also available. Financial award application deadline: 5/1. *Faculty research:* Classical and functional analysis, algebra, differential equations, geometry. *Unit head:* Dr. Anthony To-Ming Lau, Chair, 403-492-5799, E-mail: tlau@math.ualberta.ca. *Application contact:* Dr. Yau Shu Wong, Associate Chair, Graduate Studies, 403-492-5799, Fax: 403-492-6828, E-mail: gradstudies@math.ualberta.ca.

University of California, Berkeley, Graduate Division, School of Public Health, Division of Biostatistics, Group in Biostatistics, Berkeley, CA 94720-1500. Offers MA, PhD. *Students:* 35 (22 women); includes 5 minority (all Asian Americans or Pacific Islanders) 19 international. 94 applicants, 17% accepted, 7 enrolled. In 2003, 5 master's, 2 doctorates awarded. *Degree requirements:* For master's, comprehensive exam; for doctorate, thesis/dissertation, qualifying exam. *Entrance requirements:* For master's and doctorate, GRE General Test, minimum GPA of 3.0. Additional exam requirements/recommendations for international students: Required—TOEFL. *Application deadline:* For fall admission, 12/1 for domestic students. Applications are processed on a rolling basis. Application fee: $60. International tuition: $12,491 full-time. Required fees: $5,484. *Financial support:* In 2003–04, 5 fellowships with full and partial tuition reimbursements, 2 research assistantships with full tuition reimbursements (averaging $13,000 per year), 4 teaching assistantships with partial tuition reimbursements (averaging $14,445 per year) were awarded. Career-related internships or fieldwork, Federal Work-Study, institutionally sponsored loans, and unspecified assistantships also available. Financial award application deadline: 12/1; financial award applicants required to submit FAFSA. *Faculty research:* Applied statistics, risk research, clinical trials, nonparametrics. *Unit head:* Nicholas P. Jewell, Chair, 510-642-4627, E-mail: jewell@uclink4.berkeley.edu. *Application contact:* Bonnie Hutchings, Graduate Assistant, 510-642-3241, E-mail: bjh@stat.berkeley.edu.

University of California, Davis, Graduate Studies, Graduate Group in Biostatistics, Davis, CA 95616. Offers MS, PhD. *Faculty:* 22. *Students:* 12 full-time (10 women); includes 2 minority (both American Indian/Alaska Native), 8 international. Average age 27. 72 applicants, 42% accepted, 6 enrolled. *Entrance requirements:* Additional exam requirements/recommendations for international students: Required—TOEFL (minimum score 550 paper-based; 213 computer-based). *Application deadline:* For fall admission, 1/15 for domestic students, 1/15 for international students. Applications are processed on a rolling basis. Application fee: $60. Electronic applications accepted. Tuition, nonresident: full-time $12,245. Required fees: $7,062. *Financial support:* In 2003–04, 11 students received support, including 2 research assistantships with full and partial tuition reimbursements available (averaging $8,511 per year), 4 teaching assistantships with partial tuition reimbursements available (averaging $12,545 per year); fellowships with full and partial tuition reimbursements available, Federal Work-Study, institutionally sponsored loans, scholarships/grants, tuition waivers (full and partial), and unspecified assistantships also available. Financial award application deadline: 1/15. *Unit head:* Hans-Georg Mueller, Graduate Group Chair, 530-752-1629, E-mail: hgmueller@ucdavis.edu. *Application contact:* Effie Kolbeins, Administrative Assistant, 530-752-2632, Fax: 530-752-7099, E-mail: grad-staff@wald.ucdavis.edu.

University of California, Los Angeles, Graduate Division, School of Public Health, Department of Biostatistics, Los Angeles, CA 90095. Offers MS, PhD. *Degree requirements:* For master's, comprehensive exam; for doctorate, thesis/dissertation, oral and written qualifying exams. *Entrance requirements:* For master's, GRE General Test, minimum GPA of 3.0; for doctorate, GRE General Test, minimum undergraduate GPA of 3.0. Electronic applications accepted. Tuition, nonresident: full-time $12,245. Required fees: $6,318.

University of Cincinnati, Division of Research and Advanced Studies, College of Medicine, Graduate Programs in Medicine, Department of Environmental Health, Cincinnati, OH 45267. Offers environmental and industrial hygiene (MS, PhD); environmental and occupational medicine (MS); epidemiology and biostatistics (MS, PhD); occupational safety and ergonomics (MS, PhD); toxicology (MS, PhD). *Accreditation:* ABET (one or more programs are accredited). Terminal master's awarded for partial completion of doctoral program. *Degree requirements:* For master's, thesis; for doctorate, thesis/dissertation, qualifying exam. *Entrance requirements:* For master's, GRE General Test, bachelor's degree in science; for doctorate, GRE General Test. Additional exam requirements/recommendations for international students: Required—TOEFL (minimum score 580 paper-based; 237 computer-based). Electronic applications accepted. *Faculty research:* Carcinogens and mutagenesis, pulmonary studies, reproduction and development.

University of Illinois at Chicago, Graduate College, School of Public Health, Biostatistics Section, Chicago, IL 60607-7128. Offers MS, PhD. Part-time programs available. *Students:* 10 full-time (6 women), 11 part-time (6 women); includes 6 minority (1 African American, 5 Asian Americans or Pacific Islanders), 14 international. Average age 32. 57 applicants, 19% accepted, 5 enrolled. In 2003, 10 degrees awarded. Terminal master's awarded for partial completion of doctoral program. *Degree requirements:* For master's, thesis, field practicum; for doctorate, thesis/dissertation, independent research, internship. *Entrance requirements:* For master's and doctorate, GRE General Test, minimum GPA of 3.75 on a 5.0 scale. Additional exam requirements/recommendations for international students: Required—TOEFL. *Application deadline:* For fall admission, 2/1 for domestic students, 1/1 for international students. Application fee: $40 ($50 for international students). Electronic applications accepted. *Expenses:* Tuition, state resident: part-time $941 per semester. Tuition, nonresident: part-time $2,338 per semester. *Financial support:* Fellowships with full tuition reimbursements, research assistantships with full tuition reimbursements, teaching assistantships with full tuition reimbursements, career-related internships or fieldwork, Federal Work-Study, institutionally sponsored loans, scholarships/grants, traineeships, tuition waivers (full), and unspecified assistantships available. Support available to part-time students. Financial award application deadline: 3/1; financial award applicants required to submit FAFSA. *Application contact:* Dr. Sylvia Furner, Director of Graduate Studies, 312-996-5013.

The University of Iowa, Graduate College, College of Public Health, Department of Biostatistics, Iowa City, IA 52242-1316. Offers MS, PhD. *Faculty:* 8 full-time, 1 part-time/adjunct. *Students:* 30 full-time (18 women), 8 part-time (1 woman); includes 3 minority (all Asian Americans or Pacific Islanders), 27 international. 75 applicants, 49% accepted, 8 enrolled. In 2003, 5 master's, 1 doctorate awarded. *Degree requirements:* For master's, exam, thesis optional; for doctorate, thesis/dissertation, comprehensive exam, registration. *Entrance requirements:* For master's and doctorate, GRE General Test, minimum GPA of 3.0. Additional exam requirements/recommendations for international students: Required—TOEFL (minimum score 550 paper-based; 213 computer-based). *Application deadline:* For fall admission, 1/15 priority date for domestic students, 1/15 priority date for international students; for spring admission, 10/1 priority date for domestic students. Applications are processed on a rolling basis. Application fee: $50 ($75 for international students). Electronic applications accepted. *Expenses:* Tuition, state resident: full-time $5,038. Tuition, nonresident: full-time $15,072. Tuition and fees vary according to course load and program. *Financial support:* In 2003–04, 1 fellowship, 22 research assistantships, 8 teaching assistantships were awarded. Financial award applicants required to submit FAFSA. *Unit head:* Kathryn Chaloner, Head, 319-384-5029, Fax: 319-384-5018.

University of Louisville, Graduate School, School of Public Health, Program in Bioinformatics and Biostatistics, Louisville, KY 40292-0001. Offers MS, PhD. *Students:* 12 full-time (5 women), 5 part-time (1 woman), 5 international. In 2003, 6 degrees awarded. Application fee: $50. *Expenses:* Tuition, state resident: full-time $4,842. Tuition, nonresident: full-time $13,338. *Unit head:* Dr. Richard D. Clover, Dean, School of Public Health, 502-852-3297, Fax: 502-852-3291, E-mail: rdclov01@gwise.louisville.edu.

University of Michigan, School of Public Health, Department of Biostatistics, Ann Arbor, MI 48109. Offers MPH, MS, PhD. MS and PhD offered through the Horace H. Rackham School of Graduate Studies. *Faculty:* 15 full-time (3 women), 11 part-time/adjunct (5 women). *Students:* 76 full-time (43 women), 1 (woman) part-time; includes 4 minority (1 African American, 2 Asian Americans or Pacific Islanders, 1 Hispanic American), 42 international. Average age 27. 277 applicants, 36% accepted. *Median time to degree:* Master's–2 years full-time; doctorate–4.75 years full-time. *Degree requirements:* For doctorate, oral defense of dissertation, preliminary exam. *Entrance requirements:* For master's, GRE General Test, MCAT; for doctorate, GRE General Test, MCAT, master's degree. Additional exam requirements/recommendations for international students: Required—TOEFL (minimum score 560 paper-based; 220 computer-based). *Application deadline:* For fall admission, 2/1 for domestic students. Applications are processed on a rolling basis. Application fee: $60 ($75 for international students). Electronic applications accepted. *Expenses:* Tuition, state resident: full-time $7,463. Tuition, nonresident: full-time $13,913. Full-time tuition and fees vary according to course load, degree level and program. *Financial support:* In 2003–04, 67 students received support, including 3 fellowships with full tuition reimbursements available (averaging $12,853 per year), 45 research assistantships with full tuition reimbursements available (averaging $12,853 per year), 12 teaching assistantships with full tuition reimbursements available (averaging $12,853 per year); scholarships/grants, traineeships, and tuition waivers (partial) also available. Financial award application deadline: 2/1. *Faculty research:* Statistical genetics, categorical data analysis, incomplete data, survival analysis, modeling. Total annual research expenditures: $4.7 million. *Unit head:* Dr. John David Kalbfleisch, Chair, 734-615-7067, Fax: 734-763-2215, E-mail: jdkalbfl@umich.edu. *Application contact:* Heonia Hillock, Student Services Assistant, 734-615-9812, Fax: 734-763-2215, E-mail: sph.bio.inquiries@umich.edu.

University of Michigan, School of Public Health, Interdepartmental Program in Clinical Research Design and Statistical Analysis, Ann Arbor, MI 48109. Offers MS. Offered through the Horace H. Rackham School of Graduate Studies; program admits applicants in odd calendar years. Part-time and evening/weekend programs available. *Faculty:* 6. *Students:* 42 full-time. 49 applicants, 92% accepted. *Degree requirements:* For master's, thesis. *Entrance requirements:* For master's, GRE General Test. *Application deadline:* For fall admission, 2/1 for domestic students. Applications are processed on a rolling basis. Application fee: $60 ($75 for international students). Electronic applications accepted. *Expenses:* Tuition, state resident: full-time $7,463. Tuition, nonresident: full-time $13,913. Full-time tuition and fees vary according to course load, degree level and program. *Unit head:* Rod Little, Director, 734-936-1009. *Application contact:* Amanda Cumming, Information Contact, 734-615-9817, E-mail: sph.bio.inquiries@umich.edu.

University of Minnesota, Twin Cities Campus, School of Public Health, Major in Biostatistics, Minneapolis, MN 55455-0213. Offers MPH, MS, PhD. Part-time programs available. *Faculty:* 18 full-time (9 women). *Students:* 47 full-time (31 women), 7 part-time (all women); includes 1 minority (Asian American or Pacific Islander), 42 international. 89 applicants, 38% accepted. In 2003, 18 master's, 1 doctorate awarded. Terminal master's awarded for partial completion of doctoral program. *Degree requirements:* For master's, comprehensive exam; for doctorate, thesis/dissertation, comprehensive exam. *Entrance requirements:* For master's, GRE General Test, coursework in applied statistics, computer programming, multivariable calculus, linear algebra; for doctorate, GRE General Test, M.S. in statistics, biostatistics, or applied statistics, coursework in real analysis, math statistics. Additional exam requirements/recommendations for international students: Required—TOEFL (minimum score 600 paper-based; 250 computer-based). *Application deadline:* For fall admission, 12/31 for domestic students. Applications are processed on a rolling basis. Application fee: $55 ($75 for international students). Electronic applications accepted. *Expenses:* Tuition, state resident: full-time $3,681; part-time $614 per credit. Tuition, nonresident: full-time $7,231; part-time $1,205 per credit. *Financial support:* In 2003–04, research assistantships with partial tuition reimbursements (averaging $16,500 per year), teaching assistantships with partial tuition reimbursements (averaging $16,500 per year) were awarded. Fellowships with partial tuition reimbursements, institutionally sponsored loans and traineeships also available. *Faculty research:* Analysis of spatial and longitudinal data, Bayes/Empirical Bayes methods, survival analysis, longitudinal models, generalized linear models. *Unit head:* Dr. John E. Connett, Division Head, 612-626-3699, Fax: 612-626-0660, E-mail: john-c@ccbr.umn.edu. *Application contact:* Sally Olander, Coordinator, 612-625-9185, Fax: 612-624-0660, E-mail: sally@biostat.umn.edu.

The University of North Carolina at Chapel Hill, Graduate School, School of Public Health, Department of Biostatistics, Chapel Hill, NC 27599. Offers MPH, MS, Dr PH, PhD. Part-time programs available. *Faculty:* 36 full-time (10 women), 39 part-time/adjunct. *Students:* 95 full-time (47 women); includes 47 minority (6 African Americans, 2 American Indian/Alaska Native, 34 Asian Americans or Pacific Islanders, 5 Hispanic Americans). Average age 27. 218 applicants, 23% accepted, 18 enrolled. In 2003, 23 master's, 9 doctorates awarded. *Median time to degree:* Master's–2 years full-time; doctorate–4 years full-time. *Degree requirements:* For master's, thesis, major paper, comprehensive exam; for doctorate, thesis/dissertation, comprehensive exam. *Entrance requirements:* For master's and doctorate, GRE General Test, minimum GPA of 3.0. Additional exam requirements/recommendations for international students: Required—TOEFL. *Application deadline:* For fall admission, 1/1 for domestic students, 1/1 for international students. Applications are processed on a rolling basis. Application fee: $60. Electronic applications accepted. *Expenses:* Tuition, state resident: full-time $3,163. Tuition, nonresident: full-time $15,161. *Financial support:* In 2003–04, 60 students received support, including 28 fellowships with full tuition reimbursements available (averaging $11,732 per year), 32 research assistantships with full tuition reimbursements available (averaging $12,738 per year); teaching assistantships with full tuition reimbursements available, Federal Work-Study, institutionally sponsored loans, and unspecified assistantships also available. Financial award application deadline: 1/1; financial award applicants required to submit FAFSA. *Faculty research:* Cancer, cardiovascular, environmental biostatistics; AIDS and other infectious diseases;

statistical genetics; demography and population studies. Total annual research expenditures: $10 million. *Unit head:* Dr. Clarence E. Davis, Chair, 919-966-7254, Fax: 919-966-3804, E-mail: ed_davis@unc.edu. *Application contact:* Melissa Hobgood, Registrar, 919-966-7256, Fax: 919-966-3804, E-mail: hobgood@unc.edu.

University of North Texas Health Science Center at Fort Worth, School of Public Health, Fort Worth, TX 76107-2699. Offers biostatistics (MPH); community health (MPH); disease control and prevention (Dr PH); environmental health (MPH); epidemiology (MPH); health behavior (MPH); health policy and management (MPH, Dr PH). *Accreditation:* CEPH. Part-time and evening/weekend programs available. *Faculty:* 26 full-time (6 women). *Students:* 121 full-time (73 women), 123 part-time (78 women); includes 95 minority (35 African Americans, 3 American Indian/Alaska Native, 22 Asian Americans or Pacific Islanders, 35 Hispanic Americans), 46 international. Average age 33. 229 applicants, 48% accepted, 48 enrolled. In 2003, 36 degrees awarded. *Degree requirements:* For master's, thesis or alternative, supervised internship; for doctorate, thesis/dissertation, supervised internship. *Entrance requirements:* For master's, GRE General Test. Additional exam requirements/recommendations for international students: Required—TOEFL. *Application deadline:* For fall admission, 6/1 for domestic students. Applications are processed on a rolling basis. Application fee: $25 ($50 for international students). Electronic applications accepted. *Expenses:* Tuition, state resident: full-time $6,550. *Financial support:* In 2003–04, 9 research assistantships with partial tuition reimbursements (averaging $16,000 per year), 2 teaching assistantships (averaging $8,100 per year) were awarded. Fellowships, Federal Work-Study, institutionally sponsored loans, and scholarships/grants also available. Support available to part-time students. Financial award application deadline: 4/1; financial award applicants required to submit FAFSA. *Unit head:* Dr. Fernando Treviño, Dean, 817-735-2401, Fax: 817-735-0243, E-mail: sph@hsc.unt.edu. *Application contact:* Thomas Moorman, Director of Student Affairs, 817-735-0302, Fax: 817-735-0324, E-mail: tmoorman@hsc.unt.edu.

University of Oklahoma Health Sciences Center, Graduate College, College of Public Health, Program in Biostatistics and Epidemiology, Oklahoma City, OK 73190. Offers biostatistics (MPH, MS, Dr PH, PhD); epidemiology (MPH, MS, Dr PH, PhD). *Accreditation:* CEPH (one or more programs are accredited). Part-time programs available. *Faculty:* 12 full-time (7 women), 13 part-time/adjunct (8 women). *Students:* 49 full-time (24 women), 34 part-time (22 women); includes 16 minority (7 African Americans, 4 American Indian/Alaska Native, 4 Asian Americans or Pacific Islanders, 1 Hispanic American), 33 international. Average age 32. 144 applicants, 24% accepted, 16 enrolled. In 2003, 15 master's, 3 doctorates awarded. *Degree requirements:* For master's, thesis (for some programs), comprehensive exam; for doctorate, thesis/dissertation, comprehensive exam. *Entrance requirements:* For master's, letters of recommendation; for doctorate, GRE, letters of recommendation. Additional exam requirements/recommendations for international students: Required—TOEFL, TWE. *Application deadline:* For fall admission, 7/1 for domestic students; for spring admission, 12/1 for domestic students. Applications are processed on a rolling basis. Application fee: $50. *Expenses:* Tuition, state resident: full-time $2,081; part-time $156 per credit. Tuition, nonresident: part-time $284 per credit. International tuition: $5,103 full-time. *Financial support:* In 2003–04, 7 research assistantships (averaging $14,000 per year) were awarded; career-related internships or fieldwork, institutionally sponsored loans, and traineeships also available. Support available to part-time students. Financial award application deadline: 5/1. *Faculty research:* Statistical methodology, applied statistics, acute and chronic disease epidemiology. *Unit head:* Dr. Willis Owen, Interim Chair, 405-271-2229, E-mail: willis-owen@ouhsc.edu.

University of Pennsylvania, School of Medicine, Biomedical Graduate Studies, Graduate Group in Epidemiology and Biostatistics, Philadelphia, PA 19104. Offers biostatistics (MS, PhD). Part-time programs available. *Faculty:* 80. *Students:* 24 full-time (12 women); includes 3 minority (all Asian Americans or Pacific Islanders), 11 international. Average age 25. In 2003, 5 degrees awarded. *Degree requirements:* For master's, thesis, evaluations examination; for doctorate, thesis/dissertation, evaluations exam, preliminary exam. *Entrance requirements:* For master's and doctorate, GRE, one year of calculus, one semester of linear algebra, working knowledge of programming language. *Application deadline:* For fall admission, 1/5 for domestic students. Application fee: $70. *Expenses:* Tuition: Full-time $28,040; part-time $3,550 per course. Required fees: $1,750; $214 per course. Tuition and fees vary according to degree level, program and student level. *Financial support:* In 2003–04, 1 fellowship, 21 research assistantships with full tuition reimbursements were awarded. Scholarships/grants, unspecified assistantships, and faculty/staff benefits provide partial tuition coverage also available. Financial award application deadline: 1/5. *Faculty research:* Randomized clinical trials, data coordinating centers, methodological approaches to non-experimental epidemiologic studies, theoretical research in biostatistics. Total annual research expenditures: $16.1 million. *Unit head:* Dr. Brian L. Strom, Chair, 215-898-2368, Fax: 215-573-5315, E-mail: bstrom@cceb.med.upenn.edu. *Application contact:* Anne Facciolo, Program Coordinator, 215-573-3881, Fax: 215-573-4865, E-mail: afacciol@cceb.upenn.edu.

University of Pittsburgh, Graduate School of Public Health, Department of Biostatistics, Pittsburgh, PA 15260. Offers MPH, MS, Dr PH, PhD. Part-time programs available. *Faculty:* 20 full-time (6 women). *Students:* 52 full-time (35 women), 25 part-time (15 women); includes 12 minority (3 African Americans, 8 Asian Americans or Pacific Islanders, 1 Hispanic American), 36 international. Average age 30. 122 applicants, 57% accepted, 25 enrolled. In 2003, 5 master's, 8 doctorates awarded. Terminal master's awarded for partial completion of doctoral program. *Degree requirements:* For master's, thesis; for doctorate, one foreign language, thesis/dissertation. *Entrance requirements:* For master's and doctorate, GRE General Test, previous course work in biology, calculus, and fortran. Additional exam requirements/recommendations for international students: Required—TOEFL (minimum score 550 paper-based; 213 computer-based). *Application deadline:* For fall admission, 3/30 priority date for domestic students, 3/1 priority date for international students; for spring admission, 11/30 for domestic students, 5/1 for international students. Applications are processed on a rolling basis. Application fee: $50 ($60 for international students). Electronic applications accepted. *Expenses:* Tuition, state resident: full-time $11,744; part-time $479 per credit. Tuition, nonresident: full-time $22,910; part-time $941 per credit. Required fees: $560. Tuition and fees vary according to degree level and program. *Financial support:* In 2003–04, 31 students received support, including 30 research assistantships with tuition reimbursements available (averaging $18,324 per year), 3 teaching assistantships with tuition reimbursements available (averaging $19,158 per year); career-related internships or fieldwork, Federal Work-Study, institutionally sponsored loans, and tuition waivers (partial) also available. Support available to part-time students. Financial award application deadline: 2/28. *Faculty research:* Survival analysis, environmental risk assessment, statistical computing, longitudinal data analysis, experimental design. Total annual research expenditures: $8.6 million. *Unit head:* Dr. Howard E. Rockette, Chairperson, 412-624-3022, Fax: 412-624-2183, E-mail: herbst@pitt.edu. *Application contact:* Dr. Lisa Weissfeld, Professor, 412-624-3023, Fax: 412-624-2183, E-mail: lweis@pitt.edu.

University of Puerto Rico, Medical Sciences Campus, Graduate School of Public Health, Department of Biostatistics and Epidemiology, Program in Biostatistics, San Juan, PR 00936-5067. Offers MPH. Part-time programs available. *Students:* 10 (7 women). 27 applicants, 44% accepted. In 2003, 13 degrees awarded. *Entrance requirements:* For master's, GRE, previous course work in algebra. *Application deadline:* For fall admission, 3/15 for domestic students. Application fee: $15. Nonresident students who are US citizens pay tuition and fees equal to the amount they would pay in their home state. Required fees: $1,192. One-time fee: $50 part-time. Tuition and fees vary according to class time, degree level and program. *Financial support:* Research assistantships, teaching assistantships, career-related internships or fieldwork, Federal Work-Study, and institutionally sponsored loans available. Financial award application deadline: 4/30. *Unit head:* Prof. Rodolfo Vargas, Coordinator, 787-758-2525 Ext. 1428, Fax: 787-759-6719, E-mail: rvargas@rcm.upr.edu. *Application contact:* Prof. Mayra E. Santiago-Vargas, Counselor, 787-756-5244, Fax: 787-759-6719, E-mail: msantiago@rcm.upr.edu.

University of Rochester, School of Medicine and Dentistry, Graduate Programs in Medicine and Dentistry, Department of Biostatistics and Computational Biology, Rochester, NY 14627-0250. Offers medical statistics (MS); statistics (MA, PhD). *Faculty:* 10. *Students:* 9 full-time (6 women); includes 2 minority (1 American Indian/Alaska Native, 1 Asian American or Pacific Islander), 4 international. 92 applicants, 5% accepted, 3 enrolled. In 2003, 3 master's, 4 doctorates awarded. Terminal master's awarded for partial completion of doctoral program. *Degree requirements:* For doctorate, thesis/dissertation, qualifying exam. *Entrance requirements:* For master's and doctorate, GRE General Test. Additional exam requirements/recommendations for international students: Required—TOEFL. *Application deadline:* For fall admission, 2/1 for domestic students. Application fee: $25. *Expenses:* Tuition: Part-time $880 per credit hour. Required fees: $522. *Financial support:* Fellowships, research assistantships, teaching assistantships, tuition waivers (full and partial) available. Financial award application deadline: 2/1. *Unit head:* Dr. Andrei Yakovlev, Chair, 585-275-2404. *Application contact:* Patti Kolomic, Administrative Assistant, 585-275-6696, E-mail: kolomic@metro.bst.rochester.edu.

University of South Carolina, The Graduate School, Norman J. Arnold School of Public Health, Department of Epidemiology/Biostatistics, Program in Biostatistics, Columbia, SC 29208. Offers MPH, MSPH, Dr PH, PhD. Part-time programs available. *Faculty:* 9 full-time (3 women), 7 part-time/adjunct (1 woman). *Students:* 12 full-time (7 women), 5 part-time (3 women), 11 international. Average age 32. 26 applicants, 85% accepted, 6 enrolled. In 2003, 8 degrees awarded. *Degree requirements:* For master's, thesis (for some programs), practicum (MPH), comprehensive exam; for doctorate, thesis/dissertation, comprehensive exam. *Entrance requirements:* For master's and doctorate, GRE General Test. Additional exam requirements/recommendations for international students: Required—TOEFL (minimum score 570 paper-based; 230 computer-based). *Application deadline:* For fall admission, 2/1 for domestic students; for spring admission, 10/1 for domestic students. Application fee: $40. Electronic applications accepted. *Expenses:* Tuition, state resident: part-time $308 per hour. Tuition, nonresident: part-time $655 per hour. *Financial support:* Research assistantships, teaching assistantships, traineeships available. *Faculty research:* Bayesian methods, biometric modeling, nonlinear regression, health survey methodology, measurement of health status. *Application contact:* Dr. Cheryl Addy, Graduate Director, 803-777-7353, Fax: 803-777-2524, E-mail: caddy@gwm.sc.edu.

University of Southern California, Keck School of Medicine and Graduate School, Graduate Programs in Medicine, Department of Preventive Medicine, Division of Biostatistics, Los Angeles, CA 90089. Offers applied biostatistics/epidemiology (MS); biostatistics (MS, PhD); epidemiology (PhD); genetic epidemiology and statistical genetics (PhD); molecular epidemiology (MS, PhD). *Faculty:* 60 full-time (25 women). *Students:* 88 full-time (60 women); includes 23 minority (2 African Americans, 19 Asian Americans or Pacific Islanders, 2 Hispanic Americans), 43 international. Average age 30. 98 applicants, 57% accepted, 21 enrolled. In 2003, 13 master's, 4 doctorates awarded. Terminal master's awarded for partial completion of doctoral program. *Median time to degree:* Master's–5 years part-time; doctorate–4 years full-time, 6 years part-time. *Degree requirements:* For master's and doctorate, thesis/dissertation. *Entrance requirements:* For master's, GRE General Test, GRE Subject Test, minimum GPA of 3.0; for doctorate, GRE General Test, GRE Subject Test, minimum GPA of 3.5. Additional exam requirements/recommendations for international students: Required—TOEFL. *Application deadline:* For fall admission, 1/15 for domestic students. Applications are processed on a rolling basis. Application fee: $65 ($75 for international students). Electronic applications accepted. *Expenses:* Tuition: Full-time $32,784; part-time $949 per unit. Tuition and fees vary according to course load and program. *Financial support:* In 2003–04, 46 students received support, including 1 fellowship (averaging $30,000 per year), 27 research assistantships with tuition reimbursements available (averaging $23,000 per year), 18 teaching assistantships with tuition reimbursements available (averaging $23,000 per year); career-related internships or fieldwork, Federal Work-Study, and institutionally sponsored loans also available. Financial award application deadline: 4/1. *Faculty research:* Clinical trials in ophthalmology and cancer research, methods of analysis for epidemiological studies, genetic epidemiology. Total annual research expenditures: $1.3 million. *Unit head:* Dr. Stanley P. Azen, Co-Director, 323-442-1810, Fax: 323-442-2993, E-mail: mtrujill@usc.edu. *Application contact:* Mary L. Trujillo, Student Adviser, 323-442-1810, Fax: 323-442-2993, E-mail: mtrujill@usc.edu.

See in-depth description on page 611.

University of South Florida, College of Graduate Studies, College of Public Health, Department of Epidemiology and Biostatistics, Tampa, FL 33620-9951. Offers MPH, MSPH, PhD. *Accreditation:* CEPH (one or more programs are accredited). Part-time and evening/weekend programs available. *Faculty:* 14 full-time (5 women). *Students:* 8 full-time (5 women), 2 part-time (both women); includes 4 minority (1 African American, 2 Asian Americans or Pacific Islanders, 1 Hispanic American), 1 international. In 2003, 1 degree awarded. *Degree requirements:* For master's and doctorate, thesis/dissertation. *Entrance requirements:* For master's and doctorate, GRE General Test, minimum GPA of 3.0 in upper-level course work. Additional exam requirements/recommendations for international students: Required—TOEFL (minimum score 550 paper-based). *Application deadline:* For fall admission, 6/1 for domestic students; for spring admission, 10/15 for domestic students. Applications are processed on a rolling basis. Application fee: $30. *Financial support:* In 2003–04, 1 fellowship with full tuition reimbursement (averaging $5,250 per year) was awarded; research assistantships with full and partial tuition reimbursements, Federal Work-Study and institutionally sponsored loans also available. Support available to part-time students. Financial award applicants required to submit FAFSA. *Faculty research:* Dementia, mental illness, mental health preventative trails, rural health outreach, clinical and administrative studies. Total annual research expenditures: $1.9 million. *Unit head:* Heather Stockwell, Chairperson, 813-974-4860, Fax: 813-974-4719, E-mail: stockwell@hsc.usf.edu. *Application contact:* Magdalene Argiry, Director of Student Services, 813-974-6665, Fax: 813-974-4718, E-mail: margiry@com1.med.usf.edu.

University of Utah, School of Medicine and Graduate School, Graduate Programs in Medicine, Programs in Public Health, Salt Lake City, UT 84112-1107. Offers biostatistics (M Stat); public health (MPH, MSPH, PhD). *Accreditation:* CEPH (one or more programs are accredited). Part-time programs available. *Faculty:* 5 full-time (1 woman), 28 part-time/adjunct (5 women). *Students:* 38 full-time (18 women), 56 part-time (32 women); includes 13 minority (3 African Americans, 8 Asian Americans or Pacific Islanders, 2 Hispanic Americans). Average age 30. 102 applicants, 43% accepted, 39 enrolled. In 2003, 46 degrees awarded. *Degree requirements:* For master's, thesis (for some programs), thesis or project (MSPH), comprehensive exam, registration. *Entrance requirements:* For master's, GRE General Test, interview, minimum GPA of 3.0. *Application deadline:* For fall admission, 4/1 for domestic students. Applications are processed on a rolling basis. Application fee: $45 ($65 for international students). Electronic applications accepted. Tuition, nonresident: full-time $2,483. International tuition: $8,768 full-time. *Financial support:* In 2003–04, 2 fellowships (averaging $5,200 per year) were awarded; research assistantships with full and partial tuition reimbursements, teaching assistantships with full and partial tuition reimbursements, career-related internships or fieldwork, institutionally sponsored loans, scholarships/grants, traineeships, and tuition waivers also available. Support available to part-time students. *Faculty research:* Health services research, occupational and environmental exposures to toxic substances, risk assessment, health policy, epidemiology of chronic disease. *Unit head:* Dr. George L. White, Director, 801-587-3315, Fax: 801-587-3353, E-mail: gwhite@dfpm.utah.edu. *Application contact:* Peggy Christensen, Administrative Program Coordinator, 801-587-3315, Fax: 801-587-3353, E-mail: pchristensen@dfpm.utah.edu.

University of Vermont, Graduate College, College of Engineering and Mathematics, Department of Mathematics and Statistics, Program in Biostatistics, Burlington, VT 05405. Offers MS. *Students:* 6 (2 women) 2 international. 11 applicants, 82% accepted, 2 enrolled. In 2003, 5 degrees awarded. *Degree requirements:* For master's, thesis or alternative. *Entrance requirements:* Additional exam requirements/recommendations for international students: Required—TOEFL. *Application deadline:* For fall admission, 4/1 for domestic students. Applications are processed on a rolling basis. Application fee: $25. *Expenses:* Tuition, state resident: part-time $362 per credit hour. Tuition, nonresident: part-time $906 per credit hour. *Financial*

Biostatistics

University of Vermont (continued)
support: Fellowships, research assistantships, teaching assistantships available. Financial award application deadline: 3/1. *Unit head:* Dr. J. Buzas, Coordinator, 802-656-2940.

University of Washington, Graduate School, Interdisciplinary Graduate Program in Quantitative Ecology and Resource Management, Seattle, WA 98195. Offers MS, PhD. *Degree requirements:* For master's and doctorate, thesis/dissertation. *Entrance requirements:* For master's and doctorate, GRE General Test, minimum GPA of 3.0. Additional exam requirements/recommendations for international students: Required—TOEFL. Electronic applications accepted. *Faculty research:* Population dynamics, statistical analysis, ecological modeling and systems analysis of aquatic and terrestrial ecosystems.

University of Washington, Graduate School, School of Public Health and Community Medicine, Department of Biostatistics, Seattle, WA 98195. Offers biostatistics (MPH, MS, PhD); statistical genetics (PhD). *Faculty:* 71 full-time (31 women), 8 part-time/adjunct (5 women). *Students:* 71 full-time (38 women), 5 part-time (1 woman); includes 11 minority (1 African American, 1 American Indian/Alaska Native, 8 Asian Americans or Pacific Islanders, 1 Hispanic American), 26 international. Average age 24. 69 applicants, 51% accepted, 20 enrolled. In 2003, 10 master's awarded, leading to business/industry 100%, 6 doctorates awarded, leading to university research/teaching 66%, business/industry 33%. Terminal master's awarded for partial completion of doctoral program. *Median time to degree:* Master's–3 years full-time; doctorate–6 years full-time. Of those who began their doctoral program in fall 1995, 85% received their degree in 8 years or less. *Degree requirements:* For master's, thesis/dissertation, departmental qualifying exams; for doctorate, thesis/dissertation, departmental qualifying exams, comprehensive exam, registration. *Entrance requirements:* For master's and doctorate, GRE General Test, 2 years of advanced calculus, 1 course in linear algebra, 1 course in mathematical probability; minimum GPA of 3.0. Additional exam requirements/recommendations for international students: Required—TOEFL, TSE. *Application deadline:* For fall admission, 1/3 for domestic students. Application fee: $50. Electronic applications accepted. *Financial support:* In 2003–04, 64 students received support, including 1 fellowship with partial tuition reimbursement available (averaging $19,000 per year), 36 research assistantships with full tuition reimbursements available (averaging $16,000 per year), 5 teaching assistantships with full tuition reimbursements available (averaging $16,000 per year); career-related internships or fieldwork, traineeships, and unspecified assistantships also available. Financial award application deadline: 1/3. *Faculty research:* Statistical methods for survival data analysis, clinical trials, epidemiological case control and cohort studies, statistical genetics. *Unit head:* Dr. Thomas Fleming, Chair, 206-543-1044. *Application contact:* Alex Mackenzie, Program Coordinator, 206-543-1044, Fax: 206-543-3286, E-mail: alexam@u.washington.edu.

University of Waterloo, Graduate Studies, Faculty of Mathematics, Department of Statistics and Actuarial Science, Waterloo, ON N2L 3G1, Canada. Offers actuarial science (M Math); statistics (M Math, PhD); statistics-biostatistics (M Math); statistics-computing (M Math); statistics-finance (M Math). *Faculty:* 33 full-time (6 women), 21 part-time/adjunct (5 women). *Students:* 93 full-time (50 women), 5 part-time. 308 applicants, 24% accepted, 34 enrolled. In 2003, 18 master's, 3 doctorates awarded. *Degree requirements:* For master's, research paper or thesis; for doctorate, thesis/dissertation. *Entrance requirements:* For master's, honors degree in field, minimum B+ average; for doctorate, master's degree, minimum B+ average. Additional exam requirements/recommendations for international students: Required—TOEFL, TWE. *Application deadline:* For fall admission, 3/31 for domestic students; for winter admission, 8/31 for domestic students; for spring admission, 12/31 for domestic students. Applications are processed on a rolling basis. Application fee: $75 Canadian dollars. Electronic applications accepted. Tuition and fees charges are reported in Canadian dollars. *Expenses:* Tuition, state resident: full-time $3,632 Canadian dollars. International tuition: $9,180 Canadian dollars full-time. Required fees: $406 Canadian dollars. *Financial support:* In 2003–04, 30 teaching assistantships were awarded; fellowships, research assistantships, career-related internships or fieldwork and scholarships/grants also available. *Faculty research:* Data analysis, risk theory, inference, stochastic processes, quantitative finance. *Unit head:* Dr. D. E. Matthews, Chair, 519-888-4567 Ext. 5530, Fax: 519-746-1875, E-mail: dematthe@uwaterloo.ca. *Application contact:* L. Clarke, Graduate Studies Secretary, 519-888-4567 Ext. 6532, Fax: 519-746-1875, E-mail: sasgrad@math.uwaterloo.ca.

The University of Western Ontario, Faculty of Graduate Studies, Biosciences Division, Department of Epidemiology and Biostatistics, London, ON N6A 5B8, Canada. Offers M Sc, PhD. *Accreditation:* CEPH (one or more programs are accredited). Part-time programs available. *Degree requirements:* For master's, thesis; for doctorate, thesis proposal defense. *Entrance requirements:* For master's, BA or B Sc honors degree, minimum B+ average in last 10 courses; for doctorate, M Sc or equivalent, minimum B+ average in last 10 courses. *Faculty research:* Chronic disease epidemiology, clinical epidemiology.

Virginia Commonwealth University, Medical College of Virginia-Professional Programs, School of Medicine and Graduate Programs, School of Medicine Graduate Programs, Department of Biostatistics, Richmond, VA 23284-9005. Offers MS, PhD, MD/PhD. Part-time programs available. *Faculty:* 10 full-time (2 women). *Students:* 17 full-time (14 women), 15 part-time (8 women); includes 8 minority (6 African Americans, 2 Asian Americans or Pacific Islanders), 6 international. 33 applicants, 45% accepted, 5 enrolled. In 2003, 3 master's, 5 doctorates awarded. Terminal master's awarded for partial completion of doctoral program. *Degree requirements:* For master's, thesis; for doctorate, thesis/dissertation, comprehensive oral and written exams. *Entrance requirements:* For master's, DAT, GRE General Test, or MCAT; for doctorate, GRE General Test, MCAT, DAT. *Application deadline:* For fall admission, 2/15 for domestic students. Application fee: $30. *Expenses:* Tuition, state resident: full-time $2,889; part-time $321 per credit hour. Tuition, nonresident: full-time $7,952; part-time $884 per credit hour. Required fees: $42 per credit hour. *Financial support:* Fellowships, teaching assistantships, career-related internships or fieldwork available. *Faculty research:* Health services, linear models, response surfaces, design and analysis of drug/chemical combinations, clinical trials. *Unit head:* Dr. W. Hans Carter, Chair, 804-827-2042, Fax: 804-828-8900, E-mail: whcarter@vcu.edu. *Application contact:* Dr. Ronald K. Elswick, Director, 804-827-2037, E-mail: rkelswic@vcu.edu.

Western Michigan University, Graduate College, College of Arts and Sciences, Department of Statistics, Program in Biostatistics, Kalamazoo, MI 49008-5202. Offers MS. *Degree requirements:* For master's, written exams, internship.

Yale University, School of Medicine, School of Public Health, Division of Biostatistics, New Haven, CT 06520. Offers MPH, MS, PhD. MS and PhD offered through the Graduate School. Part-time programs available. *Faculty:* 8 full-time (2 women), 6 part-time/adjunct (3 women). *Students:* 22 full-time (11 women), 2 part-time (1 woman); includes 5 minority (all Asian Americans or Pacific Islanders), 14 international. Average age 28. In 2003, 2 degrees awarded. Terminal master's awarded for partial completion of doctoral program. *Degree requirements:* For master's, thesis, internship. *Entrance requirements:* For master's, GMAT, GRE, or MCAT, previous undergraduate course work in mathematics and science. Additional exam requirements/recommendations for international students: Required—TOEFL. *Application deadline:* For fall admission, 3/1 for domestic students. Applications are processed on a rolling basis. Application fee: $60. Electronic applications accepted. *Expenses:* Tuition: Full-time $25,600; part-time $6,400 per term. *Financial support:* Career-related internships or fieldwork, Federal Work-Study, institutionally sponsored loans, and scholarships/grants available. Support available to part-time students. Financial award application deadline: 4/1. *Faculty research:* Statistical and genetic epidemiology, population models for chronic and infectious diseases, clinical trials, regression methods. *Unit head:* Dr. Robert W. Makuch, Division Head, 203-785-2838, Fax: 203-785-6912, E-mail: robert.makuch@yale.edu. *Application contact:* Jacqui Comshaw, Director of Admissions, 203-785-2844, Fax: 203-785-4845, E-mail: eph.admissions@yale.edu.

Computational Sciences

Arizona State University, Graduate College, College of Liberal Arts and Sciences, Department of Biology, Program in Computational, Statistical, and Mathematical Biology, Tempe, AZ 85287. Offers MS, PhD. *Entrance requirements:* Additional exam requirements/recommendations for international students: Required—TOEFL (minimum score 600 paper-based); Recommended—TSE. *Expenses:* Tuition, state resident: full-time $3,708; part-time $194 per credit hour. Tuition, nonresident: full-time $12,228; part-time $510 per credit hour. Required fees: $87; $22 per semester. Part-time tuition and fees vary according to program.

California Institute of Technology, Division of Engineering and Applied Science, Option in Computation and Neural Systems, Pasadena, CA 91125-0001. Offers MS, PhD. *Faculty:* 3 full-time (0 women), 1 part-time/adjunct (0 women). *Students:* 47 full-time (12 women); includes 3 minority (1 African American, 1 Asian American or Pacific Islander, 1 Hispanic American), 20 international. 122 applicants, 15% accepted, 3 enrolled.Terminal master's awarded for partial completion of doctoral program. *Degree requirements:* For doctorate, thesis/dissertation, qualifying exam. *Entrance requirements:* For doctorate, GRE General Test. *Application deadline:* For fall admission, 1/15 for domestic students. Application fee: $0. *Financial support:* In 2003–04, 2 research assistantships were awarded; fellowships, teaching assistantships, Federal Work-Study and institutionally sponsored loans also available. Financial award application deadline: 1/15. *Faculty research:* Biological and artificial computational devices, modeling of sensory processes and learning, theory of collective computation. *Unit head:* Dr. Christof Koch, Executive Officer, 626-395-6855.

Carnegie Mellon University, Graduate School of Industrial Administration, Program in Algorithms, Combinatorics, and Optimization, Pittsburgh, PA 15213-3891. Offers MS, PhD. *Degree requirements:* For doctorate, thesis/dissertation. *Entrance requirements:* For master's, GMAT; for doctorate, GRE General Test. *Expenses:* Tuition: Full-time $28,200; part-time $392 per unit. Required fees: $220.

Carnegie Mellon University, Mellon College of Science, Department of Biological Sciences, Program in Computational Biology, Pittsburgh, PA 15213-3891. Offers MS. *Entrance requirements:* For master's, GRE General Test, GRE Subject Test, interview. *Expenses:* Tuition: Full-time $28,200; part-time $392 per unit. Required fees: $220.

Claremont Graduate University, Graduate Programs, School of Mathematical Sciences, Claremont, CA 91711-6160. Offers computational science (PhD); engineering mathematics (PhD); financial engineering (MS); operations research and statistics (MA, MS); physical applied mathematics (MA, MS); pure mathematics (MA, MS, PhD); scientific computing (MA, MS); systems and control theory (MA, MS). Part-time programs available. *Faculty:* 2 full-time (0 women), 3 part-time/adjunct (0 women). *Students:* 41 full-time (8 women), 11 part-time (3 women). Average age 36. In 2003, 9 master's, 4 doctorates awarded. Terminal master's awarded for partial completion of doctoral program. *Degree requirements:* For doctorate, 2 foreign languages, thesis/dissertation. *Entrance requirements:* For master's and doctorate, GRE General Test. *Application deadline:* For fall admission, 2/15 for domestic students. Applications are processed on a rolling basis. Electronic applications accepted. *Expenses:* Tuition: Full-time $25,250; part-time $1,099 per semester. *Financial support:* Fellowships, research assistantships, career-related internships or fieldwork, Federal Work-Study, institutionally sponsored loans, and tuition waivers (full and partial) available. Support available to part-time students. Financial award application deadline: 2/15; financial award applicants required to submit FAFSA. *Unit head:* John Angus, Chair, 909-621-8080, Fax: 909-607-8261, E-mail: john.angus@cgu.edu. *Application contact:* Mary Solberg, Administrative Assistant, 909-621-8080, Fax: 909-607-8261, E-mail: math@cgu.edu.

Clemson University, Graduate School, College of Engineering and Science, Department of Mathematical Sciences, Clemson, SC 29634. Offers applied and pure mathematics (MS, PhD); computational mathematics (MS, PhD); management science (PhD); operations research (MS, PhD); statistics (MS, PhD). Part-time programs available. *Students:* 73 full-time (25 women), 5 part-time (1 woman); includes 3 minority (2 African Americans, 1 Asian American or Pacific Islander), 33 international. Average age 29. 116 applicants, 74% accepted, 31 enrolled. In 2003, 25 master's, 5 doctorates awarded. *Degree requirements:* For master's, final project, thesis optional; for doctorate, thesis/dissertation, qualifying exams. *Entrance requirements:* For master's and doctorate, GRE General Test. Additional exam requirements/recommendations for international students: Required—TOEFL. *Application deadline:* For fall admission, 6/1 for domestic students. Application fee: $40. *Expenses:* Tuition, state resident: full-time $7,432. Tuition, nonresident: full-time $14,732. *Financial support:* Fellowships, research assistantships, teaching assistantships available. Financial award application deadline: 4/15; financial award applicants required to submit FAFSA. *Faculty research:* Applied and computational analysis, discrete mathematics, mathematical programming statistics. *Unit head:* Dr. Perino Dearing, Interim Dean, 864-656-5240, Fax: 864-656-5230, E-mail: pmdrn@clemson.edu. *Application contact:* Dr. Douglas Shier, Graduate Coordinator, 864-656-1100, Fax: 864-656-5230, E-mail: shierd@clemson.edu.

The College of William and Mary, Faculty of Arts and Sciences, Department of Computer Science, Program in Computational Operations Research, Williamsburg, VA 23187-8795. Offers MS. Part-time programs available. *Degree requirements:* For master's, research project, thesis optional. *Entrance requirements:* For master's, GRE General Test, minimum GPA of 2.5. *Application deadline:* For fall admission, 1/15 for domestic students; for spring admission, 11/1 for domestic students. Applications are processed on a rolling basis. Application fee: $30. *Expenses:* Tuition, state resident: full-time $4,858; part-time $222 per credit hour. Tuition, nonresident: full-time $16,440; part-time $618 per credit hour. Required fees: $2,674. Tuition and fees vary according to program. *Financial support:* Teaching assistantships with full tuition reimbursements, scholarships/grants and tuition waivers (full) available. Financial award application deadline: 3/3; financial award applicants required to submit FAFSA. *Faculty research:* Metaheuristics, reliability, optimization, statistics. *Unit head:* Dr. Rex Kincaid, Professor, 757-221-2038, Fax: 757-221-1717, E-mail: rrkinc@math.wm.edu. *Application contact:* Vanessa Godwin, Administrative Director, 757-221-3455, Fax: 757-221-1717, E-mail: gradinfo@cs.wm.edu.

Cornell University, Graduate School, Graduate Fields of Engineering, Field of Chemical Engineering, Ithaca, NY 14853-0001. Offers advanced materials processing (M Eng, MS, PhD); applied mathematics and computational methods (M Eng, MS, PhD); biochemical engineering (M Eng, MS, PhD); chemical reaction engineering (M Eng, MS, PhD); classical and statistical thermodynamics (M Eng, MS, PhD); fluid dynamics, rheology and biorheology (M Eng, MS, PhD); heat and mass transfer (M Eng, MS, PhD); kinetics and catalysis (M Eng,

MS, PhD); polymers (M Eng, MS, PhD); surface science (M Eng, MS, PhD). *Faculty:* 23 full-time. *Students:* 92 full-time (22 women); includes 13 minority (11 Asian Americans or Pacific Islanders, 2 Hispanic Americans), 43 international. 321 applicants, 29% accepted, 36 enrolled. In 2003, 17 master's, 8 doctorates awarded. *Degree requirements:* For master's, thesis (MS); for doctorate, thesis/dissertation, comprehensive exam. *Entrance requirements:* For master's and doctorate, GRE General Test, pre-application, 2 letters of recommendation. Additional exam requirements/recommendations for international students: Required—TOEFL (minimum score 580 paper-based; 237 computer-based). *Application deadline:* For fall admission, 1/15 for domestic students. Application fee: $60. Electronic applications accepted. *Expenses:* Tuition: Full-time $28,630. One-time fee: $50 full-time. *Financial support:* In 2003–04, 72 students received support, including 19 fellowships with full tuition reimbursements available, 43 research assistantships with full tuition reimbursements available, 10 teaching assistantships with full tuition reimbursements available; institutionally sponsored loans, scholarships/grants, health care benefits, tuition waivers (full and partial), and unspecified assistantships also available. Financial award applicants required to submit FAFSA. *Faculty research:* Biochemical, biomedical and metabolic engineering; fluid and polymer dynamics; surface science and chemical kinetics; electronics materials; microchemical systems and nanotechnology. *Unit head:* Director of Graduate Studies, 607-255-4550. *Application contact:* Graduate Field Assistant, 607-255-4550, E-mail: dgs@cheme.cornell.edu.

George Mason University, School of Computational Sciences, Fairfax, VA 22030. Offers computational sciences (MS); computational sciences and informatics (PhD); computational techniques and applications (Certificate). Part-time and evening/weekend programs available. *Faculty:* 42 full-time (6 women), 17 part-time/adjunct (0 women). *Students:* 62 full-time (23 women), 218 part-time (70 women); includes 46 minority (10 African Americans, 33 Asian Americans or Pacific Islanders, 3 Hispanic Americans), 102 international. Average age 30. 91 applicants, 81% accepted. In 2003, 14 master's, 12 doctorates, 1 other advanced degree awarded. *Degree requirements:* For doctorate, thesis/dissertation, comprehensive exam, registration. *Entrance requirements:* For master's and doctorate, GRE General Test, minimum GPA of 3.0 in last 60 hours. Additional exam requirements/recommendations for international students: Required—TOEFL. *Application deadline:* For fall admission, 3/1 for domestic students; for spring admission, 11/1 priority date for domestic students. Applications are processed on a rolling basis. Application fee: $60. Electronic applications accepted. *Expenses:* Tuition, state resident: full-time $4,398. Tuition, nonresident: full-time $14,952. Required fees: $1,482. *Financial support:* In 2003–04, 22 fellowships with tuition reimbursements (averaging $2,800 per year), 56 research assistantships with full tuition reimbursements (averaging $12,600 per year) were awarded. Teaching assistantships, career-related internships or fieldwork, Federal Work-Study, institutionally sponsored loans, and tuition waivers (partial) also available. Financial award application deadline: 2/1; financial award applicants required to submit FAFSA. *Faculty research:* Space sciences and astrophysics, fluid dynamics, materials modeling and simulation, bioinformatics, global changes and statistics. *Unit head:* Dr. Menas Kafatos, Dean, 703-993-1990, Fax: 703-993-1993, E-mail: mkafatos@gmu.edu. *Application contact:* Dr. Peter A. Becker, Associate Dean for Graduate Studies, 703-993-3619, Fax: 703-993-1980, E-mail: pbecker@gmu.edu.

See in-depth description on page 541.

Iowa State University of Science and Technology, Graduate College, Interdisciplinary Programs, Bioinformatics and Computational Biology Program, Ames, IA 50011-3260. Offers MS, PhD. *Students:* 50 full-time (14 women), 2 part-time; includes 3 minority (all Asian Americans), 25 international. 276 applicants, 7% accepted, 7 enrolled. In 2003, 5 master's, 4 doctorates awarded. *Degree requirements:* For doctorate, thesis/dissertation. *Entrance requirements:* For doctorate, GRE General Test. Additional exam requirements/recommendations for international students: Required—TOEFL or IELTS. *Application deadline:* For fall admission, 2/1 priority date for domestic students, 2/1 priority date for international students. Application fee: $30 ($70 for international students). Electronic applications accepted. Tuition, nonresident: part-time $560 per credit. Required fees: $38 per unit. *Financial support:* In 2003–04, 14 fellowships with full tuition reimbursements (averaging $23,250 per year), 35 research assistantships with full and partial tuition reimbursements (averaging $18,240 per year) were awarded. Scholarships/grants, traineeships, health care benefits, and unspecified assistantships also available. *Faculty research:* Functional and structural genomics, genome evolution, macromolecular structure and function, mathematical biology and biological statistics, metabolic and developmental networks. *Unit head:* Dr. Vasant Honavar, Chair, Supervising Committee, 515-294-5122, Fax: 515-294-6790, E-mail: bcb@cs.iastate.edu. *Application contact:* Tori Frjelich, Program Assistant, 888-569-8509, Fax: 515-294-6790, E-mail: bcb@iastate.edu.

Kean University, School of Natural, Applied and Health Sciences, Department of Mathematics and Computer Science, Program in Computing, Statistics and Mathematics, Union, NJ 07083. Offers MS. Part-time and evening/weekend programs available. *Faculty:* 25 full-time (7 women). *Students:* 2 full-time (1 woman), 7 part-time (3 women); includes 4 minority (1 African American, 3 Asian Americans or Pacific Islanders). Average age 41. 11 applicants, 55% accepted, 3 enrolled. In 2003, 2 degrees awarded. *Degree requirements:* For master's, thesis or alternative. *Entrance requirements:* For master's, GRE General Test, 2 letters of recommendation, interview. *Application deadline:* For fall admission, 6/15 for domestic students; for spring admission, 11/15 for domestic students. Application fee: $60. *Expenses:* Tuition, state resident: full-time $7,488; part-time $312 per credit. Tuition, nonresident: full-time $9,528; part-time $397 per credit. Required fees: $1,814; $76 per credit. *Financial support:* In 2003–04, research assistantships with full tuition reimbursements (averaging $2,700 per year) *Application contact:* Joanne Morris, Director of Graduate Admissions, 908-527-2665, Fax: 908-527-2286, E-mail: grad_adm@turbo.kean.edu.

Louisiana Tech University, Graduate School, College of Engineering and Science, Department of Physics, Ruston, LA 71272. Offers applied computational analysis and modeling (PhD); physics (MS). Part-time programs available. *Degree requirements:* For master's, thesis or alternative; for doctorate, thesis/dissertation. *Entrance requirements:* For master's, GRE General Test, minimum GPA of 3.0 in last 60 hours. Additional exam requirements/recommendations for international students: Required—TOEFL. *Expenses:* Tuition, state resident: full-time $3,120. Tuition, nonresident: full-time $9,120. Tuition and fees vary according to course load. *Faculty research:* Experimental high energy physics, laser/optics, computational physics, quantum gravity.

Massachusetts Institute of Technology, School of Science, Department of Brain and Cognitive Sciences, Cambridge, MA 02139-4307. Offers cellular/molecular neuroscience (PhD); cognitive neuroscience (PhD); cognitive science (PhD); computational cognitive science (PhD); computational neuroscience (PhD); systems neuroscience (PhD). *Faculty:* 30 full-time (6 women). *Students:* 70 full-time (30 women); includes 12 minority (3 African Americans, 1 American Indian/Alaska Native, 6 Asian Americans or Pacific Islanders, 2 Hispanic Americans), 17 international. Average age 26. 303 applicants, 10% accepted, 15 enrolled. In 2003, 7 doctorates awarded. *Degree requirements:* For doctorate, thesis/dissertation, qualifying exam, comprehensive exam. *Entrance requirements:* For doctorate, GRE General Test. Additional exam requirements/recommendations for international students: Required—TOEFL. *Application deadline:* For fall admission, 1/2 for domestic students, 1/2 for international students. Application fee: $70. Electronic applications accepted. *Expenses:* Tuition: Full-time $29,400. Required fees: $200. *Financial support:* In 2003–04, 68 students received support, including 48 fellowships with tuition reimbursements available, 14 research assistantships with tuition reimbursements available (averaging $23,760 per year), 12 teaching assistantships with tuition reimbursements available (averaging $18,270 per year); Federal Work-Study, institutionally sponsored loans, scholarships/grants, traineeships, health care benefits, and unspecified assistantships also available. *Faculty research:* Vision, learning and memory, motor control, plasticity. Total annual research expenditures: $17.5 million. *Unit head:* Prof. Mriganka Sur, Head, 617-253-5748, E-mail: bcs-info@mit.edu. *Application contact:* Brain and Cognitive Sciences Graduate Office, 617-253-7403, E-mail: bcs-admissions@mit.edu.

Memorial University of Newfoundland, School of Graduate Studies, Interdisciplinary Program in Computational Science, St. John's, NL A1C 5S7, Canada. Offers computational science (M Sc); computational science (cooperative) (M Sc). *Students:* 7 full-time, 1 part-time. 25 applicants, 12% accepted, 2 enrolled. In 2003, 1 degree awarded. *Degree requirements:* For master's, thesis (for some programs). *Entrance requirements:* For master's, honors B Sc or significant background in the field. *Application deadline:* Applications are processed on a rolling basis. Application fee: $40. Electronic applications accepted. Tuition and fees charges are reported in Canadian dollars. *Expenses:* Tuition, state resident: part-time $733 Canadian dollars per semester. Tuition, nonresident: part-time $953 Canadian dollars per semester. Required fees: $194 Canadian dollars per year. Tuition and fees vary according to degree level and program. *Faculty research:* Scientific computing, modeling and simulation, computational fluid dynamics, polymer physics, computational chemistry. *Unit head:* Dr. George Miminis, Chair, 709-737-8635, E-mail: george@cs.mun.ca. *Application contact:* Gail Kenny, Secretary, 709-737-3444, Fax: 709-737-3316, E-mail: gkenny@mun.ca.

Michigan Technological University, Graduate School, College of Engineering, Department of Electrical and Computer Engineering, Program in Computational Science and Engineering, Houghton, MI 49931-1295. Offers PhD. Part-time programs available. *Faculty:* 20 full-time (2 women). *Students:* 4 full-time (1 woman), 4 part-time (1 woman), 5 international. Average age 31. 7 applicants, 57% accepted, 2 enrolled. In 2003, 2 degrees awarded. *Degree requirements:* For doctorate, thesis/dissertation, comprehensive exam, registration. *Application deadline:* For fall admission, 3/15 for domestic students. Applications are processed on a rolling basis. Application fee: $40 ($45 for international students). Electronic applications accepted. Tuition, nonresident: full-time $9,552; part-time $398 per credit. Required fees: $768. *Financial support:* In 2003–04, 4 fellowships with full tuition reimbursements (averaging $13,500 per year), 3 research assistantships with full tuition reimbursements (averaging $8,950 per year), 2 teaching assistantships with full tuition reimbursements (averaging $8,950 per year) were awarded. Career-related internships or fieldwork, Federal Work-Study, institutionally sponsored loans, scholarships/grants, traineeships, unspecified assistantships, and co-op also available. Support available to part-time students. Financial award application deadline: 3/1; financial award applicants required to submit FAFSA. *Application contact:* Dr. Phillip R. Merkey, Research Assistant Professor, 906-487-2220, Fax: 906-487-2283, E-mail: merk@mtu.edu.

See in-depth description on page 555.

New Jersey Institute of Technology, Office of Graduate Studies, College of Computing Science, Program in Computational Biology, Newark, NJ 07102. Offers MS. Part-time and evening/weekend programs available. *Students:* 20 full-time (9 women), 38 part-time (16 women); includes 31 minority (1 African American, 27 Asian Americans or Pacific Islanders, 3 Hispanic Americans), 8 international. Average age 31. 100 applicants, 66% accepted, 21 enrolled. In 2003, 9 degrees awarded. *Entrance requirements:* For master's, GRE General Test. *Application deadline:* For fall admission, 6/5 for domestic students; for spring admission, 10/15 for domestic students. Applications are processed on a rolling basis. Application fee: $50. Electronic applications accepted. *Expenses:* Tuition, state resident: full-time $9,620; part-time $520 per credit. Tuition, nonresident: full-time $13,542; part-time $715 per credit. Tuition and fees vary according to course load. *Financial support:* Fellowships with full and partial tuition reimbursements, research assistantships with full and partial tuition reimbursements, teaching assistantships with full and partial tuition reimbursements, career-related internships or fieldwork, Federal Work-Study, institutionally sponsored loans, and unspecified assistantships available. Financial award application deadline: 3/15. *Faculty research:* Technological, computational, and mathematical aspects of biology and bioengineering. *Unit head:* Dr. Michael L. Recce, Director, 973-596-5535, E-mail: michael.l.recce@njit.edu. *Application contact:* Kathryn Kelly, Director of Admissions, 973-596-3300, Fax: 973-596-3461, E-mail: admissions@njit.edu.

Princeton University, Graduate School, Department of Mathematics, Princeton, NJ 08544-1019. Offers applied and computational mathematics (PhD); mathematical physics (PhD); mathematics (PhD). *Faculty:* 47 full-time (5 women), 9 part-time/adjunct (1 woman). *Students:* 58 full-time (12 women); includes 6 minority (1 African American, 5 Asian Americans or Pacific Islanders), 36 international. 202 applicants, 14% accepted, 14 enrolled. *Median time to degree:* Doctorate–4.64 years full-time. *Degree requirements:* For doctorate, 2 foreign languages, thesis/dissertation. *Entrance requirements:* For doctorate, GRE General Test, GRE Subject Test. Additional exam requirements/recommendations for international students: Required—TOEFL (minimum score 600 paper-based; 250 computer-based). *Application deadline:* For fall admission, 12/31 for domestic students, 12/1 for international students. Application fee: $80 ($55 for international students). Electronic applications accepted. *Expenses:* Tuition: Full-time $29,910. Required fees: $810. *Financial support:* Fellowships with full tuition reimbursements, research assistantships with full tuition reimbursements, teaching assistantships with full tuition reimbursements, Federal Work-Study and institutionally sponsored loans available. Financial award application deadline: 1/2. *Unit head:* Prof. Sergiu Klainerman, Director of Graduate Studies, 609-258-4188, Fax: 609-258-1367, E-mail: seri@princeton.edu. *Application contact:* Janice Yip, Director of Graduate Admissions, 609-258-3034, Fax: 609-258-6180, E-mail: gsadmit@princeton.edu.

Princeton University, Graduate School, Department of Physics, Princeton, NJ 08544-1019. Offers applied and computational mathematics (PhD); mathematical physics (PhD); physics (PhD); physics and chemical physics (PhD). *Faculty:* 42 full-time (2 women), 2 part-time/adjunct (0 women). *Students:* 103 full-time (13 women); includes 11 minority (10 Asian Americans or Pacific Islanders, 1 Hispanic American), 48 international. Average age 22. 425 applicants, 12% accepted, 26 enrolled. In 2003, 14 degrees awarded, leading to continued full-time study 86%. *Median time to degree:* Doctorate–5 years full-time. *Degree requirements:* For doctorate, thesis/dissertation, qualifying exam. *Entrance requirements:* For doctorate, GRE General Test, GRE Subject Test. Additional exam requirements/recommendations for international students: Required—TOEFL (minimum score 600 paper-based; 250 computer-based). *Application deadline:* For fall admission, 12/31 for domestic students, 12/1 for international students. Application fee: $80 ($55 for international students). Electronic applications accepted. *Expenses:* Tuition: Full-time $29,910. Required fees: $810. *Financial support:* In 2003–04, 100 students received support, including 40 fellowships with full tuition reimbursements available (averaging $19,360 per year), 30 research assistantships with full tuition reimbursements available (averaging $18,100 per year), 30 teaching assistantships with full tuition reimbursements available (averaging $19,625 per year); Federal Work-Study and institutionally sponsored loans also available. Financial award application deadline: 1/2. Total annual research expenditures: $10.7 million. *Unit head:* Prof. Chiana Nappi, Director of Graduate Studies, 609-258-4322, Fax: 609-258-1549, E-mail: cnappi@princeton.edu. *Application contact:* Janice Yip, Director of Graduate Admissions, 609-258-3034, Fax: 609-258-6180, E-mail: gsadmit@princeton.edu.

Princeton University, Graduate School, Program in Applied and Computational Mathematics, Princeton, NJ 08544-1019. Offers PhD. *Students:* 19 full-time (5 women), 11 international. 76 applicants, 12% accepted, 5 enrolled. In 2003, 4 degrees awarded, leading to university research/teaching 25%, continued full-time study 50%. *Median time to degree:* Doctorate–4.28 years full-time. *Degree requirements:* For doctorate, thesis/dissertation. *Entrance requirements:* For doctorate, GRE General Test, GRE Subject Test. Additional exam requirements/recommendations for international students: Required—TOEFL (minimum score 600 paper-based; 250 computer-based). *Application deadline:* For fall admission, 12/31 for domestic students, 12/1 for international students. Application fee: $80 ($55 for international students). Electronic applications accepted. *Expenses:* Tuition: Full-time $29,910. Required fees: $810. *Financial support:* In 2003–04, 8 fellowships with full tuition reimbursements (averaging $19,218 per year), 3 research assistantships with full tuition reimbursements (averaging $31,467 per year), 3 teaching assistantships with full tuition reimbursements (averaging $19,000 per year) were awarded. Federal Work-Study and institutionally sponsored loans also available. Financial award application deadline: 1/2. Total annual research expenditures: $1.1 million. *Unit head:* Prof. Paul Seymour, Director of Graduate Studies, 609-258-4685, Fax: 609-258-1735, E-mail: pds@princeton.edu. *Application contact:* Janice Yip, Director of Graduate Admissions, 609-258-3034, Fax: 609-258-6180, E-mail: gsadmit@princeton.edu.

Computational Sciences

Rice University, Graduate Programs, George R. Brown School of Engineering, Department of Computational and Applied Mathematics, Houston, TX 77251-1892. Offers MA, MCAM, MCSE, PhD. *Faculty:* 9 full-time (1 woman). *Students:* 34 full-time (13 women); includes 13 minority (6 African Americans, 3 Asian Americans or Pacific Islanders, 4 Hispanic Americans), 10 international. Average age 28. 110 applicants, 16% accepted, 6 enrolled. In 2003, 8 master's awarded, leading to continued full-time study 50%, business/industry 50%; 5 doctorates awarded, leading to university research/teaching 20%, business/industry 20%, government 60%. *Median time to degree:* Master's–2 years full-time; doctorate–5 years full-time. Of those who began their doctoral program in fall 1995, 100% received their degree in 8 years or less. *Degree requirements:* For master's, thesis (for some programs), comprehensive exam (for some programs), registration; for doctorate, thesis/dissertation, comprehensive exam, registration. *Entrance requirements:* For master's and doctorate, GRE General Test, minimum GPA of 3.0. Additional exam requirements/recommendations for international students: Required—TOEFL (minimum score 600 paper-based; 250 computer-based). *Application deadline:* For fall admission, 2/1 priority date for domestic students, 2/1 priority date for international students; for spring admission, 11/1 for domestic students, 11/1 for international students. Applications are processed on a rolling basis. Application fee: $35. Electronic applications accepted. *Expenses:* Tuition: Full-time $19,700; part-time $1,096 per hour. *Financial support:* In 2003–04, 16 fellowships with full tuition reimbursements (averaging $18,666 per year), 11 research assistantships with full tuition reimbursements (averaging $18,660 per year), 4 teaching assistantships with full tuition reimbursements (averaging $7,500 per year) were awarded. *Faculty research:* Inverse problems, partial differential equations, computer algorithms, computational modeling, optimization theory. Total annual research expenditures: $2.3 million. *Unit head:* Dr. William W. Symes, Chairman, 713-348-4805, Fax: 713-348-5318, E-mail: symes@caam.rice.edu. *Application contact:* Daria A. Lawrence, Graduate Secretary, 713-348-4657, Fax: 713-348-5318, E-mail: gradapps@caam.rice.edu.

Rutgers, The State University of New Jersey, Newark, Graduate School, Program in Computational Biology, Newark, NJ 07102. Offers MS. *Students:* 1 applicant, 0% accepted. In 2003, 1 degree awarded. *Entrance requirements:* For master's, GRE, minimum undergraduate B average. Additional exam requirements/recommendations for international students: Required—TOEFL. *Application deadline:* For fall admission, 6/1 for domestic students, 6/1 for international students; for spring admission, 12/1 for domestic students, 12/1 for international students. Application fee: $50. *Expenses:* Tuition, state resident: full-time $10,030. Tuition, nonresident: full-time $14,202. *Application contact:* Amy Trimarco, Department Administrator, 973-353-1235, Fax: 973-353-5518, E-mail: trimarco@andromeda.rutgers.edu.

Sam Houston State University, College of Arts and Sciences, Department of Computer Science, Huntsville, TX 77341. Offers computing and information science (MS). *Students:* 8 full-time (1 woman), 15 part-time (6 women); includes 1 minority (Hispanic American), 17 international. In 2003, 11 degrees awarded. Application fee: $35. *Expenses:* Tuition, state resident: part-time $243 per semester hour. Tuition, nonresident: part-time $479 per semester hour. *Unit head:* Dr. Peter Cooper, Chair, 936-294-1564, Fax: 936-294-1882, E-mail: css_pac@shsu.edu. *Application contact:* Dr. Jiuhung Ji, Advisor, 936-294-1579, E-mail: csc_jxj@shsu.edu.

San Diego State University, Graduate and Research Affairs, College of Sciences, Program in Computational Science, San Diego, CA 92182. Offers MS, PhD. *Students:* 12 full-time (2 women), 16 part-time (4 women); includes 3 minority (2 Asian Americans or Pacific Islanders, 1 Hispanic American), 13 international. 28 applicants, 71% accepted, 4 enrolled. *Degree requirements:* For master's and doctorate, thesis/dissertation. *Entrance requirements:* For master's, GRE General Test. *Application deadline:* For fall admission, 5/1 for domestic students, 5/1 for international students; for spring admission, 11/1 for domestic students, 10/1 for international students. Applications are processed on a rolling basis. Application fee: $55. Electronic applications accepted. Tuition, nonresident: part-time $282 per unit. Required fees: $1,349; $875 per year. *Financial support:* Applicants required to submit FAFSA. *Unit head:* Jose Castillo, Director, 619-594-3430, Fax: 619-594-5291, E-mail: castillo@sdsu.edu.

Southern Methodist University, Dedman College, Department of Mathematics, Dallas, TX 75275. Offers computational and applied mathematics (MS, PhD). *Faculty:* 20 full-time (3 women). *Students:* 12 full-time (3 women), 5 part-time (3 women); includes 4 minority (1 African American, 3 Asian Americans or Pacific Islanders), 11 international. Average age 30. In 2003, 7 master's, 2 doctorates awarded. *Degree requirements:* For doctorate, thesis/dissertation, oral and written exams. *Entrance requirements:* For master's and doctorate, GRE General Test, minimum GPA of 3.0, 18 undergraduate hours in mathematics beyond first and second year calculus. Additional exam requirements/recommendations for international students: Required—TOEFL. *Application deadline:* For fall admission, 6/30 for domestic students; for winter admission, 11/30 for domestic students. Applications are processed on a rolling basis. Application fee: $60. Electronic applications accepted. *Expenses:* Tuition: Full-time $11,362; part-time $874 per credit. Required fees: $112 per credit. Tuition and fees vary according to course load and program. *Financial support:* In 2003–04, 7 teaching assistantships with full tuition reimbursements (averaging $14,000 per year) were awarded; career-related internships or fieldwork, scholarships/grants, and tuition waivers (partial) also available. Support available to part-time students. Financial award applicants required to submit FAFSA. *Faculty research:* Numerical analysis, scientific computation, fluid dynamics, software development, differential equations. Total annual research expenditures: $195,000. *Unit head:* Dr. Douglas Reinelt, Chairman, 214-768-2506, Fax: 214-768-2355, E-mail: mathchair@mail.smu.edu. *Application contact:* Dr. Zhangxin Chen, Director of Graduate Studies, 214-768-4338, E-mail: math@mail.smu.edu.

Stanford University, School of Engineering, Program in Scientific Computing and Computational Mathematics, Stanford, CA 94305-9991. Offers MS, PhD. *Students:* 52 full-time (10 women), 14 part-time (4 women); includes 10 minority (9 Asian Americans or Pacific Islanders, 1 Hispanic American), 35 international. Average age 28. 38 applicants, 66% accepted. In 2003, 14 master's, 8 doctorates awarded. Terminal master's awarded for partial completion of doctoral program. *Degree requirements:* For doctorate, thesis/dissertation, qualifying exam. *Entrance requirements:* For master's, GRE General Test; for doctorate, GRE General Test, GRE Subject Test. Additional exam requirements/recommendations for international students: Required—TOEFL. *Application deadline:* For fall admission, 2/15 for domestic students. Application fee: $65 ($80 for international students). Electronic applications accepted. *Expenses:* Tuition: Full-time $28,563. *Unit head:* Dr. Gene H. Golub, Director, 650-723-3124, Fax: 650-723-2411, E-mail: golub@sccm.stanford.edu. *Application contact:* Admissions Coordinator, 650-723-0572.

State University of New York College at Brockport, School of Letters and Sciences, Department of Computational Science, Brockport, NY 14420-2997. Offers MS. Part-time programs available. *Students:* 6 full-time (1 woman), 3 part-time, 4 international. 7 applicants, 86% accepted, 6 enrolled. In 2003, 4 degrees awarded. *Degree requirements:* For master's, thesis or alternative. *Entrance requirements:* For master's, minimum GPA of 3.0, letters of recommendation. Additional exam requirements/recommendations for international students: Required—TOEFL (minimum score 550 paper-based; 213 computer-based). *Application deadline:* For fall admission, 4/15 for domestic students, 4/15 for international students; for spring admission, 10/15 for domestic students, 10/15 for international students. Application fee: $50. *Expenses:* Tuition, state resident: full-time $6,910; part-time $288 per credit hour. Tuition, nonresident: full-time $10,500; part-time $438 per credit hour. Required fees: $26 per credit. *Financial support:* Federal Work-Study and scholarships/grants available. Financial award application deadline: 3/15. *Faculty research:* Parallel computing, fluid and particle dynamics, molecular simulation, engine combustion, linear algebra software. *Unit head:* Dr. Osman Yasar, Chairperson, 585-395-2021, Fax: 585-395-5020, E-mail: oyasar@brockport.edu. *Application contact:* Dr. Robert Tuzun, Graduate Program Director, 585-395-5365, E-mail: rtuzun@brockport.edu.

Temple University, Graduate School, College of Science and Technology, Department of Mathematics, Philadelphia, PA 19122-6096. Offers applied and computational mathematics (MA, PhD); pure mathematics (MA, PhD). Part-time and evening/weekend programs available. Terminal master's awarded for partial completion of doctoral program. *Degree requirements:* For master's, written exam, thesis optional; for doctorate, 2 foreign languages, thesis/dissertation, oral and written exams. *Entrance requirements:* For master's and doctorate, GRE General Test, GRE Subject Test, minimum GPA of 3.0 during previous 2 years, 2.8 overall. *Faculty research:* Differential geometry, numerical analysis.

University of California, Santa Barbara, Graduate Division, College of Engineering, Department of Computer Science, Computational Science and Technology Integrative Graduate Education and Research Traineeship Program, Santa Barbara, CA 93106. Offers computer science (PhD); electrical and computer engineering (PhD); mathematics (PhD); mechanical and environmental engineering (PhD). Program offered jointly with the Departments of Chemical Engineering, Mathematics, and Mechanical and Environmental Engineering. *Students:* 5 applicants, 80% accepted, 3 enrolled. *Degree requirements:* For doctorate, contact department. *Entrance requirements:* For doctorate, contact department, contact department. *Application deadline:* Applications are processed on a rolling basis. Application fee: $60. Electronic applications accepted. *Expenses:* Tuition, state resident: full-time $7,188. Tuition, nonresident: full-time $19,608. *Financial support:* In 2003–04, 3 students received support, including fellowships with full tuition reimbursements available (averaging $27,500 per year); research assistantships, teaching assistantships, career-related internships or fieldwork, scholarships/grants, traineeships, and health care benefits also available. *Faculty research:* Microscale engineering, complex fluids, materials science, systems biology. *Unit head:* Loren A. Banner, Education Coordinator, 805-893-8334, Fax: 805-893-5435, E-mail: loren@cs.ucsb.edu.

University of Colorado at Denver, Graduate School, College of Engineering and Applied Science, Department of Computer Science and Engineering, Program in Computer Science and Information Systems, Denver, CO 80217-3364. Offers computational biology (PhD); computer science and information systems (PhD). *Faculty:* 11 full-time (3 women). *Students:* 2 full-time (0 women), 10 part-time (3 women); includes 2 minority (1 African American, 1 Asian American or Pacific Islander), 3 international. Average age 36. 14 applicants, 64% accepted, 6 enrolled. *Entrance requirements:* For doctorate, GRE General Test. *Expenses:* Tuition, state resident: part-time $255 per credit hour. Tuition, nonresident: part-time $1,025 per credit hour. *Application contact:* Laura Cuellar, Program Assistant, 303-556-4083, Fax: 303-556-8369, E-mail: laura.cuellar@cudenver.edu.

University of Idaho, College of Graduate Studies, College of Science, Department of Biological Sciences, Programs in Bioinformatics and Computational Biology, Moscow, ID 83844-2282. Offers MS, PhD. *Entrance requirements:* For master's, GRE, minimum GPA of 2.8. *Application deadline:* For fall admission, 8/1 for domestic students; for spring admission, 12/15 for domestic students. Application fee: $55 ($60 for international students). *Expenses:* Tuition, state resident: full-time $3,348. Tuition, nonresident: full-time $10,740. Required fees: $540. *Financial support:* Application deadline: 2/15. *Unit head:* Larry J. Forney, Head, Department of Biological Sciences, 208-885-6280.

The University of Iowa, Graduate College, Program in Applied Mathematical and Computational Sciences, Iowa City, IA 52242-1316. Offers PhD. *Students:* 12 full-time (5 women), 16 part-time (6 women); includes 8 minority (3 African Americans, 5 Hispanic Americans), 16 international. 41 applicants, 34% accepted, 4 enrolled. In 2003, 5 degrees awarded. *Degree requirements:* For doctorate, thesis/dissertation, comprehensive exam, registration. *Entrance requirements:* For doctorate, GRE General Test, minimum GPA of 3.0. Additional exam requirements/recommendations for international students: Required—TOEFL (minimum score 600 paper-based; 250 computer-based). *Application deadline:* For fall admission, 1/15 for domestic students, 1/15 for international students; for spring admission, 10/1 priority date for domestic students. Application fee: $50 ($75 for international students). Electronic applications accepted. *Expenses:* Tuition, state resident: full-time $5,038. Tuition, nonresident: full-time $15,072. Tuition and fees vary according to course load and program. *Financial support:* In 2003–04, 6 fellowships, 3 research assistantships, 21 teaching assistantships were awarded. Financial award applicants required to submit FAFSA. *Unit head:* Herbert W. Hethcote, Chair, 319-335-0790.

University of Manitoba, Faculty of Graduate Studies, Faculty of Science, Department of Mathematical, Computational and Statistical Sciences, Winnipeg, MB R3T 2N2, Canada. Offers MMCSS. Tuition charges are reported in Canadian dollars. Tuition, nonresident: full-time $3,878 Canadian dollars.

University of Massachusetts Lowell, Graduate School, College of Arts and Sciences, Department of Mathematics, Lowell, MA 01854-2881. Offers applied mathematics (MS); computational mathematics (PhD); mathematics (MS). Part-time programs available. *Entrance requirements:* For master's, GRE General Test.

University of Michigan–Dearborn, College of Arts, Sciences, and Letters, Program in Applied and Computational Mathematics, Dearborn, MI 48128-1491. Offers MS. Part-time and evening/weekend programs available. *Faculty:* 2 full-time (0 women), 8 part-time/adjunct (3 women). *Students:* 2 full-time (1 woman), 10 part-time (6 women), 2 international. Average age 31. 5 applicants, 100% accepted, 3 enrolled. In 2003, 3 degrees awarded. *Median time to degree:* Master's–2 years part-time. *Degree requirements:* For master's, thesis or alternative. *Entrance requirements:* For master's, 3 letters of recommendation, minimum GPA of 3.0, 2 years of math. *Application deadline:* For fall admission, 8/1 for domestic students; for winter admission, 12/1 for domestic students; for spring admission, 4/1 for domestic students. Applications are processed on a rolling basis. Application fee: $60 ($75 for international students). Electronic applications accepted. *Expenses:* Tuition, state resident: part-time $357 per credit hour. Tuition, nonresident: part-time $820 per credit hour. Required fees: $107. *Financial support:* Federal Work-Study and scholarships/grants available. Support available to part-time students. Financial award application deadline: 4/1; financial award applicants required to submit FAFSA. *Faculty research:* Partial differential equations, statisitics, discrete optimization, approximation theory. *Unit head:* Dr. Frank Massey, Director, 313-593-5198, E-mail: fmassey@umd.umich.edu. *Application contact:* Carol Ligienza, Administrative Assistant, 313-593-1183, Fax: 313-593-5552, E-mail: cligienz@umd.umich.edu.

University of Minnesota, Duluth, Graduate School, College of Science and Engineering, Department of Mathematics and Statistics, Duluth, MN 55812-2496. Offers applied and computational mathematics (MS). Part-time programs available. *Faculty:* 16 full-time (3 women). *Students:* 25 full-time (11 women), 13 international. Average age 24. 25 applicants, 80% accepted, 11 enrolled. In 2003, 9 degrees awarded, leading to university research/teaching 20%, continued full-time study60%, business/industry 20%. *Median time to degree:* Master's–2 years full-time, 6 years part-time. *Degree requirements:* For master's, thesis or alternative. *Entrance requirements:* For master's, GRE General Test, minimum GPA of 3.0. Additional exam requirements/recommendations for international students: Required—TOEFL (minimum score 550 paper-based; 213 computer-based); Recommended—TWE, TSE. *Application deadline:* For fall admission, 3/1 priority date for domestic students, 3/1 priority date for international students; for spring admission, 11/15 for domestic students, 9/1 for international students. Applications are processed on a rolling basis. Application fee: $55 ($75 for international students). *Expenses:* Tuition, state resident: part-time $614 per credit. Tuition, nonresident: part-time $1,205 per credit. *Financial support:* In 2003–04, 6 research assistantships with full tuition reimbursements (averaging $11,154 per year), 20 teaching assistantships with full tuition reimbursements (averaging $11,154 per year) were awarded. Fellowships, scholarships/grants, health care benefits, unspecified assistantships, and summer fellowships also available. Financial award application deadline: 3/1. *Faculty research:* Discrete mathematics, diagnostic markers, combinatorics, biostatistics, mathematical modeling and scientific computation. Total annual research expenditures: $137,193. *Unit head:* Dr. Zhuangyi Liu, Director of Graduate Studies, 218-726-7179, Fax: 218-726-8399, E-mail: zliu@d.umn.edu.

University of Minnesota, Twin Cities Campus, Graduate School, Scientific Computation Program, Minneapolis, MN 55455-0213. Offers MS, PhD. Part-time programs available. *Faculty:*

41 full-time (2 women), 2 part-time/adjunct (0 women). *Students:* 12 full-time (2 women), 4 part-time (1 woman), 6 international. 13 applicants, 62% accepted, 2 enrolled. In 2003, 1 degree awarded. *Degree requirements:* For master's and doctorate, thesis/dissertation. *Entrance requirements:* For doctorate, GRE General Test. *Application deadline:* For fall admission, 6/15 for domestic students; for spring admission, 10/15 for domestic students. Applications are processed on a rolling basis. Application fee: $50 ($55 for international students). Electronic applications accepted. *Expenses:* Tuition, state resident: full-time $3,681; part-time $614 per credit. Tuition, nonresident: full-time $7,231; part-time $1,205 per credit. *Financial support:* In 2003–04, 2 fellowships with full tuition reimbursements were awarded; research assistantships with full tuition reimbursements, institutionally sponsored loans, health care benefits, and unspecified assistantships also available. *Faculty research:* Parallel computations, quantum mechanical dynamics, computational materials science, computational fluid dynamics, computational neuroscience. *Unit head:* Prof. Jiali Gao, Director of Graduate Studies, 612-625-0769, Fax: 612-625-9442, E-mail: gao@chem.umn.edu. *Application contact:* Kathleen Clinton, Graduate Program Administrator, 612-625-8424, Fax: 612-625-9442, E-mail: clinton@compneuro.umn.edu.

University of Mississippi, Graduate School, School of Engineering, Oxford, University, MS 38677. Offers computational engineering science (MS, PhD); engineering science (MS, PhD). *Faculty:* 49 full-time (4 women). *Students:* 158 full-time (42 women), 33 part-time (7 women); includes 12 minority (10 African Americans, 2 Asian Americans or Pacific Islanders), 130 international. In 2003, 58 master's, 7 doctorates awarded. *Degree requirements:* For master's, thesis (for some programs); for doctorate, thesis/dissertation. *Entrance requirements:* For master's, GRE General Test, minimum GPA of 3.0; for doctorate, GRE General Test. Additional exam requirements/recommendations for international students: Required—TOEFL. *Application deadline:* For fall admission, 4/1 for domestic students; for spring admission, 10/1 for domestic students. Applications are processed on a rolling basis. Application fee: $25. *Expenses:* Tuition, state resident: part-time $218 per hour. Tuition, nonresident: part-time $273 per hour. *Financial support:* Scholarships/grants available. Financial award application deadline: 3/1; financial award applicants required to submit FAFSA. *Unit head:* Dr. Kai-Fong Lee, Dean, 662-915-7407, Fax: 662-915-1287, E-mail: engineer@olemiss.edu.

University of Puerto Rico, Mayagüez Campus, Graduate Studies, College of Arts and Sciences, Department of Mathematics, Mayagüez, PR 00681-9000. Offers applied mathematics (MS); computational sciences (MS); pure mathematics (MS); statistics (MS). Part-time programs available. *Degree requirements:* For master's, one foreign language, comprehensive exam. *Faculty research:* Automata theory, linear algebra, logic.

University of South Florida, College of Medicine and College of Graduate Studies, Graduate Programs in Medical Sciences, Tampa, FL 33620-9951. Offers anatomy (PhD); biochemistry and molecular biology (MS, PhD), including biochemistry and molecular biology (PhD), bioinformatics and computational biology (MS); medical microbiology and immunology (PhD); pathology (PhD); pharmacology and therapeutics (PhD), including medical sciences; physiology and biophysics (PhD). *Students:* 88 full-time (38 women), 20 part-time (10 women); includes 18 minority (3 African Americans, 4 Asian Americans or Pacific Islanders, 11 Hispanic Americans), 14 international. 145 applicants, 30% accepted, 34 enrolled. In 2003, 3 master's, 3 doctorates awarded. *Degree requirements:* For doctorate, thesis/dissertation. *Entrance requirements:* For doctorate, GRE General Test, minimum GPA of 3.0. Application fee: $30. *Expenses:* Contact institution. *Financial support:* Institutionally sponsored loans and scholarships/grants available. Financial award application deadline: 4/1; financial award applicants required to submit FAFSA. *Unit head:* Dr. Joseph J. Krzanowski, Associate Dean for Research and Graduate Affairs, 813-974-4181, Fax: 813-974-4317, E-mail: jkrzanow@com1.med.usf.edu.

The University of Texas at Austin, Graduate School, Program in Computational and Applied Mathematics, Austin, TX 78712-1111. Offers MA, PhD. Terminal master's awarded for partial completion of doctoral program. *Degree requirements:* For master's, thesis optional; for doctorate, thesis/dissertation, 3 area qualifying exams. Electronic applications accepted.

Virginia Polytechnic Institute and State University, Graduate School, Program in Genetics, Bioinformatics and Computational Biology, Blacksburg, VA 24061. Offers PhD. *Students:* 15 full-time (5 women), 2 part-time; includes 2 minority (both Asian Americans or Pacific Islanders), 12 international. *Entrance requirements:* For doctorate, GRE. Additional exam requirements/recommendations for international students: Required—TOEFL (minimum score 550 paper-based; 213 computer-based). *Application deadline:* Applications are processed on a rolling basis. Application fee: $45. Electronic applications accepted. Tuition, area resident: Full-time $6,039; part-time $336 per credit. Tuition, nonresident: full-time $9,708; part-time $539 per credit. Required fees: $905; $130 per credit. *Financial support:* Fellowships with full tuition reimbursements, research assistantships with full tuition reimbursements, teaching assistantships with full tuition reimbursements, career-related internships or fieldwork, Federal Work-Study, scholarships/grants, and unspecified assistantships available. *Unit head:* Dr. David Bevan, Chair, 540-231-5040, Fax: 540-231-2606, E-mail: drbevan@vt.edu. *Application contact:* Debi Darnell, Information Contact, 540-231-2026, Fax: 540-231-2606, E-mail: gbcb@vbi.vt.edu.

Washington University in St. Louis, Graduate School of Arts and Sciences, Division of Biology and Biomedical Sciences, Program in Computational Biology, St. Louis, MO 63130-4899. Offers PhD. *Degree requirements:* For doctorate, thesis/dissertation. *Application deadline:* For fall admission, 1/1 for domestic students. Applications are processed on a rolling basis. Application fee: $0. Electronic applications accepted. *Expenses:* Tuition: Full-time $28,300; part-time $1,180 per credit. *Unit head:* Dr. Gary Stormo, Head. *Application contact:* Jenny Lawler, Admissions and Recruitment Coordinator, 800-852-9074, E-mail: admissions@dbbs.wustl.edu.

Western Michigan University, Graduate College, College of Arts and Sciences, Department of Mathematics, Program in Computational Mathematics, Kalamazoo, MI 49008-5202. Offers MS.

Yale University, School of Medicine and Graduate School of Arts and Sciences, Combined Program in Biological and Biomedical Sciences (BBS), Computational Biology and Bioinformatics Track, New Haven, CT 06520. Offers PhD, MD/PhD. *Students:* 7 full-time. *Entrance requirements:* Additional exam requirements/recommendations for international students: Required—TOEFL. *Application deadline:* For fall admission, 12/15 for domestic students, 12/15 for international students. *Unit head:* Dr. Perry Miller, Director of Graduate Studies, 203-432-8189, E-mail: dgs.bioinfo@yale.edu.

Mathematical and Computational Finance

Bernard M. Baruch College of the City University of New York, Weissman School of Arts and Sciences, Program in Applied Mathematics for Finance, New York, NY 10010-5585. Offers MS. *Entrance requirements:* For master's, GRE General Test or GMAT, GRE Mathematics Subject Test optional, 3 recommendations. Additional exam requirements/recommendations for international students: Required—TOEFL, TWE. *Application deadline:* For fall admission, 6/30 for domestic students, 5/31 for international students. Application fee: $40. *Expenses:* Tuition, state resident: full-time $7,500; part-time $330 per credit. Tuition, nonresident: full-time $15,540; part-time $555 per credit. Required fees: $218; $72 per semester. Tuition and fees vary according to course load and program. *Unit head:* Warren B. Gordon, Chair, 646-312-4110, Fax: 646-312-4111. *Application contact:* 646-312-4490, Fax: 646-312-4491, E-mail: wsas_graduate_studies@baruch.cuny.edu.

Announcement: Baruch College's MS in Applied Mathematics for Finance is a unique program for recent college graduates interested in a career in quantitative finance as well as for practitioners seeking to enhance their mathematical foundation. The curriculum comprises the fundamental tools of mathematical finance, combining rigorous mathematical theory with hands-on computational experience.

Boston University, Graduate School of Arts and Sciences, Department of Mathematics and Statistics, Boston, MA 02215. Offers mathematical finance (MA); mathematics (MA, PhD). *Students:* 69 full-time (27 women), 9 part-time (2 women); includes 5 minority (1 African American, 2 Asian Americans or Pacific Islanders, 2 Hispanic Americans), 36 international. Average age 28. 269 applicants, 29% accepted, 38 enrolled. In 2003, 16 master's, 8 doctorates awarded. Terminal master's awarded for partial completion of doctoral program. *Degree requirements:* For master's, one foreign language, comprehensive exam, registration; for doctorate, one foreign language, thesis/dissertation, comprehensive exam, registration. *Entrance requirements:* For master's and doctorate, GRE General Test, GRE Subject Test, 3 letters of recommendation. Additional exam requirements/recommendations for international students: Required—TOEFL (minimum score 600 paper-based; 250 computer-based). *Application deadline:* For fall admission, 1/15 for domestic students, 1/15 for international students; for spring admission, 10/15 for domestic students, 10/15 for international students. Application fee: $60. *Expenses:* Tuition: Full-time $28,512; part-time $891 per credit hour. *Financial support:* In 2003–04, 50 students received support, including 4 fellowships with full tuition reimbursements available (averaging $15,500 per year), 23 research assistantships with full tuition reimbursements available (averaging $15,000 per year), 23 teaching assistantships with full tuition reimbursements available (averaging $15,000 per year); Federal Work-Study and scholarships/grants also available. Support available to part-time students. Financial award application deadline: 1/15; financial award applicants required to submit FAFSA. *Unit head:* Steven Rosenberg, Chairman, 617-353-9556, Fax: 617-353-8100, E-mail: sr@bu.edu. *Application contact:* Angela M. Silva, Staff Coordinator, 617-353-2560, Fax: 617-353-8100, E-mail: amsilva@bu.edu.

Carnegie Mellon University, Graduate School of Industrial Administration, Pittsburgh, PA 15213-3891. Offers accounting (PhD); algorithms, combinatorics, and optimization (MS, PhD); business management and software engineering (MBMSE); civil engineering and industrial management (MS); computational finance (MSCF); economics (MS, PhD); electronic commerce (MS); environmental engineering and management (MEEM); finance (PhD); financial economics (PhD); industrial administration (MBA), including administration and public management; information systems (PhD); management of manufacturing and automation (MOM, PhD), including industrial administration (PhD), manufacturing (MOM); marketing (PhD); mathematical finance (PhD); operations research (PhD); organizational behavior and theory (PhD); political economy (PhD); production and operations management (PhD); public policy and management (MS, MSED); software engineering and business management (MS). Part-time programs available. Terminal master's awarded for partial completion of doctoral program. *Degree requirements:* For doctorate, thesis/dissertation. *Entrance requirements:* For master's, GMAT. Additional exam requirements/recommendations for international students: Required—TOEFL. Expenses: Contact institution.

Carnegie Mellon University, Mellon College of Science, Department of Mathematical Sciences, Pittsburgh, PA 15213-3891. Offers algorithms, combinatorics, and optimization (PhD); mathematical finance (PhD); mathematical sciences (MS, DA, PhD); pure and applied logic (PhD). Part-time programs available. Terminal master's awarded for partial completion of doctoral program. *Degree requirements:* For doctorate, thesis/dissertation. *Entrance requirements:* For master's and doctorate, GRE General Test, GRE Subject Test. Additional exam requirements/recommendations for international students: Required—TOEFL. Electronic applications accepted. *Expenses:* Tuition: Full-time $28,200; part-time $392 per unit. Required fees: $220. *Faculty research:* Continuum mechanics, discrete mathematics, applied and computational mathematics.

Florida State University, Graduate Studies, College of Arts and Sciences, Department of Mathematics, Tallahassee, FL 32306. Offers applied mathematics (MA, MS, PhD); financial mathematics (PhD); mathematical sciences (MA, MS); pure mathematics (MA, MS, PhD). Part-time programs available. *Faculty:* 35 full-time (3 women), 8 part-time/adjunct (4 women). *Students:* 110 full-time (36 women), 7 part-time (3 women); includes 54 minority (4 African Americans, 45 Asian Americans or Pacific Islanders, 5 Hispanic Americans), 4 international. Average age 26. 250 applicants, 60% accepted, 50 enrolled. In 2003, 18 master's, 3 doctorates awarded. Terminal master's awarded for partial completion of doctoral program. *Degree requirements:* For master's, thesis optional; for doctorate, thesis/dissertation. *Entrance requirements:* For master's and doctorate, GRE General Test, minimum GPA of 3.0. *Application deadline:* For fall admission, 2/1 priority date for domestic students, 1/1 priority date for international students; for winter admission, 7/1 for domestic students. Applications are processed on a rolling basis. Application fee: $20. Electronic applications accepted. *Expenses:* Tuition, state resident: part-time $196 per credit hour. Tuition, nonresident: part-time $731 per credit hour. Part-time tuition and fees vary according to campus/location. *Financial support:* In 2003–04, 2 fellowships with full tuition reimbursements (averaging $15,000 per year), 10 research assistantships with full tuition reimbursements, 78 teaching assistantships with full tuition reimbursements (averaging $15,000 per year) were awarded. Institutionally sponsored loans also available. Financial award application deadline: 3/1. *Unit head:* Dr. Dewitt Sumners, Chairperson, 850-644-4406, Fax: 850-644-4053, E-mail: sumners@math.fsu.edu. *Application contact:* Dr. Sam Huckaba, Director of Graduate Studies, 850-644-1479, Fax: 850-644-4053, E-mail: huckaba@math.fsu.edu.

Georgia Institute of Technology, Graduate Studies and Research, College of Management, Program in Management, Atlanta, GA 30332-0001. Offers accounting (PhD); finance (PhD); information technology management (PhD); marketing (PhD); operations management (PhD); organizational behavior (PhD); quantitative and computational finance (MS); strategic management (PhD). *Accreditation:* AACSB. *Degree requirements:* For doctorate, thesis/dissertation, oral exams, comprehensive exam. *Entrance requirements:* For master's and doctorate, GMAT. Additional exam requirements/recommendations for international students: Required—TOEFL. *Application deadline:* For fall admission, 3/1 for domestic students. Applications are processed on a rolling basis. Application fee: $50. *Expenses:* Tuition, state resident: part-time $1,925 per semester. Tuition, nonresident: part-time $7,700 per semester. Required fees: $434 per semester. Full-time tuition and fees vary according to program. *Financial support:* Research assistantships, teaching assistantships, career-related internships or fieldwork, Federal Work-Study, institutionally sponsored loans, and tuition waivers (partial) available. Support available to part-time students. *Faculty research:* MIS, management of technology, international business, entrepreneurship, operations management. *Application contact:* Ann Johnston Scott, Director, 404-894-8722.

Georgia Institute of Technology, Graduate Studies and Research, College of Sciences, School of Mathematics, Atlanta, GA 30332-0001. Offers algorithms, combinatorics, and optimization (PhD); applied mathematics (MS); bioinformatics (PhD); mathematics (PhD); quantitative

Mathematical and Computational Finance

Georgia Institute of Technology (continued)

and computational finance (MS); statistics (MS Stat). *Faculty:* 50 full-time (3 women). *Students:* 59 full-time (17 women), 8 part-time (2 women); includes 3 minority (2 African Americans, 1 Hispanic American), 32 international. Average age 25. In 2003, 20 master's, 7 doctorates awarded, leading to university research/teaching 55%, business/industry 30%, government 15%. Terminal master's awarded for partial completion of doctoral program. *Degree requirements:* For master's, thesis or alternative; for doctorate, one foreign language, thesis/dissertation. *Entrance requirements:* For master's, GRE General Test, minimum GPA of 3.0; for doctorate, GRE General Test, GRE Subject Test, minimum GPA of 3.0. Additional exam requirements/recommendations for international students: Required—TOEFL. *Application deadline:* For fall admission, 3/1 priority date for domestic students, 3/1 priority date for international students; for spring admission, 10/1 priority date for domestic students, 10/1 priority date for international students. Applications are processed on a rolling basis. Application fee: $50. Electronic applications accepted. *Expenses:* Tuition, state resident: part-time $1,925 per semester. Tuition, nonresident: part-time $7,700 per semester. Required fees: $434 per semester. Full-time tuition and fees vary according to program. *Financial support:* In 2003–04, 7 fellowships with tuition reimbursements, 20 research assistantships with tuition reimbursements, 40 teaching assistantships with tuition reimbursements were awarded. Career-related internships or fieldwork, Federal Work-Study, institutionally sponsored loans, tuition waivers (partial), and supplements also available. Financial award application deadline: 2/1. *Faculty research:* Dynamical systems, discrete mathematics, probability and statistics, mathematical physics. Total annual research expenditures: $1.1 million. *Unit head:* Dr. William Thomas Trotter, Chair, 404-894-2700. *Application contact:* Dr. Evans Harrell, Graduate Coordinator, 404-894-9203, Fax: 404-894-4409, E-mail: grad.coordinator@math.gatech.edu.

New York University, Graduate School of Arts and Science, Courant Institute of Mathematical Sciences, Department of Mathematics, New York, NY 10012-1019. Offers atmosphere-ocean science and mathematics (PhD); mathematics (MS, PhD); mathematics and statistics/operations research (MS); mathematics in finance (MS); scientific computing (MS). Part-time and evening/weekend programs available. *Faculty:* 46 full-time (0 women). *Students:* 135 full-time (24 women), 83 part-time (28 women); includes 28 minority (2 African Americans, 23 Asian Americans or Pacific Islanders, 3 Hispanic Americans), 76 international. Average age 28. 742 applicants, 41% accepted. In 2003, 40 master's, 25 doctorates awarded. *Degree requirements:* For master's, thesis optional; for doctorate, one foreign language, thesis/dissertation, oral and written exams. *Entrance requirements:* For master's and doctorate, GRE General Test, GRE Subject Test. Additional exam requirements/recommendations for international students: Required—TOEFL. *Application deadline:* For fall admission, 1/4 for domestic students; for spring admission, 11/1 for domestic students. Application fee: $75. *Expenses:* Tuition: Full-time $22,056; part-time $919 per credit. Required fees: $1,664; $49 per credit. Tuition and fees vary according to course load and program. *Financial support:* Fellowships with tuition reimbursements, research assistantships with tuition reimbursements, teaching assistantships with tuition reimbursements, Federal Work-Study and institutionally sponsored loans available. Financial award application deadline: 1/4; financial award applicants required to submit FAFSA. *Faculty research:* Partial differential equations, computational science, applied mathematics, geometry and topology, probability and stochastic processes. *Unit head:* Mel Hausner, Chairman, 212-998-3238, Fax: 212-995-4121. *Application contact:* Fedor Bogomolov, Director of Graduate Studies, 212-998-3238, Fax: 212-995-4121, E-mail: admissions@math.nyu.edu.

See in-depth description on page 559.

North Carolina State University, Graduate School, College of Agriculture and Life Sciences and College of Engineering and College of Physical and Mathematical Sciences, Program in Financial Mathematics, Raleigh, NC 27695. Offers MFM. Part-time programs available. *Faculty:* 14 full-time (1 woman). *Students:* 8 full-time (1 woman), 3 international. Average age 27. 21 applicants, 24% accepted. *Degree requirements:* For master's, project/internship, thesis optional. *Entrance requirements:* For master's, GRE General Test, GRE Subject Test (recommended). Additional exam requirements/recommendations for international students: Required—TOEFL (minimum score 550 paper-based; 213 computer-based). *Application deadline:* For fall admission, 6/25 for domestic students, 3/1 for international students; for spring admission, 11/25 for domestic students, 7/15 for international students. Applications are processed on a rolling basis. Application fee: $55 ($65 for international students). Electronic applications accepted. *Expenses:* Tuition, state resident: part-time $396 per hour. Tuition, nonresident: part-time $1,895 per hour. *Financial support:* In 2003–04, 4 students received support, including 5 teaching assistantships with full tuition reimbursements available (averaging $6,226 per year); research assistantships with full tuition reimbursements available Financial award application deadline: 2/1; financial award applicants required to submit FAFSA. *Faculty research:* Financial mathematics modeling and computation, futures, options and commodities markets, real options, credit risk, portfolio optimization. *Unit head:* Jean-Pierre Fouque, Director of Graduate Programs, 919-515-8588, Fax: 919-515-3798, E-mail: fouque@math.ncsu.edu.

See in-depth description on page 561.

OGI School of Science & Engineering at Oregon Health & Science University, Graduate Studies, Department of Computer Science and Engineering, Beaverton, OR 97006-8921. Offers computational finance (MS, Certificate); computer science (PhD); computer science and engineering (MS, PhD). Part-time and evening/weekend programs available. Terminal master's awarded for partial completion of doctoral program. *Degree requirements:* For master's, thesis optional; for doctorate, oral defense of dissertation. *Entrance requirements:* For master's and doctorate, GRE General Test. Additional exam requirements/recommendations for international students: Required—TOEFL. Electronic applications accepted. *Faculty research:* Computer systems architecture, intelligent and interactive systems, programming models and systems, theory of computation.

OGI School of Science & Engineering at Oregon Health & Science University, Graduate Studies, Department of Management in Science and Technology, Beaverton, OR 97006-8921. Offers computational finance (Certificate); management in science and technology (MS, Certificate), including health care management (Certificate), management in science and technology. Part-time and evening/weekend programs available. *Entrance requirements:* Additional exam requirements/recommendations for international students: Required—TOEFL. Electronic applications accepted.

Polytechnic University, Westchester Graduate Center, Graduate Programs, Department of Management, Major in Financial Engineering, Hawthorne, NY 10532-1507. Offers capital markets (MS); computational finance (MS); financial engineering (AC); financial technology (MS); financial technology management (AC); information management (AC). *Students:* 2 applicants, 50% accepted, 0 enrolled.Application fee: $55. *Expenses:* Tuition: Part-time $855 per credit. Required fees: $320 per term. *Application contact:* Anthea Jeffrey, Graduate Admissions, 718-260-3200, Fax: 718-260-3624, E-mail: gradinfo@poly.edu.

Purdue University, Graduate School, School of Science, Department of Statistics, West Lafayette, IN 47907. Offers applied statistics (MS); statistics (PhD); statistics and computer science (MS); statistics/computational finance (MS); theoretical statistics (MS). *Degree requirements:* For doctorate, thesis/dissertation. *Entrance requirements:* For master's and doctorate, GRE General Test. Additional exam requirements/recommendations for international students: Required—TOEFL. Electronic applications accepted. *Faculty research:* Nonparametric models, computational finance, design of experiments, probability theory, bioinformatics.

See in-depth description on page 579.

Rice University, Graduate Programs, George R. Brown School of Engineering, Department of Statistics, Houston, TX 77251-1892. Offers biostatistics (PhD); computational finance (PhD); statistics (M Stat, MA, PhD). *Faculty:* 9 full-time (2 women), 17 part-time/adjunct (1 woman). *Students:* 44 full-time (17 women), 1 (woman) part-time; includes 12 minority (5 African Americans, 2 Asian Americans or Pacific Islanders, 5 Hispanic Americans), 12 international. Average age 28. 130 applicants, 10% accepted, 9 enrolled. In 2003, 4 master's, 1 doctorate awarded. Terminal master's awarded for partial completion of doctoral program. *Median time to degree:* Of those who began their doctoral program in fall 1995, 90% received their degree in 8 years or less. *Degree requirements:* For master's, thesis/dissertation; for doctorate, thesis/dissertation, comprehensive exam. *Entrance requirements:* For master's and doctorate, GRE General Test, GRE Subject Test, minimum GPA of 3.0. Additional exam requirements/recommendations for international students: Required—TOEFL (minimum score 630 paper-based; 250 computer-based). *Application deadline:* For fall admission, 2/1 priority date for domestic students, 2/1 priority date for international students; for spring admission, 11/1 for domestic students, 11/1 for international students. Applications are processed on a rolling basis. Application fee: $35. Electronic applications accepted. *Expenses:* Tuition: Full-time $19,700; part-time $1,096 per hour. *Financial support:* In 2003–04, 15 fellowships with tuition reimbursements (averaging $20,000 per year), 15 research assistantships with tuition reimbursements (averaging $20,000 per year), 5 teaching assistantships with tuition reimbursements (averaging $20,000 per year) were awarded. Career-related internships or fieldwork, institutionally sponsored loans, scholarships/grants, traineeships, health care benefits, tuition waivers (full), and unspecified assistantships also available. Financial award application deadline: 1/15. *Faculty research:* Statistical genetics, non parametric function estimation, computational statistics and visualization, stochastic processes. Total annual research expenditures: $800,000. *Unit head:* Dr. Katherine B. Ensor, Chair, 713-527-6032, Fax: 713-348-5476, E-mail: kathy@rice.edu. *Application contact:* Leticia Gonzales, Recruiting Assistant, 713-348-6032, Fax: 713-348-5476, E-mail: lgonzale@rice.edu.

Stanford University, School of Humanities and Sciences, Department of Mathematics, Stanford, CA 94305-9991. Offers financial mathematics (MS); mathematics (MS, PhD). *Faculty:* 34 full-time (2 women). *Students:* 59 full-time (14 women), 10 part-time (2 women); includes 6 minority (1 African American, 3 Asian Americans or Pacific Islanders, 2 Hispanic Americans), 42 international. Average age 26. 186 applicants, 28% accepted. In 2003, 9 master's, 5 doctorates awarded. Terminal master's awarded for partial completion of doctoral program. *Degree requirements:* For doctorate, 2 foreign languages, thesis/dissertation, oral exam. *Entrance requirements:* For master's, GRE General Test; for doctorate, GRE General Test, GRE Subject Test. Additional exam requirements/recommendations for international students: Required—TOEFL. *Application deadline:* For fall admission, 1/4 for domestic students. Application fee: $65 ($80 for international students). Electronic applications accepted. *Expenses:* Tuition: Full-time $28,563. *Unit head:* Leon Simon, Chair, 650-725-6284, Fax: 650-725-4066, E-mail: lms@math.stanford.edu. *Application contact:* Graduate Administrator, 650-723-2601.

University of Alberta, Faculty of Graduate Studies and Research, Department of Mathematical and Statistical Sciences, Edmonton, AB T6G 2E1, Canada. Offers applied mathematics (M Sc, PhD); biostatistics (M Sc); mathematical finance (M Sc, PhD); mathematical physics (M Sc, PhD); mathematics (M Sc, PhD); statistics (M Sc, PhD, Postgraduate Diploma). Part-time programs available. *Faculty:* 48 full-time (4 women). *Students:* 112 full-time (41 women), 5 part-time. Average age 24. 776 applicants, 5% accepted, 34 enrolled. In 2003, 12 master's, 10 doctorates awarded. Terminal master's awarded for partial completion of doctoral program. *Median time to degree:* Master's–2 years full-time; doctorate–5 years full-time. Of those who began their doctoral program in fall 1995, 100% received their degree in 8 years or less. *Degree requirements:* For master's, thesis (for some programs); for doctorate, thesis/dissertation, comprehensive exam. *Entrance requirements:* Additional exam requirements/recommendations for international students: Required—TOEFL (minimum score 580 paper-based; 237 computer-based). *Application deadline:* For fall admission, 3/1 for domestic students, 2/1 for international students. Applications are processed on a rolling basis. Application fee: $0. Electronic applications accepted. Tuition charges are reported in Canadian dollars. Tuition, nonresident: full-time $3,921 Canadian dollars. International tuition: $7,113 Canadian dollars full-time. *Financial support:* In 2003–04, 51 research assistantships, 88 teaching assistantships with full and partial tuition reimbursements were awarded. Scholarships/grants also available. Financial award application deadline: 5/1. *Faculty research:* Classical and functional analysis, algebra, differential equations, geometry. *Unit head:* Dr. Anthony To-Ming Lau, Chair, 403-492-5799, E-mail: tlau@math.ualberta.ca. *Application contact:* Dr. Yau Shu Wong, Associate Chair, Graduate Studies, 403-492-5799, Fax: 403-492-6828, E-mail: gradstudies@math.ualberta.ca.

University of Chicago, Division of the Physical Sciences, Department of Mathematics, Program in Financial Mathematics, Chicago, IL 60637-1513. Offers MS. Part-time and evening/weekend programs available. *Faculty:* 4 full-time (0 women), 11 part-time/adjunct (0 women). *Students:* 27 full-time (7 women), 28 part-time (5 women). Average age 30. 223 applicants, 46% accepted. In 2003, 43 degrees awarded. *Entrance requirements:* For master's, GRE General Test, GRE Subject Test. Additional exam requirements/recommendations for international students: Required—TOEFL (minimum score 600 paper-based; 250 computer-based). *Application deadline:* For fall admission, 1/5 priority date for domestic students, 1/5 priority date for international students. Application fee: $55. Electronic applications accepted. *Financial support:* Institutionally sponsored loans available. Financial award applicants required to submit FAFSA. *Unit head:* Niels Nygaard, Director, 773-702-7391, Fax: 773-834-4386, E-mail: niels@math.uchicago.edu. *Application contact:* Alice Brugman, Administrator, 773-834-4385, Fax: 773-834-4386, E-mail: alice@math.uchicago.edu.

University of Connecticut, Graduate School, College of Liberal Arts and Sciences, Department of Mathematics, Field of Applied Financial Mathematics, Storrs, CT 06269. Offers MS. *Faculty:* 8 full-time (0 women). *Students:* 2 full-time (0 women), 3 part-time (1 woman), 3 international. Average age 36. 9 applicants, 67% accepted, 5 enrolled. *Degree requirements:* For master's, comprehensive exam. *Entrance requirements:* Additional exam requirements/recommendations for international students: Required—TOEFL (minimum score 550 paper-based; 213 computer-based). *Application deadline:* For fall admission, 2/1 priority date for domestic students, 2/1 priority date for international students; for spring admission, 11/1 for domestic students, 10/1 for international students. Applications are processed on a rolling basis. Application fee: $55. Electronic applications accepted. *Expenses:* Tuition, state resident: part-time $3,860 per semester. Tuition, nonresident: part-time $9,036 per semester. *Financial support:* Federal Work-Study and scholarships/grants available. Financial award application deadline: 2/1; financial award applicants required to submit FAFSA. *Unit head:* James Bridgeman, Chairperson, 860-486-8382, Fax: 860-486-4283, E-mail: james.bridgeman@uconn.edu. *Application contact:* Sharon McDermott, Administrative Assistant, 860-486-6452, Fax: 860-486-4283, E-mail: gradadm@math.uconn.edu.

University of Connecticut, Graduate School, College of Liberal Arts and Sciences, Department of Mathematics, Field of Mathematics, Storrs, CT 06269. Offers actuarial science (MS, PhD); applied mathematics (MS); financial mathematics (MS); mathematics (MS); mathematics and computer science (MS). *Faculty:* 32 full-time (4 women). *Students:* 68 full-time (27 women), 39 part-time (19 women); includes 5 minority (1 African American, 4 Asian Americans or Pacific Islanders), 62 international. Average age 29. 235 applicants, 53% accepted, 50 enrolled. In 2003, 37 master's, 5 doctorates awarded. Terminal master's awarded for partial completion of doctoral program. *Degree requirements:* For master's, comprehensive exam; for doctorate, thesis/dissertation. *Entrance requirements:* For master's and doctorate, GRE General Test. Additional exam requirements/recommendations for international students: Required—TOEFL (minimum score 550 paper-based; 213 computer-based). *Application deadline:* For fall admission, 2/1 priority date for domestic students, 2/1 priority date for international students; for spring admission, 11/1 for domestic students, 10/1 for international students. Applications are processed on a rolling basis. Application fee: $55. Electronic applications accepted. *Expenses:* Tuition, state resident: part-time $3,860 per semester. Tuition, nonresident: part-time $9,036 per semester. *Financial support:* In 2003–04, 7 research assistantships with full tuition reimbursements, 51 teaching assistantships with full tuition reimbursements were awarded. Fellowships, Federal Work-Study, scholarships/grants, health care benefits, and unspecified assistantships also available. Financial award application deadline: 2/1; financial award applicants required to submit FAFSA. *Unit head:* Eugene Spiegel, Chairperson, 860-486-3844, Fax:

860-486-4283, E-mail: eugene.spiegel@uconn.edu. *Application contact:* Sharon McDermott, Administrative Assistant, 860-486-6452, Fax: 860-486-4283, E-mail: gradadm@math.uconn.edu.

The University of North Carolina at Charlotte, Graduate School, Belk College of Business Administration, Program in Mathematical Finance, Charlotte, NC 28223-0001. Offers MS. *Students:* 1 (woman) full-time; minority (Asian American or Pacific Islander) Average age 40. 1 applicant, 100% accepted, 1 enrolled. *Entrance requirements:* For master's, GRE General Test or GMAT, minimum GPA of 2.75 overall. Additional exam requirements/recommendations for international students: Required—TOEFL (minimum score 557 paper-based; 220 computer-based). *Application deadline:* For fall admission, 7/15 for domestic students, 5/1 for international students; for spring admission, 11/15 for domestic students, 10/1 for international students. Applications are processed on a rolling basis. Application fee: $35. Electronic applications accepted. *Expenses:* Tuition, state resident: full-time $1,979. Tuition, nonresident: full-time $12,111. Required fees: $1,201. Tuition and fees vary according to course load. *Financial support:* Career-related internships or fieldwork, Federal Work-Study, institutionally sponsored loans, scholarships/grants, and unspecified assistantships available. Support available to part-time students. Financial award application deadline: 4/1; financial award applicants required to submit FAFSA. *Unit head:* Dr. Richard J. Buttimer, Director, 704-687-6219, Fax: 704-687-6987, E-mail: buttimer@email.uncc.edu. *Application contact:* Kathy B. Giddings, Director of Graduate Admissions, 704-687-3366, Fax: 704-687-3279, E-mail: gradadm@email.uncc.edu.

University of Pittsburgh, School of Arts and Sciences, Department of Mathematics, Pittsburgh, PA 15260. Offers applied mathematics (MA, MS); financial mathematics (PMS); mathematics (MA, MS, PhD). Part-time programs available. *Faculty:* 35 full-time (5 women), 13 part-time/adjunct (5 women). *Students:* 66 full-time (27 women), 10 part-time (3 women); includes 4 minority (3 African Americans, 1 Asian American or Pacific Islander), 30 international. 167 applicants, 42% accepted, 23 enrolled. In 2003, 8 master's, 5 doctorates awarded, leading to university research/teaching 100%. Terminal master's awarded for partial completion of doctoral program. *Median time to degree:* Doctorate–6 years full-time, 9.5 years part-time. *Degree requirements:* For master's, thesis (for some programs), comprehensive exam; for doctorate, thesis/dissertation, preliminary exams, comprehensive exam. *Entrance requirements:* For master's and doctorate, GRE General Test, GRE Subject Test (recommended), minimum GPA of 3.0. Additional exam requirements/recommendations for international students: Required—TOEFL (minimum score 550 paper-based; 213 computer-based). *Application deadline:* For fall admission, 1/15 priority date for domestic students, 1/15 priority date for international students; for spring admission, 9/1 for domestic students, 9/1 for international students. Applications are processed on a rolling basis. Application fee: $40. Electronic applications accepted. *Expenses:* Tuition, state resident: full-time $11,744; part-time $479 per credit. Tuition, nonresident: full-time $22,910; part-time $941 per credit. Required fees: $560. Tuition and fees vary according to degree level and program. *Financial support:* In 2003–04, 61 students received support, including 6 fellowships with full and partial tuition reimbursements available (averaging $14,700 per year), 6 research assistantships with full and partial tuition reimbursements available (averaging $12,400 per year), 48 teaching assistantships with full and partial tuition reimbursements available (averaging $12,775 per year); Federal Work-Study, institutionally sponsored loans, scholarships/grants, tuition waivers (partial), and unspecified assistantships also available. Financial award application deadline: 1/15. *Faculty research:* Computational math, mathbiology, math finance, algebra, analysis. Total annual research expenditures: $700,000. *Unit head:* John Chadam, Chairman, 412-624-8361, Fax: 412-624-8397, E-mail: chadam@pitt.edu. *Application contact:* Molly Williams, Administrator, 412-624-1175, Fax: 412-624-8397, E-mail: mollyw@pitt.edu.

Mathematics

Alabama State University, School of Graduate Studies, College of Arts and Sciences, Department of Mathematics, Computers, and Physical Science, Montgomery, AL 36101-0271. Offers mathematics (Ed S). Part-time programs available. *Degree requirements:* For Ed S, thesis. *Entrance requirements:* For master's, GRE, GRE Subject Test, graduate writing competence test; for Ed S, graduate writing competency test, GRE, MAT. Additional exam requirements/recommendations for international students: Required—TOEFL (minimum score 500 paper-based; 173 computer-based). *Faculty research:* Discrete mathematics, symbolic dynamics, mathematical social sciences.

American University, College of Arts and Sciences, Department of Mathematics and Statistics, Program in Mathematics, Washington, DC 20016-8001. Offers MA. Part-time and evening/weekend programs available. *Students:* 1 full-time (0 women), 2 part-time. Average age 48. In 2003, 2 degrees awarded. *Degree requirements:* For master's, one foreign language, thesis or alternative. *Entrance requirements:* For master's, GRE, BA in mathematics. *Application deadline:* For fall admission, 2/1 for domestic students; for spring admission, 10/1 for domestic students. Application fee: $50. *Expenses:* Tuition: Full-time $15,786; part-time $877 per credit hour. Required fees: $300. Tuition and fees vary according to course load and program. *Financial support:* Fellowships, teaching assistantships, career-related internships or fieldwork, Federal Work-Study, and institutionally sponsored loans available. Support available to part-time students. Financial award application deadline: 2/1. *Unit head:* Dr. Dan Kalman, Chair, Department of Mathematics and Statistics, 202-885-3122, Fax: 202-885-3155.

Andrews University, School of Graduate Studies, College of Arts and Sciences, Interdisciplinary Studies in Mathematics and Physical Science Program, Berrien Springs, MI 49104. Offers MS. *Application deadline:* Applications are processed on a rolling basis. Application fee: $40. *Expenses:* Tuition: Full-time $15,230; part-time $620 per credit. Required fees: $350. *Unit head:* Dr. Margarita Mattingly, Chairman, 269-471-3431. *Application contact:* Carolyn Hurst, Supervisor of Graduate Admission, 800-253-3430, Fax: 269-471-3228, E-mail: enroll@andrews.edu.

Appalachian State University, Cratis D. Williams Graduate School, College of Arts and Sciences, Department of Mathematics, Boone, NC 28608. Offers mathematics (MA); mathematics education (MA). Part-time programs available. *Faculty:* 12 full-time (5 women). *Students:* 19 full-time (10 women), 12 part-time (9 women). 10 applicants, 100% accepted, 7 enrolled. In 2003, 3 degrees awarded. *Degree requirements:* For master's, one foreign language, comprehensive exam, registration. *Entrance requirements:* For master's, GRE General Test. Additional exam requirements/recommendations for international students: Required—TOEFL (minimum score 570 paper-based; 230 computer-based). *Application deadline:* For fall admission, 7/1 for domestic students, 1/1 for international students; for spring admission, 11/1 for domestic students, 6/1 for international students. Application fee: $35. *Expenses:* Tuition, state resident: full-time $1,668; part-time $208 per credit. Tuition, nonresident: full-time $11,176; part-time $1,397 per credit. Required fees: $1,361; $196 per term. *Financial support:* In 2003–04, 5 students received support, including 7 research assistantships (averaging $8,000 per year), 1 teaching assistantship (averaging $8,000 per year); fellowships, career-related internships or fieldwork, Federal Work-Study, scholarships/grants, and unspecified assistantships also available. Support available to part-time students. Financial award application deadline: 7/1. *Faculty research:* Graph theory, differential equations, logic, geometry, complex analysis. Total annual research expenditures: $19,139. *Unit head:* Dr. William Bauldry, Chair, 828-262-3050, Fax: 828-265-8617, E-mail: wmcb@math.appstate.edu. *Application contact:* Dr. Holly Hirst, Graduate Director, 828-262-3050, E-mail: hirsthp@math.appstate.edu.

Arizona State University, Graduate College, College of Liberal Arts and Sciences, Department of Mathematics, Tempe, AZ 85287. Offers applied mathematics (MA, PhD); mathematics (MA, MNS, PhD); statistics (MA, PhD). *Degree requirements:* For master's, thesis or alternative; for doctorate, one foreign language, thesis/dissertation. *Entrance requirements:* For master's and doctorate, GRE General Test. *Expenses:* Tuition, state resident: full-time $3,708; part-time $194 per credit hour. Tuition, nonresident: full-time $12,228; part-time $510 per credit hour. Required fees: $87; $22 per semester. Part-time tuition and fees vary according to program. *Faculty research:* Mathematical biology, ordinary and partial differential equations, calculus of variations.

Arkansas State University, Graduate School, College of Sciences and Mathematics, Department of Computer Sciences, Jonesboro, State University, AR 72467. Offers computer science (MS). Part-time programs available. *Faculty:* 9 full-time (6 women). *Students:* 6 full-time (0 women), 8 part-time; includes 1 minority (Asian American or Pacific Islander), 6 international. Average age 28. In 2003, 6 degrees awarded. *Degree requirements:* For master's, thesis or alternative, comprehensive exam. *Entrance requirements:* For master's, GRE General Test or MAT, appropriate bachelor's degree. Additional exam requirements/recommendations for international students: Required—TOEFL (minimum score 213 computer-based). *Application deadline:* For fall admission, 7/1 for domestic students; for spring admission, 11/15 priority date for domestic students. Applications are processed on a rolling basis. Application fee: $15 ($25 for international students). Electronic applications accepted. *Expenses:* Tuition, state resident: full-time $2,844; part-time $158 per hour. Tuition, nonresident: full-time $7,200; part-time $400 per hour. Required fees: $644; $33 per hour. $25 per semester. Tuition and fees vary according to course load. *Financial support:* Teaching assistantships, Federal Work-Study and scholarships/grants available. Support available to part-time students. Financial award application deadline: 7/1; financial award applicants required to submit FAFSA. *Unit head:* Dr. Jeff Jenness, Chair, 870-972-3978, Fax: 870-972-3950, E-mail: jeffj@astate.edu.

Arkansas State University, Graduate School, College of Sciences and Mathematics, Department of Mathematics and Statistics, Jonesboro, State University, AR 72467. Offers mathematics (MS, MSE). Part-time programs available. *Faculty:* 6 full-time (1 woman). *Students:* 3 full-time (all women), 11 part-time (6 women); includes 2 minority (1 African American, 1 Asian American or Pacific Islander), 1 international. Average age 33. In 2003, 4 degrees awarded. *Degree requirements:* For master's, thesis or alternative, comprehensive exam. *Entrance requirements:* For master's, GRE General Test or MAT, appropriate bachelor's degree. Additional exam requirements/recommendations for international students: Required—TOEFL (minimum score 213 computer-based). *Application deadline:* For fall admission, 7/1 for domestic students; for spring admission, 11/15 priority date for domestic students. Applications are processed on a rolling basis. Application fee: $15 ($25 for international students). Electronic applications accepted. *Expenses:* Tuition, state resident: full-time $2,844; part-time $158 per hour. Tuition, nonresident: full-time $7,200; part-time $400 per hour. Required fees: $644; $33 per hour. $25 per semester. Tuition and fees vary according to course load. *Financial support:* Teaching assistantships, Federal Work-Study and scholarships/grants available. Support available to part-time students. Financial award application deadline: 7/1; financial award applicants required to submit FAFSA. *Unit head:* Dr. Jerry Linnstaedter, Chair, 870-972-3090, Fax: 870-972-3950, E-mail: linnstaedter@astate.edu.

Auburn University, Graduate School, College of Sciences and Mathematics, Department of Mathematics, Auburn University, AL 36849. Offers MAM, MS, PhD. *Faculty:* 36 full-time (3 women). *Students:* 29 full-time (14 women), 7 part-time (3 women); includes 5 minority (4 African Americans, 1 Asian American or Pacific Islander), 15 international. 41 applicants, 68% accepted. In 2003, 6 master's, 2 doctorates awarded. *Degree requirements:* For doctorate, thesis/dissertation. *Entrance requirements:* For master's, GRE General Test, undergraduate mathematics background; for doctorate, GRE General Test, GRE Subject Test. *Application deadline:* For fall admission, 7/7 for domestic students; for spring admission, 11/24 for domestic students. Applications are processed on a rolling basis. Application fee: $25 ($50 for international students). Electronic applications accepted. *Expenses:* Tuition, state resident: part-time $175 per credit hour. Tuition, nonresident: part-time $525 per credit hour. *Financial support:* Fellowships, teaching assistantships, special tuition awards available. *Faculty research:* Pure and applied mathematics. *Unit head:* Dr. Michel Smith, Chair, 334-844-4290, Fax: 334-844-6655.

Ball State University, Graduate School, College of Sciences and Humanities, Department of Mathematical Sciences, Program in Mathematics, Muncie, IN 47306-1099. Offers mathematics (MA, MS); mathematics education (MAE). *Accreditation:* NCATE (one or more programs are accredited). *Students:* 3 full-time (2 women), 6 part-time (2 women), 2 international. Average age 39. 6 applicants, 83% accepted, 4 enrolled. In 2003, 3 degrees awarded. Application fee: $25 ($35 for international students). *Expenses:* Tuition, state resident: full-time $5,748. Tuition, nonresident: full-time $14,166. *Financial support:* Research assistantships with full tuition reimbursements, teaching assistantships with tuition reimbursements available. Financial award application deadline: 3/1. *Unit head:* Dr. Sheryl Stump, Director, 765-285-8662, Fax: 765-285-1721.

Baylor University, Graduate School, College of Arts and Sciences, Department of Mathematics, Waco, TX 76798. Offers MS, PhD. *Students:* 14 full-time (4 women), 2 part-time; includes 1 minority (Asian American or Pacific Islander), 5 international. In 2003, 6 master's, 1 doctorate awarded. *Degree requirements:* For master's, thesis (for some programs), final oral exam. *Entrance requirements:* For master's, GRE General Test. *Application deadline:* For fall admission, 8/1 for domestic students. Applications are processed on a rolling basis. Application fee: $25. *Expenses:* Tuition: Part-time $698 per hour. *Financial support:* Teaching assistantships, career-related internships or fieldwork, Federal Work-Study, and institutionally sponsored loans available. Support available to part-time students. Financial award application deadline: 5/1. *Faculty research:* Algebra, statistics, probability, applied mathematics, numerical analysis. *Unit head:* Dr. Frank Mathis, Graduate Program Director, 254-710-3561, Fax: 254-710-3569, E-mail: frank_mathis@baylor.edu. *Application contact:* Suzanne Keener, Administrative Assistant, 254-710-3588, Fax: 254-710-3870, E-mail: pauline_johnson@baylor.edu.

Boston College, Graduate School of Arts and Sciences, Department of Mathematics, Chestnut Hill, MA 02467-3800. Offers MA, MBA/MA. Part-time programs available. *Students:* 10 full-time (4 women), 2 part-time. 50 applicants, 54% accepted, 9 enrolled. In 2003, 7 degrees awarded. *Degree requirements:* For master's, oral presentation, thesis optional. *Entrance requirements:* For master's, GRE General Test. Additional exam requirements/recommendations for international students: Required—TOEFL (minimum score 550 paper-based; 213 computer-based). *Application deadline:* For fall admission, 1/15 for domestic students. Application fee: $60. Electronic applications accepted. *Expenses:* Tuition: Part-time $810 per credit. *Financial support:* Fellowships, teaching assistantships, Federal Work-Study and scholarships/grants available. Support available to part-time students. Financial award application deadline: 3/1; financial award applicants required to submit FAFSA. *Faculty research:* Abstract algebra and number theory, topology, probability and statistics, computer science, analysis. *Unit head:* Dr. Gerald Keough, Chairperson, 617-552-3750, E-mail: gerald.

Mathematics

Boston College (continued)

keough@bc.edu. *Application contact:* Dr. Dan Chambers, Graduate Program Director, 617-552-3756, E-mail: daniel.chambers@bc.edu.

Boston University, Graduate School of Arts and Sciences, Department of Mathematics and Statistics, Boston, MA 02215. Offers mathematical finance (MA); mathematics (MA, PhD). *Students:* 69 full-time (27 women), 9 part-time (2 women); includes 5 minority (1 African American, 2 Asian Americans or Pacific Islanders, 2 Hispanic Americans), 36 international. Average age 28. 269 applicants, 29% accepted, 38 enrolled. In 2003, 16 master's, 8 doctorates awarded. Terminal master's awarded for partial completion of doctoral program. *Degree requirements:* For master's, one foreign language, comprehensive exam, registration; for doctorate, one foreign language, thesis/dissertation, comprehensive exam, registration. *Entrance requirements:* For master's and doctorate, GRE General Test, GRE Subject Test, 3 letters of recommendation. Additional exam requirements/recommendations for international students: Required—TOEFL (minimum score 600 paper-based; 250 computer-based). *Application deadline:* For fall admission, 1/15 for domestic students, 1/15 for international students; for spring admission, 10/15 for domestic students, 10/15 for international students. Application fee: $60. *Expenses:* Tuition: Full-time $28,512; part-time $891 per credit hour. *Financial support:* In 2003–04, 50 students received support, including 4 fellowships with full tuition reimbursements available (averaging $15,500 per year), 23 research assistantships with full tuition reimbursements available (averaging $15,000 per year), 23 teaching assistantships with full tuition reimbursements available (averaging $15,000 per year); Federal Work-Study and scholarships/grants also available. Support available to part-time students. Financial award application deadline: 1/15; financial award applicants required to submit FAFSA. *Unit head:* Steven Rosenberg, Chairman, 617-353-9556, Fax: 617-353-8100, E-mail: sr@bu.edu. *Application contact:* Angela M. Silva, Staff Coordinator, 617-353-2560, Fax: 617-353-8100, E-mail: amsilva@bu.edu.

Bowling Green State University, Graduate College, College of Arts and Sciences, Department of Mathematics and Statistics, Bowling Green, OH 43403. Offers applied statistics (MS); mathematics (MA, MAT, PhD); mathematics supervision (Ed S); statistics (MA, MAT, PhD). Part-time programs available. *Faculty:* 22 full-time. *Students:* 56 full-time (18 women), 12 part-time (6 women); includes 6 minority (4 Asian Americans or Pacific Islanders, 2 Hispanic Americans), 25 international. Average age 28. 195 applicants, 79% accepted, 6 enrolled. In 2003, 15 master's, 1 doctorate awarded. *Degree requirements:* For master's, thesis or alternative; for doctorate, thesis/dissertation, comprehensive exam; for Ed S, internship. *Entrance requirements:* For master's and doctorate, GRE General Test. Additional exam requirements/recommendations for international students: Required—TOEFL. Application fee: $30. Electronic applications accepted. *Expenses:* Tuition, state resident: part-time $436 per hour. Tuition, nonresident: part-time $768 per hour. *Financial support:* In 2003–04, 7 research assistantships with full tuition reimbursements (averaging $10,857 per year), 43 teaching assistantships with full tuition reimbursements (averaging $11,881 per year) were awarded. Federal Work-Study, institutionally sponsored loans, and unspecified assistantships also available. Financial award applicants required to submit FAFSA. *Faculty research:* Statistics and probability, algebra, analysis. *Unit head:* Dr. Neal Carothers, Chair, 419-372-7453. *Application contact:* Dr. Hanfeng Chen, Graduate Coordinator, 419-372-2179, Fax: 419-372-6092.

See in-depth description on page 521.

Brandeis University, Graduate School of Arts and Sciences, Department of Mathematics, Waltham, MA 02454-9110. Offers MA, PhD. *Faculty:* 15 full-time (2 women), 2 part-time/adjunct (0 women). *Students:* 31 full-time (4 women), 22 international. Average age 25. 66 applicants, 15% accepted. In 2003, 3 master's, 5 doctorates awarded. *Degree requirements:* For doctorate, 2 foreign languages, thesis/dissertation. *Entrance requirements:* For doctorate, GRE General Test, GRE Subject Test, resumé, transcripts, letters of recommendation. Additional exam requirements/recommendations for international students: Required—TOEFL (minimum score 600 paper-based; 250 computer-based). *Application deadline:* For fall admission, 2/15 for domestic students. Application fee: $60. Electronic applications accepted. *Expenses:* Tuition: Full-time $28,999; part-time $4,867 per course. Required fees: $175. *Financial support:* In 2003–04, 22 students received support, including 21 fellowships with full tuition reimbursements available (averaging $9,000 per year), 14 teaching assistantships with full tuition reimbursements available (averaging $6,000 per year); research assistantships, scholarships/grants and tuition waivers (full) also available. Financial award application deadline: 4/15; financial award applicants required to submit CSS PROFILE or FAFSA. *Faculty research:* Algebra, analysis, number theory, combinatorics, topology. *Unit head:* Dr. Bong Lian, Chair, 781-736-3069, Fax: 781-736-3085, E-mail: lian@brandeis.edu. *Application contact:* Prof. Fred Diamond, Graduate Advisor, 781-736-3063, Fax: 781-736-3085, E-mail: fdiamond@brandeis.edu.

Announcement: Program directed primarily toward PhD in pure mathematics. Benefits from informality, flexibility, and warmth of small department and from intellectual vigor of faculty well known for research accomplishments. Brandeis-Harvard-MIT-Northeastern Colloquium and many joint seminars provide opportunities for contact with other Boston-area mathematicians. Students normally receive full-tuition scholarship and teaching assistantship or fellowship. Contact Professor Fred Diamond, Graduate Adviser, 781-736-3063. E-mail: fdiamond@brandeis.edu. Web site: http://www.math.brandeis.edu/

Brigham Young University, Graduate Studies, College of Physical and Mathematical Sciences, Department of Mathematics, Provo, UT 84602-1001. Offers MS, PhD. Part-time programs available. *Faculty:* 35 full-time (1 woman). *Students:* 23 full-time (3 women), 5 part-time (3 women); includes 1 minority (Asian American or Pacific Islander) Average age 23. 28 applicants, 61% accepted, 14 enrolled. In 2003, 7 degrees awarded, leading to university research/teaching 33%, continued full-time study33%. Terminal master's awarded for partial completion of doctoral program. *Median time to degree:* Master's–2 years full-time, 4 years part-time. *Degree requirements:* For master's, project or thesis, written exams; for doctorate, 2 foreign languages, thesis/dissertation, qualifying exams. *Entrance requirements:* For master's, GRE General Test, GRE Subject Test, minimum GPA of 3.0 in last 60 hours, bachelor's degree in mathematics; for doctorate, GRE General Test, GRE Subject Test, master's degree in mathematics or related field. Additional exam requirements/recommendations for international students: Required—TOEFL. *Application deadline:* For fall admission, 3/1 priority date for domestic students, 3/1 priority date for international students; for winter admission, 9/15 for domestic students; for spring admission, 2/15 for domestic students. Applications are processed on a rolling basis. Application fee: $50. Electronic applications accepted. *Expenses:* Tuition: Part-time $221 per hour. *Financial support:* In 2003–04, 2 research assistantships with full tuition reimbursements (averaging $14,500 per year), 17 teaching assistantships with full tuition reimbursements (averaging $14,500 per year) were awarded. Institutionally sponsored loans also available. Support available to part-time students. Financial award application deadline: 3/1. *Faculty research:* Algebraic geometry/number theory, applied math/nonlinear PDEs, combinatorics/matrix theory, geometric group theory/topology. Total annual research expenditures: $12,000. *Unit head:* Dr. Lynn E. Garner, Chairperson, 801-422-6153, Fax: 801-422-0504, E-mail: lynng@math.byu.edu. *Application contact:* Lonette Stoddard, Graduate Secretary, 801-422-2062, Fax: 801-422-0504, E-mail: gradschool@math.byu.edu.

Brooklyn College of the City University of New York, Division of Graduate Studies, Department of Mathematics, Brooklyn, NY 11210-2889. Offers mathematics (MA, PhD); secondary mathematics education (MA). The department offers courses at Brooklyn College that are creditable toward the CUNY doctoral degree (with permission of the executive officer of the doctoral program). Part-time and evening/weekend programs available. *Students:* 8 applicants, 0% accepted, 0 enrolled. In 2003, 1 degree awarded. *Degree requirements:* For master's, comprehensive exam (mathematics). *Entrance requirements:* For master's, minimum GPA of 3.0. Additional exam requirements/recommendations for international students: Required—TOEFL. *Application deadline:* For fall admission, 3/1 for domestic students, 2/1 for international students; for spring admission, 11/1 for domestic students, 10/1 for international students. Application fee: $50. *Expenses:* Tuition, state resident: full-time $5,440; part-time $230 per credit. Tuition, nonresident: full-time $10,200; part-time $425 per credit. Required fees: $280; $103 per term. *Financial support:* Federal Work-Study, institutionally sponsored loans, and scholarships/grants available. Support available to part-time students. Financial award application deadline: 5/1; financial award applicants required to submit FAFSA. *Faculty research:* Differential geometry, gauge theory, complex analysis, orthogonal functions. *Unit head:* Dr. George Shapiro, Chairperson, 718-951-5246, E-mail: gshapiro@brooklyn.cuny.edu. *Application contact:* Michael Lovaglio, Assistant Director of Graduate Admissions, 718-951-5001, E-mail: adminqry@brooklyn.cuny.edu.

Brown University, Graduate School, Department of Mathematics, Providence, RI 02912. Offers M Sc, MA, PhD. *Faculty:* 22 full-time (2 women). *Students:* 36 full-time (10 women), 12 international. Average age 27. 162 applicants, 19% accepted, 4 enrolled. In 2003, 7 master's, 6 doctorates awarded, leading to university research/teaching 100%. *Median time to degree:* Doctorate–5 years full-time. Of those who began their doctoral program in fall 1995, 100% received their degree in 8 years or less. *Degree requirements:* For doctorate, one foreign language, thesis/dissertation. *Entrance requirements:* For doctorate, GRE. Additional exam requirements/recommendations for international students: Required—TOEFL (minimum score 550 paper-based; 173 computer-based). *Application deadline:* For fall admission, 1/1 priority date for domestic students, 1/1 priority date for international students. Application fee: $70. Electronic applications accepted. *Financial support:* In 2003–04, 36 students received support, including 12 fellowships with full tuition reimbursements available (averaging $14,750 per year), 5 research assistantships with full tuition reimbursements available (averaging $15,000 per year), 19 teaching assistantships with full tuition reimbursements available (averaging $15,250 per year); Federal Work-Study, institutionally sponsored loans, and tuition waivers (full and partial) also available. Financial award application deadline: 1/1; financial award applicants required to submit FAFSA. *Faculty research:* Algebraic geometry, number theory, functional analysis, geometry, topology. Total annual research expenditures: $729,892. *Unit head:* Prof. Joseph H. Silverman, Chairman, 401-863-3319, Fax: 401-863-9471, E-mail: jhs@math.brown.edu. *Application contact:* Prof. Thomas G. Goodwillie, Graduate Advisor, 401-863-2590, Fax: 401-863-9013, E-mail: tomg@math.brown.edu.

Bryn Mawr College, Graduate School of Arts and Sciences, Department of Mathematics, Bryn Mawr, PA 19010-2899. Offers MA, PhD. Part-time programs available. *Students:* 6 full-time (5 women), 9 part-time (5 women); includes 2 minority (both Asian Americans or Pacific Islanders), 3 international. 4 applicants, 50% accepted, 2 enrolled. In 2003, 5 degrees awarded. *Degree requirements:* For master's, one foreign language, thesis, registration; for doctorate, 2 foreign languages, thesis/dissertation, comprehensive exam, registration. *Entrance requirements:* For master's and doctorate, GRE General Test. Additional exam requirements/recommendations for international students: Required—TOEFL (minimum score 600 paper-based; 200 computer-based). *Application deadline:* For fall admission, 1/15 for domestic students, 1/15 for international students. Application fee: $30. *Expenses:* Tuition: Full-time $24,540; part-time $4,150 per unit. One-time fee: $60 part-time. *Financial support:* In 2003–04, 4 teaching assistantships with partial tuition reimbursements were awarded; research assistantships with full tuition reimbursements, Federal Work-Study, scholarships/grants, tuition waivers (full and partial), unspecified assistantships, and tuition awards also available. Support available to part-time students. Financial award application deadline: 1/15. *Unit head:* Dr. Helen Grundman, Chair, 610-526-5348, E-mail: hgrundma@brynmawr.edu. *Application contact:* Lea R. Miller, Secretary, 610-526-5072, Fax: 610-526-5076, E-mail: lrmiller@brynmawr.edu.

Bucknell University, Graduate Studies, College of Arts and Sciences, Department of Mathematics, Lewisburg, PA 17837. Offers MA, MS. Part-time programs available. *Entrance requirements:* For master's, GRE General Test, GRE Subject Test, minimum GPA of 2.8. Additional exam requirements/recommendations for international students: Required—TOEFL.

California Institute of Technology, Division of Physics, Mathematics and Astronomy, Department of Mathematics, Pasadena, CA 91125-0001. Offers PhD. *Degree requirements:* For doctorate, one foreign language, thesis/dissertation, candidacy and final exams. *Entrance requirements:* For doctorate, GRE General Test, GRE Subject Test. Additional exam requirements/recommendations for international students: Required—TOEFL. *Faculty research:* Number theory, combinatorics, differential geometry, dynamical systems, finite groups.

California Polytechnic State University, San Luis Obispo, College of Science and Mathematics, Department of Mathematics, San Luis Obispo, CA 93407. Offers MS. *Faculty:* 34 full-time (4 women), 31 part-time/adjunct (10 women). *Students:* 3 full-time (1 woman), 6 part-time (1 woman). Average age 17. 17 applicants, 59% accepted. In 2003, 5 degrees awarded. *Degree requirements:* For master's, qualifying exams, thesis optional. *Entrance requirements:* For master's, minimum GPA of 2.5 in last 90 quarter units. *Application deadline:* For fall admission, 7/1 for domestic students. Applications are processed on a rolling basis. Application fee: $55. Tuition, nonresident: part-time $188 per unit. Required fees: $3,732. *Financial support:* In 2003–04, teaching assistantships (averaging $8,000 per year); career-related internships or fieldwork and Federal Work-Study also available. Support available to part-time students. Financial award application deadline: 3/2; financial award applicants required to submit FAFSA. *Unit head:* Dr. Kent Morrison, Chair, 805-756-2206, Fax: 805-756-6537, E-mail: kmorriso@calpoly.edu. *Application contact:* Myron Hood, Graduate Coordinator, 805-756-2352, Fax: 805-756-6537, E-mail: mhood@calpoly.edu.

California State Polytechnic University, Pomona, Academic Affairs, College of Science, Program in Mathematics, Pomona, CA 91768-2557. Offers applied mathematics (MS); pure mathematics (MS). Part-time programs available. *Students:* 24 full-time (12 women), 24 part-time (8 women); includes 21 minority (2 African Americans, 13 Asian Americans or Pacific Islanders, 6 Hispanic Americans), 3 international. Average age 29. 35 applicants, 80% accepted, 15 enrolled. In 2003, 5 degrees awarded. *Degree requirements:* For master's, thesis or alternative. *Entrance requirements:* For master's, GRE General Test. *Application deadline:* For fall admission, 5/1 for domestic students; for winter admission, 10/15 for domestic students; for spring admission, 1/20 for domestic students. Applications are processed on a rolling basis. Application fee: $55. Electronic applications accepted. Tuition, nonresident: full-time $6,016; part-time $188 per unit. Required fees: $2,256. *Financial support:* Career-related internships or fieldwork, Federal Work-Study, and institutionally sponsored loans available. Support available to part-time students. Financial award application deadline: 3/2; financial award applicants required to submit FAFSA. *Unit head:* Dr. Alan C. Krinik, Graduate Coordinator, 909-869-3479, E-mail: ackrinik@csupomona.edu.

California State University, Fresno, Division of Graduate Studies, College of Science and Mathematics, Department of Mathematics, Fresno, CA 93740-8027. Offers mathematics (MA); teaching (MA). Part-time programs available. *Degree requirements:* For master's, thesis or alternative. *Entrance requirements:* For master's, GRE General Test, minimum GPA of 2.5. Additional exam requirements/recommendations for international students: Required—TOEFL. Electronic applications accepted. *Faculty research:* Diagnostic testing project.

California State University, Fullerton, Graduate Studies, College of Natural Science and Mathematics, Department of Mathematics, Fullerton, CA 92834-9480. Offers applied mathematics (MA); mathematics (MA); mathematics for secondary school teachers (MA). Part-time programs available. *Faculty:* 33 full-time (8 women), 71 part-time/adjunct. *Students:* 8 full-time (3 women), 70 part-time (34 women); includes 40 minority (3 African Americans, 26 Asian Americans or Pacific Islanders, 11 Hispanic Americans). Average age 32. 64 applicants, 86% accepted, 44 enrolled. In 2003, 19 degrees awarded. *Degree requirements:* For master's, comprehensive exam or project. *Entrance requirements:* For master's, minimum GPA of 2.5 in last 60 units, major in mathematics or related field. Application fee: $55. Tuition, nonresident: part-time $282 per unit. Required fees: $889 per semester. *Financial support:* Research assistantships, teaching assistantships, career-related internships or fieldwork, Federal Work-Study, institutionally sponsored loans, and scholarships/grants available. Support available to part-time students. Financial award application deadline: 3/1. *Unit head:* Dr. James Friel, Chair, 714-278-3631.

California State University, Hayward, Academic Programs and Graduate Studies, College of Science, Department of Mathematics and Computer Science, Mathematics Program, Hayward, CA 94542-3000. Offers MS. *Students:* 37 full-time (19 women), 29 part-time (12 women); includes 21 minority (2 African Americans, 14 Asian Americans or Pacific Islanders, 5 Hispanic Americans), 8 international. 30 applicants, 90% accepted. *Degree requirements:* For master's, comprehensive exam or thesis. *Entrance requirements:* For master's, minimum GPA of 3.0 in field. Additional exam requirements/recommendations for international students: Required—TOEFL (minimum score 550 paper-based; 213 computer-based). *Application deadline:* For fall admission, 5/31 for domestic students, 2/29 for international students; for winter admission, 9/30 for domestic students. Applications are processed on a rolling basis. Application fee: $55. Electronic applications accepted. Tuition, nonresident: part-time $188 per unit. Required fees: $560 per quarter hour. *Financial support:* Career-related internships or fieldwork, Federal Work-Study, and institutionally sponsored loans available. Support available to part-time students. Financial award application deadline: 3/2. *Unit head:* Donald L. Wolitzer, Coordinator, 510-885-3467. *Application contact:* Jennifer Cason, Graduate Program Coordinator/Operations Analyst, 510-885-3286, Fax: 510-885-4777, E-mail: jcason@csuhayward.edu.

California State University, Long Beach, Graduate Studies, College of Natural Sciences, Department of Mathematics, Long Beach, CA 90840. Offers applied mathematics (MA); mathematics (MA). Part-time programs available. *Faculty:* 20 full-time (1 woman). *Students:* 21 full-time (6 women), 43 part-time (16 women); includes 34 minority (3 African Americans, 19 Asian Americans or Pacific Islanders, 12 Hispanic Americans), 2 international. Average age 33. 46 applicants, 54% accepted, 15 enrolled. In 2003, 8 degrees awarded. *Degree requirements:* For master's, comprehensive exam or thesis. *Application deadline:* For fall admission, 7/1 for domestic students; for spring admission, 12/1 for domestic students. Applications are processed on a rolling basis. Application fee: $55. Electronic applications accepted. Tuition, nonresident: part-time $282 per unit. Required fees: $504 per semester. *Financial support:* Teaching assistantships, Federal Work-Study, institutionally sponsored loans, scholarships/grants, and traineeships available. Financial award application deadline: 3/2. *Faculty research:* Algebra, functional analysis, partial differential equations, operator theory, numerical analysis. *Unit head:* Dr. Arthur Wayman, Chair, 562-985-4721, Fax: 562-985-8227, E-mail: away@csulb.edu. *Application contact:* Dr. Ngo N.P. Viet, Graduate Coordinator, 562-985-5610, Fax: 562-985-8227, E-mail: viet@csulb.edu.

California State University, Los Angeles, Graduate Studies, College of Natural and Social Sciences, Department of Mathematics, Los Angeles, CA 90032-8530. Offers mathematics (MS), including applied mathematics, mathematics. Part-time and evening/weekend programs available. *Faculty:* 22 full-time, 43 part-time/adjunct. *Students:* 31 full-time (10 women), 41 part-time (13 women); includes 47 minority (3 African Americans, 26 Asian Americans or Pacific Islanders, 18 Hispanic Americans), 9 international. In 2003, 2 degrees awarded. *Degree requirements:* For master's, comprehensive exam or thesis. *Entrance requirements:* For master's, previous course work in mathematics. Additional exam requirements/recommendations for international students: Required—TOEFL. *Application deadline:* For fall admission, 6/30 for domestic students; for spring admission, 2/1 for domestic students. Applications are processed on a rolling basis. Application fee: $55. Tuition, nonresident: part-time $188 per unit. Required fees: $2,477. *Financial support:* Teaching assistantships, Federal Work-Study available. Support available to part-time students. Financial award application deadline: 3/1. *Faculty research:* Group theory, functional analysis, convexity theory, ordered geometry. *Unit head:* Dr. P. K. Subramanian, Chair, 323-343-2150.

California State University, Northridge, Graduate Studies, College of Science and Mathematics, Department of Mathematics, Northridge, CA 91330. Offers MS. Part-time and evening/weekend programs available. *Faculty:* 38 full-time, 45 part-time/adjunct. *Students:* 22 full-time (8 women), 52 part-time (22 women); includes 27 minority (6 African Americans, 11 Asian Americans or Pacific Islanders, 10 Hispanic Americans), 5 international. Average age 34. 52 applicants, 85% accepted. In 2003, 15 degrees awarded. *Degree requirements:* For master's, thesis (for some programs). *Entrance requirements:* Additional exam requirements/recommendations for international students: Required—TOEFL. *Application deadline:* For fall admission, 11/30 for domestic students. Application fee: $55. Required fees: $1,327; $853 per year. *Financial support:* Teaching assistantships, Federal Work-Study and institutionally sponsored loans available. Support available to part-time students. Financial award application deadline: 3/1. *Unit head:* Dr. Magnhild Lien, Chair, 818-677-2721. *Application contact:* Dr. David Protas, Graduate Coordinator, 818-677-5079.

California State University, Sacramento, Graduate Studies, College of Natural Sciences and Mathematics, Department of Mathematics and Statistics, Sacramento, CA 95819-6048. Offers MA. Part-time programs available. *Students:* 4 full-time (1 woman), 14 part-time (7 women); includes 4 minority (2 Asian Americans or Pacific Islanders, 2 Hispanic Americans). *Degree requirements:* For master's, thesis or alternative, writing proficiency exam. *Entrance requirements:* For master's, minimum GPA of 3.0 in mathematics, 2.5 overall during previous 2 years; BA in mathematics or equivalent. Additional exam requirements/recommendations for international students: Required—TOEFL. *Application deadline:* For fall admission, 5/1 for domestic students; for spring admission, 11/1 for domestic students. Application fee: $55. *Expenses:* Tuition, state resident: full-time $2,256. Tuition, nonresident: full-time $10,716. *Financial support:* Research assistantships, teaching assistantships, career-related internships or fieldwork and Federal Work-Study available. Support available to part-time students. Financial award application deadline: 3/1. *Unit head:* Dr. Doraiswamy Ramachandran, Chair, 916-278-6534, Fax: 916-278-5586.

California State University, San Bernardino, Graduate Studies, College of Natural Sciences, Program in Mathematics, San Bernardino, CA 92407-2397. Offers MA. Part-time programs available. *Faculty:* 24 full-time. *Students:* 17 full-time (10 women), 28 part-time (10 women); includes 13 minority (1 African American, 6 Asian Americans or Pacific Islanders, 6 Hispanic Americans), 1 international. Average age 30. 39 applicants, 59% accepted, 11 enrolled. In 2003, 2 degrees awarded. *Entrance requirements:* For master's, minor in mathematics. Application fee: $55. Tuition, nonresident: part-time $188 per unit. Required fees: $657 per quarter. *Financial support:* Teaching assistantships available. *Faculty research:* Mathematics education, technology in education, algebra, combinatorics, real analysis. *Unit head:* Dr. Peter D. Williams, Chair, 909-880-5361, Fax: 909-880-7119, E-mail: pwilliam@csusb.edu.

California State University, San Marcos, College of Arts and Sciences, Program in Mathematics, San Marcos, CA 92096-0001. Offers MS. Part-time and evening/weekend programs available. *Faculty:* 11 full-time (3 women), 5 part-time/adjunct (4 women). *Students:* 2 full-time (1 woman), 11 part-time (6 women); includes 2 minority (1 Asian American or Pacific Islander, 1 Hispanic American). Average age 33. 14 applicants, 64% accepted. In 2003, 3 degrees awarded. *Degree requirements:* For master's, thesis optional. *Entrance requirements:* Additional exam requirements/recommendations for international students: Required—TOEFL, TWE. *Application deadline:* For fall admission, 3/15 for domestic students; for spring admission, 1/1 for domestic students. Applications are processed on a rolling basis. Application fee: $55. Tuition, nonresident: part-time $282 per unit. Required fees: $838 per semester. *Financial support:* Teaching assistantships, career-related internships or fieldwork and Federal Work-Study available. Support available to part-time students. Financial award applicants required to submit FAFSA. *Faculty research:* Combinatorics, graph theory, partial differential equations, numerical analysis, computational linear algebra. *Unit head:* Dr. Linda Holt, Department Chair, 760-750-4092, E-mail: lholt@csusm.edu. *Application contact:* Carrie Dyal, Administrative Coordinator, 760-750-8059, Fax: 760-750-3439, E-mail: chunting@csusm.edu.

Carleton University, Faculty of Graduate Studies, Faculty of Science, School of Mathematics and Statistics, Ottawa, ON K1S 5B6, Canada. Offers information and systems science (PhD); mathematics (M Sc, PhD). *Students:* Average age 30. *Degree requirements:* For master's, thesis optional; for doctorate, one foreign language, thesis/dissertation, comprehensive exam. *Entrance requirements:* For master's, honors degree; for doctorate, master's degree. Additional exam requirements/recommendations for international students: Required—TOEFL. Application fee: $60 Canadian dollars. *Expenses:* Tuition, state resident: part-time $2,052 per term. Tuition, nonresident: part-time $4,266 per term. Full-time tuition and fees vary according to course load, degree level and program. *Financial support:* Fellowships, research assistantships, teaching assistantships, institutionally sponsored loans, scholarships/grants, and unspecified assistantships available. *Faculty research:* Pure mathematics, applied mathematics, probability and statistics. *Unit head:* Cyril Garner, Director, 613-520-2600 Ext. 2155, Fax: 613-520-3536, E-mail: mathstat@carleton.ca. *Application contact:* Sam Melkonian, Supervisor of Graduate Studies, 613-520-2600 Ext. 2152, E-mail: mathstat@carleton.ca.

Carnegie Mellon University, Mellon College of Science, Department of Mathematical Sciences, Pittsburgh, PA 15213-3891. Offers algorithms, combinatorics, and optimization (PhD); mathematical finance (PhD); mathematical sciences (MS, DA, PhD); pure and applied logic (PhD). Part-time programs available. Terminal master's awarded for partial completion of doctoral program. *Degree requirements:* For doctorate, thesis/dissertation. *Entrance requirements:* For master's and doctorate, GRE General Test, GRE Subject Test. Additional exam requirements/recommendations for international students: Required—TOEFL. Electronic applications accepted. *Expenses:* Tuition: Full-time $28,200; part-time $392 per unit. Required fees: $220. *Faculty research:* Continuum mechanics, discrete mathematics, applied and computational mathematics.

Case Western Reserve University, School of Graduate Studies, Department of Mathematics, Cleveland, OH 44106. Offers applied mathematics (MS, PhD); mathematics (MS, PhD). Part-time programs available. *Faculty:* 14 full-time (1 woman). *Students:* 9 full-time (2 women), 1 part-time, 5 international. Average age 25. 77 applicants, 3% accepted, 1 enrolled. In 2003, 1 degree awarded. Terminal master's awarded for partial completion of doctoral program. *Degree requirements:* For master's, thesis (applied mathematics); for doctorate, one foreign language, thesis/dissertation. *Entrance requirements:* For master's and doctorate, GRE General Test. Additional exam requirements/recommendations for international students: Required—TOEFL. *Application deadline:* For fall admission, 6/25 for domestic students; for spring admission, 11/12 for domestic students. Applications are processed on a rolling basis. Application fee: $50. *Expenses:* Tuition: Full-time $26,900. *Financial support:* In 2003–04, 7 students received support, including 5 teaching assistantships. Financial award application deadline: 4/15. *Faculty research:* Probability theory, differential equations and control theory, differential geometry and topology, Lie groups, functional and harmonic analysis. Total annual research expenditures: $268,000. *Unit head:* Dr. James G. Alexander, Chair, 216-368-2882, Fax: 216-368-5163, E-mail: jcal0@case.edu. *Application contact:* Gaythresa Lewis, Admissions, 216-368-5014, Fax: 216-368-5163, E-mail: gxl34@case.edu.

Central Connecticut State University, School of Graduate Studies, School of Arts and Sciences, Department of Mathematics, New Britain, CT 06050-4010. Offers data mining (MS); mathematics (MA, MS), including actuarial (MA), operations research (MA), statistics (MA). Part-time and evening/weekend programs available. *Faculty:* 26 full-time (10 women), 48 part-time/adjunct (22 women). *Students:* 17 full-time (13 women), 77 part-time (40 women); includes 3 minority (1 African American, 2 Asian Americans or Pacific Islanders), 4 international. Average age 35. 84 applicants, 70% accepted, 41 enrolled. In 2003, 10 degrees awarded. *Degree requirements:* For master's, thesis or alternative, comprehensive exam or special project. *Entrance requirements:* For master's, minimum GPA of 2.7. Additional exam requirements/recommendations for international students: Required—TOEFL. *Application deadline:* For fall admission, 8/1 for domestic students; for spring admission, 12/1 for domestic students. Applications are processed on a rolling basis. Application fee: $50. *Expenses:* Tuition, state resident: full-time $3,298. Tuition, nonresident: full-time $9,190. *Financial support:* Teaching assistantships available. Financial award application deadline: 3/15; financial award applicants required to submit FAFSA. *Faculty research:* Statistics, actuarial mathematics, computer systems and engineering, computer programming techniques, operations research. *Unit head:* Dr. Jeffrey McGowan, Interim Chair, 860-832-2835.

Central Michigan University, College of Graduate Studies, College of Science and Technology, Department of Mathematics, Mount Pleasant, MI 48859. Offers MA, MAT, PhD. *Faculty:* 32 full-time (6 women). *Students:* 8 full-time (6 women), 13 part-time (3 women). Average age 35. In 2003, 3 degrees awarded. *Degree requirements:* For master's, thesis or alternative; for doctorate, thesis/dissertation. *Entrance requirements:* For master's, minimum GPA of 2.5, 20 hours in mathematics; for doctorate, GRE, minimum GPA of 3.0, 20 hours in mathematics. Additional exam requirements/recommendations for international students: Required—TOEFL. *Application deadline:* Applications are processed on a rolling basis. Application fee: $35 ($45 for international students). *Expenses:* Tuition, state resident: part-time $200 per credit hour. Tuition, nonresident: part-time $397 per credit hour. *Financial support:* In 2003–04, 5 fellowships with tuition reimbursements, 1 research assistantship with tuition reimbursement, 23 teaching assistantships with tuition reimbursements were awarded. Career-related internships or fieldwork and Federal Work-Study also available. Financial award application deadline: 3/7. *Faculty research:* Combinatorics, approximation theory, operations theory, functional analysis, statistics. *Unit head:* Dr. Sidney Graham, Chairperson, 989-774-3596, Fax: 989-774-2414, E-mail: sidney.w.graham@cmich.edu.

Central Missouri State University, School of Graduate Studies, College of Arts and Sciences, Department of Mathematics and Computer Science, Warrensburg, MO 64093. Offers applied mathematics (MS); mathematics (MS); mathematics education (MSE), including elementary mathematics, secondary mathematics. *Accreditation:* NCATE (one or more programs are accredited). Part-time programs available. *Faculty:* 12 full-time (4 women), 1 part-time/adjunct (0 women). *Students:* 3 full-time (2 women), 7 part-time (2 women); includes 1 minority (Hispanic American), 1 international. Average age 27. 3 applicants, 67% accepted. In 2003, 5 degrees awarded. *Degree requirements:* For master's, thesis (MS); comprehensive exam or thesis (MSE). *Entrance requirements:* For master's, GRE General Test (MSE), bachelor's degree in mathematics, minimum GPA of 3.0 (MS); minimum GPA of 2.75, teaching certificate (MSE). Additional exam requirements/recommendations for international students: Required—TOEFL (minimum score 500 paper-based; 173 computer-based). *Application deadline:* For fall admission, 6/1 priority date for domestic students, 5/1 priority date for international students; for spring admission, 10/1 priority date for domestic students, 10/1 priority date for international students. Applications are processed on a rolling basis. Application fee: $25 ($50 for international students). *Expenses:* Tuition, state resident: part-time $198 per credit hour. Tuition, nonresident: part-time $396 per credit hour. Required fees: $12 per credit hour. *Financial support:* In 2003–04, 4 teaching assistantships (averaging $8,670 per year) were awarded; Federal Work-Study, scholarships/grants, unspecified assistantships, and administrative assistantships also available. Support available to part-time students. Financial award application deadline: 3/1; financial award applicants required to submit FAFSA. *Faculty research:* Graph theory, topology, applied statistics, risk theory, mathematics education. *Unit head:* Dr. Edward W. Davenport, Chair, 660-543-4931, Fax: 660-543-8006, E-mail: davenport@cmsu1.cmsu.edu.

Central Washington University, Graduate Studies, Research and Continuing Education, College of the Sciences, Department of Mathematics, Ellensburg, WA 98926. Offers MAT. MAT offered during summer only. *Faculty:* 11 full-time (0 women). In 2003, 5 degrees awarded. *Degree requirements:* For master's, thesis or alternative. *Entrance requirements:* For master's, minimum GPA of 3.0 (summer only). Application fee: $35. *Expenses:* Tuition, state resident: part-time $183 per credit. Tuition, nonresident: part-time $381 per credit. Required fees: $369. *Financial support:* Teaching assistantships, Federal Work-Study available. Financial award application deadline: 3/1; financial award applicants required to submit FAFSA. *Unit head:* Dr. Scott Lewis, Chair, 509-963-2103. *Application contact:* Barbara Sisko, Office Assistant, Graduate Studies, Research and Continuing Education, 509-963-3103, Fax: 509-963-1799, E-mail: masters@cwu.edu.

Chicago State University, School of Graduate and Professional Studies, College of Arts and Sciences, Department of Mathematics and Computer Science, Chicago, IL 60628. Offers MS.

Mathematics

Chicago State University (continued)

Faculty: 5 full-time (1 woman). *Students:* 29 (15 women); includes 22 minority (17 African Americans, 1 American Indian/Alaska Native, 2 Asian Americans or Pacific Islanders, 2 Hispanic Americans) 2 international. *Degree requirements:* For master's, oral exam, thesis optional. *Entrance requirements:* For master's, minimum GPA of 2.75. *Application deadline:* For fall admission, 7/1 for domestic students; for spring admission, 11/10 for domestic students. Application fee: $25. *Financial support:* Research assistantships available. *Unit head:* Dr. Howard Silver, Chairperson, 773-995-2102, Fax: 773-995-3767, E-mail: h-silver@csu.edu. *Application contact:* Anika Miller, Graduate Studies Office, 773-995-2404, E-mail: g-studies1@csu.edu.

City College of the City University of New York, Graduate School, College of Liberal Arts and Science, Division of Science, Department of Mathematics, New York, NY 10031-9198. Offers MA. Part-time programs available. *Students:* 4 full-time (1 woman), 28 part-time (5 women); includes 19 minority (8 African Americans, 7 Asian Americans or Pacific Islanders, 4 Hispanic Americans), 6 international. 18 applicants, 72% accepted, 7 enrolled. In 2003, 6 degrees awarded. *Degree requirements:* For master's, one foreign language. *Entrance requirements:* Additional exam requirements/recommendations for international students: Required—TOEFL. *Application deadline:* For fall admission, 5/1 for domestic students; for spring admission, 11/1 for domestic students. Application fee: $50. *Expenses:* Tuition, state resident: full-time $5,440; part-time $230 per credit. Tuition, nonresident: part-time $425 per credit. Required fees: $63 per semester. *Financial support:* Teaching assistantships, Federal Work-Study available. Support available to part-time students. Financial award application deadline: 5/1. *Faculty research:* Group theory, number theory, logic, statistics, computational geometry. *Unit head:* Edward Grossman, Chair, 212-650-5173, E-mail: egross@sci.ccny.cuny.edu. *Application contact:* K. Hrbacek, Adviser, 212-650-5101.

Claremont Graduate University, Graduate Programs, School of Mathematical Sciences, Claremont, CA 91711-6160. Offers computational science (PhD); engineering mathematics (PhD); financial engineering (MS); operations research and statistics (MA, MS); physical applied mathematics (MA, MS); pure mathematics (MA, MS, PhD); scientific computing (MA, MS); systems and control theory (MA, MS). Part-time programs available. *Faculty:* 2 full-time (0 women), 3 part-time/adjunct (0 women). *Students:* 41 full-time (8 women), 11 part-time (3 women). Average age 36. In 2003, 9 master's, 4 doctorates awarded. Terminal master's awarded for partial completion of doctoral program. *Degree requirements:* For doctorate, 2 foreign languages, thesis/dissertation. *Entrance requirements:* For master's and doctorate, GRE General Test. *Application deadline:* For fall admission, 2/15 for domestic students. Applications are processed on a rolling basis. Electronic applications accepted. *Expenses:* Tuition: Full-time $25,250; part-time $1,099 per semester. *Financial support:* Fellowships, research assistantships, career-related internships or fieldwork, Federal Work-Study, institutionally sponsored loans, and tuition waivers (full and partial) available. Support available to part-time students. Financial award application deadline: 2/15; financial award applicants required to submit FAFSA. *Unit head:* John Angus, Chair, 909-621-8080, Fax: 909-607-8261, E-mail: john.angus@cgu.edu. *Application contact:* Mary Solberg, Administrative Assistant, 909-621-8080, Fax: 909-607-8261, E-mail: math@cgu.edu.

Clarkson University, Graduate School, School of Arts and Sciences, Department of Mathematics and Computer Science, Potsdam, NY 13699. Offers mathematics (MS, PhD). *Faculty:* 11 full-time (2 women), 1 part-time/adjunct (0 women). *Students:* 9 full-time (3 women), 7 international. Average age 26. 28 applicants, 75% accepted. In 2003, 1 degree awarded. Terminal master's awarded for partial completion of doctoral program. *Median time to degree:* Master's–2.5 years full-time. *Degree requirements:* For doctorate, thesis/dissertation, departmental qualifying exam. *Entrance requirements:* For master's, GRE. Additional exam requirements/recommendations for international students: Required—TOEFL. *Application deadline:* For fall admission, 5/15 for domestic students; for spring admission, 10/15 priority date for domestic students. Applications are processed on a rolling basis. Application fee: $25 ($35 for international students). *Expenses:* Tuition: Full-time $19,272; part-time $803 per credit. Tuition and fees vary according to course load. *Financial support:* In 2003–04, 7 students received support, including 1 research assistantship (averaging $18,000 per year), 6 teaching assistantships (averaging $18,000 per year); fellowships, scholarships/grants also available. *Faculty research:* Fiber optics, hydrodynamics, inverse scattering, nonlinear optics, nonlinear waves. Total annual research expenditures: $276,791. *Unit head:* Dr. Peter Turner, Division Head, 315-268-2334, Fax: 315-268-2371, E-mail: pturner@clarkson.edu. *Application contact:* Donna Brockway, Assistant to Dean/Foreign Student Advisor, 315-268-6447, Fax: 315-268-7994, E-mail: brockway@clarkson.edu.

Clemson University, Graduate School, College of Engineering and Science, Department of Mathematical Sciences, Clemson, SC 29634. Offers applied and pure mathematics (MS, PhD); computational mathematics (MS, PhD); management science (PhD); operations research (MS, PhD); statistics (MS, PhD). Part-time programs available. *Students:* 73 full-time (25 women), 5 part-time (1 woman); includes 3 minority (2 African Americans, 1 Asian American or Pacific Islander), 33 international. Average age 29. 116 applicants, 74% accepted, 31 enrolled. In 2003, 25 master's, 5 doctorates awarded. *Degree requirements:* For master's, final project, thesis optional; for doctorate, thesis/dissertation, qualifying exams. *Entrance requirements:* For master's and doctorate, GRE General Test. Additional exam requirements/recommendations for international students: Required—TOEFL. *Application deadline:* For fall admission, 6/1 for domestic students. Application fee: $40. *Expenses:* Tuition, state resident: full-time $7,432. Tuition, nonresident: full-time $14,732. *Financial support:* Fellowships, research assistantships, teaching assistantships available. Financial award application deadline: 4/15; financial award applicants required to submit FAFSA. *Faculty research:* Applied and computational analysis, discrete mathematics, mathematical programming statistics. *Unit head:* Dr. Perino Dearing, Interim Dean, 864-656-5240, Fax: 864-656-5230, E-mail: pmdrn@clemson.edu. *Application contact:* Dr. Douglas Shier, Graduate Coordinator, 864-656-1100, Fax: 864-656-5230, E-mail: shierd@clemson.edu.

Cleveland State University, College of Graduate Studies, College of Arts and Sciences, Department of Mathematics, Cleveland, OH 44115. Offers applied mathematics (MS); mathematics (MA). Part-time programs available. *Faculty:* 15 full-time (5 women). *Students:* 3 full-time (1 woman), 16 part-time (3 women); includes 4 minority (1 African American, 3 Asian Americans or Pacific Islanders), 1 international. Average age 32. 18 applicants, 67% accepted, 3 enrolled. In 2003, 6 degrees awarded. *Degree requirements:* For master's, exit project. *Entrance requirements:* For master's, GRE. Additional exam requirements/recommendations for international students: Required—TOEFL (minimum score 515 paper-based; 197 computer-based). *Application deadline:* For fall admission, 6/15 for domestic students. Applications are processed on a rolling basis. Application fee: $30. Tuition, area resident: Full-time $8,258; part-time $344 per credit hour. Tuition, nonresident: full-time $16,352; part-time $681 per credit hour. *Financial support:* In 2003–04, 6 students received support, including 1 teaching assistantship with full and partial tuition reimbursement available (averaging $5,000 per year); Federal Work-Study, institutionally sponsored loans, and tuition waivers (full and partial) also available. Financial award application deadline: 3/15. *Unit head:* Dr. Sherwood D. Silliman, Chairperson, 216-687-4681, Fax: 216-523-7340, E-mail: silliman@csuohio.edu. *Application contact:* Dr. John F. Oprea, Director, 216-687-4702, Fax: 216-523-7340, E-mail: oprea@csuohio.edu.

College of Charleston, Graduate School, School of Sciences and Mathematics, Department of Mathematics, Charleston, SC 29424-0001. Offers MS. *Faculty:* 28 full-time (5 women). *Students:* 5 full-time (4 women), 15 part-time (3 women); includes 2 minority (both African Americans), 1 international. Average age 29. 14 applicants, 93% accepted, 12 enrolled. In 2003, 7 degrees awarded. *Entrance requirements:* For master's, GRE, BS in mathematics or equivalent. Additional exam requirements/recommendations for international students: Required—TOEFL. *Application deadline:* For fall admission, 4/30 for domestic students; for spring admission, 11/15 for domestic students. Applications are processed on a rolling basis. Application fee: $35. *Expenses:* Tuition, state resident: full-time $2,175; part-time $238 per credit hour. Tuition, nonresident: full-time $4,902; part-time $541 per credit hour. Required fees: $2 per credit hour. $15 per term. One-time fee: $45 full-time. *Financial support:* Research assistantships, Federal Work-Study available. Support available to part-time students. Financial award applicants required to submit FAFSA. *Faculty research:* Algebra and discrete mathematics, dynamical systems, probability and statistics, analysis and topology, applied mathematics. *Unit head:* Dr. Rohn England, Program Director, 843-953-5730, Fax: 843-953-1410.

Colorado School of Mines, Graduate School, Department of Mathematical and Computer Sciences, Golden, CO 80401-1887. Offers MS, PhD. Part-time programs available. *Faculty:* 16 full-time (2 women). *Students:* 29 full-time (12 women), 15 part-time (3 women); includes 4 minority (3 Asian Americans or Pacific Islanders, 1 Hispanic American), 14 international. 40 applicants, 93% accepted, 16 enrolled. In 2003, 10 master's, 3 doctorates awarded. *Degree requirements:* For master's, thesis/dissertation; for doctorate, thesis/dissertation, comprehensive exam. *Entrance requirements:* For master's and doctorate, GRE General Test. Additional exam requirements/recommendations for international students: Required—TOEFL (minimum score 550 paper-based; 213 computer-based). *Application deadline:* For fall admission, 12/1 priority date for domestic students, 12/1 priority date for international students; for spring admission, 5/1 priority date for domestic students, 5/1 priority date for international students. Application fee: $45. Electronic applications accepted. *Expenses:* Tuition, state resident: full-time $5,700; part-time $285 per credit hour. Tuition, nonresident: full-time $19,040; part-time $952 per credit hour. Required fees: $733. *Financial support:* In 2003–04, 9 students received support, including fellowships with full tuition reimbursements available (averaging $12,500 per year), 10 research assistantships with full tuition reimbursements available (averaging $10,000 per year), 14 teaching assistantships with full tuition reimbursements available (averaging $10,000 per year); scholarships/grants and unspecified assistantships also available. Financial award applicants required to submit FAFSA. *Faculty research:* Applied statistics, numerical computation, artificial intelligence, linear optimization. Total annual research expenditures: $671,211. *Unit head:* Dr. Graeme Fairweather, Head, 303-273-3502, Fax: 303-273-3875, E-mail: gfairwea@mines.edu. *Application contact:* Tracy Camp, Professor, 303-384-2184, Fax: 303-273-3875, E-mail: tcamp@mines.edu.

Colorado State University, Graduate School, College of Natural Sciences, Department of Mathematics, Fort Collins, CO 80523. Offers MS, PhD. Part-time programs available. *Faculty:* 27 full-time (5 women), 6 part-time/adjunct (0 women). *Students:* 40 full-time (17 women), 17 part-time (6 women); includes 3 minority (1 African American, 1 American Indian/Alaska Native, 1 Hispanic American), 16 international. Average age 29. 88 applicants, 42% accepted, 13 enrolled. In 2003, 10 master's, 1 doctorate awarded. Terminal master's awarded for partial completion of doctoral program. *Median time to degree:* Of those who began their doctoral program in fall 1995, 99% received their degree in 8 years or less. *Degree requirements:* For master's, thesis (for some programs); for doctorate, thesis/dissertation, comprehensive exam. *Entrance requirements:* For master's and doctorate, GRE General Test or GMAT, minimum GPA of 3.0. Additional exam requirements/recommendations for international students: Required—TOEFL (minimum score 550 paper-based; 213 computer-based). *Application deadline:* For fall admission, 2/15 for domestic students, 2/15 for international students; for spring admission, 9/1 for domestic students, 9/1 for international students. Applications are processed on a rolling basis. Application fee: $50. Electronic applications accepted. *Expenses:* Tuition, state resident: full-time $4,156. Tuition, nonresident: full-time $14,762. Required fees: $205. Tuition and fees vary according to course load, campus/location, program and reciprocity agreements. *Financial support:* In 2003–04, 5 fellowships, 3 research assistantships with full tuition reimbursements (averaging $15,000 per year), 34 teaching assistantships with full tuition reimbursements (averaging $13,200 per year) were awarded. Career-related internships or fieldwork, Federal Work-Study, institutionally sponsored loans, traineeships, and tuition waivers (partial) also available. Financial award application deadline: 3/1. *Faculty research:* Applied mathematics, numerical analysis, algebraic geometry, combinatorics. Total annual research expenditures: $250,000. *Unit head:* Simon Tavener, Chair, 970-491-1303, Fax: 970-491-2161, E-mail: tavener@math.colostate.edu. *Application contact:* Michael Kirby, Director, Graduate Program, 970-491-6852, Fax: 970-491-2161, E-mail: grad_program@math.colostate.edu.

Columbia University, Graduate School of Arts and Sciences, Division of Natural Sciences, Department of Mathematics, New York, NY 10027. Offers M Phil, MA, PhD. *Faculty:* 30 full-time. *Students:* 126 full-time (38 women), 66 part-time (15 women). Average age 28. 548 applicants, 29% accepted. In 2003, 73 master's, 10 doctorates awarded. *Degree requirements:* For master's, written exam; for doctorate, 2 foreign languages, thesis/dissertation. *Entrance requirements:* For master's and doctorate, GRE General Test, major in mathematics. Additional exam requirements/recommendations for international students: Required—TOEFL. Application fee: $75. *Expenses:* Tuition: Full-time $14,820. *Financial support:* Fellowships, teaching assistantships, Federal Work-Study and institutionally sponsored loans available. Support available to part-time students. Financial award application deadline: 1/5; financial award applicants required to submit FAFSA. *Faculty research:* Algebra, topology, analysis. *Unit head:* Robert Friedman, Chair, 212-854-4355, Fax: 212-854-8962.

See in-depth description on page 531.

Concordia University, School of Graduate Studies, Faculty of Arts and Science, Department of Mathematics and Statistics, Montréal, QC H3G 1M8, Canada. Offers mathematics (M Sc, MA, PhD); teaching of mathematics (MTM). *Students:* 42 full-time, 18 part-time. In 2003, 6 master's, 3 doctorates awarded. *Degree requirements:* For master's, thesis optional; for doctorate, thesis/dissertation, comprehensive exam. *Entrance requirements:* For master's, honors degree in mathematics or equivalent. *Application deadline:* For fall admission, 5/1 for domestic students; for winter admission, 3/31 for domestic students; for spring admission, 10/31 for domestic students. Application fee: $50. *Expenses:* Tuition, state resident: full-time $2,140. Tuition, nonresident: full-time $4,190. International tuition: $8,449 full-time. Tuition and fees vary according to course load, degree level and program. *Financial support:* Fellowships, research assistantships, teaching assistantships available. Financial award application deadline: 2/1. *Faculty research:* Number theory, computational algebra, mathematical physics, differential geometry, dynamical systems and statistics. *Unit head:* Dr. Hershy Kisilevsky, Chair, 514-848-2424 Ext. 3234, Fax: 514-848-2831. *Application contact:* Dr. Chris Cummins, Director, 514-848-2424 Ext. 3250, Fax: 514-848-2831.

Cornell University, Graduate School, Graduate Fields of Arts and Sciences, Field of Mathematics, Ithaca, NY 14853-0001. Offers PhD. *Faculty:* 41 full-time. *Students:* 76 full-time (11 women); includes 4 minority (1 Asian American or Pacific Islander, 3 Hispanic Americans), 33 international. 235 applicants, 11% accepted, 12 enrolled. In 2003, 4 doctorates awarded. *Degree requirements:* For doctorate, one foreign language, thesis/dissertation, teaching experience, comprehensive exam. *Entrance requirements:* For doctorate, GRE General Test, GRE Subject Test (mathematics), 3 letters of recommendation. Additional exam requirements/recommendations for international students: Required—TOEFL (minimum score 600 paper-based; 250 computer-based). *Application deadline:* For fall admission, 1/15 for domestic students. Application fee: $60. Electronic applications accepted. *Expenses:* Tuition: Full-time $28,630. One-time fee: $50 full-time. *Financial support:* In 2003–04, 76 students received support, including 20 fellowships with full tuition reimbursements available, 1 research assistantship with full tuition reimbursement available, 55 teaching assistantships with full tuition reimbursements available; institutionally sponsored loans, scholarships/grants, health care benefits, tuition waivers (full and partial), and unspecified assistantships also available. Financial award applicants required to submit FAFSA. *Faculty research:* Analysis, dynamical systems, Lie theory, logic, topology and geometry. *Unit head:* Director of Graduate Studies, 607-255-6757, Fax: 607-255-7149. *Application contact:* Graduate Field Assistant, 607-255-6757, Fax: 607-255-7149, E-mail: gradinfo@math.cornell.edu.

Dalhousie University, Faculty of Graduate Studies, College of Arts and Science, Faculty of Science, Department of Mathematics and Statistics, Program in Mathematics, Halifax, NS B3H

4R2, Canada. Offers M Sc, PhD. *Degree requirements:* For master's and doctorate, thesis/dissertation. *Entrance requirements:* Additional exam requirements/recommendations for international students: Required—TOEFL. *Faculty research:* Applied mathematics, category theory, algebra, analysis, graph theory.

Dartmouth College, School of Arts and Sciences, Department of Mathematics, Hanover, NH 03755. Offers PhD. *Faculty:* 12 full-time (1 woman). *Students:* 24 full-time (11 women), 1 part-time; includes 2 minority (1 Asian American or Pacific Islander, 1 Hispanic American), 4 international. Average age 26. 143 applicants, 10% accepted, 6 enrolled. In 2003, 3 degrees awarded. *Degree requirements:* For doctorate, 2 foreign languages, thesis/dissertation. *Entrance requirements:* For doctorate, GRE General Test, GRE Subject Test. Additional exam requirements/recommendations for international students: Required—TOEFL. *Application deadline:* For fall admission, 2/15 for domestic students. Application fee: $0. *Expenses:* Tuition: Full-time $28,965. *Financial support:* In 2003–04, 25 students received support, including fellowships with full tuition reimbursements available (averaging $18,528 per year), research assistantships with full tuition reimbursements available (averaging $18,528 per year); institutionally sponsored loans, scholarships/grants, tuition waivers (full and partial), and unspecified assistantships also available. *Faculty research:* Mathematical logic, set theory, combinations, number theory. Total annual research expenditures: $444,536. *Unit head:* Dr. Dana Williams, Chair, 603-646-2990, Fax: 603-646-1312, E-mail: dana.williams@dartmouth.edu. *Application contact:* Carol Fine, Graduate Program Secretary, 603-646-3722, Fax: 603-646-1312, E-mail: carol.fine@dartmouth.edu.

See in-depth description on page 533.

Delaware State University, Graduate Programs, Department of Mathematics, Dover, DE 19901-2277. Offers MS.

DePaul University, College of Liberal Arts and Sciences, Department of Mathematical Sciences, Chicago, IL 60604-2287. Offers applied statistics (MS); mathematics education (MA). Part-time and evening/weekend programs available. *Faculty:* 23 full-time (6 women), 18 part-time/adjunct (5 women). *Students:* 86 full-time (46 women), 59 part-time (27 women); includes 28 minority (10 African Americans, 13 Asian Americans or Pacific Islanders, 5 Hispanic Americans), 8 international. Average age 30. 40 applicants, 100% accepted. In 2003, 30 degrees awarded. *Application deadline:* Applications are processed on a rolling basis. Application fee: $25. *Expenses:* Tuition: Part-time $395 per hour. *Financial support:* In 2003–04, 8 students received support, including research assistantships with partial tuition reimbursements available (averaging $3,700 per year); teaching assistantships, tuition waivers (full and partial) also available. *Faculty research:* Verbally prime algebras, enveloping algebras of Lie, superalgebras and related rings, harmonic analysis, estimation theory. *Unit head:* Dr. Susanna Epp, Chairperson, 773-325-7806.

See in-depth description on page 535.

Dowling College, Programs in Arts and Sciences, Oakdale, NY 11769-1999. Offers integrated math and science (MS); liberal studies (MA). Part-time and evening/weekend programs available. *Students:* 2 full-time (both women), 6 part-time (3 women). Average age 26. *Degree requirements:* For master's, thesis. *Entrance requirements:* For master's, minimum undergraduate GPA of 3.0, 2 letters of recommendation. Additional exam requirements/recommendations for international students: Required—TOEFL (minimum score 550 paper-based). *Application deadline:* For fall admission, 9/1 for domestic students; for winter admission, 1/1 for domestic students; for spring admission, 2/1 for domestic students. Applications are processed on a rolling basis. Application fee: $25. Electronic applications accepted. *Expenses:* Tuition: Part-time $565 per credit. Required fees: $770; $258 per term. *Financial support:* Federal Work-Study, scholarships/grants, and unspecified assistantships available. Support available to part-time students. Financial award application deadline: 6/30; financial award applicants required to submit FAFSA. *Unit head:* Dr. Richard Resch, Provost, 631-244-3495, E-mail: reschr@dowling.edu. *Application contact:* Amy Stier, Director of Enrollment Services for Admissions, 631-244-5010, Fax: 631-563-3827, E-mail: stiera@dowling.edu.

Drexel University, College of Arts and Sciences, Department of Mathematics, Program in Mathematics, Philadelphia, PA 19104-2875. Offers MS, PhD. *Degree requirements:* For doctorate, one foreign language, thesis/dissertation. *Entrance requirements:* For master's and doctorate, GRE. Additional exam requirements/recommendations for international students: Required—TOEFL, TSE (financial award applicants for teaching assistantships). Electronic applications accepted.

Duke University, Graduate School, Department of Mathematics, Durham, NC 27708-0586. Offers PhD. *Faculty:* 30 full-time. *Students:* 45 full-time (5 women); includes 2 minority (1 Asian American or Pacific Islander, 1 Hispanic American), 15 international. 173 applicants, 16% accepted, 8 enrolled. In 2003, 4 doctorates awarded. *Degree requirements:* For doctorate, 2 foreign languages, thesis/dissertation. *Entrance requirements:* For doctorate, GRE General Test, GRE Subject Test. Additional exam requirements/recommendations for international students: Required—IELT (preferred) or TOEFL. *Application deadline:* For fall admission, 12/31 for domestic students. Application fee: $75. *Expenses:* Tuition: Full-time $23,280; part-time $835 per unit. *Financial support:* Fellowships, research assistantships, teaching assistantships, Federal Work-Study available. Financial award application deadline: 12/31. *Unit head:* John Trangenstein, Director of Graduate Studies, 919-660-2801, Fax: 919-660-2821, E-mail: barnes@math.duke.edu.

Duquesne University, Graduate School of Liberal Arts, Program in Computational Mathematics, Pittsburgh, PA 15282-0001. Offers MA. *Faculty:* 18 full-time (5 women), 19 part-time/adjunct (7 women). *Students:* 7 full-time (4 women), 5 part-time (2 women), 3 international. Average age 23. 17 applicants, 76% accepted, 4 enrolled. In 2003, 2 degrees awarded. *Median time to degree:* Master's–3 years full-time, 6 years part-time. *Degree requirements:* For master's, thesis, registration. *Entrance requirements:* For master's, GRE General Test. Additional exam requirements/recommendations for international students: Required—TOEFL. *Application deadline:* For fall admission, 8/1 for domestic students, 5/1 for international students. Applications are processed on a rolling basis. Application fee: $50. *Expenses:* Tuition: Part-time $626 per credit. Required fees: $62 per credit. Tuition and fees vary according to degree level and program. *Financial support:* In 2003–04, 2 teaching assistantships with full tuition reimbursements (averaging $9,000 per year) were awarded; Federal Work-Study, institutionally sponsored loans, scholarships/grants, and unspecified assistantships also available. Financial award application deadline: 5/1. *Unit head:* Dr. Frank D'Amico, Chair, 412-396-6467. *Application contact:* Dr. Kathleen Taylor, Professor, 412-396-6472, Fax: 412-396-5265, E-mail: compmath@mathcs.duq.edu.

East Carolina University, Graduate School, Thomas Harriot College of Arts and Sciences, Department of Mathematics, Greenville, NC 27858-4353. Offers applied mathematics (MA); mathematics (MA). Part-time and evening/weekend programs available. *Faculty:* 15 full-time (4 women). *Students:* 2 full-time (1 woman), 4 part-time (3 women), 1 international. Average age 30. 4 applicants, 100% accepted. In 2003, 3 degrees awarded. *Degree requirements:* For master's, comprehensive exam. *Entrance requirements:* For master's, GRE General Test, MAT. Additional exam requirements/recommendations for international students: Required—TOEFL. *Application deadline:* For fall admission, 6/1 for domestic students; for spring admission, 10/15 for domestic students. Applications are processed on a rolling basis. Application fee: $50. *Expenses:* Tuition, state resident: full-time $1,991; part-time $249 per hour. Tuition, nonresident: full-time $12,232; part-time $1,529 per hour. Required fees: $1,221; $153 per hour. *Financial support:* Research assistantships with partial tuition reimbursements, teaching assistantships with partial tuition reimbursements available. Financial award application deadline: 6/1. *Unit head:* Dr. John Daughtry, Director of Graduate Studies, 252-328-6415, Fax: 252-328-6414, E-mail: daughtryj@mail.ecu.edu. *Application contact:* Dr. Paul D. Tschetter, Interim Dean of Graduate School, 252-328-6012, Fax: 252-328-6071, E-mail: gradschool@mail.ecu.edu.

Eastern Illinois University, Graduate School, College of Sciences, Department of Mathematics and Computer Science, Charleston, IL 61920-3099. Offers mathematics (MA); mathematics education (MA). *Faculty:* 30 full-time (6 women). In 2003, 3 degrees awarded. *Entrance requirements:* For master's, GRE General Test. *Application deadline:* For fall admission, 7/31 for domestic students. Applications are processed on a rolling basis. Application fee: $30. *Expenses:* Tuition, state resident: part-time $125 per semester hour. Tuition, nonresident: part-time $375 per semester hour. Required fees: $53 per semester hour. $698 per semester. *Financial support:* In 2003–04, research assistantships with tuition reimbursements (averaging $6,300 per year), 8 teaching assistantships with tuition reimbursements (averaging $6,300 per year) were awarded. *Unit head:* Dr. Peter Andrews, Chair, 217-581-6275, Fax: 217-581-6284, E-mail: cfpga@eiu.edu. *Application contact:* Dr. Patrick Coulton, Coordinator, 217-581-6275, Fax: 217-581-6284, E-mail: cfprc@eiu.edu.

Eastern Kentucky University, The Graduate School, College of Arts and Sciences, Department of Mathematics and Statistics, Richmond, KY 40475-3102. Offers mathematical sciences (MS). Part-time programs available. *Faculty:* 17 full-time (5 women), 1 (woman) part-time/adjunct. *Students:* 9 full-time (3 women), 5 part-time (1 woman); includes 1 minority (Asian American or Pacific Islander), 2 international. Average age 35. 18 applicants, 44% accepted, 7 enrolled. In 2003, 5 degrees awarded. *Entrance requirements:* For master's, GRE General Test, minimum GPA of 2.5. Application fee: $0. *Expenses:* Tuition, state resident: full-time $3,550; part-time $197 per credit. Tuition, nonresident: full-time $9,752; part-time $542 per credit. *Financial support:* Research assistantships, teaching assistantships, Federal Work-Study available. Support available to part-time students. *Faculty research:* Graph theory, number theory, ring theory, topology, statistics. *Unit head:* Dr. Patrick James Costello, Chair, 859-622-5942, Fax: 859-622-3051, E-mail: pat.costello@eku.edu.

Eastern Michigan University, Graduate School, College of Arts and Sciences, Department of Mathematics, Ypsilanti, MI 48197. Offers computer science (M Math); mathematics education (M Math); statistics (M Math). Evening/weekend programs available. *Faculty:* 29 full-time. *Students:* 26 full-time (12 women), 45 part-time (22 women); includes 51 minority (3 African Americans, 46 Asian Americans or Pacific Islanders, 2 Hispanic Americans). *Degree requirements:* For master's, thesis optional. *Entrance requirements:* Additional exam requirements/recommendations for international students: Required—TOEFL. *Application deadline:* For fall admission, 5/15 for domestic students; for spring admission, 3/15 for domestic students. Applications are processed on a rolling basis. Application fee: $30. *Expenses:* Tuition, state resident: full-time $4,324. Tuition, nonresident: full-time $8,769. Required fees: $496. Tuition and fees vary according to course level. *Financial support:* In 2003–04, fellowships (averaging $4,000 per year), research assistantships (averaging $7,770 per year), teaching assistantships (averaging $7,770 per year) were awarded. Support available to part-time students. Financial award application deadline: 3/15; financial award applicants required to submit FAFSA. *Unit head:* Dr. Betty Warren, Head, 734-487-1444. *Application contact:* Dr. Kenneth Shiskowski, Coordinator, 734-487-1444.

Eastern New Mexico University, Graduate School, College of Liberal Arts and Sciences, Department of Mathematical Sciences, Portales, NM 88130. Offers MA. Part-time programs available. *Faculty:* 7 full-time (3 women), 1 part-time/adjunct (0 women). *Students:* 1 full-time (0 women), 4 part-time (1 woman). Average age 25. 3 applicants, 33% accepted. *Degree requirements:* For master's, thesis optional. *Entrance requirements:* For master's, minimum GPA of 2.5. *Application deadline:* For fall admission, 8/20 for domestic students. Applications are processed on a rolling basis. Application fee: $10. Electronic applications accepted. *Expenses:* Tuition, state resident: full-time $2,064; part-time $86 per credit hour. Tuition, nonresident: full-time $7,620; part-time $318 per credit hour. Required fees: $29 per credit hour. *Financial support:* In 2003–04, 1 research assistantship (averaging $7,700 per year), 3 teaching assistantships (averaging $7,700 per year) were awarded. Career-related internships or fieldwork and Federal Work-Study also available. Support available to part-time students. Financial award application deadline: 3/1. *Faculty research:* Applied mathematics, graph theory. *Unit head:* Dr. Regina Aragon, Graduate Coordinator, 505-562-2328, E-mail: regina.aragon@enmu.edu.

Eastern Washington University, Graduate School Studies, College of Science, Mathematics and Technology, Department of Mathematics, Cheney, WA 99004-2431. Offers MS. *Accreditation:* NCATE. Part-time programs available. *Faculty:* 14 full-time (6 women). *Students:* 3 full-time (2 women), 15 part-time (6 women). Average age 30. 1 applicant, 100% accepted. In 2003, 7 degrees awarded. *Degree requirements:* For master's, thesis (for some programs), comprehensive exam. *Entrance requirements:* For master's, GRE General Test, departmental qualifying exam, minimum GPA of 3.0. *Application deadline:* For fall admission, 4/1 for domestic students; for spring admission, 1/15 for domestic students. Applications are processed on a rolling basis. Application fee: $35. *Expenses:* Tuition, state resident: part-time $385 per credit. Tuition, nonresident: part-time $1,139 per credit. *Financial support:* In 2003–04, 14 teaching assistantships with partial tuition reimbursements (averaging $12,000 per year) were awarded; career-related internships or fieldwork, Federal Work-Study, institutionally sponsored loans, scholarships/grants, health care benefits, tuition waivers (partial), and unspecified assistantships also available. Support available to part-time students. Financial award application deadline: 2/1; financial award applicants required to submit FAFSA. *Unit head:* Dr. Christian Hansen, Chair, 509-359-6225, Fax: 509-359-4700. *Application contact:* Dr. Yves Nievergelt, Adviser, 509-359-2219.

East Tennessee State University, School of Graduate Studies, College of Arts and Sciences, Department of Mathematics, Johnson City, TN 37614. Offers MS. Part-time and evening/weekend programs available. *Faculty:* 15 full-time (5 women). *Students:* 15 full-time (3 women), 3 part-time (1 woman); includes 1 minority (African American), 5 international. Average age 27. 15 applicants, 80% accepted, 6 enrolled. In 2003, 7 degrees awarded. *Degree requirements:* For master's, thesis or alternative, comprehensive exam. *Entrance requirements:* For master's, GRE General Test. Additional exam requirements/recommendations for international students: Required—TOEFL (minimum score 550 paper-based; 213 computer-based). *Application deadline:* For fall admission, 7/15 for domestic students; for spring admission, 11/1 for domestic students. Applications are processed on a rolling basis. Application fee: $25 ($35 for international students). *Expenses:* Tuition, state resident: part-time $222 per hour. Tuition, nonresident: part-time $344 per hour. Required fees: $264 per hour. *Financial support:* In 2003–04, 12 teaching assistantships with full tuition reimbursements (averaging $7,700 per year) were awarded; research assistantships with full tuition reimbursements, unspecified assistantships and laboratory assistantships also available. Financial award application deadline: 7/1; financial award applicants required to submit FAFSA. *Faculty research:* Graph theory and combinatorics, probability and statistics, analysis, numerical and applied math, algebra. Total annual research expenditures: $197,750. *Unit head:* Dr. Anant Godbole, Chair, 423-439-5359, Fax: 423-439-8361, E-mail: godbolea@etsu.edu.

École Polytechnique de Montréal, Graduate Programs, Department of Mathematics, Montréal, QC H3C 3A7, Canada. Offers mathematical method in CA engineering (M Eng, M Sc A, PhD); operational research (M Eng, M Sc A, PhD). Part-time programs available. *Degree requirements:* For master's and doctorate, one foreign language, thesis/dissertation. *Entrance requirements:* For master's, minimum GPA of 2.75; for doctorate, minimum GPA of 3.0. *Faculty research:* Statistics and probability, fractal analysis, optimization.

Emory University, Graduate School of Arts and Sciences, Department of Mathematics and Computer Science, Atlanta, GA 30322-1100. Offers mathematics (PhD); mathematics/computer science (MS). *Faculty:* 29 full-time (3 women). *Students:* 44 full-time (15 women), 1 part-time; includes 8 minority (2 African Americans, 5 Asian Americans or Pacific Islanders, 1 Hispanic American), 19 international. Average age 23. 115 applicants, 24% accepted, 16 enrolled. In 2003, 9 master's, 3 doctorates awarded. Terminal master's awarded for partial completion of doctoral program. *Median time to degree:* Master's–1 year full-time; doctorate–3 years full-time. *Degree requirements:* For master's, thesis, registration; for doctorate, one foreign language, thesis/dissertation, comprehensive exam, registration. *Entrance requirements:* For master's

Mathematics

Emory University (continued)

and doctorate, GRE General Test. *Application deadline:* For fall admission, 1/20 for domestic students, 1/20 for international students. Application fee: $50. Electronic applications accepted. *Expenses:* Tuition: Part-time $1,115 per hour. Required fees: $5 per hour. $125 per term. *Financial support:* In 2003–04, fellowships (averaging $12,550 per year), teaching assistantships (averaging $16,000 per year) were awarded. Scholarships/grants also available. Financial award application deadline: 1/20. Total annual research expenditures: $1.1 million. *Unit head:* Dr. Dwight Duffus, Chairman, 404-727-7580, Fax: 404-727-5611. *Application contact:* Dr. James G. Nagy, Director of Graduate Studies, 404-727-7580, Fax: 404-727-5611, E-mail: dgs@mathcs.emory.edu.

Announcement: The department offers a PhD in mathematics and an MS in mathematics or computer science. Research specialties in mathematics include algebra, computational algebra, applied math, combinatorics, complex analysis, differential equations, dynamical systems, topology, numerical analysis, scientific computation, and mathematical physics. Full tuition and funding are available in both the math PhD and computer science MS programs.

Emporia State University, School of Graduate Studies, College of Liberal Arts and Sciences, Department of Mathematics and Computer Science, Emporia, KS 66801-5087. Offers mathematics (MS). Part-time programs available. *Faculty:* 14 full-time (2 women), 5 part-time/adjunct (4 women). *Students:* 3 full-time (2 women), 12 part-time (9 women); includes 2 minority (both Hispanic Americans) 7 applicants. In 2003, 1 degree awarded. *Degree requirements:* For master's, comprehensive exam or thesis. *Entrance requirements:* For master's, appropriate undergraduate degree. Additional exam requirements/recommendations for international students: Required—TOEFL (minimum score 450 paper-based; 133 computer-based). *Application deadline:* For fall admission, 8/15 for domestic students. Applications are processed on a rolling basis. Application fee: $30 ($75 for international students). Electronic applications accepted. *Expenses:* Tuition, state resident: full-time $2,640; part-time $110 per credit hour. Tuition, nonresident: full-time $8,454; part-time $352 per credit hour. Required fees: $576; $35 per credit hour. Tuition and fees vary according to campus/location. *Financial support:* In 2003–04, 3 teaching assistantships with full tuition reimbursements (averaging $6,225 per year) were awarded; career-related internships or fieldwork, Federal Work-Study, institutionally sponsored loans, health care benefits, and unspecified assistantships also available. Financial award application deadline: 3/15; financial award applicants required to submit FAFSA. *Unit head:* Dr. Larry Scott, Chair, 620-341-5281, Fax: 620-341-6055, E-mail: scottlar@emporia.edu. *Application contact:* Dr. Joe Yanik, Graduate Coordinator, 620-341-5639, E-mail: yanikjoe@emporia.edu.

Fairfield University, College of Arts and Sciences, Program in Mathematics and Quantitative Methods, Fairfield, CT 06824-5195. Offers MS. Part-time and evening/weekend programs available. *Faculty:* 14 full-time (3 women). *Students:* 4 full-time (1 woman), 24 part-time (9 women); includes 4 minority (2 African Americans, 2 Asian Americans or Pacific Islanders), 4 international. Average age 38. 5 applicants, 100% accepted, 5 enrolled. In 2003, 4 degrees awarded. *Degree requirements:* For master's, Capstone Course. *Entrance requirements:* For master's, minimum GPA of 3.0, 2 letters of recommendation, resumé. Additional exam requirements/recommendations for international students: Required—TOEFL (minimum score 550 paper-based; 213 computer-based). *Application deadline:* For fall admission, 7/1 for domestic students, 6/15 for international students; for spring admission, 12/1 for domestic students, 10/15 for international students. Applications are processed on a rolling basis. Application fee: $55. *Expenses:* Tuition: Full-time $10,125; part-time $540 per credit hour. Tuition and fees vary according to program. *Financial support:* Unspecified assistantships available. Financial award applicants required to submit FAFSA. *Unit head:* Dr. Benjamin Fine, Co-Director, 203-254-4000 Ext. 2197, E-mail: fine@fair1.fairfield.edu. *Application contact:* Marianne Gumpper, Director of Graduate Admissions, 203-254-4184, Fax: 203-254-4073, E-mail: gradadmis@mail.fairfield.edu.

Fayetteville State University, Graduate School, Department of Mathematics and Computer Science, Fayetteville, NC 28301-4298. Offers mathematics (MS). Part-time and evening/weekend programs available. *Degree requirements:* For master's, thesis or alternative, internship, comprehensive exam. *Entrance requirements:* For master's, GRE General Test.

Florida Atlantic University, Charles E. Schmidt College of Science, Department of Mathematical Science, Boca Raton, FL 33431-0991. Offers applied mathematics and statistics (MS); mathematics (MS, MST, PhD). Part-time programs available. *Faculty:* 25 full-time (2 women), 3 part-time/adjunct (0 women). *Students:* 31 full-time (11 women), 18 part-time (12 women); includes 12 minority (4 African Americans, 8 Hispanic Americans), 18 international. Average age 32. 36 applicants, 67% accepted, 16 enrolled. In 2003, 6 master's, 1 doctorate awarded. Terminal master's awarded for partial completion of doctoral program. *Degree requirements:* For master's, thesis (for some programs), comprehensive exam (for some programs), registration; for doctorate, thesis/dissertation, comprehensive exam, registration. *Entrance requirements:* For master's and doctorate, GRE General Test, minimum GPA of 3.0. Additional exam requirements/recommendations for international students: Required—TOEFL (minimum score 500 paper-based; 173 computer-based). *Application deadline:* For fall admission, 6/1 priority date for domestic students, 2/15 priority date for international students; for spring admission, 10/20 priority date for domestic students, 8/15 priority date for international students. Applications are processed on a rolling basis. Application fee: $30. Electronic applications accepted. *Expenses:* Tuition, state resident: full-time $3,777. Tuition, nonresident: full-time $13,953. *Financial support:* In 2003–04, fellowships with partial tuition reimbursements (averaging $20,000 per year), 20 teaching assistantships with partial tuition reimbursements (averaging $20,000 per year) were awarded. Federal Work-Study also available. Financial award application deadline: 4/1. *Faculty research:* Cryptography, statistics, algebra, analysis, combinatorics. Total annual research expenditures: $550,000. *Unit head:* Dr. Yoram Sagher, Chair, 561-297-3341, Fax: 561-297-2436, E-mail: sagher@fau.edu. *Application contact:* Dr. Heinrich Niederhausen, Graduate Director, 561-297-3237, Fax: 561-297-2436, E-mail: grad@math.fau.edu.

Florida International University, College of Arts and Sciences, Department of Mathematics, Miami, FL 33199. Offers mathematical sciences (MS). Part-time and evening/weekend programs available. *Faculty:* 29 full-time (7 women). *Students:* 6 full-time (2 women), 4 part-time (3 women); includes 5 minority (1 Asian American or Pacific Islander, 4 Hispanic Americans), 2 international. Average age 35. 12 applicants, 75% accepted, 5 enrolled. *Degree requirements:* For master's, thesis, project. *Entrance requirements:* For master's, GRE General Test, 3 letters of recommendation. Additional exam requirements/recommendations for international students: Required—TOEFL. *Application deadline:* For fall admission, 4/1 for domestic students; for spring admission, 10/1 for domestic students. Applications are processed on a rolling basis. Application fee: $20. *Expenses:* Tuition, state resident: part-time $202 per credit. Tuition, nonresident: part-time $771 per credit. Required fees: $112 per semester. *Financial support:* Application deadline: 4/1. *Unit head:* Dr. Enrique Villamor, Chairperson, 305-348-2742, Fax: 305-348-6158, E-mail: villamor@fiu.edu.

Florida State University, Graduate Studies, College of Arts and Sciences, Department of Mathematics, Tallahassee, FL 32306. Offers applied mathematics (MA, MS, PhD); financial mathematics (PhD); mathematical sciences (MA, MS); pure mathematics (MA, MS, PhD). Part-time programs available. *Faculty:* 35 full-time (3 women), 8 part-time/adjunct (4 women). *Students:* 110 full-time (36 women), 7 part-time (3 women); includes 54 minority (4 African Americans, 45 Asian Americans or Pacific Islanders, 5 Hispanic Americans), 4 international. Average age 26. 250 applicants, 60% accepted, 50 enrolled. In 2003, 18 master's, 3 doctorates awarded. Terminal master's awarded for partial completion of doctoral program. *Degree requirements:* For master's, thesis optional; for doctorate, thesis/dissertation. *Entrance requirements:* For master's and doctorate, GRE General Test, minimum GPA of 3.0. *Application deadline:* For fall admission, 2/1 priority date for domestic students, 1/1 priority date for international students; for winter admission, 7/1 for domestic students. Applications are processed on a rolling basis. Application fee: $20. Electronic applications accepted. *Expenses:* Tuition, state resident: part-time $196 per credit hour. Tuition, nonresident: part-time $731 per credit hour. Part-time tuition and fees vary according to campus/location. *Financial support:* In 2003–04, 2 fellowships with full tuition reimbursements (averaging $15,000 per year), 10 research assistantships with full tuition reimbursements, 78 teaching assistantships with full tuition reimbursements (averaging $15,000 per year) were awarded. Institutionally sponsored loans also available. Financial award application deadline: 3/1. *Unit head:* Dr. Dewitt Sumners, Chairperson, 850-644-4406, Fax: 850-644-4053, E-mail: sumners@math.fsu.edu. *Application contact:* Dr. Sam Huckaba, Director of Graduate Studies, 850-644-1479, Fax: 850-644-4053, E-mail: huckaba@math.fsu.edu.

George Mason University, College of Arts and Sciences, Department of Mathematical Sciences, Fairfax, VA 22030. Offers mathematics (MS). Evening/weekend programs available. *Faculty:* 34 full-time (9 women), 7 part-time/adjunct (1 woman). *Students:* 1 full-time (0 women), 10 part-time (4 women); includes 1 minority (Hispanic American), 2 international. Average age 35. 17 applicants, 47% accepted, 4 enrolled. In 2003, 5 degrees awarded. *Degree requirements:* For master's, thesis optional. *Entrance requirements:* For master's, minimum GPA of 3.0 in last 60 hours. *Application deadline:* For fall admission, 5/1 for domestic students; for spring admission, 11/1 for domestic students. Application fee: $60. Electronic applications accepted. *Expenses:* Tuition, state resident: full-time $4,398. Tuition, nonresident: full-time $14,952. Required fees: $1,482. *Financial support:* Fellowships, research assistantships, teaching assistantships, career-related internships or fieldwork available. Support available to part-time students. Financial award application deadline: 3/1; financial award applicants required to submit FAFSA. *Unit head:* Robert Sachs, Chair, 703-993-1462, Fax: 703-993-1491, E-mail: rsachs@gmu.edu. *Application contact:* Dr. David Walnut, Information Contact, 703-993-1460, E-mail: mathgrad@gmu.edu.

The George Washington University, Columbian College of Arts and Sciences, Department of Mathematics, Washington, DC 20052. Offers applied mathematics (MA, MS); pure mathematics (MA, PhD). Part-time and evening/weekend programs available. *Faculty:* 8 full-time (2 women). *Students:* 14 full-time (7 women), 6 part-time (2 women); includes 1 minority (Hispanic American), 7 international. Average age 31. 33 applicants, 76% accepted. In 2003, 4 degrees awarded. Terminal master's awarded for partial completion of doctoral program. *Degree requirements:* For master's, comprehensive exam; for doctorate, one foreign language, thesis/dissertation, general exam. *Entrance requirements:* For master's and doctorate, GRE General Test, minimum GPA of 3.0, interview. Additional exam requirements/recommendations for international students: Required—TOEFL (minimum score 550 paper-based; 213 computer-based). *Application deadline:* For fall admission, 2/1 priority date for domestic students, 2/1 priority date for international students; for spring admission, 10/1 priority date for domestic students, 10/1 priority date for international students. Applications are processed on a rolling basis. Application fee: $60. Electronic applications accepted. *Expenses:* Tuition: Part-time $876 per credit. Required fees: $1 per credit. Tuition and fees vary according to campus/location. *Financial support:* In 2003–04, fellowships with full tuition reimbursements (averaging $10,000 per year), teaching assistantships with tuition reimbursements (averaging $5,000 per year) were awarded. Federal Work-Study also available. Financial award application deadline: 2/1. *Unit head:* Dr. Daniel Ullman, Chair, 202-994-6235.

Georgia Institute of Technology, Graduate Studies and Research, College of Sciences, School of Mathematics, Atlanta, GA 30332-0001. Offers algorithms, combinatorics, and optimization (PhD); applied mathematics (MS); bioinformatics (PhD); mathematics (PhD); quantitative and computational finance (MS); statistics (MS Stat). *Faculty:* 50 full-time (3 women). *Students:* 59 full-time (17 women), 8 part-time (2 women); includes 3 minority (2 African Americans, 1 Hispanic American), 32 international. Average age 25. In 2003, 20 master's, 7 doctorates awarded, leading to university research/teaching 55%, business/industry 30%, government 15%. Terminal master's awarded for partial completion of doctoral program. *Degree requirements:* For master's, thesis or alternative; for doctorate, one foreign language, thesis/dissertation. *Entrance requirements:* For master's, GRE General Test, minimum GPA of 3.0; for doctorate, GRE General Test, GRE Subject Test, minimum GPA of 3.0. Additional exam requirements/recommendations for international students: Required—TOEFL. *Application deadline:* For fall admission, 3/1 priority date for domestic students, 3/1 priority date for international students; for spring admission, 10/1 priority date for domestic students, 10/1 priority date for international students. Applications are processed on a rolling basis. Application fee: $50. Electronic applications accepted. *Expenses:* Tuition, state resident: part-time $1,925 per semester. Tuition, nonresident: part-time $7,700 per semester. Required fees: $434 per semester. Full-time tuition and fees vary according to program. *Financial support:* In 2003–04, 7 fellowships with tuition reimbursements, 20 research assistantships with tuition reimbursements, 40 teaching assistantships with tuition reimbursements were awarded. Career-related internships or fieldwork, Federal Work-Study, institutionally sponsored loans, tuition waivers (partial), and supplements also available. Financial award application deadline: 2/1. *Faculty research:* Dynamical systems, discrete mathematics, probability and statistics, mathematical physics. Total annual research expenditures: $1.1 million. *Unit head:* Dr. William Thomas Trotter, Chair, 404-894-2700. *Application contact:* Dr. Evans Harrell, Graduate Coordinator, 404-894-9203, Fax: 404-894-4409, E-mail: grad.coordinator@math.gatech.edu.

Georgia Institute of Technology, Graduate Studies and Research, Multidisciplinary Program in Algorithms, Combinatorics, and Optimization, Atlanta, GA 30332-0001. Offers PhD. *Degree requirements:* For doctorate, thesis/dissertation. *Entrance requirements:* For doctorate, GRE General Test, GRE Subject Test (computer science or mathematics). Additional exam requirements/recommendations for international students: Required—TOEFL. Electronic applications accepted. *Expenses:* Tuition, state resident: part-time $1,925 per semester. Tuition, nonresident: part-time $7,700 per semester. Required fees: $434 per semester. Full-time tuition and fees vary according to program. *Faculty research:* Complexity, graph minors, combinatorial optimization, mathematical programming, probabilistic methods.

Georgian Court University, School of Sciences and Mathematics, Lakewood, NJ 08701-2697. Offers biology (MS); counseling psychology (MA); holistic health (Certificate); holistic health studies (MA); mathematics (MA); professional counselor (Certificate); school psychology (Certificate). Part-time and evening/weekend programs available. *Faculty:* 15 full-time (10 women), 6 part-time/adjunct (4 women). *Students:* 28 full-time (27 women), 133 part-time (124 women); includes 9 minority (3 African Americans, 1 Asian American or Pacific Islander, 5 Hispanic Americans). Average age 37. 57 applicants, 79% accepted, 38 enrolled. In 2003, 20 degrees awarded. *Degree requirements:* For master's, thesis (for some programs), comprehensive exam (for some programs). *Entrance requirements:* For master's, GRE General Test and Subject Test in biology (MS), GRE General Test (psychology), 3 letters of recommendation. Additional exam requirements/recommendations for international students: Required—TOEFL (minimum score 550 paper-based; 213 computer-based). *Application deadline:* For fall admission, 8/1 priority date for domestic students, 4/1 priority date for international students; for spring admission, 1/1 priority date for domestic students, 7/1 priority date for international students. Applications are processed on a rolling basis. Application fee: $40. Electronic applications accepted. *Expenses:* Tuition: Full-time $8,496; part-time $472 per credit. Required fees: $200 per semester. Tuition and fees vary according to course load. *Financial support:* In 2003–04, 60 students received support. Scholarships/grants, health care benefits, and unspecified assistantships available. Financial award application deadline: 4/15; financial award applicants required to submit FAFSA. *Unit head:* Dr. Linda James, Dean, 732-364-2200 Ext. 2671. *Application contact:* Kathie DeBona, Director of Admissions, 732-364-2200 Ext. 2760, Fax: 732-364-4442, E-mail: admissions@georgian.edu.

Georgia Southern University, Jack N. Averitt College of Graduate Studies, Allen E. Paulson College of Science and Technology, Department of Mathematical Sciences, Statesboro, GA 30460. Offers mathematics (MS). Part-time programs available. *Students:* 9 full-time (4 women), 8 part-time (4 women); includes 4 minority (3 African Americans, 1 Asian American or Pacific Islander), 3 international. Average age 30. 4 applicants, 100% accepted, 4 enrolled. In 2003, 3 degrees awarded. *Degree requirements:* For master's, terminal exam, project. *Entrance* *requirements:* For master's, GRE, BS in engineering, science, or mathematics; previous course work in calculus, probability, linear algebra; proficiency in a computer programming language. Additional exam requirements/recommendations for international students: Required—TOEFL (minimum score 550 paper-based; 213 computer-based). *Application deadline:* For fall admission, 3/1 priority date for domestic students, 6/1 priority date for international students; for spring admission, 10/1 priority date for domestic students, 10/1 priority date for international students. Applications are processed on a rolling basis. Application fee: $30. Electronic applications accepted. *Expenses:* Tuition, state resident: full-time $1,998; part-time $111 per credit hour. Tuition, nonresident: full-time $7,974; part-time $443 per credit hour. Required fees: $700. Full-time tuition and fees vary according to course load and campus/location. *Financial support:* In 2003–04, 12 students received support, including research assistantships with partial tuition reimbursements available (averaging $5,500 per year), teaching assistantships with partial tuition reimbursements available (averaging $5,500 per year); career-related internships or fieldwork, Federal Work-Study, scholarships/grants, and unspecified assistantships also available. Support available to part-time students. Financial award application deadline: 4/15; financial award applicants required to submit FAFSA. *Faculty research:* Analysis of numerical, interval, and fuzzy data; approximation theory; computational mathematics; parallel computation; applied statistic and emphasis on biological models. Total annual research expenditures: $23,426. *Unit head:* Dr. Xiezhang Li, Acting Chair, 912-681-5132, Fax: 912-681-0654, E-mail: xli@georgiasouthern.edu. *Application contact:* 912-681-5384, Fax: 912-681-0740, E-mail: gradschool@georgiasouthern.edu.

Georgia State University, College of Arts and Sciences, Department of Mathematics and Statistics, Atlanta, GA 30303-3083. Offers mathematics (MA, MAT, MS). Part-time and evening/weekend programs available. *Faculty:* 22 full-time (5 women). *Students:* 15 full-time (10 women), 9 part-time (3 women); includes 12 minority (7 African Americans, 5 Asian Americans or Pacific Islanders). 53 applicants, 32% accepted. In 2003, 6 degrees awarded. *Degree requirements:* For master's, thesis or alternative, exam. *Entrance requirements:* For master's, GRE. Additional exam requirements/recommendations for international students: Required—TOEFL. *Application deadline:* For fall admission, 8/1 for domestic students; for spring admission, 12/1 for domestic students. Applications are processed on a rolling basis. Application fee: $25. Electronic applications accepted. *Financial support:* In 2003–04, 15 research assistantships with full tuition reimbursements (averaging $6,000 per year), 10 teaching assistantships with full tuition reimbursements (averaging $2,700 per year) were awarded. Federal Work-Study and scholarships/grants also available. Financial award applicants required to submit FAFSA. *Faculty research:* Analysis, biostatistics, discrete mathematics, linear algebra, statistics. *Unit head:* Dr. Johannes Hattingh, Acting Chair, 404-651-2245, Fax: 404-651-2246, E-mail: jhhattingh@gsu.edu. *Application contact:* Dr. George Davis, Director of Graduate Studies, 404-651-2253, Fax: 404-651-2246, E-mail: gdavis@gsu.edu.

Graduate School and University Center of the City University of New York, Graduate Studies, Program in Mathematics, New York, NY 10016-4039. Offers PhD. *Faculty:* 43 full-time (2 women). *Students:* 74 full-time (17 women), 8 part-time; includes 11 minority (5 African Americans, 3 Asian Americans or Pacific Islanders, 3 Hispanic Americans), 21 international. Average age 35. 91 applicants, 79% accepted, 16 enrolled. In 2003, 8 degrees awarded. *Degree requirements:* For doctorate, 2 foreign languages, thesis/dissertation. *Entrance requirements:* For doctorate, GRE General Test. *Application deadline:* For fall admission, 4/15 for domestic students. Application fee: $50. *Expenses:* Tuition, state resident: part-time $2,435 per semester. Tuition, nonresident: part-time $475 per credit. *Financial support:* In 2003–04, 47 students received support, including 36 fellowships, 2 research assistantships, 10 teaching assistantships; career-related internships or fieldwork, Federal Work-Study, institutionally sponsored loans, and tuition waivers (full and partial) also available. Financial award application deadline: 2/1; financial award applicants required to submit FAFSA. *Unit head:* Dr. Alvany Rocha, Executive Officer, 212-817-8530, Fax: 212-817-1527, E-mail: arocha@gc.cuny.edu.

Harvard University, Graduate School of Arts and Sciences, Department of Mathematics, Cambridge, MA 02138. Offers AM, PhD. *Degree requirements:* For doctorate, 2 foreign languages, thesis/dissertation, qualifying exam. *Entrance requirements:* For master's, GRE General Test; for doctorate, GRE General Test, GRE Subject Test. Additional exam requirements/recommendations for international students: Required—TOEFL. *Expenses:* Tuition: Full-time $26,066. Full-time tuition and fees vary according to program and student level.

Hofstra University, College of Liberal Arts and Sciences, Division of Natural Sciences, Mathematics, Engineering, and Computer Science, Department of Mathematics, Hempstead, NY 11549. Offers applied mathematics (MS); mathematics (MA). Part-time and evening/weekend programs available. *Faculty:* 4 full-time (1 woman). *Students:* 5 full-time (4 women), 10 part-time (3 women); includes 1 minority (Asian American or Pacific Islander), 1 international. Average age 28. 15 applicants, 60% accepted, 8 enrolled. In 2003, 2 degrees awarded. *Entrance requirements:* For master's, bachelor's degree in related field. Additional exam requirements/recommendations for international students: Required—TOEFL (minimum score 550 paper-based; 213 computer-based). *Application deadline:* Applications are processed on a rolling basis. Application fee: $60. Electronic applications accepted. *Expenses:* Tuition: Full-time $10,800; part-time $600 per credit. Required fees: $910; $155 per semester. Tuition and fees vary according to course load and program. *Financial support:* In 2003–04, 8 students received support; research assistantships with partial tuition reimbursements available, tuition waivers (partial) available. Financial award applicants required to submit FAFSA. *Faculty research:* Dynamical systems, algebraic topology, set theory, number theory, mathematical biology. Total annual research expenditures: $200,000. *Unit head:* Dr. Maryisa T. Weiss, Chairperson, 516-463-5580, Fax: 516-463-6596, E-mail: matmtw@hofstra.edu. *Application contact:* Dr. Tina Montgomery-Sneed, Dean of Graduate Admissions, 516-463-4876, Fax: 516-463-4664, E-mail: gradstudent@hofstra.edu.

Howard University, Graduate School of Arts and Sciences, Department of Mathematics, Washington, DC 20059-0002. Offers applied mathematics (MS, PhD); mathematics (MS, PhD). Part-time programs available. *Faculty:* 29. *Students:* 19 full-time (8 women), 8 part-time (1 woman); includes 18 minority (all African Americans), 8 international. Average age 29. In 2003, 2 master's, 1 doctorate awarded. Terminal master's awarded for partial completion of doctoral program. *Degree requirements:* For master's, thesis or alternative, qualifying exam, comprehensive exam; for doctorate, 2 foreign languages, thesis/dissertation, qualifying exams, comprehensive exam. *Entrance requirements:* For master's, GRE General Test, minimum GPA of 3.0; for doctorate, GRE General Test. Additional exam requirements/recommendations for international students: Required—TOEFL. *Application deadline:* For fall admission, 2/15 for domestic students; for spring admission, 11/1 for domestic students. Application fee: $45. *Financial support:* In 2003–04, fellowships with full tuition reimbursements (averaging $16,000 per year), 2 research assistantships with full tuition reimbursements (averaging $15,000 per year), 5 teaching assistantships with full tuition reimbursements (averaging $13,000 per year) were awarded. Institutionally sponsored loans and scholarships/grants also available. Financial award application deadline: 4/1. Total annual research expenditures: $95,000. *Unit head:* Dr. Louis W. Shapiro, Interim Chairman, 202-806-6830. *Application contact:* Dr. Neil Hindman, Information Contact, 202-806-5927, Fax: 202-806-6831, E-mail: nhindman@howard.edu.

Hunter College of the City University of New York, Graduate School, School of Arts and Sciences, Department of Mathematics and Statistics, New York, NY 10021-5085. Offers applied mathematics (MA); mathematics for secondary education (MA); pure mathematics (MA). Part-time and evening/weekend programs available. *Faculty:* 7 full-time (2 women). *Students:* 4 full-time (all women), 39 part-time (22 women); includes 9 minority (2 African Americans, 6 Asian Americans or Pacific Islanders, 1 Hispanic American). Average age 34. 12 applicants, 75% accepted. In 2003, 14 degrees awarded. *Degree requirements:* For master's, one foreign language, thesis (for some programs), comprehensive exam. *Entrance requirements:* For master's, GRE General Test, 24 credits in mathematics, minimum B average. Additional exam requirements/recommendations for international students: Required—TOEFL. *Application deadline:* For fall admission, 4/1 for domestic students, 2/1 for international students; for spring admission, 11/1 for domestic students, 9/1 for international students. Application fee: $50. *Expenses:* Tuition, state resident: part-time $230 per credit. Tuition, nonresident: part-time $425 per credit. *Financial support:* Institutionally sponsored loans and tuition waivers (partial) available. Support available to part-time students. *Faculty research:* Data analysis, dynamical systems, computer graphics, topology, statistical decision theory. *Unit head:* Ada Peluso, Chairperson, 212-772-5300, Fax: 212-772-4858, E-mail: peluso@math.hunter.cuny.edu. *Application contact:* William Zlata, Director for Graduate Admissions, 212-772-4482, Fax: 212-650-3336, E-mail: admissions@hunter.cuny.edu.

Idaho State University, Office of Graduate Studies, College of Arts and Sciences, Department of Mathematics, Pocatello, ID 83209. Offers mathematics (MS, DA). *Faculty:* 16 full-time (3 women). *Students:* 9 full-time (3 women), 4 part-time (2 women); includes 1 minority (Hispanic American), 1 international. Average age 36. In 2003, 2 master's, 1 doctorate awarded. *Degree requirements:* For master's, thesis (for some programs), comprehensive exam, registration; for doctorate, thesis/dissertation, teaching internships, comprehensive exam, registration. *Entrance requirements:* For master's, GRE General Test, GRE Subject Test, course work in modern algebra, differential equations, advanced calculus, introductory analysis; for doctorate, GRE General Test, GRE Subject Test, minimum PGA of 3.5 (graduate), MS in mathematics, teaching experience. Additional exam requirements/recommendations for international students: Required—TOEFL (minimum score 550 paper-based; 213 computer-based). *Application deadline:* For fall admission, 7/1 priority date for domestic students, 7/1 priority date for international students; for spring admission, 12/1 priority date for domestic students, 12/1 priority date for international students. Applications are processed on a rolling basis. Application fee: $35. *Expenses:* Tuition, state resident: part-time $205 per credit. Tuition, nonresident: full-time $6,600; part-time $300 per credit. Required fees: $4,108. One-time fee: $35 full-time. *Financial support:* Fellowships with full and partial tuition reimbursements, research assistantships, teaching assistantships with full and partial tuition reimbursements available. Financial award application deadline: 1/1. *Faculty research:* Algebra, analysis geometry, statistics, applied mathematics. Total annual research expenditures: $57,302. *Unit head:* Dr. Dennis Stowe, Chairman, 208-282-3350.

See in-depth description on page 543.

Idaho State University, Office of Graduate Studies, Department of Interdisciplinary Studies, Pocatello, ID 83209. Offers biology (MNS); chemistry (MNS); general interdisciplinary (M Ed, MA); geology (MNS); mathematics (MNS); physics (MNS); waste management and environmental science (MS). Part-time programs available. *Students:* 3 full-time, 337 part-time; includes 7 minority (1 African American, 1 Asian American or Pacific Islander, 5 Hispanic Americans). Average age 45. In 2003, 7 degrees awarded. *Degree requirements:* For master's, thesis optional. *Entrance requirements:* For master's, GRE General Test or MAT, minimum GPA of 3.0. Additional exam requirements/recommendations for international students: Required—TOEFL (minimum score 550 paper-based; 213 computer-based). *Application deadline:* For fall admission, 7/1 priority date for domestic students, 7/1 priority date for international students; for spring admission, 12/1 priority date for domestic students, 12/1 priority date for international students. Applications are processed on a rolling basis. Application fee: $35. *Expenses:* Tuition, state resident: part-time $205 per credit. Tuition, nonresident: full-time $6,600; part-time $300 per credit. Required fees: $4,108. One-time fee: $35 full-time. *Financial support:* Research assistantships, teaching assistantships, career-related internships or fieldwork, Federal Work-Study, scholarships/grants, and tuition waivers (full and partial) available. Support available to part-time students. Financial award application deadline: 1/1. Total annual research expenditures: $1.7 million. *Unit head:* Dr. Edwin House, Chief Research Officer/Department Chair, 208-282-2714, Fax: 208-282-4529.

Illinois State University, Graduate School, College of Arts and Sciences, Department of Mathematics, Program in Mathematics, Normal, IL 61790-2200. Offers MA, MS. *Students:* 18 full-time (11 women), 14 part-time (7 women); includes 2 minority (both Asian Americans or Pacific Islanders), 14 international. 48 applicants, 83% accepted. In 2003, 13 degrees awarded. *Degree requirements:* For master's, thesis or alternative. *Entrance requirements:* For master's, GRE General Test, minimum GPA of 2.8 in last 60 hours. *Application deadline:* Applications are processed on a rolling basis. Application fee: $30. *Expenses:* Tuition, state resident: full-time $3,322; part-time $138 per hour. Tuition, nonresident: full-time $6,922; part-time $288 per hour. Required fees: $974; $41 per hour. *Financial support:* In 2003–04, 6 research assistantships (averaging $16,371 per year), 11 teaching assistantships (averaging $8,399 per year) were awarded. Tuition waivers (full) and unspecified assistantships also available. Financial award application deadline: 4/1. *Unit head:* Dr. George Seelinger, Chairperson, Department of Mathematics, 309-438-8781.

Indiana State University, School of Graduate Studies, College of Arts and Sciences, Department of Mathematics and Computer Science, Terre Haute, IN 47809-1401. Offers MA, MS. *Faculty:* 6 full-time (1 woman). *Students:* 22 full-time (4 women), 13 part-time (4 women); includes 3 minority (all African Americans), 30 international. Average age 29. In 2003, 20 degrees awarded. *Degree requirements:* For master's, thesis or alternative. *Application deadline:* For fall admission, 7/1 for domestic students; for spring admission, 11/1 priority date for domestic students. Applications are processed on a rolling basis. Application fee: $35. Electronic applications accepted. *Expenses:* Tuition, state resident: full-time $4,356; part-time $242 per credit. Tuition, nonresident: full-time $8,658; part-time $481 per credit. Required fees: $50 per term. *Financial support:* In 2003–04, 8 research assistantships with partial tuition reimbursements (averaging $4,280 per year), 1 teaching assistantship with partial tuition reimbursement (averaging $4,280 per year) were awarded. Tuition waivers (partial) also available. Financial award application deadline: 3/1; financial award applicants required to submit FAFSA. *Unit head:* Dr. Richard Easton, Chairperson, 812-237-2130.

Indiana University Bloomington, Graduate School, College of Arts and Sciences, Department of Mathematics, Bloomington, IN 47405. Offers applied mathematics–numerical analysis (MA, PhD); mathematics education (MAT); probability-statistics (MA, PhD). PhD offered through the University Graduate School. *Faculty:* 36 full-time (1 woman). *Students:* 102 full-time (33 women), 31 part-time (7 women); includes 5 minority (all Asian Americans or Pacific Islanders), 76 international. Average age 27. In 2003, 14 master's, 13 doctorates awarded. Terminal master's awarded for partial completion of doctoral program. *Degree requirements:* For doctorate, one foreign language, thesis/dissertation. *Entrance requirements:* For master's and doctorate, GRE General Test, GRE Subject Test. Additional exam requirements/recommendations for international students: Required—TOEFL. *Application deadline:* For fall admission, 1/15 priority date for domestic students, 12/15 priority date for international students; for spring admission, 9/1 priority date for domestic students, 9/1 priority date for international students. Applications are processed on a rolling basis. Application fee: $45 ($55 for international students). Electronic applications accepted. *Expenses:* Tuition, state resident: full-time $4,908; part-time $205 per credit. Tuition, nonresident: full-time $14,298; part-time $596 per credit. Required fees: $661. Tuition and fees vary according to campus/location and program. *Financial support:* In 2003–04, 8 fellowships with full tuition reimbursements (averaging $15,000 per year), 101 teaching assistantships with full tuition reimbursements (averaging $12,200 per year) were awarded. Research assistantships, Federal Work-Study also available. Support available to part-time students. Financial award application deadline: 2/1. *Faculty research:* Topology, geometry, algebra. *Unit head:* Daniel Maki, Chair, 812-855-2200, Fax: 812-855-0046, E-mail: maki@indiana.edu. *Application contact:* Misty Cummings, Graduate Secretary, 812-855-2645, Fax: 812-855-0046, E-mail: gradmath@indiana.edu.

Indiana University of Pennsylvania, Graduate School and Research, College of Natural Sciences and Mathematics, Department of Mathematics, Indiana, PA 15705-1087. Offers applied mathematics (MS); elementary and middle school mathematics education (M Ed); mathematics education (M Ed). Part-time programs available. *Faculty:* 15 full-time (3 women). *Students:* 12 full-time (3 women), 27 part-time (21 women), 2 international. Average age 27. 29 applicants, 86% accepted. In 2003, 8 degrees awarded. *Degree requirements:* For master's, thesis optional. *Entrance requirements:* For master's, 2 letters of recommendation. Additional exam requirements/recommendations for international students: Required—TOEFL. *Applica-*

Mathematics

Indiana University of Pennsylvania (continued)

tion deadline: For fall admission, 7/1 for domestic students; for spring admission, 11/1 for domestic students. Applications are processed on a rolling basis. Application fee: $30. *Expenses:* Tuition, state resident: full-time $5,518; part-time $307 per credit. Tuition, nonresident: full-time $8,830; part-time $491 per credit. Required fees: $31 per credit. $111 per semester. Tuition and fees vary according to degree level. *Financial support:* In 2003–04, 8 research assistantships were awarded; career-related internships or fieldwork and Federal Work-Study also available. Support available to part-time students. Financial award application deadline: 3/15; financial award applicants required to submit FAFSA. *Unit head:* Dr. Gary S. Stoudt, Chairperson, 724-357-2608, E-mail: gsstoudt@iup.edu.

Indiana University–Purdue University Fort Wayne, School of Arts and Sciences, Department of Mathematical Sciences, Fort Wayne, IN 46805-1499. Offers applied mathematics (MS); mathematics (MS); operations research (MS). Part-time and evening/weekend programs available. *Faculty:* 6 full-time (2 women). *Students:* 2 full-time (0 women), 11 part-time (6 women); includes 1 minority (Asian American or Pacific Islander) Average age 33. 10 applicants, 90% accepted, 2 enrolled. In 2003, 6 degrees awarded. *Entrance requirements:* For master's, minimum GPA of 3.0, major or minor in mathematics. *Application deadline:* For fall admission, 7/1 for domestic students; for spring admission, 12/1 for domestic students. Applications are processed on a rolling basis. Application fee: $30. *Expenses:* Tuition, state resident: full-time $3,443; part-time $191 per credit hour. Tuition, nonresident: full-time $7,760; part-time $431 per credit hour. Required fees: $344; $19 per credit hour. *Financial support:* In 2003–04, 8 teaching assistantships with partial tuition reimbursements (averaging $7,350 per year) were awarded; Federal Work-Study, scholarships/grants, and unspecified assistantships also available. Support available to part-time students. Financial award application deadline: 3/1; financial award applicants required to submit FAFSA. *Faculty research:* Graph theory, biostatistics, statistical design, mathematics education, partial differential equations. *Unit head:* Dr. David A. Legg, Chair, 260-481-6821, Fax: 260-481-6880, E-mail: legg@ipfw.edu. *Application contact:* Dr. W. Douglas Weakley, Director of Graduate Studies, 260-481-6821, Fax: 260-481-6880, E-mail: weakley@ipfw.edu.

Indiana University–Purdue University Indianapolis, School of Science, Department of Mathematical Sciences, Indianapolis, IN 46202-3216. Offers applied mathematics (MS, PhD); applied statistics (MS); mathematics (MS, PhD). Part-time programs available. *Faculty:* 10 full-time (0 women), 1 part-time/adjunct (0 women). *Students:* 20 full-time (10 women), 40 part-time (19 women); includes 4 minority (all Asian Americans or Pacific Islanders), 20 international. Average age 32. In 2003, 13 degrees awarded. Terminal master's awarded for partial completion of doctoral program. *Degree requirements:* For master's, thesis optional; for doctorate, one foreign language, thesis/dissertation. *Entrance requirements:* For doctorate, GRE. Additional exam requirements/recommendations for international students: Required—TOEFL. *Application deadline:* For fall admission, 2/1 for domestic students. Application fee: $45 ($55 for international students). *Expenses:* Tuition, state resident: full-time $4,658; part-time $194 per credit. Tuition, nonresident: full-time $13,444; part-time $560 per credit. Required fees: $571. Tuition and fees vary according to campus/location and program. *Financial support:* In 2003–04, 14 students received support, including 2 research assistantships with tuition reimbursements available (averaging $11,000 per year), 10 teaching assistantships with tuition reimbursements available (averaging $11,000 per year); fellowships with tuition reimbursements available, career-related internships or fieldwork, Federal Work-Study, and tuition waivers (full and partial) also available. Financial award application deadline: 3/1. *Faculty research:* Mathematical physics, analysis, operator theory, functional analysis, integrated systems. *Unit head:* Benzion Boukai, Chair, 317-274-6918, Fax: 317-274-3460, E-mail: bboukai@math.iupui.edu. *Application contact:* Joan Morand, Student Services Specialist, 317-274-4127, Fax: 317-274-3460.

Iowa State University of Science and Technology, Graduate College, College of Liberal Arts and Sciences, Department of Mathematics, Ames, IA 50011. Offers applied mathematics (MS, PhD); mathematics (MS, PhD); school mathematics (MSM). *Faculty:* 45 full-time. *Students:* 48 full-time (13 women), 14 part-time (4 women); includes 1 minority (Asian American or Pacific Islander), 29 international. 72 applicants, 44% accepted, 14 enrolled. In 2003, 17 master's, 2 doctorates awarded. *Median time to degree:* Master's–3 years full-time; doctorate–5.3 years full-time. *Degree requirements:* For master's, thesis or alternative; for doctorate, thesis/dissertation. *Entrance requirements:* For master's and doctorate, GRE General Test. Additional exam requirements/recommendations for international students: Required—TOEFL (paper score 550; computer score 213) or IELTS (score 6.5). *Application deadline:* For fall admission, 2/1 priority date for domestic students, 2/1 priority date for international students. Application fee: $30 ($70 for international students). Electronic applications accepted. Tuition, nonresident: part-time $560 per credit. Required fees: $38 per unit. *Financial support:* In 2003–04, 6 research assistantships with full and partial tuition reimbursements (averaging $15,996 per year), 48 teaching assistantships with full and partial tuition reimbursements (averaging $18,756 per year) were awarded. Fellowships, scholarships/grants, health care benefits, and unspecified assistantships also available. *Unit head:* Dr. Justin R. Peters, Chair, 515-294-1752, Fax: 515-294-5454, E-mail: gradmath@iastate.edu. *Application contact:* Dr. Jonathan Smith, Director of Graduate Education, 515-294-8172, E-mail: gradmath@iastate.edu.

Jackson State University, Graduate School, School of Science and Technology, Department of Mathematics, Jackson, MS 39217. Offers mathematics (MS); mathematics education (MST). Part-time and evening/weekend programs available. *Degree requirements:* For master's, thesis (for some programs), comprehensive exam. *Entrance requirements:* For master's, GRE General Test. Additional exam requirements/recommendations for international students: Required—TOEFL.

Jacksonville State University, College of Graduate Studies and Continuing Education, College of Arts and Sciences, Department of Mathematics, Jacksonville, AL 36265-1602. Offers MS. *Faculty:* 7 full-time (0 women). *Students:* 6 full-time (4 women), 20 part-time (15 women); includes 2 minority (both African Americans), 2 international. In 2003, 4 degrees awarded. *Degree requirements:* For master's, thesis optional. *Entrance requirements:* For master's, GRE General Test or MAT. *Application deadline:* Applications are processed on a rolling basis. Application fee: $20. *Expenses:* Tuition, state resident: full-time $4,040; part-time $202 per credit hour. Tuition, nonresident: full-time $8,080; part-time $404 per credit hour. One-time fee: $20 part-time. *Financial support:* In 2003–04, 3 teaching assistantships were awarded Support available to part-time students. Financial award application deadline: 4/1. *Unit head:* Jeff Dodd, Head, 256-782-5112. *Application contact:* 256-782-5329.

John Carroll University, Graduate School, Department of Mathematics, University Heights, OH 44118-4581. Offers MA, MS. Part-time and evening/weekend programs available. *Faculty:* 15 full-time (2 women). *Students:* 5 full-time (3 women), 15 part-time (12 women). Average age 27. 2 applicants, 100% accepted, 2 enrolled. In 2003, 4 degrees awarded. *Median time to degree:* Master's–2 years full-time, 4 years part-time. *Degree requirements:* For master's, research essay. *Entrance requirements:* For master's, minimum GPA of 2.5, teaching certificate (MA). *Application deadline:* For fall admission, 8/15 for domestic students; for spring admission, 1/3 for domestic students. Applications are processed on a rolling basis. Application fee: $25 ($35 for international students). *Expenses:* Tuition: Part-time $600 per semester hour. Tuition and fees vary according to program. *Financial support:* In 2003–04, 5 students received support, including 5 teaching assistantships with full tuition reimbursements available (averaging $9,700 per year); tuition waivers (partial) also available. Financial award application deadline: 3/1; financial award applicants required to submit FAFSA. *Faculty research:* Algebraic topology, algebra, differential geometry, combinatorics, Lie groups. *Unit head:* Dr. Douglas A. Norris, Chairperson, 216-397-4687, Fax: 216-397-3033, E-mail: norris@jcu.edu. *Application contact:* Dr. David L. Stenson, Coordinator of Student Services, 216-397-4686, Fax: 216-397-3033, E-mail: stenson@jcu.edu.

The Johns Hopkins University, G. W. C. Whiting School of Engineering, Department of Mathematical Sciences, Baltimore, MD 21218-2699. Offers discrete mathematics (MA, MSE, PhD); operations research/optimization/decision science (MA, MSE, PhD); statistics/probability/stochastic processes (MA, MSE, PhD). Terminal master's awarded for partial completion of doctoral program. *Degree requirements:* For master's, thesis (for some programs); for doctorate, thesis/dissertation, oral exam. *Entrance requirements:* For master's and doctorate, GRE General Test, GRE Subject Test. Additional exam requirements/recommendations for international students: Required—TOEFL. Electronic applications accepted. *Expenses:* Tuition: Full-time $28,730; part-time $1,490 per course. Part-time tuition and fees vary according to course load, campus/location and program. *Faculty research:* Discrete mathematics, probability, statistics, optimization and operations research, matrix and numerical analysis.

The Johns Hopkins University, Zanvyl Krieger School of Arts and Sciences, Department of Mathematics, Baltimore, MD 21218-2699. Offers PhD. *Faculty:* 17 full-time (1 woman). *Students:* 30 full-time (5 women); includes 16 minority (all Asian Americans or Pacific Islanders) Average age 26. 95 applicants, 28% accepted, 11 enrolled. In 2003, 4 doctorates awarded. *Degree requirements:* For doctorate, one foreign language, thesis/dissertation, language and 3 qualifying exams. *Entrance requirements:* Additional exam requirements/recommendations for international students: Required—TOEFL. *Application deadline:* For fall admission, 1/15 priority date for domestic students, 1/15 priority date for international students. Application fee: $55. Electronic applications accepted. *Expenses:* Tuition: Full-time $28,730; part-time $1,490 per course. Part-time tuition and fees vary according to course load, campus/location and program. *Financial support:* In 2003–04, 3 fellowships with full tuition reimbursements (averaging $5,000 per year), 30 teaching assistantships with full tuition reimbursements (averaging $15,000 per year) were awarded. Federal Work-Study, institutionally sponsored loans, and tuition waivers (partial) also available. Financial award application deadline: 4/15; financial award applicants required to submit FAFSA. *Faculty research:* Algebraic geometry, number theory, algebraic topology, differential geometry, partial differential equations. Total annual research expenditures: $472,126. *Unit head:* Dr. Christopher Sogge, Chair, 410-516-7397, Fax: 410-516-5549, E-mail: grad@math.jhu.edu. *Application contact:* Charlene Poole, Graduate Program Assistant, 410-516-7399, Fax: 410-516-5549, E-mail: grad@math.jhu.edu.

Kansas State University, Graduate School, College of Arts and Sciences, Department of Mathematics, Manhattan, KS 66506. Offers MS, PhD. Part-time programs available. *Faculty:* 31 full-time (3 women). *Students:* 39 full-time (7 women). Average age 25. 48 applicants, 79% accepted, 13 enrolled. In 2003, 6 master's, 1 doctorate awarded. Terminal master's awarded for partial completion of doctoral program. *Degree requirements:* For master's, thesis or alternative; for doctorate, one foreign language, thesis/dissertation. *Entrance requirements:* For master's, GRE, bachelor's degree in mathematics; for doctorate, master's degree in mathematics. *Application deadline:* For fall admission, 2/1 for domestic students; for spring admission, 10/31 priority date for domestic students. Applications are processed on a rolling basis. Application fee: $0 ($25 for international students). Electronic applications accepted. *Expenses:* Tuition, state resident: part-time $155 per credit hour. Tuition, nonresident: part-time $428 per credit hour. Required fees: $11 per credit hour. *Financial support:* In 2003–04, 36 teaching assistantships with full tuition reimbursements (averaging $13,005 per year) were awarded; Federal Work-Study, institutionally sponsored loans, and scholarships/grants also available. Support available to part-time students. Financial award application deadline: 3/1; financial award applicants required to submit FAFSA. *Faculty research:* Low-dimensional topology, geometry, complex and harmonic analysis, group and representation theory, noncommunicative spaces. Total annual research expenditures: $4.4 million. *Unit head:* Dr. Louis Pigno, Head, 785-532-0559, Fax: 785-532-0546, E-mail: lpigno@ksu.edu. *Application contact:* Pietro Poggi-Corrandi, Director, 785-532-0569, Fax: 785-532-0546, E-mail: pietro@math.ksu.edu.

Kean University, School of Natural, Applied and Health Sciences, Department of Mathematics and Computer Science, Program in Computing, Statistics and Mathematics, Union, NJ 07083. Offers MS. Part-time and evening/weekend programs available. *Faculty:* 25 full-time (7 women). *Students:* 2 full-time (1 woman), 7 part-time (3 women); includes 4 minority (1 African American, 3 Asian Americans or Pacific Islanders). Average age 41. 11 applicants, 55% accepted, 3 enrolled. In 2003, 2 degrees awarded. *Degree requirements:* For master's, thesis or alternative. *Entrance requirements:* For master's, GRE General Test, 2 letters of recommendation, interview. *Application deadline:* For fall admission, 6/15 for domestic students; for spring admission, 11/15 for domestic students. Application fee: $60. *Expenses:* Tuition, state resident: full-time $7,488; part-time $312 per credit. Tuition, nonresident: full-time $9,528; part-time $397 per credit. Required fees: $1,814; $76 per credit. *Financial support:* In 2003–04, research assistantships with full tuition reimbursements (averaging $2,700 per year) *Application contact:* Joanne Morris, Director of Graduate Admissions, 908-527-2665, Fax: 908-527-2286, E-mail: grad_adm@turbo.kean.edu.

Kent State University, College of Arts and Sciences, Department of Mathematical Sciences, Kent, OH 44242-0001. Offers applied mathematics (MA, MS, PhD); pure mathematics (MA, MS, PhD). Part-time programs available. *Degree requirements:* For master's, thesis optional; for doctorate, one foreign language, thesis/dissertation. Electronic applications accepted. *Expenses:* Tuition, state resident: part-time $334 per hour. Tuition, nonresident: part-time $627 per hour. *Faculty research:* Approximation theory, measure theory, ring theory, functional analysis, complex analysis.

See in-depth description on page 545.

Kutztown University of Pennsylvania, College of Graduate Studies and Extended Learning, College of Liberal Arts and Sciences, Program in Mathematics and Computer Science, Kutztown, PA 19530-0730. Offers MS. Part-time and evening/weekend programs available. *Faculty:* 4 part-time/adjunct (2 women). *Students:* 4 full-time (1 woman), 10 part-time (7 women); includes 4 minority (1 African American, 1 American Indian/Alaska Native, 2 Asian Americans or Pacific Islanders), 3 international. Average age 35. In 2003, 10 degrees awarded. *Degree requirements:* For master's, comprehensive exam or thesis. *Entrance requirements:* For master's, GRE General Test. Additional exam requirements/recommendations for international students: Required—TOEFL. *Application deadline:* Applications are processed on a rolling basis. Application fee: $35. Electronic applications accepted. *Expenses:* Tuition, state resident: full-time $5,518; part-time $307 per credit. Tuition, nonresident: full-time $8,830; part-time $491 per credit. Required fees: $1,098. *Financial support:* Career-related internships or fieldwork, Federal Work-Study, and unspecified assistantships available. Financial award application deadline: 3/15; financial award applicants required to submit FAFSA. *Faculty research:* Artificial intelligence, expert systems, neural networks. *Unit head:* William Bateman, Chairperson, 610-683-4410, E-mail: bateman@kutztown.edu.

Lakehead University, Graduate Studies, School of Mathematical Sciences, Thunder Bay, ON P7B 5E1, Canada. Offers computer science (M Sc, MA); mathematics and statistics (M Sc, MA). Part-time and evening/weekend programs available. *Degree requirements:* For master's, thesis optional. *Entrance requirements:* For master's, minimum B average, honours degree in mathematics or computer science. Additional exam requirements/recommendations for international students: Required—TOEFL. *Faculty research:* Numerical analysis, classical analysis, theoretical computer science, abstract harmonic analysis, functional analysis.

Lamar University, College of Graduate Studies, College of Engineering, Department of Mathematics, Beaumont, TX 77710. Offers MS. *Faculty:* 4 full-time (0 women). *Students:* 8 full-time (2 women), (all international). Average age 31. 12 applicants, 17% accepted, 1 enrolled. In 2003, 2 degrees awarded. *Entrance requirements:* For master's, GRE General Test, minimum GPA of 2.5 in last 60 hours of undergraduate course work. Additional exam requirements/recommendations for international students: Required—TOEFL. *Application deadline:* For fall admission, 5/15 for domestic students; for spring admission, 10/1 priority date for domestic students. Applications are processed on a rolling basis. Application fee: $25 ($50 for international students). *Expenses:* Tuition, state resident: part-time $170 per semester hour. Tuition, nonresident: part-time $351 per semester hour. Required fees: $174 per semester hour. One-time fee: $10 part-time. *Financial support:* In 2003–04, 2 research assistantships, 3 teaching assistantships (averaging $6,000 per year) were awarded. Financial award application deadline: 4/1. *Faculty research:* Complex analysis, functional analysis, wavelets, differential equations. Total annual research expenditures: $43,585. *Unit head:* John F. Harvill, Chair, 409-880-8792, Fax: 409-880-8794, E-mail: chair@math.lamar.edu. *Application contact:* Dr. Paul Chiou, Professor, 409-880-8800, Fax: 409-880-8794, E-mail: chiou@math.lamar.edu.

Lehigh University, College of Arts and Sciences, Department of Mathematics, Bethlehem, PA 18015-3094. Offers applied mathematics (MS, PhD); mathematics (MS, PhD); statistics (MS). Part-time programs available. *Faculty:* 17 full-time (1 woman). *Students:* 24 full-time (11 women), 4 part-time (all women); includes 4 minority (2 African Americans, 2 Hispanic Americans), 4 international. Average age 26. 17 applicants, 65% accepted, 8 enrolled. In 2003, 4 master's, 2 doctorates awarded. Terminal master's awarded for partial completion of doctoral program. *Median time to degree:* Master's–2 years full-time; doctorate–6 years full-time. *Degree requirements:* For master's, comprehensive exam; for doctorate, one foreign language, thesis/dissertation, qualifying exams, comprehensive exam. *Entrance requirements:* For master's and doctorate, minimum GPA of 3.0. Additional exam requirements/recommendations for international students: Required—TOEFL. *Application deadline:* For fall admission, 7/15 for domestic students; for spring admission, 12/7 priority date for domestic students. Applications are processed on a rolling basis. Application fee: $50. Electronic applications accepted. *Expenses:* Tuition: Full-time $16,920; part-time $940 per credit hour. Required fees: $200. Tuition and fees vary according to degree level and program. *Financial support:* In 2003–04, 24 students received support, including 1 fellowship with full tuition reimbursement available (averaging $13,000 per year), 2 research assistantships with full tuition reimbursements available (averaging $13,000 per year), 20 teaching assistantships with full tuition reimbursements available (averaging $13,000 per year); scholarships/grants, tuition waivers (partial), and unspecified assistantships also available. Financial award application deadline: 1/15. *Faculty research:* Probability and statistics, differential geometry, set theory, algebra, differential equations. *Unit head:* Dr. Steven Weintraub, Chairman, 610-758-3730, Fax: 610-758-3767, E-mail: shw2@lehigh.edu. *Application contact:* Dr. Garth Isaak, Graduate Coordinator, 610-758-3734, Fax: 610-758-3767, E-mail: mathgrad@lehigh.edu.

See in-depth description on page 547.

Lehman College of the City University of New York, Division of Natural and Social Sciences, Department of Mathematics and Computer Science, Program in Mathematics, Bronx, NY 10468-1589. Offers MA. Part-time and evening/weekend programs available. *Degree requirements:* For master's, one foreign language, thesis or alternative.

Long Island University, C.W. Post Campus, College of Liberal Arts and Sciences, Department of Mathematics, Brookville, NY 11548-1300. Offers applied mathematics (MS); mathematics education (MS); mathematics for secondary school teachers (MS). Part-time and evening/weekend programs available. *Faculty:* 14 full-time (3 women). *Students:* 26 full-time (14 women), 35 part-time (26 women); includes 5 minority (1 African American, 2 Asian Americans or Pacific Islanders, 2 Hispanic Americans). Average age 25. 32 applicants, 81% accepted, 13 enrolled. In 2003, 21 degrees awarded. *Degree requirements:* For master's, thesis or alternative, oral presentation. *Entrance requirements:* Additional exam requirements/recommendations for international students: Required—TOEFL. *Application deadline:* Applications are processed on a rolling basis. Application fee: $30. Electronic applications accepted. *Expenses:* Tuition: Part-time $658 per credit. Tuition and fees vary according to course load, degree level and program. *Financial support:* In 2003–04, 10 students received support. Career-related internships or fieldwork, Federal Work-Study, institutionally sponsored loans, tuition waivers (full and partial), and unspecified assistantships available. Support available to part-time students. Financial award application deadline: 5/15; financial award applicants required to submit CSS PROFILE or FAFSA. *Faculty research:* Differential geometry, topological groups, general topology, number theory, analysis and statistics, numerical analysis. *Unit head:* Dr. Neo Cleopa, Chair, 516-299-2448, Fax: 516-299-4049, E-mail: ncleopa@liu.edu. *Application contact:* Dr. Shahla Ahdout, Graduate Adviser, 516-299-2043, Fax: 516-299-4049, E-mail: sahdout@liu.edu.

Louisiana State University and Agricultural and Mechanical College, Graduate School, College of Arts and Sciences, Department of Mathematics, Baton Rouge, LA 70803. Offers MS, PhD. *Faculty:* 42 full-time (1 woman). *Students:* 69 full-time (17 women), 2 part-time (1 woman); includes 4 minority (2 African Americans, 2 Hispanic Americans), 39 international. Average age 29. 107 applicants, 39% accepted, 12 enrolled. In 2003, 11 master's, 5 doctorates awarded. Terminal master's awarded for partial completion of doctoral program. *Degree requirements:* For doctorate, 2 foreign languages, thesis/dissertation. *Entrance requirements:* For master's and doctorate, GRE General Test, minimum GPA of 3.0. Additional exam requirements/recommendations for international students: Required—TOEFL (minimum score 550 paper-based; 213 computer-based). *Application deadline:* For fall admission, 1/25 priority date for domestic students, 5/15 priority date for international students. Applications are processed on a rolling basis. Application fee: $25. Electronic applications accepted. *Expenses:* Tuition, state resident: part-time $337 per hour. Tuition, nonresident: part-time $577 per hour. *Financial support:* In 2003–04, 34 students received support, including 9 fellowships (averaging $19,361 per year), 7 research assistantships with partial tuition reimbursements available (averaging $16,686 per year), 47 teaching assistantships with partial tuition reimbursements available (averaging $17,751 per year); institutionally sponsored loans, tuition waivers (full), and unspecified assistantships also available. Financial award application deadline: 3/1; financial award applicants required to submit FAFSA. *Faculty research:* Algebra, graph theory and combinatorics, algebraic topology, analysis and probability, topological algebra. Total annual research expenditures: $839,267. *Unit head:* Dr. Lawrence Smolinksy, Associate Chair, 225-578-1570, Fax: 225-578-4276, E-mail: mmsmol@lsu.edu. *Application contact:* Dr. Leonard F. Richardson, Director of Graduate Studies and Assistant Chairman, 225-578-1568, Fax: 225-578-4276, E-mail: rich@math.lsu.edu.

Louisiana Tech University, Graduate School, College of Engineering and Science, Department of Mathematics and Statistics, Ruston, LA 71272. Offers MS. Part-time programs available. *Degree requirements:* For master's, thesis or alternative. *Entrance requirements:* For master's, GRE General Test, minimum GPA of 3.0 in last 60 hours. Additional exam requirements/recommendations for international students: Required—TOEFL. *Expenses:* Tuition, state resident: full-time $3,120. Tuition, nonresident: full-time $9,120. Tuition and fees vary according to course load.

Loyola University Chicago, Graduate School, Department of Mathematical Sciences and Statistics, Chicago, IL 60611-2196. Offers mathematics (MS), including computer science, operations research, pure mathematics, statistics and probability. Part-time and evening/weekend programs available. *Faculty:* 29 full-time (4 women), 18 part-time/adjunct (7 women). *Students:* 11 full-time (7 women), 10 part-time (6 women); includes 4 minority (2 Asian Americans or Pacific Islanders, 2 Hispanic Americans), 9 international. Average age 30. 30 applicants, 83% accepted. In 2003, 7 degrees awarded. *Entrance requirements:* For master's, GRE General Test, minimum B average. Additional exam requirements/recommendations for international students: Required—TOEFL. *Application deadline:* For fall admission, 8/1 for domestic students; for spring admission, 12/1 for domestic students. Application fee: $40. *Expenses:* Tuition: Part-time $578 per credit hour. Tuition and fees vary according to course level and program. *Financial support:* In 2003–04, 8 students received support, including 4 teaching assistantships with tuition reimbursements available (averaging $8,000 per year); career-related internships or fieldwork, Federal Work-Study, institutionally sponsored loans, and tuition waivers (partial) also available. *Faculty research:* Computer science, probability and statistics, differential equations, algebra. Total annual research expenditures: $300,000. *Unit head:* Dr. Joseph H. Mayne, Chair, 773-508-3574, Fax: 773-508-2123, E-mail: jhm@math.luc.edu. *Application contact:* Dr. Anthony Giaquinto, Graduate Director, 773-508-8520, Fax: 773-508-2123.

Marquette University, Graduate School, College of Arts and Sciences, Department of Mathematics, Statistics, and Computer Science, Milwaukee, WI 53201-1881. Offers algebra (PhD); bio-mathematical modeling (PhD); computers (MS); mathematics (MS); mathematics education (MS); statistics (MS). Part-time programs available. *Faculty:* 27 full-time (9 women), 11 part-time/adjunct (5 women). *Students:* 22 full-time (10 women), 12 part-time (4 women), 22 international. Average age 32. 43 applicants, 84% accepted, 11 enrolled. In 2003, 12 degrees awarded. Terminal master's awarded for partial completion of doctoral program. *Degree requirements:* For master's, thesis or alternative, comprehensive exam; for doctorate, 2 foreign languages, thesis/dissertation, comprehensive exam. *Entrance requirements:* For doctorate, sample of scholarly writing. Additional exam requirements/recommendations for international students: Required—TOEFL. Application fee: $40. *Expenses:* Tuition: Full-time $10,080; part-time $630 per credit. Tuition and fees vary according to program. *Financial support:* In 2003–04, 2 research assistantships, 20 teaching assistantships were awarded. Federal Work-Study, institutionally sponsored loans, scholarships/grants, and tuition waivers (full and partial) also available. Support available to part-time students. Financial award application deadline: 2/15. *Faculty research:* Models of physiological systems, mathematical immunology, computational group theory, mathematical logic. Total annual research expenditures: $77,233. *Unit head:* Dr. Peter Jones, Chairman, 414-288-7573, Fax: 414-288-1578. *Application contact:* Dr. Gary Krenz, Director of Graduate Studies, 414-288-6345.

Marshall University, Academic Affairs Division, Graduate College, College of Science, Department of Mathematics, Huntington, WV 25755. Offers MA, MS. *Faculty:* 8 full-time (3 women). *Students:* 8 full-time (4 women), 4 part-time (2 women), 2 international. Average age 32. In 2003, 5 degrees awarded. *Degree requirements:* For master's, thesis (for some programs). *Entrance requirements:* For master's, GRE General Test. Tuition, area resident: Part-time $1,730 per semester. *Expenses:* Tuition, state resident: part-time $3,295 per semester. Tuition, nonresident: part-time $5,003 per semester. *Unit head:* Dr. Ralph Oberste-Vorth, Chairperson, 304-696-6010, E-mail: oberstevorth@marshall.edu. *Application contact:* Information Contact, 304-746-1900, Fax: 304-746-1902, E-mail: services@marshall.edu.

Massachusetts Institute of Technology, School of Science, Department of Mathematics, Cambridge, MA 02139-4307. Offers PhD. *Faculty:* 52 full-time (2 women), 1 part-time/adjunct (0 women). *Students:* 116 full-time (23 women); includes 7 minority (2 African Americans, 4 Asian Americans or Pacific Islanders, 1 Hispanic American), 67 international. Average age 25. 410 applicants, 9% accepted, 19 enrolled. In 2003, 19 doctorates awarded. *Degree requirements:* For doctorate, one foreign language, thesis/dissertation, qualifying exam, comprehensive exam. *Entrance requirements:* For doctorate, GRE General Test, GRE Subject Test in mathematics. Additional exam requirements/recommendations for international students: Required—TOEFL. *Application deadline:* For fall admission, 1/2 for domestic students, 1/1 for international students. Application fee: $70. Electronic applications accepted. *Expenses:* Tuition: Full-time $29,400. Required fees: $200. *Financial support:* In 2003–04, 30 fellowships with tuition reimbursements, 21 research assistantships with tuition reimbursements (averaging $23,760 per year), 65 teaching assistantships with tuition reimbursements (averaging $18,270 per year) were awarded. Federal Work-Study, institutionally sponsored loans, scholarships/grants, traineeships, health care benefits, unspecified assistantships, and graduate instructorships also available. *Faculty research:* Analysis, topology, algebraic geometry, logic, Lie theory, combinatorics, fluid dynamics, theoretical computer science. Total annual research expenditures: $3.1 million. *Unit head:* Prof. David A. Vogan, Head, 617-253-4381, Fax: 617-253-4358, E-mail: dept@math.mit.edu. *Application contact:* Linda Okun, Graduate Administrator, 617-253-2689, Fax: 617-253-4358, E-mail: gradofc@math.mit.edu.

McGill University, Faculty of Graduate and Postdoctoral Studies, Faculty of Science, Department of Mathematics and Statistics, Montréal, QC H3A 2T5, Canada. Offers M Sc, MA, PhD. Part-time programs available. *Faculty:* 39 full-time (2 women). *Students:* 69 full-time, 5 part-time. 294 applicants, 32% accepted, 30 enrolled. In 2003, 12 master's, 1 doctorate awarded. *Degree requirements:* For master's, thesis; for doctorate, one foreign language, thesis/dissertation, comprehensive exam. *Entrance requirements:* For master's, minimum GPA of 3.0. Additional exam requirements/recommendations for international students: Required—TOEFL. *Application deadline:* For fall admission, 3/1 for domestic students; for winter admission, 10/1 for domestic students. Applications are processed on a rolling basis. Application fee: $60 Canadian dollars. Electronic applications accepted. Tuition, area resident: Full-time $1,668. *Expenses:* Tuition, state resident: full-time $4,173. Tuition, nonresident: full-time $9,468. Required fees: $1,081. *Financial support:* In 2003–04, 21 fellowships, 27 research assistantships, 31 teaching assistantships (averaging $6,000 per year) were awarded. *Unit head:* K. N. Gowrisankaran, Chair, 514-398-7373, Fax: 514-398-3899, E-mail: gowri@math.mcgill.ca. *Application contact:* Carmen Baldonado, Graduate Program Coordinator, 514-398-0503, Fax: 514-398-3899, E-mail: gradprog@math.mcgill.ca.

McMaster University, School of Graduate Studies, Faculty of Science, Department of Mathematics and Statistics, Hamilton, ON L8S 4M2, Canada. Offers mathematics (PhD); mathematics and statistics (M Sc). Part-time programs available. *Degree requirements:* For master's, thesis or alternative, oral exam; for doctorate, thesis/dissertation, comprehensive exam. *Entrance requirements:* For master's, minimum B+ average in last year of honors degree; for doctorate, minimum B+ average, M Sc in mathematics or statistics. Additional exam requirements/recommendations for international students: Required—TOEFL (minimum score 550 paper-based; 213 computer-based). *Faculty research:* Algebra, analysis, applied mathematics, geometry and topology, probability and statistics.

McNeese State University, Graduate School, College of Science, Department of Mathematics, Computer Science, and Statistics, Lake Charles, LA 70609. Offers computer science (MS); mathematics (MS); statistics (MS). Evening/weekend programs available. *Degree requirements:* For master's, thesis or alternative, written exam, comprehensive exam. *Entrance requirements:* For master's, GRE General Test.

Memorial University of Newfoundland, School of Graduate Studies, Department of Mathematics and Statistics, St. John's, NL A1C 5S7, Canada. Offers mathematics (M Sc, PhD); statistics (MAS, PhD). Part-time programs available. *Students:* 31 full-time, 1 part-time. 113 applicants, 15% accepted, 14 enrolled. In 2003, 6 master's, 1 doctorate awarded. *Degree requirements:* For master's, thesis, practicum and report (MAS); for doctorate, thesis/dissertation, oral defense of thesis, comprehensive exam. *Entrance requirements:* For doctorate, MAS or M Sc in mathematics and statistics. *Application deadline:* Applications are processed on a rolling basis. Application fee: $40. Electronic applications accepted. Tuition and fees charges are reported in Canadian dollars. *Expenses:* Tuition, state resident: part-time $733 Canadian dollars per semester. Tuition, nonresident: part-time $953 Canadian dollars per semester. Required fees: $194 Canadian dollars per year. Tuition and fees vary according to degree level and program. *Financial support:* Fellowships, teaching assistantships available. Financial award application deadline: 1/31. *Faculty research:* Algebra, topology, applied mathematics, mathematical statistics, applied statistics and probability. *Unit head:* Dr. Bruce Watson, Interim Head, 709-737-8783, Fax: 709-787-3010, E-mail: head@math.mun.ca. *Application contact:* Dr. Wanda Heath, Secretary to Department Head, 709-737-8783, Fax: 709-737-3010, E-mail: mathstat@math.mun.ca.

Miami University, Graduate School, College of Arts and Sciences, Department of Mathematics and Statistics, Program in Mathematics, Oxford, OH 45056. Offers mathematics (MA, MAT, MS); mathematics/operations research (MS). Part-time programs available. *Students:* 21 full-time (7 women), 1 (woman) part-time, 2 international. 23 applicants, 83% accepted, 8 enrolled. In 2003, 11 degrees awarded. *Degree requirements:* For master's, final exam. *Entrance requirements:* For master's, minimum undergraduate GPA of 3.0 during previous 2 years or 2.75 overall. Additional exam requirements/recommendations for international students: Required—TOEFL, TWE. *Application deadline:* For fall admission, 3/1 priority date for domestic students, 3/1 priority date for international students. Applications are processed on a rolling basis. Application fee: $35. Electronic applications accepted. Tuition, area resident: Full-time $9,346. International tuition: $19,924 full-time. Full-time tuition and fees vary according to

Mathematics

Miami University (continued)

course level and campus/location. *Financial support:* Fellowships, research assistantships, teaching assistantships, Federal Work-Study and tuition waivers (full) available. Financial award application deadline: 3/1. *Application contact:* Dr. Robert Schaefer, Director of Graduate Studies, 513-529-5818, E-mail: math@muohio.edu.

See in-depth description on page 551.

Michigan State University, Graduate School, College of Natural Science, Department of Mathematics, East Lansing, MI 48824. Offers applied mathematics (MS, PhD); industrial mathematics (MS); mathematics (MAT, MS, PhD); mathematics education (PhD). *Faculty:* 58 full-time (11 women). *Students:* 124 full-time (41 women), 10 part-time (4 women); includes 7 minority (2 African Americans, 3 Asian Americans or Pacific Islanders, 2 Hispanic Americans), 86 international. Average age 29. 185 applicants, 17% accepted. In 2003, 24 master's, 8 doctorates awarded. *Degree requirements:* For master's, certifying exam, thesis optional; for doctorate, one foreign language, thesis/dissertation, qualifying exam, seminar presentations, comprehensive exam. *Entrance requirements:* For master's, GRE General Test, bachelor's degree in mathematics, physics, or engineering, mathematics course work beyond calculus, 3 letters of recommendation; for doctorate, GRE General Test, minimum GPA of 3.0, MS in mathematics or equivalent, 3 letters of recommendation. Additional exam requirements/recommendations for international students: Required—TOEFL (minimum score 550 paper-based; 213 computer-based), Michigan State University ELT (85), Michigan ELAB (83). *Application deadline:* For fall admission, 2/1 for domestic students. Application fee: $50. Electronic applications accepted. *Expenses:* Tuition, state resident: part-time $291 per hour. Tuition, nonresident: part-time $589 per hour. *Financial support:* In 2003–04, 17 fellowships with tuition reimbursements (averaging $3,321 per year), 31 research assistantships with tuition reimbursements (averaging $13,512 per year), 87 teaching assistantships with tuition reimbursements (averaging $12,854 per year) were awarded. Financial award applicants required to submit FAFSA. *Faculty research:* Applied and industrial mathematics, analysis, geometry and topology, logic, combinatorics and graph theory. Total annual research expenditures: $2.3 million. *Unit head:* Dr. Peter W. Bates, Chairperson, 517-353-9680, Fax: 517-432-1562, E-mail: bates@math.msu.edu. *Application contact:* Zhengfang Zhou, Graduate Director, 517-353-4650, Fax: 517-432-1562, E-mail: grad@mth.msu.edu.

Michigan Technological University, Graduate School, College of Sciences and Arts, Department of Mathematical Sciences, Houghton, MI 49931-1295. Offers mathematical sciences (PhD); mathematics (MS). Part-time programs available. *Faculty:* 27 full-time (5 women), 1 part-time/adjunct (0 women). *Students:* 32 full-time (16 women), 3 part-time (1 woman), 19 international. Average age 28. 74 applicants, 49% accepted, 9 enrolled. In 2003, 5 master's, 2 doctorates awarded. *Degree requirements:* For master's, thesis/dissertation, comprehensive exam, registration; for doctorate, thesis/dissertation, comprehensive exam, registration (for some programs). *Entrance requirements:* Additional exam requirements/recommendations for international students: Required—TOEFL. *Application deadline:* For fall admission, 3/15 for domestic students. Applications are processed on a rolling basis. Application fee: $40 ($45 for international students). Electronic applications accepted. Tuition, nonresident: full-time $9,552; part-time $398 per credit. Required fees: $768. *Financial support:* In 2003–04, 19 students received support, including 1 fellowship with full tuition reimbursement available (averaging $13,500 per year), research assistantships with full tuition reimbursements available (averaging $8,950 per year), 18 teaching assistantships with full tuition reimbursements available (averaging $8,950 per year); career-related internships or fieldwork, Federal Work-Study, institutionally sponsored loans, scholarships/grants, traineeships, unspecified assistantships, and co-op also available. Support available to part-time students. Financial award application deadline: 4/1; financial award applicants required to submit FAFSA. *Faculty research:* Combinatorics, statistics and probability, discrete structures, fluid dynamics, mathematical modeling. Total annual research expenditures: $209,633. *Unit head:* Dr. Alphonse H. Baartmans, Chair, 906-487-2068, Fax: 906-487-3133, E-mail: baartman@mtu.edu. *Application contact:* Denise J. Laux, Office Assistant 5, 906-487-2068, Fax: 906-487-3133, E-mail: djlaux@mtu.edu.

Announcement: Graduate Teaching Assistants receive comprehensive training, including a course entitled "Teaching College Mathematics" and a teaching seminar. Each new GTA has a mentor chosen from the department's most popular teachers. This program has led to striking decreases in student complaints and striking increases in GTAs' teaching evaluations.

See in-depth description on page 557.

Middle Tennessee State University, College of Graduate Studies, College of Basic and Applied Sciences, Department of Mathematical Sciences, Murfreesboro, TN 37132. Offers mathematics (MS); mathematics education (MST). Part-time and evening/weekend programs available. *Faculty:* 19 full-time (8 women). *Students:* Average age 33. 5 applicants, 100% accepted. In 2003, 13 degrees awarded. *Degree requirements:* For master's, comprehensive exam. *Entrance requirements:* For master's, GRE General Test or MAT. Additional exam requirements/recommendations for international students: Required—TOEFL (minimum score 525 paper-based; 195 computer-based). *Application deadline:* For fall admission, 8/1 for domestic students. Applications are processed on a rolling basis. Application fee: $25. Electronic applications accepted. *Expenses:* Tuition, state resident: full-time $4,206. Tuition, nonresident: full-time $12,138. *Financial support:* In 2003–04, 9 students received support; teaching assistantships, institutionally sponsored loans available. Support available to part-time students. Financial award application deadline: 5/1; financial award applicants required to submit FAFSA. Total annual research expenditures: $7,876. *Unit head:* Dr. Curtis K. Church, Chair, 615-898-2669, Fax: 615-898-5422, E-mail: jallbritten@mtsu.edu.

Minnesota State University Mankato, College of Graduate Studies, College of Science, Engineering and Technology, Department of Mathematics and Statistics, Program in Computers, Mankato, MN 56001. Offers mathematics: computer science (MS). *Students:* 4 full-time (0 women), 1 part-time. Average age 32. *Degree requirements:* For master's, one foreign language, thesis or alternative, comprehensive exam. *Entrance requirements:* For master's, GRE General Test, GRE Subject Test, minimum GPA of 3.0 during previous 2 years. *Application deadline:* For fall admission, 7/9 for domestic students; for spring admission, 11/27 for domestic students. Applications are processed on a rolling basis. Application fee: $40. *Expenses:* Tuition, state resident: part-time $226 per credit hour. Tuition, nonresident: part-time $339 per credit hour. Tuition and fees vary according to reciprocity agreements. *Financial support:* Fellowships with full tuition reimbursements, research assistantships with full tuition reimbursements, teaching assistantships with full tuition reimbursements, Federal Work-Study and institutionally sponsored loans available. Support available to part-time students. Financial award application deadline: 3/15; financial award applicants required to submit FAFSA. *Unit head:* Dr. Lee Cornell, Chairperson, 507-389-2968. *Application contact:* Joni Roberts, Admissions Coordinator, 507-389-5244, Fax: 507-389-5974, E-mail: grad@mankato.msus.edu.

Minnesota State University Mankato, College of Graduate Studies, College of Science, Engineering and Technology, Department of Mathematics and Statistics, Program in Mathematics, Mankato, MN 56001. Offers MA, MS. *Faculty:* 13 full-time (3 women). *Students:* 8 full-time (4 women), 7 part-time (1 woman). Average age 32. *Degree requirements:* For master's, one foreign language, thesis or alternative, comprehensive exam. *Entrance requirements:* For master's, GRE General Test, minimum GPA of 3.0 during previous 2 years. *Application deadline:* For fall admission, 7/9 for domestic students; for spring admission, 11/27 for domestic students. Applications are processed on a rolling basis. Application fee: $40. *Expenses:* Tuition, state resident: part-time $226 per credit hour. Tuition, nonresident: part-time $339 per credit hour. Tuition and fees vary according to reciprocity agreements. *Financial support:* Research assistantships with partial tuition reimbursements, teaching assistantships with partial tuition reimbursements available. Financial award application deadline: 3/15; financial award applicants required to submit FAFSA. *Application contact:* Joni Roberts, Admissions Coordinator, 507-389-5244, Fax: 507-389-5974, E-mail: grad@mankato.msus.edu.

Mississippi College, Graduate School, College of Arts and Sciences, Department of Mathematics and Computer Science, Clinton, MS 39058. Offers computer science (MS); mathematics (MS). *Degree requirements:* For master's, comprehensive exam. *Entrance requirements:* For master's, minimum GPA of 2.5.

Mississippi College, Graduate School, College of Arts and Sciences, Program in Combined Sciences, Clinton, MS 39058. Offers biology (MCS); chemistry (MCS); mathematics (MCS). *Degree requirements:* For master's, thesis or alternative, comprehensive exam. *Entrance requirements:* For master's, GRE General Test, minimum GPA of 2.5.

Mississippi State University, College of Arts and Sciences, Department of Mathematics and Statistics, Mississippi State, MS 39762. Offers mathematical sciences (PhD); mathematics (MS); statistics (MS). Part-time programs available. *Faculty:* 35 full-time (16 women). *Students:* 30 full-time (15 women), 6 part-time (4 women); includes 1 minority (African American), 25 international. Average age 30. 46 applicants, 35% accepted, 9 enrolled. In 2003, 7 master's, 2 doctorates awarded. Terminal master's awarded for partial completion of doctoral program. *Degree requirements:* For master's, comprehensive oral or written exam, thesis optional; for doctorate, one foreign language, thesis/dissertation, comprehensive oral and written exam. *Entrance requirements:* For master's, minimum GPA of 2.75; for doctorate, GRE. Additional exam requirements/recommendations for international students: Required—TOEFL. *Application deadline:* For fall admission, 3/15 for domestic students; for spring admission, 11/1 for domestic students. Applications are processed on a rolling basis. Application fee: $25 for international students. *Expenses:* Tuition, state resident: full-time $3,874; part-time $215 per hour. Tuition, nonresident: full-time $8,780; part-time $488 per hour. International tuition: $9,105 full-time. Tuition and fees vary according to course load. *Financial support:* In 2003–04, 17 teaching assistantships with full tuition reimbursements (averaging $9,284 per year) were awarded; Federal Work-Study, institutionally sponsored loans, tuition waivers (partial), and unspecified assistantships also available. Financial award applicants required to submit FAFSA. *Faculty research:* Differential equations, algebra, numerical analysis, functional analysis, applied statistics. Total annual research expenditures: $107,993. *Unit head:* Dr. Michael Neuman, Interim Head and Professor, 662-325-3414, Fax: 662-325-0005, E-mail: office@math.msstate.edu. *Application contact:* Diane D. Wolfe, Director of Admissions, 662-325-2224, Fax: 662-325-7360, E-mail: admit@admissions.msstate.edu.

Montana State University–Bozeman, College of Graduate Studies, College of Letters and Science, Department of Mathematical Sciences, Bozeman, MT 59717. Offers mathematics (MS, PhD); statistics (MS, PhD). Part-time programs available. Postbaccalaureate distance learning degree programs offered (minimal on-campus study). *Faculty:* 31 full-time (8 women), 12 part-time/adjunct (6 women). *Students:* 9 full-time (5 women), 65 part-time (28 women); includes 2 minority (both Asian Americans or Pacific Islanders), 7 international. Average age 30. 31 applicants, 84% accepted, 21 enrolled. In 2003, 20 master's, 6 doctorates awarded. *Degree requirements:* For master's, thesis (for some programs), comprehensive exam, registration; for doctorate, thesis/dissertation, comprehensive exam, registration. *Entrance requirements:* For master's and doctorate, GRE General Test. Additional exam requirements/recommendations for international students: Required—TOEFL (minimum score 550 paper-based; 213 computer-based). *Application deadline:* For fall admission, 7/15 priority date for domestic students, 5/15 priority date for international students; for spring admission, 12/1 priority date for domestic students, 10/1 priority date for international students. Applications are processed on a rolling basis. Application fee: $50. Electronic applications accepted. *Expenses:* Tuition, state resident: full-time $3,907; part-time $163 per credit. Tuition, nonresident: full-time $12,383; part-time $516 per credit. Required fees: $890; $445 per term. Tuition and fees vary according to course load and program. *Financial support:* In 2003–04, 55 students received support, including 5 research assistantships with full tuition reimbursements available (averaging $14,000 per year), 47 teaching assistantships with full tuition reimbursements available (averaging $12,500 per year); career-related internships or fieldwork, scholarships/grants, health care benefits, tuition waivers (full), and unspecified assistantships also available. Support available to part-time students. Financial award application deadline: 3/1; financial award applicants required to submit FAFSA. *Faculty research:* Applied mathematics, dynamical systems, statistics, mathematics education, mathematical and computational biology. Total annual research expenditures: $402,126. *Unit head:* Dr. Kenneth Bowers, Head, 406-994-3604, Fax: 406-994-1789, E-mail: grad@math.montana.edu.

Montclair State University, The Graduate School, College of Science and Mathematics, Department of Mathematics, Programs in Mathematics, Upper Montclair, NJ 07043-1624. Offers computer science (MS); mathematics education (MS); pure and applied mathematics (MS); statistics (MS). Part-time and evening/weekend programs available. *Faculty:* 31 full-time (13 women), 25 part-time/adjunct. *Students:* 10 full-time (5 women), 40 part-time (24 women); includes 3 minority (1 African American, 2 Asian Americans or Pacific Islanders), 3 international. 40 applicants, 73% accepted, 19 enrolled. In 2003, 50 degrees awarded. *Degree requirements:* For master's, comprehensive exam. *Entrance requirements:* For master's, GRE General Test, minimum GPA of 2.67, 2 letters of recommendation. Additional exam requirements/recommendations for international students: Required—TOEFL (minimum score 550 paper-based; 213 computer-based). *Application deadline:* Applications are processed on a rolling basis. Application fee: $60. Electronic applications accepted. *Expenses:* Tuition, state resident: full-time $8,771; part-time $323 per credit. Tuition, nonresident: full-time $10,365; part-time $470 per credit. Required fees: $42 per credit. Tuition and fees vary according to degree level and program. *Financial support:* In 2003–04, research assistantships with full tuition reimbursements (averaging $5,000 per year); Federal Work-Study, scholarships/grants, and unspecified assistantships also available. Support available to part-time students. Financial award application deadline: 3/1; financial award applicants required to submit FAFSA. *Unit head:* Dr. Ted Williamson, Advisor, 973-655-5146, E-mail: williamsont@mail.montclair.edu.

Morgan State University, School of Graduate Studies, School of Computer, Mathematical, and Natural Sciences, Department of Mathematics, Baltimore, MD 21251. Offers MA. Part-time and evening/weekend programs available. *Faculty:* 7 full-time (1 woman). *Students:* 5 full-time (2 women), 5 part-time (1 woman); includes 5 minority (all African Americans), 2 international. *Degree requirements:* For master's, thesis, comprehensive exam. *Entrance requirements:* For master's, GRE. Additional exam requirements/recommendations for international students: Required—TOEFL (minimum score 550 paper-based; 213 computer-based). *Application deadline:* For fall admission, 2/1 for domestic students; for spring admission, 10/1 for domestic students. Applications are processed on a rolling basis. Application fee: $0. *Expenses:* Tuition, state resident: part-time $215 per credit hour. Tuition, nonresident: part-time $409 per credit hour. Required fees: $48 per credit hour. *Financial support:* Application deadline: 4/1. *Faculty research:* Number theory, semigroups, analysis, operations research. *Unit head:* Dr. Gaston M. Guerekata, Chairman, 443-885-3965. *Application contact:* Dr. James E. Waller, Admissions and Programs Officer, 443-885-3185, Fax: 443-885-8226, E-mail: jwaller@moac.morgan.edu.

Murray State University, College of Science, Engineering and Technology, Department of Mathematics, Murray, KY 42071-0009. Offers MA, MAT, MS. Part-time programs available. *Degree requirements:* For master's, thesis (for some programs). *Entrance requirements:* For master's, GRE General Test. Additional exam requirements/recommendations for international students: Required—TOEFL.

Naval Postgraduate School, Graduate Programs, Department of Mathematics, Monterey, CA 93943. Offers MS, PhD. Program only open to commissioned officers of the United States and friendly nations and selected United States federal civilian employees. Part-time programs available. *Degree requirements:* For master's, thesis; for doctorate, one foreign language, thesis/dissertation.

New Jersey Institute of Technology, Office of Graduate Studies, College of Science and Liberal Arts, Department of Mathematical Sciences, Program in Mathematics Science, Newark, NJ 07102. Offers PhD. Part-time and evening/weekend programs available. *Students:* 31 full-time (10 women), 4 part-time; includes 4 minority (all Asian Americans or Pacific

Islanders), 22 international. Average age 30. 44 applicants, 73% accepted, 15 enrolled. *Entrance requirements:* For doctorate, GRE General Test, minimum graduate GPA of 3.5. *Application deadline:* For fall admission, 6/5 for domestic students; for spring admission, 10/15 for domestic students. Applications are processed on a rolling basis. Application fee: $50. Electronic applications accepted. *Expenses:* Tuition, state resident: full-time $9,620; part-time $520 per credit. Tuition, nonresident: full-time $13,542; part-time $715 per credit. Tuition and fees vary according to course load. *Financial support:* Fellowships with full and partial tuition reimbursements, research assistantships with full and partial tuition reimbursements, teaching assistantships with full and partial tuition reimbursements, career-related internships or fieldwork, Federal Work-Study, institutionally sponsored loans, and unspecified assistantships available. Financial award application deadline: 3/15. *Application contact:* Kathryn Kelly, Director of Admissions, 973-596-3300, Fax: 973-596-3461, E-mail: admissions@njit.edu.

New Mexico Institute of Mining and Technology, Graduate Studies, Department of Mathematics, Socorro, NM 87801. Offers applied math (PhD); mathematics (MS); operations research (MS). *Faculty:* 11 full-time (0 women), 2 part-time/adjunct (1 woman). *Students:* 9 full-time (4 women), 3 part-time; includes 2 minority (both Hispanic Americans), 5 international. Average age 26. 18 applicants, 6 enrolled. In 2003, 3 degrees awarded. *Degree requirements:* For master's, thesis optional; for doctorate, thesis/dissertation. *Entrance requirements:* For master's, GRE General Test. Additional exam requirements/recommendations for international students: Required—TOEFL (minimum score 540 paper-based; 207 computer-based). *Application deadline:* For fall admission, 3/1 for domestic students; for spring admission, 6/1 for domestic students. Applications are processed on a rolling basis. Application fee: $16 ($30 for international students). *Expenses:* Tuition, state resident: full-time $2,276; part-time $126 per credit. Tuition, nonresident: full-time $9,170; part-time $509 per credit. Required fees: $924; $27 per credit. $214 per term. Part-time tuition and fees vary according to course load. *Financial support:* In 2003–04, 8 teaching assistantships with full and partial tuition reimbursements (averaging $10,888 per year) were awarded; fellowships, research assistantships, Federal Work-Study and institutionally sponsored loans also available. Financial award application deadline: 3/1; financial award applicants required to submit CSS PROFILE or FAFSA. *Faculty research:* Applied mathematics, differential equations, industrial mathematics, numerical analysis, stochastic processes. *Unit head:* Brian Borchers, Chairman, 505-835-5393, Fax: 505-835-5813, E-mail: borchers@nmt.edu. *Application contact:* Dr. David B. Johnson, Dean of Graduate Studies, 505-835-5513, Fax: 505-835-5476, E-mail: graduate@nmt.edu.

New Mexico State University, Graduate School, College of Arts and Sciences, Department of Mathematical Sciences, Las Cruces, NM 88003-8001. Offers MS, PhD. Part-time programs available. *Faculty:* 29 full-time (9 women), 3 part-time/adjunct (1 woman). *Students:* 32 full-time (8 women), 7 part-time (3 women); includes 7 minority (1 African American, 2 Asian Americans or Pacific Islanders, 4 Hispanic Americans), 19 international. Average age 31. 31 applicants, 81% accepted, 5 enrolled. In 2003, 4 master's, 1 doctorate awarded. *Degree requirements:* For master's, final oral exam, thesis optional; for doctorate, one foreign language, thesis/dissertation, final oral exam, comprehensive exam. *Entrance requirements:* Additional exam requirements/recommendations for international students: Required—TOEFL (minimum score 530 paper-based; 197 computer-based). *Application deadline:* For fall admission, 7/1 priority date for domestic students, 3/1 priority date for international students; for spring admission, 11/1 for domestic students, 10/1 for international students. Applications are processed on a rolling basis. Application fee: $30 ($50 for international students). Electronic applications accepted. *Expenses:* Tuition, state resident: full-time $2,670; part-time $151 per credit. Tuition, nonresident: full-time $10,596; part-time $481 per credit. Required fees: $954. *Financial support:* In 2003–04, 1 research assistantship, 30 teaching assistantships were awarded. Fellowships, scholarships/grants and unspecified assistantships also available. Financial award application deadline: 3/15. *Faculty research:* Commutative algebra, mathematics education, dynamical systems, harmonic analysis and applications, algebraic topology. *Unit head:* Dr. Ross Staffeldt, Head, 505-646-3901, Fax: 505-646-1064, E-mail: ross@nmsu.edu. *Application contact:* Dr. Irena Swanson, Professor, 505-646-3901, Fax: 505-646-1064, E-mail: gradcomm@nmsu.edu.

New York University, Graduate School of Arts and Science, Courant Institute of Mathematical Sciences, Department of Mathematics, New York, NY 10012-1019. Offers atmosphere-ocean science and mathematics (PhD); mathematics (MS, PhD); mathematics and statistics/operations research (MS); mathematics in finance (MS); scientific computing (MS). Part-time and evening/weekend programs available. *Faculty:* 46 full-time (0 women). *Students:* 135 full-time (24 women), 83 part-time (28 women); includes 28 minority (2 African Americans, 23 Asian Americans or Pacific Islanders, 3 Hispanic Americans), 76 international. Average age 28. 742 applicants, 41% accepted. In 2003, 40 master's, 25 doctorates awarded. *Degree requirements:* For master's, thesis optional; for doctorate, one foreign language, thesis/dissertation, oral and written exams. *Entrance requirements:* For master's and doctorate, GRE General Test, GRE Subject Test. Additional exam requirements/recommendations for international students: Required—TOEFL. *Application deadline:* For fall admission, 1/4 for domestic students; for spring admission, 11/1 for domestic students. Application fee: $75. *Expenses:* Tuition: Full-time $22,056; part-time $919 per credit. Required fees: $1,664; $49 per credit. Tuition and fees vary according to course load and program. *Financial support:* Fellowships with tuition reimbursements, research assistantships with tuition reimbursements, teaching assistantships with tuition reimbursements, Federal Work-Study and institutionally sponsored loans available. Financial award application deadline: 1/4; financial award applicants required to submit FAFSA. *Faculty research:* Partial differential equations, computational science, applied mathematics, geometry and topology, probability and stochastic processes. *Unit head:* Mel Hausner, Chairman, 212-998-3238, Fax: 212-995-4121. *Application contact:* Fedor Bogomolov, Director of Graduate Studies, 212-998-3238, Fax: 212-995-4121, E-mail: admissions@math.nyu.edu.

See in-depth description on page 559.

Nicholls State University, Graduate Studies, College of Arts and Sciences, Department of Mathematics, Thibodaux, LA 70310. Offers applied mathematics (MS). Part-time and evening/weekend programs available. *Faculty:* 5 full-time (0 women). *Students:* 15 full-time (7 women), 1 (woman) part-time; includes 2 minority (both Asian Americans or Pacific Islanders) Average age 23. 7 applicants, 100% accepted, 7 enrolled. In 2003, 4 degrees awarded. *Median time to degree:* Master's–2 years full-time. *Degree requirements:* For master's, comprehensive exam. *Entrance requirements:* For master's, GRE General Test. *Application deadline:* For fall admission, 6/17 for domestic students; for spring admission, 11/15 priority date for domestic students. Applications are processed on a rolling basis. Application fee: $20 ($30 for international students). Electronic applications accepted. Tuition, area resident: Part-time $341 per course. *Expenses:* Tuition, state resident: full-time $2,681. Tuition, nonresident: full-time $8,129. International tuition: $8,249 full-time. Tuition and fees vary according to course load. *Financial support:* In 2003–04, 12 students received support, including teaching assistantships with full tuition reimbursements available (averaging $10,000 per year); Federal Work-Study, scholarships/grants, and unspecified assistantships also available. Support available to part-time students. Financial award application deadline: 6/17. *Faculty research:* Operations research, statistics, numerical analysis, algebra. *Unit head:* Dr. Donald M. Bardwell, Head, 985-448-4380, E-mail: math-dmb@nicholls.edu.

North Carolina Central University, Division of Academic Affairs, College of Arts and Sciences, Department of Mathematics, Durham, NC 27707-3129. Offers MS. Part-time and evening/weekend programs available. *Faculty:* 15 full-time (2 women), 10 part-time/adjunct (2 women). *Students:* 6 full-time (2 women), 9 part-time (3 women); includes 10 minority (7 African Americans, 3 Asian Americans or Pacific Islanders), 1 international. Average age 33. 2 applicants, 100% accepted, 0 enrolled. In 2003, 1 degree awarded. *Degree requirements:* For master's, one foreign language, thesis, comprehensive exam. *Entrance requirements:* For master's, minimum GPA of 3.0 in major, 2.5 overall. Additional exam requirements/recommendations for international students: Required—TOEFL. *Application deadline:* For fall admission, 8/1 for domestic students. Application fee: $30. *Expenses:* Tuition, state resident: full-time $3,366. Tuition, nonresident: full-time $12,872. *Financial support:* Research assistantships, Federal Work-Study, institutionally sponsored loans, and unspecified assistantships available. Support available to part-time students. Financial award application deadline: 5/1; financial award applicants required to submit FAFSA. *Faculty research:* Structure theorems for Lie algebra, Kleene monoids and semi-groups, theoretical computer science, mathematics education. *Unit head:* Dr. Alade O. Tokuta, Chairperson, 919-560-6315, E-mail: atokuta@wpo.nccu.edu. *Application contact:* Dr. Mattie Moss, Dean, 919-560-6368, Fax: 919-530-5361, E-mail: mmoss@wpo.nccu.edu.

North Carolina State University, Graduate School, College of Physical and Mathematical Sciences, Department of Mathematics, Program in Mathematics, Raleigh, NC 27695. Offers MS, PhD. *Faculty:* 66 full-time (8 women), 20 part-time/adjunct (1 woman). *Students:* 56 full-time (20 women), 5 part-time (1 woman); includes 6 minority (5 African Americans, 1 Asian American or Pacific Islander), 5 international. Average age 29. 81 applicants, 28% accepted. In 2003, 14 master's, 5 doctorates awarded. *Degree requirements:* For master's, thesis (for some programs). *Entrance requirements:* For master's, GRE, GRE Subject Test. *Application deadline:* For fall admission, 6/25 for domestic students, 3/1 for international students; for spring admission, 11/25 for domestic students, 7/15 for international students. *Expenses:* Tuition, state resident: part-time $396 per hour. Tuition, nonresident: part-time $1,895 per hour. *Financial support:* In 2003–04, 1 fellowship with tuition reimbursement (averaging $11,106 per year), 5 research assistantships with tuition reimbursements (averaging $7,304 per year), 47 teaching assistantships with tuition reimbursements (averaging $6,591 per year) were awarded. *Unit head:* Dr. Stephen L. Campbell, Director of Graduate Programs, 919-515-3300, Fax: 919-515-3798, E-mail: s_campbell@ncsu.edu.

North Dakota State University, The Graduate School, College of Science and Mathematics, Department of Mathematics, Fargo, ND 58105. Offers applied mathematics (MS, PhD); mathematics (MS, PhD). *Faculty:* 14 full-time (1 woman). *Students:* 21 full-time (7 women), 3 part-time (1 woman), 13 international. Average age 30. 18 applicants, 56% accepted. In 2003, 3 master's awarded. *Median time to degree:* Master's–3.5 years full-time; doctorate–7 years full-time. *Degree requirements:* For master's, thesis, comprehensive exam, registration; for doctorate, one foreign language, thesis/dissertation, comprehensive exam, registration. *Entrance requirements:* For master's and doctorate, GRE General Test. Additional exam requirements/recommendations for international students: Required—TOEFL. *Application deadline:* For fall admission, 3/15 for domestic students. Applications are processed on a rolling basis. Application fee: $35 ($50 for international students). Tuition, nonresident: full-time $4,071. Required fees: $493. *Financial support:* In 2003–04, 16 students received support, including 1 fellowship with tuition reimbursement available, 1 research assistantship with tuition reimbursement available, 16 teaching assistantships with tuition reimbursements available; Federal Work-Study, institutionally sponsored loans, and tuition waivers (full) also available. Support available to part-time students. Financial award application deadline: 3/31. *Faculty research:* Differential equations, discrete mathematics, number theory, ergodic theory, algebra. Total annual research expenditures: $37,284. *Unit head:* Dr. Warren Shreve, Chair, 701-231-7707, Fax: 701-231-7598.

Northeastern Illinois University, Graduate College, College of Arts and Sciences, Department of Mathematics, Programs in Mathematics, Chicago, IL 60625-4699. Offers mathematics for elementary school teachers (MA). Part-time and evening/weekend programs available. *Degree requirements:* For master's, project, thesis optional. *Entrance requirements:* For master's, minimum GPA of 2.75, 6 undergraduate courses in mathematics. *Faculty research:* Numerical analysis, mathematical biology, operations research, statistics, geometry and mathematics of finance.

Northeastern University, College of Arts and Sciences, Department of Mathematics, Boston, MA 02115-5096. Offers mathematics (MS, PhD); operations research (MSOR). Part-time and evening/weekend programs available. *Faculty:* 41 full-time (6 women), 13 part-time/adjunct (2 women). *Students:* 34 full-time (9 women), 6 part-time (1 woman). Average age 32. 45 applicants, 60% accepted. In 2003, 8 master's, 6 doctorates awarded. *Degree requirements:* For doctorate, thesis/dissertation, qualifying exams. *Entrance requirements:* For master's and doctorate, GRE Subject Test. Additional exam requirements/recommendations for international students: Required—TOEFL. *Application deadline:* For fall admission, 5/15 for domestic students. Applications are processed on a rolling basis. Application fee: $50. *Expenses:* Tuition: Part-time $790 per credit hour. Tuition and fees vary according to course load and program. *Financial support:* In 2003–04, 26 teaching assistantships with tuition reimbursements (averaging $15,190 per year) were awarded; research assistantships with tuition reimbursements, Federal Work-Study, institutionally sponsored loans, tuition waivers (full and partial), and unspecified assistantships also available. Financial award application deadline: 3/15; financial award applicants required to submit FAFSA. *Faculty research:* Algebra and singularities, combinatorics, topology, probability and statistics, geometric analysis and partial differential equations. *Unit head:* Dr. Robert McOwen, Chairperson, 617-373-2450, Fax: 617-373-5658, E-mail: mathdept@neu.edu. *Application contact:* Dr. Alex Suciu, Graduate Coordinator, 617-373-2450, Fax: 617-373-5658, E-mail: mathdept@neu.edu.

See in-depth description on page 563.

Northern Arizona University, Graduate College, College of Arts and Sciences, Department of Mathematics, Flagstaff, AZ 86011. Offers mathematics (MAT, MS); statistics (MS). Part-time programs available. *Students:* 19 full-time (7 women), 4 part-time (1 woman); includes 3 minority (1 African American, 2 Asian Americans or Pacific Islanders). Average age 25. 19 applicants, 68% accepted. In 2003, 7 degrees awarded. *Degree requirements:* For master's, thesis optional. *Application deadline:* For fall admission, 3/15 for domestic students. Applications are processed on a rolling basis. Application fee: $45. *Expenses:* Tuition, state resident: full-time $5,103. Tuition, nonresident: full-time $12,623. *Financial support:* In 2003–04, 10 teaching assistantships were awarded; Federal Work-Study and tuition waivers (full and partial) also available. Financial award application deadline: 3/15. *Faculty research:* Topology, statistics, groups, ring theory, number theory. *Unit head:* Dr. Roy St. Laurent, Chair, 928-523-3481. *Application contact:* Dr. Brent Burch, Graduate Coordinator, 928-523-6875, E-mail: grad@math.nau.edu.

Northern Illinois University, Graduate School, College of Liberal Arts and Sciences, Department of Mathematical Sciences, De Kalb, IL 60115-2854. Offers mathematical sciences (PhD); mathematics (MS); statistics (MS). Part-time programs available. *Faculty:* 43 full-time (10 women), 4 part-time/adjunct (0 women). *Students:* 70 full-time (23 women), 28 part-time (12 women); includes 8 minority (3 African Americans, 5 Asian Americans or Pacific Islanders), 40 international. Average age 30. 107 applicants, 68% accepted, 32 enrolled. In 2003, 8 master's, 2 doctorates awarded. Terminal master's awarded for partial completion of doctoral program. *Degree requirements:* For master's, thesis optional; for doctorate, one foreign language, thesis/dissertation, candidacy exam, dissertation defense, internship. *Entrance requirements:* For master's, GRE General Test, minimum GPA of 2.75; for doctorate, GRE General Test, minimum GPA of 2.75 (undergraduate), 3.2 (graduate). Additional exam requirements/recommendations for international students: Required—TOEFL (minimum score 550 paper-based; 213 computer-based). *Application deadline:* For fall admission, 6/1 for domestic students, 5/1 for international students; for spring admission, 11/1 for domestic students, 10/1 for international students. Applications are processed on a rolling basis. Application fee: $30. Electronic applications accepted. *Expenses:* Tuition, state resident: full-time $3,968; part-time $165 per credit hour. Tuition, nonresident: full-time $7,936; part-time $330 per credit hour. Required fees: $1,255; $52 per credit hour. *Financial support:* In 2003–04, 41 teaching assistantships with full tuition reimbursements were awarded; fellowships with full tuition reimbursements, research assistantships with full tuition reimbursements, career-related internships or fieldwork, Federal Work-Study, scholarships/grants, tuition waivers (full), and unspecified assistantships also available. Support available to part-time students. Financial award applicants required to submit FAFSA. *Unit head:* Dr. William D. Blair, Chair, 815-753-0566, Fax: 815-753-1112. *Application contact:* Dr. Bernard Harris, Director, Graduate Studies, 815-753-6775.

Mathematics

Northwestern University, The Graduate School, Judd A. and Marjorie Weinberg College of Arts and Sciences, Department of Mathematics, Evanston, IL 60208. Offers PhD. Admissions and degrees offered through The Graduate School. Part-time programs available. *Degree requirements:* For doctorate, thesis/dissertation, preliminary exam. *Entrance requirements:* For doctorate, GRE General Test, GRE Subject Test. Additional exam requirements/recommendations for international students: Required—TOEFL. *Faculty research:* Algebra, algebraic topology, analysis dynamical systems, partial differential equations.

Oakland University, Graduate Study and Lifelong Learning, College of Arts and Sciences, Department of Mathematical Sciences, Program in Mathematics, Rochester, MI 48309-4401. Offers MA. *Students:* 2 full-time (1 woman), 6 part-time (1 woman); includes 2 minority (both African Americans) Average age 36. 4 applicants, 100% accepted. In 2003, 1 degree awarded. *Entrance requirements:* Additional exam requirements/recommendations for international students: Required—TOEFL (minimum score 550 paper-based; 213 computer-based). *Application deadline:* For fall admission, 7/15 priority date for domestic students, 5/1 priority date for international students; for winter admission, 12/1 for domestic students; for spring admission, 3/15 for domestic students. Applications are processed on a rolling basis. Application fee: $30. Electronic applications accepted. *Expenses:* Contact institution. *Financial support:* Application deadline: 3/1; *Unit head:* Dr. Meir Shillor, Coordinator, Graduate Programs, 248-370-3439, Fax: 248-370-4184, E-mail: shillor@oakland.edu.

The Ohio State University, Graduate School, College of Mathematical and Physical Sciences, Department of Mathematics, Columbus, OH 43210. Offers MA, MS, PhD. *Faculty:* 98. *Students:* 96 full-time (19 women), 22 part-time (4 women); includes 2 minority (1 Asian American or Pacific Islander, 1 Hispanic American), 71 international. 239 applicants, 28% accepted. In 2003, 15 master's, 10 doctorates awarded. *Degree requirements:* For master's, thesis optional; for doctorate, 2 foreign languages, thesis/dissertation. *Entrance requirements:* For master's and doctorate, GRE General Test, GRE Subject Test. Additional exam requirements/recommendations for international students: Required—TOEFL. *Application deadline:* For fall admission, 8/15 for domestic students. Applications are processed on a rolling basis. Application fee: $40 ($50 for international students). *Expenses:* Tuition, state resident: full-time $7,233. Tuition, nonresident: full-time $18,489. *Financial support:* Fellowships, research assistantships, teaching assistantships, Federal Work-Study, institutionally sponsored loans, and unspecified assistantships available. Support available to part-time students. *Unit head:* Dr. Peter D. March, Chair, Fax: 614-292-1479, E-mail: march.2@osu.edu. *Application contact:* Dr. Saleh Tanveer, Graduate Studies Committee Chair, 614-292-5710, Fax: 614-292-1479, E-mail: tanveer.1@osu.edu.

See in-depth description on page 567.

Ohio University, Graduate Studies, College of Arts and Sciences, Department of Mathematics, Athens, OH 45701-2979. Offers MS, PhD. Part-time and evening/weekend programs available. *Faculty:* 25 full-time (4 women). *Students:* 55 full-time (17 women), 11 part-time (3 women); includes 1 minority (Asian American or Pacific Islander), 55 international. 136 applicants, 60% accepted, 38 enrolled. In 2003, 27 master's, 1 doctorate awarded. *Degree requirements:* For master's, thesis or alternative; for doctorate, thesis/dissertation, comprehensive exam. *Entrance requirements:* For master's and doctorate, minimum GPA of 3.0. Additional exam requirements/recommendations for international students: Required—TOEFL. *Application deadline:* For fall admission, 2/1 for domestic students. Applications are processed on a rolling basis. Application fee: $45. *Expenses:* Tuition, state resident: full-time $2,651; part-time $328 per credit. Tuition, nonresident: full-time $5,095; part-time $632 per credit. Tuition and fees vary according to program. *Financial support:* In 2003–04, 44 students received support, including 3 fellowships with full tuition reimbursements available (averaging $15,000 per year), 33 teaching assistantships with full tuition reimbursements available (averaging $12,500 per year); Federal Work-Study, institutionally sponsored loans, and tuition waivers (full and partial) also available. Financial award application deadline: 2/1. *Faculty research:* Algebra (group and ring theory), functional analysis, topology, differential equations, computational math. *Unit head:* Dr. Sergiu Aizicovici, Chair, 740-593-1254, Fax: 740-593-9805, E-mail: aizicovi@math.ohio.edu. *Application contact:* Dr. M. S. K. Sastry, Admissions Officer, 740-593-1277, Fax: 740-593-9805, E-mail: sastry@bing.math.ohiou.edu.

Oklahoma State University, Graduate College, College of Arts and Sciences, Department of Mathematics, Stillwater, OK 74078. Offers applied mathematics (MS); mathematics (MS, Ed D, PhD). *Faculty:* 36 full-time (6 women), 9 part-time/adjunct (5 women). *Students:* 14 full-time (6 women), 25 part-time (6 women), 13 international. Average age 30. 44 applicants, 68% accepted. In 2003, 8 degrees awarded. *Degree requirements:* For doctorate, one foreign language, thesis/dissertation. *Entrance requirements:* For master's, GRE. Additional exam requirements/recommendations for international students: Required—TOEFL. *Application deadline:* For fall admission, 6/1 for domestic students. Applications are processed on a rolling basis. Application fee: $25 ($50 for international students). Electronic applications accepted. *Expenses:* Tuition, state resident: full-time $3,752; part-time $118 per credit hour. Tuition, nonresident: full-time $10,346; part-time $393 per credit hour. Tuition and fees vary according to course load. *Financial support:* In 2003–04, 1 research assistantship (averaging $18,000 per year), 37 teaching assistantships (averaging $15,906 per year) were awarded. Career-related internships or fieldwork, Federal Work-Study, and tuition waivers (partial) also available. Support available to part-time students. Financial award application deadline: 3/1. *Unit head:* Dr. Alan Adolphson, Head, 405-744-5688, Fax: 405-744-8275.

See in-depth description on page 569.

Old Dominion University, College of Sciences, Programs in Computational and Applied Mathematics, Norfolk, VA 23529. Offers MS, PhD. Part-time programs available. *Faculty:* 22 full-time (1 woman). *Students:* 25 full-time (7 women), 14 part-time (9 women); includes 6 minority (all African Americans), 15 international. Average age 31. 15 applicants, 87% accepted. In 2003, 8 master's, 2 doctorates awarded. Terminal master's awarded for partial completion of doctoral program. *Degree requirements:* For master's, comprehensive exam; for doctorate, thesis/dissertation, candidacy exam. *Entrance requirements:* For master's, minimum GPA of 3.0 in major, 2.5 overall; for doctorate, GRE General Test. Additional exam requirements/recommendations for international students: Required—TOEFL. *Application deadline:* For fall admission, 7/1 for domestic students. Applications are processed on a rolling basis. Application fee: $30. *Expenses:* Tuition, state resident: part-time $235 per credit hour. Tuition, nonresident: part-time $603 per credit hour. Part-time tuition and fees vary according to campus/location. *Financial support:* In 2003–04, 20 students received support, including 3 research assistantships with tuition reimbursements available (averaging $16,000 per year), 15 teaching assistantships with tuition reimbursements available (averaging $10,507 per year); fellowships, scholarships/grants also available. Financial award application deadline: 2/15; financial award applicants required to submit FAFSA. *Faculty research:* Numerical analysis, integral equations, continuum mechanics. Total annual research expenditures:$747,000. *Unit head:* Dr. D. Glenn Lasseigne, Graduate Program Director, 757-683-3891, Fax: 757-683-3885, E-mail: mathgpd@odu.edu.

Old Dominion University, Darden College of Education, Programs in Secondary Education, Norfolk, VA 23529. Offers biology (MS Ed); chemistry (MS Ed); English (MS Ed); instructional technology (MS Ed); library science (MS Ed); mathematics (MS Ed); secondary education (MS Ed); social studies (MS Ed). *Accreditation:* NASM; NCATE. Part-time and evening/weekend programs available. Postbaccalaureate distance learning degree programs offered (minimal on-campus study). *Faculty:* 28 full-time (11 women). *Students:* 59 full-time (39 women), 158 part-time (94 women); includes 27 minority (20 African Americans, 2 Asian Americans or Pacific Islanders, 5 Hispanic Americans), 1 international. Average age 36. 44 applicants, 95% accepted. In 2003, 114 degrees awarded. *Degree requirements:* For master's, candidacy exam, thesis optional. *Entrance requirements:* For master's, GRE General Test, or MAT, PRAXIS I for master's with licensure, minimum GPA of 2.8, teaching certificate. *Application deadline:* Applications are processed on a rolling basis. Application fee: $30. Electronic applications accepted. *Expenses:* Tuition, state resident: part-time $235 per credit hour. Tuition, nonresident: part-time $603 per credit hour. Part-time tuition and fees vary according to campus/location. *Financial support:* In 2003–04, 58 students received support, including 2 research assistantships with tuition reimbursements available (averaging $6,777 per year), 3 teaching assistantships with tuition reimbursements available (averaging $5,333 per year); fellowships, career-related internships or fieldwork, Federal Work-Study, institutionally sponsored loans, scholarships/grants, and tuition waivers (partial) also available. Support available to part-time students. Financial award application deadline: 2/15; financial award applicants required to submit FAFSA. *Faculty research:* Mathematics retraining, writing project for teachers, geography teaching, reading. *Unit head:* Dr. Murray Rudisill, Graduate Program Director, 757-683-3300, Fax: 757-683-5862, E-mail: ecisgpd@odu.edu.

Oregon State University, Graduate School, College of Science, Department of Mathematics, Corvallis, OR 97331. Offers MA, MAIS, MS, PhD. *Faculty:* 33 full-time (11 women), 1 (woman) part-time/adjunct. *Students:* 43 full-time (14 women), 5 part-time (1 woman); includes 3 minority (2 Asian Americans or Pacific Islanders, 1 Hispanic American), 11 international. Average age 30. In 2003, 7 master's, 2 doctorates awarded. Terminal master's awarded for partial completion of doctoral program. *Degree requirements:* For master's, variable foreign language requirement, thesis or alternative; for doctorate, one foreign language, thesis/dissertation, qualifying exams. *Entrance requirements:* For master's and doctorate, minimum GPA of 3.0 in last 90 hours. Additional exam requirements/recommendations for international students: Required—TOEFL. *Application deadline:* For fall admission, 3/1 for domestic students. Applications are processed on a rolling basis. Application fee: $50. *Expenses:* Tuition, state resident: full-time $8,139; part-time $301 per credit. Tuition, nonresident: full-time $14,376; part-time $532 per credit. Required fees: $1,227. *Financial support:* Research assistantships, teaching assistantships, Federal Work-Study and institutionally sponsored loans available. Support available to part-time students. Financial award application deadline: 2/1. *Unit head:* Dr. Harold R. Parks, Chair, 541-737-5766, Fax: 541-737-0517, E-mail: hal.parks@orst.edu.

Paper Science and Engineering Program, Graduate Studies and Research, College of Engineering, School of Chemical and Biomolecular Engineering, Graduate Programs, Program in Physics/Mathematics, Atlanta, GA 30318-5794. Offers MS, PhD. Part-time programs available. Terminal master's awarded for partial completion of doctoral program. *Degree requirements:* For master's, industrial experience, research project; for doctorate, thesis/dissertation. *Entrance requirements:* For master's and doctorate, GRE, minimum GPA of 3.0.

The Pennsylvania State University University Park Campus, Graduate School, Eberly College of Science, Department of Mathematics, State College, University Park, PA 16802-1503. Offers mathematics (M Ed, MA, D Ed, PhD), including applied mathematics (MA, PhD). *Students:* 94 full-time (22 women), 2 part-time (1 woman); includes 4 minority (1 African American, 3 Asian Americans or Pacific Islanders), 44 international. *Entrance requirements:* For master's and doctorate, GRE General Test. Application fee: $45. *Unit head:* Dr. Nigel D. Higson, Head, 814-865-7527, Fax: 814-865-3735, E-mail: higson@psu.edu. *Application contact:* Information Contact, E-mail: gradstudies@math.psu.edu.

See in-depth description on page 573.

Pittsburg State University, Graduate School, College of Arts and Sciences, Department of Mathematics, Pittsburg, KS 66762. Offers MS. *Degree requirements:* For master's, thesis or alternative. *Faculty research:* Operations research, numerical analysis, applied analysis, applied algebra.

Polytechnic University, Brooklyn Campus, Department of Applied Mathematics, Major in Mathematics, Brooklyn, NY 11201-2990. Offers MS, PhD. Part-time and evening/weekend programs available. *Faculty:* 2 full-time (0 women). *Students:* 2 full-time (0 women), 7 part-time (2 women); includes 2 minority (1 African American, 1 Asian American or Pacific Islander), 1 international. Average age 32. 13 applicants, 69% accepted, 5 enrolled. In 2003, 3 master's, 1 doctorate awarded. *Degree requirements:* For master's, thesis or alternative; for doctorate, one foreign language, thesis/dissertation. *Application deadline:* Applications are processed on a rolling basis. Application fee: $55. Electronic applications accepted. *Expenses:* Tuition: Full-time $16,416; part-time $855 per credit. Required fees: $320 per term. *Financial support:* Fellowships, research assistantships, teaching assistantships, institutionally sponsored loans available. Support available to part-time students. Financial award applicants required to submit FAFSA. *Faculty research:* Isoperimetric inequalities, problems arising from theoretical physics. Total annual research expenditures: $101,648.

Portland State University, Graduate Studies, College of Liberal Arts and Sciences, Department of Mathematical Sciences, Portland, OR 97207-0751. Offers mathematical sciences (MA, MAT, MS, MST, PhD); mathematics education (PhD). *Faculty:* 27 full-time (6 women), 14 part-time/adjunct (6 women). *Students:* 39 full-time (21 women), 37 part-time (12 women); includes 5 minority (3 African Americans, 2 Asian Americans or Pacific Islanders), 6 international. Average age 32. 44 applicants, 89% accepted, 29 enrolled. In 2003, 9 degrees awarded. *Degree requirements:* For master's, variable foreign language requirement, thesis or alternative, exams; for doctorate, 2 foreign languages, thesis/dissertation, exams. *Entrance requirements:* For master's, minimum GPA of 3.0 in upper-division course work or 2.75 overall; for doctorate, GRE General Test. Additional exam requirements/recommendations for international students: Required—TOEFL. *Application deadline:* For fall admission, 4/1 for domestic students; for spring admission, 11/1 for domestic students. Applications are processed on a rolling basis. Application fee: $50. *Expenses:* Tuition, state resident: full-time $6,588. Tuition, nonresident: full-time $12,060; part-time $298 per credit. Required fees: $1,041; $19 per credit. $35 per term. *Financial support:* In 2003–04, 18 teaching assistantships with full tuition reimbursements (averaging $7,639 per year) were awarded; research assistantships, Federal Work-Study, scholarships/grants, tuition waivers (partial), and unspecified assistantships also available. Support available to part-time students. Financial award application deadline: 3/1; financial award applicants required to submit FAFSA. *Faculty research:* Algebra, topology, statistical distribution theory, control theory, statistical robustness. Total annual research expenditures: $721,069. *Unit head:* Dr. Eugene Enneking, Head, 503-725-3621, Fax: 503-725-3661, E-mail: ennekinge@pdx.edu. *Application contact:* John Erdman, Coordinator, 503-725-3621, Fax: 503-725-3661, E-mail: erdman@mth.pdx.edu.

Portland State University, Graduate Studies, Systems Science Program, Portland, OR 97207-0751. Offers computational intelligence (Certificate); computer modeling and simulation (Certificate); systems science (MS); systems science/anthropology (PhD); systems science/business administration (PhD); systems science/civil engineering (PhD); systems science/economics (PhD); systems science/engineering management (PhD); systems science/general (PhD); systems science/mathematical sciences (PhD); systems science/mechanical engineering (PhD); systems science/psychology (PhD); systems science/sociology (PhD). *Faculty:* 2 full-time (0 women), 2 part-time/adjunct (0 women). *Students:* 71 full-time (36 women), 31 part-time (7 women); includes 13 minority (4 American Indian/Alaska Native, 5 Asian Americans or Pacific Islanders, 4 Hispanic Americans), 25 international. Average age 35. 98 applicants, 31% accepted, 23 enrolled. In 2003, 4 master's, 8 doctorates awarded. *Degree requirements:* For doctorate, variable foreign language requirement, thesis/dissertation. *Entrance requirements:* For doctorate, GMAT, GRE General Test, minimum undergraduate GPA of 3.0. Additional exam requirements/recommendations for international students: Required—TOEFL. *Application deadline:* For fall admission, 2/1 for domestic students; for spring admission, 11/1 for domestic students. Application fee: $50. *Expenses:* Tuition, state resident: full-time $6,588. Tuition, nonresident: full-time $12,060; part-time $298 per credit. Required fees: $1,041; $19 per credit. $35 per term. *Financial support:* In 2003–04, 8 research assistantships with full tuition reimbursements (averaging $4,420 per year), 1 teaching assistantship with full tuition reimbursement (averaging $3,294 per year) were awarded. Career-related internships or fieldwork, Federal Work-Study, scholarships/grants, and unspecified assistantships also available. Support available to part-time students. Financial award application deadline: 3/1; financial award applicants required to submit FAFSA. *Faculty research:* Systems theory and methodology, artificial intelligence neural networks, information theory, nonlinear dynamics/chaos, modeling and simulation. Total annual research expenditures: $121,699. *Unit head:* George Lendaris,

Acting Director, 503-725-4960. *Application contact:* Dawn Sharafi, Coordinator, 503-725-4960, E-mail: dawn@sysc.pdx.edu.

Prairie View A&M University, Graduate School, College of Arts and Sciences, Department of Mathematics, Prairie View, TX 77446-0519. Offers MS. Part-time and evening/weekend programs available. *Faculty:* 9 full-time (2 women). *Students:* 4 full-time (1 woman), 6 part-time (3 women); includes 5 minority (all African Americans), 3 international. Average age 35. *Degree requirements:* For master's, thesis, comprehensive exam. *Entrance requirements:* For master's, GRE General Test, bachelor's degree in mathematics. *Application deadline:* Applications are processed on a rolling basis. Application fee: $50. *Expenses:* Tuition, state resident: part-time $50 per credit hour. Tuition, nonresident: part-time $282 per credit hour. Required fees: $36 per credit hour. $51 per term. *Financial support:* In 2003–04, 2 research assistantships (averaging $14,400 per year), 1 teaching assistantship (averaging $12,000 per year) were awarded. Fellowships, career-related internships or fieldwork, Federal Work-Study, and institutionally sponsored loans also available. Support available to part-time students. Financial award application deadline: 4/1; financial award applicants required to submit FAFSA. *Faculty research:* Stochastic processor, queuing theory, waveler numeric analyses, delay systems mathematic modeling. Total annual research expenditures: $35,000. *Unit head:* Dr. Aliakbar Haghighi, Head, 936-857-2026, Fax: 936-857-2019, E-mail: aliakbar_haghighi@pvamu.edu. *Application contact:* Dr. G. A. Roberts, Graduate Adviser, 936-857-3807, Fax: 936-857-2019, E-mail: george_roberts@pvamu.edu.

Princeton University, Graduate School, Department of Mathematics, Princeton, NJ 08544-1019. Offers applied and computational mathematics (PhD); mathematical physics (PhD); mathematics (PhD). *Faculty:* 47 full-time (5 women), 9 part-time/adjunct (1 woman). *Students:* 58 full-time (12 women); includes 6 minority (1 African American, 5 Asian Americans or Pacific Islanders), 36 international. 202 applicants, 14% accepted, 14 enrolled. *Median time to degree:* Doctorate–4.64 years full-time. *Degree requirements:* For doctorate, 2 foreign languages, thesis/dissertation. *Entrance requirements:* For doctorate, GRE General Test, GRE Subject Test. Additional exam requirements/recommendations for international students: Required—TOEFL (minimum score 600 paper-based; 250 computer-based). *Application deadline:* For fall admission, 12/31 for domestic students, 12/1 for international students. Application fee: $80 ($55 for international students). Electronic applications accepted. *Expenses:* Tuition: Full-time $29,910. Required fees: $810. *Financial support:* Fellowships with full tuition reimbursements, research assistantships with full tuition reimbursements, teaching assistantships with full tuition reimbursements, Federal Work-Study and institutionally sponsored loans available. Financial award application deadline: 1/2. *Unit head:* Prof. Sergiu Klainerman, Director of Graduate Studies, 609-258-4188, Fax: 609-258-1367, E-mail: seri@princeton.edu. *Application contact:* Janice Yip, Director of Graduate Admissions, 609-258-3034, Fax: 609-258-6180, E-mail: gsadmit@princeton.edu.

Purdue University, Graduate School, School of Science, Department of Mathematics, West Lafayette, IN 47907. Offers MS, PhD. *Faculty:* 55 full-time (4 women). *Students:* 159 full-time (46 women); includes 3 minority (1 African American, 1 Asian American or Pacific Islander, 1 Hispanic American), 111 international. Average age 26. 296 applicants, 9% accepted. In 2003, 21 master's, 11 doctorates awarded. Terminal master's awarded for partial completion of doctoral program. *Median time to degree:* Master's–2 years full-time; doctorate–7 years full-time. Of those who began their doctoral program in fall 1995, 35% received their degree in 8 years or less. *Degree requirements:* For doctorate, one foreign language, thesis/dissertation, oral and written exams. *Entrance requirements:* Additional exam requirements/recommendations for international students: Required—TOEFL (minimum score 570 paper-based; 230 computer-based). *Application deadline:* For fall admission, 3/1 for domestic students, 3/1 for international students. Application fee: $55. Electronic applications accepted. *Financial support:* In 2003–04, 19 fellowships with full and partial tuition reimbursements (averaging $18,000 per year), 14 research assistantships with partial tuition reimbursements (averaging $15,000 per year), 192 teaching assistantships with partial tuition reimbursements (averaging $15,500 per year) were awarded. Support available to part-time students. Financial award application deadline: 3/1; financial award applicants required to submit FAFSA. *Faculty research:* Algebra, analysis, topology, differential equations, applied mathematics. Total annual research expenditures: $2.4 million. *Unit head:* Dr. Leonard Lipshitz, Head, 765-494-1908, Fax: 765-494-0548, E-mail: lipshitz@math.purdue.edu. *Application contact:* Dr. Johnny E. Brown, Graduate Committee Chair, 765-494-961, Fax: 765-494-0548, E-mail: gcomm@math.purdue.edu.

See in-depth description on page 577.

Purdue University Calumet, Graduate School, School of Engineering, Mathematics, and Science, Department of Mathematics, Computer Science, and Statistics, Hammond, IN 46323-2094. Offers mathematics (MAT, MS). Part-time programs available. *Entrance requirements:* Additional exam requirements/recommendations for international students: Required—TOEFL. *Faculty research:* Topology, analysis, algebra, mathematics education.

Queens College of the City University of New York, Division of Graduate Studies, Mathematics and Natural Sciences Division, Department of Mathematics, Flushing, NY 11367-1597. Offers MA. Part-time and evening/weekend programs available. *Faculty:* 25 full-time (1 woman). *Students:* 5 full-time (2 women), 32 part-time (11 women). 42 applicants, 95% accepted. In 2003, 4 degrees awarded. *Degree requirements:* For master's, comprehensive exam. *Entrance requirements:* For master's, minimum GPA of 3.0. Additional exam requirements/recommendations for international students: Required—TOEFL. *Application deadline:* For fall admission, 4/1 for domestic students; for spring admission, 11/1 for domestic students. Applications are processed on a rolling basis. Application fee: $50. *Expenses:* Tuition, state resident: full-time $7,130; part-time $230 per credit. Tuition, nonresident: full-time $11,880; part-time $425 per credit. Required fees: $66; $38 per semester. *Financial support:* Career-related internships or fieldwork, Federal Work-Study, institutionally sponsored loans, tuition waivers (partial), and adjunct lectureships available. Support available to part-time students. Financial award application deadline: 4/1; financial award applicants required to submit FAFSA. *Faculty research:* Topology, differential equations, combinatorics. *Unit head:* Dr. Wallace Goldberg, Chairperson, 718-997-5800, E-mail: wallace_goldberg@qc.edu. *Application contact:* Dr. Nick Metas, Graduate Adviser, 718-997-5800, E-mail: nick_metas@qc.edu.

Queen's University at Kingston, School of Graduate Studies and Research, Faculty of Arts and Sciences, Department of Mathematics and Statistics, Kingston, ON K7L 3N6, Canada. Offers mathematics (M Sc, M Sc Eng, PhD); statistics (M Sc, M Sc Eng, PhD). Part-time programs available. *Degree requirements:* For master's, thesis/dissertation; for doctorate, thesis/dissertation, comprehensive exam. *Entrance requirements:* Additional exam requirements/recommendations for international students: Required—TOEFL. *Faculty research:* Algebra, analysis, applied mathematics, statistics.

Rensselaer Polytechnic Institute, Graduate School, School of Science, Department of Mathematical Sciences, Program in Mathematics, Troy, NY 12180-3590. Offers MS, PhD. Part-time programs available. *Faculty:* 24 full-time (3 women), 3 part-time/adjunct (1 woman). *Students:* 45 full-time (13 women), 3 part-time (1 woman); includes 3 minority (2 African Americans, 1 Asian American or Pacific Islander), 13 international. 56 applicants, 54% accepted, 12 enrolled. In 2003, 5 master's awarded, leading to continued full-time study 60%, business/industry 40%; 5 doctorates awarded, leading to university research/teaching 60%, business/industry 40%. Terminal master's awarded for partial completion of doctoral program. *Median time to degree:* Master's–2 years full-time. Of those who began their doctoral program in fall 1995, 100% received their degree in 8 years or less. *Degree requirements:* For master's, registration; for doctorate, thesis/dissertation, preliminary exam, candidacy presentation, comprehensive exam, registration. *Entrance requirements:* For master's and doctorate, GRE General Test. Additional exam requirements/recommendations for international students: Required—TOEFL. *Application deadline:* For fall admission, 1/15 for domestic students. Applications are processed on a rolling basis. Application fee: $45. Electronic applications accepted. *Expenses:* Tuition: Full-time $27,700; part-time $1,320 per credit. Required fees: $1,470. *Financial support:* In 2003–04, 42 students received support, including 9 fellowships, 11 research assistantships, 34 teaching assistantships; institutionally sponsored loans also available. Financial award application deadline: 2/1. *Faculty research:* Inverse problems, biomathematics, operations research, applied mathematics, mathematical modeling. *Application contact:* Dawnmarie Robens, Graduate Student Coordinator, 518-276-6414, Fax: 518-276-4824, E-mail: robensd@rpi.edu.

Rhode Island College, School of Graduate Studies, Faculty of Arts and Sciences, Department of Mathematics, Providence, RI 02908-1991. Offers MA, MAT, CAGS. Evening/weekend programs available. *Faculty:* 15 full-time (5 women). *Students:* Average age 32. *Degree requirements:* For CAGS, thesis. *Entrance requirements:* For master's, GRE General Test or MAT. *Application deadline:* For fall admission, 4/1 for domestic students. Applications are processed on a rolling basis. Application fee: $35. *Expenses:* Tuition, state resident: part-time $194 per credit hour. Tuition, nonresident: part-time $410 per credit hour. Required fees: $50 per semester. *Financial support:* Career-related internships or fieldwork available. Financial award application deadline: 4/1. *Unit head:* Prof. Helen E. Salzberg, Chair, 401-456-8038.

Rice University, Graduate Programs, Wiess School of Natural Sciences, Department of Mathematics, Houston, TX 77251-1892. Offers MA, PhD. *Faculty:* 18 full-time (1 woman). *Students:* 28 full-time (10 women); includes 6 minority (all Asian Americans or Pacific Islanders) 85 applicants, 13% accepted. In 2003, 3 degrees awarded, leading to university research/teaching 3%. *Degree requirements:* For master's, one foreign language, thesis, oral defense of thesis; for doctorate, one foreign language, thesis/dissertation, qualifying exams, oral exam. *Entrance requirements:* For master's and doctorate, GRE General Test, minimum GPA of 3.0. Additional exam requirements/recommendations for international students: Required—TOEFL. *Application deadline:* For fall admission, 2/1 for domestic students, 2/1 for international students; for spring admission, 11/1 for domestic students, 11/1 for international students. Applications are processed on a rolling basis. Application fee: $35. *Expenses:* Tuition: Full-time $19,700; part-time $1,096 per hour. *Financial support:* In 2003–04, 28 students received support, including 14 fellowships with full tuition reimbursements available (averaging $15,500 per year), 11 research assistantships with full tuition reimbursements available (averaging $15,500 per year); tuition waivers (full and partial) also available. *Faculty research:* Geometry, topology, ergodic theory, knot theory. Total annual research expenditures: $471,201. *Unit head:* Dr. Robin Forman, Chair, 713-348-4835, Fax: 713-348-5231, E-mail: forman@rice.edu. *Application contact:* Dr. Bob Hardt, Professor, 713-348-5265, Fax: 713-348-5231, E-mail: hardt@rice.edu.

Rivier College, School of Graduate Studies, Department of Computer Science and Mathematics, Nashua, NH 03060-5086. Offers computer science (MS); mathematics (MAT). Part-time and evening/weekend programs available. *Faculty:* 5 full-time (2 women), 3 part-time/adjunct (1 woman). *Students:* 22 full-time (9 women), 58 part-time (32 women); includes 9 minority (1 American Indian/Alaska Native, 8 Asian Americans or Pacific Islanders), 19 international. Average age 36. In 2003, 53 degrees awarded. *Degree requirements:* For master's, registration. *Entrance requirements:* For master's, GRE Subject Test. *Application deadline:* Applications are processed on a rolling basis. Application fee: $25. Electronic applications accepted. *Expenses:* Tuition: Part-time $393 per credit. *Financial support:* Available to part-time students. Application deadline: 2/1; *Unit head:* Dr. Mihaela Sabin, Director, 603-888-1311, E-mail: msabin@rivier.edu. *Application contact:* Diane Monahan, Director of Graduate Admissions, 603-897-8129, Fax: 603-897-8810, E-mail: gradadm@rivier.edu.

Roosevelt University, Graduate Division, College of Arts and Sciences, School of Science and Mathematics, Program in Mathematics, Chicago, IL 60605-1394. Offers mathematical sciences (MS), including actuarial science. Part-time and evening/weekend programs available. *Students:* 7 full-time (5 women), 16 part-time (11 women); includes 4 minority (1 African American, 2 Asian Americans or Pacific Islanders, 1 Hispanic American), 5 international. Average age 32. 31 applicants, 65% accepted, 10 enrolled. In 2003, 2 degrees awarded. *Median time to degree:* Master's–2 years full-time, 3 years part-time. *Application deadline:* For fall admission, 6/1 for domestic students. Applications are processed on a rolling basis. Application fee: $25 ($35 for international students). *Expenses:* Tuition: Part-time $624 per semester hour. Required fees: $150 per semester. *Financial support:* Research assistantships, career-related internships or fieldwork and tuition waivers (partial) available. Support available to part-time students. Financial award application deadline: 2/15. *Faculty research:* Statistics, mathematics education, finite groups, computers in mathematics. *Application contact:* Joanne Canyon-Heller, Coordinator of Graduate Admission, 312-281-3250, Fax: 312-281-3356, E-mail: applyru@roosevelt.edu.

Rowan University, Graduate School, College of Liberal Arts and Sciences, Department of Mathematics, Glassboro, NJ 08028-1701. Offers MA. Part-time and evening/weekend programs available. *Students:* 4 full-time (1 woman), 5 part-time (4 women); includes 1 minority (Asian American or Pacific Islander) Average age 32. 2 applicants, 100% accepted, 2 enrolled. In 2003, 2 degrees awarded. *Entrance requirements:* Additional exam requirements/recommendations for international students: Required—TOEFL. *Application deadline:* Applications are processed on a rolling basis. Application fee: $50. Electronic applications accepted. *Expenses:* Tuition, state resident: full-time $8,476; part-time $385 per credit hour. Tuition, nonresident: full-time $13,576; part-time $617 per credit hour. Required fees: $1,438; $65 per credit hour. Tuition and fees vary according to degree level. *Financial support:* Career-related internships or fieldwork, Federal Work-Study, and unspecified assistantships available. Support available to part-time students. *Unit head:* Dr. Marcus Wright, Adviser, 856-256-4500 Ext. 3873.

Royal Military College of Canada, Division of Graduate Studies and Research, Science Division, Department of Mathematics and Computer Science, Kingston, ON K7K 7B4, Canada. Offers computer science (M Sc); mathematics (M Sc). *Degree requirements:* For master's, thesis, registration. Electronic applications accepted.

Rutgers, The State University of New Jersey, Camden, Graduate School, Program in Mathematical Sciences, Camden, NJ 08102-1401. Offers mathematics (MS). Part-time and evening/weekend programs available. *Degree requirements:* For master's, survey paper, thesis optional. *Entrance requirements:* For master's, BS/BA in math or related subject. Additional exam requirements/recommendations for international students: Recommended—TOEFL (minimum score 550 paper-based; 213 computer-based). Electronic applications accepted. *Faculty research:* Differential geometry, dynamical systems, vertex operator algebra, automorphic forms, CR-structures.

Rutgers, The State University of New Jersey, Camden, Graduate School, Program in Mathematics, Camden, NJ 08102-1401. Offers MS. Part-time and evening/weekend programs available. *Degree requirements:* For master's, thesis optional. *Entrance requirements:* For master's, GRE General Test. Electronic applications accepted. *Faculty research:* Differential geometry, automorphic forms, several complex variables, dynamical systems, mathematical computer science.

Rutgers, The State University of New Jersey, Newark, Graduate School, Program in Mathematical Sciences, Newark, NJ 07102. Offers PhD. *Faculty:* 13 full-time (2 women). *Students:* 9 full-time (2 women), 1 (woman) part-time; includes 4 minority (3 Asian Americans or Pacific Islanders, 1 Hispanic American). 25 applicants, 24% accepted, 4 enrolled. *Degree requirements:* For doctorate, thesis/dissertation, written qualifying exam. *Entrance requirements:* For doctorate, GRE General Test, minimum B average. Additional exam requirements/recommendations for international students: Required—TOEFL. *Application deadline:* For fall admission, 6/15 for domestic students. Applications are processed on a rolling basis. Application fee: $50. Electronic applications accepted. *Expenses:* Tuition, state resident: full-time $10,030. Tuition, nonresident: full-time $14,202. *Financial support:* In 2003–04, 1 fellowship with full tuition reimbursement (averaging $14,000 per year), 8 teaching assistantships with full tuition reimbursements (averaging $14,300 per year) were awarded. Tuition waivers (full and partial) also available. Financial award application deadline: 3/1. *Faculty research:* Number theory, automorphic form, low-dimensional topology, Kleinian groups, representation theory.

Mathematics

Rutgers, The State University of New Jersey, Newark (continued)
Unit head: Dr. Robert Sczech, Program Coordinator, 973-353-5156 Ext. 17, Fax: 973-353-5270, E-mail: sczech@andromeda.rutgers.edu.

Rutgers, The State University of New Jersey, New Brunswick/Piscataway, Graduate School, Program in Mathematics, New Brunswick, NJ 08901-1281. Offers applied mathematics (MS, PhD); mathematics (MS, PhD). Part-time programs available. *Faculty:* 113 full-time (12 women). *Students:* 65 full-time (15 women), 10 part-time; includes 8 minority (1 African American, 3 Asian Americans or Pacific Islanders, 4 Hispanic Americans), 30 international. Average age 28. 271 applicants, 10% accepted, 16 enrolled. In 2003, 1 master's awarded, leading to business/industry 100%, 7 doctorates. *Median time to degree:* Master's–3 years full-time; doctorate–5 years full-time. Of those who began their doctoral program in fall 1995, 88% received their degree in 8 years or less. *Degree requirements:* For doctorate, one foreign language, thesis/dissertation, comprehensive exam. *Entrance requirements:* For master's and doctorate, GRE General Test, GRE Subject Test. Additional exam requirements/recommendations for international students: Required—TOEFL. *Application deadline:* For fall admission, 2/1 for domestic students; for spring admission, 11/1 for domestic students. Application fee: $50. *Expenses:* Tuition, state resident: full-time $10,030. Tuition, nonresident: full-time $14,202. *Financial support:* In 2003–04, 49 students received support, including 6 fellowships with full tuition reimbursements available (averaging $16,000 per year), 9 research assistantships with full tuition reimbursements available (averaging $13,700 per year), 34 teaching assistantships with full tuition reimbursements available (averaging $13,800 per year); tuition waivers (full) also available. Financial award application deadline: 2/1; financial award applicants required to submit FAFSA. *Faculty research:* Logic and set theory, number theory, mathematical physics, control theory, partial differential equations. *Unit head:* Prof. Charles A. Weibel, Director, 732-445-3864, Fax: 732-445-5530, E-mail: grad-director@math.rutgers.edu. *Application contact:* Carla I. Ortiz, Graduate Secretary, 732-445-3864, Fax: 732-445-5530, E-mail: ortizc@math.rutgers.edu.

St. Cloud State University, School of Graduate Studies, College of Science and Engineering, Department of Mathematics, St. Cloud, MN 56301-4498. Offers MS. *Faculty:* 18 full-time (4 women). *Students:* 6 (4 women). 3 applicants, 100% accepted. In 2003, 1 degree awarded. *Degree requirements:* For master's, thesis or alternative, comprehensive exam (for some programs). *Entrance requirements:* For master's, GRE General Test, minimum GPA of 2.75. Additional exam requirements/recommendations for international students: Required—TOEFL (minimum score 550 paper-based; 213 computer-based). *Application deadline:* For fall admission, 6/1 for domestic students; for spring admission, 10/1 for domestic students. Applications are processed on a rolling basis. Application fee: $35. Electronic applications accepted. *Expenses:* Tuition, state resident: part-time $203 per credit. Tuition, nonresident: part-time $317 per credit. Required fees: $24 per credit. Tuition and fees vary according to campus/location and reciprocity agreements. *Financial support:* Federal Work-Study and unspecified assistantships available. Financial award application deadline: 3/1. *Unit head:* Dr. Daniel Scully, Chairperson, 320-255-3001, E-mail: mathdept@stcloudstate.edu. *Application contact:* Linda Lou Krueger, School of Graduate Studies, 320-255-2113, Fax: 320-654-5371, E-mail: lekrueger@stcloudstate.edu.

St. John's University, St. John's College of Liberal Arts and Sciences, Department of Mathematics and Computer Science, Jamaica, NY 11439. Offers algebra (MA); analysis (MA); applied mathematics (MA); computer science (MA); geometry-topology (MA); logic and foundations (MA); probability and statistics (MA). Part-time and evening/weekend programs available. *Faculty:* 20 full-time (2 women), 18 part-time/adjunct (8 women). *Students:* 4 full-time (3 women), 3 part-time (1 woman); includes 2 minority (1 African American, 1 Hispanic American). 16 applicants, 63% accepted, 5 enrolled. In 2003, 4 degrees awarded. *Degree requirements:* For master's, thesis optional. *Entrance requirements:* For master's, minimum GPA of 3.0. Additional exam requirements/recommendations for international students: Required—TOEFL (minimum score 500 paper-based). *Application deadline:* Applications are processed on a rolling basis. Application fee: $40. Electronic applications accepted. *Expenses:* Tuition: Full-time $15,840; part-time $8,320 per year. Tuition and fees vary according to course load, degree level, program and student level. *Financial support:* Research assistantships, scholarships/grants available. Support available to part-time students. Financial award application deadline: 3/1; financial award applicants required to submit FAFSA. *Faculty research:* Development of a computerized metabolic map. *Unit head:* Dr. Charles Traina, Chair, 718-990-6166, E-mail: trainac@stjohns.edu. *Application contact:* Matthew Whelan, Director, Office of Admission, 718-990-2000, Fax: 718-990-2096, E-mail: admissions@stjohns.edu.

Saint Louis University, Graduate School, College of Arts and Sciences and Graduate School, Department of Mathematics and Mathematical Computer Science, St. Louis, MO 63103-2097. Offers mathematics (MA, MA(R), PhD). Part-time programs available. *Faculty:* 27 full-time (4 women), 9 part-time/adjunct (4 women). *Students:* 15 full-time (6 women), 2 part-time (1 woman); includes 4 minority (1 African American, 2 Asian Americans or Pacific Islanders, 1 Hispanic American), 2 international. Average age 29. 11 applicants, 73% accepted, 6 enrolled. In 2003, 7 master's, 2 doctorates awarded. *Degree requirements:* For master's, thesis (for some programs), comprehensive exam; for doctorate, one foreign language, thesis/dissertation, preliminary exams. *Entrance requirements:* For master's and doctorate, GRE General Test. Additional exam requirements/recommendations for international students: Required—TOEFL (minimum score 550 paper-based; 213 computer-based). *Application deadline:* For fall admission, 7/1 for domestic students; for spring admission, 11/1 for domestic students. Applications are processed on a rolling basis. Application fee: $40. *Expenses:* Tuition: Part-time $690 per credit hour. Required fees: $59 per semester. Tuition and fees vary according to program. *Financial support:* In 2003–04, 16 students received support, including 15 teaching assistantships with tuition reimbursements available Financial award application deadline: 6/1; financial award applicants required to submit FAFSA. *Faculty research:* Geometric topology, lie groups, algebra and group theory, differential geometry, wavelet analysis. Total annual research expenditures: $102,000. *Unit head:* Dr. Jim Hebda, Interim Chairperson, 314-977-3146, E-mail: hedbajj@slu.edu. *Application contact:* Gary Behrman, Associate Dean of the Graduate School, 314-977-3827, Fax: 314-977-3943, E-mail: behrmang@slu.edu.

Saint Xavier University, Graduate Studies, School of Arts and Sciences, Department of Mathematics and Computer Science, Chicago, IL 60655-3105. Offers applied computer science in Internet information systems (MS); mathematics and computer science (MA). *Faculty:* 1 (woman) full-time. *Students:* 11 full-time (4 women), 5 part-time (4 women); includes 4 minority (1 African American, 3 Hispanic Americans). Average age 32. *Degree requirements:* For master's, thesis optional. *Application deadline:* For fall admission, 8/15 for domestic students. Application fee: $35. *Expenses:* Tuition: Part-time $525 per semester hour. *Unit head:* Dr. Florence Appel, Associate Professor and Associate Chair/Computer Science, 773-298-3398, Fax: 773-779-9061, E-mail: appel@sxu.edu. *Application contact:* Beth Gierach, Managing Director of Admission, 773-298-3053, Fax: 773-298-3076, E-mail: gierach@sxu.edu.

Salem State College, Graduate School, Department of Mathematics, Salem, MA 01970-5353. Offers mathematics (MAT, MS). *Faculty:* 1 part-time/adjunct (0 women). *Students:* Average age 34. In 2003, 4 degrees awarded. *Entrance requirements:* For master's, GRE General Test, MAT. *Application deadline:* Applications are processed on a rolling basis. Application fee: $25. *Expenses:* Tuition, state resident: full-time $2,520; part-time $225 per credit. Tuition, nonresident: full-time $4,140; part-time $315 per credit. Required fees: $1,530. *Unit head:* Dr. Arthur J. Rosenthal, Coordinator, 978-542-6392, Fax: 978-542-7175, E-mail: arthur.rosenthal@salemstate.edu.

Sam Houston State University, College of Arts and Sciences, Department of Mathematics and Statistics, Huntsville, TX 77341. Offers mathematics (MA, MS); statistics (MS). Part-time programs available. *Students:* 8 full-time (4 women), 19 part-time (12 women); includes 2 minority (both Hispanic Americans), 5 international. In 2003, 8 degrees awarded. *Entrance requirements:* For master's, GRE General Test. Additional exam requirements/recommendations for international students: Required—TOEFL. *Application deadline:* For fall admission, 8/1 for domestic students; for spring admission, 12/1 for domestic students. Applications are processed on a rolling basis. Application fee: $35. *Expenses:* Tuition, state resident: part-time $243 per semester hour. Tuition, nonresident: part-time $479 per semester hour. *Financial support:* Teaching assistantships, institutionally sponsored loans available. Support available to part-time students. Financial award application deadline: 5/31; financial award applicants required to submit FAFSA. *Unit head:* Dr. Jaimie Hebert, Chair, 936-294-1563, Fax: 936-294-1882, E-mail: mth_jlh@shsu.edu. *Application contact:* Anita Shipman, Advisor, 936-294-3962.

San Diego State University, Graduate and Research Affairs, College of Sciences, Department of Mathematical Sciences, San Diego, CA 92182. Offers applied mathematics (MS); mathematics (MA); mathematics and science education (PhD); statistics (MS). Part-time programs available. *Students:* 33 full-time (23 women), 49 part-time (15 women); includes 17 minority (14 Asian Americans or Pacific Islanders, 3 Hispanic Americans), 19 international. 88 applicants, 66% accepted, 9 enrolled. In 2003, 14 master's, 1 doctorate awarded. *Degree requirements:* For doctorate, thesis/dissertation. *Entrance requirements:* For master's, GRE General Test. Additional exam requirements/recommendations for international students: Required—TOEFL. *Application deadline:* For fall admission, 5/1 for domestic students, 5/1 for international students; for spring admission, 11/1 for domestic students, 10/1 for international students. Applications are processed on a rolling basis. Application fee: $55. Electronic applications accepted. Tuition, nonresident: part-time $282 per unit. Required fees: $1,349; $875 per year. *Financial support:* Applicants required to submit FAFSA. *Faculty research:* Teacher education in mathematics. Total annual research expenditures: $1.3 million. *Unit head:* David Lesley, Chair, 619-594-6191, Fax: 619-594-6746, E-mail: lesley@math.sdsu.edu. *Application contact:* Larry Sowder, Graduate Coordinator, 619-594-7246, Fax: 619-594-6746, E-mail: lsowder@sciences.sdsu.edu.

San Francisco State University, Division of Graduate Studies, College of Science and Engineering, Department of Mathematics, San Francisco, CA 94132-1722. Offers MA. *Faculty:* 7 full-time (2 women). In 2003, 4 degrees awarded. *Degree requirements:* For master's, oral exam, thesis optional. *Entrance requirements:* For master's, minimum GPA of 2.5 in last 60 units. *Application deadline:* For fall admission, 11/30 for domestic students. Applications are processed on a rolling basis. Application fee: $55. *Expenses:* Tuition, state resident: part-time $871 per unit. Tuition, nonresident: part-time $1,093 per unit. *Financial support:* In 2003–04, 8 teaching assistantships were awarded. Financial award application deadline: 3/1. *Faculty research:* Fuzzy logic, software development, number theory, complex analysis, mathematics education. *Unit head:* Dr. Sheldon Axler, Dean, 415-338-1571, Fax: 415-338-6136, E-mail: axler@sfsu.edu. *Application contact:* Dr. David Meredith, Graduate Coordinator, 415-338-2199, E-mail: meredith@sfsu.edu.

San Jose State University, Graduate Studies and Research, College of Science, Department of Mathematics, San Jose, CA 95192-0001. Offers mathematics (MA, MS); mathematics education (MA). Part-time and evening/weekend programs available. *Students:* 15 full-time (5 women), 30 part-time (15 women); includes 24 minority (1 African American, 1 American Indian/Alaska Native, 18 Asian Americans or Pacific Islanders, 4 Hispanic Americans). Average age 36. 28 applicants, 68% accepted, 11 enrolled. In 2003, 4 degrees awarded. *Degree requirements:* For master's, thesis (for some programs), comprehensive exam. *Entrance requirements:* For master's, GRE Subject Test. *Application deadline:* For fall admission, 6/29 for domestic students; for spring admission, 11/30 for domestic students. Applications are processed on a rolling basis. Application fee: $59. Electronic applications accepted. Tuition, nonresident: part-time $282 per unit. Required fees: $654 per semester. *Financial support:* In 2003–04, 20 teaching assistantships were awarded; career-related internships or fieldwork and Federal Work-Study also available. Support available to part-time students. Financial award applicants required to submit FAFSA. *Faculty research:* Artificial intelligence, algorithms, numerical analysis, software database, number theory. *Unit head:* Roger Alperin, Chair, 408-924-5100, Fax: 408-924-5080. *Application contact:* Fernanda Karp, Department Manager, 408-924-5100.

Simon Fraser University, Graduate Studies, Faculty of Science, Department of Mathematics, Burnaby, BC V5A 1S6, Canada. Offers applied mathematics (M Sc, PhD); pure mathematics (M Sc, PhD); statistics and actuarial science (M Sc, PhD). *Degree requirements:* For master's and doctorate, thesis/dissertation. *Entrance requirements:* For master's, GRE Subject Test, minimum GPA of 3.0; for doctorate, GRE Subject Test, minimum GPA of 3.5. Additional exam requirements/recommendations for international students: Required—TWE or IELTS. *Faculty research:* Semi-groups, number theory, optimization, combinations.

South Dakota State University, Graduate School, College of Engineering, Department of Mathematics, Brookings, SD 57007. Offers MS. *Degree requirements:* For master's, thesis, oral exam. *Entrance requirements:* Additional exam requirements/recommendations for international students: Required—TOEFL. *Faculty research:* Numerical linear algebra, statistics, applied quality number theory, abstract algebra, actuarial mathematics.

Southeast Missouri State University, School of Graduate and University Studies, Department of Mathematics, Cape Girardeau, MO 63701-4799. Offers MNS. Part-time programs available. *Faculty:* 14 full-time (2 women). *Students:* 3 full-time (2 women), 4 part-time (3 women), 1 international. Average age 32. *Degree requirements:* For master's, thesis or alternative. *Entrance requirements:* For master's, GRE General Test, minimum GPA of 3.0 in mathematics. Additional exam requirements/recommendations for international students: Required—TOEFL (minimum score 550 paper-based; 213 computer-based). *Application deadline:* For fall admission, 4/1 priority date for domestic students, 4/1 priority date for international students; for spring admission, 11/1 priority date for domestic students, 9/1 priority date for international students. Applications are processed on a rolling basis. Application fee: $20 ($100 for international students). Electronic applications accepted. *Expenses:* Tuition, state resident: full-time $4,061; part-time $180 per credit hour. Tuition, nonresident: full-time $7,514; part-time $324 per credit hour. One-time fee: $257. *Financial support:* In 2003–04, 5 students received support, including research assistantships with full tuition reimbursements available (averaging $6,100 per year), 6 teaching assistantships with full tuition reimbursements available (averaging $6,100 per year) Financial award applicants required to submit FAFSA. *Unit head:* Dr. Victor Gummersheimer, Chairperson, 573-651-2164, Fax: 573-986-6811, E-mail: vgummersheimer@semo.edu. *Application contact:* Marsha L. Arant, Office of Graduate Studies, 573-651-2192, Fax: 573-651-2001, E-mail: marant@semovm.semo.edu.

Southern Connecticut State University, School of Graduate Studies, School of Arts and Sciences, Department of Mathematics, New Haven, CT 06515-1355. Offers MS. Part-time and evening/weekend programs available. *Faculty:* 2 full-time. *Students:* 14 full-time (6 women), 22 part-time (9 women); includes 2 minority (both Hispanic Americans) 34 applicants, 26% accepted. In 2003, 4 degrees awarded. *Degree requirements:* For master's, thesis or alternative. *Entrance requirements:* For master's, interview. *Application deadline:* For fall admission, 7/15 for domestic students. Applications are processed on a rolling basis. Application fee: $40. Electronic applications accepted. *Expenses:* Tuition, state resident: full-time $3,298. Tuition, nonresident: full-time $9,190. Full-time tuition and fees vary according to program. *Financial support:* Application deadline: 4/15; *Unit head:* Dr. Ross Gingrich, Chairperson, 203-392-5581, Fax: 203-392-6805, E-mail: gingrichr1@southernct.edu. *Application contact:* Dr. Richard Decesare, Graduate Coordinator, 203-392-5596, Fax: 203-392-6805, E-mail: decesarer1@southernct.edu.

Southern Illinois University Carbondale, Graduate School, College of Science, Department of Mathematics, Carbondale, IL 62901-4701. Offers mathematics (MA, MS, PhD); statistics (MS). Part-time programs available. *Faculty:* 32 full-time (2 women), 1 part-time/adjunct (0 women). *Students:* 24 full-time (8 women), 15 part-time (5 women); includes 2 minority (both African Americans), 23 international. Average age 26. 48 applicants, 33% accepted, 8 enrolled. In 2003, 13 master's, 3 doctorates awarded. *Degree requirements:* For master's, thesis; for doctorate, 2 foreign languages, thesis/dissertation. *Entrance requirements:* For master's, minimum GPA of 2.7; for doctorate, minimum GPA of 3.25. Additional exam requirements/recommendations for international students: Required—TOEFL. *Application deadline:* Applications are processed on a rolling basis. Application fee: $0. *Expenses:* Tuition, state resident:

part-time $478 per hour. Tuition, nonresident: part-time $657 per hour. *Financial support:* In 2003–04, 28 students received support, including 24 teaching assistantships with full tuition reimbursements available; fellowships with full tuition reimbursements available, research assistantships with full tuition reimbursements available, Federal Work-Study, institutionally sponsored loans, and tuition waivers (full) also available. Support available to part-time students. *Faculty research:* Differential equations, combinatorics, probability, algebra, numerical analysis. *Unit head:* Andrew Earnest, Chairperson, 618-453-6522, Fax: 618-453-5300, E-mail: chairman@math.siu.edu. *Application contact:* William T. Patula, Director of Graduate Studies, 618-453-5302, Fax: 618-453-5300, E-mail: wpatula@math.siu.edu.

Announcement: The computational facilities provided by the Math Computer Lab have recently been updated with state-of-the-art computer hardware and software through a grant from the National Science Foundation. All graduate students have 24-hour access to the lab for work on class or research projects, theses, and dissertations.

See in-depth description on page 581.

Southern Illinois University Edwardsville, Graduate Studies and Research, College of Arts and Sciences, Department of Mathematics and Statistics, Edwardsville, IL 62026-0001. Offers MS. Part-time programs available. *Degree requirements:* For master's, thesis or alternative, final exam. *Entrance requirements:* For master's, undergraduate major in related area, programming language, minimum GPA of 2.7. Additional exam requirements/recommendations for international students: Required—TOEFL.

Southern Methodist University, Dedman College, Department of Mathematics, Dallas, TX 75275. Offers computational and applied mathematics (MS, PhD). *Faculty:* 20 full-time (3 women). *Students:* 12 full-time (3 women), 5 part-time (3 women); includes 4 minority (1 African American, 3 Asian Americans or Pacific Islanders), 11 international. Average age 30. In 2003, 7 master's, 2 doctorates awarded. *Degree requirements:* For doctorate, thesis/dissertation, oral and written exams. *Entrance requirements:* For master's and doctorate, GRE General Test, minimum GPA of 3.0, 18 undergraduate hours in mathematics beyond first and second year calculus. Additional exam requirements/recommendations for international students: Required—TOEFL. *Application deadline:* For fall admission, 6/30 for domestic students; for winter admission, 11/30 for domestic students. Applications are processed on a rolling basis. Application fee: $60. Electronic applications accepted. *Expenses:* Tuition: Full-time $11,362; part-time $874 per credit. Required fees: $112 per credit. Tuition and fees vary according to course load and program. *Financial support:* In 2003–04, 7 teaching assistantships with full tuition reimbursements (averaging $14,000 per year) were awarded; career-related internships or fieldwork, scholarships/grants, and tuition waivers (partial) also available. Support available to part-time students. Financial award applicants required to submit FAFSA. *Faculty research:* Numerical analysis, scientific computation, fluid dynamics, software development, differential equations. Total annual research expenditures: $195,000. *Unit head:* Dr. Douglas Reinelt, Chairman, 214-768-2506, Fax: 214-768-2355, E-mail: mathchair@mail.smu.edu. *Application contact:* Dr. Zhangxin Chen, Director of Graduate Studies, 214-768-4338, E-mail: math@mail.smu.edu.

Southern Oregon University, Graduate Office, School of Sciences, Ashland, OR 97520. Offers environmental education (MA, MS); mathematics/computer science (MA, MS); science (MA, MS). Part-time programs available. *Faculty:* 46 full-time (9 women), 5 part-time/adjunct (3 women). *Students:* 15 full-time (9 women), 14 part-time (8 women); includes 1 minority (Hispanic American), 3 international. Average age 35. 26 applicants, 77% accepted, 12 enrolled. In 2003, 17 degrees awarded. *Degree requirements:* For master's, thesis (for some programs), comprehensive exam (MA). *Entrance requirements:* For master's, GRE General Test, minimum GPA of 3.0. *Application deadline:* For fall admission, 4/15 for domestic students; for winter admission, 10/15 for domestic students; for spring admission, 1/15 for domestic students. Application fee: $50. *Expenses:* Tuition, state resident: full-time $7,326. Tuition, nonresident: full-time $12,573. *Financial support:* In 2003–04, 5 teaching assistantships with tuition reimbursements (averaging $3,519 per year) were awarded; institutionally sponsored loans and unspecified assistantships also available. *Faculty research:* Ferroelectric, ecology environmental science, biotechnology, material science. Total annual research expenditures: $318,923. *Unit head:* Dr. Joseph Graf, Dean, 541-552-6474. *Application contact:* Susan Koralek, Administrative Assistant, 541-552-6474.

Southern University and Agricultural and Mechanical College, Graduate School, College of Sciences, Department of Mathematics, Baton Rouge, LA 70813. Offers MS. *Degree requirements:* For master's, thesis optional. *Entrance requirements:* For master's, GMAT, GRE. Additional exam requirements/recommendations for international students: Required—TOEFL. *Faculty research:* Algebraic number theory, abstract algebra, computer analysis, probability, mathematics education.

Southwest Missouri State University, Graduate College, College of Natural and Applied Sciences, Department of Mathematics, Springfield, MO 65804-0094. Offers MS. Part-time programs available. *Faculty:* 22 full-time (4 women). *Students:* 7 full-time (3 women), 10 part-time (6 women), 1 international. Average age 29. 12 applicants, 92% accepted, 7 enrolled. In 2003, 1 degree awarded. *Degree requirements:* For master's, thesis or alternative, comprehensive exam. *Entrance requirements:* For master's, GRE General Test, minimum undergraduate GPA of 2.75, 3.0 in upper-level math courses. *Application deadline:* For fall admission, 8/5 for domestic students; for spring admission, 12/20 priority date for domestic students. Applications are processed on a rolling basis. Application fee: $30. Electronic applications accepted. *Expenses:* Tuition, state resident: full-time $2,862. Tuition, nonresident: full-time $5,724. *Financial support:* In 2003–04, 1 research assistantship with full tuition reimbursement (averaging $8,400 per year), 13 teaching assistantships with full tuition reimbursements (averaging $8,400 per year) were awarded. Federal Work-Study, scholarships/grants, and unspecified assistantships also available. Financial award application deadline: 3/31. *Faculty research:* Harmonic analysis, commutative algebra, number theory, K-theory, probability. *Unit head:* Dr. Yungchen Cheng, Head, 417-836-5112, Fax: 417-836-5610, E-mail: yuc471f@smsu.edu.

Stanford University, School of Engineering, Program in Scientific Computing and Computational Mathematics, Stanford, CA 94305-9991. Offers MS, PhD. *Students:* 52 full-time (10 women), 14 part-time (4 women); includes 10 minority (9 Asian Americans or Pacific Islanders, 1 Hispanic American), 35 international. Average age 28. 38 applicants, 66% accepted. In 2003, 14 master's, 8 doctorates awarded. Terminal master's awarded for partial completion of doctoral program. *Degree requirements:* For doctorate, thesis/dissertation, qualifying exam. *Entrance requirements:* For master's, GRE General Test; for doctorate, GRE General Test, GRE Subject Test. Additional exam requirements/recommendations for international students: Required—TOEFL. *Application deadline:* For fall admission, 2/15 for domestic students. Application fee: $65 ($80 for international students). Electronic applications accepted. *Expenses:* Tuition: Full-time $28,563. *Unit head:* Dr. Gene H. Golub, Director, 650-723-3124, Fax: 650-723-2411, E-mail: golub@sccm.stanford.edu. *Application contact:* Admissions Coordinator, 650-723-0572.

Stanford University, School of Humanities and Sciences, Department of Mathematics, Stanford, CA 94305-9991. Offers financial mathematics (MS); mathematics (MS, PhD). *Faculty:* 34 full-time (2 women). *Students:* 59 full-time (14 women), 10 part-time (2 women); includes 6 minority (1 African American, 3 Asian Americans or Pacific Islanders, 2 Hispanic Americans), 42 international. Average age 26. 186 applicants, 28% accepted. In 2003, 9 master's, 5 doctorates awarded. Terminal master's awarded for partial completion of doctoral program. *Degree requirements:* For doctorate, 2 foreign languages, thesis/dissertation, oral exam. *Entrance requirements:* For master's, GRE General Test; for doctorate, GRE General Test, GRE Subject Test. Additional exam requirements/recommendations for international students: Required—TOEFL. *Application deadline:* For fall admission, 1/4 for domestic students. Application fee: $65 ($80 for international students). Electronic applications accepted. *Expenses:* Tuition: Full-time $28,563. *Unit head:* Leon Simon, Chair, 650-725-6284, Fax: 650-725-4066, E-mail: lms@math.stanford.edu. *Application contact:* Graduate Administrator, 650-723-2601.

State University of New York at Binghamton, Graduate School, School of Arts and Sciences, Department of Mathematical Sciences, Binghamton, NY 13902-6000. Offers computer science (MA, PhD); probability and statistics (MA, PhD). Part-time programs available. Terminal master's awarded for partial completion of doctoral program. *Degree requirements:* For master's, thesis or alternative; for doctorate, 2 foreign languages, thesis/dissertation. *Entrance requirements:* For master's and doctorate, GRE General Test, GRE Subject Test. Additional exam requirements/recommendations for international students: Required—TOEFL. Electronic applications accepted.

State University of New York at New Paltz, Graduate School, School of Science and Engineering, Department of Mathematics, New Paltz, NY 12561. Offers MA, MAT, MS Ed. Part-time and evening/weekend programs available. *Faculty:* 13 full-time (5 women), 20 part-time/adjunct (11 women). In 2003, 1 degree awarded. *Degree requirements:* For master's, thesis (for some programs), comprehensive exam (for some programs). *Entrance requirements:* For master's, GRE General Test, minimum GPA of 3.0. Additional exam requirements/recommendations for international students: Required—TOEFL (minimum score 550 paper-based; 213 computer-based). *Application deadline:* For fall admission, 3/1 priority date for domestic students, 3/1 priority date for international students; for spring admission, 10/1 for domestic students, 10/1 for international students. Application fee: $50. *Expenses:* Tuition, state resident: full-time $6,900; part-time $288 per credit hour. Tuition, nonresident: full-time $10,500; part-time $438 per credit hour. Tuition and fees vary according to program. *Financial support:* Teaching assistantships, Federal Work-Study, institutionally sponsored loans, and tuition waivers (full) available. *Faculty research:* Universal algebra, lattice theory, mathematical logic, operator theory, combinatorics. *Unit head:* Dr. David Hobby, Chair, 845-257-3564. *Application contact:* Dr. Donald Silberger, Coordinator, 845-257-3537, E-mail: silberger@mcs.newpaltz.edu.

State University of New York College at Brockport, School of Letters and Sciences, Department of Mathematics, Brockport, NY 14420-2997. Offers MA. Part-time programs available. *Students:* 5 full-time (4 women), 9 part-time (6 women); includes 2 minority (both Asian Americans or Pacific Islanders), 1 international. 6 applicants, 100% accepted, 4 enrolled. In 2003, 5 degrees awarded. *Degree requirements:* For master's, comprehensive exam. *Entrance requirements:* For master's, minimum GPA of 3.0, letters of recommendation. Additional exam requirements/recommendations for international students: Required—TOEFL (minimum score 550 paper-based; 213 computer-based). *Application deadline:* For fall admission, 7/15 for domestic students, 7/15 for international students; for spring admission, 11/15 for domestic students, 11/15 for international students. Applications are processed on a rolling basis. Application fee: $50. *Expenses:* Tuition, state resident: full-time $6,910; part-time $288 per credit hour. Tuition, nonresident: full-time $10,500; part-time $438 per credit hour. Required fees: $26 per credit. *Financial support:* In 2003–04, 5 students received support, including 3 teaching assistantships with tuition reimbursements available (averaging $6,000 per year); Federal Work-Study, scholarships/grants, and unspecified assistantships also available. Financial award application deadline: 3/15; financial award applicants required to submit FAFSA. *Faculty research:* Complex analysis, topological graph theory, number theory, mathematical modeling, algebra. *Unit head:* Dr. Charles Sommer, Chairperson, 585-395-2036, E-mail: csommer@brockport.edu. *Application contact:* Dr. Dawn M. Jones, Graduate Director, 585-395-5174, E-mail: djones@brockport.edu.

Announcement: Flexible program leading to MA in mathematics. Three required courses in algebra, analysis, and statistics. Four additional elective courses in mathematics or computer science. The remaining 3 courses may be chosen from other departments, including education. Several assistantships, which include a stipend of $6000 and a tuition waiver, are available.

State University of New York College at Cortland, Graduate Studies, School of Arts and Sciences, Department of Mathematics, Cortland, NY 13045. Offers MAT, MS Ed. *Expenses:* Tuition, state resident: full-time $2,592; part-time $288 per credit. Tuition, nonresident: full-time $3,942; part-time $438 per credit. Required fees: $36 per credit. Part-time tuition and fees vary according to course load and campus/location. *Unit head:* Dr. Bruce Mattingly, Head, 607-753-4326.

State University of New York College at Potsdam, School of Arts and Sciences, Department of Mathematics, Potsdam, NY 13676. Offers MA. Part-time and evening/weekend programs available. *Faculty:* 5 full-time (1 woman), 1 part-time/adjunct (0 women). *Students:* 3 full-time (1 woman); includes 1 minority (African American) In 2003, 6 degrees awarded. *Degree requirements:* For master's, comprehensive exam. *Entrance requirements:* For master's, minimum GPA of 3.0. Additional exam requirements/recommendations for international students: Required—TOEFL (minimum score 550 paper-based; 220 computer-based). *Application deadline:* Applications are processed on a rolling basis. Application fee: $50. *Expenses:* Tuition, state resident: full-time $6,900; part-time $288 per credit hour. Tuition, nonresident: full-time $10,500; part-time $438 per credit hour. Required fees: $710; $29 per credit hour. One-time fee: $5 part-time. *Financial support:* Teaching assistantships with full tuition reimbursements, Federal Work-Study available. Support available to part-time students. Financial award application deadline: 3/1. *Unit head:* Dr. Laura J. Person, Chairperson, 315-267-2005, Fax: 315-267-3176, E-mail: personlj@potsdam.edu. *Application contact:* Dr. William Amoriell, Dean of Education and Graduate Studies, 315-267-2515, Fax: 315-267-4802, E-mail: amoriewj@potsdam.edu.

Stephen F. Austin State University, Graduate School, College of Sciences and Mathematics, Department of Mathematics and Statistics, Nacogdoches, TX 75962. Offers mathematics (MS); mathematics education (MS); statistics (MS). *Faculty:* 20 full-time (5 women). *Students:* 14 full-time (10 women), 50 part-time (41 women); includes 7 minority (5 African Americans, 2 Hispanic Americans), 2 international. 42 applicants, 88% accepted. In 2003, 4 degrees awarded. *Degree requirements:* For master's, thesis optional. *Entrance requirements:* For master's, GRE General Test, minimum GPA of 2.8 in last 60 hours, 2.5 overall. Additional exam requirements/recommendations for international students: Required—TOEFL. *Application deadline:* For fall admission, 8/1 for domestic students; for spring admission, 12/15 for domestic students. Applications are processed on a rolling basis. Application fee: $0 ($50 for international students). *Expenses:* Tuition, state resident: part-time $46 per hour. Tuition, nonresident: part-time $282 per hour. Required fees: $71 per hour. Tuition and fees vary according to reciprocity agreements. *Financial support:* In 2003–04, 8 teaching assistantships (averaging $10,000 per year) were awarded; Federal Work-Study, health care benefits, and unspecified assistantships also available. Financial award application deadline: 3/1. *Faculty research:* Kernel type estimators, fractal mappings, spline curve fitting, robust regression continua theory. *Unit head:* Dr. Jasper Adams, Chair, 936-468-3805.

Stevens Institute of Technology, Graduate School, School of Applied Sciences and Liberal Arts, Department of Mathematical Sciences, Program in Mathematics, Hoboken, NJ 07030. Offers algebra (PhD); analysis (PhD); applied mathematics (PhD); mathematics (MS). *Degree requirements:* For master's, thesis optional; for doctorate, one foreign language, thesis/dissertation. *Entrance requirements:* For master's and doctorate, GRE. Additional exam requirements/recommendations for international students: Required—TOEFL. Electronic applications accepted.

Stony Brook University, State University of New York, Graduate School, College of Arts and Sciences, Department of Mathematics, Stony Brook, NY 11794. Offers MA, PhD. *Faculty:* 25 full-time (2 women), 2 part-time/adjunct (0 women). *Students:* 69 full-time (9 women), 18 part-time (8 women); includes 5 minority (2 African Americans, 3 Asian Americans or Pacific Islanders), 47 international. 157 applicants, 32% accepted. In 2003, 13 master's, 6 doctorates awarded. *Degree requirements:* For doctorate, 2 foreign languages, thesis/dissertation. *Entrance requirements:* For master's and doctorate, GRE General Test. Additional exam

Mathematics

Stony Brook University, State University of New York (continued)
requirements/recommendations for international students: Required—TOEFL. *Application deadline:* For fall admission, 1/15 for domestic students. Application fee: $50. *Expenses:* Tuition, state resident: full-time $6,900; part-time $288 per credit hour. Tuition, nonresident: full-time $10,500; part-time $438 per credit hour. Required fees: $22. *Financial support:* In 2003–04, 7 fellowships, 12 research assistantships, 45 teaching assistantships were awarded. *Faculty research:* Real analysis, relativity and mathematical physics, complex analysis, topology, combinatorics. Total annual research expenditures: $1.1 million. *Unit head:* Dr. Detlef Gromall, Chair, 631-632-8250. *Application contact:* Dr. Leon Takhtajan, Director, 631-632-8258, Fax: 631-632-7631, E-mail: leontak@math.sunysb.edu.

Announcement: The Stony Brook Mathematics Department is about 40 years old, but it has already achieved a world-class reputation. Recipients of Stony Brook doctorates now hold tenured positions at leading universities in the United States and abroad. Ranked among the top departments in the country, the faculty includes a Fields medalist and several members of the National Academy of Sciences. There are about 60 doctoral students whose specialties include most branches of mathematics.

See in-depth description on page 583.

Syracuse University, Graduate School, College of Arts and Sciences, Department of Mathematics, Syracuse, NY 13244-0003. Offers mathematics (MS, PhD). Part-time programs available. *Faculty:* 35. *Students:* 36 full-time (8 women); includes 2 minority (both Asian Americans or Pacific Islanders), 21 international. 97 applicants, 26% accepted, 13 enrolled. Terminal master's awarded for partial completion of doctoral program. *Degree requirements:* For doctorate, 2 foreign languages, thesis/dissertation, qualifying exam. *Entrance requirements:* For master's and doctorate, GRE General Test, GRE Subject Test. Additional exam requirements/recommendations for international students: Required—TOEFL. *Application deadline:* Applications are processed on a rolling basis. Application fee: $65. *Expenses:* Tuition: Full-time $13,356; part-time $742 per credit. Required fees: $482. *Financial support:* Fellowships with full tuition reimbursements, research assistantships with full tuition reimbursements, teaching assistantships with full and partial tuition reimbursements, tuition waivers (partial) available. *Faculty research:* Pure mathematics, numerical mathematics, computing statistics. *Unit head:* Dr. Douglas Anderson, Chair, 315-443-1472, Fax: 315-443-1475, E-mail: danderso@syr.edu. *Application contact:* Mark Kleiner, Graduate Program Director, 315-443-1499, Fax: 315-443-1475, E-mail: mkleiner@syr.edu.

Tarleton State University, College of Graduate Studies and Academic Affairs, College of Sciences and Technology, Department of Mathematics, Physics and Engineering, Stephenville, TX 76402. Offers mathematics (MS). Part-time and evening/weekend programs available. *Students:* 3 full-time (2 women), 14 part-time (11 women); includes 5 minority (3 African Americans, 1 Asian American or Pacific Islander, 1 Hispanic American). 3 applicants, 100% accepted. In 2003, 4 degrees awarded. *Degree requirements:* For master's, thesis (for some programs), comprehensive exam. *Entrance requirements:* For master's, GRE General Test, minimum GPA of 3.0. Additional exam requirements/recommendations for international students: Required—TOEFL (minimum score 550 paper-based; 220 computer-based). *Application deadline:* For fall admission, 8/5 for domestic students; for spring admission, 12/1 for domestic students. Applications are processed on a rolling basis. Application fee: $25 ($75 for international students). *Expenses:* Tuition, state resident: part-time $99 per credit hour. Tuition, nonresident: part-time $325 per credit hour. One-time fee: $52 part-time. *Financial support:* In 2003–04, 1 research assistantship (averaging $12,000 per year), 2 teaching assistantships (averaging $12,000 per year) were awarded. Career-related internships or fieldwork and Federal Work-Study also available. Support available to part-time students. Financial award application deadline: 5/1; financial award applicants required to submit FAFSA. *Unit head:* Dr. Jim McCoy, Head, 254-968-9168.

Temple University, Graduate School, College of Science and Technology, Department of Mathematics, Philadelphia, PA 19122-6096. Offers applied and computational mathematics (MA, PhD); pure mathematics (MA, PhD). Part-time and evening/weekend programs available. Terminal master's awarded for partial completion of doctoral program. *Degree requirements:* For master's, written exam, thesis optional; for doctorate, 2 foreign languages, thesis/dissertation, oral and written exams. *Entrance requirements:* For master's and doctorate, GRE General Test, GRE Subject Test, minimum GPA of 3.0 during previous 2 years, 2.8 overall. *Faculty research:* Differential geometry, numerical analysis.

Tennessee State University, Graduate School, College of Arts and Sciences, Department of Physics and Mathematics, Nashville, TN 37209-1561. Offers mathematics (MS). Part-time and evening/weekend programs available. *Faculty:* 10 full-time (2 women). *Students:* 5 full-time (2 women), 8 part-time (2 women); includes 7 minority (all African Americans), 1 international. Average age 23. 15 applicants, 53% accepted. In 2003, 5 degrees awarded. *Degree requirements:* For master's, thesis, comprehensive exam. *Entrance requirements:* For master's, GRE General Test, GRE Subject Test, minimum GPA of 2.5. *Application deadline:* Applications are processed on a rolling basis. Application fee: $15. *Financial support:* In 2003–04, 1 research assistantship (averaging $1,906 per year), 2 teaching assistantships (averaging $8,886 per year) were awarded. Unspecified assistantships also available. Financial award application deadline: 5/1. *Faculty research:* Chaos theory, semi-coherent light scattering, lattices of topologies, Ramsey Theory, K theory. Total annual research expenditures: $60,000. *Unit head:* Dr. Sandra Scheick, Head, 615-963-5811.

Tennessee Technological University, Graduate School, College of Arts and Sciences, Department of Mathematics, Cookeville, TN 38505. Offers MS. Part-time programs available. *Faculty:* 17 full-time (4 women). *Students:* 8 full-time (3 women), 2 part-time; includes 4 minority (all Asian Americans or Pacific Islanders) Average age 27. 13 applicants, 69% accepted, 2 enrolled. In 2003, 6 degrees awarded. *Degree requirements:* For master's, thesis. *Entrance requirements:* For master's, GRE General Test. Additional exam requirements/recommendations for international students: Required—TOEFL. *Application deadline:* For fall admission, 3/1 for domestic students; for spring admission, 8/1 for domestic students. Application fee: $25 ($30 for international students). *Expenses:* Tuition, state resident: full-time $7,410; part-time $263 per semester hour. Tuition, nonresident: full-time $19,134; part-time $607 per semester hour. *Financial support:* In 2003–04, research assistantships (averaging $7,500 per year), 7 teaching assistantships (averaging $7,500 per year) were awarded. Financial award application deadline: 4/1. *Unit head:* Dr. Rafal Ablamowicz, Chairperson, 931-372-3441, Fax: 931-372-6353, E-mail: rablamowicz@tntech.edu. *Application contact:* Dr. Francis O. Otuonye, Associate Vice President for Research and Graduate Studies, 931-372-3233, Fax: 931-372-3497, E-mail: fotuonye@tntech.edu.

Texas A&M International University, Division of Graduate Studies, College of Arts and Sciences, Department of Math and Physical Science, Laredo, TX 78041-1900. Offers MAIS. *Students:* 1 (woman) full-time, 4 part-time (2 women); all Hispanic Americans *Application deadline:* For fall admission, 7/15 for domestic students; for spring admission, 11/12 for domestic students. Applications are processed on a rolling basis. Application fee: $0. *Expenses:* Tuition, state resident: part-time $158 per hour. Tuition, nonresident: part-time $394 per hour. *Financial support:* Application deadline: 11/1. *Unit head:* Dr. Juan H. Hinojosa, Dean, 956-326-2440, Fax: 956-326-2439, E-mail: jhhinojosa@tamiu.edu. *Application contact:* Veronica Gonzalez, Director of Enrollment Management and School Relations, 956-326-2270, Fax: 956-326-2269, E-mail: enroll@tamiu.edu.

Texas A&M International University, Division of Graduate Studies, Program in Interdisciplinary Studies, Laredo, TX 78041-1900. Offers biology (MAIS); mathematics (MAIS). *Students:* 1 (woman) full-time, 5 part-time (3 women); all Hispanic Americans In 2003, 1 degree awarded. *Expenses:* Tuition, state resident: part-time $158 per hour. Tuition, nonresident: part-time $394 per hour. *Application contact:* Veronica Gonzalez, Director of Enrollment Management and School Relations, 956-326-2270, Fax: 956-326-2269, E-mail: enroll@tamiu.edu.

Texas A&M University, College of Science, Department of Mathematics, College Station, TX 77843. Offers MS, PhD. Part-time programs available. Postbaccalaureate distance learning degree programs offered (minimal on-campus study). *Faculty:* 58 full-time (4 women), 2 part-time/adjunct (0 women). *Students:* 111 full-time (30 women), 59 part-time (33 women); includes 11 minority (1 African American, 1 American Indian/Alaska Native, 2 Asian Americans or Pacific Islanders, 7 Hispanic Americans), 64 international. Average age 27. 155 applicants, 50% accepted, 42 enrolled. In 2003, 18 master's, 8 doctorates awarded. Terminal master's awarded for partial completion of doctoral program. *Median time to degree:* Master's–1.5 years full-time; doctorate–5 years full-time. Of those who began their doctoral program in fall 1995, 100% received their degree in 8 years or less. *Degree requirements:* For master's, thesis optional; for doctorate, one foreign language, thesis/dissertation, comprehensive exam. *Entrance requirements:* For master's and doctorate, GRE General Test. Additional exam requirements/recommendations for international students: Required—TOEFL (minimum score 550 paper-based; 213 computer-based). *Application deadline:* For fall admission, 3/1 for domestic students, 3/1 for international students; for spring admission, 8/1 for domestic students, 8/1 for international students. Applications are processed on a rolling basis. Application fee: $50 ($75 for international students). Electronic applications accepted. *Expenses:* Tuition, state resident: full-time $3,420. Tuition, nonresident: full-time $9,084. Required fees: $1,861. *Financial support:* In 2003–04, 76 students received support, including 17 fellowships with partial tuition reimbursements available (averaging $17,850 per year), 7 research assistantships with partial tuition reimbursements available (averaging $17,850 per year), 62 teaching assistantships with partial tuition reimbursements available (averaging $17,850 per year); career-related internships or fieldwork, institutionally sponsored loans, scholarships/grants, health care benefits, and unspecified assistantships also available. Financial award application deadline: 3/1; financial award applicants required to submit FAFSA. *Faculty research:* Functional analysis, numerical analysis, algebra, geometry/topology, applied mathematics. *Unit head:* Dr. Albert Boggess, Head, 979-845-3261, Fax: 979-845-6028. *Application contact:* Monique Stewart, Academic Advisor I, 979-862-4137, Fax: 979-862-4190, E-mail: gstudies@math.tamu.edu.

Texas A&M University–Commerce, Graduate School, College of Arts and Sciences, Department of Mathematics, Commerce, TX 75429-3011. Offers MA, MS. Part-time programs available. *Degree requirements:* For master's, thesis (for some programs), comprehensive exam. *Entrance requirements:* For master's, GRE General Test. Electronic applications accepted.

Texas A&M University–Kingsville, College of Graduate Studies, College of Arts and Sciences, Department of Mathematics, Kingsville, TX 78363. Offers MS. Part-time programs available. *Degree requirements:* For master's, thesis or alternative, comprehensive exam. *Entrance requirements:* For master's, GRE General Test. Additional exam requirements/recommendations for international students: Required—TOEFL. *Faculty research:* Complex analysis, multivariate analysis, algebra, numerical analysis, applied statistics.

Texas Christian University, College of Science and Engineering, Department of Mathematics, Fort Worth, TX 76129-0002. Offers MAT. Part-time and evening/weekend programs available. *Application deadline:* For fall admission, 3/1 for domestic students; for spring admission, 12/1 for domestic students. Applications are processed on a rolling basis. Application fee: $0. *Expenses:* Tuition: Part-time $640 per credit hour. Tuition and fees vary according to program. *Financial support:* Application deadline: 3/1. *Unit head:* Dr. Bob Doran, Chairperson, 817-257-7335, E-mail: r.doran@tcu.edu. *Application contact:* Dr. Bonnie Melhart, Associate Dean, College of Science and Engineering, E-mail: b.melhart@tcu.edu.

Texas Southern University, Graduate School, School of Science and Technology, Department of Mathematics, Houston, TX 77004-4584. Offers MA, MS. Part-time and evening/weekend programs available. *Faculty:* 3 full-time (1 woman), 1 part-time/adjunct (0 women). *Students:* 1 full-time (0 women), 3 part-time (1 woman); all minorities (all African Americans) Average age 37. 1 applicant, 100% accepted, 1 enrolled. *Degree requirements:* For master's, thesis, comprehensive exam. *Entrance requirements:* For master's, GRE General Test, minimum GPA of 2.5. Additional exam requirements/recommendations for international students: Required—TOEFL. *Application deadline:* For fall admission, 7/15 for domestic students. Applications are processed on a rolling basis. Application fee: $50 ($75 for international students). *Expenses:* Tuition, state resident: full-time $1,656. Tuition, nonresident: full-time $5,940. Required fees: $1,314; $689 per semester. Tuition and fees vary according to course load and degree level. *Financial support:* In 2003–04, fellowships (averaging $1,200 per year) Financial award application deadline: 5/1. *Faculty research:* Statistics, number theory, topology, differential equations, numerical analysis. *Unit head:* Dr. Nathaniel Dean, Head, 713-313-7002. *Application contact:* Linda Williams, Secretary, 713-313-7602, E-mail: williams_km@tsu.edu.

Texas State University-San Marcos, Graduate School, College of Science, Department of Mathematics, San Marcos, TX 78666. Offers industrial mathematics (MS); mathematics (MA); middle school mathematics teaching (M Ed). Part-time programs available. *Faculty:* 11 full-time (3 women). *Students:* 30 full-time (14 women), 49 part-time (35 women); includes 16 minority (2 African Americans, 5 Asian Americans or Pacific Islanders, 9 Hispanic Americans), 4 international. Average age 33. 45 applicants, 82% accepted, 17 enrolled. In 2003, 10 degrees awarded. *Degree requirements:* For master's, thesis (for some programs), comprehensive exam. *Entrance requirements:* For master's, GRE General Test, minimum GPA of 2.75 in last 60 hours. Additional exam requirements/recommendations for international students: Required—TOEFL. *Application deadline:* For fall admission, 6/15 for domestic students; for spring admission, 10/15 priority date for domestic students. Applications are processed on a rolling basis. Application fee: $40 ($90 for international students). *Expenses:* Tuition, state resident: full-time $2,484; part-time $138 per semester hour. Tuition, nonresident: full-time $6,732; part-time $374 per semester hour. Required fees: $948; $31 per semester hour. $195 per term. Tuition and fees vary according to course load. *Financial support:* In 2003–04, 62 students received support, including 2 research assistantships (averaging $10,580 per year), 18 teaching assistantships (averaging $12,430 per year); Federal Work-Study and institutionally sponsored loans also available. Support available to part-time students. Financial award application deadline: 4/1; financial award applicants required to submit FAFSA. *Faculty research:* Differential equations, geometric topology, number theory, mathematics education, graph theory. *Unit head:* Dr. Stanley G. Wayment, Chair, 512-245-2551, Fax: 512-245-3425, E-mail: sw05@txstate.edu. *Application contact:* Dr. Maria Acosta, Graduate Adviser, 512-245-2497, E-mail: ma05@txstate.edu.

Texas Tech University, Graduate School, College of Arts and Sciences, Department of Mathematics and Statistics, Lubbock, TX 79409. Offers mathematics (MA, MS, PhD); statistics (MS). Part-time programs available. *Faculty:* 42 full-time (8 women), 1 part-time/adjunct (0 women). *Students:* 82 full-time (35 women), 14 part-time (6 women); includes 10 minority (3 African Americans, 3 Asian Americans or Pacific Islanders, 4 Hispanic Americans), 27 international. Average age 28. 79 applicants, 62% accepted, 14 enrolled. In 2003, 24 master's, 6 doctorates awarded. *Degree requirements:* For master's, thesis or alternative; for doctorate, one foreign language, thesis/dissertation. *Entrance requirements:* For master's and doctorate, GRE General Test. Additional exam requirements/recommendations for international students: Required—TOEFL (minimum score 550 paper-based; 213 computer-based). *Application deadline:* Applications are processed on a rolling basis. Application fee: $50 ($60 for international students). Electronic applications accepted. *Expenses:* Tuition, state resident: full-time $3,312. Tuition, nonresident: full-time $8,976. Required fees: $1,745. Tuition and fees vary according to program. *Financial support:* In 2003–04, 61 students received support, including 7 research assistantships with partial tuition reimbursements available (averaging $14,324 per year), 73 teaching assistantships with partial tuition reimbursements available (averaging $14,602 per year); fellowships, Federal Work-Study and institutionally sponsored loans also available. Support available to part-time students. Financial award application deadline: 5/1; financial award applicants required to submit FAFSA. *Faculty research:* Numerical analysis; control and systems theory; mathematical biology; mechanics; algebra and geometry. Total annual research expenditures: $520,256. *Unit head:* Dr. Lawrence Schovanec, Chair, 806-742-2566, Fax: 806-742-1112, E-mail: schov@math.ttu.edu. *Applica-*

tion contact: Dr. Alex Wang, Graduate Adviser, 806-742-2566, Fax: 806-742-1112, E-mail: awang@matt.ttu.edu.

Texas Woman's University, Graduate School, College of Arts and Sciences, Department of Mathematics and Computer Science, Denton, TX 76201. Offers mathematics (MA, MS); mathematics teaching (MS). Part-time and evening/weekend programs available. *Students:* 8 full-time (6 women), 8 part-time (7 women); includes 4 minority (1 African American, 2 Asian Americans or Pacific Islanders, 1 Hispanic American), 4 international. Average age 37. In 2003, 4 degrees awarded. *Degree requirements:* For master's, thesis (for some programs), comprehensive exam. *Entrance requirements:* For master's, GRE General Test, 2 letters of reference. Additional exam requirements/recommendations for international students: Required—TOEFL (minimum score 550 paper-based; 213 computer-based). *Application deadline:* Applications are processed on a rolling basis. Application fee: $30 ($50 for international students). Electronic applications accepted. *Expenses:* Tuition, state resident: part-time $66 per credit. Tuition, nonresident: part-time $302 per credit. Full-time tuition and fees vary according to reciprocity agreements. *Financial support:* In 2003–04, 3 research assistantships (averaging $7,722 per year), 4 teaching assistantships (averaging $7,722 per year) were awarded. Career-related internships or fieldwork, Federal Work-Study, institutionally sponsored loans, scholarships/grants, traineeships, health care benefits, and unspecified assistantships also available. Support available to part-time students. Financial award application deadline: 3/1; financial award applicants required to submit FAFSA. *Faculty research:* Biopharmaceutical statistics, dynamical systems and control theory, Bayesian inference, math and computer science curriculum innovation, computer modeling of physical phenomenon. *Unit head:* Dr. Don E. Edwards, Chair, 940-898-2166, Fax: 940-898-2179, E-mail: f_edwards@twu.edu. *Application contact:* Holly Kiser, Coordinator of Graduate Admissions, 940-898-3188, Fax: 940-898-3081, E-mail: hkiser@twu.edu.

Tufts University, Graduate School of Arts and Sciences, Department of Mathematics, Medford, MA 02155. Offers MA, MS, PhD. *Faculty:* 21 full-time, 8 part-time/adjunct. *Students:* 18 (5 women); includes 1 American Indian/Alaska Native 7 international. 57 applicants, 44% accepted, 9 enrolled. In 2003, 7 master's, 1 doctorate awarded. Terminal master's awarded for partial completion of doctoral program. *Degree requirements:* For master's, one foreign language, thesis; for doctorate, 2 foreign languages, thesis/dissertation. *Entrance requirements:* Additional exam requirements/recommendations for international students: Required—TOEFL (minimum score 550 paper-based; 213 computer-based). *Application deadline:* For fall admission, 2/15 for domestic students, 12/30 for international students. Applications are processed on a rolling basis. Application fee: $60. Electronic applications accepted. *Expenses:* Tuition: Full-time $29,949. *Financial support:* Teaching assistantships with full and partial tuition reimbursements, Federal Work-Study, scholarships/grants, and tuition waivers (partial) available. Financial award application deadline: 2/15; financial award applicants required to submit FAFSA. *Unit head:* Christoph Borgers, Chair, 617-627-3234, E-mail: mathgrad@tufts.edu. *Application contact:* Montserrat Teixidor, Head, 617-627-3234, E-mail: mathgrad@tufts.edu.

Tulane University, Graduate School, Department of Mathematics, New Orleans, LA 70118-5669. Offers applied mathematics (MS); mathematics (MS, PhD); statistics (MS). *Faculty:* 24 full-time. *Students:* 29 full-time (15 women), 1 part-time; includes 7 minority (2 African Americans, 2 Asian Americans or Pacific Islanders, 3 Hispanic Americans), 8 international. 68 applicants, 26% accepted, 9 enrolled. In 2003, 5 master's, 2 doctorates awarded. *Degree requirements:* For master's, thesis (for some programs); for doctorate, thesis/dissertation. *Entrance requirements:* For master's, GRE General Test, minimum B average in undergraduate course work; for doctorate, GRE General Test. Additional exam requirements/recommendations for international students: Required—TOEFL; Recommended—TSE. *Application deadline:* For fall admission, 2/1 for domestic students, 2/1 for international students. Application fee: $45. *Financial support:* Fellowships with full tuition reimbursements, research assistantships with full tuition reimbursements, teaching assistantships with full tuition reimbursements, career-related internships or fieldwork, Federal Work-Study, and institutionally sponsored loans available. Financial award application deadline: 2/1. *Unit head:* Dr. Morris Kalka, Chair, 504-865-5727. *Application contact:* Dr. Ricardo Cortez, Graduate Adviser, 504-865-5727.

Université de Moncton, Faculty of Science, Department of Mathematics and Statistics, Moncton, NB E1A 3E9, Canada. Offers mathematics (M Sc). *Degree requirements:* For master's, one foreign language, thesis. *Entrance requirements:* For master's, minimum GPA of 3.0. *Faculty research:* Statistics, numerical analysis, fixed point theory, mathematical physics.

Université de Montréal, Faculty of Graduate Studies, Faculty of Arts and Sciences, Department of Mathematics and Statistics, Montréal, QC H3C 3J7, Canada. Offers mathematics (M Sc, PhD); statistics (M Sc, PhD). *Faculty:* 33 full-time (5 women), 15 part-time/adjunct (1 woman). *Students:* 92 full-time (30 women), 1 part-time. 73 applicants, 30% accepted, 19 enrolled. In 2003, 21 master's, 3 doctorates awarded. *Degree requirements:* For master's, thesis; for doctorate, thesis/dissertation, general exam. *Entrance requirements:* For master's and doctorate, proficiency in French. *Application deadline:* For fall and spring admission, 2/1; for winter admission, 11/1 for domestic students. Application fee: $30. Electronic applications accepted. *Expenses:* Tuition, state resident: full-time $834. Tuition, nonresident: full-time $1,253. International tuition: $3,900 full-time. Tuition and fees vary according to program. *Financial support:* Fellowships, research assistantships, teaching assistantships, monitorships available. Financial award application deadline: 4/1. *Faculty research:* Pure and applied mathematics, actuarial mathematics. *Unit head:* Yvan St-Aubin, Chair, 514-343-6710, Fax: 514-343-5700. *Application contact:* Liliane Badier, Student Files Management Technician, 514-343-6111 Ext. 1695, Fax: 514-343-5700.

Université de Sherbrooke, Faculty of Sciences, Department of Mathematics and Informatics, Sherbrooke, QC J1K 2R1, Canada. Offers M Sc, PhD. *Degree requirements:* For master's and doctorate, thesis/dissertation. *Entrance requirements:* For doctorate, master's degree. *Faculty research:* Measure theory, differential equations, probability, statistics, error control codes.

Université du Québec à Montréal, Graduate Programs, Program in Mathematics, Montréal, QC H3C 3P8, Canada. Offers M Sc, PhD. Part-time programs available. *Degree requirements:* For master's and doctorate, thesis/dissertation. *Entrance requirements:* For master's, appropriate bachelor's degree or equivalent, proficiency in French; for doctorate, appropriate master's degree or equivalent, proficiency in French.

Université du Québec à Trois-Rivières, Graduate Programs, Program in Mathematics and Computer Science, Trois-Rivières, QC G9A 5H7, Canada. Offers M Sc. *Faculty research:* Probability, statistics.

Université Laval, Faculty of Sciences and Engineering, Department of Mathematics and Statistics, Programs in Mathematics, Québec, QC G1K 7P4, Canada. Offers M Sc, PhD. Terminal master's awarded for partial completion of doctoral program. *Degree requirements:* For master's, thesis (for some programs); for doctorate, thesis/dissertation, comprehensive exam. *Entrance requirements:* For master's and doctorate, knowledge of French and English. Electronic applications accepted.

University at Albany, State University of New York, College of Arts and Sciences, Department of Mathematics and Statistics, Albany, NY 12222-0001. Offers mathematics (PhD); secondary teaching (MA); statistics (MA). Evening/weekend programs available. *Students:* 34 full-time (11 women), 9 part-time (3 women). Average age 32. 37 applicants, 43% accepted, 12 enrolled. In 2003, 7 master's, 1 doctorate awarded. *Degree requirements:* For doctorate, one foreign language, thesis/dissertation. *Entrance requirements:* For doctorate, GRE General Test. Additional exam requirements/recommendations for international students: Required—TOEFL (minimum score 550 paper-based; 213 computer-based). *Application deadline:* For fall admission, 8/1 for domestic students, 5/1 for international students; for spring admission, 11/1 for domestic students, 11/1 for international students. Applications are processed on a rolling basis. Application fee: $50. Electronic applications accepted. *Expenses:* Tuition, state resident: part-time $288 per credit. Tuition, nonresident: part-time $438 per credit. Required fees: $495 per semester. *Financial support:* Fellowships, research assistantships, teaching assistantships, minority assistantships available. Financial award application deadline: 3/15. *Unit head:* Timothy Lance, Chair, 518-442-4602.

University at Buffalo, The State University of New York, Graduate School, College of Arts and Sciences, Department of Mathematics, Buffalo, NY 14260. Offers MA, PhD. Part-time programs available. *Faculty:* 36 full-time (1 woman), 10 part-time/adjunct (2 women). *Students:* 63 full-time (19 women), 6 part-time; includes 7 minority (3 African Americans, 1 American Indian/Alaska Native, 3 Asian Americans or Pacific Islanders), 40 international. Average age 29. 138 applicants, 27% accepted, 15 enrolled. In 2003, 4 master's, 2 doctorates awarded. Terminal master's awarded for partial completion of doctoral program. *Degree requirements:* For master's, thesis (for some programs), comprehensive exam (for some programs); for doctorate, thesis/dissertation, comprehensive exam. *Entrance requirements:* Additional exam requirements/recommendations for international students: Required—TOEFL (minimum score 550 paper-based; 213 computer-based). *Application deadline:* For fall admission, 1/15 priority date for domestic students, 1/15 priority date for international students; for spring admission, 10/15 priority date for domestic students, 10/15 priority date for international students. Applications are processed on a rolling basis. Application fee: $35. Electronic applications accepted. *Expenses:* Tuition, state resident: full-time $7,110. Tuition, nonresident: full-time $10,920. Tuition and fees vary according to program. *Financial support:* In 2003–04, 55 students received support, including fellowships with full tuition reimbursements available (averaging $4,500 per year), 47 teaching assistantships with full tuition reimbursements available (averaging $11,375 per year); research assistantships, Federal Work-Study, institutionally sponsored loans, and unspecified assistantships also available. Financial award application deadline: 1/15; financial award applicants required to submit FAFSA. *Faculty research:* Algebra, analysis, applied mathematics, logic, number theory, topology. Total annual research expenditures: $172,334. *Unit head:* Dr. Samuel D. Schack, Chairman, 716-645-6284 Ext. 103, Fax: 716-645-5039, E-mail: chair@math.buffalo.edu. *Application contact:* Dr. James F. Reineck, Director of Graduate Studies, 716-645-6284 Ext. 109, Fax: 716-645-5039, E-mail: graduatedirector@math.buffalo.edu.

The University of Akron, Graduate School, Buchtel College of Arts and Sciences, Department of Theoretical and Applied Mathematics, Program in Mathematics, Akron, OH 44325-0001. Offers MS. Part-time and evening/weekend programs available. *Students:* 8 full-time (4 women), 2 part-time; includes 1 minority (Asian American or Pacific Islander), 2 international. Average age 30. 6 applicants, 50% accepted, 3 enrolled. In 2003, 4 degrees awarded. *Degree requirements:* For master's, seminar and comprehensive exam or thesis, thesis optional. *Entrance requirements:* For master's, minimum GPA of 2.75. Additional exam requirements/recommendations for international students: Required—TOEFL (minimum score 550 paper-based; 213 computer-based), Michigan English Language Assessment Battery. *Application deadline:* For fall admission, 3/1 for domestic students. Applications are processed on a rolling basis. Application fee: $40 ($60 for international students). *Expenses:* Tuition, state resident: part-time $277 per credit hour. Tuition, nonresident: part-time $476 per credit hour. *Financial support:* Teaching assistantships with tuition reimbursements available. Financial award application deadline: 3/1. *Faculty research:* Topology analysis. *Unit head:* Dr. Ali Hajjafar, Coordinator, 330-972-8018.

The University of Alabama, Graduate School, College of Arts and Sciences, Department of Mathematics, Tuscaloosa, AL 35487. Offers applied mathematics (PhD); mathematics (MA); pure mathematics (PhD). *Faculty:* 26 full-time (1 woman). *Students:* 28 full-time (13 women), 6 part-time (1 woman); includes 9 minority (all African Americans), 19 international. Average age 30. 32 applicants, 25% accepted, 6 enrolled. In 2003, 3 master's, 4 doctorates awarded. Terminal master's awarded for partial completion of doctoral program. *Degree requirements:* For master's, thesis or alternative; for doctorate, one foreign language, thesis/dissertation, teaching experience. *Entrance requirements:* For master's and doctorate, GRE General Test, minimum GPA of 3.0. Additional exam requirements/recommendations for international students: Required—TOEFL. *Application deadline:* For fall admission, 7/1 for domestic students. Applications are processed on a rolling basis. Application fee: $25. Electronic applications accepted. *Expenses:* Tuition, state resident: full-time $4,134; part-time $230 per credit hour. Tuition, nonresident: full-time $11,294; part-time $627 per credit hour. Part-time tuition and fees vary according to course load. *Financial support:* In 2003–04, 3 fellowships with full tuition reimbursements (averaging $14,834 per year), 21 teaching assistantships with full tuition reimbursements (averaging $10,209 per year) were awarded. Research assistantships with full tuition reimbursements, Federal Work-Study and institutionally sponsored loans also available. Support available to part-time students. Financial award application deadline: 7/1. *Faculty research:* Analysis, topology, algebra, fluid mechanics and system control theory, optimization, stochastic processes. *Unit head:* Dr. Zhijian Wu, Chair, 205-348-5080, Fax: 205-348-7067, E-mail: zwu@gp.as.ua.edu. *Application contact:* Dr. Tan Yu Lee, Director, Graduate Programs in Mathematics, 205-348-5155, Fax: 205-348-7067, E-mail: tlee@gp.as.ua.edu.

The University of Alabama at Birmingham, School of Natural Sciences and Mathematics, Department of Mathematics, Birmingham, AL 35294. Offers applied mathematics (PhD); mathematics (MS). *Students:* 22 full-time (10 women), 6 part-time (4 women); includes 3 minority (all African Americans), 14 international. 58 applicants, 64% accepted. In 2003, 5 degrees awarded. Terminal master's awarded for partial completion of doctoral program. *Degree requirements:* For master's, thesis optional; for doctorate, one foreign language, thesis/dissertation, comprehensive exam. *Entrance requirements:* For master's and doctorate, GRE General Test. *Application deadline:* Applications are processed on a rolling basis. Application fee: $35 ($60 for international students). Electronic applications accepted. *Expenses:* Tuition, state resident: full-time $4,142; part-time $141 per credit hour. Tuition, nonresident: full-time $9,230; part-time $353 per credit hour. Required fees: $4 per credit hour. *Financial support:* In 2003–04, 18 teaching assistantships with tuition reimbursements (averaging $14,000 per year) were awarded; fellowships, research assistantships, career-related internships or fieldwork, Federal Work-Study, institutionally sponsored loans, tuition waivers (full and partial), and unspecified assistantships also available. Support available to part-time students. Financial award application deadline: 3/31; financial award applicants required to submit FAFSA. *Faculty research:* Differential equations, topology, mathematical physics, dynamic systems. *Unit head:* Dr. Rudi Weikard, Chair, 205-934-2154, Fax: 205-934-9025, E-mail: weikard@uab.edu.

The University of Alabama in Huntsville, School of Graduate Studies, College of Science, Department of Mathematical Sciences, Huntsville, AL 35899. Offers applied mathematics (PhD); mathematics (MA, MS). Part-time and evening/weekend programs available. *Faculty:* 13 full-time (1 woman), 2 part-time/adjunct (0 women). *Students:* 14 full-time (7 women), 10 part-time (4 women); includes 1 minority (Asian American or Pacific Islander), 3 international. Average age 33. 25 applicants, 84% accepted, 14 enrolled. In 2003, 4 degrees awarded. *Degree requirements:* For master's, thesis or alternative, oral and written exams, comprehensive exam, registration; for doctorate, one foreign language, thesis/dissertation, oral and written exams, comprehensive exam, registration. *Entrance requirements:* For master's and doctorate, GRE General Test, minimum GPA of 3.0. Additional exam requirements/recommendations for international students: Required—TOEFL (minimum score 550 paper-based; 213 computer-based). *Application deadline:* For fall admission, 5/30 priority date for domestic students, 2/30 priority date for international students; for spring admission, 10/10 priority date for domestic students, 7/10 priority date for international students. Applications are processed on a rolling basis. Application fee: $35. *Expenses:* Tuition, state resident: full-time $5,168; part-time $211 per hour. Tuition, nonresident: full-time $10,620; part-time $447 per hour. Tuition and fees vary according to course load. *Financial support:* In 2003–04, 17 students received support, including 1 research assistantship with full and partial tuition reimbursement available (averaging $4,766 per year), 15 teaching assistantships with full and partial tuition reimbursements available (averaging $7,753 per year); fellowships with full and partial tuition reimbursements available, career-related internships or fieldwork, Federal Work-Study, institutionally sponsored loans, scholarships/grants, health care benefits, tuition waivers (full and partial), and unspecified assistantships also available. Support available to part-time students. Financial award application deadline: 4/1; financial award applicants required to submit FAFSA. *Faculty*

Mathematics

The University of Alabama in Huntsville (continued)
research: Statistical modeling, stochastic processes, numerical analysis, combinatorics, fracture mechanics. Total annual research expenditures: $232,708. *Unit head:* Dr. Kyle Siegrist, Chair, 256-824-6470, Fax: 256-824-6173, E-mail: chair@math.uah.edu.

University of Alaska Fairbanks, College of Science, Engineering and Mathematics, Department of Mathematical Sciences, Fairbanks, AK 99775-7520. Offers computer science (MS); mathematics (MS, PhD); software engineering (MSE); statistics (MS). Part-time programs available. Terminal master's awarded for partial completion of doctoral program. *Degree requirements:* For master's, thesis or alternative, comprehensive exam, registration; for doctorate, thesis/dissertation, comprehensive exam, registration. *Entrance requirements:* For master's and doctorate, GRE General Test, GRE Subject Test. Additional exam requirements/recommendations for international students: Required—TOEFL (minimum score 600 paper-based). Electronic applications accepted. *Faculty research:* Blackbox kriging (statistics), interaction with a virtual reality environment (computer), arrangements of hyperplanes (topology), bifurcation analysis of time-periodic differential-delay equations, synthetic aperture radar interferometry software (computer).

University of Alberta, Faculty of Graduate Studies and Research, Department of Mathematical and Statistical Sciences, Edmonton, AB T6G 2E1, Canada. Offers applied mathematics (M Sc, PhD); biostatistics (M Sc); mathematical finance (M Sc, PhD); mathematical physics (M Sc, PhD); mathematics (M Sc, PhD); statistics (M Sc, PhD, Postgraduate Diploma). Part-time programs available. *Faculty:* 48 full-time (4 women). *Students:* 112 full-time (41 women), 5 part-time. Average age 24. 776 applicants, 5% accepted, 34 enrolled. In 2003, 12 master's, 10 doctorates awarded. Terminal master's awarded for partial completion of doctoral program. *Median time to degree:* Master's–2 years full-time; doctorate–5 years full-time. Of those who began their doctoral program in fall 1995, 100% received their degree in 8 years or less. *Degree requirements:* For master's, thesis (for some programs); for doctorate, thesis/dissertation, comprehensive exam. *Entrance requirements:* Additional exam requirements/recommendations for international students: Required—TOEFL (minimum score 580 paper-based; 237 computer-based). *Application deadline:* For fall admission, 3/1 for domestic students, 2/1 for international students. Applications are processed on a rolling basis. Application fee: $0. Electronic applications accepted. Tuition charges are reported in Canadian dollars. Tuition, nonresident: full-time $3,921 Canadian dollars. International tuition: $7,113 Canadian dollars full-time. *Financial support:* In 2003–04, 51 research assistantships, 88 teaching assistantships with full and partial tuition reimbursements were awarded. Scholarships/grants also available. Financial award application deadline: 5/1. *Faculty research:* Classical and functional analysis, algebra, differential equations, geometry. *Unit head:* Dr. Anthony To-Ming Lau, Chair, 403-492-5799, E-mail: tlau@math.ualberta.ca. *Application contact:* Dr. Yau Shu Wong, Associate Chair, Graduate Studies, 403-492-5799, Fax: 403-492-6828, E-mail: gradstudies@math.ualberta.ca.

The University of Arizona, Graduate College, College of Science, Department of Mathematics, Mathematical Sciences, Professional Program, Tucson, AZ 85721. Offers PMS. Part-time programs available. *Degree requirements:* For master's, thesis, internships, colloquium, business courses. *Entrance requirements:* For master's, GRE General Test, 3 letters of recommendations. *Expenses:* Tuition, state resident: part-time $196 per unit. Tuition, nonresident: part-time $326 per unit. *Faculty research:* Algebra, coding theory, graph theory, combinatorics, probability.

The University of Arizona, Graduate College, Graduate Interdisciplinary Programs, Graduate Interdisciplinary Program in Applied Mathematics, Tucson, AZ 85721. Offers applied mathematics (MS, PhD); mathematical sciences (PMS). *Faculty:* 34. *Students:* 44 full-time (15 women), 3 part-time (1 woman); includes 6 minority (2 Asian Americans or Pacific Islanders, 4 Hispanic Americans), 15 international. Average age 26. 72 applicants, 28% accepted, 10 enrolled. In 2003, 2 master's awarded, leading to university research/teaching 50%, business/industry 50%; 4 doctorates awarded, leading to university research/teaching 25%, continued full-time study 50%, business/industry 25%. Terminal master's awarded for partial completion of doctoral program. *Median time to degree:* Master's–2 years full-time; doctorate–6 years full-time. Of those who began their doctoral program in fall 1995, 100% received their degree in 8 years or less. *Degree requirements:* For master's, thesis (for some programs), registration; for doctorate, one foreign language, thesis/dissertation, comprehensive exam, registration. *Entrance requirements:* For master's and doctorate, GRE. Additional exam requirements/recommendations for international students: Required—TOEFL (minimum score 575 paper-based; 230 computer-based), TSE(minimum score 45). *Application deadline:* For fall admission, 1/30 priority date for domestic students, 2/15 priority date for international students. Applications are processed on a rolling basis. Application fee: $50. *Expenses:* Tuition, state resident: part-time $196 per unit. Tuition, nonresident: part-time $326 per unit. *Financial support:* In 2003–04, 42 students received support, including 4 fellowships with full tuition reimbursements available (averaging $27,500 per year), 21 research assistantships with full tuition reimbursements available (averaging $15,400 per year), 17 teaching assistantships with full tuition reimbursements available (averaging $15,400 per year); institutionally sponsored loans, scholarships/grants, health care benefits, tuition waivers (full), and unspecified assistantships also available. Financial award application deadline: 3/1. *Faculty research:* Dynamical systems and chaos, partial differential equations, pattern formation, fluid dynamics and turbulence, scientific computation, mathematical physics, mathematical biology, medical imaging, applied probability and stochastic processes. *Unit head:* Dr. Michael Tabor, Head, 520-621-4664, Fax: 520-626-5048, E-mail: tabor@math.arizona.edu. *Application contact:* Linda Silverman, Graduate Coordinator, 520-621-2016, Fax: 520-626-5048, E-mail: applmath@u.arizona.edu.

See in-depth description on page 587.

University of Arkansas, Graduate School, J. William Fulbright College of Arts and Sciences, Department of Mathematical Sciences, Program in Mathematics, Fayetteville, AR 72701-1201. Offers MS, PhD. *Students:* 29 full-time (14 women), 4 part-time; includes 4 minority (1 African American, 2 Asian Americans or Pacific Islanders, 1 Hispanic American), 10 international. 42 applicants, 74% accepted. In 2003, 4 degrees awarded. *Degree requirements:* For master's, thesis or alternative; for doctorate, 2 foreign languages, thesis/dissertation. Application fee: $40 ($50 for international students). *Expenses:* Tuition, state resident: full-time $4,032; part-time $224 per credit hour. Tuition, nonresident: full-time $9,540; part-time $530 per credit hour. Tuition and fees vary according to course load and program. *Financial support:* In 2003–04, 8 fellowships, 23 teaching assistantships were awarded. Career-related internships or fieldwork and Federal Work-Study also available. Support available to part-time students. Financial award application deadline: 4/1; financial award applicants required to submit FAFSA. *Unit head:* Dr. Mark Arnold, Chair of Studies, 479-575-3351, E-mail: gradmath@comp.uark.edu.

The University of British Columbia, Faculty of Graduate Studies, Faculty of Science, Department of Mathematics, Vancouver, BC V6T 1Z1, Canada. Offers M Sc, MA, PhD. *Faculty:* 44 full-time (5 women). *Students:* 63 full-time (16 women). Average age 24. 180 applicants, 32% accepted, 29 enrolled. In 2003, 17 master's, 5 doctorates awarded. *Median time to degree:* Master's–2 years full-time; doctorate–4 years full-time. *Degree requirements:* For master's, thesis or alternative, essay, qualifying exam; for doctorate, thesis/dissertation, qualifying exam. *Entrance requirements:* For master's and doctorate, first class standing. Additional exam requirements/recommendations for international students: Required—TOEFL (minimum score 600 paper-based; 250 computer-based), TSE. *Application deadline:* For fall admission, 2/29 for domestic students. Application fee: $90 Canadian dollars ($150 Canadian dollars for international students). Electronic applications accepted. *Financial support:* In 2003–04, 15 students received support; fellowships, research assistantships, teaching assistantships, institutionally sponsored loans, scholarships/grants, health care benefits, tuition waivers (full and partial), and unspecified assistantships available. *Faculty research:* Applied mathematics, financial mathematics, pure mathematics. *Unit head:* Brian Marcus, Head, 604-822-2771, Fax: 604-822-9479, E-mail: marcus@math.ubc.ca. *Application contact:* Lee Yupitun, Graduate Secretary, 604-822-3079, Fax: 604-822-6074, E-mail: admiss@math.ubc.ca.

University of Calgary, Faculty of Graduate Studies, Faculty of Science, Department of Mathematics and Statistics, Calgary, AB T2N 1N4, Canada. Offers M Sc, PhD. *Faculty:* 37 full-time (3 women), 2 part-time/adjunct (0 women). *Students:* 34 full-time (13 women), 2 part-time. Average age 30. 48 applicants, 46% accepted, 15 enrolled. In 2003, 9 master's, 2 doctorates awarded, leading to university research/teaching 50%, business/industry 50%. *Median time to degree:* Master's–2 years full-time, 5 years part-time; doctorate–5 years full-time. Of those who began their doctoral program in fall 1995, 100% received their degree in 8 years or less. *Degree requirements:* For master's, thesis, comprehensive exam; for doctorate, thesis/dissertation, candidacy exam, preliminary exams. *Entrance requirements:* For master's, honors degree in applied math, pure math, or statistics; for doctorate, MA or M Sc. Additional exam requirements/recommendations for international students: Required—TOEFL (paper score 600; computer score 250) or IELTS (paper score 7). *Application deadline:* For fall admission, 2/1 for domestic students. Applications are processed on a rolling basis. Application fee: $60. Tuition, nonresident: full-time $4,765. Tuition and fees vary according to degree level, program and student level. *Financial support:* In 2003–04, 32 students received support, including 10 research assistantships with partial tuition reimbursements available (averaging $4,000 per year), 29 teaching assistantships with partial tuition reimbursements available (averaging $12,500 per year); fellowships, scholarships/grants and unspecified assistantships also available. *Faculty research:* Combinatorics, applied mathematics, statistics, probability, analysis. Total annual research expenditures: $1.1 million. *Unit head:* T. Bisztriczky, Head, 403-220-6312, Fax: 403-282-5150, E-mail: tbisztri@math.ucalgary.ca. *Application contact:* Joanne Mellard, Graduate Secretary, 403-220-6299, Fax: 403-282-5150, E-mail: gradapps@math.ucalgary.ca.

University of California, Berkeley, Graduate Division, College of Letters and Science, Department of Mathematics, Berkeley, CA 94720-1500. Offers applied mathematics (PhD); mathematics (MA, PhD). *Students:* 173 (30 women); includes 26 minority (4 African Americans, 1 American Indian/Alaska Native, 14 Asian Americans or Pacific Islanders, 7 Hispanic Americans) 43 international. Average age 23. 491 applicants, 13% accepted, 20 enrolled. In 2003, 10 master's, 19 doctorates awarded. Terminal master's awarded for partial completion of doctoral program. *Degree requirements:* For master's, exam or thesis; for doctorate, 2 foreign languages, thesis/dissertation, qualifying exam. *Entrance requirements:* For master's and doctorate, GRE General Test, GRE Subject Test, minimum GPA of 3.0. *Application deadline:* For fall admission, 1/15 for domestic students. Application fee: $60. International tuition: $12,491 full-time. Required fees: $5,484. *Financial support:* Fellowships, research assistantships, teaching assistantships, institutionally sponsored loans and unspecified assistantships available. Financial award application deadline: 12/15. *Faculty research:* Algebra, analysis, logic, geometry/topology. *Unit head:* Calvin C. Moore, Chair, 510-642-4129. *Application contact:* Graduate Assistant for Admission, 510-642-0665, Fax: 510-642-8204, E-mail: brown@math.berkeley.edu.

University of California, Davis, Graduate Studies, Program in Mathematics, Davis, CA 95616. Offers MA, MAT, PhD. *Faculty:* 37 full-time. *Students:* 59 full-time (12 women); includes 6 minority (3 African Americans, 2 Asian Americans or Pacific Islanders, 1 Hispanic American), 11 international. Average age 28. 94 applicants, 48% accepted, 25 enrolled. In 2003, 4 master's, 4 doctorates awarded. Terminal master's awarded for partial completion of doctoral program. *Degree requirements:* For doctorate, one foreign language, thesis/dissertation. *Entrance requirements:* For master's and doctorate, GRE General Test, GRE Subject Test, minimum GPA of 3.0. Additional exam requirements/recommendations for international students: Required—TOEFL (minimum score 550 paper-based; 213 computer-based). *Application deadline:* For fall admission, 1/15 for domestic students, 1/15 for international students. Application fee: $60. Electronic applications accepted. Tuition, nonresident: full-time $12,245. Required fees: $7,062. *Financial support:* In 2003–04, 55 students received support, including 15 fellowships with full and partial tuition reimbursements available (averaging $8,387 per year), 8 research assistantships with full and partial tuition reimbursements available (averaging $9,516 per year), 19 teaching assistantships with partial tuition reimbursements available (averaging $12,762 per year); Federal Work-Study, institutionally sponsored loans, scholarships/grants, and tuition waivers (full and partial) also available. Financial award application deadline: 1/15; financial award applicants required to submit FAFSA. *Faculty research:* Mathematical physics, geometric topology, probability, partial differential equations, applied mathematics. *Unit head:* John K. Hunter, Chair, 530-752-4487, E-mail: jkhunter@ucdavis.edu. *Application contact:* Celia Davis, Administrative Assistant, 530-752-8131, Fax: 530-752-6635, E-mail: davis@math.ucdavis.edu.

University of California, Irvine, Office of Graduate Studies, School of Physical Sciences, Department of Mathematics, Irvine, CA 92697. Offers MS, PhD. *Students:* 80. In 2003, 8 master's, 5 doctorates awarded. *Degree requirements:* For doctorate, thesis/dissertation. *Entrance requirements:* For master's and doctorate, GRE General Test, GRE Subject Test, minimum GPA of 3.0. Additional exam requirements/recommendations for international students: Required—TOEFL (minimum score 550 paper-based; 213 computer-based), TSE. *Application deadline:* For fall admission, 1/15 for domestic students; for winter admission, 10/15 for domestic students. Applications are processed on a rolling basis. Application fee: $60. Electronic applications accepted. Tuition, nonresident: full-time $12,245. Required fees: $5,219. Tuition and fees vary according to degree level and program. *Financial support:* Fellowships, research assistantships with full tuition reimbursements, teaching assistantships, institutionally sponsored loans, traineeships, health care benefits, and unspecified assistantships available. Financial award application deadline: 3/1; financial award applicants required to submit FAFSA. *Faculty research:* Algebra and logic, geometry and topology, probability, mathematical physics. *Unit head:* Bernard Russo, Chair, 949-824-5510, Fax: 949-824-7993, E-mail: brusso@uci.edu. *Application contact:* Jennifer Dugan, Graduate Coordinator, 949-824-5544, Fax: 949-824-7993, E-mail: jdugan@math.uci.edu.

University of California, Los Angeles, Graduate Division, College of Letters and Science, Department of Mathematics, Los Angeles, CA 90095. Offers MA, MAT, PhD. *Degree requirements:* For master's, essay; for doctorate, one foreign language, thesis/dissertation, oral and written qualifying exams. *Entrance requirements:* For master's, GRE General Test, GRE Subject Test, minimum GPA of 3.2 in mathematics; for doctorate, GRE General Test, GRE Subject Test, minimum GPA of 3.5 in mathematics. Electronic applications accepted. Tuition, nonresident: full-time $12,245. Required fees: $6,318.

University of California, Riverside, Graduate Division, Department of Mathematics, Riverside, CA 92521-0102. Offers applied mathematics (MS); mathematics (MA, MS, PhD). Part-time programs available. *Faculty:* 22 full-time (2 women), 4 part-time/adjunct (1 woman). *Students:* 43 full-time (14 women), 4 part-time (2 women); includes 13 minority (1 African American, 7 Asian Americans or Pacific Islanders, 5 Hispanic Americans), 7 international. Average age 29. 38 applicants, 97% accepted, 19 enrolled. In 2003, 7 master's, 3 doctorates awarded. Terminal master's awarded for partial completion of doctoral program. *Median time to degree:* Master's–1.5 years full-time; doctorate–6 years full-time. *Degree requirements:* For master's, comprehensive exam; for doctorate, thesis/dissertation, qualifying exams. *Entrance requirements:* For master's and doctorate, GRE General Test, minimum GPA of 3.2. Additional exam requirements/recommendations for international students: Required—TOEFL (minimum score 550 paper-based; 213 computer-based); Recommended—TSE. *Application deadline:* For fall admission, 5/1 for domestic students, 2/1 for international students; for winter admission, 9/1 for domestic students; for spring admission, 12/1 for domestic students. Applications are processed on a rolling basis. Application fee: $60. Electronic applications accepted. Tuition, nonresident: part-time $4,082 per quarter. *Financial support:* In 2003–04, 9 students received support, including fellowships with tuition reimbursements available (averaging $12,000 per year), teaching assistantships with full and partial tuition reimbursements available (averaging $14,375 per year); research assistantships, career-related internships or fieldwork, Federal Work-Study, institutionally sponsored loans, and tuition waivers (full and partial) also available. Financial award application deadline: 1/5; financial award applicants required to submit FAFSA. *Faculty research:* Algebraic geometry, commutative algebra, Lie algebra, differential equations, differential geometry. *Unit head:* Dr. Bun Wong, Chair, 951-827-6459, Fax: 951-827-

7314. *Application contact:* Bonnie Anketell, Graduate Program Assistant, 951-827-7378, Fax: 951-827-7314, E-mail: gradprog@math.ucr.edu.

University of California, San Diego, Graduate Studies and Research, Department of Mathematics, La Jolla, CA 92093. Offers applied mathematics (MA); mathematics (MA, PhD); statistics (MS). *Faculty:* 63. *Students:* 91 (25 women); includes 11 minority (2 African Americans, 6 Asian Americans or Pacific Islanders, 3 Hispanic Americans) 14 international. 294 applicants, 27% accepted. In 2003, 20 master's, 10 doctorates awarded. *Degree requirements:* For doctorate, thesis/dissertation. *Entrance requirements:* For master's and doctorate, GRE General Test, GRE Subject Test. Application fee: $60. Electronic applications accepted. Tuition, nonresident: full-time $12,245. Required fees: $6,959. *Unit head:* James Bunch, Chair, E-mail: jbunch@ucsd.edu. *Application contact:* Lois Stewart, Graduate Coordinator, 858-534-6887, E-mail: lstewart@ucsd.edu.

University of California, Santa Barbara, Graduate Division, College of Engineering, Department of Computer Science, Computational Science and Technology Integrative Graduate Education and Research Traineeship Program, Santa Barbara, CA 93106. Offers computer science (PhD); electrical and computer engineering (PhD); mathematics (PhD); mechanical and environmental engineering (PhD). Program offered jointly with the Departments of Chemical Engineering, Mathematics, and Mechanical and Environmental Engineering. *Students:* 5 applicants, 80% accepted, 3 enrolled. *Degree requirements:* For doctorate, contact department. *Entrance requirements:* For doctorate, contact department, contact department. *Application deadline:* Applications are processed on a rolling basis. Application fee: $60. Electronic applications accepted. *Expenses:* Tuition, state resident: full-time $7,188. Tuition, nonresident: full-time $19,608. *Financial support:* In 2003–04, 3 students received support, including fellowships with full tuition reimbursements available (averaging $27,500 per year); research assistantships, teaching assistantships, career-related internships or fieldwork, scholarships/grants, traineeships, and health care benefits also available. *Faculty research:* Microscale engineering, complex fluids, materials science, systems biology. *Unit head:* Loren A. Banner, Education Coordinator, 805-893-8334, Fax: 805-893-5435, E-mail: loren@cs.ucsb.edu.

University of California, Santa Barbara, Graduate Division, College of Letters and Sciences, Division of Mathematics, Life, and Physical Sciences, Department of Mathematics, Program in Mathematics, Santa Barbara, CA 93106. Offers MA, PhD. Terminal master's awarded for partial completion of doctoral program. *Degree requirements:* For master's, thesis or alternative, comprehensive exam (for some programs), registration; for doctorate, thesis/dissertation, comprehensive exam. *Entrance requirements:* For master's and doctorate, GRE General Test, GRE Subject Test. Additional exam requirements/recommendations for international students: Required—TOEFL (minimum score 550 paper-based; 213 computer-based); Recommended—TSE. *Application deadline:* For fall admission, 1/1 for domestic students, 1/1 for international students. Application fee: $60. Electronic applications accepted. *Expenses:* Tuition, state resident: full-time $7,188. Tuition, nonresident: full-time $19,608. *Financial support:* Fellowships with full tuition reimbursements, teaching assistantships with partial tuition reimbursements, Federal Work-Study, institutionally sponsored loans, and health care benefits available. Financial award application deadline: 1/1; financial award applicants required to submit FAFSA. *Application contact:* Medina Teel, Staff Graduate Adviser, 805-893-8192, Fax: 805-893-2385, E-mail: teel@math.ucsb.edu.

University of California, Santa Cruz, Division of Graduate Studies, Division of Physical and Biological Sciences, Department of Mathematics, Santa Cruz, CA 95064. Offers applied mathematics (MA, PhD); mathematics (MA, PhD). *Faculty:* 15 full-time (2 women). *Students:* 32 full-time (7 women); includes 3 minority (2 Asian Americans or Pacific Islanders, 1 Hispanic American), 6 international. 59 applicants, 0% accepted. In 2003, 4 master's, 1 doctorate awarded. *Median time to degree:* Master's–2.17 years full-time; doctorate–5.75 years full-time. *Degree requirements:* For doctorate, one foreign language, thesis/dissertation, qualifying exam. *Entrance requirements:* For doctorate, GRE General Test, GRE Subject Test. *Application deadline:* For fall admission, 2/1 for domestic students. Application fee: $60. Tuition, nonresident: full-time $12,492. *Financial support:* Fellowships, research assistantships, teaching assistantships, Federal Work-Study and institutionally sponsored loans available. Financial award application deadline: 2/1. *Unit head:* Dr. Tony Tromba, Chair, 831-459-2215, E-mail: gem@cats.ucsc.edu. *Application contact:* James M. Moore, Graduate Admissions, Director, 831-459-2301, Fax: 831-459-4843, E-mail: gradadm@ucsc.edu.

University of Central Arkansas, Graduate School, College of Natural Sciences and Math, Department of Mathematics, Conway, AR 72035-0001. Offers MA. Part-time programs available. *Faculty:* 13 full-time (6 women). *Students:* 9 full-time (5 women), 10 part-time (7 women); includes 2 minority (1 American Indian/Alaska Native, 1 Hispanic American). In 2003, 10 degrees awarded, leading to university research/teaching 71%, continued full-time study10%. *Median time to degree:* Master's–1 year full-time. *Degree requirements:* For master's, thesis optional. *Entrance requirements:* For master's, GRE General Test, minimum GPA of 2.7. *Application deadline:* For fall admission, 3/1 for domestic students; for spring admission, 10/1 priority date for domestic students. Applications are processed on a rolling basis. Application fee: $25 ($40 for international students). *Expenses:* Tuition, state resident: full-time $3,677; part-time $204 per hour. Tuition, nonresident: full-time $6,455; part-time $362 per hour. Required fees: $130; $52 per semester. *Financial support:* In 2003–04, 11 teaching assistantships with partial tuition reimbursements (averaging $8,500 per year) were awarded; research assistantships with partial tuition reimbursements, Federal Work-Study and unspecified assistantships also available. Financial award application deadline: 2/15. *Faculty research:* Nonlinear wave equation. Total annual research expenditures: $207,823. *Unit head:* Dr. Donna Foss, Chair, 501-450-3147, Fax: 501-450-5084, E-mail: donnaf@mail.uca.edu. *Application contact:* Nancy Gage, Co-Admissions Secretary, 501-450-3124, Fax: 501-450-5066, E-mail: nancyg@mail.uca.edu.

University of Central Florida, College of Arts and Sciences, Department of Mathematics, Orlando, FL 32816. Offers mathematical science (MS); mathematics (PhD). Part-time and evening/weekend programs available. *Faculty:* 40 full-time (7 women), 1 part-time/adjunct (0 women). *Students:* 29 full-time (6 women), 20 part-time (9 women); includes 11 minority (2 African Americans, 5 Asian Americans or Pacific Islanders, 4 Hispanic Americans), 12 international. Average age 33. 51 applicants, 86% accepted, 18 enrolled. In 2003, 10 degrees awarded. *Degree requirements:* For master's, thesis or alternative; for doctorate, thesis/dissertation, candidacy exam. *Entrance requirements:* For master's, GRE General Test, minimum GPA of 3.0 in last 60 hours; for doctorate, GRE Subject Test, minimum GPA of 3.0 in last 60 hours or master's qualifying exam. Additional exam requirements/recommendations for international students: Required—TOEFL. *Application deadline:* For fall admission, 7/15 for domestic students; for spring admission, 12/1 for domestic students. Application fee: $30. Electronic applications accepted. *Expenses:* Tuition, state resident: full-time $4,968; part-time $171 per credit hour. Tuition, nonresident: full-time $18,630; part-time $713 per credit hour. *Financial support:* In 2003–04, 13 fellowships with partial tuition reimbursements (averaging $5,285 per year), 7 research assistantships with partial tuition reimbursements (averaging $9,313 per year), 33 teaching assistantships with partial tuition reimbursements (averaging $10,230 per year) were awarded. Career-related internships or fieldwork, Federal Work-Study, institutionally sponsored loans, tuition waivers (partial), and unspecified assistantships also available. Financial award application deadline: 3/1; financial award applicants required to submit FAFSA. *Faculty research:* Applied mathematics, analysis, approximation theory, graph theory, mathematical statistics. *Unit head:* Dr. Nashed M. Zuhair, Chair, 407-823-0445, Fax: 407-823-6253, E-mail: znashed@mail.ucf.edu. *Application contact:* Dr. Ram Mohapatra, Coordinator, 407-823-5080, Fax: 407-823-6253, E-mail: ramm@pegasus.cc.ucf.edu.

University of Central Oklahoma, College of Graduate Studies and Research, College of Mathematics and Science, Department of Mathematics and Statistics, Edmond, OK 73034-5209. Offers applied mathematical sciences (MS), including computer science, mathematics, mathematics/computer science teaching, statistics. *Accreditation:* NCATE. Part-time programs available. *Degree requirements:* For master's, thesis. *Faculty research:* Curvature, FAA, math education.

University of Chicago, Division of the Physical Sciences, Department of Mathematics, Chicago, IL 60637-1513. Offers applied mathematics (SM, PhD); financial mathematics (MS); mathematics (SM, PhD). *Faculty:* 59 full-time (3 women). *Students:* 107 full-time (27 women), 38 international. 299 applicants, 12% accepted. In 2003, 15 master's, 12 doctorates awarded. *Degree requirements:* For doctorate, one foreign language, thesis/dissertation, 2 qualifying exams. *Entrance requirements:* For master's and doctorate, GRE General Test, GRE Subject Test. Additional exam requirements/recommendations for international students: Required—TOEFL (minimum score 600 paper-based; 250 computer-based). *Application deadline:* For fall admission, 1/5 for domestic students. Application fee: $55. Electronic applications accepted. *Financial support:* In 2003–04, 60 fellowships, 47 teaching assistantships were awarded. Research assistantships, career-related internships or fieldwork, institutionally sponsored loans, and scholarships/grants also available. Financial award application deadline: 1/5; financial award applicants required to submit CSS PROFILE or FAFSA. *Faculty research:* Analysis, differential geometry, algebra number theory, topology, algebraic geometry. *Unit head:* Dr. Kevin Corlette, Chair, 773-702-0702, Fax: 773-702-9787, E-mail: kevin@math.uchicago.edu. *Application contact:* Laurie Wail, Graduate Studies Assistant, 773-702-7358, Fax: 773-702-9787, E-mail: lwail@math.uchicago.edu.

University of Cincinnati, Division of Research and Advanced Studies, McMicken College of Arts and Sciences, Department of Mathematical Sciences, Cincinnati, OH 45221. Offers applied mathematics (MS, PhD); mathematics education (MAT); pure mathematics (MS, PhD); statistics (MS, PhD). *Accreditation:* NCATE (one or more programs are accredited). Part-time programs available. Terminal master's awarded for partial completion of doctoral program. *Degree requirements:* For master's, thesis or alternative, comprehensive exam; for doctorate, one foreign language, thesis/dissertation, comprehensive exam. *Entrance requirements:* For master's, GRE, teacher certification (MAT); for doctorate, GRE. Additional exam requirements/recommendations for international students: Required—TOEFL. Electronic applications accepted. *Faculty research:* Algebra, analysis, differential equations, numerical analysis, statistics.

University of Colorado at Boulder, Graduate School, College of Arts and Sciences, Department of Mathematics, Boulder, CO 80309. Offers MA, MS, PhD. *Faculty:* 28 full-time (5 women). *Students:* 56 full-time (15 women), 7 part-time (3 women); includes 6 minority (1 American Indian/Alaska Native, 2 Asian Americans or Pacific Islanders, 3 Hispanic Americans), 6 international. Average age 30. 17 applicants, 71% accepted. In 2003, 4 master's, 6 doctorates awarded. Terminal master's awarded for partial completion of doctoral program. *Degree requirements:* For master's, thesis or alternative, comprehensive exam; for doctorate, one foreign language, thesis/dissertation, 2 preliminary exams, comprehensive exam. *Entrance requirements:* For master's, minimum undergraduate GPA of 2.75. *Application deadline:* For fall admission, 2/15 for domestic students. Applications are processed on a rolling basis. Application fee: $50 ($60 for international students). *Expenses:* Tuition, state resident: full-time $2,122. Tuition, nonresident: full-time $9,754. Tuition and fees vary according to course load and program. *Financial support:* In 2003–04, 2 fellowships (averaging $5,250 per year), 47 teaching assistantships (averaging $20,220 per year) were awarded. Research assistantships, scholarships/grants and tuition waivers (full) also available. Support available to part-time students. Financial award application deadline: 3/1. *Faculty research:* Pure mathematics, applied mathematics and mathematical physics (including algebra, algebraic geometry, differential equations, differential geometry, logic and foundations). Total annual research expenditures: $404,312. *Unit head:* Peter Elliott, Chair, 303-492-8566, Fax: 303-492-7707, E-mail: peter.elliott@colorado.edu. *Application contact:* Carol Deckert, Graduate Administrative Assistant, 303-492-3161, Fax: 303-492-7707, E-mail: deckert@euclid.colorado.edu.

University of Colorado at Denver, Graduate School, College of Liberal Arts and Sciences, Program in Integrated Science, Denver, CO 80217-3364. Offers applied science (MIS); computer science (MIS); mathematics (MIS). *Students:* 3 full-time (2 women), 10 part-time (6 women), 1 international. 1 applicant, 100% accepted, 1 enrolled. In 2003, 5 degrees awarded. *Expenses:* Tuition, state resident: part-time $255 per credit hour. Tuition, nonresident: part-time $1,025 per credit hour. *Financial support:* Research assistantships, teaching assistantships available. *Application contact:* Jana Everett, Associate Dean, 303-556-3513, Fax: 303-556-4681, E-mail: jana.everett@cudenver.edu.

University of Connecticut, Graduate School, College of Liberal Arts and Sciences, Department of Mathematics, Field of Mathematics, Storrs, CT 06269. Offers actuarial science (MS, PhD); applied mathematics (MS); financial mathematics (MS); mathematics (MS); mathematics and computer science (MS). *Faculty:* 32 full-time (4 women). *Students:* 68 full-time (27 women), 39 part-time (19 women); includes 5 minority (1 African American, 4 Asian Americans or Pacific Islanders), 62 international. Average age 29. 235 applicants, 53% accepted, 50 enrolled. In 2003, 37 master's, 5 doctorates awarded. Terminal master's awarded for partial completion of doctoral program. *Degree requirements:* For master's, comprehensive exam; for doctorate, thesis/dissertation. *Entrance requirements:* For master's and doctorate, GRE General Test. Additional exam requirements/recommendations for international students: Required—TOEFL (minimum score 550 paper-based; 213 computer-based). *Application deadline:* For fall admission, 2/1 priority date for domestic students, 2/1 priority date for international students; for spring admission, 11/1 for domestic students, 10/1 for international students. Applications are processed on a rolling basis. Application fee: $55. Electronic applications accepted. *Expenses:* Tuition, state resident: part-time $3,860 per semester. Tuition, nonresident: part-time $9,036 per semester. *Financial support:* In 2003–04, 7 research assistantships with full tuition reimbursements, 51 teaching assistantships with full tuition reimbursements were awarded. Fellowships, Federal Work-Study, scholarships/grants, health care benefits, and unspecified assistantships also available. Financial award application deadline: 2/1; financial award applicants required to submit FAFSA. *Unit head:* Eugene Spiegel, Chairperson, 860-486-3844, Fax: 860-486-4283, E-mail: eugene.spiegel@uconn.edu. *Application contact:* Sharon McDermott, Administrative Assistant, 860-486-6452, Fax: 860-486-4283, E-mail: gradadm@math.uconn.edu.

University of Delaware, College of Arts and Sciences, Department of Mathematical Sciences, Newark, DE 19716. Offers applied mathematics (MS, PhD); mathematics (MS, PhD). Part-time programs available. *Faculty:* 40 full-time (5 women). *Students:* 42 full-time (17 women), 1 part-time; includes 1 minority (Asian American or Pacific Islander), 26 international. Average age 25. 146 applicants, 17% accepted, 16 enrolled. In 2003, 7 master's, 3 doctorates awarded. Terminal master's awarded for partial completion of doctoral program. *Degree requirements:* For master's, thesis (for some programs); for doctorate, one foreign language, thesis/dissertation, qualifying exam. *Entrance requirements:* For master's and doctorate, GRE General Test. Additional exam requirements/recommendations for international students: Required—TOEFL. *Application deadline:* For fall admission, 3/1 for domestic students; for spring admission, 12/15 priority date for domestic students. Applications are processed on a rolling basis. Application fee: $60. Electronic applications accepted. *Expenses:* Tuition, state resident: full-time $5,890; part-time $327 per credit. Tuition, nonresident: full-time $15,420; part-time $857 per credit. Required fees: $968. *Financial support:* In 2003–04, 4 fellowships with tuition reimbursements (averaging $15,000 per year), 3 research assistantships with tuition reimbursements (averaging $13,000 per year), 27 teaching assistantships with tuition reimbursements (averaging $12,240 per year) were awarded. Career-related internships or fieldwork, institutionally sponsored loans, scholarships/grants, and tuition waivers (full and partial) also available. Financial award application deadline: 3/1. *Faculty research:* Scattering theory, inverse problems, fluid dynamics, numerical analysis, combinatorics. Total annual research expenditures:$600,000. *Unit head:* Dr. Philip Broadbridge, Chair, 302-831-2652, E-mail: pbroad@math.udel.edu. *Application contact:* Dr. Robert Gilbert, Graduate Chair, 302-831-2315, Fax: 302-831-4511, E-mail: gilbert@math.udel.edu.

See in-depth description on page 593.

University of Denver, Graduate Studies, Faculty of Natural Sciences and Mathematics, Department of Mathematics, Denver, CO 80208. Offers applied mathematics (MA, MS); computer science (MS). Part-time programs available. *Faculty:* 18 full-time (7 women), 1 (woman)

Mathematics

University of Denver (continued)
part-time/adjunct. *Students:* 6 (5 women) 1 international. 7 applicants, 86% accepted. In 2003, 2 degrees awarded. Terminal master's awarded for partial completion of doctoral program. *Degree requirements:* For master's, computer language, foreign language, or laboratory experience, one foreign language. *Entrance requirements:* For master's, GRE General Test. Additional exam requirements/recommendations for international students: Required—TOEFL. *Application deadline:* Applications are processed on a rolling basis. Application fee: $45. *Expenses:* Tuition: Full-time $24,264. *Financial support:* In 2003–04, 21 students received support, including 5 fellowships with full and partial tuition reimbursements available, 2 research assistantships with full and partial tuition reimbursements available (averaging $9,081 per year), 14 teaching assistantships with full and partial tuition reimbursements available (averaging $9,972 per year); career-related internships or fieldwork, Federal Work-Study, institutionally sponsored loans, and scholarships/grants also available. Support available to part-time students. Financial award application deadline: 3/1; financial award applicants required to submit FAFSA. *Faculty research:* Real-time software, convex bodies, multidimensional data, parallel computer clusters. Total annual research expenditures: $163,312. *Unit head:* Dr. Scott Leutenegger, Chairperson, 303-871-2821. *Application contact:* Roy James Rosa, Graduate Secretary, 303-871-3017.

University of Denver, School of Engineering and Computer Science, Department of Computer Science, Denver, CO 80208. Offers computer science (MS); math and computer science (PhD). Part-time programs available. *Faculty:* 10. *Students:* 42 (11 women); includes 5 minority (4 Asian Americans or Pacific Islanders, 1 Hispanic American) 23 international. Average age 28. 74 applicants, 82% accepted, 21 enrolled. In 2003, 17 degrees awarded. *Degree requirements:* For doctorate, thesis/dissertation, comprehensive exam. *Entrance requirements:* For master's, GRE General Test. Additional exam requirements/recommendations for international students: Required—TOEFL (minimum score 550 paper-based; 213 computer-based), TSE(minimum score 50). *Application deadline:* Applications are processed on a rolling basis. Application fee: $50. Electronic applications accepted. *Expenses:* Tuition: Full-time $24,264. *Financial support:* In 2003–04, fellowships with full and partial tuition reimbursements (averaging $6,000 per year), 9 teaching assistantships with full and partial tuition reimbursements were awarded. Career-related internships or fieldwork, Federal Work-Study, institutionally sponsored loans, and scholarships/grants also available. Financial award application deadline: 3/1; financial award applicants required to submit FAFSA. *Unit head:* Dr. Joel S. Cohen, Associate Chair, 303-871-2458, Fax: 303-871-3010, E-mail: jscohen@cs.du.edu.

University of Detroit Mercy, College of Engineering and Science, Department of Mathematics and Computer Science, Detroit, MI 48219-0900. Offers computer science (MSCS); elementary mathematics education (MATM); junior high mathematics education (MATM); secondary mathematics education (MATM); teaching of mathematics (MATM). Evening/weekend programs available. *Entrance requirements:* For master's, minimum GPA of 3.0.

University of Florida, Graduate School, College of Liberal Arts and Sciences, Department of Mathematics, Gainesville, FL 32611. Offers applied mathematics (MS, PhD); mathematics (MA, MS, PhD); mathematics teaching (MAT, MST). *Accreditation:* NCATE (one or more programs are accredited). Part-time programs available. *Faculty:* 58. *Students:* 75 full-time (21 women), 3 part-time; includes 4 minority (1 Asian American or Pacific Islander, 3 Hispanic Americans), 47 international. In 2003, 11 master's, 2 doctorates awarded. Terminal master's awarded for partial completion of doctoral program. *Degree requirements:* For master's, thesis optional; for doctorate, one foreign language, thesis/dissertation. *Entrance requirements:* For master's and doctorate, GRE General Test, minimum GPA of 3.0. Additional exam requirements/recommendations for international students: Required—TOEFL (minimum score 550 paper-based; 213 computer-based). *Application deadline:* For fall admission, 6/1 for domestic students. Applications are processed on a rolling basis. Application fee: $30. Electronic applications accepted. *Expenses:* Tuition, state resident: part-time $205 per credit hour. Tuition, nonresident: part-time $775 per credit hour. *Financial support:* In 2003–04, 65 students received support, including 3 fellowships, 2 research assistantships, 61 teaching assistantships; career-related internships or fieldwork and unspecified assistantships also available. Financial award application deadline: 3/1. *Faculty research:* Combinatorics and number theory, group theory, probability theory, logic, differential geometry and mathematical physics. *Unit head:* Dr. Krishnaswani Alladi, Chairman, 352-392-0281 Ext. 236, Fax: 352-392-8357, E-mail: alladi@math.ufl.edu. *Application contact:* Dr. Paul Robinson, Coordinator, 352-392-0281 Ext. 273, Fax: 352-392-8357, E-mail: robinson@math.ufl.edu.

University of Georgia, Graduate School, College of Arts and Sciences, Department of Mathematics, Athens, GA 30602. Offers applied mathematical science (MAMS); mathematics (MA, PhD). *Faculty:* 42 full-time (3 women). *Students:* 45 full-time (11 women), 2 part-time; includes 3 minority (1 African American, 1 Asian American or Pacific Islander, 1 Hispanic American), 23 international. 97 applicants, 16% accepted. In 2003, 2 master's, 4 doctorates awarded. *Degree requirements:* For master's, one foreign language, thesis (for some programs); for doctorate, 2 foreign languages, thesis/dissertation. *Entrance requirements:* For master's and doctorate, GRE General Test. *Application deadline:* For fall admission, 7/1 for domestic students; for spring admission, 11/15 for domestic students. Application fee: $50. Electronic applications accepted. *Expenses:* Tuition, state resident: part-time $161 per hour. Tuition, nonresident: part-time $690 per hour. One-time fee: $435 part-time. *Financial support:* Fellowships, research assistantships, teaching assistantships, unspecified assistantships available. *Unit head:* Dr. Dan Kannan, Head, 706-542-2643, Fax: 706-542-2573, E-mail: kannan@math.uga.edu. *Application contact:* Dr. Joe Fu, Graduate Coordinator, 706-542-2562, Fax: 706-542-5907, E-mail: fu@math.uga.edu.

University of Guelph, Graduate Program Services, College of Physical and Engineering Science, Department of Mathematics and Statistics, Guelph, ON N1G 2W1, Canada. Offers applied mathematics (PhD); applied statistics (PhD); mathematics and statistics (M Sc). Part-time programs available. *Faculty:* 26 full-time (5 women), 5 part-time/adjunct (1 woman). *Students:* 46 full-time, 2 part-time, 10 international. Average age 22. 96 applicants, 30% accepted, 22 enrolled. In 2003, 15 master's, 6 doctorates awarded. *Median time to degree:* Of those who began their doctoral program in fall 1995, 88% received their degree in 8 years or less. *Degree requirements:* For master's, thesis (for some programs); for doctorate, thesis/dissertation. *Entrance requirements:* For master's, minimum B- average during previous 2 years; for doctorate, minimum B average. Additional exam requirements/recommendations for international students: Required—TOEFL (minimum score 550 paper-based; 210 computer-based). *Application deadline:* For fall admission, 3/1 for domestic students, 2/1 for international students. Application fee: $75. Tuition and fees charges are reported in Canadian dollars. Tuition, nonresident: full-time $3,440 Canadian dollars. International tuition: $5,432 Canadian dollars full-time. Required fees: $753 Canadian dollars. *Financial support:* In 2003–04, 20 students received support, including 29 research assistantships (averaging $2,200 per year), 32 teaching assistantships (averaging $11,000 per year); fellowships, scholarships/grants also available. *Faculty research:* Dynamical systems, mathematical biology, numerical analysis, linear and nonlinear models, reliability and bioassay. Total annual research expenditures: $315,000. *Unit head:* Dr. O. Brian Allen, Chair, 519-824-4120 Ext. 56556, Fax: 519-837-0221, E-mail: chair@uoguelph.ca. *Application contact:* Susan McCormick, Graduate Administrative Assistant, 519-824-4120 Ext. 56553, Fax: 519-837-0221, E-mail: smccormi@uoguelph.ca.

University of Hawaii at Manoa, Graduate Division, Colleges of Arts and Sciences, College of Natural Sciences, Department of Mathematics, Honolulu, HI 96822. Offers MA, PhD. Part-time programs available. *Faculty:* 28 full-time (1 woman). *Students:* 15 full-time (2 women), 4 part-time (1 woman); includes 3 minority (2 Asian Americans or Pacific Islanders, 1 Hispanic American), 5 international. Average age 30. 24 applicants, 38% accepted, 5 enrolled. In 2003, 4 master's, 16 doctorates awarded. Terminal master's awarded for partial completion of doctoral program. *Median time to degree:* Master's–4 years full-time; doctorate–8 years full-time. *Degree requirements:* For master's, comprehensive exam; for doctorate, 2 foreign languages, thesis/dissertation, comprehensive exam. *Entrance requirements:* For master's and doctorate, GRE General Test, minimum GPA of 3.0. Additional exam requirements/recommendations for international students: Required—TOEFL. *Application deadline:* For fall admission, 3/1 for domestic students, 2/1 for international students; for spring admission, 9/1 for domestic students, 8/1 for international students. Applications are processed on a rolling basis. Application fee: $50. *Expenses:* Tuition, state resident: full-time $4,464; part-time $186 per credit hour. Tuition, nonresident: full-time $10,608; part-time $442 per credit hour. Tuition and fees vary according to program. *Financial support:* In 2003–04, 12 teaching assistantships (averaging $14,675 per year) were awarded; research assistantships, institutionally sponsored loans, tuition waivers (full and partial), and unspecified assistantships also available. Support available to part-time students. Financial award application deadline: 3/1. *Faculty research:* Analysis, algebra, lattice theory, logic topology, differential geometry. *Unit head:* Dr. Thomas Craven, Chair, 808-956-8792, Fax: 808-956-9139. *Application contact:* Dr. Robert Little, Graduate Chair, 808-956-7951, Fax: 808-956-9139, E-mail: little@math.hawaii.edu.

University of Houston, College of Natural Sciences and Mathematics, Department of Mathematics, Houston, TX 77204. Offers applied mathematics (MSAM); mathematics (MSM, PhD). Part-time and evening/weekend programs available. *Faculty:* 23 full-time (2 women), 2 part-time/adjunct (0 women). *Students:* 79 full-time (30 women), 34 part-time (15 women); includes 20 minority (2 African Americans, 11 Asian Americans or Pacific Islanders, 7 Hispanic Americans), 46 international. Average age 29. 61 applicants, 87% accepted, 27 enrolled. In 2003, 15 master's, 7 doctorates awarded. *Degree requirements:* For master's, thesis optional; for doctorate, thesis/dissertation. *Entrance requirements:* For master's, GRE General Test, minimum GPA of 3.0 in last 60 hours, bachelor's degree in mathematics or related area; for doctorate, GRE General Test, MS in mathematics or equivalent, minimum GPA of 3.0 in last 60 hours. Additional exam requirements/recommendations for international students: Required—TOEFL. *Application deadline:* For fall admission, 7/3 for domestic students; for spring admission, 12/4 for domestic students. Applications are processed on a rolling basis. Application fee: $0 ($75 for international students). *Expenses:* Tuition, state resident: full-time $1,656; part-time $92 per credit hour. Tuition, nonresident: full-time $5,904; part-time $328 per credit hour. Required fees: $1,704. *Financial support:* In 2003–04, 41 students received support, including 13 research assistantships with tuition reimbursements available (averaging $12,000 per year), 41 teaching assistantships (averaging $12,000 per year); fellowships with tuition reimbursements available, institutionally sponsored loans, tuition waivers (partial), and teaching fellowships also available. Support available to part-time students. Financial award application deadline: 3/15. *Faculty research:* Applied mathematics, modern analysis, computational science, geometry, dynamical systems. Total annual research expenditures: $310,295. *Unit head:* Dr. William E. Fitzgibbon, Chair, 713-743-3465, Fax: 713-743-3505, E-mail: fitz@math.uh.edu. *Application contact:* Pamela K. Draughn, Graduate Adviser, 713-743-3517, Fax: 713-743-3505, E-mail: pamela@math.uh.edu.

University of Houston–Clear Lake, School of Science and Computer Engineering, Program in Mathematical Sciences, Houston, TX 77058-1098. Offers MS. Part-time and evening/weekend programs available. *Students:* 8 full-time (2 women), 6 part-time (3 women); includes 2 minority (1 African American, 1 Hispanic American), 2 international. Average age 38. In 2003, 3 degrees awarded. *Entrance requirements:* For master's, GRE General Test. Additional exam requirements/recommendations for international students: Required—TOEFL (minimum score 550 paper-based; 213 computer-based). *Application deadline:* For fall admission, 8/1 for domestic students, 6/1 for international students; for spring admission, 12/1 for domestic students, 10/1 for international students. Applications are processed on a rolling basis. Application fee: $35 ($75 for international students). *Expenses:* Tuition, state resident: full-time $2,484; part-time $414 per course. Tuition, nonresident: full-time $6,318; part-time $1,053 per course. Required fees: $12 per course. $199 per semester. *Financial support:* In 2003–04, 2 teaching assistantships were awarded; fellowships, research assistantships, career-related internships or fieldwork, Federal Work-Study, institutionally sponsored loans, and scholarships/grants also available. Support available to part-time students. Financial award application deadline: 5/1; financial award applicants required to submit FAFSA. *Unit head:* Dr. Lie-Jane Shiau, Chair, 281-283-3850, Fax: 281-283-3707, E-mail: shiau@cl.uh.edu. *Application contact:* Dr. Robert Ferebee, Associate Dean, 281-283-3700, Fax: 281-283-3707, E-mail: ferebee@cl.uh.edu.

University of Idaho, College of Graduate Studies, College of Science, Department of Mathematics, Program in Mathematics, Moscow, ID 83844-2282. Offers mathematics (MS, PhD); mathematics education (MAT). *Accreditation:* NCATE (one or more programs are accredited). *Degree requirements:* For doctorate, 2 foreign languages, thesis/dissertation. *Entrance requirements:* For master's, minimum GPA of 2.8; for doctorate, minimum undergraduate GPA of 2.8, 3.0 graduate. *Application deadline:* For fall admission, 8/1 for domestic students; for spring admission, 12/15 for domestic students. Application fee: $55 ($60 for international students). *Expenses:* Tuition, state resident: full-time $3,348. Tuition, nonresident: full-time $10,740. Required fees: $540. *Financial support:* Teaching assistantships available. Financial award application deadline: 2/15. *Faculty research:* Algebra, topology, analysis. *Unit head:* Dr. Monte Boisen, Chair, Department of Mathematics, 208-885-6742.

See in-depth description on page 595.

University of Illinois at Chicago, Graduate College, College of Liberal Arts and Sciences, Department of Mathematics, Statistics, and Computer Science, Chicago, IL 60607-7128. Offers applied mathematics (MS, DA, PhD); computer science (MS, DA, PhD); math and information science for the industry (MS); probability and statistics (MS, DA, PhD); pure mathematics (MS, DA, PhD); teaching of mathematics (MST). Part-time programs available. *Faculty:* 69 full-time (4 women). *Students:* 145 full-time (61 women), 62 part-time (34 women); includes 41 minority (13 African Americans, 21 Asian Americans or Pacific Islanders, 7 Hispanic Americans), 86 international. Average age 32. 285 applicants, 30% accepted, 36 enrolled. In 2003, 38 master's, 14 doctorates awarded. *Median time to degree:* Of those who began their doctoral program in fall 1995, 50% received their degree in 8 years or less. *Degree requirements:* For master's, comprehensive exam; for doctorate, one foreign language, thesis/dissertation. *Entrance requirements:* For master's and doctorate, GRE General Test, minimum GPA of 3.75 on a 5.0 scale. Additional exam requirements/recommendations for international students: Required—TOEFL. *Application deadline:* For fall admission, 1/9 for domestic students, 1/9 for international students; for spring admission, 10/1 for domestic students. Applications are processed on a rolling basis. Application fee: $40 ($50 for international students). Electronic applications accepted. *Expenses:* Tuition, state resident: part-time $941 per semester. Tuition, nonresident: part-time $2,338 per semester. *Financial support:* In 2003–04, 118 students received support; fellowships with full tuition reimbursements available, research assistantships with full tuition reimbursements available, teaching assistantships with full tuition reimbursements available, Federal Work-Study, scholarships/grants, traineeships, tuition waivers (full), and unspecified assistantships available. Financial award application deadline: 3/1; financial award applicants required to submit FAFSA. *Unit head:* Jerry Bona, Head, 312-996-3044. *Application contact:* Charles Knessl, Director of Graduate Studies, 312-996-3041, E-mail: knessl@uic.edu.

See in-depth description on page 599.

University of Illinois at Urbana–Champaign, Graduate College, College of Liberal Arts and Sciences, Department of Mathematics, Champaign, IL 61820. Offers applied mathematics (MS); mathematics (MS, PhD); teaching of mathematics (MS). *Faculty:* 73 full-time (6 women), 7 part-time/adjunct (3 women). *Students:* 201 full-time (55 women); includes 15 minority (2 African Americans, 10 Asian Americans or Pacific Islanders, 3 Hispanic Americans), 122 international. 388 applicants, 13% accepted, 37 enrolled. In 2003, 42 master's, 23 doctorates awarded. *Degree requirements:* For doctorate, 2 foreign languages, thesis/dissertation. *Entrance requirements:* For master's, GRE, minimum GPA of 3.0. *Application deadline:* For fall admission, 1/15 for domestic students. Applications are processed on a rolling basis. Application fee: $40 ($50 for international students). Electronic applications accepted. *Expenses:* Tuition, state resident: full-time $6,692. Tuition, nonresident: full-time $18,692. *Financial support:*

In 2003–04, 26 fellowships, 24 research assistantships, 113 teaching assistantships were awarded. Tuition waivers (full and partial) also available. Financial award application deadline: 2/15. *Unit head:* Joseph Rosenblatt, Chair, 217-333-3352, Fax: 217-333-9576, E-mail: jrsnbltt@math.uiuc.edu. *Application contact:* Lori Dick, Staff Secretary, 217-244-0539, Fax: 217-333-9576, E-mail: ldick@math.uiuc.edu.

The University of Iowa, Graduate College, College of Liberal Arts and Sciences, Department of Mathematics, Iowa City, IA 52242-1316. Offers MS, PhD. *Faculty:* 49 full-time, 2 part-time/adjunct. *Students:* 48 full-time (16 women), 34 part-time (15 women); includes 14 minority (2 African Americans, 1 Asian American or Pacific Islander, 11 Hispanic Americans), 30 international. 101 applicants, 44% accepted, 22 enrolled. In 2003, 13 master's, 14 doctorates awarded. *Degree requirements:* For master's, exam, thesis optional; for doctorate, thesis/dissertation, comprehensive exam, registration. *Entrance requirements:* For master's and doctorate, GRE General Test, minimum GPA of 3.0. Additional exam requirements/recommendations for international students: Required—TOEFL (minimum score 575 paper-based; 232 computer-based). *Application deadline:* For fall admission, 1/15 priority date for domestic students, 1/15 priority date for international students. Applications are processed on a rolling basis. Application fee: $50 ($75 for international students). Electronic applications accepted. *Expenses:* Tuition, state resident: full-time $5,038. Tuition, nonresident: full-time $15,072. Tuition and fees vary according to course load and program. *Financial support:* In 2003–04, 11 fellowships, 3 research assistantships, 58 teaching assistantships were awarded. Financial award applicants required to submit FAFSA. *Unit head:* David Manderscheid, Chair, 319-335-0714, Fax: 319-335-0627.

University of Kansas, Graduate School, College of Liberal Arts and Sciences, Department of Mathematics, Lawrence, KS 66045. Offers applied mathematics and statistics (MA, PhD); mathematics (MA, PhD). *Faculty:* 41. *Students:* 55 full-time (21 women), 12 part-time (5 women); includes 4 minority (1 American Indian/Alaska Native, 2 Asian Americans or Pacific Islanders, 1 Hispanic American), 29 international. Average age 29. 57 applicants, 49% accepted, 16 enrolled. In 2003, 10 master's, 4 doctorates awarded. Terminal master's awarded for partial completion of doctoral program. *Median time to degree:* Master's–2.5 years full-time; doctorate–5.5 years full-time. *Degree requirements:* For master's, thesis or alternative; for doctorate, 2 foreign languages, thesis/dissertation, comprehensive exam. *Entrance requirements:* For master's and doctorate, GRE. Additional exam requirements/recommendations for international students: Required—TOEFL. *Application deadline:* For fall admission, 3/1 priority date for domestic students, 3/1 priority date for international students. Applications are processed on a rolling basis. Application fee: $55 ($60 for international students). Electronic applications accepted. *Expenses:* Tuition, state resident: full-time $3,745. Tuition, nonresident: full-time $10,075. Required fees: $574. *Financial support:* In 2003–04, 2 research assistantships with full and partial tuition reimbursements (averaging $14,180 per year), 44 teaching assistantships with full and partial tuition reimbursements (averaging $14,845 per year) were awarded. Fellowships, institutionally sponsored loans also available. Support available to part-time students. Financial award application deadline: 2/1. *Faculty research:* Commutative algebra/algebraic geometry; stochastic adaptive control/stochastic processes analysis/harmonic analysis/PDES; numerical analysis/dynamical systems; topology/set theory. Total annual research expenditures: $801,000. *Unit head:* Jack Porter, Chair, 785-864-3651, Fax: 785-864-5255, E-mail: porter@math.ukans.edu. *Application contact:* David Lerner, Graduate Director, 785-864-3651, E-mail: lerner@ukans.edu.

University of Kentucky, Graduate School, Graduate School Programs from the College of Arts and Sciences, Program in Mathematics, Lexington, KY 40506-0032. Offers MA, MS, PhD. *Faculty:* 39 full-time (2 women). *Students:* 67 full-time (21 women), 2 part-time (both women); includes 3 minority (1 Asian American or Pacific Islander, 2 Hispanic Americans), 15 international. 113 applicants, 28% accepted, 17 enrolled. In 2003, 14 master's, 6 doctorates awarded. *Degree requirements:* For master's, thesis optional; for doctorate, one foreign language, thesis/dissertation, comprehensive exam. *Entrance requirements:* For master's, GRE General Test, minimum undergraduate GPA of 2.5; for doctorate, GRE General Test, minimum graduate GPA of 3.0. Additional exam requirements/recommendations for international students: Required—TOEFL (minimum score 550 paper-based; 213 computer-based). *Application deadline:* For fall admission, 7/18 for domestic students, 2/1 for international students. Applications are processed on a rolling basis. Application fee: $35 ($45 for international students). *Expenses:* Tuition, state resident: full-time $4,975; part-time $261 per credit hour. Tuition, nonresident: full-time $12,315; part-time $668 per credit hour. *Financial support:* Fellowships, research assistantships, teaching assistantships, Federal Work-Study and institutionally sponsored loans available. Support available to part-time students. *Faculty research:* Numerical analysis, combinatorics, partial differential equations, algebra and number theory, real and complex analysis. *Unit head:* Dr. Russell C. Brown, Director of Graduate Studies, 859-257-3951, Fax: 859-257-4078. *Application contact:* Dr. Brian Jackson, Associate Dean, 859-257-4905, Fax: 859-323-1928.

The University of Lethbridge, School of Graduate Studies, Lethbridge, AB T1K 3M4, Canada. Offers accounting (MScM); agricultural biotechnology (M Sc); agricultural studies (M Sc, MA); anthropology (MA); archaeology (MA); art (MA); biochemistry (M Sc); biological sciences (M Sc); Canadian studies (MA); chemistry (M Sc); computer science (M Sc); counseling psychology (M Ed); dramatic arts (MA); economics (MA); English (MA); environmental science (M Sc); exercise science (M Sc); finance (MScM); French (MA); French/German (MA); French/Spanish (MA); general education (M Ed); general management (MScM); geography (M Sc, MA); German (MA); health sciences (M Sc, MA); history (MA); human resources/management and labor relations (MScM); information systems (MScM); international management (MScM); kinesiology (M Sc, MA); management (M Sc, MA); marketing (MScM); mathematics (M Sc); music (MA); Native American studies (MA, MScM); neuroscience (M Sc, PhD); nursing (M Sc); philosophy (MA); physics (M Sc); political science (MA); psychology (M Sc, MA); religious studies (MA); sociology (MA); urban and regional studies (MA). Part-time and evening/weekend programs available. *Faculty:* 250. *Students:* 317 (126 women). Average age 39. 35 applicants, 100% accepted, 35 enrolled. In 2003, 40 degrees awarded. *Degree requirements:* For doctorate, thesis/dissertation, comprehensive exam. *Entrance requirements:* For master's, bachelor's degree in related field, minimum GPA of 3.0 (during previous 20 graded semester courses), two years teaching or related experience (M Ed), GMAT for M Sc (management); for doctorate, master's degree, minimum graduate GPA of 3.5. Additional exam requirements/recommendations for international students: Required—TOEFL. Application fee: $60 Canadian dollars. *Expenses:* Tuition, state resident: part-time $475 per course. *Financial support:* Fellowships, research assistantships, teaching assistantships, scholarships/grants, health care benefits, and unspecified assistantships available. *Faculty research:* Movement and brain plasticity, gibberellin physiology, photosynthesis, carbon cycling, molecular properties of main-group ring components. *Unit head:* Dr. Shamsul Alam, Dean, 403-329-2121, Fax: 403-329-2097, E-mail: inquiries@uleth.ca. *Application contact:* Kathy Schrage, Administrative Assistant, Office of the Academic Vice President, 403-329-2121, Fax: 403-329-2097, E-mail: inquiries@uleth.ca.

University of Louisiana at Lafayette, Graduate School, College of Sciences, Department of Mathematics, Lafayette, LA 70504. Offers MS, PhD. *Faculty:* 18 full-time (4 women). *Students:* 34 full-time (17 women), 1 part-time; includes 1 minority (African American), 24 international. Average age 32. 22 applicants, 55% accepted, 9 enrolled. In 2003, 2 master's, 3 doctorates awarded. Terminal master's awarded for partial completion of doctoral program. *Degree requirements:* For master's, thesis or alternative; for doctorate, 2 foreign languages, thesis/dissertation. *Entrance requirements:* For master's, GRE General Test, minimum GPA of 2.75; for doctorate, GRE General Test, minimum GPA of 3.0. Additional exam requirements/recommendations for international students: Required—TOEFL (minimum score 550 paper-based; 213 computer-based). *Application deadline:* For fall admission, 5/15 for domestic students, 5/15 for international students; for spring admission, 10/1 for domestic students, 10/1 for international students. Applications are processed on a rolling basis. Application fee: $20 ($30 for international students). Electronic applications accepted. *Expenses:* Tuition, state resident: full-time $2,786; part-time $85 per credit. Tuition, nonresident: full-time $8,966; part-time $343 per credit. International tuition: $9,102 full-time. *Financial support:* In 2003–04, 2 fellowships with full tuition reimbursements (averaging $17,000 per year), 11 research assistantships with full tuition reimbursements (averaging $9,045 per year), 17 teaching assistantships with full tuition reimbursements (averaging $10,447 per year) were awarded. Tuition waivers (full) also available. Financial award application deadline: 3/1. *Faculty research:* Topology, algebra, applied mathematics, analysis. *Unit head:* Dr. Roger Waggoner, Head, 337-482-6702, Fax: 337-482-6587, E-mail: kje2027@louisiana.edu. *Application contact:* Dr. Nabendu Pal, Coordinator, 337-482-5279, Fax: 337-482-6587, E-mail: nxp3695@louisiana.edu.

University of Louisville, Graduate School, College of Arts and Sciences, Department of Mathematics, Louisville, KY 40292-0001. Offers applied and industrial mathematics (PhD); mathematics (MA). Evening/weekend programs available. *Students:* 28 full-time (10 women), 14 part-time (4 women); includes 2 minority (1 African American, 1 Asian American or Pacific Islander), 10 international. Average age 30. In 2003, 4 degrees awarded. *Degree requirements:* For master's, thesis optional; for doctorate, thesis/dissertation, internship, project, comprehensive exam. *Entrance requirements:* For master's and doctorate, GRE General Test. *Application deadline:* Applications are processed on a rolling basis. Application fee: $50. *Expenses:* Tuition, state resident: full-time $4,842. Tuition, nonresident: full-time $13,338. *Financial support:* In 2003–04, 25 teaching assistantships with full tuition reimbursements (averaging $12,500 per year) were awarded *Unit head:* Dr. Kevin Clancey, Chair, 502-852-5974, Fax: 802-852-7132, E-mail: kfclan01@louisville.edu. *Application contact:* Dr. Lee M. Larson, Graduate Studies Director, 502-852-6826, Fax: 502-852-7132, E-mail: llarson@louisville.edu.

University of Maine, Graduate School, College of Liberal Arts and Sciences, Department of Mathematics and Statistics, Orono, ME 04469. Offers mathematics (MA). *Faculty:* 15 full-time (1 woman). *Students:* 10 full-time (7 women), 1 (woman) part-time; includes 1 minority (Hispanic American), 4 international. Average age 36. 12 applicants, 67% accepted, 4 enrolled. In 2003, 2 degrees awarded. *Degree requirements:* For master's, thesis optional. *Entrance requirements:* For master's, GRE General Test. Additional exam requirements/recommendations for international students: Required—TOEFL. *Application deadline:* For fall admission, 2/1 for domestic students. Applications are processed on a rolling basis. Application fee: $50. Electronic applications accepted. *Expenses:* Tuition, state resident: part-time $235 per credit. Tuition, nonresident: part-time $670 per credit. Tuition and fees vary according to course load. *Financial support:* In 2003–04, 7 teaching assistantships with tuition reimbursements (averaging $9,416 per year) were awarded; research assistantships with tuition reimbursements, tuition waivers (full and partial) also available. Financial award application deadline: 3/1. *Unit head:* Dr. William Bray, Chair, 207-581-3901, Fax: 207-581-4977. *Application contact:* Scott G. Delcourt, Associate Dean of the Graduate School, 207-581-3218, Fax: 207-581-3232, E-mail: graduate@maine.edu.

University of Manitoba, Faculty of Graduate Studies, Faculty of Science, Department of Mathematical, Computational and Statistical Sciences, Winnipeg, MB R3T 2N2, Canada. Offers MMCSS. Tuition charges are reported in Canadian dollars. Tuition, nonresident: full-time $3,878 Canadian dollars.

University of Manitoba, Faculty of Graduate Studies, Faculty of Science, Department of Mathematics, Winnipeg, MB R3T 2N2, Canada. Offers M Sc, PhD. *Degree requirements:* For master's, one foreign language, thesis or alternative; for doctorate, one foreign language, thesis/dissertation. Tuition charges are reported in Canadian dollars. Tuition, nonresident: full-time $3,878 Canadian dollars.

University of Maryland, College Park, Graduate Studies and Research, College of Computer, Mathematical and Physical Sciences, Department of Mathematics, Program in Mathematics, College Park, MD 20742. Offers MA, PhD. Part-time and evening/weekend programs available. *Students:* 79 full-time (20 women), 13 part-time (4 women); includes 9 minority (3 African Americans, 2 Asian Americans or Pacific Islanders, 4 Hispanic Americans), 19 international. 168 applicants, 54% accepted. In 2003, 6 master's, 3 doctorates awarded. Terminal master's awarded for partial completion of doctoral program. *Median time to degree:* Of those who began their doctoral program in fall 1995, 52% received their degree in 8 years or less. *Degree requirements:* For master's, thesis or alternative; for doctorate, one foreign language, thesis/dissertation, written exam, oral exam. *Entrance requirements:* For master's, GRE General Test, GRE Subject Test, minimum GPA of 3.0, 3 letters of recommendation. *Application deadline:* For fall admission, 5/1 for domestic students, 2/1 for international students; for spring admission, 10/1 for domestic students, 6/1 for international students. Applications are processed on a rolling basis. Application fee: $50. Electronic applications accepted. *Expenses:* Tuition, state resident: part-time $349 per credit hour. Tuition, nonresident: part-time $602 per credit hour. *Financial support:* Fellowships, research assistantships, teaching assistantships available. Financial award applicants required to submit FAFSA. *Unit head:* Darcy Conant, Coordinator, 301-405-5058. *Application contact:* Trudy Lindsey, Director, Graduate Enrollment Management Services, 301-405-4190, Fax: 301-314-9305, E-mail: tlindsey@gradschool.umd.edu.

University of Massachusetts Amherst, Graduate School, College of Natural Sciences and Mathematics, Department of Mathematics and Statistics, Program in Mathematics and Statistics, Amherst, MA 01003. Offers MS, PhD. *Students:* 53 full-time (22 women), 4 part-time (2 women); includes 5 minority (1 African American, 3 Asian Americans or Pacific Islanders, 1 Hispanic American), 20 international. Average age 28. 233 applicants, 18% accepted, 19 enrolled. In 2003, 11 master's, 2 doctorates awarded. *Degree requirements:* For doctorate, 2 foreign languages, thesis/dissertation. *Entrance requirements:* Additional exam requirements/recommendations for international students: Required—TOEFL (minimum score 530 paper-based; 197 computer-based). *Application deadline:* For fall admission, 2/1 priority date for domestic students, 2/1 priority date for international students; for spring admission, 10/1 for domestic students, 10/1 for international students. Applications are processed on a rolling basis. Application fee: $40 ($50 for international students). *Expenses:* Tuition, state resident: full-time $1,320; part-time $110 per credit. Tuition, nonresident: full-time $4,969; part-time $414 per credit. Required fees: $2,626 per term. Tuition and fees vary according to course load. *Financial support:* Fellowships with full tuition reimbursements, research assistantships with full tuition reimbursements, teaching assistantships with full tuition reimbursements, career-related internships or fieldwork, Federal Work-Study, scholarships/grants, traineeships, and unspecified assistantships available. Support available to part-time students. Financial award application deadline: 2/1. *Unit head:* Dr. Eduardo Cattani, Director, 413-545-2282, Fax: 413-545-1801, E-mail: cattani@math.umass.edu.

University of Massachusetts Lowell, Graduate School, College of Arts and Sciences, Department of Mathematics, Lowell, MA 01854-2881. Offers applied mathematics (MS); computational mathematics (PhD); mathematics (MS). Part-time programs available. *Entrance requirements:* For master's, GRE General Test.

The University of Memphis, Graduate School, College of Arts and Sciences, Department of Mathematical Sciences, Memphis, TN 38152-3420. Offers applied mathematics (MS); applied statistics (PhD); bioinformatics (MS); computer science (PhD); computer sciences (MS); mathematics (MS, PhD); statistics (MS, PhD). Part-time programs available. *Faculty:* 24 full-time (5 women), 3 part-time/adjunct (0 women). *Students:* 106 full-time (40 women), 42 part-time (15 women); includes 8 minority (5 African Americans, 3 Asian Americans or Pacific Islanders), 108 international. Average age 30. 139 applicants, 37% accepted. In 2003, 31 master's, 8 doctorates awarded. Terminal master's awarded for partial completion of doctoral program. *Median time to degree:* Master's–2 years full-time, 4 years part-time; doctorate–2 years full-time, 4 years part-time. *Degree requirements:* For master's, comprehensive exam; for doctorate, one foreign language, thesis/dissertation, oral exams. *Entrance requirements:* For master's and doctorate, GRE General Test, minimum GPA of 2.5. Additional exam requirements/recommendations for international students: Required—TOEFL (minimum score 550 paper-based; 210 computer-based), WES evaluation of transcript. *Application deadline:* For fall admission, 8/1 for domestic students, 5/1 for international students; for spring

Mathematics

The University of Memphis (continued)

admission, 12/1 for domestic students, 9/1 for international students. Applications are processed on a rolling basis. Application fee: $25 ($50 for international students). Electronic applications accepted. *Expenses:* Tuition, state resident: full-time $5,142. Tuition, nonresident: full-time $13,296. *Financial support:* In 2003–04, 58 students received support, including fellowships with full tuition reimbursements available (averaging $17,500 per year), 9 research assistantships with full tuition reimbursements available (averaging $9,000 per year), 30 teaching assistantships with full tuition reimbursements available (averaging $9,000 per year); career-related internships or fieldwork, Federal Work-Study, scholarships/grants, unspecified assistantships, and minority scholarships also available. Financial award application deadline: 2/2. *Faculty research:* Combinatorics, ergodic theory, graph theory, Ramsey theory, applied statistics. Total annual research expenditures: $1.5 million. *Unit head:* Dr. James E. Jamison, Chairman, 901-678-2482, Fax: 901-678-2480, E-mail: jjamison@memphis.edu. *Application contact:* Coordinator of Graduate Studies, 901-678-2482, Fax: 901-678-2480, E-mail: dfwilson@memphis.edu.

University of Miami, Graduate School, College of Arts and Sciences, Department of Mathematics, Coral Gables, FL 33124. Offers MA, MS, DA, PhD. Part-time and evening/weekend programs available. *Faculty:* 25 full-time (2 women). *Students:* 22 full-time (8 women), 11 part-time (3 women); includes 12 minority (2 African Americans, 2 Asian Americans or Pacific Islanders, 8 Hispanic Americans), 10 international. Average age 30. 53 applicants, 57% accepted, 9 enrolled. In 2003, 5 master's, 1 doctorate awarded. Terminal master's awarded for partial completion of doctoral program. *Degree requirements:* For master's, qualifying exams; for doctorate, one foreign language, thesis/dissertation, qualifying exams. *Entrance requirements:* For master's and doctorate, GRE General Test, minimum GPA of 3.0. Additional exam requirements/recommendations for international students: Required—TOEFL (minimum score 550 paper-based; 213 computer-based). *Application deadline:* For fall admission, 7/1 for domestic students, 7/1 for international students; for spring admission, 12/1 for domestic students, 12/1 for international students. Applications are processed on a rolling basis. Application fee: $50. Electronic applications accepted. *Expenses:* Tuition: Full-time $19,526. *Financial support:* In 2003–04, 22 students received support, including fellowships with tuition reimbursements available (averaging $17,000 per year), 22 teaching assistantships with tuition reimbursements available (averaging $14,850 per year); career-related internships or fieldwork and institutionally sponsored loans also available. Support available to part-time students. Financial award application deadline: 2/1; financial award applicants required to submit FAFSA. *Faculty research:* Applied mathematics, probability, geometric analysis, differential equations, algebraic combinatorics. *Unit head:* Dr. Alan Zame, Chairman, 305-284-2348, Fax: 305-284-2848, E-mail: zame@math.miami.edu. *Application contact:* Dr. Marvin Mielke, Graduate Adviser, 305-284-2348, Fax: 305-284-2848, E-mail: m.mielke@math.miami.edu.

University of Michigan, Horace H. Rackham School of Graduate Studies, College of Literature, Science, and the Arts, Department of Mathematics, Ann Arbor, MI 48109. Offers AM, MS, PhD. Part-time programs available. *Faculty:* 63 full-time (5 women). *Students:* 128 full-time (28 women); includes 12 minority (1 African American, 9 Asian Americans or Pacific Islanders, 2 Hispanic Americans), 49 international. Average age 26. 418 applicants, 25% accepted, 38 enrolled. In 2003, 14 master's, 15 doctorates awarded. *Median time to degree:* Master's–2 years full-time; doctorate–5 years full-time. Of those who began their doctoral program in fall 1995, 48% received their degree in 8 years or less. *Degree requirements:* For doctorate, one foreign language, thesis/dissertation, oral defense of dissertation, preliminary exam, comprehensive exam, registration. *Entrance requirements:* For master's and doctorate, GRE General Test, GRE Subject Test. Additional exam requirements/recommendations for international students: Required—TOEFL (minimum score 580 paper-based; 220 computer-based). *Application deadline:* For fall admission, 1/22 for domestic students, 1/15 for international students. Applications are processed on a rolling basis. Application fee: $55. Electronic applications accepted. *Expenses:* Tuition, state resident: full-time $7,463. Tuition, nonresident: full-time $13,913. Full-time tuition and fees vary according to course load, degree level and program. *Financial support:* In 2003–04, 123 students received support, including 5 fellowships with full tuition reimbursements available (averaging $13,200 per year), 13 research assistantships with full tuition reimbursements available (averaging $13,570 per year), 65 teaching assistantships with full tuition reimbursements available (averaging $13,570 per year) Financial award application deadline: 3/15. *Faculty research:* Algebra, analysis, topology, applied mathematics, geometry. *Unit head:* Prof. Trevor Wooley, Chair, 734-936-1310, Fax: 734-763-0937, E-mail: math-chair@umich.edu. *Application contact:* Prof. Juha Heinonen, Associate Chairman for Graduate Studies, 734-764-7436, Fax: 734-763-0937, E-mail: math.acgs@umich.edu.

University of Minnesota, Twin Cities Campus, Graduate School, Institute of Technology, School of Mathematics, Minneapolis, MN 55455-0213. Offers MS, PhD. Part-time programs available. Terminal master's awarded for partial completion of doctoral program. *Degree requirements:* For master's, thesis (for some programs); for doctorate, 2 foreign languages, thesis/dissertation. *Entrance requirements:* For master's, GRE Subject Test (recommended); for doctorate, GRE Subject Test. Additional exam requirements/recommendations for international students: Required—TOEFL. *Expenses:* Tuition, state resident: full-time $3,681; part-time $614 per credit. Tuition, nonresident: full-time $7,231; part-time $1,205 per credit. *Faculty research:* Partial and ordinary differential equations, algebra and number theory, geometry, combinatorics, numerical analysis.

University of Mississippi, Graduate School, College of Liberal Arts, Department of Mathematics, Oxford, University, MS 38677. Offers MA, MS, PhD. *Faculty:* 20 full-time (5 women). *Students:* 25 full-time (12 women), 6 part-time (3 women); includes 10 minority (9 African Americans, 1 Asian American or Pacific Islander), 5 international. In 2003, 11 master's, 2 doctorates awarded. *Degree requirements:* For master's, thesis (for some programs); for doctorate, thesis/dissertation. *Entrance requirements:* For master's, GRE General Test, minimum GPA of 3.0; for doctorate, GRE General Test. Additional exam requirements/recommendations for international students: Required—TOEFL. *Application deadline:* For fall admission, 4/1 for domestic students; for spring admission, 10/1 for domestic students. Applications are processed on a rolling basis. Application fee: $25. *Expenses:* Tuition, state resident: part-time $218 per hour. Tuition, nonresident: part-time $273 per hour. *Financial support:* Scholarships/grants available. Financial award application deadline: 3/1; financial award applicants required to submit FAFSA. *Unit head:* Dr. Tristan Denley, Chairman, 662-915-7071, Fax: 662-915-5491, E-mail: tdenley@olemiss.edu.

University of Missouri–Columbia, Graduate School, College of Arts and Sciences, Department of Mathematics, Columbia, MO 65211. Offers applied mathematics (MS); mathematics (MA, MST, PhD). *Faculty:* 41 full-time (6 women). *Students:* 62 full-time (16 women), 5 part-time (2 women); includes 1 minority (Asian American or Pacific Islander), 31 international. In 2003, 18 master's, 2 doctorates awarded. *Degree requirements:* For doctorate, 2 foreign languages, thesis/dissertation. *Entrance requirements:* For master's and doctorate, GRE General Test, minimum GPA of 3.0. *Application deadline:* Applications are processed on a rolling basis. Application fee: $45 ($60 for international students). *Expenses:* Tuition, state resident: full-time $5,205. Tuition, nonresident: full-time $14,058. *Financial support:* Fellowships, research assistantships, teaching assistantships, institutionally sponsored loans available. *Unit head:* Dr. Yuri Latushkin, Director of Graduate Studies, 573-882-8275, E-mail: yuri@math.missouri.edu.

University of Missouri–Kansas City, College of Arts and Sciences, Department of Mathematics and Statistics, Kansas City, MO 64110-2499. Offers MA, MS, PhD. PhD offered through the School of Graduate Studies. Part-time programs available. *Faculty:* 6 full-time (2 women), 1 part-time/adjunct (0 women). *Students:* 2 full-time (1 woman), 13 part-time (7 women); includes 4 minority (2 African Americans, 1 Asian American or Pacific Islander, 1 Hispanic American), 2 international. Average age 36. In 2003, 4 master's, 1 doctorate awarded. Terminal master's awarded for partial completion of doctoral program. *Degree requirements:* For master's, written exam; for doctorate, 2 foreign languages, thesis/dissertation, oral and written exams. *Entrance requirements:* For master's, bachelor's degree in mathematics, minimum GPA of 3.0; for doctorate, GMAT or GRE General Test. *Application deadline:* For fall admission, 5/1 for domestic students. Applications are processed on a rolling basis. Application fee: $35 ($50 for international students). *Financial support:* In 2003–04, 6 students received support, including 6 teaching assistantships; Federal Work-Study, institutionally sponsored loans, and tuition waivers (full and partial) also available. Support available to part-time students. Financial award application deadline: 4/1. *Faculty research:* Classical real variables, matrix theory, ring theory, linear numerical analysis, statistics. *Unit head:* Dr. Bruce Wenner, Chairperson, 816-235-2853.

University of Missouri–Rolla, Graduate School, College of Arts and Sciences, Department of Mathematics and Statistics, Program in Mathematics, Rolla, MO 65409-0910. Offers mathematics (PhD); mathematics education (MST). *Students:* 12 full-time (3 women), 5 part-time (2 women), 8 international. Average age 32. 38 applicants, 55% accepted, 4 enrolled. In 2003, 2 degrees awarded. *Median time to degree:* Doctorate–5.5 years part-time. *Degree requirements:* For master's, thesis or alternative; for doctorate, one foreign language, thesis/dissertation. *Entrance requirements:* For master's and doctorate, GRE General Test. *Application deadline:* For fall admission, 7/1 for domestic students. Applications are processed on a rolling basis. Application fee: $50. Electronic applications accepted. *Expenses:* Tuition, state resident: full-time $5,871. Tuition, nonresident: full-time $13,114. Required fees: $820. Tuition and fees vary according to course load. *Financial support:* In 2003–04, research assistantships with partial tuition reimbursements (averaging $13,250 per year), 6 teaching assistantships with partial tuition reimbursements (averaging $13,250 per year) were awarded. Fellowships, institutionally sponsored loans also available. *Faculty research:* Analysis, differential equations, topology, statistics. *Application contact:* Dr. V. A. Samaranayake, Director of Graduate Studies, 573-341-4658, Fax: 573-341-4741, E-mail: vsam@umr.edu.

University of Missouri–St. Louis, Graduate School, College of Arts and Sciences, Department of Mathematical Sciences, St. Louis, MO 63121-4499. Offers applied mathematics (MA, PhD); computer science (MS); telecommunications science (Certificate). Part-time and evening/weekend programs available. *Faculty:* 15 full-time (0 women). *Students:* 36 full-time (13 women), 75 part-time (29 women); includes 20 minority (1 African American, 1 American Indian/Alaska Native, 18 Asian Americans or Pacific Islanders), 35 international. In 2003, 43 degrees awarded. *Degree requirements:* For master's, thesis optional; for doctorate, thesis/dissertation. *Entrance requirements:* For master's, GRE if no BS in computer science; for doctorate, GRE General Test. Additional exam requirements/recommendations for international students: Required—TOEFL (minimum score 550 paper-based; 213 computer-based). *Application deadline:* For fall admission, 5/1 for domestic students; for spring admission, 12/1 for domestic students. Applications are processed on a rolling basis. Application fee: $35 ($40 for international students). Electronic applications accepted. *Expenses:* Tuition, state resident: part-time $237 per credit hour. Tuition, nonresident: part-time $639 per credit hour. Required fees: $10 per credit hour. *Financial support:* In 2003–04, 9 teaching assistantships with full and partial tuition reimbursements (averaging $13,500 per year) were awarded; fellowships with full tuition reimbursements, research assistantships with full tuition reimbursements *Faculty research:* Applied mathematics, statistics, algebra, analysis, computer science. *Unit head:* Dr. Haiyun Cai, Director of Graduate Studies, 314-516-5741, Fax: 314-516-5400, E-mail: caih@msx.umsl.edu. *Application contact:* 314-516-5458, Fax: 314-516-5310, E-mail: gradadm@umsl.edu.

The University of Montana–Missoula, Graduate School, College of Arts and Sciences, Department of Mathematical Sciences, Missoula, MT 59812-0002. Offers mathematics (MA, PhD), including college teaching (PhD), traditional research (PhD). Part-time programs available. *Faculty:* 20 full-time (3 women). *Students:* 16 full-time (6 women), 2 part-time, 3 international. Average age 28. 9 applicants, 67% accepted, 6 enrolled. In 2003, 5 degrees awarded. Terminal master's awarded for partial completion of doctoral program. *Degree requirements:* For doctorate, thesis/dissertation. *Entrance requirements:* For master's and doctorate, GRE General Test. Additional exam requirements/recommendations for international students: Required—TOEFL (minimum score 525 paper-based; 195 computer-based). *Application deadline:* For fall admission, 2/1 for domestic students. Application fee: $45. *Expenses:* Tuition, state resident: full-time $1,848; part-time $221 per credit. Tuition, nonresident: full-time $4,880; part-time $333 per credit. Required fees: $2,200. *Financial support:* In 2003–04, 15 teaching assistantships with full tuition reimbursements were awarded; Federal Work-Study and unspecified assistantships also available. Financial award application deadline: 3/1; financial award applicants required to submit FAFSA. Total annual research expenditures: $716,087. *Unit head:* Dr. James Hirstein, Chair, 406-243-5311.

University of Nebraska at Omaha, Graduate Studies and Research, College of Arts and Sciences, Department of Mathematics, Omaha, NE 68182. Offers MA, MAT, MS. Part-time programs available. *Faculty:* 15 full-time (2 women). *Students:* 10 full-time (5 women), 26 part-time (9 women); includes 4 minority (2 African Americans, 2 Asian Americans or Pacific Islanders), 2 international. Average age 27. 15 applicants, 87% accepted, 10 enrolled. In 2003, 8 degrees awarded. *Degree requirements:* For master's, thesis (for some programs), comprehensive exam. *Entrance requirements:* For master's, minimum GPA of 3.0. Additional exam requirements/recommendations for international students: Required—TOEFL (minimum score 500 paper-based; 173 computer-based). *Application deadline:* For fall admission, 7/1 for domestic students; for spring admission, 12/1 priority date for domestic students. Applications are processed on a rolling basis. Application fee: $45. Electronic applications accepted. *Expenses:* Tuition, state resident: full-time $3,504. Tuition, nonresident: full-time $9,216. Required fees: $516. *Financial support:* In 2003–04, 19 students received support; research assistantships with tuition reimbursements available, teaching assistantships with tuition reimbursements available, Federal Work-Study, institutionally sponsored loans, traineeships, tuition waivers (partial), and unspecified assistantships available. Support available to part-time students. Financial award application deadline: 3/1; financial award applicants required to submit FAFSA. *Unit head:* Dr. Jack W. Heidel, Chairperson, 402-554-3430.

University of Nebraska–Lincoln, Graduate College, College of Arts and Sciences, Department of Mathematics and Statistics, Lincoln, NE 68588. Offers M Sc T, MA, MAT, MS, PhD. *Degree requirements:* For master's, thesis optional; for doctorate, variable foreign language requirement, thesis/dissertation, comprehensive exam. *Entrance requirements:* Additional exam requirements/recommendations for international students: Required—TOEFL (minimum score 550 paper-based; 213 computer-based), GRE General Test (international applicants). Electronic applications accepted. *Faculty research:* Applied mathematics, commutative algebra, algebraic geometry, Bayesian statistics, biostatistics.

University of Nevada, Las Vegas, Graduate College, College of Science, Department of Mathematical Sciences, Las Vegas, NV 89154-9900. Offers applied mathematics (MS); applied statistics (MS); pure mathematics (MS). Part-time programs available. *Faculty:* 28 full-time (6 women). *Students:* 28 full-time (9 women), 21 part-time (9 women); includes 12 minority (1 African American, 7 Asian Americans or Pacific Islanders, 4 Hispanic Americans), 16 international. 35 applicants, 69% accepted, 16 enrolled. In 2003, 8 degrees awarded. *Degree requirements:* For master's, thesis (for some programs), oral exam, comprehensive exam (for some programs). *Entrance requirements:* For master's, minimum GPA of 3.0 during previous 2 years, 2.75 overall. Additional exam requirements/recommendations for international students: Required—TOEFL (minimum score 550 paper-based; 213 computer-based). *Application deadline:* For fall admission, 6/15 for domestic students, 5/1 for international students; for spring admission, 11/15 for domestic students, 10/1 for international students. Application fee: $60 ($75 for international students). *Expenses:* Tuition, state resident: part-time $115 per credit. Tuition, nonresident: part-time $242 per credit. Required fees: $8 per semester. Tuition and fees vary according to course load. *Financial support:* In 2003–04, 36 teaching assistantships with partial tuition reimbursements (averaging $10,000 per year) were awarded. Financial award application deadline: 3/1. *Unit head:* Dr. Dieudonne Phanord, Head, 702-895-3567. *Application contact:* Graduate College Admissions Evaluator, 702-895-3320, Fax: 702-895-4180, E-mail: gradcollege@ccmail.nevada.edu.

University of Nevada, Reno, Graduate School, College of Science, Department of Mathematics, Reno, NV 89557. Offers mathematics (MS); teaching mathematics (MATM). *Faculty:* 17. *Students:* 13 full-time (7 women), 4 part-time (1 woman), 2 international. Average age 31. In 2003, 6 degrees awarded. *Degree requirements:* For master's, thesis optional. *Entrance requirements:* For master's, GRE General Test, minimum GPA of 2.75. Additional exam requirements/recommendations for international students: Required—TOEFL. *Application deadline:* For fall admission, 3/1 for domestic students; for spring admission, 11/1 for domestic students. Applications are processed on a rolling basis. Application fee: $60 ($95 for international students). *Expenses:* Tuition, state resident: part-time $119 per credit. Tuition, nonresident: part-time $127 per credit. Required fees: $20 per term. Tuition and fees vary according to course load. *Financial support:* In 2003–04, 2 research assistantships, 6 teaching assistantships were awarded. Institutionally sponsored loans also available. Financial award application deadline: 3/1. *Faculty research:* Operator algebra, nonlinear systems, differential equations. *Unit head:* Dr. Anna Panorska, Graduate Program Director, 775-784-6773.

University of New Brunswick Fredericton, School of Graduate Studies, Faculty of Science, Department of Mathematics and Statistics, Fredericton, NB E3B 5A3, Canada. Offers M Sc, PhD. Part-time programs available. *Degree requirements:* For master's, thesis or alternative; for doctorate, thesis/dissertation. *Entrance requirements:* For master's and doctorate, minimum GPA of 3.0. Additional exam requirements/recommendations for international students: Required—TOEFL, TWE.

University of New Hampshire, Graduate School, College of Engineering and Physical Sciences, Department of Mathematics and Statistics, Durham, NH 03824. Offers applied mathematics (MS); mathematics (MS, MST, PhD); mathematics education (PhD); statistics (MS). *Faculty:* 26 full-time. *Students:* 18 full-time (6 women), 30 part-time (12 women); includes 2 minority (1 African American, 1 Hispanic American), 17 international. Average age 28. 39 applicants, 79% accepted, 11 enrolled. In 2003, 16 master's, 1 doctorate awarded. Terminal master's awarded for partial completion of doctoral program. *Degree requirements:* For doctorate, 2 foreign languages, thesis/dissertation. *Entrance requirements:* Additional exam requirements/recommendations for international students: Required—TOEFL (minimum score 550 paper-based; 213 computer-based); Recommended—TSE. *Application deadline:* For fall admission, 4/1 for domestic students; for winter admission, 12/1 for domestic students. Applications are processed on a rolling basis. Application fee: $50. Electronic applications accepted. Tuition, area resident: Full-time $7,070. *Expenses:* Tuition, state resident: full-time $10,605. Tuition, nonresident: full-time $17,430. Required fees: $15. *Financial support:* In 2003–04, 1 fellowship, 27 teaching assistantships were awarded. Research assistantships, Federal Work-Study, scholarships/grants, and tuition waivers (full and partial) also available. Support available to part-time students. Financial award application deadline: 2/15. *Faculty research:* Operator theory, complex analysis, algebra, nonlinear dynamics, statistics. *Unit head:* Dr. Eric Grinberg, Chairperson, 603-862-2320. *Application contact:* Jan Jankawski, Graduate Coordinator, 603-862-2688, E-mail: janj@cisunix.unh.edu.

University of New Mexico, Graduate School, College of Arts and Sciences, Department of Mathematics and Statistics, Albuquerque, NM 87131-2039. Offers mathematics (MS, PhD); statistics (MS, PhD). Part-time programs available. *Students:* 73 full-time (31 women), 27 part-time (12 women); includes 19 minority (2 African Americans, 1 American Indian/Alaska Native, 5 Asian Americans or Pacific Islanders, 11 Hispanic Americans), 32 international. Average age 33. 50 applicants, 100% accepted, 31 enrolled. In 2003, 15 master's, 9 doctorates awarded. Terminal master's awarded for partial completion of doctoral program. *Degree requirements:* For master's, thesis or alternative, comprehensive exam (for some programs); for doctorate, one foreign language, thesis/dissertation, 4 department seminars, comprehensive exam. *Entrance requirements:* For master's, minimum GPA of 3.0, 3 letters of recommendation; for doctorate, GRE General Test, minimum GPA of 3.0, 3 letters of recommendation. *Application deadline:* For fall admission, 7/1 for domestic students; for spring admission, 11/1 for domestic students. Applications are processed on a rolling basis. Application fee: $40. *Expenses:* Tuition, state resident: full-time $1,802; part-time $152 per credit hour. Tuition, nonresident: full-time $6,135; part-time $513 per credit hour. Tuition and fees vary according to program. *Financial support:* In 2003–04, 4 fellowships (averaging $4,000 per year), 24 research assistantships with tuition reimbursements (averaging $11,745 per year), 45 teaching assistantships with tuition reimbursements (averaging $11,448 per year) were awarded. Health care benefits, tuition waivers (full and partial), and unspecified assistantships also available. Financial award application deadline: 3/1; financial award applicants required to submit FAFSA. *Faculty research:* Pure and applied mathematics, applied statistics, numerical analysis, biostatistics, differential geometry. Total annual research expenditures: $601,138. *Unit head:* Dr. Alejandro Aceves, Chair, 505-277-4613, Fax: 505-277-5505, E-mail: aceves@math.unm.edu. *Application contact:* Donna George, Program Advisement Coordinator, 505-277-5250, Fax: 505-277-5505, E-mail: dgeorge@unm.edu.

University of New Orleans, Graduate School, College of Sciences, Department of Mathematics, New Orleans, LA 70148. Offers MS. Part-time programs available. *Faculty:* 10 full-time (1 woman). *Students:* 29 full-time (15 women), 6 part-time (4 women); includes 9 minority (6 African Americans, 3 Asian Americans or Pacific Islanders), 14 international. Average age 29. 35 applicants, 63% accepted, 14 enrolled. In 2003, 8 degrees awarded. *Entrance requirements:* For master's, BA or BS in mathematics. Additional exam requirements/recommendations for international students: Required—TOEFL (minimum score 550 paper-based; 213 computer-based). *Application deadline:* For fall admission, 7/1 priority date for domestic students, 6/1 priority date for international students; for spring admission, 11/15 priority date for domestic students, 10/1 priority date for international students. Applications are processed on a rolling basis. Application fee: $20. Electronic applications accepted. *Expenses:* Tuition, state resident: part-time $488 per semester hour. Tuition, nonresident: part-time $1,826 per semester hour. *Financial support:* Teaching assistantships available. Financial award application deadline: 5/15; financial award applicants required to submit FAFSA. *Faculty research:* Differential equations, combinatorics, statistics, complex analysis, algebra. *Unit head:* Dr. Carroll Blakemore, Chairperson, 504-280-6125, Fax: 504-280-5516, E-mail: cblakemo@uno.edu. *Application contact:* Dr. Linxiong Li, Graduate Coordinator, 504-280-6040, Fax: 504-280-5516, E-mail: lli@math.uno.edu.

The University of North Carolina at Chapel Hill, Graduate School, College of Arts and Sciences, Department of Mathematics, Chapel Hill, NC 27599. Offers MA, MS, PhD. *Faculty:* 34 full-time (2 women). *Students:* 56 full-time (30 women). Average age 25. 142 applicants, 28% accepted, 16 enrolled. In 2003, 5 master's, 3 doctorates awarded. *Degree requirements:* For master's, thesis or alternative, computer proficiency, comprehensive exam; for doctorate, 2 foreign languages, thesis/dissertation, 3 comprehensive exams, computer proficiency. *Entrance requirements:* For master's and doctorate, GRE General Test, minimum GPA of 3.0. Additional exam requirements/recommendations for international students: Required—TOEFL. *Application deadline:* For fall admission, 1/1 for domestic students; for spring admission, 10/15 priority date for domestic students. Application fee: $60. Electronic applications accepted. *Expenses:* Tuition, state resident: full-time $3,163. Tuition, nonresident: full-time $15,161. *Financial support:* In 2003–04, 9 fellowships with full tuition reimbursements (averaging $18,000 per year), 2 research assistantships (averaging $15,000 per year), 44 teaching assistantships with full tuition reimbursements (averaging $14,750 per year) were awarded. Scholarships/grants and unspecified assistantships also available. Financial award application deadline: 3/1; financial award applicants required to submit FAFSA. *Faculty research:* Algebraic geometry, topology, analysis, lie theory, applied math. Total annual research expenditures: $550,076. *Unit head:* Dr. Chris Jones, Chairman, 919-962-1295, Fax: 919-962-2568. *Application contact:* Brenda Bethea, Student Services Manager, 919-962-4178, Fax: 919-962-2568, E-mail: bbethea@email.unc.edu.

Announcement: The department, with 34 faculty members and 57 graduate students, offers special opportunities for student-faculty interaction in master's and doctoral programs. Faculty includes distinguished, active researchers in most subfields of mathematics, including a strong new group in applied mathematics. Nearby resources are North Carolina State, Duke, and the Research Triangle Park.

The University of North Carolina at Charlotte, Graduate School, College of Arts and Sciences, Department of Mathematics, Charlotte, NC 28223-0001. Offers applied math (PhD); applied mathematics (MS); mathematics (MA, MS); mathematics education (MA). *Accreditation:* NCATE (one or more programs are accredited). Part-time and evening/weekend programs available. *Faculty:* 38 full-time (5 women), 5 part-time/adjunct (3 women). *Students:* 35 full-time (10 women), 23 part-time (10 women); includes 7 minority (5 African Americans, 2 Asian Americans or Pacific Islanders), 23 international. Average age 31. 25 applicants, 96% accepted, 14 enrolled. In 2003, 8 master's, 1 doctorate awarded. *Degree requirements:* For master's, comprehensive exam; for doctorate, thesis/dissertation. *Entrance requirements:* For master's, GRE General Test or MAT, minimum GPA of 3.0 in undergraduate major, 2.75 overall. Additional exam requirements/recommendations for international students: Required—TOEFL (minimum score 557 paper-based; 220 computer-based). *Application deadline:* For fall admission, 7/1 for domestic students, 5/1 for international students; for spring admission, 11/1 for domestic students, 10/1 for international students. Applications are processed on a rolling basis. Application fee: $35. Electronic applications accepted. *Expenses:* Tuition, state resident: full-time $1,979. Tuition, nonresident: full-time $12,111. Required fees: $1,201. Tuition and fees vary according to course load. *Financial support:* In 2003–04, 6 research assistantships (averaging $8,568 per year), 66 teaching assistantships (averaging $8,531 per year) were awarded. Fellowships, career-related internships or fieldwork, Federal Work-Study, institutionally sponsored loans, scholarships/grants, and unspecified assistantships also available. Support available to part-time students. Financial award application deadline: 4/1; financial award applicants required to submit FAFSA. *Faculty research:* Numerical analysis, inverse problems, partial differential equations, applied probability. *Unit head:* Dr. Alan S. Dow, Chair, 704-687-4551, Fax: 704-687-0415, E-mail: adow@email.uncc.edu. *Application contact:* Kathy B. Giddings, Director of Graduate Admissions, 704-687-3366, Fax: 704-687-3279, E-mail: gradadm@email.uncc.edu.

See in-depth description on page 605.

The University of North Carolina at Greensboro, Graduate School, College of Arts and Sciences, Department of Mathematics, Greensboro, NC 27412-5001. Offers computer science (MA); mathematical science (M Ed, MA). Part-time programs available. *Faculty:* 16 full-time (6 women). *Students:* 19 full-time (12 women), 31 part-time (12 women); includes 7 minority (1 African American, 6 Asian Americans or Pacific Islanders), 13 international. 54 applicants, 56% accepted. In 2003, 11 degrees awarded. *Degree requirements:* For master's, thesis (for some programs), comprehensive exam. *Entrance requirements:* For master's, GRE General Test. Additional exam requirements/recommendations for international students: Required—TOEFL. *Application deadline:* For fall admission, 6/15 for domestic students; for spring admission, 11/1 for domestic students. Applications are processed on a rolling basis. Application fee: $35. *Expenses:* Tuition, state resident: part-time $1,887 per unit. Tuition, nonresident: part-time $12,862 per unit. *Financial support:* In 2003–04, 8 research assistantships with full tuition reimbursements (averaging $6,188 per year), 4 teaching assistantships with full tuition reimbursements (averaging $6,563 per year) were awarded. Career-related internships or fieldwork, Federal Work-Study, scholarships/grants, traineeships, and unspecified assistantships also available. Support available to part-time students. *Faculty research:* General and geometric topology, statistics, computer networks, symbolic logic, mathematics education. *Unit head:* Dr. Paul Duvall, Head, 336-334-5836, Fax: 336-334-5949, E-mail: duvallp@uncg.edu. *Application contact:* Michelle Harkleroad, Director of Graduate Admissions, 336-334-4886, Fax: 336-334-4424, E-mail: mbharkle@office.uncg.edu.

The University of North Carolina at Wilmington, College of Arts and Sciences, Department of Mathematical Sciences, Wilmington, NC 28403-3297. Offers MA, MS. *Faculty:* 15 full-time (2 women). *Students:* 10 full-time (4 women), 7 part-time (4 women); includes 2 minority (both African Americans), 6 international. Average age 29. 18 applicants, 67% accepted, 7 enrolled. In 2003, 7 degrees awarded. *Degree requirements:* For master's, thesis, comprehensive exam. *Entrance requirements:* For master's, GRE General Test, GRE Subject Test, minimum B average in undergraduate major. *Application deadline:* For fall admission, 3/15 for domestic students. Applications are processed on a rolling basis. Application fee: $45. *Expenses:* Tuition, state resident: full-time $2,282. Tuition, nonresident: full-time $11,980. Required fees: $1,659. Tuition and fees vary according to course load. *Financial support:* In 2003–04, 12 teaching assistantships were awarded; career-related internships or fieldwork and Federal Work-Study also available. Support available to part-time students. Financial award application deadline: 3/15. *Unit head:* Dr. Wei Feng, Chair, 910-962-3290, Fax: 910-962-7107. *Application contact:* Dr. Robert D. Roer, Dean, Graduate School, 910-962-4117, Fax: 910-962-3787, E-mail: roer@uncw.edu.

University of North Dakota, Graduate School, College of Arts and Sciences, Department of Mathematics, Grand Forks, ND 58202. Offers M Ed, MS. Part-time programs available. *Faculty:* 14 full-time (2 women). *Students:* 4 applicants, 100% accepted, 4 enrolled. In 2003, 6 degrees awarded. *Degree requirements:* For master's, thesis or alternative, final exam. *Entrance requirements:* For master's, minimum GPA of 3.0. Additional exam requirements/recommendations for international students: Required—TOEFL (minimum score 550 paper-based; 213 computer-based). *Application deadline:* For fall admission, 3/1 priority date for domestic students, 3/1 priority date for international students. Applications are processed on a rolling basis. Application fee: $35. Electronic applications accepted. *Expenses:* Tuition, state resident: part-time $235 per credit. Tuition, nonresident: part-time $535 per credit. Tuition and fees vary according to course level, course load, program and reciprocity agreements. *Financial support:* In 2003–04, 10 teaching assistantships with full tuition reimbursements (averaging $9,540 per year) were awarded; fellowships, research assistantships, Federal Work-Study, institutionally sponsored loans, scholarships/grants, and tuition waivers (full and partial) also available. Support available to part-time students. Financial award application deadline: 3/15; financial award applicants required to submit FAFSA. *Faculty research:* Statistics, measure theory, topological vector spaces, algebras, applied math. *Unit head:* Dr. Thomas E. Gilsdorf, Chairperson, 701-777-2881, Fax: 701-777-3619, E-mail: thomas.gilsdorf@und.nodak.edu.

University of Northern British Columbia, Office of Graduate Studies, Prince George, BC V2N 4Z9, Canada. Offers community health science (M Sc); disability management (MA); education (M Ed); first nations studies (MA); gender studies (MA); history (MA); interdisciplinary studies (MA); international studies (MA); mathematical, computer and physical sciences (M Sc); natural resources and environmental studies (M Sc, MA, MNRES, PhD); political science (MA); psychology (M Sc, PhD); social work (MSW). Part-time and evening/weekend programs available. Postbaccalaureate distance learning degree programs offered (no on-campus study). *Students:* 293 full-time (187 women), 77 part-time (62 women). 290 applicants, 31% accepted, 80 enrolled. In 2003, 61 master's, 2 doctorates awarded. *Degree requirements:* For master's and doctorate, thesis/dissertation. *Entrance requirements:* For master's, GRE, minimum B average in undergraduate course work; for doctorate, candidacy exam, minimum A average in graduate course work. *Application deadline:* For fall and spring admission, 2/15; for winter admission, 9/15 for domestic students. Applications are processed on a rolling basis. Application fee: $50 ($250 for international students). *Expenses:* Tuition, state resident: full-time $2,272. *Financial support:* In 2003–04, 4 fellowships (averaging $7,750 per year), 250 research assistantships (averaging $12,000 per year), 60 teaching assistantships (averaging $8,000 per year) were awarded. Career-related internships or fieldwork, institutionally sponsored loans, and scholarships/grants also available. Support available to part-time students. Financial award application deadline: 2/15. *Unit head:* Dr. Robert W. Tait, Dean of Graduate Studies, 250-960-5726, Fax: 250-960-5362, E-mail: tait@unbc.ca. *Application contact:* Susan Deevy, Graduate Studies Officer, 250-960-6336, Fax: 250-960-6330, E-mail: deevys@unbc.ca.

University of Northern Colorado, Graduate School, College of Arts and Sciences, Department of Mathematics, Greeley, CO 80639. Offers educational mathematics (MA, PhD);

Mathematics

University of Northern Colorado (continued)

mathematics (MA, PhD). *Accreditation:* NCATE (one or more programs are accredited). *Faculty:* 11 full-time (2 women). *Students:* 15 full-time (8 women), 16 part-time (7 women); includes 2 minority (1 African American, 1 Asian American or Pacific Islander), 2 international. Average age 30. 12 applicants, 75% accepted, 7 enrolled. In 2003, 1 degree awarded. *Degree requirements:* For master's, thesis or alternative, comprehensive exam; for doctorate, thesis/dissertation, comprehensive exam. *Entrance requirements:* For master's and doctorate, GRE General Test. *Application deadline:* Applications are processed on a rolling basis. Application fee: $50 ($60 for international students). *Expenses:* Tuition, state resident: full-time $2,980; part-time $166 per semester. Tuition, nonresident: full-time $12,396; part-time $689 per semester. Required fees: $627; $35 per semester. *Financial support:* In 2003–04, 13 students received support, including 4 fellowships (averaging $1,463 per year), 1 research assistantship (averaging $18,000 per year), 9 teaching assistantships (averaging $14,147 per year); unspecified assistantships also available. Financial award application deadline: 3/1; financial award applicants required to submit FAFSA. *Unit head:* Dr. Richard Grassl, Chairperson, 970-351-2820.

University of Northern Iowa, Graduate College, College of Natural Sciences, Department of Mathematics, Cedar Falls, IA 50614. Offers mathematics (MA); mathematics for middle grades (MA). Part-time programs available. *Students:* 2 full-time (1 woman), 10 part-time (5 women). 3 applicants, 100% accepted. In 2003, 15 degrees awarded. *Degree requirements:* For master's, thesis or alternative, comprehensive exam (for some programs). *Entrance requirements:* Additional exam requirements/recommendations for international students: Required—TOEFL (minimum score 500 paper-based; 180 computer-based). *Application deadline:* For fall admission, 8/1 for domestic students. Applications are processed on a rolling basis. Application fee: $30 ($50 for international students). Electronic applications accepted. *Expenses:* Tuition, state resident: full-time $2,519. Tuition, nonresident: full-time $6,056. *Financial support:* Career-related internships or fieldwork, Federal Work-Study, scholarships/grants, and tuition waivers (full and partial) available. Support available to part-time students. Financial award application deadline: 2/1. *Unit head:* Dr. Jerry Ridenhour, Interim Head, 319-273-2631, Fax: 319-273-2546, E-mail: jerry.ridenhour@uni.edu.

University of North Florida, College of Arts and Sciences, Department of Mathematics and Statistics, Jacksonville, FL 32224-2645. Offers mathematical sciences (MS); statistics (MS). Part-time and evening/weekend programs available. *Faculty:* 20 full-time (5 women). *Students:* 12 full-time (7 women), 4 part-time (2 women), 1 international. Average age 29. 24 applicants, 42% accepted, 3 enrolled. In 2003, 2 degrees awarded. *Degree requirements:* For master's, thesis optional. *Entrance requirements:* For master's, GRE General Test, minimum GPA of 3.0 in last 60 hours. Additional exam requirements/recommendations for international students: Required—TOEFL (minimum score 500 paper-based; 173 computer-based). *Application deadline:* For fall admission, 7/6 priority date for domestic students, 5/1 priority date for international students; for winter admission, 11/2 for domestic students; for spring admission, 3/10 for domestic students. Applications are processed on a rolling basis. Application fee: $20. Electronic applications accepted. *Expenses:* Tuition, state resident: full-time $3,050; part-time $169 per semester hour. Tuition, nonresident: full-time $12,672; part-time $704 per semester hour. Required fees: $702; $39 per semester hour. *Financial support:* In 2003–04, 14 students received support, including 12 teaching assistantships (averaging $5,789 per year); Federal Work-Study and tuition waivers (partial) also available. Support available to part-time students. Financial award application deadline: 4/1; financial award applicants required to submit FAFSA. *Faculty research:* Real analysis, number theory, Euclidean geometry. Total annual research expenditures: $103,442. *Unit head:* Dr. Scott H. Hochwald, Chair, 904-620-2653, E-mail: shochwal@unf.edu. *Application contact:* Dr. Champak Panchal, Coordinator, 904-620-2469, E-mail: cpanchal@unf.edu.

University of North Texas, Robert B. Toulouse School of Graduate Studies, College of Arts and Sciences, Department of Mathematics, Denton, TX 76203. Offers MA, MS, PhD. Part-time programs available. *Faculty:* 31 full-time (5 women). *Students:* 48 full-time (13 women), 23 part-time (12 women). Average age 27. In 2003, 6 master's, 3 doctorates awarded. Terminal master's awarded for partial completion of doctoral program. *Degree requirements:* For master's, one foreign language; for doctorate, 2 foreign languages, thesis/dissertation. *Entrance requirements:* For master's and doctorate, GRE General Test. Additional exam requirements/recommendations for international students: Recommended—TOEFL (minimum score 550 paper-based; 213 computer-based). *Application deadline:* For fall admission, 7/17 for domestic students. Application fee: $50 ($75 for international students). Tuition, area resident: Full-time $4,087. Tuition, nonresident: full-time $8,730. Tuition and fees vary according to course load. *Financial support:* Research assistantships, teaching assistantships, Federal Work-Study and institutionally sponsored loans available. Financial award application deadline: 6/1. *Faculty research:* Differential equations, descriptive set theory, combinatorics, functional analysis, algebra. *Unit head:* Dr. Neal Brand, Chair, 940-565-2155, Fax: 940-565-4805, E-mail: neal@unt.edu. *Application contact:* Dr. Matt Douglass, Graduate Adviser, 940-565-2570, Fax: 940-565-4805, E-mail: douglass@unt.edu.

University of Notre Dame, Graduate School, College of Science, Department of Mathematics, Notre Dame, IN 46556. Offers algebra (PhD); algebraic geometry (PhD); applied mathematics (MSAM); complex analysis (PhD); differential geometry (PhD); logic (PhD); partial differential equations (PhD); topology (PhD). *Faculty:* 45 full-time (5 women). *Students:* 40 full-time (14 women). 153 applicants, 12% accepted, 6 enrolled. In 2003, 2 master's, 4 doctorates awarded. Terminal master's awarded for partial completion of doctoral program. *Degree requirements:* For doctorate, one foreign language, thesis/dissertation, qualifying exam. *Entrance requirements:* For master's and doctorate, GRE General Test, GRE Subject Test. Additional exam requirements/recommendations for international students: Required—TOEFL. *Application deadline:* For fall admission, 2/1 for domestic students. Applications are processed on a rolling basis. Application fee: $50. Electronic applications accepted. *Expenses:* Tuition: Full-time $29,375. *Financial support:* In 2003–04, 37 students received support, including 4 fellowships with full tuition reimbursements available (averaging $20,000 per year), 4 research assistantships with full tuition reimbursements available (averaging $12,000 per year), 29 teaching assistantships with full tuition reimbursements available (averaging $17,500 per year); tuition waivers (full) also available. Financial award application deadline: 2/1. *Faculty research:* Algebra, analysis, geometry/topology, logic, applied math. Total annual research expenditures: $1.5 million. *Unit head:* Dr. Julia Knight, Director of Graduate Studies, 574-631-7484, E-mail: mathgrad@nd.edu. *Application contact:* Dr. Terrence J. Akai, Director of Graduate Admissions, 574-631-7706, Fax: 574-631-4183, E-mail: gradad@nd.edu.

See in-depth description on page 607.

University of Oklahoma, Graduate College, College of Arts and Sciences, Department of Mathematics, Norman, OK 73019-0390. Offers MA, MS, PhD, MBA/MS. Part-time programs available. *Faculty:* 31 full-time (3 women). *Students:* 59 full-time (23 women), 7 part-time (5 women); includes 4 minority (1 African American, 1 American Indian/Alaska Native, 2 Asian Americans or Pacific Islanders), 28 international. 40 applicants, 85% accepted, 19 enrolled. In 2003, 2 master's, 2 doctorates awarded. Terminal master's awarded for partial completion of doctoral program. *Degree requirements:* For master's, thesis optional; for doctorate, 2 foreign languages, thesis/dissertation, qualifying exam. *Entrance requirements:* Additional exam requirements/recommendations for international students: Required—TOEFL (minimum score 550 paper-based; 213 computer-based), TSE. *Application deadline:* For fall admission, 6/1 priority date for domestic students, 4/1 priority date for international students; for spring admission, 11/1 for domestic students, 9/1 for international students. Applications are processed on a rolling basis. Application fee: $25 ($75 for international students). *Expenses:* Tuition, state resident: full-time $2,774; part-time $116 per credit hour. Tuition, nonresident: full-time $9,571; part-time $399 per credit hour. Required fees: $953; $33 per credit hour. Full-time tuition and fees vary according to course level, course load and program. *Financial support:* In 2003–04, 11 students received support, including 12 fellowships with full tuition reimbursements available (averaging $3,167 per year), 1 research assistantship (averaging $11,250 per year), 58 teaching assistantships with partial tuition reimbursements available (averaging $11,147 per year); scholarships/grants and unspecified assistantships also available. Financial award applicants required to submit FAFSA. *Faculty research:* Topology, geometry, algebra, analysis, mathematics education. Total annual research expenditures: $114,380. *Unit head:* Paul Goodey, Chair, 405-325-6711, Fax: 405-325-7484. *Application contact:* Dr. Murad Ozaydin, Director of Graduate Studies, 405-325-6711, Fax: 405-325-7484, E-mail: mozaydin@ou.edu.

Announcement: The Graduate Mathematics Program at the University of Oklahoma offers students a supportive environment and the opportunity for individual interaction with faculty members involved in broadly diversified research programs. Flexible degree programs allow students to concentrate in pure mathematics, applied mathematics, or research in undergraduate mathematics curriculum and pedagogy. WWW: http:/www.math.ou.edu/.

University of Oregon, Graduate School, College of Arts and Sciences, Department of Mathematics, Eugene, OR 97403. Offers MA, MS, PhD. Part-time programs available. *Faculty:* 23 full-time (3 women), 5 part-time/adjunct (1 woman). *Students:* 58 full-time (10 women), 2 part-time (1 woman); includes 4 minority (all Asian Americans or Pacific Islanders), 5 international. 35 applicants, 31% accepted. In 2003, 9 master's, 5 doctorates awarded. Terminal master's awarded for partial completion of doctoral program. *Degree requirements:* For doctorate, 2 foreign languages, thesis/dissertation. *Entrance requirements:* For master's and doctorate, GRE General Test, GRE Subject Test. Additional exam requirements/recommendations for international students: Required—TOEFL, TSE. *Application deadline:* For fall admission, 3/1 for domestic students. Application fee: $50. *Expenses:* Tuition, state resident: part-time $8,910 per term. Tuition, nonresident: part-time $13,689 per term. *Financial support:* In 2003–04, 38 teaching assistantships were awarded; Federal Work-Study also available. Support available to part-time students. Financial award application deadline: 3/1. *Faculty research:* Algebra, topology, analytic geometry, numerical analysis, statistics. *Unit head:* Brad Shelton, Head, 541-346-4705. *Application contact:* Judy Perkins, Admissions Contact, 541-346-0988.

University of Ottawa, Faculty of Graduate and Postdoctoral Studies, Faculty of Science, Ottawa-Carleton Institute of Mathematics and Statistics, Ottawa, ON K1N 6N5, Canada. Offers M Sc, PhD. Part-time programs available. *Faculty:* 31. *Students:* 41 full-time (15 women), 10 part-time (2 women). 63 applicants, 48% accepted, 16 enrolled. In 2003, 3 master's, 5 doctorates awarded. *Degree requirements:* For master's, thesis optional; for doctorate, one foreign language, thesis/dissertation, comprehensive exam. *Entrance requirements:* For master's, honors B Sc degree or equivalent, minimum B average; for doctorate, M Sc with minimum B+ average. *Application deadline:* For fall admission, 3/1 for domestic students. Applications are processed on a rolling basis. Application fee: $60. *Expenses:* Tuition, state resident: full-time $4,467. International tuition: $4,574 full-time. Tuition and fees vary according to program. *Financial support:* Fellowships, research assistantships, teaching assistantships, Federal Work-Study available. Financial award application deadline: 2/15. *Faculty research:* Pure mathematics, applied mathematics, probability. *Unit head:* Dr. Philip Scott, Chair, 613-562-5864, Fax: 613-562-5776. *Application contact:* Lise Maisonneuve, Graduate Studies Administrator, 613-562-5800 Ext. 6050, Fax: 613-562-5486, E-mail: lise@science.uottawa.ca.

University of Pennsylvania, School of Arts and Sciences, Graduate Group in Mathematics, Philadelphia, PA 19104. Offers AM, PhD. *Faculty:* 31 full-time (4 women), 17 part-time/adjunct (2 women). *Students:* 62 full-time (16 women), 1 part-time; includes 3 minority (all Asian Americans or Pacific Islanders), 32 international. 204 applicants, 21% accepted, 18 enrolled. In 2003, 9 master's, 5 doctorates awarded. Terminal master's awarded for partial completion of doctoral program. *Degree requirements:* For master's, one foreign language, thesis or alternative; for doctorate, 2 foreign languages, thesis/dissertation. *Entrance requirements:* For master's and doctorate, GRE General Test, GRE Subject Test. Additional exam requirements/recommendations for international students: Required—TOEFL. *Application deadline:* For fall admission, 12/1 for domestic students. Application fee: $70. Electronic applications accepted. *Expenses:* Tuition: Full-time $28,040; part-time $3,550 per course. Required fees: $1,750; $214 per course. Tuition and fees vary according to degree level, program and student level. *Financial support:* In 2003–04, 13 fellowships, 27 teaching assistantships were awarded. Institutionally sponsored loans also available. Financial award application deadline: 12/15. *Faculty research:* Geometry-topology, analysis, algebra, logic, combinatorics. *Application contact:* Patricia Rea, Coordinator for Admissions, 215-573-5816, Fax: 215-573-8068, E-mail: gdasadmis@sas.upenn.edu.

University of Pittsburgh, School of Arts and Sciences, Department of Mathematics, Pittsburgh, PA 15260. Offers applied mathematics (MA, MS); financial mathematics (PMS); mathematics (MA, MS, PhD). Part-time programs available. *Faculty:* 35 full-time (5 women), 13 part-time/adjunct (5 women). *Students:* 66 full-time (27 women), 10 part-time (3 women); includes 4 minority (3 African Americans, 1 Asian American or Pacific Islander), 30 international. 167 applicants, 42% accepted, 23 enrolled. In 2003, 8 master's, 5 doctorates awarded, leading to university research/teaching 100%. Terminal master's awarded for partial completion of doctoral program. *Median time to degree:* Doctorate–6 years full-time, 9.5 years part-time. *Degree requirements:* For master's, thesis (for some programs), comprehensive exam; for doctorate, thesis/dissertation, preliminary exams, comprehensive exam. *Entrance requirements:* For master's and doctorate, GRE General Test, GRE Subject Test (recommended), minimum GPA of 3.0. Additional exam requirements/recommendations for international students: Required—TOEFL (minimum score 550 paper-based; 213 computer-based). *Application deadline:* For fall admission, 1/15 priority date for domestic students, 1/15 priority date for international students; for spring admission, 9/1 for domestic students, 9/1 for international students. Applications are processed on a rolling basis. Application fee: $40. Electronic applications accepted. *Expenses:* Tuition, state resident: full-time $11,744; part-time $479 per credit. Tuition, nonresident: full-time $22,910; part-time $941 per credit. Required fees: $560. Tuition and fees vary according to degree level and program. *Financial support:* In 2003–04, 61 students received support, including 6 fellowships with full and partial tuition reimbursements available (averaging $14,700 per year), 6 research assistantships with full and partial tuition reimbursements available (averaging $12,400 per year), 48 teaching assistantships with full and partial tuition reimbursements available (averaging $12,775 per year); Federal Work-Study, institutionally sponsored loans, scholarships/grants, tuition waivers (partial), and unspecified assistantships also available. Financial award application deadline: 1/15. *Faculty research:* Computational math, mathbiology, math finance, algebra, analysis. Total annual research expenditures: $700,000. *Unit head:* John Chadam, Chairman, 412-624-8361, Fax: 412-624-8397, E-mail: chadam@pitt.edu. *Application contact:* Molly Williams, Administrator, 412-624-1175, Fax: 412-624-8397, E-mail: mollyw@pitt.edu.

University of Puerto Rico, Mayagüez Campus, Graduate Studies, College of Arts and Sciences, Department of Mathematics, Mayagüez, PR 00681-9000. Offers applied mathematics (MS); computational sciences (MS); pure mathematics (MS); statistics (MS). Part-time programs available. *Degree requirements:* For master's, one foreign language, comprehensive exam. *Faculty research:* Automata theory, linear algebra, logic.

University of Puerto Rico, Río Piedras, Faculty of Natural Sciences, Department of Mathematics, San Juan, PR 00931. Offers MS, PhD. Part-time and evening/weekend programs available. *Students:* 32 full-time (15 women), 15 part-time (4 women); includes 46 minority (2 Asian Americans or Pacific Islanders, 44 Hispanic Americans). 16 applicants, 100% accepted, 16 enrolled. In 2003, 4 degrees awarded. *Degree requirements:* For master's, one foreign language, thesis, comprehensive exam. *Entrance requirements:* For master's, GRE, EXADEP, interview, minimum GPA of 3.0, letter of recommendation. *Application deadline:* For fall admission, 2/1 for domestic students, 2/1 for international students. Application fee: $17. *Expenses:* Tuition, state resident: part-time $75 per credit. Tuition, nonresident: full-time $1,200; part-time $218 per credit. International tuition: $3,500 full-time. Required fees: $70; $35 per term. *Financial support:* Fellowships, research assistantships, teaching assistantships, Federal Work-Study, institutionally sponsored loans, and tuition waivers (partial) available. Financial award application deadline: 5/31. *Faculty research:* Investigation of database logistics, cryptograph systems, distribution and spectral theory, Boolean function, differential equations. *Unit head:* Dr. Jorge Punchín, Coordinator, 787-764-0000 Ext. 4676, Fax: 787-281-0651.

University of Regina, Faculty of Graduate Studies and Research, Faculty of Science, Department of Mathematics and Statistics, Regina, SK S4S 0A2, Canada. Offers mathematics (M Sc, MA, PhD); statistics (M Sc, MA). *Faculty:* 21 full-time (4 women), 2 part-time/adjunct (0 women). *Students:* 7 full-time (2 women), 3 part-time (1 woman). 7 applicants. In 2003, 1 degree awarded. *Degree requirements:* For master's, thesis optional; for doctorate, variable foreign language requirement, thesis/dissertation, comprehensive exam. *Entrance requirements:* Additional exam requirements/recommendations for international students: Required—TOEFL. *Application deadline:* Applications are processed on a rolling basis. Application fee: $60. *Expenses:* Tuition, state resident: part-time $130 per credit hour. Tuition and fees vary according to course load and program. *Financial support:* In 2003–04, 4 fellowships, 1 research assistantship, 2 teaching assistantships were awarded. Scholarships/grants also available. Financial award application deadline: 6/15. *Faculty research:* Pure and applied mathematics, statistics and probability. *Unit head:* Dr. E. Ahmed, Head, 306-585-4351, E-mail: ahmed@math.uregina.ca. *Application contact:* Dr. Chua-Hua Guo, Graduate Program Coordinator, 306-585-4423, Fax: 306-585-4020, E-mail: chguo@math.uregina.ca.

University of Rhode Island, Graduate School, College of Arts and Sciences, Department of Mathematics, Kingston, RI 02881. Offers MS, PhD. In 2003, 2 master's, 2 doctorates awarded. *Degree requirements:* For master's, thesis optional; for doctorate, one foreign language, thesis/dissertation. *Application deadline:* For fall admission, 4/15 for domestic students. Applications are processed on a rolling basis. Application fee: $35. *Expenses:* Tuition, state resident: full-time $4,338; part-time $281 per credit. Tuition, nonresident: full-time $12,438; part-time $704 per credit. Required fees: $1,840. *Unit head:* Dr. Lewis Pakula, Chairman, 401-874-5955.

University of Rochester, The College, Arts and Sciences, Department of Mathematics, Rochester, NY 14627-0250. Offers MA, MS, PhD. *Faculty:* 17. *Students:* 37 full-time (14 women); includes 3 minority (1 American Indian/Alaska Native, 1 Asian American or Pacific Islander, 1 Hispanic American), 23 international. 195 applicants, 10% accepted, 13 enrolled. In 2003, 8 master's, 4 doctorates awarded. Terminal master's awarded for partial completion of doctoral program. *Degree requirements:* For master's, thesis (for some programs); for doctorate, thesis/dissertation, qualifying exam. *Entrance requirements:* For master's and doctorate, GRE General Test. Additional exam requirements/recommendations for international students: Required—TOEFL. *Application deadline:* For fall admission, 2/1 for domestic students. Application fee: $25. *Expenses:* Tuition: Part-time $880 per credit hour. Required fees: $522. *Financial support:* Fellowships, research assistantships, teaching assistantships, tuition waivers (full and partial) available. Financial award application deadline: 2/1. *Unit head:* Douglas Ravenel, Chair, 585-275-9421. *Application contact:* Joan Robinson, Graduate Program Secretary, 585-275-4411.

University of Saskatchewan, College of Graduate Studies and Research, College of Arts and Sciences, Department of Mathematics and Statistics, Saskatoon, SK S7N 5A2, Canada. Offers M Math, MA, PhD. *Faculty:* 24. *Students:* 9. *Degree requirements:* For master's, thesis (for some programs), registration; for doctorate, thesis/dissertation, registration. *Entrance requirements:* Additional exam requirements/recommendations for international students: Required—TOEFL. *Application deadline:* For fall admission, 7/1 for domestic students. Applications are processed on a rolling basis. Application fee: $50. Tuition charges are reported in Canadian dollars. *Expenses:* Tuition, state resident: part-time $483 Canadian dollars per course. *Financial support:* Fellowships, research assistantships, teaching assistantships available. Financial award application deadline: 1/31. *Unit head:* Dr. Lawrence Martz, Acting Head, 306-966-6089, Fax: 306-966-6086, E-mail: lawrence.martz@usask.ca. *Application contact:* Dr. John Martin, Graduate Chair, 306-966-6099, Fax: 306-966-6086, E-mail: karen@math.usask.ca.

University of South Alabama, Graduate School, College of Arts and Sciences, Department of Mathematics/Statistics, Mobile, AL 36688-0002. Offers MS. Part-time and evening/weekend programs available. *Degree requirements:* For master's, comprehensive exam. *Entrance requirements:* For master's, GRE, minimum B average. *Faculty research:* Knot theory, chaos theory.

University of South Carolina, The Graduate School, College of Science and Mathematics, Department of Mathematics, Columbia, SC 29208. Offers mathematics (MA, MS, PhD); mathematics education (M Math, MAT). MAT offered in cooperation with the College of Education. *Accreditation:* NCATE. Part-time programs available. Terminal master's awarded for partial completion of doctoral program. *Degree requirements:* For master's, thesis; for doctorate, one foreign language, thesis/dissertation. *Entrance requirements:* For master's and doctorate, GRE General Test. Electronic applications accepted. *Expenses:* Tuition, state resident: part-time $308 per hour. Tuition, nonresident: part-time $655 per hour. *Faculty research:* Applied mathematics, analysis, discrete mathematics, algebra, topology.

The University of South Dakota, Graduate School, College of Arts and Sciences, Department of Mathematics, Vermillion, SD 57069-2390. Offers MA, MNS. Part-time programs available. *Degree requirements:* For master's, thesis (for some programs). *Entrance requirements:* For master's, GRE. Additional exam requirements/recommendations for international students: Required—TOEFL (minimum score 550 paper-based; 213 computer-based).

University of Southern California, Graduate School, College of Letters, Arts and Sciences, Department of Mathematics, Program in Mathematics, Los Angeles, CA 90089. Offers MA, PhD. *Students:* 24 full-time (8 women), 3 part-time (1 woman); includes 2 minority (both Asian Americans or Pacific Islanders), 16 international. In 2003, 1 degree awarded. *Degree requirements:* For doctorate, thesis/dissertation. *Entrance requirements:* For master's and doctorate, GRE General Test. *Application deadline:* For fall admission, 12/15 for domestic students; for spring admission, 11/1 for domestic students. Application fee: $65 ($75 for international students). *Expenses:* Tuition: Full-time $32,784; part-time $949 per unit. Tuition and fees vary according to course load and program. *Financial support:* Fellowships, research assistantships, teaching assistantships, Federal Work-Study, institutionally sponsored loans, and scholarships/grants available. Support available to part-time students. Financial award application deadline: 2/15; financial award applicants required to submit FAFSA. *Application contact:* Amy Yung, Information Contact, 213-740-2400.

University of Southern Mississippi, Graduate School, College of Science and Technology, Department of Mathematics, Hattiesburg, MS 39406-0001. Offers MS. Part-time programs available. *Faculty:* 13 full-time (5 women), 2 part-time/adjunct (1 woman). *Students:* 6 full-time (4 women), 3 part-time (1 woman); includes 2 minority (1 African American, 1 Asian American or Pacific Islander). Average age 28. 13 applicants, 62% accepted, 6 enrolled. In 2003, 5 degrees awarded. *Degree requirements:* For master's, thesis or alternative, comprehensive exam. *Entrance requirements:* For master's, GRE General Test, minimum GPA of 2.75 in last 60 hours. Additional exam requirements/recommendations for international students: Required—TOEFL. *Application deadline:* For fall admission, 3/15 for domestic students. Applications are processed on a rolling basis. Application fee: $25. *Expenses:* Tuition, state resident: part-time $1,967 per semester. Tuition, nonresident: part-time $4,376 per semester. *Financial support:* In 2003–04, 9 teaching assistantships with full tuition reimbursements (averaging $7,500 per year) were awarded; research assistantships with full tuition reimbursements, Federal Work-Study and institutionally sponsored loans also available. Financial award application deadline: 3/15. *Faculty research:* Dynamical systems, numerical analysis and multigrid methods, random number generation, matrix theory, group theory. *Unit head:* Dr. Wallace C. Pye, Chair, 601-266-4289, Fax: 601-266-5818, E-mail: wallace.pye@usm.edu.

University of South Florida, College of Graduate Studies, College of Arts and Sciences, Department of Mathematics, Tampa, FL 33620-9951. Offers applied mathematics (PhD); mathematics (MA, PhD). Part-time and evening/weekend programs available. *Faculty:* 34 full-time (2 women). *Students:* 55 full-time (23 women), 17 part-time (8 women); includes 10 minority (1 African American, 6 Asian Americans or Pacific Islanders, 3 Hispanic Americans), 32 international. 78 applicants, 38% accepted, 21 enrolled. In 2003, 2 degrees awarded. Terminal master's awarded for partial completion of doctoral program. *Degree requirements:* For master's, one foreign language, thesis optional; for doctorate, 2 foreign languages, thesis/dissertation. *Entrance requirements:* For master's, GRE General Test, minimum GPA of 3.0 in mathematics course work (undergraduate), 3.5 (graduate); for doctorate, GRE General Test. *Application deadline:* For fall admission, 6/1 for domestic students; for spring admission, 10/15 for domestic students. Application fee: $30. Electronic applications accepted. *Financial support:* In 2003–04, 48 students received support, including 34 teaching assistantships with full tuition reimbursements available (averaging $12,290 per year); unspecified assistantships also available. Financial award application deadline: 3/1. *Faculty research:* Approximation theory, differential equations, discrete mathematics, functional analysis topology. Total annual research expenditures: $129,212. *Unit head:* Marcus McWaters, Chairperson, 813-974-9530, Fax: 813-974-2700, E-mail: marcus@chuma.cas.usf.edu. *Application contact:* James Tremmel, Graduate Program Assistant, 813-974-5329, Fax: 813-974-2700, E-mail: ga@math.usf.edu.

The University of Tennessee, Graduate School, College of Arts and Sciences, Department of Mathematics, Knoxville, TN 37996. Offers applied mathematics (MS); mathematical ecology (PhD); mathematics (M Math, MS, PhD). Part-time programs available. *Degree requirements:* For master's, thesis or alternative; for doctorate, one foreign language, thesis/dissertation. *Entrance requirements:* For master's and doctorate, minimum GPA of 2.7. Additional exam requirements/recommendations for international students: Required—TOEFL. Electronic applications accepted.

The University of Texas at Arlington, Graduate School, College of Science, Department of Mathematics, Arlington, TX 76019. Offers mathematical sciences (PhD); mathematics (MS). Part-time and evening/weekend programs available. *Faculty:* 12 full-time (2 women). *Students:* 34 full-time (13 women), 37 part-time (23 women); includes 15 minority (6 African Americans, 1 American Indian/Alaska Native, 7 Asian Americans or Pacific Islanders, 1 Hispanic American), 19 international. 28 applicants, 96% accepted, 13 enrolled. In 2003, 11 master's, 3 doctorates awarded. *Median time to degree:* Of those who began their doctoral program in fall 1995, 95% received their degree in 8 years or less. *Degree requirements:* For master's, thesis or alternative, comprehensive exam; for doctorate, thesis/dissertation, comprehensive exam. *Entrance requirements:* For master's, GRE General Test; for doctorate, GRE General Test, 30 hours of graduate course work in mathematics, minimum GPA of 3.0 in last 60 hours of course work. Additional exam requirements/recommendations for international students: Required—TOEFL. *Application deadline:* For fall admission, 6/16 for domestic students. Applications are processed on a rolling basis. Application fee: $35 ($50 for international students). *Expenses:* Tuition, state resident: full-time $3,042. Tuition, nonresident: full-time $8,712. Required fees: $1,269. Tuition and fees vary according to course load. *Financial support:* In 2003–04, 30 students received support, including 4 fellowships (averaging $1,000 per year), 23 teaching assistantships (averaging $15,600 per year); Federal Work-Study, institutionally sponsored loans, scholarships/grants, health care benefits, and unspecified assistantships also available. Financial award application deadline: 6/1; financial award applicants required to submit FAFSA. *Unit head:* Dr. Danny Dyer, Chair, 817-272-3262, Fax: 817-272-5802, E-mail: dyer@exchange.uta.edu. *Application contact:* Dr. Tie Luo, Graduate Adviser, 817-272-3261, Fax: 817-272-5802, E-mail: luo@uta.edu.

The University of Texas at Austin, Graduate School, College of Natural Sciences, Department of Mathematics, Austin, TX 78712-1111. Offers mathematics (MA, PhD); statistics (MS Stat). *Entrance requirements:* For master's and doctorate, GRE General Test. Electronic applications accepted.

The University of Texas at Dallas, School of Natural Sciences and Mathematics, Programs in Mathematical Sciences, Richardson, TX 75083-0688. Offers applied mathematics (MS, PhD); engineering mathematics (MS); mathematical science (MS); statistics (MS, PhD). Part-time and evening/weekend programs available. *Faculty:* 10 full-time (1 woman), 2 part-time/adjunct (0 women). *Students:* 37 full-time (13 women), 19 part-time (8 women); includes 14 minority (5 African Americans, 7 Asian Americans or Pacific Islanders, 2 Hispanic Americans), 20 international. Average age 33. 118 applicants, 58% accepted. In 2003, 13 master's, 3 doctorates awarded. *Degree requirements:* For master's, thesis optional; for doctorate, thesis/dissertation. *Entrance requirements:* For master's, GRE General Test, minimum GPA of 3.0 in upper-level course work in field; for doctorate, GRE General Test, minimum GPA of 3.5 in upper-level course work in field. Additional exam requirements/recommendations for international students: Required—TOEFL (minimum score 550 paper-based; 213 computer-based). *Application deadline:* For fall admission, 7/15 for domestic students; for spring admission, 11/15 for domestic students. Applications are processed on a rolling basis. Application fee: $50 ($100 for international students). Electronic applications accepted. *Expenses:* Tuition, state resident: full-time $1,656; part-time $92 per credit. Tuition, nonresident: full-time $5,904; part-time $328 per credit. Required fees: $2,161; $275 per credit. $334 per term. *Financial support:* In 2003–04, 1 research assistantship (averaging $6,975 per year), 29 teaching assistantships with tuition reimbursements (averaging $5,625 per year) were awarded. Fellowships, career-related internships or fieldwork, Federal Work-Study, institutionally sponsored loans, and scholarships/grants also available. Support available to part-time students. Financial award application deadline: 4/30; financial award applicants required to submit FAFSA. *Faculty research:* Statistical methods, control theory, mathematical modeling and analyses of biological and physical systems. Total annual research expenditures: $151,159. *Unit head:* Dr. M. Ali Hooshyar, Head, 972-883-2171, Fax: 972-883-6622, E-mail: utdmath@utdallas.edu. *Application contact:* Joan Gladwell, Information Contact, 972-883-6432, Fax: 972-883-6622, E-mail: gladwell@utdallas.edu.

See in-depth description on page 613.

The University of Texas at El Paso, Graduate School, College of Science, Department of Mathematical Sciences, El Paso, TX 79968-0001. Offers mathematical sciences (MAT); mathematics (MS); statistics (MS). Part-time and evening/weekend programs available. *Students:* 55 (25 women); includes 25 minority (1 African American, 4 Asian Americans or Pacific Islanders, 20 Hispanic Americans) 15 international. Average age 34. 19 applicants, 89% accepted. In 2003, 3 degrees awarded. *Degree requirements:* For master's, thesis optional. *Entrance requirements:* For master's, GRE, minimum GPA of 3.0. Additional exam requirements/recommendations for international students: Required—TOEFL. *Application deadline:* For fall admission, 7/1 priority date for domestic students, 3/1 priority date for international students; for spring admission, 11/1 priority date for domestic students, 9/1 priority date for international students. Applications are processed on a rolling basis. Application fee: $15 ($65 for international students). Electronic applications accepted. *Expenses:* Tuition, state resident: full-time $1,388; part-time $160 per hour. Tuition, nonresident: full-time $3,440; part-time $388 per hour. Tuition and fees vary according to course load, degree level and program. *Financial support:* In 2003–04, 10 students received support, including research assistantships with partial tuition reimbursements available (averaging $21,812 per year), teaching assistantships with partial tuition reimbursements available (averaging $17,450 per year); career-related internships or fieldwork, Federal Work-Study, institutionally sponsored loans, scholarships/grants, and tuition waivers (partial) also available. Financial award application deadline: 3/15; financial award applicants required to submit FAFSA. *Unit head:* Dr. Joe Guthrie, Chairperson, 915-747-5761, Fax: 915-747-6202, E-mail: joe@math.utep.edu. *Application contact:* Dr. Charles H. Ambler, Dean of the Graduate School, 915-747-5491 Ext. 7886, Fax: 915-747-5788, E-mail: cambler@utep.edu.

The University of Texas at Tyler, Graduate Studies, College of Arts and Sciences, Department of Mathematics, Tyler, TX 75799-0001. Offers MAT, MS, MSIS. *Faculty:* 7 full-time (3 women). *Students:* 5 full-time (2 women). Average age 24. 3 applicants, 100% accepted, 3 enrolled. *Degree requirements:* For master's, comprehensive exam. *Entrance requirements:* For master's, GRE General Test. *Application deadline:* Applications are processed on a rolling basis. Application fee: $0. *Expenses:* Tuition, state resident: full-time $4,270. Tuition,

Mathematics

The University of Texas at Tyler (continued)
nonresident: full-time $12,766. *Financial support:* In 2003–04, 4 teaching assistantships (averaging $8,000 per year) were awarded; unspecified assistantships also available. Financial award application deadline: 7/1; financial award applicants required to submit FAFSA. *Faculty research:* Graph theory, abstract algebra, biomathematics. *Unit head:* Dr. Robert H. Cranford, Chair, 903-566-7210, Fax: 903-566-7189, E-mail: rcranfor@mail.uttyl.edu. *Application contact:* Carol A. Hodge, Office of Graduate Studies, 903-566-5642, Fax: 903-566-7068, E-mail: chodge@mail.uttyl.edu.

The University of Texas–Pan American, College of Science and Engineering, Department of Mathematics, Edinburg, TX 78541-2999. Offers MS. Part-time and evening/weekend programs available. *Degree requirements:* For master's, comprehensive exam. *Entrance requirements:* For master's, GRE General Test, minimum GPA of 3.0. *Expenses:* Tuition, state resident: part-time $165 per semester hour. Tuition, nonresident: part-time $381 per semester hour. *Faculty research:* Boundary value problems in differential equations, training of public school teachers in methods of presenting mathematics, harmonic analysis, inverse problems, commulative algebra.

University of the District of Columbia, College of Arts and Sciences, Division of Science and Mathematics, Department of Mathematics, Washington, DC 20008-1175. Offers MST. Part-time and evening/weekend programs available. *Students:* 4 full-time (2 women), 2 part-time (1 woman); includes 2 minority (both African Americans), 4 international. Average age 29. 33 applicants, 30% accepted, 4 enrolled. In 2003, 1 degree awarded. *Degree requirements:* For master's, comprehensive exam. *Entrance requirements:* For master's, GRE General Test, writing proficiency exam. *Application deadline:* For fall admission, 6/15 for domestic students; for spring admission, 11/1 for domestic students. Applications are processed on a rolling basis. Application fee: $20. *Expenses:* Tuition, state resident: part-time $198 per credit hour. Tuition, nonresident: part-time $329 per credit hour. *Unit head:* Dr. Lorenzo Hilliard, Chair, 202-274-5153. *Application contact:* LaVerne Hill Flannigan, Director of Admission, 202-274-6069.

University of the Incarnate Word, School of Graduate Studies and Research, School of Mathematics, Sciences, and Engineering, Program in Mathematics, San Antonio, TX 78209-6397. Offers MA, MS. Part-time and evening/weekend programs available. *Faculty:* 4 full-time (3 women). *Students:* Average age 34. In 2003, 1 degree awarded. *Entrance requirements:* For master's, GRE General Test. Additional exam requirements/recommendations for international students: Required—TOEFL. *Application deadline:* For fall admission, 8/15 for domestic students; for spring admission, 12/31 for domestic students. Applications are processed on a rolling basis. Application fee: $20. *Expenses:* Tuition: Full-time $9,360; part-time $520 per hour. Required fees: $630; $35 per hour. One-time fee: $30 full-time. *Faculty research:* Topology, set theory, mathematics education. Total annual research expenditures: $65,000. *Unit head:* Dr. Reginald Traylor, Chair, 210-829-3160, Fax: 210-829-3153, E-mail: traylor@universe.uiwtx.edu. *Application contact:* Andrea Cyterski-Acosta, Director of Admissions, 210-829-6005, Fax: 210-829-3921, E-mail: cyterski@universe.uiwtx.edu.

University of Toledo, Graduate School, College of Arts and Sciences, Department of Mathematics, Toledo, OH 43606-3390. Offers applied mathematics (MS); mathematics (MA, PhD); statistics (MS). Part-time programs available. *Students:* 32 full-time (12 women), 11 part-time (3 women), 32 international. Average age 29. 74 applicants, 53% accepted. In 2003, 19 master's, 1 doctorate awarded. *Degree requirements:* For doctorate, 2 foreign languages, thesis/dissertation. *Entrance requirements:* For master's and doctorate, GRE General Test, GRE Subject Test. *Application deadline:* For fall admission, 8/1 for domestic students. Application fee: $40. Electronic applications accepted. Tuition, area resident: Part-time $3,817 per semester. *Expenses:* Tuition, state resident: part-time $8,177 per semester. Required fees: $502 per semester. *Financial support:* In 2003–04, 6 research assistantships, 27 teaching assistantships were awarded. Federal Work-Study and institutionally sponsored loans also available. Support available to part-time students. Financial award application deadline: 4/1; financial award applicants required to submit FAFSA. *Faculty research:* Topology. *Unit head:* Dr. Geoffrey Martin, Chair, 419-530-2569, Fax: 419-530-4720. *Application contact:* Dr. Robert Ochs, Advising Coordinator, 419-530-2069, Fax: 419-530-4720, E-mail: rochs@math.utoledo.edu.

Announcement: The Department of Mathematics features the close student-faculty contact and informal atmosphere of a small department while at the same time providing facilities and opportunities comparable to those at larger institutions. Research is conducted in a variety of specialties, including algebra, harmonic analysis, differential geometry, dynamical systems and partial differential equations, optimal control, and statistics.

See in-depth description on page 617.

University of Toronto, School of Graduate Studies, Physical Sciences Division, Department of Mathematics, Toronto, ON M5S 1A1, Canada. Offers M Sc, MMF, PhD. Part-time programs available. *Faculty:* 70 full-time (3 women), 1 part-time/adjunct. *Students:* 78, 29 international. 113 applicants, 42% accepted. In 2003, 15 master's, 9 doctorates awarded. *Degree requirements:* For master's, research project, thesis optional; for doctorate, thesis/dissertation. *Entrance requirements:* For master's, minimum B average in final year, bachelor's degree in mathematics or a related area, 3 letters of reference; for doctorate, master's degree in mathematics or a related area, minimum A– average, 3 letters of reference. *Application deadline:* For fall admission, 2/1 for domestic students. Application fee: $90 Canadian dollars. Tuition, nonresident: full-time $4,185. International tuition: $10,739 full-time. *Financial support:* Teaching assistantships available. *Unit head:* J. S. Bland, Chair, 416-978-3320, Fax: 416-978-4107. *Application contact:* Ida Bulat, Assistant to Associate Chair and to Graduate Coordinator, 416-978-7894, Fax: 416-978-4107, E-mail: ida@math.toronto.edu.

University of Tulsa, Graduate School, College of Business Administration and College of Engineering and Natural Sciences, Department of Engineering and Technology Management, Tulsa, OK 74104-3189. Offers chemical engineering (METM); computer science (METM); electrical engineering (METM); geological science (METM); mathematics (METM); mechanical engineering (METM); petroleum engineering (METM). Part-time and evening/weekend programs available. *Students:* 1 full-time (0 women), 1 part-time, 1 international. Average age 32. 3 applicants, 100% accepted, 2 enrolled. In 2003, 1 degree awarded. *Entrance requirements:* For master's, GRE General Test or GMAT. Additional exam requirements/recommendations for international students: Required—TOEFL. *Application deadline:* Applications are processed on a rolling basis. Application fee: $30. Electronic applications accepted. *Expenses:* Tuition: Full-time $10,584; part-time $588 per credit hour. Required fees: $60; $3 per credit hour. *Financial support:* In 2003–04, 1 research assistantship with full and partial tuition reimbursement (averaging $6,250 per year) was awarded; fellowships, teaching assistantships, Federal Work-Study, scholarships/grants, tuition waivers (full and partial), and unspecified assistantships also available. Support available to part-time students. Financial award application deadline: 2/1; financial award applicants required to submit FAFSA. *Unit head:* Dr. Rebecca Holland, Director of Graduate Business Studies, 918-631-2242, Fax: 918-631-2142, E-mail: rebecca-holland@utulsa.edu. *Application contact:* Information Contact, E-mail: graduate-business@utulsa.edu.

University of Tulsa, Graduate School, College of Engineering and Natural Sciences, Department of Mathematical and Computer Sciences, Program in Mathematical Sciences, Tulsa, OK 74104-3189. Offers MS. Part-time programs available. *Faculty:* 12 full-time (2 women). *Students:* 4 full-time (2 women), 1 part-time; includes 2 minority (1 American Indian/Alaska Native, 1 Hispanic American). Average age 29. 4 applicants, 25% accepted, 1 enrolled. In 2003, 2 degrees awarded. *Median time to degree:* Master's–2 years full-time, 3 years part-time. *Degree requirements:* For master's, thesis optional. *Entrance requirements:* For master's, GRE General Test. Additional exam requirements/recommendations for international students: Required—TOEFL. *Application deadline:* Applications are processed on a rolling basis. Application fee: $30. Electronic applications accepted. *Expenses:* Tuition: Full-time $10,584; part-time $588 per credit hour. Required fees: $60; $3 per credit hour. *Financial support:* In 2003–04, 1 fellowship with full and partial tuition reimbursement (averaging $9,900 per year), 1 research assistantship with full and partial tuition reimbursement (averaging $7,600 per year), 1 teaching assistantship with full and partial tuition reimbursement (averaging $7,200 per year) were awarded. Federal Work-Study, scholarships/grants, tuition waivers (full and partial), and unspecified assistantships also available. Financial award application deadline: 2/1; financial award applicants required to submit FAFSA. *Faculty research:* Optimization theory, numerical analysis, mathematical physics, modeling, bayesian statistical inference. *Application contact:* Dr. Kevin A. O'Neil, Adviser, 918-631-2984, Fax: 918-631-3077, E-mail: grad@utulsa.edu.

University of Utah, Graduate School, College of Science, Department of Mathematics, Salt Lake City, UT 84112-1107. Offers M Phil, M Stat, MA, MS, PhD. Part-time programs available. *Faculty:* 37 full-time (2 women). *Students:* 61 full-time (17 women), 16 part-time (7 women); includes 4 minority (1 Asian American or Pacific Islander, 3 Hispanic Americans), 21 international. Average age 27. 124 applicants, 52% accepted, 31 enrolled. In 2003, 19 master's, 3 doctorates awarded. Terminal master's awarded for partial completion of doctoral program. *Degree requirements:* For master's, thesis or alternative, written or oral exam; for doctorate, thesis/dissertation, written and oral exams. *Entrance requirements:* Additional exam requirements/recommendations for international students: Required—TOEFL. *Application deadline:* For fall admission, 3/15 for domestic students, 3/15 for international students; for spring admission, 11/1 for domestic students, 11/1 for international students. Application fee: $45 ($60 for international students). Tuition, nonresident: full-time $2,483. International tuition: $8,768 full-time. *Financial support:* In 2003–04, 59 students received support, including 1 fellowship with full tuition reimbursement available (averaging $10,000 per year), 10 research assistantships with full tuition reimbursements available (averaging $14,900 per year), 48 teaching assistantships with full tuition reimbursements available (averaging $14,000 per year) Financial award application deadline: 3/15. *Faculty research:* Algebraic geometry, differential geometry, scientific computing, topology, mathematical biology. Total annual research expenditures: $2 million. *Unit head:* Graeme Milton, Chairman, 801-581-7870, Fax: 801-581-4148, E-mail: milton@math.utah.edu. *Application contact:* Peter C. Trombi, Director of Graduate Studies, 801-581-8005, Fax: 801-581-4148, E-mail: trombi@math.utah.edu.

See in-depth description on page 619.

University of Vermont, Graduate College, College of Engineering and Mathematics, Department of Mathematics and Statistics, Program in Mathematics, Burlington, VT 05405. Offers mathematics (MS, PhD); mathematics education (MAT, MST). *Accreditation:* NCATE (one or more programs are accredited). *Students:* 25 (9 women); includes 1 minority (Asian American or Pacific Islander) 8 international. 49 applicants, 71% accepted, 12 enrolled. In 2003, 6 degrees awarded. *Degree requirements:* For doctorate, thesis/dissertation. *Entrance requirements:* For master's and doctorate, GRE General Test. Additional exam requirements/recommendations for international students: Required—TOEFL (minimum score 550 paper-based; 213 computer-based). *Application deadline:* For fall admission, 4/1 for domestic students. Applications are processed on a rolling basis. Application fee: $25. Electronic applications accepted. *Expenses:* Tuition, state resident: part-time $362 per credit hour. Tuition, nonresident: part-time $906 per credit hour. *Financial support:* Fellowships, research assistantships, teaching assistantships available. Financial award application deadline: 3/1. *Unit head:* Dr. J. Sands, Coordinator, 802-656-2940.

University of Victoria, Faculty of Graduate Studies, Faculty of Science, Department of Mathematics and Statistics, Victoria, BC V8W 2Y2, Canada. Offers applied mathematics (M Sc, MA, PhD); pure mathematics (M Sc, MA, PhD); statistics (M Sc, MA). Part-time programs available. *Degree requirements:* For doctorate, one foreign language, thesis/dissertation, 3 qualifying exams. *Entrance requirements:* Additional exam requirements/recommendations for international students: Required—TOEFL. *Faculty research:* Functional analysis and operator theory, applied ordinary and partial differential equations, discrete mathematics and graph theory.

University of Virginia, College and Graduate School of Arts and Sciences, Department of Mathematics, Charlottesville, VA 22903. Offers MA, MS, PhD. *Faculty:* 34 full-time (7 women), 3 part-time/adjunct (2 women). *Students:* 47 full-time (19 women); includes 3 minority (2 African Americans, 1 Asian American or Pacific Islander), 11 international. Average age 25. 57 applicants, 18% accepted, 2 enrolled. In 2003, 10 master's, 5 doctorates awarded. *Degree requirements:* For master's, one foreign language, comprehensive exam; for doctorate, 2 foreign languages, thesis/dissertation, comprehensive exam. *Entrance requirements:* For master's and doctorate, GRE General Test, GRE Subject Test. *Application deadline:* For fall admission, 7/15 for domestic students; for spring admission, 12/1 for domestic students. Applications are processed on a rolling basis. Application fee: $40. Electronic applications accepted. *Expenses:* Tuition, state resident: full-time $6,476. Tuition, nonresident: full-time $18,534. Required fees: $1,380. *Financial support:* Fellowships, teaching assistantships, unspecified assistantships available. Financial award application deadline: 2/1; financial award applicants required to submit FAFSA. *Unit head:* James S. Howland, Chairman, 434-924-4919, Fax: 434-982-3084. *Application contact:* Peter C. Brunjes, Associate Dean for Graduate Programs and Research, 434-924-7184, Fax: 434-924-6737, E-mail: grad-a-s@virginia.edu.

University of Washington, Graduate School, College of Arts and Sciences, Department of Mathematics, Seattle, WA 98195. Offers MA, MS, PhD. Part-time programs available. Terminal master's awarded for partial completion of doctoral program. *Degree requirements:* For master's, thesis optional; for doctorate, 2 foreign languages, thesis/dissertation, registration. *Entrance requirements:* For master's, GRE, minimum GPA of 3.0; for doctorate, GRE General Test, GRE Subject Test (mathematics), minimum GPA of 3.0. Additional exam requirements/recommendations for international students: Required—TOEFL. Electronic applications accepted. *Faculty research:* Algebra, analysis, probability, combinatorics and geometry.

University of Washington, Graduate School, Interdisciplinary Graduate Program in Quantitative Ecology and Resource Management, Seattle, WA 98195. Offers MS, PhD. *Degree requirements:* For master's and doctorate, thesis/dissertation. *Entrance requirements:* For master's and doctorate, GRE General Test, minimum GPA of 3.0. Additional exam requirements/recommendations for international students: Required—TOEFL. Electronic applications accepted. *Faculty research:* Population dynamics, statistical analysis, ecological modeling and systems analysis of aquatic and terrestrial ecosystems.

University of Waterloo, Graduate Studies, Faculty of Mathematics, Department of Combinatorics and Optimization, Waterloo, ON N2L 3G1, Canada. Offers M Math, PhD. *Faculty:* 28 full-time (4 women), 14 part-time/adjunct (1 woman). *Students:* 46 full-time (13 women), 2 part-time. 63 applicants, 51% accepted, 19 enrolled. In 2003, 11 master's, 5 doctorates awarded. *Degree requirements:* For master's, research paper or thesis; for doctorate, thesis/dissertation, comprehensive exam. *Entrance requirements:* For master's, GRE General Test, honors degree in field, minimum B+ average; for doctorate, GRE General Test, master's degree, minimum A average. Additional exam requirements/recommendations for international students: Required—TOEFL, TWE. *Application deadline:* For fall admission, 4/15 for domestic students; for spring admission, 12/1 priority date for domestic students. Applications are processed on a rolling basis. Application fee: $75 Canadian dollars. Electronic applications accepted. Tuition and fees charges are reported in Canadian dollars. *Expenses:* Tuition, state resident: full-time $3,632 Canadian dollars. International tuition: $9,180 Canadian dollars full-time. Required fees: $406 Canadian dollars. *Financial support:* Research assistantships, teaching assistantships, career-related internships or fieldwork and scholarships/grants available. *Faculty research:* Algebraic and enumerative combinatorics, continuous optimization, cryptography, discrete optimization and graph theory. *Unit head:* Dr. W. H. Cunningham, Chair, 519-888-4567 Ext. 3482, Fax: 519-725-5441, E-mail: whcunnin@uwaterloo.ca. *Application contact:* Dr. R. B. Richter, Associate Chair, 519-888-4567 Ext. 2696, Fax: 519-725-5441, E-mail: cograd@uwaterloo.ca.

University of Waterloo, Graduate Studies, Faculty of Mathematics, Department of Pure Mathematics, Waterloo, ON N2L 3G1, Canada. Offers M Math, PhD. Part-time programs available. *Faculty:* 21 full-time (2 women), 15 part-time/adjunct (0 women). *Students:* 24 full-time (4 women), 2 part-time. 55 applicants, 42% accepted, 10 enrolled. In 2003, 6 degrees awarded. Terminal master's awarded for partial completion of doctoral program. *Degree requirements:* For master's, thesis/dissertation; for doctorate, thesis/dissertation, comprehensive exam, registration. *Entrance requirements:* For master's, honors degree in field, minimum B+ average; for doctorate, master's degree, minimum B+ average. Additional exam requirements/recommendations for international students: Required—TOEFL (minimum score 580 paper-based; 237 computer-based), TWE(minimum score 4). *Application deadline:* For fall admission, 2/1 priority date for domestic students, 2/1 priority date for international students; for winter admission, 7/1 for domestic students; for spring admission, 10/1 for domestic students. Applications are processed on a rolling basis. Application fee: $75 Canadian dollars. Electronic applications accepted. Tuition and fees charges are reported in Canadian dollars. *Expenses:* Tuition, state resident: full-time $3,632 Canadian dollars. International tuition: $9,180 Canadian dollars full-time. Required fees: $406 Canadian dollars. *Financial support:* Research assistantships, teaching assistantships, scholarships/grants and unspecified assistantships available. *Faculty research:* Algebra, algebraic and differential geometry, functional and harmonic analysis, logic and universal algebra, number theory. *Unit head:* Dr. Frank Zorzitto, Chair, 519-888-4567 Ext. 3484, Fax: 519-725-0160. *Application contact:* Dr. C. T. Ng, Graduate Officer, 519-888-4567 Ext. 4085, Fax: 519-725-0160, E-mail: ctng@math.uwaterloo.ca.

The University of Western Ontario, Faculty of Graduate Studies, Physical Sciences Division, Department of Mathematics, London, ON N6A 5B8, Canada. Offers M Sc, PhD. Terminal master's awarded for partial completion of doctoral program. *Degree requirements:* For master's, thesis or alternative; for doctorate, one foreign language, thesis/dissertation, qualifying exam, comprehensive exam. *Entrance requirements:* For master's, minimum B average, honors degree; for doctorate, master's degree. Additional exam requirements/recommendations for international students: Required—TOEFL (minimum score 550 paper-based; 213 computer-based). *Faculty research:* Algebra and number theory, analysis, geometry and topology.

University of West Florida, College of Arts and Sciences: Sciences, Department of Mathematics and Statistics, Program in Mathematics, Pensacola, FL 32514-5750. Offers MA. *Students:* 5 full-time (3 women), 10 part-time (6 women); includes 2 minority (1 African American, 1 Asian American or Pacific Islander), 1 international. Average age 29. 13 applicants, 77% accepted, 7 enrolled. In 2003, 6 degrees awarded. *Degree requirements:* For master's, thesis optional. *Entrance requirements:* For master's, GRE General Test, minimum GPA of 3.0. Additional exam requirements/recommendations for international students: Required—TOEFL (minimum score 550 paper-based; 213 computer-based). *Application deadline:* For fall admission, 6/1 for domestic students, 5/15 for international students; for spring admission, 11/1 for domestic students, 10/1 for international students. Applications are processed on a rolling basis. Application fee: $20. *Expenses:* Tuition, state resident: full-time $4,986; part-time $208 per credit hour. Tuition, nonresident: full-time $18,649; part-time $777 per credit hour. Tuition and fees vary according to course load, campus/location and reciprocity agreements. *Financial support:* Fellowships, teaching assistantships, career-related internships or fieldwork and institutionally sponsored loans available. Support available to part-time students. Financial award application deadline: 4/15; financial award applicants required to submit FAFSA. *Unit head:* Dr. Kuiyuan Li, Chairperson, Department of Mathematics and Statistics, 850-474-2287.

University of Windsor, Faculty of Graduate Studies and Research, Faculty of Science, Department of Mathematics and Statistics, Windsor, ON N9B 3P4, Canada. Offers mathematics (M Sc, PhD); statistics (M Sc, PhD). *Faculty:* 12 full-time (2 women). *Students:* 28 full-time (6 women), 1 part-time. 90 applicants, 24% accepted. In 2003, 9 master's, 1 doctorate awarded. *Degree requirements:* For master's, thesis or alternative; for doctorate, thesis/dissertation. *Entrance requirements:* For master's, minimum B average; for doctorate, minimum A average. Additional exam requirements/recommendations for international students: Required—TOEFL. *Application deadline:* For fall admission, 7/1 for domestic students; for winter admission, 11/1 for domestic students. Applications are processed on a rolling basis. Application fee: $55. Tuition charges are reported in Canadian dollars. *Expenses:* Tuition, state resident: full-time $1,704 Canadian dollars. Tuition, nonresident: full-time $2,126 Canadian dollars. International tuition: $2,976 Canadian dollars full-time. *Financial support:* In 2003–04, 20 teaching assistantships (averaging $8,000 per year) were awarded; Federal Work-Study, scholarships/grants, tuition waivers (full and partial), unspecified assistantships, and bursaries also available. Financial award application deadline: 2/15. *Unit head:* Dr. Ejaz Ahmed, Head, 519-253-3000 Ext. 3017, Fax: 519-971-3649, E-mail: seahmed@uwindsor.ca. *Application contact:* Applicant Services, 519-253-3000 Ext. 6459, Fax: 519-971-3653, E-mail: gradadmit@uwindsor.ca.

University of Wisconsin–Madison, Graduate School, College of Letters and Science, Department of Mathematics, Madison, WI 53706-1380. Offers MA, PhD. *Faculty:* 54 full-time (3 women). *Students:* 147 full-time (33 women); includes 43 minority (35 Asian Americans or Pacific Islanders, 8 Hispanic Americans). Average age 24. 419 applicants, 22% accepted, 32 enrolled. In 2003, 24 master's, 11 doctorates awarded. Terminal master's awarded for partial completion of doctoral program. *Median time to degree:* Master's–2 years full-time; doctorate–6 years full-time. Of those who began their doctoral program in fall 1995, 35% received their degree in 8 years or less. *Degree requirements:* For master's, registration; for doctorate, thesis/dissertation, comprehensive exam, registration. *Entrance requirements:* For master's and doctorate, GRE General Test, GRE Subject Test. Additional exam requirements/recommendations for international students: Required—TOEFL (minimum score 580 paper-based; 237 computer-based); Recommended—TSE(minimum score 45). *Application deadline:* For fall admission, 12/31 priority date for domestic students, 12/31 priority date for international students. Application fee: $45. Electronic applications accepted. Tuition, area resident: Full-time $7,593; part-time $476 per credit. Tuition, nonresident: full-time $22,824; part-time $1,430 per credit. Required fees: $292; $38 per credit. Part-time tuition and fees vary according to course load and reciprocity agreements. *Financial support:* In 2003–04, 128 students received support, including 11 fellowships with full tuition reimbursements available (averaging $18,000 per year), 5 research assistantships with full tuition reimbursements available (averaging $14,526 per year), 121 teaching assistantships with full tuition reimbursements available (averaging $12,100 per year); institutionally sponsored loans, scholarships/grants, health care benefits, and unspecified assistantships also available. Support available to part-time students. Financial award application deadline: 12/31. *Faculty research:* Applied mathematics, analysis, algebra, logic, topology. Total annual research expenditures: $2.3 million. *Unit head:* David Griffeath, Chair, 608-263-3051, Fax: 608-263-8891, E-mail: griffeat@math.wisc.edu. *Application contact:* Sherry M. Lange, Graduate Program Administrator, 608-263-8884, Fax: 608-263-8891, E-mail: lange@math.wisc.edu.

University of Wisconsin–Milwaukee, Graduate School, College of Letters and Sciences, Department of Mathematical Sciences, Milwaukee, WI 53201-0413. Offers mathematics (MS, PhD). *Faculty:* 35 full-time (2 women). *Students:* 54 full-time (15 women), 12 part-time (2 women); includes 1 minority (Asian American or Pacific Islander), 30 international. 67 applicants, 63% accepted, 27 enrolled. In 2003, 15 master's, 1 doctorate awarded. *Degree requirements:* For doctorate, 2 foreign languages, thesis/dissertation. *Application deadline:* For fall admission, 1/1 for domestic students; for spring admission, 9/1 for domestic students. Applications are processed on a rolling basis. Application fee: $45 ($75 for international students). *Expenses:* Tuition, state resident: part-time $634 per credit. Tuition, nonresident: part-time $1,531 per credit. Part-time tuition and fees vary according to course load, campus/location, program and reciprocity agreements. *Financial support:* In 2003–04, 8 fellowships, 48 teaching assistantships were awarded. Research assistantships, career-related internships or fieldwork also available. Support available to part-time students. Financial award application deadline: 4/15. *Unit head:* Mark Teply, Representative, 414-229-5264, Fax: 414-229-4907, E-mail: mlteply@uwm.edu.

University of Wyoming, Graduate School, College of Arts and Sciences, Department of Mathematics, Laramie, WY 82070. Offers mathematics (MA, MAT, MS, MST, PhD); mathematics/computer science (PhD). Part-time programs available. *Faculty:* 26 full-time (4 women). *Students:* 21 full-time (7 women), 7 part-time (2 women); includes 1 minority (American Indian/Alaska Native), 9 international. 9 applicants, 100% accepted. In 2003, 3 master's, 3 doctorates awarded. Terminal master's awarded for partial completion of doctoral program. *Median time to degree:* Master's–2.3 years full-time; doctorate–4.6 years full-time. *Degree requirements:* For master's, thesis or alternative, qualifying exam; for doctorate, one foreign language, thesis/dissertation, preliminary exam. *Entrance requirements:* For master's and doctorate, GRE General Test, minimum GPA of 3.0. *Application deadline:* For fall admission, 3/1 for domestic students. Applications are processed on a rolling basis. Application fee: $40. *Expenses:* Tuition, state resident: part-time $142 per credit hour. Tuition, nonresident: part-time $408 per credit hour. Required fees: $134 per semester. Tuition and fees vary according to course load, campus/location, program and student level. *Financial support:* In 2003–04, 2 research assistantships with full tuition reimbursements (averaging $12,032 per year), 19 teaching assistantships with full tuition reimbursements (averaging $12,032 per year) were awarded. Institutionally sponsored loans also available. Financial award application deadline: 3/1. *Faculty research:* Numerical analysis, classical analysis, mathematical modeling, algebraic combinations. *Unit head:* Dr. Sivaguru Sritharon, Head, 307-766-4221. *Application contact:* Jeanette Reisenburg, Office Associate, 307-766-6577.

Utah State University, School of Graduate Studies, College of Science, Department of Mathematics and Statistics, Logan, UT 84322. Offers industrial mathematics (MS); mathematical sciences (PhD); mathematics (M Math, MS); statistics (MS). Part-time programs available. *Faculty:* 30 full-time (5 women). *Students:* 30 full-time (12 women), 6 part-time, 24 international. Average age 29. 68 applicants, 19% accepted, 8 enrolled. In 2003, 9 degrees awarded. Terminal master's awarded for partial completion of doctoral program. *Degree requirements:* For master's, qualifying exam, thesis optional; for doctorate, one foreign language, thesis/dissertation, comprehensive exam. *Entrance requirements:* For master's and doctorate, GRE General Test, minimum GPA of 3.0. Additional exam requirements/recommendations for international students: Required—TOEFL. *Application deadline:* For fall admission, 6/15 for domestic students; for spring admission, 10/15 for domestic students. Applications are processed on a rolling basis. Application fee: $50 ($60 for international students). *Expenses:* Tuition, state resident: part-time $270 per credit hour. Tuition, nonresident: part-time $946 per credit hour. Required fees: $173 per credit hour. *Financial support:* In 2003–04, 1 fellowship with partial tuition reimbursement (averaging $12,000 per year), 17 teaching assistantships with partial tuition reimbursements (averaging $14,500 per year) were awarded. Research assistantships with partial tuition reimbursements Support available to part-time students. Financial award application deadline: 4/1. *Faculty research:* Differential equations, computational mathematics, dynamical systems, probability and statistics, pure mathematics. *Unit head:* Dr. Russell C. Thompson, Head, 435-797-2810, Fax: 435-797-1822, E-mail: thompson@math.usu.edu. *Application contact:* Dr. Joseph Koebbe, Graduate Chairman, 435-797-2825, Fax: 435-797-1822, E-mail: koebbe@math.usu.edu.

Vanderbilt University, Graduate School, Department of Mathematics, Nashville, TN 37240-1001. Offers MA, MAT, MS, PhD. *Degree requirements:* For master's, thesis or alternative; for doctorate, one foreign language, thesis/dissertation, final and qualifying exams. *Entrance requirements:* For master's and doctorate, GRE General Test, GRE Subject Test. Electronic applications accepted. *Expenses:* Tuition: Part-time $1,155 per semester hour. Required fees: $1,538. *Faculty research:* Algebra, topology, applied mathematics, graph theory, analytical mathematics.

Villanova University, Graduate School of Liberal Arts and Sciences, Department of Mathematical Sciences, Program in Mathematical Sciences, Villanova, PA 19085-1699. Offers MA. Part-time and evening/weekend programs available. *Students:* 5 full-time (3 women), 27 part-time (11 women); includes 1 minority (Asian American or Pacific Islander), 3 international. Average age 32. 14 applicants, 71% accepted. In 2003, 10 degrees awarded. *Entrance requirements:* For master's, minimum GPA of 3.0. *Application deadline:* For fall admission, 8/1 for domestic students; for spring admission, 12/1 for domestic students. Application fee: $40. *Expenses:* Tuition: Part-time $750 per credit. *Financial support:* Research assistantships, Federal Work-Study available. Financial award applicants required to submit FAFSA. *Unit head:* Dr. Robert Styer, Chair, Department of Mathematical Sciences, 610-519-4850.

Virginia Commonwealth University, School of Graduate Studies, College of Humanities and Sciences, Department of Mathematical Sciences, Richmond, VA 23284-9005. Offers applied mathematics (MS); mathematics (MS); operations research (MS); statistics (MS, Certificate). *Faculty:* 15 full-time (2 women). *Students:* 11 full-time (7 women), 12 part-time (3 women); includes 4 minority (2 African Americans, 1 American Indian/Alaska Native, 1 Asian American or Pacific Islander), 7 international. 23 applicants, 74% accepted, 10 enrolled. In 2003, 9 degrees awarded. *Degree requirements:* For master's, thesis optional. *Entrance requirements:* For master's, GRE General Test, GRE Subject Test. Additional exam requirements/recommendations for international students: Required—TOEFL. *Application deadline:* For fall admission, 7/1 for domestic students; for spring admission, 11/15 for domestic students. Applications are processed on a rolling basis. Application fee: $30. *Expenses:* Tuition, state resident: full-time $2,889; part-time $321 per credit hour. Tuition, nonresident: full-time $7,952; part-time $884 per credit hour. Required fees: $42 per credit hour. *Financial support:* Fellowships, research assistantships, teaching assistantships, Federal Work-Study and institutionally sponsored loans available. Support available to part-time students. *Unit head:* Dr. Andrew M. Lewis, Chair, 804-828-1301 Ext. 102, Fax: 804-828-8785, E-mail: amlewis@vcu.edu. *Application contact:* Dr. James A. Wood, Information Contact, 804-828-1301, E-mail: jawood@vcu.edu.

Virginia Polytechnic Institute and State University, Graduate School, College of Science, Department of Mathematics, Blacksburg, VA 24061. Offers applied mathematics (MS, PhD); mathematical physics (MS, PhD); pure mathematics (MS, PhD). *Faculty:* 66 full-time (18 women), 1 (woman) part-time/adjunct. *Students:* 65 full-time (22 women), 50 part-time (35 women); includes 13 minority (5 African Americans, 3 Asian Americans or Pacific Islanders, 5 Hispanic Americans), 17 international. Average age 31. 152 applicants, 47% accepted, 51 enrolled. In 2003, 24 master's, 2 doctorates awarded. *Entrance requirements:* For master's and doctorate, GRE. Additional exam requirements/recommendations for international students: Required—TOEFL (minimum score 550 paper-based; 213 computer-based). *Application deadline:* Applications are processed on a rolling basis. Application fee: $45. Electronic applications accepted. Tuition, area resident: Full-time $6,039; part-time $336 per credit. Tuition, nonresident: full-time $9,708; part-time $539 per credit. Required fees: $905; $130 per credit. *Financial support:* In 2003–04, 3 fellowships with full tuition reimbursements (averaging $4,000 per year), 6 research assistantships with full tuition reimbursements (averaging $14,752 per year), 36 teaching assistantships with full tuition reimbursements (averaging $12,858 per year) were awarded. Career-related internships or fieldwork, Federal Work-Study, scholarships/grants, and unspecified assistantships also available. *Faculty research:* Differential equations, operator theory, numerical analysis, algebra, control theory. *Unit head:* Dr. John Rossi, Head, 540-231-6536, Fax: 540-231-5960, E-mail: rossi@math.vt.edu. *Application contact:* Hannah Swiger, Information Contact, 540-231-6537, Fax: 540-231-5960, E-mail: hsswiger@math.vt.edu.

Virginia State University, School of Graduate Studies, Research, and Outreach, School of Engineering, Science and Technology, Department of Mathematics, Petersburg, VA 23806-0001. Offers mathematics (MS); mathematics education (M Ed). *Accreditation:* NCATE (one or more programs are accredited). *Degree requirements:* For master's, thesis (for some programs).

Wake Forest University, Graduate School, Department of Mathematics, Winston-Salem, NC 27109. Offers MA. Part-time programs available. *Faculty:* 15 full-time (2 women). *Students:* 14 full-time (9 women), 3 international. Average age 25. 14 applicants, 71% accepted, 8 enrolled. In 2003, 3 degrees awarded. *Degree requirements:* For master's, one foreign language, registration. *Entrance requirements:* For master's, GRE General Test, GRE Subject Test. Additional exam requirements/recommendations for international students: Required—TOEFL

Mathematics

Wake Forest University (continued)
(minimum score 213 computer-based). *Application deadline:* For fall admission, 1/15 for domestic students, 1/15 for international students. Application fee: $25. Electronic applications accepted. *Expenses:* Tuition: Full-time $26,500. *Financial support:* In 2003–04, 14 students received support, including 2 fellowships with full tuition reimbursements available (averaging $4,000 per year), 11 teaching assistantships with full tuition reimbursements available (averaging $10,000 per year); scholarships/grants and tuition waivers (full and partial) also available. Support available to part-time students. Financial award application deadline: 1/15; financial award applicants required to submit FAFSA. *Faculty research:* Algebra, ring theory, topology, differential equations. *Unit head:* Dr. Stephen Robinson, Director, 336-758-4887.

Washington State University, Graduate School, College of Sciences, Department of Mathematics, Pullman, WA 99164. Offers MS, PhD. *Faculty:* 32 full-time (5 women), 6 part-time/adjunct (3 women). *Students:* 37; includes 1 minority (African American), 19 international. Average age 29. 56 applicants. In 2003, 2 master's, 2 doctorates awarded. *Degree requirements:* For master's, oral exam, project; for doctorate, 2 foreign languages, thesis/dissertation, oral exam, written exam. *Entrance requirements:* For master's and doctorate, GRE General Test, GRE Subject Test, minimum GPA of 3.0. Additional exam requirements/recommendations for international students: Required—TOEFL (minimum score 600 paper-based; 250 computer-based). *Application deadline:* For fall admission, 3/15 priority date for domestic students, 4/1 priority date for international students. Applications are processed on a rolling basis. Application fee: $35. Electronic applications accepted. *Expenses:* Tuition, state resident: full-time $6,278; part-time $314 per hour. Tuition, nonresident: full-time $15,514; part-time $765 per hour. Required fees: $444. Full-time tuition and fees vary according to campus/location, program and student level. Part-time tuition and fees vary according to course load. *Financial support:* In 2003–04, fellowships with tuition reimbursements (averaging $3,000 per year), 4 research assistantships with full and partial tuition reimbursements (averaging $14,268 per year), 28 teaching assistantships with full and partial tuition reimbursements (averaging $12,730 per year) were awarded. Career-related internships or fieldwork, Federal Work-Study, institutionally sponsored loans, and tuition waivers (partial) also available. Financial award application deadline: 4/1; financial award applicants required to submit FAFSA. *Faculty research:* Computational mathematics, operations research, modeling in the natural sciences, applied statistics. Total annual research expenditures: $178,395. *Unit head:* Dr. Alan Genz, Chair, 509-335-4918, Fax: 509-335-1188, E-mail: chair@math.wsu.edu. *Application contact:* Pam Guptill, Coordinator, 509-335-6868, Fax: 509-335-1188, E-mail: pguptill@wsu.edu.

See in-depth description on page 623.

Washington University in St. Louis, Graduate School of Arts and Sciences, Department of Mathematics, St. Louis, MO 63130-4899. Offers mathematics (MA, PhD); mathematics education (MAT); statistics (MA, PhD). *Students:* 38 full-time (15 women); includes 1 minority (Asian American or Pacific Islander), 14 international. 124 applicants, 22% accepted, 8 enrolled. In 2003, 13 master's, 1 doctorate awarded. Terminal master's awarded for partial completion of doctoral program. *Degree requirements:* For master's, thesis or alternative; for doctorate, thesis/dissertation. *Entrance requirements:* For master's and doctorate, GRE General Test. *Application deadline:* For fall admission, 1/15 for domestic students. Applications are processed on a rolling basis. Application fee: $35. Electronic applications accepted. *Expenses:* Tuition: Full-time $28,300; part-time $1,180 per credit. *Financial support:* Fellowships, research assistantships, teaching assistantships, Federal Work-Study, institutionally sponsored loans, and tuition waivers (full and partial) available. Support available to part-time students. Financial award application deadline: 1/15. *Unit head:* Dr. Steven Krantz, Chairman, 314-935-6760.

Washington University in St. Louis, Henry Edwin Sever Graduate School of Engineering and Applied Science, Department of Electrical and Systems Engineering, St. Louis, MO 63130-4899. Offers electrical engineering (MS, D Sc); systems science and mathematics (MS, D Sc). Part-time programs available. *Entrance requirements:* For doctorate, GRE. Additional exam requirements/recommendations for international students: Required—TOEFL. Electronic applications accepted. *Expenses:* Tuition: Full-time $28,300; part-time $1,180 per credit. *Faculty research:* Linear and nonlinear control systems, robotics and automation, scheduling and transportation systems, biocybernetics, computational mathematics.

Wayne State University, Graduate School, College of Science, Department of Mathematics, Program in Mathematics, Detroit, MI 48202. Offers MA, PhD. *Students:* 26 full-time (8 women), 19 part-time (7 women); includes 8 minority (7 African Americans, 1 Hispanic American), 20 international. 73 applicants, 36% accepted, 13 enrolled. In 2003, 2 master's, 1 doctorate awarded. *Degree requirements:* For doctorate, 2 foreign languages, thesis/dissertation. *Entrance requirements:* Additional exam requirements/recommendations for international students: Required—TOEFL (minimum score 550 paper-based; 213 computer-based); Recommended—TWE(minimum score 6). *Application deadline:* For fall admission, 7/1 for domestic students, 6/1 for international students. Applications are processed on a rolling basis. Application fee: $30 ($50 for international students). Electronic applications accepted. *Expenses:* Tuition, state resident: part-time $263 per credit hour. Tuition, nonresident: part-time $580 per credit hour. Required fees: $21 per credit hour. *Application contact:* Dr. Tze-Chien Sun, Graduate Director, 313-577-8840, Fax: 313-577-7596, E-mail: tsun@wayne.edu.

Wesleyan University, Graduate Programs, Department of Mathematics, Middletown, CT 06459-0260. Offers MA, PhD. *Faculty:* 15 full-time (2 women). *Students:* 20 full-time (4 women); includes 1 minority (Hispanic American), 12 international. Average age 28. In 2003, 1 master's, 4 doctorates awarded. Terminal master's awarded for partial completion of doctoral program. *Degree requirements:* For master's, one foreign language, thesis; for doctorate, 2 foreign languages, thesis/dissertation. *Entrance requirements:* For master's, GRE General Test, GRE Subject Test; for doctorate, GRE Subject Test. *Application deadline:* For fall admission, 2/15 for domestic students. Applications are processed on a rolling basis. Application fee: $0. *Expenses:* Tuition: Full-time $22,338. Required fees: $20. *Financial support:* Teaching assistantships, tuition waivers (full and partial) available. *Faculty research:* Topology, analysis. *Unit head:* Carol Wood, Chair, 860-685-2196. *Application contact:* Nancy Procyk, Information Contact, 860-685-2620, Fax: 860-685-2571, E-mail: nprocyk@wesleyan.edu.

See in-depth description on page 627.

West Chester University of Pennsylvania, Graduate Studies, College of Arts and Sciences, Department of Mathematics, West Chester, PA 19383. Offers MA. Part-time and evening/weekend programs available. *Students:* Average age 38. 9 applicants, 100% accepted. In 2003, 2 degrees awarded. *Degree requirements:* For master's, comprehensive exam. *Entrance requirements:* For master's, GRE General Test, interview. *Application deadline:* For fall admission, 4/15 for domestic students; for spring admission, 10/15 for domestic students. Applications are processed on a rolling basis. Application fee: $35. *Expenses:* Tuition, state resident: full-time $5,518; part-time $307 per credit. Tuition, nonresident: full-time $8,830; part-time $491 per credit. Required fees: $902; $52 per credit. One-time fee: $35 part-time. *Financial support:* In 2003–04, 1 research assistantship with full tuition reimbursement (averaging $5,000 per year) was awarded; unspecified assistantships also available. Support available to part-time students. Financial award application deadline: 2/15; financial award applicants required to submit FAFSA. *Faculty research:* Teachers teaching with technology in service training program. *Unit head:* Dr. Richard Branton, Chair, 610-436-2440. *Application contact:* Dr. John Kerrigan, Graduate Coordinator, 610-436-2351, E-mail: jkerrigan@wcupa.edu.

Western Carolina University, Graduate School, College of Arts and Sciences, Department of Mathematics and Computer Science, Cullowhee, NC 28723. Offers applied mathematics (MS); comprehensive education-mathematics (MA Ed); mathematics (MAT). Part-time and evening/weekend programs available. *Faculty:* 11 full-time (4 women). *Students:* 10 full-time (7 women), 16 part-time (10 women); includes 2 minority (both African Americans) 12 applicants, 100% accepted, 10 enrolled. In 2003, 3 degrees awarded. *Degree requirements:* For master's, thesis optional. *Entrance requirements:* For master's, GRE General Test, GRE Subject Test (MS). Additional exam requirements/recommendations for international students: Required—TOEFL (minimum score 550 paper-based; 213 computer-based). *Application deadline:* For fall admission, 5/1 for domestic students; for spring admission, 10/1 priority date for domestic students. Applications are processed on a rolling basis. Application fee: $40. *Expenses:* Tuition, state resident: full-time $1,426. Tuition, nonresident: full-time $10,787. Required fees: $1,558. *Financial support:* In 2003–04, 9 students received support, including 9 research assistantships with full and partial tuition reimbursements available (averaging $6,500 per year); fellowships, teaching assistantships with full and partial tuition reimbursements available, Federal Work-Study, institutionally sponsored loans, and scholarships/grants also available. Financial award application deadline: 3/15; financial award applicants required to submit FAFSA. *Unit head:* Dr. Kathy Ivey, Head, 828-227-7245, Fax: 828-227-7240, E-mail: kivey@email.wcu.edu. *Application contact:* Josie Bewsey, Assistant to the Dean, 828-227-7398, Fax: 828-227-7480, E-mail: jbewsey@email.wcu.edu.

Western Connecticut State University, Division of Graduate Studies, School of Arts and Sciences, Department of Mathematics and Computer Science, Danbury, CT 06810-6885. Offers mathematics and computer science (MA); theoretical mathematics (MA). Part-time and evening/weekend programs available. *Faculty:* 1 full-time (0 women). *Students:* Average age 34. In 2003, 1 degree awarded. *Degree requirements:* For master's, thesis or research project. *Entrance requirements:* For master's, minimum GPA of 2.5. *Application deadline:* For fall admission, 8/1 for domestic students. Applications are processed on a rolling basis. Application fee: $40. *Expenses:* Tuition, state resident: full-time $3,263. Tuition, nonresident: full-time $6,742. *Financial support:* Fellowships, career-related internships or fieldwork available. Support available to part-time students. Financial award application deadline: 5/1; financial award applicants required to submit FAFSA. *Unit head:* Dr. C. Edward Sandifer, Professor, 203-837-9351. *Application contact:* Chris Shankle, Associate Director of Graduate Admissions, 203-837-8244, Fax: 203-837-8338, E-mail: shanklec@wcsu.edu.

Western Illinois University, School of Graduate Studies, College of Arts and Sciences, Department of Mathematics, Macomb, IL 61455-1390. Offers MS. Part-time programs available. *Faculty:* 21 full-time (2 women). *Students:* 13 full-time (4 women), 2 part-time (1 woman), 7 international. Average age 31. 8 applicants, 100% accepted. In 2003, 5 degrees awarded. *Degree requirements:* For master's, thesis or alternative. *Entrance requirements:* Additional exam requirements/recommendations for international students: Required—TOEFL (minimum score 500 paper-based; 173 computer-based). *Application deadline:* Applications are processed on a rolling basis. Application fee: $30. Electronic applications accepted. Tuition, area resident: Part-time $144 per credit hour. Tuition, nonresident: part-time $288 per credit hour. *Financial support:* In 2003–04, 10 students received support, including 10 research assistantships with full tuition reimbursements available (averaging $5,864 per year) Financial award applicants required to submit FAFSA. *Faculty research:* National Council of Teachers of Mathematics standards in geometry and mathematics, mobile computer laboratories, algebra, computational mathematics. *Unit head:* Dr. Iraj Kalantari, Chairperson, 309-298-1054. *Application contact:* Dr. Barbara Baily, Director of Graduate Studies/Associate Provost, 309-298-1806, Fax: 309-298-2345, E-mail: grad-office@wiu.edu.

Western Kentucky University, Graduate Studies, Ogden College of Science, and Engineering, Department of Mathematics, Bowling Green, KY 42101-3576. Offers MA Ed, MS. *Degree requirements:* For master's, written exam, thesis optional. *Entrance requirements:* For master's, GRE General Test, minimum GPA of 2.75. Additional exam requirements/recommendations for international students: Required—TOEFL (minimum score 555 paper-based; 213 computer-based). *Faculty research:* Differential equations numerical analysis, probability statistics, algebra, typology, knot theory.

Western Michigan University, Graduate College, College of Arts and Sciences, Department of Mathematics, Programs in Mathematics, Kalamazoo, MI 49008-5202. Offers mathematics (MA); mathematics education (MA, PhD). *Accreditation:* NCATE (one or more programs are accredited). *Degree requirements:* For master's, oral exams; for doctorate, one foreign language, thesis/dissertation, oral exams, 3 comprehensive exams, internship. *Entrance requirements:* For doctorate, GRE General Test.

Western Washington University, Graduate School, College of Sciences and Technology, Department of Mathematics, Bellingham, WA 98225-5996. Offers MS. Part-time programs available. *Faculty:* 23. *Students:* 18 full-time (6 women), 2 part-time; includes 1 minority (African American) 18 applicants, 94% accepted, 14 enrolled. In 2003, 10 degrees awarded. *Degree requirements:* For master's, thesis (for some programs), project, qualifying examination. *Entrance requirements:* For master's, GRE General Test, minimum GPA of 3.0 in last 60 semester hours or last 90 quarter hours. Additional exam requirements/recommendations for international students: Required—TOEFL. *Application deadline:* For fall admission, 6/1 for domestic students; for winter admission, 10/1 for domestic students; for spring admission, 2/1 for domestic students. Applications are processed on a rolling basis. Application fee: $35. *Expenses:* Tuition, state resident: full-time $5,694; part-time $172 per credit. Tuition, nonresident: full-time $16,221; part-time $523 per credit. *Financial support:* In 2003–04, 17 teaching assistantships with partial tuition reimbursements (averaging $9,852 per year) were awarded; Federal Work-Study, institutionally sponsored loans, scholarships/grants, and tuition waivers (partial) also available. Support available to part-time students. Financial award application deadline: 2/15; financial award applicants required to submit FAFSA. *Unit head:* Dr. Tjalling Ypma, Chair, 360-650-3785. *Application contact:* Dr. Edoh Amiran, Graduate Adviser, 360-650-3487.

West Texas A&M University, College of Agriculture, Nursing, and Natural Sciences, Department of Mathematics, Physical Sciences and Engineering Technology, Program in Mathematics, Canyon, TX 79016-0001. Offers MS. Part-time programs available. *Faculty:* 4 full-time (1 woman), 2 part-time/adjunct (both women). *Students:* Average age 34. 8 applicants, 88% accepted, 7 enrolled. In 2003, 3 degrees awarded. *Median time to degree:* Master's–3 years full-time, 6 years part-time. *Degree requirements:* For master's, thesis optional. *Entrance requirements:* For master's, GRE General Test. Additional exam requirements/recommendations for international students: Required—TOEFL (minimum score 550 paper-based). *Application deadline:* Applications are processed on a rolling basis. Application fee: $25 ($75 for international students). Electronic applications accepted. *Expenses:* Tuition, state resident: part-time $56 per credit hour. Tuition, nonresident: part-time $292 per credit hour. Full-time tuition and fees vary according to course level, degree level and program. *Financial support:* In 2003–04, research assistantships (averaging $6,500 per year), 6 teaching assistantships (averaging $6,750 per year) were awarded. Federal Work-Study, institutionally sponsored loans, scholarships/grants, and tuition waivers (partial) also available. Support available to part-time students. Financial award applicants required to submit FAFSA. Total annual research expenditures: $3,600. *Application contact:* Dr. Pamela Lockwood-Cooke, Graduate Adviser, 806-651-2531, Fax: 806-651-2536, E-mail: pcooke@mail.wtamu.edu.

West Virginia University, Eberly College of Arts and Sciences, Department of Mathematics, Morgantown, WV 26506. Offers applied mathematics (MS, PhD); discrete mathematics (PhD); interdisciplinary mathematics (MS); mathematics for secondary education (MS); pure mathematics (MS). Part-time programs available. *Faculty:* 28 full-time (1 woman), 11 part-time/adjunct (3 women). *Students:* 33 full-time (15 women), 8 part-time (2 women); includes 3 minority (1 African American, 2 Asian Americans or Pacific Islanders), 23 international. Average age 29. 30 applicants, 100% accepted, 16 enrolled. In 2003, 5 master's awarded, leading to continued full-time study 80%, business/industry 20%; 6 doctorates awarded, leading to university research/teaching 100%. Terminal master's awarded for partial completion of doctoral program. *Median time to degree:* Master's–2 years full-time; doctorate–4 years full-time. *Degree requirements:* For master's, thesis optional; for doctorate, one foreign language, thesis/dissertation, comprehensive exam. *Entrance requirements:* For master's, minimum GPA of 2.5; for doctorate, master's degree in mathematics. Additional exam requirements/recommendations for international students: Required—TOEFL (paper score 550; computer score 213) or IELTS (paper score 6). *Application deadline:* For fall admission, 2/15 priority date for domestic students, 2/15 priority date for international students. Applications are processed on a rolling basis. Application fee: $50. *Expenses:* Tuition, state resident: full-time $4,332. Tuition, nonresident: full-time $12,442. *Financial support:* In 2003–04, 25 students received support, including 6 research assistantships with full tuition reimbursements available (averaging $1,000 per year), 18 teaching assistantships with full tuition reimbursements available (averaging $9,500 per year); Federal Work-Study, institutionally sponsored loans, and tuition waivers (full and partial) also available. Financial award application deadline: 2/15; financial award applicants required to submit FAFSA. *Faculty research:* Combinatorics and graph theory, topology, differential equations, applied and computational mathematics. Total annual research expenditures: $80,423. *Unit head:* Dr. Sherman Riemenschneider, Chair, 304-293-2011 Ext. 2322, Fax: 304-293-3982, E-mail: sherm.riemenschneider@mail.wvu.edu. *Application contact:* Dr. Harvey R. Diamond, Director of Graduate Studies, 304-293-2011 Ext. 2347, Fax: 304-293-3982, E-mail: gradprog@math.wvu.edu.

Wichita State University, Graduate School, Fairmount College of Liberal Arts and Sciences, Department of Mathematics and Statistics, Wichita, KS 67260. Offers applied mathematics (PhD); mathematics (MS); statistics (MS). Part-time programs available. *Faculty:* 22 full-time (0 women). *Students:* 17 full-time (5 women), 9 part-time (4 women); includes 1 minority (Hispanic American), 12 international. Average age 33. 20 applicants, 70% accepted. In 2003, 3 master's, 2 doctorates awarded. *Degree requirements:* For master's, thesis optional; for doctorate, thesis/dissertation. *Entrance requirements:* For master's, GRE; for doctorate, GRE Subject Test. Additional exam requirements/recommendations for international students: Required—TOEFL. *Application deadline:* For fall admission, 7/1 for domestic students; for spring admission, 1/1 for domestic students. Applications are processed on a rolling basis. Application fee: $35 ($50 for international students). Electronic applications accepted. *Expenses:* Tuition, state resident: full-time $2,457; part-time $137 per credit hour. Tuition, nonresident: full-time $7,371; part-time $410 per credit hour. Required fees: $364; $20 per credit hour. Tuition and fees vary according to course load. *Financial support:* In 2003–04, 1 research assistantship (averaging $14,000 per year), 15 teaching assistantships with full tuition reimbursements (averaging $11,027 per year) were awarded. Fellowships, Federal Work-Study, institutionally sponsored loans, scholarships/grants, traineeships, and unspecified assistantships also available. Support available to part-time students. Financial award application deadline: 4/1; financial award applicants required to submit FAFSA. *Faculty research:* Partial differential equations, combinatorics, ring theory, minimal surfaces, several complex variables. *Unit head:* Dr. Buma Fridman, Chair, 316-978-3160, Fax: 316-978-3748, E-mail: buma.fridman@wichita.edu.

Wilkes University, Graduate Programs, Department of Mathematics and Computer Science, Wilkes-Barre, PA 18766-0002. Offers mathematics (MS, MS Ed). *Students:* Average age 34. *Degree requirements:* For master's, thesis or alternative. *Entrance requirements:* For master's, GRE General Test. *Application deadline:* Applications are processed on a rolling basis. Application fee: $35. *Expenses:* Tuition: Part-time $650 per credit hour. Required fees: $13 per credit hour. Tuition and fees vary according to program. *Financial support:* Federal Work-Study and unspecified assistantships available. Financial award application deadline: 3/1; financial award applicants required to submit FAFSA. *Unit head:* Dr. Louise Berard, Chair, 570-408-4830, Fax: 570-408-7883, E-mail: lberard@wilkes.edu. *Application contact:* Kathleen Diekhaus, Coordinator of Graduate Studies, 570-408-4160, Fax: 570-408-7860, E-mail: diekhaus@wilkes.edu.

Winthrop University, College of Arts and Sciences, Department of Mathematics, Rock Hill, SC 29733. Offers M Math. Part-time programs available. *Faculty:* 5 full-time (2 women). *Students:* 4 full-time (2 women), 2 part-time (1 woman); includes 1 minority (African American), 1 international. Average age 28. *Entrance requirements:* For master's, GRE General Test, minimum GPA of 3.0. *Application deadline:* For fall admission, 7/15 for domestic students; for spring admission, 12/1 for domestic students. Applications are processed on a rolling basis. Application fee: $35 ($50 for international students). Electronic applications accepted. *Expenses:* Tuition, state resident: full-time $3,203; part-time $268 per credit hour. Tuition, nonresident: full-time $5,891; part-time $492 per credit hour. Required fees: $10 per semester. *Financial support:* Federal Work-Study, scholarships/grants, and unspecified assistantships available. Support available to part-time students. Financial award application deadline: 2/1; financial award applicants required to submit FAFSA. *Unit head:* Dr. Gary T. Brooks, Chair, 803-232-2175, E-mail: brooksg@winthrop.edu. *Application contact:* Sharon B. Johnson, Director of Graduate Studies, 800-411-7041, Fax: 803-323-2292, E-mail: johnsons@winthrop.edu.

Worcester Polytechnic Institute, Graduate Studies and Enrollment, Department of Mathematical Science, Worcester, MA 01609-2280. Offers applied mathematics (MS); applied statistics (MS); financial mathematics (MS); industrial mathematics (MS); mathematical science (PhD, Certificate); mathematics (MME). Part-time and evening/weekend programs available. *Faculty:* 28 full-time (2 women), 1 (woman) part-time/adjunct. *Students:* 26 full-time (13 women), 27 part-time (12 women); includes 2 minority (1 African American, 1 Asian American or Pacific Islander), 17 international. 71 applicants, 93% accepted, 19 enrolled. In 2003, 18 degrees awarded. *Degree requirements:* For master's, thesis optional; for doctorate, thesis/dissertation, comprehensive exam. *Entrance requirements:* Additional exam requirements/recommendations for international students: Required—TOEFL (minimum score 550 paper-based; 213 computer-based). *Application deadline:* For fall admission, 2/1 for domestic students; for spring admission, 10/15 priority date for domestic students. Applications are processed on a rolling basis. Application fee: $70. Electronic applications accepted. *Expenses:* Tuition: Part-time $897 per credit. *Financial support:* In 2003–04, 10 students received support, including 6 fellowships with full tuition reimbursements available, 9 research assistantships, 10 teaching assistantships with full tuition reimbursements available; career-related internships or fieldwork, institutionally sponsored loans, scholarships/grants, health care benefits, and unspecified assistantships also available. Financial award application deadline: 2/15; financial award applicants required to submit FAFSA. *Faculty research:* Applied mathematical modeling and analysis, computational mathematics, discrete mathematics, applied and computational statistics, industrial and financial mathematics. Total annual research expenditures: $592,514. *Unit head:* Dr. Bogdan Vernesca, Head, 508-831-5316, Fax: 508-831-5824. *Application contact:* Dr. Joseph Petruccelli, Graduate Coordinator, 508-831-5362, Fax: 508-831-5824, E-mail: jdp@wpi.edu.

See in-depth description on page 631.

Wright State University, School of Graduate Studies, College of Science and Mathematics, Department of Mathematics and Statistics, Program in Mathematics, Dayton, OH 45435. Offers MS. *Students:* 3 full-time (0 women), 3 part-time (1 woman), 1 international. Average age 33. 3 applicants, 100% accepted. In 2003, 1 degree awarded. *Degree requirements:* For master's, comprehensive exam. *Entrance requirements:* For master's, previous course work in mathematics beyond calculus. Additional exam requirements/recommendations for international students: Required—TOEFL. Application fee: $25. *Expenses:* Tuition, state resident: full-time $8,112; part-time $255 per quarter hour. Tuition, nonresident: full-time $14,127; part-time $442 per quarter hour. International tuition: $14,283 full-time. Tuition and fees vary according to course load, degree level and program. *Financial support:* Fellowships, research assistantships, teaching assistantships available. Support available to part-time students. Financial award applicants required to submit FAFSA. *Faculty research:* Analysis, algebraic combinatorics, graph theory, operator theory. *Unit head:* Dr. Joanne M. Dombrowski, Director, 937-775-2785, Fax: 937-775-3068, E-mail: joanne.dombrowski@wright.edu.

Yale University, Graduate School of Arts and Sciences, Department of Mathematics, New Haven, CT 06520. Offers MS, PhD. *Degree requirements:* For doctorate, 2 foreign languages, thesis/dissertation. *Entrance requirements:* For doctorate, GRE General Test, GRE Subject Test. *Expenses:* Tuition: Full-time $25,600; part-time $6,400 per term.

York University, Faculty of Graduate Studies, Faculty of Arts, Program in Mathematics and Statistics, Toronto, ON M3J 1P3, Canada. Offers industrial and applied mathematics (M Sc); mathematics and statistics (MA, PhD). Part-time programs available. *Degree requirements:* For master's, thesis optional; for doctorate, one foreign language, thesis/dissertation, comprehensive exam. *Entrance requirements:* For master's, minimum B average; for doctorate, minimum B+ average. Electronic applications accepted. *Expenses:* Tuition, area resident: Full-time $5,431; part-time $905 per term. Tuition, nonresident: part-time $1,987 per term. International tuition: $11,918 full-time. Required fees: $287. Tuition and fees vary according to program.

Youngstown State University, Graduate School, College of Arts and Sciences, Department of Mathematics, Youngstown, OH 44555-0001. Offers MS. Part-time programs available. *Degree requirements:* For master's, thesis optional. *Entrance requirements:* For master's, minimum GPA of 2.7 in computer science and mathematics. Additional exam requirements/recommendations for international students: Required—TOEFL. *Expenses:* Tuition, state resident: full-time $4,194; part-time $233 per credit. Tuition, nonresident: full-time $8,352; part-time $464 per credit. Required fees: $42 per credit. Tuition and fees vary according to course load and reciprocity agreements. *Faculty research:* Regression analysis, numerical analysis, statistics, Markov chain, topology and fuzzy sets.

Statistics

Acadia University, Faculty of Pure and Applied Science, Department of Mathematics and Statistics, Wolfville, NS B4P 2R6, Canada. Offers applied mathematics and statistics (M Sc). *Faculty:* 12 full-time (1 woman). *Degree requirements:* For master's, thesis, 4-8 month industry internship. *Entrance requirements:* For master's, honors, degree in mathematics or statistics or equivalent. Additional exam requirements/recommendations for international students: Required—TOEFL (minimum score 550 paper-based). *Application deadline:* For fall admission, 2/1 priority date for domestic students, 2/1 priority date for international students. Applications are processed on a rolling basis. Application fee: $50. *Expenses:* Tuition, state resident: full-time $5,611. *Financial support:* Career-related internships or fieldwork and unspecified assistantships available. *Faculty research:* Geophysical fluid dynamics, machine scheduling problems, control theory, stochastic optimization, survival analysis. *Unit head:* Tom Archibald, Acting Head, 902-585-1382, Fax: 902-585-1074, E-mail: tom.archibald@acadiau.ca. *Application contact:* Dr. Richard H. Karsten, Professor, 902-585-1608, Fax: 902-585-1074, E-mail: richard.karsten@acadiau.ca.

American University, College of Arts and Sciences, Department of Mathematics and Statistics, Program in Statistics, Washington, DC 20016-8001. Offers applied statistics (Certificate); statistics (MS). Part-time and evening/weekend programs available. *Students:* 2 full-time (1 woman), 16 part-time (7 women); includes 4 minority (2 African Americans, 2 Asian Americans or Pacific Islanders), 9 international. Average age 35. In 2003, 2 degrees awarded. *Degree requirements:* For master's, one foreign language, thesis or alternative, comprehensive exam. *Entrance requirements:* For master's, GRE. *Application deadline:* For fall admission, 2/1 for domestic students; for spring admission, 10/1 for domestic students. Application fee: $50. *Expenses:* Tuition: Full-time $15,786; part-time $877 per credit hour. Required fees: $300. Tuition and fees vary according to course load and program. *Financial support:* Fellowships, teaching assistantships, career-related internships or fieldwork, Federal Work-Study, and institutionally sponsored loans available. Support available to part-time students. Financial award application deadline: 2/1. *Faculty research:* Statistical computing; data analysis; random processes; environmental, meteorological, and biological applications.

American University, College of Arts and Sciences, Department of Mathematics and Statistics, Program in Statistics for Policy Analysis, Washington, DC 20016-8001. Offers MS. Part-time programs available. *Students:* 1 (woman) full-time, 3 part-time (all women); includes 3 minority (1 African American, 2 Asian Americans or Pacific Islanders). Average age 39. In 2003, 2 degrees awarded. *Entrance requirements:* For master's, GRE. *Application deadline:* For fall admission, 2/1 for domestic students; for spring admission, 10/1 for domestic students. Application fee: $50. *Expenses:* Tuition: Full-time $15,786; part-time $877 per credit hour. Required fees: $300. Tuition and fees vary according to course load and program. *Financial support:* Application deadline: 2/1.

Arizona State University, Graduate College, College of Liberal Arts and Sciences, Department of Mathematics, Tempe, AZ 85287. Offers applied mathematics (MA, PhD); mathematics (MA, MNS, PhD); statistics (MA, PhD). *Degree requirements:* For master's, thesis or alternative; for doctorate, one foreign language, thesis/dissertation. *Entrance requirements:* For master's and doctorate, GRE General Test. *Expenses:* Tuition, state resident: full-time $3,708; part-time $194 per credit hour. Tuition, nonresident: full-time $12,228; part-time $510 per credit hour. Required fees: $87; $22 per semester. Part-time tuition and fees vary according to program. *Faculty research:* Mathematical biology, ordinary and partial differential equations, calculus of variations.

Arizona State University, Graduate College, Interdisciplinary Program in Statistics, Tempe, AZ 85287. Offers MS. *Entrance requirements:* For master's, GRE. *Expenses:* Tuition, state resident: full-time $3,708; part-time $194 per credit hour. Tuition, nonresident: full-time $12,228; part-time $510 per credit hour. Required fees: $87; $22 per semester. Part-time tuition and fees vary according to program. *Faculty research:* Regression, variance components, linear models, biostatistics, decision-theoretic methods.

Auburn University, Graduate School, College of Sciences and Mathematics, Department of Discrete and Statistical Sciences, Auburn University, AL 36849. Offers M Prob S, MAM, MS, PhD. *Faculty:* 12 full-time (0 women). *Students:* 13 full-time (9 women), 12 part-time (6 women); includes 4 minority (3 African Americans, 1 Hispanic American), 3 international. 20 applicants, 50% accepted. In 2003, 5 master's, 2 doctorates awarded. *Degree requirements:* For doctorate, thesis/dissertation. *Entrance requirements:* For master's and doctorate, GRE General Test. *Application deadline:* For fall admission, 7/7 for domestic students; for spring admission, 11/24 for domestic students. Applications are processed on a rolling basis. Application fee: $25 ($50 for international students). Electronic applications accepted. *Expenses:* Tuition, state resident: part-time $175 per credit hour. Tuition, nonresident: part-time $525 per credit hour. *Financial support:* Fellowships, teaching assistantships available. Financial award application deadline: 3/15. *Faculty research:* Discrete mathematics, applied probability, differential equations, cryptography. *Unit head:* Dr. Kevin T. Phelps, Head, 334-844-5111, Fax: 334-844-3611, E-mail: phelpkt@mail.auburn.edu.

Ball State University, Graduate School, College of Sciences and Humanities, Department of Mathematical Sciences, Program in Mathematical Statistics, Muncie, IN 47306-1099. Offers MA. *Students:* 2 full-time (1 woman), 3 part-time (1 woman), (all international). Average age 27. 8 applicants, 63% accepted, 1 enrolled. In 2003, 3 degrees awarded. Application fee: $25 ($35 for international students). *Expenses:* Tuition, state resident: full-time $5,748. Tuition, nonresident: full-time $14,166. *Financial support:* Research assistantships with full tuition reimbursements, teaching assistantships with tuition reimbursements available. Financial award application

Statistics

Ball State University (continued)

deadline: 3/1. *Faculty research:* Robust methods. *Unit head:* Dr. Mir Ali, Director, 765-285-8640, Fax: 765-285-1721, E-mail: mali@bsu.edu.

Baylor University, Graduate School, Institute of Statistics, Waco, TX 76798. Offers MA, PhD. *Faculty:* 7 full-time (1 woman), 4 part-time/adjunct (1 woman). *Students:* 21 full-time (10 women), 4 part-time (3 women); includes 4 minority (1 Asian American or Pacific Islander, 3 Hispanic Americans), 6 international. Average age 24. 38 applicants, 16% accepted. In 2003, 5 master's, 6 doctorates awarded. *Degree requirements:* For doctorate, thesis/dissertation. *Entrance requirements:* For master's, GRE General Test, 3 semesters of calculus; for doctorate, GRE General Test. *Application deadline:* Applications are processed on a rolling basis. Application fee: $25. *Expenses:* Tuition: Part-time $698 per hour. *Financial support:* In 2003–04, 1 fellowship, 5 research assistantships, 7 teaching assistantships were awarded. Institutionally sponsored loans also available. *Faculty research:* Mathematical statistics, probability theory, biostatistics, linear models, time series. *Unit head:* Dr. Tom Bratcher, Graduate Program Director, 254-710-1699, Fax: 254-710-3033, E-mail: tom_bratcher@baylor.edu. *Application contact:* Suzanne Keener, Administrative Assistant, 254-710-3588, Fax: 254-710-3870, E-mail: pauline_johnson@baylor.edu.

Bernard M. Baruch College of the City University of New York, Zicklin School of Business, Department of Statistics and Computer Information Systems, Program in Statistics, New York, NY 10010-5585. Offers MBA, MS. Part-time and evening/weekend programs available. *Entrance requirements:* For master's, GMAT, 2 letters of recommendation, resumé, 2 years of work experience. Additional exam requirements/recommendations for international students: Required—TOEFL (minimum score 590 paper-based; 243 computer-based), TWE. *Application deadline:* For fall admission, 5/31 for domestic students, 4/30 for international students; for spring admission, 10/31 for domestic students, 10/31 for international students. Application fee: $50. *Expenses:* Tuition, state resident: full-time $7,500; part-time $330 per credit. Tuition, nonresident: full-time $15,540; part-time $555 per credit. Required fees: $218; $72 per semester. Tuition and fees vary according to course load and program. *Financial support:* Fellowships, research assistantships, career-related internships or fieldwork, Federal Work-Study, scholarships/grants, and unspecified assistantships available. Financial award application deadline: 4/30; financial award applicants required to submit FAFSA. *Unit head:* Ann Brandwein, Head, 646-312-3065, E-mail: ann_brandwein@baruch.cuny.edu. *Application contact:* Frances Murphy, Office of Graduate Admissions, 646-312-1300, Fax: 646-312-1301, E-mail: zicklingradadmissions@baruch.cuny.edu.

Bowling Green State University, Graduate College, College of Arts and Sciences, Department of Mathematics and Statistics, Bowling Green, OH 43403. Offers applied statistics (MS); mathematics (MA, MAT, PhD); mathematics supervision (Ed S); statistics (MA, MAT, PhD). Part-time programs available. *Faculty:* 22 full-time. *Students:* 56 full-time (18 women), 12 part-time (6 women); includes 6 minority (4 Asian Americans or Pacific Islanders, 2 Hispanic Americans), 25 international. Average age 28. 195 applicants, 79% accepted, 6 enrolled. In 2003, 15 master's, 1 doctorate awarded. *Degree requirements:* For master's, thesis or alternative; for doctorate, thesis/dissertation, comprehensive exam; for Ed S, internship. *Entrance requirements:* For master's and doctorate, GRE General Test. Additional exam requirements/recommendations for international students: Required—TOEFL. Application fee: $30. Electronic applications accepted. *Expenses:* Tuition, state resident: part-time $436 per hour. Tuition, nonresident: part-time $768 per hour. *Financial support:* In 2003–04, 7 research assistantships with full tuition reimbursements (averaging $10,857 per year), 43 teaching assistantships with full tuition reimbursements (averaging $11,881 per year) were awarded. Federal Work-Study, institutionally sponsored loans, and unspecified assistantships also available. Financial award applicants required to submit FAFSA. *Faculty research:* Statistics and probability, algebra, analysis. *Unit head:* Dr. Neal Carothers, Chair, 419-372-7453. *Application contact:* Dr. Hanfeng Chen, Graduate Coordinator, 419-372-2179, Fax: 419-372-6092.

See in-depth description on page 521.

Bowling Green State University, Graduate College, College of Business Administration, Department of Applied Statistics and Operations Research, Bowling Green, OH 43403. Offers applied statistics (MS). Part-time programs available. *Faculty:* 9 full-time. *Students:* 20 full-time (12 women), 1 (woman) part-time, 17 international. Average age 27. 37 applicants, 86% accepted, 6 enrolled. In 2003, 6 degrees awarded. *Degree requirements:* For master's, thesis or alternative. *Entrance requirements:* For master's, GRE General Test. Additional exam requirements/recommendations for international students: Required—TOEFL. Application fee: $30. Electronic applications accepted. *Expenses:* Tuition, state resident: part-time $436 per hour. Tuition, nonresident: part-time $768 per hour. *Financial support:* In 2003–04, 5 research assistantships with full tuition reimbursements (averaging $6,656 per year), 16 teaching assistantships with full tuition reimbursements (averaging $6,213 per year) were awarded. Career-related internships or fieldwork, institutionally sponsored loans, and unspecified assistantships also available. Financial award applicants required to submit FAFSA. *Faculty research:* Reliability, linear models, time series, statistical quality control. *Unit head:* Dr. B. Madhu Rao, Chair, 419-372-8011. *Application contact:* Arthur Yeh, Associate Professor, 419-372-8386.

Brigham Young University, Graduate Studies, College of Physical and Mathematical Sciences, Department of Statistics, Provo, UT 84602-1001. Offers applied statistics (MS). *Faculty:* 13 full-time (1 woman). *Students:* 13 full-time (4 women), 6 part-time (4 women); includes 2 minority (both Asian Americans or Pacific Islanders) Average age 27. 31 applicants, 23% accepted, 7 enrolled. In 2003, 10 degrees awarded. *Degree requirements:* For master's, thesis (for some programs), comprehensive exam. *Entrance requirements:* For master's, GRE General Test, minimum GPA of 3.3 in last 60 hours. Additional exam requirements/recommendations for international students: Required—TOEFL. *Application deadline:* For fall admission, 2/1 for domestic students. Applications are processed on a rolling basis. Application fee: $50. Electronic applications accepted. *Expenses:* Tuition: Part-time $221 per hour. *Financial support:* In 2003–04, 17 students received support, including 7 research assistantships with partial tuition reimbursements available (averaging $6,400 per year), 7 teaching assistantships with partial tuition reimbursements available (averaging $6,400 per year); career-related internships or fieldwork and tuition waivers (partial) also available. Financial award application deadline: 2/1. *Faculty research:* Statistical education, combining multiple data sets, industrial quality improvement, spatial analysis, sports statistics. Total annual research expenditures: $2,085. *Unit head:* Dr. Howard B. Christensen, Chair, 801-422-4505, Fax: 801-378-5722, E-mail: howardc@byu.edu. *Application contact:* Dr. G. Bruce Schaalje, Graduate Coordinator, 801-422-3996, Fax: 801-422-0635, E-mail: schaalje@byu.edu.

California State University, Fullerton, Graduate Studies, College of Business and Economics, Department of Information Systems and Decision Sciences, Fullerton, CA 92834-9480. Offers management information systems (MS); management science (MBA, MS); operations research (MS); statistics (MS). Part-time and evening/weekend programs available. *Faculty:* 28 full-time (5 women), 11 part-time/adjunct. *Students:* 35 full-time (17 women), 38 part-time (16 women); includes 25 minority (1 American Indian/Alaska Native, 24 Asian Americans or Pacific Islanders), 33 international. Average age 30. 66 applicants, 35% accepted, 14 enrolled. In 2003, 47 degrees awarded. *Degree requirements:* For master's, project or thesis. *Entrance requirements:* For master's, GMAT, minimum AACSB index of 950. Application fee: $55. Tuition, nonresident: part-time $282 per unit. Required fees: $889 per semester. *Financial support:* Teaching assistantships, Federal Work-Study, institutionally sponsored loans, and scholarships/grants available. Support available to part-time students. Financial award application deadline: 3/1. *Unit head:* Dr. Barry Pasternack, Chair, 714-278-2221.

California State University, Hayward, Academic Programs and Graduate Studies, College of Science, Department of Statistics, Hayward, CA 94542-3000. Offers MS. *Students:* 43 full-time (27 women), 18 part-time (12 women); includes 17 minority (12 Asian Americans or Pacific Islanders, 5 Hispanic Americans), 21 international. 35 applicants, 97% accepted. *Degree requirements:* For master's, comprehensive exam. *Entrance requirements:* For master's, minimum GPA of 2.5 during previous 2 years. Additional exam requirements/recommendations for international students: Required—TOEFL (minimum score 550 paper-based; 213 computer-based). *Application deadline:* For fall admission, 5/31 for domestic students, 2/29 for international students; for winter admission, 9/30 for domestic students. Application fee: $55. Tuition, nonresident: part-time $188 per unit. Required fees: $560 per quarter hour. *Financial support:* Federal Work-Study and institutionally sponsored loans available. Support available to part-time students. Financial award application deadline: 3/2. *Unit head:* Dr. Julia Norton, Chair, 510-885-3435. *Application contact:* Jennifer Cason, Graduate Program Coordinator/Operations Analyst, 510-885-3286, Fax: 510-885-4777, E-mail: jcason@csuhayward.edu.

California State University, Sacramento, Graduate Studies, College of Natural Sciences and Mathematics, Department of Mathematics and Statistics, Sacramento, CA 95819-6048. Offers MA. Part-time programs available. *Students:* 4 full-time (1 woman), 14 part-time (7 women); includes 4 minority (2 Asian Americans or Pacific Islanders, 2 Hispanic Americans). *Degree requirements:* For master's, thesis or alternative, writing proficiency exam. *Entrance requirements:* For master's, minimum GPA of 3.0 in mathematics, 2.5 overall during previous 2 years; BA in mathematics or equivalent. Additional exam requirements/recommendations for international students: Required—TOEFL. *Application deadline:* For fall admission, 5/1 for domestic students; for spring admission, 11/1 for domestic students. Application fee: $55. *Expenses:* Tuition, state resident: full-time $2,256. Tuition, nonresident: full-time $10,716. *Financial support:* Research assistantships, teaching assistantships, career-related internships or fieldwork and Federal Work-Study available. Support available to part-time students. Financial award application deadline: 3/1. *Unit head:* Dr. Doraiswamy Ramachandran, Chair, 916-278-6534, Fax: 916-278-5586.

Carnegie Mellon University, College of Humanities and Social Sciences, Department of Statistics, Pittsburgh, PA 15213-3891. Offers mathematical finance (PhD); statistics (MS, PhD), including applied statistics (PhD), computational statistics (PhD), theoretical statistics (PhD). Terminal master's awarded for partial completion of doctoral program. *Degree requirements:* For doctorate, thesis/dissertation, comprehensive exam. *Entrance requirements:* For master's and doctorate, GRE General Test. Additional exam requirements/recommendations for international students: Required—TOEFL. *Expenses:* Tuition: Full-time $28,200; part-time $392 per unit. Required fees: $220. *Faculty research:* Stochastic processes, Bayesian statistics, statistical computing, decision theory, psychiatric statistics.

See in-depth description on page 527.

Case Western Reserve University, School of Graduate Studies, Department of Statistics, Cleveland, OH 44106. Offers MS, PhD. *Faculty:* 6 full-time (2 women), 2 part-time/adjunct (1 woman). *Students:* 13 full-time (2 women), 4 part-time (2 women), 11 international. Average age 31. 89 applicants, 10% accepted, 3 enrolled. In 2003, 2 master's, 5 doctorates awarded. *Degree requirements:* For master's, thesis (for some programs); for doctorate, thesis/dissertation. *Entrance requirements:* Additional exam requirements/recommendations for international students: Required—TOEFL. Application fee: $50. *Expenses:* Tuition: Full-time $26,900. *Financial support:* In 2003–04, 6 students received support, including 5 teaching assistantships; career-related internships or fieldwork also available. Support available to part-time students. *Faculty research:* Generalized linear models, asymptotics for restricted MLE Bayesian inference, sample survey theory and methodology, statistical computing, nonparametric inference, projection pursuit, stochastic processes, dynamical systems and chaotic behavior, Bayesian inference, sample survey theory, industrial statistics. *Unit head:* Wojror Woyczynski, Chairman, 216-368-6942, Fax: 216-368-0257, E-mail: waw@case.edu. *Application contact:* Sharon Dingess, Admissions, 216-368-6941, Fax: 216-368-0252, E-mail: skd@case.edu.

Central Connecticut State University, School of Graduate Studies, School of Arts and Sciences, Department of Mathematics, New Britain, CT 06050-4010. Offers data mining (MS); mathematics (MA, MS), including actuarial (MA), operations research (MA), statistics (MA). Part-time and evening/weekend programs available. *Faculty:* 26 full-time (10 women), 48 part-time/adjunct (22 women). *Students:* 17 full-time (13 women), 77 part-time (40 women); includes 3 minority (1 African American, 2 Asian Americans or Pacific Islanders), 4 international. Average age 35. 84 applicants, 70% accepted, 41 enrolled. In 2003, 10 degrees awarded. *Degree requirements:* For master's, thesis or alternative, comprehensive exam or special project. *Entrance requirements:* For master's, minimum GPA of 2.7. Additional exam requirements/recommendations for international students: Required—TOEFL. *Application deadline:* For fall admission, 8/1 for domestic students; for spring admission, 12/1 for domestic students. Applications are processed on a rolling basis. Application fee: $50. *Expenses:* Tuition, state resident: full-time $3,298. Tuition, nonresident: full-time $9,190. *Financial support:* Teaching assistantships available. Financial award application deadline: 3/15; financial award applicants required to submit FAFSA. *Faculty research:* Statistics, actuarial mathematics, computer systems and engineering, computer programming techniques, operations research. *Unit head:* Dr. Jeffrey McGowan, Interim Chair, 860-832-2835.

Claremont Graduate University, Graduate Programs, School of Mathematical Sciences, Claremont, CA 91711-6160. Offers computational science (PhD); engineering mathematics (PhD); financial engineering (MS); operations research and statistics (MA, MS); physical applied mathematics (MA, MS); pure mathematics (MA, MS, PhD); scientific computing (MA, MS); systems and control theory (MA, MS). Part-time programs available. *Faculty:* 2 full-time (0 women), 3 part-time/adjunct (0 women). *Students:* 41 full-time (8 women), 11 part-time (3 women). Average age 36. In 2003, 9 master's, 4 doctorates awarded. Terminal master's awarded for partial completion of doctoral program. *Degree requirements:* For doctorate, 2 foreign languages, thesis/dissertation. *Entrance requirements:* For master's and doctorate, GRE General Test. *Application deadline:* For fall admission, 2/15 for domestic students. Applications are processed on a rolling basis. Electronic applications accepted. *Expenses:* Tuition: Full-time $25,250; part-time $1,099 per semester. *Financial support:* Fellowships, research assistantships, career-related internships or fieldwork, Federal Work-Study, institutionally sponsored loans, and tuition waivers (full and partial) available. Support available to part-time students. Financial award application deadline: 2/15; financial award applicants required to submit FAFSA. *Unit head:* John Angus, Chair, 909-621-8080, Fax: 909-607-8261, E-mail: john.angus@cgu.edu. *Application contact:* Mary Solberg, Administrative Assistant, 909-621-8080, Fax: 909-607-8261, E-mail: math@cgu.edu.

Clemson University, Graduate School, College of Engineering and Science, Department of Mathematical Sciences, Clemson, SC 29634. Offers applied and pure mathematics (MS, PhD); computational mathematics (MS, PhD); management science (PhD); operations research (MS, PhD); statistics (MS, PhD). Part-time programs available. *Students:* 73 full-time (25 women), 5 part-time (1 woman); includes 3 minority (2 African Americans, 1 Asian American or Pacific Islander), 33 international. Average age 29. 116 applicants, 74% accepted, 31 enrolled. In 2003, 25 master's, 5 doctorates awarded. *Degree requirements:* For master's, final project, thesis optional; for doctorate, thesis/dissertation, qualifying exams. *Entrance requirements:* For master's and doctorate, GRE General Test. Additional exam requirements/recommendations for international students: Required—TOEFL. *Application deadline:* For fall admission, 6/1 for domestic students. Application fee: $40. *Expenses:* Tuition, state resident: full-time $7,432. Tuition, nonresident: full-time $14,732. *Financial support:* Fellowships, research assistantships, teaching assistantships available. Financial award application deadline: 4/15; financial award applicants required to submit FAFSA. *Faculty research:* Applied and computational analysis, discrete mathematics, mathematical programming statistics. *Unit head:* Dr. Perino Dearing, Interim Dean, 864-656-5240, Fax: 864-656-5230, E-mail: pmdrn@clemson.edu. *Application contact:* Dr. Douglas Shier, Graduate Coordinator, 864-656-1100, Fax: 864-656-5230, E-mail: shierd@clemson.edu.

Colorado State University, Graduate School, College of Natural Sciences, Department of Statistics, Fort Collins, CO 80523-0015. Offers MS, PhD. Part-time and evening/weekend programs available. Postbaccalaureate distance learning degree programs offered (no on-campus study). *Faculty:* 13 full-time (1 woman), 2 part-time/adjunct (0 women). *Students:* 27 full-time (10 women), 35 part-time (6 women); includes 3 minority (2 African Americans, 1

American Indian/Alaska Native), 21 international. Average age 32. 182 applicants, 19% accepted, 17 enrolled. In 2003, 9 master's, 5 doctorates awarded. *Degree requirements:* For master's, project, seminar, thesis optional; for doctorate, thesis/dissertation, candidacy exam, preliminary exam, seminar. *Entrance requirements:* For master's and doctorate, GRE General Test, minimum GPA of 3.0. Additional exam requirements/recommendations for international students: Required—TOEFL (minimum score 550 paper-based; 213 computer-based). *Application deadline:* For fall admission, 2/15 priority date for domestic students, 2/15 priority date for international students. Applications are processed on a rolling basis. Application fee: $50. Electronic applications accepted. *Expenses:* Tuition, state resident: full-time $4,156. Tuition, nonresident: full-time $14,762. Required fees: $205. Tuition and fees vary according to course load, campus/location, program and reciprocity agreements. *Financial support:* In 2003–04, 3 fellowships with tuition reimbursements (averaging $10,310 per year), 4 research assistantships with tuition reimbursements (averaging $15,675 per year), 16 teaching assistantships with tuition reimbursements (averaging $14,575 per year) were awarded. Career-related internships or fieldwork, Federal Work-Study, institutionally sponsored loans, traineeships, and unspecified assistantships also available. Support available to part-time students. Financial award application deadline: 2/15; financial award applicants required to submit FAFSA. *Faculty research:* Applied probability, linear models, experimental design, time-series analysis, statistical inference. Total annual research expenditures: $1.1 million. *Unit head:* Richard A. Davis, Chair, 970-491-5269, Fax: 970-491-7895, E-mail: stats@colostate.edu. *Application contact:* Graduate Coordinator, 970-491-5269, Fax: 970-491-7895, E-mail: stats@colostate.edu.

Columbia University, Graduate School of Arts and Sciences, Division of Natural Sciences, Department of Statistics, New York, NY 10027. Offers M Phil, MA, PhD, MD/PhD. Part-time programs available. *Faculty:* 10 full-time, 1 part-time/adjunct. *Students:* 25 full-time (8 women), 50 part-time (17 women); includes 15 minority (3 African Americans, 9 Asian Americans or Pacific Islanders, 3 Hispanic Americans), 37 international. Average age 28. 98 applicants, 52% accepted. In 2003, 29 degrees awarded. *Degree requirements:* For doctorate, thesis/dissertation. *Entrance requirements:* For master's and doctorate, GRE General Test, GRE Subject Test. Additional exam requirements/recommendations for international students: Required—TOEFL. Application fee: $75. *Expenses:* Tuition: Full-time $14,820. *Financial support:* Fellowships, teaching assistantships, Federal Work-Study and institutionally sponsored loans available. Support available to part-time students. Financial award application deadline: 1/5; financial award applicants required to submit FAFSA. *Unit head:* Shaw-Hwa Lo, Chair, 212-854-2432, Fax: 212-663-2454.

Columbia University, Graduate School of Arts and Sciences, Program in Quantitative Methods in the Social Sciences, New York, NY 10027. Offers MA. Part-time programs available. Application fee: $75. *Expenses:* Tuition: Full-time $14,820. *Unit head:* Peter Bearman, Adviser, 212-854-3094, Fax: 212-854-8925.

Cornell University, Graduate School, Graduate Fields of Engineering, Field of Operations Research and Industrial Engineering, Ithaca, NY 14853-0001. Offers applied probability and statistics (PhD); manufacturing systems engineering (PhD); mathematical programming (PhD); operations research and industrial engineering (M Eng). *Faculty:* 31 full-time. *Students:* 110 full-time (32 women); includes 22 minority (1 African American, 18 Asian Americans or Pacific Islanders, 3 Hispanic Americans), 62 international. 493 applicants, 40% accepted, 67 enrolled. In 2003, 96 master's, 5 doctorates awarded. *Degree requirements:* For doctorate, thesis/dissertation, comprehensive exam. *Entrance requirements:* For master's and doctorate, GRE General Test, 3 letters of recommendation. Additional exam requirements/recommendations for international students: Required—TOEFL (minimum score 600 paper-based; 250 computer-based). *Application deadline:* For fall admission, 1/15 for domestic students. Application fee: $60. Electronic applications accepted. *Expenses:* Tuition: Full-time $28,630. One-time fee: $50 full-time. *Financial support:* In 2003–04, 41 students received support, including 5 fellowships with full tuition reimbursements available, 6 research assistantships with full tuition reimbursements available, 30 teaching assistantships with full tuition reimbursements available; institutionally sponsored loans, scholarships/grants, health care benefits, tuition waivers (full and partial), and unspecified assistantships also available. Financial award applicants required to submit FAFSA. *Faculty research:* Mathematical programming and combinatorial optimization, statistics, stochastic processes, mathematical finance, simulation, manufacturing, and e-commerce. *Unit head:* Director of Graduate Studies, 607-255-9128, Fax: 607-255-9129. *Application contact:* Graduate Field Assistant, 607-255-9128, Fax: 607-255-9129, E-mail: orphd@cornell.edu.

Cornell University, Graduate School, Graduate Fields of Industrial and Labor Relations, Field of Statistics, Ithaca, NY 14853-0001. Offers applied statistics (MPS); biometry (MS, PhD); decision theory (MS, PhD); economic and social statistics (MS, PhD); engineering statistics (MS, PhD); experimental design (MS, PhD); mathematical statistics (MS, PhD); probability (MS, PhD); sampling (MS, PhD); statistical computing (MS, PhD); stochastic processes (MS, PhD). *Faculty:* 23 full-time. *Students:* 37 full-time (17 women); includes 6 minority (5 Asian Americans or Pacific Islanders, 1 Hispanic American), 22 international. 265 applicants, 19% accepted, 16 enrolled. In 2003, 20 master's, 2 doctorates awarded. Terminal master's awarded for partial completion of doctoral program. *Median time to degree:* Master's–1 year full-time. Of those who began their doctoral program in fall 1995, 100% received their degree in 8 years or less. *Degree requirements:* For master's, project (MPS), thesis (MS); for doctorate, one foreign language, thesis/dissertation. *Entrance requirements:* For master's, GRE General Test (MS), 2 letters of recommendation (MS and MPS); for doctorate, GRE General Test, 2 letters of recommendation. Additional exam requirements/recommendations for international students: Required—TOEFL (minimum score 550 paper-based; 213 computer-based). *Application deadline:* For fall admission, 1/15 for domestic students. Applications are processed on a rolling basis. Application fee: $60. Electronic applications accepted. *Expenses:* Tuition: Full-time $28,630. One-time fee: $50 full-time. *Financial support:* In 2003–04, 18 students received support, including 4 fellowships with full tuition reimbursements available, 1 research assistantship with full tuition reimbursement available, 13 teaching assistantships with full tuition reimbursements available; institutionally sponsored loans, scholarships/grants, tuition waivers (full and partial), and unspecified assistantships also available. Financial award applicants required to submit FAFSA. *Faculty research:* Bayesian analysis, survival analysis, nonparametric statistics, stochastic processes, mathematical statistics. *Unit head:* Director of Graduate Studies, 607-255-8066. *Application contact:* Graduate Field Assistant, 607-255-8066, E-mail: csc@cornell.edu.

Dalhousie University, Faculty of Graduate Studies, College of Arts and Science, Faculty of Science, Department of Mathematics and Statistics, Program in Statistics, Halifax, NS B3H 4R2, Canada. Offers M Sc, PhD. *Degree requirements:* For master's and doctorate, thesis/dissertation, 50 hours of consulting. *Entrance requirements:* Additional exam requirements/recommendations for international students: Required—TOEFL. *Faculty research:* Data analysis, multivariate analysis, robustness, time series, statistical genetics.

DePaul University, College of Liberal Arts and Sciences, Department of Mathematical Sciences, Program in Applied Statistics, Chicago, IL 60604-2287. Offers MS. *Students:* 6 full-time (3 women), 8 part-time (3 women); includes 4 minority (1 African American, 2 Asian Americans or Pacific Islanders, 1 Hispanic American), 1 international. Average age 35. 16 applicants, 100% accepted. In 2003, 9 degrees awarded. *Degree requirements:* For master's, comprehensive exam. *Application deadline:* Applications are processed on a rolling basis. Application fee: $25. *Expenses:* Tuition: Part-time $395 per hour. *Unit head:* Dr. Effat Moussa, Director, 312-325-7000 Ext. 1343.

Duke University, Graduate School, Institute of Statistics and Decision Sciences, Durham, NC 27708-0586. Offers PhD. Part-time programs available. *Faculty:* 13 full-time. *Students:* 28 full-time (12 women), 15 international. 134 applicants, 11% accepted, 10 enrolled. In 2003, 9 doctorates awarded. *Degree requirements:* For doctorate, thesis/dissertation. *Entrance requirements:* For doctorate, GRE General Test. Additional exam requirements/recommendations for international students: Required—IELT (preferred) or TOEFL. *Application deadline:* For fall admission, 12/31 for domestic students. Application fee: $75. *Expenses:* Tuition: Full-time $23,280; part-time $835 per unit. *Financial support:* Fellowships, research assistantships, teaching assistantships available. Financial award application deadline: 12/31. *Unit head:* Alan Gelfand, Director of Graduate Studies, 919-684-8029, Fax: 919-684-8594, E-mail: dgs@stat.duke.edu.

Eastern Michigan University, Graduate School, College of Arts and Sciences, Department of Mathematics, Ypsilanti, MI 48197. Offers computer science (M Math); mathematics education (M Math); statistics (M Math). Evening/weekend programs available. *Faculty:* 29 full-time. *Students:* 26 full-time (12 women), 45 part-time (22 women); includes 51 minority (3 African Americans, 46 Asian Americans or Pacific Islanders, 2 Hispanic Americans). *Degree requirements:* For master's, thesis optional. *Entrance requirements:* Additional exam requirements/recommendations for international students: Required—TOEFL. *Application deadline:* For fall admission, 5/15 for domestic students; for spring admission, 3/15 for domestic students. Applications are processed on a rolling basis. Application fee: $30. *Expenses:* Tuition, state resident: full-time $4,324. Tuition, nonresident: full-time $8,769. Required fees: $496. Tuition and fees vary according to course level. *Financial support:* In 2003–04, fellowships (averaging $4,000 per year), research assistantships (averaging $7,770 per year), teaching assistantships (averaging $7,770 per year) were awarded. Support available to part-time students. Financial award application deadline: 3/15; financial award applicants required to submit FAFSA. *Unit head:* Dr. Betty Warren, Head, 734-487-1444. *Application contact:* Dr. Kenneth Shiskowski, Coordinator, 734-487-1444.

Florida International University, College of Arts and Sciences, Department of Statistics, Miami, FL 33199. Offers MS. *Faculty:* 10 full-time (2 women), 1 (woman) part-time/adjunct. *Students:* 4 full-time (0 women), 1 part-time; includes 4 minority (2 Asian Americans or Pacific Islanders, 2 Hispanic Americans), 1 international. 8 applicants, 75% accepted, 3 enrolled. In 2003, 3 degrees awarded. *Degree requirements:* For master's, thesis optional. *Entrance requirements:* For master's, GRE General Test, minimum GPA of 3.0, 3 letters of recommendation. Additional exam requirements/recommendations for international students: Required—TOEFL. Application fee: $20. *Expenses:* Tuition, state resident: part-time $202 per credit. Tuition, nonresident: part-time $771 per credit. Required fees: $112 per semester. *Unit head:* Dr. Jie Mi, Chairperson, 305-348-2745, Fax: 305-348-6895, E-mail: mi@fiu.edu.

Florida State University, Graduate Studies, College of Arts and Sciences, Department of Statistics, Tallahassee, FL 32306. Offers applied statistics (MS); mathematical statistics (MS, PhD). Part-time programs available. *Faculty:* 15 full-time (1 woman). *Students:* 33 full-time (17 women), 1 part-time. Average age 30. 232 applicants, 10% accepted, 12 enrolled. In 2003, 8 master's, 4 doctorates awarded, leading to university research/teaching 75%, business/industry 25%. Terminal master's awarded for partial completion of doctoral program. *Median time to degree:* Master's–2 years full-time; doctorate–4 years full-time. Of those who began their doctoral program in fall 1995, 100% received their degree in 8 years or less. *Degree requirements:* For master's, comprehensive exam (mathematical statistics); for doctorate, thesis/dissertation, departmental qualifying exam. *Entrance requirements:* For master's, GRE General Test, previous course work in calculus, minimum GPA of 3.0; for doctorate, GRE General Test, minimum GPA of 3.0, one course in linear algebra (preferred), Calculus I-III. Additional exam requirements/recommendations for international students: Required—TOEFL (minimum score 600 paper-based; 250 computer-based). *Application deadline:* For fall admission, 7/1 for domestic students, 5/2 for international students; for spring admission, 11/1 for domestic students, 9/1 for international students. Applications are processed on a rolling basis. Application fee: $20. Electronic applications accepted. *Expenses:* Tuition, state resident: part-time $196 per credit hour. Tuition, nonresident: part-time $731 per credit hour. Part-time tuition and fees vary according to campus/location. *Financial support:* In 2003–04, 1 fellowship with full tuition reimbursement (averaging $6,300 per year), 8 research assistantships with full tuition reimbursements (averaging $16,301 per year), 25 teaching assistantships with full tuition reimbursements (averaging $16,301 per year) were awarded. Federal Work-Study, institutionally sponsored loans, scholarships/grants, and unspecified assistantships also available. Support available to part-time students. Financial award application deadline: 2/15; financial award applicants required to submit FAFSA. *Faculty research:* Statistical inference, probability theory, spatial statistics, nonparametric estimation, automatic target recognition. Total annual research expenditures: $626,760. *Unit head:* Dr. Myles Hollander, Chairman, 850-644-3218, Fax: 850-644-5271, E-mail: info@stat.fsu.edu. *Application contact:* Pamela McGhee, Program Assistant, 850-644-3218, Fax: 850-644-5271, E-mail: info@stat.fsu.edu.

Florida State University, Graduate Studies, College of Education, Department of Educational Psychology and Learning Systems, Program in Measurement and Statistics, Tallahassee, FL 32306. Offers MS, PhD. *Faculty:* 2 full-time (0 women), 1 part-time/adjunct (0 women). *Students:* 12 full-time (7 women), 5 part-time (1 woman); includes 10 minority (9 Asian Americans or Pacific Islanders, 1 Hispanic American). 12 applicants, 25% accepted, 3 enrolled. In 2003, 1 master's, 2 doctorates awarded. *Application deadline:* For fall admission, 7/1 for domestic students; for spring admission, 11/1 for domestic students. Application fee: $20. *Expenses:* Tuition, state resident: part-time $196 per credit hour. Tuition, nonresident: part-time $731 per credit hour. Part-time tuition and fees vary according to campus/location. *Application contact:* Dorothy LaSeur, Program Assistant, 850-644-4592, Fax: 850-644-8776.

George Mason University, School of Information Technology and Engineering, Department of Applied and Engineering Statistics, Fairfax, VA 22030. Offers statistical science (MS). Part-time and evening/weekend programs available. *Faculty:* 7 full-time (0 women), 5 part-time/adjunct (2 women). *Students:* 8 full-time (4 women), 66 part-time (32 women); includes 16 minority (4 African Americans, 10 Asian Americans or Pacific Islanders, 2 Hispanic Americans), 11 international. Average age 36. 50 applicants, 78% accepted, 28 enrolled. In 2003, 13 degrees awarded. *Degree requirements:* For master's, thesis optional. *Entrance requirements:* For master's, GMAT or GRE General Test, previous course work in calculus, probability, and statistics; minimum GPA of 3.0 in last 60 hours. Additional exam requirements/recommendations for international students: Required—TOEFL. *Application deadline:* For fall admission, 5/1 for domestic students; for spring admission, 11/1 for domestic students. Application fee: $60. Electronic applications accepted. *Expenses:* Tuition, state resident: full-time $4,398. Tuition, nonresident: full-time $14,952. Required fees: $1,482. *Financial support:* Fellowships, research assistantships, teaching assistantships, career-related internships or fieldwork and Federal Work-Study available. Support available to part-time students. Financial award application deadline: 3/1; financial award applicants required to submit FAFSA. *Faculty research:* Computational statistics, nonparametric function estimation, scientific and statistical visualization, statistical applications to engineering, survey research. Total annual research expenditures: $436,000. *Unit head:* Dr. Richard A. Bolstein, Head, 703-993-3645, Fax: 703-993-1700, E-mail: statistics@gmu.edu.

The George Washington University, Columbian College of Arts and Sciences, Department of Statistics, Washington, DC 20052. Offers biostatistics (MS, PhD); industrial and engineering statistics (MS); statistics (MS, PhD). Part-time and evening/weekend programs available. *Faculty:* 13 full-time (2 women), 1 part-time/adjunct (0 women). *Students:* 12 full-time (7 women), 23 part-time (9 women); includes 8 minority (3 African Americans, 5 Asian Americans or Pacific Islanders), 15 international. Average age 29. 80 applicants, 61% accepted. In 2003, 6 master's, 2 doctorates awarded. Terminal master's awarded for partial completion of doctoral program. *Degree requirements:* For master's, comprehensive exam; for doctorate, thesis/dissertation, general exam. *Entrance requirements:* For master's and doctorate, GRE General Test, interview, minimum GPA of 3.0. Additional exam requirements/recommendations for international students: Required—TOEFL (minimum score 550 paper-based; 213 computer-based). *Application deadline:* For fall admission, 2/1 priority date for domestic students, 2/1 priority date for international students; for spring admission, 10/1 priority date for domestic students, 10/1 priority date for international students. Applications are processed on a rolling basis. Application fee: $60. Electronic applications accepted. *Expenses:* Tuition: Part-time $876 per credit. Required fees: $1 per credit. Tuition and fees vary according to campus/location. *Financial support:* In 2003–04, 8 fellowships with tuition reimbursements (averaging

Statistics

The George Washington University (continued)

$10,000 per year), 8 teaching assistantships with tuition reimbursements (averaging $5,000 per year) were awarded. Federal Work-Study also available. Financial award application deadline: 2/1. *Unit head:* Dr. Tapan Nayak, Chair, 202-994-6356, Fax: 202-994-6917. *Application contact:* Information Contact, 202-994-6356, Fax: 202-994-6917.

Georgia Institute of Technology, Graduate Studies and Research, College of Sciences, School of Mathematics, Atlanta, GA 30332-0001. Offers algorithms, combinatorics, and optimization (PhD); applied mathematics (MS); bioinformatics (PhD); mathematics (PhD); quantitative and computational finance (MS); statistics (MS Stat). *Faculty:* 50 full-time (3 women). *Students:* 59 full-time (17 women), 8 part-time (2 women); includes 3 minority (2 African Americans, 1 Hispanic American), 32 international. Average age 25. In 2003, 20 master's, 7 doctorates awarded, leading to university research/teaching 55%, business/industry 30%, government 15%. Terminal master's awarded for partial completion of doctoral program. *Degree requirements:* For master's, thesis or alternative; for doctorate, one foreign language, thesis/dissertation. *Entrance requirements:* For master's, GRE General Test, minimum GPA of 3.0; for doctorate, GRE General Test, GRE Subject Test, minimum GPA of 3.0. Additional exam requirements/recommendations for international students: Required—TOEFL. *Application deadline:* For fall admission, 3/1 priority date for domestic students, 3/1 priority date for international students; for spring admission, 10/1 priority date for domestic students, 10/1 priority date for international students. Applications are processed on a rolling basis. Application fee: $50. Electronic applications accepted. *Expenses:* Tuition, state resident: part-time $1,925 per semester. Tuition, nonresident: part-time $7,700 per semester. Required fees: $434 per semester. Full-time tuition and fees vary according to program. *Financial support:* In 2003–04, 7 fellowships with tuition reimbursements, 20 research assistantships with tuition reimbursements, 40 teaching assistantships with tuition reimbursements were awarded. Career-related internships or fieldwork, Federal Work-Study, institutionally sponsored loans, tuition waivers (partial), and supplements also available. Financial award application deadline: 2/1. *Faculty research:* Dynamical systems, discrete mathematics, probability and statistics, mathematical physics. Total annual research expenditures: $1.1 million. *Unit head:* Dr. William Thomas Trotter, Chair, 404-894-2700. *Application contact:* Dr. Evans Harrell, Graduate Coordinator, 404-894-9203, Fax: 404-894-4409, E-mail: grad.coordinator@math.gatech.edu.

Georgia Institute of Technology, Graduate Studies and Research, Multidisciplinary Program in Statistics, Atlanta, GA 30332-0001. Offers MS Stat. Part-time programs available. *Degree requirements:* For master's, thesis optional. *Entrance requirements:* For master's, GRE General Test, minimum GPA of 3.0. Additional exam requirements/recommendations for international students: Required—TOEFL. *Expenses:* Tuition, state resident: part-time $1,925 per semester. Tuition, nonresident: part-time $7,700 per semester. Required fees: $434 per semester. Full-time tuition and fees vary according to program. *Faculty research:* Statistical control procedures, statistical modeling of transportation systems.

Harvard University, Graduate School of Arts and Sciences, Department of Statistics, Cambridge, MA 02138. Offers AM, PhD. Terminal master's awarded for partial completion of doctoral program. *Degree requirements:* For master's, one foreign language; for doctorate, one foreign language, thesis/dissertation, exam, qualifying paper. *Entrance requirements:* For master's and doctorate, GRE General Test, GRE Subject Test (recommended). Additional exam requirements/recommendations for international students: Required—TOEFL. *Expenses:* Tuition: Full-time $26,066. Full-time tuition and fees vary according to program and student level. *Faculty research:* Interactive graphic analysis of multidimensional data, data analysis, modeling and inference, statistical modeling of U.S. economic time series.

Indiana University Bloomington, Graduate School, College of Arts and Sciences, Department of Mathematics, Bloomington, IN 47405. Offers applied mathematics–numerical analysis (MA, PhD); mathematics education (MAT); probability-statistics (MA, PhD). PhD offered through the University Graduate School. *Faculty:* 36 full-time (1 woman). *Students:* 102 full-time (33 women), 31 part-time (7 women); includes 5 minority (all Asian Americans or Pacific Islanders), 76 international. Average age 27. In 2003, 14 master's, 13 doctorates awarded. Terminal master's awarded for partial completion of doctoral program. *Degree requirements:* For doctorate, one foreign language, thesis/dissertation. *Entrance requirements:* For master's and doctorate, GRE General Test, GRE Subject Test. Additional exam requirements/recommendations for international students: Required—TOEFL. *Application deadline:* For fall admission, 1/15 priority date for domestic students, 12/15 priority date for international students; for spring admission, 9/1 priority date for domestic students, 9/1 priority date for international students. Applications are processed on a rolling basis. Application fee: $45 ($55 for international students). Electronic applications accepted. *Expenses:* Tuition, state resident: full-time $4,908; part-time $205 per credit. Tuition, nonresident: full-time $14,298; part-time $596 per credit. Required fees: $661. Tuition and fees vary according to campus/location and program. *Financial support:* In 2003–04, 8 fellowships with full tuition reimbursements (averaging $15,000 per year), 101 teaching assistantships with full tuition reimbursements (averaging $12,200 per year) were awarded. Research assistantships, Federal Work-Study also available. Support available to part-time students. Financial award application deadline: 2/1. *Faculty research:* Topology, geometry, algebra. *Unit head:* Daniel Maki, Chair, 812-855-2200, Fax: 812-855-0046, E-mail: maki@indiana.edu. *Application contact:* Misty Cummings, Graduate Secretary, 812-855-2645, Fax: 812-855-0046, E-mail: gradmath@indiana.edu.

Indiana University–Purdue University Indianapolis, School of Science, Department of Mathematical Sciences, Indianapolis, IN 46202-3216. Offers applied mathematics (MS, PhD); applied statistics (MS); mathematics (MS, PhD). Part-time programs available. *Faculty:* 10 full-time (0 women), 1 part-time/adjunct (0 women). *Students:* 20 full-time (10 women), 40 part-time (19 women); includes 4 minority (all Asian Americans or Pacific Islanders), 20 international. Average age 32. In 2003, 13 degrees awarded. Terminal master's awarded for partial completion of doctoral program. *Degree requirements:* For master's, thesis optional; for doctorate, one foreign language, thesis/dissertation. *Entrance requirements:* For doctorate, GRE. Additional exam requirements/recommendations for international students: Required—TOEFL. *Application deadline:* For fall admission, 2/1 for domestic students. Application fee: $45 ($55 for international students). *Expenses:* Tuition, state resident: full-time $4,658; part-time $194 per credit. Tuition, nonresident: full-time $13,444; part-time $560 per credit. Required fees: $571. Tuition and fees vary according to campus/location and program. *Financial support:* In 2003–04, 14 students received support, including 2 research assistantships with tuition reimbursements available (averaging $11,000 per year), 10 teaching assistantships with tuition reimbursements available (averaging $11,000 per year); fellowships with tuition reimbursements available, career-related internships or fieldwork, Federal Work-Study, and tuition waivers (full and partial) also available. Financial award application deadline: 3/1. *Faculty research:* Mathematical physics, analysis, operator theory, functional analysis, integrated systems. *Unit head:* Benzion Boukai, Chair, 317-274-6918, Fax: 317-274-3460, E-mail: bboukai@math.iupui.edu. *Application contact:* Joan Morand, Student Services Specialist, 317-274-4127, Fax: 317-274-3460.

Instituto Tecnológico y de Estudios Superiores de Monterrey, Campus Monterrey, Graduate and Research Division, Programs in Engineering, Monterrey, , Mexico. Offers applied statistics (M Eng); artificial intelligence (PhD); automation engineering (M Eng); chemical engineering (M Eng); civil engineering (M Eng); electrical engineering (M Eng); electronic engineering (M Eng); environmental engineering (M Eng); industrial engineering (M Eng, PhD); manufacturing engineering (M Eng); mechanical engineering (M Eng); systems and quality engineering (M Eng). Part-time and evening/weekend programs available. Terminal master's awarded for partial completion of doctoral program. *Degree requirements:* For master's and doctorate, one foreign language, thesis/dissertation. *Entrance requirements:* For master's, PAEG; for doctorate, GRE, master's degree in related field. Additional exam requirements/recommendations for international students: Required—TOEFL. *Faculty research:* Flexible manufacturing cells, materials, statistical methods, environmental prevention, control and evaluation.

Iowa State University of Science and Technology, Graduate College, College of Liberal Arts and Sciences, Department of Statistics, Ames, IA 50011. Offers MS, PhD, MBA/MS. *Faculty:* 26 full-time, 3 part-time/adjunct. *Students:* 77 full-time (48 women), 48 part-time (26 women); includes 9 minority (3 African Americans, 6 Asian Americans or Pacific Islanders), 63 international. 202 applicants, 21% accepted, 27 enrolled. In 2003, 39 master's, 8 doctorates awarded. *Median time to degree:* Master's–2.9 years full-time; doctorate–6.1 years full-time. *Degree requirements:* For master's, thesis or alternative; for doctorate, thesis/dissertation. *Entrance requirements:* For master's and doctorate, GRE General Test. Additional exam requirements/recommendations for international students: Required—TOEFL (paper score 550; computer score 213) or IELTS (score 6.5). *Application deadline:* For fall admission, 3/15 priority date for domestic students, 3/15 priority date for international students; for spring admission, 10/31 for domestic students, 10/31 for international students. Applications are processed on a rolling basis. Application fee: $30 ($70 for international students). Tuition, nonresident: part-time $560 per credit. Required fees: $38 per unit. *Financial support:* In 2003–04, 62 research assistantships with full and partial tuition reimbursements (averaging $17,700 per year), 39 teaching assistantships with full and partial tuition reimbursements (averaging $18,300 per year) were awarded. Fellowships, scholarships/grants, health care benefits, and unspecified assistantships also available. *Unit head:* Dr. Kenneth Koehler, Chair, 515-294-4181, Fax: 515-294-4040, E-mail: statistics@iastate.edu.

The Johns Hopkins University, G. W. C. Whiting School of Engineering, Department of Mathematical Sciences, Baltimore, MD 21218-2699. Offers discrete mathematics (MA, MSE, PhD); operations research/optimization/decision science (MA, MSE, PhD); statistics/probability/stochastic processes (MA, MSE, PhD). Terminal master's awarded for partial completion of doctoral program. *Degree requirements:* For master's, thesis (for some programs); for doctorate, thesis/dissertation, oral exam. *Entrance requirements:* For master's and doctorate, GRE General Test, GRE Subject Test. Additional exam requirements/recommendations for international students: Required—TOEFL. Electronic applications accepted. *Expenses:* Tuition: Full-time $28,730; part-time $1,490 per course. Part-time tuition and fees vary according to course load, campus/location and program. *Faculty research:* Discrete mathematics, probability, statistics, optimization and operations research, matrix and numerical analysis.

Kansas State University, Graduate School, College of Arts and Sciences, Department of Statistics, Manhattan, KS 66506. Offers MS, PhD. *Faculty:* 12 full-time (1 woman). *Students:* 39 full-time (19 women), 2 part-time (both women); includes 2 minority (1 Asian American or Pacific Islander, 1 Hispanic American), 24 international. Average age 24. 62 applicants, 32% accepted, 17 enrolled. In 2003, 10 master's, 2 doctorates awarded. Terminal master's awarded for partial completion of doctoral program. *Degree requirements:* For master's, thesis optional; for doctorate, thesis/dissertation, qualifying and preliminary exams. *Entrance requirements:* For master's, GRE; for doctorate, previous course work in statistics and mathematics. Additional exam requirements/recommendations for international students: Required—TOEFL. *Application deadline:* For fall admission, 2/1 for domestic students; for spring admission, 10/1 priority date for domestic students. Applications are processed on a rolling basis. Application fee: $0 ($25 for international students). *Expenses:* Tuition, state resident: part-time $155 per credit hour. Tuition, nonresident: part-time $428 per credit hour. Required fees: $11 per credit hour. *Financial support:* In 2003–04, fellowships (averaging $15,000 per year), 4 research assistantships (averaging $12,486 per year), 26 teaching assistantships with full tuition reimbursements (averaging $13,383 per year) were awarded. Federal Work-Study, institutionally sponsored loans, and scholarships/grants also available. Support available to part-time students. Financial award application deadline: 3/1; financial award applicants required to submit FAFSA. *Faculty research:* Linear and nonlinear statistical models, design analysis of experiments, nonparametric methods for reliability and survival data, resampling methods and their application, categorical data analysis. Total annual research expenditures: $140,000. *Unit head:* John Boyer, Head, 785-532-0518, Fax: 785-532-7336, E-mail: jboyer@stat.ksu.edu. *Application contact:* James Neill, Director, 785-532-0516, E-mail: jwneill@ksu.edu.

Kean University, School of Natural, Applied and Health Sciences, Department of Mathematics and Computer Science, Program in Computing, Statistics and Mathematics, Union, NJ 07083. Offers MS. Part-time and evening/weekend programs available. *Faculty:* 25 full-time (7 women). *Students:* 2 full-time (1 woman), 7 part-time (3 women); includes 4 minority (1 African American, 3 Asian Americans or Pacific Islanders). Average age 41. 11 applicants, 55% accepted, 3 enrolled. In 2003, 2 degrees awarded. *Degree requirements:* For master's, thesis or alternative. *Entrance requirements:* For master's, GRE General Test, 2 letters of recommendation, interview. *Application deadline:* For fall admission, 6/15 for domestic students; for spring admission, 11/15 for domestic students. Application fee: $60. *Expenses:* Tuition, state resident: full-time $7,488; part-time $312 per credit. Tuition, nonresident: full-time $9,528; part-time $397 per credit. Required fees: $1,814; $76 per credit. *Financial support:* In 2003–04, research assistantships with full tuition reimbursements (averaging $2,700 per year) *Application contact:* Joanne Morris, Director of Graduate Admissions, 908-527-2665, Fax: 908-527-2286, E-mail: grad_adm@turbo.kean.edu.

Lakehead University, Graduate Studies, School of Mathematical Sciences, Thunder Bay, ON P7B 5E1, Canada. Offers computer science (M Sc, MA); mathematics and statistics (M Sc, MA). Part-time and evening/weekend programs available. *Degree requirements:* For master's, thesis optional. *Entrance requirements:* For master's, minimum B average, honours degree in mathematics or computer science. Additional exam requirements/recommendations for international students: Required—TOEFL. *Faculty research:* Numerical analysis, classical analysis, theoretical computer science, abstract harmonic analysis, functional analysis.

Lehigh University, College of Arts and Sciences, Department of Mathematics, Program in Statistics, Bethlehem, PA 18015-3094. Offers MS. *Degree requirements:* For master's, comprehensive exam. *Entrance requirements:* For master's, minimum GPA of 3.0. Additional exam requirements/recommendations for international students: Required—TOEFL. *Application deadline:* For fall admission, 7/15 for domestic students; for spring admission, 12/1 for domestic students. Applications are processed on a rolling basis. Application fee: $40. *Expenses:* Tuition: Full-time $16,920; part-time $940 per credit hour. Required fees: $200. Tuition and fees vary according to degree level and program. *Financial support:* Application deadline: 1/15. *Application contact:* Dr. Garth Isaak, Graduate Coordinator, 610-758-3734, Fax: 610-758-3767, E-mail: mathgrad@lehigh.edu.

Louisiana State University and Agricultural and Mechanical College, Graduate School, College of Agriculture, Department of Experimental Statistics, Baton Rouge, LA 70803. Offers applied statistics (M App St). Part-time programs available. *Faculty:* 7 full-time (0 women). *Students:* 23 full-time (18 women), 2 part-time (both women); includes 2 minority (1 African American, 1 Asian American or Pacific Islander), 15 international. Average age 32. 24 applicants, 46% accepted, 3 enrolled. In 2003, 13 degrees awarded. *Degree requirements:* For master's, project. *Entrance requirements:* For master's, GRE General Test, minimum GPA of 3.0. Additional exam requirements/recommendations for international students: Required—TOEFL (minimum score 550 paper-based; 213 computer-based). *Application deadline:* For fall admission, 1/25 priority date for domestic students, 5/15 priority date for international students; for spring admission, 10/15 priority date for domestic students, 10/15 priority date for international students. Applications are processed on a rolling basis. Application fee: $25. Electronic applications accepted. *Expenses:* Tuition, state resident: part-time $337 per hour. Tuition, nonresident: part-time $577 per hour. *Financial support:* In 2003–04, 12 students received support, including 8 research assistantships with partial tuition reimbursements available (averaging $12,738 per year), 3 teaching assistantships with partial tuition reimbursements available (averaging $9,500 per year); fellowships, career-related internships or fieldwork, institutionally sponsored loans, and unspecified assistantships also available. Financial award application deadline: 4/1; financial award applicants required to submit FAFSA. *Faculty research:* Linear models, statistical computing, ecological statistics. Total annual research expenditures: $58,687. *Unit head:* Dr. E. Barry Moser, Head, 225-578-8303, Fax: 225-578-8344, E-mail: head@stat.lsu.edu. *Application contact:* Dr. James Geaghan, Graduate Adviser, 225-578-8303, E-mail: jgeaghan@lsu.edu.

Louisiana Tech University, Graduate School, College of Engineering and Science, Department of Mathematics and Statistics, Ruston, LA 71272. Offers MS. Part-time programs available. *Degree requirements:* For master's, thesis or alternative. *Entrance requirements:* For master's, GRE General Test, minimum GPA of 3.0 in last 60 hours. Additional exam requirements/recommendations for international students: Required—TOEFL. *Expenses:* Tuition, state resident: full-time $3,120. Tuition, nonresident: full-time $9,120. Tuition and fees vary according to course load.

Loyola University Chicago, Graduate School, Department of Mathematical Sciences and Statistics, Chicago, IL 60611-2196. Offers mathematics (MS), including computer science, operations research, pure mathematics, statistics and probability. Part-time and evening/weekend programs available. *Faculty:* 29 full-time (4 women), 18 part-time/adjunct (7 women). *Students:* 11 full-time (7 women), 10 part-time (6 women); includes 4 minority (2 Asian Americans or Pacific Islanders, 2 Hispanic Americans), 9 international. Average age 30. 30 applicants, 83% accepted. In 2003, 7 degrees awarded. *Entrance requirements:* For master's, GRE General Test, minimum B average. Additional exam requirements/recommendations for international students: Required—TOEFL. *Application deadline:* For fall admission, 8/1 for domestic students; for spring admission, 12/1 for domestic students. Application fee: $40. *Expenses:* Tuition: Part-time $578 per credit hour. Tuition and fees vary according to course level and program. *Financial support:* In 2003–04, 8 students received support, including 4 teaching assistantships with tuition reimbursements available (averaging $8,000 per year); career-related internships or fieldwork, Federal Work-Study, institutionally sponsored loans, and tuition waivers (partial) also available. *Faculty research:* Computer science, probability and statistics, differential equations, algebra. Total annual research expenditures: $300,000. *Unit head:* Dr. Joseph H. Mayne, Chair, 773-508-3574, Fax: 773-508-2123, E-mail: jhm@math.luc.edu. *Application contact:* Dr. Anthony Giaquinto, Graduate Director, 773-508-8520, Fax: 773-508-2123.

Marquette University, Graduate School, College of Arts and Sciences, Department of Mathematics, Statistics, and Computer Science, Milwaukee, WI 53201-1881. Offers algebra (PhD); bio-mathematical modeling (PhD); computers (MS); mathematics (MS); mathematics education (MS); statistics (MS). Part-time programs available. *Faculty:* 27 full-time (9 women), 11 part-time/adjunct (5 women). *Students:* 22 full-time (10 women), 12 part-time (4 women), 22 international. Average age 32. 43 applicants, 84% accepted, 11 enrolled. In 2003, 12 degrees awarded. Terminal master's awarded for partial completion of doctoral program. *Degree requirements:* For master's, thesis or alternative, comprehensive exam; for doctorate, 2 foreign languages, thesis/dissertation, comprehensive exam. *Entrance requirements:* For doctorate, sample of scholarly writing. Additional exam requirements/recommendations for international students: Required—TOEFL. Application fee: $40. *Expenses:* Tuition: Full-time $10,080; part-time $630 per credit. Tuition and fees vary according to program. *Financial support:* In 2003–04, 2 research assistantships, 20 teaching assistantships were awarded. Federal Work-Study, institutionally sponsored loans, scholarships/grants, and tuition waivers (full and partial) also available. Support available to part-time students. Financial award application deadline: 2/15. *Faculty research:* Models of physiological systems, mathematical immunology, computational group theory, mathematical logic. Total annual research expenditures: $77,233. *Unit head:* Dr. Peter Jones, Chairman, 414-288-7573, Fax: 414-288-1578. *Application contact:* Dr. Gary Krenz, Director of Graduate Studies, 414-288-6345.

McGill University, Faculty of Graduate and Postdoctoral Studies, Faculty of Arts, Department of Sociology, Montréal, QC H3A 2T5, Canada. Offers medical sociology (MA); neotropical environment (MA); social statistics (MA); sociology (MA, PhD). Part-time programs available. *Faculty:* 15 full-time (5 women). *Students:* 30 full-time, 4 part-time. 101 applicants, 23% accepted, 12 enrolled. In 2003, 9 master's, 1 doctorate awarded. Terminal master's awarded for partial completion of doctoral program. *Degree requirements:* For master's, thesis (for some programs), registration; for doctorate, one foreign language, thesis/dissertation, comprehensive exam, registration. *Entrance requirements:* For master's and doctorate, GRE, minimum GPA of 3.3. Additional exam requirements/recommendations for international students: Required—TOEFL (minimum score 580 paper-based; 237 computer-based). *Application deadline:* For fall admission, 2/15 for domestic students; for winter admission, 10/1 for domestic students. Applications are processed on a rolling basis. Application fee: $60 Canadian dollars. Electronic applications accepted. Tuition, area resident: Full-time $1,668. *Expenses:* Tuition, state resident: full-time $4,173. Tuition, nonresident: full-time $9,468. Required fees: $1,081. *Financial support:* In 2003–04, 6 fellowships (averaging $7,500 per year), 7 research assistantships (averaging $4,000 per year), 18 teaching assistantships with partial tuition reimbursements (averaging $6,656 per year) were awarded. Federal Work-Study, institutionally sponsored loans, scholarships/grants, health care benefits, tuition waivers (full and partial), and unspecified assistantships also available. Financial award application deadline: 2/15. *Faculty research:* Deviance and social control, states and social movements; economy and society; social inequality (class, ethnicity and gender); medical sociology. *Unit head:* Suzanne Staggenborg, Chair, 514-398-6854, Fax: 514-398-3403, E-mail: suzanne.staggenburg@mcgill.ca. *Application contact:* Rolanda Taylor, Graduate Program Coordinator, 514-398-6847, Fax: 514-398-3403, E-mail: rolanda.taylor@mcgill.ca.

McGill University, Faculty of Graduate and Postdoctoral Studies, Faculty of Science, Department of Mathematics and Statistics, Montréal, QC H3A 2T5, Canada. Offers M Sc, MA, PhD. Part-time programs available. *Faculty:* 39 full-time (2 women). *Students:* 69 full-time, 5 part-time. 294 applicants, 32% accepted, 30 enrolled. In 2003, 12 master's, 1 doctorate awarded. *Degree requirements:* For master's, thesis; for doctorate, one foreign language, thesis/dissertation, comprehensive exam. *Entrance requirements:* For master's, minimum GPA of 3.0. Additional exam requirements/recommendations for international students: Required—TOEFL. *Application deadline:* For fall admission, 3/1 for domestic students; for winter admission, 10/1 for domestic students. Applications are processed on a rolling basis. Application fee: $60 Canadian dollars. Electronic applications accepted. Tuition, area resident: Full-time $1,668. *Expenses:* Tuition, state resident: full-time $4,173. Tuition, nonresident: full-time $9,468. Required fees: $1,081. *Financial support:* In 2003–04, 21 fellowships, 27 research assistantships, 31 teaching assistantships (averaging $6,000 per year) were awarded. *Unit head:* K. N. Gowrisankaran, Chair, 514-398-7373, Fax: 514-398-3899, E-mail: gowri@math.mcgill.ca. *Application contact:* Carmen Baldonado, Graduate Program Coordinator, 514-398-0503, Fax: 514-398-3899, E-mail: gradprog@math.mcgill.ca.

McMaster University, School of Graduate Studies, Faculty of Science, Department of Mathematics and Statistics, Hamilton, ON L8S 4M2, Canada. Offers mathematics (PhD); mathematics and statistics (M Sc). Part-time programs available. *Degree requirements:* For master's, thesis or alternative, oral exam; for doctorate, thesis/dissertation, comprehensive exam. *Entrance requirements:* For master's, minimum B+ average in last year of honors degree; for doctorate, minimum B+ average, M Sc in mathematics or statistics. Additional exam requirements/recommendations for international students: Required—TOEFL (minimum score 550 paper-based; 213 computer-based). *Faculty research:* Algebra, analysis, applied mathematics, geometry and topology, probability and statistics.

McMaster University, School of Graduate Studies, Program in Statistics, Hamilton, ON L8S 4M2, Canada. Offers applied statistics (M Sc); medical statistics (M Sc); statistical theory (M Sc). *Degree requirements:* For master's, thesis or alternative. *Entrance requirements:* For master's, honors degree background in mathematics and statistics. Additional exam requirements/recommendations for international students: Required—TOEFL (minimum score 550 paper-based; 213 computer-based). *Faculty research:* Development of polymer production technology, quality of life in patients who use pharmaceutical agents, mathematical modeling, order statistics from progressively censored samples, nonlinear stochastic model in genetics.

McNeese State University, Graduate School, College of Science, Department of Mathematics, Computer Science, and Statistics, Lake Charles, LA 70609. Offers computer science (MS); mathematics (MS); statistics (MS). Evening/weekend programs available. *Degree requirements:* For master's, thesis or alternative, written exam, comprehensive exam. *Entrance requirements:* For master's, GRE General Test.

Memorial University of Newfoundland, School of Graduate Studies, Department of Mathematics and Statistics, St. John's, NL A1C 5S7, Canada. Offers mathematics (M Sc, PhD); statistics (MAS, PhD). Part-time programs available. *Students:* 31 full-time, 1 part-time. 113 applicants, 15% accepted, 14 enrolled. In 2003, 6 master's, 1 doctorate awarded. *Degree requirements:* For master's, thesis, practicum and report (MAS); for doctorate, thesis/dissertation, oral defense of thesis, comprehensive exam. *Entrance requirements:* For doctorate, MAS or M Sc in mathematics and statistics. *Application deadline:* Applications are processed on a rolling basis. Application fee: $40. Electronic applications accepted. Tuition and fees charges are reported in Canadian dollars. *Expenses:* Tuition, state resident: part-time $733 Canadian dollars per semester. Tuition, nonresident: part-time $953 Canadian dollars per semester. Required fees: $194 Canadian dollars per year. Tuition and fees vary according to degree level and program. *Financial support:* Fellowships, teaching assistantships available. Financial award application deadline: 1/31. *Faculty research:* Algebra, topology, applied mathematics, mathematical statistics, applied statistics and probability. *Unit head:* Dr. Bruce Watson, Interim Head, 709-737-8783, Fax: 709-787-3010, E-mail: head@math.mun.ca. *Application contact:* Dr. Wanda Heath, Secretary to Department Head, 709-737-8783, Fax: 709-737-3010, E-mail: mathstat@math.mun.ca.

Miami University, Graduate School, College of Arts and Sciences, Department of Mathematics and Statistics, Program in Statistics, Oxford, OH 45056. Offers MS Stat. Part-time programs available. *Students:* 9 full-time (3 women), 1 part-time; includes 2 minority (1 African American, 1 Asian American or Pacific Islander), 2 international. 26 applicants, 35% accepted, 5 enrolled. In 2003, 6 degrees awarded. *Degree requirements:* For master's, final exam. *Entrance requirements:* For master's, minimum undergraduate GPA of 3.0 during previous 2 years or 2.75 overall. Additional exam requirements/recommendations for international students: Required—TOEFL, TWE. *Application deadline:* For fall admission, 3/1 priority date for domestic students, 3/1 priority date for international students; for spring admission, 12/15 for domestic students. Applications are processed on a rolling basis. Application fee: $35. Electronic applications accepted. Tuition, area resident: Full-time $9,346. International tuition: $19,924 full-time. Full-time tuition and fees vary according to course level and campus/location. *Financial support:* Fellowships, research assistantships, teaching assistantships, Federal Work-Study and tuition waivers (full) available. Financial award application deadline: 3/1. *Unit head:* Dr. Zevi Miller, Director of Graduate Studies, 513-529-5818, E-mail: math@muohio.edu.

Michigan State University, Graduate School, College of Natural Science, Department of Statistics and Probability, East Lansing, MI 48824. Offers applied statistics (MS); statistics (MA, MS, PhD). *Faculty:* 17 full-time (3 women). *Students:* 41 full-time (25 women), 10 part-time (5 women); includes 3 minority (2 African Americans, 1 Hispanic American), 43 international. Average age 29. 170 applicants, 22% accepted. In 2003, 27 master's, 1 doctorate awarded. *Degree requirements:* For master's, thesis optional; for doctorate, thesis/dissertation, written preliminary exam. *Entrance requirements:* For master's, GRE General Test, minimum GPA of 3.0 in mathematics and statistics courses, 3 letters of recommendation, course work in mathematics and statistics; for doctorate, GRE General Test, master's degree in statistics or equivalent, minimum GPA of 3.0 in mathematics, 3 letters of recommendation. Additional exam requirements/recommendations for international students: Required—TOEFL (minimum score 520 paper-based; 190 computer-based). *Application deadline:* For fall admission, 1/1 for domestic students. Application fee: $50. Electronic applications accepted. *Expenses:* Tuition, state resident: part-time $291 per hour. Tuition, nonresident: part-time $589 per hour. *Financial support:* In 2003–04, 6 fellowships with tuition reimbursements (averaging $4,106 per year), 8 research assistantships with tuition reimbursements (averaging $12,254 per year), 16 teaching assistantships with tuition reimbursements (averaging $12,354 per year) were awarded. Financial award applicants required to submit FAFSA. *Faculty research:* Stochastic processes, applied statistics, operational research, probability theory. Total annual research expenditures: $114,619. *Unit head:* Dr. Habib Salehi, Chairperson, 517-355-9589, Fax: 517-432-1405. *Application contact:* Dr. James Stapleton, Graduate Program Director, 517-355-9589, Fax: 517-432-1405, E-mail: sparks@stt.msu.edu.

Minnesota State University Mankato, College of Graduate Studies, College of Science, Engineering and Technology, Department of Mathematics and Statistics, Program in Statistics, Mankato, MN 56001. Offers MS. *Students:* 2 full-time (0 women), 2 part-time (both women). In 2003, 1 degree awarded. *Degree requirements:* For master's, one foreign language, thesis or alternative, comprehensive exam. *Entrance requirements:* For master's, GRE General Test, minimum GPA of 3.0 during previous 2 years. *Application deadline:* For fall admission, 7/9 for domestic students; for spring admission, 11/27 for domestic students. Applications are processed on a rolling basis. Application fee: $40. *Expenses:* Tuition, state resident: part-time $226 per credit hour. Tuition, nonresident: part-time $339 per credit hour. Tuition and fees vary according to reciprocity agreements. *Financial support:* Research assistantships with partial tuition reimbursements, teaching assistantships with partial tuition reimbursements available. Financial award application deadline: 3/15; financial award applicants required to submit FAFSA. *Application contact:* Joni Roberts, Admissions Coordinator, 507-389-5244, Fax: 507-389-5974, E-mail: grad@mankato.msus.edu.

Mississippi State University, College of Arts and Sciences, Department of Mathematics and Statistics, Mississippi State, MS 39762. Offers mathematical sciences (PhD); mathematics (MS); statistics (MS). Part-time programs available. *Faculty:* 35 full-time (16 women). *Students:* 30 full-time (15 women), 6 part-time (4 women); includes 1 minority (African American), 25 international. Average age 30. 46 applicants, 35% accepted, 9 enrolled. In 2003, 7 master's, 2 doctorates awarded. Terminal master's awarded for partial completion of doctoral program. *Degree requirements:* For master's, comprehensive oral or written exam, thesis optional; for doctorate, one foreign language, thesis/dissertation, comprehensive oral and written exam. *Entrance requirements:* For master's, minimum GPA of 2.75; for doctorate, GRE. Additional exam requirements/recommendations for international students: Required—TOEFL. *Application deadline:* For fall admission, 3/15 for domestic students; for spring admission, 11/1 for domestic students. Applications are processed on a rolling basis. Application fee: $25 for international students. *Expenses:* Tuition, state resident: full-time $3,874; part-time $215 per hour. Tuition, nonresident: full-time $8,780; part-time $488 per hour. International tuition: $9,105 full-time. Tuition and fees vary according to course load. *Financial support:* In 2003–04, 17 teaching assistantships with full tuition reimbursements (averaging $9,284 per year) were awarded; Federal Work-Study, institutionally sponsored loans, tuition waivers (partial), and unspecified assistantships also available. Financial award applicants required to submit FAFSA. *Faculty research:* Differential equations, algebra, numerical analysis, functional analysis, applied statistics. Total annual research expenditures: $107,993. *Unit head:* Dr. Michael Neuman, Interim Head and Professor, 662-325-3414, Fax: 662-325-0005, E-mail: office@math.msstate.edu. *Application contact:* Diane D. Wolfe, Director of Admissions, 662-325-2224, Fax: 662-325-7360, E-mail: admit@admissions.msstate.edu.

Montana State University–Bozeman, College of Graduate Studies, College of Letters and Science, Department of Mathematical Sciences, Bozeman, MT 59717. Offers mathematics (MS, PhD); statistics (MS, PhD). Part-time programs available. Postbaccalaureate distance learning degree programs offered (minimal on-campus study). *Faculty:* 31 full-time (8 women), 12 part-time/adjunct (6 women). *Students:* 9 full-time (5 women), 65 part-time (28 women); includes 2 minority (both Asian Americans or Pacific Islanders), 7 international. Average age 30. 31 applicants, 84% accepted, 21 enrolled. In 2003, 20 master's, 6 doctorates awarded. *Degree requirements:* For master's, thesis (for some programs), comprehensive exam, registration; for doctorate, thesis/dissertation, comprehensive exam, registration. *Entrance requirements:* For master's and doctorate, GRE General Test. Additional exam requirements/recommendations for international students: Required—TOEFL (minimum score 550 paper-based; 213 computer-based). *Application deadline:* For fall admission, 7/15 priority date for domestic students, 5/15 priority date for international students; for spring admission, 12/1 priority date for domestic students, 10/1 priority date for international students. Applications are processed on a roll-

Statistics

Montana State University–Bozeman (continued)

ing basis. Application fee: $50. Electronic applications accepted. *Expenses:* Tuition, state resident: full-time $3,907; part-time $163 per credit. Tuition, nonresident: full-time $12,383; part-time $516 per credit. Required fees: $890; $445 per term. Tuition and fees vary according to course load and program. *Financial support:* In 2003–04, 55 students received support, including 5 research assistantships with full tuition reimbursements available (averaging $14,000 per year), 47 teaching assistantships with full tuition reimbursements available (averaging $12,500 per year); career-related internships or fieldwork, scholarships/grants, health care benefits, tuition waivers (full), and unspecified assistantships also available. Support available to part-time students. Financial award application deadline: 3/1; financial award applicants required to submit FAFSA. *Faculty research:* Applied mathematics, dynamical systems, statistics, mathematics education, mathematical and computational biology. Total annual research expenditures: $402,126. *Unit head:* Dr. Kenneth Bowers, Head, 406-994-3604, Fax: 406-994-1789, E-mail: grad@math.montana.edu.

Montclair State University, The Graduate School, College of Science and Mathematics, Department of Computer Science, Upper Montclair, NJ 07043-1624. Offers applied mathematics (MS); applied statistics (MS); informatics (MS); object oriented computing (Certificate). Part-time and evening/weekend programs available. *Faculty:* 14 full-time (1 woman), 10 part-time/adjunct. *Students:* 18 full-time (4 women), 35 part-time (6 women); includes 8 minority (2 African Americans, 5 Asian Americans or Pacific Islanders, 1 Hispanic American), 18 international. 60 applicants, 33% accepted, 9 enrolled. In 2003, 51 degrees awarded. *Degree requirements:* For master's, comprehensive exam. *Entrance requirements:* For master's, GRE General Test, minimum GPA of 2.67, 15 undergraduate math credits, bachelors degree in computer science, math, science or engineering, 2 letters of recommendation. Additional exam requirements/recommendations for international students: Required—TOEFL (minimum score 550 paper-based; 213 computer-based). *Application deadline:* Applications are processed on a rolling basis. Application fee: $60. Electronic applications accepted. *Expenses:* Tuition, state resident: full-time $8,771; part-time $323 per credit. Tuition, nonresident: full-time $10,365; part-time $470 per credit. Required fees: $42 per credit. Tuition and fees vary according to degree level and program. *Financial support:* In 2003–04, 4 research assistantships with full tuition reimbursements (averaging $5,000 per year) were awarded; Federal Work-Study, scholarships/grants, and unspecified assistantships also available. Support available to part-time students. Financial award application deadline: 3/1; financial award applicants required to submit FAFSA. *Unit head:* Dr. Dorothy Deremer, Chairperson, 973-655-4166. *Application contact:* Dr. James Benham, Adviser, 973-655-3746, E-mail: benham@pegasus.montclair.edu.

Montclair State University, The Graduate School, College of Science and Mathematics, Department of Mathematics, Upper Montclair, NJ 07043-1624. Offers mathematics (MS), including computer science, mathematics education, pure and applied mathematics, statistics. Part-time and evening/weekend programs available. *Faculty:* 31 full-time (12 women), 20 part-time/adjunct. *Students:* 12 full-time (7 women), 46 part-time (28 women); includes 6 minority (4 African Americans, 2 Asian Americans or Pacific Islanders), 3 international. 40 applicants, 73% accepted, 19 enrolled. In 2003, 50 degrees awarded. *Degree requirements:* For master's, comprehensive exam. *Entrance requirements:* For master's, GRE General Test, minimum GPA of 2.67, 2 letters of recommendation. Additional exam requirements/ recommendations for international students: Required—TOEFL (minimum score 550 paper-based; 213 computer-based). *Application deadline:* Applications are processed on a rolling basis. Application fee: $60. *Expenses:* Tuition, state resident: full-time $8,771; part-time $323 per credit. Tuition, nonresident: full-time $10,365; part-time $470 per credit. Required fees: $42 per credit. Tuition and fees vary according to degree level and program. *Financial support:* In 2003–04, 9 research assistantships with full tuition reimbursements (averaging $5,000 per year) were awarded; Federal Work-Study, scholarships/grants, and unspecified assistantships also available. Support available to part-time students. Financial award application deadline: 3/1; financial award applicants required to submit FAFSA. *Unit head:* Dr. Helen Roberts, Chairperson, 973-655-5132. *Application contact:* Dr. Ted Williamson, Advisor, 973-655-5146, E-mail: williamsont@mail.montclair.edu.

Montclair State University, The Graduate School, College of Science and Mathematics, Department of Mathematics, Programs in Mathematics, Program in Statistics, Upper Montclair, NJ 07043-1624. Offers MS. Part-time and evening/weekend programs available. *Faculty:* 31 full-time (12 women), 20 part-time/adjunct. *Students:* 10 applicants, 70% accepted, 1 enrolled. In 2003, 4 degrees awarded. *Degree requirements:* For master's, comprehensive exam. *Entrance requirements:* For master's, GRE General Test, minimum GPA of 2.67, undergraduate major in computer science, mathematics, science, engineering, 18 undergraduate credits in mathematics, 2 letters of recommendation. Additional exam requirements/recommendations for international students: Required—TOEFL (minimum score 550 paper-based; 213 computer-based). *Application deadline:* Applications are processed on a rolling basis. Application fee: $60. Electronic applications accepted. *Expenses:* Tuition, state resident: full-time $8,771; part-time $323 per credit. Tuition, nonresident: full-time $10,365; part-time $470 per credit. Required fees: $42 per credit. Tuition and fees vary according to degree level and program. *Financial support:* In 2003–04, research assistantships with full tuition reimbursements (averaging $5,000 per year); Federal Work-Study, scholarships/grants, and unspecified assistantships also available. Support available to part-time students. Financial award application deadline: 3/1; financial award applicants required to submit FAFSA. *Application contact:* Dr. Ted Williamson, Advisor, 973-655-5146, E-mail: williamsont@mail.montclair.edu.

New Jersey Institute of Technology, Office of Graduate Studies, College of Science and Liberal Arts, Department of Mathematical Sciences, Program in Applied Statistics, Newark, NJ 07102. Offers MS. Part-time and evening/weekend programs available. *Students:* 8 full-time (4 women), 13 part-time (8 women); includes 12 minority (2 African Americans, 9 Asian Americans or Pacific Islanders, 1 Hispanic American), 2 international. Average age 30. 39 applicants, 74% accepted, 9 enrolled. In 2003, 4 degrees awarded. *Entrance requirements:* For master's, GRE General Test. *Application deadline:* For fall admission, 6/5 for domestic students; for spring admission, 10/15 for domestic students. Applications are processed on a rolling basis. Application fee: $50. Electronic applications accepted. *Expenses:* Tuition, state resident: full-time $9,620; part-time $520 per credit. Tuition, nonresident: full-time $13,542; part-time $715 per credit. Tuition and fees vary according to course load. *Financial support:* Fellowships with full and partial tuition reimbursements, research assistantships with full and partial tuition reimbursements, teaching assistantships with full and partial tuition reimbursements, career-related internships or fieldwork, Federal Work-Study, institutionally sponsored loans, and unspecified assistantships available. Financial award application deadline: 3/15. *Application contact:* Kathryn Kelly, Director of Admissions, 973-596-3300, Fax: 973-596-3461, E-mail: admissions@njit.edu.

New Mexico State University, Graduate School, College of Business Administration and Economics, Department of Economics and International Business, Las Cruces, NM 88003-8001. Offers economics (MA); experimental statistics (MS). Part-time programs available. *Faculty:* 17 full-time (2 women), 3 part-time/adjunct (1 woman). *Students:* 20 full-time (9 women), 5 part-time (4 women); includes 6 minority (2 African Americans, 4 Hispanic Americans), 10 international. Average age 28. 17 applicants, 88% accepted, 6 enrolled. In 2003, 12 degrees awarded. *Degree requirements:* For master's, thesis or alternative. *Entrance requirements:* For master's, minimum GPA of 3.0. Additional exam requirements/ recommendations for international students: Required—TOEFL. *Application deadline:* Applications are processed on a rolling basis. Application fee: $30 ($50 for international students). Electronic applications accepted. *Expenses:* Tuition, state resident: full-time $2,670; part-time $151 per credit. Tuition, nonresident: full-time $10,596; part-time $481 per credit. Required fees: $954. *Financial support:* In 2003–04, 2 research assistantships, 16 teaching assistantships were awarded. Career-related internships or fieldwork and Federal Work-Study also available. Support available to part-time students. Financial award application deadline: 3/1. *Faculty research:* Public utilities, environment, border demographics, linear models, biological sampling. *Unit head:* Dr. Michael Ellis, Head, 505-646-2113, Fax: 505-646-1915, E-mail: mellis@nmsu.edu. *Application contact:* Dr. Anthony Popp, Graduate Adviser, 505-646-5198, Fax: 505-646-1915, E-mail: apopp@nmsu.edu.

New York University, Leonard N. Stern School of Business, Department of Information Operations and Management Sciences, New York, NY 10006. Offers information sysetms (PhD); information systems (MBA); operations management (MBA, PhD); statistics (MBA, PhD). In 2003, 131 master's, 2 doctorates awarded. *Degree requirements:* For doctorate, thesis/dissertation. *Entrance requirements:* For master's and doctorate, GMAT. Additional exam requirements/recommendations for international students: Required—TOEFL. *Application deadline:* For fall admission, 3/15 for domestic students. Applications are processed on a rolling basis. Application fee: $150. Electronic applications accepted. *Expenses:* Tuition: Full-time $22,056; part-time $919 per credit. Required fees: $1,664; $49 per credit. Tuition and fees vary according to course load and program. *Financial support:* Fellowships with full tuition reimbursements, research assistantships, teaching assistantships with partial tuition reimbursements, career-related internships or fieldwork and scholarships/grants available. Financial award application deadline: 2/15; financial award applicants required to submit FAFSA. *Faculty research:* Knowledge management, economics of information, computer-supported groups and communities, financial information systems, data mining, business intelligence. Total annual research expenditures: $200,000. *Unit head:* Eitan Zemel, Deputy Chair, 212-998-0280, Fax: 212-995-4227. *Application contact:* Julia Minn, Assistant Dean, 212-998-0600, Fax: 212-995-4231, E-mail: sternmba@stern.nyu.edu.

North Carolina State University, Graduate School, College of Physical and Mathematical Sciences, Department of Statistics, Raleigh, NC 27695. Offers biomathematics (M Biomath, MS, PhD), including biomathematics, ecology (PhD); statistics (M Stat, MS, PhD). Part-time programs available. *Students:* 155 full-time (89 women), 13 part-time (8 women); includes 15 minority (6 African Americans, 7 Asian Americans or Pacific Islanders, 2 Hispanic Americans), 93 international. Average age 29. 327 applicants, 23% accepted. In 2003, 46 master's, 19 doctorates awarded. *Degree requirements:* For master's, thesis (for some programs), final oral exam, comprehensive exam; for doctorate, thesis/dissertation, final oral and written exams, written and oral preliminary exams. *Entrance requirements:* For master's and doctorate, GRE General Test. Additional exam requirements/recommendations for international students: Required—TOEFL. *Application deadline:* For fall admission, 6/25 for domestic students, 3/1 for international students; for spring admission, 11/25 for domestic students, 7/15 for international students. Applications are processed on a rolling basis. Application fee: $55 ($65 for international students). *Expenses:* Tuition, state resident: part-time $396 per hour. Tuition, nonresident: part-time $1,895 per hour. *Financial support:* In 2003–04, 2 fellowships with tuition reimbursements (averaging $5,552 per year), 60 research assistantships with tuition reimbursements (averaging $7,078 per year), 55 teaching assistantships with tuition reimbursements (averaging $6,581 per year) were awarded. Career-related internships or fieldwork, health care benefits, and tuition waivers (full) also available. Financial award application deadline: 3/1. *Faculty research:* Biostatistics; time series; spatial, inference, environmental, industrial, genetics applications; nonlinear models; DOE. Total annual research expenditures: $1.5 million. *Unit head:* Dr. Sastry G. Pantula, Head, 919-515-1949, Fax: 919-515-7591, E-mail: head@stat.ncsu.edu. *Application contact:* Dr. William Swallow, Director of Graduate Programs, 919-515-1916, Fax: 919-515-7591, E-mail: stat_dgp@stat.ncsu.edu.

North Dakota State University, The Graduate School, College of Science and Mathematics, Department of Statistics, Fargo, ND 58105. Offers applied statistics (MS); computer science and statistics (MS); statistics (PhD). *Degree requirements:* For master's and doctorate, thesis/ dissertation, comprehensive exam. *Entrance requirements:* Additional exam requirements/ recommendations for international students: Required—TOEFL. Tuition, nonresident: full-time $4,071. Required fees: $493. *Faculty research:* Nonparametric statistics, survival analysis, multivariate analysis, distribution theory, inference modeling, biostatistics.

Northern Arizona University, Graduate College, College of Arts and Sciences, Department of Mathematics, Flagstaff, AZ 86011. Offers mathematics (MAT, MS); statistics (MS). Part-time programs available. *Students:* 19 full-time (7 women), 4 part-time (1 woman); includes 3 minority (1 African American, 2 Asian Americans or Pacific Islanders). Average age 25. 19 applicants, 68% accepted. In 2003, 7 degrees awarded. *Degree requirements:* For master's, thesis optional. *Application deadline:* For fall admission, 3/15 for domestic students. Applications are processed on a rolling basis. Application fee: $45. *Expenses:* Tuition, state resident: full-time $5,103. Tuition, nonresident: full-time $12,623. *Financial support:* In 2003–04, 10 teaching assistantships were awarded; Federal Work-Study and tuition waivers (full and partial) also available. Financial award application deadline: 3/15. *Faculty research:* Topology, statistics, groups, ring theory, number theory. *Unit head:* Dr. Roy St. Laurent, Chair, 928-523-3481. *Application contact:* Dr. Brent Burch, Graduate Coordinator, 928-523-6875, E-mail: grad@math.nau.edu.

Northern Illinois University, Graduate School, College of Liberal Arts and Sciences, Department of Mathematical Sciences, Division of Statistics, De Kalb, IL 60115-2854. Offers MS. Part-time programs available. *Faculty:* 8 full-time (1 woman), 1 part-time/adjunct (0 women). *Students:* 17 full-time (7 women), 9 part-time (4 women); includes 2 minority (both Asian Americans or Pacific Islanders), 16 international. Average age 29. 28 applicants, 61% accepted, 9 enrolled. In 2003, 3 degrees awarded. *Degree requirements:* For master's, thesis optional. *Entrance requirements:* For master's, GRE General Test, minimum GPA of 2.75, course work in statistics, calculus, linear algebra. Additional exam requirements/recommendations for international students: Required—TOEFL (minimum score 550 paper-based; 213 computer-based). *Application deadline:* For fall admission, 6/1 for domestic students, 5/1 for international students; for spring admission, 11/1 for domestic students, 10/1 for international students. Applications are processed on a rolling basis. Application fee: $30. Electronic applications accepted. *Expenses:* Tuition, state resident: full-time $3,968; part-time $165 per credit hour. Tuition, nonresident: full-time $7,936; part-time $330 per credit hour. Required fees: $1,255; $52 per credit hour. *Financial support:* In 2003–04, 14 teaching assistantships with full tuition reimbursements were awarded; fellowships with full tuition reimbursements, research assistantships with full tuition reimbursements, career-related internships or fieldwork, Federal Work-Study, scholarships/grants, tuition waivers (full), and unspecified assistantships also available. Support available to part-time students. Financial award applicants required to submit FAFSA. *Unit head:* Dr. Sudhir Gupta, Director, Division of Statistics, 815-753-6773, Fax: 815-753-6776. *Application contact:* Dr. Alan Polansky, Director, Graduate Studies, 815-753-6864.

Northwestern University, The Graduate School, Judd A. and Marjorie Weinberg College of Arts and Sciences, Department of Statistics, Evanston, IL 60208. Offers MS, PhD. Admissions and degrees offered through The Graduate School. Part-time programs available. Terminal master's awarded for partial completion of doctoral program. *Degree requirements:* For master's, final exam; for doctorate, thesis/dissertation, preliminary exam, final exam. *Entrance requirements:* For master's and doctorate, GRE General Test. Additional exam requirements/ recommendations for international students: Required—TOEFL. *Faculty research:* Theoretical statistics, applied statistics, computational methods, statistical designs, complex models.

Oakland University, Graduate Study and Lifelong Learning, College of Arts and Sciences, Department of Mathematical Sciences, Program in Applied Statistics, Rochester, MI 48309-4401. Offers MS, PhD. Part-time and evening/weekend programs available. *Students:* 19 full-time (9 women), 17 part-time (5 women); includes 5 minority (1 African American, 4 Asian Americans or Pacific Islanders), 12 international. Average age 33. 17 applicants, 76% accepted. In 2003, 3 master's, 1 doctorate awarded. *Degree requirements:* For doctorate, thesis/ dissertation. *Entrance requirements:* For master's, minimum GPA of 3.0 for unconditional admission; for doctorate, GRE Subject Test, GRE General Test, minimum GPA of 3.0 for unconditional admission. Additional exam requirements/recommendations for international students: Required—TOEFL (minimum score 550 paper-based; 213 computer-based). *Application deadline:* For fall admission, 7/15 priority date for domestic students, 5/1 priority date for international students; for winter admission, 12/1 for domestic students; for spring admission, 3/15 for domestic students. Applications are processed on a rolling basis. Application fee: $30.

Electronic applications accepted. *Expenses:* Contact institution. *Financial support:* Career-related internships or fieldwork and tuition waivers (full) available. Financial award application deadline: 3/1; financial award applicants required to submit FAFSA. *Unit head:* Dr. Meir Shillor, Coordinator, Graduate Programs, 248-370-3439, Fax: 248-370-4184, E-mail: shillor@oakland.edu.

Oakland University, Graduate Study and Lifelong Learning, College of Arts and Sciences, Department of Mathematical Sciences, Program in Statistical Methods, Rochester, MI 48309-4401. Offers Certificate. *Students:* 3 full-time (1 woman), 3 part-time (1 woman); includes 2 minority (1 African American, 1 Asian American or Pacific Islander), 1 international. Average age 33. 3 applicants, 100% accepted. *Entrance requirements:* Additional exam requirements/recommendations for international students: Required—TOEFL (minimum score 550 paper-based; 213 computer-based). *Application deadline:* For fall admission, 7/15 priority date for domestic students, 5/1 priority date for international students; for winter admission, 12/1 for domestic students; for spring admission, 3/15 for domestic students. Application fee: $30. *Expenses:* Contact institution. *Financial support:* Federal Work-Study, institutionally sponsored loans, and tuition waivers (full) available. Financial award application deadline: 3/1; financial award applicants required to submit FAFSA. *Unit head:* Dr. Meir Shillor, Coordinator, Graduate Programs, 248-370-3439, Fax: 248-370-4184, E-mail: shillor@oakland.edu.

The Ohio State University, Graduate School, College of Mathematical and Physical Sciences, Department of Statistics, Columbus, OH 43210. Offers biostatistics (PhD); statistics (M Appl Stat, MS, PhD). *Faculty:* 29. *Students:* 82 full-time (43 women), 21 part-time (11 women); includes 3 minority (1 African American, 2 Asian Americans or Pacific Islanders), 64 international. 433 applicants, 21% accepted. In 2003, 40 master's, 11 doctorates awarded. *Degree requirements:* For master's, thesis optional; for doctorate, thesis/dissertation. *Entrance requirements:* For master's and doctorate, GRE General Test. Additional exam requirements/recommendations for international students: Required—TOEFL. *Application deadline:* For fall admission, 8/15 for domestic students. Applications are processed on a rolling basis. Application fee: $40 ($50 for international students). *Expenses:* Tuition, state resident: full-time $7,233. Tuition, nonresident: full-time $18,489. *Financial support:* Fellowships, research assistantships, teaching assistantships, Federal Work-Study and institutionally sponsored loans available. Support available to part-time students. *Unit head:* Dr. Douglas A. Wolfe, Chair, 614-292-0293, Fax: 614-292-2096, E-mail: wolfe.9@osu.edu. *Application contact:* Dr. Elizabeth A. Stasny, Graduate Studies Committee Chair, 614-292-0784, Fax: 614-292-2096, E-mail: stasny.1@osu.edu.

Oklahoma State University, Graduate College, College of Arts and Sciences, Department of Statistics, Stillwater, OK 74078. Offers MS, PhD. *Faculty:* 8 full-time (2 women), 1 (woman) part-time/adjunct. *Students:* 13 full-time (7 women), 12 part-time (9 women), 12 international. Average age 30. 27 applicants, 81% accepted. In 2003, 4 degrees awarded. *Degree requirements:* For doctorate, thesis/dissertation. *Entrance requirements:* Additional exam requirements/recommendations for international students: Required—TOEFL. *Application deadline:* For fall admission, 7/1 for domestic students. Applications are processed on a rolling basis. Application fee: $25 ($50 for international students). Electronic applications accepted. *Expenses:* Tuition, state resident: full-time $3,752; part-time $118 per credit hour. Tuition, nonresident: full-time $10,346; part-time $393 per credit hour. Tuition and fees vary according to course load. *Financial support:* In 2003–04, 17 teaching assistantships (averaging $13,889 per year) were awarded; research assistantships, Federal Work-Study and tuition waivers (partial) also available. Support available to part-time students. Financial award application deadline: 3/1. *Faculty research:* Linear models, sampling methods, ranking and selections procedures, categorical data, multiple comparisons. *Unit head:* Dr. William Warde, Head, 405-744-5684, E-mail: billw@okstate.edu.

Oregon State University, Graduate School, College of Science, Department of Statistics, Corvallis, OR 97331. Offers applied statistics (MA, MS, PhD); biometry (MA, MS, PhD); environmental statistics (MA, MS, PhD); mathematical statistics (MA, MS, PhD); operations research (MA, MAIS, MS); statistics (MA, MS, PhD). Part-time programs available. *Faculty:* 11 full-time (4 women), 1 part-time/adjunct (0 women). *Students:* 29 full-time (16 women), 9 part-time (3 women); includes 6 minority (4 Asian Americans or Pacific Islanders, 2 Hispanic Americans), 13 international. Average age 30. In 2003, 8 degrees awarded. *Degree requirements:* For master's, consulting experience; for doctorate, thesis/dissertation, consulting experience. *Entrance requirements:* For master's and doctorate, minimum GPA of 3.0 in last 90 hours. Additional exam requirements/recommendations for international students: Required—TOEFL. *Application deadline:* For fall admission, 2/15 for domestic students. Applications are processed on a rolling basis. Application fee: $50. *Expenses:* Tuition, state resident: full-time $8,139; part-time $301 per credit. Tuition, nonresident: full-time $14,376; part-time $532 per credit. Required fees: $1,227. *Financial support:* In 2003–04, 8 research assistantships, 19 teaching assistantships were awarded. Federal Work-Study and institutionally sponsored loans also available. Financial award application deadline: 2/15. *Faculty research:* Analysis of enumerative data, nonparametric statistics, asymptotics, experimental design, generalized regression models, linear model theory, reliability theory, survival analysis, wildlife and general survey methodology. *Unit head:* Dr. Robert T. Smythe, Chair, 541-737-3480, Fax: 541-737-3489, E-mail: symthe@stat.orst.edu. *Application contact:* Dr. Daniel W. Schafer, Director of Graduate Studies, 541-737-3366, Fax: 541-737-3489, E-mail: statoff@stat.orst.edu.

The Pennsylvania State University University Park Campus, Graduate School, Eberly College of Science, Department of Statistics, Program in Applied Statistics, State College, University Park, PA 16802-1503. Offers MAS. Postbaccalaureate distance learning degree programs offered (no on-campus study). *Students:* 10 full-time (7 women), 1 (woman) part-time; includes 1 minority (Asian American or Pacific Islander), 6 international. *Unit head:* Dr. Mosuk Chow, Admissions Chairman, 814-863-8128, E-mail: mxc18@psu.edu. *Application contact:* Jennifer Parkes, Information Contact, 814-865-1348, E-mail: jqp4@psu.edu.

The Pennsylvania State University University Park Campus, Graduate School, Eberly College of Science, Department of Statistics, Program in Statistics, State College, University Park, PA 16802-1503. Offers MA, MS, PhD. Postbaccalaureate distance learning degree programs offered (minimal on-campus study). *Students:* 50 full-time (25 women), 1 part-time; includes 3 minority (all Asian Americans or Pacific Islanders), 41 international. *Unit head:* Dr. Bing Li, Associate Professor of Statistics, 814-865-1952.

Princeton University, Graduate School, Department of Civil and Environmental Engineering, Princeton, NJ 08544-1019. Offers environmental engineering and water resources (PhD); mechanics, materials, and structures (M Eng, MSE, PhD); statistics and operations research (MSE, PhD); transportation systems (MSE, PhD). *Faculty:* 12 full-time (3 women), 8 part-time/adjunct (1 woman). *Students:* 34 full-time (17 women); includes 3 minority (1 African American, 1 Asian American or Pacific Islander, 1 Hispanic American), 15 international. 116 applicants, 23% accepted, 12 enrolled.Terminal master's awarded for partial completion of doctoral program. *Median time to degree:* Doctorate–4.62 years full-time. *Degree requirements:* For master's and doctorate, thesis/dissertation. *Entrance requirements:* For master's and doctorate, GRE General Test, GRE Subject Test. Additional exam requirements/recommendations for international students: Required—TOEFL (minimum score 600 paper-based; 250 computer-based). *Application deadline:* For fall admission, 12/31 for domestic students, 12/1 for international students. Application fee: $80 ($55 for international students). Electronic applications accepted. *Expenses:* Tuition: Full-time $29,910. Required fees: $810. *Financial support:* Fellowships with full tuition reimbursements, research assistantships with full tuition reimbursements, teaching assistantships with full tuition reimbursements, Federal Work-Study and institutionally sponsored loans available. Financial award application deadline: 1/2. *Unit head:* Prof. Jeane-Herve Prevost, Director of Graduate Studies, 609-258-5424, Fax: 609-258-1270, E-mail: prevost@princeton.edu. *Application contact:* Janice Yip, Director of Graduate Admissions, 609-258-3034, Fax: 609-258-6180, E-mail: gsadmit@princeton.edu.

Purdue University, Graduate School, School of Science, Department of Statistics, West Lafayette, IN 47907. Offers applied statistics (MS); statistics (PhD); statistics and computer science (MS); statistics/computational finance (MS); theoretical statistics (MS). *Degree requirements:* For doctorate, thesis/dissertation. *Entrance requirements:* For master's and doctorate, GRE General Test. Additional exam requirements/recommendations for international students: Required—TOEFL. Electronic applications accepted. *Faculty research:* Nonparametric models, computational finance, design of experiments, probability theory, bioinformatics.

See in-depth description on page 579.

Queen's University at Kingston, School of Graduate Studies and Research, Faculty of Arts and Sciences, Department of Mathematics and Statistics, Kingston, ON K7L 3N6, Canada. Offers mathematics (M Sc, M Sc Eng, PhD); statistics (M Sc, M Sc Eng, PhD). Part-time programs available. *Degree requirements:* For master's, thesis/dissertation; for doctorate, thesis/dissertation, comprehensive exam. *Entrance requirements:* Additional exam requirements/recommendations for international students: Required—TOEFL. *Faculty research:* Algebra, analysis, applied mathematics, statistics.

Rensselaer Polytechnic Institute, Graduate School, School of Engineering, Department of Decision Sciences and Engineering Systems, Program in Operations Research and Statistics, Troy, NY 12180-3590. Offers M Eng, MS, MBA/M Eng. Part-time programs available. *Faculty:* 17 full-time (1 woman), 2 part-time/adjunct (1 woman). *Students:* 6 full-time (1 woman); includes 1 minority (Asian American or Pacific Islander), 1 international. 20 applicants, 45% accepted, 5 enrolled. In 2003, 10 degrees awarded. *Degree requirements:* For master's, thesis (for some programs). *Entrance requirements:* For master's, GRE General Test. Additional exam requirements/recommendations for international students: Required—TOEFL (minimum score 570 paper-based). *Application deadline:* For fall admission, 1/15 for domestic students. Applications are processed on a rolling basis. Application fee: $45. Electronic applications accepted. *Expenses:* Tuition: Full-time $27,700; part-time $1,320 per credit. Required fees: $1,470. *Financial support:* Fellowships with full tuition reimbursements, research assistantships with full tuition reimbursements, teaching assistantships with full tuition reimbursements, career-related internships or fieldwork and institutionally sponsored loans available. Financial award application deadline: 1/15. *Faculty research:* Manufacturing, MIS, statistical consulting, education services, production, logistics, inventory. Total annual research expenditures:$797,000. *Application contact:* Lee Vilardi, Graduate Coordinator, 518-276-6681, Fax: 518-276-8227, E-mail: dsesgr@rpi.edu.

Rice University, Graduate Programs, George R. Brown School of Engineering, Department of Statistics, Houston, TX 77251-1892. Offers biostatistics (PhD); computational finance (PhD); statistics (M Stat, MA, PhD). *Faculty:* 9 full-time (2 women), 17 part-time/adjunct (1 woman). *Students:* 44 full-time (17 women), 1 (woman) part-time; includes 12 minority (5 African Americans, 2 Asian Americans or Pacific Islanders, 5 Hispanic Americans), 12 international. Average age 28. 130 applicants, 10% accepted, 9 enrolled. In 2003, 4 master's, 1 doctorate awarded. Terminal master's awarded for partial completion of doctoral program. *Median time to degree:* Of those who began their doctoral program in fall 1995, 90% received their degree in 8 years or less. *Degree requirements:* For master's, thesis/dissertation; for doctorate, thesis/dissertation, comprehensive exam. *Entrance requirements:* For master's and doctorate, GRE General Test, GRE Subject Test, minimum GPA of 3.0. Additional exam requirements/recommendations for international students: Required—TOEFL (minimum score 630 paper-based; 250 computer-based). *Application deadline:* For fall admission, 2/1 priority date for domestic students, 2/1 priority date for international students; for spring admission, 11/1 for domestic students, 11/1 for international students. Applications are processed on a rolling basis. Application fee: $35. Electronic applications accepted. *Expenses:* Tuition: Full-time $19,700; part-time $1,096 per hour. *Financial support:* In 2003–04, 15 fellowships with tuition reimbursements (averaging $20,000 per year), 15 research assistantships with tuition reimbursements (averaging $20,000 per year), 5 teaching assistantships with tuition reimbursements (averaging $20,000 per year) were awarded. Career-related internships or fieldwork, institutionally sponsored loans, scholarships/grants, traineeships, health care benefits, tuition waivers (full), and unspecified assistantships also available. Financial award application deadline: 1/15. *Faculty research:* Statistical genetics, non parametric function estimation, computational statistics and visualization, stochastic processes. Total annual research expenditures: $800,000. *Unit head:* Dr. Katherine B. Ensor, Chair, 713-527-6032, Fax: 713-348-5476, E-mail: kathy@rice.edu. *Application contact:* Leticia Gonzales, Recruiting Assistant, 713-348-6032, Fax: 713-348-5476, E-mail: lgonzale@rice.edu.

Rochester Institute of Technology, Graduate Enrollment Services, College of Engineering, Center of Quality and Applied Statistics, Rochester, NY 14623-5603. Offers applied statistics (MS); statistical quality (AC). Part-time and evening/weekend programs available. *Students:* 9 full-time (5 women), 59 part-time (18 women); includes 7 minority (3 African Americans, 2 Asian Americans or Pacific Islanders, 2 Hispanic Americans), 5 international. 48 applicants, 63% accepted, 19 enrolled. In 2003, 9 master's, 5 other advanced degrees awarded. *Degree requirements:* For master's, oral exam. *Entrance requirements:* For master's, previous course work in calculus, minimum GPA of 3.0. Additional exam requirements/recommendations for international students: Required—TOEFL. *Application deadline:* For fall admission, 3/1 for domestic students. Applications are processed on a rolling basis. Application fee: $50. *Expenses:* Tuition: Full-time $22,965; part-time $644 per hour. Required fees: $174; $29 per quarter. *Financial support:* Research assistantships available. *Unit head:* Dr. Donald Baker, Director, 585-475-5070, E-mail: ddbcqa@rit.edu.

Rutgers, The State University of New Jersey, New Brunswick/Piscataway, Graduate School, Program in Statistics, New Brunswick, NJ 08901-1281. Offers quality and productivity management (MS); statistics (MS, PhD), including biostatistics (PhD), data mining (PhD). Part-time programs available. *Faculty:* 20 full-time (2 women). *Students:* 56 full-time (35 women), 90 part-time (56 women); includes 39 minority (36 Asian Americans or Pacific Islanders, 3 Hispanic Americans), 62 international. Average age 30. 253 applicants, 11% accepted, 18 enrolled. In 2003, 22 master's, 3 doctorates awarded. Terminal master's awarded for partial completion of doctoral program. *Degree requirements:* For master's, essay, exam, non-thesis essay paper; for doctorate, one foreign language, thesis/dissertation, qualifying oral and written exams. *Entrance requirements:* For master's, GRE General Test; for doctorate, GRE General Test, GRE Subject Test (recommended). Additional exam requirements/recommendations for international students: Required—TOEFL (minimum score 550 paper-based; 213 computer-based). *Application deadline:* For fall admission, 5/1 for domestic students; for spring admission, 12/1 priority date for domestic students. Applications are processed on a rolling basis. Application fee: $50. Electronic applications accepted. *Expenses:* Tuition, state resident: full-time $10,030. Tuition, nonresident: full-time $14,202. *Financial support:* In 2003–04, 16 students received support, including 4 fellowships with full tuition reimbursements available (averaging $16,000 per year), research assistantships with full tuition reimbursements available (averaging $14,500 per year), 11 teaching assistantships with full tuition reimbursements available (averaging $14,300 per year); career-related internships or fieldwork, Federal Work-Study, institutionally sponsored loans, scholarships/grants, health care benefits, unspecified assistantships, and grant/tuition remission also available. Financial award application deadline: 3/1; financial award applicants required to submit FAFSA. *Faculty research:* Probability, decision theory, linear models, multivariate statistics, statistical computing. *Unit head:* Dr. Cuh-Hui Zhang, Director, 732-445-2693, Fax: 732-445-3428, E-mail: czhang@stat.rutgers.edu. *Application contact:* Angela T. Klein, Department Secretary, 732-445-2693, Fax: 732-445-3428, E-mail: aklein@stat.rutgers.edu.

St. John's University, St. John's College of Liberal Arts and Sciences, Department of Mathematics and Computer Science, Jamaica, NY 11439. Offers algebra (MA); analysis (MA); applied mathematics (MA); computer science (MA); geometry-topology (MA); logic and foundations (MA); probability and statistics (MA). Part-time and evening/weekend programs available. *Faculty:* 20 full-time (2 women), 18 part-time/adjunct (8 women). *Students:* 4 full-time (3 women), 3 part-time (2 woman); includes 2 minority (1 African American, 1 Hispanic American). 16 applicants, 63% accepted, 5 enrolled. In 2003, 4 degrees awarded. *Degree requirements:*

Statistics

St. John's University (continued)

For master's, thesis optional. *Entrance requirements:* For master's, minimum GPA of 3.0. Additional exam requirements/recommendations for international students: Required—TOEFL (minimum score 500 paper-based). *Application deadline:* Applications are processed on a rolling basis. Application fee: $40. Electronic applications accepted. *Expenses:* Tuition: Full-time $15,840; part-time $8,320 per year. Tuition and fees vary according to course load, degree level, program and student level. *Financial support:* Research assistantships, scholarships/grants available. Support available to part-time students. Financial award application deadline: 3/1; financial award applicants required to submit FAFSA. *Faculty research:* Development of a computerized metabolic map. *Unit head:* Dr. Charles Traina, Chair, 718-990-6166, E-mail: trainac@stjohns.edu. *Application contact:* Matthew Whelan, Director, Office of Admission, 718-990-2000, Fax: 718-990-2096, E-mail: admissions@stjohns.edu.

Sam Houston State University, College of Arts and Sciences, Department of Mathematics and Statistics, Huntsville, TX 77341. Offers mathematics (MA, MS); statistics (MS). Part-time programs available. *Students:* 8 full-time (4 women), 19 part-time (12 women); includes 2 minority (both Hispanic Americans), 5 international. In 2003, 8 degrees awarded. *Entrance requirements:* For master's, GRE General Test. Additional exam requirements/recommendations for international students: Required—TOEFL. *Application deadline:* For fall admission, 8/1 for domestic students; for spring admission, 12/1 for domestic students. Applications are processed on a rolling basis. Application fee: $35. *Expenses:* Tuition, state resident: part-time $243 per semester hour. Tuition, nonresident: part-time $479 per semester hour. *Financial support:* Teaching assistantships, institutionally sponsored loans available. Support available to part-time students. Financial award application deadline: 5/31; financial award applicants required to submit FAFSA. *Unit head:* Dr. Jaimie Hebert, Chair, 936-294-1563, Fax: 936-294-1882, E-mail: mth_jlh@shsu.edu. *Application contact:* Anita Shipman, Advisor, 936-294-3962.

San Diego State University, Graduate and Research Affairs, College of Sciences, Department of Mathematical Sciences, Program in Statistics, San Diego, CA 92182. Offers MS. Part-time programs available. *Students:* 25 full-time (17 women), 29 part-time (10 women); includes 11 minority (9 Asian Americans or Pacific Islanders, 2 Hispanic Americans), 15 international. Average age 30. 53 applicants, 85% accepted, 7 enrolled. In 2003, 9 degrees awarded. *Degree requirements:* For master's, comprehensive exam. *Entrance requirements:* For master's, GRE General Test. Additional exam requirements/recommendations for international students: Required—TOEFL. *Application deadline:* For fall admission, 5/1 for domestic students, 5/1 for international students; for spring admission, 11/1 for domestic students, 10/1 for international students. Applications are processed on a rolling basis. Application fee: $55. Electronic applications accepted. Tuition, nonresident: part-time $282 per unit. Required fees: $1,349; $875 per year. *Financial support:* Applicants required to submit FAFSA. *Unit head:* K. J. Lui, Graduate Advisor, 619-594-7239, Fax: 619-594-6746, E-mail: kil@rohan.sdsu.edu.

Simon Fraser University, Graduate Studies, Faculty of Science, Department of Mathematics, Department of Statistics and Actuarial Science, Burnaby, BC V5A 1S6, Canada. Offers M Sc, PhD. Part-time programs available. *Degree requirements:* For master's, thesis, participation in consulting; for doctorate, thesis/dissertation, comprehensive exam. *Entrance requirements:* For master's, minimum GPA of 3.0; for doctorate, minimum GPA of 3.5. Additional exam requirements/recommendations for international students: Required—TOEFL. *Faculty research:* Biostatistics, experimental design, envirometrics, statistical computing, statistical theory.

Southern Illinois University Carbondale, Graduate School, College of Science, Department of Mathematics, Carbondale, IL 62901-4701. Offers mathematics (MA, MS, PhD); statistics (MS). Part-time programs available. *Faculty:* 32 full-time (2 women), 1 part-time/adjunct (0 women). *Students:* 24 full-time (8 women), 15 part-time (5 women); includes 2 minority (both African Americans), 23 international. Average age 26. 48 applicants, 33% accepted, 8 enrolled. In 2003, 13 master's, 3 doctorates awarded. *Degree requirements:* For master's, thesis; for doctorate, 2 foreign languages, thesis/dissertation. *Entrance requirements:* For master's, minimum GPA of 2.7; for doctorate, minimum GPA of 3.25. Additional exam requirements/recommendations for international students: Required—TOEFL. *Application deadline:* Applications are processed on a rolling basis. Application fee: $0. *Expenses:* Tuition, state resident: part-time $478 per hour. Tuition, nonresident: part-time $657 per hour. *Financial support:* In 2003–04, 28 students received support, including 24 teaching assistantships with full tuition reimbursements available; fellowships with full tuition reimbursements available, research assistantships with full tuition reimbursements available, Federal Work-Study, institutionally sponsored loans, and tuition waivers (full) also available. Support available to part-time students. *Faculty research:* Differential equations, combinatorics, probability, algebra, numerical analysis. *Unit head:* Andrew Earnest, Chairperson, 618-453-6522, Fax: 618-453-5300, E-mail: chairman@math.siu.edu. *Application contact:* William T. Patula, Director of Graduate Studies, 618-453-5302, Fax: 618-453-5300, E-mail: wpatula@math.siu.edu.

See in-depth description on page 581.

Southern Illinois University Edwardsville, Graduate Studies and Research, College of Arts and Sciences, Department of Mathematics and Statistics, Edwardsville, IL 62026-0001. Offers MS. Part-time programs available. *Degree requirements:* For master's, thesis or alternative, final exam. *Entrance requirements:* For master's, undergraduate major in related area, programming language, minimum GPA of 2.7. Additional exam requirements/recommendations for international students: Required—TOEFL.

Southern Methodist University, Dedman College, Department of Statistical Science, Dallas, TX 75275. Offers MS, PhD. Part-time programs available. *Faculty:* 10 full-time (4 women). *Students:* 18 full-time (9 women), 7 part-time (3 women); includes 2 minority (both Asian Americans or Pacific Islanders), 19 international. Average age 31. 48 applicants, 75% accepted. In 2003, 3 master's, 6 doctorates awarded. *Degree requirements:* For master's and doctorate, thesis/dissertation, oral and written exams. *Entrance requirements:* For master's, GRE General Test, 12 hours in advanced math courses; for doctorate, GRE General Test, minimum GPA of 3.0. Additional exam requirements/recommendations for international students: Required—TOEFL. *Application deadline:* For fall admission, 6/30 for domestic students; for spring admission, 11/30 priority date for domestic students. Applications are processed on a rolling basis. Application fee: $60. Electronic applications accepted. *Expenses:* Tuition: Full-time $11,362; part-time $874 per credit. Required fees: $112 per credit. Tuition and fees vary according to course load and program. *Financial support:* In 2003–04, 3 research assistantships with full tuition reimbursements (averaging $15,000 per year), 18 teaching assistantships with full tuition reimbursements (averaging $13,500 per year) were awarded. Financial award application deadline: 4/30; financial award applicants required to submit FAFSA. *Faculty research:* Regression, time series, linear models sampling, nonparametrics. Total annual research expenditures: $185,000. *Unit head:* Richard F. Gunst, Chair, 214-768-2441, Fax: 214-768-4035, E-mail: rgunst@mail.smu.edu. *Application contact:* Wayne Woodward, Graduate Advisor, 214-768-2457, Fax: 214-768-4035, E-mail: waynew@mail.smu.edu.

Stanford University, School of Humanities and Sciences, Department of Statistics, Stanford, CA 94305-9991. Offers MS, PhD. *Faculty:* 14 full-time (0 women). *Students:* 83 full-time (29 women), 10 part-time (4 women); includes 8 minority (6 Asian Americans or Pacific Islanders, 2 Hispanic Americans), 59 international. Average age 27. 91 applicants, 32% accepted. In 2003, 31 master's, 13 doctorates awarded. Terminal master's awarded for partial completion of doctoral program. *Degree requirements:* For doctorate, thesis/dissertation, oral exam, qualifying exams. *Entrance requirements:* For master's, GRE General Test; for doctorate, GRE General Test, GRE Subject Test. Additional exam requirements/recommendations for international students: Required—TOEFL. *Application deadline:* For fall admission, 1/5 for domestic students. Application fee: $65 ($80 for international students). Electronic applications accepted. *Expenses:* Tuition: Full-time $28,563. *Unit head:* David O. Siegmund, Chair, 650-723-2620, Fax: 650-725-8977, E-mail: dos@stat.stanford.edu. *Application contact:* Graduate Administrator, 650-723-2625, Fax: 650-725-8977.

State University of New York at Binghamton, Graduate School, School of Arts and Sciences, Department of Mathematical Sciences, Binghamton, NY 13902-6000. Offers computer science (MA, PhD); probability and statistics (MA, PhD). Part-time programs available. Terminal master's awarded for partial completion of doctoral program. *Degree requirements:* For master's, thesis or alternative; for doctorate, 2 foreign languages, thesis/dissertation. *Entrance requirements:* For master's and doctorate, GRE General Test, GRE Subject Test. Additional exam requirements/recommendations for international students: Required—TOEFL. Electronic applications accepted.

Stephen F. Austin State University, Graduate School, College of Sciences and Mathematics, Department of Mathematics and Statistics, Nacogdoches, TX 75962. Offers mathematics (MS); mathematics education (MS); statistics (MS). *Faculty:* 20 full-time (5 women). *Students:* 14 full-time (10 women), 50 part-time (41 women); includes 7 minority (5 African Americans, 2 Hispanic Americans), 2 international. 42 applicants, 88% accepted. In 2003, 4 degrees awarded. *Degree requirements:* For master's, thesis optional. *Entrance requirements:* For master's, GRE General Test, minimum GPA of 2.8 in last 60 hours, 2.5 overall. Additional exam requirements/recommendations for international students: Required—TOEFL. *Application deadline:* For fall admission, 8/1 for domestic students; for spring admission, 12/15 for domestic students. Applications are processed on a rolling basis. Application fee: $0 ($50 for international students). *Expenses:* Tuition, state resident: part-time $46 per hour. Tuition, nonresident: part-time $282 per hour. Required fees: $71 per hour. Tuition and fees vary according to reciprocity agreements. *Financial support:* In 2003–04, 8 teaching assistantships (averaging $10,000 per year) were awarded; Federal Work-Study, health care benefits, and unspecified assistantships also available. Financial award application deadline: 3/1. *Faculty research:* Kernel type estimators, fractal mappings, spline curve fitting, robust regression continua theory. *Unit head:* Dr. Jasper Adams, Chair, 936-468-3805.

Stevens Institute of Technology, Graduate School, School of Applied Sciences and Liberal Arts, Department of Mathematical Sciences, Program in Applied Statistics, Hoboken, NJ 07030. Offers MS, Certificate. *Degree requirements:* For master's, thesis optional. *Entrance requirements:* For master's, GRE. Additional exam requirements/recommendations for international students: Required—TOEFL. Electronic applications accepted.

Stony Brook University, State University of New York, Graduate School, College of Engineering and Applied Sciences, Department of Applied Mathematics and Statistics, Stony Brook, NY 11794. Offers MS, PhD. *Faculty:* 21 full-time (3 women), 1 part-time/adjunct (0 women). *Students:* 135 full-time (67 women), 19 part-time (5 women); includes 25 minority (5 African Americans, 15 Asian Americans or Pacific Islanders, 5 Hispanic Americans), 88 international. 219 applicants, 30% accepted. In 2003, 35 master's, 14 doctorates awarded. *Degree requirements:* For master's, thesis or alternative; for doctorate, one foreign language, thesis/dissertation, comprehensive exam. *Entrance requirements:* For master's and doctorate, GRE General Test. Additional exam requirements/recommendations for international students: Required—TOEFL. *Application deadline:* For fall admission, 1/15 for domestic students. Application fee: $50. *Expenses:* Tuition, state resident: full-time $6,900; part-time $288 per credit hour. Tuition, nonresident: full-time $10,500; part-time $438 per credit hour. Required fees: $22. *Financial support:* In 2003–04, 12 fellowships, 35 research assistantships, 31 teaching assistantships were awarded. *Faculty research:* Biostatistics, combinatorial analysis, differential equations, modeling. Total annual research expenditures: $3 million. *Unit head:* Dr. J. Glimm, Chairman, 631-632-8360. *Application contact:* Dr. Woo Jong Kim, Director, 631-632-8360, Fax: 631-632-8490, E-mail: wjkim@ccmail.sunysb.edu.

See in-depth description on page 585.

Syracuse University, Graduate School, College of Arts and Sciences, Program in Applied Statistics, Syracuse, NY 13244-0003. Offers MS. Part-time programs available. *Faculty:* 1 full-time (0 women), 1 part-time/adjunct (0 women). *Students:* 3 full-time (all women); includes 1 minority (Asian American or Pacific Islander), 1 international. 18 applicants, 28% accepted, 3 enrolled. *Entrance requirements:* For master's, GRE. Additional exam requirements/recommendations for international students: Required—TOEFL. *Application deadline:* Applications are processed on a rolling basis. Application fee: $65. *Expenses:* Tuition: Full-time $13,356; part-time $742 per credit. Required fees: $482. *Financial support:* Fellowships with full tuition reimbursements, teaching assistantships with full tuition reimbursements, tuition waivers available. *Unit head:* Dr. Pinyuen Chen, Director, Program on Applied Statistics, 315-443-1577, Fax: 315-443-1475, E-mail: pinchen@syr.edu.

Temple University, Graduate School, Fox School of Business and Management, Doctoral Programs in Business, Philadelphia, PA 19122-6096. Offers accounting (PhD); economics (PhD); finance (PhD); general and strategic management (PhD); healthcare management (PhD); human resource administration (PhD); international business administration (PhD); management information systems (PhD); management science/operations research (PhD); marketing (PhD); risk, insurance, and health-care management (PhD); statistics (PhD); tourism (PhD). *Accreditation:* AACSB. *Students:* 151 full-time (74 women); includes 22 minority (8 African Americans, 1 American Indian/Alaska Native, 12 Asian Americans or Pacific Islanders, 1 Hispanic American), 80 international. Average age 35. 291 applicants, 38% accepted. In 2003, 17 degrees awarded. *Entrance requirements:* For doctorate, GRE General Test, minimum GPA of 3.0, master's degree. Additional exam requirements/recommendations for international students: Required—TOEFL. *Application deadline:* For fall admission, 1/15 for domestic students, 1/15 for international students. Applications are processed on a rolling basis. Application fee: $40. *Unit head:* Natale Butto, Director of Graduate Admissions, 215-204-7678, Fax: 215-204-8300, E-mail: butto@sbm.temple.edu.

Temple University, Graduate School, Fox School of Business and Management, Masters Programs in Business, MBA Programs, Philadelphia, PA 19122-6096. Offers accounting (MBA); business administration (EMBA, MBA); e-business (MBA); economics (MBA); finance (MBA); general and strategic management (MBA); healthcare management (MBA); human resource administration (MBA); international business (IMBA); management information systems (MBA); management science/operations management (MBA); marketing (MBA); risk management and insurance (MBA); statistics (MBA). EMBA offered in Philadelphia, PA and Tokyo, Japan. *Accreditation:* AACSB. *Students:* 255 full-time (70 women), 458 part-time (173 women); includes 79 minority (32 African Americans, 2 American Indian/Alaska Native, 38 Asian Americans or Pacific Islanders, 7 Hispanic Americans), 117 international. Average age 31. 458 applicants, 55% accepted. In 2003, 344 degrees awarded. *Median time to degree:* Master's–2 years full-time, 3 years part-time. *Entrance requirements:* For master's, GMAT, minimum undergraduate GPA of 3.0. Additional exam requirements/recommendations for international students: Required—TOEFL. *Application deadline:* For fall admission, 4/15 for domestic students, 1/15 for international students; for spring admission, 9/30 for domestic students, 9/1 for international students. Application fee: $40. *Application contact:* Natale Butto, Director of Graduate Admissions, 215-204-7678, Fax: 215-204-8300, E-mail: butto@sbm.temple.edu.

Temple University, Graduate School, Fox School of Business and Management, Masters Programs in Business, MS Programs, Philadelphia, PA 19122-6096. Offers accounting and financial management (MS); actuarial science (MS); e-business (MS); finance (MS); healthcare financial management (MS); human resource administration (MS); management information systems (MS); management science/operations management (MS); marketing (MS); statistics (MS). *Students:* 59 full-time (26 women), 82 part-time (39 women); includes 18 minority (6 African Americans, 12 Asian Americans or Pacific Islanders), 62 international. Average age 31. 260 applicants, 65% accepted. In 2003, 61 degrees awarded. *Entrance requirements:* For master's, GRE General Test, minimum undergraduate GPA of 3.0. Additional exam requirements/recommendations for international students: Required—TOEFL. *Application deadline:* For fall admission, 4/15 for domestic students, 1/15 for international students; for spring admission, 9/30 for domestic students, 9/1 for international students. Application fee: $40. *Application contact:* Natale Butto, Director of Graduate Admissions, 215-204-7678, Fax: 215-204-8300, E-mail: butto@sbm.temple.edu.

Texas A&M University, College of Science, Department of Statistics, College Station, TX 77843. Offers MS, PhD. Part-time programs available. *Faculty:* 20 full-time (3 women). *Students:* 69 full-time (36 women), 12 part-time (8 women); includes 4 minority (3 Asian Americans or Pacific Islanders, 1 Hispanic American), 53 international. Average age 29. 406 applicants, 5% accepted, 18 enrolled. In 2003, 16 master's, 6 doctorates awarded. Terminal master's awarded for partial completion of doctoral program. *Degree requirements:* For doctorate, thesis/dissertation. *Entrance requirements:* For master's and doctorate, GRE General Test. Additional exam requirements/recommendations for international students: Required—TOEFL. *Application deadline:* For fall admission, 3/1 for domestic students; for spring admission, 8/1 for domestic students. Applications are processed on a rolling basis. Application fee: $50 ($75 for international students). *Expenses:* Tuition, state resident: full-time $3,420. Tuition, nonresident: full-time $9,084. Required fees: $1,861. *Financial support:* Fellowships, research assistantships, teaching assistantships, career-related internships or fieldwork available. Financial award application deadline: 3/1. *Faculty research:* Time series, chemometrics, biometrics, smoothing, linear models. *Unit head:* Dr. Michael T. Longnecker, Head, 979-845-3141, Fax: 979-845-3144. *Application contact:* P. Fred Dahm, Graduate Adviser, 800-826-8009, Fax: 979-845-3144, E-mail: fdahm@stat.tamu.edu.

Tulane University, Graduate School, Department of Mathematics, New Orleans, LA 70118-5669. Offers applied mathematics (MS); mathematics (MS, PhD); statistics (MS). *Faculty:* 24 full-time. *Students:* 29 full-time (15 women), 1 part-time; includes 7 minority (2 African Americans, 2 Asian Americans or Pacific Islanders, 3 Hispanic Americans), 8 international. 68 applicants, 26% accepted, 9 enrolled. In 2003, 5 master's, 2 doctorates awarded. *Degree requirements:* For master's, thesis (for some programs); for doctorate, thesis/dissertation. *Entrance requirements:* For master's, GRE General Test, minimum B average in undergraduate course work; for doctorate, GRE General Test. Additional exam requirements/recommendations for international students: Required—TOEFL; Recommended—TSE. *Application deadline:* For fall admission, 2/1 for domestic students, 2/1 for international students. Application fee: $45. *Financial support:* Fellowships with full tuition reimbursements, research assistantships with full tuition reimbursements, teaching assistantships with full tuition reimbursements, career-related internships or fieldwork, Federal Work-Study, and institutionally sponsored loans available. Financial award application deadline: 2/1. *Unit head:* Dr. Morris Kalka, Chair, 504-865-5727. *Application contact:* Dr. Ricardo Cortez, Graduate Adviser, 504-865-5727.

Université de Montréal, Faculty of Graduate Studies, Faculty of Arts and Sciences, Department of Mathematics and Statistics, Montréal, QC H3C 3J7, Canada. Offers mathematics (M Sc, PhD); statistics (M Sc, PhD). *Faculty:* 33 full-time (5 women), 15 part-time/adjunct (1 woman). *Students:* 92 full-time (30 women), 1 part-time. 73 applicants, 30% accepted, 19 enrolled. In 2003, 21 master's, 3 doctorates awarded. *Degree requirements:* For master's, thesis; for doctorate, thesis/dissertation, general exam. *Entrance requirements:* For master's and doctorate, proficiency in French. *Application deadline:* For fall and spring admission, 2/1; for winter admission, 11/1 for domestic students. Application fee: $30. Electronic applications accepted. *Expenses:* Tuition, state resident: full-time $834. Tuition, nonresident: full-time $1,253. International tuition: $3,900 full-time. Tuition and fees vary according to program. *Financial support:* Fellowships, research assistantships, teaching assistantships, monitorships available. Financial award application deadline: 4/1. *Faculty research:* Pure and applied mathematics, actuarial mathematics. *Unit head:* Yvan St-Aubin, Chair, 514-343-6710, Fax: 514-343-5700. *Application contact:* Liliane Badier, Student Files Management Technician, 514-343-6111 Ext. 1695, Fax: 514-343-5700.

Université Laval, Faculty of Sciences and Engineering, Department of Mathematics and Statistics, Program in Statistics, Québec, QC G1K 7P4, Canada. Offers M Sc. *Degree requirements:* For master's, thesis (for some programs). *Entrance requirements:* For master's, knowledge of French and English. Electronic applications accepted.

University at Albany, State University of New York, College of Arts and Sciences, Department of Mathematics and Statistics, Albany, NY 12222-0001. Offers mathematics (PhD); secondary teaching (MA); statistics (MA). Evening/weekend programs available. *Students:* 34 full-time (11 women), 9 part-time (3 women). Average age 32. 37 applicants, 43% accepted, 12 enrolled. In 2003, 7 master's, 1 doctorate awarded. *Degree requirements:* For doctorate, one foreign language, thesis/dissertation. *Entrance requirements:* For doctorate, GRE General Test. Additional exam requirements/recommendations for international students: Required—TOEFL (minimum score 550 paper-based; 213 computer-based). *Application deadline:* For fall admission, 8/1 for domestic students, 5/1 for international students; for spring admission, 11/1 for domestic students, 11/1 for international students. Applications are processed on a rolling basis. Application fee: $50. Electronic applications accepted. *Expenses:* Tuition, state resident: part-time $288 per credit. Tuition, nonresident: part-time $438 per credit. Required fees: $495 per semester. *Financial support:* Fellowships, research assistantships, teaching assistantships, minority assistantships available. Financial award application deadline: 3/15. *Unit head:* Timothy Lance, Chair, 518-442-4602.

University at Albany, State University of New York, School of Education, Department of Educational and Counseling Psychology, Albany, NY 12222-0001. Offers counseling psychology (MS, PhD, CAS); educational psychology (Ed D); educational psychology and statistics (MS); measurements and evaluation (Ed D); rehabilitation counseling (MS), including counseling psychology; school counselor (CAS); school psychology (Psy D, CAS); special education (MS); statistics and research design (Ed D). *Accreditation:* APA (one or more programs are accredited). Evening/weekend programs available. *Students:* 187 full-time (151 women), 100 part-time (74 women). Average age 30. 246 applicants, 29% accepted, 52 enrolled. In 2003, 70 master's, 23 doctorates, 27 other advanced degrees awarded. *Degree requirements:* For doctorate, thesis/dissertation. *Entrance requirements:* For doctorate, GRE General Test. Additional exam requirements/recommendations for international students: Required—TOEFL (minimum score 550 paper-based; 213 computer-based). Application fee: $50. Electronic applications accepted. *Expenses:* Tuition, state resident: part-time $288 per credit. Tuition, nonresident: part-time $438 per credit. Required fees: $495 per semester. *Financial support:* Fellowships, career-related internships or fieldwork available. *Unit head:* Deborah May, Chair, 518-442-5050.

University at Albany, State University of New York, School of Public Health, Department of Biometry and Statistics, Albany, NY 12222-0001. Offers MS, PhD. *Students:* 20 full-time (10 women), 21 part-time (10 women). Average age 31. 41 applicants, 39% accepted, 11 enrolled. In 2003, 17 degrees awarded. *Degree requirements:* For doctorate, thesis/dissertation. *Entrance requirements:* For master's and doctorate, GRE General Test. Additional exam requirements/recommendations for international students: Required—TOEFL (minimum score 550 paper-based; 213 computer-based). *Application deadline:* For fall admission, 6/30 for domestic students, 5/1 for international students; for spring admission, 11/1 for domestic students, 11/1 for international students. Applications are processed on a rolling basis. Application fee: $50. Electronic applications accepted. *Expenses:* Tuition, state resident: part-time $288 per credit. Tuition, nonresident: part-time $438 per credit. Required fees: $495 per semester. *Financial support:* Application deadline: 4/1. *Unit head:* Dr. David Strogatz, Chair, 518-402-0400.

The University of Akron, Graduate School, Buchtel College of Arts and Sciences, Department of Statistics, Akron, OH 44325-0001. Offers MS. Part-time and evening/weekend programs available. *Faculty:* 6 full-time (0 women). *Students:* 19 full-time (9 women), 5 part-time; includes 1 minority (African American), 13 international. Average age 30. 32 applicants, 69% accepted, 9 enrolled. In 2003, 11 degrees awarded. *Degree requirements:* For master's, thesis optional. *Entrance requirements:* For master's, minimum GPA of 2.75. Additional exam requirements/recommendations for international students: Required—TOEFL (minimum score 550 paper-based; 213 computer-based), Michigan English Language Assessment Battery. *Application deadline:* For fall admission, 3/1 for domestic students. Applications are processed on a rolling basis. Application fee: $40 ($60 for international students). *Expenses:* Tuition, state resident: part-time $277 per credit hour. Tuition, nonresident: part-time $476 per credit hour. *Financial support:* In 2003–04, 15 teaching assistantships with full tuition reimbursements were awarded. Financial award application deadline: 3/1. *Faculty research:* Experimental design, sampling biostatistics. Total annual research expenditures: $9,566. *Unit head:* Dr. Chand Midha, Chair, 330-972-7128, E-mail: cmidha@uakron.edu.

The University of Alabama, Graduate School, Culverhouse College of Commerce and Business Administration, Department of Information Systems, Statistics, and Management Science, Tuscaloosa, AL 35487. Offers applied statistics (MS, PhD); management science (MA, MBA, MSC, PhD), including management science, manufacturing management (MA, MBA, PhD), production management (MA, MBA, PhD). *Accreditation:* AACSB. Part-time programs available. *Faculty:* 17 full-time (3 women). *Students:* 43 full-time (18 women), 9 part-time (4 women); includes 1 minority (African American), 36 international. Average age 29. 63 applicants, 32% accepted, 14 enrolled. In 2003, 13 master's, 5 doctorates awarded. Terminal master's awarded for partial completion of doctoral program. *Degree requirements:* For master's, thesis optional; for doctorate, thesis/dissertation, comprehensive exam. *Entrance requirements:* Additional exam requirements/recommendations for international students: Required—TOEFL. *Application deadline:* For fall admission, 7/6 for domestic students. Applications are processed on a rolling basis. Application fee: $25. Electronic applications accepted. *Financial support:* In 2003–04, 2 fellowships with full tuition reimbursements (averaging $12,000 per year), 6 research assistantships with full tuition reimbursements (averaging $12,450 per year), 11 teaching assistantships with full tuition reimbursements (averaging $12,450 per year) were awarded. Career-related internships or fieldwork also available. *Faculty research:* Data mining, production and inventory modeling, regression analysis, statistical quality control, supply chain management. *Unit head:* Dr. Edward R. Mansfield, Chairman, 205-348-8908, Fax: 205-348-0560, E-mail: emansfie@cba.ua.edu.

University of Alaska Fairbanks, College of Science, Engineering and Mathematics, Department of Mathematical Sciences, Fairbanks, AK 99775-7520. Offers computer science (MS); mathematics (MS, PhD); software engineering (MSE); statistics (MS). Part-time programs available. Terminal master's awarded for partial completion of doctoral program. *Degree requirements:* For master's, thesis or alternative, comprehensive exam, registration; for doctorate, thesis/dissertation, comprehensive exam, registration. *Entrance requirements:* For master's and doctorate, GRE General Test, GRE Subject Test. Additional exam requirements/recommendations for international students: Required—TOEFL (minimum score 600 paper-based). Electronic applications accepted. *Faculty research:* Blackbox kriging (statistics), interaction with a virtual reality environment (computer), arrangements of hyperplanes (topology), bifurcation analysis of time-periodic differential-delay equations, synthetic aperture radar interferometry software (computer).

University of Alberta, Faculty of Graduate Studies and Research, Department of Mathematical and Statistical Sciences, Edmonton, AB T6G 2E1, Canada. Offers applied mathematics (M Sc, PhD); biostatistics (M Sc); mathematical finance (M Sc, PhD); mathematical physics (M Sc, PhD); mathematics (M Sc, PhD); statistics (M Sc, PhD, Postgraduate Diploma). Part-time programs available. *Faculty:* 48 full-time (4 women). *Students:* 112 full-time (41 women), 5 part-time. Average age 24. 776 applicants, 5% accepted, 34 enrolled. In 2003, 12 master's, 10 doctorates awarded. Terminal master's awarded for partial completion of doctoral program. *Median time to degree:* Master's–2 years full-time; doctorate–5 years full-time. Of those who began their doctoral program in fall 1995, 100% received their degree in 8 years or less. *Degree requirements:* For master's, thesis (for some programs); for doctorate, thesis/dissertation, comprehensive exam. *Entrance requirements:* Additional exam requirements/recommendations for international students: Required—TOEFL (minimum score 580 paper-based; 237 computer-based). *Application deadline:* For fall admission, 3/1 for domestic students, 2/1 for international students. Applications are processed on a rolling basis. Application fee: $0. Electronic applications accepted. Tuition charges are reported in Canadian dollars. Tuition, nonresident: full-time $3,921 Canadian dollars. International tuition: $7,113 Canadian dollars full-time. *Financial support:* In 2003–04, 51 research assistantships, 88 teaching assistantships with full and partial tuition reimbursements were awarded. Scholarships/grants also available. Financial award application deadline: 5/1. *Faculty research:* Classical and functional analysis, algebra, differential equations, geometry. *Unit head:* Dr. Anthony To-Ming Lau, Chair, 403-492-5799, E-mail: tlau@math.ualberta.ca. *Application contact:* Dr. Yau Shu Wong, Associate Chair, Graduate Studies, 403-492-5799, Fax: 403-492-6828, E-mail: gradstudies@math.ualberta.ca.

University of Arkansas, Graduate School, J. William Fulbright College of Arts and Sciences, Department of Mathematical Sciences, Program in Statistics, Fayetteville, AR 72701-1201. Offers MS. *Students:* 19 full-time (8 women); includes 1 minority (African American), 13 international. 26 applicants, 58% accepted. In 2003, 5 degrees awarded. *Degree requirements:* For master's, thesis. Application fee: $40 ($50 for international students). *Expenses:* Tuition, state resident: full-time $4,032; part-time $224 per credit hour. Tuition, nonresident: full-time $9,540; part-time $530 per credit hour. Tuition and fees vary according to course load and program. *Financial support:* In 2003–04, 8 teaching assistantships were awarded; career-related internships or fieldwork and Federal Work-Study also available. Support available to part-time students. Financial award application deadline: 4/1; financial award applicants required to submit FAFSA. *Unit head:* Dr. Laurie Meaux, Chair of Studies, 479-575-3351, E-mail: gradmath@comp.uark.edu.

University of Arkansas at Little Rock, Graduate School, College of Science and Mathematics, Department of Mathematics and Statistics, Little Rock, AR 72204-1099. Offers applied mathematics (MS), including applied analysis, mathematical statistics. Part-time and evening/weekend programs available. *Students:* 2 full-time (1 woman), 7 part-time (5 women); includes 2 minority (both African Americans), 3 international. Average age 28. 7 applicants, 86% accepted. In 2003, 4 degrees awarded. *Degree requirements:* For master's, comprehensive exam. *Entrance requirements:* For master's, GRE General Test, GRE Subject Test, minimum GPA of 2.7, previous course work in advanced mathematics. *Application deadline:* For fall admission, 8/1 for domestic students; for spring admission, 11/1 for domestic students. Application fee: $25 ($30 for international students). Tuition, nonresident: part-time $177 per credit hour. *Financial support:* Research assistantships, teaching assistantships, Federal Work-Study, institutionally sponsored loans, and unspecified assistantships available. Support available to part-time students. Financial award application deadline: 8/1. *Unit head:* Dr. Timothy McMillan, Chairperson, 501-569-8100. *Application contact:* Dr. Alan M. Johnson, Coordinator, 501-569-8100.

The University of British Columbia, Faculty of Graduate Studies, Faculty of Science, Department of Statistics, Vancouver, BC V6T 1Z1, Canada. Offers M Sc, PhD. Part-time programs available. *Degree requirements:* For master's, thesis/dissertation; for doctorate, thesis/dissertation, comprehensive exam. *Entrance requirements:* Additional exam requirements/recommendations for international students: Required—TOEFL. *Faculty research:* Theoretical, applied, biostatistical, and computational statistics.

University of Calgary, Faculty of Graduate Studies, Faculty of Science, Department of Mathematics and Statistics, Calgary, AB T2N 1N4, Canada. Offers M Sc, PhD. *Faculty:* 37 full-time (3 women), 2 part-time/adjunct (0 women). *Students:* 34 full-time (13 women), 2 part-time. Average age 30. 48 applicants, 46% accepted, 15 enrolled. In 2003, 9 master's, 2 doctorates awarded, leading to university research/teaching 50%, business/industry 50%. *Median time to degree:* Master's–2 years full-time, 5 years part-time; doctorate–5 years full-time. Of those who began their doctoral program in fall 1995, 100% received their degree in 8 years or less. *Degree requirements:* For master's, thesis, comprehensive exam; for doctorate, thesis/dissertation, candidacy exam, preliminary exams. *Entrance requirements:* For master's, honors degree in applied math, pure math, or statistics; for doctorate, MA or M Sc. Additional exam requirements/recommendations for international students: Required—TOEFL (paper score 600; computer score 250) or IELTS (paper score 7). *Application deadline:* For fall admission, 2/1 for domestic students. Applications are processed on a rolling basis. Application fee: $60. Tuition, nonresident: full-time $4,765. Tuition and fees vary according to degree level, program and student level. *Financial support:* In 2003–04, 32 students received support, including 10 research assistantships with partial tuition reimbursements available

Statistics

University of Calgary (continued)
(averaging $4,000 per year), 29 teaching assistantships with partial tuition reimbursements available (averaging $12,500 per year); fellowships, scholarships/grants and unspecified assistantships also available. *Faculty research:* Combinatorics, applied mathematics, statistics, probability, analysis. Total annual research expenditures: $1.1 million. *Unit head:* T. Bisztriczky, Head, 403-220-6312, Fax: 403-282-5150, E-mail: tbisztri@math.ucalgary.ca. *Application contact:* Joanne Mellard, Graduate Secretary, 403-220-6299, Fax: 403-282-5150, E-mail: gradapps@math.ucalgary.ca.

University of California, Berkeley, Graduate Division, College of Letters and Science, Department of Statistics, Berkeley, CA 94720-1500. Offers MA, PhD. *Students:* 45 (11 women); includes 6 minority (all Asian Americans or Pacific Islanders) 28 international. 191 applicants, 13% accepted, 16 enrolled. In 2003, 17 master's, 8 doctorates awarded. *Degree requirements:* For doctorate, thesis/dissertation, qualifying exam, written preliminary exam. *Entrance requirements:* For master's and doctorate, GRE General Test, minimum GPA of 3.0. *Application deadline:* For fall admission, 12/15 for domestic students, 12/15 for international students. Application fee: $60. International tuition: $12,491 full-time. Required fees: $5,484. *Financial support:* Fellowships, research assistantships, teaching assistantships, unspecified assistantships available. Financial award application deadline: 12/15. *Unit head:* Dr. John Rice, Chair, 510-642-4272. *Application contact:* Angie Fong, Student Affairs Officer, 510-642-5361, Fax: 510-642-7892, E-mail: sao@stat.berkeley.edu.

University of California, Davis, Graduate Studies, Program in Statistics, Davis, CA 95616. Offers MS, PhD. *Faculty:* 22 full-time. *Students:* 45 full-time (26 women); includes 6 minority (1 African American, 5 Asian Americans or Pacific Islanders), 27 international. Average age 29. 132 applicants, 24% accepted, 8 enrolled. In 2003, 9 master's, 3 doctorates awarded. *Degree requirements:* For doctorate, thesis/dissertation. *Entrance requirements:* For master's and doctorate, GRE General Test, minimum GPA of 3.0. Additional exam requirements/recommendations for international students: Required—TOEFL (minimum score 550 paper-based; 213 computer-based). *Application deadline:* For fall admission, 1/15 for domestic students, 1/15 for international students. Application fee: $60. Electronic applications accepted. Tuition, nonresident: full-time $12,245. Required fees: $7,062. *Financial support:* In 2003–04, 44 students received support, including 1 fellowship with full and partial tuition reimbursement available (averaging $4,714 per year), 20 research assistantships with full and partial tuition reimbursements available (averaging $10,302 per year), 21 teaching assistantships with partial tuition reimbursements available (averaging $11,283 per year); Federal Work-Study, institutionally sponsored loans, scholarships/grants, and tuition waivers (full and partial) also available. Financial award application deadline: 1/15; financial award applicants required to submit FAFSA. *Faculty research:* Nonparametric analysis, time series analysis, biostatistics, curve estimation, reliability. *Unit head:* Rudolph Beran, Chair, 530-754-7765, E-mail: bearn@wald.ucdavis.edu. *Application contact:* Effie Kolbeins, Administrative Assistant, 530-752-2632, Fax: 530-752-7099, E-mail: grad-staff@wald.ucdavis.edu.

University of California, Los Angeles, Graduate Division, College of Letters and Science, Department of Statistics, Los Angeles, CA 90095. Offers MS, PhD. Tuition, nonresident: full-time $12,245. Required fees: $6,318.

University of California, Riverside, Graduate Division, Department of Statistics, Riverside, CA 92521-0102. Offers applied statistics (PhD); statistics (MS). Part-time programs available. *Faculty:* 8 full-time (1 woman). *Students:* 31 full-time (16 women); includes 4 minority (all Asian Americans or Pacific Islanders), 21 international. Average age 31. 50 applicants, 32% accepted. In 2003, 5 master's, 2 doctorates awarded. *Median time to degree:* Master's–2.5 years full-time; doctorate–5 years full-time. *Degree requirements:* For master's, comprehensive exam; for doctorate, thesis/dissertation, qualifying exams, 3 quarters of teaching experience. *Entrance requirements:* For master's and doctorate, GRE General Test, minimum GPA of 3.2. Additional exam requirements/recommendations for international students: Required—TOEFL (minimum score 550 paper-based; 213 computer-based); Recommended—TSE. *Application deadline:* For fall admission, 5/1 for domestic students, 2/1 for international students; for winter admission, 9/1 for domestic students; for spring admission, 12/1 for domestic students. Applications are processed on a rolling basis. Application fee: $60. Electronic applications accepted. Tuition, nonresident: part-time $4,082 per quarter. *Financial support:* In 2003–04, fellowships with full and partial tuition reimbursements (averaging $12,000 per year); research assistantships with partial tuition reimbursements, teaching assistantships with partial tuition reimbursements, career-related internships or fieldwork, Federal Work-Study, institutionally sponsored loans, and tuition waivers (full and partial) also available. Financial award application deadline: 2/1; financial award applicants required to submit FAFSA. *Faculty research:* Design and analysis of experiments, statistical modeling, stochastic models, paired comparisons, statistical design of experiments and linear models. *Unit head:* Dr. Keh-shin Lii, Chair, 951-827-3836, Fax: 951-827-3286, E-mail: ksl@ucrstat.ucr.edu. *Application contact:* Peggy Franklin, Graduate Secretary, 951-827-3774, Fax: 951-827-3286, E-mail: stat@ucr.edu.

University of California, San Diego, Graduate Studies and Research, Department of Mathematics, La Jolla, CA 92093. Offers applied mathematics (MA); mathematics (MA, PhD); statistics (MS). *Faculty:* 63. *Students:* 91 (25 women); includes 11 minority (2 African Americans, 6 Asian Americans or Pacific Islanders, 3 Hispanic Americans) 14 international. 294 applicants, 27% accepted. In 2003, 20 master's, 10 doctorates awarded. *Degree requirements:* For doctorate, thesis/dissertation. *Entrance requirements:* For master's and doctorate, GRE General Test, GRE Subject Test. Application fee: $60. Electronic applications accepted. Tuition, nonresident: full-time $12,245. Required fees: $6,959. *Unit head:* James Bunch, Chair, E-mail: jbunch@ucsd.edu. *Application contact:* Lois Stewart, Graduate Coordinator, 858-534-6887, E-mail: lstewart@ucsd.edu.

University of California, Santa Barbara, Graduate Division, College of Letters and Sciences, Division of Mathematics, Life, and Physical Sciences, Statistics and Applied Probability Department, Santa Barbara, CA 93106. Offers statistics (MA, PhD). *Students:* 49 full-time (19 women); includes 4 minority (all Hispanic Americans), 13 international. Average age 25. 103 applicants, 36% accepted, 18 enrolled. In 2003, 12 master's, 4 doctorates awarded. Terminal master's awarded for partial completion of doctoral program. *Median time to degree:* Master's–2 years full-time; doctorate–5 years full-time. Of those who began their doctoral program in fall 1995, 99% received their degree in 8 years or less. *Degree requirements:* For master's, thesis or alternative, comprehensive exam; for doctorate, thesis/dissertation, comprehensive exam. *Entrance requirements:* For master's and doctorate, GRE General Test. Additional exam requirements/recommendations for international students: Required—TOEFL (minimum score 550 paper-based; 213 computer-based). *Application deadline:* For fall admission, 5/1 for domestic students, 5/1 for international students; for winter admission, 11/1 for domestic students; for spring admission, 2/1 for domestic students. Applications are processed on a rolling basis. Application fee: $60. Electronic applications accepted. *Expenses:* Tuition, state resident: full-time $7,188. Tuition, nonresident: full-time $19,608. *Financial support:* In 2003–04, 32 students received support, including 3 fellowships with partial tuition reimbursements available (averaging $14,000 per year), 2 research assistantships with partial tuition reimbursements available (averaging $9,393 per year), 28 teaching assistantships with partial tuition reimbursements available (averaging $14,147 per year); Federal Work-Study, institutionally sponsored loans, scholarships/grants, health care benefits, tuition waivers (partial), and unspecified assistantships also available. Financial award application deadline: 5/1; financial award applicants required to submit FAFSA. *Faculty research:* Theoretical statistics, applied statistics, stochastic modeling, mathematical finance. Total annual research expenditures: $300,000. *Unit head:* Dr. Raya E. Feldman, Chairman, 805-893-2826, Fax: 805-893-2334. *Application contact:* Gail Kelley Murray, Graduate Program Assistant, 805-893-4857, Fax: 805-893-2334, E-mail: kelley@pstat.ucsb.edu.

University of Central Florida, College of Arts and Sciences, Department of Statistics and Actuarial Science, Orlando, FL 32816. Offers actuarial studies (MS); data mining (MS); statistical computing (MS). Part-time and evening/weekend programs available. *Faculty:* 18 full-time (5 women). *Students:* 38 full-time (18 women), 19 part-time (6 women); includes 4 minority (1 African American, 3 Asian Americans or Pacific Islanders), 25 international. Average age 31. 91 applicants, 53% accepted, 28 enrolled. In 2003, 13 degrees awarded. *Degree requirements:* For master's, comprehensive exam. *Entrance requirements:* For master's, GRE General Test, minimum GPA of 3.0 in last 60 hours. Additional exam requirements/recommendations for international students: Required—TOEFL. *Application deadline:* For fall admission, 7/15 for domestic students; for spring admission, 12/1 for domestic students. Application fee: $30. Electronic applications accepted. *Expenses:* Tuition, state resident: full-time $4,968; part-time $171 per credit hour. Tuition, nonresident: full-time $18,630; part-time $713 per credit hour. *Financial support:* In 2003–04, 7 fellowships with partial tuition reimbursements (averaging $3,600 per year), 14 research assistantships with partial tuition reimbursements (averaging $5,700 per year), 27 teaching assistantships with partial tuition reimbursements (averaging $7,570 per year) were awarded. Career-related internships or fieldwork, Federal Work-Study, institutionally sponsored loans, tuition waivers (partial), and unspecified assistantships also available. Financial award application deadline: 3/1; financial award applicants required to submit FAFSA. *Faculty research:* Multivariate analysis, quality control, shrinkage estimation. *Unit head:* Dr. Ibrahim Ahmad, Chair, 407-823-5528, Fax: 407-823-5419. *Application contact:* Dr. James R. Schott, Graduate Coordinator, 407-823-3323, Fax: 407-823-5419, E-mail: jschott@pegasus.cc.ucf.edu.

University of Central Oklahoma, College of Graduate Studies and Research, College of Mathematics and Science, Department of Mathematics and Statistics, Edmond, OK 73034-5209. Offers applied mathematical sciences (MS), including computer science, mathematics, mathematics/computer science teaching, statistics. *Accreditation:* NCATE. Part-time programs available. *Degree requirements:* For master's, thesis. *Faculty research:* Curvature, FAA, math education.

University of Chicago, Division of the Physical Sciences, Department of Statistics, Chicago, IL 60637-1513. Offers SM, PhD. *Faculty:* 16 full-time (3 women). *Students:* 65 full-time (28 women), 10 part-time (6 women); includes 6 minority (1 African American, 5 Asian Americans or Pacific Islanders), 50 international. Average age 25. 230 applicants, 26% accepted, 30 enrolled. In 2003, 13 master's, 6 doctorates awarded. Terminal master's awarded for partial completion of doctoral program. *Median time to degree:* Master's–1 year full-time, 2 years part-time; doctorate–5 years full-time. Of those who began their doctoral program in fall 1995, 100% received their degree in 8 years or less. *Degree requirements:* For master's and doctorate, thesis/dissertation, registration. *Entrance requirements:* For master's and doctorate, GRE General Test, GRE Subject Test. Additional exam requirements/recommendations for international students: Required—TOEFL. *Application deadline:* For fall admission, 6/15 for domestic students, 6/15 for international students. Application fee: $55. Electronic applications accepted. *Financial support:* In 2003–04, 60 students received support, including fellowships with full tuition reimbursements available (averaging $16,700 per year), research assistantships with full tuition reimbursements available (averaging $16,700 per year), teaching assistantships with full tuition reimbursements available (averaging $16,700 per year); tuition waivers (partial) also available. Financial award application deadline: 2/1. *Faculty research:* Genetics, econometrics, generalized linear models, history of statistics, probability theory. *Unit head:* Dr. Steven P. Lalley, Chairman, 773-702-8335. *Application contact:* Dr. Michael Winchura, Admissions Chair, 773-702-8329, E-mail: winchura@uchicago.edu.

University of Cincinnati, Division of Research and Advanced Studies, McMicken College of Arts and Sciences, Department of Mathematical Sciences, Cincinnati, OH 45221. Offers applied mathematics (MS, PhD); mathematics education (MAT); pure mathematics (MS, PhD); statistics (MS, PhD). *Accreditation:* NCATE (one or more programs are accredited). Part-time programs available. Terminal master's awarded for partial completion of doctoral program. *Degree requirements:* For master's, thesis or alternative, comprehensive exam; for doctorate, one foreign language, thesis/dissertation, comprehensive exam. *Entrance requirements:* For master's, GRE, teacher certification (MAT); for doctorate, GRE. Additional exam requirements/recommendations for international students: Required—TOEFL. Electronic applications accepted. *Faculty research:* Algebra, analysis, differential equations, numerical analysis, statistics.

University of Connecticut, Graduate School, College of Liberal Arts and Sciences, Department of Statistics, Field of Statistics, Storrs, CT 06269. Offers MS, PhD. *Faculty:* 10 full-time (2 women). *Students:* 41 full-time (22 women), 12 part-time (4 women); includes 1 minority (African American), 34 international. Average age 31. 165 applicants, 48% accepted, 19 enrolled. In 2003, 8 master's, 3 doctorates awarded. Terminal master's awarded for partial completion of doctoral program. *Degree requirements:* For master's, comprehensive exam; for doctorate, thesis/dissertation. *Entrance requirements:* For master's and doctorate, GRE General Test. Additional exam requirements/recommendations for international students: Required—TOEFL (minimum score 550 paper-based; 213 computer-based). *Application deadline:* For fall admission, 2/1 priority date for domestic students, 2/1 priority date for international students; for spring admission, 11/1 for domestic students, 10/1 for international students. Applications are processed on a rolling basis. Application fee: $55. Electronic applications accepted. *Expenses:* Tuition, state resident: part-time $3,860 per semester. Tuition, nonresident: part-time $9,036 per semester. *Financial support:* In 2003–04, 10 research assistantships with full tuition reimbursements, 27 teaching assistantships with full tuition reimbursements were awarded. Fellowships, Federal Work-Study, scholarships/grants, health care benefits, and unspecified assistantships also available. Financial award application deadline: 2/1; financial award applicants required to submit FAFSA. *Application contact:* Tracy Burke, Information Contact, 860-486-3413, Fax: 860-486-4113, E-mail: statadm2@uconnvm.uconn.edu.

University of Delaware, College of Agriculture and Natural Resources, Program in Statistics, Newark, DE 19716. Offers MS. Part-time programs available. *Faculty:* 7 full-time (2 women). *Students:* 15 full-time (10 women), 3 part-time (1 woman); includes 2 minority (both Asian Americans or Pacific Islanders), 12 international. 53 applicants, 38% accepted, 13 enrolled. In 2003, 7 degrees awarded. *Entrance requirements:* For master's, GRE General Test, letters of recommendation (3). Additional exam requirements/recommendations for international students: Required—TOEFL (minimum score 550 paper-based; 213 computer-based). Application fee: $60. *Expenses:* Tuition, state resident: full-time $5,890; part-time $327 per credit. Tuition, nonresident: full-time $15,420; part-time $857 per credit. Required fees: $968. *Financial support:* In 2003–04, 11 students received support, including 6 research assistantships with full tuition reimbursements available (averaging $12,860 per year), 2 teaching assistantships with full tuition reimbursements available (averaging $12,250 per year); career-related internships or fieldwork, scholarships/grants, tuition waivers (full), and unspecified assistantships also available. Financial award application deadline: 7/1. Total annual research expenditures: $60,000. *Unit head:* Dr. Thomas W. Ilvento, Chair, 302-831-6773, Fax: 302-831-6243, E-mail: ilvento@udel.edu. *Application contact:* Vicki Lynn Taylor, Office Coordinator, 302-831-2511, Fax: 302-831-6243, E-mail: vtaylor@udel.edu.

University of Florida, Graduate School, College of Liberal Arts and Sciences, Department of Statistics, Gainesville, FL 32611. Offers M Stat, MS Stat, PhD. *Faculty:* 41. *Students:* 59 full-time (31 women), 1 (woman) part-time; includes 5 minority (1 African American, 2 Asian Americans or Pacific Islanders, 2 Hispanic Americans), 44 international. In 2003, 22 master's, 1 doctorate awarded. *Degree requirements:* For master's, variable foreign language requirement, thesis or alternative, final oral exam, comprehensive exam; for doctorate, variable foreign language requirement, thesis/dissertation. *Entrance requirements:* For master's and doctorate, GRE General Test, minimum GPA of 3.0. Additional exam requirements/recommendations for international students: Required—TOEFL (minimum score 550 paper-based; 213 computer-based). *Application deadline:* For fall admission, 6/1 for domestic students. Applications are processed on a rolling basis. Application fee: $30. Electronic applications accepted. *Expenses:* Tuition, state resident: part-time $205 per credit hour. Tuition, nonresident: part-time $775 per credit hour. *Financial support:* In 2003–04, 40 students received support, including 1 fellowship, 28 research assistantships (averaging $11,500 per year), 16 teaching assistantships (averaging $11,500 per year); unspecified assistantships also available. Financial award application deadline: 2/1. *Faculty research:* Categorical data, time series, Bayesian analysis, nonparametrics, sampling. *Unit head:* Dr. George Casella, Chair, 352-392-1941 Ext. 204, Fax: 352-392-5175, E-mail: casella@stat.ufl.edu. *Application contact:* Dr. James P. Hobert, Coordinator, 352-392-1941 Ext. 229, Fax: 352-392-5175, E-mail: jhobert@stat.ufl.edu.

University of Georgia, Graduate School, College of Arts and Sciences, Department of Statistics, Athens, GA 30602. Offers applied mathematical science (MAMS); statistics (MS, PhD). *Faculty:* 14 full-time (3 women). *Students:* 46 full-time (23 women), 8 part-time (3 women); includes 3 minority (all African Americans), 38 international. 154 applicants, 12% accepted. In 2003, 28 master's, 1 doctorate awarded. *Degree requirements:* For master's, thesis (for some programs), technical report (MAMS); for doctorate, one foreign language, thesis/dissertation. *Entrance requirements:* For master's and doctorate, GRE General Test. *Application deadline:* For fall admission, 7/1 for domestic students; for spring admission, 11/15 for domestic students. Application fee: $50. Electronic applications accepted. *Expenses:* Tuition, state resident: part-time $161 per hour. Tuition, nonresident: part-time $690 per hour. One-time fee: $435 part-time. *Financial support:* Fellowships, research assistantships, teaching assistantships, unspecified assistantships available. *Unit head:* Dr. Ishwar V. Basawa, Head, 706-542-3309, Fax: 706-542-3391, E-mail: ishwar@stat.uga.edu. *Application contact:* Dr. Lynn Seymour, Graduated Coordinator, 706-542-3307, Fax: 706-542-3391, E-mail: seymour@stat.uga.edu.

University of Guelph, Graduate Program Services, College of Physical and Engineering Science, Department of Mathematics and Statistics, Guelph, ON N1G 2W1, Canada. Offers applied mathematics (PhD); applied statistics (PhD); mathematics and statistics (M Sc). Part-time programs available. *Faculty:* 26 full-time (5 women), 5 part-time/adjunct (1 woman). *Students:* 46 full-time, 2 part-time, 10 international. Average age 22. 96 applicants, 30% accepted, 22 enrolled. In 2003, 15 master's, 6 doctorates awarded. *Median time to degree:* Of those who began their doctoral program in fall 1995, 88% received their degree in 8 years or less. *Degree requirements:* For master's, thesis (for some programs); for doctorate, thesis/dissertation. *Entrance requirements:* For master's, minimum B- average during previous 2 years; for doctorate, minimum B average. Additional exam requirements/recommendations for international students: Required—TOEFL (minimum score 550 paper-based; 210 computer-based). *Application deadline:* For fall admission, 3/1 for domestic students, 2/1 for international students. Application fee: $75. Tuition and fee charges are reported in Canadian dollars. Tuition, nonresident: full-time $3,440 Canadian dollars. International tuition: $5,432 Canadian dollars full-time. Required fees: $753 Canadian dollars. *Financial support:* In 2003–04, 20 students received support, including 29 research assistantships (averaging $2,200 per year), 32 teaching assistantships (averaging $11,000 per year); fellowships, scholarships/grants also available. *Faculty research:* Dynamical systems, mathematical biology, numerical analysis, linear and nonlinear models, reliability and bioassay. Total annual research expenditures: $315,000. *Unit head:* Dr. O. Brian Allen, Chair, 519-824-4120 Ext. 56556, Fax: 519-837-0221, E-mail: chair@uoguelph.ca. *Application contact:* Susan McCormick, Graduate Administrative Assistant, 519-824-4120 Ext. 56553, Fax: 519-837-0221, E-mail: smccormi@uoguelph.ca.

University of Houston–Clear Lake, School of Science and Computer Engineering, Program in Statistics, Houston, TX 77058-1098. Offers MS. *Students:* 9 full-time (4 women), 5 part-time (1 woman); includes 4 minority (1 African American, 3 Asian Americans or Pacific Islanders), 6 international. Average age 34. In 2003, 2 degrees awarded. *Entrance requirements:* For master's, GRE General Test. Additional exam requirements/recommendations for international students: Required—TOEFL (minimum score 550 paper-based; 213 computer-based). *Application deadline:* For fall admission, 8/1 for domestic students, 6/1 for international students; for spring admission, 12/1 for domestic students, 10/1 for international students. Applications are processed on a rolling basis. Application fee: $35 ($75 for international students). *Expenses:* Tuition, state resident: full-time $2,484; part-time $414 per course. Tuition, nonresident: full-time $6,318; part-time $1,053 per course. Required fees: $12 per course. $199 per semester. *Financial support:* In 2003–04, 2 teaching assistantships were awarded. Financial award application deadline: 5/1; financial award applicants required to submit FAFSA. *Unit head:* Dr. Raj Chhikara, Chair, 281-283-3850, Fax: 281-283-3707. *Application contact:* Dr. Robert Ferebee, Associate Dean, 281-283-3700, Fax: 281-283-3707, E-mail: ferebee@cl.uh.edu.

University of Idaho, College of Graduate Studies, College of Science, Department of Mathematics, Program in Statistics, Moscow, ID 83844-2282. Offers MS. *Students:* 6 full-time (1 woman), 6 part-time (4 women); includes 1 minority (Asian American or Pacific Islander), 8 international. Average age 38. *Entrance requirements:* For master's, minimum GPA of 2.8. *Application deadline:* For fall admission, 8/1 for domestic students; for spring admission, 12/15 for domestic students. Application fee: $55 ($60 for international students). *Expenses:* Tuition, state resident: full-time $3,348. Tuition, nonresident: full-time $10,740. Required fees: $540. *Financial support:* Research assistantships, teaching assistantships available. Financial award application deadline: 2/15. *Unit head:* Dr. Chris Williams, Chair, 208-885-2929.

See in-depth description on page 597.

University of Illinois at Chicago, Graduate College, College of Liberal Arts and Sciences, Department of Mathematics, Statistics, and Computer Science, Chicago, IL 60607-7128. Offers applied mathematics (MS, DA, PhD); computer science (MS, DA, PhD); math and information science for the industry (MS); probability and statistics (MS, DA, PhD); pure mathematics (MS, DA, PhD); teaching of mathematics (MST). Part-time programs available. *Faculty:* 69 full-time (4 women). *Students:* 145 full-time (61 women), 62 part-time (34 women); includes 41 minority (13 African Americans, 21 Asian Americans or Pacific Islanders, 7 Hispanic Americans), 86 international. Average age 32. 285 applicants, 30% accepted, 36 enrolled. In 2003, 38 master's, 14 doctorates awarded. *Median time to degree:* Of those who began their doctoral program in fall 1995, 50% received their degree in 8 years or less. *Degree requirements:* For master's, comprehensive exam; for doctorate, one foreign language, thesis/dissertation. *Entrance requirements:* For master's and doctorate, GRE General Test, minimum GPA of 3.75 on a 5.0 scale. Additional exam requirements/recommendations for international students: Required—TOEFL. *Application deadline:* For fall admission, 1/9 for domestic students, 1/9 for international students; for spring admission, 10/1 for domestic students. Applications are processed on a rolling basis. Application fee: $40 ($50 for international students). Electronic applications accepted. *Expenses:* Tuition, state resident: part-time $941 per semester. Tuition, nonresident: part-time $2,338 per semester. *Financial support:* In 2003–04, 118 students received support; fellowships with full tuition reimbursements available, research assistantships with full tuition reimbursements available, teaching assistantships with full tuition reimbursements available, Federal Work-Study, scholarships/grants, traineeships, tuition waivers (full), and unspecified assistantships available. Financial award application deadline: 3/1; financial award applicants required to submit FAFSA. *Unit head:* Jerry Bona, Head, 312-996-3044. *Application contact:* Charles Knessl, Director of Graduate Studies, 312-996-3041, E-mail: knessl@uic.edu.

See in-depth description on page 599.

University of Illinois at Urbana–Champaign, Graduate College, College of Liberal Arts and Sciences, Department of Statistics, Champaign, IL 61820. Offers MS, PhD. *Faculty:* 7 full-time (1 woman), 1 part-time/adjunct (0 women). *Students:* 27 full-time (17 women), 23 international. 203 applicants, 1% accepted, 3 enrolled. In 2003, 9 master's, 2 doctorates awarded. Terminal master's awarded for partial completion of doctoral program. *Degree requirements:* For doctorate, thesis/dissertation. *Entrance requirements:* For master's, minimum GPA of 3.0. Additional exam requirements/recommendations for international students: Required—TOEFL. *Application deadline:* For fall admission, 2/15 for domestic students; for spring admission, 9/15 priority date for domestic students. Applications are processed on a rolling basis. Application fee: $40 ($50 for international students). Electronic applications accepted. *Expenses:* Tuition, state resident: full-time $6,692. Tuition, nonresident: full-time $18,692. *Financial support:* In 2003–04, 14 research assistantships, 12 teaching assistantships were awarded. Fellowships, tuition waivers (full) also available. Financial award application deadline: 2/15. *Faculty research:* Statistical decision theory, sequential analysis, computer-aided stochastic modeling. *Unit head:* Douglas G. Simpson, Chair, 217-333-2167, Fax: 217-244-7190. *Application contact:* Jennifer Suits, Secretary, 217-333-2167, Fax: 217-244-7190, E-mail: jmsuits@uiuc.edu.

The University of Iowa, Graduate College, College of Education, Division of Psychological and Quantitative Foundations, Iowa City, IA 52242-1316. Offers counseling psychology (PhD); educational measurement and statistics (MA, PhD); educational psychology (MA, PhD); school psychology (PhD); schoold psychology (Ed S). *Faculty:* 24 full-time, 3 part-time/adjunct. *Students:* 77 full-time (52 women), 73 part-time (49 women); includes 31 minority (15 African Americans, 1 American Indian/Alaska Native, 7 Asian Americans or Pacific Islanders, 8 Hispanic Americans), 34 international. 193 applicants, 35% accepted, 26 enrolled. In 2003, 8 master's, 15 doctorates, 6 other advanced degrees awarded. *Degree requirements:* For master's, exam, thesis optional; for doctorate, thesis/dissertation, comprehensive exam, registration; for Ed S, exam. *Entrance requirements:* For master's, doctorate, and Ed S, GRE General Test, minimum GPA of 3.0. Additional exam requirements/recommendations for international students: Required—TOEFL (minimum score 550 paper-based; 213 computer-based). Application fee: $50 ($75 for international students). Electronic applications accepted. *Expenses:* Tuition, state resident: full-time $5,038. Tuition, nonresident: full-time $15,072. Tuition and fees vary according to course load and program. *Financial support:* In 2003–04, 5 fellowships, 73 research assistantships, 20 teaching assistantships were awarded. *Unit head:* Thomas Rocklin, Chair, 319-335-5570, Fax: 319-335-6145.

The University of Iowa, Graduate College, College of Liberal Arts and Sciences, Department of Statistics and Actuarial Science, Iowa City, IA 52242-1316. Offers MS, PhD. *Faculty:* 16 full-time, 3 part-time/adjunct. *Students:* 75 full-time (41 women), 13 part-time (6 women); includes 4 minority (1 African American, 3 Asian Americans or Pacific Islanders), 69 international. 333 applicants, 64% accepted, 30 enrolled. In 2003, 11 master's, 2 doctorates awarded. *Degree requirements:* For master's, exam, thesis optional; for doctorate, thesis/dissertation, comprehensive exam, registration. *Entrance requirements:* For master's and doctorate, GRE General Test, minimum GPA of 3.0. Additional exam requirements/recommendations for international students: Required—TOEFL (minimum score 550 paper-based; 213 computer-based). *Application deadline:* Applications are processed on a rolling basis. Application fee: $50 ($75 for international students). Electronic applications accepted. *Expenses:* Tuition, state resident: full-time $5,038. Tuition, nonresident: full-time $15,072. Tuition and fees vary according to course load and program. *Financial support:* In 2003–04, 2 fellowships, 13 research assistantships, 49 teaching assistantships were awarded. Financial award applicants required to submit FAFSA. *Unit head:* James D. Broffitt, Chair, 319-335-0712, Fax: 319-335-3017.

See in-depth description on page 601.

University of Kansas, Graduate School, College of Liberal Arts and Sciences, Department of Mathematics, Lawrence, KS 66045. Offers applied mathematics and statistics (MA, PhD); mathematics (MA, PhD). *Faculty:* 41. *Students:* 55 full-time (21 women), 12 part-time (5 women); includes 4 minority (1 American Indian/Alaska Native, 2 Asian Americans or Pacific Islanders, 1 Hispanic American), 29 international. Average age 29. 57 applicants, 49% accepted, 16 enrolled. In 2003, 10 master's, 4 doctorates awarded. Terminal master's awarded for partial completion of doctoral program. *Median time to degree:* Master's–2.5 years full-time; doctorate–5.5 years full-time. *Degree requirements:* For master's, thesis or alternative; for doctorate, 2 foreign languages, thesis/dissertation, comprehensive exam. *Entrance requirements:* For master's and doctorate, GRE. Additional exam requirements/recommendations for international students: Required—TOEFL. *Application deadline:* For fall admission, 3/1 priority date for domestic students, 3/1 priority date for international students. Applications are processed on a rolling basis. Application fee: $55 ($60 for international students). Electronic applications accepted. *Expenses:* Tuition, state resident: full-time $3,745. Tuition, nonresident: full-time $10,075. Required fees: $574. *Financial support:* In 2003–04, 2 research assistantships with full and partial tuition reimbursements (averaging $14,180 per year), 44 teaching assistantships with full and partial tuition reimbursements (averaging $14,845 per year) were awarded. Fellowships, institutionally sponsored loans also available. Support available to part-time students. Financial award application deadline: 2/1. *Faculty research:* Commutative algebra/algebraic geometry; stochastic adaptive control/stochastic processes analysis/harmonic analysis/PDES; numerical analysis/dynamical systems; topology/set theory. Total annual research expenditures: $801,000. *Unit head:* Jack Porter, Chair, 785-864-3651, Fax: 785-864-5255, E-mail: porter@math.ukans.edu. *Application contact:* David Lerner, Graduate Director, 785-864-3651, E-mail: lerner@ukans.edu.

University of Kentucky, Graduate School, Graduate School Programs from the College of Arts and Sciences, Program in Statistics, Lexington, KY 40506-0032. Offers MS, PhD. *Faculty:* 11 full-time (1 woman). *Students:* 38 full-time (20 women), 9 part-time (6 women); includes 1 minority (American Indian/Alaska Native), 24 international. 112 applicants, 17% accepted, 10 enrolled. In 2003, 6 degrees awarded. *Degree requirements:* For master's, thesis optional; for doctorate, thesis/dissertation, comprehensive exam. *Entrance requirements:* For master's, GRE General Test, minimum undergraduate GPA of 2.5; for doctorate, GRE General Test, minimum graduate GPA of 3.0. Additional exam requirements/recommendations for international students: Required—TOEFL (minimum score 550 paper-based; 213 computer-based). *Application deadline:* For fall admission, 7/18 for domestic students, 2/1 for international students. Applications are processed on a rolling basis. Application fee: $35 ($45 for international students). *Expenses:* Tuition, state resident: full-time $4,975; part-time $261 per credit hour. Tuition, nonresident: full-time $12,315; part-time $668 per credit hour. *Financial support:* Fellowships, research assistantships, teaching assistantships, Federal Work-Study and institutionally sponsored loans available. Support available to part-time students. *Faculty research:* Computer intensive statistical inference, biostatistics, mathematical and applied statistics, applied probability. Total annual research expenditures: $77,000. *Unit head:* Dr. Arnold Stromberg, Director of Graduate Studies, 859-257-6903, Fax: 859-323-1973, E-mail: astro@ms.uky.edu. *Application contact:* Dr. Brian Jackson, Associate Dean, 859-257-4905, Fax: 859-323-1928.

University of Manitoba, Faculty of Graduate Studies, Faculty of Science, Department of Mathematical, Computational and Statistical Sciences, Winnipeg, MB R3T 2N2, Canada. Offers MMCSS. Tuition charges are reported in Canadian dollars. Tuition, nonresident: full-time $3,878 Canadian dollars.

University of Manitoba, Faculty of Graduate Studies, Faculty of Science, Department of Statistics, Winnipeg, MB R3T 2N2, Canada. Offers M Sc, PhD. *Degree requirements:* For master's, thesis or alternative; for doctorate, one foreign language, thesis/dissertation. Tuition charges are reported in Canadian dollars. Tuition, nonresident: full-time $3,878 Canadian dollars.

University of Maryland, Baltimore County, Graduate School, Department of Mathematics and Statistics, Program in Statistics, Baltimore, MD 21250. Offers MS, PhD. Part-time and evening/weekend programs available. *Faculty:* 8 full-time (1 woman). *Students:* 19 full-time (6 women), 21 part-time (11 women); includes 6 minority (all African Americans), 20 international. Average age 23. 45 applicants, 42% accepted, 5 enrolled. In 2003, 2 master's awarded, leading to continued full-time study 100%; 2 doctorates awarded, leading to business/industry 50%, government 50%. Terminal master's awarded for partial completion of doctoral program. *Median time to degree:* Master's–2 years full-time, 4 years part-time; doctorate–4 years full-time, 6 years part-time. Of those who began their doctoral program in fall 1995, 80% received their degree in 8 years or less. *Degree requirements:* For master's, thesis (for some programs), comprehensive exam (for some programs), registration; for doctorate, thesis/dissertation, comprehensive exam, registration. *Entrance requirements:* For master's and doctorate, GRE General Test, minimum GPA of 3.0. Additional exam requirements/recommendations for international students: Required—TOEFL. *Application deadline:* For fall admission, 2/15 priority date for domestic students, 1/1 priority date for international students; for spring admission, 10/15 priority date for domestic students, 9/15 priority date for international students. Applications are processed on a rolling basis. Application fee: $50. Electronic applications accepted. *Expenses:* Tuition, state resident: full-time $7,000. Tuition, nonresident:

Statistics

University of Maryland, Baltimore County (continued)
full-time $11,400. Required fees: $1,440. *Financial support:* In 2003–04, 20 students received support, including 4 research assistantships with full tuition reimbursements available (averaging $15,000 per year), 16 teaching assistantships with full tuition reimbursements available (averaging $15,000 per year); career-related internships or fieldwork, scholarships/grants, health care benefits, tuition waivers (full), and unspecified assistantships also available. Support available to part-time students. Financial award application deadline: 2/15. *Faculty research:* Design of experiments, statistical decision theory and inference, time series analysis, biostatistics and environmental statistics, bioinformatics. Total annual research expenditures: $627,000. *Application contact:* Dr. Rouben Rostamian, Director of Graduate Programs, 410-455-2412, Fax: 410-455-1066, E-mail: rostamian@umbc.edu.

University of Maryland, College Park, Graduate Studies and Research, College of Computer, Mathematical and Physical Sciences, Department of Mathematics, Program in Mathematical Statistics, College Park, MD 20742. Offers MA, PhD. Part-time and evening/weekend programs available. *Students:* 29 full-time (15 women), 5 part-time (1 woman); includes 3 minority (1 African American, 2 Asian Americans or Pacific Islanders), 23 international. 104 applicants, 19% accepted. In 2003, 9 degrees awarded. Terminal master's awarded for partial completion of doctoral program. *Degree requirements:* For master's, thesis or comprehensive exams, scholarly paper; for doctorate, one foreign language, thesis/dissertation, written and oral exams. *Entrance requirements:* For master's, GRE General Test, GRE Subject Test, minimum GPA of 3.0, 3 letters of recommendation; for doctorate, GRE General Test, GRE Subject Test, minimum GPA of 3.0. *Application deadline:* For fall admission, 5/1 for domestic students, 2/1 for international students; for spring admission, 10/1 for domestic students, 6/1 for international students. Applications are processed on a rolling basis. Application fee: $50. Electronic applications accepted. *Expenses:* Tuition, state resident: part-time $349 per credit hour. Tuition, nonresident: part-time $602 per credit hour. *Financial support:* Fellowships, research assistantships, teaching assistantships available. Financial award applicants required to submit FAFSA. *Faculty research:* Statistics and probability, stochastic processes, nonparametric statistics, space-time statistics. *Unit head:* Dr. Benjamin Kedem, Director, 301-405-5112, Fax: 301-314-0827. *Application contact:* Trudy Lindsey, Director, Graduate Enrollment Management Services, 301-405-4190, Fax: 301-314-9305, E-mail: tlindsey@gradschool.umd.edu.

University of Massachusetts Amherst, Graduate School, College of Natural Sciences and Mathematics, Department of Mathematics and Statistics, Program in Mathematics and Statistics, Amherst, MA 01003. Offers MS, PhD. *Students:* 53 full-time (22 women), 4 part-time (2 women); includes 5 minority (1 African American, 3 Asian Americans or Pacific Islanders, 1 Hispanic American), 20 international. Average age 28. 233 applicants, 18% accepted, 19 enrolled. In 2003, 11 master's, 2 doctorates awarded. *Degree requirements:* For doctorate, 2 foreign languages, thesis/dissertation. *Entrance requirements:* Additional exam requirements/recommendations for international students: Required—TOEFL (minimum score 530 paper-based; 197 computer-based). *Application deadline:* For fall admission, 2/1 priority date for domestic students, 2/1 priority date for international students; for spring admission, 10/1 for domestic students, 10/1 for international students. Applications are processed on a rolling basis. Application fee: $40 ($50 for international students). *Expenses:* Tuition, state resident: full-time $1,320; part-time $110 per credit. Tuition, nonresident: full-time $4,969; part-time $414 per credit. Required fees: $2,626 per term. Tuition and fees vary according to course load. *Financial support:* Fellowships with full tuition reimbursements, research assistantships with full tuition reimbursements, teaching assistantships with full tuition reimbursements, career-related internships or fieldwork, Federal Work-Study, scholarships/grants, traineeships, and unspecified assistantships available. Support available to part-time students. Financial award application deadline: 2/1. *Unit head:* Dr. Eduardo Cattani, Director, 413-545-2282, Fax: 413-545-1801, E-mail: cattani@math.umass.edu.

The University of Memphis, Graduate School, College of Arts and Sciences, Department of Mathematical Sciences, Memphis, TN 38152-3420. Offers applied mathematics (MS); applied statistics (PhD); bioinformatics (MS); computer science (PhD); computer sciences (MS); mathematics (MS, PhD); statistics (MS, PhD). Part-time programs available. *Faculty:* 24 full-time (5 women), 3 part-time/adjunct (0 women). *Students:* 106 full-time (40 women), 42 part-time (15 women); includes 8 minority (5 African Americans, 3 Asian Americans or Pacific Islanders), 108 international. Average age 30. 139 applicants, 37% accepted. In 2003, 31 master's, 8 doctorates awarded. Terminal master's awarded for partial completion of doctoral program. *Median time to degree:* Master's–2 years full-time, 4 years part-time; doctorate–2 years full-time, 4 years part-time. *Degree requirements:* For master's, comprehensive exam; for doctorate, one foreign language, thesis/dissertation, oral exams. *Entrance requirements:* For master's and doctorate, GRE General Test, minimum GPA of 2.5. Additional exam requirements/recommendations for international students: Required—TOEFL (minimum score 550 paper-based; 210 computer-based), WES evaluation of transcript. *Application deadline:* For fall admission, 8/1 for domestic students, 5/1 for international students; for spring admission, 12/1 for domestic students, 9/1 for international students. Applications are processed on a rolling basis. Application fee: $25 ($50 for international students). Electronic applications accepted. *Expenses:* Tuition, state resident: full-time $5,142. Tuition, nonresident: full-time $13,296. *Financial support:* In 2003–04, 58 students received support, including fellowships with full tuition reimbursements available (averaging $17,500 per year), 9 research assistantships with full tuition reimbursements available (averaging $9,000 per year), 30 teaching assistantships with full tuition reimbursements available (averaging $9,000 per year); career-related internships or fieldwork, Federal Work-Study, scholarships/grants, unspecified assistantships, and minority scholarships also available. Financial award application deadline: 2/2. *Faculty research:* Combinatorics, ergodic theory, graph theory, Ramsey theory, applied statistics. Total annual research expenditures: $1.5 million. *Unit head:* Dr. James E. Jamison, Chairman, 901-678-2482, Fax: 901-678-2480, E-mail: jjamison@memphis.edu. *Application contact:* Coordinator of Graduate Studies, 901-678-2482, Fax: 901-678-2480, E-mail: dfwilson@memphis.edu.

University of Miami, Graduate School, School of Business Administration, Department of Management Science, Coral Gables, FL 33124. Offers management science (MS, PhD), including applied statistics (MS), operations research (MS). Part-time and evening/weekend programs available. Postbaccalaureate distance learning degree programs offered. *Faculty:* 10 full-time (2 women). *Students:* 10 full-time (6 women); includes 7 minority (1 African American, 3 Asian Americans or Pacific Islanders, 3 Hispanic Americans). Average age 30. 8 applicants, 75% accepted. In 2003, 2 degrees awarded. Terminal master's awarded for partial completion of doctoral program. *Degree requirements:* For master's, thesis optional; for doctorate, thesis/dissertation, comprehensive exam. *Entrance requirements:* For master's and doctorate, GRE General Test. Additional exam requirements/recommendations for international students: Required—TOEFL. *Application deadline:* For fall admission, 6/30 for domestic students; for spring admission, 10/31 for domestic students. Applications are processed on a rolling basis. Application fee: $50. *Expenses:* Tuition: Full-time $19,526. *Financial support:* Career-related internships or fieldwork and Federal Work-Study available. Financial award application deadline: 3/1. *Faculty research:* Mathematical programming, applied statistics, applied probability, logistics, statistical process control. Total annual research expenditures: $20,000. *Unit head:* Dr. Anuj Mehrotra, Chairman, 305-284-6595, Fax: 305-284-2321, E-mail: anuj@miami.edu. *Application contact:* Dr. Howard Gitlow, Director, 305-284-4296, Fax: 305-284-2321, E-mail: hgitlow@miami.edu.

University of Michigan, Horace H. Rackham School of Graduate Studies, College of Literature, Science, and the Arts, Department of Statistics, Ann Arbor, MI 48109. Offers applied statistics (AM); statistics (AM, PhD). *Faculty:* 27 full-time (7 women), 1 part-time/adjunct (0 women). *Students:* 98 full-time (47 women); includes 4 minority (1 African American, 2 Asian Americans or Pacific Islanders, 1 Hispanic American), 57 international. Average age 28. 311 applicants, 19% accepted, 33 enrolled. In 2003, 30 master's, 6 doctorates awarded. Terminal master's awarded for partial completion of doctoral program. *Median time to degree:* Master's–1.5 years full-time; doctorate–6.5 years full-time. Of those who began their doctoral program in fall 1995, 44% received their degree in 8 years or less. *Degree requirements:* For master's, registration; for doctorate, one foreign language, thesis/dissertation, oral defense of dissertation, preliminary exam. *Entrance requirements:* For master's and doctorate, GRE General Test. Additional exam requirements/recommendations for international students: Required—TOEFL (minimum score 560 paper-based; 220 computer-based). *Application deadline:* For fall admission, 1/31 priority date for domestic students, 1/15 priority date for international students. Applications are processed on a rolling basis. Application fee: $60 ($75 for international students). Electronic applications accepted. *Expenses:* Tuition, state resident: full-time $7,463. Tuition, nonresident: full-time $13,913. Full-time tuition and fees vary according to course load, degree level and program. *Financial support:* In 2003–04, 67 students received support, including 8 fellowships with full and partial tuition reimbursements available, 13 research assistantships with full and partial tuition reimbursements available, 46 teaching assistantships with full and partial tuition reimbursements available (averaging $13,570 per year); career-related internships or fieldwork, Federal Work-Study, institutionally sponsored loans, scholarships/grants, health care benefits, and unspecified assistantships also available. Support available to part-time students. Financial award application deadline: 1/31. *Faculty research:* Sequential analysis, Bayesian statistics, multivariate analysis, statistical computing, bioinformation. *Unit head:* Vijayan Nair, Chair, 734-763-3519, Fax: 734-763-4676, E-mail: vnn@umich.edu. *Application contact:* Lu Ann Custer, Graduate Secretary, 734-763-3520, Fax: 734-763-4676, E-mail: stat-admission@umich.edu.

University of Minnesota, Twin Cities Campus, Graduate School, College of Liberal Arts, School of Statistics, Minneapolis, MN 55455-0213. Offers MS, PhD. Part-time programs available. *Faculty:* 19 full-time (2 women), 2 part-time/adjunct (0 women). *Students:* 65 full-time (30 women), 11 part-time (5 women); includes 7 minority (4 African Americans, 3 Asian Americans or Pacific Islanders), 44 international. Average age 24. 194 applicants, 81% accepted, 20 enrolled. In 2003, 7 master's, 7 doctorates awarded. Terminal master's awarded for partial completion of doctoral program. *Median time to degree:* Master's–2.5 years full-time; doctorate–5.5 years full-time. Of those who began their doctoral program in fall 1995, 100% received their degree in 8 years or less. *Degree requirements:* For master's, comprehensive exam, registration; for doctorate, thesis/dissertation, comprehensive exam, registration. *Entrance requirements:* For master's and doctorate, GRE General Test. Additional exam requirements/recommendations for international students: Required—TOEFL (minimum score 550 paper-based; 213 computer-based). *Application deadline:* For fall admission, 1/1 priority date for domestic students, 1/1 priority date for international students. Applications are processed on a rolling basis. Application fee: $55 ($75 for international students). Electronic applications accepted. *Expenses:* Tuition, state resident: full-time $3,681; part-time $614 per credit. Tuition, nonresident: full-time $7,231; part-time $1,205 per credit. *Financial support:* In 2003–04, 3 fellowships with full tuition reimbursements (averaging $12,847 per year), 6 research assistantships with full tuition reimbursements (averaging $12,847 per year), 37 teaching assistantships with full tuition reimbursements (averaging $12,847 per year) were awarded. Scholarships/grants, health care benefits, and tuition waivers (partial) also available. *Faculty research:* Data analysis, statistical computing, experimental design, probability theory, Bayesian inference. Total annual research expenditures: $166,909. *Unit head:* Glen Meeden, Director, 612-625-8046, Fax: 612-624-8868, E-mail: glen@stat.umn.edu. *Application contact:* Mary Hildre, Executive Administrative Specialist, 612-625-7300, Fax: 612-624-8868, E-mail: mary@stat.umn.edu.

University of Missouri–Columbia, Graduate School, College of Arts and Sciences, Department of Statistics, Columbia, MO 65211. Offers MA, PhD. *Faculty:* 10 full-time (3 women). *Students:* 40 full-time (16 women), 5 part-time (4 women); includes 1 minority (Hispanic American), 31 international. In 2003, 6 master's, 2 doctorates awarded. *Degree requirements:* For doctorate, thesis/dissertation. *Entrance requirements:* For master's and doctorate, GRE General Test, minimum GPA of 3.0. *Application deadline:* For fall admission, 2/15 for domestic students; for winter admission, 10/15 for domestic students. Applications are processed on a rolling basis. Application fee: $45 ($60 for international students). *Expenses:* Tuition, state resident: full-time $5,205. Tuition, nonresident: full-time $14,058. *Financial support:* Research assistantships, teaching assistantships, institutionally sponsored loans and tuition waivers (full and partial) available. *Unit head:* Dr. Paul L. Speckman, Director of Graduate Studies, 573-882-7082, E-mail: speckmanp@missouri.edu.

University of Missouri–Kansas City, College of Arts and Sciences, Department of Mathematics and Statistics, Kansas City, MO 64110-2499. Offers MA, MS, PhD. PhD offered through the School of Graduate Studies. Part-time programs available. *Faculty:* 6 full-time (2 women), 1 part-time/adjunct (0 women). *Students:* 2 full-time (1 woman), 13 part-time (7 women); includes 4 minority (2 African Americans, 1 Asian American or Pacific Islander, 1 Hispanic American), 2 international. Average age 36. In 2003, 4 master's, 1 doctorate awarded. Terminal master's awarded for partial completion of doctoral program. *Degree requirements:* For master's, written exam; for doctorate, 2 foreign languages, thesis/dissertation, oral and written exams. *Entrance requirements:* For master's, bachelor's degree in mathematics, minimum GPA of 3.0; for doctorate, GMAT or GRE General Test. *Application deadline:* For fall admission, 5/1 for domestic students. Applications are processed on a rolling basis. Application fee: $35 ($50 for international students). *Financial support:* In 2003–04, 6 students received support, including 6 teaching assistantships; Federal Work-Study, institutionally sponsored loans, and tuition waivers (full and partial) also available. Support available to part-time students. Financial award application deadline: 4/1. *Faculty research:* Classical real variables, matrix theory, ring theory, linear numerical analysis, statistics. *Unit head:* Dr. Bruce Wenner, Chairperson, 816-235-2853.

University of Nebraska–Lincoln, Graduate College, College of Arts and Sciences, Department of Mathematics and Statistics, Lincoln, NE 68588. Offers M Sc T, MA, MAT, MS, PhD. *Degree requirements:* For master's, thesis optional; for doctorate, variable foreign language requirement, thesis/dissertation, comprehensive exam. *Entrance requirements:* Additional exam requirements/recommendations for international students: Required—TOEFL (minimum score 550 paper-based; 213 computer-based), GRE General Test (international applicants). Electronic applications accepted. *Faculty research:* Applied mathematics, commutative algebra, algebraic geometry, Bayesian statistics, biostatistics.

University of Nevada, Las Vegas, Graduate College, College of Science, Department of Mathematical Sciences, Las Vegas, NV 89154-9900. Offers applied mathematics (MS); applied statistics (MS); pure mathematics (MS). Part-time programs available. *Faculty:* 28 full-time (6 women). *Students:* 28 full-time (9 women), 21 part-time (9 women); includes 12 minority (1 African American, 7 Asian Americans or Pacific Islanders, 4 Hispanic Americans), 16 international. 35 applicants, 69% accepted, 16 enrolled. In 2003, 8 degrees awarded. *Degree requirements:* For master's, thesis (for some programs), oral exam, comprehensive exam (for some programs). *Entrance requirements:* For master's, minimum GPA of 3.0 during previous 2 years, 2.75 overall. Additional exam requirements/recommendations for international students: Required—TOEFL (minimum score 550 paper-based; 213 computer-based). *Application deadline:* For fall admission, 6/15 for domestic students, 5/1 for international students; for spring admission, 11/15 for domestic students, 10/1 for international students. Application fee: $60 ($75 for international students). *Expenses:* Tuition, state resident: part-time $115 per credit. Tuition, nonresident: part-time $242 per credit. Required fees: $8 per semester. Tuition and fees vary according to course load. *Financial support:* In 2003–04, 36 teaching assistantships with partial tuition reimbursements (averaging $10,000 per year) were awarded. Financial award application deadline: 3/1. *Unit head:* Dr. Dieudonne Phanord, Head, 702-895-3567. *Application contact:* Graduate College Admissions Evaluator, 702-895-3320, Fax: 702-895-4180, E-mail: gradcollege@ccmail.nevada.edu.

University of New Brunswick Fredericton, School of Graduate Studies, Faculty of Science, Department of Mathematics and Statistics, Fredericton, NB E3B 5A3, Canada. Offers M Sc, PhD. Part-time programs available. *Degree requirements:* For master's, thesis or alternative; for doctorate, thesis/dissertation. *Entrance requirements:* For master's and doctorate, minimum GPA of 3.0. Additional exam requirements/recommendations for international students: Required—TOEFL, TWE.

University of New Hampshire, Graduate School, College of Engineering and Physical Sciences, Department of Mathematics and Statistics, Durham, NH 03824. Offers applied mathematics (MS); mathematics (MS, MST, PhD); mathematics education (PhD); statistics (MS). *Faculty:* 26 full-time. *Students:* 18 full-time (6 women), 30 part-time (12 women); includes 2 minority (1 African American, 1 Hispanic American), 17 international. Average age 28. 39 applicants, 79% accepted, 11 enrolled. In 2003, 16 master's, 1 doctorate awarded. Terminal master's awarded for partial completion of doctoral program. *Degree requirements:* For doctorate, 2 foreign languages, thesis/dissertation. *Entrance requirements:* Additional exam requirements/recommendations for international students: Required—TOEFL (minimum score 550 paper-based; 213 computer-based); Recommended—TSE. *Application deadline:* For fall admission, 4/1 for domestic students; for winter admission, 12/1 for domestic students. Applications are processed on a rolling basis. Application fee: $50. Electronic applications accepted. Tuition, area resident: Full-time $7,070. *Expenses:* Tuition, state resident: full-time $10,605. Tuition, nonresident: full-time $17,430. Required fees: $15. *Financial support:* In 2003–04, 1 fellowship, 27 teaching assistantships were awarded. Research assistantships, Federal Work-Study, scholarships/grants, and tuition waivers (full and partial) also available. Support available to part-time students. Financial award application deadline: 2/15. *Faculty research:* Operator theory, complex analysis, algebra, nonlinear dynamics, statistics. *Unit head:* Dr. Eric Grinberg, Chairperson, 603-862-2320. *Application contact:* Jan Jankawski, Graduate Coordinator, 603-862-2688, E-mail: janj@cisunix.unh.edu.

University of New Mexico, Graduate School, College of Arts and Sciences, Department of Mathematics and Statistics, Albuquerque, NM 87131-2039. Offers mathematics (MS, PhD); statistics (MS, PhD). Part-time programs available. *Students:* 73 full-time (31 women), 27 part-time (12 women); includes 19 minority (2 African Americans, 1 American Indian/Alaska Native, 5 Asian Americans or Pacific Islanders, 11 Hispanic Americans), 32 international. Average age 33. 50 applicants, 100% accepted, 31 enrolled. In 2003, 15 master's, 9 doctorates awarded. Terminal master's awarded for partial completion of doctoral program. *Degree requirements:* For master's, thesis or alternative, comprehensive exam (for some programs); for doctorate, one foreign language, thesis/dissertation, 4 department seminars, comprehensive exam. *Entrance requirements:* For master's, minimum GPA of 3.0, 3 letters of recommendation; for doctorate, GRE General Test, minimum GPA of 3.0, 3 letters of recommendation. *Application deadline:* For fall admission, 7/1 for domestic students; for spring admission, 11/1 for domestic students. Applications are processed on a rolling basis. Application fee: $40. *Expenses:* Tuition, state resident: full-time $1,802; part-time $152 per credit hour. Tuition, nonresident: full-time $6,135; part-time $513 per credit hour. Tuition and fees vary according to program. *Financial support:* In 2003–04, 4 fellowships (averaging $4,000 per year), 24 research assistantships with tuition reimbursements (averaging $11,745 per year), 45 teaching assistantships with tuition reimbursements (averaging $11,448 per year) were awarded. Health care benefits, tuition waivers (full and partial), and unspecified assistantships also available. Financial award application deadline: 3/1; financial award applicants required to submit FAFSA. *Faculty research:* Pure and applied mathematics, applied statistics, numerical analysis, biostatistics, differential geometry. Total annual research expenditures: $601,138. *Unit head:* Dr. Alejandro Aceves, Chair, 505-277-4613, Fax: 505-277-5505, E-mail: aceves@math.unm.edu. *Application contact:* Donna George, Program Advisement Coordinator, 505-277-5250, Fax: 505-277-5505, E-mail: dgeorge@unm.edu.

The University of North Carolina at Chapel Hill, Graduate School, College of Arts and Sciences, Department of Statistics, Chapel Hill, NC 27599. Offers MS, PhD. *Faculty:* 12 full-time (0 women), 7 part-time/adjunct (0 women). *Students:* 29 full-time (9 women); includes 4 minority (2 Asian Americans or Pacific Islanders, 2 Hispanic Americans), 13 international. Average age 29. 141 applicants, 18% accepted, 8 enrolled. In 2003, 1 master's, 6 doctorates awarded. *Degree requirements:* For master's, essay, or thesis; for doctorate, thesis/dissertation, comprehensive exam. *Entrance requirements:* For master's and doctorate, GRE General Test, GRE Subject Test, minimum GPA of 3.0. Additional exam requirements/recommendations for international students: Required—TOEFL. *Application deadline:* For fall admission, 1/1 for domestic students. Application fee: $60. *Expenses:* Tuition, state resident: full-time $3,163. Tuition, nonresident: full-time $15,161. *Financial support:* In 2003–04, 2 fellowships with full tuition reimbursements (averaging $14,000 per year), 3 research assistantships with full tuition reimbursements (averaging $13,500 per year), 14 teaching assistantships with full tuition reimbursements (averaging $12,000 per year) were awarded. Career-related internships or fieldwork, scholarships/grants, and tuition waivers (full) also available. Financial award application deadline: 3/1. *Unit head:* Dr. Vidyadhar Kulkarni, Chairman, 919-962-8343, Fax: 919-962-1279. *Application contact:* Prof. Chuanshu Ji, Director of Admissions, 919-962-3917, Fax: 919-962-1279, E-mail: cji@stat.unc.edu.

University of North Florida, College of Arts and Sciences, Department of Mathematics and Statistics, Jacksonville, FL 32224-2645. Offers mathematical sciences (MS); statistics (MS). Part-time and evening/weekend programs available. *Faculty:* 20 full-time (5 women). *Students:* 12 full-time (7 women), 4 part-time (2 women), 1 international. Average age 29. 24 applicants, 42% accepted, 3 enrolled. In 2003, 2 degrees awarded. *Degree requirements:* For master's, thesis optional. *Entrance requirements:* For master's, GRE General Test, minimum GPA of 3.0 in last 60 hours. Additional exam requirements/recommendations for international students: Required—TOEFL (minimum score 500 paper-based; 173 computer-based). *Application deadline:* For fall admission, 7/6 priority date for domestic students, 5/1 priority date for international students; for winter admission, 11/2 for domestic students; for spring admission, 3/10 for domestic students. Applications are processed on a rolling basis. Application fee: $20. Electronic applications accepted. *Expenses:* Tuition, state resident: full-time $3,050; part-time $169 per semester hour. Tuition, nonresident: full-time $12,672; part-time $704 per semester hour. Required fees: $702; $39 per semester hour. *Financial support:* In 2003–04, 14 students received support, including 12 teaching assistantships (averaging $5,789 per year); Federal Work-Study and tuition waivers (partial) also available. Support available to part-time students. Financial award application deadline: 4/1; financial award applicants required to submit FAFSA. *Faculty research:* Real analysis, number theory, Euclidean geometry. Total annual research expenditures: $103,442. *Unit head:* Dr. Scott H. Hochwald, Chair, 904-620-2653, E-mail: shochwal@unf.edu. *Application contact:* Dr. Champak Panchal, Coordinator, 904-620-2469, E-mail: cpanchal@unf.edu.

University of Ottawa, Faculty of Graduate and Postdoctoral Studies, Faculty of Science, Ottawa-Carleton Institute of Mathematics and Statistics, Ottawa, ON K1N 6N5, Canada. Offers M Sc, PhD. Part-time programs available. *Faculty:* 31. *Students:* 41 full-time (15 women), 10 part-time (2 women). 63 applicants, 48% accepted, 16 enrolled. In 2003, 3 master's, 5 doctorates awarded. *Degree requirements:* For master's, thesis optional; for doctorate, one foreign language, thesis/dissertation, comprehensive exam. *Entrance requirements:* For master's, honors B Sc degree or equivalent, minimum B average; for doctorate, M Sc with minimum B+ average. *Application deadline:* For fall admission, 3/1 for domestic students. Applications are processed on a rolling basis. Application fee: $60. *Expenses:* Tuition, state resident: full-time $4,467. International tuition: $4,574 full-time. Tuition and fees vary according to program. *Financial support:* Fellowships, research assistantships, teaching assistantships, Federal Work-Study available. Financial award application deadline: 2/15. *Faculty research:* Pure mathematics, applied mathematics, probability. *Unit head:* Dr. Philip Scott, Chair, 613-562-5864, Fax: 613-562-5776. *Application contact:* Lise Maisonneuve, Graduate Studies Administrator, 613-562-5800 Ext. 6050, Fax: 613-562-5486, E-mail: lise@science.uottawa.ca.

University of Pennsylvania, Wharton School, Department of Statistics, Philadelphia, PA 19104. Offers MBA, PhD. *Degree requirements:* For doctorate, thesis/dissertation, comprehensive exam. *Entrance requirements:* For master's and doctorate, GRE. Additional exam requirements/recommendations for international students: Required—TOEFL, TWE, TSE. *Faculty research:* Nonparametric function estimation, analysis of algorithms, time series analysis, observational studies, inference.

University of Pittsburgh, School of Arts and Sciences, Department of Statistics, Pittsburgh, PA 15260. Offers applied statistics (MA, MS); statistics (MA, MS, PhD). Part-time programs available. *Faculty:* 11 full-time (2 women). *Students:* 35 full-time (19 women), 1 part-time; includes 2 minority (1 Asian American or Pacific Islander, 1 Hispanic American), 28 international. Average age 23. 257 applicants, 18% accepted, 8 enrolled. In 2003, 8 master's, 5 doctorates awarded, leading to continued full-time study 100%. Terminal master's awarded for partial completion of doctoral program. *Median time to degree:* Master's–2 years full-time, 3 years part-time; doctorate–5 years full-time. *Degree requirements:* For master's, thesis (for some programs), comprehensive exam, registration; for doctorate, thesis/dissertation, comprehensive exam, registration. *Entrance requirements:* For master's, 3 semesters of calculus, 1 semester of linear algebra, 1 year of mathematical statistics; for doctorate, 3 semesters of calculus, 1 semester of linear algebra, 1 year of mathematical statistics, 1 semester of advanced calculus. Additional exam requirements/recommendations for international students: Required—TOEFL (minimum score 550 paper-based; 213 computer-based); Recommended—TSE. *Application deadline:* For fall admission, 2/1 priority date for domestic students, 2/1 priority date for international students; for spring admission, 10/1 priority date for domestic students, 9/1 priority date for international students. Applications are processed on a rolling basis. Application fee: $40. Electronic applications accepted. *Expenses:* Tuition, state resident: full-time $11,744; part-time $479 per credit. Tuition, nonresident: full-time $22,910; part-time $941 per credit. Required fees: $560. Tuition and fees vary according to degree level and program. *Financial support:* In 2003–04, 29 students received support, including 1 fellowship with tuition reimbursement available (averaging $13,240 per year), 9 research assistantships with tuition reimbursements available (averaging $13,290 per year), 18 teaching assistantships with tuition reimbursements available (averaging $12,775 per year); career-related internships or fieldwork, Federal Work-Study, institutionally sponsored loans, scholarships/grants, and health care benefits also available. Financial award application deadline: 2/1; financial award applicants required to submit FAFSA. *Faculty research:* Multivariate statistics, time series, reliability, meta-analysis, linear and nonlinear regression modeling. Total annual research expenditures: $665,000. *Unit head:* Henry Block, Chairman, 412-624-8280, Fax: 412-648-8814, E-mail: si@stat.pitt.edu. *Application contact:* Leon J. Gleser, Director of Graduate Studies, 412-624-3925, Fax: 412-648-8814, E-mail: ljg@stat.pitt.edu.

University of Puerto Rico, Mayagüez Campus, Graduate Studies, College of Arts and Sciences, Department of Mathematics, Mayagüez, PR 00681-9000. Offers applied mathematics (MS); computational sciences (MS); pure mathematics (MS); statistics (MS). Part-time programs available. *Degree requirements:* For master's, one foreign language, comprehensive exam. *Faculty research:* Automata theory, linear algebra, logic.

University of Regina, Faculty of Graduate Studies and Research, Faculty of Science, Department of Mathematics and Statistics, Regina, SK S4S 0A2, Canada. Offers mathematics (M Sc, MA, PhD); statistics (M Sc, MA). *Faculty:* 21 full-time (4 women), 2 part-time/adjunct (0 women). *Students:* 7 full-time (2 women), 3 part-time (1 woman). 7 applicants. In 2003, 1 degree awarded. *Degree requirements:* For master's, thesis optional; for doctorate, variable foreign language requirement, thesis/dissertation, comprehensive exam. *Entrance requirements:* Additional exam requirements/recommendations for international students: Required—TOEFL. *Application deadline:* Applications are processed on a rolling basis. Application fee: $60. *Expenses:* Tuition, state resident: part-time $130 per credit hour. Tuition and fees vary according to course load and program. *Financial support:* In 2003–04, 4 fellowships, 1 research assistantship, 2 teaching assistantships were awarded. Scholarships/grants also available. Financial award application deadline: 6/15. *Faculty research:* Pure and applied mathematics, statistics and probability. *Unit head:* Dr. E. Ahmed, Head, 306-585-4351, E-mail: ahmed@math.uregina.ca. *Application contact:* Dr. Chua-Hua Guo, Graduate Program Coordinator, 306-585-4423, Fax: 306-585-4020, E-mail: chguo@math.uregina.ca.

University of Rhode Island, Graduate School, College of Arts and Sciences, Department of Computer Science and Statistics, Kingston, RI 02881. Offers MS, PhD. In 2003, 4 degrees awarded. *Degree requirements:* For master's, thesis optional; for doctorate, one foreign language, thesis/dissertation. *Entrance requirements:* For master's, GRE Subject Test. *Application deadline:* For fall admission, 4/15 for domestic students. Applications are processed on a rolling basis. Application fee: $35. *Expenses:* Tuition, state resident: full-time $4,338; part-time $281 per credit. Tuition, nonresident: full-time $12,438; part-time $704 per credit. Required fees: $1,840. *Financial support:* Unspecified assistantships available. *Unit head:* Dr. James Kowalski, Chair, 401-874-2701.

University of Rochester, School of Medicine and Dentistry, Graduate Programs in Medicine and Dentistry, Department of Biostatistics and Computational Biology, Rochester, NY 14627-0250. Offers medical statistics (MS); statistics (MA, PhD). *Faculty:* 10. *Students:* 9 full-time (6 women); includes 2 minority (1 American Indian/Alaska Native, 1 Asian American or Pacific Islander), 4 international. 92 applicants, 5% accepted, 3 enrolled. In 2003, 3 master's, 4 doctorates awarded. Terminal master's awarded for partial completion of doctoral program. *Degree requirements:* For doctorate, thesis/dissertation, qualifying exam. *Entrance requirements:* For master's and doctorate, GRE General Test. Additional exam requirements/recommendations for international students: Required—TOEFL. *Application deadline:* For fall admission, 2/1 for domestic students. Application fee: $25. *Expenses:* Tuition: Part-time $880 per credit hour. Required fees: $522. *Financial support:* Fellowships, research assistantships, teaching assistantships, tuition waivers (full and partial) available. Financial award application deadline: 2/1. *Unit head:* Dr. Andrei Yakovlev, Chair, 585-275-2404. *Application contact:* Patti Kolomic, Administrative Assistant, 585-275-6696, E-mail: kolomic@metro.bst.rochester.edu.

University of Saskatchewan, College of Graduate Studies and Research, College of Arts and Sciences, Department of Mathematics and Statistics, Saskatoon, SK S7N 5A2, Canada. Offers M Math, MA, PhD. *Faculty:* 24. *Students:* 9. *Degree requirements:* For master's, thesis (for some programs), registration; for doctorate, thesis/dissertation, registration. *Entrance requirements:* Additional exam requirements/recommendations for international students: Required—TOEFL. *Application deadline:* For fall admission, 7/1 for domestic students. Applications are processed on a rolling basis. Application fee: $50. Tuition charges are reported in Canadian dollars. *Expenses:* Tuition, state resident: part-time $483 Canadian dollars per course. *Financial support:* Fellowships, research assistantships, teaching assistantships available. Financial award application deadline: 1/31. *Unit head:* Dr. Lawrence Martz, Acting Head, 306-966-6089, Fax: 306-966-6086, E-mail: lawrence.martz@usask.ca. *Application contact:* Dr. John Martin, Graduate Chair, 306-966-6099, Fax: 306-966-6086, E-mail: karen@math.usask.ca.

University of South Carolina, The Graduate School, College of Science and Mathematics, Department of Statistics, Columbia, SC 29208. Offers applied statistics (CAS); statistics (MIS, MS, PhD). Part-time and evening/weekend programs available. Postbaccalaureate distance learning degree programs offered (minimal on-campus study). Terminal master's awarded for partial completion of doctoral program. *Degree requirements:* For master's, thesis/dissertation; for doctorate, thesis/dissertation, comprehensive exam. *Entrance requirements:* For master's, GRE General Test or GMAT, 2 years of work experience, (MIS); for doctorate, GRE General Test; for CAS, GRE General Test, or GMAT. Electronic applications accepted. Expenses: Contact institution. *Faculty research:* Reliability, environmentrics, statistics computing, psychometrics, bioinformatics.

University of Southern California, Graduate School, College of Letters, Arts and Sciences, Department of Mathematics, Program in Statistics, Los Angeles, CA 90089. Offers MS. *Degree requirements:* For master's, thesis. *Entrance requirements:* For master's, GRE General Test. *Application deadline:* For fall admission, 12/15 for domestic students. Application fee: $65 ($75 for international students). *Expenses:* Tuition: Full-time $32,784; part-time $949 per unit. Tuition and fees vary according to course load and program. *Financial support:* Fellowships, research assistantships, teaching assistantships, Federal Work-Study and institutionally sponsored loans available. Support available to part-time students. Financial award application deadline: 2/15; financial award applicants required to submit FAFSA.

University of Southern Maine, College of Arts and Science, Portland, ME 04104-9300. Offers American and New England studies (MA); biology (MS); creative writing (MFA); social

Statistics

University of Southern Maine (continued)
work (MSW); statistics (MS). Part-time and evening/weekend programs available. Post-baccalaureate distance learning degree programs offered (minimal on-campus study). *Faculty:* 43 full-time (19 women), 26 part-time/adjunct (19 women). *Students:* 202 full-time (136 women), 40 part-time (22 women). Average age 37. 158 applicants, 68% accepted. In 2003, 387 degrees awarded. *Degree requirements:* For master's, thesis optional. *Entrance requirements:* For master's, GRE General Test or MAT. Additional exam requirements/recommendations for international students: Required—TOEFL. *Application deadline:* For fall admission, 3/15 priority date for domestic students, 3/15 priority date for international students; for spring admission, 10/1 priority date for domestic students, 10/1 priority date for international students. Application fee: $50. Electronic applications accepted. Tuition, area resident: Part-time $215 per credit. *Expenses:* Tuition, state resident: part-time $323 per credit. Tuition, nonresident: part-time $602 per credit. Required fees: $18 per credit hour. Tuition and fees vary according to reciprocity agreements. *Financial support:* In 2003–04, 3 research assistantships were awarded; career-related internships or fieldwork and Federal Work-Study also available. Support available to part-time students. *Unit head:* Dr. Luisa Deprez, Dean, 207-780-4221. *Application contact:* Mary Sloan, Director of Graduate Admissions, 207-780-4386, Fax: 207-780-4969, E-mail: gradstudies@usm.maine.edu.

The University of Tennessee, Graduate School, College of Business Administration, Department of Statistics, Knoxville, TN 37996. Offers industrial statistics (MS); statistics (MS). Part-time programs available. *Degree requirements:* For master's, thesis or alternative. *Entrance requirements:* For master's, GMAT or GRE General Test, minimum GPA of 2.7. Additional exam requirements/recommendations for international students: Required—TOEFL. Electronic applications accepted.

The University of Tennessee, Graduate School, College of Business Administration, Program in Business Administration, Knoxville, TN 37996. Offers accounting (PhD); finance (MBA, PhD); logistics and transportation (MBA, PhD); management (PhD); marketing (MBA, PhD); operations management (MBA); professional business administration (MBA); statistics (PhD). *Accreditation:* AACSB. Postbaccalaureate distance learning degree programs offered. *Degree requirements:* For master's, thesis or alternative; for doctorate, thesis/dissertation. *Entrance requirements:* For master's and doctorate, GMAT, minimum GPA of 2.7. Additional exam requirements/recommendations for international students: Required—TOEFL. Electronic applications accepted.

The University of Texas at Austin, Graduate School, College of Natural Sciences, Department of Mathematics, Program in Statistics, Austin, TX 78712-1111. Offers MS Stat. *Entrance requirements:* For master's, GRE General Test.

The University of Texas at Dallas, School of Natural Sciences and Mathematics, Programs in Mathematical Sciences, Richardson, TX 75083-0688. Offers applied mathematics (MS, PhD); engineering mathematics (MS); mathematical science (MS); statistics (MS, PhD). Part-time and evening/weekend programs available. *Faculty:* 10 full-time (1 woman), 2 part-time/adjunct (0 women). *Students:* 37 full-time (13 women), 19 part-time (8 women); includes 14 minority (5 African Americans, 7 Asian Americans or Pacific Islanders, 2 Hispanic Americans), 20 international. Average age 33. 118 applicants, 58% accepted. In 2003, 13 master's, 3 doctorates awarded. *Degree requirements:* For master's, thesis optional; for doctorate, thesis/dissertation. *Entrance requirements:* For master's, GRE General Test, minimum GPA of 3.0 in upper-level course work in field; for doctorate, GRE General Test, minimum GPA of 3.5 in upper-level course work in field. Additional exam requirements/recommendations for international students: Required—TOEFL (minimum score 550 paper-based; 213 computer-based). *Application deadline:* For fall admission, 7/15 for domestic students; for spring admission, 11/15 for domestic students. Applications are processed on a rolling basis. Application fee: $50 ($100 for international students). Electronic applications accepted. *Expenses:* Tuition, state resident: full-time $1,656; part-time $92 per credit. Tuition, nonresident: full-time $5,904; part-time $328 per credit. Required fees: $2,161; $275 per credit. $334 per term. *Financial support:* In 2003–04, 1 research assistantship (averaging $6,975 per year), 29 teaching assistantships with tuition reimbursements (averaging $5,625 per year) were awarded. Fellowships, career-related internships or fieldwork, Federal Work-Study, institutionally sponsored loans, and scholarships/grants also available. Support available to part-time students. Financial award application deadline: 4/30; financial award applicants required to submit FAFSA. *Faculty research:* Statistical methods, control theory, mathematical modeling and analyses of biological and physical systems. Total annual research expenditures: $151,159. *Unit head:* Dr. M. Ali Hooshyar, Head, 972-883-2171, Fax: 972-883-6622, E-mail: utdmath@utdallas.edu. *Application contact:* Joan Gladwell, Information Contact, 972-883-6432, Fax: 972-883-6622, E-mail: gladwell@utdallas.edu.

See in-depth description on page 613.

The University of Texas at El Paso, Graduate School, College of Science, Department of Mathematical Sciences, El Paso, TX 79968-0001. Offers mathematical sciences (MAT); mathematics (MS); statistics (MS). Part-time and evening/weekend programs available. *Students:* 55 (25 women); includes 25 minority (1 African American, 4 Asian Americans or Pacific Islanders, 20 Hispanic Americans) 15 international. Average age 34. 19 applicants, 89% accepted. In 2003, 3 degrees awarded. *Degree requirements:* For master's, thesis optional. *Entrance requirements:* For master's, GRE, minimum GPA of 3.0. Additional exam requirements/recommendations for international students: Required—TOEFL. *Application deadline:* For fall admission, 7/1 priority date for domestic students, 3/1 priority date for international students; for spring admission, 11/1 priority date for domestic students, 9/1 priority date for international students. Applications are processed on a rolling basis. Application fee: $15 ($65 for international students). Electronic applications accepted. *Expenses:* Tuition, state resident: full-time $1,388; part-time $160 per hour. Tuition, nonresident: full-time $3,440; part-time $388 per hour. Tuition and fees vary according to course load, degree level and program. *Financial support:* In 2003–04, 10 students received support, including research assistantships with partial tuition reimbursements available (averaging $21,812 per year), teaching assistantships with partial tuition reimbursements available (averaging $17,450 per year); career-related internships or fieldwork, Federal Work-Study, institutionally sponsored loans, scholarships/grants, and tuition waivers (partial) also available. Financial award application deadline: 3/15; financial award applicants required to submit FAFSA. *Unit head:* Dr. Joe Guthrie, Chairperson, 915-747-5761, Fax: 915-747-6202, E-mail: joe@math.utep.edu. *Application contact:* Dr. Charles H. Ambler, Dean of the Graduate School, 915-747-5491 Ext. 7886, Fax: 915-747-5788, E-mail: cambler@utep.edu.

The University of Texas at San Antonio, College of Business, Department of Management Science and Statistics, San Antonio, TX 78249-0617. Offers management science (MBA); statistics (MS). *Accreditation:* AACSB. *Faculty:* 7 full-time (2 women), 2 part-time/adjunct (1 woman). *Students:* 8 full-time (5 women), 17 part-time (8 women); includes 11 minority (all Hispanic Americans), 2 international. Average age 31. 6 applicants, 67% accepted, 4 enrolled. In 2003, 8 degrees awarded. *Degree requirements:* For master's, thesis optional. *Entrance requirements:* For master's, GMAT, minimum GPA of 3.0. Additional exam requirements/recommendations for international students: Required—TOEFL (minimum score 500 paper-based; 173 computer-based). *Application deadline:* For fall admission, 7/1 for domestic students, 4/1 for international students; for spring admission, 11/1 for domestic students, 9/1 for international students. Applications are processed on a rolling basis. Application fee: $40 ($75 for international students). Electronic applications accepted. *Expenses:* Tuition, state resident: part-time $153 per hour. Tuition, nonresident: part-time $625 per hour. Total annual research expenditures: $61,116. *Unit head:* Dr. Jerry Keating, Chair, 210-458-6345, Fax: 210-458-6350, E-mail: jkeating@utsa.edu.

University of Toledo, Graduate School, College of Arts and Sciences, Department of Mathematics, Toledo, OH 43606-3390. Offers applied mathematics (MS); mathematics (MA, PhD); statistics (MS). Part-time programs available. *Students:* 32 full-time (12 women), 11 part-time (3 women), 32 international. Average age 29. 74 applicants, 53% accepted. In 2003, 19 master's, 1 doctorate awarded. *Degree requirements:* For doctorate, 2 foreign languages, thesis/dissertation. *Entrance requirements:* For master's and doctorate, GRE General Test, GRE Subject Test. *Application deadline:* For fall admission, 8/1 for domestic students. Application fee: $40. Electronic applications accepted. Tuition, area resident: Part-time $3,817 per semester. *Expenses:* Tuition, state resident: part-time $8,177 per semester. Required fees: $502 per semester. *Financial support:* In 2003–04, 6 research assistantships, 27 teaching assistantships were awarded. Federal Work-Study and institutionally sponsored loans also available. Support available to part-time students. Financial award application deadline: 4/1; financial award applicants required to submit FAFSA. *Faculty research:* Topology. *Unit head:* Dr. Geoffrey Martin, Chair, 419-530-2569, Fax: 419-530-4720. *Application contact:* Dr. Robert Ochs, Advising Coordinator, 419-530-2069, Fax: 419-530-4720, E-mail: rochs@math.utoledo.edu.

See in-depth description on page 617.

University of Toronto, School of Graduate Studies, Physical Sciences Division, Department of Statistics, Toronto, ON M5S 1A1, Canada. Offers M Sc, PhD. Part-time programs available. *Faculty:* 18 full-time (1 woman). *Students:* 45 full-time (18 women), 9 part-time, 5 international. 79 applicants, 39% accepted. In 2003, 18 master's, 3 doctorates awarded. *Median time to degree:* Master's–1 year full-time. *Degree requirements:* For doctorate, thesis/dissertation, comprehensive exam. *Entrance requirements:* For master's, GRE (recommended for students educated outside of Canada), 3 letters of reference, minimum B+ average, exposure to statistics and mathematics; for doctorate, GRE (recommended for students educated outside of Canada), 3 letters of reference, M Stat or equivalent, minimum B+ average. *Application deadline:* For fall admission, 1/5 for domestic students. Application fee: $90 Canadian dollars. Tuition, nonresident: full-time $4,185. International tuition: $10,739 full-time. *Unit head:* Keith Knight, Chair, 416-978-4461, Fax: 416-978-5133, E-mail: keith@utstat.toronto.edu. *Application contact:* Laura Kerr, Secretary, 416-978-5136, Fax: 416-978-5133, E-mail: grad-info@utstat.utoronto.ca.

University of Utah, Graduate School, Interdepartmental Program in Statistics, Salt Lake City, UT 84112-1107. Offers M Stat. Part-time programs available. *Students:* 3 full-time (2 women), 9 part-time (4 women); includes 2 minority (both Asian Americans or Pacific Islanders), 1 international. Average age 35. 20 applicants, 75% accepted. *Degree requirements:* For master's, projects. *Entrance requirements:* For master's, minimum GPA of 3.0, previous course work in calculus, matrix theory, statistics. Additional exam requirements/recommendations for international students: Required—TOEFL. *Application deadline:* For fall admission, 7/1 for domestic students. Applications are processed on a rolling basis. Application fee: $45 ($60 for international students). Tuition, nonresident: full-time $2,483. International tuition: $8,768 full-time. *Financial support:* Career-related internships or fieldwork available. *Faculty research:* Biostatistics, management, economics, educational psychology, mathematics. *Unit head:* Marlene Egger, Chair, University Statistics Committee, 801-581-6830, E-mail: megger@dfpm.utah.edu. *Application contact:* Glenda Pruemper, Administrative Assistant, 801-581-7148, Fax: 801-581-5566, E-mail: pruemper@ed.utah.edu.

University of Utah, Graduate School, Program in Science and Technology, Salt Lake City, UT 84112-1107. Offers statistics (MST). *Students:* 15 full-time (3 women), 12 part-time (3 women); includes 3 minority (2 Asian Americans or Pacific Islanders, 1 Hispanic American), 4 international. Tuition, nonresident: full-time $2,483. International tuition: $8,768 full-time. *Application contact:* Jennifer Schmidt, Director, 801-585-5630, E-mail: jennifer.schmidt@admin.utah.edu.

University of Vermont, Graduate College, College of Engineering and Mathematics, Department of Mathematics and Statistics, Program in Statistics, Burlington, VT 05405. Offers MS. *Students:* 7 (3 women) 2 international. 21 applicants, 67% accepted, 4 enrolled. In 2003, 3 degrees awarded. *Entrance requirements:* Additional exam requirements/recommendations for international students: Required—TOEFL (minimum score 550 paper-based; 213 computer-based). *Application deadline:* For fall admission, 4/1 for domestic students. Applications are processed on a rolling basis. Application fee: $25. *Expenses:* Tuition, state resident: part-time $362 per credit hour. Tuition, nonresident: part-time $906 per credit hour. *Financial support:* Fellowships, research assistantships, teaching assistantships available. Financial award application deadline: 3/1. *Faculty research:* Applied statistics. *Unit head:* Dr. J. Buzas, Coordinator, 802-656-2940.

University of Victoria, Faculty of Graduate Studies, Faculty of Science, Department of Mathematics and Statistics, Victoria, BC V8W 2Y2, Canada. Offers applied mathematics (M Sc, MA, PhD); pure mathematics (M Sc, MA, PhD); statistics (M Sc, MA). Part-time programs available. *Degree requirements:* For doctorate, one foreign language, thesis/dissertation, 3 qualifying exams. *Entrance requirements:* Additional exam requirements/recommendations for international students: Required—TOEFL. *Faculty research:* Functional analysis and operator theory, applied ordinary and partial differential equations, discrete mathematics and graph theory.

University of Virginia, College and Graduate School of Arts and Sciences, Department of Statistics, Charlottesville, VA 22903. Offers MS, PhD. *Faculty:* 5 full-time (1 woman). *Students:* 8 full-time (1 woman), 1 (woman) part-time; includes 1 minority (Asian American or Pacific Islander), 2 international. Average age 31. 39 applicants, 0% accepted. In 2003, 4 master's, 2 doctorates awarded. *Degree requirements:* For master's and doctorate, thesis/dissertation. *Entrance requirements:* For master's and doctorate, GRE General Test, GRE Subject Test. *Application deadline:* For fall admission, 7/15 for domestic students; for spring admission, 12/1 for domestic students. Applications are processed on a rolling basis. Application fee: $40. Electronic applications accepted. *Expenses:* Tuition, state resident: full-time $6,476. Tuition, nonresident: full-time $18,534. Required fees: $1,380. *Financial support:* Application deadline: 2/1; *Unit head:* Jeff Holt, Chairman, 434-924-3222, Fax: 434-924-3076, E-mail: gradapp1@pitman.stat.virginia.edu. *Application contact:* Peter C. Brunjes, Associate Dean for Graduate Programs and Research, 434-924-7184, Fax: 434-924-6737, E-mail: grad-a-s@virginia.edu.

University of Washington, Graduate School, College of Arts and Sciences, Department of Statistics, Seattle, WA 98195. Offers MS, PhD. Terminal master's awarded for partial completion of doctoral program. *Degree requirements:* For master's, thesis optional; for doctorate, one foreign language, thesis/dissertation. *Entrance requirements:* For master's and doctorate, GRE General Test, minimum GPA of 3.0. Additional exam requirements/recommendations for international students: Required—TOEFL. *Faculty research:* Mathematical statistics, stochastic modeling, spatial statistics, statistical computing.

University of Washington, Graduate School, School of Public Health and Community Medicine, Department of Biostatistics, Seattle, WA 98195. Offers biostatistics (MPH, MS, PhD); statistical genetics (PhD). *Faculty:* 71 full-time (31 women), 8 part-time/adjunct (5 women). *Students:* 71 full-time (38 women), 5 part-time (1 woman); includes 11 minority (1 African American, 1 American Indian/Alaska Native, 8 Asian Americans or Pacific Islanders, 1 Hispanic American), 26 international. Average age 24. 69 applicants, 51% accepted, 20 enrolled. In 2003, 10 master's awarded, leading to business/industry 100%, 6 doctorates awarded, leading to university research/teaching 66%, business/industry 33%. Terminal master's awarded for partial completion of doctoral program. *Median time to degree:* Master's–3 years full-time; doctorate–6 years full-time. Of those who began their doctoral program in fall 1995, 85% received their degree in 8 years or less. *Degree requirements:* For master's, thesis/dissertation, departmental qualifying exams; for doctorate, thesis/dissertation, departmental qualifying exams, comprehensive exam, registration. *Entrance requirements:* For master's and doctorate, GRE General Test, 2 years of advanced calculus, 1 course in linear algebra, 1 course in mathematical probability; minimum GPA of 3.0. Additional exam requirements/recommendations for international students: Required—TOEFL, TSE. *Application deadline:* For fall admission, 1/3 for domestic students. Application fee: $50. Electronic applications accepted. *Financial support:* In 2003–04, 64 students received support, including 1 fellowship with partial tuition reimbursement available (averaging $19,000 per year), 36 research assistantships with full tuition reimbursements available (averaging $16,000 per year), 5 teaching assistantships with full tuition reimbursements available (averaging $16,000 per year); career-related internships or fieldwork, traineeships, and unspecified assistantships also available. Financial award application deadline: 1/3. *Faculty research:* Statistical methods for survival data analysis, clinical trials, epidemiological case control and cohort studies, statistical genetics. *Unit head:* Dr. Thomas Fleming, Chair, 206-543-1044. *Application contact:* Alex Mackenzie, Program Coordinator, 206-543-1044, Fax: 206-543-3286, E-mail: alexam@u.washington.edu.

University of Waterloo, Graduate Studies, Faculty of Mathematics, Department of Statistics and Actuarial Science, Waterloo, ON N2L 3G1, Canada. Offers actuarial science (M Math); statistics (M Math, PhD); statistics-biostatistics (M Math); statistics-computing (M Math); statistics-finance (M Math). *Faculty:* 33 full-time (6 women), 21 part-time/adjunct (5 women). *Students:* 93 full-time (50 women), 5 part-time. 308 applicants, 24% accepted, 34 enrolled. In 2003, 18 master's, 3 doctorates awarded. *Degree requirements:* For master's, research paper or thesis; for doctorate, thesis/dissertation. *Entrance requirements:* For master's, honors degree in field, minimum B+ average; for doctorate, master's degree, minimum B+ average. Additional exam requirements/recommendations for international students: Required—TOEFL, TWE. *Application deadline:* For fall admission, 3/31 for domestic students; for winter admission, 8/31 for domestic students; for spring admission, 12/31 for domestic students. Applications are processed on a rolling basis. Application fee: $75 Canadian dollars. Electronic applications accepted. Tuition and fees charges are reported in Canadian dollars. *Expenses:* Tuition, state resident: full-time $3,632 Canadian dollars. International tuition: $9,180 Canadian dollars full-time. Required fees: $406 Canadian dollars. *Financial support:* In 2003–04, 30 teaching assistantships were awarded; fellowships, research assistantships, career-related internships or fieldwork and scholarships/grants also available. *Faculty research:* Data analysis, risk theory, inference, stochastic processes, quantitative finance. *Unit head:* Dr. D. E. Matthews, Chair, 519-888-4567 Ext. 5530, Fax: 519-746-1875, E-mail: dematthe@uwaterloo.ca. *Application contact:* L. Clarke, Graduate Studies Secretary, 519-888-4567 Ext. 6532, Fax: 519-746-1875, E-mail: sasgrad@math.uwaterloo.ca.

The University of Western Ontario, Faculty of Graduate Studies, Physical Sciences Division, Department of Statistical and Actuarial Sciences, London, ON N6A 5B8, Canada. Offers M Sc, PhD. *Degree requirements:* For master's, thesis (for some programs); for doctorate, thesis/dissertation, comprehensive exam. *Faculty research:* Statistical theory, statistical applications, probability, actuarial science.

University of West Florida, College of Arts and Sciences: Sciences, Department of Mathematics and Statistics, Pensacola, FL 32514-5750. Offers mathematics (MA); mathematics education (MAT); statistics (MA). *Accreditation:* NCATE (one or more programs are accredited). Part-time and evening/weekend programs available. *Faculty:* 8 full-time (1 woman), 1 part-time/adjunct (0 women). *Students:* 6 full-time (4 women), 12 part-time (7 women); includes 3 minority (1 African American, 1 American Indian/Alaska Native, 1 Asian American or Pacific Islander), 1 international. Average age 32. 14 applicants, 79% accepted, 8 enrolled. In 2003, 8 degrees awarded. *Degree requirements:* For master's, thesis optional. *Entrance requirements:* For master's, GRE General Test, minimum GPA of 3.0. Additional exam requirements/recommendations for international students: Required—TOEFL (minimum score 550 paper-based; 213 computer-based). *Application deadline:* For fall admission, 6/1 for domestic students, 5/15 for international students; for spring admission, 11/1 for domestic students, 10/1 for international students. Applications are processed on a rolling basis. Application fee: $20. *Expenses:* Tuition, state resident: full-time $4,986; part-time $208 per credit hour. Tuition, nonresident: full-time $18,649; part-time $777 per credit hour. Tuition and fees vary according to course load, campus/location and reciprocity agreements. *Financial support:* In 2003–04, 6 teaching assistantships with partial tuition reimbursements (averaging $4,000 per year) were awarded; fellowships, career-related internships or fieldwork, Federal Work-Study, institutionally sponsored loans, and tuition waivers (full and partial) also available. Support available to part-time students. Financial award application deadline: 4/15; financial award applicants required to submit FAFSA. *Unit head:* Dr. Kuiyuan Li, Chairperson, 850-474-2287.

University of Windsor, Faculty of Graduate Studies and Research, Faculty of Science, Department of Mathematics and Statistics, Windsor, ON N9B 3P4, Canada. Offers mathematics (M Sc, PhD); statistics (M Sc, PhD). *Faculty:* 12 full-time (2 women). *Students:* 28 full-time (6 women), 1 part-time. 90 applicants, 24% accepted. In 2003, 9 master's, 1 doctorate awarded. *Degree requirements:* For master's, thesis or alternative; for doctorate, thesis/dissertation. *Entrance requirements:* For master's, minimum B average; for doctorate, minimum A average. Additional exam requirements/recommendations for international students: Required—TOEFL. *Application deadline:* For fall admission, 7/1 for domestic students; for winter admission, 11/1 for domestic students. Applications are processed on a rolling basis. Application fee: $55. Tuition charges are reported in Canadian dollars. *Expenses:* Tuition, state resident: full-time $1,704 Canadian dollars. Tuition, nonresident: full-time $2,126 Canadian dollars. International tuition: $2,976 Canadian dollars full-time. *Financial support:* In 2003–04, 20 teaching assistantships (averaging $8,000 per year) were awarded; Federal Work-Study, scholarships/grants, tuition waivers (full and partial), unspecified assistantships, and bursaries also available. Financial award application deadline: 2/15. *Unit head:* Dr. Ejaz Ahmed, Head, 519-253-3000 Ext. 3017, Fax: 519-971-3649, E-mail: seahmed@uwindsor.ca. *Application contact:* Applicant Services, 519-253-3000 Ext. 6459, Fax: 519-971-3653, E-mail: gradadmit@uwindsor.ca.

University of Wisconsin–Madison, Graduate School, College of Letters and Science, Department of Statistics, Madison, WI 53706-1380. Offers MS, PhD. Part-time programs available. *Degree requirements:* For master's, exam; for doctorate, thesis/dissertation. *Entrance requirements:* For master's and doctorate, GRE. Additional exam requirements/recommendations for international students: Required—TOEFL. Electronic applications accepted. Tuition, area resident: Full-time $7,593; part-time $476 per credit. Tuition, nonresident: full-time $22,824; part-time $1,430 per credit. Required fees: $292; $38 per credit. Part-time tuition and fees vary according to course load and reciprocity agreements. *Faculty research:* Biostatistics, bootstrap and other resampling theory and methods, linear and nonlinear models, nonparametrics, time series and stochastic processes.

University of Wyoming, Graduate School, College of Arts and Sciences, Department of Statistics, Laramie, WY 82070. Offers MS, PhD. *Faculty:* 7 full-time (1 woman). *Students:* 17 full-time (12 women), 4 part-time (1 woman), 9 international. Average age 33. 2 applicants, 100% accepted. In 2003, 1 degree awarded. Terminal master's awarded for partial completion of doctoral program. *Degree requirements:* For master's, thesis (for some programs), comprehensive exam (for some programs); for doctorate, thesis/dissertation, comprehensive exam. *Entrance requirements:* For master's, GMAT, GRE General Test, minimum GPA of 3.0; for doctorate, GRE General Test, minimum GPA of 3.0. Additional exam requirements/recommendations for international students: Required—TOEFL; Recommended—TWE. *Application deadline:* For fall admission, 3/1 for domestic students. Application fee: $40. Electronic applications accepted. *Expenses:* Tuition, state resident: part-time $142 per credit hour. Tuition, nonresident: part-time $408 per credit hour. Required fees: $134 per semester. Tuition and fees vary according to course load, campus/location, program and student level. *Financial support:* In 2003–04, 9 teaching assistantships with full tuition reimbursements (averaging $10,062 per year) were awarded; research assistantships with full tuition reimbursements, Federal Work-Study and institutionally sponsored loans also available. Financial award application deadline: 3/1. *Faculty research:* Mining impacts, biotic integrity. Total annual research expenditures: $25,000. *Unit head:* Dr. Stephen Bieber, Head, 307-766-4229, Fax: 307-766-3927, E-mail: barbr@uwyo.edu.

Utah State University, School of Graduate Studies, College of Science, Department of Mathematics and Statistics, Logan, UT 84322. Offers industrial mathematics (MS); mathematical sciences (PhD); mathematics (M Math, MS); statistics (MS). Part-time programs available. *Faculty:* 30 full-time (5 women). *Students:* 30 full-time (12 women), 6 part-time, 24 international. Average age 29. 68 applicants, 19% accepted, 8 enrolled. In 2003, 9 degrees awarded. Terminal master's awarded for partial completion of doctoral program. *Degree requirements:* For master's, qualifying exam, thesis optional; for doctorate, one foreign language, thesis/dissertation, comprehensive exam. *Entrance requirements:* For master's and doctorate, GRE General Test, minimum GPA of 3.0. Additional exam requirements/recommendations for international students: Required—TOEFL. *Application deadline:* For fall admission, 6/15 for domestic students; for spring admission, 10/15 for domestic students. Applications are processed on a rolling basis. Application fee: $50 ($60 for international students). *Expenses:* Tuition, state resident: part-time $270 per credit hour. Tuition, nonresident: part-time $946 per credit hour. Required fees: $173 per credit hour. *Financial support:* In 2003–04, 1 fellowship with partial tuition reimbursement (averaging $12,000 per year), 17 teaching assistantships with partial tuition reimbursements (averaging $14,500 per year) were awarded. Research assistantships with partial tuition reimbursements Support available to part-time students. Financial award application deadline: 4/1. *Faculty research:* Differential equations, computational mathematics, dynamical systems, probability and statistics, pure mathematics. *Unit head:* Dr. Russell C. Thompson, Head, 435-797-2810, Fax: 435-797-1822, E-mail: thompson@math.usu.edu. *Application contact:* Dr. Joseph Koebbe, Graduate Chairman, 435-797-2825, Fax: 435-797-1822, E-mail: koebbe@math.usu.edu.

Villanova University, Graduate School of Liberal Arts and Sciences, Department of Mathematical Sciences, Program in Applied Statistics, Villanova, PA 19085-1699. Offers MS. Part-time and evening/weekend programs available. *Students:* 2 full-time (1 woman), 42 part-time (24 women); includes 3 minority (all Asian Americans or Pacific Islanders), 8 international. Average age 32. 34 applicants, 50% accepted. In 2003, 14 degrees awarded. *Degree requirements:* For master's, comprehensive exam. *Entrance requirements:* For master's, minimum GPA of 3.0. *Application deadline:* For fall admission, 8/1 for domestic students; for spring admission, 12/1 for domestic students. Application fee: $40. *Expenses:* Tuition: Part-time $750 per credit. *Financial support:* Research assistantships, Federal Work-Study available. Financial award applicants required to submit FAFSA. *Unit head:* Dr. Thomas Short, Director.

Virginia Commonwealth University, School of Graduate Studies, College of Humanities and Sciences, Department of Mathematical Sciences, Program in Statistics, Richmond, VA 23284-9005. Offers MS, Certificate. *Students:* 2 full-time (both women), 5 part-time (1 woman); includes 2 minority (both African Americans), 3 international. 7 applicants, 71% accepted, 2 enrolled. In 2003, 4 degrees awarded. *Entrance requirements:* For master's, GRE General Test, GRE Subject Test. Additional exam requirements/recommendations for international students: Required—TOEFL. *Application deadline:* For fall admission, 7/1 for domestic students; for spring admission, 11/15 for domestic students. Applications are processed on a rolling basis. Application fee: $30. *Expenses:* Tuition, state resident: full-time $2,889; part-time $321 per credit hour. Tuition, nonresident: full-time $7,952; part-time $884 per credit hour. Required fees: $42 per credit hour. *Application contact:* Dr. James A. Wood, Information Contact, 804-828-1301, E-mail: jawood@vcu.edu.

Virginia Polytechnic Institute and State University, Graduate School, College of Science, Department of Statistics, Blacksburg, VA 24061. Offers MS, PhD. *Entrance requirements:* Additional exam requirements/recommendations for international students: Required—TOEFL. *Application deadline:* Applications are processed on a rolling basis. Application fee: $45. Tuition, area resident: Full-time $6,039; part-time $336 per credit. Tuition, nonresident: full-time $9,708; part-time $539 per credit. Required fees: $905; $130 per credit. *Financial support:* Fellowships, research assistantships with full tuition reimbursements, teaching assistantships with full tuition reimbursements, career-related internships or fieldwork, Federal Work-Study, scholarships/grants, and unspecified assistantships available. Financial award application deadline: 4/1. *Faculty research:* Design and sampling theory, computing and simulation, nonparametric statistics, robust and multivariate methods, biostatistics quality. *Unit head:* Dr. Geoff Vining, Head, 540-231-5657, Fax: 540-231-3863, E-mail: vining@vt.edu. *Application contact:* Dr. Jeffrey B. Birch, Director of Graduate Programs, 540-231-7934, Fax: 540-231-3863, E-mail: jbbirch@vt.edu.

Washington University in St. Louis, Graduate School of Arts and Sciences, Department of Mathematics, St. Louis, MO 63130-4899. Offers mathematics (MA, PhD); mathematics education (MAT); statistics (MA, PhD). *Students:* 38 full-time (15 women); includes 1 minority (Asian American or Pacific Islander), 14 international. 124 applicants, 22% accepted, 8 enrolled. In 2003, 13 master's, 1 doctorate awarded. Terminal master's awarded for partial completion of doctoral program. *Degree requirements:* For master's, thesis or alternative; for doctorate, thesis/dissertation. *Entrance requirements:* For master's and doctorate, GRE General Test. *Application deadline:* For fall admission, 1/15 for domestic students. Applications are processed on a rolling basis. Application fee: $35. Electronic applications accepted. *Expenses:* Tuition: Full-time $28,300; part-time $1,180 per credit. *Financial support:* Fellowships, research assistantships, teaching assistantships, Federal Work-Study, institutionally sponsored loans, and tuition waivers (full and partial) available. Support available to part-time students. Financial award application deadline: 1/15. *Unit head:* Dr. Steven Krantz, Chairman, 314-935-6760.

Wayne State University, Graduate School, College of Science, Department of Mathematics, Program in Statistics, Detroit, MI 48202. Offers MA, PhD. *Students:* 8 full-time (5 women), 1 (woman) part-time, 8 international. 12 applicants, 25% accepted, 1 enrolled. In 2003, 1 degree awarded. *Degree requirements:* For doctorate, thesis/dissertation. *Entrance requirements:* Additional exam requirements/recommendations for international students: Required—TOEFL (minimum score 550 paper-based; 213 computer-based); Recommended—TWE(minimum score 6). *Application deadline:* For fall admission, 7/1 for domestic students, 6/1 for international students. Applications are processed on a rolling basis. Application fee: $30 ($50 for international students). Electronic applications accepted. *Expenses:* Tuition, state resident: part-time $263 per credit hour. Tuition, nonresident: part-time $580 per credit hour. Required fees: $21 per credit hour. *Application contact:* Dr. Tze-Chien Sun, Graduate Director, 313-577-8840, Fax: 313-577-7596, E-mail: tsun@wayne.edu.

Western Michigan University, Graduate College, College of Arts and Sciences, Department of Statistics, Kalamazoo, MI 49008-5202. Offers biostatistics (MS).

West Virginia University, College of Business and Economics, Division of Economics and Finance, Morgantown, WV 26506. Offers business analysis (MA); econometrics (PhD); industrial economics (PhD); international economics (PhD); labor economics (PhD); mathematical economics (MA, PhD); monetary economics (PhD); public finance (PhD); public policy (MA); regional and urban economics (PhD); statistics and economics (MA). *Faculty:* 21 full-time (3 women), 2 part-time/adjunct (1 woman). *Students:* 48 full-time (15 women), 10 part-time (2 women); includes 1 minority (Asian American or Pacific Islander), 38 international. Average age 30. 120 applicants, 25% accepted, 12 enrolled. In 2003, 6 degrees awarded, leading to continued full-time study 84%, business/industry 16%. Terminal master's awarded for partial completion of doctoral program. *Degree requirements:* For master's, thesis optional; for doctorate, thesis/dissertation, comprehensive exam. *Entrance requirements:* For master's and doctorate, GRE General Test, minimum GPA of 3.0, course work in intermediate microeconomics, intermediate macroeconomics, calculus, and statistics. Additional exam requirements/recommendations for international students: Required—TOEFL. *Application deadline:* For fall admission, 3/1 priority date for domestic students, 3/1 priority date for international students. Applications are processed on a rolling basis. Application fee: $50. Electronic applications accepted. *Expenses:* Tuition, state resident: full-time $4,332. Tuition, nonresident: full-time $12,442. *Financial support:* In 2003–04, 50 students received support, including 1 fellowship with full tuition reimbursement available (averaging $15,000 per year), 8 research assistantships with full tuition reimbursements available (averaging $9,300 per year), 23 teaching assistantships with full tuition reimbursements available (averaging $9,300 per year); Federal Work-Study, institutionally sponsored loans, and tuition waivers (full and partial) also available. Financial award applicants required to submit FAFSA. *Faculty research:* Financial economics, regional/urban development and problems, public economics. *Unit head:* Dr. William N. Trumbull, Director, 304-293-7860, Fax: 304-293-5652, E-mail: william.trumbull@mail.wvu.edu. *Application contact:* Dr.

Statistics

West Virginia University (continued)
Brian Cushing, Director of Admissions and Financial Awards, 304-293-7881, Fax: 304-293-5652, E-mail: brian.cushing@mail.wvu.edu.

West Virginia University, Eberly College of Arts and Sciences, Department of Statistics, Morgantown, WV 26506. Offers MS. *Faculty:* 7 full-time (0 women), 2 part-time/adjunct (0 women). *Students:* 29 full-time (22 women), 15 part-time (9 women); includes 5 minority (all Asian Americans or Pacific Islanders), 35 international. Average age 32. 31 applicants, 94% accepted, 15 enrolled. In 2003, 18 degrees awarded. *Median time to degree:* Master's–2 years full-time, 3 years part-time. *Degree requirements:* For master's, thesis, comprehensive exam. *Entrance requirements:* For master's, minimum GPA of 3.0, course work in linear multivanate calculus and algebra. Additional exam requirements/recommendations for international students: Required—TOEFL. *Application deadline:* For fall admission, 3/15 priority date for domestic students, 3/15 priority date for international students; for spring admission, 10/15 priority date for domestic students, 10/15 priority date for international students. Applications are processed on a rolling basis. Application fee: $45. *Expenses:* Tuition, state resident: full-time $4,332. Tuition, nonresident: full-time $12,442. *Financial support:* In 2003–04, 7 research assistantships with full tuition reimbursements (averaging $8,554 per year), 11 teaching assistantships with full tuition reimbursements (averaging $8,554 per year) were awarded. Federal Work-Study, institutionally sponsored loans, and tuition waivers (full and partial) also available. Financial award application deadline: 2/1; financial award applicants required to submit FAFSA. *Faculty research:* Linear models, categorical data analysis, statistical computing, experimental design, non parametric analysis. Total annual research expenditures: $404,000. *Unit head:* E. James Harner, Chair, 304-293-3607 Ext. 1051, Fax: 304-293-2272, E-mail: jim.harner@mail.wvu.edu.

Wichita State University, Graduate School, Fairmount College of Liberal Arts and Sciences, Department of Mathematics and Statistics, Wichita, KS 67260. Offers applied mathematics (PhD); mathematics (MS); statistics (MS). Part-time programs available. *Faculty:* 22 full-time (0 women). *Students:* 17 full-time (5 women), 9 part-time (4 women); includes 1 minority (Hispanic American), 12 international. Average age 33. 20 applicants, 70% accepted. In 2003, 3 master's, 2 doctorates awarded. *Degree requirements:* For master's, thesis optional; for doctorate, thesis/dissertation. *Entrance requirements:* For master's, GRE; for doctorate, GRE Subject Test. Additional exam requirements/recommendations for international students: Required—TOEFL. *Application deadline:* For fall admission, 7/1 for domestic students; for spring admission, 1/1 for domestic students. Applications are processed on a rolling basis. Application fee: $35 ($50 for international students). Electronic applications accepted. *Expenses:* Tuition, state resident: full-time $2,457; part-time $137 per credit hour. Tuition, nonresident: full-time $7,371; part-time $410 per credit hour. Required fees: $364; $20 per credit hour. Tuition and fees vary according to course load. *Financial support:* In 2003–04, 1 research assistantship (averaging $14,000 per year), 15 teaching assistantships with full tuition reimbursements (averaging $11,027 per year) were awarded. Fellowships, Federal Work-Study, institutionally sponsored loans, scholarships/grants, traineeships, and unspecified assistantships also available. Support available to part-time students. Financial award application deadline: 4/1; financial award applicants required to submit FAFSA. *Faculty research:* Partial differential equations, combinatorics, ring theory, minimal surfaces, several complex variables. *Unit head:* Dr. Buma Fridman, Chair, 316-978-3160, Fax: 316-978-3748, E-mail: buma.fridman@wichita.edu.

Worcester Polytechnic Institute, Graduate Studies and Enrollment, Department of Mathematical Science, Worcester, MA 01609-2280. Offers applied mathematics (MS); applied statistics (MS); financial mathematics (MS); industrial mathematics (MS); mathematical science (PhD, Certificate); mathematics (MME). Part-time and evening/weekend programs available. *Faculty:* 28 full-time (2 women), 1 (woman) part-time/adjunct. *Students:* 26 full-time (13 women), 27 part-time (12 women); includes 2 minority (1 African American, 1 Asian American or Pacific Islander), 17 international. 71 applicants, 93% accepted, 19 enrolled. In 2003, 18 degrees awarded. *Degree requirements:* For master's, thesis optional; for doctorate, thesis/dissertation, comprehensive exam. *Entrance requirements:* Additional exam requirements/recommendations for international students: Required—TOEFL (minimum score 550 paper-based; 213 computer-based). *Application deadline:* For fall admission, 2/1 for domestic students; for spring admission, 10/15 priority date for domestic students. Applications are processed on a rolling basis. Application fee: $70. Electronic applications accepted. *Expenses:* Tuition: Part-time $897 per credit. *Financial support:* In 2003–04, 10 students received support, including 6 fellowships with full tuition reimbursements available, 9 research assistantships, 10 teaching assistantships with full tuition reimbursements available; career-related internships or fieldwork, institutionally sponsored loans, scholarships/grants, health care benefits, and unspecified assistantships also available. Financial award application deadline: 2/15; financial award applicants required to submit FAFSA. *Faculty research:* Applied mathematical modeling and analysis, computational mathematics, discrete mathematics, applied and computational statistics, industrial and financial mathematics. Total annual research expenditures: $592,514. *Unit head:* Dr. Bogdan Vernesca, Head, 508-831-5316, Fax: 508-831-5824. *Application contact:* Dr. Joseph Petruccelli, Graduate Coordinator, 508-831-5362, Fax: 508-831-5824, E-mail: jdp@wpi.edu.

See in-depth description on page 631.

Wright State University, School of Graduate Studies, College of Science and Mathematics, Department of Mathematics and Statistics, Program in Applied Statistics, Dayton, OH 45435. Offers MS. *Students:* 3 full-time (all women), 4 part-time (2 women), 2 international. Average age 30. 6 applicants, 100% accepted. In 2003, 5 degrees awarded. *Degree requirements:* For master's, comprehensive exam. *Entrance requirements:* For master's, 1 year of course work in calculus and matrix algebra, previous course work in computer programming and statistics. Additional exam requirements/recommendations for international students: Required—TOEFL. Application fee: $25. *Expenses:* Tuition, state resident: full-time $8,112; part-time $255 per quarter hour. Tuition, nonresident: full-time $14,127; part-time $442 per quarter hour. International tuition: $14,283 full-time. Tuition and fees vary according to course load, degree level and program. *Financial support:* Fellowships, research assistantships, teaching assistantships available. Support available to part-time students. Financial award applicants required to submit FAFSA. *Faculty research:* Reliability theory, stochastic process, nonparametric statistics, design of experiments, multivariate statistics. *Unit head:* Dr. Munsup Seoh, Director, 937-775-2785, Fax: 937-775-3068, E-mail: munsup.seoh@wright.edu.

Yale University, Graduate School of Arts and Sciences, Department of Statistics, New Haven, CT 06520. Offers MS, PhD. Terminal master's awarded for partial completion of doctoral program. *Degree requirements:* For doctorate, thesis/dissertation. *Entrance requirements:* For doctorate, GRE General Test, GRE Subject Test. *Expenses:* Tuition: Full-time $25,600; part-time $6,400 per term.

York University, Faculty of Graduate Studies, Faculty of Arts, Program in Mathematics and Statistics, Toronto, ON M3J 1P3, Canada. Offers industrial and applied mathematics (M Sc); mathematics and statistics (MA, PhD). Part-time programs available. *Degree requirements:* For master's, thesis optional; for doctorate, one foreign language, thesis/dissertation, comprehensive exam. *Entrance requirements:* For master's, minimum B average; for doctorate, minimum B+ average. Electronic applications accepted. Tuition, area resident: Full-time $5,431; part-time $905 per term. Tuition, nonresident: part-time $1,987 per term. International tuition: $11,918 full-time. Required fees: $287. Tuition and fees vary according to program.

Cross-Discipline Announcements

Northeastern University, College of Computer and Information Science, Boston, MA 02115-5096.

The College of Computer and Information Science offers programs leading to the MS and PhD degrees. The MS program prepares students for challenging technical positions in the software industry. The PhD program equips its graduates with the depth of knowledge and experience needed to conduct advanced research in either academia or industry.

Northwestern University, McCormick School of Engineering and Applied Science, Department of Industrial Engineering and Management Sciences, Evanston, IL 60208.

The department offers a doctoral program for studies in applied probability and simulation, economics and decision analysis, production and logistics, optimization, organization theory and systems analysis, and statistics and decision analysis. For further information, see In-Depth Description in Book 5, Industrial Engineering section, or visit www.iems.nwu.edu/programs/doctoral/.

BOWLING GREEN STATE UNIVERSITY

Department of Mathematics and Statistics

Programs of Study

The Department of Mathematics and Statistics offers a full range of graduate degrees. Degree options at the master's level include the M.A., with concentrations in pure mathematics, scientific computation, and probability and statistics, and the M.S. in applied statistics. These programs are offered with a thesis option and a comprehensive examination option. The department also offers a Master of Arts in Teaching (M.A.T.) in mathematics for those interested in teaching at the secondary level or at two- and four-year colleges. M.A.T. course work is tailored to the individual and may be supplemented by an internship or other field experience. The master's degree programs are two-year programs of study, but well-qualified students can complete a degree in three semesters.

The Ph.D. program combines advanced study with individual research; a dissertation consisting of original research is required. Strong research areas include probability and statistics, algebra, analysis, and scientific computation. The research environment is further enhanced by the department's active program of seminars and colloquia. Weekly seminars are conducted in algebra, analysis, mathematics education, scientific computation, and statistics. The department has 27 full-time faculty members, all of whom hold Ph.D. degrees. The department hosts several distinguished visiting scholars each year, including a Lukacs Distinguished Professor in Probability and Statistics. In addition to working with advanced graduate students, the Lukacs Professor organizes the Annual Lukacs Symposium, which attracts leading statisticians from around the world. As part of the department's continuing commitment to quality instruction, all students are given opportunities for a variety of training and mentoring experiences that are designed to enhance their effectiveness both as students and as teachers.

Research Facilities

Faculty member and graduate student offices are located in the Mathematical Sciences Building, which also houses the Frank C. Ogg Science Library and the Scientific Computing Laboratory. The Science Library, in addition to its extensive holdings, maintains subscriptions to approximately 400 journals, both paper and electronic, in mathematics and statistics. Further, the interlibrary OhioLink program provides access to the holdings of all other state-funded university libraries in Ohio. The Scientific Computing Laboratory offers microcomputer access with fast Internet connections and a wealth of software, UNIX/X11 access, and a full-time staff to provide assistance to users. Additional computing resources include a network of UNIX workstations that are maintained by the department and available to students at all times. The University also maintains several systems for student use, including a four-processor SGI Power Challenge, a DEC Alpha 2100 5/250, a DEC VAX 6620, two IBM mainframes, and various graphics workstations. Each graduate student office is furnished with a microcomputer with network access.

Financial Aid

The department provides approximately fifty-six teaching assistantships with stipends of $10,000 for master's students for the academic year and $12,623 for doctoral students for the academic year. Also offered are three nonservice fellowships of $15,779 for the calendar year. Instructional and nonresident fees are waived. The department also provides summer support through a variety of fellowships and assistantships that range from $1594 to $3550. In addition, all new students are encouraged to accept Summer Fellowships of $1800 for an initial six-week summer program.

Teaching assistants serve as instructors for small individual classes that consist of about 30 students. This involves five or six contact hours per week with undergraduate students. The University's Statistical Consulting Center also provides consultantships for graduate assistants with appropriate backgrounds. These positions provide valuable experience for those preparing for careers in statistics. The stipends offered by the Statistical Consulting Center are the same amount as those awarded to teaching assistants. For further information, students should consult the department's Web site (address below).

Cost of Study

Tuition and nonresident fees for the 2004–05 academic year (fall, spring, and summer) are $22,614. Tuition and nonresident fees and most other fees are covered by the assistantship package. Students are also required to have adequate health insurance, which may be purchased through the University at a nominal fee. Students must purchase their own books and pay any applicable thesis or dissertation fees.

Living and Housing Costs

As a small town, Bowling Green offers a modest cost of living. Most graduate students choose to live off campus. The city of Bowling Green offers a wide variety of rental housing, with prices beginning at $150 and averaging $350 per month. A limited number of rooms in on-campus residence halls are set aside for graduate students.

Student Group

There are currently 57 full-time graduate students in the department. Of these, 29 are international students, 18 are women, 26 are in the master's programs, and 31 are in the Ph.D. program.

Student Outcomes

Bowling Green State University (BGSU) graduates enjoy a very high placement rate. At the Ph.D. level, for instance, 56 students have graduated since 1990; of the 35 respondents to a recent survey of graduates, all report that they are meaningfully employed in academic or industrial research positions.

Location

Bowling Green is a peaceful semirural community in historic northwest Ohio. Founded in 1833, the city's early growth was greatly influenced by the prosperous oil-boom era of the late 1800s, evident today through downtown Bowling Green's stately architecture. Bowling Green is conveniently located on Interstate 75, just 20 miles south of Toledo, Ohio, and 90 miles south of Detroit, Michigan. The average temperature in August is 71.1°F (21.7°C); the average temperature in January is 25.5°F (-3.6°C).

The University

Established in 1910 as a teacher-training college, BGSU attained full university status in 1935 and has since grown into a multidimensional institution that offers approximately 200 different degree programs from the bachelor's through doctoral levels. The intellectual climate—in the University generally and in the department particularly—combines the warmth and collegiality of a liberal arts atmosphere with the resources and opportunities of a research institution.

Applying

Application (for both admission and financial assistance) consists of a completed application and financial disclosure forms, which are available by request; a brief personal statement that indicates the applicant's goals and academic interests; three letters of reference; two copies of official transcripts from each institution attended; test scores on the GRE General Test; a $30 check or money order made payable to the Graduate College, Bowling Green State University; and, if the applicant's native language is not English, test scores on the TOEFL or MELAB. The deadline for applications is March 1. Late applications are considered if positions are still available. Full instructions for applying, along with an online application form, can be found at the department's Web site. Application materials may also be requested via e-mail (address below).

Correspondence and Information

Graduate Coordinator
Department of Mathematics and Statistics
Bowling Green State University
Bowling Green, Ohio 43403-0221

Telephone: 419-372-7463
Fax: 419-372-6092
E-mail: hchen@bgnet.bgsu.edu
World Wide Web: http://www.bgsu.edu/departments/math/

Bowling Green State University

THE FACULTY AND THEIR RESEARCH

James H. Albert, Professor; Ph.D., Purdue. Bayesian analysis, analysis of categorical data.
Juan Bes, Assistant Professor; Ph.D., Kent State. Operator theory.
Neal Carothers, Professor and Chair; Ph.D., Ohio State. Functional analysis, Banach space theory, real analysis.
Kit Chan, Professor; Ph.D., Michigan. Functional analysis, function theory.
Hanfeng Chen, Professor and Graduate Coordinator; Ph.D., Wisconsin–Madison. Transformed data analysis, finite mixture models.
John T. Chen, Associate Professor; Ph.D., Sydney (Australia). Multivariate statistics, probability inequalities, biostatistics.
So-Hsiang Chou, Professor; Ph.D., Pittsburgh. Numerical analysis, fluid mechanics.
Humphrey S. Fong, Associate Professor; Ph.D., Ohio State. Probability, real analysis.
John T. Gresser, Associate Professor; Ph.D., Wisconsin–Milwaukee. Complex analysis.
Arjun K. Gupta, Distinguished University Professor; Ph.D., Purdue. Multivariate statistical analysis, analysis of categorical data.
Corneliu Hoffman, Associate Professor; Ph.D., USC. Representations of finite groups, inverse Galois problems.
Alexander Izzo, Associate Professor; Ph.D., Berkeley. Complex analysis, functional analysis.
Warren W. McGovern, Assistant Professor; Ph.D., Florida. Ordered algebraic structures.
David E. Meel, Associate Professor; Ed.D., Pittsburgh. Mathematics education.
Barbara E. Moses, Professor; Ph.D., Indiana. Mathematics education, problem solving.
Diem Nguyen, Assistant Professor; Ph.D., Texas A&M. Mathematics education.
Truc T. Nguyen, Professor; Ph.D., Pittsburgh. Mathematical statistics.
Steven M. Seubert, Professor; Ph.D., Virginia. Functional analysis, operator theory, complex analysis.
Sergey Shpectorov, Professor; Ph.D., Moscow State. Groups and geometries.
Tong Sun, Associate Professor; Ph.D., Texas A&M. Numerical analysis, partial differential equations.
Gábor Székely, Professor; Ph.D., Eötvös Loránd (Budapest). Probability and statistics.
J. Gordon Wade, Associate Professor; Ph.D., Brown. Numerical analysis, inverse problems.
Dale Winter, Director of Service Mathematics; Ph.D., Michigan. Mathematics education.
Craig L. Zirbel, Associate Professor; Ph.D., Princeton. Probability, stochastic processes.

Mathematical Sciences Building.

Bowling Green State University

SELECTED PUBLICATIONS

Albert, J. H. Bayesian testing and estimation of association in a two-way contingency table. *J. Am. Stat. Assoc.* 92:685–93, 1997.

Albert, J. H. Bayesian selection of log-linear modes. *Can. J. Stat.* 24:327–47, 1996.

Albert, J. H., and S. Chib. Bayesian residual analysis for binary response regression models. *Biometrika* 82:747–59, 1995.

Bes, J., and **K. C. Chan.** Approximation by chaotic operators and by conjugate classes. *J. Math. Analysis Applications* 284:206–12, 2001.

Bes, J., K. C. Chan, and **S. Seubert.** Chaotic unbounded differentiation operators. *Integral Equations Operator Theory* 40:257–67, 2001.

Carothers, N. L. *A Short Course on Banach Space Theory.* New York: Cambridge University Press, 2004.

Carothers, N. L., S. Dilworth, and D. Sobecki. Splittings of Banach spaces induced by Clifford algebras. *Proc. Am. Math. Soc.* 128:1347–56, 2000.

Carothers, N. L. *Real Analysis.* New York: Cambridge University Press, 2000.

Chan, K. C., and R. Sanders. A weakly hypercyclic operator that is not norm hypercyclic. *J. Operator Theory,* in press.

Chan, K. C. The density of hypercyclic operators on a Hilbert space. *J. Operator Theory* 47:131–43, 2002.

Chan, K. C., and R. Taylor. Hypercyclic subspaces of a Banach space. *Integral Equations Operator Theory* 41:381–8, 2001.

Chen, H., J. Chen, and J. D. Kalbfleisch. Testing for a finite mixture model with two components. *J. Royal Stat. Soc., Ser B.* 66(1):95–115, 2004.

Chen, H., and J. Chen. Tests for homogeneity in normal mixtures in the presence of a structural parameter. *Stat. Sin.* 13(2):351–65, 2003.

Chen, H., J. Chen, and J. D. Kalbfleisch. A modified likelihood ratio test for homogeneity in finite mixture models. *J. Royal Stat. Soc., Ser. B* 63(1):19–29, 2001.

Kamburowska, G., and **H. Chen.** Fitting data to the Johnson system. *J. Stat. Comput. Simulation* 69:21–32, 2001.

Chen, J. T. A lower bound using Hamilton-type circuit and its applications. *J. Appl. Probability* 40:1121–32, 2003.

Chen, J. T., F. M. Hoppe, S. Iyengar, and D. Brent. A hybrid logistic regression model for case-control studies. *Methodology Computing Appl. Probability* 5:419–26, 2003.

Chen, J. T., and F. M. Hopper. A connection between successive comparisons and ranking procedures. *Stat. Probability Lett.* 67:19–25, 2004.

Chen, J. T., A. K. Gupta, and C. Troskie. Distribution of stock returns when the market is up (down). *Commun. Stat. Theory Methods* 32:1541–58, 2003.

Chou, S.-H., D. Y. Kwak, and P. S. Vassilevski. Mixed covolume methods for elliptic problems on triangular grids. *SIAM J. Numerical Anal.* 35(5):1850–61, 1998.

Chou, S.-H., and D. Y. Kwak. A covolume method based on rotated bilinears for the generalized Stokes problem. *SIAM J. Numerical Anal.* 35(2):497–507, 1998.

Chou, S.-H. Analysis and convergence of a covolume method for the generalized Stokes problem. *Math. Comput.* 217(66):85–104, 1997.

Gresser, J. *A Maple Approach to Calculus,* 2nd ed. Englewood Cliffs, N.J.: Prentice Hall Publishing Company, 2002.

Gresser, J. *A Mathematica Approach to Calculus,* 2nd ed. Englewood Cliffs, N.J.: Prentice Hall Publishing Company, 2002.

Chen, J., and **A. K. Gupta.** Information theoretic approach for detecting change in the parameters of a normal model. *Math. Methods Stat.* 12:116–30, 2004.

Gupta, A. K., N. Henze, and B. Klar. Testing for affine equivalence of elliptically symmetric distributions. *J. Multivariate Analysis* 88:222–42, 2004.

Gupta, A. K., G. Gonzalez-Farias, and J. A. Dominguez-Molina. A multivariate skew normal distribution. *J. Multivariate Analysis* 89:181–90, 2004.

Gupta, A. K. Multivariate skew t-distribution. *Statistics* 37:359–63, 2003.

Izzo, A. C^r convergence of Picard's successive approximations. *Proc. Am. Math. Soc.* 127:2059–63, 1999.

Izzo, A. A characterization of *C(K)* among the uniform algebras containing *A(K)*. *Indiana University Math. J.* 46:771–88, 1997.

Izzo, A. Failure of polynomial approximation on polynomially convex subsets of the sphere. *Bull. London Math. Soc.* 28:393–7, 1996.

Hager, A. W., C. M. Kimber, and **W. Wm. McGovern.** Weakly least integer closed groups. *Rendiconti Circolo Matematico Palermo* 52:453–80, 2003.

McGovern, W. W. Clean semiprime *f*-rings with bounded inversion. *Commun. Algebra* 31(7):3295–304, 2003.

McGovern, W. W. Free topological groups over weak P-spaces. *Top. Appl.* 112(2):175–80, 2001.

Hager, A. W., C. M. Kimber, and **W. Wm. McGovern.** Least integer closed groups. In *Proceedings of the Conference on Lattice Ordered Groups and f-Rings,* pp. 245–60. Gainesville, Fla.: Kluwer Academic Publishers, 2001.

Meel, D. E. Honor students' calculus understandings: Comparing Calculus and Mathematica and traditional calculus students. In *Research in Collegiate Mathematics Education III,* pp. 163–215, eds. A. H. Schoenfeld, J. Kaput, and E. Dubinsky. Providence, R.I.: American Mathematical Society, 1998.

Meel, D. E. Calculator-available assessments: The why, what, and how. *Educ. Assess.* 4(3):149–75, 1997.

Meel, D. E. A mis-generalization in calculus: Searching for the origins. In *Proceedings of the Nineteenth Annual Meeting of the North American Chapter of the International Group for the Psychology of Mathematics Education,* pp. 23–9, eds. J. A. Dossey, J. O. Swafford, M. Parmantie, and A. E. Dossey. Columbus, Ohio: ERIC Clearinghouse for Science, Mathematics, and Environmental Education, 1997.

Moses, B. E. Beyond problem solving: Problem posing. In *Problem Posing: Reflections and Applications,* eds. S. Brown and M. Walter. Mahwah, N.J.: Lawrence Erlbaum Associates, 1993.

Moses, B. E. IDEAS: Mathematics and music. *Arithmetic Teacher* 40(4):215–25, 1992.

Moses, B. E. Developing spatial thinking in the middle grades. *Arithmetic Teacher* 37(6):59–63, 1990.

Nguyen, T. T., and K. T. Dinh. Characterizations of normal distributions and EDF goodness-of-fit tests. *Metrika* 58:149–57, 2003.

Nguyen, T. T., and K. T. Dinh. A regression characterization of inverse Gaussian distributions and application to EDF goodness-of-fit tests. *Int. J. Math. Math. Sci.* 9:587–92, 2003.

Nguyen, T. T., J. T. Chen, A. K. Gupta, and K. T. Dinh. A proof of the conjecture on positive skewness of generalised inverse Gaussian distributions. *Biometrika* 90:245–50, 2003.

Bowling Green State University

Selected Publications (continued)

Nguyen, T. T., and K. T. Dinh. Exact EDF goodness-of-fit tests for inverse Gaussian distributions. *Commun. Stat. Simulation Comput.* 32:505–16, 2003.

Seubert, S. M. Semigroups of compressed toeplitz operators and Nevanlinna-Pick interpolation. *Houston J. Math.,* in press.

Seubert, S. M., and **J. G. Wade.** Frechet differentiability of parameter-dependent analytic semigroups. *J. Math. Anal. Applications* 232:119–37, 1999.

Lesko, J., and **S. M. Seubert.** Cyclicity results for Jordan and compressed Toeplitz operators. *Integral Equations Operator Theory* 31:338–52, 1998.

Cheng, R., and **S. M. Seubert.** Weakly outer polynomials. *Mich. J. Math.* 41:235–46, 1994.

Ivanov, A., and **S. Shpectorov.** The universal non-abelian representation of the Peterson type geometry related to J-4. *J. Algebra* 191:541–67, 1997.

Ivanov, A., D. Pasechnik, and **S. Shpectorov.** Non-abelian embeddings of some sporadic geometries. *J. Algebra* 181:523–57, 1996.

Del Fra, A., A. Pasini, and **S. Shpectorov.** Geometries with bi-affine and bi-linear diagrams. *Eur. J. Combinatorics* 16:439–59, 1995.

Székely, G. J., and M. Rizzo. Mean distance test of Poisson distribution. *Stat. Probability Lett.* 67(3):241–7, 2004.

Bennett, C., A. Glass, and **G. J. Székely.** Fermat's last theorem for rational exponents. *Am. Math. Monthly* 111(4):322–9, 2004.

Székely, G. J., and N. K. Bakrov. Extremal probabilities for Gaussian quadratic forms. *Probability Theory Related Fields* 126:184–202, 2003.

Rao, C. R., and **G. J. Székely.** *Statistics for the 21st Century.* New York: Dekker, 2000.

Filippova, D. V., and **J. G. Wade.** A preconditioner for regularized inverse problems. *SIAM J. Sci. Computation,* in press.

Wade, J. G., and P. S. Vassilevski. A comparison of multilevel methods for total variation regularization. *Elec. Trans. Numerical Anal.* 6:225–70, 1997.

Wade, J. G., and C. R. Vogel. Analysis of costate discretizations in parameter estimation for linear evolution equations. *SIAM J. Control Optimization* 33(1):227–54, 1995.

DeLong, M., **D. Winter,** and C. A. Yackel. Motivation, management, and student-centered instruction I: Analytical framework. *PRIMUS* 13(2):97–123, 2003.

DeLong, M., **D. Winter,** and C. A. Yackel. Motivation, management and student-centered instruction II: Analytical framework. *PRIMUS* 13(3):223–47, 2003.

DeLong, M., and **D. Winter.** *Learning to Teach and Teaching to Learn Mathematics.* MAA Notes #57, Washington, D.C.: Mathematical Association of America, 2002.

Winter, D., P. Lemons, J. Bookman, and W. Hoese. Novice instructors and student-centered instruction: Identifying and addressing obstacles to learning in the college science laboratory. *J. Scholarship Teaching Learning* 2(1):14–42, 2001.

Bennett, C. D., and **C. L. Zirbel.** Discrete velocity fields with explicitly computable Lagrangian law. *J. Stat. Phys.* 111:681–701, 2003.

Woyczynski, W. A., and **C. L. Zirbel.** Rotation of particles in polarized Brownian flows. *Stochastics Dynamics* 2:109–29, 2002.

Jordan, R., B. Turkington, and **C. L. Zirbel.** A mean-field statistical theory for the nonlinear Schrodinger equation. *Physica D* 137:353–78, 2000.

BROWN UNIVERSITY

Division of Applied Mathematics

Programs of Study

The Division of Applied Mathematics offers graduate programs leading to the Ph.D. and Sc.M. degrees.

The emphasis of the Ph.D. program is on both thesis research and obtaining a solid foundation for future work. Course programs are designed to suit each individual's needs. Admission to Ph.D. candidacy is based on a preliminary examination designed individually for each student in light of his or her interests. Research interests of the faculty can be gauged from the list on the reverse of this page and include partial differential equations and dynamical systems, stochastic systems (including stochastic control), probability and statistics, numerical analysis and scientific computation, continuum and fluid mechanics, computer vision, image reconstruction and speech recognition, pattern theory, and computational neuroscience and computational biology. A wide spectrum of graduate courses is offered, reflecting the broad interests of the faculty in the different areas of applied mathematics. Relevant courses are also offered by the Departments of Mathematics, Physics, Computer Sciences, Economics, Geological Sciences, Linguistics, and Psychology and the Divisions of Engineering and of Biology and Medicine.

The Sc.M. program does not require a thesis, and students with sound preparation usually complete it in one year.

Research Facilities

The University's science library houses an outstanding collection in mathematics and its applications. The computer center is equipped with an IBM SP2 with ninety-six thin nodes, and the University maintains access to supercomputing installations and other facilities. The Division has a network of Sun, SGI, Compaq, and PC desktops for instructional and research activities. An IBM SP2, composed of twenty-four thin nodes, two 12-node Linux clusters, and more than ten Compaq, Sun, and Intel-based SMP class workstations, serves intensive scientific computing. The Division is also equipped with state-of-the-art backup facilities and central file servers. All computer systems on campus are interconnected via a high-speed network.

Financial Aid

Fellowships, scholarships, and research and teaching assistantships, which cover tuition and living expenses, are available for qualified full-time graduate students. Exceptional candidates receive guaranteed support for four years, provided that they make satisfactory progress toward the degree. Summer support can usually be arranged.

Cost of Study

Tuition fees for full-time students are $30,672 per year in 2004–05. Teaching assistants and research assistants are not charged for tuition.

Living and Housing Costs

The cost of living in Providence is somewhat lower than the national average. Housing for graduate students in Miller Hall is available at $5302 for the 2004–05 academic year. Numerous off-campus apartments are available for students to rent.

Student Group

Brown University has approximately 5,600 undergraduates and 1,300 graduate students. The Division of Applied Mathematics has 57 full-time graduate students, of whom 51 receive financial support from the University. A number of other students hold outside fellowships.

Location

Brown University is located on a hill overlooking Providence, the capital of Rhode Island and one of America's oldest cities. The proximity of Providence to the excellent beaches and ocean ports of Rhode Island and Massachusetts provides considerable recreational opportunities. Numerous nearby ski facilities are available for winter recreation. The libraries, theaters, museums, and historic sites in Providence and Newport offer an abundance of cultural resources. In addition, Providence is only an hour from Boston and 4 hours from New York City by auto or train.

The University and The Division

Brown University was founded in 1764 in Warren, Rhode Island, as Rhode Island College. It is the seventh-oldest college in America and the third-oldest in New England. In 1770, the College was moved to College Hill, high above the city of Providence, where it has remained ever since. The name was changed to Brown University in 1804 in honor of Nicholas Brown, son of one of the founders of the College. The University awarded its first Doctor of Philosophy degree in 1889. The University attracts many distinguished lecturers both in the sciences and in the arts. Brown is a member of the Ivy League and participates in all intercollegiate sports.

Brown has the oldest tradition and one of the strongest programs in applied mathematics of all universities in the country. Based on a wartime program instituted in 1942, the Division of Applied Mathematics at Brown was established in 1946 as a center of graduate education and fundamental research. It includes several research centers, has cooperative programs with many other universities, and attracts many scientific visitors.

Applying

The preferred method of application for admission is via the electronic application on the Internet at http://apply.embark.com/grad/brown/.

Correspondence and Information

Professor Chi-Wang Shu, Chair
Division of Applied Mathematics
Brown University
Providence, Rhode Island 02912
World Wide Web: http://www.dam.brown.edu

Brown University

THE FACULTY AND THEIR RESEARCH

Elie Bienenstock, Associate Professor of Applied Mathematics and Neuroscience; Ph.D., Brown. Computer vision, brain models.
Frederic E. Bisshopp, Emeritus Professor of Applied Mathematics; Ph.D., Chicago. Asymptotics, nonlinear wave propagation, fluid mechanics.
Dorothy Buck, Assistant Professor of Applied Mathematics; Ph.D., Texas at Austin. Mathematical molecular biology.
Constantine M. Dafermos, Professor of Applied Mathematics, Alumni-Alumnae University Professor, and Chair, Graduate Program in Applied Mathematics; Ph.D., Johns Hopkins. Continuum mechanics, differential equations.
Philip J. Davis, Emeritus Professor of Applied Mathematics; Ph.D., Harvard. Numerical analysis, approximation theory, philosophy of mathematics.
Paul G. Dupuis, Professor of Applied Mathematics; Ph.D., Brown. Stochastic control and probability theory.
Peter L. Falb, Professor of Applied Mathematics; Ph.D., Harvard. Control and stability theory, mathematics of finance.
Wendell H. Fleming, Emeritus Professor of Applied Mathematics and Mathematics; Ph.D., Wisconsin. Stochastic differential equations, stochastic control theory.
Walter F. Freiberger, Emeritus Professor of Applied Mathematics; Ph.D., Cambridge. Statistics, biostatistics.
Constantine Gatsonis, Professor of Medical Science and Applied Mathematics; Ph.D., Cornell. Bayesian statistical inference, biostatistics.
Stuart Geman, Professor of Applied Mathematics and James Manning Professor; Ph.D., MIT. Probability and statistics, natural and computer vision.
Basilis Gidas, Professor of Applied Mathematics; Ph.D., Michigan. Mathematical physics, computer vision, speech recognition, computational molecular biology.
David Gottlieb, Professor of Applied Mathematics and Ford Foundation Professor; Ph.D., Tel-Aviv. Numerical methods, scientific computation.
Ulf Grenander, Emeritus Professor of Applied Mathematics; Ph.D., Stockholm. Probability and statistics, pattern theory.
Yan Guo, Associate Professor of Applied Mathematics; Ph.D., Brown. Partial differential equations and kinetic theory.
Jan S. Hesthaven, Associate Professor of Applied Mathematics; Ph.D., Denmark Technical. Numerical analysis, spectral and high-order methods, scientific computing, computational electromagnetics, optics, and fluid dynamics.
Din-Yu Hsieh, Emeritus Professor of Applied Mathematics; Ph.D., Caltech. Fluid mechanics, mathematical physics.
George Em Karniadakis, Professor of Applied Mathematics; Ph.D., MIT. Computational fluid dynamics, scientific computing, turbulence modeling, stochastic differential equations.
Ioannis Kontoyiannis, Assistant Professor of Applied Mathematics and Computer Science; Ph.D., Stanford. Information theory, probability, statistics, mathematical biology.
Harold J. Kushner, Emeritus Professor of Applied Mathematics and Engineering; Ph.D., Wisconsin. Stochastic systems theory and applications.
John Mallet-Paret, Professor of Applied Mathematics, George I. Chase Professor of the Physical Sciences, and Director, Lefschetz Center for Dynamical Systems; Ph.D., Minnesota. Differential equations, dynamical systems.
Martin Maxey, Professor of Applied Mathematics and Engineering; Ph.D., Cambridge. Dynamics of two-phase flow, turbulence, turbulent mixing and dispersion of particles or bubbles.
Donald E. McClure, Professor of Applied Mathematics; Ph.D., Brown. Pattern analysis, image processing, mathematical statistics.
David Mumford, University Professor; Ph.D., Harvard. Pattern theory, biological and computer vision.
Chi-Wang Shu, Professor of Applied Mathematics and Chair; Ph.D., UCLA. Numerical analysis, scientific computation, computational physics.
Walter Strauss, Professor of Mathematics and Applied Mathematics and L. Herbert Ballou University Professor; Ph.D., MIT. Nonlinear waves, scattering theory, partial differential equations.
Chau-Hsing Su, Professor of Applied Mathematics; Ph.D., Princeton. Fluid mechanics, mathematical physics.
Hui Wang, Assistant Professor of Applied Mathematics; Ph.D., Columbia. Stochastic optimization, probability theory.

CARNEGIE MELLON UNIVERSITY

Department of Statistics

Programs of Study

Statisticians apply rigorous thinking and modern computational methods to help scientists, engineers, computer scientists, and policymakers draw reliable inferences from quantitative information. The program at Carnegie Mellon prepares students for such work by providing them with collaborative experience while they master technical skills based on a solid conceptual foundation. The faculty members are all very active in research and professional endeavors yet put a high priority on graduate training. The moderate size of the department and its congenial and supportive environment foster close working relationships between the faculty and students. The outstanding success of the department's graduates, when they take positions in industry, government, and academic institutions, may be attributed to their unusual abilities, the state-of-the-art training given to them, and the dedication they develop during their studies.

In pursuing graduate degrees, students follow programs that may be tailored to suit individual interests. The master's degree program trains students in applied statistics by imparting knowledge of the theory and practice of statistics. Requirements are satisfactory completion of course work and a written comprehensive examination. There is no thesis requirement. Students complete the program in 1, 1½, or 2 years, depending on their previous preparation.

The Ph.D. program is structured to prepare students for careers in university teaching and research and for industrial and government positions that involve consulting and research in new statistical methods. Doctoral candidates first complete the requirements for the M.S. in statistics. They then typically complete another year of courses in probability and statistics. A written Ph.D. comprehensive examination and an oral thesis proposal presentation and defense are required. Proficiency in the use of the computer is required. There are no foreign language requirements.

The department also offers two cross-disciplinary Ph.D. programs. The first leads to a Ph.D. in statistics and public policy and is sponsored jointly with the H. John Heinz III School of Public Policy and Management. The second is a joint program with the Center for Automated Learning and Discovery. Students can obtain additional information by visiting the Web site.

Research Facilities

The computational resources available to students at Carnegie Mellon are unsurpassed and are a major strength of the program. The Department of Statistics operates its own computer facilities, which provide students with experience using advanced graphics workstations. The facilities consist of fifty-four Linux workstations of various compatible models, eight HP workstations, one SGI workstation, about ten PCs, nine monochrome laser printers, and one laser color printer. The department also maintains a 128-processor Beowulf Linux cluster, a high-performance parallel computer. The workstations are interconnected by a departmental Ethernet network, which, in turn, is connected to University and worldwide networks. The department also has a graphics laboratory with equipment for producing computer-animated videotapes and for digitizing video images.

Financial Aid

The department attempts to provide financial aid for all of its students, both master's and Ph.D. candidates. Tuition scholarships are usually granted in conjunction with graduate assistantships, which currently offer a stipend of $12,600 for nine months in return for duties as teaching or research assistants. Students who receive both tuition scholarships and graduate assistantships are expected to maintain a full course load and devote effort primarily to their studies and assigned duties. These duties require, on average, no more than 12 hours per week. Exceptionally well qualified candidates may qualify for a fellowship that pays tuition and a stipend and requires no assistantship duties.

Cost of Study

The tuition fee for full-time graduate students in 2003–04 was $28,200 per academic year.

Living and Housing Costs

Pittsburgh has attractive, reasonably priced neighborhoods where students attending Carnegie Mellon University can live comfortably.

Student Group

Carnegie Mellon University has 4,823 undergraduate and 2,809 graduate students. The teaching faculty numbers approximately 620. During 2003–04, there were 49 full-time students in the graduate program; 28 were working toward a Ph.D. degree. Roughly 33 percent of the statistics graduate students are U.S. citizens and one half are women. Graduate students in statistics have diverse backgrounds, with typical preparation being an undergraduate program in mathematics or in engineering, science, economics, or management. All had outstanding undergraduate records, and many have won nationally competitive fellowships.

Location

Located in a metropolitan area of more than 2 million people, Pittsburgh is the headquarters of many of the nation's largest corporations. There is an unusually large concentration of research laboratories in the area. Carnegie Mellon is located in Oakland, the cultural center of the city. The campus is within walking distance of museums and libraries and is close to the many cultural and sports activities of the city.

The University

One of the leading universities in the country, Carnegie Mellon has long been devoted to liberal professional education. Five colleges—the Carnegie Institute of Technology, the College of Fine Arts, the College of Humanities and Social Sciences, the Mellon College of Science, and the School of Computer Science—offer both undergraduate and graduate programs. The Graduate School of Industrial Administration and the H. John Heinz III School of Public Policy and Management offer graduate programs only.

Applying

The application deadline is January 1 and students are encouraged to apply even earlier, if possible. A course in probability and statistics at the level of DeGroot's *Probability and Statistics* is highly desirable, but excellence and promise always balance a lack of formal preparation. The General Test of the Graduate Record Examinations is required of all applicants. International applicants are also required to take the TOEFL and the Test of Spoken English and should further document their ability to speak English, if possible.

Correspondence and Information

Department of Statistics
Carnegie Mellon University
Pittsburgh, Pennsylvania 15213-3890
Telephone: 412-268-8588
Fax: 412-268-7828
E-mail: admissions@stat.cmu.edu
World Wide Web: http://www.stat.cmu.edu/www/cmu-stats/GSS/

Carnegie Mellon University

THE FACULTY AND THEIR RESEARCH

Anthony Brockwell, Assistant Professor of Statistics; Ph.D., Melbourne, 1998. Stochastic processes, control theory, time-series analysis, Monte Carlo methods, statistics in cognitive neuroscience.

Bernie Devlin, Adjunct Senior Research Scientist (primary appointment with the University of Pittsburgh School of Medicine); Ph.D., Penn State, 1986. Statistical genetics, genetic epidemiology, genomics.

George T. Duncan, Professor of Statistics, H. John Heinz III School of Public Policy and Management (primary appointment); Ph.D., Minnesota, 1970. Confidentiality of databases, mediation and negotiation, Bayesian decision making.

William F. Eddy, Professor of Statistics; Ph.D., Yale, 1976. Neuroimaging, data mining, visualization, proteomics, image processing.

Stephen E. Fienberg, Maurice Falk University Professor of Statistics and Social Science; Ph.D., Harvard, 1968. Categorical data, data mining, confidentiality and disclosure limitation, federal statistics, multivariate data analysis, sampling and the census, statistical inference.

Christopher R. Genovese, Associate Professor of Statistics; Ph.D., Berkeley, 1994. Statistical inverse problems, magnetic resonance imaging, inference from spatio-temporal processes, model selection, functional inference, statistical cosmology.

Joel B. Greenhouse, Professor of Statistics; Ph.D., Michigan, 1982. General methodology, biostatistics, applied Bayesian methods.

Brian W. Junker, Professor of Statistics and Associate Head; Ph.D., Illinois, 1988. Mixture and hierarchical models for multivariate discrete measures, nonparametric and semiparametric inference for latent variables, applications in education, psychology, the social sciences, and biostatistics.

Joseph B. Kadane, Leonard J. Savage University Professor of Statistics and Social Science (joint appointment with Department of Social and Decision Sciences and with the Graduate School of Industrial Administration); Ph.D., Stanford, 1966. Statistical inference, econometrics, statistical methods in social sciences, sequential problems, statistics and the law, clinical trials.

Robert E. Kass, Professor of Statistics; Ph.D., Chicago, 1980. Bayesian inference, statistical methods in neuroscience.

Nicole Lazar, Associate Professor of Statistics; Ph.D., Chicago, 1996. Likelihood theory, functional neuroimaging, model selection and interpretation, statistics in the social sciences.

John P. Lehoczky, Thomas Lord Professor of Statistics and Mathematics and Dean, College of Humanities and Social Sciences; Ph.D., Stanford, 1969. Stochastic processes with applications in real-time computer systems, computational finance, biostatistics.

Kathryn Roeder, Professor of Statistics; Ph.D., Penn State, 1988. Statistical models in genetics and molecular biology, mixture models, semiparametric inference.

Mark J. Schervish, Professor of Statistics; Ph.D., Illinois at Urbana-Champaign, 1979. Statistical computing, foundations of statistics, multivariate analysis, statistical methods in engineering, environmental statistics.

Teddy Seidenfeld, Herbert A. Simon Professor of Philosophy and Statistics (primary appointment in Department of Philosophy); Ph.D., Columbia, 1976. Foundations of statistical inference and decision theory.

Howard Seltman, Research Scientist in Statistics; M.D., Medical College of Pennsylvania, 1979; Ph.D., Carnegie Mellon, 1999. Psychiatric studies, biological modeling, genetics, Bayesian methods.

Valérie Ventura, Research Scientist in Statistics; D.Phil., Oxford (England), 1997. Bootstrap methods, efficient simulations, statistics in cognitive neuroscience.

Isabella Verdinelli, Professor in Residence; Ph.D., Carnegie Mellon, 1996. Bayesian design of experiments, multiple testing, tissue engineering, statistical models in engineering.

Pantelis K. Vlachos, Research Scientist in Statistics; Ph.D., Connecticut, 1996. Bayesian inference, biostatistics, multivariate analysis, text mining.

Larry A. Wasserman, Professor of Statistics; Ph.D., Toronto, 1988. Nonparametric inference, astrophysics, causality, bioinformatics.

Lan Zhang, Assistant Professor of Statistics; Ph.D., Chicago, 2001. Inference for stochastic processes, statistical arbitrage and trading, analysis of high-frequency data, statistics in finance.

Carnegie Mellon University

SELECTED PUBLICATIONS

Brockwell, A. E., N. H. Chan, and P. K. Lee. A class of models for aggregated traffic volume time series. *J. Royal Statist. Soc., Ser. C* 52(4):417–30, 2003.

Brockwell, A. E., and **J. B. Kadane.** A gridding method for Bayesian sequential decision problems. *J. Computat. Graphic. Stat.* 12(3): 566–84, 2003.

Brockwell, A. A regulator for a class of unknown continuous-time nonlinear systems. *Syst. Control Lett.* 44:405–12, 2001.

Brockwell, A. E., and P. J. Brockwell. A class of non-embeddable ARMA processes. *J. Time Ser. Analysis* 20(5):483–6, 1999.

Tzeng, J.-Y., et al. **(B. Devlin, K. Roeder,** and **L. Wasserman).** Outlier detection and false discovery rates for whole-genome DNA matching. *JASA,* in press.

Devlin, B., K. Roeder, and **L. Wasserman.** Genomic control for association studies: A semiparametric test to detect excess-haplotype sharing. *Biostatistics* 1:369–87, 2002.

Devlin, B., K. Roeder, and **L. Wasserman.** Genomic control, a new approach to genetic-based association studies. *Theor. Pop. Biol.* 60:156–66, 2001.

Devlin, B., and **K. Roeder.** Genomic control for association studies. *Biometrics* 55:997–1004, 1999.

Duncan, G., and S. Roehrig. Mediating the tension between information, privacy, and information access: The role of digital government. In *Public Information Technology: Policy and Management Issues,* pp. 94–129, ed. G. David Garson. Hershey and London: Idea Group Publishing, 2003.

Duncan, G., et al. **(S. E. Fienberg).** Disclosure limitation methods and information loss for tabular data. In *Confidentiality, Disclosure, and Data Access,* pp. 135–66, eds. P. Doyle et al. Amsterdam: North Holland, 2001.

Duncan, G., and S. Mukherjee. Optimal disclosure limitation strategy in statistical databases: Deterring tracker attacks through additive noise. *JASA* 95:720–8, 2000.

Duncan, G., et al. Disclosure detection in multivariate categorical databases: Auditing confidentiality protection through two new matrix operators. *Mgmt. Sci.* 45, 1999.

Rosano, C., et al. **(W. F. Eddy).** Pursuit and saccadic eye movement subregions in human frontal eye field: A high resolution fMRI investigation. *Cereb. Cortex* 12(2):107–15, 2002.

McNamee, R. L., and **W. F. Eddy.** Visual analysis of variance: A tool for quantitative assessment of fMRI data processing and analysis. *Magn. Reson. Med.* 46:1202–8, 2001.

Eddy, W. F., and T. K. Young. Optimizing the resampling of registered images. In *Handbook of Medical Image Processing, Processing and Analysis,* pp. 603–12, ed. I. N. Bankman. Academic Press, 2000.

Carpenter, P. A., et al. **(W. F. Eddy).** Time course of fMRI-activation in language and spatial networks during sentence comprehension. *NeuroImage* 10:216–24, 1999.

Eddy, W. F., et al. **(C. R. Genovese** and **N. Lazar).** The challenge of functional magnetic resonance imaging. *J. Computat. Graphic. Stat.* 8(3):545–58, 1999.

Fienberg, S. E., et al. *The Polygraph and Lie Detection.* Washington, D.C.: National Academy Press, 2003.

Dobra, A., **S. E. Fienberg,** and M. Trottini. Assessing the risk of disclosure of confidential categorical data. In *Bayesian Statistics 7,* eds. J. Bernardo, et al. Clarendon: Oxford University Press.

Fienberg, S. E., and **N. A. Lazar.** "William Sealy Gossett, 1876–1937." In *Statisticians of the Centuries,* eds. C. C. Hyder and E. Seneta. New York: Springer.

Anderson, M., and **S. E. Fienberg.** *Who Counts? The Politics of Census-Taking in Contemporary America.* New York: Russell Sage Foundation, 2001.

Fienberg, S. E. Contingency tables and log-linear models: Basic results and new developments. *JASA* 95:643–7, 2000.

Anderson, M., et al. **(S. E. Fienberg** and **J. B. Kadane).** Sample-based adjustment of the 2000 census—A balanced perspective. *Jurimetrics* 40:341–56, 2000.

Dobra, A., and **S. E. Fienberg.** Bounds for cell entries in contingency tables given marginal totals and decomposable graphs. *Proc. Nat. Acad. Sci.* 97(22):11885–92, 2000.

Genovese, C. R., and **L. Wasserman.** Rates of convergence for the Gaussian mixture sieve. *Ann. Stat.,* in press.

Genovese, C. R. A Bayesian time-course model for functional Magnetic Resonance Imaging data. *JASA,* in press.

Perone Pacifico, M., **C. Genovese, I. Verdinelli,** and **L. Wasserman.** False discovery rates for random fields. Technical Report 771, Department of Statistics, Carnegie Mellon University, 2003.

Luna, B., et al. **(C. R. Genovese** and **W. F. Eddy).** Maturation of widely distributed brain function subserves cognitive development. *NeuroImage* 13:786–93, 2001.

Diggs, B., **C. R. Genovese, J. B. Kadane,** and R. H. Swendsen. Bayesian analysis of series expansions. *Comput. Phys. Commun.* 121–2:1–4, 1999.

Genovese, C. R., and J. A. Sweeney. Functional connectivity in the cortical regions subserving eye movements. In *Case Studies in Bayesian Statistics* vol. 4, pp. 59–132, eds. **R. E. Kass** et al. **(I. Verdinelli).** New York: Springer-Verlag, 1999.

Genovese, C. R., P. B. Stark, and M. J. Thompson. Uncertainties for two-dimensional models of solar rotation from helioseismic eigenfrequency splitting. *Astrophys. J.* 443:843–54, 1995.

Erosheva, E. A., P. D. Kroboth, and **J. B. Greenhouse.** Characterizing the diurnal rhythm of DHEA. *Amer. Stat.* 56:273–83, 2002.

Greenhouse, J. Meta-analysis: In practice. In *International Encyclopedia of the Social and Behavioral Sciences,* pp. 9713–71, eds. Neil Smelser and Paul Baltes. Elsevier, 2001.

Greenhouse, J. B. On clinical trials in psychiatry. *Bio. Psych.* 48:433–5, 2000.

Lovett, M., and **J. Greenhouse.** Applying cognitive theory to statistics instruction. *Amer. Stat.* 54:196–206, 2000.

Johnson, M. S., and **B. W. Junker.** Using data augmentation and Markov chain Monte Carlo for the estimation of unfolding response models. *J. Educ. Behav. Stat.* 28:195–30, 2003.

Patz, R. J., **B. W. Junker,** M. S. Johnson, and L. T. Mariano. The hierarchical rater model for rated test items and its application to large-scale educational assessment data. *J. Educ. Behav. Stat.* 27:341–84, 2002.

Junker, B. W., and K. Sijtsma. Cognitive assessment models with few assumptions, and connections with nonparametric item response theory. *Appl. Psychol. Meas.* 25:258–72, 2001.

Kadane, J. B., and **N. A. Lazar.** Methods and criteria for model selection. *JASA,* in press.

Boatwright, P., S. Borle, and **J. B. Kadane.** A model of the joint distribution of purchase quantity and timing. *JASA,* 2003.

London, A., and **J. B. Kadane.** Placebos that harm: Sham surgery controls in clinical trials. *Stat. Methods Med. Res.* 11(5):413–27, 2002.

Ware, M. J., and **J. B. Kadane.** Chance and skill in games: Electronic draw poker. *Jurimetrics* 43(1):129–34, 2002.

Kadane, J. B. Crossing lines in a patent case. *Chance* 15(4):27–32, 2002.

Kass, R. E., and **V. Ventura.** A spike train oribability model. *Neural Computat.* 13:1713–20.

Kass, R. E., and **L. Wasserman.** The selection of prior distributions by formal rules. *JASA* 91:1343–70, 1996.

Kass, R. E., and A. E. Raftery. Bayes factors. *JASA* 90:773–95, 1995.

Carnegie Mellon University

Selected Publications (continued)

Lazar, N. A. A short survey of causal inference, with implications for context of learning studies of second language acquisition. *Stud. Second Lang. Acquisition,* in press.

Lazar, N. A. Bayesian empirical likelihood. *Biometrika* 90:319–26, 2003.

Lazar, N. A., and **J. B. Kadane.** Movies for the visualization of MCMC output. *J. Computat. Graphic. Statist.* 11:863–74, 2002.

Lazar, N. A., B. Luna, J. A. Sweeney, and **W. F. Eddy.** Combining brains: A survey of methods for statistical pooling of information. *NeuroImage* 16:538–50, 2002.

Lazar, N. A., W. F. Eddy, C. R. Genovese, and J. Welling. Statistical issues in fMRI for brain imaging. *Int. Stat. Rev.* 69:105–27, 2001.

Lazar, N. A., and P. A. Mykland. Empirical likelihood in the presence of nuisance parameters. *Biometrika* 86:203–11, 1999.

Kruk, L., **J. Lehoczky,** S. Shreve, and S-N Yeung. Multiple-input heavy traffic real-time queues. *Ann. Appl. Prob.* 13(1):54–99, 2003.

Yeung, S. N., and **J. P. Lehoczky.** End to end delay analysis for real time distributed networks. *IEEE Real-Time Systems Symposiums,* pp. 299–309, 2001.

Akesson, F., and **J. P. Lehoczky.** Path generation for quasi-Monte Carlo simulation of mortgage-backed securities. *Mgmt. Sci.* 46(9): 1171–87, 2000.

Lehoczky, J. Simulation methods for option pricing. In *Mathematics of Derivative Securities,* pp. 528–44, eds. M. A. Dempster and S. R. Plisha. Cambridge University Press, 1997.

Roeder, K., R. G. Carroll, and B. G. Lindsay. A nonparametric maximum likelihood approach to case-control studies with errors in covariables. *JASA* 91:722–32, 1996.

Schervish, M. J., T. Seidenfeld, and **J. B. Kadane.** How sets of coherent probabilities may serve as models for degrees of incoherence. *J. Uncertainty Fuzziness Knowledge-Based Sys.,* in press.

Schervish, M. J., T. Seidenfeld, J. B. Kadane, and I. Levi. Extensions of expected utility theory and some limitations of pairwise comparisons. *ISIPTA-03 Conference Proceedings,* 2003.

DeGroot, M. H., and **M. J. Schervish.** *Elementary Probability and Statistics,* 3rd ed. Addison-Wesley, 2002.

Lockwood, J. R., **M. J. Schervish,** P. Gurian, and M. J. Small. Characterization of forensic occurrence in U.S. drinking water treatment facility source waters. *JASA* 96:1184–93, 2001.

Schervish, M. J., T. Seidenfeld, and **J. B. Kadane.** Improper regular conditional distributions. *Ann. Prob.* 29:1612–24, 2001.

Lavine, M., and **M. J. Schervish.** Bayes factors: What they are and what they are not. *Am. Statist.* 53:119–22, 1999.

Barron, A., **M. J. Schervish,** and **L. Wasserman.** The consistency of posterior distributions in nonparametric problems. *Ann. Stat.* 27:536–61, 1999.

Schervish, M. J. P-values: What they are and what they are not. *Am. Statist.* 50:203–6, 1996.

Schervish, M. J. *Theory of Statistics.* New York: Springer-Verlag, 1995.

Seidenfeld, T. Remarks on the theory of conditional probability. In *Statistics—Philosophy, Recent History, and Relations to Science,* eds. V. F. Hendricks, S. A. Pedersen, and K. F. Jorgensen. Kluwer Academic Publishing, in press.

Geisser, S., and **T. Seidenfeld.** Remarks on the Bayesian method of moments. *J. Appl. Stat.* 26:97–101, 1999.

Seidenfeld, T., M. J. Schervish, and **J. B. Kadane.** Non-conglomerability for finite-valued, finitely additive probability. *Sankhya* 60(3):476–91, 1998.

Heron, T., **T. Seidenfeld,** and **L. Wasserman.** Divisive conditioning: Further results on dilation. *Phil. Sci.* 411–4, 1997.

Seidenfeld, T., M. J. Schervish, and **J. B. Kadane.** A representation of partially ordered preferences. *Ann. Stat.* 23:2168–74, 1995.

Seltman, H., B. Devlin, and **K. Roeder.** Evolutionary-based association analysis using haplotype data. *Gent. Epid.* 25:48–59, 2003.

Seltman, H., J. Greenhouse, and **L. Wasserman.** Bayesian model selection: Analysis of a survival model with a surviving fraction. *Stat. Med.* 20(11):1681–91, 2001.

Seltman, H. "Hidden Markov models for analysis of biological rhythm data." In *Case Studies in Bayesian Statistics,* vol. 5, pp. 398–406, New York: Springer Verlag, 2001.

Seltman, H., K. Roeder, and **B. Devlin.** TDT meets MHA: Family-based association analysis guided by evolution of haplotypes. *Am. J. Hum. Genet.* 68(5):1250–63, 2001.

Ventura, V. Nonparametric bootstrap recycling. *Stat. Comput.,* in press.

Robins, J. M., A. W. van der Vaart, and **V. Ventura.** The asymptotic distribution of p-values in composite null models. *JASA* 62:452, 2000.

Olson, C. R., et al. **(V. Ventura** and **R. E. Kass).** Neuronal activity in macaque supplementary eye field during planning of saccades in response to pattern and spatial cues. *J. Neurophysiol.* 84:1369–84, 2000.

Ventura, V., A. C. Davison, and S. J. Boniface. Statistical inference for the effect of magnetic brain stimulation on a motoneurone. *Appl. Stat.* 47:77–94, 1998.

Verdinelli, I. Bayesian design for the normal linear model with unknown error variance. *Biometrika* 87:222–7, 2000.

Verdinelli, I., and **L. A. Wasserman.** Bayesian goodness of fit testing using infinite dimensional exponential families. *Ann. Stat.* 26:1215–41, 1998.

Verdinelli, I., and **L. A. Wasserman.** Bayes factors, nuisance parameters, and imprecise tests. In *Bayesian Statistics,* 5:765–71, eds. J. M. Bernardo, J. O. Berger, A. P. Dawid, and A. F. M. Smith, Oxford: Claredon Press, 1996.

Verdinelli, I., and **L. A. Wasserman.** Computing Bayes factors by using a generalization of the Savage-Dickey density ratio. *JASA* 90:614–8, 1995.

Vlachos, P. K., and A. E. Gelfand. On the calibration of Bayesian model choice criteria. *J. Stat. Plan. Inf.* 111:223–34, 2003.

Vlachos, P. K., and A. E. Gelfand. *Practical nonparametric and semiparametric Bayesian statistics,* pp. 115–32, eds. Dey et al., 1998.

Shen, X., and **L. A. Wasserman.** Rates of convergence of posterior distributions. *Ann. Stat.,* in press.

Wasserman, L. A. Asymptotic inference for mixture models using data dependent priors. *J. Roy. Stat. Soc. B* 62:159–80, 2000.

Wasserman, L. A. Asymptotic properties of nonparametric Bayesian procedures. In *Practical Nonparametric and Semiparametric Bayesian Statistics,* eds. D. Dey, P. Muller, and D. Sinha. New York: Springer-Verlag, 1998.

Zhang, L., P. A. Mykland, and Y. At-Sahalia. A tale of two time scales: Determining integrated volatility with noisy high frequency data. NBER working paper series 10111, 2003.

At-Sahalia, Y., P. A. Mykland, and **L. Zhang.** How often to sample a continuous-time process in the presence of market microstructure noise. Technical Report, Princeton University, 2003.

Mykland, P. A., and **L. Zhang.** ANOVA for diffusions. Technical Report 784, Department of Statistics, Carnegie Mellon University, 2003.

COLUMBIA UNIVERSITY

Graduate School of Arts and Sciences
Department of Mathematics

Programs of Study

The Department of Mathematics offers programs leading to the degrees of Doctor of Philosophy and Master of Arts.

The Ph.D. program is an intensive course of study designed for the full-time student planning a career in research and teaching at the university level or in basic research in a nonacademic setting. Admission is limited and selective. Applicants should present an undergraduate major in mathematics from a college with strong mathematics offerings. In the first year, students must pass written qualifying examinations in areas chosen from a first-year core curriculum, which offers courses in modern geometry, arithmetic and algebraic geometry, complex analysis, analysis and probability, groups and representations, and algebraic topology. Most of the formal course work is completed in the second year, when an oral examination in two selected topics must be passed. Also required is a reading knowledge of one language, chosen from French, German, and Russian. The third and fourth years are devoted to seminars and the preparation of a dissertation. Students are required to serve as teaching assistants for three years beginning with the second year of study. A number of students are selected for NSF funding and are exempt from one or two years of teaching duties.

The M.A. in mathematics of finance is a ten-course program that can be completed in one year of full-time study or two years of part-time study. All courses are offered in the evening. Six core courses are required, and four can be selected from statistics, economics, and the business school. Graduates of the program work in financial firms and investment banking institutions.

There are allied graduate programs available in mathematical statistics and in computer science.

Research Facilities

The mathematics department is housed in a comfortable building containing an excellent Mathematics Library, computing facilities, graduate student offices, a lounge for tea and conversation, and numerous seminar and lecture rooms.

Financial Aid

The department has a broad fellowship program designed to enable qualified students to achieve the Ph.D. degree in the shortest practicable time. Each student admitted to the Ph.D. program is appointed a fellow in the Department of Mathematics for the duration of his or her doctoral candidacy, up to a total of five years. A fellow receives a stipend of at least $19,646 for the 2004–05 nine-month academic year and is exempt from payment of tuition and fees. An additional $3600 of NSF summer support is available to a number of selected students. Financial aid is generally not available to M.A. students.

A fellow in the Department of Mathematics may hold a fellowship from a source outside Columbia University. When not prohibited by the terms of the outside fellowship, the University supplements the outside stipend to bring it up to the level of the University fellowship. Candidates for admission are urged to apply for fellowships for which they are eligible (e.g., National Science Foundation, New York State Regents).

Cost of Study

All students admitted to the Ph.D. program become fellows in the department and are exempt from fees, as explained above.

Living and Housing Costs

Students in the program have managed to live comfortably in the University neighborhood on their fellowship stipends.

Student Group

The Ph.D. program in mathematics has an enrollment of approximately 55 students. Normally, 8 to 12 students enter each year. While students come from all over the world, they have always been socially as well as scientifically cohesive and mutually supportive.

Location

New York City is America's major center of culture. Columbia University's remarkably pleasant and sheltered campus, near the Hudson River and Riverside Park, is situated within 20 minutes of Lincoln Center, Broadway theaters, Greenwich Village, and major museums. Most department members live within a short walk of the University.

The University

Since receiving its charter from King George II in 1754, Columbia University has played an eminent role in American education. In addition to its various faculties and professional schools (such as Engineering, Law, and Medicine), the University has close ties with nearby museums, schools of music and theology, the United Nations, and the city government.

Applying

The application deadline is December 31; however, applicants of unusual merit are considered beyond the application deadline. Applicants who expect to be in the New York vicinity are encouraged to arrange a department visit and interview.

Correspondence and Information

For information on the department and program:
Chairman
Department of Mathematics
Mail Code 4406
Columbia University
New York, New York 10027
Telephone: 212-854-4112
E-mail: ref8@columbia.edu
World Wide Web: http://www.math.columbia.edu

For applications:
Graduate School of Arts and Sciences
Office of Student Affairs
Mail Code 4304
107 Low Memorial Library
Columbia University
New York, New York 10027
Telephone: 212-854-4737

Columbia University

THE FACULTY AND THEIR RESEARCH

Peter M. Bank, Assistant Professor; Ph.D., Berlin, 2000. Mathematical finance.
David A. Bayer, Professor; Ph.D., Harvard, 1982. Algebraic geometry.
Joel Bellaiche, Ritt Assistant Professor; Ph.D., Paris XI (South), 2002. Number theory.
Hubert Bray, Associate Professor; Ph.D., Stanford, 1997. Differential geometry, geometrical analysis.
Xiaodong Cao, Ritt Assistant Professor; Ph.D., MIT, 2002. Differential geometry.
Panagiota Daskalopoulos, Professor; Ph.D., Chicago, 1992. Partial differential equations, differential geometry, harmonic analysis.
Robert Friedman, Professor; Ph.D., Harvard, 1981. Algebraic geometry.
Patrick X. Gallagher, Professor; Ph.D., Princeton, 1959. Analytic number theory, group theory.
Darren Glass, VIGRE Assistant Professor; Ph.D., Pennsylvania, 2002. Algebraic geometry.
Dorian Goldfeld, Professor; Ph.D., Columbia, 1969. Number theory.
Brian Greene, Professor; D.Phil., Oxford, 1987. Mathematical physics, string theory.
Richard Hamilton, Professor; Ph.D., Princeton, 1966. Differential geometry.
Zuoliang Hou, Ritt Assistant Professor; Ph.D., MIT, 2003. Algebraic geometry.
Tom Ilmanen, Eilenberg Visiting Professor (fall); Ph.D., Berkeley, 1991. Geometric analysis and partial differential equations.
Stanislav Jabuka, VIGRE Assistant Professor; Ph.D., Michigan State, 2002. Gauge theory.
Hervé Jacquet, Professor; Dr.Sci.Math., Paris, 1967. Representation theory, automorphic functions.
Troels Jorgensen, Professor; Cand.Scient., Copenhagen, 1970. Hyperbolic geometry, complex analysis.
Ioannis Karatzas, Professor; Ph.D., Columbia, 1980. Probability, mathematical finance.
Ilya S. Kofman, Assistant Professor; Ph.D., Maryland, 2000. Knot theory, Vassiliev invariants.
Igor Krichever, Professor; Ph.D., Moscow State, 1972. Integrable systems, algebraic geometry.
Kimball Martin, Ritt Assistant Professor; Ph.D., Caltech, 2004. Number theory.
John W. Morgan, Professor and Chair; Ph.D., Rice, 1969. Geometric topology, manifold theory.
Walter Neumann, Professor; Ph.D., Bonn (Germany), 1969. Geometry/topology.
Peter S. Ozsváth, Associate Professor; Ph.D., Princeton, 1994. Gauge theory, low-dimensional topology.
Sean Paul, Ritt Assistant Professor; Ph.D., Princeton, 2000. Differential geometry, algebraic geometry, partial differential equations.
Duong H. Phong, Professor; Ph.D., Princeton, 1977. Analysis.
Henry C. Pinkham, Professor and Dean; Ph.D., Harvard, 1974. Algebraic geometry.
Julius Ross, Ritt Assistant Professor; Ph.D., Imperial College (London), 2003. Geometric analysis, algebraic geometry.
Mihai Sirbu, Ritt Assistant Professor; Ph.D., Carnegie Mellon, 2004. Mathematical finance.
Mikhail Smirnov, Assistant Professor; Ph.D., Princeton, 1995. Differential and integral geometry.
Michael Thaddeus, Associate Professor; D.Phil., Oxford, 1992. Algebraic geometry.
Mao-Pei Tsui, Assistant Professor; Ph.D., Brandeis, 2001. Differential geometry.
Eric Urban, Associate Professor; Ph.D., Paris XI (South), 1995. Number theory.
Mu-Tao Wang, Assistant Professor; Ph.D., Harvard, 1998. Differential geometry.
Peter Woit, Director of Instruction; Ph.D., Princeton, 1985. Mathematical physics, topology.
Shing Ting Yau, Eilenberg Visiting Professor; Ph.D., Berkeley, 1971. Differential geometry.
Shou-Wu Zhang, Professor; Ph.D., Columbia, 1991. Number theory, arithmetic geometry.

DARTMOUTH COLLEGE

Department of Mathematics

Program of Study

The Dartmouth Ph.D. program in mathematics is designed to develop mathematicians highly qualified for both teaching and research at the college or university level or for research in the mathematical sciences in industry or government. Students earn a master's degree as part of becoming a candidate for the Ph.D. degree but should not apply to study only for a master's degree. During the first six terms (eighteen months) of residence, the student develops a strong basic knowledge of algebra, analysis, topology, and a fourth area of mathematics chosen by the student. Areas recently chosen for this fourth area include applied mathematics, combinatorics, geometry, logic, number theory, probability, and statistics. Rather than using traditional qualifying exams, the department requires that 2 faculty members certify that the student knows the material on the departmental syllabus in each of the four areas. This certification may be based on a formal oral exam, course work, informal discussions, supervised independent study, seminar presentations, informal oral exams, or any means that seems appropriate. Students and faculty usually find a formal oral exam to be the most efficient route to certification.

After completion of at least eight graduate courses and certification, students are awarded the master's degree and, subject to departmental approval, are admitted to candidacy for the Ph.D. degree. This normally occurs by the end of the second year of graduate study. After admission to candidacy, the student chooses a thesis adviser and thesis area and begins in-depth study of the chosen area. Normally, the thesis is completed during the fourth or fifth year of graduate study. The typical thesis consists of publishable original work. Areas recently chosen for thesis research include algebra, analysis, applied mathematics, combinatorics, geometry, logic, number theory, set theory, and topology. Students continue taking courses according to their interests and demonstrate competence in one foreign language while doing their thesis research.

Dartmouth is committed to helping its graduate students develop as teachers by providing examples of effective teaching, by instruction in a graduate course on teaching mathematics, and by provision of carefully chosen opportunities to gain realistic teaching experience. These opportunities begin as tutorial or discussion leader positions for courses taught by senior faculty. They culminate in the third and fourth years, after completion of the graduate course, in the opportunity to teach one course for one term each year. The first of these courses is normally a section of a multisection course supervised by a senior faculty member, and the second is chosen to fit the interests and needs of the students and the department. All students are required to participate in these teaching experiences.

Research Facilities

The department has an outstanding library and abundant computer resources and office, laboratory, seminar, and lounge space. More specifically, the already excellent collection of mathematics books and journals is supplemented by online access to the collections from a consortium of peer institutions. Significant digital resources are also available. Graduate students have offices, many equipped with personal computers, and other computers (Mac, Windows, Linux) are available in adjacent lab space. There are lounges for graduate and undergraduate use. The department maintains its own Web, print, and mail servers, and significant technology is available for both computational research and also for use in the classroom. There is a computer store on campus offering discounted prices for computers, software, and supplies.

Financial Aid

Students receive a full tuition scholarship and the Dartmouth College fellowship, for which the stipend in 2004–05 is $1585 per month. This stipend continues for twelve months per year through the fourth year of graduate study and is generally renewable for a fifth year as well. In addition to the stipend, the College provides a $1045 health benefit that is paid for students requiring health insurance (i.e., students who do not provide a waiver form).

Cost of Study

With the exception of textbooks, all costs of study are covered by the scholarship.

Living and Housing Costs

Students find that $1585 per month suffices comfortably for living in College housing, renting local apartments, or sharing a locally rented house with other students. A married student whose spouse does not work or hold a similar fellowship can maintain a spartan life in College-owned married student housing.

Student Group

Dartmouth attracts and admits students from colleges and universities of all types. About 50 percent are women, the percentage of married students has varied from 5 to 35, 1 or 2 often are not recent graduates, and 1 or 2 often are not from North America. The department has about 20 graduate students, and it offers an effective placement program for its Ph.D. graduates. Recipients of the Ph.D. degree from Dartmouth have found employment at a broad cross section of academic institutions, including Ivy League institutions, major state universities, and outstanding four-year liberal arts colleges, and some are working as research mathematicians in industry and government.

Location

Dartmouth is in a small town that has an unusual metropolitan flavor. There are adequate shopping facilities but no large cities nearby. Hiking, boating, fishing, swimming, ski touring, and Alpine skiing are all available in the immediate area. A car is a pleasant luxury, but many students find it unnecessary.

The College

Dartmouth has about 4,000 undergraduate students, who are among the most talented and motivated in the nation. There are under 1,000 graduate students in the College (arts and sciences faculty) and in associated professional schools in engineering, medicine, and business. With a faculty–graduate student ratio close to 1:1, the department is a friendly place where student-faculty interaction is encouraged.

Applying

Application forms are available from the department. Applicants should send to the address below a completed application form, an undergraduate transcript, and three letters of recommendation that describe their mathematical background and ability, estimate their potential as teachers, and compare them with a peer group of the recommender's choice. Applicants must take both the General Test and Subject Test of the Graduate Record Examinations and have the official scores sent to the department. All sections of the TOEFL are required of applicants whose native language is not English. Applicants whose files are complete by February 15 receive first consideration.

Correspondence and Information

Graduate Admissions Committee Chair
Ph.D. Program in Mathematics
Department of Mathematics, 6188 Bradley Hall
Dartmouth College
Hanover, New Hampshire 03755-3551
Telephone: 603-646-3722 or 603-646-2415
E-mail: mathphd@dartmouth.edu
World Wide Web: http://www.math.dartmouth.edu/

Dartmouth College

THE FACULTY AND THEIR RESEARCH

Professors

Martin Arkowitz, Ph.D., Cornell, 1960. Algebraic topology and differential geometry. Provides thesis supervision in these areas.
Kenneth P. Bogart, Ph.D., Caltech, 1968. Combinatorial mathematics and algebra and their applications. Current research in ordered sets, the theory of generating functions, algebraic coding theory, and database design. Provides thesis supervision in algebra and combinatorics and their applications.
Peter Doyle, Ph.D., Dartmouth, 1982. Geometry.
Carolyn Gordon, Ph.D., Washington (St. Louis), 1979. Geometry. Provides thesis supervision in differential geometry.
Marcia Groszek, Ph.D., Harvard, 1981. Logic. Provides thesis supervision in logic.
Charles Dwight Lahr, Ph.D., Syracuse, 1971. Analysis, especially functional analysis. Provides thesis supervision in functional analysis.
Carl Pomerance, Ph.D., Harvard, 1972. Number theory. Provides thesis supervision in number theory.
Daniel Rockmore, Ph.D., Harvard, 1989. Representation theory, fast transforms, group theoretic transforms, dynamical systems, signal processing, data analysis. Provides thesis supervision in analysis and representation theory.
Thomas R. Shemanske, Ph.D., Rochester, 1979. Number theory and modular forms. Currently interested in Hilbert/Siegel modular forms and theta series. Provides thesis supervision in number theory and related areas of mathematics.
Dorothy Wallace, Ph.D., California, San Diego, 1982. Number theory, especially analytic number theory. Provides thesis supervision in number theory.
David L. Webb, Ph.D., Cornell, 1983. Algebraic K theory. Provides thesis supervision in algebra.
Dana P. Williams, Department Chair; Ph.D., Berkeley, 1979. Analysis. Provides thesis supervision in analysis.
Peter Winkler, Ph.D., Yale, 1975. Discrete mathematics, pure and applied; probability; theory of computing. Provides thesis supervision in these areas.

Associate Professor

John Trout, Ph.D., Penn State, 1995. Analysis, functional analysis, operator algebras and noncommutative topology/geometry. Provides thesis supervision in analysis.

Assistant Professors

Vladimir Chernov, Ph.D., Uppsala, 1998. Contact and symplectic geometry, geometric and low-dimensional topology. Provides thesis supervision in topology and geometry.
Rosa Orellana, Ph.D., California, San Diego, 1999. Finite dimensional representations of braid groups of type B, algebraic combinatorics. Provides thesis supervision in combinatorics.
Scott Pauls, Ph.D., Pennsylvania, 1998. Geometry and analysis of Carnot-Carathéodory manifolds. Provides thesis supervision in geometry.

John Wesley Young Research Instructors

The JWY Research Instructorship is a two-year visiting position; the people involved and their fields thus change from year to year.
Ryan Daileda, Ph.D., UCLA, 2004. Number theory, particularly automorphic L-.
Robert Hladky, Ph.D., Washington (Seattle), 2004. Geometry.
Alexander Shumakovitch, Ph.D., Uppsala, 1996. Low-dimensional topology.
Mark Skandera, Ph.D., MIT, 2000. Algebraic combinatorics.

Visiting and Adjunct Faculty

Bernard Cole, Ph.D., Boston University, 1992. Biostatistics.
Eugene Demidenko, Adjunct Associate Professor, Department of Mathematics; Ph.D., Central Institute of Mathematics and Economics of Academy of Sciences of the U.S.S.R. (Moscow), 1975. Statistics.

DEPAUL UNIVERSITY

Graduate Program in Mathematical Sciences

Programs of Study

The Department of Mathematical Sciences offers courses in pure and applied mathematics to help students reach a wide variety of intellectual, academic, and career goals. Many students come to the department to obtain the mathematical background needed to be successful in programs in the natural sciences, computer science, social sciences, and business.

Students may obtain master's degrees in four areas of concentration in mathematical sciences: applied mathematics with a concentration in actuarial science, applied mathematics with a concentration in statistics, applied statistics, or mathematics education. Students with a bachelor's degree may also enroll in the department's certificate program in applied statistics.

Applied mathematics and statistics degrees are designed to provide students with the necessary quantitative background for employment in business, industry, or government and to provide a solid foundation for students who are interested in pursuing a Ph.D. degree in statistics.

The Master of Arts in Mathematics Education operates slightly differently from the other mathematical sciences programs. DePaul University offers the only graduate program in the area for teachers and prospective teachers of mathematics that meets on the weekends and can be completed in a year and a half. The curriculum of twelve carefully articulated courses is directly tied to secondary and middle school teaching strategies. Each course meets for five weekend days. The program can either be completed in six quarters over eighteen months or over a longer period of time, depending upon the needs of the individual.

Courses for the applied mathematics and applied statistics mathematical sciences degrees are most often offered at the Lincoln Park campus. Some may also be taken at the Naperville campus.

Courses for the Master of Arts in Mathematics Education are all offered on the weekends at DePaul's Lincoln Park campus.

Research Facilities

DePaul University offers extensive advising, content area tutoring, and computer lab facilities and workshops to assist students. The two main campuses have significantly expanded their facilities within the past decade, increasing both library and lab space.

Opportunities for research are extensive at DePaul. The on-site library system includes facilities on each of its six campuses. The library offers access to the holdings of more than forty Illinois libraries through ILLINET Online and the catalogs of more than 800 Illinois libraries. Electronic resources such as e-journals, database access, online research assistance, and book ordering are available through the University Web site.

In addition, the online mathematical sciences career information Web site is available for all students to help them find out how others in their course of study are utilizing their advanced degrees.

Financial Aid

The U.S. Department of Education's Free Application for Federal Student Aid (FAFSA) and other financial aid links for graduate students are available on DePaul's graduate programs Web site.

Cost of Study

Full-time tuition for the academic year 2004–05 is $407 per credit hour.

Living and Housing Costs

Graduate students are welcome at the new University Center of Chicago, just one block from DePaul's Loop Campus in the heart of Chicago. The eighteen-story building features studios and two- and four-bedroom apartments with kitchens as well as residence hall-style semisuites with semiprivate bathrooms. The building offers a food court, workout center, rooftop garden, laundry facilities, meeting and study rooms, and many other amenities. Per-person rates range from $6678 to $10,526 annually.

Location

Students enrolled in graduate programs at DePaul reap many benefits from the University's location in one of the most dynamic cities in the world. Chicago is one of the nation's largest business and cultural centers, with a wide array of academic and entertainment resources. Graduate students can tap into internships and permanent positions and network with industry professionals while earning their degrees.

The University

Founded in 1898 by Vincentians to ensure that immigrants had access to a high-quality education, DePaul has grown to become the nation's largest Catholic university. Its mission of providing an unparalleled educational experience accessible to all is accomplished through a learn-by-doing approach with an urban flare.

Many graduate programs schedule classes in the evening and on weekends. DePaul's two urban campuses are easily reached by public transportation; the Loop campus is at the south end of Chicago's downtown area, and the 32-acre Lincoln Park campus is located on the city's North Side. There are suburban satellite campuses as well: O'Hare, Naperville, South/Oak Forest, and Rolling Meadows.

Numerous student organizations offer extensive opportunities for participation in both community and University activities. There are music performance groups, theater groups, student publications, sports, and honor and service societies. Athletic facilities include two gymnasiums, a swimming pool, racquetball courts, and extensive physical education equipment.

Applying

Prospective graduate students may apply online by going to http://www.depaul.edu/admission/graduate_admission.asp and then selecting the Graduate College of Liberal Arts and Sciences division. For full admission, students must submit the following credentials: a bachelor's degree from an accredited university, two years of calculus and linear algebra, a course in statistics, and a course in scientific computer programming other than COBOL. Applicants who do not have this preparation may be admitted on a conditional basis until they have completed the requirements with minimum grades of B.

Correspondence and Information

Department of Mathematical Sciences
College of Liberal Arts and Sciences
DePaul University
2320 North Kenmore Avenue
Chicago, Illinois 60614
Telephone: 312-362-5551
Fax: 312-362-8521
E-mail: gradprograms@depaul.edu
World Wide Web: http://www.depaul.edu/gradlisting/

DePaul University

THE FACULTY AND THEIR RESEARCH

Ahmed A. Zayed, Ph.D., Professor and Chair.
J. Marshall Ash, Ph.D., Professor.
Allan Berele, Ph.D., Professor.
Jeffrey Bergen, Ph.D., Professor.
Stefan Catoiu, Ph.D., Assistant Professor.
William Chin, Ph.D., Professor.
Jonathan Cohen, Ph.D., Professor.
Barbara Cortzen, Ph.D., Associate Professor.
Susanna S. Epp, Ph.D., Professor.
Eduardo A. Gatto, Ph.D., Associate Professor.
Constantine Georgakis, Ph.D., Associate Professor.
Lawrence Gluck, Ph.D., Associate Professor.
Sigrun Goes, Ph.D., Associate Professor.
Jerry Goldman, Ph.D., Professor.
Roger Jones, Ph.D., Professor.
Yevgenia Kashina, Ph.D., Assistant Professor.
Leonid Krop, Ph.D., Associate Professor.
Jeanne LaDuke, Ph.D., Associate Professor.
Effat Moussa, Ph.D., Professor.
Lynn Narasimhan, Ph.D., Associate Professor.
Ayse A. Sahin, Ph.D., Associate Professor.
Claudia Schmegner, Ph.D., Assistant Professor.
Alexander Stokolos, Ph.D., Assistant Professor.
Eric Vestrup, Ph.D., Assistant Professor.
Gang Wang, Ph.D., Associate Professor.
Yuen F. Wong, Ph.D., Professor.

EMORY UNIVERSITY

Graduate School of Arts and Sciences
Rollins School of Public Health
Department of Biostatistics

Programs of Study

Biostatistics is the science that applies statistical theory and methods to the solution of problems in the biological and health sciences. The Department of Biostatistics at Emory University offers programs of study leading to the Master of Science and Doctor of Philosophy degrees in biostatistics through the Graduate School of Arts and Sciences. In addition, the department offers study leading to the Master of Public Health and the Master of Science in Public Health degrees in biostatistics through the Rollins School of Public Health. The programs are designed for individuals with a strong background in the mathematical sciences and an interest in the biological or health sciences. Graduates have pursued a wide variety of career options in academia; federal, state, and local government; health agencies; health insurance organizations; the pharmaceutical industry; and other public and private research organizations. The department also offers the M.S.P.H. degree in public health informatics. Public health informatics is a combination of computer science, information science, and public health science in the management and processing of public health data, information, and knowledge supporting effective public health practice. This term has been defined as the application of information science and technology to public health science and practice. Graduates of this program will possess the knowledge and skills necessary to introduce new technology and distribute information systems to support public health decision making.

The Department of Biostatistics is situated within a rich environment of collaborative institutes. Many active research and employment opportunities for students are available at the Rollins School of Public Health, the Emory Medical School, the neighboring Centers for Disease Control and Prevention (CDC)—the federal institute responsible for disease surveillance and control; the Carter Center; the American Cancer Society; the Georgia Department of Human Resources; and local health departments. The department coordinates the activities of the Biostatistics Consulting Center, which serves as a resource for advice on the design, conduct, and analysis of studies in the health sciences. Students may get hands-on experience in practical biostatistical problems through working with faculty members on real-life consulting problems.

Students are required to complete a core curriculum that consists of graduate courses in biostatistics. Advanced course work and research are tailored to the experience, training, area of concentration, and degree objective of each student. The M.S., M.S.P.H., and M.P.H. programs usually include four semesters of course work and generally take two years to complete. The Ph.D. degree program normally requires four calendar years to complete, including four to six semesters of course work.

Research Facilities

The Department of Biostatistics conducts active research programs in biostatistics, public health informatics, categorical data analysis, complex sample survey methods, spatial statistics, and methods for infectious disease epidemiology. The Rollins School of Public Health is equipped with state-of-the-art computers and numerous microcomputers. A network of mainframe computers is accessible to the School through high-speed telecommunications lines. Extensive analytical research laboratories are housed in the School and at the CDC. Health sciences libraries are conveniently located at Emory University, the national headquarters of the American Cancer Society, and the CDC.

Financial Aid

Qualified Ph.D. students are supported by nationally competitive graduate school fellowships that include full tuition coverage and a stipend. Research assistantships may be available to M.S.P.H. and M.P.H. students. Financial aid information is available through the Office of Financial Aid.

Cost of Study

Tuition for M.S. and Ph.D. students in 2004–05 is $13,885 per semester for full-time study or $1157 per credit hour. For M.S.P.H. and M.P.H. students, the cost is $10,140 per semester for full-time students or $845 per credit hour. The student activity and athletic fees total $186 per semester. In addition, the cost of books and supplies averages $1000 per year.

Living and Housing Costs

Living expenses for a single person are estimated to be $14,000 per year. Interested students may obtain information regarding University and off-campus housing by contacting the Housing Office.

Student Group

Emory University has a total enrollment of about 11,600 students. Enrollments in the various schools of the University are restricted in order to maintain a favorable balance between resources, faculty members, and students. There are approximately 6,285 students in the undergraduate college and 5,315 in the eight graduate and professional schools. The student body represents all areas of the United States and more than 100 nations.

Location

The Atlanta metropolitan area has a population of nearly 4.5 million. It is the academic center in the Southeast: there are eight major universities in the metropolitan area. Atlanta is green the year round, with numerous parks and a temperate climate. Professional, athletic, cultural, and recreational activities are available throughout the year. Atlanta is one of the leading convention centers in the United States, and the city is served by one of the busiest airports in the world, providing convenient access to national and international destinations. Atlanta was the site of the 1996 Summer Olympics.

The University and The School

Emory University ranks among the twenty-five most distinguished centers for higher education in the United States. The heavily wooded 631-acre campus features a blend of traditional and contemporary architecture. A main corridor through the campus incorporates the expanding health sciences complex with the headquarters of the CDC and the American Cancer Society. Within a short drive from the main campus are a variety of affiliated resources, such as the Georgia Mental Health Institute, the Georgia Department of Human Resources, the Carter Center of Emory University, and Grady Memorial Hospital.

The Rollins School of Public Health has six academic departments, which offer M.P.H. and M.S.P.H. degrees—Behavioral Sciences and Health Education, Biostatistics, Environmental/Occupational Health, Epidemiology, Health Policy and Management, and International Health.

The Rollins School of Public Health is ranked ninth in the nation by public health deans, faculty members, and administrators of accredited graduate programs of public health. Research strengths in the School make it the second-highest-ranked school at Emory in terms of research funding. In 2003, *U.S. News & World Report* ranked Emory ninth among Health Disciplines: Public Health (Master's/Doctorate).

Applying

Minimum requirements for admission include a baccalaureate degree from an accredited college or university and satisfactory performance on the GRE. Prerequisites for the M.P.H., M.S.P.H., M.S., and Ph.D. program include at least two semesters of college-level calculus and one semester of college-level linear and matrix algebra. International students whose schooling has not been in English must submit a TOEFL score. Application forms for admission to the M.S./Ph.D. program may be obtained from the Graduate School of Arts and Sciences, Emory University, Atlanta, Georgia 30322. Admissions information on the M.S.P.H. and M.P.H. degrees may be obtained from the Office of Admissions, Rollins School of Public Health, Emory University, Atlanta, Georgia 30322.

Correspondence and Information

John J. Hanfelt, Ph.D., Director of Graduate Studies
Department of Biostatistics
Rollins School of Public Health
Emory University
1518 Clifton Road, NE
Atlanta, Georgia 30322

Telephone: 404-727-2876
E-mail: biosadmit@sph.emory.edu
World Wide Web: http://www.sph.emory.edu/hpbios.html

Emory University

THE FACULTY AND THEIR RESEARCH

José N. G. Binongo, Lecturer; Ph.D., Ulster (Northern Ireland), 2000.
F. DuBois Bowman, Assistant Professor; Ph.D., North Carolina at Chapel Hill, 2000. Analysis of longitudinal data, missing data, and the application of statistical methods to medical imaging studies. Dr. Bowman is currently involved in collaborative neuro-imaging research at the Positron Emission Tomography (PET) Center of Emory University.
Donna J. Brogan, Professor Emerita; Ph.D., Iowa State, 1967. Sample survey design and analysis, both theory and application. Dr. Brogan conducts courses and workshops on specialized techniques for analyzing data from complex sample surveys. Current interests include comparison of random digit dialing sampling to area probability sampling.
Ying Guo, Research Assistant Professor; Ph.D., Emory, 2004. Logistic regression.
Michael J. Haber, Professor; Ph.D., Hebrew (Jerusalem), 1976. Categorical data analysis, models of infectious diseases. Dr. Haber conducts research in categorical data analysis and statistical methods for the analysis of infectious disease data. In categorical data analysis, Dr. Haber generalizes existing models and develops new methods for investigating particular types of data. He also explores the properties of methods for 2x2 tables and developed an exact unconditional test for comparing two proportions. In the area of analyzing infectious disease data, Dr. Haber, in collaboration with Drs. Longini and Halloran, develops methods for estimation of transmission probabilities and for evaluating the efficacy and effectiveness of vaccines. These methods are applied to data on influenza, measles, mumps, and AIDS.
M. Elizabeth Halloran, Professor; M.D., Berlin, 1983; D.Sc., Harvard, 1989. Causal inference, epidemiologic methods for infectious disease, Bayesian methods, vaccine evaluation. Her research interests encompass methodological problems in studying and evaluating effects of interventions against infectious disease, especially vector-borne and parasitic diseases. Dr. Halloran draws on Bayesian methods and paradigms of causal inference. She has also worked on spatial mapping and inference for phylogenetic trees.
John J. Hanfelt, Associate Professor; Ph.D., Johns Hopkins, 1994. Dr. Hanfelt's research interests are in the design and analysis of familial aggregation studies, genetic studies, longitudinal data analysis, the theory of estimating functions, and approximate likelihood inference.
Vicki Stover Hertzberg, Associate Professor; Ph.D., Washington (Seattle), 1980. Categorical data analysis, clinical trials, reproductive epidemiology. Dr. Hertzberg's research interests include categorical data analysis, especially for clustered binary data, as result from a variety of clinical trials and reproductive epidemiology studies. She works especially closely with neurologists involved in stroke research.
Andrew N. Hill, Lecturer; Ph.D., Canterbury (New Zealand), 1996. Semi-parametric methods, Markov models, epidemic theory, spatial spread of infectious diseases.
Yijian (Eugene) Huang Associate Professor; Ph.D., Minnesota, 1997. Survival analysis: multistate process, quality adjusted survival time, lifetime medical cost, and recurrent events; covariate measurement error; semiparametric and nonparametric inferences.
Mary E. Kelley, Research Assistant Professor; Ph.D., Pittsburgh, 2004. Managing and analyzing research data, research design and statistical analysis.
Michael H. Kutner, Rollins Professor and Chair; Ph.D., Texas A&M, 1971. Linear models, model diagnostics, clinical trials, statistical education. Dr. Kutner's research interests involve estimation and hypothesis testing for analysis of variance models with missing cells, clinical trials methodology, and textbook writing in applied linear statistical models.
Ira M. Longini Jr., Professor; Ph.D., Minnesota, 1977. Stochastic processes, models of infectious diseases. Dr. Longini's research interests are in the area of stochastic processes applied to epidemiological problems. He has specialized in the mathematical and statistical theory of epidemics—a process that involves constructing and analyzing mathematical models of infectious disease transmission and the analysis of infectious disease data based on these models. This work has been carried out jointly with other faculty members and collaborators at other universities and at the CDC. He has worked extensively on the analysis of epidemics of influenza, dengue fever, rhinovirus, rotavirus, measles, cholera, and HIV.
Robert H. Lyles, Associate Professor, Ph.D., North Carolina at Chapel Hill, 1996. Longitudinal data analysis, prediction of random effects, measurement error models, missing and censored data problems. Dr. Lyles' research has investigated applications in the areas of occupational and HIV epidemiology, and his collaborative work includes data analysis for studies of cancer and diabetes.
Amita K. Manatunga, Professor; Ph.D., Rochester, 1990. Multivariate survival analysis, frailty models, categorical data analysis, longitudinal data. Dr. Manatunga's research interests focus on theory and application of survival data analysis. She has worked on multivariate survival data where the interest centers on estimating the covariate effects as well as the correlation between outcomes of survival times. She is interested in developing statistical methodologies based on frailty models and their application in genetics. Dr. Manatunga also has worked closely with medical researchers in the fields of hypertension and pharmacology. She is the biostatistician at the General Clinical Research Center of Emory University.
Bindu Viswanatha, Visiting Assistant Professor; Ph.D, Emory, 1999. Clinical trials, anvanced survival analysis, statistical education.
Lance A. Waller, Professor; Ph.D., Cornell, 1992. Spatial statistics, point process models, environmental statistics. Dr. Waller's research interests involve statistical analysis of spatial patterns in public health data. Past investigations include development of statistical tests of spatial clustering in disease incidence data and implementation of spatial and space-time Markov random field models for maps of disease rates. He is currently investigating statistical methods to analyze environmental exposure, demographic, and disease incidence data linked through geographic information systems (GIS's).
Zheng (Lily) Zhang Assistant Professor; Ph.D., Washington (Seattle), 2004. Collaborative research in clinical and laboratory medicine.

Adjunct Faculty

Huiman X. Barnhart, Associate Professor, Department of Biostatistics and Bioinformatics, Duke University; Ph.D., Pittsburgh, 1992. Analysis for repeated measures, categorical data analysis, clinical trials. Dr. Barnhart's research interests are in the areas of analysis for repeated measures, categorical data analysis, GEE modeling for correlated data, and diagnostic testing. She is currently investigating statistical methods for randomly repeated measures and for evaluation of diagnostic testing.
Carol A. Gotway Crawford, Mathematical Statistician, National Center for Environmental Health, Biometry Branch, Centers for Disease Control and Prevention; Ph.D., Iowa State, 1989. Spatial prediction and mapping, geostatistics, time series analysis, mixed model applications.
Owen J. Devine, Senior Statistician, National Center for Birth Defects and Developmental Disabilities, Office of the Director, Centers for Disease Control and Prevention; Ph.D., Emory, 1992. Use of stochastic methods in mathematical modeling of human health risks related to sexually transmitted diseases and exposure to environmental contaminants, mapping and spatial analyses of indicator of disease risks, methods for addressing uncertainty in measures of potential exposure in the planning and analysis of human health studies.
Andrew Friede, Physician Executive, Cerner Corporation, Southeast Region (Atlanta); M.D., Johns Hopkins, 1981. Public health informatics, clinical and management information systems.
Andrzej S. Kosinski, Assistant Professor, Department of Biostatistics and Bioinformatics, Duke University; Ph.D., Washington (Seattle), 1990. Linear models, cardiovascular clinical trials, statistical computing, survival analysis. Dr. Kosinski's interests are in undue influence of groups of observations on the estimation process and in diagnostic procedures to detect such influence. His work involves cardiovascular clinical trials, including the Emory Angioplasty-Surgery Trial (EAST).
Lillian S. Lin, Mathematical Statistician, National Center for HIV, STD, and TB Prevention, Division of HIV/AIDS Prevention: Surveillance and Epidemiology, Centers for Disease Control and Prevention; Ph.D., Washington (Seattle), 1990. Cluster-randomized studies, social and behavioral sciences applied to HIV/AIDS prevention.
Philip H. Rhodes, Mathematical Statistician, National Immunization Program, Epidemiology Surveillance Division, Centers for Disease Control and Prevention; Ph.D., Emory, 1992. Survival analysis, models for infectious disease data.
Glen A. Satten, Mathematical Statistician, National Center for Environmental Health, Divisions of Environmental Health Lab Sciences, Centers for Disease Control and Prevention; Ph.D., Harvard, 1985. Stochastic processes, HIV/AIDS modeling.
Maya R. Sternberg, Mathematical Statistician, National Center for HIV, STD, and TB Prevention, Division of Sexually Transmitted Diseases Prevention, Centers for Disease Control and Prevention; Ph.D., Emory, 1996.
Donna F. Stroup, Associate Director for Science, National Center for Chronic Disease Prevention and Health Promotion, Office of the Director, Centers for Disease Control and Prevention; Ph.D., Princeton, 1980. Stopping rules for stochastic approximation procedures; public health surveillance; Bayesian approaches to detecting aberrations in public health surveillance data; ethical issues in public health; epidemiology curriculum for students; methods for pooling results of studies, including meta-analysis.
Brani Vidakovic, Professor, School of Industrial and Systems Engineering, Georgia Institute of Technology; Ph.D., Purdue, 1992.
G. David Williamson, Director, Office of the Assistant Administrator of Health Sciences, Agency for Toxic Substances and Disease Registry (ATSDR); Ph.D., Emory, 1987. Methods for disease surveillance, epidemiologic studies.
John M. Williamson, Mathematical Statistician, National Center for HIV, STD, and TB Prevention, Division of HIV/AIDS Prevention: Surveillance and Epidemiology, Centers for Disease Control and Prevention; Sc.D., Harvard, 1993. Clustered correlated data, Interrater agreement, HIV/AIDS modeling.
William A. Yasnoff, Professor and Associate Director of Science, Public Health Practice Program Office, Centers for Disease Control and Prevention; M.D., Northwestern, 1975. Public health informatics.

Associate Faculty

George Cotsonis, Senior Associate; M.S., West Florida, 1978. Statistical computing and clinical trials.
Kirk A. Easley, Senior Associate; M.A., LSU, 1981. Statistical applications in clinical research.
Lisa K. Elon, Senior Associate; M.P.H., Emory, 1997. Sample survey analysis, longitudinal study of health promotion in medical education.
Jennifer Favaloro-Sabatier, Associate; M.S., LSU, 2002. Applied statistics.
Angelita Gordon, Associate; M.S., North Carolina at Chapel Hill, 2000. Statistical education, data analysis.
Michael J. Lynn, Senior Associate; M.S., Mississippi State, 1976. Clinical trials, statistical applications in ophthalmic research, statistical computing.
Azhar Nizam, Senior Associate; M.S., South Carolina, 1987. Statistical education.
Paul S. Weiss, Associate; M.S., Michigan, 1997. Survey sampling design, research methodologies, statistical computing.
Rebecca H. Zhang, Senior Associate; M.S., Florida State, 1994. Data management, statistical analysis.

Jointly Appointed Faculty

Michael P. Epstein, Assistant Professor (joint appointment with Department of Human Genetics); Ph.D., Michigan, 2002.
W. Dana Flanders, Professor (joint appointment with Department of Epidemiology); D.Sc., Harvard, 1982.

SELECTED PUBLICATIONS

Barnhart, H X., and **J. M. Williamson**. Goodness-of-fit tests for GEE modeling with binary response. *Biometrics* 54:720–9, 1998.

Wolf, S. L., and **H. X. Barnhart** et al. The effect of Tai Chi Quan and computerized balance training on postural stability in older subjects. *Phys. Ther.*, 77:371–84, 1997.

Albert, P. S., D. Follman, and **H. X. Barnhart.** A generalized estimating equation approach for modeling random-length binary vector data. *Biometrics* 53:1116–24, 1997.

Wolf, S. L., and **H. X. Barnhart** et al. Reducing frailty and falls in older persons: An investigation of Tai Chi and computerized balance training. *J. Am. Geriatr. Soc.* 44(5):489–97, 1996.

Barnhart, H. X., et al. Natural history of HIV disease in perinatally infected children: An analysis from the Pediatric Spectrum of Disease Project. *Pediatrics* 97:710–6, 1996.

Barnhart, H. X., and A. R. Sampson. Multiple population models for multivariate random-length data with applications in clinical trials. *Biometrics* 51(1):195–204, 1995.

Barnhart, H. X., and A. R. Sampson. Overview of multinomial models for ordinal data. *Commun. Stat.* 23(12):3395–416, 1994.

Barnhart, H. X. Models for multivariate random length data with applications in clinical trials. *Drug Information J.* 27:1147–57, 1993.

Brogan, D., K. O'Hanlan, **L. Elon**, and E. Frank. Health and professional characteristics of lesbian vs. heterosexual women physicians. *J. Am. Med. Wom. Assoc.* 58:10–9, 2003.

Brogan, D., E. Frank, **L. Elon**, and K. O'Hanlan. Methodological concerns for defining lesbian for health research. *Epidemiology* 12(1):109–13, 2001.

Brogan, D., H. M. Haber, and N. Kutner. Functional decline among older adults: Comparing a chronic disease cohort and controls when mortality rates are markedly different. *J. Clin. Epidemiol.* 53(8):847–51, 2000.

Brogan, D. J., et al. **(L. Elon)**. Harassment of lesbians as medical students and physicians. *JAMA*, 282:1290–2, 1999.

Brogan, D. J. Software for sample survey data: Misuse of standard packages. Invited chapter in *Encyclopedia of Biostatistics*, editors-in-chief P. Armitage and T. Colton. New York: John Wiley, 5:4167–74, 1998.

Brogan, D., E. Flagg, M. Deming, and R. Waldman. Increasing the accuracy of the expanded programme on immunization's cluster survey design. *Ann. Epidemiol.* 4(4):302–11, 1994.

Flanders, W. D., C. D. Drews, and **A. S. Kosinski.** Methodology to correct for differential misclassification. *Epidemiology* 6(2):152–6, 1995.

Haber, M. J. Estimation of the population effectiveness of vaccination. *Statistics Med.* 16:601–10, 1997.

Haber, M. J., W. A. Orenstein, **M. E. Halloran,** and **I. M. Longini Jr.** The effect of disease prior to an outbreak on estimation of vaccine efficacy following the outbreak. *Am. J. Epidemiol.* 141:980–90, 1995.

Haber, M. J., L. Watelet, and **M. E. Halloran.** On individual and population effectiveness of vaccination. *Int. J. Epidemiol.* 24:1249–60, 1995.

Haber, M., I. M. Longini Jr., and **M. E. Halloran.** Measures of the effects of vaccination in a randomly mixing population. *Int. J. Epidemiol.* 20:300–10, 1991.

Haber, M., I. M. Longini Jr., and **G. A. Cotsonis.** Models for the statistical analysis of infectious data. *Biometrics* 44:163–73, 1988.

Haber, M., and M. B. Brown. Maximum likelihood methods for log-linear models when expected frequencies are subject to linear constraints. *J. Am. Stat. Assoc.* 81:477–82, 1986.

Haber, M. J. Testing for pairwise independence. *Biometrics* 42:429–35, 1986.

Haber, M. J. Maximum likelihood methods for linear and log-linear models in categorical data. *Comput. Stat. Data Anal.* 3:1–10, 1985.

Haber, M. J. Log-linear models for linked loci. *Biometrics* 40:189–98, 1984.

Golm, G. T., **M. E. Halloran**, and **I. M. Longini Jr.** Semiparametric models for mismeasured exposure information in vaccine trials. *Statistics Med.*, in press.

Halloran, M. E., M.-P. Préziosi, and H. Chu. Estimating vaccine efficacy from secondary attach rates. *J. Am. Stat. Assoc.* 98:38–46, 2003.

Halloran, M. E., I. M. Longini Jr., A. Nizam, and Y. Yang. Containing bioterrorist smallpox. *Science* 298:1428–32, 2002.

Halloran, M. E., I. M. Longini Jr., D. M. Cowart, and **A. Nizam.** Community trials of vaccination and the epidemic prevention potential. *Vaccine* 20:3254–62, 2002.

Golm, G. T., **M. E. Halloran**, and **I. M. Longini Jr.** Semiparametric methods for multiple exposure mismeasurement and a bivariate outcome in HIV vaccine trials. *Biometrics* 55:94–101, 1999.

Halloran, M. E., I. M. Longini Jr., and C. J. Strichiner. Design and interpretation of vaccine field studies. *Epidemiol. Rev.* 21(1):73–88, 1999.

Golm, G. T., **M. E. Halloran**, and **I. M. Longini Jr.** Semi-parametric models for mismeasured exposure information in vaccine trials. *Statistics Med.* 17:2335–532, 1998.

Halloran, M. E., and C. J. Struchiner. Causal inference for interventions in infectious diseases. *Epidemiology* 6:142–51, 1995.

Hanfelt, J. J., S. Slack, and E. G. Gehan. A modification of Simon's optimal design for phase II trials when the criterion is median sample size. *Controlled Clin. Trials* 20:555–66, 1999.

Hanfelt, J. J. Optimal multi-stage designs for a phase II trial that permits one dose escalation. *Statistics Med.* 18:1323–39, 1999.

Hanfelt, J. J., and K.-Y. Liang. Inference for odds ratio regression models with sparse dependent data. *Biometrics* 54:136–47, 1998.

Hanfelt, J. J. Statistical approaches to experimental design and data analysis of in vivo studies. *Breast Cancer Res. Treatment* 46:279–302, 1997.

Hanfelt, J. J., and K.-Y. Liang. Approximate likelihoods for generalized linear errors-in-variables models. *J. R. Stat. Soc. B* 59:627–37, 1997.

Liang, K.-Y., C. A. Rohde, and **J. J. Hanfelt.** Instrumental variable estimation and estimating functions. *Statistica Applicata* 8:43–58, 1996.

Hanfelt, J. J., and K.-Y Liang. Approximate likelihood ratios for general estimating functions. *Biometrika* 82:461–77, 1995.

Liang, K.-Y., and **J. J. Hanfelt.** On the use of the quasi-likelihood method in tautological experiments. *Biometrics* 50:872–80, 1994.

Hertzberg, V. S. Simulation evaluation of three models for correlated binary data with covariates specific to each binary observation. *Commun. Stat.* 26:375–96, 1997.

Rosenman, K., et al. **(V. S. Hertzberg).** Silicosis among foundry workers: Implication for the need to revise the OSHA standard. *Am. J. Epidemiol.* 144:890–900, 1996.

Reilly, M. J., et al. **(V. S. Hertzberg).** Ocular effects of exposure to triethylamine in a foundry sand core cold box operation. *Occup. Environ. Med.* 52:337–43, 1995.

Hertzberg, V. S. Utilization 2: Special datasets. *Statistics Med.* 14:693, 1995.

Hertzberg, V. S., C. Rice, S. Pinney, and D. Linz. Occupational epidemiology in the era of TQM: Challenges for the future. In *1994 Proceedings of the Epidemiology Section, American Statistical Association.*

Hertzberg, V. S., G. K. Lemasters, K. Hansen, and H. M. Zenick. Statistical issues in risk assessment of reproductive outcomes with chemical mixtures. *Environ. Health Perspect.* 90:171–5, 1991.

Hertzberg, V. S., and L. D. Fisher. A model for variability in arteriographic reading. *Statistics Med.* 5:619–27, 1986.

King, S. B., III, **A. S. Kosinski,** and W. S. Weintraub. Eight year outcome in the Emory Angioplasty vs. Surgery Trial. *J. Am. Coll. Cardiol.,* in press.

Kosinski, A. S., and **W. D. Flanders**. Regression model for estimating for odds ratios with misclassified exposure. *Statistics Med.* 18:2795–808, 1999.

Kosinski, A. S. A procedure for the detection of multivariate outliers. *Computational Stat. Data Anal.* 29(2):199–211, 1999.

Barnhart, H. X., A. S. Kosinski, and A. Sampson. A regression model for multivariate random length data. *Statistics Med.* 18(2):199–211, 1999.

Deyi, B. A., **A. S. Kosinski,** and S. S. Snapinn. Power considerations when a continuous outcome variable is dichotomized. *J. Biopharm. Statistics* 8(2):337–52, 1998.

Stiger, T. R., **A. S. Kosinski, H. X. Barnhart,** and D. G. Kleinbaum. ANOVA for repeated ordinal data with small sample size? A comparison of ANOVA, MANOVA, WLS and GEE methods by simulation. In *Commun. Statistics Simulation Computation* 27(2): 357–75, 1998.

Cecil, M. C., and **A. S. Kosinski** et al. The importance of work-up (verification) bias correction in assessing the accuracy of SPECT thallium-201 testing for the diagnosis of coronary artery disease. *J. Clin. Epidemiol.* 49(7):735–42, 1996.

King, S. B.,III, et al. **(A. S. Kosinski** and **H. X. Barnhart).** A randomized trial comparing coronary angioplasty with coronary bypass surgery: Emory Angioplasty Versus Surgery Trial (EAST). *N. Engl. J. Med.* 331(16):1044–50, 1994.

Weintraub, W. S., et al. **(A. S. Kosinski).** Lack of effect of lovastatin on restenosis after coronary angioplasty. *N. Engl. J. Med.* 331(20):1331–7, 1994.

Tan, M., X. Xiong, and **M. H. Kutner.** Clinical trial designs based on sequential conditional probability ratio tests and reverse stochastic curtailing. *Biometrics,* 54:684–697, 1998.

Tan, M., Y. Qu, and **M. H. Kutner.** Model diagnostics for marginal regression analysis of correlated binary data. *Commun. Statistics Ser. B,* 23:539–58, 1997.

Emory University

Selected Publications (continued)

Qu, Y., M. Tan, and **M. H. Kutner.** Random effects models in latent class analysis for evaluating accuracy of diagnostic tests. *Biometrics,* 52:797–810, 1996.

Neter, J., **M. H. Kutner,** C. J. Nachsheim, and W. Wasserman. *Appl. Linear Regression Models* (3rd ed.). Chicago: Richard D. Irwin, Inc., 1996.

Neter, J., **M. H. Kutner,** C. J. Nachtsheim, and W. Wasserman. *Appl. Linear Stat. Models* (4th ed.). Chicago: Richard D. Irwin, Inc., 1996.

Kutner, M. H. The computer analysis of factorial experiments with nested factors. Invited response to Dallah, G. E., *Am. Statistician* 42:420, 1992.

Hocking, R. R., and **M. H. Kutner.** Some analytical and numerical comparisons of estimators for the mixed A.O.V. model. *Biometrics,* 3:19–27, 1975.

Frome, E. L., **M. H. Kutner,** and J. J. Beauchamp. Regression analysis of Poisson distributed data. *J. Am. Stat. Assoc.* 68:935–40, 1973.

Longini, I. M., M. E. Halloran, and A. Nizam et al. Estimation of the efficacy of live, attenuated influenza vaccine from a two-year multi-center vaccine trial: Implications for influenza epidemic control. *Vaccine* 18:1902–9, 2000.

Longini, I. M., M. G. Hudgens, **M. E. Halloran,** and K. Sagatelian. A Markov model for measuring vaccine efficacy for both susceptibility to infection and reduction in infectiousness for prophylactic HIV vaccines. *Statistics Med.* 18:53–68. 1999.

Durham, L. K., et al. **(I. M. Longini Jr., M. E. Halloran,** and **A. Nizam).** Estimation of vaccine efficacy in the presence of waning: Application to cholera vaccines. *Am. J. Epidemiol.,* in press.

Longini, I. M., S. Datta, and **M. E. Halloran.** Measuring vaccine efficacy for both susceptibility to infection and reduction in infectiousness for prophylactic HIV-1 vaccines. *J. Acquired Immun. Defic. Syndromes Hum. Retrovirol.* 13:440–7, 1996.

Longini, I. M., and **M. E. Halloran.** A frailty mixture model for estimating vaccine efficacy. *Appl. Stat.* 45:165–73, 1996.

Longini, I. M., and **M. E. Halloran.** AIDS: Modeling epidemic control. Letter to the editor. *Science* 267:1250–1, 1995.

Longini, I. M., M. E. Halloran, and **M. J. Haber.** Estimation of vaccine efficacy from epidemics of acute infectious agents under vaccine-related heterogeneity. *Math. Biosci.* 117:271–81, 1993.

Longini, I. M., W. S. Clark, and J. M. Karon. Effect of routine use of therapy in slowing the clinical course of human immunodeficiency virus infection in a population-based cohort. *Am. J. Epidemiol.* 137:1229–40, 1993.

Longini, I. M., M. E. Halloran, M. Haber, and R. T. Chen. Methods for estimating vaccine efficacy from outbreaks of acute infectious agents. *Statistics Med.* 12:249–63, 1993.

Longini, I. M., R. H. Byers, N. A. Hessol, and W. Y. Tan. Estimating the stage-specific numbers of HIV infection using a Markov model and back-calculation. *Statistics Med.* 11:831–43, 1992.

Longini, I. M., W. S. Clark, L. I. Gardner, and J. F. Brundage. The dynamics of CD4+ T-lymphocyte decline in HIV-infected individuals: A Markov modeling approach. *J. AIDS* 4:1141–7, 1991.

Longini, I. M., and **W. S. Clark** et al. Statistical analysis of the stages of HIV infection using a Markov model. *Statistics Med.* 8:831–43, 1989.

Longini, I. M. A mathematical model for predicting the geographic spread of new infectious agents. *Math. Biosci.* 90:367–83, 1988.

Lyles, R. H., D. Fan, and R. Chuachoowong. Correlation coefficient estimation involving a left-censored laboratory assay variable. *Statistics Med.,* in press.

Lyles, R. H., and G. McFarlane. Effects of covariate measurement error in the initial level and rate of change of an exposure variable. *Biometrics* 56:634–39, 2000.

Lyles, R. H., C. M. Lyles, and D. J. Taylor. Randomized regression models for HIV RNA data subject to left censoring and informative dropouts. *Appl. Stat.* 49:485–97, 2000.

Lyles, R. H., and L. L. Kupper. A note of confidence interval estimation in measurement error adjustment. *Am. Statistician* 53:247–53, 1999.

Lyles, R. H., et al. Prognostic value of HIV RNA in the natural history of *Pneumocystis carinii* pneumonia, cytomegalovirus, and *Mycobacterium avium* complex disease. *AIDS* 13:341–50, 1999.

Lyles, R. H., et al. Adjusting for measurement error to assess health effects of variability in biomarkers. *Statistics Med.* 18:1069–86, 1999.

Lyles, R. H., and J. Xu. Classifying individuals based on predictors of random effects. *Statistics Med.* 18:35–52, 1999.

Lyles, R. H., and L. L. Kupper. A detailed evaluation of adjustment methods for multiplicative measurement error in multiple linear regression, with applications in occupational epidemiology. *Biometrics* 53:1008–25, 1997.

Lyles, R. H., L. L. Kupper, and S. M. Rappaport. On prediction of lognormal-scale mean exposure levels in epidemiologic studies, *J. Agric. Biol. Environ. Stats.* 2:417–39, 1997.

Price, D. L., and **A. K. Manatunga.** Modeling survival data with a cured fraction using frailty models. *Statistics Med.,* in press.

Manatunga, A. K., and S. Chen. Sample size estimation for survival outcomes in cluster randomized studies with small cluster sizes. *Biometrics,* in press.

Manatunga, A. K., and D. Oakes. Parametric analysis for matched paid data. *Life Time Data Anal.* 5:371–87, 1999.

Durham, K. L., **M. E. Halloran, I. M. Longini Jr.,** and **A. K. Manatunga.** Comparison of two smoothing methods for exploring waning vaccine effects. *Appl. Statistics* 48:395–407, 1999.

Chen, M.-H., **A. K. Manatunga,** and C. J. Williams. Heritability estimates from human twin data by incorporating historical prior information. *Biometrics* 54:1348–62, 1998.

Sun, F., et al. **(M. E. Halloran** and **A. K. Manatunga).** Testing for contribution of mitochondrial DNA mutations to complex diseases. *Genet. Epidemiol.* 15:451–469, 1998.

Manatunga, A. K., and D. Oakes. A measure of association for bivariate frailty distributions. *J. Multivar. Analysis* 56:60–74, 1996.

Manatunga, A. K., J. J. Jones, and J. H. Pratt. Longitudinal assessment of blood pressures in black and white children. *J. Hypertension* 22:84–89, 1993.

Oakes, D., and **A. K. Manatunga.** Fisher information for a bivariate extreme value distribution. *Biometrika* 79:827–32, 1992.

Oakes, D., and **A. K. Manatunga.** A new representation of Cox's score statistic and its variance. *Stat. Probab. Lett.* 14:107–10, 1992.

Manatunga, A. K., T. K. Reister, J. Z. Miller, and J. H. Pratt. Genetic influences on the urinary excretion of aldosterone in children. *J. Hypertension* 19:192–7, 1992.

Rhodes, P., M. E. Halloran, and **I. M. Longini Jr.**. Counting process models for infectious disease data: Distinguishing exposure to infection from susceptibility. *J. R. Stat. Soc. B* 58:751–62, 1997.

Satten, G. A., and **I. M. Longini Jr.** Markov chains with measurement error: Estimating the "true" course of a marker on HIV disease progression (with discussion). *Appl. Stat.* 45:275–309, 1996.

Satten, G. A., and **I. M. Longini Jr.** Estimation of incidence of HIV infection using cross-sectional marker surveys. *Biometrics* 50:675–88, 1994.

Satten, G. A., T. D. Mastro, and **I. M. Longini Jr.** Estimating the heterosexual transmission probability of HIV-1 in Thailand. *Statistics Med.* 13:2097–106, 1994.

Smith, D., et al. **(L. A. Waller).** Predicting the spatial dynamics of rabies epidemics on heterogeneous landscapes. *Proc. Natl. Acad. Sci. U.S.A.* 99:3668–72, 2002.

Wakefield, J., N. Best, and **L. A. Waller.** Bayesian approaches to disease mapping. In *Spatial Epidemiology: Methods and Applications,* pp. 106–27, eds. P. Elliott, J. D. Wakefield, N. G. Best, and D. J. Briggs. Oxford: Oxford University Press, 2000.

Best, N. G., et al. **(L. A. Waller).** Bayesian models for spatially correlated disease and exposure data. *Bayesian Statistics 6,* eds. J. M. Bernardo, J. O. Berger, A. P. Dawid, and A. F. M. Smith. Oxford: Oxford University Press, 1999.

English, P. R., et al. **(L. Waller).** Examining associations between childhood asthma and traffic flow using a geographic information system. *Environ. Health Perspect.* 107:761–7, 1999.

Waller, L. A., T. A. Louis, and B. P. Carlin. Environmental justice and statistical summaries of differences in exposure distributions. *J. Exposure Anal. Environ. Epidemiol.* 9:56–65, 1999.

Yu, C., **L. A. Waller,** and D. Zelterman. A discrete distribution for use in twin studies. *Biometrics* 54:546–57, 1998.

Waller, L. A., and R. B. McMaster. Incorporating indirect standardization in tests for disease clustering in a GIS environment. *Geog. Systems* 4:327–42, 1997.

Waller, L. A., T. A. Louis, and B. P. Carlin. Bayes methods for combining disease and exposure data in assessing environmental justice. *Environ. Ecol. Statistics* 4:267–81, 1997.

Waller, L. A., and D. Zelterman. Log-linear modeling with the negative multinomial distribution. *Biometrics* 53:971–82, 1997.

Waller, L. A., B. P. Carlin, H. Xia, and A. Gelfand. Hierarchical spatio-temporal mapping of disease rates. *J. Am. Stat. Assoc.* 92:607–17, 1997.

Lawson, A. B., and **L. A. Waller.** A review of point pattern methods for spatial modeling of events around sources of pollution. *Environmetrics* 7:471–88, 1996.

Waller, L. A., Does the characteristic function numerically distinguish distributions? *Am. Statistician* 49:150–2, 1995.

Waller, L. A., and G. M. Jacquez. Disease models implicit in statistical tests of disease clustering. *Epidemiology* 6:584–90, 1995.

Williamson, G. D., and **M. J. Haber.** Models for three-dimensional contingency tables with completely and partially cross-classified data. *Biometrics* 50:194–203, 1994.

Williamson, J. M., and **A. K. Manatunga.** Assessing interrater agreement from dependent data. *Biometrics* 53(2):707–14, 1997.

GEORGE MASON UNIVERSITY

School of Computational Sciences

Program of Study

The School of Computational Sciences (SCS) offers doctoral and master's programs in the broad area of computational sciences, which is defined as the systematic development and application of computational methodologies and techniques to understand, model, and simulate phenomena in the natural sciences and engineering. SCS currently offers a doctoral program in computational sciences and informatics (CSI), a doctoral program in climate dynamics, a master's program in computational science, and a master's program in earth systems science.

The CSI doctoral program provides interdisciplinary research opportunities in several computational areas, including astrophysics, materials science, biology, chemistry, fluid dynamics, applied mathematics, physics, space sciences, statistics, and earth observing/remote sensing. The program combines three intellectual elements: core computational science topics, computationally intensive courses in specific science areas, and research leading to the dissertation. The doctoral program includes 12 hours of core computational classes (numerical methods, scientific computing, databases, visualization), 12 hours from courses in one of the science areas, 12 hours in electives from science courses, 12 hours from general electives, and 24 hours in dissertation research.

The Ph.D. program in climate dynamics is designed to train the next generation of world leaders in the science of climate dynamics. Understanding climate variability and predictability poses difficult mathematical, computational, and observational questions that have generated increasing intellectual excitement in recent years. Because atmospheric behavior is strongly coupled to the oceans and land surface, physical oceanography and land surface physics can also be considered part of the science of climate dynamics. The curriculum is divided into four logical areas: 12 credit hours of fundamental climate science courses, 9 credit hours of core computational methods, 3 credit hours of seminar, a minimum of 24 credit hours of electives, and a minimum of 24 credit hours of dissertation research.

Students interested in the computational science M.S. degree should have backgrounds that include courses in differential equations, computer programming, and natural science. Students interested in the earth systems science M.S. degree should have backgrounds that include courses in chemistry, calculus, and physics.

Research Facilities

The SCS Computing Facility houses a massively parallel Beowolf PC cluster with 120 processors, 1 gigabyte RAM, and a high-performance symmetric multiprocessor computer, the Silicon Graphics Origin 2000, with 16 nodes and 4 gigabytes RAM. There is also a Pentium Linux cluster consisting of twenty-four workstations. In addition, there are several research computer platforms available to advanced students actively pursuing research in collaboration with faculty members. General University facilities are available to SCS students. SCS program information can be accessed on the World Wide Web (http://www.scs.gmu.edu).

Financial Aid

A limited number of highly competitive research assistantships are available carrying a full tuition waiver and a stipend. The minimum stipend in 2003–04 was $13,000 for the fiscal year. Assistantships in research, fellowships, and student loans are available. Further information can be obtained from SCS.

Cost of Study

Full-time students take at least 9 credit hours per semester. In 2003–04, out-of-state tuition was $623 per credit hour, and in-state tuition was $245 per credit hour.

Living and Housing Costs

Approximately 3,000 students live on campus in six residential areas. Most graduate students prefer off-campus housing. Estimated costs per year are $3200–$4000 for room, $1500–$1800 for board, and $600 for books and supplies. Further information can be obtained by calling the Office of Housing at 703-993-2720.

Student Group

The total number of doctoral students at SCS is currently 180. Full-time students number about 56, and the remainder are part-time students. A wide variety of age groups and academic, ethnic, and national backgrounds are represented among these students.

Location

George Mason University and the surrounding community together provide an ideal environment for learning and research. The campus is located 15 miles from Washington, D.C., on 583 wooded acres in Fairfax, northern Virginia. The setting combines the quietness of a residential suburban area with access to Fairfax County's high-technology firms; to Washington, D.C.'s libraries, galleries, museums, and national and federal laboratories; and to Virginia's historical sites. The Patriot Center and the Performing Arts Center house continuous community activities and recreational events. The 2,000-seat Concert Hall is host to full-scale music, dance, opera, and theater of the most renowned productions. The Sports and Recreational Complex and the three student unions available on campus also offer a variety of recreational activities.

The University and The School

In the last decade, George Mason University has emerged as a major academic institution offering nationally recognized programs in advanced technology and science, among others. From its origins in 1957, George Mason has grown into a medium-sized state university in northern Virginia with innovative programs that have attracted a faculty of world-renowned scholars and teachers. In 1979, George Mason received doctoral status approval. SCS is a dynamic and forward-looking school with a strong commitment to developing a diverse and innovative research curriculum.

Applying

A bachelor's degree in mathematics, engineering, computer science, or any natural science with a minimum GPA of 3.0 is needed to apply. The GRE is required. A TOEFL score of 575 is required for international students. All international transcripts must be evaluated by a U.S. evaluation service. These are listed in the Application for Admission. Applications should be received by February 1 for the fall semester and by November 1 for the spring semester. Applications requesting financial support should be received by February 1 for the fall semester, and GRE scores are part of the consideration for financial support.

Correspondence and Information

Office of the Graduate Coordinator
SCS/School of Computational Sciences
George Mason University MS 5C3
Fairfax, Virginia 22030-4444

Telephone: 703-993-1990
Fax: 703-993-1980
E-mail: pbecker@science.gmu.edu

George Mason University

THE FACULTY AND THEIR RESEARCH

Dean

Menas Kafatos, University Professor and Dean, School of Computational Sciences; Ph.D., MIT, 1972. Astrophysics, space sciences, Earth observing, informatics.

SCS Full-time Faculty

Sheryl Beach, Associate Professor; Ph.D., Minnesota, 1990. Physical geography, hydrology, ground water, GIS.
Peter A. Becker, Associate Professor and Associate Dean for Graduate Studies, School of Computational Sciences; Ph.D., Colorado, 1987. Astrophysics, computational mathematics.
Avrama L. Blackwell, Associate Professor; Ph. D., Pennsylvania, 1988. Computational neurobiology.
Estela Blaisten-Barojas, Professor; Ph.D., Paris VI, 1974. Computational physics, condensed-matter physics.
Juan Raul Cebral, Associate Professor; Ph.D., George Mason, 1996. Computational fluid dynamics.
Long S. Chiu, Associate Professor; Ph.D., MIT, 1980. Earth observation, meteorology.
Claudio Cioffi-Revilla, Professor of Computational Social Sciences; Ph.D., Florence, 1977. Complexity theory, social science, computational modeling.
James E. Gentle, University Professor and Assistant Dean for Faculty, School of Computational Sciences; Ph.D., Texas A&M, 1974. Computational statistics, numerical analysis.
John J. Grefenstette, Associate Professor; Ph.D., Pittsburgh, 1980. Bioinformatics, computational biology.
Mohin Saleet Jafri, Associate Professor; Ph.D., CUNY, Mount Sinai, 1993. Cellular signaling, protein structure, high-performance computing.
D. Curtis Jamison, Associate Professor; Ph.D., Denver, 1992. Bioinformatics.
Jason M. Kinser, Associate Professor; D.Sc., South Eastern Institute of Technology, 1993. Bioinformatics, computational biology.
Ben Kirtman, Associate Professor of Climate Dynamics; Ph.D., Maryland, 1992. Climate dynamics, coupled ocean-atmosphere predictability.
Barry Klinger, Associate Professor; Ph.D., MIT and Woods Hole Oceanographic Institute, 1992. Oceanography.
Rainald Lohner, Professor; Ph.D., University College of Swansea (Wales), 1984. Computational fluid dynamics.
Keith McKenney, Associate Professor; Ph.D., Johns Hopkins, 1982. Microbial genomics and diversity.
Ryszard S. Michalski, Planning Research Corporation Professor of Computational Sciences and Information Technology; Ph.D., Silesian University of Technology, 1969. Machine learning and inference, knowledge mining, computational intelligence.
Yuri Mishin, Associate Professor; Ph.D., Moscow Institute of Steel and Alloys, 1985. Computational materials science.
Rita Sambruna, Assistant Professor; Ph.D., International School for Advanced Studies, Trieste, Italy, 1994. Astrophysics, X-ray astronomy.
Edwin K. Schneider, Professor of Climate Dynamics; Ph.D., Harvard, 1976. Climate dynamics, climate system modeling.
Paul S. Schopf, Professor and Assistant Dean for Research, School of Computational Sciences; Ph.D., Princeton, 1978. Oceanography, climate dynamics.
Donald Seto, Associate Professor; Ph.D., Johns Hopkins, 1987. Microbial genomics and diversity, applied cell biology and genetics.
Jagadish Shukla, Professor; Ph.D., Banaras Hindu (India), 1971; Sc.D., MIT, 1976. Climate dynamics, global change.
David M. Straus, Professor of Climate Dynamics; Ph.D., Cornell, 1977. Atmospheric dynamics, atmospheric predictability, atmospheric waves.
Michael E. Summers, Associate Professor; Ph.D., Caltech, 1985. Atmospheric physics.
George E. Taylor Jr., Professor and Assistant Dean for Administration, School of Computational Sciences; Ph.D., Emory, 1976. Environmental sciences, ecology, air quality.
Iosif Vaisman, Associate Professor; Ph.D., Academy of Sciences (Moscow), 1990. Bioinformatics.
John F. Wallin, Associate Professor; Ph.D., Iowa State, 1989. Astronomy, astrophysics.
Edward J. Wegman, Dunn Professor; Ph.D., Iowa, 1968. Computational statistics.
Jennifer Weller, Associate Professor; Ph.D. Bioinformatics.
James Willett, Professor; Ph.D., MIT, 1965. Biochemistry, applied cell biology, genetics.
David W. Wong, Associate Professor; Ph.D., SUNY at Buffalo, 1990. Geography, spatial analysis and statistics, GIS.
Chi Yang, Associate Professor; Ph.D., Shanghai Jiao Tong, 1988. Computational fluid dynamics, numerical ship hydrodynamics.
Ruixin Yang, Assistant Professor; Ph.D., USC, 1990. Data information systems.
Stanley M. Zoltek, Associate Professor; Ph.D., SUNY, 1976. Differential geometry.

SCS Part-time Faculty

James H. Beall, Senior Contract Professor; Ph.D., Maryland, 1979. Astrophysics, space sciences.
Timothy DelSole, Associate Professor of Climate Dynamics; Ph.D., Harvard, 1993. Climate dynamics.
John Guillory, Senior Contract Professor; Ph.D., California, 1970. Plasma science.
Bohua Huang, Associate Professor; Ph.D., Maryland, 1992. General circulation models, seasonal variability.
James L. Kinter III, Associate Professor; Ph.D., Princeton, 1984. General circulation modeling.
V. Krishnamurthy, Contract Professor of Climate Dynamics; Ph.D., MIT, 1985. Climate dynamics, chaos.
Dimitrios Papaconstantopoulos, Senior Contract Professor; Ph.D., London, 1967. Solid-state physics.
Jeffrey L. Solka, Contract Assistant Professor; Ph.D., George Mason, 1995. Computational statistics.
Kent S. Wood, Senior Contract Professor; Ph.D., MIT, 1973. Astrophysics, space sciences.

SCS Research Faculty

Zafer Boybeyi, Research Professor; Ph.D., North Carolina State, 1993. Atmospheric dispersion.
Liping Di, Research Professor; Ph.D., Nebraska–Lincoln, 1991. Remote sensing.
Richard B. Gomez, Research Professor; Ph.D., New Mexico State, 1976. Hyperspectral imaging, remote sensing.
Yimin Ji, Research Scientist; Ph.D., Maryland, 1995. Remote sensing.
Kenneth Kaufman, Research Associate Professor; Ph.D., George Mason, 1998. Data mining and knowledge discovery, machine learning.
John M. Kwiatkowski, Principal Research Scientist; Ph.D., Michigan Tech, 1995. Remote sensing.
John Qu, Principal Research Scientist; Ph.D., Colorado State, 1997. Remote sensing.
Lev Titarchuk, Research Professor, Ph.D., Space Research Institute (Moscow), 1972. Astrophysics.
Chaowei Yang, Research Scientist; Ph.D., Peking University, 2000. Cartography, GIS.
Wenli Yang, Principal Research Scientist; Ph.D., Nebraska–Lincoln. Remote sensing.

SCS Affiliate Faculty

Giorgio Ascoli, Associate Professor; Ph.D., Scuola Normale Superiore de Pisa, 1996. Computational neuroanatomy.
W. Murray Black, Professor and Founding Dean, School of Computational Sciences; Ph.D., Penn State, 1971. Electrical engineering, materials science.
Daniel Carr, Professor; Ph.D., Wisconsin, 1976. Computational statistics.
Patrick Gillevet, Research Associate Professor; Ph.D., Manitoba, 1982. Bioinformatics.
Larry Kerschberg, Professor; Ph.D., Case Western Reserve, 1969. Software engineering, intelligent databases.
B. Joseph Lieb, Professor; Ph.D., William and Mary, 1971. Experimental nuclear physics.
Jeng-Eng Lin, Associate Professor; Ph.D., Brown, 1976. Nonlinear partial differential equations.
James L. Olds, Shelley Krasnow University Professor of Neuroscience and Director and CEO Krasnow Institute for Advanced Study; Ph.D., Michigan, 1987. Neuroscience.
Shobita Satyapal, Assistant Professor; Ph.D., Rochester, 1995. Infrared astronomy and instrumentation.
Timothy D. Sauer, Professor; Ph.D., California, 1982. Chaos, dynamical systems.
David A. Schum, Professor; Ph.D., Methodist University, 1964. Operations research.
Xiaoyang Wang, Associate Professor; Ph.D., California, 1982. Chaos, dynamical systems.

IDAHO STATE UNIVERSITY

Department of Mathematics

Programs of Study

The Department of Mathematics offers the Doctor of Arts and Master of Science degrees. It also participates in the Ph.D. program in engineering and applied science.

The Doctor of Arts program is designed to prepare the student for a teaching career in institutions of higher learning. The program emphasizes broad competence in mathematics rather than specialization and provides classroom teaching experience. It requires 48 credits of course work, distributed among mathematics, interdisciplinary, and education components; teaching internships; an expository or research thesis in mathematics or mathematics education; and written and oral examinations. Three years is a typical time to degree, although the time depends on the student's background.

The Master of Science program is a two-year program that provides a broad, in-depth background in mathematics. It prepares students for further study at the doctoral level or for an industrial or academic career. The nonthesis option involves 30 hours of graduate course work and written and oral examinations. The thesis option involves 24 hours of classroom work, a written examination, and an oral thesis defense.

The Ph.D. in engineering and applied science is an interdisciplinary program administered by the College of Engineering. Students in the subsurface science emphasis area may conduct their research under the direction of a mathematics faculty member.

Research Facilities

Idaho State University's Oboler Library holds monographs and a wide range of research journals in pure and applied mathematics. Faculty members and students also have access to other resources for research through electronic journals and interlibrary loan. Graduate students in mathematics have access to a departmental computer lab as well as a University-wide system of computer labs. Software includes Maple, Matlab, and statistics packages.

Financial Aid

The Department of Mathematics supports its graduate students through graduate teaching assistantships and Doctor of Arts fellowships. In the 2004–05 academic year, stipends for graduate assistantships range from $8276 to $10,803, and stipends for Doctor of Arts fellowships are $11,579. Grant-supported thesis work and contract teaching provide further opportunities.

Cost of Study

In 2004–05, fees for full-time graduate study are $4380 for Idaho residents and an additional $7080 for nonresidents. Those fees include mandatory student health insurance. A waiver of nonresident tuition accompanies all graduate assistantships and Doctor of Arts fellowships, and the department routinely supplements those awards with a scholarship waiving all tuition and fees. Both waivers are in the form of nontaxable scholarships. Stipends for assistantships and Doctor of Arts fellowships are subject to tax.

Living and Housing Costs

Although some student housing is available, most graduate students at Idaho State rent apartments or houses near the campus. One-bedroom apartments are typically $350 to $450 per month. The cost of living in Pocatello is generally low.

Student Group

The department's full-time graduate student population has averaged about 5 doctoral students and 8 master's students in recent years, with a men-women ratio of about 2:1. Students come from a variety of backgrounds. Many in the Doctor of Arts program have come to Idaho State to improve their credentials after a few years' college teaching with a master's degree. Those in the master's programs often enter directly from a baccalaureate program.

Student Outcomes

The Doctor of Arts program is particularly successful at placing graduates in academic positions at two- and four-year colleges such as Nebraska Wesleyan University, Pacific Union College, the University of La Verne, the University of Southern Maine, and Walla Walla College. Master of Science recipients have gone on to Ph.D. programs or taken jobs in industry.

Location

Pocatello, a city of 50,000, is located on the southeast edge of the Snake River Plain. It is served by its own airport and the Salt Lake City airport 150 miles to the south. The surroundings provide opportunities for many outdoor activities, such as fishing, hiking, mountain biking, and skiing.

The University

Idaho State University is the state university for eastern Idaho. Beyond its growing reputation in mathematics, it is known for its research in pharmacy, geoscience, and biology.

Applying

Applicants to the Doctor of Arts program should have completed the requirements for a master's degree equivalent to the M.S. in mathematics at Idaho State University, with a minimum 3.5 GPA in all graduate work. Applicants to the Master of Science program must have completed all requirements for a bachelor's degree in mathematics at an accredited institution, with a minimum 3.0 GPA in the last two years of undergraduate work. Both programs require satisfactory scores on the Graduate Record Examinations. Applications requesting financial aid should be submitted by March 15. Applications can be submitted online at the graduate department's Web site.

Correspondence and Information

Inquiries may be directed to:
Graduate School
Campus Box 8075
Idaho State University
Pocatello, Idaho 83209
Telephone: 208-282-2150
World Wide Web: http://www.isu.edu/departments/graduate/

For specific information about degree programs in mathematics, applicants should contact:
Chair, Department of Mathematics
Campus Box 8085
Idaho State University
Pocatello, Idaho 83209
Telephone: 208-282-3350

Idaho State University

THE FACULTY AND THEIR RESEARCH

Yu Chen, Assistant Professor; Ph.D., Notre Dame, 2002. Algebra and representation theory.
Alan Egger, Professor; Ph.D., Colorado State, 1981. Approximation theory.
Robert J. Fisher, Professor; Ph.D., Massachusetts Amherst, 1981. Differential geometry.
Lawrence Ford, Associate Professor; Ph.D., Caltech, 1974. Harmonic analysis, voting theory, number theory.
Ann Gironella, Assistant Professor; Ph.D., Kansas State, 1978. Statistics.
Yuriy Gryazin, Assistant Professor; Ph.D., Novosibirsk State (Russia), 1996. Numerical analysis.
Leonid Hanin, Associate Professor; Ph.D., Steklov Institute of Mathematics (Russia), 1985. Biomathematics, probability and stochastic processes, functional analysis.
Linda Hill, Associate Professor; Ph.D., Rochester, 1973. Commutative algebra.
Richard Hill, Professor; Ph.D., Oregon State, 1968. Matrix theory.
Lawrence Kratz, Professor; Ph.D., Utah, 1975. Enumerative combinatorics.
Catherine Kriloff, Associate Professor; Ph.D., Michigan, 1995. Representation theory of Hecke algebras, Lie theory.
Patrick Lang, Professor; Ph.D., Colorado State, 1985. Biased regression techniques.
H. Turner Laquer, Professor; Ph.D., Harvard, 1982. Differential geometry.
Terry Lay, Associate Professor; Ph.D., Tennessee, 1980. Topology.
Bennett Palmer, Associate Professor; Ph.D., Stanford, 1986. Differential geometry.
Tracy Payne, Assistant Professor; Ph.D., Michigan, 1995. Differential geometry, dynamical systems.
Dennis Stowe, Professor; Ph.D., Berkeley, 1980. Differential geometry, complex analysis.
Rob Van Kirk, Assistant Professor; Ph.D., Utah, 1995. Applied mathematics, mathematical biology.
James Wolper, Professor; Ph.D., Brown, 1981. Algebraic geometry, algebraic groups, coding theory, geometric control theory, pattern recognition, navigation.

KENT STATE UNIVERSITY

College of Arts and Sciences
Department of Mathematical Sciences

Programs of Study

The Department of Mathematical Sciences at Kent State University offers courses and research in both pure mathematics and applied mathematics leading to the M.A., M.S., and Ph.D. degrees. The master's program is intended for those who want a professional education beyond the bachelor's level. It is designed for students who wish to enter mathematically oriented careers in various industries and businesses, or more advanced research and study in mathematics. The Ph.D. program, in contrast, is designed for students interested in becoming professional scholars, college or university professors, or conducting independent research at private, industrial, or government institutions.

Research Facilities

Through research, advanced degree programs, technology transfer, and workforce development, Kent State promotes economic development in Ohio and beyond. Faculty researchers actively engage in nanotechnology, biotechnology, and information technology projects related to Governor Taft's "Third Frontier" plan. The University is a Carnegie Foundation Doctoral/Research University–Extensive, one of ninety public institutions to be so designated. This year, the Division of Research and Graduate Studies has helped faculty and staff members secure $29 million in extramural funding to support research, instructional, and public service projects. Department research focuses on areas such as finite groups, numerical and scientific computation, probability, and stochastic processes. The department has its own library, which houses 270 journal titles in the areas of both mathematics and computer science. Monographs, reference materials, and related journal titles that support these subject areas are housed in the main library. Graduate students are assigned office space as well as their own computers for conducting research.

Financial Aid

Graduate students receive financial aid in the form of teaching assistantships, research assistantships, and teaching fellowships. Assistantships currently provide nine-month stipends of $13,300 for master's-level students and $14,300 to $15,300 for Ph.D. students, with an exemption from all instructional and out-of-state fees. Summer support is available for those making solid progress. Research assistantships provide twelve-month stipends with a full fee exemption and no service obligation. Application for financial aid must be received by January 15 for September admission.

Cost of Study

For fall 2003 semester, the graduate tuition per credit was $334 for an Ohio resident and $627 for a nonresident.

Living and Housing Costs

Rooms in the graduate hall of residence are $1475 to $2455 per semester; married students' apartments may be rented for $525 to $550 per month (all utilities included). Information concerning off-campus housing may be obtained from the University housing office. Costs vary widely, but apartments typically rent for $450 to $550 per month.

Student Group

Approximately 30 graduate students are enrolled in the program.

Student Outcomes

The majority of students have assumed academic positions, while others have found employment in industry.

Location

Kent, a city of about 30,000, is located 35 miles southeast of Cleveland and 12 miles east of Akron in a peaceful suburban setting. Kent offers the cultural advantages of a major metropolitan complex as well as the relaxed pace of semirural living. There are a number of theater and art groups at the University and in the community. Blossom Music Center, the summer home of the Cleveland Orchestra and the site of Kent State's cooperative programs in art, music, and theater, is only 15 miles from the main campus. The Akron and Cleveland art museums are also within easy reach of the campus. There are a wide variety of recreational facilities available on the campus and within the local area, including West Branch State Park and the Cuyahoga Valley National Recreation Area. Opportunities for outdoor activities such as summer sports, ice skating, swimming, and downhill and cross-country skiing abound.

The University and The Department

Established in 1910, Kent State University is one of Ohio's largest state universities. The campus is situated on 866 acres and includes an airport and an eighteen-hole golf course. Bachelor's, master's, and doctoral degrees are offered in more than thirty subject areas. The faculty numbers approximately 800 members.

Applying

Prospective students need to file a completed application to the Office of Graduate Study, which forwards the materials to the Department Graduate Office for evaluation. There are prerequisites for admission, while conditional admission to the master's program is offered in certain circumstances. More admissions information can be found at http://www.mathsrv2.math.kent.edu/grad/apply/admis-reg.html.

Correspondence and Information

Mathematics Graduate Office
Department of Mathematics and Computer Science
Kent State University
Kent, Ohio 44242-0001
Telephone: 330-672-9045
E-mail: math-gradinfo@mcs.kent.edu
World Wide Web: http://www.math.kent.edu/grad/graduate.html

Kent State University

THE FACULTY AND THEIR RESEARCH

Hassan Allouba, Ph.D., Cornell, 1996. SPDEs, probability PDEs, applied math, stochastic analysis.
Volodymyr Andriyevskyy, Ph.D., Institute of Applied Mathematics and Mechanics, Ukranian Academy of Sciences, 1980. Geometric function theory, approximation theory, potential theory.
Richard M. Aron, Ph.D., Rochester, 1971. Functional analysis, complex analysis.
Alfred S. Cavaretta Jr., Ph.D., Wisconsin, 1970. Approximation theory.
Morley Davidson, Ph.D., Michigan, 1995. Number theory.
Joseph Diestel, Ph.D., Catholic University, 1968. Functional analysis.
Per H. Enflo, University Professor; Ph.D., Stockholm, 1967. Analysis and analytic number theory.
Stephen M. Gagola Jr., Ph.D., Wisconsin, 1974. Group theory.
Eugene C. Gartland Jr., Ph.D., Purdue, 1980. Applied mathematics, numerical analysis.
Mohammad K. Khan, Ph.D., Case Western Reserve, 1980. Statistics.
Michal Kowalczyk, Ph.D., Tennessee, Knoxville, 1995. Dynamical systems, PDE.
Mark Lewis, Ph.D., Wisconsin, 1995. Character theory of finite groups.
Austin Melton, Ph.D., Kansas State, 1980. Lattice theory, math education.
John P. Neuzil, Ph.D., Iowa, 1969. Geometric topology.
Lothar Reichel, Ph.D., Stockholm, 1982. Numerical analysis.
Frank Smith, Ph.D., Purdue, 1965. General topology and partially ordered algebra.
Laura Smithies, Ph.D., Utah, 1997. Lie group representation theory.
Andrew Tonge, Ph.D., Cambridge, 1976. Harmonic analysis.
Richard S. Varga, University Professor; Ph.D., Harvard, 1954. Numerical analysis, approximation theory, linear algebra.
Ulrike Vorhauer, Ph.D., Ulm (Germany), 1996. Number theory, math education.
Donald L. White, Ph.D., Yale, 1987. Group representation theory.

LEHIGH UNIVERSITY

College of Arts and Sciences
Department of Mathematics

Programs of Study

Graduate study in mathematics at Lehigh University covers a broad spectrum of pure mathematics, applied mathematics, and statistics. The department offers programs of study leading to the M.S. and Ph.D. degrees in mathematics and in applied mathematics as well as the M.S. in statistics. The department has been awarding graduate degrees for more than sixty years, and more than 250 M.S. and 150 Ph.D. degrees in mathematics have been awarded in the past thirty-five years. Graduate courses are offered in algebra, real analysis, complex analysis, topology, differential geometry, functional analysis, differential equations, combinatorics, number theory, set theory, numerical analysis, wavelets, probability, financial mathematics, and statistics. In addition, advanced seminars are offered in research areas of current faculty interest. Topics of recent seminars have included algebraic topology, differential geometry, discrete mathematics, financial mathematics, number theory, and probability.

All entering graduate students take a comprehensive examination during their first year of graduate work. Thirty credit hours are needed for the M.S., and up to 6 of these may be used for research and the writing of a thesis. To be admitted to candidacy for a doctoral degree, the student who has passed the comprehensive examination must take a qualifying examination consisting of three exams chosen from eleven areas of mathematics. Doctoral students also must pass a general examination and a language examination and complete and publicly defend a dissertation.

The department conducts the prestigious Pitcher Lecture series, an annual program given by a distinguished mathematician and directed at graduate students and faculty members. Recent speakers include Peter Shor (2001), Joan Birman (2002), and James Arthur (2003). In addition, the department offers a weekly colloquium featuring invited speakers and an annual Geometry/Topology Conference. Proximity to Philadelphia, New York, and Princeton provides students with ample opportunities to participate in outside mathematical activities.

The University publishes the *Journal of Differential Geometry.* Members of the faculty are on the editorial boards of *Annals of Applied Probability; Advances in Geometry; Current Index to Statistics; Homology, Homotopy and Applications; Journal of Differential Geometry; Interstat;* and *Sequential Analysis.*

Research Facilities

More than 22,000 volumes in the mathematical sciences, including monographs and bound periodicals, are part of the mathematics collection. Computing resources include a Silicon Graphics (SGI) Origin 3800 symmetric multiprocessor computer well suited for large-scale scientific computing, more than 400 PCs at public sites running Windows XP, and forty high-end SGI work stations for public use. The principal programming languages used are FORTRAN, C, Pascal, C++, Reduce, and Maple, for which Lehigh has a campuswide license. Students may obtain personal copies of the microcomputer versions. The University libraries contain one of the most technologically advanced information systems in the U.S. Through the campus network, all services are received electronically in offices, classrooms, and laboratories. The collection includes 1 million volumes, 10,000 serials, 1.7 million microforms, and 550,000 government documents plus audiovisual, CD-ROM databases, a media production center, and listening and viewing facilities.

Financial Aid

The Department of Mathematics has appointed 23 teaching assistants for 2004–05, with a $13,500–$14,000 stipend plus tuition remission for the academic year. The University awards approximately forty-five fellowships in various amounts and forty tuition scholarships to graduate students on a competitive basis.

Cost of Study

Tuition for 2004–05 is $970 per credit. The University pays tuition expenses for students awarded teaching assistantships and research assistantships in the Department of Mathematics. Most students without an assistantship receive matching tuition aid, effectively making the cost $485 per credit.

Living and Housing Costs

Students live in a wide variety of accommodations, and expenses can be reasonable, especially if shared. Lehigh operates a 148-unit garden apartment complex for single and married students, located in nearby Saucon Valley. Rent for a one-bedroom unfurnished apartment is $460 per month. Day care is available nearby, and hourly bus service is provided. Private rental units are also available. Costs average $6000 per year.

Student Group

The department has about 30 full-time students. University-wide, students come from many states and other countries. It is the policy of the University to provide equal opportunity based on merit and without discrimination due to race, color, religion, gender, age, national origin, citizenship, status, handicap, or veteran status.

Student Outcomes

A typical group of new graduate students consists of approximately 7 individuals, with about half of these admitted into the Ph.D. program. Recent graduates of the master's degree programs have pursued further graduate work at Lehigh and other institutions or have entered careers in secondary education, the insurance industry, and the government. The department has had great success in placing its Ph.D. graduates in academic positions. Several graduates have gone on to major postdoctoral research positions and some to positions in industry.

Location

Bethlehem, Pennsylvania (population 72,000), is located 50 miles north of Philadelphia and 90 miles west of New York City; the best access is via Interstate 78, U.S. Route 22, or the Lehigh Valley International Airport. Founded in 1741, Bethlehem has a rich cultural heritage in the Moravian tradition. Historical buildings have been well preserved, giving the community a charming Colonial atmosphere. The Lehigh Valley (Allentown, Bethlehem, and Easton), with a population exceeding 750,000, is the chief commercial and industrial center for east central Pennsylvania.

The University

Lehigh is an independent, nondenominational, coeducational university. Founded in 1865, it has approximately 4,800 undergraduates within its three major colleges: Arts and Sciences, Engineering and Applied Science, and Business and Economics. There are approximately 2,000 students enrolled in various graduate programs and in the graduate-only College of Education. The beautiful 700-acre campus includes superb athletic facilities, a fitness center, and cultural venues, including a $33-million arts center.

Applying

Applications for admission as a regular graduate student are accepted until July 15 for the fall term, December 1 for the spring term, April 30 for the first summer term, and May 30 for the second summer term. For first consideration for financial aid for the following academic year, the College of Arts and Sciences Graduate Office must receive completed applications by January 15. Prospective students should send all admission forms to CAS Graduate Study, Maginnes Hall, Lehigh University, 9 West Packer Avenue, Bethlehem, Pennsylvania 18015. Forms are also available at http://www3.lehigh.edu/arts-sciences/casgacademics.asp. The TOEFL is required of all students whose native language is not English, and the TSE is required for teaching assistants from non-English-speaking countries. A minimum score of 230 on the computer-based TOEFL is required for consideration for financial aid. The GRE General Test and Subject Test in mathematics are recommended for all applicants.

Correspondence and Information

Garth Isaak, Graduate Coordinator
Department of Mathematics, Christmas-Saucon Hall
Lehigh University
14 East Packer Avenue
Bethlehem, Pennsylvania 18015-3174
Telephone: 610-758-3731
Fax: 610-758-3767
E-mail: mathgrad@lehigh.edu
World Wide Web: http://www.lehigh.edu/math

Lehigh University

THE FACULTY AND THEIR RESEARCH

Steven H. Weintraub, Professor and Chair; Ph.D., Princeton, 1974. Topology, geometry. (610-758-3731, shw2@lehigh.edu)
Garth Isaak, Associate Professor and Graduate Coordinator; Ph.D., Rutgers, 1990. Discrete mathematics. (610-758-3754, gisaak@lehigh.edu)

Huai-Dong Cao, Pitcher Professor; Ph.D., Princeton, 1986. Differential geometry.
Gautam Chinta, Assistant Professor; Ph.D., Columbia, 2000. Automorphic forms, number theory.
Donald M. Davis, Professor; Ph.D., Stanford, 1972. Algebraic topology, homotopy theory.
Vladimir Dobric, Professor; Ph.D., Zagreb (Croatia), 1985. Analysis, probability, financial mathematics.
Bruce A. Dodson, Associate Professor; Ph.D., SUNY at Stony Brook, 1976. Algebra, computational arithmetic geometry.
Bennett Eisenberg, Professor; Ph.D., MIT, 1968. Probability, mathematical statistics.
Howard Fegan, Adjunct Professor; Ph.D., Oxford, 1977. Differential geometry, Lie groups.
Bhaskar K. Ghosh, Professor; Ph.D., London, 1959. Statistics.
Wei-Min Huang, Professor; Ph.D., Rochester, 1982. Statistics, probability.
David L. Johnson, Associate Professor; Ph.D., MIT, 1977. Differential geometry, algebraic geometry.
Samir A. Khabbaz, Professor; Ph.D., Kansas, 1960. Algebra, topology, singularities.
Jerry P. King, Professor; Ph.D., Kentucky, 1962. Complex analysis, summability.
Gabriele La Nave, A. Everett Pitcher Visiting Assistant Professor; Ph.D., Brandeis, 2000. Algebraic and differential geometry.
Terrence Napier, Associate Professor; Ph.D., Chicago, 1989. Complex geometry, several complex variables.
Dmitry Ostrovsky, C. C. Hsiung Visiting Assistant Professor; Ph.D., Yale, 2004. Probability theory.
Clifford S. Queen, Associate Professor; Ph.D., Ohio State, 1969. Algebra, number theory.
Eric P. Salathe, Professor; Ph.D., Brown, 1965. Applied mathematics, physiological transport phenomena.
Lee J. Stanley, Professor; Ph.D., Berkeley, 1977. Set theory, mathematical logic.
Susan Szczepanski, Associate Professor; Ph.D., Rutgers, 1980. Algebraic topology, geometric topology.
Ramamirtham Vankataraman, Associate Professor; Ph.D., Brown, 1968. Applied mathematics, fluid mechanics.
Joseph E. Yukich, Professor; Ph.D., MIT, 1982. Probability, analysis.
Linghai Zhang, Assistant Professor; Ph.D., Ohio State, 1999. Partial differential equations, mathematical biology.

Mathematics Ph.D. Theses Since 1994

Matthew Haines, 1994, "Ranks of Degenerate, Primitive CM Types" (adviser Dodson), now at Augsburg College.
Margaret Dodson, 1994, "Extended Runge-Kufta Monte-Cado Methods" (adviser Stengle), now at Muhlenberg College, Pennsylvania.
Robert Stolz, 1995, "Radon-Nikodym Property and Law of Large Numbers" (adviser Dobric), now at University of the Virgin Islands, U.S. Virgin Islands.
Cathy Liebars, 1995, "Stochastic Differentiability in Maximum Likelihood Theory" (adviser Dobric), now at The College of New Jersey.
Huajian Yang, 1995, "Stable Homotopy Types of Stunted Lens Spaces Mod 4" (adviser Davis), now at Toronto Dominion Bank.
Maureen Carroll, 1995, "Biorthogonal Systems, Bases, and the Invariance of the Wilansky Property" (adviser Snyder), now at University of Scranton, Pennsylvania.
Rosemary Sullivan, 1996, "Crofton's Theorem for Parametrized Families of Convex Polygons" (adviser Eisenberg), now at Widener University, Pennsylvania.
Ismet Karaca, 1996, "Nilpotence in the mod p Steenrod Algebra" (adviser Davis), now at University of Ege, Turkey.
Kate McGivney, 1997, "Probabilistic Limit Theorems for Combinatorial Optimization Problems" (adviser Yukich), now at Shippensburg University.
Kuntal McElroy, 1997, "Stochastic Analysis of Euclidean Functionals" (adviser Yukich), now at PriceWaterhouseCoopers.
Theresa Friedman, 1998, "Relating Embedding Properties with Certain Operator-Theoretic Properties" (adviser Snyder), now at Willamette University.
Vitaly Zelov, 1998, "Immersions and Embeddings of Real Projective Spaces" (adviser Davis), now at Microsoft Corp.
George Tessaro, 1999, "Some Conditions in which a Sequence Space Fails to Have the Wilansky Property" (adviser Snyder), now at Lehigh University as adjunct.
Elizabeth Kuehner Mauch, 1999, "Representations of Schmudgen Type for Semidefinite Functions" (adviser Stengle), now at Bloomsburg University of Pennsylvania.
Julie Belock, 1999, "Random Variable Dilation Equations and Multidimensional Prescale Functions" (adviser Dobric), now at Salem State University.
Darren Narayan, 2000, "The Reversing Number of a Digraph" (adviser Isaak), now at Rochester Institute of Technology.
Lyn Phy, 2000, "Applications of Weak*-basic Sequences and Biorthogonal Systems to Questions in Banach Space Theory" (adviser Snyder), now at Kutztown University.
Daniel Rose, 2000, "Asymptotic Behavior of Combinatorial Optimization and Proximity Graphs on Random Point Sets" (adviser Yukich), now at Educational Testing Service.
Michael Fisher, 2001, "Topics in v1-Periodic Homotopy Theory" (adviser Davis), now at California State University, Fresno.
Lisa Marano, 2001, "On the Global and Local Moduli of Continuity of Brownian Motion with Applications to Mathematical Finance" (adviser Dobric), now at West Chester University.
Thomas Shimkus, 2002, "Immersions of 2-Torsion Lens Spaces" (adviser Davis), now at University of Scranton.
Michael Fraboni, 2002, "Some q-Convexity Properties of Coverings of Complex Manifolds" (adviser Napier), now at Moravian College.
Leyla Batakci, 2002, "Cohomology of the Steenrod Algebra Mod Nilpotents" (adviser Davis), now at Elizabethtown College.
John Frommeyer, 2003, "Arithmetic on Free Abelian Groups" (adviser Queen).
Miranda Teboh-Ewungkem, 2003, "Mathematical Analysis or Oxygen and Substrate Transport within a Multicapillary System in Skeletal Muscle" (adviser Salathe), now at Lafayette College.
Tracy Bowers, 2003, "Characterization of Minimal Submanifolds by Total Gaussian Curvature" (adviser Johnson), now at Muhlenberg College.
Katarzyna Potocka, 2004, "Number of Summands in v1-Periodic Homotopy Groups of SU(n)" (adviser Davis), now at Ramapo College.
Beth Shimkus, 2004, "Limit Theory for Functionals on Random Bipartite Sets" (adviser Yukich).
Trisha Moller, 2004, "t-Split Interval Orders" (adviser Isaak), now at DeSales University.

MEDICAL COLLEGE OF WISCONSIN

Graduate School of Biomedical Sciences
Division of Biostatistics

Program of Study The Division of Biostatistics offers a program leading to the Ph.D. The program is designed for students with strong undergraduate preparation in mathematics and trains students in biostatistical methodology, theory, and practice. Emphasis is placed on sound theoretical understanding of statistical principles, research in the development of applied methodology, and collaborative research with biomedical scientists and clinicians. In addition, students gain substantial training and experience in statistical computing and in the use of software packages. Courses in the program are offered in collaboration with the Department of Mathematics at the University of Wisconsin–Milwaukee. The degree requirements, including the dissertation research, are typically completed in five years beyond a bachelor's degree that includes strong mathematical preparation.

Faculty members are engaged in a number of collaborative research projects at the International Bone Marrow Transplant Registry, the General Clinical Research Center, the Center for AIDS Intervention Research, the Center for Patient Care and Outcomes Research, the Human and Molecular Genetics Center, and the Cancer Center, as well as medical imaging, clinical trials, and pharmacologic modeling. Students participate in these projects under faculty supervision. Dissertation research topics in statistical methodology often evolve from such participation, and students usually become coauthors on medically oriented papers arising from these projects.

Research Facilities The Division of Biostatistics is located in the Health Policy Institute of the Medical College of Wisconsin (MCW). The Medical College has extensive research laboratories and facilities available for faculty and student use. The Division has an up-to-date network of Sun workstations, PCs, Macintoshes, and peripherals. This network is linked with the campus backbone, providing direct access to the Internet. The Division's network is equipped with all leading statistical software and tools needed for the development of statistical methodology. The MCW libraries' holdings are among the largest health sciences collections in the Midwest, with more than 244,700 volumes and subscriptions to 1,905 journals. The libraries operate the Medical Information Network, a remote-access computer network that includes the full MEDLINE database along with other medical science databases. The libraries also provide access to several bibliographic databases on compact disc workstations as well as the Internet and the World Wide Web. Students also have access to the University of Wisconsin–Milwaukee's extensive library, and the Division maintains its own library of statistical journals, books, and monographs.

The Epidemiologic Data Service provides access to national data on health and health care and special clinical data sets collected locally (the Medical College is a repository for the National Center for Health Statistics). The Biostatistics Consulting Service provides students with extensive experience in biomedical research.

Financial Aid Students are supported by fellowships and research assistantships. Each includes tuition and a stipend. The stipend for 2002–03 was $19,845 per year. The research assistantships provide students with the opportunity to gain experience in statistical consulting and collaborative research.

Cost of Study Tuition is $9900 per year. Tuition and health insurance are included in the fellowships and research assistantships.

Living and Housing Costs Many rental units are available in pleasant residential neighborhoods surrounding the Medical College. Housing costs begin at about $550 per month for a married couple or 2 students sharing an apartment. The usual stipend supports a modest standard of living.

Student Group There are 249 degree-seeking graduate students, 665 residents and fellows, 812 medical students, and 390 M.P.H. students at the Medical College. A low student-faculty ratio fosters individual attention and a close working relationship between students and faculty members. Graduates pursue academic positions and jobs in government and industry.

Location Milwaukee has long been noted for its old-world image. Its many ethnic traditions, especially from Middle Europe, give the city this distinction. Cultural opportunities are numerous and include museums, concert halls, art centers, and theaters. Milwaukee has a well-administered government, a low crime rate, and excellent schools. It borders Lake Michigan and lies within commuting distance of 200 inland lakes. Outdoor activities may be pursued year-round.

The College The College was established in 1913 as the Marquette University School of Medicine. It was reorganized in 1967 as an independent corporation and renamed the Medical College of Wisconsin in 1970. There are 868 full-time faculty and 86 part-time and visiting faculty members; they are assisted by more than 1,700 physicians who practice in the Milwaukee community and participate actively in the College's teaching programs. MCW is one of seven organizations working in partnership on the Milwaukee Regional Medical Complex (MRMC) campus. Most physicians who staff the clinics and hospitals are full-time faculty physicians of MCW. Other MRMC member organizations include the Froedtert Memorial Lutheran Hospital, Children's Hospital of Wisconsin, the Blood Center of Southeastern Wisconsin, Curative Rehabilitation Services, and the Milwaukee County Mental Health Complex. Full-time students in any department may enroll in graduate courses in other departments and in programs of the University of Wisconsin–Milwaukee and Marquette University without any increase in basic tuition. The College ranks in the top 40 percent of all American medical schools in NIH research funding.

Applying Prerequisites for admission to the program include the baccalaureate degree, satisfactory GRE scores on the General Test, and adequate preparation in mathematics. A complete description of the graduate program and application forms may be obtained by writing to the Graduate Program Director at the address given below or downloaded from the Graduate School Web site. Complete application materials should be submitted by February 15.

Correspondence and Information

Dr. Prakash Laud
Graduate Program Director
Division of Biostatistics
Medical College of Wisconsin
Milwaukee, Wisconsin 53226-0509
Telephone: 414-456-8280
Fax: 414-456-6513
E-mail: meijie@mcw.edu
World Wide Web: http://www.biostat.mcw.edu/

Send completed applications to:
Graduate Admissions
Graduate School of Biomedical Sciences
Medical College of Wisconsin
Milwaukee, Wisconsin 53226-0509
Telephone: 414-456-8218
E-mail: gradschool@mcw.edu
World Wide Web: http://www.mcw.edu/gradschool/

Medical College of Wisconsin

THE FACULTY AND THEIR RESEARCH

John P. Klein, Professor and Head; Ph.D., Missouri–Columbia. Survival analysis, dependent, competing risks theory, and design and analysis of clinical trials. Research methods have been applied to transplant data, data from the Framingham Heart Study, and the Danish Breast Cancer Cooperative Group. Dr. Klein also serves as the Statistical Director of the International Bone Marrow Transplant Registry at the Medical College. He is an elected member of the International Statistical Institute and fellow of ASA.

Keiding N., **J. P. Klein,** and M. M. Horowitz. Multistate models and outcome prediction in bone marrow transplantation. *Stat. Med.* 20:1871–85, 2001.

Klein, J. P., J. D. Rizzo, M. J. Zhang, and N. Keiding. Statistical methods for the analysis and presentation of the results of bone marrow transplants. Part II: Regression modeling. *Bone Marrow Transplantation* 28:1001–11, 2001.

Christian Boudreau, Assistant Professor; Ph.D. Waterloo. Longitudinal data and survival analysis. Dr. Boudreau also serves as the codirector of the Division of Biostatistics' Consulting Center.

Boudreau, C. and J. F. Lawless. Survival analysis based on survey data. *Proc. Int. Conf. Res. Adv. Survey Sampling,* in press.

Sun-Wei Guo, Professor; Ph.D., Washington. Stochastic modeling, statistical methods in genetics and genetic epidemiology. Positioned in the forefront of revolutionary changes in biomedical research brought about by rapid advances in genomics, Dr. Guo and his lab have been involved with molecular genetic studies of endometriosis and of prostate cancer and in genetic epidemiologic studies of diabetes.

Guo, S. W. Does higher concordance in monozygotic twins than in dizygotic twins suggest for a genetic component? *Hum. Heredity* 51:121–32, 2001.

Raymond G. Hoffmann, Professor; Ph.D., Johns Hopkins. Linear and nonlinear time series; GLM models for sexual behavior data; methods for identifying changes in fMRI images of the brain, spatial patterns of disease, and neural networks. Dr. Hoffman is the chair of the Statistics in Epidemiology Section of the American Statistical Association.

Warren, S. J., et al. **(R. G. Hoffmann).** The prevalence of antibodies against desmoglein 1 in endemic pemphigus foliaceus in Brazil. Cooperative Group on Fogo Selvagem Research (comments). *N. Engl. J. Med.* 343(1):23–30, 2000.

Nattinger, A. B., **R. G. Hoffmann,** R. T. Kneusel, and M. M. Schapira. Relation between appropriateness of primary therapy for early-stage breast carcinoma and increased use of breast-conserving surgery. *Lancet* 356(9236):1148–53, 2000.

Purushottam W. Laud, Associate Professor; Ph.D., Missouri–Columbia. Bayesian statistical methods in biomedical sciences; Bayesian inference and model selection in linear, nonlinear, generalized linear, hierarchical, bioassay, and survival methods; Markov chain Monte Carlo methods; statistical models and inference for genetic epidemiology. Dr. Laud also serves as the faculty biostatistician in the Center for Patient Care and Outcomes Research at the Medical College.

Meyer, M. C., and **P. W. Laud.** Predictive variable selection in generalized linear models. *JASA* 97:859–71, 2002.

George, V., and **P. W. Laud.** A Bayesian approach to the transmission/disequilibrium test for binary traits. *Genet. Epidemiol.* 22:41–51, 2002.

Brent R. Logan, Assistant Professor; Ph.D., Northwestern. Multiple comparison procedures, methods for analyzing multiple endpoints in clinical trials, inference in dose-response studies.

Tamhane, A. C., and **B. R. Logan.** Multiple test procedures for identifying the minimum effective and maximum safe doses of drug. *JASA* 97:293–301, 2002.

Tamhane, A. C., and **B. R. Logan.** Accurate critical constants for the one sided approximate likelihood ratio test of a normal mean vector when the covariance matrix is estimated. *Biometrics* 58:650–6, 2002.

Timothy L. McAuliffe, Associate Professor; Ph.D., UCLA. Epidemiological methods, clinical trials, group-randomized trials, space-time clustering. Dr. McAuliffe also serves as Director of the Analysis Core of the Center for AIDS Intervention Research at the Medical College.

Nattinger, A. B., **T. L. McAuliffe,** and M. M. Schapira. Generalizability of the surveillance, epidemiology, and end results registry population: Factors relevant to epidemiologic and health-care research. *J. Clin. Epidemiol.* 50:939–45, 1997.

Daniel B. Rowe, Assistant Professor; Ph.D., California, Riverside. Mathematical and statistical methods in fMRI, Bayesian factor analysis and latent variables.

Rowe, D. B. *Multivariate Bayesian Statistics: Models for Source Separation and Signal Unmixing.* Boca Raton, Fla.: CRC Press, 2002.

Rowe, D. B. Bayesian source separation for reference function determination in fMRI. *Magn. Reson. Med.* 46, 2001.

Tao Wang, Assistant Professor; Ph.D., North Carolina State. Statistical genetics, linkage disequilibrium mapping of quantitative trait loci, SNP blocks. Dr. Wang also serves as an adjunct faculty member at the Human Molecular Genetic Center at the Medical College.

Wang, T., and H. Jacob. Linkage disequilibrium mapping using genotype data from unrelated individuals. *Am. J. Hum. Genet.* 4:451, 2002.

Wang, T., and Z. B. Zeng. A multipoint likelihood method to infer quantitative trait loci using data from unrelated individuals. *ENAR Spring Meeting, Crystal City, Virginia,* 2002.

Hyun Ja (Lim) Yun, Assistant Professor; Ph.D., Case Western Reserve. Survival analysis, multiple/recurrent failure time analysis, clinical trials, epidemiologic studies. Dr. Yun also serves as the Director of the Statistics Consulting Center at the Medical College.

Albert, J. M., and **H. J. Yun.** Statistical advances from AIDS therapy trials. Stat. Methods Med. Res. 10:85–100, 2001.

Johnson, J. J., et al. **(H. J. Yun).** Duration of efficacy of treatment of latent tuberculosis infection in HIV-infected adults. *AIDS* 15:1–11, 2001.

Mei-Jie Zhang, Associate Professor; Ph.D., Florida State. Survival analysis, inference for stochastic processes, nonlinear models. As a biostatistician for the International Bone Marrow Transplant Registry at the Medical College, Dr. Zhang is interested in developing statistical models and methodology for analyzing complex transplant data.

Scheike, T. H., and **M. J. Zhang.** An additive multiplicative Cox-Aslen regression model. *Scand. J. Stat.* 29 75–88, 2002.

Zhang, M. J., and J. P. Klein. Confidence bands for the difference of two survival curves under proportional hazards model. *Lifetime Data Analysis* 7(3):243–54, 2001.

Adjunct Faculty

Jay Beder, Associate Professor; Ph.D., George Washington. Gaussian processes, factorial experiments, categorical data analysis.

Vytaras Brazauskas, Assistant Professor; Ph.D., Texas at Dallas. Robust and nonparametric estimation, extreme value theory, risk theory.

Jugal Ghorai, Professor; Ph.D., Purdue. Nonparametric estimation, density and survival function estimation, censored data analysis.

Eric Key, Associate Professor; Ph.D., Cornell. Probability theory and stochastic processes, ergodic theory.

Tom O'Bryan, Associate Professor; Ph.D., Michigan State. Empirical Bayes, decision theory.

MIAMI UNIVERSITY

College of Arts and Science
Department of Mathematics and Statistics

Programs of Study

The purpose of the department's several master's degree programs is to prepare students for a variety of careers in mathematics and statistics in industry and government or for further study at the Ph.D. level in these areas. This is accomplished by giving the student a broad base in the core foundations as well as a set of focused experiences in more advanced studies. The student chooses the program that best fits their interests.

The Master of Arts in mathematics prepares students for subsequent doctoral study in mathematics, having a required core of pure mathematics courses. The Master of Science in mathematics, with an option in operations research, is a concentration in modern applicable mathematics, including discrete mathematics, optimization, and statistics. The Master of Science in mathematics is a flexible program that is designed by the student, subject to some very basic requirements, and allows the student to explore a number of different areas. The Master of Science in statistics gives students a solid foundation in both applied and theoretical statistics. The program features opportunities to participate in data analysis projects of the Statistics Consulting Center and to combine statistics course work with study in related fields. The Master of Arts in Teaching (M.A.T.) is designed to strengthen and broaden the mathematical knowledge of secondary school teachers.

The course work in each program consists of the standard first two years of graduate study in the area covered. All programs except the M.A.T. have a 32-hour requirement, and the M.A.T. has a 30-hour requirement. Students must pass a set of three comprehensive examinations, each exam covering a graduate two-course sequence in some area. Of the 32 hours, at least 15 are at the second-year graduate level. Students complete these programs in two years.

The research strength of the faculty opens up many opportunities for advanced independent study and even original research for those students who are far enough along in their studies. By the second year, many students take reading courses in subjects outside their formal course work. Some have gone on to do original research work during the time of their master's studies.

Research Facilities

The department houses a computer laboratory with access to Maple, MatLab, and several statistical computing software packages such as SAS and S-Plus. There is also access to a computing cluster on the campus and to the Ohio Supercomputing Center at Ohio State University.

The Hughes Science Library has an extensive collection of books and research journals covering all areas of mathematics and statistics. Miami also has a site license for online versions of many of these journals. Articles not available in the library can be obtained through the OhioLink program.

Financial Aid

The department offers graduate assistantships (GA), which, in 2004–05, provide a stipend of $13,500 for the academic year and $1800 for those taking summer classes. GA duties involve teaching precalculus, calculus, or introductory statistics courses or assisting faculty members teaching those courses, through grading and work at help sessions. These assistantships carry a waiver of tuition and half the general fee.

Cost of Study

The 2003–04 graduate tuition was $6560.40, and the general fee was $1213.92 (of which graduate students paid $607). Tuition is waived for graduate assistants.

Living and Housing Costs

Housing for the fall semester should be arranged no later than the preceding midsummer. Monthly cost of housing ranges from $325 to $450 for single rooms or apartments and $325 to $525 for shared apartments. Monthly individual total living expenses average about $925.

Student Group

The roughly 26 full-time graduate students, both men and women, come from all over the United States, and some are international students. The majority come from the Midwest.

Student Outcomes

A recent survey of students in the M.A. and various M.S. programs over a five-year period showed that after graduation 8 went into teaching at the small-college level, 20 went on to a Ph.D. program, 32 went into business or industry, and 2 went into government. Specific examples include instructor at Taylor University; analyst for the Census Bureau in Washington, D.C.; systems programmer for Meditech. Corp. in Boston; consultant for PricewaterhouseCoopers in Washington, D.C.; and Ph.D. students at Penn State, Ohio State, and North Carolina.

Location

Oxford is a typical, very pretty college town, with a population of roughly 20,000, with commercial establishments surrounding the campus. The city is 35 miles from Cincinnati and 45 miles from Dayton.

The University and The Department

Miami is a state-assisted university serving roughly 14,000 students, founded under the Northwest Charter in 1809. It is frequently cited as a public ivy and ranked as one of the leading undergraduate institutions in the United States. This tradition of excellence in teaching carries over to its graduate programs. In mathematics and statistics, one finds a faculty of accomplished scholars with national and international reputations, who are also committed to significant effort in teaching and to working one on one with students in independent studies and research. This combination of research strength and outstanding teaching typifies Miami and the department in particular.

Applying

Applications for admission and assistantships should be sent in by February 1. There are two separate applications, one for admission that is sent to the Graduate School and one for a graduate assistantship that is sent to the Director of Graduate Studies in the department, as listed below. Paper copies of the applications can be obtained by contacting the Graduate Director. The applications can also be obtained and completed online. The application for admission to the Graduate School can be found at http://www.miami.muohio.edu/academics/graduateprograms/index.cfm and the one for an assistantship at the Web site listed below. International students must submit TOEFL scores.

Correspondence and Information

Dr. Zevi Miller
Director of Graduate Studies
Department of Mathematics and Statistics
Miami University
Oxford, Ohio 45056

Telephone: 513-529-3520
E-mail: millerz@muohio.edu
World Wide Web: http://www.muohio.edu/mathstat/graduate

Miami University

THE FACULTY AND THEIR RESEARCH

Reza Akhtar, Assistant Professor; Ph.D., Brown. Algebraic geometry (algebraic cycles, Chow groups, motives, K-theory).
A. John Bailer, Professor; Ph.D., North Carolina. Biostatistics, quantitative risk estimation, statistical methods for the design and analysis of environmental and occupational health studies.
Olga Brezhneva, Assistant Professor; Ph.D., Russian Academy of Sciences. Optimization, numerical analysis.
Dennis Burke, Professor; Ph.D., Washington State. Set-theoretic topology (study of general topological spaces with the use of techniques and notation of modern set-theory as tools).
Dennis Davenport, Associate Professor; Ph.D., Howard. Topological semigroups.
Sheldon Davis, Professor; Ph.D., Ohio. Set theoretic topology.
Patrick N. Dowling, Professor; Ph.D., Kent State. Functional analysis: in particular, geometry of Banach spaces with applications to metric fixed point theory and harmonic analysis.
Charles L. Dunn, Professor; Ph.D., Texas A&M. Multivariate statistics, simulation of percentile points.
Thomas Farmer, Associate Professor; Ph.D., Minnesota. Algebra, undergraduate mathematics.
Frederick Gass, Professor; Ph.D., Dartmouth. Logic, mathematics education.
David Groggel, Associate Professor; Ph.D., Florida. Nonparametric statistics, statistical education, statistics in sports.
Suzanne Harper, Assistant Professor; Ph.D., Viriginia. Appropriate use of technology to teach K–12 mathematics, the content knowledge of prospective mathematics teachers, and the teaching and learning of geometry.
Charles S. Holmes, Professor; Ph.D., Michigan. Relationship between the structure of the subgroup lattice of a group G and the structure of the group G itself.
Tao Jiang, Assistant Professor; Ph.D., Illinois at Urbana-Champaign. Graph theory and combinatorics.
Dennis Keeler, Assistant Professor; Ph.D., Michigan. Noncommutative algebraic geometry: Using the techniques of algebraic geometry to study noncommutative rings; vanishing theorems in algebraic geometry.
Jane Keiser, Associate Professor; Ph.D., Indiana. Mathematics education.
Dave Kullman, Professor; Ph.D., Kansas. History of mathematics and mathematics education.
Paul Larson, Assistant Professor; Ph.D., Berkely. Set theory.
Bruce Magurn, Professor; Ph.D., Northwestern. Algebra, number theory, K-theory.
Zevi Miller, Professor; Ph.D., Michigan. Graph theory, combinatorics, graph algorithms.
Emily Murphree, Associate Professor; Ph.D., North Carolina. Statistics, probability.
Robert Noble, Assistant Professor; Ph.D., Virginia Tech. Application of Bayesian model averaging to multivariate models, environmental statistical applications, statistical procedures associated with stability analysis.
Ivonne Ortiz, Assistant Professor; Ph.D., SUNY at Binghamton. Algebraic K-theory.
Daniel Pritikin, Professor; Ph.D., Wisconsin. Graph theory, combinatorics.
Beata Randrianantoanina, Associate Professor; Ph.D., Missouri. Functional analysis, linear and nonlinear problems in geometry of Banach spaces.
Narcisse Randrianantoanina, Associate Professor; Ph.D., Missouri. Banach space structures of noncommutative Lp-spaces, noncommutative Hardy spaces, roles of noncommutative martingales in quantum probability theory.
Robert Schaefer, Professor; Ph.D., Michigan. Biostatistics, statistical computing.
Kyoungah See, Associate Professor; Ph.D., Viriginia Tech. Sampling designs, principal component analysis, environmental toxicity studies.
John Skillings, Professor; Ph.D., Ohio State. Statistics, experimental design.
Mark Smith, Professor; Ph.D., Illinois at Urbana-Champaign. Functional analysis, geometry of Banach spaces.
Robert Smith, Professor; Ph.D., Penn State. Mathematics education, algebra.
Jerry Stonewater, Associate Professor; Ph.D., Michigan State. Mathematics education.
Vasant Waikar, Professor; Ph.D., Florida State. Distribution of characteristic roots of random matrices, two-stage estimation, application of bootstrap sampling to estimation.
Douglas Ward, Professor; Ph.D., Dalhousie. Optimization, operations research.
John Westman, Assistant Professor; Ph.D., Illinois at Chicago. Stochastic optimal control, computational finance, applications of biomathematics.
Stephen Wright, Associate Professor; Ph.D., Washington (Seattle). Mathematical programming, applications of convex optimization to analysis of scientific data, decomposition algorithms for large-scale optimization.

SELECTED PUBLICATIONS

Akhtar, R. Zero-cycles on varieties over finite fields. *Commun. Algebra,* in press.

Akhtar, R. Torsion in mixed K-groups. *Commun. Algebra,* in press.

Bailer, A. J., et al. **(K. See** and **R. S. Schaefer).** Defining and evaluating impact in environmental toxicology. *Environmetrics* 14:235–43, 2003.

Bailer, A. J., and W. W. Piegorsch. From quantal response to mechanisms and systems: The past, present, and future of biometrics in environmental toxicology. *Biometrics* 56:327–36, 2000.

Brezhneva, O. A., and A. A. Tretyakov. Optimality conditions for degenerate extremum problems with equality constraints. *SIAM J. Control Optimization* 42(2):729–45, 2003.

Brezhneva, O. A., and A. F. Izmailov. Construction of defining systems for finding singular solutions to nonlinear equations. *Computational Mathematics Math. Phys.* 42(1):8–19, 2002.

Burke, D. K., and R. Pol. On nonmeasurability of L^∞/C_0 in its second dual. *Proc. Am. Math. Soc.*, in press.

Burke, D. K., and L. D. Ludwig. Hereditarily α-normal spaces and infinite products. *Top. Proc.* 25:291–9, 2002.

Davis, S., et al. Strongly almost disjoint sets and weakly uniform bases. *Trans. AMS* 4971–87, 2000.

Davis, S., D. K. Burke, and Z. Balogh. A ZFC nonseparable Lindel of symmetrizable Hausdorff space. *C.R. Bulgarian Acad. Sci.* 11–12, 1989.

Dowling, P., B. Turett, and C. J. Lennard. Characterizations of weakly compact sets and new fixed point free maps in c_0. *Studia Math.* 154:277–93, 2003.

Dowling, P., and **N. Randriantoanina.** Riemann-Lebesgue properties of Banach spaces associated with subsets of countable discrete Abelian groups. *Glasgow Math. J.* 45:159–166, 2003.

Dunn, C. L. Precise similated percentiles in a pinch. *Am. Statistician* 45(3):201–11, 1991.

Dunn, C. L. Application of multiple comparison type procedures to the eigenvalues of $\Sigma_1^{-1}\Sigma_2$. *Commun. Statistics: Theory Methods* A15(2):451–71, 1986.

Harper, S. R. Enhancing elementary preservice teachers' knowledge of geometric transformations through the use of dynamic geometry computer software. In *Society for Information Technology and Teacher Education International Conference Annual*, pp. 2909–16, eds. C. Crawford et al. Norfolk, VA: Association for the Advancement of Computing in Education, 2003.

Harper, S. R., S. O. Schirack, H. D. Stohl, and J. Garofalo. Learning mathematics and developing pedagogy with technology: A reply to Browning and Klespis. *Contemp. Issues Technol. Teacher Educ.* 1(3):346–54, 2001 (online).

Holmes, C. S., M. Costantini, and G. Zacher. A representation theorem for the group of autoprojectivities of an Abelian p-group of finite exponent. *Ann. Matematica (IV)* CLXXV:119–40, 1988.

Holmes, C. S. Generalized Rottlaender, Honda, Yff groups. *Houston J. Math.* 10:405–14, 1984.

Jiang, T. Anti-Ramsey numbers of subdivided graphs. *J. Combinatorial Theory Ser. B* 85:361–6, 2002.

Jiang, T. On a conjecture about trees in graphs with large girth. *J. Combinatorial Theory Ser. B* 83:221–32, 2001.

Jiang, T., and D. Mubayi. New upper bounds for a canonical Ramsey problem. *Combinatorica* 20:141–6, 2000.

Keeler, D. Noncommutative ampleness for multiple divisors. *J. Algebra*, in press.

Keeler, D. Criteria for σ-ampleness. *J. Am. Math. Soc.* 13(3):517–32, 2000.

Kullman, D. Stories about story problems. *Centroid* 29(1):10–14, 2003.

Kullman, D. Undergraduate Mathematics in the Old Northwest. In *Proceedings of the History of Undergraduate Mathematics in America Conference*, pp. 195–208, 2002.

Larson, P. A uniqueness theorem for iterations. *J. Symbolic Logic*, in press.

Larson, P., and S. Todorevic. Katetov's problem. *Trans. AMS* 354:1783–91, 2002.

Miller, Z., L. Gardner, **D. Pritikin,** and I. H. Sudborough. One-to-many embeddings of hypercubes into cayley graphs generated by reversals. *Theory Computing Syst.* 34:399–431, 2001.

Miller, Z., and **D. Pritikin.** On randomized greedy matchings. *Random Struct. Algorithms* 10:353–83, 1997.

Noble, B. Model selection in canonical correlation analysis (CCA) using Bayesian model averaging. *Environmetrics*, in press.

Noble, B. An alternative model for cylindrical data. *Nonlinear Analysis Ser. A* 47:2011–22, 2001.

Randrianantoanina, B. On the structure of level sets of uniform and Lipschitz quotient mappings from R^n to R. *Geometric Functional Analysis*, in press.

Randrianantoanina, B. On isometric stability of complemented subspaces of L^P. *Israel J. Math.* 113:45–60, 1999.

Randrianantoanina, N. Noncommutative martingale transforms. *J. Funct. Anal.* 194:181–212, 2002.

Randrianantoanina, N. Factorizations of operators on C^*-algebras. *Studia Math.* 128:273–85, 1998.

See, K., J. Stufken, S. Y. Song, and **A. J. Bailer**. Relative efficiencies of sampling plans for selecting a small number of units from a rectangular region. *J. Stat. Computation Simulation* 66:273–294, 2000.

See, K., and S. Y. Song. Association schemes of small order. *J. Stat. Plann. Inferences* 73(1/2):225–71, 1998.

Smith, M. A., P. Dowling, and Z. Hu. Geometry of spaces of vector-valued harmonic functions. *Can. J. Math.* 46:274–283, 1994.

Smith, M. A., and B. Turett. Normal structure in Bochner L^P-spaces *Pacific J. Math.* 142:347–56, 1990.

Waikar, V., F. Schuurman, and S. R. Adke. A two-stage shrinkage testimator for the mean of an exponential distribution. *Commun. Statistics* 16:1821–34, 1987.

Waikar, V., F. Schuurman, and T. E. Raghunathan. On a two-stage shrinkage testimator for the mean of a normal distribution. *Commun. Statistics* 13:1901–13, 1984.

Ward, D., and M. Studniarski. Weak sharp minima: characterizations and sufficient conditions. *SIAM J. Control Optimization* 38:219–36, 1999.

Ward, D. Dini derivatives of the marginal function of a non-Lipschitzian program. *SIAM J. Optimization* 6:198–211, 1996.

Westman, J. J., and F. B. Hanson. Optimal portfolio and consumption policies subject to Rishel's important jump events model: Computational methods. *Trans. Automatic Control*, in press.

Westman, J. J., F. B. Hanson, and E. K. Boukas. Optimal Production Scheduling for Manufacturing Systems with Preventive Maintenance in an Uncertain Environment. In *Proceedings of 2001 American Control Conference,* 25 June 2001, pp. 1375–80.

Wright, S. E., J. A. Foley, and J. M. Hughes. Optimization of site-occupancies in minerals using quadratic programming. *Am. Mineral.* 85:524–31, 2000.

Wright, S. E. A general primal-dual envelope method for convex programming problems. *SIAM J. Optimization* 10:405–14, 2000.

MichiganTech

MICHIGAN TECHNOLOGICAL UNIVERSITY

Computational Science and Engineering

Program of Study

The Computational Science and Engineering (CS&E) Ph.D. program is a nondepartmental, multidisciplinary program that fosters computationally intensive research and graduate education in the sciences and engineering. The student's plan of study combines core computer science and mathematics courses with research and course work in his or her specific discipline. Students are required to take 30 credits. These courses are chosen from a list of core courses in computer science and mathematics, along with courses from the student's major department. Students take comprehensive exams or preliminaries, which consist of two parts: the computational exams to verify broadbase proficiency and the speciality exam, which displays a deep understanding in the student's specialty area.

Each student is advised and supported by the department in which his or her research is conducted. In addition, a student's advisory committee plays an active role in the student's course of study, providing the diverse skill set needed to mentor a multidisciplinary student.

Research Facilities

The CS&E program's participants currently share the largest concentration of computational resources available at Michigan Technological University (MTU). Students work in a multidisciplinary environment. Their environment is a combination of the discipline-specific resources and the shared computational resources maintained by CS&E. CS&E currently maintains a Sun Enterprise 4500 and two Beowulf clusters. Access to larger machines is obtained through MTU's relationship with vendors, national laboratories, and supercomputing sites.

Financial Aid

Financial aid is available to a limited number of qualified full-time students in the form of fellowships, research assistantships, and teaching assistantships. Aid packages include a stipend, tuition, and some student fees. The stipend for M.S. candidates is currently $4328 per semester and for Ph.D. candidates, $5025 per semester. In addition, a health insurance supplement is provided by the University. Funding may be available on a competitive basis for students to travel to professional conferences.

Cost of Study

Tuition for full-time graduate students (resident and nonresident) for the 2003–04 academic year was $3582 per semester; engineering and computer science majors paid $3982 per semester. All students are responsible for a student activity fee of approximately $135 per semester. Health insurance is required for all graduate students; a supplement is subject to financial aid status.

Living and Housing Costs

Michigan Tech residence halls have accommodations for single students, and applications may be obtained from the Director of Residential Services. For married students, Michigan Tech has one- and two-bedroom furnished apartments; applications may be obtained from the manager of Daniell Heights Apartments. Because the cost of housing is subject to change, representative costs cannot be stated. There is also off-campus housing available in the surrounding community. Yahoo! lists the overall cost-of-living index for Houghton as 83 (national average is 100). Interested students should visit the Web site at http://list.realestate.yahoo.com/realestate/neighborhood/main.html for more information.

Student Group

There are currently 6 students enrolled in the CS&E Ph.D. program. These students are supported by graduate teaching or research assistantships or other forms of University-funded support.

Student Outcomes

The CS&E program prepares students for careers in academia, national laboratories, or industry. An increasing number of positions in computational science are becoming available in academia and industry in addition to the opportunities that have traditionally been provided by national labs.

Location

Michigan Tech is located in Houghton on Michigan's scenic Keweenaw Peninsula. The Keweenaw stretches about 70 miles into Lake Superior, and the surrounding area is perfect for any outdoor activity. The campus is a 15-minute walk from downtown Houghton; public transportation is available from Houghton and Hancock. Houghton has been listed as the safest college town in Michigan and was ranked 8 out of 467 nationwide in the report, "Crime at College: Student Guide to Personal Safety." The Houghton County Memorial Airport (CMX) serves the area with direct flights to Minneapolis and Detroit on Northwest Airlink.

The University

Michigan Tech was founded in 1885 as the Michigan Mining School to serve the nation's first major mining enterprises focused on copper and iron. Several name changes tracked the growth and diversification of the institution, and it was named Michigan Technological University in 1964. Today, the University offers a full range of associate, bachelor's, master's, and doctoral degrees in the sciences, engineering, forestry, business, communication, and technology. MTU has been rated one of the nation's "Top Ten" best buys for science and technology by *U.S. News & World Report.*

Applying

Students who wish to apply for admission to the CS&E program should obtain an application from the address given below. The enclosed forms should be completed and returned to the Graduate School Office, along with a nonrefundable application fee. The registrar of each college or university the student attended should send official transcripts directly to the Graduate School Office. International students must submit TOEFL scores. All students are required to take the GRE General Test. Applicants with an undergraduate major in all areas of science and engineering are encouraged to apply.

Correspondence and Information

Computational Science and Engineering
Computer Science Department
Michigan Technological University
1400 Townsend Drive
Houghton, Michigan 49931
E-mail: cse@mtu.edu
World Wide Web: http://www.cse.mtu.edu

Michigan Technological University

THE FACULTY AND THEIR RESEARCH

Gregg Bluth, Associate Professor of Geological Sciences and Engineering; Ph.D., Penn State, 1990. Remote sensing of natural hazards and volcanic emissions, quantitative methods in satellite-based sensor data to study phenomena such as volcanic ash and gas clouds in atmosphere, watershed geochemistry. (gbluth@mtu.edu; http://www.geo.mtu.edu/~gbluth/)

Judith W. Budd, Research Assistant Professor of Geological Sciences and Engineering; Ph.D., Michigan Tech, 1997. Remote sensing of surface water quality: visible and thermal infrared remote sensing, lake optical properties, data visualization, and numerical modeling; study of surface temperatures, suspended sediments cycling, and temporal changes in chlorophyll concentrations in the Great Lakes. (jrbudd@mtu.edu; http://www.geo.mtu.edu/~jrbudd/)

Kathleen Feigl, Associate Professor of Mathematical Sciences; Ph.D., IIT, 1991. Modeling and simulation of complex fluids; development and use of finite element methods to solve viscoelastic flow problems, stochastic simulation techniques to compute polymer stress, and boundary integral methods to calculate the deformation and breakup of liquid droplets in a flow field. (feigl@mtu.edu; http://www.math.mtu.edu/~feigl/)

Mark S. Gockenbach, Associate Professor of Mathematical Sciences; Ph.D., Rice, 1994. Inverse problems in partial differential equations, numerical methods and software for large-scale optimization problems. (msgocken@mtu.edu; http://www.math.mtu.edu/~msgocken/)

John A. Jaszczak, Associate Professor of Physics; Ph.D., Ohio State, 1989. Monte Carlo and molecular dynamics simulation of materials, dynamics and roughening of crystal surfaces, surface dynamics and morphology of graphite. (jaszczak@mtu.edu; http://www.phy.mtu.edu/~jaszczak/)

Alex Mayer, Associate Professor of Geological Sciences and Engineering; Ph.D., North Carolina, 1988. Simulations for predicting groundwater contaminant transport and remediation at the field scale, mathematical optimization of groundwater remediation systems. (asmayer@mtu.edu; http://www.geo.mtu.edu/profile/ASMAYER.HTM)

Phil Merkey, Research Assistant Professor of Computer Science; Ph.D., Illinois, 1986. Application of advanced computational techniques to new problems in mathematics, science, and engineering; development of system software for cluster computers; performance prediction for NASA's earth and space sciences grand challenge problems. (merk@mtu.edu; http://www.cs.mtu.edu/~merk/)

Donna Michalek, Assistant Professor of Mechanical Engineering and Engineering Mechanics; Ph.D., Texas at Arlington, 1992. Algorithms for multidimensional solvers for Euler equations, using structured and unstructured grids; analysis of fluid flow through fuel injectors. (donna@mtu.edu)

Robert J. Nemiroff, Professor of Physics; Ph.D., Pennsylvania, 1987. Analysis and processing of astronomical image data; time series analysis of astronomical phenomena; computer modeling of general relativistic optics. (nemiroff@mtu.edu; http://www.phy.mtu.edu/faculty/Nemiroff.html)

Nilufer Onder, Assistant Professor of Computer Science; Ph.D., Pittsburgh, 1999. Artificial intelligence; planning and scheduling; decision-theoretic planning; reasoning under uncertainty; planning applications in chemical, civil, and electrical engineering; machine learning; data mining. (nilufer@mtu.edu; http://www.cs.mtu.edu/~nilufer/)

Warren F. Perger, Associate Professor of Electrical and Computer Engineering and of Physics (joint appointment); Ph.D., Colorado State, 1987. Theoretical atomic physics. (wfp@mtu.edu; http://www.ee.mtu.edu/faculty/wfp/wfp2.html)

Steve Seidel, Associate Professor of Computer Science; Ph.D., Iowa, 1979. Parallel algorithms, interprocessor communication for parallel computation, unified parallel C run-time system development. (steve@mtu.edu; http://www.cs.mtu.edu/~steve/)

Franz X. Tanner, Associate Professor of Mathematical Sciences; Ph.D., Illinois at Urbana-Champaign, 1988. Mathematical modeling and numerical simulation of turbulent reacting multiphase flows, with applications to engines; scientific computing; optimal control. (tanner@mtu.edu; http://www.math.mtu.edu/~tanner/)

MICHIGAN TECHNOLOGICAL UNIVERSITY

Department of Mathematical Sciences

Programs of Study

The department awards M.S. and Ph.D. degrees with concentrations in applied mathematics, discrete mathematics, pure mathematics (M.S. only), and statistics. Both the M.S. and Ph.D. degrees are research-based degrees (although a course work–only M.S. is available), and students work closely with a faculty member to plan and conduct the research. Michigan Tech faculty members investigate a number of exciting areas, including coding theory, cryptography, financial mathematics, imaging, laser optics, materials science, mathematical software, modeling (diesel engines, food processing, nonlinear fluid dynamics), statistical genetics, and wildlife statistics.

An M.S. typically requires 21–24 courses credits (seven or eight courses) and 6–9 research credits and can be completed in two academic years. A Ph.D. typically requires three to four years beyond the M.S. A Ph.D. student must pass the proficiency and comprehensive examinations and write and defend a dissertation describing original research of high quality.

The Department of Mathematical Sciences prepares students for careers in either academia or industry. Ph.D. students are encouraged to complete an internship of one or two semesters at a company or national lab or to work on an industry-sponsored research project. Many of the department's core courses are cross-listed with the program in Computational Science and Engineering (CS&E) and prepare students for careers in this new and exciting field. In addition, the department runs one of the most thorough graduate teaching assistant training programs in the nation, preparing students to teach in classrooms and computer labs.

Research Facilities

Graduate students and faculty members use state-of-the-art computer workstations and have access to parallel computers through the program in CS&E. In addition, students working on interdisciplinary research topics have access to the facilities of the Engineering College, home of some of the nation's top engineering programs.

Discrete mathematics faculty members and students are housed in the Combinatorics Research Institute, a separate facility, encouraging collaboration between students and faculty members.

Financial Aid

Financial aid is available to a limited number of qualified full-time students in the form of fellowships, research assistantships, and teaching assistantships. Aid packages include a stipend, tuition, and some student fees. The stipend for M.S. candidates is currently $4415 per semester and for Ph.D. candidates, $5126 per semester. In addition, a health insurance supplement is provided by the University. Funding may be available on a competitive basis for students to travel to professional conferences.

Cost of Study

Tuition for full-time graduate students (resident and nonresident) for the 2004–05 academic year is $3888 per semester; engineering and computer science majors pay $4288 per semester. All students are responsible for a student activity fee of approximately $135 per semester. Health insurance is required for all graduate students; a supplement is subject to financial aid status.

Living and Housing Costs

Michigan Tech residence halls have accommodations for single students; applications may be obtained from the Director of Residential Services. For married students, Michigan Tech has one- and two-bedroom furnished apartments; applications may be obtained from the manager of Daniell Heights Apartments. Because the cost of housing is subject to change, representative costs cannot be stated. There is also off-campus housing available in the surrounding community. Yahoo! lists the overall cost-of-living index for Houghton as 83 (national average is 100). Visit http://list.realestate.yahoo.com/realestate/neighborhood/main.html.

Student Group

Michigan Tech has about 6,610 students in residence, approximately 672 of whom are graduate students. The Department of Mathematical Sciences typically has 30 to 35 graduate students.

Location

Michigan Tech is located in Houghton on Michigan's scenic Keweenaw Peninsula, which stretches about 70 miles into Lake Superior. The surrounding area is perfect for any outdoor activity. The campus is a 15-minute walk from downtown Houghton; public transportation is available from Houghton and Hancock. Houghton has been listed as the safest college town in Michigan and was ranked 8 out of 467 nationwide in the report, "Crime at College: Student Guide to Personal Safety." The Houghton County Memorial Airport (CMX) serves the area with direct flights to Minneapolis via Northwest Airlink. Marquette K. I. Sawyer (SAW, an approximate 2-hour drive from Houghton) serves the area via Detroit.

The University

Michigan Tech was founded in 1885 as the Michigan Mining School to serve the nation's first major mining enterprises focused on copper and iron. Several name changes tracked the growth and diversification of the institution, and it was named Michigan Technological University in 1964. Today, the University offers a full range of associate, bachelor's, master's, and doctoral degrees in the sciences, engineering, forestry, business, communication, and technology. MTU has been rated one of the nation's "Top Ten" best buys for science and technology by *U.S. News & World Report.*

Applying

Application packets are available from the Department of Mathematical Sciences and online or downloadable applications can be found on the Web at http://www.phy.mtu.edu/physicsgradprog.html. Completed applications should be sent to the Graduate School along with the nonrefundable application fee. Official transcripts should be sent to the Graduate School from all colleges or universities previously attended. All students are required to take the GRE General Test and have official scores sent to the Graduate School. International students must also submit TOEFL scores. Three letters of recommendation may be sent directly to the Department of Mathematical Sciences.

Correspondence and Information

Jianping Dong, Ph.D.
Department of Mathematical Sciences
Michigan Technological University
1400 Townsend Drive
Houghton, Michigan 49931
Telephone: 906-487-2068
E-mail: jdong@mtu.edu

Michigan Technological University

FACULTY

Alphonse H. Baartmans, Professor and Department Chair; Ph.D., Michigan State. Combinatorics, design theory, algebra.
Beverly J. Baartmans, Professor; Ph.D., Colorado. Mathematical problem-solving strategies, instructional technology, spatial visualization.
John P. Beckwith, Associate Professor; Ph.D., Wayne State. Statistics.
Barbara S. Bertram, Professor; Ph.D., New Mexico. Singular integral equations, numerical analysis.
Juergen Bierbrauer, Professor; Ph.D., Mainz (Germany). Combinatorics, cryptology, algebra.
Huann-Sheng Chen, Associate Professor; Ph.D., Illinois. Statistical genetics, survival data analysis, applied and computational statistics.
Jianping Dong, Associate Professor; Ph.D., NYU. Statistics, statistical genetics.
Thomas D. Drummer, Associate Professor; Ph.D., Wyoming. Statistical ecology, model-based sampling, applications of statistics to wildlife management.
Lee Erlebach, Associate Professor; Ph.D., Washington (Seattle). 2-Person game theory.
Kathleen A. Feigl, Professor; Ph.D., Illinois Tech. Applied mathematics, numerical methods, finite element methods for fluids, simulation and modeling of viscoelastic fluids.
William P. Francis, Associate Professor; Ph.D., Cornell. Applied mathematics, cosmology, field theories.
Michael J. Gilpin, Professor; Ph.D., Oregon. Combinatorics, discrete mathematics.
Clark Givens, Professor; M.S., Michigan. Applied linear algebra, signal processing, differential geometry, mathematical physics.
Mark S. Gockenbach, Associate Professor and Director of Graduate Studies; Ph.D., Rice. Inverse problems, computational optimization, mathematical software.
Konrad J. Heuvers, Professor; Ph.D., Ohio State. Functional equations, linear algebra, combinatorics, group theory.
John W. Hilgers, Associate Professor; Ph.D., Wisconsin–Madison. Integral equations, functional analysis, signal processing, EM-wave generation and propagation, astrophysics, cosmology.
Renfang Jiang, Associate Professor; Ph.D., Columbia. Statistical genetics, density estimation, smoothing techniques.
Robert W. Kolkka, Associate Professor, Adjunct Associate Professor of Chemistry and Chemical Engineering, and Director, Fluids Research Oriented Group; Ph.D., Lehigh. Bifurcation and stability theory, viscoelasticity, non-Newtonian fluid mechanics, polymer rheology, constitutive equations.
Igor L. Kliakhandler, Associate Professor; Ph.D., Tel-Aviv. Financial mathematics, fluid dynamics, computational mathematics.
Donald L. Kreher, Professor; Ph.D., Nebraska–Lincoln. Combinatorics, computational combinatorics, combinatorial designs, coding theory, algorithms, cryptography.
Gilbert N. Lewis, Associate Professor; Ph.D., Wisconsin–Milwaukee. Asymptotics, singular perturbations, numerical solutions of ordinary differential equations, boundary value problems, cosmology.
Phillip Merkey, Assistant Professor; Ph.D., Illinois. Computational science and engineering.
Tamara Olson, Associate Professor; Ph.D., NYU. Applied mathematics, continuum mechanics, composites.
Iosif Pinelis, Professor; Ph.D., Institute of Mathematics, Novosibirsk (Russia). Probability and statistics.
Allan A. Struthers, Associate Professor; Ph.D., Carnegie-Mellon. Applied mathematics, continuum mechanics, constitutive theory, phase transitions.
Franz X. Tanner, Professor; Ph.D., Illinois. Applied mathematics, computational reacting multiphase flows, scientific computing, optimal control.
Vladimir D. Tonchev, Professor; D.M.Sc., Bulgarian Academy of Sciences; Ph.D., Sofia (Bulgaria). Algorithms, computing, coding theory, combinatorics, finite geometry.
Shuanglin Zhang, Associate Professor; Ph.D., Beijing. Statistical genetics, nonparametric function estimation.

NEW YORK UNIVERSITY

Courant Institute of Mathematical Sciences
Department of Mathematics

Program of Study

The graduate program offers a balanced array of options, with special focus on mathematical analysis and on applications of mathematics in the broadest sense. It includes computational applied mathematics as well as strong interactions with neural science and other science departments. The program of study leads to the M.S. and Ph.D. degrees in mathematics. A special Ph.D. degree in atmosphere/ocean science and mathematics is also offered in cooperation with the Center for Atmosphere-Ocean Studies, and a Ph.D. in computational biology is planned. It is possible to earn both degrees by part-time study, but most students in the Ph.D. program are full-time. In addition to the standard M.S. degree, special career-oriented programs are available in financial mathematics and scientific computing. The M.S. degree can be completed in the equivalent of three or four terms of full-time study. Doctoral students obtain the M.S. degree as they fulfill the requirements for the Ph.D. Students must earn 72 course and research points for the Ph.D., but no specific courses are required. One requirement is the Written Comprehensive Examination, often taken during the first year of full-time study. A second requirement is the Oral Preliminary Examination, which serves as the threshold between course work and thesis research. Thereafter, students engage in research under the supervision of a faculty adviser, leading to the writing and defense of a doctoral dissertation. Students are encouraged from the outset to participate in the Institute's extensive research activities and to use its sophisticated computing environment.

The department occupies a leading position in applied mathematics, differential equations, geometry/topology, probability, and scientific computing. In applied mathematics, the department's activities go beyond differential equations and numerical analysis to encompass many topics not commonly found in a mathematics department, including neural science, atmosphere/ocean science, computational fluid dynamics, financial mathematics, materials science, mathematical physiology, plasma physics, and statistical physics.

The department has been successful in helping its Ph.D. graduates find desirable positions at universities or in nonacademic employment. Those interested may visit the department's job placement Web page at http://www.math.nyu.edu/degree/guide/job_placement.htm.

Research Facilities

The Courant Institute Library, located in the same building as the department, has one of the nation's most complete mathematics collections; it receives more than 275 journals and holds more than 64,000 volumes. Students have access to MathSciNet and Web of Science (Science Citation Index) and an increasing number of electronic journals. The Institute's computer network is fully equipped with scientific software; X-terminals are available in public locations and in every graduate student office. The Courant Applied Mathematics Laboratory comprises an experimental facility in fluid mechanics and other applied areas, coupled with a visualization and simulation facility.

Financial Aid

Financial support is awarded to students who engage in full-time Ph.D. study; they cover tuition, fees, and NYU's individual comprehensive insurance plan, and, in 2004–05, provide a stipend of $19,500 for the nine-month academic year. Some summer positions associated with Courant Institute research projects are available to assistants with computational skills. Because the department is unable to support all qualified students, applicants should apply for other support as well. Federally funded low-interest loans are available to qualified U.S. citizens on the basis of need.

Cost of Study

In 2004–05, tuition is calculated at $971 per point. Associated fees are calculated at $292 for the first point in fall 2004, $305 for the first point in spring 2005, and $52 per point thereafter in both terms. A full-time program of study normally consists of 24 points per year (four 3-point courses each term).

Living and Housing Costs

University housing for graduate students is limited. It consists mainly of shared studio apartments in buildings adjacent to Warren Weaver Hall and shared suites in residence halls within walking distance of the University. University housing rents in the 2004–05 academic year range from $8800 to $16,040.

Student Group

In 2003–04, the department had 250 graduate students. More than half were full-time students.

Location

New York City is a world capital for art, music, and drama and for the financial and communications industries. NYU is located at Washington Square in Greenwich Village, just north of SoHo and Tribeca in a residential neighborhood consisting of apartments, lofts, art galleries, theaters, restaurants, and shops.

The University and The Institute

New York University, founded in 1831, enrolls about 50,000 students and is one of the major private universities in the world. Its various schools offer a wide range of undergraduate, graduate, and professional degrees. Among its internationally known divisions is the Courant Institute of Mathematical Sciences. Named for its founder, Richard Courant, the Institute combines research in the mathematical sciences with advanced training at the graduate and postdoctoral levels. Its activities are supported by the University, government, industry, and private foundations and individuals. The graduate program in mathematics is conducted by the faculty of the Courant Institute. The mathematics department ranks among leading departments in the country and is the only highly distinguished department to have made applications a focal concern of its programs. Eleven members of the Courant Institute faculty are members of the National Academy of Sciences.

Applying

The graduate program is open to students with strong mathematical interests, regardless of their undergraduate major. They are expected to have a knowledge of the elements of mathematical analysis. Applications for admission are evaluated throughout the year, but a major annual review of applications to the Ph.D. program occurs in February, and most awards for the succeeding academic year are made by early March. Ph.D. applications must include GRE scores on both the General and Subject tests and must be received by January 4. The application deadline for the M.S. programs is June 1, except for the Mathematics in Finance program, which is March 1.

Correspondence and Information

For program and financial aid information:
Fellowship Committee
Courant Institute
New York University
251 Mercer Street
New York, New York 10012
Telephone: 212-998-3238
E-mail: admissions@math.nyu.edu
World Wide Web: http://www.math.nyu.edu

For application forms and a Graduate School bulletin:
Graduate Enrollment Services
Graduate School of Arts and Science
New York University
P.O. Box 907, Cooper Station
New York, New York 10276-0907
Telephone: 212-998-8050
E-mail: gsas.admissions@nyu.edu
World Wide Web: http://www.nyu.edu/gsas

New York University

THE FACULTY AND THEIR RESEARCH

Professors

Marco M. Avellaneda, Ph.D. Applied mathematics, mathematical modeling in finance, probability.
Gerard Ben Arous, Ph.D. Probability theory and applications, large deviations, statistical mechanics, spectra of random matrices, stochastic processes in random media, partial differential equations.
Simeon M. Berman, Ph.D. Stochastic processes, probability theory, applications.
Fedor A. Bogomolov, Ph.D. Algebraic geometry and related problems in algebra, topology, symplectic geometry, and number theory.
Sylvain E. Cappell, Ph.D. Algebraic and geometric topology, symplectic and algebraic geometry.
Jeff Cheeger, Ph.D. Differential geometry and its connections to analysis and topology.
W. Stephen Childress, Ph.D. Fluid dynamics, magnetohydrodynamics, biological fluid dynamics.
Tobias H. Colding, Ph.D. Differential geometry, geometric analysis, partial differential equations, three-dimensional topology.
Percy A. Deift, Ph.D. Spectral theory and inverse spectral theory, integrable systems, Riemann-Hilbert problems, random matrix theory.
Paul R. Garabedian, Ph.D. Complex analysis, computational fluid dynamics, plasma physics.
Jonathan Goodman, Ph.D. Fluid dynamics, computational physics, computational finance.
Leslie Greengard, Ph.D. Applied and computational mathematics, partial differential equations, computational chemistry, mathematical biology, optics.
Frederick P. Greenleaf, Ph.D. Noncommutative harmonic analysis, Lie groups and group representations, invariant partial differential operators.
Mikhael Gromov, Ph.D. Riemannian manifolds, symplectic manifolds, infinite groups, mathematical models of biomolecular systems.
Eliezer Hameiri, Ph.D. Applied mathematics, magnetohydrodynamics, plasma physics.
Melvin Hausner, Ph.D. Combinatorics, geometry, nonstandard analysis.
Helmut Hofer, Ph.D. Symplectic geometry, dynamical systems, partial differential equations.
Robert V. Kohn, Ph.D. Nonlinear partial differential equations, materials science, mathematical finance.
Fang-Hua Lin, Ph.D. Partial differential equations, geometric measure theory.
Andrew J. Majda, Ph.D. Modern applied mathematics, atmosphere/ocean science, partial differential equations.
Henry P. McKean, Ph.D. Probability, partial differential equations, complex function theory.
David W. McLaughlin, Ph.D. Applied mathematics, nonlinear wave equations, visual neural science.
Charles M. Newman, Ph.D. Probability theory, statistical physics, stochastic models.
Albert B. J. Novikoff, Ph.D. Analysis, history of mathematics, pedagogy.
Jerome K. Percus, Ph.D. Chemical physics, mathematical biology.
Charles S. Peskin, Ph.D. Applications of mathematics and computing to problems in medicine and biology: cardiac fluid dynamics, molecular machinery within biological cells, mathematical/computational neuroscience.
Richard M. Pollack, Ph.D. Algorithms in real algebraic geometry, discrete geometry, computational geometry.
John Rinzel, Ph.D. Computational neuroscience, nonlinear dynamics of neurons and neural circuits, sensory processing.
Peter Sarnak, Ph.D. Analysis; number theory, especially L-functions and related automorphic form theory.
Jacob T. Schwartz, Ph.D. Robotics, computational geometry, analysis of algorithms.
Jalal M. I. Shatah, Ph.D. Partial differential equations, analysis.
Michael Shelley, Ph.D. Applied mathematics and modeling, visual neuroscience, fluid dynamics, computational physics and neuroscience.
Joel H. Spencer, Ph.D. Discrete mathematics, theoretical computer science.
Srinivasa S. R. Varadhan, Ph.D. Probability theory, stochastic processes, partial differential equations.
Harold Weitzner, Ph.D. Plasma physics, fluid dynamics, differential equations.
Olof Widlund, Ph.D. Numerical analysis, partial differential equations, parallel computing.
Horng-tzer Yau, Ph.D. Probability theory, statistical mechanics, quantum mechanics.
Lai-Sang Young, Ph.D. Dynamical systems and ergodic theory.

Associate Professors

David Cai, Ph.D. Nonlinear stochastic behavior in physical and biological systems.
Yu Chen, Ph.D. Numerical scattering theory, ill-posed problems, scientific computing.
David M. Holland, Ph.D. Ocean-ice studies, climate theory and modeling.
Richard Kleeman, Ph.D. Predictability of dynamical systems relevant to the atmosphere and the ocean, climate dynamics.
Nader Masmoudi, Ph.D. Nonlinear partial differential equations.
Sylvia Serfaty, Ph.D. Partial differential equations, variational problems with applications to physics.
Esteban G. Tabak, Ph.D. Physical processes in the atmosphere and ocean, turbulence.
Daniel Tranchina, Ph.D. Mathematical modeling in neuroscience.
Eric Vanden-Eijnden, Ph.D. Applied mathematics, stochastic processes, statistical physics.

Assistant Professors

Oliver Buhler, Ph.D. Geophysical fluid dynamics, interactions between waves and vortices, acoustics, statistical mechanics.
Sinan Gunturk, Ph.D. Harmonic analysis, information theory, signal processing.
K. Shafer Smith, Ph.D. Geophysical fluid dynamics, physical oceanography and climate.
Anna-Karin Tornberg, Ph.D., Numerical analysis, computational fluid dynamics, moving boundary problems.
Jun Zhang, Ph.D. Fluid dynamics, biophysics, complex systems.

Associated Faculty

Marsha J. Berger (Computer Science), Kit Fine (Philosophy), Michael L. Overton (Computer Science), Nicolaus Rajewsky (Biology), Tamar Schlick (Chemistry, Computer Science).

Affiliated Faculty

Bhubaneswar Mishra (Computer Science), Robert Shapley (Computer Science), Eero P. Simoncelli (Neural Science), Alan Sokal (Physics), Demetri Terzopoulos (Computer Science), George Zaslavsky (Physics).

NC STATE UNIVERSITY

NORTH CAROLINA STATE UNIVERSITY

Master of Financial Mathematics

Program of Study

The financial mathematics program at North Carolina State University (NCSU) provides a structured program to help students develop their skills in preparation for entering the workplace or for further study in related Ph.D. programs. Employment opportunities exist with banks, investment firms, financial trading companies and financial exchanges, insurance companies, power companies, natural resource–based firms, agribusinesses, and government regulatory institutions.

This program is limited to a master's degree, but is closely related to research programs and Ph.D. degrees conducted in participating departments. This two-year program provides an integrated set of tools for students seeking careers in quantitative financial analysis. After taking six core courses in the first year to provide a common foundation, students have the flexibility in the second year either to pursue a broad view of the subject or specialize on a topic of their choice. This second year consists of four elective courses and a project/internship, which provides students with experience working on real-world problems in financial mathematics under the guidance of faculty members who are actively engaged in research.

The core courses have been chosen to provide students with a strong mathematical background, statistical and computational tools, and a comprehensive description of financial markets. The departments participating in the core requirements are mathematics, industrial engineering, statistics, economics, and agricultural and resource economics. Elective courses are offered by these departments and others, including business management and computer science. In addition, a seminar series organized in conjunction with this program exposes students to the ideas of outside academics and practitioners.

Research Facilities

The students in the program have access to the facilities offered by the participating departments.

Financial Aid

Federally funded low-interest loans are available to qualified U.S. citizens on the basis of need.

Cost of Study

For each semester of the 2003–04 academic year, full-time students paid tuition in the amount of $1581.50 (in state) or $7580.50 (out of state) plus $513 for student fees. In-state residency can be established after one year. These figures do not include the cost of textbooks or other supplies.

Living and Housing Costs

One-bedroom apartments or shared larger apartments can cost $400 to $700 (per person) near campus. Graduate housing is available on campus and in the E. S. King Village, an apartment complex designed for graduate students and for family housing.

Student Group

The 2002–03 academic year represented the first year of the financial mathematics program at NCSU. The class size is kept small to ensure that each student obtains the individual attention he or she needs. There are 11 students currently enrolled.

Student Outcomes

Student placement is aimed at obtaining various jobs in the private sector as well as at gaining advanced academic degrees.

Location

Raleigh, North Carolina, is only a short drive from Duke University, the University of North Carolina at Chapel Hill, and Research Triangle Park. Raleigh is home to a symphony, ballet, opera, and theater as well as museums and historic sites. Raleigh lies only a few hours away from the majestic Appalachian Mountains and the lovely beaches of the Atlantic Ocean.

The University

As a land-grant university, North Carolina State has historic strengths in agriculture, technology, and engineering and has demonstrated strengths in emerging fields, such as the computational sciences. The Master of Financial Mathematics degree program combines these strengths to train students in the new discipline of quantitative finance and risk analysis. NCSU has a graduate student-faculty ratio of 3.5:1 to allow students to work closely with faculty members, and is recognized nationally and internationally as a top teaching and research university.

Applying

Selection is based on scholastic records, as reflected by the courses chosen and quality of performance; evaluation of former teachers and advisers; and Graduate Record Examinations (GRE) General Test scores. Applicants should have an undergraduate degree in mathematics or in a closely related field with a strong mathematical background. A GPA of at least 3.0 (out of 4.0) in the sciences is required. The TOEFL is required of international students; TOEFL scores of at least 550 are preferred. For most favorable consideration for the fall term, all application materials should be received by February 1.

Correspondence and Information

Financial Math Program
North Carolina State University
Campus Box 7640
Raleigh, North Carolina 27695-7640

Telephone: 919-513-2287
Fax: 919-513-1991
E-mail: jmjones4@math.ncsu.edu
World Wide Web: http://www.math.ncsu.edu/finmath

North Carolina State University

THE FACULTY AND THEIR RESEARCH

Richard H. Bernhard, Professor, Department of Industrial Engineering; Ph.D., Cornell, 1961. Capital investment economic analysis, Bayesian decision analysis, multiattribute decision making, financial engineering.

Peter Bloomfield, Professor, Department of Statistics; Ph.D., London, 1970. Time series, credit risk.

Xiuli Chao, Professor, Department of Industrial Engineering; Ph.D., Columbia, 1989. Stochastic modeling and analysis, investment analysis, stochastic optimization, queueing and stochastic service systems, production and inventory systems, Markovian decision processes, supply chain and value chain management.

David Dickey, Professor, Department of Statistics; Ph.D., Iowa State, 1976. Time series, regression, general statistical methodology.

Salah E. Elmaghraby, Professor, Departments of Industrial Engineering and Operations Research; Ph.D., Cornell, 1958.

Edward W. Erickson, Professor, Department of Economics; Ph.D., Vanderbilt, 1968.

Paul L. Fackler, Associate Professor, Department of Agricultural and Resource Economics; Ph.D., Minnesota, 1986. Futures and options markets, commodity market analysis, risk analysis and management, computational economics.

Jean-Pierre Fouque, Professor, Department of Mathematics, and Director, Financial Mathematics Program; Ph.D., Paris VI (Curie), 1979. Stochastic processes, stochastic partial differential equations, random media, financial mathematics.

Marc Genton, Associate Professor, Department of Statistics; Ph.D., Swiss Federal Institute of Technology, 1996. Time series, multivariate analysis, data mining.

Sujit Ghosh, Associate Professor, Department of Statistics; Ph.D., Connecticut, 1996. Bayesian inference and applications.

Atsushi Inoue, Assistant Professor, Department of Agricultural and Resource Economics; Ph.D., Pennsylvania, 1998. Theoretical and applied econometrics.

Kazufumi Ito, Professor, Department of Mathematics.

Min Kang, Assistant Professor, Department of Mathematics; Ph.D., Cornell. Probability theory and partial differential equations, stochastic partial differential equations.

Tao Pang, Assistant Professor, Department of Mathematics; Ph.D., Brown, 2002. Financial engineering, stochastic control, operations research.

Sastry Pantula, Professor, Department of Statistics; Ph.D., Iowa State, 1982. Time series, spatial statistics, nonlinear models.

Jeffrey S. Scroggs, Associate Professor, Department of Mathematics; Ph.D., Illinois at Urbana-Champaign, 1988. Numerical methods for partial differential equations, fluid dynamics, scientific computing, financial mathematics.

John J. Seater, Professor, Department of Economics and Business; Ph.D., Brown, 1975. Macroeconomics, monetary economics, stability and control of dynamical systems.

Charles E. Smith, Associate Professor, Department of Statistics; Ph.D., Chicago. Poisson-driven stochastic differential equations, level crossing and first passage times.

Thomislav Vukina, Associate Professor, Department of Agricultural and Resource Economics; Ph.D., Rhode Island, 1991.

Jim Wilson, Professor, Department of Industrial Engineering; Ph.D., Rice, 1970. Probabilistic and statistical issues in the design and analysis of large-scale simulation experiments, analysis of output processes, improving simulating efficiency using variance reduction techniques, optimization using multiple-comparison and search procedures, applications to production systems engineering and financial engineering.

NORTHEASTERN UNIVERSITY

Department of Mathematics
Graduate Programs in Mathematics

Programs of Study

The Department of Mathematics at Northeastern University offers M.S. and Ph.D. degrees in mathematics and an M.S. degree in operations research (in conjunction with the Department of Mechanical, Industrial, and Manufacturing Engineering). The department offers both full- and part-time M.S. programs and a full-time Ph.D. program. The programs are designed to provide students with a broad overview of current mathematics and a strong command of an area of specialization. In addition to the course requirements, a thesis is required for the Ph.D. program. A thesis is optional in place of two electives in all master's-level programs.

Graduate students work with internationally recognized faculty members in a range of research programs in both pure and applied mathematics. In addition, numerous seminars and colloquia at Northeastern and in the Boston area give students ample opportunity to learn about important recent advances in mathematics. The department is an active participant in the Brandeis-Harvard-MIT-Northeastern Colloquium.

Mathematical sciences research at Northeastern is concentrated in three main areas: algebra-singularities-combinatorics, analysis-geometry-topology, and probability-statistics.

The algebra-singularities-combinatorics group includes strong researchers in areas covering discrete geometry, algebraic geometry, representation theory, K-theory, and singularities of mappings. Some of the concrete topics being studied are cluster algebras, regular tilings of Euclidean spaces, representations of algebraic and quantum groups, representations of quivers, Schubert varieties, motives, hyperplane arrangements, Koszul algebras, and commutative rings and their deformations. All these topics have combinatorial and computational components, which makes it possible to involve graduate students in calculating examples, bringing them quickly to the frontiers of modern research.

The analysis-geometry-topology group encompasses a wide range of research interests and activities in areas that include partial differential equations, geometric analysis, differential geometry, mathematical physics, algebraic topology, and geometric topology. Topics include index theory of elliptic operators, Schrödinger operators, conformal metrics, noncommutative geometry, integrable Hamiltonian systems, Maxwell Higgs systems, delay equations, geometry and topology of manifolds and submanifolds, topology of knots and links, and group cohomology.

The probability-statistics group is involved in a wide variety of research activities, ranging from basic research to industrial collaborations. This broad and varied program is made possible by the interdisciplinary interests of the faculty members in the group, who are involved in projects with the physics, engineering, computer science, pharmacology, and medical departments. The research areas include theoretical statistics, applied statistics, biostatistics, industrial statistics, information theory, and quantum computing.

Research Facilities

Students have access to Compaq Alpha systems, public-access microcomputer labs (PC and Macintosh), a conferencing system, multimedia labs, and specialized computing equipment. Northeastern is also an Internet2 site.

University libraries contain 984,443 volumes, 2,260,556 microforms, 160,834 government documents, 7,654 serial subscriptions, and 22,205 audio, video, and software titles. The libraries have licensed access to more than 12,950 electronic information sources. Central and branch libraries contain technologically sophisticated services, including Web-based catalog and circulation systems and a Web portal to licensed electronic resources. The University is a member of the Boston Library Consortium and the Boston Regional Library System, giving students and faculty members access to the region's collections and information resources.

Financial Aid

Each year, the department offers a limited number of Research Assistantships (RAs), Teaching Assistantships (TAs), and Northeastern University Tuition Assistantships (NUTAs) to promising full-time students. An RA includes tuition and a stipend, and a recipient is required to complete a project for a professor each quarter. A TA includes tuition and a stipend, and a recipient is required to teach a basic undergraduate course each quarter. For this reason, international students receiving a TA should be able to speak English fluently. A NUTA covers tuition only, and a recipient is required to assist with grading and tutoring each quarter.

Cost of Study

The tuition rate for 2003–04 was $850 per semester hour. There are special tuition charges for theses and dissertations, where applicable. The Student Center fee and health and accident insurance fee required for all full-time students were approximately $1600 per academic year.

Living and Housing Costs

Living expenses both on and off campus are estimated to be between $1200 and $1500 per month. A public transportation system serves the greater Boston area, and there are subway and bus services nearby.

Student Group

For the 2003–04 academic year, the department had 29 full-time graduate students and 40 part-time graduate students.

Student Outcomes

The majority of graduates find employment in various high-technology industries across the United States. Ph.D. graduates are also employed by academic institutions in teaching and research.

Location

Northeastern University is located in the heart of Boston, a city that has played a pioneering role in American education. Within a 25-mile radius of the campus, there are more than fifty degree-granting institutions. Within walking distance of the campus, there are numerous renowned cultural centers, such as the Museum of Fine Arts, Isabella Stewart Gardner Museum, Symphony Hall, Horticultural Hall, and Boston Public Library. Theater in Boston includes everything from pre-Broadway to experimental and college productions. The Boston area is also the site of all home games of the Red Sox, Celtics, Bruins, and Patriots.

The University

Northeastern University is among the nation's largest private universities, with an international reputation as a leader in cooperative education. The cooperative plan of education, initiated by the College of Engineering in 1909 and subsequently adopted by the other colleges of the University, enables students to alternate periods of work and study. Today, Northeastern has eight undergraduate colleges, eight graduate and professional schools, several suburban campuses, and an extensive research division.

Applying

Applicants must have a bachelor's degree in mathematics or a closely related field. Applicants to the Ph.D. program must, in addition, have a master's degree in mathematics or a closely related field. Applicants must have taken the Graduate Record Examinations (GRE) Subject Test in Mathematics, and international students must demonstrate proficiency in English. An applicant's undergraduate course work should include linear algebra, combinatorics, differential and integral calculus, differential equations, real analysis, and some computer programming. Students who are deficient in any of these areas may be accepted provisionally if their overall college work is particularly strong, but they must eliminate the deficiency either before enrollment (summer courses are available) or within their first two quarters at Northeastern. Placement exams in algebra and analysis are given to all entering students.

All applicants must submit a completed application form, including official transcripts of all previous undergraduate and graduate course work and a nonrefundable $50 processing fee. All documents submitted must be originals. Letters of recommendation should be completed by someone acquainted with the applicant's academic and personal qualifications. Only those documents required to complete the application package should be sent, as unsolicited documents do not improve the applicant's chances for admission.

The application deadline for fall admission to the full-time program is April 15. To be considered for an assistantship, the application must be submitted by February 15. Applications received after the stated deadline but before the start of the semester are processed; however, it may not be possible to have a decision rendered prior to the beginning of classes.

Correspondence and Information

Alexandru I. Suciu, Graduate Director
441 Lake Hall
Northeastern University
Boston, Massachusetts 02115
Telephone: 617-373-4456
E-mail: a.suciu@neu.edu
World Wide Web: http://www.math.neu.edu/grad/

Northeastern University

THE FACULTY AND THEIR RESEARCH

Professors

Samuel J. Blank, Ph.D., Brandeis, 1967. Differential topology.
Bohumil Cenkl, D.Sc., Charles (Prague), 1968. Differential geometry, algebraic topology.
Stanley J. Eigen, Undergraduate Director; Ph.D., McGill, 1982. Ergodic theory, measure theory, number theory, dynamical systems.
Terence Gaffney, Ph.D., Brandeis, 1976. Singularities of mappings and its application to algebraic and differential geometry.
Maurice E. Gilmore, Ph.D., Berkeley, 1967. Geometric topology, secondary education.
Arshag Hajian, Ph.D., Yale, 1957. Ergodic theory, analysis.
Anthony Iarrobino, Ph.D., MIT, 1970. Algebraic geometry, commutative rings and their deformations, singularities of maps, families of points on a variety, Gorenstein algebras.
Christopher King, Ph.D., Harvard, 1984. Mathematical physics.
V. Lakshmibai, Ph.D., Tata (Bombay), 1976. Algebraic geometry, algebraic groups, representation theory.
Marc N. Levine, Ph.D., Brandeis, 1979. Algebraic geometry, algebraic K-theory, motives, motivic cohomology.
Mikhail B. Malioutov, D.Sc., Moscow State, 1983. Statistics, probability, experimental design, information theory.
Robert C. McOwen, Chairman; Ph.D., Berkeley, 1978. Partial differential equations, with applications to problems in differential geometry.
Richard D. Porter, Ph.D., Yale, 1971. Algebraic and differential topology; Massey products; deRham theory, with applications to the fundamental group and group cohomology.
Egon Schulte, Ph.D., Dortmund (Germany), 1980. Discrete geometry, combinatorics, group theory.
Jayant M. Shah, Ph.D., MIT, 1974. Computer vision.
Mikhail A. Shubin, Matthews Distinguished Professor; Ph.D., Moscow State, 1969. Partial differential equations, geometric analysis, spectral theory, mathematical physics.
Alexandru I. Suciu, Graduate Director; Ph.D., Columbia, 1984. Algebraic topology, geometric topology.
Chuu-Lian Terng, Ph.D., Brandeis, 1976. Differential geometry, Lie groups, integrable systems.
Jerzy Weyman, Ph.D., Brandeis, 1980. Commutative algebra, algebraic geometry, representation theory.
Andrei Zelevinsky, Ph.D., Moscow State, 1978. Representation theory, algebraic geometry, algebraic combinatorics, discrete geometry, special functions.

Associate Professors

Mark Bridger, Ph.D., Brandeis, 1967. Mathematics education, computer-assisted instruction, numerical and constructive algebra, commutative algebra.
Robert W. Case, Ph.D., Yeshiva, 1966. Mathematical logic, Socratic teaching of mathematics.
Adam Ding, Ph.D., Cornell, 1996. Artificial neural networks, high-dimensional empirical linear prediction (HELP), biostatistics, prediction and confidence intervals.
John N. Frampton, Ph.D., Yale, 1965. Artificial intelligence, natural language.
Eugene H. Gover, Ph.D., Brandeis, 1970. Commutative algebra, homology of local rings.
Samuel Gutmann, Ph.D., MIT, 1977. Quantum computing, statistical decision theory, probability, syntax.
Solomon M. Jekel, Ph.D., Dartmouth, 1974. Classifying spaces, homeomorphism groups, homology of groups, foliations.
Donald R. King, Vice Chairman; Ph.D., MIT, 1979. Lie groups, Lie algebras, Weyl groups, Lie algebra cohomology, noncommutative ring theory.
Nishan Krikorian, Ph.D., Cornell, 1969. Low-dimensional dynamical systems, numerical analysis.
Alex Martsinkovsky, Ph.D., Brandeis, 1987. Functorial and homological methods in representation theory, homological algebra, homotopy theory and applications, industrial mathematics.
David B. Massey, Ph.D., Duke, 1986. Complex analytic singularities, stratified spaces.
Mark B. Ramras, Ph.D., Brandeis, 1967. Commutative algebra, graph theory.
Martin Schwarz Jr., Ph.D., NYU, 1981. Nonlinear analysis, nonlinear differential equations, mathematical problems in science.
Thomas O. Sherman, Undergraduate Head Advisor; Ph.D., MIT, 1964. Noncommutative harmonic analysis, symmetric spaces, Lie groups, numerical analysis.
Gordana G. Todorov, Ph.D., Brandeis, 1979. Representation theory of Artin algebras, noncommutative algebra.

Assistant Professor

Maxim Braverman, Ph.D., Tel Aviv, 1997. Symplectic geometry, partial differential equations.

Stone Visiting Professor

Alexander Voronov, Ph.D., Moscow State, 1988. Mathematical physics, algebra, algebraic geometry, algebraic topology, representation theory.

Clinical Assistant Professor

Carla B. Oblas, M.S., California, Davis, 1972.

NORTHWESTERN UNIVERSITY

Program in Applied Mathematics

Programs of Study

Graduate programs leading to the M.S. and Ph.D. degrees in applied mathematics are offered by the Department of Engineering Sciences and Applied Mathematics. Qualified students with backgrounds in engineering, mathematics, or natural science are eligible for admission to these programs. Study plans are drawn up to meet the needs of the individual student; they encompass courses in mathematical methods and in one or more fields of science or engineering, where significant applications of mathematics are made.

A student can obtain the M.S. degree in one academic year of full-time study. This entails the successful completion of an approved program of courses, followed by an examination relative to the work. No thesis is required for the M.S. degree. The Ph.D. program takes a minimum of three years beyond the B.S. degree. For the Ph.D. degree, the student must achieve a distinguished record in an approved program of courses and pass both a preliminary and a qualifying examination in the general research area to be followed in the doctoral dissertation. A final examination on the doctoral dissertation is required upon its completion.

Research Facilities

The department maintains a number of UNIX workstations for graduate student research, and computational time is available both on computers maintained on campus and at the National Supercomputer Centers. All of Northwestern's buildings have high-speed fiber-optic network connections to the Internet for convenient access to such facilities (through the vBNS, the very high-speed Backbone Network Service). In addition, the University has a number of laboratories with workstation-class machines available for classroom work and computers that provide access to electronic mail, Usenet, the World Wide Web, and various other networked information servers.

Financial Aid

Students who have been accepted for graduate study toward the Ph.D. in applied mathematics are eligible for various forms of financial support. University scholarships and fellowships as well as teaching and research assistantships cover tuition costs and provide a monthly stipend for living expenses. Some students may also qualify for a University loan. All full-time students are entitled to the benefits of the University Health Service as well as hospitalization and surgical insurance coverage.

Cost of Study

Tuition totals $29,940 for the academic year 2004–05, with varying rates applicable during the summer quarter.

Living and Housing Costs

A variety of housing is available in the area. In addition to University-owned dwellings, there are apartments and rooms to be rented in the surrounding community. Costs vary according to the type of housing and the location.

Student Group

Graduate students in the applied mathematics program come from all parts of the United States and from various other countries. There are 35–40 students in the program.

Student Outcomes

Graduates have been successfully placed in industry, government, and academic positions, both postdoctoral and tenure track. Recent postdoctoral placements include Cambridge, Harvard, Princeton, and Stanford Universities. Recent tenure-track positions include Colgate University, Courant Institute, and the Universities of Delaware, Maryland, Michigan, Minnesota, and Washington. Graduates have recently obtained corporate and government placements at NIH, NIST, IBM, Naval Research Lab, 3M Corporation, Aerospace Corporation, Argonne National Lab, Los Alamos National Lab, and Merrill Lynch.

Location

The main campus of the University is located in the residential suburb of Evanston, immediately north of Chicago. It occupies some 170 acres, partly bounded by a mile of Lake Michigan shoreline. This location provides the combined advantages of a lovely suburban community and the many cultural opportunities of Metropolitan Chicago. The University maintains its own beach and sailing club for use by students, faculty, and staff.

The University

Northwestern University was founded in 1851 and is a privately supported school in the Big Ten. It is a coeducational institution that offers a full range of educational opportunities. Research awards at the University exceeded $170 million last year.

Applying

Northwestern University operates on the quarter system. It is usual practice for new students to enter at the beginning of the fall quarter. Admissions applications that request financial aid should be completed by January 31. Application forms can be requested directly through e-mail at gradapp@nwu.edu.

Correspondence and Information

Director of Applied Mathematics
Department of Engineering Sciences and Applied Mathematics
McCormick School of Engineering and Applied Science
Northwestern University
Evanston, Illinois 60208-3125
Telephone: 847-491-5397
Fax: 847-491-2178
World Wide Web: http://www.esam.northwestern.edu

Northwestern University

THE FACULTY AND THEIR RESEARCH

Jan D. Achenbach, Ph.D., Stanford. Theoretical and applied mechanics.
Alvin Bayliss, Ph.D., NYU (Courant). Numerical analysis, scientific computations.
David Chopp, Ph.D., Berkeley. Numerical methods for PDEs, evolution of fronts, scientific computing.
Stephen H. Davis, Ph.D., Rensselaer. Hydrodynamic stability, interfacial phenomena, phase-change phenomena.
Alexander Golovin, Ph.D., Karpov (Russia). Materials science, physicochemical hydrodynamics, chemically reacting systems.
William L. Kath, Ph.D., Caltech. Wave propagation and optics.
Moshe Matalon, Ph.D., Cornell. Combustion theory, chemically reacting flows.
Bernard J. Matkowsky, Ph.D., NYU (Courant). Bifurcation and stability, combustion, pattern formation, nonlinear dynamics.
Michael J. Miksis, Ph.D., NYU (Courant). Interfacial phenomena, multiphase flow, scientific computations.
Toshio Mura, Ph.D., Tokyo. Micromechanics.
W. Edward Olmstead, Ph.D., Northwestern. Reaction-diffusion theory, shear localization effects, blow-up phenomena.
Hermann Riecke, Ph.D., Bayreuth (Germany). Extended dynamical systems, pattern formation.
Mary Silber, Ph.D., Berkeley. Dynamical systems, symmetry-breaking bifurcations, pattern formation.
Sara Solla, Ph.D., Washington (Seattle). Theoretical statistical mechanics.
Vladimir A. Volpert, Ph.D., USSR Academy of Sciences. Dynamical systems, pattern formation, combustion, reaction-diffusion systems.

Selected Recent Doctoral Dissertations

"Asymptotic analysis of random wave selections," Rachel A. Kuske.
"Morphological instability and the effect of elastic stresses," Brian J. Spencer.
"Premixed flame propagation in closed tubes," Jennifer Levin McGreevy.
"A class of integral equations which model explosion phenomena," Catherine A. Roberts.
"Bifurcation analysis of multimode instabilities in class B lasers," Thomas W. Carr.
"Numerical studies of nonlinear optical pulse propagation," Cheryl V. Hile.
"Thermal effects in rapid directional solidification," Douglas A. Huntley.
"Adaptive pseudo-spectral methods with applications to sheer band formation in viscoplastic materials," Dawn A. L. Crumpler.
"Domain structures and their stability," David Raitt.
"Stability of two-layer fluid flow in an inclined channel," Burt S. Tilley.
"Numerical solution of free boundary problems with surface tension at low Reynolds number," T.-M. Tsai.
"Interaction of a dislocation with an imperfectly bonded anchor in an anisotrophic bimaterial," Tom A. Homulka.
"Pulse propagation in nonlinear optical fibers using phase-sensitive amplifiers," J. Nathan Kutz.
"Shear stabilization of morphological instability during directional solidification," Timothy P. Schulze.
"Shear-diffusion mixing of passive scalars and vorticity in monopoles and dipoles," Joseph F. Lingevitch.
"The dynamics of thin liquid films," Michael P. Ida.
"Filtration combustion with applications to smoldering and combustion synthesis of materials," Daniel A. Schult.
"Soliton dynamics in optical fibers," Anne Niculae.

THE OHIO STATE UNIVERSITY

Department of Mathematics

Programs of Study The Department of Mathematics offers programs leading to the M.S. and Ph.D. degrees. Courses of study are available in all of the principal branches of mathematics: algebra, analysis, applied mathematics, combinatorics, geometry, logic, group theory, number theory, probability, ergodic theory, representation theory, and topology.

Research Facilities The Ohio State libraries have more than 4 million volumes and are served by a campuswide automated circulation system. In addition to the main library, there are eighteen departmental libraries. The Science and Engineering Library serves the College of Mathematics and Physical Sciences and the College of Engineering. This library contains more than 350,000 volumes and currently receives more than 2,750 serial titles. Students have ready access to microcomputers and the University mainframes. The Department of Mathematics has a National Science Foundation (NSF)–funded VIGRE program, seeking to vertically integrate research and education. Special features include Working Group Rotations, involving students and faculty members in an informal setting exploring research problems in different areas. The mathematics department, jointly with the statistics department, is the home of the NSF Mathematical Biosciences Institute (MBI). The Office of Information Technology is a research and service facility that serves all departments, offering short-term seminars and noncredit courses directed to the needs of faculty and staff members and graduate students. The Department of Mathematics is home to the International Mathematics Research Institute.

Financial Aid Financial assistance is offered to nearly every mathematics graduate student attending Ohio State, in the form of fellowship and/or teaching associateship. Both forms of support carry a stipend plus total waiver of all regular tuition and fees. In 2004–05, stipends for entering graduate students range from $15,300 to $16,020 for a nine-month appointment. The work load of teaching associates involves 6 hours per week of student contact, plus preparation and grading. Each new graduate student at Ohio State is encouraged to accept an initial Early Start Summer Fellowship, which carries a stipend of at least $2700 in 2004. Most continuing students receive summer-quarter support in the form of either fellowships or research associate or teaching associate appointments. Graduate teaching associate positions are renewable depending on the progress of the student. VIGRE fellowships are awarded to qualified U.S. citizens and permanent residents, while University fellowships are open to both domestic and international students.

Cost of Study In 2004, tuition for full-time graduate study is $2204 per quarter for Ohio residents and $5729 for nonresidents. Tuition is waived for students with teaching associateships, research associateships, or fellowships.

Living and Housing Costs Convenient housing is located on and near the Columbus campus. Two dormitories house graduate students exclusively, at a cost of $389 per person per month. Ohio State maintains an apartment complex for married students; monthly rent ranges from $501 for a one-bedroom unit to $660 for a two-bedroom unit, including gas and water. The Off-Campus Student Center keeps files of available off-campus housing as a free service and prospective students can visit their Web site (http://www.osuoffcampus.com) for additional information. Monthly rent in Columbus ranges from $400 to $650.

Student Group The Department of Mathematics has approximately 100 graduate students, representing about twenty states and fifteen countries. Over the past four years, the department has averaged fourteen Ph.D. degrees and ten M.S. degrees per year. Most Ph.D. recipients seek and find employment in academic institutions, whereas M.S. recipients are employed, for the most part, by business, industry, or government.

Location Columbus is centrally located in the eastern half of the country, 316 miles from Chicago, 555 miles from New York City, 560 miles from Atlanta, and 404 miles from St. Louis. The Columbus metropolitan area has approximately 1.25 million residents. It is the only major population center in Ohio to have gained residents since 1970. Columbus has a wide variety of fine restaurants and cultural activities. The city supports its own art museum and symphony orchestra and is home to one of the premier zoos in the nation. Temperatures average 73.5°F in August and 30.1°F in January. The average annual precipitation is 36.29 inches.

The University The Ohio State University, comprising seventeen colleges, nine schools, four regional campuses, and the Graduate School, is the principal center for graduate and professional study in Ohio and one of the leading institutions of higher education in the United States. Approximately 48,500 students are enrolled in the University, more than 13,000 of them pursuing graduate or professional degrees. Each year the University attracts a large number of visiting scholars (about 40 in mathematics) who contribute to the intellectual vigor of the Ohio State community. Many Ohio State faculty members play important roles as consultants to federal and state government bodies and to private enterprise.

Applying Candidates for graduate admission to Ohio State must send an application form (applications for fellowships or teaching associateships may be made on the same form) along with all college transcripts to the Ohio State Admissions Office, 320 Lincoln Tower, 1800 Cannon Drive, Columbus, Ohio 43210-1174. In addition, applicants must forward to the address below three letters of recommendation, an autobiography, and scores on the GRE General Test (required of all fellowship nominees). Candidates for admission to the graduate program in mathematics must also submit a GRE Subject Test score.

Applicants from non-English-speaking countries must take the TOEFL. Applications for fellowships must be completed by January 15.

Correspondence and Information

Saleh Tanveer, Vice-Chair of Graduate Studies
The Ohio State University
231 West 18th Avenue
Columbus, Ohio 43210-1174

Telephone: 614-292-5710
Fax: 614-292-1479
E-mail: gradinfo@math.ohio-state.edu (Re: graduate applications)
World Wide Web: http://www.math.ohio-state.edu
http:/www.applyweb.com/apply/osu (for online application)

The Ohio State University

THE FACULTY AND THEIR RESEARCH

Algebra
Harry Allen, Ph.D., Yale.
Robert Brown, Ph.D., Chicago.
Daniel Shapiro, Ph.D., Berkeley.

Algebraic Geometry
Linda Chen, Ph.D., Chicago.
Herb Clemens, Ph.D., Berkeley.
Roy Joshua, Ph.D., Northwestern.
Andras Nemethi, Ph.D., Romanian Academy.

Applied Mathematics
Gregory Baker, Ph.D., Caltech.
Avner Friedman, Ph.D., Hebrew (Jerusalem).
Yuji Kodama, Ph.D., Clarkson.
Yuan Lou, Ph.D., Minnesota.
Vladimir Maz'ya, Ph.D., Moscow State.
Edward Overman, Ph.D., Arizona.
Bjorn Sandstede, Ph.D., Stuttgart (Germany).
Saleh Tanveer, Ph.D., Caltech.
David Terman, Ph.D., Minnesota.
Fei Ran Tian, Ph.D., Courant.

Combinatorics
Thomas Dowling, Ph.D., North Carolina.
Cai-Heng Li, Ph.D., Western Australia.
Stephen Milne, Ph.D., Caltech.
Neil Robertson, Ph.D., Waterloo.
Akos Seress, Ph.D., Ohio State.

Differential Geometry
Andrzej Derdzinski, Ph.D., Wroclaw (Poland).
Fangyang Zheng, Ph.D., Harvard.

Ergodic Theory and Probability
Vitaly Bergelson, Ph.D., Hebrew (Jerusalem).
Neil Falkner, Ph.D., British Columbia.
Alexander Leibman, Ph.D., Technion (Israel).
Peter March, Ph.D., Minnesota.
Boris Pittel, Ph.D., Leningrad.
Michel Talagrand, Ph.D., Paris.

Group Theory
Koichiro Harada, Ph.D., Tokyo.
Radha Kessar, Ph.D., Ohio State.
Markus Linckelmann, Ph.D., Paris.
Ronald Solomon, Ph.D., Yale.
Sia Wong, Ph.D., Monash (Australia).

Harmonic Analysis and Representation Theory
Luis Casian, Ph.D., MIT.
Yuval Flicker, Ph.D., Cambridge.
Henri Moscovici, Ph.D., Bucharest.
Steve Rallis, Ph.D., MIT.
Robert Stanton, Ph.D., Cornell.

Logic
Timothy Carlson, Ph.D., Minnesota.
Harvey Friedman, Ph.D., MIT.
Chris Miller, Ph.D., Illinois at Urbana-Champaign.
Michael Rathjen, Ph.D., Munster (Germany).

Math Education
Herbert C. Clemens, Ph.D., Berkeley.

Mathematical Physics
Alexander Dynin, Ph.D., Moscow.
Ulrich Gerlach, Ph.D., Princeton.

Number Theory
James Cogdell, Ph.D., Yale.
David Goss, Ph.D., Harvard.
Wenzhi Luo, Ph.D., Rutgers.
Alayne Parson, Ph.D., Illinois at Chicago.
Paul Ponomarev, Ph.D., Yale.
Alice Silverberg, Ph.D., Princeton.
Warren Sinnott, Ph.D., Stanford.

Partial Differential Equations
Avner Friedman, Ph.D., Hebrew (Jerusalem).
Bo Guan, Ph.D., Massachusetts.
Yuan Lou, Ph.D., Minnesota.
Vladimir Maz'ya, Ph.D., Moscow State.

Real and Complex Analysis
Zita Divis, Ph.D., Heidelberg (Germany).
Gerald Edgar, Ph.D., Harvard.
Bo Guan, Ph.D., Massachusetts.
Kenneth Koenig, Ph.D., Princeton.
Vladimir Maz'ya, Ph.D., Moscow State.
Jeffery McNeal, Ph.D., Purdue.
Boris Mityagin, Ph.D., Moscow.
Paul Nevai, Ph.D., Szeged (Hungary).
Tatyana Shaposhnikova, Ph.D., St. Petersburg (Russia).

System/Control Theory
Bostwick Wyman, Ph.D., Berkeley.

Topology
Dan Burghelea, Ph.D., Romanian Academy.
Michael Davis, Ph.D., Princeton.
Zbigniew Fiedorowicz, Ph.D., Chicago.
Henry Glover, Ph.D., Michigan.
Thomas Kerler, Ph.D., Zurich.
Ian Leary, Ph.D., Cambridge.
Crichton Ogle, Ph.D., Brandeis.

OKLAHOMA STATE UNIVERSITY

Department of Mathematics

Programs of Study The Department of Mathematics offers programs leading to the Master of Science and Doctor of Philosophy degrees. There are three Master of Science degree options, pure mathematics, applied mathematics, and mathematics education, each requiring 32 credit hours of graduate course work in mathematics and/or related subjects. Students must receive a grade of A or B in 18 hours of core courses of the appropriate option and write a thesis, a report, or a creative component. Students with a good background in mathematics should expect to complete all requirements within two years. The Doctor of Philosophy program accepts only students with superior records in their graduate or undergraduate study. There are three options in the doctoral program: pure mathematics, applied mathematics, and mathematics education. The options are designed to prepare students for faculty positions at major research universities or for positions in industry. The mathematics education option is a blend of traditional foundational course work in mathematics and work in mathematics education and is designed to prepare students for positions in which mathematics teaching and educational concerns are a primary focus. A minimum of 90 credit hours of graduate credit beyond the bachelor's degree is required for each option, with 15 to 24 hours credited for a thesis. A minimum of 60 hours is required beyond the master's degree. Students must pass a written comprehensive exam covering core courses and embark on a study of a chosen area of mathematics, pass an oral qualifying examination, and complete the foreign language requirement. The most important requirement is the preparation of an acceptable thesis, which must demonstrate the candidate's ability to do independent, original work in mathematics or mathematics education. A well-prepared, motivated student should expect to complete all requirements within five to six years (or three to four years beyond the master's).

Research Facilities The department operates a network of microcomputer workstations and personal computers with several file servers. Computing is available for all graduate students. Through this network, access to the University Computer Center is available. The department also houses current issues of important mathematics journals in a reading room. This makes about 100 journals available in a very convenient location. Electronic access is available for the Math Reviews, tables of contents of many journals, and the library catalog and database resources.

Financial Aid Teaching assistantships are available to qualified students, with appointments covering the fall and spring semesters (renewed each year based on satisfactory progress). Students do not teach in their first semester and are provided with training to enhance their instructional skills. Subsequently, students normally have 5 to 6 hours of instructional duties per week. Some reduction in teaching is available to doctoral candidates making good progress toward their degree. Nine-month stipends are $12,000 for pre-master's students and $13,500 for students with a master's degree. Some summer appointments, as well as scholarships, fellowships, and assistantships that enhance the stipend, are available.

Cost of Study Tuition is reduced to the in-state level for all assistants, with full tuition waivers given to some exceptional incoming students. In-state tuition and fees are approximately $140 per credit hour.

Living and Housing Costs On-campus housing is available in residence halls and in several apartment complexes. It is recommended that prospective students contact the Office of Residential Life (telephone: 405-744-5592; e-mail: reslife@okway.okstate.edu; World Wide Web: http://www.reslife.okstate.edu) for information. Most students live in apartment complexes in the surrounding community, which cost $300 and up per month.

Student Group Of the current student body of about 50 students, 40 percent are women and 30 percent are international students. Almost all are full-time students on teaching assistantships. The department seeks highly motivated students without regard to race, color, national origin, religion, sex, or handicap.

Student Outcomes The department has been very successful in having all its recent doctoral students obtain positions in higher education institutions across the country. Master's students have placed very well in industry, community colleges, and schools. Many master's students go on to pursue doctoral degrees. Many doctoral students are appointed to prestigious postdoctoral positions.

Location Stillwater, a small city of about 40,000, is a safe, friendly, and lively community. The cost of living is relatively low, and affordable housing is plentiful. The city offers most of the cultural and recreational opportunities of a college town and is just an hour's drive from both Oklahoma City and Tulsa.

The University Oklahoma State University, a comprehensive research university with more than 22,000 students and almost 1,000 faculty members, is located on a scenic campus in Stillwater, Oklahoma. Founded in 1890, the University has developed an international reputation for excellence in teaching and research, especially in the basic and applied sciences. Students come to OSU from fifty states and more than fifty countries. The Graduate College has about 4,000 students.

Applying An application package may be obtained from the Mathematics Department. Applicants should plan to have three letters of recommendation sent to the department. GRE scores are not required, but they are strongly recommended. The Graduate Committee in the Mathematics Department begins deliberations in early December and continues the process until March. It is recommended that applicants read the departmental World Wide Web page for a detailed description.

Correspondence and Information

Director of Graduate Studies
Department of Mathematics
Oklahoma State University
Stillwater, Oklahoma 74078-1058
E-mail: graddir@math.okstate.edu
World Wide Web: http://mathgrad.okstate.edu

Oklahoma State University

THE FACULTY AND THEIR RESEARCH

Alan Adolphson, Regents Professor and Head; Ph.D., Princeton, 1973. Number theory, arithmetical algebraic geometry.
Douglas Aichele, Professor; Ed.D., Missouri, 1969. Mathematics education.
Dale Alspach, Professor; Ph.D., Ohio State, 1976. Functional analysis, Banach space theory.
Leticia Barchini, Southwestern Bell Professor; Ph.D., National University (Argentina), 1987. Representations of Lie groups.
Dennis Bertholf, Professor; Ph.D., New Mexico State, 1968. Abelian group theory, mathematics education.
Birne Binegar, Associate Professor; Ph.D., UCLA, 1982. Representations of Lie groups and Lie algebras, mathematical physics.
Hermann Burchard, Professor; Ph.D., Purdue, 1968. Approximation theory, numerical analysis.
James Choike, Noble Professor; Ph.D., Wayne State, 1970. Complex analysis, mathematics education.
J. Brian Conrey, Professor; Ph.D., Michigan, 1980. Number theory, automorphic forms.
Bruce Crauder, Professor; Ph.D., Columbia, 1981. Algebraic geometry.
Benny Evans, Professor; Ph.D., Michigan, 1971. Topology of low-dimensional manifolds, mathematics education.
Amit Ghosh, Professor; Ph.D., Nottingham, 1981. Number theory, automorphic forms.
Richard Paul Horja, Assistant Professor; Ph.D., Duke, 1999. Algebraic geometry and mirror.
William Jaco, G. B. Kerr Professor; Ph.D., Wisconsin, 1968. Topology of low-dimensional manifolds.
Ning Ju, Assistant Professor; Ph.D., Indiana, 1999. Applied mathematics, partial differential equations.
Anthony Kable, Assistant Professor; Ph.D., Oklahoma State, 1997. Number theory.
Ralph Kaufmann, Assistant Professor; Ph.D., Bonn (Germany), 1997. Algebraic geometry.
Marvin Keener, Professor; Ph.D., Missouri, 1970. Ordinary differential equations.
Tao Li, Assistant Professor; Ph.D., Caltech, 2000. Low-dimensional topology.
Weiping Li, Associate Professor; Ph.D., Michigan State, 1992. Low-dimensional topology, gauge theory, differential geometry.
Lisa Mantini, Associate Professor; Ph.D., Harvard, 1983. Representations of Lie groups, integral geometry.
Anvar Mavlyutov, Assistant Professor; Ph.D., Massachusetts, 2002. Algeraic geometry and mirror.
J. Robert Myers, Associate Professor; Ph.D., Rice, 1977. Topology of low-dimensional manifolds.
Alan Noell, Associate Professor; Ph.D., Princeton, 1983. Several complex variables.
Igor Pritsker, Assistant Professor; Ph.D., South Florida, 1995. Complex analysis, potential theory, approximation theory.
David Ullrich, Professor; Ph.D., Wisconsin, 1986. Harmonic analysis.
John Wolfe, Professor; Ph.D., Berkeley, 1971. Functional analysis, mathematics education.
David J. Wright, Associate Professor; Ph.D., Harvard, 1982. Algebraic number theory, Riemann surfaces.
Jiahong Wu, Associate Professor; Ph.D., Chicago, 1996. Fluid mechanics, partial differential equations.
Roger Zierau, Associate Professor; Ph.D., Berkeley, 1985. Representations of Lie groups.

RESEARCH ACTIVITIES

Algebraic Geometry: three-dimensional algebraic varieties, birational geometry, degenerations of surfaces, geometry of resolutions, birational geometry of projective spaces; enumerative geometry, interaction of algebraic geometry with theoretical physics; complex holomorphic vector bundles over algebraic varieties, intersection theory on the moduli space of curves.
Analysis: functional analysis, geometry of Banach spaces; approximation theory, numerical analysis, optimization; several complex variables, convexity properties of pseudoconvex domains; harmonic analysis, random Fourier series, boundary behavior of harmonic and analytic functions; Riemann surfaces.
Lie Groups: representation theory of semisimple and reductive Lie groups, analysis and geometry of homogeneous spaces, symmetry and groups of transformations, algebraic aspects of the study of Lie groups and arithmetic groups.
Mathematics Education: school mathematics curriculum, professional development of mathematics teachers, technology in the classroom and applications in the curriculum, mathematics reform issues, equity and minority issues, early intervention testing programs.
Number Theory: L-functions of algebraic varieties over finite fields and cohomological techniques, automorphic representations and L-functions, analytic number theory and the distribution of zeros of the Riemann zeta function, algebraic number theory and cubic extensions of number fields, algebraic groups over algebraic number fields and geometric invariant theory.
Topology: structure and classification of compact 3-manifolds; normal, incompressible, and Heegaard surfaces; laminations and foliations; algorithms and computation in low-dimensional topology; relations with combinatorial and geometric group theory; structure of noncompact 3-manifolds; covering spaces of 3-manifolds; Casson invariants, Floer homology, symplectic topology, dynamical systems.
Partial Differential Equations: theoretical and numerical studies of the Navier-Stokes equations, the 2D quasi-geostrophic equations, nonlinear wave equations, and other model equations arising in fluid mechanics; qualitative and quantitative analysis of turbulent dynamics.

SELECTED PUBLICATIONS

Adolphson, A., and S. Sperber. Exponential sums on A^n, III. *Manuscripta Mathematica* 102(4):429–46, 2000.

Adolphson, A., and S. Sperber. Dwork cohomology, de Rham cohomology, and hypergeometric functions. *Am. J. Math.* 122(2): 319–48, 2000.

Adolphson, A. Higher solutions of hypergeometric systems and Dwork cohomology. *Rend. Sem. Mat. Univ. Padova* 101:179–90, 1999.

Adolphson, A., and S. Sperber. A remark on local cohomology. *J. Algebra* 206(2):555–67, 1998.

Adolphson, A., and S. Sperber. On twisted de Rham cohomology. *Nagoya Math. J.* 146:55–81, 1997.

Adolphson, A., and S. Sperber. On the zeta function of a complete intersection. *Ann. Sci. Ecole Norm. Suppl. (4)* 29(3), 1996.

Adolphson, A., and B. Dwork. Contiguity relations for generalized hypergeometric functions. *Trans. Am. Math. Soc.* 347(2), 1995.

Aichele, D. B., et al. *Geometry—Explorations and Applications.* Boston: Houghton Mifflin/McDougal Littell, 1997.

Aichele, D. B., and S. Gay. Middle school students' understanding of number sense related to percent. *Sch. Sci. Math.* 97(1):27–36, 1997.

Aichele, D. B., ed. *Professional Development for Teachers of Mathematics—1994 Yearbook,* Reston, VA: NCTM, 1994.

Alspach, D., and S. Tong. Subspaces of L_p, p 2, determined by partitions and weights. *Studia Math.* 159:207–27, 2003.

Alspach, D., and E. Odell. L_p spaces. In *Handbook of the Geometry of Banach Spaces,* vol. 1, pp. 123–60, eds. W. B. Johnson and J. Lindenstrauss. Amsterdam: North-Holland, 2001.

Alspach, D. The dual of the Bourgain-Delbaen space. *Israel J. Math.* 117:239–59, 2000.

Alspach, D. Tensor products and independent sums of L_p-spaces, $1<p<\infty$. *Mem. Am. Math. Soc.* 138(660):77, 1999.

Barchini, L. Stein extensions of real symmetric spaces and the geometry of the flag manifold. *Math Annalen* 326:331–46, 2003.

Barchini, L., and M. Sepanski. Finite-reductive dual pairs in G2. *Linear Algebra Appl.* 340:123–36, 2002.

Barchini, L., C. Leslie, and **R. Zierau.** Domains of holomorphy and representations of SL $(n,\mathbf{R})$. *Manuscripta Mathmatica 106(4):411–27, 2001.*

Barchini, L., and **R. Zierau.** The mathematical legacy of Harish-Chandra. In *Proceedings of Symposia in Pure Mathematics,* vol. 68, eds. R. S. Doran and V. S. Varadarajan. Providence, R.I.: American Math Society, 2000.

Barchini, L. Strongly harmonic forms for representations in the discrete series. *J. Funct. Anal.* 161(1):111–31, 1999.

Barchini, L., and **R. Zierau.** Square integrable harmonic forms and representation theory. *Duke Math. J.* 92(3):645–64, 1998.

Binegar, B., and **R. Zierau.** A singular representation of E_6. *Trans. Am. Math. Soc.* 341(2):771–85, 1994.

Binegar, B., and **R. Zierau.** Unitarization of a singular representation of $SO_{(p,q)}$. *Comm. Math. Phys.* 138(2):245–58, 1991.

Binegar, B. Cohomology and deformations of Lie superalgebras. *Lett. Math. Phys.* 12(4):201–308, 1986.

Binegar, B. Conformal superalgebras, massless representations, and hidden symmetries. *Phys. Rev. D* 3-34(2):525–32, 1986.

Binegar, B. Unitarity of conformal supergravity. *Phys. Rev. D* 3-31(10):2497–502, 1985.

Binegar, B. On the state space of the dipole ghost. *Lett. Math. Phys.* 8(2):149–58, 1984.

Binegar, B., C. Fronsdal, and W. Heidenreich. Conformal QED. *J. Math. Phys.* 24(12):2828–46, 1983.

Binegar, B., C. Fronsdal, and W. Heidenreich. Linear conformal quantum gravity. *Phys. Rev. D* 3(10):2249–61, 1983.

Binegar, B., C. Fronsdal, and W. Heidenreich. de Sitter QED. *Ann. Phys.* 149(2):254–72, 1983.

Binegar, B. Relativistic field theories in three dimensions. *J. Math. Phys.* 23(8):1511–7, 1982.

Binegar, B., C. Fronsdale, M. Flato, and S. Salamo. de Sitter and conformal field theories. In *Proceedings of the International Symposium "Selected Topics in Quantum Field Thoery and Mathematics Physics"* (Bechnyle, 1981). *Czechoslovak J. Phys. B* 32(4):439–71, 1982.

Burchard, H. G., and J. Lei. Coordinate order of approximation by functional-based approximation operators. *J. Approx. Theory* 82(2), 1995.

Burchard, H. G., J. A. Ayers, W. H. Frey, and N. S. Sapidis. Approximation with aesthetic constraints. Designing fair curves and surfaces. In *Geometric Design Publishing,* pp. 3–28. Philadelphia: SIAM, 1994.

Burchard, H. G. Discrete curves and curvature constraints. In *Curves and Surfaces II,* ed. L. L. Schumaker et al. Boston: AK Peters, 1994.

Conrey, J. B., A. Granville, B. Poonen, and K. Soundararajan. Zeros of Fekete polynomials. *Ann. Inst. Fourier* (Grenoble) 50(3):865–89, 2000.

Conrey, J. B., and H. Iwaniec. The cubic moment of central values of automorphic L-functions. *Ann. Math.* (2) 151(3):1175–216, 2000.

Conrey, J. B., and D. Farmer. Mean values of L-functions and symmetry. *Int. Math. Res. Notices* 17:883–908, 2000.

Conrey, J. B., D. Farmer, and K. Soundararajan. Transition mean values of real characters. *J. Number Theory* 82(1):109–120, 2000.

Conrey, J. B., and D. W. Farmer. Hecke operators and the nonvanishing of L-functions. *Math. Appl.* 467:143–50, 1999.

Conrey, J. B., **A. Ghosh**, and S. M. Gonek. Simple zeros of the Riemann zeta-function. *Proc. London Math. Soc.* 76(3):497–522, 1998.

Conrey, J. B., and **A. Ghosh.** A conjecture for the sixth power moment of the Riemann zeta-function. *Int. Math. Res. Notices* 15:775–80, 1998.

Crauder, B., and R. Miranda. Quantum cohomology of rational surfaces. In *The Moduli Space of Curves* (Texel Island, 1994) *Progr. Math.,* 129. Boston: Birkhäuser Boston, 1995.

Crauder, B., and D. R. Morrison. Minimal models and degenerations of surfaces with Kodaira number zero. *Trans. Am. Math. Soc.* 343(2), 1994.

Crauder, B., and S. Katz. Cremona transformers and Hartshorne's conjecture. *Am. J. Math.* 113(2), 1991.

Crauder, B. Degenerations of minimal ruled surfaces. *Ark. Mat.* 28(2), 1990.

Evans, B., and J. Johnson. *Linear Algebra with MAPLE.* John Wiley and Sons, 1994.

Evans, B. DERIVE in linear algebra. In *Proc. Fifth Intl. Conf. Technol. Coll. Math.,* 1993.

Evans, B., and J. Johnson. *Discovering Calculus with DERIVE.* John Wiley and Sons, 1992.

Evans, B. The long annulus theorem. *Can. Math. Bull.* 29(3), 1986.

Jaco, W., and J. H. Rubinstein. 0-efficient triangulations of 3-manifolds. *J. Differential Geometry* 65, 2003.

Jaco, W. and E. Sedgwick. Decision problems in the space of Dehn fillings. *Topology* 42, 2003.

Jaco, W., D. Letscher, and J. H. Rubinstein. Algorithms for essential surfaces in 3-manifolds. *Contemp. Math.* 314, 2002.

Jaco, W., and J. L. Tollefson. Algorithms for the complete decomposition of a closed 3-manifold. *Illinois J. Math.* 39(3), 1995.

Jaco, W., and J. H. Rubinstein. PL equivariant surgery and invariant decompositions of 3-manifolds. *Adv. Math.* 73(2), 1989.

Jaco, W. Lectures on three-manifold topology. *CBMS Reg. Conf. Ser. Math. 43,* Providence, R.I.: American Mathematical Society, 1980.

Kable, A. C., and A. Yukie. The mean value of the product of class numbers of paired quadratic fields. I. *Tohoku Math. J.* 54(4):513–65, 2002.

Oklahoma State University

Selected Publications (continued)

Kable, A. C. The tensor product of exceptional representations on the general linear group. *Ann. Sci. Ecole Norm. Suppl.* 34(5):741–69, 2001.

Kable, A. C., and A. Yukie. Prehomogeneous vector spaces and field extensions. II. *Invent. Math.* 130(2):315–44, 1997.

Li, W. A module structure on the symplectic Floer cohomology. *Comm. Math. Phys.* 211(1):137–51, 2000.

Li, W. Knneth formula for SO(3) Floer homology. *Topology* 38(6):1209–37, 1999.

Li, W. The symplectic Floer homology of composite knots. *Forum Math.* 11(5):617–46, 1999.

Li, W. The symplectic Floer homology of the square knot and granny knots. *Acta Math. Sin.* (Engl. ser.) 15(1):1–10, 1999.

Li, W. Künneth formula for SO(3) Floer homology. *Topology* 38(6):1209–37, 1999.

Li, W., and Z. Qin. On blowup formulae for the S-duality conjecture of Vafa and Witten. *Invent. Math.* 136(2):451–82, 1999.

Li, W., and Z. Qin. Vertex operator algebras and the blowup formula for the S-duality conjecture of Vafa and Witten. *Math. Res. Lett.* 5(6):791–8, 1998.

Li, W., and Z. Qin. On blowup formulae for the S-duality conjecture of Vafa and Witten. II. The universal functions. *Math. Res. Lett.* 5(4):439–53, 1998.

Li, W. Singular connections and Riemann theta functions. *Topol. Appl.* 90(1–3):149–63, 1998.

Lorch, J. D., and **L. A. Mantini.** Inversion of an integral transform and ladder representations of U(1,q). In *Representation Theory and Harmonic Analysis* (Cincinnati, Ohio, 1994); *Contemp. Math.,* 191; *Am. Math. Soc.* Providence, R.I., 1995.

Mantini, L. A. An L^2-cohomology construction of unitary highest weight modules for U(p,q). *Trans. Am. Math. Soc.* 323(2), 1991.

Mantini, L. A. An L^2-cohomology construction of negative spin mass zero equations for U(p,q). *Math. Anal. Appl.* 136(2), 1988.

Mantini, L. A. An L^2-cohomology analogue of the Penrose transform for the oscillator representation. In *Integral Geometry* (Brunswick, Maine, 1984); *Contemp. Math.,* 63; *Am. Math. Soc.* Providence, R.I., 1987.

Myers, R. Splitting homomorphisms and the geometrization conjecture. *Math. Proc. Cambridge Philos. Soc.* 129(2):291–300, 2000.

Myers, R. Uncountably many arcs in S^3 whose complements have non-isomorphic, indecomposable fundamental groups. *J. Knot Theory Ramifications* 9(4):505–21, 2000.

Myers, R. On covering translations and homeotopy groups of contractible open n-manifolds. *Proc. Amer. Math. Sci.* 128(5):1563–6, 2000.

Myers, R. Compactifying sufficiently regular covering spaces of compact 3-manifolds. *Proc. Am. Math. Soc.* 128:1507–13, 2000.

Myers, R. On covering translations and homeotopy groups of contractible open n-manifolds. *Proc. Am. Math. Soc.* 128:1563–6, 2000.

Myers, R. Contractible open 3-manifolds which non-trivially cover only non-compact 3-manifolds. *Topology* 38(1):85–94, 1999.

Myers, R. Contractible open 3-manifolds with free covering translation groups. *Topol. Appl.* 96(2):97–108, 1999.

Noell, A., and R. Belhachemi. Global plurisubharmonicdefining functions. *Mich. Math. J.* 47:377–84, 2000.

Noell, A. Local and global plurisubharmonic defining functions. *Pacific J. Math.* 176(2):421–6, 1996.

Noell, A. Peak functions for pseudoconvex domains in C^n. In *Several Complex Variables: Proceedings of the Mittag-leffler Institute,* 1987–88, *Math. Notes* 38. Princeton, N.J.: Princeton University Press, 1993.

Noell, A. Local versus global convexity of pseudoconvex domains. In *Several Complex Variables and Complex Geometry, Proc. Sympos. Pure Math.* 52. Providence, R.I.: American Mathematics Society, 1991.

Noell, A. Interpolation from curves in pseudoconvex boundaries. *Mich. Math. J.* 37(2), 1990.

Noell, A., and B. Stensones. Proper holomorphic maps from weakly pseudoconvex domains. *Duke Math. J.* 60:363–88, 1990.

Noell, A., and T. Wolff. On peak sets for Lip α classes. *J. Funct. Anal.* 86:136–79, 1989.

Laugesen, R. S., and **I. E. Pritsker.** Potential theory of the farthest-point distance function. *Can. Math. Bull.* 46:373–87, 2003.

Pritsker, I. E. Products of polynomials in uniform norms. *Trans. Am. Math. Soc.* 353:3971–93, 2001.

Andrievskii, V. V., **I. E. Pritsker,** and R. S. Varga. Simultaneous approximation and interpolation of functions on continua in the complex plane. *J. Math. Pures Appl.* 80:373–88, 2001.

Pritsker, I. E. An inequality for the norm of a polynomial factor. *Proc. Am. Math. Soc.* 129:2283–91, 2001.

Andrievskii, V. V., and **I. E. Pritsker.** Convergence of Bieberbach polynomials in domains with interior cusps. *J. d'Analyse Math.* 82:315–32, 2000.

Kroó, A., and **I. E. Pritsker.** A sharp version of Mahler's inequality for products of polynomials. *Bull. London Math. Soc.* 31(3):269–78, 1999.

Pritsker, I. E., and R. S. Varga. Weighted rational approximation in the complex plane. *J. Math. Pures Appl.* 78(2):177–202, 1999.

Pritsker, I. E., and R. S. Varga. The Szego curve, zero distribution and weighted approximation. *Trans. Am. Math. Soc.* 349:4085–105, 1997.

Choe, B. R., W. Ramey, and **D. C. Ullrich.** Bloch-to-BMOA pullbacks on the disk. *Proc. Am. Math. Soc.* 125(10):2987–96, 1997.

Stegenga, D. A., and **D. C. Ullrich.** Superharmonic functions in Hölder domains. *Rocky Mtn. J. Math.* 25(4), 1995.

Ullrich, D. C. Radial divergence in BMOA. *Proc. London Math. Soc. (3)* 68(1), 1994.

Ullrich, D. C. Recurrence for lacunary cosine series. In *The Madison Symposium on Complex Analysis* (Madison, Wisc., 1991); *Contemp. Math.,* 137; *Am. Math. Soc.* Providence, R.I., 1992.

Wright, D. J., and A. Yukie. Prehomogeneous vector spaces and field extensions. *Invent. Math.* 110(2), 1992.

Wright D. J. Twists of the Iwasawa-Tate zeta function. *Math. Z.* 200(2), 1989.

Wright D. J. Distribution of discriminants of abelian extensions. *Proc. London Math. Soc. 3* 58(1), 1989.

Wu, J. Regularity results for weak solutions of the 3D MHD equations. Partial differential equations and applications. *Discrete Contin. Dyn. Syst.* 10(1–2):543–56, 2004.

Wu, J. Generalized MHD equations. *J. Differential Equations* 195(2):284–312, 2003.

Bona, J. L., and **J. Wu.** The zero-viscosity limit of the 2D Navier-Stokes equations. *Stud. Appl. Math.* 109(4):265–78, 2002.

Wu, J. The quasi-geostrophic equation and its two regularizations. *Comm. Partial Differential Equations* 27(5–6):1161–81, 2002.

Constantin, P., D. Cordoba, and **J. Wu.** On the critical dissipative quasi-geostrophic equation. Dedicated to Professors Ciprian Foias and Roger Temam (Bloomington, Indiana, 2000). *Indiana Univ. Math. J.* (special issue) 50:97–107, 2001.

Wu, J. Analytic results related to magneto-hydrodynamic turbulence. *Physica D* 136(3–4):353–72, 2000.

Mehdi, S., and **R. Zierau.** Harmonic spinors on semisimple symmetric spaces. *J. Funct. Anal.* 198(2):536–57, 2003.

Zierau, A. Representations in Dolbeault cohornology. In *Representation Theory of Lie Groups,* Park City Math Institute, vol. 8; *Am. Math. Soc.,* Providence, R.I., 2000.

Wolf, J. A., and **R. Zierau.** Linear cycle spaces in flag domains. *Math. Ann.* 316(3):529–45, 2000.

Dunne, E. G., and **R. Zierau.** The automorphism groups of complex homogeneous spaces. *Math. Ann.* 307(3):489–503, 1997.

PENNSYLVANIA STATE UNIVERSITY

Department of Mathematics

Programs of Study

The Department of Mathematics offers Ph.D., D.Ed., M.A., and M.Ed. degree programs. A wide range of faculty interests provides a broad spectrum of areas of specialization in which students may choose their course work and research topics. There are several areas of mathematics in which Penn State has groups of world-class researchers on faculty. These areas include the theory of operator algebras, K-theory, and related areas; dynamical systems, ergodic theory, and related areas; number theory and arithmetical algebraic geometry; differential geometry, algebraic geometry, and Lie groups; set theory and mathematical logic; numerical analysis; and applied mathematics. The Pritchard Fluid Mechanics Laboratory provides a unique opportunity for students specializing in applied mathematics to carry out mathematical research starting from experimental grounds. In addition, the University has recently founded three research centers within the Department of Mathematics: the Center for Dynamical Systems, the Center for Geometry and Mathematical Physics, and the Center for Computational Mathematics and Applications.

In a typical year, the department admits about 20 students, almost all to the Ph.D. program. All doctoral students are required to pass three qualifying examinations. The qualifying examinations are in the areas of analysis, algebra, and topology/geometry unless a student chooses to enroll in the Applied Mathematics Option or the Logic and Foundations Option. For the Applied Mathematics Option, the qualifying examinations are in the areas of analysis, numerical analysis, and partial differential equations, and for the Logic and Foundations Option, the areas are analysis, algebra, and logic and foundations. Among other requirements for the Ph.D. are at least eleven 3-credit graduate courses, passing a comprehensive examination, writing a thesis, and passing a final oral examination based on the thesis. The length of time it takes students to complete their Ph.D. degree is typically between 5½ and six years.

Research Facilities

The Department of Mathematics is housed in McAllister Building, a large four-story structure located in the heart of the Penn State campus. The Physical and Mathematical Sciences Library is conveniently located across the street in Davey Laboratory. It is a first-rate library, containing more than 45,000 volumes and receiving almost 600 mathematical journals and serials. The library also subscribes to *MathSci,* the Web-based edition of *Math Reviews.*

The department maintains a network of nearly 150 Sun Workstations, together with specialized machines to support very high-speed computation, high-resolution three-dimensional visualization, and specialized software. The network is readily accessible to graduate students, with workstations in graduate student offices. Supported software includes TeX, MACSYMA, Maple, Mathematica, Matlab, and more specialized packages such as Pari, GAP, and DSLIB. The network has an excellent Internet connection via a fiber-optic link to the Penn State data backbone. Through it, faculty members and graduate students access Penn State's 50-node SP-2 parallel computer and the national supercomputer centers.

Financial Aid

Most of the graduate students are supported by teaching assistantships. In addition to the tuition waiver, the stipend for a half-time teaching assistantship is $13,185 (for ten months) prior to admittance to candidacy, after which time it increases to $14,175. A half-time assistantship requires the student to teach 3 hours per week in the first year and 4½ hours per week in subsequent years. The other sources of support are Curry Fellowships, which are awarded to incoming doctoral students based on their performance in Ph.D. qualifying examinations taken upon arrival in August and that carry a stipend of $16,470 for ten months, and various Graduate School and Eberly College of Science fellowships. These fellowships give students one or two semesters free of teaching. Summer teaching assistantships are also available to many students.

Cost of Study

Students holding any of the fellowships or assistantships described above receive a tuition waiver (in 2003–04, $4175 per semester).

Living and Housing Costs

For a single student, a room in a University residence hall and board are available for about $2000 per semester. For married students, 358 family units are available, with monthly rates that range from $325 to $485. The town of State College also provides attractive and reasonably priced off-campus living within walking distance of the campus.

Student Group

As of September 2003, the department had 99 mathematics graduate students. Of these, 85 were doctoral students, with the remaining students seeking a master's degree. Sixty-two percent were international students from all over the world. Teaching assistantships were provided for 92 students.

Student Outcomes

In spite of the very difficult job market in mathematics in general over the past years, graduates have been successfully placed in academic positions and industry. Recent academic placements include tenure-track and postdoctoral positions at Princeton, MSRI, Caltech, UCLA, Dartmouth, SUNY, Purdue, Rutgers, University of Minnesota, University of Pennsylvania, and University of Georgia. Corporate placements include (Bellcore) Lucent Technologies; Parametric Technology Corporation; Electronic Digital System; HRB Systems; Micro Strategy, Inc.; and CVC International.

Location

The University Park Campus of Penn State is in the town of State College—a metropolitan area of more than 100,000 people in the center of the commonwealth. Located in a rural and scenic part of the Appalachian Mountains, it is only 3 to 4 hours from Pittsburgh, Philadelphia, and Washington, D.C. Various cultural, educational, and athletic activities are available throughout the year.

The University

Founded in 1855, Penn State is the land-grant university of Pennsylvania. It is one of the largest universities in the country, with twenty-three campuses. The University Park Campus is the center of most of the graduate studies at the University. University enrollment is approximately 70,000, including 60,000 undergraduates and 10,000 graduate students. The graduate faculty has about 1,800 members. Enrollment at the University Park Campus is about 39,000.

Applying

The Graduate School at Penn State now has an electronic application online. Applications processed electronically require a $45 application fee. Admission information may be accessed at http://www.math.psu.edu/Grad/Admissions.html. Two official transcripts, test scores (GRE and TOEFL, if applicable), visa application (if applicable), three letters of recommendation, a statement of purpose, and a brief description of junior, senior, and graduate-level mathematics courses that the applicant will have completed upon entering graduate school must be sent to the Department of Mathematics by February 1. A minimum TOEFL score of 213 (computer-based test) or 550 (paper-based test) is required for all applicants whose native language is not English.

Correspondence and Information

Director of Graduate Studies
Department of Mathematics
Pennsylvania State University
University Park, Pennsylvania 16802

Telephone: 814-865-7529
E-mail: gradstudies@math.psu.edu
World Wide Web: http://www.math.psu.edu/Grad/

Pennsylvania State University

THE FACULTY AND THEIR RESEARCH

Joel H. Anderson, Professor of Mathematics; Ph.D., Indiana, 1971. Operator algebras.
George E. Andrews, Evan Pugh Professor of Mathematics; Ph.D., Pennsylvania, 1964. Number theory, partitions.
Augustin Banyaga, Professor of Mathematics; Ph.D., Geneva, 1976. Symplectic, contact geometry and topology.
Jesse Barlow, Professor of Mathematics and Computer Science and Engineering; Ph.D., Northwestern, 1981. Numerical linear algebra, concurrent scientific computing, accuracy of computation.
Paul F. Baum, Evan Pugh Professor of Mathematics; Ph.D., Princeton, 1963. Topology and operator algebras.
Gregory Bell, S. Chowla Research Postdoctoral Scholar; Ph.D. Florida, 2002. Geometric group theory.
Andrew Belmonte, Associate Professor of Mathematics; Ph.D., Princeton, 1994. Experimental fluid dynamics, viscoelastic materials and applied mathematics.
Leonid Berlyand, Professor of Mathematics and Materials Science; Ph.D., Kharkov (Russia), 1984. Partial differential equations and applications in materials science, homogenization theory, mathematical physics.
Nathanial P. Brown, Assistant Professor of Mathematics; Ph.D., Purdue, 1999. Operator algebras.
W. Dale Brownawell, Distinguished Professor of Mathematics; Ph.D., Cornell, 1970. Number theory, transcendence.
Dmitri Burago, Professor of Mathematics; Ph.D., St. Petersburg (Russia), 1992. Differential and Riemannian geometry.
Wenwu Cao, Professor of Mathematics and Materials Science; Ph.D., Penn State, 1987. Applied mathematics, computer simulations, materials sciences.
John D. Clemens, Assistant Professor of Mathematics; Ph.D., Berkeley, 2001. Mathematical logic, descriptive set theory.
Qiang Du, Professor of Mathematics; Ph.D., Carnegie Mellon, 1988. Computational and applied mathematics, partial differential equations and parallel computation.
Edward Formanek, Professor of Mathematics; Ph.D., Rice, 1970. Algebra, ring theory.
Moses Glasner, Associate Professor of Mathematics; Ph.D., UCLA, 1966. Potential theory, complex variables and differential geometry.
Diane M. Henderson, Associate Professor of Mathematics; Ph.D., California, San Diego, 1989. Fluid dynamics, applied mathematics.
Nigel Higson, Distinguished Professor of Mathematics; Ph.D., Dalhousie, 1986. Operator algebras and K-theory.
Joseph Hundley, S. Chowla Research Postdoctoral Scholar; Ph.D., Columbia, 2002. Automorphic forms.
Robert P. Hunter, Professor of Mathematics; Ph.D., LSU, 1958. Transformation groups, abstract semigroups.
Katherine Hurley, S. Chowla Research Postdoctoral Scholar; Ph.D., California, Santa Cruz, 2002. Vertex operator algebras, infinite dimensional Lie algebras and modular forms.
Anatole Katok, Raymond N. Shibley Professor of Mathematics; Ph.D., Moscow State, 1968. Dynamical systems, ergodic theory and differential geometry.
Svetlana Katok, Professor of Mathematics; Ph.D., Maryland, 1983. Automorphic forms, analysis on manifolds, dynamical systems.
Bryna Kra, Associate Professor of Mathematics; Ph.D., Stanford, 1995. Ergodic theory, dynamical systems, topological dynamics.
Gerard Lallement, Professor of Mathematics; Doctorat es Mathematiques, Paris, 1966. Algebraic and combinatorial semigroup theory.
Mark Levi, Professor of Mathematics; Ph.D., NYU (Courant), 1978. Dynamical systems and their applications in physics and engineering.
Jenny Xiaoe Li, Associate Professor of Mathematics and Economics; Ph.D., Cornell, 1993. Mathematical economics, mathematical finance, computational economics.
L. C. Li, Associate Professor of Mathematics; Ph.D., NYU (Courant), 1983. Differential equations, completely integrable Hamiltonian systems.
W. C. Winnie Li, Professor of Mathematics; Ph.D., Berkeley, 1974. Automorphic forms, representation theory, number theory, algebra and combinatorics.
Chun Liu, Associate Professor of Mathematics; Ph.D., NYU (Courant), 1995. Partial differential equations, calculus of variations, applied mathematics.
Anna Mazzucato, Assistant Professor of Mathematics; Ph.D., North Carolina, Chapel Hill, 2000. Partial differential equations, fluid mechanics, harmonic and microlocal anlysis.
Eric Mortenson, S. Chowla Research Postdoctoral Scholar; Ph.D., Wisconsin, 2003. Combinatorics, modular forms, number theory.
Gary L. Mullen, Professor of Mathematics; Ph.D., Penn State, 1974. Finite fields and combinatorics.
Victor Nistor, Professor of Mathematics; Ph.D., Berkeley, 1992. Partial differential equations, analysis on singular spaces, applications.
Alexei Novikov, Assistant Professor of Mathematics; Ph.D., Stanford, 1999. Applied mathematics, analysis.
Adrian Ocneanu, Professor of Mathematics; Ph.D., Warwick (England), 1983. Operator algebras.
Yakov Pesin, Distinguished Professor of Mathematics; Ph.D., Moscow State, 1979. Dynamical systems and applications of dynamical systems to statistical physics, population dynamics, mathematical ecology, and geometry.
Anton Petrunin, Assistant Professor of Mathematics; Ph.D., Illinois, 1995. Singular geometry, analysis, topology, combinatorial geometry.
John Roe, Professor of Mathematics; D.Phil., Oxford, 1984. Index theory, coarse geometry, C*-algebras, topology.
James A. Sellers, Associate Professor of Mathematics; Ph.D., Penn State, 1992. Number theory, combinatorics.
Stephen G. Simpson, Professor of Mathematics; Ph.D., MIT, 1971. Mathematical logic, foundations of mathematics.
Gregory Swiatek, Professor of Mathematics; Ph.D., Warsaw, 1987. Dynamical systems.
Sergei Tabachnikov, Professor of Mathematics; Ph.D., Moscow State, 1987. Dynamical systems, symplectic geometry, low-dimensional topology.
Arkady Tempelman, Professor of Mathematics and Statistics; Ph.D., Vilnius, 1975. Ergodic theory, statistics.
David Terhune, S. Chowla Research Postdoctoral Scholar; Ph.D., Texas at Austin, 2002. Number theory, multiple L-function theory.
Leonid N. Vaserstein, Professor of Mathematics; Ph.D., Moscow State, 1969. Classical groups over rings and algebraic K-theory, number theory, operations research, systems with local interactions.
Robert C. Vaughan, Professor of Mathematics; Ph.D., London, 1970. Analytic number theory.
Aissa Wade, Assistant Professor of Mathematics; Ph.D., Montpellier, 1996. Differential geometry, symplectic geometry.
William C. Waterhouse, Professor of Mathematics; Ph.D., Harvard, 1968. Algebra, number theory, affine group schemes, history of mathematics.
Howard Weiss, Professor of Mathematics; Ph.D., Maryland, 1986. Dynamical systems and applications of dynamical systems to problems in statistical physics, population dynamics, mathematical ecology, and geometry.
Kris Wysocki, Associate Professor of Mathematics; Ph.D., Rutgers, 1989. Symplectic and contact topology, Hamiltonian dynamics.
Jinchao Xu, Professor of Mathematics; Ph.D., Cornell, 1989. Numerical partial differential equations, multigrid methods.
Ping Xu, Professor of Mathematics; Ph.D., Berkeley, 1990. Symplectic geometry and mathematical physics.
Ae Ja Yee, Associate Professor of Mathematics; Ph.D., Korea Advanced Institute of Science and Technology, 2000. Partitions, q-series and combinatorics.
Peng Yu, S. Chowla Research Assistant Professor; Ph.D., Carnegie Mellon, 2003. Mathematical modeling, scientific computing, applications in materials science.
Yuri Zarhin, Professor of Mathematics; Ph.D., Leningrad (Russia), 1986. Algebraic geometry.
Yuxi Zheng, Professor of Mathematics; Ph.D., Berkeley, 1990. Partial differential equations from physical world.
Ludmil Zikatanov, Assistant Professor of Mathematics; Ph.D., Sofia, 1995. Discretization methods for differential equations, algebraic multigrid methods and their applications.

SELECTED PUBLICATIONS

Andrews, G. Umbral calculus, Bailey chains and pentagonal number theorems. *J. Combinatorial Theory* (A)91:464–75, 2000.

Andrews, G., O. Warnaar, and A. Schilling. An A2 Bailey lemma and Rogers-Ramanujan-type identities. *J. Am. Math. Soc.* 12:677–702, 1999.

Banyaga, A. The geometry surrounding the Arnold-Liouville theorem. In *Advances in Geometry,* 53–69, Progr. Math., 172, Boston: Birkhaüser, 1999.

Banyaga, A. The structure of classical diffeomorphism groups. In *Mathematics and Its Applications,* vol. 400. Dordrecht: Kluwer Academic Publishers, 1997.

Banyaga, A., R. de la Llave, and C. E. Wayne. Cohomology equations near hyperbolic points and geometric versions of Sternberg linearization theorem. J. Geom. Anal. 4:613–49, 1997.

Baum, P., A. Connes, and **N. Higson.** Classifying space for proper actions and K-theory of group C* algebras. In *C*-Algebras: 1943–1993 A Fifty Year Celebration, Contemporary Mathematics,* 167:241–91, ed. R. Doran. Providence: AMS, 1994.

Baum, P., and R. Douglas. K homology and index theory. *Proc. Symp. Pure Math.,* 38:117–73. Providence: AMS, 1982.

Baum, P., W. Fulton, and R. MacPherson. Riemann-Roch for singular varieties. *Publ. Math. IHES.* 45:101–67, 1975.

Bell, G., and A. Dranishnikov. On asymptotic dimension of groups acting on trees. *Geom. Dedicata* 103:89–101, 2004.

Bell, G. Property A for groups acting on metric spaces. *Topol. Appl.* 130:239–51, 2003.

Bell, G., and A. Dranishnikov. On asymptotic dimension of groups. *Algebra Geom. Topol.* 1:57–71, 2001.

Belmonte, A., and M. C. Sostarecz. Motion and shape of a viscoelastic drop falling through a viscous fluid. *J. Fluid Mech.* 497:235–52, 2003.

Belmonte, A., and L. B. Smolka. Drop pinch-off and filament dynamics of wormlike micellar fluids. *J. Non-Newtonian Fluid Mech.* 115:1–25, 2003.

Belmonte, A., M. J. Shelley, S. T. Eldakar, and C. H. Wiggins. Dynamic patterns and self-knotting of a driven hanging chain. *Phys. Rev. Lett.* 87:114301–4, 2001.

Berlyand, L., and P. Mironescu. Ginzburg-Landau minimizers with prescribed degrees: Dependence on domain. *C. R. Acad. Sci., Paris* 337(6):375–80, 2003.

Berlyand, L., and **A. Novikov.** Error of the network approximation for densely packed composites with irregular geometry. *SIAM J. Math. Anal.* 34(2):385–408, 2002.

Berlyand, L., and V. Mityushev. Generalized Clausius-Mosotti formula for random composites with circular fibers. *J. Stat. Phys.*102(1/2):115–45, 2001.

Brown, N., K. Dykema, and D. Shlyakhtenko. Topological entropy of free product automorphisms. *Acta Math.* 189:1–35, 2002.

Brown, N. Herrero's approximation problem for quasidiagonal operators. *J. Funct. Anal.* 186:360–5, 2001.

Brownawell, W. D. Bounds for the degrees in the Nullstellensatz. *Ann. Math.* 126:577–91, 1987.

Beukers, F., **W. D. Brownawell,** and G. Heckman. Siegel normality. *Ann. Math.* 127:279–308, 1987.

Burago, D., S. Ferleger, and A. Kononenko. Uniform estimates for the number of collisions in semi-dispersing billiards. *Ann. Math.* 147:695–708, 1998.

Burago, D., and S. Ivanov. Riemannian Tori without conjugate points are flat. *Geom. Funct. Anal.* 3(4):259–69, 1994.

Burago, D. Periodic metrics. In *Progress in Nonlinear Differential Equations,* pp. 90–5, ed. H. Brezis. Boston: Birkhaüser, 1993.

Cao, W., and L. E. Cross. Theory of tetragonal twin structure in ferroelectric perovskite with first order phase transition. *Phys. Rev. B* 44:5–12, 1991.

Cao, W., and G. R. Barsch. Landau-Ginzburg model of interface boundaries in improper ferroelastic perovskites of D4h symmetry. *Phys. Rev. B* 41:4334–48, 1990.

Cao, W., and J. A. Krumhansl. Continuum theory of 4mm-2mm proper ferroelastic transition under inhomogeneous stress. *Phys. Rev. B* 42:4334–40, 1990.

Clemens, J. D., S. Gao, and A. S. Kechris. Polish metric spaces: Their classification and isometry groups. *Bull. Symb. Logic* 7(3):361–75, 2001.

Du, Q., C. Liu, and **P. Yu.** From micro to macro dynamics via a new moment closure approximation to the FENE model of polymeric fluids. *SIAM J. Multiscale Modeling Simulation,* in press.

Du, Q., V. Faber, and M. Gunzberger. Centroidal voronoi diagrams and its applications. *SIAM Review* 41:627–76, 1999.

Du, Q. Discrete gauge invariant approximations of a time-dependent Ginzburg-Landau model of superconductivity. *Math. Computation* 67:965–86, 1998.

Du, Q., M. Gunzburger, and J. Peterson. Analysis and approximation of the Ginzburg-Landau model of superconductivity. *SIAM Review* 34:54–81, 1992.

Formanek, E. Braid group representations of low degree. *Proc. London Math. Soc.* 73:279–322, 1996.

Formanek, E., and C. Procesi. The automorphism group of a free group is not linear. *J. Algebra* 149:494–9, 1992.

Henderson, D. M., H. Segur, L. Smolka, and M. Wadati. The motion of falling liquid filaments. *Phys. Fluids* A12:550, 2000.

Henderson, D. M. Effects of surfactants on Faraday-wave dynamics. *J. Fluid Mech.* 365:89–107, 1998.

Henderson, D. M., and J. L. Hammack. Experiments on ripple instabilities. Part 1. Resonant triads. *J. Fluid Mech.* 184:15–41, 1987.

Higson, N., and **J. Roe.** Amenable group actions and the Novikov conjecture. *Journal fur die reine und angewandte Mathematik* 519:143–53, 2000.

Higson, N., and G. Kasparov. Operator K-theory for groups which act properly and isometrically on Hilbert space. *ERA Am. Math. Soc.* 3:131–42, 1997.

Hurley, K. Highest-weight vectors of the moonshine module with non-zero graded trace. *J. Algebra* 261:411–33, 2003.

Hunter, R. P. Embeddings into 2 generator semigroups. *Semigroup Forum* 47:96–100, 1993.

Hunter, R. P. On infinite words and dimension raising homomorphisms. *Fundam. Math.* 129:211–4, 1989.

Hunter, R. P. Total subgroups lying in the centralizer of the group of units. *Proc. Am. Math. Soc.* 79:113–22, 1980.

Katok, A., S. Katok, and K. Schmidt. Rigidity of measurable structure for Z^d actions by automorphisms of a torus. *Comment. Math. Helv.* 77(4):418–745, 2002.

Katok, A., and B. Hasselblatt. *Introduction to the Modern Theory of Smooth Dynamical Systems.* 820 pp. Cambridge: Cambridge University Press, 1995; paperback edition, 1996.

Katok, A. Entropy and closed geodesics. *Erg. Th. Dynam. Sys.* 2(3-4):339–66, 1982.

Gurevich, B., and **S. Katok.** Arithmetic coding and entropy for the positive geodesic flow on the modular surface. *Moscow Math. J.* 1(4):569–82, 2001.

Katok, S. *Fuchsian Groups.* Chicago: University of Chicago Press, 1992.

Kra, B., and J. Schmeling. Diophantine numbers, dimension and Denjoy maps. *Acta Arith.* 105:323–40, 2002.

Kra, B., and B. Host. Convergence of Conze-Lesigne Averages. *Erg. Th. Dynam. Sys.* 21:493–509, 2001.

Kra, B. Commutative groups of circle diffeomorphisms. *Isr. J. Math.* 93:303–16, 1996.

Levi, M. Geometry and physics of averaging with applications. *Physica* D(132):150–64, 1999.

Levi, M. A new randomness-generating phenomenon in forced relaxation oscillations. *Physica* D(114):230–6, 1998.

Levi, M., and H. Broer. Geometrical aspect of stability theory for Hill's equations. *Arch. Rational Mech. Anal.* 131:225–40, 1995.

Li, J. X. Non-steady-state equilibrium solution of a class of dynamic models. *J. Econ. Dynamics Control* 25:967–78, 2001.

Li, J. X., with Jerry L. Bona. Stabilization, monetary injection policies, *J. Econ. Theory* 98:127–57, 2001.

Li, L. C. Classical r-matrices and compatible Poisson structures for Lax equations on Poisson algebras. *Commun. Math. Phys.* 203:573–92, 1999.

Li, L. C. The SVD flows on generic symplectic leaves are completely integrable. *Adv. Math.* 128:82–118, 1997.

Li, L. C. On the complete integrability of some Lax equations on a periodic lattice. *Trans. Am. Math. Soc.* 349:331–72, 1997.

Li, W., and H. Maharaj. Coverings of curves with asymptotically many rational points. *J. Number Theory* 96:232–56, 2002.

Li, W. *Number Theory with Applications.* Singapore: World Scientific, 1996.

Li, W. Character sums and abelian Ramanujan graphs. *J. Number Theory* 41:199–214, 1992.

Du, Q., C. Liu, and **P. Yu.** From micro to macro dynamics via a new moment closure approximation to the FENE model of polymeric fluids. *SIAM J. Multiscale Modeling Simulation,* in press.

Liu, C., M. C. Calderer, and K. Voss. Radical configurations of smectic A materials and focal conics. *Phys. D* 124:11–22, 1998.

Liu, C., and F.-H. Lin. Nonlinear dissipative systems modeling the flow of liquid crystals. *Commun. Pure Appl. Math.* XLVIII:501–37, 1995.

Mazzucato, A. Besov-Morrey spaces: Function space theory and applications to non-linear PDE. *Trans. Amer. Math. Soc.* 355:(4): 1297–364, 2003.

Mazzucato, A. Decomposition of Besov-Morrey spaces. In *Harmonic Analysis at Mount Holyoke,* 16 pp., eds. W. Beckner et al. Providence, R.I.: American Mathematical Society, 2003.

Mortenson, E. Supercongruences between truncated 2F1

Pennsylvania State University

Selected Publications (continued)

hypergeometric functions and their Gaussian analogs. *Trans. Am. Math. Soc.* 355(3):987–1007, 2003.
Mortenson, E. A supercongruence conjecture of Rodriguez-Villegas for a certain truncated hypergeometric function. *J. Number Theory* 99(1):139–47, 2003.
Mullen, G., B. Bajnok, S. B. Damelin, and **J. X. Li.** A constructive finite field method for scattering points on the surface of d-dimensional spheres. *Computing* 68(2):97–109, 2002.
Mullen, G. Permutation polynomials: A matrix analogue of Schur's conjecture and a survey of recent results. *Finite Fields Appl.* 1:242–58, 1995.
Nistor, V. Cyclic cohomology of crossed products by algebraic groups. *Invent. Math.* 112:615–38, 1993.
Nistor, V. A bivariant Chern-Connes character. *Ann. Math.* 138:555–90, 1993.
Nistor, V. Group cohomology and the cyclic cohomology of crossed products. *Invent. Math.* 99:411–24, 1990.
Novikov, A., and G. Papanicolaou. Eddy viscosity of cellular flows. *J. Fluid Mech.* 446:173–98, 2001.
Novikov, A., and W. Pfeffer. An invariant Riemann type integral defined by figures. *Proc. Am. Math. Soc.* 120:849–54, 1994.
Barreira, L., and **Y. Pesin.** Lyapunov exponents and smooth ergodic theory. Publication of the AMS, *University Lecture Series,* 2001.
Pesin, Y. General theory of smooth dynamical systems. Encyclopedia of Mathematical Sciences, in *Dynamical Systems II: Ergodic Theory with Applications to Dynamical Systems and Statistical Mechanics,* 2nd edition, ed. Y. Sinai. New York–Berlin: Springer-Verlag, 1999.
Pesin, Y. *Dimension theory in dynamical systems: Contemporary views and applications.* Chicago Lectures in Mathematics Series. Chicago: University of Chicago Press, 1997.
Petrunin, A., X. Rong, and W. Tuschmann. Collapsing vs. positive pinching. *Geom. Funct. Anal.* 9(4):699–735, 1999.
Petrunin, A., and W. Tuschmann. Diffeomorphism finiteness, positive pinching, and second homotopy. *Geom. Funct. Anal.* 9(4):736–74, 1999.
Petrunin, A. Application of quasigeodesics and gradient curves, In *Comparison Geometry,* pp. 203-219, eds. K. Grove et al., Math. Sci. Res. Inst. Publ. 30, Cambridge Univ. Press, 1998.
Roe, J. *Elliptic Operators, Topology, and Asymptotic Methods,* Second Edition. CRC Press, 1999.
Roe, J. *Index Theory, Coarse Geometry, and the Topology of Manifolds.* Providence, Am. Math. Soc., 1996.
Rodseth, O., and **J. A. Sellers.** On m-ary partition function congruences: A fresh look at a past problem. *J. Number Theory* 87(2):270–81, 2001.
Hirschhorn, M. D., and **J. A. Sellers.** On representations of a number as a sum of three triangles. *Acta Arithmetica* 77:289–301, 1996.
Sellers, J. A. New congruences for generalized Frobenius partitions with 2 or 3 colors. *Discrete Math.* 367–74, 1994.
Simpson, S. G. *Subsystems of Second Order Arithmetic.* XIV + 445 pp. Springer-Verlag, 1999.
Humphreys, A. J., and **S. G. Simpson.** Separable Banach space theory needs strong set existence axioms. *Trans. Am. Math. Soc.* 348:4231–55, 1996.
Simpson, S. G. On the strength of König's duality theorem for countable bipartite graphs. *J. Symbolic Logic* 59:113–23, 1994.
Graczyk, J., and **G. Swiątek.** Induced expansion for quadratic polynomials. *Ann. Scient. Éc. Norm. Sup.* 29:399–482, 1996.
Graczyk, J., and **G. Swiatek.** Critical circle maps near bifurcation. *Commun. Math. Phys.* 176:227–60, 1996.
Swiatek, G. Rational rotation numbers for maps of the circle. *Commun. Math. Phys.* 119:109–28, 1988.
Tabachnikov, S., and M. Farber. Topology of cyclic configuration spaces and periodic orbits of multi-dimensional billards. *Topology* 41:553–89, 2002.
Fuchs, D., and **S. Tabachnikov**. Invariants of Legendrian and transverse knots in the standard contact space. *Topology* 36:1025–53, 1997.
Tabachnikov, S. *Billiards.* SMF "Panoramas et Syntheses," N1, 1995.
Tempelman, A. A. Dimension of random fractals in metric spaces. *Theory Probability Applications* 44(3)537–57, 2000.
Tempelman, A. A. Ergodic Theorems for Group Actions, Netherlands: Kluwer Academic Publishers, 1992.
Tempelman, A. A. Specific characteristics and variational principle for homogeneous random fields. *Zeits. Wahrscheinlichkeitstheorie Verw. Gebiete* 65:341–65, 1984.
Vaserstein, L. N., and E. Wheland. Two-dimensional representations of the free group in two generators over an arbitrary field. *Linear Algebra* 307:145–50, 2000.
Vaserstein, L. N. Quantum (abc)-theorems. *J. Number Theory* 81(2):351–68, 2000.
Vaserstein, L. N., and H. You. Normal subgroups of classical groups over rings. *J. P. Appl. Algebra* 105(1):93–106, 1995.
Vaughan, R. On a variance associated with the distribution of general sequences in arithmetic progressions II. *Phil. Trans. Royal Soc. Lond.* A 356:793–809, 1998.
Vaughan, R., and T. D. Wooley. Further improvements in Waring's problem, I. *Acta Math.* 174:147–240, 1995.
Montgomery, H. L., and **R. Vaughan.** On the distribution of reduced residues. *Ann. Math.* 123:311–33, 1986.
Wade, A. A generalization of Poisson-Nijenhuis structures. *J. Geom. Phys.* 39:217–32, 2001.
Wade, A. Conformal Dirac structures. *Lett. Math. Phys.* 53:331–48, 2000.
Wade, A. Modèles locaux de structures de Poisson singulières en dimension 3. *Bull. Soc. Math. Fr.* 125:573–618, 1997.
Waterhouse, W. Automorphism groups schemes of basic matrix invariants. *Trans. Am. Math. Soc.* 347:3859–72, 1995.
Waterhouse, W. A counterexample for Germain. *Am. Math. Monthly* 101:140–50, 1994.
Ugarcovici, I., and **H. Weiss.** Remarkable dynamics of an overcompensatory Leslie population model. *Nonlinearity,* in press.
Pollicott, M., and **H. Weiss.** Free energy as a dynamical invariant (or can you hear the shape of a potential?). *Comm. Math. Phys.* 240:457–82, 2003.
Knieper, G., and **H. Weiss.** Genericity of positive topological entropy for geodesic flows on the two-sphere. *J. Diff. Geometry* 62:127–41, 2003.
Hofer, H., **K. Wysocki,** and E. Zehnder. Foliations of the tight three sphere. *Ann. Math.* 157(1):125–255, 2003.
Floer, A., H. Hofer, and **K. Wysocki.** Applications of symplectic homology. *Math. Z.* 217(4):577–606, 1994.
Hofer, H., **K. Wysocki,** and E. Zehnder. The dynamics on a strictly convex energy surface in R^4. *Ann. Math.* 148:197–289, 1988.
Xu, J., and **L. Zikatanov.** The method of alternating projections and the method of subspace corrections in Hilbert space. *J. Am. Math. Soc.,* in press.
Xu, J., and **L. Zikatanov.** A monotone finite element scheme for convection diffusion equations. *Math. Comp.* 68:1429–46, 1999.
Chan, T. F., **J. Xu,** and **L. Zikatanov.** An agglomeration multigrid method for unstructured grids. *Contemp. Math.* 218:67–81, 1998.
Xu, P. Noncommutative Poisson algebras. *Am. J. Math.* 116:101–25, 1994.
Xu, P., and A. Weinstein. Classical solutions of the quantum Yang-Baxter equations. *Commun. Math. Phys.* 148:309–43, 1992.
Xu, P. Morita equivalence of Poisson manifolds. *Commun. Math. Phys.* 142:493–509, 1991.
Yee, A. J. A combinatorial proof of Andrews' partition functions related to Schur's partition theorem. *Proc. Amer. Math. Soc.* 130:2229–35, 2002.
Berndt, B. C., P. R. Bialek, and **A. J. Yee.** Formulas of Ramanujan for the power series coefficients of certain quotients of Eisenstein series. *Int. Math. Res. Notices* 21:1077–109, 2002.
Berndt, B. C., and **A. J. Yee.** Congruences for the coefficients of quotients of Eisenstein series. *Acta Arithmetica* 104:297–308, 2002.
Du, Q., C. Liu, and **P. Yu.** From micro to macro dynamics via a new moment closure approximation to the FENE model of polymeric fluids. *SIAM J. Multiscale Modeling Simulation,* in press.
Ta'asan, S., and **P. Yu.** Bridging micro and macro scales in fluids. *Proc. Tenth Int. Symp. Continuum Models Discrete Syst.,* Shoresh, Israel, June 30–July 4, 2003, in press.
Kinderlehrer, D., et al. **(P. Yu).** Multiscale modeling and simulation of grain boundary evolution. *Proceedings of the 44th AIAA/ASME/ ASCE.AHS Structures, Structural Dynamics, and Materials Conference,* Norfolk, Va., April 7–10, 2003, in press.
Zarhin, Y. G. Cyclic covers, their Jacobians and endomorphisms. *J. Reine Angew. Math.* 544:91–110, 2002.
Silverberg, A., and **Y. G. Zarhin.** Polarizations on abelian varieties and self-dual l-adic representations. *Compositio Math.* 126:25–45, 2001.
Zarhin, Y. G. Hyperelliptical Jacobians without complex multiplication. *Math. Res. Lett.* 7:123–32, 2000.
Zhang, P., and **Y. Zheng.** Weak solutions to a nonlinear variational wave equation. *Arch. Rat. Mech. Anal.* 166:303–19, 2003.
Mauser, N. J., P. Zhang, and **Y. Zheng.** The limit from the Schrodinger-Poisson to the Vlasov-Poisson equations with general data in one dimension. *Comm. Pure Appl. Math.* LV:582–632, 2002.
Zheng, Y. *Systems of Conservation Laws: Two-Dimensional Riemann Problems.* Birkhauser, 2001.

PURDUE UNIVERSITY

School of Science
Department of Mathematics

Program of Study

The Department of Mathematics offers programs leading to the degrees of Master of Science (M.S.) and Doctor of Philosophy (Ph.D.). There are several programs leading to the Master of Science degree, some of which prepare the student to seek nonacademic employment; others prepare the students to continue to the Ph.D. degree. The interdisciplinary computational science and engineering program gives students the opportunity to study mathematics and computing in a multidisciplinary environment. The master's degree program requires 30 hours of course work. The other programs include the new computational finance program, which requires 34 hours of course work. There are no required oral or written examinations, and a thesis is not required. A student with a half-time teaching assistantship normally takes two years to complete the master's degree program.

Among the requirements for the Ph.D. are a minimum of 42 hours of graduate work, reading knowledge in one foreign language, passing written qualifying examinations and an oral specialty examination, writing a thesis, and passing a final oral examination based on the thesis. A student with a half-time teaching assistantship would require a minimum of four years to complete the Ph.D. program, and most students spend five or six years in the program.

Research Facilities

The Mathematics Library features an outstanding collection of research journals and reference material in pure and applied mathematics. The department maintains a network of more than sixty Sun Workstations, several high-performance scientific computing and graphics workstations, and equipment for high-quality graphics output. Supported software includes TEX, Macaulay, MACSYMA, Maple, Mathematica, and MATLAB. University facilities for research computing include an Intel Paragon parallel supercomputer.

Financial Aid

Beginning graduate students who intend to work toward the Ph.D. degree and who supply application material by February 1 are considered for a fellowship. Andrews Fellowships provide a tax-free stipend of at least $18,000 for twelve months with all fees remitted except for $478 per semester. This fellowship is renewable for a second year. An additional stipend is provided to cover insurance costs. The department also makes nominations for Master's and Doctoral Purdue Fellowships. These fellowships provide a tax-free stipend of $18,000 for twelve months with all fees remitted except for $478 per semester. An additional stipend is provided to cover insurance costs. Both of these fellowships are renewable for a second year contingent upon satisfactory academic progress. Final selection of these fellows is made by the University committee.

The Department of Mathematics has been awarded VIGRE and GAANN grants that have created several graduate fellowships available to U.S. citizens and permanent residents. These fellowships carry a stipend of at least $18,000 per year for five years and greatly reduced teaching responsibilities. Fellows have the opportunity to involve themselves in innovative research structures. The Department of Mathematics anticipates awarding several of these fellowships to first-year graduate students. The department encourage all students with any interest in graduate study to consider applying to its program.

Graduate teaching assistantships are available with stipends ranging from $13,000 to $14,200 per academic year with a minimum of $14,200 for the most successful applicants who can be assigned to classroom teaching. Half-time assistants usually teach 4 hours per week. Fees are remitted to $478 per semester and $239 for the summer session. Several departmental fellowships with reduced teaching are given to outstanding candidates. Research fellowships are available for advanced students for both the summer and the academic year.

Purdue University is a tenable school under the provisions set forth by the Fannie and John Hertz Foundation. Hertz Fellowships cover tuition and all fees plus a $20,000 annual stipend.

Cost of Study

In 2004–05, tuition is $6092 per year for Indiana residents and $18,700 per year for out-of-state students. Students with assistantships do not pay tuition, but they do pay an annual fee of $992 per academic year. In 2005–06, the tuition and fees are expected to increase slightly. For the most current information, students should visit http://www.adpc.purdue.edu/Bursar.

Living and Housing Costs

The cost of dormitory rooms in University-supervised graduate residences ranges from $335 to $585 per month in 2004–05. The cost of one- or two-bedroom unfurnished apartments in Purdue Village ranges from $492 to $632 per month. Off-campus rates are comparable. For more detailed housing information, students should visit http://www.adpc.purdue.edu/HFS.

Student Group

Purdue's main campus has approximately 39,000 undergraduate students and 7,100 graduate students. There are 158 graduate students in mathematics, all of whom receive financial support.

Location

Purdue University is located in West Lafayette, Indiana, which lies on the banks of the Wabash River and has a population of approximately 29,000. Lafayette can be reached by car from Indianapolis in 1 hour and from downtown Chicago in 2 hours. The Purdue airport provides scheduled air service to St. Louis. The Lafayette–West Lafayette area (population 85,000 not including students) is nestled in a predominantly rural area. The local area has shopping malls, restaurants of note, two hospitals, two large municipal parks, and five golf courses. Two of Indiana's larger bodies of water, Lake Schafer and Lake Freeman, are a half hour away and feature water sports and beaches. Community groups that offer theatrical and musical programs include the Bach Chorale Singers, the Civic Theater, and the Lafayette Symphony Orchestra. The University offers musical, dramatic, and athletic events that may be attended by the general public.

The University and The Department

Purdue University, the land-grant college of Indiana, has achieved international recognition in the areas of agriculture, engineering, and science. Since 1960, the University has greatly expanded its efforts in the humanities but it remains a predominantly technical and scientific institution. The West Lafayette campus of Purdue enrolls about 39,000 students. The Purdue Department of Mathematics is one of the seven departments of Purdue's School of Sciences and consists of approximately 65 professors who are actively involved in the latest developments of every major area of mathematics. The department is one of the leading mathematical establishments in the United States and has earned an international reputation for its research and teaching excellence.

Applying

There is a $55 application fee. Completed applications for assistantships beginning in the fall semester should be received before March 15. Completed applications for fellowships should be received by February 1. Applicants should arrange to take the General Test and the Subject Test in mathematics of the Graduate Record Examinations so that scores are received by the department before February 1. A minimum TOEFL score of 570 on the written test (or 230 on the computer-based test) is required for all applicants whose native language is not English. An official score report not more than two years old must be submitted.

Correspondence and Information

Graduate Committee Chairman
Department of Mathematics
Purdue University
150 North University Street
West Lafayette, Indiana 47907-2067

Telephone: 765-494-1961
Fax: 765-494-0548
E-mail: gcomm@math.purdue.edu
World Wide Web: http://www.math.purdue.edu/academics/graduateProgram/

Purdue University

THE FACULTY AND THEIR RESEARCH

Algebra and Commutative Algebra
Sangki Choi, Visiting Scholar; Purdue, 1989. Commutative algebra, algebraic geometry.
Michael Drazin, Professor Emeritus of Mathematics; Cambridge, 1953. Noncommutative algebra.
William Heinzer, Professor of Mathematics; Florida State, 1966. Commutative algebra.
Jooyoun Hong, Visiting Assistant Professor; Rutgers, 2003. Commutative algebra.
Bernd Ulrich, Professor of Mathematics; Saarland, 1980. Commutative algebra.
Hans Ulrich Walther, Assistant Professor of Mathematics; Minnesota, 1999. Algebraic geometry, commutative algebra.

Algebraic Geometry
Shreeram Abhyankar, Marshall Distinguished Professor of Mathematics; Harvard, 1955. Algebraic geometry.
Donu Arapura, Professor of Mathematics; Columbia, 1985. Algebraic geometry.
Andrei Gabrielov, Professor of Mathematics and Earth and Atmospheric Sciences; Moscow State, 1973. Real algebraic and analytic geometry.
Joseph Lipman, Professor of Mathematics; Harvard, 1965. Algebraic geometry, commutative algebra.
Kenji Matsuki, Professor of Mathematics; Columbia, 1988. Algebraic geometry.
Tzuong-Tsieng Moh, Professor of Mathematics; Purdue, 1969. Algebraic geometry.
Jaroslaw Wisniewski, Visiting Associate Professor of Mathematics; Notre Dame, 1987. Algebraic geometry.
Jaroslaw Wlodarczyk, Associate Professor of Mathematics; Warsaw, 1993. Algebraic geometry.

Automorphic Forms, Lie Groups, and Representation Theory
David Goldberg, Associate Professor of Mathematics; Maryland, 1991. Representation theory.
Volker Heiermann, Visiting Professor of Mathematics; Provence (France), 1994. Representation theory.
Mark McKee, Research Assistant Professor; Princeton, 2002. Number theory, L-functions.
Dominic Naughton, Visiting Assistant Professor; Auburn, 1999. Representation theory of Lie algebras.
Richard Penney, Professor of Mathematics; MIT, 1971. Group representations, harmonic analysis, several complex variables.
Freydoon Shahidi, Distinguished Professor of Mathematics; Johns Hopkins, 1975. Automorphic forms.
John Wang, Professor of Mathematics; Cornell, 1966. Lie groups.
Jiu-Kang Yu, Associate Professor; Harvard, 1994. Representation theory, number theory, algebraic geometry.

Complex Analysis
Johnny Brown, Professor of Mathematics; Michigan, 1979. Complex variables.
Arsalan Chademan, Visiting Scholar; Paris, 1970. Complex analysis.
David Drasin, Professor of Mathematics; Cornell, 1966. Complex variables, potential theory.
Alexandre Eremenko, Professor of Mathematics; Rostov State, 1979. Complex analysis, dynamical systems.
Alexandre Fryntov, Visiting Associate Professor; Rostov State, 1977. Complex analysis.
Sam Perlis, Professor Emeritus of Mathematics; Chicago, 1938. Structure of analysis, theory of fields.
Grigore Tataru, Visiting Assistant Professor of Mathematics; MIT, 2003. Global analysis, pseudodifferential operators.
Allen Weitsman, Professor of Mathematics; Syracuse, 1968. Complex variables.

Complex Manifolds and Differential Geometry
Harold Donnelly, Professor of Mathematics; Berkeley, 1974. Differential geometry.
Yue Lin Tong, Professor of Mathematics; Johns Hopkins, 1970. Complex manifolds.
William Ugalde, Research Assistant Professor; Iowa, 2003. Conformal differential geometry.
Sai Kee Yeung, Professor of Mathematics; Columbia, 1989. Differential geometry, complex manifolds.

Functional Analysis, Operator Theory, and Operator Algebras
Aliprantis Charalambos, Professor of Economics and Mathematics; Caltech, 1973. Functional analysis, mathematical economics.
Lawrence Brown, Professor of Mathematics; Harvard, 1968. Operator algebras, operator theory.
Carl Cowen, Professor of Mathematics; Berkeley, 1976. Operator theory, complex analysis, linear algebra.
Marius Dadarlat, Professor of Mathematics; UCLA, 1991. Operator algebras, K-theory.
Louis de Branges de Bourcia, Edward C. Elliott Distinguished Professor of Mathematics; Cornell, 1957. Linear analysis, complex analysis, number theory.
Michael Jury, Research Assistant Professor of Mathematics; Washington (St. Louis), 2002. Operator theory.
Eung Il Ko, Visiting Scholar; Indiana, 1993. Operator theory.
Oana Mocioalca, Visiting Assistant Professor; Florida, 2002. Functional analysis/math finance.
Robert Zink, Professor Emeritus of Mathematics; Minnesota, 1953. Functional analysis.

Inverse Problems, Mathematical Physics, and Control Theory
Leonard Berkovitz, Professor Emeritus of Mathematics; Chicago, 1951. Control theory.

Logic and Set Theory
Leonard Lipshitz, Professor of Mathematics; Princeton, 1972. Logic, algebra.

Mathematical Biology
Zhilan Feng, Associate Professor of Mathematics; Arizona State, 1994. Mathematical biology, applied mathematics.
Fabio Milner, Professor of Mathematics; Chicago, 1983. Numerical analysis, applied mathematics.

Mathematics Education
Justin Price, Professor of Mathematics; Pennsylvania, 1956. Orthogonal expansions.

Numerical Methods
Zhiqiang Cai, Professor of Mathematics; Colorado, 1990. Numerical analysis, applied mathematics.
Min Chen, Associate Professor of Mathematics; Indiana, 1991. Numerical analysis, pde, scientific computing.
John Cushman, Professor of Agronomy and Mathematics; Iowa State, 1978. Applied mathematics.
Jim Douglas, Compere and Marcella Loveless Distinguished Professor Emeritus of Computational Mathematics; Rice, 1952. Computational modeling, numerical analysis.
Bradley Lucier, Professor of Mathematics and Computer Science; Chicago, 1981. Numerical analysis, wavelets.
Jae-Hong Pyo, Visiting Assistant Professor; Maryland, 2002. Finite element methods, fluid dynamics.
John Rice, Professor of Computer Sciences and Mathematics; Caltech, 1959. Applied mathematics, numerical analysis.
Juan Santos, Professor of Mathematics; Chicago, 1983. Numerical analysis, applied mathematics.
Jie Shen, Professor; Paris XI (South), 1987. Numerical analysis, pde, scientific computing.
LiLian, Wang, Postdoctoral Research Associate; Shanghai, 2002. Math analysis, numerical analysis.

Ordinary Differential Equations
William Fuller, Professor Emeritus of Mathematics; Purdue, 1957. Nonlinear differential equations.
Felix Haas, Professor Emeritus of Mathematics; MIT, 1952. Nonlinear differential equations, transformation groups.
Dmitry Novikov, Visiting Assistant Professor; Weizmann (Israel), 1998. Ordinary differential equations.

Partial Differential Equations
Patricia Bauman, Professor of Mathematics; Minnesota, 1982. Partial differential equations, applied mathematics.
Donatella Danielli, Assistant Professor of Mathematics; Purdue, 1999. Partial differential equations, applied mathematics, harmonic analysis.
Nicola Garofalo, Professor of Mathematics; Minnesota, 1987. Partial differential equations, harmonic analysis and geometry.
Michael Golomb, Professor Emeritus of Mathematics; Berlin, 1933. Approximation theory, differential equations.
Hala Jadallah, Research Assistant Professor of Mathematics; Indiana, 2001. Partial differential equations, calculus of variations.
Arshak Petrosyan, Assistant Professor; Royal Institute of Technology (Stockholm), 2000. Partial differential equations.
Daniel Phillips, Professor of Mathematics; Minnesota, 1981. Partial differential equations, applied mathematics.
Antonio Sa Barreto, Professor of Mathematics; MIT, 1988. Partial differential equations.
Plamen Stefanov, Associate Professor of Mathematics; Sofia (Bulgaria), 1988. Partial differential equations, math physics.
Federico Tournier, Visiting Assistant Professor; Temple, 2002. Partial differential equations.
Nung Kwan Yip, Associate Professor of Mathematics; Princeton, 1996. Partial differential equations.
Eleftherios Zachmanoglou, Professor of Mathematics; Berkeley, 1962. Partial differential equations.

Probability and Harmonic Analysis
Bañuelos, Rodrigo, Professor of Mathematics; UCLA, 1984. Probability and its applications to harmonic analysis, pde, spectral theory and geometry.
Burgess Davis, Professor of Mathematics and Statistics; Illinois, 1968. Probability.
Jin Ma, Professor of Mathematics; Minnesota, 1992. Probability.
Christoph Neugebauer, Professor of Mathematics; Ohio State, 1954. Harmonic analysis.
Mihai Pascu, Research Assistant Professor of Mathematics; Connecticut, 2001. Probability theory, stochastic processes.
Anastasia Ruzmaikina, Assistant Professor of Statistics and Mathematics; Princeton, 1999. Probability theory, ergodic theory, pde.
Frederi Viens, Associate Professor of Statistics and Mathematics; California, Irvine, 1996. Probability, stochastic processes, mathematical finance.

Several Complex Variables
Steven Bell, Professor of Mathematics; MIT, 1979. Several complex variables.
Gregery Buzzard, Associate Professor; Michigan, 1995. Several complex variables.
David Catlin, Professor of Mathematics; Princeton, 1978. Several complex variables.
Sanghyun Cho, Visiting Scholar; Purdue, 1991. Several complex variables.
Laszlo Lempert, Professor of Mathematics; Eötvös Lorand (Budapest), 1979. Complex analysis.
Malgorzata Stawiska, Research Assistant Professor of Mathematics; Northwestern, 2001. Several complex variables, dynamical systems.

Statistics
Herman Rubin, Professor of Statistics and Mathematics; Chicago, 1948. Statistics.
William Studden, Professor of Statistics and Mathematics; Stanford, 1962. Probability and statistics.

Topology
James Becker, Professor of Mathematics; Michigan, 1964. Algebraic topology.
Daniel Davis, Research Assistant Professor of Mathematics; Northwestern, 2003. Algebraic topology.
Daniel Gottlieb, Professor of Mathematics; UCLA, 1962. Algebraic topology, mathematical physics.
Andrew Mauer-Oats, Research Assistant Professor; Illinois, 2001. Algebraic topology.
James McClure, Professor of Mathematics; Chicago, 1978. Topology.
Jeffrey Smith, Professor of Mathematics; MIT, 1981. Algebraic topology.
Stephen Weingram, Associate Professor of Mathematics; Princeton, 1962. Algebraic topology.
Clarence Wilkerson, Professor of Mathematics; Rice, 1970. Algebraic topology.

PURDUE UNIVERSITY

Department of Statistics

Programs of Study The Master of Science programs in statistics with emphases in applied statistics, statistics and computer science, or computational finance serve students' interests in careers as statisticians in industry and government. These degree programs do not require a thesis and are usually completed in two years. Students in the programs are encouraged to participate in the department's consulting service.

The Doctor of Philosophy program in statistics prepares students for careers in university teaching and research or in government or industrial research. Students take a three-semester core program in probability and theoretical and applied statistics in preparation for general examinations. Specialized study and thesis research in the student's chosen area follows. Students are encouraged to strengthen their training through advanced courses and participation in statistical consulting. Completion of the Ph.D. program normally takes four or five years.

Research Facilities The Department of Statistics is housed in the Mathematical Sciences Building along with the Department of Mathematics. This building contains faculty and graduate student offices, seminar rooms, classrooms, the Mathematical Sciences Library. The library contains 57,000 volumes and subscribes to 550 journals in mathematics and related fields.

The Statistics Department has a network of IBM RS/6000 servers and workstations and Windows NT PCs. Graduate students can access the departmental IBM RS/6000 servers using X terminals in their offices, through one of the X terminals or PCs in one of the Stat Labs elsewhere on campus, through dial-up access, or from anywhere on the Internet. Access to Windows-based applications is available via the Windows NT labs or X terminals in student offices via a Windows Terminal Server. Statistical software packages maintained on departmental computers include SAS, SPSS, S-Plus, R Mathematica, Maple, and Matlab. Other software packages are available through the Information Technology at Purdue (ITaP). The equipment is maintained by ITaP, a full-time computer systems administrator, a Webmaster, and 2 part-time assistant computer systems administrators.

Financial Aid Most students have half-time teaching assistantships. For 2004–05, half-time teaching assistantships have a minimum stipend of $15,000 for the fall and spring semesters, plus reduction of tuition and fees to $992 per academic year and $261 for the summer session. Purdue University assistantships are available to entering students on a competitive basis; the assistantship stipend for 2004–05 is at least $24,000 for one year, with tuition and fees reduced as above. The assistantships may be renewed for one year for students with good records.

Cost of Study In 2004–05, tuition is $6092 per year for Indiana residents and $18,700 per year for out-of-state students. Students with assistantships do not pay tuition, but they do pay a fee of $992 per academic year. In 2005–06, the tuition and fees are expected to increase slightly. For the most current information, students should visit http://www.adpc.purdue.edu/Bursar.

Living and Housing Costs The cost of dormitory rooms in University-supervised graduate residences ranges from $335 to $585 per month in 2004–05. The cost of one- or two-bedroom unfurnished apartments in Purdue Village ranges from $492 to $632 per month. Off-campus rates are comparable. For more detailed housing information, students should visit http://www.adpc.purdue.edu/HFS.

Student Group Purdue University has about 7,100 graduate students. The Department of Statistics has 97 graduate students, with 64 working toward the Ph.D. About two fifths are women and about two thirds are international students. Many of the American students begin graduate work immediately after the B.S. Some enter after the M.S., and a few have some work experience.

The Graduate Student Organization (GSO) is a group concerned with the input and opinions of graduate students on matters such as department policy, course requirements, and new course creation. All students admitted to the department are automatically members. The organization also serves as a social group, introducing new members to each other and to previous members related to Purdue University and the immediate area.

Location Purdue University is the principal institution in West Lafayette, Indiana, which has a population of 30,000. In the larger Lafayette–West Lafayette area (population, 140,000), there are several other large organizations. Although Lafayette is an industrial town, it retains the atmosphere of an agricultural county seat. However, there are shopping malls, restaurants of note, two hospitals, and two large municipal parks. The Purdue University Airport (LAF) is served by American Airlines. Community groups present plays, operettas, and musical programs several times each year, and the University offers musical, dramatic, and athletic events that may be attended by the general public. Several state parks are close to Lafayette.

The University and The Department Purdue University, the land-grant college of Indiana, has achieved international recognition in the areas of agriculture, engineering, and science. The West Lafayette campus of Purdue enrolls about 39,000 students. Purdue University is an Equal Opportunity/Affirmative Action employer.

The Department of Statistics is one of the seven departments that constitute Purdue's School of Science. The department's faculty members interact with other faculty members and graduate students through teaching, research, and a statistical consulting service. The faculty quality has been consistently ranked among the top ten statistics departments in the country by the National Research Council Surveys.

Applying Applicants should submit their application online at http://www.stat.purdue.edu/academics/graduateProgram or http://www.stat.edu/GradSchool/Admissions. An applicant's mathematical training should include linear algebra and advanced calculus; probability and mathematical statistics are desirable.

Applications for Purdue University fellowships and assistantships have the best chance of acceptance if received before January 15. Other applications are considered at any time, although the availability of assistantships becomes limited after mid-April. Other helpful Web sites include Purdue Graduate School (http://www.purdue.edu/GradSchool), International Students and Scholars (http://www.purdue.edu/OIP/iss), and American Statistical Association (http://www.amstat.org).

Correspondence and Information

Department of Statistics
Mathematical Sciences Building
Purdue University
150 North University
West Lafayette, Indiana 47907-2067

Telephone: 765-494-5794
E-mail: graduate@stat.purdue.edu
World Wide Web: http://www.stat.purdue.edu

Purdue University

THE FACULTY AND THEIR RESEARCH

Mary Ellen Bock, Head (Illinois at Urbana-Champaign). Nonparmetric regression, statistical computing, genome analysis.
Bill Cleveland (Yale). Computer networking, machine learning, data mining, statistical models and model building, time series, data visualization.
Bruce Craig (Wisconsin–Madison). Bayesian hierarchical models, Markov chain Monte Carlo methods, experimental design, statistical genetics.
Anirban DasGupta (Indian Statistical Institute). Mathematical statistics, applied probability.
Burgess Davis (Illinois at Urbana-Champaign). Probability.
Rebecca Doerge (North Carolina State). Statistical issues in quantitative genetics, resampling methods, regression.
Jayanta K. Ghosh (Calcutta). Bayesian analysis, asymptotics, stochastic modeling.
Chong Gu (Wisconsin–Madison). Statistical computing, nonparametric estimation.
Kristofer Jennings (Stanford). Statistical computing nonparametric estimation.
Thomas Kuczek (Purdue). Experimental design, response surface alternatives to Taguchi, probability models in biology.
Mihails Levins (Pennsylvania). Nonparametric regression, variance estimation in the empirical finance context, nonlinear time series.
George P. McCabe (Columbia). Applications of statistics.
Herman Rubin (Chicago). Mathematical statistics, probability theory, numerical methods, robustness, decision theory.
Anastasia Rumzaikina (Princeton). Mathematical physics, probability theory, stochastic processes, large deviations, PDE's dynamical systems and statistical mechanics.
Thomas Sellke (Stanford). Sequential analysis, probability theory.
Katy L. Simonsen (Cornell). Statistical genetics, coalescent models, linkage analysis.
Jongwoo Song (Chicago). Statistical genetics, microarray data analysis, clustering/classification, semiparametric mixture model, dissimilarity measure in time series data.
Seongjoo Song (Chicago). Pricing and hedging of derivative securities in an imcomplete market, convergence of stochastic processes.
William J. Studden (Stanford). Optimal designs, spline smoothing, canonical moments.
Frederi Viens (California, Irvine). Probability, theory, stochastic PDEs, applications to finance, filtering, fluid dynamics.
Jing Wu (USC). Bioinformatics.
Bowei Xi (Michigan). Internet tomography, computer networking, combinatorial and global optimization.
Jun Xie (UCLA). Computational statistics, Markov chain Monte Carlo methods, bioinformatics and computational biology.
Tonglin Zhang (Michigan). Problems in restricted parameter spaces, statistical problems in clinical trial, spatial data analysis.
Michael Zhu (Michigan). Developing and applying statistical methodology to industrial applications, including manufacturing, computer software engineering, and drug discovery.

RECENT PUBLICATIONS

Bock, M. E., A. Apostolico, S. Lonardi, and X. Xu. Efficient detection of unusual words. *J. Comput. Biol.* 7:71–94, 2000.
Craig, B. A., W. Gu, and Z. Feng. Developing an integrated model of land-use/land-cover change. In *Conserving Biodiversity in Agricultural Landscapes: Model-Based Planning Tools,* eds. R. K. Swihart and J. E. Moore. West Lafayette, Ind.: Purdue University Press, in press.
DasGupta, A., W. Wang, and J. T. Hwang. Statistical tests for multivariate bioequivalence. *Biometricka* 86, 395–402, 1999.
Davis, B. Brownian motion and random walk perturbed at extrema. *Probability Theory Related Fields* 113:501–18, 1999.
Doerge, R., B. A. Craig, and M. A. Black. Gene expression data: The technology and statistical analysis. *J. Agric. Biol. Environ. Stat.* 8(1):1–28, 2003.
Ghosh, J. K., and B. Clarke. Convergence of posterior given sample mean. *Ann. Stat.* 23:2116–44, 1995.
Gu, C. Smoothing spline density estimation: Conditional distribution. *Stat. Sin.* 5:709–26, 1995.
Kuczek, T., and T. C. K. Chan. The rate-normal model for tumor drug resistance. *Cancer Chemo. Pharm.* 30:355–9, 1992.
McCabe, G. P., and G. H. Beaton. Efficacy of intermittent iron supplementation in the control of iron deficiency anemia in developing countries. *Report to the Micronutrient Initiative and the Canadian International Development Agency,* 1999.
Moore, D. S. Undergraduate programs and the future of academic statistics. *Am. Statistician* 55:1–6, 2001.
Rubin, H., and K. S. Song. Exact computation of the asymptotic efficiency of maximum likelihood estimators of discontinuous signal in a Gaussian white noise. *Ann. Stat.* 23:732–9, 1995.
Samuels, S. M. A Bayesian species-sampling-inspired approach to the uniques problem in microdata disclosure risk assessment. *J. Official Stats.* 14:1998.
Sellke, T., and S. P. Lalley. Hyperbolic branching Brownian motion. *Probability Theory Related Fields* 108:171–92, 1997.
Simonsen, K., and G. A. Churchill. A Markov chain model of coalescence with recombination. *Theoretical Popul. Biol.* 52:43–59, 1997.
Studden, W. J., and H. Dette. *The Theory of Canonical Moments.* New York: John Wiley & Sons, 1997.
Viens, F., and D. Nualart. Evolution equation of a stochastic semigroup with white-noise drift. *Ann. Prob.* 28(1):36–73, 2000.
Xie, J., O. Catoni, and D. Chen. The reduction method, the loop erase exit path, and the meta-stability of the biased majority vote process. *Stochastic Processes Appl.* 86(2):231–61, 2000.

SOUTHERN ILLINOIS UNIVERSITY CARBONDALE

Department of Mathematics
Doctoral Program

Program of Study

The Department of Mathematics of Southern Illinois University Carbondale (SIUC) offers a degree program leading to the Doctor of Philosophy (Ph.D.) degree in mathematics. This program, which was established in 1964, is designed to prepare students for careers in business, industry, government, and academia requiring advanced training in mathematics and statistics.

Students in the program work closely with members of the faculty in course work and research in a wide variety of fields of pure and applied mathematics. The graduate adviser works directly with each student in the program to develop an individualized plan of study. Recent graduates have written doctoral dissertations in the areas of algebra and number theory, combinatorics, differential equations, numerical analysis, probability and stochastic analysis, and statistics. There is also a concentration in computational mathematics, in which the student completes courses in both computer science and mathematics. Graduate students are encouraged to participate in the variety of research seminars organized by Department faculty members. An active colloquium program regularly brings outside speakers into the Department.

Roughly half of the students in the doctoral program are admitted directly into the program; the other half enter the Department in the master's program and are accepted into the doctoral program upon successful completion of the requirements for that degree.

Research Facilities

The Department of Mathematics maintains a computer lab that was equipped with the support of a grant from the National Science Foundation. The thirty PCs in this lab are programmed with sophisticated mathematical software and are networked for access to the Internet and to high-speed laser printers, and the lab is equipped with a projection panel for instructional purposes. Graduate students have 24-hour access to the lab for use in their research or for the preparation of papers and reports. Graduate student offices are also equipped with PCs that are connected to the Department network. The American Mathematical Society's Mathematical Reviews and other resources can be accessed directly through the network. Morris Library, the main library on campus, has extensive collections of books and journals in mathematics and related disciplines; additional materials can be retrieved via interlibrary loan. The Department also maintains a small independent reading library where students can read current journals and access copies of theses and dissertations of former students.

Financial Aid

Nearly all students in the program receive financial assistance, primarily in the form of teaching assistantships. Assistantship responsibilities include direct classroom teaching and/or a combination of teaching support duties. Some assistantship support is usually available during the summer term. Strong applicants are nominated by the Department for fellowships. Teaching assistantships and fellowships both include a tuition waiver. Information on other forms of financial aid, such as student loans or work-study programs, is available from the Financial Aid Office (telephone: 618-453-4334; e-mail: fao@siu.edu).

Cost of Study

In-state tuition is $192 per semester credit hour in 2004–05. Out-of-state tuition is 2.5 times the in-state tuition rate. Fees vary from $356 (1 credit hour) to $707 (12 credit hours).

Living and Housing Costs

For married couples, students with families, and single graduate students, the University has 589 efficiency and one-, two-, and three-bedroom apartments that rent for $374 to $458 per month in 2004–05. Residence halls for single graduate students are also available, as are accessible residence hall rooms and apartments for students with disabilities.

Student Group

Applicants are considered for acceptance into the doctoral program if they have completed with distinction a program comparable to that for the master's degree in mathematics, statistics, or computer science at SIUC. Additional evidence of outstanding scholarly ability or achievement (e.g., a high score on the advanced section of the GRE or published research papers of high quality) lends strength to the application.

Student Outcomes

On average, between 2 and 3 students earn their Ph.D. degrees in the program each year. Among the most recent graduates of the program, more than half are employed in a variety of research-oriented positions in private industry, business, and government, and the others are employed in positions involving research and/or teaching in colleges and universities throughout the U.S. Graduates hold tenured faculty positions at such institutions as the University of Memphis, James Madison University, the University of Dayton, and Tennessee Technological University.

Location

SIUC is 350 miles south of Chicago and 100 miles southeast of St. Louis. Nestled in rolling hills bordered by the Ohio and Mississippi Rivers and enhanced by a mild climate, the area has state parks, national forests and wildlife refuges, and large lakes for outdoor recreation. Cultural offerings include theater, opera, concerts, art exhibits, and cinema. Educational facilities for the families of students are excellent.

The University

Southern Illinois University Carbondale is a comprehensive public university with a variety of general and professional education programs. The University offers associate, bachelor's, master's, and doctoral degrees; the J.D. degree; and the M.D. degree. The University is fully accredited by the North Central Association of Colleges and Schools. The graduate school has an essential role in the development and coordination of graduate instruction and research programs. The Graduate Council has academic responsibility for determining graduate standards, recommending new graduate programs and research centers, and establishing policies to facilitate the research effort.

Applying

The forms needed to apply for admission to the program can be accessed through the department's Web site listed below. All applications for admission are considered for financial support, unless requested otherwise. In order to be considered for a fellowship, the applicant must take the GRE General Test. Review of applications for the fall semester begins around February 1. There is no application fee.

Correspondence and Information

Applications and supporting documents should be sent to:

Director of Graduate Studies
c/o Graduate Admissions Secretary
Department of Mathematics
Southern Illinois University
Carbondale, Illinois 62902-4408
World Wide Web:
http://www.math.siu.edu/gradprogs.html

Specific questions or inquiries or further information regarding the department and its programs may be directed to:

Professor S. Jeyaratnam
Director of Graduate Studies
Department of Mathematics
Southern Illinois University
Carbondale, Illinois 62901-4408
Telephone: 618-453-5302
E-mail: gradinfo@math.siu.edu
World Wide Web: http://www.math.siu.edu

Southern Illinois University Carbondale

THE FACULTY AND THEIR RESEARCH

Dubravka Ban, Assistant Professor; Dr.Sci., Zagreb (Croatia), 1998. Algebra, number theory, automorphic forms.
Bhaskar Bhattacharya, Associate Professor; Ph.D., Iowa, 1993. Order restricted statistical inference, I-projections, linear models, multivariate analysis.
Gregory Budzban, Associate Professor; Ph.D., South Florida, 1991. Probability on algebraic structures, stochastic methods in image processing.
Lane Clark, Professor; Ph.D., New Mexico, 1980. Extremal graph theory, random graphs and enumeration.
Andrew Earnest, Professor; Ph.D., Ohio State, 1975. Algebra, algebraic number theory, arithmetic theory of quadratic forms.
Philip Feinsilver, Professor; Ph.D., NYU (Courant), 1975. Probability theory, representation theory.
Robert Fitzgerald, Professor; Ph.D., UCLA, 1980. Quadratic forms and algebra.
John Gregory, Professor; Ph.D., UCLA, 1969. Optimization theory, numerical analysis, applied functional analysis.
Ronald Grimmer, Professor; Ph.D., Iowa, 1967. Differential equations, integral equations, operator semigroups, applied mathematics.
H. Randolph Hughes, Associate Professor; Ph.D., Northwestern, 1988. Stochastic processes, stochastic differential geometry.
Sakthivel Jeyaratnam, Professor; Ph.D., Colorado State, 1978. Statistics, linear models, variance components, robust inference.
David Kammler, Professor; Ph.D., Michigan, 1971. Approximation theory, Fourier analysis, numerical analysis, applications of mathematics.
Jerzy Kocik, Assistant Professor; Ph.D., Southern Illinois at Carbondale, 1989. Mathematical physics, lie algebras, differential-geometric structures, symplectic geometry.
Donald Mills, Assistant Professor; Ph.D., Clemson, 1999. Algebra, number theory, finite fields.
Salah-Eldin Mohammed, Professor; Ph.D., Warwick (England), 1976. Stochastic analysis, deterministic and stochastic hereditary dynamical systems, probabilistic analysis of PDEs.
Abdel-Razzaq Mugdadi, Assistant Professor; Ph.D., Northern Illinois, 1999. Statistics.
Edward Neuman, Professor; Ph.D., Wroclaw (Poland), 1972. Numerical analysis, spline functions, approximation theory, special functions.
David Olive, Assistant Professor; Ph.D., Minnesota, 1998. Applications of high breakdown robust statistics, regression graphics, applied probability theory.
George Parker, Associate Professor; Ph.D., California, San Diego, 1971. Differential geometry, classical geometry, linear programming.
Kathleen Pericak-Spector, Professor; Ph.D., Carnegie Mellon, 1980. Hyperbolic PDEs, continuum mechanics, science education.
Thomas Porter, Associate Professor; Ph.D., New Mexico, 1990. Combinatorial analysis and graph theory.
Don Redmond, Associate Professor; Ph.D., Illinois, 1976. Analytic and elementary number theory, classical analysis, history of mathematics.
Henri Schurz, Professor; Ph.D., Humboldt University Berlin, 1997. Stochastic analysis, stochastic dynamical systems, mathematical finance.
Scott Spector, Professor; Ph.D., Carnegie Mellon, 1978. Elasticity and continuum mechanics.
Michael Sullivan, Associate Professor; Ph.D., Texas at Austin, 1992. Topological dynamical systems and knot theory.
Walter Wallis, Professor; Ph.D., Sydney, 1968. Combinatorics and combinatorial computing.
Mary Wright, Professor; Ph.D., McGill Montreal, 1980. Rings and modules.
MingQuing Xiao, Assistant Professor; Ph.D., Illinois, 1997. Partial differential equations, control theory, optimization theory, dynamical systems, computational science.
Joseph Yucas, Professor; Ph.D., Penn State, 1978. Algebra and combinatorics.
Marvin Zeman, Professor; Ph.D., NYU, 1974. Partial differential equations, integro-differential equations, numerical analysis.

STONY BROOK UNIVERSITY, STATE UNIVERSITY OF NEW YORK

College of Arts and Sciences
Department of Mathematics

Programs of Study

Both the Master of Arts and Ph.D., professional option, and Master of Arts, secondary teacher option, are offered by the Department of Mathematics.

The professional option is designed for students who plan careers as professional mathematicians in research or teaching at colleges and universities or in finance, industry, or government. Almost all students in this option are full-time. At least one year of full-time study is required. The secondary teacher option is a two-year, part-time program designed for secondary teachers who seek permanent certification. The courses are given in the evenings and in the summer in a two-year cycle, each being offered once every two years.

Research Facilities

The department has an extensive computer network, primarily using Linux and Solaris platforms, but also PCs and Macintoshes. There are computers in the offices of both faculty members and graduate students, as well as a number of workstations in public areas for use by students, faculty members, and visitors. In addition, there is an instructional lab with 30 Sun workstations and 25 Windows machines in which computer-related courses are taught. Several faculty members and many graduate students use computation as part of their research.

Financial Aid

Because Stony Brook is committed to attracting quality students, the graduate school provides two competitive fellowships for U.S. citizens and permanent residents. Graduate Council fellowships are for outstanding doctoral candidates studying in any discipline, and the W. Burghardt Turner Fellowships target outstanding African-American, Hispanic-American, and Native American students entering either a doctoral or master's degree program. For doctoral students, both fellowships provide a minimum annual stipend of $20,850 for up to five years, as well as a full tuition scholarship. For master's students, the Turner Fellowship provides an annual stipend of $10,000 for up to two years with a full tuition scholarship. Health insurance subsidies are also provided within a scale depending on the size of the fellow's dependent family. Departments and degree programs award approximately 900 teaching and graduate assistantships and approximately 600 research assistantships on an annual basis. Full assistantships carry a stipend amount that usually ranges from $11,260 to $18,000, depending on the department.

Cost of Study

In 2003–04, full-time tuition was $3450 per semester for state residents and $5250 per semester for nonresidents. Part-time tuition was $288 per credit hour for residents and $438 per credit hour for nonresidents. Additional charges included an activity fee of $22 and a comprehensive fee of $242.50 per semester.

Living and Housing Costs

University apartments range in cost from approximately $208 per month to approximately $1180 per month, depending on the size of the unit. Off-campus housing options include furnished rooms to rent and houses and/or apartments to share that can be rented for $350 to $550 per month.

Location

Stony Brook's campus is approximately 50 miles east of Manhattan on the north shore of Long Island. The cultural offerings of New York City and Suffolk County's countryside and seashore are conveniently located nearby. Cold Spring Harbor Laboratories and Brookhaven National Laboratories are easily accessible from, and have close relationships with, the University.

The University

The University, established in 1957, achieved national stature within a generation. Founded at Oyster Bay, Long Island, the school moved to its present location in 1962. Stony Brook has grown to encompass more than 110 buildings on 1,100 acres. There are approximately 1,568 faculty members, and the annual budget is more than $805 million. The Graduate Student Organization oversees the spending of the student activity fee for graduate student campus events. International students find the additional four-week Summer Institute in American Living very helpful. The Intensive English Center offers classes in English as a second language. The Career Development Office assists with career planning and has information on permanent full-time employment. Disabled Student Services has a Resource Center that offers placement testing, tutoring, vocational assessment, and psychological counseling. The Counseling Center provides individual, group, family, and marital counseling and psychotherapy. Day-care services are provided in four on-campus facilities. The Writing Center offers tutoring in all phases of writing.

Applying

Applicants are judged on the basis of distinguished undergraduate records (and graduate records, if applicable), thorough preparation for advanced study and research in the field of interest, candid appraisals from those familiar with the applicant's academic/professional work, potential for graduate study, and a clearly defined statement of purpose and scholarly interest germane to the program. For the professional option, a baccalaureate degree with a major in mathematics or the equivalent is required, with a minimum overall grade point average of 2.75 and an average grade of B in the major and related courses. For the secondary teacher option, a baccalaureate degree, two years of college-level mathematics, including one year of single variable calculus, one semester of linear algebra and one more semester of mathematics beyond single variable calculus are required, in addition to a 3.0 grade point average in all calculus and post-calculus mathematics courses, and a New York State certification for teaching mathematics. Students should submit admission and financial aid applications by January 15 for the fall semester and by October 1 for the spring semester. Decisions are made on a rolling basis as space permits.

Correspondence and Information

Lowell E. Jones, Graduate Program Director
Department of Mathematics
Stony Brook University, State University of New York
Stony Brook, New York 11790-3651
Telephone: 631-632-8248
Fax: 631-632-7631
E-mail: gpd@math.sunysb.edu
World Wide Web: http://www.math.sunysb.edu

Stony Brook University, State University of New York

THE FACULTY AND THEIR RESEARCH

Michael Anderson, Professor; Ph.D., Indiana, 1981. Differential geometry.
Christopher Bishop, Professor; Ph.D., Chicago, 1987. Complex analysis.
Araceli M. Bonifant, IMS Lecturer; Ph.D., CUNY, City College, 1995. Dynamical systems.
Alastair Craw, James H. Simons Instructor; Ph.D., University of Warwick, 2001. Algebraic geometry.
Mark Andrea de Cataldo, Assistant Professor; Ph.D., Notre Dame, 1995. Algebraic geometry.
David Ebin, Professor; Ph.D., MIT, 1967. Global analysis, mathematics of continuum mechanics, partial differential equations.
Daryl Geller, Professor; Ph.D., Princeton, 1977. Partial differential equations, harmonic analysis, several complex variables, lie groups.
James Glimm, Professor; Ph.D., Columbia, 1959. Applied mathematics, numerical analysis, mathematical physics.
Detlef Gromoll, Leading Professor; Ph.D., Bonn, 1964. Differential geometry.
Basak Gurel, James H. Simons Instructor; Ph.D., California, Santa Cruz, 2003. Hamiltonian dynamical systems, symplectic geometry and topology.
C. Denson Hill, Professor; Ph.D., NYU, 1966. Partial differential equations, several complex variables.
Lowell Jones, Professor; Ph.D., Yale, 1970. Topology, geometry.
Alexander Kirillov Jr., Associate Professor; Ph.D., Yale, 1995. Algebra, representation theory.
Anthony Knapp, Professor Emeritus; Ph.D., Princeton, 1965. Lie groups, representation theory.
Irwin Kra, Distinguished Service Professor; Ph.D., Columbia, 1966. Complex analysis, Kleinian groups.
Matthew Kuzdin, VIGRE Fellow; Ph.D., Indiana, 2002. Riemannian geometry.
Paul G. Kumpel, Professor; Ph.D., Brown, 1964. Algebraic topology.
H. Blaine Lawson Jr., Distinguished Professor; Ph.D., Stanford, 1968. Differential geometry, topology, geometric measure theory, several complex variables, algebraic geometry.
Neil Portnoy, Assistant Professor; Ph.D., New Hampshire, 1998. Operator theory on spaces of analytic functions, mathematics education.
Justin Sawon, James H. Simons Instructor; Ph.D., Trinity (Hartford), Cambridge College, 2000. Geometry.
Santiago Simanca, Director of Mathematical Computing; Ph.D., MIT, 1985. Differential geometry, analysis.
Rasul Shafikov, James H. Simons Instructor; Ph.D., Indiana, 2001. Several complex variables.
Dennis Sullivan, Distinguished Professor; Ph.D., Princeton, 1965. Theory of manifolds, triangulations, and algebraic topology; differential forms and homotopy theory; foliations, laminations and low dimensional dynamical systems; Riemann surfaces and Kleinian groups; fluid evolution and computation; quantum theory; topology.
Scott Sutherland, Associate Professor; Ph.D., Boston University, 1989. Dynamical systems, root-finding algorithms, computing.
Leon Takhtajan, Professor; Ph.D., Steklova Institute of Mathematics, 1975. Mathematical physics.
John Terilla, VIGRE Fellow; Ph.D., North Carolina at Chapel Hill, 2001. Deformation theory, mathematical physics.

STONY BROOK UNIVERSITY, STATE UNIVERSITY OF NEW YORK

College of Engineering and Applied Sciences
Department of Applied Mathematics and Statistics

Programs of Study

The Department of Applied Mathematics and Statistics offers programs leading to the master's and Doctor of Philosophy degrees. Special strengths in applied mathematics and statistics include computational fluid dynamics, operations research, applied statistics, numerical analysis, and bioinformatics. All students receive a broad range of basic and advanced training in mathematics and applied mathematics.

The Ph.D. program consists of an individually designed selection of advanced courses followed by a program of research leading to a dissertation. Students are required to pass a written comprehensive examination and an oral preliminary examination.

The master's degree program focuses on specific mathematical sciences skills needed for a career as a teacher or an industrial mathematician.

All students receive personal attention and advising at all levels. There are numerous seminars and colloquia, featuring both distinguished guest speakers and Stony Brook faculty members. These present both accelerated background knowledge and ongoing research. The Institute for Mathematical Modeling is under the direction of James Glimm. The department has close ties and joint activities with many units on campus, including the Institute for Theoretical Physics, Harriman College of Management, and the Computer Science Department as well as nearby Brookhaven National Laboratory and Cold Spring Harbor Laboratory.

Research Facilities

The department is housed in the Mathematics Building. Each graduate student shares an office with at least one other student. The mathematics-physics library, located in an adjoining building, contains 50,000 books and subscribes to about 500 journals. The department has about 150 Sun Workstations and state-of-the-art PCs, most available to graduate students.

Financial Aid

The department is currently supporting 10 students on various fellowships, with stipends ranging from $18,000 to $30,000; 28 students on teaching assistantships; and 25 students on research assistantships. The assistantship stipends range from $11,650 to $18,000. All students supported by the department also receive tuition remission. Summer support is available in certain research areas.

Cost of Study

In 2003–04, tuition was $288 and $438 per credit hour for state and out-of-state residents, respectively. Full-time tuition per semester was $3450 for state residents and $5250 for out-of-state residents. Additional charges include an activity fee of $5 and a comprehensive fee of $80 per semester.

Living and Housing Costs

Monthly rents at the University apartments range from $320 to $1000 per month, depending on the locations and the size of the room. The off-campus housing office assists in locating available apartments or houses to share, which can be rented for $350 to $550 per month.

Student Group

The number of full-time graduate students in the Department of Applied Mathematics and Statistics is about 140. The department awards about eleven Ph.D.'s and thirty M.S.'s annually. In spring 2003, the department had 149 students, of whom 93 percent were full-time, 35 percent were master's, and 65 percent were doctoral students; 45 percent were women.

Student Outcomes

Recent graduates have found positions as faculty members and postdoctoral fellows in academia, financial and risk analysts in the financial sector, biostatisticians in medical and research centers, research scientists in industrial and national laboratories, and actuaries in insurance companies. Their places of employment include Harvard University; New York University's Courant Institute; Rutgers University; Franklin and Marshall College; Worcester Polytechnic Institute; Eli Lilly Pharmaceuticals; M. D. Anderson Cancer Center; Bell Labs; IBM Watson Research Center; Los Alamos National Laboratory; Chase Manhattan Bank; Bear, Stearns & Co.; American Express; Metropolitan Life Insurance Company; and the U.S. Department of Transportation.

Location

Stony Brook's campus is approximately 50 miles east of Manhattan on the North Shore of Long Island. The cultural offerings of New York City and Suffolk County's countryside and seashore are conveniently located nearby. Cold Spring Harbor Laboratories and Brookhaven National Laboratory are easily accessible and have close relationships with the University.

The University and The Department

The University, established in 1957, achieved national stature within a generation. Founded in Oyster Bay, Long Island, the school moved to its present location in 1962. Stony Brook has grounds that encompass more than 110 buildings on 1,100 acres. The University enrolls about 21,000 students, including 7,000 graduate students. There are more than 1,565 faculty members, and the annual budget is more than $805 million. The Graduate Student Organization oversees the spending of the student activity fee for graduate student campus events. International students find the additional four-week Summer Institute in American Living very helpful. The Intensive English Center offers classes in English as a second language. The Career Development Office offers career planning and has information on permanent full-time employment. Disabled students have a resource center that offers placement testing, tutoring, vocational assessment, counseling, and psychotherapy. Day-care services are provided in four on-campus facilities. The Writing Center offers tutoring in all phases of writing.

The department's 21 regular faculty members and 22 affiliated faculty members include 2 National Academy of Sciences members and recipients of several prestigious professional honors. Special strengths are computational fluid dynamics, applied statistics, and computational geometry. The department's Institute for Mathematical Modeling supports extensive computing facilities and an active program of conferences and visiting scholars. The focus on problem-driven research includes a diverse array of interdisciplinary projects spanning the biomedical, physical, and social sciences.

Applying

Applications for admission are welcome at all times. Transcripts, GRE General Test scores, and three letters of recommendation are required. Completed applications for fall admission should be received by March 1; the deadline for those applying for financial aid is January 15. For more information and application forms, students should visit the department's Web site, listed below.

Correspondence and Information

Director of Graduate Program
Department of Applied Mathematics and Statistics
Stony Brook University, State University of New York
Stony Brook, New York 11794-3600
Telephone: 631-632-8360
World Wide Web: http://www.ams.sunysb.edu

Stony Brook University, State University of New York

THE FACULTY AND THEIR RESEARCH

Hongshik Ahn, Associate Professor; Ph.D., Wisconsin. Biostatistics.
Esther Arkin, Professor; Ph.D., Stanford. Combinatorial optimization, computational geometry.
Edward Beltrami, Professor Emeritus; Ph.D., Adelphi. Nonlinear models, stochastic models.
Yung Ming Chen, Professor Emeritus; Ph.D., Columbia. Computational fluid dynamics, parallel computing.
Yuefan Deng, Professor; Ph.D., Columbia. Computational fluid dynamics, parallel computing.
Daniel Dicker, Professor Emeritus; Ph.D., Columbia. Porous flow problems.
Vaclav Dolezal, Professor Emeritus; Ph.D., Czechoslovak Academy of Sciences. Mathematical systems theory.
Eugene Feinberg, Professor; Ph.D., Vilnius State (Lithuania). Applied probability.
Stephen Finch, Associate Professor; Ph.D., Princeton. Applied statistics.
Charles Fortmann, Visiting Associate Professor; Ph.D., Stanford. Computational biophysics, photonics.
Robert Frey, Adjunct Assistant Professor (Renaissance Technologies); Ph.D., SUNY at Stony Brook. Operations research.
James Glimm, Distinguished Professor, Chair, and Director, Institute for Mathematical Modeling; Ph.D., Columbia. Computational fluid dynamics, conservation laws, mathematical physics.
John Grove, Adjunct Professor; Ph.D., Ohio State. Computational fluid dynamics.
Woo Jong Kim, Professor; Ph.D., Carnegie Mellon. Ordinary differential equations.
Xiaolin Li, Professor; Ph.D., Columbia. Computational fluid dynamics.
Brent Lindquist, Professor; Ph.D., Cornell. Computational fluid dynamics, reservoir modeling.
Nancy Mendell, Professor; Ph.D., North Carolina. Applied statistics.
Joseph Mitchell, Professor; Ph.D., Stanford. Computational geometry.
Wonho Oh, Assistant Professor; Ph.D., SUNY at Stony Brook. Computational fluid dynamics.
Bradley Plohr, Adjunct Professor; Ph.D., Princeton. Computational fluid dynamics.
John Reinitz, Associate Professor; Ph.D., Yale. Bioinformatics.
David Sharp, Adjunct Professor (Los Alamos National Lab); Ph.D., Princeton. Nonlinear analysis.
Steven Skiena, Associate Professor; Ph.D., Illinois. Combinatorial algorithms.
Jadranka Skorin-Kapov, Professor; Ph.D., British Columbia. Mathematical programming.
Ram Srivastav, Professor; Dc.S., Glasgow. Numerical analysis, integral equations.
Reginald Tewarson, Professor Emeritus; Ph.D., Boston University. Numerical analysis, biomathematics.
Alan Tucker, Distinguished Teaching Professor; Ph.D., Stanford. Combinatorial optimization.
Ilya Vaksar, Associate Professor; Ph.D., Moscow. Bioinformatics.
Kenny Ye, Assistant Professor; Ph.D., Michigan. Applied statistics.
E. Alper Yildirim, Assistant Professor; Ph.D., Cornell. Mathematical programming.
Yongmin Zhang, Assistant Professor; Ph.D., Chicago. Computational fluid dynamics.
Wei Zhu, Associate Professor; Ph.D., UCLA. Biostatistics.

THE UNIVERSITY OF ARIZONA

Program in Applied Mathematics

Programs of Study

The Program in Applied Mathematics offers flexible courses of study leading to M.S. and Ph.D. degrees in applied mathematics. It encourages research in many areas of the mathematical, physical, biological, and engineering sciences involving mathematical modeling and the development of mathematical and computational methods. First-year students take a sequence of core courses on numerical analysis, principles of analysis, and methods of applied mathematics, and participate in research tutorial groups. In subsequent years, students can choose from a broad variety of courses suited to their evolving research interests. Very importantly, the Program in Applied Mathematics operates as an interdisciplinary program that enables its students to carry out research under the supervision of faculty members from many different disciplines and departments around the University of Arizona.

The Program in Applied Mathematics also offers a separate professional master's degree in mathematical science designed for individuals intending careers in industry, commerce, or the public sector. The flexible program of study includes course work in mathematics and the sciences, special business courses, a colloquium, an internship, and a master's thesis or project.

Program faculty members are actively involved in supervising and teaching the Program's graduate students. In addition, the program has a substantial body of affiliate members who are involved in research with a strong applied mathematics component and who are potential research advisers. The combined network of program faculty members and affiliate members creates an unusually broad base of interdisciplinary research opportunities in applied mathematics. A list of faculty members is given below, and a list of the affiliate members can be found on the program's Web site, listed below.

Research Facilities

The Program in Applied Mathematics is housed in the mathematics building on the main campus of the University of Arizona. In addition to classrooms, seminar rooms, and student offices, there are two computer laboratories in the building reserved for the exclusive use of graduate students. Students also have access to supercomputer clusters, a graphics laboratory, and other computational resources at the University's Center for Computing and Information Technology (CCIT).

The Program in Applied Mathematics also operates two unique experimental laboratories. The Applied Mathematics Laboratory was designed for advanced mathematical modeling courses and research projects in condensed-matter physics and fluid dynamics, and the Biophysics Training Laboratory has state-of-the-art equipment for courses and research problems in the biological sciences.

The University has extensive library facilities. Most of the journals, monographs, and texts in applied mathematics are housed in the University's Science Library.

Financial Aid

Teaching assistantships are available for qualified graduate students. The academic year stipends for 2003–04 ranged from $14,743 to $16,120 for teaching 4 class hours per week. Many program students eventually receive financial support in the form of research assistantships. Both types of assistantships include valuable health insurance and out-of-state tuition waivers. All students are required to pay in-state registration fees of approximately $1800 per semester. There are also many opportunities for program students to receive summer support. Fellowships from the program's IGERT and VIGRE grants are available, on a competitive basis, for students who are U.S. citizens or permanent residents.

Cost of Study

In addition to registration fees, full-time out-of-state students are required to pay out-of-state tuition fees of approximately $4100 each semester. The program makes every effort to provide students whose out-of-state tuition costs are not covered by an assistantship with a tuition scholarship to cover this expense.

Living and Housing Costs

Housing for graduate students is available on campus. There are also several apartment complexes and many rental homes within walking or biking distance of campus. The campus can also be accessed via public bus transportation from nearly all areas of Tucson. Excluding registration/tuition fees, the approximate living expenses for a graduate student have been estimated to be $4000 per semester.

Student Group

The University of Arizona has approximately 37,000 students, including more than 8,500 graduate students. Total enrollment in the Program in Applied Mathematics is currently 48 students, of whom more than 25 percent are women. There is a long tradition of collegiality among program students and friendly relations with program faculty members. Each year, the students elect a Graduate Student Representative who acts as a liaison with the Program Directorate. Nearly all students receive financial aid.

Student Outcomes

The program has produced more than 100 Ph.D.s over the last twenty years, many of whom now hold faculty positions in leading universities or research positions in national laboratories and industry. Prospective students should visit the alumni section of the program's Web site for an up-to-date list of graduates and their current career information.

Location

Tucson is located in southern Arizona in a valley surrounded by mountain ranges, some rising 9,000 feet above the city. The population is approximately 850,000. The University is located 65 miles from the Mexican border, 120 miles from Phoenix, and approximately 400 miles from San Diego. The climate lends itself to outstanding outdoor recreational activities, while Tucson offers a rich and varied cultural life.

The University and The Program

The Program in Applied Mathematics was established in 1976 and is the University of Arizona's leading interdisciplinary program with a highly ranked national and international reputation. The University of Arizona, located in the city of Tucson, was founded in 1885 and is the state's only land-grant university. It is a leading public research university with noted strengths in the sciences, and is the only one of seventeen public universities with both a medical school and a college of agriculture.

Applying

Application forms are available from the Program in Applied Mathematics' Graduate Office (contact information listed below). GRE scores are required. The Subject Test in mathematics is optional. International students must ensure that their complete applications for admission and financial aid are received by February 1, and must include TOEFL scores and a Test of Spoken English (TSE) score if their primary language is not English. Applications from U.S. students can be accepted somewhat later.

Correspondence and Information

Graduate Committee
Program in Applied Mathematics
The University of Arizona
617 North Santa Rita
Tucson, Arizona 85721-0089

Telephone 520-621-2016
Fax: 520-626-5048
E-mail: applmath@u.arizona.edu
World Wide Web: http://appliedmath.arizona.edu/

The University of Arizona

THE FACULTY

Key to abbreviations: A.M.E.—Aerospace and Mechanical Engineering; E.C.E.—Electrical and Computer Engineering; E.E.B.—Ecology and Evolutionary Biology; S.I.E.—Systems and Industrial Engineering.

G. R. Andrews (Computer Science). Software for parallel computing.
B. R. Barrett (Physics). Nuclear many-body theory, structure finite nuclei, interacting boson model.
H. H. Barrett (Radiology and Optics). Inverse problems in medicine.
J. C. Baygents (Chemical Engineering). Fluid mechanics, colloidal phenomena and bioseparations.
M. Brio (Mathematics). Numerical solution of partial differential equations.
W. J. Cocke (Astronomy). Turbulence theory, general relativity, cosmology, nature of the redshift.
*J. M. Cushing (Mathematics). Differential equations, integral equations, population dynamics and ecology.
*P. Deymier (M.S.E.). Materials theory, modeling and simulation, structural defects.
N. M. Ercolani (Mathematics). Applications of algebraic geometry, nonlinear analysis.
G. L. Eyink (Mathematics). Mathematical physics, fluid mechanics, turbulence, dynamical systems, equilibrium and nonequilibrium statistical physics.
W. G. Faris (Mathematics). Operator theory, quantum mechanics, probability, statistical mechanics.
H. Flaschka (Mathematics). Nonlinear waves, dynamical systems.
L. Friedlander (Mathematics). Spectral geometry, spectrum of differential operators and geometry of manifolds.
I. Gabitov (Mathematics). Mathematical and theoretical physics, nonlinear optics, solitons and their applications, theory of integrability, inverse scattering transform.
K. Glasner (Mathematics). Fluid mechanics, dynamics of interfaces and computation.
R. T. Goldstein (Physics). Condensed-matter theory, nonlinear dynamics, pattern formation, fluid dynamics, experimental and theoretical biological physics.
A. Goriely (Mathematics). Dynamical systems (pure and applied), elasticity theory, biology.
R. J. Greenberg (Lunar and Planetary Science). Planetary dynamics and celestial mechanics.
*T. G. Kennedy (Mathematics). Statistical mechanics, condensed-matter theory.
*E. J. Kerschen (A.M.E.). Aeroacoustics, fluid mechanics, singular perturbations.
J. Lega (Mathematics). Nonlinear dynamics (pattern formation, envelope equations, weak turbulence) and applications to hydrodynamics, optics, and biology.
J. I. Lunine (Planetary Science). Theoretical studies of outer solar system bodies.
M. W. Marcellin (E.C.E.). Digital communication/data storage systems, data compression, digital signal/image processing.
P. B. Mirchandani (S.I.E.). Operational research, traffic flow.
J. V. Moloney (Mathematics and Optics). Nonlinear optics, instability and chaos in lasers.
W. R. Montfort (Biochemistry). Protein structure.
S. P. Neuman (Hydrology). Subsurface hydrology and underground transport, computer simulation.
A. C. Newell (Mathematics). Nonlinear processes, waves, cooperative phenomena, numerical analysis.
J. Restrepo (Mathematics). Geophysical fluid dynamics, large-scale computing and numerical analysis, nonlinear waves.
*T. W. Secomb (Physiology). Fluid mechanics, microcirculation, blood rheology.
*D. L. Stein (Physics). Disordered systems, biophysics.
*M. Tabor (Applied Mathematics). Nonlinear dynamics, condensed-matter physics, elasticity theory, biology.
H. S. Tharp (E.C.E.). Control systems.
*L. P. Tolbert (Neurobiology). Developmental neurobiology.
A. Tumin (S.I.E.). Fluid dynamics, hydrodynamic stability, heat transfer.
Q. D. Wang (Mathematics). Dynamical systems, Hamiltonian systems, N-body problem, twist maps.
A. W. Warrick (Soils, Water, and Environment). Soil physics, soil water flow, quantifying soil variability and sampling.
J. C. Watkins (Mathematics). Probability theory and stochastic processes, particularly limit theorems and models of random processes in biology and physics.
J. Wehr (Mathematics). Mathematical physics, probability, differential equations.

A list of affiliate faculty members is available upon request.

*Steering Committee Member.

UNIVERSITY OF CALIFORNIA, LOS ANGELES

School of Medicine
Department of Biomathematics

Programs of Study

The Department of Biomathematics offers a graduate program leading to the Master of Science and Doctor of Philosophy degrees in biomathematics. The goal of the doctoral program is to train creative, fully independent investigators who can initiate research in both applied mathematics and their chosen biomedical specialty. The department's orientation is away from abstract modeling and toward theoretical and applied research vital to the advancement of current biomedical frontiers. This is reflected in a curriculum providing a high level of competence in a biomedical specialty; substantial training in applied mathematics, statistics, and computing; and appropriate biomathematics courses and research experience. A low student-faculty ratio permits close and frequent contact between students and faculty throughout the training and research years. Biomathematics also participates in UCLA bioinformatics programs.

Entering students come from a variety of backgrounds in mathematics, biology, the physical sciences, and computer science. Some of the students are enrolled in the UCLA M.D./Ph.D. program. Doctoral students generally use the first two years to take the core sequence and electives in biomathematics, to broaden their backgrounds in biology and mathematics, and to begin directed individual study or research. Comprehensive examinations in biomathematics are taken after this period, generally followed by the choice of a major field and dissertation area. Individualized programs permit students to select graduate courses in applied mathematics, biomathematics, and statistics appropriate to their area of research and to choose among diverse biomedical specialties. At present, approved fields of special emphasis for which courses of study and qualifying examinations have been developed include genetics, physiology, neurosciences, pharmacology, immunology, and molecular biology. Other major fields can be added to the list by petition.

The master's program can be a step to further graduate work in biomathematics, but it also can be adapted to the needs of researchers desiring supplemental biomathematical training or of individuals wishing to provide methodologic support to biomedical researchers. The M.S. program requires at least five graduate biomathematics courses and either a thesis or comprehensive examination plan. The master's degree can be completed in one or two years.

Research Facilities

The department is situated in the Center for the Health Sciences, close to UCLA's rich research and educational resources in the School of Medicine; the Departments of Mathematics, Biology, Computer Science, Engineering, Chemistry, and Physics; the Institute for Pure and Applied Mathematics; and the Molecular Biology Institute. The department has for many years housed multidisciplinary research programs comprising innovative modeling, statistical, and computing methods directed to many areas of biomedical research. It was the original home of the BMDP statistical programs and has an active consulting clinic for biomedical researchers. Computers within the department and graduate student offices include Macintosh units, Pentium PCs, and UNIX-based workstations. Nearby are terminals to UCLA's supercomputing resources (SP/2 cluster) and access to networked SUN computers and University-wide supercomputing. The Biomedical Library is one of the finest libraries of its kind in the country, and nearby are the Engineering and Mathematical Sciences Library and other subject libraries of the renowned nineteen-branch University Library. The department maintains a small library with selected titles in mathematical biology and statistics.

Financial Aid

Financial support is provided from a variety of sources, including University-sponsored fellowships, affiliated training grants, research assistantships, and other merit-based funds. Supplementation is also possible from consulting and teaching assistantships.

Cost of Study

The 2004–05 registration and other fees for California residents are estimated to be $7480 50 and for nonresidents, $7725. Nonresident tuition is projected to be $14,695. Domestic students may attain residency status after one year. The University's fee proposal is subject to change based on state budget decisions.

Living and Housing Costs

The estimated cost of living varies. (The cost of living is in addition to the cost of study.) For additional housing information, students can go to the Web site (http://www.housing.ucla.edu/housing/housing.htm).

Student Group

Currently, 17 graduate students are enrolled in the department's program. About a fifth of the students are international. An NIH predoctoral training grant supports up to 6 students. Most other students are also receiving financial support and/or are employed on campus in the area of their research. Many graduates hold tenure-track appointments at leading universities, research appointments at the National Institutes of Health, or in industry.

Location

UCLA's 411 acres are cradled in rolling green hills just 5 miles inland from the ocean, in one of the most attractive areas of southern California. The campus is bordered on the north by the protected wilderness of the Santa Monica Mountains and at its southern gate by Westwood Village, one of the entertainment magnets of Los Angeles.

The University

UCLA is one of America's most prestigious and influential public universities, serving more than 33,000 students. The Department of Biomathematics is one of ten basic science departments in the School of Medicine. The medical school, regarded by many to be among the best in the nation, is situated on the south side of the UCLA campus, just adjacent to the Life Sciences Building and the Court of Sciences. For more information, students can visit the University's Web site (http://www.ucla.edu).

Applying

Most students enter in the fall quarter, but applications for winter or spring quarter entry are considered. However, it is advantageous for candidates applying for financial support to initiate the application by the middle of January for decisions for the following fall. The department expects applicants for direct admission to the doctoral program to submit scores on the General Test of the Graduate Record Examinations and on one GRE Subject Test of the student's choice. Inquiries are welcome from students early in their undergraduate training. The department supports minority recruitment.

Correspondence and Information

Admissions Committee Chair
Department of Biomathematics
UCLA School of Medicine
Los Angeles, California 90095-1766
Telephone: 310-825-5554
Fax: 310-825-8685
E-mail: gradprog@biomath.ucla.edu
World Wide Web: http://www.biomath.ucla.edu/

University of California, Los Angeles

THE FACULTY AND THEIR RESEARCH

A. A. Afifi, Professor of Biostatistics and Biomathematics; Ph.D. (statistics), Berkeley, 1965. Multivariate statistical analysis, with applications to biomedical and public health problems.

Sally M. Blower, Professor of Biomathematics; Ph.D. (biology), Stanford, 1987. Population and evolutionary biology; mathematical models of disease transmission dynamics; uncertainty and sensitivity techniques; epidemic control strategies and applications to HIV, tuberculosis, and herpes.

Tom Chou, Assistant Professor of Biomathematics; Ph.D. (physics), Harvard, 1995. Theoretical biophysics, cellular and molecular modeling, transport, bioenergetics.

Wilfrid J. Dixon, Professor of Biomathematics, Biostatistics, and Psychiatry (Emeritus); Ph.D. (statistics), Princeton, 1944. Statistical computation, statistical theory, biological applications, data analysis, psychiatric research.

Robert M. Elashoff, Professor of Biomathematics and Biostatistics; Chair of Biostatistics; Ph.D. (statistics), Harvard, 1963. Markov renewal models in survival analysis, random coefficient regression models.

Eli Engel, Adjunct Associate Professor of Biomathematics; M.D., Buffalo, 1951; Ph.D. (physiology), UCLA, 1975. Mechanisms for acid neutralization in gastric mucus, facilitated transport of oxygen, theory of intracellular microelectrodes.

Alan B. Forsythe, Adjunct Professor of Biomathematics and Dentistry (Emeritus); Ph.D. (biometry), Yale, 1967. Methods development in robust regression and hypothesis testing, design and analysis of clinical and epidemiological studies, computer systems design.

Sanjiv Sam Gambhir, Professor, Department of Molecular and Medical Pharmacology and Biomathematics and Director, Crump Institute for Molecular Imaging; Ph.D. (biomathematics), UCLA, 1990; M.D., UCLA, 1993. Positron emission tomography (PET), deterministic modeling, medical imaging, neural networks, imaging gene expression, nuclear medicine, and optical imaging.

Sung-Cheng (Henry) Huang, Professor of Medical Pharmacology and Biomathematics; D.Sc. (electrical engineering), Washington (St. Louis), 1973. Positron emission computed tomography and physiological modeling.

Donald J. Jenden, Professor of Pharmacology and Biomathematics (Emeritus); M.B./B.S. (pharmacology and therapeutics), Westminster (London), 1950. Pharmacokinetic modeling, chemical pharmacology, analysis of GC/MS data, neuropharmacology.

Robert I. Jennrich, Professor of Mathematics, Biomathematics, and Biostatistics (Emeritus); Ph.D. (mathematics), UCLA, 1960. Statistical methodology, computational algorithms, nonlinear regression, factor analysis, compartment analysis.

Elliot M. Landaw, Professor and Chair of Biomathematics; M.D., Chicago, 1972; Ph.D. (biomathematics), UCLA, 1980. Identifiability and optimal experiment design for compartmental models; nonlinear regression; modeling/estimation applications in pharmacokinetics, ligand-receptor analysis, transport, and molecular biology.

Kenneth L. Lange, Professor of Biomathematics, Human Genetics, and Statistics; Ph.D. (mathematics), MIT, 1971. Statistical and mathematical methods for human genetics, demography, medical imaging, probability, optimization theory.

Carol M. Newton, Professor of Biomathematics and Radiation Oncology; Ph.D. (physics and mathematics), Stanford, 1956; M.D., Chicago, 1960. Simulation; cellular models for hematopoiesis, cancer treatment strategies, optimization; interactive graphics for modeling; model-based exploration of complex data structures.

Michael E. Phelps, Norton Simon Professor; Chair, Department of Molecular and Medical Pharmacology; Professor of Biomathematics; Chief, Division of Nuclear Medicine; and Associate Director, Laboratory of Structural Biology and Molecular Medicine; Ph.D. (nuclear chemistry), Washington (St. Louis), 1970. Positron emission tomography (PET), tracer kinetic modeling of biochemical and pharmacokinetic processes; biological imaging of human disease.

Janet S. Sinsheimer, Associate Professor of Biomathematics, Biostatistics, and Human Genetics; Ph.D. (biomathematics), UCLA, 1994. Statistical models of molecular evolution and genetics.

Marc A. Suchard, Assistant Adjunct Professor of Biomathematics; Ph.D. (biomathematics), UCLA, 2002. Evolutionary reconstruction, sequence analysis, medical time series.

University of California, Los Angeles

SELECTED PUBLICATIONS

Blower, S. M., A. N. Aschenbach, H. B. Gershegorn, and J. O. Kahn. Predicting the unpredictable: Transmission of drug-resistant HIV. *Nature Med.* 7(9):1016–20, 2001.

Blower, S. M., K. Koelle, D. E. Kirschner, and J. Mills. Live attenuated HIV vaccine: Predicting the trade off between efficacy and safety. *Proc. Natl. Acad. Sci. U.S.A.* 98(6):3618–23, 2001.

Blower, S. M., H. Gershengorn, and R. M. Grant. A tale of two futures: HIV and antiretroviral therapy in San Francisco. *Science* 287:650–4, 2000.

Lietman, T., T. Porco, T. Dawson, and **S. M. Blower.** Global elimination of Trachoma: How frequently should we administer mass chemotherapy? *Nature Med.* 5(5):572–6, 1999.

Blower, S. M., and J. L. Gerberding. Understanding, predicting & controlling the emergence of drug-resistant tuberculosis: A theoretical framework. *J. Mol. Med.* 76:624–36, 1998.

Blower, S. M., T. Porco, and G. Darby. Predicting & preventing the emergence of antiviral drug resistance in HSV-2. *Nature Med.* 4(6):673–8, 1998.

Porco, T. C., and **S. M. Blower.** Quantifying the intrinsic transmission dynamics of tuberculosis. *Theor. Popul. Biol.* 54:117–32, 1998.

Blower, S. M., P. M. Small, and P. Hopewell. Control strategies for tuberculosis epidemics: New models for old problems. *Science* 273:497–500, 1996.

D'Orsogna, M. R., and **T. Chou.** Chiral molecule adsorption on helical polymers. *Phys. Rev. E* 69:021805, 2004.

Lakatos, G. W., and **T. Chou.** Totally asymmetric exclusion process with particles of arbitrary size. *J. Phys. A: Math. Gen.* 36:2027–41, 2003.

Chou, T. An exact theory of histone-DNA adsorption and wrapping. *Europhys. Lett.* 62:753–9, 2003.

Chou, T. Ribosome recycling, diffusion, and MRNA loop formation in translational regulation. *Biophys. J.* 85:755–73, 2003.

Chou, T. An interacting spin-flip model for one-dimensional proton conduction. *J. Phys. A: Math. Gen.* 35:4515–26, 2002.

Bal, G., and **T. Chou.** Capillary-gravity wave transport over spatially random drift. *Wave Motion* 35:107–24, 2002.

Chou, T. Geometry-dependent electrostatics near contact lines. *Phys. Rev. Lett.* 87(10):106101, 2001.

McGee, M. P., and **T. Chou.** Surface-dependent electrostatics near contact lines. *J. Biol. Chem.* 276:7827–35, 2001.

Chou, T., K. S. Kim, and G. Oster. Statistical thermodynamics of membrane bending mediated protein-protein interactions. *Biophys. J.* 80:1075–87, 2001.

Chou, T., and D. Lohse. Entropy-driven pumping in zeolites and ion channels. *Phys. Rev. Lett.* 110:606–15, 1999.

Chou, T. Kinetics and thermodynamics across single-file pores: Solute permeability and rectified osmosis. *J. Chem. Phys.* 110:606–15, 1999.

Leung, K. M., and **R. M. Elashoff.** A three-state disease model with application to AIDS and melanoma. *J. Lifetime Anal.* 1996.

Leung, K. M., **R. M. Elashoff,** and **A. A. Afifi.** On censoring. *Am. J. Public Health Mono.* 1996.

Leung, K. M., and **R. M. Elashoff.** Generalized linear mixed-effects models with finite-support random-effects distribution: A maximum-penalized likelihood approach. *Biometr. J.* 1995.

Leung, K. M., and **R. M. Elashoff.** Estimation of generalized linear mixed-effects models with finite-support random-effects distribution via Gibbs sampling. *Biometr. J.* 1995.

Wanek, L. A., and **R. M. Elashoff** et al. Application of multistage Markov modeling to malignant melanoma progression. *Cancer* 73(2):336–43, 1994.

Livingston, E. H., and **E. Engel.** Modeling of the gastric gel mucus layer: Application to the measured pH gradient. *J. Clin. Gastroenterol.* 21:S120–4, 1995.

Engel, E., P. H. Guth, Y. Nishizaki, and J. D. Kaunitz. Barrier function of the gastric mucus gel. *Am. J. Physiol.* (Gastrointest. Liver Physiol. 32) 269:G994–9, 1995.

Livingston, E. H., J. Miller, and **E. Engel.** Bicarbonate diffusion through mucus. *Am. J. Physiol.* (Gastrointest. Liver Physiol. 32) 269:G453–7, 1995.

Engel, E., A. Peskoff, G. L. Kauffman, and M. I. Grossman. Analysis of hydrogen ion concentration in the gastric gel mucus layer. *Am. J. Physiol.* (Gastrointest. Liver Physiol. 10) 247:G321–38, 1984.

Engel, E., V. Barcilon, and R. S. Eisenberg. The interpretation of current-voltage relations recorded from a spherical cell with a single microelectrode. *Biophys. J.* 12(4):384–403, 1972.

Eisenberg, R. S., and **E. Engel.** The spatial variation of membrane potential near a small source of current in a spherical cell. *J. Gen. Physiol.* 55(6):736–57, 1970.

Yee, R. E., and **S. C. Huang** et al. Imaging and therapeutics: The role of neuronal transport in the regional specificity of L-DOPA accumulation in brain. *Mol. Imaging Biol.* 4:208218, 2002.

McElroy, D. P., **S. C. Huang,** and E. J. Hoffman. The use of retro-reflective tape for improving spatial resolution of scintillation detectors. *IEEE Trans. Nucl. Sci.* 49:165–71, 2002.

Zhou, Y., **S. C. Huang,** M. Bergsneider, and D. F. Wong. Improved parametric image generation using spatial-temporal analysis of dynamic PET studies. *Neuroimaging* 15:697–707, 2002.

Liao, W.-H., **S. C. Huang, K. Lange,** and M. Bergesneider. Use of MM algorithm for regularization of parametric images in dynamic PET. In *Brain Imaging Using PET,* pp. 107–14, eds. M. Senda, Y. Kimura, P. Herscovitch, and Y. Kimura. New York: Academic Press, 2002.

Shoghi-Jadid, K., and **S. C. Huang** et al. **(M. E. Phelps).** Striatal kinetic modeling of FDOPA with a cerebellar-derived constraint on the distribution volume of 3OFMD: A positron emission topography (PET) investigation using nonhuman primates. *J. Cereb. Blood Flow Metab.* 20:1134–48, 2000.

Stout, D. B., and **S. C. Huang** et al. Distribution volume of 3-O-methyl-6-[F-18]FDOPA in rat brain. *J. Cereb. Blood F. Metab.* 20:1717–24, 2000.

Huang, S. C., et al. Distribution volume of radiolabeled large neutral amino acid in brain tissue. *J. Cereb. Blood Flow Metab.* 18:1288–93, 1998.

Yu, R. C., D. Hattis, **E. M. Landaw,** and J. R. Froines. Toxicokinetic interaction of 2,5-hexanedione and methyl ethyl ketone. *Arch. Toxicol.* 75:643–52, 2002.

Lopez, A. M., M. D. Pegram, D. J. Slamon, and **E. M. Landaw.** A model-based approach for assessing in vivo combination therapy interactions. *Proc. Natl. Acad. Sci. U.S.A.* 96:13023–8, 1999.

Greenword, A. C., **E. M. Landaw,** and T. H. Brown. Testing the fit of a quantal model of neurotransmission. *Biophys. J.* 76:1847–55, 1999.

Walker, W. L., D. S. Goodsell, and **E. M. Landaw.** An analysis of a class of DNA sequence reading molecules. *J. Comput. Biol.* 5:571–83, 1998.

Walker, W. L., **E. M. Landaw,** R. E. Dickerson, and D. S. Goodsell. The theoretical limits of DNA sequence discrimination by linked polyamides. *Proc. Natl. Acad. Sci. U.S.A.* 95:4315–20, 1998.

Walker, W. L., **E. M. Landaw,** R. E. Dickerson, and D. S. Goodsell. Estimation of the DNA sequence discriminatory ability of hairpin-linked lexitropsins. *Proc. Natl. Acad. Sci. U.S.A.* 94:5634–9, 1997.

Landaw, E. M. Model-based adaptive control for cancer chemotherapy with suramin. In *Proceedings of the Simulation in Health Sciences Conferences,* pp. 93–8, eds. J. G. Anderson and M. Katzper. San Diego: Society for Computer Simulation, 1994.

Marino, A. T., J. J. Distefano III, and **E. M. Landaw.** DIMSUM: An expert system for multiexponential model discrimination. *Am. J. Physiol.* (Endocrinol. Metab. 25) 262:E546–56, 1992.

Landaw, E. M. Optimal multicompartmental sampling designs for parameter estimation-practical aspects of the identification problem. *Math. Comp. Simul.* 24:525–30, 1982.

Liao, W.-H., **K. Lange,** M. Bergsneider, and **S. C. Huang.** Optimal design in PET data acquisition: A new approach using simulated annealing and component-wise metropolis updating. *IEEE Trans. Nucl. Sci.* 49:2291–6, 2002.

University of California, Los Angeles

Selected Publications (continued)

Lange, K. *Mathematical and Statistical Methods for Genetic Analysis,* 2nd ed. New York: Springer-Verlag, 2002.

Sabbati, C., and **K. Lange.** Genomewide motif identification using a dictionary model. *Proc. IEEE* 90:1803–10, 2002.

Schadt, E. E., and **K. Lange.** Codon rate variation models in molecular phylogeny. *Mol. Biol. Evol.* 19:1534–49, 2002.

Berloff, N., M. Perola, and **K. Lange.** Spline methods for comparison of physical and genetic maps. *J. Comp. Biol.* 9:465–76, 2002.

Liao, W.-H., **K. Lange, S. C. Huang,** and M. Bergsneider. Optimal design in PET data acquisition: A new approach using simulated annealing and component-wise Metropolis updating. *Nuclear Science Symposium Conference Record, 2001 IEEE* 4:1979–83, 2002.

Sobel, E., J. Papp, and **K. Lange.** Detection and integration of genotyping errors in statistical genetics. *Am. J. Hum. Genet.* 70:496–508, 2002.

Ro, K. M., R. M. Cantor, **K. Lange,** and S. S. Ahn. Palmer hyperhidrosis: Evidence of genetic transmission. *J. Vascular Surg.* 35:382–86, 2002.

Hunter, D. R., and **K. Lange.** Computing estimates in the proportional odds model. *Ann. Inst. Stat. Math.* 54:155–68, 2002.

Lange, K., and B. Redelings. Disease gene dynamics in a population isolate. In *An Introduction to Mathematical Modeling in Physiology, Cell Biology, and Immunology,* pp. 119–38, ed. J. Sneyd. Providence, R.I.: American Mathematical Society, 2002.

Perola, M., et al. **(K. Lange).** Quantitative-trait locus analysis of body mass index and stature, by combined analysis of genome scans of five Finnish study groups. *Am. J. Hum. Genet.* 69:117–23, 2001.

Peltonen, L., A. Palotie, and **K. Lange.** The use of population isolates for mapping complex traits. *Nature Genet. Rev.* 1:182–90, 2000.

Douglas, J. A., M. Boehnke, and **K. Lange.** A multipoint method for detecting genotyping errors and mutations in sibling-pair linkage data. *Am. J. Hum. Genet.* 66:1287–97, 2000.

Dorman, K. S., A. H. Kaplan, **K. Lange,** and **J. S. Sinsheimer.** Mutation takes no vacation: Can structured treatment interruptions increase the risk of drug resistant HIV-1? *J. AIDS* 25:398–402, 2000.

Guo, S-W., and **K. Lange.** Genetic mapping of complex traits: Promises, problems, and prospects. *Theor. Popul. Biol.* 57:1–11, 2000.

Newton, C. M. An interactive graphics system for real-time investigation and multivariate data portrayal for complex pedigree data systems. *Comp. Biomed. Res.* 26:327–43, 1993.

Newton, C. M. Exploring categorical and scalar data interactions: Another graphical approach. *Proc. Am. Stat. Assoc. Meet. (Section on Statistical Graphics),* pp. 49–54, Boston, August 1992.

Newton, C. M. Conference retrospective: An appropriate modeling infrastructure for cancer research. *Bull. Math. Biol.* 48(3/4):443–52, 1986.

Ray, P., et al. **(M. E. Phelps** and **S. S. Gambhir).** Monitoring gene therapy with reporter gene imaging. *Semin. Nucl. Med.* 31(4):312–20, 2001.

Yaghoubi, S. S., et al. **(M. E. Phelps** and **S. S. Gambhir).** Human pharmacokinetic and dosimetry studies of [18F]-FHBG: A reporter probe for imaging herpes simplex virus 1 thymidine kinase (HSV1-tk) reporter gene expression. *J. Nucl. Med.* 42(8):1225–34, 2001.

Huebner, R. H., et al. **(M. E. Phelps** and **S. S. Gambhir).** A meta-analysis of the literature for whole-body FDG PET in the detection of recurrent colorectal cancer. *J. Nucl. Med.* 41:1177–89, 2000.

M. E. Phelps. Positron emission tomography provides molecular imaging of biological processes. *Proc. Natl. Acad. Sci. U.S.A.* 97:9226–33, 2000.

Wu, A., et al. **(M. E. Phelps** and **S. S. Gambhir).** High-resolution microPET imaging of carcinoembryonic antigen-positive xenografts by using copper-64-labeled engineered antibody fragments. *Proc. Natl. Acad. Sci. U.S.A.* 97(5):8495–500, 2000.

Yu, Y., et al. **(M. E. Phelps** and **S. S. Gambhir).** Quantification of target gene expression by imaging reporter gene expression in living animals. *Nature Med.* 6(8):933–7, 2000.

Kraft, P., and **J. S. Sinsheimer** et al. RHD Maternal-fetal genotype incompatibility and schizophrenia: Extending the MFG test to include multiple siblings and birth order. *Eur. J. Hum. Genet.* 12:192–8, 2004.

Dorman K., **J. S. Sinsheimer,** and **K. Lange.** In the garden of branching processes. *SIAM Rev.* 46:202–29, 2004.

Sinsheimer, J. S., and **M. A. Suchard** et al. Are you my mother? Bayesian phylogenetic models to detect recombination among putative parental strains. *Appl. Bioinformatics* 2:131–44, 2003.

Sinsheimer, J. S., C. G. S. Palmer, and J. A. Woodward. The maternal-fetal genotype incompatibility test: Detecting genotype combinations that increase risk for disease. *Genet. Epidemiol.* 24:1–13 2003.

Dorman, K. S., A. H. Kaplan, and **J. S. Sinsheimer.** Bootstrap confidence levels for HIV-1 recombinants. *J. Mol. Evol.* 54(2):200–9, 2002.

Sinsheimer, J. S., C. A. McKenzie, B. Keavney, and **K. Lange.** SNPs and snails and puppy dog tails: Analysis of SNP haplotype data using the gamete competition model. *Ann. Hum. Genet.* 65:483–90, 2001.

Sinsheimer, J. S., J. Blangero, and **K. Lange.** Gamete competition models. *Am. J. Hum. Genet.* 66:1168–72, 2000.

D'Orsogna, M. R., **M. A. Suchard,** and **T. Chou.** Interplay of chemotaxis and chemokinesis mechanisms in bacterial dynamics. *Phys. Rev. E* 68:021925, 2003.

Suchard, M. A., C. M. R. Kitchen, **J. S. Sinsheimer,** and R. E. Weiss. Hierarchical phylogenetic models for analyzing multipartite sequence data. *Syst. Biol.* 52:649–64, 2003.

Suchard, M. A., et al. Evolutionary similarity among genes. *J. Am. Stat. Assoc.* 98:653–62, 2003.

Suchard, M. A., R. E. Weiss, K. S. Dorman and **J. S. Sinsheimer.** Inferring spatial phylogenetic variation along nucleotide sequences: A multiple change-point model. *J. Am. Stat. Assoc.* 98:427–37, 2003.

Suchard, M. A., R. E. Weiss, and **J. S. Sinsheimer.** Testing a molecular clock without an outgroup: Derivations of induced priors on branch length restrictions in a Bayesian framework. *Syst. Biol.* 52:48–54, 2003.

Chan J. L., et al. **(M. A. Suchard).** Regulation of circulating soluble leptin receptor levels by gender, adiposity, sex steroids and leptin: Observational and interventional studies in humans. *Diabetes* 51:2105–12, 2002.

Suchard, M. A., R. E. Weiss, K. S. Dorman, and **J. S. Sinsheimer.** Oh brother, where art thou? A Bayes factor test for recombination with uncertain heritage. *Syst. Biol.* 51:715–28, 2002.

Suchard, M. A., R. E. Weiss, and **J. S. Sinsheimer.** Bayesian selection of continuous-time Markov chain evolutionary models. *Mol. Biol. Evol.* 18:1001–13, 2001.

Suchard, M. A., P. Yudkin, and **J. S. Sinsheimer.** Are general practitioners willing and able to provide genetic services for common diseases? *J. Genet. Couns.* 8:301–11, 1999.

UNIVERSITY OF DELAWARE

Department of Mathematical Sciences

Programs of Study

The Department of Mathematical Sciences offers master's and Ph.D. programs in mathematics and applied mathematics. Students receive instruction in a broad range of courses and may specialize in many areas of mathematics. Strong departmental research groups exist in analysis, applied mathematics, partial differential equations, combinatorics, inverse problems, topology, probability, and numerical analysis. Master's programs normally require two years for completion, while the Ph.D. usually takes five years. Internships are encouraged.

Research Facilities

The University libraries contain 2 million volumes and documents and subscribe to 24,000 periodicals and serials. The University library belongs to the Association of Research Libraries.

The University Information Technologies Department provides e-mail and network access via central Sun servers. The Department of Mathematical Sciences has its own network of three-computer classrooms, a microcomputer laboratory, and a Silicon Graphics Origin 2000 parallel computer. All graduate students have personal workstations in their offices with network access.

The department fosters an active research environment, with numerous seminars and colloquia and many national and international visitors.

Financial Aid

Graduate assistantships and fellowships are available on a competitive basis. Teaching assistantships in 2002–03 ranged from $12,240 to $13,260 for nine months (two semesters), plus tuition remission. Additional winter and summer session teaching stipends are sometimes available. Currently, most full-time students receive full financial support. Some research assistantships and fellowships are also available.

Cost of Study

Course fees for full-time students in 2004–05 were $6304 per academic year for residents of Delaware and $15,990 per academic year for out-of-state students. Tuition for the summer sessions and for part-time students was $327 per credit for Delaware residents and $857 per credit for nonresidents. The graduation fee was $35 for the master's degree and $95 for the Ph.D.

Living and Housing Costs

While prices vary widely throughout the area, average monthly rent for a one-bedroom apartment is $710 plus utilities.

Student Group

There are approximately 36 full-time graduate students in the Department of Mathematical Sciences. About one quarter of these are international students and one third are women.

Location

The University is located in Newark, Delaware, a pleasant college community of about 30,000 people. Newark is 14 miles southwest of Wilmington and halfway between Philadelphia and Baltimore. It offers the advantages of a small community yet is within easy driving distance of Philadelphia, New York, Baltimore, and Washington, D.C. It is also close to the recreational areas on the Atlantic Ocean and Chesapeake Bay.

The University

The University of Delaware grew out of a small academy founded in 1743. It has been a degree-granting institution since 1834. In 1867, an act of the Delaware General Assembly made the University a part of the nationwide system of land-grant colleges and universities. Delaware College and the Women's College, an affiliate, were combined under the name of the University of Delaware in 1921. In 1950, the Graduate College was organized to administer the existing graduate programs and to develop new ones.

Applying

Application forms may be obtained from the address below. Completed applications, including letters of recommendation, a $60 application fee, GRE General Test scores, and transcripts of previous work, should be submitted as early as possible but no later than March 1 to be considered for financial aid for the fall semester.

Correspondence and Information

Coordinator of Graduate Studies
Department of Mathematical Sciences
University of Delaware
Newark, Delaware 19716

Telephone: 302-831-2346
E-mail: see@math.udel.edu
World Wide Web: http://www.math.udel.edu

University of Delaware

THE FACULTY AND THEIR RESEARCH

Thomas S. Angell, Professor; Ph.D., Michigan. Optimal control theory, differential equations.
Constantin Bacuta, Assistant Professor; Ph.D., Texas A&M. Numerical analysis.
Willard E. Baxter, Professor Emeritus; Ph.D., Pennsylvania. Algebra.
David P. Bellamy, Professor; Ph.D., Michigan State. Topology.
John G. Bergman, Associate Professor; Ph.D., Illinois at Urbana-Champaign. Functional analysis, probability.
Richard J. Braun, Professor; Ph.D., Northwestern. Applied mathematics.
Philip Broadbridge, Professor and Chair; Ph.D., Adelaide. Applied nonlinear PDEs.
Michael Brook, Instructor; Ph.D., Delaware. Mathematics education.
Jinfa Cai, Professor; Ph.D., Pittsburgh. Mathematics education.
Fioralba Cakoni, Assistant Professor; Ph.D., Tirana University (Albania). Direct and inverse scattering theory.
Antonio Ciro, Instructor; M.S., Drexel. Mathematics education.
David L. Colton, Unidel Professor; Ph.D., D.Sc., Edinburgh. Partial differential equations, integral equations.
L. Pamela Cook-Ioannidis, Professor; Ph.D., Cornell. Applied mathematics, perturbation theory, transonic flow.
Robert Couter, Assistant Professor: Queensland (Australia). Finite fields, combinatorics.
Bryan Crissinger, Instructor; M.S., Penn State. Statistics.
Bettyann Daley, Instructor; M.S., Vermont. Math education.
Margaret Donlan, Instructor; M.S., Toledo. Mathematics for the liberal arts student, quantitative literacy.
Tobin A. Driscoll, Associate Professor; Ph.D., Cornell. Numerical analysis, applied mathematics.
Christine Ebert, Assistant Professor; Ph.D., Delaware. Investigation of pedagogical content knowledge for pre-service and in-service teachers, the cognitive development of the concept of function, the use of technology.
Gary L. Ebert, Professor; Ph.D., Wisconsin–Madison. Combinatorics.
David A. Edwards, Associate Professor; Ph.D., Caltech. Applied math.
Robert P. Gilbert, Unidel Chair Professor; Ph.D., Carnegie Mellon. Homogenization, inverse problems, partial differential equations.
David J. Hallenbeck, Professor Emeritus; Ph.D., SUNY at Albany. Function theory.
George C. Hsiao, Professor; Ph.D., Carnegie Mellon. Differential and integral equations, perturbation theory, fluid dynamics.
Mary Ann Huntley, Assistant Professor; Ph.D., Maryland. Research and evaluation of teacher preparation, induction, and enhancement.
Judy A. Kennedy, Professor; Ph.D., Auburn. Topology and dynamical systems.
Felix Lazebnik, Professor; Ph.D., Pennsylvania. Graph theory, combinatorics, algebra.
Yuk J. Leung, Associate Professor; Ph.D., Michigan. Function theory.
Wenbo Li, Professor; Ph.D., Wisconsin–Madison. Probability theory, stochastic processes, statistics.
Richard J. Libera, Professor Emeritus; Ph.D., Rutgers. Function theory.
Albert E. Livingston, Professor Emeritus; Ph.D., Rutgers. Function theory.
David Russell Luke, Assistant Professor; Ph.D., Washington (Seattle). Optimization and inverse problems.
Peter Monk, Unidel Professor; Ph.D., Rutgers. Numerical analysis.
Patrick F. Mwerinde, Assistant Professor; Ph.D., Columbia. Math education, conceptual learning theory, active learning, experimental design, statistical inference.
David Olagunju, Associate Professor; Ph.D., Northwestern. Applied mathematics.
John Pelesko, Assistant Professor; Ph.D., NJIT. Applied mathematics.
Geraldine Prange, Instructor; M.S., St. Louis. Math education for liberal arts majors, cooperative learning.
Georgia B. Pyrros, Instructor; M.S., McMaster. Nuclear physics.
Rakesh, Associate Professor; Ph.D., Cornell. Partial differential equations.
David P. Roselle, Professor and President of the University; Ph.D., Duke. Combinatorics.
Louis F. Rossi, Associate Professor; Ph.D., Arizona. Fluid dynamics, numerical analysis, vorticity dynamics.
Lillian M. Russell, Instructor; M.S., Delaware. Statistics.
Gilberto Schleiniger, Associate Professor; Ph.D., UCLA. Scientific computing, numerical analysis.
Anthony Seraphin, Instructor; B.S., Florida State. Boundary layer flow, turbulent diffusion and dispersion within and above canopie wind and water tunnel flow simulations, air pollution climatology and its precursors.
Clifford W. Sloyer, Professor and Associate Chair; Ph.D., Lehigh. Topology, mathematics education.
Ivar Stakgold, Professor Emeritus; Ph.D., Harvard. Nonlinear boundary-value problems.
Robert M. Stark, Professor Emeritus; Ph.D., Delaware. Applied probability, operations research, civil engineering systems.
Anja Sturm, Assistant Professor; Ph.D., Oxford (England). Branching and interacting particle systems.
Richard J. Weinacht, Professor Emeritus; Ph.D., Maryland. Partial differential equations.
Ronald H. Wenger, Associate Professor; Ph.D., Michigan State. Algebra, mathematics education.
Qing Xiang, Associate Professor; Ph.D., Ohio State. Combinatorics.
Shangyou Zhang, Associate Professor; Ph.D., Penn State. Numerical analysis and scientific computation.

Joint Appointments with Other Departments

Morris W. Brooks, Ph.D., Harvard. Computer-based instruction.
Bobby F. Caviness, Ph.D., Carnegie Mellon. Computer algebra.
Kathleen Hollowell, Ed.D., Boston University. Mathematics education.
William B. Moody, Ed.D., Maryland. Mathematics education.
Richard S. Sacher, Ph.D., Stanford. Scientific computing, operations research.
David Saunders, Ph.D., Wisconsin–Madison. Computer algebra.
Leonard W. Schwartz, Ph.D., Stanford. Fluid mechanics.

Adjunct Faculty and Their Affiliations

Alan Jeffrey, University of Newcastle-upon-Tyne. Wave propagation.
Rainer Kress, University of Göttingen. Integral equations, scattering theory.
Emeka Nwanko, DuPont Company.
Lassi Paivarinta, University of Oulu (Finland).
Gary Roach, University of Strathclyde. Operator theory, scattering theory.
Wolfgang Wendland, University of Stuttgart (Germany). Integral equations and analysis.

UNIVERSITY OF IDAHO

College of Science
Programs in Mathematics

Programs of Study

The University of Idaho (UI) offers the Master of Science in Mathematics, the Master of Arts in Teaching in Mathematics, and the Ph.D. in mathematics. The M.S. degree in mathematics can be pursued with two different career goals in mind: One aims to develop a strong base in the traditional areas of algebra, topology, analysis, or discrete mathematics. It is designed for students who wish to teach in a two-year college or to pursue a Ph.D. degree in mathematics. The other is intended to serve as a strong background in mathematics and applications to computer science, for an individual who sees the M.S. in mathematics as a terminal degree and seeks employment in the high-technology sector. It is highly recommended that this option be combined with an internship with industry through the University of Idaho Cooperative Education Office. The Master of Arts in Teaching (M.A.T.) gives secondary mathematics teachers a broad background of course work in mathematics that is relevant to their teaching needs. This degree is also available via distance learning. The M.A.T. program has grown to more than 30 students. The Ph.D. in mathematics is a program that has a strong core of course work in the traditional areas of pure and applied math and gives graduate students an opportunity to become experienced college-level teachers with potential to carry out original research. Graduate students develop strong teaching skills.

Research Facilities

The UI libraries contain approximately 2.5 million items, including more than 12,000 serial titles. The main library recently had a major expansion and renovation. The University of Idaho features a strong balance of basic and applied research. As a Carnegie Research II institution, one of fewer than 130 in the nation, the University conducts theoretical research as its contribution to the advance of knowledge. As a Morrill Act land-grant institution, the University fulfills its responsibility to the local, national, and international communities by conducting applied research to improve the way people work and live and to improve the economic returns of research. Departmental research is conducted in the areas of algebra, combinatorics, convex geometry and discrete optimization, differential equations, discrete mathematics, mathematical biology, mathematics education, and probability.

Financial Aid

Many departments offer teaching assistantships or research assistantships, which include a waiver of nonresident tuition. Information on assistantships may be obtained directly from the appropriate department director of graduate studies. Financial aid is also available through the Federal Perkins Loan Program, the Federal Stafford Student Loan Program, and work-study grants. Information and applications can be provided by the Student Financial Aid Office.

Cost of Study

For 2004–05, full-time graduate fees are $2086 per semester for Idaho residents, with an additional fee of $4010 per semester for nonresidents. Resident students enrolled part-time pay $205 per credit; nonresidents pay an additional $123 per credit for part-time work. There is no additional fee charged for nonresident credits for credits during the summer session. Full-time fees are charged for 8 credits or more. Fees are subject to change.

Living and Housing Costs

Graduate student housing is available through the University for $462 to $684 per month for apartments ranging in size from efficiencies to four-bedroom units. Potential graduate students are advised to reserve housing early. Off-campus housing lists are available at http://www.asui.uidaho.edu.

Student Group

Total graduate enrollment at UI is about 2,700. UI enrolls students from fifty states and from seventy-eight other countries, providing cultural diversity as part of its educational mission.

Student Outcomes

During the past five years, the department has produced 4 Ph.D.'s, all of whom are employed in academic teaching positions.

Location

Moscow is located in the Idaho panhandle among the rolling hills of the Palouse. It is an agricultural and recreational area and is the cultural center of the region. Local music and theater productions have received international acclaim. Skiing and lake and river sports are within easy drives. Spokane is 88 miles north, and Seattle and Portland are both 6 hours west.

The University

The University of Idaho was created in 1889, a year before Idaho became a state. UI is a publicly supported, comprehensive land-grant institution with principal responsibility in Idaho for performing research and granting the Ph.D. degree. More than 750 faculty members participate in teaching and research. In addition to the accreditation of individual programs, the University is accredited by the Northwest Association of Schools and Colleges.

Applying

Applicants must submit three letters of recommendation, official transcripts of all undergraduate and graduate work, a letter of intent, an application form, and the application fee. For more information, prospective students should visit the Graduate Admissions Office's Web site at http://www.uidaho.edu/cogs/. International applicants must take the TOEFL and submit a score of 525 or higher. Deadlines for all applicants are as follows: fall admission, August 1; spring admission, December 15; and summer admission, April 1. Students who wish to apply for a departmental assistantship should consult with the department regarding the process and the deadline date, which may be earlier than the application deadline date.

Correspondence and Information

Monte Boisen
Department of Mathematics
College of Science
300 Brink Hall
University of Idaho
P.O. Box 441103
Moscow, Idaho, 83844-1103
Telephone: 208-885-6742
Fax: 208-885-5843
E-mail: math@uidaho.edu
World Wide Web: http://www.uidaho.edu/math/

University of Idaho

THE FACULTY AND THEIR RESEARCH

Arie Bialostocki, Ph.D., Combinatorics.
Dora Bialostocki, M.S., Differential equations.
Monte Boisen, Ph.D. Algebra.
Willy Brandal, Ph.D., Algebra.
John Cobb, Ph.D., Topology.
Frank Gao, Ph.D., Functional analysis, probability.
Paul Joyce, Ph.D., Probability and stochastic processes.
Steve Krone, Ph.D., Probability and stochastic processes.
Ralph Neuhaus, Ph.D., Algebra.
Mark Nielsen, Ph.D., Convex geometry and discrete optimization.
Cynthia Piez, M.S., Mathematics education.
Brooks Roberts, Ph.D., Algebra.
Tony Shaska, Ph.D., Algebra.
Hunter Snevily, Ph.D., Combinatorics.
Dave Thomas, Ph.D., Mathematics education and geometry.
Kirk Trigsted, M.S.
Hong Wang, Ph.D., Combinatorics.

UNIVERSITY OF IDAHO

Department of Statistics

Programs of Study

The Department of Statistics at the University of Idaho (UI) offers graduate training leading to the degree of Master of Science (M.S.) in statistics. The objective is to provide sound training in the fundamental principles and techniques of statistics. Graduates are equipped for a variety of statistical careers in industry, business, natural resources, agriculture, and government or to engage in further study at the doctoral level.

The UI statistics group is an intercollegiate, interdisciplinary team that emphasizes broad applications as well as theoretical aspects of statistics. In addition to research within the discipline, faculty members collaborate actively with researchers from the physical, biological, and social sciences, promoting campuswide cooperation in the investigation of statistical problems. There is also close academic liaison with the Department of Statistics at nearby Washington State University.

An M.S. candidate must complete 30 credits of course work and either a thesis, a comprehensive exam, or an internship report. Prerequisites for admission are multivariable calculus; 6 credits of statistics course work, including statistical methods; and course work or experience in computer programming. A student can normally complete the M.S. program in four semesters.

Research Facilities

Statistics graduate students have a private computer lab available that contains several Pentium PCs and a UNIX workstations. Students may also use any of the student computer labs distributed throughout the campus. These labs are equipped with Pentium-class computers and Power Macintosh computers and have access to the University system of UNIX workstations, laser printers, and scanners. Available software includes the latest versions of SAS, S-PLUS, R, SPSS, and SYSTAT, as well as other productivity software and access to the Internet.

The statistics graduate student computer lab also has a library of statistical references and manuals for many statistics programs, such as SAS and S-PLUS.

Financial Aid

Several teaching assistantships (TAs) are available, beginning in the fall semester, and include a waiver of nonresident tuition. Only students with completed application files for admission are considered for teaching assistantships. TA applications are available online at http://www.sci.uidaho.edu/stat/Forms/tara-app.htm and in hard copy. TA awards are determined in March for the following academic year. TA applications should be received by March 1 for fullest consideration. Financial aid is also available through the Federal Perkins Loan Program and work-study grants. The Student Financial Aid Office can provide information and applications.

Research assistantships (RAs) are also available on a limited basis. TA applicants are automatically considered for any available RA positions.

Cost of Study

For 2004–05, full-time graduate fees are $2086 per semester for Idaho residents, with an additional $4010 per semester for nonresidents. Resident students enrolled part-time paid $205 per credit; nonresidents paid an additional $123 per credit for part-time work. Full-time fees are charged for 8 credits or more.

Living and Housing Costs

Graduate student housing is available through the University for $346 to $629 per month for apartments ranging in size from efficiencies to four-bedroom units. Potential graduate students are advised to reserve housing early. Off-campus housing lists are available at http://www.asui.uidaho.edu.

Student Group

There are approximately 20 students in the department; 45 percent are women and 85 percent are international students. There are 16 full-time and 4 part-time students.

Student Outcomes

Alumni may be found working in government agencies, industry, and higher education. Graduates have a variety of employment opportunities. Employers of recent M.S. graduates include the Cleveland Clinic, the U.S. Fish and Wildlife Service, Blue Cross Blue Shield, and the Indiana University School of Medicine. Alumni have also gone on to complete Ph.D. programs in statistics and other fields at the University of Minnesota, Purdue University, Boston University, and others.

Location

Moscow, located in the Idaho panhandle among the rolling hills of the Palouse, is an agricultural and recreational area and is the cultural center of the region. Local music and theater productions have received international acclaim. Skiing and lake and river sports are within easy drives. Spokane is 88 miles north, and Seattle and Portland are each 6 hours west.

The Department

The Department of Statistics is a vital part of the University of Idaho and is a key component in the University's strategic plan to become a premier research institution. Faculty members offer service courses to all departments in addition to conducting their own research and teaching and guiding master's degree students in statistics. The department also operates the Statistical Consulting Center (SCC), which is available to all faculty and staff members and graduate students at the University. The SCC offers free advice on design of surveys and experiments, analysis of data, proposal preparation, and other statistical questions.

Applying

Students seeking admission to graduate study in statistics at UI are required to submit official transcripts of all undergraduate and graduate work, three letters of recommendation, a statement of purpose, an application form, and the application fee to Graduate Admissions by July 1 for fall semester entrance, by November 1 for spring semester entrance, and by April 1 for summer session entrance. Applications and credentials from international applicants have earlier deadlines. International applicants must take the TOEFL and achieve a score of 525 or higher. Students who wish to apply for a departmental assistantship should consult with the department regarding the process and deadline date, which may be earlier than the application deadline. For more information and application materials, prospective students should visit the Graduate Admissions Office Web site at http://www.students.uidaho.edu/gradadmissions.

Correspondence and Information

Department of Statistics
Brink Hall, Room 415A
University of Idaho
P.O. Box 441104
Moscow, Idaho 83844-4266

Telephone: 208-885-2929
Fax: 208-885-4406
E-mail: stat@uidaho.edu
World Wide Web: http://www.sci.uidaho.edu/stat

University of Idaho

THE FACULTY AND THEIR RESEARCH

Raymond Dacey, Professor; Ph.D., Purdue, 1970. Decision theory, game theory, international interactions.
Brian C. Dennis, Professor; Ph.D., Penn State, 1981. Statistical ecology, stochastic population models.
Rick L. Edgeman, Professor and Chair; Ph.D. Wyoming, 1983. Six sigma, quality and reliability engineering, sustainable development, business excellence.
Edward O. Garton, Professor; Ph.D., California, Davis, 1976. Quantitative population ecology and biostatistics.
Ismail H. Genc, Assistant Professor; Ph.D., Texas A&M, 1999. Econometrics methods.
Timothy R. Johnson, Assistant Professor; Ph.D., Illinois at Urbana-Champaign, 2001. Behavioral statistics, psychometrics and statistical computing.
Paul Joyce, Professor; Ph.D., Utah, 1988. Probability, stochastic processes, mathematical population genetics, mathematical statistics.
John J. Lawrence, Associate Professor; Ph.D., Penn State, 1993. Quality control, total quality management, business statistics.
Sauchi Stephen Lee, Associate Professor; Ph.D., Florida State, 1991. Classification, regression, neural networks, pattern recognition, and prediction, Bayesian methods.
R. Ashley Lyman, Associate Professor; Ph.D., Northwestern, 1972. Econometrics methods, microeconomics, demand and project analysis.
Andrew Robinson, Assistant Professor; Ph.D., Minnesota, 1998. Model building and testing and natural resource applications.
Bahman Shafii, Director of Statistical Programs, AG Experiment Station; Ph.D., Idaho, 1988. Design and analysis of experiments, empirical model building, linear and nonlinear regression applications, statistical computing.
R. Kirk Steinhorst, Professor; Ph.D., Colorado State, 1971. Linear models, multivariate analysis, biometry.
Christopher J. Williams, Professor; Ph.D., Georgia, 1988. Biostatistics, statistical genetics, statistical computing and Bayesian methods.

UIC

UNIVERSITY OF ILLINOIS AT CHICAGO

Department of Mathematics, Statistics, and Computer Science

Programs of Study

The department, which ranks in the top thirty-five research mathematics departments nationwide, offers a wide variety of programs of study leading to degrees at the master's and doctoral levels.

The Master of Science (M.S.) degree program in mathematics is designed to lay foundations for doctoral work and also to prepare students for careers in business, government, and industry. The M.S. and Ph.D. degrees in mathematics can be earned with a concentration in applied mathematics, pure mathematics, computer science, or statistics. Also available are the M.S. degree in Mathematics and Information Sciences for Industry (M.I.S.I.), the Master of Science in Teaching (M.S.T.) of mathematics, and the Doctor of Arts (D.A.) degree programs.

Students in the M.S. program have the option of passing a cumulative exam or writing a thesis. Students from other institutions seeking admission to the department's doctoral program must complete the work equivalent to that of the department's M.S. program. They may be required to pass a departmental exam to fully satisfy this requirement.

Two written preliminary exams must be passed and a minor course sequence must be successfully completed for the Ph.D. degree. The Ph.D. dissertation is expected to be a significant contribution to original mathematical research.

The M.I.S.I. program offers a core curriculum with group projects focused on industrial problems with practical deliverables. Emphasis is placed on applications in science, engineering, health care, and business.

The M.S.T. program is designed to strengthen the preparation and background of secondary school and primary school teachers. The program is arranged on an individual basis and has no thesis requirement. Students who are teaching can complete it through evening and summer courses.

The D.A. program is designed to prepare students for instruction at two- and four-year colleges. It includes study and research in methodology and techniques for successful teaching of college mathematics. A dissertation is required.

Research Facilities

The University Library houses more than 1.5 million volumes and specialized collections. The Mathematics Library, located in the department, has more than 20,000 volumes and maintains more than 240 journals. In addition, students have access to the library resources of nearby institutions and the University of Illinois at Urbana-Champaign.

The University offers state-of-the-art computing facilities and Internet access. Resources include an IBM mainframe, a Convex mini-supercomputer, and an extensive network of UNIX workstations and PCs.

The department operates a diverse computing environment with UNIX workstations and PCs available for graduate student use. Graduate students have access to the department's Laboratory for Advanced Computing for research-related programming, supercomputers through specific departmental courses, and a statistical laboratory for research in statistics.

Financial Aid

The department awards a large number of teaching assistantships, some research assistantships, and a few tuition and fee waivers. Some summer support is available. The 2003–04 stipend for the full-time, nine-month teaching assistantship (4–6 contact hours per week) was $12,942. The campus awards a limited number of University fellowships for graduate study, with a 2003–04 stipend of $15,000.

Cost of Study

Semester tuition and fees for 2003–04 were $3774 for Illinois residents and $7965 for all others. Tuition and the service fee are waived for those holding teaching assistantships or fellowships as well as for those on tuition and fee waivers.

Living and Housing Costs

Some of UIC's residence halls are exclusively for graduate students. Rooms and apartments are available near campus and throughout the city at widely varying costs. The campus is easily accessible by public transportation.

Student Group

Approximately 25,000 students are enrolled at UIC, nearly 5,000 of whom are graduate students. They come from all parts of Illinois and the United States as well as from many other countries. The department has about 200 full-time students, of whom approximately 75 are in the doctoral program.

Location

UIC is located just west of the Loop, Chicago's downtown center, which is 5 minutes away by public transportation. Adjacent to campus are the Jane Addams's Hull House and two historic landmark residential areas. The city is well-known for its concerts, theater, galleries and museums, parks, ethnic restaurants, and lakefront recreation. There are other distinguished institutions of higher learning in the metropolitan area, which, along with UIC, contribute to an exciting atmosphere for the study of mathematics.

The University

UIC is the largest institution of higher learning in the Chicago area, and it is grouped in the top 100 research universities in the United States. The University offers bachelor's degrees in ninety-eight fields, master's degrees in seventy-nine, and doctoral degrees in forty-six.

Applying

Applicants are required to take the GRE General Test and a Subject Test in mathematics or computer science. The department requires three letters of recommendation and at least a B average in mathematics beyond calculus. Applications for fall admission should be submitted no later than January 1 for consideration for a fall teaching assistantship or research assistantship or a University Fellowship. Study may also begin in the spring or summer semesters.

Correspondence and Information

Director of Graduate Studies
Department of Mathematics, Statistics, and Computer Science (Mail Code 249)
University of Illinois at Chicago
851 South Morgan Street
Chicago, Illinois 60607-7045
Telephone: 312-996-3041
Fax: 312-996-1491
E-mail: dgs@math.uic.edu
World Wide Web: http://www.math.uic.edu/programs/gradstudies

University of Illinois at Chicago

THE FACULTY AND THEIR RESEARCH

Algebra

A. O. L. Atkin (Emeritus), Ph.D., Cambridge, 1952. Modular forms, number theory.
Daniel Bernstein, Ph.D., Berkeley, 1995. Number theory.
Paul Fong (Emeritus), Ph.D., Harvard, 1959. Group theory, representation theory of finite groups.
Ju-Lee Kim, Ph.D., Yale, 1997. Representation theory of p-adic groups.
Richard G. Larson, Ph.D., Chicago, 1965. Hopf algebras, application of computers to algebra, algorithms.
David E. Radford, Ph.D., North Carolina at Chapel Hill, 1970. Hopf algebras, algebraic groups.
Mark A. Ronan, Ph.D., Oregon, 1978. Buildings, geometries of finite groups.
Fredrick L. Smith, Ph.D., Ohio State, 1972. Group theory.
Stephen D. Smith, D.Phil., Oxford, 1973. Finite groups, representation theory.
Bhama Srinivasan, Ph.D., Manchester, 1960. Representation theory of finite and algebraic groups.
Jeremy Teitelbaum, Ph.D., Harvard, 1986. Number theory.

Analysis

Calixto P. Calderon (Emeritus), Ph.D., Buenos Aires, 1969. Harmonic analysis, differentiation theory.
Alexander Furman, Ph.D., Hebrew, 1996. Ergodic theories, dynamical systems, lie groups.
Shmuel Friedland, D.Sc., Technion (Israel), 1971. Matrix theory and its applications.
Melvin L. Heard, Ph.D., Purdue, 1967. Integrodifferential equations.
Jeff E. Lewis, Ph.D., Rice, 1966. Partial differential equations, microlocal analysis.
Charles S. C. Lin (Emeritus), Ph.D., Berkeley, 1967. Operator theory, perturbation theory, functional analysis.
Howard A. Masur, Ph.D., Minnesota, 1974. Quasiconformal mappings, Teichmuller spaces.
Yoram Sagher, Ph.D., Chicago, 1967. Harmonic analysis, interpolation theory.
Zbigniew Slodkowski, D.Sc., Warsaw, 1981. Several complex variables.
David S. Tartakoff, Ph.D., Berkeley, 1969. Partial differential equations, several complex variables.

Applied Mathematics

Jerry Bona, Ph.D., Harvard, 1971. Applied mathematics.
Susan Friedlander, Ph.D., Princeton, 1972. Geophysical and fluid dynamics.
Floyd B. Hanson, Ph.D., Brown, 1968. Numerical methods, asymptotic methods, stochastic bioeconomics.
Charles Knessl, Ph.D., Northwestern, 1986. Stochastic models, perturbation methods, queuing theory.
Roman Shvydkoy, Ph.D., Missouri–Columbia, 2001. Fluid mechanics, topology.
Charles Tier, Ph.D., NYU, 1976. Analysis of stochastic models, queuing theory.

Computer Science and Combinatorics

Robert Grossman, Ph.D., Princeton, 1985. Applications of computers to analysis, symbolic computation.
Jeffrey S. Leon, Ph.D., Caltech, 1971. Computer methods in group theory and combinatorics, algorithms.
Anton Leykin, Ph.D., Minnesota, 2003. Algebraic analysis, computer algebra, computer science.
Glenn Manacher, Ph.D., Carnegie Tech, 1961. Algorithms, complexity, computer language design.
Dhruv Mubayi, Ph.D., Illinois at Urbana-Champaign, 1998. Combinatorics.
Uri N. Peled, Ph.D., Waterloo, 1976. Optimization, combinatorial algorithms, computational complexity.
Vera Pless, Ph.D., Northwestern, 1957. Coding theory, combinatorics.
Gyorgy Turan, Ph.D., Attila József (Hungary), 1982. Complexity theory, logic, combinatorics.
Jan Verschelde, Ph.D., Katholieke (Belgium), 1996. Computational algebraic geometry, combinatorial and polyhedral methods.
Yi Zhao, Ph.D., Rutgers, 2001. Graph theory, combinatorics, discrete mathematics.

Geometry and Topology

Ian Agol, Ph.D., San Diego, 1998. Knot theory, three manifold topology.
A. K. Bousfield (Emeritus), Ph.D., MIT, 1966. Algebraic topology, homotopy theory.
Marc Culler, Ph.D., Berkeley, 1978. Low-dimensional topology, group theory.
Lawrence Ein, Ph.D., Berkeley, 1981. Algebraic geometry.
Henri Gillet, Ph.D., Harvard, 1978. Algebraic K-theory, algebraic geometry.
Yair Glasner, Ph.D., Hebrew (Jerusalem), 2002. P-adic Lie groups, group theory.
Brayton I. Gray, Ph.D., Chicago, 1965. Homotopy theory, cobordism theory.
James L. Heitsch, Ph.D., Chicago, 1971. Differential topology, theory of foliations.
John Holt, Ph.D., Michigan, 2000. Hyperbolic three manifolds, Kleinian groups, low-dimensional topology.
Steven Hurder, Ph.D., Illinois at Urbana-Champaign, 1980. Differential topology, theory of foliations.
Louis Kauffman, Ph.D., Princeton, 1972. Differential topology, knot theory of singularities.
Anatoly S. Libgober, Ph.D., Tel-Aviv, 1977. Topology of varieties, theory of singularities.
Wei-Dong Ruan, Ph.D., Harvard, 1995. Differential geometry, symplectic geometry, algebraic geometry.
Peter Shalen, Ph.D., Harvard, 1972. Low-dimensional topology, group theory.
Brooke Shipley, Ph.D., MIT, 1995. Algebraic topology, homological algebra.
Martin C. Tangora, Ph.D., Northwestern, 1966. Algebraic topology, homotopy theory.
Kevin Whyte, Ph.D., Chicago, 1998. Geometry of groups and group actions.
John W. Wood, Ph.D., Berkeley, 1968. Differential topology, topology of varieties.
Stephen S.-T. Yau, Ph.D., SUNY at Stony Brook, 1976. Complex geometry, singularities of complex algebraic varieties.

Logic and Universal Algebra

Matthias Aschenbrenner, Ph.D., Illinois at Urbana-Champaign, 2001. Model theory and its applications to algebra and analysis.
John T. Baldwin, Ph.D., Simon Fraser, 1971. Model theory, universal algebra.
Joel D. Berman, Ph.D., Washington (Seattle), 1970. Lattice theory, universal algebra.
Willem J. Blok, Ph.D., Amsterdam, 1976. Algebraic logic, universal algebra, nonclassical logics.
William A. Howard (Emeritus), Ph.D., Chicago, 1956. Foundations of mathematics, proof theory.
David Marker, Ph.D., Yale, 1983. Model theory and applications to algebra.

Mathematics Education

Steven L. Jordan, Ph.D., Berkeley, 1970. Education, computer graphics, computational geometry.
David A. Page, M.A., Illinois, 1950. Elementary mathematics education.
Philip Wagreich, Ph.D., Columbia, 1966. Algebraic geometry, discrete groups, mathematics education.
A. I. Weinzweig, Ph.D., Harvard, 1957. Teaching and learning of mathematics, microcomputers in education.

Probability and Statistics

Emad El-Neweihi, Ph.D., Florida State, 1973. Reliability theory, probability, stochastic processes.
Nasrollah Etemadi, Ph.D., Minnesota, 1974. Probability theory, stochastic processes.
Samad Hedayat, Ph.D., Cornell, 1969. Optimal designs, sampling theory, linear models, discrete optimization.
Dibyen Majumdar, Ph.D., Indian Statistical Institute, 1981. Optimal designs, linear models.
Klaus J. Miescke, Dr.rer.nat., Heidelberg, 1972. Statistics, decision theory, selection procedures.
T. E. S. Raghavan, Ph.D., Indian Statistical Institute, 1966. Game theory, optimization methods in matrices, statistics.

THE UNIVERSITY OF IOWA

Department of Statistics and Actuarial Science

Programs of Study

The department offers graduate programs leading to a Doctor of Philosophy (Ph.D.) in statistics, which may include an emphasis in actuarial science; a Master of Science (M.S.) in statistics; and a Master of Science in actuarial science. Most students earn a master's degree before continuing to the Ph.D. Students usually complete the master's degree in two years; however, well-prepared actuarial science students sometimes finish in three semesters.

The M.S. in actuarial science prepares students for actuarial careers in insurance or consulting companies or other financial institutions. Course work greatly aids students in preparing for the professional exams given by the Society of Actuaries and the Casualty Actuarial Society. The program is designed for graduate students to complete SOA/CAS exams 1 through 4 and also learn the mathematical portions for SOA exam 6 and the finance track of exam 8. The department reimburses exam fees for students who pass professional exams.

The M.S. program in statistics includes a solid foundation in statistical computing, regression analysis, experimental design, and mathematical statistics, plus electives in statistical applications and/or theory. All students gain experience in statistical consulting. This degree is a stepping stone for either a career as an applied statistician or for entry into a Ph.D. program.

The Ph.D. program prepares students for careers in research, applications, and teaching. In addition to required core courses, students take courses in one of four possible areas of concentration: biostatistics, statistical modeling, probability/mathematical statistics, or actuarial science/financial mathematics. The Ph.D. comprehensive exam is usually taken after 2½ years of graduate study.

Research Facilities

The department is housed in Schaeffer Hall, adjacent to the Old Capitol Building, a national historic landmark and the academic center of the campus. All graduate teaching assistants enjoy modern offices in Schaeffer Hall, which are equipped with PCs. The department operates the Statistical Consulting Center, which provides students with important experience in data analysis, consulting, and interdisciplinary research. The department operates two instructional computing labs. One lab, which also is used as an electronic classroom, contains twenty-eight PCs running the Windows operating system. The second lab houses eighteen Linux workstations. Graduate students use these labs for both classwork and research. A Beowulf cluster is also available for graduate students doing highly computer-intensive research.

Financial Aid

Most qualified graduate students are appointed as either teaching or research assistants. For 2004–05, beginning half-time teaching assistants earn an academic-year salary of $15,490. This award is further enhanced by a partial tuition scholarship.

Cost of Study

For 2003–04, tuition and fees for one semester of full-time graduate study totaled $2844.50 for Iowa residents and $7861.50 for nonresidents. Additional fees of $325.50 must be paid. Graduate assistants who are supported at least quarter-time pay the same tuition as Iowa residents.

Living and Housing Costs

Graduate students may request accommodations in University residence halls; however, nearly all choose to live in private apartments or University-owned family housing. For information on University residence halls, students should call 319-335-3000. For information on University apartments, students should call 319-335-9199. There is a wide array of off-campus housing. Many affordable apartments are within walking distance of the campus.

Student Group

The department has a diverse group of 88 graduate students, 57 percent of whom are actuarial science majors and 43 percent of whom are statistics majors. Approximately 53 percent are women, 47 percent are men, and 82 percent are international students. The camaraderie is excellent, and Graduate Students in Statistics and Actuarial Science (GSSAS) meet periodically for parties, pizza, and picnics. Ph.D. students are allocated funds for travel to professional meetings.

Student Outcomes

Iowa students are well educated and in high demand. Graduates from the statistics program find employment in a variety of industrial fields, such as medical, pharmaceutical, electronics, manufacturing, and software. Others select academic careers. A few employers of recent statistics graduates include Alaska Department of Fish and Game, Chung Yuan Christian University, St. Ambrose University, University of Iowa, Wyeth Research, Icelandic Heart Association, Soongsil University, Loyola University, CAN Insurance Co., General Motors, Emmes Corporation, and the Food and Drug Administration.

The demand for actuarial science students is exceptionally high, and the University of Iowa produces excellent actuarial graduates. Twenty-one Iowa students passed the Society of Actuaries/Casualty Actuarial Society's challenging Exam 4 in May 2002. In November 2002, 22 Iowa students passed Exam 3. The department's pass rate for these two exams is about 76 percent. Twenty-four Iowa actuarial students are scheduled to have internships during the summer of 2004, and 16 of the 30 May 2003 actuarial graduates accepted permanent actuarial employment in insurance or consulting companies.

Location

The University of Iowa is nestled in the rolling hills of eastern Iowa along the banks of the Iowa River. Iowa City is a clean, attractive community of approximately 70,000 people. It is noted for its public schools, medical and athletic facilities, attractive business district, parks, and excellent mass transit system. Iowa City is within 300 miles of Chicago, St. Louis, Kansas City, and Minneapolis. In 1999, *Editor & Market Guide* rated Iowa City as the best metropolitan area in which to live in the United States.

The University and The Department

Approximately 30,000 students are enrolled at the University. Iowa is known for its fine arts, and a variety of touring dance, musical, and theatrical groups perform on campus. As a member of the Big Ten Conference, Iowa hosts many outstanding athletic events.

Degree programs are designed to be career oriented and to provide a good balance between theory and practice. High-quality teaching has been a hallmark of the department since it was formed in 1965. Several faculty members have won teaching awards and research awards, and at least eighteen texts have been authored by department faculty members.

Applying

Application deadlines for fall admission are April 15 for international students and July 15 for domestic students. For spring admission, the corresponding dates are October 1 and December 1. For electronic applications, students should go to the Web site at http://www.uiowa.edu/admissions/applications/graduate.html. The Graduate Record Examinations (verbal, quantitative, and analytical writing) are required. International students whose TOEFL scores are below 550 (213 for the computer-based exam) are not eligible for admission.

Correspondence and Information

Students should specify whether they are interested in statistics or actuarial science.

Graduate Information
Department of Statistics and Actuarial Science
University of Iowa
Iowa City, Iowa 52242
Telephone: 319-335-0712
Fax: 319-335-3017
E-mail: stat_info@stat.uiowa.edu
World Wide Web: http://www.stat.uiowa.edu

The University of Iowa

THE FACULTY AND THEIR RESEARCH

Research strengths of the faculty include statistical genetics, spatial and environmental statistics, chaos, time series, Markov chain Monte Carlo simulation, Bayesian statistics, computational statistics, computing environments for statistics, survival analysis, linear models, categorical data analysis, dynamic graphics, multivariate analysis, law and justice statistics, financial mathematics, and various other areas of probability, mathematical statistics, and actuarial science.

James D. Broffitt, Professor and Chair; Ph.D., Colorado State, 1969; Associate, Society of Actuaries. Actuarial science, mathematical statistics.

Joseph E. Cavanaugh, Associate Professor (primary appointment in biostatistics); Ph.D., California, Davis, 1993. Model selection, time-series analysis, state-space modeling, linear models, modeling diagnostics, computational statistics, discrimination and classification, missing data applications, wavelets.

Kathryn Chaloner, Professor and Chair of Biostatistics (primary appointment in biostatistics); Ph.D., Carnegie-Mellon, 1982; Fellow, American Statistical Association; elected member, International Statistical Institute. Bayesian statistics, experimental design, HIV research, clinical trials, biostatistics.

Grace Chan, Assistant Professor; Ph.D., Australian National, 1995. Stochastic simulation and modeling fractal surfaces.

Kung-Sik Chan, Professor; Ph.D., Princeton, 1986; Fellow, American Statistical Association; elected member, International Statistical Institute. Time-series analysis, sampling-based inference, stochastic processes, chaos, statistical ecology.

Mary Kathryn Cowles, Associate Professor, Ph.D., Minnesota, 1994. Bayesian methods in biostatistics and environmental science, statistical computing.

Richard L. Dykstra, Professor; Ph.D., Iowa, 1968; Fellow, American Statistical Association; Fellow, Institute of Mathematical Statistics; elected member, International Statistical Institute. Constrained optimization, order-restricted inference, statistical duality, inequalities, mathematical statistics.

John Geweke, Professor; Ph.D., Minnesota, 1975; Harlan E. McGregor Chair in Economic Theory; Fellow, Econometric Society; Fellow, American Statistical Association. Bayesian statistics, econometrics, time-series analysis.

Jian Huang, Associate Professor; Ph.D., Washington (Seattle), 1994. Statistical genetics, empirical processes, nonparametrics and semiparametrics, survival analysis.

Michael P. Jones, Professor (primary appointment in biostatistics); Ph.D., Washington (Seattle), 1986. Survival analysis.

Gordon Klein, Instructor; B.S., Northeast Missouri State, 1985; Fellow, Society of Actuaries; Enrolled Actuary. Actuarial science.

Joseph B. Lang, Associate Professor; Ph.D., Florida, 1992. Categorical data analysis.

Johannes Ledolter, Professor (primary appointment in management sciences); Ph.D., Wisconsin–Madison, 1975. Time-series analysis, statistical applications in business and engineering.

Russell V. Lenth, Associate Professor; Ph.D. New Mexico, 1975; Director, Statistical Consulting Center; Fellow, American Statistical Association. Experimental design, statistical computing, power and sample size, quality improvement.

Paul Muhly, Professor (primary appointment in mathematics); Ph.D., Michigan, 1969. Functional analysis and operator theory.

Ralph P. Russo, Professor; Ph.D., SUNY at Binghamton, 1980. Probability theory and stochastic processes.

Elias S. W. Shiu, Professor; Ph.D., Caltech, 1975; Principal Financial Group Foundation Professor of Actuarial Science; Associate, Society of Actuaries. Actuarial science, mathematical finance.

Osnat Stramer, Associate Professor; Ph.D., Colorado State, 1993. Time series, probability, stochastic processes.

Luke Tierney, Professor and Ralph E. Wareham Professor of Mathematical Sciences; Ph.D., Cornell, 1980; Fellow, American Statistical Association; Fellow, Institute for Mathematical Statistics; elected member, International Statistical Institute. Bayesian inference, approximate Bayesian methods, Markov chain Monte Carlo methods, statistical computing, computing environments for statistics, dynamic graphics.

George G. Woodworth, Professor; Ph.D., Minnesota, 1966; Fellow, American Statistical Association. Law and justice statistics, multivariate analysis, statistical computing, choice modeling.

Jun Yan, Assistant Professor; Ph.D., Wisconsin–Madison, 2003. Functional data analysis, generalized linear models, multistate survival analysis.

Dale L. Zimmerman, Professor; Ph.D., Iowa State, 1986; Fellow, American Statistical Association. Linear models, experimental design, spatial statistics.

Schaeffer Hall is the home of the Department of Statistics and Actuarial Science.

The University of Iowa

SELECTED PUBLICATIONS

Broffitt, J. D. On smoothness terms in multidimensional Whittaker graduation. *Insur. Math. Econ.* 18:13–27, 1996.

Broffitt, J. D. Maximum likelihood alternatives to actuarial estimators of mortality rates. *Trans. Soc. Actuaries* XXXVI:77–122, 1984.

Broffitt, J. D. A Bayes Estimator for ordered parameters and isotonic Bayesian graduation. *Scand. Actuarial J.* 231–47, 1984.

Cavanaugh, J. E., Y. Wang, and J. W. Davis. Locally self-similar processes and their wavelet analysis. In *Stochastic Processes: Modeling and Simulation* (Handbook of Statistics, Volume 21), pp. 93–135, eds. D. N. Shanbhag and C. R. Rao. Amsterdam: Elsevier Science, 2003.

Neath, A. A., and **J. E. Cavanaugh.** A regression model selection criterion based on bootstrap bumping for use with resistant fitting. *Comput. Stat. Data Anal.* 35:155–69, 2000.

Cavanaugh, J. E., and W. O. Johnson. Assessing the predictive influence of cases in a state-space process. *Biometrika* 86:183–90, 1999.

Chaloner, K., and F. S. Rhame. Quantifying and documenting prior beliefs in clinical trials. *Stat. Med.* 20:581–600, 2001.

Shlay, J., and **K. Chaloner** et al. A randomized placebo controlled trial of a standardized acupuncture regimen, and amitriptyline, for pain caused by HIV-related peripheral neuropathy. *J. Am. Med. Assoc.* 280:1590–5, 1998.

Clyde, M. A., and **K. Chaloner.** The equivalence of constrained and weighted designs in multiple objective design problems. *J. Am. Stat. Assoc.* 91:1236–44, 1996.

Chaloner, K., and I. Verdinelli. Bayesian experimental design: A review. *Stat. Sci.* 10:273–304, 1995.

Chaloner, K. Bayesian residual analysis in the presence of censoring. *Biometrika* 78:637–44, 1991.

Chan, G., and A. T. A. Wood. Increment-based estimators of fractal dimension for two-dimensional surface data. *Stat. Sin.* 10:343–76, 2000.

Chan, G., and A. T. A. Wood. Simulation of stationary Gaussian vector fields. *Stat. Comput.* 9:265–8, 1999.

Chan, G., and A. T. A. Wood. Simulation of multifractional Brownian motion. *Proc. Comput. Stat.,* pp. 233–8, eds. R. Payne and P. J. Green. Physica-Verlag, 1998.

Stenseth, N. C., et al. **(K. S. Chan).** Ecological effects of large-scale climate functions. *Science* 297:1292–6, 2002.

Chan, K. S., and H. Tong. *Chaos: A Statistical Perspective.* New York: Springer-Verlag, 2001.

Tsai, H., and **K. S. Chan.** Testing for nonlinearity with partially observed time series. *Biometrika* 87:805–21, 2000.

Cowles, M. K. Bayesian estimation of the proportion of treatment effect captured by a surrogate marker. *Stat. Med.* 21(6):811–34, 2002.

Cowles, M. K., D. L. Zimmerman, A. Christ, and D. L. McGinnis. Combining snow water equivalent data from multiple sources to estimate spatio-temporal trends and compare measurement systems. *J. Agric. Biol. Environ. Stat.* 7:536–57, 2002.

Cowles, M. K. Accelerating Markov chain Monte Carlo convergence for cumulative-link generalized linear model. *Stat. Comput.* 6:101–11, 2002.

Dykstra, R. L., J. B. Lang, M. Oh, and T. Robertson. Order restricted inference for hypotheses concerning qualitative dispersion. *J. Stat. Plann. Inference* 107:249–65, 2002.

Dykstra, R., and C. Carolan. Marginal densities of the least concave majorant of Brownian motion. *Ann. Stat.* 29:1732–49, 2001.

Dykstra, R., and Y.-F. Chen. The distribution of sizes of ordered level sets. *Stat. Prob. Lett.* 53:339–46, 2001.

Dykstra, R., J. Hewett, and T. Robertson. Nonparametric, isotonic, discriminant procedures. *Biometrika* 86:429–38, 1999.

Geweke, J., and M. Keane. An empirical analysis of income dynamics among men in the PSID: 1968–1989. *J. Econometrics* 96:293–356, 2000.

Geweke, J., and S. Porter-Hudak. The estimation and application of long memory times series models. *J. Time Ser. Anal.* 4:221–38, 1984.

Huang, J. Efficient estimation of the partly linear additive Cox Model. *Ann. Stat.* 27:1536–63, 1999.

Huang, J., and Y. Jiang. Linkage Detection Adaptive to Linkage disequilibrium: The disequilibrium-maximum-likelihood-binomial test for affected sibship data. *Am. J. Human Genet.* 65:1741–59, 1999.

Huang, J. Efficient estimation for the proportional hazards model with interval censoring. *Ann. Stat.* 24:540–68, 1996.

Jones, M. P. Unmasking the trend sought by Jonckheere-type tests for right-censored data. *Scand. J. Stat.* 28:527–36, 2001.

Jones, M. P. Nonrobustness of the information test in detecting heterogeneity. *Can. J. Stat.* 27:771–9, 1999.

Jones, M. P. A class of semiparametric regressions for the accelerated failure time model. *Biometrika* 84:73–84, 1997.

Klein, G., and G. R. Barnes. *How to Pass Exam 2.* Published by the author, 2002.

Klein, G. *How to Pass Exam 3, How to Pass Exam 4, How to Pass Exam 140.* Published by the author, 2000.

Klein, G. A note on annuities payable at a different frequency than interest is compounded. *Actuarial Research Clearing House* 2:221–9, 1994.

Lang, J. B., and T. Aspelund. Binormal association-marginal models for empirically evaluating and comparing diagnostics. *Stat. Modeling: Int. J.* 1:49–64, 2001.

Ledolter, J., and C. W. Burrill. *Statistical Quality Control: Strategies and Tools for Continual Improvement.* John Wiley & Sons, 1999.

Burrill, C. W., and **J. Ledolter.** *Achieving Quality Through Continual Improvement.* John Wiley & Sons, 1999.

Tsimikas, J., and **J. Ledolter.** Analysis of multi-unit variance components models with state space profiles. *Ann. Inst. Stat. Math.* 50:147–64, 1998.

Lenth, R. Some practical guidelines for effective sample-size determination. *Am. Stat.* 55:187–93, 2001.

Sauter, R. M., and **R. Lenth.** Experimental design for process settings in aircraft manufacturing. *Soc. Ind. Appl. Math.,* 1998.

Lenth, R. Quick and easy analysis of unreplicated factorials. *Technometrics,* 1989.

Muhly, P. S., and B. Solel. Quantum Markov Processes (correspondences and dilations). *Int. J. Math.* 13:863–906, 2002.

Muhly, P. S., R. Curto, and J. Xia. Random Toeplitz operators. *Proc. Symp. Pure Math.* 51(1):147–69, 1990.

Muhly, P. S. The function algebraic ramifications of Wieners work on prediction theory and random analysis. In *Norbert Wiener: Collected Works with Commentaries, III,* pp. 339–70. MIT Press, 1981.

Rothmann, M. D., and **R. P. Russo.** Laws of large numbers for observations that change with time. *J. Theor. Prob.* 13, 2000.

The University of Iowa

Selected Publications (continued)

Appel, M. J. B., M. Klass, and **R. P. Russo.** A series criterion for the almost-sure growth rate of the generalized diameter of an increasing sequence of random points. *J. Theor. Prob.* 12:27–47, 1999.

Gerber, H. U., and **E. S. W. Shiu.** Pricing perpetual fund protection with withdrawal option. *North Am. Actuarial J.* 7(2):60–77, 2003.

Gerber, H. U., and **E. S. W. Shiu.** On the time value of ruin. *North Am. Actuarial J.* 2(1):48–72, 1998.

Gerber, H. U., and **E. S. W. Shiu.** Actuarial bridges to dynamic hedging and option pricing. *Insur. Math. Econ.* 18:183–218, 1996.

Roberts, G. O., and **O. Stramer.** Langevin diffusions and Metropolis–Hastings algorithms. *Methodology Comput. Appl. Prob.* 4(4):337–57, 2002.

Stramer, O., and Y. J. Lin. On inference for threshold autoregressive models using the reversible jump sampler. *Test* 11:55–71, 2002.

Roberts, G. O., and **O. Stramer.** On inference for nonlinear diffusion models using the Hastings-Metropolis algorithms. *Biometrika* 88(3):603–21, 2001.

Mira, A., and **L. Tierney.** Efficiency and convergence properties of slice samplers. *Scand. J. Stat.* 29:1–12, 2002.

Tierney, L. Markov chains for exploring posterior distributions, with discussion. *Ann. Stat.* 22:1701–62, 1994.

Tierney, L. *LISP-STAT: An Object-Oriented Environment for Statistical Computing and Dynamic Graphics.* New York: Wiley, 1990.

Woodworth, G., D. Baldus, and C. Pulaski. *Equal Justice and the Death Penalty.* Boston: Northeastern University Press, 1990.

Woodworth, G., D. Baldus, and C. Pulaski. Monitoring and evaluating contemporary death sentencing systems: Lessons from Georgia. *U. C. Davis Law Review* 18, 1985.

Woodworth, G., and J. Louviere. Design and analysis of simulated consumer choice or allocation experiments: An approach based on aggregate data. *J. Marketing Res.,* 1983.

Zimmerman, D. L. Viewing the correlation structure of longitudinal data through a PRISM. *Am. Stat.* 54:310–8, 2000.

Isaacson, J. D., and **D. Zimmerman.** Combining temporally correlated environmental data from two measurement systems. *J. Agric. Biol. Environ. Syst.* 5:64–83, 2000.

Zimmerman, D., and V. Nunez-Anton. Modeling nonstationary longitudinal data. *Biometrics* 56:93–9, 2000.

UNIVERSITY OF NORTH CAROLINA AT CHARLOTTE

Department of Mathematics

Programs of Study

The Department of Mathematics offers programs that lead to the M.S. in mathematics, the Ph.D. in applied mathematics, and the M.A. in math education. These programs are designed to develop advanced skills, knowledge, and critical-thinking abilities that are directly applicable to a wide variety of positions in industry, business, government, and teaching at the secondary school, community college, and/or university level. The department also participates in the interdisciplinary M.S. in mathematical finance and Ph.D. in curriculum and instruction programs. The department has active research programs in commutative algebra; computational fluid dynamics, combustion, and electromagnetics; numerical analysis; dynamical systems; operator algebras, Banach space geometry, and wavelets; partial differential equations and mathematical physics; probability and stochastic processes; and statistics.

The M.S. in mathematics is divided into three concentrations: applied mathematics, statistics, and general. Applied mathematics and statistics require nine and ten courses, respectively, and a project. The programs follow a rigorously structured framework of analytical and applied subjects. General mathematics requires ten courses and offers a good deal of flexibility to a student who wants a broad background of pure and applied courses. The M.A. in math education is primarily designed for secondary school teachers who are interested in professional growth and graduate certification. It requires twelve courses, with at least six in mathematics and the other six chosen from mathematics, mathematics education, and education. All master's programs require a comprehensive oral exam; completion of a thesis is optional.

After their first year, students in the Ph.D. program are required to pass a preliminary exam based on a yearlong advanced real analysis sequence and a yearlong basic course sequence in an applied area of their choice. By the end of their third year, Ph.D. students are expected to pass a qualifying exam for admission to candidacy; the qualifying exam is based on advanced topics in their area of specialization. In addition, Ph.D. students are required to pass a foreign language reading proficiency exam and complete a two- to three-course interdisciplinary minor. The latter can often be coordinated via the department's external consulting activities. Finally, Ph.D. students are required to complete a Ph.D. dissertation that comprises a substantial and original contribution to their area of study.

Research Facilities

The Department of Mathematics provides state-of-the-art computing facilities in its two UNIX workstation labs, which house thirty-five Sun workstations (with nine additional Silicon Graphics workstations in the department). Three PC labs with 105 Pentium-class PCs are conveniently located in the Fretwell building, the home of the Department of Mathematics. In addition, state-of-the-art laptops equipped with the latest multimedia are available for in-class lecture demonstration. All graduate student and faculty member offices are equipped with either a PC or a workstation. In addition, for computationally intensive projects, faculty members and students have fast access to the North Carolina Supercomputing Center's CRAY T916, 32-node CRAY T3E, and visualization facilities. The J. Murrey Atkins University Library contains 750,000 bound volumes (including 13,000 monograph holdings in mathematics, computer science, and statistics) as well as more than 200 mathematics research journals and more than 1 million units in microfilm. The J. Murrey Atkins Library has completed a three-year expansion project that has added more than 11,000 square feet for its holding and reading areas and upgraded its information-searching capabilities.

Financial Aid

Most students accepted into mathematics graduate programs are supported by teaching assistantships, which pay $10,200 for master's students and start at $12,500 for Ph.D. students. Assistantships for advanced Ph.D. students pay $13,500 to $15,000. A limited number of fellowship awards can be applied to supplement the above stipends for especially qualified students. Some students are supported by project-specific externally funded research assistantships, with stipends starting at $13,500. Virtually all out-of-state teaching and research assistants receive waivers for their out-of-state tuition, and a few in-state tuition waivers are available for especially qualified North Carolina residents.

Cost of Study

Tuition and academic fees for 2003–04 were $1071–$1605 per semester for North Carolina residents and $4871–$6671 for nonresidents without assistantships and out-of-state tuition waivers. Graduate students who are U.S. citizens or permanent residents normally become residents of North Carolina after their first year.

Living and Housing Costs

Typical room and board expenses for students living off campus are about $4550 per semester. Off-campus rents average about $400 per month for a two- to four-bedroom apartment. A limited amount of on-campus housing is available with somewhat lower rents.

Student Group

Of 55 mathematics graduate students in spring 2004, 18 were women and 27 were international. Thirty-three were teaching assistants, 5 held research assistantships, and 6 held stipend increases from fellowship sources.

Student Outcomes

Students who successfully complete the master's and Ph.D. programs find challenging and rewarding jobs in academia and business and industry, particularly in the financial and technological sectors, with organizations such as Arbitrade, Duke Power, and Moody Investment Corporation. Recent master's graduates have secured academic positions at regional community colleges and statistical analysis and management positions with Bank of America and First Union Corporation, two of the largest banks in the nation. The most recent Ph.D. graduates include a postdoctoral fellow at Duke University, Department of Electrical Engineering; a vice president of Bank America; an instructor at Pfeiffer University, Department of Mathematics; and a tenure-track professor at Clarkson University, Department of Mathematics and Computer Science.

Location

The city of Charlotte is the hub of a dynamic and growing metropolitan area in terms of economic and cultural development. The city features two major sports franchises, an internationally renowned symphony orchestra, Opera Carolina, and the North Carolina Dance Theater. Specialty shops, galleries, and restaurants reflect the tastes and culture of an ethnically diverse multinational community. Recreational opportunities include biking, boating, and fishing at and around nearby Lake Norman, Lake Lure, and Mountain Island Lake. Many parks and uptown areas host yearly festivals. Mountain recreation areas and ocean beaches are within a 2½- to 4½-hour drive.

The University

The University of North Carolina (UNC) at Charlotte is located in the largest urban center in the Carolinas. Its campus occupies 1,000 wooded acres in the University City area, which also includes University Place, University Hospital, and University Research Park, the nation's sixth-largest university-affiliated research park. The Research Park has more than 11,000 employees and a number of large firms, including AT&T, IBM, Duke Power, Nations Bank, First Union, and the *Wall Street Journal*. The University maintains many professional contacts with several of the firms, and graduate students are very often involved. Of the University's nearly 19,000 students who represent forty-six states and sixty-five countries, about 3,800 are graduate students. UNC Charlotte is known for its academic excellence and is distinguished by its commitment to scholarly activities and teaching accomplishments.

Applying

Application forms may be obtained from the Department of Mathematics. All students must take the General Test of the Graduate Record Examinations (GRE). The Subject Test is recommended but not required. International applicants must take the TOEFL and score above 550 or have received a degree from an American institution. For full consideration for financial support, applicants for the fall semester should submit all materials by January 15.

Correspondence and Information

Joel Avrin
Graduate Coordinator
Department of Mathematics
University of North Carolina at Charlotte
Charlotte, North Carolina 28223-0001

Telephone: 704-687-4929
Fax: 704-687-6415
E-mail: jdavrin@email.uncc.edu
World Wide Web: http://www.math.uncc.edu/grad/

University of North Carolina at Charlotte

THE FACULTY AND THEIR RESEARCH

Robert Anderson, Associate Professor; Ph.D., Minnesota, 1972. Probability.
Joel Avrin, Professor; Ph.D., Berkeley, 1982. Partial differential equations and mathematical physics.
Auimikh Biswas, Assistant Professor; Ph.D., Indiana, 2000. Functional analysis and partial differential equations.
Charles Burnap, Associate Professor; Ph.D., Harvard, 1976. Mathematical physics.
Wei Cai, Professor; Ph.D., Brown, 1989. Computational fluid dynamics and electromagnetics.
Zongwu Cai, Assistant Professor; Ph.D., California, Davis, 1995. Statistics.
Vic Cifarelli, Associate Professor; Ph.D., Purdue, 1988. Mathematics education.
Xingde Dai, Associate Professor; Ph.D., Texas A&M, 1990. Operator algebras.
Yuanan Diao, Associate Professor; Ph.D., Florida State, 1990. Topology.
Jacek Dmochowski, Research Assistant Professor; Ph.D., Purdue, 1995. Statistics.
Alan Dow, Professor; Ph.D., Manitoba, 1980. Topology.
Yuri Godin, Ph.D., Technion (Israel), 1994. Mathematical physics.
Kim Harris, Associate Professor; Ph.D., Georgia, 1985. Mathematics education.
Gabor Hetyei, Assistant Professor; Ph.D., MIT, 1994. Combinatorics.
Evan Houston, Professor; Ph.D., Texas at Austin, 1973. Commutative algebra.
Phillip Johnson, Associate Professor; Ph.D., Vanderbilt, 1968. Mathematics education.
John Kawczak, Assistant Professor; Ph.D., Western Ontario, 1998. Statistics.
Mohammad Kazemi, Professor; Ph.D., Michigan, 1982. Control theory.
Michael Kilbanov, Professor; Ph.D., Ural State (Russia), 1977. Inverse problems.
Alan Lambert, Professor; Ph.D., Michigan, 1970. Operator theory.
Thomas G. Lucas, Professor; Ph.D., Missouri, 1983. Commutative algebra.
Thomas R. Lucas, Professor; Ph.D., Georgia Tech, 1970. Numerical analysis.
Stanislav Molchanov, Professor; Ph.D., Moscow State, 1967. Probability/mathematical physics.
Wanda Nabors, Assistant Professor; Ph.D., Georgia. Mathematics education.
Hae-Soo Oh, Associate Professor; Ph.D., Michigan, 1980. Numerical analysis.
Alexander Papadopoulos, Professor; Ph.D., Virginia Tech, 1972. Statistics.
Joseph Quinn, Professor; Ph.D., Michigan State, 1970. Stochastic processes.
Harold Reiter, Associate Professor; Ph.D., Clemson, 1969. Combinatorics.
Franz Rothe, Associate Professor; Ph.D., Tübingen (Germany), 1975. Partial differential equations.
David C. Royster, Associate Professor; Ph.D., LSU, 1978. Differential topology.
Adalira Saenz-Ludlow, Associate Professor; Ph.D., Florida State, 1990. Mathematics education.
Douglas Shafer, Professor; Ph.D., North Carolina at Chapel Hill, 1978. Dynamical systems.
Isaac Sonin, Professor; Ph.D., Moscow State, 1971. Probability/operations research.
Nicholas Stavrakas, Professor; Ph.D., Clemson, 1973. Convexity.
Yanqing Sun, Associate Professor; Ph.D., Florida State, 1992. Statistics.
Rajeshwari Sundaram, Assistant Professor; Ph.D., Michigan State, 1999. Statistics.
Boris Vainberg, Professor; Ph.D., Moscow State, 1963. Partial differential equations and mathematical physics.
Barnet Weinstock, Professor; Ph.D., MIT, 1966. Several complex variables.
Volker Wihstutz, Professor; Ph.D., Bremen (Germany), 1975. Stochastic dynamical systems.
Alexander Yushkevich, Professor; Ph.D., Moscow State, 1956. Probability/operations research.
Zhi-Yi Zhang, Associate Professor; Ph.D., Rutgers, 1990. Statistics.
You-Lan Zhu, Professor; Ph.D., Qinghau (China), 1963. Computational fluid dynamics.

UNIVERSITY OF NOTRE DAME

Graduate Studies in Mathematics

Program of Study The purpose of the graduate program in mathematics is to give students the opportunity to develop into educated and creative mathematicians. In most instances, the doctoral program starts with two years of basic training, including supervised teaching experience and introductory and advanced course work in the fundamentals of algebra, analysis, geometry, and topology. This is followed by thesis work done in close association with one or more members of the faculty. Limited enrollment and the presence of several active groups of research mathematicians provide thesis opportunities in many areas of algebra, algebraic geometry, applied mathematics, complex analysis, differential geometry, logic, partial differential equations, and topology.

Research Facilities Every effort is made to enable students to avail themselves of the opportunities provided by the excellent mathematics faculty at Notre Dame. The Department of Mathematics has its own building with all modern facilities, including a comprehensive research library of 35,000 volumes that subscribes to 290 current journals. All graduate students have comfortable offices. Students are ensured a stimulating and challenging intellectual experience.

Financial Aid In 2002–03, all new students received a twelve-month stipend of more than $17,000; they have no teaching duties the first year. Next, they become teaching assistants and begin the three stages of supervised teaching provided by the department. A teaching assistant usually starts by doing tutorial work in freshman and sophomore calculus courses (4 classroom hours per week); this is followed by a variety of duties in advanced undergraduate courses; the final, lecturing stage involves independent teaching in the classroom. All doctoral students in mathematics also receive a full tuition fellowship. Support is available for citizens and noncitizens.

Cost of Study All graduate students in mathematics are supported by fellowships or assistantships, which include tuition scholarships.

Living and Housing Costs University housing includes two-bedroom apartments for single men and women, four-bedroom town houses for single men and women, and two- and four-bedroom apartments for married students at rents that ranged from $400 to $700 per month in 2000–01. Comfortable and attractive off-campus rooms normally cost between $300 and $500 per month. Other expenses are lower than in most metropolitan areas.

Student Group The carefully selected men and women who make up the student body of the University come from every state in the Union and sixty-six countries. There are about 38 graduate students working for their doctorate in mathematics. The faculty-student ratio is greater than 1:1.

Location The University is just north of South Bend, a pleasant Midwestern city with a population of about 110,000. The Notre Dame campus is exceptionally rich in active cultural programs, and the wide variety of cultural, educational, and recreational facilities of Chicago and Lake Michigan are less than 2 hours away by car.

The University Founded in 1842, the University of Notre Dame has a 1,250-acre campus. Much of the campus is heavily wooded, and two delightful lakes lie entirely within it. Total enrollment for fall 2002 was 11,311; approximately one fourth of these are graduate students. The University is proud of its tradition as a Catholic university with a profound commitment to intellectual freedom in every area of contemporary thought. The students and faculty represent a rich diversity of religious, racial, and ethnic backgrounds.

Applying All applicants are required to take the General Test of the Graduate Record Examinations and are required to take the Subject Test in mathematics. Application for these tests should be made to Educational Testing Service in Princeton, New Jersey 08541, or at 1947 Center Street, Berkeley, California 94704. The application fee is $50 for all applications submitted after December 1. The fee for applications submitted by December 1 for the following fall semester is $35. The application deadline for students who wish to be considered for financial aid is February 1. All applicants are considered without regard to race, sex, or religious affiliation.

Correspondence and Information

Director of Graduate Studies
Department of Mathematics
University of Notre Dame
255 Hurley Building
Notre Dame, Indiana 46556-4618
Telephone: 219-631-7245
Fax: 219-631-6579
E-mail: mathgrad.1@nd.edu
World Wide Web: http://www.science.nd.edu/math

University of Notre Dame

THE FACULTY AND THEIR RESEARCH

Algebra
Mario Borelli, Ph.D., Indiana. Algebraic geometry, computer graphics.
Matthew Dyer, Ph.D., Sydney. Representation theory, algebraic groups.
Samuel R. Evens, Ph.D., MIT. Geometry of Lie groups and homogeneous spaces and representation theory.
Alexander J. Hahn, Ph.D., Notre Dame. Linear groups, theories of algebras, quadratic forms.
Warren J. Wong, Ph.D., Harvard. Theory of finite groups and their representations.

Algebraic Geometry/Commutative Algebra
Karen Chandler, Ph.D., Harvard. Castelnuovo theory, zero-dimensional schemes.
Juan C. Migliore, Ph.D., Brown. Liaison theory, minimal free resolutions.
Claudia Polini, Ph.D., Rutgers. Commutative and homological algebra, blowup algebras, linkage and residual intersection theory.

Applied Mathematics
Mark Alber, Ph.D., Pennsylvania. Nonlinear dynamical systems and nonlinear partial differential equations and applications to biology.
Leonid Faybusovich, Ph.D., Harvard. Optimization, optimal control theory.
Bei Hu, Ph.D., Minnesota. Nonlinear partial differential equations.
David Nicholls, Ph.D., Brown. Free boundary problems, partial differential equations, numerical analysis.
Joachim Rosenthal, Ph.D., Arizona State. Control theory, coding theory and cryptography.
Israel Michael Sigal, Ph.D., Tel-Aviv. Mathematical physics, applied mathematics, partial differential equations.

Complex Analysis
Jeffrey A. Diller, Ph.D., Michigan. Several complex variables.
Mei-Chi Shaw, Ph.D., Princeton. Partial differential equations and several complex variables.
Dennis M. Snow, Ph.D., Notre Dame. Homogeneous complex manifolds, group actions.
Pit-Mann Wong, Ph.D., Notre Dame. Several complex variables.

Computational Mathematics
Andrew J. Sommese, Ph.D., Princeton. Numerical analysis of polynomial systems.

Differential Geometry
Jianguo Cao, Ph.D., Pennsylvania. Differential geometry.
Matthew Gursky, Ph.D., Caltech. Geometric analysis.
Richard Hind, Ph.D., Stanford. Symplectic geometry.
Alan Howard, Ph.D., Brown. Complex manifolds.
Xiaobo Liu, Ph.D., Pennsylvania. Differential geometry.
Brian Smyth, Ph.D., Brown. Differential geometry.
Frederico J. Xavier, Ph.D., Rochester. Differential geometry.

Logic
Steven A. Buechler, Ph.D., Maryland. Model theory.
Peter Cholak, Ph.D., Wisconsin. Computability theory.
Julia Knight, Ph.D., Berkeley. Computability, computable structures.
Sergei Starchenko, Ph.D., Novosibirsk (Russia). Model theory.

Mathematical Physics
Katrina Barron, Ph.D., Rutgers. Vertex operator superalgebras and superconformal field theory.
Michael Gekhtman, Ph.D., Ukrainian Academy of Sciences. Integrable models, Poisson geometry.
Brian C. Hall, Ph.D., Cornell. Quantization and coherent states, analysis on Lie groups.
Israel Michael Sigal, Ph.D., Tel-Aviv. Mathematical physics, applied mathematics, partial differential equations.

Partial Differential Equations
Qing Han, Ph.D., NYU (Courant). Partial differential equations.
A. Alexandrou Himonas, Ph.D., Purdue. Partial differential equations.
Gerard Misiolek, Ph.D., SUNY at Stony Brook. Geometric and nonlinear functional analysis and partial differential equations.
Israel Michael Sigal, Ph.D., Tel-Aviv. Mathematical physics, applied mathematics, partial differential equations.
Nancy K. Stanton, Ph.D., MIT. Differential geometry, complex manifolds.

Topology
Francis X. Connolly, Ph.D., Rochester. Differential and algebraic topology.
John E. Derwent, Ph.D., Notre Dame. Differential and algebraic topology.
William G. Dwyer, Ph.D., MIT. Algebraic topology.
Liviu Nicolaescu, Ph.D., Michigan State. Gauge theory.
Stephan A. Stolz, Ph.D., Mainz (Germany). Algebraic topology and differential geometry.
Laurence R. Taylor, Ph.D., Berkeley. Geometric and algebraic topology.
E. Bruce Williams, Ph.D., MIT. Geometric and algebraic topology, K-theory.

University of Notre Dame

SELECTED PUBLICATIONS

Alber, M. S., et al. The complex geometry of weak piecewise smooth solutions of integrable nonlinear PDE's of shallow water and Dym type. *Commun. Math. Phys.* 221:197–227, 2001.

Alber, M. S., and Y. N. Fedorov. Algebraic geometrical solutions for certain evolution equations and Hamiltonian flows on nonlinear subvarieties of generalized Jacobians. *Inverse Problems* 17:1017–42, 2001.

Alber, M. S., G. G. Luther, and C. Miller. On soliton-type solutions of the equations associated with N-component systems. *J. Math. Phys.* 41:1284–316, 2000.

Barron, K. The notion of N=1 supergeometric vertex operator superalgebra and the isomorphism theorem. *Commun. Contemp. Math.* 5(4):481–567, 2003.

Barron, K. The moduli space of N=1 superspheres with tubes and the sewing operation. *Mem. Am. Math. Soc.* 162(772), 2003.

Barron, K., C. Dong, G. Mason. Twisted sectors for tensor product vertex operator algebras associated to permutation groups. *Commun. Math. Phys.* 227:349–84, 2002.

Borelli, M. Variedades casi-proyectivas y divisoriales. *Publicationes del Institutio de Matematicas de la Universidad Nacional Interamericana,* Lima, Peru, in press.

Borelli, M. The cohomology of divisorial schemes. *Pacific J. Math.* 37:1–7, 1971.

Borelli, M. Affine complements of divisors. *Pacific J. Math.* 31:595–605, 1969.

Buechler, S., and C. Hoover. Classification of small types of rank ω, part I. *J. Symbol. Logic,* in press.

Buechler, S., A. Pillay, and F. Wagner. Supersimple theories. *J. Am. Math. Soc. No. 1* 14:109–24, 2000.

Buechler, S. Lascar strong types in some simple theories. *J. Symbol. Logic* 64(2):817–24, 1999.

Cao, J., and **F. J. Xavier.** Kahler parabolicity and the Euler number of compact manifolds of nonpositive sectional curvature. *Math. Ann. No. 3* 319:493–91, 2001.

Cao, J., J. Cheeger, and X. Rong. Splittings and Cr-structures for manifolds with nonpositive sectional curvature. *Inventiones Math.* 144:139–67, 2001.

Cao, J. Cheeger isoperimetric constants of Gromov-hyperbolic spaces with quasi-pole. *Commun. Contemp. Math. No. 4* 2:511–33, 2000.

Chandler, K. A. A brief proof of a maximal rank theorem for generic double points in projective spaces. *Trans. Am. Math. Soc. No. 5* 353:1907–20, 2001.

Chandler, K. A., A. Howard, and **A. J. Sommese.** Reducible hyperphase sections I. *J. Math. Soc. Japan* 51(4):887–910, 1999.

Chandler, K. A. Higher infinitesimal neighborhoods. *J. Algebra No. 2* 205:460–79, 1998.

Chandler, K. A. Geometry of dots and ropes. *Trans. Am. Math. Soc.* 347(3):767–84, 1995.

Cholak, P., and L. Harrington. On the definability of the double jump in the computably enumerable sets. *J. Math. Logic* 2(2):261–96, 2002.

Cholak, P., R. Coles, R. Downey, and E. Herrmann. Automorphisms of the lattice of Pi_1^0 classes; prefect thin classes and anc degrees. *Trans. Am. Math. Soc.* 353:4899–924, 2001.

Cholak, P., C. Jockusch, and T. Slaman. The strength of Ramsey's theorem for pairs. *J. Symbol. Logic* 66(1):1–55, 2001.

Connolly, F. X., and D. Anderson. Finiteness obstructions to cocompact actions on S^m x $\hat{A}^n$. *Comment. Math. Helv.* 68:85–110, 1993.

Connolly, F. X., and T. Kozniewski. Examples of lack of rigidity in crystallographic groups. In *Lecture Notes in Mathematics—Algebraic Topology,* Poznan, 1989, vol. 1474, pp. 139–45. Berlin/Heidelberg: Springer-Verlag, 1991.

Connolly, F. X., and T. Kozniewski. Rigidity and crystallographic groups I. *Inventiones Math.* 99:25–48, 1990.

Derwent, J. E. A note on numerable covers. *Proc. Am. Math. Soc.* 19:1130–2, 1968.

Derwent, J. E. Inverses for fiber spaces. *Proc. Am. Math. Soc.* 19:1491–4, 1968.

Derwent, J. E. Handle decompositions of manifolds. *J. Math. Mech.* 15:329–46, 1966.

Diller, J., and C. Faure. Dynamics of bimeromorphic maps of surfaces. *Am. J. Math.,* in press.

Diller, J., and M. Jonsson. Topological entropy on saddle sets in **P** 2. *Duke Math. J. No. 2* 103:261–78, 2000.

Barrett, D. and **J. Diller.** A new construction of Riemann surfaces with corona. *J. Geom. Anal. No. 3* 8:341–7, 1998.

Dwyer, W. G., and C. W. Wilkerson. The elementary geometric structure of compact Lie groups. *Bull. London Math. Soc.* 30:337–64, 1998.

Dwyer, W. G. Transfer maps for fibrations. *Math. Proc. Cambridge Philos. Soc.* 120:221–35, 1996.

Dwyer, W. G., and J. Spalinski. Homotopy theories and model categories. In *Handbook of Algebraic Topology,* pp. 73–126, ed. I. M. James. Amsterdam: Elsevier, 1995.

Dyer, M. J. Representation theories from coxeter groups. *Can. Math. Soc. Conf. Proc.* 16:105–39, 1995.

Dyer, M. J. Bruhat intervals, polyhedral cones and Kazhdan-Lusztig-Stanley polynomials. *Math. Z.* 215:223–36, 1994.

Dyer, M. J. The nil Hecke ring and Deodhar's conjecture on Bruhat intervals. *Inventiones Math.* III:571–4, 1993.

Evens, S., and J.-H. Lu. Poisson harmonic forms, Kostant harmonic forms, and the S1-equivariant cohomology of K/T. *Adv. Math.* 142:171–220, 1999.

Evens, S., and I. Mirkovic. Characteristic cycles for the loop Grassmannian and nilpotent orbits. *Duke Math. J.* 97:109–26, 1999.

Evens, S., and I. Mirkovic. Fourier transform and the Iwahori-Matsumoto involution. *Duke Math. J.* 86:435–64, 1997.

Faybusovich, L. Jordan-algebraic approach to potential-reduction algorithms. *Math. Z.* 239:117–29, 2002.

Faybusovich, L. Self-concordan barriers for cones generated by Chebyshev systems. *SIAM J. Optimization* 12:770–81, 2002.

Faybusovich, L. On Nesterov's approach to semiinfinite programming. *Acta Appl. Math.* 74:195–215, 2002.

Gekhtman, M., and M. Shapiro. Noncommutative and commutative integrability of generic Toda flows in simple Lie algebras. *Commun. Pure Appl. Math.* 52:53–84, 1999.

Bloch, A., and **M. Gekhtman.** Hamiltonian and gradient structures in the Toda flows. *J. Geom. Phys.* 27:230–48, 1998.

Gekhtman, M. Hamiltonian structure of nonabelian Toda lattice. *Lett. Math. Phys.* 46:189–205, 1998.

Gursky, M. J., and J. Viaclovsky. A new variational characterization of three-dimensional space forms. *Inventiones Math.* 145:251–78, 2001.

Gursky, M. J. The Weyl functional, deRham cohomology, and Kahler-Einstein metrics. *Ann. Math.* 148:315–37, 1998.

Gursky, M. J., and C. LeBrun. Yamabe invariants and spin^c structures. *Geom. Funct. Anal.* 8:965–77, 1998.

Hahn, A. J. The elements of the orthogonal group Ω_n (V) as products of commutators of symmetries. *J. Algebra* 184:927–44, 1996.

Hahn, A. J. Quadratic algebras, Clifford algebras and arithmetic Witt groups. In *UNIVERSITEXT Series.* Berlin and New York: Springer-Verlag, 1994.

Hahn, A. J., and O. T. O'Meara. The classical groups and K-theory. In *Grundlehren der Mathematik,* vol. 291. Berlin and New York: Springer-Verlag, 1989.

Hall, B. C. Geometric quantization and generalized Segal-Bargmann transform for Lie groups of compact type. *Commun. Math. Phys.* 226:233–68, 2002.

Hall, B. C. Harmonic analysis with respect to heat kernel measure. *Bull. Am. Math. Soc.* 38:43–78, 2001.

Hall, B. C. The Segal-Bargmann "coherent state" transform for compact Lie groups. *J. Funct. Anal.* 122:103–51, 1994.

Han, Q., R. Hardt, and F.-H. Lin. Geometric measure of singular sets of elliptic equations. *Comm. Pure Appl. Math.* 51:1425–43, 1998.

Han, Q. On the Schauder estimates of solutions to parabolic equations. *Ann. Sculo Di Pisa* 27:1–26, 1998.

Han, Q., Singular sets of solutions to elliptic equations. *Indiana J. Math.* 43:983–1002, 1994.

Himonas, A. A., and **G. Misiolek.** A priori estimates for higher order multipliers on a circle. *Proc. Am. Math. Soc.* 130(10):3043–50, 2002.

Himonas, A. A., and **G. Misiolek.** The Cauchy problem for a shallow-water equation. *Differential Integral Equations* 14(7):821–31, 2001.

Himonas, A. A., and G. Petronilho. Global hypoellipticity and simultaneous approximability. *J. Funct. Anal.* 170(2):356–65, 2000.

Burnes, D., S. Halverscheid, and **R. Hind.** The geometry of Grauert tubes and complexification of symmetric spaces. *Duke Math. J.* 118(3):465–91, 2003.

Burnes, D., and **R. Hind.** Symplectic geometry and the uniqueness of Grauert tubes. *J. Geom. Funct. Anal.* 11:1–10, 2001.

Hind, R. Holomorphic filing of RP^3. *Comm. Contemp. Math.* 3:349–63, 2000.

Hind, R. Filling by holomorphic disks with weakly pseudoconvex boundary conditions. *J. Geom. Funct. Anal.* 7:462–95, 1997.

Beltrametti, M. C., **A. Howard**, M. Schneider, and **A. J. Sommese.**

University of Notre Dame

Selected Publications (continued)

Projections from subvarieties. In *Complex Analysis and Algebraic Geometry: A Volume in Memory of Michael Schneider,* 406 pp., eds., T. Peternell and F. O. Schreyer. Berlin: de Gruyter, 2000.

Howard, A., and **A. J. Sommese.** On the theorem of DeFranchis. *Ann. Scuola Norm. Supp. Pisa* 10(3):429–36, 1983.

Friedman, A., **B. Hu,** and J. J. L. Valazquez. The evolution of stress intensity factors in the propagation of cracks in elastic media. *Arch. Ration. Mech. Anal.* 152:103–39, 2000.

Friedman, A., and **B. Hu.** Head-media interaction in magnetic recording. *Arch. Ration. Mech. Anal.* 140:79–101, 1997.

Hu, B., and H.-M. Yin. The profile near blowup time for solutions of the heat equation with a nonlinear boundary condition. *Trans. Am. Math. Soc.* 346(1):117–35, 1994.

Goncharov, S. S., V. S. Harizanov, **J. F. Knight,** and C. McCoy. Simple and immune relations. *Arch. Math. Logic* 42:279–91, 2003.

Harizanov, V. S., **J. F. Knight,** and A. S. Morozov. Sequences of n-diagrams. *J. Symbol. Logic* 67:1227–47, 2002.

Goncharov, S. S., and **J. F. Knight.** Computable structure and non-structure theorems. *Algebra Logic* 41:351–73, 2002.

Heintze, E., and **X. Liu.** Homogeneity of infinite dimensional isoparametric submanifolds. *Ann. Math.* 149:149–81, 1999.

Liu, X., and G. Tian. Virasoro constraints for quantum cohomology. *J. Differential Geom.* 50:537–91, 1998.

Liu, X. Volume minimizing cycles in compact Lie groups. *Am. J. Math.* 117:1203–48, 1995.

Migliore, J., and R. Miro-Roig. On the minimal free resolution of n+1 generic forms. *Trans. Am. Math. Soc.* 355:1–36, 2003.

Kleppe, R. M., and **J. Migliore** et al. Gorenstein liaison, complete intersection liaison invariants and unobstructedness. *Mem. Am. Math. Soc.,* vol. 154, 2001.

Migliore, J. Introduction to liaison theory and deficiency modules. In *Progress in Mathematics,* vol. 165. Boston: Birkhäuser, 1998.

Khesin, B., and **G. Misiolek.** Euler equations on homogeneous spaces and Virasoro Orbits. *Adv. Math.,* in press.

Misiolek, G. Classical solutions of the Camassa-Holm "equation." *Geom. Funct. Anal.,* in press.

Misiolek, G. The exponential map on the free loop space is Fredholm. *Geom. Funct. Anal.* 7:954–69, 1997.

Nicholls, D. P., and F. Reitich. A new approach to analyticity of Dirichlet-Neumann operators. *Proc. R. Soc. Edinburgh, Ser. A* 131(6):1411–33, 2001.

Nicholls, D. P., and F. Reitich. A stable high-order perturbative method for the computation of Dirichlet-Neumann operators. *J. Computational Phys. No. 1* 170:276–98, 2001.

Craig, W., and **D. P. Nicholls.** Traveling two- and three-dimensional capillary gravity water waves. *SIAM J. Math. Anal. No. 2* 32:232–59, 2000.

Nicolaescu, L. Adiabatic limits of the Seiberg-Witten equations on Seifert manifolds. *Commun. Anal. Geom.* 6:301–62, 1998.

Nicolaescu, L. Generalized symplectic geometries and the index of families of elliptic problems. *Mem. Am. Math. Soc.* 128(609), 1997.

Nicolaescu, L. The spectral flow, the Maslov index and decompositions of manifolds. *Duke Univ. J.* 80:485–534, 1995.

Corso, A., **C. Polini,** and B. Ulrich. The structure of the core of ideals. *Math. Ann.* 321:89–105, 2001.

Polini, C., and B. Ulrich. Necessary and sufficient conditions for the Cohen-Macaulayness of blowup algebras. *Composition Math.* 119:189–211, 1999.

Polini, C., and B. Ulrich. Linkage and reduction numbers. *Math. Ann.* 310:631–51, 1998.

Marcus, B., and **J. Rosenthal.** Codes systems and graphical models. In *Mathematics and Its Applications, IMA,* vol. 123. Springer-Verlag, 2001.

Rosenthal, J., and X. Wang. The multiplicative inverse eigenvalue problem over an algebraically closed field. *SIAM J. Matrix Anal. Appl. No. 2* 23:517–23, 2001.

Rosenthal, J., and R. Smarandache. Maximum distance separable convolutional codes. *Applicable Algebra Eng. Commun. Computing No. 1* 10:15–32, 1999.

Chen, S.-C., and **M.-C. Shaw.** *Partial Differential Equations in Several Complex Variables,* vol. 19. Providence: AMS International Press, 2001.

Michel, J., and **M.-C. Shaw.** The $\bar{\partial}$ problem on domains with piecewise smooth boundaries with applications. *Trans. Am. Math. Soc.* 311:4365–80, 1999.

Michel, J., and **M.-C. Shaw.** C^∞-regularity of solutions of the tangential CR-equations on weakly pseudoconvex manifolds. *Math. Ann.* 311:147–62, 1998.

Sigal, I. M., and B. Vasilijevic. Mathematical theory of tunneling at positive temperatures. *Ann. Inst. Henri Poincaré* 3:1–41, 2002.

Gustafson, S., and **I. M. Sigal.** The stability of magnetic vortices. *Comm. Math. Phys.* 212(2):257–75, 2000.

Bach, V., J. Fröhlich, and **I. M. Sigal.** Return to equilibrium. *J. Math. Phys.* 41:3985–4060, 2000.

Smyth, B., and **F. J. Xavier.** Eigenvalue estimates and the index of Hessiau fields. *Bull. London Math. Soc.* 32:1–4, 2000.

Smyth, B., and **F. J. Xavier.** Real solvability of the equation $\partial 2/z\ \omega$ = pg and the topology of isolated umbilics. *J. Geom. Anal.* 8:655–71, 1998.

Snow, D. M., and J. Winkelmann. Compact complex homogeneous manifolds with large automorphism groups. *Inventiones Math.* 134:139–44, 1998.

Snow, D. M., and L. Manivel. A Borel-Weil theorem for holomorphic forms. *Compositio Math.* 103:351–65, 1996.

Snow, D. M. The nef value of homogeneous line bundles and related vanishing theorems. *Forum Math.* 7:385–92, 1995.

Sommese, A. J., J. Verschelde, and C. W. Wampler. Symmetric functions applied to decomposing solution sets of polynomial systems. *SIAM J. Numerical Anal.* 40:2026–46, 2002.

Sommese, A. J., J. Verschelde, and C. W. Wampler. Numerical decomposition of the solution sets of polynomial systems into irreducible components. *SIAM J. Numerical Anal.* 38:2022–46, 2001.

Kebekus, S., T. Peternell, **A. J. Sommese,** and J. A. Wisniewski. Projective contact manifolds. *Inventiones Math.* 142:1–15, 2000.

Morgan, A., **A. J. Sommese,** and C. Wampler. A product-decomposition bound for Bezout numbers. *SIAM J. Numerical Anal.* 32:1308–25, 1995.

Stanton, N. K. Infinitesimal automorphisms of real hypersurfaces. *Am. J. Math.* 118:209–33, 1996.

Stanton, N. K. Spectral invariants of pseudoconformal manifolds. *Proc. Symp. Pure Math.* 54(2):551–7, 1993.

Stanton, N. K. The Riemann mapping non-theorem. *Math. Intelligencer* 14:32–6, 1992.

Stolz, S., Multiplicities of Dupin hypersurfaces. *Inv. Math.* 138:253–79, 1999.

Stolz, S. A conjecture concerning positive Ricci curvature and the Witten genus. *Math. Ann.* 304:785–800, 1996.

Stolz, S. Simply connected manifolds of positive scalar curvature. *Ann. Math.* 136:511–40, 1992.

Hughes, B., **L. R. Taylor,** S. Weinberger, and **B. Williams.** Neighborhoods in stratified spaces with two strata. *Topology* 39:873–919, 2000.

Hambleton, I., and **L. R. Taylor.** A guide to the calculation of surgery obstruction groups. Surveys on Surgery Theory, Volume I. In *Annals of Mathematical Studies 145,* pp. 225–74, eds. S. Cappell, A. Ranicki, and J. Rosenberg. Princeton University Press, 2000.

Taylor, L. R. Taut codimension one spheres of odd order, "Geometry and Topology: Aarhus." *Contemp. Math., Am. Math Soc.* 258:369–375, 2000.

Dwyer, W., M. Weiss, and **B. Williams.** A parametrized index theorem for the algebraic K-theory Euler class. *Acta Math.,* 2003.

Weiss, M., and **B. Williams.** Automorphisms of manifolds. *Ann. Math. Stud.* 149:165–220, 2001.

Williams, B. Bivariant Riemann Roch theorems. *Geometry Topology: Aarhus* 258:377–93, 2000.

Wong, P.-M. Holomorphic curves into spaces of constant curvature. In *Complex Geometry,* eds. G. Komatsu and Y. Sakane. New York: Marcel Dekker, 1992.

Wong, P.-M. Diophantine approximation and the theory of holomorphic curves. In *Proceedings of the Symposium on Value Distribution Theory in Several Complex Variables, Notre Dame Mathematics Lectures,* vol. 12, pp. 115–56, ed. W. Stoll, 1992.

Ru, M., and **P.-M. Wong.** Integral points of $\mathbf{P}^n$-{2n+1 hyperplanes in general position}. *Inventiones Math.* 106:195–216, 1991.

Xavier, F. J. Embedded, simply connected, minimal surfaces with bounded curvature. *GAFA,* in press.

Xavier, F. J., and S. Nollet. Global inversion via the Palais-Smale condition. *Discrete Continuous Dynamical Syst.,* in press.

Xavier, F. J., and V. Nitica. Schrodinger operators and topological pressure on manifolds of negative curvature. *Proc. Symp. Pure Math. Am. Math. Soc.* 2001.

UNIVERSITY OF SOUTHERN CALIFORNIA

Division of Biostatistics

Programs of Study

Graduate education at the University of Southern California (USC) prepares students for leadership in research, teaching, or professional practice in the private or public sector. Rigorous, individually tailored course work and research forms the basis for the program.

Graduate studies in biostatistics are contained within USC's Keck School of Medicine. The University offers the Master of Science (M.S.) and Doctor of Philosophy (Ph.D.) degrees. The Ph.D. in biostatistics is designed to produce a biostatistician with a deep knowledge of statistical theory and methodology. The Ph.D. in statistical genetics and genetic epidemiology is a joint effort to combine biostatistics, epidemiology, statistical and molecular genetics, and computational methods in order to develop new and cutting-edge statistical methodology appropriate for human genomic studies.

Master's degree studies in biostatistics focus on the theory of biostatistics, data analytic methods, experimental design (including clinical trials), statistical methods in human genetics, biomedical informatics, and statistical computing methods. The master's degree in applied biostatistics and epidemiology includes applied biostatistics, epidemiological research methods, and research applications, including cancer, infectious disease, chronic disease, and environmental epidemiology. Doctoral studies cover the areas of biostatistics and data analysis; descriptive, genetic, and molecular epidemiology; computational methods; clinical trial methodology; and related fields of field research, such as population disease and treatment trials.

The Division of Biostatistics also offers a joint degree program in either the M.S. or Ph.D. in molecular epidemiology in conjunction with the Department of Biochemistry and Molecular Biology. The objective of the M.S. degree is to train students in the application of statistical methods to the design of biomedical research. The objective of the doctoral degree is to produce a molecular epidemiologist with in-depth laboratory, statistical, and analytical skills in both epidemiology and the molecular biosciences.

Research Facilities

Hands-on research alongside a faculty mentor is the norm at USC. Graduate students work alongside colleagues as co-investigators on epidemiological, clinical trial, and environmental research projects. Graduate students have myriad opportunities to participate in the latest medical methods. Research teams gain expertise on study design as well as statistical methodology and data analysis. The University's Health Sciences Campus contains the Norris Cancer Center, the General Clinical Research Center, and the Doheny Eye Institute Vision Research Center.

USC has a dozen libraries to serve all the varied needs of its graduate students. Primary source materials include ongoing research projects and recent faculty and staff members' publications. In addition, electronic resources in hundreds of subjects plus online archives and Internet access is available for students through the library system.

Financial Aid

Most graduate students who demonstrate financial need qualify for low-interest loans, work-study, or assistantships. Graduate assistantships are awarded on the basis of scholastic accomplishment and competence. Students exchange teaching and laboratory assistant time for tuition waivers and stipends.

The Sponsored Projects Information Network (SPIN) is a computerized database of funding opportunities—federal, private, and corporate—created to help faculty members identify external financial support for research and education. SPIN funds that are directed toward USC programs in biostatistics result in research funds and fellowships for graduate students.

Cost of Study

Costs for 2004–05 are estimated as follows: tuition and mandatory fees, $19,448; room and board (on-campus or off-campus), $9258; books and supplies, $962; other miscellaneous expenses, $1754.

Living and Housing Costs

Estimated housing costs for the Los Angeles area are approximately $9200 per year. Housing costs vary greatly, depending on the location and type of accomodations. There are ample housing facilities in the many communities surrounding the medical school.

Student Group

There are approximately 1500 graduate students at USC and 100 in the biostatistics and genetics program. The relatively small size of the program facilitates student-faculty member interchange and good accessibility for students to their professors and mentors.

Location

University of Southern California campuses are mostly centered around Los Angeles, with other facilities in nearby Alhambra, Pasadena, Marina del Rey, on Catalina Island, and further away in Orange County to the south and Sacramento to the north. Los Angeles is the second largest city in the U.S. and the nucleus of Southern California. The scenic, sunny, and culturally diverse area of Los Angeles boasts miles of beaches, acres of recreational and park areas, and some of the finest arts and cultural opportunities in the nation.

The University

USC is the oldest and largest independent coeducational university in the West. The campus is composed of 169 buildings located in a 150-acre parklike setting near downtown Los Angeles. USC is among the ten most successful private universities in the country in attracting research support from external sources (more than 100 million annually). Graduate students in the Division of Biostatistics take the majority of their courses at the Health Sciences campus, 3 miles northeast of downtown Los Angeles and 7 miles from the USC University Park Campus. The Health Sciences Campus is adjacent to the Los Angeles County–USC Medical Center, one of the nation's largest teaching hospitals. The surrounding neighborhoods are among the most historically significant in the city, with rich educational resources.

Applying

For the M.S. degree, an undergraduate degree in mathematics, statistics, biostatistics, or computer science is most helpful. Undergraduate preparation should include differential and integral calculus, mathematical statistics, and basic computer programming. The Ph.D. requires successful scores on a screening examination (the M.S. prepares students for this exam). Students may apply online or by mail. An application booklet, plus forms and other application materials, may be found on the University's Web site.

Correspondence and Information

Graduate Programs in Biostatistics and Epidemiology
Division of Biostatistics
Department of Preventive Medicine
Keck School of Medicine
Center for Health Professions, 218
University of Southern California
1540 Alcazar
Los Angeles, California 90089-9010
Telephone: 323-442-1810
Fax: 323-442-2993
E-mail: mtrujill@usc.edu
World Wide Web: http://www.usc.edu

University of Southern California

THE FACULTY AND THEIR RESEARCH

Todd Alonzo, Assistant Professor; Ph.D., Washington (Seattle), 2000. Design and analysis of clinical trials, pediatric oncology, statistical methodology and missing data methodology.
Edward Avol, Associate Professor; M.S., Caltech, 1974. Chronic respiratory effects of airborne pollutants in populations.
Stanley Azen, Professor and Co-director; Ph.D., UCLA, 1969. Biostatisticsal methodology.
Lourdes Baezconde-Garbanati, Assistant Professor; Ph.D., UCLA, 1994. Cancer control research.
Kiros Berhane, Associate Professor; Ph.D., Toronto, 1994. Analysis of health effects of environmental exposures.
Leslie Bernstein, Professor and AFLAC, Inc. Chair in Cancer Research; Ph.D., USC, 1981. Epidemiology of breast cancer and non-Hodgkin's lymphoma.
Jonathan Buckley, Professor; Ph.D., Melbourne, 1981. Epidemiology of childhood cancer, clinical trials; molecular epidemiology.
John Casagrande, Associate Professor; D.Ph., UCLA, 1978. Computer applications in research.
Chih-Ping Chou, Associate Professor; Ph.D., UCLA, 1983. Evaluation of approaches to substance abuse prevention among adolescents, statistical methods in prevention research.
Miles Cockburn, Assistant Professor; Ph.D., Otago (New Zealand), 1998. Epidemiology of melanoma, gastric cancer, and *Heliobacter pylori;* computational methods; geographical information systems (GIS).
David Conti, Assistant Professor; Ph.D., Case Western Reserve, 2002. Statistical methods in genetic association studies, use of hierarchical models in epidemiology.
Victoria Cortessis, Assistant Professor; Ph.D., UCLA, 1993. Genetic-epidemiologic and molecular genetic studies of congenital disorders, adult-onset cancers and etiologic relationships among these entities.
Wendy Cozen, Assistant Professor; M.P.H., UCLA, 1989. Epidemiology of hemetologic neoplasms, Hodgkin's disease, non-Hodgkin's lymphoma.
Martha Cruz, Research Associate, Ph.D., Oxford, 2000. Insulin resistance and its relationship to type 2 diabetes and cardiovascular disease.
N. Tess Cruz, Assistant Professor; Ph.D., Massachusetts, 1993. Public health communications research, anti-tobacco media and pro-tobacco marketing effects.
Dennis Deapen, Professor; Dr.Ph., UCLA, 1982. Cancer outcomes among breast implant patients; lupus erythematosus, diabetes, multiple sclerosis, and Alzheimer's disease.
Clyde Dent, Associate Professor; Ph.D., North Carolina, 1984. Prevention and cessation of tobacco, alcohol, and other drug use in school-based, medical clinic, and worksite contexts.
James Dwyer, Professor; Ph.D., California, Santa Cruz, 1975. Cardiovascular and atherosclerosis.
W. James Gauderman, Associate Professor; Ph.D., USC, 1992. Biostatistical methodology, genetic-epidemiological analysis of pedigree data, health outcomes to environmental exposure.
Frank Gilliand, Associate Professor; Ph.D., Minnesota, 1992. Environmental exposures on air pollution.
Michael I. Goran, Professor; Ph.D., Manchester (England), 1986. Biophysics etiology prevention of obesity, type 2 diabetes in children.
Susan Groshen, Professor; Ph.D., Rutgers, 1980. New drugs and treating cancer.
Robert Haile, Professor; Ph.D., UCLA, 1979. Genetic epidemiology of breast, colon, and prostate cancers.
Ann Hamilton, Assistant Professor; Ph.D., UCLA, 1987. Breast, prostate, and testicular cancer; Kaposi's sarcoma, cancers in twins.
Brian Henderson, Professor; M.D., Chicago, 1962. Cancers of the breast, prostate, ovary, testes, and endometrium in different ethnic groups.
Annlia Hill, Professor; Ph.D., UCLA, 1974. Cancer, cardiovascular, diabetes.
Andrea Hricko, Associate Professor; M.P.H., North Carolina, 1971. Outreach and education techniques, translational and community-based participatory research.
Sue A. Ingles, Assistant Professor; D.P.H., UCLA, 1993. Nutritional genetics and breast, prostate, and colorectal cancer.
Michael Jerrett, Associate Professor; Ph.D., Toronto, 1996. Mapping, health air pollution.
Carl Anderson Johnson, Professor; Ph.D., Duke, 1974. Tobacco, alcohol, and other drug use prevention; nutritional; physical exercise; health promotion.
Carol Koprowski, Assistant Professor; Ph.D., USC, 1998. Diet and physical activity.
Mark Krailo, Professor; Ph.D., Waterloo, 1981. Clinical trials on cancer treatment.
Nino Kuenzli, Associate Professor; Ph.D., Berkeley, 1996. Air pollution.
Peter W. Laird, Associate Professor; Ph.D., Amsterdam (Netherlands Cancer Institute), 1988. Biochemistry and molecular biology, cancer genetics, gene regulation.
Bryan Langholz, Professor; Ph.D., Washington (Seattle), 1984. Cancer and other chronic diseases, cohort studies.
Thomas Mack, Professor; M.P.H., Harvard, 1969. Chronic disease in twins.
Wendy Mack, Associate Professor; Ph.D., USC, 1989. Biostatistical methodology in cardiovascular research, clinical trials using angiographic and ultrasound endpoints.
Paul Marjoram, Assistant Professor; Ph.D., University College (London), 1992. Computational biology, the coalescent, probabilistic models, microarray data.
Rob McConnell, Associate Professor; M.D., California, San Francisco, 1980. Environmental exposures, air pollution.
Roberta McKean-Cowdin, Assistant Professor; Ph.D., 1996. Breast, brain, and endometrial cancer.
Elaine Nezami, Assistant Professor; Ph.D., USC, 1994. Chronic disease, cancer; cardiovascular.
Paula Palmer, Assistant Professor; Ph.D., California School of Professional Psychology, 1998. Social and cultural determinants of health in ethnically diverse populations, school and community-based research.
Mary Ann Pentz, Professor; Syracuse, Ph.D., 1978. Development and testing of school/community-based prevention intervention for adolescents.
John Peters, Professor; S.C.D., Harvard, 1966. Environmental exposures on air pollution.
Malcolm Pike, Professor; Ph.D., Aberdeen (England), 1963. Hormonal, endometrial, and ovarian cancer.
Susan Preston-Martin, Professor; Ph.D., UCLA, 1978. Central nervous system tumors, myeloid leukemia, and other radiogenic cancers; HIV infection in women.
Juergen K. V. Reichardt, Associate Professor; Ph.D., Stanford, 1989. Biochemistry and molecular biology, preventive medicine, cancer epiemiology, molecular epidemiology.
Kim Reynolds, Associate Professor; Ph.D., Arizona State, 1987. Prevention and control of chronic disease; dietary behavior, physical activity, and obesity in school.
Jean Richardson, Professor; M.P.H., UCLA, 1971. Cancer control, behavioral and epidemiological research methods.
Phyllis Rideout, Associate Professor; Ph.D., Florida State, 1981. Cancer education.
Louise Rohrbach, Assistant Professor; Ph.D., USC, 1989. Community-based interventions for disease prevention and health promotion; prevention of tobacco, alcohol, and other drug abuse.
Ronald Ross, Professor; M.D., Iowa, 1975. Hormone cancers, international collaborative efforts to identify dietary causes of cancer.
Harland Sather, Associate Professor; Ph.D., UCLA, 1975. Clinical trials in pediatric cancer.
Kimberly Siegmund, Assistant Professor; Ph.D., Washington (Seattle), 1995. Statistical methods for genetics.
Janet Sobell, Associate Professor; Ph.D., 1991. Multifactorial neurological, neurodegenerative, and neuropsychiatric disorders.
Richard Sposto, Associate Professor; Ph.D., UCLA, 1981. Biostatistics, clinical trials in pediatric oncology, Bayesian analysis of survival data.
Donna Spruijt-Metz, Assistant Professor; Ph.D., Amsterdam Vrije University, 1996. Obesity and type 2 diabetes, smoking prevention.
Alan Stacy, Associate Professor; Ph.D., California, Riverside, 1986. Addiction, prevention.
Michael R. Stallcup, Professor; Ph.D., Berkeley, 1977. Cancer cell biology, signal transduction, genes.
Mariana Stern, Assistant Professor; Ph.D., Texas Health Science Center, 1997. Colorectal and breast cancer, gene-diet, gene-smoking.
Daniel Stram, Associate Professor; Ph.D., Temple, 1983. Modern statistical methods; measurement error methods in cancer epidemiology, repeated measures data; human genetics data.
Ping Sun, Research Associate; Ph.D., USC, 1999. Cardiovascular disease and cancer.
Steven Sussman, Professor; Ph.D., Illinois at Chicago, 1984. Drug abuse, cessation, school-based alcohol, tobacco.
Duncan Thomas, Professor; Ph.D., McGill, 1976. Statistical methods, occupational and environmental health.
Jennifer Unger, Associate Professor; Ph.D., USC, 1996. Psychosocial and cultural factors in adolescent.
Giska Ursin, Associate Professor; Ph.D., UCLA, 1992. Breast cancer.
Thomas Valente, Associate Professor; Ph.D., USC, 1991. Health promotion, substance abuse.
Richard Watanabe, Assistant Professor; Ph.D., USC, 1995. Type 2 diabetes, biologic systems, positional cloning and gene characterization in complex disease.
Anna Wu, Professor; Ph.D., UCLA, 1983. Various cancers among Asian migrants to the U.S.
Anny Xiang, Assistant Professor; Ph.D., USC, 1995. Clinical collaboration and statistical methodology, noninsulin-dependent diabetes (NIDDM).
Mimi Yu, Professor; Ph.D., UCLA, 1977. Cancer epidemiology, nasopharyngeal and liver cancers, large-scale cohort study in Singapore in cancer causation.
Jian-Min Yuan, Assistant Professor; Ph.D., USC, 1996. Cancer epidemiology, cohort study in Shanghai aimed at investigating roles of dietary, environmental exposures, and gene-environment interaction in cancer.
Tianni Zhou, Associate Professor; Ph.D., 2002. Clinical trials in pediatric oncology.

THE UNIVERSITY OF TEXAS AT DALLAS

Mathematical Sciences

Programs of Study

The mathematical sciences department at the University of Texas at Dallas (UT Dallas) offers the Master of Science degree in four specializations: applied mathematics, engineering mathematics, mathematics, and statistics. The Doctor of Philosophy degree is offered in applied mathematics and in statistics. The program has major research faculty and thrusts in the latter two areas. The degree programs are designed to prepare graduates for careers in mathematical sciences or in related fields for which these disciplines provide indispensable foundations and tools. There is no language requirement.

The Master of Science degree requires 33–36 semester hours of course work, consisting of core courses and approved electives. The student may choose a thesis plan or a nonthesis plan. In the thesis plan, the thesis replaces 6 semester hours of course work.

The Ph.D. program is tailored to the student, who arranges a course program with the guidance and approval of the graduate adviser. Adjustments can be made as the student's interests develop and a specific dissertation topic is chosen. Approximately 39 hours of core courses and 18–24 hours of elective courses are required for a typical degree program. After completion of about two years of course work, the student must undertake and pass a Ph.D. qualifying examination in order to continue in the program. The program culminates in the preparation of a dissertation, which must be approved by the graduate program. The topic may be in mathematical sciences exclusively or may involve considerable work in an area of application. Typical areas of concentrations within applied mathematics include, but are not restricted to, applied analysis, computational and mathematical biology, relativity theory, differential equations, scattering theory, systems theory, control theory, signal processing, and differential geometry. In the area of statistics, concentrations are offered in mathematical statistics, applied statistics, statistical computing, probability, stochastic processes, linear models, time series analysis, statistical classification, multivariate analysis, robust statistics, statistical inference, and asymptotic theory.

In addition to a wide range of courses in mathematics and statistics, the mathematical sciences program offers a unique selection of courses that consider theoretical and computational aspects of engineering and scientific problems.

Research Facilities

Faculty members and students in mathematical sciences have access to state-of-the-art scientific workstations and computers. Faculty and staff offices in mathematical sciences are equipped with Pentium II or III workstations, and all teaching assistant offices are equipped with Pentium III workstations that run current versions of Linux. These machines are connected via Ethernet to the campus network, giving faculty members and students access to all of the software tools and machines on campus for research and educational use.

Financial Aid

Graduate Studies Scholarship (GSS) covers the full cost of tuition and fees for up to 9 credit hours per semester; the total GSS value is $6070 per academic year. In addition to GSS, full-time graduate students qualify for teaching assistantships. The full teaching assistantship stipend for 2004–05 is $9286; the value of the total package is $15,365 per academic year. Support for summer study is usually available. In addition to the GSS and teaching assistantships, applicants may also be awarded an Excellence in Education Fellowship for up to two years at a rate of $8000 per year. UT Dallas has also developed a comprehensive program of grants, scholarships, loans, and employment opportunities to assist students in meeting the cost of their education.

Cost of Study

Nonresidents holding teaching assistantships are eligible to pay tuition at the lower rate applicable to Texas residents. The rates for 2003–04 for a 9-hour course load were $1981.40 for Texas residents and $4105.40 for nonresidents. In past years, the University has provided additional financial assistance to teaching assistants in an amount that covers much of the nonresident tuition cost. It is anticipated that this will continue.

Living and Housing Costs

Students in the program typically live in a nearby apartment complex that offers comfortable accommodations at attractive rates. In fall 2003, monthly rates ranged from $426 to $610 for one-bedroom, $796 to $872 for two-bedroom, and $1072 for four-bedroom apartments, some including washer and dryer.

Student Group

The total enrollment at the University is 13,718, including 5,030 graduate students. The mathematical sciences program has 29 master's students and 27 Ph.D. candidates, some of whom attend part-time while employed full-time with companies in the Dallas area.

Student Outcomes

The most recent 6 Ph.D. graduates of the program have secured employment in both industrial and academic positions. Of the program's 3 most recent Ph.D. students in applied mathematics, 1 is now employed by Convex Computer Corporation (a manufacturer of high-end computers), 1 has joined the faculty at Virginia Tech, and the third has joined the faculty of the University of Houston. In statistics, the 2 most recent Ph.D. graduates have joined the faculties of Northern Arizona University and Depaul University.

Location

UT Dallas is located in Richardson, a quiet suburb of North Dallas, which is easily accessible to the more than 800 high-technology companies located in the Dallas–Fort Worth area. Many of these companies are located within 10 miles of UT Dallas, providing graduates with numerous career opportunities. The Dallas metropolitan area also offers a wide range of cultural, social, and sports activities.

The University and The Program

The University of Texas at Dallas was created in 1969 when the privately funded Southwest Center for Advanced Studies was transferred to the state of Texas. In 1972 the Program in Mathematical Sciences was introduced and in 1975 became part of the School of Natural Sciences and Mathematics. Research at the graduate level has continued to represent a major thrust of the University and of the program.

Applying

Applications are considered at any time until vacancies are filled. For consideration for teaching assistantships, the deadline of January 15 is set for first-round consideration. Applicants should arrange for GRE scores and (for international students) TOEFL scores to be included as early as possible in the application materials. Applications not complete before March 15 receive relatively late consideration for teaching assistantships.

Correspondence and Information

Head
Mathematical Sciences
The University of Texas at Dallas
P.O. Box 830688, MS EC35
Richardson, Texas 75083-0688

Telephone: 972-883-2161
Fax: 972-883-6622
E-mail: utdmath@utdallas.edu
World Wide Web: http://www.utdallas.edu/dept/math

The University of Texas at Dallas

THE FACULTY AND THEIR RESEARCH

Larry P. Ammann, Professor; Ph.D., Florida State, 1976. Robust multivariate statistical methods, signal processing, statistical computing, applied probability, remote sensing.

Michael Baron, Associate Professor; Ph.D., Maryland, 1995. Sequential analysis, Bayesian inference, change-point problems, applications in semiconductor manufacturing, psychology, energy finance.

Pankaj Choudhary, Assistant Professor; Ph.D., Ohio State, 2002. Biostatistics, statistical inference, method comparison studies.

Tiberiu Constantinescu, Associate Professor; Ph.D., Bucharest, 1989. Functional analysis, operator theory, linear and multilinear algebra, matrix theory, combinatorics, system theory and control.

Mieczyslaw K. Dabkowski, Assistant Professor; Ph.D., George Washington, 2003. Knot invariants and 3-manifold invariants, applications of topology to biology, recursion theory.

M. Ali Hooshyar, Professor; Ph.D., Indiana, 1970. Scattering theory, inverse scattering theory with geophysical and optical applications, fission.

Istvan Ozsvath, Professor; Ph.D., Hamburg, 1960. Relativistic cosmology, differential geometry.

Viswanath Ramakrishna, Associate Professor; Ph.D., Washington (St. Louis), 1991. Control, optimization, computation, applications in material and molecular sciences.

Ivor Robinson, Professor; B.A., Cambridge, 1947. General relativity theory, particularly exact solutions to Einstein's equations of gravitation.

Robert Serfling, Professor; Ph.D., North Carolina, 1967. Probability theory, statistical inference, robust and nonparametric methods, asymptotic theory, stochastic processes, applications in bioscience and finance. (Web site: http://www.utdallas.edu/~serfling)

Janos Turi, Professor, Ph.D., Virginia Tech, 1986. Functional differential equations, integral equations, approximation theory, optimal control theory, numerical analysis, applied functional analysis.

John Van Ness, Professor; Ph.D., Brown, 1964. Robust linear models, statistical classification, multivariate analysis, applications of statistics to the physical and medical sciences.

John Wiorkowski, Professor; Ph.D., Chicago, 1972. Statistical time series, forecasting, applied statistics, regression analysis, multivariate techniques.

SELECTED PUBLICATIONS

Ammann, L., E. M. Dowling, and R. D. DeGroat. A TQR-iteration based adaptive SVD for real-time angle and frequency tracking. *IEEE Trans. Signal Processing* 42:914–26, 1994.

Ammann, L. Robust singular value decompositions: A new approach to projection pursuit. *J. Am. Stat. Assoc.* 88:504–14, 1993.

Baron, M. Bayes stopping rules in a change-point model with a random hazard rate. *Sequential Anal.* 20(3):147–63, 2001.

Baron, M., C. K. Lakshminarayan, and Z. Chen. Markov random fields in pattern recognition for semiconductor manufacturing. *Technometrics* 43(1):66–72, 2001.

Baron, M. Nonparametric adaptive change-point estimation and on-line detection. *Sequential Anal.* 19(1–2):1–23, 2000.

Choudhary, P. K., and H. N. Nagaraja. Number of records in a bivariate sample with application to Missouri river flood data. *Methodology Computing Appl. Probability,* in press.

Choudhary, P. K., N. Misra, I. D. Dhariyal, and D. Kundu. Smooth estimators for estimating order restricted scale parameters of two gamma distributions. *Metrika* 56:143–61, 2002.

Choudhary, P. K., D. Kundu, and N. Misra. Likelihood ratio test for simultaneous testing of mean and variance in a normal distribution. *J. Stat. Computation Simulation* 71:313–33, 2001.

Constantinescu, T. *Schur Parameters, Factorization and Dilation Problems.* Birkhäuser, 1996.

Dabkowski, Mieczyslaw K., and Jozef H. Przytycki. Burnside obstructions to the Montesinos-Nakanishi 3-move conjecture. *Geom. Topol.* 6:355–60, 2002.

Hooshyar, M. A. An inverse problem of electromagnetic scattering and the method of lines. *Microwave Opt. Technol. Lett.* 29:420–6, 2001.

Hooshyar, M. A. Variation principles and the one-dimensional profile reconstruction. *J. Opt. Soc. Am.* 15:1867–76, 1998.

Ozsvath, I., and E. Schucking. Approaches to Godel's rotating universe. *Class Quantum Gravity* 18:2243–52, 2001.

Ozsvath, I., and E. Schucking. The world viewed from outside. *J. Geometry Phys.* 24:303–333, 1998.

Ozsvath, I. The finite rotating universe revisited. *Class Quantum Gravity* 14:A291–7, 1997.

Ramakrishna, V. Local solvability of degenerate, overdetermined systems—a control-theoretic perspective. *J. Differential Equations,* in press.

Ramakrishna, V. Controlled invariance for singular distributions. *SIAM J. Control Optimization* 32:790–807, 1994.

Robinson, I. On the Bel-Robinson tensor. *Classical Quantum Gravity,* in press.

Robinson, I., and I. Trautman. The conformal geometry of complex quadrics and the fractional-linear form of Mobius transformations. *J. Math. Phys.* 34:5391, 1993.

Serfling, R. Nonparametric multivariate descriptive measures based on spatial quantiles. *J. Stat. Plann. Inference,* in press.

Serfling, R. Efficient and robust fitting of lognormal distributions. *North Am. Actuarial J.,* 6:95–109, 2002.

Serfling, R., and F. Ramirez-Perez. Shot noise on cluster processes with cluster marks, and studies of long range dependence. *Adv. Appl. Probability* 33:631–51, 2001.

Turi, J., and F. Hartung. Linearized stability in functional differential equations with state-dependent delays. *Dynamical Syst. Differential Equations* (an added volume to *Discrete Continuous Dynamical Syst.)* 416–25, 2001.

Turi, J., F. Hartung, and T. L. Herdman. Parameter identification in classes of neutral differential equations with state-dependent delays. *J. Nonlinear Analysis Theory Methods Appl.* 39:305–25, 2000.

Turi, J., and W. Desch. The stop operator related to a convex polyhedron. *J. Differential Equations* 157:329–47, 1999.

Van Ness, J. Recent results in clustering admissibility. In *Applied Stochastic Models and Data Analysis.* Lisbon: Instituto Nacional del Estatistica, 1999.

Van Ness, J., and C. L. Cheng. *Statistical Regression with Measurement Error.* London: Edward Arnold Publishers, 1999.

Van Ness, J. and J. Yang. Robust discriminant analysis: Training data breakdown point. *J. Stat. Plann. Inference* 1:67–84, 1998.

Wiorkowski, J. A lightly annotated bibliography of the publications of the American Statistical Association. *Am. Statistician* 44:106–13, 1990.

Wiorkowski, J. Fitting of growth curves over time when the data are obtained from a single realization. *J. Forecasting* 7:259–72, 1988.

THE UNIVERSITY OF TEXAS GRADUATE SCHOOL OF BIOMEDICAL SCIENCES AT HOUSTON

UT Health Science Center at Houston and M. D. Anderson Cancer Center
Program in Biomathematics and Biostatistics

Program of Study

The Program in Biomathematics and Biostatistics leads to a Ph.D. degree with specialization in quantitative areas of biomedical research. It combines course work with an active research environment, providing an integrative approach to graduate education. Training stresses biomedical applications as well as probability and statistical theory, mathematical modeling, and numerical methods. The program faculty includes members from the M. D. Anderson Cancer Center, the Human Genetics Center of the School of Public Health, and the Medical School.

In the first year, students begin taking required and recommended basic courses and spend part of the year completing three research tutorials. The program's course requirements provide students with an opportunity to acquire breadth and depth in biomathematics or biostatistics as well as in the areas of molecular, cellular, and systems biology to meet basic breadth requirements of the Graduate School of Biomedical Sciences. Faculty members and students also participate in regular seminars, a journal club, and research meetings.

The diversity of the faculty members allows each student to develop his or her own course of study, choosing from a wide range of advanced courses and research areas with the assistance of his or her advisory committee and other faculty members. Under the direction of an adviser, students carry out independent research, culminating in the Ph.D. dissertation. The dissertation must be submitted in writing and presented at a public seminar. Example areas of research include Bayesian methods, bioinformatics, clinical trials, health economics, health services research, longitudinal and repeated measures, mathematical modeling of biological processes, medical decision making, nonlinear dynamics, proteomics, statistical computing, statistical genetics, survival analysis, and tumor growth modeling.

Research Facilities

The School is located in the Texas Medical Center (TMC) in Houston, which includes the University of Texas Health Science Center (Medical School, Dental Branch, School of Public Health, and Graduate School of Biomedical Sciences (GSBS)), the affiliated Hermann Hospital, Baylor College of Medicine, and several other hospitals.

The Department of Biostatistics and Applied Mathematics at the University of Texas M. D. Anderson Cancer Center maintains a close relationship with the Department of Statistics of Rice University, including coordinated teaching of classes and jointly sponsoring seminars during the year. State-of-the-art computing facilities are available for research work. The Houston Academy of Medicine–Texas Medical Center Library includes more than 330,000 books and bound journals as well as more than 3,200 current biomedical periodicals and other serial publications, many of which are available online.

Financial Aid

All Ph.D. students are supported throughout their studies by research assistantships and traineeships, which include stipends ($20,800 in 2004–05), required fees, medical insurance, and tuition. More than $100,000 of supplemental scholarships and fellowships are available each year, as are teaching assistantships and internships for those who want the experience. Travel awards are available for GSBS students to attend scientific meetings.

Cost of Study

Tuition for full-time students is $738 per semester for Texas residents and $2862 for nonresidents in 2004–05. Research assistants and trainees are considered state residents for the purpose of tuition assessment. Tuition and fees are provided for all full-time Ph.D. students.

Living and Housing Costs

Safe, convenient, and affordable housing, beginning at $500 per month for a single apartment, is available within a mile of the campus, and University housing is available. Houston has the second-lowest cost of living among major American cities and the lowest cost of housing of the ten largest metropolitan areas in the country.

Student Group

Currently, 489 students are enrolled, of whom 55 percent are women. The multiethnic student population consists of 190 Texas residents, 149 students from other states, and 150 students from two dozen other countries.

Location

The GSBS campus is the TMC, among the world's largest and most modern facilities for biomedical education and research. It is 2 miles from downtown Houston, immediately adjacent to Rice University and a large, student-friendly area for shopping and dining. Houston, the cultural center of the Southwest, is ethnically diverse and within 1 hour of the Gulf of Mexico.

The School

The GSBS was established in 1963 and has awarded more than 1,500 M.S. and Ph.D. degrees in the biomedical sciences since its inception. Alumni currently work as faculty members at major universities and undergraduate colleges and also hold positions at pharmaceutical, biotechnology, and other industries and government or private institutes. They are involved in research, teaching, scientific administration, and other activities, such as patent law and scientific journalism. GSBS provides numerous career development activities as well as scientific training.

Applying

The **preferred** application date for U.S. citizens seeking fall admission is January 15. Applications for the fall, spring, or summer terms must be completed two months prior to the anticipated enrollment date. All credentials from U.S. applicants should be forwarded to the Office of the Registrar.

Applicants who are not U.S. citizens or permanent residents **must** submit the International Student Application by December 15.

Correspondence and Information

For application materials:
Office of the Registrar
UT–Houston Health Science Center
P.O. Box 20036
Houston, Texas 77225-0036
Telephone: 713-500-3333
E-mail: registrar@uth.tmc.edu
WWW: http://gsbs.uth.tmc.edu/pro_admission.htm

For program information:
Dr. Gary L. Rosner
Department of Biostatistics and Applied Mathematics
M. D. Anderson Cancer Center
1515 Holcombe Boulevard, Unit 447
Houston, Texas 77030
Telephone: 713-794-1798
E-mail: glrosner@mdanderson.org

The University of Texas Graduate School of Biomedical Sciences at Houston

THE FACULTY AND THEIR RESEARCH

Christopher I. Amos, Professor; Ph.D., LSU Medical Center, 1988. Mathematical genetics, cancer genetics, genetics of common diseases, genetic risk assessment.

Keith A. Baggerly, Assistant Professor; Ph.D., Rice, 1995. Proteomics (mass spectrometry), microarrays, serial analysis of gene expression.

Donald A. Berry, Professor; Ph.D., Yale, 1971. Theory and applications of Bayesian statistics, particularly sequential design of experiments; design and analysis of clinical trials; statistical genetics; medical decision making.

Eric Boerwinkle, Professor; Ph.D., Michigan, 1985. Human genetics, epidemiology, heart disease, lipid metabolism, apolipoprotein genes, DNA variation.

Molly S. Bray, Assistant Professor; Ph.D., Texas–Houston Health Science Center, 1998. Molecular and genetic basis of obesity, genetic analysis of complex traits, gene-environment interaction, physical activity/exercise physiology/adipogenesis.

Lyle D. Broemeling, Professor; Ph.D., Texas A&M, 1966. Statistical interpretations of the medical literature.

Scott B. Cantor, Associate Professor; Ph.D., Harvard, 1991. Medical decision making, clinical decision analysis, cost-effectiveness analysis, psychology of decision making, technology assessment, cancer prevention.

Kevin R. Coombes, Associate Professor; Ph.D., Chicago, 1982. Statistical, mathematical, and computational models of gene expression profiles; cDNA microarrays and SAGE.

E. Warwick Daw, Assistant Professor; Ph.D., UCLA, 1992. Statistical genetics, identification of genetic risk factors for common diseases, oligogenic models for linkage analysis in large families, gene-environment interactions.

Kim-Anh Do, Associate Professor; Ph.D., Stanford, 1990. Computational statistics and biostatistics; statistical genetics; nonparametric statistical methods, including the bootstrap.

Linda S. Elting, Associate Professor; Ph.D., Texas–Houston Health Science Center, 1988. Outcomes and cost of cancer screening, treatment, and supportive care; access to cancer care; disparities in cancer care; health policy; health-care quality.

Yun-Xin Fu, Professor; Ph.D., Reading (England), 1988. Molecular evolution, population genetics, bioinformatics, computational genomics.

Lincoln C. Gray, Professor; Ph.D., Michigan State, 1977. Development of hearing, stereo hearing.

Kenneth R. Hess, Associate Professor; Ph.D., Texas–Houston Health Science Center, 1992. Design and analysis of cancer clinical trials, design and analysis of cDNA microarrays, survival analysis, prognostic factor studies.

Xuelin Huang, Assistant Professor; Ph.D., Michigan, 2002. Survival analysis, longitudinal studies, statistical genetics, bioinformatics, clinical trial design.

Yuan Ji, Assistant Professor; Ph.D., Wisconsin, 2003. Bayesian methodologies, bioinformatics.

Terri King, Assistant Professor; Ph.D., Johns Hopkins, 1993. Bioinformatics, genetic epidemiology, statistical genetics.

J. Jack Lee, Professor; Ph.D., UCLA, 1989. Biostatistics, design and analysis of clinical trials, longitudinal data analysis, statistical computing and graphics, chemoprevention.

Jeffrey S. Morris, Assistant Professor; Ph.D., Texas A&M, 2000. Functional data analysis, linear mixed models, nonparametric regression, wavelets, multivariate methods, Bayesian methods, proteomics, carcinogenesis.

Mandri Obeyeskere, Assistant Professor; Ph.D., Texas Tech, 1989. Nonlinear dynamics, cell-cycle regulation, brain tumor growth, irradiation effects, hematopoietic dynamics.

Gary L. Rosner, Professor; Sc.D., Harvard, 1985. Bayesian methods, clinical trial design and analysis, longitudinal data models, population pharmacokinetics and pharmacodynamics.

Yu Shen, Associate Professor; Ph.D., Washington (Seattle), 1994. Design and analysis of clinical trials, modeling dynamic process of cancer screening, survival analysis, estimation of natural history of diseases.

Sanjay S. Shete, Assistant Professor; Ph.D., Georgia, 1998. Statistical genetics, cancer genetics, segregation and linkage analysis, affected sib-pair methods.

Ya-Chen (Tina) Shih, Associate Professor; Ph.D., Stanford, 1997. Statistical/econometric methods in health services research, Bayesian methods in economic evaluations, health inequality in health-care access and utilization.

George Starkschall, Professor; Ph.D., Harvard, 1972. Radiation treatment planning, radiation oncology imaging, gated radiation therapy.

Peter F. Thall, Professor; Ph.D., Florida State, 1975. Clinical trial design, survival analysis, statistical modeling, nonlinear regression, longitudinal and repeated measures data, computer-intensive methods in statistics, applied Bayesian methods.

R. Allen White, Professor; Ph.D., Chicago, 1970. Computer analysis of DNA sequence data, cell kinetics, mathematical modeling.

Momiao Xiong, Assistant Professor; Ph.D., Georgia, 1993. Bioinformatics, statistical genetics, genetic epidemiology, mapping complex trait, mapping QTL, functional genomics, human gene expression maps and gene expression database, genetic circuits.

Li Zhang, Assistant Professor; Ph.D., North Carolina, 1995. Computational genome biology, gene expression microarray data modeling, networks of gene expression regulation.

Ming Zhang, Assistant Professor; Ph.D., Rice, 2000. Docking, protein folding, computer-assisted drug design, mathematical modeling and algorithms.

Z. Hong Zhou, Associate Professor; Ph.D., Baylor College of Medicine, 1995. Structural basis of functions and pathogenesis of viruses and supramolecular assemblies, electron cryomicroscopy and computer image processing, bioinformatics, computational modeling.

Supporting Faculty

Rudy Guerra, Associate Professor; Ph.D., Berkeley, 1992. Bioinformatics, statistical genetics.

Peter Müller, Professor; Ph.D., Purdue, 1991. Bayesian statistics, numerical integration in Bayesian statistics, Markov chain Monte Carlo methods, simulation-based optimal design, neural network models, longitudinal data models, hierarchical models.

UNIVERSITY OF TOLEDO

Department of Mathematics

Programs of Study

The Ph.D. program trains mathematicians and statisticians who intend to make research in these areas their life work. The Ph.D. requires a minimum of 90 credit hours, of which 18 to 36 are for the dissertation. Students must enroll in abstract algebra, real analysis, and topology in the first year and successfully complete a yearlong sequence in complex analysis, plus two other yearlong sequences. Students must demonstrate the ability to read mathematical literature in one foreign language, ordinarily chosen from among French, German, and Russian, and spend two consecutive semesters in supervised teaching.

For full-time students, the written qualifying examination must be passed by the end of the student's second year and a topic-specific oral exam must be passed within a year of passing the qualifying exam. A completed dissertation must be approved by an outside examiner, then defended by the student before a faculty committee. Typically, students take two to three years to complete their dissertations.

The M.A. in mathematics requires at least 30 credit hours, including course work in algebra, topology, real analysis, and complex analysis, and at least one 2-semester sequence in a single discipline. Students must either pass a comprehensive examination or write a thesis to complete the degree. The M.S. in applied mathematics requires 30 credits, culminating in a written thesis or examination. The M.S. in statistics requires 35 credit hours and passing a two-part examination in statistical theory and applied statistics. At least 32 credit hours are required for the M.S. in education, including at least 18 in mathematics and 9 in education.

Research Facilities

The William S. Carlson Library houses more than 1.6 million volumes and over 3,000 periodicals. The library has a large, current collection of mathematical texts and monographs and subscribes to more than 200 mathematical journals. The University Libraries have a fully electronic catalog and circulation service that is available through any terminal on or off campus. The University Library network is connected to a statewide university library network, which provides access to the collections of all other university and college libraries in the state of Ohio, as well as numerous research databases, such as ISI. A network-based computing facility is built around a Sun Ultra-Enterprise server and two Dell PowerEdge servers running Linux. The department also maintains two instructional computing laboratories equipped with projectors and containing about forty PCs each, as well as a smaller computing lab.

Financial Aid

Graduate teaching and research assistantships provide a stipend and a fee waiver of up to 12 credit hours in exchange for approximately 20 hours of work per week. A limited number of fellowships are available to doctoral students; these include a stipend of $15,000 plus remission of various fees as well as a subsidy for health insurance. Several scholarships are available for both part-time and full-time students based on academic merit or financial need; amounts and eligibility requirements vary. Loans are also available.

Cost of Study

In the 2004–05 academic year, full-time tuition (12 credits) is $4165.68 per semester for Ohio residents and $8571.48 for out-of-state students. In-state and out-of-state students taking fewer than 12 credits pay $372.14 or $714.29 per credit hour, respectively. Other fees include general fees, technology fees, health insurance, and other miscellaneous fees.

Living and Housing Costs

On-campus housing is available for $2400 to $3500 per semester, depending on the type of housing. Meal plans are available for $775 to $1350 per semester, depending on the number of meals purchased per week. Off-campus housing is also available. Students can expect to pay $300 to $600 per month for a one-bedroom apartment and $500 to $800 per month for a two bedroom apartment.

Student Group

The doctoral program is designed for students who want to pursue careers in academic mathematical research. The master's programs are designed for students who want to pursue a Ph.D. or teach mathematics. Approximately 40 full-time students are enrolled in the graduate programs.

Student Outcomes

Graduates of the program occupy academic positions in colleges and universities around the world. Graduates from the master's programs are well prepared both for doctoral studies and for employment in academic and nonacademic settings.

Location

The University is located just 6 miles from downtown Toledo, which offers numerous business, social, industrial, and cultural opportunities. In addition to numerous attractions, including the zoo, art museum, arboretum, and cultural events, Toledo provides students with cooperative educational experiences, internships, and a diverse job market. The campus is also considered one of the safest in the nation.

The University

The University of Toledo began in 1872 as a private arts and trades school that offered painting and architectural drawing as its only subjects. Today, the University offers more than 250 undergraduate and graduate programs through eight colleges to more than 20,000 students from around the world. The University ranks fiftieth among all colleges and universities in terms of National Merit Scholars enrolled, and its schools of law and pharmacy are among the top ranked in the nation.

Applying

Admission to the program requires a completed application form, a statement of purpose, three sets of transcripts of all undergraduate and prior graduate work, at least three letters of recommendation, and an application fee of $40. There is no formal deadline for receipt of applications, but candidates for the fall semester whose applications are complete by mid-February have the best chance of success. Applications should be sent to the Graduate School rather than to the department.

Correspondence and Information

Geoffrey K. Martin, Chair
Department of Mathematics
University of Toledo
2040 University Hall
2801 West Bancroft Street
Toledo, Ohio 43606-3390
Telephone: 419-530-2568
Fax: 419-530-4720
World Wide Web: http://www.math.utoledo.edu/

University of Toledo

THE FACULTY AND THEIR RESEARCH

James Anderson, Assistant Professor.
H. Lamar Bentley, Professor; Ph.D., Rensselaer. Extensions of topological spaces by means of nearness structures, using primarily the methods of category theory.
Dean A. Carlson, Professor; Ph.D., Delaware. Investigation of noncooperative dynamic games on an unbounded time horizon, using classical and nonclassical methods of analysis to provide conditions when a given class of dynamic games has equilibrium.
Zeljko Cuckovic, Associate Professor; Ph.D., Michigan State. Algebraic properties of Toeplitz operators and harmonic function theory, as specialized subfields of functional analysis and complex analysis.
Mohamed S. Elbialy, Professor; Ph.D., Minnesota. Dynamical systems, Hamiltonian systems, celestial mechanics, and differential equations involving methods from nonlinear functional analysis, real analysis, and differential geometry.
Donald Greco, Professor.
David Hemmer, Assistant Professor; Ph.D., Chicago. Group theory; representation theory of finite groups, especially the symmetric and general linear groups.
Paul R. Hewitt, Associate Professor; Ph.D., Michigan State. Group theory, especially intrinsic and extrinsic structures, typically from geometry, topology, and logic, reflected in algebraic properties of the group.
Marie Hoover, Associate Professor and Associate Chair.
En-Bing Lin, Professor; Ph.D., Johns Hopkins. Wavelet theory and applications; geometric and hadronic quantization in mathematical physics; domain characterizations in complex manifolds by means of algebraic and geometric structures, using primarily analytic methods.
Geoffrey K. Martin, Associate Professor and Chair; Ph.D., SUNY at Stony Brook. Symplectic geometry over determined systems of partial differential equations, geometric algebra in eight dimensions, triality, foundations of electromagnetism and relativity, geometric mathematical physics, Lie groups and indefinite symmetric domains, general geometric structure and partial differential relations.
Elaine Miller, Associate Professor.
Rao V. Nagisetty, Professor; Ph.D., Steklov Institute (Moscow). Theory of approximation, functional analysis, complex function theory and Toeplitz operators, Liouville's theory on function fields.
Robert L. Ochs Jr., Associate Professor; Ph.D., Delaware. Applied mathematics of wave propagation.
Charles J. Odenthal, Associate Professor; Ph.D., Wisconsin. Representations of Noetherian and Artinian rings.
Biao Ou, Associate Professor; Ph.D., Minnesota. Partial differential equations in applied area and differential geometry.
Martin R. Pettet, Professor; Ph.D., Yale. Theory of groups, with particular focus on relationships between structure and properties of a group and those of its automorphisms.
Friedhelm Schwarz, Professor; Ph.D., Bremen (Germany). Categorical topology, especially Cartesian closedness, exponentiability, and topological universes; teaching with technology, especially calculus with MAPLE, the World Wide Web, and distance learning.
Qin Shao, Assistant Professor; Ph.D., Georgia. Time series, experimental design.
Ivie Stein Jr., Associate Professor; Ph.D., UCLA. Optimization, calculus of variations, numerical analysis.
Stuart A. Steinberg, Professor; Ph.D., Illinois. Ordered structures and ring theory.
Gwen Terwilliger, Associate Professor; Ph.D., Toledo.
William Thomas, Associate Professor.
Gerard Thompson, Professor; Ph.D., Open University; Ph.D., North Carolina. Application of differential geometry, Lagrangian and Hamiltonian mechanics and symplectic geometry.
H. Westcott Vayo, Professor; Ph.D., Illinois. Applications of differential equations to biology and medicine.
Henry C. Wente, Distinguished University Professor; Ph.D., Harvard. Calculus of variations and elliptic partial differential equations as they apply to minimal surface theory, immersions of constant mean curvature, and capillary theory.
Denis A. White, Professor; Ph.D., Northwestern. Schroedinger operators and their application to quantum mechanical scattering theory, using functional analysis and partial differential equations.
Donald B. White, Associate Professor; Ph.D., California, Irvine. Applications of statistics to various scientific areas, especially medicine and pharmacology; statistical areas, including nonlinear models and population modeling in pharmacokinetics and pharmacodynamics.
Harvey E. Wolff, Professor; Ph.D., Illinois. Category theory, with applications to algebra and topology.
Biao Zhang, Professor; Ph.D., Chicago. Density estimation and empirical likelihood.

UNIVERSITY OF UTAH

Department of Mathematics

Programs of Study

The Department of Mathematics offers programs leading to the degrees of Doctor of Philosophy (Ph.D.), Master of Arts (M.A.), and Master of Science (M.S.) in mathematics and a certificate in computational engineering and science (CES) and a Professional Master of Science and Technology degree (PMST).

The master's degree requires 30 hours of course work beyond certain basic prerequisites. The candidate for the M.A. degree must satisfy the standard proficiency requirement in one foreign language; a further requirement is an expository thesis of good quality or an approved two-semester graduate course sequence.

The doctoral degree carries a minimum course requirement designed to prepare the student to pass a written qualifying examination in the basic fields of mathematics. An oral examination, with emphasis on the candidate's area of specialization, is also required. A dissertation describing independent and original work is required. The Department of Mathematics stresses excellence in research.

Research Facilities

The Mathematics Branch Library collection in theoretical mathematics consists of 190 journal subscriptions, 15,000 bound journals, and 12,000 books. In addition, the Marriott Library collection includes numerous books and journals of interest to mathematics researchers and scholars. There are extensive interactive computing and computer graphics facilities available in the department.

Financial Aid

Approximately 70 percent of the mathematics graduate students are supported by fellowships. There are teaching fellowships that grant from a minimum of $14,000 to $15,500 plus tuition and fees. Application for University research fellowships can be made through the University Research Fellowship Office, 310 Park Building, at the University of Utah. These fellowships are available to both U.S. and international students.

The department currently offers VIGRE and IGERT Teaching Assistantships to U.S. citizens and permanent residents, with a stipend of $16,500 for a VIGRE award and $25,200 for an IGERT award.

The normal teaching load for a teaching assistant and teaching fellow is one course per semester. Summer teaching is available. The stipend for one course during the summer is $3500.

Cost of Study

For 2004–05, tuition is $1320.28 per semester for Utah residents and $4661.84 per semester for nonresidents (9 credit hours). All tuition fees are waived for teaching assistants and teaching fellows (except for a small computer fee).

Living and Housing Costs

A wide variety of housing is offered by the University on or near the campus. University Village, for married students, is operated by the University. One-, two-, and three-bedroom apartments range from $409 to $701 per month, including heat, hot water, electricity, range, and refrigerator. (These rates may change without notice.) There is a waiting period of about four to six months for the University's married-student housing. Privately owned housing near the campus is also available. For details and complete listings of on-campus housing, students should visit the Web site http://www.apartments.utah.edu.

Student Group

The University's total enrollment is currently 27,225. The Department of Mathematics has 86 graduate students; 58 receive financial support.

Student Outcomes

Graduates typically go on to postdoctoral research appointments followed by academic careers in teaching and research or careers in government and industry. In the past two years, 13 graduates took positions at various universities, including Johns Hopkins, Minnesota, Purdue, Tulane, Virginia Tech, Washington (St. Louis), the Institute for Theoretical Dynamics, and Lawrence Livermore National Laboratory.

Location

The Salt Lake City metropolitan area has a population of about 1 million and is the cultural, economic, and educational center of the Intermountain West. The Utah Symphony and Ballet West are located in Salt Lake City. The Delta Center is the home of the Utah Jazz basketball team. Climate and geography combine in the Salt Lake environs to provide ideal conditions for outdoor sports. Some of the world's best skiing is available less than an hour's drive from the University campus.

The University and The Department

The University of Utah is a state-supported coeducational public institution. Founded in 1850, it is the oldest state university west of the Missouri River.

In the last five years, the Department of Mathematics has awarded 105 master's degrees. In recent years, the Graduate School has been awarding about 205 doctoral degrees per year. The University faculty has 1,350 members.

Applying

Admission to graduate status requires that students hold a bachelor's degree or its equivalent and that they show promise for success in graduate work. Applicants are urged to take the mathematics Subject Test of the Graduate Record Examinations.

Students are normally admitted at the beginning of the autumn (fall) term. It is desirable that applications for teaching fellowships, as well as for other financial grants, be submitted as early as possible (after December 15). All applications received before March 15 are automatically considered for financial assistance. All program information and application materials can be accessed from the Web address below.

Correspondence and Information

Graduate Admissions
Department of Mathematics
University of Utah
155 South 1400 East, JWB 233
Salt Lake City, Utah 84112-0090
World Wide Web: http://www.math.utah.edu/grad

University of Utah

THE FACULTY AND THEIR RESEARCH

Distinguished Professor
G. Milton, Ph.D., Cornell, 1985. Materials science.
J. P. Keener, Ph.D., Caltech, 1972. Applied mathematics.

Professors
P. W. Alfeld, Ph.D., Dundee (Scotland), 1977. Numerical analysis.
A. Bertram, Ph.D., UCLA, 1989. Algebraic geometry and physics.
M. Bestvina, Ph.D., Tennessee, 1984. Topology.
P. Bressloff, Ph.D., King's College (London), 1988. Mathematical biology.
R. M. Brooks, Ph.D., LSU, 1963. Topological algebras.
J. A. Carlson, Ph.D., Princeton, 1971. Algebraic geometry.
A. V. Cherkaev, Ph.D., St. Petersburg Technical (Russia), 1979. Applied math.
D. Dobson, Ph.D., Rice, 1990. Partial differential equations.
S. N. Ethier, Ph.D., Wisconsin–Madison, 1975. Probability and statistics.
A. L. Fogelson, Ph.D., NYU, 1982. Computational fluids.
E. S. Folias, Ph.D., Caltech, 1963. Applied mathematics, elasticity.
S. M. Gersten, Ph.D., Cambridge, 1965. Algebra.
K. M. Golden, Ph.D., NYU, 1984. Applied math.
F. I. Gross, Ph.D., Caltech, 1964. Algebra.
G. B. Gustafson, Ph.D., Arizona State, 1968. Ordinary differential equations.
H. Hecht, Ph.D., Columbia, 1974. Lie groups.
L. Horvath, Ph.D., Szeged (Hungary), 1982. Probability, statistics.
M. Kapovich, Ph.D., Russian Academy of Science, 1988. Geometry.
D. Khoshnevisan, Ph.D., Berkeley, 1989. Probability.
N. J. Korevaar, Ph.D., Stanford, 1981. Partial differential equations.
J. D. Mason, Ph.D., California, Riverside, 1968. Probability.
D. Milicic, Ph.D., Zagreb (Yugoslavia), 1973. Lie groups.
P. C. Roberts, Ph.D., McGill, 1974. Commutative algebra, algebraic geometry.
G. Savin, Ph.D., Harvard, 1988. Group representation.
K. Schmitt, Ph.D., Nebraska, 1967. Differential equations.
N. Smale, Ph.D., Berkeley, 1987. Differential geometry.
J. L. Taylor, Ph.D., LSU, 1964. Abstract analysis.
D. Toledo, Ph.D., Cornell, 1972. Algebraic and differential geometry.
A. E. Treibergs, Ph.D., Stanford, 1980. Differential geometry.
P. C. Trombi, Ph.D., Illinois at Urbana–Champaign, 1970. Lie groups.
D. H. Tucker, Ph.D., Texas, 1958. Differential equations, functional analysis.

Professor (Lecturer)
A. D. Roberts, Ph.D., McGill, 1972. Analysis.

Emeritus Professors
C. E. Burgess, Ph.D., Texas, 1951. Topology.
W. J. Coles, Ph.D., Duke, 1954. Ordinary differential equations.
P. Fife, Ph.D., NYU, 1959. Applied mathematics.
L. C. Glaser, Ph.D., Wisconsin–Madison, 1964. Geometric topology.
H. R. Rossi, Ph.D., MIT, 1960. Complex analysis.
J. E. Wolfe, Ph.D., Harvard, 1948. Geometric integration theory.

Associate Professors
F. Adler, Ph.D., Cornell, 1991. Mathematical biology.
A. Balk, Ph.D., Moscow Institute of Physics, 1988. Nonlinear phenomena.
C. Khare, Ph.D., Caltech, 1995. Algebraic number theory.
W. Niziol, Ph.D., Chicago, 1991. Arithmetical algebraic geometry.
J. Zhu, Ph.D., NYU (Courant), 1989. Computational fluid dynamics.

Assistant Professors
K. Bromberg, Berkeley, 1998. Topology.
C. Hacon, Ph.D., UCLA, 1998. Algebraic geometry.
Y. P. Lee, Ph.D., Berkeley, 1999. Algebraic geometry.
P. Trapa, Ph.D., MIT, 1998. Representation theory.

Research Professors
N. Beebe, Ph.D., Florida, 1972. Numerical analysis.
E. Cherkaev, Ph.D., St. Petersburg (Russia), 1988. Partial differential equations.
R. Horn, Ph.D., Stanford, 1967. Matrix analysis.

Assistant Professors (Lecturers)
D. Arcara, Ph.D., Georgia, 2003. Algebraic geometry.
A. Aue, Ph.D., Cologne (Germany), 2004. Probability and statistics.
R. W. Bell, Ph.D., Ohio State, 2003. Topology.
M. Bocea, Ph.D., Carnegie Mellon, 2004. Partial differential equations.
S. K. Chaudhary, Ph.D., UCLA, 2004. Applied mathematics.
B. H. Im, Ph.D., Indiana, 2004. Number theory.
K. H. Kim, Ph.D., Minnesota, 2004. Partial differential equations.
M. J. Kim, Ph.D., Brown, 2004. Mathematical biology.
D. Margalit, Ph.D., Chicago, 2003. Topology.
L. Miller, Ph.D., NYU (Courant), 2004. Mathematical biology.
K. Montgomery, Ph.D., Northwestern, 2004. Mathematical biology.
S. Spiroff, Ph.D., Illinois at Urbana-Champaign, 2003. Commutative algebra.
F. vanHeerden, Ph.D., Utah State, 2003, Partial differential equations.
M. vanOpstall, Ph.D., Washington (Seattle), 2004. Algebraic geometry.
O. Veliche, Ph.D., Purdue, 2004. Commutative algebra.
G. Wright, Ph.D., Colorado at Boulder, 2003. Numerical analysis.

SELECTED PUBLICATIONS

Adler, F. R., and D. M. Gordon. Optimization, conflict, and non-overlapping foraging ranges in ants. *Am. Naturalist* 162:529–43, 2003.

Adler, F. R., and T. T. Hills. Time's crooked arrow: Rate-biased time perception and optimal foraging. *Anim. Behav.* 64:589–97, 2002.

Alfeld, P. W., and L. L. Schumaker. Upper and lower bounds on the dimension of superspline spaces. *Constructive Approximation* 19:145–61, 2003.

Alfeld, P. W., and L. L. Schumaker. Smooth macro-elements based on Clough-Tocher triangle splits. *Numerische Mathematik* 90:597–616, 2002.

Balk, A. Propagation in multiscale media. *Physica B* 338:1–3, 2003.

Balk, A., A. Cherkaev, and L. Slepyan. Dynamics of chains with nonmonotone stress-strain relations. *J. Mech. Phys. Solids* 49:131–71, 2001.

Bertram, A. Another way to enumerate rational curves with torus actions. *Inventiones Mathematicae* 142:487–512, 2000.

Bertram, A. Some applications of localization to enumerative problems. *Mich. Math. J.* 48:65–75, 2000.

Bestvina, M., and M. Handel. Train-tracks and automorphisms of free groups. *Ann. Math.* 135:1–51, 2002.

Bestvina, M., and M. Feighn. A combination theorem for negatively curved groups. *J. Diff. Geometry* 35(1):85–101, 1992.

Bressloff, P. C., and S. Coombes. Saltatory waves in the spike-diffuse-spike model of active dendritic spines. *Phys. Rev. Lett.* 91:028102, 2003.

Bressloff, P. C., S. Folias, A. Prat, and Y-X. Li. Oscillatory waves in inhomogeneous neural media. *Phys. Rev. Lett.* 91:178101, 2003.

Bromberg, K. Rigidity of geometrically finite hyperbolic cone-manifolds. Preprint, 2000.

Bromberg, K. Hyperbolic Dehn surgery on geometrically infinite 3-manifolds. Preprint, 2000.

Brooks, R. M. Analytic structure in the spectra of certain uF-algebras. *Math. Ann.* 240:27–33, 1979.

Brooks, R. M. On the spectrum of an inverse limit of holomorphic function algebras. *Adv. Math.* 19:238–44, 1976.

Carlson, J. A., D. Toledo, and D. Allcock. The complex hyperbolic geometry of the moduli space of cubic surfaces. *J. Alg. Geom.*, in press.

Carlson, J. A., D. Allcock, and **D. Toledo.** Complex hyperbolic structures for moduli of cubic surfaces. *Comptes Rendus Acad. Sci. Paris Ser. I* 326:49–54, 1998.

Cherkaev, A. V., and I. Kucuk. Detecting stress fields in an optimal structure. *Int. J. Struct. Multidisciplinary Optimization* 26(1):1–27, 2004.

Cherkaev, A. V. *Variational Methods for Structural Optimization.* Springer-Verlag, 2000.

Coles, W. J., D. Hughell, and W. D. Smith. An optimal foraging model for the red-cockaded woodpecker. In *Proceedings of the Seventh Symposium on Systems Analysis in Forest Resources, USDA Technical Report*, vol. NC-205, pp. 118–21, 2000.

Coles, W. J., and M. K. Kinyon. Some oscillation results for second order matrix differential equations. *Rocky Mtn. J. Math.* 1:19–36, 1994.

Dobson, D. C., and F. Santosa. Optimal localization of eigenfunctions in an inhomogeneous medium. *SIAM, J. App. Math.*, in press.

Dobson, D. C., and S. J. Cox. Maximizing band gaps in two-dimensional photonic crystals. *SIAM J. Appl. Math.* 59:2108–20, 1999.

Ethier, S. N., and S. Wang. A generalized likelihood ratio test to identify differentially expressed genes from microarray data. *Bioinformatics* 20:100–4, 2004.

Ethier, S. N., and **D. Khoshnevisan.** Bounds on gambler's ruin probabilities in terms of moments. *Methodology Computing Appl. Probability* 4(1):55–68, 2002.

Fife, P. C. Some nonclassical trends in parabolic and parabolic-like evolutions. In *Trends in Nonlinear Analysis,* Springer-Verlag, in press.

Fife, P. C., J. Cahn, and C. Elliott. A free boundary model for diffusion-induced grain boundary motion. *Interfaces Free Boundaries* 3:291–336, 2001.

Fogelson, A. L., and R. Guy. Probabilistic modeling of platelet aggregation: Effects of activation time and receptor occupancy. *J. Theor. Biol.* 219:33–53, 2002.

Fogelson, A. L., and A. Kuharsky. Surface-mediated control of blood coagulation: The role of binding site densities and platelet deposition. *Biophys. J.* 80:1050–74, 2001.

Folias, E. S., and M. Hohn. Predicting crach initiation in composite material systems due to a thermal expansion mismatch. *Int. J. Fracture* 93(1/4):335–49, 1999.

Folias, E. S., and L. Perry. Fast fracture of a threaded pressurized vessel. *Int. J. Press. Vess. Pipe.* 76(10):685–92, 1999.

Gersten, S. M. Filling length in finitely presentable groups. *Geometriae Dedicata,* in press.

Gersten, S. M., D. Holt, and T. Riley. Isopemetric inequalities for nilpotent groups. Preprint, 2002.

Glaser, L. C., and T. B. Rushing. Geometric topology. *Proceedings of the Geometric Topology Conference,* Park City, Utah, February 1974; in *Lectures in Mathematics*, vol. 438, p. 459. New York: Springer-Verlag, 1975.

Glaser, L. C. On tame Cantor sets in spheres having the same projection in each direction. *Pacific J. Math.* 60:87–102, 1975.

Golden, K. M., et al. Inverse electromagnetic scattering models for sea ice. *IEEE Trans. Geosci. Remote Sensing,* in press.

Golden, K. M. Critical behavior of transport in lattice and continuum percolation models. *Phys. Rev. Lett.* 78:3935–8, 1997.

Gross, F. I. Odd order Hall subgroups of the classical linear groups. *Math. Z.* 220:317–36, 1995.

Gross, F. I. Hall subgroups of order not divisible by 3. *Rocky Mtn. J. Math.* 23:569–91, 1993.

Gustafson, G. B., and M. Laitoch. The inverse carrier problem. *Czech. Math. J.* 52(127):439–46, 2002.

Gustafson, G. B. Three papers of C. de la Vallée Poussin on linear boundary value problems. *Charles-Jean de la Vallée Poussin Collected Works,* vol. II, pp. 315–55. Académie Royale de Belgique, 2001.

Hacon, C., and H. Clemens. Deformations of flat line bundles and their metrics. *Am. J. Math.* 124.4:769–815, 2002.

Hacon, C., and J. A. Chen. Characterization of Abelian varieties. *Inventiones Mathematicae* 143(2):435–47, 2001.

Hecht, H. On Casselman's compatibility theorem for n-homology. In *Proceedings of Cordoba Conference, Reductive Lie Groups*. Boston: Birkhäuser, 1997.

University of Utah

Selected Publications (continued)

Hecht, H., and **J. L. Taylor.** A comparison theorem for n-homology. *Compositio Mathematica* 86:189–207, 1993.

Horn, R., and G. G. Piepmeyer. Two applications of primary matrix functions. *Linear Algebra Appl.* 361:99–106, 2003.

Horn, R., G. Goodson, and D. Merino. Quasi-real normal matrices and eigenvalue pairings. *Linear Algebra Appl.* 369:279–94, 2003.

Horvath, L., and M. Csorgo. *Limit Theorems in Change-Point Analysis.* New York: John Wiley & Sons, 1997.

Horvath, L., and M. Csorgo. *Weighted Approximations in Probability and Statistics.* New York: John Wiley & Sons, 1993.

Kapovich, M., D. Gallo, and A. Marden. On monodromy of Schwarzian differential equation on Riemann surfaces. *Ann. Math.* 151(N2):625–704, 2000.

Kapovich, M. Hyperbolic manifolds and discrete groups. In *Progress in Mathematics,* vol. 183. Boston: Birkhäuser, 2000.

Keener, J. P., and E. Cytrynbaum. The effect of spatial scale resistive inhomogeneity on defibrillation of cardiac tissue. *J. Theor. Biol.* 223:233–48, 2003.

Keener, J. P. Model for the onset of fibrillation following a coronary occlasion. *J. Cardiovasc. Electro Phys.* 14:1225–32, 2003.

Khoshnevisan, D., Y. Xiao, and Y. Zhang. Measuring the range of an additive Lévy process. *Ann. Probability* 31(2):1097–141 2003.

Khoshnevisan, D. *Multiparameter Processes: An Introduction to Random Fields.* New York: Springer, 2002.

Korevaar, N. J., R. Mazzco, F. Pacard, and R. M. Schoen. Refined asymptotics for constant scalar curvature metrics with isolated singularities. *Inventiones Mathematicae* 135:233–72, 1999.

Korevaar, N. J., and R. M. Schoen. Harmonic maps to non-locally compact spaces. *Commun. Anal. Geom.* 5(2):333–87, 1997.

Lee, Y. P., and A. Givental. Quantum K-theory on flag manifolds, finite difference Toda lattices and quantum groups. *Inventiones Mathematicae* 151:193–219, 2003.

Lee, Y. P. Quantum Lefschetz hyperplane theorem. *Inventiones Mathematicae* 145(1):121–49, 2001.

Mason, J. D., and T. Burns. A structural equations approach to combining data sets. Accepted as a paper for *International Congress of Sociologists,* 1994.

Mason, J. D., and Z. J. Jurek. *Operator-Limit Distribution in Probability Theory.* New York: John Wiley & Sons, 1993.

Mikhalkin, G. Counting curves via lattice paths in polygons. *Comptes Rendus Acad. Sci. Paris,* in press.

Mikhalkin, G. Decomposition into pairs-of-pants for complex algebraic hypersurfaces. *http://arxiv.org/abs/math.GT/0205011*

Milicic, D., and P. Pandzic. Equivariant derived categories, Zuckerman functors and localization. In the *Progress in Mathematics* series, *Geometry and Representation Theory of Real and p-adic Lie Groups,* vol. 158, pp. 209–42, eds. J. Tirao, D. Vogan, and J. A. Wolfe. Boston: Birkhäuser, 1997.

Milicic, D., and P. Pandzic. On degeneration of the spectral sequence for the composition of Zuckerman functors. *Glasnik Matematicki* 32(52):179–99, 1997.

Milton, G. W., S. K. Serkov, and A. B. Morchan. Realizable (average stress, average strain) pairs in a plate with holes. *SIAM J. Appl. Math.* 63(3):987–1028, 2003.

Milton, G. W., Y. Grabovsky, and D. S. Sage. Exact relations for effective tensors of composites: Necessary conditions and sufficient conditions. *Comm. Pure Appl. Math.* 53(3):300–53, 2000.

Niziol, W. Crystalline conjecture via K-theory. *Ann. Sci. Ecole Norm. Suppl.* 31:659–81, 1998.

Niziol, W. On the image of *p*-adic regulators. *Inventiones Mathematicae* 127:375–400, 1997.

Roberts, P. C., and V. Srinivas. Modules of finite length and finite projective dimension. *Inventiones Mathematicae,* in press.

Roberts, P. C., and K. Kurano. The positivity of intersection multiplicities and symbolic powers of prime ideals. *Compositio Mathematica* 122:165–82, 2000.

Rossi, H., and C. Patton. Unitary structures on cohomology. *Trans. Am. Math. Soc.* 290:235–58, 1985.

Rossi, H. LeBrun's nonrealizability theorem in higher dimensions. *Duke Math. J.* 52:457–525, 1985.

Savin, G., and B. Gross. The dual pair $PGL_3 \times G_2$. *Can. Math. Bull.* 40:376–84, 1997.

Savin, G., J. S. Huang, and P. Pandzic. New dual pair correspondences. *Duke Math. J.* 82:447–71, 1996.

Schmitt, K., M. Poppenberg, and Z.Q. Wang. On the existence of soliton solutions of quasilinear Schrodinger equations. *Calc. Var. PDE* 14:329–44, 2002.

Schmitt, K., and J. Jacobsen. The Liouville-Brata-Gelfand problem for radical operators. *J. Differential Equations* 114:283–98, 2002.

Smale, N. A construction of homologically area minimizing hypersurfaces with higher dimensional singular sets. *Trans. Am. Math. Soc.*, in press.

Smale, N. Singular homologically area minimizing surfaces of codimension one in Riemannian manifolds. *Inventiones Mathematicae* 135:145–83, 1999.

Taylor, J. L. Several complex variables with connections to algebraic geometry and Lie groups. *AMS Graduate Studies Math.* 46, 2002.

Taylor, J. L., and L. Smithies. An analytic Riemann-Hilbert correspondence. *J. Representation Theor.* 4:466–73, 2000.

Toledo, D. Maps between complex hyperbolic surfaces. *Geom. Dedicata* 97:115–28, 2003.

Toledo, D., D. Allcock, and J. Carlson. Real cubic surfaces and real hyperbolic geometry. *Comptes Rendus Acad. Sci. Paris Ser. I* 337:185–8, 2003.

Treibergs, A. E. Instability in a buoyant chemical front driven by curvature. Preprint, 2001.

Treibergs, A. E., and H. Chan. Nonpositively curved surfaces in $\mathbf{R}^3$. *J. Differential Geometry* 57:389–407, 2001.

Trombi, P. C. Uniform asymptotics for real reductive Lie groups. *Pacific J. Math.* 146:131–99, 1990.

Trombi, P. C. Invariant harmonic analysis on split rank one groups with applications. *Pacific J. Math.* 100:80–102, 1982.

Tucker, D. H., and J. F. Gold. A new vector product. In *Proceedings of the 10th National Conference on Undergraduate Research,* 1996.

Tucker, D. H., and D. T. M. Ha. Concerning differential type operators: A preliminary report. In *Proceedings of the International Conference on Analysis and Mechanics of Continuous Media,* Ho Chi Minh City, December 27–29, 1995.

Zhu, J., and M. Avellaneda. J. modeling the distance-to-default process of a firm. *Risk* 149(12):125–9, 2001.

Zhu, J. A numerical study of chemical front propagation in a Hele-Shaw flow under buoyancy effects. *Phys. Fluids* 10(4):775–88, 1998.

WASHINGTON STATE UNIVERSITY

College of Sciences
Department of Mathematics

Programs of Study

The Department of Mathematics offers graduate programs leading to the M.S., Ph.D., and Ph.D with teaching emphasis, as well as an M.S. in applied mathematics tailored to industrial employment. Courses of study are available in all of the principal branches of mathematics with special emphases in the applied areas of operations research, computational mathematics, applied statistics, and mathematical modeling as well as in the more traditional fields of number theory, finite geometry, general topology, algebra, and analysis. The Ph.D. program combines the more traditional orientations usually associated with university teaching and research with options specifically directed toward careers in industry and government. The Ph.D. with teaching emphasis program is designed to prepare exceptionally well qualified teachers of undergraduate mathematics. The degree program is distinguished from that of the traditional Ph.D. by a greater emphasis on breadth of course work and a critical, historical, or expository thesis.

Research Facilities

All mathematics faculty members and graduate students are housed in Neill Hall. These modern and spacious facilities include offices, seminar rooms, classrooms, consulting rooms, student computer laboratories, and computing facilities. An outstanding collection of mathematics books and journals are housed in the nearby Owen Science and Engineering Library. The department operates a high-speed network of UNIX and Windows computers for research and instruction. Offices of the graduate students are equipped with computers connected to the network. The University operates a gigabit backbone with high-speed connection to the Internet.

Financial Aid

More than 90 percent of the mathematics graduate students are supported by teaching assistantships; stipends ranged from $12,730.50 to $13,387.50 for the 2003–04 academic year. Normal duties are 20 hours per week teaching classes or assisting a faculty member. Summer teaching assignments for an additional stipend are usually available as are a few annual research assistantships for advanced students. Federal and state-supported work-study and loan programs are also available. Three special scholarships are granted each year: the Distinguished TA, the Abelson, and the Hacker, which carry stipends of $5000, $3000, and $2000, respectively.

Cost of Study

Tuition for full-time study (more than 6 credit hours) is $3139 per semester for Washington residents and $7647 for nonresidents. Part-time and summer students pay on a per-credit-hour basis. There are tuition waivers for teaching and research assistants.

Living and Housing Costs

The University maintains a residence center strictly for graduate students as well as a wide variety of single-student and family apartments. University-owned apartments rent for $350 to $670 per month, including utilities; room and board at the graduate center are $5876 to $6470 per academic year. Private apartments are readily available at slightly higher rates.

Student Group

Washington State University has an enrollment of approximately 17,500, including about 3,000 graduate students; 33 of the latter are in mathematics. The mathematics graduate students come from many areas of the United States and several other countries, and about a dozen complete an advanced degree each year.

Student Outcomes

Recent recipients of advanced degrees have taken positions in academic institutions, in the private sector, and in governmental agencies. The academic appointments include teaching and research at both comprehensive universities and four-year liberal arts colleges. The nonacademic positions include systems analyst, actuary, program manager, senior scientist, research mathematician, reliability analyst, and computer consultant.

Location

Pullman, a city of about 25,000, is located in the heart of the Palouse region in southeastern Washington. It is a rich agricultural area that enjoys clean air and a generally dry, "continental" climate. The area offers easy access to outdoor recreational opportunities such as fishing, hiking, camping, sailing, skiing, and white-water rafting in three states—Washington, Idaho, and Oregon. The on-campus activities both at WSU and at the University of Idaho (8 miles away) contribute greatly to the cultural, athletic, and scientific life of the area.

The University and The Department

The University was founded in 1890 and was the first land-grant institution to establish a chapter of Phi Beta Kappa. Today, the core of the Pullman campus covers nearly 600 acres, and some 100 major buildings house the faculty members and students associated with the more than fifty academic disciplines. Mathematics is the largest department in the Division of Sciences, with a faculty of 40. Master's degrees were first awarded in 1912, and more than 100 mathematics Ph.D.'s have been hooded since 1960.

Applying

Requests for information or applications for admission and financial support should be directed to the department. Completed applications and other necessary credentials should be submitted as early as possible, preferably by February 1 for fall admission. Applicants are advised to take the Graduate Record Examinations General Test and the Subject Test in mathematics. Also required are copies of transcripts of all previous college work and three letters of recommendation. TOEFL scores must be submitted to the Graduate School by all students whose native language is not English.

Correspondence and Information

Graduate Studies Committee
Department of Mathematics
Washington State University
Pullman, Washington 99164-3113

Telephone: 509-335-6868
E-mail: gradinfo@math.wsu.edu
World Wide Web: http://www.math.wsu.edu

Washington State University

THE FACULTY AND THEIR RESEARCH

Algebra and Number Theory
J. J. McDonald, Ph.D., Wisconsin–Madison, 1993. Matrix analysis, linear algebra.
D. Ng, Ph.D., Oregon State, 1973. Algebra.
M. J. Tsatsomeros, Ph.D., Connecticut, 1990. Linear algebra, matrix analysis, dynamical systems.
W. A. Webb, Ph.D., Penn State, 1968. Number theory, fair division problems, combinatorics, cryptography.

Analysis
S. C. Cooper, Ph.D., Colorado State, 1988. Approximation theory.
D. W. DeTemple, Ph.D., Stanford, 1970. Combinatorics, graph theory, analysis, elementary geometry, mathematics education.
J. E. Kucera, Ph.D., Czechoslovak Academy of Sciences, 1966. Functional analysis, distributions.

Applied Analysis
J. A. Cochran, Ph.D., Stanford, 1964. Differential and integral equations, electromagnetics, special functions, operator theory, asymptotics.
A. Y. Khapalov, Ph.D., Russian Academy of Sciences, 1982. Applied partial differential equations, control theory.
A. N. Panchenko, Ph.D., Delaware, 2000. Partial differential equations of continuum mechanics, homogenization, inverse problems.
H. Yin, Ph.D., Washington State, 1986. Applied partial differential equations.

Modeling
R. H. Dillon, Ph.D., Utah, 1993. Numerical analysis, modeling biological processes.
R. S. Gomulkiewicz, Ph.D., California, Davis, 1989. Theoretical population biology.
V. S. Manoranjan, Ph.D., Dundee (Scotland), 1982. Mathematical modeling, biomathematics, numerical analysis, nonlinear waves.
E. F. Pate, Ph.D., RPI, 1976. Mathematical modeling, biomathematics.
M. F. Schumaker, Ph.D., Texas at Austin, 1987. Mathematical modeling, biomathematics.
D. J. Wollkind, Ph.D., RPI, 1968. Continuum mechanics, asymptotic methods, stability techniques and mathematical modeling.

Numerical Analysis and Operations Research
K. A. Ariyawansa, Ph.D., Toronto, 1983. Mathematical programming and optimization, high-performance computing, operations research, applied statistical inference.
A. Genz, Ph.D., Kent (England), 1976. Numerical analysis, numerical integration, scientific computing.
R. B. Mifflin, Ph.D., Berkeley, 1971. Operations research, nonsmooth optimization.
D. S. Watkins, Ph.D., Calgary, 1974. Numerical analysis, scientific computing.

Probability and Applied Statistics
M. A. Jacroux, Ph.D., Oregon State, 1976. Experimental design, optimal experimental design, estimation in linear and nonlinear models.
V. K. Jandhyala, Ph.D., Western Ontario, 1986. Statistical inference, stochastic processes.
H. Li, Ph.D., Arizona, 1994. Stochastic orderings, statistical theory of reliability, stochastic convexity, probabilistic modeling.
F. Pascual, Ph.D., Iowa State, 1997. Statistical reliability, optimal experimental design.

Topology and Geometry
M. Hudelson, Ph.D., Washington (Seattle), 1995. Combinatorics, discrete geometry.
M. J. Kallaher, Ph.D., Syracuse, 1967. Algebra, projective geometry, finite geometries.
D. C. Kent, Ph.D., New Mexico, 1963. General topology.

Thesis Titles and Current Positions of Recent Graduates

B. Blitz. *Topics Concerning Regular Maps.* Assistant Professor of Mathematics, University of Alaska Southeast.
R. Drake. *A Dynamically Adaptive Method and Spectrum Enveloping Technique.* Research Scientist, SANDIA National Laboratory.
A. J. Felt. *A Computational Evaluation of Interior Point Cutting Plane Algorithms for Stochastic Programs.* Assistant Professor of Mathematics, University of Wisconsin–Stevens Point.
C. Gómez-Wulschner. *Compactness of Inductive Limits.* Assistant Professor of Mathematics, Departamento de Mathematicas, Instituto Technológico Autónomo de México.
P. L. Jiang. *Polynomial Cutting Plane Algorithms for Stochastic Programming and Related Problems.* Research Manager, Professional Services, Delta Dental Plan of Minnesota.
B. E. Peterson. *Integer Polyhedra and the Perfect Box.* Assistant Professor of Mathematics, Oregon State University.
L. E. Stephenson. *Weekly Nonlinear Stability Analyses of Turing Pattern Formation in the CIMA/Starch Reaction Diffusion Model System.* Senior Engineer/Scientist, United Defense LP.
M. Tian. *Pattern Formation Analysis of Thin Liquid Films.* Assistant Professor of Mathematics, Wright State University.
M. Zhu. *Techniques for Large-Scale Nonlinear Optimization: Principles and Practice.* Software Design Engineer, Multimedia Applications Group, Microsoft Corporation.

Washington State University

SELECTED PUBLICATIONS

Ariyawansa, K. A., and W. L. Tabor. A note on line search termination criteria for collinear scaling algorithms. *Computing, Computing* 70:25–39, 2003.

Ariyawansa, K. A., W. C. Davidon, and K. D. McKennon. A characterization of convexity-preserving maps from a subset of a vector space into another. *J. London Math. Soc.* 64:179–90, 2001.

Ariyawansa, K. A., W. C. Davidon, and K. D. McKennon. On a characterization of convexity-preserving maps, Davidon's collinear scalings and Karmarkar's projective transformations. *Math. Programming A* 90:153–68, 2001.

Ariyawansa, K. A., and P. L. Jiang. On the complexity of the translational-cut algorithm for convex minimax problems. *J. Opt. Th. Appl.* 107:223–43, 2000.

Cochran, J., A. D. Klemm, A. J. Gilks, D. Rhodes. Pair-correlation functions of hard spheres from Green's functions, in press.

Cochran, J., and Z. Y. Cai. Mode bifurcation in corrugated waveguides. In *Mathematical and Numerical Aspects of Wave Propagation Phenomena,* pp. 651–9, eds. G. Cohen, L. Halpern, and P. Joly. Philadelphia: SIAM, 1991.

Cochran, J., and L. M. Ciasullo. Accelerating the convergence of the Chebyshev series. In *Asymptotic and Computational Analysis,* pp. 95–136, ed. R. Wong. New York: Marcel Dekker, 1990.

Cooper, S. C., and P. Gustafson. The strong Chebyshev and orthogonal Laurent polynomials. *J. Approximation Theory* 92:361–78, 1998.

Cooper, S. C., and P. Gustafson. Extremal properties of strong quadrative weights and maximal mass results for truncated strong moment problems. *JCAM* 80:197–208, 1997.

DeTemple, D. W., and C. T. Long. *Mathematical Reasoning for Elementary School Teachers,* 3rd ed. Reading: Addison Wesley Longman, 2003.

DeTemple, D. W., and M. Hudelson. Square-banded polygons and affine regularity, *Amer. Math. Monthly* 108:100–14, 2001.

DeTemple, D. W., C. Anbeek, K. McAvaney, and J. Robertson. When are chordal graphs also partition graphs. *Australasian J. Combinatorics* 16:285–93, 1997.

Dillon, R., and L. Fauci. An integrative model of internal axoneme mechanics and external fluid dynamics in cilliary beating. *J. Theor. Biol.* in press.

Dillon, R., and L. Fauci. A microscale model of bacterial and biofilm dynamics in porous media. *Biotechnology and Bioengineering* 68:536–47, 2000.

Dillon, R., and H. G. Othmer. A mathematical model for outgrowth and spatial patterning of the vertebrate limb bud. *J. Theor. Biol.* 197:295–300, 1999.

Genz, A., and F. Bretz. Methods for the computation of multivariate t probabilities. *J. Comp. Graph. Stat.,* in press.

Bretz, F., A. J. Hayter, and **A. Genz.** Critical point and power calculations for the studentised range test. *J. Stat. Comp. Simul.,* in press.

Genz, A., and K-S. Kwong. Numerical evaluation of singular multivariate Normal probabilities. *J. Stat. Comp. Simul.* 68:1–21, 2000.

Holt, R. D., **R. Gomulkiewicz,** and M. Barfield. The phenomenology of niche evolution via quantitative traits in a black-hole sink: A mechanism for punctuated evolution? *Proc. Royal Soc. London B* 270:215–24, 2003.

Nuismer, S. L., **R. Gomulkiewicz,** and M. T. Morgan. Coevolution in temporally variable environments. *The American Naturalist* 162: 195–204, 2003.

Kingsolver, J., **R. Gomulkiewicz,** and P. A. Carter. Variation, selection, and evolution of function-valued traits. *Genetica* 112/113: 87–104, 2001.

Gomulkiewicz, R., et al. Hot spots, cold spots, and the geographic mosaic theory of coevolution. *The American Naturalist,* 156:156–74, 2000.

Hudelson, M. Recurrences Modulo P. *Fibonacci Quarterly,* in press.

Hudelson, M. Periodic omnihedral billiards in regular polyhedra and polytopes. *J. Geometry,* in press.

Hudelson, M. A solution to the generalized Cevian problem using forest polynomials. *J. Combinatorial Theory Ser. A* 88:297–305, 1999.

Jacroux, M. A note on the construction of magic rectangles of higher order. *ARS Combinatorica,* in press.

Jacroux, M. On the determination and construction of A- and MU-optimal block designs for comparing a set of treatments to a set of standard treatments. *J. Stat. Plann. Inf.,* in press.

Jacroux, M. Some optimal orthogonal and nearly-orthogonal block designs for comparing a set of a set of test treatments to a set of standard treatments. *Sankhya B* 62:276–89, 2000.

Jandhyala, V. K., N. E. Evaggelopoulos, and S. B. Fotopoulos. A comparison of unconditional and conditional solutions to the maximum likelihood estimation of a change-point. *Computational Statistics and Data Analysis,* in press.

Jandhyala, V. K., and J. A. Alsaleh. Parameter changes at unknown times in non-linear regression. *Environmetrics* 10:711–24, 1999.

Jandhyala, V. K., S. B. Fotopoulos, and N. Evaggelopoulos. Change-point methods for Weibull models with applications to detection of trends in extreme temperatures. *Environmetrics* 10:547–64, 1999.

Kallaher, M. Translation planes. In *Handbook of Geometry,* pp. 137–92, ed. F. Buckenhout, 1995 (an invited review chapter).

Hanson, J., and **M. Kallaher.** Finite Bol quasifields are nearfields. *Utilitas Math.* 37:45–64, 1990.

Kent, D., and W. K. Min. Neighborhood spaces. *Int. J. Math. Sci.* 32:387–99, 2002.

Kent, D., and J. Wig. P-regular Cauchy completions. *Int. J. Math. Math. Sci.* 24:275–304, 2000.

Kent, D., and S. A. Wilde. P-topological and p-regular: Dual notions in convergence theory. *Int. J. Math. Math. Sci.* 22:1–12, 1999.

Kent, D., and G. Richardson. Completions of probabilistic convergence spaces. *Mathematica Jpn.* 48:399–407, 1998.

Khapalov, A. Y. Controllability of the semilinear parabolic equation governed by a multiplicative control in the reaction term: A qualitative approach. *SIAM J. Control Optim.* 41:1886–900, 2003.

Khapalov, A. Y. Global non-negative controllability of the semilinear parabolic equation governed by bilinear control. *ESAIM: COCV* 7:269–83, 2002.

Khapalov, A. Y. Mobile point controls versus locally distributed ones for the controllability of the semilinear parabolic equation. *SIAM J. Control Optim.* 40:231–52, 2001.

Khapalov, A. Y. Observability and stabilization for the vibrating string equipped with bouncing point sensors and actuators. *Math. Methods Appl. Sci.* 24:1055–72, 2001.

Kucera, J. Sequential completeness of LF-spaces. *Czech. Math. J.* 51(126):181–3, 2001.

Gómez, C., and **J. Kucera.** Sequential completeness of inductive limits. *Int. J. Math.* 24:419–21, 2000.

Kucera, J. Regularity of conservative inductive limits. *Int. J. Math.* 22(4):705–7, 1999.

Li, H. Stochastic models for dependent life lengths induced by common pure jump shock environments. *J. Appl. Prob.* 37:453–69, 2000.

Xu, S., and **H. Li.** Majorization of weighted trees: A new tool to study correlated stochastic systems. *Math. Oper. Res.* 35:298–323, 2000.

Li, H., and M. Shaked. On the first passage times for Markov processes with monotone convex transition kernels. *Stochastic Proc. Appl.* 58:205–216, 1995.

Song, Y., D. Edwards, and **V. S. Manoranjan.** Fuzzy cell mapping applied to autonomous systems. *ASME J. Computing Information Sci. Eng.,* in press.

Patton, R. L., **V. S. Manoranjan,** and A. J. Watkinson. Plate formation at the surface of a convecting fluid. *Proc. XIII Int. Congress Rheology, British Society of Rheology,* 167–9, 2000.

Manoranjan, V. S. Qualitative study of differential equations. In *MAA Notes No. 50, Revolutions in Differential Equations—Exploring ODEs with Modern Technology,* pp. 59–65, ed. M. J. Kallaher, 1999.

Washington State University

Selected Publications (continued)

Zaslavsky, B. G., and **J. J. McDonald.** A characterization of Jordan Canonical Forms which are similar to eventually nonnegative matrices with the properties of nonnegative matrices. *Linear Algebra Applications,* in press.

McDonald, J. J. The peripheral spectrum of a nonnegative matrix. *Linear Algebra Applications* 363:217–35, 2003.

Carnochan Naqvi, S., and **J. J. McDonald.** The combinatorial structure of eventually nonnegative matrices. *Electronic J. Linear Algebra* 9:255–69, 2002.

McDonald, J. J., and M. Neumann. The Soules approach to the inverse eigenvalue problem for nonnegative symmetric matrices of order $n \leq 5$. *Contemp. Math.* 259:387–90, 2000.

Mifflin, R., and C. Sagastizabel. Primal-dual gradient structured functions: Second order results; links to epiderivatives and partially smooth functions. *SIAM J. Optimization* 13:1174–94, 2002.

Mifflin, R., and C. Sagastizabal. Proximal points on the fast track. *J. Convex Anal.* 9:563–79, 2002.

Mifflin, R., and C. Sagastizabal. On VU-theory for functions with primal-dual gradient structure. *SIAM J. Optimization* 11:547–71, 2000.

Pascual, F. G. Theory for optimal test plans for the random fatigue-limit model. *Technometrics* 45:130–41, 2003.

Pascual, F. G., and G. Montepiedra. Model-robust test plans with applications in accelerated life testing. *Technometrics* 45:47–57, 2002.

Pascual, F., and W. Q. Meeker. Estimating fatigue curves with the random fatigue-limit model. *Technometrics* 41:277–90, 1999.

Pate, E., et al. A structural change in the kinesin motor that drives motility. *Nature* 402:778–84, 1999.

Pate, E., K. Francis-Skiba, and R. Cooke. Depletion of phosphate in active muscle fibers probes actmyosin states within the powerstroke. *Biophys. J.* 74:369–80, 1998.

Pate, E., et al. Opening of the myosin nucleotide triphosphate binding domain during the hydrolysis cycle. *Biochemistry* 36:12155–66, 1997.

Gowen, J. A., et al. **(M. F. Schumaker).** The role of trp side chains in tuning single proton conduction through gramicidin channels. *Biophys. J.* 83(2):880–98, 2002.

Schumaker, M. F. Boundary conditions and trajectories of diffusion processes. *J. Chem. Phys.* 117(6):2469–73, 2002.

Psarrakos, P. J., and **M. J. Tsatsomeros.** On the stability radius of matrix polynomials. *Linear Multilinear Algebra* 50:151–65, 2002.

Tsatsomeros, M. J. Matrices with a common nontrivial invariant subspace. *Linear Algebra Applications* 322:51–9, 2001.

Tsatsomeros, M. J., and L. Li. A recursive test for *P*-matrices. *BIT* 40:404–8, 2000.

Tsatsomeros, M. J. Principal pivot transforms: Properties and applications. *Linear Algebra Applications* 300:151–65, 2000.

Watkins, D. S. *Fundamentals of Matrix Computations,* 2nd Ed. New York: John Wiley and Sons, 2002.

Mehrmann, V., and **D. S. Watkins.** Structure-preserving methods for computing eigenpairs of large, sparse skew-Hamiltonian/Hamiltonian pencils. *SIAM J. Sci. Comput.* 22:1905–25, 2001.

Watkins, D. S. Performance of the QZ algorithm in the presence of infinite eigenvalues. *SIAM J. Matrix Anal. Appl.* 22:364–75, 2000.

Webb, W., and H. Yokota. Polynomial Pell's Equation. *Proc. Amer. Math. Soc.* 131(4):993–1006, 2003.

Webb, W., and M. Caragiu. Invariants for linear recurrences. In *Applications of Fibonacci Numbers,* Vol. 8, pp. 75–81. Dordecht: Kluwer, 1999.

Webb, W. An algorithm for super envy-free cake division. *J. Math. Anal. Appl.* 239:175–79, 1999.

Webb, W., and J. M. Robertson. *Cake Cutting Algorithms.* Natick, Mass.: A. K. Peters, 1998.

Tian, E. M., and **D. J. Wollkind.** A nonlinear stability analysis of pattern formation in thin liquid films. *Interfaces Free Boundaries* 5:1–25, 2003.

Wollkind, D. J., and L. E. Stephenson. Chemical Turing patterns: A model system of a paradigm for morphogenesis. In *Mathematical Models of Biological Pattern Formation,* pp. 113–42, eds. P. K. Maini and H. G. Othmer. New York: Springer-Verlag, 2001.

Wollkind, D. J., V. S. Manoranjan, and L. Zhang. Weakly nonlinear stability analyses of prototype reaction-diffusion model equations. *SIAM Rev.* 36:176–214, 1994.

Wollkind, D. J., and L. Zhang. The effect of suspended particles on Rayleigh-Bénard convection II. A nonlinear stability analysis of a thermal disequilibrium model. *Math. Comput. Modelling* 19:43–74, 1994.

Yin, H. On a free boundary problem with superheating arising in microwave heating processes. *Adv. Math. Sci. Appl.* 12:409–33, 2002.

Yin, H., B. Q. Li, and J. Zou. A degenerate evolution system modeling Bean's critical-state type-II superconductors. *Discrete Continuous Dynamical Syst.* 8:781–94, 2002.

Yin, H. On a p-Laplacian type of evolution system and applications to the Bean model in the type-II superconductivity theory. *Q. Appl. Math.* LIX:47–66, 2001.

Yin, H. On a singular limit problem for nonlinear Maxwell's equations. *J. Differential Equations* 156:355–75, 1999.

WESLEYAN UNIVERSITY

Department of Mathematics

Programs of Study

The Department of Mathematics offers a program of courses and research leading to the degrees of Master of Arts and Doctor of Philosophy.

The Ph.D. degree demands breadth of knowledge, intensive specialization in one field, original contribution to that field, and expository skill. First-year courses are designed to provide a strong foundation in algebra, analysis, topology, combinatorics, logic, and computer science. Written preliminary examinations are normally taken after the first year. During the second year, the student continues with a variety of courses, sampling areas of possible concentration. By the start of the third year, the student chooses a specialty and begins research work under the guidance of a thesis adviser. Also required is the ability to read mathematics in at least two of the following languages: French, German, and Russian. The usual time required for completion of all requirements for a Ph.D., including the dissertation, is four to five years.

After passing the preliminary examinations, most Ph.D. candidates teach one course per year, typically a small section (fewer than 20 students) of calculus.

The M.A. degree is designed to ensure basic knowledge and the capacity for sustained scholarly study; requirements are six semester courses at the graduate level and the writing and oral presentation of a thesis. The thesis requires (at least) independent search and study of the literature.

Students are also involved in a variety of departmental activities, including seminars and colloquia. The small size of the program contributes to an atmosphere of informality and accessibility.

The emphasis at Wesleyan is in pure mathematics and theoretical computer science, and most Wesleyan Ph.D.s have chosen academic careers.

Research Facilities

The department is housed in the Science Center, where all graduate students and faculty members have offices. Computer facilities are available for both learning and research purposes. The Science Library collection has about 120,000 volumes, with extensive mathematics holdings; there are more than 200 subscriptions to mathematics journals, and approximately 60 new mathematics books arrive each month. The proximity of students and faculty and the daily gatherings at teatime are also key elements of the research environment.

Financial Aid

Each applicant for admission is automatically considered for appointment to an assistantship. For the 2004–05 academic year, the stipend is $14,748, plus a dependency allowance when appropriate, and about one-third more is usually available for the student who wishes to remain on campus to study during the summer. Costs of tuition and health fees are borne by the University. All students in good standing are given financial support for the duration of their studies.

Cost of Study

The only academic costs to the student are books and other educational materials.

Living and Housing Costs

The University provides some subsidized housing and assists in finding private housing. The academic-year cost of a single student's housing (a private room in a 2- or 4-person house, with common kitchen and living area) is about $3880.

Student Group

The number of graduate students in mathematics ranges from 18 to 24, with an entering class of 4 to 8 each year. There have always been both male and female students, graduates of small colleges and large universities, and U.S. and international students, including, in recent years, students from China, Germany, Hungary, India, Korea, Mexico, Peru, and Yugoslavia.

All of the department's recent Ph.D. recipients have obtained academic employment. Some of these have subsequently taken positions as industrial mathematicians.

Location

Middletown, Connecticut, is a small city of 40,000 on the Connecticut River, about 19 miles southeast of Hartford and 25 miles northeast of New Haven, midway between New York and Boston. The University provides many cultural and recreational opportunities, supplemented by those in the countryside and in larger cities nearby. Several members of the mathematical community are actively involved in sports, including distance running, golf, handball, hiking, softball, squash, table tennis, volleyball, and cycling.

The University

Founded in 1831, Wesleyan is an independent coeducational institution of liberal arts and sciences, with Ph.D. programs in biology, chemistry, ethnomusicology, mathematics, and physics and master's programs in a number of departments. Current enrollments show about 2,800 undergraduates and 145 graduate students.

Applying

No specific courses are required for admission, but it is expected that the equivalent of an undergraduate major in mathematics will have been completed. The complete application consists of the application form, transcripts of all previous academic work at or beyond the college level, letters of recommendation from three college instructors familiar with the applicant's mathematical ability and performance, and GRE scores (if available). Applications should be submitted by February 15 in order to receive adequate consideration, but requests for admission from outstanding candidates are welcome at any time. Preference is given to Ph.D. candidates. A visit to the campus is strongly recommended for its value in determining the suitability of the program for the applicant.

Correspondence and Information

Department of Mathematics and Computer Science
Graduate Education Committee
Wesleyan University
Middletown, Connecticut 06459-0128
Telephone: 860-685-2620
E-mail: nprocyk@wesleyan.edu
World Wide Web: http://math.wesleyan.edu

Wesleyan University

THE FACULTY AND THEIR RESEARCH

Professors
Karen Collins, Ph.D., MIT. Combinatorics.
W. Wistar Comfort, Ph.D., Washington (Seattle). Point-set topology, ultrafilters, set theory, topological groups.
Adam Fieldsteel, Ph.D., Berkeley. Ergodic theory.
Anthony W. Hager, Ph.D., Penn State. Lattice-ordered algebraic structures, general and categorical topology.
Michael S. Keane, Dr.rer.nat., Erlangen. Ergodic theory, random walks, statistical physics.
F. E. J. Linton, Ph.D., Columbia. Categorical algebra, functorial semantics, topoi.
Philip H. Scowcroft, Ph.D., Cornell. Foundations of mathematics, model-theoretic algebra.
Carol Wood, Ph.D., Yale. Mathematical logic, applications of model theory to algebra.

Associate Professor
Mark Hovey, Ph.D., MIT. Algebraic topology and homological algebra.

Assistant Professors
Petra Bonfert-Taylor, Ph.D., Berlin Technical. Complex analysis, complex dynamics, geometric function theory, discrete groups.
Wai Kiu Chan, Ph.D., Ohio State. Arithmetic theory of quadratic forms, arithmetic of algebraic groups, combinatorics.
David Pollack, Ph.D., Harvard. Number theory, automorphic forms, representation of *p-adic* groups.
Edward C. Taylor, Ph.D., SUNY at Stony Brook. Analysis, low-dimensional geometry and topology.

Van Vleck Visiting Professor (Fall)
Richard Canary, Ph.D., Princeton. Low dimensional topology, Kleiman groups.

Van Vleck Visiting Researchers (Spring)
Richard Mauldin, Ph.D., Texas at Austin.
Marcus Pivato, Ph.D., Toronto. Dynamical systems/ergodic theory.
Reem Yassawi, Ph.D., McGill. Analysis, ergodic dynamic systems/theory.

Professor of Computer Science
Michael Rice, Ph.D., Wesleyan. Parallel computing, formal specification methods.

Associate Professors of Computer Science
Danny Krizanc, Ph.D., Harvard. Theoretical computer science.
James Lipton, Ph.D., Cornell. Logic and computation, logic programming, type theory, linear logic.

Assistant Professor of Computer Science
Norman Danner, Ph.D., Indiana (Bloomington). Logic, theoretical computer science.

Visiting Instructor in Computer Science
John V. E. Ridgway, M.Sc., Massachusetts Amherst. Programming languages/databases.

Professors Emeriti
Ethan M. Coven, Ph.D., Yale. Dynamical systems.
James D. Reid, Ph.D., Washington (Seattle). Abelian groups, module theory.
Lewis C. Robertson, Ph.D., UCLA. Lie groups, topological groups, representation theory.
Robert A. Rosenbaum, Ph.D., Yale. Geometry, mathematics and science education.

Visiting Scholar
George Maltese, Ph.D., Yale. Functional analysis.

Faculty-student conferences, daily gatherings at teatime, and discussions in graduate students' offices are key ingredients of the research environment in the Department of Mathematics.

SELECTED PUBLICATIONS

Bonfert-Taylor, P., and **E. C. Taylor**. Patterson-Sullivan theory and the local analysis of limit sets. *Trans. Am. Math. Soc.* 355(2):787–811, 2003.

Bonfert-Taylor, P., and **E. C. Taylor**. The exponent of convergence and a theorem of Astala. *Indiana Univ. Math. J.* 51:607–23, 2002.

Bonfert-Taylor, P., and G. Martin. Quasiconformal groups with small dilatation I. *Proc. Am. Math. Soc.* 129:2019–29, 2001.

Bonfert-Taylor, P., and **E. C. Taylor.** Hausdorff dimension and limit sets of quasiconformal groups. *Mich. Math. J.* 49:243–57, 2001.

Bonfert-Taylor, P. Jørgensen's inequality for discrete convergence groups. *Ann. Acad. Sci. Fenn.* 26:131–50, 2000.

Chan, W. K., and F. Xu. On representations of spinor genera. *Compositio Math.* 140:287–300, 2004.

Chan, W. K., and M. Peters. Quaternary quadratic forms and Hilbert modular surfaces. *Contemporary Math.* 344: AMS 85–97, 2004.

Chan, W. K., and B.-K. Oh. Positive ternary quadratic forms with finitely many exceptions. *Proc. Am. Math. Soc.* 132(6):1567–73, 2004.

Chan, W. K., and B.-K. Oh. Finiteness theorems for positive definite n-regular quadratic forms. *Trans. Am. Math. Soc.* 355(6):2385–96, 2003.

Chan, W. K., and J. S. Hsia. On almost strong approximation for algebraic groups. *J. Algebra* 254:441–61, 2002.

Collins, K. L. Factoring distance matrix polynomials. *Discrete Math.* 122:103–12, 1993.

Collins, K. L. Planar lattices are lexicographically shellable. *Order* 8:375–81, 1992.

Comfort, W. W., S. Hernandez, and F. J. Trigos-Arrieta. Relating a locally compact Abelian group to its Bohr compactification. *Adv. in Math.* 120:322-44, 1996.

Comfort, W. W., and **L. C. Robertson.** Extremal phenomena in certain classes of topological groups. *Dissertations Math.* 272:1–41, 1988.

Comfort, W. W. Topological groups. In *Handbook of General Topology,* eds. K. Kunen and J. Vaughan, pp. 1143–1263. Amsterdam: North-Holland Publishing Company, Inc., 1984.

Comfort, W. W., and S. Negrepontis. The theory of ultrafilters. *Grundlehren der Math.* Wissenschaften Band 211, Springer-Verlag, Berlin-Heidelberg, 1974.

Comfort, W. W., and K. A. Ross. Pseudocompactness and uniform continuity in topological groups. *Pacific J. Math.* 16:483–96, 1966.

Coven, E. M., and N. Jonoska. DNA hybridization, shifts of finite type, and tiling of the integers. Gheorghe Paun Festschrift volume, *Romanian Acad. Sci.*, in press.

Coven, E. M., and A. Meyerowitz. Tiling the integers with translates of one finite set. *J. Algebra* 212:161–74, 1999.

Coven, E. M., and A. M. Blokh. Sharkovskii type of cycles. *Bull. London Math. Soc.* 28, 1996.

Danner, N., and C. Pollett. Minimization and NP-multifunctions. *Theor. Comp. Sci.*, in press.

Danner, N. Ramified recurrence with dependent types. In *Typed λ-calculi and applications, Proceedings of the 5th International Conference,* Krakow, Poland, May 2001; in *Lecture Notes in Computer Science,* vol. 2044, pp. 91–105, ed. S. Abramsky. Berlin: Springer-Verlag, 2001.

Danner, N., and D. Leivant. Stratified polymorphism and primitive recursion. *Math. Struct. Comput. Sci.* 9(4):507–22, 1999.

Fieldsteel, A., A. del Junco, and D. J. Rudolph. α-equivalence: A refinement of Kakutani equivalence. *Ergod. Theory Dynamical Syst.*, in press.

Hagar, A. W., C. M. Kimber, and W. W. McGovern. Weakly least integer closed groups. *Rendiconti Circolo Matemàtico Palermo* 52:453–80, 2003.

Hager, A.W., and J. Martinez. α-Specker spaces. *Top. Applications* 131:57–77, 2003.

Hager, A. W., and J. Martinez. *C*-epic compacitifications. *Top. Applications* 117:113–38, 2002.

Hager, A. W., and R. N. Ball. The relative uniform density of the continuous functions in the Baire functions, and of a divisible Archimedean *I*-group in any epicompletion. *Top. Applications* 97:109–26, 1999.

Hager, A. W. Alpha-cut complete Boolean algebras. *Algebra Universalis* 39:57–70, 1998.

Hovey, M., B. Shipley, and J. Smith. Symmetric spectra. *J. Am. Math. Soc.* 13(1):149–208, 2000.

Hovey, M. Model categories. In *Mathematical Surveys and Monographs 63*, Providence: American Mathematical Society, 1999.

Hovey, M., and N. Strickland. Morava K-theories and localization. *Mem. Am. Math. Soc.* 139(666), 1999.

Hovey, M., J. H. Palmieri, and N. Strickland. Axiomatic stable homotopy theory. *Mem. Am. Math. Soc.* 128(610), 1997.

Hovey, M. Morita theory for Hopf algebroids and presheaves of groupoids. *Am. J. Math.* 124:1289–1318, 2002.

Keane, M. S., and S. W. W. Rolles. Tubular recurrence. *Acta Mathematica Hungarica.* 97:207–21, 2003.

Keane, M. S., and J. E. Steif. Finitary coding for the 1-D T,T^{-1}-process with drift. *Ann. Probability* 31:1979–85, 2003.

Keane, M. S., F. den Hollander, J. Serafin, and J. E. Steif. Weak Bernoullicity of random walk in random scenery. *Jpn. J. Math.* 29:389–406, 2003.

Keane, M. S. Marches Aléatoires Renforceés. In *Leçons de Mathématiques d' Aujourd'hui,* Paris: Cassini. 2:347–60, 2003.

Keane, M. S. Entropy in ergodic theory. In *Entropy,* eds. A. Greven, G. Keller, G. Warnecke. Princeton: Princeton University Press, 2003.

Maltese, G. The role of convexity in existence theorems for invariant and hyperinvariant subspaces in Hilbert space. *Rendiconti Circolo Matemàtico Palermo* 49(2):381–90, 2000.

Maltese, G. Some remarks on the Riesz representation theorem in Hilbert space. *Boll. Un. Mater. Ital. B (7)* 11(4):903–7, 1997.

Maltese, G. *Series of the Mathematical Institute of the University of Munster. Series 3. Vol. 17.* Universitat Munster, Mathematisches Institut, Munster, 1996.

Maltese, G. A representation theorem for positive functionals on involution algebras (revisited). *Boll. Un. Mater. Ital. A (7)* 8(3):431–8, 1994.

Maltese, G., and R. Wille-Fier. A characterization of homomorphisms in certain Banach involution algebras. *Studia Math.* 89(2):133–43, 1988.

Pollack, D. J., and J. Lansky. Hecke algebras in automorphic forms. *Comp. Math.,* in press.

Pollack, D. J., A. Ash, and D. Doud. Galois representations with conjectural connections to arithmetic cohomology. *Duke Math. J.*, in press.

Wesleyan University

Selected Publications (continued)

Reid, J. D. Some matrix groups associated with ACD groups. *Abelian Groups and Modules (Proceedings Dublin)*, Birkhauser, 1999.

Reid, J. D. Abelian groups cyclic over their endomorphism rings. *Abelian Group Theory (Proceedings Honolulu)*, Springer, 1983.

Reid, J. D. Abelian groups finitely generated over their endomorphism rings. In *Abelian Group Theory (Proceedings Oberwolfach)*, Springer, 1981.

Rice, M. D., and M. Weir. Ordered partitioning reveals extended splice site consensus information. *Genome Res.* 14:67–78, 2004.

Rice, M. D., and M. Siff. Clusters, concepts, and pseudometrics. In *Proceedings First Irish Conference on Mathematical Foundations of Computer Science and Information Technology*, 2001. Elsevier - ENTCS 40, 2002.

Rice, M. D. Continuous Algorithms. *Top. Applications* 85(1–3):299–318, 1998.

Rice, M. D., and S. B. Seidman. A formal model for module interconnection languages. *IEEE Trans. Software Eng.* 20(1):88–101, 1994.

Robertson, L., and G. Liu. Free subgroups of $SO_3(Q)$. *Commun. Algebra* 27(4):1555–70, 1999.

Robertson, L., R. M. Shortt, and S. Landry. Dice with fair sums. *Am. Math. Monthly* 95:316–28, 1988.

Robertson, L., and **W. W. Comfort.** Images and quotients of SO (3,R): Remarks on a theorem of van der Waerden. *Rocky Mountain J. Math.* 17:1–13, 1987.

Robertson, L., and **A. W. Hager.** Extremal units in an Archimedean Riesz space. *Rend. Sem. Mat. Univ. Padova* 59:97–115, 1978.

Robertson, L. Connectivity, divisibility, and torsion. *Trans. Am. Math. Soc.* 128:482–505, 1967.

Scowcroft, P. H. Some purely topological models for intuitionistic analysis. *Ann. Pure Appl. Logic* 98:173–215, 1999.

Scowcroft, P. H. Cross-sections for p-adically closed fields. *J. Algebra* 183:913–28, 1996.

Scowcroft, P. H., and A. Macintyre. On the elimination of imaginaries from certain valued fields. *Ann. Pure Appl. Logic* 61:241–76, 1993.

Scowcroft, P. H., and L. van den Dries. On the structure of semialgebraic sets over p-adic fields. *J. Symbolic Logic* 53:1138–64, 1988.

Scowcroft, P. H. A transfer theorem in constructive real algebra. *Ann. Pure Appl. Logic* 40:29–87, 1988.

Taylor, E. C., J. Anderson, and **P. Bonfert-Taylor.** Convergence groups, Hausdorff dimension, and a theorem of Sullivan and Tukia. *Geometriae Dedicata.* 130:51–67, 2004.

Taylor, E. C., and M. Bridgeman. Length distortion and the Hausdorff dimension of limit sets. *Am. J. Math.* 122:465–82, 2000.

Taylor, E. C., and R. Canary. Hausdorff dimension and limits of Kleinian groups. *Geom. Funct. Anal.* 9:283–97, 1999.

Taylor, E. C. Geometric finiteness and the convergence of Kleinian groups. *Commun. Anal. Geom.* 5(3):497–533, 1997.

Wood, C., and Z. Chatzidakis. Minimal types in separably closed fields. *J. Symbolic Logic,* in press.

Wood, C. Differentially closed fields. In *Model Theory and Algebraic Geometry,* ed. E. Bouscaren. *Springer Lecture Notes* 1696:129–42, 1998.

Wood, C., and D. Saracino. Homogeneous finite rings in characteristic 2^n. *Ann. Pure Appl. Logic* 40:11–28, 1998.

Wood, C., and D. Saracino. Partially homogeneous partially ordered sets. *J. Combinatorial Theory A* 62:216–24, 1993.

Wood, C., G. Cherlin, and D. Saracino. On homogeneous nilpotent groups and rings. *Proc. Am. Math. Soc.* 119:1289–306, 1993.

WORCESTER POLYTECHNIC INSTITUTE

Department of Mathematical Sciences

Programs of Study

The Mathematical Sciences Department at Worcester Polytechnic Institute (WPI) offers two programs leading to the degree of Master of Science (M.S.), two professional science master's programs, a program leading to the degree of Master of Mathematics for Educators (M.M.E.), and a program leading to the degree of Doctor of Philosophy (Ph.D.).

The Master of Science in applied mathematics is a 36-credit program that gives students a broad background in mathematics, placing an emphasis on numerical methods and scientific computation, mathematical modeling, discrete mathematics, optimization and operations research. Students have a choice of completing their master's thesis or project in cooperation with one department's established industrial partners.

The Master of Science in applied statistics is a 36-credit program that gives graduates the knowledge and experience to tackle problems of statistical design, analysis, and control that is likely to be encountered in business, industry, or academia. Professional experience is provided by a statistical consulting course and master's project, often done with local industry.

The Master of Science in financial mathematics (supported by the Alfred P. Sloan Foundation) is a 30-credit program that offers an efficient, practice-oriented track to prepare students for quantitative careers in the financial industry. The mathematical knowledge is complemented by studies in financial management, information technology, and/or computer science. The bridge from the academic environment to the professional workplace is provided by a professional master's project that involves the solution of a concrete, real-world problem directly originating from the financial industry.

The Master of Science in industrial mathematics (supported by the Alfred P. Sloan Foundation) is a 30-credit practice-oriented program that prepares students for successful careers in industry. The program aims at developing the analysis, modeling, and computational skills needed by mathematicians who work in industrial environments. The connection between academic training and industrial experience is provided by an industrial professional master's project that involves the solution of a concrete, real-world problem originating in industry, and by summer internships.

The Master of Mathematics for Educators is a two-year program designed primarily for secondary mathematics teachers. The program provides teachers with an understanding of the fundamental principles of mathematics through courses and project work that model diverse pedagogical methods. All program requirements also incorporate appropriate technologies, as well as relevant results from research in mathematics education.

The Doctor of Philosophy in mathematical sciences produces active and creative problem solvers capable of contributing in academic and industrial environments. One distinguishing feature of this program is a 9-credit-hour project to be completed under the guidance of an external sponsor, either from industry or a national research center. The intention of this project is to connect theoretical knowledge with the relevant applications and to introduce the candidate to potential employers.

Research Facilities

The Department of Mathematical Sciences boasts a full-time faculty of 28 members with a research focus in applied and computational mathematics and statistics. The George C. Gordon Library is committed to supporting the research information needs of WPI's graduate community. The collection currently numbers 270,000 bound volumes and includes subscriptions to 1,400 periodicals. In addition, hundreds of databases can be researched with the library's On-Line Search Services. Computing facilities in the Department of Mathematical Sciences include a network of high-performance work stations, two computer labs, and a 16-node (32-processor) IBM RS/6000 SP supercomputer for parallel computation.

Financial Aid

Teaching assistantships and research assistantships are available on a competitive basis. Full assistantships provide tuition plus a stipend of approximately $13,500 for the nine-month academic year. U.S. citizens with exceptional qualifications are encouraged to apply for the Robert F. Goddard Fellowships. Other fellowship opportunities are also available. Information may be found online at http://www.wpi.edu/Admin/GAO/fellowships.html.

Cost of Study

Tuition for all courses taken by graduate students is based on a fee per credit hour. The 2003–04 academic year tuition was $858 per credit hour. The tuition rate for individuals auditing a course is 50 percent of the normal tuition.

Living and Housing Costs

In general, graduate students live in private homes or apartments in residential areas near the campus. Listings of off-campus accommodations are maintained in the Office of Residential Life. Depending on living arrangements, students may spend $700 to $900 per month for food, rent, and utilities.

Student Group

The current WPI student body of about 4,000 includes 1,300 full- and part-time graduate students. Presently, 65 graduate students are enrolled in the Department of Mathematical Sciences programs. Of these, 36 are part-time students, 28 are women, 21 are international students, and 44 are receiving financial aid from the university.

Location

WPI is attractively located on a 62-acre campus in a residential section of Worcester, Massachusetts. Worcester (population 165,000) is New England's third-largest city and is the home of ten colleges. Worcester is also well-known for its art museum, the historic Higgins Armory, the New England Science Center, the world-renowned American Antiquarian Society (adjacent to WPI campus), an outstanding downtown shopping mall, and the 14,000-seat Centrum, venue for various sporting and musical events. Worcester is centrally located within an hour's drive of cultural and academic centers in Boston, Providence, Hartford, Amherst, and Storrs.

The Institute

Founded in 1865, WPI is a pioneer in technological higher education. WPI was the first university to understand that students learn best when they have the opportunity to apply the knowledge they gain in the classroom to the solution of important problems. Today its students, working in teams at more than twenty project centers around the globe, put their knowledge and skills to work as they complete professional-level work that can have an immediate positive impact on society. WPI's innovative, globally focused curriculum has been recognized by leaders in industry, government, and academia as the model for the technological education of tomorrow. Students emerge from this program as true technological humanists, well-rounded, with the confidence, the interpersonal skills, and the commitment to innovation they need to make a real difference in their professional and personal lives. The university awarded its first advanced degree in 1898. Today, its first-rate research laboratories support master's and Ph.D. programs in more than thirty disciplines in engineering, science, and the management of technology. Located in the heart of the region's biotechnology and high-technology sectors, WPI has built research programs—including the largest industry/university alliance in North America—that have won it worldwide recognition.

Applying

Applicants must submit WPI application forms, official college transcript(s), three letters of recommendation, and a $60 application fee (waived for WPI alumni). Submission of GRE scores is recommended. International students must also submit a paper-based TOEFL score of at least 550 (at least 213, computer-based). Applications for admission are accepted at any time. However, in order to receive full consideration for financial support, the application file should be completed by February 1. Application forms for admission and financial support, as well as additional information about the program, can be obtained from the Department of Mathematical Sciences at the address below.

Correspondence and Information

For program information and application forms, interested students should contact:

Graduate Committee
Department of Mathematical Sciences
Worcester Polytechnic Institute
100 Institute Road
Worcester, Massachusetts 01609-2280
Telephone: 508-831-5241
Fax: 508-831-5824
E-mail: ma-grad-p@wpi.edu
World Wide Web: http://www.wpi.edu/Academics/Depts/Math/Programs/

Worcester Polytechnic Institute

THE FACULTY AND THEIR RESEARCH

Florin Catrina, Visiting Assistant Professor; Ph.D., Utah State, 2000. Partial differential equations, variational methods.
Peter R. Christopher, Professor; Ph.D., Clark, 1982. Graph theory, group theory, algebraic graph theory, combinatorics, linear algebra, discrete mathematics.
Paul W. Davis, Professor; Ph.D., Rensselaer, 1970. Unit commitment, optimal power flow, economic dispatch, state estimation, and other control and measurement problems for electric power networks.
Bogdan Doytchinov, Assistant Professor; Ph.D., Carnegie Mellon, 1997. Applied probability, queueing systems, reliability.
William W. Farr, Associate Professor; Ph.D., Minnesota, 1986. Ordinary and partial differential equations, dynamical systems, local bifurcation theory with symmetry and its application to problems involving chemical reactions and/or fluid mechanics.
Joseph D. Fehribach, Associate Professor; Ph.D., Duke, 1985. Partial differential equations and scientific computing, free and moving boundary problems (crystal growth), nonequilibrium thermodynamics and averaging (molten carbonate fuel cells).
John Goulet, Coordinator, Master of Mathematics for Educators Program; Ph.D., Rensselaer, 1976. Applications of linear algebra, educational and industrial assessment, development of educational software.
Arthur C. Heinricher Jr., Associate Professor; Ph.D., Carnegie Mellon, 1986. Applied probability, stochastic processes and optimal control theory.
Mayer Humi, Professor; Ph.D., Weizmann (Israel), 1969. Mathematical physics, applied mathematics and modeling, lie groups, differential equations, numerical analysis, turbulence and chaos, continuum mechanics, control theory, artificial intelligence.
Christopher J. Larsen, Assistant Professor; Ph.D., Carnegie Mellon, 1996. Calculus of variations, partial differential equations, and geometric measure theory, with focus on free discontinuity problems modeling fracture mechanics, image segmentation (computer vision), and optimal design.
Roger Lui, Professor; Ph.D., Minnesota, 1981. Nonlinear partial differential equations, mathematical biology, nonlinear analysis.
Konstantin A. Lurie, Professor; Ph.D., A. F. Ioffe Physical-Technical Institute (Russia), 1964; D.Sc., Russian Academy of Sciences, 1972. Control theory for the distributed parameter systems, optimization and nonconvex variational calculus, optimal design.
William Martin, Associate Professor; Ph.D., Waterloo, 1992. Applications of algebra and combinatorics to problems in computer science and mathematics designs and codes in association schemes, error-correcting codes, cryptography, and combinatorial designs.
Carlos Morales, Assistant Professor; Ph.D., Boston University, 2002. Statistics, wavelets, fractal time-series analysis.
Balgobin Nandram, Associate Professor; Ph.D., Iowa, 1989. Applied Bayesian statistics, small-area estimation and computational methods, categorical data analysis, predictive and restrictive inference.
Daniel Pasca, Visiting Assistant Professor; Ph.D., Bucharest, 1999. Variational methods, critical point theory, and bifurcation theory for ODE and PDE, with applications to nonlinear problems in fluid mechanics and Hamiltonian systems, hydrodynamic and hydromagnetic stability of fluid motions, biomechanics.
Joseph D. Petruccelli, Professor; Ph.D., Purdue, 1978. Time series, optimal stopping, statistics, statistics education, biomedical applications of statistics.
Luis Roman, Visiting Assistant Professor; Ph.D., Minnesota, 2000. Stochastic partial differential equations, stochastic control.
Marcus Sarkis, Assistant Professor; Ph.D., NYU (Courant), 1994. Domain decomposition methods, numerical analysis, parallel computing, computational fluid dynamics, preconditioned iterative methods for linear and nonlinear problems, numerical partial differential equations, mixed and nonconforming finite methods, overlapping nonmatching grids, mortar finite elements, eigenvalue solvers, aeroelasticity, porous media reservoir.
Brigitte Servatius, Associate Professor; Ph.D., Syracuse, 1987. Combinatorics, rigidity of structures, geometric foundations of computer-aided design, symmetry and duality, the history and philosophy of mathematics.
Dewon Shon, Visiting Assistant Professor; Ph.D., SUNY at Stony Brook, 2002. Biostatistics, genetic epidemiology, financial statistics.
Andrew Swift, Visiting Assistant Professor; D.Sc., George Washington, 2001. Stochastic modeling, statistical forecasting, Bayesian inference, data analysis, quality control, reliability, risk analysis, sports statistics.
Dalin Tang, Professor; Ph.D., Wisconsin–Madison, 1988. Biomechanics, blood flow, applied fluid mechanics, nonlinear analysis, numerical methods, biological fluid dynamics, transport theory.
Domokos Vermes, Associate Professor; Ph.D., Szeged (Hungary), 1975; Habilitation in Mathematics, Hungarian Academy of Sciences. Optimal stochastic control theory, nonsmooth analysis, stochastic processes with discontinuous dynamics, optimal scheduling under uncertainty, adaptive control in medical decision making.
Bogdan Vernescu, Professor; Ph.D., Institute of Mathematics, Bucharest, 1989. Partial differential equations, phase transitions and free boundaries, viscous flow in porous media and homogenization.
Homer F. Walker, Professor and Department Head; Ph.D., NYU (Courant), 1970. Numerical analysis, especially numerical solution of large-scale linear and nonlinear systems, unconstrained optimization, and applications to differential equations and statistical estimation; applied mathematics.
Suzanne Weekes, Assistant Professor; Ph.D., Michigan, 1995. Numerical analysis, computational fluid dynamics, porous media flow, hyperbolic conservation laws, shock capturing schemes.
Jayson Wilbur, Assistant Professor; Ph.D., Purdue, 2002. Applied statistics, resampling methods, multivariate statistical analysis, model selection, Bayesian inference, statistical issues in molecular biology and ecology.
Eugene Yablonski, Visiting Assistant Professor; Ph.D., Ohio State, 2003. Infinite dimensional analysis.
Vadim Yakovlev, Visiting Associate Professor; Ph.D. Institute of Radio Engineering and Electronics, Moscow, 1991. Electromagnetic fields in transmission lines and near interfaces; atmospheric wave propagation; microwave thermoprocessing; coupled electromagnetic/thermal boundary problems; control and optimization of electric and temperature fields; numerical methods, CAD tools, and computation.

ACADEMIC AND PROFESSIONAL PROGRAMS IN THE AGRICULTURAL SCIENCES

Section 8
Agricultural and Food Sciences

This section contains a directory of institutions offering graduate work in agricultural and food sciences, followed by in-depth entries submitted by institutions that chose to prepare detailed program descriptions. Additional information about programs listed in the directory but not augmented by an in-depth entry may be obtained by writing directly to the dean of a graduate school or chair of a department at the address given in the directory.

For programs offering related work, see also in this book Natural Resources. In Book 2, see Architecture (Landscape Architecture) and Economics (Agricultural Economics and Agribusiness); in Book 3, see Biological and Biomedical Sciences; Botany and Plant Biology; Ecology, Environmental Biology, and Evolutionary Biology; Entomology; Genetics, Developmental Biology, and Reproductive Biology; Nutrition; Pathology and Pathobiology; Physiology; and Zoology; in Book 5, see Agricultural Engineering and Bioengineering, Biomedical Engineering, and Biotechnology; and in Book 6, see Education (Agricultural Education) and Veterinary Medicine and Sciences.

CONTENTS

Program Directories

Announcement

In-Depth Descriptions

Agricultural Sciences—General

Alabama Agricultural and Mechanical University, School of Graduate Studies, School of Agricultural and Environmental Sciences, Huntsville, AL 35811. Offers MS, MURP, PhD. Part-time and evening/weekend programs available. *Faculty:* 30 full-time (6 women). *Students:* 42 full-time (26 women), 68 part-time (49 women); includes 98 minority (88 African Americans, 4 American Indian/Alaska Native, 6 Asian Americans or Pacific Islanders). Terminal master's awarded for partial completion of doctoral program. *Degree requirements:* For doctorate, one foreign language, thesis/dissertation. *Entrance requirements:* For master's, GRE General Test; for doctorate, GRE General Test, MS. *Application deadline:* For fall admission, 5/1 for domestic students. Applications are processed on a rolling basis. Application fee: $25. Electronic applications accepted. *Expenses:* Tuition, state resident: full-time $3,250; part-time $370 per credit hour. Tuition, nonresident: full-time $6,490; part-time $740 per credit hour. *Financial support:* Fellowships, research assistantships, teaching assistantships, career-related internships or fieldwork and Federal Work-Study available. Support available to part-time students. Financial award application deadline: 4/1. *Faculty research:* Remote sensing, environmental pollutants, food biotechnology, plant growth. Total annual research expenditures: $5 million. *Unit head:* Dr. James W. Shuford, Dean, 256-372-5783, Fax: 256-372-5906.

Alcorn State University, School of Graduate Studies, School of Agriculture and Applied Science, Alcorn State, MS 39096-7500. Offers agricultural economics (MS Ag); agronomy (MS Ag); animal science (MS Ag). *Faculty:* 11 full-time (2 women). *Students:* 9 full-time (2 women), 7 part-time (2 women); includes 12 minority (all African Americans), 3 international. *Degree requirements:* For master's, thesis optional. *Application deadline:* For fall admission, 7/15 for domestic students; for spring admission, 11/25 for domestic students. Applications are processed on a rolling basis. Application fee: $0 ($10 for international students). *Expenses:* Tuition, state resident: full-time $3,192. Tuition, nonresident: full-time $7,698. *Financial support:* Career-related internships or fieldwork available. Support available to part-time students. *Faculty research:* Aquatic systems, dairy herd improvement, fruit production, alternative farming practices. *Unit head:* Napoleon Moses, Dean, 601-877-6137, Fax: 601-877-6219.

Angelo State University, Graduate School, College of Sciences, Department of Agriculture, San Angelo, TX 76909. Offers animal science (MS). Part-time and evening/weekend programs available. *Faculty:* 7 full-time (2 women), 2 part-time/adjunct (0 women). *Students:* 8 full-time (0 women), 13 part-time (1 woman); includes 1 minority (Hispanic American), 1 international. Average age 27. 10 applicants, 100% accepted, 8 enrolled. In 2003, 11 degrees awarded. *Degree requirements:* For master's, thesis optional. *Entrance requirements:* For master's, GRE General Test, minimum GPA of 2.5. Additional exam requirements/recommendations for international students: Required—TOEFL (minimum score 550 paper-based; 213 computer-based). *Application deadline:* For fall admission, 7/15 priority date for domestic students, 6/15 priority date for international students; for spring admission, 12/8 for domestic students, 11/1 for international students. Applications are processed on a rolling basis. Application fee: $25 ($50 for international students). Electronic applications accepted. *Expenses:* Tuition, state resident: part-time $204 per semester hour. Tuition, nonresident: part-time $440 per semester hour. *Financial support:* In 2003–04, 6 students received support, including 8 fellowships, 2 research assistantships; teaching assistantships, career-related internships or fieldwork, Federal Work-Study, scholarships/grants, tuition waivers (partial), and unspecified assistantships also available. Support available to part-time students. Financial award application deadline: 8/1. *Faculty research:* Effect of protein and energy on feedlot performance, bitterweed toxicosis in sheep, meat laboratory, North Concho watershed project, baseline vegetation. *Unit head:* Dr. Gilbert R. Engdahl, Head, 325-942-2027 Ext. 227, E-mail: gil.engdahl@angelo.edu. *Application contact:* Dr. Cody B. Scott, Graduate Advisor, 325-942-2027 Ext. 284, E-mail: cody.scott@angelo.edu.

Arkansas State University, Graduate School, College of Agriculture, Jonesboro, State University, AR 72467. Offers agricultural education (MSA, SCCT); agriculture (MSA); vocational-technical administration (MS, SCCT). Part-time programs available. *Faculty:* 11 full-time (1 woman). *Students:* 8 full-time (6 women), 31 part-time (13 women); includes 1 minority (African American) Average age 35. In 2003, 11 degrees awarded. *Degree requirements:* For master's, thesis or alternative, comprehensive exam. *Entrance requirements:* For master's, GRE General Test or MAT, appropriate bachelor's degree; for SCCT, GRE General Test or MAT, interview, master's degree. Additional exam requirements/recommendations for international students: Required—TOEFL (minimum score 213 computer-based). *Application deadline:* For fall admission, 7/1 for domestic students; for spring admission, 11/15 priority date for domestic students. Applications are processed on a rolling basis. Application fee: $15 ($25 for international students). Electronic applications accepted. *Expenses:* Tuition, state resident: full-time $2,844; part-time $158 per hour. Tuition, nonresident: full-time $7,200; part-time $400 per hour. Required fees: $644; $33 per hour. $25 per semester. Tuition and fees vary according to course load. *Financial support:* Teaching assistantships, Federal Work-Study and scholarships/grants available. Support available to part-time students. Financial award application deadline: 7/1; financial award applicants required to submit FAFSA. *Unit head:* Dr. Gregory Phillips, Dean, 870-972-2085, Fax: 870-972-3885, E-mail: gphillips@astate.edu.

Auburn University, Graduate School, College of Agriculture, Auburn University, AL 36849. Offers M Ag, M Aq, MS, PhD. Part-time programs available. *Faculty:* 131 full-time (19 women). *Students:* 122 full-time (47 women), 89 part-time (28 women); includes 12 minority (6 African Americans, 1 American Indian/Alaska Native, 3 Asian Americans or Pacific Islanders, 2 Hispanic Americans), 62 international. 112 applicants, 60% accepted. In 2003, 46 master's, 15 doctorates awarded. *Degree requirements:* For doctorate, thesis/dissertation. *Entrance requirements:* For master's and doctorate, GRE General Test. *Application deadline:* For fall admission, 7/7 for domestic students; for spring admission, 11/24 for domestic students. Applications are processed on a rolling basis. Application fee: $25 ($50 for international students). Electronic applications accepted. *Expenses:* Tuition, state resident: part-time $175 per credit hour. Tuition, nonresident: part-time $525 per credit hour. *Financial support:* Fellowships, research assistantships, teaching assistantships, Federal Work-Study available. Support available to part-time students. Financial award application deadline: 3/15. *Unit head:* Dr. John W. Jensen, Interim Dean, 334-844-2345. *Application contact:* Dr. John F. Pritchett, Dean of the Graduate School, 334-844-4700, E-mail: hatchlb@mail.auburn.edu.

Brigham Young University, Graduate Studies, College of Biological and Agricultural Sciences, Provo, UT 84602-1001. Offers MS, PhD. Part-time programs available. *Faculty:* 93 full-time (9 women), 1 (woman) part-time/adjunct. *Students:* 106 full-time (50 women), 15 part-time (8 women); includes 12 minority (1 African American, 5 Asian Americans or Pacific Islanders, 6 Hispanic Americans), 4 international. Average age 26. 77 applicants, 57% accepted, 38 enrolled. In 2003, 35 master's awarded, leading to continued full-time study 22%, business/industry 84%; 4 doctorates. Terminal master's awarded for partial completion of doctoral program. *Degree requirements:* For master's, thesis, comprehensive exam, registration. *Entrance requirements:* For master's and doctorate, GRE General Test. Additional exam requirements/recommendations for international students: Required—TOEFL. *Application deadline:* For fall admission, 1/31 for domestic students, 1/31 for international students. Application fee: $50. Electronic applications accepted. *Expenses:* Tuition: Part-time $221 per hour. *Financial support:* In 2003–04, 94 students received support, including 6 fellowships with full and partial tuition reimbursements available (averaging $9,750 per year), 38 research assistantships with full and partial tuition reimbursements available (averaging $14,400 per year), 71 teaching assistantships with full and partial tuition reimbursements available (averaging $10,750 per year); career-related internships or fieldwork, institutionally sponsored loans, scholarships/grants, and tuition awards also available. Support available to part-time students. Total annual research expenditures: $2.3 million. *Unit head:* Dr. R. Kent Crookston, Dean, 801-422-2007, Fax: 801-422-0050.

California Polytechnic State University, San Luis Obispo, College of Agriculture, San Luis Obispo, CA 93407. Offers agriculture (MS); forestry sciences (MS). Part-time programs available. *Faculty:* 5 full-time (1 woman), 2 part-time/adjunct (1 woman). *Students:* 90 full-time (50 women), 41 part-time (22 women); includes 13 Hispanic Americans. 105 applicants, 72% accepted, 45 enrolled. In 2003, 34 degrees awarded. *Degree requirements:* For master's, thesis, comprehensive exam. *Entrance requirements:* For master's, minimum GPA of 2.5 in last 90 quarter units. Additional exam requirements/recommendations for international students: Required—TOEFL, TWE. *Application deadline:* For fall admission, 7/1 for domestic students; for winter admission, 11/1 for domestic students; for spring admission, 3/1 for domestic students. Applications are processed on a rolling basis. Application fee: $55. Electronic applications accepted. Tuition, nonresident: part-time $188 per unit. Required fees: $3,732. *Financial support:* In 2003–04, 40 students received support, including 6 fellowships (averaging $2,000 per year), 20 research assistantships (averaging $10,000 per year), 10 teaching assistantships (averaging $2,000 per year); career-related internships or fieldwork, Federal Work-Study, institutionally sponsored loans, and scholarships/grants also available. Support available to part-time students. Financial award application deadline: 3/2; financial award applicants required to submit FAFSA. *Faculty research:* Soils, food processing, forestry, dairy products development, irrigation. *Unit head:* Dr. David J. Wehner, Dean, 805-756-5072, Fax: 805-756-6577, E-mail: dwehner@calpoly.edu. *Application contact:* Jim Maraviglia, Admissions Office, 805-756-2311, E-mail: admissions@calpoly.edu.

California State Polytechnic University, Pomona, Academic Affairs, College of Agriculture, Pomona, CA 91768-2557. Offers agricultural science (MS); animal science (MS); foods and nutrition (MS). Part-time programs available. *Faculty:* 43 full-time (15 women), 15 part-time/adjunct (6 women). *Students:* 24 full-time (18 women), 24 part-time (19 women); includes 14 minority (1 African American, 6 Asian Americans or Pacific Islanders, 7 Hispanic Americans), 6 international. Average age 30. 66 applicants, 55% accepted, 26 enrolled. In 2003, 19 degrees awarded. *Degree requirements:* For master's, thesis or alternative. *Application deadline:* For fall admission, 5/1 for domestic students; for winter admission, 10/15 for domestic students; for spring admission, 1/2 for domestic students. Applications are processed on a rolling basis. Application fee: $55. Electronic applications accepted. Tuition, nonresident: full-time $6,016; part-time $188 per unit. Required fees: $2,256. *Financial support:* Career-related internships or fieldwork, Federal Work-Study, and institutionally sponsored loans available. Support available to part-time students. Financial award application deadline: 3/2; financial award applicants required to submit FAFSA. *Faculty research:* Equine nutrition, physiology, and reproduction; leadership development; bioartificial pancreas; plant science; ruminant and human nutrition. *Unit head:* Dr. Wayne R. Bidlack, Dean, 909-869-2200, E-mail: wrbidlack@csupomona.edu.

California State University, Fresno, Division of Graduate Studies, College of Agricultural Sciences and Technology, Fresno, CA 93740-8027. Offers MS. Part-time and evening/weekend programs available. *Entrance requirements:* For master's, GRE General Test. Additional exam requirements/recommendations for international students: Required—TOEFL. Electronic applications accepted.

Central Missouri State University, School of Graduate Studies, College of Applied Sciences and Technology, Department of Agriculture, Warrensburg, MO 64093. Offers agriculture technology (MS). *Faculty:* 4 full-time (0 women), 1 part-time/adjunct (0 women). *Students:* 1 full-time (0 women), 1 international. Average age 31. *Entrance requirements:* Additional exam requirements/recommendations for international students: Required—TOEFL (minimum score 500 paper-based; 173 computer-based). *Application deadline:* For fall admission, 6/1 priority date for domestic students, 5/1 priority date for international students; for spring admission, 10/1 priority date for domestic students, 10/1 priority date for international students. Application fee: $25 ($50 for international students). *Expenses:* Tuition, state resident: part-time $198 per credit hour. Tuition, nonresident: part-time $396 per credit hour. Required fees: $12 per credit hour. *Faculty research:* Passive irrigation systems in greenhouse and nursery production, characterization of ovarian follicular development using transrectal ultrasound in cyclic quilts, fertility management for eastern gamagram. Total annual research expenditures:$1,500. *Unit head:* Dr. Fred Worman, Chair, 660-543-4240, E-mail: worman@cmsu1.cmsu.edu.

Clemson University, Graduate School, College of Agriculture, Forestry and Life Sciences, Clemson, SC 29634. Offers M Ag Ed, M Engr, MFR, MS, PhD. Part-time programs available. *Faculty:* 198 full-time (30 women), 27 part-time/adjunct (8 women). *Students:* 293 full-time (133 women), 85 part-time (40 women); includes 25 minority (15 African Americans, 4 American Indian/Alaska Native, 1 Asian American or Pacific Islander, 5 Hispanic Americans), 97 international. 445 applicants, 50% accepted, 66 enrolled. In 2003, 70 master's, 37 doctorates awarded. Terminal master's awarded for partial completion of doctoral program. *Degree requirements:* For master's, thesis (for some programs); for doctorate, thesis/dissertation. *Entrance requirements:* For master's and doctorate, GRE General Test. Additional exam requirements/recommendations for international students: Required—TOEFL. *Application deadline:* Applications are processed on a rolling basis. Application fee: $40. Electronic applications accepted. *Expenses:* Tuition, state resident: full-time $7,432. Tuition, nonresident: full-time $14,732. *Financial support:* Fellowships, research assistantships, teaching assistantships, career-related internships or fieldwork, Federal Work-Study, institutionally sponsored loans, scholarships/grants, and unspecified assistantships available. Financial award applicants required to submit FAFSA. *Unit head:* Dr. Calvin Schoulties, Interim Dean, 864-656-7592, Fax: 864-656-1286, E-mail: cshlts@clemson.edu.

Colorado State University, Graduate School, College of Agricultural Sciences, Fort Collins, CO 80523-0015. Offers M Agr, MS, PhD. Part-time programs available. Postbaccalaureate distance learning degree programs offered. *Faculty:* 101 full-time (15 women). *Students:* 131 full-time (52 women), 128 part-time (57 women); includes 10 minority (1 African American, 1 American Indian/Alaska Native, 4 Asian Americans or Pacific Islanders, 4 Hispanic Americans), 40 international. Average age 31. 238 applicants, 45% accepted, 60 enrolled. In 2003, 57 master's, 12 doctorates awarded. *Degree requirements:* For master's, thesis (for some programs); for doctorate, thesis/dissertation, comprehensive exam (for some programs). *Entrance requirements:* For master's and doctorate, GRE General Test, minimum GPA of 3.0. Additional exam requirements/recommendations for international students: Required—TOEFL. *Application deadline:* For fall admission, 4/1 priority date for domestic students, 4/1 priority date for international students; for spring admission, 9/1 priority date for domestic students, 9/1 priority date for international students. Applications are processed on a rolling basis. Application fee: $50. Electronic applications accepted. *Expenses:* Tuition, state resident: full-time $4,156. Tuition, nonresident: full-time $14,762. Required fees: $205. Tuition and fees vary according to course load, campus/location, program and reciprocity agreements. *Financial support:* In 2003–04, 14 fellowships, 34 research assistantships, 21 teaching assistantships were awarded. Career-related internships or fieldwork, Federal Work-Study, institutionally sponsored loans, and traineeships also available. Support available to part-time students. *Faculty research:* Systems methodology, biotechnology, plant and animal breeding, water management, plant protection. Total annual research expenditures: $5 million. *Unit head:* Dr. Marc A. Johnson, Dean, 970-491-6274, Fax: 970-491-4895, E-mail: m.johnson@colostate.edu.

Dalhousie University, Faculty of Graduate Studies, Nova Scotia Agricultural College, Halifax, NS B3H 4R2, Canada. Offers M Sc. Part-time programs available. *Degree requirements:* For master's, thesis, candidacy exam. *Entrance requirements:* For master's, minimum GPA of 3.0. Additional exam requirements/recommendations for international students: Required—TOEFL. *Faculty research:* Biology, soil science, animal science, plant science, environmental science, biotechnology.

Illinois State University, Graduate School, College of Applied Science and Technology, Department of Agriculture, Normal, IL 61790-2200. Offers agribusiness (MS). *Faculty:* 12 full-time (1 woman). *Students:* 18 full-time (3 women), 4 part-time (1 woman); includes 1 minority (Hispanic American), 13 international. 14 applicants, 93% accepted. In 2003, 8 degrees awarded. *Degree requirements:* For master's, thesis optional. *Entrance requirements:* For master's, GRE General Test, minimum GPA of 3.0 in last 60 hours. *Application deadline:* Applications are processed on a rolling basis. Application fee: $30. *Expenses:* Tuition, state resident: full-time $3,322; part-time $138 per hour. Tuition, nonresident: full-time $6,922; part-time $288 per hour. Required fees: $974; $41 per hour. *Financial support:* In 2003–04, 17 research assistantships (averaging $5,851 per year), 1 teaching assistantship (averaging $6,750 per year) were awarded. Tuition waivers (full) and unspecified assistantships also available. Financial award application deadline: 4/1. *Faculty research:* Transferring on-farm composting technology for swine waste to Illinois producers, genetic selection for improved swine performance, landscape waste disposal. Total annual research expenditures: $410,788. *Unit head:* Dr. J. R. Winter, Chairperson, 309-438-5654.

Instituto Tecnológico y de Estudios Superiores de Monterrey, Campus Monterrey, Graduate and Research Division, Program in Agriculture, Monterrey, , Mexico. Offers agricultural parasitology (PhD); agricultural sciences (MS); farming productivity (MS); food processing engineering (MS); phytopathology (MS). Part-time programs available. *Degree requirements:* For master's and doctorate, one foreign language, thesis/dissertation. *Entrance requirements:* For master's, PAEG; for doctorate, GMAT or GRE, master's degree in related field. Additional exam requirements/recommendations for international students: Required—TOEFL. *Faculty research:* Animal embryos and reproduction, crop entomology, tropical agriculture, agricultural productivity, induced mutation in oleaginous plants.

Iowa State University of Science and Technology, Graduate College, College of Agriculture, Ames, IA 50011. Offers M Ag, MS, PhD. Part-time programs available. Postbaccalaureate distance learning degree programs offered (no on-campus study). *Faculty:* 229 full-time, 21 part-time/adjunct. *Students:* 418 full-time (177 women), 216 part-time (68 women); includes 30 minority (18 African Americans, 2 American Indian/Alaska Native, 3 Asian Americans or Pacific Islanders, 7 Hispanic Americans), 172 international. 501 applicants, 26% accepted, 100 enrolled. In 2003, 73 master's, 50 doctorates awarded. *Degree requirements:* For doctorate, thesis/dissertation. *Entrance requirements:* Additional exam requirements/recommendations for international students: Required—TOEFL. *Application deadline:* Applications are processed on a rolling basis. Application fee: $50 ($70 for international students). Electronic applications accepted. Tuition, nonresident: part-time $560 per credit. Required fees: $38 per unit. *Financial support:* In 2003–04, 361 research assistantships with full and partial tuition reimbursements (averaging $16,320 per year), 41 teaching assistantships with full and partial tuition reimbursements (averaging $16,686 per year) were awarded. Fellowships, Federal Work-Study, scholarships/grants, health care benefits, and unspecified assistantships also available. Support available to part-time students. *Unit head:* Dr. Catherine E. Woteki, Dean, 515-294-2518, Fax: 515-294-6800.

Kansas State University, Graduate School, College of Agriculture, Manhattan, KS 66506. Offers MAB, MS, PhD. Part-time programs available. Postbaccalaureate distance learning degree programs offered (minimal on-campus study). *Faculty:* 240. *Students:* 406 full-time (143 women), 24 part-time (12 women); includes 27 minority (6 African Americans, 2 American Indian/Alaska Native, 7 Asian Americans or Pacific Islanders, 12 Hispanic Americans), 122 international. 192 applicants, 62% accepted, 72 enrolled. In 2003, 48 master's, 40 doctorates awarded. Terminal master's awarded for partial completion of doctoral program. *Entrance requirements:* For master's, minimum undergraduate GPA of 3.0; for doctorate, minimum undergraduate GPA of 3.5. Additional exam requirements/recommendations for international students: Required—TOEFL. *Application deadline:* For fall admission, 2/1 for domestic students; for spring admission, 10/1 for domestic students. Application fee: $0 ($25 for international students). Electronic applications accepted. *Expenses:* Tuition, state resident: part-time $155 per credit hour. Tuition, nonresident: part-time $428 per credit hour. Required fees: $11 per credit hour. *Financial support:* In 2003–04, 229 research assistantships (averaging $14,399 per year), 16 teaching assistantships (averaging $6,842 per year) were awarded. Fellowships, career-related internships or fieldwork, Federal Work-Study, institutionally sponsored loans, scholarships/grants, and tuition waivers (partial) also available. Support available to part-time students. Financial award application deadline: 3/1; financial award applicants required to submit FAFSA. *Unit head:* Marc Johnson, Dean, 785-532-7137, Fax: 785-532-6563, E-mail: mjohnson@ksu.edu.

Louisiana State University and Agricultural and Mechanical College, Graduate School, College of Agriculture, Baton Rouge, LA 70803. Offers M App St, MS, MSBAE, PhD. Part-time programs available. *Faculty:* 219 full-time (33 women). *Students:* 388 full-time (197 women), 171 part-time (92 women); includes 38 minority (25 African Americans, 3 American Indian/Alaska Native, 2 Asian Americans or Pacific Islanders, 8 Hispanic Americans), 159 international. Average age 30. 268 applicants, 42% accepted, 48 enrolled. In 2003, 81 master's, 33 doctorates awarded. Terminal master's awarded for partial completion of doctoral program. *Degree requirements:* For doctorate, thesis/dissertation. *Entrance requirements:* For master's and doctorate, GRE General Test, minimum GPA of 3.0. Additional exam requirements/recommendations for international students: Required—TOEFL (minimum score 550 paper-based; 213 computer-based). *Application deadline:* Applications are processed on a rolling basis. Application fee: $25. *Expenses:* Tuition, state resident: part-time $337 per hour. Tuition, nonresident: part-time $577 per hour. *Financial support:* In 2003–04, 14 fellowships with full tuition reimbursements (averaging $18,102 per year), 196 research assistantships with partial tuition reimbursements (averaging $14,668 per year), 33 teaching assistantships with partial tuition reimbursements (averaging $12,315 per year) were awarded. Career-related internships or fieldwork, Federal Work-Study, institutionally sponsored loans, tuition waivers (full), and unspecified assistantships also available. Support available to part-time students. Financial award applicants required to submit FAFSA. *Faculty research:* Biotechnology, resource economics and marketing, aquaculture, food science and technology. Total annual research expenditures: $159,403. *Unit head:* Dr. Kenneth Koonce, Dean, 225-578-2362, Fax: 225-578-2526, E-mail: kkoonce@lsu.edu. *Application contact:* Paula Beecher, Recruiting Coordinator, 225-578-2468, E-mail: pbeeche@lsu.edu.

McGill University, Faculty of Graduate and Postdoctoral Studies, Faculty of Agricultural and Environmental Sciences, Montréal, QC H3A 2T5, Canada. Offers M Sc, M Sc A, PhD, Certificate, MBA/M Sc. Part-time programs available. *Faculty:* 90 full-time (20 women). *Students:* 322 full-time, 11 part-time. Average age 28. 360 applicants, 41% accepted, 86 enrolled. In 2003, 72 master's, 22 doctorates awarded. *Degree requirements:* For doctorate, thesis/dissertation. *Entrance requirements:* For doctorate, M Sc, minimum GPA of 3.0; for Certificate, minimum GPA of 3.0, B Sc in biological sciences. Additional exam requirements/recommendations for international students: Required—TOEFL (paper score 550; computer score 213) or IELTS (paper score 6). *Application deadline:* For fall admission, 6/1 for domestic students, 3/1 for international students; for winter admission, 10/1 for domestic students; for spring admission, 2/1 for domestic students. Applications are processed on a rolling basis. Application fee: $60 Canadian dollars. Tuition, area resident: Full-time $1,668. *Expenses:* Tuition, state resident: full-time $4,173. Tuition, nonresident: full-time $9,468. Required fees: $1,081. *Financial support:* In 2003–04, fellowships (averaging $9,000 per year), 55 research assistantships (averaging $10,800 per year), 84 teaching assistantships (averaging $1,300 per year) were awarded. Career-related internships or fieldwork, institutionally sponsored loans, scholarships/grants, and tuition waivers also available. *Faculty research:* Agriculture, environmental, food sciences, nutrition and molecular biology, biosystems and agricultural engineering. *Unit head:* Dr. Deborah J. Buszard, Dean, 514-398-7707, Fax: 514-398-7766, E-mail: buszard@macdonald.mcgill.ca. *Application contact:* Student Affairs Office, 514-398-7925, Fax: 514-398-7968, E-mail: grad@macdonald.mcgill.ca.

Michigan State University, Graduate School, College of Agriculture and Natural Resources, East Lansing, MI 48824. Offers MS, PhD. *Faculty:* 285 full-time (51 women), 1 part-time/adjunct (0 women). *Students:* 526 full-time (248 women), 164 part-time (68 women); includes 57 minority (21 African Americans, 5 American Indian/Alaska Native, 9 Asian Americans or Pacific Islanders, 22 Hispanic Americans), 270 international. Average age 31. 702 applicants, 29% accepted. In 2003, 159 master's, 74 doctorates awarded. Application fee: $50. *Expenses:* Tuition, state resident: part-time $291 per hour. Tuition, nonresident: part-time $589 per hour. *Financial support:* In 2003–04, 188 fellowships with tuition reimbursements (averaging $4,345 per year), 434 research assistantships with tuition reimbursements (averaging $12,199 per year), 26 teaching assistantships with tuition reimbursements (averaging $11,811 per year) were awarded. Career-related internships or fieldwork, Federal Work-Study, institutionally sponsored loans, and tuition waivers (partial) also available. Support available to part-time students. *Faculty research:* Plant science, animal sciences, forestry, fisheries and wildlife, recreation and tourism. Total annual research expenditures: $30.5 million. *Unit head:* Dr. Jeffrey D. Armstrong, Dean, 517-355-0232, Fax: 517-353-9896. *Application contact:* Dr. Thomas G. Coon, Associate Dean, Graduate and International Programs, 517-353-8858, Fax: 517-353-9896.

Mississippi State University, College of Agriculture and Life Sciences, Mississippi State, MS 39762. Offers MABM, MLA, MS, PhD. Part-time programs available. *Faculty:* 142 full-time (27 women), 6 part-time/adjunct (5 women). *Students:* 143 full-time (61 women), 91 part-time (45 women); includes 12 minority (10 African Americans, 2 Asian Americans or Pacific Islanders), 60 international. Average age 30. 139 applicants, 38% accepted, 27 enrolled. In 2003, 65 master's, 13 doctorates awarded. *Degree requirements:* For doctorate, thesis/dissertation. *Entrance requirements:* Additional exam requirements/recommendations for international students: Required—TOEFL. *Application deadline:* For fall admission, 7/1 for domestic students; for spring admission, 11/1 for domestic students. Applications are processed on a rolling basis. Application fee: $25 for international students. *Expenses:* Tuition, state resident: full-time $3,874; part-time $215 per hour. Tuition, nonresident: full-time $8,780; part-time $488 per hour. International tuition: $9,105 full-time. Tuition and fees vary according to course load. *Financial support:* In 2003–04, 28 research assistantships with full tuition reimbursements (averaging $11,451 per year), 16 teaching assistantships with full tuition reimbursements (averaging $9,963 per year) were awarded. Career-related internships or fieldwork, Federal Work-Study, institutionally sponsored loans, scholarships/grants, tuition waivers (partial), and unspecified assistantships also available. Financial award applicants required to submit FAFSA. *Faculty research:* Animal and dairy sciences-biochemistry, molecular biology, biological engineering, human sciences, food sciences, economics. Total annual research expenditures: $17 million. *Unit head:* Dr. Vance Watson, Dean and Vice President, 662-325-2110, E-mail: vwatson@dafvm.msstate.edu. *Application contact:* Diane D. Wolfe, Director of Admissions, 662-325-2224, Fax: 662-325-7360, E-mail: admit@admissions.msstate.edu.

Montana State University–Bozeman, College of Graduate Studies, College of Agriculture, Bozeman, MT 59717. Offers MS, PhD. Part-time programs available. *Faculty:* 84 full-time (12 women), 14 part-time/adjunct (7 women). *Students:* 37 full-time (20 women), 115 part-time (66 women); includes 3 minority (2 American Indian/Alaska Native, 1 Hispanic American), 16 international. Average age 30. 61 applicants, 75% accepted, 33 enrolled. In 2003, 32 master's, 2 doctorates awarded. *Degree requirements:* For master's, comprehensive exam, registration; for doctorate, thesis/dissertation, comprehensive exam, registration. *Entrance requirements:* For master's and doctorate, GRE General Test. Additional exam requirements/recommendations for international students: Required—TOEFL (minimum score 550 paper-based; 213 computer-based). *Application deadline:* For fall admission, 7/15 priority date for domestic students, 5/15 priority date for international students; for spring admission, 12/1 priority date for domestic students, 10/1 priority date for international students. Applications are processed on a rolling basis. Application fee: $50. Electronic applications accepted. *Expenses:* Tuition, state resident: full-time $3,907; part-time $163 per credit. Tuition, nonresident: full-time $12,383; part-time $516 per credit. Required fees: $890; $445 per term. Tuition and fees vary according to course load and program. *Financial support:* Research assistantships with full and partial tuition reimbursements, teaching assistantships with full and partial tuition reimbursements, scholarships/grants, health care benefits, and unspecified assistantships available. Financial award application deadline: 3/1; financial award applicants required to submit FAFSA. Total annual research expenditures: $20.2 million. *Unit head:* Dr. Jeffrey S. Jacobsen, Interim Dean, 406-994-7060, Fax: 406-994-3933, E-mail: lresinfo@montana.edu.

Murray State University, School of Agriculture, Murray, KY 42071-0009. Offers MS. Part-time programs available. *Entrance requirements:* For master's, GRE General Test. Additional exam requirements/recommendations for international students: Required—TOEFL.

New Mexico State University, Graduate School, College of Agriculture and Home Economics, Las Cruces, NM 88003-8001. Offers M Ag, MA, MS, PhD. Part-time and evening/weekend programs available. *Faculty:* 93 full-time (28 women), 25 part-time/adjunct (3 women). *Students:* 150 full-time (76 women), 91 part-time (54 women); includes 64 minority (3 African Americans, 8 American Indian/Alaska Native, 5 Asian Americans or Pacific Islanders, 48 Hispanic Americans), 33 international. Average age 30. 125 applicants, 70% accepted, 35 enrolled. In 2003, 57 master's, 12 doctorates awarded. *Degree requirements:* For master's, thesis, comprehensive exam, registration; for doctorate, one foreign language, thesis/dissertation. *Application deadline:* For fall admission, 7/1 for domestic students; for spring admission, 11/1 for domestic students. Applications are processed on a rolling basis. Application fee: $30 ($50 for international students). Electronic applications accepted. *Expenses:* Tuition, state resident: full-time $2,670; part-time $151 per credit. Tuition, nonresident: full-time $10,596; part-time $481 per credit. Required fees: $954. *Financial support:* In 2003–04, 64 research assistantships, 49 teaching assistantships were awarded. Career-related internships or fieldwork and Federal Work-Study also available. Support available to part-time students. Financial award application deadline: 3/1. *Faculty research:* Biological control, competitiveness in agricultural business, family social issues, management of natural resources, plant and animal improvement. *Unit head:* Dr. Jerry Schickedanz, Dean, 505-646-1806, Fax: 505-646-5975, E-mail: agdean@nmsu.edu.

North Carolina Agricultural and Technical State University, Graduate School, School of Agriculture and Environmental and Allied Sciences, Greensboro, NC 27411. Offers MS. Part-time and evening/weekend programs available. *Degree requirements:* For master's, qualifying exam. *Entrance requirements:* For master's, GRE General Test. *Faculty research:* Aid for small farmers, agricultural technology, housing, food science, nutrition.

North Carolina State University, Graduate School, College of Agriculture and Life Sciences, Raleigh, NC 27695. Offers M Econ, M Tox, MAEE, MB, MBAE, MFG, MFM, MFS, MG, MMB, MN, MP, MS, PhD. Part-time programs available. *Faculty:* 470 full-time (82 women), 310 part-time/adjunct (28 women). *Students:* 653 full-time (356 women), 147 part-time (82 women); includes 87 minority (37 African Americans, 2 American Indian/Alaska Native, 35 Asian Americans or Pacific Islanders, 13 Hispanic Americans), 134 international. Average age 30. 818 applicants, 34% accepted. In 2003, 124 master's, 83 doctorates awarded. *Application deadline:* For fall admission, 6/25 for domestic students, 3/1 for international students; for spring admission, 11/25 for domestic students, 7/15 for international students. Application fee: $45. *Expenses:* Tuition, state resident: part-time $396 per hour. Tuition, nonresident: part-time $1,895 per hour. *Financial support:* In 2003–04, 58 fellowships with tuition reimbursements (averaging $8,266 per year), 418 research assistantships with tuition reimbursements (averaging $5,965 per year), 66 teaching assistantships with tuition reimbursements (averaging $5,842 per year) were awarded. Career-related internships or fieldwork, Federal Work-Study, institutionally sponsored loans, traineeships, and tuition waivers (partial) also available. Support available to part-time students. Total annual research expenditures: $39 million. *Unit head:* Dr. Johnny C. Wynne, Interim Dean, 919-515-2668, Fax: 919-515-6980, E-mail: johnny_wynne@ncsu.edu. *Application contact:* Cheri Hitt, Administrative Assistant, 919-515-6210, Fax: 919-515-6980, E-mail: cheri_hitt@ncsu.edu.

North Dakota State University, The Graduate School, College of Agriculture, Food Systems, and Natural Resources, Fargo, ND 58105. Offers MS, PhD. Part-time programs available. *Faculty:* 122. *Students:* 237 (98 women); includes 6 minority (2 African Americans, 1 American Indian/Alaska Native, 1 Asian American or Pacific Islander, 2 Hispanic Americans) 105 international. In 2003, 46 master's, 7 doctorates awarded. *Median time to degree:* Master's–7 years part-time; doctorate–3 years full-time, 7 years part-time. *Degree requirements:* For doctorate, thesis/dissertation. *Entrance requirements:* Additional exam requirements/

Agricultural Sciences—General

North Dakota State University (continued)
recommendations for international students: Required—TOEFL. *Application deadline:* Applications are processed on a rolling basis. Application fee: $35 ($50 for international students). Electronic applications accepted. Tuition, nonresident: full-time $4,071. Required fees: $493. *Financial support:* Fellowships with full tuition reimbursements, research assistantships with full tuition reimbursements, teaching assistantships with full tuition reimbursements, career-related internships or fieldwork, Federal Work-Study, and institutionally sponsored loans available. Support available to part-time students. *Faculty research:* Horticulture and forestry, plant and wheat breeding, diseases of insects, animal and range sciences, soil science, veterinary medicine. Total annual research expenditures: $13.7 million. *Unit head:* Dr. James R. Venette, Associate Dean for Academic Programs, 701-231-8790, Fax: 701-231-8520, E-mail: james.venette@ndsu.nodak.edu.

Northwest Missouri State University, Graduate School, College of Arts and Sciences, Department of Agriculture, Maryville, MO 64468-6001. Offers agriculture (MS); teaching agriculture (MS Ed). Part-time programs available. *Faculty:* 5 full-time (0 women). *Students:* 5 full-time (0 women), 4 part-time (1 woman), 1 international. 6 applicants, 83% accepted, 2 enrolled. In 2003, 4 degrees awarded. *Degree requirements:* For master's, thesis (for some programs), comprehensive exam. *Entrance requirements:* For master's, GRE General Test, minimum undergraduate GPA of 2.5, writing sample. Additional exam requirements/recommendations for international students: Required—TOEFL (minimum score 550 paper-based; 213 computer-based). *Application deadline:* For fall admission, 7/1 for domestic students, 7/1 for international students; for spring admission, 11/15 for domestic students, 11/15 for international students. Applications are processed on a rolling basis. Application fee: $0 ($50 for international students). *Expenses:* Tuition, state resident: full-time $1,815; part-time $202 per credit. Tuition, nonresident: full-time $3,177; part-time $354 per credit. Tuition and fees vary according to course level and course load. *Financial support:* In 2003–04, research assistantships with full tuition reimbursements (averaging $5,500 per year), teaching assistantships with full tuition reimbursements (averaging $5,500 per year) were awarded. Unspecified assistantships also available. Financial award application deadline: 3/1; financial award applicants required to submit FAFSA. *Unit head:* Dr. Arley Larson, Chairperson, 660-562-1161. *Application contact:* Dr. Frances Shipley, Dean of Graduate School, 660-562-1145, Fax: 660-562-1096, E-mail: gradsch@mail.nwmissouri.edu.

Nova Scotia Agricultural College, Research and Graduate Studies, Truro, NS B2N 5E3, Canada. Offers agriculture (M Sc), including air quality, animal behavior, animal molecular genetics, animal nutrition, animal technology, aquaculture, botany, crop management, crop physiology, ecology, environmental microbiology, food science, horticulture, nutrient management, pest management, physiology, plant biotechnology, plant pathology, soil chemistry, soil fertility, waste management and composting, water quality. Part-time programs available. *Faculty:* 38 full-time (5 women), 13 part-time/adjunct (1 woman). *Students:* 46 full-time (27 women), 21 part-time (13 women); includes 13 minority (10 African Americans, 2 American Indian/Alaska Native, 1 Asian American or Pacific Islander). 45 applicants, 58% accepted, 16 enrolled. In 2003, 11 degrees awarded, leading to university research/teaching 18%, continued full-time study36%, business/industry 9%, government 27%. *Median time to degree:* Master's–2.25 years full-time, 4 years part-time. *Degree requirements:* For master's, thesis, candidacy exam. *Entrance requirements:* For master's, B.Sc. honors degree, minimum GPA of 3.0. Additional exam requirements/recommendations for international students: Required—TOEFL (minimum score 580 paper-based; 237 computer-based), Michigan English Language Assessment Battery. *Application deadline:* For fall admission, 6/1 for domestic students, 4/1 for international students; for winter admission, 11/15 for domestic students; for spring admission, 2/28 for domestic students. Applications are processed on a rolling basis. Application fee: $70. *Expenses:* Tuition, state resident: full-time $6,270. Tuition, nonresident: full-time $9,270. Required fees: $402. Tuition and fees vary according to student level. *Financial support:* In 2003–04, 63 students received support, including research assistantships (averaging $15,000 per year), teaching assistantships (averaging $900 per year); career-related internships or fieldwork, scholarships/grants, and unspecified assistantships also available. *Faculty research:* Organogenesis, somatic embryogenesis, composting, sustainable agriculture, ecotoxicology. Total annual research expenditures: $2 million. *Unit head:* Jill L. Rogers, Manager, 902-893-6360, Fax: 902-893-3430, E-mail: jrogers@nsac.ns.ca. *Application contact:* Marie Law, Administrative Assistant, 902-893-6502, Fax: 902-893-3430, E-mail: mlaw@nsac.ns.ca.

The Ohio State University, Graduate School, College of Food, Agricultural, and Environmental Sciences, Columbus, OH 43210. Offers MS, PhD. Part-time programs available. *Faculty:* 313. *Students:* 346 full-time (179 women), 101 part-time (54 women); includes 30 minority (15 African Americans, 2 American Indian/Alaska Native, 5 Asian Americans or Pacific Islanders, 8 Hispanic Americans), 178 international. 713 applicants, 28% accepted. In 2003, 96 master's, 43 doctorates awarded. *Degree requirements:* For doctorate, thesis/dissertation. *Application deadline:* For fall admission, 8/15 for domestic students. Applications are processed on a rolling basis. Application fee: $40 ($50 for international students). *Expenses:* Tuition, state resident: full-time $7,233. Tuition, nonresident: full-time $18,489. *Financial support:* Fellowships, research assistantships, teaching assistantships, career-related internships or fieldwork, Federal Work-Study, institutionally sponsored loans, and unspecified assistantships available. Support available to part-time students. *Unit head:* Dr. Bobby D. Moser, Dean, 614-292-6891, Fax: 614-292-1218, E-mail: moser.2@osu.edu.

Oklahoma State University, Graduate College, College of Agricultural Sciences and Natural Resources, Stillwater, OK 74078. Offers M Ag, M Bio E, MS, Ed D, PhD. Part-time programs available. *Faculty:* 233 full-time (37 women), 13 part-time/adjunct (2 women). *Students:* 149 full-time (62 women), 208 part-time (71 women); includes 19 minority (5 African Americans, 10 American Indian/Alaska Native, 1 Asian American or Pacific Islander, 3 Hispanic Americans), 158 international. Average age 30. 213 applicants, 58% accepted. In 2003, 79 master's, 32 doctorates awarded. *Degree requirements:* For doctorate, thesis/dissertation. *Entrance requirements:* Additional exam requirements/recommendations for international students: Required—TOEFL. *Application deadline:* Applications are processed on a rolling basis. Application fee: $25 ($50 for international students). Electronic applications accepted. *Expenses:* Tuition, state resident: full-time $3,752; part-time $118 per credit hour. Tuition, nonresident: full-time $10,346; part-time $393 per credit hour. Tuition and fees vary according to course load. *Financial support:* In 2003–04, 245 students received support, including 227 research assistantships (averaging $13,541 per year), 29 teaching assistantships (averaging $12,480 per year); fellowships, career-related internships or fieldwork, Federal Work-Study, and tuition waivers (partial) also available. Support available to part-time students. Financial award application deadline: 3/1. *Unit head:* Dr. Samuel E. Curl, Dean, 405-744-5398, Fax: 405-744-5339, E-mail: securl@okstate.edu.

Oregon State University, Graduate School, College of Agricultural Sciences, Corvallis, OR 97331. Offers M Ag, M Agr, MA, MAIS, MAT, MS, PhD. Part-time programs available. *Faculty:* 217 full-time (49 women), 21 part-time/adjunct (3 women). *Students:* 309 full-time (154 women), 35 part-time (13 women); includes 19 minority (1 African American, 4 American Indian/Alaska Native, 11 Asian Americans or Pacific Islanders, 3 Hispanic Americans), 126 international. Average age 31. In 2003, 73 master's, 32 doctorates awarded. Terminal master's awarded for partial completion of doctoral program. *Degree requirements:* For doctorate, thesis/dissertation. *Entrance requirements:* For master's and doctorate, GRE, minimum GPA of 3.0 in last 90 hours. Additional exam requirements/recommendations for international students: Required—TOEFL. Application fee: $50. *Expenses:* Tuition, state resident: full-time $8,139; part-time $301 per credit. Tuition, nonresident: full-time $14,376; part-time $532 per credit. Required fees: $1,227. *Financial support:* Fellowships, research assistantships, teaching assistantships, career-related internships or fieldwork, Federal Work-Study, and institutionally sponsored loans available. Support available to part-time students. Financial award application deadline: 2/1. *Faculty research:* Fish and wildlife biology, food science, soil/water/plant relationships, natural resources, animal biochemistry. *Unit head:* Dr. Thayne R. Dutson, Dean, 541-737-2331, Fax: 541-737-4574, E-mail: thayne.dutson@orst.edu. *Application contact:* Dr. Michael J. Burke, Associate Dean, 541-737-2211, Fax: 541-737-2256, E-mail: mike.burke@orst.edu.

The Pennsylvania State University University Park Campus, Graduate School, College of Agricultural Sciences, State College, University Park, PA 16802-1503. Offers M Agr, M Ed, MFR, MS, D Ed, PhD. *Students:* 440. Average age 30. 538 applicants, 36% accepted. In 2003, 65 master's, 38 doctorates awarded. *Entrance requirements:* For master's and doctorate, GRE General Test. Additional exam requirements/recommendations for international students: Required—TOEFL (minimum score 550 paper-based; 213 computer-based). *Application deadline:* Applications are processed on a rolling basis. Application fee: $45. Electronic applications accepted. *Expenses:* Tuition, state resident: full-time $10,010; part-time $417 per credit. Tuition, nonresident: full-time $19,830; part-time $826 per credit. Full-time tuition and fees vary according to course level, course load, campus/location and program. *Financial support:* In 2003–04, 7 fellowships, 231 research assistantships, 23 teaching assistantships were awarded. Health care benefits and unspecified assistantships also available. Financial award applicants required to submit FAFSA. Total annual research expenditures: $24.5 million. *Unit head:* Dr. Robert D. Steele, Dean, 814-865-2541, Fax: 814-865-3103, E-mail: rsteele@psu.edu.

Prairie View A&M University, Graduate School, College of Agriculture and Human Sciences, Prairie View, TX 77446-0519. Offers agricultural economics (MS); animal sciences (MS); interdisciplinary human sciences (MS); marriage and family therapy (MS); soil science (MS). Part-time and evening/weekend programs available. *Faculty:* 15 full-time (3 women). *Students:* 49 full-time (31 women), 71 part-time (59 women); includes 104 minority (101 African Americans, 2 Asian Americans or Pacific Islanders, 1 Hispanic American), 11 international. Average age 33. *Degree requirements:* For master's, thesis (for some programs), field placement, comprehensive exam. *Entrance requirements:* For master's, GRE General Test. *Application deadline:* Applications are processed on a rolling basis. Application fee: $50. *Expenses:* Tuition, state resident: part-time $50 per credit hour. Tuition, nonresident: part-time $282 per credit hour. Required fees: $36 per credit hour. $51 per term. *Financial support:* In 2003–04, 8 fellowships with tuition reimbursements (averaging $12,000 per year), 10 research assistantships with tuition reimbursements (averaging $15,000 per year) were awarded. Career-related internships or fieldwork, Federal Work-Study, institutionally sponsored loans, and tuition waivers (partial) also available. Financial award application deadline: 4/1; financial award applicants required to submit FAFSA. *Faculty research:* Domestic violence prevention, water quality, food growth regulators. Total annual research expenditures: $4 million. *Unit head:* Dr. Elizabeth Noel, Dean, 936-857-2996, Fax: 936-857-2998, E-mail: elizabeth_noel@pvamu.edu.

Purdue University, Graduate School, College of Agriculture, West Lafayette, IN 47907. Offers EMBA, M Agr, MS, MSF, PhD. Part-time programs available. *Degree requirements:* For doctorate, thesis/dissertation. *Entrance requirements:* Additional exam requirements/recommendations for international students: Required—TOEFL. Application fee: $30. Electronic applications accepted. *Financial support:* Fellowships with tuition reimbursements, research assistantships with tuition reimbursements, teaching assistantships with tuition reimbursements, career-related internships or fieldwork and tuition waivers (partial) available. Support available to part-time students. Financial award applicants required to submit FAFSA. *Unit head:* Dr. Victor L. Lechtenberg, Dean, 765-494-8392.

Sam Houston State University, College of Arts and Sciences, Department of Agricultural Sciences, Huntsville, TX 77341. Offers agricultural business (MS); agricultural education (M Ed, MA); agricultural mechanization (MS); agriculture (MS); industrial education (M Ed, MA); industrial technology (MA); vocational education (M Ed). Part-time and evening/weekend programs available. *Students:* 18 full-time (10 women), 15 part-time (11 women); includes 2 minority (both African Americans) In 2003, 10 degrees awarded. *Degree requirements:* For master's, thesis optional. *Entrance requirements:* For master's, GRE General Test, minimum GPA of 2.5. *Application deadline:* For fall admission, 8/1 for domestic students; for spring admission, 12/1 for domestic students. Application fee: $35. *Expenses:* Tuition, state resident: part-time $243 per semester hour. Tuition, nonresident: part-time $479 per semester hour. *Financial support:* Teaching assistantships, career-related internships or fieldwork available. Financial award application deadline: 5/31; financial award applicants required to submit FAFSA. *Unit head:* Dr. Robert A. Lane, Chair, 936-294-1225, Fax: 936-294-1232, E-mail: agr_ral@shsu.edu.

South Dakota State University, Graduate School, College of Agriculture and Biological Sciences, Brookings, SD 57007. Offers MS, PhD. Part-time programs available. *Degree requirements:* For master's, thesis, oral exam; for doctorate, thesis/dissertation, preliminary oral and written exams. *Entrance requirements:* Additional exam requirements/recommendations for international students: Required—TOEFL.

Southern Illinois University Carbondale, Graduate School, College of Agriculture, Carbondale, IL 62901-4701. Offers MS, MBA/MS. Part-time programs available. *Faculty:* 51 full-time (8 women). *Students:* 39 full-time (21 women), 101 part-time (44 women); includes 8 minority (1 African American, 3 Asian Americans or Pacific Islanders, 4 Hispanic Americans), 7 international. 52 applicants, 58% accepted, 7 enrolled. In 2003, 33 degrees awarded. *Entrance requirements:* For master's, minimum GPA of 2.7. Additional exam requirements/recommendations for international students: Required—TOEFL. *Application deadline:* Applications are processed on a rolling basis. Application fee: $0. *Expenses:* Tuition, state resident: part-time $478 per hour. Tuition, nonresident: part-time $657 per hour. *Financial support:* In 2003–04, 35 students received support, including 31 research assistantships; fellowships, teaching assistantships, career-related internships or fieldwork, Federal Work-Study, institutionally sponsored loans, and tuition waivers (full) also available. Support available to part-time students. *Faculty research:* Production and studies in crops, animal nutrition, agribusiness economics and management, forest biology and ecology, microcomputers in agriculture. *Unit head:* David Shoup, Dean.

Southern University and Agricultural and Mechanical College, Graduate School, College of Agricultural, Family and Consumer Sciences, Baton Rouge, LA 70813. Offers urban forestry (MS). *Degree requirements:* For master's, thesis. *Entrance requirements:* For master's, GRE, minimum GPA of 3.0. Additional exam requirements/recommendations for international students: Required—TOEFL. *Faculty research:* Urban forest interactions with environment, social and economic impacts of urban forests, tree biology/pathology, development of urban forest management tools.

Southwest Missouri State University, Graduate College, College of Natural and Applied Sciences, Department of Agriculture, Springfield, MO 65804-0094. Offers agriculture (MS Ed); plant science (MS). *Faculty:* 10 full-time (1 woman). *Students:* 4 full-time (3 women), 1 part-time, 3 international. Average age 27. 7 applicants, 57% accepted, 1 enrolled. In 2003, 2 degrees awarded. *Application deadline:* For fall admission, 8/5 for domestic students; for spring admission, 12/20 for domestic students. Applications are processed on a rolling basis. Application fee: $30. Electronic applications accepted. *Expenses:* Tuition, state resident: full-time $2,862. Tuition, nonresident: full-time $5,724. *Financial support:* In 2003–04, 1 research assistantship (averaging $8,400 per year) was awarded *Unit head:* Dr. W. Anson Elliott, Head, 417-836-5638.

Tarleton State University, College of Graduate Studies and Academic Affairs, College of Agriculture and Human Sciences, Stephenville, TX 76402. Offers MS. Part-time and evening/weekend programs available. Postbaccalaureate distance learning degree programs offered (minimal on-campus study). *Faculty:* 18 full-time (2 women). *Students:* 22 full-time (9 women), 14 part-time (4 women). 12 applicants, 92% accepted. In 2003, 32 degrees awarded. *Degree requirements:* For master's, thesis (for some programs), comprehensive exam. *Entrance requirements:* For master's, GRE General Test, minimum GPA of 3.0. Additional exam requirements/recommendations for international students: Required—TOEFL (minimum score 550 paper-based; 220 computer-based). *Application deadline:* For fall admission, 8/5 for domestic students; for spring admission, 12/1 for domestic students. Applications are processed on a rolling basis. Application fee: $25 ($75 for international students). *Expenses:* Tuition, state resident: part-time $99 per credit hour. Tuition, nonresident: part-time $325 per credit hour. One-time fee: $52 part-time. *Financial support:* In 2003–04, 5 research assistantships (averaging $12,000 per year), 4 teaching assistantships (averaging $12,000 per year) were awarded. Career-related internships or fieldwork, Federal Work-Study, and institutionally sponsored loans also available. Support available to part-time students. Financial award application deadline: 5/1; financial award applicants required to submit FAFSA. *Unit head:* Dr. Don Cawthon, Acting Dean, 254-968-9227.

Tennessee State University, Graduate School, School of Agriculture and Family Services, Nashville, TN 37209-1561. Offers MS, PhD. Part-time and evening/weekend programs available. *Faculty:* 8 full-time (5 women), 5 part-time/adjunct (1 woman). *Students:* 12 full-time (7 women), 6 part-time (3 women); includes 14 minority (all African Americans), 2 international. Average age 31. 25 applicants, 44% accepted. In 2003, 4 degrees awarded. *Degree requirements:* For master's, thesis. *Entrance requirements:* For master's, GRE General Test, GRE Subject Test, MAT. *Application deadline:* Applications are processed on a rolling basis. Application fee: $15. Electronic applications accepted. *Financial support:* In 2003–04, 2 research assistantships (averaging $7,929 per year), 1 teaching assistantship (averaging $3,501 per year) were awarded. *Faculty research:* Small farm economics, ornamental horticulture, beef cattle production, rural elderly. *Unit head:* Dr. Troy Wakefield, Dean, 615-963-7620, E-mail: twakefield@tnstate.edu.

Texas A&M University, College of Agriculture and Life Sciences, College Station, TX 77843. Offers M Agr, M Ed, M Eng, MAB, MS, DE, Ed D, PhD. Part-time programs available. Postbaccalaureate distance learning degree programs offered (minimal on-campus study). *Faculty:* 216 full-time (30 women), 7 part-time/adjunct (1 woman). *Students:* 940 full-time (438 women), 318 part-time (121 women); includes 85 minority (12 African Americans, 1 American Indian/Alaska Native, 23 Asian Americans or Pacific Islanders, 49 Hispanic Americans), 403 international. Average age 29. *Entrance requirements:* Additional exam requirements/recommendations for international students: Required—TOEFL (minimum score 550 paper-based; 213 computer-based). *Application deadline:* For fall admission, 7/21 priority date for domestic students, 6/1 priority date for international students; for spring admission, 12/1 priority date for domestic students, 10/1 priority date for international students. Applications are processed on a rolling basis. Application fee: $50 ($75 for international students). Electronic applications accepted. *Expenses:* Tuition, state resident: full-time $3,420. Tuition, nonresident: full-time $9,084. Required fees: $1,861. *Financial support:* Fellowships, research assistantships, teaching assistantships, career-related internships or fieldwork, Federal Work-Study, institutionally sponsored loans, scholarships/grants, tuition waivers (partial), and unspecified assistantships available. Support available to part-time students. Financial award applicants required to submit FAFSA. *Faculty research:* Plant sciences, animal sciences, environmental natural resources, biological and agricultural engineering, agricultural economics. *Unit head:* Dr. Edward A. Hiler, Dean, 979-845-4747, Fax: 979-845-9938, E-mail: e-hiler@tamu.edu.

Texas A&M University–Commerce, Graduate School, College of Arts and Sciences, Department of Agriculture, Commerce, TX 75429-3011. Offers agricultural education (M Ed, MS); agricultural sciences (M Ed, MS). Part-time programs available. *Degree requirements:* For master's, thesis (for some programs), comprehensive exam. *Entrance requirements:* For master's, GRE General Test. Electronic applications accepted. *Faculty research:* Soil conservation, retention.

Texas A&M University–Kingsville, College of Graduate Studies, College of Agriculture and Home Economics, Kingsville, TX 78363. Offers MS, PhD. Part-time and evening/weekend programs available. *Degree requirements:* For master's, thesis or alternative, comprehensive exam; for doctorate, one foreign language, thesis/dissertation, comprehensive exam. *Entrance requirements:* For master's, GRE General Test, minimum GPA of 3.0; for doctorate, GRE General Test, minimum GPA of 3.5. Additional exam requirements/recommendations for international students: Required—TOEFL. *Faculty research:* Mesquite cloning; genesis of soil salinity; dove management; bone development; egg, meat, and milk consumption versus price.

Texas Tech University, Graduate School, College of Agricultural Sciences and Natural Resources, Lubbock, TX 79409. Offers M Agr, MLA, MS, Ed D, PhD, JD/MS. Part-time and evening/weekend programs available. *Faculty:* 65 full-time (9 women), 3 part-time/adjunct (0 women). *Students:* 162 full-time (62 women), 87 part-time (29 women); includes 5 minority (1 Asian American or Pacific Islander, 4 Hispanic Americans), 40 international. Average age 30. 160 applicants, 63% accepted, 59 enrolled. In 2003, 65 master's, 19 doctorates awarded. *Degree requirements:* For doctorate, thesis/dissertation. *Entrance requirements:* For master's and doctorate, GRE General Test. Additional exam requirements/recommendations for international students: Required—TOEFL (minimum score 550 paper-based; 213 computer-based). *Application deadline:* Applications are processed on a rolling basis. Application fee: $50 ($60 for international students). Electronic applications accepted. *Expenses:* Contact institution. Tuition and fees vary according to program. *Financial support:* In 2003–04, 157 students received support, including 113 research assistantships with partial tuition reimbursements available (averaging $11,461 per year), 19 teaching assistantships with partial tuition reimbursements available (averaging $11,052 per year); career-related internships or fieldwork, Federal Work-Study, and institutionally sponsored loans also available. Support available to part-time students. Financial award application deadline: 5/1; financial award applicants required to submit FAFSA. Total annual research expenditures: $9.1 million. *Unit head:* Dr. Marvin R. Cepica, Interim Dean, 806-742-2810, Fax: 806-742-2836. *Application contact:* Graduate Adviser, 806-742-2808, Fax: 806-742-2836.

Tuskegee University, Graduate Programs, College of Agricultural, Environmental and Natural Sciences, Department of Agricultural Sciences, Tuskegee, AL 36088. Offers agricultural and resource economics (MS); animal and poultry sciences (MS); environmental sciences (MS); plant and soil sciences (MS). *Faculty:* 26 full-time (12 women), 1 part-time/adjunct (0 women). *Students:* 25 full-time (11 women), 13 part-time (5 women); includes 17 minority (all African Americans), 18 international. Average age 30. In 2003, 5 degrees awarded. *Degree requirements:* For master's, thesis. *Entrance requirements:* For master's, GRE General Test. *Application deadline:* For fall admission, 7/15 for domestic students. Applications are processed on a rolling basis. Application fee: $25 ($35 for international students). *Expenses:* Tuition: Full-time $11,060; part-time $655 per credit hour. Required fees: $250. Tuition and fees vary according to course load. *Financial support:* In 2003–04, 5 fellowships, 4 research assistantships were awarded. Financial award application deadline: 4/15. *Unit head:* Dr. P. K. Biswas, Head, 334-727-8632.

Université Laval, Faculty of Agricultural and Food Sciences, Québec, QC G1K 7P4, Canada. Offers M Sc, PhD, Diploma. Part-time programs available. *Degree requirements:* For doctorate, thesis/dissertation, comprehensive exam. Electronic applications accepted.

University of Alberta, Faculty of Graduate Studies and Research, Department of Agricultural, Food and Nutritional Science, Edmonton, AB T6G 2E1, Canada. Offers M Ag, M Eng, M Sc, PhD, MBA/M Ag. *Faculty:* 44 full-time (14 women). *Students:* 76 full-time (42 women), 49 part-time (29 women), 23 international. 143 applicants, 22% accepted. In 2003, 16 master's, 6 doctorates awarded. *Median time to degree:* Master's–2 years full-time; doctorate–5 years full-time. Of those who began their doctoral program in fall 1995, 100% received their degree in 8 years or less. *Degree requirements:* For master's, thesis/dissertation; for doctorate, thesis/dissertation, comprehensive exam. *Entrance requirements:* For master's, minimum GPA of 3.0; for doctorate, minimum GPA of 3.5. Additional exam requirements/recommendations for international students: Required—TOEFL (paper score 550; computer score 213) or IELTS (paper score 6). *Application deadline:* Applications are processed on a rolling basis. Tuition charges are reported in Canadian dollars. Tuition, nonresident: full-time $3,921 Canadian dollars. International tuition: $7,113 Canadian dollars full-time. *Financial support:* In 2003–04, 65 students received support, including 6 fellowships, 17 research assistantships with partial tuition reimbursements available (averaging $7,000 per year), 37 teaching assistantships (averaging $3,600 per year); scholarships/grants and unspecified assistantships also available. *Faculty research:* Animal science, food science, nutrition and metabolism, bioresource engineering, plant science and range management. Total annual research expenditures: $12.6 million. *Unit head:* Dr. Peter Sporns, Graduate Coordinator, 780-492-5131, Fax: 780-492-4265, E-mail: peter.sporns@ualberta.ca. *Application contact:* Jody Forslund, Student Support, 780-492-5131, Fax: 780-492-4265, E-mail: jody.forslund@ualberta.ca.

The University of Arizona, Graduate College, College of Agriculture and Life Sciences, Tucson, AZ 85721. Offers M Ag Ed, MHE Ed, MS, PhD. Part-time programs available. *Faculty:* 248. *Students:* Average age 32. 246 applicants, 47% accepted, 90 enrolled. In 2003, 64 master's, 22 doctorates awarded. *Degree requirements:* For doctorate, thesis/dissertation. *Entrance requirements:* Additional exam requirements/recommendations for international students: Required—TOEFL. *Application deadline:* Applications are processed on a rolling basis. Application fee: $50. *Expenses:* Tuition, state resident: part-time $196 per unit. Tuition, nonresident: part-time $326 per unit. *Financial support:* Fellowships, research assistantships, teaching assistantships, career-related internships or fieldwork, Federal Work-Study, institutionally sponsored loans, scholarships/grants, and tuition waivers (full and partial) available. Total annual research expenditures: $31 million. *Unit head:* Dr. Eugene G. Sander, Dean, 520-621-7621, Fax: 520-621-7196. *Application contact:* Dr. David E. Cox, Associate Dean, 520-621-3612, Fax: 520-621-8662.

University of Arkansas, Graduate School, Dale Bumpers College of Agricultural, Food and Life Sciences, Fayetteville, AR 72701-1201. Offers MAT, MS, PhD. *Students:* 304 full-time (133 women), 137 part-time (51 women). 355 applicants, 46% accepted. In 2003, 89 master's, 29 doctorates awarded. *Degree requirements:* For doctorate, thesis/dissertation. Application fee: $40 ($50 for international students). *Expenses:* Tuition, state resident: full-time $4,032; part-time $224 per credit hour. Tuition, nonresident: full-time $9,540; part-time $530 per credit hour. Tuition and fees vary according to course load and program. *Financial support:* In 2003–04, 47 fellowships, 198 research assistantships, 13 teaching assistantships were awarded. Career-related internships or fieldwork, Federal Work-Study, scholarships/grants, and unspecified assistantships also available. Support available to part-time students. Financial award application deadline: 4/1; financial award applicants required to submit FAFSA. *Unit head:* Dr. Greg Weideman, Dean, 479-575-2252.

The University of British Columbia, Faculty of Graduate Studies, Faculty of Agricultural Sciences, Vancouver, BC V6T 1Z1, Canada. Offers M Sc, MASLA, MLA, PhD. *Faculty:* 54 full-time (14 women), 10 part-time/adjunct (4 women). *Students:* 235 full-time (161 women). Average age 24. 274 applicants, 28% accepted, 53 enrolled. In 2003, 19 master's, 4 doctorates awarded. *Degree requirements:* For master's, thesis/dissertation; for doctorate, thesis/dissertation, comprehensive exam. *Entrance requirements:* Additional exam requirements/recommendations for international students: Required—TOEFL (minimum score 560 paper-based; 220 computer-based). *Application deadline:* For fall admission, 3/30 for domestic students, 2/28 for international students; for winter admission, 8/31 for domestic students; for spring admission, 12/31 for domestic students. Applications are processed on a rolling basis. Application fee: $90 Canadian dollars ($150 Canadian dollars for international students). Electronic applications accepted. *Financial support:* In 2003–04, 91 students received support, including 91 fellowships with partial tuition reimbursements available (averaging $9,104 per year), 49 research assistantships with partial tuition reimbursements available (averaging $14,000 per year), 87 teaching assistantships with partial tuition reimbursements available (averaging $2,200 per year); career-related internships or fieldwork, Federal Work-Study, institutionally sponsored loans, scholarships/grants, and tuition waivers (full and partial) also available. Total annual research expenditures: $4.6 million Canadian dollars. *Unit head:* Dr. Mahesh Upadhyaya, Associate Dean, Research/Graduate Programs, 604-822-4593, Fax: 604-822-4400, E-mail: gradapp@interchange.ubc.ca. *Application contact:* Alina Yuhymets, Graduate Programs Manager, 604-822-4593, Fax: 604-822-4400, E-mail: yuhymets@interchange.ubc.ca.

University of California, Davis, Graduate Studies, Graduate Group in International Agricultural Development, Davis, CA 95616. Offers MS. *Faculty:* 85 full-time. *Students:* 40 full-time (24 women); includes 4 minority (3 Asian Americans or Pacific Islanders, 1 Hispanic American), 2 international. Average age 30. 44 applicants, 91% accepted, 19 enrolled. In 2003, 7 degrees awarded. *Degree requirements:* For master's, thesis optional. *Entrance requirements:* For master's, GRE General Test, minimum GPA of 3.0. Additional exam requirements/recommendations for international students: Required—TOEFL (minimum score 550 paper-based; 213 computer-based). *Application deadline:* For fall admission, 1/15 for domestic students, 12/15 for international students. Application fee: $60. Electronic applications accepted. Tuition, nonresident: full-time $12,245. Required fees: $7,062. *Financial support:* In 2003–04, 28 students received support, including 7 fellowships with full and partial tuition reimbursements available (averaging $7,797 per year), 13 research assistantships with full and partial tuition reimbursements available (averaging $9,347 per year), 2 teaching assistantships with partial tuition reimbursements available (averaging $14,145 per year); Federal Work-Study, institutionally sponsored loans, scholarships/grants, and tuition waivers (full and partial) also available. Financial award application deadline: 1/15; financial award applicants required to submit FAFSA. *Faculty research:* Aspects of agricultural, environmental and social sciences on agriculture and related issues in developing countries. *Unit head:* William Rains, Graduate Chair, 530-752-1711, Fax: 530-752-5660, E-mail: derains@ucdavis.edu. *Application contact:* Judy Erwin, Graduate Assistant, 530-752-1926, Fax: 530-752-5660, E-mail: gjerwin@ucdavis.edu.

University of Connecticut, Graduate School, College of Agriculture and Natural Resources, Storrs, CT 06269. Offers MS, PhD. *Faculty:* 63 full-time (17 women). *Students:* 152 full-time (78 women), 42 part-time (26 women); includes 6 minority (2 Asian Americans or Pacific Islanders, 4 Hispanic Americans), 79 international. Average age 31. 174 applicants, 48% accepted, 52 enrolled. In 2003, 35 master's, 20 doctorates awarded. Terminal master's awarded for partial completion of doctoral program. *Degree requirements:* For master's, comprehensive exam; for doctorate, thesis/dissertation, comprehensive exam. *Entrance requirements:* For master's and doctorate, GRE General Test. Additional exam requirements/recommendations for international students: Required—TOEFL (minimum score 550 paper-based; 213 computer-based). *Application deadline:* For fall admission, 2/1 priority date for domestic students, 2/1 priority date for international students; for spring admission, 11/1 for domestic students, 10/1 for international students. Applications are processed on a rolling basis. Application fee: $55. Electronic applications accepted. *Expenses:* Tuition, state resident: part-time $3,860 per semester. Tuition, nonresident: part-time $9,036 per semester. *Financial support:* In 2003–04, 122 research assistantships with full tuition reimbursements, 18 teaching assistantships with full tuition reimbursements were awarded. Fellowships, Federal Work-Study, scholarships/grants, health care benefits, and unspecified assistantships also available. Financial award application deadline: 2/1; financial award applicants required to submit FAFSA. *Unit head:* Kirklyn M. Kerr, Dean, 860-486-2917, Fax: 860-486-5113, E-mail: kirklyn.ker@uconn.edu. *Application contact:* Larissa Hull, Assistant, 860-486-2918, Fax: 860-486-5113, E-mail: larissa.hull@uconn.edu.

University of Delaware, College of Agriculture and Natural Resources, Newark, DE 19716. Offers MS, PhD. Part-time programs available. *Faculty:* 79 full-time (14 women), 1 part-time/adjunct (0 women). *Students:* 115 full-time (64 women), 12 part-time (5 women); includes 6 minority (1 African American, 1 American Indian/Alaska Native, 4 Asian Americans or Pacific Islanders), 45 international. Average age 28. 285 applicants, 33% accepted, 68 enrolled. In 2003, 37 master's, 6 doctorates awarded. *Degree requirements:* For master's and doctorate, thesis/dissertation. *Entrance requirements:* For master's and doctorate, GRE General Test. Application fee: $60. Electronic applications accepted. *Expenses:* Tuition, state resident: full-time $5,890; part-time $327 per credit. Tuition, nonresident: full-time $15,420; part-time $857 per credit. Required fees: $968. *Financial support:* In 2003–04, 100 students received support, including 14 fellowships with full tuition reimbursements available (averaging $14,355 per year), 47 research assistantships with full tuition reimbursements available (averaging $12,625 per year), 17 teaching assistantships with full tuition reimbursements available (averaging $11,185 per year); career-related internships or fieldwork, Federal Work-Study, institution-

Agricultural Sciences—General

University of Delaware (continued)
ally sponsored loans, and tuition waivers (full) also available. Total annual research expenditures: $11.8 million. *Unit head:* Dr. Robin Morgan, Dean, 302-831-2501. *Application contact:* Karen Roth Aniunas, Assistant Dean of Student Services, 302-831-2508, Fax: 302-831-6758, E-mail: kra@udel.edu.

University of Florida, Graduate School, College of Agricultural and Life Sciences, Gainesville, FL 32611. Offers M Ag, MAB, MFAS, MFRC, MS, DPM, PhD, JD/MFRC, JD/MS, JD/PhD. Part-time programs available. *Faculty:* 709. *Students:* 634 full-time (302 women), 181 part-time (66 women); includes 91 minority (23 African Americans, 6 American Indian/Alaska Native, 22 Asian Americans or Pacific Islanders, 40 Hispanic Americans), 188 international. In 2003, 114 master's, 39 doctorates awarded. *Degree requirements:* For doctorate, thesis/dissertation. *Entrance requirements:* For master's and doctorate, GRE General Test, minimum GPA of 3.0. Additional exam requirements/recommendations for international students: Required—TOEFL. *Application deadline:* Applications are processed on a rolling basis. Application fee: $20. Electronic applications accepted. *Expenses:* Tuition, state resident: part-time $205 per credit hour. Tuition, nonresident: part-time $775 per credit hour. *Financial support:* In 2003–04, 390 students received support, including 22 fellowships with tuition reimbursements available; research assistantships with tuition reimbursements available, teaching assistantships with tuition reimbursements available, career-related internships or fieldwork, Federal Work-Study, institutionally sponsored loans, and unspecified assistantships also available. Support available to part-time students. *Unit head:* Dr. Jimmy G. Cheek, Dean, 352-392-1961, Fax: 352-392-8988, E-mail: jgcheek@ufl.edu. *Application contact:* Dr. E. Jane Luzar, Associate Dean for Academic Programs, 352-392-2251, Fax: 352-392-8988, E-mail: ejluzar@ufl.edu.

University of Georgia, Graduate School, College of Agricultural and Environmental Sciences, Athens, GA 30602. Offers MA Ext, MADS, MAE, MAL, MCCS, MFT, MPPPM, MS, PhD. *Faculty:* 246 full-time (28 women). *Students:* 300 full-time (141 women), 79 part-time (43 women); includes 24 minority (19 African Americans, 5 Asian Americans or Pacific Islanders), 140 international. 402 applicants, 35% accepted. In 2003, 70 master's, 41 doctorates awarded. *Degree requirements:* For doctorate, thesis/dissertation. *Entrance requirements:* For master's and doctorate, GRE General Test. *Application deadline:* For fall admission, 7/1 for domestic students; for spring admission, 11/15 for domestic students. Application fee: $50. Electronic applications accepted. *Expenses:* Tuition, state resident: part-time $161 per hour. Tuition, nonresident: part-time $690 per hour. One-time fee: $435 part-time. *Financial support:* Fellowships, research assistantships, teaching assistantships, career-related internships or fieldwork and unspecified assistantships available. *Unit head:* Dr. Gale A. Buchanan, Dean, 706-542-3924, Fax: 706-542-0803, E-mail: caesdean@uga.edu.

University of Guelph, Graduate Program Services, Ontario Agricultural College, Guelph, ON N1G 2W1, Canada. Offers M Sc, MLA, PhD, Diploma. Part-time programs available. Postbaccalaureate distance learning degree programs offered (minimal on-campus study). *Students:* 509. In 2003, 116 master's, 35 doctorates awarded. *Degree requirements:* For doctorate, thesis/dissertation. Application fee: $75. Tuition and fees charges are reported in Canadian dollars. Tuition, nonresident: full-time $3,440 Canadian dollars. International tuition: $5,432 Canadian dollars full-time. Required fees: $753 Canadian dollars. *Financial support:* Fellowships, research assistantships, teaching assistantships, scholarships/grants and unspecified assistantships available. Support available to part-time students. *Unit head:* Dr. Craig J. Pearson, Dean, 519-824-4120 Ext. 52285, Fax: 519-766-1423, E-mail: cpearson@uoguelph.ca.

University of Hawaii at Manoa, Graduate Division, College of Tropical Agriculture and Human Resources, Honolulu, HI 96822. Offers MS, PhD. Part-time programs available. *Faculty:* 276 full-time (39 women), 78 part-time/adjunct (17 women). *Students:* 140 full-time (73 women), 35 part-time (14 women); includes 38 minority (2 African Americans, 32 Asian Americans or Pacific Islanders, 4 Hispanic Americans), 73 international. 150 applicants, 53% accepted, 48 enrolled. *Median time to degree:* Master's–3 years full-time; doctorate–6 years full-time. *Degree requirements:* For doctorate, thesis/dissertation. *Entrance requirements:* For doctorate, GRE. Application fee: $50. *Expenses:* Tuition, state resident: full-time $4,464; part-time $186 per credit hour. Tuition, nonresident: full-time $10,608; part-time $442 per credit hour. Tuition and fees vary according to program. *Financial support:* In 2003–04, 97 research assistantships (averaging $16,124 per year), 21 teaching assistantships (averaging $13,597 per year) were awarded. Fellowships, career-related internships or fieldwork, Federal Work-Study, institutionally sponsored loans, tuition waivers (full and partial), and unspecified assistantships also available. *Unit head:* Dr. Andrew Hashimoto, Dean, 808-956-8234, Fax: 808-956-9105, E-mail: dean@ctahr.hawaii.edu.

See in-depth description on page 675.

University of Idaho, College of Graduate Studies, College of Agriculture and Life Sciences, Department of Agricultural and Extension Education, Moscow, ID 83844-2282. Offers MS. *Accreditation:* NCATE. *Students:* 2 full-time (1 woman), 7 part-time (4 women). Average age 31. *Entrance requirements:* For master's, minimum GPA of 2.8. *Application deadline:* For fall admission, 8/1 for domestic students; for spring admission, 12/15 for domestic students. Application fee: $55 ($60 for international students). *Expenses:* Tuition, state resident: full-time $3,348. Tuition, nonresident: full-time $10,740. Required fees: $540. *Financial support:* Application deadline: 2/15. *Unit head:* Dr. Louis E. Riesenberg, Head, 208-885-6358.

University of Illinois at Urbana–Champaign, Graduate College, College of Agricultural, Consumer and Environmental Sciences, Champaign, IL 61820. Offers AM, MS, PhD, MD/PhD. *Faculty:* 219 full-time (46 women), 10 part-time/adjunct (5 women). *Students:* 557 full-time (286 women); includes 45 minority (9 African Americans, 3 American Indian/Alaska Native, 19 Asian Americans or Pacific Islanders, 14 Hispanic Americans), 211 international. 664 applicants, 23% accepted, 125 enrolled. In 2003, 140 master's, 47 doctorates awarded. *Degree requirements:* For doctorate, thesis/dissertation. *Entrance requirements:* For master's, minimum GPA of 3.0. *Application deadline:* Applications are processed on a rolling basis. Application fee: $40 ($50 for international students). Electronic applications accepted. *Expenses:* Tuition, state resident: full-time $6,692. Tuition, nonresident: full-time $18,692. *Financial support:* In 2003–04, 87 fellowships, 334 research assistantships, 58 teaching assistantships were awarded. Career-related internships or fieldwork and tuition waivers (full and partial) also available. Financial award application deadline: 2/15. *Unit head:* Robert A. Easter, Dean, 217-333-0460, Fax: 217-244-2911, E-mail: r_easter@uiuc.edu. *Application contact:* Mary McElzain, Information Contact, 217-333-3380, Fax: 217-244-6537.

University of Kentucky, Graduate School, Graduate School Programs in the College of Agriculture, Lexington, KY 40506-0032. Offers MS, MS Ag, MSAE, MSFOR, PhD. Part-time programs available. *Students:* 363 applicants, 44% accepted, 57 enrolled. In 2003, 43 master's, 16 doctorates awarded. Terminal master's awarded for partial completion of doctoral program. *Degree requirements:* For master's, thesis (for some programs), comprehensive exam; for doctorate, thesis/dissertation, comprehensive exam. *Entrance requirements:* For master's and doctorate, GRE General Test. Additional exam requirements/recommendations for international students: Required—TOEFL (minimum score 550 paper-based; 213 computer-based). *Application deadline:* For fall admission, 7/18 for domestic students, 2/1 for international students. Application fee: $35 ($45 for international students). *Expenses:* Tuition, state resident: full-time $4,975; part-time $261 per credit hour. Tuition, nonresident: full-time $12,315; part-time $668 per credit hour. *Financial support:* Fellowships, research assistantships, teaching assistantships, career-related internships or fieldwork, Federal Work-Study, institutionally sponsored loans, and unspecified assistantships available. Support available to part-time students. *Unit head:* Dr. M. Scott Smith, Dean, 859-257-4772. *Application contact:* Dr. Brian Jackson, Associate Dean, 859-257-4905, Fax: 859-323-1928.

The University of Lethbridge, School of Graduate Studies, Lethbridge, AB T1K 3M4, Canada. Offers accounting (MScM); agricultural biotechnology (M Sc); agricultural studies (M Sc, MA); anthropology (MA); archaeology (MA); art (MA); biochemistry (M Sc); biological sciences (M Sc); Canadian studies (MA); chemistry (M Sc); computer science (M Sc); counseling psychology (M Ed); dramatic arts (MA); economics (MA); English (MA); environmental science (M Sc); exercise science (M Sc); finance (MScM); French (MA); French/German (MA); French/Spanish (MA); general education (M Ed); general management (MScM); geography (M Sc, MA); German (MA); health sciences (M Sc, MA); history (MA); human resources/management and labor relations (MScM); information systems (MScM); international management (MScM); kinesiology (M Sc, MA); management (M Sc, MA); marketing (MScM); mathematics (M Sc); music (MA); Native American studies (MA, MScM); neuroscience (M Sc, PhD); nursing (M Sc); philosophy (MA); physics (M Sc); political science (MA); psychology (M Sc, MA); religious studies (MA); sociology (MA); urban and regional studies (MA). Part-time and evening/weekend programs available. *Faculty:* 250. *Students:* 317 (126 women). Average age 39. 35 applicants, 100% accepted, 35 enrolled. In 2003, 40 degrees awarded. *Degree requirements:* For doctorate, thesis/dissertation, comprehensive exam. *Entrance requirements:* For master's, bachelor's degree in related field, minimum GPA of 3.0 (during previous 20 graded semester courses), two years teaching or related experience (M Ed), GMAT for M Sc (management); for doctorate, master's degree, minimum graduate GPA of 3.5. Additional exam requirements/recommendations for international students: Required—TOEFL. Application fee: $60 Canadian dollars. *Expenses:* Tuition, state resident: part-time $475 per course. *Financial support:* Fellowships, research assistantships, teaching assistantships, scholarships/grants, health care benefits, and unspecified assistantships available. *Faculty research:* Movement and brain plasticity, gibberellin physiology, photosynthesis, carbon cycling, molecular properties of main-group ring components. *Unit head:* Dr. Shamsul Alam, Dean, 403-329-2121, Fax: 403-329-2097, E-mail: inquiries@uleth.ca. *Application contact:* Kathy Schrage, Administrative Assistant, Office of the Academic Vice President, 403-329-2121, Fax: 403-329-2097, E-mail: inquiries@uleth.ca.

University of Maine, Graduate School, College of Natural Sciences, Forestry, and Agriculture, Orono, ME 04469. Offers MF, MPS, MS, MWC, PhD. *Accreditation:* SAF (one or more programs are accredited). Part-time and evening/weekend programs available. *Students:* 282 full-time (170 women), 92 part-time (53 women); includes 7 minority (2 African Americans, 4 Asian Americans or Pacific Islanders, 1 Hispanic American), 68 international. Average age 30. 371 applicants, 40% accepted, 86 enrolled. In 2003, 64 master's, 13 doctorates awarded. *Degree requirements:* For doctorate, thesis/dissertation. *Entrance requirements:* For master's and doctorate, GRE General Test. Additional exam requirements/recommendations for international students: Required—TOEFL. *Application deadline:* For fall admission, 2/1 for domestic students. Applications are processed on a rolling basis. Application fee: $50. Electronic applications accepted. *Expenses:* Tuition, state resident: part-time $235 per credit. Tuition, nonresident: part-time $670 per credit. Tuition and fees vary according to course load. *Financial support:* Fellowships, research assistantships, teaching assistantships, career-related internships or fieldwork, Federal Work-Study, institutionally sponsored loans, scholarships/grants, tuition waivers (full and partial), and unspecified assistantships available. Support available to part-time students. Financial award application deadline: 3/1. *Unit head:* Dr. G. Bruce Wiersma, Dean, 207-581-3202, Fax: 207-581-3207. *Application contact:* Scott G. Delcourt, Associate Dean of the Graduate School, 207-581-3218, Fax: 207-581-3232, E-mail: graduate@maine.edu.

University of Manitoba, Faculty of Graduate Studies, Faculty of Agriculture, Winnipeg, MB R3T 2N2, Canada. Offers M Sc, PhD. *Degree requirements:* For master's, thesis or alternative; for doctorate, variable foreign language requirement, thesis/dissertation. Tuition charges are reported in Canadian dollars. Tuition, nonresident: full-time $3,878 Canadian dollars.

University of Maryland, College Park, Graduate Studies and Research, College of Agriculture and Natural Resources, College Park, MD 20742. Offers DVM, MS, PhD. Part-time and evening/weekend programs available. *Faculty:* 346 full-time (130 women), 32 part-time/adjunct (19 women). *Students:* 312 full-time (214 women), 35 part-time (19 women); includes 32 minority (16 African Americans, 1 American Indian/Alaska Native, 11 Asian Americans or Pacific Islanders, 4 Hispanic Americans), 102 international. 319 applicants, 35% accepted. In 2003, 29 first professional degrees, 25 master's, 15 doctorates awarded. *Median time to degree:* Of those who began their doctoral program in fall 1995, 32% received their degree in 8 years or less. *Degree requirements:* For DVM, thesis, oral exam, public seminar; for doctorate, thesis/dissertation. *Entrance requirements:* For DVM, GRE General Test; for master's, minimum GPA of 3.0. Additional exam requirements/recommendations for international students: Required—TOEFL. *Application deadline:* Applications are processed on a rolling basis. Application fee: $50 ($70 for international students). Electronic applications accepted. *Expenses:* Tuition, state resident: part-time $349 per credit hour. Tuition, nonresident: part-time $602 per credit hour. *Financial support:* In 2003–04, 15 fellowships with full tuition reimbursements (averaging $10,901 per year), 122 research assistantships with tuition reimbursements (averaging $16,030 per year), 41 teaching assistantships with tuition reimbursements (averaging $14,398 per year) were awarded. Career-related internships or fieldwork, Federal Work-Study, and scholarships/grants also available. Support available to part-time students. Financial award applicants required to submit FAFSA. Total annual research expenditures: $28.3 million. *Unit head:* Dr. Bruce L. Gardner, Interim Dean, 301-405-2072, Fax: 301-314-9146, E-mail: bgardner@umd.edu. *Application contact:* Trudy Lindsey, Director, Graduate Enrollment Management Services, 301-405-4190, Fax: 301-314-9305, E-mail: tlindsey@gradschool.umd.edu.

University of Maryland Eastern Shore, Graduate Programs, Department of Agriculture, Princess Anne, MD 21853-1299. Offers agriculture education and extension (MS); food and agricultural sciences (MS). *Degree requirements:* For master's, thesis (for some programs), oral exam. *Entrance requirements:* For master's, GRE, minimum GPA of 3.0. Additional exam requirements/recommendations for international students: Required—TOEFL. Electronic applications accepted. *Faculty research:* Poultry and swine nutrition and management, soybean specialty products, farm management practices, aquaculture technology.

University of Minnesota, Twin Cities Campus, Graduate School, College of Agricultural, Food, and Environmental Sciences, Minneapolis, MN 55455-0213. Offers MA, MBAE, MS, MSBAE, PhD. Part-time and evening/weekend programs available. *Students:* 337 full-time (183 women), 145 part-time (81 women); includes 26 minority (6 African Americans, 14 Asian Americans or Pacific Islanders, 6 Hispanic Americans), 171 international. Average age 31. 457 applicants, 32% accepted. In 2003, 65 master's, 55 doctorates awarded. Application fee: $50 ($55 for international students). *Expenses:* Tuition, state resident: full-time $3,681; part-time $614 per credit. Tuition, nonresident: full-time $7,231; part-time $1,205 per credit. *Financial support:* Fellowships, research assistantships, teaching assistantships, career-related internships or fieldwork, Federal Work-Study, institutionally sponsored loans, and tuition waivers (full) available. Support available to part-time students. *Unit head:* Dr. Charles C. Muscoplat, Dean, 612-624-5387. *Application contact:* Steve Gillard, Information Contact, 612-625-6792, E-mail: sgillard@umn.edu.

University of Missouri–Columbia, Graduate School, College of Agriculture, Food and Natural Resources, Columbia, MO 65211. Offers MS, PhD, MD/PhD. Part-time programs available. *Faculty:* 192 full-time (36 women). *Students:* 188 full-time (79 women), 117 part-time (45 women); includes 20 minority (11 African Americans, 2 American Indian/Alaska Native, 2 Asian Americans or Pacific Islanders, 5 Hispanic Americans), 118 international. In 2003, 53 master's, 34 doctorates awarded. *Degree requirements:* For doctorate, thesis/dissertation. *Entrance requirements:* For master's and doctorate, GRE General Test, minimum GPA of 3.0. *Application deadline:* Applications are processed on a rolling basis. Application fee: $45 ($60 for international students). *Expenses:* Tuition, state resident: full-time $5,205. Tuition, nonresident: full-time $14,058. *Financial support:* Fellowships, research assistantships, teaching assistantships, institutionally sponsored loans available. *Unit head:* Dr. Thomas T. Payne, Dean, 573-882-3846, E-mail: paynet@missouri.edu.

University of Nebraska–Lincoln, Graduate College, College of Agricultural Sciences and Natural Resources, Lincoln, NE 68588. Offers M Ag, MA, MS, PhD. *Degree requirements:* For doctorate, thesis/dissertation, comprehensive exam. *Entrance requirements:* Additional exam requirements/recommendations for international students: Required—TOEFL. Electronic applications accepted. *Faculty research:* Environmental sciences, animal sciences, human resources and family sciences, plant breeding and genetics, food and nutrition.

University of Nevada, Reno, Graduate School, College of Agriculture and Natural Resources, Reno, NV 89557. Offers MS, PhD. *Faculty:* 38. *Students:* 66 full-time (38 women), 17 part-time (8 women); includes 3 minority (1 African American, 2 Asian Americans or Pacific Islanders), 17 international. Average age 30. In 2003, 22 master's, 8 doctorates awarded. *Degree requirements:* For master's, thesis optional. *Entrance requirements:* For master's, GRE General Test, minimum GPA of 2.75. Additional exam requirements/recommendations for international students: Required—TOEFL. *Application deadline:* For fall admission, 3/1 for domestic students. Applications are processed on a rolling basis. Application fee: $60 ($95 for international students). *Expenses:* Tuition, state resident: part-time $119 per credit. Tuition, nonresident: part-time $127 per credit. Required fees: $20 per term. Tuition and fees vary according to course load. *Financial support:* In 2003–04, 4 teaching assistantships were awarded; research assistantships, Federal Work-Study and institutionally sponsored loans also available. Financial award application deadline: 3/1. *Unit head:* Dr. David Trawley, Dean, 775-784-1660.

University of Puerto Rico, Mayagüez Campus, Graduate Studies, College of Agricultural Sciences, Mayagüez, PR 00681-9000. Offers MS. Part-time programs available. *Degree requirements:* For master's, thesis, comprehensive exam.

University of Saskatchewan, College of Graduate Studies and Research, College of Agriculture, Saskatoon, SK S7N 5A2, Canada. Offers M Ag, M Sc, MA, PhD. Part-time programs available. *Faculty:* 51. *Students:* 172. *Degree requirements:* For master's, thesis (for some programs), registration; for doctorate, thesis/dissertation, registration. *Entrance requirements:* Additional exam requirements/recommendations for international students: Required—TOEFL. *Application deadline:* For fall admission, 7/1 for domestic students. Applications are processed on a rolling basis. Application fee: $50. Tuition charges are reported in Canadian dollars. *Expenses:* Tuition, state resident: part-time $483 Canadian dollars per course. *Financial support:* Fellowships, research assistantships, teaching assistantships, career-related internships or fieldwork available. Financial award application deadline: 1/31. *Unit head:* Dr. J. E.M. Barber, Dean, 306-966-4050, Fax: 306-966-8894, E-mail: ernie.barber@usask.ca.

The University of Tennessee, Graduate School, College of Agricultural Sciences and Natural Resources, Knoxville, TN 37996. Offers MS, PhD. Part-time programs available. Postbaccalaureate distance learning degree programs offered (minimal on-campus study). *Degree requirements:* For master's, thesis (for some programs); for doctorate, thesis/dissertation. *Entrance requirements:* For master's and doctorate, minimum GPA of 2.7. Additional exam requirements/recommendations for international students: Required—TOEFL. Electronic applications accepted.

University of Vermont, Graduate College, College of Agriculture and Life Sciences, Burlington, VT 05405. Offers M Ext Ed, MAT, MPA, MS, MST, PhD. Part-time programs available. *Students:* 101 (59 women); includes 5 minority (2 African Americans, 3 Hispanic Americans) 17 international. 152 applicants, 51% accepted, 44 enrolled. In 2003, 21 master's, 2 doctorates awarded. *Degree requirements:* For doctorate, one foreign language, thesis/dissertation. *Entrance requirements:* For master's and doctorate, GRE General Test. Additional exam requirements/recommendations for international students: Required—TOEFL. Application fee: $25. *Expenses:* Tuition, state resident: part-time $362 per credit hour. Tuition, nonresident: part-time $906 per credit hour. *Financial support:* Fellowships, research assistantships, teaching assistantships, career-related internships or fieldwork, Federal Work-Study, and tuition waivers (full and partial) available. Financial award application deadline: 3/1. *Unit head:* Dr. R. K. Johnson, Dean, 802-656-2980.

University of Wisconsin–Madison, Graduate School, College of Agricultural and Life Sciences, Madison, WI 53706-1380. Offers MA, MS, PhD. Part-time programs available. *Faculty:* 305 full-time (59 women). *Students:* 932 full-time (467 women), 83 part-time (53 women); includes 82 minority (13 African Americans, 9 American Indian/Alaska Native, 26 Asian Americans or Pacific Islanders, 34 Hispanic Americans). Average age 30. 2,155 applicants, 22% accepted, 256 enrolled. In 2003, 106 master's, 92 doctorates awarded. *Entrance requirements:* For master's and doctorate, GRE. Additional exam requirements/recommendations for international students: Required—TOEFL. Application fee: $45. Electronic applications accepted. Tuition, area resident: Full-time $7,593; part-time $476 per credit. Tuition, nonresident: full-time $22,824; part-time $1,430 per credit. Required fees: $292; $38 per credit. Part-time tuition and fees vary according to course load and reciprocity agreements. *Financial support:* Fellowships, research assistantships, teaching assistantships, career-related internships or fieldwork, Federal Work-Study, institutionally sponsored loans, traineeships, health care benefits, tuition waivers (full and partial), and project assistantships available. Support available to part-time students. Financial award applicants required to submit FAFSA. Total annual research expenditures: $58.1 million. *Unit head:* Elton D. Aberle, Dean and Director, 608-262-4930, Fax: 608-262-4556, E-mail: eaberle@cals.wisc.edu.

University of Wisconsin–River Falls, Outreach and Graduate Studies, College of Agriculture, Food, and Environmental Sciences, River Falls, WI 54022-5001. Offers MS. Part-time programs available. *Degree requirements:* For master's, thesis (for some programs), comprehensive exam. *Entrance requirements:* For master's, minimum GPA of 2.75. Electronic applications accepted.

University of Wyoming, Graduate School, College of Agriculture, Laramie, WY 82070. Offers MS, PhD. Part-time programs available. *Faculty:* 102 full-time (11 women), 9 part-time/adjunct (2 women). *Students:* 88 full-time (40 women), 53 part-time (30 women); includes 4 minority (1 American Indian/Alaska Native, 2 Asian Americans or Pacific Islanders, 1 Hispanic American), 31 international. Average age 29. 77 applicants, 48% accepted. In 2003, 28 master's, 6 doctorates awarded. Terminal master's awarded for partial completion of doctoral program. *Degree requirements:* For doctorate, thesis/dissertation. *Entrance requirements:* For master's and doctorate, GRE General Test, minimum GPA of 3.0. *Application deadline:* Applications are processed on a rolling basis. Application fee: $40. Electronic applications accepted. *Expenses:* Tuition, state resident: part-time $142 per credit hour. Tuition, nonresident: part-time $408 per credit hour. Required fees: $134 per semester. Tuition and fees vary according to course load, campus/location, program and student level. *Financial support:* In 2003–04, 3 fellowships, 15 research assistantships, 32 teaching assistantships were awarded. Career-related internships or fieldwork, Federal Work-Study, institutionally sponsored loans, scholarships/grants, tuition waivers (partial), and unspecified assistantships also available. Financial award application deadline: 3/1. *Faculty research:* Nutrition, molecular biology, animal science, plant science, entomology. *Unit head:* Dr. Frank D. Galey, Dean, 307-766-4133, E-mail: fgaley@uwyo.edu.

Utah State University, School of Graduate Studies, College of Agriculture, Logan, UT 84322. Offers MDA, MFMS, MS, PhD. Part-time programs available. Postbaccalaureate distance learning degree programs offered (minimal on-campus study). *Faculty:* 92 full-time (19 women), 19 part-time/adjunct (0 women). *Students:* 81 full-time (35 women), 28 part-time (9 women); includes 2 minority (both African Americans), 21 international. Average age 27. 66 applicants, 52% accepted, 20 enrolled. In 2003, 30 master's, 11 doctorates awarded. Terminal master's awarded for partial completion of doctoral program. *Degree requirements:* For doctorate, thesis/dissertation. *Entrance requirements:* For master's and doctorate, GRE General Test, minimum GPA of 3.0. Additional exam requirements/recommendations for international students: Required—TOEFL. *Application deadline:* For fall admission, 6/15 for domestic students; for spring admission, 10/15 for domestic students. Applications are processed on a rolling basis. Application fee: $50 ($60 for international students). *Expenses:* Tuition, state resident: part-time $270 per credit hour. Tuition, nonresident: part-time $946 per credit hour. Required fees: $173 per credit hour. *Financial support:* In 2003–04, fellowships (averaging $15,000 per year), research assistantships (averaging $13,000 per year), teaching assistantships (averaging $8,000 per year) were awarded. Career-related internships or fieldwork, Federal Work-Study, institutionally sponsored loans, scholarships/grants, and tuition waivers (full and partial) also available. Support available to part-time students. *Faculty research:* Low-input agriculture, anti-viral chemotherapy, lactic culture, environmental biophysics and climate. *Unit head:* Noelle E. Crocket, Dean, 435-797-2215.

Virginia Polytechnic Institute and State University, Graduate School, College of Agriculture and Life Sciences, Blacksburg, VA 24061. Offers M Eng, MS, PhD. *Faculty:* 216 full-time (44 women). *Students:* 265 full-time (145 women), 56 part-time (27 women); includes 17 minority (7 African Americans, 1 American Indian/Alaska Native, 6 Asian Americans or Pacific Islanders, 3 Hispanic Americans), 97 international. Average age 28. 339 applicants, 34% accepted, 81 enrolled. In 2003, 53 master's, 20 doctorates awarded. *Entrance requirements:* Additional exam requirements/recommendations for international students: Required—TOEFL. *Application deadline:* Applications are processed on a rolling basis. Application fee: $45. Electronic applications accepted. Tuition, area resident: Full-time $6,039; part-time $336 per credit. Tuition, nonresident: full-time $9,708; part-time $539 per credit. Required fees: $905; $130 per credit. *Financial support:* In 2003–04, 20 fellowships with full tuition reimbursements (averaging $11,203 per year), 101 research assistantships with full tuition reimbursements (averaging $14,426 per year), 62 teaching assistantships with full tuition reimbursements (averaging $11,801 per year) were awarded. Career-related internships or fieldwork, Federal Work-Study, scholarships/grants, and unspecified assistantships also available. Financial award application deadline: 4/1. *Faculty research:* Biotechnology, plant pathology, animal nutrition, agribusiness. *Unit head:* Dr. Sharron Quisenberry, Dean, 540-231-4152.

Washington State University, Graduate School, College of Agricultural, Human, and Natural Resource Sciences, Pullman, WA 99164. Offers MA, MLA, MS, PhD. Part-time programs available. *Students:* 244 full-time (123 women), 36 part-time (18 women); includes 19 minority (3 African Americans, 6 American Indian/Alaska Native, 6 Asian Americans or Pacific Islanders, 4 Hispanic Americans), 97 international. In 2003, 77 master's, 13 doctorates awarded. Terminal master's awarded for partial completion of doctoral program. *Degree requirements:* For master's, oral exam; for doctorate, thesis/dissertation, oral exam. *Entrance requirements:* For master's and doctorate, minimum GPA of 3.0. *Application deadline:* Applications are processed on a rolling basis. Application fee: $35. Electronic applications accepted. *Expenses:* Tuition, state resident: full-time $6,278; part-time $314 per hour. Tuition, nonresident: full-time $15,514; part-time $765 per hour. Required fees: $444. Full-time tuition and fees vary according to campus/location, program and student level. Part-time tuition and fees vary according to course load. *Financial support:* In 2003–04, 146 research assistantships with full and partial tuition reimbursements (averaging $11,500 per year), 38 teaching assistantships with full and partial tuition reimbursements (averaging $11,500 per year) were awarded. Fellowships, career-related internships or fieldwork, Federal Work-Study, institutionally sponsored loans, tuition waivers (partial), unspecified assistantships, and staff assistantships, teaching associateships also available. Financial award application deadline: 4/1; financial award applicants required to submit FAFSA. Total annual research expenditures: $25 million. *Unit head:* Dr. James R. Cook, Interim Dean, 509-335-4561. *Application contact:* Broderick Gant, Assistant to the Associate Dean and Director of Recruitment, 509-335-4562, Fax: 509-335-1065, E-mail: bgant@wsu.edu.

Western Kentucky University, Graduate Studies, Ogden College of Science, and Engineering, Department of Agriculture, Bowling Green, KY 42101-3576. Offers MA Ed, MS. Part-time and evening/weekend programs available. *Degree requirements:* For master's, thesis optional. *Entrance requirements:* For master's, GRE General Test, minimum GPA of 2.75. Additional exam requirements/recommendations for international students: Required—TOEFL (minimum score 555 paper-based; 213 computer-based). *Faculty research:* Establishment of warm season grasses, heat composting, enrichment activities in agricultural education.

West Texas A&M University, College of Agriculture, Nursing, and Natural Sciences, Division of Agriculture, Canyon, TX 79016-0001. Offers agricultural business and economics (MS); agriculture (PhD); animal science (MS); plant science (MS). Part-time programs available. *Faculty:* 17 full-time (2 women), 16 part-time/adjunct (2 women). *Students:* 35 full-time (13 women), 17 part-time (8 women); includes 1 minority (Hispanic American), 16 international. Average age 34. 43 applicants, 77% accepted. In 2003, 18 degrees awarded. *Median time to degree:* Master's–3 years full-time, 6 years part-time. *Degree requirements:* For master's, thesis optional. *Entrance requirements:* For master's, GRE General Test. Additional exam requirements/recommendations for international students: Required—TOEFL (minimum score 550 paper-based). *Application deadline:* Applications are processed on a rolling basis. Application fee: $25 ($75 for international students). Electronic applications accepted. *Expenses:* Tuition, state resident: part-time $56 per credit hour. Tuition, nonresident: part-time $292 per credit hour. Full-time tuition and fees vary according to course level, degree level and program. *Financial support:* In 2003–04, 23 research assistantships with tuition reimbursements (averaging $6,500 per year), 16 teaching assistantships with tuition reimbursements (averaging $6,750 per year) were awarded. Federal Work-Study, institutionally sponsored loans, scholarships/grants, traineeships, and tuition waivers (partial) also available. Support available to part-time students. Financial award applicants required to submit FAFSA. *Faculty research:* Pest management, high plains green beans production and management, expected revenue for fixed cow/calf, digestibility and retention, inorganic/organic forms of copper zinc in mature horses . Total annual research expenditures: $1.4 million. *Unit head:* Dr. Donald Topliff, Head, 806-651-2550, Fax: 806-651-2938, E-mail: dtopliff@mail.wtamu.edu.

West Virginia University, Davis College of Agriculture, Forestry and Consumer Sciences, Morgantown, WV 26506. Offers M Agr, MS, MSF, MSFCS, PhD. Part-time programs available. *Faculty:* 87 full-time (19 women), 16 part-time/adjunct (10 women). *Students:* 172 full-time (92 women), 79 part-time (34 women); includes 7 minority (1 African American, 4 Asian Americans or Pacific Islanders, 2 Hispanic Americans), 42 international. Average age 28. 136 applicants, 75% accepted, 75 enrolled. In 2003, 72 master's, 15 doctorates awarded. *Median time to degree:* Master's–2 years full-time, 4 years part-time; doctorate–5 years full-time. *Entrance requirements:* Additional exam requirements/recommendations for international students: Required—TOEFL. *Application deadline:* For fall admission, 6/1 priority date for domestic students, 6/1 priority date for international students; for spring admission, 1/5 for domestic students, 1/5 for international students. Applications are processed on a rolling basis. Application fee: $45. Electronic applications accepted. *Expenses:* Tuition, state resident: full-time $4,332. Tuition, nonresident: full-time $12,442. *Financial support:* In 2003–04, 8 fellowships (averaging $2,000 per year), 105 research assistantships (averaging $9,936 per year), 25 teaching assistantships (averaging $7,452 per year) were awarded. Career-related internships or fieldwork, Federal Work-Study, institutionally sponsored loans, tuition waivers (full and partial), and unspecified assistantships also available. Financial award application deadline: 2/1; financial award applicants required to submit FAFSA. *Faculty research:* Reproductive physiology, soil and water quality, human nutrition, aquaculture, wildlife management. *Unit head:* Dr. Cameron R. Hackney, Dean, 304-293-2395 Ext. 4530, Fax: 304-293-3740, E-mail: cameron.hackney@mail.wvu.edu. *Application contact:* Dr. Dennis K. Smith, Associate Dean, 304-293-2691 Ext. 4521, Fax: 304-293-3740, E-mail: denny.smith@mail.wvu.edu.

Agronomy and Soil Sciences

Alabama Agricultural and Mechanical University, School of Graduate Studies, School of Agricultural and Environmental Sciences, Department of Plant and Soil Sciences, Huntsville, AL 35811. Offers animal sciences (MS); environmental science (MS); plant and soil science (PhD). Evening/weekend programs available. *Faculty:* 18 full-time (2 women), 6 part-time/adjunct (0 women). *Students:* 28 full-time (16 women), 53 part-time (30 women); includes 70 minority (53 African Americans, 4 American Indian/Alaska Native, 13 Asian Americans or Pacific Islanders). In 2003, 6 degrees awarded. Terminal master's awarded for partial completion of doctoral program. *Degree requirements:* For master's, thesis; for doctorate, one foreign language, thesis/dissertation. *Entrance requirements:* For master's, GRE General Test, BS in agriculture; for doctorate, GRE General Test, master's degree. *Application deadline:* For fall admission, 5/1 for domestic students. Applications are processed on a rolling basis. Application fee: $25. Electronic applications accepted. *Expenses:* Tuition, state resident: full-time $3,250; part-time $370 per credit hour. Tuition, nonresident: full-time $6,490; part-time $740 per credit hour. *Financial support:* In 2003–04, 1 fellowship with tuition reimbursement (averaging $18,000 per year), 9 research assistantships with tuition reimbursements (averaging $9,000 per year) were awarded. Career-related internships or fieldwork and Federal Work-Study also available. Financial award application deadline: 4/1. *Faculty research:* Plant breeding, cytogenetics, crop production, soil chemistry and fertility, remote sensing. Total annual research expenditures: $113,000. *Unit head:* Dr. Govind Sharma, Chair, 256-372-4173.

Alcorn State University, School of Graduate Studies, School of Agriculture and Applied Science, Alcorn State, MS 39096-7500. Offers agricultural economics (MS Ag); agronomy (MS Ag); animal science (MS Ag). *Faculty:* 11 full-time (2 women). *Students:* 9 full-time (2 women), 7 part-time (2 women); includes 12 minority (all African Americans), 3 international. *Degree requirements:* For master's, thesis optional. *Application deadline:* For fall admission, 7/15 for domestic students; for spring admission, 11/25 for domestic students. Applications are processed on a rolling basis. Application fee: $0 ($10 for international students). *Expenses:* Tuition, state resident: full-time $3,192. Tuition, nonresident: full-time $7,698. *Financial support:* Career-related internships or fieldwork available. Support available to part-time students. *Faculty research:* Aquatic systems, dairy herd improvement, fruit production, alternative farming practices. *Unit head:* Napoleon Moses, Dean, 601-877-6137, Fax: 601-877-6219.

Auburn University, Graduate School, College of Agriculture, Department of Agronomy and Soils, Auburn University, AL 36849. Offers M Ag, MS, PhD. Part-time programs available. *Faculty:* 22 full-time (3 women). *Students:* 19 full-time (4 women), 11 part-time (2 women); includes 1 minority (African American), 10 international. 8 applicants, 100% accepted. In 2003, 4 master's, 4 doctorates awarded. *Degree requirements:* For master's, thesis (for some programs); for doctorate, thesis/dissertation. *Entrance requirements:* For master's and doctorate, GRE General Test. *Application deadline:* For fall admission, 7/7 for domestic students; for spring admission, 11/24 for domestic students. Applications are processed on a rolling basis. Application fee: $25 ($50 for international students). Electronic applications accepted. *Expenses:* Tuition, state resident: part-time $175 per credit hour. Tuition, nonresident: part-time $525 per credit hour. *Financial support:* Research assistantships, teaching assistantships, Federal Work-Study available. Support available to part-time students. Financial award application deadline: 3/15. *Faculty research:* Plant breeding and genetics; weed science; crop production; soil fertility and plant nutrition; soil genesis, morphology, and classification. *Unit head:* Dr. Joseph T. Touchton, Head, 334-844-4100, E-mail: jtouchto@ag.auburn.edu. *Application contact:* Dr. John F. Pritchett, Dean of the Graduate School, 334-844-4700, E-mail: hatchlb@mail.auburn.edu.

Brigham Young University, Graduate Studies, College of Biological and Agricultural Sciences, Department of Plant and Animal Sciences, Provo, UT 84602-1001. Offers agronomy (MS); horticulture (MS). *Faculty:* 16 full-time (2 women), 1 (woman) part-time/adjunct. *Students:* 11 full-time (5 women), 2 part-time (1 woman); includes 1 minority (African American) Average age 26. 7 applicants, 43% accepted, 3 enrolled. In 2003, 7 degrees awarded. *Degree requirements:* For master's, thesis, comprehensive exam, registration. *Entrance requirements:* For master's, GRE General Test, minimum GPA of 3.0 during previous 2 years. *Application deadline:* For fall admission, 2/15 for domestic students, 2/15 for international students. Applications are processed on a rolling basis. Application fee: $50. Electronic applications accepted. *Expenses:* Tuition: Part-time $221 per hour. *Financial support:* In 2003–04, 11 students received support, including 1 research assistantship with partial tuition reimbursement available (averaging $15,000 per year), 10 teaching assistantships with partial tuition reimbursements available (averaging $15,000 per year); institutionally sponsored loans, scholarships/grants, and tuition waivers (partial) also available. Financial award application deadline: 4/15. *Faculty research:* Iron nutrition in plants–mode of uptake, photosynthesis, forage quality, seed physiology/modeling, cytogenetics. Total annual research expenditures: $13,500. *Unit head:* Dr. Sheldon D. Nelson, Chair, 801-422-2760, Fax: 801-378-7499, E-mail: sheldon_nelson@byu.edu. *Application contact:* Dr. Richard E. Terry, Graduate Coordinator, 801-422-2421, Fax: 801-378-7499, E-mail: richard_terry@byu.edu.

Colorado State University, Graduate School, College of Agricultural Sciences, Department of Soil and Crop Sciences, Fort Collins, CO 80523-0015. Offers crop science (MS, PhD); plant genetics (MS, PhD); soil science (MS, PhD). Part-time programs available. *Faculty:* 23 full-time (4 women). *Students:* 15 full-time (3 women), 21 part-time (7 women); includes 2 minority (1 Asian American or Pacific Islander, 1 Hispanic American), 9 international. Average age 35. 27 applicants, 33% accepted, 5 enrolled. In 2003, 4 master's, 3 doctorates awarded. *Degree requirements:* For master's, thesis (for some programs), comprehensive exam, registration; for doctorate, thesis/dissertation, comprehensive exam, registration. *Entrance requirements:* For master's, minimum GPA of 3.0, appropriate bachelor's degree; for doctorate, minimum GPA of 3.0, appropriate master's degree. Additional exam requirements/recommendations for international students: Required—TOEFL. *Application deadline:* For fall admission, 2/1 for domestic students; for spring admission, 8/1 priority date for domestic students. Applications are processed on a rolling basis. Application fee: $50. Electronic applications accepted. *Expenses:* Tuition, state resident: full-time $4,156. Tuition, nonresident: full-time $14,762. Required fees: $205. Tuition and fees vary according to course load, campus/location, program and reciprocity agreements. *Financial support:* In 2003–04, 1 fellowship with partial tuition reimbursement (averaging $15,600 per year), 14 research assistantships with partial tuition reimbursements (averaging $15,600 per year), 2 teaching assistantships with partial tuition reimbursements (averaging $15,600 per year) were awarded. Career-related internships or fieldwork and traineeships also available. *Faculty research:* Water quality, soil fertility, soil/plant ecosystems, plant breeding and genetics, information systems/technology. Total annual research expenditures: $4.8 million. *Unit head:* Dr. Gary A. Peterson, Head, 970-491-6501, Fax: 970-491-0564, E-mail: gary.peterson@colostate.edu. *Application contact:* Dr. Dan H. Smith, Graduate Studies Coordinator, 970-491-6371, Fax: 970-491-0564, E-mail: dsmith@ceres.agsci.colostate.edu.

Cornell University, Graduate School, Graduate Fields of Agriculture and Life Sciences, Department of Soil and Crop Sciences, Ithaca, NY 14853. Offers agronomy (MPS, MS, PhD); atmospheric sciences (MPS, MS, PhD); environmental information science (MPS, MS, PhD); environmental management (MPS); field crop science (MPS, MS, PhD); soil science (MPS, MS, PhD). Terminal master's awarded for partial completion of doctoral program. *Degree requirements:* For master's, thesis (MS), project paper (MPS); for doctorate, thesis/dissertation. *Entrance requirements:* For master's and doctorate, GRE General Test. Additional exam requirements/recommendations for international students: Required—TOEFL. Electronic applications accepted. Expenses: Contact institution. One-time fee: $50 full-time. *Faculty research:* Environmental modeling, soil chemistry and physics, international agriculture, weather and climate, crop physiology.

Cornell University, Graduate School, Graduate Fields of Agriculture and Life Sciences, Field of Soil and Crop Sciences, Ithaca, NY 14853-0001. Offers agronomy (MS, PhD); environmental information science (MS, PhD); environmental management (MPS); field crop science (MS, PhD); soil science (MS, PhD). *Faculty:* 32 full-time. *Students:* 44 full-time (17 women); includes 1 minority (Hispanic American), 24 international. 40 applicants, 43% accepted, 14 enrolled. In 2003, 9 master's, 7 doctorates awarded. *Degree requirements:* For master's, thesis (MS); for doctorate, thesis/dissertation, comprehensive exam. *Entrance requirements:* For master's and doctorate, GRE General Test, 2 letters of recommendation. Additional exam requirements/recommendations for international students: Required—TOEFL (minimum score 550 paper-based; 213 computer-based). *Application deadline:* For fall admission, 2/1 for domestic students. Applications are processed on a rolling basis. Application fee: $60. Electronic applications accepted. *Expenses:* Tuition: Full-time $28,630. One-time fee: $50 full-time. *Financial support:* In 2003–04, 36 students received support, including 8 fellowships with full tuition reimbursements available, 21 research assistantships with full tuition reimbursements available, 7 teaching assistantships with full tuition reimbursements available; institutionally sponsored loans, traineeships, health care benefits, tuition waivers (full and partial), and unspecified assistantships also available. *Faculty research:* Soil chemistry, physics and biology; crop physiology and management; environmental information science and modeling; international agriculture; weed science. *Unit head:* Director of Graduate Studies, 607-255-3267, Fax: 607-255-8615. *Application contact:* Graduate Field Assistant, 607-255-3267, Fax: 607-255-8615, E-mail: jae2@cornell.edu.

Cornell University, Graduate School, Graduate Fields of Agriculture and Life Sciences, Field of Vegetable Crops, Ithaca, NY 14853-0001. Offers MPS, MS, PhD. *Faculty:* 15 full-time. *Students:* 6 full-time (3 women); includes 1 minority (Asian American or Pacific Islander), 3 international. 5 applicants, 80% accepted, 1 enrolled. In 2003, 2 master's, 2 doctorates awarded. *Degree requirements:* For master's, thesis (MS), project paper (MPS); for doctorate, thesis/dissertation, teaching experience. *Entrance requirements:* For master's and doctorate, GRE General Test (recommended), letters of recommendation (3). Additional exam requirements/recommendations for international students: Required—TOEFL (minimum score 550 paper-based; 213 computer-based). *Application deadline:* Applications are processed on a rolling basis. Application fee: $60. Electronic applications accepted. *Expenses:* Tuition: Full-time $28,630. One-time fee: $50 full-time. *Financial support:* In 2003–04, 6 students received support, including 6 research assistantships with full tuition reimbursements available; fellowships with full tuition reimbursements available, teaching assistantships with full tuition reimbursements available, institutionally sponsored loans, health care benefits, tuition waivers (full and partial), and unspecified assistantships also available. Financial award applicants required to submit FAFSA. *Faculty research:* Vegetable nutrition and physiology, post-harvest physiology and storage, application of new technologies, sustainable vegetable production, weed management and IPM. *Unit head:* Director of Graduate Studies, 607-255-4568. *Application contact:* Graduate Field Assistant, 607-255-4568, E-mail: hortgrad@cornell.edu.

Iowa State University of Science and Technology, Graduate College, College of Agriculture, Department of Agronomy, Ames, IA 50011. Offers agricultural meteorology (MS, PhD); agronomy (MS); crop production and physiology (MS, PhD); plant breeding (MS, PhD); soil science (MS, PhD). Postbaccalaureate distance learning degree programs offered (no on-campus study). *Faculty:* 66 full-time, 8 part-time/adjunct. *Students:* 103 full-time (37 women), 98 part-time (24 women); includes 7 minority (5 African Americans, 1 Asian American or Pacific Islander, 1 Hispanic American), 46 international. 88 applicants, 51% accepted, 39 enrolled. In 2003, 25 master's, 19 doctorates awarded. *Median time to degree:* Master's–2.7 years full-time; doctorate–4.9 years full-time. *Degree requirements:* For master's, thesis or alternative; for doctorate, thesis/dissertation. *Entrance requirements:* Additional exam requirements/recommendations for international students: Required—TOEFL (paper score 530; computer score 197) or IELTS (score 6). *Application deadline:* For fall admission, 1/1 priority date for domestic students, 1/1 priority date for international students; for spring admission, 9/1 priority date for domestic students, 9/1 priority date for international students. Applications are processed on a rolling basis. Application fee: $30 ($70 for international students). Electronic applications accepted. Tuition, nonresident: part-time $560 per credit. Required fees: $38 per unit. *Financial support:* In 2003–04, 83 research assistantships with full and partial tuition reimbursements (averaging $15,924 per year), 3 teaching assistantships with full and partial tuition reimbursements (averaging $15,924 per year) were awarded. Fellowships, scholarships/grants, health care benefits, and unspecified assistantships also available. *Unit head:* Dr. Steven Fales, Head, 515-294-7636, Fax: 515-294-3163. *Application contact:* Jacquelyn Severson, Information Contact, 515-294-1361, E-mail: director@agron.iastate.edu.

Kansas State University, Graduate School, College of Agriculture, Department of Agronomy, Manhattan, KS 66506. Offers crop science (MS, PhD); range management (MS, PhD); soil science (MS, PhD); weed science (MS, PhD). Part-time programs available. *Faculty:* 63 full-time (11 women). *Students:* 40 full-time (13 women), 12 part-time (5 women); includes 12 minority (3 African Americans, 5 Asian Americans or Pacific Islanders, 4 Hispanic Americans). 26 applicants, 92% accepted, 5 enrolled. In 2003, 11 master's, 7 doctorates awarded. Terminal master's awarded for partial completion of doctoral program. *Degree requirements:* For master's, thesis or alternative, oral exam; for doctorate, thesis/dissertation, preliminary exams. *Entrance requirements:* For master's, minimum GPA of 3.0 in B.S. For doctorate, minimum GPA of 3.5 in masters program, transcripts. Additional exam requirements/recommendations for international students: Required—TOEFL. *Application deadline:* For fall admission, 2/1 for domestic students; for spring admission, 10/1 for domestic students. Applications are processed on a rolling basis. Application fee: $0 ($25 for international students). Electronic applications accepted. *Expenses:* Tuition, state resident: part-time $155 per credit hour. Tuition, nonresident: part-time $428 per credit hour. Required fees: $11 per credit hour. *Financial support:* In 2003–04, 34 research assistantships (averaging $15,264 per year), 6 teaching assistantships with partial tuition reimbursements (averaging $2,763 per year) were awarded. Institutionally sponsored loans and scholarships/grants also available. Support available to part-time students. Financial award application deadline: 3/1; financial award applicants required to submit FAFSA. *Faculty research:* Plant breeding, weed science, environmental soil science, crop and water management, range science. Total annual research expenditures: $3 million. *Unit head:* Dr. David B. Mengel, Head, 785-532-6101, Fax: 785-532-6094, E-mail: dmengel@ksu.edu. *Application contact:* Dr. Gerard Kluitenberg, Director, 785-532-7215, E-mail: gjk@ksu.edu.

Louisiana State University and Agricultural and Mechanical College, Graduate School, College of Agriculture, Department of Agronomy and Environmental Management, Baton Rouge, LA 70803. Offers agronomy (MS, PhD). Part-time programs available. *Faculty:* 29 full-time (0 women). *Students:* 31 full-time (5 women), 17 part-time (3 women); includes 3 minority (2 African Americans, 1 American Indian/Alaska Native), 21 international. Average age 32. 14 applicants, 36% accepted, 1 enrolled. In 2003, 4 master's, 4 doctorates awarded. *Degree requirements:* For master's, thesis or alternative; for doctorate, thesis/dissertation. *Entrance requirements:* For master's and doctorate, GRE General Test, minimum GPA of 3.0. Additional exam requirements/recommendations for international students: Required—TOEFL (minimum score 550 paper-based; 213 computer-based). *Application deadline:* For fall admission, 1/25 priority date for domestic students, 5/15 priority date for international students. Applications are processed on a rolling basis. Application fee: $25. Electronic applications accepted. *Expenses:* Tuition, state resident: part-time $337 per hour. Tuition, nonresident: part-time $577 per hour. *Financial support:* In 2003–04, 26 research assistantships with partial tuition reimbursements (averaging $16,169 per year), 1 teaching assistantship with partial tuition reimbursement (averaging $17,000 per year) were awarded. Fellowships, tuition waivers (full) also available. Financial award applicants required to submit FAFSA. *Faculty research:* Crop production, resource management, environmental studies, soil science, plant genetics. *Unit head:* Dr. Freddie A. Martin, Head, 225-578-2110, Fax: 225-578-1403, E-mail: fmartin@agctr.lsu.edu. *Application contact:* Magdi Selim, Graduate Coordinator, 225-578-1332, Fax: 225-578-1403, E-mail: mselim@agctr.lsu.edu.

McGill University, Faculty of Graduate and Postdoctoral Studies, Faculty of Agricultural and Environmental Sciences, Department of Bioresource Engineering, Montréal, QC H3A

2T5, Canada. Offers computer applications (M Sc, M Sc A, PhD); food engineering (M Sc, M Sc A, PhD); grain drying (M Sc, M Sc A, PhD); irrigation and drainage (M Sc, M Sc A, PhD); machinery (M Sc, M Sc A, PhD); pollution control (M Sc, M Sc A, PhD); postharvest (M Sc, M Sc A, PhD); soil dynamics (M Sc, M Sc A, PhD); structure and environment (M Sc, M Sc A, PhD); vegetable and fruit storage (M Sc, M Sc A, PhD). Part-time programs available. *Faculty:* 11 full-time (2 women). *Students:* 54 full-time. Average age 26. 62 applicants, 63% accepted, 20 enrolled. In 2003, 11 master's, 3 doctorates awarded. *Degree requirements:* For master's and doctorate, thesis/dissertation. *Entrance requirements:* For master's, minimum GPA of 3.0; for doctorate, M Sc, minimum GPA of 3.0. Additional exam requirements/recommendations for international students: Required—TOEFL (paper score 550; computer score 213) or IELTS (paper score 6). *Application deadline:* For fall admission, 6/1 for domestic students, 3/1 for international students; for winter admission, 10/15 for domestic students; for spring admission, 2/15 for domestic students. Applications are processed on a rolling basis. Application fee: $60 Canadian dollars. Electronic applications accepted. Tuition, area resident: Full-time $1,668. *Expenses:* Tuition, state resident: full-time $4,173. Tuition, nonresident: full-time $9,468. Required fees: $1,081. *Financial support:* Fellowships, research assistantships, teaching assistantships, institutionally sponsored loans available. *Faculty research:* Postharvest technology, geotextiles for soil-lined manure reservoirs, groundwater transport of contaminants, insect protein for human food. *Unit head:* Dr. Robert Kok, Chair, 514-398-7775, Fax: 514-398-8387, E-mail: kok@macdonald.mcgill.ca. *Application contact:* Susan Gregus, Graduate Program Secretary, 514-398-7925, Fax: 514-398-7968, E-mail: susan.gregus@mcgill.ca.

McGill University, Faculty of Graduate and Postdoctoral Studies, Faculty of Agricultural and Environmental Sciences, Department of Natural Resource Sciences, Montréal, QC H3A 2T5, Canada. Offers agrometeorology (M Sc, PhD); entomology (M Sc, PhD); forest science (M Sc, PhD); microbiology (M Sc, PhD); neotropical environment (M Sc, PhD); soil science (M Sc, PhD); wildlife biology (M Sc, PhD). *Faculty:* 18 full-time (1 woman). *Students:* 69 full-time, 2 part-time. 51 applicants, 37% accepted, 15 enrolled. In 2003, 12 master's, 4 doctorates awarded. *Degree requirements:* For master's and doctorate, thesis/dissertation. *Entrance requirements:* For master's, minimum GPA of 3.0; for doctorate, M Sc, minimum GPA of 3.0. Additional exam requirements/recommendations for international students: Required—TOEFL (paper score 550; computer score 213) or IELTS (paper score 6). *Application deadline:* For fall admission, 6/1 for domestic students, 3/1 for international students; for winter admission, 10/15 for domestic students; for spring admission, 2/15 for domestic students. Applications are processed on a rolling basis. Application fee: $60 Canadian dollars. Electronic applications accepted. Tuition, area resident: Full-time $1,668. *Expenses:* Tuition, state resident: full-time $4,173. Tuition, nonresident: full-time $9,468. Required fees: $1,081. *Financial support:* In 2003–04, 2 fellowships with partial tuition reimbursements (averaging $8,000 per year), 34 teaching assistantships were awarded. Institutionally sponsored loans also available. *Faculty research:* Toxicology, reproductive physiology, parasites, wildlife management, genetics. *Unit head:* Dr. Benoit Côté, Chair, 514-398-7952, Fax: 514-398-7990, E-mail: coteb@nrs.mcgill.ca. *Application contact:* Marie Kubecki, Graduate Student Coordinator, 514-398-7991, Fax: 514-398-7990, E-mail: kubecki@nrs.mcgill.ca.

Michigan State University, Graduate School, College of Agriculture and Natural Resources, Department of Crop and Soil Sciences, East Lansing, MI 48824. Offers crop and soil sciences (MS, PhD); crop and soil sciences-environmental toxicology (PhD); plant breeding and genetics-crop and soil sciences (MS, PhD). *Faculty:* 31 full-time (5 women), 1 part-time/adjunct (0 women). *Students:* 66 full-time (28 women), 13 part-time (7 women); includes 7 minority (2 African Americans, 5 Hispanic Americans), 33 international. Average age 30. 49 applicants, 35% accepted. In 2003, 11 master's, 8 doctorates awarded. *Degree requirements:* For master's, thesis or alternative, oral final exam; for doctorate, thesis/dissertation, oral final exam in defense of dissertation, 1 year of residence, comprehensive exam. *Entrance requirements:* For master's, GRE General Test, minimum GPA of 3.0, bachelor's degree in crop and soil sciences or related field; for doctorate, GRE General Test, minimum GPA of 3.0. Additional exam requirements/recommendations for international students: Required—TOEFL (minimum score 550 paper-based; 213 computer-based), Michigan State University ELT (85), Michigan ELAB (83). *Application deadline:* For fall admission, 12/23 for domestic students. Application fee: $50. Electronic applications accepted. *Expenses:* Tuition, state resident: part-time $291 per hour. Tuition, nonresident: part-time $589 per hour. *Financial support:* In 2003–04, 19 fellowships with tuition reimbursements (averaging $6,861 per year), 53 research assistantships with tuition reimbursements (averaging $12,151 per year) were awarded. Financial award applicants required to submit FAFSA. *Faculty research:* Turfgrass management, environmental toxicology, integrated pest management, water science, plant breeding and genetics. Total annual research expenditures: $7.5 million. *Unit head:* Dr. Douglas Buhler, Chairperson, 517-355-0271, Fax: 517-353-5174, E-mail: buhler@msu.edu. *Application contact:* Taylor Johnston, Graduate Programs Coordinator, 517-355-2234, Fax: 517-353-5174, E-mail: johnsto4@msu.edu.

Michigan State University, Graduate School, College of Agriculture and Natural Resources, Program in Plant Breeding and Genetics, East Lansing, MI 48824. Offers plant breeding and genetics (MS, PhD), including botany and plant pathology, crop and soil sciences, forestry, horticulture. *Faculty:* 22 full-time (5 women). *Students:* 22 full-time (12 women), 5 part-time (3 women); includes 1 minority (Hispanic American), 12 international. Average age 30. 29 applicants, 17% accepted. In 2003, 3 master's, 2 doctorates awarded. *Degree requirements:* For master's, thesis; for doctorate, thesis/dissertation, oral examination, comprehensive exam. *Entrance requirements:* For master's and doctorate, GRE, minimum GPA of 3.0, 3 letters of recommendation. Additional exam requirements/recommendations for international students: Required—TOEFL (minimum score 550 paper-based; 213 computer-based). *Application deadline:* For fall admission, 12/23 for domestic students. Application fee: $50. *Expenses:* Tuition, state resident: part-time $291 per hour. Tuition, nonresident: part-time $589 per hour. *Financial support:* Applicants required to submit FAFSA. *Unit head:* Dr. Jim Hancock, Director, 517-355-4598, Fax: 517-353-0890, E-mail: hancock@msu.edu. *Application contact:* Program Office, 517-353-2913.

Michigan State University, Graduate School, College of Natural Science, Plant Research Laboratory, East Lansing, MI 48824. Offers biochemistry and molecular biology (PhD); cellular and molecular biology (PhD); crop and soil sciences (PhD); genetics (PhD); microbiology and molecular genetics (PhD); plant biology (PhD); plant physiology (PhD). Offered jointly with the Department of Energy. *Faculty:* 10 full-time (1 woman). *Students:* 19 full-time (6 women); includes 1 minority (Asian American or Pacific Islander), 6 international. Average age 27. *Degree requirements:* For doctorate, thesis/dissertation, laboratory rotation, defense of dissertation, comprehensive exam. *Entrance requirements:* For doctorate, GRE General Test, acceptance into one of the affiliated department programs; 3 letters of recommendation; bachelor's degree or equivalent in life sciences, chemistry, biochemistry, or biophysics; research experience. Additional exam requirements/recommendations for international students: Required—TOEFL (minimum score 550 paper-based; 213 computer-based), Michigan State University ELT (85), Michigan ELAB (83). *Application deadline:* For fall admission, 1/15 for domestic students. Application fee: $50. Electronic applications accepted. *Expenses:* Tuition, state resident: part-time $291 per hour. Tuition, nonresident: part-time $589 per hour. *Financial support:* Research assistantships with tuition reimbursements available. Financial award applicants required to submit FAFSA. *Faculty research:* Role of hormones in the regulation of plant development and physiology, molecular mechanisms associated with signal recognition, development and application of genetic methods and materials, protein routing and function. Total annual research expenditures: $6.6 million. *Unit head:* Dr. Kenneth Keegstra, Director, 517-353-2270, Fax: 517-353-9168, E-mail: keegstra@msu.edu. *Application contact:* Zita Schneider, Information Contact, 517-353-2270, Fax: 517-353-9168, E-mail: prl@msu.edu.

Mississippi State University, College of Agriculture and Life Sciences, Department of Plant and Soil Sciences, Mississippi State, MS 39762. Offers agronomy (MS, PhD); horticulture (MS, PhD); weed science (MS, PhD). Part-time programs available. *Faculty:* 31 full-time (2 women), 1 part-time/adjunct (0 women). *Students:* 36 full-time (10 women), 25 part-time (6 women); includes 1 minority (Asian American or Pacific Islander), 16 international. Average age 31. 16 applicants, 38% accepted, 3 enrolled. In 2003, 9 master's, 3 doctorates awarded. *Degree requirements:* For master's and doctorate, thesis/dissertation, comprehensive oral or written exam. *Entrance requirements:* Additional exam requirements/recommendations for international students: Required—TOEFL. *Application deadline:* For fall admission, 7/1 for domestic students; for spring admission, 11/1 for domestic students. Applications are processed on a rolling basis. Application fee: $25 for international students. *Expenses:* Tuition, state resident: full-time $3,874; part-time $215 per hour. Tuition, nonresident: full-time $8,780; part-time $488 per hour. International tuition: $9,105 full-time. Tuition and fees vary according to course load. *Financial support:* In 2003–04, 12 research assistantships with full tuition reimbursements (averaging $12,423 per year), 3 teaching assistantships with full tuition reimbursements (averaging $13,696 per year) were awarded. Career-related internships or fieldwork, Federal Work-Study, institutionally sponsored loans, and unspecified assistantships also available. Financial award applicants required to submit FAFSA. *Faculty research:* Metabolism, morphology, growth regulators, biotechnology, stress physiology. Total annual research expenditures: $874,795. *Unit head:* Dr. Frank Matta, Interim Head, 662-325-2352, Fax: 662-325-8742, E-mail: fmatta@pss.msstate.edu. *Application contact:* Diane D. Wolfe, Director of Admissions, 662-325-2224, Fax: 662-325-7360, E-mail: admit@admissions.msstate.edu.

New Mexico State University, Graduate School, College of Agriculture and Home Economics, Department of Agronomy and Horticulture, Las Cruces, NM 88003-8001. Offers general agronomy (MS, PhD); horticulture (MS). Part-time programs available. *Faculty:* 24 full-time (3 women), 6 part-time/adjunct (1 woman). *Students:* 33 full-time (10 women), 15 part-time (7 women); includes 13 minority (2 American Indian/Alaska Native, 11 Hispanic Americans), 18 international. Average age 34. 24 applicants, 71% accepted, 2 enrolled. In 2003, 6 master's, 8 doctorates awarded. *Median time to degree:* Of those who began their doctoral program in fall 1995, 90% received their degree in 8 years or less. *Degree requirements:* For master's, thesis; for doctorate, one foreign language, thesis/dissertation. *Entrance requirements:* For master's, minimum GPA of 3.0; for doctorate, minimum GPA of 3.3. *Application deadline:* For fall admission, 7/1 for domestic students; for spring admission, 11/1 for domestic students. Applications are processed on a rolling basis. Application fee: $30 ($50 for international students). Electronic applications accepted. *Expenses:* Tuition, state resident: full-time $2,670; part-time $151 per credit. Tuition, nonresident: full-time $10,596; part-time $481 per credit. Required fees: $954. *Financial support:* In 2003–04, 15 research assistantships, 10 teaching assistantships were awarded. Career-related internships or fieldwork and Federal Work-Study also available. Support available to part-time students. Financial award application deadline: 3/1. *Faculty research:* Plant breeding and genetics, molecular biology, plant physiology, soil science and environmental remediation, urban horticulture. *Unit head:* Dr. James T. Fisher, Head, 505-646-3406, Fax: 505-646-6041, E-mail: jtfisher@nmsu.edu.

North Carolina State University, Graduate School, College of Agriculture and Life Sciences, Department of Crop Science, Raleigh, NC 27695. Offers MS, PhD. Part-time programs available. *Faculty:* 57 full-time (6 women), 26 part-time/adjunct (0 women). *Students:* 59 full-time (23 women), 4 part-time; includes 4 minority (2 African Americans, 1 Asian American or Pacific Islander, 1 Hispanic American), 13 international. Average age 29. 37 applicants, 49% accepted. In 2003, 4 master's, 8 doctorates awarded. Terminal master's awarded for partial completion of doctoral program. *Degree requirements:* For master's, thesis (MS); for doctorate, thesis/dissertation. *Entrance requirements:* For master's and doctorate, GRE. *Application deadline:* For fall admission, 6/25 for domestic students, 3/1 for international students; for spring admission, 11/25 for domestic students, 7/15 for international students. Application fee: $45. *Expenses:* Tuition, state resident: part-time $396 per hour. Tuition, nonresident: part-time $1,895 per hour. *Financial support:* In 2003–04, 2 fellowships with tuition reimbursements (averaging $5,892 per year), 45 research assistantships with tuition reimbursements (averaging $6,492 per year), 3 teaching assistantships with tuition reimbursements (averaging $6,392 per year) were awarded. Career-related internships or fieldwork, Federal Work-Study, and institutionally sponsored loans also available. Support available to part-time students. Financial award application deadline: 6/25. *Faculty research:* Crop breeding and genetics, application of biotechnology to crop improvement, plant physiology, crop physiology and management, agroecology. Total annual research expenditures: $2.8 million. *Unit head:* Dr. H. Thomas Stalker, Interim Head, 919-515-2647, Fax: 919-515-7959, E-mail: tom_stalker@ncsu.edu. *Application contact:* Dr. Randy Wells, Director of Graduate Programs, 919-515-4062, Fax: 919-515-7959, E-mail: randy_wells@ncsu.edu.

North Carolina State University, Graduate School, College of Agriculture and Life Sciences, Department of Soil Science, Raleigh, NC 27695. Offers MS, PhD. Part-time programs available. *Faculty:* 25 full-time (1 woman), 22 part-time/adjunct (1 woman). *Students:* 37 full-time (12 women), 12 part-time (6 women); includes 5 minority (2 African Americans, 3 Asian Americans or Pacific Islanders), 9 international. Average age 30. 35 applicants, 37% accepted. In 2003, 10 master's, 4 doctorates awarded. *Degree requirements:* For master's, thesis (for some programs); for doctorate, thesis/dissertation. *Entrance requirements:* For master's and doctorate, minimum GPA of 3.0. *Application deadline:* For fall admission, 6/25 for domestic students, 3/1 for international students; for spring admission, 11/25 for domestic students, 7/15 for international students. Application fee: $45. *Expenses:* Tuition, state resident: part-time $396 per hour. Tuition, nonresident: part-time $1,895 per hour. *Financial support:* In 2003–04, 1 fellowship with tuition reimbursement (averaging $8,039 per year), 31 research assistantships with tuition reimbursements (averaging $5,368 per year) were awarded. Teaching assistantships with tuition reimbursements, Federal Work-Study and institutionally sponsored loans also available. Support available to part-time students. Financial award application deadline: 6/25. *Faculty research:* Soil management, soil-environmental relations, chemical and physical properties of soils, nutrient and water management, land use. Total annual research expenditures: $1.8 million. *Unit head:* Dr. D. Keith Cassel, Interim Head, 919-515-2655, Fax: 919-515-2167, E-mail: keith_cassel@ncsu.edu. *Application contact:* Dr. Michael G. Wagger, Director of Graduate Programs, 919-515-4269, Fax: 919-515-2167, E-mail: michael_wagger@ncsu.edu.

North Dakota State University, The Graduate School, College of Agriculture, Food Systems, and Natural Resources, Department of Soil Science, Fargo, ND 58105. Offers natural resources management (MS); soil sciences (MS, PhD). Part-time programs available. *Faculty:* 11 full-time (0 women), 4 part-time/adjunct (0 women). *Students:* 7 full-time (3 women), 3 part-time (1 woman), 3 international. Average age 23. 4 applicants, 75% accepted, 2 enrolled. In 2003, 1 degree awarded, leading to business/industry 100%. *Median time to degree:* Master's–2 years full-time. *Degree requirements:* For master's and doctorate, thesis/dissertation, classroom teaching, comprehensive exam, registration. *Entrance requirements:* For master's and doctorate, GRE General Test. Additional exam requirements/recommendations for international students: Required—TOEFL (minimum score 525 paper-based; 193 computer-based). *Application deadline:* Applications are processed on a rolling basis. Application fee: $35. Tuition, nonresident: full-time $4,071. Required fees: $493. *Financial support:* In 2003–04, 1 student received support, including 1 fellowship with full tuition reimbursement available (averaging $16,000 per year), 3 research assistantships with full tuition reimbursements available (averaging $13,500 per year); Federal Work-Study, institutionally sponsored loans, and scholarships/grants also available. Financial award application deadline: 3/15. *Faculty research:* Microclimate, nitrogen management, landscape studies, water quality, soil management. *Unit head:* Dr. Jimmie L. Richardson, Chair, 701-231-8903, Fax: 701-231-7861, E-mail: jimmie.richardson@ndsu.nodak.edu.

Nova Scotia Agricultural College, Research and Graduate Studies, Truro, NS B2N 5E3, Canada. Offers agriculture (M Sc), including air quality, animal behavior, animal molecular genetics, animal nutrition, animal technology, aquaculture, botany, crop management, crop physiology, ecology, environmental microbiology, food science, horticulture, nutrient management, pest management, physiology, plant biotechnology, plant pathology, soil chemistry, soil fertility, waste management and composting, water quality. Part-time programs available. *Faculty:* 38 full-time (5 women), 13 part-time/adjunct (1 woman). *Students:* 46 full-time (27 women), 21 part-time (13 women); includes 13 minority (10 African Americans, 2 American Indian/Alaska Native, 1 Asian American or Pacific Islander). 45 applicants, 58% accepted, 16

Agronomy and Soil Sciences

Nova Scotia Agricultural College (continued)

enrolled. In 2003, 11 degrees awarded, leading to university research/teaching 18%, continued full-time study36%, business/industry 9%, government 27%. *Median time to degree:* Master's–2.25 years full-time, 4 years part-time. *Degree requirements:* For master's, thesis, candidacy exam. *Entrance requirements:* For master's, B.Sc. honors degree, minimum GPA of 3.0. Additional exam requirements/recommendations for international students: Required—TOEFL (minimum score 580 paper-based; 237 computer-based), Michigan English Language Assessment Battery. *Application deadline:* For fall admission, 6/1 for domestic students, 4/1 for international students; for winter admission, 11/15 for domestic students; for spring admission, 2/28 for domestic students. Applications are processed on a rolling basis. Application fee: $70. *Expenses:* Tuition, state resident: full-time $6,270. Tuition, nonresident: full-time $9,270. Required fees: $402. Tuition and fees vary according to student level. *Financial support:* In 2003–04, 63 students received support, including research assistantships (averaging $15,000 per year), teaching assistantships (averaging $900 per year); career-related internships or fieldwork, scholarships/grants, and unspecified assistantships also available. *Faculty research:* Organogenesis, somatic embryogenesis, composting, sustainable agriculture, ecotoxicology. Total annual research expenditures: $2 million. *Unit head:* Jill L. Rogers, Manager, 902-893-6360, Fax: 902-893-3430, E-mail: jrogers@nsac.ns.ca. *Application contact:* Marie Law, Administrative Assistant, 902-893-6502, Fax: 902-893-3430, E-mail: mlaw@nsac.ns.ca.

The Ohio State University, Graduate School, College of Food, Agricultural, and Environmental Sciences, School of Natural Resources, Program in Soil Science, Columbus, OH 43210. Offers MS, PhD. *Faculty:* 17. *Students:* 12 full-time (5 women), 2 part-time (both women), 6 international. 29 applicants, 31% accepted. In 2003, 1 master's, 1 doctorate awarded. *Degree requirements:* For doctorate, thesis/dissertation. *Entrance requirements:* For master's and doctorate, GRE General Test. *Application deadline:* For fall admission, 8/15 for domestic students. Applications are processed on a rolling basis. Application fee: $40 ($50 for international students). *Expenses:* Tuition, state resident: full-time $7,233. Tuition, nonresident: full-time $18,489. *Unit head:* Dr. Warren A. Dick, Graduate Studies Committee Chair, 614-263-3877, Fax: 614-292-7162, E-mail: dick.5@osu.edu.

Oklahoma State University, Graduate College, College of Agricultural Sciences and Natural Resources, Department of Horticulture and Landscape Architecture, Stillwater, OK 74078. Offers crop science (PhD); horticulture (M Ag, MS). *Faculty:* 20 full-time (1 woman), 3 part-time/adjunct (1 woman). *Students:* 4 full-time (2 women), 4 part-time (1 woman); includes 2 minority (1 African American, 1 American Indian/Alaska Native), 4 international. Average age 27. 7 applicants, 29% accepted. In 2003, 2 degrees awarded. *Degree requirements:* For master's, thesis or alternative. *Entrance requirements:* Additional exam requirements/recommendations for international students: Required—TOEFL. *Application deadline:* For fall admission, 6/1 for domestic students. Applications are processed on a rolling basis. Application fee: $25 ($50 for international students). Electronic applications accepted. *Expenses:* Tuition, state resident: full-time $3,752; part-time $118 per credit hour. Tuition, nonresident: full-time $10,346; part-time $393 per credit hour. Tuition and fees vary according to course load. *Financial support:* In 2003–04, 9 research assistantships (averaging $12,043 per year) were awarded; teaching assistantships, career-related internships or fieldwork, Federal Work-Study, and tuition waivers (partial) also available. Support available to part-time students. Financial award application deadline: 3/1. *Faculty research:* Stress and postharvest physiology; water utilization and runoff; IPM systems and nursery, turf, floriculture, vegetable, net and fruit produces and natural resources, food extraction, and processing; public garden management. *Unit head:* Dr. Dale Maronek, Head, 405-744-5414, Fax: 405-744-9709, E-mail: maronek@okstate.edu.

Oklahoma State University, Graduate College, College of Agricultural Sciences and Natural Resources, Department of Plant and Soil Sciences, Stillwater, OK 74078. Offers agronomy (M Ag, MS, PhD); crop science (PhD); soil science (PhD). *Faculty:* 34 full-time (1 woman), 2 part-time/adjunct (0 women). *Students:* 18 full-time (6 women), 26 part-time (7 women); includes 1 minority (Hispanic American), 24 international. Average age 31. 20 applicants, 25% accepted. In 2003, 12 master's, 8 doctorates awarded. *Degree requirements:* For master's and doctorate, thesis/dissertation. *Entrance requirements:* Additional exam requirements/recommendations for international students: Required—TOEFL. *Application deadline:* For fall admission, 6/1 for domestic students. Applications are processed on a rolling basis. Application fee: $25 ($50 for international students). Electronic applications accepted. *Expenses:* Tuition, state resident: full-time $3,752; part-time $118 per credit hour. Tuition, nonresident: full-time $10,346; part-time $393 per credit hour. Tuition and fees vary according to course load. *Financial support:* In 2003–04, 49 research assistantships (averaging $14,340 per year), 3 teaching assistantships (averaging $14,773 per year) were awarded. Career-related internships or fieldwork, Federal Work-Study, and tuition waivers (partial) also available. Support available to part-time students. Financial award application deadline: 3/1. *Faculty research:* Crop science, weed science, rangeland ecology and management, biotechnology, breeding and genetics. *Unit head:* Dr. James H. Stiegler, Head, 405-744-6425, Fax: 405-744-5269.

Oregon State University, Graduate School, College of Agricultural Sciences, Department of Crop and Soil Science, Program in Crop Science, Corvallis, OR 97331. Offers M Agr, MAIS, MS, PhD. Part-time programs available. *Students:* 28 full-time (13 women), 3 part-time; includes 2 minority (1 Asian American or Pacific Islander, 1 Hispanic American), 13 international. Average age 29. In 2003, 3 master's, 1 doctorate awarded. *Degree requirements:* For master's, thesis (for some programs); for doctorate, variable foreign language requirement, thesis/dissertation. *Entrance requirements:* For master's and doctorate, GRE, minimum GPA of 3.0 in last 90 hours. Additional exam requirements/recommendations for international students: Required—TOEFL. *Application deadline:* For fall admission, 3/1 for domestic students. Applications are processed on a rolling basis. Application fee: $50. *Expenses:* Tuition, state resident: full-time $8,139; part-time $301 per credit. Tuition, nonresident: full-time $14,376; part-time $532 per credit. Required fees: $1,227. *Financial support:* Fellowships, research assistantships, teaching assistantships, career-related internships or fieldwork, Federal Work-Study, and institutionally sponsored loans available. Support available to part-time students. Financial award application deadline: 2/1. *Faculty research:* Cereal and new crops breeding and genetics; weed science; seed technology and production; potato, new crops, and general crop production; plant physiology. *Unit head:* Patrick Hayes, Head, 541-737-5878, E-mail: hayesp@bcc.orst.edu. *Application contact:* Dr. Alvin Mosely, Associate Professor, 541-737-5835, Fax: 541-737-1589, E-mail: alvin.r.mosely@orst.edu.

Oregon State University, Graduate School, College of Agricultural Sciences, Department of Crop and Soil Science, Program in Soil Science, Corvallis, OR 97331. Offers M Agr, MAIS, MS, PhD. Part-time programs available. *Students:* 22 full-time (11 women), 3 part-time (2 women), 11 international. Average age 29. In 2003, 12 master's, 1 doctorate awarded. *Degree requirements:* For master's, thesis (for some programs); for doctorate, variable foreign language requirement, thesis/dissertation. *Entrance requirements:* For master's and doctorate, GRE, minimum GPA of 3.0 in last 90 hours. Additional exam requirements/recommendations for international students: Required—TOEFL. *Application deadline:* For fall admission, 3/1 for domestic students. Applications are processed on a rolling basis. Application fee: $50. *Expenses:* Tuition, state resident: full-time $8,139; part-time $301 per credit. Tuition, nonresident: full-time $14,376; part-time $532 per credit. Required fees: $1,227. *Financial support:* Fellowships, research assistantships, teaching assistantships, career-related internships or fieldwork, Federal Work-Study, and institutionally sponsored loans available. Support available to part-time students. Financial award application deadline: 2/1. *Faculty research:* Soil physics, chemistry, biology, fertility, and genesis. *Unit head:* David Myrold, Head, 541-737-5737, E-mail: david.myrold@orst.edu. *Application contact:* Dr. Neil W. Christensen, Professor, 541-737-5733, Fax: 541-737-5725, E-mail: neil.w.christensen@orst.edu.

The Pennsylvania State University University Park Campus, Graduate School, College of Agricultural Sciences, Department of Crop and Soil Sciences, Program in Agronomy, State College, University Park, PA 16802-1503. Offers M Agr, MS, PhD. *Students:* 8 full-time (3 women), 3 part-time, 5 international. *Entrance requirements:* For master's and doctorate, GRE General Test. Application fee: $45. *Expenses:* Tuition, state resident: full-time $10,010; part-time $417 per credit. Tuition, nonresident: full-time $19,830; part-time $826 per credit. Full-time tuition and fees vary according to course level, course load, campus/location and program. *Unit head:* Dr. Dan P. Knievel, Associate Professor, 814-865-1547, Fax: 814-863-7043, E-mail: dpk@psu.edu.

The Pennsylvania State University University Park Campus, Graduate School, College of Agricultural Sciences, Department of Crop and Soil Sciences, Program in Soil Science, State College, University Park, PA 16802-1503. Offers M Agr, MS, PhD. *Students:* 14 full-time (6 women), 4 part-time (2 women); includes 1 minority (African American), 8 international. *Entrance requirements:* For master's and doctorate, GRE General Test. Application fee: $45. *Expenses:* Tuition, state resident: full-time $10,010; part-time $417 per credit. Tuition, nonresident: full-time $19,830; part-time $826 per credit. Full-time tuition and fees vary according to course level, course load, campus/location and program. *Unit head:* Dr. Gary R. Peterson, Distinguished Professor, 814-865-0970, Fax: 814-863-7043, E-mail: gwp2@psu.edu.

Prairie View A&M University, Graduate School, College of Agriculture and Human Sciences, Prairie View, TX 77446-0519. Offers agricultural economics (MS); animal sciences (MS); interdisciplinary human sciences (MS); marriage and family therapy (MS); soil science (MS). Part-time and evening/weekend programs available. *Faculty:* 15 full-time (3 women). *Students:* 49 full-time (31 women), 71 part-time (59 women); includes 104 minority (101 African Americans, 2 Asian Americans or Pacific Islanders, 1 Hispanic American), 11 international. Average age 33. *Degree requirements:* For master's, thesis (for some programs), field placement, comprehensive exam. *Entrance requirements:* For master's, GRE General Test. *Application deadline:* Applications are processed on a rolling basis. Application fee: $50. *Expenses:* Tuition, state resident: part-time $50 per credit hour. Tuition, nonresident: part-time $282 per credit hour. Required fees: $36 per credit hour. $51 per term. *Financial support:* In 2003–04, 8 fellowships with tuition reimbursements (averaging $12,000 per year), 10 research assistantships with tuition reimbursements (averaging $15,000 per year) were awarded. Career-related internships or fieldwork, Federal Work-Study, institutionally sponsored loans, and tuition waivers (partial) also available. Financial award application deadline: 4/1; financial award applicants required to submit FAFSA. *Faculty research:* Domestic violence prevention, water quality, food growth regulators. Total annual research expenditures: $4 million. *Unit head:* Dr. Elizabeth Noel, Dean, 936-857-2996, Fax: 936-857-2998, E-mail: elizabeth_noel@pvamu.edu.

Purdue University, Graduate School, College of Agriculture, Department of Agronomy, West Lafayette, IN 47907. Offers MS, PhD. Part-time programs available. *Degree requirements:* For doctorate, thesis/dissertation. *Entrance requirements:* For master's and doctorate, GRE General Test. Additional exam requirements/recommendations for international students: Required—TOEFL. Electronic applications accepted. *Faculty research:* Plant genetics and breeding, crop physiology and ecology, agricultural meteorology, soil microbiology.

South Dakota State University, Graduate School, College of Agriculture and Biological Sciences, Department of Plant Science, Program in Agronomy, Brookings, SD 57007. Offers MS, PhD. *Degree requirements:* For master's, thesis, oral exam; for doctorate, thesis/dissertation, preliminary oral and written exams. *Entrance requirements:* For master's and doctorate, GRE General Test. Additional exam requirements/recommendations for international students: Required—TOEFL. *Faculty research:* Breeding/genetics, weed science, soil science, production agronomy, molecular biology.

Southern Illinois University Carbondale, Graduate School, College of Agriculture, Department of Plant, Soil, and General Agriculture, Carbondale, IL 62901-4701. Offers horticultural science (MS); plant and soil science (MS). *Faculty:* 20 full-time (1 woman). *Students:* 11 full-time (5 women), 34 part-time (11 women), 2 international. 9 applicants, 56% accepted, 1 enrolled. In 2003, 10 degrees awarded. *Degree requirements:* For master's, thesis. *Entrance requirements:* For master's, minimum GPA of 2.7. Additional exam requirements/recommendations for international students: Required—TOEFL. *Application deadline:* Applications are processed on a rolling basis. Application fee: $0. *Expenses:* Tuition, state resident: part-time $478 per hour. Tuition, nonresident: part-time $657 per hour. *Financial support:* In 2003–04, 22 students received support, including 15 research assistantships with full tuition reimbursements available, 6 teaching assistantships with full tuition reimbursements available; fellowships with full tuition reimbursements available, Federal Work-Study, institutionally sponsored loans, and tuition waivers (full) also available. Support available to part-time students. *Faculty research:* Herbicides, fertilizers, agriculture education, landscape design, plant breeding. Total annual research expenditures: $2 million. *Unit head:* John Russin, Chairperson, 618-453-2496.

Southwest Missouri State University, Graduate College, College of Natural and Applied Sciences, Department of Fruit Science, Springfield, MO 65804-0094. Offers MS. *Faculty:* 6 full-time (0 women). *Expenses:* Tuition, state resident: full-time $2,862. Tuition, nonresident: full-time $5,724. *Unit head:* Dr. James Moore, Head, 417-926-4125.

Texas A&M University, College of Agriculture and Life Sciences, Department of Soil and Crop Sciences, College Station, TX 77843. Offers agronomy (M Agr, MS, PhD); food science and technology (M Agr, MS, PhD); genetics (MS, PhD); molecular and environmental plant sciences (MS, PhD); plant breeding (MS, PhD); soil science (MS, PhD). *Faculty:* 20 full-time (0 women). *Students:* 95 full-time (27 women), 33 part-time (4 women); includes 4 minority (2 African Americans, 2 Hispanic Americans), 48 international. Average age 26. 24 applicants, 58% accepted. In 2003, 12 master's, 12 doctorates awarded. *Degree requirements:* For master's and doctorate, thesis/dissertation. *Entrance requirements:* For master's and doctorate, GRE General Test. Additional exam requirements/recommendations for international students: Required—TOEFL. *Application deadline:* For fall admission, 3/1 for domestic students; for spring admission, 8/1 for domestic students. Applications are processed on a rolling basis. Application fee: $50 ($75 for international students). *Expenses:* Tuition, state resident: full-time $3,420. Tuition, nonresident: full-time $9,084. Required fees: $1,861. *Financial support:* In 2003–04, 6 fellowships (averaging $16,000 per year), 49 research assistantships with partial tuition reimbursements (averaging $15,000 per year) were awarded. Career-related internships or fieldwork, Federal Work-Study, institutionally sponsored loans, and health care benefits also available. *Faculty research:* Soil and crop management, turfgrass science, weed science, cereal chemistry, food protein chemistry. *Unit head:* Dr. Mark Hussey, Head, 979-845-3342.

Texas A&M University–Kingsville, College of Graduate Studies, College of Agriculture and Home Economics, Program in Plant and Soil Sciences, Kingsville, TX 78363. Offers MS, PhD. *Degree requirements:* For master's, thesis or alternative, comprehensive exam. *Entrance requirements:* For master's, GRE General Test, minimum GPA of 3.0. Additional exam requirements/recommendations for international students: Required—TOEFL.

Texas Tech University, Graduate School, College of Agricultural Sciences and Natural Resources, Department of Plant and Soil Science, Lubbock, TX 79409. Offers agronomy (PhD); crop science (MS); entomology (MS); horticulture (MS); soil science (MS). Part-time programs available. *Faculty:* 12 full-time (2 women), 1 part-time/adjunct (0 women). *Students:* 39 full-time (13 women), 21 part-time (8 women); includes 1 minority (Asian American or Pacific Islander), 14 international. Average age 32. 18 applicants, 78% accepted, 10 enrolled. In 2003, 13 master's, 6 doctorates awarded. *Degree requirements:* For doctorate, thesis/dissertation. *Entrance requirements:* For master's and doctorate, GRE General Test. Additional exam requirements/recommendations for international students: Required—TOEFL (minimum score 550 paper-based; 213 computer-based). *Application deadline:* Applications are processed on a rolling basis. Application fee: $50 ($60 for international students). Electronic applications accepted. *Expenses:* Tuition, state resident: full-time $3,312. Tuition, nonresident: full-time $8,976. Required fees: $1,745. Tuition and fees vary according to program. *Financial support:* In 2003–04, 44 students received support, including 21 research assistantships with partial tuition reimbursements available (averaging $13,555 per year); teaching assistantships with partial tuition reimbursements available, Federal Work-Study and institutionally sponsored loans also available. Support available to part-time students. Financial award application deadline: 5/1; financial award applicants required to submit FAFSA. *Faculty research:* Molecular and cellular biology of plant stress, physiology/genetics of crop production in semiarid conditions, agricultural bioterrorism, improvement of native plants. Total annual research expenditures: $2.1 million. *Unit head:* Dr. Dick L. Auld, Chair, 806-742-2837, Fax: 806-742-0775, E-mail: dick.auld@ttu.edu. *Application contact:* Dr. Richard E. Zartman, Graduate Adviser, 806-742-2837, Fax: 806-742-0775, E-mail: richard.zartman@ttu.edu.

Tuskegee University, Graduate Programs, College of Agricultural, Environmental and Natural Sciences, Department of Agricultural Sciences, Program in Plant and Soil Sciences, Tuskegee, AL 36088. Offers MS. *Faculty:* 13 full-time (1 woman), 2 part-time/adjunct (1 woman). *Students:* 6 full-time (3 women), 4 part-time (3 women); includes 3 minority (all African Americans), 7 international. Average age 28. *Degree requirements:* For master's, thesis. *Entrance requirements:* For master's, GRE General Test. *Application deadline:* For fall admission, 7/15 for domestic students. Applications are processed on a rolling basis. Application fee: $25 ($35 for international students). *Expenses:* Tuition: Full-time $11,060; part-time $655 per credit hour. Required fees: $250. Tuition and fees vary according to course load. *Financial support:* Application deadline: 4/15.

Université Laval, Faculty of Agricultural and Food Sciences, Department of Soils and Agricultural Engineering, Programs in Soils and Environment Science, Québec, QC G1K 7P4, Canada. Offers environmental technology (M Sc); soils and environment science (M Sc, PhD). Terminal master's awarded for partial completion of doctoral program. *Degree requirements:* For master's, thesis (for some programs); for doctorate, thesis/dissertation, comprehensive exam. *Entrance requirements:* For master's and doctorate, knowledge of French and English. Electronic applications accepted.

Université Laval, Faculty of Forestry and Geomatics, Program in Agroforestry, Québec, QC G1K 7P4, Canada. Offers M Sc. *Degree requirements:* For master's, thesis (for some programs). *Entrance requirements:* For master's, English exam (comprehension of English), knowledge of French, knowledge of a third language. Electronic applications accepted.

University of Alberta, Faculty of Graduate Studies and Research, Department of Renewable Resources, Edmonton, AB T6G 2E1, Canada. Offers agroforestry (M Ag, M Sc, MF); conservation biology (M Sc, PhD); forest biology and management (M Sc, PhD); land reclamation and remediation (M Sc, PhD); protected areas and wildlands management (M Sc, PhD); soil science (M Ag, M Sc, PhD); water and land resources (M Ag, M Sc, PhD); wildlife ecology and management (M Sc, PhD). Part-time programs available. *Faculty:* 26 full-time (4 women), 22 part-time/adjunct (3 women). *Students:* 63 full-time (33 women), 50 part-time (20 women), 14 international. 122 applicants, 24% accepted, 22 enrolled. In 2003, 16 master's, 8 doctorates awarded. *Median time to degree:* Of those who began their doctoral program in fall 1995, 100% received their degree in 8 years or less. *Degree requirements:* For master's, thesis (for some programs); for doctorate, thesis/dissertation, comprehensive exam. *Entrance requirements:* For master's, 2-3 years of relevant professional experiences, minimum GPA of 3.0; for doctorate, minimum GPA of 3.0. Additional exam requirements/recommendations for international students: Required—TOEFL (minimum score 550 paper-based; 213 computer-based). *Application deadline:* For fall admission, 7/1 priority date for domestic students, 6/1 priority date for international students. Applications are processed on a rolling basis. Application fee: $0. Electronic applications accepted. Tuition charges are reported in Canadian dollars. Tuition, nonresident: full-time $3,921 Canadian dollars. International tuition: $7,113 Canadian dollars full-time. *Financial support:* In 2003–04, 63 students received support, including 21 research assistantships with partial tuition reimbursements available (averaging $2,800 per year), 28 teaching assistantships with partial tuition reimbursements available (averaging $1,900 per year); scholarships/grants and unspecified assistantships also available. *Faculty research:* Natural and managed landscapes. Total annual research expenditures: $6.1 million. *Unit head:* Dr. John R. Spence, Chair, 780-492-1426, Fax: 780-492-4323, E-mail: john.spence@ualberta.ca. *Application contact:* Sandy Nakashima, Graduate Program Secretary, 780-492-2820, Fax: 780-492-4323, E-mail: sandy.nakashima@ualberta.ca.

The University of Arizona, Graduate College, College of Agriculture and Life Sciences, Department of Soil, Water and Environmental Science, Tucson, AZ 85721. Offers MS, PhD. *Faculty:* 18 full-time (2 women). *Students:* 58 full-time (28 women), 15 part-time (7 women); includes 8 minority (2 African Americans, 2 Asian Americans or Pacific Islanders, 4 Hispanic Americans). Average age 32. 29 applicants, 52% accepted, 9 enrolled. In 2003, 6 master's, 3 doctorates awarded. *Degree requirements:* For master's, thesis; for doctorate, one foreign language, thesis/dissertation. *Entrance requirements:* Additional exam requirements/recommendations for international students: Required—TOEFL. *Application deadline:* For fall admission, 3/1 for domestic students. Applications are processed on a rolling basis. Application fee: $50. *Expenses:* Tuition, state resident: part-time $196 per unit. Tuition, nonresident: part-time $326 per unit. *Financial support:* In 2003–04, 5 students received support, including research assistantships (averaging $16,000 per year), teaching assistantships (averaging $16,000 per year); Federal Work-Study, institutionally sponsored loans, scholarships/grants, and tuition waivers (full and partial) also available. Financial award application deadline: 5/1. *Faculty research:* Plant production, environmental microbiology, contaminant flow and transport. Total annual research expenditures: $2.8 million. *Unit head:* Dr. Jeffery C. Silvertooth, Head, 520-621-7228, Fax: 520-621-1647, E-mail: silver@ag.arizona.edu. *Application contact:* Judi Ellwanger, Graduate Coordinator, 520-621-1646, Fax: 520-621-1647, E-mail: ellwangr@ag.arizona.edu.

University of Arkansas, Graduate School, Dale Bumpers College of Agricultural, Food and Life Sciences, Department of Crop, Soil and Environmental Sciences, Fayetteville, AR 72701-1201. Offers agronomy (MS, PhD). *Students:* 35 full-time (8 women), 15 part-time (4 women); includes 4 minority (3 African Americans, 1 Asian American or Pacific Islander), 13 international. 39 applicants, 36% accepted. In 2003, 3 master's, 6 doctorates awarded. *Degree requirements:* For master's, thesis optional; for doctorate, variable foreign language requirement, thesis/dissertation. Application fee: $40 ($50 for international students). *Expenses:* Tuition, state resident: full-time $4,032; part-time $224 per credit hour. Tuition, nonresident: full-time $9,540; part-time $530 per credit hour. Tuition and fees vary according to course load and program. *Financial support:* In 2003–04, 9 fellowships, 32 research assistantships, 2 teaching assistantships were awarded. Career-related internships or fieldwork and Federal Work-Study also available. Support available to part-time students. Financial award application deadline: 4/1; financial award applicants required to submit FAFSA. *Unit head:* Dr. James Barrentine, Chair, 479-575-2347, E-mail: gfry@comp.uark.edu.

The University of British Columbia, Faculty of Graduate Studies, Faculty of Agricultural Sciences, Program in Soil Science, Vancouver, BC V6T 1Z1, Canada. Offers M Sc, PhD. *Faculty:* 8 full-time (0 women), 5 part-time/adjunct (2 women). *Students:* 11 full-time (7 women). Average age 25. 9 applicants, 22% accepted, 2 enrolled. In 2003, 2 master's, 1 doctorate awarded. *Median time to degree:* Doctorate–5 years full-time. *Degree requirements:* For master's, thesis/dissertation, registration; for doctorate, thesis/dissertation, comprehensive exam, registration. *Entrance requirements:* Additional exam requirements/recommendations for international students: Required—TOEFL (minimum score 560 paper-based; 220 computer-based). *Application deadline:* For fall admission, 3/30 for domestic students, 2/28 for international students; for winter admission, 8/31 for domestic students; for spring admission, 12/31 for domestic students. Applications are processed on a rolling basis. Application fee: $90 Canadian dollars ($150 Canadian dollars for international students). Electronic applications accepted. *Financial support:* In 2003–04, 4 fellowships (averaging $17,925 per year) were awarded; research assistantships, teaching assistantships, institutionally sponsored loans, scholarships/grants, and tuition waivers (full and partial) also available. *Faculty research:* Soil and water conservation, land use, land use and land classification, remote sensing, soil physics, soil chemistry and mineralogy. Total annual research expenditures: $522,194. *Unit head:* Dr. Chris Chanway, Graduate Advisor, Fax: 604-822-4400, E-mail: gradapp@interchange.ubc.ca. *Application contact:* Alina Yuhymets, Graduate Programs Manager, 604-822-4593, Fax: 604-822-4400, E-mail: yuhymets@interchange.ubc.ca.

University of California, Davis, Graduate Studies, Graduate Group in Horticulture and Agronomy, Davis, CA 95616. Offers MS. *Faculty:* 90 full-time. *Students:* 43 full-time (28 women); includes 2 minority (1 American Indian/Alaska Native, 1 Asian American or Pacific Islander), 12 international. Average age 31. 41 applicants, 46% accepted, 13 enrolled. In 2003, 8 degrees awarded. *Degree requirements:* For master's, thesis optional. *Entrance requirements:* For master's, GRE General Test. Additional exam requirements/recommendations for international students: Required—TOEFL (minimum score 550 paper-based; 213 computer-based). *Application deadline:* For fall admission, 4/1 for domestic students, 3/1 for international students. Applications are processed on a rolling basis. Application fee: $60. Electronic applications accepted. Tuition, nonresident: full-time $12,245. Required fees: $7,062. *Financial support:* In 2003–04, 36 students received support, including 21 fellowships with full and partial tuition reimbursements available (averaging $2,249 per year), 23 research assistantships with full and partial tuition reimbursements available (averaging $9,988 per year), 6 teaching assistantships with partial tuition reimbursements available (averaging $11,788 per year); career-related internships or fieldwork, Federal Work-Study, institutionally sponsored loans, scholarships/grants, and tuition waivers (full and partial) also available. Financial award application deadline: 1/15; financial award applicants required to submit FAFSA. *Faculty research:* Postharvest physiology, mineral nutrition, crop improvement, plant growth and development. *Unit head:* M. Andrew Walker, Chairperson, 530-752-0902, Fax: 530-752-0382, E-mail: awalker@ucdavis.edu. *Application contact:* Lisa Brown, Graduate Group Secretary, 530-752-7738, Fax: 530-752-1819, E-mail: lfbrown@ucdavis.edu.

University of California, Davis, Graduate Studies, Graduate Group in Soil Science, Davis, CA 95616. Offers MS, PhD. *Faculty:* 45 full-time. *Students:* 40 full-time (20 women); includes 4 minority (2 Asian Americans or Pacific Islanders, 2 Hispanic Americans), 5 international. Average age 30. 27 applicants, 67% accepted, 17 enrolled. In 2003, 3 master's, 2 doctorates awarded. Terminal master's awarded for partial completion of doctoral program. *Degree requirements:* For master's, thesis optional; for doctorate, thesis/dissertation. *Entrance requirements:* For master's, minimum GPA of 3.3; for doctorate, GRE, minimum GPA of 3.3. Additional exam requirements/recommendations for international students: Required—TOEFL (minimum score 550 paper-based; 213 computer-based). *Application deadline:* For fall admission, 1/15 for domestic students, 1/15 for international students. Applications are processed on a rolling basis. Application fee: $60. Electronic applications accepted. Tuition, nonresident: full-time $12,245. Required fees: $7,062. *Financial support:* In 2003–04, 36 students received support, including 1 fellowship with full and partial tuition reimbursement available (averaging $20,000 per year), 27 research assistantships with full and partial tuition reimbursements available (averaging $11,410 per year), 2 teaching assistantships with partial tuition reimbursements available (averaging $14,145 per year); career-related internships or fieldwork, Federal Work-Study, institutionally sponsored loans, scholarships/grants, and tuition waivers (full and partial) also available. Support available to part-time students. Financial award application deadline: 1/15; financial award applicants required to submit FAFSA. *Faculty research:* Rhizosphere ecology, soil transport processes, biogeochemical cycling, sustainable agriculture. *Unit head:* William Horwath, Chair, 530-752-6029, Fax: 530-752-5262, E-mail: wrhorwath@ucdavis.edu. *Application contact:* Noeu Leung, Graduate Staff Adviser, 530-752-1669, Fax: 530-752-1552, E-mail: lawradvising@ucdavis.edu.

University of California, Riverside, Graduate Division, Program in Soil and Water Sciences, Riverside, CA 92521-0102. Offers MS, PhD. *Faculty:* 26 full-time (4 women). *Students:* 14 full-time (6 women); includes 3 minority (1 Asian American or Pacific Islander, 2 Hispanic Americans), 1 international. Average age 26. 22 applicants, 50% accepted, 6 enrolled. In 2003, 4 master's, 4 doctorates awarded. *Median time to degree:* Master's–3 years full-time; doctorate–5 years full-time. *Entrance requirements:* For master's and doctorate, minimum GPA of 3.2. Additional exam requirements/recommendations for international students: Required—TOEFL (minimum score 550 paper-based; 213 computer-based); Recommended—TSE. *Application deadline:* For fall admission, 5/1 for domestic students, 2/1 for international students; for winter admission, 9/1 for domestic students; for spring admission, 12/1 for domestic students. Application fee: $60. Electronic applications accepted. Tuition, nonresident: part-time $4,082 per quarter. *Financial support:* In 2003–04, fellowships (averaging $12,000 per year) *Unit head:* Dr. Walter J. Farmer, Chair, 951-827-5116, Fax: 951-827-3993, E-mail: wfarmer@citrus.ucr.edu. *Application contact:* Mari Ridgeway, Student Affairs Officer, 951-827-5103, Fax: 951-827-3993, E-mail: soilwatr@ucr.edu.

University of Connecticut, Graduate School, College of Agriculture and Natural Resources, Department of Plant Science, Field of Plant Science, Storrs, CT 06269. Offers plant and soil sciences (MS, PhD). *Faculty:* 25 full-time (5 women). *Students:* 18 full-time (8 women), 8 part-time (3 women), 11 international. Average age 33. 15 applicants, 73% accepted, 4 enrolled. In 2003, 4 master's, 4 doctorates awarded. Terminal master's awarded for partial completion of doctoral program. *Degree requirements:* For master's, comprehensive exam; for doctorate, thesis/dissertation. *Entrance requirements:* For master's and doctorate, GRE General Test, GRE Subject Test. Additional exam requirements/recommendations for international students: Required—TOEFL (minimum score 550 paper-based; 213 computer-based). *Application deadline:* For fall admission, 2/1 priority date for domestic students, 2/1 priority date for international students; for spring admission, 11/1 for domestic students, 10/1 for international students. Applications are processed on a rolling basis. Application fee: $55. Electronic applications accepted. *Expenses:* Tuition, state resident: part-time $3,860 per semester. Tuition, nonresident: part-time $9,036 per semester. *Financial support:* In 2003–04, 13 research assistantships with full tuition reimbursements, 5 teaching assistantships with full tuition reimbursements were awarded. Fellowships, Federal Work-Study, scholarships/grants, health care benefits, and unspecified assistantships also available. Financial award application deadline: 2/1; financial award applicants required to submit FAFSA. *Application contact:* George C. Elliott, Chairperson, 860-486-1938, Fax: 860-486-0682, E-mail: george.elliott@uconn.edu.

University of Delaware, College of Agriculture and Natural Resources, Department of Plant and Soil Sciences, Newark, DE 19716. Offers MS, PhD. Part-time programs available. *Students:* 35 full-time (18 women), 4 part-time (2 women), 9 international. Average age 29. 34 applicants, 41% accepted, 12 enrolled. In 2003, 4 master's, 4 doctorates awarded. Terminal master's awarded for partial completion of doctoral program. *Degree requirements:* For master's and doctorate, thesis/dissertation. *Entrance requirements:* For master's and doctorate, GRE General Test. Additional exam requirements/recommendations for international students: Required—TOEFL (minimum score 550 paper-based; 213 computer-based). *Application deadline:* For fall admission, 7/1 for domestic students. Application fee: $60. Electronic applications accepted. *Expenses:* Tuition, state resident: full-time $5,890; part-time $327 per credit. Tuition, nonresident: full-time $15,420; part-time $857 per credit. Required fees: $968. *Financial support:* In 2003–04, 26 students received support, including 1 fellowship with full tuition reimbursement available (averaging $15,000 per year), 19 research assistantships with full tuition reimbursements available (averaging $13,500 per year), 3 teaching assistantships with full tuition reimbursements available (averaging $11,000 per year); career-related internships or fieldwork also available. Financial award application deadline: 3/1. *Faculty research:* Soil chemistry, plant and cell tissue culture, plant breeding and genetics, soil physics, soil biochemistry, plant molecular biology, soil microbiology. Total annual research expenditures: $3.8 million. *Unit head:* Dr. Donald L. Sparks, Chair, 302-831-2532, Fax: 302-831-3651, E-mail: dlsparks@udel.edu. *Application contact:* Dr. Robert Carroll, Graduate Coordinator, 302-831-2534, E-mail: rbc@udel.edu.

University of Florida, Graduate School, College of Agricultural and Life Sciences, Department of Agronomy, Gainesville, FL 32611. Offers MS, PhD. *Faculty:* 50. *Students:* 27 full-time (10 women), 6 part-time (2 women), 14 international. 20 applicants, 65% accepted. In 2003, 10 master's, 3 doctorates awarded. *Degree requirements:* For master's, thesis optional; for doctorate, thesis/dissertation. *Entrance requirements:* For master's and doctorate, GRE General Test, minimum GPA of 3.0. Additional exam requirements/recommendations for international

Agronomy and Soil Sciences

University of Florida (continued)

students: Required—TOEFL. *Application deadline:* For fall admission, 6/1 for domestic students. Applications are processed on a rolling basis. Application fee: $20. Electronic applications accepted. *Expenses:* Tuition, state resident: part-time $205 per credit hour. Tuition, nonresident: part-time $775 per credit hour. *Financial support:* In 2003–04, 1 fellowship, 15 research assistantships were awarded. Teaching assistantships, career-related internships or fieldwork, institutionally sponsored loans, and unspecified assistantships also available. *Faculty research:* Genetics and plant breeding, aquatic and terrestrial weed science, plant physiology, molecular biology, forage and crop production. *Unit head:* Dr. J. M. Bennett, Chair, 352-392-1811 Ext. 202, Fax: 352-392-1840, E-mail: jmbt@gnv.ifas.ufl.edu. *Application contact:* Dr. D. S. Wofford, Coordinator, 352-392-1823 Ext. 205, Fax: 352-392-7248, E-mail: dsw@mail.ifas.ufl.edu.

University of Florida, Graduate School, College of Agricultural and Life Sciences, Department of Soil and Water Science, Gainesville, FL 32611. Offers M Ag, MS, PhD. Part-time programs available. *Faculty:* 53. *Students:* 62 full-time (24 women), 16 part-time (2 women); includes 6 minority (3 African Americans, 3 Hispanic Americans), 33 international. 27 applicants, 78% accepted. In 2003, 11 master's, 1 doctorate awarded. Terminal master's awarded for partial completion of doctoral program. *Degree requirements:* For master's, thesis optional; for doctorate, thesis/dissertation. *Entrance requirements:* For master's and doctorate, GRE General Test, minimum GPA of 3.0. Additional exam requirements/recommendations for international students: Required—TOEFL. *Application deadline:* For fall admission, 6/1 for domestic students; for spring admission, 9/14 for domestic students. Applications are processed on a rolling basis. Application fee: $20. Electronic applications accepted. *Expenses:* Tuition, state resident: part-time $205 per credit hour. Tuition, nonresident: part-time $775 per credit hour. *Financial support:* In 2003–04, 33 students received support, including 24 research assistantships, 2 teaching assistantships; fellowships, career-related internships or fieldwork, Federal Work-Study, institutionally sponsored loans, and unspecified assistantships also available. Support available to part-time students. *Faculty research:* Environmental fate and transport of pesticides, conservation, wetlands, land application of nonhazardous waste, soil/water agrochemical management. *Unit head:* Dr. K. Ramesh Reddy, Chair and Graduate Research Professor, 352-392-1803 Ext. 341, Fax: 352-392-3399, E-mail: krr@ufl.edu. *Application contact:* Dr. Nicholas B. Comerford, Graduate Coordinator and Professor, 352-392-1951 Ext. 248, Fax: 352-392-3902, E-mail: nbc@mail.ifas.ufl.edu.

University of Georgia, Graduate School, College of Agricultural and Environmental Sciences, Department of Crop and Soil Sciences, Athens, GA 30602. Offers agronomy (MS, PhD); crop and soil sciences (MCCS); plant protection and pest management (MPPPM). Part-time programs available. *Faculty:* 17 full-time (2 women). *Students:* 23 full-time (9 women), 5 part-time (2 women); includes 1 minority (Asian American or Pacific Islander), 8 international. Average age 24. 13 applicants, 38% accepted, 4 enrolled. In 2003, 7 master's, 4 doctorates awarded. *Median time to degree:* Master's–2.1 years full-time; doctorate–4.1 years full-time. *Degree requirements:* For master's, thesis (MS); for doctorate, thesis/dissertation, comprehensive exam. *Entrance requirements:* For master's and doctorate, GRE General Test. Additional exam requirements/recommendations for international students: Required—TOEFL (minimum score 550 paper-based; 213 computer-based). *Application deadline:* For fall admission, 7/1 priority date for domestic students, 4/15 priority date for international students; for spring admission, 11/15 for domestic students, 10/15 for international students. Applications are processed on a rolling basis. Application fee: $50. Electronic applications accepted. *Expenses:* Tuition, state resident: part-time $161 per hour. Tuition, nonresident: part-time $690 per hour. One-time fee: $435 part-time. *Financial support:* In 2003–04, research assistantships with full tuition reimbursements (averaging $14,600 per year), teaching assistantships with full tuition reimbursements (averaging $15,350 per year) were awarded. Fellowships, scholarships/grants, tuition waivers (full), and unspecified assistantships also available. *Faculty research:* Plant breeding, genomics, nutrient management, water quality, soil chemistry. *Unit head:* Dr. Donn Shilling, Head, 706-542-0906, Fax: 706-542-0914. *Application contact:* Dr. Miquel L. Cabrera, Graduate Coordinator, 706-542-1242, Fax: 706-542-0914, E-mail: mcabrera@uga.edu.

University of Guelph, Graduate Program Services, Ontario Agricultural College, Department of Land Resource Science, Guelph, ON N1G 2W1, Canada. Offers atmospheric science (M Sc, PhD); environmental and agricultural earth sciences (M Sc, PhD); land resources management (M Sc, PhD); soil science (M Sc, PhD). Part-time programs available. *Faculty:* 19 full-time (5 women), 3 part-time/adjunct (0 women). *Students:* 47 full-time (24 women), 3 part-time; includes 1 African American, 6 Asian Americans or Pacific Islanders, 2 Hispanic Americans, 2 international. Average age 28. 24 applicants, 46% accepted. In 2003, 9 master's, 4 doctorates awarded. *Degree requirements:* For master's and doctorate, thesis/dissertation. *Entrance requirements:* For master's, minimum B- average during previous 2 years; for doctorate, minimum B average during previous 2 years. Additional exam requirements/recommendations for international students: Required—TOEFL (minimum score 550 paper-based; 213 computer-based). *Application deadline:* For fall admission, 7/1 priority date for domestic students, 5/1 priority date for international students; for winter admission, 10/1 for domestic students; for spring admission, 3/1 for domestic students. Applications are processed on a rolling basis. Application fee: $75 Canadian dollars. Electronic applications accepted. Tuition and fees charges are reported in Canadian dollars. Tuition, nonresident: full-time $3,440 Canadian dollars. International tuition: $5,432 Canadian dollars full-time. Required fees: $753 Canadian dollars. *Financial support:* In 2003–04, 30 students received support, including 40 research assistantships (averaging $16,500 Canadian dollars per year), 15 teaching assistantships (averaging $3,800 Canadian dollars per year); fellowships, scholarships/grants also available. *Faculty research:* Soil science, environmental earth science, land resource management. Total annual research expenditures: $2.1 million Canadian dollars. *Unit head:* Dr. S. Hilts, Chairman, 519-824-4120 Ext. 52447, Fax: 519-824-5730, E-mail: shilts@uoguelph.ca. *Application contact:* Dr. T. J. Gillespie, Graduate Coordinator, 519-824-4120 Ext. 54276, Fax: 519-824-5730, E-mail: tgillesp@lrs.uoguelph.ca.

University of Idaho, College of Graduate Studies, College of Agriculture and Life Sciences, Department of Plant, Soil, and Entomological Sciences, Moscow, ID 83844-2282. Offers entomology (MS, PhD); plant protection (MS, PhD); plant science (MS, PhD); soil science (MS, PhD). *Students:* 51 full-time (18 women), 23 part-time (5 women); includes 4 minority (all Hispanic Americans), 16 international. Average age 29. *Degree requirements:* For doctorate, thesis/dissertation. *Entrance requirements:* For master's and doctorate, GRE General Test, minimum GPA of 3.0. *Application deadline:* For fall admission, 7/1 for domestic students; for spring admission, 11/1 for domestic students. Application fee: $55 ($60 for international students). *Expenses:* Tuition, state resident: full-time $3,348. Tuition, nonresident: full-time $10,740. Required fees: $540. *Financial support:* Research assistantships, teaching assistantships available. Financial award application deadline: 2/15. *Application contact:* Dr. Joseph McCaffrey, Graduate Director, 208-885-7548.

See in-depth description on page 683.

University of Illinois at Urbana–Champaign, Graduate College, College of Agricultural, Consumer and Environmental Sciences, Department of Crop Sciences, Champaign, IL 61820. Offers MS, PhD. *Faculty:* 35 full-time (4 women). *Students:* 64 full-time (25 women), 24 international. 45 applicants, 36% accepted, 15 enrolled. In 2003, 28 master's, 8 doctorates awarded. *Degree requirements:* For master's and doctorate, thesis/dissertation, comprehensive exam. *Entrance requirements:* For master's, GRE, minimum GPA of 3.0. *Application deadline:* For fall admission, 2/15 for domestic students. Applications are processed on a rolling basis. Application fee: $40 ($50 for international students). Electronic applications accepted. *Expenses:* Tuition, state resident: full-time $6,692. Tuition, nonresident: full-time $18,692. *Financial support:* In 2003–04, 10 fellowships, 47 research assistantships, 2 teaching assistantships were awarded. Tuition waivers (full and partial) also available. Financial award application deadline: 2/15. *Faculty research:* Plant breeding and genetics, molecular biology, crop production, plant physiology, weed science. *Unit head:* Gary H. Heichel, Head, 217-333-9480, Fax: 217-333-9817, E-mail: gheichel@uiuc.edu. *Application contact:* Carol A. Phillippe, Secretary, 217-244-0396, Fax: 217-333-9187, E-mail: cphilli1@uiuc.edu.

University of Kentucky, Graduate School, Graduate School Programs in the College of Agriculture, Program in Crop Science, Lexington, KY 40506-0032. Offers MS, MS Ag, PhD. *Faculty:* 18 full-time (0 women). *Students:* 11 full-time (6 women), 8 part-time (2 women), 12 international. 22 applicants, 45% accepted, 1 enrolled. In 2003, 2 master's, 3 doctorates awarded. *Degree requirements:* For master's, thesis optional; for doctorate, thesis/dissertation, comprehensive exam. *Entrance requirements:* For master's, GRE General Test, minimum GPA of 2.5; for doctorate, GRE General Test, minimum GPA of 3.0. Additional exam requirements/recommendations for international students: Required—TOEFL (minimum score 550 paper-based; 213 computer-based). *Application deadline:* For fall admission, 7/18 for domestic students, 2/1 for international students. Applications are processed on a rolling basis. Application fee: $35 ($45 for international students). *Expenses:* Tuition, state resident: full-time $4,975; part-time $261 per credit hour. Tuition, nonresident: full-time $12,315; part-time $668 per credit hour. *Financial support:* Fellowships, research assistantships available. *Faculty research:* Crop physiology, crop ecology, crop management, crop breeding and genetics, weed science. Total annual research expenditures: $8 million. *Unit head:* Dr. David Van Sanford, Director of Graduate Studies, 859-257-5811, E-mail: agr038@pop.uky.edu. *Application contact:* Dr. Brian Jackson, Associate Dean, 859-257-4905, Fax: 859-323-1928.

University of Kentucky, Graduate School, Graduate School Programs in the College of Agriculture, Program in Plant and Soil Science, Lexington, KY 40506-0032. Offers MS. *Faculty:* 26 full-time (2 women). *Students:* 22 full-time (12 women), 7 part-time (3 women), 6 international. 30 applicants, 40% accepted, 10 enrolled. In 2003, 10 degrees awarded. *Degree requirements:* For master's, thesis optional. *Entrance requirements:* For master's, GRE General Test, minimum GPA of 2.5 (undergraduate), 3.0 (graduate). Additional exam requirements/recommendations for international students: Required—TOEFL (minimum score 550 paper-based; 213 computer-based). *Application deadline:* For fall admission, 7/18 for domestic students, 2/1 for international students. Application fee: $35 ($45 for international students). *Expenses:* Tuition, state resident: full-time $4,975; part-time $261 per credit hour. Tuition, nonresident: full-time $12,315; part-time $668 per credit hour. *Financial support:* Fellowships, research assistantships, unspecified assistantships available. *Unit head:* Dr. Michael Collins, Director of Graduate Studies, 859-257-3358, Fax: 859-323-1952, E-mail: mcollins@ca.uky.edu. *Application contact:* Dr. Brian Jackson, Associate Dean, 859-257-4905, Fax: 859-323-1928.

University of Kentucky, Graduate School, Graduate School Programs in the College of Agriculture, Program in Soil Science, Lexington, KY 40506-0032. Offers PhD. *Faculty:* 3 full-time (0 women). *Students:* 7 full-time (3 women), 4 part-time (2 women), 6 international. 12 applicants, 33% accepted, 2 enrolled. In 2003, 2 degrees awarded. *Degree requirements:* For doctorate, thesis/dissertation, comprehensive exam. *Entrance requirements:* For doctorate, GRE General Test, minimum graduate GPA of 3.0. Additional exam requirements/recommendations for international students: Required—TOEFL (minimum score 550 paper-based; 213 computer-based). *Application deadline:* For fall admission, 7/18 for domestic students, 2/1 for international students. Applications are processed on a rolling basis. Application fee: $35 ($45 for international students). *Expenses:* Tuition, state resident: full-time $4,975; part-time $261 per credit hour. Tuition, nonresident: full-time $12,315; part-time $668 per credit hour. *Financial support:* Fellowships, research assistantships, teaching assistantships, Federal Work-Study and institutionally sponsored loans available. Support available to part-time students. *Faculty research:* Soil fertility and plant nutrition, soil chemistry and physics, soil genesis and morphology, soil management and conservation, water and environmental quality. *Unit head:* Dr. John Grove, Director of Graduate Studies, 859-257-5852, Fax: 859-257-2185, E-mail: jgrove@ca.uky.edu. *Application contact:* Dr. Brian Jackson, Associate Dean, 859-257-4905, Fax: 859-323-1928.

University of Maine, Graduate School, College of Natural Sciences, Forestry, and Agriculture, Department of Plant, Soil, and Environmental Sciences, Orono, ME 04469. Offers biological sciences (PhD); ecology and environmental sciences (MS, PhD); forest resources (PhD); horticulture (MS); plant science (PhD); plant, soil, and environmental sciences (MS); resource utilization (MS). *Students:* 20 full-time (14 women), 8 part-time (5 women); includes 1 minority (Asian American or Pacific Islander), 2 international. Average age 31. 12 applicants, 42% accepted, 5 enrolled. In 2003, 2 degrees awarded. *Entrance requirements:* For master's and doctorate, GRE General Test. Additional exam requirements/recommendations for international students: Required—TOEFL. *Application deadline:* Applications are processed on a rolling basis. Application fee: $50. Electronic applications accepted. *Expenses:* Tuition, state resident: part-time $235 per credit. Tuition, nonresident: part-time $670 per credit. Tuition and fees vary according to course load. *Financial support:* In 2003–04, 9 research assistantships with tuition reimbursements (averaging $12,180 per year) were awarded; teaching assistantships, scholarships/grants, tuition waivers (full and partial), and unspecified assistantships also available. *Unit head:* Dr. M. Susan Erich, Chair, 207-581-2938, Fax: 207-581-3207. *Application contact:* Scott G. Delcourt, Associate Dean of the Graduate School, 207-581-3218, Fax: 207-581-3232, E-mail: graduate@maine.edu.

University of Manitoba, Faculty of Graduate Studies, Faculty of Agriculture, Department of Soil Science, Winnipeg, MB R3T 2N2, Canada. Offers M Sc, PhD. *Degree requirements:* For master's, thesis; for doctorate, one foreign language, thesis/dissertation. Tuition charges are reported in Canadian dollars. Tuition, nonresident: full-time $3,878 Canadian dollars.

University of Maryland, College Park, Graduate Studies and Research, College of Agriculture and Natural Resources, Department of Natural Resource Sciences and Landscape Architecture, Program in Agronomy, College Park, MD 20742. Offers MS, PhD. *Students:* 4 full-time (3 women), 3 part-time (2 women); includes 1 minority (Asian American or Pacific Islander), 1 international. In 2003, 2 degrees awarded. *Degree requirements:* For doctorate, written and oral exams. *Entrance requirements:* Additional exam requirements/recommendations for international students: Required—TOEFL. *Application deadline:* For fall admission, 5/1 for domestic students, 2/1 for international students; for spring admission, 10/1 for domestic students, 6/1 for international students. Applications are processed on a rolling basis. Application fee: $50. Electronic applications accepted. *Expenses:* Tuition, state resident: part-time $349 per credit hour. Tuition, nonresident: part-time $602 per credit hour. *Financial support:* Fellowships, research assistantships, teaching assistantships, career-related internships or fieldwork available. Financial award applicants required to submit FAFSA. *Faculty research:* Cereal crop production, soil and water conservation, turf management, x-ray defraction. *Application contact:* Trudy Lindsey, Director, Graduate Enrollment Management Services, 301-405-4190, Fax: 301-314-9305, E-mail: tlindsey@gradschool.umd.edu.

University of Massachusetts Amherst, Graduate School, College of Natural Resources and the Environment, Department of Plant and Soil Sciences, Amherst, MA 01003. Offers plant science (PhD); soil science (MS, PhD). *Faculty:* 19 full-time (4 women). *Students:* 17 full-time (6 women), 20 part-time (14 women); includes 2 minority (1 African American, 1 Hispanic American), 9 international. Average age 37. 19 applicants, 37% accepted, 6 enrolled. In 2003, 10 master's, 2 doctorates awarded. Terminal master's awarded for partial completion of doctoral program. *Degree requirements:* For master's, thesis optional; for doctorate, thesis/dissertation. *Entrance requirements:* For master's and doctorate, GRE General Test. Additional exam requirements/recommendations for international students: Required—TOEFL (minimum score 530 paper-based; 197 computer-based). *Application deadline:* For fall admission, 2/1 priority date for domestic students, 2/1 priority date for international students; for spring admission, 10/1 for domestic students, 10/1 for international students. Applications are processed on a rolling basis. Application fee: $40 ($50 for international students). *Expenses:* Tuition, state resident: full-time $1,320; part-time $110 per credit. Tuition, nonresident: full-time $4,969; part-time $414 per credit. Required fees: $2,626 per term. Tuition and fees vary according to course load. *Financial support:* In 2003–04, 21 research assistantships with full tuition reimbursements (averaging $5,942 per year), 15 teaching assistantships with full tuition reimbursements (averaging $5,522 per year) were awarded. Fellowships with full tuition reimbursements, career-related internships or fieldwork, Federal Work-Study, scholarships/grants, traineeships, and unspecified assistantships also available. Support available to part-time students. Financial award application deadline: 2/1. *Unit head:* Dr. Petrus Veneman, Director, 413-545-2242, Fax: 413-545-3075, E-mail: veneman@pssci.umass.edu.

University of Minnesota, Twin Cities Campus, Graduate School, College of Agricultural, Food, and Environmental Sciences, Department of Soil, Water, and Climate, Minneapolis, MN 55455-0213. Offers MS, PhD. *Faculty:* 28 full-time (1 woman), 8 part-time/adjunct (0 women). *Students:* 26 full-time (12 women), 2 part-time (both women); includes 1 African American, 6 Asian Americans or Pacific Islanders, 4 Hispanic Americans. Average age 25. 19 applicants, 58% accepted, 9 enrolled. In 2003, 5 degrees awarded. *Median time to degree:* Master's–2.5 years full-time. *Degree requirements:* For master's, thesis or alternative; for doctorate, thesis/dissertation. *Entrance requirements:* For master's and doctorate, GRE General Test, minimum GPA of 3.0. Additional exam requirements/recommendations for international students: Required—TOEFL (minimum score 550 paper-based; 213 computer-based). *Application deadline:* For fall admission, 6/15 for domestic students; for spring admission, 10/15 for domestic students. Applications are processed on a rolling basis. Application fee: $55 ($75 for international students). Electronic applications accepted. *Expenses:* Tuition, state resident: full-time $3,681; part-time $614 per credit. Tuition, nonresident: full-time $7,231; part-time $1,205 per credit. *Financial support:* In 2003–04, 2 fellowships with full tuition reimbursements (averaging $17,000 per year), 24 research assistantships with full and partial tuition reimbursements (averaging $16,000 per year), 2 teaching assistantships with full tuition reimbursements (averaging $16,000 per year) were awarded. Federal Work-Study, scholarships/grants, health care benefits, tuition waivers (full), and unspecified assistantships also available. Support available to part-time students. *Faculty research:* Soil water and atmospheric resources, soil physical management, agricultural chemicals and their management, plant nutrient management, biological nitrogen fixation. *Unit head:* Dr. Edward A. Nater, Head, 612-625-9734, Fax: 612-625-2208, E-mail: enater@umn.edu. *Application contact:* Dr. Deborah L. Allan, Professor and Director of Graduate Studies, 612-625-3158, Fax: 612-625-2208, E-mail: dallan@umn.edu.

University of Missouri–Columbia, Graduate School, College of Agriculture, Food and Natural Resources, Program in Agronomy, Columbia, MO 65211. Offers MS, PhD. *Faculty:* 24 full-time (3 women). *Students:* 20 full-time (7 women), 14 part-time (3 women); includes 1 minority (Hispanic American), 14 international. In 2003, 4 master's, 3 doctorates awarded. Terminal master's awarded for partial completion of doctoral program. *Degree requirements:* For master's and doctorate, thesis/dissertation. *Entrance requirements:* For master's and doctorate, GRE General Test, minimum GPA of 3.0. *Application deadline:* Applications are processed on a rolling basis. Application fee: $45 ($60 for international students). *Expenses:* Tuition, state resident: full-time $5,205. Tuition, nonresident: full-time $14,058. *Financial support:* Research assistantships, teaching assistantships, institutionally sponsored loans available. *Unit head:* Dr. Dale G. Blevins, Director of Graduate Studies, 573-882-4819, E-mail: blevinsd@missouri.edu.

University of Missouri–Columbia, Graduate School, School of Natural Resources, Department of Soil, Environmental, and Atmospheric Sciences, Columbia, MO 65211. Offers atmospheric science (MS); soil science (PhD); spo scoemce (MS); stmospheric science (PhD). *Faculty:* 7 full-time (0 women). *Students:* 12 full-time (3 women), 15 part-time (6 women); includes 1 minority (Asian American or Pacific Islander), 13 international. In 2003, 1 master's, 1 doctorate awarded. *Degree requirements:* For doctorate, thesis/dissertation. *Entrance requirements:* For master's and doctorate, GRE General Test, minimum GPA of 3.0. *Application deadline:* Applications are processed on a rolling basis. Application fee: $45 ($60 for international students). *Expenses:* Tuition, state resident: full-time $5,205. Tuition, nonresident: full-time $14,058. *Financial support:* Fellowships, research assistantships, teaching assistantships, institutionally sponsored loans and scholarships/grants available. *Unit head:* Dr. Anthony Lupo, Director of Graduate Studies, 573-884-1638.

University of Nebraska–Lincoln, Graduate College, College of Agricultural Sciences and Natural Resources, Department of Agronomy and Horticulture, Program in Agronomy, Lincoln, NE 68588. Offers MS, PhD. *Degree requirements:* For master's, thesis/dissertation; for doctorate, thesis/dissertation, comprehensive exam. *Entrance requirements:* Additional exam requirements/recommendations for international students: Required—TOEFL (minimum score 500 paper-based; 173 computer-based). Electronic applications accepted. *Faculty research:* Crop physiology and production, plant breeding and genetics, range and forage management, soil and water science, weed science.

University of New Hampshire, Graduate School, College of Life Sciences and Agriculture, Department of Natural Resources, Durham, NH 03824. Offers environmental conservation (MS); forestry (MS); soil science (MS); water resources management (MS); wildlife (MS). Part-time programs available. *Faculty:* 40 full-time. *Students:* 25 full-time (11 women), 31 part-time (21 women), 5 international. Average age 32. 74 applicants, 38% accepted, 16 enrolled. In 2003, 13 degrees awarded. *Degree requirements:* For master's, thesis or alternative. *Entrance requirements:* For master's, GRE General Test. Additional exam requirements/recommendations for international students: Required—TOEFL (minimum score 550 paper-based; 213 computer-based); Recommended—TSE. *Application deadline:* For fall admission, 4/1 for domestic students; for winter admission, 12/1 for domestic students. Applications are processed on a rolling basis. Application fee: $50. Electronic applications accepted. Tuition, area resident: Full-time $7,070. *Expenses:* Tuition, state resident: full-time $10,605. Tuition, nonresident: full-time $17,430. Required fees: $15. *Financial support:* In 2003–04, 3 fellowships, 15 research assistantships, 12 teaching assistantships were awarded. Career-related internships or fieldwork, Federal Work-Study, scholarships/grants, and tuition waivers (full and partial) also available. Support available to part-time students. Financial award application deadline: 2/15. *Unit head:* Dr. William H. McDowell, Chairperson, 603-862-2249, E-mail: tehoward@cisunix.unh.edu. *Application contact:* Linda Scogin, Administrative Assistant, 603-862-3932, E-mail: natural.resources @unh.edu.

University of Puerto Rico, Mayagüez Campus, Graduate Studies, College of Agricultural Sciences, Department of Agronomy, Mayagüez, PR 00681-9000. Offers crops (MS); soils (MS). Part-time programs available. *Degree requirements:* For master's, thesis, comprehensive exam. *Faculty research:* Soil physics and chemistry, soil management, plant physiology, ecology, plant breeding.

University of Puerto Rico, Mayagüez Campus, Graduate Studies, College of Agricultural Sciences, Department of Crop Protection, Mayagüez, PR 00681-9000. Offers MS. Part-time programs available. *Degree requirements:* For master's, thesis, comprehensive exam. *Faculty research:* Nematology, virology, plant pathology, weed control, peas and soybean seed diseases.

University of Saskatchewan, College of Graduate Studies and Research, College of Agriculture, Department of Soil Science, Saskatoon, SK S7N 5A2, Canada. Offers M Ag, M Sc, PhD. *Faculty:* 27. *Students:* 24. *Degree requirements:* For master's, thesis (for some programs), registration; for doctorate, thesis/dissertation, registration. *Entrance requirements:* Additional exam requirements/recommendations for international students: Required—TOEFL. *Application deadline:* For fall admission, 7/1 for domestic students. Applications are processed on a rolling basis. Application fee: $50. Tuition charges are reported in Canadian dollars. *Expenses:* Tuition, state resident: part-time $483 Canadian dollars per course. *Financial support:* Fellowships, research assistantships, teaching assistantships available. Financial award application deadline: 1/31. *Unit head:* Dr. J. Germida, Head, 306-966-6836, Fax: 306-966-6881, E-mail: germida@sask.usask.ca. *Application contact:* Dr. Fran Walley, Graduate Chair, 306-966-6854, Fax: 306-966-6881, E-mail: walley@sask.usask.ca.

University of Vermont, Graduate College, College of Agriculture and Life Sciences, Department of Plant and Soil Science, Burlington, VT 05405. Offers MS, PhD. *Students:* 18 (8 women); includes 1 minority (Hispanic American) 2 international. 12 applicants, 75% accepted, 3 enrolled. In 2003, 2 degrees awarded. *Degree requirements:* For master's, thesis; for doctorate, one foreign language, thesis/dissertation. *Entrance requirements:* For master's and doctorate, GRE General Test. Additional exam requirements/recommendations for international students: Required—TOEFL (minimum score 550 paper-based; 213 computer-based). *Application deadline:* For fall admission, 4/1 for domestic students; for spring admission, 11/15 for domestic students. Applications are processed on a rolling basis. Application fee: $25. Electronic applications accepted. *Expenses:* Tuition, state resident: part-time $362 per credit hour. Tuition, nonresident: part-time $906 per credit hour. *Financial support:* Fellowships, research assistantships, teaching assistantships available. Financial award application deadline: 3/1. *Faculty research:* Soil chemistry, plant nutrition. *Unit head:* Dr. A. Gotlieb, Chairperson, 802-656-2630. *Application contact:* Dr. M. Starrett, Coordinator, 802-656-2630.

University of Wisconsin–Madison, Graduate School, College of Agricultural and Life Sciences, Department of Agronomy, Madison, WI 53706-1380. Offers MS, PhD. *Faculty:* 21 full-time (2 women). *Students:* 15 full-time (6 women); includes 3 minority (all Hispanic Americans), 1 international. Average age 25. 26 applicants, 12% accepted. In 2003, 2 master's, 2 doctorates awarded. *Degree requirements:* For master's, thesis or alternative; for doctorate, thesis/dissertation. *Entrance requirements:* For master's and doctorate, GRE. Additional exam requirements/recommendations for international students: Required—TOEFL. *Application deadline:* Applications are processed on a rolling basis. Application fee: $45. Electronic applications accepted. Tuition, area resident: Full-time $7,593; part-time $476 per credit. Tuition, nonresident: full-time $22,824; part-time $1,430 per credit. Required fees: $292; $38 per credit. Part-time tuition and fees vary according to course load and reciprocity agreements. *Financial support:* Fellowships, research assistantships available. *Faculty research:* Plant breeding and genetics, plant molecular biology and physiology, cropping systems and management, weed science. *Unit head:* Stanley H. Duke, Chair, 608-262-1390, Fax: 608-262-5217. *Application contact:* Colleen Smith, Graduate Secretary, 608-262-7702, Fax: 608-262-5217, E-mail: clsmith8@facstaff.wisc.edu.

University of Wisconsin–Madison, Graduate School, College of Agricultural and Life Sciences, Department of Soil Science, Madison, WI 53706-1380. Offers MS, PhD. *Faculty:* 22 full-time (4 women). *Students:* 15 full-time (8 women), 2 part-time (1 woman); includes 3 minority (2 African Americans, 1 Hispanic American), 3 international. Average age 29. 30 applicants, 20% accepted, 5 enrolled. In 2003, 8 master's awarded, leading to university research/teaching 25%, continued full-time study37%, business/industry 25%, government 13%; 3 doctorates awarded, leading to university research/teaching 67%, business/industry 33%. *Median time to degree:* Master's–2 years full-time; doctorate–4 years full-time. Of those who began their doctoral program in fall 1995, 100% received their degree in 8 years or less. *Degree requirements:* For master's and doctorate, thesis/dissertation, comprehensive exam, registration. *Entrance requirements:* For master's and doctorate, GRE General Test. Additional exam requirements/recommendations for international students: Required—TOEFL. Application fee: $45. Electronic applications accepted. Tuition, area resident: Full-time $7,593; part-time $476 per credit. Tuition, nonresident: full-time $22,824; part-time $1,430 per credit. Required fees: $292; $38 per credit. Part-time tuition and fees vary according to course load and reciprocity agreements. *Financial support:* In 2003–04, 2 fellowships with full tuition reimbursements (averaging $18,720 per year), 20 research assistantships with full tuition reimbursements (averaging $17,430 per year) were awarded. Federal Work-Study, scholarships/grants, and health care benefits also available. *Faculty research:* Physical chemistry of soil colloids/surfaces, forest biogeochemistry, soil-plant-atmosphere interactions, organic byproducts recycling, microbial metabolism in soil. *Unit head:* Birl Lowery, Chair, 608-263-5691, Fax: 608-265-2595, E-mail: blowery@wisc.edu. *Application contact:* Ann M. Curtis, Information Contact, 608-262-2633, Fax: 608-265-2595, E-mail: amcurtis@wisc.edu.

University of Wyoming, Graduate School, College of Agriculture, Department of Plant Sciences, Program in Agronomy, Laramie, WY 82070. Offers MS, PhD. *Faculty:* 5 full-time (0 women). *Students:* 11 full-time (4 women), 5 part-time (4 women), 3 international. 11 applicants, 73% accepted. In 2003, 3 degrees awarded. *Degree requirements:* For master's and doctorate, thesis/dissertation. *Entrance requirements:* For master's and doctorate, GRE General Test, minimum GPA of 3.0. Additional exam requirements/recommendations for international students: Required—TOEFL (minimum score 525 paper-based; 197 computer-based). *Application deadline:* For fall admission, 6/1 for domestic students. Applications are processed on a rolling basis. Application fee: $40. Electronic applications accepted. *Expenses:* Tuition, state resident: part-time $142 per credit hour. Tuition, nonresident: part-time $408 per credit hour. Required fees: $134 per semester. Tuition and fees vary according to course load, campus/location, program and student level. *Financial support:* In 2003–04, 9 research assistantships with full tuition reimbursements (averaging $10,062 per year) were awarded Financial award application deadline: 3/1. *Faculty research:* Plant biology, molecular biology/physiology/morphology, production, genetics/breeding, weed control. Total annual research expenditures: $610,000. *Unit head:* Dr. Ron H. Delaney, Head, Department of Plant Sciences, 307-766-3103, Fax: 307-766-5549, E-mail: rdelaney@uwyo.edu.

University of Wyoming, Graduate School, College of Agriculture, Department of Renewable Resources, Laramie, WY 82070. Offers entomology (MS, PhD); rangeland ecology and watershed management (MS, PhD), including soil sciences (PhD), soil sciences and water resources (MS), water resources. *Faculty:* 22 full-time (1 woman). *Students:* 20 full-time (7 women), 10 part-time (3 women), 7 international. 8 applicants. In 2003, 11 master's, 3 doctorates awarded. *Degree requirements:* For master's, thesis (for some programs); for doctorate, 2 foreign languages, thesis/dissertation. *Entrance requirements:* For master's and doctorate, GRE General Test, minimum GPA of 3.0. *Application deadline:* For fall admission, 6/1 for domestic students; for spring admission, 12/1 priority date for domestic students. Applications are processed on a rolling basis. Application fee: $40. *Expenses:* Tuition, state resident: part-time $142 per credit hour. Tuition, nonresident: part-time $408 per credit hour. Required fees: $134 per semester. Tuition and fees vary according to course load, campus/location, program and student level. *Financial support:* In 2003–04, 8 students received support, including 8 research assistantships with full tuition reimbursements available (averaging $10,062 per year); career-related internships or fieldwork and Federal Work-Study also available. Financial award application deadline: 3/1. *Faculty research:* Plant control, grazing management, riparian restoration, riparian management, reclamation. *Unit head:* Dr. Thomas L. Thurow, Head, 307-766-2263, Fax: 307-766-6403, E-mail: thurow@uwyo.edu. *Application contact:* Kimm Mann-Malody, Office Assistant, Sr., 307-766-2263, Fax: 307-766-6403, E-mail: kimmmann@uwyo.edu.

Utah State University, School of Graduate Studies, College of Agriculture, Department of Plants, Soils, and Biometeorology, Logan, UT 84322. Offers biometeorology (MS, PhD); ecology (MS, PhD); plant science (MS, PhD); soil science (MS, PhD). Part-time programs available. *Faculty:* 31 full-time (4 women), 13 part-time/adjunct (0 women). *Students:* 29 full-time (9 women), 5 part-time; includes 1 minority (African American), 6 international. Average age 26. 18 applicants, 50% accepted, 2 enrolled. In 2003, 10 master's, 4 doctorates awarded. Terminal master's awarded for partial completion of doctoral program. *Median time to degree:* Of those who began their doctoral program in fall 1995, 100% received their degree in 8 years or less. *Degree requirements:* For master's and doctorate, thesis/dissertation. *Entrance requirements:* For master's, GRE General Test, BS in plant, soil, atmospheric science, or related field, minimum GPA of 3.0; for doctorate, GRE General Test, minimum GPA of 3.0. Additional exam requirements/recommendations for international students: Required—TOEFL. *Application deadline:* For fall admission, 6/15 priority date for domestic students, 3/15 priority date for international students; for spring admission, 10/15 for domestic students, 9/15 for international students. Applications are processed on a rolling basis. Application fee: $50 ($60 for international students). *Expenses:* Tuition, state resident: part-time $270 per credit hour. Tuition, nonresident: part-time $946 per credit hour. Required fees: $173 per credit hour. *Financial support:* In 2003–04, 23 research assistantships with partial tuition reimbursements (averaging $15,000 per year) were awarded; Federal Work-Study, institutionally sponsored loans, and tuition waivers (full) also available. Support available to part-time students. Financial award application deadline: 3/1. *Faculty research:* Biotechnology and genomics, plant physiology and biology, nutrient and water efficient landscapes, physical-chemical-biological processes in soil,

Agronomy and Soil Sciences

Utah State University (continued)
environmental biophysics and climate. Total annual research expenditures: $4.5 million. *Unit head:* Dr. Larry A. Rupp, Head, 435-797-2099, Fax: 435-797-3376, E-mail: larryr@ext.usu.edu. *Application contact:* Dr. Janis L. Boettinger, Graduate Program Coordinator, 435-797-4026, Fax: 435-797-3376, E-mail: janis.boettinger@usu.edu.

Virginia Polytechnic Institute and State University, Graduate School, College of Agriculture and Life Sciences, Department of Crop and Soil Environmental Sciences, Blacksburg, VA 24061. Offers MS, PhD. *Faculty:* 22 full-time (1 woman). *Students:* 29 full-time (14 women), 6 part-time (1 woman); includes 3 minority (2 African Americans, 1 Hispanic American), 5 international. Average age 28. 17 applicants, 35% accepted, 6 enrolled. In 2003, 5 master's, 3 doctorates awarded. *Entrance requirements:* For master's and doctorate, GRE. Additional exam requirements/recommendations for international students: Required—TOEFL (minimum score 550 paper-based; 213 computer-based). *Application deadline:* Applications are processed on a rolling basis. Application fee: $45. Electronic applications accepted. Tuition, area resident: Full-time $6,039; part-time $336 per credit. Tuition, nonresident: full-time $9,708; part-time $539 per credit. Required fees: $905; $130 per credit. *Financial support:* In 2003–04, 13 research assistantships with full tuition reimbursements (averaging $14,545 per year), 7 teaching assistantships with full tuition reimbursements (averaging $11,727 per year) were awarded. Career-related internships or fieldwork, Federal Work-Study, scholarships/grants, and unspecified assistantships also available. Financial award application deadline: 4/1. *Faculty research:* Environmental soil chemistry, waste management, soil fertility, plant molecular genetics, turfgrass management. *Unit head:* Dr. Steven Clarke Hodges, Head, 540-231-6305, Fax: 540-231-3431, E-mail: hodges@vt.edu. *Application contact:* Dr. M. Alley, Research and Graduate Coordinator, 540-231-9777, Fax: 540-231-3431, E-mail: malley@vt.edu.

Washington State University, Graduate School, College of Agricultural, Human, and Natural Resource Sciences, Department of Crop and Soil Sciences, Program in Crop Sciences, Pullman, WA 99164. Offers MS, PhD. *Faculty:* 11 full-time (2 women), 6 part-time/adjunct (2 women). *Students:* 19 full-time (6 women), 1 part-time; includes 1 minority (American Indian/Alaska Native), 9 international. Average age 28. 31 applicants, 61% accepted, 9 enrolled. In 2003, 2 degrees awarded. Terminal master's awarded for partial completion of doctoral program. *Degree requirements:* For master's, oral exam, thesis optional; for doctorate, thesis/dissertation, oral exam, written exam. *Entrance requirements:* For master's and doctorate, GRE General Test, minimum GPA of 3.0. Additional exam requirements/recommendations for international students: Required—TOEFL (minimum score 550 paper-based; 213 computer-based). *Application deadline:* For fall admission, 3/1 priority date for domestic students, 3/1 priority date for international students; for spring admission, 10/1 priority date for domestic students, 7/1 priority date for international students. Applications are processed on a rolling basis. Application fee: $35. Electronic applications accepted. *Expenses:* Tuition, state resident: full-time $6,278; part-time $314 per hour. Tuition, nonresident: full-time $15,514; part-time $765 per hour. Required fees: $444. Full-time tuition and fees vary according to campus/location, program and student level. Part-time tuition and fees vary according to course load. *Financial support:* In 2003–04, 16 research assistantships with full and partial tuition reimbursements (averaging $11,791 per year), 1 teaching assistantship with full and partial tuition reimbursement (averaging $11,961 per year) were awarded. Fellowships, career-related internships or fieldwork, Federal Work-Study, institutionally sponsored loans, tuition waivers (partial), and teaching associateships also available. Financial award application deadline: 2/1; financial award applicants required to submit FAFSA. *Faculty research:* Plant breeding, plant genetics, plant nutrition/nutrient cycling, plant/seed metabolism, turfgrass management. *Unit head:* Dr. Steve Ullrin, Coordinator, 509-335-7247, Fax: 509-335-8674. *Application contact:* Lynn Kamal, Academic Programs Coordinator, 509-335-2615, Fax: 509-335-8674, E-mail: lpounds@wsu.edu.

Washington State University, Graduate School, College of Agricultural, Human, and Natural Resource Sciences, Department of Crop and Soil Sciences, Program in Soil Sciences, Pullman, WA 99164. Offers MS, PhD. *Faculty:* 11 full-time (1 woman), 4 part-time/adjunct (1 woman). *Students:* 14 full-time (10 women), 3 part-time (2 women), 6 international. Average age 29. 32 applicants, 22% accepted, 3 enrolled. In 2003, 3 master's, 1 doctorate awarded. Terminal master's awarded for partial completion of doctoral program. *Degree requirements:* For master's, oral exam, thesis optional; for doctorate, thesis/dissertation, oral exam, written exam. *Entrance requirements:* For master's and doctorate, minimum GPA of 3.0. Additional exam requirements/recommendations for international students: Required—TOEFL (minimum score 550 paper-based; 213 computer-based), GRE. *Application deadline:* For fall admission, 3/1 priority date for domestic students, 3/1 priority date for international students; for spring admission, 8/1 priority date for domestic students, 7/1 priority date for international students. Applications are processed on a rolling basis. Application fee: $35. Electronic applications accepted. *Expenses:* Tuition, state resident: full-time $6,278; part-time $314 per hour. Tuition, nonresident: full-time $15,514; part-time $765 per hour. Required fees: $444. Full-time tuition and fees vary according to campus/location, program and student level. Part-time tuition and fees vary according to course load. *Financial support:* In 2003–04, 11 research assistantships with full and partial tuition reimbursements (averaging $11,848 per year), 2 teaching assistantships with full and partial tuition reimbursements (averaging $11,792 per year) were awarded. Career-related internships or fieldwork, Federal Work-Study, institutionally sponsored loans, tuition waivers (partial), and teaching associateships also available. Financial award application deadline: 4/1; financial award applicants required to submit FAFSA. *Faculty research:* Environmental soils, soil/water quality, soil microbiology, soil physics. *Unit head:* Dr. David F. Bezdicek, Soil Science Graduate Coordinator, 509-335-3644, Fax: 509-335-8674, E-mail: bezdicek@wsu.edu. *Application contact:* Lynn Kamal, Academic Programs Coordinator, 509-335-2615, Fax: 509-335-8674, E-mail: lpounds@wsu.edu.

West Virginia University, Davis College of Agriculture, Forestry and Consumer Sciences, Division of Animal and Veterinary Sciences, Program in Agricultural Sciences, Morgantown, WV 26506. Offers animal and food sciences (PhD); plant and soil sciences (PhD). *Degree requirements:* For doctorate, thesis/dissertation, oral and written exams. *Entrance requirements:* Additional exam requirements/recommendations for international students: Required—TOEFL. Application fee: $45. *Expenses:* Tuition, state resident: full-time $4,332. Tuition, nonresident: full-time $12,442. *Financial support:* Research assistantships with tuition reimbursements, teaching assistantships with tuition reimbursements, Federal Work-Study, institutionally sponsored loans, and tuition waivers (full and partial) available. Financial award application deadline: 2/1; financial award applicants required to submit FAFSA. *Faculty research:* Ruminant nutrition, metabolism, forage utilization, physiology, reproduction. *Application contact:* Dr. Hillar Klandorf, Professor, 304-293-2631 Ext. 4436, Fax: 304-293-3676, E-mail: hillar.klandorf@mail.wvu.edu.

West Virginia University, Davis College of Agriculture, Forestry and Consumer Sciences, Division of Plant and Soil Sciences, Morgantown, WV 26506. Offers agronomy (MS); entomology (MS); environmental microbiology (MS); horticulture (MS); plant pathology (MS). *Faculty:* 18 full-time (1 woman), 1 part-time/adjunct (0 women). *Students:* 17 full-time (11 women), 3 part-time (2 women), 2 international. Average age 27. In 2003, 5 degrees awarded. *Degree requirements:* For master's, thesis. *Entrance requirements:* For master's, GRE, minimum GPA of 2.5. Additional exam requirements/recommendations for international students: Required—TOEFL. *Application deadline:* Applications are processed on a rolling basis. Application fee: $45. *Expenses:* Tuition, state resident: full-time $4,332. Tuition, nonresident: full-time $12,442. *Financial support:* In 2003–04, 13 research assistantships with full tuition reimbursements (averaging $9,936 per year), 4 teaching assistantships with full tuition reimbursements (averaging $9,936 per year) were awarded. Federal Work-Study, institutionally sponsored loans, and tuition waivers (full and partial) also available. Financial award application deadline: 2/1; financial award applicants required to submit FAFSA. *Faculty research:* Water quality, reclamation of disturbed land, crop production, pest control, environmental protection. Total annual research expenditures: $1 million. *Unit head:* Dr. Barton S. Baker, Chair, 304-293-6131 Ext. 4341, Fax: 304-293-2960, E-mail: barton.baker@mail.wvu.edu.

Animal Sciences

Alabama Agricultural and Mechanical University, School of Graduate Studies, School of Agricultural and Environmental Sciences, Department of Plant and Soil Sciences, Huntsville, AL 35811. Offers animal sciences (MS); environmental science (MS); plant and soil science (PhD). Evening/weekend programs available. *Faculty:* 18 full-time (2 women), 6 part-time/adjunct (0 women). *Students:* 28 full-time (16 women), 53 part-time (30 women); includes 70 minority (53 African Americans, 4 American Indian/Alaska Native, 13 Asian Americans or Pacific Islanders). In 2003, 6 degrees awarded. Terminal master's awarded for partial completion of doctoral program. *Degree requirements:* For master's, thesis; for doctorate, one foreign language, thesis/dissertation. *Entrance requirements:* For master's, GRE General Test, BS in agriculture; for doctorate, GRE General Test, master's degree. *Application deadline:* For fall admission, 5/1 for domestic students. Applications are processed on a rolling basis. Application fee: $25. Electronic applications accepted. *Expenses:* Tuition, state resident: full-time $3,250; part-time $370 per credit hour. Tuition, nonresident: full-time $6,490; part-time $740 per credit hour. *Financial support:* In 2003–04, 1 fellowship with tuition reimbursement (averaging $18,000 per year), 9 research assistantships with tuition reimbursements (averaging $9,000 per year) were awarded. Career-related internships or fieldwork and Federal Work-Study also available. Financial award application deadline: 4/1. *Faculty research:* Plant breeding, cytogenetics, crop production, soil chemistry and fertility, remote sensing. Total annual research expenditures: $113,000. *Unit head:* Dr. Govind Sharma, Chair, 256-372-4173.

Alcorn State University, School of Graduate Studies, School of Agriculture and Applied Science, Alcorn State, MS 39096-7500. Offers agricultural economics (MS Ag); agronomy (MS Ag); animal science (MS Ag). *Faculty:* 11 full-time (2 women). *Students:* 9 full-time (2 women), 7 part-time (2 women); includes 12 minority (all African Americans), 3 international. *Degree requirements:* For master's, thesis optional. *Application deadline:* For fall admission, 7/15 for domestic students; for spring admission, 11/25 for domestic students. Applications are processed on a rolling basis. Application fee: $0 ($10 for international students). *Expenses:* Tuition, state resident: full-time $3,192. Tuition, nonresident: full-time $7,698. *Financial support:* Career-related internships or fieldwork available. Support available to part-time students. *Faculty research:* Aquatic systems, dairy herd improvement, fruit production, alternative farming practices. *Unit head:* Napoleon Moses, Dean, 601-877-6137, Fax: 601-877-6219.

Angelo State University, Graduate School, College of Sciences, Department of Agriculture, San Angelo, TX 76909. Offers animal science (MS). Part-time and evening/weekend programs available. *Faculty:* 7 full-time (2 women), 2 part-time/adjunct (0 women). *Students:* 8 full-time (0 women), 13 part-time (1 woman); includes 1 minority (Hispanic American), 1 international. Average age 27. 10 applicants, 100% accepted, 8 enrolled. In 2003, 11 degrees awarded. *Degree requirements:* For master's, thesis optional. *Entrance requirements:* For master's, GRE General Test, minimum GPA of 2.5. Additional exam requirements/recommendations for international students: Required—TOEFL (minimum score 550 paper-based; 213 computer-based). *Application deadline:* For fall admission, 7/15 priority date for domestic students, 6/15 priority date for international students; for spring admission, 12/8 for domestic students, 11/1 for international students. Applications are processed on a rolling basis. Application fee: $25 ($50 for international students). Electronic applications accepted. *Expenses:* Tuition, state resident: part-time $204 per semester hour. Tuition, nonresident: part-time $440 per semester hour. *Financial support:* In 2003–04, 6 students received support, including 8 fellowships, 2 research assistantships; teaching assistantships, career-related internships or fieldwork, Federal Work-Study, scholarships/grants, tuition waivers (partial), and unspecified assistantships also available. Support available to part-time students. Financial award application deadline: 8/1. *Faculty research:* Effect of protein and energy on feedlot performance, bitterweed toxicosis in sheep, meat laboratory, North Concho watershed project, baseline vegetation. *Unit head:* Dr. Gilbert R. Engdahl, Head, 325-942-2027 Ext. 227, E-mail: gil.engdahl@angelo.edu. *Application contact:* Dr. Cody B. Scott, Graduate Advisor, 325-942-2027 Ext. 284, E-mail: cody.scott@angelo.edu.

Auburn University, Graduate School, College of Agriculture, Department of Animal Sciences, Auburn University, AL 36849. Offers M Ag, MS, PhD. Part-time programs available. *Faculty:* 20 full-time (2 women). *Students:* 11 full-time (8 women), 7 part-time (4 women), 2 international. 23 applicants, 52% accepted. In 2003, 8 master's, 1 doctorate awarded. *Degree requirements:* For master's, thesis (for some programs); for doctorate, thesis/dissertation. *Entrance requirements:* For master's and doctorate, GRE General Test. *Application deadline:* For fall admission, 7/7 for domestic students; for spring admission, 11/24 for domestic students. Applications are processed on a rolling basis. Application fee: $25 ($50 for international students). Electronic applications accepted. *Expenses:* Tuition, state resident: part-time $175 per credit hour. Tuition, nonresident: part-time $525 per credit hour. *Financial support:* Research assistantships, teaching assistantships, Federal Work-Study available. Support available to part-time students. Financial award application deadline: 3/15. *Faculty research:* Animal breeding and genetics, animal biochemistry and nutrition, physiology of reproduction, animal production. *Unit head:* Dr. Lowell T. Frobish, Head, 334-844-4160. *Application contact:* Dr. John F. Pritchett, Dean of the Graduate School, 334-844-4700, E-mail: hatchlb@mail.auburn.edu.

Auburn University, Graduate School, College of Agriculture, Department of Poultry Science, Auburn University, AL 36849. Offers M Ag, MS, PhD. Part-time programs available. *Faculty:* 10 full-time (1 woman). *Students:* 12 full-time (6 women), 8 part-time (4 women); includes 2 minority (1 African American, 1 Asian American or Pacific Islander), 9 international. 7 applicants, 57% accepted. In 2003, 2 master's, 1 doctorate awarded. *Degree requirements:* For master's, thesis (for some programs); for doctorate, thesis/dissertation. *Entrance requirements:* For master's, GRE General Test; for doctorate, GRE General Test, MS. *Application deadline:* For fall admission, 7/7 for domestic students; for spring admission, 11/24 for domestic students. Applications are processed on a rolling basis. Application fee: $25 ($50 for international students). Electronic applications accepted. *Expenses:* Tuition, state resident: part-time $175 per credit hour. Tuition, nonresident: part-time $525 per credit hour. *Financial support:* Research assistantships, Federal Work-Study available. Support available to part-time students. Financial award application deadline: 3/15. *Faculty research:* Poultry nutrition, poultry breeding, poultry physiology, poultry diseases and parasites, processing/food science. *Unit head:* Dr. Donald E. Conner, Head, 334-844-4133, E-mail: connede@auburn.edu. *Application contact:* Dr. John F. Pritchett, Dean of the Graduate School, 334-844-4700, E-mail: hatchlb@mail.auburn.edu.

Brigham Young University, Graduate Studies, College of Biological and Agricultural Sciences, Department of Plant and Animal Sciences, Provo, UT 84602-1001. Offers agronomy

(MS); horticulture (MS). *Faculty:* 16 full-time (2 women), 1 (woman) part-time/adjunct. *Students:* 11 full-time (5 women), 2 part-time (1 woman); includes 1 minority (African American) Average age 26. 7 applicants, 43% accepted, 3 enrolled. In 2003, 7 degrees awarded. *Degree requirements:* For master's, thesis, comprehensive exam, registration. *Entrance requirements:* For master's, GRE General Test, minimum GPA of 3.0 during previous 2 years. *Application deadline:* For fall admission, 2/15 for domestic students, 2/15 for international students. Applications are processed on a rolling basis. Application fee: $50. Electronic applications accepted. *Expenses:* Tuition: Part-time $221 per hour. *Financial support:* In 2003–04, 11 students received support, including 1 research assistantship with partial tuition reimbursement available (averaging $15,000 per year), 10 teaching assistantships with partial tuition reimbursements available (averaging $15,000 per year); institutionally sponsored loans, scholarships/grants, and tuition waivers (partial) also available. Financial award application deadline: 4/15. *Faculty research:* Iron nutrition in plants–mode of uptake, photosynthesis, forage quality, seed physiology/modeling, cytogenetics. Total annual research expenditures: $13,500. *Unit head:* Dr. Sheldon D. Nelson, Chair, 801-422-2760, Fax: 801-378-7499, E-mail: sheldon_nelson@byu.edu. *Application contact:* Dr. Richard E. Terry, Graduate Coordinator, 801-422-2421, Fax: 801-378-7499, E-mail: richard_terry@byu.edu.

California State Polytechnic University, Pomona, Academic Affairs, College of Agriculture, Pomona, CA 91768-2557. Offers agricultural science (MS); animal science (MS); foods and nutrition (MS). Part-time programs available. *Faculty:* 43 full-time (15 women), 15 part-time/adjunct (6 women). *Students:* 24 full-time (18 women), 24 part-time (19 women); includes 14 minority (1 African American, 6 Asian Americans or Pacific Islanders, 7 Hispanic Americans), 6 international. Average age 30. 66 applicants, 55% accepted, 26 enrolled. In 2003, 19 degrees awarded. *Degree requirements:* For master's, thesis or alternative. *Application deadline:* For fall admission, 5/1 for domestic students; for winter admission, 10/15 for domestic students; for spring admission, 1/2 for domestic students. Applications are processed on a rolling basis. Application fee: $55. Electronic applications accepted. Tuition, nonresident: full-time $6,016; part-time $188 per unit. Required fees: $2,256. *Financial support:* Career-related internships or fieldwork, Federal Work-Study, and institutionally sponsored loans available. Support available to part-time students. Financial award application deadline: 3/2; financial award applicants required to submit FAFSA. *Faculty research:* Equine nutrition, physiology, and reproduction; leadership development; bioartificial pancreas; plant science; ruminant and human nutrition. *Unit head:* Dr. Wayne R. Bidlack, Dean, 909-869-2200, E-mail: wrbidlack@csupomona.edu.

California State University, Fresno, Division of Graduate Studies, Department of Animal Science and Agricultural Education, Fresno, CA 93740-8027. Offers animal science (MA). Part-time and evening/weekend programs available. *Degree requirements:* For master's, thesis. *Entrance requirements:* For master's, GRE General Test, minimum GPA of 3.0 in last 60 hours. Additional exam requirements/recommendations for international students: Required—TOEFL. Electronic applications accepted. *Faculty research:* Horse nutrition, animal health and welfare, electronic monitoring.

Colorado State University, Graduate School, College of Agricultural Sciences, Department of Animal Sciences, Fort Collins, CO 80523-0015. Offers animal breeding and genetics (MS, PhD); animal nutrition (MS, PhD); animal reproduction (MS, PhD); animal sciences (M Agr); integrated resource management (M Agr); livestock handling (MS, PhD); meats (MS, PhD); production management (MS, PhD). Part-time programs available. *Faculty:* 21 full-time (2 women). *Students:* 34 full-time (15 women), 16 part-time (9 women); includes 1 minority (Hispanic American), 10 international. Average age 28. 65 applicants, 26% accepted, 13 enrolled. In 2003, 13 master's, 3 doctorates awarded. *Degree requirements:* For master's, thesis, publishable paper; for doctorate, thesis/dissertation, 2 publishable papers. *Entrance requirements:* For master's and doctorate, GRE General Test, minimum GPA of 3.0. Additional exam requirements/recommendations for international students: Required—TOEFL. *Application deadline:* For fall admission, 2/1 for domestic students. Applications are processed on a rolling basis. Application fee: $50. Electronic applications accepted. *Expenses:* Tuition, state resident: full-time $4,156. Tuition, nonresident: full-time $14,762. Required fees: $205. Tuition and fees vary according to course load, campus/location, program and reciprocity agreements. *Financial support:* In 2003–04, 16 research assistantships with full and partial tuition reimbursements (averaging $14,100 per year), 3 teaching assistantships with full tuition reimbursements (averaging $13,200 per year) were awarded. Fellowships, traineeships also available. *Faculty research:* Efficiency, food safety, beef management. Total annual research expenditures: $1.5 million. *Unit head:* William R. Wailes, Interim Department Head, 970-491-5390, Fax: 970-491-5326, E-mail: wwailes@ceres.agsci.colostate.edu. *Application contact:* Cheryl Lee Miller, Graduate Coordinator, 970-491-1442, Fax: 970-491-5326, E-mail: cheryl.miller@colostate.edu.

Cornell University, Graduate School, Graduate Fields of Agriculture and Life Sciences, Field of Animal Breeding, Ithaca, NY 14853-0001. Offers animal breeding (MS, PhD); animal genetics (MS, PhD). *Faculty:* 7 full-time. *Students:* 3 full-time (0 women). 4 applicants, 25% accepted, 1 enrolled. *Degree requirements:* For master's, thesis/dissertation, teaching experience; for doctorate, thesis/dissertation, teaching experience, comprehensive exam. *Entrance requirements:* For master's and doctorate, 2 letters of recommendation. Additional exam requirements/recommendations for international students: Required—TOEFL (minimum score 550 paper-based; 213 computer-based). *Application deadline:* For fall admission, 4/1 for domestic students; for spring admission, 9/1 for domestic students. Application fee: $60. Electronic applications accepted. *Expenses:* Tuition: Full-time $28,630. One-time fee: $50 full-time. *Financial support:* In 2003–04, 3 students received support, including 3 research assistantships with full tuition reimbursements available; fellowships with full tuition reimbursements available, teaching assistantships with full tuition reimbursements available, institutionally sponsored loans, scholarships/grants, health care benefits, tuition waivers (full and partial), and unspecified assistantships also available. Financial award applicants required to submit FAFSA. *Faculty research:* Quantitative genetics, genetic improvement of animal populations, statistical genetics. *Unit head:* Director of Graduate Studies, 607-255-4416, Fax: 607-254-5413, E-mail: shh4@cornell.edu. *Application contact:* Graduate Field Assistant, 607-255-4416, Fax: 607-254-5413, E-mail: shh4@cornell.edu.

Cornell University, Graduate School, Graduate Fields of Agriculture and Life Sciences, Field of Animal Science, Ithaca, NY 14853-0001. Offers animal nutrition (MPS, MS, PhD); animal science (MPS, MS, PhD); physiology of reproduction (MPS, MS, PhD). *Faculty:* 38 full-time. *Students:* 38 full-time (24 women); includes 1 minority (Asian American or Pacific Islander), 14 international. 46 applicants, 20% accepted, 5 enrolled. In 2003, 7 master's, 8 doctorates awarded. *Degree requirements:* For master's, teaching experience, thesis (MS); for doctorate, thesis/dissertation, teaching experience, comprehensive exam. *Entrance requirements:* For master's and doctorate, GRE General Test, 2 letters of recommendation. Additional exam requirements/recommendations for international students: Required—TOEFL (minimum score 550 paper-based; 213 computer-based). *Application deadline:* For fall admission, 3/1 for domestic students; for spring admission, 11/1 for domestic students. Application fee: $60. Electronic applications accepted. *Expenses:* Tuition: Full-time $28,630. One-time fee: $50 full-time. *Financial support:* In 2003–04, 37 students received support, including 2 fellowships with full tuition reimbursements available, 25 research assistantships with full tuition reimbursements available, 10 teaching assistantships with full tuition reimbursements available; institutionally sponsored loans, scholarships/grants, health care benefits, tuition waivers (full and partial), and unspecified assistantships also available. Financial award applicants required to submit FAFSA. *Faculty research:* Animal growth and development, dairy science, animal nutrition, physiology of reproduction. *Unit head:* Director of Graduate Studies, 607-255-4416, Fax: 607-254-5413. *Application contact:* Graduate Field Assistant, 607-255-4416, Fax: 607-254-5413, E-mail: shh4@cornell.edu.

Florida Agricultural and Mechanical University, Division of Graduate Studies, Research, and Continuing Education, College of Engineering Science, Technology, and Agriculture, Division of Agricultural Sciences, Tallahassee, FL 32307-3200. Offers agribusiness (MS); animal science (MS); engineering technology (MS); entomology (MS); food science (MS); international programs (MS); plant science (MS). *Faculty:* 31 full-time (2 women). *Students:* 14 full-time (8 women), 8 part-time (4 women); includes 17 minority (16 African Americans, 1 Asian American or Pacific Islander), 3 international. In 2003, 7 degrees awarded. *Degree requirements:* For master's, thesis. *Entrance requirements:* For master's, GRE General Test, minimum GPA of 3.0. Additional exam requirements/recommendations for international students: Required—TOEFL (minimum score 500 paper-based). *Application deadline:* For fall admission, 5/18 for domestic students, 12/18 for international students; for spring admission, 11/12 for domestic students, 5/12 for international students. Application fee: $20. *Expenses:* Tuition, state resident: part-time $192 per credit. Tuition, nonresident: part-time $727 per credit. Tuition and fees vary according to course load. *Financial support:* Application deadline: 2/15. *Unit head:* Dr. Mitwe N. Musingo, Graduate Coordinator, 850-561-2309, Fax: 850-599-8821.

Fort Valley State University, College of Graduate Studies and Extended Education, Program in Animal Science, Fort Valley, GA 31030-4313. Offers MS. *Students:* 3 full-time (1 woman). In 2003, 3 degrees awarded. *Degree requirements:* For master's, thesis, registration. *Entrance requirements:* For master's, GRE General Test. *Application deadline:* For fall admission, 8/23 for domestic students. Application fee: $20. *Expenses:* Tuition, state resident: part-time $111 per credit hour. Tuition, nonresident: part-time $402 per credit hour. Required fees: $32 per credit hour. *Financial support:* Federal Work-Study and unspecified assistantships available. Support available to part-time students. *Unit head:* Dr. Seyoum Gelaye, Acting Dean, 478-825-6338, Fax: 478-825-6533, E-mail: gelayes@fvsu.edu. *Application contact:* Wallace Keese, Dean of Admissions and Enrollment Management, 478-825-6307, E-mail: keesew@fvsu.edu.

Iowa State University of Science and Technology, Graduate College, College of Agriculture, Department of Animal Science, Ames, IA 50011. Offers animal breeding and genetics (MS, PhD); animal nutrition (MS, PhD); animal physiology (MS); animal psychology (PhD); animal science (MS, PhD); meat science (MS, PhD). *Faculty:* 56 full-time, 3 part-time/adjunct. *Students:* 76 full-time (34 women), 23 part-time (7 women); includes 5 minority (1 African American, 1 American Indian/Alaska Native, 3 Hispanic Americans), 25 international. 72 applicants, 26% accepted, 12 enrolled. In 2003, 16 master's, 12 doctorates awarded. *Median time to degree:* Master's–2.2 years full-time; doctorate–5.3 years full-time. *Degree requirements:* For master's, thesis or alternative; for doctorate, thesis/dissertation. *Entrance requirements:* For master's and doctorate, GRE General Test. Additional exam requirements/recommendations for international students: Required—TOEFL (paper score 550; computer score 213) or IELTS (score 6.5). *Application deadline:* For fall admission, 3/1 priority date for domestic students, 3/1 priority date for international students; for spring admission, 10/1 priority date for domestic students, 10/1 priority date for international students. Application fee: $30 ($70 for international students). Electronic applications accepted. Tuition, nonresident: part-time $560 per credit. Required fees: $38 per unit. *Financial support:* In 2003–04, 67 research assistantships with full and partial tuition reimbursements (averaging $16,248 per year), 2 teaching assistantships with full and partial tuition reimbursements (averaging $12,480 per year) were awarded. Fellowships, scholarships/grants, health care benefits, and unspecified assistantships also available. *Faculty research:* Animal breeding, animal nutrition, meat science, muscle biology, nutritional physiology. *Unit head:* Dr. Maynard Hogberg, Head, 515-294-2160, Fax: 515-294-6994. *Application contact:* Charles Sauer, Information Contact, 515-294-4524, E-mail: csauer@iastate.edu.

Iowa State University of Science and Technology, Graduate College, College of Agriculture, Department of Natural Resource Ecology and Management, Ames, IA 50011. Offers animal ecology (MS, PhD), including animal ecology, fisheries biology, wildlife biology; forestry (MS, PhD). *Faculty:* 23 full-time, 7 part-time/adjunct. *Students:* 36 full-time (13 women), 7 part-time (2 women), 8 international. 44 applicants, 36% accepted, 12 enrolled. In 2003, 6 master's, 4 doctorates awarded. *Median time to degree:* Master's–2.7 years full-time; doctorate–4.5 years full-time. *Degree requirements:* For master's, thesis (for some programs); for doctorate, thesis/dissertation. *Entrance requirements:* For master's and doctorate, GRE General Test. Additional exam requirements/recommendations for international students: Required—TOEFL (paper score 547; computer score 210) or IELTS (score 6). *Application deadline:* For fall admission, 1/1 priority date for domestic students, 1/1 priority date for international students; for spring admission, 9/1 priority date for domestic students, 9/1 priority date for international students. Application fee: $30 ($70 for international students). Electronic applications accepted. Tuition, nonresident: part-time $560 per credit. Required fees: $38 per unit. *Financial support:* In 2003–04, 35 research assistantships with full and partial tuition reimbursements (averaging $17,496 per year), 4 teaching assistantships with full and partial tuition reimbursements (averaging $17,496 per year) were awarded. *Unit head:* Dr. J. Michael Kelly, Chair, 515-294-1166. *Application contact:* Lyn Van De Pol, Information Contact, 515-294-6148, E-mail: lvdp@iastate.edu.

Kansas State University, Graduate School, College of Agriculture, Department of Animal Sciences and Industry, Manhattan, KS 66506. Offers animal nutrition (MS, PhD); animal reproduction (MS, PhD); animal sciences and industry (MS, PhD); genetics (MS, PhD); meat science (MS, PhD). *Faculty:* 47 full-time (11 women). *Students:* 48 full-time (19 women), 9 international. 39 applicants, 77% accepted, 13 enrolled. In 2003, 11 master's, 8 doctorates awarded. *Degree requirements:* For master's, thesis, oral exam; for doctorate, thesis/dissertation, preliminary exams. *Application deadline:* For fall admission, 2/1 for domestic students; for spring admission, 10/1 for domestic students. Applications are processed on a rolling basis. Application fee: $0 ($25 for international students). Electronic applications accepted. *Expenses:* Tuition, state resident: part-time $155 per credit hour. Tuition, nonresident: part-time $428 per credit hour. Required fees: $11 per credit hour. *Financial support:* In 2003–04, 44 research assistantships (averaging $11,726 per year), 4 teaching assistantships with full tuition reimbursements (averaging $9,702 per year) were awarded. Federal Work-Study, institutionally sponsored loans, and scholarships/grants also available. Support available to part-time students. Financial award application deadline: 3/1; financial award applicants required to submit FAFSA. *Faculty research:* Nutritional management, reproductive and genetic management, managing health and well-being of animals in production systems, managing the environmental aspects of production systems, converting animals and products into safe products. Total annual research expenditures: $3.3 million. *Unit head:* Jack G. Riley, Head, 785-532-7624, Fax: 785-532-7059, E-mail: jriley@oznet.ksu.edu. *Application contact:* J. Ernest Minton, Coordinator, 785-532-1238, Fax: 785-532-7059, E-mail: eminton@oznet.ksu.edu.

Louisiana State University and Agricultural and Mechanical College, Graduate School, College of Agriculture, Department of Animal Sciences, Baton Rouge, LA 70803. Offers MS, PhD. Part-time programs available. *Faculty:* 16 full-time (2 women). *Students:* 29 full-time (12 women), 12 part-time (6 women); includes 2 minority (1 African American, 1 Hispanic American), 12 international. Average age 28. 23 applicants, 52% accepted, 4 enrolled. In 2003, 1 master's, 4 doctorates awarded. Terminal master's awarded for partial completion of doctoral program. *Degree requirements:* For master's and doctorate, thesis/dissertation. *Entrance requirements:* For master's and doctorate, GRE General Test, minimum GPA of 3.0. Additional exam requirements/recommendations for international students: Required—TOEFL (minimum score 550 paper-based; 213 computer-based). *Application deadline:* For fall admission, 1/25 priority date for domestic students, 5/15 priority date for international students. Applications are processed on a rolling basis. Application fee: $25. Electronic applications accepted. *Expenses:* Tuition, state resident: part-time $337 per hour. Tuition, nonresident: part-time $577 per hour. *Financial support:* In 2003–04, 2 research assistantships with partial tuition reimbursements (averaging $16,250 per year), 18 teaching assistantships with partial tuition reimbursements (averaging $12,718 per year) were awarded. Fellowships, Federal Work-Study and institutionally sponsored loans also available. Support available to part-time students. Financial award applicants required to submit FAFSA. *Faculty research:* Breeding and genetics, nutrition, reproduction, meats, biotechnology. Total annual research expenditures: $6,195. *Unit head:* Dr. Paul E. Humes, Head, 225-578-3241, Fax: 225-578-3279, E-mail: phumes@agctr.lsu.edu. *Application contact:* Dr. Donald L. Thompson, Graduate Coordinator, 225-578-3445, Fax: 225-578-3279, E-mail: dthompson@agctr.lsu.edu.

Louisiana State University and Agricultural and Mechanical College, Graduate School, College of Agriculture, Department of Dairy Science, Baton Rouge, LA 70803. Offers MS, PhD.

Animal Sciences

Louisiana State University and Agricultural and Mechanical College (continued)

Faculty: 7 full-time (1 woman). *Students:* 5 full-time (2 women), 2 part-time (1 woman), 1 international. Average age 27. 6 applicants, 67% accepted, 0 enrolled. In 2003, 3 master's, 2 doctorates awarded. *Degree requirements:* For master's and doctorate, thesis/dissertation. *Entrance requirements:* For master's and doctorate, GRE General Test, minimum GPA of 3.0. Additional exam requirements/recommendations for international students: Required—TOEFL (minimum score 550 paper-based; 213 computer-based). *Application deadline:* For fall admission, 1/25 priority date for domestic students, 5/15 priority date for international students. Applications are processed on a rolling basis. Application fee: $25. Electronic applications accepted. *Expenses:* Tuition, state resident: part-time $337 per hour. Tuition, nonresident: part-time $577 per hour. *Financial support:* In 2003–04, 4 research assistantships with partial tuition reimbursements (averaging $13,875 per year) were awarded; fellowships, teaching assistantships with partial tuition reimbursements, unspecified assistantships also available. Financial award applicants required to submit FAFSA. *Faculty research:* Nutrition physiology, genetics, dairy foods technology, dairy management, dairy microbiology. Total annual research expenditures: $2,550. *Unit head:* Dr. Bruce Jenny, Head, 225-578-4411, Fax: 225-578-4008, E-mail: bjenny@agctr.lsu.edu. *Application contact:* John Chandler, Graduate Coordinator, 225-578-3292, Fax: 225-578-4008, E-mail: jchandler@agctr.lsu.edu.

McGill University, Faculty of Graduate and Postdoctoral Studies, Faculty of Agricultural and Environmental Sciences, Department of Animal Science, Montréal, QC H3A 2T5, Canada. Offers M Sc, M Sc A, PhD. *Faculty:* 15 full-time (0 women). *Students:* 24 full-time. Average age 28. 28 applicants, 25% accepted, 3 enrolled. In 2003, 5 master's, 2 doctorates awarded. *Degree requirements:* For master's, thesis (for some programs); for doctorate, thesis/dissertation. *Entrance requirements:* For master's, minimum GPA of 3.0; for doctorate, M Sc, minimum GPA of 3.0. Additional exam requirements/recommendations for international students: Required—TOEFL (paper score 550; computer score 213) or IELTS (paper score 6). *Application deadline:* For fall admission, 6/1 for domestic students, 3/1 for international students; for winter admission, 10/15 for domestic students; for spring admission, 2/15 for domestic students. Applications are processed on a rolling basis. Application fee: $60 Canadian dollars. Electronic applications accepted. Tuition, area resident: Full-time $1,668. *Expenses:* Tuition, state resident: full-time $4,173. Tuition, nonresident: full-time $9,468. Required fees: $1,081. *Financial support:* In 2003–04, 15 research assistantships with full tuition reimbursements (averaging $13,000 per year), 13 teaching assistantships were awarded. Fellowships, institutionally sponsored loans, scholarships/grants, and tuition waivers (full) also available. *Faculty research:* Animal nutrition, genetics, embryo transfer, DNA fingerprinting, dairy, milk recording, biochemistry, biotechnology, information systems. *Unit head:* Dr. Xin Zhao, Chair, 514-398-7975, Fax: 514-398-7964, E-mail: zhao@macdonald.mcgill.ca. *Application contact:* Leslie Laduke, Graduate Program Secretary, 514-398-7792, Fax: 514-398-7964, E-mail: leslie.laduke@mcgill.ca.

Michigan State University, College of Veterinary Medicine and Graduate School, Graduate Programs in Veterinary Medicine, Department of Large Animal Clinical Sciences, East Lansing, MI 48824. Offers MS, PhD. *Faculty:* 26 full-time (9 women), 4 part-time/adjunct (1 woman). *Students:* 23 full-time (12 women); includes 3 minority (all Asian Americans or Pacific Islanders), 7 international. Average age 32. 4 applicants, 75% accepted, 3 enrolled. In 2003, 12 master's, 5 doctorates awarded. *Degree requirements:* For master's, thesis or alternative; for doctorate, thesis/dissertation. *Entrance requirements:* For master's and doctorate, 3 letters of recommendation. *Application deadline:* For fall admission, 6/30 for domestic students; for spring admission, 11/1 priority date for domestic students. Applications are processed on a rolling basis. Application fee: $50. Electronic applications accepted. *Expenses:* Tuition, state resident: part-time $291 per hour. Tuition, nonresident: part-time $589 per hour. *Financial support:* In 2003–04, 15 fellowships with tuition reimbursements (averaging $3,315 per year), 12 research assistantships with tuition reimbursements (averaging $13,495 per year) were awarded. *Faculty research:* Pulmonary and exercise physiology, surgery, theriogenology, epidemiology and production medicine. Total annual research expenditures: $2.4 million. *Unit head:* Dr. Thomas H. Herdt, Chairperson, 517-355-9593, Fax: 517-432-1042, E-mail: herdt@cvm.msu.edu. *Application contact:* Faith L. Peterson, Secretary, 517-353-3064, Fax: 517-432-1042, E-mail: lcsinfo@cvm.msu.edu.

Michigan State University, College of Veterinary Medicine and Graduate School, Graduate Programs in Veterinary Medicine, Department of Small Animal Clinical Sciences, East Lansing, MI 48824. Offers MS. *Faculty:* 20 full-time (5 women), 1 part-time/adjunct (0 women). *Students:* 2 full-time (1 woman); includes 1 minority (Hispanic American) 6 applicants, 17% accepted, 1 enrolled. *Degree requirements:* For master's, thesis or alternative. *Entrance requirements:* For master's, DVM residency. Application fee: $50. *Expenses:* Tuition, state resident: part-time $291 per hour. Tuition, nonresident: part-time $589 per hour. *Financial support:* Research assistantships available. *Faculty research:* Molecular genetics, comparative orthopedics, dermatology, cardiology, anesthesiology. Total annual research expenditures: $930,076. *Unit head:* Dr. Charles E. DeCamp, Chairperson, 517-355-5199, Fax: 517-355-5164, E-mail: decampc@cvm.msu.edu.

Michigan State University, Graduate School, College of Agriculture and Natural Resources, Department of Animal Science, East Lansing, MI 48824. Offers animal science (MS, PhD); animal science-environmental toxicology (PhD). *Faculty:* 38 full-time (8 women). *Students:* 40 full-time (19 women), 7 part-time (5 women); includes 5 minority (1 African American, 4 Hispanic Americans), 14 international. Average age 29. 53 applicants, 11% accepted. In 2003, 18 master's, 6 doctorates awarded. *Degree requirements:* For master's, thesis or alternative, presentation of thesis/project and oral exam; for doctorate, thesis/dissertation, defense of dissertation, year of residence, comprehensive exam. *Entrance requirements:* For master's and doctorate, GRE General Test, minimum GPA of 3.0 in last 2 undergraduate years, references. Additional exam requirements/recommendations for international students: Required—TOEFL (minimum score 550 paper-based; 213 computer-based), Michigan State University ELT (85), Michigan ELAB (83). *Application deadline:* For fall admission, 12/23 for domestic students. Applications are processed on a rolling basis. Application fee: $50. Electronic applications accepted. *Expenses:* Tuition, state resident: part-time $291 per hour. Tuition, nonresident: part-time $589 per hour. *Financial support:* In 2003–04, 7 fellowships with tuition reimbursements (averaging $8,153 per year), 41 research assistantships with tuition reimbursements (averaging $12,155 per year) were awarded. Financial award applicants required to submit FAFSA. *Faculty research:* Breeding and genetics, management and systems, meats and growth biology, reproductive and mammary physiology, microbiology and molecular biology. Total annual research expenditures: $6.8 million. *Unit head:* Dr. Margaret Benson, Acting Chairperson, 517-355-8383, Fax: 517-353-1699. *Application contact:* Jacqueline Kay Christie, Graduate Program Contact, 517-353-8383, E-mail: christi7@msu.edu.

Mississippi State University, College of Agriculture and Life Sciences, Department of Poultry Science, Mississippi State, MS 39762. Offers MS. *Faculty:* 10 full-time (2 women). *Students:* 6 full-time (4 women), 3 part-time (2 women), 3 international. Average age 28. 2 applicants, 50% accepted, 0 enrolled. In 2003, 2 degrees awarded. *Degree requirements:* For master's, thesis. *Entrance requirements:* Additional exam requirements/recommendations for international students: Required—TOEFL. *Application deadline:* For fall admission, 7/1 for domestic students; for spring admission, 11/1 for domestic students. Applications are processed on a rolling basis. Application fee: $25 for international students. Electronic applications accepted. *Expenses:* Contact institution. Tuition and fees vary according to course load. *Financial support:* In 2003–04, 1 research assistantship with full tuition reimbursement (averaging $11,455 per year), 1 teaching assistantship with full tuition reimbursement (averaging $9,818 per year) were awarded. Federal Work-Study, institutionally sponsored loans, scholarships/grants, and unspecified assistantships also available. Financial award applicants required to submit FAFSA. *Faculty research:* Physiology, nutrition management, food science. Total annual research expenditures: $283,064. *Unit head:* Dr. G. Wallace Morgan, Head, 662-325-3416, Fax: 662-325-8292, E-mail: wmorgan@poultry.msstate.edu. *Application contact:* Diane D. Wolfe, Director of Admissions, 662-325-2224, Fax: 662-325-7360, E-mail: admit@admissions.msstate.edu.

Montana State University–Bozeman, College of Graduate Studies, College of Agriculture, Department of Animal and Range Sciences, Bozeman, MT 59717. Offers MS, PhD. Part-time programs available. *Faculty:* 13 full-time (3 women), 5 part-time/adjunct (2 women). *Students:* 5 full-time (2 women), 18 part-time (10 women); includes 1 minority (American Indian/Alaska Native), 1 international. Average age 28. 10 applicants, 70% accepted, 6 enrolled. In 2003, 7 degrees awarded. *Degree requirements:* For master's, comprehensive exam, registration; for doctorate, thesis/dissertation, comprehensive exam, registration. *Entrance requirements:* For master's and doctorate, GRE General Test. Additional exam requirements/recommendations for international students: Required—TOEFL (minimum score 550 paper-based; 213 computer-based). *Application deadline:* For fall admission, 7/15 priority date for domestic students, 5/15 priority date for international students; for spring admission, 12/1 priority date for domestic students, 10/1 priority date for international students. Applications are processed on a rolling basis. Application fee: $50. Electronic applications accepted. *Expenses:* Tuition, state resident: full-time $3,907; part-time $163 per credit. Tuition, nonresident: full-time $12,383; part-time $516 per credit. Required fees: $890; $445 per term. Tuition and fees vary according to course load and program. *Financial support:* In 2003–04, 12 students received support, including 6 research assistantships with partial tuition reimbursements available (averaging $12,000 per year), 1 teaching assistantship with partial tuition reimbursement available (averaging $12,000 per year); scholarships/grants and unspecified assistantships also available. Financial award application deadline: 3/1; financial award applicants required to submit FAFSA. *Faculty research:* Range nutrition, genetics, reproductive physiology, range ecology, livestock management, invasive species management. Total annual research expenditures: $2 million. *Unit head:* Dr. Michael Tess, Head, 406-994-5610, Fax: 406-994-5589, E-mail: mwtess@montana.edu.

New Mexico State University, Graduate School, College of Agriculture and Home Economics, Department of Animal and Range Sciences, Las Cruces, NM 88003-8001. Offers animal science (M Ag, MS, PhD); range science (M Ag, MS, PhD). Part-time programs available. *Faculty:* 17 full-time (1 woman), 7 part-time/adjunct (0 women). *Students:* 33 full-time (15 women), 12 part-time (6 women); includes 12 minority (3 American Indian/Alaska Native, 9 Hispanic Americans), 6 international. Average age 29. 27 applicants, 63% accepted, 11 enrolled. In 2003, 4 master's, 4 doctorates awarded. *Degree requirements:* For master's, thesis, seminar; for doctorate, thesis/dissertation, research tool. *Entrance requirements:* For master's, minimum GPA of 3.0 in last 60 hours of undergraduate course work (MS); for doctorate, minimum graduate GPA of 3.2. *Application deadline:* For fall admission, 7/1 for domestic students; for spring admission, 11/1 for domestic students. Applications are processed on a rolling basis. Application fee: $30 ($50 for international students). Electronic applications accepted. *Expenses:* Tuition, state resident: full-time $2,670; part-time $151 per credit. Tuition, nonresident: full-time $10,596; part-time $481 per credit. Required fees: $954. *Financial support:* In 2003–04, 5 research assistantships, 17 teaching assistantships were awarded. Federal Work-Study also available. Support available to part-time students. Financial award application deadline: 3/1. *Faculty research:* Reproductive physiology, ruminant nutrition, nutrition toxicology, range ecology, wildland hydrology. *Unit head:* Dr. Mark Wise, Head, 505-646-2514, Fax: 505-646-5441, E-mail: mawise@nmsu.edu.

North Carolina State University, Graduate School, College of Agriculture and Life Sciences, Department of Animal Science, Raleigh, NC 27695. Offers MS, PhD. *Faculty:* 35 full-time (7 women), 25 part-time/adjunct (0 women). *Students:* 29 full-time (22 women), 7 part-time (4 women), 4 international. Average age 27. 47 applicants, 47% accepted. In 2003, 6 master's, 4 doctorates awarded. *Degree requirements:* For master's, thesis (for some programs); for doctorate, thesis/dissertation. *Entrance requirements:* For master's and doctorate, GRE, minimum GPA of 3.0. *Application deadline:* For fall admission, 6/25 for domestic students, 3/1 for international students; for spring admission, 11/25 for domestic students, 7/15 for international students. Application fee: $45. *Expenses:* Tuition, state resident: part-time $396 per hour. Tuition, nonresident: part-time $1,895 per hour. *Financial support:* In 2003–04, 18 research assistantships with tuition reimbursements (averaging $5,057 per year), 3 teaching assistantships with tuition reimbursements (averaging $5,713 per year) were awarded. Financial award application deadline: 4/1. *Faculty research:* Nutrient utilization, mineral nutrition, genomics, transgenics, neuroendocrinology. Total annual research expenditures: $536,684. *Unit head:* Dr. Roger McCraw, Interim Department Head, 919-515-2755, Fax: 919-515-6884, E-mail: roger_mccraw@ncsu.edu. *Application contact:* Dr. Eugene J. Eisen, Director of Graduate Programs, 919-515-4017, Fax: 919-515-7780, E-mail: gene_eisen@ncsu.edu.

North Carolina State University, Graduate School, College of Agriculture and Life Sciences, Department of Poultry Science, Raleigh, NC 27695. Offers MS. Part-time programs available. *Faculty:* 23 full-time (1 woman), 21 part-time/adjunct (3 women). *Students:* 10 full-time (8 women); includes 1 minority (Hispanic American), 3 international. Average age 30. 6 applicants, 67% accepted. In 2003, 3 degrees awarded. *Degree requirements:* For master's, thesis. *Application deadline:* For fall admission, 6/25 for domestic students, 3/1 for international students; for spring admission, 11/25 for domestic students, 7/15 for international students. Applications are processed on a rolling basis. Application fee: $45. *Expenses:* Tuition, state resident: part-time $396 per hour. Tuition, nonresident: part-time $1,895 per hour. *Financial support:* In 2003–04, 6 research assistantships with tuition reimbursements (averaging $5,909 per year), 2 teaching assistantships with tuition reimbursements (averaging $6,301 per year) were awarded. Fellowships with tuition reimbursements, career-related internships or fieldwork and institutionally sponsored loans also available. *Faculty research:* Reproductive physiology, nutrition, toxicology, immunology, molecular biology. Total annual research expenditures: $2.2 million. *Unit head:* Dr. Gerald B. Havenstein, Head, 919-515-5555, Fax: 919-515-2625, E-mail: gerald_havenstein@ncsu.edu. *Application contact:* Dr. John T. Brake, Director of Graduate Programs, 919-515-5060, Fax: 919-515-2625, E-mail: jbrake@ncsu.edu.

North Dakota State University, The Graduate School, College of Agriculture, Food Systems, and Natural Resources, Department of Animal and Range Sciences, Fargo, ND 58105. Offers animal science (MS, PhD); natural resources management (MS, PhD); range science (MS, PhD). *Degree requirements:* For master's and doctorate, thesis/dissertation. *Entrance requirements:* For master's and doctorate, GRE General Test. Additional exam requirements/recommendations for international students: Required—TOEFL. Tuition, nonresident: full-time $4,071. Required fees: $493. *Faculty research:* Reproduction, nutrition, meat and muscle biology, breeding/genetics.

Nova Scotia Agricultural College, Research and Graduate Studies, Truro, NS B2N 5E3, Canada. Offers agriculture (M Sc), including air quality, animal behavior, animal molecular genetics, animal nutrition, animal technology, aquaculture, botany, crop management, crop physiology, ecology, environmental microbiology, food science, horticulture, nutrient management, pest management, physiology, plant biotechnology, plant pathology, soil chemistry, soil fertility, waste management and composting, water quality. Part-time programs available. *Faculty:* 38 full-time (5 women), 13 part-time/adjunct (1 woman). *Students:* 46 full-time (27 women), 21 part-time (13 women); includes 13 minority (10 African Americans, 2 American Indian/Alaska Native, 1 Asian American or Pacific Islander). 45 applicants, 58% accepted, 16 enrolled. In 2003, 11 degrees awarded, leading to university research/teaching 18%, continued full-time study36%, business/industry 9%, government 27%. *Median time to degree:* Master's–2.25 years full-time, 4 years part-time. *Degree requirements:* For master's, thesis, candidacy exam. *Entrance requirements:* For master's, B.Sc. honors degree, minimum GPA of 3.0. Additional exam requirements/recommendations for international students: Required—TOEFL (minimum score 580 paper-based; 237 computer-based), Michigan English Language Assessment Battery. *Application deadline:* For fall admission, 6/1 for domestic students, 4/1 for international students; for winter admission, 11/15 for domestic students; for spring admission, 2/28 for domestic students. Applications are processed on a rolling basis. Application fee: $70. *Expenses:* Tuition, state resident: full-time $6,270. Tuition, nonresident: full-time $9,270. Required fees: $402. Tuition and fees vary according to student level. *Financial support:* In 2003–04, 63 students received support, including research assistantships (averaging $15,000 per year), teaching assistantships (averaging $900 per year); career-related internships or fieldwork, scholarships/grants, and unspecified assistantships also available. *Faculty research:*

Organogenesis, somatic embryogenesis, composting, sustainable agriculture, ecotoxicology. Total annual research expenditures: $2 million. *Unit head:* Jill L. Rogers, Manager, 902-893-6360, Fax: 902-893-3430, E-mail: jrogers@nsac.ns.ca. *Application contact:* Marie Law, Administrative Assistant, 902-893-6502, Fax: 902-893-3430, E-mail: mlaw@nsac.ns.ca.

The Ohio State University, Graduate School, College of Food, Agricultural, and Environmental Sciences, Department of Animal Sciences, Columbus, OH 43210. Offers MS, PhD. *Faculty:* 47. *Students:* 31 full-time (13 women), 9 part-time (4 women); includes 3 minority (all African Americans), 14 international. 52 applicants, 33% accepted. In 2003, 11 master's, 7 doctorates awarded. *Degree requirements:* For master's and doctorate, thesis/dissertation. *Entrance requirements:* For master's and doctorate, GRE General Test. *Application deadline:* For fall admission, 8/15 for domestic students. Applications are processed on a rolling basis. Application fee: $40 ($50 for international students). *Expenses:* Tuition, state resident: full-time $7,233. Tuition, nonresident: full-time $18,489. *Financial support:* Fellowships, research assistantships, teaching assistantships, Federal Work-Study and institutionally sponsored loans available. Support available to part-time students. *Unit head:* Dr. James E. Kinder, Chair, 614-292-3232, Fax: 614-292-2929, E-mail: kinder.15@osu.edu. *Application contact:* Dr. Jeffrey L. Firkins, Graduate Studies Committee Chair, 614-688-3089, Fax: 614-292-2929, E-mail: firkins.1@osu.edu.

Oklahoma State University, Graduate College, College of Agricultural Sciences and Natural Resources, Department of Animal Sciences, Stillwater, OK 74078. Offers animal breeding (PhD); animal nutrition (PhD); animal sciences (M Ag, MS); food science (MS, PhD). *Faculty:* 30 full-time (2 women). *Students:* 28 full-time (15 women), 49 part-time (18 women); includes 1 minority (African American), 27 international. Average age 29. 55 applicants, 31% accepted, 13 enrolled. In 2003, 20 master's, 4 doctorates awarded. *Degree requirements:* For master's and doctorate, thesis/dissertation. *Entrance requirements:* Additional exam requirements/recommendations for international students: Required—TOEFL. *Application deadline:* For fall admission, 6/1 for domestic students. Applications are processed on a rolling basis. Application fee: $25 ($50 for international students). Electronic applications accepted. *Expenses:* Tuition, state resident: full-time $3,752; part-time $118 per credit hour. Tuition, nonresident: full-time $10,346; part-time $393 per credit hour. Tuition and fees vary according to course load. *Financial support:* In 2003–04, 39 research assistantships (averaging $11,176 per year), 7 teaching assistantships (averaging $12,639 per year) were awarded. Career-related internships or fieldwork, Federal Work-Study, and tuition waivers (partial) also available. Support available to part-time students. Financial award application deadline: 3/1. *Faculty research:* Quantitative trait loci identification for economical traits in swing/beef; quantitative genetic selection in farm animals; waste management strategies in livestock; endocrine control of reproductive processes in farm animals; cholesterol synthesis, inhibition, and reduction; food safety research for E. Coli and Listeria. *Unit head:* Dr. Donald G. Wagner, Head, 405-744-6062, Fax: 405-744-7390, E-mail: wagner@okstate.edu.

Oregon State University, Graduate School, College of Agricultural Sciences, Department of Animal Sciences, Corvallis, OR 97331. Offers animal science (M Agr, MAIS, MS, PhD); poultry science (M Agr, MAIS, MS, PhD). *Faculty:* 26 full-time (4 women). *Students:* 18 full-time (7 women), 3 part-time (all women), 7 international. Average age 29. In 2003, 13 master's, 1 doctorate awarded. Terminal master's awarded for partial completion of doctoral program. *Degree requirements:* For master's, thesis (for some programs); for doctorate, thesis/dissertation. *Entrance requirements:* For master's and doctorate, GRE General Test, minimum GPA of 3.0 in last 90 hours. Additional exam requirements/recommendations for international students: Required—TOEFL. *Application deadline:* For fall admission, 3/1 for domestic students. Applications are processed on a rolling basis. Application fee: $50. *Expenses:* Tuition, state resident: full-time $8,139; part-time $301 per credit. Tuition, nonresident: full-time $14,376; part-time $532 per credit. Required fees: $1,227. *Financial support:* Fellowships, research assistantships, career-related internships or fieldwork, Federal Work-Study, and institutionally sponsored loans available. Support available to part-time students. Financial award application deadline: 2/1. *Faculty research:* Reproductive physiology, population genetics, general nutrition of ruminants and nonruminants, embryo physiology, endocrinology. *Unit head:* James R. Males, Head, 541-737-1891, Fax: 541-737-4174, E-mail: james.males@orst.edu.

The Pennsylvania State University University Park Campus, Graduate School, College of Agricultural Sciences, Department of Dairy and Animal Science, State College, University Park, PA 16802-1503. Offers animal science (M Agr, MS, PhD). *Students:* 15 full-time (7 women), 5 part-time (3 women), 7 international. *Entrance requirements:* For master's and doctorate, GRE General Test. Application fee: $45. *Expenses:* Tuition, state resident: full-time $10,010; part-time $417 per credit. Tuition, nonresident: full-time $19,830; part-time $826 per credit. Full-time tuition and fees vary according to course level, course load, campus/location and program. *Unit head:* Dr. Terry D. Etherton, Head, 814-863-3665, Fax: 814-863-6042, E-mail: tetherton@psu.edu. *Application contact:* Dr. Daniel R. Hagen, Graduate Officer, 814-863-0723, Fax: 814-863-6042, E-mail: drh@psu.edu.

Prairie View A&M University, Graduate School, College of Agriculture and Human Sciences, Prairie View, TX 77446-0519. Offers agricultural economics (MS); animal sciences (MS); interdisciplinary human sciences (MS); marriage and family therapy (MS); soil science (MS). Part-time and evening/weekend programs available. *Faculty:* 15 full-time (3 women). *Students:* 49 full-time (31 women), 71 part-time (59 women); includes 104 minority (101 African Americans, 2 Asian Americans or Pacific Islanders, 1 Hispanic American), 11 international. Average age 33. *Degree requirements:* For master's, thesis (for some programs), field placement, comprehensive exam. *Entrance requirements:* For master's, GRE General Test. *Application deadline:* Applications are processed on a rolling basis. Application fee: $50. *Expenses:* Tuition, state resident: part-time $50 per credit hour. Tuition, nonresident: part-time $282 per credit hour. Required fees: $36 per credit hour. $51 per term. *Financial support:* In 2003–04, 8 fellowships with tuition reimbursements (averaging $12,000 per year), 10 research assistantships with tuition reimbursements (averaging $15,000 per year) were awarded. Career-related internships or fieldwork, Federal Work-Study, institutionally sponsored loans, and tuition waivers (partial) also available. Financial award application deadline: 4/1; financial award applicants required to submit FAFSA. *Faculty research:* Domestic violence prevention, water quality, food growth regulators. Total annual research expenditures: $4 million. *Unit head:* Dr. Elizabeth Noel, Dean, 936-857-2996, Fax: 936-857-2998, E-mail: elizabeth_noel@pvamu.edu.

Purdue University, Graduate School, College of Agriculture, Department of Animal Sciences, West Lafayette, IN 47907. Offers MS, PhD. Part-time programs available. Terminal master's awarded for partial completion of doctoral program. *Degree requirements:* For master's, thesis optional; for doctorate, thesis/dissertation. *Entrance requirements:* For master's and doctorate, GRE General Test. Additional exam requirements/recommendations for international students: Required—TOEFL, TWE. Electronic applications accepted. *Faculty research:* Genetics, meat science, nutrition, management, ethology.

Rutgers, The State University of New Jersey, New Brunswick/Piscataway, Graduate School, Program in Animal Sciences, New Brunswick, NJ 08901-1281. Offers endocrine control of growth and metabolism (MS, PhD); nutrition of ruminant and nonruminant animals (MS, PhD); reproductive endocrinology and neuroendocrinology (MS, PhD). *Faculty:* 20 full-time (7 women), 8 part-time/adjunct (3 women). *Students:* 17 full-time (9 women), 6 part-time (5 women); includes 1 minority (Asian American or Pacific Islander), 7 international. Average age 28. 35 applicants, 20% accepted, 4 enrolled. In 2003, 1 master's awarded. Terminal master's awarded for partial completion of doctoral program. *Median time to degree:* Master's–3 years full-time; doctorate–5 years full-time. Of those who began their doctoral program in fall 1995, 100% received their degree in 8 years or less. *Degree requirements:* For master's, thesis/dissertation; for doctorate, thesis/dissertation, comprehensive exam. *Entrance requirements:* For master's, GRE General Test; for doctorate, GRE General Test. *Application deadline:* For fall admission, 3/15 for domestic students, 1/15 for international students. Applications are processed on a rolling basis. Application fee: $50. Electronic applications accepted. *Expenses:* Tuition, state resident: full-time $10,030. Tuition, nonresident: full-time $14,202. *Financial support:* In 2003–04, 12 students received support, including 1 fellowship with full tuition reimbursement available (averaging $21,500 per year), 2 research assistantships with full tuition reimbursements available (averaging $16,550 per year), 9 teaching assistantships with full tuition reimbursements available (averaging $14,300 per year); unspecified assistantships also available. Financial award application deadline: 1/15; financial award applicants required to submit FAFSA. *Faculty research:* Equine exercise physiology and nutrition, alcohol and stress, reproductive biology and endocrinology, mammary gland biology and lactation reproductive behavior. Total annual research expenditures: $1.1 million. *Unit head:* Dr. Henry B. John-Alder, Director, 732-932-3229, Fax: 732-932-6996, E-mail: henry@aesop.rutgers.edu. *Application contact:* Dr. Katherine A. Manger, Administrator, 732-932-3879, Fax: 732-932-6996, E-mail: manger@aesop.rutgers.edu.

South Dakota State University, Graduate School, College of Agriculture and Biological Sciences, Department of Animal Science and Range Science, Brookings, SD 57007. Offers animal science (MS, PhD). *Degree requirements:* For master's, thesis, oral exam; for doctorate, thesis/dissertation, preliminary oral and written exams. *Entrance requirements:* Additional exam requirements/recommendations for international students: Required—TOEFL. *Faculty research:* Ruminant and nonruminant nutrition, meat science, reproductive physiology, range utilization, ecology genetics.

South Dakota State University, Graduate School, College of Agriculture and Biological Sciences, Department of Dairy Science, Brookings, SD 57007. Offers MS, PhD. *Degree requirements:* For master's, thesis, oral exam; for doctorate, thesis/dissertation, preliminary oral and written exams. *Entrance requirements:* Additional exam requirements/recommendations for international students: Required—TOEFL. *Faculty research:* Dairy cattle nutrition, energy metabolism, lowfat cheese technology, food safety, sensory evaluation of dairy products.

Southern Illinois University Carbondale, Graduate School, College of Agriculture, Department of Animal Science, Food and Nutrition, Program in Animal Science, Carbondale, IL 62901-4701. Offers MS. *Faculty:* 15 full-time (6 women). *Students:* 4 full-time (all women), 11 part-time (8 women); includes 2 minority (1 Asian American or Pacific Islander, 1 Hispanic American). Average age 29. 7 applicants, 29% accepted, 0 enrolled. In 2003, 5 degrees awarded. *Degree requirements:* For master's, thesis. *Entrance requirements:* For master's, minimum GPA of 2.7. Additional exam requirements/recommendations for international students: Required—TOEFL. *Application deadline:* Applications are processed on a rolling basis. Application fee: $0. *Expenses:* Tuition, state resident: part-time $478 per hour. Tuition, nonresident: part-time $657 per hour. *Financial support:* In 2003–04, 13 research assistantships with full tuition reimbursements, 2 teaching assistantships with full tuition reimbursements were awarded. Fellowships with full tuition reimbursements, career-related internships or fieldwork, Federal Work-Study, institutionally sponsored loans, and tuition waivers (full) also available. Support available to part-time students. *Faculty research:* Nutrition, reproductive physiology, animal biotechnology, phytoestrogens and animal reproduction. Total annual research expenditures: $300,000. *Unit head:* Patricia Welch, Chair, Department of Animal Science, Food and Nutrition, 618-453-7516, Fax: 618-453-5231.

Sul Ross State University, Division of Agricultural and Natural Resource Science, Program in Animal Science, Alpine, TX 79832. Offers M Ag, MS. Part-time programs available. *Degree requirements:* For master's, thesis (for some programs). *Entrance requirements:* For master's, GRE General Test, minimum GPA of 2.5 in last 60 hours of undergraduate work. *Faculty research:* Reproductive physiology, meat processing, animal nutrition, equine foot and motion studies, Spanish goat and Barbido sheep studies.

Tarleton State University, College of Graduate Studies and Academic Affairs, College of Agriculture and Human Sciences, Department of Animal Sciences, Stephenville, TX 76402. Offers MS. Part-time and evening/weekend programs available. Postbaccalaureate distance learning degree programs offered (minimal on-campus study). *Faculty:* 18 full-time (2 women). *Students:* 22 full-time (9 women), 14 part-time (4 women), 1 international. 12 applicants, 92% accepted. In 2003, 11 degrees awarded. *Degree requirements:* For master's, thesis (for some programs), comprehensive exam. *Entrance requirements:* For master's, GRE General Test, minimum GPA of 3.0. Additional exam requirements/recommendations for international students: Required—TOEFL (minimum score 550 paper-based; 220 computer-based). *Application deadline:* For fall admission, 8/5 for domestic students; for spring admission, 12/1 for domestic students. Applications are processed on a rolling basis. Application fee: $25 ($75 for international students). *Expenses:* Tuition, state resident: part-time $99 per credit hour. Tuition, nonresident: part-time $325 per credit hour. One-time fee: $52 part-time. *Financial support:* In 2003–04, 5 research assistantships (averaging $12,000 per year), 4 teaching assistantships (averaging $12,000 per year) were awarded. Career-related internships or fieldwork, Federal Work-Study, and institutionally sponsored loans also available. Support available to part-time students. Financial award application deadline: 5/1; financial award applicants required to submit FAFSA. *Unit head:* Dr. David A. Snyder, Head, 254-968-9222.

Texas A&M University, College of Agriculture and Life Sciences, Department of Animal Science, College Station, TX 77843. Offers animal breeding (MS, PhD); animal science (M Agr, MS, PhD); dairy science (M Agr, MS); food science and technology (MS, PhD); genetics (MS, PhD); nutrition (MS, PhD); physiology of reproduction (MS, PhD). *Faculty:* 34 full-time (6 women). *Students:* 116 full-time (70 women), 44 part-time (21 women); includes 8 minority (5 Asian Americans or Pacific Islanders, 3 Hispanic Americans), 29 international. Average age 26. *Degree requirements:* For master's and doctorate, thesis/dissertation, registration. *Entrance requirements:* For master's and doctorate, GRE General Test. Additional exam requirements/recommendations for international students: Required—TOEFL. *Application deadline:* For fall admission, 2/1 for domestic students; for spring admission, 10/1 priority date for domestic students. Applications are processed on a rolling basis. Application fee: $50 ($75 for international students). *Expenses:* Tuition, state resident: full-time $3,420. Tuition, nonresident: full-time $9,084. Required fees: $1,861. *Financial support:* In 2003–04, fellowships (averaging $15,000 per year), research assistantships (averaging $12,950 per year), teaching assistantships (averaging $11,500 per year) were awarded. Career-related internships or fieldwork, Federal Work-Study, institutionally sponsored loans, and scholarships/grants also available. Financial award application deadline: 2/1; financial award applicants required to submit FAFSA. *Faculty research:* Genetic engineering/gene markers, dietary effects on colon cancer, biotechnology. *Unit head:* Dr. John McNeill, Head, 979-845-1541. *Application contact:* Ronnie Edwards, Graduate Advisor, 979-845-1542, Fax: 979-845-6433, E-mail: r-edwards@tamu.edu.

Texas A&M University, College of Agriculture and Life Sciences, Department of Poultry Science, College Station, TX 77843. Offers M Agr, MS, PhD. Part-time and evening/weekend programs available. Postbaccalaureate distance learning degree programs offered (no on-campus study). *Faculty:* 7 full-time (1 woman). *Students:* 29 full-time (12 women), 13 part-time (6 women); includes 3 minority (all Hispanic Americans), 21 international. Average age 29. In 2003, 9 master's, 5 doctorates awarded. Terminal master's awarded for partial completion of doctoral program. *Median time to degree:* Of those who began their doctoral program in fall 1995, 100% received their degree in 8 years or less. *Degree requirements:* For master's, thesis (for some programs); for doctorate, thesis/dissertation. *Entrance requirements:* For master's and doctorate, GRE General Test. Additional exam requirements/recommendations for international students: Required—TOEFL. Application fee: $50 ($75 for international students). Electronic applications accepted. *Expenses:* Tuition, state resident: full-time $3,420. Tuition, nonresident: full-time $9,084. Required fees: $1,861. *Financial support:* In 2003–04, 25 students received support, including 4 fellowships with partial tuition reimbursements available (averaging $18,000 per year), 23 research assistantships with partial tuition reimbursements available; teaching assistantships, scholarships/grants, health care benefits, and unspecified assistantships also available. Financial award application deadline: 4/1; financial award applicants required to submit FAFSA. *Faculty research:* Poultry diseases and immunology, avian genetics and physiology, nutrition and metabolism, poultry processing and food safety, waste management. *Unit head:* Dr. Alan Sams, Head, 979-845-1931, Fax: 979-845-1921, E-mail: asams@

Animal Sciences

Texas A&M University (continued)
poultry.tamu.edu. *Application contact:* Dr. Jerry Daniels, Advisor/Lecturer, 979-845-1654, Fax: 979-845-1931, E-mail: jdaniels@poultry.tamu.edu.

Texas A&M University–Kingsville, College of Graduate Studies, College of Agriculture and Home Economics, Program in Animal Sciences, Kingsville, TX 78363. Offers MS. *Degree requirements:* For master's, thesis or alternative, comprehensive exam. *Entrance requirements:* For master's, GRE General Test, minimum GPA of 3.0. Additional exam requirements/recommendations for international students: Required—TOEFL.

Texas Tech University, Graduate School, College of Agricultural Sciences and Natural Resources, Department of Animal and Food Sciences, Lubbock, TX 79409. Offers agriculture (M Agr); animal science (MS, PhD); food technology (MS). Part-time programs available. *Faculty:* 14 full-time (4 women), 2 part-time/adjunct (0 women). *Students:* 42 full-time (19 women), 12 part-time (3 women); includes 1 minority (Hispanic American), 2 international. Average age 27. 41 applicants, 56% accepted, 14 enrolled. In 2003, 11 master's, 7 doctorates awarded. *Degree requirements:* For master's, thesis, internship (M Agr); for doctorate, thesis/dissertation. *Entrance requirements:* For master's and doctorate, GRE General Test. Additional exam requirements/recommendations for international students: Required—TOEFL (minimum score 550 paper-based; 213 computer-based). *Application deadline:* Applications are processed on a rolling basis. Application fee: $50 ($60 for international students). Electronic applications accepted. *Expenses:* Tuition, state resident: full-time $3,312. Tuition, nonresident: full-time $8,976. Required fees: $1,745. Tuition and fees vary according to program. *Financial support:* In 2003–04, 29 students received support, including 34 research assistantships with partial tuition reimbursements available (averaging $10,630 per year), 5 teaching assistantships with partial tuition reimbursements available (averaging $10,740 per year); Federal Work-Study and institutionally sponsored loans also available. Support available to part-time students. Financial award application deadline: 5/1; financial award applicants required to submit FAFSA. *Faculty research:* Animal growth composition and product acceptability, animal nutrition and utilization, animal physiology and adaptation to stress, food microbiology, food safety and security. Total annual research expenditures: $2.5 million. *Unit head:* Dr. Kevin R. Pond, Chairman, 806-742-2513, Fax: 806-742-0898, E-mail: asft.grad@ttu.edu. *Application contact:* Diane Reid, Graduate Secretary, 806-742-2814, Fax: 806-742-2427, E-mail: diane.reid@ttu.edu.

Tuskegee University, Graduate Programs, College of Agricultural, Environmental and Natural Sciences, Department of Agricultural Sciences, Program in Animal and Poultry Sciences, Tuskegee, AL 36088. Offers MS. *Faculty:* 13 full-time (1 woman), 2 part-time/adjunct (1 woman). *Students:* 4 full-time (3 women), 4 part-time (1 woman); includes 3 minority (all African Americans), 3 international. Average age 27. *Degree requirements:* For master's, thesis. *Entrance requirements:* For master's, GRE General Test. *Application deadline:* For fall admission, 7/15 for domestic students. Applications are processed on a rolling basis. Application fee: $25 ($35 for international students). *Expenses:* Tuition: Full-time $11,060; part-time $655 per credit hour. Required fees: $250. Tuition and fees vary according to course load. *Financial support:* Application deadline: 4/15. *Unit head:* Dr. P. K. Biswas, Head, Department of Agricultural Sciences, 334-727-8632.

Université Laval, Faculty of Agricultural and Food Sciences, Department of Animal Sciences, Programs in Animal Sciences, Québec, QC G1K 7P4, Canada. Offers M Sc, PhD. Part-time programs available. Terminal master's awarded for partial completion of doctoral program. *Degree requirements:* For master's, thesis/dissertation; for doctorate, thesis/dissertation, comprehensive exam. *Entrance requirements:* For master's and doctorate, knowledge of French and English. Electronic applications accepted.

The University of Arizona, Graduate College, College of Agriculture and Life Sciences, Department of Animal Sciences, Tucson, AZ 85721. Offers MS, PhD. Part-time programs available. *Faculty:* 11 full-time (0 women), 5 part-time/adjunct (2 women). *Students:* 13 full-time (4 women), 4 part-time (2 women); includes 3 minority (all Hispanic Americans), 2 international. Average age 28. 12 applicants, 50% accepted, 5 enrolled. In 2003, 2 degrees awarded. *Degree requirements:* For master's and doctorate, thesis/dissertation. *Entrance requirements:* For master's, GRE Subject Test, 3 letters of recommendation; for doctorate, GRE Subject Test (biology or chemistry recommended), 3 letters of recommendation. Additional exam requirements/recommendations for international students: Required—TOEFL (minimum score 550 paper-based; 213 computer-based). *Application deadline:* For fall admission, 4/1 for domestic students, 2/1 for international students; for spring admission, 8/1 for domestic students, 8/1 for international students. Applications are processed on a rolling basis. Application fee: $50. *Expenses:* Tuition, state resident: part-time $196 per unit. Tuition, nonresident: part-time $326 per unit. *Financial support:* In 2003–04, 10 students received support, including 6 research assistantships with partial tuition reimbursements available (averaging $18,640 per year), 4 teaching assistantships with partial tuition reimbursements available (averaging $15,644 per year); fellowships, scholarships/grants, health care benefits, and unspecified assistantships also available. Financial award application deadline: 4/1. *Faculty research:* Nutrition of beef and dairy cattle, reproduction and breeding, muscle growth and function, animal stress, meat science. Total annual research expenditures: $543,938. *Unit head:* Dr. Robert J. Collier, Professor and Head, 520-621-1322, Fax: 520-621-9435. *Application contact:* Alberta Rettig, Administrative Assistant, 520-621-7623, Fax: 520-621-9435, E-mail: ans@ag.arizona.edu.

University of Arkansas, Graduate School, Dale Bumpers College of Agricultural, Food and Life Sciences, Department of Animal Science, Fayetteville, AR 72701-1201. Offers MS, PhD. *Students:* 17 full-time (9 women), 8 part-time (1 woman); includes 3 minority (2 African Americans, 1 Hispanic American), 3 international. 16 applicants, 69% accepted. In 2003, 6 master's, 8 doctorates awarded. *Degree requirements:* For master's, thesis; for doctorate, variable foreign language requirement, thesis/dissertation. Application fee: $40 ($50 for international students). *Expenses:* Tuition, state resident: full-time $4,032; part-time $224 per credit hour. Tuition, nonresident: full-time $9,540; part-time $530 per credit hour. Tuition and fees vary according to course load and program. *Financial support:* In 2003–04, 2 fellowships, 14 research assistantships, 2 teaching assistantships were awarded. Career-related internships or fieldwork and Federal Work-Study also available. Support available to part-time students. Financial award application deadline: 4/1; financial award applicants required to submit FAFSA. *Unit head:* Dr. Keith Lusby, Chair, 479-575-4351. *Application contact:* Dr. Wayne Kellogg, Graduate Coordinator, E-mail: wkellogg@comp.uark.edu.

University of Arkansas, Graduate School, Dale Bumpers College of Agricultural, Food and Life Sciences, Department of Poultry Science, Fayetteville, AR 72701-1201. Offers MS, PhD. *Faculty:* 15 full-time (3 women). *Students:* 33 full-time (13 women), 10 part-time (3 women); includes 3 minority (1 African American, 2 Asian Americans or Pacific Islanders), 17 international. 26 applicants, 62% accepted. In 2003, 7 master's, 5 doctorates awarded. *Degree requirements:* For master's, thesis; for doctorate, variable foreign language requirement, thesis/dissertation. Application fee: $40 ($50 for international students). *Expenses:* Tuition, state resident: full-time $4,032; part-time $224 per credit hour. Tuition, nonresident: full-time $9,540; part-time $530 per credit hour. Tuition and fees vary according to course load and program. *Financial support:* In 2003–04, 3 fellowships, 33 research assistantships were awarded. Teaching assistantships, career-related internships or fieldwork and Federal Work-Study also available. Support available to part-time students. Financial award application deadline: 4/1; financial award applicants required to submit FAFSA. *Unit head:* Walter Bottje, Head, 479-575-4952.

The University of British Columbia, Faculty of Graduate Studies, Faculty of Agricultural Sciences, Animal Science Graduate Program, Vancouver, BC V6T 1Z1, Canada. Offers M Sc, PhD. *Faculty:* 10 full-time (1 woman), 4 part-time/adjunct (0 women). *Students:* 41 full-time (25 women). Average age 24. 25 applicants, 20% accepted, 4 enrolled. In 2003, 2 master's, 1 doctorate awarded. *Median time to degree:* Master's–3.5 years full-time; doctorate–6 years full-time. *Degree requirements:* For master's, thesis/dissertation, registration; for doctorate, thesis/dissertation, comprehensive exam, registration. *Entrance requirements:* Additional exam requirements/recommendations for international students: Required—TOEFL (minimum score 560 paper-based; 220 computer-based). *Application deadline:* For fall admission, 3/30 for domestic students, 2/28 for international students; for winter admission, 8/31 for domestic students; for spring admission, 12/31 for domestic students. Applications are processed on a rolling basis. Application fee: $90 Canadian dollars ($150 Canadian dollars for international students). Electronic applications accepted. *Financial support:* In 2003–04, 22 fellowships with tuition reimbursements (averaging $14,149 per year) were awarded; research assistantships, teaching assistantships, career-related internships or fieldwork, Federal Work-Study, institutionally sponsored loans, scholarships/grants, and tuition waivers (full and partial) also available. *Faculty research:* Nutrition and metabolism, animal production, animal behavior and welfare, reproductive physiology, animal genetics, aquaculture and fish physiology. Total annual research expenditures: $797,021. *Unit head:* Dr. Marina von Keyserlingk, Graduate Advisor, Fax: 604-822-4400, E-mail: gradapp@interchange.ubc.ca. *Application contact:* Alina Yuhymets, Graduate Programs Manager, 604-822-4593, Fax: 604-822-4400, E-mail: yuhymets@interchange.ubc.ca.

University of California, Davis, Graduate Studies, Program in Animal Science, Davis, CA 95616. Offers MAM, MS. *Faculty:* 34 full-time. *Students:* 30 full-time (21 women); includes 4 minority (3 Asian Americans or Pacific Islanders, 1 Hispanic American), 3 international. Average age 25. 46 applicants, 48% accepted, 14 enrolled. In 2003, 15 degrees awarded. *Degree requirements:* For master's, thesis optional. *Entrance requirements:* For master's, GRE General Test, minimum GPA of 3.0. Additional exam requirements/recommendations for international students: Required—TOEFL (minimum score 550 paper-based; 213 computer-based). *Application deadline:* For fall admission, 1/15 for domestic students, 1/15 for international students. Application fee: $60. Electronic applications accepted. Tuition, nonresident: full-time $12,245. Required fees: $7,062. *Financial support:* In 2003–04, 29 students received support, including 9 fellowships with full and partial tuition reimbursements available (averaging $5,857 per year), 4 research assistantships with full and partial tuition reimbursements available (averaging $8,228 per year), 15 teaching assistantships with partial tuition reimbursements available (averaging $14,145 per year); Federal Work-Study, institutionally sponsored loans, and tuition waivers (full and partial) also available. Financial award application deadline: 1/15; financial award applicants required to submit FAFSA. *Faculty research:* Genetics, nutrition, physiology and behavior in domestic and aquatic animals. *Unit head:* Gary B. Anderson, Graduate Chair, 530-752-1252, E-mail: gbanderson@ucdavis.edu. *Application contact:* Alisha L. Nork, Administrative Assistant, 530-752-2382, E-mail: alnork@ucdavis.edu.

University of Connecticut, Graduate School, College of Agriculture and Natural Resources, Department of Animal Science, Field of Animal Science, Storrs, CT 06269. Offers MS, PhD. *Faculty:* 17 full-time (3 women). *Students:* 31 full-time (13 women), 7 part-time (5 women), 21 international. Average age 30. 26 applicants, 46% accepted, 10 enrolled. In 2003, 9 master's, 8 doctorates awarded. Terminal master's awarded for partial completion of doctoral program. *Degree requirements:* For master's and doctorate, thesis/dissertation, comprehensive exam. *Entrance requirements:* For master's and doctorate, GRE General Test. Additional exam requirements/recommendations for international students: Required—TOEFL (minimum score 550 paper-based; 213 computer-based). *Application deadline:* For fall admission, 2/1 priority date for domestic students, 2/1 priority date for international students; for spring admission, 11/1 for domestic students, 10/1 for international students. Applications are processed on a rolling basis. Application fee: $55. Electronic applications accepted. *Expenses:* Tuition, state resident: part-time $3,860 per semester. Tuition, nonresident: part-time $9,036 per semester. *Financial support:* In 2003–04, 24 research assistantships with tuition reimbursements, 3 teaching assistantships with tuition reimbursements were awarded. Fellowships, Federal Work-Study, scholarships/grants, health care benefits, and unspecified assistantships also available. Financial award application deadline: 2/1; financial award applicants required to submit FAFSA. *Application contact:* Larry Silbart, Chairperson, 860-486-6073, Fax: 860-486-4375, E-mail: lawrence.silbart@uconn.edu.

University of Florida, Graduate School, College of Agricultural and Life Sciences, Department of Animal Sciences, Gainesville, FL 32611. Offers M Ag, MS, PhD. *Faculty:* 58. *Students:* 53 full-time (26 women), 12 part-time (7 women); includes 9 minority (1 African American, 1 Asian American or Pacific Islander, 7 Hispanic Americans), 18 international. 28 applicants, 68% accepted. In 2003, 14 master's, 9 doctorates awarded. *Degree requirements:* For master's, variable foreign language requirement, thesis optional; for doctorate, variable foreign language requirement, thesis/dissertation. *Entrance requirements:* For master's and doctorate, GRE General Test, minimum GPA of 3.0. Additional exam requirements/recommendations for international students: Required—TOEFL. *Application deadline:* For fall admission, 6/1 for domestic students. Applications are processed on a rolling basis. Application fee: $20. Electronic applications accepted. *Expenses:* Tuition, state resident: part-time $205 per credit hour. Tuition, nonresident: part-time $775 per credit hour. *Financial support:* In 2003–04, 32 students received support, including 1 fellowship, 26 research assistantships, 2 teaching assistantships. *Faculty research:* Meat science, breeding and genetics, animal physiology, molecular biology, animal nutrition. Total annual research expenditures: $4.1 million. *Unit head:* Dr. F. G. Hembry, Chair, 352-392-1911, Fax: 352-392-5595, E-mail: hembry@animal.ufl.edu. *Application contact:* Dr. Joel Brendemuhl, Assistant Chair, 352-392-2186, Fax: 352-392-1913, E-mail: brendemuhl@animal.ufl.edu.

University of Georgia, Graduate School, College of Agricultural and Environmental Sciences, Department of Animal and Dairy Sciences, Athens, GA 30602. Offers animal and dairy science (PhD); animal and dairy sciences (MADS); animal science (MS); dairy science (MS). *Faculty:* 26 full-time (1 woman). *Students:* 28 full-time (18 women), 8 part-time (6 women); includes 1 minority (African American), 10 international. 40 applicants, 33% accepted. In 2003, 8 master's, 3 doctorates awarded. *Degree requirements:* For master's, thesis; for doctorate, one foreign language, thesis/dissertation. *Entrance requirements:* For master's and doctorate, GRE General Test. *Application deadline:* For fall admission, 7/1 for domestic students; for spring admission, 11/15 for domestic students. Application fee: $50. Electronic applications accepted. *Expenses:* Tuition, state resident: part-time $161 per hour. Tuition, nonresident: part-time $690 per hour. One-time fee: $435 part-time. *Financial support:* Fellowships, research assistantships, teaching assistantships, unspecified assistantships available. *Unit head:* Dr. Joe W. West, Head, 706-542-6259, E-mail: ads-info@ads.uga.edu. *Application contact:* Dr. Mark A. Froetschel, Graduate Coordinator, 706-542-0985, Fax: 706-583-0274, E-mail: markf@uga.edu.

University of Georgia, Graduate School, College of Agricultural and Environmental Sciences, Department of Poultry Science, Athens, GA 30602. Offers animal nutrition (PhD); poultry science (MS, PhD). *Faculty:* 13 full-time (1 woman). *Students:* 18 full-time (6 women), 2 part-time (both women), 7 international. 12 applicants, 50% accepted. In 2003, 4 master's, 3 doctorates awarded. *Degree requirements:* For master's, thesis; for doctorate, one foreign language, thesis/dissertation. *Entrance requirements:* For master's and doctorate, GRE General Test. *Application deadline:* For fall admission, 7/1 for domestic students; for spring admission, 11/15 for domestic students. Application fee: $50. Electronic applications accepted. *Expenses:* Tuition, state resident: part-time $161 per hour. Tuition, nonresident: part-time $690 per hour. One-time fee: $435 part-time. *Financial support:* Fellowships, research assistantships, teaching assistantships, unspecified assistantships available. *Unit head:* Dr. Michael Lacy, Head, 706-542-8383, Fax: 706-542-1827, E-mail: mlacy@uga.edu. *Application contact:* Dr. Daniel Fletcher, Graduate Coordinator, 706-542-2476, Fax: 706-542-1827, E-mail: fletcher@uga.edu.

University of Guelph, Graduate Program Services, Ontario Agricultural College, Department of Animal and Poultry Science, Guelph, ON N1G 2W1, Canada. Offers animal science (M Sc, PhD); poultry science (M Sc, PhD). *Faculty:* 34 full-time (2 women), 1 (woman) part-time/adjunct. *Students:* 90. In 2003, 16 master's, 8 doctorates awarded. *Degree requirements:* For master's, thesis (for some programs); for doctorate, thesis/dissertation. *Entrance requirements:* For master's, minimum B- average during previous 2 years; for doctorate, minimum B average. *Application deadline:* Applications are processed on a rolling basis. Application fee: $75.

Tuition and fees charges are reported in Canadian dollars. Tuition, nonresident: full-time $3,440 Canadian dollars. International tuition: $5,432 Canadian dollars full-time. Required fees: $753 Canadian dollars. *Financial support:* Fellowships, research assistantships, teaching assistantships available. *Faculty research:* Animal breeding and genetics (quantitative or molecular), animal nutrition (monogastric or ruminant), animal physiology (environmental, reproductive or behavioral), growth and metabolism (meat science). Total annual research expenditures: $5 million. *Unit head:* Dr. Steve Leeson, Chair, 519-824-4120 Ext. 53681, E-mail: sleeson@uoguelph.ca. *Application contact:* Dr. Andy Robinson, Graduate Coordinator, 519-824-4120 Ext. 53679, E-mail: andyr@uoguelph.ca.

University of Hawaii at Manoa, Graduate Division, College of Tropical Agriculture and Human Resources, Department of Human Nutrition, Food and Animal Sciences, Program in Animal Sciences, Honolulu, HI 96822. Offers MS. Part-time programs available. *Students:* Average age 30. *Degree requirements:* For master's, thesis (for some programs). *Entrance requirements:* For master's, GRE General Test. *Application deadline:* For fall admission, 3/1 for domestic students, 1/15 for international students; for spring admission, 9/1 for domestic students, 8/1 for international students. Application fee: $50. *Expenses:* Tuition, state resident: full-time $4,464; part-time $186 per credit hour. Tuition, nonresident: full-time $10,608; part-time $442 per credit hour. Tuition and fees vary according to program. *Financial support:* In 2003–04, research assistantships (averaging $14,958 per year), teaching assistantships (averaging $12,786 per year) were awarded. Tuition waivers (full) also available. *Faculty research:* Nutritional biochemistry, food composition, nutrition education, nutritional epidemiology, international nutrition, food toxicology. *Unit head:* Dr. James Carpenter, Graduate Chairperson, 808-956-8393, Fax: 808-956-7095, E-mail: cjim@hawaii.edu.

University of Idaho, College of Graduate Studies, College of Agriculture and Life Sciences, Department of Animal and Veterinary Science, Moscow, ID 83844-2282. Offers animal physiology (PhD); veterinary science (MS). *Students:* 13 full-time (6 women), 5 part-time (2 women), 3 international. Average age 36. *Degree requirements:* For doctorate, thesis/dissertation. *Entrance requirements:* For master's, GRE General Test, minimum GPA of 2.8; for doctorate, minimum undergraduate GPA of 2.8, graduate GPA of 3.0. *Application deadline:* For fall admission, 8/1 for domestic students; for spring admission, 12/15 for domestic students. Application fee: $55 ($60 for international students). *Expenses:* Tuition, state resident: full-time $3,348. Tuition, nonresident: full-time $10,740. Required fees: $540. *Financial support:* Research assistantships, teaching assistantships available. Financial award application deadline: 2/15. *Faculty research:* Agribusiness, range-livestock management. *Unit head:* Dr. Richard A. Battaglia, Head, 208-885-6345.

See in-depth description on page 679.

University of Illinois at Urbana–Champaign, Graduate College, College of Agricultural, Consumer and Environmental Sciences, Department of Animal Sciences, Champaign, IL 61820. Offers MS, PhD. *Faculty:* 38 full-time (4 women), 4 part-time/adjunct (2 women). *Students:* 102 full-time (53 women); includes 6 minority (2 African Americans, 2 Asian Americans or Pacific Islanders, 2 Hispanic Americans), 24 international. 69 applicants, 32% accepted, 20 enrolled. In 2003, 17 master's, 17 doctorates awarded. *Degree requirements:* For doctorate, thesis/dissertation. *Entrance requirements:* For master's, GRE, minimum GPA of 3.0. *Application deadline:* For fall admission, 2/15 for domestic students. Applications are processed on a rolling basis. Application fee: $40 ($50 for international students). Electronic applications accepted. *Expenses:* Tuition, state resident: full-time $6,692. Tuition, nonresident: full-time $18,692. *Financial support:* In 2003–04, 22 fellowships, 72 research assistantships, 4 teaching assistantships were awarded. Tuition waivers (full and partial) also available. Financial award application deadline: 2/15. *Unit head:* Neal R. Merchen, Head, 217-333-3462, Fax: 217-333-2871, E-mail: nmerchen@uiuc.edu. *Application contact:* Sharon E. Franks, Staff Secretary, 217-333-1045, Fax: 217-333-8804, E-mail: s-franks@uiuc.edu.

University of Kentucky, Graduate School, Graduate School Programs in the College of Agriculture, Program in Animal Sciences, Lexington, KY 40506-0032. Offers MS, PhD. *Faculty:* 47 full-time (5 women). *Students:* 50 full-time (24 women), 8 part-time (5 women); includes 1 minority (African American), 13 international. 66 applicants, 33% accepted, 14 enrolled. In 2003, 9 master's, 2 doctorates awarded. Terminal master's awarded for partial completion of doctoral program. *Degree requirements:* For master's, thesis optional; for doctorate, thesis/dissertation, comprehensive exam. *Entrance requirements:* For master's, GRE General Test, minimum undergraduate GPA of 2.5; for doctorate, GRE General Test, minimum graduate GPA of 3.0. Additional exam requirements/recommendations for international students: Required—TOEFL (minimum score 550 paper-based; 213 computer-based). *Application deadline:* For fall admission, 7/18 for domestic students, 2/1 for international students. Applications are processed on a rolling basis. Application fee: $35 ($45 for international students). *Expenses:* Tuition, state resident: full-time $4,975; part-time $261 per credit hour. Tuition, nonresident: full-time $12,315; part-time $668 per credit hour. *Financial support:* Fellowships, research assistantships, teaching assistantships, Federal Work-Study and institutionally sponsored loans available. Support available to part-time students. *Faculty research:* Nutrition of horses, cattle, swine, poultry, and sheep; physiology of reproduction and lactation; food science; microbiology. Total annual research expenditures: $2.8 million. *Unit head:* Dr. David Harmon, Director of Graduate Studies, 859-257-7516, Fax: 859-257-3412. *Application contact:* Dr. Brian Jackson, Associate Dean, 859-257-4905, Fax: 859-323-1928.

University of Maine, Graduate School, College of Natural Sciences, Forestry, and Agriculture, Department of Animal and Veterinary Sciences, Program in Animal Sciences, Orono, ME 04469. Offers MPS, MS. *Students:* 4 full-time (1 woman), 2 part-time (both women). Average age 28. 3 applicants, 67% accepted, 2 enrolled. In 2003, 1 degree awarded. *Degree requirements:* For master's, thesis. *Entrance requirements:* For master's, GRE General Test, BS in animal sciences or related area. Additional exam requirements/recommendations for international students: Required—TOEFL. *Application deadline:* For fall admission, 2/1 for domestic students. Applications are processed on a rolling basis. Application fee: $50. Electronic applications accepted. *Expenses:* Tuition, state resident: part-time $235 per credit. Tuition, nonresident: part-time $670 per credit. Tuition and fees vary according to course load. *Financial support:* Research assistantships with tuition reimbursements, teaching assistantships with tuition reimbursements available. Financial award application deadline: 3/1. *Unit head:* Dr. Charles Wallace, Coordinator, 207-581-2737. *Application contact:* Scott G. Delcourt, Associate Dean of the Graduate School, 207-581-3218, Fax: 207-581-3232, E-mail: graduate@maine.edu.

University of Manitoba, Faculty of Graduate Studies, Faculty of Agriculture, Department of Animal Science, Winnipeg, MB R3T 2N2, Canada. Offers M Sc, PhD. *Degree requirements:* For master's, thesis; for doctorate, one foreign language, thesis/dissertation. Tuition charges are reported in Canadian dollars. Tuition, nonresident: full-time $3,878 Canadian dollars.

University of Maryland, College Park, Graduate Studies and Research, College of Agriculture and Natural Resources, Department of Animal and Avian Sciences, Program in Animal Sciences, College Park, MD 20742. Offers MS, PhD. *Students:* 31 full-time (16 women), 6 part-time (5 women); includes 6 minority (5 African Americans, 1 Asian American or Pacific Islander), 14 international. 48 applicants, 25% accepted. In 2003, 5 master's, 6 doctorates awarded. *Degree requirements:* For master's, thesis, oral exam or written comprehensive exam; for doctorate, thesis/dissertation, journal publication, scientific paper. *Entrance requirements:* For master's, GRE General Test, minimum GPA of 3.0; for doctorate, GRE General Test. Additional exam requirements/recommendations for international students: Required—TOEFL. *Application deadline:* For fall admission, 5/1 for domestic students, 2/1 for international students; for spring admission, 10/1 for domestic students, 6/1 for international students. Applications are processed on a rolling basis. Application fee: $50. Electronic applications accepted. *Expenses:* Tuition, state resident: part-time $349 per credit hour. Tuition, nonresident: part-time $602 per credit hour. *Financial support:* Fellowships, research assistantships, teaching assistantships available. Financial award applicants required to submit FAFSA. *Faculty research:* Animal physiology, cell biology and biochemistry, reproduction, biometrics, animal behavior. *Application contact:* Trudy Lindsey, Director, Graduate Enrollment Management Services, 301-405-4190, Fax: 301-314-9305, E-mail: tlindsey@gradschool.umd.edu.

University of Maryland, College Park, Graduate Studies and Research, College of Agriculture and Natural Resources, Department of Animal and Avian Sciences, Program in Poultry Science, College Park, MD 20742. Offers MS, PhD. *Degree requirements:* For master's, thesis, annual seminar; for doctorate, thesis/dissertation, annual seminar, qualifying/oral exam. *Entrance requirements:* For master's, GRE General Test, minimum GPA of 3.0; for doctorate, GRE General Test. *Application deadline:* For fall admission, 5/1 for domestic students, 2/1 for international students; for spring admission, 10/1 for domestic students, 6/1 for international students. Application fee: $50. *Expenses:* Tuition, state resident: part-time $349 per credit hour. Tuition, nonresident: part-time $602 per credit hour. *Financial support:* Fellowships, research assistantships, teaching assistantships available. Financial award applicants required to submit FAFSA. *Faculty research:* Amino acids, atomic absorption, histology and histochemistry, tissue culture, monoclonal antibody production. *Application contact:* Trudy Lindsey, Director, Graduate Enrollment Management Services, 301-405-4190, Fax: 301-314-9305, E-mail: tlindsey@gradschool.umd.edu.

University of Massachusetts Amherst, Graduate School, College of Natural Resources and the Environment, Department of Animal Biotechnology and Biomedical Science, Amherst, MA 01003. Offers mammalian and avian biology (MS, PhD). Part-time programs available. *Faculty:* 16 full-time (7 women). *Students:* 23 full-time (14 women); includes 2 minority (1 African American, 1 Hispanic American), 5 international. Average age 27. 20 applicants, 65% accepted, 11 enrolled. In 2003, 2 master's, 5 doctorates awarded. Terminal master's awarded for partial completion of doctoral program. *Degree requirements:* For master's, thesis or alternative; for doctorate, thesis/dissertation. *Entrance requirements:* For master's and doctorate, GRE General Test. Additional exam requirements/recommendations for international students: Required—TOEFL (minimum score 530 paper-based; 197 computer-based). *Application deadline:* For fall admission, 2/1 priority date for domestic students, 2/1 priority date for international students; for spring admission, 10/1 for domestic students, 10/1 for international students. Applications are processed on a rolling basis. Application fee: $40 ($50 for international students). *Expenses:* Tuition, state resident: full-time $1,320; part-time $110 per credit. Tuition, nonresident: full-time $4,969; part-time $414 per credit. Required fees: $2,626 per term. Tuition and fees vary according to course load. *Financial support:* In 2003–04, research assistantships with full tuition reimbursements (averaging $10,439 per year), teaching assistantships with full tuition reimbursements (averaging $6,707 per year) were awarded. Fellowships with full tuition reimbursements, career-related internships or fieldwork, Federal Work-Study, scholarships/grants, traineeships, and unspecified assistantships also available. Support available to part-time students. Financial award application deadline: 2/1. *Unit head:* Dr. Sam Black, Director, 413-545-2312, Fax: 413-545-6326, E-mail: sblack@vasci.umass.edu.

University of Minnesota, Twin Cities Campus, Graduate School, College of Agricultural, Food, and Environmental Sciences, Department of Animal Science, Minneapolis, MN 55455-0213. Offers MS, PhD. Part-time programs available. *Faculty:* 39 full-time (7 women). *Students:* 30 full-time (12 women); includes 12 minority (8 Asian Americans or Pacific Islanders, 4 Hispanic Americans). 30 applicants, 57% accepted, 6 enrolled. In 2003, 2 master's, 3 doctorates awarded. *Degree requirements:* For master's and doctorate, thesis/dissertation. *Entrance requirements:* For master's and doctorate, GRE. Additional exam requirements/recommendations for international students: Required—TOEFL. *Application deadline:* For fall admission, 6/15 priority date for domestic students, 6/15 priority date for international students; for spring admission, 10/15 priority date for domestic students, 10/15 priority date for international students. Applications are processed on a rolling basis. Application fee: $55 ($75 for international students). *Expenses:* Tuition, state resident: full-time $3,681; part-time $614 per credit. Tuition, nonresident: full-time $7,231; part-time $1,205 per credit. *Financial support:* In 2003–04, 25 research assistantships, 2 teaching assistantships were awarded. *Faculty research:* Physiology, growth biology, nutrition, genetics, production systems. *Unit head:* Dr. F. Abel Ponce de León, Head, 612-624-1205, Fax: 612-625-5789, E-mail: apl@umn.edu. *Application contact:* Kimberly A. Reno, Student Support Services Assistant, 612-624-3491, Fax: 612-625-5789, E-mail: renox001@umn.edu.

University of Missouri–Columbia, Graduate School, College of Agriculture, Food and Natural Resources, Department of Animal Sciences, Columbia, MO 65211. Offers MS, PhD. *Faculty:* 37 full-time (2 women). *Students:* 45 full-time (17 women), 17 part-time (7 women); includes 1 minority (Hispanic American), 14 international. In 2003, 7 master's, 8 doctorates awarded. Terminal master's awarded for partial completion of doctoral program. *Degree requirements:* For doctorate, 2 foreign languages, thesis/dissertation. *Entrance requirements:* For master's and doctorate, GRE General Test, minimum GPA of 3.0. *Application deadline:* Applications are processed on a rolling basis. Application fee: $45 ($60 for international students). *Expenses:* Tuition, state resident: full-time $5,205. Tuition, nonresident: full-time $14,058. *Financial support:* Research assistantships, teaching assistantships, institutionally sponsored loans available. *Unit head:* Dr. Bill Lamberson, Director of Graduate Studies, 573-882-8234, E-mail: lamersonw@missouri.edu.

University of Nebraska–Lincoln, Graduate College, College of Agricultural Sciences and Natural Resources, Department of Animal Science, Lincoln, NE 68588. Offers MS, PhD. *Degree requirements:* For master's, thesis/dissertation; for doctorate, thesis/dissertation, comprehensive exam. *Entrance requirements:* For master's and doctorate, GRE General Test. Additional exam requirements/recommendations for international students: Required—TOEFL (minimum score 525 paper-based; 195 computer-based). Electronic applications accepted. *Faculty research:* Animal breeding and genetics, meat and poultry products, nonruminant and ruminant nutrition, physiology.

University of Nevada, Reno, Graduate School, College of Agriculture and Natural Resources, Program in Animal Science, Reno, NV 89557. Offers MS. *Faculty:* 10. *Students:* 15 full-time (12 women), 1 (woman) part-time; includes 1 minority (African American), 2 international. Average age 26. In 2003, 5 degrees awarded. *Degree requirements:* For master's, thesis optional. *Entrance requirements:* For master's, GRE, minimum GPA of 2.75. Additional exam requirements/recommendations for international students: Required—TOEFL. *Application deadline:* For fall admission, 3/1 for domestic students; for spring admission, 11/1 for domestic students. Applications are processed on a rolling basis. Application fee: $60 ($95 for international students). *Expenses:* Tuition, state resident: part-time $119 per credit. Tuition, nonresident: part-time $127 per credit. Required fees: $20 per term. Tuition and fees vary according to course load. *Financial support:* In 2003–04, 5 research assistantships were awarded. Financial award application deadline: 3/1. *Faculty research:* Sperm fertility, embryo development, ruminant utilization of forages. *Unit head:* Dr. Graca Almeida–Porana, Director, 775-784-6135.

University of New Hampshire, Graduate School, College of Life Sciences and Agriculture, Department of Animal and Nutritional Sciences, Program in animal and Nutritional Sciences, Durham, NH 03824. Offers PhD. *Students:* 3 full-time (2 women), 3 part-time (1 woman). 3 applicants, 100% accepted, 1 enrolled.Tuition, area resident: Full-time $7,070. *Expenses:* Tuition, state resident: full-time $10,605. Tuition, nonresident: full-time $17,430. Required fees: $15. *Financial support:* In 2003–04, 4 teaching assistantships were awarded *Application contact:* Ann Barbarits, Administrative Assistant, 603-862-2178, E-mail: ansc.grad@unh.edu.

University of New Hampshire, Graduate School, College of Life Sciences and Agriculture, Department of Animal and Nutritional Sciences, Program in Animal Science, Durham, NH 03824. Offers MS. Part-time programs available. *Faculty:* 23 full-time. *Students:* 6 full-time (5 women), 6 part-time (5 women). 7 applicants, 71% accepted, 4 enrolled. In 2003, 4 degrees awarded. *Degree requirements:* For master's, registration. *Entrance requirements:* For master's, GRE General Test. Additional exam requirements/recommendations for international students: Required—TOEFL (minimum score 550 paper-based; 213 computer-based); Recommended—TSE. *Application deadline:* For fall admission, 4/1 for domestic students; for winter admission, 12/1 for domestic students. Applications are processed on a

Animal Sciences

University of New Hampshire (continued)
rolling basis. Application fee: $50. Electronic applications accepted. Tuition, area resident: Full-time $7,070. *Expenses:* Tuition, state resident: full-time $10,605. Tuition, nonresident: full-time $17,430. Required fees: $15. *Financial support:* In 2003–04, 2 research assistantships, 6 teaching assistantships were awarded. Fellowships, career-related internships or fieldwork, Federal Work-Study, scholarships/grants, and tuition waivers (full and partial) also available. Support available to part-time students. Financial award application deadline: 2/15.

University of Puerto Rico, Mayagüez Campus, Graduate Studies, College of Agricultural Sciences, Department of Animal Industry, Mayagüez, PR 00681-9000. Offers MS. Part-time programs available. *Degree requirements:* For master's, thesis, comprehensive exam. *Faculty research:* Swine production and nutrition, poultry production, dairy science and technology, microbiology.

University of Rhode Island, Graduate School, College of the Environment and Life Sciences, Department of Fisheries, Aquaculture and Pathology, Kingston, RI 02881. Offers animal science (MS). In 2003, 6 degrees awarded. *Application deadline:* For fall admission, 4/15 for domestic students. Applications are processed on a rolling basis. Application fee: $35. *Expenses:* Tuition, state resident: full-time $4,338; part-time $281 per credit. Tuition, nonresident: full-time $12,438; part-time $704 per credit. Required fees: $1,840. *Unit head:* Dr. Michael Rice, Chairperson, 401-874-2477.

University of Saskatchewan, College of Graduate Studies and Research, College of Agriculture, Department of Animal and Poultry Science, Saskatoon, SK S7N 5A2, Canada. Offers M Ag, M Sc, PhD. *Faculty:* 11. *Students:* 34. *Degree requirements:* For master's and doctorate, thesis/dissertation, registration. *Entrance requirements:* Additional exam requirements/recommendations for international students: Required—TOEFL. *Application deadline:* For fall admission, 7/1 for domestic students. Applications are processed on a rolling basis. Application fee: $50. Tuition charges are reported in Canadian dollars. *Expenses:* Tuition, state resident: part-time $483 Canadian dollars per course. *Financial support:* Fellowships, research assistantships, teaching assistantships available. Financial award application deadline: 1/31. *Unit head:* Dr. B. Laarveld, Head, 306-966-4972, Fax: 306-966-4151, E-mail: laarveld@sask.usask.ca. *Application contact:* Dr. Fiona Buchanan, Graduate Chair, 306-966-4151, Fax: 306-966-4151, E-mail: fiona.buchanan@usask.ca.

University of Saskatchewan, Western College of Veterinary Medicine and College of Graduate Studies and Research, Graduate Programs in Veterinary Medicine, Department of Large Animal Clinical Sciences, Saskatoon, SK S7N 5A2, Canada. Offers herd medicine and theriogenology (M Sc, M Vet Sc, PhD). *Faculty:* 9 full-time (1 woman). *Students:* 14 full-time (6 women); includes 4 minority (all African Americans) In 2003, 4 master's, 2 doctorates awarded. *Degree requirements:* For master's, thesis (for some programs); for doctorate, thesis/dissertation. Tuition charges are reported in Canadian dollars. *Expenses:* Tuition, state resident: part-time $483 Canadian dollars per course. *Faculty research:* Reproduction, infectious diseases, epidemiology, food safety. Total annual research expenditures: $2 million. *Unit head:* Dr. David Wilson, Acting Head, 306-966-7087, Fax: 306-966-7159, E-mail: david.wilson@usask.ca.

University of Saskatchewan, Western College of Veterinary Medicine and College of Graduate Studies and Research, Graduate Programs in Veterinary Medicine, Department of Small Animal Clinical Sciences, Saskatoon, SK S7N 5A2, Canada. Offers small animal clinical sciences (M Sc, PhD); veterinary anesthesiology, radiology and surgery (M Vet Sc); veterinary internal medicine (M Vet Sc). *Faculty:* 5 full-time (2 women). *Students:* 7 full-time (6 women). In 2003, 4 degrees awarded. *Degree requirements:* For master's, thesis (for some programs); for doctorate, thesis/dissertation. Tuition charges are reported in Canadian dollars. *Expenses:* Tuition, state resident: part-time $483 Canadian dollars per course. *Faculty research:* Orthopedics, wildlife, cardiovascular exercise/myelopathy, ophthalmology. *Unit head:* Dr. Klaas Post, Head, 306-966-7084, Fax: 306-966-7174, E-mail: klaas.post@usask.ca.

The University of Tennessee, Graduate School, College of Agricultural Sciences and Natural Resources, Department of Animal Science, Knoxville, TN 37996. Offers animal anatomy (PhD); breeding (MS, PhD); management (MS, PhD); nutrition (MS, PhD); physiology (MS, PhD). Part-time programs available. *Degree requirements:* For master's and doctorate, thesis/dissertation. *Entrance requirements:* For master's and doctorate, GRE General Test, minimum GPA of 2.7. Additional exam requirements/recommendations for international students: Required—TOEFL. Electronic applications accepted.

University of Vermont, Graduate College, College of Agriculture and Life Sciences, Department of Animal Sciences, Burlington, VT 05405. Offers MS, PhD. *Students:* 13 (7 women); includes 1 minority (African American) 6 international. 16 applicants, 38% accepted, 5 enrolled. In 2003, 1 master's, 1 doctorate awarded. *Degree requirements:* For master's, thesis; for doctorate, one foreign language, thesis/dissertation. *Entrance requirements:* For master's and doctorate, GRE General Test. Additional exam requirements/recommendations for international students: Required—TOEFL (minimum score 550 paper-based; 213 computer-based). *Application deadline:* For fall admission, 4/1 for domestic students. Applications are processed on a rolling basis. Application fee: $25. Electronic applications accepted. *Expenses:* Tuition, state resident: part-time $362 per credit hour. Tuition, nonresident: part-time $906 per credit hour. *Financial support:* Fellowships, research assistantships, teaching assistantships available. Financial award application deadline: 3/1. *Faculty research:* Animal nutrition, dairy production. *Unit head:* Dr. K. Plaut, Chairperson, 802-656-2070. *Application contact:* Dr. T. McFadden, Coordinator, 802-656-0142.

University of Wisconsin–Madison, Graduate School, College of Agricultural and Life Sciences, Department of Animal Sciences, Madison, WI 53706-1380. Offers MS, PhD. Part-time programs available. *Faculty:* 18 full-time (0 women), 2 part-time/adjunct (0 women). *Students:* 14 full-time (5 women), 5 part-time (3 women), 7 international. Average age 29. 57 applicants, 11% accepted, 6 enrolled. In 2003, 3 master's, 1 doctorate awarded. Terminal master's awarded for partial completion of doctoral program. *Median time to degree:* Master's–2 years full-time; doctorate–7 years full-time. *Degree requirements:* For master's and doctorate, thesis/dissertation. *Entrance requirements:* For master's and doctorate, GRE. Additional exam requirements/recommendations for international students: Required—TOEFL (minimum score 550 paper-based; 213 computer-based). *Application deadline:* For fall admission, 1/2 priority date for domestic students, 1/2 priority date for international students; for winter admission, 8/15 for domestic students; for spring admission, 3/1 for domestic students. Applications are processed on a rolling basis. Application fee: $45. Electronic applications accepted. Tuition, area resident: Full-time $7,593; part-time $476 per credit. Tuition, nonresident: full-time $22,824; part-time $1,430 per credit. Required fees: $292; $38 per credit. Part-time tuition and fees vary according to course load and reciprocity agreements. *Financial support:* In 2003–04, 2 fellowships with full tuition reimbursements, 9 research assistantships with full tuition reimbursements (averaging $17,430 per year) were awarded. Career-related internships or fieldwork and scholarships/grants also available. *Faculty research:* Animal biology, immunity and toxicology, endocrinology and reproductive physiology, genetics-animal breeding, meat science muscle biology. *Unit head:* Daniel M. Schaefer, Chair, 608-262-4300, Fax: 608-262-5157, E-mail: schaederd@ansci.wisc.edu. *Application contact:* Kathy A. Monson, Student Services, 608-263-5225, Fax: 608-262-5157, E-mail: kmonson@calshp.cals.wisc.edu.

University of Wisconsin–Madison, Graduate School, College of Agricultural and Life Sciences, Department of Dairy Science, Madison, WI 53706-1380. Offers MS, PhD. Part-time programs available. *Faculty:* 14 full-time (1 woman), 2 part-time/adjunct (0 women). *Students:* 41 full-time (21 women), 3 part-time (2 women), 21 international. 23 applicants, 22% accepted, 5 enrolled. In 2003, 6 master's, 4 doctorates awarded. *Degree requirements:* For master's, thesis (for some programs); for doctorate, thesis/dissertation. *Entrance requirements:* For master's and doctorate, GRE General Test. Additional exam requirements/recommendations for international students: Required—TOEFL. *Application deadline:* For fall admission, 10/1 for domestic students. Applications are processed on a rolling basis. Application fee: $45. Electronic applications accepted. Tuition, area resident: Full-time $7,593; part-time $476 per credit. Tuition, nonresident: full-time $22,824; part-time $1,430 per credit. Required fees: $292; $38 per credit. Part-time tuition and fees vary according to course load and reciprocity agreements. *Financial support:* In 2003–04, 27 research assistantships with full tuition reimbursements (averaging $17,772 per year), 1 teaching assistantship with full tuition reimbursement were awarded. Fellowships, Federal Work-Study also available. Support available to part-time students. Financial award applicants required to submit FAFSA. *Faculty research:* Genetics, nutrition, lactation, reproduction, management of dairy cattle. Total annual research expenditures: $2.5 million. *Unit head:* Louis E. Armentano, Chair, 608-263-3308, Fax: 608-263-9412.

University of Wyoming, Graduate School, College of Agriculture, Department of Animal Sciences, Program in Animal Sciences, Laramie, WY 82070. Offers MS, PhD. *Faculty:* 14 full-time (1 woman), 3 part-time/adjunct (0 women). *Students:* 10 full-time (4 women), 6 part-time (2 women), 2 international. Average age 31. 14 applicants, 43% accepted. *Median time to degree:* Doctorate–4 years full-time. *Degree requirements:* For master's and doctorate, thesis/dissertation. *Entrance requirements:* For master's and doctorate, GRE General Test, minimum GPA of 3.0. Additional exam requirements/recommendations for international students: Required—TOEFL (minimum score 525 paper-based). *Application deadline:* For fall admission, 2/1 priority date for domestic students, 2/1 priority date for international students; for spring admission, 9/1 priority date for domestic students, 9/1 priority date for international students. Applications are processed on a rolling basis. Application fee: $40. *Expenses:* Tuition, state resident: part-time $142 per credit hour. Tuition, nonresident: part-time $408 per credit hour. Required fees: $134 per semester. Tuition and fees vary according to course load, campus/location, program and student level. *Financial support:* In 2003–04, 4 students received support, including research assistantships with tuition reimbursements available (averaging $12,000 per year); career-related internships or fieldwork, Federal Work-Study, institutionally sponsored loans, scholarships/grants, and unspecified assistantships also available. Financial award application deadline: 3/1. *Application contact:* Office Assistant, Senior, 307-766-2224, Fax: 307-766-2355, E-mail: animalscience@uwyo.edu.

Utah State University, School of Graduate Studies, College of Agriculture, Department of Animal, Dairy and Veterinary Sciences, Logan, UT 84322. Offers animal science (MS, PhD); bioveterinary science (MS, PhD); dairy science (MS). Part-time programs available. *Faculty:* 19 full-time (1 woman). *Students:* 16 full-time (7 women), 2 part-time (1 woman), 1 international. Average age 25. 9 applicants, 56% accepted, 4 enrolled. In 2003, 2 degrees awarded. *Degree requirements:* For master's, thesis (for some programs), registration; for doctorate, thesis/dissertation, comprehensive exam, registration. *Entrance requirements:* For master's and doctorate, GRE General Test, minimum GPA of 3.0. Additional exam requirements/recommendations for international students: Required—TOEFL. *Application deadline:* For fall admission, 5/15 for domestic students; for spring admission, 10/15 for domestic students. Applications are processed on a rolling basis. Application fee: $50 ($60 for international students). *Expenses:* Tuition, state resident: part-time $270 per credit hour. Tuition, nonresident: part-time $946 per credit hour. Required fees: $173 per credit hour. *Financial support:* In 2003–04, 7 students received support, including 10 fellowships with full and partial tuition reimbursements available (averaging $12,000 per year), 4 research assistantships with full and partial tuition reimbursements available (averaging $13,300 per year), 3 teaching assistantships with full and partial tuition reimbursements available (averaging $13,300 per year); career-related internships or fieldwork, Federal Work-Study, institutionally sponsored loans, scholarships/grants, and tuition waivers (partial) also available. Financial award application deadline: 3/15. *Faculty research:* Monoclonal antibodies, antiviral chemotherapy, management systems, biotechnology, rumen fermentation manipulation. *Unit head:* Dr. Mark C. Healey, Head, 435-797-2162, Fax: 435-797-2118, E-mail: mchealey@cc.usu.edu. *Application contact:* Dr. Jeffrey L. Walters, Graduate Program Coordinator, 435-797-2161, Fax: 435-797-2118, E-mail: jwalters@cc.usu.edu.

Virginia Polytechnic Institute and State University, Graduate School, College of Agriculture and Life Sciences, Department of Animal and Poultry Sciences, Blacksburg, VA 24061. Offers animal science (MS, PhD); poultry science (MS, PhD), including behavior, genetics, management, nutrition, physiology. *Faculty:* 21 full-time (5 women). *Students:* 33 full-time (18 women), 7 part-time (4 women); includes 3 minority (2 Asian Americans or Pacific Islanders, 1 Hispanic American), 13 international. Average age 27. 32 applicants, 41% accepted, 12 enrolled. In 2003, 11 master's, 1 doctorate awarded. *Entrance requirements:* For master's and doctorate, GRE. Additional exam requirements/recommendations for international students: Required—TOEFL (minimum score 550 paper-based; 213 computer-based). *Application deadline:* Applications are processed on a rolling basis. Application fee: $45. Electronic applications accepted. Tuition, area resident: Full-time $6,039; part-time $336 per credit. Tuition, nonresident: full-time $9,708; part-time $539 per credit. Required fees: $905; $130 per credit. *Financial support:* In 2003–04, 12 fellowships with full tuition reimbursements (averaging $14,244 per year), 5 research assistantships with full tuition reimbursements (averaging $16,470 per year), 10 teaching assistantships with full tuition reimbursements (averaging $11,784 per year) were awarded. Career-related internships or fieldwork, Federal Work-Study, scholarships/grants, and unspecified assistantships also available. Financial award application deadline: 4/1. *Faculty research:* Quantitative genetics of cattle and sheep, swine nutrition and management, animal molecular biology, nutrition of grazing livestock. *Unit head:* Dr. Mark A. McCann, Head, 540-231-9157, Fax: 540-231-3010, E-mail: mmccnn@vt.edu. *Application contact:* Dr. David R. Notter, Professor, 540-231-5135, Fax: 540-231-3010, E-mail: drnotter@vt.edu.

Virginia Polytechnic Institute and State University, Graduate School, College of Agriculture and Life Sciences, Department of Dairy Science, Blacksburg, VA 24061. Offers animal science (MS, PhD). *Faculty:* 12 full-time (1 woman). *Students:* 14 full-time (11 women), 4 part-time (1 woman), 3 international. Average age 25. 14 applicants, 50% accepted, 6 enrolled. In 2003, 4 master's, 2 doctorates awarded. *Entrance requirements:* For master's and doctorate, GRE. Additional exam requirements/recommendations for international students: Required—TOEFL (minimum score 550 paper-based; 213 computer-based). *Application deadline:* Applications are processed on a rolling basis. Application fee: $45. Electronic applications accepted. Tuition, area resident: Full-time $6,039; part-time $336 per credit. Tuition, nonresident: full-time $9,708; part-time $539 per credit. Required fees: $905; $130 per credit. *Financial support:* In 2003–04, 5 research assistantships with full tuition reimbursements (averaging $11,967 per year), 2 teaching assistantships with full tuition reimbursements (averaging $12,073 per year) were awarded. Career-related internships or fieldwork, Federal Work-Study, scholarships/grants, and unspecified assistantships also available. Financial award application deadline: 4/1. *Faculty research:* Genetics, nutrition, reproduction, lactation. *Unit head:* Dr. Mike Akers, Head, 540-231-4757, Fax: 540-231-5014, E-mail: rma@vt.edu. *Application contact:* Julie Shumaker, Professor, 540-231-6331, Fax: 540-231-5014, E-mail: shumaker@vt.edu.

Washington State University, Graduate School, College of Agricultural, Human, and Natural Resource Sciences, Department of Animal Sciences, Pullman, WA 99164. Offers MS, PhD. *Faculty:* 20 full-time (4 women). *Students:* 21 full-time (14 women), 1 (woman) part-time; includes 4 minority (1 African American, 1 American Indian/Alaska Native, 1 Asian American or Pacific Islander, 1 Hispanic American), 4 international. 35 applicants, 26% accepted, 8 enrolled. In 2003, 6 master's, 1 doctorate awarded. *Degree requirements:* For master's, thesis, oral exam; for doctorate, thesis/dissertation, oral and written exam. *Entrance requirements:* For master's and doctorate, GRE General Test, minimum GPA of 3.0. *Application deadline:* For fall admission, 3/1 for domestic students; for spring admission, 11/15 priority date for domestic students. Applications are processed on a rolling basis. Application fee: $35. Electronic applications accepted. *Expenses:* Tuition, state resident: full-time $6,278; part-time $314 per hour. Tuition, nonresident: full-time $15,514; part-time $765 per hour. Required fees: $444. Full-time tuition and fees vary according to campus/location, program and student level. Part-time tuition and fees vary according to course load. *Financial support:* In 2003–04, 13 research assistantships with full and partial tuition reimbursements, 4 teaching assistantships with full and partial tuition reimbursements were awarded. Fellowships, career-related internships or fieldwork,

Federal Work-Study, institutionally sponsored loans, scholarships/grants, tuition waivers (partial), and teaching associateships also available. Financial award application deadline: 4/1; financial award applicants required to submit FAFSA. *Faculty research:* Reproduction, genetics. Total annual research expenditures: $1.8 million. *Unit head:* Dr. Raymond W. Wright, Chair, 509-335-5523, Fax: 509-335-4815, E-mail: raywright@wsu.edu.

West Texas A&M University, College of Agriculture, Nursing, and Natural Sciences, Division of Agriculture, Emphasis in Animal Science, Canyon, TX 79016-0001. Offers MS. Part-time programs available. *Faculty:* 4 full-time (0 women), 5 part-time/adjunct (1 woman). *Students:* 13 full-time (6 women), 9 part-time (4 women); includes 1 minority (Hispanic American), 2 international. Average age 34. 18 applicants, 78% accepted, 14 enrolled. In 2003, 4 degrees awarded. *Median time to degree:* Master's–3 years full-time, 6 years part-time. *Degree requirements:* For master's, thesis optional. *Entrance requirements:* For master's, GRE General Test. Additional exam requirements/recommendations for international students: Required—TOEFL (minimum score 550 paper-based). *Application deadline:* Applications are processed on a rolling basis. Application fee: $25 ($75 for international students). Electronic applications accepted. *Expenses:* Tuition, state resident: part-time $56 per credit hour. Tuition, nonresident: part-time $292 per credit hour. Full-time tuition and fees vary according to course level, degree level and program. *Financial support:* In 2003–04, research assistantships (averaging $6,500 per year), 10 teaching assistantships (averaging $6,750 per year) were awarded. Career-related internships or fieldwork, Federal Work-Study, institutionally sponsored loans, scholarships/grants, traineeships, health care benefits, and tuition waivers (partial) also available. Support available to part-time students. *Faculty research:* Nutrition, animal breeding, meat science, reproduction physiology, feedlots. Total annual research expenditures: $414,026. *Application contact:* Dr. Ted Montgomery, Graduate Adviser, 806-651-2560, Fax: 806-651-2938, E-mail: tmontgomery@mail.wtamu.edu.

West Virginia University, Davis College of Agriculture, Forestry and Consumer Sciences, Division of Animal and Veterinary Sciences, Program in Agricultural Sciences, Morgantown, WV 26506. Offers animal and food sciences (PhD); plant and soil sciences (PhD). *Degree requirements:* For doctorate, thesis/dissertation, oral and written exams. *Entrance requirements:* Additional exam requirements/recommendations for international students: Required—TOEFL. Application fee: $45. *Expenses:* Tuition, state resident: full-time $4,332. Tuition, nonresident: full-time $12,442. *Financial support:* Research assistantships with tuition reimbursements, teaching assistantships with tuition reimbursements, Federal Work-Study, institutionally sponsored loans, and tuition waivers (full and partial) available. Financial award application deadline: 2/1; financial award applicants required to submit FAFSA. *Faculty research:* Ruminant nutrition, metabolism, forage utilization, physiology, reproduction. *Application contact:* Dr. Hillar Klandorf, Professor, 304-293-2631 Ext. 4436, Fax: 304-293-3676, E-mail: hillar.klandorf@mail.wvu.edu.

West Virginia University, Davis College of Agriculture, Forestry and Consumer Sciences, Division of Animal and Veterinary Sciences, Program in Animal and Veterinary Sciences, Morgantown, WV 26506. Offers breeding (MS); food sciences (MS); nutrition (MS); physiology (MS); production management (MS); reproduction (MS). Part-time programs available. *Degree requirements:* For master's, thesis, oral and written exams. *Entrance requirements:* For master's, minimum GPA of 2.5. Additional exam requirements/recommendations for international students: Required—TOEFL. Application fee: $45. *Expenses:* Tuition, state resident: full-time $4,332. Tuition, nonresident: full-time $12,442. *Financial support:* Research assistantships, teaching assistantships, Federal Work-Study, institutionally sponsored loans, and tuition waivers (full and partial) available. Financial award application deadline: 2/1; financial award applicants required to submit FAFSA. *Faculty research:* Animal nutrition, reproductive physiology, food science. *Unit head:* Dr. Hillar Klandorf, Coordinator, 304-293-2631 Ext. 4436, Fax: 304-293-3676, E-mail: hillar.klandorf@mail.wvu.edu.

Aquaculture

Auburn University, Graduate School, College of Agriculture, Department of Fisheries and Allied Aquacultures, Auburn University, AL 36849. Offers M Aq, MS, PhD. Part-time programs available. *Faculty:* 18 full-time (3 women). *Students:* 33 full-time (9 women), 37 part-time (11 women); includes 5 minority (1 African American, 1 American Indian/Alaska Native, 1 Asian American or Pacific Islander, 2 Hispanic Americans), 20 international. 33 applicants, 52% accepted. In 2003, 21 master's, 6 doctorates awarded. *Degree requirements:* For master's, thesis (for some programs); for doctorate, 2 foreign languages, thesis/dissertation. *Entrance requirements:* For master's and doctorate, GRE General Test. *Application deadline:* For fall admission, 7/7 for domestic students; for spring admission, 11/24 for domestic students. Applications are processed on a rolling basis. Application fee: $25 ($50 for international students). Electronic applications accepted. *Expenses:* Tuition, state resident: part-time $175 per credit hour. Tuition, nonresident: part-time $525 per credit hour. *Financial support:* Fellowships, research assistantships, teaching assistantships, Federal Work-Study available. Support available to part-time students. Financial award application deadline: 3/15. *Faculty research:* Channel catfish production; aquatic animal health; community and population ecology; pond management; production hatching, breeding and genetics. Total annual research expenditures: $8 million. *Unit head:* Dr. David B. Rouse, Interim Head, 334-844-4786. *Application contact:* Dr. John F. Pritchett, Dean of the Graduate School, 334-844-4700, E-mail: hatchlb@mail.auburn.edu.

Clemson University, Graduate School, College of Agriculture, Forestry and Life Sciences, Department of Forestry and Natural Resources, Program in Aquaculture, Fisheries, and Wildlife, Clemson, SC 29634. Offers MS, PhD. *Students:* 11 full-time (2 women), 7 part-time (4 women); includes 3 minority (1 African American, 1 American Indian/Alaska Native, 1 Hispanic American), 2 international. Average age 25. 17 applicants, 6% accepted, 1 enrolled. In 2003, 7 master's, 2 doctorates awarded. *Degree requirements:* For master's and doctorate, thesis/dissertation. *Entrance requirements:* For master's, GRE General Test, minimum undergraduate GPA of 3.0. Additional exam requirements/recommendations for international students: Required—TOEFL. *Application deadline:* For fall admission, 6/1 for domestic students. Application fee: $40. *Expenses:* Tuition, state resident: full-time $7,432. Tuition, nonresident: full-time $14,732. *Financial support:* Fellowships, research assistantships, teaching assistantships, career-related internships or fieldwork available. Financial award applicants required to submit FAFSA. *Faculty research:* Intensive freshwater culture systems, conservation biology, stream management, applied wildlife management. Total annual research expenditures: $1 million. *Unit head:* Dr. Dave Guynn, Coordinator, 864-656-4803, Fax: 864-656-3304, E-mail: dguynn@clemson.edu.

Kentucky State University, College of Arts and Sciences, Frankfort, KY 40601. Offers aquaculture (MS). Part-time programs available. *Faculty:* 6 part-time/adjunct (0 women). *Students:* 6 full-time (2 women), 5 part-time; includes 3 minority (2 African Americans, 1 Hispanic American). Average age 25. *Degree requirements:* For master's, thesis optional. *Entrance requirements:* For master's, GRE General Test. *Application deadline:* For fall admission, 7/15 for domestic students. Applications are processed on a rolling basis. Application fee: $17. *Expenses:* Tuition, state resident: full-time $3,096. Tuition, nonresident: full-time $9,332. Tuition and fees vary according to course level, degree level and program. *Financial support:* In 2003–04, 7 research assistantships with full tuition reimbursements (averaging $13,000 per year) were awarded Financial award applicants required to submit FAFSA. *Unit head:* Dr. Paul Bibbins, Dean, 502-597-5911, Fax: 502-597-6405, E-mail: pbibbins@gwmail.kysu.edu. *Application contact:* Tamera Thomas, Administrative Specialist, 502-597-5977, Fax: 502-597-6405, E-mail: tthomas@gwmail.kysu.edu.

Memorial University of Newfoundland, School of Graduate Studies, Interdisciplinary Program in Aquaculture, St. John's, NL A1C 5S7, Canada. Offers M Sc. Part-time programs available. *Students:* 12 full-time, 3 part-time. 5 applicants, 20% accepted, 1 enrolled. In 2003, 2 degrees awarded. *Degree requirements:* For master's, thesis. *Entrance requirements:* For master's, honors B Sc or diploma in aquaculture from the Marine Institute of Memorial University of Newfoundland. *Application deadline:* Applications are processed on a rolling basis. Application fee: $40 Canadian dollars. Electronic applications accepted. Tuition and fees charges are reported in Canadian dollars. *Expenses:* Tuition, state resident: part-time $733 Canadian dollars per semester. Tuition, nonresident: part-time $953 Canadian dollars per semester. Required fees: $194 Canadian dollars per year. Tuition and fees vary according to degree level and program. *Financial support:* Fellowships, research assistantships, teaching assistantships available. *Faculty research:* Marine fish larval biology, fin fish nutrition, shellfish culture, fin fish virology, fin fish reproductive biology. *Unit head:* Dr. Joe Brown, Acting Co-Chair, 709-737-3252, Fax: 709-737-3220, E-mail: jabrown@mun.ca. *Application contact:* Gail Kenny, Secretary, 709-737-3444, Fax: 709-737-3316, E-mail: gkenny@mun.ca.

Nova Scotia Agricultural College, Research and Graduate Studies, Truro, NS B2N 5E3, Canada. Offers agriculture (M Sc), including air quality, animal behavior, animal molecular genetics, animal nutrition, animal technology, aquaculture, botany, crop management, crop physiology, ecology, environmental microbiology, food science, horticulture, nutrient management, pest management, physiology, plant biotechnology, plant pathology, soil chemistry, soil fertility, waste management and composting, water quality. Part-time programs available. *Faculty:* 38 full-time (5 women), 13 part-time/adjunct (1 woman). *Students:* 46 full-time (27 women), 21 part-time (13 women); includes 13 minority (10 African Americans, 2 American Indian/Alaska Native, 1 Asian American or Pacific Islander). 45 applicants, 58% accepted, 16 enrolled. In 2003, 11 degrees awarded, leading to university research/teaching 18%, continued full-time study36%, business/industry 9%, government 27%. *Median time to degree:* Master's–2.25 years full-time, 4 years part-time. *Degree requirements:* For master's, thesis, candidacy exam. *Entrance requirements:* For master's, B.Sc. honors degree, minimum GPA of 3.0. Additional exam requirements/recommendations for international students: Required—TOEFL (minimum score 580 paper-based; 237 computer-based), Michigan English Language Assessment Battery. *Application deadline:* For fall admission, 6/1 for domestic students, 4/1 for international students; for winter admission, 11/15 for domestic students; for spring admission, 2/28 for domestic students. Applications are processed on a rolling basis. Application fee: $70. *Expenses:* Tuition, state resident: full-time $6,270. Tuition, nonresident: full-time $9,270. Required fees: $402. Tuition and fees vary according to student level. *Financial support:* In 2003–04, 63 students received support, including research assistantships (averaging $15,000 per year), teaching assistantships (averaging $900 per year); career-related internships or fieldwork, scholarships/grants, and unspecified assistantships also available. *Faculty research:* Organogenesis, somatic embryogenesis, composting, sustainable agriculture, ecotoxicology. Total annual research expenditures: $2 million. *Unit head:* Jill L. Rogers, Manager, 902-893-6360, Fax: 902-893-3430, E-mail: jrogers@nsac.ns.ca. *Application contact:* Marie Law, Administrative Assistant, 902-893-6502, Fax: 902-893-3430, E-mail: mlaw@nsac.ns.ca.

Purdue University, Graduate School, College of Agriculture, Department of Forestry and Natural Resources, West Lafayette, IN 47907. Offers aquaculture, fisheries, aquatic science (MSF); aquaculture, fisheries, aquatic sciences (MS, PhD); forest biology (MS, MSF, PhD); natural resources and environmental policy (MS, MSF); natural resources environmental policy (PhD); quantitative resource analysis (MS, MSF, PhD); wildlife science (MS, MSF, PhD); wood science and technology (MS, MSF, PhD). *Faculty:* 28 full-time (3 women), 3 part-time/adjunct (1 woman). *Students:* 67 full-time (28 women), 3 part-time (all women); includes 3 minority (1 African American, 2 Hispanic Americans), 24 international. Average age 30. 44 applicants, 23% accepted, 9 enrolled. In 2003, 7 master's, 6 doctorates awarded. *Degree requirements:* For master's and doctorate, thesis/dissertation. *Entrance requirements:* For master's and doctorate, GRE General Test, minimum B+ average in undergraduate course work. Additional exam requirements/recommendations for international students: Required—TOEFL. *Application deadline:* For fall admission, 1/5 for domestic students; for spring admission, 9/15 for domestic students. Applications are processed on a rolling basis. Application fee: $55. Electronic applications accepted. *Financial support:* In 2003–04, 10 research assistantships (averaging $15,259 per year) were awarded; fellowships, teaching assistantships, career-related internships or fieldwork and scholarships/grants also available. Support available to part-time students. Financial award application deadline: 1/5; financial award applicants required to submit FAFSA. *Faculty research:* Wildlife management, forest management, forest ecology, forest soils, limnology. Total annual research expenditures: $200,000. *Unit head:* Dr. Robert K. Swihart, Interim Head, 765-494-3590, Fax: 765-494-9461, E-mail: rswihart@purdue.edu. *Application contact:* Kelly Garrett, Graduate Secretary, 765-494-3572, Fax: 765-494-9461, E-mail: kgarrett@purdue.edu.

See in-depth description on page 795.

University of Florida, Graduate School, College of Agricultural and Life Sciences, Department of Fisheries and Aquatic Science, Gainesville, FL 32611. Offers MFAS, MS, PhD. *Faculty:* 30. *Students:* 33 full-time (12 women), 21 part-time (9 women); includes 6 minority (3 African Americans, 1 American Indian/Alaska Native, 2 Asian Americans or Pacific Islanders), 2 international. 29 applicants, 31% accepted. In 2003, 8 master's, 1 doctorate awarded. *Degree requirements:* For master's, thesis optional; for doctorate, thesis/dissertation. *Entrance requirements:* For master's and doctorate, GRE General Test, minimum GPA of 3.0. Additional exam requirements/recommendations for international students: Required—TOEFL. *Application deadline:* For fall admission, 6/1 for domestic students. Applications are processed on a rolling basis. Application fee: $20. Electronic applications accepted. *Expenses:* Tuition, state resident: part-time $205 per credit hour. Tuition, nonresident: part-time $775 per credit hour. *Financial support:* In 2003–04, 1 fellowship, 18 research assistantships were awarded. Unspecified assistantships also available. *Unit head:* Dr. Randall Stocker, Interim Chair, 352-392-9613, Fax: 352-392-3672, E-mail: aqplants@ifas.ufl.edu. *Application contact:* Dr. Ed Phlips, Graduate Coordinator, 352-392-9617 Ext. 248, Fax: 352-392-3672, E-mail: phlips@ufl.edu.

University of Guelph, Graduate Program Services, Program in Aquaculture, Guelph, ON N1G 2W1, Canada. Offers M Sc. *Faculty:* 14 full-time (3 women). *Students:* 2 full-time (1 woman). Average age 24. 8 applicants, 25% accepted. In 2003, 5 degrees awarded. *Entrance requirements:* For master's, minimum B- average during previous 2 years. *Application deadline:* For fall admission, 5/31 for domestic students. Applications are processed on a rolling basis. Application fee: $75. Tuition and fees charges are reported in Canadian dollars. Tuition, nonresident: full-time $3,440 Canadian dollars. International tuition: $5,432 Canadian dollars full-time. Required fees: $753 Canadian dollars. *Financial support:* Teaching assistantships, career-related internships or fieldwork available. *Faculty research:* Protein and amino acid metabolism, genetics, gamete cryogenics, pathology, epidemiology. *Unit head:* R. D. Moccia, Co-Coordinator, 519-824-4120 Ext. 56216, Fax: 519-767-0573, E-mail: rmoccia@uoguelph.ca.

University of Rhode Island, Graduate School, College of the Environment and Life Sciences, Department of Fisheries, Aquaculture and Pathology, Kingston, RI 02881. Offers animal

Aquaculture

University of Rhode Island (continued)
science (MS). In 2003, 6 degrees awarded. *Application deadline:* For fall admission, 4/15 for domestic students. Applications are processed on a rolling basis. Application fee: $35. *Expenses:* Tuition, state resident: full-time $4,338; part-time $281 per credit. Tuition, nonresident: full-time $12,438; part-time $704 per credit. Required fees: $1,840. *Unit head:* Dr. Michael Rice, Chairperson, 401-874-2477.

Food Science and Technology

Alabama Agricultural and Mechanical University, School of Graduate Studies, School of Agricultural and Environmental Sciences, Department of Family and Consumer Sciences, Huntsville, AL 35811. Offers family and consumer sciences (MS); food science (MS, PhD). Part-time and evening/weekend programs available. *Faculty:* 4 full-time (all women), 3 part-time/adjunct (1 woman). *Students:* 7 full-time (6 women), 18 part-time (all women); includes 19 minority (all African Americans) In 2003, 11 degrees awarded. *Degree requirements:* For master's, thesis optional; for doctorate, one foreign language, thesis/dissertation. *Entrance requirements:* For master's, GRE General Test; for doctorate, GRE General Test, MS. *Application deadline:* For fall admission, 5/1 for domestic students. Applications are processed on a rolling basis. Application fee: $25. Electronic applications accepted. *Expenses:* Tuition, state resident: full-time $3,250; part-time $370 per credit hour. Tuition, nonresident: full-time $6,490; part-time $740 per credit hour. *Financial support:* In 2003–04, 2 research assistantships with tuition reimbursements (averaging $9,000 per year), teaching assistantships with tuition reimbursements (averaging $9,000 per year) were awarded. Career-related internships or fieldwork, Federal Work-Study, and traineeships also available. Financial award application deadline: 4/1. *Faculty research:* Food biotechnology, nutrition, food microbiology, food engineering, food chemistry. *Unit head:* Dr. Bernice Richardson, Chair, 256-372-5455, Fax: 256-372-5433.

Auburn University, Graduate School, College of Human Sciences, Department of Nutrition and Food Science, Auburn University, AL 36849. Offers MS, PhD. Part-time programs available. *Faculty:* 13 full-time (9 women). *Students:* 20 full-time (14 women), 12 part-time (9 women); includes 5 minority (3 African Americans, 1 American Indian/Alaska Native, 1 Asian American or Pacific Islander), 14 international. 28 applicants, 64% accepted. In 2003, 6 master's, 2 doctorates awarded. *Degree requirements:* For master's, thesis (for some programs); for doctorate, thesis/dissertation. *Entrance requirements:* For master's and doctorate, GRE General Test. *Application deadline:* For fall admission, 7/7 for domestic students; for spring admission, 11/24 for domestic students. Applications are processed on a rolling basis. Application fee: $25 ($50 for international students). Electronic applications accepted. *Expenses:* Tuition, state resident: part-time $175 per credit hour. Tuition, nonresident: part-time $525 per credit hour. *Financial support:* Research assistantships, teaching assistantships, career-related internships or fieldwork and Federal Work-Study available. Support available to part-time students. Financial award application deadline: 3/15. *Faculty research:* Food quality and safety, diet, food supply, physical activity in maintenance of health, prevention of selected chronic disease states. *Unit head:* Dr. Robert E. Keith, Acting Head, 334-844-4261. *Application contact:* Dr. John F. Pritchett, Dean of the Graduate School, 334-844-4700, E-mail: hatchlb@mail.auburn.edu.

Brigham Young University, Graduate Studies, College of Biological and Agricultural Sciences, Department of Nutrition, Dietetics and Food Science, Provo, UT 84602-1001. Offers food science (MS); nutrition (MS). *Faculty:* 12. *Students:* 12 full-time (8 women); includes 1 minority (Hispanic American) Average age 27. 10 applicants, 60% accepted, 6 enrolled. In 2003, 6 degrees awarded, leading to continued full-time study 20%, business/industry 80%. *Degree requirements:* For master's, thesis, comprehensive exam, registration. *Entrance requirements:* For master's, GRE General Test, minimum GPA of 3.0 during previous 2 years. *Application deadline:* For fall admission, 2/1 for domestic students; for winter admission, 6/30 for domestic students. Application fee: $50. Electronic applications accepted. *Expenses:* Tuition: Part-time $221 per hour. *Financial support:* In 2003–04, 7 students received support, including 5 research assistantships (averaging $15,400 per year), 4 teaching assistantships (averaging $15,400 per year); career-related internships or fieldwork, institutionally sponsored loans, and scholarships/grants also available. *Faculty research:* Dairy foods, lipid oxidation, food processes, magnesium and selenium nutrition, nutrient effect on gene expression. Total annual research expenditures: $223,955. *Unit head:* Dr. Lynn V. Ogden, Chair, 801-422-3912, Fax: 801-422-0258, E-mail: lynn_ogden@byu.edu. *Application contact:* Dr. Merrill J. Christensen, Graduate Coordinator, 801-422-5255, Fax: 801-422-0258, E-mail: merrill_christensen@byu.edu.

California State Polytechnic University, Pomona, Academic Affairs, College of Agriculture, Pomona, CA 91768-2557. Offers agricultural science (MS); animal science (MS); foods and nutrition (MS). Part-time programs available. *Faculty:* 43 full-time (15 women), 15 part-time/adjunct (6 women). *Students:* 24 full-time (18 women), 24 part-time (19 women); includes 14 minority (1 African American, 6 Asian Americans or Pacific Islanders, 7 Hispanic Americans), 6 international. Average age 30. 66 applicants, 55% accepted, 26 enrolled. In 2003, 19 degrees awarded. *Degree requirements:* For master's, thesis or alternative. *Application deadline:* For fall admission, 5/1 for domestic students; for winter admission, 10/15 for domestic students; for spring admission, 1/2 for domestic students. Applications are processed on a rolling basis. Application fee: $55. Electronic applications accepted. Tuition, nonresident: full-time $6,016; part-time $188 per unit. Required fees: $2,256. *Financial support:* Career-related internships or fieldwork, Federal Work-Study, and institutionally sponsored loans available. Support available to part-time students. Financial award application deadline: 3/2; financial award applicants required to submit FAFSA. *Faculty research:* Equine nutrition, physiology, and reproduction; leadership development; bioartificial pancreas; plant science; ruminant and human nutrition. *Unit head:* Dr. Wayne R. Bidlack, Dean, 909-869-2200, E-mail: wrbidlack@csupomona.edu.

California State University, Fresno, Division of Graduate Studies, College of Agricultural Sciences and Technology, Department of Food Science and Nutritional Sciences, Fresno, CA 93740-8027. Offers MS. Part-time programs available. *Degree requirements:* For master's, thesis, registration. *Entrance requirements:* For master's, GRE General Test, minimum GPA of 3.0 in last 60 hours. Additional exam requirements/recommendations for international students: Required—TOEFL. Electronic applications accepted. *Faculty research:* Liquid foods, agroecosystems, pruning evaluations, characterization of juice concentrates, evaluation of root systems.

Chapman University, Graduate Studies, Department of Physical Sciences, Orange, CA 92866. Offers food science and nutrition (MS). Part-time and evening/weekend programs available. *Faculty:* 4 full-time (2 women), 3 part-time/adjunct (1 woman). *Students:* 6 full-time (5 women), 13 part-time (10 women); includes 5 minority (4 Asian Americans or Pacific Islanders, 1 Hispanic American), 5 international. Average age 29. 17 applicants, 71% accepted, 7 enrolled. In 2003, 4 degrees awarded. *Degree requirements:* For master's, thesis, comprehensive exam, registration. *Entrance requirements:* For master's, GRE General Test, minimum undergraduate GPA of 3.0. Additional exam requirements/recommendations for international students: Required—TOEFL (minimum score 550 paper-based). *Application deadline:* Applications are processed on a rolling basis. Application fee: $40. Electronic applications accepted. *Expenses:* Contact institution. *Financial support:* In 2003–04, 6 students received support; fellowships, Federal Work-Study available. Financial award application deadline: 6/30; financial award applicants required to submit FAFSA. *Unit head:* Dr. Anuradha Prakash, Chair, 714-744-7826, E-mail: prakash@chapman.edu. *Application contact:* Jojo Delfin, Information Contact, 714-997-6786, Fax: 714-997-6713, E-mail: delfin@chapman.edu.

Clemson University, Graduate School, College of Agriculture, Forestry and Life Sciences, Department of Food Science and Human Nutrition, Program in Food, Nutrition, and Culinary Science, Clemson, SC 29634. Offers MS. Offered in cooperation with the Departments of Food Science and Poultry Science. *Students:* 8 full-time (4 women), 4 part-time (3 women), 4 international. 24 applicants, 63% accepted, 3 enrolled. In 2003, 2 degrees awarded. *Degree requirements:* For master's, thesis. *Entrance requirements:* For master's, GRE General Test. Additional exam requirements/recommendations for international students: Required—TOEFL. *Application deadline:* For fall admission, 6/1 for domestic students. Applications are processed on a rolling basis. Application fee: $40. Electronic applications accepted. *Expenses:* Tuition, state resident: full-time $7,432. Tuition, nonresident: full-time $14,732. *Financial support:* Fellowships with partial tuition reimbursements, research assistantships with partial tuition reimbursements, teaching assistantships with partial tuition reimbursements available. Financial award applicants required to submit FAFSA. *Unit head:* Dr. Paul Dawson, Coordinator, 864-656-1138, Fax: 864-656-3131, E-mail: pdawson@clemson.edu.

Clemson University, Graduate School, College of Agriculture, Forestry and Life Sciences, Department of Food Science and Human Nutrition and Department of Animal and Veterinary Sciences, Program in Food Technology, Clemson, SC 29634. Offers PhD. *Students:* 9 full-time (5 women), 1 part-time; includes 1 minority (African American), 7 international. 21 applicants, 57% accepted, 1 enrolled. In 2003, 3 degrees awarded. *Degree requirements:* For doctorate, thesis/dissertation. *Entrance requirements:* For doctorate, GRE General Test. Additional exam requirements/recommendations for international students: Required—TOEFL. *Application deadline:* For fall admission, 6/1 for domestic students. Application fee: $40. *Expenses:* Tuition, state resident: full-time $7,432. Tuition, nonresident: full-time $14,732. *Financial support:* Applicants required to submit FAFSA. *Unit head:* Dr. Paul Dawson, Coordinator, 864-656-1138, Fax: 864-656-3131, E-mail: pdawson@clemson.edu.

Colorado State University, Graduate School, College of Applied Human Sciences, Department of Food Science and Human Nutrition, Fort Collins, CO 80523-0015. Offers food science (MS, PhD); nutrition (MS, PhD). Part-time programs available. *Faculty:* 13 full-time (5 women). *Students:* 41 full-time (35 women), 17 part-time (all women); includes 3 minority (1 Asian American or Pacific Islander, 2 Hispanic Americans), 5 international. Average age 30. 121 applicants, 36% accepted, 17 enrolled. In 2003, 14 master's, 1 doctorate awarded. *Degree requirements:* For master's, thesis optional; for doctorate, thesis/dissertation, registration. *Entrance requirements:* For master's and doctorate, GRE General Test, minimum GPA of 3.0. Additional exam requirements/recommendations for international students: Required—TOEFL (minimum score 550 paper-based; 213 computer-based). *Application deadline:* For fall admission, 2/1 priority date for domestic students, 2/1 priority date for international students; for spring admission, 8/1 priority date for domestic students, 8/1 priority date for international students. Applications are processed on a rolling basis. Application fee: $50. Electronic applications accepted. *Expenses:* Tuition, state resident: full-time $4,156. Tuition, nonresident: full-time $14,762. Required fees: $205. Tuition and fees vary according to course load, campus/location, program and reciprocity agreements. *Financial support:* In 2003–04, 3 fellowships (averaging $4,000 per year), 15 research assistantships with full and partial tuition reimbursements (averaging $13,608 per year), 6 teaching assistantships with full and partial tuition reimbursements (averaging $10,206 per year) were awarded. Career-related internships or fieldwork, Federal Work-Study, institutionally sponsored loans, scholarships/grants, traineeships, and unspecified assistantships also available. Financial award application deadline: 4/1. *Faculty research:* Metabolic regulation, nutrition education, nutritional epidemiology, food safety, obesity and diabetes. Total annual research expenditures: $2.9 million. *Unit head:* Dr. Christopher Melby, Head, 970-491-1944, Fax: 970-491-7252, E-mail: christopher.melby@colostate.edu. *Application contact:* Dr. Jennifer Anderson, Graduate Coordinator, 970-491-7334, Fax: 970-491-3875, E-mail: anderson@cahs.colostate.edu.

Cornell University, Graduate School, Graduate Fields of Agriculture and Life Sciences, Field of Food Science and Technology, Ithaca, NY 14853-0001. Offers dairy science (MPS, MS, PhD); food chemistry (MPS, MS, PhD); food engineering (MPS, MS, PhD); food microbiology (MPS, MS, PhD); food processing waste technology (MPS, MS, PhD); food science (MPS, MPS, MS, PhD); international food science (MPS, MS, PhD); sensory evaluation (MPS, MS, PhD). *Faculty:* 38 full-time. *Students:* 81 full-time (45 women); includes 7 minority (5 Asian Americans or Pacific Islanders, 2 Hispanic Americans), 56 international. 131 applicants, 30% accepted, 15 enrolled. In 2003, 13 master's, 15 doctorates awarded. Terminal master's awarded for partial completion of doctoral program. *Degree requirements:* For master's, thesis (MS), teaching experience; for doctorate, thesis/dissertation, teaching experience, comprehensive exam. *Entrance requirements:* For master's and doctorate, GRE General Test, letters of recommendation (3). Additional exam requirements/recommendations for international students: Required—TOEFL (minimum score 550 paper-based; 213 computer-based). *Application deadline:* For fall admission, 1/30 for domestic students. Application fee: $60. Electronic applications accepted. *Expenses:* Tuition: Full-time $28,630. One-time fee: $50 full-time. *Financial support:* In 2003–04, 62 students received support, including 5 fellowships with full tuition reimbursements available, 44 research assistantships with full tuition reimbursements available, 13 teaching assistantships with full tuition reimbursements available; institutionally sponsored loans, scholarships/grants, health care benefits, tuition waivers (full and partial), and unspecified assistantships also available. Financial award applicants required to submit FAFSA. *Faculty research:* Food microbiology/biotechnology, food engineering/processing, food safety/toxicology, sensory science/flavor chemistry, food packaging. *Unit head:* Director of Graduate Studies, 607-255-7637, Fax: 607-254-4868. *Application contact:* Graduate Field Assistant, 607-255-7637, Fax: 607-254-4868, E-mail: fdscigrad@cornell.edu.

Dalhousie University, Faculty of Graduate Studies, DalTech, Faculty of Engineering, Department of Food Science and Technology, Halifax, NS B3H 4R2, Canada. Offers M Sc, PhD. *Degree requirements:* For master's and doctorate, thesis/dissertation. *Entrance requirements:* Additional exam requirements/recommendations for international students: Required—TOEFL. *Faculty research:* Food microbiology, food safety/HALLP, rheology and rheometry, food processing, seafood processing.

Drexel University, College of Arts and Sciences, Department of Bioscience and Biotechnology, Program in Nutrition and Food Sciences, Philadelphia, PA 19104-2875. Offers food science (MS); nutrition science (PhD). Part-time programs available. Terminal master's awarded for partial completion of doctoral program. *Degree requirements:* For master's and doctorate, thesis/dissertation. *Entrance requirements:* For master's and doctorate, GRE General Test. Additional exam requirements/recommendations for international students: Required—TOEFL. Electronic applications accepted. *Faculty research:* Metabolism of lipids, W-3 fatty acids, obesity, diabetes and heart disease, mineral metabolism.

Florida Agricultural and Mechanical University, Division of Graduate Studies, Research, and Continuing Education, College of Engineering Science, Technology, and Agriculture, Division of Agricultural Sciences, Tallahassee, FL 32307-3200. Offers agribusiness (MS);

animal science (MS); engineering technology (MS); entomology (MS); food science (MS); international programs (MS); plant science (MS). *Faculty:* 31 full-time (2 women). *Students:* 14 full-time (8 women), 8 part-time (4 women); includes 17 minority (16 African Americans, 1 Asian American or Pacific Islander), 3 international. In 2003, 7 degrees awarded. *Degree requirements:* For master's, thesis. *Entrance requirements:* For master's, GRE General Test, minimum GPA of 3.0. Additional exam requirements/recommendations for international students: Required—TOEFL (minimum score 500 paper-based). *Application deadline:* For fall admission, 5/18 for domestic students, 12/18 for international students; for spring admission, 11/12 for domestic students, 5/12 for international students. Application fee: $20. *Expenses:* Tuition, state resident: part-time $192 per credit. Tuition, nonresident: part-time $727 per credit. Tuition and fees vary according to course load. *Financial support:* Application deadline: 2/15. *Unit head:* Dr. Mitwe N. Musingo, Graduate Coordinator, 850-561-2309, Fax: 850-599-8821.

Florida State University, Graduate Studies, College of Human Sciences, Department of Nutrition, Food, and Exercise Sciences, Tallahassee, FL 32306. Offers exercise science (PhD), including exercise physiology (MS, PhD), motor learning and control (MS, PhD); movement science (MS), including exercise physiology (MS, PhD), motor learning and control (MS, PhD); nutrition and food science (PhD); nutrition and food sciences (MS), including clinical nutrition, food science, nutrition and sport, nutrition science, nutrition, education and health promotion. *Faculty:* 14 full-time (10 women). *Students:* 48 full-time (29 women), 19 part-time (8 women); includes 11 minority (6 African Americans, 3 Asian Americans or Pacific Islanders, 2 Hispanic Americans), 10 international. 97 applicants, 45% accepted, 14 enrolled. In 2003, 21 master's, 2 doctorates awarded. *Degree requirements:* For master's, thesis optional; for doctorate, thesis/dissertation. *Entrance requirements:* For master's and doctorate, GRE General Test, minimum GPA of 3.0. Additional exam requirements/recommendations for international students: Required—TOEFL. Application fee: $20. Electronic applications accepted. *Expenses:* Tuition, state resident: part-time $196 per credit hour. Tuition, nonresident: part-time $731 per credit hour. Part-time tuition and fees vary according to campus/location. *Financial support:* In 2003–04, 43 students received support, including 3 fellowships with partial tuition reimbursements available (averaging $10,000 per year), 9 research assistantships with partial tuition reimbursements available (averaging $8,000 per year), 22 teaching assistantships with partial tuition reimbursements available (averaging $8,000 per year); career-related internships or fieldwork, Federal Work-Study, institutionally sponsored loans, scholarships/grants, and unspecified assistantships also available. Financial award applicants required to submit FAFSA. *Faculty research:* Nutrition and exercise, vitamin A deficiency, protein biochemistry, cardiovascular responses to exercises, physiological effects of cigarette smoking related to health and wellness. *Unit head:* Dr. J. Michael Overton, Chair, 850-644-1828, Fax: 850-644-0700, E-mail: moverton@mailer.fsu.edu. *Application contact:* Dr. Doris Abood, Graduate Coordinator, 850-644-4800, Fax: 850-644-0700, E-mail: dabood@mailer.fsu.edu.

Framingham State College, Graduate Programs, Department of Chemistry and Food Science, Framingham, MA 01701-9101. Offers food science and nutrition science (MS). Part-time and evening/weekend programs available. *Entrance requirements:* For master's, GRE General Test.

Announcement: The MS program in food science and nutrition science focuses on analytical food chemistry, nutritional biochemistry, basic food processing technology, chemical and microbiological food safety, and food formulation. Thesis and nonthesis options exist for full- and part-time study, using up-to-date laboratory facilities, instrumentation, and food pilot plant capabilities. E-mail: crussel@frc.mass.edu; WWW: http://www.framingham.edu.

Illinois Institute of Technology, Graduate College, College of Science and Letters, Department of Food Safety and Technology, Chicago, IL 60616-3793. Offers MS. Part-time and evening/weekend programs available. *Faculty:* 4 full-time (2 women), 2 part-time/adjunct (0 women). *Students:* 5 full-time (2 women), 9 part-time (4 women), 8 international. Average age 30. 25 applicants, 52% accepted, 2 enrolled. In 2003, 7 degrees awarded. *Degree requirements:* For master's, thesis (for some programs), project, comprehensive exam. *Entrance requirements:* For master's, GRE General Test, minimum undergraduate GPA of 3.0. Additional exam requirements/recommendations for international students: Required—TOEFL (minimum score 550 paper-based; 213 computer-based). *Application deadline:* For fall admission, 5/1 for domestic students, 5/1 for international students; for spring admission, 10/15 for domestic students, 10/15 for international students. Applications are processed on a rolling basis. Application fee: $40. Electronic applications accepted. *Expenses:* Tuition: Part-time $628 per credit. Tuition and fees vary according to course load and program. *Financial support:* Fellowships, research assistantships, teaching assistantships, career-related internships or fieldwork, Federal Work-Study, and institutionally sponsored loans available. Financial award application deadline: 3/1; financial award applicants required to submit FAFSA. *Faculty research:* Food biotechnology, food science, microbiology, food preservation, food processing. Total annual research expenditures: $6 million. *Unit head:* Dr. Darsh Wasan, Interim Director, National Center for Food Safety and Technology, E-mail: wasan@iit.edu. *Application contact:* Beverly Wolak, Faculty Secretary, 708-563-8153, Fax: 708-563-1873, E-mail: wolak@iit.edu.

Iowa State University of Science and Technology, Graduate College, College of Family and Consumer Sciences and College of Agriculture, Department of Food Science and Human Nutrition, Ames, IA 50011. Offers food science and technology (MS, PhD); nutrition (MS, PhD). *Faculty:* 31 full-time, 1 part-time/adjunct. *Students:* 56 full-time (39 women), 7 part-time (all women); includes 8 minority (3 African Americans, 1 Asian American or Pacific Islander, 4 Hispanic Americans), 27 international. 117 applicants, 11% accepted, 10 enrolled. In 2003, 11 master's, 3 doctorates awarded. *Median time to degree:* Master's–2.7 years full-time; doctorate–5.2 years full-time. *Degree requirements:* For master's and doctorate, thesis/dissertation. *Entrance requirements:* For master's and doctorate, GRE General Test. Additional exam requirements/recommendations for international students: Required—TOEFL (paper score 550; computer score 213) or IELTS (score 6.5). *Application deadline:* For fall admission, 2/1 priority date for domestic students, 2/1 priority date for international students. Applications are processed on a rolling basis. Application fee: $50 ($70 for international students). Electronic applications accepted. Tuition, nonresident: part-time $560 per credit. Required fees: $38 per unit. *Financial support:* In 2003–04, 49 research assistantships with full and partial tuition reimbursements (averaging $17,748 per year) were awarded; fellowships, teaching assistantships, scholarships/grants also available. *Unit head:* Dr. Diane F. Birt, Chair, 515-294-3011, Fax: 515-294-8181. *Application contact:* Dr. Wendy S. White, Director of Graduate Education, 515-294-6442.

See in-depth description on page 671.

Kansas State University, Graduate School, College of Human Ecology, Department of Human Nutrition, Manhattan, KS 66506. Offers food science (MS, PhD); nutrition (MS, PhD); public health (MS). Part-time programs available. *Faculty:* 19 full-time (9 women). *Students:* 29 full-time (26 women), 6 part-time (3 women); includes 2 minority (both African Americans), 13 international. Average age 25. 18 applicants, 89% accepted, 16 enrolled. In 2003, 2 degrees awarded. *Degree requirements:* For master's, thesis or alternative, residency; for doctorate, thesis/dissertation, residency. *Entrance requirements:* For master's, GRE General Test, minimum undergraduate GPA of 3.0; for doctorate, GRE General Test, minimum graduate GPA of 3.5, previous course work in biochemistry and statistics. Additional exam requirements/recommendations for international students: Required—TOEFL. *Application deadline:* For fall admission, 2/1 for domestic students; for spring admission, 10/1 for domestic students. Applications are processed on a rolling basis. Application fee: $0 ($25 for international students). Electronic applications accepted. *Expenses:* Tuition, state resident: part-time $155 per credit hour. Tuition, nonresident: part-time $428 per credit hour. Required fees: $11 per credit hour. *Financial support:* In 2003–04, fellowships (averaging $15,000 per year), 22 research assistantships (averaging $12,279 per year), 5 teaching assistantships with full tuition reimbursements (averaging $16,185 per year) were awarded. Career-related internships or fieldwork, Federal Work-Study, institutionally sponsored loans, scholarships/grants, and tuition waivers (full) also available. Support available to part-time students. Financial award application deadline: 3/1; financial award applicants required to submit FAFSA. *Faculty research:* Assessment of food portion size, bone mineral density and turnover in post menopausal women, weight maintenance in cancer prevention, dietary antioxidants and age related macular degeneration, food consumption and nutrient intakes of older women living alone. Total annual research expenditures: $1.4 million. *Unit head:* Dr. Denis Medeiros, Head, 785-532-0150, Fax: 785-532-3132, E-mail: medeiros@ksu.edu. *Application contact:* Janet Finney, Office Specialist, 785-532-5508, Fax: 785-532-3132, E-mail: finney@humec.ksu.edu.

Kansas State University, Graduate School, Food Science Program, Manhattan, KS 66506. Offers MS, PhD. Part-time programs available. Postbaccalaureate distance learning degree programs offered (minimal on-campus study). *Students:* 51 full-time (34 women), 10 part-time (6 women); includes 6 minority (4 Asian Americans or Pacific Islanders, 2 Hispanic Americans), 23 international. Average age 30. 24 applicants, 50% accepted, 10 enrolled. In 2003, 14 master's, 7 doctorates awarded. *Degree requirements:* For master's, thesis, residency; for doctorate, thesis/dissertation, preliminary exams, residency. *Entrance requirements:* For master's, GRE General Test, minimum GPA of 3.0 in undergraduate course work, previous course work in mathematics; for doctorate, GRE General Test, minimum GPA of 3.5 in master's course work. Additional exam requirements/recommendations for international students: Required—TOEFL. *Application deadline:* For fall admission, 2/1 for domestic students; for spring admission, 10/1 priority date for domestic students. Applications are processed on a rolling basis. Application fee: $0 ($25 for international students). *Expenses:* Tuition, state resident: part-time $155 per credit hour. Tuition, nonresident: part-time $428 per credit hour. Required fees: $11 per credit hour. *Financial support:* In 2003–04, 46 research assistantships with partial tuition reimbursements (averaging $8,000 per year), teaching assistantships with partial tuition reimbursements (averaging $8,000 per year) were awarded. Federal Work-Study, institutionally sponsored loans, and scholarships/grants also available. Support available to part-time students. Financial award application deadline: 3/1; financial award applicants required to submit FAFSA. *Faculty research:* Develop systems to insure food safety, determine nutrients and bioactive compounds in fruits, etc., develop new processes to modigy ag-based materials into higher food values, develop and implement sensory evaluation strategies for food, develop and implement hazard analysis and critical control point systems. Total annual research expenditures: $5.3 million. *Unit head:* Tom Herald, Director, 785-532-1221, Fax: 785-532-5681, E-mail: therald@ksu.edu. *Application contact:* Elsa Toburen, Information Contact, 785-532-1057, E-mail: etoburen@oznet.ksu.edu.

Louisiana State University and Agricultural and Mechanical College, Graduate School, College of Agriculture, Department of Food Science, Baton Rouge, LA 70803. Offers MS, PhD. Part-time programs available. *Faculty:* 10 full-time (3 women). *Students:* 20 full-time (15 women), 6 part-time (all women); includes 5 minority (4 African Americans, 1 Hispanic American), 18 international. Average age 30. 41 applicants, 12% accepted, 3 enrolled. In 2003, 5 master's, 1 doctorate awarded. *Degree requirements:* For master's and doctorate, thesis/dissertation. *Entrance requirements:* For master's and doctorate, GRE General Test, minimum GPA of 3.0. Additional exam requirements/recommendations for international students: Required—TOEFL (minimum score 550 paper-based; 213 computer-based). *Application deadline:* For fall admission, 1/25 priority date for domestic students, 5/15 priority date for international students. Applications are processed on a rolling basis. Application fee: $25. Electronic applications accepted. *Expenses:* Tuition, state resident: part-time $337 per hour. Tuition, nonresident: part-time $577 per hour. *Financial support:* In 2003–04, 1 fellowship (averaging $14,333 per year), 14 research assistantships with partial tuition reimbursements (averaging $17,057 per year) were awarded. Teaching assistantships with partial tuition reimbursements, institutionally sponsored loans also available. Financial award application deadline: 4/1; financial award applicants required to submit FAFSA. *Faculty research:* Food toxicology, food microbiology, food quality, food safety, food processing. *Unit head:* Dr. Michael Moody, Head, 225-578-5206, Fax: 225-578-5300, E-mail: mmoody@agctr.lsu.edu. *Application contact:* Dr. Witoon Prinyawiwatkul, Graduate Coordinator, 225-578-5192, Fax: 225-578-5300, E-mail: wprinya@lsu.edu.

Marywood University, Academic Affairs, College of Health and Human Services, Department of Nutrition and Dietetics, Program in Foods and Nutrition, Scranton, PA 18509-1598. Offers MS. *Students:* 6 full-time (all women), 8 part-time (6 women); includes 2 minority (1 African American, 1 Hispanic American). Average age 30. In 2003, 9 degrees awarded. *Degree requirements:* For master's, thesis. *Entrance requirements:* For master's, GRE General Test or MAT. Application fee: $30. *Expenses:* Tuition: Part-time $584 per credit. *Unit head:* Dr. Marianne Borja, Chairperson, 570-348-6211.

McGill University, Faculty of Graduate and Postdoctoral Studies, Faculty of Agricultural and Environmental Sciences, Department of Food Science and Agricultural Chemistry, Montréal, QC H3A 2T5, Canada. Offers M Sc, PhD. *Faculty:* 9 full-time (0 women). *Students:* 40 full-time, 3 part-time. 53 applicants, 28% accepted, 9 enrolled. In 2003, 14 master's, 6 doctorates awarded. *Degree requirements:* For master's, thesis/dissertation, registration; for doctorate, thesis/dissertation, comprehensive exam, registration. *Entrance requirements:* For master's, B Sc in related discipline, minimum GPA of 3.0; for doctorate, M Sc, minimum GPA of 3.0. Additional exam requirements/recommendations for international students: Required—TOEFL (paper score 550; computer score 213) or IELTS (paper score 6). *Application deadline:* For fall admission, 6/1 for domestic students, 3/1 for international students; for winter admission, 10/15 for domestic students; for spring admission, 2/15 for domestic students. Applications are processed on a rolling basis. Application fee: $60. Electronic applications accepted. Tuition, area resident: Full-time $1,668. *Expenses:* Tuition, state resident: full-time $4,173. Tuition, nonresident: full-time $9,468. Required fees: $1,081. *Financial support:* Research assistantships, teaching assistantships, institutionally sponsored loans available. *Faculty research:* Food processing, food biotechnology/enzymology, food microbiology/packaging, food analysis, food chemistry/biochemistry. *Unit head:* Dr. William D. Marshall, Chair, 514-398-7898, Fax: 514-398-7977, E-mail: william.marshall@mcgill.ca. *Application contact:* Lise Stiebel, Graduate Program Secretary, 514-398-7898, Fax: 514-398-7977, E-mail: lise.stiebel@mcgill.ca.

Memorial University of Newfoundland, School of Graduate Studies, Department of Biochemistry, St. John's, NL A1C 5S7, Canada. Offers biochemistry (M Sc, PhD); food science (M Sc, PhD). Part-time programs available. *Students:* 25 full-time. 69 applicants, 9% accepted, 6 enrolled. In 2003, 8 degrees awarded. *Degree requirements:* For master's, thesis; for doctorate, thesis/dissertation, oral defense of thesis, comprehensive exam. *Entrance requirements:* For master's, 2nd class degree in related field; for doctorate, M Sc. *Application deadline:* Applications are processed on a rolling basis. Application fee: $40. Electronic applications accepted. Tuition and fees charges are reported in Canadian dollars. *Expenses:* Tuition, state resident: part-time $733 Canadian dollars per semester. Tuition, nonresident: part-time $953 Canadian dollars per semester. Required fees: $194 Canadian dollars per year. Tuition and fees vary according to degree level and program. *Financial support:* Fellowships, research assistantships, teaching assistantships available. *Faculty research:* Toxicology, cell and molecular biology, food engineering, marine biotechnology, lipid biology. Total annual research expenditures: $1.1 million. *Unit head:* Dr. Martin Mulligan, Head, 709-737-8530, E-mail: mulligan@mun.ca. *Application contact:* Dr. Sukhinder Kaur, Graduate Officer, 709-737-8545, Fax: 709-737-2422, E-mail: biochem@mun.ca.

Michigan State University, College of Veterinary Medicine and Graduate School, Graduate Programs in Veterinary Medicine, National Food Safety and Toxicology Center, East Lansing, MI 48824. Offers food safety (MS). Part-time programs available. Postbaccalaureate distance learning degree programs offered (minimal on-campus study). *Students:* 11 applicants, 9% accepted, 1 enrolled. *Entrance requirements:* For master's, minimum GPA of 3.0, 2 letters of recommendation. *Application deadline:* Applications are processed on a rolling basis. Application fee: $50. Electronic applications accepted. *Expenses:* Contact institution. *Unit head:* Dr. Edward C. Mather, Director, 517-432-3100, Fax: 517-432-2310, E-mail: mather@cvm.msu.edu. *Application contact:* Pattie McNiel, Distance Learning Program Coordinator, 517-432-3100, Fax: 517-432-2310, E-mail: mcnielpa@msu.edu.

Food Science and Technology

Michigan State University, Graduate School, College of Human Ecology and College of Agriculture and Natural Resources, Department of Food Science and Human Nutrition, East Lansing, MI 48824. Offers food science (MS, PhD); food science—environmental toxicology (PhD); human nutrition (MS, PhD); human nutrition-environmental toxicology (PhD). *Faculty:* 22 full-time (8 women). *Students:* 39 full-time (27 women), 17 part-time (12 women); includes 4 minority (2 African Americans, 1 Asian American or Pacific Islander, 1 Hispanic American), 24 international. Average age 32. 148 applicants, 9% accepted. In 2003, 13 master's, 8 doctorates awarded. *Degree requirements:* For master's, thesis optional; for doctorate, thesis/dissertation, 1 term assistant teaching, 1 year residency, oral presentation and defense of dissertation, comprehensive exam. *Entrance requirements:* For master's, GRE General Test, minimum GPA of 3.0 in last 2 years of undergraduate course work, 3 letters of recommendation; for doctorate, GRE General Test, minimum GPA of 3.0, 3 letters of recommendation. Additional exam requirements/recommendations for international students: Required—TOEFL (minimum score 550 paper-based; 213 computer-based), Michigan State University ELT (85), Michigan ELAB (83). *Application deadline:* For fall admission, 1/15 for domestic students. Application fee: $50. Electronic applications accepted. *Expenses:* Tuition, state resident: part-time $291 per hour. Tuition, nonresident: part-time $589 per hour. *Financial support:* In 2003–04, 7 fellowships with tuition reimbursements (averaging $4,102 per year), 35 research assistantships with tuition reimbursements (averaging $11,821 per year), 3 teaching assistantships with tuition reimbursements (averaging $11,784 per year) were awarded. Financial award applicants required to submit FAFSA. *Faculty research:* Food safety and toxicology; food processing and quality enhancement; biochemical nutrition; comunity nutrition. Total annual research expenditures: $3.4 million. *Unit head:* Dr. Mark A. Uebersax, Chairperson, 517-355-8474 Ext. 100, Fax: 517-353-8963, E-mail: uebersax@msu.edu. *Application contact:* Dr. Zeynep Ustunol, Graduate Program Contact, 517-355-8474 Ext. 184, Fax: 517-353-8963, E-mail: ustunol@msu.edu.

Mississippi State University, College of Agriculture and Life Sciences, Department of Food Science and Technology, Mississippi State, MS 39762. Offers MS, PhD. *Faculty:* 7 full-time (2 women). *Students:* 17 full-time (7 women), 11 part-time (5 women); includes 1 minority (African American), 19 international. Average age 29. 31 applicants, 29% accepted, 4 enrolled. In 2003, 6 master's, 7 doctorates awarded. *Degree requirements:* For master's and doctorate, thesis/dissertation, comprehensive exam, registration. *Entrance requirements:* For master's, GRE General Test, minimum GPA of 2.8; for doctorate, GRE General Test, minimum GPA of 3.0. Additional exam requirements/recommendations for international students: Required—TOEFL. *Application deadline:* For fall admission, 7/1 for domestic students; for spring admission, 11/1 for domestic students. Applications are processed on a rolling basis. Application fee: $25 for international students. Electronic applications accepted. *Expenses:* Tuition, state resident: full-time $3,874; part-time $215 per hour. Tuition, nonresident: full-time $8,780; part-time $488 per hour. International tuition: $9,105 full-time. Tuition and fees vary according to course load. *Financial support:* In 2003–04, 1 research assistantship with full tuition reimbursement (averaging $9,360 per year), 1 teaching assistantship with full tuition reimbursement (averaging $9,000 per year) were awarded. Federal Work-Study, institutionally sponsored loans, scholarships/grants, and unspecified assistantships also available. Financial award application deadline: 4/1; financial award applicants required to submit FAFSA. *Faculty research:* Food preservation, food chemistry, food safety, food processing, product development. Total annual research expenditures: $1.5 million. *Unit head:* Dr. Charles H. White, Head, 662-325-3200, Fax: 662-325-8728, E-mail: chwhite@ra.msstate.edu. *Application contact:* Diane D. Wolfe, Director of Admissions, 662-325-2224, Fax: 662-325-7360, E-mail: admit@admissions.msstate.edu.

North Carolina State University, Graduate School, College of Agriculture and Life Sciences, Department of Food Science, Raleigh, NC 27695. Offers MFS, MS, PhD. *Faculty:* 30 full-time (5 women), 19 part-time/adjunct (2 women). *Students:* 62 full-time (34 women), 5 part-time (all women); includes 11 minority (5 African Americans, 6 Asian Americans or Pacific Islanders), 20 international. Average age 29. 92 applicants, 29% accepted. In 2003, 8 master's, 7 doctorates awarded. *Degree requirements:* For master's, thesis (for some programs); for doctorate, thesis/dissertation. *Entrance requirements:* For master's, GRE. *Application deadline:* For fall admission, 6/25 for domestic students, 3/1 for international students; for spring admission, 11/25 for domestic students, 7/15 for international students. Applications are processed on a rolling basis. Application fee: $45. *Expenses:* Tuition, state resident: part-time $396 per hour. Tuition, nonresident: part-time $1,895 per hour. *Financial support:* In 2003–04, 4 fellowships with tuition reimbursements (averaging $8,126 per year), 51 research assistantships with tuition reimbursements (averaging $5,401 per year), 1 teaching assistantship with tuition reimbursement (averaging $6,301 per year) were awarded. Federal Work-Study also available. *Faculty research:* Food safety, value-added food products, environmental quality, nutrition and health, biotechnology. Total annual research expenditures: $2.6 million. *Unit head:* Dr. Kenneth R. Swartzel, Head, 919-515-7435, Fax: 919-515-4694, E-mail: ken_swartzel@ncsu.edu. *Application contact:* Dr. Jonathan C. Allen, Director of Graduate Programs, 919-513-2257, Fax: 919-515-7124, E-mail: jon_allen@ncsu.edu.

North Dakota State University, The Graduate School, Interdisciplinary Program in Food Safety, Fargo, ND 58105. Offers MS, PhD. Part-time programs available. *Faculty:* 10 full-time (5 women), 3 part-time/adjunct (2 women). *Students:* 8 full-time (6 women), 5 international. 5 applicants, 40% accepted, 0 enrolled. *Degree requirements:* For master's, thesis/dissertation; for doctorate, thesis/dissertation, comprehensive exam. *Entrance requirements:* For doctorate, preliminary exam. Additional exam requirements/recommendations for international students: Required—TOEFL (minimum score 525 paper-based), TWE(minimum score 5), GRE. *Application deadline:* Applications are processed on a rolling basis. Application fee: $35 ($50 for international students). Tuition, nonresident: full-time $4,071. Required fees: $493. *Financial support:* In 2003–04, 8 research assistantships with full tuition reimbursements (averaging $16,000 per year) were awarded; scholarships/grants also available. *Faculty research:* Myco toxins in grain, pathogens in meat systems, benson development for food pathogens. *Unit head:* Dr. Clifford Hall, Head, 701-231-6359, E-mail: clifford.hall@ndsu.nodak.edu.

Nova Scotia Agricultural College, Research and Graduate Studies, Truro, NS B2N 5E3, Canada. Offers agriculture (M Sc), including air quality, animal behavior, animal molecular genetics, animal nutrition, animal technology, aquaculture, botany, crop management, crop physiology, ecology, environmental microbiology, food science, horticulture, nutrient management, pest management, physiology, plant biotechnology, plant pathology, soil chemistry, soil fertility, waste management and composting, water quality. Part-time programs available. *Faculty:* 38 full-time (5 women), 13 part-time/adjunct (1 woman). *Students:* 46 full-time (27 women), 21 part-time (13 women); includes 13 minority (10 African Americans, 2 American Indian/Alaska Native, 1 Asian American or Pacific Islander). 45 applicants, 58% accepted, 16 enrolled. In 2003, 11 degrees awarded, leading to university research/teaching 18%, continued full-time study36%, business/industry 9%, government 27%. *Median time to degree:* Master's–2.25 years full-time, 4 years part-time. *Degree requirements:* For master's, thesis, candidacy exam. *Entrance requirements:* For master's, B.Sc. honors degree, minimum GPA of 3.0. Additional exam requirements/recommendations for international students: Required—TOEFL (minimum score 580 paper-based; 237 computer-based), Michigan English Language Assessment Battery. *Application deadline:* For fall admission, 6/1 for domestic students, 4/1 for international students; for winter admission, 11/15 for domestic students; for spring admission, 2/28 for domestic students. Applications are processed on a rolling basis. Application fee: $70. *Expenses:* Tuition, state resident: full-time $6,270. Tuition, nonresident: full-time $9,270. Required fees: $402. Tuition and fees vary according to student level. *Financial support:* In 2003–04, 63 students received support, including research assistantships (averaging $15,000 per year), teaching assistantships (averaging $900 per year); career-related internships or fieldwork, scholarships/grants, and unspecified assistantships also available. *Faculty research:* Organogenesis, somatic embryogenesis, composting, sustainable agriculture, ecotoxicology. Total annual research expenditures: $2 million. *Unit head:* Jill L. Rogers, Manager, 902-893-6360, Fax: 902-893-3430, E-mail: jrogers@nsac.ns.ca. *Application contact:* Marie Law, Administrative Assistant, 902-893-6502, Fax: 902-893-3430, E-mail: mlaw@nsac.ns.ca.

The Ohio State University, Graduate School, College of Food, Agricultural, and Environmental Sciences, Program in Food Science and Nutrition, Columbus, OH 43210. Offers MS, PhD. *Faculty:* 23. *Students:* 53 full-time (36 women), 6 part-time (4 women); includes 6 minority (3 African Americans, 2 Asian Americans or Pacific Islanders, 1 Hispanic American), 27 international. 160 applicants, 20% accepted. In 2003, 12 master's, 7 doctorates awarded. *Degree requirements:* For master's, thesis optional; for doctorate, thesis/dissertation. *Entrance requirements:* For master's and doctorate, GRE General Test. *Application deadline:* For fall admission, 8/15 for domestic students. Applications are processed on a rolling basis. Application fee: $40 ($50 for international students). *Expenses:* Tuition, state resident: full-time $7,233. Tuition, nonresident: full-time $18,489. *Financial support:* Fellowships, research assistantships, Federal Work-Study and institutionally sponsored loans available. Support available to part-time students. *Unit head:* Dr. Kenneth Lee, Graduate Studies Committee Chair, 614-292-7797, Fax: 614-292-0218, E-mail: lee.133@osu.edu.

Oklahoma State University, Graduate College, College of Agricultural Sciences and Natural Resources, Department of Animal Sciences, Program in Food Science, Stillwater, OK 74078. Offers MS, PhD. *Degree requirements:* For master's and doctorate, thesis/dissertation. *Entrance requirements:* Additional exam requirements/recommendations for international students: Required—TOEFL. *Application deadline:* For fall admission, 6/1 for domestic students. Application fee: $25 ($50 for international students). *Expenses:* Tuition, state resident: full-time $3,752; part-time $118 per credit hour. Tuition, nonresident: full-time $10,346; part-time $393 per credit hour. Tuition and fees vary according to course load. *Financial support:* Research assistantships, teaching assistantships, career-related internships or fieldwork, Federal Work-Study, and tuition waivers (partial) available. Support available to part-time students. Financial award application deadline: 3/1. *Unit head:* Dr. Gerald Horn, Coordinator, 405-744-6621, E-mail: horngw@okstate.edu.

Oklahoma State University, Graduate College, College of Agricultural Sciences and Natural Resources and College of Engineering, Architecture and Technology, School of Biosystems and Agricultural Engineering, Stillwater, OK 74078. Offers biosystems engineering (M Bio E); environmental and natural resources (MS, PhD); food and bioprocessing (MS, PhD). *Faculty:* 21 full-time (2 women), 1 part-time/adjunct (0 women). *Students:* 8 full-time (1 woman), 20 part-time (7 women); includes 1 minority (American Indian/Alaska Native), 19 international. Average age 32. 25 applicants, 60% accepted. In 2003, 6 master's, 3 doctorates awarded. *Degree requirements:* For master's and doctorate, thesis/dissertation. *Entrance requirements:* Additional exam requirements/recommendations for international students: Required—TOEFL. *Application deadline:* For fall admission, 6/1 for domestic students. Applications are processed on a rolling basis. Application fee: $25 ($50 for international students). Electronic applications accepted. *Expenses:* Tuition, state resident: full-time $3,752; part-time $118 per credit hour. Tuition, nonresident: full-time $10,346; part-time $393 per credit hour. Tuition and fees vary according to course load. *Financial support:* In 2003–04, 26 research assistantships (averaging $11,850 per year), 1 teaching assistantship (averaging $11,400 per year) were awarded. Career-related internships or fieldwork, Federal Work-Study, and tuition waivers (partial) also available. Support available to part-time students. Financial award application deadline: 3/1. *Unit head:* Dr. Ronald L. Elliot, Head, 405-744-5431, Fax: 405-744-6059.

Oregon State University, Graduate School, College of Agricultural Sciences, Department of Food Science and Technology, Corvallis, OR 97331. Offers M Agr, MAIS, MS, PhD. *Faculty:* 14 full-time (3 women). *Students:* 35 full-time (23 women), 4 part-time (2 women); includes 1 minority (Asian American or Pacific Islander), 29 international. Average age 29. In 2003, 11 master's, 4 doctorates awarded. *Degree requirements:* For master's, thesis (for some programs); for doctorate, thesis/dissertation. *Entrance requirements:* For master's and doctorate, GRE General Test, minimum GPA of 3.0 in last 90 hours. Additional exam requirements/recommendations for international students: Required—TOEFL. *Application deadline:* For fall admission, 3/1 for domestic students. Applications are processed on a rolling basis. Application fee: $50. *Expenses:* Tuition, state resident: full-time $8,139; part-time $301 per credit. Tuition, nonresident: full-time $14,376; part-time $532 per credit. Required fees: $1,227. *Financial support:* Fellowships, research assistantships, teaching assistantships, career-related internships or fieldwork, Federal Work-Study, and institutionally sponsored loans available. Support available to part-time students. Financial award application deadline: 2/1. *Faculty research:* Diet, cancer, and anticarcinogenesis; sensory analysis; chemistry and biochemistry. *Unit head:* Dr. Robert McGorrin, Head, 541-737-8737, Fax: 541-737-1877, E-mail: robert.mcgorrin@orst.edu. *Application contact:* 541-737-6486, Fax: 541-737-1877.

The Pennsylvania State University University Park Campus, Graduate School, College of Agricultural Sciences, Department of Food Science, State College, University Park, PA 16802-1503. Offers MS, PhD. *Students:* 37 full-time (23 women), 4 part-time (3 women); includes 3 minority (1 African American, 1 Asian American or Pacific Islander, 1 Hispanic American), 26 international. *Entrance requirements:* For master's and doctorate, GRE General Test. Application fee: $45. *Expenses:* Tuition, state resident: full-time $10,010; part-time $417 per credit. Tuition, nonresident: full-time $19,830; part-time $826 per credit. Full-time tuition and fees vary according to course level, course load, campus/location and program. *Unit head:* Dr. John D. Floros, Head, 814-863-2950, Fax: 814-863-6132, E-mail: jdf10@psu.edu. *Application contact:* Juanita Wolfe, Information Contact, E-mail: jmw5@psu.edu.

Purdue University, Graduate School, College of Agriculture, Department of Food Science, West Lafayette, IN 47907. Offers MS, PhD. *Degree requirements:* For master's, thesis (for some programs); for doctorate, thesis/dissertation, teaching assistantship. *Entrance requirements:* For master's and doctorate, GRE General Test. Additional exam requirements/recommendations for international students: Required—TOEFL, TWE. Electronic applications accepted. *Faculty research:* Processing, technology, microbiology, chemistry of foods, carbohydrate chemistry.

Purdue University, Graduate School, School of Consumer and Family Sciences, Department of Foods and Nutrition, West Lafayette, IN 47907. Offers food sciences (MS, PhD); nutrition (MS, PhD). *Degree requirements:* For master's and doctorate, thesis/dissertation. *Entrance requirements:* For master's and doctorate, GRE General Test. Additional exam requirements/recommendations for international students: Required—TOEFL. Electronic applications accepted. *Faculty research:* Nutrient requirements, nutrient metabolism, nutrition and disease prevention.

Rutgers, The State University of New Jersey, New Brunswick/Piscataway, Graduate School, Program in Food Science, New Brunswick, NJ 08901-1281. Offers M Phil, MS, PhD. Part-time and evening/weekend programs available. Postbaccalaureate distance learning degree programs offered (minimal on-campus study). *Degree requirements:* For master's, thesis or alternative; for doctorate, thesis/dissertation. *Entrance requirements:* For master's and doctorate, GRE General Test. *Expenses:* Tuition, state resident: full-time $10,030. Tuition, nonresident: full-time $14,202. *Faculty research:* Nutraceuticals and functional foods, food and flavor analysis, food chemistry and biochemistry, food nanotechnology, food engineering and processing.

Texas A&M University, College of Agriculture and Life Sciences, Department of Animal Science, Intercollegiate Faculty of Food Science and Technology, College Station, TX 77843. Offers MS, PhD. *Students:* 61. Average age 28. *Degree requirements:* For master's and doctorate, thesis/dissertation. *Entrance requirements:* For master's and doctorate, GRE General Test. Additional exam requirements/recommendations for international students: Required—TOEFL. *Application deadline:* For fall admission, 2/1 for domestic students; for spring admission, 10/1 priority date for domestic students. Applications are processed on a rolling basis. Application fee: $50 ($75 for international students). *Expenses:* Tuition, state resident: full-time $3,420. Tuition, nonresident: full-time $9,084. Required fees: $1,861. *Financial support:* Fellowships, research assistantships, teaching assistantships, career-related internships or fieldwork and scholarships/grants available. *Faculty research:* Food safety, microbiology, product development. *Unit head:* Ronnie Edwards, Graduate Advisor, 979-845-1542, Fax: 979-845-6433, E-mail: r-edwards@tamu.edu.

Texas Tech University, Graduate School, College of Agricultural Sciences and Natural Resources, Department of Animal and Food Sciences, Lubbock, TX 79409. Offers agriculture (M Agr); animal science (MS, PhD); food technology (MS). Part-time programs available. *Faculty:* 14 full-time (4 women), 2 part-time/adjunct (0 women). *Students:* 42 full-time (19 women), 12 part-time (3 women); includes 1 minority (Hispanic American), 2 international. Average age 27. 41 applicants, 56% accepted, 14 enrolled. In 2003, 11 master's, 7 doctorates awarded. *Degree requirements:* For master's, thesis, internship (M Agr); for doctorate, thesis/dissertation. *Entrance requirements:* For master's and doctorate, GRE General Test. Additional exam requirements/recommendations for international students: Required—TOEFL (minimum score 550 paper-based; 213 computer-based). *Application deadline:* Applications are processed on a rolling basis. Application fee: $50 ($60 for international students). Electronic applications accepted. *Expenses:* Tuition, state resident: full-time $3,312. Tuition, nonresident: full-time $8,976. Required fees: $1,745. Tuition and fees vary according to program. *Financial support:* In 2003–04, 29 students received support, including 34 research assistantships with partial tuition reimbursements available (averaging $10,630 per year), 5 teaching assistantships with partial tuition reimbursements available (averaging $10,740 per year); Federal Work-Study and institutionally sponsored loans also available. Support available to part-time students. Financial award application deadline: 5/1; financial award applicants required to submit FAFSA. *Faculty research:* Animal growth composition and product acceptability, animal nutrition and utilization, animal physiology and adaptation to stress, food microbiology, food safety and security. Total annual research expenditures: $2.5 million. *Unit head:* Dr. Kevin R. Pond, Chairman, 806-742-2513, Fax: 806-742-0898, E-mail: asft.grad@ttu.edu. *Application contact:* Diane Reid, Graduate Secretary, 806-742-2814, Fax: 806-742-2427, E-mail: diane.reid@ttu.edu.

Texas Woman's University, Graduate School, College of Health Sciences, Department of Nutrition and Food Sciences, Denton, TX 76201. Offers exercise and sports nutrition (MS); food science (MS); institutional administration (MS); nutrition (MS, PhD). Part-time and evening/weekend programs available. *Students:* 63 full-time (57 women), 72 part-time (68 women); includes 33 minority (11 African Americans, 6 Asian Americans or Pacific Islanders, 16 Hispanic Americans), 13 international. Average age 31. In 2003, 28 master's, 2 doctorates awarded. *Degree requirements:* For master's, comprehensive exam; for doctorate, thesis/dissertation, qualifying exam, comprehensive exam. *Entrance requirements:* For master's, GRE General Test, minimum GPA of 3.25, resumé; for doctorate, GRE General Test, minimum GPA of 3.5, letters of reference. Additional exam requirements/recommendations for international students: Required—TOEFL (minimum score 550 paper-based; 213 computer-based). *Application deadline:* Applications are processed on a rolling basis. Application fee: $30 ($50 for international students). Electronic applications accepted. *Expenses:* Tuition, state resident: part-time $66 per credit. Tuition, nonresident: part-time $302 per credit. Full-time tuition and fees vary according to reciprocity agreements. *Financial support:* In 2003–04, 13 research assistantships (averaging $6,369 per year), 6 teaching assistantships (averaging $6,369 per year) were awarded. Career-related internships or fieldwork, Federal Work-Study, institutionally sponsored loans, scholarships/grants, traineeships, health care benefits, and unspecified assistantships also available. Support available to part-time students. Financial award application deadline: 3/1; financial award applicants required to submit FAFSA. *Faculty research:* Food science, food safety, clinical nutrition, nutrition and cancer, weight management. *Unit head:* Dr. Carolyn M. Bednar, Chair, 940-898-2636, Fax: 940-898-2634, E-mail: cbednar@twu.edu. *Application contact:* Holly Kiser, Coordinator of Graduate Admissions, 940-898-3188, Fax: 940-898-3081, E-mail: hkiser@twu.edu.

Tuskegee University, Graduate Programs, College of Agricultural, Environmental and Natural Sciences, Department of Food and Nutritional Sciences, Tuskegee, AL 36088. Offers MS. *Faculty:* 4 full-time (3 women). *Students:* 14 full-time (12 women), 5 part-time (all women); includes 11 minority (all African Americans), 5 international. Average age 30. In 2003, 6 degrees awarded. *Degree requirements:* For master's, thesis. *Entrance requirements:* For master's, GRE General Test. *Application deadline:* For fall admission, 7/15 for domestic students. Applications are processed on a rolling basis. Application fee: $25 ($35 for international students). *Expenses:* Tuition: Full-time $11,060; part-time $655 per credit hour. Required fees: $250. Tuition and fees vary according to course load. *Financial support:* Application deadline: 4/15. *Unit head:* Dr. Ralphenia Pace, Head, 334-727-8162.

Universidad de las Américas–Puebla, Division of Graduate Studies, School of Engineering, Program in Chemical Engineering, Puebla, , Mexico. Offers chemical engineering (MS); food technology (MS). Part-time and evening/weekend programs available. *Faculty:* 10 full-time (0 women), 2 part-time/adjunct (0 women). *Students:* 7 full-time (3 women); all minorities (all Hispanic Americans) Average age 29. 5 applicants, 80% accepted. In 2003, 16 degrees awarded. *Degree requirements:* For master's, one foreign language, thesis. *Application deadline:* For fall admission, 7/19 for domestic students. Applications are processed on a rolling basis. Application fee: $0. *Expenses:* Tuition: Part-time $148 per credit. *Financial support:* In 2003–04, 8 research assistantships were awarded Support available to part-time students. Financial award application deadline: 5/15. *Faculty research:* Food science, reactors, oil industry, biotechnology. Total annual research expenditures: $75,000. *Unit head:* Dr. René Reyes Mazzoco, Coordinator, 292126, Fax: 292032. *Application contact:* Ing. Gladis Avendaño, Chair of Admissions Office, 22292017, Fax: 22292018, E-mail: admission@mail.udlap.mx.

Universidad de las Américas–Puebla, Division of Graduate Studies, School of Engineering, Program in Food Sciences, Puebla, , Mexico. Offers MS. *Faculty:* 10 full-time (0 women), 2 part-time/adjunct (0 women). *Students:* 20 full-time (18 women); all minorities (all Hispanic Americans) 66 applicants, 70% accepted. In 2003, 8 degrees awarded. Application fee: $0. *Expenses:* Tuition: Part-time $148 per credit. *Financial support:* In 2003–04, 5 research assistantships were awarded Total annual research expenditures: $33,000. *Unit head:* Dr. Aurelio López Maco, Coordinator, 22292409, Fax: 22292032, E-mail: amalo@mail.udlap.mx. *Application contact:* Ing. Gladis Avendaño, Chair of Admissions Office, 22292017, Fax: 22292018, E-mail: admission@mail.udlap.mx.

Université de Moncton, School of Food Science, Nutrition and Family Studies, Moncton, NB E1A 3E9, Canada. Offers family studies (M Sc); foods/nutrition (M Sc). Part-time programs available. *Degree requirements:* For master's, one foreign language, thesis. *Entrance requirements:* For master's, previous course work in statistics. Electronic applications accepted. *Faculty research:* Clinic nutrition (anemia, elderly, osteoporosis), applied nutrition, assessment of microbial safety of fresh fruits and vegetables, metabolic activities of lactic bacterias, solubility of low density lipoproteins.

Université Laval, Faculty of Agricultural and Food Sciences, Department of Food Sciences and Nutrition, Programs in Food Sciences and Technology, Québec, QC G1K 7P4, Canada. Offers M Sc, PhD. Terminal master's awarded for partial completion of doctoral program. *Degree requirements:* For master's, thesis (for some programs); for doctorate, thesis/dissertation, comprehensive exam. *Entrance requirements:* For master's and doctorate, knowledge of French and English. Electronic applications accepted.

The University of Akron, Graduate School, College of Fine and Applied Arts, School of Family and Consumer Sciences, Program in Food Science, Akron, OH 44325-0001. Offers MA. *Students:* Average age 43. *Degree requirements:* For master's, project or thesis, thesis optional. *Entrance requirements:* For master's, GRE General Test, minimum GPA of 2.75, letters of reference. Additional exam requirements/recommendations for international students: Required—TOEFL (minimum score 550 paper-based; 213 computer-based), Michigan English Language Assessment Battery. *Application deadline:* For fall admission, 8/15 for domestic students. Applications are processed on a rolling basis. Application fee: $40 ($60 for international students). *Expenses:* Tuition, state resident: part-time $277 per credit hour. Tuition, nonresident: part-time $476 per credit hour. *Financial support:* Application deadline: 3/1. *Unit head:* Dr. Deborah Marino, Associate Professor, 330-972-6322, E-mail: debora7@uakron.edu.

University of Arkansas, Graduate School, Dale Bumpers College of Agricultural, Food and Life Sciences, Department of Food Science, Fayetteville, AR 72701-1201. Offers MS, PhD. *Students:* 33 full-time (15 women), 10 part-time (4 women); includes 5 minority (1 African American, 4 Asian Americans or Pacific Islanders), 26 international. 59 applicants, 25% accepted. In 2003, 9 master's, 3 doctorates awarded. *Degree requirements:* For master's and doctorate, thesis/dissertation. Application fee: $40 ($50 for international students). *Expenses:* Tuition, state resident: full-time $4,032; part-time $224 per credit hour. Tuition, nonresident: full-time $9,540; part-time $530 per credit hour. Tuition and fees vary according to course load and program. *Financial support:* In 2003–04, 1 fellowship, 33 research assistantships were awarded. Teaching assistantships, career-related internships or fieldwork, Federal Work-Study, scholarships/grants, and unspecified assistantships also available. Support available to part-time students. Financial award application deadline: 4/1; financial award applicants required to submit FAFSA. *Unit head:* Dr. Ron Buescher, Head, 479-575-4605. *Application contact:* Navam Hettiarachchy, Graduate Coordinator, E-mail: nhettiar@comp.uark.edu.

The University of British Columbia, Faculty of Graduate Studies, Faculty of Agricultural Sciences, Program in Food Science, Vancouver, BC V6T 1Z1, Canada. Offers M Sc, PhD. *Faculty:* 8 full-time (2 women), 8 part-time/adjunct (2 women). *Students:* 25 full-time (16 women). Average age 25. 49 applicants, 10% accepted, 3 enrolled. In 2003, 5 degrees awarded. *Degree requirements:* For master's, thesis/dissertation, registration; for doctorate, thesis/dissertation, comprehensive exam, registration. *Entrance requirements:* Additional exam requirements/recommendations for international students: Required—TOEFL (minimum score 560 paper-based; 220 computer-based). *Application deadline:* For fall admission, 3/30 for domestic students, 2/28 for international students; for winter admission, 8/31 for domestic students; for spring admission, 12/31 for domestic students. Application fee: $90 Canadian dollars ($150 Canadian dollars for international students). Electronic applications accepted. *Financial support:* In 2003–04, 10 fellowships (averaging $9,075 per year) were awarded; research assistantships, teaching assistantships, institutionally sponsored loans, scholarships/grants, and tuition waivers (partial) also available. *Faculty research:* Food chemistry and biochemistry, food process science, food toxicology and safety, food microbiology, food biotechnology. Total annual research expenditures: $1.6 million. *Unit head:* Dr. Eunice Li-Chan, Graduate Advisor, Fax: 604-822-4400, E-mail: gradapp@interchange.ubc.ca. *Application contact:* Alina Yuhymets, Graduate Programs Manager, 604-822-4593, Fax: 604-822-4400, E-mail: yuhymets@interchange.ubc.ca.

University of California, Davis, Graduate Studies, Graduate Group in Food Science, Davis, CA 95616. Offers MS, PhD. *Faculty:* 53 full-time. *Students:* 52 full-time (34 women); includes 6 minority (1 African American, 4 Asian Americans or Pacific Islanders, 1 Hispanic American), 25 international. Average age 28. 115 applicants, 27% accepted, 22 enrolled. In 2003, 11 master's, 4 doctorates awarded. Terminal master's awarded for partial completion of doctoral program. *Degree requirements:* For master's, thesis optional; for doctorate, thesis/dissertation. *Entrance requirements:* For master's and doctorate, GRE General Test, minimum GPA of 3.0. Additional exam requirements/recommendations for international students: Required—TOEFL (minimum score 550 paper-based; 213 computer-based). *Application deadline:* For fall admission, 1/15 for domestic students, 1/15 for international students. Application fee: $60. Electronic applications accepted. Tuition, nonresident: full-time $12,245. Required fees: $7,062. *Financial support:* In 2003–04, 42 students received support, including 5 fellowships with full and partial tuition reimbursements available (averaging $9,381 per year), 21 research assistantships with full and partial tuition reimbursements available (averaging $11,809 per year), 10 teaching assistantships with partial tuition reimbursements available (averaging $14,145 per year); Federal Work-Study, institutionally sponsored loans, scholarships/grants, and tuition waivers (full and partial) also available. Financial award application deadline: 1/15; financial award applicants required to submit FAFSA. *Unit head:* Stephanie Dungan, Graduate Group Chair, 530-752-5447, E-mail: srdungan@ucdavis.edu. *Application contact:* Karen Jo Hunter, Administrative Assistant, 530-752-1466, Fax: 530-752-4759, E-mail: kjhunter@ucdavis.edu.

University of Delaware, College of Agriculture and Natural Resources, Department of Animal and Food Sciences, Newark, DE 19716. Offers animal sciences (MS, PhD); food sciences (MS). Part-time programs available. *Faculty:* 17 full-time (5 women). *Students:* 25 full-time (10 women), 2 part-time; includes 2 minority (1 African American, 1 Hispanic American), 5 international. Average age 28. 57 applicants, 21% accepted, 10 enrolled. In 2003, 5 master's, 1 doctorate awarded. Terminal master's awarded for partial completion of doctoral program. *Degree requirements:* For master's and doctorate, thesis/dissertation. *Entrance requirements:* For master's and doctorate, GRE General Test. Additional exam requirements/recommendations for international students: Required—TOEFL. *Application deadline:* For fall admission, 7/1 for domestic students; for spring admission, 12/1 for domestic students. Applications are processed on a rolling basis. Application fee: $60. Electronic applications accepted. *Expenses:* Tuition, state resident: full-time $5,890; part-time $327 per credit. Tuition, nonresident: full-time $15,420; part-time $857 per credit. Required fees: $968. *Financial support:* In 2003–04, 17 students received support, including 10 research assistantships with full tuition reimbursements available (averaging $15,736 per year), 7 teaching assistantships with full tuition reimbursements available (averaging $11,755 per year); fellowships with full tuition reimbursements available, scholarships/grants and tuition waivers (full) also available. Financial award application deadline: 3/1. *Faculty research:* Food chemistry, food microbiology, process engineering technology, packaging, food analysis, microbial genetics, molecular endocrinology, growth physiology, avian immunology and virology, monogastric nutrition, avian genomics. Total annual research expenditures: $1.5 million. *Unit head:* Dr. John K. Rosenberger, Chair, 302-831-2524, Fax: 302-831-2822, E-mail: john.rosenberger@mvs.udel.edu. *Application contact:* Dr. Jack Gelb, Graduate Program Coordinator, 302-831-2524, Fax: 302-831-2822, E-mail: jgelb@udel.edu.

University of Florida, Graduate School, College of Agricultural and Life Sciences, Department of Food Science and Human Nutrition, Gainesville, FL 32611. Offers MS, PhD. *Faculty:* 37. *Students:* 55 full-time (37 women), 14 part-time (8 women); includes 12 minority (5 African Americans, 4 Asian Americans or Pacific Islanders, 3 Hispanic Americans), 9 international. 84 applicants, 61% accepted. In 2003, 5 master's, 2 doctorates awarded. *Degree requirements:* For master's, variable foreign language requirement, thesis optional; for doctorate, thesis/dissertation. *Entrance requirements:* For master's and doctorate, GRE General Test, minimum GPA of 3.0. Additional exam requirements/recommendations for international students: Required—TOEFL. *Application deadline:* For fall admission, 6/1 for domestic students. Applications are processed on a rolling basis. Application fee: $20. Electronic applications accepted. *Expenses:* Tuition, state resident: part-time $205 per credit hour. Tuition, nonresident: part-time $775 per credit hour. *Financial support:* In 2003–04, 37 students received support, including 9 fellowships, 24 research assistantships, 7 teaching assistantships; career-related internships or fieldwork also available. *Faculty research:* Pesticide research, nutritional biochemistry and microbiology, food safety and toxicology assessment and dietetics, food chemistry. *Unit head:* Dr. Charles A. Sims, Chair, 352-392-1991 Ext. 202, Fax: 352-392-9467, E-mail: casims@ifas.ufl.edu. *Application contact:* Dr. Harry Sitren, Coordinator, 352-392-1991 Ext. 216, Fax: 352-392-9467, E-mail: hssitren@ifas.ufl.edu.

University of Georgia, Graduate School, College of Agricultural and Environmental Sciences, Department of Food Science, Athens, GA 30602. Offers food science (MS, PhD); food technology (MFT). Part-time programs available. *Faculty:* 25 full-time (5 women), 7 part-time/adjunct (1 woman). *Students:* 65 full-time (39 women), 27 part-time (17 women); includes 11 minority (8 African Americans, 3 Asian Americans or Pacific Islanders), 45 international. 75 applicants, 43% accepted. In 2003, 17 master's, 12 doctorates awarded. *Degree requirements:* For master's and doctorate, thesis/dissertation. *Entrance requirements:* For master's and doctorate, GRE General Test. Additional exam requirements/recommendations for international students: Required—TOEFL (minimum score 550 paper-based; 213 computer-based). *Application deadline:* For fall admission, 7/1 for domestic students, 5/1 for international students; for spring admission, 11/15 for domestic students, 10/1 for international students. Applications are processed on a rolling basis. Application fee: $50. Electronic applications accepted. *Expenses:* Tuition, state resident: part-time $161 per hour. Tuition, nonresident: part-time $690 per hour. One-time fee: $435 part-time. *Financial support:* Fellowships, research assistantships, teaching assistantships, unspecified assistantships available. Total annual research expenditures: $1.5 million. *Unit head:* Dr. Rakesh K. Singh, Head, 706-542-2286,

Food Science and Technology

University of Georgia (continued)

Fax: 706-542-1050, E-mail: rsingh@uga.edu. *Application contact:* Dr. Philip E. Koehler, Graduate Coordinator, 706-542-1099, Fax: 706-542-1050, E-mail: pkoehler@uga.edu.

University of Guelph, Graduate Program Services, Ontario Agricultural College, Department of Food Science, Guelph, ON N1G 2W1, Canada. Offers M Sc, PhD. *Faculty:* 14 full-time (1 woman). *Students:* 57 full-time (31 women), 1 part-time; includes 30 minority (1 African American, 19 Asian Americans or Pacific Islanders, 10 Hispanic Americans). Average age 27. 59 applicants, 22% accepted, 12 enrolled. In 2003, 15 master's awarded, leading to university research/teaching 7%, continued full-time study26%, business/industry 60%, government 7%; 4 doctorates awarded, leading to university research/teaching 50%, business/industry 50%. *Median time to degree:* Master's–2.3 years full-time; doctorate–3.75 years full-time. *Degree requirements:* For master's and doctorate, thesis/dissertation. *Entrance requirements:* For master's, minimum B- average during previous 2 years of honors B Sc degree; for doctorate, minimum B average. Additional exam requirements/recommendations for international students: Required—TOEFL (minimum score 550 paper-based; 213 computer-based). *Application deadline:* For fall admission, 8/1 priority date for domestic students, 6/1 priority date for international students; for winter admission, 12/1 for domestic students; for spring admission, 4/1 for domestic students. Applications are processed on a rolling basis. Application fee: $75. Electronic applications accepted. Tuition and fees charges are reported in Canadian dollars. Tuition, nonresident: full-time $3,440 Canadian dollars. International tuition: $5,432 Canadian dollars full-time. Required fees: $753 Canadian dollars. *Financial support:* In 2003–04, 36 students received support, including 52 research assistantships (averaging $15,800 per year), 14 teaching assistantships (averaging $4,429 per year); scholarships/grants, unspecified assistantships, and bursaries also available. *Faculty research:* Food chemistry, food microbiology, food processing, preservation and utilization. Total annual research expenditures: $3.7 million. *Unit head:* Dr. P. Purslow, Chair, 519-824-4120 Ext. 52099, Fax: 519-824-6631, E-mail: ppurslow@uoguelph.ca. *Application contact:* Dr. Y. Kakuda, Graduate Coordinator, 519-824-4120 Ext. 52260, Fax: 519-824-6631, E-mail: ykakuda@uoguelph.ca.

University of Guelph, Graduate Program Services, Program in Food Safety and Quality Assurance, Guelph, ON N1G 2W1, Canada. Offers M Sc. Part-time programs available. *Faculty:* 22 full-time (3 women). *Students:* 31 full-time (17 women), 10 part-time (6 women); includes 3 African Americans, 19 Asian Americans or Pacific Islanders, 4 Hispanic Americans. Average age 25. 31 applicants, 35% accepted, 7 enrolled. In 2003, 17 degrees awarded, leading to continued full-time study 5%, business/industry 83%, government 12%. *Median time to degree:* Master's–1.67 years full-time, 3.8 years part-time. *Degree requirements:* For master's, major project. *Entrance requirements:* For master's, minimum B average in last 2 years of honors B Sc degree. Additional exam requirements/recommendations for international students: Required—TOEFL (minimum score 550 paper-based; 213 computer-based). *Application deadline:* For fall admission, 5/1 for domestic students, 5/1 for international students; for winter admission, 10/1 for domestic students; for spring admission, 2/1 for domestic students. Application fee: $75. Electronic applications accepted. Tuition and fees charges are reported in Canadian dollars. Tuition, nonresident: full-time $3,440 Canadian dollars. International tuition: $5,432 Canadian dollars full-time. Required fees: $753 Canadian dollars. *Financial support:* In 2003–04, 13 students received support, including 1 research assistantship (averaging $15,000 per year), 3 teaching assistantships (averaging $4,429 per year); scholarships/grants and bursaries also available. *Faculty research:* Food microbiology, food chemistry, food engineering, food processing, veterinary microbiology. *Unit head:* Dr. M. W. Griffiths, Graduate Coordinator, 519-824-4120 Ext. 52269, Fax: 519-824-6631, E-mail: mgriffit@uoguelph.ca. *Application contact:* Judy A. Campbell, Graduate Student Secretary, 519-824-4120 Ext. 56983, Fax: 519-824-6631, E-mail: jacampbe@uoguelph.ca.

University of Hawaii at Manoa, Graduate Division, College of Tropical Agriculture and Human Resources, Department of Human Nutrition, Food and Animal Sciences, Program in Food Science, Honolulu, HI 96822. Offers MS. *Students:* Average age 27. *Entrance requirements:* For master's, GRE General Test. *Application deadline:* For fall admission, 2/1 for domestic students, 2/1 for international students; for spring admission, 9/1 for domestic students, 9/1 for international students. Application fee: $50. *Expenses:* Tuition, state resident: full-time $4,464; part-time $186 per credit hour. Tuition, nonresident: full-time $10,608; part-time $442 per credit hour. Tuition and fees vary according to program. *Financial support:* In 2003–04, research assistantships (averaging $14,958 per year), teaching assistantships (averaging $12,786 per year) were awarded. *Faculty research:* Biochemistry of natural products, sensory evaluation, food processing, food chemistry, food safety. *Unit head:* Wayne Iwaoka, Graduate Chair, 808-956-6456, Fax: 808-956-3894, E-mail: iwaoka@hawaii.edu.

See in-depth description on page 675.

University of Idaho, College of Graduate Studies, College of Agriculture and Life Sciences, Department of Food Science and Toxicology, Moscow, ID 83844-2282. Offers food science (MS); food science and toxicology (MAT). *Students:* 6 full-time (2 women), 7 part-time (3 women), 7 international. Average age 27. *Entrance requirements:* For master's, minimum GPA of 2.8. *Application deadline:* For fall admission, 8/1 for domestic students; for spring admission, 12/15 for domestic students. Application fee: $55 ($60 for international students). *Expenses:* Tuition, state resident: full-time $3,348. Tuition, nonresident: full-time $10,740. Required fees: $540. *Financial support:* Research assistantships, teaching assistantships available. Financial award application deadline: 2/15. *Unit head:* Denise M. Smith, Head, 208-885-7081.

See in-depth description on page 681.

University of Illinois at Urbana–Champaign, Graduate College, College of Agricultural, Consumer and Environmental Sciences, Department of Food Science and Human Nutrition, Champaign, IL 61820. Offers MS, PhD, MD/PhD. *Faculty:* 25 full-time (9 women), 3 part-time/adjunct (all women). *Students:* 57 full-time (38 women); includes 5 minority (all Asian Americans or Pacific Islanders), 28 international. 116 applicants, 17% accepted, 16 enrolled. In 2003, 28 master's, 4 doctorates awarded. *Degree requirements:* For doctorate, one foreign language, thesis/dissertation. *Entrance requirements:* For master's, minimum GPA of 3.0. *Application deadline:* Applications are processed on a rolling basis. Application fee: $40 ($50 for international students). Electronic applications accepted. *Expenses:* Tuition, state resident: full-time $6,692. Tuition, nonresident: full-time $18,692. *Financial support:* In 2003–04, 7 fellowships, 27 research assistantships, 12 teaching assistantships were awarded. Tuition waivers (full and partial) also available. Financial award application deadline: 2/15. Total annual research expenditures: $4.4 million. *Unit head:* Faye Dong, Head, 217-244-4498, Fax: 217-244-2455, E-mail: fayedong@uiuc.edu. *Application contact:* Crystal Howard, Secretary, 217-333-1326, Fax: 217-244-2455, E-mail: clperkns@uiuc.edu.

University of Maine, Graduate School, College of Natural Sciences, Forestry, and Agriculture, Department of Food Science and Human Nutrition, Orono, ME 04469. Offers food and nutritional sciences (PhD); food science and human nutrition (MS). Part-time programs available. *Faculty:* 4 full-time (1 woman). *Students:* 27 full-time (22 women), 5 part-time (all women); includes 3 minority (2 African Americans, 1 Asian American or Pacific Islander), 5 international. Average age 28. 27 applicants, 37% accepted, 9 enrolled. In 2003, 10 master's, 3 doctorates awarded. *Degree requirements:* For master's and doctorate, thesis/dissertation. *Entrance requirements:* For master's, GRE General Test, minimum GPA of 3.0; for doctorate, GRE General Test. Additional exam requirements/recommendations for international students: Required—TOEFL. *Application deadline:* For fall admission, 2/1 for domestic students. Applications are processed on a rolling basis. Application fee: $50. Electronic applications accepted. *Expenses:* Tuition, state resident: part-time $235 per credit. Tuition, nonresident: part-time $670 per credit. Tuition and fees vary according to course load. *Financial support:* In 2003–04, 9 research assistantships with tuition reimbursements (averaging $13,500 per year), 4 teaching assistantships with tuition reimbursements (averaging $12,000 per year) were awarded. Scholarships/grants and tuition waivers (full and partial) also available. Financial award application deadline: 3/1. *Faculty research:* Product development of fruit and vegetables, lipid oxidation in fish and meat, analytical methods development, metabolism of potato glycoalkaloids, seafood quality. *Unit head:* Dr. Rodney Bushway, Chair, 207-581-1626, Fax: 207-581-1636. *Application contact:* Scott G. Delcourt, Associate Dean of the Graduate School, 207-581-3218, Fax: 207-581-3232, E-mail: graduate@maine.edu.

University of Manitoba, Faculty of Graduate Studies, Faculty of Agriculture, Department of Food Science, Winnipeg, MB R3T 2N2, Canada. Offers M Sc. *Degree requirements:* For master's, thesis. Tuition charges are reported in Canadian dollars. Tuition, nonresident: full-time $3,878 Canadian dollars.

University of Maryland, College Park, Graduate Studies and Research, College of Agriculture and Natural Resources, Department of Nutrition and Food Science, Program in Food Science, College Park, MD 20742. Offers MS, PhD. *Students:* 17 full-time (10 women), 3 part-time (2 women); includes 1 minority (Asian American or Pacific Islander), 13 international. 37 applicants, 24% accepted. In 2003, 1 degree awarded. *Degree requirements:* For master's, research-based thesis or equivalent paper; for doctorate, thesis/dissertation, comprehensive exam. *Entrance requirements:* For master's, GRE General Test, minimum GPA of 3.0, professional experience, 3 letters of recommendation; for doctorate, GRE General Test, minimum GPA of 3.0. Additional exam requirements/recommendations for international students: Required—TOEFL. *Application deadline:* For fall admission, 5/1 for domestic students, 2/1 for international students; for spring admission, 10/1 for domestic students, 6/1 for international students. Applications are processed on a rolling basis. Application fee: $50. Electronic applications accepted. *Expenses:* Tuition, state resident: part-time $349 per credit hour. Tuition, nonresident: part-time $602 per credit hour. *Financial support:* Fellowships, research assistantships, teaching assistantships available. Financial award applicants required to submit FAFSA. *Faculty research:* Food chemistry, engineering, microbiology, and processing technology; quality assurance; membrane separations, rheology and texture measurement. *Unit head:* Dr. Jianghong Meng, Director, 301-405-4521, Fax: 301-405-7980, E-mail: jm332@umail.umd.edu. *Application contact:* Trudy Lindsey, Director, Graduate Enrollment Management Services, 301-405-4190, Fax: 301-314-9305, E-mail: tlindsey@gradschool.umd.edu.

University of Maryland Eastern Shore, Graduate Programs, Department of Agriculture, Program in Food and Agricultural Sciences, Princess Anne, MD 21853-1299. Offers MS. *Degree requirements:* For master's, thesis (for some programs), oral exams. *Entrance requirements:* For master's, GRE General Test, interview, minimum GPA of 3.0. Additional exam requirements/recommendations for international students: Required—TOEFL. Electronic applications accepted. *Faculty research:* Poultry and swine nutrition and management, soybean specialty products, farm management practices, agriculture technology.

University of Massachusetts Amherst, Graduate School, College of Natural Resources and the Environment, Department of Food Science, Amherst, MA 01003. Offers MS, PhD. Part-time programs available. *Faculty:* 11 full-time (2 women). *Students:* 13 full-time (9 women), 23 part-time (8 women); includes 1 minority (Asian American or Pacific Islander), 28 international. Average age 29. 85 applicants, 16% accepted, 9 enrolled. In 2003, 5 master's, 2 doctorates awarded. Terminal master's awarded for partial completion of doctoral program. *Degree requirements:* For master's, thesis or alternative; for doctorate, thesis/dissertation. *Entrance requirements:* For master's and doctorate, GRE General Test. Additional exam requirements/recommendations for international students: Required—TOEFL (minimum score 530 paper-based; 197 computer-based). *Application deadline:* For fall admission, 2/1 priority date for domestic students, 2/1 priority date for international students; for spring admission, 10/1 for domestic students, 10/1 for international students. Applications are processed on a rolling basis. Application fee: $40 ($50 for international students). *Expenses:* Tuition, state resident: full-time $1,320; part-time $110 per credit. Tuition, nonresident: full-time $4,969; part-time $414 per credit. Required fees: $2,626 per term. Tuition and fees vary according to course load. *Financial support:* In 2003–04, 23 research assistantships with full tuition reimbursements (averaging $9,560 per year), 7 teaching assistantships with full tuition reimbursements (averaging $3,912 per year) were awarded. Fellowships with full tuition reimbursements, career-related internships or fieldwork, Federal Work-Study, scholarships/grants, traineeships, and unspecified assistantships also available. Support available to part-time students. Financial award application deadline: 2/1. *Unit head:* Dr. Fergus Clydesdale, Head, 413-545-2277, Fax: 413-545-1262, E-mail: fergc@foodsci.umass.edu.

University of Minnesota, Twin Cities Campus, Graduate School, College of Agricultural, Food, and Environmental Sciences, Program in Food Science, Minneapolis, MN 55455-0213. Offers MS, PhD. Part-time programs available. *Faculty:* 18 full-time (5 women), 8 part-time/adjunct (2 women). *Students:* 24 full-time (12 women), 22 part-time (15 women); includes 14 minority (13 Asian Americans or Pacific Islanders, 1 Hispanic American). Average age 25. 63 applicants, 24% accepted, 6 enrolled. In 2003, 14 master's, 2 doctorates awarded. Terminal master's awarded for partial completion of doctoral program. *Degree requirements:* For master's, thesis (for some programs); for doctorate, thesis/dissertation. *Entrance requirements:* For master's and doctorate, GRE General Test, previous course work in general chemistry, organic chemistry, calculus, and physics. Additional exam requirements/recommendations for international students: Required—TOEFL. *Application deadline:* For fall admission, 6/15 for domestic students; for spring admission, 10/15 priority date for domestic students. Applications are processed on a rolling basis. Application fee: $55 ($75 for international students). Electronic applications accepted. *Expenses:* Tuition, state resident: full-time $3,681; part-time $614 per credit. Tuition, nonresident: full-time $7,231; part-time $1,205 per credit. *Financial support:* In 2003–04, 6 fellowships with full tuition reimbursements (averaging $19,800 per year), 32 research assistantships with full and partial tuition reimbursements (averaging $16,006 per year), 2 teaching assistantships with full and partial tuition reimbursements (averaging $16,006 per year) were awarded. Career-related internships or fieldwork, Federal Work-Study, institutionally sponsored loans, and scholarships/grants also available. Support available to part-time students. Financial award applicants required to submit FAFSA. *Faculty research:* Food chemistry, food microbiology, food technology, grain science, dairy science. Total annual research expenditures: $4.4 million. *Unit head:* Dr. Larry L. McKay, Director of Graduate Studies, 612-624-3090, Fax: 612-625-5272, E-mail: lmckay@umn.edu. *Application contact:* Susan K. Viker, Assistant Coordinator, 612-624-6753, Fax: 612-625-5272, E-mail: sviker@umn.edu.

University of Missouri–Columbia, Graduate School, College of Agriculture, Food and Natural Resources, Department of Food Science and Human Nutrition, Columbia, MO 65211. Offers food science (MS, PhD); foods and food systems management (MS); human nutrition (MS). *Faculty:* 8 full-time (5 women), 1 part-time/adjunct (0 women). *Students:* 15 full-time (9 women), 10 part-time (7 women); includes 2 minority (1 African American, 1 Hispanic American), 20 international. In 2003, 5 master's, 3 doctorates awarded. Terminal master's awarded for partial completion of doctoral program. *Degree requirements:* For doctorate, thesis/dissertation. *Entrance requirements:* For master's and doctorate, GRE General Test, minimum GPA of 3.0. *Application deadline:* For fall admission, 4/1 for domestic students. Applications are processed on a rolling basis. Application fee: $45 ($60 for international students). *Expenses:* Tuition, state resident: full-time $5,205. Tuition, nonresident: full-time $14,058. *Financial support:* Research assistantships, teaching assistantships, institutionally sponsored loans available. *Unit head:* Dr. Andrew D. Clarke, Director of Graduate Studies, 573-882-2610, E-mail: clakrea@missouri.edu.

University of Nebraska–Lincoln, Graduate College, College of Agricultural Sciences and Natural Resources, Department of Food Science and Technology, Lincoln, NE 68588. Offers MS, PhD. *Degree requirements:* For master's, thesis optional; for doctorate, thesis/dissertation, comprehensive exam. *Entrance requirements:* For master's and doctorate, GRE General Test. Additional exam requirements/recommendations for international students: Required—TOEFL (minimum score 505 paper-based; 213 computer-based). Electronic applications accepted. *Faculty research:* Food chemistry, microbiology, processing, engineering, and biotechnology.

University of Puerto Rico, Mayagüez Campus, Graduate Studies, College of Agricultural Sciences, Department of Food Technology, Mayagüez, PR 00681-9000. Offers MS. *Degree* *requirements:* For master's, thesis, comprehensive exam. *Entrance requirements:* For master's, minimum GPA of 2.5. *Faculty research:* Food microbiology, food science, seafood technology, food engineering and packaging, fermentation.

University of Rhode Island, Graduate School, College of the Environment and Life Sciences, Department of Food Science and Nutrition, Kingston, RI 02881. Offers food and nutrition science (MS, PhD); food science and technology, nutrition and dietetics (MS, PhD). In 2003, 2 degrees awarded. *Entrance requirements:* For master's and doctorate, GRE General Test. Additional exam requirements/recommendations for international students: Required—TOEFL. *Application deadline:* For fall admission, 4/15 for domestic students. Applications are processed on a rolling basis. Application fee: $35. *Expenses:* Tuition, state resident: full-time $4,338; part-time $281 per credit. Tuition, nonresident: full-time $12,438; part-time $704 per credit. Required fees: $1,840. *Unit head:* Dr. Marjorie Caldwell, Graduate Coordinator, 401-874-2253.

University of Saskatchewan, College of Graduate Studies and Research, College of Agriculture, Department of Applied Microbiology and Food Science, Saskatoon, SK S7N 5A2, Canada. Offers M Ag, M Sc, PhD. *Faculty:* 19. *Students:* 22. *Degree requirements:* For master's and doctorate, thesis/dissertation, registration. *Entrance requirements:* Additional exam requirements/recommendations for international students: Required—TOEFL. *Application deadline:* For fall admission, 7/1 for domestic students. Applications are processed on a rolling basis. Application fee: $50. Tuition charges are reported in Canadian dollars. *Expenses:* Tuition, state resident: part-time $483 Canadian dollars per course. *Financial support:* Fellowships, research assistantships, teaching assistantships available. Financial award application deadline: 1/31. *Unit head:* Dr. G. G. Khachatourians, Chair, 306-966-5032, Fax: 306-966-8898, E-mail: george.khachatourians@usask.ca.

University of Southern Mississippi, Graduate School, College of Health, Center for Nutrition and Food Systems, Hattiesburg, MS 39406-0001. Offers MS, PhD. *Faculty:* 7 full-time (6 women). *Students:* 17 full-time (14 women), 32 part-time (30 women); includes 7 minority (all African Americans), 2 international. Average age 31. 5 applicants, 80% accepted, 4 enrolled. Application fee: $25. *Expenses:* Tuition, state resident: part-time $1,967 per semester. Tuition, nonresident: part-time $4,376 per semester. *Unit head:* Dr. Kathleen Yadrick, Director, 601-266-5377, Fax: 601-266-6343.

The University of Tennessee, Graduate School, College of Agricultural Sciences and Natural Resources, Department of Food Science and Technology, Knoxville, TN 37996. Offers food science and technology (MS, PhD), including food chemistry (PhD), food microbiology (PhD), food processing (PhD), sensory evaluation of foods (PhD). Part-time programs available. *Degree requirements:* For master's, thesis or alternative; for doctorate, thesis/dissertation. *Entrance requirements:* For master's and doctorate, GRE General Test, minimum GPA of 2.7. Additional exam requirements/recommendations for international students: Required—TOEFL. Electronic applications accepted.

The University of Tennessee at Martin, Graduate Studies, College of Agriculture and Applied Sciences, Department of Family and Consumer Sciences, Martin, TN 38238-1000. Offers child development and family relations (MSFCS); food science and nutrition (MSFCS). Part-time programs available. *Faculty:* 7. *Students:* 23. 19 applicants, 100% accepted, 15 enrolled. In 2003, 12 degrees awarded. *Degree requirements:* For master's, thesis optional. *Entrance requirements:* For master's, GRE General Test, minimum GPA of 2.5. Additional exam requirements/recommendations for international students: Required—TOEFL (minimum score 525 paper-based; 197 computer-based). *Application deadline:* For fall admission, 8/1 for domestic students; for spring admission, 1/1 for domestic students. Applications are processed on a rolling basis. Application fee: $25 ($50 for international students). *Expenses:* Tuition, state resident: part-time $251 per credit hour. Tuition, nonresident: part-time $676 per credit hour. *Financial support:* In 2003–04, 3 students received support. Scholarships/grants, tuition waivers (partial), and unspecified assistantships available. Financial award application deadline:3/1. *Faculty research:* Children with developmental disabilities, regional food product development and marketing, parent education. *Unit head:* Dr. Lisa LeBleu, Coordinator, 731-587-7116, E-mail: llebleu@utm.edu. *Application contact:* Linda L. Arant, Administrative Services Assistant, 731-587-7012, Fax: 731-587-7499, E-mail: larant@utm.edu.

University of Wisconsin–Madison, Graduate School, College of Agricultural and Life Sciences, Department of Food Science, Madison, WI 53706-1380. Offers MS, PhD. Part-time programs available. *Faculty:* 14 full-time (2 women). *Students:* 40 full-time (22 women); includes 30 minority (26 Asian Americans or Pacific Islanders, 4 Hispanic Americans). Average age 28. 102 applicants, 9% accepted, 8 enrolled. In 2003, 3 master's, 7 doctorates awarded. *Median time to degree:* Of those who began their doctoral program in fall 1995, 90% received their degree in 8 years or less. *Degree requirements:* For master's and doctorate, thesis/dissertation. *Entrance requirements:* For master's and doctorate, GRE General Test. Additional exam requirements/recommendations for international students: Required—TOEFL. *Application deadline:* For fall admission, 6/15 priority date for domestic students, 6/15 priority date for international students; for winter admission, 11/15 for domestic students; for spring admission, 5/5 for domestic students. Applications are processed on a rolling basis. Application fee: $45. Electronic applications accepted. Tuition, area resident: Full-time $7,593; part-time $476 per credit. Tuition, nonresident: full-time $22,824; part-time $1,430 per credit. Required fees: $292; $38 per credit. Part-time tuition and fees vary according to course load and reciprocity agreements. *Financial support:* In 2003–04, 37 students received support, including 1 fellowship with full tuition reimbursement available (averaging $17,940 per year), 30 research assistantships with full tuition reimbursements available (averaging $16,350 per year), 3 teaching assistantships with full tuition reimbursements available (averaging $10,476 per year); scholarships/grants also available. Financial award application deadline: 6/15. *Faculty research:* Food chemistry, food engineering, food microbiology, food processing. Total annual research expenditures: $2.1 million. *Unit head:* Dr. William L. Wendorff, Chair, 608-263-2015, Fax: 608-262-6872, E-mail: wlwendor@facstaff.wisc.edu. *Application contact:* Sarah M. Grant, Graduate Admissions Coordinator, 608-262-3046, Fax: 608-262-6872, E-mail: smgrant@wisc.edu.

University of Wisconsin–Stout, Graduate School, College of Human Development, Program in Food and Nutritional Sciences, Menomonie, WI 54751. Offers MS. Part-time programs available. *Degree requirements:* For master's, thesis.

University of Wyoming, Graduate School, College of Agriculture, Department of Animal Sciences, Program in Food Science and Human Nutrition, Laramie, WY 82070. Offers MS. *Faculty:* 6 full-time (0 women). *Students:* 3 full-time (2 women), 4 part-time (3 women), 1 international. Average age 35. 2 applicants, 50% accepted, 0 enrolled. In 2003, 2 degrees awarded. *Median time to degree:* Master's–2 years full-time. *Degree requirements:* For master's, thesis. *Entrance requirements:* For master's, GRE General Test, minimum GPA of 3.0. Additional exam requirements/recommendations for international students: Required—TOEFL (minimum score 525 paper-based). *Application deadline:* For fall admission, 2/1 priority date for domestic students, 2/1 priority date for international students; for spring admission, 9/1 for domestic students, 9/1 for international students. Applications are processed on a rolling basis. Application fee: $40. *Expenses:* Tuition, state resident: part-time $142 per credit hour. Tuition, nonresident: part-time $408 per credit hour. Required fees: $134 per semester. Tuition and fees vary according to course load, campus/location, program and student level. *Financial support:* In 2003–04, 1 student received support, including research assistantships with tuition reimbursements available (averaging $7,000 per year); career-related internships or fieldwork, Federal Work-Study, institutionally sponsored loans, scholarships/grants, and unspecified assistantships also available. Financial award application deadline:2/1. *Faculty research:* Protein and lipid metabolism, food microbiology, food safety, meat science. *Unit head:* Daniel Rule, Professor, 307-766-3404, Fax: 307-766-2355. *Application contact:* Office Assistant, Senior, 307-766-2224, Fax: 307-766-2355, E-mail: animalscience@uwyo.edu.

Utah State University, School of Graduate Studies, College of Agriculture, Department of Nutrition and Food Sciences, Logan, UT 84322. Offers dietetic administration (MDA); food microbiology and safety (MFMS); molecular biology (MS, PhD); nutrition and food sciences (MS, PhD). *Faculty:* 18 full-time (9 women), 2 part-time/adjunct (0 women). *Students:* 23 full-time (15 women), 9 part-time (5 women); includes 1 minority (African American), 13 international. Average age 27. 39 applicants, 28% accepted, 7 enrolled. In 2003, 4 master's, 7 doctorates awarded. *Degree requirements:* For master's, thesis; for doctorate, thesis/dissertation, teaching experience. *Entrance requirements:* For master's, GRE General Test, minimum GPA of 3.0, previous course work in chemistry; for doctorate, GRE General Test, minimum GPA of 3.2, previous course work in chemistry. Additional exam requirements/recommendations for international students: Required—TOEFL. *Application deadline:* For fall admission, 2/1 for domestic students; for spring admission, 10/15 priority date for domestic students. Applications are processed on a rolling basis. Application fee: $50 ($60 for international students). *Expenses:* Tuition, state resident: part-time $270 per credit hour. Tuition, nonresident: part-time $946 per credit hour. Required fees: $173 per credit hour. *Financial support:* In 2003–04, 22 students received support, including 22 research assistantships with partial tuition reimbursements available (averaging $12,600 per year), 3 teaching assistantships with partial tuition reimbursements available (averaging $3,750 per year); fellowships with partial tuition reimbursements available, Federal Work-Study, institutionally sponsored loans, and tuition waivers (full and partial) also available. Financial award application deadline: 2/1. *Faculty research:* Mineral balance, meat microbiology and nitrate interactions, milk ultrafiltration, lactic culture, milk coagulation. Total annual research expenditures: $319,280. *Unit head:* Dr. Charles C. Carpenter, Head, 435-797-2126, Fax: 435-797-2379, E-mail: chuck@cc.usu.edu. *Application contact:* Pam Zetterquist, Staff Assistant II, 435-797-4041, E-mail: pzett@cc.usu.edu.

Virginia Polytechnic Institute and State University, Graduate School, College of Agriculture and Life Sciences, Department of Food Science and Technology, Blacksburg, VA 24061. Offers MS, PhD. *Faculty:* 10 full-time (2 women). *Students:* 25 full-time (19 women), 1 part-time; includes 3 minority (1 African American, 2 Asian Americans or Pacific Islanders), 5 international. Average age 27. 36 applicants, 19% accepted, 3 enrolled. In 2003, 9 master's, 3 doctorates awarded. *Degree requirements:* For doctorate, thesis/dissertation optional. *Entrance requirements:* For master's and doctorate, GRE General Test. Additional exam requirements/recommendations for international students: Required—TOEFL (minimum score 570 paper-based; 230 computer-based). *Application deadline:* Applications are processed on a rolling basis. Application fee: $45. Electronic applications accepted. Tuition, area resident: Full-time $6,039; part-time $336 per credit. Tuition, nonresident: full-time $9,708; part-time $539 per credit. Required fees: $905; $130 per credit. *Financial support:* In 2003–04, 13 research assistantships with full tuition reimbursements (averaging $15,593 per year), 4 teaching assistantships with full tuition reimbursements (averaging $12,978 per year) were awarded. Fellowships, career-related internships or fieldwork, Federal Work-Study, scholarships/grants, and unspecified assistantships also available. Financial award application deadline: 4/1. *Faculty research:* Food microbiology, food chemistry, food processing, engineering, muscle foods. *Unit head:* Dr. S. Sumner, Head, 540-231-6806, Fax: 540-231-9293, E-mail: sumners@vt.edu. *Application contact:* Jennifer Carr, Professor, 540-231-6806, Fax: 540-231-9293, E-mail: jjc@vt.edu.

Washington State University, Graduate School, College of Agricultural, Human, and Natural Resource Sciences, Department of Food Science and Human Nutrition, Program in Food Science, Pullman, WA 99164. Offers MS, PhD. *Faculty:* 10 full-time (3 women). *Students:* 26 full-time (14 women), 3 part-time (1 woman); includes 4 minority (1 American Indian/Alaska Native, 2 Asian Americans or Pacific Islanders, 1 Hispanic American), 16 international. 52 applicants, 46% accepted. In 2003, 5 degrees awarded. *Degree requirements:* For master's and doctorate, thesis/dissertation, oral exam, written exam. *Entrance requirements:* For master's and doctorate, GRE General Test, minimum GPA of 3.0. Additional exam requirements/recommendations for international students: Required—TOEFL. *Application deadline:* For fall admission, 3/1 for domestic students; for spring admission, 7/1 priority date for domestic students. Applications are processed on a rolling basis. Application fee: $35. Electronic applications accepted. *Expenses:* Tuition, state resident: full-time $6,278; part-time $314 per hour. Tuition, nonresident: full-time $15,514; part-time $765 per hour. Required fees: $444. Full-time tuition and fees vary according to campus/location, program and student level. Part-time tuition and fees vary according to course load. *Financial support:* In 2003–04, 17 research assistantships with full and partial tuition reimbursements, 2 teaching assistantships with full and partial tuition reimbursements were awarded. Fellowships, career-related internships or fieldwork, Federal Work-Study, institutionally sponsored loans, scholarships/grants, tuition waivers (partial), and unspecified assistantships also available. Financial award application deadline: 2/1; financial award applicants required to submit FAFSA. *Faculty research:* Sports anemia, lipid chemistry, malfunction of edible oils and fats, Malolactic fermentation, wine microbiology. *Application contact:* Jodi Anderson, Coordinator, 509-335-4763, Fax: 509-335-4815, E-mail: jlanderson@wsu.edu.

Wayne State University, Graduate School, College of Science, Department of Nutrition and Food Science, Detroit, MI 48202. Offers MA, MS, PhD, Certificate. *Faculty:* 7 full-time. *Students:* 25 full-time (21 women), 3 part-time (all women); includes 6 minority (4 African Americans, 2 Asian Americans or Pacific Islanders), 9 international. Average age 30. 35 applicants, 34% accepted, 6 enrolled. In 2003, 4 master's, 1 doctorate, 4 other advanced degrees awarded. Terminal master's awarded for partial completion of doctoral program. *Degree requirements:* For master's, thesis (for some programs); for doctorate, thesis/dissertation. *Entrance requirements:* For master's and doctorate, GRE General Test, minimum GPA of 3.0. Additional exam requirements/recommendations for international students: Required—TOEFL (minimum score 550 paper-based; 213 computer-based); Recommended—TWE(minimum score 6). *Application deadline:* For fall admission, 7/1 for domestic students, 6/1 for international students. Applications are processed on a rolling basis. Application fee: $30 ($50 for international students). Electronic applications accepted. *Expenses:* Tuition, state resident: part-time $263 per credit hour. Tuition, nonresident: part-time $580 per credit hour. Required fees: $21 per credit hour. *Financial support:* In 2003–04, 10 students received support, including 1 fellowship, 7 teaching assistantships; research assistantships, career-related internships or fieldwork and Federal Work-Study also available. Financial award application deadline: 4/1. *Faculty research:* Nutrition and cancer, food microbiology and food safety, lipoprotein metabolism, etiology of obesity, nutrition and gene expression. Total annual research expenditures: $191,000. *Unit head:* Dr. David M. Klurfeld, Professor, 313-577-2459, Fax: 313-577-8616, E-mail: david.klurfeld@wayne.edu. *Application contact:* Thomas Fungwe, Graduate Director, 313-577-2941, Fax: 313-577-8616.

West Virginia University, Davis College of Agriculture, Forestry and Consumer Sciences, Division of Animal and Veterinary Sciences, Program in Agricultural Sciences, Morgantown, WV 26506. Offers animal and food sciences (PhD); plant and soil sciences (PhD). *Degree requirements:* For doctorate, thesis/dissertation, oral and written exams. *Entrance requirements:* Additional exam requirements/recommendations for international students: Required—TOEFL. Application fee: $45. *Expenses:* Tuition, state resident: full-time $4,332. Tuition, nonresident: full-time $12,442. *Financial support:* Research assistantships with tuition reimbursements, teaching assistantships with tuition reimbursements, Federal Work-Study, institutionally sponsored loans, and tuition waivers (full and partial) available. Financial award application deadline: 2/1; financial award applicants required to submit FAFSA. *Faculty research:* Ruminant nutrition, metabolism, forage utilization, physiology, reproduction. *Application contact:* Dr. Hillar Klandorf, Professor, 304-293-2631 Ext. 4436, Fax: 304-293-3676, E-mail: hillar.klandorf@mail.wvu.edu.

West Virginia University, Davis College of Agriculture, Forestry and Consumer Sciences, Division of Animal and Veterinary Sciences, Program in Animal and Veterinary Sciences, Morgantown, WV 26506. Offers breeding (MS); food sciences (MS); nutrition (MS); physiology (MS); production management (MS); reproduction (MS). Part-time programs available. *Degree requirements:* For master's, thesis, oral and written exams. *Entrance requirements:* For master's, minimum GPA of 2.5. Additional exam requirements/recommendations for international students:

Food Science and Technology

West Virginia University (continued)

Required—TOEFL. Application fee: $45. *Expenses:* Tuition, state resident: full-time $4,332. Tuition, nonresident: full-time $12,442. *Financial support:* Research assistantships, teaching assistantships, Federal Work-Study, institutionally sponsored loans, and tuition waivers (full and partial) available. Financial award application deadline: 2/1; financial award applicants required to submit FAFSA. *Faculty research:* Animal nutrition, reproductive physiology, food science. *Unit head:* Dr. Hillar Klandorf, Coordinator, 304-293-2631 Ext. 4436, Fax: 304-293-3676, E-mail: hillar.klandorf@mail.wvu.edu.

Horticulture

Auburn University, Graduate School, College of Agriculture, Department of Horticulture, Auburn University, AL 36849. Offers M Ag, MS, PhD. Part-time programs available. *Faculty:* 18 full-time (2 women). *Students:* 10 full-time (6 women), 13 part-time (2 women), 3 international. 15 applicants, 47% accepted. In 2003, 3 master's, 2 doctorates awarded. *Degree requirements:* For master's, thesis (for some programs); for doctorate, thesis/dissertation. *Entrance requirements:* For master's and doctorate, GRE General Test. *Application deadline:* For fall admission, 7/7 for domestic students; for spring admission, 11/24 for domestic students. Applications are processed on a rolling basis. Application fee: $25 ($50 for international students). Electronic applications accepted. *Expenses:* Tuition, state resident: part-time $175 per credit hour. Tuition, nonresident: part-time $525 per credit hour. *Financial support:* Research assistantships, teaching assistantships, Federal Work-Study available. Support available to part-time students. Financial award application deadline: 3/15. *Faculty research:* Environmental regulators, water quality, weed control, growth regulators, plasticulture. *Unit head:* Dr. Charles H. Gilliam, Chair, 334-844-4862. *Application contact:* Dr. John F. Pritchett, Dean of the Graduate School, 334-844-4700, E-mail: hatchlb@mail.auburn.edu.

Brigham Young University, Graduate Studies, College of Biological and Agricultural Sciences, Department of Plant and Animal Sciences, Provo, UT 84602-1001. Offers agronomy (MS); horticulture (MS). *Faculty:* 16 full-time (2 women), 1 (woman) part-time/adjunct. *Students:* 11 full-time (5 women), 2 part-time (1 woman); includes 1 minority (African American) Average age 26. 7 applicants, 43% accepted, 3 enrolled. In 2003, 7 degrees awarded. *Degree requirements:* For master's, thesis, comprehensive exam, registration. *Entrance requirements:* For master's, GRE General Test, minimum GPA of 3.0 during previous 2 years. *Application deadline:* For fall admission, 2/15 for domestic students, 2/15 for international students. Applications are processed on a rolling basis. Application fee: $50. Electronic applications accepted. *Expenses:* Tuition: Part-time $221 per hour. *Financial support:* In 2003–04, 11 students received support, including 1 research assistantship with partial tuition reimbursement available (averaging $15,000 per year), 10 teaching assistantships with partial tuition reimbursements available (averaging $15,000 per year); institutionally sponsored loans, scholarships/grants, and tuition waivers (partial) also available. Financial award application deadline: 4/15. *Faculty research:* Iron nutrition in plants–mode of uptake, photosynthesis, forage quality, seed physiology/modeling, cytogenetics. Total annual research expenditures: $13,500. *Unit head:* Dr. Sheldon D. Nelson, Chair, 801-422-2760, Fax: 801-378-7499, E-mail: sheldon_nelson@byu.edu. *Application contact:* Dr. Richard E. Terry, Graduate Coordinator, 801-422-2421, Fax: 801-378-7499, E-mail: richard_terry@byu.edu.

Colorado State University, Graduate School, College of Agricultural Sciences, Department of Horticulture and Landscape Architecture, Fort Collins, CO 80523-0015. Offers floriculture (M Agr, MS, PhD); horticultural food crops (M Agr, MS, PhD); nursery and landscape management (M Agr, MS, PhD); plant genetics (MS, PhD); plant physiology (MS, PhD); turf management (M Agr, MS, PhD). Part-time programs available. *Faculty:* 12 full-time (0 women). *Students:* 8 full-time (3 women), 13 part-time (5 women); includes 1 minority (Hispanic American), 8 international. Average age 35. 22 applicants, 36% accepted, 3 enrolled. In 2003, 4 master's, 1 doctorate awarded. *Degree requirements:* For master's, thesis optional; for doctorate, thesis/dissertation. *Entrance requirements:* For master's and doctorate, GRE General Test, minimum GPA of 3.0. Additional exam requirements/recommendations for international students: Required—TOEFL. *Application deadline:* For fall admission, 2/1 for domestic students. Applications are processed on a rolling basis. Application fee: $50. Electronic applications accepted. *Expenses:* Tuition, state resident: full-time $4,156. Tuition, nonresident: full-time $14,762. Required fees: $205. Tuition and fees vary according to course load, campus/location, program and reciprocity agreements. *Financial support:* In 2003–04, 2 fellowships with full tuition reimbursements, 3 research assistantships with partial tuition reimbursements, 6 teaching assistantships with partial tuition reimbursements were awarded. Career-related internships or fieldwork, Federal Work-Study, institutionally sponsored loans, and traineeships also available. Total annual research expenditures: $600,000. *Unit head:* Dr. Stephen J. Wallner, Head, 970-491-7018, Fax: 970-491-7745. *Application contact:* Judith A. Croissant, Administrative Assistant III, 970-491-7018, Fax: 970-491-7745, E-mail: jcroissa@ceres.agsci.colostate.edu.

Cornell University, Graduate School, Graduate Fields of Agriculture and Life Sciences, Field of Floriculture and Ornamental Horticulture, Ithaca, NY 14853-0001. Offers controlled environment agriculture (MPS, PhD); controlled environment horticulture (MS); greenhouse crops (MPS, MS, PhD); horticultural business management (MPS, MS, PhD); horticultural physiology (MPS, MS, PhD); landscape horticulture (MPS, MS, PhD); nursery crops (MPS, MS, PhD); nutrition of horticultural crops (MPS, MS, PhD); plant propagation (MPS, MS, PhD); public garden management (MPS, MS, PhD); restoration ecology (MPS, MS, PhD); taxonomy of ornamental plants (MPS, MS, PhD); turfgrass science (MPS, MS, PhD); urban horticulture (MPS, MS, PhD); weed science (MPS, MS, PhD). *Faculty:* 14 full-time. *Students:* 30 full-time (13 women); includes 1 minority (Hispanic American), 12 international. 48 applicants, 46% accepted, 6 enrolled. In 2003, 4 master's, 4 doctorates awarded. *Degree requirements:* For master's, thesis (MS); for doctorate, thesis/dissertation, comprehensive exam. *Entrance requirements:* For master's and doctorate, GRE General Test, letters of recommendation (3). Additional exam requirements/recommendations for international students: Required—TOEFL (minimum score 550 paper-based; 213 computer-based). *Application deadline:* For fall admission, 1/15 for domestic students; for spring admission, 8/15 for domestic students. Application fee: $60. Electronic applications accepted. *Expenses:* Tuition: Full-time $28,630. One-time fee: $50 full-time. *Financial support:* In 2003–04, 18 students received support, including 2 fellowships with full tuition reimbursements available, 15 research assistantships with full tuition reimbursements available, 1 teaching assistantship with full tuition reimbursement available; institutionally sponsored loans, scholarships/grants, health care benefits, tuition waivers (full and partial), and unspecified assistantships also available. Financial award applicants required to submit FAFSA. *Faculty research:* Plant selection/plant materials, greenhouse management, greenhouse crop production, urban landscape management, turfgrass management. *Unit head:* Director of Graduate Studies, 607-255-4568, Fax: 607-255-0599. *Application contact:* Graduate Field Assistant, 607-255-4568, Fax: 607-255-0599, E-mail: hortgrad@cornell.edu.

Cornell University, Graduate School, Graduate Fields of Agriculture and Life Sciences, Field of Pomology, Ithaca, NY 14853-0001. Offers MPS, MS, PhD. *Faculty:* 17 full-time. *Students:* 19 full-time (10 women), 11 international. 5 applicants, 60% accepted, 3 enrolled. In 2003, 1 degree awarded. *Degree requirements:* For master's, thesis (MS), project paper (MPS); for doctorate, thesis/dissertation, comprehensive exam. *Entrance requirements:* For master's and doctorate, GRE General Test, interview (recommended), letters of recommendation (3). Additional exam requirements/recommendations for international students: Required—TOEFL (minimum score 550 paper-based; 213 computer-based). *Application deadline:* For fall admission, 1/15 for domestic students; for spring admission, 8/15 for domestic students. Application fee: $60. Electronic applications accepted. *Expenses:* Tuition: Full-time $28,630. One-time fee: $50 full-time. *Financial support:* In 2003–04, 17 students received support, including 1 fellowship with full tuition reimbursement available, 16 research assistantships with full tuition reimbursements available; teaching assistantships with full tuition reimbursements available, institutionally sponsored loans, scholarships/grants, health care benefits, tuition waivers (full and partial), and unspecified assistantships also available. Financial award applicants required to submit FAFSA. *Faculty research:* Fruit breeding and biotechnology, fruit crop physiology, orchard management, orchard ecology and IPM, post-harvest physiology. *Unit head:* Director of Graduate Studies, 607-255-4568, Fax: 607-255-0599. *Application contact:* Graduate Field Assistant, 607-255-4568, Fax: 607-255-0599, E-mail: hortgrad@cornell.edu.

Cornell University, Graduate School, Graduate Fields of Agriculture and Life Sciences, Field of Vegetable Crops, Ithaca, NY 14853-0001. Offers MPS, MS, PhD. *Faculty:* 15 full-time. *Students:* 6 full-time (3 women); includes 1 minority (Asian American or Pacific Islander), 3 international. 5 applicants, 80% accepted, 1 enrolled. In 2003, 2 master's, 2 doctorates awarded. *Degree requirements:* For master's, thesis (MS), project paper (MPS); for doctorate, thesis/dissertation, teaching experience. *Entrance requirements:* For master's and doctorate, GRE General Test (recommended), letters of recommendation (3). Additional exam requirements/recommendations for international students: Required—TOEFL (minimum score 550 paper-based; 213 computer-based). *Application deadline:* Applications are processed on a rolling basis. Application fee: $60. Electronic applications accepted. *Expenses:* Tuition: Full-time $28,630. One-time fee: $50 full-time. *Financial support:* In 2003–04, 6 students received support, including 6 research assistantships with full tuition reimbursements available; fellowships with full tuition reimbursements available, teaching assistantships with full tuition reimbursements available, institutionally sponsored loans, health care benefits, tuition waivers (full and partial), and unspecified assistantships also available. Financial award applicants required to submit FAFSA. *Faculty research:* Vegetable nutrition and physiology, post-harvest physiology and storage, application of new technologies, sustainable vegetable production, weed management and IPM. *Unit head:* Director of Graduate Studies, 607-255-4568. *Application contact:* Graduate Field Assistant, 607-255-4568, E-mail: hortgrad@cornell.edu.

Iowa State University of Science and Technology, Graduate College, College of Agriculture, Department of Horticulture, Ames, IA 50011. Offers MS, PhD. *Faculty:* 17 full-time. *Students:* 20 full-time (9 women), 6 part-time (2 women); includes 2 minority (1 African American, 1 Hispanic American), 9 international. 15 applicants, 27% accepted, 4 enrolled. In 2003, 3 master's, 1 doctorate awarded. *Median time to degree:* Master's–3.2 years full-time; doctorate–4.9 years full-time. *Degree requirements:* For master's and doctorate, thesis/dissertation. *Entrance requirements:* For master's and doctorate, GRE General Test. Additional exam requirements/recommendations for international students: Required—TOEFL (paper score 530; computer score 197) or IELTS (score 6). *Application deadline:* For fall admission, 1/1 priority date for domestic students, 1/1 priority date for international students; for spring admission, 9/1 priority date for domestic students, 9/1 priority date for international students. Applications are processed on a rolling basis. Application fee: $30 ($70 for international students). Electronic applications accepted. Tuition, nonresident: part-time $560 per credit. Required fees: $38 per unit. *Financial support:* In 2003–04, 19 research assistantships with partial tuition reimbursements (averaging $15,072 per year), 1 teaching assistantship with full and partial tuition reimbursement (averaging $15,072 per year) were awarded. Fellowships, scholarships/grants, health care benefits, and unspecified assistantships also available. *Unit head:* Dr. Jeffrey Iles, Head, 515-294-3718, E-mail: hortgrad@iastate.edu. *Application contact:* William R. Graves, Information Contact, 515-294-2751, E-mail: hortgrade@iastate.edu.

Kansas State University, Graduate School, College of Agriculture, Department of Horticulture, Forestry and Recreation Resources, Manhattan, KS 66506. Offers horticulture (MS, PhD). *Faculty:* 21 full-time (6 women). *Students:* 28 full-time (15 women), 1 part-time, 15 international. Average age 25. 9 applicants, 67% accepted, 5 enrolled. In 2003, 2 master's, 4 doctorates awarded. *Degree requirements:* For master's, thesis, oral exam; for doctorate, thesis/dissertation, preliminary exams. *Entrance requirements:* For master's and doctorate, GRE General Test. Additional exam requirements/recommendations for international students: Required—TOEFL. *Application deadline:* For fall admission, 2/1 for domestic students; for spring admission, 10/1 for domestic students. Applications are processed on a rolling basis. Application fee: $0 ($25 for international students). Electronic applications accepted. *Expenses:* Tuition, state resident: part-time $155 per credit hour. Tuition, nonresident: part-time $428 per credit hour. Required fees: $11 per credit hour. *Financial support:* In 2003–04, 15 research assistantships (averaging $10,584 per year), 1 teaching assistantship were awarded. Career-related internships or fieldwork, Federal Work-Study, institutionally sponsored loans, and scholarships/grants also available. Support available to part-time students. Financial award application deadline: 3/1; financial award applicants required to submit FAFSA. *Faculty research:* Environmental stress, turfgrass management, vegetable alternate crop production, floriculture-pest and nutrition, horticulture therapy. Total annual research expenditures: $1 million. *Unit head:* Thomas Warner, Head, 785-532-1413, Fax: 785-532-6949, E-mail: twarner@oz.oznet.ksu.edu. *Application contact:* Dr. Channa Rajashekar, Director, 785-532-1427, Fax: 785-532-6949, E-mail: crajashe@oznet.ksu.edu.

Louisiana State University and Agricultural and Mechanical College, Graduate School, College of Agriculture, Department of Horticulture, Baton Rouge, LA 70803. Offers MS, PhD. Part-time programs available. *Faculty:* 9 full-time (0 women). *Students:* 15 full-time (5 women), 9 part-time (2 women); includes 1 minority (Hispanic American), 11 international. Average age 36. 9 applicants, 67% accepted, 4 enrolled. In 2003, 7 master's, 1 doctorate awarded. Terminal master's awarded for partial completion of doctoral program. *Degree requirements:* For master's, thesis (for some programs); for doctorate, thesis/dissertation. *Entrance requirements:* For master's and doctorate, GRE General Test, minimum GPA of 3.0. Additional exam requirements/recommendations for international students: Required—TOEFL (minimum score 550 paper-based; 213 computer-based). *Application deadline:* For fall admission, 7/1 priority date for domestic students, 5/15 priority date for international students. Applications are processed on a rolling basis. Application fee: $25. Electronic applications accepted. *Expenses:* Tuition, state resident: part-time $337 per hour. Tuition, nonresident: part-time $577 per hour. *Financial support:* In 2003–04, 13 research assistantships with partial tuition reimbursements (averaging $14,238 per year) were awarded; fellowships, teaching assistantships with partial tuition reimbursements, Federal Work-Study and unspecified assistantships also available. Financial award application deadline: 4/15; financial award applicants required to submit FAFSA. *Faculty research:* Plant breeding, stress physiology, postharvest physiology, biotechnology. *Unit head:* Dr. David G. Himelrick, Head, 225-578-2158, Fax: 225-578-1068, E-mail: dhimelrick@agctr.lsu.edu. *Application contact:* Dr. Paul Wilson, Graduate Coordinator, 225-578-1025, Fax: 225-578-1068, E-mail: pwilson@agctr.lsu.edu.

Michigan State University, Graduate School, College of Agriculture and Natural Resources, Department of Horticulture, East Lansing, MI 48824. Offers horticulture (MS, PhD); plant breeding and genetics-horticulture (MS, PhD). *Faculty:* 32 full-time (6 women). *Students:* 44 full-time (25 women), 8 part-time (5 women); includes 4 minority (2 African Americans, 1 Asian

American or Pacific Islander, 1 Hispanic American), 22 international. Average age 29. 31 applicants, 32% accepted. In 2003, 11 master's, 5 doctorates awarded. *Degree requirements:* For master's, teaching experience, thesis optional; for doctorate, thesis/dissertation, oral defense of dissertation, teaching/ extension experience, comprehensive exam. *Entrance requirements:* For master's and doctorate, GRE General Test, minimum GPA of 3.0, 3 letters of recommendation. Additional exam requirements/recommendations for international students: Required—TOEFL (minimum score 580 paper-based; 237 computer-based). *Application deadline:* For fall admission, 12/23 for domestic students. Applications are processed on a rolling basis. Application fee: $50. Electronic applications accepted. *Expenses:* Tuition, state resident: part-time $291 per hour. Tuition, nonresident: part-time $589 per hour. *Financial support:* In 2003–04, 12 fellowships with tuition reimbursements (averaging $4,656 per year), 49 research assistantships with tuition reimbursements (averaging $11,568 per year), 1 teaching assistantship with tuition reimbursement (averaging $12,252 per year) were awarded. Financial award applicants required to submit FAFSA. *Faculty research:* Natural products chemistry, plant breeding and genetics, floriculture and perennial fruit production, post-harvest crop and plant physiology. Total annual research expenditures: $5.1 million. *Unit head:* Dr. Ronald Perry, Chairperson, 517-355-5191 Ext. 361, Fax: 517-353-0890, E-mail: hrt@msu.edu. *Application contact:* Kristi Lowrie, Information Contact, 517-355-8393, E-mail: hrtgrad@msu.edu.

Michigan State University, Graduate School, College of Agriculture and Natural Resources, Program in Plant Breeding and Genetics, East Lansing, MI 48824. Offers plant breeding and genetics (MS, PhD), including botany and plant pathology, crop and soil sciences, forestry, horticulture. *Faculty:* 22 full-time (5 women). *Students:* 22 full-time (12 women), 5 part-time (3 women); includes 1 minority (Hispanic American), 12 international. Average age 30. 29 applicants, 17% accepted. In 2003, 3 master's, 2 doctorates awarded. *Degree requirements:* For master's, thesis; for doctorate, thesis/dissertation, oral examination, comprehensive exam. *Entrance requirements:* For master's and doctorate, GRE, minimum GPA of 3.0, 3 letters of recommendation. Additional exam requirements/recommendations for international students: Required—TOEFL (minimum score 550 paper-based; 213 computer-based). *Application deadline:* For fall admission, 12/23 for domestic students. Application fee: $50. *Expenses:* Tuition, state resident: part-time $291 per hour. Tuition, nonresident: part-time $589 per hour. *Financial support:* Applicants required to submit FAFSA. *Unit head:* Dr. Jim Hancock, Director, 517-355-4598, Fax: 517-353-0890, E-mail: hancock@msu.edu. *Application contact:* Program Office, 517-353-2913.

New Mexico State University, Graduate School, College of Agriculture and Home Economics, Department of Agronomy and Horticulture, Las Cruces, NM 88003-8001. Offers general agronomy (MS, PhD); horticulture (MS). Part-time programs available. *Faculty:* 24 full-time (3 women), 6 part-time/adjunct (1 woman). *Students:* 33 full-time (10 women), 15 part-time (7 women); includes 13 minority (2 American Indian/Alaska Native, 11 Hispanic Americans), 18 international. Average age 34. 24 applicants, 71% accepted, 2 enrolled. In 2003, 6 master's, 8 doctorates awarded. *Median time to degree:* Of those who began their doctoral program in fall 1995, 90% received their degree in 8 years or less. *Degree requirements:* For master's, thesis; for doctorate, one foreign language, thesis/dissertation. *Entrance requirements:* For master's, minimum GPA of 3.0; for doctorate, minimum GPA of 3.3. *Application deadline:* For fall admission, 7/1 for domestic students; for spring admission, 11/1 for domestic students. Applications are processed on a rolling basis. Application fee: $30 ($50 for international students). Electronic applications accepted. *Expenses:* Tuition, state resident: full-time $2,670; part-time $151 per credit. Tuition, nonresident: full-time $10,596; part-time $481 per credit. Required fees: $954. *Financial support:* In 2003–04, 15 research assistantships, 10 teaching assistantships were awarded. Career-related internships or fieldwork and Federal Work-Study also available. Support available to part-time students. Financial award application deadline: 3/1. *Faculty research:* Plant breeding and genetics, molecular biology, plant physiology, soil science and environmental remediation, urban horticulture. *Unit head:* Dr. James T. Fisher, Head, 505-646-3406, Fax: 505-646-6041, E-mail: jtfisher@nmsu.edu.

North Carolina State University, Graduate School, College of Agriculture and Life Sciences, Department of Horticultural Science, Raleigh, NC 27695. Offers MS, PhD. *Faculty:* 42 full-time (9 women), 17 part-time/adjunct (1 woman). *Students:* 41 full-time (22 women), 7 part-time (5 women); includes 3 minority (1 African American, 2 Hispanic Americans), 6 international. Average age 32. 31 applicants, 39% accepted. In 2003, 10 master's, 3 doctorates awarded. Terminal master's awarded for partial completion of doctoral program. *Degree requirements:* For master's and doctorate, thesis/dissertation. *Entrance requirements:* For master's and doctorate, GRE General Test, bachelor's degree in agriculture or biology, minimum GPA of 3.0. *Application deadline:* For fall admission, 6/25 for domestic students, 3/1 for international students; for spring admission, 11/25 for domestic students, 7/15 for international students. Applications are processed on a rolling basis. Application fee: $45. *Expenses:* Tuition, state resident: part-time $396 per hour. Tuition, nonresident: part-time $1,895 per hour. *Financial support:* In 2003–04, 33 research assistantships with tuition reimbursements (averaging $5,289 per year), 4 teaching assistantships with tuition reimbursements (averaging $5,696 per year) were awarded. Fellowships with tuition reimbursements Financial award application deadline: 6/25. *Faculty research:* Plant physiology, breeding and genetics, tissue culture, herbicide physiology, propagation. Total annual research expenditures: $1.4 million. *Unit head:* Dr. Julia L. Kornegay, Head, 919-515-3131, Fax: 919-515-3191, E-mail: julia_kornegay@ncsu.edu. *Application contact:* Dr. John M. Dole, Director of Graduate Programs, 919-515-3537, Fax: 919-515-7747, E-mail: john_dole@ncsu.edu.

Nova Scotia Agricultural College, Research and Graduate Studies, Truro, NS B2N 5E3, Canada. Offers agriculture (M Sc), including air quality, animal behavior, animal molecular genetics, animal nutrition, animal technology, aquaculture, botany, crop management, crop physiology, ecology, environmental microbiology, food science, horticulture, nutrient management, pest management, physiology, plant biotechnology, plant pathology, soil chemistry, soil fertility, waste management and composting, water quality. Part-time programs available. *Faculty:* 38 full-time (5 women), 13 part-time/adjunct (1 woman). *Students:* 46 full-time (27 women), 21 part-time (13 women); includes 13 minority (10 African Americans, 2 American Indian/Alaska Native, 1 Asian American or Pacific Islander). 45 applicants, 58% accepted, 16 enrolled. In 2003, 11 degrees awarded, leading to university research/teaching 18%, continued full-time study36%, business/industry 9%, government 27%. *Median time to degree:* Master's–2.25 years full-time, 4 years part-time. *Degree requirements:* For master's, thesis, candidacy exam. *Entrance requirements:* For master's, B.Sc. honors degree, minimum GPA of 3.0. Additional exam requirements/recommendations for international students: Required—TOEFL (minimum score 580 paper-based; 237 computer-based), Michigan English Language Assessment Battery. *Application deadline:* For fall admission, 6/1 for domestic students, 4/1 for international students; for winter admission, 11/15 for domestic students; for spring admission, 2/28 for domestic students. Applications are processed on a rolling basis. Application fee: $70. *Expenses:* Tuition, state resident: full-time $6,270. Tuition, nonresident: full-time $9,270. Required fees: $402. Tuition and fees vary according to student level. *Financial support:* In 2003–04, 63 students received support, including research assistantships (averaging $15,000 per year), teaching assistantships (averaging $900 per year); career-related internships or fieldwork, scholarships/grants, and unspecified assistantships also available. *Faculty research:* Organogenesis, somatic embryogenesis, composting, sustainable agriculture, ecotoxicology. Total annual research expenditures: $2 million. *Unit head:* Jill L. Rogers, Manager, 902-893-6360, Fax: 902-893-3430, E-mail: jrogers@nsac.ns.ca. *Application contact:* Marie Law, Administrative Assistant, 902-893-6502, Fax: 902-893-3430, E-mail: mlaw@nsac.ns.ca.

The Ohio State University, Graduate School, College of Food, Agricultural, and Environmental Sciences, Department of Horticulture and Crop Science, Columbus, OH 43210. Offers MS, PhD. *Faculty:* 51. *Students:* 50 full-time (29 women), 10 part-time (6 women); includes 3 minority (2 African Americans, 1 Hispanic American), 23 international. 69 applicants, 29% accepted. In 2003, 16 master's, 5 doctorates awarded. *Degree requirements:* For master's, thesis optional; for doctorate, thesis/dissertation. *Entrance requirements:* For master's and doctorate, GRE General Test. *Application deadline:* For fall admission, 8/15 for domestic students. Applications are processed on a rolling basis. Application fee: $40 ($50 for international students). *Expenses:* Tuition, state resident: full-time $7,233. Tuition, nonresident: full-time $18,489. *Financial support:* Fellowships, research assistantships, teaching assistantships, Federal Work-Study and institutionally sponsored loans available. Support available to part-time students. *Unit head:* Dr. Stephen C. Myers, Chair, 614-292-1399, Fax: 614-292-7162, E-mail: myers.603@osu.edu. *Application contact:* Dr. Claudio C. Pasian, Graduate Studies Committee Chair, 614-292-3864, Fax: 614-292-7162, E-mail: pasia.1@osu.edu.

Oklahoma State University, Graduate College, College of Agricultural Sciences and Natural Resources, Department of Horticulture and Landscape Architecture, Stillwater, OK 74078. Offers crop science (PhD); horticulture (M Ag, MS). *Faculty:* 20 full-time (1 woman), 3 part-time/adjunct (1 woman). *Students:* 4 full-time (2 women), 4 part-time (1 woman); includes 2 minority (1 African American, 1 American Indian/Alaska Native), 4 international. Average age 27. 7 applicants, 29% accepted. In 2003, 2 degrees awarded. *Degree requirements:* For master's, thesis or alternative. *Entrance requirements:* Additional exam requirements/recommendations for international students: Required—TOEFL. *Application deadline:* For fall admission, 6/1 for domestic students. Applications are processed on a rolling basis. Application fee: $25 ($50 for international students). Electronic applications accepted. *Expenses:* Tuition, state resident: full-time $3,752; part-time $118 per credit hour. Tuition, nonresident: full-time $10,346; part-time $393 per credit hour. Tuition and fees vary according to course load. *Financial support:* In 2003–04, 9 research assistantships (averaging $12,043 per year) were awarded; teaching assistantships, career-related internships or fieldwork, Federal Work-Study, and tuition waivers (partial) also available. Support available to part-time students. Financial award application deadline: 3/1. *Faculty research:* Stress and postharvest physiology; water utilization and runoff; IPM systems and nursery, turf, floriculture, vegetable, net and fruit produces and natural resources, food extraction, and processing; public garden management. *Unit head:* Dr. Dale Maronek, Head, 405-744-5414, Fax: 405-744-9709, E-mail: maronek@okstate.edu.

Oregon State University, Graduate School, College of Agricultural Sciences, Department of Horticulture, Corvallis, OR 97331. Offers M Ag, MAIS, MS, PhD. *Faculty:* 40 full-time (14 women), 1 part-time/adjunct (0 women). *Students:* 30 full-time (15 women), 2 part-time; includes 1 minority (Asian American or Pacific Islander), 16 international. Average age 30. In 2003, 2 master's, 1 doctorate awarded. *Degree requirements:* For master's, thesis (for some programs); for doctorate, thesis/dissertation. *Entrance requirements:* For master's and doctorate, GRE General Test, minimum GPA of 3.0 in last 90 hours. Additional exam requirements/recommendations for international students: Required—TOEFL. *Application deadline:* For fall admission, 3/1 for domestic students. Applications are processed on a rolling basis. Application fee: $50. *Expenses:* Tuition, state resident: full-time $8,139; part-time $301 per credit. Tuition, nonresident: full-time $14,376; part-time $532 per credit. Required fees: $1,227. *Financial support:* Research assistantships, teaching assistantships, career-related internships or fieldwork, Federal Work-Study, and institutionally sponsored loans available. Support available to part-time students. Financial award application deadline: 2/1. *Unit head:* Anita Azarenko, Interim Head, 541-737-5457, Fax: 541-737-3479. *Application contact:* Machteld C. Mok, Graduate Coordinator, 541-737-5456, E-mail: mokm@bcc.orst.edu.

The Pennsylvania State University University Park Campus, Graduate School, College of Agricultural Sciences, Department of Horticulture, State College, University Park, PA 16802-1503. Offers M Agr, MS, PhD. *Students:* 21 full-time (10 women), 2 part-time (1 woman), 10 international. *Entrance requirements:* For master's and doctorate, GRE General Test. Application fee: $45. *Expenses:* Tuition, state resident: full-time $10,010; part-time $417 per credit. Tuition, nonresident: full-time $19,830; part-time $826 per credit. Full-time tuition and fees vary according to course level, course load, campus/location and program. *Unit head:* Dr. Dennis R. Decoteau, Head, 814-865-2572, Fax: 814-863-6139, E-mail: drd10@psu.edu. *Application contact:* Dr. Kathleen Brown, Coordinator, 814-863-2260, Fax: 814-863-6139, E-mail: kbe@psu.edu.

Purdue University, Graduate School, College of Agriculture, Department of Horticulture and Landscape Architecture, West Lafayette, IN 47907. Offers horticulture (M Agr, MS, PhD). Part-time programs available. Terminal master's awarded for partial completion of doctoral program. *Degree requirements:* For doctorate, thesis/dissertation. *Entrance requirements:* Additional exam requirements/recommendations for international students: Required—TOEFL. Electronic applications accepted. *Faculty research:* Plant physiology, plant genetics and breeding, plant molecular biology and cell physiology, environmental and production horticulture.

Rutgers, The State University of New Jersey, New Brunswick/Piscataway, Graduate School, Program in Plant Biology, New Brunswick, NJ 08901-1281. Offers horticulture (MS, PhD); molecular biology and biochemistry (MS, PhD); pathology (MS, PhD); plant ecology (MS, PhD); plant genetics (PhD); plant physiology (MS, PhD); production and management (MS); structure and plant groups (MS, PhD). Part-time programs available. *Faculty:* 59 full-time (14 women), 1 part-time/adjunct (0 women). *Students:* 44 full-time (17 women), 5 part-time (2 women); includes 5 minority (3 African Americans, 2 Asian Americans or Pacific Islanders), 17 international. Average age 27. 49 applicants, 33% accepted, 8 enrolled. In 2003, 6 master's, 2 doctorates awarded. Terminal master's awarded for partial completion of doctoral program. *Median time to degree:* Master's–3 years full-time; doctorate–5.5 years full-time. Of those who began their doctoral program in fall 1995, 90% received their degree in 8 years or less. *Degree requirements:* For master's, thesis or alternative, comprehensive exam; for doctorate, thesis/dissertation, comprehensive exam. *Entrance requirements:* For master's and doctorate, GRE General Test, GRE Subject Test (recommended). Additional exam requirements/recommendations for international students: Required—TOEFL (minimum score 600 paper-based; 250 computer-based). *Application deadline:* For fall admission, 4/1 for domestic students, 4/1 for international students. Application fee: $50. Electronic applications accepted. *Expenses:* Tuition, state resident: full-time $10,030. Tuition, nonresident: full-time $14,202. *Financial support:* In 2003–04, 42 students received support, including 9 fellowships with full tuition reimbursements available (averaging $20,000 per year), 22 research assistantships with full tuition reimbursements available (averaging $16,500 per year), 10 teaching assistantships with full tuition reimbursements available (averaging $15,100 per year) Financial award application deadline: 1/15; financial award applicants required to submit FAFSA. *Faculty research:* Molecular biology and biochemistry of plants, plant development and genomics, plant protection, plant improvement, plant management of horticultural and field crops. Total annual research expenditures: $10 million. *Unit head:* Dr. Thomas Leustek, Director, 732-932-8165 Ext. 326, Fax: 732-932-9377, E-mail: leustek@aesop.rutgers.edu. *Application contact:* Barbara Mulder, Program Associate, 732-932-9375 Ext. 358, Fax: 732-932-9377, E-mail: plantbio@aesop.rutgers.edu.

Southern Illinois University Carbondale, Graduate School, College of Agriculture, Department of Plant, Soil, and General Agriculture, Carbondale, IL 62901-4701. Offers horticultural science (MS); plant and soil science (MS). *Faculty:* 20 full-time (1 woman). *Students:* 11 full-time (5 women), 34 part-time (11 women), 2 international. 9 applicants, 56% accepted, 1 enrolled. In 2003, 10 degrees awarded. *Degree requirements:* For master's, thesis. *Entrance requirements:* For master's, minimum GPA of 2.7. Additional exam requirements/recommendations for international students: Required—TOEFL. *Application deadline:* Applications are processed on a rolling basis. Application fee: $0. *Expenses:* Tuition, state resident: part-time $478 per hour. Tuition, nonresident: part-time $657 per hour. *Financial support:* In 2003–04, 22 students received support, including 15 research assistantships with full tuition reimbursements available, 6 teaching assistantships with full tuition reimbursements available; fellowships with full tuition reimbursements available, Federal Work-Study, institutionally sponsored loans, and tuition waivers (full) also available. Support available to part-time students. *Faculty research:* Herbicides, fertilizers, agriculture education, landscape design, plant breeding. Total annual research expenditures: $2 million. *Unit head:* John Russin, Chairperson, 618-453-2496.

Texas A&M University, College of Agriculture and Life Sciences, Department of Horticultural Sciences, College Station, TX 77843. Offers horticulture (PhD); horticulture and floriculture

Horticulture

Texas A&M University (continued)

(M Agr, MS). *Faculty:* 11 full-time (2 women). *Students:* 45 full-time (25 women), 11 part-time (6 women); includes 1 minority (Asian American or Pacific Islander), 22 international. Average age 29. 40 applicants, 50% accepted, 15 enrolled. In 2003, 14 master's, 5 doctorates awarded. Terminal master's awarded for partial completion of doctoral program. *Degree requirements:* For master's, thesis (for some programs), professional internship; for doctorate, thesis/dissertation. *Entrance requirements:* For master's and doctorate, GRE General Test. Additional exam requirements/recommendations for international students: Required—TOEFL. Application fee: $50 ($75 for international students). Electronic applications accepted. *Expenses:* Tuition, state resident: full-time $3,420. Tuition, nonresident: full-time $9,084. Required fees: $1,861. *Financial support:* In 2003–04, 30 students received support, including 2 fellowships with full tuition reimbursements available (averaging $15,000 per year), 16 research assistantships with partial tuition reimbursements available (averaging $14,000 per year), 14 teaching assistantships with partial tuition reimbursements available (averaging $14,000 per year); career-related internships or fieldwork and tuition waivers (partial) also available. Financial award application deadline: 4/1. *Faculty research:* Plant breeding, molecular biology, plant nutrition, postharvest physiology, plant physiology. *Unit head:* Dr. Tim D. Davis, Head, 979-845-9341, Fax: 979-845-0627, E-mail: t-davis5@tamu.edu. *Application contact:* Dr. Michael A. Arnold, Associate Head for Research, 979-845-1499, Fax: 979-845-0627, E-mail: ma-arnold@tamu.edu.

Texas Tech University, Graduate School, College of Agricultural Sciences and Natural Resources, Department of Plant and Soil Science, Lubbock, TX 79409. Offers agronomy (PhD); crop science (MS); entomology (MS); horticulture (MS); soil science (MS). Part-time programs available. *Faculty:* 12 full-time (2 women), 1 part-time/adjunct (0 women). *Students:* 39 full-time (13 women), 21 part-time (8 women); includes 1 minority (Asian American or Pacific Islander), 14 international. Average age 32. 18 applicants, 78% accepted, 10 enrolled. In 2003, 13 master's, 6 doctorates awarded. *Degree requirements:* For doctorate, thesis/dissertation. *Entrance requirements:* For master's and doctorate, GRE General Test. Additional exam requirements/recommendations for international students: Required—TOEFL (minimum score 550 paper-based; 213 computer-based). *Application deadline:* Applications are processed on a rolling basis. Application fee: $50 ($60 for international students). Electronic applications accepted. *Expenses:* Tuition, state resident: full-time $3,312. Tuition, nonresident: full-time $8,976. Required fees: $1,745. Tuition and fees vary according to program. *Financial support:* In 2003–04, 44 students received support, including 21 research assistantships with partial tuition reimbursements available (averaging $13,555 per year); teaching assistantships with partial tuition reimbursements available, Federal Work-Study and institutionally sponsored loans also available. Support available to part-time students. Financial award application deadline: 5/1; financial award applicants required to submit FAFSA. *Faculty research:* Molecular and cellular biology of plant stress, physiology/genetics of crop production in semiarid conditions, agricultural bioterrorism, improvement of native plants. Total annual research expenditures: $2.1 million. *Unit head:* Dr. Dick L. Auld, Chair, 806-742-2837, Fax: 806-742-0775, E-mail: dick.auld@ttu.edu. *Application contact:* Dr. Richard E. Zartman, Graduate Adviser, 806-742-2837, Fax: 806-742-0775, E-mail: richard.zartman@ttu.edu.

University of Arkansas, Graduate School, Dale Bumpers College of Agricultural, Food and Life Sciences, Department of Horticulture, Fayetteville, AR 72701-1201. Offers MS. *Students:* 8 full-time (3 women), 6 part-time (2 women), 3 international. 7 applicants, 43% accepted. In 2003, 3 degrees awarded. *Degree requirements:* For master's, thesis. Application fee: $40 ($50 for international students). *Expenses:* Tuition, state resident: full-time $4,032; part-time $224 per credit hour. Tuition, nonresident: full-time $9,540; part-time $530 per credit hour. Tuition and fees vary according to course load and program. *Financial support:* In 2003–04, 7 research assistantships were awarded; fellowships, teaching assistantships, career-related internships or fieldwork and Federal Work-Study also available. Support available to part-time students. Financial award application deadline: 4/1; financial award applicants required to submit FAFSA. *Unit head:* Dr. David Hensley, Head, 479-575-2603. *Application contact:* Dr. J. Brad Murphy, Graduate Coordinator, 479-575-2446, E-mail: jbmurph@comp.uark.edu.

University of California, Davis, Graduate Studies, Graduate Group in Horticulture and Agronomy, Davis, CA 95616. Offers MS. *Faculty:* 90 full-time. *Students:* 43 full-time (28 women); includes 2 minority (1 American Indian/Alaska Native, 1 Asian American or Pacific Islander), 12 international. Average age 31. 41 applicants, 46% accepted, 13 enrolled. In 2003, 8 degrees awarded. *Degree requirements:* For master's, thesis optional. *Entrance requirements:* For master's, GRE General Test. Additional exam requirements/recommendations for international students: Required—TOEFL (minimum score 550 paper-based; 213 computer-based). *Application deadline:* For fall admission, 4/1 for domestic students, 3/1 for international students. Applications are processed on a rolling basis. Application fee: $60. Electronic applications accepted. Tuition, nonresident: full-time $12,245. Required fees: $7,062. *Financial support:* In 2003–04, 36 students received support, including 21 fellowships with full and partial tuition reimbursements available (averaging $2,249 per year), 23 research assistantships with full and partial tuition reimbursements available (averaging $9,988 per year), 6 teaching assistantships with partial tuition reimbursements available (averaging $11,788 per year); career-related internships or fieldwork, Federal Work-Study, institutionally sponsored loans, scholarships/grants, and tuition waivers (full and partial) also available. Financial award application deadline: 1/15; financial award applicants required to submit FAFSA. *Faculty research:* Postharvest physiology, mineral nutrition, crop improvement, plant growth and development. *Unit head:* M. Andrew Walker, Chairperson, 530-752-0902, Fax: 530-752-0382, E-mail: awalker@ucdavis.edu. *Application contact:* Lisa Brown, Graduate Group Secretary, 530-752-7738, Fax: 530-752-1819, E-mail: lfbrown@ucdavis.edu.

University of Delaware, College of Agriculture and Natural Resources, Longwood Graduate Program in Public Horticulture, Newark, DE 19716. Offers MS. *Faculty:* 1 full-time (0 women). *Students:* 15 full-time (8 women); includes 1 minority (African American), 2 international. Average age 23. 22 applicants, 23% accepted, 5 enrolled. In 2003, 2 degrees awarded. *Degree requirements:* For master's, thesis, internship. *Entrance requirements:* For master's, GRE General Test, introductory taxonomy course. Additional exam requirements/recommendations for international students: Required—TOEFL. *Application deadline:* For fall admission, 11/30 for domestic students, 11/30 for international students. Application fee: $60. Electronic applications accepted. *Expenses:* Tuition, state resident: full-time $5,890; part-time $327 per credit. Tuition, nonresident: full-time $15,420; part-time $857 per credit. Required fees: $968. *Financial support:* In 2003–04, 11 fellowships with full tuition reimbursements (averaging $18,000 per year) were awarded; career-related internships or fieldwork also available. Financial award application deadline: 3/1. *Faculty research:* Management and engineering of publicly oriented horticultural institutions. *Unit head:* Dr. James E. Swasey, Coordinator, 302-831-2517, Fax: 302-831-3651, E-mail: j.swasey@mvs.udel.edu.

University of Florida, Graduate School, College of Agricultural and Life Sciences, Department of Environmental Horticulture, Gainesville, FL 32611. Offers MS, PhD. *Faculty:* 38. *Students:* 21 full-time (9 women), 5 part-time (3 women); includes 1 minority (Asian American or Pacific Islander), 5 international. 11 applicants, 45% accepted. In 2003, 3 master's, 1 doctorate awarded. *Degree requirements:* For master's, thesis optional; for doctorate, thesis/dissertation. *Entrance requirements:* For master's and doctorate, GRE General Test, minimum GPA of 3.0. *Application deadline:* For fall admission, 6/1 for domestic students; for spring admission, 11/1 for domestic students. Applications are processed on a rolling basis. Application fee: $20. Electronic applications accepted. *Expenses:* Tuition, state resident: part-time $205 per credit hour. Tuition, nonresident: part-time $775 per credit hour. *Financial support:* In 2003–04, 14 students received support, including 5 research assistantships, 2 teaching assistantships; fellowships, unspecified assistantships also available. Financial award application deadline: 6/1. *Faculty research:* Production and genetics, landscape horticulture, turf grass, foliage, floriculture. *Unit head:* Dr. T. Nell, Chair, 352-392-1831 Ext. 377, Fax: 352-392-3870, E-mail: tnell@mail.ifas.ufl.edu. *Application contact:* Grady L. Miller, Coordinator, 352-392-1831 Ext. 375, Fax: 352-392-3870, E-mail: gmiller@mail.ifas.ufl.edu.

University of Florida, Graduate School, College of Agricultural and Life Sciences, Department of Horticultural Sciences, Gainesville, FL 32611. Offers fruit crops (MS, PhD); vegetable crops and crop science (MS, PhD). *Faculty:* 77. *Students:* 34 full-time (12 women), 8 part-time (1 woman); includes 4 minority (1 African American, 1 Asian American or Pacific Islander, 2 Hispanic Americans), 16 international. 51 applicants, 33% accepted. *Degree requirements:* For master's, variable foreign language requirement, thesis optional; for doctorate, variable foreign language requirement, thesis/dissertation. *Entrance requirements:* For master's and doctorate, GRE General Test, minimum GPA of 3.0. *Application deadline:* For fall admission, 6/1 for domestic students. Applications are processed on a rolling basis. Application fee: $20. Electronic applications accepted. *Expenses:* Tuition, state resident: part-time $205 per credit hour. Tuition, nonresident: part-time $775 per credit hour. *Financial support:* In 2003–04, 26 students received support, including 1 fellowship, 19 research assistantships; teaching assistantships, institutionally sponsored loans also available. Financial award application deadline: 6/1. *Faculty research:* Genetics, plant nutrition, stress physiology, biotechnology, postharvest physiology. *Unit head:* Dr. D. J. Cantliffe, Chair, 352-392-1928 Ext. 203, Fax: 352-392-6479, E-mail: djc@mail.ifas.ufl.edu. *Application contact:* Dr. Donald J. Huber, Coordinator, 352-392-1928 Ext. 217, Fax: 352-392-6479, E-mail: djh@mail.ifas.ufl.edu.

University of Georgia, Graduate School, College of Agricultural and Environmental Sciences, Department of Horticulture, Athens, GA 30602. Offers horticulture (MS, PhD); plant protection and pest management (MPPPM). Part-time programs available. *Faculty:* 23 full-time (4 women). *Students:* 17 full-time (8 women), 3 part-time (2 women), 8 international. Average age 0. 18 applicants, 28% accepted. In 2003, 4 master's, 3 doctorates awarded. *Degree requirements:* For master's, thesis (MS); for doctorate, one foreign language, thesis/dissertation. *Entrance requirements:* For master's and doctorate, GRE General Test. *Application deadline:* For fall admission, 7/1 for domestic students; for spring admission, 11/15 for domestic students. Application fee: $50. Electronic applications accepted. *Expenses:* Tuition, state resident: part-time $161 per hour. Tuition, nonresident: part-time $690 per hour. One-time fee: $435 part-time. *Financial support:* In 2003–04, fellowships with partial tuition reimbursements (averaging $1,338 per year), research assistantships with partial tuition reimbursements (averaging $1,338 per year), teaching assistantships with partial tuition reimbursements (averaging $1,338 per year) were awarded. Unspecified assistantships also available. *Unit head:* Dr. Douglas A. Bailey, Head, 706-542-2471, Fax: 706-542-0624, E-mail: dabailey@uga.edu. *Application contact:* Dr. Harry Mills, Graduate Coordinator, 706-542-0794, Fax: 706-542-0624, E-mail: hmills@uga.edu.

University of Guelph, Graduate Program Services, Ontario Agricultural College, Department of Plant Agriculture, Guelph, ON N1G 2W1, Canada. Offers M Sc, PhD. Part-time programs available. *Faculty:* 43 full-time (5 women), 7 part-time/adjunct (2 women). *Students:* 81 full-time (33 women), 5 part-time (1 woman); includes 8 minority (4 Asian Americans or Pacific Islanders, 4 Hispanic Americans), 5 international. 30 applicants, 53% accepted, 14 enrolled. In 2003, 12 master's, 8 doctorates awarded. *Median time to degree:* Master's–2.6 years full-time; doctorate–4.6 years full-time. Of those who began their doctoral program in fall 1995, 100% received their degree in 8 years or less. *Degree requirements:* For master's, thesis/dissertation; for doctorate, thesis/dissertation, comprehensive exam. *Entrance requirements:* For master's, minimum B average during previous 2 years; for doctorate, minimum B average. Additional exam requirements/recommendations for international students: Required—TOEFL (minimum score 550 paper-based; 213 computer-based), Michigan English Language Assessment Battery (score 85). *Application deadline:* For fall admission, 4/30 priority date for domestic students, 2/28 priority date for international students; for winter admission, 8/31 for domestic students; for spring admission, 12/24 for domestic students. Applications are processed on a rolling basis. Application fee: $75. Electronic applications accepted. Tuition and fees charges are reported in Canadian dollars. Tuition, nonresident: full-time $3,440 Canadian dollars. International tuition: $5,432 Canadian dollars full-time. Required fees: $753 Canadian dollars. *Financial support:* In 2003–04, 10 students received support, including 60 fellowships (averaging $4,100 Canadian dollars per year), 62 research assistantships (averaging $16,500 Canadian dollars per year), 9 teaching assistantships (averaging $4,134 Canadian dollars per year); scholarships/grants and unspecified assistantships also available. Financial award application deadline: 4/30. *Faculty research:* Plant physiology, biochemistry, taxonomy, morphology, genetics, production, ecology, breeding and biotechnology. Total annual research expenditures: $12 million. *Unit head:* Dr. C. J. Swanton, Chair, 519-824-4120 Ext. 53386, Fax: 519-763-8933, E-mail: cswanton@uoguelph.ca. *Application contact:* Dr. J. A. Sullivan, Graduate Coordinator, 519-842-4120 Ext. 52792, Fax: 519-767-0755, E-mail: asulliva@uoguelph.ca.

University of Hawaii at Manoa, Graduate Division, College of Tropical Agriculture and Human Resources, Department of Tropical Plant and Soil Sciences, Honolulu, HI 96822. Offers MS, PhD. *Faculty:* 31 full-time (4 women), 14 part-time/adjunct (3 women). *Students:* 20 full-time (12 women), 2 part-time (1 woman); includes 5 minority (all Asian Americans or Pacific Islanders), 10 international. Average age 31. 27 applicants, 67% accepted, 9 enrolled. *Median time to degree:* Master's–3 years full-time; doctorate–5 years full-time. *Degree requirements:* For master's, thesis (for some programs); for doctorate, thesis/dissertation. *Entrance requirements:* For doctorate, GRE. *Application deadline:* For fall admission, 3/1 for domestic students, 1/15 for international students; for spring admission, 9/1 for domestic students, 8/1 for international students. Application fee: $50. *Expenses:* Tuition, state resident: full-time $4,464; part-time $186 per credit hour. Tuition, nonresident: full-time $10,608; part-time $442 per credit hour. Tuition and fees vary according to program. *Financial support:* In 2003–04, 19 research assistantships (averaging $16,508 per year), 3 teaching assistantships (averaging $13,658 per year) were awarded. Tuition waivers (full and partial) also available. *Faculty research:* Genetics and breeding; physiology, culture, and management; weed science; turfgrass and landscape; sensory evaluation. *Unit head:* Robert E. Paull, Chairman, 808-956-5900, Fax: 808-956-3894, E-mail: paull@hawaii.edu.

See in-depth description on page 675.

University of Maine, Graduate School, College of Natural Sciences, Forestry, and Agriculture, Department of Plant, Soil, and Environmental Sciences, Program in Horticulture, Orono, ME 04469. Offers MS. *Faculty:* 5 full-time (0 women). *Students:* 3 full-time (all women), 1 (woman) part-time, 1 international. Average age 40. 1 applicant, 0% accepted. *Entrance requirements:* For master's, GRE General Test. Additional exam requirements/recommendations for international students: Required—TOEFL. *Application deadline:* For fall admission, 2/1 for domestic students. Applications are processed on a rolling basis. Application fee: $50. Electronic applications accepted. *Expenses:* Tuition, state resident: part-time $235 per credit. Tuition, nonresident: part-time $670 per credit. Tuition and fees vary according to course load. *Financial support:* In 2003–04, 2 research assistantships with tuition reimbursements (averaging $12,180 per year) were awarded; teaching assistantships with tuition reimbursements, tuition waivers (full and partial) also available. Financial award application deadline: 3/1. *Unit head:* Dr. Tsutomu Ohno, Coordinator, 207-584-2975. *Application contact:* Scott G. Delcourt, Associate Dean of the Graduate School, 207-581-3218, Fax: 207-581-3232, E-mail: graduate@maine.edu.

University of Manitoba, Faculty of Graduate Studies, Faculty of Agriculture, Department of Plant Science, Winnipeg, MB R3T 2N2, Canada. Offers horticulture (M Sc, PhD). *Degree requirements:* For master's, thesis; for doctorate, one foreign language, thesis/dissertation. Tuition charges are reported in Canadian dollars. Tuition, nonresident: full-time $3,878 Canadian dollars.

University of Maryland, College Park, Graduate Studies and Research, College of Agriculture and Natural Resources, Department of Natural Resource Sciences and Landscape Architecture, Program in Horticulture, College Park, MD 20742. Offers PhD. *Students:* 6 full-time (4 women), 3 international. *Entrance requirements:* For doctorate, GRE General Test. *Application deadline:* For fall admission, 5/1 for domestic students, 2/1 for international students; for spring admission, 10/1 for domestic students, 6/1 for international students. Applications are processed on a rolling basis. Application fee: $50. Electronic applications accepted. *Expenses:* Tuition, state resident: part-time $349 per credit hour. Tuition, nonresident: part-time $602 per credit hour.

Financial support: Fellowships, research assistantships, teaching assistantships, career-related internships or fieldwork available. Financial award applicants required to submit FAFSA. *Faculty research:* Mineral nutrition, genetics and breeding, chemical growth, histochemistry, postharvest physiology. *Application contact:* Trudy Lindsey, Director, Graduate Enrollment Management Services, 301-405-4190, Fax: 301-314-9305, E-mail: tlindsey@gradschool.umd.edu.

University of Missouri–Columbia, Graduate School, College of Agriculture, Food and Natural Resources, Program in Horticulture, Columbia, MO 65211. Offers MS, PhD. *Faculty:* 6 full-time (2 women). *Students:* 2 full-time (1 woman), 2 part-time (both women); includes 1 minority (African American) In 2003, 2 degrees awarded. *Degree requirements:* For master's, thesis; for doctorate, variable foreign language requirement, thesis/dissertation. *Entrance requirements:* For master's and doctorate, GRE General Test, minimum GPA of 3.0. *Application deadline:* Applications are processed on a rolling basis. Application fee: $45 ($60 for international students). *Expenses:* Tuition, state resident: full-time $5,205. Tuition, nonresident: full-time $14,058. *Financial support:* Research assistantships, teaching assistantships, institutionally sponsored loans available. *Unit head:* Dr. Michele Warmund, Director of Graduate Studies, 573-882-9632, E-mail: warmundm@missouri.edu.

University of Nebraska–Lincoln, Graduate College, College of Agricultural Sciences and Natural Resources, Department of Agronomy and Horticulture, Program in Horticulture, Lincoln, NE 68588. Offers MS, PhD. *Degree requirements:* For master's, thesis optional. *Entrance requirements:* For master's, GRE General Test. Additional exam requirements/recommendations for international students: Required—TOEFL (minimum score 600 paper-based; 250 computer-based). Electronic applications accepted. *Faculty research:* Horticultural crops: production, management, cultural, and ecological aspects; tissue and cell culture; plant nutrition and anatomy; postharvest physiology and ecology.

University of Puerto Rico, Mayagüez Campus, Graduate Studies, College of Agricultural Sciences, Department of Horticulture, Mayagüez, PR 00681-9000. Offers MS. Part-time programs available. *Degree requirements:* For master's, thesis, comprehensive exam. *Faculty research:* Growth regulators, floriculture, starchy crops, coffee and fruit technology.

The University of Tennessee, Graduate School, College of Agricultural Sciences and Natural Resources, Department of Plant Sciences and Landscape Systems, Knoxville, TN 37996. Offers floriculture (MS); landscape design (MS); public horticulture (MS); turfgrass (MS); woody ornamentals (MS). Part-time programs available. *Degree requirements:* For master's, thesis or alternative. *Entrance requirements:* For master's, minimum GPA of 2.7. Additional exam requirements/recommendations for international students: Required—TOEFL. Electronic applications accepted.

University of Washington, Graduate School, College of Forest Resources, Seattle, WA 98195. Offers forest economics (MS, PhD); forest ecosystem analysis (MS, PhD); forest engineering/forest hydrology (MS, PhD); forest products marketing (MS, PhD); forest soils (MS, PhD); paper science and engineering (MS, PhD); quantitative resource management (MS, PhD); silviculture (MFR); silviculture and forest protection (MS, PhD); social sciences (MS, PhD); urban horticulture (MFR, MS, PhD); wildlife science (MS, PhD). *Degree requirements:* For master's, thesis (for some programs), registration; for doctorate, thesis/dissertation, comprehensive exam (for some programs), registration. *Entrance requirements:* For master's and doctorate, GRE, minimum GPA of 3.0. Additional exam requirements/recommendations for international students: Required—TOEFL. Electronic applications accepted. *Faculty research:* Ecosystem analysis, silviculture and forest protection, paper science and engineering, environmental horticulture and urban forestry, natural resource policy and economics.

University of Wisconsin–Madison, Graduate School, College of Agricultural and Life Sciences, Department of Horticulture, Madison, WI 53706-1380. Offers horticulture (MS, PhD); plant breeding and plant genetics (MS, PhD). Part-time programs available. *Faculty:* 21 full-time (4 women). *Students:* 14 full-time (3 women), 6 part-time (4 women); includes 3 minority (all Asian Americans or Pacific Islanders) Average age 34. 28 applicants, 36% accepted, 10 enrolled. In 2003, 2 master's awarded, leading to continued full-time study 100%; 3 doctorates awarded. Terminal master's awarded for partial completion of doctoral program. *Median time to degree:* Master's–2.5 years full-time; doctorate–4.3 years full-time. Of those who began their doctoral program in fall 1995, 100% received their degree in 8 years or less. *Degree requirements:* For master's, thesis (for some programs), comprehensive exam; for doctorate, thesis/dissertation, comprehensive exam. *Entrance requirements:* For master's and doctorate, minimum GPA of 3.0. Additional exam requirements/recommendations for international students: Required—TOEFL (minimum score 580 paper-based; 213 computer-based). *Application deadline:* For fall admission, 1/2 for domestic students, 1/2 for international students; for spring admission, 10/30 for domestic students, 10/30 for international students. Applications are processed on a rolling basis. Application fee: $45. Electronic applications accepted. Tuition, area resident: Full-time $7,593; part-time $476 per credit. Tuition, nonresident: full-time $22,824; part-time $1,430 per credit. Required fees: $292; $38 per credit. Part-time tuition and fees vary according to course load and reciprocity agreements. *Financial support:* In 2003–04, 2 fellowships with tuition reimbursements (averaging $18,720 per year), 9 research assistantships with full tuition reimbursements (averaging $17,430 per year), 2 teaching assistantships with full tuition reimbursements (averaging $24,200 per year) were awarded. Career-related internships or fieldwork, Federal Work-Study, and tuition waivers (partial) also available. Financial award application deadline: 1/2. *Faculty research:* Biotechnology, crop breeding/genetics, environmental physiology, crop management, cytogenetics. *Unit head:* Dr. Dennis P. Stimart, Chair, 608-262-8406, Fax: 608-262-4743, E-mail: dstimart@facstaff.wisc.edu. *Application contact:* Dr. Sara Patterson, Professor, 608-262-1543, Fax: 608-262-4743.

Virginia Polytechnic Institute and State University, Graduate School, College of Agriculture and Life Sciences, Department of Horticulture, Blacksburg, VA 24061. Offers MS, PhD. *Faculty:* 15 full-time (2 women). *Students:* 15 full-time (5 women), 17 part-time (9 women); includes 1 minority (Asian American or Pacific Islander), 3 international. Average age 35. 25 applicants, 44% accepted, 7 enrolled. In 2003, 5 master's, 1 doctorate awarded. *Entrance requirements:* Additional exam requirements/recommendations for international students: Required—TOEFL (minimum score 550 paper-based; 213 computer-based). *Application deadline:* Applications are processed on a rolling basis. Application fee: $45. Electronic applications accepted. Tuition, area resident: Full-time $6,039; part-time $336 per credit. Tuition, nonresident: full-time $9,708; part-time $539 per credit. Required fees: $905; $130 per credit. *Financial support:* In 2003–04, 4 research assistantships with full tuition reimbursements (averaging $12,455 per year), 4 teaching assistantships with full tuition reimbursements (averaging $11,067 per year) were awarded. Career-related internships or fieldwork, Federal Work-Study, scholarships/grants, and unspecified assistantships also available. Financial award application deadline:6/1. *Unit head:* Dr. Jerzy Nowak, Head, 540-231-5451, Fax: 540-231-3083, E-mail: jenowak@vt.edu. *Application contact:* Karen Veilleux, Professor, 540-231-5584, Fax: 540-231-3083, E-mail: potato@vt.edu.

Washington State University, Graduate School, College of Agricultural, Human, and Natural Resource Sciences, Department of Horticulture and Landscape Architecture, Pullman, WA 99164. Offers horticulture (MS, PhD); landscape architecture (MLA). Part-time programs available. *Faculty:* 26 full-time (3 women). *Students:* 23 full-time (9 women), 4 part-time (1 woman); includes 1 minority (Asian American or Pacific Islander), 8 international. In 2003, 6 master's, 1 doctorate awarded. *Degree requirements:* For master's, oral exam, thesis optional; for doctorate, thesis/dissertation, oral exam, written exam. *Entrance requirements:* For master's and doctorate, GRE General Test, GRE Subject Test, minimum GPA of 3.0. *Application deadline:* For fall admission, 4/1 priority date for domestic students, 3/1 priority date for international students; for spring admission, 8/1 for domestic students, 7/1 for international students. Applications are processed on a rolling basis. Application fee: $35. Electronic applications accepted. *Expenses:* Tuition, state resident: full-time $6,278; part-time $314 per hour. Tuition, nonresident: full-time $15,514; part-time $765 per hour. Required fees: $444. Full-time tuition and fees vary according to campus/location, program and student level. Part-time tuition and fees vary according to course load. *Financial support:* In 2003–04, 8 research assistantships with full and partial tuition reimbursements (averaging $11,533 per year), 6 teaching assistantships with full and partial tuition reimbursements were awarded. Career-related internships or fieldwork, Federal Work-Study, institutionally sponsored loans, and health care benefits also available. Financial award application deadline: 4/1; financial award applicants required to submit FAFSA. *Faculty research:* Post-harvest physiology, genetics/plant breeding, molecular biology. *Unit head:* Dr. William Hendrix, Chair and Professor, 509-335-9502, Fax: 509-335-8690. *Application contact:* Judy Hobart, Coordinator, 509-335-9504, Fax: 509-335-8690.

West Virginia University, Davis College of Agriculture, Forestry and Consumer Sciences, Division of Plant and Soil Sciences, Morgantown, WV 26506. Offers agronomy (MS); entomology (MS); environmental microbiology (MS); horticulture (MS); plant pathology (MS). *Faculty:* 18 full-time (1 woman), 1 part-time/adjunct (0 women). *Students:* 17 full-time (11 women), 3 part-time (2 women), 2 international. Average age 27. In 2003, 5 degrees awarded. *Degree requirements:* For master's, thesis. *Entrance requirements:* For master's, GRE, minimum GPA of 2.5. Additional exam requirements/recommendations for international students: Required—TOEFL. *Application deadline:* Applications are processed on a rolling basis. Application fee: $45. *Expenses:* Tuition, state resident: full-time $4,332. Tuition, nonresident: full-time $12,442. *Financial support:* In 2003–04, 13 research assistantships with full tuition reimbursements (averaging $9,936 per year), 4 teaching assistantships with full tuition reimbursements (averaging $9,936 per year) were awarded. Federal Work-Study, institutionally sponsored loans, and tuition waivers (full and partial) also available. Financial award application deadline: 2/1; financial award applicants required to submit FAFSA. *Faculty research:* Water quality, reclamation of disturbed land, crop production, pest control, environmental protection. Total annual research expenditures: $1 million. *Unit head:* Dr. Barton S. Baker, Chair, 304-293-6131 Ext. 4341, Fax: 304-293-2960, E-mail: barton.baker@mail.wvu.edu.

Plant Sciences

Alabama Agricultural and Mechanical University, School of Graduate Studies, School of Agricultural and Environmental Sciences, Department of Plant and Soil Sciences, Huntsville, AL 35811. Offers animal sciences (MS); environmental science (MS); plant and soil science (PhD). Evening/weekend programs available. *Faculty:* 18 full-time (2 women), 6 part-time/adjunct (0 women). *Students:* 28 full-time (16 women), 53 part-time (30 women); includes 70 minority (53 African Americans, 4 American Indian/Alaska Native, 13 Asian Americans or Pacific Islanders). In 2003, 6 degrees awarded. Terminal master's awarded for partial completion of doctoral program. *Degree requirements:* For master's, thesis; for doctorate, one foreign language, thesis/dissertation. *Entrance requirements:* For master's, GRE General Test, BS in agriculture; for doctorate, GRE General Test, master's degree. *Application deadline:* For fall admission, 5/1 for domestic students. Applications are processed on a rolling basis. Application fee: $25. Electronic applications accepted. *Expenses:* Tuition, state resident: full-time $3,250; part-time $370 per credit hour. Tuition, nonresident: full-time $6,490; part-time $740 per credit hour. *Financial support:* In 2003–04, 1 fellowship with tuition reimbursement (averaging $18,000 per year), 9 research assistantships with tuition reimbursements (averaging $9,000 per year) were awarded. Career-related internships or fieldwork and Federal Work-Study also available. Financial award application deadline: 4/1. *Faculty research:* Plant breeding, cytogenetics, crop production, soil chemistry and fertility, remote sensing. Total annual research expenditures: $113,000. *Unit head:* Dr. Govind Sharma, Chair, 256-372-4173.

Brigham Young University, Graduate Studies, College of Biological and Agricultural Sciences, Department of Plant and Animal Sciences, Provo, UT 84602-1001. Offers agronomy (MS); horticulture (MS). *Faculty:* 16 full-time (2 women), 1 (woman) part-time/adjunct. *Students:* 11 full-time (5 women), 2 part-time (1 woman); includes 1 minority (African American) Average age 26. 7 applicants, 43% accepted, 3 enrolled. In 2003, 7 degrees awarded. *Degree requirements:* For master's, thesis, comprehensive exam, registration. *Entrance requirements:* For master's, GRE General Test, minimum GPA of 3.0 during previous 2 years. *Application deadline:* For fall admission, 2/15 for domestic students, 2/15 for international students. Applications are processed on a rolling basis. Application fee: $50. Electronic applications accepted. *Expenses:* Tuition: Part-time $221 per hour. *Financial support:* In 2003–04, 11 students received support, including 1 research assistantship with partial tuition reimbursement available (averaging $15,000 per year), 10 teaching assistantships with partial tuition reimbursements available (averaging $15,000 per year); institutionally sponsored loans, scholarships/grants, and tuition waivers (partial) also available. Financial award application deadline: 4/15. *Faculty research:* Iron nutrition in plants–mode of uptake, photosynthesis, forage quality, seed physiology/modeling, cytogenetics. Total annual research expenditures: $13,500. *Unit head:* Dr. Sheldon D. Nelson, Chair, 801-422-2760, Fax: 801-378-7499, E-mail: sheldon_nelson@byu.edu. *Application contact:* Dr. Richard E. Terry, Graduate Coordinator, 801-422-2421, Fax: 801-378-7499, E-mail: richard_terry@byu.edu.

California State University, Fresno, Division of Graduate Studies, College of Agricultural Sciences and Technology, Department of Plant Science, Fresno, CA 93740-8027. Offers MS. Part-time programs available. *Degree requirements:* For master's, thesis. *Entrance requirements:* For master's, GRE General Test, minimum GPA of 2.50. Additional exam requirements/recommendations for international students: Required—TOEFL. Electronic applications accepted. *Faculty research:* Crop patterns, small watershed management, postharvest techniques, larval control, electronic monitoring of feedlot cattle, disease control.

Colorado State University, Graduate School, College of Agricultural Sciences, Department of Bioagricultural Sciences and Pest Management, Program in Plant Pathology and Weed Science, Fort Collins, CO 80523-0015. Offers plant pathology (MS, PhD); weed science (MS, PhD). *Faculty:* 14 full-time (3 women). *Students:* 14 full-time (6 women), 5 part-time (3 women); includes 2 minority (1 African American, 1 Asian American or Pacific Islander). Average age 30. 16 applicants, 25% accepted, 4 enrolled. In 2003, 3 degrees awarded. *Degree requirements:* For master's, thesis (for some programs); for doctorate, thesis/dissertation. *Entrance requirements:* For master's and doctorate, GRE General Test, minimum GPA of 3.0. Additional exam requirements/recommendations for international students: Required—TOEFL. *Application deadline:* For fall admission, 4/1 priority date for domestic students, 4/1 priority date for international students; for spring admission, 9/1 for domestic students, 9/1 for international students. Applications are processed on a rolling basis. Application fee: $50. Electronic applications accepted. *Expenses:* Tuition, state resident: full-time $4,156. Tuition, nonresident: full-time $14,762. Required fees: $205. Tuition and fees vary according to course load, campus/location, program and reciprocity agreements. *Financial support:* In 2003–04, 1 fellowship, 11 research assistantships with full tuition reimbursements

Plant Sciences

Colorado State University (continued)

(averaging $16,200 per year), 7 teaching assistantships with full tuition reimbursements (averaging $16,200 per year) were awarded. Traineeships also available. Financial award application deadline: 4/1; financial award applicants required to submit FAFSA. *Faculty research:* Biological control of plant pathogens and weeds, integrated pest management, weed ecology/biology, seed physiology/technology, molecular biology of plant stress. Total annual research expenditures: $2 million. *Unit head:* Thomas O. Holtzer, Head, 970-491-5261, Fax: 970-491-3862, E-mail: tholtzer@lamar.colostate.edu. *Application contact:* Janet Dill, Administrative Assistant, 970-491-4140, Fax: 970-491-3862, E-mail: dillj@lamar.colostate.edu.

Cornell University, Graduate School, Graduate Fields of Agriculture and Life Sciences, Field of Plant Breeding, Ithaca, NY 14853-0001. Offers plant breeding (MPS, MS, PhD); plant genetics (MPS, MS, PhD). *Faculty:* 22 full-time. *Students:* 32 full-time (11 women); includes 3 minority (1 African American, 1 Asian American or Pacific Islander, 1 Hispanic American), 18 international. 41 applicants, 34% accepted, 8 enrolled. In 2003, 1 master's, 7 doctorates awarded. Terminal master's awarded for partial completion of doctoral program. *Degree requirements:* For master's, thesis (MS), project paper (MPS); for doctorate, thesis/dissertation, comprehensive exam. *Entrance requirements:* For master's and doctorate, GRE General Test, GRE Subject Test (recommended), 3 letters of recommendation. Additional exam requirements/recommendations for international students: Required—TOEFL (minimum score 550 paper-based; 213 computer-based). *Application deadline:* For fall admission, 1/15 for domestic students. Application fee: $60. Electronic applications accepted. *Expenses:* Tuition: Full-time $28,630. One-time fee: $50 full-time. *Financial support:* In 2003–04, 24 students received support, including 2 fellowships with full tuition reimbursements available, 17 research assistantships with full tuition reimbursements available, 5 teaching assistantships with full tuition reimbursements available; institutionally sponsored loans, scholarships/grants, health care benefits, tuition waivers (full and partial), and unspecified assistantships also available. Financial award applicants required to submit FAFSA. *Faculty research:* Crop breeding for improved yield, stress resistance and quality; genetics and genomics of crop plants; applications of moelcular biology and bioinformatics to crop improvement; genetic diversity and utilization of wild germplasm; international agriculture. *Unit head:* Director of Graduate Studies, 607-255-2180. *Application contact:* Graduate Field Assistant, 607-255-2180, E-mail: plbrgrad@cornell.edu.

Cornell University, Graduate School, Graduate Fields of Agriculture and Life Sciences, Field of Plant Protection, Ithaca, NY 14853-0001. Offers MPS. *Faculty:* 21 full-time. *Students:* 1 (woman) full-time. 2 applicants, 50% accepted, 1 enrolled. *Degree requirements:* For master's, internship, final exam. *Entrance requirements:* For master's, GRE General Test, 3 letters of recommendation. Additional exam requirements/recommendations for international students: Required—TOEFL (minimum score 550 paper-based; 213 computer-based). *Application deadline:* For fall admission, 4/1 for domestic students. Application fee: $60. Electronic applications accepted. *Expenses:* Tuition: Full-time $28,630. One-time fee: $50 full-time. *Financial support:* Fellowships with full tuition reimbursements, research assistantships with full tuition reimbursements, teaching assistantships with full tuition reimbursements, institutionally sponsored loans, scholarships/grants, health care benefits, tuition waivers (full and partial), and unspecified assistantships available. Financial award applicants required to submit FAFSA. *Faculty research:* Fruit and vegetable crop insects and diseases, systems modeling, biological control, plant protection economics, integrated pest management. *Unit head:* Director of Graduate Studies, 315-787-2323, Fax: 315-787-2326. *Application contact:* Graduate Field Assistant, 315-787-2323, Fax: 315-787-2326, E-mail: plprotection@cornell.edu.

Cornell University, Graduate School, Graduate Fields of Agriculture and Life Sciences, Field of Pomology, Ithaca, NY 14853-0001. Offers MPS, MS, PhD. *Faculty:* 17 full-time. *Students:* 19 full-time (10 women), 11 international. 5 applicants, 60% accepted, 3 enrolled. In 2003, 1 degree awarded. *Degree requirements:* For master's, thesis (MS), project paper (MPS); for doctorate, thesis/dissertation, comprehensive exam. *Entrance requirements:* For master's and doctorate, GRE General Test, interview (recommended), letters of recommendation (3). Additional exam requirements/recommendations for international students: Required—TOEFL (minimum score 550 paper-based; 213 computer-based). *Application deadline:* For fall admission, 1/15 for domestic students; for spring admission, 8/15 for domestic students. Application fee: $60. Electronic applications accepted. *Expenses:* Tuition: Full-time $28,630. One-time fee: $50 full-time. *Financial support:* In 2003–04, 17 students received support, including 1 fellowship with full tuition reimbursement available, 16 research assistantships with full tuition reimbursements available; teaching assistantships with full tuition reimbursements available, institutionally sponsored loans, scholarships/grants, health care benefits, tuition waivers (full and partial), and unspecified assistantships also available. Financial award applicants required to submit FAFSA. *Faculty research:* Fruit breeding and biotechnology, fruit crop physiology, orchard management, orchard ecology and IPM, post-harvest physiology. *Unit head:* Director of Graduate Studies, 607-255-4568, Fax: 607-255-0599. *Application contact:* Graduate Field Assistant, 607-255-4568, Fax: 607-255-0599, E-mail: hortgrad@cornell.edu.

Cornell University, Graduate School, Graduate Fields of Agriculture and Life Sciences, Field of Vegetable Crops, Ithaca, NY 14853-0001. Offers MPS, MS, PhD. *Faculty:* 15 full-time. *Students:* 6 full-time (3 women); includes 1 minority (Asian American or Pacific Islander), 3 international. 5 applicants, 80% accepted, 1 enrolled. In 2003, 2 master's, 2 doctorates awarded. *Degree requirements:* For master's, thesis (MS), project paper (MPS); for doctorate, thesis/dissertation, teaching experience. *Entrance requirements:* For master's and doctorate, GRE General Test (recommended), letters of recommendation (3). Additional exam requirements/recommendations for international students: Required—TOEFL (minimum score 550 paper-based; 213 computer-based). *Application deadline:* Applications are processed on a rolling basis. Application fee: $60. Electronic applications accepted. *Expenses:* Tuition: Full-time $28,630. One-time fee: $50 full-time. *Financial support:* In 2003–04, 6 students received support, including 6 research assistantships with full tuition reimbursements available; fellowships with full tuition reimbursements available, teaching assistantships with full tuition reimbursements available, institutionally sponsored loans, health care benefits, tuition waivers (full and partial), and unspecified assistantships also available. Financial award applicants required to submit FAFSA. *Faculty research:* Vegetable nutrition and physiology, post-harvest physiology and storage, application of new technologies, sustainable vegetable production, weed management and IPM. *Unit head:* Director of Graduate Studies, 607-255-4568. *Application contact:* Graduate Field Assistant, 607-255-4568, E-mail: hortgrad@cornell.edu.

Florida Agricultural and Mechanical University, Division of Graduate Studies, Research, and Continuing Education, College of Engineering Science, Technology, and Agriculture, Division of Agricultural Sciences, Tallahassee, FL 32307-3200. Offers agribusiness (MS); animal science (MS); engineering technology (MS); entomology (MS); food science (MS); international programs (MS); plant science (MS). *Faculty:* 31 full-time (2 women). *Students:* 14 full-time (8 women), 8 part-time (4 women); includes 17 minority (16 African Americans, 1 Asian American or Pacific Islander), 3 international. In 2003, 7 degrees awarded. *Degree requirements:* For master's, thesis. *Entrance requirements:* For master's, GRE General Test, minimum GPA of 3.0. Additional exam requirements/recommendations for international students: Required—TOEFL (minimum score 500 paper-based). *Application deadline:* For fall admission, 5/18 for domestic students, 12/18 for international students; for spring admission, 11/12 for domestic students, 5/12 for international students. Application fee: $20. *Expenses:* Tuition, state resident: part-time $192 per credit. Tuition, nonresident: part-time $727 per credit. Tuition and fees vary according to course load. *Financial support:* Application deadline: 2/15. *Unit head:* Dr. Mitwe N. Musingo, Graduate Coordinator, 850-561-2309, Fax: 850-599-8821.

Lehman College of the City University of New York, Division of Natural and Social Sciences, Department of Biological Sciences, Program in Plant Sciences, Bronx, NY 10468-1589. Offers PhD. *Degree requirements:* For doctorate, 2 foreign languages, thesis/dissertation. *Entrance requirements:* For doctorate, GRE General Test.

McGill University, Faculty of Graduate and Postdoctoral Studies, Faculty of Agricultural and Environmental Sciences, Department of Plant Science, Montréal, QC H3A 2T5, Canada. Offers M Sc, M Sc A, PhD. Part-time programs available. *Faculty:* 15 full-time (9 women). *Students:* 31 full-time, 1 part-time. 43 applicants, 26% accepted, 8 enrolled. In 2003, 6 master's, 3 doctorates awarded. Terminal master's awarded for partial completion of doctoral program. *Degree requirements:* For master's and doctorate, thesis/dissertation. *Entrance requirements:* For master's, minimum GPA of 3.0; for doctorate, M Sc, minimum GPA of 3.0. Additional exam requirements/recommendations for international students: Required—TOEFL (paper score 550; computer score 213) or IELTS (paper score 6). *Application deadline:* For fall admission, 6/1 for domestic students, 3/1 for international students; for winter admission, 10/15 for domestic students; for spring admission, 2/15 for domestic students. Applications are processed on a rolling basis. Application fee: $60 Canadian dollars. Electronic applications accepted. Tuition, area resident: Full-time $1,668. *Expenses:* Tuition, state resident: full-time $4,173. Tuition, nonresident: full-time $9,468. Required fees: $1,081. *Financial support:* In 2003–04, 1 fellowship (averaging $8,000 per year) was awarded; research assistantships, teaching assistantships, institutionally sponsored loans also available. *Faculty research:* Plant breeding, cytogenetics, crop physiology, bioherbicides, production. *Unit head:* Dr. Marc Fortin, Chair, 514-398-8384, Fax: 514-398-7897, E-mail: marc.fortin@mcgill.ca. *Application contact:* Carolyn Bowes, Graduate Program Secretary, 514-398-7560, Fax: 514-398-7897, E-mail: carolyn.bowes@mcgill.ca.

Michigan State University, Graduate School, College of Agriculture and Natural Resources, Program in Plant Breeding and Genetics, East Lansing, MI 48824. Offers plant breeding and genetics (MS, PhD), including botany and plant pathology, crop and soil sciences, forestry, horticulture. *Faculty:* 22 full-time (5 women). *Students:* 22 full-time (12 women), 5 part-time (3 women); includes 1 minority (Hispanic American), 12 international. Average age 30. 29 applicants, 17% accepted. In 2003, 3 master's, 2 doctorates awarded. *Degree requirements:* For master's, thesis; for doctorate, thesis/dissertation, oral examination, comprehensive exam. *Entrance requirements:* For master's and doctorate, GRE, minimum GPA of 3.0, 3 letters of recommendation. Additional exam requirements/recommendations for international students: Required—TOEFL (minimum score 550 paper-based; 213 computer-based). *Application deadline:* For fall admission, 12/23 for domestic students. Application fee: $50. *Expenses:* Tuition, state resident: part-time $291 per hour. Tuition, nonresident: part-time $589 per hour. *Financial support:* Applicants required to submit FAFSA. *Unit head:* Dr. Jim Hancock, Director, 517-355-4598, Fax: 517-353-0890, E-mail: hancock@msu.edu. *Application contact:* Program Office, 517-353-2913.

Michigan State University, Graduate School, College of Natural Science, Plant Research Laboratory, East Lansing, MI 48824. Offers biochemistry and molecular biology (PhD); cellular and molecular biology (PhD); crop and soil sciences (PhD); genetics (PhD); microbiology and molecular genetics (PhD); plant biology (PhD); plant physiology (PhD). Offered jointly with the Department of Energy. *Faculty:* 10 full-time (1 woman). *Students:* 19 full-time (6 women); includes 1 minority (Asian American or Pacific Islander), 6 international. Average age 27. *Degree requirements:* For doctorate, thesis/dissertation, laboratory rotation, defense of dissertation, comprehensive exam. *Entrance requirements:* For doctorate, GRE General Test, acceptance into one of the affiliated department programs; 3 letters of recommendation; bachelor's degree or equivalent in life sciences, chemistry, biochemistry, or biophysics; research experience. Additional exam requirements/recommendations for international students: Required—TOEFL (minimum score 550 paper-based; 213 computer-based), Michigan State University ELT (85), Michigan ELAB (83). *Application deadline:* For fall admission, 1/15 for domestic students. Application fee: $50. Electronic applications accepted. *Expenses:* Tuition, state resident: part-time $291 per hour. Tuition, nonresident: part-time $589 per hour. *Financial support:* Research assistantships with tuition reimbursements available. Financial award applicants required to submit FAFSA. *Faculty research:* Role of hormones in the regulation of plant development and physiology, molecular mechanisms associated with signal recognition, development and application of genetic methods and materials, protein routing and function. Total annual research expenditures: $6.6 million. *Unit head:* Dr. Kenneth Keegstra, Director, 517-353-2270, Fax: 517-353-9168, E-mail: keegstra@msu.edu. *Application contact:* Zita Schneider, Information Contact, 517-353-2270, Fax: 517-353-9168, E-mail: prl@msu.edu.

Mississippi State University, College of Agriculture and Life Sciences, Department of Plant and Soil Sciences, Mississippi State, MS 39762. Offers agronomy (MS, PhD); horticulture (MS, PhD); weed science (MS, PhD). Part-time programs available. *Faculty:* 31 full-time (2 women), 1 part-time/adjunct (0 women). *Students:* 36 full-time (10 women), 25 part-time (6 women); includes 1 minority (Asian American or Pacific Islander), 16 international. Average age 31. 16 applicants, 38% accepted, 3 enrolled. In 2003, 9 master's, 3 doctorates awarded. *Degree requirements:* For master's and doctorate, thesis/dissertation, comprehensive oral or written exam. *Entrance requirements:* Additional exam requirements/recommendations for international students: Required—TOEFL. *Application deadline:* For fall admission, 7/1 for domestic students; for spring admission, 11/1 for domestic students. Applications are processed on a rolling basis. Application fee: $25 for international students. *Expenses:* Tuition, state resident: full-time $3,874; part-time $215 per hour. Tuition, nonresident: full-time $8,780; part-time $488 per hour. International tuition: $9,105 full-time. Tuition and fees vary according to course load. *Financial support:* In 2003–04, 12 research assistantships with full tuition reimbursements (averaging $12,423 per year), 3 teaching assistantships with full tuition reimbursements (averaging $13,696 per year) were awarded. Career-related internships or fieldwork, Federal Work-Study, institutionally sponsored loans, and unspecified assistantships also available. Financial award applicants required to submit FAFSA. *Faculty research:* Metabolism, morphology, growth regulators, biotechnology, stress physiology. Total annual research expenditures: $874,795. *Unit head:* Dr. Frank Matta, Interim Head, 662-325-2352, Fax: 662-325-8742, E-mail: fmatta@pss.msstate.edu. *Application contact:* Diane D. Wolfe, Director of Admissions, 662-325-2224, Fax: 662-325-7360, E-mail: admit@admissions.msstate.edu.

Montana State University–Bozeman, College of Graduate Studies, College of Agriculture, Department of Plant Sciences and Plant Pathology, Bozeman, MT 59717. Offers plant pathology (MS); plant science (MS, PhD). Part-time programs available. Postbaccalaureate distance learning degree programs offered. *Faculty:* 21 full-time (2 women), 1 part-time/adjunct (0 women). *Students:* 6 full-time (3 women), 16 part-time (6 women), 6 international. Average age 31. 6 applicants, 100% accepted, 4 enrolled. In 2003, 6 master's, 1 doctorate awarded. *Degree requirements:* For master's, thesis (for some programs), comprehensive exam, registration; for doctorate, thesis/dissertation, comprehensive exam, registration. *Entrance requirements:* For master's and doctorate, GRE General Test. Additional exam requirements/recommendations for international students: Required—TOEFL (minimum score 550 paper-based; 213 computer-based). *Application deadline:* For fall admission, 7/15 priority date for domestic students, 5/15 priority date for international students; for spring admission, 12/1 priority date for domestic students, 10/1 priority date for international students. Applications are processed on a rolling basis. Application fee: $50. Electronic applications accepted. *Expenses:* Tuition, state resident: full-time $3,907; part-time $163 per credit. Tuition, nonresident: full-time $12,383; part-time $516 per credit. Required fees: $890; $445 per term. Tuition and fees vary according to course load and program. *Financial support:* In 2003–04, research assistantships with full tuition reimbursements (averaging $12,500 per year), 1 teaching assistantship with full tuition reimbursement (averaging $12,000 per year) were awarded. Health care benefits and unspecified assistantships also available. Financial award application deadline: 3/1; financial award applicants required to submit FAFSA. *Faculty research:* Plant genetics, plant microbe interactives, plant physiology, plant taxonomy. Total annual research expenditures: $4.3 million. *Unit head:* Dr. John Sherwood, Head, 406-994-5153, Fax: 406-994-1848, E-mail: sherwood@montana.edu.

New Mexico State University, Graduate School, College of Agriculture and Home Economics, Department of Entomology, Plant Pathology and Weed Science, Las Cruces, NM 88003-8001. Offers MS. Part-time programs available. *Faculty:* 12 full-time (5 women), 2 part-time/adjunct (0 women). *Students:* 11 full-time (6 women), 8 part-time (4 women); includes 3 minority (1 African American, 1 American Indian/Alaska Native, 1 Hispanic American). Average age 30. 4 applicants, 100% accepted, 3 enrolled. In 2003, 2 degrees awarded. *Degree* *requirements:* For master's, thesis, comprehensive exam, registration. *Entrance requirements:* For master's, GRE General Test. *Application deadline:* For fall admission, 7/1 for domestic students; for spring admission, 11/1 priority date for domestic students. Applications are processed on a rolling basis. Application fee: $30 ($50 for international students). Electronic applications accepted. *Expenses:* Tuition, state resident: full-time $2,670; part-time $151 per credit. Tuition, nonresident: full-time $10,596; part-time $481 per credit. Required fees: $954. *Financial support:* In 2003–04, 14 research assistantships with partial tuition reimbursements were awarded; teaching assistantships with partial tuition reimbursements, career-related internships or fieldwork also available. Financial award application deadline: 3/1. *Faculty research:* Integrated pest management, pesticide application and safety, livestock ectoparasite research, biotechnology, nematology. *Unit head:* Dr. Grant Kinzer, Head, 505-646-3225, Fax: 505-646-8087, E-mail: gkinzer@nmsu.edu.

North Carolina Agricultural and Technical State University, Graduate School, School of Agriculture and Environmental and Allied Sciences, Department of Natural Resources and Environmental Design, Greensboro, NC 27411. Offers plant science (MS). Part-time and evening/weekend programs available. *Degree requirements:* For master's, qualifying exam, thesis optional. *Entrance requirements:* For master's, GRE General Test, minimum GPA of 3.0. *Faculty research:* Soil parameters and compaction of forest site, controlled traffic effects on soil, improving soybean and vegetable crops.

North Dakota State University, The Graduate School, College of Agriculture, Food Systems, and Natural Resources, Department of Plant Sciences, Fargo, ND 58105. Offers crop and weed sciences (MS); horticulture (MS); natural resources management (MS); plant sciences (PhD). Part-time programs available. *Faculty:* 39 full-time (3 women), 19 part-time/adjunct (1 woman). *Students:* 63 full-time (30 women), 8 part-time (2 women); includes 1 minority (Asian American or Pacific Islander), 37 international. Average age 26. 40 applicants, 50% accepted. In 2003, 1 master's, 2 doctorates awarded. *Degree requirements:* For master's and doctorate, thesis/dissertation. *Entrance requirements:* Additional exam requirements/recommendations for international students: Required—TOEFL. *Application deadline:* Applications are processed on a rolling basis. Application fee: $35 ($50 for international students). Electronic applications accepted. Tuition, nonresident: full-time $4,071. Required fees: $493. *Financial support:* In 2003–04, 1 student received support, including 2 fellowships (averaging $19,950 per year), 60 research assistantships; teaching assistantships, Federal Work-Study and institutionally sponsored loans also available. Financial award application deadline: 4/15. *Faculty research:* Biotechnology, weed control science, plant breeding, plant genetics, crop physiology. Total annual research expenditures: $880,000. *Unit head:* Dr. Al Schneiter, Chair, 701-231-7971, Fax: 701-231-8474, E-mail: albert.schneiter@ndsu.nodak.edu.

Oklahoma State University, Graduate College, Program in Plant Science, Stillwater, OK 74078. Offers PhD. *Application deadline:* Applications are processed on a rolling basis. Application fee: $25 ($50 for international students). Electronic applications accepted. *Expenses:* Tuition, state resident: full-time $3,752; part-time $118 per credit hour. Tuition, nonresident: full-time $10,346; part-time $393 per credit hour. Tuition and fees vary according to course load. *Financial support:* Research assistantships available. *Unit head:* Dr. Charles Tauer, Coordinator, 405-744-5462.

Rutgers, The State University of New Jersey, New Brunswick/Piscataway, Graduate School, Program in Plant Biology, New Brunswick, NJ 08901-1281. Offers horticulture (MS, PhD); molecular biology and biochemistry (MS, PhD); pathology (MS, PhD); plant ecology (MS, PhD); plant genetics (PhD); plant physiology (MS, PhD); production and management (MS); structure and plant groups (MS, PhD). Part-time programs available. *Faculty:* 59 full-time (14 women), 1 part-time/adjunct (0 women). *Students:* 44 full-time (17 women), 5 part-time (2 women); includes 5 minority (3 African Americans, 2 Asian Americans or Pacific Islanders), 17 international. Average age 27. 49 applicants, 33% accepted, 8 enrolled. In 2003, 6 master's, 2 doctorates awarded. Terminal master's awarded for partial completion of doctoral program. *Median time to degree:* Master's–3 years full-time; doctorate–5.5 years full-time. Of those who began their doctoral program in fall 1995, 90% received their degree in 8 years or less. *Degree requirements:* For master's, thesis or alternative, comprehensive exam; for doctorate, thesis/dissertation, comprehensive exam. *Entrance requirements:* For master's and doctorate, GRE General Test, GRE Subject Test (recommended). Additional exam requirements/recommendations for international students: Required—TOEFL (minimum score 600 paper-based; 250 computer-based). *Application deadline:* For fall admission, 4/1 for domestic students, 4/1 for international students. Application fee: $50. Electronic applications accepted. *Expenses:* Tuition, state resident: full-time $10,030. Tuition, nonresident: full-time $14,202. *Financial support:* In 2003–04, 42 students received support, including 9 fellowships with full tuition reimbursements available (averaging $20,000 per year), 22 research assistantships with full tuition reimbursements available (averaging $16,500 per year), 10 teaching assistantships with full tuition reimbursements available (averaging $15,100 per year) Financial award application deadline: 1/15; financial award applicants required to submit FAFSA. *Faculty research:* Molecular biology and biochemistry of plants, plant development and genomics, plant protection, plant improvement, plant management of horticultural and field crops. Total annual research expenditures: $10 million. *Unit head:* Dr. Thomas Leustek, Director, 732-932-8165 Ext. 326, Fax: 732-932-9377, E-mail: leustek@aesop.rutgers.edu. *Application contact:* Barbara Mulder, Program Associate, 732-932-9375 Ext. 358, Fax: 732-932-9377, E-mail: plantbio@aesop.rutgers.edu.

South Dakota State University, Graduate School, College of Agriculture and Biological Sciences, Department of Plant Science, Brookings, SD 57007. Offers agronomy (MS, PhD); biological sciences (PhD); entomology (MS); plant pathology (MS). *Degree requirements:* For master's, thesis, oral exam; for doctorate, thesis/dissertation, preliminary oral and written exams. *Entrance requirements:* For master's and doctorate, GRE General Test. Additional exam requirements/recommendations for international students: Required—TOEFL.

Southern Illinois University Carbondale, Graduate School, College of Agriculture, Department of Plant, Soil, and General Agriculture, Carbondale, IL 62901-4701. Offers horticultural science (MS); plant and soil science (MS). *Faculty:* 20 full-time (1 woman). *Students:* 11 full-time (5 women), 34 part-time (11 women), 2 international. 9 applicants, 56% accepted, 1 enrolled. In 2003, 10 degrees awarded. *Degree requirements:* For master's, thesis. *Entrance requirements:* For master's, minimum GPA of 2.7. Additional exam requirements/recommendations for international students: Required—TOEFL. *Application deadline:* Applications are processed on a rolling basis. Application fee: $0. *Expenses:* Tuition, state resident: part-time $478 per hour. Tuition, nonresident: part-time $657 per hour. *Financial support:* In 2003–04, 22 students received support, including 15 research assistantships with full tuition reimbursements available, 6 teaching assistantships with full tuition reimbursements available; fellowships with full tuition reimbursements available, Federal Work-Study, institutionally sponsored loans, and tuition waivers (full) also available. Support available to part-time students. *Faculty research:* Herbicides, fertilizers, agriculture education, landscape design, plant breeding. Total annual research expenditures: $2 million. *Unit head:* John Russin, Chairperson, 618-453-2496.

Southwest Missouri State University, Graduate College, College of Natural and Applied Sciences, Department of Agriculture, Program in Plant Science, Springfield, MO 65804-0094. Offers MS. *Students:* 4 full-time (3 women), 1 part-time, 3 international. Average age 27. 7 applicants, 57% accepted, 1 enrolled. In 2003, 2 degrees awarded. *Degree requirements:* For master's, thesis, comprehensive exam. *Entrance requirements:* For master's, GRE General Test, minimum undergraduate GPA of 3.0. *Application deadline:* For fall admission, 8/5 for domestic students; for spring admission, 12/20 priority date for domestic students. Applications are processed on a rolling basis. Application fee: $30. Electronic applications accepted. *Expenses:* Tuition, state resident: full-time $2,862. Tuition, nonresident: full-time $5,724. *Financial support:* Research assistantships with full tuition reimbursements, teaching assistantships with full tuition reimbursements, Federal Work-Study and unspecified assistantships available. Financial award application deadline: 3/31. *Unit head:* Dr. William Cheek, Director, 417-836-5249, Fax: 417-836-6934.

State University of New York College of Environmental Science and Forestry, Faculty of Environmental and Forest Biology, Syracuse, NY 13210-2779. Offers chemical ecology (MPS, MS, PhD); conservation biology (MPS, MS, PhD); ecology (MPS, MS, PhD); entomology (MPS, MS, PhD); environmental interpretation (MPS, MS, PhD); environmental physiology (MPS, MS, PhD); fish and wildlife biology (MPS, MS, PhD); forest pathology and mycology (MPS, MS, PhD); plant science and biotechnology (MPS, MS, PhD). *Faculty:* 32 full-time (3 women), 1 (woman) part-time/adjunct. *Students:* 93 full-time (53 women), 53 part-time (23 women); includes 4 minority (1 Asian American or Pacific Islander, 3 Hispanic Americans), 16 international. Average age 30. 100 applicants, 52% accepted, 25 enrolled. In 2003, 28 master's, 7 doctorates awarded. *Degree requirements:* For master's, thesis (for some programs), registration; for doctorate, thesis/dissertation, comprehensive exam, registration. *Entrance requirements:* For master's and doctorate, GRE General Test, GRE Subject Test, minimum GPA of 3.0. Additional exam requirements/recommendations for international students: Required—TOEFL (minimum score 550 paper-based; 213 computer-based). *Application deadline:* For fall admission, 2/1 priority date for domestic students, 2/1 priority date for international students; for spring admission, 11/1 priority date for domestic students, 11/1 priority date for international students. Applications are processed on a rolling basis. Application fee: $50. Tuition, area resident: Part-time $288 per credit hour. Tuition, nonresident: part-time $438 per credit hour. Required fees: $300; $5 per credit hour. $18 per semester. One-time fee: $25 full-time. *Financial support:* In 2003–04, 86 students received support, including 17 fellowships with full and partial tuition reimbursements available (averaging $9,446 per year), 41 research assistantships with full and partial tuition reimbursements available (averaging $11,000 per year), 34 teaching assistantships with full and partial tuition reimbursements available (averaging $9,446 per year); Federal Work-Study, institutionally sponsored loans, scholarships/grants, health care benefits, and unspecified assistantships also available. *Faculty research:* Ecology, fish and wildlife biology and management, plant science, entomology. Total annual research expenditures: $2.6 million. *Unit head:* Dr. Neil H. Ringler, Chair, 315-470-6770, Fax: 315-470-6934, E-mail: neilringler@esf.edu. *Application contact:* Dr. Dudley J. Raynal, Dean, Instruction and Graduate Studies, 315-470-6599, Fax: 315-470-6978, E-mail: esfgrad@esf.edu.

Texas A&M University, College of Agriculture and Life Sciences, Department of Soil and Crop Sciences, Intercollegiate Program in Molecular and Environmental Plant Sciences, College Station, TX 77843. Offers MS, PhD. *Students:* Average age 29. 23 applicants, 17% accepted. In 2003, 2 master's, 1 doctorate awarded. *Median time to degree:* Master's–2 years full-time; doctorate–4 years full-time. *Degree requirements:* For master's and doctorate, thesis/dissertation, seminar. *Entrance requirements:* For master's and doctorate, GRE General Test, letters of reference. Additional exam requirements/recommendations for international students: Required—TOEFL. *Application deadline:* For fall admission, 3/1 for domestic students; for spring admission, 8/1 for domestic students. Applications are processed on a rolling basis. Application fee: $50 ($75 for international students). Electronic applications accepted. *Expenses:* Tuition, state resident: full-time $3,420. Tuition, nonresident: full-time $9,084. Required fees: $1,861. *Financial support:* In 2003–04, fellowships with tuition reimbursements (averaging $20,000 per year), research assistantships (averaging $17,000 per year), teaching assistantships (averaging $18,200 per year) were awarded. Financial award application deadline: 3/1; financial award applicants required to submit FAFSA. *Faculty research:* Functional genomics, bioremediation, physiological ecology, transformation systems, abiotic stress. *Unit head:* Dr. Marla L. Binzel, Chair, 979-845-8938, Fax: 979-458-0533, E-mail: m-binzel@tamu.edu. *Application contact:* Dr. Jean Gould, Admissions Chair, 979-845-5078, Fax: 979-845-6049, E-mail: gould@tamu.edu.

Texas A&M University–Kingsville, College of Graduate Studies, College of Agriculture and Home Economics, Program in Plant and Soil Sciences, Kingsville, TX 78363. Offers MS, PhD. *Degree requirements:* For master's, thesis or alternative, comprehensive exam. *Entrance requirements:* For master's, GRE General Test, minimum GPA of 3.0. Additional exam requirements/recommendations for international students: Required—TOEFL.

Texas Tech University, Graduate School, College of Agricultural Sciences and Natural Resources, Department of Plant and Soil Science, Lubbock, TX 79409. Offers agronomy (PhD); crop science (MS); entomology (MS); horticulture (MS); soil science (MS). Part-time programs available. *Faculty:* 12 full-time (2 women), 1 part-time/adjunct (0 women). *Students:* 39 full-time (13 women), 21 part-time (8 women); includes 1 minority (Asian American or Pacific Islander), 14 international. Average age 32. 18 applicants, 78% accepted, 10 enrolled. In 2003, 13 master's, 6 doctorates awarded. *Degree requirements:* For doctorate, thesis/dissertation. *Entrance requirements:* For master's and doctorate, GRE General Test. Additional exam requirements/recommendations for international students: Required—TOEFL (minimum score 550 paper-based; 213 computer-based). *Application deadline:* Applications are processed on a rolling basis. Application fee: $50 ($60 for international students). Electronic applications accepted. *Expenses:* Tuition, state resident: full-time $3,312. Tuition, nonresident: full-time $8,976. Required fees: $1,745. Tuition and fees vary according to program. *Financial support:* In 2003–04, 44 students received support, including 21 research assistantships with partial tuition reimbursements available (averaging $13,555 per year); teaching assistantships with partial tuition reimbursements available, Federal Work-Study and institutionally sponsored loans also available. Support available to part-time students. Financial award application deadline: 5/1; financial award applicants required to submit FAFSA. *Faculty research:* Molecular and cellular biology of plant stress, physiology/genetics of crop production in semiarid conditions, agricultural bioterrorism, improvement of native plants. Total annual research expenditures: $2.1 million. *Unit head:* Dr. Dick L. Auld, Chair, 806-742-2837, Fax: 806-742-0775, E-mail: dick.auld@ttu.edu. *Application contact:* Dr. Richard E. Zartman, Graduate Adviser, 806-742-2837, Fax: 806-742-0775, E-mail: richard.zartman@ttu.edu.

Tuskegee University, Graduate Programs, College of Agricultural, Environmental and Natural Sciences, Department of Agricultural Sciences, Program in Plant and Soil Sciences, Tuskegee, AL 36088. Offers MS. *Faculty:* 13 full-time (1 woman), 2 part-time/adjunct (1 woman). *Students:* 6 full-time (3 women), 4 part-time (3 women); includes 3 minority (all African Americans), 7 international. Average age 28. *Degree requirements:* For master's, thesis. *Entrance requirements:* For master's, GRE General Test. *Application deadline:* For fall admission, 7/15 for domestic students. Applications are processed on a rolling basis. Application fee: $25 ($35 for international students). *Expenses:* Tuition: Full-time $11,060; part-time $655 per credit hour. Required fees: $250. Tuition and fees vary according to course load. *Financial support:* Application deadline: 4/15.

The University of Arizona, Graduate College, College of Agriculture and Life Sciences, Department of Plant Sciences, Tucson, AZ 85721. Offers MS, PhD. Part-time programs available. *Degree requirements:* For master's, thesis or alternative; for doctorate, thesis/dissertation. *Entrance requirements:* For master's and doctorate, GRE General Test, GRE Subject Test (biology or chemistry) (recommended), minimum GPA of 3.0. Additional exam requirements/recommendations for international students: Required—TOEFL. Electronic applications accepted. *Expenses:* Tuition, state resident: part-time $196 per unit. Tuition, nonresident: part-time $326 per unit. *Faculty research:* Molecular/cell biology, plant genetics and physiology, agronomic and horticultural production (including turf and ornamentals).

University of Arkansas, Graduate School, Dale Bumpers College of Agricultural, Food and Life Sciences, Interdepartmental Program in Plant Science, Fayetteville, AR 72701-1201. Offers PhD. *Students:* 13 full-time (4 women), 2 part-time, 9 international. 9 applicants, 11% accepted. In 2003, 1 degree awarded. *Degree requirements:* For doctorate, thesis/dissertation. Application fee: $40 ($50 for international students). *Expenses:* Tuition, state resident: full-time $4,032; part-time $224 per credit hour. Tuition, nonresident: full-time $9,540; part-time $530 per credit hour. Tuition and fees vary according to course load and program. *Financial support:* In 2003–04, 3 fellowships, 13 research assistantships were awarded. Teaching assistantships, career-related internships or fieldwork and Federal Work-Study also available. Support avail-

Plant Sciences

University of Arkansas (continued)

able to part-time students. Financial award application deadline: 4/1; financial award applicants required to submit FAFSA. *Unit head:* Dr. Brad Murphy, Chair, 479-575-2678.

The University of British Columbia, Faculty of Graduate Studies, Faculty of Agricultural Sciences, Plant Science Program, Vancouver, BC V6T 1Z1, Canada. Offers M Sc, PhD. *Faculty:* 7 full-time (1 woman), 4 part-time/adjunct (1 woman). *Students:* 31 full-time (17 women). Average age 24. 21 applicants, 33% accepted, 7 enrolled. In 2003, 1 master's, 1 doctorate awarded. *Median time to degree:* Master's–4 years full-time; doctorate–6 years full-time. *Degree requirements:* For master's, comprehensive exam or thesis; for doctorate, thesis/dissertation, comprehensive exam, registration. *Entrance requirements:* Additional exam requirements/recommendations for international students: Required—TOEFL (minimum score 560 paper-based; 220 computer-based). *Application deadline:* For fall admission, 3/30 for domestic students, 2/28 for international students; for winter admission, 8/31 for domestic students; for spring admission, 12/31 for domestic students. Application fee: $90 Canadian dollars ($150 Canadian dollars for international students). Electronic applications accepted. *Financial support:* In 2003–04, 9 fellowships (averaging $12,157 per year) were awarded; research assistantships, teaching assistantships, institutionally sponsored loans, scholarships/grants, and tuition waivers (full and partial) also available. *Faculty research:* Plant physiology and biochemistry, biotechnology, plant protection (insect, weeds, and diseases), plant protection, plant-environment interaction. Total annual research expenditures: $542,829. *Unit head:* Dr. Murray Isman, Graduate Adviser, Fax: 604-822-4400, E-mail: gradapp@interchange.ubc.ca. *Application contact:* Alina Yuhymets, Graduate Programs Manager, 604-822-4593, Fax: 604-822-4400, E-mail: yuhymets@interchange.ubc.ca.

University of California, Riverside, Graduate Division, Department of Botany and Plant Sciences, Riverside, CA 92521-0102. Offers plant biology (MS, PhD); plant biology (plant genetics) (PhD). Part-time programs available. *Faculty:* 40 full-time (12 women). *Students:* 52 full-time (25 women); includes 4 minority (2 Asian Americans or Pacific Islanders, 2 Hispanic Americans), 24 international. Average age 31. In 2003, 2 master's, 10 doctorates awarded. Terminal master's awarded for partial completion of doctoral program. *Median time to degree:* Master's–2.5 years full-time; doctorate–5.5 years full-time. *Degree requirements:* For master's, comprehensive exams or thesis; for doctorate, thesis/dissertation, qualifying exams. *Entrance requirements:* For master's and doctorate, GRE General Test, minimum GPA of 3.2. Additional exam requirements/recommendations for international students: Required—TOEFL (minimum score 550 paper-based; 213 computer-based); Recommended—TSE. *Application deadline:* For fall admission, 5/1 for domestic students, 2/1 for international students; for spring admission, 12/1 for domestic students, 10/1 for international students. Applications are processed on a rolling basis. Application fee: $60. Electronic applications accepted. Tuition, nonresident: part-time $4,082 per quarter. *Financial support:* Fellowships, research assistantships, teaching assistantships, career-related internships or fieldwork, Federal Work-Study, institutionally sponsored loans, scholarships/grants, and tuition waivers (full and partial) available. Financial award application deadline: 2/1; financial award applicants required to submit FAFSA. *Faculty research:* Plant molecular biology, plant cell and developmental biology, plant systematics and evolution, ecology and natural resources, agriculture and crop physiology. *Unit head:* Dr. Jodie S. Holt, Chair. *Application contact:* 800-735-0717, Fax: 951-827-5517, E-mail: plantbio@citrus.ucr.edu.

University of Connecticut, Graduate School, College of Agriculture and Natural Resources, Department of Plant Science, Field of Plant Science, Storrs, CT 06269. Offers plant and soil sciences (MS, PhD). *Faculty:* 25 full-time (5 women). *Students:* 18 full-time (8 women), 8 part-time (3 women), 11 international. Average age 33. 15 applicants, 73% accepted, 4 enrolled. In 2003, 4 master's, 4 doctorates awarded. Terminal master's awarded for partial completion of doctoral program. *Degree requirements:* For master's, comprehensive exam; for doctorate, thesis/dissertation. *Entrance requirements:* For master's and doctorate, GRE General Test, GRE Subject Test. Additional exam requirements/recommendations for international students: Required—TOEFL (minimum score 550 paper-based; 213 computer-based). *Application deadline:* For fall admission, 2/1 priority date for domestic students, 2/1 priority date for international students; for spring admission, 11/1 for domestic students, 10/1 for international students. Applications are processed on a rolling basis. Application fee: $55. Electronic applications accepted. *Expenses:* Tuition, state resident: part-time $3,860 per semester. Tuition, nonresident: part-time $9,036 per semester. *Financial support:* In 2003–04, 13 research assistantships with full tuition reimbursements, 5 teaching assistantships with full tuition reimbursements were awarded. Fellowships, Federal Work-Study, scholarships/grants, health care benefits, and unspecified assistantships also available. Financial award application deadline: 2/1; financial award applicants required to submit FAFSA. *Application contact:* George C. Elliott, Chairperson, 860-486-1938, Fax: 860-486-0682, E-mail: george.elliott@uconn.edu.

University of Delaware, College of Agriculture and Natural Resources, Department of Plant and Soil Sciences, Newark, DE 19716. Offers MS, PhD. Part-time programs available. *Students:* 35 full-time (18 women), 4 part-time (2 women), 9 international. Average age 29. 34 applicants, 41% accepted, 12 enrolled. In 2003, 4 master's, 4 doctorates awarded. Terminal master's awarded for partial completion of doctoral program. *Degree requirements:* For master's and doctorate, thesis/dissertation. *Entrance requirements:* For master's and doctorate, GRE General Test. Additional exam requirements/recommendations for international students: Required—TOEFL (minimum score 550 paper-based; 213 computer-based). *Application deadline:* For fall admission, 7/1 for domestic students. Application fee: $60. Electronic applications accepted. *Expenses:* Tuition, state resident: full-time $5,890; part-time $327 per credit. Tuition, nonresident: full-time $15,420; part-time $857 per credit. Required fees: $968. *Financial support:* In 2003–04, 26 students received support, including 1 fellowship with full tuition reimbursement available (averaging $15,000 per year), 19 research assistantships with full tuition reimbursements available (averaging $13,500 per year), 3 teaching assistantships with full tuition reimbursements available (averaging $11,000 per year); career-related internships or fieldwork also available. Financial award application deadline: 3/1. *Faculty research:* Soil chemistry, plant and cell tissue culture, plant breeding and genetics, soil physics, soil biochemistry, plant molecular biology, soil microbiology. Total annual research expenditures: $3.8 million. *Unit head:* Dr. Donald L. Sparks, Chair, 302-831-2532, Fax: 302-831-3651, E-mail: dlsparks@udel.edu. *Application contact:* Dr. Robert Carroll, Graduate Coordinator, 302-831-2534, E-mail: rbc@udel.edu.

University of Florida, Graduate School, College of Agricultural and Life Sciences, Program in Plant Medicine, Gainesville, FL 32611. Offers DPM. *Entrance requirements:* For doctorate, bachelor's degree in agricultural science. *Expenses:* Tuition, state resident: part-time $205 per credit hour. Tuition, nonresident: part-time $775 per credit hour. *Unit head:* Dr. Robert McGovern, Director, 352-392-3631.

University of Hawaii at Manoa, Graduate Division, College of Tropical Agriculture and Human Resources, Department of Plant and Environmental Protection Sciences, Honolulu, HI 96822. Offers botanical sciences (MS, PhD); entomology (MS, PhD); plant pathology (MS, PhD); tropical plant pathology (MS, PhD). Part-time programs available. *Faculty:* 55 full-time (10 women), 23 part-time/adjunct (6 women). *Students:* 16 full-time (9 women), 6 part-time (1 woman); includes 5 minority (1 African American, 4 Asian Americans or Pacific Islanders), 7 international. Average age 32. 11 applicants, 73% accepted, 4 enrolled.Terminal master's awarded for partial completion of doctoral program. *Median time to degree:* Master's–4 years full-time; doctorate–7 years full-time. *Degree requirements:* For master's, thesis optional; for doctorate, thesis/dissertation. *Entrance requirements:* For master's and doctorate, GRE General Test. Application fee: $50. *Expenses:* Tuition, state resident: full-time $4,464; part-time $186 per credit hour. Tuition, nonresident: full-time $10,608; part-time $442 per credit hour. Tuition and fees vary according to program. *Financial support:* In 2003–04, 12 research assistantships (averaging $16,613 per year), 2 teaching assistantships (averaging $13,296 per year) were awarded. Tuition waivers (full) also available. *Faculty research:* Nematology, virology, mycology, bacteriology, epidemiology. Total annual research expenditures: $1.9 million. *Unit head:* Dr. Kenneth Rohrbach, Chairperson, 808-956-7096, Fax: 808-956-2428. *Application contact:* Dr. John Hu, Graduate Chairperson, 808-956-8329, Fax: 808-956-2832.

University of Idaho, College of Graduate Studies, College of Agriculture and Life Sciences, Department of Plant, Soil, and Entomological Sciences, Moscow, ID 83844-2282. Offers entomology (MS, PhD); plant protection (MS, PhD); plant science (MS, PhD); soil science (MS, PhD). *Students:* 51 full-time (18 women), 23 part-time (5 women); includes 4 minority (all Hispanic Americans), 16 international. Average age 29. *Degree requirements:* For doctorate, thesis/dissertation. *Entrance requirements:* For master's and doctorate, GRE General Test, minimum GPA of 3.0. *Application deadline:* For fall admission, 7/1 for domestic students; for spring admission, 11/1 for domestic students. Application fee: $55 ($60 for international students). *Expenses:* Tuition, state resident: full-time $3,348. Tuition, nonresident: full-time $10,740. Required fees: $540. *Financial support:* Research assistantships, teaching assistantships available. Financial award application deadline: 2/15. *Application contact:* Dr. Joseph McCaffrey, Graduate Director, 208-885-7548.

See in-depth description on page 683.

University of Kentucky, Graduate School, Graduate School Programs in the College of Agriculture, Program in Plant and Soil Science, Lexington, KY 40506-0032. Offers MS. *Faculty:* 26 full-time (2 women). *Students:* 22 full-time (12 women), 7 part-time (3 women), 6 international. 30 applicants, 40% accepted, 10 enrolled. In 2003, 10 degrees awarded. *Degree requirements:* For master's, thesis optional. *Entrance requirements:* For master's, GRE General Test, minimum GPA of 2.5 (undergraduate), 3.0 (graduate). Additional exam requirements/recommendations for international students: Required—TOEFL (minimum score 550 paper-based; 213 computer-based). *Application deadline:* For fall admission, 7/18 for domestic students, 2/1 for international students. Application fee: $35 ($45 for international students). *Expenses:* Tuition, state resident: full-time $4,975; part-time $261 per credit hour. Tuition, nonresident: full-time $12,315; part-time $668 per credit hour. *Financial support:* Fellowships, research assistantships, unspecified assistantships available. *Unit head:* Dr. Michael Collins, Director of Graduate Studies, 859-257-3358, Fax: 859-323-1952, E-mail: mcollins@ca.uky.edu. *Application contact:* Dr. Brian Jackson, Associate Dean, 859-257-4905, Fax: 859-323-1928.

University of Maine, Graduate School, College of Natural Sciences, Forestry, and Agriculture, Department of Biological Sciences, Orono, ME 04469. Offers biological sciences (PhD); botany and plant pathology (MS); ecology and environmental science (MS, PhD); entomology (MS); plant science (PhD); zoology (MS, PhD). Part-time programs available. *Students:* 36 full-time (20 women), 16 part-time (11 women), 7 international. Average age 31. 33 applicants, 36% accepted, 3 enrolled. In 2003, 3 master's, 4 doctorates awarded. *Degree requirements:* For doctorate, thesis/dissertation. *Entrance requirements:* For master's and doctorate, GRE General Test. Additional exam requirements/recommendations for international students: Required—TOEFL. *Application deadline:* For fall admission, 2/1 for domestic students. Applications are processed on a rolling basis. Application fee: $50. Electronic applications accepted. *Expenses:* Tuition, state resident: part-time $235 per credit. Tuition, nonresident: part-time $670 per credit. Tuition and fees vary according to course load. *Financial support:* In 2003–04, 1 fellowship with tuition reimbursement (averaging $15,000 per year), 17 research assistantships with tuition reimbursements (averaging $13,650 per year), 20 teaching assistantships with tuition reimbursements (averaging $9,634 per year) were awarded. Career-related internships or fieldwork, Federal Work-Study, institutionally sponsored loans, and tuition waivers (full and partial) also available. Financial award application deadline: 3/1. *Unit head:* Dr. Susan Hunter, Chair, 207-581-2540, Fax: 207-581-2537. *Application contact:* Scott G. Delcourt, Associate Dean of the Graduate School, 207-581-3218, Fax: 207-581-3232, E-mail: graduate@maine.edu.

University of Maine, Graduate School, College of Natural Sciences, Forestry, and Agriculture, Department of Plant, Soil, and Environmental Sciences, Orono, ME 04469. Offers biological sciences (PhD); ecology and environmental sciences (MS, PhD); forest resources (PhD); horticulture (MS); plant science (PhD); plant, soil, and environmental sciences (MS); resource utilization (MS). *Students:* 20 full-time (14 women), 8 part-time (5 women); includes 1 minority (Asian American or Pacific Islander), 2 international. Average age 31. 12 applicants, 42% accepted, 5 enrolled. In 2003, 2 degrees awarded. *Entrance requirements:* For master's and doctorate, GRE General Test. Additional exam requirements/recommendations for international students: Required—TOEFL. *Application deadline:* Applications are processed on a rolling basis. Application fee: $50. Electronic applications accepted. *Expenses:* Tuition, state resident: part-time $235 per credit. Tuition, nonresident: part-time $670 per credit. Tuition and fees vary according to course load. *Financial support:* In 2003–04, 9 research assistantships with tuition reimbursements (averaging $12,180 per year) were awarded; teaching assistantships, scholarships/grants, tuition waivers (full and partial), and unspecified assistantships also available. *Unit head:* Dr. M. Susan Erich, Chair, 207-581-2938, Fax: 207-581-3207. *Application contact:* Scott G. Delcourt, Associate Dean of the Graduate School, 207-581-3218, Fax: 207-581-3232, E-mail: graduate@maine.edu.

University of Massachusetts Amherst, Graduate School, College of Natural Resources and the Environment, Department of Plant and Soil Sciences, Amherst, MA 01003. Offers plant science (PhD); soil science (MS, PhD). *Faculty:* 19 full-time (4 women). *Students:* 17 full-time (6 women), 20 part-time (14 women); includes 2 minority (1 African American, 1 Hispanic American), 9 international. Average age 37. 19 applicants, 37% accepted, 6 enrolled. In 2003, 10 master's, 2 doctorates awarded. Terminal master's awarded for partial completion of doctoral program. *Degree requirements:* For master's, thesis optional; for doctorate, thesis/dissertation. *Entrance requirements:* For master's and doctorate, GRE General Test. Additional exam requirements/recommendations for international students: Required—TOEFL (minimum score 530 paper-based; 197 computer-based). *Application deadline:* For fall admission, 2/1 priority date for domestic students, 2/1 priority date for international students; for spring admission, 10/1 for domestic students, 10/1 for international students. Applications are processed on a rolling basis. Application fee: $40 ($50 for international students). *Expenses:* Tuition, state resident: full-time $1,320; part-time $110 per credit. Tuition, nonresident: full-time $4,969; part-time $414 per credit. Required fees: $2,626 per term. Tuition and fees vary according to course load. *Financial support:* In 2003–04, 21 research assistantships with full tuition reimbursements (averaging $5,942 per year), 15 teaching assistantships with full tuition reimbursements (averaging $5,522 per year) were awarded. Fellowships with full tuition reimbursements, career-related internships or fieldwork, Federal Work-Study, scholarships/grants, traineeships, and unspecified assistantships also available. Support available to part-time students. Financial award application deadline: 2/1. *Unit head:* Dr. Petrus Veneman, Director, 413-545-2242, Fax: 413-545-3075, E-mail: veneman@pssci.umass.edu.

University of Minnesota, Twin Cities Campus, Graduate School, College of Agricultural, Food, and Environmental Sciences, Program in Applied Plant Sciences, Minneapolis, MN 55455-0213. Offers MS, PhD. *Faculty:* 23 full-time (2 women), 7 part-time/adjunct (0 women). *Students:* 54 full-time (25 women), 2 part-time (1 woman); includes 2 minority (1 African American, 1 Asian American or Pacific Islander), 19 international. Average age 24. 42 applicants, 19% accepted. In 2003, 7 master's, 2 doctorates awarded. *Degree requirements:* For master's and doctorate, thesis/dissertation. *Entrance requirements:* For master's and doctorate, GRE General Test. Additional exam requirements/recommendations for international students: Required—TOEFL. *Application deadline:* Applications are processed on a rolling basis. Application fee: $55 ($75 for international students). *Expenses:* Tuition, state resident: full-time $3,681; part-time $614 per credit. Tuition, nonresident: full-time $7,231; part-time $1,205 per credit. *Financial support:* In 2003–04, research assistantships with tuition reimbursements (averaging $16,500 per year). *Faculty research:* Weed science, crop management, sustainable agriculture, biotechnology, plant breeding. *Unit head:* Dr. Nancy J. Elke, Head, 612-625-8761, Fax: 612-625-1268.

University of Rhode Island, Graduate School, College of the Environment and Life Sciences, Department of Plant Sciences, Program in Plant Science, Kingston, RI 02881. Offers MS, PhD. *Degree requirements:* For master's, thesis, professional seminar; for doctorate, one foreign language, thesis/dissertation, professional seminar. *Entrance requirements:* For master's, GRE General Test. *Application deadline:* For fall admission, 4/15 for domestic students. Application fee: $35. *Expenses:* Tuition, state resident: full-time $4,338; part-time $281 per credit. Tuition, nonresident: full-time $12,438; part-time $704 per credit. Required fees: $1,840. *Financial support:* Unspecified assistantships available. *Faculty research:* Ecology, physiology, improvement of turf, ornamental and food-crop plants.

University of Saskatchewan, College of Graduate Studies and Research, College of Agriculture, Department of Plant Sciences, Saskatoon, SK S7N 5A2, Canada. Offers M Ag, M Sc, PhD. *Faculty:* 16. *Students:* 43. *Degree requirements:* For master's and doctorate, thesis/dissertation, registration. *Entrance requirements:* Additional exam requirements/recommendations for international students: Required—TOEFL. *Application deadline:* For fall admission, 7/1 for domestic students. Applications are processed on a rolling basis. Application fee: $50. Tuition charges are reported in Canadian dollars. *Expenses:* Tuition, state resident: part-time $483 Canadian dollars per course. *Financial support:* Fellowships, research assistantships, teaching assistantships available. Financial award application deadline: 1/31. *Unit head:* Dr. G. R. Hughes, Head, 306-966-5857, Fax: 306-966-5015, E-mail: geoff.hughes@usask.ca. *Application contact:* Dr. Pierre Hucl, Graduate Chair, 306-966-5015, Fax: 306-966-5015, E-mail: pierre.hucl@usask.ca.

University of Vermont, Graduate College, College of Agriculture and Life Sciences, Department of Plant and Soil Science, Burlington, VT 05405. Offers MS, PhD. *Students:* 18 (8 women); includes 1 minority (Hispanic American) 2 international. 12 applicants, 75% accepted, 3 enrolled. In 2003, 2 degrees awarded. *Degree requirements:* For master's, thesis; for doctorate, one foreign language, thesis/dissertation. *Entrance requirements:* For master's and doctorate, GRE General Test. Additional exam requirements/recommendations for international students: Required—TOEFL (minimum score 550 paper-based; 213 computer-based). *Application deadline:* For fall admission, 4/1 for domestic students; for spring admission, 11/15 for domestic students. Applications are processed on a rolling basis. Application fee: $25. Electronic applications accepted. *Expenses:* Tuition, state resident: part-time $362 per credit hour. Tuition, nonresident: part-time $906 per credit hour. *Financial support:* Fellowships, research assistantships, teaching assistantships available. Financial award application deadline: 3/1. *Faculty research:* Soil chemistry, plant nutrition. *Unit head:* Dr. A. Gotlieb, Chairperson, 802-656-2630. *Application contact:* Dr. M. Starrett, Coordinator, 802-656-2630.

The University of Western Ontario, Faculty of Graduate Studies, Biosciences Division, Department of Plant Sciences, London, ON N6A 5B8, Canada. Offers plant and environmental sciences (M Sc); plant sciences (M Sc, PhD); plant sciences and environmental sciences (PhD); plant sciences and molecular biology (M Sc, PhD). *Degree requirements:* For master's and doctorate, thesis/dissertation. *Entrance requirements:* For doctorate, M Sc or equivalent. *Faculty research:* Ecology systematics, plant biochemistry and physiology, yeast genetics, molecular biology.

University of Wisconsin–Madison, Graduate School, College of Agricultural and Life Sciences, Department of Horticulture, Plant Breeding and Plant Genetics Program, Madison, WI 53706-1380. Offers MS, PhD. Part-time programs available. *Faculty:* 38 full-time (4 women). *Students:* 47 full-time (15 women), 2 part-time; includes 25 minority (13 Asian Americans or Pacific Islanders, 12 Hispanic Americans). Average age 30. 55 applicants, 11% accepted, 6 enrolled. In 2003, 3 master's awarded, leading to university research/teaching 33%, continued full-time study33%, business/industry 33%; 2 doctorates awarded, leading to university research/teaching 50%, government 50%. Terminal master's awarded for partial completion of doctoral program. *Median time to degree:* Of those who began their doctoral program in fall 1995, 100% received their degree in 8 years or less. *Degree requirements:* For master's, thesis (for some programs), comprehensive exam; for doctorate, thesis/dissertation, comprehensive exam. *Entrance requirements:* For master's and doctorate, GRE, minimum GPA of 3.0. Additional exam requirements/recommendations for international students: Required—TOEFL (minimum score 580 paper-based; 213 computer-based). *Application deadline:* For fall admission, 1/2 for domestic students, 1/2 for international students; for spring admission, 10/30 for domestic students, 10/30 for international students. Applications are processed on a rolling basis. Application fee: $45. Electronic applications accepted. Tuition, area resident: Full-time $7,593; part-time $476 per credit. Tuition, nonresident: full-time $22,824; part-time $1,430 per credit. Required fees: $292; $38 per credit. Part-time tuition and fees vary according to course load and reciprocity agreements. *Financial support:* In 2003–04, 4 fellowships with full tuition reimbursements (averaging $18,720 per year), 38 research assistantships with full tuition reimbursements (averaging $17,430 per year), 1 teaching assistantship with full tuition reimbursement (averaging $24,200 per year) were awarded. Career-related internships or fieldwork, Federal Work-Study, and tuition waivers (partial) also available. Financial award application deadline: 1/2. *Faculty research:* Classical and molecular genetics. Total annual research expenditures: $5,000. *Unit head:* Dr. Irwin Goldman, Professor, 608-262-7781, Fax: 608-262-4743. *Application contact:* Catherine A. Pryes, Program Assistant, 608-262-8406, Fax: 608-262-4743, E-mail: capryes@wisc.edu.

Utah State University, School of Graduate Studies, College of Agriculture, Department of Plants, Soils, and Biometeorology, Logan, UT 84322. Offers biometeorology (MS, PhD); ecology (MS, PhD); plant science (MS, PhD); soil science (MS, PhD). Part-time programs available. *Faculty:* 31 full-time (4 women), 13 part-time/adjunct (0 women). *Students:* 29 full-time (9 women), 5 part-time; includes 1 minority (African American), 6 international. Average age 26. 18 applicants, 50% accepted, 2 enrolled. In 2003, 10 master's, 4 doctorates awarded. Terminal master's awarded for partial completion of doctoral program. *Median time to degree:* Of those who began their doctoral program in fall 1995, 100% received their degree in 8 years or less. *Degree requirements:* For master's and doctorate, thesis/dissertation. *Entrance requirements:* For master's, GRE General Test, BS in plant, soil, atmospheric science, or related field, minimum GPA of 3.0; for doctorate, GRE General Test, minimum GPA of 3.0. Additional exam requirements/recommendations for international students: Required—TOEFL. *Application deadline:* For fall admission, 6/15 priority date for domestic students, 3/15 priority date for international students; for spring admission, 10/15 for domestic students, 9/15 for international students. Applications are processed on a rolling basis. Application fee: $50 ($60 for international students). *Expenses:* Tuition, state resident: part-time $270 per credit hour. Tuition, nonresident: part-time $946 per credit hour. Required fees: $173 per credit hour. *Financial support:* In 2003–04, 23 research assistantships with partial tuition reimbursements (averaging $15,000 per year) were awarded; Federal Work-Study, institutionally sponsored loans, and tuition waivers (full) also available. Support available to part-time students. Financial award application deadline: 3/1. *Faculty research:* Biotechnology and genomics, plant physiology and biology, nutrient and water efficient landscapes, physical-chemical-biological proceses in soil, environmental biophysics and climate. Total annual research expenditures: $4.5 million. *Unit head:* Dr. Larry A. Rupp, Head, 435-797-2099, Fax: 435-797-3376, E-mail: larryr@ext.usu.edu. *Application contact:* Dr. Janis L. Boettinger, Graduate Program Coordinator, 435-797-4026, Fax: 435-797-3376, E-mail: janis.boettinger@usu.edu.

West Texas A&M University, College of Agriculture, Nursing, and Natural Sciences, Division of Agriculture, Emphasis in Plant Science, Canyon, TX 79016-0001. Offers MS. Part-time programs available. *Faculty:* 7 full-time (2 women), 5 part-time/adjunct (1 woman). *Students:* 13 full-time (3 women), 6 part-time (2 women), 13 international. Average age 34. 15 applicants, 80% accepted. In 2003, 9 degrees awarded. *Median time to degree:* Master's–3 years full-time, 6 years part-time. *Degree requirements:* For master's, thesis optional. *Entrance requirements:* For master's, GRE General Test. Additional exam requirements/recommendations for international students: Required—TOEFL (minimum score 550 paper-based). *Application deadline:* Applications are processed on a rolling basis. Application fee: $25 ($75 for international students). Electronic applications accepted. *Expenses:* Tuition, state resident: part-time $56 per credit hour. Tuition, nonresident: part-time $292 per credit hour. Full-time tuition and fees vary according to course level, degree level and program. *Financial support:* In 2003–04, 2 research assistantships with tuition reimbursements (averaging $6,500 per year), 2 teaching assistantships with tuition reimbursements (averaging $6,750 per year) were awarded. Career-related internships or fieldwork, Federal Work-Study, institutionally sponsored loans, scholarships/grants, health care benefits, and unspecified assistantships also available. Support available to part-time students. *Faculty research:* Crop and soil disciplines. Total annual research expenditures: $45,000. *Application contact:* Dr. Ronald Thomason, Graduate Adviser, 806-651-2554, Fax: 806-651-2938, E-mail: rthomason@mail.wtamu.edu.

West Virginia University, Davis College of Agriculture, Forestry and Consumer Sciences, Division of Animal and Veterinary Sciences, Program in Agricultural Sciences, Morgantown, WV 26506. Offers animal and food sciences (PhD); plant and soil sciences (PhD). *Degree requirements:* For doctorate, thesis/dissertation, oral and written exams. *Entrance requirements:* Additional exam requirements/recommendations for international students: Required—TOEFL. Application fee: $45. *Expenses:* Tuition, state resident: full-time $4,332. Tuition, nonresident: full-time $12,442. *Financial support:* Research assistantships with tuition reimbursements, teaching assistantships with tuition reimbursements, Federal Work-Study, institutionally sponsored loans, and tuition waivers (full and partial) available. Financial award application deadline: 2/1; financial award applicants required to submit FAFSA. *Faculty research:* Ruminant nutrition, metabolism, forage utilization, physiology, reproduction. *Application contact:* Dr. Hillar Klandorf, Professor, 304-293-2631 Ext. 4436, Fax: 304-293-3676, E-mail: hillar.klandorf@mail.wvu.edu.

West Virginia University, Davis College of Agriculture, Forestry and Consumer Sciences, Division of Plant and Soil Sciences, Morgantown, WV 26506. Offers agronomy (MS); entomology (MS); environmental microbiology (MS); horticulture (MS); plant pathology (MS). *Faculty:* 18 full-time (1 woman), 1 part-time/adjunct (0 women). *Students:* 17 full-time (11 women), 3 part-time (2 women), 2 international. Average age 27. In 2003, 5 degrees awarded. *Degree requirements:* For master's, thesis. *Entrance requirements:* For master's, GRE, minimum GPA of 2.5. Additional exam requirements/recommendations for international students: Required—TOEFL. *Application deadline:* Applications are processed on a rolling basis. Application fee: $45. *Expenses:* Tuition, state resident: full-time $4,332. Tuition, nonresident: full-time $12,442. *Financial support:* In 2003–04, 13 research assistantships with full tuition reimbursements (averaging $9,936 per year), 4 teaching assistantships with full tuition reimbursements (averaging $9,936 per year) were awarded. Federal Work-Study, institutionally sponsored loans, and tuition waivers (full and partial) also available. Financial award application deadline: 2/1; financial award applicants required to submit FAFSA. *Faculty research:* Water quality, reclamation of disturbed land, crop production, pest control, environmental protection. Total annual research expenditures: $1 million. *Unit head:* Dr. Barton S. Baker, Chair, 304-293-6131 Ext. 4341, Fax: 304-293-2960, E-mail: barton.baker@mail.wvu.edu.

IOWA STATE UNIVERSITY

Department of Food Science and Human Nutrition

Programs of Study The Department of Food Science and Human Nutrition is jointly administered by the Colleges of Agriculture and of Family and Consumer Sciences. The department offers M.S. and Ph.D. degrees in food science and technology and in nutrition. Graduate work in meat science is offered as a co-major with the Department of Animal Science. The department participates in the interdepartmental majors of molecular, cellular, and developmental biology and of toxicology. The graduate programs provide breadth of knowledge and perspective in food chemistry, food safety, fermentation, food engineering, commodity processing technology, food microbiology, nutritional science, basic and clinical human nutrition, community nutrition, and education. Current research areas include physicochemical characteristics of proteins, carbohydrates, and lipids; food safety and toxicology; nutritional effects on carcinogenesis; nutritive quality of food; chemical and microbiological changes in foods during processing and storage; processing commodities to nonfood products; and nutritional science with an emphasis on molecular, cellular, metabolic, community, and educational approaches to improve health. Programs of Study (POS) are developed by the graduate student and major professor with the POS committee. M.S. students take 30 credits, with approximately 20 in course work, and write a thesis. Ph.D. students take 70 credits of course work, including M.S. credits, with approximately 40 course credits, and defend a dissertation. All graduate students are required to complete a teaching function.

Research Facilities The department is housed in the Food Sciences Building, the Human Nutritional Sciences Building, and MacKay Hall. The Center for Crop Utilization Research (CCUR), the Center for Designing Foods to Improve Nutrition (CDFIN), the Center for Research on Dietary Botanical Supplements, and the NASA Food Technology Commercial Space Center are affiliated with the department. The research budget is in excess of $7.6 million, with more than $4.3 million in external funding. The Meat Laboratory houses a Department of Energy project linear accelerator irradiation facility. CCUR has more than 14,000 square feet of pilot plants with extruders (food and nonfood), mills, grinders, fermenters, retorts, supercritical fluid extraction systems, and a countercurrent solvent extractor. The CDFIN opened in 1992, and contains state-of-the-art animal-care and diet-making facilities; sensory evaluation and food analysis laboratories; a Fisons Optima GC-C-IRMS with breath gas manifold and elemental analyzer interfaces; Fisons Trio GC-MS with EI and CI; toxicology, cell culture, and other analytical instrumentation; TOBEC and DEXA for assessment of human body composition and energy metabolism; and facilities for large-scale human feeding trials.

Financial Aid Research assistantships are available for most students from faculty research grants and the Experiment Station. All students on at least quarter-time assistantships are assessed as in-state residents. Students with half-time assistantships receive full tuition scholarships.

Cost of Study In 2002–03, graduate fees for a semester of full-time study totaled $2519 for in-state residents and $7107 for nonresidents.

Living and Housing Costs The University provides housing facilities for single and married graduate students. Costs for 2002–03 ranged from $400 per month for double-occupancy residence halls to $499 per month for University student apartments. The Off-Campus Center assists students seeking rooms, apartments, or duplexes in Ames or in surrounding communities.

Student Group There are approximately 80 graduate students in the department. About 60 percent are food science majors, 34 percent are nutrition majors, and the balance are in toxicology. Thirty percent men, and 60 percent are international students. There are 250 undergraduates in the department.

Student Outcomes Nearly all graduates find employment upon or soon after graduation in postdoctoral positions, academic positions, federal laboratories (such as the USDA, DOE, and FDA), state laboratories, or the food industry. Employment examples for 2002 graduates include General Mills, GPC, Red Star Yeast, McCormick, Burnes-Philp-Tones, ConAgra, Pillsbury, Pepsi, and U.S. and international academic institutions.

Location The University is situated on a 1,000-acre tract in Ames, Iowa (population 50,000). It is located 35 miles north of Des Moines (population 500,000), the state capital, on I-35 and U.S. Highway 30, near I-80. The city offers social, cultural, and athletic events that surpass those of some metropolitan areas. The Ames-University community is cosmopolitan, representing more than 100 countries. The city maintains more than 700 acres of parks. The atmosphere is relaxed and friendly.

The University Iowa State University (ISU) was chartered in 1858 and is the land-grant institution in Iowa. The first graduate degree was conferred in 1877. George Washington Carver was one of the early graduates. Currently, the enrollment is approximately 25,000, including 4,500 graduate students.

Applying A baccalaureate degree in food science/technology, nutrition or other physical or biological science, or engineering that is substantially equivalent to those at Iowa State is a prerequisite to major work. Applications for fall semester admission and assistantships should be completed by January 1 for consideration. For admission to other terms, materials should be completed as soon as possible before the beginning of that term. Application materials can be obtained by writing to the address below or to the Graduate Admissions Office, Alumni Hall, ISU, Ames, Iowa 50011. Application fees are $20 for domestic students, $50 for international students, and $50 for international nonimmigrants. The department requires the scores of the General Test of the Graduate Record Examinations, three letters of reference, transcripts of previous academic work, a statement of purpose, and a department application.

Correspondence and Information

Dr. Pamela J. White, Director of Graduate Education
Department of Food Science and Human Nutrition
2312 Food Sciences Building
Iowa State University
Ames, Iowa 50011
Telephone: 515-294-6442
Fax: 515-294-8181
E-mail: gradsecretary@iastate.edu
World Wide Web: http://www.fcs.iastate.edu/fshn/grad/

Iowa State University

THE FACULTY AND THEIR RESEARCH

D. L. Alekel, Assistant Professor; Ph.D., Illinois, 1993. Dietary- and physical activity-related factors as they impact the physical health of midlife women, particularly osteoporosis prevention; reducing overall disease risk and promoting women's health by focusing on effect of isoflavone-rich soy protein on bone, body composition, menopausal symptoms, and the cardiovascular health of postmenopausal women.
S. E. Beattie, Assistant Professor; Ph.D., Oregon State, 1990. Food and agricultural mycology, with an emphasis on mycotoxigenic molds; food safety and security issues for food processors and consumers.
D. F. Birt, Professor and Chairman; Ph.D., Purdue, 1975. Assessing mechanisms for cancer prevention by novel dietary constituents and studying mechanisms for cancer enhancement by overeating and obesity, identifying the bioactive and toxic constituents in dietary botanical supplements and assessing mechanisms of action.
T. D. Boylston, Assistant Professor; Ph.D., Michigan State, 1988. Effects of processing and storage on the lipid and flavor composition of foods, effects of incorporation of probiotic bacteria into foods on the flavor and sensory quality, effects of irradiation on flavor quality.
P. Flakoll, Professor and Director of Center for Designing Foods to Improve Nutrition; Ph.D., Iowa State, 1988. Protein and amino acid metabolism, macronutrient substrate interaction, endocrinology and regulation of growth, nutrition and composition of growth.
C. Ford, Associate Professor; Ph.D., Iowa, 1981. Genetic engineering of the starch-processing enzyme glucoamylase to improve its industrial performance: thermostability and substrate specificity.
B. A. Glatz, University Professor and Associate DEO; Ph.D., Wisconsin, 1975. Production of antimicrobials (acids, bacteriocins) by beneficial microorganisms, microbiological quality and safety of apples and apple cider.
R. Gonzalez, Assistant Professor; Ph.D., Chile, 2001. Metabolic engineering, functional genomics, microbial fermentations.
C. M. Hansen, Assistant Professor; Ph.D., Oregon State, 1995. Vitamin B-6 metabolism, bioavailability, requirements; role in one-carbon metabolism; and effects of intake and status on immunity and chronic disease risk.
S. Hendrich, Professor; Ph.D., Berkeley, 1985. Food toxicology, health effects and bioavailability of soybean isoflavones and saponins, gut microbial ecology, and fungal toxicants.
J. Jane, Professor; Ph.D., Iowa State, 1984. Biosynthesis and genetic modification of starch; chemical and physical structures, properties, and utilization of starch; protein-based biodegradable plastics.
L. A. Johnson, Professor; Ph.D., Kansas State, 1978. Value-added processing of cereals and legumes, especially corn and soybeans; extraction, plant separations; wet and dry milling; processing transgenic crops with enhanced end-use traits; food and industrial product applications of proteins, oils, and starch.
M. L. Kaplan, Professor; Ph.D., CUNY, 1972. Diet and endocrine interactions in the regulation of biosynthetic and oxidative processes of carbohydrate, lipid, and energy metabolism during postnatal development in adipose tissue, muscle, and liver.
R. Litchfield, Assistant Professor; Ph.D., Iowa State, 2000. Dietetic education, distance education, nutrition and exercise science, educational pedagogy, sports nutrition.
J. A. Love, Associate Professor; Ph.D., Michigan State, 1973. Lipid oxidation in meats, functional properties of plant proteins, sensory evaluation methodology.
M. H. Love, Associate Professor; Ph.D., Michigan State, 1975. Nutrient retention in processed foods, physicochemical determinants of texture in processed vegetables.
G. S. Marquis, Assistant Professor; Ph.D., Cornell, 1996. Infant and child nutrition in the international and domestic setting, with emphasis on the interactions among breast-feeding, dietary intakes, morbidity, and growth.
A. F. Mendonca, Assistant Professor; Ph.D., Iowa State, 1992. Survival, injury, and destruction of foodborne pathogens as influenced by chemical treatment, heating, or irradiation of foods; conventional and molecular techniques for detection of foodborne pathogens; novel methods for recovery of foodborne pathogens sublethally injured by food processing treatments.
P. A. Murphy, Professor; Ph.D., Michigan State, 1979. Soy isoflavone analysis and health benefits, fumonisin toxicology, soy storage proteins, Echinacea and Hypericum fractionation.
D. J. Myers, Professor; Ph.D., Iowa State, 1984. Utilization of legume and cereal proteins in nonfood and food applications and their functionality.
M. J. Oakland, Associate Professor; Ph.D., Iowa State, 1985. Nutrition education and community nutrition, including nutrition/health status of elderly and children with disabilities.
A. L. Pometto III, Professor and Director of the NASA Food Technology Commercial Space Center; Ph.D., Idaho, 1987. Microbial degradation of degradable plastics, bioconversion of agricultural commodities into value-added products via fermentation, development of novel bioreactors, production of enzymes for the food industry, utilization of food industrial wastes.
K. J. Prusa, Professor; Ph.D., Kansas State, 1983. Preharvest treatment of pigs for the improvement of pork quality and safety.
M. B. Reddy, Associate Professor; Ph.D., Texas A&M, 1987. Bioavailability of iron in foods; iron deficiency and overload assessment, consequences, and prevention; effect of isoflavones and phytate on reducing oxidative stress and cardiovascular disease risk.
C. A. Reitmeier, Associate Professor; Ph.D., Iowa State, 1988. Quality attributes of small fruit, irradiation of fruit, food safety, apple cider.
K. L. Schalinske, Assistant Professor; Ph.D., Wisconsin, 1992. Regulation of folate/methyl group metabolism relevant to health and disease, molecular regulation of iron homeostasis.
J. G. Sebranek, University Professor; Ph.D., Wisconsin, 1974. Meat processing and preservation; influence of additives, new technology, and processing techniques on quality.
T. Wang, Assistant Professor; Ph.D., Iowa State, 1998. Lipid chemistry, oilseed processing and value-added utilization, vegetable oil refining and industrial application.
P. J. White, Professor; Ph.D., Iowa State, 1981. Oxidation of edible oils and their sensory and chemical changes, uses of antioxidants in oils, lipid-carbohydrate interactions, starch structure and function in food and industrial products, genetic variation of fatty acid composition in corn and soybeans and of starch structure in corn, beta-glucan structure and function in foods and in human health.
W. S. White, Associate Professor; Ph.D., Cornell, 1990. Bioavailability and metabolism of beta-carotene and other carotenoids, health protective effects of carotenoids, molecular biology and nutritional modulation of carotene 15,15'-dioxygenase activity.
L. A. Wilson, Professor; Ph.D., California, Davis, 1975. Interactions between processing/storage/food chemistry and their influence on the quality of food, with special emphasis on quality evaluation, food safety, and process control standards; predicting process/consumer acceptance from raw product data; food flavor.

Courtesy Faculty

C. R. Hurburgh Jr., Professor; Ph.D., Iowa State, 1981. Grain quality, marketing, and distribution; value-added to grain through quality specification and traceability.

Iowa State University

SELECTED PUBLICATIONS

Moeller, L. E., et al. **(D. L. Alekel).** Isoflavone-rich soy protein prevents loss of hip lean mass, but does not prevent the shift in regional fat distribution in menopausal women. *Menopause* 10(4): 322–31, 2003.

Beattie, S. Cheese. In *Food Processing: Principles and Applications,* chap. 14, eds. H. Y. Hui and J. S. Smith. Ames, Iowa: Blackwell Publishing, 2004.

Beattie, S. Cheddar cheese. In *Food Chemistry: Principles and Applications, a Workbook,* 1st ed., chap. 5, eds. G. Christen and J. S. Smith. Sacramento, Calif.: STS Publishers, 2002.

Luick, B., and **S. Beattie.** *Preservation of Alaskan Salmon.* Salmon Preservation url: 137.229.28.37/salmon and CD, 2001.

Lee, C. J., **D. F. Birt,** A. Kirksey, and C. Weaver. Helen E. Clark (1912–2001) *J. Nutr.* 133:1773–5, 2003.

Liu, Y., W. Wang, J. Hawley, and **D. F. Birt.** Adrenalectomy abrogates reduction of TPA-induced ERK activity in the epidermis of dietary energy restricted SENCAR mice: Implications of glucocorticoid hormone. *Cancer Epidemiol. Biomarkers Prev.* 11:299–304, 2002.

Liu, Y., et al. **(D. F. Birt).** Dietary energy restriction inhibits ERK but not JNK or p38 activity in the epidermis of SENCAR mice. *Carcinogenesis* 22:607–12, 2001.

Boylston, T. D., H. Wang, **C. A. Reitmeier,** and **B. A. Glatz.** Irradiation of apple cider: Impact on flavor quality. In *Quality of Fresh and Processed Foods,* pp. 281–8, eds. F. Shahidi, A. M. Spanier, C.-T. Ho, and T. Braggins. New York: Kluwer Academic/Plenum Publishers, 2003.

Boylston, T. D., H. Wang, **C. A. Reitmeier,** and **B. A. Glatz.** Effects of processing treatment and sorbate addition on the flavor characteristics of apple cider. *J. Agric. Food Chem.* 51(7):1924–31, 2003.

Boylston, T. D., and **T. Wang.** Integration of team-building skills into food chemistry team research projects. *J. Food Sci. Educ.* 2:18–24, 2003.

Boylston, T. D., and **C. A. Reitmeier** et al. Sensory quality and nutrient composition of three Hawaiian fruits treated by X-irradiation. *J. Food. Qual.* 25:419–33, 2002.

Flakoll P. J., M. D. Jensen, and A. C. Cherrington. Physiological action of insulin. In *Diabetes Mellitus: A Fundamental and Clinical Text,* 3rd ed., pp. 165–81, eds. D. Leroith, S. I. Taylor, and J. Olefsky. Philadelphia: Lippcott Williams & Wilkins, 2004.

Flakoll P. J., et al. Bioelectrical impedance versus air displacement plethysmography and dual-energy X-ray absorptiometry to determine body composition in patients with end stage renal disease. *J. Parenter. Enter. Nutr.* 28:13–21, 2004.

Hemmafarb, J., **P. J. Flakoll,** R. Hakim., and A. Ikizler. Urea space and total body water measurements by stable isotopes in patients with acute renal failure. *Kidney Int.* 65:725–32, 2004.

Cornett, C. A. G., T.-Y. Fang, P. J. Reilly, and **C. F. Ford.** Starch-binding domain shuffling in *Aspergillus niger* glucoamylase. *Protein Eng.* 16:521–9, 2003.

Allen, M. J., E. B. Fuchs, and **C. F. Ford.** Asp238→Asn creates a novel consensus *N*-glycosylation site in *Aspergillus awamori* glucoamylase. *Starch/Stärke* 54:385–92, 2002.

Khan, S. M., P. J. Reilly, and **C. F. Ford.** Thermal and molecular characterization of *Aspergillus awamori* glucoamylase catalytic and starch-binding domains. *Starch/Stärke* 52:385–97, 2000.

Gonzalez, R., et al. Gene array–based identification of changes that contribute to ethanol tolerance in ethanologenic *Escherichia coli:* Comparison of KO11 (parent) to LYO1 (resistant mutant). *Biotechnol. Prog.* 19(2):612–23, 2003.

Gonzalez, R., B. A. Andrews, J. Molitor, and J. A. Asenjo. Metabolic analysis of the synthesis of high levels of intracellular human SOD in *S. cerevisiae* rhSOD 2060 411 SGA122. *Biotechnol. Bioeng.* 82:152–69, 2003.

Gonzalez, R., J. C. Gentina, and F. Acevedo. Optimization of the solids suspension conditions in the biooxidation of gold concentrates in continuous stirred tank reactors. *Electron. J. Biotechnol.* 6(3):184, 2003. (Web site: http://www.ejbiotechnology.info/content/next/index.html)

Kwak, H. K., et al. **(C. M. Hansen).** Improved vitamin B-6 status is positively related to lymphocyte proliferation in young women consuming a controlled diet. *J. Nutr.* 132:3308–13, 2002.

Hansen, C. M., et al. Assessment of vitamin B-6 status in young women consuming a controlled diet containing four levels of vitamin B-6 provides an Estimated Average Requirement and Recommended Dietary Allowance. *J. Nutr.* 131:1777–86, 2001.

Hansen, C. M., and T. D. Schultz. Stability of vitamin B-6 dependent aminotransferase activity in frozen packed erythrocytes is dependent on storage temperature. *J. Nutr.* 131:1581–3, 2001.

Hendrich, S. Bioavailability of isoflavones. *J. Chromatog. B* 777:203–10, 2002.

Lu, Y., et al. **(S. Hendrich** and **P. A. Murphy).** Characterization of fumonisin B_1-glucose reaction kinetics and products. *J. Agric. Food Chem.* 50:4726–33, 2002.

Siska, J., **C. R. Hurburgh Jr.,** and P. Siska. The standardization of near-infrared instruments using master selection and Wiener filter methods. *JNIRS,* in press.

Siska, J., **C. R. Hurburgh Jr.,** and P. Siska. The impact of engineering parameters on the accuracy of calibration transfer. *JNIRS,* in press.

Westgate, M. E., E. Piper, W. D. Batchelor, and **C. R. Hurburgh Jr.** Effect of cultural and environmental conditions during soybean growth on nutritive value of soy products. *Proc. Soy Swine Symposium, Global Soybean Forum, United Soybean Board, St. Louis, Missouri,* 2000.

Ji, Y., et al. **(J. Jane** and **P. J. White).** Structure and function of starch from advanced generations of new corn lines. *Carbohydr. Polym.* 54:305–19, 2003.

Yoo, S.-H., and **J. Jane.** Molecular weights and gyration radii of amylopectins determined by high-performance size-exclusion chromatography equipped with multi-angle laser light scattering and refractive index detection. *Carbohydr. Polym.* 49:307–14, 2002.

Katopo, H., Y. Song, and **J. Jane.** Effect and mechanism of ultrahigh-hydrostatic pressure on the structure and properties of starches. *Carbohydr. Polym.* 47:233–44, 2002.

Hammond, E. G., **L. A. Johnson,** and **P. A. Murphy.** Soy (soya) beans: Properties and analysis. In *Encyclopaedia of Food Sciences and Nutrition,* 2nd ed., eds. B. Caballero, L. Trugo, and P. Finglas. London: Academic Press, 2003.

Wang, C., **L. A. Johnson,** and **L. A. Wilson.** Calcium coagulation properties of hydrothermally processed soymilk. *JAOCS* 80(12):1225–9, 2003.

Crowe, T. D., T. W. Crowe, **L. A. Johnson,** and **P. J. White.** Impact of extractions method on lipid oxidation products from oxidized and unoxidized walnuts. *J. Am. Oil Chem. Soc.* 79:453–6, 2002.

Stewart, J. W., **M. L. Kaplan,** and D. C. Beitz. Pork with high content of polyunsaturated fatty acids lowers LDL-cholesterol in women. *Am. J. Clin. Nutr.* 74:179–87, 2001.

Li, Z., **M. L. Kaplan,** and D. L. Hachey. Hepatic microsomal and perosixomal docosahexaenoate biosynthesis during piglet development. *Lipids* 35:1325–33, 2000.

Zhou, X., and **M. L. Kaplan.** Soluble amylose corn starch is more digestible than soluble amylopectin potato starch in rats. *J. Nutr.* 127:1349–56, 1997.

Kruzich, L. A., et al. **(R. E. Litchfield** and **M. J. Oakland).** A preceptor focus group approach to evaluation of a dietetic internship. *J. Am. Diet. Assoc.* 103(7):884–6, 2003.

Litchfield, R. E., M. J. Oakland, and J. A. Anderson. Promoting and evaluating competence in dietetic education. *J. Am. Diet. Assoc.* 102(10):1455–8, 2002.

Anderson, J. A., **R. E. Litchfield,** and **M. J. Oakland.** Professional development rubric: An evaluation tool to facilitate self-assessment of professional development among dietetic interns. *J. Am. Diet. Assoc.* 102(9S):A62 (abstract), 2002.

Litchfield, R. E., M. J. Oakland, and J. A. Anderson. Improving dietetic education with interactive communication technology. *J. Am. Diet. Assoc.* 100:1191–4, 2000.

Vidal-Quantanar, R. L., **J. A. Love,** and **L. A. Johnson.** Role of oil on physical properties of corn masa flours and sensory characteristics of corn tortillas. *J. Food Process. Preservation* 25:1–14, 2001.

Vidal-Quintanar, R. L., **M. H. Love, J. A. Love, P. J. White,** and **L. A. Johnson.** Lipid-autooxidation-limited shelf-life of nixtamalized instant corn masa. *J. Food Lipids* 10:153–63, 2003.

Marquis, G. S., et al. An overlap of breastfeeding during late pregnancy is associated with subsequent changes in colostrum composition and morbidity rates among Peruvian infants and their mothers. *J. Nutr.* 133:2585–91, 2003.

Iowa State University

Selected Publications (continued)

Mazur, R. E., **G. S. Marquis,** and H. H. Jensen. Diet, nutrition, and food insufficiency among Hispanic youth: Acculturation and socioeconomic determinants in NHANES III. *Am. J. Clin. Nutr.* 78:1120–7, 2003.

Drammeh, B., et al. **(G. S. Marquis).** The effect of dried mangoes in a randomized 4-mo trial to improve vitamin A status among young Gambian children. *J. Nutr.* 132:3693–9, 2002.

Mendonca, A. F., et al. Radiation resistance and virulence of Listeria monocytogenes Scott A following starvation in physiological saline. *J. Food Prot.* 67:470–4, 2004.

Zhu, M., et al. **(A. F. Mendonca).** Dietary vitamin E improved the immune responses and accelerated the clearance of inoculated Listeria monocytogenes in turkeys. *Poultry Sci.* 82(10):1559–64, 2003.

Zheng, Y. L., et al. **(P. A. Murphy, D. L. Alekel,** and **S. Hendrich).** Rapid gut transit time and slow fecal isoflavone disappearance phenotype are associated with greater genistein bioavailability in women. *J. Nutr.* 133:3110–6, 2003.

Song, T. T., S. O. Lee, **P. A. Murphy,** and **S. Hendrich.** Soy protein with or without isoflavones, soy germ and soy germ extract, and daidzein lessen plasma cholesterol levels in golden Syrian hamsters. *Exp. Biol. Med.* 228:1063–68, 2003.

Lang'at-Thoruwa, C., et al. **(P. A. Murphy).** A simple synthesis of 7,4'-dihydroxy-6-methoxy isoflavone, glycitein, the third soybean isoflavone. *J. Nat. Prod.* 66:149–51, 2003.

Fehr, W. R., J. A. Hoeck, S. L. Johnson, and **P. A. Murphy.** Genotype and environment influence on protein components of soybean. *Crop Sci.* 43:511–4, 2003.

Zhang, Y., **P. A. Murphy,** and **S. Hendrich.** Glucuronides are the main isoflavone metabolites in women. *J. Nutr.* 133:399–404, 2003.

Dias, K., and **D. J. Myers** et al. **(P. A. Murphy).** Functional properties of the acidic and basic subunits of the glycinin (11S) soy protein fraction. *JAOCS* 80(6):551–5, 2002.

Bian, Y., and **D. J. Myers** et al. **(P. A. Murphy).** Functional properties of pilot plant produced soybean fractions. *JAOCS* 80(6):545–9, 2002.

Brunt, A. R., E. Schafer, and **M. J. Oakland.** Ability of social support to predict at-risk dietary intake and anthropometric measures in white, rural, community-dwelling elderly women. *J. Nutr. Elderly* 19(1):49–69, 2000.

Kennedy, T. S., **M. J. Oakland,** and R. D. Shaw. A community nutrition intervention with families of preterm low birth weight infants. *Nutr. Clin. Pract.* 15(2):30–5, 2000.

Urbance, S. E., **A. L. Pometto III,** A. A. DiSpirito, and A. Demirci. Medium evaluation and plastic composite support ingredient selection for biofilm formation and succinic acid production by *Actinobacillus succinogenes. Food Biotech.* 17:53–65, 2003.

Demirci, A., et al. **(A. L. Pometto III).** Resistance of *Lactobacillus casei* in PCS biofilm reactors during liquid membrane extraction and optimization of the extraction system. *Biotechnol. Bioeng.* 83:749–59, 2003.

Van Leeuwen, J., et al. **(A. L. Pometto III).** Kinetic model for selective cultivation of microfungi in a microscreen process for food processing wastewater treatment in biomass production. *Acta Biotechnol.* 23(2–3):289–300, 2003.

Nam, K. C., **K. J. Prusa,** and D. U. Ahn. Addition of antioxidants to improve quality and sensory characteristics of irradiated pork patties. *J. Food Sci.* 67:2625–30, 2002.

Lonergan, S. M., et al. **(K. J. Prusa).** Correlation among selected pork quality traits. *J. Anim. Sci.* 80:617–27, 2002.

Malek, M., et al. **(K. J. Prusa).** A molecular genome scan analysis to identify chromosal regions influencing economic traits in the pig. II. Meat and muscle composition. *Mammalian Genome* 12:637–45, 2001.

Hurrell R. F., **M. B. Reddy,** M.-A. Juillerat, and J. D. Cook. Degradation of phytic acid in cereal porridges improved iron absorption in humans. *Am. J. Clin. Nutr.* 77:1213–9, 2003.

Serfass, R. E., and **M. B. Reddy.** Breast milk fractions solubilize Fe(III) and enhance iron flux across Caco2 cells. *J. Nutr.* 133:449–55, 2003.

Hurrell, R. F., **M. B. Reddy,** J. Burri, and J. D. Cook. Effect of industrial processing and home cooking on iron absorption from cereal-based food. *Br. J. Nutr.* 76:165–71, 2002.

Swain, J. H., et al. **(M. B. Reddy).** Iron indices and antioxidant status in response to soy protein intake in perimenopausal women. *Am. J. Clin. Nutr.* 76:165–71, 2002.

Wang, H., **C. A. Reitmeier, B. A. Glatz,** and A. L. Carriquiry. Mixed model analysis of sensory characteristics of irradiated apple cider. *J. Food Sci.* 68:1498-1503, 2003.

Cummins, A., **C. A. Reitmeier, L. Wilson, and B. Glatz.** A survey of apple cider production practices and microbial loads in cider in the state of Iowa. *Dairy, Food, Environ. Sanit.* 22:745–51, 2002.

Ozias, M. K., and **K. L. Schalinske.** All-trans-retinoic acid rapidly induces glycine N-methyltrasferase in a dose-dependent manner and reduces circulating methionine and homocysteine levels in rats. *J. Nutr.* 133:4090–4, 2003.

Rowling, M. J., and **K. L. Schalinske.** Retinoic acid and glucocorticoid treatment induces hepatic glycine N-methyltransferase and lowers plasma homocysteine concentrations in the rat and rat hepatoma cells. *J. Nutr.* 133:3392–8, 2003.

Schalinske, K. L. Interrelationship between diabetes and homocysteine metabolism: Hormonal regulation of cystathionine β-synthase. *Nutr. Rev.* 61:136–8, 2003.

Davis, K. J., **J. G. Sebranek,** E. Huff-Lonergan, and S. M. Lonergan. The effects of aging on moisture-enhanced pork loins. *Meat Sci.* 66:519, 2004.

Sebranek, J. G. Semi-dry fermented sausages. In *Handbook of Food and Beverage Fermentation Technology,* ed. Y. H. Hui. New York: Marcel Dekker, Inc., 2003.

Sebranek, J. G. Chemical analysis—raw material composition analyses. In *Encyclopedia of Meat Sciences,* eds. W. Jensen, C. Devine, and M. Dikeman. London: Academic Press, Elsevier, Ltd., Oxford, 2003.

Steenblock, R. L., **J. G. Sebranek,** D. G. Olson, and **J. A. Love.** The effects of oat fiber on the properties of light bologna and fat-free frankfurters. *J. Food Sci.* 66:1409–15, 2001.

Briggs, J. L., and **T. Wang.** Influence of shearing and time on the rheological properties of milk chocolate during tempering. *J. Am. Oil Chem. Soc.* 81:117–21, 2004.

Wang, T. Use of fats and oils in candle production. *Lipid Technol.* 15:131–4, 2003.

Wu, Y. Z., and **T. Wang.** Total and polar lipids in soybean protein meals. *J. Am. Oil Chem. Soc.* 80:983–5, 2003.

Ji, Y., et al. **(P. J. White).** Gelatinization properties of starches from three successive generations of six exotic corn lines grown in two locations. *Cereal Chem.* 81:59–64, 2004.

Ji, Y., K. Seetharaman, and **P. J. White.** Optimizing a small-scale corn-starch extraction method for use in the laboratory. *Cereal Chem.* 81:55-58, 2004.

White, P. J., and **L. A. Johnson,** eds. *Corn: Chemistry and Technology,* 2nd ed., 892 pp. St. Paul, Minn.: American Association of Cereal Chemists, Inc., 2003.

White, P. J. Lipids of the kernel. In *Corn: Chemistry and Technology,* 2nd ed., chap. 10, pp. 355–95, eds. **P. J. White** and **L. A. Johnson.** St. Paul, Minn.: American Association of Cereal Chemists, Inc., 2003.

Brown M. J., et al. **(W. S. White).** The bioavailability of carotenoids is higher in salads ingested with full-fat versus fat-reduced salad dressings as measured by using electrochemical detection. *Am. J. Clin. Nutr.,* in press.

Barr J., and **W. S. White** et al. The GHOST terminal oxidase regulates developmental programming in tomato fruit. *Plant Cell Environ.,* in press.

Yao, L., et al. **(W. S. White).** Use of a 13C tracer to quantify the plasma appearance of a physiological dose of lutein in humans. *Lipids* 35:339–48, 2000.

Hu, X., R. J. Jandacek, and **W. S. White**. Intestinal absorption of beta-carotene ingested with a meal rich in sunflower oil or beef tallow: Postprandial appearance in triacylglycerol-rich lipoproteins in women. *Am. J. Clin. Nutr.* 71:1170–80, 2000.

Wilson, L. A. Spices and flavourings (flavouring) crops—use of spices in the food industry. *Encyclopedia Food Sci. Nutr.* 5460–6, 2003.

Geater, C. W., W. R. Fehr, **L. A. Wilson,** and J. F. Robyt. A more rapid method of total sugar analysis for soybean seed. *Crop Sci.* 41:250–2, 2001.

UNIVERSITY OF HAWAII AT MANOA

College of Tropical Agriculture and Human Resources

Programs of Study

The College of Tropical Agriculture and Human Resources (CTAHR) is known nationally and internationally as a leader in tropical agriculture. The College belongs to the nationwide network of land-grant universities, and CTAHR's tripartite mission is visible in its separate but interacting programs in teaching, research, and public service. CTAHR offers the M.S. and Ph.D. degrees in the following graduate programs: entomology, molecular biosciences and bioengineering, natural resources and environmental management, tropical plant pathology, tropical plant and soil sciences, and tropical plant and soil sciences (horticulture). CTAHR also offers the M.S. degree in animal sciences, bioengineering, food science, and nutritional sciences. Three of the College's graduate programs in tropical agriculture—entomology, natural resources and environmental management, and tropical plant and soil sciences—have been recognized as distinctive programs by WICHE, the Western Interstate Commission for Higher Education; qualified graduate students from participating states (Alaska, Arizona, Colorado, Idaho, Montana, Nevada, New Mexico, Oregon, Utah, Washington, and Wyoming) may enroll in these Western Regional Graduate Programs at resident tuition rates.

Upon acceptance, the student and his or her adviser develop a program of study that generally includes required and elective courses and seminars, written and oral examinations, and original research guided by a major professor. At the master's level, both Plan A (thesis) and Plan B (nonthesis) programs are offered.

Research Facilities

CTAHR shares in the use of general University facilities, including the libraries, which offer extensive collections and information services, and the computing center, which provides a full range of computers, from individual computers to large mainframes. It jointly sponsors, with the Pacific Biomedical Research Center, the Biotechnology–Molecular Biology Instrumentation Facility for the benefit of researchers throughout the University of Hawaii. The College's facilities include a microcomputer laboratory, several research stations, and specialized laboratories with state-of-the-art equipment, all of which support research and instruction in the agricultural sciences. On-campus affiliations with the Hawaii Institute of Marine Biology, Water Research Center, East-West Center, Harold L. Lyon Arboretum, Sea Grant College Program, and Hawaii Natural Energy Institute extend CTAHR's resources. The College also is affiliated closely with off-campus institutions, such as the Bernice P. Bishop Museum, USDA/ARS Tropical Fruit and Vegetable Research Laboratory, Hawaii Agricultural Research Center, U.S. Geological Survey, National Marine Fisheries Service, and Hawaii State Department of Agriculture.

Financial Aid

Students may contact individual departments (listed on the reverse of this page), the Graduate Division (2540 Maile Way, Spalding Hall, Honolulu, Hawaii 96822), or the Financial Aid Services (2600 Campus Road, Honolulu, Hawaii 96822) for information on grants, fellowships, assistantships, scholarships, tuition waivers, loans, work-study programs, and job opportunities. Graduate assistantships start at $15,558 per year for M.S. candidates and $16,824 per year for Ph.D. candidates for eleven-month half-time appointments.

Cost of Study

In 2004–05, estimated tuition for full-time study (12 or more credit hours) is $2316 per semester for residents of Hawaii and $5424 for nonresidents. Part-time graduate students are assessed $193 per credit hour for Hawaii residents and $452 for nonresidents.

Living and Housing Costs

Dormitory rooms and apartments, ranging from approximately $1402 to $2828 per person per semester, are available to single and married graduate students. These accommodations are on campus within walking distance of classrooms and laboratories. Meal plans are available through the University food service for $765 to $1183 a semester. Most graduate students elect to live off campus in shared apartments and houses, the costs of which vary widely.

Student Group

There are 4,834 graduate students at Manoa. The College's 154 graduate students come from throughout the United States and many countries, as well as from Hawaii, and represent a diversity of educational, cultural, and academic backgrounds.

Location

The University of Hawaii is located in Manoa Valley, a residential section close to the heart of Metropolitan Honolulu, the capital of the state of Hawaii. The campus is a short distance from the center of the commercial, cultural, and political life of Hawaii, and a variety of recreational, athletic, and social activities are available to students throughout the year. Hawaii's population is diverse, and its climate moderate and tropical. Hawaii provides CTAHR with a living laboratory that cannot be duplicated elsewhere: a full range of the soils and climates found throughout the world; tropical plants, animals, and organisms; and a location as the gateway to Asia and the Pacific Basin.

The University

The University of Hawaii at Manoa was founded in 1907 as a land-grant college of agriculture and mechanic arts. Today, it is a major comprehensive research institution with more than 18,700 students and offers course work leading to bachelor's degrees in ninety fields of study, master's degrees in eighty-nine, doctorates in fifty-seven, first professional degrees in law and medicine, and a number of certificates. It is accredited by the Accrediting Commission for Senior Colleges and Universities of the Western Association of Schools and Colleges.

Applying

Applications, transcripts, GRE scores, and letters of recommendation must be submitted. Applications are processed as early as October 1 for the fall semester and May 1 for the spring semester. The deadline for international students is January 15 and August 1 for fall and spring semesters, respectively. International students must submit Test of English as a Foreign Language (TOEFL) scores in addition to the items mentioned above. Information regarding the program, admission criteria, and financial assistance is available from the individual departments (the names and addresses of the departmental chairs are listed on the reverse side). Additional information may be obtained from the individual departments.

Correspondence and Information

Associate Dean for Academic and Student Affairs
College of Tropical Agriculture and Human Resources
University of Hawaii
3050 Maile Way, Gilmore 211
Honolulu, Hawaii 96822
E-mail: acadaff@ctahr.hawaii.edu
World Wide Web: http://www.ctahr.hawaii.edu

University of Hawaii at Manoa

THE FACULTY

The addresses at which the department chairs may be contacted are given in parentheses for each chair; the street address should be preceded by the name of the department and the University.

Graduate Program in Animal Sciences
Rachel Novotny, Chair; Ph.D., Cornell, 1986; RD. (1955 East-West Road Agricultural Science 216B, Honolulu, Hawaii 96822)
James R. Carpenter, Chair of Graduate Program; Ph.D., Cornell, 1976. (1955 East-West Road Agricultural Science 314E, Honolulu, Hawaii 96822)

Brent A. Buckley, Ph.D., Nebraska, 1985. Joan C. Dobbs, Ph.D., California, Davis, 1983. Yong-Soo Kim, Ph.D., California, Davis, 1978. Chin Nyean Lee, Ph.D., Wisconsin, 1984. Spencer R. Malecha, Ph.D., Hawaii, 1971. Douglas L. Vincent, Ph.D., Illinois, 1983. Charles W. Weems, Ph.D., West Virginia, 1975. Yoshie S. Weems, Ph.D., Hawaii, 1994. Jinzeng Yang, Ph.D., Alberta, 1999. Halina Zaleski, Ph.D., Guelph, 1992.

Cooperating Graduate Faculty: Shannon Atkinson, Ph.D., Murdoch (Australia), 1985. E. Gordon Grau, Ph.D., Delaware, 1984.

Affiliate Graduate Faculty: Brad Argue, Ph.D., Auburn, 1996. William C. Bergin, D.V.M., Kansas State, 1967. James A. Brock, D.V.M., Washington State, 1977. Olivier Decamp, Ph.D., Leicester (England), 1996. Ian Foster, Ph.D., Washington, 1993. Charles Laidley, Ph.D., Texas, 1995. Bruce Mathews, Ph.D., Florida, 1992. Shaun Moss, Ph.D., Hawaii, 1993. Ben Okimoto, D.V.M., Kansas State, 1980. Anthony Ostrewski, Ph.D., Michigan State, 1987. Barbara A. Rasco, Ph.D., Massachusetts, 1983. Larry Rawson, D.V.M., Kansas State, 1983. Alfred Tacon, Ph.D., Wales, 1978. Lee Ann Woodward, Ph.D., California, Davis, 1999. Thierry M. Work, D.V.M., California, Davis, 1988.

Graduate Program in Bioengineering
Charles M. Kinoshita, Chair; Ph.D., Berkeley, 1980. (1955 East-West Road, Agricultural Science 218, Honolulu, Hawaii 96822)
P. Y. Yang, Chair of Graduate Program; Ph.D., Oklahoma State, 1972. (1955 East-West Road, Agricultural Science 218, Honolulu, Hawaii 96822)

Edmond Cheng, Ph.D., Utah State, 1969. Pengcheng Fu, Ph.D., Sydney (Australia), 1996. Loren Gautz, Ph.D., California, Davis, 1990. Andrew Hashimoto, Ph.D., Cornell, 1972. Daniel Jenkins, Ph.D., California, Davis, 2001. PingSun Leung, Ph.D., Hawaii, 1977. Clark Liu, Ph.D., Cornell, 1976. Stephen Masutani, Ph.D., Stanford, 1985. James Moy, Ph.D., Rutgers, 1965. Chittaranjan Ray, Ph.D., Illinois, 1994. Wei-Wen Su, Ph.D., Lehigh, 1991. Marcel Tsang, Ph.D., LSU, 1984. Scott Turn, Ph.D., California, Davis, 1994. Jaw-Kai Wang, Ph.D., Michigan State, 1958.

Graduate Program in Entomology
J. Kenneth Grace, Chair; Ph.D., Berkeley, 1986. (3050 Maile Way, Gilmore 310, Honolulu, Hawaii 96822)
Stephen Saul, Chair of Graduate Faculty; Ph.D., Rochester, 1970. (3050 Maile Way, Gilmore 310, Honolulu, Hawaii 96822)

Rodrigo Almeida, Ph.D., Berkeley, 2002. Lorna Arita-Tsutsumi, Ph.D., Hawaii, 1983. Arnold Hara, Ph.D., California, Davis, 1982. Kenneth Kaneshiro, Ph.D., Hawaii, 1968. Ronald F. L. Mau, Ph.D., Hawaii, 1975. Russell H. Messing, Ph.D., Oregon State, 1986. Daniel Rubinoff, Ph.D., Berkeley, 2001. Josef Seifert, Ph.D., Prague Institute of Chemical Technology, 1973. Mark G. Wright, Ph.D., Natal (South Africa), 1996. Julian R. Yates, Ph.D., Hawaii, 1988.

Graduate Program in Food Science
Rachel Novotny, Chair; Ph.D., Cornell, 1986; RD. (1955 East-West Road Agricultural Science 216B, Honolulu, Hawaii 96822)
Wayne T. Iwaoka, Chair of Graduate Program; Ph.D., Illinois, 1973. (1955 East-West Road Agricultural Science 302A, Honolulu, Hawaii 96822)

Harry Ako, Ph.D., Washington State, 1973. Anne M. Alvarez, Ph.D., Berkeley, 1972. Dulal Borthakur, Ph.D., East Anglia (England), 1987. Brent A. Buckley, Ph.D., Nebraska, 1985. Dian A. Doley, Ph.D., Wisconsin, 1988. Loren D. Gautz, Ph.D., California, Davis, 1990. Alvin S. Huang, Ph.D., Wisconsin, 1985. Yong-Soo Kim, Ph.D., California, Davis, 1988. Qing Xiao Li, Ph.D., California, Davis, 1990. James H. Moy, Ph.D., Rutgers, 1965. Robert E. Paull, Ph.D., Berkeley, 1974. Aurora Saulo, Ph.D., Massachusetts Amherst, 1978. Wei-Wen Su, Ph.D., Lehigh, 1991.

Cooperating Graduate Faculty: Roger S. Fujioka, Ph.D., Michigan, 1970. Paul Q. Patek, Ph.D., Texas at Houston, 1976. Josef Seifert, Ph.D., Prague Institute of Chemical Technology, 1963. Clyde S. Tamaru, Ph.D., Tokyo, 1988. Carol Waslien, Ph.D., Berkeley, 1968; RD.

Affiliate Graduate Faculty: Alfred Tacon, Ph.D., Wales, 1978.

Graduate Program in Molecular Biosciences and Bioengineering
Charles M. Kinoshita, Chair; Ph.D., Berkeley, 1980. (1955 East-West Road, Agricultural Science 218, Honolulu, Hawaii 96822)
Dulal Borthakur, Chair of Graduate Program; Ph.D., East Anglia (England), 1987. (1955 East-West Road, Agricultural Science 218, Honolulu, Hawaii 96822)

Harry Ako, Ph.D., Washington State, 1973. Henrik H. Albert, Ph.D., Hawaii, 1991. Anne Alvarez, Ph.D., Berkeley, 1972. Sandra Chang, Ph.D., Oregon, 1983. David Christopher, Ph.D., Arizona, 1989. Michael Cooney, Ph.D., California, Davis, 1992. Maureen M. M. Fitch, Ph.D., Hawaii, 1991. Pengcheng Fu, Ph.D., Sydney (Australia), 1996. Loren Gautz, Ph.D., California, Davis, 1990. Andrew Hashimoto, Ph.D., Cornell, 1972. John Hu, Ph.D., Cornell, 1987. Daniel Jenkins, Ph.D., California, Davis, 2001. Monto Kumagai, Ph.D., California, Davis, 1990. Qing Xiao Li, Ph.D., California, Davis, 1990. PingSun Leung, Ph.D., Hawaii, 1977. James H. Moy, Ph.D., Rutgers, 1965. Paul H. Moore, Ph.D., UCLA, 1966. Pratibha V. Nerurkar, Ph.D., Bombay, 1990. Chittaranjan Ray, Ph.D., Illinois, 1994. Wei-Wen Winston Su, Ph.D., Lehigh, 1991. C. S. Tang, Ph.D., California, Davis, 1967. Ping-Yi Yang, Ph.D., Oklahoma State, 1972. Harry Y. Yamamoto, Ph.D., California, Davis, 1962.

Graduate Program in Natural Resources and Environmental Management
S. A. El-Swaify, Chair; Ph.D., California, Davis, 1964. (1910 East-West Road, Sherman 101, Honolulu, Hawaii 96822)

Richard L. Bowen, Ph.D., Colorado State, 1982. Catherine Chan-Halbrendt, Ph.D., Missouri–Columbia, 1986. Chauncey Ching, Ph.D., California, Davis, 1967. Linda J. Cox, Ph.D., Texas A&M, 1982. Carl I. Evensen, Ph.D., Hawaii, 1989. Ali Fares, Ph.D., Florida, 1996. Carol A. Ferguson, Ph.D., Cornell, 1985. James B. Friday, Ph.D., Hawaii, 1998. Peter V. Garrod, Ph.D., Berkeley, 1972. Chennat Gopalakrishnan, Ph.D., Montana State, 1967. Travis Idol, Ph.D., Purdue, 2000. Tomoaki Miura, Ph.D., Arizona, 2000. John Yanagida, Ph.D., Illinois, 1978.

Graduate Program in Nutritional Sciences
Rachel Novotny, Chair; Ph.D., Cornell, 1986; RD. (1955 East-West Road Agricultural Science 216B, Honolulu, Hawaii 96822)
Michael A. Dunn, Chair of Graduate Program; Ph.D., Penn State. (1985 East-West Road Agricultural Science 302G, Honolulu, Hawaii 96822)

Amy C. Brown, Ph.D., Virginia Tech, 1986. James R. Carpenter, Ph.D., Cornell, 1976. Joan Dobbs, Ph.D., California, Davis, 1983. Dian A. Dooley, Ph.D., Wisconsin, 1988. Alvin S. Huang, Ph.D., Wisconsin, 1985. Wayne T. Iwaoka, Ph.D., Illinois, 1973. Yong-Soo Kim, Ph.D., California, Davis, 1978. Rachel Novotny, Ph.D., Cornell, 1986; RD. Anne C. Shovic, Ph.D., Washington State, 1982; RD. C. Alan Titchenal, Ph.D., California, Davis, 1986. Charles W. Weems, Ph.D., West Virginia, 1975. Jinzeng Yang, Ph.D., Alberta, 1999.

Cooperating Graduate Faculty: John J. Buzanoski, M.P.H., Georg-Austin (Germany), 1989; M.D., Hawaii, 2000. Andrian Franke, Ph.D., Freiburg, 1985. Karen Glanz, Ph.D., Michigan, 1979. Ronald Hetzler, Ph.D., Southern Illinois, 1988. Daniel Jenkis, Ph.D., California, Davis, 2001. David A. Lally, Ph.D., Hawaii, 1973. Loic LeMarchand, M.D., de Rennes (France); M.P.H., Hawaii, 1983; Ph.D., Hawaii, 1987. Gertraud Maskarinec, M.D., Freiburg, 1979; Ph.D., Hawaii, 1996. Suzanne Murphy, Ph.D., Berkeley, 1984; RD. Pratibha V. Nerurkar, Ph.D., Bombay (India), 1990. Claudio R. Nigg, Ph.D., Rhode Island, 1999. Sangita Sharma, Ph.D., Manchester (England), 1996. Andre G. Theriault, Ph.D., Windsor, 1994. Carol Waslien, Ph.D., Berkeley, 1968; RD.

Affiliate Graduate Faculty: Dan Galanis, Ph.D., Cornell, 1994. William D. B. Hiller, Ph.D., Thomas Jefferson, 1981. Alfred Tacon, Ph.D., Wales, 1978. Thomas Vogt, M.D., California, San Francisco, 1971.

Graduate Program in Tropical Plant and Soil Sciences
Kent D. Kobayashi, Chair; Ph.D., Oregon State, 1981. (3190 Maile Way, St. John 102, Honolulu, Hawaii 96822)

Henrik Albert, Ph.D., Hawaii, 1991. Michael Austin, Ph.D., Hawaii, 1995. Harry Bittenbender, Ph.D., Michigan State, 1977. James L. Brewbaker, Ph.D., Cornell, 1952. Catherine G. Cavaletto, M.S., Hawaii, 1968. Chian L. Chia, Ph.D., Cornell, 1975. Richard A. Criley, Ph.D., UCLA, 1968. Joseph DeFrank, Ph.D., Michigan State, 1983. Maureen M. M. Fitch, Ph.D., Hawaii, 1991. Kent D. Fleming, Ph.D., Massachusetts, 1991. Shelton C. Furutani, Ph.D., Michigan State, 1982. Mitiku Habte, Ph.D., Cornell, 1976. Nguyen V. Hue, Ph.D., Auburn, 1981. Michael K. Kawate, Ph.D., Oregon State, 1987. Bernard A. Kratky, Ph.D., Purdue, 1971. Adelheid R. Kuehnle, Ph.D., Cornell, 1988. Kenneth W. Leonhardt, Ph.D., Hawaii, 1977. Richard M. Manshardt, Ph.D., Florida, 1980. Ray R. G. Ming, Ph.D., Hawaii, 1995. Susan C. Miyasaka, Ph.D., Cornell, 1988. Paul Moore, Ph.D., UCLA, 1966. Mike A. Nagao, Ph.D., Massachusetts, 1975. Roy K. Nishimoto, Ph.D., Purdue, 1970. Robert V. Osgood, Ph.D., Hawaii, 1969. Robert E. Paull, Ph.D., Berkeley, 1974. Diane Ragone, Ph.D., Hawaii, 1991. Yoneo Sagawa, Ph.D., Connecticut, 1956. William S. Sakai, Ph.D., Hawaii, 1970. Aurora Saulo, Ph.D., Massachusetts Amherst, 1978. Terry T. Sekioka, Ph.D., Minnesota, 1969. James A. Silva, Ph.D., Iowa State, 1964. Paul W. Singleton, Ph.D., Hawaii, 1982. Christopher Smith, Ph.D., North Carolina, 1989. Michael J. Tanabe, Ph.D., Hawaii, 1976. Goro Uehara, Ph.D., Michigan State, 1959. Hector R. Valenzuela, Ph.D., Florida, 1990. Russell S. Yost, Ph.D., North Carolina State, 1977. Francis Zee, Ph.D., Cornell, 1986.

Graduate Program in Tropical Plant Pathology
J. Kenneth Grace, Chair; Ph.D., Berkeley, 1986. (3050 Maile Way, Gilmore 310, Honolulu, Hawaii 96822)
John S. Hu, Chair of Graduate Program; Ph.D., Cornell, 1987. (3190 Maile Way, St. John 310C, Honolulu, Hawaii 96822)

Anne M. Alvarez, Ph.D., Berkeley, 1972. John J. Cho, Ph.D., Berkeley, 1974. Stephen A. Ferreira, Ph.D., California, Davis, 1974. Wen-hsiung Ko, Ph.D., Michigan State, 1966. Scot C. Nelson, Ph.D., North Carolina State, 1992. Wayne T. Nishijima, Ph.D., Wisconsin, 1977. Jeri J. Ooka, Ph.D., Minnesota, 1975. Brent S. Sipes, Ph.D., North Carolina State, 1991. Eduardo E. Trujillo, Ph.D., Berkeley, 1962. Janice Y. Uchida, Ph.D., Hawaii, 1984.

SELECTED PUBLICATIONS

Almeida, R. P. P., and A. H. Purcell. Transmission of *Xylella fastidiosa* to grapevines by *Homalodisca coagulata* (Hemiptera, Cicadellidae). *J. Econ. Entomol.* 96:264–71, 2003.

Borthakur, D., M. Soedarjo, P. M. Fox, and D. T. Webb. The *mid* genes of *Rhizobium* sp. strain TAL1145 are required for degradation of mimosine into 3-hydroxy-4-pyridone and are inducible by mimosine. *Microbiology* 149:537–46, 2003.

Saafi, H., and **D. Borthakur.** In vitro plantlet regeneration from cotyledon of the tree legume *Leucaena leucocephala. Plant Growth Regul.* 38:279–85, 2002.

Bowen, R. L., and **C. A. Ferguson.** Hawaii's LESA experience in a changing policy environment. In *Agricultural Land Evaluation and Site Assessment,* eds. F. Steiner, J. Pease, and R. Coughlin. Ankeny, Iowa: Soils and Water Conservation Society, 1996.

Brown, A. C., and **C. I. Waslien.** Nutrition and stress. In *Encyclopedia of Food Science, Food Technology and Nutrition.* London: Academic Press, 2000.

Brown, A. C. Understanding food. In *Principles and Preparation.* Wadsworth Publishing, 2000.

Brown, A. C. Lupus erythematosus and nutrition: A review of the literature. *J. Renal Nutr.* 10(4):170–83, 2000.

Cox, L. J., and M. Fox. Agriculturally based leisure attractions. *J. Tourism Studies* 14(1):49–58, 2003.

Criley, R. A., N. Maciel, Z. Fu, and **J. Y. Uchida.** Productivity of three heliconia hybrids. *Bull. Heliconia Soc. Int.* 10(3):1–3, 2001.

Criley, R. A. Proteaceae: Beyond the big three. *Acta Hort.* 545:79–85, 2001.

Criley, R. A. Tropical rhododenrons as potted plants. *Acta Hort.* 513:123-127. 2000.

Criley, R. A. Ethephon forces plumeria for winter flowering. In *Proceedings Hawaii Floriculture Industry Conference 1994–1995,* pp. 11–13, eds. K. W. Leonhardt and L. L. Burnham-Larish. College of Tropical Agriculture and Human Resources Proceedings P-12/00, 2000.

Dooley, D. A., J. P. Derrickson, and **R. Novotny.** Wheel of nutrition game: Nutrition in the round. *J. Nutr. Educ.* 33(3):175–6, 2001.

Dooley, D. A. The study of ethics in the applied science curriculum: Training future science educators in the ethics of nutrition. *J. Coll. Sci. Teaching* 29(5):341–5, 2000.

Cox, K. A., and **M. A. Dunn.** Aluminum toxicity alters the regulation of calbibdin-D28k protein and mRNA expression in chick intestine. *J. Nutr.* 131:2007–13, 2001.

Han, J., J. Han, and **M. A. Dunn.** Effect of dietary aluminum on tissue nonheme iron and ferritin levels in the chick. *Toxicology* 142(2):97–109, 2000.

El-Swaify, S. A. Impact of erosion and restoration on water and nutrient use efficiency in a Hawaii Oxisol. In *Potential Use of Innovative Nutrient Management Alternatives to Increase Nutrient Use Efficiency, Reduce Losses and Protect Soil and Water Quality.* New York: Marcel Dekker. *J. Commun. Soil Sci. Plant Anal.* 32:1187–201, 2001.

El-Swaify, S. A., and D. S. Yakowitz. *Multiple Objective Decision Making for Land, Water and Environmental Management.* Delray Beach, Florida: CRC/Lewis/St. Lucie Press, 1998.

Evensen, C. I., S. A. El-Swaify, and C. W. Smith. C-factor development of sugarcane in Hawaii. In *Soil Erosion Research for the 21st Century, Proc. Int. Symp.* (a3–5 January 2001, Honolulu, HI, USA) pp. 687–90, eds. J. C. Ascough II and D. C. Flanagan. St. Joseph, Michigan: ASAE, 701P0007, 2001.

Fares, A., et al. Effect of emitter patterns on solute transport. *Soil Crop Sci. Florida Proc.* 61:46–56, 2001.

Fares, A., and A. K. Alva. Soil water balance components based on real-time multisensor capacitance probes in a sandy. *Soil Sci. Soc. Am. J.* 64:311–8, 2000.

Friday, J. B., and J. H. Fownes. Competition for light between hedgerows and maize in an alley cropping system. *Agroforestry Syst.* 55(2):125–36, 2002.

Gopalakrishnan, C., and **L. J. Cox.** Water consumption by the visitor industry: The case of Hawaii. *Int. J. Water Resource Dev.* 19(1):29–35, 2003.

Gopalakrishnan, C., ed. *Classic Papers in Natural Resource Economics.* MacMillian, 2000.

Campora, C. E., and **J. K. Grace.** Tunnel orientation and search pattern sequence of the Formosan subterranean termite (Isoptera: Rhinotermitidae). *J. Econ. Entomol.* 94:1193–9, 2001.

Sether, D. M., and **J. S. Hu.** Closterovirus infection and mealybug exposure are both necessary factors for the development of mealybug wilt of pineapple disease. *Phytopathology* 92:928–35, 2002.

Melzer, M. J., A. V. Karasev, D. M. Sether, and **J. S. Hu.** Nucleotide sequence, genome organization, and phylogenetic analysis of pineapple mealybug wilt-associated virus-2. *J. Gen. Virol.* 82:1–7, 2001.

Hue, N. V., and Y. Mai. Manganese toxicity in watermelon as affected by lime and compost amended to a Hawaii soil. *Hort. Sci.* 37:656–61, 2002.

Hue, N. V., et al. Reducing salinity and organic contaminants in the Pearl Harbor dredged material using soil amendments and plants. *J. Remediat.* 45–63, 2002.

Hue, N. V., S. Vega, and J. A. Silva. Manganese toxicity in a Hawaiian Oxisol affected by soil pH and organic amendments. *Soil Sci. Soc. Am. J.* 65:153-60, 2001.

Idol, T. W., P. E. Pope, and F. Ponder Jr. N mineralization, nitrification, and N mineralization, nitrification, and N uptake across a 100-year chronosequence of upland hardwood forests. *For. Ecol. Manage.* 176:509–18, 2003.

Idol, T. W., P. E. Pope, and F. Ponder Jr. Changes in microbial nitrogen across a 100-year chronosequence of upland hardwood forests. *Soil Sci. Soc. Am. J.* 66:1662–8, 2002.

Shimojo, R. Y., and **W. T. Iwaoka.** A rapid hemolysis assay for the detection of sodium channel-specific marine toxins. *Toxicology* 154:1–7, 2000.

Iwaoka, W. T., and S. Brewer. Toxicants. In *Food Chemistry: Principles and Application,* ch. 15, eds. G. L. Christian and J. S. Smith. West Sacramento, California: Science Technology System, 2000.

Gu, Y. H., and **W. H. Ko.** Occurrence of parasexual cycle following transfer of isolated nuclei into protoplasts of *Phytophthora parasitica. Curr. Genet.* 143:120–3, 1998.

Liu, L., and **K. D. Kobayashi.** Biomass production of four turfgrasses in different light conditions in Hawaii. *J. Hawaiian Pacific Agric.,* in press.

Kobayashi, K. D., H. C. Bittenbender, and I. S. Campbell. Farmer's bookshelf: Evolution of a horticultural information delivery system. *J. Hawaiian Pacific Agric.,* in press.

Wang, K. H., **A. R. Kuehnle,** and **B. S. Sipes.** In vitro screening for burrowing nematode, *Radopholus citrophilus,* tolerance and resistance in commercial Anthurium hybrids. *In Vitro Cell Dev. Biol.* 33:205–8, 1997.

Lee, C. N. Managing Holstein cows in the sub-tropical environment in Hawaii. *International Training on Strategies for Reducing Heat Stress in Dairy Cattle at Taiwan Livestock Research Institute, Tainan, Taiwan,* 2002.

Hillman, P., and **C. N. Lee.** Field test of a new cooling system for dairy cows in a freestall facility. *ASAE/CIGR XVth World Congress* 024065, 2002.

DeJarnette, J. M., et al. **(C. N. Lee).** Effects of sequential insemination number after batch-thaw on conception rates of cryopreserved bovine semen: A review. *NAAB Conf.,* 2002.

Campbell, S., et al. **(Q. X. Li).** Trace analysis of explosives in soil: Pressurized fluid extraction and gas and liquid chromatography mass spectrometry. *J. Chromatogr. Sci.* 41(6):284–8, 2003.

Kim, H. J., et al. **(Q. X. Li).** Development of an enzyme-linked immunosorbent assay for the insecticide thiamethoxam. *J. Agric. Food Chem.* 51(7):1823–30, 2003.

Kim, H. J., et al. **(Q. X. Li).** Improved enzyme-linked immunosorbent assay for the insecticide imidacloprid. In *Environmental Fate and*

University of Hawaii at Manoa

Selected Publications (continued)

Effects of Pesticides, pp. 30–45, eds. J. R. Coats and H. Yamamoto. ACS Symposium Series 853, Washington, D.C., 2003.

Mau, R. F. L., et al. Implementation of a geographic information system with integrated control tactics for areawide fruit fly management. In *Proceedings of the Workshop on Plant Protection Management for Sustainable Development: Technology and New Dimension,* pp. 23–33, eds. C-C. Ho et al. The Plant Protection Society of the Republic of China, 2003.

Messing, R. H., E. B. Jang, and L. M. Klungness. Response of the melon fly parasite *Psyttalia fletcheri* to host larvae in relation to odor cues, mating status and prior experience. *J. Appl. Entomol.,* in press.

Wang, X. G., and **R. H. Messing.** Newly imported larval parasitoids pose minimal competitive risk to extant egg-larval parasitoid of fruit flies in Hawaii. *Bull. Entomol. Res.,* in press.

Miura, T., A. R. Huete, L. G. Ferreira, and E. E. Sano. Discrimination and biophysical characterization of cerrado physiognomies with EO-1 hyperspectral hyperion. In *XI Simposio Brasileiro de Sensoriamento Remoto (XI SBSR),* Belo Horizonte, Minas Gerais, Brazil, April 5–10, 2003.

Miura, T., A. R. Huete, H. Yoshioka, and B. N. Holben. An error and sensitivity analysis of atmospheric resistant vegetation indices derived from dark target-based atmospheric correction. *Remote Sensing Environ.* 78:284–98, 2001.

Miyasaka, S. C., J. R. Hollyer, and L. S. Kodani. Mulch and compost effects on yield and corm rots of taro. *Field Crops Res.* 71:101–12, 2002.

Miyasaka, S. C., and M. C. Hawes. Possible role of root border cells in detection and avoidance of aluminum toxicity. *Plant Physiol.* 125:1978–87, 2001.

Miyasaka, S. C., and **M. Habte.** Plant mechanisms and mycorrhizal symbioses to increase phosphorus uptake efficiency. *Commun. Plant Soil Anal.* 32:1101–47, 2001.

Nishijima, K. A., P. A. Follet, B. C. Bushe, and **M. A. Nagao.** First report of Lasmenia sp. and two species of *Gliocephalotrichum* on rambutan in Hawaii. *Plant Disease* 86:71, 2002.

Nagao, M. A., E. B. Ho-a, M. S. Nishina, and **F. Zee.** December pruning of vegetative flushes affects flowering of 'Kaimana' lychee in Hawaii. *J. Hawaiian Pacific Agric.* 11:17–21, 2000.

Nagao, M. A., and E. B. Ho-a. Stimulating flowering of longan in Hawaii with lorate. *J. Hawaiian Pacific Agric.* 11:23–7, 2000.

Nelson, S. C. A simple analysis of disease foci. *Phytopathology* 84:332–9, 1996.

Novotny, R., et al. Calcium intake of Asian, Hispanic and White youth. *J. Am. Coll. Nutr.* 22(1):64–70, 2003.

Read, M., and **R. Novotny** et al. Age differences in milk consumption as a snack and by eating occasion. *Top. Clin. Nutr.* 17(4):55–62, 2002.

Maskarinec, G., **R. Novotny,** and K. Tasaki. Dietary patterns and body mass index in a multi-ethnic population. *J. Nutr.* 130(12):3068–72, 2000.

Novotny, R., et al. Pelvic size, measured by dual energy absorptiometry, predicts infant birth weight. *Am. J. Hum. Biol.* 12:552–7, 2000.

Bunsiri, A., S. Ketsa, and **R. E. Paull.** Phenolic metabolism and lignin synthesis in damaged pericarp of mangosteen fruit after impact. *Postharvest Biol. Technol.,* in press.

Bartholomew, D. P., **R. E. Paull,** and K. G. Rohrbach (eds.). *Pineapple: Botany, Production and Uses.* Wallingford, United Kingdom: CABI, 2002.

Kim, M. S., et al. **(R. E. Paull).** Genetic diversity of *Carica papaya* L. as revealed by AFLP markers. *Genome* 45:503–12, 2002.

Chen, C. C., and **R. E. Paull.** Fruit temperature and crown removal on the occurrence of pineapple fruit translucency. *Scientia Hort.* 88:85–96, 2001.

Paull, R. E., and T. Chantrachit. Benzyladenine and the vase life of tropical ornamentals. *Postharvest Biol. Technol.* 21:303–10, 2001.

Zhou, L., and **R. E. Paull.** Sucrose metabolism during papaya *(Carica papaya)* fruit growth and ripening. *J. Am. Soc. Hort. Sci.* 126:351–7, 2001.

Rubinoff, D., and F. A. H. Sperling. Evolution of ecological traits and wing morphology in Hemileuca (Saturniidae) based on a two gene phylogeny. *Mol. Phylogen. Evol.* 25:70–86, 2002.

Rubinoff, D. Endangered plants as guides for saving endemic insects in California. *Fremontia* 30:62–6, 2002.

Silva, J. A., et al. **(C. I. Evensen, R. Bowen,** and **R. S. Yost).** Managing nutrients to protect the environment and human health. In *Plant Nutrient Management in Hawaii's Soils: Approaches for Tropical and Subtropical Agriculture,* pp. 7–22, eds. **J. A. Silva** and R. S. Uchida. University of Hawaii, CTAHR, 2000.

Wang, K. H., **B. S. Sipes,** and D. P. Schmitt. Enhancement of *Rotylenchulus reniformis* suppressiveness by *Crotalaria juncea* amendment in pineapple soils. *Agriculture, Ecosystems Environ.* 94:197–203, 2003.

Chinnasri, B., **B. S. Sipes,** and D. P. Schmitt. Effect of acibenzolar-s-methyl application on *Rotylenchulus reniformis* and *Meloidogyne javanica. J. Nematology* 35:110–4, 2003.

Aragaki, M., and **J. Uchida.** Morphological distinction between *Phytophthora capsici* and *P. tropicalis* sp. nov. *Mycologia* 93:137–45, 2001.

Atkinson, S., et al. **(D. Vincent).** Monitoring of progesterone in captive female false killer whales, *Pseudorca crassidens. Gen. Comp. Endocrinol.* 115:323–32, 1999.

Shikuma, C. M., et al. **(C. I. Waslien).** Fasting hyperinsulinemia and increased waist-to-hip ratios in non-wasting individuals with AIDS. *AIDS* 13:1359–65, 1999.

Dufour, D. L., et al. **(C. I. Waslien).** Estimating energy and macronutrient intake in women in a developing country: Comparison of diet records and recalls. *Am. J. Phys. Anthropol.* 108:53–63, 1999.

Weems, Y. S., et al. **(C. W. Weems).** Effect of luteinizing hormone (LH), pregnancy specific protein B (PSPB), or arachidonic acid (AA) on ovine endometrium of the estrous cycle or placental secretion of prostaglandins E_2 (PGE_2) and F_2a (PGF_2a), and progesterone in vitro. *Prostaglandins Other Lipid Mediators* 71:55–73, 2003.

Weems, Y. S., et al. **(C. W. Weems).** Effects of mifepristone on pregnancy and secretion of progesterone, estaradiol-17β, pregnancy specific protein B (PSPB), and prostaglandins E and $F_{2\alpha}$ (PGE; $PGF_{2\alpha}$) in 90-day intact pregnant sheep. *Prostaglandins Other Lipid Mediators* 70:195–208, 2002.

Weems, Y. S., et al. **(C. W. Weems).** Effect of an aromatase inhibitor, CGS-16949A, on secretion of estradiol-17β, pregnancy specific protein B (PSPB), progesterone, and prostaglandins E and $F_{2\alpha}$ (PGE; $PGF_{2\alpha}$) in 90-day ovarietomized pregnant sheep. *Prostaglandins Other Lipid Mediators* 66:77–87, 2001.

Kuhar, T. P., M. P. Hoffmann, and **M. G. Wright.** Controlling European corn borer in vegetables with a parasitic wasp. *Pesticide Outlook* 14:99–101, 2003.

Yang, J., et al. Expression of myostatin pro domain results in muscular transgenic mice. *Mol. Reprod. Dev.* 60:351–61, 2001.

Yang, J., J. J. Kennelly, and V. E. Baracos. Transcription factor Stat5 responses to prolactin, growth hormone and IGF-I in rat and bovine mammary gland explant. *J. Anim. Sci.* 78:3114–25, 2000.

Yang, P. Y., and T. T. Myint. Integrating EMMC technology for treatment of wastewater containing DMSO for reuse in semiconductor industries. *Clean Technol. Environ. Policy,* in press.

Yang, P. Y., H. J. Chen, and S. J. Kim. Integrating EMMC process for biological removal of carbon and nitrogen from dilute swine wastewater for agricultural reuse. *Bioresour. Technol.* 86:245–52, 2003.

Yang, P. Y., K. Cao, and S. J. Kim. Entrapped mixed microbial cell process for combined secondary and tertiary wastewater treatment. *Water Environ. Res.* 74:226–34, 2002.

Zeller, M., et al. **(H. M. Zaleski).** Edible antibiotics in food crops. In *Life Science Ethics,* pp. 271–3, ed. G. L. Comstock. Iowa State Press, 2002.

UNIVERSITY OF IDAHO

College of Agricultural and Life Sciences
Department of Animal and Veterinary Science

Programs of Study

Graduate degree programs include an M.S. degree in animal science or veterinary science and a Ph.D. in animal physiology. Areas of study include ruminant nutrition (beef feedlot, cow/calf, and dairy), meat science, growth and development, dairy cattle management, physiology (lactation, growth, reproduction), equine reproduction, veterinary science (disease management, pathology, microbiology, and parasitology), and aquaculture. Study consists of formal course work and individual thesis research.

Students pursuing an M.S. degree typically finish in two years. The first year and a half is course work and initiation of research. The last half-year is completion and oral defense of the thesis. Students in the Ph.D. program take courses for approximately two years with written and oral qualifying exams for Ph.D. candidacy taken near the end of course work. Students may take longer than three years to complete their Ph.D., depending on the scope of their research program. A final oral defense of the dissertation is required for the Ph.D. Both M.S. and Ph.D. students are required to assist in teaching once per year.

Degree programs are designed to provide both basic and applied scientific training. An adviser directs the research of candidates while each student also has a committee to address course requirements and administer examinations. Students work closely with their adviser in the pursuit of their degree. Programs prepare students for career opportunities with private industry (feed, pharmaceutical, meats), government agencies (USDA, FDA), commercial farms, and universities (teaching, research and extension).

Research Facilities

The Department of Animal and Veterinary Science maintains laboratories on campus that are equipped to perform a broad array of research in nutrition, physiology, and meat science. The new Ag Biotech Building offers state-of-the-art facilities and equipment to explore the molecular biology of animals. Immediately adjacent to campus are the animal research centers—beef, dairy, sheep, equine reproduction, and meats and aquaculture. Students may also complete their graduate research at the following facilities, which are all located in Idaho: Caine Veterinary Teaching Center in Caldwell; Hagerman Fish Culture Experiment Station in Hagerman; Nancy M. Cummings Research, Extension, and Education Center in Salmon; and the U.S. Sheep Experiment Station in Dubois.

Financial Aid

Research and teaching assistantships are available on a competitive basis to those accepted to the graduate program in the department. In addition, financial aid is available to qualified students through various endowment and scholarship programs. Financial aid is available through the Federal Perkins Loan Program, and work-study grants are also available. The Student Financial Aid Office provides information and applications.

Cost of Study

For 2004–05, full-time graduate fees were $2086 per semester for Idaho residents, with an additional $4010 per semester for nonresidents. Resident students enrolled part-time paid $205 per credit, and nonresidents paid an additional $123 per credit for part-time work. Full-time fees are charged for 8 credits or more.

Living and Housing Costs

Graduate student housing is available through the University for $462 to $684 per month for apartments ranging in size from efficiencies to four-bedroom units. Potential graduate students are advised to reserve housing early. Off-campus housing lists are available at http://www.asui.uidaho.edu.

Student Group

Currently, there are 23 graduate students in the various programs in the department. Approximately 20 percent are from outside the U.S. There are currently two part-time students enrolled. The department seeks graduate students who possess the potential to do innovative research leading to the discovery of new knowledge as well as students who desire to enhance animal agriculture. Students are interested in a variety of careers associated with animal biology.

Student Outcomes

Graduates are prepared for a variety of opportunities. M.S. degree graduates may further pursue their education in Ph.D. and doctor of veterinary medicine (D.V.M.) programs. Graduates also enter professional positions with various allied animal industries such as pharmaceutical, nutrition/feeds, assisted reproductive technologies (e.g., artificial insemination and embryo transfer), and meats-related agribusinesses, education, extension, and other government agencies.

Location

Moscow, located in the Idaho panhandle among the rolling hills of the Palouse, is an agricultural and recreational area and is the cultural center of the region. Local music and theater productions have received international acclaim. Skiing and lake and river sports are within easy drives. Spokane is 88 miles north, and Seattle and Portland are each 6 hours west.

The Department

The Department of Animal and Veterinary Science has a proud tradition of training graduate students. Faculty members have received many recent teaching, advising, and research awards. Faculty members take great pride in preparing students for their professional careers and offer a great deal of individualized instruction and mentoring to students enrolled in the program.

Applying

Candidates are required to submit three letters of recommendation and a cover letter stating their career goals and experience in addition to the standard application. A minimum of a 3.0 grade point average is required for full acceptance with an assistantship. Provisional acceptance, temporarily without funding, is available. Applications are evaluated in March for the fall semester and October for the spring semester.

Students applying for a departmental assistantship should consult with the department regarding the process and the deadline date, which may be earlier than the other application deadlines.

Correspondence and Information

For program and application information, students may contact:

Mark A. McGuire, Chair, Graduate Committee
P.O. Box 442330
Department of Animal and Veterinary Science
College of Agricultural and Life Sciences
University of Idaho
Moscow, Idaho 83844-2330
Telephone: 208-885-7683
Fax: 208-885-7036
E-mail: mmcguire@uidaho.edu
World Wide Web: http://www.avs.uidaho.edu/

University of Idaho

THE FACULTY AND THEIR RESEARCH

Amin Ahmadzadeh, Assistant Professor; Ph.D., Virginia Tech, 1998. Dairy science, dairy management, animal reproduction.
Bruce C. Anderson, Professor; D.V.M., 1965, Ph.D., 1977, California, Davis. Veterinary pathology, parasitology.
Richard A. Battaglia, Professor and Department Head; Ph.D., Virginia Tech, 1969. Animal production.
Marie S. Bulgin, Professor; D.V.M., California, Davis, 1967. Veterinary microbiology, small ruminant management.
Joseph C. Dalton, Assistant Professor; Ph.D., Virginia Tech, 1999. Dairy management, animal reproduction.
James J. England, Professor; Ph.D., 1972, D.V.M., 1981, Colorado State. Virology, beef production medicine, diagnostic testing.
J. Benton Glaze Jr., Assistant Professor; Ph.D., Kansas State, 1998. Beef cattle management, animal breeding and genetics, range-livestock management.
Ronald W. Hardy, Professor; Ph.D., Washington (Seattle), 1978. Aquaculture, fish nutrition, nutrient management.
Rodney A. Hill, Assistant Professor; Ph.D., Central Queensland (Australia), 1995. Growth biology, muscle biology, endocrine control of growth.
Alex N. Hristov, Assistant Professor; Ph.D., Academy of Agricultural Sciences (Bulgaria), 1992. Ruminant nutrition, dairy cattle nutrition, impact of nutrients on the environment.
Carl W. Hunt, Professor; Ph.D., Missouri–Columbia, 1984. Ruminant nutrition, forage quality and utilization, beef cattle management.
Mark A. McGuire, Associate Professor; Ph.D., Cornell, 1994. Lactational physiology, nutrient partitioning, milk composition, nutrition, role of animal products in the human diet.
John Miller, Professor; Ph.D., Penn State, 1968. Meats.
Patrick A. Momont, Professor; Ph.D., South Dakota State, 1990. Beef cattle management, profit and sustainability, range cow nutrition.
Richard J. Norell, Professor; Ph.D., Minnesota, 1983. Dairy management, animal behavior.
Troy L. Ott, Assistant Professor; Ph.D., Florida, 1992. Reproductive physiology, maternal recognition of pregnancy, sheep reproduction.
Madison Powell, Assistant Professor; Ph.D., Texas Tech, 1995. Fish genetics, conservation genetics, aquaculture.
Dirk K. Vanderwall, Assistant Professor; D.V.M., Cornell, 1986; Ph.D., Idaho, 1992. Equine reproductive physiology.
Gordon L. Woods, Professor; D.V.M., Colorado State, 1978; Ph.D., Wisconsin, 1983. Equine reproductive physiology.

UNIVERSITY OF IDAHO

Department of Food Science and Toxicology

Program of Study

The Department of Food Science and Toxicology offers the M.S. and Ph.D. degrees in food science. Faculty members also advise students in the environmental science graduate program. The M.S. program in food science requires a minimum of 30 semester credits, including 20–24 credits in course work and a thesis. Ph.D. students take 78 credits beyond the B.S. degree and prepare a dissertation describing an original research project. Credits taken in an M.S. program may be applied toward the Ph.D. program with the consent of the student's advisory committee. Formal course work is taken in the department and in related scientific and engineering areas. Programs of study are designed to meet the individual needs of each student. Students with bachelor's degrees in food science, chemistry, microbiology, biochemistry, engineering, nutrition, and related areas are encouraged to apply.

Areas of research emphasis include food chemistry, food biotechnology, food safety, food engineering, and food and environmental toxicology. Departmental research programs include genetic/metabolic engineering of microorganisms, such as lactic acid bacteria, to make valuable products from renewable biomass feedstocks; development of new processes and technologies to improve the microbial safety of foods; investigations into mechanism(s) of action of food-borne anti-toxicants that may improve human health or reduce chronic human disease; investigation of soft wheat and potato quality, functionality, and end-use potential; assessment of starch behavior and function in food processing operations; investigation of the physicochemical and functional properties of dairy and meat protein ingredients; utilization of novel protein and starch ingredients in food systems; Fickian and non-Fickian transport in porous biopolymeric systems; stress-crack prediction in food materials and controlled release of drugs and flavors; and examination of natural and engineered processes in the characterization, fate, transport, and control of environmental and food system contaminants.

Research Facilities

The department faculty is housed in the Agricultural Sciences Building, Holm Research Center, and the Agricultural Biotechnology Building. Well-equipped laboratories are available for chemical, microbiological, molecular biological, and immunological research. The department oversees the Analytical Science Laboratory, a full GLP service laboratory for the state of Idaho with state-of-the-art equipment. Department researchers have access to the Laboratory Animal Research Facility, the Electron Microscopy Center, and the Meat Laboratory in the Department of Animal and Veterinary Sciences. The Department of Food Science and Toxicology and the Department of Food Science and Human Nutrition at Washington State University have a cooperative program in food science that allows graduate students to participate in a joint curriculum, with access to research facilities at both institutions. University of Idaho students also interact with faculty members at Washington State University, allowing for a more diverse education.

Financial Aid

Graduate teaching and research assistantships, from the Department of Food Science and Toxicology and faculty grants and contracts, are available to qualified applicants. Approximately 60 percent of graduate students in the department receive assistantships and pay in-state fees. Financial aid is also available through the Federal Perkins Loan Program and work-study grants. The Student Financial Aid Office can provide information and applications.

Cost of Study

For 2004–05, full-time graduate fees were $2086 per semester for Idaho residents; nonresidents paid an additional $4010 per semester. Resident students enrolled part-time paid $205 per credit; nonresidents paid an additional $123 per credit for part-time study. Full-time fees are charged for 8 credits or more.

Living and Housing Costs

Graduate student housing is available through the University for $462 to $684 per month for apartments that range in size from efficiencies to four-bedroom units. Graduate students are advised to reserve housing early. Off-campus housing lists are available at http://www.asui.uidaho.edu.

Student Group

The University of Idaho enrolls about 12,000 students, including 2,200 graduate students from eighty-two countries. The department enrolls 15–20 graduate students with diverse educational backgrounds and academic interests.

Student Outcomes

Demand for food science graduates is high. Recent graduates have found employment with major food companies, such as H. J. Heinz, J. R. Simplot, Lamb Weston, Kraft Foods, and Land O'Lakes. Students also find employment with federal agencies, such as the Food and Drug Administration (FDA) and the United States Department of Agriculture. Many M.S. graduates continue on for a Ph.D. in preparation for a career in academia.

Location

Moscow, located in the Idaho panhandle among the rolling hills of the Palouse, is an agricultural and recreational area and is the cultural center of the region. Local music and theater productions have received international acclaim. Skiing and lake and river sports are within easy drives. Spokane is 88 miles north, and Seattle and Portland are each 6 hours west.

The Department

The Department of Food Science and Toxicology is dynamic, rapidly growing department, staffed with energetic, young faculty members. Local professional development activities are sponsored by regional sections of the Institute of Food Technologists (IFT), including the Intermountain Section and the Lewis and Clark Section. Faculty members and graduate students also participate in national activities of the IFT. Students are encouraged to join other professional societies that are appropriate to their field of study, including the American Association of Cereal Chemists, American Society for Microbiology, and the Society of Toxicology.

Applying

In addition to admission requirements of the College of Graduate Studies, admission to the graduate program in food science requires a minimum GPA of 2.8, satisfactory performance on the GRE, a letter outlining research interests and career goals, and three letters of recommendation. International applicants must achieve scores of 550 or better on the TOEFL. Prospective students are encouraged to contact the department or individual faculty members to learn more about specific research opportunities.

Students applying for a departmental assistantship should consult with the department regarding the process and the deadline date, which may be earlier than the other application deadlines.

Correspondence and Information

For program information:

Dr. Denise M. Smith, Department Head
Department of Food Science and Toxicology
University of Idaho
P.O. Box 442312
Moscow, Idaho 83844-2312

Telephone: 208-885-7081
Fax: 208-885-8937
E-mail: fstasl@uidaho.edu
World Wide Web: http://www.ag.uidaho.edu/fst

University of Idaho

THE FACULTY AND THEIR RESEARCH

Jeffry D. Culbertson, Professor; Ph.D., Washington State, 1985. Food safety and quality, food processing, distance education in food science.
Jerry H. Exon, Professor; Ph.D., Idaho, 1984. Immunotoxicology, chemical food safety, anticarcinogens in natural products, carcinogenesis.
Kerry C. Huber, Associate Professor; Ph.D., Purdue, 1998. Food chemistry, starch chemistry, quality of wheat and potato products.
Gregory Möller, Associate Professor; Ph.D., California, Davis, 1985. Environmental chemistry and toxicology, biogeochemistry of selenium and arsenic, analytical chemistry, water/wastewater treatment.
Pawan P. Singh, Assistant Professor; Ph.D., Purdue, 2002. Food process engineering, food rheology, transport in biopolymeric materials, thermodynamics and heat transfer, applied mathematics.
Denise M. Smith, Professor and Head; Ph.D., Washington State, 1985. Food chemistry, food safety, meat product processing, safety and quality, protein chemistry and functionality.
Patricia A. Talcott, Associate Professor; Ph.D., Idaho, 1989. Veterinary diagnostic toxicology, immunotoxicology, food safety.
Gülhan Ünlu Yüksel, Assistant Professor; Ph.D., Wisconsin, 1998. Food microbiology, food safety, genetic and metabolic engineering of lactic acid bacteria, utilization of food and agricultural processing waste to add value, food-borne pathogens.

UNIVERSITY OF IDAHO

Department of Plant, Soil, and Entomological Sciences

Programs of Study

Plant, Soil, and Entomological Sciences (PSES) is a large and diverse department at the University of Idaho (UI) with faculty members organized into four divisions: crop and weed science, entomology, horticulture, and soil and land resources. All four divisions conduct teaching, research, and extension programs. The combined departments offer M.S. and Ph.D. degrees in plant science, soils, and entomology.

Program coordination among divisions and interdisciplinary approaches to problems are encouraged. Areas of student specialization include plant breeding and genetics, integrated pest management, precision crop management, postharvest physiology, ornamental horticulture, and environmental science.

Research Facilities

Research facilities at Moscow, Idaho, include twenty-five research laboratories; ten teaching labs; two research farms; 16,500 square feet of greenhouse space, including newly renovated, state-of-the-art laboratory units and growth chambers; and a 2-million-specimen entomological museum. The University has 1,145 acres for field crops, orchards, and livestock located close to campus. Excellent field and laboratory facilities are also available at research and extension centers at Aberdeen, Parma, and Twin Falls, Idaho. In addition, the graduate program is closely coordinated with the Departments of Entomology, Crop, and Soil Sciences; Horticulture and Landscape Architecture; and Plant Pathology at Washington State University.

Financial Aid

The department has fourteen allocated assistantships for graduate student support. Research assistantships supported by grant funds are offered as available. Ph.D. students receive funding for three years; master's degree students receive funding for two years. Part-time students are not eligible for assistantship funding. Financial aid is also available through the Federal Perkins Loan Program and work-study grants. The Student Financial Aid Office can provide information and applications.

Cost of Study

For 2004–05, full-time graduate fees are $2086 per semester for Idaho residents, with an additional fee of $4010 per semester for nonresidents. Resident students enrolled part-time paid $205 per credit; nonresidents paid an additional $123 per credit for part-time study. Nonresidents are not charged any additional fee for credits earned during the summer session. Full-time fees are charged for 8 credits or more. Fees are subject to change.

Living and Housing Costs

Graduate student housing is available through the University for $346 to $629 per month for apartments ranging in size from efficiencies to four-bedroom units. Potential graduate students are advised to reserve housing early. Off-campus housing lists are available on the Web at http://www.asui.uidaho.edu.

Student Group

Currently, there are 75 graduate students in the combined departments, with 25 percent from outside the United States. The department seeks graduate students who possess the potential to do independent and innovative research, leading to the discovery of new knowledge. Most students enter the program with the intent to enter a career in scientific research.

Student Outcomes

Graduate students seek positions in academia or industry. In the past five years, students have gone on to positions as scientists in government, education, or private institutions. Others have gone on to positions in merchandising, marketing, and private firms.

Location

Moscow is located in the Idaho panhandle among the rolling hills of the Palouse. It is an agricultural and recreational area and is the cultural center of the region. Local music and theater productions have received international acclaim. Skiing and lake and river sports are within easy drives. Spokane is 88 miles north, and Seattle and Portland are each 6 hours west.

The University

The University of Idaho was created in 1889, a year before Idaho became a state. UI is a publicly supported, comprehensive land-grant institution with principal responsibility in Idaho for performing research and granting the Ph.D. degree. More than 750 faculty members participate in teaching and research. In addition to the accreditation of individual programs, the University is accredited by the Northwest Commission on Colleges and Universities.

Applying

Applications, accepted throughout the year, are available from the department, from the University of Idaho Graduate Admissions Office, and online at http://www.uidaho.edu/cogs. Deadlines for domestic applications are July 1 for the fall semester, November 1 for the spring semester, and April 1 for the summer session. The deadlines are earlier for international applicants. Students applying for departmental assistantships must consult with the department regarding the process and deadline date, which may be earlier than the application deadline date. Application materials, official GRE scores, letters of recommendation, resume or CV, and a letter of intent should be sent directly to the Office of Graduate Admissions. Nonnative speakers of English must submit TOEFL scores with a minimum of 550 on the paper-based test or 213 on the computer-based test.

Correspondence and Information

Sonia Todd, Academic Assistant
Department of Plant, Soil, and Entomological Studies
University of Idaho
P.O. Box 442339
Moscow, Idaho 83844-2339
Telephone: 208-885-6930
Fax: 208-885-7760
E-mail: soniat@uidaho.edu
World Wide Web: http://www.ag.uidaho.edu/pses/

University of Idaho

THE FACULTY AND THEIR RESEARCH

Juan M. Alvarez, Assistant Professor of Entomology; Ph.D., Florida. IPM of cereal and potato pests.
James D. Barbour, Assistant Professor; Ph.D., North Carolina State. Insect-plant interactions, host-plant resistance and integrated pest management.
Danny L. Barney, Professor; Ph.D., Cornell. Production of small fruits, native plants as potential commercial alternative crops.
Edward J. Bechinski, Professor; Ph.D., Iowa State. Pest management and scouting tools, alternatives to traditional pesticides.
Nilsa A. Bosque-Pérez, Associate Professor; Ph.D., California, Davis. Host plant resistance to insects, insect vectors of plant pathogens, tritrophic interactions, pest management.
Bradford D. Brown, Associate Professor; Ph.D., Utah State. Soil fertility and plant nutrition, soil and plant tests for predicting irrigated crop nutrient requirements.
Jack Brown, Professor; Ph.D., St. Andrews (Scotland). Brassica crop cultivars.
Wesley W. C. Chun, Associate Professor; Ph.D., California, Riverside. Plant bacterial diseases, biological control, host range and pathogenicity determinants of phytopathogenic bacteria, seed pathology.
Sanford Eigenbrode, Associate Professor; Ph.D., Cornell. Chemical ecology of insects, plant-insect interactions, tritrophic interactions, insect behavior, plant surface waxes.
Jason Ellsworth, Assistant Professor; Ph.D., Iowa State. Nutrient management practices pertaining to southern Idaho growers.
Esmaeil Fallahi, Professor; Ph.D., Oregon State. Preharvest environmental and physiological factors influencing quality, yield, and postharvest physiology of pome and stone fruit.
John J. Gallian, Associate Professor; Ph.D., Oregon State. Sugar beets, improved stand establishment, disease etiology and control.
Stephen O. Guy, Professor; Ph.D., Wisconsin–Madison. Cereal and brassica crop management investigating practices in northern Idaho.
Saad L. Hafez, Professor; Ph.D., California, Davis. Biological control of and resistance to nematodes.
Bryan G. Hopkins, Assistant Professor; Ph.D., Kansas State. Fertilizer, irrigation, and tillage management in potato rotations.
Pamela Hutchinson, Assistant Professor; Ph.D., Nebraska. Potato cropping systems and weed biology, weed control, herbicide, and biopesticide environmental fate.
James B. "Ding" Johnson, Professor and Chair, Division of Entomology, and Interim Department Head; Ph.D., Berkeley. Aquatic entomology, biological control of aphids, taxonomy of green lacewings.
Jodi Johnson-Maynard, Associate Professor; Ph.D., California, Riverside. Residue management, soil and water quality, biogeochemical cycling in forested and agricultural environments.
Marc J. Klowden, Professor; Ph.D., Illinois. Endocrinology of insect behavior and reproduction, general entomology, insect reproduction, anatomy and physiology.
Guy R. Knudsen, Professor; Ph.D., Cornell. Soil-borne plant pathogens, soil microbiology and bioremediation of soil pollutants, genetically engineered microorganisms, fungal epizootics and insect pests.
John Lloyd, Assistant Professor; Ph.D., Ohio State. Functional ecology in ornamental landscapes.
Jim Lorenzen, Associate Professor; Ph.D., Cornell. Potato molecular biology, mechanisms of plant defense, multiple defense mechanisms in individual genotypes, molecular tools and target genes.
Stephen L. Love, Professor and Superintendent, Aberdeen R&E Center; Ph.D., Clemson. Potato germplasm.
Robert L. Mahler, Professor; Ph.D., North Carolina State. Soil-plant relationships, crop response to fertilizer placement, fertilizer biotechnology, cereal crops.
Joseph P. McCaffrey, Professor; Ph.D., Virginia Tech. Biologically based pest management systems for rapeseed, canola, and mustard; cabbage seedpod weevil.
Paul A. McDaniel, Professor; Ph.D., North Carolina State. Wind-blown materials and Idaho soils, volcanic ash and northern and central Idaho soils, wind-deposited soil parent materials of the Palouse region and upper Snake River Plain.
Jeff Miller, Assistant Professor; Ph.D., Washington State. Production and storage diseases of potatoes, developing and delivering technical information on potato diseases to Idaho potato growers.
S. Krishna Mohan, Professor; Ph.D., Indian Agricultural Research Institute. Diseases of vegetable, seed, and fruit crops.
Don W. Morishita, Professor; Ph.D., Idaho. Weed biology and management of sugar beets and small-grain cereals.
Matthew J. Morra, Professor and Chair, Division of Soil and Land Resources; Ph.D., Ohio State. Natural and synthetic organic compounds in the soil environment, chemical ecology, sulfur biogeochemistry, metal contaminants in lake ecosystems.
Thomas M. Mowry, Associate Professor; Ph.D., Michigan State. Insect vector-plant-plant pathogen interactions, disease modification of infected plants, plant viruses.
Phillip Nolte, Professor; Ph.D., North Dakota State. Seed potato production and health management.
Nora L. Olsen, Assistant Professor; Ph.D., Washington State. Seed potato production, quality and performance, potato late blight management, potato storage management.
Timothy S. Prather, Associate Professor; Ph.D., Idaho. Invasive plants, IPM techniques for management of native communities.
Mark Schwarzlaender, Assistant Professor; Ph.D., Kiel (Germany). Biological control of weeds, insect-plant interactions, specialist herbivore insect species and host plants, weeds and insect herbivore and plant competition, nontarget effects of biological control agents.
Bahman Shafii, Professor of Plant Science and Director of Statistical Programs; Ph.D., Idaho. Biometrics, ecological modeling, plant competition, Bayesian statistics.
Glenn E. Shewmaker, Assistant Professor; Ph.D., Utah State. Forage management and utilization, alfalfa and grass forage quality, intensive pasture grazing systems, nutrient management planning, environmental effects of grazing.
Shree P. Singh, Professor; Ph.D., Wisconsin. Genetics and plant breeding in production of superior dry bean germplasm and cultivars.
Edward J. Souza, Professor; Ph.D., Cornell. Development of winter wheats for southern Idaho and spring wheats for all of Idaho.
Jeffrey C. Stark, Professor and Chair, Division of Horticulture; Ph.D., California, Riverside. Water and nutrient management in irrigated cropping systems.
Robert L. Stoltz, Professor; Ph.D., California, Riverside. Crops and livestock, sampling methods, economic thresholds, beneficial insects, insect-plant interactions, sustainable agriculture.
Carl Strausbaugh, Acting Assistant Professor; Ph.D., Washington State. Plant pathogen management.
Daniel G. Strawn, Assistant Professor; Ph.D., Delaware. Contaminant and nutrient sorption and desorption in soils and soil materials.
Donald C. Thill, Professor and Chair, Division of Crops and Weed Science; Ph.D., Oregon State. Weed biology, integrated weed control practices for small-grain production systems, herbicide resistance in weeds and crops.
Michael Thornton, Associate Professor and Superintendent, Southwest Idaho Research and Extension Centers; Ph.D., Idaho. Potato physiology, with emphasis on plant growth and development as impacted by crop production practices.
Robert R. Tripepi, Professor; Ph.D., Purdue. Woody plants and in-shoot regeneration, genetic engineering, and use of herbaceous waste or by-products.
Markus Tuller, Assistant Professor; Ph.D., Vienna University of Agricultural Sciences. Flow and transport in porous media, engineered plant growth media under microgravity, flow and stability of granular materials, infiltration and runoff from frozen soil.
Michael J. Weiss, Professor; Ph.D., Nebraska. Integrated pest management and applied insect ecology.
Linda Wilson, Adjunct Assistant Professor and Research Scientist; Ph.D., Idaho. Ecology of invasive plant species, with emphasis on classical biological control.
Robert S. Zemetra, Professor; Ph.D., Colorado State. New wheat cultivars for Idaho and the Pacific Northwest.

ACADEMIC AND PROFESSIONAL PROGRAMS IN THE ENVIRONMENT AND NATURAL RESOURCES

Section 9
Environmental Sciences and Management

This section contains a directory of institutions offering graduate work in environmental sciences and management, followed by in-depth entries submitted by institutions that chose to prepare detailed program descriptions. Additional information about programs listed in the directory but not augmented by an in-depth entry may be obtained by writing directly to the dean of a graduate school or chair of a department at the address given in the directory.

For programs offering related work, see also in this book Natural Resources; in Book 2, see Political Science and International Affairs and Public, Regional, and Industrial Affairs; in Book 3, see Ecology, Environmental Biology, and Evolutionary Biology; and in Book 5, see Management of Engineering and Technology.

CONTENTS

Environmental Management and Policy

Adelphi University, Graduate School of Arts and Sciences, Program in Environmental Studies, Garden City, NY 11530. Offers MS. *Faculty:* 1 full-time (0 women). *Students:* 2 full-time (1 woman), 8 part-time (4 women); includes 1 minority (Hispanic American) Average age 29. *Degree requirements:* For master's, thesis optional. *Entrance requirements:* For master's, GRE, 3 letters of recommendation, courses in microeconomics, political science, statistics, calculus, and either chemistry or physics. Additional exam requirements/recommendations for international students: Required—TOEFL (minimum score 550 paper-based; 213 computer-based). Application fee: $50. *Expenses:* Tuition: Full-time $19,550; part-time $590 per credit hour. Required fees: $700; $200 per semester. *Financial support:* Teaching assistantships available. Financial award application deadline: 2/15; financial award applicants required to submit FAFSA. *Unit head:* Dr. Anagnostis Agelarakis, Director, 516-877-4170, E-mail: agelorak@adelphi.edu. *Application contact:* Christine Murphy, Director of Admissions, 516-877-3050, Fax: 516-877-3039, E-mail: admissions@adelphi.edu.

Air Force Institute of Technology, Graduate School of Engineering and Management, Department of Systems and Engineering Management, Dayton, OH 45433-7765. Offers environmental and engineering management (MS); information resource management (MS); systems acquisition management (MS). Part-time programs available. *Degree requirements:* For master's, thesis. *Entrance requirements:* For master's, GRE, GMAT, minimum GPA of 3.0.

American University, College of Arts and Sciences, Department of Biology, Environmental Science Program, Washington, DC 20016-8001. Offers MS. *Students:* 8 full-time (7 women), 1 part-time; includes 1 minority (Asian American or Pacific Islander), 1 international. Average age 24. In 2003, 7 degrees awarded. *Degree requirements:* For master's, thesis or alternative, comprehensive exam. *Entrance requirements:* For master's, GRE General Test, GRE Subject Test, minimum GPA of 3.0. Additional exam requirements/recommendations for international students: Required—TOEFL. *Application deadline:* For fall admission, 2/1 for domestic students; for spring admission, 10/1 for domestic students. Application fee: $50. *Expenses:* Tuition: Full-time $15,786; part-time $877 per credit hour. Required fees: $300. Tuition and fees vary according to course load and program. *Financial support:* Research assistantships, teaching assistantships available. Financial award application deadline: 2/1. *Unit head:* Dr. David Culver, Director, 202-885-2176, Fax: 202-885-2182.

American University, School of International Service, Washington, DC 20016-8001. Offers comparative and regional studies (MA); cross-cultural communication (Certificate); development management (MS); environmental policy (MA); ethics and peace (MA); global environmental policy (MA); international communication (MA); international development (MA); international development management (Certificate); international economic policy (MA); international economic relations (Certificate); international peace and conflict resolution (MA); international politics (MA); international relations (PhD); international service (MIS); the Americas (Certificate); U.S. foreign policy (MA). Part-time and evening/weekend programs available. *Faculty:* 59 full-time (23 women), 42 part-time/adjunct (17 women). *Students:* 582 full-time (371 women), 292 part-time (189 women); includes 85 minority (31 African Americans, 2 American Indian/Alaska Native, 23 Asian Americans or Pacific Islanders, 29 Hispanic Americans), 130 international. Average age 26. 1,923 applicants, 66% accepted, 361 enrolled. In 2003, 249 master's, 8 doctorates awarded. Terminal master's awarded for partial completion of doctoral program. *Degree requirements:* For master's, one foreign language, thesis or alternative, comprehensive exam; for doctorate, one foreign language, thesis/dissertation, comprehensive exam. *Entrance requirements:* For master's, GRE General Test, 24 credits in related social sciences, minimum of 3.3; 2 letter of recommendations; for doctorate, GRE General Test, 2 letters of recommendations; 24 credits in related social sciences. Additional exam requirements/recommendations for international students: Required—TOEFL (minimum score 550 paper-based; 213 computer-based). *Application deadline:* For fall admission, 1/15 for domestic students; for spring admission, 10/1 priority date for domestic students. Applications are processed on a rolling basis. Application fee: $50. *Expenses:* Tuition: Full-time $15,786; part-time $877 per credit hour. Required fees: $300. Tuition and fees vary according to course load and program. *Financial support:* Career-related internships or fieldwork, Federal Work-Study, and institutionally sponsored loans available. Financial award application deadline: 1/15. *Faculty research:* International intellectual property, international environmental issues, international law and legal order, international telecommunications/technology, international sustainable development. *Unit head:* Dr. Louis W. Goodman, Dean, 202-885-1600, Fax: 202-885-2494. *Application contact:* Amanda Taylor, Director of Graduate Admissions and Financial Aid, 202-885-1599, Fax: 202-885-2494.

Antioch New England Graduate School, Graduate School, Department of Environmental Studies, Doctoral Program in Environmental Studies, Keene, NH 03431-3552. Offers PhD. *Faculty:* 4 full-time (2 women), 2 part-time/adjunct (both women). *Students:* 38 full-time (27 women), 15 part-time (9 women); includes 2 minority (1 Asian American or Pacific Islander, 1 Hispanic American), 1 international. Average age 41. 22 applicants, 86% accepted. In 2003, 4 degrees awarded. *Degree requirements:* For doctorate, thesis/dissertation, practicum. *Entrance requirements:* For doctorate, master's degree and previous experience in the environmental field. *Application deadline:* For fall admission, 2/1 for domestic students. Application fee: $75. *Expenses:* Tuition: Part-time $5,650 per semester. *Financial support:* In 2003–04, 31 students received support, including 2 fellowships (averaging $8,450 per year), 3 research assistantships (averaging $1,551 per year), 2 teaching assistantships (averaging $488 per year); Federal Work-Study and scholarships/grants also available. *Faculty research:* Environmental history, green politics, ecopsychology. *Unit head:* Dr. Beth Kaplin, Head, 603-357-3122 Ext. 238. *Application contact:* Leatrice A. Johnson, Director of Admissions, 603-357-6265 Ext. 287, Fax: 603-357-0718, E-mail: ljohnson@antiochne.edu.

Antioch New England Graduate School, Graduate School, Department of Environmental Studies, Program in Environmental Studies, Keene, NH 03431-3552. Offers conservation biology (MS); environmental advocacy (MS); environmental education (MS); teacher certification in biology (7th-12th grade) (MS); teacher certification in general science (5th-9th grade) (MS). *Faculty:* 12 full-time (5 women), 10 part-time/adjunct (3 women). *Students:* 119 full-time (78 women), 19 part-time (13 women); includes 2 minority (1 American Indian/Alaska Native, 1 Hispanic American). Average age 31. 120 applicants, 78% accepted. In 2003, 51 degrees awarded. *Degree requirements:* For master's, practicum. *Entrance requirements:* For master's, previous undergraduate course work in biology, chemistry, mathematics (environmental biology). *Application deadline:* For fall admission, 8/1 for domestic students. Applications are processed on a rolling basis. Application fee: $40. *Expenses:* Tuition: Part-time $5,650 per semester. *Financial support:* In 2003–04, 114 students received support, including 2 fellowships (averaging $750 per year), 5 research assistantships (averaging $795 per year), 4 teaching assistantships (averaging $598 per year); Federal Work-Study and scholarships/grants also available. Financial award applicants required to submit FAFSA. *Faculty research:* Sustainability, natural resources inventory. *Unit head:* Dr. Jimmy Karlan, Academic Director, 603-357-3122 Ext. 329, Fax: 603-357-0718, E-mail: jkarlan@antiochne.edu. *Application contact:* Leatrice A. Johnson, Director of Admissions, 603-357-6265 Ext. 287, Fax: 603-357-0718, E-mail: ljohnson@antiochne.edu.

Announcement: Master of Science in environmental studies with a concentration in environmental advocacy and organizing is a one-of-a-kind master's program that prepares students for careers as environmental activists. This 2-year, 50-credit program emphasizes ecological literacy, political analysis, organization building, personal transformation, and social action.

Antioch New England Graduate School, Graduate School, Department of Environmental Studies, Program in Resource Management and Administration, Keene, NH 03431-3552. Offers MS. *Faculty:* 12 full-time (5 women), 10 part-time/adjunct (3 women). *Students:* 35 full-time (24 women), 4 part-time (1 woman); includes 1 minority (African American) Average age 31. 23 applicants, 91% accepted. In 2003, 13 degrees awarded. *Degree requirements:* For master's, practicum, thesis optional. *Entrance requirements:* For master's, previous undergraduate course work in science and math. *Application deadline:* For fall admission, 8/1 for domestic students. Applications are processed on a rolling basis. Application fee: $40. *Expenses:* Tuition: Part-time $5,650 per semester. *Financial support:* In 2003–04, 26 students received support. Federal Work-Study and scholarships/grants available. Financial award applicants required to submit FAFSA. *Faculty research:* Waste management, land use. *Unit head:* Michael Simpson, Co-Director, 603-357-3122 Ext. 252, Fax: 603-357-0718, E-mail: msimpson@antiochne.edu. *Application contact:* Leatrice A. Johnson, Director of Admissions, 603-357-6265 Ext. 287, Fax: 603-357-0718, E-mail: ljohnson@antiochne.edu.

Announcement: The Master of Science in Resource Management and Administration Program provides practice-oriented training in environmental policy, science, and organizational management. The program prepares individuals for leadership in organizations that manage, conserve, and restore natural systems and trains professionals to understand environmental issues while working effectively to implement change within organizational settings.

Antioch University Seattle, Graduate Programs, Center for Creative Change, Seattle, WA 98121-1814. Offers environment and community (MA); management (MS); organizational psychology (MA); whole system design (MA). Evening/weekend programs available. Expenses: Contact institution.

Arizona State University East, Morrison School of Agribusiness and Resource Management, Mesa, AZ 85212. Offers agribusiness (MS); environmental resources (MS). Part-time and evening/weekend programs available. *Faculty:* 12 full-time (1 woman). *Students:* 12 full-time (5 women), 18 part-time (7 women); includes 2 minority (1 American Indian/Alaska Native, 1 Hispanic American), 8 international. Average age 34. 27 applicants, 59% accepted, 6 enrolled. In 2003, 14 degrees awarded. *Median time to degree:* Master's–1.9 years full-time, 3.2 years part-time. *Degree requirements:* For master's, thesis, oral defense. *Entrance requirements:* For master's, GMAT, GRE General Test, MAT, minimum GPA of 3.0, 3 letters of recommendation, resumé. Additional exam requirements/recommendations for international students: Required—TOEFL (minimum score 550 paper-based; 213 computer-based); Recommended—TWE, TSE. *Application deadline:* Applications are processed on a rolling basis. Application fee: $50. Electronic applications accepted. *Expenses:* Tuition, state resident: full-time $3,708; part-time $194 per credit hour. Tuition, nonresident: full-time $12,228; part-time $510 per credit hour. Required fees: $37. Tuition and fees vary according to course load and program. *Financial support:* In 2003–04, 11 research assistantships with partial tuition reimbursements (averaging $4,415 per year), 1 teaching assistantship with partial tuition reimbursement (averaging $8,405 per year) were awarded. Fellowships, career-related internships or fieldwork, Federal Work-Study, institutionally sponsored loans, scholarships/grants, health care benefits, and tuition waivers (full and partial) also available. Support available to part-time students. Financial award application deadline: 3/1; financial award applicants required to submit CSS PROFILE or FAFSA. *Faculty research:* Agribusiness marketing, management and financial structuring. Total annual research expenditures: $1 million. *Unit head:* Dr. Raymond Marquardt, Dean, 480-727-1585, Fax: 480-727-1961, E-mail: ray.marquardt@asu.edu.

Bard College, Bard Center for Environmental Policy, Annandale-on-Hudson, NY 12504. Offers MS, Professional Certificate, MS/JD, MS/MA. Masters international is offered with the Peace Corps. Part-time programs available. *Faculty:* 5 full-time (3 women), 14 part-time/adjunct (7 women). *Students:* 36 full-time. Average age 28. *Degree requirements:* For master's, thesis, internship within U.S. or abroad, master's project. *Entrance requirements:* For master's, GRE (if out of school more than 5 years), statement, written work, curriculum vitae, transcripts, letters of recommendations (3); for Professional Certificate, statement, written work, curriculum vitae, transcripts, letters of recommendations (3). Additional exam requirements/recommendations for international students: Required—TOEFL. *Application deadline:* For fall admission, 1/15 priority date for domestic students, 1/15 priority date for international students. Applications are processed on a rolling basis. Application fee: $50. *Expenses:* Contact institution. *Financial support:* In 2003–04, 10 students received support, including 6 fellowships (averaging $6,000 per year); scholarships/grants also available. Financial award application deadline: 2/15; financial award applicants required to submit FAFSA. *Faculty research:* Agricultural practices, fisheries management, international agreements, decision making under uncertainty, energy. *Unit head:* Dr. Joanne Fox-Przeworski, Director, 845-758-7071, Fax: 845-758-7636, E-mail: jfp@bard.edu. *Application contact:* Jacqui Burke, Assistant to the Director, 845-758-7073, Fax: 845-758-7636, E-mail: cep@bard.edu.

See in-depth description on page 721.

Baylor University, Graduate School, College of Arts and Sciences, Department of Environmental Studies, Waco, TX 76798. Offers MES, MS. *Students:* 17 full-time (12 women), 4 part-time (all women), 3 international. In 2003, 6 degrees awarded. *Degree requirements:* For master's, thesis. *Entrance requirements:* For master's, GRE General Test. *Application deadline:* For fall admission, 8/1 for domestic students; for spring admission, 1/1 for domestic students. Applications are processed on a rolling basis. Application fee: $25. *Expenses:* Tuition: Part-time $698 per hour. *Financial support:* Research assistantships, teaching assistantships, career-related internships or fieldwork, Federal Work-Study, and institutionally sponsored loans available. *Faculty research:* Renewable energy/waste management policies, Third World environmental problem solving, ecotourism. *Unit head:* Dr. Susan Bratton, Graduate Program Director, 254-710-3405, Fax: 254-710-3409. *Application contact:* Suzanne Keener, Administrative Assistant, 254-710-3588, Fax: 254-710-3870, E-mail: pauline_johnson@baylor.edu.

Bemidji State University, Graduate Studies, College of Social and Natural Sciences, Center for Environmental Studies, Bemidji, MN 56601-2699. Offers MS. Part-time programs available. *Faculty:* 4 part-time/adjunct (0 women). *Students:* 5 full-time (3 women), 1 (woman) part-time. Average age 28. *Degree requirements:* For master's, thesis or alternative. *Entrance requirements:* For master's, GRE General Test. *Application deadline:* For fall admission, 5/1 for domestic students. Applications are processed on a rolling basis. Application fee: $20. Electronic applications accepted. *Expenses:* Tuition, state resident: part-time $217 per credit. Tuition, nonresident: part-time $344 per credit. Required fees: $7 per credit. $245 per semester. *Financial support:* In 2003–04, 1 research assistantship with partial tuition reimbursement (averaging $8,000 per year) was awarded; career-related internships or fieldwork, Federal Work-Study, scholarships/grants, and unspecified assistantships also available. Support available to part-time students. Financial award application deadline: 5/1. *Unit head:* Dr. Fu-Hsian Chang, Director, 218-755-4104, Fax: 218-755-4107.

Boise State University, Graduate College, College of Social Science and Public Affairs, Program in Public Policy and Administration, Boise, ID 83725. Offers environmental and natural resources policy and administration (MPA); general public administration (MPA); state and local government policy and administration (MPA). *Accreditation:* NASPAA. Part-time programs available. *Faculty:* 11 full-time (3 women), 6 part-time/adjunct (1 woman). *Students:* 17 full-time (10 women), 53 part-time (31 women); includes 4 minority (1 African American, 3 Hispanic Americans). Average age 37. In 2003, 10 degrees awarded. *Degree requirements:* For master's, directed research project, internship. *Entrance requirements:* For master's, GRE General Test, minimum GPA of 3.0. Additional exam requirements/recommendations for international students: Required—TOEFL. *Application deadline:* For fall admission, 7/17 for domestic students; for spring admission, 12/5 priority date for domestic students. Applications are processed on a rolling basis. Application fee: $30. Electronic applications accepted. *Expenses:* Tuition, state resident: full-time $4,668. Tuition, nonresident: full-time $11,388. *Financial support:* In 2003–04, 4 students received support; research assistantships with full tuition reimbursements available, Federal Work-Study, institutionally sponsored loans, and unspecified assistantships available. Support available to part-time students. Financial award application deadline: 3/1. *Unit head:* Dr. James D. Weatherby, Chair, 208-426-4018, Fax: 208-426-4370.

Boston University, Graduate School of Arts and Sciences, Department of International Relations, Boston, MA 02215. Offers African studies (Certificate); international relations (MA); international relations and environmental policy management (MA); international relations and international communication (MA). *Students:* 69 full-time (38 women), 19 part-time (11 women); includes 10 minority (2 African Americans, 7 Asian Americans or Pacific Islanders, 1 Hispanic American), 16 international. Average age 27. 337 applicants, 64% accepted, 48 enrolled. In 2003, 35 degrees awarded. *Degree requirements:* For master's, one foreign language, thesis, comprehensive exam, registration. *Entrance requirements:* For master's, GRE General Test, 3 letters of recommendation; for Certificate, GRE General Test. Additional exam requirements/recommendations for international students: Required—TOEFL (minimum score 600 paper-based; 250 computer-based). *Application deadline:* For fall admission, 4/15 for domestic students, 4/15 for international students; for spring admission, 10/15 for domestic students, 10/15 for international students. Application fee: $60. *Expenses:* Tuition: Full-time $28,512; part-time $891 per credit hour. *Financial support:* In 2003–04, 20 students received support. Federal Work-Study, scholarships/grants, and unspecified assistantships available. Support available to part-time students. Financial award application deadline: 1/15; financial award applicants required to submit FAFSA. *Unit head:* Dr. Joachim Maitre, Chairman, 617-353-9390, Fax: 617-353-9290, E-mail: yomaitre@bu.edu. *Application contact:* Nicole Janelle, Graduate Program Administrator, 617-353-9349, Fax: 617-353-9290, E-mail: njanelle@bu.edu.

Boston University, Graduate School of Arts and Sciences, Program in Energy and Environmental Studies, Boston, MA 02215. Offers energy and environmental analysis (MA); environmental remote sensing and geographic information systems (MA); international relations and environmental policy (MA). *Students:* 15 full-time (9 women), 5 part-time (1 woman); includes 1 minority (African American), 3 international. Average age 26. 67 applicants, 69% accepted, 12 enrolled. *Degree requirements:* For master's, one foreign language, comprehensive exam, registration, research paper. *Entrance requirements:* For master's, GRE General Test, 2 letters of recommendation. Additional exam requirements/recommendations for international students: Required—TOEFL (minimum score 550 paper-based; 213 computer-based). *Application deadline:* For fall admission, 7/1 for domestic students, 7/1 for international students; for spring admission, 11/15 for domestic students, 11/15 for international students. Application fee: $60. *Expenses:* Tuition: Full-time $28,512; part-time $891 per credit hour. *Financial support:* In 2003–04, 8 students received support, including 4 research assistantships with full tuition reimbursements available (averaging $15,000 per year); fellowships, career-related internships or fieldwork and Federal Work-Study also available. Support available to part-time students. Financial award application deadline: 1/15; financial award applicants required to submit FAFSA. *Unit head:* Cutler J. Cleveland, Director, 617-353-7552, Fax: 617-353-5986, E-mail: cutler@bu.edu. *Application contact:* Alpana Roy, Administrative Assistant, 617-353-3083, Fax: 617-353-5986, E-mail: alpana@bu.edu.

Brown University, Graduate School, Center for Environmental Studies, Providence, RI 02912. Offers AM. Part-time programs available. *Faculty:* 5 full-time (3 women), 9 part-time/adjunct (4 women). *Students:* 25 full-time (16 women); includes 1 minority (Asian American or Pacific Islander), 6 international. Average age 28. 44 applicants, 55% accepted, 17 enrolled. In 2003, 10 degrees awarded. *Median time to degree:* Master's–2 years full-time. *Degree requirements:* For master's, thesis. *Entrance requirements:* For master's, GRE, writing sample. Additional exam requirements/recommendations for international students: Required—TOEFL. *Application deadline:* For fall admission, 1/2 priority date for domestic students, 1/2 priority date for international students. Applications are processed on a rolling basis. Application fee: $60. Electronic applications accepted. *Financial support:* In 2003–04, 25 students received support, including 2 teaching assistantships with full tuition reimbursements available (averaging $14,000 per year); career-related internships or fieldwork, Federal Work-Study, health care benefits, and tuition waivers (partial) also available. Financial award application deadline: 1/2; financial award applicants required to submit FAFSA. *Faculty research:* Solid waste management, risk management policy (environmental health), resource management policy (water/fisheries), climate change, environmental justice. *Unit head:* Harold Ward, Director, 401-863-3449, Fax: 401-863-3503, E-mail: harold_ward@brown.edu. *Application contact:* Patricia-Ann Caton, Administrative Manager, 401-863-3449, Fax: 401-863-3503, E-mail: patti_caton@brown.edu.

California State University, Fullerton, Graduate Studies, College of Humanities and Social Sciences, Program in Environmental Studies, Fullerton, CA 92834-9480. Offers environmental education and communication (MS); environmental policy and planning (MS); environmental sciences (MS); technological studies (MS). Part-time programs available. *Faculty:* 2 full-time (1 woman), 2 part-time/adjunct. *Students:* 19 full-time (11 women), 47 part-time (24 women); includes 20 minority (5 African Americans, 10 Asian Americans or Pacific Islanders, 5 Hispanic Americans), 2 international. Average age 33. 48 applicants, 83% accepted, 26 enrolled. In 2003, 36 degrees awarded. *Degree requirements:* For master's, thesis. *Entrance requirements:* For master's, minimum GPA of 2.5 in last 60 units. Application fee: $55. Tuition, nonresident: part-time $282 per unit. Required fees: $889 per semester. *Financial support:* Career-related internships or fieldwork, Federal Work-Study, institutionally sponsored loans, and scholarships/grants available. Support available to part-time students. Financial award application deadline: 3/1. *Unit head:* Dr. Robert Voeks, Coordinator, 714-278-2228.

Central European University, Graduate Studies, Department of Environmental Sciences and Policy, Budapest, , Hungary. Offers MS, PhD. *Faculty:* 7 full-time (1 woman), 1 part-time/adjunct (0 women). *Students:* 60 full-time (27 women), 8 part-time (6 women). Average age 26. 374 applicants, 20% accepted, 49 enrolled. In 2003, 28 degrees awarded, leading to university research/teaching 36%, continued full-time study36%, business/industry 9%, government 18%. *Median time to degree:* Master's–1 year full-time. *Degree requirements:* For master's, one foreign language, thesis/dissertation, registration; for doctorate, one foreign language, thesis/dissertation, comprehensive exam, registration. *Entrance requirements:* For master's and doctorate, interview. Additional exam requirements/recommendations for international students: Required—TOEFL (minimum score 570 paper-based; 230 computer-based). *Application deadline:* For fall admission, 1/5 for domestic students, 1/5 for international students. Application fee: $0. Electronic applications accepted. *Expenses:* Tuition: Full-time $11,300; part-time $2,550 per semester. Required fees: $500. Full-time tuition and fees vary according to program and reciprocity agreements. *Financial support:* In 2003–04, 49 students received support, including 49 fellowships with full and partial tuition reimbursements available (averaging $5,000 per year); career-related internships or fieldwork, institutionally sponsored loans, and scholarships/grants also available. *Faculty research:* Management of ecological systems; environmental impact assessment; energy conservation; climate change policy; forest policy in countries in transition. Total annual research expenditures: $16,127. *Unit head:* Dr. Ruben Mnatsakanian, Head, 361-327-3021, Fax: 361-327-3031, E-mail: envsci@ceu.hu. *Application contact:* Krisztina Szabados, Coordinator, 361-327-3021, Fax: 361-327-3031, E-mail: envsci@ceu.hu.

Central Washington University, Graduate Studies, Research and Continuing Education, College of the Sciences, Program in Resource Management, Ellensburg, WA 98926. Offers MS. *Faculty:* 21 full-time (7 women). *Students:* 42 full-time (23 women), 9 part-time (5 women); includes 15 minority (1 African American, 13 American Indian/Alaska Native, 1 Asian American or Pacific Islander). 37 applicants, 70% accepted, 20 enrolled. In 2003, 13 degrees awarded. *Degree requirements:* For master's, thesis. *Entrance requirements:* For master's, minimum GPA of 3.0. Additional exam requirements/recommendations for international students: Required—TOEFL (minimum score 550 paper-based; 213 computer-based). *Application deadline:* For fall admission, 4/1 for domestic students; for spring admission, 1/1 for domestic students. Applications are processed on a rolling basis. Application fee: $35. Electronic applications accepted. *Expenses:* Tuition, state resident: part-time $183 per credit. Tuition, nonresident: part-time $381 per credit. Required fees: $369. *Financial support:* In 2003–04, 10 research assistantships with partial tuition reimbursements (averaging $7,120 per year), 6 teaching assistantships with partial tuition reimbursements (averaging $7,120 per year) were awarded. Career-related internships or fieldwork, Federal Work-Study, and unspecified assistantships also available. Financial award application deadline: 3/1; financial award applicants required to submit FAFSA. *Unit head:* Dr. Steven Hackenberger, Co-Director, 509-963-1166, Fax: 509-963-3224. *Application contact:* Barbara Sisko, Office Assistant, Graduate Studies, Research and Continuing Education, 509-963-3103, Fax: 509-963-1799, E-mail: masters@cwu.edu.

Clark University, Graduate School, Department of International Development, Community, and Environment, Program in Environmental Science and Policy, Worcester, MA 01610-1477. Offers MA. Part-time programs available. *Students:* 29 full-time (22 women), 1 part-time; includes 1 minority (African American), 7 international. Average age 28. 47 applicants, 98% accepted, 18 enrolled. In 2003, 6 degrees awarded. *Degree requirements:* For master's, thesis. *Entrance requirements:* For master's, GRE General Test. Additional exam requirements/recommendations for international students: Required—TOEFL. *Application deadline:* For fall admission, 2/15 for domestic students. Application fee: $40. *Expenses:* Tuition: Full-time $26,700. *Financial support:* In 2003–04, research assistantships with full and partial tuition reimbursements (averaging $9,250 per year), teaching assistantships with full and partial tuition reimbursements (averaging $9,250 per year) were awarded. Fellowships, career-related internships or fieldwork and tuition waivers (partial) also available. *Faculty research:* Water resources, environmental management, natural and man-made hazards, health risks, public health policy, hazard management, energy and environmental systems analysis, technology and environmental assessment, global climate change. *Unit head:* Dr. William F. Fisher, Director, 508-421-3765, Fax: 508-793-8820, E-mail: wfisher@clarku.edu. *Application contact:* Liz Owens, IDCE Graduate Admissions, 508-793-7201, Fax: 508-793-8820, E-mail: idce@clarku.edu.

Clark University, Graduate School, Department of International Development, Community, and Environment, Program in Geographic Information Science for Development and Environment, Worcester, MA 01610-1477. Offers MA. *Students:* 24 full-time (7 women), 5 part-time (2 women), 13 international. Average age 31. 56 applicants, 88% accepted, 19 enrolled. In 2003, 12 degrees awarded. *Degree requirements:* For master's, thesis. *Application deadline:* For fall admission, 2/1 for domestic students. Application fee: $40. *Expenses:* Tuition: Full-time $26,700. *Financial support:* In 2003–04, research assistantships with full and partial tuition reimbursements (averaging $9,250 per year), teaching assistantships with full and partial tuition reimbursements (averaging $9,250 per year) were awarded. Fellowships, tuition waivers (full and partial) also available. *Unit head:* Dr. William F. Fisher, Director, 508-421-3765, Fax: 508-793-8820, E-mail: wfisher@clarku.edu. *Application contact:* Liz Owens, IDCE Graduate Admissions, 508-793-7201, Fax: 508-793-8820, E-mail: idce@clarku.edu.

Clemson University, Graduate School, College of Agriculture, Forestry and Life Sciences, Department of Biological Sciences, Program in Plant and Environmental Sciences, Clemson, SC 29634. Offers MS, PhD. *Students:* 35 full-time (14 women), 7 part-time (4 women); includes 2 minority (1 American Indian/Alaska Native, 1 Hispanic American), 5 international. 28 applicants, 46% accepted, 10 enrolled. In 2003, 6 degrees awarded. *Degree requirements:* For master's, thesis. *Entrance requirements:* For master's, GRE General Test, bachelor's degree in biological science or chemistry. Additional exam requirements/recommendations for international students: Required—TOEFL. *Application deadline:* For fall admission, 6/1 for domestic students. Application fee: $40. *Expenses:* Tuition, state resident: full-time $7,432. Tuition, nonresident: full-time $14,732. *Financial support:* Teaching assistantships available. Financial award application deadline: 3/15; financial award applicants required to submit FAFSA. *Faculty research:* Systematics, aquatic botany, plant ecology, plant-fungus interactions, plant developmental genetics. *Unit head:* Dr. Nancy Walker, Coordinator, 864-656-3510, Fax: 864-656-7594, E-mail: nwalker@clemson.edu.

Cleveland State University, College of Graduate Studies, Maxine Goodman Levin College of Urban Affairs, Program in Environmental Studies, Cleveland, OH 44115. Offers MAES, JD/MAES. Tuition, area resident: Full-time $8,258; part-time $344 per credit hour. Tuition, nonresident: full-time $16,352; part-time $681 per credit hour. *Application contact:* Graduate Programs Coordinator, 216-523-7522, Fax: 216-687-5398, E-mail: gradprog@wolf.csuohio.edu.

College of the Atlantic, Program in Human Ecology, Bar Harbor, ME 04609-1198. Offers M Phil. *Faculty:* 22 full-time (6 women), 6 part-time/adjunct (3 women). *Students:* 12 full-time (10 women). Average age 25. 10 applicants, 20% accepted. In 2003, 2 degrees awarded. *Degree requirements:* For master's, thesis. *Application deadline:* For fall admission, 2/15 for domestic students. Applications are processed on a rolling basis. Application fee: $40. *Expenses:* Tuition: Full-time $12,225. *Financial support:* In 2003–04, 3 students received support, including 1 fellowship (averaging $7,000 per year), 1 research assistantship with partial tuition reimbursement available (averaging $1,000 per year), 2 teaching assistantships with partial tuition reimbursements available (averaging $2,000 per year); career-related internships or fieldwork, Federal Work-Study, institutionally sponsored loans, scholarships/grants, tuition waivers (partial), and unspecified assistantships also available. Financial award application deadline: 2/15; financial award applicants required to submit FAFSA. *Faculty research:* Conservation of endangered species, public policy/community planning, environmental education, history, philosophy. *Unit head:* Dr. John G. Anderson, Dean for Advanced Studies, 207-288-5015 Ext. 269, Fax: 207-288-3780, E-mail: jga@ecology.coa.edu.

Colorado State University, Graduate School, College of Liberal Arts, Department of Political Science, Fort Collins, CO 80523-0015. Offers environmental politics and policy (PhD); political science (MA, PhD). Part-time programs available. *Faculty:* 14 full-time (5 women). *Students:* 17 full-time (6 women), 18 part-time (5 women), 2 international. Average age 32. 41 applicants, 51% accepted, 9 enrolled. In 2003, 5 master's, 5 doctorates awarded. *Degree requirements:* For master's, thesis (for some programs), comprehensive exam; for doctorate, thesis/dissertation, comprehensive exam. *Entrance requirements:* For master's, GRE General Test, minimum GPA of 3.0; for doctorate, GRE General Test, MA, minimum GPA of 3.0. Additional exam requirements/recommendations for international students: Required—TOEFL. *Application deadline:* For fall admission, 2/15 for domestic students; for spring admission, 10/15 for domestic students. Applications are processed on a rolling basis. Application fee: $50. Electronic applications accepted. *Expenses:* Tuition, state resident: full-time $4,156. Tuition, nonresident: full-time $14,762. Required fees: $205. Tuition and fees vary according to course load, campus/location, program and reciprocity agreements. *Financial support:* In 2003–04, 12 students received support, including 1 fellowship (averaging $4,500 per year), 11 teaching assistantships with full tuition reimbursements available (averaging $9,720 per year); research assistantships, career-related internships or fieldwork, Federal Work-Study, institutionally sponsored loans, and traineeships also available. Financial award application deadline: 2/15; financial award applicants required to submit FAFSA. *Faculty research:* Environmental politics and policy, international relations, politics of developing nations, state and local politics and administration, political behavior. *Unit head:* Dr. William Chaloupka, Chair, 970-491-5157, Fax: 970-491-2490, E-mail: williamc@colostate.edu. *Application contact:* Dr. Robert Duffy, Coordinator, 970-491-6225, Fax: 970-491-2490, E-mail: robert.duffy@colostate.edu.

Colorado State University, Graduate School, College of Natural Resources, Department of Natural Resource Recreation and Tourism, Fort Collins, CO 80523-0015. Offers commercial recreation and tourism (MS); human dimensions in natural resources (PhD); recreation resource management (MS, PhD); resource interpretation (MS). *Faculty:* 8 full-time (2 women). *Students:* 19 full-time (13 women), 16 part-time (7 women); includes 1 minority (Asian American or Pacific Islander), 6 international. Average age 30. 50 applicants, 20% accepted, 6 enrolled. In 2003, 3 master's, 3 doctorates awarded. *Degree requirements:* For master's, thesis or alternative; for doctorate, thesis/dissertation. *Entrance requirements:* For master's and doctorate, GRE General Test, minimum GPA of 3.0. Additional exam requirements/recommendations for international students: Required—TOEFL. *Application deadline:* For fall admission, 3/1 for domestic students; for spring admission, 10/1 priority date for domestic students. Applications are processed on a rolling basis. Application fee: $50. Electronic applications accepted. *Expenses:* Tuition, state resident: full-time $4,156. Tuition, nonresident: full-time $14,762. Required fees: $205. Tuition and fees vary according to course load, campus/location, program and reciprocity agreements. *Financial support:* In 2003–04, 6 research assistantships with tuition reimbursements (averaging $13,000 per year), 8 teaching assistantships with tuition reimbursements (averaging $13,000 per year) were awarded. Fellowships, career-related

Environmental Management and Policy

Colorado State University (continued)

internships or fieldwork, Federal Work-Study, scholarships/grants, and traineeships also available. Support available to part-time students. Financial award application deadline: 2/1; financial award applicants required to submit FAFSA. *Faculty research:* International tourism, wilderness preservation, resource interpretation, human dimensions in natural resources, protected areas management. Total annual research expenditures: $257,300. *Unit head:* Dr. Michael J. Manfredo, Chair, 970-491-6591, Fax: 970-491-2255, E-mail: manfredo@cnr.colostate.edu. *Application contact:* Dr. Alan D. Bright, Graduate Program Administrator, 970-491-5487, Fax: 970-491-2255, E-mail: abright@cnr.colostate.edu.

Columbia University, School of International and Public Affairs, Program in Environmental Science and Policy, New York, NY 10027. Offers MPA. Program admits applicants in June only. *Degree requirements:* For master's, workshops. *Entrance requirements:* For master's, previous course work in biology and chemistry, or earth sciences recommended. Electronic applications accepted. *Expenses:* Tuition: Full-time $14,820. *Faculty research:* Ecological management of enclosed ecosystems vegetation dynamics; environmental policy and management; energy policy; nuclear waste policy; environmental and natural resource economics and policy.

See in-depth description on page 723.

Concordia University, School of Graduate Studies, Faculty of Arts and Science, Department of Geography, Montréal, QC H3G 1M8, Canada. Offers environmental impact assessment (Diploma). *Students:* 12 full-time, 4 part-time. In 2003, 4 degrees awarded. *Application deadline:* For fall admission, 3/1 for domestic students; for winter admission, 8/31 for domestic students. *Expenses:* Tuition, state resident: full-time $2,140. Tuition, nonresident: full-time $4,190. International tuition: $8,449 full-time. Tuition and fees vary according to course load, degree level and program. *Unit head:* Dr. P. A. Thornton, Chair, 514-848-2424 Ext. 2056, Fax: 514-848-2057. *Application contact:* Dr. Monica Mulrennan, Director, 514-848-2424 Ext. 2050, Fax: 514-848-2057.

Cornell University, Graduate School, Field of Environmental Management, Ithaca, NY 14853. Offers MPS. *Expenses:* Tuition: Full-time $28,630. One-time fee: $50 full-time. *Application contact:* Tad McGalliard, Education Coordinator, 607-255-9996, Fax: 607-255-0238, E-mail: tnm2@cornell.edu.

Cornell University, Graduate School, Graduate Fields of Agriculture and Life Sciences, Department of Soil and Crop Sciences, Ithaca, NY 14853. Offers agronomy (MPS, MS, PhD); atmospheric sciences (MPS, MS, PhD); environmental information science (MPS, MS, PhD); environmental management (MPS); field crop science (MPS, MS, PhD); soil science (MPS, MS, PhD). Terminal master's awarded for partial completion of doctoral program. *Degree requirements:* For master's, thesis (MS), project paper (MPS); for doctorate, thesis/dissertation. *Entrance requirements:* For master's and doctorate, GRE General Test. Additional exam requirements/recommendations for international students: Required—TOEFL. Electronic applications accepted. Expenses: Contact institution. One-time fee: $50 full-time. *Faculty research:* Environmental modeling, soil chemistry and physics, international agriculture, weather and climate, crop physiology.

Cornell University, Graduate School, Graduate Fields of Agriculture and Life Sciences, Field of Agricultural Economics, Ithaca, NY 14853-0001. Offers agricultural economics (MPS, MS, PhD), including agricultural finance, applied econometrics and quantitative analysis, economics of development, farm management and production economics (MPS), marketing and food distribution (MPS), public policy analysis (MPS); resource economics (MPS, MS, PhD), including environmental economics, environmental management (MPS), resource economics. *Faculty:* 43 full-time. *Students:* 71 full-time (32 women); includes 6 minority (all Asian Americans or Pacific Islanders), 42 international. 157 applicants, 58% accepted, 28 enrolled. In 2003, 10 master's, 6 doctorates awarded. Terminal master's awarded for partial completion of doctoral program. *Degree requirements:* For master's, thesis (MS); for doctorate, thesis/dissertation, comprehensive exam. *Entrance requirements:* For master's and doctorate, GRE General Test, 2 letters of recommendation. Additional exam requirements/recommendations for international students: Required—TOEFL (minimum score 550 paper-based; 213 computer-based). *Application deadline:* For fall admission, 1/15 for domestic students. Application fee: $60. Electronic applications accepted. *Expenses:* Tuition: Full-time $28,630. One-time fee: $50 full-time. *Financial support:* In 2003–04, 39 students received support, including 8 fellowships with full tuition reimbursements available, 18 research assistantships with full tuition reimbursements available, 13 teaching assistantships with full tuition reimbursements available; institutionally sponsored loans, scholarships/grants, health care benefits, tuition waivers (full and partial), and unspecified assistantships also available. Financial award applicants required to submit FAFSA. *Faculty research:* Production economics, international economic development and trade, farm management and finance, resource and environmental economics, agricultural marketing and policy. *Unit head:* Director of Graduate Studies, 607-255-8048, Fax: 607-255-9984, E-mail: aegrad@cornell.edu. *Application contact:* Graduate Field Assistant, 607-255-8048, Fax: 607-255-9984, E-mail: aegrad@cornell.edu.

Cornell University, Graduate School, Graduate Fields of Agriculture and Life Sciences, Field of Natural Resources, Ithaca, NY 14853-0001. Offers aquatic science (MPS, MS, PhD); environmental management (MPS); fishery science (MPS, MS, PhD); forest science (MPS, MS, PhD); resource policy and management (MPS, MS, PhD); wildlife science (MPS, MS, PhD). *Faculty:* 43 full-time. *Students:* 73 full-time (31 women); includes 10 minority (1 African American, 2 American Indian/Alaska Native, 5 Asian Americans or Pacific Islanders, 2 Hispanic Americans), 14 international. 107 applicants, 22% accepted, 18 enrolled. In 2003, 16 master's, 6 doctorates awarded. *Degree requirements:* For master's, thesis (MS), project paper (MPS); for doctorate, thesis/dissertation, comprehensive exam. *Entrance requirements:* For master's and doctorate, GRE General Test, 2 letters of recommendation. Additional exam requirements/recommendations for international students: Required—TOEFL (minimum score 550 paper-based; 213 computer-based). *Application deadline:* ; for spring admission, 10/30 for domestic students. Applications are processed on a rolling basis. Application fee: $60. Electronic applications accepted. *Expenses:* Tuition: Full-time $28,630. One-time fee: $50 full-time. *Financial support:* In 2003–04, 63 students received support, including 11 fellowships with full tuition reimbursements available, 27 research assistantships with full tuition reimbursements available, 25 teaching assistantships with full tuition reimbursements available; institutionally sponsored loans, scholarships/grants, health care benefits, tuition waivers (full and partial), and unspecified assistantships also available. Financial award applicants required to submit FAFSA. *Faculty research:* Ecosystem-level dynamics, systems modeling, conservation biology/management, resource management's human dimensions, biogeochemistry. *Unit head:* Director of Graduate Studies, 607-255-2807, Fax: 607-255-0349. *Application contact:* Graduate Field Assistant, 607-255-2807, Fax: 607-255-0349, E-mail: nrgrad@cornell.edu.

Cornell University, Graduate School, Graduate Fields of Agriculture and Life Sciences, Field of Soil and Crop Sciences, Ithaca, NY 14853-0001. Offers agronomy (MS, PhD); environmental information science (MS, PhD); environmental management (MPS); field crop science (MS, PhD); soil science (MS, PhD). *Faculty:* 32 full-time. *Students:* 44 full-time (17 women); includes 1 minority (Hispanic American), 24 international. 40 applicants, 43% accepted, 14 enrolled. In 2003, 9 master's, 7 doctorates awarded. *Degree requirements:* For master's, thesis (MS); for doctorate, thesis/dissertation, comprehensive exam. *Entrance requirements:* For master's and doctorate, GRE General Test, 2 letters of recommendation. Additional exam requirements/recommendations for international students: Required—TOEFL (minimum score 550 paper-based; 213 computer-based). *Application deadline:* For fall admission, 2/1 for domestic students. Applications are processed on a rolling basis. Application fee: $60. Electronic applications accepted. *Expenses:* Tuition: Full-time $28,630. One-time fee: $50 full-time. *Financial support:* In 2003–04, 36 students received support, including 8 fellowships with full tuition reimbursements available, 21 research assistantships with full tuition reimbursements available, 7 teaching assistantships with full tuition reimbursements available; institutionally sponsored loans, traineeships, health care benefits, tuition waivers (full and partial), and unspecified assistantships also available. *Faculty research:* Soil chemistry, physics and biology; crop physiology and management; environmental information science and modeling; international agriculture; weed science. *Unit head:* Director of Graduate Studies, 607-255-3267, Fax: 607-255-8615. *Application contact:* Graduate Field Assistant, 607-255-3267, Fax: 607-255-8615, E-mail: jae2@cornell.edu.

Cornell University, Graduate School, Graduate Fields of Architecture, Art and Planning, Field of Regional Science, Ithaca, NY 14853-0001. Offers environmental studies (MA, MS, PhD); international spatial problems (MA, MS, PhD); location theory (MA, MS, PhD); multiregional economic analysis (MA, MS, PhD); peace science (MA, MS, PhD); planning methods (MA, MS, PhD); urban and regional economics (MA, MS, PhD). *Faculty:* 14 full-time. *Students:* 12 full-time (2 women), (all international). 11 applicants, 73% accepted, 1 enrolled. In 2003, 2 master's, 2 doctorates awarded. Terminal master's awarded for partial completion of doctoral program. *Degree requirements:* For master's, thesis/dissertation; for doctorate, thesis/dissertation, comprehensive exam. *Entrance requirements:* For master's and doctorate, GRE General Test (native English speakers only), 2 letters of recommendation. Additional exam requirements/recommendations for international students: Required—TOEFL (minimum score 600 paper-based; 250 computer-based). *Application deadline:* For fall admission, 1/15 for domestic students. Application fee: $60. Electronic applications accepted. *Expenses:* Tuition: Full-time $28,630. One-time fee: $50 full-time. *Financial support:* In 2003–04, 1 student received support, including 1 research assistantship with full tuition reimbursement available; fellowships with full tuition reimbursements available, teaching assistantships with full tuition reimbursements available, institutionally sponsored loans, scholarships/grants, health care benefits, tuition waivers (full and partial), and unspecified assistantships also available. Financial award applicants required to submit FAFSA. *Faculty research:* Urban and regional growth, spatial economics, formation of spatial patterns by socioeconomic systems, non-linear dynamics and complex systems, environmental-economic systems. *Unit head:* Director of Graduate Studies, 607-255-6848, Fax: 607-255-1971. *Application contact:* Graduate Field Assistant, 607-255-6848, Fax: 607-255-1971, E-mail: regsci@cornell.edu.

Cornell University, Graduate School, Graduate Fields of Arts and Sciences, Field of Archaeology, Ithaca, NY 14853-0001. Offers environmental archaeology (MA); historical archaeology (MA); Latin American archaeology (MA); medieval archaeology (MA); Mediterranean and Near Eastern archaeology (MA); Stone Age archaeology (MA). *Faculty:* 13 full-time. *Students:* 5 full-time (4 women). 14 applicants, 21% accepted, 1 enrolled. *Degree requirements:* For master's, one foreign language, thesis. *Entrance requirements:* For master's, GRE General Test, 3 letters of recommendation, sample of written work. Additional exam requirements/recommendations for international students: Required—TOEFL. *Application deadline:* For fall admission, 1/15 for domestic students. Application fee: $60. Electronic applications accepted. *Expenses:* Tuition: Full-time $28,630. One-time fee: $50 full-time. *Financial support:* In 2003–04, 4 students received support, including 3 fellowships with full tuition reimbursements available, 1 teaching assistantship with full tuition reimbursement available; research assistantships with full tuition reimbursements available, institutionally sponsored loans, scholarships/grants, health care benefits, tuition waivers (full and partial), and unspecified assistantships also available. Financial award applicants required to submit FAFSA. *Faculty research:* Anatolia, Lydia, Sardis, classical and Hellenistic Greece; science in archaeology; North American Indians; Stone Age Africa; Maya trade. *Unit head:* Director of Graduate Studies, 607-255-6768. *Application contact:* Graduate Field Assistant, 607-255-6768, E-mail: bad2@cornell.edu.

Dalhousie University, Faculty of Graduate Studies, Faculty of Management, School for Resource and Environmental Studies, Halifax, NS B3H 4R2, Canada. Offers MES. Part-time programs available. *Degree requirements:* For master's, thesis. *Entrance requirements:* For master's, honors degree. Additional exam requirements/recommendations for international students: Required—TOEFL. *Faculty research:* Resource management and ecology, aboriginal resource rights, management of toxic substances, environmental impact assessment, forest management, policy, coastal zone management.

Drexel University, College of Arts and Sciences, Program in Environmental Policy, Philadelphia, PA 19104-2875. Offers MS. Part-time and evening/weekend programs available. *Degree requirements:* For master's, thesis optional. Electronic applications accepted.

Duke University, Graduate School, Department of Environment, Durham, NC 27708. Offers natural resource economics/policy (AM, PhD); natural resource science/ecology (AM, PhD); natural resource systems science (AM, PhD). Part-time programs available. *Faculty:* 35 full-time. *Students:* 64 full-time (31 women); includes 7 minority (3 African Americans, 1 Asian American or Pacific Islander, 3 Hispanic Americans), 18 international. 151 applicants, 16% accepted, 15 enrolled. In 2003, 1 master's, 7 doctorates awarded. Terminal master's awarded for partial completion of doctoral program. *Degree requirements:* For doctorate, variable foreign language requirement, thesis/dissertation. *Entrance requirements:* For master's and doctorate, GRE General Test. Additional exam requirements/recommendations for international students: Required—IELT (preferred) or TOEFL. *Application deadline:* For fall admission, 12/31 for domestic students. Application fee: $75. *Expenses:* Tuition: Full-time $23,280; part-time $835 per unit. *Financial support:* Fellowships, research assistantships, teaching assistantships, Federal Work-Study available. Financial award application deadline: 12/31. *Unit head:* Kenneth Knoerr, Director of Graduate Studies, 919-613-8002, Fax: 919-684-8741, E-mail: nmm@duke.edu.

Duke University, Nicholas School of the Environment and Earth Sciences, Durham, NC 27708-0328. Offers coastal environmental management (MEM); environmental health and security (MEM); environmental science and policy (PhD); environmental toxicology, chemistry, and risk assessment (MEM); forest resource management (MF); global environmental change (MEM); resource ecology (MEM); resource economics and policy (MEM); water and air resources (MEM). PhD offered through the Graduate School. *Accreditation:* SAF (one or more programs are accredited). Part-time programs available. Terminal master's awarded for partial completion of doctoral program. *Degree requirements:* For master's, thesis (for some programs); for doctorate, thesis/dissertation. *Entrance requirements:* For master's, GRE General Test, previous course work in biology or ecology, calculus, statistics, and microeconomics; computer familiarity with word processing and data analysis; for doctorate, GRE General Test. Additional exam requirements/recommendations for international students: Required—TOEFL (minimum score 550 paper-based; 213 computer-based). Electronic applications accepted. Expenses: Contact institution. *Faculty research:* Ecosystem management, conservation ecology, earth systems, risk assessment.

Announcement: Interdisciplinary focus of Environmental Economics and Policy Program provides excellent background for careers with a broad spectrum of employers. Opportunities for specialization in environmental management, forestry, resource ecology, coastal and marine resources, water and air resources, environmental health. Concurrent degrees available: MBA, JD in environmental law, MPP, MA in teaching. Partial fellowships for qualified students.

See in-depth description on page 787.

Duquesne University, Bayer School of Natural and Environmental Sciences, Environmental Science and Management Program, Pittsburgh, PA 15282-0001. Offers environmental management (Certificate); environmental science (Certificate); environmental science and management (MS). Part-time and evening/weekend programs available. Postbaccalaureate distance learning degree programs offered (minimal on-campus study). *Faculty:* 2 full-time (0 women), 15 part-time/adjunct (1 woman). *Students:* 14 full-time (10 women), 47 part-time (22 women), 1 international. Average age 28. 20 applicants, 75% accepted, 9 enrolled. In 2003, 20 degrees awarded, leading to continued full-time study 5%, business/industry 80%, government 15%. *Median time to degree:* Master's–2 years full-time, 3 years part-time. *Degree requirements:* For master's, thesis or internship. *Entrance requirements:* For master's, GRE General Test, previous course work in biology, calculus, chemistry, and statistics. Additional exam requirements/recommendations for international students: Required—TOEFL, TSE. *Application deadline:*

For fall admission, 4/1 priority date for domestic students, 4/1 priority date for international students; for spring admission, 10/1 priority date for domestic students, 10/1 priority date for international students. Applications are processed on a rolling basis. Application fee: $40. *Expenses:* Contact institution. *Financial support:* In 2003–04, 1 fellowship with full tuition reimbursement (averaging $14,000 per year), 2 teaching assistantships with partial tuition reimbursements (averaging $10,000 per year) were awarded. Research assistantships, career-related internships or fieldwork, institutionally sponsored loans, scholarships/grants, tuition waivers (partial), and unspecified assistantships also available. Support available to part-time students. Financial award application deadline: 5/1; financial award applicants required to submit FAFSA. *Faculty research:* Watershed management systems, environmental analytical chemistry, environmental endocrinology, environmental microbiology, aquatic biology. Total annual research expenditures: $161,550. *Unit head:* Dr. Daniel Donnelly, Director, 412-396-4367, Fax: 412-396-4092, E-mail: donnelly@duq.edu. *Application contact:* Mary Ann Quinn, Assistant to the Dean Graduate Affairs, 412-396-6339, Fax: 412-396-4881, E-mail: gradinfo@duq.edu.

East Carolina University, Graduate School, Program in Coastal Resources Management, Greenville, NC 27858-4353. Offers PhD. *Faculty:* 42 full-time (7 women), 2 part-time/adjunct (0 women). *Students:* 13 full-time (7 women), 19 part-time (6 women); includes 3 minority (1 African American, 2 Hispanic Americans). Average age 36. 18 applicants, 56% accepted. *Degree requirements:* For doctorate, thesis/dissertation, internship, comprehensive exam, registration. *Entrance requirements:* For doctorate, GRE. Additional exam requirements/recommendations for international students: Required—TOEFL. *Application deadline:* For fall admission, 3/1 for domestic students, 3/1 for international students. Application fee: $50. *Expenses:* Tuition, state resident: full-time $1,991; part-time $249 per hour. Tuition, nonresident: full-time $12,232; part-time $1,529 per hour. Required fees: $1,221; $153 per hour. *Financial support:* In 2003–04, 8 fellowships with tuition reimbursements (averaging $17,000 per year), 2 research assistantships with tuition reimbursements (averaging $17,000 per year) were awarded. Career-related internships or fieldwork and institutionally sponsored loans also available. Financial award application deadline: 3/1; financial award applicants required to submit FAFSA. *Faculty research:* Coastal geology, wetlands and coastal ecology, ecological and social networks, submerged cultural resources, coastal resources economics. Total annual research expenditures: $24,000. *Unit head:* Dr. Lauriston R. King, Director, 252-328-2484, Fax: 252-328-0381, E-mail: kingl@mail.ecu.edu. *Application contact:* Dr. Paul D. Tschetter, Interim Dean of Graduate School, 252-328-6012, Fax: 252-328-6071, E-mail: gradschool@mail.ecu.edu.

The Evergreen State College, Graduate Programs, Program in Environmental Studies, Olympia, WA 98505. Offers MES. Part-time and evening/weekend programs available. *Degree requirements:* For master's, thesis. *Entrance requirements:* For master's, minimum undergraduate GPA of 3.0; BA/BS major in biological, physical, or social science. *Application deadline:* For fall admission, 11/15 for domestic students. Applications are processed on a rolling basis. Application fee: $36. *Expenses:* Tuition, state resident: full-time $5,979; part-time $199. Tuition, nonresident: full-time $18,306; part-time $610. Required fees: $153; $39 per quarter. *Financial support:* Fellowships, research assistantships, career-related internships or fieldwork, Federal Work-Study, institutionally sponsored loans, scholarships/grants, tuition waivers (partial), and unspecified assistantships available. Support available to part-time students. Financial award application deadline: 3/15; financial award applicants required to submit FAFSA. *Faculty research:* Land and water policy, canopy studies; ecology (marine microbial, phytoplankton, of introduced Spartina cordgrass, green crabs), pesticides, bacteriophage research, international-domestic relations. Total annual research expenditures: $19,900. *Unit head:* Dr. John Perkins, Director, 360-867-6503, Fax: 360-867-5430, E-mail: perkinsj@evergreen.edu. *Application contact:* Graduate Studies Office, 360-867-6707, Fax: 360-867-5430, E-mail: graduatestudies@evergreen.edu.

See in-depth description on page 725.

Florida Gulf Coast University, College of Public and Social Services, Program in Public Administration, Fort Myers, FL 33965-6565. Offers criminal justice (MPA); environmental policy (MPA); general public administration (MPA); management (MPA). Part-time programs available. *Faculty:* 21 full-time (13 women), 13 part-time/adjunct (5 women). *Students:* 5 full-time (4 women), 42 part-time (24 women); includes 7 minority (2 African Americans, 2 Asian Americans or Pacific Islanders, 3 Hispanic Americans). Average age 37. 23 applicants, 83% accepted, 13 enrolled. In 2003, 15 degrees awarded. *Entrance requirements:* For master's, GRE General Test, MAT, minimum GPA of 3.0. *Application deadline:* For fall admission, 7/1 for domestic students; for spring admission, 11/15 for domestic students. Applications are processed on a rolling basis. Application fee: $30. Electronic applications accepted. *Expenses:* Tuition, state resident: part-time $199 per credit hour. Tuition, nonresident: part-time $733 per credit hour. *Financial support:* In 2003–04, 5 research assistantships were awarded; career-related internships or fieldwork and tuition waivers (full and partial) also available. Support available to part-time students. *Faculty research:* Personnel, public policy, public finance, housing policy. *Unit head:* Dr. Roberta Walsh, Chair, 239-590-7841, Fax: 239-590-7846, E-mail: rwalsh@fgcu.edu. *Application contact:* Roger Green, Information Contact, 239-590-7838, Fax: 239-590-7846.

Florida Institute of Technology, Graduate Programs, College of Engineering, Department of Marine and Environmental Systems, Melbourne, FL 32901-6975. Offers environmental resource management (MS); environmental science (MS, PhD); meteorology (MS); ocean engineering (MS, PhD); oceanography (MS, PhD), including biological oceanography, chemical oceanography, coastal zone management (MS), geological oceanography, physical oceanography. Part-time programs available. *Faculty:* 16 full-time (1 woman), 4 part-time/adjunct (0 women). *Students:* 42 full-time (16 women), 19 part-time (8 women); includes 1 minority (Hispanic American), 25 international. Average age 29. 129 applicants, 55% accepted, 17 enrolled. In 2003, 17 master's, 3 doctorates awarded. Terminal master's awarded for partial completion of doctoral program. *Degree requirements:* For master's, thesis, comprehensive exam, registration; for doctorate, thesis/dissertation, attendance of graduate seminar, internships (oceanography and environmental science), comprehensive exam, registration. *Entrance requirements:* For master's, GRE General Test (environmental science), letters of recommendation(3), minimum GPA of 3.0; for doctorate, GRE General Test (oceanography and environmental science), resumé, letters of recommendation (3), statement of objectives, minimum GPA of 3.2. Additional exam requirements/recommendations for international students: Required—TOEFL (minimum score 550 paper-based; 213 computer-based). *Application deadline:* Applications are processed on a rolling basis. Application fee: $50. Electronic applications accepted. *Expenses:* Tuition: Part-time $745 per credit. *Financial support:* In 2003–04, 35 students received support, including 10 fellowships with full and partial tuition reimbursements available (averaging $5,565 per year), 15 research assistantships with full and partial tuition reimbursements available (averaging $14,657 per year), 10 teaching assistantships with full and partial tuition reimbursements available (averaging $17,533 per year); career-related internships or fieldwork and tuition remissions also available. Financial award application deadline: 3/1; financial award applicants required to submit FAFSA. *Faculty research:* Environmental modeling, coastal processes, exploring marine pollution, marine geophysics, remote sensing . Total annual research expenditures: $1.9 million. *Unit head:* Dr. George Maul, Department Head, 321-674-7453, Fax: 321-674-7212, E-mail: gmaul@fit.edu. *Application contact:* Carolyn P. Farrior, Director of Graduate Admissions, 321-674-7118, Fax: 321-723-9468, E-mail: cfarrior@fit.edu.

See in-depth description on page 727.

Florida International University, College of Arts and Sciences, Department of Environmental Studies, Miami, FL 33199. Offers biological management (MS); energy (MS); pollution (MS). *Faculty:* 10 full-time (2 women). *Students:* 18 full-time (10 women), 24 part-time (13 women); includes 13 minority (1 American Indian/Alaska Native, 2 Asian Americans or Pacific Islanders, 10 Hispanic Americans), 6 international. Average age 32. 32 applicants, 41% accepted, 6 enrolled. In 2003, 18 degrees awarded. *Degree requirements:* For master's, thesis. *Entrance requirements:* For master's, GRE General Test, minimum GPA of 3.0, 3 letters of recommendation. Additional exam requirements/recommendations for international students: Required—TOEFL. *Application deadline:* For fall admission, 4/1 for domestic students; for spring admission, 10/30 for domestic students. Application fee: $20. *Expenses:* Tuition, state resident: part-time $202 per credit. Tuition, nonresident: part-time $771 per credit. Required fees: $112 per semester. *Financial support:* Research assistantships, teaching assistantships available. Financial award application deadline: 4/1. *Unit head:* Dr. Joel Heinen, Chairperson, 305-348-3732, Fax: 305-348-6137, E-mail: joel.heinen@fiu.edu.

Friends University, Graduate School, Division of Science, Arts, and Education, Program in Environmental Studies, Wichita, KS 67213. Offers MSES. Evening/weekend programs available. *Faculty:* 4 full-time, 5 part-time/adjunct. *Students:* 22 full-time. *Application deadline:* Applications are processed on a rolling basis. Application fee: $45 ($65 for international students). *Expenses:* Tuition: Part-time $429 per credit hour. *Unit head:* Dr. Alan Maccarone, Director, 800-794-6945 Ext. 5890, E-mail: alanm@friends.edu. *Application contact:* Craig Davis, Executive Director of Recruitment-Adult and Graduate Studies, 800-794-6945 Ext. 5573, Fax: 316-295-5050, E-mail: cdavis@friends.edu.

George Mason University, College of Arts and Sciences, Department of Environmental Science and Public Policy, Fairfax, VA 22030. Offers MS, PhD. Part-time programs available. *Faculty:* 27 full-time (6 women), 9 part-time/adjunct (4 women). *Students:* 9 full-time (5 women), 119 part-time (64 women); includes 25 minority (10 African Americans, 10 American Indian/Alaska Native, 5 Asian Americans or Pacific Islanders), 13 international. Average age 36. 73 applicants, 56% accepted, 33 enrolled. In 2003, 2 master's, 12 doctorates awarded. *Degree requirements:* For doctorate, thesis/dissertation, internship. *Entrance requirements:* For doctorate, GRE General Test, GRE Subject Test. *Application deadline:* For fall admission, 5/1 for domestic students; for spring admission, 11/1 for domestic students. Application fee: $60. Electronic applications accepted. *Expenses:* Tuition, state resident: full-time $4,398. Tuition, nonresident: full-time $14,952. Required fees: $1,482. *Financial support:* Fellowships, research assistantships, teaching assistantships available. Support available to part-time students. Financial award application deadline: 3/1; financial award applicants required to submit FAFSA. *Unit head:* Dr. R. Christian Jones, Interim Director, 703-963-1127, Fax: 703-993-1046, E-mail: rcjones@gmu.edu.

The George Washington University, Columbian College of Arts and Sciences, School of Public Policy and Public Administration, Washington, DC 20052. Offers public policy (MA, MPP), including environmental and resource policy (MA), philosophy and social policy (MA), women's studies (MA); public policy and administration (PhD); public policy and public administration (MPA), including budget and public finance, federal policy, politics, and management, international development management, managing public organizations, managing state and local governments and urban policy, nonprofit management, policy analysis and evaluation, public administration. Part-time and evening/weekend programs available. In 2003, 11 degrees awarded. *Degree requirements:* For doctorate, thesis/dissertation, general exam. *Entrance requirements:* For master's, GRE General Test, minimum GPA of 3.0; for doctorate, GRE General Test, interview, minimum GPA of 3.3. Additional exam requirements/recommendations for international students: Required—TOEFL (minimum score 550 paper-based; 213 computer-based). *Application deadline:* For fall admission, 2/1 priority date for domestic students, 2/1 priority date for international students; for spring admission, 10/1 priority date for domestic students, 10/1 priority date for international students. Applications are processed on a rolling basis. Application fee: $60. Electronic applications accepted. *Expenses:* Tuition: Part-time $876 per credit. Required fees: $1 per credit. Tuition and fees vary according to campus/location. *Financial support:* In 2003–04, fellowships (averaging $10,000 per year), teaching assistantships (averaging $5,000 per year) were awarded. Federal Work-Study and institutionally sponsored loans also available. Financial award application deadline: 2/1. *Application contact:* Information Contact, 202-994-8500, Fax: 202-994-8913, E-mail: pubpol@gwu.edu.

The George Washington University, Columbian College of Arts and Sciences, School of Public Policy and Public Administration, Interdisciplinary Programs in Public Policy, Program in Environmental and Resource Policy, Washington, DC 20052. Offers MA. *Students:* 8 full-time (5 women), 11 part-time (7 women); includes 3 minority (1 African American, 2 Asian Americans or Pacific Islanders), 1 international. Average age 28. 22 applicants, 82% accepted. In 2003, 5 degrees awarded. *Degree requirements:* For master's, project. *Entrance requirements:* For master's, GRE General Test, minimum GPA of 3.0. Additional exam requirements/recommendations for international students: Required—TOEFL (minimum score 550 paper-based; 213 computer-based). *Application deadline:* For fall admission, 4/1 priority date for domestic students, 4/1 priority date for international students; for spring admission, 10/1 priority date for domestic students, 10/1 priority date for international students. Applications are processed on a rolling basis. Application fee: $60. Electronic applications accepted. *Expenses:* Tuition: Part-time $876 per credit. Required fees: $1 per credit. Tuition and fees vary according to campus/location. *Financial support:* In 2003–04, 3 students received support, including 3 fellowships with tuition reimbursements available; Federal Work-Study and institutionally sponsored loans also available. Financial award application deadline: 2/1. *Unit head:* Dr. Henry C. Merchant, Academic Director, 202-994-7123.

Georgia Institute of Technology, Graduate Studies and Research, College of Architecture, City and Regional Planning Program, Atlanta, GA 30332-0001. Offers architecture (PhD); economic development (MCRP); environmental planning and management (MCRP); geographic information systems (MCRP); land development (MCRP); land use planning (MCRP); transportation (MCRP); urban design (MCRP). *Accreditation:* ACSP. *Degree requirements:* For master's, thesis, internship. *Entrance requirements:* For master's, GRE General Test, minimum GPA of 2.7. Additional exam requirements/recommendations for international students: Required—TOEFL. *Application deadline:* For fall admission, 6/1 for domestic students. Application fee: $50. Electronic applications accepted. *Expenses:* Tuition, state resident: part-time $1,925 per semester. Tuition, nonresident: part-time $7,700 per semester. Required fees: $434 per semester. Full-time tuition and fees vary according to program. *Financial support:* Fellowships, research assistantships, teaching assistantships, career-related internships or fieldwork, Federal Work-Study, institutionally sponsored loans, and tuition waivers (partial) available. Support available to part-time students. Financial award application deadline: 3/1. *Unit head:* Dr. Steven P. French, Director, 404-894-2350. *Application contact:* Dot Matthews, Academic Assistant, 404-894-2352.

Hardin-Simmons University, Graduate School, Program in Environmental Management, Abilene, TX 79698-0001. Offers MS. Part-time programs available. *Faculty:* 7 full-time (0 women), 1 part-time/adjunct (0 women). *Students:* 2 full-time (0 women), 8 part-time (4 women); includes 1 minority (Hispanic American) Average age 32. 3 applicants, 100% accepted, 2 enrolled. In 2003, 4 degrees awarded. *Degree requirements:* For master's, thesis or alternative, internship, comprehensive exam. *Entrance requirements:* For master's, minimum undergraduate GPA of 3.0 in major, 2.7 overall; 2 semesters each of biology, chemistry, and geology; interview, writing sample, occupational experience. *Application deadline:* For fall admission, 8/15 for domestic students; for spring admission, 1/5 priority date for domestic students. Applications are processed on a rolling basis. Application fee: $50 ($100 for international students). *Expenses:* Tuition: Full-time $7,020; part-time $390 per hour. Required fees: $650; $110 per year. Tuition and fees vary according to course load, degree level and program. *Financial support:* In 2003–04, 8 students received support, including 1 fellowship with partial tuition reimbursement available (averaging $675 per year); career-related internships or fieldwork, Federal Work-Study, scholarships/grants, and tuition waivers (full and partial) also available. Support available to part-time students. Financial award application deadline: 3/15; financial award applicants required to submit FAFSA. *Faculty research:* South American history, herpetology, geology, environmental education, petroleum biodegradation, environmental ecology and microbiology. *Unit head:* Dr. Mark Ouimette, Director, 325-670-1383, Fax: 325-670-1391, E-mail: ouimette@hsutx.edu. *Application contact:* Dr. Gary Stanlake, Dean of Graduate Studies, 325-670-1298, Fax: 325-670-1564, E-mail: gradoff@hsutx.edu.

Environmental Management and Policy

Harvard University, Extension School, Cambridge, MA 02138-3722. Offers applied sciences (CAS); English for graduate and professional studies (DGP); environmental management (CEM); information technology (ALM); liberal arts (ALM); museum studies (CMS); premedical studies (Diploma); public health (CPH); publication and communication (CPC); special studies in administration and management (CSS); technologies of education (CTE). Part-time and evening/weekend programs available. *Faculty:* 49 part-time/adjunct. *Students:* 154 full-time (93 women), 588 part-time (303 women); includes 178 minority (28 African Americans, 3 American Indian/Alaska Native, 101 Asian Americans or Pacific Islanders, 46 Hispanic Americans). Average age 34. In 2003, 82 master's, 246 Diplomas awarded. *Degree requirements:* For master's, thesis. *Entrance requirements:* For master's, 3 completed graduate courses with grade of B or higher. Additional exam requirements/recommendations for international students: Required—TOEFL (minimum score 600 paper-based; 250 computer-based), TWE(minimum score 5). *Application deadline:* Applications are processed on a rolling basis. Application fee: $75. *Expenses:* Contact institution. Full-time tuition and fees vary according to program and student level. *Financial support:* In 2003–04, 225 students received support. Scholarships/grants available. Support available to part-time students. Financial award application deadline: 8/6; financial award applicants required to submit FAFSA. *Unit head:* Michael Shinagel, Dean. *Application contact:* Program Director, 617-495-4024, Fax: 617-495-9176.

Illinois Institute of Technology, Graduate College, Armour College of Engineering, Department of Chemical and Environmental Engineering, Chicago, IL 60616-3793. Offers chemical engineering (M Ch E, MS, PhD); environmental engineering (M Env E, MS, PhD); environmental management (MS); food process engineering (MFPE); food processing engineering (MS); gas engineering (MGE). Part-time and evening/weekend programs available. Postbaccalaureate distance learning degree programs offered. *Faculty:* 18 full-time (0 women), 7 part-time/adjunct (0 women). *Students:* 128 full-time (32 women), 84 part-time (22 women); includes 19 minority (5 African Americans, 13 Asian Americans or Pacific Islanders, 1 Hispanic American), 149 international. Average age 28. 650 applicants, 50% accepted, 42 enrolled. In 2003, 37 master's, 17 doctorates awarded. Terminal master's awarded for partial completion of doctoral program. *Degree requirements:* For master's, thesis (for some programs), comprehensive exam; for doctorate, thesis/dissertation, comprehensive exam. *Entrance requirements:* For master's and doctorate, GRE General Test, minimum undergraduate GPA of 3.0. Additional exam requirements/recommendations for international students: Required—TOEFL (minimum score 550 paper-based; 213 computer-based). *Application deadline:* For fall admission, 5/1 for domestic students, 5/1 for international students; for spring admission, 10/15 for domestic students, 10/15 for international students. Applications are processed on a rolling basis. Application fee: $40. Electronic applications accepted. *Expenses:* Tuition: Part-time $628 per credit. Tuition and fees vary according to course load and program. *Financial support:* In 2003–04, 1 fellowship with tuition reimbursement (averaging $6,000 per year), 56 research assistantships with tuition reimbursements (averaging $4,746 per year), 23 teaching assistantships with tuition reimbursements (averaging $2,558 per year) were awarded. Federal Work-Study, institutionally sponsored loans, scholarships/grants, and unspecified assistantships also available. Support available to part-time students. Financial award application deadline: 3/1; financial award applicants required to submit FAFSA. *Faculty research:* Particle technology and crystallization, energy and environmental engineering, polymer science and engineering, bioengineering, electrodynamical science and engineering. Total annual research expenditures: $1.9 million. *Unit head:* Dr. Fouad Teymour, Chair, 312-567-3040, Fax: 312-567-8874, E-mail: teymour@iit.edu. *Application contact:* Kelly A. Cherwin, Director of Graduate Outreach, 312-567-7974, Fax: 312-567-3494, E-mail: inquiry.grad@iit.edu.

Illinois Institute of Technology, Stuart Graduate School of Business, Program in Environmental Management, Chicago, IL 60616-3793. Offers MS, JD/MS, MBA/MS. Part-time and evening/weekend programs available. *Students:* 9 full-time (4 women), 24 part-time (12 women); includes 8 minority (1 African American, 5 Asian Americans or Pacific Islanders, 2 Hispanic Americans), 6 international. Average age 30. 17 applicants, 100% accepted, 9 enrolled. In 2003, 13 degrees awarded. *Entrance requirements:* For master's, GMAT or GRE General Test. Additional exam requirements/recommendations for international students: Required—TOEFL (minimum score 550 paper-based; 213 computer-based). *Application deadline:* For fall admission, 6/1 priority date for domestic students, 6/1 priority date for international students; for spring admission, 1/1 priority date for domestic students, 1/1 priority date for international students. Applications are processed on a rolling basis. Application fee: $75. Electronic applications accepted. *Expenses:* Contact institution. *Financial support:* Fellowships, institutionally sponsored loans, scholarships/grants, and unspecified assistantships available. Support available to part-time students. Financial award application deadline: 3/1; financial award applicants required to submit FAFSA. *Faculty research:* Removal of mercury vapor, renewable energy sources, application of GIS for sustainability, applying sustainable strategies to business. *Unit head:* Dr. George P. Nassos, Director, 312-906-6543, Fax: 312-906-6549, E-mail: george.nassos@iit.edu. *Application contact:* Vizente Freeman, Admission Coordinator, 312-906-6567, Fax: 312-906-6549, E-mail: admissions@stuart.iit.edu.

Instituto Tecnológico y de Estudios Superiores de Monterrey, Campus Estado de México, Professional and Graduate Division, Estado de Mexico, 52926, Mexico. Offers administration of information technologies (MITA); architecture (M Arch); business administration (GMBA, MBA); computer sciences (MCS, PhD); education (M Ed); educational institution administration (MAD); educational technology and innovation (PhD); electronic commerce (MEC); environmental systems (MS); finance (MAF); humanistic studies (MHS); information sciences and knowledge management (MISKM); information systems (MS); manufacturing systems (MS); marketing (MEM); quality systems and productivity (MS); science and materials engineering (PhD); telecommunications management (MTM). Part-time programs available. Postbaccalaureate distance learning degree programs offered (minimal on-campus study). *Degree requirements:* For master's, one foreign language, thesis (for some programs), registration; for doctorate, one foreign language, thesis/dissertation, registration (for some programs). *Entrance requirements:* For master's, E-PAEP 500, interview; for doctorate, E-PAEP 500, research proposal. Additional exam requirements/recommendations for international students: Required—TOEFL (minimum score 550 paper-based). *Faculty research:* Surface treatments by plasmas, mechanical properties, robotics, graphical computing, mechatronics security protocols.

Instituto Tecnológico y de Estudios Superiores de Monterrey, Campus Irapuato, Graduate Programs, Irapuato, , Mexico. Offers administration (MBA); administration of information technology (MAIT); administration of telecommunications (MAT); architecture (M Arch); computer science (MCS); education (M Ed); educational administration (MEA); educational innovation and technology (DEIT); educational technology (MET); electronic commerce (MBA); environmental administration and planning (MEAP); environmental systems (MES); finances (MBA); humanistic studies (MHS); international management for Latin American executives (MIMLAE); library and information science (MLIS); manufacturing quality management (MMQM); marketing research (MBA).

Iowa State University of Science and Technology, Graduate College, College of Agriculture, Department of Natural Resource Ecology and Management, Ames, IA 50011. Offers animal ecology (MS, PhD), including animal ecology, fisheries biology, wildlife biology; forestry (MS, PhD). *Faculty:* 23 full-time, 7 part-time/adjunct. *Students:* 36 full-time (13 women), 7 part-time (2 women), 8 international. 44 applicants, 36% accepted, 12 enrolled. In 2003, 6 master's, 4 doctorates awarded. *Median time to degree:* Master's–2.7 years full-time; doctorate–4.5 years full-time. *Degree requirements:* For master's, thesis (for some programs); for doctorate, thesis/dissertation. *Entrance requirements:* For master's and doctorate, GRE General Test. Additional exam requirements/recommendations for international students: Required—TOEFL (paper score 547; computer score 210) or IELTS (score 6). *Application deadline:* For fall admission, 1/1 priority date for domestic students, 1/1 priority date for international students; for spring admission, 9/1 priority date for domestic students, 9/1 priority date for international students. Application fee: $30 ($70 for international students). Electronic applications accepted. Tuition, nonresident: part-time $560 per credit. Required fees: $38 per unit. *Financial support:* In 2003–04, 35 research assistantships with full and partial tuition reimbursements (averaging $17,496 per year), 4 teaching assistantships with full and partial tuition reimbursements (averaging $17,496 per year) were awarded. *Unit head:* Dr. J. Michael Kelly, Chair, 515-294-1166. *Application contact:* Lyn Van De Pol, Information Contact, 515-294-6148, E-mail: lvdp@iastate.edu.

The Johns Hopkins University, Zanvyl Krieger School of Arts and Sciences, Advanced Academic Programs, Baltimore, MD 21218-2699. Offers applied economics (MA); bioinformatics (MS); biotechnology (MS); communications in contemporary society (MA); environmental sciences and policy (MS); government (MA); liberal arts (MA); writing (MA). Part-time and evening/weekend programs available. Postbaccalaureate distance learning degree programs offered. *Faculty:* 27 full-time, 230 part-time/adjunct. *Students:* 43 full-time (23 women), 1,395 part-time (849 women). Average age 33. 330 applicants, 74% accepted, 243 enrolled. In 2003, 479 degrees awarded. *Median time to degree:* Master's–1.5 years full-time, 3 years part-time. *Degree requirements:* For master's, thesis (for some programs). *Entrance requirements:* For master's, minimum GPA of 3.0. Additional exam requirements/recommendations for international students: Required—TOEFL. *Application deadline:* For fall admission, 5/31 priority date for domestic students, 5/31 priority date for international students; for spring admission, 10/31 priority date for domestic students, 10/31 priority date for international students. Applications are processed on a rolling basis. Application fee: $60. Electronic applications accepted. *Expenses:* Tuition: Full-time $28,730; part-time $1,490 per course. Part-time tuition and fees vary according to course load, campus/location and program. *Financial support:* In 2003–04, 151 students received support. Scholarships/grants available. Financial award applicants required to submit FAFSA. *Unit head:* Deborah Cebula, Dean, 800-847-3330, Fax: 410-516-6017, E-mail: advanced@jhu.edu.

Kansas State University, Graduate School, College of Architecture, Planning and Design, Department of Regional and Community Planning, Manhattan, KS 66506. Offers environmental planning and management (MA); regional and community planning (MRCP). *Accreditation:* ACSP (one or more programs are accredited). Part-time and evening/weekend programs available. Postbaccalaureate distance learning degree programs offered (minimal on-campus study). *Faculty:* 22 full-time (5 women). *Students:* 17 full-time (6 women), 5 part-time (1 woman); includes 2 minority (1 African American, 1 Asian American or Pacific Islander), 4 international. 26 applicants, 65% accepted, 8 enrolled. *Degree requirements:* For master's, thesis, oral exam. *Entrance requirements:* For master's, minimum GPA of 3.0, portfolio. *Application deadline:* For fall admission, 2/1 for domestic students; for spring admission, 10/1 priority date for domestic students. Applications are processed on a rolling basis. Application fee: $30. Electronic applications accepted. *Expenses:* Tuition, state resident: part-time $155 per credit hour. Tuition, nonresident: part-time $428 per credit hour. Required fees: $11 per credit hour. *Financial support:* In 2003–04, 6 teaching assistantships with full tuition reimbursements (averaging $6,964 per year) were awarded; research assistantships, career-related internships or fieldwork, Federal Work-Study, institutionally sponsored loans, and scholarships/grants also available. Support available to part-time students. Financial award application deadline: 3/1; financial award applicants required to submit FAFSA. *Faculty research:* Community planning and design, water resource planning, golf course design, reclaimed landscapes, wind energy in Kansas. Total annual research expenditures: $50,000. *Unit head:* Prof. Dan Donelin, Head, 785-532-5961, Fax: 785-532-6722, E-mail: dandon@ksu.edu. *Application contact:* Prof. C. A. Keithley, Graduate Coordinator, 785-532-2440, Fax: 785-532-6722, E-mail: cak@ksu.edu.

Kean University, College of Business and Public Administration, Department of Public Administration, Union, NJ 07083. Offers environmental management (MPA); health services administration (MPA); public administration (MPA). *Accreditation:* NASPAA. Part-time and evening/weekend programs available. *Faculty:* 11 full-time (6 women). *Students:* 64 full-time (42 women), 88 part-time (58 women); includes 93 minority (68 African Americans, 5 Asian Americans or Pacific Islanders, 20 Hispanic Americans), 9 international. Average age 33. 74 applicants, 82% accepted, 49 enrolled. In 2003, 58 degrees awarded. *Degree requirements:* For master's, internship. *Entrance requirements:* For master's, GRE General Test, 2 letters of recommendation. *Application deadline:* For fall admission, 6/15 for domestic students; for spring admission, 11/15 for domestic students. Application fee: $60. *Expenses:* Tuition, state resident: full-time $7,488; part-time $312 per credit. Tuition, nonresident: full-time $9,528; part-time $397 per credit. Required fees: $1,814; $76 per credit. *Financial support:* In 2003–04, 23 research assistantships with full tuition reimbursements (averaging $2,700 per year) were awarded; career-related internships or fieldwork, institutionally sponsored loans, and unspecified assistantships also available. Financial award application deadline: 5/1. *Faculty research:* Fiscal impact of New Federalism, New Jersey state and local government, computer application in public management. *Unit head:* Dr. M. Laury, Coordinator, 908-737-4309, Fax: 908-737-4305. *Application contact:* Joanne Morris, Director of Graduate Admissions, 908-737-3355, Fax: 908-737-3354, E-mail: grad-adm@kean.edu.

Lamar University, College of Graduate Studies, College of Engineering, Department of Civil Engineering, Beaumont, TX 77710. Offers civil engineering (ME, MES, DE); environmental engineering (MS); environmental studies (MS). Part-time programs available. *Faculty:* 7 full-time (0 women). *Students:* 52 full-time (6 women), 10 part-time (3 women); includes 1 minority (Hispanic American), 60 international. Average age 25. 129 applicants, 62% accepted, 16 enrolled. In 2003, 54 master's, 1 doctorate awarded. *Degree requirements:* For master's, thesis optional; for doctorate, thesis/dissertation. *Entrance requirements:* For master's and doctorate, GRE General Test. Additional exam requirements/recommendations for international students: Required—TOEFL. *Application deadline:* For fall admission, 5/15 for domestic students; for spring admission, 10/1 priority date for domestic students. Applications are processed on a rolling basis. Application fee: $25 ($50 for international students). *Expenses:* Tuition, state resident: part-time $170 per semester hour. Tuition, nonresident: part-time $351 per semester hour. Required fees: $174 per semester hour. One-time fee: $10 part-time. *Financial support:* In 2003–04, 45 fellowships with partial tuition reimbursements (averaging $1,000 per year), 10 research assistantships with partial tuition reimbursements (averaging $7,200 per year), 3 teaching assistantships with partial tuition reimbursements (averaging $7,200 per year) were awarded. Scholarships/grants and tuition waivers (partial) also available. Financial award application deadline: 4/1. *Faculty research:* Environmental remediations, construction productivity, geotechnical soil stabilization, lake/reservoir hydrodynamics, air pollution. Total annual research expenditures: $47,688. *Unit head:* Dr. Enno Koehn, Chair, 409-880-8759, Fax: 409-880-8121, E-mail: koehneu@hal.lamar.edu. *Application contact:* Sandy Drane, Coordinator of Graduate Admissions, 409-880-8356, Fax: 409-880-8414, E-mail: gradmissions@hal.lamar.edu.

Long Island University, C.W. Post Campus, College of Liberal Arts and Sciences, Program in Environmental Studies, Brookville, NY 11548-1300. Offers environmental studies (MS). Part-time and evening/weekend programs available. *Faculty:* 16 full-time (3 women), 2 part-time/adjunct (0 women). *Students:* 7 full-time (5 women), 25 part-time (13 women); includes 2 minority (both Hispanic Americans) Average age 30. 21 applicants, 52% accepted, 6 enrolled. In 2003, 1 degree awarded. *Degree requirements:* For master's, internship or thesis. *Entrance requirements:* For master's, 1 year of course work in general chemistry and biology or geology; 1 semester in organic chemistry; computer proficiency. *Application deadline:* Applications are processed on a rolling basis. Application fee: $30. Electronic applications accepted. *Expenses:* Tuition: Part-time $658 per credit. Tuition and fees vary according to course load, degree level and program. *Financial support:* In 2003–04, 1 teaching assistantship was awarded; career-related internships or fieldwork, Federal Work-Study, institutionally sponsored loans, and unspecified assistantships also available. Support available to part-time students. Financial award application deadline: 5/15; financial award applicants required to submit CSS PROFILE or FAFSA. *Faculty research:* Symbiotic algae, local marine organisms, coastal processes, global tectonics, paleomagnetism. *Unit head:* Dr. Lillian Hess, Director, 516-299-2428, Fax: 516-299-3945, E-mail: lhess@liu.edu.

Louisiana State University and Agricultural and Mechanical College, Graduate School, School of the Coast and Environment, Department of Environmental Studies, Baton Rouge, LA 70803. Offers environmental planning and management (MS); environmental toxicology (MS).

Faculty: 14 full-time (3 women). *Students:* 15 full-time (6 women), 14 part-time (8 women); includes 4 minority (2 African Americans, 2 American Indian/Alaska Native), 3 international. Average age 30. 24 applicants, 38% accepted, 5 enrolled. In 2003, 9 degrees awarded. *Degree requirements:* For master's, thesis (for some programs). *Entrance requirements:* For master's, GRE General Test, minimum GPA of 3.0. Additional exam requirements/recommendations for international students: Required—TOEFL (minimum score 550 paper-based; 213 computer-based). *Application deadline:* For fall admission, 1/25 priority date for domestic students, 5/15 priority date for international students. Applications are processed on a rolling basis. Application fee: $25. Electronic applications accepted. *Expenses:* Tuition, state resident: part-time $337 per hour. Tuition, nonresident: part-time $577 per hour. *Financial support:* In 2003–04, 7 students received support, including 1 fellowship (averaging $14,000 per year), 9 research assistantships with partial tuition reimbursements available (averaging $10,478 per year); teaching assistantships with partial tuition reimbursements available, career-related internships or fieldwork and unspecified assistantships also available. Financial award applicants required to submit FAFSA. *Faculty research:* Fates and movement of pollutants, neurobiotic metabolism, application of cellular toxicity/mutagenicity testing. Total annual research expenditures: $1.1 million. *Unit head:* Dr. Ralph J. Portier, Chair, 225-578-8521, Fax: 225-578-4286, E-mail: rportie@lsu.edu.

Michigan State University, Graduate School, College of Agriculture and Natural Resources, Department of Community, Agriculture, Recreation, and Resource Studies, East Lansing, MI 48824. Offers MS, PhD. *Faculty:* 31 full-time (6 women). *Students:* 81 full-time (43 women), 53 part-time (25 women); includes 14 minority (7 African Americans, 3 American Indian/Alaska Native, 1 Asian American or Pacific Islander, 3 Hispanic Americans), 45 international. Average age 34. 109 applicants, 39% accepted. In 2003, 36 master's, 16 doctorates awarded. *Degree requirements:* For master's, thesis or alternative; for doctorate, thesis/dissertation, comprehensive exam. *Entrance requirements:* For master's and doctorate, GRE General Test, resumé, 3 letters of recommendation. Additional exam requirements/recommendations for international students: Required—TOEFL (minimum score 550 paper-based; 213 computer-based), Michigan State University ELT (80), Michigan ELAB (83). *Application deadline:* For fall admission, 12/23 for domestic students. Application fee: $50. Electronic applications accepted. *Expenses:* Tuition, state resident: part-time $291 per hour. Tuition, nonresident: part-time $589 per hour. *Financial support:* In 2003–04, 33 fellowships with tuition reimbursements (averaging $2,636 per year), 42 research assistantships with tuition reimbursements (averaging $11,661 per year) were awarded. Federal Work-Study also available. Support available to part-time students. *Faculty research:* Natural resources and the environment, recreation and tourism systems, education, communication, and leadership. Total annual research expenditures: $2 million. *Unit head:* Dr. Scott G. Witter, Acting Chairperson. *Application contact:* Cheryl Lowe, Graduate Secretary, 517-353-5190 Ext. 102, Fax: 517-432-3597, E-mail: lowec@msu.edu.

Michigan Technological University, Graduate School, College of Sciences and Arts, Department of Social Sciences, Program in Environmental Policy, Houghton, MI 49931-1295. Offers MS. Part-time programs available. *Faculty:* 15 full-time (5 women), 1 part-time/adjunct (0 women). *Students:* 7 full-time (5 women), 3 part-time (all women); includes 1 minority (Hispanic American), 4 international. Average age 26. 15 applicants, 40% accepted, 4 enrolled. In 2003, 4 degrees awarded. *Degree requirements:* For master's, comprehensive exam, registration. *Entrance requirements:* Additional exam requirements/recommendations for international students: Required—TOEFL. *Application deadline:* For fall admission, 3/1 for domestic students. Applications are processed on a rolling basis. Application fee: $40 ($45 for international students). Electronic applications accepted. Tuition, nonresident: full-time $9,552; part-time $398 per credit. Required fees: $768. *Financial support:* In 2003–04, 6 students received support, including fellowships with full tuition reimbursements available (averaging $13,500 per year), 3 research assistantships with full tuition reimbursements available (averaging $8,950 per year), 3 teaching assistantships with full tuition reimbursements available (averaging $8,950 per year); career-related internships or fieldwork, Federal Work-Study, institutionally sponsored loans, scholarships/grants, traineeships, unspecified assistantships, and co-op also available. Support available to part-time students. Financial award application deadline: 3/1; financial award applicants required to submit FAFSA. *Faculty research:* Citizen participation, pollution prevention, natural resource policy, energy policy, environmental history. *Application contact:* Dr. Kathleen E. Halvorsen, Director, 906-487-2824, Fax: 906-487-2468, E-mail: kehalvor@mtu.edu.

Announcement: Michigan Tech's Master's in Environmental Policy provides students with the intellectual framework they need to develop, implement, manage, and evaluate environmental policies and programs. EP students acquire an understanding of the social context of environmental problems and are able to move readily among science, policy, and social analysis.

See in-depth description on page 735.

Michigan Technological University, Graduate School, School of Forest Resources and Environmental Science, Program in Forest Ecology and Management, Houghton, MI 49931-1295. Offers applied ecology (MS); forest ecology and management (MS); forestry (MS). Part-time programs available. *Faculty:* 19 full-time (4 women). *Students:* 43 full-time (20 women), 10 part-time (5 women); includes 2 minority (both Hispanic Americans) Average age 27. 23 applicants, 65% accepted, 12 enrolled. In 2003, 11 degrees awarded. *Degree requirements:* For master's, thesis (for some programs), comprehensive exam, registration. *Entrance requirements:* Additional exam requirements/recommendations for international students: Required—TOEFL. *Application deadline:* For fall admission, 3/15 for domestic students. Applications are processed on a rolling basis. Application fee: $40 ($45 for international students). Electronic applications accepted. Tuition, nonresident: full-time $9,552; part-time $398 per credit. Required fees: $768. *Financial support:* In 2003–04, 23 students received support, including 2 fellowships with full tuition reimbursements available (averaging $13,500 per year), 17 research assistantships with full tuition reimbursements available (averaging $8,950 per year), 4 teaching assistantships with full tuition reimbursements available (averaging $8,950 per year); career-related internships or fieldwork, Federal Work-Study, institutionally sponsored loans, scholarships/grants, traineeships, unspecified assistantships, and co-op also available. Support available to part-time students. Financial award application deadline: 2/1; financial award applicants required to submit FAFSA. *Application contact:* Dr. Margaret R. Gale, Graduate Coordinator, 906-487-2352, Fax: 906-487-2915, E-mail: mrgale@mtu.edu.

See in-depth description on page 791.

Montana State University–Bozeman, College of Graduate Studies, College of Engineering, Department of Civil Engineering, Bozeman, MT 59717. Offers civil engineering (MS); construction engineering management (MCEM); engineering (PhD); environmental engineering (MS); land rehabilitation (interdisciplinary) (MS). Part-time programs available. *Faculty:* 20 full-time (2 women), 3 part-time/adjunct (0 women). *Students:* 20 full-time (5 women), 15 part-time (2 women), 2 international. Average age 28. 29 applicants, 90% accepted, 15 enrolled. In 2003, 18 degrees awarded. *Degree requirements:* For master's, thesis (for some programs), comprehensive exam, registration; for doctorate, thesis/dissertation, comprehensive exam, registration. *Entrance requirements:* For master's and doctorate, GRE General Test. Additional exam requirements/recommendations for international students: Required—TOEFL (minimum score 550 paper-based; 213 computer-based). *Application deadline:* For fall admission, 7/15 priority date for domestic students, 5/15 priority date for international students; for spring admission, 12/1 priority date for domestic students, 10/1 priority date for international students. Applications are processed on a rolling basis. Application fee: $50. Electronic applications accepted. *Expenses:* Tuition, state resident: full-time $3,907; part-time $163 per credit. Tuition, nonresident: full-time $12,383; part-time $516 per credit. Required fees: $890; $445 per term. Tuition and fees vary according to course load and program. *Financial support:* In 2003–04, 15 students received support, including 3 fellowships with partial tuition reimbursements available (averaging $16,200 per year), 7 research assistantships with partial tuition reimbursements available (averaging $8,100 per year), 6 teaching assistantships with partial tuition reimbursements available (averaging $9,000 per year); institutionally sponsored loans, scholarships/grants, and tuition waivers (partial) also available. Financial award application deadline: 3/1; financial award applicants required to submit FAFSA. *Faculty research:* Snow and ice mechanics, transportation systems and infrastructure, geotechnical testing and pavements, wetlands and rivers. Total annual research expenditures: $5.2 million. *Unit head:* Dr. Brett Gunnick, Head, 406-994-2111, Fax: 406-994-6105, E-mail: bgunnick@montana.edu.

Montana State University–Bozeman, College of Graduate Studies, College of Letters and Science, Department of Earth Sciences, Bozeman, MT 59717. Offers earth sciences (MS, PhD); land rehabilitation (interdisciplinary) (MS). Part-time programs available. *Faculty:* 11 full-time (1 woman), 3 part-time/adjunct (0 women). *Students:* 8 full-time (4 women), 24 part-time (10 women). Average age 29. 13 applicants, 85% accepted, 10 enrolled. In 2003, 5 degrees awarded. *Degree requirements:* For master's, thesis (for some programs), comprehensive exam, registration; for doctorate, thesis/dissertation, comprehensive exam, registration. *Entrance requirements:* For master's and doctorate, GRE General Test. Additional exam requirements/recommendations for international students: Required—TOEFL (minimum score 550 paper-based; 213 computer-based). *Application deadline:* For fall admission, 7/15 priority date for domestic students, 5/15 priority date for international students; for spring admission, 12/1 priority date for domestic students. Applications are processed on a rolling basis. Application fee: $50. Electronic applications accepted. *Expenses:* Tuition, state resident: full-time $3,907; part-time $163 per credit. Tuition, nonresident: full-time $12,383; part-time $516 per credit. Required fees: $890; $445 per term. Tuition and fees vary according to course load and program. *Financial support:* In 2003–04, 3 students received support, including 4 research assistantships (averaging $4,471 per year), 13 teaching assistantships with full tuition reimbursements available (averaging $8,787 per year); scholarships/grants and tuition waivers (partial) also available. Financial award application deadline: 3/1; financial award applicants required to submit FAFSA. *Faculty research:* Cultural geography, paleontology, GIS. Total annual research expenditures: $579,446. *Unit head:* Dr. David Lageson, Head, 406-994-3331, Fax: 406-994-6923, E-mail: lageson@montana.edu.

Montclair State University, The Graduate School, College of Science and Mathematics, Department of Earth and Environmental Studies, Program in Environmental Management, Upper Montclair, NJ 07043-1624. Offers MA, D Env M. *Faculty:* 3 full-time (2 women), 6 part-time/adjunct. *Students:* 10 full-time (3 women), 14 part-time (8 women); includes 5 minority (2 African Americans, 2 Asian Americans or Pacific Islanders, 1 Hispanic American), 2 international. 21 applicants, 76% accepted, 16 enrolled. In 2003, 21 master's, 3 doctorates awarded. *Entrance requirements:* For master's, GRE General Test, 2 letters of recommendation. Application fee: $60. *Expenses:* Tuition, state resident: full-time $8,771; part-time $323 per credit. Tuition, nonresident: full-time $10,365; part-time $470 per credit. Required fees: $42 per credit. Tuition and fees vary according to degree level and program. *Unit head:* Dr. Michael Kruge, Adviser, 973-655-7668.

See in-depth description on page 737.

Monterey Institute of International Studies, Graduate School of International Policy Studies, Program in International Environmental Policy, Monterey, CA 93940-2691. Offers MA. *Students:* 42 full-time (25 women), 2 part-time (1 woman); includes 3 minority (2 Asian Americans or Pacific Islanders, 1 Hispanic American), 8 international. Average age 29. 55 applicants, 85% accepted, 19 enrolled. In 2003, 23 degrees awarded. *Degree requirements:* For master's, one foreign language. *Entrance requirements:* For master's, minimum GPA of 3.0, proficiency in a foreign language. Additional exam requirements/recommendations for international students: Required—TOEFL. *Application deadline:* For fall admission, 3/15 for domestic students; for spring admission, 10/1 priority date for domestic students. Applications are processed on a rolling basis. Application fee: $50. Electronic applications accepted. *Expenses:* Tuition: Full-time $22,180; part-time $990 per credit. Required fees: $200. *Financial support:* Applicants required to submit FAFSA. *Unit head:* Dr. Laura Strohm, Head. *Application contact:* 831-647-4123, Fax: 831-647-6405, E-mail: admit@miis.edu.

Naropa University, Graduate Programs, Program in Environmental Leadership, Boulder, CO 80302-6697. Offers MA. *Faculty:* 3 full-time (all women), 9 part-time/adjunct (7 women). *Students:* 21 full-time (14 women), 22 part-time (16 women); includes 3 minority (all Hispanic Americans), 4 international. Average age 31. 30 applicants, 87% accepted, 15 enrolled. In 2003, 4 degrees awarded. *Degree requirements:* For master's, thesis. *Entrance requirements:* For master's, interview. Additional exam requirements/recommendations for international students: Required—TOEFL (minimum score 600 paper-based; 250 computer-based). *Application deadline:* For fall admission, 1/15 priority date for domestic students, 1/15 priority date for international students; for spring admission, 10/15 priority date for domestic students. Applications are processed on a rolling basis. Application fee: $60. Electronic applications accepted. *Expenses:* Tuition: Full-time $12,100; part-time $550 per hour. Required fees: $560. *Financial support:* In 2003–04, 13 students received support. Federal Work-Study, scholarships/grants, and tuition waivers (partial) available. Support available to part-time students. Financial award application deadline: 3/1; financial award applicants required to submit FAFSA. *Unit head:* Dr. Anne Parker, Chair, 303-546-3525. *Application contact:* Donna McIntyre, Admissions Counselor, 303-546-3555, Fax: 303-546-3583, E-mail: donna@naropa.edu.

National Technological University, Programs in Engineering, Minneapolis, MN 55401. Offers chemical engineering (MS); computer engineering (MS); computer science (MS); electrical engineering (MS); engineering management (MS); environmental systems management (MS); manufacturing systems engineering (MS); materials science and engineering (MS); mechanical engineering (MS); microelectronics and semiconductor engineering (MS); software engineering (MS); special majors (MS); systems engineering (MS). Part-time and evening/weekend programs available. Postbaccalaureate distance learning degree programs offered (no on-campus study). *Students:* Average age 30. In 2003, 132 degrees awarded. *Median time to degree:* Master's–5 years part-time. *Degree requirements:* For master's, thesis (for some programs), registration. *Entrance requirements:* For master's, BS in engineering or related field; minimum GPA of 2.9. *Application deadline:* Applications are processed on a rolling basis. Application fee: $50. Electronic applications accepted. *Expenses:* Tuition: Part-time $865 per semester hour. Required fees: $100 per semester hour. Part-time tuition and fees vary according to program. *Unit head:* Dr. James B. Patton, Provost/Chief Academic Officer, 612-312-1243, Fax: 612-312-2400, E-mail: provost@ntu.edu. *Application contact:* Kay Smith, Admissions Specialist, 800-586-9976, Fax: 410-843-6507, E-mail: kay.smith@ntu.edu.

New Jersey Institute of Technology, Office of Graduate Studies, College of Science and Liberal Arts, Department of Humanities and Social Sciences, Program in Environmental Policy Studies, Newark, NJ 07102. Offers MS, PhD. Part-time and evening/weekend programs available. *Students:* 5 full-time (3 women), 21 part-time (12 women); includes 4 minority (2 African Americans, 2 Asian Americans or Pacific Islanders), 1 international. Average age 32. 19 applicants, 58% accepted, 4 enrolled. In 2003, 2 degrees awarded. Terminal master's awarded for partial completion of doctoral program. *Degree requirements:* For master's, thesis or alternative. *Entrance requirements:* For master's, GRE General Test. *Application deadline:* For fall admission, 6/5 for domestic students; for spring admission, 10/15 for domestic students. Applications are processed on a rolling basis. Application fee: $50. Electronic applications accepted. *Expenses:* Tuition, state resident: full-time $9,620; part-time $520 per credit. Tuition, nonresident: full-time $13,542; part-time $715 per credit. Tuition and fees vary according to course load. *Financial support:* Fellowships with full and partial tuition reimbursements, research assistantships with full and partial tuition reimbursements, teaching assistantships with full and partial tuition reimbursements, career-related internships or fieldwork, Federal Work-Study, institutionally sponsored loans, and unspecified assistantships available. Financial award application deadline: 3/15. *Application contact:* Kathryn Kelly, Director of Admissions, 973-596-3300, Fax: 973-596-3461, E-mail: admissions@njit.edu.

New Mexico Highlands University, Graduate Studies, College of Arts and Sciences, Department of Natural Sciences, Las Vegas, NM 87701. Offers applied chemistry (MS); biology (MS); environmental science and management (MS). Part-time programs available. *Faculty:* 11

Environmental Management and Policy

New Mexico Highlands University (continued)

full-time (3 women), 6 part-time/adjunct (2 women). *Students:* 21 full-time (9 women), 12 part-time (7 women). Average age 30. 30 applicants, 70% accepted, 11 enrolled. In 2003, 5 degrees awarded. *Degree requirements:* For master's, thesis, comprehensive exam, registration. *Entrance requirements:* For master's, minimum undergraduate GPA of 3.0. Additional exam requirements/recommendations for international students: Required—TOEFL (minimum score 540 paper-based; 207 computer-based). *Application deadline:* For fall admission, 8/1 for domestic students. Applications are processed on a rolling basis. Application fee: $15. *Expenses:* Tuition, state resident: full-time $2,328; part-time $97 per hour. Tuition, nonresident: full-time $9,672. One-time fee: $50 full-time; $20 part-time. *Financial support:* In 2003–04, 13 students received support, including 13 teaching assistantships (averaging $11,500 per year); research assistantships with full and partial tuition reimbursements available, Federal Work-Study, institutionally sponsored loans, scholarships/grants, and unspecified assistantships also available. Support available to part-time students. Financial award application deadline: 3/1. *Unit head:* Dr. Ken Bentson, Director. *Application contact:* Dr. Linda S. LaGrange, Dean of Graduate Studies, 505-454-3194, Fax: 505-454-3558, E-mail: lagrange_l@nmhu.edu.

New York Institute of Technology, Graduate Division, School of Engineering and Technology, Program in Energy Management, Old Westbury, NY 11568-8000. Offers energy management (MS); energy technology (Advanced Certificate); environmental management (Advanced Certificate); facilities management (Advanced Certificate). Part-time and evening/weekend programs available. Postbaccalaureate distance learning degree programs offered. *Students:* 15 full-time (2 women), 61 part-time (7 women); includes 11 minority (2 African Americans, 1 American Indian/Alaska Native, 3 Asian Americans or Pacific Islanders, 5 Hispanic Americans), 17 international. Average age 35. 64 applicants, 80% accepted, 31 enrolled. In 2003, 19 degrees awarded. *Degree requirements:* For master's, thesis or alternative, comprehensive exam. *Entrance requirements:* For master's, minimum QPA of 2.85. *Application deadline:* For fall admission, 7/1 for domestic students; for spring admission, 12/1 priority date for domestic students. Applications are processed on a rolling basis. Application fee: $50. Electronic applications accepted. *Expenses:* Tuition: Part-time $598 per credit. One-time fee: $50 part-time. *Financial support:* Fellowships, research assistantships with partial tuition reimbursements, institutionally sponsored loans, tuition waivers (full and partial), and unspecified assistantships available. Support available to part-time students. Financial award applicants required to submit FAFSA. *Unit head:* Dr. Robert Amundsen, Director, 516-686-7578. *Application contact:* Jacquelyn Nealon, Dean of Admissions and Financial Aid, 516-686-7925, Fax: 516-686-7613, E-mail: jnealon@nyit.edu.

North Dakota State University, The Graduate School, College of Agriculture, Food Systems, and Natural Resources, Department of Animal and Range Sciences, Fargo, ND 58105. Offers animal science (MS, PhD); natural resources management (MS, PhD); range science (MS, PhD). *Degree requirements:* For master's and doctorate, thesis/dissertation. *Entrance requirements:* For master's and doctorate, GRE General Test. Additional exam requirements/recommendations for international students: Required—TOEFL. Tuition, nonresident: full-time $4,071. Required fees: $493. *Faculty research:* Reproduction, nutrition, meat and muscle biology, breeding/genetics.

North Dakota State University, The Graduate School, College of Agriculture, Food Systems, and Natural Resources, Department of Entomology, Fargo, ND 58105. Offers entomology (MS, PhD); environment and conservation science (MS, PhD); natural resouarce management (MS); natural resource management (PhD). Part-time programs available. *Faculty:* 8 full-time (2 women), 6 part-time/adjunct (0 women). *Students:* 20 full-time (6 women), 2 part-time (1 woman); includes 10 minority (2 African Americans, 8 Asian Americans or Pacific Islanders), 10 international. 5 applicants, 60% accepted, 3 enrolled. In 2003, 3 degrees awarded. *Median time to degree:* Master's–2.3 years full-time. *Degree requirements:* For master's, thesis/dissertation; for doctorate, thesis/dissertation, comprehensive exam. *Entrance requirements:* For master's and doctorate, minimum GPA of 3.0. Additional exam requirements/recommendations for international students: Required—TOEFL. *Application deadline:* Applications are processed on a rolling basis. Application fee: $35 ($50 for international students). Tuition, nonresident: full-time $4,071. Required fees: $493. *Financial support:* In 2003–04, 19 research assistantships with full tuition reimbursements (averaging $13,800 per year) were awarded; Federal Work-Study and institutionally sponsored loans also available. Financial award application deadline: 4/15. *Faculty research:* Insect systematics, conservation biology, integrated pest management, insect behavior, insect biology. *Unit head:* Dr. Gary J. Brewer, Chair, 701-231-7908, Fax: 701-231-8557, E-mail: gary.brewer@ndsu.nodak.edu.

North Dakota State University, The Graduate School, College of Agriculture, Food Systems, and Natural Resources, Department of Plant Sciences, Fargo, ND 58105. Offers crop and weed sciences (MS); horticulture (MS); natural resources management (MS); plant sciences (PhD). Part-time programs available. *Faculty:* 39 full-time (3 women), 19 part-time/adjunct (1 woman). *Students:* 63 full-time (30 women), 8 part-time (2 women); includes 1 minority (Asian American or Pacific Islander), 37 international. Average age 26. 40 applicants, 50% accepted. In 2003, 1 master's, 2 doctorates awarded. *Degree requirements:* For master's and doctorate, thesis/dissertation. *Entrance requirements:* Additional exam requirements/recommendations for international students: Required—TOEFL. *Application deadline:* Applications are processed on a rolling basis. Application fee: $35 ($50 for international students). Electronic applications accepted. Tuition, nonresident: full-time $4,071. Required fees: $493. *Financial support:* In 2003–04, 1 student received support, including 2 fellowships (averaging $19,950 per year), 60 research assistantships; teaching assistantships, Federal Work-Study and institutionally sponsored loans also available. Financial award application deadline: 4/15. *Faculty research:* Biotechnology, weed control science, plant breeding, plant genetics, crop physiology. Total annual research expenditures: $880,000. *Unit head:* Dr. Al Schneiter, Chair, 701-231-7971, Fax: 701-231-8474, E-mail: albert.schneiter@ndsu.nodak.edu.

North Dakota State University, The Graduate School, College of Agriculture, Food Systems, and Natural Resources, Department of Soil Science, Fargo, ND 58105. Offers natural resources management (MS); soil sciences (MS, PhD). Part-time programs available. *Faculty:* 11 full-time (0 women), 4 part-time/adjunct (0 women). *Students:* 7 full-time (3 women), 3 part-time (1 woman), 3 international. Average age 23. 4 applicants, 75% accepted, 2 enrolled. In 2003, 1 degree awarded, leading to business/industry 100%. *Median time to degree:* Master's–2 years full-time. *Degree requirements:* For master's and doctorate, thesis/dissertation, classroom teaching, comprehensive exam, registration. *Entrance requirements:* For master's and doctorate, GRE General Test. Additional exam requirements/recommendations for international students: Required—TOEFL (minimum score 525 paper-based; 193 computer-based). *Application deadline:* Applications are processed on a rolling basis. Application fee: $35. Tuition, nonresident: full-time $4,071. Required fees: $493. *Financial support:* In 2003–04, 1 student received support, including 1 fellowship with full tuition reimbursement available (averaging $16,000 per year), 3 research assistantships with full tuition reimbursements available (averaging $13,500 per year); Federal Work-Study, institutionally sponsored loans, and scholarships/grants also available. Financial award application deadline: 3/15. *Faculty research:* Microclimate, nitrogen management, landscape studies, water quality, soil management. *Unit head:* Dr. Jimmie L. Richardson, Chair, 701-231-8903, Fax: 701-231-7861, E-mail: jimmie.richardson@ndsu.nodak.edu.

North Dakota State University, The Graduate School, College of Science and Mathematics, Department of Biological Sciences, Fargo, ND 58105. Offers botany (MS, PhD); cellular and molecular biology (PhD); environmental and conservation sciences (PhD); genomics (PhD); natural resources management (MS); zoology (MS, PhD). *Degree requirements:* For master's and doctorate, thesis/dissertation. *Entrance requirements:* For master's and doctorate, GRE General Test. Additional exam requirements/recommendations for international students: Required—TOEFL. Electronic applications accepted. Tuition, nonresident: full-time $4,071. Required fees: $493. *Faculty research:* Comparative endocrinology, physiology, behavioral ecology, plant cell biology, aquatic biology.

North Dakota State University, The Graduate School, Interdisciplinary Program in Natural Resources Management, Fargo, ND 58105. Offers MS, PhD. Part-time programs available. *Faculty:* 16 full-time (1 woman). *Students:* 37 full-time (13 women); includes 1 African American, 1 American Indian/Alaska Native, 1 Asian American or Pacific Islander, 2 international. Average age 28. 12 applicants, 100% accepted. In 2003, 3 degrees awarded. *Degree requirements:* For master's, thesis/dissertation; for doctorate, thesis/dissertation, comprehensive exam. *Entrance requirements:* Additional exam requirements/recommendations for international students: Required—TOEFL. *Application deadline:* Applications are processed on a rolling basis. Application fee: $35 ($50 for international students). Electronic applications accepted. Tuition, nonresident: full-time $4,071. Required fees: $493. *Financial support:* In 2003–04, 15 students received support; research assistantships with full tuition reimbursements available, teaching assistantships with full tuition reimbursements available. Support available to part-time students. Financial award application deadline: 3/15. *Faculty research:* Natural resources economics, wetlands issues, wildlife, prairie ecology, range management. Total annual research expenditures: $500,000. *Unit head:* Dr. Carolyn Grygiel, Director, 701-231-8180, Fax: 701-231-7590, E-mail: carolyn.grygiel@ndsu.nodak.edu.

Northeastern Illinois University, Graduate College, College of Arts and Sciences, Department of Geography, Environmental Studies and Economics, Program in Geography and Environmental Studies, Chicago, IL 60625-4699. Offers MA. Part-time and evening/weekend programs available. *Degree requirements:* For master's, thesis optional. *Entrance requirements:* For master's, undergraduate minor in geography or environmental studies, minimum GPA of 2.75. *Faculty research:* Segregation and urbanization of minority groups in the Chicago area, scale dependence and parameterization in nonpoint source pollution modeling, ecological land classification and mapping, ecosystem restoration, soil-vegetation relationships.

Northern Arizona University, Graduate College, College of Arts and Sciences, Department of Environmental Sciences, Flagstaff, AZ 86011. Offers conservation ecology (Certificate); environmental sciences and policy (MS). *Accreditation:* NCA . *Students:* 15 full-time (12 women), 2 part-time (both women); includes 2 minority (both Hispanic Americans) 38 applicants, 16% accepted. In 2003, 7 degrees awarded. *Degree requirements:* For master's, thesis optional. *Entrance requirements:* For master's, GRE General Test. Application fee: $45. *Expenses:* Tuition, state resident: full-time $5,103. Tuition, nonresident: full-time $12,623. *Financial support:* In 2003–04, 14 research assistantships were awarded. Financial award application deadline: 2/15. *Unit head:* Dr. Roderic Parnell, Chair, 928-523-9333, Fax: 928-523-7423, E-mail: roderic.parnell@nau.edu. *Application contact:* Information Contact, E-mail: esf.program@nau.edu.

Nova Scotia Agricultural College, Research and Graduate Studies, Truro, NS B2N 5E3, Canada. Offers agriculture (M Sc), including air quality, animal behavior, animal molecular genetics, animal nutrition, animal technology, aquaculture, botany, crop management, crop physiology, ecology, environmental microbiology, food science, horticulture, nutrient management, pest management, physiology, plant biotechnology, plant pathology, soil chemistry, soil fertility, waste management and composting, water quality. Part-time programs available. *Faculty:* 38 full-time (5 women), 13 part-time/adjunct (1 woman). *Students:* 46 full-time (27 women), 21 part-time (13 women); includes 13 minority (10 African Americans, 2 American Indian/Alaska Native, 1 Asian American or Pacific Islander). 45 applicants, 58% accepted, 16 enrolled. In 2003, 11 degrees awarded, leading to university research/teaching 18%, continued full-time study36%, business/industry 9%, government 27%. *Median time to degree:* Master's–2.25 years full-time, 4 years part-time. *Degree requirements:* For master's, thesis, candidacy exam. *Entrance requirements:* For master's, B.Sc. honors degree, minimum GPA of 3.0. Additional exam requirements/recommendations for international students: Required—TOEFL (minimum score 580 paper-based; 237 computer-based), Michigan English Language Assessment Battery. *Application deadline:* For fall admission, 6/1 for domestic students, 4/1 for international students; for winter admission, 11/15 for domestic students; for spring admission, 2/28 for domestic students. Applications are processed on a rolling basis. Application fee: $70. *Expenses:* Tuition, state resident: full-time $6,270. Tuition, nonresident: full-time $9,270. Required fees: $402. Tuition and fees vary according to student level. *Financial support:* In 2003–04, 63 students received support, including research assistantships (averaging $15,000 per year), teaching assistantships (averaging $900 per year); career-related internships or fieldwork, scholarships/grants, and unspecified assistantships also available. *Faculty research:* Organogenesis, somatic embryogenesis, composting, sustainable agriculture, ecotoxicology. Total annual research expenditures: $2 million. *Unit head:* Jill L. Rogers, Manager, 902-893-6360, Fax: 902-893-3430, E-mail: jrogers@nsac.ns.ca. *Application contact:* Marie Law, Administrative Assistant, 902-893-6502, Fax: 902-893-3430, E-mail: mlaw@nsac.ns.ca.

OGI School of Science & Engineering at Oregon Health & Science University, Graduate Studies, Department of Environmental and Biomolecular Systems, Beaverton, OR 97006-8921. Offers biochemistry and molecular biology (MS, PhD); ecosystem management and restoration (MS); environmental engineering (MS, PhD); environmental information technology (PhD); environmental science (MS, PhD); environmental science and engineering (MS, PhD); environmental systems management (MS). Part-time programs available. Terminal master's awarded for partial completion of doctoral program. *Degree requirements:* For master's, thesis optional; for doctorate, oral defense of dissertation. *Entrance requirements:* For master's and doctorate, GRE General Test. Additional exam requirements/recommendations for international students: Required—TOEFL. Electronic applications accepted. *Faculty research:* Air and water science, hydrogeology, estuarine and coastal modeling, environmental microbiology, contaminant transport.

Ohio University, Graduate Studies, College of Arts and Sciences, Department of Geological Sciences, Athens, OH 45701-2979. Offers environmental geochemistry (MS); environmental geology (MS); environmental/hydrology (MS); geology (MS); geology education (MS); geomorphology/surficial processes (MS); geophysics (MS); hydrogeology (MS); sedimentology (MS); structure/tectonics (MS). Part-time programs available. *Faculty:* 10 full-time (3 women), 4 part-time/adjunct (1 woman). *Students:* 13 full-time (4 women), 4 part-time (1 woman); includes 1 minority (Hispanic American), 4 international. Average age 25. 11 applicants, 45% accepted, 4 enrolled. In 2003, 8 degrees awarded. *Median time to degree:* Master's–2.5 years full-time. *Degree requirements:* For master's, thesis, thesis proposal defense. *Entrance requirements:* Additional exam requirements/recommendations for international students: Required—TOEFL (minimum score 550 paper-based; 217 computer-based). *Application deadline:* For fall admission, 2/1 priority date for domestic students, 1/1 priority date for international students. Application fee: $45. *Expenses:* Tuition, state resident: full-time $2,651; part-time $328 per credit. Tuition, nonresident: full-time $5,095; part-time $632 per credit. Tuition and fees vary according to program. *Financial support:* In 2003–04, 16 students received support, including 3 research assistantships with full tuition reimbursements available (averaging $11,000 per year), 13 teaching assistantships with full tuition reimbursements available (averaging $11,000 per year); institutionally sponsored loans, scholarships/grants, tuition waivers (full), and unspecified assistantships also available. Financial award application deadline: 3/15. *Faculty research:* Geoscience education, tectonics, flurial geomorphology, invertebrate paleontology, mine/hydrology. Total annual research expenditures: $506,400. *Unit head:* Dr. Douglas Green, Chair, 740-593-6896, Fax: 740-593-0486, E-mail: green@ohio.edu. *Application contact:* Dr. Dina L. Lopez, Graduate Chair, 740-593-9435, Fax: 740-593-0486, E-mail: lopezd@ohio.edu.

Ohio University, Graduate Studies, College of Arts and Sciences, Program in Environmental Studies, Athens, OH 45701-2979. Offers MS. Part-time programs available. *Students:* 42 full-time (24 women), 10 part-time (6 women), 20 international. Average age 28. 52 applicants, 65% accepted, 16 enrolled. In 2003, 9 degrees awarded. *Median time to degree:* Master's–2 years full-time. *Degree requirements:* For master's, thesis (for some programs), written exams (if no thesis), research project, comprehensive exam (for some programs), registration. *Entrance requirements:* For master's, minimum GPA of 3.0. Additional exam requirements/recommendations for international students: Required—TOEFL (minimum score 600 paper-based; 250 computer-based). *Application deadline:* For fall admission, 1/1 for domestic students; for winter admission, 10/1 for domestic students; for spring admission, 2/1 for domestic students.

Application fee: $45. *Expenses:* Tuition, state resident: full-time $2,651; part-time $328 per credit. Tuition, nonresident: full-time $5,095; part-time $632 per credit. Tuition and fees vary according to program. *Financial support:* In 2003–04, 24 students received support, including research assistantships with tuition reimbursements available (averaging $9,810 per year), 5 teaching assistantships with tuition reimbursements available (averaging $9,810 per year); fellowships with tuition reimbursements available, career-related internships or fieldwork, Federal Work-Study, institutionally sponsored loans, scholarships/grants, tuition waivers (full), and unspecified assistantships also available. Financial award application deadline: 1/1. *Faculty research:* Air quality modeling, conservation biology, environmental policy, geographical information sytems, land management and watershed restoration. *Unit head:* Dr. Gene Mapes, Director, 740-593-9526, Fax: 740-593-0924, E-mail: mapesg@ohio.edu.

Oregon State University, Graduate School, College of Oceanic and Atmospheric Sciences, Corvallis, OR 97331. Offers atmospheric sciences (MA, MS, PhD); geophysics (MA, MS, PhD); marine resource management (MA, MS); oceanography (MA, MS, PhD). *Faculty:* 61 full-time (9 women), 5 part-time/adjunct (1 woman). *Students:* 85 full-time (42 women), 5 part-time (2 women); includes 2 minority (both Hispanic Americans), 18 international. Average age 30. In 2003, 19 master's, 5 doctorates awarded. Terminal master's awarded for partial completion of doctoral program. *Degree requirements:* For master's, thesis optional; for doctorate, thesis/dissertation. *Entrance requirements:* For master's and doctorate, GRE General Test, minimum GPA of 3.0 in last 90 hours. Additional exam requirements/recommendations for international students: Required—TOEFL. *Application deadline:* For fall admission, 2/1 for domestic students. Applications are processed on a rolling basis. Application fee: $50. *Expenses:* Tuition, state resident: full-time $8,139; part-time $301 per credit. Tuition, nonresident: full-time $14,376; part-time $532 per credit. Required fees: $1,227. *Financial support:* Fellowships, research assistantships, teaching assistantships, career-related internships or fieldwork, Federal Work-Study, and institutionally sponsored loans available. Support available to part-time students. Financial award application deadline: 2/1. *Faculty research:* Biological, chemical, geological, and physical oceanography. *Unit head:* Dr. Mark R. Abbott, Dean, 541-737-4045, Fax: 541-737-2064, E-mail: mark@oce.orst.edu. *Application contact:* Irma Delson, Assistant Director, Student Services, 541-737-5189, Fax: 541-737-2064, E-mail: student_adviser@oce.orst.edu.

The Pennsylvania State University University Park Campus, Graduate School, Intercollege Graduate Programs, Intercollege Program in Environmental Pollution Control, State College, University Park, PA 16802-1503. Offers M Eng, MEPC, MS. *Students:* 10 full-time (8 women), 2 part-time (1 woman), 3 international. *Entrance requirements:* For master's, GRE General Test. Additional exam requirements/recommendations for international students: Required—TOEFL. Application fee: $45. *Expenses:* Tuition, state resident: full-time $10,010; part-time $417 per credit. Tuition, nonresident: full-time $19,830; part-time $826 per credit. Full-time tuition and fees vary according to course level, course load, campus/location and program. *Unit head:* Dr. Herschel A. Elliott, Chair, 814-865-1417, Fax: 814-863-1031, E-mail: haelliott@psu.edu. *Application contact:* Dorcas R. Holt, Program Assistant, 814-865-1417, Fax: 814-863-1031, E-mail: drh3@psu.edu.

Polytechnic University of Puerto Rico, Graduate School, Hato Rey, PR 00919. Offers business administration (MBA); civil engineering (MCE); competitiveness manufacturing (MMC); electrical engineering (MEE); engineering management (MEM); environmental protection management (MEPM); manufacturing engineering (MME). Part-time and evening/weekend programs available. *Faculty:* 18 full-time (1 woman), 22 part-time/adjunct (7 women). *Students:* 263 full-time (120 women), 332 part-time (150 women). 167 applicants, 89% accepted, 124 enrolled. In 2003, 96 degrees awarded. *Application deadline:* For fall admission, 7/20 for domestic students; for winter admission, 10/26 for domestic students; for spring admission, 2/15 for domestic students. Application fee: $50 ($250 for international students). *Expenses:* Tuition: Full-time $3,150; part-time $1,575 per term. One-time fee: $10 full-time. *Unit head:* Dr. Miriam Pabón, Dean, 787-754-8000 Ext. 333, Fax: 787-756-7274, E-mail: mpabon@pupr.edu. *Application contact:* Sra. Rosa Belvis, Supervisor, Graduate School Integrated Services Office, 787-754-8000 Ext. 467, Fax: 787-758-7933, E-mail: rbelvis@pupr.edu.

Portland State University, Graduate Studies, College of Liberal Arts and Sciences, Interdisciplinary Program in Environmental Sciences and Resources, Portland, OR 97207-0751. Offers environmental management (MEM); environmental sciences/biology (PhD); environmental sciences/chemistry (PhD); environmental sciences/civil engineering (PhD); environmental sciences/economics (PhD); environmental sciences/geography (PhD); environmental sciences/geology (PhD); environmental sciences/physics (PhD); environmental studies (MS). Part-time programs available. *Faculty:* 8 full-time (0 women). *Students:* 77 full-time (36 women), 29 part-time (11 women); includes 6 minority (1 African American, 1 American Indian/Alaska Native, 1 Asian American or Pacific Islander, 3 Hispanic Americans), 23 international. Average age 33. 84 applicants, 71% accepted, 41 enrolled. In 2003, 12 master's, 4 doctorates awarded. *Degree requirements:* For doctorate, variable foreign language requirement, thesis/dissertation, oral and qualifying exams. *Entrance requirements:* For doctorate, minimum GPA of 3.0 in upper-division course work or 2.75 overall. Additional exam requirements/recommendations for international students: Required—TOEFL. *Application deadline:* For fall admission, 4/1 for domestic students. Applications are processed on a rolling basis. Application fee: $50. *Expenses:* Tuition, state resident: full-time $6,588. Tuition, nonresident: full-time $12,060; part-time $298 per credit. Required fees: $1,041; $19 per credit. $35 per term. *Financial support:* In 2003–04, 4 research assistantships with full tuition reimbursements (averaging $7,749 per year), 5 teaching assistantships with full tuition reimbursements (averaging $9,359 per year) were awarded. Federal Work-Study, scholarships/grants, tuition waivers (partial), and unspecified assistantships also available. Support available to part-time students. Financial award application deadline: 3/1; financial award applicants required to submit FAFSA. *Faculty research:* Environmental aspects of biology, chemistry, civil engineering, geology, physics. Total annual research expenditures: $914,700. *Unit head:* Dr. Roy Koch, Director, 503-725-4980, Fax: 503-725-3888, E-mail: kochr@mail.pdx.edu. *Application contact:* Harmony Van Eaton, Coordinator, 503-725-4982, Fax: 503-725-3888, E-mail: harmonyr@pdx.edu.

Prescott College, Graduate Programs, Program in Environmental Studies, Prescott, AZ 86301-2990. Offers agroecology (MA); ecopsychology (MA); environmental education (MA); environmental studies (MA); sustainability (MA). MA (environmental education) offered jointly with Teton Science School. Part-time programs available. Postbaccalaureate distance learning degree programs offered (minimal on-campus study). *Faculty:* 1 full-time (0 women), 29 part-time/adjunct (6 women). *Students:* 21 full-time (13 women), 15 part-time (5 women); includes 2 minority (1 Asian American or Pacific Islander, 1 Hispanic American), 2 international. Average age 47. In 2003, 4 degrees awarded. *Degree requirements:* For master's, thesis, fieldwork or internship, practicum. *Application deadline:* For fall admission, 2/15 for domestic students; for spring admission, 9/15 priority date for domestic students. Applications are processed on a rolling basis. Application fee: $40. *Expenses:* Tuition: Full-time $10,980; part-time $308 per credit hour. One-time fee: $193 full-time. *Unit head:* Dr. Paul Sneed, Head, 928-350-3204. *Application contact:* Lisa Mauldin, Admissions Counselor, 800-628-6364, Fax: 928-776-5242, E-mail: mapmail@prescott.edu.

Princeton University, Graduate School, Department of Mechanical and Aerospace Engineering, Princeton, NJ 08544. Offers applied physics (M Eng, MSE, PhD); computational methods (M Eng, MSE); dynamics and control systems (M Eng, MSE, PhD); energy and environmental policy (M Eng, MSE, PhD); energy conversion, propulsion, and combustion (M Eng, MSE, PhD); flight science and technology (M Eng, MSE, PhD); fluid mechanics (M Eng, MSE, PhD). Part-time programs available. *Faculty:* 21 full-time (2 women), 2 part-time/adjunct (0 women). *Students:* 76 full-time (13 women); includes 5 minority (1 African American, 1 Asian American or Pacific Islander, 3 Hispanic Americans), 43 international. Average age 24. 315 applicants, 17% accepted, 17 enrolled. In 2003, 7 master's, 8 doctorates awarded. Terminal master's awarded for partial completion of doctoral program. *Median time to degree:* Master's–2.4 years full-time; doctorate–5.75 years full-time. *Degree requirements:* For master's, thesis/dissertation; for doctorate, thesis/dissertation, comprehensive exam. *Entrance requirements:* For master's and doctorate, GRE General Test. Additional exam requirements/recommendations for international students: Required—TOEFL (minimum score 600 paper-based; 250 computer-based). *Application deadline:* For fall admission, 12/31 for domestic students, 12/1 for international students. Application fee: $80 ($55 for international students). Electronic applications accepted. *Expenses:* Tuition: Full-time $29,910. Required fees: $810. *Financial support:* In 2003–04, 12 fellowships with full tuition reimbursements (averaging $8,800 per year), 36 research assistantships with full tuition reimbursements (averaging $27,461 per year), 9 teaching assistantships with full tuition reimbursements (averaging $21,641 per year) were awarded. Federal Work-Study and institutionally sponsored loans also available. Financial award application deadline: 1/2. Total annual research expenditures: $6.2 million. *Unit head:* Prof. Luigi Martinelli, Director of Graduate Studies, 609-258-6652, Fax: 609-258-1918, E-mail: gigi@princeton.edu. *Application contact:* Janice Yip, Director of Graduate Admissions, 609-258-3034, Fax: 609-258-6180, E-mail: gsadmit@princeton.edu.

Purdue University, Graduate School, College of Agriculture, Department of Forestry and Natural Resources, West Lafayette, IN 47907. Offers aquaculture, fisheries, aquatic science (MSF); aquaculture, fisheries, aquatic sciences (MS, PhD); forest biology (MS, MSF, PhD); natural resources and environmental policy (MS, MSF); natural resources environmental policy (PhD); quantitative resource analysis (MS, MSF, PhD); wildlife science (MS, MSF, PhD); wood science and technology (MS, MSF, PhD). *Faculty:* 28 full-time (3 women), 3 part-time/adjunct (1 woman). *Students:* 67 full-time (28 women), 3 part-time (all women); includes 3 minority (1 African American, 2 Hispanic Americans), 24 international. Average age 30. 44 applicants, 23% accepted, 9 enrolled. In 2003, 7 master's, 6 doctorates awarded. *Degree requirements:* For master's and doctorate, thesis/dissertation. *Entrance requirements:* For master's and doctorate, GRE General Test, minimum B+ average in undergraduate course work. Additional exam requirements/recommendations for international students: Required—TOEFL. *Application deadline:* For fall admission, 1/5 for domestic students; for spring admission, 9/15 for domestic students. Applications are processed on a rolling basis. Application fee: $55. Electronic applications accepted. *Financial support:* In 2003–04, 10 research assistantships (averaging $15,259 per year) were awarded; fellowships, teaching assistantships, career-related internships or fieldwork and scholarships/grants also available. Support available to part-time students. Financial award application deadline: 1/5; financial award applicants required to submit FAFSA. *Faculty research:* Wildlife management, forest management, forest ecology, forest soils, limnology. Total annual research expenditures: $200,000. *Unit head:* Dr. Robert K. Swihart, Interim Head, 765-494-3590, Fax: 765-494-9461, E-mail: rswihart@purdue.edu. *Application contact:* Kelly Garrett, Graduate Secretary, 765-494-3572, Fax: 765-494-9461, E-mail: kgarrett@purdue.edu.

See in-depth description on page 795.

Rensselaer Polytechnic Institute, Graduate School, School of Humanities and Social Sciences, Department of Economics, Interdisciplinary Program in Ecological Economics, Troy, NY 12180-3590. Offers PhD. Part-time programs available. *Faculty:* 9 full-time (1 woman). *Students:* 13 full-time (9 women); includes 4 minority (1 African American, 2 Asian Americans or Pacific Islanders, 1 Hispanic American), 1 international. 24 applicants, 96% accepted, 4 enrolled. In 2003, 2 degrees awarded. *Median time to degree:* Doctorate–4 years full-time. *Degree requirements:* For doctorate, thesis/dissertation, comprehensive exam. *Entrance requirements:* For doctorate, GMAT or GRE General Test. Additional exam requirements/recommendations for international students: Required—TOEFL (minimum score 570 paper-based; 230 computer-based). *Application deadline:* For fall admission, 1/15 for domestic students. Applications are processed on a rolling basis. Application fee: $45. Electronic applications accepted. *Expenses:* Tuition: Full-time $27,700; part-time $1,320 per credit. Required fees: $1,470. *Financial support:* In 2003–04, 10 students received support, including 1 fellowship with full tuition reimbursement available (averaging $16,000 per year), 5 research assistantships with full tuition reimbursements available (averaging $12,000 per year), 5 teaching assistantships with full tuition reimbursements available (averaging $12,000 per year); scholarships/grants and tuition waivers (full) also available. Financial award application deadline: 2/1. *Faculty research:* Sustainable development, natural resource economics, cost-benefit analysis, social economics, regional input-output analysis. *Unit head:* Dr. John M. Gowdy, Director, 518-276-8094, Fax: 518-276-2235, E-mail: gowdyj@rpi.edu. *Application contact:* Kathy M. Keenan, Administrative Secretary, 518-276-8088, Fax: 518-276-2235, E-mail: keenak@rpi.edu.

Rensselaer Polytechnic Institute, Graduate School, School of Humanities and Social Sciences, Program in Ecological Economics, Values, and Policy, Troy, NY 12180-3590. Offers MS. Part-time programs available. *Faculty:* 8 full-time (3 women). *Students:* 2 full-time (0 women), 1 (woman) part-time. Average age 24. 9 applicants, 78% accepted, 2 enrolled. In 2003, 7 degrees awarded, leading to continued full-time study 14%, business/industry 84%. *Median time to degree:* Master's–2 years full-time, 3 years part-time. *Degree requirements:* For master's, professional project. *Entrance requirements:* For master's, GRE General Test. Additional exam requirements/recommendations for international students: Required—TOEFL (minimum score 600 paper-based; 250 computer-based). *Application deadline:* For fall admission, 1/15 priority date for domestic students, 1/15 priority date for international students. Applications are processed on a rolling basis. Application fee: $45. Electronic applications accepted. *Expenses:* Tuition: Full-time $27,700; part-time $1,320 per credit. Required fees: $1,470. *Financial support:* In 2003–04, 1 student received support, including 1 teaching assistantship with full tuition reimbursement available (averaging $12,000 per year); fellowships, research assistantships, career-related internships or fieldwork and institutionally sponsored loans also available. Financial award application deadline: 1/15. *Faculty research:* Environmental politics and policy, environmentalism, political economy, third world politics, environmental health. *Unit head:* Dr. Steve Breyman, Director of Graduate Studies, 518-276-8515, Fax: 518-276-2659, E-mail: breyms@rpi.edu.

Rice University, Graduate Programs, Wiess School of Natural Sciences, Professional Master's Program in Environmental Analysis and Decision Making, Houston, TX 77251-1892. Offers MS. Part-time programs available. *Degree requirements:* For master's, internship. *Entrance requirements:* For master's, GRE General Test, letters of recommendation (4). Additional exam requirements/recommendations for international students: Required—TOEFL (minimum score 600 paper-based; 250 computer-based). Electronic applications accepted. *Expenses:* Tuition: Full-time $19,700; part-time $1,096 per hour. *Faculty research:* Environmental biotechnology, environmental nanochemistry, environmental statistics, remote sensing.

Rochester Institute of Technology, Graduate Enrollment Services, College of Applied Science and Technology, Department of Environmental Management, Rochester, NY 14623-5603. Offers MS. *Students:* 3 full-time (2 women), 48 part-time (18 women); includes 10 minority (5 African Americans, 2 American Indian/Alaska Native, 3 Hispanic Americans), 3 international. 32 applicants, 59% accepted, 14 enrolled. In 2003, 21 degrees awarded. *Entrance requirements:* For master's, minimum GPA of 3.0. *Application deadline:* For fall admission, 3/1 for domestic students. Applications are processed on a rolling basis. Application fee: $50. Electronic applications accepted. *Expenses:* Tuition: Full-time $22,965; part-time $644 per hour. Required fees: $174; $29 per quarter. *Unit head:* Maureen Valentine, Chair, 585-475-7398, E-mail: msvite@rit.edu.

Royal Roads University, Graduate Studies, Science, Technology and Environment Program, Victoria, BC V9B 5Y2, Canada. Offers environment and management (M Sc, MA); knowledge management (MA). Postbaccalaureate distance learning degree programs offered (minimal on-campus study). *Degree requirements:* For master's, thesis. *Entrance requirements:* For master's, 5-7 years of related work experience. Electronic applications accepted. *Faculty research:* Sustainable development, atmospheric processes, sustainable communities, chemical fate and transport of persistent organic pollutants, educational technology.

St. Cloud State University, School of Graduate Studies, College of Science and Engineering, Department of Environmental and Technological Studies, St. Cloud, MN 56301-4498. Offers MS. *Faculty:* 8 full-time (0 women). *Students:* 11 (2 women); includes 5 minority (2 African Americans, 3 Asian Americans or Pacific Islanders). 13 applicants, 92% accepted. *Degree requirements:*

Environmental Management and Policy

St. Cloud State University (continued)

For master's, thesis or alternative. *Entrance requirements:* For master's, GRE General Test, minimum GPA of 2.75. Additional exam requirements/recommendations for international students: Required—TOEFL (minimum score 550 paper-based; 213 computer-based). *Application deadline:* For fall admission, 6/1 for domestic students, 6/1 for international students; for spring admission, 10/1 for domestic students. Applications are processed on a rolling basis. Application fee: $35. Electronic applications accepted. *Expenses:* Tuition, state resident: part-time $203 per credit. Tuition, nonresident: part-time $317 per credit. Required fees: $24 per credit. Tuition and fees vary according to campus/location and reciprocity agreements. *Financial support:* Federal Work-Study and unspecified assistantships available. Financial award application deadline: 3/1. *Unit head:* Dr. Anthony Schwaller, Chairperson, 320-255-3235, Fax: 320-654-5122, E-mail: ets@stcloudstate.edu. *Application contact:* Linda Lou Krueger, School of Graduate Studies, 320-255-2113, Fax: 320-654-5371, E-mail: lekrueger@stcloudstate.edu.

Saint Joseph's University, College of Arts and Sciences, Program in Environmental Protection, Philadelphia, PA 19131-1395. Offers MS. *Students:* 2 full-time (0 women), 34 part-time (10 women); includes 5 minority (4 African Americans, 1 Hispanic American). In 2003, 7 degrees awarded. *Expenses:* Tuition: Part-time $645 per credit. Part-time tuition and fees vary according to class time, course load, degree level and program. *Application contact:* Sena Owereko-Andah, Assistant Director of Graduate Admissions, 610-660-1108, Fax: 610-660-1224, E-mail: sowereko@sju.edu.

Saint Mary-of-the-Woods College, Program in Earth Literacy, Saint Mary-of-the-Woods, IN 47876. Offers MA. Part-time programs available. Postbaccalaureate distance learning degree programs offered (minimal on-campus study). *Faculty:* 11 part-time/adjunct (9 women). *Students:* 1 (woman) full-time, 31 part-time (29 women). Average age 43. 17 applicants, 100% accepted. In 2003, 3 degrees awarded. *Degree requirements:* For master's, thesis. *Application deadline:* Applications are processed on a rolling basis. Application fee: $35. Electronic applications accepted. Students attend class via distance learning. There are no campus-based graduate students. *Expenses:* Tuition: Part-time $364 per credit hour. Required fees: $90 per term. *Financial support:* Career-related internships or fieldwork available. Financial award application deadline: 3/1; financial award applicants required to submit FAFSA. *Faculty research:* Ecology, art, spirituality. *Unit head:* Dr. Mary Lou Dolan, CSJ, Director, 812-535-5160, Fax: 812-535-5127, E-mail: mldolan@smwc.edu.

Saint Mary's University of Minnesota, Graduate School, Program in Resource Analysis, Winona, MN 55987-1399. Offers business (MS); criminal justice (MS); geographic information systems (Certificate); natural resources (MS); public administration (MS). *Faculty:* 6 full-time (2 women), 1 part-time/adjunct (0 women). *Students:* 19 full-time (5 women), 12 part-time (3 women); includes 2 minority (1 African American, 1 Hispanic American). Average age 28. 26 applicants, 100% accepted, 23 enrolled. In 2003, 10 degrees awarded. *Degree requirements:* For master's, thesis or alternative. *Entrance requirements:* For master's and Certificate, letters of recommendation. *Application deadline:* Applications are processed on a rolling basis. Application fee: $25. Electronic applications accepted. *Expenses:* Tuition: Part-time $255 per credit. *Unit head:* Dr. David McConville, Professor, 507-457-1542, Fax: 507-457-1633, E-mail: dmcconvi@smumn.edu. *Application contact:* Dr. John A. Nosek, Information Contact, 507-457-6952, E-mail: janosek@smumn.edu.

San Francisco State University, Division of Graduate Studies, College of Behavioral and Social Sciences, Department of Geography and Human Environmental Studies, San Francisco, CA 94132-1722. Offers geography (MA), including environmental planning, resource management. Part-time programs available. *Faculty:* 10 full-time (3 women). In 2003, 3 degrees awarded. *Degree requirements:* For master's, thesis, exam. *Entrance requirements:* For master's, minimum GPA of 2.5 in last 60 units. *Application deadline:* For fall admission, 11/30 for domestic students. Applications are processed on a rolling basis. Application fee: $55. *Expenses:* Tuition, state resident: part-time $871 per unit. Tuition, nonresident: part-time $1,093 per unit. *Financial support:* Application deadline: 3/1. *Faculty research:* Geomorphology, remote sensing, GIS, biogeography. *Unit head:* Dr. Nancy Wilkinson, Chair, 415-338-2049. *Application contact:* Dr. Barbara Holzman, Associate Professor, 415-338-7506, E-mail: bholzman@sfsu.edu.

San Jose State University, Graduate Studies and Research, College of Social Sciences, Department of Environmental Studies, San Jose, CA 95192-0001. Offers MS. Part-time programs available. *Students:* 14 full-time (10 women), 26 part-time (18 women); includes 10 minority (1 African American, 5 Asian Americans or Pacific Islanders, 4 Hispanic Americans). Average age 32. 21 applicants, 86% accepted, 15 enrolled. In 2003, 5 degrees awarded. *Degree requirements:* For master's, thesis or alternative, comprehensive exam. *Entrance requirements:* For master's, minimum GPA of 3.0. *Application deadline:* For fall admission, 6/29 for domestic students; for spring admission, 11/30 for domestic students. Applications are processed on a rolling basis. Application fee: $59. Electronic applications accepted. Tuition, nonresident: part-time $282 per unit. Required fees: $654 per semester. *Financial support:* In 2003–04, 2 teaching assistantships were awarded; career-related internships or fieldwork, Federal Work-Study, and institutionally sponsored loans also available. Support available to part-time students. Financial award applicants required to submit FAFSA. *Faculty research:* Remote sensing, land use/land cover mapping. *Unit head:* Lynne Trulio, Chair, 408-924-5450, Fax: 408-924-5477.

Shippensburg University of Pennsylvania, School of Graduate Studies, College of Arts and Sciences, Department of Geography and Earth Science, Shippensburg, PA 17257-2299. Offers geoenvironmental studies (MS). Part-time and evening/weekend programs available. *Faculty:* 11 full-time (4 women). *Students:* 25 full-time (11 women), 20 part-time (8 women); includes 2 minority (1 African American, 1 Hispanic American), 1 international. Average age 29. 19 applicants, 95% accepted, 9 enrolled. In 2003, 21 degrees awarded. *Degree requirements:* For master's, internship or thesis. *Entrance requirements:* For master's, GRE if GPA *Application deadline:* Applications are processed on a rolling basis. Application fee: $30. Electronic applications accepted. *Expenses:* Tuition, state resident: full-time $5,518; part-time $307 per credit hour. Tuition, nonresident: full-time $8,830; part-time $491 per credit hour. Required fees: $25 per credit hour. $162 per semester. Tuition and fees vary according to course load. *Financial support:* In 2003–04, 18 research assistantships with full tuition reimbursements were awarded; career-related internships or fieldwork and unspecified assistantships also available. Support available to part-time students. Financial award application deadline: 3/1; financial award applicants required to submit FAFSA. *Unit head:* Dr. William Blewett, Acting Chairperson, 717-477-1685, Fax: 717-477-4029, E-mail: wlblew@ship.edu. *Application contact:* Renee Payne, Associate Dean of Graduate Admissions, 717-477-1213, Fax: 717-477-4016, E-mail: rmpayn@ship.edu.

Simon Fraser University, Graduate Studies, Faculty of Applied Science, School of Resource and Environmental Management, Burnaby, BC V5A 1S6, Canada. Offers MRM, PhD. *Degree requirements:* For master's, thesis or alternative, research project; for doctorate, thesis/dissertation, comprehensive exam. *Entrance requirements:* For master's, minimum GPA of 3.0; for doctorate, GRE Writing Assessment, minimum GPA of 3.5. Additional exam requirements/recommendations for international students: Required—TOEFL or IELTS. *Faculty research:* Management of resources, resource economics, regional planning, public policy analysis, tourism and parks.

Slippery Rock University of Pennsylvania, Graduate Studies (Recruitment), College of Health, Environment, and Science, Department of Parks, Recreation, and Environmental Education, Slippery Rock, PA 16057-1383. Offers environmental education (M Ed); resource management (MS); sustainable systems (MS). Part-time and evening/weekend programs available. *Faculty:* 8 full-time (2 women), 1 part-time/adjunct (0 women). *Students:* 30 full-time (20 women), 30 part-time (16 women); includes 3 minority (2 African Americans, 1 Hispanic American). Average age 28. 53 applicants, 66% accepted, 24 enrolled. In 2003, 12 degrees awarded. *Degree requirements:* For master's, thesis (for some programs), comprehensive exam (for some programs). *Entrance requirements:* For master's, GRE General Test, MAT, minimum GPA of 2.75. Additional exam requirements/recommendations for international students: Required—TOEFL (minimum score 550 paper-based; 213 computer-based). *Application deadline:* For fall admission, 7/1 for domestic students; for spring admission, 11/1 for domestic students. Applications are processed on a rolling basis. Application fee: $25. Electronic applications accepted. *Expenses:* Tuition, state resident: full-time $5,518; part-time $307 per credit hour. Tuition, nonresident: full-time $8,830; part-time $491 per credit hour. Required fees: $1,620; $106 per credit hour. Tuition and fees vary according to course load and program. *Financial support:* In 2003–04, 23 students received support, including 23 research assistantships with full and partial tuition reimbursements available (averaging $4,000 per year); career-related internships or fieldwork, Federal Work-Study, scholarships/grants, and unspecified assistantships also available. Support available to part-time students. Financial award application deadline: 5/1; financial award applicants required to submit FAFSA. *Unit head:* Dr. Daniel Dziubek, Graduate Coordinator, 724-738-2958, Fax: 724-738-2938, E-mail: daniel.dziubek@sru.edu. *Application contact:* Dr. Duncan M. Sargent, Director of Graduate Studies, 724-738-2051 Ext. 2116, Fax: 724-738-2146, E-mail: graduate.studies@sru.edu.

Southeast Missouri State University, School of Graduate and University Studies, Department of Human Environmental Studies, Cape Girardeau, MO 63701-4799. Offers home economics (MA); human environmental studies (MA). Part-time programs available. *Faculty:* 7 full-time (6 women). *Students:* 8 full-time (all women), 19 part-time (all women); includes 3 minority (all African Americans) Average age 28. 8 applicants, 100% accepted. In 2003, 3 degrees awarded. *Degree requirements:* For master's, thesis or alternative. *Entrance requirements:* For master's, GRE General Test, minimum GPA of 2.75. Additional exam requirements/recommendations for international students: Required—TOEFL (minimum score 550 paper-based; 213 computer-based). *Application deadline:* For fall admission, 8/1 priority date for domestic students, 4/1 priority date for international students; for spring admission, 11/1 priority date for domestic students, 9/1 priority date for international students. Applications are processed on a rolling basis. Application fee: $20 ($100 for international students). Electronic applications accepted. *Expenses:* Tuition, state resident: full-time $4,061; part-time $180 per credit hour. Tuition, nonresident: full-time $7,514; part-time $324 per credit hour. One-time fee: $257. *Financial support:* In 2003–04, 15 students received support, including 1 research assistantship with full tuition reimbursement available (averaging $6,100 per year), 7 teaching assistantships with full tuition reimbursements available (averaging $6,100 per year) Financial award applicants required to submit FAFSA. *Unit head:* Dr. Paula King, Chairperson, 573-651-2109, E-mail: pking@semo.edu. *Application contact:* Marsha L. Arant, Office of Graduate Studies, 573-651-2192, Fax: 573-651-2001, E-mail: marant@semovm.semo.edu.

Southeast Missouri State University, School of Graduate and University Studies, Harrison College of Business, Cape Girardeau, MO 63701-4799. Offers accounting (MBA); environmental management (MBA); finance (MBA); general management (MBA); industrial management (MBA); international business (MBA). *Accreditation:* AACSB. Part-time and evening/weekend programs available. *Faculty:* 35 full-time (10 women). *Students:* 30 full-time (15 women), 42 part-time (21 women); includes 1 minority (African American), 23 international. Average age 26. 19 applicants, 95% accepted. In 2003, 24 degrees awarded. *Degree requirements:* For master's, applied research project. *Entrance requirements:* For master's, GMAT, minimum undergraduate GPA of 3.0. Additional exam requirements/recommendations for international students: Required—TOEFL (minimum score 550 paper-based; 213 computer-based). *Application deadline:* For fall admission, 4/1 priority date for domestic students, 4/1 priority date for international students; for spring admission, 11/21 for domestic students, 9/1 for international students. Applications are processed on a rolling basis. Application fee: $20 ($100 for international students). *Expenses:* Tuition, state resident: full-time $4,061; part-time $180 per credit hour. Tuition, nonresident: full-time $7,514; part-time $324 per credit hour. One-time fee: $257. *Financial support:* In 2003–04, 49 students received support, including 18 research assistantships with full tuition reimbursements available (averaging $6,100 per year) Financial award applicants required to submit FAFSA. *Unit head:* Kenneth Heischmidt, Director, 573-651-5116, Fax: 573-651-5032, E-mail: kheischmidt@semo.edu. *Application contact:* Marsha L. Arant, Office of Graduate Studies, 573-651-2192, Fax: 573-651-2001, E-mail: marant@semovm.semo.edu.

Southwest Missouri State University, Graduate College, College of Natural and Applied Sciences, Department of Geography, Geology, and Planning, Springfield, MO 65804-0094. Offers earth science (MS Ed); geography (MS Ed); geography, geology and planning (MNAS); natural science (MS Ed); resource planning (MS). Part-time and evening/weekend programs available. *Faculty:* 15 full-time (2 women), 3 part-time/adjunct (0 women). *Students:* 16 full-time (9 women), 19 part-time (9 women); includes 4 minority (2 American Indian/Alaska Native, 1 Asian American or Pacific Islander, 1 Hispanic American), 2 international. Average age 34. 16 applicants, 88% accepted, 11 enrolled. In 2003, 5 degrees awarded. *Degree requirements:* For master's, thesis, comprehensive exam. *Entrance requirements:* For master's, GRE General Test, minimum undergraduate GPA of 3.0. *Application deadline:* For fall admission, 8/5 for domestic students; for spring admission, 12/20 priority date for domestic students. Applications are processed on a rolling basis. Application fee: $30. Electronic applications accepted. *Expenses:* Tuition, state resident: full-time $2,862. Tuition, nonresident: full-time $5,724. *Financial support:* In 2003–04, 6 research assistantships with full tuition reimbursements (averaging $8,400 per year), 9 teaching assistantships with full tuition reimbursements (averaging $6,300 per year) were awarded. Career-related internships or fieldwork, Federal Work-Study, and unspecified assistantships also available. Financial award application deadline: 3/31. *Faculty research:* Water resources, small town planning, recreation and open space planning. *Unit head:* Dr. James Skinner, Head, 417-836-5800, Fax: 417-836-6934. *Application contact:* Dr. Robert T. Pavlowsky, Graduate Adviser, 417-836-5800, Fax: 417-836-6934, E-mail: rtp138f@smsu.edu.

Southwest Missouri State University, Graduate College, Program in Administrative Studies, Springfield, MO 65804-0094. Offers community analysis (MSAS); environmental management (MSAS). Postbaccalaureate distance learning degree programs offered (no on-campus study). *Students:* 14 full-time (7 women), 60 part-time (37 women); includes 5 minority (4 African Americans, 1 Hispanic American), 2 international. Average age 37. 18 applicants, 94% accepted, 15 enrolled. In 2003, 12 degrees awarded. *Degree requirements:* For master's, thesis, comprehensive exam. *Entrance requirements:* For master's, GRE General Test, GMAT, 3 years of work experience. *Application deadline:* For fall admission, 8/5 for domestic students; for spring admission, 12/20 priority date for domestic students. Applications are processed on a rolling basis. Application fee: $30. Electronic applications accepted. *Expenses:* Tuition, state resident: full-time $2,862. Tuition, nonresident: full-time $5,724. *Financial support:* In 2003–04, 1 research assistantship with full tuition reimbursement (averaging $6,300 per year) was awarded; career-related internships or fieldwork, Federal Work-Study, institutionally sponsored loans, scholarships/grants, and unspecified assistantships also available. Support available to part-time students. Financial award application deadline: 3/31. *Unit head:* John Bourhis, Director, 417-836-6390, Fax: 417-836-5218, E-mail: jsb806@smsu.edu.

Stanford University, School of Earth Sciences, Earth Systems Program, Stanford, CA 94305-9991. Offers MS. Students admitted at the undergraduate level. *Students:* 9 full-time (4 women), 6 part-time (3 women); includes 4 minority (1 Asian American or Pacific Islander, 3 Hispanic Americans). Average age 23. In 2003, 10 degrees awarded. Application fee: $65 ($80 for international students). Electronic applications accepted. *Expenses:* Tuition: Full-time $28,563. *Unit head:* Joan Roughgarden, Director, 650-723-3648, Fax: 650-725-0958, E-mail: rough@pangea.stanford.edu.

State University of New York College of Environmental Science and Forestry, Faculty of Environmental Resources and Forest Engineering, Syracuse, NY 13210-2779. Offers environmental and resources engineering (MPS, MS, PhD). *Faculty:* 7 full-time (1 woman). *Students:* 16 full-time (6 women), 28 part-time (6 women); includes 2 minority (both Asian Americans or Pacific Islanders), 7 international. Average age 33. 25 applicants, 52% accepted, 11 enrolled. In 2003, 5 master's, 3 doctorates awarded. *Degree requirements:* For master's, thesis (for some programs), registration; for doctorate, thesis/dissertation, comprehensive exam, registration. *Entrance requirements:* For master's and doctorate, GRE General Test, minimum GPA of 3.0. Additional exam requirements/recommendations for international students: Required—TOEFL (minimum score 550 paper-based; 213 computer-based). *Application deadline:* For fall admission, 2/1 priority date for domestic students, 2/1 priority date for international students; for spring admission, 11/1 priority date for domestic students, 11/1 priority date for international students. Applications are processed on a rolling basis. Application fee: $50. Tuition, area resident: Part-time $288 per credit hour. Tuition, nonresident: part-time $438 per credit hour. Required fees: $300; $5 per credit hour. $18 per semester. One-time fee: $25 full-time. *Financial support:* In 2003–04, 20 students received support, including 2 fellowships with full and partial tuition reimbursements available (averaging $9,446 per year), 7 research assistantships with full and partial tuition reimbursements available, 8 teaching assistantships with full and partial tuition reimbursements available (averaging $9,446 per year); Federal Work-Study, institutionally sponsored loans, scholarships/grants, health care benefits, and unspecified assistantships also available. Financial award applicants required to submit FAFSA. *Faculty research:* Forest engineering, paper science and engineering, wood products engineering. Total annual research expenditures: $1.6 million. *Unit head:* Dr. James M. Hassett, Chair, 315-470-6633, Fax: 315-470-6958, E-mail: jhassett@esf.edu. *Application contact:* Dr. Dudley J. Raynal, Dean, Instruction and Graduate Studies, 315-470-6599, Fax: 315-470-6978, E-mail: esfgrad@esf.edu.

State University of New York College of Environmental Science and Forestry, Faculty of Environmental Studies, Syracuse, NY 13210-2779. Offers environmental and community land planning (MPS, MS, PhD); environmental and natural resources policy (PhD); environmental communication and participatory processes (MPS, MS, PhD); environmental policy and democratic processes (MPS, MS, PhD); environmental systems and risk management (MPS, MS, PhD); water and wetland resource studies (MPS, MS, PhD). Part-time programs available. *Faculty:* 8 full-time (4 women), 10 part-time/adjunct (8 women). *Students:* 40 full-time (24 women), 26 part-time (16 women); includes 4 minority (2 African Americans, 1 Asian American or Pacific Islander, 1 Hispanic American), 25 international. Average age 32. 72 applicants, 61% accepted, 19 enrolled. In 2003, 25 master's, 3 doctorates awarded. *Degree requirements:* For master's, thesis (for some programs), registration; for doctorate, thesis/dissertation, comprehensive exam, registration. *Entrance requirements:* For master's and doctorate, GRE General Test, minimum GPA of 3.0. Additional exam requirements/recommendations for international students: Required—TOEFL (minimum score 550 paper-based; 213 computer-based). *Application deadline:* For fall admission, 2/1 priority date for domestic students, 2/1 priority date for international students; for spring admission, 11/1 priority date for domestic students, 11/1 priority date for international students. Applications are processed on a rolling basis. Application fee: $50. Tuition, area resident: Part-time $288 per credit hour. Tuition, nonresident: part-time $438 per credit hour. Required fees: $300; $5 per credit hour. $18 per semester. One-time fee: $25 full-time. *Financial support:* In 2003–04, 25 students received support, including 16 fellowships with full and partial tuition reimbursements available (averaging $9,446 per year), 5 research assistantships with full and partial tuition reimbursements available (averaging $10,000 per year), 7 teaching assistantships with full and partial tuition reimbursements available (averaging $9,446 per year); career-related internships or fieldwork, Federal Work-Study, institutionally sponsored loans, scholarships/grants, health care benefits, and unspecified assistantships also available. Support available to part-time students. Financial award applicants required to submit FAFSA. *Faculty research:* Environmental education/communications, water resources, land resources, waste management. Total annual research expenditures: $237,610. *Unit head:* Dr. Richard Smardon, Chair, 315-470-6636, Fax: 315-470-6915, E-mail: rsmardon@syr.edu. *Application contact:* Dr. Dudley J. Raynal, Dean, Instruction and Graduate Studies, 315-470-6599, Fax: 315-470-6978, E-mail: esfgrad@esf.edu.

State University of New York College of Environmental Science and Forestry, Faculty of Forest and Natural Resources Management, Syracuse, NY 13210-2779. Offers environmental and natural resource policy (MS, PhD); environmental and natural resources policy (MPS); forest management and operations (MF); forestry ecosystems science and applications (MPS, MS, PhD); natural resources management (MPS, MS, PhD); quantitative methods and management in forest science (MPS, MS, PhD); recreation and resource management (MPS, MS, PhD); watershed management and forest hydrology (MPS, MS, PhD). *Faculty:* 28 full-time (5 women). *Students:* 48 full-time (18 women), 26 part-time (10 women); includes 2 minority (1 African American, 1 Hispanic American), 14 international. Average age 32. 47 applicants, 57% accepted, 14 enrolled. In 2003, 35 master's, 5 doctorates awarded. *Degree requirements:* For master's, thesis (for some programs), registration; for doctorate, thesis/dissertation, comprehensive exam, registration. *Entrance requirements:* For master's and doctorate, GRE General Test, minimum GPA of 3.0. Additional exam requirements/recommendations for international students: Required—TOEFL (minimum score 550 paper-based; 213 computer-based). *Application deadline:* For fall admission, 2/1 priority date for domestic students, 2/1 priority date for international students; for spring admission, 11/1 priority date for domestic students, 11/1 priority date for international students. Applications are processed on a rolling basis. Application fee: $50. Tuition, area resident: Part-time $288 per credit hour. Tuition, nonresident: part-time $438 per credit hour. Required fees: $300; $5 per credit hour. $18 per semester. One-time fee: $25 full-time. *Financial support:* In 2003–04, 43 students received support, including 9 fellowships with full and partial tuition reimbursements available (averaging $9,446 per year), 15 research assistantships with full and partial tuition reimbursements available (averaging $10,000 per year), 14 teaching assistantships with full and partial tuition reimbursements available (averaging $9,446 per year); career-related internships or fieldwork, Federal Work-Study, institutionally sponsored loans, scholarships/grants, health care benefits, and unspecified assistantships also available. Financial award applicants required to submit FAFSA. *Faculty research:* Silviculture recreation management, tree improvement, operations management, economics. Total annual research expenditures: $1.9 million. *Unit head:* Dr. Chad P. Dawson, Chair, 315-470-6536, Fax: 315-470-6535, E-mail: cpdawson@esf.edu. *Application contact:* Dr. Dudley J. Raynal, Dean, Instruction and Graduate Studies, 315-470-6599, Fax: 315-470-6978, E-mail: esfgrad@esf.edu.

Stony Brook University, State University of New York, Graduate School, College of Engineering and Applied Sciences, Department of Technology and Society, Program in Environmental and Waste Management, Stony Brook, NY 11794. Offers MS, Advanced Certificate. *Students:* 1 full-time (0 women), 5 part-time (all women). *Expenses:* Tuition, state resident: full-time $6,900; part-time $288 per credit hour. Tuition, nonresident: full-time $10,500; part-time $438 per credit hour. Required fees: $22. *Financial support:* Research assistantships, teaching assistantships, career-related internships or fieldwork available.

Announcement: Multidisciplinary perspective covers scientific, engineering, regulatory, economic, policy, and community values aspects of environmental, energy, and waste issues and technologies. Combines hands-on practical experience with emerging technologies and their applications with judicious use of risk analysis, life-cycle analysis, computer modeling, geographic information systems, and other analytical tools.

See in-depth description on page 745.

Stony Brook University, State University of New York, School of Professional Development and Continuing Studies, Stony Brook, NY 11794. Offers biology 7-12 (MAT); chemistry-grade 7-12 (MAT); coaching (Certificate); computer integrated engineering (Certificate); cultural studies (Certificate); earth science-grade 7-12 (MAT); educational computing (Certificate); English-grade 7-12 (MAT); environmental systems management (Certificate); environmental/occupational health and safety (Certificate); French-grade 7-12 (MAT); German-grade 7-12 (MAT); human resource management (Certificate); industrial management (Certificate); information systems management (Certificate); Italian-grade 7-12 (MAT); liberal studies (MA); liberal studies online (MA); Long Island regional studies (Certificate); operation research (Certificate); physics-grade 7-12 (MAT); Russian-grade 7-12 (MAT); school administration and supervision (Certificate); school district administration (Certificate); social science and the professions (MPS), including human resources management, labor management, public affairs, waste management; social studies 7-12 (MAT); waste management (Certificate); women's studies (Certificate). Part-time and evening/weekend programs available. Postbaccalaureate distance learning degree programs offered. *Faculty:* 1 full-time (0 women), 114 part-time/adjunct (52 women). *Students:* 359 full-time (201 women), 1,775 part-time (1,172 women); includes 186 minority (78 African Americans, 5 American Indian/Alaska Native, 28 Asian Americans or Pacific Islanders, 75 Hispanic Americans), 21 international. Average age 28. In 2003, 600 master's, 166 other advanced degrees awarded. *Degree requirements:* For master's, one foreign language, thesis or alternative. *Application deadline:* Applications are processed on a rolling basis. Application fee: $50. *Expenses:* Tuition, state resident: full-time $6,900; part-time $288 per credit hour. Tuition, nonresident: full-time $10,500; part-time $438 per credit hour. Required fees: $22. *Financial support:* Fellowships, research assistantships, teaching assistantships, career-related internships or fieldwork available. Support available to part-time students. *Unit head:* Dr. Paul J. Edelson, Dean, 631-632-7052, Fax: 631-632-9046, E-mail: paul.edelson@sunysb.edu. *Application contact:* Sandra Romansky, Director of Admissions and Advisement, 631-632-7050, Fax: 631-632-9046, E-mail: sandra.romansky@sunysb.edu.

Texas State University-San Marcos, Graduate School, College of Liberal Arts, Department of Geography, Program in Resource and Environmental Studies, San Marcos, TX 78666. Offers MAG. Part-time and evening/weekend programs available. *Students:* 9 full-time (6 women), 14 part-time (10 women); includes 3 minority (all Hispanic Americans), 1 international. Average age 30. 19 applicants, 84% accepted, 13 enrolled. In 2003, 11 degrees awarded. *Degree requirements:* For master's, internship or thesis. *Entrance requirements:* For master's, GRE General Test, minimum GPA of 3.0 in last 60 hours. Additional exam requirements/recommendations for international students: Required—TOEFL. *Application deadline:* For fall admission, 6/15 for domestic students; for spring admission, 10/15 priority date for domestic students. Applications are processed on a rolling basis. Application fee: $40 ($90 for international students). *Expenses:* Tuition, state resident: full-time $2,484; part-time $138 per semester hour. Tuition, nonresident: full-time $6,732; part-time $374 per semester hour. Required fees: $948; $31 per semester hour. $195 per term. Tuition and fees vary according to course load. *Financial support:* In 2003–04, 13 students received support, including 5 research assistantships (averaging $11,820 per year); teaching assistantships, career-related internships or fieldwork, Federal Work-Study, institutionally sponsored loans, and scholarships/grants also available. Support available to part-time students. Financial award application deadline: 4/1; financial award applicants required to submit FAFSA. *Unit head:* Dr. Fred Shelley, Graduate Adviser, 512-245-8704, Fax: 512-245-8353, E-mail: fs03@txstate.edu.

Texas Tech University, Graduate School, College of Architecture, Program in Land-Use Planning, Management, and Design, Lubbock, TX 79409. Offers PhD. *Students:* 6 full-time (4 women), 4 part-time (1 woman), 5 international. Average age 36. 6 applicants, 33% accepted, 0 enrolled. In 2003, 1 degree awarded. *Degree requirements:* For doctorate, thesis/dissertation. *Entrance requirements:* For doctorate, GRE General Test. Additional exam requirements/recommendations for international students: Required—TOEFL (minimum score 550 paper-based; 213 computer-based). *Application deadline:* Applications are processed on a rolling basis. Application fee: $50 ($60 for international students). Electronic applications accepted. *Expenses:* Tuition, state resident: full-time $3,312. Tuition, nonresident: full-time $8,976. Required fees: $1,745. Tuition and fees vary according to program. *Financial support:* Research assistantships with partial tuition reimbursements, teaching assistantships with partial tuition reimbursements, career-related internships or fieldwork, Federal Work-Study, and institutionally sponsored loans available. Support available to part-time students. Financial award application deadline: 5/1; financial award applicants required to submit FAFSA. *Faculty research:* Movement in designed environments, architecture, landscape architecture, urban planning, environmental engineering. *Unit head:* Dr. Saif Haq, Program Director, 806-742-3136, Fax: 806-742-2855, E-mail: saif.haq@ttu.edu. *Application contact:* Karen Brownmiller, Academic Program Assistant, 806-742-3136 Ext. 272, Fax: 806-742-2855, E-mail: karen.brownmiller@ttu.edu.

Towson University, Graduate School, Program in Geography and Environmental Planning, Towson, MD 21252-0001. Offers MA. Part-time and evening/weekend programs available. *Faculty:* 9 full-time (1 woman), 2 part-time/adjunct (0 women). *Students:* 36. Average age 30. In 2003, 3 degrees awarded. *Degree requirements:* For master's, thesis optional. *Entrance requirements:* For master's, 9 credits in geography, minimum GPA of 3.0 in geography. Additional exam requirements/recommendations for international students: Required—TOEFL. *Application deadline:* Applications are processed on a rolling basis. Application fee: $40. Electronic applications accepted. *Expenses:* Tuition, state resident: part-time $244 per unit. Tuition, nonresident: part-time $510 per unit. Required fees: $61 per unit. *Financial support:* In 2003–04, 1 teaching assistantship with full tuition reimbursement (averaging $4,000 per year) was awarded; Federal Work-Study and unspecified assistantships also available. Financial award application deadline: 4/1; financial award applicants required to submit FAFSA. *Faculty research:* Geographic information systems, regional planning, hazards, development issues, urban fluvial systems. *Unit head:* Dr. Virginia Thompson, Director, 410-704-4371, Fax: 410-704-3880, E-mail: vthompson@towson.edu. *Application contact:* 410-704-2501, Fax: 410-704-4675, E-mail: grads@towson.edu.

Trent University, Graduate Studies, Program in Watershed Ecosystems, Environmental and Resource Studies Program, Peterborough, ON K9J 7B8, Canada. Offers M Sc, PhD. *Degree requirements:* For master's and doctorate, thesis/dissertation. *Entrance requirements:* For master's, honours degree; for doctorate, master's degree. *Faculty research:* Environmental biogeochemistry, aquatic organic contaminants, fisheries, wetland ecology, renewable resource management.

Troy University, Graduate School, College of Arts and Sciences, Program in Environmental Analysis and Management, Troy, AL 36082. Offers MS. Part-time and evening/weekend programs available. *Degree requirements:* For master's, thesis, comprehensive exam. *Entrance requirements:* For master's, GRE General Test, MAT, minimum GPA of 2.5. Electronic applications accepted.

Tufts University, Graduate School of Arts and Sciences, Department of Urban and Environmental Policy and Planning, Medford, MA 02155. Offers community development (MA); environmental policy (MA); health and human welfare (MA); housing policy (MA); international environment/development policy (MA); public policy (MPP); public policy and citizen participation (MA). *Accreditation:* ACSP (one or more programs are accredited). Part-time programs available. *Faculty:* 7 full-time, 12 part-time/adjunct. *Students:* 120 (85 women); includes 17 minority (6 African Americans, 5 Asian Americans or Pacific Islanders, 6 Hispanic Americans) 5 international. 173 applicants, 76% accepted, 40 enrolled. In 2003, 30 degrees awarded. *Degree requirements:* For master's, thesis, internship. *Entrance requirements:* For master's, GRE General Test. Additional exam requirements/recommendations for international students: Required—TOEFL (minimum score 550 paper-based; 213 computer-based). *Application deadline:* For fall admission, 1/5 for domestic students, 12/30 for international students. Applications are processed on a rolling basis. Application fee: $60. Electronic applications accepted. *Expenses:* Contact institution. *Financial support:* Fellowships with full and partial tuition reimbursements, teaching assistantships with full and partial tuition reimbursements, career-related internships or fieldwork, Federal Work-Study, scholarships/grants, and tuition waivers (partial) available. Support available to part-time students. Financial award application deadline: 2/15; financial award applicants required to submit FAFSA. *Unit head:* Fran Jacobs, Chair, 617-627-3394, Fax: 617-627-3377.

Tufts University, Graduate School of Arts and Sciences, Graduate Certificate Programs, Community Environmental Studies Program, Medford, MA 02155. Offers Certificate. Part-time and evening/weekend programs available. *Students:* Average age 36. 6 applicants, 100% accepted, 4 enrolled. In 2003, 9 degrees awarded. *Application deadline:* For fall admission, 8/15 for domestic students; for spring admission, 12/12 for domestic students. Applications are processed on a rolling basis. Application fee: $60. Electronic applications accepted. *Expenses:* Contact institution. *Financial support:* Career-related internships or fieldwork available. Support available to part-time students. Financial award application deadline: 5/1; financial award

Environmental Management and Policy

Tufts University (continued)

applicants required to submit FAFSA. *Application contact:* Information Contact, 617-627-3395, Fax: 617-627-3016, E-mail: gradschool@ase.tufts.edu.

Tufts University, Graduate School of Arts and Sciences, Graduate Certificate Programs, Environmental Management Program, Medford, MA 02155. Offers Certificate. Part-time and evening/weekend programs available. *Students:* Average age 28. 6 applicants, 100% accepted, 5 enrolled. In 2003, 3 degrees awarded. *Application deadline:* For fall admission, 8/15 for domestic students; for spring admission, 12/12 priority date for domestic students. Applications are processed on a rolling basis. Application fee: $60. Electronic applications accepted. *Expenses:* Tuition: Full-time $29,949. *Financial support:* Available to part-time students. Application deadline: 5/1; *Application contact:* Information Contact, 617-627-3395, Fax: 617-627-3016, E-mail: gradschool@ase.tufts.edu.

Tufts University, School of Engineering, Department of Civil and Environmental Engineering, Medford, MA 02155. Offers civil engineering (ME, MS, PhD), including geotechnical engineering, structural engineering; environmental engineering (ME, MS, PhD), including environmental engineering and environmental sciences, environmental geotechnology, environmental health, environmental science and management, hazardous materials management, water resources engineering. Part-time programs available. *Faculty:* 13 full-time, 10 part-time/adjunct. *Students:* 61 (28 women); includes 1 minority (Asian American or Pacific Islander) 7 international. 97 applicants, 68% accepted, 27 enrolled. In 2003, 17 master's, 2 doctorates awarded. Terminal master's awarded for partial completion of doctoral program. *Degree requirements:* For master's, thesis or alternative; for doctorate, thesis/dissertation. *Entrance requirements:* Additional exam requirements/recommendations for international students: Required—TOEFL (minimum score 550 paper-based; 213 computer-based). *Application deadline:* For fall admission, 2/15 for domestic students, 12/30 for international students; for spring admission, 10/15 for domestic students, 9/15 for international students. Applications are processed on a rolling basis. Application fee: $60. Electronic applications accepted. *Expenses:* Tuition: Full-time $29,949. *Financial support:* Research assistantships with full and partial tuition reimbursements, teaching assistantships with full and partial tuition reimbursements, Federal Work-Study, scholarships/grants, and tuition waivers (partial) available. Support available to part-time students. Financial award application deadline: 2/1; financial award applicants required to submit FAFSA. *Unit head:* Dr. Christopher Swan, Chair, 617-627-3211, Fax: 617-627-3994.

Universidad del Turabo, Graduate Programs, Program in Science and Technology, Turabo, PR 00778-3030. Offers environmental studies (MES). *Entrance requirements:* For master's, GRE, PAEG, interview.

Universidad Metropolitana, School of Environmental Affairs, Program in Conservation and Management of Natural Resources, Río Piedras, PR 00928-1150. Offers MEM. Part-time programs available. *Degree requirements:* For master's, thesis. Electronic applications accepted.

Universidad Metropolitana, School of Environmental Affairs, Program in Environmental Planning, Río Piedras, PR 00928-1150. Offers MEM. Part-time programs available. *Degree requirements:* For master's, thesis. *Entrance requirements:* For master's, PAEG, interview. Electronic applications accepted.

Universidad Metropolitana, School of Environmental Affairs, Program in Environmental Risk and Assessment Management, Río Piedras, PR 00928-1150. Offers MEM. Part-time programs available. *Degree requirements:* For master's, thesis. Electronic applications accepted.

Université de Montréal, Faculty of Graduate Studies, Programs in Environment and Prevention, Montréal, QC H3C 3J7, Canada. Offers DESS. *Students:* 14 full-time (7 women), 8 part-time (6 women). 19 applicants, 47% accepted, 7 enrolled. In 2003, 2 degrees awarded. *Application deadline:* For fall and spring admission, 2/1; for winter admission, 11/1 for domestic students. Applications are processed on a rolling basis. Application fee: $30. Electronic applications accepted. *Expenses:* Tuition, state resident: full-time $834. Tuition, nonresident: full-time $1,253. International tuition: $3,900 full-time. Tuition and fees vary according to program. *Faculty research:* Health, environment, pollutants, protection, waste. *Unit head:* Joseph Zayed, Director, 514-343-5912, Fax: 514-343-6668, E-mail: joseph.zayed@umontreal.ca. *Application contact:* Micheline Dessureault, Information Contact, 514-343-2280.

Université du Québec à Chicoutimi, Graduate Programs, Program in Renewable Resources, Chicoutimi, QC G7H 2B1, Canada. Offers M Sc. Part-time programs available. *Degree requirements:* For master's, thesis. *Entrance requirements:* For master's, appropriate bachelor's degree, proficiency in French.

Université du Québec, Institut National de la Recherche Scientifique, Graduate Programs, Research Center—Earth and Environment, Ste-Foy, QC G1V 4C7, Canada. Offers earth sciences (M Sc, PhD); earth sciences-environmental technologies (M Sc); water sciences (MA, PhD). Part-time programs available. *Faculty:* 38. *Students:* 155 full-time (67 women), 10 part-time (3 women), 37 international. In 2003, 16 master's, 9 doctorates awarded. *Degree requirements:* For master's, thesis optional; for doctorate, thesis/dissertation. *Entrance requirements:* For master's, appropriate bachelor's degree, proficiency in French; for doctorate, appropriate master's degree, proficiency in French. *Application deadline:* For fall admission, 3/31 for domestic students. Application fee: $30. Tuition, area resident: Full-time $2,639. *Expenses:* Tuition, state resident: full-time $6,155. Tuition, nonresident: full-time $13,889. *Financial support:* Fellowships, research assistantships, teaching assistantships available. *Unit head:* Jean Pierre Villeneuve, Director, 418-654-2575, Fax: 418-654-2615, E-mail: jp_villeneuve@inrs.uquebec.ca. *Application contact:* Michel Barbeau, Registrar, 418-654-2518, Fax: 418-654-3858, E-mail: michel_barbeau@inrs.uquebec.ca.

Université Laval, Faculty of Agricultural and Food Sciences, Department of Soils and Agricultural Engineering, Programs in Agri-Food Engineering, Québec, QC G1K 7P4, Canada. Offers agri-food engineering (M Sc); environmental technology (M Sc). *Degree requirements:* For master's, thesis (for some programs). *Entrance requirements:* For master's, knowledge of French. Electronic applications accepted.

Université Laval, Faculty of Agricultural and Food Sciences, Department of Soils and Agricultural Engineering, Programs in Soils and Environment Science, Québec, QC G1K 7P4, Canada. Offers environmental technology (M Sc); soils and environment science (M Sc, PhD). Terminal master's awarded for partial completion of doctoral program. *Degree requirements:* For master's, thesis (for some programs); for doctorate, thesis/dissertation, comprehensive exam. *Entrance requirements:* For master's and doctorate, knowledge of French and English. Electronic applications accepted.

University at Albany, State University of New York, College of Arts and Sciences, Department of Biological Sciences, Program in Biodiversity, Conservation, and Policy, Albany, NY 12222-0001. Offers MS. *Degree requirements:* For master's, one foreign language. *Entrance requirements:* For master's, GRE General Test. Application fee: $50. *Expenses:* Tuition, state resident: part-time $288 per credit. Tuition, nonresident: part-time $438 per credit. Required fees: $495 per semester. *Faculty research:* Aquatic ecology, plant community ecology, biodiversity and public policy, restoration ecology, costal and estuarine science. *Unit head:* Gary Kleppel, Program Director, 518-442-4338.

University of Alaska Fairbanks, School of Natural Resources and Agricultural Sciences, Department of Resources Management, Fairbanks, AK 99775-7520. Offers MS. Part-time programs available. *Degree requirements:* For master's, thesis or alternative, comprehensive exam. *Entrance requirements:* For master's, GRE General Test. Additional exam requirements/recommendations for international students: Required—TOEFL. Electronic applications accepted. *Faculty research:* Wildlands management and policy, bioeconomic modeling, hydrologic modeling of land-use changes, global climate change, community ecology.

University of Alberta, Faculty of Graduate Studies and Research, Department of Economics, Edmonton, AB T6G 2E1, Canada. Offers economics (MA, PhD); economics and finance (MA); environmental and natural resource economics (PhD). Part-time programs available. *Faculty:* 25 full-time (5 women), 3 part-time/adjunct (0 women). *Students:* 33 full-time (7 women), 7 part-time (3 women). Average age 26. 112 applicants, 58% accepted, 22 enrolled. In 2003, 8 master's, 1 doctorate awarded. *Degree requirements:* For doctorate, thesis/dissertation. *Entrance requirements:* For master's and doctorate, GRE. Additional exam requirements/recommendations for international students: Required—TOEFL. *Application deadline:* For fall admission, 6/15 for domestic students. Applications are processed on a rolling basis. Tuition charges are reported in Canadian dollars. Tuition, nonresident: full-time $3,921 Canadian dollars. International tuition: $7,113 Canadian dollars full-time. *Financial support:* In 2003–04, 19 students received support, including 6 research assistantships with partial tuition reimbursements available (averaging $14,300 per year), 5 teaching assistantships with partial tuition reimbursements available (averaging $11,200 per year); career-related internships or fieldwork and scholarships/grants also available. Financial award application deadline: 3/1. *Faculty research:* Public finance, international trade, industrial organization, Pacific Rim economics, monetary economics. *Unit head:* Constance Smith, Graduate Coordinator, 780-492-7634, Fax: 780-492-3300, E-mail: constance.smith@ualberta.ca. *Application contact:* Audrey Jackson, Graduate Program Administrator, 780-492-7634, Fax: 780-492-3300, E-mail: econapps@ualberta.ca.

The University of Arizona, Graduate College, Graduate Interdisciplinary Programs, Graduate Interdisciplinary Program in Planning, Tucson, AZ 85721. Offers MS. *Accreditation:* ACSP. *Degree requirements:* For master's, thesis or alternative. *Entrance requirements:* For master's, GRE General Test, minimum B average. Additional exam requirements/recommendations for international students: Required—TOEFL. *Expenses:* Tuition, state resident: part-time $196 per unit. Tuition, nonresident: part-time $326 per unit. *Faculty research:* Environmental analysis, regional planning, land development, regional development, arid lands.

The University of British Columbia, Faculty of Graduate Studies, Resource Management and Environmental Studies Program/Institute for Resources, Environment, and Sustainability, Vancouver, BC V6T 1Z1, Canada. Offers M Sc, MA, PhD. *Faculty:* 12 full-time (1 woman), 2 part-time/adjunct (0 women). *Students:* 115 full-time (69 women). Average age 30. 126 applicants, 16% accepted, 18 enrolled. In 2003, 10 master's, 6 doctorates awarded. *Median time to degree:* Master's–3 years full-time; doctorate–5 years full-time. Of those who began their doctoral program in fall 1995, 100% received their degree in 8 years or less. *Degree requirements:* For master's, thesis/dissertation, registration; for doctorate, thesis/dissertation, comprehensive exam, registration. *Entrance requirements:* Additional exam requirements/recommendations for international students: Required—TOEFL (minimum score 600 paper-based; 250 computer-based). *Application deadline:* For fall admission, 9/1 for domestic students; for spring admission, 2/28 for domestic students. Applications are processed on a rolling basis. Application fee: $90 Canadian dollars ($150 Canadian dollars for international students). Electronic applications accepted. *Financial support:* In 2003–04, 32 students received support, including 32 fellowships with partial tuition reimbursements available (averaging $16,500 per year), 22 research assistantships with partial tuition reimbursements available (averaging $15,500 per year), 2 teaching assistantships; institutionally sponsored loans, scholarships/grants, tuition waivers (full and partial), and unspecified assistantships also available. Financial award application deadline: 10/1. *Faculty research:* Land management, water resources, energy, environmental assessment, risk evaluation. Total annual research expenditures: $8.6 million Canadian dollars. *Unit head:* Leslie M. Lavkulich, Director, 604-822-3487, Fax: 604-822-9250, E-mail: ire@ires.ubc.ca. *Application contact:* Jennifer Shaw, Graduate Admissions, 604-822-9249, Fax: 604-822-9250, E-mail: rmesgrad@interchange.ubc.ca.

University of Calgary, Faculty of Graduate Studies, Program in Resources and the Environment, Calgary, AB T2N 1N4, Canada. Offers M Sc, MA, PhD. *Students:* 25 full-time (14 women), 2 part-time (1 woman). 8 applicants, 88% accepted, 7 enrolled. In 2003, 5 master's, 1 doctorate awarded. *Degree requirements:* For master's, thesis; for doctorate, thesis/dissertation, written and oral candidacy exam. *Entrance requirements:* Additional exam requirements/recommendations for international students: Required—TOEFL. *Application deadline:* For fall admission, 4/1 for domestic students, 2/1 for international students; for winter admission, 9/1 for domestic students. Applications are processed on a rolling basis. Application fee: $60. Tuition, nonresident: full-time $4,765. Tuition and fees vary according to degree level, program and student level. *Financial support:* In 2003–04, 7 research assistantships (averaging $4,000 per year), 5 teaching assistantships (averaging $6,221 per year) were awarded. Financial award application deadline: 2/1. *Unit head:* Dr. Michael McMordie, Director, 403-220-7209, Fax: 403-284-4399, E-mail: mcmordie@ucalgary.ca. *Application contact:* Pauline Fisk, Program Administrator, 403-220-7209, Fax: 403-284-4399, E-mail: pfisk@ucalgary.ca.

University of California, Berkeley, Graduate Division, College of Natural Resources, Department of Environmental Science, Policy, and Management, Berkeley, CA 94720-1500. Offers environmental science, policy, and management (MS, PhD); forestry (MF). *Faculty:* 62 full-time (16 women), 3 part-time/adjunct (2 women). *Students:* 165 (91 women); includes 30 minority (5 African Americans, 4 American Indian/Alaska Native, 11 Asian Americans or Pacific Islanders, 10 Hispanic Americans) 31 international. 345 applicants, 14% accepted, 30 enrolled. In 2003, 10 master's, 13 doctorates awarded. Terminal master's awarded for partial completion of doctoral program. *Median time to degree:* Of those who began their doctoral program in fall 1995, 98% received their degree in 8 years or less. *Degree requirements:* For master's, thesis optional; for doctorate, thesis/dissertation, qualifying exam. *Entrance requirements:* For master's and doctorate, GRE General Test, minimum GPA of 3.0. Additional exam requirements/recommendations for international students: Required—TOEFL; Recommended—TSE. *Application deadline:* For fall admission, 12/1 for domestic students. Application fee: $60. Electronic applications accepted. International tuition: $12,491 full-time. Required fees: $5,484. *Financial support:* In 2003–04, 10 fellowships with full tuition reimbursements (averaging $15,000 per year), 34 research assistantships with full tuition reimbursements (averaging $15,000 per year), 50 teaching assistantships with full tuition reimbursements (averaging $7,175 per year) were awarded. Unspecified assistantships also available. Financial award application deadline: 12/1; financial award applicants required to submit FAFSA. *Faculty research:* Biology and ecology of insects; ecosystem function and environmental issues of soils; plant health/interactions from molecular to ecosystem levels; range management and ecology; forest and resource policy, sustainability, and management. *Unit head:* Dr. Steven R. Beissinger, Chair, 510-642-8051, Fax: 510-643-3058, E-mail: beis@nature.berkeley.edu. *Application contact:* Sue Baumgartner, Student Affairs Officer, 510-642-6410, Fax: 510-642-4034, E-mail: espmgradproginfo@nature.berkeley.edu.

See in-depth description on page 749.

University of California, Berkeley, Graduate Division, Group in Energy and Resources, Berkeley, CA 94720-1500. Offers MA, MS, PhD. *Students:* 60 (28 women); includes 6 minority (2 African Americans, 1 American Indian/Alaska Native, 1 Asian American or Pacific Islander, 2 Hispanic Americans) 9 international. 161 applicants, 11% accepted, 15 enrolled. In 2003, 14 master's, 4 doctorates awarded. *Degree requirements:* For master's, project or thesis; for doctorate, one foreign language, thesis/dissertation, qualifying exam. *Entrance requirements:* For master's and doctorate, GRE General Test, minimum GPA of 3.0. *Application deadline:* For fall admission, 1/5 for domestic students. Application fee: $60. International tuition: $12,491 full-time. Required fees: $5,484. *Financial support:* Unspecified assistantships available. Financial award application deadline: 1/5. *Faculty research:* Technical, economic, environmental, and institutional aspects of energy conservation in residential and commercial buildings; international patterns of energy use; renewable energy sources and barriers to their potential contribution to energy supplies; assessment of conventional and nonconventional valuation of energy and environmental resources pricing. *Unit head:* Per Peterson, Chair, 510-642-1640. *Application contact:* Donna Bridges, Student Affairs Officer, 510-642-1760, Fax: 510-642-1085, E-mail: dbridges@socrates.berkeley.edu.

University of California, Irvine, Office of Graduate Studies, School of Social Ecology, Department of Environmental Analysis and Design, Irvine, CA 92697. Offers environmental health science and policy (MS, PhD); social ecology (PhD). *Students:* 15. In 2003, 3 degrees awarded. *Degree requirements:* For doctorate, thesis/dissertation, research project. *Entrance requirements:* For master's and doctorate, GRE General Test, minimum GPA of 3.0. Additional exam requirements/recommendations for international students: Required—TOEFL (minimum score 550 paper-based; 213 computer-based). *Application deadline:* For fall admission, 1/15 for domestic students; for winter admission, 10/15 for domestic students. Application fee: $60. Electronic applications accepted. Tuition, nonresident: full-time $12,245. Required fees:$5,219. Tuition and fees vary according to degree level and program. *Financial support:* Fellowships, research assistantships with full tuition reimbursements, teaching assistantships, institutionally sponsored loans, traineeships, health care benefits, and unspecified assistantships available. Financial award application deadline: 3/1; financial award applicants required to submit FAFSA. *Faculty research:* Effects of environmental stressors, environmental pollution, biology and politics of water pollution, potential impacts of natural disasters, risk management. *Unit head:* Jonathon Ericson, Chair, 949-824-7261, Fax: 949-824-2056, E-mail: jeericso@uci.edu. *Application contact:* Jill Vidas, Academic Counselor, 949-824-5918, Fax: 949-824-2056, E-mail: jjvidas@uci.edu.

University of California, Santa Barbara, Graduate Division, Donald Bren School of Environmental Science and Management, Santa Barbara, CA 93106. Offers MESM, PhD. *Faculty:* 17 full-time (3 women), 3 part-time/adjunct (0 women). *Students:* 127 full-time (66 women), 6 part-time (4 women); includes 7 minority (all Asian Americans or Pacific Islanders), 16 international. Average age 25. 293 applicants, 55% accepted, 75 enrolled. In 2003, 38 master's, 4 doctorates awarded, leading to university research/teaching 50%, government 50%. *Median time to degree:* Master's–2 years full-time, 3 years part-time; doctorate–6 years full-time. *Degree requirements:* For master's, group project as student thesis; for doctorate, thesis/dissertation, comprehensive exam, registration. *Entrance requirements:* For master's and doctorate, GRE. Additional exam requirements/recommendations for international students: Required—TOEFL (minimum score 550 paper-based; 213 computer-based). *Application deadline:* For fall admission, 2/1 for domestic students, 2/1 for international students. Applications are processed on a rolling basis. Application fee: $60. Electronic applications accepted. *Expenses:* Tuition, state resident: full-time $7,188. Tuition, nonresident: full-time $19,608. *Financial support:* In 2003–04, 18 fellowships with partial tuition reimbursements, 14 research assistantships with full tuition reimbursements (averaging $11,140 per year), 12 teaching assistantships with partial tuition reimbursements (averaging $4,531 per year) were awarded. Career-related internships or fieldwork, Federal Work-Study, institutionally sponsored loans, scholarships/grants, traineeships, health care benefits, and unspecified assistantships also available. Financial award application deadline: 2/1; financial award applicants required to submit FAFSA. *Faculty research:* Hydrology, ecology, political instituting, environmental economics, biogeochemistry. *Unit head:* Dr. Dennis J. Aigner, Dean, 805-893-7363, Fax: 805-893-7612, E-mail: info@bren.ucsb.edu. *Application contact:* Graduate Program Coordinator, 805-893-7611, Fax: 805-893-7612, E-mail: gradasst@bren.ucsb.edu.

See in-depth description on page 753.

University of California, Santa Cruz, Division of Graduate Studies, Division of Social Sciences, Program in Environmental Studies, Santa Cruz, CA 95064. Offers PhD. *Faculty:* 15 full-time (5 women). *Students:* 42 full-time (24 women), 7 part-time (3 women); includes 5 minority (1 American Indian/Alaska Native, 2 Asian Americans or Pacific Islanders, 2 Hispanic Americans), 4 international. 77 applicants, 18% accepted, 9 enrolled. In 2003, 5 degrees awarded. *Median time to degree:* Doctorate–6.25 years full-time. *Degree requirements:* For doctorate, thesis/dissertation, qualifying exam. *Entrance requirements:* For doctorate, GRE General Test. *Application deadline:* For fall admission, 1/7 for domestic students. Application fee: $60. Tuition, nonresident: full-time $12,492. *Financial support:* Fellowships, research assistantships, teaching assistantships, career-related internships or fieldwork, Federal Work-Study, and institutionally sponsored loans available. Financial award application deadline: 1/7. *Faculty research:* Political economy and sustainability, conservation biology, agroecology. *Unit head:* David Goodman, Chairperson, 831-459-4561. *Application contact:* James M. Moore, Graduate Admissions, Director, 831-459-2301, Fax: 831-459-4843, E-mail: gradadm@ucsc.edu.

University of Chicago, The Irving B. Harris Graduate School of Public Policy Studies, Chicago, IL 60637-1513. Offers environmental science and policy (MS); public policy studies (AM, MPP, PhD). Part-time programs available. *Faculty:* 25 full-time (6 women), 12 part-time/adjunct (3 women). *Students:* 269 full-time, 7 part-time; includes 58 minority (15 African Americans, 34 Asian Americans or Pacific Islanders, 9 Hispanic Americans), 58 international. Average age 27. 722 applicants, 60% accepted, 141 enrolled. In 2003, 100 degrees awarded. Terminal master's awarded for partial completion of doctoral program. *Median time to degree:* Master's–2 years full-time. *Degree requirements:* For doctorate, thesis/dissertation. *Entrance requirements:* For master's and doctorate, GMAT or GRE General Test. Additional exam requirements/recommendations for international students: Required—TOEFL. *Application deadline:* For fall admission, 1/3 priority date for domestic students, 1/3 priority date for international students. Application fee: $50. Electronic applications accepted. *Expenses:* Contact institution. *Financial support:* In 2003–04, 149 fellowships with full and partial tuition reimbursements (averaging $11,000 per year) were awarded; career-related internships or fieldwork, Federal Work-Study, institutionally sponsored loans, and scholarships/grants also available. Support available to part-time students. Financial award application deadline: 1/3; financial award applicants required to submit FAFSA. *Faculty research:* Family and child policy, international security, health policy, social policy. *Unit head:* Dr. Susan E. Mayer, Dean, 773-702-9623, E-mail: s-mayer@uchicago.edu. *Application contact:* Maggie DeCarlo, Director of Admission, 773-834-0136, Fax: 773-702-0926, E-mail: mdecarlo@uchicago.edu.

University of Colorado at Boulder, Graduate School, College of Arts and Sciences, Program in Environmental Studies, Boulder, CO 80309. Offers MS, PhD. *Faculty:* 5 full-time (1 woman). *Students:* 36 full-time (19 women), 1 (woman) part-time; includes 4 minority (1 American Indian/Alaska Native, 3 Hispanic Americans), 1 international. Average age 31. 25 applicants, 60% accepted. In 2003, 2 degrees awarded. *Expenses:* Tuition, state resident: full-time $2,122. Tuition, nonresident: full-time $9,754. Tuition and fees vary according to course load and program. *Financial support:* In 2003–04, 6 fellowships (averaging $14,641 per year), 3 research assistantships (averaging $16,725 per year), 6 teaching assistantships (averaging $17,598 per year) were awarded. *Faculty research:* Climate and atmospheric chemistry, water sciences, environmental policy and sustainability, waste management and environmental remediation, biogeochemical cycles. Total annual research expenditures: $1.4 million. *Unit head:* James W. C. White, Director, 303-492-5494, Fax: 303-492-8437, E-mail: jwhite@colorado.edu. *Application contact:* Graduate Program Assistant, 303-492-5478, Fax: 303-492-5207, E-mail: envsgrad@colorado.edu.

University of Connecticut, Graduate School, College of Agriculture and Natural Resources, Department of Natural Resources Management and Engineering, Field of Natural Resources Management and Engineering, Storrs, CT 06269. Offers natural resources (MS, PhD). *Faculty:* 11 full-time (1 woman). *Students:* 21 full-time (5 women), 5 part-time (3 women), 7 international. Average age 30. 15 applicants, 40% accepted, 4 enrolled. In 2003, 4 degrees awarded. Terminal master's awarded for partial completion of doctoral program. *Degree requirements:* For master's, comprehensive exam; for doctorate, thesis/dissertation. *Entrance requirements:* For master's, GRE General Test, GRE Subject Test. Additional exam requirements/recommendations for international students: Required—TOEFL (minimum score 550 paper-based; 213 computer-based). *Application deadline:* For fall admission, 2/1 priority date for domestic students, 2/1 priority date for international students; for spring admission, 11/1 for domestic students, 10/1 for international students. Applications are processed on a rolling basis. Application fee: $55. Electronic applications accepted. *Expenses:* Tuition, state resident: part-time $3,860 per semester. Tuition, nonresident: part-time $9,036 per semester. *Financial support:* In 2003–04, 18 research assistantships with full tuition reimbursements, 2 teaching assistantships with full tuition reimbursements were awarded. Fellowships, Federal Work-Study, scholarships/grants, health care benefits, and unspecified assistantships also available. Financial award application deadline: 2/1; financial award applicants required to submit FAFSA. *Application contact:* John Clausen, Chairman, Graduate Admissions, 860-486-0139, Fax: 860-486-5408, E-mail: john.clausen@uconn.edu.

University of Delaware, College of Human Services, Education and Public Policy, Center for Energy and Environmental Policy, Newark, DE 19716. Offers environmental and energy policy (MEEP, PhD); urban affairs and public policy (MA, PhD). *Faculty:* 7 full-time (1 woman), 9 part-time/adjunct (2 women). *Students:* 52 full-time (20 women), 13 part-time (8 women); includes 12 minority (6 African Americans, 4 Asian Americans or Pacific Islanders, 2 Hispanic Americans), 29 international. 145 applicants, 18% accepted, 19 enrolled. In 2003, 6 master's awarded, leading to business/industry 33%, government 67%, 8 doctorates awarded, leading to university research/teaching 25%, business/industry 25%, government 50%. *Degree requirements:* For master's, analytical paper or thesis; for doctorate, thesis/dissertation, comprehensive exam. *Entrance requirements:* For master's, GRE General Test, minimum GPA of 3.0; for doctorate, GRE General Test, minimum GPA of 3.5. Additional exam requirements/recommendations for international students: Required—TOEFL. *Application deadline:* ; for spring admission, 2/15 for domestic students. Application fee: $60. Electronic applications accepted. *Expenses:* Tuition, state resident: full-time $5,890; part-time $327 per credit. Tuition, nonresident: full-time $15,420; part-time $857 per credit. Required fees: $968. *Financial support:* In 2003–04, 38 students received support, including 9 fellowships with tuition reimbursements available (averaging $11,000 per year), 28 research assistantships with tuition reimbursements available (averaging $11,000 per year), 1 teaching assistantship with full tuition reimbursement available (averaging $11,000 per year); career-related internships or fieldwork, Federal Work-Study, and tuition waivers (full) also available. Financial award application deadline: 2/15. *Faculty research:* Sustainable development, renewable energy, climate change, environmental policy, environmental justice, disaster policy. Total annual research expenditures: $500,000. *Unit head:* Dr. John Byrne, Director, 302-831-8405, Fax: 302-831-3098, E-mail: jbbyrne@udel.edu. *Application contact:* Terri Brower, Staff Assistant, 302-831-8405, Fax: 302-831-3098, E-mail: tbrower@udel.edu.

See in-depth description on page 757.

University of Delaware, College of Human Services, Education and Public Policy, School of Urban Affairs and Public Policy, Program in Urban Affairs and Public Policy, Newark, DE 19716. Offers community development and nonprofit leadership (MA); energy and environmental policy (MA); governance, planning and management (PhD); historic preservation (MA); social and urban policy (PhD); technology, environment and society (PhD). Part-time programs available. *Faculty:* 15 full-time (6 women). *Students:* 82 full-time (46 women), 9 part-time (5 women); includes 22 minority (15 African Americans, 2 American Indian/Alaska Native, 1 Asian American or Pacific Islander, 4 Hispanic Americans), 21 international. Average age 36. 101 applicants, 36% accepted, 25 enrolled. In 2003, 12 master's, 10 doctorates awarded. Terminal master's awarded for partial completion of doctoral program. *Degree requirements:* For master's, thesis or alternative, analytical paper or thesis; for doctorate, thesis/dissertation. *Entrance requirements:* For master's, GRE General Test, minimum GPA of 3.0; for doctorate, GRE General Test, minimum GPA of 3.5. Additional exam requirements/recommendations for international students: Required—TOEFL. *Application deadline:* For fall admission, 2/1 for domestic students; for spring admission, 12/1 for domestic students. Applications are processed on a rolling basis. Application fee: $60. Electronic applications accepted. *Expenses:* Tuition, state resident: full-time $5,890; part-time $327 per credit. Tuition, nonresident: full-time $15,420; part-time $857 per credit. Required fees: $968. *Financial support:* In 2003–04, 78 students received support, including 4 fellowships with full tuition reimbursements available (averaging $11,000 per year), 62 research assistantships with full tuition reimbursements available (averaging $11,000 per year), 4 teaching assistantships with full tuition reimbursements available (averaging $11,000 per year); career-related internships or fieldwork, Federal Work-Study, and tuition waivers (full) also available. Financial award application deadline: 2/1. *Faculty research:* Political economy; social policy analysis; technology and society; historic preservation; urban policy. Total annual research expenditures: $1 million. *Unit head:* Dr. Steven W. Peuquet, Director, 302-831-6294, Fax: 302-831-4225, E-mail: speuquet@udel.edu. *Application contact:* Diana Simmons, Information Contact, 302-831-1687, Fax: 302-831-3587, E-mail: dwalls@udel.edu.

University of Denver, University College, Denver, CO 80208. Offers alternative dispute resolution (MPS); applied communication (MAC); civic leadership and development (MPS); computer information systems (MCIS, MPS); e-commerce (MPS); environmental policy and management (MEPM); environmental policy and mangement (MPS); geographic information systems (MPS); leadership (MPS); liberal studies (MLS); organizational security (MPS); project management (MPS); technology management (MPS, MoTM); telecommunications (MPS, MTEL); training (MPS). Part-time and evening/weekend programs available. Postbaccalaureate distance learning degree programs offered (no on-campus study). *Faculty:* 167 part-time/adjunct (52 women). *Students:* 790 (431 women); includes 106 minority (33 African Americans, 4 American Indian/Alaska Native, 34 Asian Americans or Pacific Islanders, 35 Hispanic Americans) 50 international. 111 applicants, 68% accepted. In 2003, 225 degrees awarded. *Entrance requirements:* For master's, minimum undergraduate GPA of 3.0. *Application deadline:* For fall admission, 7/15 for domestic students; for winter admission, 10/14 for domestic students; for spring admission, 2/10 for domestic students. Applications are processed on a rolling basis. Application fee: $25. *Expenses:* Contact institution. *Financial support:* In 2003–04, 174 students received support. Total annual research expenditures: $59,206. *Unit head:* Dr. James Davis, Dean, 303-871-3141. *Application contact:* Cindy Kraft, Admission Coordinator, 303-871-3969.

The University of Findlay, Graduate College, College of Science, Program in Environmental Management, Findlay, OH 45840-3653. Offers MSEM. Part-time and evening/weekend programs available. Postbaccalaureate distance learning degree programs offered (no on-campus study). *Students:* 44 full-time (16 women), 91 part-time (37 women); includes 22 minority (5 African Americans, 13 Asian Americans or Pacific Islanders, 4 Hispanic Americans), 13 international. Average age 35. In 2003, 24 degrees awarded. *Degree requirements:* For master's, cumulative project. *Application deadline:* Applications are processed on a rolling basis. Application fee: $25. Electronic applications accepted. *Expenses:* Tuition: Part-time $349 per semester hour. One-time fee: $30 part-time. *Financial support:* In 2003–04, 8 students received support, including 2 teaching assistantships with full tuition reimbursements available (averaging $6,000 per year); unspecified assistantships also available. Financial award application deadline: 4/1; financial award applicants required to submit FAFSA. *Unit head:* Dr. William Carter, Graduate Director, 419-434-6919, Fax: 419-434-4822, E-mail: carter@findlay.edu.

University of Guelph, Graduate Program Services, Ontario Agricultural College, Department of Environmental Biology, Guelph, ON N1G 2W1, Canada. Offers environmental management (M Sc, PhD); plant protection (M Sc, PhD). Part-time programs available. *Faculty:* 21 full-time (2 women), 6 part-time/adjunct (1 woman). *Students:* 75 full-time (43 women), 13 part-time (9 women). 44 applicants, 20% accepted, 8 enrolled. In 2003, 15 master's, 11 doctorates awarded. *Median time to degree:* Of those who began their doctoral program in fall 1995, 79.5% received their degree in 8 years or less. *Degree requirements:* For master's, thesis/dissertation, registration; for doctorate, thesis/dissertation, comprehensive exam, registration. *Entrance requirements:* For master's, minimum B- average during previous 2 years; for doctorate, minimum B average. *Application deadline:* Applications are processed on a rolling basis. Application fee: $75. Electronic applications accepted. Tuition and fees charges are reported in Canadian dollars. Tuition, nonresident: full-time $3,440 Canadian dollars. International tuition: $5,432 Canadian dollars full-time. Required fees: $753 Canadian dollars. *Financial support:* In 2003–04, research assistantships (averaging $16,500 per year), teaching assistantships (averaging $2,214 per year) were awarded. *Faculty research:* Entomology, environmental microbiology and biotechnology, environmental toxicology, forest ecology, plant pathology. Total annual research expenditures: $3 million. *Unit head:* Dr. M. A. Dixon, Chair, 519-824-4120 Ext. 52555, Fax: 519-837-0442, E-mail: mdixon@uoguelph.ca. *Application contact:* Dr. G. J. Boland, Admissions Coordinator, 519-824-4120 Ext. 52755, Fax: 519-837-0442, E-mail: gboland@uoguelph.ca.

Environmental Management and Policy

University of Guelph, Graduate Program Services, Ontario Agricultural College, Department of Land Resource Science, Guelph, ON N1G 2W1, Canada. Offers atmospheric science (M Sc, PhD); environmental and agricultural earth sciences (M Sc, PhD); land resources management (M Sc, PhD); soil science (M Sc, PhD). Part-time programs available. *Faculty:* 19 full-time (5 women), 3 part-time/adjunct (0 women). *Students:* 47 full-time (24 women), 3 part-time; includes 1 African American, 6 Asian Americans or Pacific Islanders, 2 Hispanic Americans, 2 international. Average age 28. 24 applicants, 46% accepted. In 2003, 9 master's, 4 doctorates awarded. *Degree requirements:* For master's and doctorate, thesis/dissertation. *Entrance requirements:* For master's, minimum B- average during previous 2 years; for doctorate, minimum B average during previous 2 years. Additional exam requirements/recommendations for international students: Required—TOEFL (minimum score 550 paper-based; 213 computer-based). *Application deadline:* For fall admission, 7/1 priority date for domestic students, 5/1 priority date for international students; for winter admission, 10/1 for domestic students; for spring admission, 3/1 for domestic students. Applications are processed on a rolling basis. Application fee: $75 Canadian dollars. Electronic applications accepted. Tuition and fees charges are reported in Canadian dollars. Tuition, nonresident: full-time $3,440 Canadian dollars. International tuition: $5,432 Canadian dollars full-time. Required fees: $753 Canadian dollars. *Financial support:* In 2003–04, 30 students received support, including 40 research assistantships (averaging $16,500 Canadian dollars per year), 15 teaching assistantships (averaging $3,800 Canadian dollars per year); fellowships, scholarships/grants also available. *Faculty research:* Soil science, environmental earth science, land resource management. Total annual research expenditures: $2.1 million Canadian dollars. *Unit head:* Dr. S. Hilts, Chairman, 519-824-4120 Ext. 52447, Fax: 519-824-5730, E-mail: shilts@uoguelph.ca. *Application contact:* Dr. T. J. Gillespie, Graduate Coordinator, 519-824-4120 Ext. 54276, Fax: 519-824-5730, E-mail: tgillesp@lrs.uoguelph.ca.

University of Hawaii at Manoa, Graduate Division, College of Tropical Agriculture and Human Resources, Department of Natural Resources and Environmental Management, Honolulu, HI 96822. Offers MS, PhD. Part-time programs available. *Faculty:* 23 full-time (3 women), 8 part-time/adjunct (2 women). *Students:* 22 full-time (12 women), 3 part-time (1 woman); includes 4 minority (all Asian Americans or Pacific Islanders), 7 international. Average age 34. 36 applicants, 67% accepted, 13 enrolled.Terminal master's awarded for partial completion of doctoral program. *Median time to degree:* Doctorate–7 years full-time. *Degree requirements:* For master's, thesis or alternative; for doctorate, thesis/dissertation. *Entrance requirements:* For master's and doctorate, GRE, minimum GPA of 3.0 in last 4 semesters. Additional exam requirements/recommendations for international students: Required—TOEFL. *Application deadline:* For fall admission, 3/1 for domestic students, 1/15 for international students; for spring admission, 9/1 for domestic students, 8/1 for international students. Applications are processed on a rolling basis. Application fee: $50. *Expenses:* Tuition, state resident: full-time $4,464; part-time $186 per credit hour. Tuition, nonresident: full-time $10,608; part-time $442 per credit hour. Tuition and fees vary according to program. *Financial support:* In 2003–04, 7 research assistantships (averaging $15,746 per year), 5 teaching assistantships (averaging $14,089 per year) were awarded. Fellowships, career-related internships or fieldwork and tuition waivers (full and partial) also available. *Faculty research:* Bioeconomics, natural resource management. *Unit head:* Dr. Samir El-Swarfy, Chairperson, 808-956-6708, Fax: 808-956-2811.

University of Hawaii at Manoa, Graduate Division, Colleges of Arts and Sciences, College of Social Sciences, Department of Urban and Regional Planning, Honolulu, HI 96822. Offers community planning and social policy (MURP); environmental planning and management (MURP); land use and infrastructure planning (MURP); urban and regional planning in Asia and Pacific (MURP). *Accreditation:* ACSP. *Faculty:* 46 full-time (14 women), 4 part-time/adjunct (0 women). *Students:* 50 full-time (24 women), 25 part-time (10 women); includes 24 minority (all Asian Americans or Pacific Islanders), 22 international. Average age 31. 63 applicants, 67% accepted, 26 enrolled. In 2003, 8 degrees awarded. *Median time to degree:* Master's–2 years full-time. *Entrance requirements:* For master's, GRE, minimum GPA of 3.0. Additional exam requirements/recommendations for international students: Required—TOEFL. *Application deadline:* For fall admission, 3/1 for domestic students, 3/1 for international students; for spring admission, 9/1 for domestic students, 9/1 for international students. Application fee: $50. *Expenses:* Tuition, state resident: full-time $4,464; part-time $186 per credit hour. Tuition, nonresident: full-time $10,608; part-time $442 per credit hour. Tuition and fees vary according to program. *Financial support:* In 2003–04, 8 research assistantships (averaging $15,813 per year), 4 teaching assistantships (averaging $13,697 per year) were awarded. Career-related internships or fieldwork, Federal Work-Study, institutionally sponsored loans, and tuition waivers (full) also available. *Unit head:* Kem Lowry, Chairperson, 808-956-7381, Fax: 808-956-6870, E-mail: lowry@hawaii.edu.

University of Houston–Clear Lake, School of Business and Public Administration, Program in General Business, Houston, TX 77058-1098. Offers environmental management (MS); healthcare administration (MHA); human resource management (MA); management information systems (MS); public management (MA). *Accreditation:* ACEHSA (one or more programs are accredited). Part-time and evening/weekend programs available. *Students:* 83 full-time (36 women), 81 part-time (38 women); includes 38 minority (11 African Americans, 1 American Indian/Alaska Native, 18 Asian Americans or Pacific Islanders, 8 Hispanic Americans), 67 international. Average age 33. In 2003, 91 degrees awarded. *Degree requirements:* For master's, thesis optional. *Entrance requirements:* For master's, GMAT. Additional exam requirements/recommendations for international students: Required—TOEFL (minimum score 550 paper-based; 213 computer-based). *Application deadline:* For fall admission, 8/1 for domestic students, 6/1 for international students; for spring admission, 12/1 for domestic students, 10/1 for international students. Applications are processed on a rolling basis. Application fee: $35 ($75 for international students). Electronic applications accepted. *Expenses:* Tuition, state resident: full-time $2,484; part-time $414 per course. Tuition, nonresident: full-time $6,318; part-time $1,053 per course. Required fees: $12 per course. $199 per semester. *Financial support:* Fellowships, research assistantships, teaching assistantships, career-related internships or fieldwork, Federal Work-Study, institutionally sponsored loans, and scholarships/grants available. Support available to part-time students. Financial award application deadline: 5/1; financial award applicants required to submit FAFSA. *Unit head:* Dr. Richard Allison, Chair, 281-283-3251, E-mail: allison@cl.uh.edu. *Application contact:* Dr. Sue Neeley, Associate Professor, 281-283-3110, E-mail: neeley@cl.uh.edu.

University of Idaho, College of Graduate Studies, College of Natural Resources, Moscow, ID 83844-2282. Offers fish and wildlife resources (MS, PhD), including fishery resources, wildlife resources; forest products (MS); forest resources (MS, PhD); forestry, wildlife, and range sciences (PhD); natural resources management and administration (MNR); range science (MS, PhD); rangeland ecology and management (MS, PhD); recreation and park management (MS, PhD); resource recreation and tourism (MS, PhD). *Students:* 222 (91 women); includes 12 minority (3 American Indian/Alaska Native, 2 Asian Americans or Pacific Islanders, 7 Hispanic Americans) 33 international. *Degree requirements:* For doctorate, thesis/dissertation. *Entrance requirements:* For master's, minimum GPA of 2.8; for doctorate, minimum undergraduate GPA of 2.8, 3.0 graduate. *Application deadline:* For fall admission, 8/1 for domestic students; for spring admission, 12/15 for domestic students. Application fee: $55 ($60 for international students). *Expenses:* Tuition, state resident: full-time $3,348. Tuition, nonresident: full-time $10,740. Required fees: $540. *Financial support:* Fellowships, research assistantships, teaching assistantships, Federal Work-Study available. Support available to part-time students. Financial award application deadline: 2/15. *Unit head:* Steven B. Daley-Laursen, Dean, 208-885-6442, Fax: 208-885-6226. *Application contact:* Dr. Ali Moslemi, Graduate Coordinator, 208-885-6126.

See in-depth description on page 763.

University of Illinois at Springfield, Graduate Programs, College of Public Affairs and Administration, Program in Environmental Studies, Springfield, IL 62703-5407. Offers MA. *Faculty:* 2 full-time (1 woman), 1 (woman) part-time/adjunct. *Students:* 19 full-time (10 women), 25 part-time (14 women); includes 4 minority (3 Asian Americans or Pacific Islanders, 1 Hispanic American), 1 international. Average age 32. 28 applicants, 89% accepted, 17 enrolled. In 2003, 13 degrees awarded. *Degree requirements:* For master's, thesis or alternative. *Entrance requirements:* For master's, GRE General Test, minimum GPA of 3.0. *Application deadline:* Applications are processed on a rolling basis. Application fee: $0. *Expenses:* Tuition, state resident: full-time $3,108; part-time $130 per credit. Tuition, nonresident: full-time $9,324; part-time $389 per credit. Required fees: $860. Full-time tuition and fees vary according to student level. *Financial support:* In 2003–04, 22 students received support, including 15 research assistantships with full and partial tuition reimbursements available (averaging $6,300 per year); career-related internships or fieldwork, Federal Work-Study, scholarships/grants, tuition waivers (partial), and unspecified assistantships also available. Financial award application deadline: 6/1; financial award applicants required to submit FAFSA. *Faculty research:* Population ecology and evolution, transportation and energy resource planning, environmental economics, environmental policies, risk assessment. *Unit head:* Malcolm Levin, Chair, 217-206-6720.

University of Maine, Graduate School, College of Natural Sciences, Forestry, and Agriculture, Department of Plant, Soil, and Environmental Sciences, Orono, ME 04469. Offers biological sciences (PhD); ecology and environmental sciences (MS, PhD); forest resources (PhD); horticulture (MS); plant science (PhD); plant, soil, and environmental sciences (MS); resource utilization (MS). *Students:* 20 full-time (14 women), 8 part-time (5 women); includes 1 minority (Asian American or Pacific Islander), 2 international. Average age 31. 12 applicants, 42% accepted, 5 enrolled. In 2003, 2 degrees awarded. *Entrance requirements:* For master's and doctorate, GRE General Test. Additional exam requirements/recommendations for international students: Required—TOEFL. *Application deadline:* Applications are processed on a rolling basis. Application fee: $50. Electronic applications accepted. *Expenses:* Tuition, state resident: part-time $235 per credit. Tuition, nonresident: part-time $670 per credit. Tuition and fees vary according to course load. *Financial support:* In 2003–04, 9 research assistantships with tuition reimbursements (averaging $12,180 per year) were awarded; teaching assistantships, scholarships/grants, tuition waivers (full and partial), and unspecified assistantships also available. *Unit head:* Dr. M. Susan Erich, Chair, 207-581-2938, Fax: 207-581-3207. *Application contact:* Scott G. Delcourt, Associate Dean of the Graduate School, 207-581-3218, Fax: 207-581-3232, E-mail: graduate@maine.edu.

University of Maine, Graduate School, College of Natural Sciences, Forestry, and Agriculture, Program in Resource Utilization, Orono, ME 04469. Offers MS. *Faculty:* 10 full-time (1 woman). *Degree requirements:* For master's, thesis. *Entrance requirements:* For master's, GRE General Test. Additional exam requirements/recommendations for international students: Required—TOEFL. *Application deadline:* For fall admission, 2/1 for domestic students. Applications are processed on a rolling basis. Application fee: $50. Electronic applications accepted. *Expenses:* Tuition, state resident: part-time $235 per credit. Tuition, nonresident: part-time $670 per credit. Tuition and fees vary according to course load. *Financial support:* Research assistantships with tuition reimbursements, teaching assistantships with tuition reimbursements, career-related internships or fieldwork, Federal Work-Study, institutionally sponsored loans, scholarships/grants, and tuition waivers (full and partial) available. Financial award application deadline:3/1. *Faculty research:* Waste utilities, wildlife evaluation, tourism and recreation economics. *Unit head:* Dr. Mario Teisl, Coordinator, 207-581-3162. *Application contact:* Scott G. Delcourt, Associate Dean of the Graduate School, 207-581-3218, Fax: 207-581-3232, E-mail: graduate@maine.edu.

University of Manitoba, Faculty of Graduate Studies, Natural Resources Institute, Winnipeg, MB R3T 2N2, Canada. Offers natural resources and environmental management (PhD); natural resources management (MNRM). Tuition charges are reported in Canadian dollars. Tuition, nonresident: full-time $3,878 Canadian dollars.

University of Maryland University College, Graduate School of Management and Technology, Program in Environmental Management, Adelphi, MD 20783. Offers MS, Certificate. Offered evenings and weekends only. Part-time and evening/weekend programs available. Postbaccalaureate distance learning degree programs offered (no on-campus study). *Students:* 6 full-time (2 women), 251 part-time (119 women); includes 50 minority (31 African Americans, 1 American Indian/Alaska Native, 7 Asian Americans or Pacific Islanders, 11 Hispanic Americans), 4 international. Average age 35. 88 applicants, 99% accepted, 70 enrolled. In 2003, 35 master's, 3 other advanced degrees awarded. *Degree requirements:* For master's, thesis or alternative. *Entrance requirements:* For master's, BS/BA in social science, physical science, engineering; 6 semester hours in biology and chemistry; 1 year of experience in field. *Application deadline:* Applications are processed on a rolling basis. Application fee: $50. Electronic applications accepted. *Expenses:* Tuition, state resident: part-time $339 per semester hour. Tuition, nonresident: part-time $553 per semester hour. Tuition and fees vary according to course level and program. *Financial support:* Federal Work-Study and scholarships/grants available. Support available to part-time students. Financial award application deadline: 6/1; financial award applicants required to submit FAFSA. *Unit head:* Dr. Robert Ouellette, Acting Chair, 301-985-7200, Fax: 301-985-4611, E-mail: rouellette@umuc.edu. *Application contact:* Coordinator, Graduate Admissions, 301-985-7155, Fax: 301-985-7175, E-mail: gradinfo@nova.umuc.edu.

University of Massachusetts Lowell, Graduate School, James B. Francis College of Engineering, Department of Work Environment, Lowell, MA 01854-2881. Offers cleaner production and pollution prevention (MS, Sc D); environmental risk assessment (Certificate); identification and control of ergonomic hazards (Certificate); industrial hygiene (MS, Sc D); job stress and healthy job redesign (Certificate); occupational epidemiology (MS, Sc D); occupational ergonomics (MS, Sc D); radiological health physics and general work environment protection (Certificate); work environmental policy (MS, Sc D). *Accreditation:* ABET (one or more programs are accredited). Part-time programs available. Terminal master's awarded for partial completion of doctoral program. *Degree requirements:* For master's, thesis optional; for doctorate, thesis/dissertation. *Entrance requirements:* For master's and doctorate, GRE General Test. Additional exam requirements/recommendations for international students: Required—TOEFL. *Faculty research:* Ergonomics, industrial hygiene, epidemiology, work environment policy, pollution prevention.

University of Miami, Graduate School, School of Business Administration, Department of Economics, Coral Gables, FL 33124. Offers economic development (MA, PhD); environmental economics (PhD); human resource economics (MA, PhD); international economics (MA, PhD); macroeconomics (PhD). PhD students admitted every two years in the fall semester. *Faculty:* 13 full-time (7 women). *Students:* 13 full-time (7 women); includes 1 minority (African American), 11 international. Average age 28. 95 applicants, 14% accepted, 7 enrolled. In 2003, 7 master's, 1 doctorate awarded. Terminal master's awarded for partial completion of doctoral program. *Degree requirements:* For master's, comprehensive exam; for doctorate, thesis/dissertation, comprehensive exam. *Entrance requirements:* For master's and doctorate, GRE General Test, minimum GPA of 3.0. Additional exam requirements/recommendations for international students: Required—TOEFL. *Application deadline:* For fall admission, 3/1 for domestic students. Application fee: $50. *Expenses:* Tuition: Full-time $19,526. *Financial support:* In 2003–04, 1 fellowship with full tuition reimbursement (averaging $17,000 per year), 12 research assistantships with full tuition reimbursements (averaging $12,000 per year), 7 teaching assistantships with full tuition reimbursements (averaging $3,500 per year) were awarded. Tuition waivers (partial) and unspecified assistantships also available. Financial award application deadline: 3/1. *Faculty research:* International economics/trade, applied microeconomics, development, macroeconomics. Total annual research expenditures: $426,180. *Unit head:* Dr. Michael Connolly, Chairman, 305-284-4898, Fax: 305-284-2985, E-mail: mconnolly@miami.edu. *Application contact:* Dr. David L. Kelly, Director of Graduate Programs in Economics, 305-284-3725, Fax: 305-284-2985, E-mail: dkelly@miami.edu.

University of Michigan, School of Natural Resources and Environment, Program in Resource Ecology and Management, Ann Arbor, MI 48109. Offers natural resources and environment

(PhD); resource ecology and management (MS). Terminal master's awarded for partial completion of doctoral program. *Degree requirements:* For master's, thesis or alternative, thesis, practicum or group project; for doctorate, thesis/dissertation, oral defense of dissertation, preliminary exam, comprehensive exam, registration. *Entrance requirements:* For master's, GRE General Test; for doctorate, GRE General Test, master's degree. Additional exam requirements/recommendations for international students: Required—TOEFL (paper score 560; computer score 220) or IELTS (6.5). Electronic applications accepted. *Expenses:* Tuition, state resident: full-time $7,463. Tuition, nonresident: full-time $13,913. Full-time tuition and fees vary according to course load, degree level and program. *Faculty research:* Stream ecology, plant-insect interactions, fish biology, resource control and reproductive success, remote sensing.

University of Michigan, School of Natural Resources and Environment, Program in Resource Policy and Behavior, Ann Arbor, MI 48109. Offers natural resources and environment (PhD); resource policy and behavior (MS). Terminal master's awarded for partial completion of doctoral program. *Degree requirements:* For master's, thesis, practicum or group project; for doctorate, thesis/dissertation, oral defense of dissertation, preliminary exam, comprehensive exam, registration. *Entrance requirements:* For master's, GRE General Test; for doctorate, GRE General Test, master's degree. Additional exam requirements/recommendations for international students: Required—TOEFL (paper score 560; computer score 220) or IELTS. Electronic applications accepted. *Expenses:* Tuition, state resident: full-time $7,463. Tuition, nonresident: full-time $13,913. Full-time tuition and fees vary according to course load, degree level and program. *Faculty research:* Business and environment/sustainable systems, environmental behavior/psychology, environmental conflict management/dispute resolution, enviornmental education, environmental justice/policy planning.

University of Minnesota, Twin Cities Campus, Graduate School, College of Natural Resources, Department of Forest Resources, Minneapolis, MN 55455-0213. Offers natural resources science and management (MS, PhD). Part-time programs available. *Faculty:* 19 full-time (3 women), 26 part-time/adjunct (1 woman). *Students:* 37 full-time (18 women), 26 part-time (10 women); includes 1 minority (Asian American or Pacific Islander), 9 international. 49 applicants, 45% accepted, 13 enrolled. In 2003, 9 master's, 4 doctorates awarded. Terminal master's awarded for partial completion of doctoral program. *Degree requirements:* For master's, thesis optional; for doctorate, thesis/dissertation, comprehensive exam, registration. *Entrance requirements:* For master's and doctorate, GRE. Additional exam requirements/recommendations for international students: Required—TOEFL (minimum score 550 paper-based; 213 computer-based). *Application deadline:* For fall admission, 1/1 priority date for domestic students, 1/1 priority date for international students; for spring admission, 10/15 for domestic students, 10/15 for international students. Applications are processed on a rolling basis. Application fee: $55 ($75 for international students). Electronic applications accepted. *Expenses:* Tuition, state resident: full-time $3,681; part-time $614 per credit. Tuition, nonresident: full-time $7,231; part-time $1,205 per credit. *Financial support:* In 2003–04, 4 fellowships with full tuition reimbursements, 26 research assistantships with full and partial tuition reimbursements were awarded. Teaching assistantships with full and partial tuition reimbursements, tuition waivers (partial) also available. Financial award application deadline: 1/15. Total annual research expenditures: $2 million. *Unit head:* Dr. Alan R. Ek, Head, 612-624-3400, E-mail: aek@umn.edu. *Application contact:* Kathleen A. Walter, Student Support Services Assistant, 612-624-2748, Fax: 612-624-6282, E-mail: kwalter@umn.edu.

University of Minnesota, Twin Cities Campus, Graduate School, College of Natural Resources, Department of Wood and Paper Science, Minneapolis, MN 55455-0213. Offers natural resources science and management (MS, PhD). *Faculty:* 10 full-time (2 women), 1 part-time/adjunct (0 women). *Students:* 6 full-time (1 woman), 6 part-time (2 women), 6 international. 6 applicants, 33% accepted, 1 enrolled. In 2003, 5 master's, 3 doctorates awarded. Terminal master's awarded for partial completion of doctoral program. *Degree requirements:* For master's, thesis optional; for doctorate, thesis/dissertation, comprehensive exam, registration. *Entrance requirements:* For master's and doctorate, GRE. Additional exam requirements/recommendations for international students: Required—TOEFL (minimum score 550 paper-based; 213 computer-based). *Application deadline:* For fall admission, 1/1 priority date for domestic students, 1/1 priority date for international students; for spring admission, 10/15 for domestic students, 10/15 for international students. Applications are processed on a rolling basis. Application fee: $55 ($75 for international students). Electronic applications accepted. *Expenses:* Tuition, state resident: full-time $3,681; part-time $614 per credit. Tuition, nonresident: full-time $7,231; part-time $1,205 per credit. *Financial support:* In 2003–04, 6 research assistantships with full tuition reimbursements were awarded; fellowships with full tuition reimbursements, teaching assistantships with full tuition reimbursements, tuition waivers (partial) also available. Financial award application deadline: 1/15. Total annual research expenditures: $422,223. *Unit head:* Dr. Shri Ramaswamy, Interim Head, 612-625-5200. *Application contact:* Kathleen A. Walter, Student Support Services Assistant, 612-624-2748, Fax: 612-624-6282, E-mail: kwalter@umn.edu.

University of Minnesota, Twin Cities Campus, Graduate School, Hubert H. Humphrey Institute of Public Affairs, Program in Science, Technology, and Environmental Policy, Minneapolis, MN 55455-0213. Offers MS, JD/MS. Part-time programs available. *Faculty:* 21 full-time (7 women), 8 part-time/adjunct (3 women). *Students:* 9 full-time (4 women), 8 part-time (4 women); includes 2 minority (both African Americans), 1 international. Average age 26. In 2003, 2 degrees awarded. *Degree requirements:* For master's, thesis. *Entrance requirements:* For master's, GRE General Test, undergraduate training in the biological or physical sciences or engineering, minimum undergraduate GPA of 3.0. Additional exam requirements/recommendations for international students: Required—TOEFL (minimum score 600 paper-based; 250 computer-based). *Application deadline:* For fall admission, 4/1 for domestic students, 4/1 for international students. Applications are processed on a rolling basis. Application fee: $55 ($75 for international students). Electronic applications accepted. *Expenses:* Tuition, state resident: full-time $3,681; part-time $614 per credit. Tuition, nonresident: full-time $7,231; part-time $1,205 per credit. *Financial support:* In 2003–04, 4 students received support, including fellowships with full and partial tuition reimbursements available (averaging $8,500 per year), research assistantships with full and partial tuition reimbursements available (averaging $5,270 per year), teaching assistantships with full and partial tuition reimbursements available (averaging $5,270 per year); career-related internships or fieldwork, Federal Work-Study, scholarships/grants, health care benefits, tuition waivers (full and partial), and unspecified assistantships also available. Financial award application deadline: 1/5. *Faculty research:* Economics, history, philosophy, and politics of science and technology; organization and management of science and technology. *Unit head:* Dr. Kenneth Keller, Head, 612-624-3800, Fax: 612-626-0002, E-mail: admissions@hhh.umn.edu. *Application contact:* Julie Harrold, Director of Admissions, 612-626-9749, Fax: 612-626-0002, E-mail: admissions@hhh.umn.edu.

University of Missouri–St. Louis, Graduate School, College of Arts and Sciences, Department of Biology, St. Louis, MO 63121-4499. Offers biology (MS, PhD), including animal behavior (MS), biochemistry, biotechnology (MS), conservation biology (MS), development (MS), ecology (MS), environmental studies (PhD), evolution (MS), genetics (MS), molecular biology and biotechnology (PhD), molecular/cellular biology (MS), physiology (MS), plant systematics, population biology (MS), tropical biology (MS); biotechnology (Certificate); tropical biology and conservation (Certificate). Part-time programs available. *Faculty:* 47 full-time (14 women). *Students:* 26 full-time (15 women), 106 part-time (63 women); includes 13 minority (3 African Americans, 3 Asian Americans or Pacific Islanders, 7 Hispanic Americans), 36 international. In 2003, 21 master's, 5 doctorates awarded. *Degree requirements:* For master's, thesis or alternative; for doctorate, one foreign language, thesis/dissertation, 1 semester of teaching experience. *Entrance requirements:* For doctorate, GRE General Test. *Application deadline:* For fall admission, 7/1 for domestic students; for spring admission, 11/1 priority date for domestic students. Applications are processed on a rolling basis. Application fee: $35 ($40 for international students). Electronic applications accepted. *Expenses:* Tuition, state resident: part-time $237 per credit hour. Tuition, nonresident: part-time $639 per credit hour. Required fees: $10 per credit hour. *Financial support:* In 2003–04, 9 fellowships with full tuition reimbursements (averaging $13,644 per year), 11 research assistantships with full and partial tuition reimbursements (averaging $13,818 per year), 22 teaching assistantships with full and partial tuition reimbursements (averaging $14,805 per year) were awarded. Career-related internships or fieldwork and Federal Work-Study also available. Support available to part-time students. Financial award application deadline: 2/1. *Faculty research:* Animal behavior, biochemistry, conservation biology, molecular biology, microbial genetics. *Unit head:* Director of Graduate Studies, 314-516-6203, Fax: 314-516-6233, E-mail: icte@umsl.edu. *Application contact:* 314-516-5458, Fax: 314-516-5310, E-mail: gradadm@umsl.edu.

The University of Montana–Missoula, Graduate School, College of Arts and Sciences, Program in Environmental Studies (EVST), Missoula, MT 59812-0002. Offers MS, JD/MS. Part-time programs available. *Faculty:* 6 full-time (2 women), 3 part-time/adjunct (0 women). *Students:* 52 full-time (32 women), 46 part-time (25 women); includes 6 minority (1 American Indian/Alaska Native, 2 Asian Americans or Pacific Islanders, 3 Hispanic Americans). Average age 28. 104 applicants, 64% accepted, 37 enrolled. In 2003, 25 degrees awarded. *Median time to degree:* Master's–2.5 years full-time, 5 years part-time. *Degree requirements:* For master's, portfolio, professional paper or thesis. *Entrance requirements:* For master's, GRE General Test. Additional exam requirements/recommendations for international students: Required—TOEFL (minimum score 525 paper-based; 195 computer-based). *Application deadline:* For fall admission, 2/15 for domestic students, 2/15 for international students. Application fee: $45. *Expenses:* Tuition, state resident: full-time $1,848; part-time $221 per credit. Tuition, nonresident: full-time $4,880; part-time $333 per credit. Required fees: $2,200. *Financial support:* In 2003–04, 17 students received support, including 5 fellowships with full tuition reimbursements available (averaging $3,000 per year), 5 teaching assistantships with full tuition reimbursements available (averaging $9,000 per year); career-related internships or fieldwork and Federal Work-Study also available. Support available to part-time students. Financial award application deadline: 4/15. *Faculty research:* Pollution ecology, sustainable agriculture, environmental writing, environmental policy, habitat-land management. Total annual research expenditures: $147,033. *Unit head:* Thomas M. Roy, Director, 406-243-6273, Fax: 406-243-6090, E-mail: tom.roy@umontana.edu. *Application contact:* Karen Hurd, Administrative Assistant, 406-243-6273, Fax: 406-243-6090, E-mail: karen.hurd@umontana.edu.

The University of Montana–Missoula, Graduate School, College of Forestry and Conservation, Missoula, MT 59812-0002. Offers ecosystem management (MEM, MS); fish and wildlife biology (PhD); forestry (MS, PhD); recreation management (MS); resource conservation (MS); wildlife biology (MS). *Faculty:* 34 full-time (4 women). *Students:* 158 full-time (44 women), 49 part-time (22 women); includes 3 minority (2 American Indian/Alaska Native, 1 Hispanic American), 16 international. 175 applicants, 35% accepted, 46 enrolled. In 2003, 28 master's, 5 doctorates awarded. *Degree requirements:* For doctorate, thesis/dissertation. *Entrance requirements:* For master's and doctorate, GRE General Test. Additional exam requirements/recommendations for international students: Required—TOEFL (minimum score 575 paper-based; 213 computer-based). *Application deadline:* For fall admission, 1/31 for domestic students; for spring admission, 8/31 priority date for domestic students. Applications are processed on a rolling basis. Application fee: $45. *Expenses:* Tuition, state resident: full-time $1,848; part-time $221 per credit. Tuition, nonresident: full-time $4,880; part-time $333 per credit. Required fees: $2,200. *Financial support:* In 2003–04, 25 research assistantships with tuition reimbursements, 12 teaching assistantships with full tuition reimbursements were awarded. Fellowships, career-related internships or fieldwork and Federal Work-Study also available. Financial award application deadline: 3/1; financial award applicants required to submit FAFSA. Total annual research expenditures: $6.7 million. *Unit head:* Dr. Perry Brown, Dean, 406-243-5521, Fax: 406-243-4845, E-mail: pbrown@forestry.umt.edu.

University of Nevada, Reno, Graduate School, College of Science, Interdisciplinary Program in Land Use Planning, Reno, NV 89557. Offers MS. Offered through the College of Science, the College of Engineering, and the College of Agriculture. *Faculty:* 1. *Students:* 5 full-time (3 women), 2 part-time. Average age 43. In 2003, 1 degree awarded. *Degree requirements:* For master's, thesis. *Entrance requirements:* For master's, GRE General Test, minimum GPA of 3.0. Additional exam requirements/recommendations for international students: Required—TOEFL. *Application deadline:* For fall admission, 3/1 for domestic students. Applications are processed on a rolling basis. Application fee: $60 ($95 for international students). *Expenses:* Tuition, state resident: part-time $119 per credit. Tuition, nonresident: part-time $127 per credit. Required fees: $20 per term. Tuition and fees vary according to course load. *Financial support:* Research assistantships, teaching assistantships available. Financial award application deadline: 3/1. *Unit head:* Dr. Chris Exline, Graduate Program Director, 775-784-6999, E-mail: chexline@unr.edu.

University of New Brunswick Saint John, Faculty of Business, Saint John, NB E2L 4L5, Canada. Offers administration (MBA); electronic commerce (MBA); international business (MBA); natural resource management (MBA). Part-time programs available. *Faculty:* 14 full-time (2 women), 2 part-time/adjunct (1 woman). *Students:* 25 full-time (7 women), 19 part-time (6 women), 24 international. Average age 26. 93 applicants, 78% accepted, 25 enrolled. In 2003, 19 degrees awarded. *Median time to degree:* Master's–1 year full-time, 6 years part-time. *Degree requirements:* For master's, thesis optional. *Entrance requirements:* For master's, GMAT. Additional exam requirements/recommendations for international students: Required—TOEFL (minimum score 550 paper-based). *Application deadline:* For fall admission, 5/15 for domestic students, 5/15 for international students. Application fee: $100. *Expenses:* Contact institution. *Financial support:* In 2003–04, 4 students received support; fellowships, research assistantships, teaching assistantships, career-related internships or fieldwork and scholarships/grants available. *Unit head:* Dr. Julien Vincze, Director, 506-648-5735, Fax: 506-648-5574, E-mail: mba@unbsj.ca. *Application contact:* Dr. Jack M. Terhune, Associate Dean of Graduate Studies, 506-648-5633, Fax: 506-648-5528, E-mail: graduate@unbsj.ca.

University of New Hampshire, Graduate School, College of Life Sciences and Agriculture, Department of Natural Resources, Durham, NH 03824. Offers environmental conservation (MS); forestry (MS); soil science (MS); water resources management (MS); wildlife (MS). Part-time programs available. *Faculty:* 40 full-time. *Students:* 25 full-time (11 women), 31 part-time (21 women), 5 international. Average age 32. 74 applicants, 38% accepted, 16 enrolled. In 2003, 13 degrees awarded. *Degree requirements:* For master's, thesis or alternative. *Entrance requirements:* For master's, GRE General Test. Additional exam requirements/recommendations for international students: Required—TOEFL (minimum score 550 paper-based; 213 computer-based); Recommended—TSE. *Application deadline:* For fall admission, 4/1 for domestic students; for winter admission, 12/1 for domestic students. Applications are processed on a rolling basis. Application fee: $50. Electronic applications accepted. Tuition, area resident: Full-time $7,070. *Expenses:* Tuition, state resident: full-time $10,605. Tuition, nonresident: full-time $17,430. Required fees: $15. *Financial support:* In 2003–04, 3 fellowships, 15 research assistantships, 12 teaching assistantships were awarded. Career-related internships or fieldwork, Federal Work-Study, scholarships/grants, and tuition waivers (full and partial) also available. Support available to part-time students. Financial award application deadline: 2/15. *Unit head:* Dr. William H. McDowell, Chairperson, 603-862-2249, E-mail: tehoward@cisunix.unh.edu. *Application contact:* Linda Scogin, Administrative Assistant, 603-862-3932, E-mail: natural.resources @unh.edu.

University of New Hampshire, Graduate School, College of Life Sciences and Agriculture, Department of Resource Economics and Development, Program in Resource Administration, Durham, NH 03824. Offers MS. Part-time programs available. *Faculty:* 2 full-time. *Students:* 4 full-time (1 woman), 3 part-time (1 woman). Average age 27. 3 applicants, 100% accepted, 1 enrolled. In 2003, 5 degrees awarded. *Degree requirements:* For master's, thesis or alternative. *Entrance requirements:* For master's, GRE General Test. Additional exam requirements/recommendations for international students: Required—TOEFL (minimum score 550 paper-based; 213 computer-based); Recommended—TSE. *Application deadline:* For fall admission, 4/1 for domestic students. Applications are processed on a rolling basis. Application fee: $50. Electronic applications accepted. Tuition, area resident: Full-time $7,070. *Expenses:* Tuition,

Environmental Management and Policy

University of New Hampshire (continued)

state resident: full-time $10,605. Tuition, nonresident: full-time $17,430. Required fees: $15. *Financial support:* In 2003–04, 4 research assistantships were awarded; fellowships, teaching assistantships, career-related internships or fieldwork, Federal Work-Study, and scholarships/grants also available. Support available to part-time students. Financial award application deadline: 2/15.

University of New Hampshire, Graduate School, College of Life Sciences and Agriculture, Department of Resource Economics and Development, Program in Resource Economics, Durham, NH 03824. Offers MS. Part-time programs available. *Faculty:* 6 full-time. *Students:* Average age 26. 3 applicants, 67% accepted, 0 enrolled. *Degree requirements:* For master's, thesis or alternative. *Entrance requirements:* For master's, GRE General Test. Additional exam requirements/recommendations for international students: Required—TOEFL (minimum score 550 paper-based; 213 computer-based); Recommended—TSE. *Application deadline:* For fall admission, 4/1 for domestic students. Applications are processed on a rolling basis. Application fee: $50. Electronic applications accepted. Tuition, area resident: Full-time $7,070. *Expenses:* Tuition, state resident: full-time $10,605. Tuition, nonresident: full-time $17,430. Required fees: $15. *Financial support:* In 2003–04, 1 teaching assistantship was awarded; fellowships, research assistantships, career-related internships or fieldwork and Federal Work-Study also available. Support available to part-time students. Financial award application deadline: 2/15.

The University of North Carolina at Chapel Hill, Graduate School, School of Public Health, Department of Environmental Sciences and Engineering, Chapel Hill, NC 27599. Offers air, radiation and industrial hygiene (MPH, MS, MSEE, MSPH, PhD); aquatic and atmospheric sciences (MPH, MS, MSPH, PhD); environmental engineering (MPH, MS, MSEE, MSPH, PhD); environmental health sciences (MPH, MS, MSPH, PhD); environmental management and policy (MPH, MS, MSPH, PhD). *Accreditation:* ABET (one or more programs are accredited). *Faculty:* 34 full-time (5 women), 36 part-time/adjunct. *Students:* 153 full-time (85 women); includes 43 minority (11 African Americans, 30 Asian Americans or Pacific Islanders, 2 Hispanic Americans). Average age 26. 234 applicants, 35% accepted, 40 enrolled. In 2003, 38 master's, 13 doctorates awarded. Terminal master's awarded for partial completion of doctoral program. *Median time to degree:* Master's–2 years full-time; doctorate–4.5 years full-time. *Degree requirements:* For master's, thesis (for some programs), research paper, comprehensive exam; for doctorate, thesis/dissertation, comprehensive exam. *Entrance requirements:* For master's and doctorate, GRE General Test, minimum GPA of 3.0. Additional exam requirements/recommendations for international students: Required—TOEFL. *Application deadline:* For fall admission, 1/1 priority date for domestic students, 1/1 priority date for international students; for spring admission, 9/15 for domestic students. Applications are processed on a rolling basis. Application fee: $60. Electronic applications accepted. *Expenses:* Tuition, state resident: full-time $3,163. Tuition, nonresident: full-time $15,161. *Financial support:* In 2003–04, 120 students received support, including 44 fellowships with tuition reimbursements available (averaging $17,230 per year), 63 research assistantships with tuition reimbursements available (averaging $16,264 per year), 13 teaching assistantships with tuition reimbursements available (averaging $11,120 per year); career-related internships or fieldwork, Federal Work-Study, and traineeships also available. Support available to part-time students. Financial award application deadline: 1/1; financial award applicants required to submit FAFSA. *Faculty research:* Air, radiation and industrial hygiene, aquatic and atmospheric sciences, environmental health sciences, environmental management and policy, water resources engineering. Total annual research expenditures: $7.8 million. *Unit head:* Dr. Casey T. Miller, Chair, 919-966-1024, Fax: 919-966-7911, E-mail: casey_miller@unc.edu. *Application contact:* Jack Whaley, Assistant Registrar, 919-966-3844, Fax: 919-966-7911, E-mail: jack_whaley@unc.edu.

University of Northern British Columbia, Office of Graduate Studies, Prince George, BC V2N 4Z9, Canada. Offers community health science (M Sc); disability management (MA); education (M Ed); first nations studies (MA); gender studies (MA); history (MA); interdisciplinary studies (MA); international studies (MA); mathematical, computer and physical sciences (M Sc); natural resources and environmental studies (M Sc, MA, MNRES, PhD); political science (MA); psychology (M Sc, PhD); social work (MSW). Part-time and evening/weekend programs available. Postbaccalaureate distance learning degree programs offered (no on-campus study). *Students:* 293 full-time (187 women), 77 part-time (62 women). 290 applicants, 31% accepted, 80 enrolled. In 2003, 61 master's, 2 doctorates awarded. *Degree requirements:* For master's and doctorate, thesis/dissertation. *Entrance requirements:* For master's, GRE, minimum B average in undergraduate course work; for doctorate, candidacy exam, minimum A average in graduate course work. *Application deadline:* For fall and spring admission, 2/15; for winter admission, 9/15 for domestic students. Applications are processed on a rolling basis. Application fee: $50 ($250 for international students). *Expenses:* Tuition, state resident: full-time $2,272. *Financial support:* In 2003–04, 4 fellowships (averaging $7,750 per year), 250 research assistantships (averaging $12,000 per year), 60 teaching assistantships (averaging $8,000 per year) were awarded. Career-related internships or fieldwork, institutionally sponsored loans, and scholarships/grants also available. Support available to part-time students. Financial award application deadline: 2/15. *Unit head:* Dr. Robert W. Tait, Dean of Graduate Studies, 250-960-5726, Fax: 250-960-5362, E-mail: tait@unbc.ca. *Application contact:* Susan Deevy, Graduate Studies Officer, 250-960-6336, Fax: 250-960-6330, E-mail: deevys@unbc.ca.

University of Oregon, Graduate School, College of Arts and Sciences, Environmental Studies Program, Eugene, OR 97403. Offers environmental science, studies, and policy (PhD); environmental studies (MA, MS). *Faculty:* 11 full-time (3 women), 1 part-time/adjunct (0 women). *Students:* 22 full-time (12 women), 2 part-time, 2 international. Average age 30. 139 applicants, 14% accepted, 9 enrolled. In 2003, 11 master's, 1 doctorate awarded. *Degree requirements:* For master's, one foreign language, thesis; for doctorate, thesis/dissertation, comprehensive exam. *Entrance requirements:* For master's, GRE General Test, minimum GPA of 3.0; for doctorate, GRE General Test. Additional exam requirements/recommendations for international students: Required—TOEFL (minimum score 550 paper-based; 213 computer-based). *Application deadline:* For fall admission, 1/15 for domestic students, 1/15 for international students. Application fee: $50. Electronic applications accepted. *Expenses:* Tuition, state resident: part-time $8,910 per term. Tuition, nonresident: part-time $13,689 per term. *Financial support:* In 2003–04, 23 teaching assistantships were awarded; career-related internships or fieldwork and Federal Work-Study also available. *Unit head:* Daniel Udovic, Director, 541-346-5000, Fax: 541-346-5954, E-mail: udovic@oregon.uoregon.edu. *Application contact:* Gayla WardWell, Graduate Coordinator, 541-346-5057, Fax: 541-346-5954, E-mail: gaylaw@uoregon.edu.

Announcement: The Environmental Studies Program is supported by a full range of graduate-level courses offered by over 80 faculty members in many disciplines. The program offers a flexible, explicitly interdisciplinary, largely student-designed program that attracts exceptionally strong students, many of whom have nonacademic environmental experience (employment, volunteer work, internships, Peace Corps). Visit the Web site at http://darkwing.uoregon.edu/~ecostudy.

University of Pennsylvania, School of Arts and Sciences, College of General Studies, Philadelphia, PA 19104. Offers environmental studies (MES); individualized study (MLA). *Faculty:* 13 part-time/adjunct (5 women). *Students:* 18 full-time (7 women), 34 part-time (15 women); includes 4 minority (1 African American, 3 Asian Americans or Pacific Islanders), 4 international. In 2003, 16 degrees awarded. *Application deadline:* For fall admission, 12/1 for domestic students. Application fee: $70. Electronic applications accepted. *Expenses:* Tuition: Full-time $28,040; part-time $3,550 per course. Required fees: $1,750; $214 per course. Tuition and fees vary according to degree level, program and student level. *Application contact:* Patricia Rea, Coordinator for Admissions, 215-573-5816, Fax: 215-573-8068, E-mail: gdasadmis@sas.upenn.edu.

University of Pittsburgh, Graduate School of Public and International Affairs, Division of International Development, Pittsburgh, PA 15260. Offers development planning and environmental sustainability (MPIA); governmental organizations and civil society (MPIA); international development (MID). Part-time programs available. *Faculty:* 31 full-time (8 women), 18 part-time/adjunct (10 women). *Students:* 54 full-time (40 women), 9 part-time (7 women); includes 13 minority (9 African Americans, 4 Hispanic Americans), 17 international. Average age 26. 109 applicants, 91% accepted, 32 enrolled. In 2003, 27 degrees awarded. *Degree requirements:* For master's, internship, thesis optional. *Entrance requirements:* For master's, 3 letters of recommendation, minimum GPA of 3.0. Additional exam requirements/recommendations for international students: Required—TOEFL (minimum score 550 paper-based; 213 computer-based), TWE(minimum score 4). *Application deadline:* For fall admission, 3/1 for domestic students, 3/1 for international students; for spring admission, 10/1 for domestic students, 8/1 for international students. Application fee: $40. Electronic applications accepted. *Expenses:* Tuition, state resident: full-time $11,744; part-time $479 per credit. Tuition, nonresident: full-time $22,910; part-time $941 per credit. Required fees: $560. Tuition and fees vary according to degree level and program. *Financial support:* In 2003–04, 31 students received support, including 16 fellowships (averaging $15,725 per year), 3 research assistantships; career-related internships or fieldwork, scholarships/grants, tuition waivers (full and partial), and unspecified assistantships also available. Financial award application deadline:2/1. *Faculty research:* Project/program evaluation, population and environment, international development, development economics, civil society. Total annual research expenditures: $1 million. *Unit head:* Dr. Paul J. Nelson, Director, International Development Division, 412-648-7645, Fax: 412-648-2605, E-mail: pjnelson@birch.gspia.pitt.edu. *Application contact:* Maureen O'Malley, Admissions Counselor, 412-648-7646, Fax: 412-648-7641, E-mail: pronobis@birch.gspia.pitt.edu.

University of Rhode Island, Graduate School, College of the Environment and Life Sciences, Department of Environmental and Natural Resource Economics, Kingston, RI 02881. Offers resource economics and marine resources (MS, PhD). In 2003, 15 master's, 1 doctorate awarded. *Degree requirements:* For master's, thesis optional; for doctorate, thesis/dissertation. *Entrance requirements:* For master's and doctorate, GRE General Test. Additional exam requirements/recommendations for international students: Required—TOEFL. *Application deadline:* For fall admission, 4/15 for domestic students. Applications are processed on a rolling basis. *Expenses:* Tuition, state resident: full-time $4,338; part-time $281 per credit. Tuition, nonresident: full-time $12,438; part-time $704 per credit. Required fees: $1,840. *Unit head:* Dr. James Anderson, Chairperson, 401-874-2471. *Application contact:* Dr. Tim Tyrrell, Graduate Admissions Committee, 401-874-2472, Fax: 401-782-4766, E-mail: renri@uriacc.uri.edu.

University of St. Thomas, Graduate Studies, College of Business, Evening MBA Program, St. Paul, MN 55105-1096. Offers accounting (MBA); electronic commerce (MBA); environmental management (MBA); finance (MBA); financial services management (MBA); franchise management (MBA); government contracts (MBA); health care management (MBA); human resource management (MBA); insurance and risk management (MBA); management (MBA); manufacturing systems (MBA); marketing (MBA); nonprofit management (MBA); real estate (MBA); sports and entertainment management (MBA); venture management (MBA). Part-time and evening/weekend programs available. *Degree requirements:* For master's, registration. *Entrance requirements:* For master's, GMAT, 2 years full time work experience. *Application deadline:* For fall admission, 8/1 for domestic students; for spring admission, 1/1 priority date for domestic students. Applications are processed on a rolling basis. Application fee: $30. Electronic applications accepted. *Financial support:* Fellowships, research assistantships, career-related internships or fieldwork, institutionally sponsored loans, and scholarships/grants available. Support available to part-time students. Financial award application deadline: 4/1; financial award applicants required to submit FAFSA. *Application contact:* Martha Ballard, Director of Faculty and Student Services, 651-962-4226, Fax: 651-962-4260, E-mail: mbballard@stthomas.edu.

University of St. Thomas, Graduate Studies, College of Business, UST MBA Program, St. Paul, MN 55105-1096. Offers accounting (MBA); environmental management (MBA); finance (MBA); financial services management (MBA); franchise management (MBA); government contracts (MBA); health care management (MBA); human resource management (MBA); information management (MBA); insurance and risk management (MBA); management (MBA); manufacturing systems (MBA); marketing (MBA); nonprofit management (MBA); sports and entertainment management (MBA); venture management (MBA). *Degree requirements:* For master's, registration. *Entrance requirements:* For master's, GMAT. *Application deadline:* For fall admission, 4/1 for domestic students. Applications are processed on a rolling basis. Application fee: $30. Electronic applications accepted. *Expenses:* Contact institution. *Financial support:* Fellowships, research assistantships, career-related internships or fieldwork, institutionally sponsored loans, and scholarships/grants available. Support available to part-time students. Financial award application deadline: 4/1; financial award applicants required to submit FAFSA. *Unit head:* Dr. Teresa Rothausen, Director, 651-962-8805. *Application contact:* James P. O'Connor, Application Coordinator, 651-962-4233, Fax: 651-962-4260, E-mail: jpoconnor@stthomas.edu.

University of San Francisco, College of Arts and Sciences, Program in Environmental Management, San Francisco, CA 94117-1080. Offers MS. Evening/weekend programs available. *Faculty:* 13 full-time (2 women), 18 part-time/adjunct (4 women). *Students:* 73 full-time (41 women), 21 part-time (9 women); includes 12 minority (1 African American, 8 Asian Americans or Pacific Islanders, 3 Hispanic Americans), 31 international. Average age 32. 81 applicants, 90% accepted, 30 enrolled. In 2003, 41 degrees awarded. *Degree requirements:* For master's, thesis. *Entrance requirements:* For master's, 3 semesters of chemistry, minimum GPA of 2.7, work experience in environmental field. *Application deadline:* For fall admission, 3/1 for domestic students. Applications are processed on a rolling basis. Application fee: $55 ($65 for international students). *Expenses:* Tuition: Full-time $15,840; part-time $880 per unit. Tuition and fees vary according to degree level, campus/location and program. *Financial support:* In 2003–04, 41 students received support; teaching assistantships, career-related internships or fieldwork available. Financial award application deadline: 3/2; financial award applicants required to submit FAFSA. *Faculty research:* Problems of environmental managers, water quality, hazardous materials, environmental health. *Unit head:* Dr. Thomas MacDonald, Director, 415-422-6553, Fax: 415-422-6363, E-mail: msem@usfca.edu.

University of South Carolina, The Graduate School, School of the Environment, Program in Earth and Environmental Resources Management, Columbia, SC 29208. Offers MEERM, JD/MEERM. Part-time programs available. Postbaccalaureate distance learning degree programs offered (no on-campus study). *Faculty:* 151. *Students:* 18 full-time (8 women), 19 part-time (12 women); includes 5 minority (4 African Americans, 1 Asian American or Pacific Islander), 6 international. 24 applicants, 58% accepted, 5 enrolled. In 2003, 16 degrees awarded. *Degree requirements:* For master's, thesis optional. *Entrance requirements:* For master's, GRE General Test. Additional exam requirements/recommendations for international students: Required—TOEFL. *Application deadline:* For fall admission, 7/15 for domestic students; for spring admission, 11/15 for domestic students. Applications are processed on a rolling basis. Application fee: $40. Electronic applications accepted. *Expenses:* Tuition, state resident: part-time $308 per hour. Tuition, nonresident: part-time $655 per hour. *Financial support:* In 2003–04, 2 fellowships with partial tuition reimbursements, 8 research assistantships with partial tuition reimbursements, 2 teaching assistantships with partial tuition reimbursements were awarded. Career-related internships or fieldwork and scholarships/grants also available. *Faculty research:* Hydrology, sustainable development, environmental geology and engineering, energy/environmental resources management. *Application contact:* Dr. Kirk Karwan, Graduate Director, 803-777-1325, Fax: 803-777-5715, E-mail: meerm@environ.sc.edu.

University of South Florida, College of Graduate Studies, College of Arts and Sciences, Department of Environmental Science and Policy, Tampa, FL 33620-9951. Offers MS, PhD. *Faculty:* 28 full-time (20 women), 2 part-time/adjunct (both women). *Students:* 16 full-time (10 women), 12 part-time (7 women); includes 3 minority (1 African American, 2 Hispanic Americans), 2 international. 255 applicants, 32% accepted, 62 enrolled. In 2003, 9 master's, 2 doctorates awarded. *Degree requirements:* For master's, thesis optional. *Entrance requirements:* For master's, GRE General Test, minimum GPA 3.0 in last 60 hours. *Application deadline:* For fall admission, 5/1 for domestic students; for spring admission, 9/15 for domestic students. Application fee: $30. *Financial support:* In 2003–04, 9 students received support, including 2 fellowships with tuition reimbursements available (averaging $10,800 per year), 2 research assistantships with full tuition reimbursements available (averaging $8,977 per year), 5 teaching assistantships with full tuition reimbursements available (averaging $10,800 per year); scholarships/grants and unspecified assistantships also available. Support available to part-time students. Financial award application deadline: 5/1. Total annual research expenditures: $1,588. *Unit head:* Rick Oches, Interim Director, 813-974-2978. *Application contact:* Dr. Ingrid Bartsch, Information Contact, 813-974-3069, E-mail: klschrad@chumal.cas.usf.edu.

The University of Tennessee, Graduate School, College of Arts and Sciences, Department of Sociology, Knoxville, TN 37996. Offers criminology (MA, PhD); energy, environment, and resource policy (MA, PhD); political economy (MA, PhD). Part-time programs available. *Degree requirements:* For master's, thesis or alternative; for doctorate, thesis/dissertation. *Entrance requirements:* For master's, GRE General Test, minimum GPA of 3.0; for doctorate, GRE General Test, minimum GPA of 3.5. Additional exam requirements/recommendations for international students: Required—TOEFL. Electronic applications accepted.

The University of Texas at Austin, Graduate School, College of Engineering, Department of Petroleum and Geosystems Engineering, Program in Energy and Mineral Resources, Austin, TX 78712-1111. Offers MA, MS. *Degree requirements:* For master's, thesis, seminar. *Entrance requirements:* For master's, GRE General Test. Additional exam requirements/recommendations for international students: Required—TOEFL. Electronic applications accepted.

University of Vermont, Graduate College, School of Natural Resources, Program in Natural Resources Planning, Burlington, VT 05405. Offers MS, PhD. *Students:* 55 (26 women); includes 1 minority (Asian American or Pacific Islander) 4 international. 120 applicants, 33% accepted, 24 enrolled. In 2003, 9 master's, 6 doctorates awarded. *Degree requirements:* For master's, thesis or alternative; for doctorate, thesis/dissertation. *Entrance requirements:* For master's and doctorate, GRE General Test. Additional exam requirements/recommendations for international students: Required—TOEFL (minimum score 550 paper-based; 213 computer-based). *Application deadline:* For fall admission, 3/1 for domestic students. Applications are processed on a rolling basis. Application fee: $25. Electronic applications accepted. *Expenses:* Tuition, state resident: part-time $362 per credit hour. Tuition, nonresident: part-time $906 per credit hour. *Financial support:* Fellowships, research assistantships, teaching assistantships available. Financial award application deadline: 3/1. *Unit head:* Dr. C. Newton, Chairperson, 802-656-2620. *Application contact:* D. Wang, Coordinator, 802-656-2620.

University of Washington, Graduate School, College of Forest Resources, Seattle, WA 98195. Offers forest economics (MS, PhD); forest ecosystem analysis (MS, PhD); forest engineering/forest hydrology (MS, PhD); forest products marketing (MS, PhD); forest soils (MS, PhD); paper science and engineering (MS, PhD); quantitative resource management (MS, PhD); silviculture (MFR); silviculture and forest protection (MS, PhD); social sciences (MS, PhD); urban horticulture (MFR, MS, PhD); wildlife science (MS, PhD). *Degree requirements:* For master's, thesis (for some programs), registration; for doctorate, thesis/dissertation, comprehensive exam (for some programs), registration. *Entrance requirements:* For master's and doctorate, GRE, minimum GPA of 3.0. Additional exam requirements/recommendations for international students: Required—TOEFL. Electronic applications accepted. *Faculty research:* Ecosystem analysis, silviculture and forest protection, paper science and engineering, environmental horticulture and urban forestry, natural resource policy and economics.

University of Washington, Graduate School, Interdisciplinary Graduate Program in Quantitative Ecology and Resource Management, Seattle, WA 98195. Offers MS, PhD. *Degree requirements:* For master's and doctorate, thesis/dissertation. *Entrance requirements:* For master's and doctorate, GRE General Test, minimum GPA of 3.0. Additional exam requirements/recommendations for international students: Required—TOEFL. Electronic applications accepted. *Faculty research:* Population dynamics, statistical analysis, ecological modeling and systems analysis of aquatic and terrestrial ecosystems.

Announcement: Application of statistical, mathematical, and decision sciences to terrestrial and marine ecology, natural resource management, and biometrical and mathematical biology problems. MS and PhD program designed for students interested in contemporary ecological or resource management problems from a quantitative perspective. For more information, contact Quantitative Ecology and Resource Management, University of Washington, Box 352182, Seattle, WA 98195-2182; 206-616-9571; e-mail: qerm@u.washington.edu; WWW: http://depts.washington.edu/qerm.

University of Waterloo, Graduate Studies, Faculty of Environmental Studies, Program in Environment and Resource Studies, Waterloo, ON N2L 3G1, Canada. Offers MES. Part-time programs available. *Faculty:* 10 full-time (2 women), 12 part-time/adjunct (5 women). *Students:* 15 full-time (10 women), 3 part-time (all women). 62 applicants, 27% accepted, 8 enrolled. In 2003, 10 degrees awarded. *Degree requirements:* For master's, thesis. *Entrance requirements:* For master's, honors degree, minimum B average, resumé. Additional exam requirements/recommendations for international students: Required—TOEFL, TWE. *Application deadline:* For fall admission, 1/31 for domestic students. Application fee: $75 Canadian dollars. Electronic applications accepted. Tuition and fees charges are reported in Canadian dollars. *Expenses:* Tuition, state resident: full-time $3,632 Canadian dollars. International tuition: $9,180 Canadian dollars full-time. Required fees: $406 Canadian dollars. *Financial support:* Research assistantships, teaching assistantships, scholarships/grants available. *Faculty research:* Sustainable development, water conservation, native issues, environmental assessment. *Unit head:* Dr. Susan K. Wismer, Chair, 519-888-4567, Fax: 519-746-0292, E-mail: skwismer@fes.uwaterloo.ca. *Application contact:* Dr. Robert Gibson, Graduate Officer, 519-888-4567 Ext. 3407, Fax: 519-746-0292, E-mail: rbgibson@watserv1.uwaterloo.ca.

University of Waterloo, Graduate Studies, Faculty of Environmental Studies, Program in Local Economic Development/Tourism Policy and Planning, Waterloo, ON N2L 3G1, Canada. Offers MAES. Part-time programs available. *Faculty:* 19 part-time/adjunct (3 women). *Students:* 18 full-time (10 women), 10 part-time (5 women). Average age 31. 42 applicants, 43% accepted, 15 enrolled. In 2003, 10 degrees awarded. *Degree requirements:* For master's, research paper. *Entrance requirements:* For master's, honors degree in related field, minimum B average. Additional exam requirements/recommendations for international students: Required—TOEFL, TWE. *Application deadline:* For fall admission, 3/1 for domestic students. Applications are processed on a rolling basis. Application fee: $75 Canadian dollars. Electronic applications accepted. Tuition and fees charges are reported in Canadian dollars. *Expenses:* Tuition, state resident: full-time $3,632 Canadian dollars. International tuition: $9,180 Canadian dollars full-time. Required fees: $406 Canadian dollars. *Financial support:* Research assistantships, career-related internships or fieldwork, institutionally sponsored loans, and scholarships/grants available. Support available to part-time students. *Faculty research:* Urban and regional economics, regional economic development, strategic planning, environmental economics, economic geography. *Unit head:* Dr. Paul Parker, Graduate Officer, 519-888-4567 Ext. 3610, Fax: 519-746-2031, E-mail: pparker@fes.uwaterloo.ca.

University of Wisconsin–Green Bay, Graduate Studies, Program in Environmental Science and Policy, Green Bay, WI 54311-7001. Offers MS. Part-time programs available. *Faculty:* 22 full-time (4 women), 2 part-time/adjunct (0 women). *Students:* 28 full-time (14 women), 33 part-time (18 women); includes 6 minority (3 American Indian/Alaska Native, 3 Asian Americans or Pacific Islanders), 1 international. Average age 30. 50 applicants, 78% accepted, 19 enrolled. In 2003, 12 degrees awarded. *Degree requirements:* For master's, thesis. *Entrance requirements:* For master's, GRE General Test, minimum GPA of 3.0. *Application deadline:* For fall admission, 8/1 for domestic students; for spring admission, 11/1 for domestic students. Applications are processed on a rolling basis. Application fee: $45. *Expenses:* Tuition, state resident: full-time $5,996; part-time $333 per credit. Tuition, nonresident: full-time $16,606; part-time $922 per credit. Full-time tuition and fees vary according to program and reciprocity agreements. Part-time tuition and fees vary according to course load and reciprocity agreements. *Financial support:* In 2003–04, 3 research assistantships with full tuition reimbursements, 9 teaching assistantships with full tuition reimbursements were awarded. Career-related internships or fieldwork, Federal Work-Study, and institutionally sponsored loans also available. Financial award application deadline: 7/15; financial award applicants required to submit FAFSA. *Faculty research:* Bald eagle, parasitic population of domestic and wild animals, resource recovery, anaerobic digestion of organic waste. *Unit head:* Dr. John Stoll, Coordinator, 920-465-2358, E-mail: stollj@uwgb.edu. *Application contact:* Ronald D. Stieglitz, Associate Dean, 920-465-2123, Fax: 920-465-2718, E-mail: stieglir@uwgb.edu.

University of Wisconsin–Madison, Graduate School, College of Agricultural and Life Sciences, School of Natural Resources, Madison, WI 53706-1380. Offers MA, MS, PhD. Part-time programs available. *Degree requirements:* For doctorate, thesis/dissertation. *Entrance requirements:* For doctorate, GRE. Application fee: $45. Electronic applications accepted. Tuition, area resident: Full-time $7,593; part-time $476 per credit. Tuition, nonresident: full-time $22,824; part-time $1,430 per credit. Required fees: $292; $38 per credit. Part-time tuition and fees vary according to course load and reciprocity agreements. *Financial support:* Fellowships, research assistantships, teaching assistantships, career-related internships or fieldwork, Federal Work-Study, and institutionally sponsored loans available. Support available to part-time students. *Unit head:* Kevin McSweeney, Director, 608-262-6968, Fax: 608-262-6055.

University of Wisconsin–Madison, Graduate School, Gaylord Nelson Institute for Environmental Studies, Land Resources Program, Madison, WI 53706-1380. Offers MS, PhD. Part-time programs available. *Faculty:* 2 full-time (1 woman), 104 part-time/adjunct (21 women). *Students:* 72 full-time (44 women), 24 part-time (14 women); includes 5 minority (1 African American, 1 American Indian/Alaska Native, 2 Asian Americans or Pacific Islanders, 1 Hispanic American), 7 international. Average age 32. 105 applicants, 50% accepted, 28 enrolled. In 2003, 17 master's, 10 doctorates awarded. *Degree requirements:* For master's and doctorate, thesis/dissertation. *Entrance requirements:* For master's and doctorate, GRE General Test. Additional exam requirements/recommendations for international students: Required—TOEFL (minimum score 550 paper-based; 213 computer-based). *Application deadline:* For fall admission, 2/1 for domestic students, 2/1 for international students; for spring admission, 10/15 for domestic students, 10/15 for international students. Application fee: $45. Electronic applications accepted. Tuition, area resident: Full-time $7,593; part-time $476 per credit. Tuition, nonresident: full-time $22,824; part-time $1,430 per credit. Required fees: $292; $38 per credit. Part-time tuition and fees vary according to course load and reciprocity agreements. *Financial support:* In 2003–04, 53 students received support, including 7 fellowships with full tuition reimbursements available (averaging $14,400 per year), 16 research assistantships with full tuition reimbursements available (averaging $14,250 per year), 18 teaching assistantships with full tuition reimbursements available (averaging $11,260 per year); career-related internships or fieldwork, Federal Work-Study, scholarships/grants, health care benefits, unspecified assistantships, and project assistantships also available. Financial award application deadline: 1/2. *Faculty research:* Land use issues, soil science/watershed management, geographic information systems, environmental law/justice, waste management. *Unit head:* Stephen J. Ventura, Chair, 608-262-6416, Fax: 608-262-2273, E-mail: sventura@wisc.edu. *Application contact:* James E. Miller, Associate Student Services Coordinator, 608-263-4373, Fax: 608-262-2273, E-mail: jemiller@wisc.edu.

Utah State University, School of Graduate Studies, College of Natural Resources, Department of Environment and Society, Logan, UT 84322. Offers bioregional planning (MS); geography (MA, MS); human dimensions of ecosystem science and management (MS, PhD); recreation resource management (MS, PhD). *Faculty:* 16 full-time (3 women), 7 part-time/adjunct (3 women). *Students:* 33 full-time (14 women), 13 part-time (4 women), 5 international. Average age 32. 37 applicants, 51% accepted, 16 enrolled. In 2003, 4 degrees awarded. *Degree requirements:* For master's, thesis (for some programs), comprehensive exam. *Entrance requirements:* For master's and doctorate, GRE General Test, minimum GPA of 3.0. Additional exam requirements/recommendations for international students: Required—TOEFL. *Application deadline:* For fall admission, 6/15 for domestic students; for spring admission, 10/15 for domestic students. Applications are processed on a rolling basis. Application fee: $50 ($60 for international students). *Expenses:* Tuition, state resident: part-time $270 per credit hour. Tuition, nonresident: part-time $946 per credit hour. Required fees: $173 per credit hour. *Financial support:* In 2003–04, 14 research assistantships with partial tuition reimbursements (averaging $11,000 per year), 1 teaching assistantship with partial tuition reimbursement (averaging $10,000 per year) were awarded. Fellowships with partial tuition reimbursements, career-related internships or fieldwork, Federal Work-Study, tuition waivers (full and partial), and unspecified assistantships also available. *Faculty research:* Geographic information systems/geographic and environmental education, bioregional planning, natural resource and environmental policy, outdoor recreation and tourism, natural resource and environmental management. Total annual research expenditures: $1.4 million. *Unit head:* Dr. Terry L. Sharik, Head, 435-797-3270, Fax: 435-797-4048, E-mail: tlsharik@cc.usu.edu. *Application contact:* Dr. Cliff B. Craig, Information Contact, 435-797-1790, Fax: 435-797-4048, E-mail: envs.info@cnr.usu.edu.

Vanderbilt University, School of Engineering, Department of Civil and Environmental Engineering, Program in Environmental Engineering, Nashville, TN 37240-1001. Offers environmental engineering (M Eng); environmental management (MS, PhD). MS and PhD offered through the Graduate School. Part-time programs available. *Faculty:* 16 full-time (1 woman), 2 part-time/adjunct (0 women). *Students:* 23 full-time (14 women), 10 international. Average age 27. 135 applicants, 10% accepted, 7 enrolled. In 2003, 3 degrees awarded. Terminal master's awarded for partial completion of doctoral program. *Degree requirements:* For master's, thesis or alternative; for doctorate, thesis/dissertation. *Entrance requirements:* For master's and doctorate, GRE General Test. Additional exam requirements/recommendations for international students: Required—TOEFL. *Application deadline:* For fall admission, 1/15 for domestic students; for spring admission, 11/1 for domestic students. Applications are processed on a rolling basis. Application fee: $40. Electronic applications accepted. *Expenses:* Tuition: Part-time $1,155 per semester hour. Required fees: $1,538. *Financial support:* In 2003–04, 22 students received support, including 6 fellowships with full tuition reimbursements available (averaging $22,750 per year), 16 research assistantships with full tuition reimbursements available (averaging $18,885 per year), 7 teaching assistantships with full tuition reimbursements available (averaging $11,157 per year); career-related internships or fieldwork, institutionally sponsored loans, and tuition waivers (full and partial) also available. Financial award application deadline: 1/15. *Faculty research:* Waste treatment, hazardous waste management, chemical waste treatment, water quality. *Application contact:* Dr. James H. Clarke, Graduate Program Administrator, 615-322-3897, Fax: 615-322-3365.

Vermont Law School, Law School, Environmental Law Center, South Royalton, VT 05068-0096. Offers LL M, MSEL, JD/MSEL. Part-time programs available. *Faculty:* 12 full-time (6 women), 8 part-time/adjunct (4 women). *Students:* 60 full-time; includes 3 minority (1 African American, 1 American Indian/Alaska Native, 1 Hispanic American), 2 international. Average age 31. 94 applicants, 72% accepted, 42 enrolled. *Entrance requirements:* For master's, GRE General Test or LSAT. Additional exam requirements/recommendations for international students: Required—TOEFL. *Application deadline:* For fall admission, 3/15 for domestic students. Applications are processed on a rolling basis. Application fee: $50. *Expenses:* Tuition: Full-time $25,020. *Financial support:* In 2003–04, 40 students received support, including 2 fellowships with full tuition reimbursements available (averaging $5,000 per year); career-related internships or fieldwork, Federal Work-Study, institutionally sponsored loans, scholarships/grants, and tuition waivers (partial) also available. Support available to part-time students. Financial award application deadline: 2/15; financial award applicants required to submit FAFSA. *Faculty research:* Environment and technology; takings; international environmental law; interaction among

Environmental Management and Policy

Vermont Law School (continued)
science, law, and environmental policy; air pollution. Total annual research expenditures: $52,000. *Unit head:* Karin Sheldon, Associate Dean, 802-763-8303 Ext. 2201, Fax: 802-763-2490, E-mail: elcinfo@vermontlaw.edu. *Application contact:* Anne Mansfield, Assistant Director, 802-763-8303 Ext. 2338, Fax: 802-763-2940, E-mail: elcinfo@vermontlaw.edu.

Virginia Commonwealth University, School of Graduate Studies, College of Humanities and Sciences, Center for Environmental Studies, Richmond, VA 23284-9005. Offers environmental communication (MIS); environmental health (MIS); environmental policy (MIS); environmental sciences (MIS). *Students:* 33 full-time (25 women), 28 part-time (15 women); includes 5 minority (4 African Americans, 1 Hispanic American), 2 international. Average age 33. 24 applicants, 96% accepted, 13 enrolled. In 2003, 13 degrees awarded. *Degree requirements:* For master's, thesis. *Entrance requirements:* For master's, GRE General Test. Application fee: $30. *Expenses:* Tuition, state resident: full-time $2,889; part-time $321 per credit hour. Tuition, nonresident: full-time $7,952; part-time $884 per credit hour. Required fees: $42 per credit hour. *Unit head:* Dr. Gregory C. Garman, Director, 804-828-1574, Fax: 804-828-0503, E-mail: gcgarman@vcu.edu.

Webster University, School of Business and Technology, Department of Management, St. Louis, MO 63119-3194. Offers business and organizational security management (MA); computer resources and information management (MA); environmental management (MS); health care management (MA); health services management (MA); human resources development (MA); human resources management (MA); management (MA, DM); marketing (MA); procurement and acquisitions management (MA); public administration (MA); security management (MA); space systems management (MA, MS); telecommunications management (MA). *Students:* 1,589 full-time (799 women), 3,681 part-time (1,894 women); includes 2,479 minority (1,948 African Americans, 35 American Indian/Alaska Native, 127 Asian Americans or Pacific Islanders, 369 Hispanic Americans), 142 international. Average age 36. In 2003, 1,552 master's, 6 doctorates awarded. *Median time to degree:* Master's–2.4 years part-time; doctorate–8.3 years part-time. *Degree requirements:* For doctorate, thesis/dissertation, written exam. *Entrance requirements:* For doctorate, GMAT, 3 years of work experience, MBA. *Application deadline:* Applications are processed on a rolling basis. Application fee: $25 ($50 for international students). *Expenses:* Tuition: Full-time $7,740; part-time $430 per credit. Tuition and fees vary according to degree level, campus/location and program. *Financial support:* Federal Work-Study available. Support available to part-time students. Financial award application deadline: 4/1; financial award applicants required to submit FAFSA. *Unit head:* Dr. John Robinson, Director, 314-961-5929, Fax: 314-968-7077, E-mail: robinsjo@webster.edu. *Application contact:* Director of Graduate and Evening Student Admissions, Fax: 314-968-7116, E-mail: gadmit@webster.edu.

West Virginia University, College of Engineering and Mineral Resources, Department of Industrial and Management Systems Engineering, Program in Safety and Environmental Management, Morgantown, WV 26506. Offers safety management (MS). *Accreditation:* ABET. *Students:* 48 full-time (6 women), 29 part-time (4 women); includes 2 minority (1 African American, 1 Hispanic American), 5 international. Average age 29. In 2003, 39 degrees awarded. *Expenses:* Tuition, state resident: full-time $4,332. Tuition, nonresident: full-time $12,442. *Financial support:* In 2003–04, 12 research assistantships, 1 teaching assistantship were awarded. *Unit head:* Gary Winn, Coordinator, 304-293-2742 Ext. 3744, E-mail: gary.winn@mail.wvu.edu.

West Virginia University, Davis College of Agriculture, Forestry and Consumer Sciences, Division of Resource Management, Program in Natural Resource Economics, Morgantown, WV 26506. Offers PhD. Part-time programs available. *Students:* 7 full-time (4 women), 3 part-time (2 women); includes 1 minority (Asian American or Pacific Islander), 7 international. Average age 34. 18 applicants, 56% accepted. In 2003, 4 degrees awarded. *Degree requirements:* For doctorate, thesis/dissertation. *Entrance requirements:* For doctorate, GRE General Test. Additional exam requirements/recommendations for international students: Required—TOEFL. Application fee: $45. *Expenses:* Tuition, state resident: full-time $4,332. Tuition, nonresident: full-time $12,442. *Financial support:* In 2003–04, 4 research assistantships, 1 teaching assistantship were awarded. Federal Work-Study, institutionally sponsored loans, and tuition waivers (partial) also available. Financial award application deadline: 2/1; financial award applicants required to submit FAFSA. *Unit head:* Dr. Gerard E. D'Souza, Graduate Coordinator, 304-293-4832 Ext. 4471, Fax: 304-293-3740.

West Virginia University, Eberly College of Arts and Sciences, Department of Geology and Geography, Program in Geography, Morgantown, WV 26506. Offers energy and environmental resources (MA); geographic information systems (PhD); geography-regional development (PhD); GIS/cartographic analysis (MA); regional development (MA). Part-time programs available. *Students:* 8 full-time (4 women), 6 part-time (4 women); includes 1 minority (Hispanic American), 2 international. Average age 30. 40 applicants, 25% accepted, 5 enrolled. In 2003, 7 degrees awarded. *Median time to degree:* Master's–2.5 years full-time, 4 years part-time. *Degree requirements:* For master's, thesis/dissertation, oral and written exams; for doctorate, thesis/dissertation, oral and written exams, comprehensive exam. *Entrance requirements:* For master's, GRE General Test, minimum GPA of 3.0; for doctorate, GRE General Test. Additional exam requirements/recommendations for international students: Required—TOEFL. *Application deadline:* For fall admission, 2/14 priority date for domestic students, 11/14 priority date for international students; for spring admission, 10/1 priority date for domestic students, 7/1 priority date for international students. Applications are processed on a rolling basis. Application fee: $45. Electronic applications accepted. *Expenses:* Tuition, state resident: full-time $4,332. Tuition, nonresident: full-time $12,442. *Financial support:* In 2003–04, 13 students received support, including 1 research assistantship with full tuition reimbursement available (averaging $9,185 per year), 6 teaching assistantships with full tuition reimbursements available (averaging $9,185 per year); career-related internships or fieldwork, Federal Work-Study, institutionally sponsored loans, health care benefits, and tuition waivers (partial) also available. Financial award application deadline: 2/1; financial award applicants required to submit FAFSA. *Faculty research:* Resources, regional development, geographic information systems, gender geography, environmental geography. Total annual research expenditures: $1.5 million. *Unit head:* Dr. Kenneth Martis, Associate Chair, 304-293-5603 Ext. 4350, Fax: 304-293-6522, E-mail: ken.martis@mail.wvu.edu. *Application contact:* Dr. Timothy Warner, Associate Professor, 304-293-5603 Ext. 4328, Fax: 304-293-6522, E-mail: tim.warner@mail.wvu.edu.

Wright State University, School of Graduate Studies, College of Science and Mathematics, Department of Geological Sciences, Program in Geological Sciences, Dayton, OH 45435. Offers environmental geochemistry (MS); environmental geology (MS); environmental sciences (MS); geological sciences (MS); geophysics (MS); hydrogeology (MS); petroleum geology (MS). Part-time programs available. *Students:* 22 full-time (4 women), 9 part-time (4 women), 2 international. Average age 26. 21 applicants, 100% accepted. In 2003, 15 degrees awarded. *Degree requirements:* For master's, thesis. *Entrance requirements:* Additional exam requirements/recommendations for international students: Required—TOEFL. Application fee: $25. *Expenses:* Tuition, state resident: full-time $8,112; part-time $255 per quarter hour. Tuition, nonresident: full-time $14,127; part-time $442 per quarter hour. International tuition: $14,283 full-time. Tuition and fees vary according to course load, degree level and program. *Financial support:* Fellowships, research assistantships, teaching assistantships, Federal Work-Study and unspecified assistantships available. Support available to part-time students. Financial award application deadline: 3/1; financial award applicants required to submit FAFSA. *Application contact:* Deborah L. Cowles, Assistant to Chair, 937-775-3455, Fax: 937-775-3462, E-mail: deborah.cowles@wright.edu.

Yale University, Graduate School of Arts and Sciences, Department of Forestry and Environmental Studies, New Haven, CT 06520. Offers environmental sciences (PhD); forestry (PhD). *Students:* 43 full-time (22 women); includes 6 minority (5 Asian Americans or Pacific Islanders, 1 Hispanic American), 9 international. 97 applicants, 10% accepted, 8 enrolled. In 2003, 4 degrees awarded. *Degree requirements:* For doctorate, thesis/dissertation. *Entrance requirements:* For doctorate, GRE General Test. *Application deadline:* For fall admission, 1/2 for domestic students. Application fee: $80. *Expenses:* Tuition: Full-time $25,600; part-time $6,400 per term. *Financial support:* Fellowships, Federal Work-Study and institutionally sponsored loans available. Support available to part-time students. *Unit head:* Dean, School of Forestry and Environmental Studies, 203-432-5109. *Application contact:* Admissions Information, 203-432-2770.

See in-depth description on page 805.

Yale University, School of Forestry and Environmental Studies, New Haven, CT 06511. Offers MES, MF, MFS, DFES, PhD, JD/MES, MBA/MES, MBA/MF, MES/MA, MES/MPH, MF/MA. *Accreditation:* SAF (one or more programs are accredited). Part-time programs available. Terminal master's awarded for partial completion of doctoral program. *Degree requirements:* For doctorate, thesis/dissertation. *Entrance requirements:* For master's and doctorate, GRE General Test. *Expenses:* Contact institution. *Faculty research:* Ecosystem science and management, coastal and watershed systems, environmental policy and management, social ecology and community development, conservation biology.

See in-depth description on page 805.

York University, Faculty of Graduate Studies, Faculty of Environmental Studies, Toronto, ON M3J 1P3, Canada. Offers MES, PhD, MES/LL B, MES/MA. Part-time programs available. *Degree requirements:* For master's, thesis optional; for doctorate, thesis/dissertation, research seminar, comprehensive exam. *Entrance requirements:* For master's and doctorate, minimum B average. Electronic applications accepted. *Expenses:* Tuition, area resident: Full-time $5,431; part-time $905 per term. Tuition, nonresident: part-time $1,987 per term. International tuition: $11,918 full-time. Required fees: $287. Tuition and fees vary according to program.

Youngstown State University, Graduate School, College of Arts and Sciences, Program in Environmental Studies, Youngstown, OH 44555-0001. Offers environmental studies (MS); industrial/institutional management (Certificate); risk management (Certificate). *Degree requirements:* For master's, thesis, minimum GPA of 3.0, oral defense of dissertation, comprehensive exam. *Entrance requirements:* For master's, GRE General Test or minimum GPA of 2.7. Additional exam requirements/recommendations for international students: Required—TOEFL. *Expenses:* Tuition, state resident: full-time $4,194; part-time $233 per credit. Tuition, nonresident: full-time $8,352; part-time $464 per credit. Required fees: $42 per credit. Tuition and fees vary according to course load and reciprocity agreements.

Environmental Sciences

Alabama Agricultural and Mechanical University, School of Graduate Studies, School of Agricultural and Environmental Sciences, Department of Plant and Soil Sciences, Huntsville, AL 35811. Offers animal sciences (MS); environmental science (MS); plant and soil science (PhD). Evening/weekend programs available. *Faculty:* 18 full-time (2 women), 6 part-time/adjunct (0 women). *Students:* 28 full-time (16 women), 53 part-time (30 women); includes 70 minority (53 African Americans, 4 American Indian/Alaska Native, 13 Asian Americans or Pacific Islanders). In 2003, 6 degrees awarded. Terminal master's awarded for partial completion of doctoral program. *Degree requirements:* For master's, thesis; for doctorate, one foreign language, thesis/dissertation. *Entrance requirements:* For master's, GRE General Test, BS in agriculture; for doctorate, GRE General Test, master's degree. *Application deadline:* For fall admission, 5/1 for domestic students. Applications are processed on a rolling basis. Application fee: $25. Electronic applications accepted. *Expenses:* Tuition, state resident: full-time $3,250; part-time $370 per credit hour. Tuition, nonresident: full-time $6,490; part-time $740 per credit hour. *Financial support:* In 2003–04, 1 fellowship with tuition reimbursement (averaging $18,000 per year), 9 research assistantships with tuition reimbursements (averaging $9,000 per year) were awarded. Career-related internships or fieldwork and Federal Work-Study also available. Financial award application deadline: 4/1. *Faculty research:* Plant breeding, cytogenetics, crop production, soil chemistry and fertility, remote sensing. Total annual research expenditures: $113,000. *Unit head:* Dr. Govind Sharma, Chair, 256-372-4173.

Alaska Pacific University, Graduate Programs, Environmental Science Department, Anchorage, AK 99508-4672. Offers MSES. Part-time programs available. *Faculty:* 5 full-time (0 women). *Students:* 18 full-time (9 women), 6 part-time (5 women); includes 1 minority (American Indian/Alaska Native), 1 international. Average age 27. In 2003, 12 degrees awarded. *Degree requirements:* For master's, comprehensive exam or thesis. *Entrance requirements:* For master's, GRE General Test, minimum GPA of 3.0, resumé. *Application deadline:* For fall admission, 4/1 for domestic students; for spring admission, 12/15 for domestic students. Applications are processed on a rolling basis. Application fee: $25. *Expenses:* Tuition: Full-time $11,400; part-time $475 per semester hour. Required fees: $110. *Financial support:* Research assistantships, career-related internships or fieldwork, Federal Work-Study, and scholarships/grants available. Support available to part-time students. Financial award application deadline: 3/15; financial award applicants required to submit FAFSA. *Faculty research:* Animal-plant interactions, public attitudes towards native and wildlife, species-area relationships, conservation biology, forest canopy ecology. *Unit head:* Roman Dial, Director, 907-564-8252, Fax: 907-562-4276. *Application contact:* Jessica Carr, Co-Director of Admissions, 907-564-8248, Fax: 907-564-8317, E-mail: jessica@alaskapacific.edu.

American University, College of Arts and Sciences, Department of Biology, Environmental Science Program, Washington, DC 20016-8001. Offers MS. *Students:* 8 full-time (7 women), 1 part-time; includes 1 minority (Asian American or Pacific Islander), 1 international. Average age 24. In 2003, 7 degrees awarded. *Degree requirements:* For master's, thesis or alternative, comprehensive exam. *Entrance requirements:* For master's, GRE General Test, GRE Subject Test, minimum GPA of 3.0. Additional exam requirements/recommendations for international students: Required—TOEFL. *Application deadline:* For fall admission, 2/1 for domestic students; for spring admission, 10/1 for domestic students. Application fee: $50. *Expenses:* Tuition: Full-time $15,786; part-time $877 per credit hour. Required fees: $300. Tuition and fees vary according to course load and program. *Financial support:* Research assistantships, teaching assistantships available. Financial award application deadline: 2/1. *Unit head:* Dr. David Culver, Director, 202-885-2176, Fax: 202-885-2182.

Antioch New England Graduate School, Graduate School, Department of Environmental Studies, Doctoral Program in Environmental Studies, Keene, NH 03431-3552. Offers PhD. *Faculty:* 4 full-time (2 women), 2 part-time/adjunct (both women). *Students:* 38 full-time (27 women), 15 part-time (9 women); includes 2 minority (1 Asian American or Pacific Islander, 1 Hispanic American), 1 international. Average age 41. 22 applicants, 86% accepted. In 2003, 4 degrees awarded. *Degree requirements:* For doctorate, thesis/dissertation, practicum. *Entrance requirements:* For doctorate, master's degree and previous experience in the environmental field. *Application deadline:* For fall admission, 2/1 for domestic students. Application fee: $75. *Expenses:* Tuition: Part-time $5,650 per semester. *Financial support:* In 2003–04, 31 students received support, including 2 fellowships (averaging $8,450 per year), 3 research assistantships (averaging $1,551 per year), 2 teaching assistantships (averaging $488 per year); Federal Work-Study and scholarships/grants also available. *Faculty research:* Environmental history, green politics, ecopsychology. *Unit head:* Dr. Beth Kaplin, Head, 603-357-3122 Ext. 238. *Application contact:* Leatrice A. Johnson, Director of Admissions, 603-357-6265 Ext. 287, Fax: 603-357-0718, E-mail: ljohnson@antiochne.edu.

Announcement: The Doctoral Program in Environmental Studies is an interdisciplinary program for those committed to scholarly excellence who wish to design, implement, and evaluate research regarding crucial environmental issues. The program cultivates a dynamic learning community of environmental scholars and practitioners who combine scope, vision, depth, and precision to implement research strategies that contribute to solving regional, national, and global environmental problems.

Antioch New England Graduate School, Graduate School, Department of Environmental Studies, Program in Environmental Studies, Keene, NH 03431-3552. Offers conservation biology (MS); environmental advocacy (MS); environmental education (MS); teacher certification in biology (7th-12th grade) (MS); teacher certification in general science (5th-9th grade) (MS). *Faculty:* 12 full-time (5 women), 10 part-time/adjunct (3 women). *Students:* 119 full-time (78 women), 19 part-time (13 women); includes 2 minority (1 American Indian/Alaska Native, 1 Hispanic American). Average age 31. 120 applicants, 78% accepted. In 2003, 51 degrees awarded. *Degree requirements:* For master's, practicum. *Entrance requirements:* For master's, previous undergraduate course work in biology, chemistry, mathematics (environmental biology). *Application deadline:* For fall admission, 8/1 for domestic students. Applications are processed on a rolling basis. Application fee: $40. *Expenses:* Tuition: Part-time $5,650 per semester. *Financial support:* In 2003–04, 114 students received support, including 2 fellowships (averaging $750 per year), 5 research assistantships (averaging $795 per year), 4 teaching assistantships (averaging $598 per year); Federal Work-Study and scholarships/grants also available. Financial award applicants required to submit FAFSA. *Faculty research:* Sustainability, natural resources inventory. *Unit head:* Dr. Jimmy Karlan, Academic Director, 603-357-3122 Ext. 329, Fax: 603-357-0718, E-mail: jkarlan@antiochne.edu. *Application contact:* Leatrice A. Johnson, Director of Admissions, 603-357-6265 Ext. 287, Fax: 603-357-0718, E-mail: ljohnson@antiochne.edu.

Arkansas State University, Graduate School, College of Sciences and Mathematics, Program in Environmental Sciences, Jonesboro, State University, AR 72467. Offers PhD. *Expenses:* Tuition, state resident: full-time $2,844; part-time $158 per hour. Tuition, nonresident: full-time $7,200; part-time $400 per hour. Required fees: $644; $33 per hour. $25 per semester. Tuition and fees vary according to course load. *Unit head:* Dr. Jerry Farris, Director, 870-972-2007.

California State University, Chico, Graduate School, College of Natural Sciences, Department of Geological and Environmental Sciences, Program in Environmental Science, Chico, CA 95929-0722. Offers MS. Part-time programs available. *Students:* 7 full-time (6 women), 2 part-time. Average age 28. 4 applicants, 100% accepted, 3 enrolled. *Degree requirements:* For master's, thesis. *Entrance requirements:* For master's, GRE. Additional exam requirements/recommendations for international students: Required—TOEFL (minimum score 550 paper-based; 213 computer-based). *Application deadline:* For fall admission, 3/1 for domestic students, 3/1 for international students; for spring admission, 9/15 for domestic students, 9/15 for international students. Applications are processed on a rolling basis. Application fee: $55. Electronic applications accepted. Tuition, nonresident: part-time $282 per semester hour. Required fees: $1,029 per semester. *Unit head:* David L. Brown, Graduate Coordinator, 530-898-5163.

California State University, Fullerton, Graduate Studies, College of Humanities and Social Sciences, Program in Environmental Studies, Fullerton, CA 92834-9480. Offers environmental education and communication (MS); environmental policy and planning (MS); environmental sciences (MS); technological studies (MS). Part-time programs available. *Faculty:* 2 full-time (1 woman), 2 part-time/adjunct. *Students:* 19 full-time (11 women), 47 part-time (24 women); includes 20 minority (5 African Americans, 10 Asian Americans or Pacific Islanders, 5 Hispanic Americans), 2 international. Average age 33. 48 applicants, 83% accepted, 26 enrolled. In 2003, 36 degrees awarded. *Degree requirements:* For master's, thesis. *Entrance requirements:* For master's, minimum GPA of 2.5 in last 60 units. Application fee: $55. Tuition, nonresident: part-time $282 per unit. Required fees: $889 per semester. *Financial support:* Career-related internships or fieldwork, Federal Work-Study, institutionally sponsored loans, and scholarships/grants available. Support available to part-time students. Financial award application deadline: 3/1. *Unit head:* Dr. Robert Voeks, Coordinator, 714-278-2228.

Christopher Newport University, Graduate Studies, Department of Biology, Chemistry and Environmental Science, Newport News, VA 23606-2998. Offers environmental science (MS). Part-time and evening/weekend programs available. *Faculty:* 9 full-time (1 woman). *Students:* 10 full-time (8 women), 17 part-time (11 women); includes 1 minority (African American) Average age 31. 5 applicants, 100% accepted. In 2003, 5 degrees awarded. *Degree requirements:* For master's, thesis, comprehensive exam. *Entrance requirements:* For master's, GRE General Test, minimum GPA of 3.0. *Application deadline:* For fall admission, 5/1 for domestic students; for spring admission, 11/1 for domestic students. Applications are processed on a rolling basis. Application fee: $40. Electronic applications accepted. *Expenses:* Tuition, state resident: part-time $139 per credit hour. Tuition, nonresident: part-time $448 per credit hour. Required fees: $74 per credit hour. *Financial support:* In 2003–04, 2 fellowships with full tuition reimbursements (averaging $6,500 per year), 3 research assistantships with full tuition reimbursements (averaging $1,500 per year), 3 teaching assistantships (averaging $10,000 per year) were awarded. Career-related internships or fieldwork, Federal Work-Study, institutionally sponsored loans, and scholarships/grants also available. Support available to part-time students. Financial award application deadline: 3/1; financial award applicants required to submit FAFSA. *Faculty research:* Wetlands ecology and restoration, aquatic ecology, wetlands mitigation, greenhouse gases. *Unit head:* Dr. Gary Whiting, Coordinator, 757-594-7613, Fax: 757-594-7209, E-mail: gwhiting@cnu.edu. *Application contact:* Susan R. Chittenden, Graduate Admissions, 757-594-7359, Fax: 757-594-7333, E-mail: gradstdy@cnu.edu.

City College of the City University of New York, Graduate School, College of Liberal Arts and Science, Division of Science, Department of Earth and Atmospheric Sciences, New York, NY 10031-9198. Offers earth and environmental science (PhD); earth systems science (MA). *Students:* 10 applicants, 70% accepted, 5 enrolled. In 2003, 2 degrees awarded. *Degree requirements:* For master's, thesis, comprehensive exam. *Entrance requirements:* For master's, appropriate bachelor's degree. Additional exam requirements/recommendations for international students: Required—TOEFL. *Application deadline:* For fall admission, 5/1 for domestic students; for spring admission, 11/1 for domestic students. Application fee: $50. *Expenses:* Tuition, state resident: full-time $5,440; part-time $230 per credit. Tuition, nonresident: part-time $425 per credit. Required fees: $63 per semester. *Financial support:* Fellowships, career-related internships or fieldwork available. *Faculty research:* Water resources, high-temperature geochemistry, sedimentary basin analysis, tectonics. *Unit head:* Jeffrey Steiner, Chair, 212-650-6984. *Application contact:* O. Lehn Franke, Adviser, 212-650-6984.

Clarkson University, Graduate School, Interdisciplinary Studies, Program in Environmental Science and Engineering, Potsdam, NY 13699. Offers MS, PhD. *Students:* 3 full-time (1 woman). Average age 23. 6 applicants, 83% accepted. *Expenses:* Tuition: Full-time $19,272; part-time $803 per credit. Tuition and fees vary according to course load. *Financial support:* In 2003–04, 2 students received support, including 1 research assistantship (averaging $18,000 per year), 1 teaching assistantship (averaging $18,000 per year); tuition waivers (partial) also available. *Unit head:* Dr. Susan E. Powers, Director, Center for the Environment, 315-268-6542, Fax: 315-268-4291, E-mail: sep@clarkson.edu.

Clemson University, Graduate School, College of Agriculture, Forestry and Life Sciences, Department of Environmental Toxicology, Clemson, SC 29634. Offers MS, PhD. *Students:* 31 full-time (18 women), 5 part-time (3 women); includes 2 minority (1 African American, 1 Asian American or Pacific Islander), 6 international. Average age 25. 31 applicants, 26% accepted, 6 enrolled. In 2003, 5 master's, 4 doctorates awarded. *Degree requirements:* For master's, thesis; for doctorate, one foreign language, thesis/dissertation. *Entrance requirements:* For master's and doctorate, GRE General Test. Additional exam requirements/recommendations for international students: Required—TOEFL. *Application deadline:* For fall admission, 6/1 for domestic students. Application fee: $40. *Expenses:* Tuition, state resident: full-time $7,432. Tuition, nonresident: full-time $14,732. *Financial support:* Fellowships, research assistantships, teaching assistantships, career-related internships or fieldwork, Federal Work-Study, and institutionally sponsored loans available. Financial award applicants required to submit FAFSA. *Faculty research:* Biochemical toxicology, analytical toxicology, ecological risk assessment, wildlife toxicology, mathematical modeling. Total annual research expenditures: $3 million. *Unit head:* Dr. Steve Klaine, Coordinator, 864-646-2188, Fax: 864-646-2277, E-mail: sklaine@clemson.edu.

Cleveland State University, College of Graduate Studies, College of Arts and Sciences, Department of Biological, Geological, and Environmental Sciences, Cleveland, OH 44115. Offers MS, PhD. Part-time programs available. *Faculty:* 19 full-time (5 women), 3 part-time/adjunct (0 women). *Students:* 47 full-time (25 women), 24 part-time (13 women); includes 6 minority (5 African Americans, 1 Asian American or Pacific Islander), 26 international. Average age 31. 71 applicants, 48% accepted, 20 enrolled. In 2003, 5 master's, 5 doctorates awarded, leading to university research/teaching 80%, business/industry 20%. Terminal master's awarded for partial completion of doctoral program. *Median time to degree:* Doctorate–5 years full-time. *Degree requirements:* For master's, thesis (for some programs); for doctorate, thesis/dissertation, comprehensive exam. *Entrance requirements:* For master's and doctorate, GRE General Test, essay on career goals and research interests, two letters of recommendation. Additional exam requirements/recommendations for international students: Required—TOEFL (minimum score 525 paper-based; 197 computer-based); Recommended—TSE. *Application deadline:* For fall admission, 4/1 priority date for domestic students, 4/1 priority date for international students; for spring admission, 12/1 priority date for domestic students. Applications are processed on a rolling basis. Application fee: $30. Electronic applications accepted. Tuition, area resident: Full-time $8,258; part-time $344 per credit hour. Tuition, nonresident: full-time $16,352; part-time $681 per credit hour. *Financial support:* In 2003–04, 36 students received support, including 21 research assistantships with full and partial tuition reimbursements available (averaging $6,134 per year), 21 teaching assistantships with full and partial tuition reimbursements available (averaging $5,810 per year); institutionally sponsored loans and unspecified assistantships also available. *Faculty research:* Molecular and cell biology, immunology, molecular medicine, environmental/science. *Unit head:* Dr. Michael Gates, Chairperson, 216-687-3917, Fax: 216-687-6972, E-mail: m.gates@csuohio.edu. *Application contact:* Dr. Jeffrey Dean, Graduate Program Director, 216-687-2440, Fax: 216-687-6972, E-mail: gpd.bges@csuohio.edu.

College of Charleston, Graduate School, School of Sciences and Mathematics, Program in Environmental Studies, Charleston, SC 29424-0001. Offers MS. *Faculty:* 32 full-time (9 women), 14 part-time/adjunct (4 women). *Students:* 57 full-time (34 women), 30 part-time (15 women); includes 2 minority (1 African American, 1 Asian American or Pacific Islander), 1 international. Average age 29. 54 applicants, 76% accepted, 25 enrolled. In 2003, 22 degrees awarded. *Entrance requirements:* For master's, GRE. Additional exam requirements/recommendations for international students: Required—TOEFL. *Application deadline:* For fall admission, 7/1 for domestic students; for spring admission, 11/1 for domestic students. Application fee: $35. *Expenses:* Contact institution. One-time fee: $45 full-time. *Unit head:* Angela C. Halfacre, Director, 843-727-6483, Fax: 843-953-5546. *Application contact:* Dodie Weise, Administrative Assistant, 843-727-6483, Fax: 843-727-2012, E-mail: dodie_weise@smtpgw.musc.edu.

College of Staten Island of the City University of New York, Graduate Programs, Program in Environmental Science, Staten Island, NY 10314-6600. Offers MS. Part-time and evening/weekend programs available. *Faculty:* 3 full-time (0 women), 1 (woman) part-time/adjunct. *Students:* Average age 32. 10 applicants, 70% accepted, 3 enrolled. In 2003, 4 degrees awarded. *Median time to degree:* Master's–3 years part-time. *Degree requirements:* For master's, thesis. *Entrance requirements:* For master's, GRE General Test, 1 year of course work in chemistry, physics, calculus, and ecology, minimum GPA of 3.0. Additional exam requirements/recommendations for international students: Required—TOEFL. *Application deadline:* For fall admission, 8/15 for domestic students; for spring admission, 1/15 for domestic students. Applications are processed on a rolling basis. Application fee: $50. *Expenses:* Tuition, state resident: full-time $5,440; part-time $230 per credit. Tuition, nonresident: full-time $10,200; part-time $425 per credit. Required fees: $154 per semester. Tuition and fees vary according to course load. *Financial support:* In 2003–04, 1 research assistantship, 3 teaching assistantships were awarded. Fellowships, career-related internships or fieldwork and Federal Work-Study also available. Support available to part-time students. Total annual research expenditures: $51,600. *Unit head:* Dr. Alfred Levine, Director, 718-982-3921, Fax: 718-982-3923, E-mail: levine@postbox.csi.cuny.edu. *Application contact:* Mary Beth Reilly, Director of Admissions, 718-982-2010, Fax: 718-982-2500, E-mail: reilly@postbox.csi.cuny.edu.

Colorado School of Mines, Graduate School, Division of Environmental Science and Engineering, Golden, CO 80401-1887. Offers MS, PhD. Part-time programs available. *Faculty:* 9 full-time (4 women), 3 part-time/adjunct (0 women). *Students:* 44 full-time (24 women), 34 part-time (19 women). 65 applicants, 94% accepted, 24 enrolled. In 2003, 28 master's, 4 doctorates awarded. *Degree requirements:* For master's, thesis (for some programs); for doctorate, thesis/dissertation, comprehensive exam. *Entrance requirements:* For master's and doctorate, GRE General Test. Additional exam requirements/recommendations for international students: Required—TOEFL (minimum score 550 paper-based; 213 computer-based). *Application deadline:* For fall admission, 12/1 priority date for domestic students, 12/1 priority date for international students; for spring admission, 5/1 priority date for domestic students, 5/1 priority date for international students. Application fee: $45. Electronic applications accepted. *Expenses:* Tuition, state resident: full-time $5,700; part-time $285 per credit hour. Tuition, nonresident: full-time $19,040; part-time $952 per credit hour. Required fees: $733. *Financial support:* In 2003–04, 41 students received support, including 2 fellowships with full tuition reimbursements available (averaging $12,500 per year), 28 research assistantships with full tuition reimbursements available (averaging $10,000 per year), 4 teaching assistantships with full tuition reimbursements available (averaging $10,000 per year); scholarships/grants and unspecified assistantships also available. Financial award applicants required to submit FAFSA. *Faculty research:* Treatment of water and wastes, environmental law–policy and practice, natural environment systems, hazardous waste management, environmental data analysis. Total annual research expenditures: $2 million. *Unit head:* Dr. Robert Seigrist, Director, 303-273-3473, Fax: 303-273-3413, E-mail: rseigris@mines.edu. *Application contact:* Tim VanHaverbeke, Coordinator, 303-273-3467, Fax: 303-273-3413, E-mail: tvanhave@mines.edu.

Columbus State University, Graduate Studies, College of Science, Department of Environmental Science and Public Health, Columbus, GA 31907-5645. Offers environmental science (MS). Part-time and evening/weekend programs available. *Faculty:* 2 full-time (1 woman), 1 (woman) part-time/adjunct. *Students:* 9 full-time (6 women), 6 part-time (1 woman); includes 4 minority (all African Americans), 3 international. Average age 37. 7 applicants, 57% accepted, 3 enrolled. In 2003, 3 degrees awarded. *Degree requirements:* For master's, thesis. *Entrance requirements:* For master's, GRE General Test, MAT, minimum GPA of 3.0. Additional exam requirements/recommendations for international students: Required—TOEFL (minimum score 550 paper-based; 213 computer-based). *Application deadline:* For fall admission, 7/1 priority date for domestic students, 7/1 priority date for international students; for spring admission, 12/12 for domestic students, 12/12 for international students. Applications are processed on a rolling basis. Application fee: $25. Electronic applications accepted. *Expenses:* Tuition, state resident: part-time $110 per semester hour. Tuition, nonresident: part-time $443 per

Environmental Sciences

Columbus State University (continued)
semester hour. Required fees: $168 per semester hour. *Financial support:* In 2003–04, 5 students received support, including 8 research assistantships with partial tuition reimbursements available (averaging $3,000 per year); career-related internships or fieldwork, Federal Work-Study, institutionally sponsored loans, scholarships/grants, and unspecified assistantships also available. Support available to part-time students. Financial award application deadline: 5/1; financial award applicants required to submit FAFSA. *Unit head:* Dr. James A. Gore, Acting Chair, 706-568-2067, E-mail: gore_james@colstate.edu. *Application contact:* Katie Thornton, Graduate Admissions Specialist, 706-568-2035, Fax: 706-568-2462, E-mail: thornton_katie@colstate.edu.

Cornell University, Graduate School, Graduate Fields of Agriculture and Life Sciences, Field of Soil and Crop Sciences, Ithaca, NY 14853-0001. Offers agronomy (MS, PhD); environmental information science (MS, PhD); environmental management (MPS); field crop science (MS, PhD); soil science (MS, PhD). *Faculty:* 32 full-time. *Students:* 44 full-time (17 women); includes 1 minority (Hispanic American), 24 international. 40 applicants, 43% accepted, 14 enrolled. In 2003, 9 master's, 7 doctorates awarded. *Degree requirements:* For master's, thesis (MS); for doctorate, thesis/dissertation, comprehensive exam. *Entrance requirements:* For master's and doctorate, GRE General Test, 2 letters of recommendation. Additional exam requirements/recommendations for international students: Required—TOEFL (minimum score 550 paper-based; 213 computer-based). *Application deadline:* For fall admission, 2/1 for domestic students. Applications are processed on a rolling basis. Application fee: $60. Electronic applications accepted. *Expenses:* Tuition: Full-time $28,630. One-time fee: $50 full-time. *Financial support:* In 2003–04, 36 students received support, including 8 fellowships with full tuition reimbursements available, 21 research assistantships with full tuition reimbursements available, 7 teaching assistantships with full tuition reimbursements available; institutionally sponsored loans, traineeships, health care benefits, tuition waivers (full and partial), and unspecified assistantships also available. *Faculty research:* Soil chemistry, physics and biology; crop physiology and management; environmental information science and modeling; international agriculture; weed science. *Unit head:* Director of Graduate Studies, 607-255-3267, Fax: 607-255-8615. *Application contact:* Graduate Field Assistant, 607-255-3267, Fax: 607-255-8615, E-mail: jae2@cornell.edu.

Drexel University, College of Arts and Sciences, Program in Environmental Science, Philadelphia, PA 19104-2875. Offers MS, PhD. Part-time and evening/weekend programs available. Terminal master's awarded for partial completion of doctoral program. *Degree requirements:* For master's, thesis optional; for doctorate, thesis/dissertation. Electronic applications accepted.

Duke University, Graduate School, Department of Environment, Durham, NC 27708. Offers natural resource economics/policy (AM, PhD); natural resource science/ecology (AM, PhD); natural resource systems science (AM, PhD). Part-time programs available. *Faculty:* 35 full-time. *Students:* 64 full-time (31 women); includes 7 minority (3 African Americans, 1 Asian American or Pacific Islander, 3 Hispanic Americans), 18 international. 151 applicants, 16% accepted, 15 enrolled. In 2003, 1 master's, 7 doctorates awarded. Terminal master's awarded for partial completion of doctoral program. *Degree requirements:* For doctorate, variable foreign language requirement, thesis/dissertation. *Entrance requirements:* For master's and doctorate, GRE General Test. Additional exam requirements/recommendations for international students: Required—IELT (preferred) or TOEFL. *Application deadline:* For fall admission, 12/31 for domestic students. Application fee: $75. *Expenses:* Tuition: Full-time $23,280; part-time $835 per unit. *Financial support:* Fellowships, research assistantships, teaching assistantships, Federal Work-Study available. Financial award application deadline: 12/31. *Unit head:* Kenneth Knoerr, Director of Graduate Studies, 919-613-8002, Fax: 919-684-8741, E-mail: nmm@duke.edu.

Duke University, Nicholas School of the Environment and Earth Sciences, Durham, NC 27708-0328. Offers coastal environmental management (MEM); environmental health and security (MEM); environmental science and policy (PhD); environmental toxicology, chemistry, and risk assessment (MEM); forest resource management (MF); global environmental change (MEM); resource ecology (MEM); resource economics and policy (MEM); water and air resources (MEM). PhD offered through the Graduate School. *Accreditation:* SAF (one or more programs are accredited). Part-time programs available. Terminal master's awarded for partial completion of doctoral program. *Degree requirements:* For master's, thesis (for some programs); for doctorate, thesis/dissertation. *Entrance requirements:* For master's, GRE General Test, previous course work in biology or ecology, calculus, statistics, and microeconomics; computer familiarity with word processing and data analysis; for doctorate, GRE General Test. Additional exam requirements/recommendations for international students: Required—TOEFL (minimum score 550 paper-based; 213 computer-based). Electronic applications accepted. Expenses: Contact institution. *Faculty research:* Ecosystem management, conservation ecology, earth systems, risk assessment.

See in-depth description on page 787.

Duquesne University, Bayer School of Natural and Environmental Sciences, Environmental Science and Management Program, Pittsburgh, PA 15282-0001. Offers environmental management (Certificate); environmental science (Certificate); environmental science and management (MS). Part-time and evening/weekend programs available. Postbaccalaureate distance learning degree programs offered (minimal on-campus study). *Faculty:* 2 full-time (0 women), 15 part-time/adjunct (1 woman). *Students:* 14 full-time (10 women), 47 part-time (22 women), 1 international. Average age 28. 20 applicants, 75% accepted, 9 enrolled. In 2003, 20 degrees awarded, leading to continued full-time study 5%, business/industry 80%, government 15%. *Median time to degree:* Master's–2 years full-time, 3 years part-time. *Degree requirements:* For master's, thesis or internship. *Entrance requirements:* For master's, GRE General Test, previous course work in biology, calculus, chemistry, and statistics. Additional exam requirements/recommendations for international students: Required—TOEFL, TSE. *Application deadline:* For fall admission, 4/1 priority date for domestic students, 4/1 priority date for international students; for spring admission, 10/1 priority date for domestic students, 10/1 priority date for international students. Applications are processed on a rolling basis. Application fee: $40. *Expenses:* Contact institution. *Financial support:* In 2003–04, 1 fellowship with full tuition reimbursement (averaging $14,000 per year), 2 teaching assistantships with partial tuition reimbursements (averaging $10,000 per year) were awarded. Research assistantships, career-related internships or fieldwork, institutionally sponsored loans, scholarships/grants, tuition waivers (partial), and unspecified assistantships also available. Support available to part-time students. Financial award application deadline: 5/1; financial award applicants required to submit FAFSA. *Faculty research:* Watershed management systems, environmental analytical chemistry, environmental endocrinology, environmental microbiology, aquatic biology. Total annual research expenditures: $161,550. *Unit head:* Dr. Daniel Donnelly, Director, 412-396-4367, Fax: 412-396-4092, E-mail: donnelly@duq.edu. *Application contact:* Mary Ann Quinn, Assistant to the Dean Graduate Affairs, 412-396-6339, Fax: 412-396-4881, E-mail: gradinfo@duq.edu.

Florida Agricultural and Mechanical University, Division of Graduate Studies, Research, and Continuing Education, Environmental Sciences Institute, Tallahassee, FL 32307-3200. Offers MS, PhD. *Faculty:* 6 full-time (2 women). *Students:* 23 full-time (17 women), 19 part-time (14 women); includes 39 minority (38 African Americans, 1 American Indian/Alaska Native). In 2003, 8 master's, 2 doctorates awarded. *Degree requirements:* For master's, thesis/dissertation; for doctorate, thesis/dissertation, comprehensive exam. *Entrance requirements:* For master's and doctorate, GRE General Test, minimum GPA of 3.0. Additional exam requirements/recommendations for international students: Required—TOEFL. *Application deadline:* For fall admission, 5/18 for domestic students, 12/18 for international students; for spring admission, 11/12 for domestic students, 5/12 for international students. Application fee: $20. *Expenses:* Tuition, state resident: part-time $192 per credit. Tuition, nonresident: part-time $727 per credit. Tuition and fees vary according to course load. *Faculty research:* Statistical mechanics and quantum chemistry, aquatic microbial ecology, contaminant transport, modeling, bio-conversion of agricultural waste. *Unit head:* Dr. Richard Gragg, Interim Director, 850-599-3550.

Florida Atlantic University, Charles E. Schmidt College of Science, Environmental Sciences Program, Boca Raton, FL 33431-0991. Offers MS. *Faculty:* 23 part-time/adjunct (4 women). *Students:* 15 full-time (9 women), 11 part-time (8 women); includes 2 minority (1 African American, 1 Hispanic American), 3 international. Average age 35. 15 applicants, 67% accepted, 8 enrolled. In 2003, 2 degrees awarded. *Degree requirements:* For master's, thesis. *Entrance requirements:* For master's, GRE General Test, minimum GPA of 3.0. Additional exam requirements/recommendations for international students: Required—TOEFL. *Application deadline:* For fall admission, 6/1 for domestic students. Application fee: $30. *Expenses:* Tuition, state resident: full-time $3,777. Tuition, nonresident: full-time $13,953. *Financial support:* In 2003–04, 8 teaching assistantships were awarded; career-related internships or fieldwork and Federal Work-Study also available. *Faculty research:* Tropical and terrestrial ecology, coastal/marine/wetlands ecology, hydrogeology, tropical botany. *Unit head:* John Volin, Director, 561-297-4473, Fax: 561-297-2067, E-mail: jvolin@fau.edu. *Application contact:* Gina Fourreau, Coordinator for Academic Programs, 561-297-2625, Fax: 561-297-2067, E-mail: gfourreau@fau.edu.

Florida Gulf Coast University, College of Arts and Sciences, Program in Environmental Science, Fort Myers, FL 33965-6565. Offers MS. Part-time programs available. *Faculty:* 72 full-time (27 women), 109 part-time/adjunct (45 women). *Students:* 11 full-time (5 women), 7 part-time (3 women). Average age 32. 12 applicants, 83% accepted, 10 enrolled. *Entrance requirements:* For master's, GRE General Test, minimum GPA of 3.0. *Application deadline:* For fall admission, 7/1 for domestic students; for spring admission, 11/15 for domestic students. Applications are processed on a rolling basis. Application fee: $30. Electronic applications accepted. *Expenses:* Tuition, state resident: part-time $199 per credit hour. Tuition, nonresident: part-time $733 per credit hour. *Faculty research:* Political issues in environmental science, recycling, environmental friendly buildings, pathophysiology, immunotoxicology of marine organisms. *Unit head:* Dr. Win Everham, Chair, 239-590-7231, Fax: 239-590-7200. *Application contact:* Mikele Meether, Adviser, 239-590-7204, Fax: 239-590-7200, E-mail: mmeether@fgcu.edu.

Florida Institute of Technology, Graduate Programs, College of Engineering, Department of Marine and Environmental Systems, Melbourne, FL 32901-6975. Offers environmental resource management (MS); environmental science (MS, PhD); meteorology (MS); ocean engineering (MS, PhD); oceanography (MS, PhD), including biological oceanography, chemical oceanography, coastal zone management (MS), geological oceanography, physical oceanography. Part-time programs available. *Faculty:* 16 full-time (1 woman), 4 part-time/adjunct (0 women). *Students:* 42 full-time (16 women), 19 part-time (8 women); includes 1 minority (Hispanic American), 25 international. Average age 29. 129 applicants, 55% accepted, 17 enrolled. In 2003, 17 master's, 3 doctorates awarded. Terminal master's awarded for partial completion of doctoral program. *Degree requirements:* For master's, thesis, comprehensive exam, registration; for doctorate, thesis/dissertation, attendance of graduate seminar, internships (oceanography and environmental science), comprehensive exam, registration. *Entrance requirements:* For master's, GRE General Test (environmental science), letters of recommendation(3), minimum GPA of 3.0; for doctorate, GRE General Test (oceanography and environmental science), resumé, letters of recommendation (3), statement of objectives, minimum GPA of 3.2. Additional exam requirements/recommendations for international students: Required—TOEFL (minimum score 550 paper-based; 213 computer-based). *Application deadline:* Applications are processed on a rolling basis. Application fee: $50. Electronic applications accepted. *Expenses:* Tuition: Part-time $745 per credit. *Financial support:* In 2003–04, 35 students received support, including 10 fellowships with full and partial tuition reimbursements available (averaging $5,565 per year), 15 research assistantships with full and partial tuition reimbursements available (averaging $14,657 per year), 10 teaching assistantships with full and partial tuition reimbursements available (averaging $17,533 per year); career-related internships or fieldwork and tuition remissions also available. Financial award application deadline: 3/1; financial award applicants required to submit FAFSA. *Faculty research:* Environmental modeling, coastal processes, exploring marine pollution, marine geophysics, remote sensing . Total annual research expenditures: $1.9 million. *Unit head:* Dr. George Maul, Department Head, 321-674-7453, Fax: 321-674-7212, E-mail: gmaul@fit.edu. *Application contact:* Carolyn P. Farrior, Director of Graduate Admissions, 321-674-7118, Fax: 321-723-9468, E-mail: cfarrior@fit.edu.

See in-depth description on page 727.

Florida International University, College of Arts and Sciences, Department of Environmental Studies, Miami, FL 33199. Offers biological management (MS); energy (MS); pollution (MS). *Faculty:* 10 full-time (2 women). *Students:* 18 full-time (10 women), 24 part-time (13 women); includes 13 minority (1 American Indian/Alaska Native, 2 Asian Americans or Pacific Islanders, 10 Hispanic Americans), 6 international. Average age 32. 32 applicants, 41% accepted, 6 enrolled. In 2003, 18 degrees awarded. *Degree requirements:* For master's, thesis. *Entrance requirements:* For master's, GRE General Test, minimum GPA of 3.0, 3 letters of recommendation. Additional exam requirements/recommendations for international students: Required—TOEFL. *Application deadline:* For fall admission, 4/1 for domestic students; for spring admission, 10/30 for domestic students. Application fee: $20. *Expenses:* Tuition, state resident: part-time $202 per credit. Tuition, nonresident: part-time $771 per credit. Required fees: $112 per semester. *Financial support:* Research assistantships, teaching assistantships available. Financial award application deadline: 4/1. *Unit head:* Dr. Joel Heinen, Chairperson, 305-348-3732, Fax: 305-348-6137, E-mail: joel.heinen@fiu.edu.

George Mason University, College of Arts and Sciences, Department of Environmental Science and Public Policy, Fairfax, VA 22030. Offers MS, PhD. Part-time programs available. *Faculty:* 27 full-time (6 women), 9 part-time/adjunct (4 women). *Students:* 9 full-time (5 women), 119 part-time (64 women); includes 25 minority (10 African Americans, 10 American Indian/Alaska Native, 5 Asian Americans or Pacific Islanders), 13 international. Average age 36. 73 applicants, 56% accepted, 33 enrolled. In 2003, 2 master's, 12 doctorates awarded. *Degree requirements:* For doctorate, thesis/dissertation, internship. *Entrance requirements:* For doctorate, GRE General Test, GRE Subject Test. *Application deadline:* For fall admission, 5/1 for domestic students; for spring admission, 11/1 for domestic students. Application fee: $60. Electronic applications accepted. *Expenses:* Tuition, state resident: full-time $4,398. Tuition, nonresident: full-time $14,952. Required fees: $1,482. *Financial support:* Fellowships, research assistantships, teaching assistantships available. Support available to part-time students. Financial award application deadline: 3/1; financial award applicants required to submit FAFSA. *Unit head:* Dr. R. Christian Jones, Interim Director, 703-963-1127, Fax: 703-993-1046, E-mail: rcjones@gmu.edu.

Georgia Institute of Technology, Graduate Studies and Research, College of Sciences, School of Earth and Atmospheric Sciences, Atlanta, GA 30332-0001. Offers atmospheric chemistry and air pollution (MS, PhD); atmospheric dynamics and climate (MS, PhD); geochemistry (MS, PhD); hydrologic cycle (MS, PhD); ocean sciences (MS, PhD); solid-earth and environmental geophysics (PhD); solid-earth and environmental geophysics (MS). Part-time programs available. *Students:* 80 full-time (40 women); includes 39 minority (5 African Americans, 31 Asian Americans or Pacific Islanders, 3 Hispanic Americans). 143 applicants, 18% accepted, 15 enrolled. In 2003, 14 master's, 6 doctorates awarded. Terminal master's awarded for partial completion of doctoral program. *Median time to degree:* Of those who began their doctoral program in fall 1995, 78% received their degree in 8 years or less. *Degree requirements:* For master's, thesis or alternative; for doctorate, thesis/dissertation, comprehensive exam. *Entrance requirements:* For master's and doctorate, GRE General Test, minimum GPA of 2.7. Additional exam requirements/recommendations for international students: Required—TOEFL (minimum score 550 paper-based; 213 computer-based). *Application deadline:* For fall admission, 1/15 priority date for domestic students, 1/15 priority date for international students; for spring admission, 1/1 for domestic students. Applications are processed on a rolling basis. Application fee: $50. *Expenses:* Tuition, state resident: part-time $1,925 per semester. Tuition, nonresident: part-time $7,700 per semester. Required fees: $434 per semester. Full-time tuition and fees vary according to program. *Financial support:* In 2003–04, 3 fellowships, 52 research assistantships (averaging $20,000 per year), 8 teaching assistantships were awarded. Career-related internships or fieldwork, Federal Work-Study, and institutionally sponsored loans also available. Financial award application deadline: 2/15. *Faculty research:* Geophysics, atmospheric chemistry, atmospheric dynamics, seismology. Total annual research expenditures: $5 million. *Unit head:* Dr. Judith A. Curry, Chair, 404-894-3948, Fax: 404-894-5638. *Application contact:* Derek M. Cunnold, Graduate Coordinator, 404-894-3814, Fax: 404-894-5638, E-mail: cunnold@eas.gatech.edu.

See in-depth description on page 237.

Graduate School and University Center of the City University of New York, Graduate Studies, Program in Earth and Environmental Sciences, New York, NY 10016-4039. Offers PhD. *Faculty:* 36 full-time (5 women). *Students:* 46 full-time (18 women), 4 part-time (1 woman); includes 10 minority (3 African Americans, 2 Asian Americans or Pacific Islanders, 5 Hispanic Americans), 17 international. Average age 36. 25 applicants, 76% accepted, 11 enrolled. In 2003, 2 degrees awarded. *Degree requirements:* For doctorate, one foreign language, thesis/dissertation, comprehensive exam. *Entrance requirements:* For doctorate, GRE General Test. *Application deadline:* For fall admission, 4/15 for domestic students. Application fee: $50. *Expenses:* Tuition, state resident: part-time $2,435 per semester. Tuition, nonresident: part-time $475 per credit. *Financial support:* In 2003–04, 30 students received support, including 28 fellowships, 2 research assistantships, 1 teaching assistantship; career-related internships or fieldwork, Federal Work-Study, institutionally sponsored loans, and tuition waivers (full and partial) also available. Financial award application deadline: 2/1; financial award applicants required to submit FAFSA. *Unit head:* Dr. Yehuda Klein, Acting Executive Officer, 212-817-8241, Fax: 212-817-1513.

Harvard University, School of Public Health, Department of Environmental Health, Boston, MA 02115-6096. Offers environmental epidemiology (SM, DPH, SD); environmental health (SM); environmental science and engineering (SM, SD); occupational health (MOH, SM, DPH, SD); physiology (SD). *Accreditation:* ABET (one or more programs are accredited); CEPH. Part-time programs available. *Degree requirements:* For doctorate, thesis/dissertation, qualifying exam. *Entrance requirements:* For master's and doctorate, GRE. Additional exam requirements/recommendations for international students: Required—TOEFL (minimum score 560 paper-based; 220 computer-based). Electronic applications accepted. *Expenses:* Tuition: Full-time $26,066. Full-time tuition and fees vary according to program and student level. *Faculty research:* Industrial hygiene and occupational safety, population genetics, indoor and outdoor air pollution, cell and molecular biology of the lungs, infectious diseases.

Howard University, Graduate School of Arts and Sciences, Department of Chemistry, Washington, DC 20059-0002. Offers analytical chemistry (MS, PhD); atmospheric (MS, PhD); biochemistry (MS, PhD); environmental (MS, PhD); inorganic chemistry (MS, PhD); organic chemistry (MS, PhD); physical chemistry (MS, PhD); polymer chemistry (MS, PhD). Part-time programs available. *Degree requirements:* For master's, one foreign language, thesis, teaching experience, comprehensive exam, registration; for doctorate, 2 foreign languages, thesis/dissertation, teaching experience, comprehensive exam, registration. *Entrance requirements:* For master's, GRE General Test, minimum GPA of 2.7; for doctorate, GRE General Test, minimum GPA of 3.0. *Faculty research:* Stratospheric aerosols, liquid crystals, polymer coatings, terrestrial and extraterrestrial atmospheres, amidogen reaction.

Humboldt State University, Graduate Studies, College of Natural Resources and Sciences, Programs in Environmental Systems, Arcata, CA 95521-8299. Offers MS. *Faculty:* 37 full-time (8 women), 19 part-time/adjunct (8 women). *Students:* 25 full-time (5 women), 18 part-time (8 women), 2 international. Average age 29. 28 applicants, 82% accepted, 13 enrolled. In 2003, 7 degrees awarded. *Degree requirements:* For master's, thesis. *Entrance requirements:* For master's, GRE, appropriate bachelor's degree, minimum GPA of 2.5. Additional exam requirements/recommendations for international students: Required—TOEFL. *Application deadline:* Applications are processed on a rolling basis. Application fee: $55. *Expenses:* Tuition, state resident: full-time $2,539. *Financial support:* Application deadline: 3/1. *Faculty research:* Mathematical modeling, international development technology, geology, environmental resources engineering. *Unit head:* Dr. Roland Lamberson, Coordinator, 707-826-4926.

Hunter College of the City University of New York, Graduate School, School of Arts and Sciences, Department of Geography, New York, NY 10021-5085. Offers analytical geography (MA); earth system science (MA); environmental and social issues (MA); geographic information science (Certificate); geographic information systems (MA); teaching earth science (MA). Part-time and evening/weekend programs available. *Faculty:* 11 full-time (5 women), 2 part-time/adjunct (0 women). *Students:* 3 full-time (1 woman), 29 part-time (13 women); includes 5 minority (3 African Americans, 1 Asian American or Pacific Islander, 1 Hispanic American). Average age 35. 12 applicants, 75% accepted. *Degree requirements:* For master's, comprehensive exam or thesis. *Entrance requirements:* For master's, GRE General Test, minimum B average in major, B- overall; 18 credits in geography, 2 letters of recommendation; for Certificate, minimum of B average in major, B- overall. Additional exam requirements/recommendations for international students: Required—TOEFL. *Application deadline:* For fall admission, 4/1 for domestic students; for spring admission, 11/1 for domestic students. Applications are processed on a rolling basis. Application fee: $50. *Expenses:* Tuition, state resident: part-time $230 per credit. Tuition, nonresident: part-time $425 per credit. *Financial support:* In 2003–04, 1 fellowship (averaging $3,000 per year), 2 research assistantships (averaging $10,000 per year), 10 teaching assistantships (averaging $6,000 per year) were awarded. Career-related internships or fieldwork, Federal Work-Study, institutionally sponsored loans, and unspecified assistantships also available. Financial award application deadline: 3/1. *Faculty research:* Urban geography, economic geography, geographic information science, demographic methods, climate change. *Unit head:* Prof. Charles A. Heatwole, Chair, 212-772-5265, Fax: 212-772-5268, E-mail: cah@geo.hunter.cuny.edu. *Application contact:* Prof. Marianna Pavlovskaya, Graduate Adviser, 212-772-5320, Fax: 212-772-5268, E-mail: mpavlov@geo.hunter.cuny.edu.

Idaho State University, Office of Graduate Studies, Department of Interdisciplinary Studies, Pocatello, ID 83209. Offers biology (MNS); chemistry (MNS); general interdisciplinary (M Ed, MA); geology (MNS); mathematics (MNS); physics (MNS); waste management and environmental science (MS). Part-time programs available. *Students:* 3 full-time, 337 part-time; includes 7 minority (1 African American, 1 Asian American or Pacific Islander, 5 Hispanic Americans). Average age 45. In 2003, 7 degrees awarded. *Degree requirements:* For master's, thesis optional. *Entrance requirements:* For master's, GRE General Test or MAT, minimum GPA of 3.0. Additional exam requirements/recommendations for international students: Required—TOEFL (minimum score 550 paper-based; 213 computer-based). *Application deadline:* For fall admission, 7/1 priority date for domestic students, 7/1 priority date for international students; for spring admission, 12/1 priority date for domestic students, 12/1 priority date for international students. Applications are processed on a rolling basis. Application fee: $35. *Expenses:* Tuition, state resident: part-time $205 per credit. Tuition, nonresident: full-time $6,600; part-time $300 per credit. Required fees: $4,108. One-time fee: $35 full-time. *Financial support:* Research assistantships, teaching assistantships, career-related internships or fieldwork, Federal Work-Study, scholarships/grants, and tuition waivers (full and partial) available. Support available to part-time students. Financial award application deadline: 1/1. Total annual research expenditures: $1.7 million. *Unit head:* Dr. Edwin House, Chief Research Officer/Department Chair, 208-282-2714, Fax: 208-282-4529.

Indiana University Bloomington, School of Public and Environmental Affairs, Environmental Science Programs, Bloomington, IN 47405. Offers MSES, PhD, JD/MSES, MSES/MA, MSES/MPA, MSES/MS. Part-time programs available. *Students:* 106 full-time (60 women), 17 part-time (8 women); includes 8 minority (2 African Americans, 2 Asian Americans or Pacific Islanders, 4 Hispanic Americans), 27 international. Average age 27. In 2003, 28 degrees awarded. Terminal master's awarded for partial completion of doctoral program. *Degree requirements:* For doctorate, thesis/dissertation. *Entrance requirements:* For master's, GRE General Test, LSAT (JD/MSES); for doctorate, GRE General Test. *Application deadline:* For fall admission, 2/1 priority date for domestic students, 1/15 priority date for international students. Applications are processed on a rolling basis. Application fee: $45 ($55 for international students). *Expenses:* Tuition, state resident: full-time $4,908; part-time $205 per credit. Tuition, nonresident: full-time $14,298; part-time $596 per credit. Required fees: $661. Tuition and fees vary according to campus/location and program. *Financial support:* Fellowships, research assistantships, teaching assistantships, career-related internships or fieldwork, Federal Work-Study, institutionally sponsored loans, and minority fellowships, Peace Corps assistantships available. Financial award application deadline: 2/1; financial award applicants required to submit FAFSA. *Faculty research:* Applied ecology, environmental chemistry, hazardous materials management, water resources. *Application contact:* Charles A. Johnson, Coordinator of Student Recruitment, 800-765-7755, Fax: 812-855-7802, E-mail: speainfo@indiana.edu.

See in-depth description on page 729.

Instituto Tecnológico y de Estudios Superiores de Monterrey, Campus Ciudad de México, Virtual University Division, Ciudad de Mexico, , Mexico. Offers administration of information technologies (MA); computer sciences (MA); education (MA, PhD); educational technology (MA); environmental engineering (MA); environmental systems (MA); humanistics studies (MA); industrial engineering (MA); international business for Latin America (MA); quality systems (MA); quality systems and productivity (MA). Part-time and evening/weekend programs available. Postbaccalaureate distance learning degree programs offered (minimal on-campus study). *Entrance requirements:* For master's and doctorate, Instituto entrance exam. Additional exam requirements/recommendations for international students: Required—TOEFL.

Inter American University of Puerto Rico, San Germán Campus, Graduate Studies Center, Graduate Program in Environmental Sciences, San Germán, PR 00683-5008. Offers MS. Part-time and evening/weekend programs available. *Faculty:* 3 full-time (all women), 2 part-time/adjunct (0 women). *Students:* 47; all minorities (all Hispanic Americans) Average age 27. In 2003, 10 degrees awarded. *Degree requirements:* For master's, thesis, comprehensive exam. *Entrance requirements:* For master's, GRE General Test, or EXADEP, minimum GPA of 3.0. *Application deadline:* For fall admission, 4/30 for domestic students; for spring admission, 11/15 for domestic students. Applications are processed on a rolling basis. Application fee: $31. *Expenses:* Tuition: Part-time $170 per credit. *Financial support:* Fellowships, research assistantships, teaching assistantships available. *Faculty research:* Environmental biology, environmental chemistry, water resources and unit operations. *Application contact:* Prof. Jaime Galarza, Graduate Coordinator, 787-264-1912 Ext. 7471, Fax: 787-892-7510, E-mail: rjegl@sg.inter.edu.

Jackson State University, Graduate School, School of Science and Technology, Department of Biology, Jackson, MS 39217. Offers biology education (MST); environmental science (MS, PhD). Part-time and evening/weekend programs available. *Degree requirements:* For master's, thesis (alternative accepted for MST); for doctorate, thesis/dissertation, comprehensive exam. *Entrance requirements:* For master's, GRE General Test; for doctorate, MAT. Additional exam requirements/recommendations for international students: Required—TOEFL. *Faculty research:* Comparative studies on the carbohydrate composition of marine macroalgae, host-parasite relationship between the spruce budworm and entomepathogen fungus.

Lehigh University, College of Arts and Sciences, Department of Earth and Environmental Sciences, Bethlehem, PA 18015-3094. Offers MS, PhD. *Faculty:* 14 full-time (2 women). *Students:* 27 full-time (14 women), 2 part-time; includes 3 minority (all Asian Americans or Pacific Islanders) Average age 26. 35 applicants, 40% accepted, 9 enrolled. In 2003, 6 master's, 1 doctorate awarded. Terminal master's awarded for partial completion of doctoral program. *Degree requirements:* For master's, thesis, registration; for doctorate, thesis/dissertation, language at the discretion of the PhD committee, comprehensive exam, registration. *Entrance requirements:* For master's and doctorate, GRE General Test, 2 letters of recommendation. Additional exam requirements/recommendations for international students: Required—TOEFL. *Application deadline:* For fall admission, 1/15 for domestic students; for spring admission, 10/15 priority date for domestic students. Applications are processed on a rolling basis. Application fee: $40. *Expenses:* Tuition: Full-time $16,920; part-time $940 per credit hour. Required fees: $200. Tuition and fees vary according to degree level and program. *Financial support:* In 2003–04, 3 fellowships with full tuition reimbursements (averaging $13,670 per year), 4 research assistantships with full tuition reimbursements (averaging $13,670 per year), 8 teaching assistantships with full tuition reimbursements (averaging $13,670 per year) were awarded. Federal Work-Study, institutionally sponsored loans, and tuition waivers (full and partial) also available. Financial award application deadline: 1/15. *Faculty research:* Tectonics, surficial processes, aquatic ecology. Total annual research expenditures: $1.5 million. *Unit head:* Dr. Anne S. Meltzer, Chairman, 610-758-3660 Ext. 3673, Fax: 610-758-3677, E-mail: asm3@lehigh.edu. *Application contact:* Dr. Frank Jame Pazzaglia, Graduate Coordinator, 610-758-3660 Ext. 3667, Fax: 610-758-3677, E-mail: fjp3@lehigh.edu.

See in-depth description on page 731.

Louisiana State University and Agricultural and Mechanical College, Graduate School, College of Agriculture, School of Renewable Natural Resources, Baton Rouge, LA 70803. Offers fisheries (MS); forestry (MS, PhD); wildlife (MS); wildlife and fisheries science (PhD). *Faculty:* 30 full-time (0 women). *Students:* 56 full-time (12 women), 16 part-time (7 women); includes 42 minority (1 American Indian/Alaska Native, 41 Hispanic Americans), 27 international. Average age 30. 34 applicants, 50% accepted, 11 enrolled. In 2003, 20 master's, 9 doctorates awarded. *Degree requirements:* For master's and doctorate, thesis/dissertation. *Entrance requirements:* For master's, GRE General Test, minimum GPA of 3.0; for doctorate, GRE General Test, MS, minimum GPA of 3.0. Additional exam requirements/recommendations for international students: Required—TOEFL (minimum score 550 paper-based; 213 computer-based). *Application deadline:* For fall admission, 1/25 priority date for domestic students, 5/15 priority date for international students. Applications are processed on a rolling basis. Application fee: $25. Electronic applications accepted. *Expenses:* Tuition, state resident: part-time $337 per hour. Tuition, nonresident: part-time $577 per hour. *Financial support:* In 2003–04, 2 fellowships (averaging $18,750 per year), 50 research assistantships with partial tuition reimbursements (averaging $15,766 per year), 2 teaching assistantships with partial tuition reimbursements (averaging $16,375 per year) were awarded. Federal Work-Study also available. Financial award application deadline: 4/15; financial award applicants required to submit FAFSA. *Faculty research:* Forest biology and management, aquaculture, fisheries biology and ecology, upland and wetlands wildlife. Total annual research expenditures: $7,325. *Unit head:* Dr. Bob G. Blackmon, Director, 225-578-4131, Fax: 225-578-4227, E-mail: bblackmon@agctr.lsu.edu. *Application contact:* Dr. Allen Rutherford, Coordinator of Graduate Studies, 225-578-4187, Fax: 225-578-4227, E-mail: druther@lsu.edu.

See in-depth description on page 789.

Loyola Marymount University, Graduate Division, College of Science and Engineering, Department of Civil Engineering and Environmental Science, Program in Environmental Science, Los Angeles, CA 90045-2659. Offers MS. Part-time and evening/weekend programs available. *Students:* 4 full-time (1 woman), 11 part-time (4 women); includes 8 minority (2 African Americans, 3 Asian Americans or Pacific Islanders, 3 Hispanic Americans), 3 international. Average age 25. 6 applicants, 67% accepted, 3 enrolled. In 2003, 1 degree awarded. *Degree requirements:* For master's, thesis or alternative, comprehensive exam. *Entrance requirements:* Additional exam requirements/recommendations for international students: Required—TOEFL (minimum score 550 paper-based; 213 computer-based). Application fee: $50. *Expenses:* Tuition: Part-time $664 per unit. Tuition and fees vary according to course load, degree level and program. *Financial support:* In 2003–04, 6 students received support; research assistantships, Federal Work-Study, scholarships/grants, and unspecified assistantships available. Support available to part-time students. Financial award application deadline: 6/1; financial award applicants required to submit FAFSA. *Unit head:* Prof. Joe Reichenberger, Professor, Depart-

Environmental Sciences

Loyola Marymount University (continued)
ment of Civil Engineering and Environmental Science, 310-338-2830, Fax: 310-338-5896, E-mail: jreichen@lmu.edu.

Marshall University, Academic Affairs Division, Graduate College, College of Information, Technology and Engineering, Division of Environmental Science and Safety Technology, Program in Environmental Science and Safety Technology, Huntington, WV 25755. Offers MS. Part-time and evening/weekend programs available. *Students:* 18 full-time (7 women), 28 part-time (9 women); includes 1 minority (Asian American or Pacific Islander), 2 international. Average age 32. In 2003, 4 degrees awarded. *Degree requirements:* For master's, final project, oral exam. *Entrance requirements:* For master's, GRE General Test or MAT, minimum GPA of 2.5, previous course work in calculus. Tuition, area resident: Part-time $1,730 per semester. *Expenses:* Tuition, state resident: part-time $3,295 per semester. Tuition, nonresident: part-time $5,003 per semester. *Financial support:* Tuition waivers (full) available. Support available to part-time students. Financial award application deadline: 8/1; financial award applicants required to submit FAFSA. *Application contact:* Information Contact, 304-746-1900, Fax: 304-746-1902, E-mail: services@marshall.edu.

Massachusetts Institute of Technology, School of Engineering, Department of Civil and Environmental Engineering, Cambridge, MA 02139-4307. Offers biological oceanography (PhD, Sc D); chemical oceanography (PhD, Sc D); civil and environmental engineering (M Eng, SM, PhD, Sc D, CE, Env E); civil engineering (PhD, Sc D); coastal engineering (Sc D); construction engineering and management (PhD, Sc D); costal engineering (PhD); environmental biology (PhD, Sc D); environmental chemistry (PhD, Sc D); environmental engineering (PhD, Sc D); environmental fluid mechanics (PhD, Sc D); geotechnical and geoenvironmental engineering (PhD, Sc D); hydrology (PhD, Sc D); information technology (PhD, Sc D); oceanographic engineering (PhD); oceonographic engineering (Sc D); structures and materials (PhD, Sc D); transportation (PhD, Sc D). *Faculty:* 36 full-time (4 women). *Students:* 239 full-time (70 women); includes 17 minority (1 African American, 10 Asian Americans or Pacific Islanders, 6 Hispanic Americans), 147 international. Average age 26. 591 applicants, 37% accepted, 90 enrolled. In 2003, 149 master's, 27 doctorates awarded. *Degree requirements:* For master's and other advanced degree, thesis/dissertation; for doctorate, thesis/dissertation, comprehensive exam. *Entrance requirements:* For master's and doctorate, GRE General Test. Additional exam requirements/recommendations for international students: Required—TOEFL (minimum score 577 paper-based; 233 computer-based). *Application deadline:* For fall admission, 1/2 for domestic students, 1/2 for international students. Application fee: $70. Electronic applications accepted. *Expenses:* Tuition: Full-time $29,400. Required fees: $200. *Financial support:* In 2003–04, 214 students received support, including 42 fellowships with tuition reimbursements available, 112 research assistantships with tuition reimbursements available (averaging $22,740 per year), 29 teaching assistantships with tuition reimbursements available (averaging $17,370 per year); career-related internships or fieldwork, Federal Work-Study, institutionally sponsored loans, scholarships/grants, health care benefits, and unspecified assistantships also available. *Faculty research:* Environmental chemistry and biology, environmental fluid dynamics and hydrodynamics, geoenvironment and geotechnology, surface and groundwater hydrology, materials and structures. Total annual research expenditures: $10.9 million. *Unit head:* Prof. Patrick Jaillet, Head, 617-452-3379, Fax: 617-452-3294, E-mail: jaillet@mit.edu. *Application contact:* Graduate Admissions, 617-253-7101, E-mail: ceed@mit.edu.

McNeese State University, Graduate School, College of Science, Department of Biological and Environmental Sciences, Lake Charles, LA 70609. Offers biology (MS); environmental and chemical sciences (MS); environmental sciences (MS). Evening/weekend programs available. *Degree requirements:* For master's, thesis or alternative, comprehensive exam. *Entrance requirements:* For master's, GRE General Test.

McNeese State University, Graduate School, College of Science, Department of Chemistry, Lake Charles, LA 70609. Offers chemistry (PhD); environmental and chemical sciences (MS, PhD). Evening/weekend programs available. *Degree requirements:* For master's, thesis or alternative, comprehensive exam. *Entrance requirements:* For master's, GRE General Test. *Faculty research:* Environmental studies, carotenoids, polymers, chemical education.

Memorial University of Newfoundland, School of Graduate Studies, Interdisciplinary Program in Environmental Science, St. John's, NL A1C 5S7, Canada. Offers M Env Sc, M Sc. Part-time programs available. *Students:* 25 full-time, 7 part-time. 77 applicants, 17% accepted, 13 enrolled. In 2003, 13 degrees awarded. *Degree requirements:* For master's, thesis (M Sc), project (M Env Sci). *Entrance requirements:* For master's, honors B Sc or 2nd class B Eng. *Application deadline:* Applications are processed on a rolling basis. Application fee: $40. Electronic applications accepted. Tuition and fees charges are reported in Canadian dollars. *Expenses:* Tuition, state resident: part-time $733 Canadian dollars per semester. Tuition, nonresident: part-time $953 Canadian dollars per semester. Required fees: $194 Canadian dollars per year. Tuition and fees vary according to degree level and program. *Financial support:* Fellowships, research assistantships, teaching assistantships available. Financial award application deadline: 3/1. *Faculty research:* Earth and ocean systems, environmental chemistry and toxicology, environmental engineering. *Unit head:* Dr. John D. Jacobs, Co-Chair, 709-737-2331, E-mail: jjacobs@mun.ca. *Application contact:* Gail Kenny, Secretary, 709-737-3444, Fax: 709-737-3316, E-mail: gkenny@mun.ca.

Miami University, Graduate School, Institute of Environmental Sciences, Oxford, OH 45056. Offers M En S. Part-time programs available. *Faculty:* 1 full-time (0 women), 2 part-time/adjunct (1 woman). *Students:* 66 full-time (29 women), 4 part-time (all women); includes 1 minority (African American), 17 international. 58 applicants, 60% accepted, 12 enrolled. In 2003, 11 degrees awarded. *Degree requirements:* For master's, thesis, final exam, comprehensive exam. *Entrance requirements:* For master's, minimum undergraduate GPA of 3.0 during previous 2 years or 2.75 overall. Additional exam requirements/recommendations for international students: Required—TOEFL, TWE. *Application deadline:* For fall admission, 2/1 priority date for domestic students, 2/1 priority date for international students. Applications are processed on a rolling basis. Application fee: $35. Electronic applications accepted. Tuition, area resident: Full-time $9,346. International tuition: $19,924 full-time. Full-time tuition and fees vary according to course level and campus/location. *Financial support:* In 2003–04, 9 fellowships with partial tuition reimbursements (averaging $6,807 per year) were awarded; research assistantships, teaching assistantships, career-related internships or fieldwork, Federal Work-Study, tuition waivers (full), and unspecified assistantships also available. Financial award application deadline: 2/1. *Unit head:* Dr. Gene Willeke, Director, 513-529-5811, Fax: 513-529-5814, E-mail: environ@muohio.edu.

Michigan State University, Graduate School, College of Natural Science, Department of Geological Sciences, East Lansing, MI 48824. Offers environmental geosciences (MS, PhD); environmental geosciences-environmental toxicology (PhD); geological sciences (MS, PhD). Part-time programs available. *Faculty:* 12 full-time (2 women). *Students:* 24 full-time (11 women), 4 part-time (2 women); includes 1 minority (Asian American or Pacific Islander), 3 international. Average age 28. 47 applicants, 62% accepted, 7 enrolled. In 2003, 8 master's, 2 doctorates awarded. *Median time to degree:* Master's–3.1 years full-time; doctorate–3.3 years full-time. *Degree requirements:* For master's and doctorate, thesis/dissertation, registration. *Entrance requirements:* For master's, GRE General Test, minimum GPA of 3.0, geoscience coursework, 3 letters of recommendation; for doctorate, GRE General Test, 3 letters of recommendation. Additional exam requirements/recommendations for international students: Required—TOEFL (minimum score 575 paper-based; 232 computer-based), TSE required only for teaching positions. *Application deadline:* For fall admission, 1/15 priority date for domestic students, 6/1 priority date for international students; for spring admission, 10/15 priority date for domestic students, 11/1 priority date for international students. Applications are processed on a rolling basis. Application fee: $50. Electronic applications accepted. *Expenses:* Tuition, state resident: part-time $291 per hour. Tuition, nonresident: part-time $589 per hour. *Financial support:* In 2003–04, 9 research assistantships with full tuition reimbursements (averaging $11,376 per year), 23 teaching assistantships with full tuition reimbursements (averaging $11,376 per year) were awarded. Fellowships with tuition reimbursements, Federal Work-Study, institutionally sponsored loans, scholarships/grants, health care benefits, and unspecified assistantships also available. Financial award application deadline: 1/15; financial award applicants required to submit CSS PROFILE or FAFSA. *Faculty research:* Water in the environment, biogeochemical cycles, paleobiology and paleoenvironmental change, crystal dynamics. Total annual research expenditures: $841,206. *Unit head:* Dr. Michael A. Velbel, Chairperson, 517-355-4626, Fax: 517-353-8787, E-mail: geosci@msu.edu.

Minnesota State University Mankato, College of Graduate Studies, College of Science, Engineering and Technology, Department of Biological Sciences, Program in Environmental Science, Mankato, MN 56001. Offers ecology (MS); economic and political systems (MS); human ecosystems (MS); physical science (MS); technology (MS). *Faculty:* 1 (woman) full-time. *Students:* 3 full-time (all women), 4 part-time (3 women). Average age 31. In 2003, 4 degrees awarded. *Degree requirements:* For master's, one foreign language, thesis or alternative, comprehensive exam. *Entrance requirements:* For master's, minimum GPA of 3.0 during previous 2 years. *Application deadline:* For fall admission, 7/9 for domestic students; for spring admission, 11/27 for domestic students. Applications are processed on a rolling basis. Application fee: $40. *Expenses:* Tuition, state resident: part-time $226 per credit hour. Tuition, nonresident: part-time $339 per credit hour. Tuition and fees vary according to reciprocity agreements. *Financial support:* Research assistantships with partial tuition reimbursements, teaching assistantships with partial tuition reimbursements, career-related internships or fieldwork, Federal Work-Study, and institutionally sponsored loans available. Financial award application deadline: 3/15; financial award applicants required to submit FAFSA. *Unit head:* Dr. Beth Proctor, Graduate Coordinator, 507-389-5697. *Application contact:* Joni Roberts, Admissions Coordinator, 507-389-5244, Fax: 507-389-5974, E-mail: grad@mankato.msus.edu.

Montana State University–Bozeman, College of Graduate Studies, College of Agriculture, Department of Land Resources and Environmental Sciences, Bozeman, MT 59717. Offers land rehabilitation (interdisciplinary) (MS); land resources and environmental sciences (MS, PhD). Part-time programs available. *Faculty:* 13 full-time (1 woman), 2 part-time/adjunct (1 woman). *Students:* 13 full-time (9 women), 48 part-time (28 women); includes 1 minority (American Indian/Alaska Native), 2 international. Average age 32. 22 applicants, 73% accepted, 12 enrolled. In 2003, 12 master's, 1 doctorate awarded. *Degree requirements:* For master's, thesis (for some programs), comprehensive exam, registration; for doctorate, thesis/dissertation, comprehensive exam, registration. *Entrance requirements:* For master's and doctorate, GRE General Test. Additional exam requirements/recommendations for international students: Required—TOEFL (minimum score 550 paper-based; 213 computer-based). *Application deadline:* For fall admission, 7/15 priority date for domestic students, 5/15 priority date for international students; for spring admission, 12/1 priority date for domestic students, 10/1 priority date for international students. Applications are processed on a rolling basis. Application fee: $50. Electronic applications accepted. *Expenses:* Tuition, state resident: full-time $3,907; part-time $163 per credit. Tuition, nonresident: full-time $12,383; part-time $516 per credit. Required fees: $890; $445 per term. Tuition and fees vary according to course load and program. *Financial support:* Application deadline: 3/1; Total annual research expenditures: $4 million. *Unit head:* Dr. John Wraith, Interim Head, 406-994-4605, Fax: 406-994-3933, E-mail: jwraith@montana.edu.

Montclair State University, The Graduate School, College of Science and Mathematics, Department of Earth and Environmental Studies, Upper Montclair, NJ 07043-1624. Offers environmental management (MA, D Env M); environmental studies (MS), including environmental education, environmental health, environmental management, environmental science; geoscience (MS, Certificate), including geoscience (MS), water resource management (Certificate). Part-time and evening/weekend programs available. *Faculty:* 13 full-time (2 women), 6 part-time/adjunct. *Students:* 17 full-time (8 women), 39 part-time (18 women); includes 8 minority (3 African Americans, 3 Asian Americans or Pacific Islanders, 2 Hispanic Americans), 3 international. 27 applicants, 59% accepted, 12 enrolled. In 2003, 53 master's, 3 doctorates awarded. *Degree requirements:* For master's, comprehensive exam. *Entrance requirements:* For master's, GRE General Test, 2 letters of recommendation. Additional exam requirements/recommendations for international students: Required—TOEFL (minimum score 550 paper-based; 213 computer-based). *Application deadline:* Applications are processed on a rolling basis. Application fee: $60. Electronic applications accepted. *Expenses:* Tuition, state resident: full-time $8,771; part-time $323 per credit. Tuition, nonresident: full-time $10,365; part-time $470 per credit. Required fees: $42 per credit. Tuition and fees vary according to degree level and program. *Financial support:* In 2003–04, 7 research assistantships with full tuition reimbursements (averaging $5,000 per year) were awarded; Federal Work-Study, scholarships/grants, and unspecified assistantships also available. Support available to part-time students. Financial award application deadline: 3/1; financial award applicants required to submit FAFSA. Total annual research expenditures: $127,880. *Unit head:* Dr. Gregory Pope, Chairperson, 973-655-7385. *Application contact:* Dr. Harbans Singh, Adviser, 973-655-7383.

New Jersey Institute of Technology, Office of Graduate Studies, College of Science and Liberal Arts, Department of Chemistry and Environmental Science, Program in Environmental Science, Newark, NJ 07102. Offers MS, PhD. Part-time and evening/weekend programs available. *Students:* 18 full-time (10 women), 35 part-time (15 women); includes 9 minority (4 African Americans, 2 Asian Americans or Pacific Islanders, 3 Hispanic Americans), 12 international. Average age 31. 33 applicants, 45% accepted, 9 enrolled. In 2003, 10 master's, 6 doctorates awarded. *Degree requirements:* For doctorate, thesis/dissertation. *Entrance requirements:* For master's, GRE General Test; for doctorate, GRE General Test, minimum graduate GPA of 3.5. *Application deadline:* For fall admission, 6/5 for domestic students; for spring admission, 10/15 for domestic students. Applications are processed on a rolling basis. Application fee: $50. Electronic applications accepted. *Expenses:* Tuition, state resident: full-time $9,620; part-time $520 per credit. Tuition, nonresident: full-time $13,542; part-time $715 per credit. Tuition and fees vary according to course load. *Financial support:* Fellowships with full and partial tuition reimbursements, research assistantships with full and partial tuition reimbursements, teaching assistantships with full and partial tuition reimbursements, career-related internships or fieldwork, Federal Work-Study, institutionally sponsored loans, and unspecified assistantships available. Financial award application deadline: 3/15. *Application contact:* Kathryn Kelly, Director of Admissions, 973-596-3300, Fax: 973-596-3461, E-mail: admissions@njit.edu.

New Mexico Institute of Mining and Technology, Graduate Studies, Department of Chemistry, Socorro, NM 87801. Offers biochemistry (MS); chemistry (MS); environmental chemistry (PhD); explosives technology and atmospheric chemistry (PhD). Part-time programs available. *Faculty:* 9 full-time (1 woman), 4 part-time/adjunct (1 woman). *Students:* 14 full-time (6 women), 11 international. Average age 28. 20 applicants, 5 enrolled. In 2003, 1 degree awarded. *Degree requirements:* For master's and doctorate, thesis/dissertation. *Entrance requirements:* For master's, GRE General Test; for doctorate, GRE General Test, GRE Subject Test. Additional exam requirements/recommendations for international students: Required—TOEFL (minimum score 540 paper-based; 207 computer-based). *Application deadline:* For fall admission, 3/1 for domestic students; for spring admission, 6/1 priority date for domestic students. Applications are processed on a rolling basis. Application fee: $16 ($30 for international students). Electronic applications accepted. *Expenses:* Tuition, state resident: full-time $2,276; part-time $126 per credit. Tuition, nonresident: full-time $9,170; part-time $509 per credit. Required fees: $924; $27 per credit. $214 per term. Part-time tuition and fees vary according to course load. *Financial support:* In 2003–04, 6 research assistantships (averaging $5,492 per year), 13 teaching assistantships with full and partial tuition reimbursements (averaging $10,384 per year) were awarded. Fellowships, Federal Work-Study, institutionally sponsored loans, and unspecified assistantships also available. Financial award application deadline: 3/1; financial award applicants required to submit CSS PROFILE or FAFSA. *Faculty research:* Organic, analytical, environmental, and explosives chemistry. *Unit head:* Dr. Tanja Pietrass, Chairman,

505-835-5586, Fax: 505-835-5364, E-mail: tanja@nmt.edu. *Application contact:* Dr. David B. Johnson, Dean of Graduate Studies, 505-835-5513, Fax: 505-835-5476, E-mail: graduate@nmt.edu.

North Carolina Agricultural and Technical State University, Graduate School, School of Agriculture and Environmental and Allied Sciences, Greensboro, NC 27411. Offers MS. Part-time and evening/weekend programs available. *Degree requirements:* For master's, qualifying exam. *Entrance requirements:* For master's, GRE General Test. *Faculty research:* Aid for small farmers, agricultural technology, housing, food science, nutrition.

North Dakota State University, The Graduate School, College of Science and Mathematics, Department of Biological Sciences, Fargo, ND 58105. Offers botany (MS, PhD); cellular and molecular biology (PhD); environmental and conservation sciences (PhD); genomics (PhD); natural resources management (MS); zoology (MS, PhD). *Degree requirements:* For master's and doctorate, thesis/dissertation. *Entrance requirements:* For master's and doctorate, GRE General Test. Additional exam requirements/recommendations for international students: Required—TOEFL. Electronic applications accepted. Tuition, nonresident: full-time $4,071. Required fees: $493. *Faculty research:* Comparative endocrinology, physiology, behavioral ecology, plant cell biology, aquatic biology.

Northern Arizona University, Graduate College, College of Arts and Sciences, Department of Environmental Sciences, Flagstaff, AZ 86011. Offers conservation ecology (Certificate); environmental sciences and policy (MS). *Accreditation:* NCA . *Students:* 15 full-time (12 women), 2 part-time (both women); includes 2 minority (both Hispanic Americans) 38 applicants, 16% accepted. In 2003, 7 degrees awarded. *Degree requirements:* For master's, thesis optional. *Entrance requirements:* For master's, GRE General Test. Application fee: $45. *Expenses:* Tuition, state resident: full-time $5,103. Tuition, nonresident: full-time $12,623. *Financial support:* In 2003–04, 14 research assistantships were awarded. Financial award application deadline: 2/15. *Unit head:* Dr. Roderic Parnell, Chair, 928-523-9333, Fax: 928-523-7423, E-mail: roderic.parnell@nau.edu. *Application contact:* Information Contact, E-mail: esf.program@nau.edu.

Nova Scotia Agricultural College, Research and Graduate Studies, Truro, NS B2N 5E3, Canada. Offers agriculture (M Sc), including air quality, animal behavior, animal molecular genetics, animal nutrition, animal technology, aquaculture, botany, crop management, crop physiology, ecology, environmental microbiology, food science, horticulture, nutrient management, pest management, physiology, plant biotechnology, plant pathology, soil chemistry, soil fertility, waste management and composting, water quality. Part-time programs available. *Faculty:* 38 full-time (5 women), 13 part-time/adjunct (1 woman). *Students:* 46 full-time (27 women), 21 part-time (13 women); includes 13 minority (10 African Americans, 2 American Indian/Alaska Native, 1 Asian American or Pacific Islander). 45 applicants, 58% accepted, 16 enrolled. In 2003, 11 degrees awarded, leading to university research/teaching 18%, continued full-time study36%, business/industry 9%, government 27%. *Median time to degree:* Master's–2.25 years full-time, 4 years part-time. *Degree requirements:* For master's, thesis, candidacy exam. *Entrance requirements:* For master's, B.Sc. honors degree, minimum GPA of 3.0. Additional exam requirements/recommendations for international students: Required—TOEFL (minimum score 580 paper-based; 237 computer-based), Michigan English Language Assessment Battery. *Application deadline:* For fall admission, 6/1 for domestic students, 4/1 for international students; for winter admission, 11/15 for domestic students; for spring admission, 2/28 for domestic students. Applications are processed on a rolling basis. Application fee: $70. *Expenses:* Tuition, state resident: full-time $6,270. Tuition, nonresident: full-time $9,270. Required fees: $402. Tuition and fees vary according to student level. *Financial support:* In 2003–04, 63 students received support, including research assistantships (averaging $15,000 per year), teaching assistantships (averaging $900 per year); career-related internships or fieldwork, scholarships/grants, and unspecified assistantships also available. *Faculty research:* Organogenesis, somatic embryogenesis, composting, sustainable agriculture, ecotoxicology. Total annual research expenditures: $2 million. *Unit head:* Jill L. Rogers, Manager, 902-893-6360, Fax: 902-893-3430, E-mail: jrogers@nsac.ns.ca. *Application contact:* Marie Law, Administrative Assistant, 902-893-6502, Fax: 902-893-3430, E-mail: mlaw@nsac.ns.ca.

Nova Southeastern University, Oceanographic Center, Program in Marine Environmental Science, Fort Lauderdale, FL 33314-7796. Offers MS. *Students:* 1 (woman) full-time, 16 part-time (9 women). 8 applicants, 63% accepted, 5 enrolled. In 2003, 2 degrees awarded. *Degree requirements:* For master's, thesis. *Entrance requirements:* For master's, GRE. Additional exam requirements/recommendations for international students: Required—TOEFL (minimum score 550 paper-based). *Application deadline:* Applications are processed on a rolling basis. Application fee: $50. *Expenses:* Tuition: Full-time $8,715; part-time $484 per credit. Required fees: $75. Full-time tuition and fees vary according to degree level and program. *Application contact:* Dr. Andrew Rogerson, Associate Dean, 954-262-3600, Fax: 954-262-4020, E-mail: arogerso@nsu.nova.edu.

Oakland University, Graduate Study and Lifelong Learning, College of Arts and Sciences, Department of Chemistry, Rochester, MI 48309-4401. Offers chemistry (MS, PhD); health and environmental chemistry (PhD). *Faculty:* 19 full-time (6 women). *Students:* 6 full-time (2 women), 22 part-time (8 women); includes 3 minority (all Asian Americans or Pacific Islanders), 5 international. Average age 29. 15 applicants, 100% accepted, 9 enrolled. In 2003, 6 master's, 2 doctorates awarded. *Degree requirements:* For master's and doctorate, thesis/dissertation. *Entrance requirements:* For master's, minimum GPA of 3.0 for unconditional admission; for doctorate, GRE Subject Test, minimum GPA of 3.0 for unconditional admission. *Application deadline:* For fall admission, 7/15 for domestic students; for winter admission, 12/1 for domestic students; for spring admission, 3/15 for domestic students. Applications are processed on a rolling basis. Application fee: $30. Electronic applications accepted. *Expenses:* Tuition, state resident: full-time $7,032; part-time $293 per credit. Tuition, nonresident: full-time $12,804; part-time $534 per credit. *Financial support:* Federal Work-Study, institutionally sponsored loans, and tuition waivers (full) available. Financial award application deadline: 3/1; financial award applicants required to submit FAFSA. *Faculty research:* C-3 nucleic acid radicals, radiation damage to DNA multidimensional gas chromotograph for toxological analyses, research excellence fund. Total annual research expenditures: $472,159. *Unit head:* Dr. Mark W. Severson, Chair, 248-370-2327, Fax: 248-370-2321, E-mail: severson@oakland.edu. *Application contact:* Dr. Kathleen W. Moore, Coordinator, 248-370-2338, Fax: 248-370-2321, E-mail: kmoore@oakland.edu.

OGI School of Science & Engineering at Oregon Health & Science University, Graduate Studies, Department of Environmental and Biomolecular Systems, Program in Environmental Science and Engineering, Beaverton, OR 97006-8921. Offers MS, PhD. *Entrance requirements:* For master's and doctorate, GRE General Test. Additional exam requirements/recommendations for international students: Required—TOEFL (minimum score 600 paper-based; 250 computer-based).

See in-depth description on page 739.

The Ohio State University, Graduate School, College of Biological Sciences, Program in Environmental Science, Columbus, OH 43210. Offers MS, PhD. *Faculty:* 89. *Students:* 44 full-time (28 women), 9 part-time (3 women); includes 7 minority (1 African American, 6 Hispanic Americans), 19 international. 157 applicants, 25% accepted. In 2003, 15 master's, 7 doctorates awarded. *Degree requirements:* For master's, one foreign language, thesis optional; for doctorate, one foreign language, thesis/dissertation. *Entrance requirements:* For master's and doctorate, GRE General Test. *Application deadline:* For fall admission, 8/15 for domestic students. Applications are processed on a rolling basis. Application fee: $40 ($50 for international students). *Expenses:* Tuition, state resident: full-time $7,233. Tuition, nonresident: full-time $18,489. *Financial support:* Fellowships, research assistantships, teaching assistantships, Federal Work-Study and institutionally sponsored loans available. Support available to part-time students. *Unit head:* Dr. Mohan K. Wali, Director, 614-292-9814, E-mail: wali.1@osu.edu. *Application contact:* Dr. Anand Desai, Graduate Studies Committee Chair, 614-292-9814, E-mail: desai.1@osu.edu.

Ohio University, Graduate Studies, College of Arts and Sciences, Program in Environmental Studies, Athens, OH 45701-2979. Offers MS. Part-time programs available. *Students:* 42 full-time (24 women), 10 part-time (6 women), 20 international. Average age 28. 52 applicants, 65% accepted, 16 enrolled. In 2003, 9 degrees awarded. *Median time to degree:* Master's–2 years full-time. *Degree requirements:* For master's, thesis (for some programs), written exams (if no thesis), research project, comprehensive exam (for some programs), registration. *Entrance requirements:* For master's, minimum GPA of 3.0. Additional exam requirements/recommendations for international students: Required—TOEFL (minimum score 600 paper-based; 250 computer-based). *Application deadline:* For fall admission, 1/1 for domestic students; for winter admission, 10/1 for domestic students; for spring admission, 2/1 for domestic students. Application fee: $45. *Expenses:* Tuition, state resident: full-time $2,651; part-time $328 per credit. Tuition, nonresident: full-time $5,095; part-time $632 per credit. Tuition and fees vary according to program. *Financial support:* In 2003–04, 24 students received support, including research assistantships with tuition reimbursements available (averaging $9,810 per year), 5 teaching assistantships with tuition reimbursements available (averaging $9,810 per year); fellowships with tuition reimbursements available, career-related internships or fieldwork, Federal Work-Study, institutionally sponsored loans, scholarships/grants, tuition waivers (full), and unspecified assistantships also available. Financial award application deadline: 1/1. *Faculty research:* Air quality modeling, conservation biology, environmental policy, geographical information sytems, land management and watershed restoration. *Unit head:* Dr. Gene Mapes, Director, 740-593-9526, Fax: 740-593-0924, E-mail: mapesg@ohio.edu.

Oklahoma State University, Graduate College, Program in Environmental Sciences, Stillwater, OK 74078. Offers MS, PhD. *Degree requirements:* For master's and doctorate, thesis/dissertation. *Entrance requirements:* For master's and doctorate, GRE, minimum GPA of 3.0. Additional exam requirements/recommendations for international students: Required—TOEFL. *Application deadline:* For fall admission, 7/1 for domestic students. Applications are processed on a rolling basis. Application fee: $25 ($50 for international students). Electronic applications accepted. *Expenses:* Tuition, state resident: full-time $3,752; part-time $118 per credit hour. Tuition, nonresident: full-time $10,346; part-time $393 per credit hour. Tuition and fees vary according to course load. *Financial support:* Research assistantships, teaching assistantships, tuition waivers (partial) available. Support available to part-time students. Financial award application deadline: 3/1. *Unit head:* Dr. Will Focht, Director, 405-744-9994.

Oregon State University, Graduate School, College of Agricultural Sciences, Department of Environmental and Molecular Toxicology, Corvallis, OR 97331. Offers toxicology (MS, PhD). Application fee: $50. *Expenses:* Tuition, state resident: full-time $8,139; part-time $301 per credit. Tuition, nonresident: full-time $14,376; part-time $532 per credit. Required fees: $1,227. *Unit head:* Dr. Lawrence R. Curtis, Head, 541-737-1764, Fax: 541-737-0497, E-mail: larry.curtis@orst.edu.

Oregon State University, Graduate School, College of Science, Program in Environmental Sciences, Corvallis, OR 97331. Offers MA, MS, PhD. Application fee: $50. *Expenses:* Tuition, state resident: full-time $8,139; part-time $301 per credit. Tuition, nonresident: full-time $14,376; part-time $532 per credit. Required fees: $1,227. *Unit head:* Dr. Kate Lajtha, Interim Director, 541-737-1745.

Pace University, White Plains Campus, Dyson College of Arts and Sciences, Program in Environmental Science, White Plains, NY 10606. Offers MS. *Faculty:* 7 full-time (3 women), 4 part-time/adjunct (0 women). *Students:* 3 full-time (2 women), 2 part-time (1 woman); includes 1 minority (African American), 1 international. Average age 31. 22 applicants, 55% accepted, 5 enrolled. In 2003, 5 degrees awarded. *Degree requirements:* For master's, research project. *Entrance requirements:* For master's, GRE. *Application deadline:* For fall admission, 8/1 for domestic students; for spring admission, 12/1 priority date for domestic students. Applications are processed on a rolling basis. Application fee: $65. Electronic applications accepted. *Expenses:* Tuition: Part-time $710 per credit. Tuition and fees vary according to course load and program. *Unit head:* Dr. Ellen Weiser, Director, 914-773-3656, E-mail: eweiser@pace.edu. *Application contact:* Joanna Broda, Director of Admissions, 914-422-4283, Fax: 914-422-4287, E-mail: gradwp@pace.edu.

See in-depth description on page 741.

The Pennsylvania State University Harrisburg Campus of the Capital College, Graduate School, School of Science, Engineering and Technology, Program in Environmental Pollution Control, Middletown, PA 17057-4898. Offers M Eng, MEPC, MS. Evening/weekend programs available. *Students:* 10 full-time (3 women), 16 part-time (5 women); includes 2 minority (1 African American, 1 Asian American or Pacific Islander), 3 international. Average age 33. *Degree requirements:* For master's, thesis. *Entrance requirements:* For master's, GRE General Test, minimum GPA of 2.75. Additional exam requirements/recommendations for international students: Required—TOEFL. Application fee: $45. *Expenses:* Tuition, state resident: full-time $10,010; part-time $417 per credit. Tuition, nonresident: full-time $16,512; part-time $668 per credit. *Unit head:* Dr. Charles A. Cole, Professor, 717-948-6133, E-mail: cac7@psu.edu.

The Pennsylvania State University University Park Campus, Graduate School, Intercollege Graduate Programs, Intercollege Program in Environmental Pollution Control, State College, University Park, PA 16802-1503. Offers M Eng, MEPC, MS. *Students:* 10 full-time (8 women), 2 part-time (1 woman), 3 international. *Entrance requirements:* For master's, GRE General Test. Additional exam requirements/recommendations for international students: Required—TOEFL. Application fee: $45. *Expenses:* Tuition, state resident: full-time $10,010; part-time $417 per credit. Tuition, nonresident: full-time $19,830; part-time $826 per credit. Full-time tuition and fees vary according to course level, course load, campus/location and program. *Unit head:* Dr. Herschel A. Elliott, Chair, 814-865-1417, Fax: 814-863-1031, E-mail: haelliott@psu.edu. *Application contact:* Dorcas R. Holt, Program Assistant, 814-865-1417, Fax: 814-863-1031, E-mail: drh3@psu.edu.

Polytechnic University, Brooklyn Campus, Department of Humanities and Social Sciences, Major in Environment Behavior Studies, Brooklyn, NY 11201-2990. Offers MS. Part-time and evening/weekend programs available. *Students:* Average age 32. *Application deadline:* Applications are processed on a rolling basis. Application fee: $55. Electronic applications accepted. *Expenses:* Tuition: Full-time $16,416; part-time $855 per credit. Required fees: $320 per term.

Portland State University, Graduate Studies, College of Liberal Arts and Sciences, Interdisciplinary Program in Environmental Sciences and Resources, Portland, OR 97207-0751. Offers environmental management (MEM); environmental sciences/biology (PhD); environmental sciences/chemistry (PhD); environmental sciences/civil engineering (PhD); environmental sciences/economics (PhD); environmental sciences/geography (PhD); environmental sciences/geology (PhD); environmental sciences/physics (PhD); environmental studies (MS). Part-time programs available. *Faculty:* 8 full-time (0 women). *Students:* 77 full-time (36 women), 29 part-time (11 women); includes 6 minority (1 African American, 1 American Indian/Alaska Native, 1 Asian American or Pacific Islander, 3 Hispanic Americans), 23 international. Average age 33. 84 applicants, 71% accepted, 41 enrolled. In 2003, 12 master's, 4 doctorates awarded. *Degree requirements:* For doctorate, variable foreign language requirement, thesis/dissertation, oral and qualifying exams. *Entrance requirements:* For doctorate, minimum GPA of 3.0 in upper-division course work or 2.75 overall. Additional exam requirements/recommendations for international students: Required—TOEFL. *Application deadline:* For fall admission, 4/1 for domestic students. Applications are processed on a rolling basis. Application fee: $50. *Expenses:* Tuition, state resident: full-time $6,588. Tuition, nonresident: full-time $12,060; part-time $298 per credit. Required fees: $1,041; $19 per credit. $35 per term. *Financial support:* In 2003–04, 4 research assistantships with full tuition reimbursements (averaging $7,749 per year), 5 teaching assistantships with full tuition reimbursements (averaging $9,359 per year) were awarded. Federal Work-Study, scholarships/grants, tuition waivers (partial), and unspecified assistantships also available. Support available to part-time students. Financial award application deadline: 3/1; financial award applicants required to submit FAFSA. *Faculty research:* Environmental aspects of biology, chemistry, civil engineering, geology, physics. Total annual research

Environmental Sciences

Portland State University (continued)
expenditures: $914,700. *Unit head:* Dr. Roy Koch, Director, 503-725-4980, Fax: 503-725-3888, E-mail: kochr@mail.pdx.edu. *Application contact:* Harmony Van Eaton, Coordinator, 503-725-4982, Fax: 503-725-3888, E-mail: harmonyr@pdx.edu.

Queens College of the City University of New York, Division of Graduate Studies, Mathematics and Natural Sciences Division, School of Earth and Environmental Science, Flushing, NY 11367-1597. Offers MA. Part-time and evening/weekend programs available. *Faculty:* 11 full-time (3 women). *Students:* 8 applicants, 88% accepted. *Degree requirements:* For master's, thesis, comprehensive exam. *Entrance requirements:* For master's, GRE, previous course work in calculus, physics, and chemistry; minimum GPA of 3.0. Additional exam requirements/recommendations for international students: Required—TOEFL. *Application deadline:* For fall admission, 4/1 for domestic students; for spring admission, 11/1 for domestic students. Applications are processed on a rolling basis. Application fee: $50. *Expenses:* Tuition, state resident: full-time $7,130; part-time $230 per credit. Tuition, nonresident: full-time $11,880; part-time $425 per credit. Required fees: $66; $38 per semester. *Financial support:* Career-related internships or fieldwork, Federal Work-Study, institutionally sponsored loans, tuition waivers (partial), unspecified assistantships, and adjunct lectureships available. Support available to part-time students. Financial award application deadline: 4/1; financial award applicants required to submit FAFSA. *Faculty research:* Sedimentology/stratigraphy, paleontology, field petrology. *Unit head:* Dr. Daniel Habib, Chairperson, 718-997-3300, E-mail: daniel_habib@qc.edu. *Application contact:* Dr. Hannes Brueckner, Graduate Adviser, 718-997-3300, E-mail: hannes_brueckner@qc.edu.

Rensselaer Polytechnic Institute, Graduate School, School of Science, Department of Earth and Environmental Sciences, Troy, NY 12180-3590. Offers environmental chemistry (MS, PhD); geochemistry (MS, PhD); geology (MS, PhD); geophysics (MS, PhD); petrology (MS, PhD). Part-time programs available. *Faculty:* 7 full-time (0 women). *Students:* 15 full-time (7 women); includes 3 minority (all Asian Americans or Pacific Islanders) Average age 24. 35 applicants, 11% accepted. In 2003, 4 master's, 1 doctorate awarded. Terminal master's awarded for partial completion of doctoral program. *Degree requirements:* For master's, thesis (for some programs), comprehensive exam; for doctorate, thesis/dissertation, comprehensive exam. *Entrance requirements:* For master's and doctorate, GRE General Test. Additional exam requirements/recommendations for international students: Required—TOEFL. *Application deadline:* For fall admission, 1/15 for domestic students. Applications are processed on a rolling basis. Application fee: $45. Electronic applications accepted. *Expenses:* Tuition: Full-time $27,700; part-time $1,320 per credit. Required fees: $1,470. *Financial support:* In 2003–04, 9 research assistantships with full tuition reimbursements (averaging $12,000 per year), 5 teaching assistantships with full tuition reimbursements (averaging $12,000 per year) were awarded. Fellowships with full tuition reimbursements, career-related internships or fieldwork, institutionally sponsored loans, and scholarships/grants also available. Financial award application deadline: 2/1; financial award applicants required to submit FAFSA. *Faculty research:* Mantel geochemistry, contaminant geochemistry, seismology, GPS geodesy, remote sensing petrology. Total annual research expenditures: $1.3 million. *Unit head:* Dr. Frank Spear, Chair, 518-276-6474, Fax: 518-276-6680, E-mail: ees@rpi.edu. *Application contact:* Dr. Steven Roecker, Professor, 518-276-6474, Fax: 518-276-6680, E-mail: ees@rpi.edu.

Rice University, Graduate Programs, George R. Brown School of Engineering, Department of Civil and Environmental Engineering, Houston, TX 77251-1892. Offers civil engineering (MCE, MS, PhD); environmental engineering (MEE, MES, MS, PhD); environmental science (MEE, MES, MS, PhD). Part-time programs available. *Faculty:* 11 full-time (0 women), 15 part-time/adjunct (1 woman). *Students:* 34 full-time (15 women), 5 part-time (1 woman); includes 10 minority (6 Asian Americans or Pacific Islanders, 4 Hispanic Americans), 16 international. Average age 23. 131 applicants, 10% accepted, 9 enrolled. In 2003, 8 degrees awarded, leading to continued full-time study 50%. *Median time to degree:* Master's–2 years full-time. *Degree requirements:* For master's, thesis (for some programs); for doctorate, thesis/dissertation. *Entrance requirements:* For master's and doctorate, GRE General Test, GRE Subject Test, minimum GPA of 3.25. Additional exam requirements/recommendations for international students: Required—TOEFL. *Application deadline:* For fall admission, 2/1 priority date for domestic students, 2/1 priority date for international students; for spring admission, 11/1 for domestic students, 11/1 for international students. Applications are processed on a rolling basis. Application fee: $35. Electronic applications accepted. *Expenses:* Tuition: Full-time $19,700; part-time $1,096 per hour. *Financial support:* In 2003–04, 2 fellowships with full tuition reimbursements (averaging $18,672 per year), 20 research assistantships with full and partial tuition reimbursements (averaging $18,672 per year) were awarded. Scholarships/grants, traineeships, and tuition waivers (full) also available. *Faculty research:* Biology and chemistry of groundwater, pollutant fate in groundwater systems, water quality monitoring, urban storm water runoff, urban air quality. Total annual research expenditures: $1.1 million. *Unit head:* Dr. C. H. Ward, Chair, 713-348-4086, Fax: 713-348-5203, E-mail: wardch@rice.edu. *Application contact:* Emily J.P. Hall, Department Coordinator, 713-348-4951, Fax: 713-348-5203, E-mail: envi@rice.edu.

Royal Military College of Canada, Division of Graduate Studies and Research, Engineering Division, Program in Environmental Science, Kingston, ON K7K 7B4, Canada. Offers M Sc, PhD. *Degree requirements:* For master's, thesis/dissertation, registration; for doctorate, thesis/dissertation, comprehensive exam, registration. Electronic applications accepted.

Rutgers, The State University of New Jersey, Newark, Graduate School, Program in Environmental Science, Newark, NJ 07102. Offers MS, PhD. *Faculty:* 6 full-time (1 woman), 1 part-time/adjunct (0 women). *Students:* 8 full-time (3 women), 3 part-time (1 woman); includes 7 minority (1 African American, 3 Asian Americans or Pacific Islanders, 3 Hispanic Americans). In 2003, 2 degrees awarded. *Entrance requirements:* For master's and doctorate, GRE, minimum B average. *Application deadline:* For fall admission, 4/1 for domestic students; for spring admission, 12/1 for domestic students. *Expenses:* Tuition, state resident: full-time $10,030. Tuition, nonresident: full-time $14,202. *Financial support:* Federal Work-Study and tuition waivers (full and partial) available. Support available to part-time students. *Unit head:* Dr. Alex Gates, Program Coordinator and Adviser, 973-353-5034, Fax: 973-353-5100, E-mail: agates@andromeda.rutgers.edu.

Rutgers, The State University of New Jersey, New Brunswick/Piscataway, Graduate School, Program in Environmental Sciences, New Brunswick, NJ 08901-1281. Offers air resources (MS, PhD); aquatic biology (MS, PhD); aquatic chemistry (MS, PhD); atmospheric science (MS, PhD); chemistry and physics of aerosol and hydrosol systems (MS, PhD); environmental chemistry (MS, PhD); environmental microbiology (MS, PhD); environmental toxicology (PhD); exposure assessment (PhD); fate and effects of pollutants (MS, PhD); pollution prevention and control (MS, PhD); water and wastewater treatment (MS, PhD); water resources (MS, PhD). *Faculty:* 62 full-time (12 women), 6 part-time/adjunct (1 woman). *Students:* 50 full-time (23 women), 57 part-time (27 women); includes 7 minority (1 African American, 4 Asian Americans or Pacific Islanders, 2 Hispanic Americans), 37 international. Average age 32. 110 applicants, 11% accepted, 8 enrolled. In 2003, 9 master's, 4 doctorates awarded. Terminal master's awarded for partial completion of doctoral program. *Degree requirements:* For master's, thesis or alternative, oral final exam, comprehensive exam; for doctorate, thesis/dissertation, thesis defense, qualifying exam, comprehensive exam. *Entrance requirements:* For master's and doctorate, GRE General Test. Additional exam requirements/recommendations for international students: Required—TOEFL. *Application deadline:* For fall admission, 3/1 for domestic students; for spring admission, 11/1 for domestic students. Applications are processed on a rolling basis. Application fee: $50. Electronic applications accepted. *Expenses:* Tuition, state resident: full-time $10,030. Tuition, nonresident: full-time $14,202. *Financial support:* In 2003–04, 10 fellowships with full tuition reimbursements (averaging $19,000 per year), 34 research assistantships with full tuition reimbursements (averaging $16,400 per year), 3 teaching assistantships with full tuition reimbursements (averaging $14,300 per year) were awarded. Career-related internships or fieldwork and Federal Work-Study also available. Financial award application deadline: 1/15; financial award applicants required to submit FAFSA. *Faculty research:* Atmospheric sciences; biological waste treatment; contaminant fate and transport; exposure assessment; air, soil and water quality. Total annual research expenditures: $5.7 million. *Unit head:* Dr. Barbara Turpin, Director, 732-932-9540, Fax: 732-932-8644, E-mail: env_gradpgm@envsci.rutgers.edu. *Application contact:* Dr. Paul J. Lioy, Graduate Admissions Committee, 732-932-0150, Fax: 732-445-0116, E-mail: plioy@eohsi.rutgers.edu.

South Dakota School of Mines and Technology, Graduate Division, Joint PhD Program in Atmospheric, Environmental, and Water Resources, Rapid City, SD 57701-3995. Offers PhD. *Students:* 3 full-time (1 woman), 9 part-time (2 women); includes 1 minority (American Indian/Alaska Native), 3 international. In 2003, 2 degrees awarded. *Degree requirements:* For doctorate, thesis/dissertation. *Entrance requirements:* For doctorate, GRE General Test, GRE Subject Test. Additional exam requirements/recommendations for international students: Required—TOEFL, TWE. *Application deadline:* For fall admission, 6/15 for domestic students; for spring admission, 10/15 for domestic students. Applications are processed on a rolling basis. Application fee: $35. Electronic applications accepted. *Expenses:* Tuition, state resident: part-time $109 per credit hour. Tuition, nonresident: part-time $323 per credit hour. Required fees: $100 per credit hour. *Financial support:* In 2003–04, 5 research assistantships with partial tuition reimbursements (averaging $23,500 per year) were awarded; teaching assistantships with partial tuition reimbursements *Unit head:* Dr. Andrew Detwiler, Chair, 605-394-2291. *Application contact:* Brenda Brown, Secretary, 800-454-8162 Ext. 2493, Fax: 605-394-5360, E-mail: graduate_admissions@silver.sdsmt.edu.

See in-depth description on page 313.

South Dakota State University, Graduate School, College of Engineering, Joint PhD Program in Atmospheric, Environmental, and Water Resources, Brookings, SD 57007. Offers PhD. Postbaccalaureate distance learning degree programs offered (minimal on-campus study). *Degree requirements:* For doctorate, thesis/dissertation, preliminary oral and written exams. *Entrance requirements:* Additional exam requirements/recommendations for international students: Required—TOEFL (minimum score 525 paper-based). Expenses: Contact institution.

See in-depth description on page 313.

Southern Illinois University Carbondale, Graduate School, College of Science, Department of Geology and Department of Geography, Program in Environmental Resources and Policy, Carbondale, IL 62901-4701. Offers PhD. *Students:* 7 full-time (2 women), 18 part-time (4 women), 9 international. 31 applicants, 26% accepted, 5 enrolled. *Entrance requirements:* For doctorate, GRE. *Expenses:* Tuition, state resident: part-time $478 per hour. Tuition, nonresident: part-time $657 per hour. *Application contact:* Jean Stricklin, ER&P Program Office, 618-453-7328, E-mail: jstrick@siu.edu.

Announcement: SIU's Environmental Resources and Policy PhD Program provides interdisciplinary perspectives regarding public policy and social institutions that shape reactions to environmental issues. The degree is organized by the Departments of Geography and Geology and the College of Agriculture, in cooperation with the School of Law and College of Engineering.

See in-depth description on page 743.

Southern Illinois University Edwardsville, Graduate Studies and Research, College of Arts and Sciences, Program in Environmental Sciences, Edwardsville, IL 62026-0001. Offers MS. Part-time programs available. *Degree requirements:* For master's, thesis or alternative, final exam, oral exam. *Entrance requirements:* For master's, GRE General Test. Additional exam requirements/recommendations for international students: Required—TOEFL.

Southern Methodist University, School of Engineering, Department of Environmental and Civil Engineering, Dallas, TX 75275. Offers applied science (MS, PhD); civil engineering (MS, PhD); environmental engineering (MS); environmental science (MS), including environmental systems management, hazardous and waste materials management; facilities management (MS). Part-time and evening/weekend programs available. Postbaccalaureate distance learning degree programs offered (no on-campus study). *Faculty:* 3 full-time (0 women). *Students:* 5 full-time (1 woman), 24 part-time (10 women); includes 3 minority (2 African Americans, 1 Asian American or Pacific Islander), 5 international. Average age 33. In 2003, 8 degrees awarded. Terminal master's awarded for partial completion of doctoral program. *Degree requirements:* For master's, thesis optional; for doctorate, thesis/dissertation, oral and written qualifying exams. *Entrance requirements:* For master's, GRE General Test, minimum GPA of 3.0 in last 2 years; bachelor's degree in engineering, mathematics, or sciences; for doctorate, bachelor's degree in related field. Additional exam requirements/recommendations for international students: Required—TOEFL. *Application deadline:* For fall admission, 7/1 for domestic students, 5/15 for international students; for spring admission, 11/15 for domestic students, 9/1 for international students. Applications are processed on a rolling basis. Application fee: $60. *Expenses:* Tuition: Full-time $11,362; part-time $874 per credit. Required fees: $112 per credit. Tuition and fees vary according to course load and program. *Financial support:* In 2003–04, 5 students received support, including 1 research assistantship with full tuition reimbursement available (averaging $11,700 per year), 2 teaching assistantships with full tuition reimbursements available (averaging $18,000 per year); career-related internships or fieldwork, tuition waivers (full and partial), and unspecified assistantships also available. *Faculty research:* Human and environmental health effects of endocrine disrupters, development of air pollution control systems for diesel engines, structural analysis and design, modeling and design of waste treatment systems. Total annual research expenditures:$100,000. *Unit head:* Dr. Bijan Mohraz, Head, 214-768-3123, Fax: 214-768-2164, E-mail: bmohraz@engr.smu.edu. *Application contact:* Marc Valerin, Associate Director of Graduate Admissions, 214-768-3484, Fax: 214-768-3778, E-mail: valerin@seas.smu.edu.

Southern University and Agricultural and Mechanical College, Graduate School, College of Sciences, Department of Chemistry, Baton Rouge, LA 70813. Offers analytical chemistry (MS); biochemistry (MS); environmental sciences (MS); inorganic chemistry (MS); organic chemistry (MS); physical chemistry (MS). *Degree requirements:* For master's, thesis. *Entrance requirements:* For master's, GMAT or GRE General Test. Additional exam requirements/recommendations for international students: Required—TOEFL. *Faculty research:* Synthesis of macrocyclic ligands, latex accelerators, anticancer drugs, biosensors, absorption isotheums, isolation of specific enzymes from plants.

Stanford University, School of Earth Sciences, Department of Geological and Environmental Sciences, Stanford, CA 94305-9991. Offers MS, PhD, Eng. *Faculty:* 22 full-time (4 women). *Students:* 69 full-time (27 women), 31 part-time (11 women); includes 3 minority (1 African American, 2 Asian Americans or Pacific Islanders), 24 international. Average age 28. 102 applicants, 23% accepted. In 2003, 4 master's, 19 doctorates awarded. Terminal master's awarded for partial completion of doctoral program. *Degree requirements:* For masters, doctorate, and Eng, thesis/dissertation. *Entrance requirements:* For master's, doctorate, and Eng, GRE General Test. Additional exam requirements/recommendations for international students: Required—TOEFL. *Application deadline:* For fall admission, 1/15 for domestic students. Application fee: $65 ($80 for international students). Electronic applications accepted. *Expenses:* Tuition: Full-time $28,563. *Unit head:* Jonathan Stebbins, Chair, 650-723-1140, Fax: 650-725-2199, E-mail: stebbins@pangea.stanford.edu. *Application contact:* Graduate Admissions Coordinator, 650-725-0574.

Stanford University, School of Earth Sciences, Earth Systems Program, Stanford, CA 94305-9991. Offers MS. Students admitted at the undergraduate level. *Students:* 9 full-time (4 women), 6 part-time (3 women); includes 4 minority (1 Asian American or Pacific Islander, 3 Hispanic Americans). Average age 23. In 2003, 10 degrees awarded. Application fee: $65 ($80 for international students). Electronic applications accepted. *Expenses:* Tuition: Full-time $28,563. *Unit head:* Joan Roughgarden, Director, 650-723-3648, Fax: 650-725-0958, E-mail: rough@pangea.stanford.edu.

State University of New York College of Environmental Science and Forestry, Faculty of Environmental and Forest Biology, Syracuse, NY 13210-2779. Offers chemical ecology (MPS, MS, PhD); conservation biology (MPS, MS, PhD); ecology (MPS, MS, PhD); entomology (MPS, MS, PhD); environmental interpretation (MPS, MS, PhD); environmental physiology (MPS, MS, PhD); fish and wildlife biology (MPS, MS, PhD); forest pathology and mycology (MPS, MS, PhD); plant science and biotechnology (MPS, MS, PhD). *Faculty:* 32 full-time (3 women), 1 (woman) part-time/adjunct. *Students:* 93 full-time (53 women), 53 part-time (23 women); includes 4 minority (1 Asian American or Pacific Islander, 3 Hispanic Americans), 16 international. Average age 30. 100 applicants, 52% accepted, 25 enrolled. In 2003, 28 master's, 7 doctorates awarded. *Degree requirements:* For master's, thesis (for some programs), registration; for doctorate, thesis/dissertation, comprehensive exam, registration. *Entrance requirements:* For master's and doctorate, GRE General Test, GRE Subject Test, minimum GPA of 3.0. Additional exam requirements/recommendations for international students: Required—TOEFL (minimum score 550 paper-based; 213 computer-based). *Application deadline:* For fall admission, 2/1 priority date for domestic students, 2/1 priority date for international students; for spring admission, 11/1 priority date for domestic students, 11/1 priority date for international students. Applications are processed on a rolling basis. Application fee: $50. Tuition, area resident: Part-time $288 per credit hour. Tuition, nonresident: part-time $438 per credit hour. Required fees: $300; $5 per credit hour. $18 per semester. One-time fee: $25 full-time. *Financial support:* In 2003–04, 86 students received support, including 17 fellowships with full and partial tuition reimbursements available (averaging $9,446 per year), 41 research assistantships with full and partial tuition reimbursements available (averaging $11,000 per year), 34 teaching assistantships with full and partial tuition reimbursements available (averaging $9,446 per year); Federal Work-Study, institutionally sponsored loans, scholarships/grants, health care benefits, and unspecified assistantships also available. *Faculty research:* Ecology, fish and wildlife biology and management, plant science, entomology. Total annual research expenditures: $2.6 million. *Unit head:* Dr. Neil H. Ringler, Chair, 315-470-6770, Fax: 315-470-6934, E-mail: neilringler@esf.edu. *Application contact:* Dr. Dudley J. Raynal, Dean, Instruction and Graduate Studies, 315-470-6599, Fax: 315-470-6978, E-mail: esfgrad@esf.edu.

State University of New York College of Environmental Science and Forestry, Faculty of Environmental Studies, Syracuse, NY 13210-2779. Offers environmental and community land planning (MPS, MS, PhD); environmental and natural resources policy (PhD); environmental communication and participatory processes (MPS, MS, PhD); environmental policy and democratic processes (MPS, MS, PhD); environmental systems and risk management (MPS, MS, PhD); water and wetland resource studies (MPS, MS, PhD). Part-time programs available. *Faculty:* 8 full-time (4 women), 10 part-time/adjunct (8 women). *Students:* 40 full-time (24 women), 26 part-time (16 women); includes 4 minority (2 African Americans, 1 Asian American or Pacific Islander, 1 Hispanic American), 25 international. Average age 32. 72 applicants, 61% accepted, 19 enrolled. In 2003, 25 master's, 3 doctorates awarded. *Degree requirements:* For master's, thesis (for some programs), registration; for doctorate, thesis/dissertation, comprehensive exam, registration. *Entrance requirements:* For master's and doctorate, GRE General Test, minimum GPA of 3.0. Additional exam requirements/recommendations for international students: Required—TOEFL (minimum score 550 paper-based; 213 computer-based). *Application deadline:* For fall admission, 2/1 priority date for domestic students, 2/1 priority date for international students; for spring admission, 11/1 priority date for domestic students, 11/1 priority date for international students. Applications are processed on a rolling basis. Application fee: $50. Tuition, area resident: Part-time $288 per credit hour. Tuition, nonresident: part-time $438 per credit hour. Required fees: $300; $5 per credit hour. $18 per semester. One-time fee: $25 full-time. *Financial support:* In 2003–04, 25 students received support, including 16 fellowships with full and partial tuition reimbursements available (averaging $9,446 per year), 5 research assistantships with full and partial tuition reimbursements available (averaging $10,000 per year), 7 teaching assistantships with full and partial tuition reimbursements available (averaging $9,446 per year); career-related internships or fieldwork, Federal Work-Study, institutionally sponsored loans, scholarships/grants, health care benefits, and unspecified assistantships also available. Support available to part-time students. Financial award applicants required to submit FAFSA. *Faculty research:* Environmental education/communications, water resources, land resources, waste management. Total annual research expenditures: $237,610. *Unit head:* Dr. Richard Smardon, Chair, 315-470-6636, Fax: 315-470-6915, E-mail: rsmardon@syr.edu. *Application contact:* Dr. Dudley J. Raynal, Dean, Instruction and Graduate Studies, 315-470-6599, Fax: 315-470-6978, E-mail: esfgrad@esf.edu.

Stephen F. Austin State University, Graduate School, College of Sciences and Mathematics, Divison of Environmental Science, Nacogdoches, TX 75962. Offers MS. *Faculty:* 2 full-time (0 women), 37 part-time/adjunct (9 women). *Students:* 20 full-time (8 women), 9 part-time (6 women); includes 4 minority (3 African Americans, 1 Asian American or Pacific Islander), 6 international. 23 applicants, 87% accepted. In 2003, 3 degrees awarded. *Degree requirements:* For master's, comprehensive exam. *Entrance requirements:* For master's, GRE General Test, minimum GPA of 2.8 in last 60 hours, 2.5 overall. Additional exam requirements/recommendations for international students: Required—TOEFL. *Application deadline:* For fall admission, 8/1 for domestic students; for spring admission, 12/15 for domestic students. Applications are processed on a rolling basis. Application fee: $0 ($50 for international students). *Expenses:* Tuition, state resident: part-time $46 per hour. Tuition, nonresident: part-time $282 per hour. Required fees: $71 per hour. Tuition and fees vary according to reciprocity agreements. *Financial support:* In 2003–04, 15 research assistantships (averaging $7,066 per year) were awarded; Federal Work-Study, health care benefits, and unspecified assistantships also available. Financial award application deadline: 3/1. *Unit head:* Dr. Kenneth Farrish, Director, 936-468-4582, E-mail: kfarrish@sfasu.edu.

Tarleton State University, College of Graduate Studies and Academic Affairs, College of Sciences and Technology, Program in Environmental Science, Stephenville, TX 76402. Offers MS. Part-time and evening/weekend programs available. *Students:* 2 full-time (0 women), 4 part-time (3 women). 3 applicants, 100% accepted. In 2003, 4 degrees awarded. *Degree requirements:* For master's, thesis optional. *Entrance requirements:* For master's, GRE General Test, minimum GPA of 3.0. Additional exam requirements/recommendations for international students: Required—TOEFL (minimum score 550 paper-based; 220 computer-based). *Application deadline:* For fall admission, 8/5 for domestic students; for spring admission, 12/1 for domestic students. Applications are processed on a rolling basis. Application fee: $25 ($75 for international students). *Expenses:* Tuition, state resident: part-time $99 per credit hour. Tuition, nonresident: part-time $325 per credit hour. One-time fee: $52 part-time. *Financial support:* Research assistantships, teaching assistantships, career-related internships or fieldwork and Federal Work-Study available. Support available to part-time students. Financial award application deadline: 5/1; financial award applicants required to submit FAFSA. *Unit head:* Dr. Carol Thompson, Director, 254-968-9863.

Taylor University, Program in Environmental Science, Upland, IN 46989-1001. Offers MES. *Faculty research:* Environmental assessment.

Tennessee Technological University, Graduate School, College of Arts and Sciences, Department of Environmental Sciences, Cookeville, TN 38505. Offers PhD. *Students:* 7 full-time (3 women), 9 part-time (4 women); includes 5 minority (all Asian Americans or Pacific Islanders) 24 applicants, 33% accepted, 3 enrolled. In 2003, 3 degrees awarded. *Degree requirements:* For doctorate, one foreign language, thesis/dissertation. *Entrance requirements:* For doctorate, GRE. Additional exam requirements/recommendations for international students: Required—TOEFL. *Application deadline:* For fall admission, 3/1 for domestic students; for spring admission, 8/1 for domestic students. Application fee: $25 ($30 for international students). Electronic applications accepted. *Expenses:* Tuition, state resident: full-time $7,410; part-time $263 per semester hour. Tuition, nonresident: full-time $19,134; part-time $607 per semester hour. *Financial support:* In 2003–04, 5 research assistantships (averaging $10,000 per year), 4 teaching assistantships (averaging $10,000 per year) were awarded. Financial award application deadline: 4/1. *Unit head:* Dr. Jeffrey Boles, Director, 931-372-3844, Fax: 931-372-3434, E-mail: jboles@tntech.edu. *Application contact:* Dr. Francis O. Otuonye, Associate Vice President for Research and Graduate Studies, 931-372-3233, Fax: 931-372-3497, E-mail: fotuonye@tntech.edu.

See in-depth description on page 747.

Texas A&M University–Corpus Christi, Graduate Studies and Research, College of Science and Technology, Program in Sciences, Corpus Christi, TX 78412-5503. Offers biology (MS); environmental sciences (MS); mariculture (MS). Part-time and evening/weekend programs available. In 2003, 19 degrees awarded. *Degree requirements:* For master's, thesis (for some programs), comprehensive exam, registration. *Entrance requirements:* For master's, GRE General Test. Additional exam requirements/recommendations for international students: Required—TOEFL. *Application deadline:* For fall admission, 7/15 priority date for domestic students, 5/1 priority date for international students; for spring admission, 11/15 priority date for domestic students, 9/1 priority date for international students. Applications are processed on a rolling basis. Application fee: $30 ($50 for international students). Electronic applications accepted. *Expenses:* Tuition, state resident: part-time $58 per credit hour. Tuition, nonresident: part-time $294 per credit hour. *Financial support:* Research assistantships, teaching assistantships, career-related internships or fieldwork, Federal Work-Study, institutionally sponsored loans, scholarships/grants, health care benefits, and unspecified assistantships available. Support available to part-time students. Financial award application deadline: 3/15; financial award applicants required to submit FAFSA. *Unit head:* Dr. Grady Price-Blount, Head, 361-825-2358. *Application contact:* Maria Martinez, Records Evaluator, 361-825-5740, Fax: 361-825-2755, E-mail: maria.martinez@mail.tamucc.edu.

Texas Christian University, College of Science and Engineering, Department of Biology, Program in Environmental Sciences, Fort Worth, TX 76129-0002. Offers earth sciences (MS); ecology (MS). Part-time and evening/weekend programs available. *Degree requirements:* For master's, thesis optional. *Entrance requirements:* For master's, GRE General Test, GRE Subject Test, 1 year of biology and chemistry; 1 semester of calculus, government, and physical geology. Additional exam requirements/recommendations for international students: Required—TOEFL. *Application deadline:* For fall admission, 3/1 for domestic students; for spring admission, 12/1 for domestic students. Applications are processed on a rolling basis. Application fee: $0. *Expenses:* Tuition: Part-time $640 per credit hour. Tuition and fees vary according to program. *Financial support:* Unspecified assistantships available. Financial award application deadline: 3/1. *Unit head:* Dr. Mike Slattery, Director, 817-257-7506. *Application contact:* Dr. Bonnie Melhart, Associate Dean, College of Science and Engineering, E-mail: b.melhart@tcu.edu.

Texas Tech University, Graduate School, College of Arts and Sciences, Department of Environmental Toxicology, Lubbock, TX 79409. Offers MS, PhD. Part-time programs available. *Faculty:* 11 full-time (0 women), 2 part-time/adjunct (0 women). *Students:* 43 full-time (20 women), 5 part-time (2 women); includes 4 minority (1 African American, 3 Hispanic Americans), 18 international. Average age 29. 26 applicants, 65% accepted, 13 enrolled. In 2003, 6 master's, 2 doctorates awarded. *Degree requirements:* For master's and doctorate, thesis/dissertation. *Entrance requirements:* For master's and doctorate, GRE General Test. Additional exam requirements/recommendations for international students: Required—TOEFL (minimum score 550 paper-based; 213 computer-based). *Application deadline:* Applications are processed on a rolling basis. Application fee: $50 ($60 for international students). Electronic applications accepted. *Expenses:* Tuition, state resident: full-time $3,312. Tuition, nonresident: full-time $8,976. Required fees: $1,745. Tuition and fees vary according to program. *Financial support:* In 2003–04, 27 students received support; teaching assistantships with partial tuition reimbursements available. Financial award application deadline: 5/1. *Faculty research:* Terrestrial and aquatic toxicology, biochemical and developmental toxicology, advanced materials and high performance computing, countermeasures to biologic and chemical threats, molecular epidemiology and modeling. *Unit head:* Dr. Ronald J. Kendall, Professor, 806-885-4567, Fax: 806-885-2132, E-mail: ron.kendall@tiehh.ttu.edu. *Application contact:* Dr. Todd A. Anderson, Graduate Program Adviser, 806-885-4567 Ext. 231, Fax: 806-885-2132, E-mail: todd.anderson@tiehh.ttu.edu.

Towson University, Graduate School, Program in Environmental Science, Towson, MD 21252-0001. Offers MS, Certificate. Part-time and evening/weekend programs available. *Students:* 22. *Application deadline:* Applications are processed on a rolling basis. Application fee: $40. Electronic applications accepted. *Expenses:* Tuition, state resident: part-time $244 per unit. Tuition, nonresident: part-time $510 per unit. Required fees: $61 per unit. *Financial support:* Application deadline: 4/1; *Unit head:* Dr. Jane Wolfson, Director, 410-704-4920, Fax: 410-704-2604, E-mail: jwolfson@towson.edu. *Application contact:* 410-704-2501, Fax: 410-704-4675, E-mail: grads@towson.edu.

Tufts University, School of Engineering, Department of Civil and Environmental Engineering, Medford, MA 02155. Offers civil engineering (ME, MS, PhD), including geotechnical engineering, structural engineering; environmental engineering (ME, MS, PhD), including environmental engineering and environmental sciences, environmental geotechnology, environmental health, environmental science and management, hazardous materials management, water resources engineering. Part-time programs available. *Faculty:* 13 full-time, 10 part-time/adjunct. *Students:* 61 (28 women); includes 1 minority (Asian American or Pacific Islander) 7 international. 97 applicants, 68% accepted, 27 enrolled. In 2003, 17 master's, 2 doctorates awarded. Terminal master's awarded for partial completion of doctoral program. *Degree requirements:* For master's, thesis or alternative; for doctorate, thesis/dissertation. *Entrance requirements:* Additional exam requirements/recommendations for international students: Required—TOEFL (minimum score 550 paper-based; 213 computer-based). *Application deadline:* For fall admission, 2/15 for domestic students, 12/30 for international students; for spring admission, 10/15 for domestic students, 9/15 for international students. Applications are processed on a rolling basis. Application fee: $60. Electronic applications accepted. *Expenses:* Tuition: Full-time $29,949. *Financial support:* Research assistantships with full and partial tuition reimbursements, teaching assistantships with full and partial tuition reimbursements, Federal Work-Study, scholarships/grants, and tuition waivers (partial) available. Support available to part-time students. Financial award application deadline: 2/1; financial award applicants required to submit FAFSA. *Unit head:* Dr. Christopher Swan, Chair, 617-627-3211, Fax: 617-627-3994.

Tuskegee University, Graduate Programs, College of Agricultural, Environmental and Natural Sciences, Department of Agricultural Sciences, Program in Environmental Sciences, Tuskegee, AL 36088. Offers MS. *Faculty:* 13 full-time (1 woman), 2 part-time/adjunct (1 woman). *Students:* 5 full-time (0 women), 2 part-time; includes 3 minority (all African Americans), 2 international. Average age 28. In 2003, 4 degrees awarded. *Degree requirements:* For master's, thesis. *Entrance requirements:* For master's, GRE General Test. *Application deadline:* For fall admission, 7/15 for domestic students. Applications are processed on a rolling basis. Application fee: $25 ($35 for international students). *Expenses:* Tuition: Full-time $11,060; part-time $655 per credit hour. Required fees: $250. Tuition and fees vary according to course load. *Financial support:* Application deadline: 4/15. *Unit head:* Dr. P. K. Biswas, Head, Department of Agricultural Sciences, 334-727-8632.

Université de Sherbrooke, Faculty of Sciences, Diplôme de gestion de l'environement, Sherbrooke, QC J1K 2R1, Canada. Offers Diploma. Postbaccalaureate distance learning degree programs offered (no on-campus study).

Université de Sherbrooke, Faculty of Sciences, Program in the Environment, Sherbrooke, QC J1K 2R1, Canada. Offers M Env. *Degree requirements:* For master's, thesis.

Université du Québec à Montréal, Graduate Programs, Program in Environmental Sciences, Montréal, QC H3C 3P8, Canada. Offers M Sc, PhD. Part-time programs available. *Degree requirements:* For master's, research report; for doctorate, thesis/dissertation. *Entrance requirements:* For master's, appropriate bachelor's degree or equivalent, proficiency in French; for doctorate, appropriate master's degree or equivalent, proficiency in French.

Environmental Sciences

Université du Québec à Trois-Rivières, Graduate Programs, Program in Environmental Sciences, Trois-Rivières, QC G9A 5H7, Canada. Offers M Sc, PhD. Part-time programs available. *Degree requirements:* For master's, thesis. *Entrance requirements:* For master's, appropriate bachelor's degree, proficiency in French.

Université Laval, Faculty of Sciences and Engineering, Department of Geology and Geological Engineering, Programs in Earth Sciences, Québec, QC G1K 7P4, Canada. Offers earth sciences (M Sc, PhD); environmental technologies (M Sc). Offered jointly with INRS-Géressources. Terminal master's awarded for partial completion of doctoral program. *Degree requirements:* For master's, thesis (for some programs); for doctorate, thesis/dissertation, comprehensive exam. *Entrance requirements:* For master's and doctorate, knowledge of French. Electronic applications accepted.

University at Albany, State University of New York, College of Arts and Sciences, Department of Biological Sciences, Program in Biodiversity, Conservation, and Policy, Albany, NY 12222-0001. Offers MS. *Degree requirements:* For master's, one foreign language. *Entrance requirements:* For master's, GRE General Test. Application fee: $50. *Expenses:* Tuition, state resident: part-time $288 per credit. Tuition, nonresident: part-time $438 per credit. Required fees: $495 per semester. *Faculty research:* Aquatic ecology, plant community ecology, biodiversity and public policy, restoration ecology, costal and estuarine science. *Unit head:* Gary Kleppel, Program Director, 518-442-4338.

The University of Alabama in Huntsville, School of Graduate Studies, College of Science, Department of Atmospheric and Environmental Science, Huntsville, AL 35899. Offers MS, PhD. Part-time and evening/weekend programs available. *Faculty:* 6 full-time (0 women), 7 part-time/adjunct (1 woman). *Students:* 30 full-time (13 women), 5 part-time (4 women); includes 2 minority (1 African American, 1 Hispanic American), 13 international. Average age 27. 23 applicants, 91% accepted, 10 enrolled. In 2003, 3 master's, 2 doctorates awarded. *Degree requirements:* For master's, thesis or alternative, oral and written exams, comprehensive exam, registration; for doctorate, thesis/dissertation, oral and written exams, comprehensive exam, registration. *Entrance requirements:* For master's and doctorate, GRE General Test, minimum GPA of 3.0. Additional exam requirements/recommendations for international students: Required—TOEFL (minimum score 550 paper-based; 213 computer-based). *Application deadline:* For fall admission, 5/30 priority date for domestic students, 2/30 priority date for international students; for spring admission, 10/10 priority date for domestic students, 7/10 priority date for international students. Applications are processed on a rolling basis. Application fee: $35. *Expenses:* Tuition, state resident: full-time $5,168; part-time $211 per hour. Tuition, nonresident: full-time $10,620; part-time $447 per hour. Tuition and fees vary according to course load. *Financial support:* In 2003–04, 27 students received support, including 26 research assistantships with full and partial tuition reimbursements available (averaging $12,473 per year), 1 teaching assistantship with full and partial tuition reimbursement available (averaging $12,600 per year); fellowships with full and partial tuition reimbursements available, career-related internships or fieldwork, Federal Work-Study, institutionally sponsored loans, scholarships/grants, health care benefits, tuition waivers (full and partial), and unspecified assistantships also available. Support available to part-time students. Financial award application deadline: 4/1; financial award applicants required to submit FAFSA. Total annual research expenditures: $648,082. *Unit head:* Dr. Ronald Welch, Chair, 256-961-7754, Fax: 256-961-7755, E-mail: ron.welch@atmos.uah.edu.

University of Alaska Anchorage, School of Engineering, Program in Environmental Quality Engineering, Anchorage, AK 99508-8060. Offers MS. Part-time and evening/weekend programs available. *Entrance requirements:* For master's, GRE General Test, BS in engineering. *Faculty research:* Wastewater treatment, environmental regulations, water resources management, justification of public facilities, rural sanitation, biological treatment process.

University of Alaska Anchorage, School of Engineering, Program in Environmental Quality Science, Anchorage, AK 99508-8060. Offers MS. *Entrance requirements:* For master's, GRE General Test, BS in engineering or scientific field. *Faculty research:* Waste water treatment, environmental regulations, water resources management, justification of public facilities, rural sanitation, biological treatment process.

University of Alaska Fairbanks, College of Science, Engineering and Mathematics, Department of Civil and Environmental Engineering, Fairbanks, AK 99775-7520. Offers arctic engineering (MS); civil engineering (MCE, MS); engineering (PhD); engineering and science management (MS); environmental quality engineering (MS); environmental quality science (MS). Part-time programs available. Terminal master's awarded for partial completion of doctoral program. *Degree requirements:* For master's, thesis or alternative, comprehensive exam, registration; for doctorate, thesis/dissertation, comprehensive exam, registration. *Entrance requirements:* For master's and doctorate, GRE General Test. Additional exam requirements/recommendations for international students: Required—TOEFL (minimum score 575 paper-based). Electronic applications accepted. *Faculty research:* Soils, structures, culvert thawing with solar power, pavement drainage, contaminant hydrogeology.

University of Alberta, Faculty of Graduate Studies and Research, Department of Civil and Environmental Engineering, Edmonton, AB T6G 2E1, Canada. Offers construction engineering and management (M Eng, M Sc, PhD); environmental engineering (M Eng, M Sc, PhD); environmental science (M Sc, PhD); geoenvironmental engineering (M Eng, M Sc, PhD); geotechnical engineering (M Eng, M Sc, PhD); mining engineering (M Eng, M Sc, PhD); petroleum engineering (M Eng, M Sc, PhD); structural engineering (M Eng, M Sc, PhD); water resources (M Eng, M Sc, PhD). Part-time programs available. Postbaccalaureate distance learning degree programs offered (minimal on-campus study). *Faculty:* 44 full-time (3 women), 2 part-time/adjunct (0 women). *Students:* 215 full-time (49 women), 99 part-time (19 women). 1,428 applicants, 15% accepted, 123 enrolled. In 2003, 124 master's, 34 doctorates awarded. *Degree requirements:* For master's, thesis (for some programs); for doctorate, thesis/dissertation. *Entrance requirements:* For master's, minimum GPA of 3.0 in last two years of undergraduate studies; for doctorate, minimum GPA of 3.0. Additional exam requirements/recommendations for international students: Required—TOEFL (minimum score 550 paper-based; 213 computer-based). *Application deadline:* For fall admission, 6/1 priority date for domestic students, 6/1 priority date for international students; for winter admission, 11/1 for domestic students. Applications are processed on a rolling basis. Application fee: $0 Canadian dollars. Electronic applications accepted. Tuition charges are reported in Canadian dollars. Tuition, nonresident: full-time $3,921 Canadian dollars. International tuition: $7,113 Canadian dollars full-time. *Financial support:* In 2003–04, 88 research assistantships with full and partial tuition reimbursements, 134 teaching assistantships with full and partial tuition reimbursements were awarded. Scholarships/grants and tuition waivers (full and partial) also available. Financial award application deadline: 4/1. *Faculty research:* Mining. Total annual research expenditures: $6,791 Canadian dollars. *Unit head:* Dr. Dave Chan, Associate Chair, Graduate Studies, 780-492-4725, Fax: 403-492-8198, E-mail: dchan@civil.ualberta.ca. *Application contact:* Gwen Mendoza, Student Services Officer, 403-492-1539, Fax: 403-492-0249, E-mail: graduate_studies@civil.ualberta.ca.

The University of Arizona, Graduate College, College of Agriculture and Life Sciences, Department of Soil, Water and Environmental Science, Tucson, AZ 85721. Offers MS, PhD. *Faculty:* 18 full-time (2 women). *Students:* 58 full-time (28 women), 15 part-time (7 women); includes 8 minority (2 African Americans, 2 Asian Americans or Pacific Islanders, 4 Hispanic Americans). Average age 32. 29 applicants, 52% accepted, 9 enrolled. In 2003, 6 master's, 3 doctorates awarded. *Degree requirements:* For master's, thesis; for doctorate, one foreign language, thesis/dissertation. *Entrance requirements:* Additional exam requirements/recommendations for international students: Required—TOEFL. *Application deadline:* For fall admission, 3/1 for domestic students. Applications are processed on a rolling basis. Application fee: $50. *Expenses:* Tuition, state resident: part-time $196 per unit. Tuition, nonresident: part-time $326 per unit. *Financial support:* In 2003–04, 5 students received support, including research assistantships (averaging $16,000 per year), teaching assistantships (averaging $16,000 per year); Federal Work-Study, institutionally sponsored loans, scholarships/grants, and tuition waivers (full and partial) also available. Financial award application deadline: 5/1. *Faculty research:* Plant production, environmental microbiology, contaminant flow and transport. Total annual research expenditures: $2.8 million. *Unit head:* Dr. Jeffery C. Silvertooth, Head, 520-621-7228, Fax: 520-621-1647, E-mail: silver@ag.arizona.edu. *Application contact:* Judi Ellwanger, Graduate Coordinator, 520-621-1646, Fax: 520-621-1647, E-mail: ellwangr@ag.arizona.edu.

The University of Arizona, Graduate College, Graduate Interdisciplinary Programs, Graduate Interdisciplinary Program in Arid Land Resource Sciences, Tucson, AZ 85721. Offers PhD. *Degree requirements:* For doctorate, one foreign language, thesis/dissertation. *Entrance requirements:* For doctorate, GRE. Additional exam requirements/recommendations for international students: Required—TOEFL (minimum score 550 paper-based; 213 computer-based). *Expenses:* Tuition, state resident: part-time $196 per unit. Tuition, nonresident: part-time $326 per unit.

University of California, Berkeley, Graduate Division, College of Natural Resources, Department of Environmental Science, Policy, and Management, Berkeley, CA 94720-1500. Offers environmental science, policy, and management (MS, PhD); forestry (MF). *Faculty:* 62 full-time (16 women), 3 part-time/adjunct (2 women). *Students:* 165 (91 women); includes 30 minority (5 African Americans, 4 American Indian/Alaska Native, 11 Asian Americans or Pacific Islanders, 10 Hispanic Americans) 31 international. 345 applicants, 14% accepted, 30 enrolled. In 2003, 10 master's, 13 doctorates awarded. Terminal master's awarded for partial completion of doctoral program. *Median time to degree:* Of those who began their doctoral program in fall 1995, 98% received their degree in 8 years or less. *Degree requirements:* For master's, thesis optional; for doctorate, thesis/dissertation, qualifying exam. *Entrance requirements:* For master's and doctorate, GRE General Test, minimum GPA of 3.0. Additional exam requirements/recommendations for international students: Required—TOEFL; Recommended—TSE. *Application deadline:* For fall admission, 12/1 for domestic students. Application fee: $60. Electronic applications accepted. International tuition: $12,491 full-time. Required fees: $5,484. *Financial support:* In 2003–04, 10 fellowships with full tuition reimbursements (averaging $15,000 per year), 34 research assistantships with full tuition reimbursements (averaging $15,000 per year), 50 teaching assistantships with full tuition reimbursements (averaging $7,175 per year) were awarded. Unspecified assistantships also available. Financial award application deadline: 12/1; financial award applicants required to submit FAFSA. *Faculty research:* Biology and ecology of insects; ecosystem function and environmental issues of soils; plant health/interactions from molecular to ecosystem levels; range management and ecology; forest and resource policy, sustainability, and management. *Unit head:* Dr. Steven R. Beissinger, Chair, 510-642-8051, Fax: 510-643-3058, E-mail: beis@nature.berkeley.edu. *Application contact:* Sue Baumgartner, Student Affairs Officer, 510-642-6410, Fax: 510-642-4034, E-mail: espmgradproginfo@nature.berkeley.edu.

See in-depth description on page 749.

University of California, Berkeley, Graduate Division, College of Natural Resources, Group in Agricultural and Environmental Chemistry, Berkeley, CA 94720-1500. Offers MS, PhD. *Students:* 3, 2 international. 6 applicants, 17% accepted, 0 enrolled.Terminal master's awarded for partial completion of doctoral program. *Degree requirements:* For master's, exam or thesis; for doctorate, thesis/dissertation, qualifying exam, seminar presentation. *Entrance requirements:* For master's and doctorate, GRE General Test, minimum GPA of 3.0. *Application deadline:* For fall admission, 1/5 for domestic students. Application fee: $60. International tuition: $12,491 full-time. Required fees: $5,484. *Financial support:* Research assistantships, Federal Work-Study, institutionally sponsored loans, and unspecified assistantships available. Financial award application deadline: 1/5. *Unit head:* Dr. Isao Kubo, Chair, 510-642-5167. *Application contact:* Kyle Dukart, Graduate Assistant for Admission, 510-642-5167, Fax: 510-642-4995, E-mail: kdukart@nature.berkeley.edu.

University of California, Davis, Graduate Studies, Graduate Group in Soil Science, Davis, CA 95616. Offers MS, PhD. *Faculty:* 45 full-time. *Students:* 40 full-time (20 women); includes 4 minority (2 Asian Americans or Pacific Islanders, 2 Hispanic Americans), 5 international. Average age 30. 27 applicants, 67% accepted, 17 enrolled. In 2003, 3 master's, 2 doctorates awarded. Terminal master's awarded for partial completion of doctoral program. *Degree requirements:* For master's, thesis optional; for doctorate, thesis/dissertation. *Entrance requirements:* For master's, minimum GPA of 3.3; for doctorate, GRE, minimum GPA of 3.3. Additional exam requirements/recommendations for international students: Required—TOEFL (minimum score 550 paper-based; 213 computer-based). *Application deadline:* For fall admission, 1/15 for domestic students, 1/15 for international students. Applications are processed on a rolling basis. Application fee: $60. Electronic applications accepted. Tuition, nonresident: full-time $12,245. Required fees: $7,062. *Financial support:* In 2003–04, 36 students received support, including 1 fellowship with full and partial tuition reimbursement available (averaging $20,000 per year), 27 research assistantships with full and partial tuition reimbursements available (averaging $11,410 per year), 2 teaching assistantships with partial tuition reimbursements available (averaging $14,145 per year); career-related internships or fieldwork, Federal Work-Study, institutionally sponsored loans, scholarships/grants, and tuition waivers (full and partial) also available. Support available to part-time students. Financial award application deadline: 1/15; financial award applicants required to submit FAFSA. *Faculty research:* Rhizosphere ecology, soil transport processes, biogeochemical cycling, sustainable agriculture. *Unit head:* William Horwath, Chair, 530-752-6029, Fax: 530-752-5262, E-mail: wrhorwath@ucdavis.edu. *Application contact:* Noeu Leung, Graduate Staff Adviser, 530-752-1669, Fax: 530-752-1552, E-mail: lawradvising@ucdavis.edu.

University of California, Los Angeles, Graduate Division, School of Public Health, Program in Environmental Science and Engineering, Los Angeles, CA 90095. Offers D Env. *Degree requirements:* For doctorate, thesis/dissertation, oral and written qualifying exams. *Entrance requirements:* For doctorate, GRE General Test, minimum undergraduate GPA of 3.0, master's degree or equivalent in a natural science, engineering, or public health. Electronic applications accepted. Tuition, nonresident: full-time $12,245. Required fees: $6,318. *Faculty research:* Toxic and hazardous substances, air and water pollution, risk assessment/management, water resources, marine science.

See in-depth description on page 751.

University of California, Riverside, Graduate Division, Department of Environmental Sciences, Riverside, CA 92521-0102. Offers MS, PhD. Part-time programs available. *Faculty:* 47 full-time (6 women), 1 part-time/adjunct (0 women). *Students:* 19 full-time (11 women); includes 1 minority (Asian American or Pacific Islander), 6 international. Average age 28. In 2003, 3 degrees awarded. Terminal master's awarded for partial completion of doctoral program. *Median time to degree:* Master's–2 years full-time. *Degree requirements:* For master's, thesis; for doctorate, thesis/dissertation, oral and written qualifying exams. *Entrance requirements:* For master's and doctorate, GRE General Test, bachelor's degree in natural and physical sciences, engineering, or economics, minimum GPA of 3.2. Additional exam requirements/recommendations for international students: Required—TOEFL (minimum score 550 paper-based; 213 computer-based); Recommended—TSE. *Application deadline:* For fall admission, 5/1 for domestic students, 2/1 for international students; for winter admission, 9/1 for domestic students; for spring admission, 12/1 for domestic students. Applications are processed on a rolling basis. Application fee: $60. Electronic applications accepted. Tuition, nonresident: part-time $4,082 per quarter. *Financial support:* In 2003–04, fellowships (averaging $12,000 per year); research assistantships, teaching assistantships, career-related internships or fieldwork, Federal Work-Study, institutionally sponsored loans, and tuition waivers (full and partial) also available. Financial award application deadline: 2/1; financial award applicants required to submit FAFSA. *Faculty research:* Atmospheric processes, biogeochemical cycling and bioaccumulation, contaminant fate and transport in soil and water systems, environmental management and policy, environmental monitoring and risk assessment. *Unit head:* Dr. William A. Jury, Chair, 951-827-5116, Fax: 951-827-4652, E-mail: william.jury@ucr.edu. *Applica-*

tion contact: Daniel Schlenk, Admissions Committee Chair, 951-827-2441, Fax: 951-827-3993, E-mail: envisci@citrus.ucr.edu.

University of California, Santa Barbara, Graduate Division, Donald Bren School of Environmental Science and Management, Santa Barbara, CA 93106. Offers MESM, PhD. *Faculty:* 17 full-time (3 women), 3 part-time/adjunct (0 women). *Students:* 127 full-time (66 women), 6 part-time (4 women); includes 7 minority (all Asian Americans or Pacific Islanders), 16 international. Average age 25. 293 applicants, 55% accepted, 75 enrolled. In 2003, 38 master's, 4 doctorates awarded, leading to university research/teaching 50%, government 50%. *Median time to degree:* Master's–2 years full-time, 3 years part-time; doctorate–6 years full-time. *Degree requirements:* For master's, group project as student thesis; for doctorate, thesis/dissertation, comprehensive exam, registration. *Entrance requirements:* For master's and doctorate, GRE. Additional exam requirements/recommendations for international students: Required—TOEFL (minimum score 550 paper-based; 213 computer-based). *Application deadline:* For fall admission, 2/1 for domestic students, 2/1 for international students. Applications are processed on a rolling basis. Application fee: $60. Electronic applications accepted. *Expenses:* Tuition, state resident: full-time $7,188. Tuition, nonresident: full-time $19,608. *Financial support:* In 2003–04, 18 fellowships with partial tuition reimbursements, 14 research assistantships with full tuition reimbursements (averaging $11,140 per year), 12 teaching assistantships with partial tuition reimbursements (averaging $4,531 per year) were awarded. Career-related internships or fieldwork, Federal Work-Study, institutionally sponsored loans, scholarships/grants, traineeships, health care benefits, and unspecified assistantships also available. Financial award application deadline: 2/1; financial award applicants required to submit FAFSA. *Faculty research:* Hydrology, ecology, political instituting, environmental economics, biogeochemistry. *Unit head:* Dr. Dennis J. Aigner, Dean, 805-893-7363, Fax: 805-893-7612, E-mail: info@bren.ucsb.edu. *Application contact:* Graduate Program Coordinator, 805-893-7611, Fax: 805-893-7612, E-mail: gradasst@bren.ucsb.edu.

See in-depth description on page 753.

University of Chicago, The Irving B. Harris Graduate School of Public Policy Studies, Chicago, IL 60637-1513. Offers environmental science and policy (MS); public policy studies (AM, MPP, PhD). Part-time programs available. *Faculty:* 25 full-time (6 women), 12 part-time/adjunct (3 women). *Students:* 269 full-time, 7 part-time; includes 58 minority (15 African Americans, 34 Asian Americans or Pacific Islanders, 9 Hispanic Americans), 58 international. Average age 27. 722 applicants, 60% accepted, 141 enrolled. In 2003, 100 degrees awarded. Terminal master's awarded for partial completion of doctoral program. *Median time to degree:* Master's–2 years full-time. *Degree requirements:* For doctorate, thesis/dissertation. *Entrance requirements:* For master's and doctorate, GMAT or GRE General Test. Additional exam requirements/recommendations for international students: Required—TOEFL. *Application deadline:* For fall admission, 1/3 priority date for domestic students, 1/3 priority date for international students. Application fee: $50. Electronic applications accepted. *Expenses:* Contact institution. *Financial support:* In 2003–04, 149 fellowships with full and partial tuition reimbursements (averaging $11,000 per year) were awarded; career-related internships or fieldwork, Federal Work-Study, institutionally sponsored loans, and scholarships/grants also available. Support available to part-time students. Financial award application deadline: 1/3; financial award applicants required to submit FAFSA. *Faculty research:* Family and child policy, international security, health policy, social policy. *Unit head:* Dr. Susan E. Mayer, Dean, 773-702-9623, E-mail: s-mayer@uchicago.edu. *Application contact:* Maggie DeCarlo, Director of Admission, 773-834-0136, Fax: 773-702-0926, E-mail: mdecarlo@uchicago.edu.

University of Cincinnati, Division of Research and Advanced Studies, College of Engineering, Department of Civil and Environmental Engineering, Program in Environmental Sciences, Cincinnati, OH 45221. Offers MS, PhD. Part-time programs available. *Degree requirements:* For master's, thesis or alternative; for doctorate, one foreign language, thesis/dissertation. *Entrance requirements:* For master's and doctorate, GRE General Test. Additional exam requirements/recommendations for international students: Required—TOEFL (minimum score 580 paper-based; 237 computer-based). Electronic applications accepted.

University of Colorado at Colorado Springs, Graduate School, College of Letters, Arts and Sciences, Department of Geography and Environmental Studies, Colorado Springs, CO 80918. Offers MA. *Faculty:* 6 full-time (1 woman), 1 part-time/adjunct (0 women). *Students:* 10 full-time (7 women), 9 part-time (3 women). Average age 39. In 2003, 3 degrees awarded. *Expenses:* Tuition, state resident: full-time $3,745; part-time $226 per semester hour. Tuition, nonresident: full-time $13,602; part-time $804 per semester hour. Required fees: $19 per semester hour. $135 per semester. One-time fee: $40 full-time. Tuition and fees vary according to course load and program. *Unit head:* Dr. Steve Jennings, Chair, 719-262-4056.

University of Colorado at Denver, Graduate School, College of Liberal Arts and Sciences, Program in Environmental Science, Denver, CO 80217-3364. Offers MS. Part-time and evening/weekend programs available. *Students:* 19 full-time (10 women), 20 part-time (10 women); includes 7 minority (1 African American, 2 Asian Americans or Pacific Islanders, 4 Hispanic Americans), 6 international. Average age 30. 14 applicants, 71% accepted, 7 enrolled. In 2003, 4 degrees awarded. *Degree requirements:* For master's, thesis or alternative. *Entrance requirements:* For master's, GRE General Test. *Application deadline:* For fall admission, 4/1 for domestic students; for spring admission, 10/15 for domestic students. Applications are processed on a rolling basis. Application fee: $50 ($60 for international students). Electronic applications accepted. *Expenses:* Tuition, state resident: part-time $255 per credit hour. Tuition, nonresident: part-time $1,025 per credit hour. *Financial support:* Research assistantships, teaching assistantships, Federal Work-Study available. Financial award application deadline: 3/1; financial award applicants required to submit FAFSA. Total annual research expenditures: $147,543. *Unit head:* John Wyckoff, Associate Professor, 303-556-2590, Fax: 303-556-6197, E-mail: jwyckoff@carbon.cudenver.edu. *Application contact:* Rosemary Wormington, Coordinator, 303-556-4520, Fax: 303-556-4292, E-mail: fworming@carbon.cudenver.edu.

University of Guam, Graduate School and Research, College of Arts and Sciences, Program in Environmental Science, Mangilao, GU 96923. Offers MS. Part-time programs available. *Degree requirements:* For master's, thesis. *Entrance requirements:* For master's, GRE General Test. Additional exam requirements/recommendations for international students: Required—TOEFL. *Faculty research:* Water resources, ecology, karst formations, hydrogeology, meteorology.

University of Guelph, Graduate Program Services, Ontario Agricultural College, Department of Land Resource Science, Guelph, ON N1G 2W1, Canada. Offers atmospheric science (M Sc, PhD); environmental and agricultural earth sciences (M Sc, PhD); land resources management (M Sc, PhD); soil science (M Sc, PhD). Part-time programs available. *Faculty:* 19 full-time (5 women), 3 part-time/adjunct (0 women). *Students:* 47 full-time (24 women), 3 part-time; includes 1 African American, 6 Asian Americans or Pacific Islanders, 2 Hispanic Americans, 2 international. Average age 28. 24 applicants, 46% accepted. In 2003, 9 master's, 4 doctorates awarded. *Degree requirements:* For master's and doctorate, thesis/dissertation. *Entrance requirements:* For master's, minimum B- average during previous 2 years; for doctorate, minimum B average during previous 2 years. Additional exam requirements/recommendations for international students: Required—TOEFL (minimum score 550 paper-based; 213 computer-based). *Application deadline:* For fall admission, 7/1 priority date for domestic students, 5/1 priority date for international students; for winter admission, 10/1 for domestic students; for spring admission, 3/1 for domestic students. Applications are processed on a rolling basis. Application fee: $75 Canadian dollars. Electronic applications accepted. Tuition and fees charges are reported in Canadian dollars. Tuition, nonresident: full-time $3,440 Canadian dollars. International tuition: $5,432 Canadian dollars full-time. Required fees: $753 Canadian dollars. *Financial support:* In 2003–04, 30 students received support, including 40 research assistantships (averaging $16,500 Canadian dollars per year), 15 teaching assistantships (averaging $3,800 Canadian dollars per year); fellowships, scholarships/grants also available. *Faculty research:* Soil science, environmental earth science, land resource management. Total annual research expenditures: $2.1 million Canadian dollars. *Unit head:* Dr. S. Hilts, Chairman, 519-824-4120 Ext. 52447, Fax: 519-824-5730, E-mail: shilts@uoguelph.ca. *Application contact:* Dr. T. J. Gillespie, Graduate Coordinator, 519-824-4120 Ext. 54276, Fax: 519-824-5730, E-mail: tgillesp@lrs.uoguelph.ca.

University of Houston–Clear Lake, School of Science and Computer Engineering, Program in Environmental Science, Houston, TX 77058-1098. Offers MS. Part-time and evening/weekend programs available. *Students:* 8 full-time (4 women), 37 part-time (20 women); includes 11 minority (5 African Americans, 1 American Indian/Alaska Native, 1 Asian American or Pacific Islander, 4 Hispanic Americans). Average age 32. In 2003, 16 degrees awarded. *Entrance requirements:* For master's, GRE General Test. Additional exam requirements/recommendations for international students: Required—TOEFL (minimum score 550 paper-based; 213 computer-based). *Application deadline:* For fall admission, 8/1 for domestic students, 6/1 for international students; for spring admission, 12/1 for domestic students, 10/1 for international students. Applications are processed on a rolling basis. Application fee: $35 ($75 for international students). *Expenses:* Tuition, state resident: full-time $2,484; part-time $414 per course. Tuition, nonresident: full-time $6,318; part-time $1,053 per course. Required fees: $12 per course. $199 per semester. *Financial support:* In 2003–04, 1 teaching assistantship was awarded; fellowships, research assistantships, career-related internships or fieldwork, Federal Work-Study, institutionally sponsored loans, and scholarships/grants also available. Support available to part-time students. Financial award application deadline: 5/1; financial award applicants required to submit FAFSA. *Unit head:* Dr. Theron Sage, Chair, 281-283-3770, Fax: 281-283-3776, E-mail: sage@cl.uh.edu. *Application contact:* Dr. Robert Ferebee, Associate Dean, 281-283-3700, Fax: 281-283-3707, E-mail: ferebee@cl.uh.edu.

University of Idaho, College of Graduate Studies, Program in Environmental Science, Moscow, ID 83844-2282. Offers MS. *Students:* 40 full-time (18 women), 24 part-time (9 women); includes 1 minority (Asian American or Pacific Islander), 11 international. Average age 27. *Application deadline:* For fall admission, 8/1 for domestic students; for spring admission, 12/15 for domestic students. Applications are processed on a rolling basis. Application fee: $55 ($60 for international students). *Expenses:* Tuition, state resident: full-time $3,348. Tuition, nonresident: full-time $10,740. Required fees: $540. *Financial support:* Research assistantships, teaching assistantships available. Financial award application deadline: 2/15. *Unit head:* Dr. Margrit von Braun, Associate Dean of the College of Graduate Studies, 208-885-6243, Fax: 208-885-6198, E-mail: uigrad@uidaho.edu.

See in-depth description on page 761.

University of Illinois at Urbana–Champaign, Graduate College, College of Agricultural, Consumer and Environmental Sciences, Department of Natural Resources and Environmental Science, Champaign, IL 61820. Offers MS, PhD. *Faculty:* 47 full-time (5 women), 1 part-time/adjunct (0 women). *Students:* 130 full-time (54 women); includes 5 minority (2 Asian Americans or Pacific Islanders, 3 Hispanic Americans), 38 international. 138 applicants, 22% accepted, 26 enrolled. In 2003, 24 master's, 8 doctorates awarded. *Degree requirements:* For master's and doctorate, thesis/dissertation. *Entrance requirements:* For master's and doctorate, GRE, minimum GPA of 3.0. *Application deadline:* For fall admission, 2/1 for domestic students. Applications are processed on a rolling basis. Application fee: $40 ($50 for international students). Electronic applications accepted. *Expenses:* Tuition, state resident: full-time $6,692. Tuition, nonresident: full-time $18,692. *Financial support:* In 2003–04, 7 fellowships, 79 research assistantships, 10 teaching assistantships were awarded. Tuition waivers (full and partial) also available. Financial award application deadline: 2/15. *Unit head:* Wesley M. Jarrell, Head, 217-333-2770, Fax: 217-244-3219. *Application contact:* Mary Lowry, Resident Specialist, 217-244-5761, Fax: 217-244-3219, E-mail: lowry@uiuc.edu.

University of Illinois at Urbana–Champaign, Graduate College, College of Engineering, Department of Civil and Environmental Engineering, Program in Civil and Environmental Engineering, Champaign, IL 61820. Offers environmental engineering (MS, PhD); environmental science (MS, PhD). *Students:* 70 full-time (29 women); includes 5 minority (4 Asian Americans or Pacific Islanders, 1 Hispanic American), 45 international. *Degree requirements:* For master's, thesis or alternative; for doctorate, thesis/dissertation. *Application deadline:* Applications are processed on a rolling basis. Application fee: $40 ($50 for international students). Electronic applications accepted. *Expenses:* Tuition, state resident: full-time $6,692. Tuition, nonresident: full-time $18,692. *Financial support:* Application deadline: 2/15. *Unit head:* Mark Rood, Coordinator, 217-333-6963, Fax: 217-333-9464, E-mail: m-rood@uiuc.edu. *Application contact:* Dr. Frederick V. Lawrence, Director of Graduate Studies, 217-333-6928, Fax: 217-333-9464, E-mail: flawrenc@uiuc.edu.

University of Kansas, Graduate School, School of Engineering, Department of Civil, Environmental, and Architectural Engineering, Lawrence, KS 66045. Offers architectural engineering (MS); civil engineering (MCE, MS, DE, PhD); construction management (MCM); environmental engineering (MS, PhD); environmental science (MS, PhD); water resources science (MS). Part-time and evening/weekend programs available. *Faculty:* 27. *Students:* 42 full-time (12 women), 108 part-time (28 women); includes 5 minority (2 African Americans, 2 American Indian/Alaska Native, 1 Hispanic American), 25 international. Average age 30. 119 applicants, 48% accepted, 30 enrolled. In 2003, 31 master's, 3 doctorates awarded. *Degree requirements:* For master's, thesis or alternative, exam; for doctorate, thesis/dissertation, comprehensive exam. *Entrance requirements:* For master's, GRE, minimum GPA of 3.0; for doctorate, GRE, minimum GPA of 3.5. Additional exam requirements/recommendations for international students: Required—TOEFL, Michigan English Language Assessment Battery. *Application deadline:* For fall admission, 7/1 for domestic students, 7/1 for international students; for spring admission, 12/1 for domestic students, 12/1 for international students. Applications are processed on a rolling basis. Application fee: $55 ($60 for international students). Electronic applications accepted. *Expenses:* Tuition, state resident: full-time $3,745. Tuition, nonresident: full-time $10,075. Required fees: $574. *Financial support:* In 2003–04, 18 research assistantships with full and partial tuition reimbursements (averaging $11,073 per year), 10 teaching assistantships with full and partial tuition reimbursements (averaging $9,540 per year) were awarded. Fellowships, career-related internships or fieldwork also available. Financial award application deadline: 4/1. *Faculty research:* Structures (fracture mechanics), transportation, environmental health, water resources, engineering materials. Total annual research expenditures: $2.2 million. *Unit head:* Thomas E. Mulinazzi, Chair, 785-864-3766, Fax: 785-864-5631, E-mail: tomm@ku.edu. *Application contact:* Bruce McEnroe, Graduate Director, E-mail: mcenroe@ku.edu.

The University of Lethbridge, School of Graduate Studies, Lethbridge, AB T1K 3M4, Canada. Offers accounting (MScM); agricultural biotechnology (M Sc); agricultural studies (M Sc, MA); anthropology (MA); archaeology (MA); art (MA); biochemistry (M Sc); biological sciences (M Sc); Canadian studies (MA); chemistry (M Sc); computer science (M Sc); counseling psychology (M Ed); dramatic arts (MA); economics (MA); English (MA); environmental science (M Sc); exercise science (M Sc); finance (MScM); French (MA); French/German (MA); French/Spanish (MA); general education (M Ed); general management (MScM); geography (M Sc, MA); German (MA); health sciences (M Sc, MA); history (MA); human resources/management and labor relations (MScM); information systems (MScM); international management (MScM); kinesiology (M Sc, MA); management (M Sc, MA); marketing (MScM); mathematics (M Sc); music (MA); Native American studies (MA, MScM); neuroscience (M Sc, PhD); nursing (M Sc); philosophy (MA); physics (M Sc); political science (MA); psychology (M Sc, MA); religious studies (MA); sociology (MA); urban and regional studies (MA). Part-time and evening/weekend programs available. *Faculty:* 250. *Students:* 317 (126 women). Average age 39. 35 applicants, 100% accepted, 35 enrolled. In 2003, 40 degrees awarded. *Degree requirements:* For doctorate, thesis/dissertation, comprehensive exam. *Entrance requirements:* For master's, bachelor's degree in related field, minimum GPA of 3.0 (during previous 20 graded semester courses), two years teaching or related experience (M Ed), GMAT for M Sc (management); for doctorate, master's degree, minimum graduate GPA of 3.5. Additional exam requirements/recommendations for international students: Required—TOEFL. Application fee: $60 Canadian dollars. *Expenses:* Tuition, state resident: part-time $475 per course. *Financial support:* Fellowships, research assistantships, teaching assistantships, scholarships/grants, health care benefits,

Environmental Sciences

The University of Lethbridge (continued)

and unspecified assistantships available. *Faculty research:* Movement and brain plasticity, gibberellin physiology, photosynthesis, carbon cycling, molecular properties of main-group ring components. *Unit head:* Dr. Shamsul Alam, Dean, 403-329-2121, Fax: 403-329-2097, E-mail: inquiries@uleth.ca. *Application contact:* Kathy Schrage, Administrative Assistant, Office of the Academic Vice President, 403-329-2121, Fax: 403-329-2097, E-mail: inquiries@uleth.ca.

University of Maine, Graduate School, College of Natural Sciences, Forestry, and Agriculture, Department of Biological Sciences, Program in Ecology and Environmental Science, Orono, ME 04469. Offers MS, PhD. Part-time programs available. *Students:* 37 full-time (22 women), 22 part-time (12 women); includes 1 minority (Asian American or Pacific Islander), 6 international. Average age 30. 72 applicants, 19% accepted, 13 enrolled. In 2003, 9 master's, 2 doctorates awarded. *Degree requirements:* For doctorate, thesis/dissertation. *Entrance requirements:* For master's and doctorate, GRE General Test. Additional exam requirements/recommendations for international students: Required—TOEFL. *Application deadline:* For fall admission, 2/1 for domestic students. Applications are processed on a rolling basis. Application fee: $50. Electronic applications accepted. *Expenses:* Tuition, state resident: part-time $235 per credit. Tuition, nonresident: part-time $670 per credit. Tuition and fees vary according to course load. *Financial support:* Fellowships, research assistantships with tuition reimbursements, teaching assistantships with tuition reimbursements, career-related internships or fieldwork, Federal Work-Study, institutionally sponsored loans, and tuition waivers (full) available. Financial award application deadline: 3/1. *Unit head:* Dr. Christopher Cronan, Coordinator, 207-581-3236. *Application contact:* Scott G. Delcourt, Associate Dean of the Graduate School, 207-581-3218, Fax: 207-581-3232, E-mail: graduate@maine.edu.

University of Maine, Graduate School, College of Natural Sciences, Forestry, and Agriculture, Department of Plant, Soil, and Environmental Sciences, Orono, ME 04469. Offers biological sciences (PhD); ecology and environmental sciences (MS, PhD); forest resources (PhD); horticulture (MS); plant science (PhD); plant, soil, and environmental sciences (MS); resource utilization (MS). *Students:* 20 full-time (14 women), 8 part-time (5 women); includes 1 minority (Asian American or Pacific Islander), 2 international. Average age 31. 12 applicants, 42% accepted, 5 enrolled. In 2003, 2 degrees awarded. *Entrance requirements:* For master's and doctorate, GRE General Test. Additional exam requirements/recommendations for international students: Required—TOEFL. *Application deadline:* Applications are processed on a rolling basis. Application fee: $50. Electronic applications accepted. *Expenses:* Tuition, state resident: part-time $235 per credit. Tuition, nonresident: part-time $670 per credit. Tuition and fees vary according to course load. *Financial support:* In 2003–04, 9 research assistantships with tuition reimbursements (averaging $12,180 per year) were awarded; teaching assistantships, scholarships/grants, tuition waivers (full and partial), and unspecified assistantships also available. *Unit head:* Dr. M. Susan Erich, Chair, 207-581-2938, Fax: 207-581-3207. *Application contact:* Scott G. Delcourt, Associate Dean of the Graduate School, 207-581-3218, Fax: 207-581-3232, E-mail: graduate@maine.edu.

University of Maryland, Graduate School, Program in Marine-Estuarine-Environmental Sciences, Baltimore, MD 21201. Offers MS, PhD. An intercampus, interdisciplinary program. Part-time programs available. *Faculty:* 6. *Students:* 1 (woman) full-time, 1 (woman) part-time; includes 1 minority (Hispanic American) 4 applicants, 0% accepted.Terminal master's awarded for partial completion of doctoral program. *Degree requirements:* For master's, thesis; for doctorate, thesis/dissertation, proposal defense, comprehensive exam. *Entrance requirements:* For master's and doctorate, GRE General Test, minimum GPA of 3.0. Additional exam requirements/recommendations for international students: Required—TOEFL. *Application deadline:* For fall admission, 2/1 for domestic students; for spring admission, 9/1 for domestic students. Applications are processed on a rolling basis. Application fee: $50. Electronic applications accepted. *Financial support:* Research assistantships with tuition reimbursements, teaching assistantships with tuition reimbursements, scholarships/grants and unspecified assistantships available. *Unit head:* Dr. Kennedy T. Paynter, Director, 301-405-6938, Fax: 301-314-4139, E-mail: mees@mees.umd.edu.

See in-depth description on page 291.

University of Maryland, Baltimore County, Graduate School, Department of Biological Sciences, Program in Marine-Estuarine-Environmental Sciences, Baltimore, MD 21250. Offers MS, PhD. Part-time programs available. *Faculty:* 12. *Students:* 12 (8 women); includes 1 minority (African American) 2 international. 6 applicants, 50% accepted, 3 enrolled. In 2003, 1 degree awarded. *Degree requirements:* For master's, thesis; for doctorate, thesis/dissertation, proposal defense, comprehensive exam (for some programs). *Entrance requirements:* For master's and doctorate, GRE General Test, minimum GPA of 3.0. Additional exam requirements/recommendations for international students: Required—TOEFL. *Application deadline:* For fall admission, 2/1 for domestic students, 1/1 for international students; for spring admission, 9/1 for domestic students. Applications are processed on a rolling basis. Application fee: $50. Electronic applications accepted. *Expenses:* Tuition, state resident: full-time $7,000. Tuition, nonresident: full-time $11,400. Required fees: $1,440. *Financial support:* In 2003–04, 1 fellowship with tuition reimbursement (averaging $20,000 per year), research assistantships with tuition reimbursements (averaging $19,000 per year), teaching assistantships with tuition reimbursements (averaging $19,000 per year) were awarded. Career-related internships or fieldwork, scholarships/grants, and unspecified assistantships also available. Financial award application deadline: 1/1. *Unit head:* Dr. Kennedy T. Paynter, Director, 301-405-6938, Fax: 301-314-4139, E-mail: mees@mees.umd.edu. *Application contact:* Dr. Thomas Cronin, Graduate Program Director, 410-455-3669, Fax: 410-455-3875, E-mail: biograd@umbc.edu.

University of Maryland, College Park, Graduate Studies and Research, College of Life Sciences, Program in Marine-Estuarine-Environmental Sciences, College Park, MD 20742. Offers MS, PhD. An intercampus, interdisciplinary program. Part-time programs available. *Faculty:* 139. *Students:* 180 (94 women); includes 12 minority (2 African Americans, 1 American Indian/Alaska Native, 3 Asian Americans or Pacific Islanders, 6 Hispanic Americans) 37 international. 176 applicants, 33% accepted, 43 enrolled. In 2003, 18 master's, 17 doctorates awarded. Terminal master's awarded for partial completion of doctoral program. *Degree requirements:* For master's, thesis, oral defense; for doctorate, thesis/dissertation, proposal defense, comprehensive exam. *Entrance requirements:* For master's and doctorate, GRE General Test, minimum GPA of 3.0. Additional exam requirements/recommendations for international students: Required—TOEFL. *Application deadline:* For fall admission, 2/1 for domestic students; for spring admission, 9/1 for domestic students. Applications are processed on a rolling basis. Application fee: $50. Electronic applications accepted. *Expenses:* Tuition, state resident: part-time $349 per credit hour. Tuition, nonresident: part-time $602 per credit hour. *Financial support:* In 2003–04, 9 teaching assistantships with full tuition reimbursements were awarded; fellowships with full tuition reimbursements, research assistantships with full tuition reimbursements, Federal Work-Study, scholarships/grants, traineeships, health care benefits, and unspecified assistantships also available. Financial award application deadline: 1/1; financial award applicants required to submit FAFSA. *Faculty research:* Marine and estuarine organisms, terrestrial and freshwater ecology, remote environmental sensing. *Unit head:* Dr. Kennedy T. Paynter, Director, 301-405-6938, Fax: 301-314-4139, E-mail: mees@mees.umd.edu.

University of Maryland Eastern Shore, Graduate Programs, Department of Natural Sciences, Princess Anne, MD 21853-1299. Offers marine estuarine (MS, PhD), including environmental science; toxicology (MS, PhD). *Degree requirements:* For master's, thesis/dissertation; for doctorate, thesis/dissertation, comprehensive exam. *Entrance requirements:* For master's and doctorate, GRE, minimum GPA of 3.0. Additional exam requirements/recommendations for international students: Required—TOEFL. Electronic applications accepted. *Faculty research:* Environmental chemistry (air/water pollution), fin fish ecology.

University of Maryland Eastern Shore, Graduate Programs, Program in Marine-Estuarine-Environmental Sciences, Princess Anne, MD 21853-1299. Offers MS, PhD. Part-time programs available. *Faculty:* 13. *Students:* 24 (16 women); includes 13 minority (9 African Americans, 2 Asian Americans or Pacific Islanders, 2 Hispanic Americans) 7 international. 16 applicants, 19% accepted, 2 enrolled. In 2003, 5 master's, 2 doctorates awarded. *Degree requirements:* For master's, thesis; for doctorate, thesis/dissertation, proposal defense, comprehensive exam. *Entrance requirements:* For master's and doctorate, GRE General Test, minimum GPA of 3.0. Additional exam requirements/recommendations for international students: Required—TOEFL. *Application deadline:* For fall admission, 2/1 for domestic students; for spring admission, 9/1 for domestic students. Applications are processed on a rolling basis. Application fee: $30. Electronic applications accepted. *Financial support:* In 2003–04, 30 students received support; fellowships with tuition reimbursements available, research assistantships with tuition reimbursements available, teaching assistantships with tuition reimbursements available, career-related internships or fieldwork, scholarships/grants, and unspecified assistantships available. Support available to part-time students. Financial award application deadline: 1/1. *Unit head:* Dr. Kennedy T. Paynter, Director, 301-405-6938, Fax: 301-314-4139, E-mail: mees@mees.umd.edu.

University of Massachusetts Boston, Office of Graduate Studies and Research, College of Science and Mathematics, Department of Environmental, Coastal and Ocean Sciences, Boston, MA 02125-3393. Offers environmental biology (PhD); environmental sciences (MS); environmental, coastal and ocean sciences (PhD). Part-time and evening/weekend programs available. *Students:* 26 full-time (18 women), 43 part-time (25 women); includes 5 minority (1 African American, 2 Asian Americans or Pacific Islanders, 2 Hispanic Americans), 17 international. Average age 35. 65 applicants, 31% accepted, 7 enrolled. In 2003, 2 master's, 2 doctorates awarded. *Degree requirements:* For master's, thesis; for doctorate, thesis/dissertation, oral exams, comprehensive exam. *Entrance requirements:* For master's and doctorate, GRE General Test, minimum GPA of 2.75. *Application deadline:* For fall admission, 2/1 for domestic students; for spring admission, 10/15 for domestic students. Application fee: $25 ($40 for international students). *Expenses:* Tuition, state resident: full-time $4,461. Tuition, nonresident: full-time $9,390. *Financial support:* In 2003–04, 7 research assistantships with full tuition reimbursements (averaging $8,000 per year), 9 teaching assistantships with full tuition reimbursements (averaging $8,000 per year) were awarded. Career-related internships or fieldwork, Federal Work-Study, and unspecified assistantships also available. Support available to part-time students. Financial award application deadline: 3/1; financial award applicants required to submit FAFSA. *Faculty research:* In situ instrumentation, benthic ecology, watershed, estuarine and coastal systems, functional mechanisms in aquatic toxicology, marine fisheries economics and management. *Unit head:* Robert Chen, Director, 617-287-7491. *Application contact:* Peggy Roldan, Graduate Admissions Coordinator, 617-287-6400, Fax: 617-287-6236, E-mail: bos.gadm@dpc.umassp.edu.

University of Massachusetts Lowell, Graduate School, College of Arts and Sciences, Department of Chemistry, Lowell, MA 01854-2881. Offers biochemistry (PhD); chemistry (MS, PhD); environmental studies (PhD); polymer sciences (MS, PhD). Terminal master's awarded for partial completion of doctoral program. *Degree requirements:* For master's, thesis; for doctorate, 2 foreign languages, thesis/dissertation. *Entrance requirements:* For master's and doctorate, GRE General Test. Electronic applications accepted.

University of Massachusetts Lowell, Graduate School, James B. Francis College of Engineering, Department of Civil Engineering and College of Arts and Sciences, Program in Environmental Studies, Lowell, MA 01854-2881. Offers MS Eng. Part-time programs available. *Degree requirements:* For master's, thesis optional. *Entrance requirements:* For master's, GRE General Test. *Faculty research:* Remote sensing of air pollutants, atmospheric deposition of toxic metals, contaminant transport in groundwater, soil remediation.

University of Massachusetts Lowell, Graduate School, James B. Francis College of Engineering, Department of Work Environment, Lowell, MA 01854-2881. Offers cleaner production and pollution prevention (MS, Sc D); environmental risk assessment (Certificate); identification and control of ergonomic hazards (Certificate); industrial hygiene (MS, Sc D); job stress and healthy job redesign (Certificate); occupational epidemiology (MS, Sc D); occupational ergonomics (MS, Sc D); radiological health physics and general work environment protection (Certificate); work environmental policy (MS, Sc D). *Accreditation:* ABET (one or more programs are accredited). Part-time programs available. Terminal master's awarded for partial completion of doctoral program. *Degree requirements:* For master's, thesis optional; for doctorate, thesis/dissertation. *Entrance requirements:* For master's and doctorate, GRE General Test. Additional exam requirements/recommendations for international students: Required—TOEFL. *Faculty research:* Ergonomics, industrial hygiene, epidemiology, work environment policy, pollution prevention.

University of Medicine and Dentistry of New Jersey, Graduate School of Biomedical Sciences, Graduate Programs in Biomedical Sciences–Piscataway, Program in Environmental Sciences/Exposure Assessment, Piscataway, NJ 08854-5635. Offers PhD. *Application deadline:* For fall admission, 2/1 for domestic students. Applications are processed on a rolling basis. Application fee: $40. *Financial support:* Application deadline: 5/1; *Unit head:* Dr. Clifford Wersel, Director, 732-932-5205, Fax: 732-932-3562.

University of Michigan–Dearborn, College of Arts, Sciences, and Letters, Program in Environmental Science, Dearborn, MI 48128-1491. Offers MS. Part-time and evening/weekend programs available. *Faculty:* 3 full-time (0 women), 2 part-time/adjunct (0 women). *Students:* Average age 34. 10 applicants, 80% accepted. In 2003, 2 degrees awarded. *Median time to degree:* Master's–2 years full-time. *Degree requirements:* For master's, thesis optional. *Entrance requirements:* For master's, letters of reference, minimum GPA of 3.0. *Application deadline:* For fall admission, 8/1 for domestic students; for winter admission, 12/1 for domestic students; for spring admission, 4/1 for domestic students. Applications are processed on a rolling basis. Application fee: $60 ($75 for international students). Electronic applications accepted. *Expenses:* Tuition, state resident: part-time $357 per credit hour. Tuition, nonresident: part-time $820 per credit hour. Required fees: $107. *Financial support:* In 2003–04, 1 fellowship (averaging $2,500 per year), 2 research assistantships (averaging $2,500 per year) were awarded. Financial award application deadline: 4/1; financial award applicants required to submit FAFSA. *Faculty research:* Heavy metal and PAH containment/remediation, land use and impact on ground water and surface water quality, ecosystems and management, natural resources, plant and animal diversity. *Unit head:* Dr. John C. Thomas, Associate Professor, E-mail: jcthomas@umd.umich.edu. *Application contact:* Carol Ligienza, Administrative Assistant, 313-593-1183, Fax: 313-593-5552, E-mail: cligienz@umd.umich.edu.

The University of Montana–Missoula, Graduate School, College of Arts and Sciences, Program in Environmental Studies (EVST), Missoula, MT 59812-0002. Offers MS, JD/MS. Part-time programs available. *Faculty:* 6 full-time (2 women), 3 part-time/adjunct (0 women). *Students:* 52 full-time (32 women), 46 part-time (25 women); includes 6 minority (1 American Indian/Alaska Native, 2 Asian Americans or Pacific Islanders, 3 Hispanic Americans). Average age 28. 104 applicants, 64% accepted, 37 enrolled. In 2003, 25 degrees awarded. *Median time to degree:* Master's–2.5 years full-time, 5 years part-time. *Degree requirements:* For master's, portfolio, professional paper or thesis. *Entrance requirements:* For master's, GRE General Test. Additional exam requirements/recommendations for international students: Required—TOEFL (minimum score 525 paper-based; 195 computer-based). *Application deadline:* For fall admission, 2/15 for domestic students, 2/15 for international students. Application fee: $45. *Expenses:* Tuition, state resident: full-time $1,848; part-time $221 per credit. Tuition, nonresident: full-time $4,880; part-time $333 per credit. Required fees: $2,200. *Financial support:* In 2003–04, 17 students received support, including 5 fellowships with full tuition reimbursements available (averaging $3,000 per year), 5 teaching assistantships with full tuition reimbursements available (averaging $9,000 per year); career-related internships or fieldwork and Federal Work-Study also available. Support available to part-time students. Financial award application deadline: 4/15. *Faculty research:* Pollution ecology, sustainable agriculture, environmental writing, environmental policy, habitat-land management. Total annual research expenditures: $147,033. *Unit head:* Thomas M. Roy, Director, 406-243-6273, Fax:

406-243-6090, E-mail: tom.roy@umontana.edu. *Application contact:* Karen Hurd, Administrative Assistant, 406-243-6273, Fax: 406-243-6090, E-mail: karen.hurd@umontana.edu.

Announcement: Interdisciplinary program emphasizing activism. Offerings include environmental science, policy law, public land ecosystem management, water issues, and environmental justice, thought, and writing. Seeks to provide students with the literacy and skills needed to foster a healthy natural environment and to create a more sustainable, equitable, and peaceful society. Accepts students from all disciplines. Web site: http://www.cas.umt.edu/evst.

University of Nevada, Las Vegas, Graduate College, Greenspun College of Urban Affairs, Department of Environmental Studies, Las Vegas, NV 89154-9900. Offers environmental science (MS, PhD). Part-time programs available. *Faculty:* 7 full-time (3 women), 4 part-time/adjunct (0 women). *Students:* 6 full-time (3 women), 25 part-time (14 women); includes 3 minority (2 African Americans, 1 Hispanic American), 3 international. 14 applicants, 43% accepted, 5 enrolled. In 2003, 3 degrees awarded. *Degree requirements:* For master's and doctorate, thesis/dissertation, comprehensive exam (for some programs). *Entrance requirements:* For master's and doctorate, GRE General Test, minimum GPA of 3.0. Additional exam requirements/recommendations for international students: Required—TOEFL (minimum score 550 paper-based; 213 computer-based). *Application deadline:* For fall admission, 6/15 for domestic students, 5/1 for international students; for spring admission, 11/15 for domestic students, 10/1 for international students. Application fee: $60 ($75 for international students). *Expenses:* Tuition, state resident: part-time $115 per credit. Tuition, nonresident: part-time $242 per credit. Required fees: $8 per semester. Tuition and fees vary according to course load. *Financial support:* In 2003–04, 3 teaching assistantships with partial tuition reimbursements (averaging $10,000 per year) were awarded; research assistantships with partial tuition reimbursements Financial award application deadline: 3/1. *Unit head:* Dr. Helen Neill, Interim Chair, 702-895-4440. *Application contact:* Graduate College Admissions Evaluator, 702-895-3320, Fax: 702-895-4180, E-mail: gradcollege@ccmail.nevada.edu.

University of Nevada, Reno, Graduate School, College of Agriculture and Natural Resources, Department of Environmental and Natural Resource Sciences, Reno, NV 89557. Offers environmental and natural resource science (MS). *Faculty:* 25. *Students:* 20 full-time (12 women), 8 part-time (5 women), 1 international. Average age 30. In 2003, 11 degrees awarded. *Degree requirements:* For master's, thesis optional. *Entrance requirements:* For master's, GRE, minimum GPA of 2.75. Additional exam requirements/recommendations for international students: Required—TOEFL. *Application deadline:* For fall admission, 3/1 for domestic students; for spring admission, 11/1 for domestic students. Applications are processed on a rolling basis. Application fee: $60 ($95 for international students). *Expenses:* Tuition, state resident: part-time $119 per credit. Tuition, nonresident: part-time $127 per credit. Required fees: $20 per term. Tuition and fees vary according to course load. *Financial support:* In 2003–04, 4 teaching assistantships were awarded. Financial award application deadline: 3/1. *Faculty research:* Range management, plant physiology, remote sensing, soils, wildlife. *Unit head:* Dr. Lewis Oring, Graduate Program Director, 775-784-6763.

University of Nevada, Reno, Graduate School, College of Science, Interdisciplinary Program in Environmental Sciences and Health, Reno, NV 89557. Offers MS, PhD. *Faculty:* 4. *Students:* 17 full-time (13 women), 8 part-time (4 women); includes 3 minority (1 Asian American or Pacific Islander, 2 Hispanic Americans), 5 international. Average age 33. In 2003, 6 master's, 2 doctorates awarded. *Degree requirements:* For master's and doctorate, thesis/dissertation. *Entrance requirements:* For master's, GRE General Test, minimum GPA of 2.75; for doctorate, GRE General Test, minimum GPA of 3.0. Additional exam requirements/recommendations for international students: Required—TOEFL. *Application deadline:* For fall admission, 3/1 for domestic students; for spring admission, 11/1 for domestic students. Applications are processed on a rolling basis. Application fee: $60 ($95 for international students). *Expenses:* Tuition, state resident: part-time $119 per credit. Tuition, nonresident: part-time $127 per credit. Required fees: $20 per term. Tuition and fees vary according to course load. *Financial support:* In 2003–04, 1 research assistantship was awarded. Financial award application deadline: 3/1. *Unit head:* Dr. Glenn C. Miller, Graduate Program Director, 775-784-6461, Fax: 775-784-1142, E-mail: gmiller@scs.unr.edu.

University of New Haven, Graduate School, College of Arts and Sciences, Program in Environmental Sciences, West Haven, CT 06516-1916. Offers MS. Part-time and evening/weekend programs available. *Students:* 6 full-time (3 women), 19 part-time (7 women); includes 1 minority (Asian American or Pacific Islander), 2 international. In 2003, 10 degrees awarded. *Degree requirements:* For master's, thesis or alternative. *Application deadline:* Applications are processed on a rolling basis. Application fee: $50. *Expenses:* Tuition: Part-time $520 per credit. Required fees: $35. Tuition and fees vary according to course load and program. *Financial support:* Career-related internships or fieldwork and Federal Work-Study available. Support available to part-time students. Financial award application deadline: 5/1; financial award applicants required to submit FAFSA. *Faculty research:* Mapping and assessing geological and living resources in Long Island Sound, geology, San Salvador Island, Bahamas. *Unit head:* Dr. L. Davis, Coordinator, 203-932-7108.

The University of North Carolina at Chapel Hill, Graduate School, School of Public Health, Department of Environmental Sciences and Engineering, Chapel Hill, NC 27599. Offers air, radiation and industrial hygiene (MPH, MS, MSEE, MSPH, PhD); aquatic and atmospheric sciences (MPH, MS, MSPH, PhD); environmental engineering (MPH, MS, MSEE, MSPH, PhD); environmental health sciences (MPH, MS, MSPH, PhD); environmental management and policy (MPH, MS, MSPH, PhD). *Accreditation:* ABET (one or more programs are accredited). *Faculty:* 34 full-time (5 women), 36 part-time/adjunct. *Students:* 153 full-time (85 women); includes 43 minority (11 African Americans, 30 Asian Americans or Pacific Islanders, 2 Hispanic Americans). Average age 26. 234 applicants, 35% accepted, 40 enrolled. In 2003, 38 master's, 13 doctorates awarded. Terminal master's awarded for partial completion of doctoral program. *Median time to degree:* Master's–2 years full-time; doctorate–4.5 years full-time. *Degree requirements:* For master's, thesis (for some programs), research paper, comprehensive exam; for doctorate, thesis/dissertation, comprehensive exam. *Entrance requirements:* For master's and doctorate, GRE General Test, minimum GPA of 3.0. Additional exam requirements/recommendations for international students: Required—TOEFL. *Application deadline:* For fall admission, 1/1 priority date for domestic students, 1/1 priority date for international students; for spring admission, 9/15 for domestic students. Applications are processed on a rolling basis. Application fee: $60. Electronic applications accepted. *Expenses:* Tuition, state resident: full-time $3,163. Tuition, nonresident: full-time $15,161. *Financial support:* In 2003–04, 120 students received support, including 44 fellowships with tuition reimbursements available (averaging $17,230 per year), 63 research assistantships with tuition reimbursements available (averaging $16,264 per year), 13 teaching assistantships with tuition reimbursements available (averaging $11,120 per year); career-related internships or fieldwork, Federal Work-Study, and traineeships also available. Support available to part-time students. Financial award application deadline: 1/1; financial award applicants required to submit FAFSA. *Faculty research:* Air, radiation and industrial hygiene, aquatic and atmospheric sciences, environmental health sciences, environmental management and policy, water resources engineering. Total annual research expenditures: $7.8 million. *Unit head:* Dr. Casey T. Miller, Chair, 919-966-1024, Fax: 919-966-7911, E-mail: casey_miller@unc.edu. *Application contact:* Jack Whaley, Assistant Registrar, 919-966-3844, Fax: 919-966-7911, E-mail: jack_whaley@unc.edu.

University of Northern Iowa, Graduate College, College of Natural Sciences, Environmental Programs, Cedar Falls, IA 50614. Offers MS. *Students:* 10 full-time (5 women), 4 part-time (2 women); includes 3 minority (all African Americans), 9 international. 11 applicants, 73% accepted. In 2003, 7 degrees awarded. *Degree requirements:* For master's, thesis or alternative, comprehensive exam (for some programs). *Entrance requirements:* Additional exam requirements/recommendations for international students: Required—TOEFL (minimum score 500 paper-based; 180 computer-based). *Application deadline:* For fall admission, 8/1 for domestic students. Applications are processed on a rolling basis. Application fee: $30 ($50 for international students). Electronic applications accepted. *Expenses:* Tuition, state resident: full-time $2,519. Tuition, nonresident: full-time $6,056. *Financial support:* Application deadline: 2/1. *Unit head:* Dr. James Walters, Head, 319-273-2573, Fax: 319-273-5815, E-mail: james.walters@uni.edu.

University of North Texas, Robert B. Toulouse School of Graduate Studies, College of Arts and Sciences, Department of Biological Sciences, Program in Environmental Science, Denton, TX 76203. Offers MS, PhD. *Faculty:* 6 full-time (1 woman), 2 part-time/adjunct (0 women). *Students:* 29 full-time (18 women), 22 part-time (14 women). In 2003, 5 master's, 3 doctorates awarded. *Degree requirements:* For master's, oral defense of thesis; for doctorate, one foreign language, thesis/dissertation, comprehensive exam. *Entrance requirements:* For master's and doctorate, GRE General Test. *Application deadline:* For fall admission, 7/15 for domestic students; for spring admission, 11/1 for domestic students. Application fee: $50 ($75 for international students). Tuition, area resident: Full-time $4,087. Tuition, nonresident: full-time $8,730. Tuition and fees vary according to course load. *Unit head:* Dr. Thomas W. LaPoint, Director, 940-369-7926, Fax: 940-565-4297, E-mail: lapoint@unt.edu. *Application contact:* Candy King, Graduate Adviser, 940-565-3599, E-mail: cking@unt.edu.

University of Oklahoma, Graduate College, College of Engineering, School of Civil Engineering and Environmental Science, Program in Environmental Science, Norman, OK 73019-0390. Offers air (M Env Sc); environmental science (PhD); groundwater management (M Env Sc); hazardous solid waste (M Env Sc); occupational safety and health (M Env Sc); process design (M Env Sc); water quality resources (M Env Sc). Part-time programs available. *Students:* 17 full-time (13 women), 6 part-time (3 women); includes 6 minority (2 African Americans, 3 American Indian/Alaska Native, 1 Asian American or Pacific Islander), 5 international. 17 applicants, 65% accepted, 5 enrolled. In 2003, 3 degrees awarded. Terminal master's awarded for partial completion of doctoral program. *Degree requirements:* For master's, oral exams; for doctorate, thesis/dissertation, oral, and qualifying exams, comprehensive exam. *Entrance requirements:* For master's, minimum GPA of 3.0; for doctorate, minimum graduate GPA of 3.5. Additional exam requirements/recommendations for international students: Required—TOEFL (minimum score 600 paper-based). *Application deadline:* For fall admission, 4/1 priority date for domestic students, 4/1 priority date for international students; for spring admission, 11/1 for domestic students, 9/1 for international students. Applications are processed on a rolling basis. Application fee: $25 ($75 for international students). *Expenses:* Tuition, state resident: full-time $2,774; part-time $116 per credit hour. Tuition, nonresident: full-time $9,571; part-time $399 per credit hour. Required fees: $953; $33 per credit hour. Full-time tuition and fees vary according to course level, course load and program. *Financial support:* In 2003–04, 8 students received support; fellowships, research assistantships with partial tuition reimbursements available, teaching assistantships with partial tuition reimbursements available, scholarships/grants available. Financial award application deadline: 3/1; financial award applicants required to submit FAFSA. *Application contact:* Susan Williams, Graduate Programs Specialist, 405-325-2344, Fax: 405-325-4217, E-mail: srwilliams@ou.edu.

University of South Carolina, The Graduate School, College of Science and Mathematics, Department of Geological Sciences, Columbia, SC 29208. Offers environmental geoscience (PMS); geological sciences (MS, PhD). Terminal master's awarded for partial completion of doctoral program. *Degree requirements:* For master's, thesis; for doctorate, thesis/dissertation, published paper, comprehensive exam. *Entrance requirements:* For master's and doctorate, GRE General Test. Additional exam requirements/recommendations for international students: Required—TOEFL. Electronic applications accepted. *Expenses:* Tuition, state resident: part-time $308 per hour. Tuition, nonresident: part-time $655 per hour. *Faculty research:* Environmental geology, tectonics, petrology, coastal processes, paleoclimatology.

University of South Florida, College of Graduate Studies, College of Arts and Sciences, Department of Environmental Science and Policy, Tampa, FL 33620-9951. Offers MS, PhD. *Faculty:* 28 full-time (20 women), 2 part-time/adjunct (both women). *Students:* 16 full-time (10 women), 12 part-time (7 women); includes 3 minority (1 African American, 2 Hispanic Americans), 2 international. 255 applicants, 32% accepted, 62 enrolled. In 2003, 9 master's, 2 doctorates awarded. *Degree requirements:* For master's, thesis optional. *Entrance requirements:* For master's, GRE General Test, minimum GPA 3.0 in last 60 hours. *Application deadline:* For fall admission, 5/1 for domestic students; for spring admission, 9/15 for domestic students. Application fee: $30. *Financial support:* In 2003–04, 9 students received support, including 2 fellowships with tuition reimbursements available (averaging $10,800 per year), 2 research assistantships with full tuition reimbursements available (averaging $8,977 per year), 5 teaching assistantships with full tuition reimbursements available (averaging $10,800 per year); scholarships/grants and unspecified assistantships also available. Support available to part-time students. Financial award application deadline: 5/1. Total annual research expenditures: $1,588. *Unit head:* Rick Oches, Interim Director, 813-974-2978. *Application contact:* Dr. Ingrid Bartsch, Information Contact, 813-974-3069, E-mail: klschrad@chumal.cas.usf.edu.

The University of Tennessee at Chattanooga, Graduate Division, College of Arts and Sciences, Department of Biological and Environmental Sciences, Program in Environmental Sciences, Chattanooga, TN 37403-2598. Offers MS. *Faculty:* 8 full-time (1 woman). *Students:* 14 full-time (4 women), 25 part-time (8 women); includes 3 minority (all African Americans) Average age 33. 22 applicants, 95% accepted, 13 enrolled. In 2003, 7 degrees awarded. *Median time to degree:* Master's–2 years full-time. *Degree requirements:* For master's, thesis optional. *Entrance requirements:* For master's, GRE General Test, minimum undergraduate GPA of 2.75. *Application deadline:* For fall admission, 8/1 for domestic students; for spring admission, 12/1 priority date for domestic students. Applications are processed on a rolling basis. Application fee: $25. *Expenses:* Tuition, state resident: full-time $2,228; part-time $764 per credit. Tuition, nonresident: full-time $6,054; part-time $2,039 per credit. *Financial support:* Application deadline: 4/1; *Unit head:* Dr. Gary Litchford, Coordinator, 423-425-1740, Fax: 423-425-2285, E-mail: gary-litchford@utc.edu. *Application contact:* Dr. Deborah E. Arfken, Dean of Graduate Studies, 423-425-1740, Fax: 423-425-5223, E-mail: deborah-arfken@utc.edu.

The University of Texas at Arlington, Graduate School, College of Science, Department of Geology, Arlington, TX 76019. Offers environmental science (MS, PhD); geology (MS); math: geoscience (PhD). Part-time and evening/weekend programs available. *Faculty:* 4 full-time (0 women), 2 part-time/adjunct (0 women). *Students:* 5 full-time (0 women), 6 part-time (3 women); includes 3 minority (all African Americans), 4 international. 4 applicants, 100% accepted, 4 enrolled. In 2003, 6 degrees awarded. Terminal master's awarded for partial completion of doctoral program. *Median time to degree:* Master's–2 years full-time. *Degree requirements:* For master's, thesis optional; for doctorate, thesis/dissertation, comprehensive exam. *Entrance requirements:* For master's, GRE General Test. *Application deadline:* For fall admission, 6/16 for domestic students. Applications are processed on a rolling basis. Application fee: $35 ($50 for international students). Electronic applications accepted. *Expenses:* Tuition, state resident: full-time $3,042. Tuition, nonresident: full-time $8,712. Required fees: $1,269. Tuition and fees vary according to course load. *Financial support:* In 2003–04, 7 students received support, including 4 fellowships (averaging $1,000 per year), 7 teaching assistantships (averaging $14,700 per year); career-related internships or fieldwork, Federal Work-Study, institutionally sponsored loans, scholarships/grants, health care benefits, and unspecified assistantships also available. Financial award application deadline: 6/1; financial award applicants required to submit FAFSA. *Faculty research:* Hydrology, aqueous geochemistry, biostratigraphy, structural geology, petroleum geology. Total annual research expenditures: $250,000. *Unit head:* Dr. John S. Wickham, Chair, 817-272-2987, Fax: 817-272-2628, E-mail: wickham@uta.edu. *Application contact:* Dr. William L. Balsam, Graduate Adviser, 817-272-2987, Fax: 817-272-2628, E-mail: balsam@uta.edu.

The University of Texas at Arlington, Graduate School, College of Science, Program in Environmental Science and Engineering, Arlington, TX 76019. Offers MS, PhD. Part-time programs available. *Students:* 12 full-time (8 women), 10 part-time (3 women); includes 2 minority (both Asian Americans or Pacific Islanders), 7 international. 15 applicants, 80%

Environmental Sciences

The University of Texas at Arlington (continued)

accepted, 4 enrolled. In 2003, 3 degrees awarded. Terminal master's awarded for partial completion of doctoral program. *Degree requirements:* For master's, oral defense of thesis, thesis optional; for doctorate, thesis/dissertation, oral defense of thesis, comprehensive exam. *Entrance requirements:* For master's, GRE General Test, minimum GPA of 3.0 in the last 60 hours coursework; for doctorate, GRE General Test, minimum graduate GPA of 3.0 in the last 60 hours of coursework. Additional exam requirements/recommendations for international students: Required—TOEFL. *Application deadline:* For fall admission, 6/16 for domestic students. Applications are processed on a rolling basis. Application fee: $35 ($50 for international students). Electronic applications accepted. *Expenses:* Tuition, state resident: full-time $3,042. Tuition, nonresident: full-time $8,712. Required fees: $1,269. Tuition and fees vary according to course load. *Financial support:* In 2003–04, 6 students received support, including 4 fellowships (averaging $1,000 per year), 2 research assistantships (averaging $15,500 per year); institutionally sponsored loans, scholarships/grants, health care benefits, tuition waivers (partial), and unspecified assistantships also available. Financial award application deadline: 6/1; financial award applicants required to submit FAFSA. *Faculty research:* Water quality, aquatic ecology, treatment systems, air quality. *Unit head:* Dr. James P. Grover, Director, 817-272-2405, Fax: 817-272-2855, E-mail: grover@uta.edu. *Application contact:* Dr. Andrew P. Kruzic, Graduate Advisor, 817-272-3822, Fax: 817-272-2830, E-mail: kruzic@uta.edu.

The University of Texas at El Paso, Graduate School, College of Science, Department of Biological Sciences, El Paso, TX 79968-0001. Offers bioinformatics (MS); biological science (MS, PhD); environmental science and engineering (PhD). Part-time and evening/weekend programs available. *Students:* 117 (44 women); includes 49 minority (4 African Americans, 2 Asian Americans or Pacific Islanders, 43 Hispanic Americans) 42 international. Average age 34. 94 applicants, 55% accepted. In 2003, 7 degrees awarded. *Degree requirements:* For master's, thesis. *Entrance requirements:* For master's, GRE General Test, minimum GPA of 3.0; for doctorate, GRE General Test. Additional exam requirements/recommendations for international students: Required—TOEFL. *Application deadline:* For fall admission, 7/1 priority date for domestic students, 3/1 priority date for international students; for spring admission, 11/1 priority date for domestic students, 9/1 priority date for international students. Applications are processed on a rolling basis. Application fee: $15 ($65 for international students). Electronic applications accepted. *Expenses:* Tuition, state resident: full-time $1,388; part-time $160 per hour. Tuition, nonresident: full-time $3,440; part-time $388 per hour. Tuition and fees vary according to course load, degree level and program. *Financial support:* In 2003–04, research assistantships with partial tuition reimbursements (averaging $22,500 per year), teaching assistantships with partial tuition reimbursements (averaging $18,000 per year) were awarded. Fellowships with partial tuition reimbursements, Federal Work-Study, institutionally sponsored loans, scholarships/grants, and tuition waivers (partial) also available. Financial award application deadline: 3/15; financial award applicants required to submit FAFSA. *Unit head:* Dr. Eppie D. Rael, Chairperson, 915-747-5844, Fax: 915-747-5808, E-mail: erael@miners.utep.edu. *Application contact:* Dr. Charles H. Ambler, Contact Information, 915-747-5844, Fax: 915-747-5808, E-mail: bioscience@utep.edu.

The University of Texas at El Paso, Graduate School, Interdisciplinary Program in Environmental Science and Engineering, El Paso, TX 79968-0001. Offers PhD. Part-time and evening/weekend programs available. *Students:* 54 (17 women); includes 17 minority (2 African Americans, 2 Asian Americans or Pacific Islanders, 13 Hispanic Americans) 27 international. Average age 34. 16 applicants, 81% accepted. In 2003, 1 degree awarded. *Degree requirements:* For doctorate, thesis/dissertation. *Entrance requirements:* For doctorate, GRE General Test, minimum GPA of 3.0. Additional exam requirements/recommendations for international students: Required—TOEFL. *Application deadline:* For fall admission, 7/1 for domestic students, 3/1 for international students; for spring admission, 11/1 for domestic students, 9/1 for international students. Applications are processed on a rolling basis. Application fee: $15 ($65 for international students). *Expenses:* Tuition, state resident: full-time $1,388; part-time $160 per hour. Tuition, nonresident: full-time $3,440; part-time $388 per hour. Tuition and fees vary according to course load, degree level and program. *Financial support:* In 2003–04, research assistantships with partial tuition reimbursements (averaging $22,500 per year), teaching assistantships with partial tuition reimbursements (averaging $18,000 per year) were awarded. Fellowships with partial tuition reimbursements, Federal Work-Study, institutionally sponsored loans, scholarships/grants, and tuition waivers (partial) also available. Financial award application deadline: 3/15; financial award applicants required to submit FAFSA. *Unit head:* Dr. Jorge Gardea-Torredey, Chairperson, 915-747-5701, Fax: 915-747-5748, E-mail: jgardea@utep.edu. *Application contact:* Dr. Charles H. Ambler, Dean of the Graduate School, 915-747-5491 Ext. 7886, Fax: 915-747-5788, E-mail: cambler@utep.edu.

The University of Texas at San Antonio, College of Sciences, Department of Earth and Environmental Sciences, San Antonio, TX 78249-0617. Offers environmental science and engineering (PhD); environmental sciences (MS); geology (MS). *Faculty:* 10 full-time (1 woman), 4 part-time/adjunct (2 women). *Students:* 32 full-time (14 women), 62 part-time (27 women); includes 17 minority (1 Asian American or Pacific Islander, 16 Hispanic Americans), 6 international. Average age 33. 41 applicants, 83% accepted, 34 enrolled. In 2003, 14 degrees awarded. *Degree requirements:* For master's, thesis optional; for doctorate, thesis/dissertation, comprehensive exam, registration. *Entrance requirements:* For master's, GRE General Test, minimum GPA of 3.0 in last 60 hours; for doctorate, GRE, resumé, 3 letters of recommendation. Additional exam requirements/recommendations for international students: Required—TOEFL (minimum score 500 paper-based; 173 computer-based). *Application deadline:* For fall admission, 7/1 for domestic students, 4/1 for international students; for spring admission, 11/1 for domestic students, 9/1 for international students. Applications are processed on a rolling basis. Application fee: $40 ($75 for international students). Electronic applications accepted. *Expenses:* Tuition, state resident: part-time $153 per hour. Tuition, nonresident: part-time $625 per hour. *Financial support:* Research assistantships, teaching assistantships available. Total annual research expenditures: $303,352. *Unit head:* Dr. Robert K. Smith, Chair, 210-458-4455.

University of Toledo, Graduate School, College of Engineering and College of Arts and Sciences, Program in Environmental Sustainability Science and Engineering, Toledo, OH 43606-3390. Offers ecology (PhD); engineering (PhD). *Faculty:* 8 full-time (2 women). *Students:* 33 full-time (9 women); includes 1 minority (Hispanic American), 26 international. *Degree requirements:* For doctorate, thesis/dissertation. *Entrance requirements:* For doctorate, GRE General Test. Additional exam requirements/recommendations for international students: Required—TOEFL. *Application deadline:* For fall admission, 5/31 for domestic students. Applications are processed on a rolling basis. Application fee: $40. Electronic applications accepted. Tuition, area resident: Part-time $3,817 per semester. *Expenses:* Tuition, state resident: part-time $8,177 per semester. Required fees: $502 per semester. *Financial support:* In 2003–04, 5 research assistantships with tuition reimbursements (averaging $16,000 per year), 19 teaching assistantships with tuition reimbursements (averaging $16,000 per year) were awarded. Fellowships, scholarships/grants, health care benefits, tuition waivers (full and partial), and unspecified assistantships also available. Support available to part-time students. Financial award application deadline: 4/1. *Faculty research:* Green engineering, phytoremediation, watershed modeling, urban environmental systems, Great Lakes ecosystem. Total annual research expenditures: $238,183. *Unit head:* Dr. Arunan Nadarajah, Interim Associate Dean of Research, 419-530-7391, Fax: 419-530-7392, E-mail: nadarajah@utoledo.edu.

Announcement: PhD in Environmental Sustainability Science and Engineering, a multidisciplinary initiative that integrates the social, physical, and biological constraints placed on an ecosystem by human activities. The program is the natural and necessary partnership in which engineers learn the science and scientists study the engineering to create a sustainable technological society.

See in-depth description on page 765.

University of Virginia, College and Graduate School of Arts and Sciences, Department of Environmental Sciences, Charlottesville, VA 22903. Offers MA, MS, PhD. *Faculty:* 28 full-time (5 women), 3 part-time/adjunct (1 woman). *Students:* 73 full-time (35 women), 2 part-time (1 woman); includes 4 minority (1 African American, 1 American Indian/Alaska Native, 2 Asian Americans or Pacific Islanders), 11 international. Average age 29. 107 applicants, 31% accepted, 16 enrolled. In 2003, 11 master's, 9 doctorates awarded. *Degree requirements:* For master's and doctorate, thesis/dissertation. *Entrance requirements:* For master's and doctorate, GRE General Test, GRE Subject Test. *Application deadline:* For fall admission, 7/15 for domestic students; for spring admission, 12/1 for domestic students. Applications are processed on a rolling basis. Application fee: $40. Electronic applications accepted. *Expenses:* Tuition, state resident: full-time $6,476. Tuition, nonresident: full-time $18,534. Required fees: $1,380. *Financial support:* Application deadline: 2/1; *Unit head:* Bruce P. Hayden, Chairman, 434-924-7761, Fax: 434-982-2137, E-mail: bph@virginia.edu. *Application contact:* Peter C. Brunjes, Associate Dean for Graduate Programs and Research, 434-924-7184, Fax: 434-924-6737, E-mail: grad-a-s@virginia.edu.

The University of Western Ontario, Faculty of Graduate Studies, Biosciences Division, Department of Plant Sciences, London, ON N6A 5B8, Canada. Offers plant and environmental sciences (M Sc); plant sciences (M Sc, PhD); plant sciences and environmental sciences (PhD); plant sciences and molecular biology (M Sc, PhD). *Degree requirements:* For master's and doctorate, thesis/dissertation. *Entrance requirements:* For doctorate, M Sc or equivalent. *Faculty research:* Ecology systematics, plant biochemistry and physiology, yeast genetics, molecular biology.

The University of Western Ontario, Faculty of Graduate Studies, Physical Sciences Division, Department of Earth Sciences, London, ON N6A 5B8, Canada. Offers geology (M Sc, PhD); geology and environmental science (M Sc, PhD); geophysics (M Sc, PhD); geophysics and environmental science (M Sc, PhD). *Degree requirements:* For master's, thesis, registration; for doctorate, thesis/dissertation, qualifying exam. *Entrance requirements:* For master's, honors in B Sc; for doctorate, M Sc. Additional exam requirements/recommendations for international students: Required—TOEFL. *Faculty research:* Geophysics, geochemistry, paleontology, sedimentology/stratigraphy, glaciology/quaternary.

University of Wisconsin–Green Bay, Graduate Studies, Program in Environmental Science and Policy, Green Bay, WI 54311-7001. Offers MS. Part-time programs available. *Faculty:* 22 full-time (4 women), 2 part-time/adjunct (0 women). *Students:* 28 full-time (14 women), 33 part-time (18 women); includes 6 minority (3 American Indian/Alaska Native, 3 Asian Americans or Pacific Islanders), 1 international. Average age 30. 50 applicants, 78% accepted, 19 enrolled. In 2003, 12 degrees awarded. *Degree requirements:* For master's, thesis. *Entrance requirements:* For master's, GRE General Test, minimum GPA of 3.0. *Application deadline:* For fall admission, 8/1 for domestic students; for spring admission, 11/1 for domestic students. Applications are processed on a rolling basis. Application fee: $45. *Expenses:* Tuition, state resident: full-time $5,996; part-time $333 per credit. Tuition, nonresident: full-time $16,606; part-time $922 per credit. Full-time tuition and fees vary according to program and reciprocity agreements. Part-time tuition and fees vary according to course load and reciprocity agreements. *Financial support:* In 2003–04, 3 research assistantships with full tuition reimbursements, 9 teaching assistantships with full tuition reimbursements were awarded. Career-related internships or fieldwork, Federal Work-Study, and institutionally sponsored loans also available. Financial award application deadline: 7/15; financial award applicants required to submit FAFSA. *Faculty research:* Bald eagle, parasitic population of domestic and wild animals, resource recovery, anaerobic digestion of organic waste. *Unit head:* Dr. John Stoll, Coordinator, 920-465-2358, E-mail: stollj@uwgb.edu. *Application contact:* Ronald D. Stieglitz, Associate Dean, 920-465-2123, Fax: 920-465-2718, E-mail: stieglir@uwgb.edu.

University of Wisconsin–Madison, Graduate School, Gaylord Nelson Institute for Environmental Studies, Environmental Monitoring Program, Madison, WI 53706-1380. Offers MS, PhD. Part-time programs available. *Faculty:* 19 part-time/adjunct (5 women). *Students:* 16 full-time (6 women), 6 part-time (2 women), 3 international. Average age 31. 55 applicants, 16% accepted, 5 enrolled. In 2003, 10 degrees awarded. *Degree requirements:* For master's, thesis or alternative; for doctorate, thesis/dissertation. *Entrance requirements:* For master's and doctorate, GRE General Test. Additional exam requirements/recommendations for international students: Required—TOEFL (minimum score 600 paper-based; 250 computer-based). *Application deadline:* For fall admission, 2/1 for domestic students, 2/1 for international students; for spring admission, 10/15 for domestic students, 10/15 for international students. Application fee: $45. Electronic applications accepted. Tuition, area resident: Full-time $7,593; part-time $476 per credit. Tuition, nonresident: full-time $22,824; part-time $1,430 per credit. Required fees: $292; $38 per credit. Part-time tuition and fees vary according to course load and reciprocity agreements. *Financial support:* In 2003–04, 14 students received support, including 2 research assistantships with full tuition reimbursements available (averaging $14,250 per year), 3 teaching assistantships with full tuition reimbursements available (averaging $11,260 per year); fellowships with full tuition reimbursements available, career-related internships or fieldwork, Federal Work-Study, scholarships/grants, health care benefits, unspecified assistantships, and project assistantships also available. Financial award application deadline: 1/2. *Faculty research:* Remote sensing, geographic information systems, climate modeling, natural resource management. *Unit head:* Thomas M. Lillesand, Chair, 608-263-3251, Fax: 608-262-2273, E-mail: tmlilles@wisc.edu. *Application contact:* James E. Miller, Associate Student Services Coordinator, 608-263-4373, Fax: 608-262-2273, E-mail: jemiller@wisc.edu.

Virginia Commonwealth University, School of Graduate Studies, College of Humanities and Sciences, Center for Environmental Studies, Richmond, VA 23284-9005. Offers environmental communication (MIS); environmental health (MIS); environmental policy (MIS); environmental sciences (MIS). *Students:* 33 full-time (25 women), 28 part-time (15 women); includes 5 minority (4 African Americans, 1 Hispanic American), 2 international. Average age 33. 24 applicants, 96% accepted, 13 enrolled. In 2003, 13 degrees awarded. *Degree requirements:* For master's, thesis. *Entrance requirements:* For master's, GRE General Test. Application fee: $30. *Expenses:* Tuition, state resident: full-time $2,889; part-time $321 per credit hour. Tuition, nonresident: full-time $7,952; part-time $884 per credit hour. Required fees: $42 per credit hour. *Unit head:* Dr. Gregory C. Garman, Director, 804-828-1574, Fax: 804-828-0503, E-mail: gcgarman@vcu.edu.

Virginia Polytechnic Institute and State University, Graduate School, College of Engineering, Department of Civil and Environmental Engineering, Blacksburg, VA 24061. Offers civil engineering (M Eng, MS, PhD); environmental engineering (MS); environmental sciences and engineering (MS). *Accreditation:* ABET (one or more programs are accredited). *Faculty:* 43 full-time (4 women). *Students:* 252 full-time (55 women), 91 part-time (25 women); includes 20 minority (6 African Americans, 11 Asian Americans or Pacific Islanders, 3 Hispanic Americans), 140 international. Average age 28. 666 applicants, 45% accepted, 102 enrolled. In 2003, 100 master's, 13 doctorates awarded. *Entrance requirements:* Additional exam requirements/recommendations for international students: Required—TOEFL (minimum score 570 paper-based; 230 computer-based), GRE. *Application deadline:* Applications are processed on a rolling basis. Application fee: $45. Electronic applications accepted. Tuition, area resident: Full-time $6,039; part-time $336 per credit. Tuition, nonresident: full-time $9,708; part-time $539 per credit. Required fees: $905; $130 per credit. *Financial support:* In 2003–04, 44 fellowships with full tuition reimbursements (averaging $7,660 per year), 65 research assistantships with full tuition reimbursements (averaging $15,727 per year), 1 teaching assistantship with full tuition reimbursement (averaging $14,298 per year) were awarded. Career-related internships or fieldwork, Federal Work-Study, scholarships/grants, and unspecified assistantships also available. Financial award application deadline: 4/1. *Faculty research:* Construction, environmental geotechnical hydrosystems, structures and transportation engineering. *Unit head:* Dr. William Knocke, Head, 540-231-6635, Fax: 540-231-7532, E-mail: knocke@vt.edu. *Application contact:* Lindy Cranwell, Information Contact, 540-231-7296, Fax: 540-231-7532, E-mail: lindycra@vt.edu.

Washington State University, Graduate School, College of Sciences, Programs in Environmental Science and Regional Planning, Program in Environmental Science and Regional

Planning, Pullman, WA 99164. Offers environmental and natural resource sciences (PhD); environmental science (MS). *Faculty:* 4 full-time (0 women), 2 part-time/adjunct (0 women). *Students:* 22 full-time (13 women), 7 part-time (2 women); includes 2 minority (1 American Indian/Alaska Native, 1 Hispanic American), 4 international. In 2003, 17 degrees awarded. *Degree requirements:* For master's, oral exam, thesis optional; for doctorate, oral exam, written exam. *Entrance requirements:* For master's and doctorate, minimum GPA of 3.0. Additional exam requirements/recommendations for international students: Required—TOEFL. *Application deadline:* For fall admission, 3/1 for domestic students. Applications are processed on a rolling basis. Application fee: $35. *Expenses:* Tuition, state resident: full-time $6,278; part-time $314 per hour. Tuition, nonresident: full-time $15,514; part-time $765 per hour. Required fees: $444. Full-time tuition and fees vary according to campus/location, program and student level. Part-time tuition and fees vary according to course load. *Financial support:* In 2003–04, 3 research assistantships with full and partial tuition reimbursements, 8 teaching assistantships with full and partial tuition reimbursements were awarded. Federal Work-Study, institutionally sponsored loans, and tuition waivers (partial) also available. Financial award application deadline: 4/1; financial award applicants required to submit FAFSA. *Application contact:* Coordinator, 509-335-8536, Fax: 509-335-7636, E-mail: esrp@wsu.edu.

Announcement: The Program in Environmental Science and Regional Planning awards the MS in environmental science and the PhD in environmental and natural resource sciences. The master's degree in environmental science is also offered at the WSU-Tri-Cities and WSU Vancouver campuses. Teaching assistantships, tuition waivers, Federal Work-Study, and institutionally sponsored loans are available. Visit the Web site at http://esrp.wsu.edu.

Washington State University Tri-Cities, Graduate Programs, Program in Environmental Science, Richland, WA 99352-1671. Offers MS. Part-time programs available. *Faculty:* 1 full-time (0 women), 53 part-time/adjunct. *Students:* 3 full-time (1 woman), 17 part-time (7 women); includes 2 minority (both Hispanic Americans) *Degree requirements:* For master's, thesis optional. *Entrance requirements:* For master's, GRE General Test, minimum GPA of 3.0. Additional exam requirements/recommendations for international students: Required—TOEFL (minimum score 550 paper-based; 213 computer-based). *Application deadline:* For fall admission, 7/15 priority date for domestic students, 3/1 priority date for international students; for spring admission, 10/15 priority date for domestic students, 7/1 priority date for international students. Application fee: $35. Tuition, area resident: Full-time $3,139; part-time $314 per credit. Tuition, nonresident: full-time $7,647; part-time $765 per credit. *Financial support:* Research assistantships with full and partial tuition reimbursements, teaching assistantships with full and partial tuition reimbursements, Federal Work-Study, scholarships/grants, health care benefits, and unspecified assistantships available. *Unit head:* Dr. Gene Schreckhise, Associate Dean and Coordinator, 509-372-7323, E-mail: gschreck@wsu.edu.

Washington State University Vancouver, Graduate Programs, Program in Environmental Science, Vancouver, WA 98686. Offers MS. *Faculty:* 7 full-time (2 women), 9 part-time/adjunct (4 women). *Students:* 12 full-time (6 women), 2 part-time (1 woman); includes 5 minority (2 American Indian/Alaska Native, 3 Hispanic Americans). *Degree requirements:* For master's, thesis or alternative, comprehensive exam, registration. *Entrance requirements:* For master's, GRE General Test, minimum GPA of 3.0. Additional exam requirements/recommendations for international students: Required—TOEFL (minimum score 550 paper-based; 213 computer-based). *Application deadline:* For fall admission, 7/15 priority date for domestic students, 3/1 priority date for international students; for spring admission, 10/15 priority date for domestic students, 7/1 priority date for international students. Application fee: $35. Tuition, area resident: Full-time $3,139; part-time $314 per credit. Tuition, nonresident: full-time $7,647; part-time $765 per credit. *Faculty research:* Conservation biology, environmental chemistry. *Unit head:* Dr. Steve Sylvester, Director, 360-546-9620.

Wesley College, Graduate Environmental Sciences Program, Dover, DE 19901-3875. Offers MS. Part-time and evening/weekend programs available. *Faculty:* 2 full-time (0 women). *Students:* Average age 30. 4 applicants, 100% accepted. In 2003, 2 degrees awarded, leading to business/industry 100%. *Median time to degree:* Master's–1.5 years full-time, 3 years part-time. *Entrance requirements:* For master's, BA/BSM in science or engineering field, portfolio. *Application deadline:* Applications are processed on a rolling basis. Application fee: $20. *Expenses:* Tuition: Full-time $5,040; part-time $280 per credit hour. Required fees: $90; $15 per course. *Financial support:* Teaching assistantships with tuition reimbursements, unspecified assistantships available. *Unit head:* Dr. Bruce Allison, Director, 302-736-2349, Fax: 302-736-2301, E-mail: allisobr@wesley.edu. *Application contact:* Arthur Jacobs, Director of Admissions, 302-736-2428, Fax: 302-736-2301, E-mail: jacobsar@mail.wesley.edu.

Western Connecticut State University, Division of Graduate Studies, School of Arts and Sciences, Department of Biological and Environmental Sciences, Danbury, CT 06810-6885. Offers MA. Part-time and evening/weekend programs available. *Faculty:* 5 full-time (2 women). *Students:* Average age 35. In 2003, 3 degrees awarded. *Degree requirements:* For master's, comprehensive exam or thesis. *Entrance requirements:* For master's, minimum GPA of 2.5. *Application deadline:* For fall admission, 8/1 for domestic students. Applications are processed on a rolling basis. Application fee: $40. *Expenses:* Tuition, state resident: full-time $3,263. Tuition, nonresident: full-time $6,742. *Financial support:* Fellowships, career-related internships or fieldwork available. Support available to part-time students. Financial award application deadline: 5/1; financial award applicants required to submit FAFSA. *Unit head:* Dr. Richard Halliburton, Professor, 203-837-8233. *Application contact:* Chris Shankle, Associate Director of Graduate Admissions, 203-837-8244, Fax: 203-837-8338, E-mail: shanklec@wcsu.edu.

Western Washington University, Graduate School, Huxley College of the Environment, Department of Environmental Sciences, Bellingham, WA 98225-5996. Offers MS. Part-time programs available. *Faculty:* 24. *Students:* 19 full-time (11 women), 5 part-time (all women); includes 1 minority (Hispanic American), 1 international. 66 applicants, 38% accepted, 17 enrolled. In 2003, 13 degrees awarded. *Degree requirements:* For master's, thesis. *Entrance requirements:* For master's, GRE General Test, minimum GPA of 3.0 in last 60 semester hours or last 90 quarter hours. Additional exam requirements/recommendations for international students: Required—TOEFL (minimum score 227 computer-based). *Application deadline:* For fall admission, 2/1 for domestic students. Application fee: $35. *Expenses:* Tuition, state resident: full-time $5,694; part-time $172 per credit. Tuition, nonresident: full-time $16,221; part-time $523 per credit. *Financial support:* In 2003–04, 5 teaching assistantships with partial tuition reimbursements (averaging $9,438 per year) were awarded; Federal Work-Study, institutionally sponsored loans, and scholarships/grants also available. Support available to part-time students. Financial award application deadline: 2/15; financial award applicants required to submit FAFSA. *Unit head:* Dr. Jack Hardy, Chair, 360-650-7585. *Application contact:* Sally Elmore, Graduate Program Coordinator, 360-650-3646.

Western Washington University, Graduate School, Huxley College of the Environment, Department of Environmental Studies, Bellingham, WA 98225-5996. Offers geography (MS); natural science/science education (M Ed), including environmental studies. Part-time programs available. *Faculty:* 24. *Students:* 29 full-time (16 women), 15 part-time (6 women); includes 1 minority (Asian American or Pacific Islander), 3 international. 28 applicants, 54% accepted, 9 enrolled. In 2003, 11 degrees awarded. *Degree requirements:* For master's, thesis. *Entrance requirements:* For master's, GRE General Test, minimum GPA of 3.0 in last 60 semester hours or last 90 quarter hours. Additional exam requirements/recommendations for international students: Required—TOEFL (minimum score 227 computer-based). *Application deadline:* For fall admission, 2/1 for domestic students. Applications are processed on a rolling basis. Application fee: $35. *Expenses:* Tuition, state resident: full-time $5,694; part-time $172 per credit. Tuition, nonresident: full-time $16,221; part-time $523 per credit. *Financial support:* In 2003–04, 9 teaching assistantships with partial tuition reimbursements (averaging $8,763 per year) were awarded; Federal Work-Study, institutionally sponsored loans, scholarships/grants, and tuition waivers (partial) also available. Support available to part-time students. Financial award application deadline: 2/15; financial award applicants required to submit FAFSA. *Unit head:* Dr. Gigi Berardi, Chair, 360-650-3284. *Application contact:* Sally Elmore, Graduate Program Coordinator, 360-650-3646.

West Texas A&M University, College of Agriculture, Nursing, and Natural Sciences, Department of Life, Earth, and Environmental Sciences, Program in Environmental Science, Canyon, TX 79016-0001. Offers MS. Part-time programs available. *Faculty:* 1 full-time (0 women), 3 part-time/adjunct (0 women). *Students:* 9 full-time (6 women), 10 part-time (2 women); includes 4 minority (1 African American, 1 American Indian/Alaska Native, 2 Hispanic Americans), 1 international. Average age 34. 19 applicants, 68% accepted, 13 enrolled. In 2003, 5 degrees awarded. *Median time to degree:* Master's–3 years full-time, 6 years part-time. *Degree requirements:* For master's, thesis optional. *Entrance requirements:* For master's, GRE General Test. Additional exam requirements/recommendations for international students: Required—TOEFL (minimum score 550 paper-based). *Application deadline:* Applications are processed on a rolling basis. Application fee: $25 ($75 for international students). Electronic applications accepted. *Expenses:* Tuition, state resident: part-time $56 per credit hour. Tuition, nonresident: part-time $292 per credit hour. Full-time tuition and fees vary according to course level, degree level and program. *Financial support:* In 2003–04, research assistantships (averaging $6,500 per year), 1 teaching assistantship (averaging $6,750 per year) were awarded. Federal Work-Study, institutionally sponsored loans, and tuition waivers (partial) also available. Support available to part-time students. Financial award applicants required to submit FAFSA. *Faculty research:* Degradation of presistant pesticides in soils and ground water, air quality. *Application contact:* Dr. Jim Rogers, Graduate Adviser, 806-651-2581, E-mail: jrogers@mail.wtamu.edu.

Wichita State University, Graduate School, Fairmount College of Liberal Arts and Sciences, Interdisciplinary Program in Liberal Studies, Wichita, KS 67260. Offers environmental science (MS). Participating faculty are from the Departments of Minority Studies, Philosophy, Religion, Social Work, and Women's Studies. Part-time programs available. *Students:* 5 full-time (all women), 15 part-time (11 women); includes 1 minority (Hispanic American), 1 international. Average age 40. 10 applicants, 70% accepted. In 2003, 8 degrees awarded. *Degree requirements:* For master's, project, thesis optional. *Entrance requirements:* For master's, GRE, minimum GPA of 2.75. Additional exam requirements/recommendations for international students: Required—TOEFL. *Application deadline:* For fall admission, 7/1 for domestic students; for spring admission, 1/1 for domestic students. Applications are processed on a rolling basis. Application fee: $35 ($50 for international students). Electronic applications accepted. *Expenses:* Tuition, state resident: full-time $2,457; part-time $137 per credit hour. Tuition, nonresident: full-time $7,371; part-time $410 per credit hour. Required fees: $364; $20 per credit hour. Tuition and fees vary according to course load. *Financial support:* In 2003–04, 1 research assistantship (averaging $8,096 per year), 6 teaching assistantships with full tuition reimbursements (averaging $9,556 per year) were awarded. Fellowships, Federal Work-Study, institutionally sponsored loans, scholarships/grants, traineeships, and unspecified assistantships also available. Support available to part-time students. Financial award application deadline: 4/1; financial award applicants required to submit FAFSA. *Unit head:* Dr. Gerald Litchi, Coordinator, 316-978-3100, Fax: 316-978-3978, E-mail: gerlad.litchi@wichita.edu.

Wright State University, School of Graduate Studies, College of Science and Mathematics, Department of Biological Sciences, Dayton, OH 45435. Offers biological sciences (MS); environmental sciences (MS). *Students:* 40 full-time (19 women), 18 part-time (13 women); includes 5 minority (4 African Americans, 1 American Indian/Alaska Native), 5 international. Average age 27. 30 applicants, 97% accepted. In 2003, 23 degrees awarded. *Degree requirements:* For master's, thesis optional. *Entrance requirements:* Additional exam requirements/recommendations for international students: Required—TOEFL. Application fee: $25. *Expenses:* Tuition, state resident: full-time $8,112; part-time $255 per quarter hour. Tuition, nonresident: full-time $14,127; part-time $442 per quarter hour. International tuition: $14,283 full-time. Tuition and fees vary according to course load, degree level and program. *Financial support:* Fellowships, research assistantships, teaching assistantships, career-related internships or fieldwork, institutionally sponsored loans, and unspecified assistantships available. Support available to part-time students. Financial award applicants required to submit FAFSA. *Unit head:* Dr. David L. Goldstein, Interim Chair, 937-775-2655, Fax: 937-775-3320, E-mail: david.goldstein@wright.edu. *Application contact:* Dr. James R. Runkle, Director, 937-775-3199, Fax: 937-775-3320, E-mail: james.runkle@wright.edu.

Wright State University, School of Graduate Studies, College of Science and Mathematics, Department of Chemistry, Dayton, OH 45435. Offers chemistry (MS); environmental sciences (MS). Part-time and evening/weekend programs available. *Students:* 23 full-time (13 women), 6 part-time (1 woman); includes 3 minority (1 African American, 2 Asian Americans or Pacific Islanders), 8 international. Average age 28. 19 applicants, 84% accepted. In 2003, 8 degrees awarded. *Degree requirements:* For master's, oral defense of thesis, seminar. *Entrance requirements:* Additional exam requirements/recommendations for international students: Required—TOEFL. *Application deadline:* For fall admission, 6/1 for domestic students. Applications are processed on a rolling basis. Application fee: $25. *Expenses:* Tuition, state resident: full-time $8,112; part-time $255 per quarter hour. Tuition, nonresident: full-time $14,127; part-time $442 per quarter hour. International tuition: $14,283 full-time. Tuition and fees vary according to course load, degree level and program. *Financial support:* Fellowships, research assistantships, teaching assistantships, unspecified assistantships available. Support available to part-time students. Financial award applicants required to submit FAFSA. *Faculty research:* Polymer synthesis and characterization, laser kinetics, organic and inorganic synthesis, analytical and environmental chemistry. Total annual research expenditures: $60,000. *Unit head:* Dr. Paul G. Seybold, Chair, 937-775-2855, Fax: 937-775-2717, E-mail: paul.seybold@wright.edu. *Application contact:* Dr. Kenneth Turnbull, Chair, Graduate Studies Committee, 937-775-2671, Fax: 937-775-2717, E-mail: kenneth.turnbull@wright.edu.

Wright State University, School of Graduate Studies, College of Science and Mathematics, Department of Geological Sciences, Program in Geological Sciences, Dayton, OH 45435. Offers environmental geochemistry (MS); environmental geology (MS); environmental sciences (MS); geological sciences (MS); geophysics (MS); hydrogeology (MS); petroleum geology (MS). Part-time programs available. *Students:* 22 full-time (4 women), 9 part-time (4 women), 2 international. Average age 26. 21 applicants, 100% accepted. In 2003, 15 degrees awarded. *Degree requirements:* For master's, thesis. *Entrance requirements:* Additional exam requirements/recommendations for international students: Required—TOEFL. Application fee: $25. *Expenses:* Tuition, state resident: full-time $8,112; part-time $255 per quarter hour. Tuition, nonresident: full-time $14,127; part-time $442 per quarter hour. International tuition: $14,283 full-time. Tuition and fees vary according to course load, degree level and program. *Financial support:* Fellowships, research assistantships, teaching assistantships, Federal Work-Study and unspecified assistantships available. Support available to part-time students. Financial award application deadline: 3/1; financial award applicants required to submit FAFSA. *Application contact:* Deborah L. Cowles, Assistant to Chair, 937-775-3455, Fax: 937-775-3462, E-mail: deborah.cowles@wright.edu.

Wright State University, School of Graduate Studies, College of Science and Mathematics, Program in Environmental Sciences, Dayton, OH 45435. Offers PhD. *Students:* 5 full-time (2 women), 2 international. *Expenses:* Tuition, state resident: full-time $8,112; part-time $255 per quarter hour. Tuition, nonresident: full-time $14,127; part-time $442 per quarter hour. International tuition: $14,283 full-time. Tuition and fees vary according to course load, degree level and program. *Unit head:* Dr. Wayne W. Carmichael, Director, 937-775-3273, Fax: 937-775-3559, E-mail: wayne.carmichael@wright.edu. *Application contact:* Hunt Brown, Associate Director, Institute for Environmental Quality, 937-775-2201, Fax: 937-775-4997, E-mail: hunt.brown@wright.edu.

Yale University, Graduate School of Arts and Sciences, Department of Forestry and Environmental Studies, New Haven, CT 06520. Offers environmental sciences (PhD); forestry (PhD). *Students:* 43 full-time (22 women); includes 6 minority (5 Asian Americans or Pacific Islanders, 1 Hispanic American), 9 international. 97 applicants, 10% accepted, 8 enrolled. In 2003, 4

Yale University (continued)

degrees awarded. *Degree requirements:* For doctorate, thesis/dissertation. *Entrance requirements:* For doctorate, GRE General Test. *Application deadline:* For fall admission, 1/2 for domestic students. Application fee: $80. *Expenses:* Tuition: Full-time $25,600; part-time $6,400 per term. *Financial support:* Fellowships, Federal Work-Study and institutionally sponsored loans available. Support available to part-time students. *Unit head:* Dean, School of Forestry and Environmental Studies, 203-432-5109. *Application contact:* Admissions Information, 203-432-2770.

See in-depth description on page 805.

Yale University, School of Forestry and Environmental Studies, New Haven, CT 06511. Offers MES, MF, MFS, DFES, PhD, JD/MES, MBA/MES, MBA/MF, MES/MA, MES/MPH, MF/MA. *Accreditation:* SAF (one or more programs are accredited). Part-time programs available. Terminal master's awarded for partial completion of doctoral program. *Degree requirements:* For doctorate, thesis/dissertation. *Entrance requirements:* For master's and doctorate, GRE General Test. Expenses: Contact institution. *Faculty research:* Ecosystem science and management, coastal and watershed systems, environmental policy and management, social ecology and community development, conservation biology.

See in-depth description on page 805.

Marine Affairs

Dalhousie University, Faculty of Graduate Studies, Program in Marine Affairs, Halifax, NS B3H 4R2, Canada. Offers MMM. *Degree requirements:* For master's, project. *Entrance requirements:* For master's, minimum GPA of 3.0. Additional exam requirements/recommendations for international students: Required—TOEFL. *Faculty research:* Integrated coastal zone management, marine law and policy, fisheries management, maritime transport, marine protected areas.

Duke University, Nicholas School of the Environment and Earth Sciences, Durham, NC 27708-0328. Offers coastal environmental management (MEM); environmental health and security (MEM); environmental science and policy (PhD); environmental toxicology, chemistry, and risk assessment (MEM); forest resource management (MF); global environmental change (MEM); resource ecology (MEM); resource economics and policy (MEM); water and air resources (MEM). PhD offered through the Graduate School. *Accreditation:* SAF (one or more programs are accredited). Part-time programs available. Terminal master's awarded for partial completion of doctoral program. *Degree requirements:* For master's, thesis (for some programs); for doctorate, thesis/dissertation. *Entrance requirements:* For master's, GRE General Test, previous course work in biology or ecology, calculus, statistics, and microeconomics; computer familiarity with word processing and data analysis; for doctorate, GRE General Test. Additional exam requirements/recommendations for international students: Required—TOEFL (minimum score 550 paper-based; 213 computer-based). Electronic applications accepted. Expenses: Contact institution. *Faculty research:* Ecosystem management, conservation ecology, earth systems, risk assessment.

See in-depth description on page 787.

East Carolina University, Graduate School, Program in Coastal Resources Management, Greenville, NC 27858-4353. Offers PhD. *Faculty:* 42 full-time (7 women), 2 part-time/adjunct (0 women). *Students:* 13 full-time (7 women), 19 part-time (6 women); includes 3 minority (1 African American, 2 Hispanic Americans). Average age 36. 18 applicants, 56% accepted. *Degree requirements:* For doctorate, thesis/dissertation, internship, comprehensive exam, registration. *Entrance requirements:* For doctorate, GRE. Additional exam requirements/recommendations for international students: Required—TOEFL. *Application deadline:* For fall admission, 3/1 for domestic students, 3/1 for international students. Application fee: $50. *Expenses:* Tuition, state resident: full-time $1,991; part-time $249 per hour. Tuition, nonresident: full-time $12,232; part-time $1,529 per hour. Required fees: $1,221; $153 per hour. *Financial support:* In 2003–04, 8 fellowships with tuition reimbursements (averaging $17,000 per year), 2 research assistantships with tuition reimbursements (averaging $17,000 per year) were awarded. Career-related internships or fieldwork and institutionally sponsored loans also available. Financial award application deadline: 3/1; financial award applicants required to submit FAFSA. *Faculty research:* Coastal geology, wetlands and coastal ecology, ecological and social networks, submerged cultural resources, coastal resources economics. Total annual research expenditures: $24,000. *Unit head:* Dr. Lauriston R. King, Director, 252-328-2484, Fax: 252-328-0381, E-mail: kingl@mail.ecu.edu. *Application contact:* Dr. Paul D. Tschetter, Interim Dean of Graduate School, 252-328-6012, Fax: 252-328-6071, E-mail: gradschool@mail.ecu.edu.

Florida Institute of Technology, Graduate Programs, College of Engineering, Department of Marine and Environmental Systems, Melbourne, FL 32901-6975. Offers environmental resource management (MS); environmental science (MS, PhD); meteorology (MS); ocean engineering (MS, PhD); oceanography (MS, PhD), including biological oceanography, chemical oceanography, coastal zone management (MS), geological oceanography, physical oceanography. Part-time programs available. *Faculty:* 16 full-time (1 woman), 4 part-time/adjunct (0 women). *Students:* 42 full-time (16 women), 19 part-time (8 women); includes 1 minority (Hispanic American), 25 international. Average age 29. 129 applicants, 55% accepted, 17 enrolled. In 2003, 17 master's, 3 doctorates awarded. Terminal master's awarded for partial completion of doctoral program. *Degree requirements:* For master's, thesis, comprehensive exam, registration; for doctorate, thesis/dissertation, attendance of graduate seminar, internships (oceanography and environmental science), comprehensive exam, registration. *Entrance requirements:* For master's, GRE General Test (environmental science), letters of recommendation(3), minimum GPA of 3.0; for doctorate, GRE General Test (oceanography and environmental science), resumé, letters of recommendation (3), statement of objectives, minimum GPA of 3.2. Additional exam requirements/recommendations for international students: Required—TOEFL (minimum score 550 paper-based; 213 computer-based). *Application deadline:* Applications are processed on a rolling basis. Application fee: $50. Electronic applications accepted. *Expenses:* Tuition: Part-time $745 per credit. *Financial support:* In 2003–04, 35 students received support, including 10 fellowships with full and partial tuition reimbursements available (averaging $5,565 per year), 15 research assistantships with full and partial tuition reimbursements available (averaging $14,657 per year), 10 teaching assistantships with full and partial tuition reimbursements available (averaging $17,533 per year); career-related internships or fieldwork and tuition remissions also available. Financial award application deadline: 3/1; financial award applicants required to submit FAFSA. *Faculty research:* Environmental modeling, coastal processes, exploring marine pollution, marine geophysics, remote sensing . Total annual research expenditures: $1.9 million. *Unit head:* Dr. George Maul, Department Head, 321-674-7453, Fax: 321-674-7212, E-mail: gmaul@fit.edu. *Application contact:* Carolyn P. Farrior, Director of Graduate Admissions, 321-674-7118, Fax: 321-723-9468, E-mail: cfarrior@fit.edu.

See in-depth description on page 727.

Louisiana State University and Agricultural and Mechanical College, Graduate School, School of the Coast and Environment, Department of Oceanography and Coastal Sciences, Baton Rouge, LA 70803. Offers MS, PhD. *Faculty:* 28 full-time (2 women), 1 part-time/adjunct (0 women). *Students:* 56 full-time (30 women), 8 part-time (1 woman); includes 2 minority (1 African American, 1 Hispanic American), 16 international. Average age 30. 32 applicants, 31% accepted, 10 enrolled. In 2003, 7 master's, 5 doctorates awarded. *Degree requirements:* For master's, thesis (for some programs); for doctorate, one foreign language, thesis/dissertation. *Entrance requirements:* For master's, GRE General Test, minimum GPA of 3.0; for doctorate, GRE General Test, MA or MS, minimum GPA of 3.0. Additional exam requirements/recommendations for international students: Required—TOEFL (minimum score 550 paper-based; 213 computer-based). *Application deadline:* For fall admission, 1/25 priority date for domestic students, 5/15 priority date for international students. Applications are processed on a rolling basis. Application fee: $25. *Expenses:* Tuition, state resident: part-time $337 per hour. Tuition, nonresident: part-time $577 per hour. *Financial support:* In 2003–04, 17 students received support, including 7 fellowships (averaging $18,071 per year), 42 research assistantships with partial tuition reimbursements available (averaging $17,897 per year), 2 teaching assistantships with partial tuition reimbursements available (averaging $9,875 per year); Federal Work-Study, institutionally sponsored loans, and unspecified assistantships also available. Financial award applicants required to submit FAFSA. *Faculty research:* Management and development of estuarine and coastal areas and resources; physical, chemical, geological, and biological research. Total annual research expenditures: $57,294. *Unit head:* Dr. Lawrence Rouse, Chair, 225-578-2453, Fax: 225-578-6307, E-mail: lrouse@lsu.edu. *Application contact:* Dr. Masamichi Inoue, Graduate Adviser, 225-578-6308, Fax: 225-578-6307, E-mail: coiino@lsu.edu.

Memorial University of Newfoundland, School of Graduate Studies, Department of Sociology, St. John's, NL A1C 5S7, Canada. Offers gender (PhD); maritime sociology (PhD); sociology (M Phil, MA); work and development (PhD). Part-time programs available. *Students:* 23 full-time, 3 part-time. 46 applicants, 35% accepted, 16 enrolled. In 2003, 10 degrees awarded. *Degree requirements:* For master's, comprehensive exam or thesis; for doctorate, one foreign language, thesis/dissertation, oral defense of thesis, comprehensive exam. *Entrance requirements:* For master's, 2nd class degree from university of recognized standing in area of study; for doctorate, MA, M Phil, or equivalent. *Application deadline:* For fall admission, 1/31 for domestic students. Applications are processed on a rolling basis. Application fee: $40. Electronic applications accepted. Tuition and fees charges are reported in Canadian dollars. *Expenses:* Tuition, state resident: part-time $733 Canadian dollars per semester. Tuition, nonresident: part-time $953 Canadian dollars per semester. Required fees: $194 Canadian dollars per year. Tuition and fees vary according to degree level and program. *Financial support:* Fellowships, research assistantships, teaching assistantships available. Financial award application deadline: 1/31. *Faculty research:* Work and development, gender, maritime sociology. *Unit head:* Dr. Judith Adler, Head, 709-737-7443, Fax: 709-737-2075, E-mail: jadler@mun.ca. *Application contact:* Stephen Crocker, Graduate Officer, 709-737-7447, Fax: 709-737-2075, E-mail: bcrocker@mun.ca.

Memorial University of Newfoundland, School of Graduate Studies, Interdisciplinary Program in Marine Studies, St. John's, NL A1C 5S7, Canada. Offers fisheries resource management (MMS). Part-time programs available. *Students:* 9 full-time, 12 part-time. 9 applicants, 44% accepted, 4 enrolled. In 2003, 2 degrees awarded. *Degree requirements:* For master's, report. Application fee: $40 Canadian dollars. Tuition and fees charges are reported in Canadian dollars. *Expenses:* Tuition, state resident: part-time $733 Canadian dollars per semester. Tuition, nonresident: part-time $953 Canadian dollars per semester. Required fees: $194 Canadian dollars per year. Tuition and fees vary according to degree level and program. *Financial support:* Fellowships, research assistantships, teaching assistantships available. *Faculty research:* Biological, ecological and oceanographic aspects of world fisheries; economics; political science; sociology. *Unit head:* Dr. Peter Fisher, Chair, 709-778-0356, Fax: 709-778-0346, E-mail: pfisher@gill.ifmt.nf.ca.

Nova Southeastern University, Oceanographic Center, Program in Coastal-Zone Management, Fort Lauderdale, FL 33314-7796. Offers MS. *Students:* 10 applicants, 80% accepted. In 2003, 6 degrees awarded. *Entrance requirements:* For master's, GRE. Additional exam requirements/recommendations for international students: Required—TOEFL (minimum score 550 paper-based). *Application deadline:* Applications are processed on a rolling basis. Application fee: $50. *Expenses:* Tuition: Full-time $8,715; part-time $484 per credit. Required fees: $75. Full-time tuition and fees vary according to degree level and program. *Application contact:* Dr. Andrew Rogerson, Associate Dean, 954-262-3600, Fax: 954-262-4020, E-mail: arogerso@nsu.nova.edu.

See in-depth description on page 281.

Oregon State University, Graduate School, College of Oceanic and Atmospheric Sciences, Program in Marine Resource Management, Corvallis, OR 97331. Offers MA, MS. *Students:* 24 full-time (14 women), 3 part-time (2 women), 5 international. Average age 30. In 2003, 8 degrees awarded. *Degree requirements:* For master's, thesis optional. *Entrance requirements:* For master's, GRE General Test, minimum GPA of 3.0 in last 90 hours. Additional exam requirements/recommendations for international students: Required—TOEFL. *Application deadline:* For fall admission, 2/1 for domestic students. Applications are processed on a rolling basis. Application fee: $50. *Expenses:* Tuition, state resident: full-time $8,139; part-time $301 per credit. Tuition, nonresident: full-time $14,376; part-time $532 per credit. Required fees: $1,227. *Financial support:* Fellowships, research assistantships, teaching assistantships, career-related internships or fieldwork, Federal Work-Study, and institutionally sponsored loans available. Support available to part-time students. Financial award application deadline: 2/1. *Faculty research:* Ocean and coastal resources, fisheries resources, marine pollution, marine recreation and tourism. *Unit head:* Dr. Jim W. Good, Director, 541-737-1339, Fax: 541-737-2064, E-mail: good@oce.orst.edu. *Application contact:* Irma Delson, Assistant Director, Student Services, 541-737-5189, Fax: 541-737-2064, E-mail: student_adviser@oce.orst.edu.

Stevens Institute of Technology, Graduate School, Charles V. Schaefer Jr. School of Engineering, Department of Civil, Environmental, and Ocean Engineering, Program in Maritime Systems, Hoboken, NJ 07030. Offers M Eng.

Université du Québec à Rimouski, Graduate Programs, Program in Management of Marine Resources, Rimouski, QC G5L 3A1, Canada. Offers M Sc. Part-time programs available. *Entrance requirements:* For master's, appropriate bachelor's degree, proficiency in French.

University of Delaware, College of Marine Studies, Newark, DE 19716. Offers marine policy (MS); marine studies (MMP, MS, PhD); oceanography (MS, PhD). *Faculty:* 36 full-time (4 women). *Students:* 101 full-time (50 women), 2 part-time (1 woman); includes 6 minority (2 African Americans, 3 Asian Americans or Pacific Islanders, 1 Hispanic American), 23 international. Average age 29. 141 applicants, 30% accepted, 29 enrolled. In 2003, 17 master's, 12 doctorates awarded. *Degree requirements:* For master's and doctorate, thesis/dissertation. *Entrance requirements:* For master's and doctorate, GRE General Test. Additional exam requirements/recommendations for international students: Required—TOEFL. *Application deadline:* For fall admission, 3/1 for domestic students; for spring admission, 10/1 for domestic students. Applications are processed on a rolling basis. Application fee: $60. Electronic applications accepted. *Expenses:* Tuition, state resident: full-time $5,890; part-time $327 per credit. Tuition, nonresident: full-time $15,420; part-time $857 per credit. Required fees: $968. *Financial support:* In 2003–04, 77 students received support, including 22 fellowships with full tuition reimbursements available (averaging $19,000 per year), 55 research assistantships with full tuition reimbursements available (averaging $19,000 per year), teaching assistantships with full tuition reimbursements available (averaging $19,000 per year); career-related internships or fieldwork, Federal Work-Study, and tuition waivers (full and partial) also available. Financial award application deadline: 3/1. *Faculty research:* Marine biology and biochemistry, oceanography, marine policy, physical ocean science and engineering, ocean engineering. Total annual research expenditures: $10.2 million. *Unit head:* Dr. Carolyn A. Thoroughgood, Dean, 302-831-2841. *Application contact:* Doris Manship, Coordinator, 302-645-4226, E-mail: dmanship@udel.edu.

University of Maine, Graduate School, College of Natural Sciences, Forestry, and Agriculture, School of Marine Sciences, Program in Marine Policy, Orono, ME 04469. Offers MS. *Students:* 10 full-time (8 women), 2 part-time. Average age 27. 19 applicants, 26% accepted, 3 enrolled. In 2003, 3 degrees awarded. *Degree requirements:* For master's, thesis. *Entrance requirements:* For master's, GRE General Test. Additional exam requirements/recommendations for international students: Required—TOEFL. *Application deadline:* For fall admission, 2/1 for domestic students. Applications are processed on a rolling basis. Application fee: $50. Electronic applications accepted. *Expenses:* Tuition, state resident: part-time $235 per credit. Tuition, nonresident: part-time $670 per credit. Tuition and fees vary according to course load. *Financial support:* Fellowships with tuition reimbursements, research assistantships with tuition reimbursements, teaching assistantships with tuition reimbursements, career-related internships or fieldwork, Federal Work-Study, and tuition waivers (full and partial) available. Support available to part-time students. Financial award application deadline: 3/1. *Unit head:* Dr. James Wilson, Coordinator, 207-581-4368. *Application contact:* Scott G. Delcourt, Associate Dean of the Graduate School, 207-581-3218, Fax: 207-581-3232, E-mail: graduate@maine.edu.

University of Miami, Graduate School, Rosenstiel School of Marine and Atmospheric Science, Division of Marine Affairs, Coral Gables, FL 33124. Offers MA, MS, JD/MA. Part-time programs available. *Faculty:* 9 full-time (3 women), 5 part-time/adjunct (0 women). *Students:* 35 full-time (23 women), 4 part-time (2 women); includes 7 minority (2 African Americans, 3 Asian Americans or Pacific Islanders, 2 Hispanic Americans), 2 international. Average age 25. 44 applicants, 84% accepted, 17 enrolled. In 2003, 9 degrees awarded. *Median time to degree:* Master's–1.9 years full-time. *Degree requirements:* For master's, internship, paper, thesis. *Entrance requirements:* For master's, GRE General Test. Additional exam requirements/recommendations for international students: Required—TOEFL (minimum score 550 paper-based; 213 computer-based). *Application deadline:* For fall admission, 6/1 priority date for domestic students, 4/1 priority date for international students. Applications are processed on a rolling basis. Application fee: $50. Electronic applications accepted. *Expenses:* Tuition: Full-time $19,526. *Financial support:* In 2003–04, 20 students received support, including 4 fellowships with partial tuition reimbursements available (averaging $20,124 per year), 12 research assistantships with partial tuition reimbursements available (averaging $20,124 per year), 4 teaching assistantships (averaging $20,124 per year); career-related internships or fieldwork, Federal Work-Study, institutionally sponsored loans, scholarships/grants, and unspecified assistantships also available. Financial award application deadline: 3/1; financial award applicants required to submit FAFSA. *Unit head:* Dr. Sarah Meltzoff, Chair, 305-361-4087, E-mail: smeltzoff@rsmas.miami.edu. *Application contact:* Dr. Frank Millero, Associate Dean, 305-361-4155, Fax: 305-361-4771, E-mail: gso@rsmas.miami.edu.

University of Rhode Island, Graduate School, College of the Environment and Life Sciences, Department of Environmental and Natural Resource Economics, Kingston, RI 02881. Offers resource economics and marine resources (MS, PhD). In 2003, 15 master's, 1 doctorate awarded. *Degree requirements:* For master's, thesis optional; for doctorate, thesis/dissertation. *Entrance requirements:* For master's and doctorate, GRE General Test. Additional exam requirements/recommendations for international students: Required—TOEFL. *Application deadline:* For fall admission, 4/15 for domestic students. Applications are processed on a rolling basis. *Expenses:* Tuition, state resident: full-time $4,338; part-time $281 per credit. Tuition, nonresident: full-time $12,438; part-time $704 per credit. Required fees: $1,840. *Unit head:* Dr. James Anderson, Chairperson, 401-874-2471. *Application contact:* Dr. Tim Tyrrell, Graduate Admissions Committee, 401-874-2472, Fax: 401-782-4766, E-mail: renri@uriacc.uri.edu.

University of Rhode Island, Graduate School, College of the Environment and Life Sciences, Department of Marine Affairs, Kingston, RI 02881. Offers MA, MMA. *Application deadline:* For fall admission, 4/15 for domestic students. Applications are processed on a rolling basis. Application fee: $35. *Expenses:* Tuition, state resident: full-time $4,338; part-time $281 per credit. Tuition, nonresident: full-time $12,438; part-time $704 per credit. Required fees: $1,840. *Unit head:* Dr. Lawrence Juda, Chairperson, 401-874-2596.

University of San Diego, College of Arts and Sciences, Program in Marine and Environmental Studies, San Diego, CA 92110-2492. Offers marine science (MS). Part-time programs available. *Faculty:* 8 full-time (5 women), 1 part-time/adjunct (0 women). *Students:* 9 full-time (5 women), 22 part-time (13 women); includes 2 minority (both Asian Americans or Pacific Islanders), 1 international. Average age 26. 34 applicants, 65% accepted, 8 enrolled. In 2003, 6 degrees awarded. *Degree requirements:* For master's, thesis. *Entrance requirements:* For master's, GRE General Test, minimum GPA of 3.0, undergraduate major in science. Additional exam requirements/recommendations for international students: Required—TOEFL (minimum score 580 paper-based; 237 computer-based), TWE. *Application deadline:* For fall admission, 5/1 for domestic students. Applications are processed on a rolling basis. Application fee: $45. Electronic applications accepted. *Expenses:* Tuition: Full-time $14,850; part-time $825 per unit. Required fees: $126. Full-time tuition and fees vary according to class time, course load, degree level and program. *Financial support:* Career-related internships or fieldwork, Federal Work-Study, institutionally sponsored loans, tuition waivers (partial), and unspecified assistantships available. Support available to part-time students. Financial award application deadline: 5/1; financial award applicants required to submit FAFSA. *Faculty research:* Marine ecology; paleoclimatology; geochemistry; functional morphology; marine zoology of mammals, birds and turtles. *Unit head:* Dr. Hugh I. Ellis, Director, 619-260-4075, Fax: 619-260-6804, E-mail: ellis@sandiego.edu. *Application contact:* Stephen Pultz, Director of Admissions, 619-260-4524, Fax: 619-260-4158, E-mail: grads@sandiego.edu.

University of Washington, Graduate School, College of Ocean and Fishery Sciences, School of Marine Affairs, Seattle, WA 98195. Offers MMA, MMA/MAIS. *Degree requirements:* For master's, thesis. *Entrance requirements:* For master's, GRE General Test, minimum GPA of 3.0. Additional exam requirements/recommendations for international students: Required—TOEFL. Electronic applications accepted. *Faculty research:* Marine pollution, port authorities, fisheries management, global climate change, marine environmental protection.

University of West Florida, College of Arts and Sciences: Sciences, Division of Life and Health Services, Specialization in Coastal Zone Studies, Pensacola, FL 32514-5750. Offers biology (MS). Part-time programs available. *Students:* 1 (woman) full-time, 5 part-time (4 women). Average age 25. *Degree requirements:* For master's, thesis or alternative. *Entrance requirements:* For master's, GRE General Test. Additional exam requirements/recommendations for international students: Required—TOEFL (minimum score 550 paper-based; 213 computer-based). *Application deadline:* For fall admission, 6/1 for domestic students, 5/15 for international students; for spring admission, 11/1 for domestic students, 10/1 for international students. Applications are processed on a rolling basis. Application fee: $20. *Expenses:* Tuition, state resident: full-time $4,986; part-time $208 per credit hour. Tuition, nonresident: full-time $18,649; part-time $777 per credit hour. Tuition and fees vary according to course load, campus/location and reciprocity agreements. *Financial support:* Application deadline: 4/15; *Unit head:* Dr. George L. Stewart, Chairperson, Division of Life and Health Services, 850-474-2748.

Cross-Discipline Announcements

Carnegie Mellon University, Carnegie Institute of Technology, Department of Engineering and Public Policy, Pittsburgh, PA 15213-3891.

PhD program addresses policy problems in which technical details are critically important by using tools of engineering, science, and the social sciences. Carnegie Mellon offers an excellent environment for interdisciplinary research. Program requires equivalent of undergraduate degree in engineering, physical science, or mathematics. See In-Depth Description in the Engineering and Applied Sciences volume (Book 5) of this series. Write to Victoria Finney, Graduate Program Administrator.

Massachusetts Institute of Technology, School of Engineering, Biological Engineering Division, Cambridge, MA 02139-4307.

Program provides opportunities for study and research at the interface of biology and engineering leading to specialization in bioengineering and applied biosciences. The areas include understanding how biological systems operate, especially when perturbed by genetic, chemical, or materials interventions or subjected to pathogens or toxins, and designing innovative biology-based technologies in diagnostics, therapeutics, materials, and devices for application to human health and diseases, as well as other societal problems and opportunities.

Tufts University, The Gerald J. and Dorothy R. Friedman School of Nutrition Science and Policy, Medford, MA 02155.

The Program in Agriculture, Food, and Environment at the Friedman School of Nutrition Science and Policy emphasizes policy aspects of the interconnections of food production and supply with environmental constraints and problems. The program draws on interdisciplinary domestic and international expertise at Tufts. Students receive an MS or PhD from the Friedman School of Nutrition Science and Policy and interact with students and faculty members at the Tufts Department of Urban and Environmental Policy through a collaborative arrangement. MS includes a field internship and directed research project.

BARD COLLEGE

Bard Center for Environmental Policy

Program of Study

The Bard Center for Environmental Policy (BCEP) offers intensive graduate studies and practical training in preparation for environmental careers at the local, national, and international levels. The innovative program, headed by the former Director for North America of the United Nations Environment Programme, is specifically designed to meet contemporary demands for environmental leadership in government, business, and nonprofit organizations. The unique course of studies, leading to a Master of Science or a Professional Certificate in Environmental Policy, features integrated application of natural and social sciences for the analysis of environmental problems and responses. Distinctive elements include its modular curriculum, multimedia communication and leadership training, an exceptional faculty, and internships in the United States and abroad.

Curriculum organization and diverse internship opportunities permit considerable flexibility to meet the specific needs and career aspirations of students. The objectives of the rigorous, interdisciplinary program are to prepare environmental leaders who understand the complex interconnections among various disciplines involved in environmental policymaking and can translate scientific results into feasible and creative strategies. Graduates are skilled at using various forms of communication to build support and consensus for effective environmental management. The second-year internship, culminating in the final project, provides hands-on experience to facilitate entry into the job market.

Several options are available to accepted students. Active professionals who have substantial experience in environment-related fields may qualify for the master's degree after completion of the first-year courses and the Master's Project. Options include a joint program leading to the Master of Science and Doctor of Jurisprudence (M.S./J.D.) degrees with Pace University School of Law; dual master's program (M.S./M.A.T.) with the Bard Center Master of Arts in Teaching program; dual master's program (M.S./M.A.) with Bard Center for Studies in the Decorative Arts, Design, and Culture; Master's International Program with the Peace Corps; and a Professional Certificate in Environmental Policy.

Research Facilities

Stevenson Library houses the latest periodicals and books dealing with environmental issues. The Jerome Levy Economics Institute offers a full array of professional journals, particularly those related to economics. Students can also draw on the New York State interlibrary loan system, online services, and Bard's ecology field station. A designated site for the National Estuarine Research Reserve, Bard is also home to the environmental research institute Hudsonia Ltd. and the Bard College Field Station. The Institute of Ecosystem Studies in nearby Millbrook is an internationally known scientific establishment dedicated to advancing the understanding of the function and development of ecological systems. In proximity is the Hastings Center, the oldest independent, nonpartisan, interdisciplinary research center in the world, which addresses fundamental ethical issues regarding health, medicine, and the environment. Several researchers from these institutions are members of BCEP's faculty, offering students access to the latest scientific results and debates pertaining to contemporary environmental problems.

Financial Aid

Financial assistance is awarded on the basis of achievement and promise and also on the basis of financial need, according to criteria determined annually by the Office of Financial Aid of Bard College. BCEP is committed to assisting qualified students whose personal financial resources are insufficient to meet the expenses of graduate study. A limited number of fellowships are available. Awards are made on an annual basis without regard to gender, sexual orientation, race, color, age, marital status, religion, ethnic or national origin, or handicapping conditions. Application must be made annually by February 1. Applications on or before the deadline receive first consideration.

Cost of Study

For full-time first-year students entering in 2005 and working toward the Master of Science in Environmental Policy, tuition is $22,250 and $16,000 for students entering their second year in 2004. For professionals admitted with the internship waiver and candidates for the Professional Certificate program, the tuition is $22,250 plus the Master's Project fee of $2400. For students admitted on a modular basis, the tuition for the four-week General Concepts Module is $3850; tuition for additional modules is $2625 each. Modest facility and registration fees apply.

Living and Housing Costs

A variety of houses and apartments for reasonable rent can be found near the Bard College campus. Limited campus housing is available for graduate students with special circumstances. Upon admission to the program, students receive a continually updated list of possible off-campus housing opportunities.

Student Group

Bard's 2,600 undergraduate and graduate students come from forty-nine states and thirty-two countries. According to the *U.S. News & World Report 2000* on America's best colleges, Bard College is second in the country for "class size" and eighth for "faculty resources." The Bard Center for Environmental Policy has a ratio of nearly 1 full-time or affiliated faculty member to each student. These numbers are highly conducive to student interaction with colleagues and faculty and staff members as well as to successful internships and career placements.

Student Outcomes

Expertise in the burgeoning field of environmental policy allows graduates to take advantage of opportunities in a wide variety of professional careers. The New England Board of Higher Education reported that an increasing number of environmental careers are now found in the arts, humanities, education, health, law, politics, social change, and forestry—fields that even a decade ago were not linked with environmental policy. Dramatic growth is especially seen in the environmental industry, estimated to reach $600 billion internationally by 2010, and in the nongovernmental sector. Close mentoring of internship partner organizations and student career preparations enhances graduates' marketability.

Location

Bard's magnificent setting along the historic Hudson River offers an unusual blend of diverse environmental, cultural, and recreational resources on campus or within 90 minutes' reach. From New York City to the Adirondacks, urban and natural wonders provide seasonal recreation. The campus lifestyle is enriched by distinguished scientists' lectures; forums on timely environmental, political, and ethical issues; and a host of visual and performing arts exhibitions, concerts, and performances in the stunning Richard B. Fisher Performing Arts Center, designed by Frank Gehry.

The College and The Center

Bard's approach to education aims to assist students in planning and achieving individual intellectual growth throughout the academic process. A hallmark of the educational experience at Bard is the intensive interaction between students and faculty members through small seminars, tutorials, and independent project work. The Bard Center for Environmental Policy builds on Bard College's tradition of creative innovation, with added emphasis on professional preparation and career development in environmental policy fields.

Applying

The ideal candidate has a strong background in sciences, math, and/or economics, although qualified students with exceptional leadership promise from other disciplines are seriously considered. Relevant activities subsequent to college graduation are given special attention in the selection process. Applications for fall 2005 admission should be received by February 1, 2005. Applications postmarked after this date are considered only if space is available in the entering class.

Correspondence and Information

Bard Center for Environmental Policy
Bard College
30 Campus Road, P.O. Box 5000
Annandale-on-Hudson, New York 12504-5000
Telephone: 845-758-7073; Fax 845-758-7636
E-mail: cep@bard.edu
World Wide Web: http://www.bard.edu/cep

Bard College

THE FACULTY

The faculty is composed of a distinguished core of full-time members and affiliated members who are eminent experts and researchers in diverse fields relating to environmental policy and current practices. Affiliated faculty members* have primary appointments at other institutions and are available for participation in courses and for advising. The high ratio of faculty members to students allows for close rapport and individualized guidance. Small classes ensure close mentoring of student career preparations. To access faculty biographies, students should refer to the faculty segment of Bard's Web site at http://www.bard.edu/cep/graduate/faculty/.

Ana Arana*, M.S., Columbia.
Mark Becker, M.A., CUNY, Hunter.
Peter Berle*, J.D., Harvard.
Daniel Berthold, Ph.D., Yale.
Hillary Brown*, M.Arch., Yale.
Allsion Morrill Chatrchyan, Ph.D., Maryland.
Allan J. Costello, B.B.A., Siena.
Paula Di Perna*, M.A., NYU.
Stuart E. G. Findlay*, Ph.D., Georgia.
Joanne Fox-Przeworski, Ph.D., Washington (St. Louis). Director, Bard Center for Environmental Policy, and former Director for North America of the United Nations Environment Programme.
Ann Goodman*, Ph.D., Chicago.
Robert Henshaw*, Ph.D., Iowa.
Lori Knowles*, LL.M., Wisconsin–Madison.
Frederic B. Mayo*, Ph.D., Johns Hopkins.
William Mullen, Ph.D., Texas.
Lee Paddock, J.D., Iowa.
Jennifer Phillips, Ph.D., Cornell.
Jerome Delli Priscolli*, Ph.D., Georgetown.
David Sampson, J.D., SUNY at Albany.
Gautam Sethi, Ph.D., Berkeley.
Elizabeth Smith.
Eleanor Sterling*, Ph.D., Yale.
Kathleen Weathers*, Ph.D., Rutgers.
Iddo Wernick*, Ph.D., Columbia.
Zywia Wojnar, M.S., Jagiellonian (Poland); M.S.M., Arthur D. Little.

SIPA

COLUMBIA UNIVERSITY

School of International and Public Affairs Master of Public Administration Program in Environmental Science and Policy

Program of Study

The Master of Public Administration (M.P.A.) Program in Environmental Science and Policy trains sophisticated public managers and policy makers, who apply innovative, systems-based thinking to environmental issues. The program challenges students to think systemically and act pragmatically. To meet this challenge, Columbia offers a top-quality graduate program in management and policy analysis that emphasizes practical skills and is enriched by ecological and planetary science.

The program's approach reflects the system-level thinking that is needed to understand ecological interactions and maintain the health of the earth's interconnected ecological, institutional, economic, and social systems. This program requires more environmental science than any other public policy master's degree in the world. The skills and concepts learned involve an understanding of scientific method, including observation, hypothesis generation, and hypothesis testing. Students also study the chemical processes affecting environmental quality and public health, methods of collection and analysis of field and laboratory data, and systems modeling.

To train effective earth systems professionals, the program focuses on the practical skills necessary to understand the formulation and management of public policy. The teaching of public policy and administration represents the core of the program. This set of classes focuses on specific professional and vocational skills, such as memo writing, oral briefings, group process and team building, spreadsheet and other forms of financial analysis, use of computer programs, case studies of earth systems issues, and the World Wide Web. The principal goal of the core curriculum is to provide students with the analytic, communication, and work skills required to be problem-solving earth systems professionals.

Research Facilities

Lamont-Doherty Earth Observatory was established in 1949 by Columbia geology professor Maurice Ewing. In the last fifty years, research from the observatory has significantly changed understanding of the earth, from the groundbreaking discovery of plate tectonics to an understanding of the ocean's role in regulating climate change. The 125-acre rural campus is connected to Morningside Heights by a regular shuttle bus that brings students, scientists, and faculty members to and from the campus. During the second semester, students take their courses on Columbia's campus in Morningside Heights, one of the richest concentrations of educational resources and academic activity in the United States. Its fifteen schools draw on a renowned faculty, making it among the country's most productive research centers. Students in the program are granted access to the extensive collections within the renowned Columbia University Libraries system, including twenty-two campus libraries, each supporting a specific academic or professional discipline. The Lehman Social Sciences Library, located in the International Affairs Building, holds a contemporary collection of more than 330,000 volumes and approximately 1,700 periodical titles. It includes materials acquired by Columbia libraries since 1974 in political science, sociology, social anthropology, political geography, and journalism, as well as a rich collection of materials on post–World War II international relations. It also houses Columbia's extensive collection of international newspapers. The Office of Information Technology and the Picker Computer Center cater to the needs of School of International and Public Affairs (SIPA) students with newly expanded, state-of-the art computer labs; digital research programs; and wireless networks at both the SIPA and the Lamont campus. Columbia's trilevel Dodge Physical Fitness Center includes more than 7,500 square feet of aerobic and anaerobic exercise equipment, an indoor running track, and a 9,000-square-foot all-purpose gymnasium and is open to all SIPA students.

Financial Aid

There are fellowships available based upon need and merit. Students who apply for admission and fellowships by the November 1 early decision deadline are notified of their status by December 1. The application deadline for all other students applying for fellowships is January 15. The final admission deadline is February 15 without fellowship. Applicants are notified of admission and fellowship decisions by March 15. Long-term loans at low interest rates are available, including Federal Stafford Student Loans and Federal Perkins Loans. The Federal Work-Study Program is also available.

Cost of Study

Tuition for the 2004–05 academic year is $14,264 per semester. The cost of tuition and fees for the complete twelve-month program is about $45,300.

Living and Housing Costs

Housing in the Morningside Heights neighborhood around SIPA in buildings owned by Columbia University may be available to entering M.P.A. students. Accommodations include apartment shares; dormitory or suite-style housing; efficiency, one-bedroom, and family-style apartments; and single rooms in the International House. Living and personal expenses vary.

Student Group

Drawn from more than seventy-five countries, SIPA students are diverse, mature (the average age is 27), and intelligent individuals. The environmental science and policy program enrolls approximately 45 to 50 students each year.

Student Outcomes

Graduates of the M.P.A. Program in Environmental Science and Policy are prepared for the roles of analyst, manager, and translator of scientific knowledge. Recent graduates have gone on to careers with NASA, the Center for Corporate Responsibility, EarthTech Environmental Consulting and Engineering, Forest Guardians, and the Agency for Toxic Substances and Disease Registry. The program prepares highly marketable students for management and leadership roles in countless arenas of the global public and private sectors.

The Office of Career Services, located in the School of International and Public Affairs, helps students in all stages of their search for employment, from career interviews to the writing of resumes and their submission to appropriate organizations. The office has a long-standing working relationship with scores of agencies and private organizations.

Location

This twelve-month program takes place at Columbia University's Morningside Heights Campus in New York City and at its Lamont-Doherty Earth Observatory in Palisades, New York, a 25-minute drive (or campus shuttle ride) from the main campus. Students enroll in their summer science course work at the beautiful Lamont campus, overlooking the Hudson River. Policy courses are held on the Morningside Heights Campus on New York City's dynamic, diverse upper west side.

The University and The School

SIPA's focus on a broad range of real-world issues is an outgrowth of the School's original mission, which was written and established in 1946: to train professionals to meet new challenges by providing an interdisciplinary curriculum that draws on Columbia's renowned faculty in the social sciences and other traditional fields. The Master of Public Administration was added to the School in 1977 to meet a growing demand for skilled professionals at home as well as abroad. Students in the M.P.A. Program in Environmental Science and Policy work closely with Columbia's Earth Institute, the world's leading academic center for the integrated study of Earth, its environment, and society. The Earth Institute builds upon excellence in core disciplines—earth sciences, biological sciences, engineering sciences, social sciences, and health sciences—and stresses cross-disciplinary approaches to complex problems.

Applying

A bachelor's degree or its equivalent is required. Advanced high school course work in chemistry and biology is strongly recommended. November 1 is the early admission deadline. Applicants who submit a completed application by that date are promised a decision by December 1 for the following June. January 15 is the application deadline for students seeking fellowships. February 15 is the final deadline for June admission. International applicants are encouraged to apply a month in advance of these deadlines. Qualification for admission is based upon the Admissions Committee's review of the applicant's file: personal statement, transcripts, and letters of appraisal.

Correspondence and Information

For information concerning admission, financial aid, curriculum, and staff members, students should write to the address below.

Louise A. Rosen
Assistant Director, Master of Public Administration Program in Environmental Science and Policy
School of International and Public Affairs
1407 International Affairs
420 West 118th Street
New York, New York 10027
Telephone: 212-854-3142
Fax: 212-864-4847
E-mail: lar46@columbia.edu
World Wide Web: http://www.columbia.edu/cu/mpaenvironment/

Columbia University

THE PROGRAM'S CORE TEACHING FACULTY

Steven A. Cohen, Director, Master of Public Administration Program in Environmental Science and Policy; Ph.D., SUNY at Buffalo, 1979.
Howard N. Apsan, Adjunct Professor of Public Affairs; Ph.D., Columbia, 1985.
Bruce P. Chadwick, Assistant Professor of Public Policy; Ph.D., Columbia, 2002.
Robert A. Cook, Adjunct Professor of Environmental Affairs; V.M.D., Pennsylvania, 1980.
David Downie, Director of Educational Partnerships, Office of Educational Programs, Columbia Earth Institute; Ph.D., North Carolina at Chapel Hill, 1996.
William Eimicke, Director of the Picker Center for Executive Education, School of International and Public Affairs; Ph.D., Syracuse, 1973.
Lewis E. Gilbert, Adjunct Professor of Environmental Policy, Columbia University; Ph.D., Columbia, 1993.
Adela J. Gondek, Adjunct Professor of Public Affairs; Ph.D., Harvard, 1980.
Tanya Heikkila, Assistant Professor of Environmental Management; Ph.D., Arizona, 2001.
Patrick Louchouarn, Professor of Environmental Science; Ph.D., Quebec at Montreal, 1997.
Alexander S. P. Pfaff, Associate Professor of Economics and International Affairs; Ph.D., MIT, 1995.
Stephanie Pfirman, Professor and Chair, Department of Environmental Science, Barnard College; Ph.D., MIT, 1995.
Jeffrey D. Sachs, Director, Earth Institute, Columbia University; Ph.D., Harvard, 1980.
Glenn Sheriff, Lecturer in Earth Systems Policy and Management; Ph.D. candidate, Maryland.
Arthur A. Small, Assistant Professor of International and Public Affairs; Ph.D., Berkeley, 1998.
Bryan Lee Williams, Adjunct Professor of Environmental Affairs, Columbia University; Ph.D., Penn State, 1992.
Paula Wilson, Assistant Professor of International and Public Affairs; M.S.W., SUNY at Albany, 1977.

THE EVERGREEN STATE COLLEGE

Graduate Program in Environmental Studies

Program of Study

The Evergreen State College (TESC) instituted an integrated, interdisciplinary course of study in 1984 leading to the degree of Master of Environmental Studies (M.E.S.). Students interested in the application of technical and management aspects of environmental studies gain the background and working skills necessary to solve a broad range of environmental problems and prepare to enter a wide variety of career areas.

The 72-quarter-hour program can be completed in two years by full-time students and in as little as three years by part-time students. The program is composed of three distinct components. The first is a core sequence of four programs: Political, Economic, and Ecological Processes; Population, Energy, and Resources; Case Studies: Environmental Assessment Policy and Management; and Quantitative Analysis and Research Methods. Each of these programs is 8 quarter hours and is offered by an interdisciplinary team of social and natural scientists. The second component is the creation of an individual program through the selection of regular electives offered by the College, as well as opportunities for internships for credit and "Individual Learning Contracts." The electives that are offered include pesticides, wetland ecology, environmental policy, environmental law, environmental philosophy and ethics, environmental health, conservation and restoration biology, environmental economics, hydrology, and salmonid ecology. The third component of the program is a thesis that consists of applied research and analysis in the form of an individual or small-group project. Full-time students carry out the parts of this plan concurrently, while part-time students complete components consecutively.

All students entering the program are expected to have had course work in both the social and natural sciences. Evergreen prides itself on its active, interdisciplinary, action-oriented teaching methods. Faculty members pursue a variety of additional relevant research and professional interests. The faculty members advise students on electives, thesis work, and professional development.

Research Facilities

The College's research facilities include chemical and biological laboratory facilities, an organic farm, 700 acres of second-growth forest, 3,000 feet of undeveloped marine shoreline, and a variety of computers with a full range of software, including GIS capability.

The College's location in the state capital provides extensive research opportunities within state government. TESC library and the nearby Washington State library provide needed reference materials. Students can make use of local and regional agencies and communities as sites to carry out research activities. The program will help coordinate such work. Evergreen is the site of the Editorial Office for *Environmental Practice,* a peer-reviewed professional journal published by Oxford University Press for the National Association of Environmental Professionals.

Financial Aid

Modest financial aid is available. Sources of support include fellowships, program assistantships, work-study positions, employment with the College, paid internships, and participation in contract research. In addition, the M.E.S. program assists students in finding external funding sources and locating part-time employment with public and private agencies. Students should also check with TESC's Financial Aid Office and file a financial aid form by February 15 for priority consideration.

Cost of Study

Full-time tuition for Washington State residents is $2167 per quarter in 2004–05. Nonresident tuition was $6646 per quarter. Fees are subject to change.

Living and Housing Costs

An estimated $5400 covers room and board for a single person living on or off campus during the nine-month academic year. Most graduate students live in or near Olympia in rental units or in apartments adjacent to the campus.

Student Group

Approximately 40 students enroll each fall quarter. Total program size is currently about 100 students. A cooperative spirit within the student group is emphasized primarily through seminars and group assignments. Another 80 graduate students in Evergreen's M.P.A. program share some space and faculty members with the M.E.S. program.

Student Outcomes

More than half of the program alumni are employed in the public sector, predominantly in state and local government agencies. Almost a quarter work in the private sector, and others work in positions in education or nongovernmental organizations or are pursuing further study. Most graduates are employed in positions that are degree related. The Assistant Director assists students in their professional development planning.

Location

Olympia lies at the southern end of Puget Sound, equidistant from the Cascade Range, the Pacific Ocean, and the Olympic Mountains. Train, bus, and highway connections provide easy access to metropolitan Seattle and Portland. Evergreen serves as a cultural and intellectual focus for Washington's capital city of Olympia. The city and surrounding area have a population of 250,000, with excellent outdoor recreation opportunities nearby.

The College

The Evergreen State College opened in 1971. Its national reputation for innovative curricular design and academic excellence have drawn a diverse faculty, staff, and student body to the 1,000-acre campus, which is located 7 miles northwest of Olympia. The most distinctive feature of the curriculum is the concept of interdisciplinary instruction carried out in coordinated study programs for a quarter or longer. This results in the student having both a single and a multifaceted academic commitment at the same time. This concept of study is the essence of the core component of the M.E.S. program.

Evergreen has the usual recreational and athletic facilities on campus, including those for tennis, swimming, racquetball, basketball, and soccer. The College's beach on Puget Sound is the focus for water recreation, and the Cascade and Olympic Mountains provide excellent hiking, climbing, and skiing.

Applying

Admission is normally granted for the fall quarter so that the student can begin the core sequence. Application forms and a catalog are available from the Assistant Director or the Graduate Studies Office.

Correspondence and Information

Assistant Director
Graduate Program in Environmental Studies
Lab I, 3022
The Evergreen State College
Olympia, Washington 98505

Telephone: 360-867-6225 or 6707
E-mail: austinj@evergreen.edu
World Wide Web: http://www.evergreen.edu/mes

The Evergreen State College

THE FACULTY

Shown below are the areas of interest in teaching and study of each faculty member.

Natural Science
Sharon Anthony. Environmental chemistry.
Frederica Bowcutt. Botany, restoration ecology, natural history.
Paul Butler. Geology, hydrology.
Gerardo Chin-Leo. Biology, marine studies.
Robert Cole. Physics, energy studies.
Amy Cook. Fish biology.
Heather Heying. Ecology and animal behavior.
Robert Knapp. Physics, energy systems.
Jack Longino. Cell biology, tropical biology.
Nalini Nadkarni. Forest ecology.
John Perkins. Biology, history of technology and environment, editor of *Environmental Practice.*
Paul Przybylowicz. Biology, ecology.
Oscar Soule. Ecology.
James Stroh. Geology.
Kenneth Tabbutt. Geology.
Erik Thuesen. Marine biology.
Alfred Wiedemann. Biology, botany.

Social Science
Carolyn Dobbs. Environmental planning, community organization.
Peter Dorman. Political economy.
Russell Fox. Community planning and development.
Martha Henderson-Tubesing. Cultural geography, human ecology, public lands management.
Cheri Lucas-Jennings. Environmental law.
Carol Minugh. Native American community-based environmental studies.
Ralph Murphy. Environmental economics, natural resource policy.
Lin Nelson. Environmental health and advocacy.
Alan Parker. Native American issues.
Matthew Smith. Political science, environmental politics.
Linda Moon Stumpff. Natural resource policy.
Ted Whitesell. Geography.
Tom Womeldorff. Environmental economics.

Contributing Adjunct Faculty
Stephen L. Beck. Environmental philosophy and ethics.
Nina Carter. Environmental management.
Jeffrey Cederholm. Fisheries biology.
Jean MacGregor. Environmental education.
Charles Newling. Wetlands ecology and management.
Tim Quinn. Habitat conservation planning.

An M.E.S. student presents his candidacy paper to fellow students and faculty members.

Every year, M.E.S. students organize the Rachel Carson forum to publicly debate an environmental issue.

Students have opportunities to study in the field, here with a forest ecologist.

INDIANA UNIVERSITY BLOOMINGTON

School of Public and Environmental Affairs
Environmental Science Graduate Programs

Programs of Study

The objective of the environmental science programs at the School of Public and Environmental Affairs (SPEA) is to provide rigorous training in a chosen environmental science specialization and an exposure to the broader interdisciplinary context necessary for developing solutions to complex environmental problems. Degree programs are offered to serve students seeking professional careers in private industry, consulting firms, nonprofit agencies, and all levels of government, as well as students seeking research training in preparation for academic careers and other research-oriented positions. Master's degree programs include the two-year, professional Master of Science in Environmental Science (M.S.E.S.) program and several joint-degree programs. The M.S.E.S. combines core courses in environmental chemistry, applied math for environmental chemistry, applied math for environmental sciences, environmental engineering and ecology with a selection of courses in environmental policy, management, law, and/or economics to provide students with an interdisciplinary foundation for environmental problem solving. Each student also completes course work in a concentration area, which provides more in-depth training in a specific area of environmental science. Concentration areas include applied ecology; environmental chemistry, toxicology, and risk assessment; and water resources. To integrate this academic training within a practical framework, students are required to complete an internship, undertake a significant research project, or complete a master's thesis. Program flexibility allows students to design individualized concentrations. Joint-degree programs are offered with SPEA's Master of Public Affairs (M.P.A.) program; the Indiana University (IU) biology, geography, and geology departments; and the Indiana University Schools of Law and Journalism. The Ph.D. program in environmental science is designed to provide rigorous and in-depth research training in a chosen area of environmental science. The program allows students to tailor their course work and research to meet their goals and needs. Admission to the program is highly competitive and requires acceptance by a faculty member or members with compatible research interests. The 22 environmental science faculty members on the Bloomington campus have active research programs within and/or between each of the following subdisciplines: groundwater flow modeling, contaminant fate and transport, environmental chemistry, subsurface bioremediation, biogeochemistry, atmospheric chemistry, global climate change, meteorology and climatology, GIS applications, toxicology, applied statistics, environmental microbiology, applied ecology, conservation biology, and wetland ecology and wetlands restoration.

Research Facilities

The research facilities and equipment available at SPEA are excellent. Equipment includes two programmable environmental chambers, three UV-visible spectrophotometers, an atomic absorption spectrophotometer with graphic furnace and flame atomization, six gas chromatographs, an ion chromatograph, HPLC, an autoanalyzer, an organic carbon analyzer, three mass spectrometers, an inductively coupled plasma analyzer, a CHN thermal analyzer, a portable photosynthesis analyzer, an anaerobic chamber, a phase contrast/epifluorescent microscope, a 2.5-liter bacterial fermentor, a high-end compound research microscope (DM) with camera attachments, two stereo microscopes, a rotary microtome, a cryostat, an Nd:YAG pumped dye laser system, and an adiabatic bomb calorimeter. SPEA also has excellent terrestrial and aquatic field sampling equipment and instruments, a 16-foot research boat, cartographic equipment and map files, and aerial photographic and photo interpretation equipment. One of only a handful of labs in the U.S. capable of multiuser training, SPEA's Geographic Information Systems (GIS) laboratory features some of the most advanced technology to manage, display, and analyze spatial data for scientific and policy research. Libraries on the Bloomington campus house more than 6 million volumes, and another 3.2 million are available through the University's seven other campuses.

Financial Aid

Departmental assistance for qualified students is awarded on a competitive basis and is determined by merit. Awards include teaching and research assistantships. Students may apply for need-based aid through IU's Office of Student Financial Assistance.

Cost of Study

Residents of Indiana paid $248 per credit hour and nonresidents paid $671 per credit hour for the master's programs in 2003–04. Resident Ph.D. students paid $205 per credit hour and nonresident Ph.D. students paid $596 per credit hour in 2003–04. Other academic fees, services, and supplies total between $600 and $700 per year.

Living and Housing Costs

On-campus room and board for single graduate students during the 2003–04 academic year ranged from $4960 to $8040. The 1,500 on-campus housing units for married students ranged in monthly rent from $541 for an efficiency to $906 for an unfurnished three-bedroom apartment. A variety of off-campus housing is available near the University. Rents are generally inexpensive, with the average two-bedroom unit renting for $500 to $700 per month.

Student Group

Forty-three students are enrolled in the M.S.E.S. program, with 31 students pursuing the joint M.P.A./M.S.E.S. program and 21 students enrolled in the Ph.D. programs in environmental science. About one tenth of these students are international, more than one half are women, and more than one tenth are members of minority groups.

Student Outcomes

SPEA maintains an outstanding placement record, which is attributed to a well-rounded curriculum, national prestige, and strong alumni support. The SPEA Career Services and Alumni Affairs Office is staffed with professionals who assist graduate students in obtaining permanent employment and internship experiences. Samples of recent placements include the U.S. Fish and Wildlife Service, U.S. Environmental Protection Agency, Radian Corporation, World Wildlife Federation, ICF Kaiser Environmental, and Upjohn Company.

Location

Bloomington, a college town of 70,000 people, was chosen as one of the top ten college towns in America for its "rich mixture of atmospherics and academia" by Edward Fiske, former education editor of the *New York Times*. It is a culturally vibrant community settled among southern Indiana's rolling hills just 45 miles south of Indianapolis, the state capital. Mild winters and warm summers are ideal for outdoor recreation in the two state forests, one national forest, and three state parks that surround Bloomington.

The University and The School

Established in 1820, Indiana University has more than 7,500 graduate students and more than 38,000 total students enrolled on the Bloomington campus. Fifty-five academic departments are ranked in the top twenty in the country, including SPEA, music, business, biology, foreign languages, political science, and chemistry. Attractions include nearly 1,000 musical performances each year, including eight full-length operas and professional Broadway plays; the IU Art Museum, designed by I. M. Pei, with more than 30,000 art objects; fifty campus and community volunteer agencies; more than 500 student clubs and organizations; two indoor student recreational facilities; and Big Ten sports. SPEA, founded in 1972, was the first school to combine public management, policy, and administration with the environmental sciences.

Applying

Applications must include the SPEA Admission and Financial Aid application form, transcripts, GRE General Test scores, and three letters of recommendation. Priority is given to applications received by February 1. School visits are encouraged. Applicants are encouraged to visit the School's World Wide Web site (http://www.spea.indiana.edu).

Correspondence and Information

For master's programs:
Graduate Programs Office
SPEA 260
Indiana University
Bloomington, Indiana 47405
Telephone: 812-855-2840
800-765-7755 (toll-free in U.S. only)
E-mail: speainfo@indiana.edu
World Wide Web: http://www.spea.indiana.edu

For doctoral programs:
Ph.D. Programs Office
SPEA 441
Indiana University
Bloomington, Indiana 47405
Telephone: 812-855-2457
800-765-7755 (toll-free in U.S. only)
E-mail: speainfo@indiana.edu
World Wide Web: http://www.indiana.edu/~speaweb/academic/science/phd.html

Indiana University Bloomington

THE GRADUATE FACULTY AND THEIR RESEARCH

The faculty members listed below are either part of the environmental policy program or associated with the environmental science graduate programs.

Matthew R. Auer, Ph.D., Yale, 1996. Environmental policy and management problems, with an international focus: international environmental assistance, comparative industrial environmental policy, international policies governing forests and forestry.

Debera Backhus, Ph.D., MIT, 1990. Environmental organic chemistry, particularly the processes controlling the fate of hazardous organic chemicals in the environment; application of research lies in understanding processes, examining exposure and risks, predicting future environmental impacts, evaluating alternative actions or remediation strategies, and designing technologies to prevent future degradation.

Randall Baker, Ph.D., London, 1968. Bridging the gap between the natural and social sciences, comparative study on different perspectives regarding the way problems are perceived and handled, historical perspectives in the analysis of contemporary environmental and policy problems.

James Barnes, J.D., Harvard, 1967. Environmental law, domestic and international environmental policy, ethics and the public official, mediation and alternative dispute resolution, law and public policy.

James Bever (Biology), Ph.D., Duke, 1992. Ecology and evolution of plants and fungi.

Ben Brabson (Physics), Ph.D., Berkeley, 1991. Environmental physics, wind energy and wind speed analysis, climate changes.

Simon Brassel (Geologic Sciences), Ph.D., Bristol, 1980. Biogeochemical responses to climatic and environmental change, abundance and isotopic composition of organic matter in sediments.

John Brothers, Emeritus (Mathematics); Ph.D., Brown, 1964. Geometric analysis.

Lynton Keith Caldwell, Emeritus; Ph.D., Chicago, 1943. Public administration, with emphasis on administrative history and theory; public policy for science and the environment.

Keith Clay (Biology), Ph.D., Duke, 1982. Plant ecology, symbiosis, disease ecology, microbial community ecology.

Clara Cotton (Biology), Ph.D., Indiana, 1985. Aquatic biology, paleolimnology, indexing of key species for environmental assessment.

Christopher Craft, Ph.D., North Carolina State, 1987. Terrestrial and wetland ecosystem restoration, wetlands ecology, soil resources, biogeochemistry, nutrient cycling and carbon sequestration of soils and sediments.

Bruce Douglas (Geological Sciences), Ph.D., Princeton, 1983. Rheological properties of rocks, deformation mechanisms active in the brittle and ductile portions of the lithosphere, development of tertiary extensional basins.

David Good, Ph.D., Pennsylvania, 1985. Quantitative policy modeling, productivity measurement in public and regulated industries, urban policy analysis.

Sue Grimmond (Geography–Atmospheric Sciences), Ph.D., British Columbia, 1989. Micrometeorology and hydroclimatology of heterogeneous terrain, especially urban areas; measurement and modeling of energy and mass (water and carbon dioxide) exchanges in areas of heterogeneous terrain (cities, forests, and wetlands).

Hendrik M. Haitjema, Ph.D., Minnesota, 1982. Groundwater flow modeling, including regional groundwater flow systems, conjunctive surface water and groundwater flow modeling, three-dimensional groundwater flow, and saltwater intrusion problems; emphasis on application of analytic functions to modeling groundwater flow, specifically the analytic element method.

Diane Henshel, Ph.D., Washington (St. Louis), 1987. Sublethal health effects of environmental pollutants, especially pollutant effects on the developing organism, including the effects of polychlorinated dibenzo-p-dioxins (PCDDs) and related congeners on the developing nervous system of birds exposed in the wild and under controlled laboratory conditions.

Gary Hieftje (Chemistry), Ph.D., Illinois, 1969. Development of spectrochemical measurements and instrumentation.

Ronald Hites, Ph.D., MIT, 1968. Applying organic analytical chemistry techniques to the analysis of trace levels of toxic pollutants, such as polychlorinated biphenyls and pesticides, with a focus on understanding the behavior of these compounds in the atmosphere and in the Great Lakes.

Claudia Johnson (Geologic Sciences), Ph.D., Colorado, 1993. Tropical paleontology, quantitative analysis of latitudinal trends in species and genetic diversity, evolutionary and extinction patterns of molluscs and corals.

William Jones, M.S., Wisconsin–Madison, 1977. Lake and watershed management, especially diagnosing lake and watershed water-quality problems; preparing management plans to address problems identified; stream ecology; Caribbean coral reef ecology; underwater archaeology; certified lake manager (CLM).

Erle Kauffman, Emeritus (Geological Sciences); Ph.D., 1961. Distribution of communities along an environmental stress gradient during the Cretaceous, systematic revision of the species-subspecies levels for the bivalvia and ammonoidea, Cretaceous climate investigations.

Ellen Ketterson (Biology), Ph.D., Indiana, 1974. Avian biology, mating systems and parental care, hormones and behavior, physiological mechanisms underlying trade-offs in life histories, using hormones to explore adaptation, dominance and aggression, population dynamics during the nonbreeding season.

Noel Krothe (Geologic Sciences), Ph.D., Penn State, 1976. Flow and chemistry of ground and surface water, carbonate hydrogeology, flow and water chemistry in fractured and solution-controlled aquifers.

Kerry Krutilla, Ph.D., Duke, 1988. Energy policy, resource management in developing countries, environmental regulation, public choice, cost-benefit analysis.

Vicky Meretsky, Ph.D., Arizona, 1995. Ecology and management of rare species, biocomplexity, landscape-level species and community conservation, temporal patterns in biodiversity, integrating ecosystem research and endangered-species management within adaptive management.

Theodore K. Miller, Ph.D., Iowa, 1970. Statistical analysis.

Emilio Moran (Anthropology), Ph.D., Florida, 1975. Tropical ecosystem ecology, Amazon basin, secondary successional forests, human ecology.

Craig Nelson (Biology), Ph.D., Texas, 1966. Evolutionary ecology, amphibian communities, sex determination in reptiles, speciation, interactions among species.

Greg Olyphant (Geologic Sciences and Geography), Ph.D., Iowa, 1979. Environmental geology, instrumentation for intensive site monitoring, numerical/statistical modeling of geospatial data, modeling of wetland hydrology.

David Parkhurst, Ph.D., Wisconsin–Madison, 1970. Physiological plant ecology, including transfers of carbon dioxide and water between leaves and atmosphere and among the cells within leaves, both in relation to leaf structure; mathematics and statistics applied to environmental issues; examples include analysis of concentrations of indicator bacteria at swimming beaches and correct interpretation of statistical hypothesis tests in decision making.

Mark Person (Geologic Sciences), Ph.D., Johns Hopkins, 1992. Groundwater flow mechanisms in different tectonic environments, mathematical modeling of subsurface and flow.

Flynn W. Picardal, Ph.D., Arizona, 1992. Bioremediation, environmental microbiology, and biogeochemistry, with a focus on the microbial reduction of iron oxides and nitrate, transformation of metals and chlorinated hydrocarbons, and combined microbial-geochemical interactions.

Lisa Pratt (Geological Sciences), Ph.D., Princeton, 1982. Biogeochemistry, stable isotopic and organic geochemical studies of sediments.

Sara Pryor (Geography–Atmospheric Sciences), Ph.D., East Anglia, 1992. Air pollution meteorology.

J. C. Randolph, Ph.D., Carleton (Ottawa), 1972. Forest ecology; ecological aspects of global environmental change, with particular interests in forestry and agriculture; applications of geographic information systems (GIS) and remote sensing in environmental and natural resources management; landscape ecology and regional-scale modeling; physiological ecology of woody plants and of small mammals.

Heather Reynolds (Biology), Ph.D., Berkeley, 1995. Plant community ecology.

Edwardo L. Rhodes, Ph.D., Carnegie-Mellon, 1978. Public policy analysis, particularly public-sector applications of management science in the evaluation and assessment of the efficiency or organization performance of public activities, including environmental and natural resource policy implementation.

Kenneth R. Richards, J.D./Ph.D., Pennsylvania, 1997. Climate change policy, carbon sequestration economics, environmental policy implementation and instrument choice.

Evan J. Ringquist, Ph.D., Wisconsin–Madison, 1990. Public policy (environmental, energy, natural resources, and regulation) research methodology, American political institutions.

Scott Robeson (Geography–Atmospheric Sciences), Ph.D., Delaware, 1992. Climate change, statistical climatology, applied climatology.

H. P. Schmid (Geography–Atmospheric Sciences), Ph.D., British Columbia, 1988. Boundary-layer meteorology and micrometeorology, turbulent exchange over inhomogeneous surfaces.

Philip S. Stevens, Ph.D., Harvard, 1990. Characterization of the chemical mechanisms that influence regional air quality and global climate change.

Lee Suttner (Geologic Sciences), Ph.D., Wisconsin, 1966. Subsurface and field-based studies of Cretaceous fluvial systems in the Rocky Mountain foreland basin of Colorado, Wyoming, and Montana; reconstructing paleochannel hydraulics and geometries and modeling the alluvial architecture; chemical stratigraphy of the Upper and Lower Cretaceous nonmarine deposits.

Maxine Watson (Biology), Ph.D., Yale, 1974. Plant developmental ecology; dynamic interaction between development and patterns of resource uptake and use; investigations of genetic variation examined through a combination of common garden, reciprocal transplant, and greenhouse studies, especially of perennial clonal systems, particularly the mayapple (*Podophyllum peltatum*); plant-mycorrhizal interactions.

Jeffrey R. White, Ph.D., Syracuse, 1984. Environmental biogeochemistry, aquatic chemistry, limnology.

LEHIGH UNIVERSITY

College of Arts and Sciences
Department of Earth and Environmental Sciences

Programs of Study

Lehigh's Department of Earth and Environmental Sciences (EES) offers programs leading to the M.S. and Ph.D. degrees in earth and environmental sciences. M.S. programs typically require two years of full-time effort; a Ph.D., about four years. Faculty research programs include aquatic ecosystems, aquatic ecology, aqueous geochemistry, geochronology, fluvial and tectonic geomorphology, glacial geology, hydrogeology, metamorphic petrology, microbial ecology, sedimentation, paleoclimatology, paleoecology, paleomagnetism, seismology, high-resolution geophysics, structural geology, tectonics, and remote sensing. Detailed information on these programs is available at the Web site listed in the Correspondence and Information section. The intermediate size of the department (14 faculty and 4 support staff members) and its range of active research programs provide an intimate atmosphere in which students receive extensive experience with diverse analytical and theoretical approaches to the study of geological, ecological, and environmental processes.

Research Facilities

The department houses a vast array of instrumentation and facilities for both field and laboratory research in earth and environmental sciences and maintains a variety of networked workstation and microcomputer laboratories. The workstations support a geographic information system for multiattribute locational database management, inquiry, and graphic information analysis and presentation. The University supports high-speed networking to offices, labs, and classrooms and provides access to high-performance workstations for computationally intensive tasks.

State-of-the-art instrumentation and laboratories exist for studies in aquatic and terrestrial ecology and ecosystems research, sediment coring and analysis, aqueous geochemistry, noble-gas and fission-track geochronology, stable-isotope geochemistry, structural geology, sedimentation, fluvial geomorphology, and DEM analysis. Complete petrographic facilities are also available, including cathodoluminescence and camera lucida digitizing apparatus. Geophysical equipment includes a complete paleomagnetism and rock magnetism laboratory; a seismology laboratory, including a multichannel seismograph and ground-penetrating radar unit for field data acquisition; and a complete computer workstation lab for data processing and analysis. Other field geophysical equipment includes a gravimeter, a portable proton precession magnetometer, and resistivity equipment. The department also maintains automated meteorological and hydrological facilities, a GPS base station and broadband seismometer, and terrestrial and water column instrumentation for measuring sedimentation and solar UV radiation.

Financial Aid

Financial assistance in the form of teaching assistantships, research assistantships, scholarships, and University and departmental fellowships is awarded to applicants on a competitive basis. Teaching assistant stipends begin at $13,800 for the nine-month academic year. In addition, teaching assistants receive tuition remission for up to 9 credits per semester and 3 credits during the summer. Fellowship and research assistantship stipends are comparable to the stipends for teaching assistants. Students making satisfactory progress are normally supported until the completion of their degree program.

Cost of Study

Tuition for the 2004–05 academic year is $950 per credit; tuition expenses are paid for teaching assistants and research assistants.

Living and Housing Costs

Students live in a wide variety of accommodations, and expenses can be reasonable, especially if shared. Lehigh operates a 148-unit garden apartment complex in nearby Saucon Valley for single and married students; rent for a one-bedroom unfurnished apartment is $510 per month. Day care is available nearby, and hourly bus service is provided. Private rental units are also available. Costs average $6000 per year.

Student Group

In 2004 there were 32 students in the EES graduate program; they came from many states and several other countries. It is the policy of the University to provide equal opportunity based on merit and without discrimination due to race, color, religion, gender, age, national origin, citizenship, status, handicap, or veteran status.

Student Outcomes

Graduates from the department typically find employment in industry, consulting firms, and governmental agencies and in academics as postdoctoral researchers and as faculty members at colleges and universities.

Location

Bethlehem, Pennsylvania, which has a population of 75,000, is located 50 miles north of Philadelphia and 90 miles west of New York City; best access is via Interstate 78, U.S. Route 22, or Lehigh Valley International Airport. Founded in 1741, Bethlehem has a rich cultural heritage in the Moravian tradition. Historical buildings have been well preserved, giving the community a charming Colonial atmosphere. The Lehigh Valley (Allentown, Bethlehem, and Easton), with a population of more than 600,000, is the chief commercial and industrial center for east-central Pennsylvania.

The University

Lehigh is an independent, nondenominational, coeducational university. Founded in 1865, it has approximately 4,500 undergraduates within its three major colleges: Arts and Sciences, Engineering and Applied Science, and Business and Economics. There are approximately 2,000 students enrolled in various graduate programs and in the graduate-only College of Education. The 700-acre campus includes superb athletic facilities, a health club, cultural venues, and an arts center.

Applying

Applicants to the Department of Earth and Environmental Sciences' graduate program typically have earned science baccalaureate degrees (e.g., geological sciences, biological sciences, environmental science, physics, or chemistry). Application for admission requires official academic transcripts, letters of recommendation from academic contacts, results from the GRE General Test, and statements of research and career interests. Results from the TOEFL exam are required of all applicants whose native language is not English. Applications for admission as a regular graduate student are accepted until July 15 for the fall term, December 1 for the spring term, April 30 for the first summer term, and May 30 for the second summer term. To be considered for financial aid, students must submit completed applications to the College of Arts and Sciences Graduate Programs Office by January 15 for the following academic year. Online applications are available at http://www.lehigh.edu/~incas/graduate/application.html. Admission forms should be sent to CAS Graduate Programs, Maginnes Hall, Lehigh University, 9 West Packer Avenue, Bethlehem, Pennsylvania 18015.

Correspondence and Information

Graduate Coordinator
Earth and Environmental Sciences
Lehigh University
31 Williams Drive
Bethlehem, Pennsylvania 18105-3188

Telephone: 610-758-3660
Fax: 610-758-3677
World Wide Web: http://www.ees.lehigh.edu

Lehigh University

THE FACULTY AND THEIR RESEARCH

Peter K. Zeitler, Professor and Chair; Ph.D., Dartmouth, 1983. Geochronology, tectonics.

David J. Anastasio, Associate Professor; Ph.D., Johns Hopkins, 1988. Structural geology, tectonics.

Gray E. Bebout, Associate Professor; Ph.D., UCLA, 1989. Metamorphic petrology, stable-isotope geochemistry.

Edward B. Evenson, Professor; Ph.D., Michigan, 1972. Glacial and Quaternary geology.

Bruce Hargreaves, Associate Professor; Ph.D., Berkeley, 1977. Bioptics, aquatic ecosystems.

Kenneth P. Kodama, Professor; Ph.D., Stanford, 1977. Paleomagnetism, rock magnetism, environmental magnetism, tectonics.

Anne S. Meltzer, Professor and Dean, College of Arts and Sciences; Ph.D., Rice, 1989. Seismology, high-resolution geophysics, tectonics.

Donald P. Morris, Associate Professor; Ph.D., Colorado, 1990. Microbial ecology, aquatic ecosystems.

Carl Moses, Associate Professor and Associate Dean, College of Arts and Sciences; Ph.D., Virginia, 1988. Aqueous geochemistry, mineral-solution interface.

Frank J. Pazzaglia, Associate Professor; Ph.D., Penn State, 1993. Fluvial and tectonic geomorphology, watershed evolution.

Steven Peters, Assistant Professor; Ph.D., Michigan, 2001. Low-temperature geochemistry, radiogenic and stable-isotope geochemistry, hydrology.

Joan Ramage, Assistant Professor; Ph.D., Cornell, 2001. Remote sensing, surface processes, hydrology, glacial geology.

Dork Sahagian, Professor; Ph.D., Chicago, 1987. Global change, hydrology, environment and human civilization.

Craig Williamson, Professor; Ph.D., Dartmouth, 1981. Aquatic ecosystems, limnology.

Zicheng Yu, Assistant Professor; Ph.D., Toronto, 1997. Paleoecology and paleoclimatology.

Lehigh University

SELECTED PUBLICATIONS

Anastasio, D. J., and J. E. Holl. Transverse fold evolution in the External Sierra, southern Pyrenees, Spain. *J. Struct. Geol.* 23:379–92, 2001.

Bebout, G. E., and E. Nakamura. Record in metamorphic tourmalines of subduction zone devolatilization and boron cycling. *Geology* 31:407–10.

Alley, R. B., et al. **(E. B. Evenson).** Stabilizing feedbacks in glacier bed erosion. *Nature* 424:758–60, 2003.

Evenson, E. B., et al. Field evidence for the recognition of glaciohydrologic supercooling. In *Glacial Processes Past and Present,* GSA Special Paper 337, pp. 11–22, eds. D. M. Mickelson and J. W. Attig. Boulder, Colorado: Geological Society of America, 1999.

Hargreaves, B. R. Water column optics and penetration of ultraviolet radiation. In *UV Effects in Aquatic Organisms and Ecosystems,* Comprehensive Series in Photochemical and Photobiological Sciences, eds. E. W. Helbling and H. E. Zagarese. Cambridge: Royal Society of Chemistry, 2003.

Tan, X., et al. **(K. P. Kodama).** Paleomagnetic and magnetic anisotropy of Cretaceous red beds from the Tarim basin, northwest China: Evidence for a rock magnetic cause of anomalously shallow paleomagnetic inclinations from central Asia. *J. Geophys. Res.* 108(B2):2107, 2003.

Kodama, K. P., and P. D. Ward. Compaction-corrected paleomagnetic paleolatitudes for Late Cretaceous rudists along the Cretaceous California margin; evidence for less than 1500 km of post–Late Cretaceous offset for Baja British Columbia. *Geol. Soc. Am. Bull.* 113:1171–8, 2001.

Gulick, S. P. S., **A. S. Meltzer,** and S. H. Clarke. Effect of the northward-migrating Mendocino Triple Junction on the Eel River forearc basin, California: Part 1. Stratigraphic development. *Geol. Soc. Am. Bull.* 114:178–91, 2002.

Meltzer, A. S., et al. Seismic characterization of an active metamorphic massif, Nanga Parbat, Pakistan, Himalaya. *Geology* 29:651–4, 2001.

Osburn, C. L., and **D. P. Morris.** Photochemistry of dissolved organic matter in natural waters. In *UV Effects in Aquatic Organisms and Ecosystems,* eds. E. W. Helbling and H. E. Zagarese. Cambridge: Royal Society of Chemistry, 2003.

Wegmann, K., and **F. Pazzaglia.** Holocene strath terraces, climate change, and active tectonics: The Clear River basin, Olympic Peninsula, Washington State. *Geol. Soc. Am. Bull.* 114:731–44, 2002.

Pazzaglia, F. J., and M. T. Brandon. A fluvial record of long-term steady-state uplift and erosion across the Cascadia forearc high, western Washington state. *Am. J. Sci.* 301:385–431, 2001.

Ramage, J. M., and B. Isacks. Interannual variations of snowmelt and refreeze timing in southeast-Alaskan icefields. *U.S.A. J. Glaciology* 49:102–16, 2003.

Sahagian, D., A. Proussevitch, and W. Carlson. Analysis of vesicular basalts and lava emplacement processes for application as a paleobarometer/paleoaltimeter: A reply. *J. Geol.* 111:502–4, 2003.

Grad, G., B. J. Burnett, and **C. E. Williamson.** UV damage and photoreaction: Timing and age are everything. *Photochem. Photobiol.* 78:225–7, 2003.

Williamson, C. E., et al. Temperature-dependent ultraviolet responses in zooplankton: Implication of climate change. *Limnology and Oceanography* 47:1844–8, 2002.

Yu, Z. C. Late Quaternary dynamics of tundra and forest vegetation in the southern Niagara Escarpment, Canada. *New Phytologist* 157:365–90, 2003.

Zeitler, P. K., et al. **(A. Meltzer).** Crustal reworking at Nanga Parbat, Pakistan: Evidence for erosional focusing of crustal strain. *Tectonics* 20:712–28, 2001.

MichiganTech
Michigan's Technological University

MICHIGAN TECHNOLOGICAL UNIVERSITY

Department of Social Sciences
Master of Science in Environmental Policy

Program of Study

The Master of Science in Environmental Policy (EP) Program links policy and science through an innovative curriculum that emphasizes collaboration of social sciences, biology, engineering, and forestry faculty members. It stresses practical training in environmental decision making and the importance of public participation in those decisions. Social sciences faculty members teach most core courses. Faculty members in other academic units provide expertise in environmental economics, communication, ecology, resource management, and other areas of environmental sciences and engineering. The M.S. in environmental policy is a professional degree. The curriculum provides students with a range of analytical skills, along with a sophisticated conceptual understanding of environmental issues and their social dimensions. Faculty members emphasize interdisciplinary research and teaching and pay careful attention to the development of students as competent professionals. Recent research opportunities have included projects on pollution control policy, emissions trading, endangered species, land use, and Great Lakes water quality.

Typically, the program involves two years in residence. First-year students study the fundamentals of environmental policy analysis, the social context of environmental issues, environmental decision making, and global environmental systems. During the summer, students are encouraged to participate in an internship with a public or private organization or conduct an independent project under faculty supervision. Most of the second year is devoted to concentration courses and a research project or thesis.

Research Facilities

Faculty members emphasize interdisciplinary research and teaching, paying careful attention to the development of students as competent professionals. Recent research opportunities include projects on pollution control policy, emissions trading, endangered species, land use, and Great Lakes water quality. During the summer between the first and second years, students are encouraged to undertake an internship, working with either a public agency, nongovernmental organization, or private firm. Ideally, these internships form the basis for the student's master's project or thesis.

Financial Aid

Financial aid is available to a limited number of qualified full-time students in the form of fellowships, research assistantships, and teaching assistantships. Aid packages include a stipend, tuition, and some student fees. The stipend for M.S. candidates is currently $4415 per semester and for Ph.D. candidates, $5126 per semester. In addition, a health insurance supplement is provided by the University. Funding may be available on a competitive basis for students to travel to professional conferences.

Cost of Study

Tuition for full-time graduate students (resident and nonresident) for the 2004–05 academic year is $3888 per semester; engineering and computer science majors pay $4288 per semester. All students are responsible for a student activity fee of approximately $135 per semester. Health insurance is required for all graduate students; a supplement is subject to financial aid status.

Living and Housing Costs

Michigan Tech residence halls have accommodations for single students, and applications may be obtained from the Director of Residential Services. For married students, Michigan Tech has one- and two-bedroom furnished apartments. Applications may be obtained from the manager of Daniell Heights Apartments. Because the cost of housing is subject to change, representative costs cannot be stated. Off-campus housing is available in the surrounding community. Yahoo! lists the overall cost-of-living index for Houghton as 83 (national average is 100). Interested students can visit http://list.realestate.yahoo.com/realestate/neighborhood/main.html for more information.

Student Group

EP students come to Michigan Tech from a variety of undergraduate fields, including environmental science, environmental engineering, biology, business, psychology, and political science. However, they share a commitment to environmental quality and enthusiasm for policies to generate environmental improvement. Most students are full-time; 50 percent are women. About 80 percent of students are funded as teaching or research assistants. Prospective students should have strong undergraduate credentials and proven written and oral communication skills.

Student Outcomes

Recent graduates have taken positions as an environmental specialist with a consulting firm, a marketing researcher with a nonprofit environmental organization, a solid-waste planner, an environmental regulation specialist, and a research forester with the U.S. Forest Service. Several others have gone on to Ph.D. programs in fields such as environmental engineering, public health, and public policy.

Location

Michigan Tech is located in Houghton on Michigan's scenic Keweenaw Peninsula, which stretches about 70 miles into Lake Superior. The surrounding area is perfect for any outdoor activity. The campus is a 15-minute walk from downtown Houghton; public transportation is available from Houghton and Hancock. Houghton has been listed as the safest college town in Michigan and was ranked 8 out of 467 nationwide in the report, "Crime at College: Student Guide to Personal Safety." The Houghton County Memorial Airport (CMX) serves the area with direct flights to Minneapolis on Northwest Airlink; Marquette K.I. Sawyer (SAW, an approximate 2-hour drive from Houghton) serves the area via Detroit.

The University

Michigan Tech was founded in 1885 as the Michigan Mining School to serve the nation's first major mining enterprises focused on copper and iron. Several name changes tracked the growth and diversification of the institution, and it was named Michigan Technological University in 1964. Today, the University offers a full range of associate, bachelor's, master's, and doctoral degrees in the sciences, engineering, forestry, business, communication, and technology. MTU has been rated one of the nation's "Top Ten" best buys for science and technology by *U.S. News & World Report.*

Applying

Students should obtain an application packet from the EP Program or apply online at http://www.mtu.edu/apply. The application should be returned to the Graduate School. Official transcripts should be forwarded directly to the Graduate School. Graduate Record Examinations (GRE) scores are required; results should be sent directly to the Graduate School. Students should request three letters of recommendation from faculty members who are familiar with their work. These letters should be returned directly to the Director of the Environmental Policy Program. Applicants whose native language is not English must submit TOEFL scores. In order for applicants to be considered for financial assistance, all application materials should be received by March 1 for admission in the fall.

Correspondence and Information

Dr. Kathy Halvorsen
Director of the Environmental Policy Program
Department of Social Sciences
Michigan Technological University
Houghton, Michigan 49931-1295

Telephone: 906-487-2824)
E-mail: kehalvor@mtu.edu
World Wide Web: http://www.ss.mtu.edu/EP/index.html

Michigan Technological University

THE CORE FACULTY AND THEIR RESEARCH

Bradley H. Baltensperger, Professor of Geography; Ph.D., Clark, 1974. Environmental perception, natural hazards, environmental history. (brad@mtu.edu)

Mary H. Durfee, Associate Professor of Political Science; Ph.D., Cornell, 1990. Environmental policy, technology policy, Great Lakes institutions. (mhdurfee@mtu.edu)

Hugh Gorman, Associate Professor of Environmental Policy and History; Ph.D., Carnegie Mellon, 1996. Environmental history, history of pollution control policy. (hsgorman@mtu.edu)

Kathleen E. Halvorsen, Associate Professor of Natural Resource Policy; Ph.D., Washington (Seattle), 1996. Environmental and natural resource policy, environmental sociology. (kehalvor@mtu.edu)

Carol A. MacLennan, Associate Professor of Anthropology; Ph.D., Berkeley, 1979. Democratic participation, environmental politics. (camac@mtu.edu)

Barry D. Solomon, Associate Professor of Geography and Environmental Policy; Ph.D., Indiana, 1983. Environmental and energy policy, air pollution, endangered species. (bdsolomo@mtu.edu)

Adjunct Faculty

Adjunct faculty members are drawn from other academic units at the University, including environmental engineering, archaeology, mechanical engineering, geology, forestry, and the humanities.

MONTCLAIR STATE UNIVERSITY

College of Science and Mathematics
Environmental Management

Program of Study

Montclair State University offers the Doctor of Environmental Management (D.Env.M.), with four concentration areas: environmental education, serving the needs of teachers; environmental health, for health professionals; environmental management, for government and business leaders; and environmental science, serving industry. The program's overall goal is to emphasize research that is grounded in an interdisciplinary, systems-based approach to address environmental management issues. Administered by the Department of Earth and Environmental Studies, the program uses facilities of the New Jersey School of Conservation, operated by the University at Stokes State Forest.

In keeping with the University's mission of teaching, research, and public service, the D.Env.M. program takes an interdisciplinary approach to the study of human impact on natural resources. Students gain an understanding of the structure and function of environmental systems as well as the causes of and responses to environmental change in major urban areas, using New Jersey as its classroom and research field. Montclair State graduates become environmental experts who influence public policy and land-water protection systems.

The doctoral program centers on three interrelated research themes and includes within several disciplines a wide range of natural, social, and environmental management scientists. The water-land systems approach focuses on interactions between hydrological systems, including water and wetland systems patterns, coastal environments, and landscape structure and human settlement patterns. The nature of water in all its forms and how its availability is protected fall within this area of study. Another research area covers sustainability, vulnerability, and equity—a critical area for understanding and managing urban environments. Research in this area includes analysis of natural systems and establishment of working models for monitoring water supply, waste systems, and material use. The study of sustainability includes research into opportunities for enhancing environmental protection through business, education, and governmental institutions. The modeling and visualization research area uses computer-assisted techniques and methods to study the process of environmental change. Data-gathering and data-processing devices become cutting-edge research tools for the analysis of how physical and human environments interact.

Working professionals need not compromise their schedules to submerge themselves in a rigorous, research-based doctoral study experience, as the program is offered part-time, with evening and weekend study. The study begins with core courses in organizational environmental management, methods of environmental research, and ecology, environmental law, or management processes, depending upon a student's choice of focus area. All students complete a minimum of 30 credits of research, with a research project and a dissertation. Elective courses are chosen with an adviser and center on the student's particular area of interest. Elective courses may cover economic problems of the Third World, natural resource management, geography and urban studies, or managing a global workforce, along with many other course work choices. This interdisciplinary study covers major themes of sociology, science, and business. Physical science courses in wetland or shoreline ecology, microbiology, geophysics, evolutionary mechanisms, and other topics are available as well. Students are encouraged to choose an area of study and research based on their professional interests and goals. Elective courses can support that choice, or students may wish to take a diversity of subjects with an interdisciplinary theme.

Research Facilities

More than fifty teaching and research labs are outfitted for research in biology, chemistry, geoscience, geology, ecology, marine and aquatic biology, and many other topics of environmental concern. Specialized facilities include two greenhouses, laboratories for environmental geophysics and soil stratigraphy, and specialized equipment for environmental analysis—earth, air, plant, animal, or water. Field testing equipment include ground-penetrating radar, current and tide gauges, and hand-held Global Positioning System units. Montclair State University's libraries maintain academic resources that include books, journals, videos, scholarly publications, and electronic databases. These provide the most up-to-date information available on any subject. The widest research facility of all—the state of New Jersey—is fertile ground for environmental studies. The state contains all manner of habitats: shoreline, wetlands, urban and suburban development, farmland, and mountain regions. Montclair State maintains professional and academic relationships with dozens of local and state organizations, providing numerous opportunities for doctoral research in a diverse and plentiful number of applications.

Financial Aid

Several types of financial aid are available to graduate students who meet Montclair State's admission requirements; for further information, students should refer to the Graduate Catalog. A limited number of graduate assistantships, including full tuition waivers, are available on a competitive basis for full-time D.Env.M. students. Applications for assistantships are included in the application packet.

Cost of Study

Doctoral tuition fees for in-state residents are $376.01 per semester hour. Out-of-state tuition is about 35 percent higher.

Living and Housing Costs

At Montclair State University, graduate students have several housing options, ranging from traditional and suite-style dorms to apartment communities. A shuttle bus that connects apartment housing with the main campus is available. Dorm rooms cost anywhere from $2000 to $3000 per year. Two-bedroom apartments for 4 residents cost $2721 per student per year. Other options may be reviewed on the University's Web site. Meal plans are available in flexible package and cost options, depending on individual need.

Student Group

Montclair State University enrolls approximately 14,000 students.

Location

In many ways, Montclair State University provides an outstanding learning environment. The University's easy access to New York City makes it a great place in which to study. The campus is near local bus and train service, major train transportation, and international airports. Montclair State's location offers diverse cultural experiences, restaurants, shopping, recreation, and entertainment. New Jersey offers beautiful shoreline and beach areas, rural and park recreation, mountain skiing and hiking, and city culture and nightlife. The state has myriad possibilities for study and exploration, both for academic and social purposes.

The University

Founded in 1908, Montclair State University was originally established for teacher training. In the 1930s, Montclair began offering master's degree programs and became accredited as a teachers' college—one of the first in the nation. The University now offers forty-four undergraduate majors, thirty-five graduate majors, and numerous interdisciplinary programs through three colleges and two schools. Its easy access to New York City, as well as the New Jersey mountains and shoreline, makes it ideal for the study of environmental disciplines. Fertile research ground in several areas can be found within proximity of the campus.

Applying

Graduate students wishing to be considered as doctoral candidates must complete an application, which may be found online at http://www.montclair.edu. In addition, applicants must write a personal essay describing their areas of potential research interest and the relevance of doctoral study to their scholarly development. Official transcripts, GRE scores, TOEFL scores (if necessary), three letters of reference, and an application fee of $60 complete the package. Applicants to this program must complete a self-managed application, meaning the applicant gathers all required documentation and then submits it in one packet for University review. The deadline for receipt of all application materials, including applications for assistantships, is February 15 for admission for the following fall semester. Applications for spring admission are considered.

Correspondence and Information

College of Science and Mathematics
Richardson Hall 262
Montclair State University
Montclair, New Jersey 07043

Telephone: 973-655-5108
Fax: 973-655-4390
E-mail: debeusb@mail.montclair.edu
World Wide Web: http://www.csam.montclair.edu/denvm/

Montclair State University

THE FACULTY AND THEIR RESEARCH

George E. Antoniou, Professor; Ph.D., National Technology University (Athens). Computer modeling.
Paul A. X. Bologna, Assistant Professor; Ph.D., South Alabama. Marine ecology, aquatic vegetation.
Stefanie A. Brachfeld, Assistant Professor; Ph.D., Minnesota. Marine geophysics, paleoclimatology, polar regions.
Mark J. Chopping, Assistant Professor; Ph.D., Nottingham. Remote sensing, GIS.
Norma C. Connolly, Professor; J.D., New York Law. Environmental law, natural resource dispute litigation.
Huan Feng, Assistant Professor; Ph.D., SUNY at Stony Brook. Estuarine and coastal environmental quality assessment and management; behavior, transport, and fate of land-based contaminants in aquatic systems and sediments; biogeochemical cycle of trace elements in riverine, estuarine, and coastal environments.
Zhaodong Feng, Associate Professor; Ph.D., Kansas. Environmental change, human-environment interactions, semiarid environments, Quaternary studies, GIS applications in geomorphology and environmental studies.
Richard R. Franke, Professor; Ph.D., Harvard. International development and planning, sustainability, South Asia.
Peter Freund, Professor; Ph.D., New School. Sociological aspects of public health, social organization of space and the environment, social impacts of the automobile.
Yuan Gao, Associate Professor; Ph.D., Rhode Island. Atmospheric chemistry.
Matthew Gorring, Assistant Professor; Ph.D., Cornell. Igneous petrology, geochronology, radiogenic isotope, geochemistry, tectonics.
Eileen Kaplan, Professor; Ph.D., Rutgers. Business administration, international human resources administration.
Scott L. Kight, Assistant Professor; Ph.D., Indiana. Evolutionary biology, entomology, ecology, animal behavior.
Michael A. Kruge, Professor and Associate Dean, College of Science and Mathematics; Ph.D., Berkeley. Geochemistry of organic contaminants in sediments.
Phillip LeBel, Professor; Ph.D., Boston University. Resource and energy economics.
Lee Lee, Professor; Ph.D., CUNY. Microbiology.
Jonathan M. Lincoln, Associate Professor and Chair, Earth and Environmental Studies; Ph.D., Northwestern. Shallow marine stratigraphy sedimentation, environmental applications of geophysics.
Bonnie Lustigman, Professor and Chair, Biology; Ph.D., Fordham. Microbiology: effect of metals on growth of microorganisms.
George T. Martin, Professor; Ph.D., Chicago. Social impacts of the automobile, globalization and consumption.
Jon Michael McCormick, Professor; Ph.D., Oregon State. Benthic and estuarine ecology, effects of heavy-metal contamination in estuarine environment.
Duke U. Ophori, Associate Professor; Ph.D., Alberta. Hydrogeology, groundwater flow modeling in fractured reservoirs, nuclear-waste disposal.
Gregory A. Pope, Associate Professor; Ph.D., Arizona State. Geomorphology, physical geography, geographic information systems applications in physical geography, human impacts on the environment, global change, geoarchaeology.
Robert S. Prezant, Professor and Dean, College of Science and Mathematics; Ph.D., Delaware. Aquatic ecology, biodiversity, malacology.
Glenville Rawlins, Associate Professor; Ph.D., NYU. International business, international development, Africa.
Stefan A. Robila, Assistant Professor; Ph.D., Syracuse. Remote sensing.
Paul Scipione, Professor; Ph.D., Rutgers. Consumer psychology, marketing, spatial analysis.
Harbans Singh, Professor; Ph.D., Rutgers. Environmental policy and problem solving.
John Smallwood, Associate Professor; Ph.D., Ohio State. Ecology and kestrel ecology, effect of land use on bird migration and nesting.
Rolf Sternberg, Professor; Ph.D., Syracuse. Geography, geopolitics, urban geography, transportation geography and world resources.
Robert W. Taylor, Professor; Ph.D., Saint Louis. Environmental public policy, regional planning and urban development, urban environmental issues, environmental communications, environmental business policy.
Dirk W. Vanderklein, Associate Professor; Ph.D., Minnesota. Tree physiological ecology, forestry and forest ecology.
Neeraj Vedwan, Assistant Professor; Ph.D., Georgia. Impact of climate change on agriculture.
Stanley Walling, Director, Center for Archaeological Studies; Ph.D., Tulane. Field and contract archaeology, geoarchaeology.
Michael Zey, Associate Professor; Ph.D., Rutgers. International business and technology development, futurist.

OGI SCHOOL OF SCIENCE & ENGINEERING

at Oregon Health & Science University

Department of Environmental and Biomolecular Systems
Environmental Science and Engineering Program

Programs of Study

Founded more than thirty years ago, the Environmental Science and Engineering (ESE) Program is one of the oldest stand-alone ESE programs in the country. It is known for its research and degree programs, which balance practical applications with fundamental investigations of the physical, chemical, and biological processes underlying environmental phenomena. The curriculum is built on a foundation of fundamental science and engineering, drawing from chemistry, hydrology, microbiology, estuarine and coastal processes, risk assessment, and environmental law. The department offers M.S. and Ph.D. degrees and a specific educational track in environmental information technology.

Ph.D. candidates must complete at least 52 credit hours of course work. Ph.D. candidates must pass a two-part comprehensive exam. The first part is a written examination covering four subject areas selected by the department. The second part is the preparation and oral defense of a proposal that defines the student's Ph.D. dissertation research. A written Ph.D. dissertation with an oral defense is required. Ph.D. students complete the majority of their course work during the first two years of their program.

Students in the M.S. program must complete at least 45 credits. Those enrolled in the thesis program earn no more than 9 credits in research, with the remainder earned through distribution courses in applied mathematics, chemistry, fluid dynamics, biology, surface waters, groundwater, and air. A comprehensive examination is required for the M.S. thesis. Nonthesis degree students must complete at least 45 credits through course work and up to 8 credits in nonthesis research or professional internship. A comprehensive examination is not required for the nonthesis degree. Students may also pursue an M.S. or Ph.D. with a concentration in environmental information technology or an M.S. with a concentration in environmental health systems.

Research Facilities

There is a strong emphasis on modern instrumentation, with state-of-the-art equipment within easy access of each laboratory. The department operates regional facilities in high-resolution mass spectroscopy, electron paramagnetic resonance spectroscopy, and Raman spectroscopy. It is also equipped with Fourier-transform nuclear magnetic resonance and Fourier-transform infrared and fluorescence spectrophotometers, as well as extensive facilities for gas chromatography, high-pressure liquid chromatography, and fast-protein liquid chromatography. The department contains a number of ultracentrifuges, scintillation counters, electrophoresis systems, laminar flow hoods, and controlled-growth chambers. Students and faculty members have access to a wide variety of computers that are interconnected through a campuswide local area network, making available powerful facilities for scientific computing, online text and document processing, and e-mail. Two research centers are housed in the department. The Center for Coastal and Land-Margin Research (CCALMR) is dedicated to regional-scale and interdisciplinary research and its applications to ecosystems at the margins of the land and the sea. Advanced modeling and scientific visualization techniques are used to integrate process-oriented research on the physics, chemistry, and biology of land-margin ecosystems. CCALMR operates CORIE, a state-of-the-art environmental observation and forecast system for the Columbia River estuary. CORIE is a multipurpose research tool addressing important ecosystem issues and is an integral component of the environmental information technology track. The Center for Groundwater Research (CGR) operates with a multidisciplinary group of scientists who conduct research on important issues related to groundwater quality and quantity. CGR operates a variety of large experimental aquifers, unlike any in the world, in which contaminant migration in groundwater can be studied in a completely controlled environment at very nearly field scale. The Samuel L. Diack Library includes more than 19,000 monographic titles and 300 current journal subscriptions and provides electronic access to many science, technology, and business-related databases through the Internet.

Financial Aid

All M.S. and Ph.D. students are eligible for financial assistance. Candidates applying to the Ph.D. program are automatically considered for fellowships that provide an annual stipend, fully paid tuition, and fully paid health insurance. Other research assistantships are available for qualified Ph.D. applicants.

Cost of Study

Tuition and fees vary by course load. Prospective students should contact the Graduate Education Office for details.

Living and Housing Costs

Graduate students live off campus. A variety of off campus housing is available near OGI, ranging from $550 to $950 per month. Housing is also available through the Portland State University housing program.

Student Group

The student population is divided equally between men and women and between individuals of U.S. and international origin.

Location

The School is located 12 miles west of downtown Portland in an area known as the Silicon Forest. The School's neighbors include Intel's largest research and development facility, Tektronix, IBM, Hewlett-Packard, Mentor Graphics, Nike, and Adidas. The greater Portland metropolitan area provides diverse cultural and recreational activities, including the largest wilderness park within the limits of any city in the United States.

The School

The OGI School of Science & Engineering is one of four schools of Oregon Health & Science University. OGI provides a graduate-level education that combines a vigorous research emphasis and state-of-the-art instrumentation with the intimacy and personal attention associated with small colleges. The research environment emphasizes the fundamentals and practical applications to solve problems in advanced technology, science, management, the environment, and health. The faculty members are internationally recognized for their research, giving students the opportunity to get involved in all aspects of the departmental research programs and have ready access to state-of-the-art research instrumentation.

Applying

For degree programs, the following items must be submitted: a completed application form, a $65 nonrefundable application fee, official transcripts from each college or university attended, three letters of recommendation, official GRE scores, and TOEFL scores, if applicable. Applications are considered on a year-round basis, and it is recommended that students submit their applications ten weeks prior to the quarter in which they would like to begin (fifteen weeks for international students). All candidates for the program must have strong quantitative skills, as well as previous course work in chemistry, biology, and mathematics, including at least one year of college-level calculus.

Correspondence and Information

Office of Graduate Education
OGI School of Science & Engineering at OHSU
20000 Northwest Walker Road
Beaverton, Oregon 97006-8921

Telephone: 503-748-1382
Fax: 503-748-1285
E-mail: admissions@admin.ogi.edu
World Wide Web: http://www.ebs.ogi.edu/

OGI School of Science & Engineering at OHSU

THE FACULTY AND THEIR RESEARCH

António M. Baptista, Professor and Department Head; Ph.D., MIT, 1987. Integrated analysis of estuarine and coastal processes, environmental observation and forecasting systems, numerical methods and grid generation.

William H. Glaze, Professor; Ph.D., Wisconsin–Madison, 1961. Structures of catalysis by organometallic compounds, viz., the determination of structure/activity relationships among group IA/IIA metal organics through spectroscopic and kinetic isotope effects.

David A. Jay, Associate Professor; Ph.D., Washington (Seattle), 1987. River basin, estuarine, and continental shelf processes; turbulent mixing; tides and tidal analysis; the influence of hydrodynamic processes on ecosystems.

Richard L. Johnson, Associate Professor; Ph.D., Oregon Graduate Center, 1985. Physical and chemical behavior of organic contaminants in the air, soil, and water; environmental analytical organic chemistry; transport and fate of contaminants at the watershed scale; modeling of contaminant transport.

James F. Pankow, Professor; Ph.D., Caltech, 1978. Physical and analytical chemistry of trace organics and metals in natural water and the atmosphere, fates of organic and inorganic compounds in the environment.

Reinhold A. Rasmussen, Professor; Ph.D., Washington (St. Louis), 1964. Measurement of trace gases, including the chlorofluorocarbons and their replacement HCFCs and HFCs, methane, nitrous oxide, carbon monoxide, hydrogen, carbonyl sulfide, and the C2-C15 hydrocarbons; both biogenic isoprene-terpenoids and anthropogenic air toxic emissions of other VOCs and their roles in stratospheric ozone destruction, greenhouse effect, and regional ozone formation.

Patricia L. Toccalino, Assistant Professor; Ph.D., Oregon Graduate Institute of Science and Technology, 1992. Human and ecological assessments, water quality assessments, contaminant fate and transport in various environmental media.

Paul G. Tratnyek, Associate Professor; Ph.D., Colorado School of Mines, 1987. Mechanistic and kinetic aspects of the fate of organic pollutants in the environment; degradation reactions involving pesticides, phenols, munitions, dyestuffs, and chlorinated hydrocarbon solvents; chemical and microbiological processes in sediments, soils, and groundwaters as well as photochemical processes in surface waters; natural and engineered remediation systems.

Karen H. Watanabe, Research Assistant Professor; Ph.D., Berkeley 1993. Bioaccumulation in aquatic environments, mathematical modeling of living systems, health and ecological risk assessment.

PACE UNIVERSITY

Dyson College of Arts and Sciences
Master of Science in Environmental Science

Program of Study

The Departments of Biological Sciences and of Chemistry and Physical Sciences offer the Master of Science in Environmental Science degree program. The 41- or 42-credit curriculum is structured so that students may encounter environmental issues from scientific, ethical, practical, and legal perspectives. Its faculty members, who are senior professionals in academe, research, industry, and law, bring an interdisciplinary approach to the program. An independent project is part of the curriculum. Specialization courses allow for additional study in either a directed scientific discipline, such as toxicology, waste treatment and management, geographical information and surveillance systems, environmental sampling and analysis, or ecology, or in areas related to public administration.

Research Facilities

The Pace University Library is a comprehensive teaching library and student learning center, a virtual library that combines strong core collections with ubiquitous access to global Internet resources to support broad and diversified curricula. Reciprocal borrowing and access accords, traditional interlibrary loan services, and commercial document-delivery options supplement the aggregate library. Pace offers instructional services librarians, a state-of-the-art electronic classroom, digital reference services, and multimedia applications. Pace's computer resource centers are linked to high-speed data networks and feature sophisticated hardware and software to facilitate active learning. Recognized as one of America's most wired universities, Pace supports high-speed Internet and Internet2 access on every campus; residence facilities are wired, and most public areas are enabled for wireless connectivity. Full-motion videoconference facilities enable remote delivery of instruction between campus sites for synchronous learning applications. Many courses are Web assisted with state-of-the-art software, and some courses and programs are completely Web based.

Financial Aid

Pace's comprehensive student financial assistance program includes scholarships, graduate assistantships, student loans, and tuition-payment plans. Scholarships are awarded to students in recognition of academic achievement and are available for full- and part-time study. Highly qualified students may be eligible for assistantships awarded by departments, which pay stipends of up to $5100 and tuition remission of up to 24 credits during the 2003–04 academic year. Pace participates in all major federal and state financial aid programs, such as Direct Loans, the New York State Tuition Assistance Program (TAP), Federal Perkins Loans, and the Federal Work-Study Program. All students are encouraged to apply for these programs by filing the Free Application for Federal Student Aid (FAFSA).

Cost of Study

Tuition for graduate courses was $700 per credit in 2003–04.

Living and Housing Costs

Residence facilities are available on campus in both New York City and Westchester. Double-occupancy rooms cost $5600 for the 2003–04 academic year. University-operated, off-campus housing is available within proximity of the New York City campus.

Student Group

Pace students represent diverse personal, cultural, and educational backgrounds. Many students are employed and pursue graduate study for personal growth and career advancement. Sixty-three percent are enrolled part-time in evening classes. Current enrollment in the graduate environmental science program is approximately 10 students.

Location

Pace University is a multicampus institution with campuses in New York City and Westchester County, New York. All locations are within reach of cultural, business, and social resources and opportunities. The downtown Manhattan campus is adjacent to Wall Street and City Hall. Pace's Midtown Center is a short distance from Times Square, theaters, and Grand Central Station. The Pleasantville/Briarcliff campus is located in a suburban setting, surrounded by towns that offer various forms of recreation. The Graduate Center and the School of Law are located in White Plains, New York, among major retail districts and many corporate headquarters. Pace also offers courses at a satellite campus in Hudson Valley, New York. All locations are accessible by public transportation. The graduate environmental science program is available at the Pleasantville campus.

The University

Founded in 1906, Pace University is a private, nonsectarian, coeducational institution. Originally founded as a school of accounting, Pace Institute was designated Pace College in 1973. Through growth and various successes, Pace College was renamed Pace University, as approved by the New York State Board of Regents. Today, Pace offers comprehensive undergraduate, graduate, doctoral, and professional programs at several campus locations through six schools and colleges.

Applying

Admission to Pace University graduate programs requires successful completion of a U.S. baccalaureate degree or its equivalent from an accredited institution. Students must submit a completed application, an application fee, official transcripts from all postsecondary institutions attended, a personal statement, a resume, and two letters of recommendation. International students must submit official TOEFL score reports and transcripts in their native language with a professional English translation.

Students must demonstrate satisfactory performance on the GRE General Test. An undergraduate major in science is not required; however, preparation should include one year of course work in general biology, general chemistry, and organic chemistry.

Applications should be submitted by August 1 for the fall semester, December 1 for the spring semester, and May 1 for summer sessions. International applications should be submitted one month prior to these dates.

Correspondence and Information

Office of Graduate Admission
Pace University
1 Pace Plaza
New York, New York 10038
Telephone: 212-346-1531
Fax: 212-346-1585
E-mail: gradnyc@pace.edu
World Wide Web: http://www.pace.edu

Office of Graduate Admission
Pace University
1 Martine Avenue
White Plains, New York 10606
Telephone: 914-422-4283
Fax: 914-422-4287
E-mail: gradwp@pace.edu
World Wide Web: http://www.pace.edu

Pace University

THE FACULTY

Carl Candioloro, Professor of Biological Sciences; Ph.D., St. John's (New York). Biotechnology.
Frank Commisso, Professor of Botany Biology; Ph.D., Fordham.
William Flank, Professor of Chemistry; Ph.D., Delaware. Field sampling, water monitoring, statistical analysis.
Margaret Minnis, Lecturer in Chemistry; Ph.D., Syracuse. Chemistry.
John Pawlowski, Professor of Biology; Ph.D., Fordham. Ecology and environmental testing.
Kevin Reilly, Professor; J.D., New York State Supreme Court. Environmental law.
Richard Schlesinger, Professor and Chair of Biological Sciences and Toxicology; Ph.D., NYU.
Joshua Schwartz, Associate Professor of Biological Sciences and Ecology; Ph.D., Connecticut.
Mary M. Timney, Professor of Political Science; Ph.D., Pittsburgh.
William Ventura, Professor of Biological Sciences and Toxicology; Ph.D., New York Medical College.
Ellen Weiser, Professor and Chair of Chemistry and Physical Sciences and Assistant Program Director; Ph.D., CUNY Graduate School. Environmental biochemistry.

SOUTHERN ILLINOIS UNIVERSITY CARBONDALE

Environmental Resources and Policy

Program of Study

The Environmental Resources and Policy (ER&P) Ph.D. degree at Southern Illinois University Carbondale (SIUC) provides students with an interdisciplinary education in natural resource and environmental processes, with a perspective on public policy and social institutions that shape societal and individual reactions to environmental issues. Students are prepared to work with multifaceted environmental problems and carry out interdisciplinary scientific research and are qualified for high-level administration positions in academia, government, and the private sector. Graduates are able to address the most compelling and daunting challenge in natural resource and environmental issues—identifying and solving problems that cross disciplinary boundaries.

The Environmental Resources and Policy Ph.D. degree is administered through the Departments of Geography and Geology and the College of Agriculture (agribusiness economics, forestry, and plant, soil, and general agriculture). The School of Law and the College of Engineering also cooperate in the program.

The course of study is composed of four interdisciplinary core courses and supplemented with the requirements and electives for each of the six areas of concentration: earth and environmental processes; energy and mineral resources; environmental policy and administration; forestry, agricultural, and rural land resources; geographic information systems and environmental modeling; and water resources. Students typically spend three years in course work and research, with oral and written preliminary examinations at the end of their course work.

Research Facilities

Students in the ER&P Ph.D. program have access to a fully equipped, state-of-the-art geographic information systems/remote sensing laboratory with a full-time supervisor and individual workstations. Cooperating departments have laboratory facilities that are used by various professors in their research.

In addition, the University's Morris Library has a general collection of 2.7 million volumes, 4.5 million microforms, and more than 26,000 current serial subscriptions, with access to Online Computer Library Center (OCLC) and ILLINET Online, the statewide automated catalog system.

Financial Aid

Students accepted into the ER&P program are eligible for financial aid on a competitive basis. Students may also be eligible for assistance through grants from research projects or other sources.

Cost of Study

In-state tuition was $192 per semester credit hour (or $3587 for 15 hours and up) in 2003–04. Out-of-state tuition was $480 per semester credit hour (or $7907 for 15 hours and up). Fees varied from $356 (1 hour) to $707 (12 hours).

Living and Housing Costs

For married couples, students with families, and single graduate students, the University had 589 efficiency and one-, two-, and three-bedroom apartments that rented for $385 to $445 per month in 2003–04. Residence halls for single graduate students are also available, as are accessible residence hall rooms and apartments for students with disabilities.

Student Group

Southern Illinois University's 21,000 undergraduate and graduate students come from many states and countries. The ER&P Ph.D. program attracts a large number of international as well as domestic students. Students are given the opportunity to work with a number of faculty members from other cooperating departments in research, teaching, and learning activities.

Location

SIUC is 350 miles south of Chicago and 100 miles southeast of St. Louis. Nestled in rolling hills bordered by the Ohio and Mississippi Rivers and enhanced by a mild climate, the area has state parks, national forests and wildlife refuges, and large lakes for outdoor recreation. Cultural offerings include theater, opera, concerts, art exhibits, and cinema. Educational facilities for the families of students are excellent.

The University

Southern Illinois University Carbondale is a comprehensive public university with a variety of general and professional education programs. The University offers bachelor's and associate degrees, master's and doctoral degrees, the J.D. degree, and the M.D. degree. The University is fully accredited by the North Central Association of Colleges and Schools. The Graduate School has an essential role in the development and coordination of graduate instruction and research programs. The Graduate Council has academic responsibility for determining graduate standards, recommending new graduate programs and research centers, and establishing policies to facilitate the research effort.

Applying

Interested students should apply directly to the ER&P Ph.D. program. Application deadlines vary. The program accepts midyear applications.

Correspondence and Information

Director
Environmental Resources and Policy
Southern Illinois University Carbondale
Carbondale, Illinois 62901-4637
Telephone: 618-453-7328
Fax: 618-453-7346
World Wide Web: http://www.siu.edu/~er&p

Southern Illinois University Carbondale

THE FACULTY AND THEIR RESEARCH

Ken Anderson, Associate Professor. Organic geochemistry.
Cem Basman, Assistant Professor. Forest recreation.
Jeff Beaulieu, Associate Professor. Environmental modeling and policy, marketing.
Roger Beck, Professor. Value-added agricultural enterprises, agribusiness firm location, land use, spatial patterns of economic activity.
Wendy Bigler, Assistant Professor. Fluvial geomorphology, rivers and society.
Jason Bond, Assistant Professor. Nematology and plant pathology.
John Burde, Professor. Policy and forest recreation.
Andrew Carver, Assistant Professor. Natural resource economics and development, land use planning, GIS/spatial analysis.
She-Kong Chong, Professor. Soil physics, turf soil management.
John Crelling, Professor. Coal geology.
Imed Dami, Assistant Professor. Viticulture.
Ken Diesburg, Assistant Professor. Turfgrass management training, breeding, and research.
Leslie Duram, Associate Professor. Population and natural resources, rural land use, conservation thought.
Benedykt Dziegielewski, Professor. Resources analysis and evaluation techniques, water resources planning and management, water conservation.
Phil Eberle, Associate Professor. Economic efficiency and viability studies of various enterprises and management practices.
Steven Esling, Associate Professor and Chair, Department of Geology. Hydrogeology.
Eric Ferré, Assistant Professor. Structural geology, rock magnetism.
Richard Fifarek, Associate Professor. Economic geology.
John Groninger, Assistant Professor. Silviculture, forest vegetation management.
Kim Harris, Associate Professor. Agriculture finance and agribusiness management.
Paul Henry, Associate Professor. Ornamental horticulture.
Bruce Hooper, Associate Professor. Watershed management, integrated water resources management and policy, floodplain management.
Scott Ishman, Associate Professor. Marine micropaleontology.
Brian Klubek, Professor. Soil microbiology.
Steven Kraft, Professor and Chair, Department of Agribusiness Economics. Soil and water conservation policy, watershed management and planning, farm policy.
Christopher L. Lant, Professor and Chair, Department of Geography. Water resources management, wetlands and nonpoint source pollution policy, sustainable development.
David Lightfoot, Professor. Plant biotechnology and genomics.
Halid Meksem, Assistant Professor. Plant genomics, genetics, and biotechnology.
Jean Mangun, Assistant Professor. Human dimensions of natural resource management.
Karen Midden, Associate Professor. Landscape design.
Wanki Moon, Assistant Professor. Public acceptance of GMOs, health information in food markets natural resources, rural land use, conservation thought.
Tonny Oyana, Assistant Professor. GIS, GIScience, cartographic and geographic visualization, environmental health and exposure.
John Phelps, Professor and Chair, Department of Forestry. Forest product marketing, wood science.
Nicholas Pinter, Associate Professor. Environmental geology, fluvial geomorphology.
John Preece, Professor. Horticulture, propagation, biotechnology.
Tiku Ravat, Professor. Potential-field geophysics.
Matt Rendleman, Associate Professor. Fuel ethanol, local enterprise impact analysis, Illinois dairy sector.
Paul L. Roth, Professor. Forest protection and forest management.
Charles Ruffner, Assistant Professor. Dendrochronology, ecology and paleoecology.
John Russin, Professor and Chair, Department of Plant and Soil Science. Plant pathology.
Dwight Sanders, Assistant Professor. Risk management, future contract design, forecasting techniques and evaluation.
Mike Schmidt, Associate Professor. Plant breeding and genetics.
John Sexton, Professor. Seismology.
Wanxiao Sun, Assistant Professor and Director of SEALab. Remote sensing, 3-D visualization and simulation, GIS.
Bradley Taylor, Associate Professor. Fruit crops.
Ed Varsa, Professor. Soil fertility, management, and testing.
Alan Walters. Vegetable production.
Karl Williard, Assistant Professor. Watershed management, forest hydrology, forest biochemistry, riparian zone management, sediment yield.
Bryan Young, Assistant Professor. Weed science.
Jim Zaczek, Assistant Professor. Ecology, biology, physiology, and genetics of trees; oak silviculture; regeneration ecology.

STONY BROOK UNIVERSITY, STATE UNIVERSITY OF NEW YORK

Department of Technology and Society
Environmental and Waste Management Program

Program of Study

The Department of Technology and Society offers graduate work leading to the Master of Science in technological systems management. The concentration in environmental and waste management is designed both for persons pursuing careers in environmental, waste, and energy management and technology assessment and for those planning environmental, waste, and energy research and technical careers. The program is particularly well suited for recent college graduates interested in studying environmental problems in a rigorous, thoroughly multidisciplinary setting and for middle career professionals who want to advance in or transfer to an environmental career or introduce environmental components into their main area of expertise. Thirty credits and a thesis are required for the master's degree. Full-time students may complete their programs of study in twelve to eighteen months; part-time students in twenty-four to thirty-six months. Most courses are taught in the evening.

Generally speaking, emphasis is placed on environmental, waste, and energy problems in industry and society at large; pollution prevention and waste minimization; environmental regulatory compliance; hazardous and radioactive waste, contamination, and cleanup; assessment of new environmental products, technologies, and policies; mathematical modeling and computer simulation; risk analysis; and the diagnosis of environmental disputes. Student theses have covered the full range of environmental, energy, and waste topics. Strong ties are maintained with area industry, Brookhaven National Laboratory, and the Waste Reduction and Management Institute.

Research Facilities

The department has advanced computer laboratories available for environmental modeling and simulation. Research projects are conducted off-site (for example, pollution and waste reduction assessments for a business). Research laboratories in other Stony Brook engineering and marine sciences departments and Brookhaven National Laboratory are available for collaborative projects.

Financial Aid

Some research assistantships and teaching assistants are available, but generally are reserved for full-time students. Many companies, government agencies, and national laboratories reimburse tuition costs. Paid internships with area industry, government agencies, and Brookhaven National Laboratory are sometimes available.

Cost of Study

Graduate courses cost $288 per credit hour for in-state residents and $438 per credit hour for out-of-state residents.

Living and Housing Costs

University apartments range in cost from $283 per month to $1302 per month, depending on the size of the unit. Off-campus housing options include furnished rooms to rent and houses and/or apartments to share that can be rented from $350 to $1500 per month.

Student Group

There are 15–20 matriculated environmental and waste management students, of whom one third are full-time and two thirds are part-time, within an overall departmental graduate program of approximately 80 students pursuing concentrations in industrial management, environmental and waste management, or educational computing. One fourth of the students come from other countries.

Student Outcomes

Graduates have established a distinguished record in their careers in environmental consulting firms; environmental technology companies; corporate environmental divisions of manufacturing and high-technology industries; American and foreign government environmental, energy, and waste management agencies; national laboratories; and research, educational, and technology assessment organizations.

Location

Stony Brook's campus is approximately 50 miles east of Manhattan on the North Shore of Long Island. The cultural offerings of New York City and Suffolk County's countryside and seashore are conveniently located nearby. Cold Spring Harbor Laboratories and Brookhaven National Laboratories are easily accessible from, and have close relationships with, the University.

The University

The University, established in 1957, achieved national stature within a generation. Founded at Oyster Bay, Long Island, the school moved to its present location in 1962. Stony Brook has grown to encompass more than 110 buildings on 1,100 acres. There are more than 1,568 faculty members, and the annual budget is more than $805 million. The Graduate Student Organization oversees the spending of the student activity fee for graduate student campus events. International students find the additional four-week Summer Institute in American Living very helpful. The Intensive English Center offers classes in English as a second language. The Career Development Office assists with career planning and has information on permanent full-time employment. Disabled Student Services has a Resource Center that offers placement testing, tutoring, vocational assessment, and psychological counseling. The Counseling Center provides individual, group, family, and marital counseling and psychotherapy. Day-care services are provided in four on-campus facilities. The Writing Center offers tutoring in all phases of writing.

Applying

For domestic students, all application materials for admission to the master's program must be received by March 1 for the summer session, March 15 for the fall semester, and October 1 for the spring semester. For international students, all application materials for admission to the master's program must be received by January 1 for the summer session, March 15 for the fall semester, and September 1 for the spring semester.

Correspondence and Information

Graduate Program Coordinator
Department of Technology and Society
347A Harriman Hall
Stony Brook University, State University of New York
Stony Brook, New York 11794-3760
Telephone: 631-632-8765

Stony Brook University, State University of New York

THE FACULTY AND THEIR RESEARCH

Distinguished Service Professors

David L. Ferguson, Chairperson; Ph.D., Berkeley, 1980. Quantitative methods, computer applications (especially intelligent tutoring systems and decision support systems); mathematics, science, and engineering education.

Lester G. Paldy, M.S., Hofstra, 1966. Nuclear arms control, science policy.

Distinguished Teaching Professors

Thomas T. Liao, Emeritus; Ed.D., Columbia, 1971. Computers in education, science, and technology education.

John G. Truxal, Emeritus; Sc.D., MIT, 1950. Control systems, technology-society issues.

Professors

Emil J. Piel, Emeritus; Ed.D., Rutgers, 1960. Decision making, technology-society issues, human-machine systems.

Tian-Lih Teng, Ph.D., Pittsburgh, 1969. Electrical engineering, computer science, management of information systems, electronics commerce.

Marian Visich Jr., Emeritus; Ph.D., Polytechnic of Brooklyn, 1956. Aerospace engineering, technology-society issues.

Associate Professors

Edward Kaplan, Visiting Associate Professor; Ph.D., Pennsylvania, 1973. Environmental systems engineering.

Samuel C. Morris, Visiting Associate Professor; Sc.D., Pittsburgh. Environmental science, risk analysis.

Sheldon J. Reaven, Graduate Program Director; Ph.D., Berkeley, 1975. Science and technology policy; energy and environmental problems and issues; waste management, recycling, and pollution prevention; risk analysis and life-cycle analysis; nuclear, chemical, and biological threats; technology assessment; homeland security.

Assistant Professor

Glenn G. Smith, Ph.D., Arizona State, 1998. Computer games and spatial visualization, distance education.

Lecturers

Joanne English Daly, M.S., SUNY at Stony Brook, 1994. Internet technology, computers in learning environments.

Herb Schiller, M.S., Polytechnic, 1973; M.S.M.E., Caltech, 1966. Operations management, manufacturing systems.

TENNESSEE TECHNOLOGICAL UNIVERSITY

Environmental Sciences Program

Programs of Study

The Environmental Sciences Program at Tennessee Technological University offers a concentration in either biology or chemistry but emphasizes the solution of complex environmental problems using an interdisciplinary approach. Course work is required in biology, chemistry, geology, agriculture, and sociology. It is an interdisciplinary degree program under the direction of interdepartmental advisory committees. The Ph.D. degree requires a minimum of 25 credit hours of course work beyond the master's degree (43 beyond the baccalaureate), satisfactory completion of a comprehensive examination, and satisfactory presentation and defense of a doctoral dissertation. The program's duration is three to four years. The interdisciplinary approach ensures that students become aware of a wide range of environmental concerns and that their research includes a breadth of environmental understanding beyond the boundaries of a particular discipline. Research areas cover a diverse array of environmental science and involve a variety of collaborative research with agencies such as the U.S. Fish and Wildlife Service, Tennessee Wildlife Resources Agency, NASA, USDA, EPA, and the National Laboratories at Oak Ridge, Los Alamos, and Brookhaven. Specific areas of emphasis are biodiversity; analytical method development; radionuliclide detection in the environment; nuclear waste treatment development; feeding ecology and habitat utilization of trout; management of endangered and threatened vertebrates; screening of environmental samples for pathogens; accelerated plant growth; surface and ground water protection; domestic, industrial, and recreational water use; wetland construction; wastewater treatment and disposal; development of new microbial aquatic toxicity assays; and the protection of aquatic organisms and other wildlife from point and non-point resources. The goal of the program is to prepare students for careers in research, management, government service, teaching, and other areas where they can make productive contributions to the solution of the ever-increasing diversity of environmental problems.

Research Facilities

Research is carried out in each of the following locations: the Department of Biology (Pennebaker Hall), the Department of Chemistry (Foster Hall), and the Center for Management, Utilization and Protection of Water Resources (Prescott Hall). The Department of Biology houses the federally and state-funded Tennessee Cooperative Fishery Research Unit. The Department of Chemistry houses the Tennessee Tech Center for Structural Chemistry (an NSF-funded research laboratory containing a diverse array of instrumentation). The Center for Management, Utilization and Protection of Water Resources is a federally and state-funded research facility that investigates all phases of water quality and resource management associated with aquatic environments. It maintains a staff with expertise in geographic information systems (GIS), modeling, and database management, and a professionally staffed laboratory, capable of general wet chemistry/physical parameter analyses, organic analyses, metal analyses, and biological/toxicity testing. Each department or center houses a wide variety of equipment and laboratories to carry out a diverse array of environmental research and analysis.

Financial Aid

Aid is available through individual departments and centers in the form of teaching or research assistantships. Full assistantships pay tuition and fees plus a stipend of $14,000 per year. Approximately 87 percent of all graduate students received either a teaching or research assistantship during the 2003–04 academic year.

Cost of Study

The 2002–03 tuition and fees for full-time graduate students were $3690 per academic year (two semesters) for Tennessee residents and $10,648 per academic year for nonresidents. A typical annual figure for books and other supplies is $600.

Living and Housing Costs

In 2003–04, dormitory accommodations were available for $990 per semester for double occupancy. The rooms are fully furnished with all utilities paid. Off-campus housing is also available. The Tech Village consists of more that 300 apartments, which have been available at approximately $250 per month. Meals on campus averaged $1330 per semester.

Student Group

The University enrolls about 9,107 undergraduate and 1,800 graduate students of whom 51 percent are men and 49 percent are women. The College of Arts and Sciences enrolled 1,347 undergraduates, 43 master's students, and 17 doctoral students in 2000–01.

Location

Cookeville is a city of about 30,000 people, located halfway between Nashville and Knoxville. The surrounding area abounds in natural beauty and includes several state parks and large lakes.

The University and The Program

Tennessee Technological University, founded in 1915, is a coeducational, state-supported university occupying a 235-acre main campus. The University comprises six colleges: Agriculture and Human Ecology, Arts and Sciences, Business Administration, Education, Engineering, and Nursing. The Environmental Sciences Program consists of faculty members from the Departments of Agriculture, Biology, Chemistry, Earth Sciences, and Sociology and Philosophy.

Applying

Students seeking admission to full standing in the chemistry concentration must have at least a bachelor's degree in chemistry that has been certified by the American Chemical Society or course work equivalent to this degree, a grade point average of 3.0 or above, and a minimum total score of 1000 on the revised GRE General Test. For questions concerning admission to the chemistry concentration, students should contact Dr. Jeffrey Boles at Jboles@tntech.edu or 931-372-3844. Students seeking admission to full standing in the biology concentration must have a bachelor's or master's degree in a biological science, a grade point average of 3.5 or above for the highest degree earned, and a minimum total score of 1000 on the GRE General Test. In addition, financial support must have been identified for a stipend and research needs, and a graduate faculty member must have agreed to direct the student's doctoral program. For financial support questions concerning admission to the biology concentration, students should contact Dr. Brad Cook at sbcook@tntech.edu or 931-372-3194. International students must have a score of 525 or above on the TOEFL. Students may be admitted to provisional standing in either concentration at the discretion of the Departmental Graduate Policies Committee and the Departmental Chairperson.

Correspondence and Information

For application requests:
Dean
Graduate School
Box 5036
Tennessee Technological University
Cookeville, Tennessee 38505
Telephone: 931-372-3233
Fax: 931-372-3497
E-mail: g_admissions@tntech.edu
World Wide Web: http://www.tntech.edu/

For other information:
Director, Environmental Sciences Ph.D. Program
College of Arts and Sciences
Box 5055
Tennessee Technological University
Cookeville, Tennessee 38505
Telephone: 931-372-3844
Fax: 931-372-3434
E-mail: Jboles@tntech.edu
World Wide Web: http://www2.tntech.edu/evs/

Tennessee Technological University

THE FACULTY AND THEIR RESEARCH

Department of Biology

S. K. Ballal, Professor; Ph.D., Tennessee, 1964. Plant cell biology.

Phillip W. Bettoli, Associate Professor; Ph.D. (wildlife and fisheries science), Texas A&M, 1987. Reservoir and tailwater fisheries management.

Chris Brown, Assistant Professor; Ph.D., Texas, 1998. Ecology, evolution, and behavior of terrestrial arthropods.

Felix G. Coe, Associate Professor; Ph.D., Connecticut, 1994. Systematics of vascular plants, floristics, economic botany, ethnobotany, phytochemistry.

Daniel L. Combs, Professor; Ph.D., Missouri–Columbia, 1987. Ecology and behavior of avian wildlife species, especially waterfowl; ecology and management of wetland ecosystems.

Steven B. Cook, Associate Professor; Ph.D. (zoology), Southern Illinois at Carbondale, 1994. Fish and benthic macroinvertebrate ecology in lotic (stream) ecosystems, feeding ecology of fishes, rainbow trout habitat utilization in stocked warmwater streams, effects of brook trout restoration on benthic macroinvertebrate communities.

John H. Gunderson, Assistant Professor; Ph.D. (zoology), Berkeley, 1981. Protistan phylogeny and microbial (primarily protistan-bacterial) interactions, characterization of prokaryotic symbionts of termite hindgut flagellates, development of 16S rRNA-based methods for the identification of protistan food vacuole contents, development of probes for tracking the abundance and distribution of parasitic dinoflagellates infecting a series of free-living dinoflagellates in Chesapeake Bay, screening of environmental samples for the presence of Legionella-like amoebal pathogens.

Michael Harvey, Ph.D. (vertebrate zoology), Kentucky, 1967. Ecology, distribution, status, and management of endangered and threatened vertebrates, especially bats and other mammals.

Steven E. Hayslette, Assistant Professor; Ph.D., Auburn, 2001. Wildlife ecology and management, avian behavior, ecology and management of doves and pigeons.

James B. Layzer, Professor; Ph.D. (zoology), Oklahoma State, 1982. Fish ecology, instream flow needs, evolutionary ecology, endangered species, mussel ecology.

Hayden Mattingly, Assistant Professor; Ph.D., Missouri–Columbia, 1999. Conservation biology, aquatic biology, ichthyology.

Eric L. Morgan, Professor; Ph.D., Virginia Tech, 1973. Aquatic biology and ecology, environmental and ecological physiology, environmental toxicology.

Thomas H. Roberts, Professor; Ph.D. (wildlife ecology), Mississippi State, 1981. Animal ecology, wetland ecology, habitat evaluation and management.

Department of Chemistry

Titus Albu, Assistant Professor; Ph.D., Case Western Reserve, 2001. Chemical reaction dynamics in gas phase and solution, algorithms for dynamical calculations.

Jeffrey O. Boles, Associate Professor; Ph.D. (biochemistry), South Carolina, 1992. Protein chemistry, enzymology, and crystallography; accelerated plant growth for environmentally friendly agriculture; isolation, purification, and regulation of plant growth factors; identification of plant growth hormones; synthesis of novel selenium and tellurium containing amino acids for bio-incorporation as X-ray labels and NMR probes.

Dale D. Ensor, Professor; Ph.D. (inorganic and radiochemistry), Florida State, 1977. Detection of radionuclides in the environment; application of ionic liquids to the development of environmentally sound separation practices; separation chemistry of lanthanides and actinides and its application to the development of advanced treatment processes of nuclear waste.

John J. Harwood, Professor; Ph.D. (analytical chemistry), Missouri–Columbia, 1984. Analytical/environmental chemistry, chemistry of natural waters, chromatographic speciation of selenium and arsenic in waters, sequestration of metal ions by polyphosphates.

Eugene Kline, Professor; Ph.D. (organic chemistry), Iowa State, 1973. Supercritical fluid extraction and chromatography, photodegradation of herbicides in soil, model compound studies of coal liquefaction and syntheses of the compounds, chemical information.

Daniel J. Swartling, Assistant Professor; Ph.D. (organic chemistry), North Dakota, 1989. Green chemistry, synthesis and characterization of non-ionic liquids.

Hong Zhang, Assistant Professor; Ph.D., Vermont, 2000. Analytical and environmental chemistry, aquatic and soil chemistry, trace metal analysis in natural waters and soils.

Center for Management, Utilization and Protection of Water Resources

Sharon Berk, Professor; Ph.D. (microbiology), Maryland, College Park, 1978. Legionella-protozoa interactions and cooling tower biocide effects, development of new microbial aquatic toxicity assays, protozoan-bacterial trophic interactions.

G. Kim Stearman, Professor; Ph.D. (plant and soil science), Tennessee, Knoxville, 1987. Accelerated solvent extraction, developing innovative extraction and analytical methods including supercritical fluid extraction and enzyme immunoassay analysis, studying fate and transport of anthropogenic chemicals in soil, developing an extraction method for analyzing phospholipids and other naturally occurring compounds in soil, developing constructed wetland systems for cleanup of water runoff in nurseries, developing best management systems for control of urban nonpoint source pollutants.

Martha Wells, Professor; Ph.D. (medicinal and analytical chemistry), Auburn, 1981. Establishment and application of emerging analytical procedures to determine the fate and transport of anthropogenic contaminants in the environment; new technologies development to prepare samples for trace enrichment of anthropogenic contaminants from environmental matrices; environmental applications of quantitative structure-activity, structure-property, and structure-retention relationships; governmental regulation and science policy accessing for chemicals in the environment.

UNIVERSITY OF CALIFORNIA, BERKELEY

Department of Environmental Science, Policy, and Management

Programs of Study

The Department of Environmental Science, Policy, and Management (ESPM) offers both the M.S. and Ph.D. degrees in environmental science, policy, and management. The degree programs address current and future anthropogenic environmental problems of major social and political impact that are based in the biological and physical sciences. Two general kinds of education are needed to produce people qualified to address these hybrid problems: 1) broadly based interdisciplinary education and 2) disciplinary education in relevant fields supplemented by exposure to cross-disciplinary communication and problem solving. The ESPM program integrates the biological, social, and physical sciences to provide advanced education in basic and applied environmental sciences; develops critical analytical abilities; and fosters the capacity to conduct research into the structure and function of ecosystems at molecular through ecosystem levels and their interlinked human social systems.

The program in ESPM requires that a student completes two core courses and course work in the following four areas: disciplinary emphasis, area of specialization, research methods, and breadth requirement, in addition to the dissertation. Working with a Graduate Advisor and a Guiding Committee, the student designs a program that fulfills the program requirements and meets the student's individual needs. The Ph.D. requires approximately five years to complete.

The research areas in ESPM vary widely but include biology and ecology of insects; ecosystem function and environmental issues of the atmosphere; soil, water, and plant health/interactions from molecular to ecosystem levels; wildlife ecology, conservation, and management; forest and resource policy, sustainability, and management; range management and ecology; and social distributions of power and resources affecting environmental dynamics and their social consequences.

Research Facilities

Departmental facilities offering state-of-the-art instrumentation and laboratories, insectary buildings, controlled-environment chambers, extensive greenhouse space, and field plots at the Oxford Tract (on campus) are available to support graduate student research and education. Field facilities available include the 3,500-acre Blodgett Forest, Whitaker's Forest (with giant sequoia stands adjacent to King's Canyon National Park), and Russell Reservation, which is located 13 miles east of the campus. Students may conduct research at any of several University of California Field Stations located throughout the state.

The University library system includes more than 8 million volumes, 90,000 current serial publications, 400,000 maps, and hundreds of thousands of government documents. The Bioscience and Natural Resources Library branch houses more than 450,000 volumes and subscribes to more than 8,300 journals, including government publications from the United States and other countries.

Financial Aid

ESPM makes every effort to support entering and continuing students from a variety of funding sources, including University Fellowships, Departmentally Restricted Fellowships, Graduate Student Research (GSR) Assistantships, and Graduate Student Instructor (GSI) positions. The stipend for the fellowships and GSR Assistantships is approximately $15,000 for ten months, and a waiver is included for fees ($8636 per year). If applicable, a nonresident tuition waiver ($14,700 per year) is provided. Offers of financial support are made at the time ESPM makes formal offers of admission.

Cost of Study

If an applicant does not receive financial support from the department, the cost for graduate study in 2004–05 is $8636 per year for fees and, when applicable, an additional $14,700 per year for nonresident tuition. Books and supplies may cost an additional $850 per year.

Living and Housing Costs

Most UC Berkeley graduate students live in rental housing in Berkeley and in communities within 5 miles of the campus. Although there are several University-provided and University-affiliated housing options to consider, space is limited; in many cases, early application is advised. For current information, students should visit the housing Web site at http://www.housing.berkeley.edu/housing/index.html.

Student Group

ESPM has 198 full-time graduate students in the program who come from a wide variety of academic, cultural, and national backgrounds. The student group consists of 47 percent men and 53 percent women, of whom approximately 15 percent are international students.

Student Outcomes

ESPM has been monitoring initial employment for graduates for several years and has found that 24 percent accept postdoctoral fellowships, 19 percent secure academic (tenure-track and non-tenure-track) positions, 12 percent are employed by nongovernmental organizations, 23 percent accept positions with government agencies, and 22 percent pursue careers in consulting, industry, or research.

Location

Berkeley is a large and complex institution surrounded by wooded rolling hills and by the city of Berkeley, which has a population of 106,500. The San Francisco Bay Area offers culture, entertainment, and natural beauty. All of northern California, with its great variety of cultural and recreational opportunities, is within easy reach.

The University

The University of California, Berkeley, was founded in 1868. Berkeley's faculty includes 8 Nobel Laureates, 19 MacArthur Fellows, 128 members of the National Academy of Sciences, and 86 members of the National Academy of Engineering. Berkeley's academic departments consistently rank among the top five in the country. The Department of Environmental Science, Policy, and Management is the largest of four academic departments in the College of Natural Resources, with 64 faculty members and affiliates, 198 graduate students, and 225 undergraduate students.

Applying

Applicants must submit a Graduate Division application form postmarked by December 1, 2004, to be considered for admission for fall 2005. ESPM accepts applications for the fall semester only. The Graduate Division application is available by contacting the department or may be downloaded from the Graduate Division home page (http://www.grad.berkeley.edu/). A nonrefundable fee of $60 is required at the time of submission.

Correspondence and Information

ESPM Graduate Student Services Office
145 Mulford Hall #3114
University of California, Berkeley
Berkeley, California 94720-3114

Telephone: 510-642-6410
Fax: 510-642-4034
E-mail: espmgradproginfo@nature.berkeley.edu
World Wide Web: http://nature.berkeley.edu/espm/

University of California, Berkeley

THE FACULTY AND THEIR RESEARCH

Barbara Allen-Díaz, Professor. Rangeland ecology and management.
Miguel A. Altieri, Professor. Biological control, agroecology.
Ronald G. Amundson, Professor. Pedology and isotope biogeochemistry.
Dennis Baldocchi, Professor. Biometeorology, biosphere-atmosphere trace gas fluxes.
Jill Banfield, Professor. Geomicrobiology and environmental biogeochemistry.
Reginald H. Barrett, Professor. Wildlife biology and management.
James W. Bartolome, Professor. Rangeland ecology and management.
John J. Battles, Associate Professor. Forest community ecology.
Frank C. Beall, Professor. Forest products and wood technology.
Steven R. Beissinger, Professor and ESPM Chair. Conservation biology.
Gregory S. Biging, Professor and Vice-Chair of Instruction. Forest biometrics and remote sensing.
Justin Brashares, Assistant Professor. Wildlife ecology, management, and conservation.
Thomas D. Bruns, Professor. Fungal molecular evolution and ecology.
Claudia J. Carr, Associate Professor. International and rural resource development.
John E. Casida, Professor. Pesticide chemistry and toxicology.
Ignacio H. Chapela, Assistant Professor. Microbial ecology.
Richard S. Dodd, Associate Professor. Tree genetics and systematics.
Harvey E. Doner, Professor. Soil chemistry, trace elements, elemental associations and distributions.
Sally K. Fairfax, Professor. Conservation policy and public land administration.
Mary K. Firestone, Professor. Soil microbial ecology, nutrient cycling.
Louise P. Fortmann, Professor. Natural resource sociology.
Gordon W. Frankie, Professor. Urban entomology.
Inez Y. Fung, Professor. Climate change, biogeochemical cycles.
Matteo Garbelotto, Adjunct Assistant Professor. Forest pathology, forest mycology, forest and tree management.
Wayne M. Getz, Professor. Population modeling, epidemiology, resource and wildlife management.
Rosemary Gillespie, Professor. Island biogeography, evolution, arthropod systematics.
J. Keith Gilless, Professor. Forest economics.
Allen H. Goldstein, Associate Professor. Biogeochemistry, atmospheric chemistry.
Peng Gong, Professor. Remote sensing and GIS.
Andrew P. Gutierrez, Professor. Systems ecology, biological control.
John Harte, Professor. Global change, ecosystem ecology, biodiversity.
Eileen Hebets, Assistant Professor. Evolution and function of complex signaling.
Oenes C. Huisman, Associate Professor. Fungal ecology, pathogen physiology.
Lynn Huntsinger, Associate Professor. Rangeland ecology and conservation.
Nina Maggi Kelly, Adjunct Associate Professor. GIS and remote sensing.
Isao Kubo, Professor. Natural products chemistry.
Robert S. Lane, Professor. Parasitology, tick biology.
Steven E. Lindow, Professor. Microbial ecology, epidemiology of bacterial plant diseases.
Joe R. McBride, Professor. Forest ecology, urban forestry.
John G. McColl, Professor. Soil science: nutrient cycling, forest soils.
Dale R. McCullough, Professor. Wildlife biology and management.
Carolyn Merchant, Professor. Environmental history, philosophy, and ethics.
Adina M. Merenlender, Adjunct Associate Professor. Ecology, conservation biology, landscape ecology.
Nicholas J. Mills, Professor. Biological control.
Katharine Milton, Professor. Tropical ecology of human/nonhuman primates, diet, parasite-host interactions.
T. N. Narasimhan, Professor. Groundwater in relation to ecosystems/environment, water policy.
Kevin L. O'Hara, Professor. Stand dynamics, silviculture, forest management.
Kate O'Neill, Assistant Professor. International environmental politics/political economy.
Dara O'Rourke, Assistant Professor. Political economy of industry and the environment.
George F. Oster, Professor. Mathematical ecology.
Per Palsbøll, Assistant Professor. Conservation genetics, molecular biology.
Nancy L. Peluso, Professor. Environmental sociology and resource policy.
Jerry A. Powell, Professor of the Graduate School. Systematic entomology.
Alexander H. Purcell, Professor. Insect vectors of plant pathogens.
Vincent H. Resh, Professor. Aquatic ecology.
George Roderick, Acting Associate Professor. Population biology, genetics, and evolution.
Jeffrey M. Romm, Professor. Natural resource and environmental policy.
Whendee L. Silver, Associate Professor. Ecosystem ecology.
Garrison Sposito, Professor. Soil physical chemistry.
Scott Stephens, Assistant Professor. Fire management.
Mark A. Tanouye, Professor. Insect neurophysiology.
Loy E. Volkman, Professor. Baculovirus pathogenesis and host interaction.
Stephen C. Welter, Professor. Plant-insect interactions and agricultural entomology.
Kipling Will, Assistant Professor. Insect systematics, taxonomy, and defensive chemistry.
David L. Wood, Professor of the Graduate School. Forest entomology and chemical ecology.

UNIVERSITY OF CALIFORNIA, LOS ANGELES

Environmental Science and Engineering Program

Program of Study

The Environmental Science and Engineering Program is an interdepartmental graduate degree curriculum administered through the School of Public Health that culminates in the award of the Doctor of Environmental Science and Engineering (D.Env.) degree. This professional degree was established in 1973 with the conviction that resolving complex environmental problems requires individuals who are not specialists in a narrow traditional sense but who have a broad understanding of the environment as well as the technical and managerial skills for environmental problem solving. The purpose of the program is to supply this much-needed kind of professional. A graduate of the D.Env. program has an area of specialization (represented by the student's master's degree), a background that includes several disciplinary areas, experience gained through working with experts in a variety of fields, and an understanding of how a particular discipline interacts with others. More than 200 students have graduated from UCLA with the D.Env. degree, and they hold leadership positions in government, industry, and private consulting firms.

Applicants must qualify for admission to the UCLA Graduate Division; hold a master's degree or the equivalent in one of the natural sciences, engineering, or public health; have a good background in basic science and mathematics; and have strong communication skills. Following admission, a student takes a program of courses to broaden his or her education in environmental problem areas. In the second year, the student enrolls in three quarters of environmental problems courses—projects that provide intensive exposure to multidisciplinary professional work. Recent problems course topics have emphasized groundwater pollution, air pollution, water quality, toxic substances, hazardous-waste control, stormwater management, and habitat restoration, and they often focus on the interaction between policy and technology. The student advances to candidacy after passing written and oral qualifying examinations. There is no language requirement. An approved internship of 1½ to 3 years with government, industry, or consulting firms follows, during which time the student completes a dissertation on a topic related to the internship experience. The candidate is required to present a written prospectus, including an outline of the dissertation, and defend it before the doctoral committee within nine months of advancement to candidacy and the beginning of the internship. Completion of the program normally requires four to five years.

Research Facilities

UCLA has some of the finest library resources and computer facilities in the nation. Several laboratories are available to support workshops and field studies, although the program is not primarily a laboratory research one. Campus organizations formally affiliated with the program are the Schools of Engineering and Applied Science, Law, Public Policy and Social Research, and Public Health and the Departments of Atmospheric Sciences, Chemistry, Earth and Space Sciences, Geography, Environmental Health Sciences, Statistics, Economics, and Organismic Biology, Ecology, and Evolution. Students, therefore, have the opportunity to take advantage of the full spectrum of campus resources.

Financial Aid

In the second year, the program offers graduate research assistantships that paid $3000 per quarter plus fee remission for 2003–04. A limited number of fellowships are available as well. Students may also be eligible for aid from funds administered through the Graduate Division. Currently, 100 percent of the students entering the program receive some form of financial aid.

Cost of Study

In 2003–04, fees for California residents were $2188.50 per quarter. Nonresident fees were an additional $12,245.

Living and Housing Costs

The University provides housing for single and married graduate students. In 2003–04, monthly rates for married student housing ranged from $556 to $875. Single graduate students were housed in a coed graduate hall at a cost of about $1633 per quarter. Early enrollment for housing is advised. There is adequate housing in the west Los Angeles area, within bicycling distance of UCLA, or on bus routes leading directly to UCLA.

Student Group

There are about 24,000 undergraduate and 10,000 graduate students enrolled at UCLA. Each year the Environmental Science and Engineering Program enrolls 6–10 doctoral students who come from many schools and hold master's degrees in science or engineering disciplines.

Student Outcomes

In the last several years, environmental science and engineering students have been successfully placed in a wide range of professional positions, such as with the U.S. EPA, California EPA, U.S. Army Corps of Engineers, California Air Resources Board, Lawrence Berkeley Laboratory, the State of Washington Department of Ecology, and Regional Water Quality Control Boards. Graduates also find employment with environmental consulting companies, industry, and nonprofit organizations. Many graduates have risen to positions of leadership in government and the private sector.

Location

UCLA is located on the west side of Los Angeles, 5 miles from the Pacific Ocean and 12 miles from downtown Los Angeles. The many diverse cultural and recreational opportunities in the region are within easy reach, and the University itself is a vigorous community center.

The University

UCLA, established in 1919, is academically ranked among the leading universities in the United States and has attracted distinguished scholars and researchers from all over the world. Undergraduate and graduate programs offered in the colleges and schools cover the academic spectrum. UCLA has also developed research programs and curricula outside the usual departmental structures. Interdisciplinary research facilities include institutes, centers, projects, bureaus, nondepartmental laboratories, stations, and museums. There are also many interdisciplinary programs of study, one of which is the Environmental Science and Engineering Program. UCLA's library is the largest in the Southwest. The University's Center for the Health Sciences contains one of the nation's leading hospitals and several nationally known institutes. UCLA's performing arts program of music, dance, theater, film, and lectures is one of the largest and most diverse offered by any university in the country.

Applying

Application forms for admission and financial aid may be obtained from the Graduate Admissions Office. The GRE General Test is required. TOEFL scores are required for international applicants whose native language is not English. The application deadline is December 15 for fall quarter admission.

Correspondence and Information

Dr. Richard F. Ambrose, Director
Environmental Science and Engineering Program
School of Public Health, Room 46-081 CHS
University of California
Los Angeles, California 90095-1772

Telephone: 310-825-9901
E-mail: app-ese@admin.ph.ucla.edu
World Wide Web: http://www.ph.ucla.edu/ese

University of California, Los Angeles

THE FACULTY

Environmental Science and Engineering is an interdepartmental program drawing faculty members from participating campus departments and organizations. This unusual structure precludes identifying faculty members as permanently associated with Environmental Science and Engineering except for 4 core faculty members. Any faculty member of the thirteen participating departments may be associated with the program, depending upon the theme of the problems courses being offered. He or she may also serve as a member of a student's doctoral committee or contribute to regularly scheduled candidacy examinations.

The program is administered through the School of Public Health by an Interdepartmental Committee appointed by the Dean of the Graduate Division. The Interdepartmental Committee determines administrative and academic policy within the program and ensures interdepartmental participation. Members of the current Interdepartmental Committee and ESE-affiliated faculty are presented below.

Richard F. Ambrose, Professor of Environmental Health Sciences and Director, ESE Program; Ph.D., UCLA, 1982.
Richard A. Berk, Professor of Sociology; Ph.D., Johns Hopkins, 1970.
Yoram Cohen, Professor of Chemical Engineering; Ph.D., Delaware, 1981.
Michael Collins, Professor of Environmental Health Sciences; Ph.D., Missouri, 1982.
Randall Crane, Professor of Urban Planning; Ph.D., MIT, 1987.
William Cumberland, Professor of Biostatistics; Ph.D., Johns Hopkins, 1975.
Climis Davos, Professor of Environmental Health Sciences; Ph.D., Michigan, 1974.
J. R. DeShazo, Assistant Professor of Policy Studies; Ph.D., Harvard, 1997.
Peggy Fong, Associate Professor of Organismic Biology, Ecology, and Evolution; Ph.D., California, Davis; San Diego State, 1991.
Jody Freeman, Professor, School of Law; S.J.D., Harvard, 1995.
John Froines, Professor of Environmental Health Sciences; Ph.D., Yale, 1967.
Malcolm S. Gordon, Professor of Organismic Biology, Ecology, and Evolution; Ph.D., Yale, 1958.
William Hinds, Professor of Environmental Health Sciences; Sc.D., Harvard, 1972.
Vasilios Manousiothakis, Professor of Chemical Engineering; Ph.D., Rensselaer, 1986.
Antony Orme, Professor of Geography; Ph.D., Birmingham (England), 1961.
Linwood Pendleton, Associate Professor of Environmental Health Sciences; D.F.E.S., Yale, 1997.
Richard L. Perrine, Professor Emeritus of Civil and Environmental Engineering; Ph.D., Stanford, 1953.
Theodore Porter, Professor of History; Ph.D., Princeton, 1991.
Shane Que Hee, Professor of Environmental Health Sciences; Ph.D., Saskatchewan, 1976.
Beate R. Ritz, Associate Professor of Epidemiology; M.D., Hamburg, 1984; Ph.D., UCLA, 1995.
Michael K. Stenstrom, Professor of Civil and Environmental Engineering; Ph.D., Clemson, 1976.
Irwin H. Suffet, Professor of Environmental Health Sciences; Ph.D., Rutgers, 1968.
Stanley W. Trimble, Professor of Geography; Ph.D., Georgia, 1973.
Richard P. Turco, Professor of Atmospheric Sciences; Ph.D., Illinois, 1971.
Arthur M. Winer, Professor of Environmental Health Sciences; Ph.D., Ohio State, 1969.

Sampling for fish using beach seines at Malibu Lagoon.

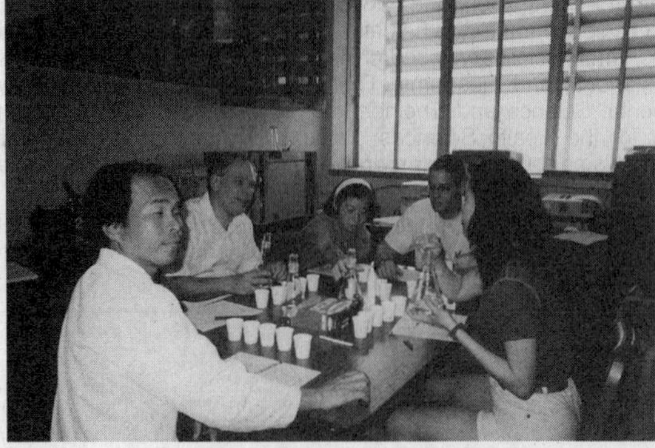

Dr. Mel Suffet and his Flavor Profile Analysis Panel test Los Angeles's water supply.

A continuous liquid extractor collects 500-liter extracts at a water reuse project at West Basin in El Segundo, California.

UNIVERSITY OF CALIFORNIA, SANTA BARBARA

Donald Bren School of Environmental Science and Management

Programs of Study

The Donald Bren School of Environmental Science and Management is committed in its research and teaching to blending natural science, social science, law and policy, and business management in ways that facilitate the solution of environmental problems. The Bren School offers both a master's (M.E.S.M.) and a Ph.D. degree in environmental science and management. The M.E.S.M., with its balanced core curriculum and the capstone group project that serves as a master's thesis, is a two-year professional degree program that trains students to approach environmental issues from an integrated perspective, accounting for the social, legal, political, and business contexts within which they arise. The M.E.S.M. degree program is enhanced by an individual program of study created by each student, which builds depth in a chosen area of specialization and adequately trains the student in technical applications.

The Bren School's approach at the Ph.D. level is multidisciplinary in nature while being very individualized. The School accommodates a wide range of Ph.D. students and interests, from those who are highly focused in a particular discipline to those who are strongly multidisciplinary. In addition, the program aims to preserve the University of California, Santa Barbara's (UCSB), mission of training high-caliber future research professors while simultaneously meeting the urgent need for highly trained personnel in the public and private sector. The Bren School has excellent research programs in natural science, social science, and information systems and recruits students to participate in these programs. The School is also interested in recruiting students to perform dissertations on policy-related implications of natural science research. In addition, in 2001 UCSB was awarded a $2-million grant from the National Science Foundation's Integrative Graduate Education and Research Traineeship (IGERT) program to support a Ph.D. training program in the integrative study of economics and environmental science. This training program is a joint venture between the Bren School and UCSB's Department of Economics and prepares the student to be an expert in economics as well as in a complementary area of natural science (applied ecology, climate, hydrology, or marine science). For more information, students should visit the Web site at http://www.ees.ucsb.edu.

Research Facilities

The Bren School has research laboratories for the disciplines of environmental microbiology, biogeochemistry, biogeography, hydrology, toxicology, and information management. The School also provides a Student Computing Facility that contains forty-one workstations with a suite of cutting-edge analytical and graphical software tools. Donald Bren Hall, where the Bren School is housed, was completed in spring 2002. The building was designed to be a model of "green" building design, not only for UCSB but also for the entire University of California (UC) system. It was awarded a "Platinum" LEED™ (Leadership in Energy and Environmental Design) rating by the U.S. Green Building Council, among many other awards and commendations from the state of California, the county of Santa Barbara, and various organizations, for its innovative and sustainable design.

Financial Aid

Sponsoring professors usually provide graduate student research assistant support for Ph.D. students. Ph.D. students may also be eligible for campus-based fellowships. In addition, the Bren School offers a Ph.D. fellowship program in economics and environmental science for students interested in a combined expertise in those areas. This fellowship program is open to U.S. citizens and permanent residents only. For more information, students should visit the Web site at http://www.ees.ucsb.edu. Loans and other federally based support are available through UCSB's Financial Aid Office. For more information on financing graduate studies, students should visit the UCSB Graduate Division's Fellowship and Financial Support Web site at http://www.graddiv.ucsb.edu/financial.

Cost of Study

Graduate student fees for the 2003–04 academic year were $7115 for California residents and $19,607 for nonresidents. These figures include registration fees, tuition, and graduate student health insurance. Fees are expected to increase by approximately $3000 for 2004–05.

Living and Housing Costs

Santa Barbara is an exceptionally beautiful place to live, and there is a high demand for rental housing. Monthly rents range from $977 for a studio to $2200 for a three-bedroom house. More information can be found at http://www.housing.ucsb.edu.

Student Group

The Bren School has 153 full-time graduate students; roughly 80 percent are master's students. Students range from those who have recently completed their undergraduate education to those who have spent years working in a variety of fields.

Student Outcomes

The Bren School operates its own career development program, which is committed to helping students develop the job search and career development skills necessary for successful transition into rewarding environmental careers. With the School's multidisciplinary approach and strong career development program, graduates have found employment in a variety of environmental positions and organizations, such as consulting firms, the public sector, nonprofit organizations, industry, and academics and research, in the U.S. and internationally. Job placement statistics for Bren School graduates can be found on the Career Services Web site at http://www.bren.ucsb.edu/career/placement.html.

Location

UCSB is located 10 miles west of downtown Santa Barbara (100 miles northwest of Los Angeles) near the city of Goleta and occupies a picturesque 989-acre palm- and eucalyptus-lined plateau overlooking the Pacific Ocean. The Santa Barbara/Goleta area is surrounded by extraordinary beauty and has a mild, Mediterranean climate. UCSB is part of a diverse ecosystem that provides an ideal setting for the study of environmental science and management.

The University and The School

Founded in 1944, UCSB has become one of the nation's most distinguished academic institutions, renowned for outstanding scientific research, interdisciplinary collaboration, and public service. The latest Graham/Diamond study of university quality ranked UCSB the second-best public research university in the nation. In 2002, *Newsweek* named UCSB one of the twelve hottest universities in the country. Since 1997, three UCSB professors have been awarded Nobel Prizes in Chemistry and Physics. The Bren School accepted its first M.E.S.M. students in 1996 and was created to fulfill the need for graduates equipped with the knowledge and tools necessary to assess and meet environmental challenges in business and government settings. The School was renamed in December 1997 after a major gift was received from the Donald Bren Foundation. The purpose of the Bren gift was to transform the School into a multicampus, interdisciplinary program that stimulates the integration of natural and social science, law, and business programs throughout the UC system. The School's intercampus program offers an emphasis in corporate environmental management to M.B.A. students in all five UC business schools (Los Angeles, Berkeley, Davis, Irvine, and Riverside). Students in the five M.B.A. programs travel to Santa Barbara three weekends during the fall and winter quarters to attend courses. Bren School M.E.S.M. and Ph.D. students have the opportunity to join the M.B.A. students in courses in law, policy, and management.

Applying

The Bren School welcomes applications from all undergraduate disciplines. Applications are available electronically (http://www.graddiv.ucsb.edu/eapp). A statement of purpose, three letters of recommendation, two copies of official transcripts for all tertiary-level institutions, an application fee (currently $60), official GRE scores, recent TOEFL scores for nonnative English speakers, and a resume must be submitted. Applications are normally accepted for the fall only. The M.E.S.M. application deadline is February 1 for primary consideration and for consideration for School-based financial support, but applications are accepted until March 1, space permitting. The Ph.D. application deadline is December 15 for primary consideration and for consideration for University-based financial support. Ph.D. applications are accepted until February 1, space permitting.

Correspondence and Information

Graduate Program Assistant
Donald Bren School of Environmental Science and Management
Donald Bren Hall, Room 2400
University of California, Santa Barbara
Santa Barbara, California 93106-5131

Telephone: 805-893-7611
Fax: 805-893-7612
E-mail: gradasst@bren.ucsb.edu
World Wide Web: http://www.bren.ucsb.edu

University of California, Santa Barbara

THE FACULTY AND THEIR RESEARCH

The Bren School has 19 permanent and 6 adjunct/affiliated faculty members from the fields of ecology, hydrology, toxicology, oceanography, business management, law, public policy, economics, and information management. The Bren School also has several visiting faculty members each year from renowned institutions across the U.S., which further diversifies and strengthens the School's teaching, research, and curriculum development.

DEANS

Dennis Aigner, Dean, Acting Bren Associate Dean for Business Management, and Donald Bren Professor of Business Management. Ph.D., Berkeley, 1963. Econometrics, corporate environmental management.

Jody Freeman, Bren Associate Dean for Law and Policy and Professor of Law (UCLA). S.J.D., Harvard, 1995. Environmental law, administrative law, toxic torts.

THE FACULTY

Antonio Bento, Assistant Professor; Ph.D., Maryland, College Park, 2000. Environmental economics, public finance, microeconomic theory, applied general equilibrium, development economics.

Christopher Costello, Assistant Professor; Ph.D., Berkeley, 2000. Environmental and resource economics, dynamic optimization, quantitative ecology, stochastic modeling.

Frank Davis, Professor; Ph.D., Johns Hopkins, 1982. Plant ecology, quantitative biogeography, vegetation remote sensing, ecological applications of remote sensing and geographic information systems, conservation planning, fire ecology.

Magali Delmas, Assistant Professor; Ph.D., H.E.C. Graduate School of Management (Paris), 1996. Corporate environmental management, impact of technological and regulatory uncertainties on industry choices.

Jeff Dozier, Professor; Ph.D., Michigan, 1973. Snow science, hydrology, hydrochemistry of Alpine regions, remote sensing, information systems.

Thomas Dunne, Professor; Ph.D., Johns Hopkins, 1969. Drainage basin and hill slope evolution, hydrology and floodplain sedimentation, applications of hydrology, geomorphology in environmental management.

James Frew, Assistant Professor; Ph.D., California, Santa Barbara, 1990. Application of computing and information science to large-scale problems in environmental science, information system specification and integration, science data management, digital libraries.

Roland Geyer, Assistant Professor; Ph.D., Surrey (England), 2003. Green supply-chain management and industrial ecology.

Patricia Holden, Assistant Professor; Ph.D., Berkeley, 1995. Pathogens in the environment, microbial ecology of pollutant biodegradation, soil microbiology.

Arturo Keller, Assistant Professor; Ph.D., Stanford, 1997. Biogeochemistry; fate and transport of pollutants in the environment; development of technologies for containment, remediation, and monitoring.

Bruce Kendall, Assistant Professor; Ph.D., Arizona, 1996. Quantitative, applied ecology with a focus on animal and plant population dynamics.

*Charles D. Kolstad, Donald Bren Professor of Environmental Economics; Ph.D., Stanford, 1982. Industrial organization and environmental/resource economics, environmental policy, structure of energy markets, environmental regulations.

Hunter Lenihan, Assistant Professor; Ph.D., North Carolina at Chapel Hill, 1996. Marine ecology and resource conservation; conserving and restoring marine populations, communities, and their habitat.

Christopher Marwood, Assistant Professor; Ph.D., Guelph, 1999. Environmental toxicology, monitoring exposure and effects of anthropogenic contaminants on fish and other aquatic organisms.

*Carol McAusland, Assistant Professor; Ph.D., Michigan, 1999. Trade and environment.

*John Melack, Professor; Ph.D., Duke, 1976. Limnology, ecology, biogeochemistry, remote sensing.

Catherine Ramus, Assistant Professor; Ph.D., Lausanne, 1999. Environmental management, organizational behavior, negotiation, public policy.

Oran Young, Professor; Ph.D., Yale, 1965. Program on Governance for Sustainable Development.

**Joint appointment with at least one other UCSB department.*

SELECTED PUBLICATIONS

Parry, I. W. H., and **A. Bento.** Estimating the welfare effect of congestion taxes: The critical importance of other distortions within the transport system. *J. Urban Econ.* 51(2):339–65, 2002.

Parry, I. W. H., and **A. Bento.** Revenue recycling and the welfare effects of road pricing. *Scan. J. Econ.* 103(4):645–72, 2001.

Costello, C., and **C. McAusland.** Protectionism, trade, and measures of damage from exotic species introduction. *Am. J. Agric. Econ.* 85(4):964–75, 2003.

Costello, C., and A. Solow. On the pattern of discovery of introduced species. *Proc. Natl. Acad. Sci. U.S.A.* 100(6):3321–3, 2003.

Moledina, A., J. Coggins, S. Polasky, and **C. Costello.** Dynamic environmental policy with strategic firms: Prices vs. quantities. *J. Environ. Econ. Manage.* 45:356–76, 2003.

Stoms, D. M., J. M. McDonald, and **F. W. Davis.** Fuzzy assessment of land suitability for scientific research reserves. *Environ. Manage.* 29:545–58, 2002.

Delmas, M. The diffusion of environmental management standards in Europe and in the United States: An institutional perspective. *Policy Sci.* 35(1):1–119, 2002.

Delmas, M., and A. Terlaak. Institutional factors and environmental voluntary agreements: The cases of the United States, Germany, The Netherlands and France. *J. Comp. Policy Anal.* 4(1):5–29, 2002.

Delmas, M. Innovating against European rigidities: Institutional environment and dynamic capabilities. *J. High Technol. Manage. Res.* 13(1):18–42, 2002.

Delmas, M. Stakeholders and competitive advantage: The case of ISO 14001. *Prod. Operation Manage.* 10(3):343–58, 2001.

Delmas, M., and B. Heiman. Government credible commitment in the French and American nuclear industry. *J. Policy Anal. Manage.* 20(3):434–56, 2001.

Delmas, M., and A. Terlaak. A framework for analyzing environmental voluntary agreements. *California Manage. Rev.* 43(3):44–63, 2001.

Green, R.O., **J. Dozier,** D. A. Roberts, and T. H. Painter. Spectral snow reflectance models for grain size and liquid water fraction in melting snow for the solar reflected spectrum. *Ann. Glaciol.* 34:71–73, 2002.

Minster, J. B., et al. **(J. Dozier** and **J. M. Melack).** *Resolving Conflicts Arising from Privitization of Environmental Data.* Committee on Geophysical and Environmental Data, National Research Council. Washington, D.C.: National Academy Press, 2002.

Painter, T. H., et al. **(J. Dozier).** Detection and quantification of snow algae with an airborne imaging spectrometer. *Appl. Environ. Microbiol.* 67(11):5267–72, 2001.

Malmon, D. V., **T. Dunne,** and S. L. Reneau. Predicting the fate of sediment and pollutants in river floodplains. *Environ. Sci. Technol.* 36(9):2026–32, 2002.

Singer, M. B., and **T. Dunne.** Identifying eroding and depositional reaches of valley by analysis of suspended-sediment transport in the Sacramento River, California. *Water Resour. Res.* 37(12):3371–81, 2002.

Alsdorf, D., et al. **(T. Dunne** and **J. Melack).** Water level changes in a large Amazon lake measured with spaceborne radar interferometry and altimetry. *Geophys. Res. Lett.* 28(14):2671–4, 2001.

Janee, G., **J. Frew,** and D. Valentine. Content access characterization in digital libraries. In *Third ACM/IEEE-CS Joint Conference on Digital Libraries.* Houston, Tex.: ACM Press, 2003.

Smith, T., et al. **(J. Frew).** *Second ACM/IEEE-CS Joint Conference on Digital Libraries.* Portland, Ore.: ACM Press, 2002.

Holden, P. A., et al. Assessing the role of *Pseudomonas aeruginosa* surface-active gene expression to hexadecane biodegradation in sand. *Appl. Environ. Microbiol.* 68:2509–18, 2002.

LaMontagne, M. G., F. C. Michel Jr., **P. A. Holden,** and C. A. Reddy. Evaluation of extraction and purification methods for obtaining PCR-amplifiable DNA from compost for microbial community analysis. *J. Microbiol. Methods* 49:255–64, 2002.

Steinberger, R. E., A. R. Allen, H. G. Hansma, and **P. A. Holden.** Elongation correlates with nutrient deprivation in *Pseudomonas aeruginosa* unsaturated biofilms. *Microb. Ecol.* 43(4), 2002.

Holden, P. A., and D. Pierce. New Environmental Scanning Electron Microscope (ESEM) observations of bacteria on simulated soil substrates. *Microsc. Microanal.* 7(Suppl. 2:Proceedings):736–7, 2001.

Holden, P. A., L. E. Hersman, and M. K. Firestone. Water content mediated microaerophilic toluene biodegradation in arid vadose zone materials. *Microb. Ecol.* 42:256–66, 2001.

Kram, M. L., **A. A. Keller,** J. Rossabi, and L. Everett. DNAPL characterization methods and approaches Part 2: Cost comparisons. *Ground Water Monit. Rem.* 22(1):46–61, 2002.

Mitani, M. M., and **A. A. Keller** et al. Kinetics and products of reactions of MTBE with ozone and ozone/hydrogen peroxide in water. *J. Hazard. Mater.* B89:197–202, 2002.

Kram, M. L., **A. A. Keller,** J. Rossabi, and L. Everett. DNAPL characterization methods and approaches Part 1: Performance comparisons. *Ground Water Monit. Rem.* 21(1):67–76, 2001.

Mitani M. M., and **A. A. Keller** et al. Low temperature catalytic decomposition and oxidation of MTBE. *Appl. Catal., B* 34:87–95, 2001.

Keller, A. A., A. Wilson, and **P. A. Holden.** Modeling the seasonal variation in bioavailability of residual NAPL in the vadose zone. In *Groundwater Quality.* Sheffield, UK: International Association of Hydrological Sciences, 2001.

Kendall, B. E., and G. A. Fox. Variation among individuals and reduced demographic stochasticity. *Conservation Biol.* 16:109–16, 2002.

Murdoch, W. W., and **B. E. Kendall** et al. Single-species models for many-species food webs. *Nature* 417:541–3, 2002.

Fox, G. A., and **B. E. Kendall.** Demographic stochasticity and the variance reduction effect. *Ecology* 83:1928–34, 2002.

Ellner, S. P., et al. **(B. E. Kendall).** Habitat structure and population persistence in an experimental community. *Nature* 412:538–43, 2001.

Xing, Y., and **C. Kolstad.** Do lax environmental regulations attract foreign investment? *Environ. Resour. Econ.* 21(1):1–22, 2002.

Braden, J., **C. Kolstad,** R. Woock, and J. Machado. Is coal desulphurisation worthwhile? Evidence from the market. *Energy Policy* 29(3):217–25, 2001.

Kelly, D. and **C. Kolstad.** Malthus and climate change: Betting on a stable population. *J. Environ. Econ. Manage.* 21(2):1–22, 2001.

Kolstad, C., and D. Kelly. Solving infinite horizon growth models with an environmental sector. *Comput. Econ.* 18:217–31, 2001.

Marwood, C. A., et al. Chlorophyll fluorescence as a bioindicator of creosote toxicity in plant growth in aquatic microcosms. *Environ. Toxicol. Chem.* 22(5):1075–85, 2003.

Marwood, C. A., K. R. Solomon, and B. M. Greenberg. Chlorophyll fluorescence as a bioindicator of growth on aquatic macrophytes from mixtures of polycyclic aromatic hydrocarbons. *Environ. Toxicol. Chem.* 20(4):890–8, 2001.

University of California, Santa Barbara

Selected Publications (continued)

McAusland, C. Voting for pollution policy: The importance of income inequality and openness to trade. *J. Int. Econ.* 61(2): 425–51, 2003.

McAusland, C. Cross-hauling of polluting factors. *J. Environ. Econ. Manage.* 44(3):448–70, 2002.

De Souza, O. C., M. R. Aruajo, L. A. K. Mertes, and **J. M. Melack.** Form and process along the Taquari River Alluvial Fan, Pantanal, Brazil. *Z. Geomorphol.*, 2002.

Gergel, S. E., et al. **(J. M. Melack).** Indicators of human impacts to river-floodplain systems: The importance of landscape context. *Aquatic Sci.* 64:118–28, 2002.

Hess, L. L., et al. **(J. M. Melack).** Geocoded digital videography for validation of land cover mapping in the Amazon Basin. *Int. J. Remote Sensing* 7:1527–56, 2002.

Richey, J. E., and **J. M. Melack** et al. Carbon dioxide evasion from water to the atmosphere in the Central Amazon Basin. *Nature* 416:617–20, 2002.

Aizen, E. M., et al. **(J. M. Melack).** Precipitation and atmospheric circulation at mid-latitudes of Asia. *Int. J. Climatol.* 21:535–56, 2001.

Alsdorf, D. E., L. C. Smith, and **J. M. Melack.** Amazon water level changes measured with interferometric SIR-C radar. *IEEE Trans. Geosci. Remote Sensing* 39:423–31, 2001.

Engle, D., and **J. M. Melack.** Ecological consequences of infrequent events in high-elevation lakes and streams of the Sierra Nevada, California. *Verh. Internat. Verein. Limnol.* 27:3761–5, 2001.

Jellison, R., and **J. M. Melack.** Nitrogen limitation and particulate elemental ratios of seston in hypersaline Mono Lake, California, U.S.A. *Hydrobiologia* 466:1–12, 2001.

Jellison, R., H. Adams, and **J. M. Melack.** Re-appearance of rotifers in hypersaline Mono Lake, California, during a period of rising lake levels and decreasing salinity. *Hydrobiologia* 466:39–43, 2001.

Leydecker, A., J. O. Sickman, and **J. M. Melack.** Spatial scaling of hydrological and biogeochemical aspects of high-altitude catchments in the Sierra Nevada, California, U.S.A. *Arctic, Antarctic Alpine Res.* 33:391–6, 2001.

Melack, J. M., and M. Gastil. Airborne remote sensing of chlorophyll distributions in Mono Lake, California. *Hydrobiologia* 466:31–8, 2001.

Saline Lakes. In *Developments in Hydrobiology,* vol. 162, p. 347, eds. **J. M. Melack,** R. Jellison, and D. Herbst. The Netherlands: Kluwer, 2001.

Sickman, J. O., A. Leydecker, and **J. M. Melack.** Nitrogen mass balances and abiotic controls on N retention and yield in high-elevation catchments of the Sierra Nevada, California, USA. *Water Resour. Res.* 37:1445–61, 2001.

Turk, J. T., et al. **(J. M. Melack).** Major-Ion chemistry of the Rocky Mountain Snowpack, USA. *Atmos. Environ.* 35:3957–66, 2001.

Williams, M. R., A. Leydecker, A. D. Brown, and **J. M. Melack.** Processes regulating the solute concentrations of snowmelt runoff in two subalpine catchments of the Sierra Nevada, California. *Water Resour. Res.* 37:1993–2008, 2001.

Ramus, C. A. Encouraging innovative environmental actions: What companies and managers must do. *J. World Business* 37:151–64, 2002.

Ramus, C. A. Organizational support for employees: Encouraging creative ideas for environmental sustainability. *California Manage. Rev.* 43(3):85–105, 2001.

Young, O. R. Taking stock: Management pitfalls in fisheries science. *Environment* 45(3):24–30, 2003.

Victor, D. G., and **O. R. Young.** The collapse of the Kyoto Protocol and the struggle to slow global warming. *Am. J. Int. Law* 96(3):736–41, 2002.

Young, O. R. Evaluating the success of international environmental regimes: Where are we now? *Global Environ. Change–Hum. Policy Dimens.* 12(1):73–7, 2002.

UNIVERSITY OF DELAWARE

Center for Energy and Environmental Policy

Programs of Study

The Center for Energy and Environmental Policy (CEEP) at the University of Delaware provides graduate instruction and conducts interdisciplinary research in the areas of energy policy, environmental policy, and sustainable development. Collaborative research and exchange agreements to foster international research and graduate study have been established with Asian, African, Latin American, and European universities and research institutes. CEEP is composed of an internationally diverse faculty and graduate student body with backgrounds in political science, economics, sociology, geography, philosophy, urban planning, environmental studies, history, anthropology, and engineering.

CEEP administers the Environmental and Energy Policy (ENEP) program. Its 7-member faculty offers a Master of Environmental and Energy Policy (M.E.E.P.) and a Doctor of Philosophy in Environmental and Energy Policy (Ph.D./ENEP). These degrees offer in-depth study in the fields of sustainable development, the political economy of energy and environment, energy policy, environmental policy, and disaster policy. The M.E.E.P. requires completion of 36 credits, of which 15 are electives; the Ph.D./ENEP normally requires completion of 45 credits, of which 24 credits are electives. In addition, CEEP sponsors a 15-credit energy, environment, and equity concentration in the M.A. in urban affairs and public policy and a 21-credit technology, environment, and society concentration in the Ph.D. in urban affairs and public policy. The latter degrees are administered by the urban affairs and public policy program faculty with the M.A. requiring completion of 36 credits (of which 15 are electives) and the Ph.D. normally requiring completion of 42 credits (including 21 elective credits).

Opportunities exist for students to participate in research projects on such topics as socioeconomic impacts of global climate change, economic and environmental evaluation of renewable energy options (especially photovoltaic technology), impacts of environmental regulations, environmental ethics, development of a sustainability index, sustainable urban development strategies, energy and poverty issues, integrated resource planning, electricity restructuring in developed and developing countries, and water conservation planning and policy. Students have obtained paid internships with the World Bank, UNDP, overseas research institutes, intergovernmental organizations, U.S. senators' offices, federal and state government agencies, and nonprofit organizations.

Research Facilities

University Libraries contain more than 2 million books and journals and serve as a depository library for U.S. government publications. The University maintains a computerized online catalog, accessible via a campus computer network, the Internet, and telephone and computer modem from anywhere in the world. The University's computing services include microcomputer laboratories, UNIX multiworkstation and time-sharing facilities, and an IBM vector processing time-sharing service.

Financial Aid

Nearly three quarters of CEEP graduate students receive financial awards. University and minority fellowships, tuition scholarships, and research assistantships are awarded on the basis of merit. Awards are made only to full-time students in good academic standing. Most students admitted to the two Ph.D. programs in research areas related to ongoing Center activity are awarded full assistantships covering tuition (up to $15,990 per year) and stipend ($11,500 in 2004–05). Funding may be provided for four years, depending upon academic performance. Students admitted to the M.A. and M.E.E.P. programs ordinarily self-fund their first year of study and receive full assistantships in their second year.

Cost of Study

In 2004–05, graduate tuition is $6304 per year for full-time resident students and $15,990 per year for full-time nonresident students. Full-time matriculated students are automatically assessed nonrefundable fees for health ($363) and student-sponsored activities ($160).

Living and Housing Costs

The University's Office of Housing and Residence Life offers graduate students a number of housing options. Single graduate student housing rates range from $350 to $700. Family housing rates range from $690 to $800. The cost includes all utilities and local telephone service. Students who are seeking accommodations in adjacent residential areas within walking or commuting distance should contact the Off-Campus Housing Office for a list of rooms, apartments, and houses to rent or share. Further information can be obtained from the Office of Housing Assignment Services (telephone: 302-831-3676).

Student Group

Enrollment at the University in 2003–04 included 16,422 undergraduate students, 3,301 graduate students, and 1,392 students in the Division of Continuing Education. Currently, the University offers eighty different programs leading to a master's degree and forty programs leading to a doctoral degree through forty-six departments in its seven instructional colleges. Spring 2004 graduate enrollment in CEEP included 38 Ph.D. and 23 M.A. students.

Location

The main campus of the University is located in the residential community of Newark. Newark is a suburban community of 30,000, located midway between Philadelphia and Baltimore and within 2 hours by train of New York City and Washington, D.C. Newark lies a short distance from the Delaware and Chesapeake Bays and from Delaware's ocean beaches.

The University

The University is a comprehensive land- and sea-grant institution of higher education. Opened in 1743, the Newark campus currently consists of 2,019 acres and a $499-million physical plant with 449 buildings, including classrooms, laboratories, athletic complexes, and student activity centers. Other land holdings include a 405-acre Marine Studies Complex and a 347-acre Agricultural Substation. The University's distinguished faculty includes internationally recognized researchers, artists, authors, and teachers. There are thirty-nine named professorships. The University community includes 1,089 faculty members, 1,322 professionals, 956 salaried staff members, and 498 hourly employees.

Applying

For the M.A. and M.E.E.P. degrees, the successful candidate for admission must have an undergraduate GPA above 3.0 (on a 4.0 scale). A combined GRE score above 1100 (math and verbal portions) is normally expected. Admission to the either of the Ph.D. programs requires a master's degree with at least a 3.5 GPA. A combined GRE score above 1150 (math and verbal portions) is normally expected. Complete applications contain three letters of recommendation, a 1,000-word statement of the applicant's research interest, academic transcript(s), and GRE scores. For students whose first language is not English, a demonstrated proficiency in English is required. This may be judged on the basis of a TOEFL score of at least 550. Ph.D. students are expected to have TOEFL scores above 600. Most students are admitted for the fall semester. A completed admission application and all credentials should be submitted by February 15 to guarantee consideration for financial aid.

Correspondence and Information

Dr. John Byrne, Director
Center for Energy and Environmental Policy
University of Delaware
Newark, Delaware 19716
Telephone: 302-831-8405
Fax: 302-831-3098
E-mail: jbbyrne@udel.edu
World Wide Web: http://www.udel.edu/ceep

University of Delaware

THE FACULTY AND THEIR RESEARCH

Core Faculty

John Byrne, Professor and Director, Center for Energy and Environmental Policy (CEEP); Ph.D., Delaware, 1980. Technology, environment and society, political ecology, climate change, renewable energy, sustainable development, environmental justice.

Paul Durbin, Professor Emeritus, Department of Philosophy and CEEP Senior Policy Fellow; Ph.D., Aquinas Institute, 1966. Technology and society, philosophy of science, environmental ethics.

Leigh Glover, Assistant Professor and CEEP Policy Fellow; Ph.D., Delaware, 2003. Environmental politics, postmodern theory, climate change, natural resource management.

William Ritter, Professor, Department of Bioresource Engineering, and CEEP Senior Policy Fellow; Ph.D., Iowa State, 1971. Water resources, soil and water conservation engineering, waste management.

Yda Schreuder, Associate Professor, Department of Geography, and CEEP Senior Policy Fellow; Ph.D., Wisconsin–Madison, 1982. Global resources, development and environment, sustainable development, growth management.

Richard T. Sylves, Professor, Department of Political Science and International Relations, and CEEP Senior Policy Fellow; Ph.D., Illinois, 1976. Environmental policy, emergency response management, energy policy.

Young-Doo Wang, Professor, CEEP Associate Director, and Environmental and Energy Policy Graduate Program Director; Ph.D., Delaware, 1980. Energy and environmental policy, water resource and watershed management, sustainable energy analysis, econometric applications.

Adjunct Faculty

Cesar Cuello, Professor, Santo Domingo Technological Institute and Universidad Autonoma (Dominican Republic) and CEEP Policy Fellow; Ph.D., Delaware, 1997. Sustainable development, science, technology and society, environmental philosophy.

J. Barry Cullingworth, Professor of Land Use Planning, Oxford University, and CEEP Senior Policy Fellow; Oxford, 1974; MRTPI, FRSA. Environmental planning, land use policy, urban management.

Steven M. Hoffman, Professor and Director, Environmental Studies Program, University of St. Thomas (Minnesota), and CEEP Senior Policy Fellow; Ph.D., Delaware, 1986. Technology and society, political economy, energy and environmental policy.

Jong-dall Kim, Associate Professor and Director, Research Institute for Energy, Environment and Economy, Kyungbuk National University (South Korea), and CEEP Policy Fellow; Ph.D., Delaware, 1991. Political economy, renewable energy, energy conservation, sustainable development.

Hoesung Lee, President, Council for Energy and Environment (South Korea), and CEEP Senior Policy Fellow; Ph.D., Rutgers, 1976. Energy and environmental economics, climate change, sustainable development.

Cecilia Martinez, Leadership Fellow, Archibald Bush Foundation (Minnesota); Research Fellow, American Indian Policy Institute; and CEEP Senior Policy Fellow; Ph.D., Delaware, 1990. Technology, environment and society, political economy, American Indian policy, environmental justice.

Hon. Russell W. Peterson, Ecologist (past president, National Audubon Society; former chairman, U.S. President's Council on Environmental Quality; former governor, State of Delaware) and CEEP Distinguished Policy Fellow. Global ecological issues.

Subodh Wagle, President, Prayas (India) and CEEP Policy Fellow; Ph.D., Delaware, 1997. Political economy, social and environmental justice, antiglobalization strategy, sustainable livelihoods.

CEEP researchers assisted an international team in an effort to change Taiwanese government plans to construct a heavy-industry complex near the nesting area of the black-faced spoonbill, an endangered bird. Of the known population of 600 birds, 400 winter along the west coast of Taiwan.

SELECTED PUBLICATIONS

Byrne, J., Y.-D. Wang, H. Lee and **J.-d. Kim.** *The Sustainable Energy Revolution: Toward an Energy-Efficient Future for South Korea.* Seoul, South Korea: Maeil Kyung Jae, 2004.

Byrne, J., et al **(L. Glover).** Reclaiming the atmospheric commons: Beyond Kyoto. In *Climate Change: Perspectives Five Years After Kyoto,* chapter 21, ed. V. I. Grover. Plymouth, UK: Science Publishers, Inc., 2004.

Byrne, J., L. Kurdgekashvili, D. Poponi, and A. Barnett. The potential of solar electric power for meeting future U.S. energy needs: A comparison of projections of solar electric energy generation and Arctic National Wildlife Refuge oil production. *Energy Policy* 32(2):289–97, 2004.

Byrne, J., and Y.-M. Mun. Rethinking reform in the electricity sector: Power liberalization or energy transformation. In *Electricity Reform: Social and Environmental Challenges*, pp. 49–76, eds. Wamunkonya and Roskilde. Denmark: UNEP-RISØ Centre, 2003.

Byrne, J., and V. Inniss. Island sustainability and sustainable development in the context of climate change. In *Sustainable Development for Island Societies and the World,* eds. H.-H. Hsiao et al. Taipei, Taiwan: Academia Sinica, 2002.

Byrne, J., C. Martinez, and **L. Glover.** *Environmental Justice: Discourses in International Political Economy.* New Brunswick, N.J., and London: Transaction Publishers, 2002.

Byrne, J., C. Martinez, and **L. Glover.** A brief on environmental justice. In *Environmental Justice: Discourses in International Political Economy,* pp. 3–17, eds. **J. Byrne** et al. New Brunswick, N.J., and London: Transaction Publishers, 2002.

Byrne, J., and **S. Hoffman.** A 'necessary sacrifice:' Industrialization and American Indian lands. In *Environmental Justice: Discourses in International Political Economy,* pp. 97–118, eds. J. Byrne et al. New Brunswick, N.J., and London: Transaction Publishers, 2002.

Byrne, J., L. Glover, and **C. Martinez.** The production of unequal nature. In *Environmental Justice: Discourses in International Political Economy,* pp. 261–91, eds. **J. Byrne** et al. New Brunswick, N.J., and London: Transaction Publishers, 2002.

Byrne, J., and **L. Glover.** A common future or towards a future commons: Globalization and sustainable development since UNCED. *Int. Rev. Environ. Strategies* 3(1):5–25, 2002.

Byrne, J., and **S. Hoffman,** eds. Energy controversy—part II: Reversing course. *Bull. Sci. Technol. Soc.* 22(2), 2002.

Zhou, A., and **J. Byrne.** Renewable energy for rural sustainability: Lessons from China. *Bull. Sci. Technol. Soc.* 22(2):123–31, 2002.

Byrne, J. (contributing author). Decision-making frameworks. In *Climate Change 2001: Mitigation,* pp. 601–88, eds. B. Metz et al. Contribution of Working Group III to the Third Assessment Report of the Intergovernmental Panel on Climate Change (IPCC). New York: Cambridge University Press, 2001.

Byrne, J., and **S. Hoffman,** eds. Energy controversy—part I: Change and resistance. *Bull. Sci. Technol. Soc.* 21(6), 2001.

Byrne, J., and **L. Glover** et al. The postmodern greenhouse: Creating virtual carbon reductions from business-as-usual energy politics. *Bull. Sci. Technol. Soc.* 21(6): 443–55, 2001.

Byrne, J., and R. Scattone. Community participation is key to environmental justice in brownfields. *Race Poverty Environ.* 3(1):6–7, 2001.

Byrne, J., and **L. Glover.** Climate shopping: Putting the atmosphere up for sale. In *TELA: Environment, Economy and Society* series, 28 pp. Melbourne, Australia: Australian Conservation Foundation, 2000.

Byrne, J., and T.-L. Lin. Beyond pollution and risk: Energy and environmental policy in the greenhouse. In *Proceedings of the International Conference on Sustainable Energy and Environmental Strategies,* Taipei, Taiwan: 1–23, 2000.

Byrne, J., et al. An international comparison of the economics of building integrated PV in different resource, pricing and policy environments: The cases of the U.S., Japan and South Korea. In *Proceedings of the American Solar Energy Society Solar 2000 Conference,* Madison, Wisc.: 81–5, 2000.

Byrne, J., and V. Inniss. Island sustainability and sustainable development in the context of global warming. In *Proceedings of the International Conference on Sustainable Development for Island Societies*, pp. 21–44. National Central University: Chungli, Taiwan, 2000.

Byrne, J., and S.-J. Yun. Efficient global warming: Contradictions in liberal democratic responses to global environmental problems. *Bull. Sci. Technol. Soc.* 19(6):493–500, 1999.

Byrne, J., and **Y.-D. Wang** et al. **(J-d. Kim).** Mitigating CO_2 emissions of the Republic of Korea: The role of energy efficiency measures. In *Proceedings of the 20th Annual North American Conference of the U.S. Association for Energy Economics,* Orlando, Fla.: 319–28, 1999.

Byrne, J. Climate change and renewable energy: Opportunities and challenges for Korea. In *Climate Change and Alternative Energy Development,* pp. 49–82, ed. S.-H. Kim. Seoul, South Korea: Environmental Forum, Korea National Assembly, 1999.

Byrne, J., Y.-D. Wang, H. Lee, and **J.-d. Kim.** An equity- and sustainability-based policy response to global climate change. *Energy Policy* 26(4):335–43, 1998.

Byrne, J. Sustainable energy and environmental futures: The implications of climate change, technological change and economic restructuring. In *Global Warming and a Sustainable Energy Future,* ed. **J.-d. Kim,** pp. 1–23. Taegu, South Korea: Research Institute for Energy, Environment and Economy, Kyungpook National University, 1998.

Byrne, J., B. Shen, and W. Wallace. The economics of sustainable energy for rural development: A study of renewable energy in rural China. *Energy Policy* 26(1):45–54, 1998.

Byrne, J., et al. Photovoltaics as an energy services technology: A case study of PV sited at the Union of Concerned Scientists headquarters. In *Proceedings of the American Solar Energy Society Solar 98 Conference,* Albuquerque, N.Mex., 1998.

Letendre, S., **J. Byrne,** C. Weinberg, and **Y.-D. Wang.** Commercializing photovoltaics: The importance of capturing distributed benefits. In *Proceedings of the American Solar Energy Society Solar 98 Conference,* Albuquerque, N.Mex., pp. 231–7, 1998.

Byrne, J. *Equity and Sustainability in the Greenhouse: Reclaiming our Atmospheric Commons.* Pune, India: Parisar, 1997.

Byrne, J., and C. Govindarajalu. Power sector reform: Elements of a regulatory framework. *Econ. Political Weekly* 32(31):1946–7, 1997.

Byrne, J., contributing author. A generic assessment of response options. In *Climate Change 1995: Economic and Social Dimensions of Climate Change,* Contribution of Working Group III to the Second Assessment Report of the Intergovernmental Panel on Climate Change, pp. 225–62. New York: Cambridge University Press, 1996.

Byrne, J., and **S. Hoffman** eds. *Governing the Atom: The Politics of Risk.* New Brunswick, N.J., and London: Transaction Publishers, 1996.

Byrne, J., and **S. Hoffman.** The ideology of progress and the globalization of nuclear power. In *Governing the Atom: The Politics of Risk,* pp. 11-45, eds. **J. Byrne** and **S. Hoffman.** New Brunswick, N.J., and London: Transaction Publishers, 1996.

Byrne, J., S. Letendre, and **Y.-D. Wang.** The distributed utility concept: Toward a sustainable electric utility sector. In *Proceedings of the ACEEE 1996 Summer Study on Energy Efficiency in Buildings,* vol. 7, pp. 7.1–8, 1996.

Byrne, J., and **S. Hoffman.** Sustainability: From concept to practice. *IEEE Technol. Soc.* 15(2):6–7, 1996.

Byrne, J., B. Shen, and X. Li. The challenge of sustainability balancing China's energy, economic and environmental goals. *Energy Policy* 24(5):455–62, 1996.

Byrne, J. and S. J. Hsu. Community versus commodity: Environmental protest in Taiwan. *Bull. Sci. Technol. Soc.* 16(5–6):329–36, 1996.

Byrne, J., et al. **(Y.-D. Wang).** Evaluating the economics of photovoltaics in a demand-side management role. *Energy Policy* 24(2):177–85, 1996.

Byrne, J., R. Nigro, and **Y.-D. Wang.** Photovoltaic technology as a dispatchable, peak-shaving option. *Public Utilities Fortnightly* September, 1995.

Byrne, J., C. Hadjilambrinos, and **S. Wagle.** Distributing costs of global climate change. *IEEE Technol. Soc.* 13(1):17–24, 1994.

Byrne, J., Y.-D. Wang, and S. Hegedus. Photovoltaics as a demand-side management technology: An analysis of peak-shaving and direct load control options. *Prog. Photovoltaics* 2:235–48, 1994.

Byrne, J., Y.-D. Wang, B. Shen, and X. Li. Sustainable urban development strategies for China. *Environ. Urbanization* 6(1):174–87, 1994.

Byrne, J., Y.-D. Wang, R. Nigro, and S. Letendre. Photovoltaics in a demand-side management role. In *Proceedings of the ACEEE 1994 Summer Study on Energy Efficiency in Buildings* vol. 2, pp. 2.43–9, 1994.

Byrne, J., B. Shen, and X. Li. Energy efficiency and renewable energy options for China's economic expansion. In *Proceedings of the ACEEE 1994 Summer Study on Energy Efficiency in Buildings* vol. 4, pp. 4.25–36, 1994.

Byrne, J., and **Y.-D. Wang** et al. Urban sustainability during industrialization: The case of China. *Bull. Sci. Technol. Soc.* 13(6):324–31, 1993.

Byrne, J., Y.-D. Wang, and **S. Wagle.** Toward a politics of sustainability: The responsibilities of industrialized countries. *Regions* 183:4–7, 1993.

Byrne, J., and D. Rich, eds. *Energy and Environment: The Policy Challenge.* New Brunswick, N.J, and London: Transaction Publishers, 1992.

Byrne, J., and D. Rich. Toward a political economy of global change: Energy, environment and development in the greenhouse. In *Energy and Environment: The Policy Challenge,* pp. 269–302, eds. **J. Byrne** and D. Rich. New Brunswick, N.J, and London: Transaction Publishers, 1992.

University of Delaware

Selected Publications (continued)

Byrne, J., and **J.-d. Kim.** City and technology in social theory: A theoretical reconstruction of postindustrialism. *Korean J. Reg. Stud.* 8(1):67–86, 1992.

Byrne, J., **S. Hoffman** and **C. R. Martinez.** Environmental commodification and the industrialization of Native American lands. In *Proceedings of the Seventh Annual Meeting of the National Association of Science, Technology and Society,* pp. 170–81, 1992.

Byrne, J., and **Y.-D. Wang.** The politics of unsustainability: The US (un)prepares for UNCED. *Regions* 178:8–11, 1992.

Byrne, J., Y.-D. Wang, J.-d. Kim, and K. Ham. The political economy of energy, environment and development. *Korean J. Environ. Stud.* 30:278–312, 1992.

Byrne, J., and **Y.-D. Wang** et al. Energy and environmental sustainability in East and Southeast Asia. *IEEE Technol. Soc.* 10(4):21–9, 1991.

Byrne, J. Meeting the certain challenge: A policy perspective on systemic energy and environmental problems. In *Energy and Environment,* pp. 40–51, eds. E. Kainlauri et al. Atlanta, Ga.: ASHRAE Special Publications, 1991.

Byrne, J., and **Y.-D. Wang** et al. Institutional strategies for sustainable development: Case studies of four Asian industrializing countries. In *Proceedings of the Interdisciplinary Conference on Preparing for a Sustainable Society,* pp. 105–15, 1991.

Byrne, J., and **S. Hoffman.** Energy, environment and sustainable world development: Options for the year 2000. *Energy Sources* 13(1):1–4, 1991.

Byrne, J., and **S. Hoffman.** The politics of alternative energy: A study of water pumping systems in developing nations. *Energy Sources* 13(1):55–66, 1991.

Byrne, J., and **S. Hoffman.** Nuclear optimism and the technological imperative: A study of the Pacific Northwest electrical network. *Bull. Sci. Technol. Soc.* 11:63–77, 1991.

Byrne, J., S. Hoffman, and **C. Martinez.** The social structure of nature. In *Proceedings of the Sixth Annual Meeting of the National Association of Science, Technology and Society,* pp. 67–76, 1991.

Byrne, J., et al. Green economics and the developing world: Institutional strategies for sustainable development. In *Proceedings of the Sixth Annual Conference of the National Association of Science, Technology and Society,* pp. 97–109, 1991.

Byrne, J., and D. Rich. The real energy crisis. *Regions* 169:2–5, 1990.

Byrne, J., and **J.-d. Kim.** Centralization, technicization and development on the semi-periphery: A study of South Korea's commitment to nuclear power. *Bull. Sci. Technol. Soc.* 10(4):212–22, 1990.

Byrne, J., D. Rich, and **C. Martinez.** Lewis Mumford and the living city. *Regions* 166:10–2, 1990.

Byrne, J., and **C. Martinez.** Ghastly science. *Society* 27(1):22–4, 1989.

Byrne, J., S. Hoffman, and **C. Martinez.** Technological politics in the nuclear age. *Bull. Sci. Technol. Soc.* 8(6):580–94, 1989.

Byrne, J., C. Martinez, and **J.-d. Kim,** et al. The city as commodity: The decline of urban vision. *Raumplannung* 46(47):174–8, 1989.

Byrne, J., and **S. Hoffman.** Nuclear power and technological authoritarianism. *Bull. Sci. Technol. Soc.* 7:658–71, 1988.

Byrne, J., Y.-D. Wang, and K. Ham. The political geography of acid rain: The U.S. case. *Regions* 157: 3–6, 1988.

Byrne, J., Y.-D. Wang, D. Rich, and I. Han. Economic and policy implications of integrated resource planning in the utility sector. In *Proceedings of the ACEEE 1988 Summer Study on Energy Efficiency in Buildings,* vol. 8, pp. 8.265–78, 1988.

Byrne, J., and D. Rich. Post-Chernobyl notes on the U.S. nuclear fizzle. *Regions* 150:3–6, 1987.

Byrne, J. Policy science and the administrative state: The political economy of cost-benefit analysis. In *Confronting Values in Policy Analysis: The Politics of Criteria,* Sage Yearbooks in Politics and Public Policy, eds. J. Forester and F. Fischer. Beverly Hills, Calif.: Sage Publications, 1987.

Byrne, J., and **C. Martinez.** Urban policy without the urban. *Regions* 148:4–7, 1987.

Byrne, J., and D. Rich, eds. *The Politics of Energy R&D.* New Brunswick, N.J., and London: Transaction Publishers, 1986.

Byrne, J., and D. Rich. In search of the abundant energy machine. In *The Politics of Energy R&D,* pp. 141–60, eds. **J. Byrne** and D. Rich. New Brunswick, N.J., and London: Transaction Publishers, 1986.

Byrne, J., and **S. Hoffman.** Some lessons in the political economy of megapower: WPPSS and the municipal bond market. *J. Urban Affairs* 8(1):35–47, 1986.

Byrne, J., and D. Rich. *Energy and Cities.* New Brunswick, N.J., and London: Transaction Publishers, 1985.

Byrne, J., C. Martinez, and D. Rich. The post-industrial imperative: Energy, cities and the featureless plain. In *Energy and Cities,* pp. 101–41, eds. **J. Byrne** and D. Rich. New Brunswick, N.J.: Transaction Publishers, 1985.

Byrne, J., and **S. Hoffman.** Efficient corporate harm: A Chicago metaphysic. In *Errant Corporations: Responsibility, Compliance and Sanctions,* eds. B. Fisse and P. French. San Antonio: Trinity University Press, 1985.

Byrne, J., and D. Rich. Deregulation and energy conservation: A reappraisal. *Policy Stud. J.* 13(2):331–44, 1984.

Byrne, J., and D. Rich. The solar energy transition as a problem of political economy. In *The Solar Energy Transition: Implementation and Policy Implications,* pp. 163–86, eds. D. Rich et al. Boulder, Colo.: Westview Press, 1983.

Rich, D., A. Barnett, J. Veigel, and **J. Byrne,** eds. *The Solar Energy Transition: Implementation and Policy Implications.* Boulder, Colo.: Westview Press for the American Association for the Advancement of Science, 1983.

Byrne, J. What's wrong with being reasonable: The politics of cost-benefit analysis. In *Ethical Theory and Business,* pp. 568–76, eds. N. E. Bowie and T. L. Beauchamp. Englewood Cliffs: Prentice-Hall, 1982.

Durbin, P. T. Environmental ethics and environmental activism. In *Technology and the Environment,* Research in Philosophy and Technology Series, vol. 12, pp. 107–17, ed. F. Ferre. New York: JAI Press Inc., 1992.

Glover, L. globalization.com vs. ecologicaljustice.org: Contesting the end of history. In *Environmental Justice: Discourses in International Political Economy,* pp. 231–60, eds. **J. Byrne** et al. New Brunswick, N.J., and London: Transaction Publishers, 2002.

Hoffman, S. Powering injustice: Hydroelectric development in northern Manitoba. In *Environmental Justice: Discourses in International Political Economy,* pp. 147–70, eds. **J. Byrne** et al. New Brunswick, N.J., and London: Transaction Publishers, 2002.

Kim, J.-d., ed. *Global Warming and a Sustainable Energy Future.* Taegu, South Korea: Research Institute for Energy, Environment and Economy, Kyungpook National University, 1998.

Kim, J.-d., and **J. Byrne.** The Asian atom: Hard-path nuclearization in East Asia. In *Governing the Atom: The Politics of Risk,* pp. 273–300, eds. **J. Byrne** and **S. Hoffman.** New Brunswick, N.J., and London: Transaction Publishers, 1996.

Martinez, C., and J. Poupart. The circle of life: Preserving American Indian traditions and facing the nuclear challenge. In *Environmental Justice: Discourses in International Political Economy,* pp. 119–46, eds. **J. Byrne** et al. New Brunswick, N.J., and London: Transaction Publishers, 2002.

Martinez, C., and **J. Byrne.** Science, society and the state: The nuclear project and the transformation of the American political economy. In *Governing the Atom: The Politics of Risk,* eds. **J. Byrne** and **S. Hoffman.** New Brunswick, N.J.: Transaction Publishers, 1996.

Schreuder, Y., and C. Sherry. Flexible mechanisms in the corporate greenhouse: Implementation of the Kyoto Protocol and the globalization of the electric power industry. *Energy Environ.* 12(5–6): 487–98, 2001.

Sylves, R. T., and W. L. Waugh. *Disaster Management in the U.S. and Canada: The Politics, Policymaking, Administration and Analysis of Emergency Management.* Springfield, Ill.: Charles C. Thomas Publishers, 1996.

Sylves, R. *The Nuclear Oracles: A Political History of the General Advisory Committee of the Atomic Energy Commission, 1947-1977.* Ames, Iowa: Iowa State University Press, 1987.

Wang, Y.-D., and **J. Byrne** et al. Designing revenue neutral and equitable water conservation-oriented rates for use during drought summer months. In *Proceedings of the Water Sources Conference.* American Water Works Association, 2002.

Wang, Y.-D., and **J. Byrne** et al. Less energy, a better economy, and a sustainable South Korea: An energy efficiency scenario analysis. *Bull. Sci. Technol. Soc.* 22(2):110–22, 2002.

Wang, Y.-D., and **J. Byrne.** Short- and mid-term prospects for world oil prices using a modified Delphi method. In *Factors Influencing World Prices: Alternative Methods of Prediction,* pp. 156–206, ed. J.-K. Kim. Seoul, South Korea: Korea Energy Economics Institute, 2001.

Wang, Y.-D., and **J. Byrne** et al. Evaluating the persistence of residential water conservation: A 1992–97 panel study of a water utility program in Delaware. *J. Am. Water Resources. Assoc.* 35(5):1269–76, 1999.

Wang, Y.-D., and W. Latham. Energy and state economic growth: Some new evidence. *J. Energy Develop.* 13(2):197–221, 1989.

Wang, Y.-D. A residential energy market model: An econometric analysis. *J. Reg. Sci.* 25(2):215–39, 1985.

UNIVERSITY OF IDAHO

Environmental Science Program

Programs of Study

The quality of life in tomorrow's world hinges on the ability to resolve very complex environmental issues. The University of Idaho (UI) Environmental Science Program emphasizes an integrated approach for students committed to studying and solving environmental issues. The Environmental Science faculty members are from throughout the University and include soil scientists, engineers, biologists, ecologists, geographers, political scientists, sociologists, economists, chemists, and hydrologists. Their goal is to work across traditional disciplines to provide a comprehensive education in the hows and whys of environmental problem solving. Students working on an M.S. or Ph.D. in environmental science can choose one of seven option areas: earth science/hydrology, ecology, environmental toxicology, natural resources management, physical science, policy and law, and waste management. The duration of the M.S. program is generally two years, with course work during three semesters, research during the summers, and one semester of thesis completion. The environmental science Ph.D. requires that the student develop a study program of at least 78 semester hours in consultation his or her major professor and supervisory committee. A major professor works closely with each student to accomplish research goals in a timely fashion. Graduates are employed in the private and public sectors in areas such as natural resource management, pollution prevention, air and water quality monitoring, hazardous waste management, planning, and environmental compliance.

The University of Idaho also offers a concurrent J.D./M.S. degree program, which gives students an opportunity to combine the study of scientific, social, philosophical, and legal aspects of environmental issues. This course of study takes place over four years, in which the first and second years are spent almost entirely in the law school, the third year taking classes that apply to both programs, and the final year finishing the M.S. work and writing a thesis.

Research Facilities

Students are able to draw on University resources, such as an extensive library, computer labs, and research facilities, including the Idaho Water Resources Research Institute, the UI Experimental Forest, the Environmental Research Institute, and the National Institute for Advanced Transportation Technology.

Financial Aid

All applicants are automatically considered for teaching and research assistantships. Both departmental teaching assistantships and Governor's Initiative/Environmental Science research assistantships are available. The teaching assistantships pay out-of-state fees and a monthly stipend. The research assistantships pay in-state and out-of-state fees and a monthly stipend. Financial aid is also available through the Federal Perkins Loan Program and work-study grants. The Student Financial Aid Office can provide information and applications.

Cost of Study

For 2004–05, full-time graduate fees are $2086 per semester for Idaho residents, with an additional fee of $4010 per semester for nonresidents. Resident students enrolled part-time pay $205 per credit; nonresidents pay an additional $123 per credit for part-time work. Full-time fees are charged for 8 credits or more. Fees are subject to change.

Living and Housing Costs

Graduate student housing is available through the University for $462 to $684 per month for apartments ranging in size from efficiencies to four-bedroom units. Potential graduate students are advised to reserve housing early. Off-campus housing lists are available on the Web at http://www.asui.uidaho.edu.

Student Group

Faculty members look for competitive applicants coming from successful undergraduate experiences who are focused individuals interested in refining their research skills. Two thirds of the 98 graduate students attend the Moscow campus; one third are part-time nontraditional students who work full-time and attend the Idaho Falls campus. Most full-time students are fully funded; 60 percent are men, 40 percent are women, and 20 percent of the graduate student population are international students from places as diverse as Siberia and Colombia.

Student Outcomes

U.S. News & World Report recently rated environmental science graduate degrees as "highly marketable," with starting salaries ranging from $35,000 to $39,000 (government) and $47,000 to $49,000 (private industry). Graduates work in challenging and high-paying jobs for state and local government, private industry, and private environmental consulting firms—as aides to U.S. congressional representatives, as water quality managers for industry, as hazardous waste supervisors, and as environmental lawyers.

Location

Moscow, located in the Idaho panhandle among the rolling hills of the Palouse, is an agricultural and recreational area and is the cultural center of the region. Local music and theater productions have received international acclaim. Skiing and lake and river sports are within an easy drive. Spokane is 88 miles north, and Seattle and Portland are each 6 hours west.

The Department

The Environmental Science Program is the largest interdisciplinary program at UI. Faculty members represent all eight colleges and twenty-six departments. The program is committed to finding venues for students to work across traditional disciplines to study complex environmental problems. The committee structure for each graduate student reflects this commitment—a biological scientist, a physical scientist, and a social scientist are included on each committee. The program has grown significantly from 27 students in 1993 to nearly 220 in 2004.

Applying

Applicants to the M.S. or Ph.D. program must take the GRE and submit three letters of recommendation and a statement of research interests. International applicants must take the TOEFL, with a score of 550 or better. Students applying to the J.D./M.S. program must apply separately to the Graduate College, College of Law, and Concurrent J.D./M.S. Degree Program. Admission into the Environmental Science Program depends upon a demonstrated ability to excel in an intense, interdisciplinary educational environment. The deadline for applications for fall semester is February 1.

Students applying for a departmental assistantship should consult with the department regarding the process and the deadline date, which may be earlier than the other application deadlines.

Correspondence and Information

Chris Dixon, Program Academic Advisor
Environmental Science Graduate Program
University of Idaho
P.O. Box 443006
Moscow, Idaho 83844-3006
Telephone: 208-885-6113
Fax: 208-885-4674
E-mail: envs@uidaho.edu
World Wide Web: http://www.webs.uidaho.edu/envs

University of Idaho

THE FACULTY AND THEIR RESEARCH

Ecology/Biological Science and Natural Resource Management

Edward Bechinski. Public education and field research about alternatives to pesticides for insect control in agricultural and urban ecosystems. (edb@uidaho.edu)
Jan Boll. Surface and sub-surface hydrology, water quality, watershed management, GIS applications, computer modeling, nondestructive measurement techniques. (jboll@uidaho.edu)
Nilsa Bosque-Peréz. Insect biodiversity, entomology, insect/plant interactions, host plant resistance. (nbosque@uidaho.edu)
Steven Brunsfeld. Ecological genetics, conservation biology, rare plant ecology. (sbruns@uidaho.edu)
Stephen Bunting. Rangeland ecology, fire ecology. (sbunting@uidaho.edu)
Jeff Braatne. Stream and riparian ecology, restoration of riparian and wetland ecosystems. (braatne@uidaho.edu)
Donald Crawford. Bioremediation of soil and water. (donc@uidaho.edu)
Ronald Crawford. Biodegradation of natural and man-made chemicals. (crawford@uidaho.edu)
Stephen Cook. Impact of standard tree harvesting practices on insect diversity. (stephenc@uidaho.edu)
Sanford Eigenbrode. Ecology and interactions between insects and plants. (seigenbrode@uidaho.edu)
Edward Garton. Population dynamics of birds and mammals. (ogarton@uidaho.edu)
Tom Hess. Wastewater treatment, land treatment of municipal wastewater and biosolids. (tfhess@uidaho.edu)
James Johnson. Aquatic entomology (djohnson@uidaho.edu)
James Kingery. Ecological restoration of altered wildlands and forest/range relationships. (jkingery@uidaho.edu)
Guy Knudsen. Soil microbioogy and microbial energy in forest, wilderness, and agricultural systems. (gknudsen@uidaho.edu)
Karen Launchbaugh. Plant-animal interactions and grazing ecology. (klaunchb@uidaho.edu)
Robert L. Mahler. Water quality, nutrient cycling in agricultural and forest systems. (bmahler@uidaho.edu)
John Marshall. Physiological ecology of trees, stable isotope methods in ecology. (jdm@uidaho.edu)
Penny Morgan. Fire ecology and management; effects of fire on individual plants, communities, and ecosystems; ecological modeling; agroforestry and silvopastoral systems for lesser developed countries. (pmorgan@uidaho.edu)
Matt Morra. Environmental organic chemistry, fate of organics in soils. (matthewm@uidaho.edu)
Kerry Reese. Avian ecology, particularly waterfowl and upland game birds. (kreese@uidaho.edu)
Ronald Robberecht. Plant response to natural and enhanced levels of UV-B radiation. (ronrobb@uidaho.edu)
Dennis Scarnecchia. Large river fisheries. (scar@uidaho.edu)
J. Michael Scott. Conservation biology, ornithology, wildlife management. (mscott@uidaho.edu)
Molly Stock. Expert systems, interactive computer programming. (mstock@uidaho.edu)
Lisette Waits. Conservation biology, conservation genetics. (lwaits@uidaho.edu)
Gerald Wright. Wildlife habitat relations, long-term vegetation change, landscape-level land use planning and protection. (gwright@uidaho.edu)
Robert Zemetra. Plant breeding/genetics, plant biotechnology, insect and disease resistance in wheat. (rzemetra@uidaho.edu)

Policy and Law and Natural Resource Management

Kathy Aiken. History of twentieth century; labor, women, and social reform; impact of new technology on management and workers. (kaiken@uidaho.edu)
Rula Awwad-Rafferty. Factors affecting quality of life in the built environment. (rulaa@uidaho.edu)
Steve Cooke. Public policy analysis, public finance and taxation. (scooke@uidaho.edu)
Donald Crowley. Judicial policy, civil liberties, public policy. (crowley@uidaho.edu)
Stephen Drown. Human behavior and environmental design. (sdrown@uidaho.edu)
Jo Ellen Force. Community social change in resource dependent communities. (joellen@uidaho.edu)
Rodney Frey. Understanding how indigenous peoples, especially American Indians, have come to perceive and interact with their "landscape." (rfrey@uidaho.edu)
Dale D. Goble. Natural resources law and policy. (gobled@uidaho.edu)
Bruce Haglund. Energy use in buildings, computer-based visualization. (bhaglund@uidaho.edu)
Chuck Harris. Nontangible/nonmarket values of amenity and natural resources. (charris@uidaho.edu)
Steve Hollenhorst. Environmental policy, wilderness and protected area management. (stevenh@uidaho.edu)
Harley Johansen. Economic geography, rural development. (johansen@uidaho.edu)
Douglas Lind. Philosophy of law, environmental ethics, environmental law. (dlind@uidaho.edu)
Gary Machlis. Environmental sociology, human ecology, conservation biology, national park management. (gmachlis@uidaho.edu)
Jon Miller. Regional economic modeling, water resources/green economics. (jrmecon@uidaho.edu)
Mike Odell. Environmental and science education. (mirodell@novell.uidaho.edu)
Gundars Rudzitis. Estimated value of environmental cleanup/amenities, public lands/wilderness policy, environmental attitudes, development and environmental amenities. (gundars@uidaho.edu)
Nick Sanyal. Human dimensions of fish and wildlife management, recreation and tourism planning. (nsanyal@uidaho.edu)
Jerry Wegman. Accountant's liability and securities regulation. (wegman@uidaho.edu)
Patrick Wilson. Natural resource and environmental policy. (pwilson@uidaho.edu)
J. D. Wulfhorst. Community sociology, natural resources policy analysis. (jd@uidaho.edu)

Waste Management, Earth Science/Hydrology, and Physical Science

Thomas Bitterwolf. Inorganic chemistry, nuclear waste. (bitterte@uidaho.edu)
Valerie Chamberlien. Adiogenic isotopes, geochronology, and geochemistry of all types of rocks related to plate tectonics; geological history; pollution and waste disposal; mineral exploration; mineralogy. (vec@uidaho.edu)
Jerry Fairley. Unsaturated zone hydrology in fractured rock, nuclear waste disposal. (jfairley@uidaho.edu)
Fritz Fiedler. Mathematical modeling of flow and transport process related to environmental hydrology, soil erosion models, surface water quality and watershed restoration, ground water quality. (fritz@uidaho.edu)
Rick Fletcher. Atmospheric chemistry, kinetics and dynamics. (fletcher@uidaho.edu)
Dennis Geist. Volcanology, hard rock petrology. (dgeist@uidaho.edu)
Mickey Gunter. X-ray and optical crystallography, health effects of minerals. (gunter@uidaho.edu)
Karen Humes. Near surface hydrology, vadose zone. (khumes@uidaho.edu)
Timothy Link. Surface hydrology, snow hydrology, interactions of vegetation and hydrologic processes, hydroclimatology, modeling land-surface processes. (tlink@uidaho.edu)
Paul McDaniel. Soil formation, mineralogy, hydrology, management, geomorphology. (pmcdaniel@uidaho.edu)
Jeanne McHale. Physical chemistry, spectroscopy. (jmchale@uidaho.edu)
Gregory Moller. Biogeochemical cycling, oxidative stress, chemical ecotoxicology. (gmoller@uidaho.edu)
James L. Osiensky. Artificial recharge, contaminant hydrogeology. (osiensky@uidaho.edu)
Batric Pesic. Wastewater treatment, heavy metal removal, soil stabilization. (pesic@uidaho.edu)
Keith Prisbrey. Remediation of acid mine drainage, transuranics. (pris@uidaho.edu)
Russell Qualls. Land surface hydrology, soil moisture and evapotranspiration modeling. (rqualls@uidaho.edu)
Dan Strawn. Soil chemistry, trace metals in soils. (dgstrawn@uidaho.edu)
Marcus Tuller. Flow and distribution of fluid phases through porous plant growth media in microgravity, angle of repose of surrogate Martian dust. (mtuller@uidaho.edu)
Ray von Wandruszka. Chemistry of humic acid, analysis of anabolic steroids. (rvw@uidaho.edu)
Chien Wai. Separation science, developing new chelating agents for selective extraction of metal ions, synthesis and characterizations of ionizable crown ethers for metal complexation, supercritical fluid extraction for recovery of metal ion, radioisotopes. (wchien@uidaho.edu)
Barbara Cooke Williams. Mine waste management of surface and groundwater. (barbwill@uidaho.edu)
Scott Wood. Aqueous geochemistry, thermodynamics. (swood@novell.uidaho.edu)

UNIVERSITY OF IDAHO

College of Natural Resources
Department of Natural Resources

Program of Study

The Master of Natural Resources (M.N.R.) is a 30-credit, professional, nonthesis degree focused on natural resource management and administration. The program is targeted to students who wish to increase their breadth and depth of technical knowledge, who wish to develop skills in management and administration rather than research as well as develop credentials that would increase their opportunities for professional advancement.

In contrast to M.S. and Ph.D. programs, which emphasize research and depth of knowledge in a particular subject area, the M.N.R. program focuses on breadth across natural resource disciplines and is designed as a terminal degree. M.N.R. students take 28 credits in four emphasis areas: policy, planning and law, human dimensions, ecology and resource management, and tools and technology, as well as 2 credits of colloquia focused on natural resource issues. The classes for this interdisciplinary degree program combine theory, field experience, and tools for quantitative and critical analysis. Topics are examined at local to landscape to regional scales and address the issues and problems of sustainable ecosystem use and management. Through interdisciplinary graduate course work, students interact with M.S. and Ph.D. students from across the College of Natural Resources. Completion of the degree typically takes from two to three semesters.

Research Facilities

The research function of the College is coordinated by the Idaho Forest, Wildlife and Range Experiment Station. The Cooperative Fish and Wildlife Research Unit and the Cooperative Park Studies Unit are joint federal-state-University units, whose federal employees hold faculty appointments. Other CNR research units are the Wilderness Research Center, the Policy Analysis Group, the Inland Empire Tree Improvement Cooperative, the Intermountain Forest Tree Nutrition Cooperative, and the offices of Extension Forestry. Research and support facilities include the 7,500-acre University of Idaho Experimental Forest; Field Campuses: McCall Field Campus, Clark Fork Field Campus, and Taylor Ranch Wilderness Field Station in the Frank Church Wilderness of No Return; the Forest Research Nursery, a teaching, research, and production nursery producing 750,000 seedlings per year with three greenhouses; and the Remote Sensing/GIS Lab, a fully equipped, state-of-the-art laboratory used for teaching and research. The University of Idaho and Washington State University share library resources through interlibrary loan.

Financial Aid

Graduate students accepted into the Master of Natural Resources program should file the Free Application for Federal Student Aid (FAFSA) prior to February 15 to identify financial resources such as loans, grants, and work-study. Nonresident M.N.R. students are considered for full out-of-state waivers by the Graduate School (worth $3696 per semester).

Cost of Study

For 2004–05, full-time graduate fees are $2086 per semester for Idaho residents, with an additional fee of $4010 per semester for nonresidents. Resident students enrolled part-time pay $205 per credit; nonresidents pay an additional $123 per credit for part-time work. Full-time fees are charged for 8 credits or more. Fees are subject to change.

Living and Housing Costs

Graduate student housing is available through the University for $462 to $684 per month for apartments ranging in size from efficiencies to four-bedroom units. Potential graduate students are advised to reserve housing early. Off-campus housing lists are available on the Web at http://www.asui.uidaho.edu.

Student Group

Successful applicants typically have a minimum 3.0 GPA with an undergraduate degree in natural resource management, ecology, or environmental science or a closely related field.

Student Outcomes

Depending on professional experience, graduates are competitive for administrative and technical positions in federal or state agencies, private companies, and nongovernmental organizations. Graduates have taken positions with the U.S. Forest Service, Bureau of Land Management, U.S. Fish and Wildlife Service, and Washington Cattleman's Association, with salaries ranging from $31,000 to $52,000.

Location

Moscow, located in the Idaho panhandle among the rolling hills of the Palouse, is an agricultural and recreational area and is the cultural center of the region. Local music and theater productions have received international acclaim. Skiing and lake and river sports are within easy drives. Spokane is 88 miles north, and Seattle and Portland are each 6 hours west.

The University

The University of Idaho was created in 1889, a year before Idaho became a state. UI is a publicly supported, comprehensive land-grant institution with principal responsibility in Idaho for performing research and granting the Ph.D. degree. More than 750 faculty members participate in teaching and research. In addition to the accreditation of individual programs, the University is accredited by the Northwest Association of Schools and Colleges.

Applying

For an application and complete information about applying to the Graduate School, prospective students should visit the Web site http://www.uidaho.edu/cogs (College of Graduate Studies).

Applicants must submit the following items to the Graduate Admissions Office: formal application with a statement of educational objectives, professional vitae or resume, official transcripts sent from each institution attended, two letters of reference, and Graduate Record Examinations (GRE) scores. Students who have not completed a B.S. degree in a natural resource or related discipline are required to take additional background courses.

Students applying for a departmental assistantship should consult with the department regarding the process and the deadline date, which may be earlier than the other application deadlines.

Correspondence and Information

Cheri Cole, Administrative Assistant
College of Natural Resources
University of Idaho
P.O. Box 441142
Moscow, Idaho 83843-1142

Telephone: 208-885-8981
Fax: 208-885-5534
E-mail: cheric@uidaho.edu
World Wide Web: http://www.cnr.uidaho.edu/cnr

University of Idaho

THE FACULTY

Dr. Charles (Chuck) Harris, Professor, Resource Recreation and Tourism and M.N.R. Program Director (e-mail: charris@uidaho.edu).
Dr. Jeffrey Braatne, Assistant Professor, Fish and Wildlife Resources (e-mail: braatne@uidaho.edu).
Dr. Han-Sup Han, Assistant Professor, Forest Products (e-mail: hanh@uidaho.edu).
Dr. Kerry Reese, Professor, Fish and Wildlife Resources (e-mail: kreese@uidaho.edu).
Dr. Ron Robberecht, Professor, Rangeland Ecology and Management (e-mail: ecology@uidaho.edu).
Dr. Dave Wenny, Professor, Forest Resources (e-mail: dwenny@uidaho.edu).

UNIVERSITY OF TOLEDO

Ph.D. Initiative: Environmental Sustainability Science and Engineering

Programs of Study

The University of Toledo Colleges of Engineering and Arts and Sciences (Departments of Civil Engineering, Chemical and Environmental Engineering, and Earth, Ecological, and Environmental Sciences) have developed a multidisciplinary initiative in environmental sustainability science and engineering. Students completing studies within this initiative can earn a Ph.D. in biological sciences (ecology track) or Ph.D. in engineering. This initiative is designed for students with a range of backgrounds in biology, geology, engineering, and environmental science and accommodates the diverse backgrounds of its students through a series of leveling courses.

The triple bottom line, a rapidly emerging business concept that considers environmental and social propriety in addition to economic measures, is an emphasis of study. Some attention to international issues of sustainability are expected, particularly in light of the global nature of environmental issues (e.g., global warming, transborder pollution) that are central to fully understanding the problems of environmental sustainability in today's world.

The Ph.D. program requires 90 semester credit hours beyond the B.S. (or 60 hours beyond the M.S.); typically 45 hours of course work and 45 hours of dissertation. Because of the multidisciplinary nature of the proposed program, each student is required to complete classes in three different aspects of sustainability: engineering, environmental sciences, and societal context. Students are required to complete three courses from each of the science and engineering cores as well as two courses from the social science core (24 hours). An additional 15 hours of elective classes are selected to enhance the research experience.

Research Facilities

Research activities may be broadly classified into three clusters: Bioremediation and Phytoremediation, Ecosystems and Watersheds, and Green Engineering. Research is supported by state-of-the-art research and computing laboratories that include the Bowman-Oddy/Wolfe Laboratory Complex and the Nitschke Engineering Complex. Laboratories are equipped with all utilities normally found in wet laboratories as appropriate for experimental research. A network of more than 250 PCs and more than thirty UNIX workstations is available for modeling studies and analysis.

The University of Toledo also houses the Lake Erie Research Center, a multidisciplinary research institution evaluating the environmental stability of Lake Erie; the Legal Institute of the Great Lakes, which provides a forum for the development and exchange of solutions to the regional problems of the Great Lakes states and provinces in areas such as environmental protection; and the Plant Sciences Research Center.

Financial Aid

Many graduate students receive financial support in the form of fellowships and teaching or research assistantships that are available on a competitive basis. Fellowships may be up to $20,000 per year plus full tuition and fees. All supported graduate students may also receive a subsidy toward the purchase of the University of Toledo Student Health Insurance.

Cost of Study

The tuition rate for the 2004–05 academic year is $347.14 per semester credit hour for in-state students and $714.29 per semester credit hour for out-of-state students. Additional fees are required and include a general fee, a technology fee, and mandatory insurance.

Living and Housing Costs

Students may choose to live in moderately priced, high-quality housing within easy walking distance of the campus. Apartments are available with average monthly rent and expenses of $412.29 per student. The University of Toledo offers shuttle bus service to many off-campus housing and apartment complexes.

Student Group

There are approximately 21,000 students at the University of Toledo. Approximately 4,400 are graduate students. The University has a rich mixture of diverse student organizations. Students join groups that are organized around common cultural, religious, athletic, and educational interests. A Graduate Student Association ensures the representation of graduate students on University committees, provides recognition to graduate students for outstanding achievement and service, and organizes social and other activities throughout the year.

Student Outcomes

Graduates of this program have the skills needed to influence both industrial and government policy decisions to effect a better society. Graduates are equipped to serve as translators between industry, government, and nongovernmental organizations to facilitate interactions that lead to sustainable systems. The University believes that its graduates can become the next generation of leaders that will provide sustainable technological systems for the twenty-first century and provide a healthier planet for future generations.

Location

The University of Toledo is located in a residential (suburban) environment inside the city of Toledo, situated on the banks of the Maumee River and on the shores of Lake Erie in northwestern Ohio. Toledo, the fiftieth-largest city in the U.S., has a population of about 325,000 and a history as an industrial center surrounded by a large agricultural enterprise that makes it ideally suited as a center for environmental research.

The University

The University of Toledo, a major comprehensive state university, stands for excellence in research and scholarship as it develops and disseminates knowledge through its academic programs. As a leading development force and center of culture, the University is dedicated to serving the urban region in which it is located, with outreach initiatives, research projects, continuing education programs, and economic development support. The University of Toledo was founded by Jessup W. Scott in 1872.

Applying

Students with a Bachelor of Science in civil engineering, chemical engineering, environmental engineering, biology, chemistry, ecology, geology, environmental science, or related areas should apply. Applicants should have a 3.0 grade point average or better, but exceptions are made for those who demonstrate ability for graduate study. Applications should be completed by March 1 for full consideration for the fall semester. Admission materials can be obtained from the graduate school office or online.

Correspondence and Information

Graduate School
University of Toledo
Toledo, Ohio 43606
Telephone: 419-530-4723
E-mail: grdsch@utnet.utoledo.edu
enviro@utoledo.edu
WWW: http://enviro.utoledo.edu

College of Engineering
1014 Nitschke Hall, MS 310
University of Toledo
Toledo, Ohio 43606
Telephone: 419-530-7391

Department of Earth, Ecological, and Environmental Sciences
MS 604
University of Toledo
Toledo, Ohio 43606
Telephone: 419-530-2009

University of Toledo

THE FACULTY AND THEIR RESEARCH

Bioremediation and Phytoremediation

Bioremediation and phytoremediation combine engineering and ecology to develop bioremediation technologies for cleanup of mixed-contaminant sites, using multiple methods that include enhanced in situ bioremediation, phytoremediation, and contaminant mobility control. The combination of multiple remediation techniques provides synergistic benefits that can enhance the rate of brownfield remediation and expand application to a greater number of potential sites that can be redeveloped for economic growth.

Daryl Dwyer, Ph.D., Michigan State: environmental microbiology, bioremediation, phytoremediation. Cyndee Gruden, Ph.D., Michigan: bioremediation, waste water, water supply. Scott Heckathorn, Ph.D., Illinois: plant biology. Steve Goldman, Ph.D., Missouri: plant genetics, genetic engineering in plants, phytoremediation. Dong-Shik Kim, Ph.D., Michigan: biotechnology, bioremediation. Alison Spongberg, Ph.D., Texas A&M: fate and transport of hazardous contaminants, environmental geochemistry. Donald Stierman, Ph.D., Stanford: applied environmental geophysics, geologic hazards mitigation. William Von Siegler, Ph.D., Purdue: agronomy, plant science.

Watersheds and Ecosystems

Watersheds across the Great Lakes and the United States are adversely affected by a number of environmental problems, including nutrient loading, sedimentation and erosion, and pesticide (insecticide and herbicide) contamination. Research integrates multiple water-flow pathways into existing watershed modeling software to predict how the interactions between various pathways are affected by land use.

Mark Camp, Ph.D., Ohio State: invertebrate paleontology, freshwater mollusks, Quaternary geology. Jiquan Chen, Ph.D., Washington (Seattle): landscape and community ecology, forest ecosystems. Isabel Escobar, Ph.D., Florida: membrane filtration in the field of pathogen rejection, AOC and BDOC rejection, organic matter rejection to minimize the potential for disinfection by-product formation, natural organic matter (NOM) fouling, and biological fouling. Johan Gottgens, Ph.D., Florida: aquatic ecology, pollution control and stability in lakes and wetlands. Andrew Heydinger, Ph.D., Houston: laboratory soil testing, field instrumentation and mathematical modeling, geoenvironmental engineering. David Krantz, Ph.D., South Carolina: coastal and marine geology, Quaternary geology. Ashok Kumar, Ph.D., Waterloo: air pollution, risk analysis and environmental information technology. James Martin-Hayden, Ph.D., Connecticut: hydrogeology, field methods, numerical groundwater modeling. Christine Mayer, Ph.D., Cornell: invertebrate biology. Daryl Moorhead, Ph.D., Tennessee: mathematical modeling of ecosystems, extreme environments and global change. Brian Randolph, Ph.D., Ohio State: subsurface instrumentation, geosynthetics, soil testing, flow modeling. Carol Stepien, Lake Erie Center Director; Ph.D., USC: evolutionary ecology, population genetics, environmental genomics. Elliot Tramer, Ph.D., Georgia: ornithology, population dynamics of vertebrates and higher plants.

Green Engineering

Green engineering is the design, commercialization, and use of processes and products, which are feasible and economical while minimizing generation of pollution at the source and risk to human health and the environment. This research initiative evaluates new manufacturing tools such as life-cycle engineering, green chemistry and benign solvents, and recycling opportunities.

Martin Abraham, Ph.D., Delaware: green engineering, reactions in benign solvents, hydrogen production, catalytic reforming, biomass conversion. Abdul-Majeed Azad, Ph.D., Madras: catalysis, fuel-cell technologies. Robert A. Bennett, Ph.D., Wayne State: plastics recycling, materials, product design, engineering economy, applied statistics. James L. Kamm, Ph.D. Ohio State: alternative energy. James P. LeSage, Ph.D., Boston College: spatial statistics and econometrics. Patrick McGuire, Director, Urban Affairs Center; Ph.D., SUNY at Stony Brook: political economy, social change theory. Walter W. Olson, Ph.D., Rensselaer: advanced manufacturing systems, computer-aided manufacturing, life-cycle analysis to manufacturing processes.

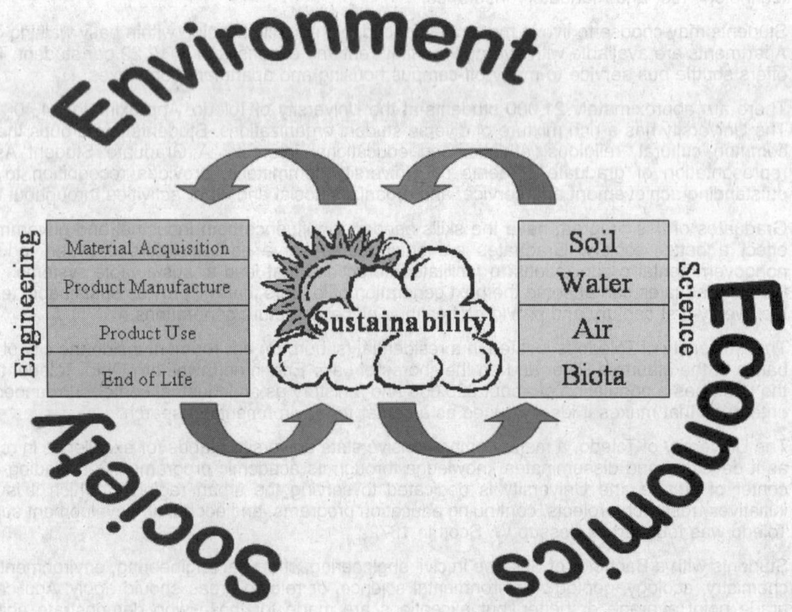

Section 10
Natural Resources

This section contains a directory of institutions offering graduate work in natural resources, followed by in-depth entries submitted by institutions that chose to prepare detailed program descriptions. Additional information about programs listed in the directory but not augmented by an in-depth entry may be obtained by writing directly to the dean of a graduate school or chair of a department at the address given in the directory.

For programs offering related work, see also in this book Environmental Sciences and Management and Meteorology and Atmospheric Sciences; in Book 2, see Architecture (Landscape Architecture) and Public, Regional, and Industrial Affairs; in Book 3, see Biological and Biomedical Sciences; Botany and Plant Biology; Ecology, Environmental Biology, and Evolutionary Biology; Entomology; Genetics, Developmental Biology, and Reproductive Biology; Nutrition; Pathology and Pathobiology; Pharmacology and Toxicology; Physiology; and Zoology; in Book 5, see Agricultural Engineering; Civil and Environmental Engineering; Geological, Mineral/Mining, and Petroleum Engineering; Management of Engineering and Technology; and Ocean Engineering; and in Book 6, see Veterinary Medicine and Sciences.

CONTENTS

Program Directories

Announcements

In-Depth Descriptions

See also:

Fish, Game, and Wildlife Management

Arkansas Tech University, Graduate Studies, School of Physical and Life Sciences, Department of Fisheries and Wildlife Biology, Russellville, AR 72801. Offers MS. *Faculty:* 5 full-time (0 women). *Students:* 10 (4 women); includes 1 minority (Hispanic American) Average age 30. 6 applicants, 50% accepted, 3 enrolled. In 2003, 4 degrees awarded. *Degree requirements:* For master's, thesis. *Entrance requirements:* For master's, GRE General Test. Additional exam requirements/recommendations for international students: Required—TOEFL (minimum score 500 paper-based; 173 computer-based). *Application deadline:* For fall admission, 3/1 priority date for domestic students, 5/1 priority date for international students; for spring admission, 10/1 priority date for domestic students, 10/1 priority date for international students. Applications are processed on a rolling basis. Application fee: $0 ($30 for international students). Electronic applications accepted. *Expenses:* Tuition, state resident: full-time $2,628; part-time $146 per credit hour. Tuition, nonresident: full-time $5,256; part-time $242 per credit hour. International tuition: $9,936 full-time. Required fees: $3 per hour. $95 per term. *Financial support:* Research assistantships with full tuition reimbursements, Federal Work-Study and health care benefits available. Support available to part-time students. Financial award application deadline: 4/15; financial award applicants required to submit FAFSA. *Unit head:* Dr. Joseph N. Stoeckel, Director, 479-964-0852, Fax: 479-964-0837, E-mail: joe.stoeckel@mail.atu.edu. *Application contact:* Dr. Eldon G. Clary, Dean, 479-968-0398, Fax: 479-964-0542, E-mail: graduate.school@mail.atu.edu.

Auburn University, Graduate School, College of Agriculture, Department of Fisheries and Allied Aquacultures, Auburn University, AL 36849. Offers M Aq, MS, PhD. Part-time programs available. *Faculty:* 18 full-time (3 women). *Students:* 33 full-time (9 women), 37 part-time (11 women); includes 5 minority (1 African American, 1 American Indian/Alaska Native, 1 Asian American or Pacific Islander, 2 Hispanic Americans), 20 international. 33 applicants, 52% accepted. In 2003, 21 master's, 6 doctorates awarded. *Degree requirements:* For master's, thesis (for some programs); for doctorate, 2 foreign languages, thesis/dissertation. *Entrance requirements:* For master's and doctorate, GRE General Test. *Application deadline:* For fall admission, 7/7 for domestic students; for spring admission, 11/24 for domestic students. Applications are processed on a rolling basis. Application fee: $25 ($50 for international students). Electronic applications accepted. *Expenses:* Tuition, state resident: part-time $175 per credit hour. Tuition, nonresident: part-time $525 per credit hour. *Financial support:* Fellowships, research assistantships, teaching assistantships, Federal Work-Study available. Support available to part-time students. Financial award application deadline: 3/15. *Faculty research:* Channel catfish production; aquatic animal health; community and population ecology; pond management; production hatching, breeding and genetics. Total annual research expenditures: $8 million. *Unit head:* Dr. David B. Rouse, Interim Head, 334-844-4786. *Application contact:* Dr. John F. Pritchett, Dean of the Graduate School, 334-844-4700, E-mail: hatchlb@mail.auburn.edu.

Auburn University, Graduate School, School of Forestry and Wildlife Sciences, Auburn University, AL 36849. Offers MF, MS, PhD. Part-time programs available. *Faculty:* 29 full-time (3 women). *Students:* 25 full-time (5 women), 21 part-time (9 women), 10 international. 29 applicants, 69% accepted. In 2003, 12 master's, 3 doctorates awarded. *Degree requirements:* For master's, oral exam (MF), thesis (MS); for doctorate, thesis/dissertation. *Entrance requirements:* For master's and doctorate, GRE General Test. *Application deadline:* For fall admission, 7/7 for domestic students; for spring admission, 11/24 for domestic students. Applications are processed on a rolling basis. Application fee: $25 ($50 for international students). Electronic applications accepted. *Expenses:* Tuition, state resident: part-time $175 per credit hour. Tuition, nonresident: part-time $525 per credit hour. *Financial support:* Fellowships, research assistantships, teaching assistantships, Federal Work-Study available. Support available to part-time students. Financial award application deadline: 3/15. *Faculty research:* Forest nursery management, silviculture and vegetation management, biological processes and ecological relationships, growth and yield of plantations and natural stands, urban forestry, forest taxation, law and policy. *Unit head:* Richard W. Brinker, Dean, 334-844-1007, Fax: 334-844-1084, E-mail: brinker@forestry.auburn.edu. *Application contact:* Dr. John F. Pritchett, Dean of the Graduate School, 334-844-4700, E-mail: hatchlb@mail.auburn.edu.

Brigham Young University, Graduate Studies, College of Biological and Agricultural Sciences, Department of Integrative Biology, Provo, UT 84602-1001. Offers biological science education (MS); integrative biology (MS, PhD); wildlife and wildland conservation (MS, PhD). *Faculty:* 33 full-time (2 women). *Students:* 50 full-time (21 women), 6 part-time; includes 2 minority (both Hispanic Americans), 4 international. Average age 31. 32 applicants, 59% accepted, 15 enrolled. In 2003, 11 master's, 1 doctorate awarded. *Median time to degree:* Of those who began their doctoral program in fall 1995, 100% received their degree in 8 years or less. *Degree requirements:* For master's and doctorate, thesis/dissertation, comprehensive exam, registration. *Entrance requirements:* For master's, GRE General Test, minimum GPA of 3.2 during previous 2 years, minimum GPA of 3.0 for last 60 credit hours; for doctorate, GRE General Test, minimum GPA of 3.0 for last 60 credit hours. Additional exam requirements/recommendations for international students: Required—TOEFL (minimum score 550 paper-based; 213 computer-based), GRE. *Application deadline:* For fall admission, 1/31 for domestic students, 1/31 for international students. Application fee: $50. Electronic applications accepted. *Expenses:* Tuition: Part-time $221 per hour. *Financial support:* In 2003–04, 53 students received support, including 3 fellowships with full and partial tuition reimbursements available (averaging $5,500 per year), 14 research assistantships with full and partial tuition reimbursements available (averaging $12,000 per year), 39 teaching assistantships with full and partial tuition reimbursements available (averaging $12,000 per year); career-related internships or fieldwork, institutionally sponsored loans, scholarships/grants, tuition waivers (full and partial), and unspecified assistantships also available. Financial award application deadline: 3/1. *Faculty research:* Systemaitcs, biofermatics, conservation. Total annual research expenditures:$375,944. *Unit head:* Dr. Larry L. St. Clair, Chair, 801-422-2582, Fax: 801-422-0090, E-mail: larry_stclair@byu.edu. *Application contact:* Dr. Keith A. Crandall, Graduate Coordinator, 801-422-3495, Fax: 801-422-0090, E-mail: keith_crandall@byu.edu.

Clemson University, Graduate School, College of Agriculture, Forestry and Life Sciences, Department of Forestry and Natural Resources, Program in Aquaculture, Fisheries, and Wildlife, Clemson, SC 29634. Offers MS, PhD. *Students:* 11 full-time (2 women), 7 part-time (4 women); includes 3 minority (1 African American, 1 American Indian/Alaska Native, 1 Hispanic American), 2 international. Average age 25. 17 applicants, 6% accepted, 1 enrolled. In 2003, 7 master's, 2 doctorates awarded. *Degree requirements:* For master's and doctorate, thesis/dissertation. *Entrance requirements:* For master's, GRE General Test, minimum undergraduate GPA of 3.0. Additional exam requirements/recommendations for international students: Required—TOEFL. *Application deadline:* For fall admission, 6/1 for domestic students. Application fee: $40. *Expenses:* Tuition, state resident: full-time $7,432. Tuition, nonresident: full-time $14,732. *Financial support:* Fellowships, research assistantships, teaching assistantships, career-related internships or fieldwork available. Financial award applicants required to submit FAFSA. *Faculty research:* Intensive freshwater culture systems, conservation biology, stream management, applied wildlife management. Total annual research expenditures: $1 million. *Unit head:* Dr. Dave Guynn, Coordinator, 864-656-4803, Fax: 864-656-3304, E-mail: dguynn@clemson.edu.

Colorado State University, Graduate School, College of Natural Resources, Department of Fishery and Wildlife Biology, Fort Collins, CO 80523-0015. Offers MS, PhD. Part-time programs available. *Faculty:* 15 full-time (2 women). *Students:* 15 full-time (5 women), 22 part-time (7 women); includes 1 minority (Asian American or Pacific Islander) Average age 29. 54 applicants, 17% accepted, 9 enrolled. In 2003, 5 master's, 2 doctorates awarded. *Degree requirements:* For master's, thesis or alternative; for doctorate, one foreign language, thesis/dissertation. *Entrance requirements:* For master's, GRE General Test, minimum GPA of 3.0, BA or BS in related field; for doctorate, GRE General Test, minimum GPA of 3.0, MS in related field. Additional exam requirements/recommendations for international students: Required—TOEFL. *Application deadline:* For fall admission, 2/15 priority date for domestic students, 2/15 priority date for international students. Application fee: $50. Electronic applications accepted. *Expenses:* Tuition, state resident: full-time $4,156. Tuition, nonresident: full-time $14,762. Required fees: $205. Tuition and fees vary according to course load, campus/location, program and reciprocity agreements. *Financial support:* In 2003–04, research assistantships with full and partial tuition reimbursements (averaging $17,628 per year), teaching assistantships with full and partial tuition reimbursements (averaging $11,340 per year) were awarded. Fellowships, career-related internships or fieldwork, Federal Work-Study, institutionally sponsored loans, scholarships/grants, and traineeships also available. Financial award application deadline: 2/15. *Faculty research:* Conservation biology, aquatic ecology, animal behavior, population modeling, habitat evaluation and management. Total annual research expenditures: $5.2 million. *Unit head:* Randall Robinette, Head, 970-491-1410, Fax: 970-491-5091, E-mail: fwb@cnr.colostate.edu. *Application contact:* Graduate Affairs Coordinator, 970-491-5020, Fax: 970-491-5091, E-mail: fwb@cnr.colostate.edu.

Cornell University, Graduate School, Graduate Fields of Agriculture and Life Sciences, Field of Natural Resources, Ithaca, NY 14853-0001. Offers aquatic science (MPS, MS, PhD); environmental management (MPS); fishery science (MPS, MS, PhD); forest science (MPS, MS, PhD); resource policy and management (MPS, MS, PhD); wildlife science (MPS, MS, PhD). *Faculty:* 43 full-time. *Students:* 73 full-time (31 women); includes 10 minority (1 African American, 2 American Indian/Alaska Native, 5 Asian Americans or Pacific Islanders, 2 Hispanic Americans), 14 international. 107 applicants, 22% accepted, 18 enrolled. In 2003, 16 master's, 6 doctorates awarded. *Degree requirements:* For master's, thesis (MS), project paper (MPS); for doctorate, thesis/dissertation, comprehensive exam. *Entrance requirements:* For master's and doctorate, GRE General Test, 2 letters of recommendation. Additional exam requirements/recommendations for international students: Required—TOEFL (minimum score 550 paper-based; 213 computer-based). *Application deadline:* ; for spring admission, 10/30 for domestic students. Applications are processed on a rolling basis. Application fee: $60. Electronic applications accepted. *Expenses:* Tuition: Full-time $28,630. One-time fee: $50 full-time. *Financial support:* In 2003–04, 63 students received support, including 11 fellowships with full tuition reimbursements available, 27 research assistantships with full tuition reimbursements available, 25 teaching assistantships with full tuition reimbursements available; institutionally sponsored loans, scholarships/grants, health care benefits, tuition waivers (full and partial), and unspecified assistantships also available. Financial award applicants required to submit FAFSA. *Faculty research:* Ecosystem-level dynamics, systems modeling, conservation biology/management, resource management's human dimensions, biogeochemistry. *Unit head:* Director of Graduate Studies, 607-255-2807, Fax: 607-255-0349. *Application contact:* Graduate Field Assistant, 607-255-2807, Fax: 607-255-0349, E-mail: nrgrad@cornell.edu.

Frostburg State University, Graduate School, College of Liberal Arts and Sciences, Department of Biology, Program in Fisheries and Wildlife Management, Frostburg, MD 21532-1099. Offers MS. Part-time and evening/weekend programs available. *Faculty:* 11. *Students:* 6 full-time (3 women), 7 part-time (5 women). Average age 27. 15 applicants, 20% accepted, 3 enrolled. In 2003, 3 degrees awarded. *Degree requirements:* For master's, thesis. *Entrance requirements:* For master's, GRE General Test, resumé. *Application deadline:* For fall admission, 7/15 for domestic students. Applications are processed on a rolling basis. Application fee: $30. Electronic applications accepted. *Expenses:* Tuition, state resident: full-time $4,212; part-time $234 per credit hour. Tuition, nonresident: full-time $4,878; part-time $271 per credit hour. *Financial support:* In 2003–04, 6 research assistantships with full tuition reimbursements (averaging $5,000 per year) were awarded; Federal Work-Study also available. Financial award application deadline: 4/1; financial award applicants required to submit FAFSA. *Faculty research:* Evolution and systematics of freshwater fishes, biochemical mechanisms of temperature adaptation in freshwater fishes, wildlife and fish parasitology, biology of freshwater invertebrates, remote sensing. *Unit head:* Dr. R. Scott Fritz, Coordinator, 301-687-4166. *Application contact:* Patricia C. Spiker, Director, Graduate Services, 301-687-7053, Fax: 301-687-4597, E-mail: pspiker@frostburg.edu.

Iowa State University of Science and Technology, Graduate College, College of Agriculture, Department of Natural Resource Ecology and Management, Ames, IA 50011. Offers animal ecology (MS, PhD), including animal ecology, fisheries biology, wildlife biology; forestry (MS, PhD). *Faculty:* 23 full-time, 7 part-time/adjunct. *Students:* 36 full-time (13 women), 7 part-time (2 women), 8 international. 44 applicants, 36% accepted, 12 enrolled. In 2003, 6 master's, 4 doctorates awarded. *Median time to degree:* Master's–2.7 years full-time; doctorate–4.5 years full-time. *Degree requirements:* For master's, thesis (for some programs); for doctorate, thesis/dissertation. *Entrance requirements:* For master's and doctorate, GRE General Test. Additional exam requirements/recommendations for international students: Required—TOEFL (paper score 547; computer score 210) or IELTS (score 6). *Application deadline:* For fall admission, 1/1 priority date for domestic students, 1/1 priority date for international students; for spring admission, 9/1 priority date for domestic students, 9/1 priority date for international students. Application fee: $30 ($70 for international students). Electronic applications accepted. Tuition, nonresident: part-time $560 per credit. Required fees: $38 per unit. *Financial support:* In 2003–04, 35 research assistantships with full and partial tuition reimbursements (averaging $17,496 per year), 4 teaching assistantships with full and partial tuition reimbursements (averaging $17,496 per year) were awarded. *Unit head:* Dr. J. Michael Kelly, Chair, 515-294-1166. *Application contact:* Lyn Van De Pol, Information Contact, 515-294-6148, E-mail: lvdp@iastate.edu.

Louisiana State University and Agricultural and Mechanical College, Graduate School, College of Agriculture, School of Renewable Natural Resources, Baton Rouge, LA 70803. Offers fisheries (MS); forestry (MS, PhD); wildlife (MS); wildlife and fisheries science (PhD). *Faculty:* 30 full-time (0 women). *Students:* 56 full-time (12 women), 16 part-time (7 women); includes 42 minority (1 American Indian/Alaska Native, 41 Hispanic Americans), 27 international. Average age 30. 34 applicants, 50% accepted, 11 enrolled. In 2003, 20 master's, 9 doctorates awarded. *Degree requirements:* For master's and doctorate, thesis/dissertation. *Entrance requirements:* For master's, GRE General Test, minimum GPA of 3.0; for doctorate, GRE General Test, MS, minimum GPA of 3.0. Additional exam requirements/recommendations for international students: Required—TOEFL (minimum score 550 paper-based; 213 computer-based). *Application deadline:* For fall admission, 1/25 priority date for domestic students, 5/15 priority date for international students. Applications are processed on a rolling basis. Application fee: $25. Electronic applications accepted. *Expenses:* Tuition, state resident: part-time $337 per hour. Tuition, nonresident: part-time $577 per hour. *Financial support:* In 2003–04, 2 fellowships (averaging $18,750 per year), 50 research assistantships with partial tuition reimbursements (averaging $15,766 per year), 2 teaching assistantships with partial tuition reimbursements (averaging $16,375 per year) were awarded. Federal Work-Study also available. Financial award application deadline: 4/15; financial award applicants required to submit FAFSA. *Faculty research:* Forest biology and management, aquaculture, fisheries biology and ecology, upland and wetlands wildlife. Total annual research expenditures: $7,325. *Unit head:* Dr. Bob G. Blackmon, Director, 225-578-4131, Fax: 225-578-4227, E-mail: bblackmon@agctr.lsu.edu. *Application contact:* Dr. Allen Rutherford, Coordinator of Graduate Studies, 225-578-4187, Fax: 225-578-4227, E-mail: druther@lsu.edu.

See in-depth description on page 789.

McGill University, Faculty of Graduate and Postdoctoral Studies, Faculty of Agricultural and Environmental Sciences, Department of Natural Resource Sciences, Montréal, QC H3A 2T5, Canada. Offers agrometeorology (M Sc, PhD); entomology (M Sc, PhD); forest science (M Sc, PhD); microbiology (M Sc, PhD); neotropical environment (M Sc, PhD); soil science (M Sc, PhD); wildlife biology (M Sc, PhD). *Faculty:* 18 full-time (1 woman). *Students:* 69 full-time, 2 part-time. 51 applicants, 37% accepted, 15 enrolled. In 2003, 12 master's, 4 doctorates awarded. *Degree requirements:* For master's and doctorate, thesis/dissertation.

Entrance requirements: For master's, minimum GPA of 3.0; for doctorate, M Sc, minimum GPA of 3.0. Additional exam requirements/recommendations for international students: Required—TOEFL (paper score 550; computer score 213) or IELTS (paper score 6). *Application deadline:* For fall admission, 6/1 for domestic students, 3/1 for international students; for winter admission, 10/15 for domestic students; for spring admission, 2/15 for domestic students. Applications are processed on a rolling basis. Application fee: $60 Canadian dollars. Electronic applications accepted. Tuition, area resident: Full-time $1,668. *Expenses:* Tuition, state resident: full-time $4,173. Tuition, nonresident: full-time $9,468. Required fees: $1,081. *Financial support:* In 2003–04, 2 fellowships with partial tuition reimbursements (averaging $8,000 per year), 34 teaching assistantships were awarded. Institutionally sponsored loans also available. *Faculty research:* Toxicology, reproductive physiology, parasites, wildlife management, genetics. *Unit head:* Dr. Benoit Côté, Chair, 514-398-7952, Fax: 514-398-7990, E-mail: coteb@nrs.mcgill.ca. *Application contact:* Marie Kubecki, Graduate Student Coordinator, 514-398-7991, Fax: 514-398-7990, E-mail: kubecki@nrs.mcgill.ca.

Memorial University of Newfoundland, School of Graduate Studies, Interdisciplinary Program in Marine Studies, St. John's, NL A1C 5S7, Canada. Offers fisheries resource management (MMS). Part-time programs available. *Students:* 9 full-time, 12 part-time. 9 applicants, 44% accepted, 4 enrolled. In 2003, 2 degrees awarded. *Degree requirements:* For master's, report. Application fee: $40 Canadian dollars. Tuition and fees charges are reported in Canadian dollars. *Expenses:* Tuition, state resident: part-time $733 Canadian dollars per semester. Tuition, nonresident: part-time $953 Canadian dollars per semester. Required fees: $194 Canadian dollars per year. Tuition and fees vary according to degree level and program. *Financial support:* Fellowships, research assistantships, teaching assistantships available. *Faculty research:* Biological, ecological and oceanographic aspects of world fisheries; economics; political science; sociology. *Unit head:* Dr. Peter Fisher, Chair, 709-778-0356, Fax: 709-778-0346, E-mail: pfisher@gill.ifmt.nf.ca.

Michigan State University, Graduate School, College of Agriculture and Natural Resources, Department of Fisheries and Wildlife, East Lansing, MI 48824. Offers fisheries and wildlife (MS, PhD), including environmental toxicology (PhD). *Faculty:* 26 full-time (6 women). *Students:* 72 full-time (41 women), 8 part-time (4 women); includes 6 minority (1 African American, 2 American Indian/Alaska Native, 2 Asian Americans or Pacific Islanders, 1 Hispanic American), 10 international. Average age 30. 62 applicants, 29% accepted. In 2003, 14 master's, 9 doctorates awarded. *Degree requirements:* For master's, thesis or alternative; for doctorate, thesis/dissertation. *Entrance requirements:* For master's, GRE General Test, minimum GPA of 3.0 in last 2 undergraduate years; for doctorate, GRE General Test. Additional exam requirements/recommendations for international students: Required—TOEFL (minimum score 550 paper-based; 213 computer-based), Michigan State University ELT (85), Michigan ELAB (83). *Application deadline:* For fall admission, 12/23 for domestic students. Applications are processed on a rolling basis. Application fee: $50. Electronic applications accepted. *Expenses:* Tuition, state resident: part-time $291 per hour. Tuition, nonresident: part-time $589 per hour. *Financial support:* In 2003–04, 39 fellowships with tuition reimbursements (averaging $5,150 per year), 67 research assistantships with tuition reimbursements (averaging $12,100 per year), 1 teaching assistantship with tuition reimbursement (averaging $11,475 per year) were awarded. Financial award applicants required to submit FAFSA. *Faculty research:* Environmental toxicology, biometry and ecological modeling, conservation biology and restoration ecology, fisheries/wildlife ecology and management, human dimensions and environmental management. Total annual research expenditures: $5.8 million. *Unit head:* Dr. William W. Taylor, Chairperson, 517-353-3048, Fax: 517-432-1699, E-mail: taylor2@msu.edu. *Application contact:* Mary Witchell, Graduate Records Secretary, 517-353-9091, Fax: 517-432-1699, E-mail: witchel1@msu.edu.

Mississippi State University, College of Forest Resources, Department of Wildlife and Fisheries, Mississippi State, MS 39762. Offers wildlife and fisheries science (MS). Part-time programs available. *Faculty:* 13 full-time (1 woman). *Students:* 27 full-time (7 women), 15 part-time (2 women); includes 4 minority (1 African American, 1 Asian American or Pacific Islander, 2 Hispanic Americans). Average age 27. 12 applicants, 42% accepted, 4 enrolled. In 2003, 12 degrees awarded. *Degree requirements:* For master's, thesis, comprehensive oral or written exam. *Entrance requirements:* For master's, GRE General Test, minimum GPA of 3.0 in last 60 undergraduate credits. Additional exam requirements/recommendations for international students: Required—TOEFL. *Application deadline:* For fall admission, 7/1 for domestic students; for spring admission, 11/1 for domestic students. Applications are processed on a rolling basis. Application fee: $0 ($25 for international students). *Expenses:* Tuition, state resident: full-time $3,874; part-time $215 per hour. Tuition, nonresident: full-time $8,780; part-time $488 per hour. International tuition: $9,105 full-time. Tuition and fees vary according to course load. *Financial support:* In 2003–04, 5 research assistantships with partial tuition reimbursements (averaging $11,128 per year), 6 teaching assistantships with partial tuition reimbursements (averaging $9,750 per year) were awarded. Fellowships, Federal Work-Study, institutionally sponsored loans, and unspecified assistantships also available. Financial award applicants required to submit FAFSA. *Faculty research:* Spatial technology, habitat restoration, aquaculture, fisheries, wildlife management. Total annual research expenditures: $756,308. *Unit head:* Dr. Bruce D. Leopold, Head, 662-325-2619, Fax: 662-325-8726, E-mail: bleopold@cfr.msstate.edu. *Application contact:* Diane D. Wolfe, Director of Admissions, 662-325-2224, Fax: 662-325-7360, E-mail: admit@admissions.msstate.edu.

Montana State University–Bozeman, College of Graduate Studies, College of Letters and Science, Department of Ecology, Bozeman, MT 59717. Offers biological sciences (MS, PhD); fish and wildlife biology (PhD); fish and wildlife management (MS); land rehabilitation (interdisciplinary) (MS). Part-time programs available. *Faculty:* 15 full-time (4 women), 2 part-time/adjunct (1 woman). *Students:* 9 full-time (2 women), 53 part-time (19 women), 1 international. Average age 30. 9 applicants, 100% accepted, 9 enrolled. In 2003, 7 master's, 5 doctorates awarded. *Degree requirements:* For master's, thesis (for some programs), comprehensive exam, registration; for doctorate, thesis/dissertation, comprehensive exam, registration. *Entrance requirements:* For master's and doctorate, GRE General Test. Additional exam requirements/recommendations for international students: Required—TOEFL (minimum score 550 paper-based; 213 computer-based). *Application deadline:* For fall admission, 7/15 priority date for domestic students, 5/15 priority date for international students; for spring admission, 12/1 priority date for domestic students, 10/1 priority date for international students. Applications are processed on a rolling basis. Application fee: $50. Electronic applications accepted. *Expenses:* Tuition, state resident: full-time $3,907; part-time $163 per credit. Tuition, nonresident: full-time $12,383; part-time $516 per credit. Required fees: $890; $445 per term. Tuition and fees vary according to course load and program. *Financial support:* Application deadline: 3/1; Total annual research expenditures: $2.5 million. *Unit head:* Dr. Scott Creel, Head, 406-994-7033, Fax: 406-994-3190, E-mail: screel@montana.edu.

New Mexico State University, Graduate School, College of Agriculture and Home Economics, Department of Fishery and Wildlife Sciences, Las Cruces, NM 88003-8001. Offers wildlife science (MS). Part-time programs available. *Faculty:* 7 full-time (1 woman), 7 part-time/adjunct (2 women). *Students:* 21 full-time (12 women), 5 part-time (1 woman); includes 6 minority (2 Asian Americans or Pacific Islanders, 4 Hispanic Americans), 2 international. Average age 28. 16 applicants, 44% accepted, 4 enrolled. In 2003, 5 degrees awarded. *Degree requirements:* For master's, thesis (for some programs). *Entrance requirements:* For master's, GRE General Test, minimum GPA of 3.0. Additional exam requirements/recommendations for international students: Required—TOEFL. *Application deadline:* For fall admission, 4/1 for domestic students; for spring admission, 11/1 priority date for domestic students. Applications are processed on a rolling basis. Application fee: $30 ($50 for international students). Electronic applications accepted. *Expenses:* Tuition, state resident: full-time $2,670; part-time $151 per credit. Tuition, nonresident: full-time $10,596; part-time $481 per credit. Required fees: $954. *Financial support:* In 2003–04, 16 research assistantships with partial tuition reimbursements, 6 teaching assistantships with partial tuition reimbursements were awarded. Career-related internships or fieldwork, Federal Work-Study, and scholarships/grants also available. Support available to part-time students. Financial award application deadline: 4/1. *Faculty research:* Ecosystems analyses, landscape and wildlife ecology, wildlife and fish population dynamics, management models, wildlife and fish habitat relationships. *Unit head:* Dr. Donald F. Caccamise, Head, 505-646-1544, Fax: 505-646-1281, E-mail: natres@nmsu.edu.

North Carolina State University, Graduate School, College of Natural Resources and College of Agriculture and Life Sciences, Program in Fisheries and Wildlife Sciences, Raleigh, NC 27695. Offers MFWS, MS. *Faculty:* 35 full-time (1 woman), 5 part-time/adjunct (0 women). *Students:* 12 full-time (8 women), 1 (woman) part-time, 1 international. Average age 28. 26 applicants, 35% accepted. In 2003, 7 degrees awarded. *Degree requirements:* For master's, thesis optional. *Entrance requirements:* For master's, GRE General Test. Additional exam requirements/recommendations for international students: Required—TOEFL. *Application deadline:* For fall admission, 6/25 for domestic students, 3/1 for international students; for spring admission, 11/25 for domestic students, 7/15 for international students. Application fee: $45. *Expenses:* Tuition, state resident: part-time $396 per hour. Tuition, nonresident: part-time $1,895 per hour. *Financial support:* In 2003–04, 1 fellowship with tuition reimbursement (averaging $4,915 per year), 8 research assistantships with tuition reimbursements (averaging $5,317 per year), 1 teaching assistantship with tuition reimbursement (averaging $5,545 per year) were awarded. *Faculty research:* Fisheries biology; ecology of marine, estuarine, and anadromous fishes; aquaculture pond water quality; larviculture of freshwater and marine finfish; predator/prey interactions. *Unit head:* Dr. James A. Rice, Director of Graduate Programs, 919-515-4542, Fax: 919-515-5327, E-mail: jim_rice@ncsu.edu. *Application contact:* Dr. Robert C. Abt, Director of Graduate Programs, 919-515-7563, Fax: 919-515-8149, E-mail: bob_abt@ncsu.edu.

Oregon State University, Graduate School, College of Agricultural Sciences, Department of Fisheries and Wildlife, Program in Fisheries Science, Corvallis, OR 97331. Offers M Agr, MAIS, MS, PhD. Part-time programs available. *Students:* 56 full-time (24 women), 6 part-time. Average age 30. In 2003, 9 master's, 7 doctorates awarded. *Degree requirements:* For master's, thesis (for some programs); for doctorate, thesis/dissertation. *Entrance requirements:* For master's and doctorate, GRE, minimum GPA of 3.0 in last 90 hours. Additional exam requirements/recommendations for international students: Required—TOEFL. *Application deadline:* For fall admission, 3/15 for domestic students; for spring admission, 12/15 for domestic students. Applications are processed on a rolling basis. Application fee: $50. *Expenses:* Tuition, state resident: full-time $8,139; part-time $301 per credit. Tuition, nonresident: full-time $14,376; part-time $532 per credit. Required fees: $1,227. *Financial support:* Fellowships, research assistantships, teaching assistantships, career-related internships or fieldwork, Federal Work-Study, and institutionally sponsored loans available. Support available to part-time students. Financial award application deadline: 2/1. *Faculty research:* Fisheries ecology, fish toxicology, stream ecology, quantitative analyses of marine and freshwater fish populations. *Application contact:* Charlotte Vickers, Advising Specialist, 541-737-1941, Fax: 541-737-3590, E-mail: charlotte.vickers@orst.edu.

Oregon State University, Graduate School, College of Agricultural Sciences, Department of Fisheries and Wildlife, Program in Wildlife Science, Corvallis, OR 97331. Offers MAIS, MS, PhD. *Students:* 35 full-time (19 women), 3 part-time (2 women); includes 4 minority (1 American Indian/Alaska Native, 2 Asian Americans or Pacific Islanders, 1 Hispanic American), 2 international. Average age 31. In 2003, 8 master's, 1 doctorate awarded. *Degree requirements:* For master's, thesis (for some programs); for doctorate, thesis/dissertation. *Entrance requirements:* For master's and doctorate, GRE, minimum GPA of 3.0 in last 90 hours. Additional exam requirements/recommendations for international students: Required—TOEFL. Application fee: $50. *Expenses:* Tuition, state resident: full-time $8,139; part-time $301 per credit. Tuition, nonresident: full-time $14,376; part-time $532 per credit. Required fees: $1,227. *Financial support:* Fellowships, research assistantships, teaching assistantships, career-related internships or fieldwork, Federal Work-Study, and institutionally sponsored loans available. Financial award application deadline: 2/1. *Application contact:* Charlotte Vickers, Advising Specialist, 541-737-1941, Fax: 541-737-3590, E-mail: charlotte.vickers@orst.edu.

The Pennsylvania State University University Park Campus, Graduate School, College of Agricultural Sciences, School of Forest Resources, Program in Wildlife and Fisheries Sciences, State College, University Park, PA 16802-1503. Offers M Agr, MFR, MS, PhD. *Students:* 17 full-time (5 women), 6 part-time (3 women); includes 1 minority (Hispanic American) *Entrance requirements:* For master's and doctorate, GRE General Test. Application fee: $45. *Expenses:* Tuition, state resident: full-time $10,010; part-time $417 per credit. Tuition, nonresident: full-time $19,830; part-time $826 per credit. Full-time tuition and fees vary according to course level, course load, campus/location and program. *Unit head:* Dr. Wayne L. Myers, Chair, 814-863-0002, Fax: 814-865-3725, E-mail: wlm@psu.edu. *Application contact:* Emily Hill, Staff Assistant, 814-863-7221, Fax: 814-865-3725, E-mail: evh2@psu.edu.

Purdue University, Graduate School, College of Agriculture, Department of Forestry and Natural Resources, West Lafayette, IN 47907. Offers aquaculture, fisheries, aquatic science (MSF); aquaculture, fisheries, aquatic sciences (MS, PhD); forest biology (MS, MSF, PhD); natural resources and environmental policy (MS, MSF); natural resources environmental policy (PhD); quantitative resource analysis (MS, MSF, PhD); wildlife science (MS, MSF, PhD); wood science and technology (MS, MSF, PhD). *Faculty:* 28 full-time (3 women), 3 part-time/adjunct (1 woman). *Students:* 67 full-time (28 women), 3 part-time (all women); includes 3 minority (1 African American, 2 Hispanic Americans), 24 international. Average age 30. 44 applicants, 23% accepted, 9 enrolled. In 2003, 7 master's, 6 doctorates awarded. *Degree requirements:* For master's and doctorate, thesis/dissertation. *Entrance requirements:* For master's and doctorate, GRE General Test, minimum B+ average in undergraduate course work. Additional exam requirements/recommendations for international students: Required—TOEFL. *Application deadline:* For fall admission, 1/5 for domestic students; for spring admission, 9/15 for domestic students. Applications are processed on a rolling basis. Application fee: $55. Electronic applications accepted. *Financial support:* In 2003–04, 10 research assistantships (averaging $15,259 per year) were awarded; fellowships, teaching assistantships, career-related internships or fieldwork and scholarships/grants also available. Support available to part-time students. Financial award application deadline: 1/5; financial award applicants required to submit FAFSA. *Faculty research:* Wildlife management, forest management, forest ecology, forest soils, limnology. Total annual research expenditures: $200,000. *Unit head:* Dr. Robert K. Swihart, Interim Head, 765-494-3590, Fax: 765-494-9461, E-mail: rswihart@purdue.edu. *Application contact:* Kelly Garrett, Graduate Secretary, 765-494-3572, Fax: 765-494-9461, E-mail: kgarrett@purdue.edu.

See in-depth description on page 795.

South Dakota State University, Graduate School, College of Agriculture and Biological Sciences, Department of Wildlife and Fisheries Sciences, Brookings, SD 57007. Offers biological sciences (PhD); wildlife and fisheries sciences (MS). *Degree requirements:* For master's, thesis, oral exam; for doctorate, thesis/dissertation, preliminary oral and written exams. *Entrance requirements:* For master's, GRE. Additional exam requirements/recommendations for international students: Required—TOEFL. *Faculty research:* Agriculture interactions, wetland conservation, biostress.

State University of New York College of Environmental Science and Forestry, Faculty of Environmental and Forest Biology, Syracuse, NY 13210-2779. Offers chemical ecology (MPS, MS, PhD); conservation biology (MPS, MS, PhD); ecology (MPS, MS, PhD); entomology (MPS, MS, PhD); environmental interpretation (MPS, MS, PhD); environmental physiology (MPS, MS, PhD); fish and wildlife biology (MPS, MS, PhD); forest pathology and mycology (MPS, MS, PhD); plant science and biotechnology (MPS, MS, PhD). *Faculty:* 32 full-time (3 women), 1 (woman) part-time/adjunct. *Students:* 93 full-time (53 women), 53 part-time (23 women); includes 4 minority (1 Asian American or Pacific Islander, 3 Hispanic Americans), 16 international. Average age 30. 100 applicants, 52% accepted, 25 enrolled. In 2003, 28 master's, 7 doctorates awarded. *Degree requirements:* For master's, thesis (for some programs), registration; for doctorate, thesis/dissertation, comprehensive exam, registration. *Entrance requirements:*

Fish, Game, and Wildlife Management

State University of New York College of Environmental Science and Forestry (continued)
For master's and doctorate, GRE General Test, GRE Subject Test, minimum GPA of 3.0. Additional exam requirements/recommendations for international students: Required—TOEFL (minimum score 550 paper-based; 213 computer-based). *Application deadline:* For fall admission, 2/1 priority date for domestic students, 2/1 priority date for international students; for spring admission, 11/1 priority date for domestic students, 11/1 priority date for international students. Applications are processed on a rolling basis. Application fee: $50. Tuition, area resident: Part-time $288 per credit hour. Tuition, nonresident: part-time $438 per credit hour. Required fees: $300; $5 per credit hour. $18 per semester. One-time fee: $25 full-time. *Financial support:* In 2003–04, 86 students received support, including 17 fellowships with full and partial tuition reimbursements available (averaging $9,446 per year), 41 research assistantships with full and partial tuition reimbursements available (averaging $11,000 per year), 34 teaching assistantships with full and partial tuition reimbursements available (averaging $9,446 per year); Federal Work-Study, institutionally sponsored loans, scholarships/grants, health care benefits, and unspecified assistantships also available. *Faculty research:* Ecology, fish and wildlife biology and management, plant science, entomology. Total annual research expenditures: $2.6 million. *Unit head:* Dr. Neil H. Ringler, Chair, 315-470-6770, Fax: 315-470-6934, E-mail: neilringler@esf.edu. *Application contact:* Dr. Dudley J. Raynal, Dean, Instruction and Graduate Studies, 315-470-6599, Fax: 315-470-6978, E-mail: esfgrad@esf.edu.

Sul Ross State University, Division of Agricultural and Natural Resource Science, Program in Range and Wildlife Management, Alpine, TX 79832. Offers M Ag, MS. Part-time programs available. *Degree requirements:* For master's, thesis (for some programs). *Entrance requirements:* For master's, GRE General Test, minimum undergraduate GPA of 2.5 in last 60 hours.

Tennessee Technological University, Graduate School, College of Arts and Sciences, Department of Biology, Cookeville, TN 38505. Offers environmental biology (MS); fish, game, and wildlife management (MS). Part-time programs available. *Faculty:* 22 full-time (2 women). *Students:* 22 full-time (7 women), 8 part-time (3 women); includes 1 minority (Asian American or Pacific Islander) Average age 25. 13 applicants, 62% accepted, 6 enrolled. In 2003, 5 degrees awarded. *Degree requirements:* For master's, thesis. *Entrance requirements:* For master's, GRE General Test. Additional exam requirements/recommendations for international students: Required—TOEFL. *Application deadline:* For fall admission, 3/1 for domestic students; for spring admission, 8/1 for domestic students. Application fee: $25 ($30 for international students). *Expenses:* Tuition, state resident: full-time $7,410; part-time $263 per semester hour. Tuition, nonresident: full-time $19,134; part-time $607 per semester hour. *Financial support:* In 2003–04, 17 research assistantships (averaging $9,000 per year), 8 teaching assistantships (averaging $7,500 per year) were awarded. Financial award application deadline: 4/1. *Faculty research:* Aquatics, environmental studies. *Unit head:* Dr. Daniel Combs, Interim Chairperson, 931-372-3134, Fax: 931-372-6257, E-mail: dcombs@tntech.edu. *Application contact:* Dr. Francis O. Otuonye, Associate Vice President for Research and Graduate Studies, 931-372-3233, Fax: 931-372-3497, E-mail: fotuonye@tntech.edu.

Texas A&M University, College of Agriculture and Life Sciences, Department of Wildlife and Fisheries Sciences, College Station, TX 77843. Offers M Agr, MS, PhD. Part-time programs available. Postbaccalaureate distance learning degree programs offered (no on-campus study). *Faculty:* 19 full-time (2 women), 1 part-time/adjunct (0 women). *Students:* 113 full-time (53 women), 60 part-time (24 women); includes 19 minority (1 American Indian/Alaska Native, 2 Asian Americans or Pacific Islanders, 16 Hispanic Americans), 23 international. Average age 26. 102 applicants, 57% accepted. In 2003, 28 master's, 12 doctorates awarded. Terminal master's awarded for partial completion of doctoral program. *Median time to degree:* Master's–3.15 years full-time, 5 years part-time; doctorate–5.2 years full-time, 9.8 years part-time. Of those who began their doctoral program in fall 1995, 43% received their degree in 8 years or less. *Degree requirements:* For master's and doctorate, thesis/dissertation, final oral defense. *Entrance requirements:* For master's and doctorate, GRE General Test, minimum GPA of 3.0. Additional exam requirements/recommendations for international students: Required—TOEFL (minimum score 550 paper-based; 213 computer-based). *Application deadline:* Applications are processed on a rolling basis. Application fee: $50 ($75 for international students). Electronic applications accepted. *Expenses:* Tuition, state resident: full-time $3,420. Tuition, nonresident: full-time $9,084. Required fees: $1,861. *Financial support:* In 2003–04, 86 students received support, including 14 fellowships with partial tuition reimbursements available (averaging $22,000 per year), 42 research assistantships (averaging $14,400 per year), 30 teaching assistantships (averaging $14,400 per year); career-related internships or fieldwork, institutionally sponsored loans, and scholarships/grants also available. Financial award application deadline: 3/1; financial award applicants required to submit FAFSA. *Faculty research:* Wildlife ecology and management, fisheries ecology and management, aquaculture, biological inventories and museum collections, biosystematics and genome analysis. *Unit head:* Dr. Robert D. Brown, Professor and Head, 979-845-5777, Fax: 979-845-3786, E-mail: r-brown@tamu.edu. *Application contact:* Janice Crenshaw, Senior Academic Advisor I, 979-845-5777, Fax: 979-845-3786, E-mail: j-crenshaw@tamu.edu.

Texas A&M University–Kingsville, College of Graduate Studies, College of Agriculture and Home Economics, Program in Range and Wildlife Management, Kingsville, TX 78363. Offers MS. *Degree requirements:* For master's, thesis or alternative, comprehensive exam. *Entrance requirements:* For master's, GRE General Test, minimum GPA of 3.0. Additional exam requirements/recommendations for international students: Required—TOEFL.

Texas A&M University–Kingsville, College of Graduate Studies, College of Agriculture and Home Economics, Program in Wildlife Science, Kingsville, TX 78363. Offers PhD. *Degree requirements:* For doctorate, one foreign language, thesis/dissertation, comprehensive exam. *Entrance requirements:* For doctorate, GRE General Test, minimum GPA of 3.5.

Texas State University-San Marcos, Graduate School, College of Science, Department of Biology, Program in Wildlife Ecology, San Marcos, TX 78666. Offers MS. *Students:* 17 full-time (11 women), 12 part-time (6 women); includes 1 minority (Hispanic American) Average age 28. 16 applicants, 88% accepted, 12 enrolled. In 2003, 6 degrees awarded. *Entrance requirements:* For master's, GRE General Test, minimum GPA of 2.75 in last 60 hours of undergraduate work. *Application deadline:* For fall admission, 6/15 for domestic students; for spring admission, 10/15 priority date for domestic students. Applications are processed on a rolling basis. Application fee: $40 ($90 for international students). *Expenses:* Tuition, state resident: full-time $2,484; part-time $138 per semester hour. Tuition, nonresident: full-time $6,732; part-time $374 per semester hour. Required fees: $948; $31 per semester hour. $195 per term. Tuition and fees vary according to course load. *Financial support:* In 2003–04, 20 students received support, including 2 research assistantships (averaging $12,190 per year), 11 teaching assistantships (averaging $8,950 per year) Financial award application deadline: 4/1. *Unit head:* Dr. John Baccus, Graduate Advisor, 512-245-2347, Fax: 512-245-8713, E-mail: jb02@txstate.edu.

Texas Tech University, Graduate School, College of Agricultural Sciences and Natural Resources, Department of Range, Wildlife, and Fisheries Management, Lubbock, TX 79409. Offers fisheries science (MS, PhD); range science (MS, PhD); wildlife science (MS, PhD). Part-time programs available. *Faculty:* 13 full-time (0 women). *Students:* 39 full-time (15 women), 10 part-time (4 women); includes 1 minority (Hispanic American), 11 international. Average age 30. 17 applicants, 47% accepted, 7 enrolled. In 2003, 14 master's, 2 doctorates awarded. *Degree requirements:* For master's and doctorate, thesis/dissertation. *Entrance requirements:* For master's and doctorate, GRE General Test. Additional exam requirements/recommendations for international students: Required—TOEFL (minimum score 550 paper-based; 213 computer-based). *Application deadline:* Applications are processed on a rolling basis. Application fee: $50 ($60 for international students). Electronic applications accepted. *Expenses:* Tuition, state resident: full-time $3,312. Tuition, nonresident: full-time $8,976. Required fees: $1,745. Tuition and fees vary according to program. *Financial support:* In 2003–04, 34 students received support, including 27 research assistantships with partial tuition reimbursements available (averaging $10,699 per year), 6 teaching assistantships with partial tuition reimbursements available (averaging $11,200 per year); Federal Work-Study and institutionally sponsored loans also available. Support available to part-time students. Financial award application deadline: 5/1; financial award applicants required to submit FAFSA. *Faculty research:* Use of fire on range lands, waterfowl, upland game birds and playa lakes in the southern Great Plains, reproductive physiology in fisheries, conservation biology. Total annual research expenditures: $1.2 million. *Unit head:* Dr. Ernest B. Fish, Chairman, 806-742-2841, Fax: 806-742-2280. *Application contact:* L. Jeannine Moerbe, Graduate Secretary, 806-742-2825, E-mail: jeannine.moerbe@ttu.edu.

Université du Québec à Rimouski, Graduate Programs, Program in Wildlife Resources Management, Rimouski, QC G5L 3A1, Canada. Offers M Sc, Diploma. *Entrance requirements:* For degree, appropriate bachelor's degree, proficiency in French.

University of Alaska Fairbanks, College of Science, Engineering and Mathematics, Department of Biology and Wildlife, Fairbanks, AK 99775-7520. Offers biological sciences (MS, PhD), including biology, botany, zoology; wildlife biology and management (MS, PhD). Part-time programs available. Terminal master's awarded for partial completion of doctoral program. *Degree requirements:* For master's, thesis, comprehensive exam; for doctorate, one foreign language, thesis/dissertation, comprehensive exam. *Entrance requirements:* For master's and doctorate, GRE General Test, GRE Subject Test. Additional exam requirements/recommendations for international students: Required—TOEFL. Electronic applications accepted. *Faculty research:* Plant-herbivore interactions, plant metabolic defenses, insect manufacture of glycerol, ice nucleators, structure and functions of arctic and subarctic freshwater ecosystems.

University of Alaska Fairbanks, School of Fisheries and Ocean Sciences, Department of Marine Sciences and Limnology, Fairbanks, AK 99775-7520. Offers marine biology (MS); oceanography (MS, PhD), including biological oceanography (PhD), chemical oceanography (PhD), fisheries (PhD), geological oceanography (PhD), physical oceanography (PhD). Part-time programs available. Terminal master's awarded for partial completion of doctoral program. *Degree requirements:* For master's and doctorate, thesis/dissertation, comprehensive exam, registration. *Entrance requirements:* For master's and doctorate, GRE General Test. Additional exam requirements/recommendations for international students: Required—TOEFL. Electronic applications accepted. *Faculty research:* Seafood science and nutrition, sustainable harvesting, chemical oceanography, marine biology, physical oceanography.

See in-depth description on page 289.

University of Alaska Fairbanks, School of Fisheries and Ocean Sciences, Program in Fisheries, Fairbanks, AK 99775-7520. Offers MS, PhD. Part-time programs available. Terminal master's awarded for partial completion of doctoral program. *Degree requirements:* For master's, thesis, comprehensive exam, registration; for doctorate, one foreign language, thesis/dissertation, comprehensive exam, registration. *Entrance requirements:* For master's and doctorate, GRE General Test. Additional exam requirements/recommendations for international students: Required—TOEFL. Electronic applications accepted. *Faculty research:* Marine stock reconstruction, oil spill research on marine life, Pacific salmon management, population dynamics of fish and major predators, ecology of marine fish.

See in-depth description on page 289.

The University of Arizona, Graduate College, College of Agriculture and Life Sciences, School of Natural Resources, Program in Wildlife, Fisheries Conservation, and Management, Tucson, AZ 85721. Offers MS, PhD. *Faculty:* 11 full-time (1 woman). *Students:* 31 full-time (17 women), 17 part-time (7 women); includes 3 minority (all Hispanic Americans) Average age 32. 33 applicants, 36% accepted, 11 enrolled. In 2003, 9 degrees awarded. *Degree requirements:* For master's, thesis/dissertation; for doctorate, thesis/dissertation, comprehensive exam. *Entrance requirements:* For master's and doctorate, GRE General Test, GRE Subject Test (biology), minimum GPA of 3.0, 3 letters of recommendation. Additional exam requirements/recommendations for international students: Required—TOEFL (minimum score 550 paper-based; 213 computer-based). *Application deadline:* For fall admission, 8/1 priority date for domestic students, 12/1 priority date for international students. Applications are processed on a rolling basis. Application fee: $50. *Expenses:* Tuition, state resident: part-time $196 per unit. Tuition, nonresident: part-time $326 per unit. *Financial support:* In 2003–04, 5 fellowships with tuition reimbursements (averaging $15,000 per year), 20 research assistantships with tuition reimbursements (averaging $15,000 per year), 2 teaching assistantships with tuition reimbursements (averaging $15,000 per year) were awarded. Career-related internships or fieldwork, scholarships/grants, health care benefits, tuition waivers (partial), and unspecified assistantships also available. *Faculty research:* Short-term effects of artificial oases on Arizona wildlife, elk response to cattle in northern Arizona, effect of reservoir operation on tailwaters, conservation of wildlife. *Unit head:* Dr. William W. Shaw, Chair, 520-621-7265, E-mail: wshaw@ag.arizona.edu. *Application contact:* Cheryl L. Craddock, Academic Coordinator, 520-621-7260, Fax: 520-621-8801, E-mail: ccraddoc@email.arizona.edu.

University of Florida, Graduate School, College of Agricultural and Life Sciences, Department of Wildlife Ecology and Conservation, Gainesville, FL 32611. Offers MS, PhD. *Faculty:* 39. *Students:* 44 full-time (23 women), 23 part-time (10 women); includes 7 minority (1 African American, 2 American Indian/Alaska Native, 4 Hispanic Americans), 12 international. 65 applicants, 29% accepted. In 2003, 13 master's, 5 doctorates awarded. *Degree requirements:* For master's, thesis optional; for doctorate, thesis/dissertation. *Entrance requirements:* For master's and doctorate, GRE General Test, minimum GPA of 3.3. *Application deadline:* For fall admission, 6/1 for domestic students; for spring admission, 12/1 for domestic students. Applications are processed on a rolling basis. Application fee: $20. Electronic applications accepted. *Expenses:* Tuition, state resident: part-time $205 per credit hour. Tuition, nonresident: part-time $775 per credit hour. *Financial support:* In 2003–04, 46 students received support, including 6 fellowships, 23 research assistantships, 17 teaching assistantships; institutionally sponsored loans also available. *Faculty research:* Wildlife biology and management, tropical ecology and conservation, conservation biology, landscape ecology and restoration, conservation education. *Unit head:* Dr. Nat Frazer, Chair, 352-846-0552, Fax: 352-392-6984, E-mail: frazern@wec.ufl.edu. *Application contact:* Dr. Wiley Kitchens, Coordinator, 352-896-0536, Fax: 352-846-0841, E-mail: kitchensw@wec.ufl.edu.

University of Idaho, College of Graduate Studies, College of Natural Resources, Department of Fish and Wildlife Resources, Moscow, ID 83844-2282. Offers fishery resources (MS, PhD); wildlife resources (MS, PhD). *Students:* 24 full-time (14 women), 26 part-time (11 women); includes 3 minority (all Hispanic Americans), 1 international. Average age 31. *Degree requirements:* For doctorate, thesis/dissertation. *Entrance requirements:* For master's, minimum GPA of 2.8; for doctorate, minimum undergraduate GPA of 2.8, 3.0 graduate. *Application deadline:* For fall admission, 8/1 for domestic students; for spring admission, 12/15 for domestic students. Application fee: $55 ($60 for international students). *Expenses:* Tuition, state resident: full-time $3,348. Tuition, nonresident: full-time $10,740. Required fees: $540. *Financial support:* Research assistantships, teaching assistantships available. Financial award application deadline: 2/15. *Unit head:* Dr. George W. LaBar, Head, 208-885-6434.

See in-depth description on page 797.

University of Idaho, College of Graduate Studies, College of Natural Resources, Program in Forestry, Wildlife, and Range Sciences, Moscow, ID 83844-2282. Offers PhD. *Degree requirements:* For doctorate, thesis/dissertation. *Entrance requirements:* For doctorate, minimum undergraduate GPA of 2.8, 3.0 graduate. *Application deadline:* For fall admission, 8/1 for domestic students; for spring admission, 12/15 for domestic students. Application fee: $55 ($60 for international students). *Expenses:* Tuition, state resident: full-time $3,348. Tuition, nonresident: full-time $10,740. Required fees: $540. *Financial support:* Fellowships, research assistantships, teaching assistantships available. Financial award application deadline: 2/15. *Application contact:* Dr. Ali Moslemi, Graduate Coordinator, 208-885-6126.

University of Maine, Graduate School, College of Natural Sciences, Forestry, and Agriculture, Department of Wildlife Ecology, Orono, ME 04469. Offers wildlife conservation (MWC); wildlife ecology (MS, PhD). Part-time programs available. *Faculty:* 6 full-time (0 women). *Students:* 17 full-time (10 women), 7 part-time (5 women), 4 international. Average age 30. 37 applicants, 22% accepted, 8 enrolled. In 2003, 2 master's, 1 doctorate awarded. *Degree requirements:* For master's, thesis (for some programs); for doctorate, one foreign language, thesis/dissertation. *Entrance requirements:* For master's and doctorate, GRE General Test. Additional exam requirements/recommendations for international students: Required—TOEFL. *Application deadline:* For fall admission, 2/1 for domestic students. Applications are processed on a rolling basis. Application fee: $50. Electronic applications accepted. *Expenses:* Tuition, state resident: part-time $235 per credit. Tuition, nonresident: part-time $670 per credit. Tuition and fees vary according to course load. *Financial support:* In 2003–04, 1 fellowship with tuition reimbursement (averaging $11,250 per year), 10 research assistantships with tuition reimbursements (averaging $15,000 per year), 3 teaching assistantships with tuition reimbursements (averaging $12,700 per year) were awarded. Career-related internships or fieldwork, Federal Work-Study, institutionally sponsored loans, and tuition waivers (full and partial) also available. Financial award application deadline: 3/1. *Faculty research:* Integration of wildlife and forest management; population dynamics; behavior, physiology and nutrition; wetland ecology and influence of environmental disturbances. *Unit head:* Dr. Frederick Servello, Chair, 207-581-2862, Fax: 207-581-2858. *Application contact:* Scott G. Delcourt, Associate Dean of the Graduate School, 207-581-3218, Fax: 207-581-3232, E-mail: graduate@maine.edu.

University of Massachusetts Amherst, Graduate School, College of Natural Resources and the Environment, Department of Natural Resources Conservation, Program in Wildlife and Fisheries Conservation, Amherst, MA 01003. Offers MS, PhD. Part-time programs available. *Faculty:* 30 full-time (4 women). *Students:* 22 full-time (10 women), 22 part-time (7 women); includes 2 minority (1 African American, 1 Asian American or Pacific Islander), 6 international. Average age 33. 55 applicants, 27% accepted, 10 enrolled. In 2003, 12 master's, 3 doctorates awarded. Terminal master's awarded for partial completion of doctoral program. *Degree requirements:* For master's, thesis optional; for doctorate, variable foreign language requirement, thesis/dissertation. *Entrance requirements:* For master's and doctorate, GRE General Test. Additional exam requirements/recommendations for international students: Required—TOEFL (minimum score 530 paper-based; 197 computer-based). *Application deadline:* For fall admission, 2/1 priority date for domestic students, 2/1 priority date for international students; for spring admission, 10/1 for domestic students, 10/1 for international students. Applications are processed on a rolling basis. Application fee: $40 ($50 for international students). *Expenses:* Tuition, state resident: full-time $1,320; part-time $110 per credit. Tuition, nonresident: full-time $4,969; part-time $414 per credit. Required fees: $2,626 per term. Tuition and fees vary according to course load. *Financial support:* Fellowships with full tuition reimbursements, research assistantships with full tuition reimbursements, teaching assistantships with full tuition reimbursements, career-related internships or fieldwork, Federal Work-Study, scholarships/grants, traineeships, and unspecified assistantships available. Support available to part-time students. Financial award application deadline: 2/1. *Unit head:* Dr. Francis Juanes, Director, 413-545-2665, Fax: 413-545-4358, E-mail: juanes@forwild.umass.edu.

University of Miami, Graduate School, Rosenstiel School of Marine and Atmospheric Science, Division of Marine Biology and Fisheries, Coral Gables, FL 33124. Offers MS, PhD. *Faculty:* 24 full-time (4 women), 19 part-time/adjunct (2 women). *Students:* 54 full-time (26 women), 1 part-time; includes 3 minority (1 African American, 2 Hispanic Americans), 11 international. Average age 28. 84 applicants, 17% accepted, 12 enrolled. In 2003, 3 master's awarded, leading to university research/teaching 67%; 6 doctorates awarded, leading to university research/teaching 67%, government 33%. Terminal master's awarded for partial completion of doctoral program. *Median time to degree:* Master's–3.5 years full-time; doctorate–6.5 years full-time. *Degree requirements:* For master's and doctorate, thesis/dissertation, comprehensive exam, registration. *Entrance requirements:* For master's and doctorate, GRE General Test, GRE Subject Test. Additional exam requirements/recommendations for international students: Required—TOEFL (minimum score 550 paper-based; 213 computer-based). *Application deadline:* For fall admission, 1/1 for domestic students. Applications are processed on a rolling basis. Application fee: $50. Electronic applications accepted. *Expenses:* Tuition: Full-time $19,526. *Financial support:* In 2003–04, 14 fellowships with tuition reimbursements (averaging $20,124 per year), 30 research assistantships with tuition reimbursements (averaging $20,124 per year), 8 teaching assistantships with tuition reimbursements (averaging $20,124 per year) were awarded. Institutionally sponsored loans and scholarships/grants also available. Financial award application deadline: 3/1; financial award applicants required to submit FAFSA. *Faculty research:* Biochemistry, physiology, plankton, coral, fisheries, biology. *Unit head:* Dr. Sharon Smith, Chairperson, 305-361-4177, E-mail: ssmith@rsmas.miami.edu. *Application contact:* Dr. Frank Millero, Associate Dean, 305-361-4155, Fax: 305-361-4771, E-mail: gso@rsmas.miami.edu.

University of Minnesota, Twin Cities Campus, Graduate School, College of Natural Resources, Department of Fisheries, Wildlife, and Conservation Biology, Minneapolis, MN 55455-0213. Offers conservation biology (MS, PhD); wildlife conservation (MS, PhD). *Faculty:* 21 full-time (4 women), 6 part-time/adjunct (0 women). *Students:* 73 full-time (41 women), 31 part-time (18 women); includes 8 minority (2 African Americans, 1 American Indian/Alaska Native, 2 Asian Americans or Pacific Islanders, 3 Hispanic Americans), 15 international. 123 applicants, 27% accepted, 21 enrolled. In 2003, 11 master's, 5 doctorates awarded. Terminal master's awarded for partial completion of doctoral program. *Degree requirements:* For master's, thesis optional; for doctorate, thesis/dissertation, comprehensive exam, registration. *Entrance requirements:* For master's and doctorate, GRE. Additional exam requirements/recommendations for international students: Required—TOEFL (minimum score 550 paper-based; 213 computer-based). *Application deadline:* For fall admission, 1/1 priority date for domestic students, 1/1 priority date for international students. Application fee: $55 ($75 for international students). *Expenses:* Tuition, state resident: full-time $3,681; part-time $614 per credit. Tuition, nonresident: full-time $7,231; part-time $1,205 per credit. *Financial support:* In 2003–04, 14 fellowships with full tuition reimbursements, 30 research assistantships with full and partial tuition reimbursements, 16 teaching assistantships with full and partial tuition reimbursements were awarded. Tuition waivers (partial) also available. Financial award application deadline: 1/1. *Faculty research:* Management, ecology, physiology, genetics, and computer modeling of fish and wildlife. Total annual research expenditures: $983,279. *Unit head:* Dr. James A. Perry, Head, 612-624-3600, E-mail: jperry@umn.edu. *Application contact:* Kathleen A. Walter, Student Support Services Assistant, 612-624-2748, Fax: 612-624-6282, E-mail: kwalter@umn.edu.

University of Missouri–Columbia, Graduate School, School of Natural Resources, Program in Fisheries and Wildlife, Columbia, MO 65211. Offers MS, PhD. *Faculty:* 10 full-time (0 women). *Students:* 10 full-time (2 women), 35 part-time (16 women); includes 5 minority (2 African Americans, 1 Asian American or Pacific Islander, 2 Hispanic Americans), 4 international. In 2003, 8 master's, 1 doctorate awarded. *Degree requirements:* For doctorate, thesis/dissertation. *Entrance requirements:* For master's and doctorate, GRE General Test, minimum GPA of 3.0. *Application deadline:* Applications are processed on a rolling basis. Application fee: $45 ($60 for international students). *Expenses:* Tuition, state resident: full-time $5,205. Tuition, nonresident: full-time $14,058. *Financial support:* Research assistantships, teaching assistantships, institutionally sponsored loans and scholarships/grants available. *Unit head:* Dr. Charles F. Rabeni, Director of Graduate Studies, 573-882-3524, E-mail: rabenic@missouri.edu.

The University of Montana–Missoula, Graduate School, College of Forestry and Conservation, Missoula, MT 59812-0002. Offers ecosystem management (MEM, MS); fish and wildlife biology (PhD); forestry (MS, PhD); recreation management (MS); resource conservation (MS); wildlife biology (MS). *Faculty:* 34 full-time (4 women). *Students:* 158 full-time (44 women), 49 part-time (22 women); includes 3 minority (2 American Indian/Alaska Native, 1 Hispanic American), 16 international. 175 applicants, 35% accepted, 46 enrolled. In 2003, 28 master's, 5 doctorates awarded. *Degree requirements:* For doctorate, thesis/dissertation. *Entrance requirements:* For master's and doctorate, GRE General Test. Additional exam requirements/recommendations for international students: Required—TOEFL (minimum score 575 paper-based; 213 computer-based). *Application deadline:* For fall admission, 1/31 for domestic students; for spring admission, 8/31 priority date for domestic students. Applications are processed on a rolling basis. Application fee: $45. *Expenses:* Tuition, state resident: full-time $1,848; part-time $221 per credit. Tuition, nonresident: full-time $4,880; part-time $333 per credit. Required fees: $2,200. *Financial support:* In 2003–04, 25 research assistantships with tuition reimbursements, 12 teaching assistantships with full tuition reimbursements were awarded. Fellowships, career-related internships or fieldwork and Federal Work-Study also available. Financial award application deadline: 3/1; financial award applicants required to submit FAFSA. Total annual research expenditures: $6.7 million. *Unit head:* Dr. Perry Brown, Dean, 406-243-5521, Fax: 406-243-4845, E-mail: pbrown@forestry.umt.edu.

University of New Hampshire, Graduate School, College of Life Sciences and Agriculture, Department of Natural Resources, Durham, NH 03824. Offers environmental conservation (MS); forestry (MS); soil science (MS); water resources management (MS); wildlife (MS). Part-time programs available. *Faculty:* 40 full-time. *Students:* 25 full-time (11 women), 31 part-time (21 women), 5 international. Average age 32. 74 applicants, 38% accepted, 16 enrolled. In 2003, 13 degrees awarded. *Degree requirements:* For master's, thesis or alternative. *Entrance requirements:* For master's, GRE General Test. Additional exam requirements/recommendations for international students: Required—TOEFL (minimum score 550 paper-based; 213 computer-based); Recommended—TSE. *Application deadline:* For fall admission, 4/1 for domestic students; for winter admission, 12/1 for domestic students. Applications are processed on a rolling basis. Application fee: $50. Electronic applications accepted. Tuition, area resident: Full-time $7,070. *Expenses:* Tuition, state resident: full-time $10,605. Tuition, nonresident: full-time $17,430. Required fees: $15. *Financial support:* In 2003–04, 3 fellowships, 15 research assistantships, 12 teaching assistantships were awarded. Career-related internships or fieldwork, Federal Work-Study, scholarships/grants, and tuition waivers (full and partial) also available. Support available to part-time students. Financial award application deadline: 2/15. *Unit head:* Dr. William H. McDowell, Chairperson, 603-862-2249, E-mail: tehoward@cisunix.unh.edu. *Application contact:* Linda Scogin, Administrative Assistant, 603-862-3932, E-mail: natural.resources@unh.edu.

University of North Dakota, Graduate School, College of Arts and Sciences, Department of Biology, Grand Forks, ND 58202. Offers botany (MS, PhD); ecology (MS, PhD); entomology (MS, PhD); environmental biology (MS, PhD); fisheries/wildlife (MS, PhD); genetics (MS, PhD); zoology (MS, PhD). *Faculty:* 16 full-time (2 women). *Students:* 1 full-time (0 women), 21 part-time (9 women). 8 applicants, 100% accepted, 6 enrolled. In 2003, 5 master's, 1 doctorate awarded. Terminal master's awarded for partial completion of doctoral program. *Degree requirements:* For master's, thesis/dissertation, final exam; for doctorate, thesis/dissertation, final exam, comprehensive exam. *Entrance requirements:* For master's, GRE General Test, GRE Subject Test, minimum GPA of 3.0; for doctorate, GRE General Test, GRE Subject Test, minimum GPA of 3.5. Additional exam requirements/recommendations for international students: Required—TOEFL (minimum score 550 paper-based; 213 computer-based). *Application deadline:* For fall admission, 2/15 for domestic students, 2/15 for international students. Application fee: $35. Electronic applications accepted. *Expenses:* Tuition, state resident: part-time $235 per credit. Tuition, nonresident: part-time $535 per credit. Tuition and fees vary according to course level, course load, program and reciprocity agreements. *Financial support:* In 2003–04, research assistantships with full tuition reimbursements (averaging $10,516 per year), teaching assistantships with full tuition reimbursements (averaging $9,668 per year) were awarded. Fellowships, Federal Work-Study, institutionally sponsored loans, scholarships/grants, and tuition waivers (full and partial) also available. Support available to part-time students. Financial award application deadline: 3/15; financial award applicants required to submit FAFSA. *Faculty research:* Population biology, wildlife ecology, RNA processing, hormonal control of behavior. *Unit head:* Dr. Richard D. Crawford, Graduate Director, 701-777-4673, Fax: 701-777-2623, E-mail: richard_crawford@und.nodak.edu.

University of Rhode Island, Graduate School, College of the Environment and Life Sciences, Department of Environmental and Natural Resource Economics, Kingston, RI 02881. Offers resource economics and marine resources (MS, PhD). In 2003, 15 master's, 1 doctorate awarded. *Degree requirements:* For master's, thesis optional; for doctorate, thesis/dissertation. *Entrance requirements:* For master's and doctorate, GRE General Test. Additional exam requirements/recommendations for international students: Required—TOEFL. *Application deadline:* For fall admission, 4/15 for domestic students. Applications are processed on a rolling basis. *Expenses:* Tuition, state resident: full-time $4,338; part-time $281 per credit. Tuition, nonresident: full-time $12,438; part-time $704 per credit. Required fees: $1,840. *Unit head:* Dr. James Anderson, Chairperson, 401-874-2471. *Application contact:* Dr. Tim Tyrrell, Graduate Admissions Committee, 401-874-2472, Fax: 401-782-4766, E-mail: renri@uriacc.uri.edu.

University of Rhode Island, Graduate School, College of the Environment and Life Sciences, Department of Fisheries, Aquaculture and Pathology, Kingston, RI 02881. Offers animal science (MS). In 2003, 6 degrees awarded. *Application deadline:* For fall admission, 4/15 for domestic students. Applications are processed on a rolling basis. Application fee: $35. *Expenses:* Tuition, state resident: full-time $4,338; part-time $281 per credit. Tuition, nonresident: full-time $12,438; part-time $704 per credit. Required fees: $1,840. *Unit head:* Dr. Michael Rice, Chairperson, 401-874-2477.

The University of Tennessee, Graduate School, College of Agricultural Sciences and Natural Resources, Department of Forestry, Wildlife, and Fisheries, Program in Wildlife and Fisheries Science, Knoxville, TN 37996. Offers MS. *Degree requirements:* For master's, thesis. *Entrance requirements:* For master's, GRE General Test, minimum GPA of 2.7. Additional exam requirements/recommendations for international students: Required—TOEFL. Electronic applications accepted.

University of Vermont, Graduate College, School of Natural Resources, Program in Wildlife and Fisheries Biology, Burlington, VT 05405. Offers MS. *Students:* 15 (4 women). 31 applicants, 13% accepted, 1 enrolled. In 2003, 4 degrees awarded. *Degree requirements:* For master's, thesis. *Entrance requirements:* For master's, GRE General Test. Additional exam requirements/recommendations for international students: Required—TOEFL. *Application deadline:* For fall admission, 3/1 for domestic students. Applications are processed on a rolling basis. Application fee: $25. *Expenses:* Tuition, state resident: part-time $362 per credit hour. Tuition, nonresident: part-time $906 per credit hour. *Financial support:* Research assistantships, teaching assistantships available. Financial award application deadline: 3/1. *Unit head:* Dr. D. Hirth, Chairperson, 802-656-2620. *Application contact:* D. Wang, Coordinator, 802-656-2620.

University of Washington, Graduate School, College of Forest Resources, Seattle, WA 98195. Offers forest economics (MS, PhD); forest ecosystem analysis (MS, PhD); forest engineering/forest hydrology (MS, PhD); forest products marketing (MS, PhD); forest soils (MS, PhD); paper science and engineering (MS, PhD); quantitative resource management (MS, PhD); silviculture (MFR); silviculture and forest protection (MS, PhD); social sciences (MS, PhD); urban horticulture (MFR, MS, PhD); wildlife science (MS, PhD). *Degree requirements:* For master's, thesis (for some programs), registration; for doctorate, thesis/dissertation, comprehensive exam (for some programs), registration. *Entrance requirements:* For master's and doctorate, GRE, minimum GPA of 3.0. Additional exam requirements/recommendations for international students: Required—TOEFL. Electronic applications accepted. *Faculty research:* Ecosystem analysis, silviculture and forest protection, paper science and engineering, environmental horticulture and urban forestry, natural resource policy and economics.

University of Washington, Graduate School, College of Ocean and Fishery Sciences, School of Aquatic and Fishery Sciences, Seattle, WA 98195. Offers MS, PhD. *Degree requirements:* For master's and doctorate, thesis/dissertation. *Entrance requirements:* For master's and doctorate, GRE General Test, minimum GPA of 3.0. Additional exam requirements/recommendations for international students: Required—TOEFL. Electronic applications accepted.

Fish, Game, and Wildlife Management

University of Washington (continued)
Faculty research: Fish and shellfish ecology, fisheries management, aquatic ecology, conservation biology, genetics.

Utah State University, School of Graduate Studies, College of Natural Resources, Department of Aquatic, Watershed, and Earth Resources, Logan, UT 84322. Offers ecology (MS, PhD); fisheries biology (MS, PhD). *Faculty:* 14 full-time (3 women), 4 part-time/adjunct (1 woman). *Students:* 45 full-time (16 women), 14 part-time (5 women); includes 2 minority (both Hispanic Americans), 3 international. Average age 33. 30 applicants, 33% accepted, 6 enrolled. In 2003, 4 master's, 1 doctorate awarded. *Median time to degree:* Master's–3.3 years full-time; doctorate–4 years full-time. *Degree requirements:* For master's, thesis (for some programs); for doctorate, thesis/dissertation. *Entrance requirements:* For master's and doctorate, GRE General Test, minimum GPA of 3.2. Additional exam requirements/recommendations for international students: Required—TOEFL. *Application deadline:* For fall admission, 2/15 for domestic students; for spring admission, 10/15 for domestic students. Applications are processed on a rolling basis. Application fee: $50 ($60 for international students). *Expenses:* Tuition, state resident: part-time $270 per credit hour. Tuition, nonresident: part-time $946 per credit hour. Required fees: $173 per credit hour. *Financial support:* In 2003–04, 2 fellowships with partial tuition reimbursements, 32 research assistantships with partial tuition reimbursements, 1 teaching assistantship with partial tuition reimbursement were awarded. Career-related internships or fieldwork, Federal Work-Study, and institutionally sponsored loans also available. Support available to part-time students. Financial award application deadline: 2/1. *Faculty research:* Behavior, population ecology, habitat, conservation biology, restoration. Total annual research expenditures: $4.7 million. *Unit head:* Chris Luecke, Head, 435-797-2463, Fax: 435-797-1871, E-mail: awerinfo@cc.usu.edu. *Application contact:* Julia Dance, Staff Assistant, 435-797-2459, Fax: 435-797-1871, E-mail: awerinfo@cc.usu.edu.

Utah State University, School of Graduate Studies, College of Natural Resources, Department of Forest, Range, and Wildlife Sciences, Logan, UT 84322. Offers ecology (MS, PhD); forestry (MS, PhD); range science (MS, PhD); wildlife biology (MS, PhD). Part-time programs available. *Faculty:* 22 full-time (4 women), 17 part-time/adjunct (3 women). *Students:* 55 full-time (21 women), 16 part-time (9 women), 7 international. Average age 24. 42 applicants, 33% accepted, 10 enrolled. In 2003, 8 master's, 2 doctorates awarded. *Degree requirements:* For master's and doctorate, thesis/dissertation. *Entrance requirements:* For master's and doctorate, GRE General Test, minimum GPA of 3.0. Additional exam requirements/recommendations for international students: Required—TOEFL. *Application deadline:* For fall admission, 6/15 for domestic students; for spring admission, 10/15 for domestic students. Applications are processed on a rolling basis. Application fee: $50 ($60 for international students). *Expenses:* Tuition, state resident: part-time $270 per credit hour. Tuition, nonresident: part-time $946 per credit hour. Required fees: $173 per credit hour. *Financial support:* In 2003–04, 14 research assistantships with partial tuition reimbursements (averaging $13,600 per year) were awarded; fellowships, teaching assistantships, career-related internships or fieldwork, Federal Work-Study, and institutionally sponsored loans also available. *Faculty research:* Range plant ecophysiology, plant community ecology, ruminant nutrition, population ecology. Total annual research expenditures: $3.5 million. *Unit head:* Dr. David W. Roberts, Interim Head, 435-797-2503, Fax: 435-797-3796, E-mail: ggriffeth@cnr.usu.edu. *Application contact:* Gaye Griffeth, Staff Assistant, 435-797-2503, Fax: 435-797-3796, E-mail: ggriffeth@cnr.usu.edu.

Virginia Polytechnic Institute and State University, Graduate School, College of Natural Resources, Department of Fisheries and Wildlife Sciences, Blacksburg, VA 24061. Offers MS, PhD. *Faculty:* 15 full-time (3 women). *Students:* 33 full-time (13 women), 15 part-time (5 women); includes 2 minority (1 African American, 1 Hispanic American), 6 international. Average age 30. 51 applicants, 27% accepted, 11 enrolled. In 2003, 9 master's, 2 doctorates awarded. *Entrance requirements:* For master's and doctorate, GRE General Test. Additional exam requirements/recommendations for international students: Required—TOEFL (minimum score 550 paper-based; 213 computer-based). *Application deadline:* Applications are processed on a rolling basis. Application fee: $45. Electronic applications accepted. Tuition, area resident: Full-time $6,039; part-time $336 per credit. Tuition, nonresident: full-time $9,708; part-time $539 per credit. Required fees: $905; $130 per credit. *Financial support:* In 2003–04, 22 research assistantships with full tuition reimbursements (averaging $14,707 per year), 5 teaching assistantships with full tuition reimbursements (averaging $12,630 per year) were awarded. Career-related internships or fieldwork, Federal Work-Study, scholarships/grants, and unspecified assistantships also available. Financial award application deadline: 4/1. *Faculty research:* Fisheries management, wildlife management, wildlife toxicology and physiology, endangered species, computer applications. *Unit head:* Dr. Donald J. Orth, Head, 540-231-5573, Fax: 540-231-7580, E-mail: dorth@vt.edu. *Application contact:* Linda D. Boothe, Assistant to the Head, 540-231-6944, Fax: 540-231-7580, E-mail: boothel@vt.edu.

West Virginia University, Davis College of Agriculture, Forestry and Consumer Sciences, Division of Forestry, Program in Wildlife and Fisheries Resources, Morgantown, WV 26506. Offers MS. Part-time programs available. *Students:* 22 full-time (8 women), 4 part-time. Average age 28. 20 applicants, 65% accepted, 13 enrolled. In 2003, 12 degrees awarded. *Median time to degree:* Master's–2.25 years full-time. *Degree requirements:* For master's, thesis, comprehensive exam. *Entrance requirements:* For master's, GRE, minimum GPA of 3.0. Additional exam requirements/recommendations for international students: Required—TOEFL. *Application deadline:* For fall admission, 7/7 for domestic students, 7/7 for international students; for spring admission, 12/1 for domestic students, 12/1 for international students. Applications are processed on a rolling basis. Application fee: $45. Electronic applications accepted. *Expenses:* Tuition, state resident: full-time $4,332. Tuition, nonresident: full-time $12,442. *Financial support:* In 2003–04, 19 research assistantships with full tuition reimbursements, 3 teaching assistantships with full tuition reimbursements were awarded. Career-related internships or fieldwork, Federal Work-Study, institutionally sponsored loans, health care benefits, tuition waivers (full and partial), and unspecified assistantships also available. Financial award application deadline: 2/1; financial award applicants required to submit FAFSA. *Faculty research:* Managing habitat for game, nongame, and fish; fish ecology; wildlife ecology. Total annual research expenditures: $2 million. *Unit head:* Dr. Kyle J. Hartman, Coordinator, 304-293-2941 Ext. 2491, Fax: 304-293-2441, E-mail: kyle.hartman@mail.wvu.edu.

Forestry

Auburn University, Graduate School, School of Forestry and Wildlife Sciences, Auburn University, AL 36849. Offers MF, MS, PhD. Part-time programs available. *Faculty:* 29 full-time (3 women). *Students:* 25 full-time (5 women), 21 part-time (9 women), 10 international. 29 applicants, 69% accepted. In 2003, 12 master's, 3 doctorates awarded. *Degree requirements:* For master's, oral exam (MF), thesis (MS); for doctorate, thesis/dissertation. *Entrance requirements:* For master's and doctorate, GRE General Test. *Application deadline:* For fall admission, 7/7 for domestic students; for spring admission, 11/24 for domestic students. Applications are processed on a rolling basis. Application fee: $25 ($50 for international students). Electronic applications accepted. *Expenses:* Tuition, state resident: part-time $175 per credit hour. Tuition, nonresident: part-time $525 per credit hour. *Financial support:* Fellowships, research assistantships, teaching assistantships, Federal Work-Study available. Support available to part-time students. Financial award application deadline: 3/15. *Faculty research:* Forest nursery management, silviculture and vegetation management, biological processes and ecological relationships, growth and yield of plantations and natural stands, urban forestry, forest taxation, law and policy. *Unit head:* Richard W. Brinker, Dean, 334-844-1007, Fax: 334-844-1084, E-mail: brinker@forestry.auburn.edu. *Application contact:* Dr. John F. Pritchett, Dean of the Graduate School, 334-844-4700, E-mail: hatchlb@mail.auburn.edu.

California Polytechnic State University, San Luis Obispo, College of Agriculture, San Luis Obispo, CA 93407. Offers agriculture (MS); forestry sciences (MS). Part-time programs available. *Faculty:* 5 full-time (1 woman), 2 part-time/adjunct (1 woman). *Students:* 90 full-time (50 women), 41 part-time (22 women); includes 13 Hispanic Americans. 105 applicants, 72% accepted, 45 enrolled. In 2003, 34 degrees awarded. *Degree requirements:* For master's, thesis, comprehensive exam. *Entrance requirements:* For master's, minimum GPA of 2.5 in last 90 quarter units. Additional exam requirements/recommendations for international students: Required—TOEFL, TWE. *Application deadline:* For fall admission, 7/1 for domestic students; for winter admission, 11/1 for domestic students; for spring admission, 3/1 for domestic students. Applications are processed on a rolling basis. Application fee: $55. Electronic applications accepted. Tuition, nonresident: part-time $188 per unit. Required fees: $3,732. *Financial support:* In 2003–04, 40 students received support, including 6 fellowships (averaging $2,000 per year), 20 research assistantships (averaging $10,000 per year), 10 teaching assistantships (averaging $2,000 per year); career-related internships or fieldwork, Federal Work-Study, institutionally sponsored loans, and scholarships/grants also available. Support available to part-time students. Financial award application deadline: 3/2; financial award applicants required to submit FAFSA. *Faculty research:* Soils, food processing, forestry, dairy products development, irrigation. *Unit head:* Dr. David J. Wehner, Dean, 805-756-5072, Fax: 805-756-6577, E-mail: dwehner@calpoly.edu. *Application contact:* Jim Maraviglia, Admissions Office, 805-756-2311, E-mail: admissions@calpoly.edu.

Clemson University, Graduate School, College of Agriculture, Forestry and Life Sciences, Department of Forestry and Natural Resources, Program in Forest Resources, Clemson, SC 29634. Offers MFR, MS, PhD. Part-time programs available. *Students:* 29 full-time (11 women), 9 part-time (2 women); includes 1 minority (African American), 2 international. Average age 25. 18 applicants, 44% accepted, 7 enrolled. In 2003, 8 master's, 3 doctorates awarded. *Degree requirements:* For master's and doctorate, thesis/dissertation. *Entrance requirements:* For master's, GRE General Test, minimum B average in last 2 years of undergraduate course work; for doctorate, GRE General Test, minimum B average in graduate course work. Additional exam requirements/recommendations for international students: Required—TOEFL. *Application deadline:* For fall admission, 3/1 for domestic students; for spring admission, 10/1 for domestic students. Application fee: $40. *Expenses:* Tuition, state resident: full-time $7,432. Tuition, nonresident: full-time $14,732. *Financial support:* Fellowships, research assistantships, teaching assistantships available. Financial award application deadline: 5/1; financial award applicants required to submit FAFSA. *Faculty research:* Wetlands management, wood technology, forest management, silviculture, economics. *Application contact:* Dr. Dave Guynn, Coordinator, 864-656-4803, Fax: 864-656-3304, E-mail: dguynn@clemson.edu.

Colorado State University, Graduate School, College of Natural Resources, Department of Forest, Rangeland, and Watershed Stewardship, Program in Forest Sciences, Fort Collins, CO 80523-0015. Offers MF, MS, PhD. *Students:* 33 full-time (14 women), 38 part-time (14 women); includes 6 minority (1 African American, 2 American Indian/Alaska Native, 3 Hispanic Americans), 6 international. Average age 33. 50 applicants, 52% accepted, 15 enrolled. In 2003, 14 master's, 2 doctorates awarded. Application fee: $50. *Expenses:* Tuition, state resident: full-time $4,156. Tuition, nonresident: full-time $14,762. Required fees: $205. Tuition and fees vary according to course load, campus/location, program and reciprocity agreements. *Application contact:* Kelley Mathers, Graduate Coordinator, 970-491-4994, Fax: 970-491-6754, E-mail: kmathers@cnr.colostate.edu.

Cornell University, Graduate School, Graduate Fields of Agriculture and Life Sciences, Field of Natural Resources, Ithaca, NY 14853-0001. Offers aquatic science (MPS, MS, PhD); environmental management (MPS); fishery science (MPS, MS, PhD); forest science (MPS, MS, PhD); resource policy and management (MPS, MS, PhD); wildlife science (MPS, MS, PhD). *Faculty:* 43 full-time. *Students:* 73 full-time (31 women); includes 10 minority (1 African American, 2 American Indian/Alaska Native, 5 Asian Americans or Pacific Islanders, 2 Hispanic Americans), 14 international. 107 applicants, 22% accepted, 18 enrolled. In 2003, 16 master's, 6 doctorates awarded. *Degree requirements:* For master's, thesis (MS), project paper (MPS); for doctorate, thesis/dissertation, comprehensive exam. *Entrance requirements:* For master's and doctorate, GRE General Test, 2 letters of recommendation. Additional exam requirements/recommendations for international students: Required—TOEFL (minimum score 550 paper-based; 213 computer-based). *Application deadline:* ; for spring admission, 10/30 for domestic students. Applications are processed on a rolling basis. Application fee: $60. Electronic applications accepted. *Expenses:* Tuition: Full-time $28,630. One-time fee: $50 full-time. *Financial support:* In 2003–04, 63 students received support, including 11 fellowships with full tuition reimbursements available, 27 research assistantships with full tuition reimbursements available, 25 teaching assistantships with full tuition reimbursements available; institutionally sponsored loans, scholarships/grants, health care benefits, tuition waivers (full and partial), and unspecified assistantships also available. Financial award applicants required to submit FAFSA. *Faculty research:* Ecosystem-level dynamics, systems modeling, conservation biology/management, resource management's human dimensions, biogeochemistry. *Unit head:* Director of Graduate Studies, 607-255-2807, Fax: 607-255-0349. *Application contact:* Graduate Field Assistant, 607-255-2807, Fax: 607-255-0349, E-mail: nrgrad@cornell.edu.

Duke University, Nicholas School of the Environment and Earth Sciences, Durham, NC 27708-0328. Offers coastal environmental management (MEM); environmental health and security (MEM); environmental science and policy (PhD); environmental toxicology, chemistry, and risk assessment (MEM); forest resource management (MF); global environmental change (MEM); resource ecology (MEM); resource economics and policy (MEM); water and air resources (MEM). PhD offered through the Graduate School. *Accreditation:* SAF (one or more programs are accredited). Part-time programs available. Terminal master's awarded for partial completion of doctoral program. *Degree requirements:* For master's, thesis (for some programs); for doctorate, thesis/dissertation. *Entrance requirements:* For master's, GRE General Test, previous course work in biology or ecology, calculus, statistics, and microeconomics; computer familiarity with word processing and data analysis; for doctorate, GRE General Test. Additional exam requirements/recommendations for international students: Required—TOEFL (minimum score 550 paper-based; 213 computer-based). Electronic applications accepted. Expenses: Contact institution. *Faculty research:* Ecosystem management, conservation ecology, earth systems, risk assessment.

See in-depth description on page 787.

Harvard University, Graduate School of Arts and Sciences, The Harvard Forest, Cambridge, MA 02138. Offers forest science (MFS). *Degree requirements:* For master's, thesis. *Entrance requirements:* For master's, GRE General Test, bachelor's degree in biology or forestry. Additional exam requirements/recommendations for international students: Required—TOEFL. *Expenses:* Tuition: Full-time $26,066. Full-time tuition and fees vary according to program and student level. *Faculty research:* Forest ecology, planning, and physiology; forest microbiology.

Iowa State University of Science and Technology, Graduate College, College of Agriculture, Department of Natural Resource Ecology and Management, Ames, IA 50011. Offers animal ecology (MS, PhD), including animal ecology, fisheries biology, wildlife biology; forestry (MS, PhD). *Faculty:* 23 full-time, 7 part-time/adjunct. *Students:* 36 full-time (13 women), 7 part-time (2 women), 8 international. 44 applicants, 36% accepted, 12 enrolled. In 2003, 6 master's, 4 doctorates awarded. *Median time to degree:* Master's–2.7 years full-time; doctorate–4.5 years full-time. *Degree requirements:* For master's, thesis (for some programs); for doctorate, thesis/dissertation. *Entrance requirements:* For master's and doctorate, GRE General Test. Additional exam requirements/recommendations for international students: Required—TOEFL (paper score 547; computer score 210) or IELTS (score 6). *Application deadline:* For fall admission, 1/1 priority date for domestic students, 1/1 priority date for international students; for spring admission, 9/1 priority date for domestic students, 9/1 priority date for international students. Application fee: $30 ($70 for international students). Electronic applications accepted. Tuition, nonresident: part-time $560 per credit. Required fees: $38 per unit. *Financial support:* In 2003–04, 35 research assistantships with full and partial tuition reimbursements (averaging $17,496 per year), 4 teaching assistantships with full and partial tuition reimbursements (averaging $17,496 per year) were awarded. *Unit head:* Dr. J. Michael Kelly, Chair, 515-294-1166. *Application contact:* Lyn Van De Pol, Information Contact, 515-294-6148, E-mail: lvdp@iastate.edu.

Lakehead University, Graduate Studies, Faculty of Forestry, Thunder Bay, ON P7B 5E1, Canada. Offers M Sc F, MF. Part-time programs available. *Degree requirements:* For master's, report (MF), thesis (M Sc F). *Entrance requirements:* For master's, minimum B average. Additional exam requirements/recommendations for international students: Required—TOEFL. *Faculty research:* Soils, silviculture, wildlife, ecology, genetics.

Louisiana State University and Agricultural and Mechanical College, Graduate School, College of Agriculture, School of Renewable Natural Resources, Baton Rouge, LA 70803. Offers fisheries (MS); forestry (MS, PhD); wildlife (MS); wildlife and fisheries science (PhD). *Faculty:* 30 full-time (0 women). *Students:* 56 full-time (12 women), 16 part-time (7 women); includes 42 minority (1 American Indian/Alaska Native, 41 Hispanic Americans), 27 international. Average age 30. 34 applicants, 50% accepted, 11 enrolled. In 2003, 20 master's, 9 doctorates awarded. *Degree requirements:* For master's and doctorate, thesis/dissertation. *Entrance requirements:* For master's, GRE General Test, minimum GPA of 3.0; for doctorate, GRE General Test, MS, minimum GPA of 3.0. Additional exam requirements/recommendations for international students: Required—TOEFL (minimum score 550 paper-based; 213 computer-based). *Application deadline:* For fall admission, 1/25 priority date for domestic students, 5/15 priority date for international students. Applications are processed on a rolling basis. Application fee: $25. Electronic applications accepted. *Expenses:* Tuition, state resident: part-time $337 per hour. Tuition, nonresident: part-time $577 per hour. *Financial support:* In 2003–04, 2 fellowships (averaging $18,750 per year), 50 research assistantships with partial tuition reimbursements (averaging $15,766 per year), 2 teaching assistantships with partial tuition reimbursements (averaging $16,375 per year) were awarded. Federal Work-Study also available. Financial award application deadline: 4/15; financial award applicants required to submit FAFSA. *Faculty research:* Forest biology and management, aquaculture, fisheries biology and ecology, upland and wetlands wildlife. Total annual research expenditures: $7,325. *Unit head:* Dr. Bob G. Blackmon, Director, 225-578-4131, Fax: 225-578-4227, E-mail: bblackmon@agctr.lsu.edu. *Application contact:* Dr. Allen Rutherford, Coordinator of Graduate Studies, 225-578-4187, Fax: 225-578-4227, E-mail: druther@lsu.edu.

See in-depth description on page 789.

McGill University, Faculty of Graduate and Postdoctoral Studies, Faculty of Agricultural and Environmental Sciences, Department of Natural Resource Sciences, Montréal, QC H3A 2T5, Canada. Offers agrometeorology (M Sc, PhD); entomology (M Sc, PhD); forest science (M Sc, PhD); microbiology (M Sc, PhD); neotropical environment (M Sc, PhD); soil science (M Sc, PhD); wildlife biology (M Sc, PhD). *Faculty:* 18 full-time (1 woman). *Students:* 69 full-time, 2 part-time. 51 applicants, 37% accepted, 15 enrolled. In 2003, 12 master's, 4 doctorates awarded. *Degree requirements:* For master's and doctorate, thesis/dissertation. *Entrance requirements:* For master's, minimum GPA of 3.0; for doctorate, M Sc, minimum GPA of 3.0. Additional exam requirements/recommendations for international students: Required—TOEFL (paper score 550; computer score 213) or IELTS (paper score 6). *Application deadline:* For fall admission, 6/1 for domestic students, 3/1 for international students; for winter admission, 10/15 for domestic students; for spring admission, 2/15 for domestic students. Applications are processed on a rolling basis. Application fee: $60 Canadian dollars. Electronic applications accepted. Tuition, area resident: Full-time $1,668. *Expenses:* Tuition, state resident: full-time $4,173. Tuition, nonresident: full-time $9,468. Required fees: $1,081. *Financial support:* In 2003–04, 2 fellowships with partial tuition reimbursements (averaging $8,000 per year), 34 teaching assistantships were awarded. Institutionally sponsored loans also available. *Faculty research:* Toxicology, reproductive physiology, parasites, wildlife management, genetics. *Unit head:* Dr. Benoit Côté, Chair, 514-398-7952, Fax: 514-398-7990, E-mail: coteb@nrs.mcgill.ca. *Application contact:* Marie Kubecki, Graduate Student Coordinator, 514-398-7991, Fax: 514-398-7990, E-mail: kubecki@nrs.mcgill.ca.

Michigan State University, Graduate School, College of Agriculture and Natural Resources, Department of Forestry, East Lansing, MI 48824. Offers forestry (MS, PhD); forestry-environmental toxicology (PhD); plant breeding and genetics-forestry (MS, PhD). *Faculty:* 18 full-time (2 women). *Students:* 31 full-time (12 women), 7 part-time (2 women); includes 1 minority (Hispanic American), 17 international. Average age 33. 30 applicants, 43% accepted. In 2003, 6 master's, 3 doctorates awarded. *Degree requirements:* For master's, thesis optional; for doctorate, thesis/dissertation. *Entrance requirements:* For master's and doctorate, GRE General Test, 3 letters of recommendation. Additional exam requirements/recommendations for international students: Required—TOEFL (minimum score 550 paper-based; 213 computer-based), Michigan State University ELT (85), Michigan ELAB (83). *Application deadline:* For fall admission, 12/23 for domestic students. Applications are processed on a rolling basis. Application fee: $50. Electronic applications accepted. *Expenses:* Tuition, state resident: part-time $291 per hour. Tuition, nonresident: part-time $589 per hour. *Financial support:* In 2003–04, 6 fellowships with tuition reimbursements (averaging $9,975 per year), 19 research assistantships with tuition reimbursements (averaging $14,314 per year) were awarded. Financial award applicants required to submit FAFSA. *Faculty research:* Silviculture, biometry and ecology, social forestry and agroforestry, tree physiology and wood science, plant breeding and genetics. Total annual research expenditures: $3.4 million. *Unit head:* Dr. Daniel Keathley, Chairperson, 517-355-0091, Fax: 517-432-1143, E-mail: keathley@msu.edu. *Application contact:* Juli Kerr, Information Contact, 517-355-0090, E-mail: kerrju@msu.edu.

Michigan State University, Graduate School, College of Agriculture and Natural Resources, Program in Plant Breeding and Genetics, East Lansing, MI 48824. Offers plant breeding and genetics (MS, PhD), including botany and plant pathology, crop and soil sciences, forestry, horticulture. *Faculty:* 22 full-time (5 women). *Students:* 22 full-time (12 women), 5 part-time (3 women); includes 1 minority (Hispanic American), 12 international. Average age 30. 29 applicants, 17% accepted. In 2003, 3 master's, 2 doctorates awarded. *Degree requirements:* For master's, thesis; for doctorate, thesis/dissertation, oral examination, comprehensive exam. *Entrance requirements:* For master's and doctorate, GRE, minimum GPA of 3.0, 3 letters of recommendation. Additional exam requirements/recommendations for international students: Required—TOEFL (minimum score 550 paper-based; 213 computer-based). *Application deadline:* For fall admission, 12/23 for domestic students. Application fee: $50. *Expenses:* Tuition, state resident: part-time $291 per hour. Tuition, nonresident: part-time $589 per hour. *Financial support:* Applicants required to submit FAFSA. *Unit head:* Dr. Jim Hancock, Director, 517-355-4598, Fax: 517-353-0890, E-mail: hancock@msu.edu. *Application contact:* Program Office, 517-353-2913.

Michigan Technological University, Graduate School, School of Forest Resources and Environmental Science, Program in Forest Ecology and Management, Houghton, MI 49931-1295. Offers applied ecology (MS); forest ecology and management (MS); forestry (MS). Part-time programs available. *Faculty:* 19 full-time (4 women). *Students:* 43 full-time (20 women), 10 part-time (5 women); includes 2 minority (both Hispanic Americans) Average age 27. 23 applicants, 65% accepted, 12 enrolled. In 2003, 11 degrees awarded. *Degree requirements:* For master's, thesis (for some programs), comprehensive exam, registration. *Entrance requirements:* Additional exam requirements/recommendations for international students: Required—TOEFL. *Application deadline:* For fall admission, 3/15 for domestic students. Applications are processed on a rolling basis. Application fee: $40 ($45 for international students). Electronic applications accepted. Tuition, nonresident: full-time $9,552; part-time $398 per credit. Required fees: $768. *Financial support:* In 2003–04, 23 students received support, including 2 fellowships with full tuition reimbursements available (averaging $13,500 per year), 17 research assistantships with full tuition reimbursements available (averaging $8,950 per year), 4 teaching assistantships with full tuition reimbursements available (averaging $8,950 per year); career-related internships or fieldwork, Federal Work-Study, institutionally sponsored loans, scholarships/grants, traineeships, unspecified assistantships, and co-op also available. Support available to part-time students. Financial award application deadline: 2/1; financial award applicants required to submit FAFSA. *Application contact:* Dr. Margaret R. Gale, Graduate Coordinator, 906-487-2352, Fax: 906-487-2915, E-mail: mrgale@mtu.edu.

Announcement: Graduate studies in forest ecology and management prepare students for leadership in either the public or private sector with rewarding careers in such areas as forest ecology, forest soils, silviculture, tree improvement, forest wildlife ecology and management, economics, inventory, growth and yield, and forest biology. Michigan Tech is located in the Upper Peninsula of Michigan, the "jewel" of the Great Lakes region.

See in-depth description on page 791.

Michigan Technological University, Graduate School, School of Forest Resources and Environmental Science, Program in Forest Molecular Genetics and Biotechnology, Houghton, MI 49931-1295. Offers PhD. *Faculty:* 19 full-time (4 women). *Students:* 10 full-time (2 women); includes 1 minority (Hispanic American), 8 international. Average age 30. 4 applicants, 100% accepted, 3 enrolled. *Degree requirements:* For doctorate, thesis/dissertation, comprehensive exam, registration. Application fee: $40 ($45 for international students). Tuition, nonresident: full-time $9,552; part-time $398 per credit. Required fees: $768. *Financial support:* Career-related internships or fieldwork, Federal Work-Study, institutionally sponsored loans, scholarships/grants, traineeships, and unspecified assistantships available. Support available to part-time students. *Application contact:* Dr. Margaret R. Gale, Graduate Coordinator, 906-487-2352, Fax: 906-487-2915, E-mail: mrgale@mtu.edu.

Michigan Technological University, Graduate School, School of Forest Resources and Environmental Science, Program in Forest Science, Houghton, MI 49931-1295. Offers PhD. Part-time programs available. *Faculty:* 19 full-time (4 women). *Students:* 12 full-time (7 women), 5 part-time (2 women); includes 1 minority (Hispanic American), 3 international. Average age 30. In 2003, 2 degrees awarded. *Degree requirements:* For doctorate, thesis/dissertation, comprehensive exam, registration. *Entrance requirements:* Additional exam requirements/recommendations for international students: Required—TOEFL. *Application deadline:* For fall admission, 3/15 for domestic students. Applications are processed on a rolling basis. Application fee: $40 ($45 for international students). Electronic applications accepted. Tuition, nonresident: full-time $9,552; part-time $398 per credit. Required fees: $768. *Financial support:* In 2003–04, 16 students received support, including 4 fellowships with full tuition reimbursements available (averaging $13,500 per year), 11 research assistantships with full tuition reimbursements available (averaging $8,950 per year), 1 teaching assistantship with full tuition reimbursement available (averaging $8,950 per year); career-related internships or fieldwork, Federal Work-Study, institutionally sponsored loans, scholarships/grants, traineeships, unspecified assistantships, and co-op also available. Support available to part-time students. Financial award application deadline: 2/1; financial award applicants required to submit FAFSA. *Application contact:* Dr. Margaret R. Gale, Graduate Coordinator, 906-487-2352, Fax: 906-487-2915, E-mail: mrgale@mtu.edu.

Announcement: Michigan Tech offers many programs in the forest sciences. The graduate program emphasizes an intensive hands-on research approach that is matched with excellent laboratory, greenhouse, and field trial facilities, producing a student with a solid understanding of growth and developmental processes in trees. Michigan Tech is located in the Upper Peninsula of Michigan, the "jewel" of the Great Lakes region.

See in-depth description on page 793.

Mississippi State University, College of Forest Resources, Department of Forest Products, Mississippi State, MS 39762. Offers MS. *Faculty:* 14 full-time (1 woman), 1 part-time/adjunct (0 women). *Students:* 4 full-time (1 woman), 3 part-time (1 woman); includes 1 minority (African American) Average age 27. 3 applicants, 33% accepted. In 2003, 1 degree awarded. *Degree requirements:* For master's, thesis, comprehensive oral or written exam. *Entrance requirements:* For master's, minimum GPA of 3.0. Additional exam requirements/recommendations for international students: Required—TOEFL. *Application deadline:* For fall admission, 7/1 for domestic students; for spring admission, 11/1 for domestic students. Applications are processed on a rolling basis. Application fee: $25 for international students. Electronic applications accepted. *Expenses:* Tuition, state resident: full-time $3,874; part-time $215 per hour. Tuition, nonresident: full-time $8,780; part-time $488 per hour. International tuition: $9,105 full-time. Tuition and fees vary according to course load. *Financial support:* In 2003–04, 3 research assistantships with full tuition reimbursements (averaging $9,627 per year) were awarded; fellowships, Federal Work-Study and institutionally sponsored loans also available. Financial award applicants required to submit FAFSA. *Faculty research:* Wood property enhancement and durability, environmental science and chemistry, wood-based composites, primary wood production, furniture manufacturing and management. Total annual research expenditures: $2.2 million. *Unit head:* Dr. Liam E. Leightley, Head, 662-325-4444, Fax: 662-325-8126, E-mail: lleightley@cfr.msstate.edu. *Application contact:* Diane D. Wolfe, Director of Admissions, 662-325-2224, Fax: 662-325-7360, E-mail: admit@admissions.msstate.edu.

Mississippi State University, College of Forest Resources, Department of Forestry, Mississippi State, MS 39762. Offers MS. Part-time programs available. *Faculty:* 22 full-time (3 women). *Students:* 21 full-time (3 women), 8 part-time (2 women); includes 1 minority (Asian American or Pacific Islander), 2 international. Average age 28. 7 applicants, 71% accepted, 5 enrolled. In 2003, 10 degrees awarded. *Degree requirements:* For master's, thesis, comprehensive oral or written exam. *Entrance requirements:* For master's, minimum GPA of 2.5. Additional exam requirements/recommendations for international students: Required—TOEFL. *Application deadline:* For fall admission, 7/1 for domestic students; for spring admission, 11/1 for domestic students. Applications are processed on a rolling basis. Application fee: $25 for international students. *Expenses:* Tuition, state resident: full-time $3,874; part-time $215 per hour. Tuition, nonresident: full-time $8,780; part-time $488 per hour. International tuition: $9,105 full-time. Tuition and fees vary according to course load. *Financial support:* In 2003–04, 10 research assistantships with full tuition reimbursements (averaging $11,258 per year), 2 teaching assistantships with full tuition reimbursements (averaging $13,428 per year) were awarded. Federal Work-Study, institutionally sponsored loans, and unspecified assistantships also available. Financial award applicants required to submit FAFSA. *Faculty research:* Forest hydrology, forest biometry, forest management/economics, forest biology, industrial forest operations. Total annual research expenditures: $1.6 million. *Unit head:* Dr. Steven H. Bullard, Interim Head, 662-325-2781, Fax: 662-325-8126, E-mail: shbullard@cfr.msstate.edu. *Application contact:* Diane D. Wolfe, Director of Admissions, 662-325-2224, Fax: 662-325-7360, E-mail: admit@admissions.msstate.edu.

North Carolina State University, Graduate School, College of Natural Resources, Department of Forestry, Raleigh, NC 27695. Offers MF, MS, PhD. Part-time programs available. *Faculty:* 64 full-time (10 women), 49 part-time/adjunct (0 women). *Students:* 82 full-time (36 women), 23 part-time (7 women); includes 6 minority (4 African Americans, 1 Asian American

Forestry

North Carolina State University (continued)
or Pacific Islander, 1 Hispanic American), 19 international. Average age 31. 59 applicants, 68% accepted. In 2003, 25 master's, 4 doctorates awarded. *Degree requirements:* For master's, thesis (for some programs), teaching experience; for doctorate, thesis/dissertation, teaching experience. *Entrance requirements:* For master's and doctorate, GRE General Test. Additional exam requirements/recommendations for international students: Required—TOEFL. *Application deadline:* For fall admission, 6/25 for domestic students, 3/1 for international students; for spring admission, 11/25 for domestic students, 7/15 for international students. Applications are processed on a rolling basis. Application fee: $45. *Expenses:* Tuition, state resident: part-time $396 per hour. Tuition, nonresident: part-time $1,895 per hour. *Financial support:* In 2003–04, 1 fellowship with tuition reimbursement (averaging $16,782 per year), 51 research assistantships with tuition reimbursements (averaging $5,639 per year), 8 teaching assistantships with tuition reimbursements (averaging $4,161 per year) were awarded. Institutionally sponsored loans also available. Financial award application deadline: 3/1. *Faculty research:* Forest genetics, forest ecology and silviculture, forest economics/management/policy, international forestry, remote sensing/geographic information systems. Total annual research expenditures: $1.8 million. *Unit head:* Dr. Frederick W. Cubbage, Head, 919-515-7789, Fax: 919-515-7231, E-mail: fred_cubbage@ncsu.edu. *Application contact:* Dr. Robert C. Abt, Director of Graduate Programs, 919-515-7563, Fax: 919-515-8149, E-mail: bob_abt@ncsu.edu.

Northern Arizona University, Graduate College, School of Forestry, Flagstaff, AZ 86011. Offers MSF, PhD. Part-time programs available. *Faculty:* 24 full-time (6 women), 14 part-time/adjunct (4 women). *Students:* 41 full-time (13 women), 26 part-time (7 women); includes 8 minority (2 African Americans, 2 American Indian/Alaska Native, 2 Asian Americans or Pacific Islanders, 2 Hispanic Americans). Average age 33. 33 applicants, 52% accepted. In 2003, 15 master's, 5 doctorates awarded. *Degree requirements:* For master's, thesis optional; for doctorate, thesis/dissertation. *Entrance requirements:* For master's and doctorate, GRE General Test. *Application deadline:* For fall admission, 3/15 for domestic students; for spring admission, 10/15 for domestic students. Applications are processed on a rolling basis. Application fee: $45. *Expenses:* Tuition, state resident: full-time $5,103. Tuition, nonresident: full-time $12,623. *Financial support:* In 2003–04, 44 research assistantships were awarded; fellowships, teaching assistantships, Federal Work-Study and tuition waivers (full and partial) also available. *Faculty research:* Multiresource management, ecology, entomology, recreation, hydrology. Total annual research expenditures: $1.4 million. *Unit head:* Dr. Thomas Kolb, Coordinator, 928-523-7491.

Oklahoma State University, Graduate College, College of Agricultural Sciences and Natural Resources, Department of Forestry, Stillwater, OK 74078. Offers M Ag, MS. *Faculty:* 15 full-time (0 women). *Students:* 3 full-time (2 women), 5 part-time (3 women); includes 2 minority (1 Asian American or Pacific Islander, 1 Hispanic American), 3 international. Average age 35. 4 applicants, 100% accepted, 2 enrolled. In 2003, 1 degree awarded. *Degree requirements:* For master's, thesis. *Entrance requirements:* Additional exam requirements/recommendations for international students: Required—TOEFL. *Application deadline:* For fall admission, 6/1 for domestic students. Applications are processed on a rolling basis. Application fee: $25 ($50 for international students). Electronic applications accepted. *Expenses:* Tuition, state resident: full-time $3,752; part-time $118 per credit hour. Tuition, nonresident: full-time $10,346; part-time $393 per credit hour. Tuition and fees vary according to course load. *Financial support:* In 2003–04, 11 research assistantships (averaging $13,783 per year) were awarded; teaching assistantships, career-related internships or fieldwork, Federal Work-Study, and tuition waivers (partial) also available. Support available to part-time students. Financial award application deadline: 3/1. *Faculty research:* Forest ecology, upland bird ecology, forest ecophysiology, urban forestry, molecular forest genetics/biotechnology/tree breeding. *Unit head:* Dr. Craig McKinley, Head, 405-744-5437.

Oregon State University, Graduate School, College of Forestry, Department of Forest Engineering, Corvallis, OR 97331. Offers MAIS, MF, MS, PhD. *Accreditation:* SAF (one or more programs are accredited). Part-time programs available. *Faculty:* 13 full-time (0 women). *Students:* 22 full-time (6 women), 1 part-time, 5 international. Average age 28. In 2003, 6 master's, 2 doctorates awarded. *Degree requirements:* For master's and doctorate, thesis/dissertation. *Entrance requirements:* For master's and doctorate, GRE General Test, minimum GPA of 3.0 in last 90 hours. Additional exam requirements/recommendations for international students: Required—TOEFL. *Application deadline:* For fall admission, 3/1 for domestic students. Applications are processed on a rolling basis. Application fee: $50. *Expenses:* Tuition, state resident: full-time $8,139; part-time $301 per credit. Tuition, nonresident: full-time $14,376; part-time $532 per credit. Required fees: $1,227. *Financial support:* Fellowships, research assistantships, career-related internships or fieldwork, Federal Work-Study, and institutionally sponsored loans available. Support available to part-time students. Financial award application deadline: 2/1. *Faculty research:* Timber harvesting systems, forest hydrology, slope stability, impacts of harvesting on soil and water, training of logging labor force. *Unit head:* Dr. Steven D. Tesch, Head, 541-737-4952, Fax: 541-737-4316, E-mail: teschs@for.orst.edu. *Application contact:* Rayetta Beall, Office Manager, 541-737-1345, Fax: 541-737-4316, E-mail: rayetta.beall@orst.edu.

Oregon State University, Graduate School, College of Forestry, Department of Forest Resources, Corvallis, OR 97331. Offers economics (MS, PhD); forest resources (MAIS, MF, MS, PhD). MS and PhD (economics) offered through the University Graduate Faculty of Economics. *Accreditation:* SAF (one or more programs are accredited). Part-time programs available. *Faculty:* 15 full-time (2 women), 3 part-time/adjunct (0 women). *Students:* 29 full-time (9 women), 1 part-time; includes 1 minority (American Indian/Alaska Native), 6 international. Average age 30. In 2003, 12 master's, 3 doctorates awarded. Terminal master's awarded for partial completion of doctoral program. *Degree requirements:* For master's, thesis (for some programs); for doctorate, thesis/dissertation. *Entrance requirements:* For master's and doctorate, GRE General Test, minimum GPA of 3.0 in last 90 hours. Additional exam requirements/recommendations for international students: Required—TOEFL. *Application deadline:* For fall admission, 2/1 for domestic students. Applications are processed on a rolling basis. Application fee: $50. *Expenses:* Tuition, state resident: full-time $8,139; part-time $301 per credit. Tuition, nonresident: full-time $14,376; part-time $532 per credit. Required fees: $1,227. *Financial support:* Fellowships, research assistantships, teaching assistantships, career-related internships or fieldwork, Federal Work-Study, and institutionally sponsored loans available. Support available to part-time students. Financial award application deadline: 2/1. *Faculty research:* Geographic information systems, long-term productivity, recreation, silviculture, biometrics, policy. *Unit head:* Dr. John D. Walstad, Head, 541-737-3607, Fax: 541-737-3049, E-mail: john.walstad@orst.edu. *Application contact:* Marty Roberts, Coordinator, 541-737-1485, Fax: 541-737-3049, E-mail: roberts@for.orst.edu.

Oregon State University, Graduate School, College of Forestry, Department of Forest Science, Corvallis, OR 97331. Offers MAIS, MF, MS, PhD. *Accreditation:* SAF (one or more programs are accredited). Part-time programs available. *Faculty:* 19 full-time (6 women), 1 (woman) part-time/adjunct. *Students:* 49 full-time (24 women), 4 part-time (1 woman); includes 4 minority (1 American Indian/Alaska Native, 3 Asian Americans or Pacific Islanders), 12 international. Average age 31. In 2003, 9 master's, 6 doctorates awarded. *Degree requirements:* For master's, thesis (for some programs); for doctorate, thesis/dissertation. *Entrance requirements:* For master's and doctorate, GRE General Test, minimum GPA of 3.0 in last 90 hours. Additional exam requirements/recommendations for international students: Required—TOEFL. *Application deadline:* For fall admission, 8/25 for domestic students; for spring admission, 3/1 for domestic students. Applications are processed on a rolling basis. Application fee: $50. *Expenses:* Tuition, state resident: full-time $8,139; part-time $301 per credit. Tuition, nonresident: full-time $14,376; part-time $532 per credit. Required fees: $1,227. *Financial support:* Fellowships, research assistantships, career-related internships or fieldwork, Federal Work-Study, and institutionally sponsored loans available. Support available to part-time students. Financial award application deadline: 2/1. *Faculty research:* Ecosystem structure and function, nutrient cycling, biotechnology, vegetation management, integrated forest protection. *Unit head:* Dr. W. Thomas Adams, Head, 541-737-6583, Fax: 541-737-1393.

Oregon State University, Graduate School, College of Forestry, Department of Wood Science and Engineering, Corvallis, OR 97331. Offers forest products (MAIS, MF, MS, PhD); wood science and technology (MF, MS, PhD). *Accreditation:* SAF (one or more programs are accredited). Part-time programs available. *Faculty:* 14 full-time (1 woman). *Students:* Average age 30. In 2003, 2 master's, 1 doctorate awarded. *Degree requirements:* For master's, thesis (for some programs); for doctorate, thesis/dissertation. *Entrance requirements:* For master's and doctorate, GRE General Test, minimum GPA of 3.0 in last 90 hours. Additional exam requirements/recommendations for international students: Required—TOEFL. *Application deadline:* For fall admission, 3/1 for domestic students. Applications are processed on a rolling basis. Application fee: $50. *Expenses:* Tuition, state resident: full-time $8,139; part-time $301 per credit. Tuition, nonresident: full-time $14,376; part-time $532 per credit. Required fees: $1,227. *Financial support:* Fellowships, research assistantships, career-related internships or fieldwork, Federal Work-Study, and institutionally sponsored loans available. Support available to part-time students. Financial award application deadline: 2/1. *Faculty research:* Biodeterioration and preservation, timber engineering, process engineering and control, composite materials science, anatomy, chemistry and physical properties. *Unit head:* Dr. Thomas E. McLain, Head, 541-737-4224, Fax: 541-737-3385, E-mail: thomas.mclain@orst.edu. *Application contact:* George Swanson, Program Support Coordinator, 541-737-4206, Fax: 541-737-3385, E-mail: george.swanson@orst.edu.

The Pennsylvania State University University Park Campus, Graduate School, College of Agricultural Sciences, School of Forest Resources, Program in Forest Resources, State College, University Park, PA 16802-1503. Offers M Agr, MFR, MS, PhD. *Students:* 28 full-time (10 women), 9 part-time (1 woman); includes 2 minority (1 African American, 1 American Indian/Alaska Native), 8 international. *Entrance requirements:* For master's and doctorate, GRE General Test. Application fee: $45. *Expenses:* Tuition, state resident: full-time $10,010; part-time $417 per credit. Tuition, nonresident: full-time $19,830; part-time $826 per credit. Full-time tuition and fees vary according to course level, course load, campus/location and program. *Unit head:* Dr. Wayne L. Myers, Chair, 814-863-0002, Fax: 814-865-3725, E-mail: wlm@psu.edu. *Application contact:* Emily Hill, Staff Assistant, 814-863-7221, Fax: 814-865-3725, E-mail: evh2@psu.edu.

Purdue University, Graduate School, College of Agriculture, Department of Forestry and Natural Resources, West Lafayette, IN 47907. Offers aquaculture, fisheries, aquatic science (MSF); aquaculture, fisheries, aquatic sciences (MS, PhD); forest biology (MS, MSF, PhD); natural resources and environmental policy (MS, MSF); natural resources environmental policy (PhD); quantitative resource analysis (MS, MSF, PhD); wildlife science (MS, MSF, PhD); wood science and technology (MS, MSF, PhD). *Faculty:* 28 full-time (3 women), 3 part-time/adjunct (1 woman). *Students:* 67 full-time (28 women), 3 part-time (all women); includes 3 minority (1 African American, 2 Hispanic Americans), 24 international. Average age 30. 44 applicants, 23% accepted, 9 enrolled. In 2003, 7 master's, 6 doctorates awarded. *Degree requirements:* For master's and doctorate, thesis/dissertation. *Entrance requirements:* For master's and doctorate, GRE General Test, minimum B+ average in undergraduate course work. Additional exam requirements/recommendations for international students: Required—TOEFL. *Application deadline:* For fall admission, 1/5 for domestic students; for spring admission, 9/15 for domestic students. Applications are processed on a rolling basis. Application fee: $55. Electronic applications accepted. *Financial support:* In 2003–04, 10 research assistantships (averaging $15,259 per year) were awarded; fellowships, teaching assistantships, career-related internships or fieldwork and scholarships/grants also available. Support available to part-time students. Financial award application deadline: 1/5; financial award applicants required to submit FAFSA. *Faculty research:* Wildlife management, forest management, forest ecology, forest soils, limnology. Total annual research expenditures: $200,000. *Unit head:* Dr. Robert K. Swihart, Interim Head, 765-494-3590, Fax: 765-494-9461, E-mail: rswihart@purdue.edu. *Application contact:* Kelly Garrett, Graduate Secretary, 765-494-3572, Fax: 765-494-9461, E-mail: kgarrett@purdue.edu.

See in-depth description on page 795.

Southern Illinois University Carbondale, Graduate School, College of Agriculture, Department of Forestry, Carbondale, IL 62901-4701. Offers MS. Part-time programs available. *Faculty:* 10 full-time (1 woman). *Students:* 10 full-time (4 women), 29 part-time (11 women); includes 3 minority (1 African American, 2 Hispanic Americans), 2 international. Average age 24. 11 applicants, 91% accepted, 1 enrolled. In 2003, 8 degrees awarded. *Degree requirements:* For master's, thesis. *Entrance requirements:* For master's, minimum GPA of 2.7. Additional exam requirements/recommendations for international students: Required—TOEFL. *Application deadline:* Applications are processed on a rolling basis. Application fee: $0. *Expenses:* Tuition, state resident: part-time $478 per hour. Tuition, nonresident: part-time $657 per hour. *Financial support:* In 2003–04, 18 students received support, including 3 fellowships with full tuition reimbursements available, 10 research assistantships with full tuition reimbursements available, 3 teaching assistantships with full tuition reimbursements available; career-related internships or fieldwork, Federal Work-Study, institutionally sponsored loans, and tuition waivers (full) also available. Support available to part-time students. *Faculty research:* Forest recreation, forest ecology, remote sensing, forest management and economics. *Unit head:* John Phelps, Chair, 618-453-3341, E-mail: jphelps@siu.edu.

Southern University and Agricultural and Mechanical College, Graduate School, College of Agricultural, Family and Consumer Sciences, Department of Urban Forestry, Baton Rouge, LA 70813. Offers MS. *Degree requirements:* For master's, thesis. *Entrance requirements:* For master's, GRE, minimum GPA of 3.0. Additional exam requirements/recommendations for international students: Required—TOEFL. *Faculty research:* Biology of plant pathogen, water resources, plant pathology.

State University of New York College of Environmental Science and Forestry, Faculty of Environmental and Forest Biology, Syracuse, NY 13210-2779. Offers chemical ecology (MPS, MS, PhD); conservation biology (MPS, MS, PhD); ecology (MPS, MS, PhD); entomology (MPS, MS, PhD); environmental interpretation (MPS, MS, PhD); environmental physiology (MPS, MS, PhD); fish and wildlife biology (MPS, MS, PhD); forest pathology and mycology (MPS, MS, PhD); plant science and biotechnology (MPS, MS, PhD). *Faculty:* 32 full-time (3 women), 1 (woman) part-time/adjunct. *Students:* 93 full-time (53 women), 53 part-time (23 women); includes 4 minority (1 Asian American or Pacific Islander, 3 Hispanic Americans), 16 international. Average age 30. 100 applicants, 52% accepted, 25 enrolled. In 2003, 28 master's, 7 doctorates awarded. *Degree requirements:* For master's, thesis (for some programs), registration; for doctorate, thesis/dissertation, comprehensive exam, registration. *Entrance requirements:* For master's and doctorate, GRE General Test, GRE Subject Test, minimum GPA of 3.0. Additional exam requirements/recommendations for international students: Required—TOEFL (minimum score 550 paper-based; 213 computer-based). *Application deadline:* For fall admission, 2/1 priority date for domestic students, 2/1 priority date for international students; for spring admission, 11/1 priority date for domestic students, 11/1 priority date for international students. Applications are processed on a rolling basis. Application fee: $50. Tuition, area resident: Part-time $288 per credit hour. Tuition, nonresident: part-time $438 per credit hour. Required fees: $300; $5 per credit hour. $18 per semester. One-time fee: $25 full-time. *Financial support:* In 2003–04, 86 students received support, including 17 fellowships with full and partial tuition reimbursements available (averaging $9,446 per year), 41 research assistantships with full and partial tuition reimbursements available (averaging $11,000 per year), 34 teaching assistantships with full and partial tuition reimbursements available (averaging $9,446 per year); Federal Work-Study, institutionally sponsored loans, scholarships/grants, health care benefits, and unspecified assistantships also available. *Faculty research:* Ecology, fish and wildlife biology and management, plant science, entomology. Total annual research expenditures: $2.6 million. *Unit head:* Dr. Neil H. Ringler, Chair, 315-470-6770, Fax: 315-470-

6934, E-mail: neilringler@esf.edu. *Application contact:* Dr. Dudley J. Raynal, Dean, Instruction and Graduate Studies, 315-470-6599, Fax: 315-470-6978, E-mail: esfgrad@esf.edu.

State University of New York College of Environmental Science and Forestry, Faculty of Forest and Natural Resources Management, Syracuse, NY 13210-2779. Offers environmental and natural resource policy (MS, PhD); environmental and natural resources policy (MPS); forest management and operations (MF); forestry ecosystems science and applications (MPS, MS, PhD); natural resources management (MPS, MS, PhD); quantitative methods and management in forest science (MPS, MS, PhD); recreation and resource management (MPS, MS, PhD); watershed management and forest hydrology (MPS, MS, PhD). *Faculty:* 28 full-time (5 women). *Students:* 48 full-time (18 women), 26 part-time (10 women); includes 2 minority (1 African American, 1 Hispanic American), 14 international. Average age 32. 47 applicants, 57% accepted, 14 enrolled. In 2003, 35 master's, 5 doctorates awarded. *Degree requirements:* For master's, thesis (for some programs), registration; for doctorate, thesis/dissertation, comprehensive exam, registration. *Entrance requirements:* For master's and doctorate, GRE General Test, minimum GPA of 3.0. Additional exam requirements/recommendations for international students: Required—TOEFL (minimum score 550 paper-based; 213 computer-based). *Application deadline:* For fall admission, 2/1 priority date for domestic students, 2/1 priority date for international students; for spring admission, 11/1 priority date for domestic students, 11/1 priority date for international students. Applications are processed on a rolling basis. Application fee: $50. Tuition, area resident: Part-time $288 per credit hour. Tuition, nonresident: part-time $438 per credit hour. Required fees: $300; $5 per credit hour. $18 per semester. One-time fee: $25 full-time. *Financial support:* In 2003–04, 43 students received support, including 9 fellowships with full and partial tuition reimbursements available (averaging $9,446 per year), 15 research assistantships with full and partial tuition reimbursements available (averaging $10,000 per year), 14 teaching assistantships with full and partial tuition reimbursements available (averaging $9,446 per year); career-related internships or fieldwork, Federal Work-Study, institutionally sponsored loans, scholarships/grants, health care benefits, and unspecified assistantships also available. Financial award applicants required to submit FAFSA. *Faculty research:* Silviculture recreation management, tree improvement, operations management, economics. Total annual research expenditures: $1.9 million. *Unit head:* Dr. Chad P. Dawson, Chair, 315-470-6536, Fax: 315-470-6535, E-mail: cpdawson@esf.edu. *Application contact:* Dr. Dudley J. Raynal, Dean, Instruction and Graduate Studies, 315-470-6599, Fax: 315-470-6978, E-mail: esfgrad@esf.edu.

Stephen F. Austin State University, Graduate School, College of Forestry, Nacogdoches, TX 75962. Offers MF, MS, PhD. Part-time programs available. *Faculty:* 19 full-time (1 woman), 24 part-time/adjunct (2 women). *Students:* 28 full-time (9 women), 47 part-time (26 women); includes 3 minority (2 African Americans, 1 Hispanic American), 1 international. 65 applicants, 63% accepted. In 2003, 7 master's, 2 doctorates awarded. *Degree requirements:* For master's and doctorate, thesis/dissertation. *Entrance requirements:* For master's and doctorate, GRE General Test. Additional exam requirements/recommendations for international students: Required—TOEFL. *Application deadline:* For fall admission, 8/1 for domestic students; for spring admission, 12/15 for domestic students. Applications are processed on a rolling basis. Application fee: $25 ($50 for international students). *Expenses:* Tuition, state resident: part-time $46 per hour. Tuition, nonresident: part-time $282 per hour. Required fees: $71 per hour. Tuition and fees vary according to reciprocity agreements. *Financial support:* In 2003–04, 20 research assistantships (averaging $13,000 per year), 4 teaching assistantships (averaging $7,066 per year) were awarded. Career-related internships or fieldwork and Federal Work-Study also available. Support available to part-time students. Financial award application deadline: 3/1. *Faculty research:* Wildlife management, basic plant science, forest recreation, multipurpose land management. *Unit head:* Dr. Scott Beasley, Dean, 936-468-3304, E-mail: sbeasley@sfasu.edu.

Texas A&M University, College of Agriculture and Life Sciences, Department of Forest Science, College Station, TX 77843. Offers forestry (MS, PhD); natural resources development (M Agr). Part-time programs available. *Faculty:* 8 full-time (4 women). *Students:* 14 full-time (3 women), 10 part-time (3 women), 11 international. Average age 27. 15 applicants, 60% accepted, 8 enrolled. In 2003, 1 master's, 3 doctorates awarded. Terminal master's awarded for partial completion of doctoral program. *Degree requirements:* For master's, thesis (for some programs); for doctorate, thesis/dissertation. *Entrance requirements:* For master's and doctorate, GRE General Test. Additional exam requirements/recommendations for international students: Required—TOEFL. *Application deadline:* For fall admission, 3/1 for domestic students; for spring admission, 11/1 priority date for domestic students. Applications are processed on a rolling basis. Application fee: $50 ($75 for international students). Electronic applications accepted. *Expenses:* Tuition, state resident: full-time $3,420. Tuition, nonresident: full-time $9,084. Required fees: $1,861. *Financial support:* In 2003–04, fellowships with partial tuition reimbursements (averaging $15,000 per year), 7 research assistantships with partial tuition reimbursements (averaging $15,000 per year), 5 teaching assistantships with partial tuition reimbursements (averaging $15,000 per year) were awarded. Career-related internships or fieldwork and institutionally sponsored loans also available. Support available to part-time students. Financial award application deadline: 3/1; financial award applicants required to submit FAFSA. *Faculty research:* Expert systems, geographic information systems, economics, biology, genetics. *Unit head:* Dr. C. T. Smith, Professor and Head, 979-845-5033, Fax: 979-845-6049, E-mail: tat-smith@tamu.edu. *Application contact:* Dr. Carol Loopstra, Associate Head for Research and Graduate Studies, 979-862-2200, Fax: 979-845-6049, E-mail: c-loopstra@tamu.edu.

Université Laval, Faculty of Forestry and Geomatics, Department of Wood and Forest Sciences, Programs in Forestry Sciences, Québec, QC G1K 7P4, Canada. Offers M Sc, PhD. Terminal master's awarded for partial completion of doctoral program. *Degree requirements:* For master's, thesis (for some programs); for doctorate, thesis/dissertation, comprehensive exam. *Entrance requirements:* For master's and doctorate, knowledge of French. Additional exam requirements/recommendations for international students: Required—TOEIC or TOEFL. Electronic applications accepted.

Université Laval, Faculty of Forestry and Geomatics, Department of Wood and Forest Sciences, Programs in Wood Sciences, Québec, QC G1K 7P4, Canada. Offers M Sc, PhD. Terminal master's awarded for partial completion of doctoral program. *Degree requirements:* For master's, thesis/dissertation; for doctorate, thesis/dissertation, comprehensive exam. *Entrance requirements:* For master's and doctorate, knowledge of French. Electronic applications accepted.

Université Laval, Faculty of Forestry and Geomatics, Program in Agroforestry, Québec, QC G1K 7P4, Canada. Offers M Sc. *Degree requirements:* For master's, thesis (for some programs). *Entrance requirements:* For master's, English exam (comprehension of English), knowledge of French, knowledge of a third language. Electronic applications accepted.

University of Alberta, Faculty of Graduate Studies and Research, Department of Rural Economy, Edmonton, AB T6G 2E1, Canada. Offers agricultural economics (M Ag, M Sc, PhD); forest economics (M Ag, M Sc, PhD); rural sociology (M Ag, M Sc). Part-time programs available. *Faculty:* 13 full-time (1 woman), 6 part-time/adjunct (0 women). *Students:* 31 full-time (13 women), 21 part-time (11 women). Average age 25. 35 applicants, 83% accepted. In 2003, 10 master's, 2 doctorates awarded. *Degree requirements:* For doctorate, thesis/dissertation. *Entrance requirements:* Additional exam requirements/recommendations for international students: Required—TOEFL. Application fee: $60. Tuition charges are reported in Canadian dollars. Tuition, nonresident: full-time $3,921 Canadian dollars. International tuition: $7,113 Canadian dollars full-time. *Financial support:* In 2003–04, 4 fellowships, 12 research assistantships, 2 teaching assistantships were awarded. Scholarships/grants also available. *Faculty research:* Agroforestry, development, extension education, marketing and trade, natural resources and environment, policy, production economics. Total annual research expenditures: $850,000. *Unit head:* Marty Luckert, Graduate Coordinator, 403-492-4225, Fax: 403-492-0268. *Application contact:* Liz Bruce, Graduate Secretary, 780-492-4225, Fax: 780-492-0268, E-mail: rural.economy@ualberta.ca.

The University of Arizona, Graduate College, College of Agriculture and Life Sciences, School of Natural Resources, Watershed Resources Program, Tucson, AZ 85721. Offers MS, PhD. *Faculty:* 8 full-time (0 women), 3 part-time/adjunct (0 women). *Students:* 15 full-time (7 women), 12 part-time (5 women); includes 3 minority (1 American Indian/Alaska Native, 2 Hispanic Americans). Average age 33. 8 applicants, 100% accepted, 6 enrolled. In 2003, 4 master's awarded, leading to continued full-time study 50%, government 50%; 1 doctorate. *Degree requirements:* For master's and doctorate, thesis/dissertation, comprehensive exam, registration. *Entrance requirements:* For master's and doctorate, GRE General Test, minimum GPA of 3.0, 3 letters of recommendation. Additional exam requirements/recommendations for international students: Required—TOEFL (minimum score 550 paper-based; 213 computer-based). *Application deadline:* For fall admission, 8/1 priority date for domestic students, 12/1 priority date for international students. Applications are processed on a rolling basis. Application fee: $50. *Expenses:* Tuition, state resident: part-time $196 per unit. Tuition, nonresident: part-time $326 per unit. *Financial support:* Research assistantships with tuition reimbursements, teaching assistantships, career-related internships or fieldwork, scholarships/grants, health care benefits, tuition waivers (partial), and unspecified assistantships available. *Faculty research:* Forest fuel characteristics, prescribed fire, tree ring-fire scar anaylsis, erosion, sedimentation. *Unit head:* Dr. Malcolm J. Zwolinski, Chair, 520-621-7255, Fax: 520-621-8801. *Application contact:* Cheryl L. Craddock, Academic Coordinator, 520-621-7260, Fax: 520-621-8801, E-mail: ccraddoc@email.arizona.edu.

University of Arkansas at Monticello, School of Forest Resources, Monticello, AR 71656. Offers MS. Part-time programs available. *Degree requirements:* For master's, thesis, comprehensive exam. *Entrance requirements:* For master's, GRE General Test, minimum GPA of 2.7. Additional exam requirements/recommendations for international students: Required—TOEFL (minimum score 550 paper-based; 213 computer-based). *Faculty research:* Geographic information systems/remote sensing, forest ecology, wildlife ecology and management.

The University of British Columbia, Faculty of Graduate Studies, Faculty of Forestry, Vancouver, BC V6T 1Z1, Canada. Offers M Sc, MA Sc, MF, PhD. Part-time programs available. *Degree requirements:* For master's, thesis, thesis or comprehensive exam (MF, M Sc); for doctorate, thesis/dissertation, comprehensive exam, registration. *Entrance requirements:* Additional exam requirements/recommendations for international students: Required—TOEFL. Electronic applications accepted. *Faculty research:* Forest sciences, forest resources management, forest operations, wood sciences, conservation.

University of California, Berkeley, Graduate Division, College of Natural Resources, Department of Environmental Science, Policy, and Management, Berkeley, CA 94720-1500. Offers environmental science, policy, and management (MS, PhD); forestry (MF). *Faculty:* 62 full-time (16 women), 3 part-time/adjunct (2 women). *Students:* 165 (91 women); includes 30 minority (5 African Americans, 4 American Indian/Alaska Native, 11 Asian Americans or Pacific Islanders, 10 Hispanic Americans) 31 international. 345 applicants, 14% accepted, 30 enrolled. In 2003, 10 master's, 13 doctorates awarded. Terminal master's awarded for partial completion of doctoral program. *Median time to degree:* Of those who began their doctoral program in fall 1995, 98% received their degree in 8 years or less. *Degree requirements:* For master's, thesis optional; for doctorate, thesis/dissertation, qualifying exam. *Entrance requirements:* For master's and doctorate, GRE General Test, minimum GPA of 3.0. Additional exam requirements/recommendations for international students: Required—TOEFL; Recommended—TSE. *Application deadline:* For fall admission, 12/1 for domestic students. Application fee: $60. Electronic applications accepted. International tuition: $12,491 full-time. Required fees: $5,484. *Financial support:* In 2003–04, 10 fellowships with full tuition reimbursements (averaging $15,000 per year), 34 research assistantships with full tuition reimbursements (averaging $15,000 per year), 50 teaching assistantships with full tuition reimbursements (averaging $7,175 per year) were awarded. Unspecified assistantships also available. Financial award application deadline: 12/1; financial award applicants required to submit FAFSA. *Faculty research:* Biology and ecology of insects; ecosystem function and environmental issues of soils; plant health/interactions from molecular to ecosystem levels; range management and ecology; forest and resource policy, sustainability, and management. *Unit head:* Dr. Steven R. Beissinger, Chair, 510-642-8051, Fax: 510-643-3058, E-mail: beis@nature.berkeley.edu. *Application contact:* Sue Baumgartner, Student Affairs Officer, 510-642-6410, Fax: 510-642-4034, E-mail: espmgradproginfo@nature.berkeley.edu.

See in-depth description on page 749.

University of California, Berkeley, Graduate Division, Group in Wood Science and Technology, Berkeley, CA 94720-1500. Offers MS, PhD. *Students:* 1, 1 international. 2 applicants, 0% accepted. In 2003, 1 master's, 2 doctorates awarded. *Degree requirements:* For doctorate, thesis/dissertation, qualifying exam. *Entrance requirements:* For master's and doctorate, GRE General Test, minimum GPA of 3.0. Additional exam requirements/recommendations for international students: Required—TOEFL. *Application deadline:* For fall admission, 2/10 for domestic students. Application fee: $60. International tuition: $12,491 full-time. Required fees: $5,484. *Financial support:* Fellowships, research assistantships, career-related internships or fieldwork, Federal Work-Study, institutionally sponsored loans, tuition waivers (full and partial), and unspecified assistantships available. Financial award application deadline: 1/5; financial award applicants required to submit FAFSA. *Unit head:* Frank Beall, Chair.

University of Florida, Graduate School, College of Agricultural and Life Sciences, School of Forest Resources and Conservation, Gainesville, FL 32611. Offers MFRC, MS, PhD, JD/MFRC, JD/MS, JD/PhD. Part-time programs available. *Faculty:* 33. *Students:* 51 full-time (29 women), 15 part-time (3 women); includes 5 minority (1 African American, 1 American Indian/Alaska Native, 2 Asian Americans or Pacific Islanders, 1 Hispanic American), 20 international. Average age 24. 101 applicants, 35% accepted. In 2003, 12 master's, 5 doctorates awarded. *Degree requirements:* For master's, project (MFRC), thesis defense (MS); for doctorate, thesis/dissertation, qualifying exams, defense. *Entrance requirements:* For master's and doctorate, GRE General Test, minimum GPA of 3.0. Additional exam requirements/recommendations for international students: Required—TOEFL. *Application deadline:* For fall admission, 6/1 for domestic students; for spring admission, 10/1 for domestic students. Applications are processed on a rolling basis. Application fee: $20. Electronic applications accepted. *Expenses:* Tuition, state resident: part-time $205 per credit hour. Tuition, nonresident: part-time $775 per credit hour. *Financial support:* In 2003–04, 3 fellowships with full tuition reimbursements, 31 research assistantships with full tuition reimbursements, 2 teaching assistantships with full tuition reimbursements were awarded. Federal Work-Study and institutionally sponsored loans also available. Support available to part-time students. *Faculty research:* Forest biology and ecology, agroforestry and tropical forestry, forest management, economics, and policy, natural resource education and ecotourism. *Unit head:* Dr. Tim White, Director, 352-846-0850, Fax: 352-392-1707, E-mail: tlwhite@ufl.edu. *Application contact:* Dr. George M. Blakeslee, Graduate Coordinator, 352-846-0845, Fax: 352-392-1707, E-mail: gb4stree@ufl.edu.

University of Georgia, Graduate School, School of Forest Resources, Athens, GA 30602. Offers MFR, MS, PhD. *Faculty:* 48 full-time (3 women). *Students:* 121 full-time (36 women), 23 part-time (7 women); includes 7 minority (4 African Americans, 2 Asian Americans or Pacific Islanders, 1 Hispanic American), 29 international. 65 applicants, 48% accepted. In 2003, 37 master's, 6 doctorates awarded. *Degree requirements:* For master's, thesis (MS); for doctorate, one foreign language, thesis/dissertation. *Entrance requirements:* For master's and doctorate, GRE General Test. *Application deadline:* For fall admission, 7/1 for domestic students; for spring admission, 11/15 for domestic students. Application fee: $50. Electronic applications accepted. *Expenses:* Tuition, state resident: part-time $161 per hour. Tuition, nonresident: part-time $690 per hour. One-time fee: $435 part-time. *Financial support:* Fellowships, research assistantships, teaching assistantships, unspecified assistantships available. *Unit head:* Dr. James M. Sweeney, Interim Dean, 706-542-2866, Fax: 706-542-2281, E-mail: jsweeney@

Forestry

University of Georgia (continued)
smokey.forestry.uga.edu. *Application contact:* Dr. Barry D. Shiver, Graduate Coordinator, 706-542-3009, Fax: 706-542-8356, E-mail: shiver@smokey.forestry.uga.edu.

University of Idaho, College of Graduate Studies, College of Natural Resources, Department of Forest Products, Moscow, ID 83844-2282. Offers MS, PhD. *Students:* 11 full-time (1 woman), 2 part-time, 5 international. Average age 29. *Degree requirements:* For doctorate, thesis/dissertation. *Entrance requirements:* For master's, minimum GPA of 2.8; for doctorate, minimum undergraduate GPA of 2.8, 3.0 graduate. *Application deadline:* For fall admission, 8/1 for domestic students; for spring admission, 12/15 for domestic students. Application fee: $55 ($60 for international students). *Expenses:* Tuition, state resident: full-time $3,348. Tuition, nonresident: full-time $10,740. Required fees: $540. *Financial support:* Research assistantships, teaching assistantships available. Financial award application deadline: 2/15. *Unit head:* Dr. Thomas M. Gorman, Head, 208-885-9663.

See in-depth description on page 799.

University of Idaho, College of Graduate Studies, College of Natural Resources, Department of Forest Resources, Moscow, ID 83844-2282. Offers MS, PhD. *Students:* 21 full-time (6 women), 12 part-time (4 women); includes 3 minority (2 American Indian/Alaska Native, 1 Hispanic American), 4 international. Average age 31. *Degree requirements:* For doctorate, thesis/dissertation. *Entrance requirements:* For master's, minimum GPA of 2.8; for doctorate, minimum undergraduate GPA of 2.8, 3.0 graduate. *Application deadline:* For fall admission, 8/1 for domestic students; for spring admission, 12/15 for domestic students. Application fee: $55 ($60 for international students). *Expenses:* Tuition, state resident: full-time $3,348. Tuition, nonresident: full-time $10,740. Required fees: $540. *Financial support:* Research assistantships, teaching assistantships available. Financial award application deadline: 2/15. *Unit head:* Dr. JoEllen Force, Head, 208-885-7952.

See in-depth description on page 801.

University of Kentucky, Graduate School, Graduate School Programs in the College of Agriculture, Program in Forestry, Lexington, KY 40506-0032. Offers MSFOR. *Faculty:* 12 full-time (1 woman). *Students:* 10 full-time (6 women), 5 part-time. 11 applicants, 64% accepted, 5 enrolled. In 2003, 7 degrees awarded. *Degree requirements:* For master's, thesis optional. *Entrance requirements:* For master's, GRE General Test, minimum undergraduate GPA of 3.0. Additional exam requirements/recommendations for international students: Required—TOEFL (minimum score 550 paper-based; 213 computer-based). *Application deadline:* For fall admission, 7/18 for domestic students, 2/1 for international students. Applications are processed on a rolling basis. Application fee: $35 ($45 for international students). *Expenses:* Tuition, state resident: full-time $4,975; part-time $261 per credit hour. Tuition, nonresident: full-time $12,315; part-time $668 per credit hour. *Financial support:* Fellowships, research assistantships, teaching assistantships, career-related internships or fieldwork, Federal Work-Study, and institutionally sponsored loans available. Support available to part-time students. *Faculty research:* Forest ecology, silviculture, watershed management, forest products utilization, wildlife habitat management. *Unit head:* Dr. David Wagner, Director of Graduate Studies, 859-257-3373, Fax: 859-323-1031. *Application contact:* Dr. Brian Jackson, Associate Dean, 859-257-4905, Fax: 859-323-1928.

University of Maine, Graduate School, College of Natural Sciences, Forestry, and Agriculture, Department of Forest Management and Forest Ecosystem Science, Orono, ME 04469. Offers forest resources (PhD); forestry (MF, MS). *Accreditation:* SAF (one or more programs are accredited). Part-time programs available. *Students:* 37 full-time (12 women), 12 part-time (5 women), 12 international. Average age 30. 21 applicants, 81% accepted, 8 enrolled. In 2003, 9 master's, 4 doctorates awarded. *Degree requirements:* For master's, thesis; for doctorate, one foreign language, thesis/dissertation. *Entrance requirements:* For master's and doctorate, GRE General Test. Additional exam requirements/recommendations for international students: Required—TOEFL. *Application deadline:* For fall admission, 2/1 for domestic students. Applications are processed on a rolling basis. Application fee: $50. Electronic applications accepted. *Expenses:* Tuition, state resident: part-time $235 per credit. Tuition, nonresident: part-time $670 per credit. Tuition and fees vary according to course load. *Financial support:* In 2003–04, research assistantships with tuition reimbursements (averaging $13,500 per year), teaching assistantships with tuition reimbursements (averaging $12,276 per year) were awarded. Fellowships, career-related internships or fieldwork, Federal Work-Study, and institutionally sponsored loans also available. Financial award application deadline: 3/1. *Faculty research:* Forest economics, engineering and operations analysis, biometrics and remote sensing, timber management, wood technology. *Unit head:* Dr. David Field, Chair, 207-581-2856, Fax: 207-581-2858. *Application contact:* Scott G. Delcourt, Associate Dean of the Graduate School, 207-581-3218, Fax: 207-581-3232, E-mail: graduate@maine.edu.

University of Maine, Graduate School, College of Natural Sciences, Forestry, and Agriculture, Department of Plant, Soil, and Environmental Sciences, Orono, ME 04469. Offers biological sciences (PhD); ecology and environmental sciences (MS, PhD); forest resources (PhD); horticulture (MS); plant science (PhD); plant, soil, and environmental sciences (MS); resource utilization (MS). *Students:* 20 full-time (14 women), 8 part-time (5 women); includes 1 minority (Asian American or Pacific Islander), 2 international. Average age 31. 12 applicants, 42% accepted, 5 enrolled. In 2003, 2 degrees awarded. *Entrance requirements:* For master's and doctorate, GRE General Test. Additional exam requirements/recommendations for international students: Required—TOEFL. *Application deadline:* Applications are processed on a rolling basis. Application fee: $50. Electronic applications accepted. *Expenses:* Tuition, state resident: part-time $235 per credit. Tuition, nonresident: part-time $670 per credit. Tuition and fees vary according to course load. *Financial support:* In 2003–04, 9 research assistantships with tuition reimbursements (averaging $12,180 per year) were awarded; teaching assistantships, scholarships/grants, tuition waivers (full and partial), and unspecified assistantships also available. *Unit head:* Dr. M. Susan Erich, Chair, 207-581-2938, Fax: 207-581-3207. *Application contact:* Scott G. Delcourt, Associate Dean of the Graduate School, 207-581-3218, Fax: 207-581-3232, E-mail: graduate@maine.edu.

University of Massachusetts Amherst, Graduate School, College of Natural Resources and the Environment, Department of Natural Resources Conservation, Program in Forestry and Wood Technology, Amherst, MA 01003. Offers MS, PhD. Part-time programs available. *Faculty:* 17 full-time (2 women). *Students:* 14 full-time (4 women), 14 part-time (5 women); includes 1 minority (African American), 6 international. Average age 34. 16 applicants, 63% accepted, 7 enrolled. In 2003, 8 degrees awarded. Terminal master's awarded for partial completion of doctoral program. *Degree requirements:* For master's, thesis or alternative; for doctorate, variable foreign language requirement, thesis/dissertation. *Entrance requirements:* For master's and doctorate, GRE General Test. Additional exam requirements/recommendations for international students: Required—TOEFL (minimum score 530 paper-based; 197 computer-based). *Application deadline:* For fall admission, 2/1 priority date for domestic students, 2/1 priority date for international students; for spring admission, 10/1 for domestic students, 10/1 for international students. Applications are processed on a rolling basis. Application fee: $40 ($50 for international students). *Expenses:* Tuition, state resident: full-time $1,320; part-time $110 per credit. Tuition, nonresident: full-time $4,969; part-time $414 per credit. Required fees: $2,626 per term. Tuition and fees vary according to course load. *Financial support:* Fellowships with full tuition reimbursements, research assistantships with full tuition reimbursements, teaching assistantships with full tuition reimbursements, career-related internships or fieldwork, Federal Work-Study, scholarships/grants, traineeships, and unspecified assistantships available. Support available to part-time students. Financial award application deadline: 2/1. *Unit head:* Dr. William Patterson, Director, 413-545-2666, Fax: 413-545-4358.

University of Michigan, School of Natural Resources and Environment, Ann Arbor, MI 48109-1115. Offers industrial ecology (Certificate); landscape architecture (MLA, PhD); resource ecology and management (MS, PhD), including natural resources and environment (PhD), resource ecology and management (MS); resource policy and behavior (MS, PhD), including natural resources and environment (PhD), resource policy and behavior (MS); spatial analysis (Certificate). MLA, MS, PhD, and JD/MS offered through the Horace H. Rackham School of Graduate Studies. *Accreditation:* ASLA (one or more programs are accredited); SAF (one or more programs are accredited). *Degree requirements:* For master's, thesis or alternative, thesis, practicum, or group project; for doctorate, thesis/dissertation, oral defense of dissertation, preliminary exam, comprehensive exam, registration. *Entrance requirements:* For master's, GRE General Test; for doctorate, GRE General Test, master's degree. Additional exam requirements/recommendations for international students: Required—TOEFL (paper score 560; computer score 220) or IELTS. Electronic applications accepted. *Expenses:* Tuition, state resident: full-time $7,463. Tuition, nonresident: full-time $13,913. Full-time tuition and fees vary according to course load, degree level and program. *Faculty research:* Ecology, environmental policy, landscape architecture, climate change, Great Lakes, sustainable systems.

University of Minnesota, Twin Cities Campus, Graduate School, College of Natural Resources, Department of Forest Resources, Minneapolis, MN 55455-0213. Offers natural resources science and management (MS, PhD). Part-time programs available. *Faculty:* 19 full-time (3 women), 26 part-time/adjunct (1 woman). *Students:* 37 full-time (18 women), 26 part-time (10 women); includes 1 minority (Asian American or Pacific Islander), 9 international. 49 applicants, 45% accepted, 13 enrolled. In 2003, 9 master's, 4 doctorates awarded. Terminal master's awarded for partial completion of doctoral program. *Degree requirements:* For master's, thesis optional; for doctorate, thesis/dissertation, comprehensive exam, registration. *Entrance requirements:* For master's and doctorate, GRE. Additional exam requirements/recommendations for international students: Required—TOEFL (minimum score 550 paper-based; 213 computer-based). *Application deadline:* For fall admission, 1/1 priority date for domestic students, 1/1 priority date for international students; for spring admission, 10/15 for domestic students, 10/15 for international students. Applications are processed on a rolling basis. Application fee: $55 ($75 for international students). Electronic applications accepted. *Expenses:* Tuition, state resident: full-time $3,681; part-time $614 per credit. Tuition, nonresident: full-time $7,231; part-time $1,205 per credit. *Financial support:* In 2003–04, 4 fellowships with full tuition reimbursements, 26 research assistantships with full and partial tuition reimbursements were awarded. Teaching assistantships with full and partial tuition reimbursements, tuition waivers (partial) also available. Financial award application deadline: 1/15. Total annual research expenditures: $2 million. *Unit head:* Dr. Alan R. Ek, Head, 612-624-3400, E-mail: aek@umn.edu. *Application contact:* Kathleen A. Walter, Student Support Services Assistant, 612-624-2748, Fax: 612-624-6282, E-mail: kwalter@umn.edu.

University of Minnesota, Twin Cities Campus, Graduate School, College of Natural Resources, Department of Wood and Paper Science, Minneapolis, MN 55455-0213. Offers natural resources science and management (MS, PhD). *Faculty:* 10 full-time (2 women), 1 part-time/adjunct (0 women). *Students:* 6 full-time (1 woman), 6 part-time (2 women), 6 international. 6 applicants, 33% accepted, 1 enrolled. In 2003, 5 master's, 3 doctorates awarded. Terminal master's awarded for partial completion of doctoral program. *Degree requirements:* For master's, thesis optional; for doctorate, thesis/dissertation, comprehensive exam, registration. *Entrance requirements:* For master's and doctorate, GRE. Additional exam requirements/recommendations for international students: Required—TOEFL (minimum score 550 paper-based; 213 computer-based). *Application deadline:* For fall admission, 1/1 priority date for domestic students, 1/1 priority date for international students; for spring admission, 10/15 for domestic students, 10/15 for international students. Applications are processed on a rolling basis. Application fee: $55 ($75 for international students). Electronic applications accepted. *Expenses:* Tuition, state resident: full-time $3,681; part-time $614 per credit. Tuition, nonresident: full-time $7,231; part-time $1,205 per credit. *Financial support:* In 2003–04, 6 research assistantships with full tuition reimbursements were awarded; fellowships with full tuition reimbursements, teaching assistantships with full tuition reimbursements, tuition waivers (partial) also available. Financial award application deadline: 1/15. Total annual research expenditures: $422,223. *Unit head:* Dr. Shri Ramaswamy, Interim Head, 612-625-5200. *Application contact:* Kathleen A. Walter, Student Support Services Assistant, 612-624-2748, Fax: 612-624-6282, E-mail: kwalter@umn.edu.

University of Missouri–Columbia, Graduate School, School of Natural Resources, Program in Forestry, Columbia, MO 65211. Offers MS, PhD. *Faculty:* 14 full-time (1 woman). *Students:* 19 full-time (7 women), 11 part-time (2 women), 7 international. In 2003, 3 degrees awarded. Terminal master's awarded for partial completion of doctoral program. *Degree requirements:* For master's and doctorate, thesis/dissertation. *Entrance requirements:* For master's and doctorate, GRE General Test, minimum GPA of 3.0. *Application deadline:* Applications are processed on a rolling basis. Application fee: $45 ($60 for international students). *Expenses:* Tuition, state resident: full-time $5,205. Tuition, nonresident: full-time $14,058. *Financial support:* Research assistantships, teaching assistantships, institutionally sponsored loans and scholarships/grants available. *Unit head:* Dr. Bruce E. Cutter, Director of Graduate Studies, 573-882-2744, E-mail: cutterb@missouri.edu.

The University of Montana–Missoula, Graduate School, College of Forestry and Conservation, Missoula, MT 59812-0002. Offers ecosystem management (MEM, MS); fish and wildlife biology (PhD); forestry (MS, PhD); recreation management (MS); resource conservation (MS); wildlife biology (MS). *Faculty:* 34 full-time (4 women). *Students:* 158 full-time (44 women), 49 part-time (22 women); includes 3 minority (2 American Indian/Alaska Native, 1 Hispanic American), 16 international. 175 applicants, 35% accepted, 46 enrolled. In 2003, 28 master's, 5 doctorates awarded. *Degree requirements:* For doctorate, thesis/dissertation. *Entrance requirements:* For master's and doctorate, GRE General Test. Additional exam requirements/recommendations for international students: Required—TOEFL (minimum score 575 paper-based; 213 computer-based). *Application deadline:* For fall admission, 1/31 for domestic students; for spring admission, 8/31 priority date for domestic students. Applications are processed on a rolling basis. Application fee: $45. *Expenses:* Tuition, state resident: full-time $1,848; part-time $221 per credit. Tuition, nonresident: full-time $4,880; part-time $333 per credit. Required fees: $2,200. *Financial support:* In 2003–04, 25 research assistantships with tuition reimbursements, 12 teaching assistantships with full tuition reimbursements were awarded. Fellowships, career-related internships or fieldwork and Federal Work-Study also available. Financial award application deadline: 3/1; financial award applicants required to submit FAFSA. Total annual research expenditures: $6.7 million. *Unit head:* Dr. Perry Brown, Dean, 406-243-5521, Fax: 406-243-4845, E-mail: pbrown@forestry.umt.edu.

University of New Brunswick Fredericton, School of Graduate Studies, Faculty of Forestry and Environmental Management, Fredericton, NB E3B 6C2, Canada. Offers ecological foundations of forest management (PhD); forest engineering (M Sc FE, MFE); forest resources (M Sc F, MF, PhD). Part-time programs available. *Degree requirements:* For master's and doctorate, thesis/dissertation. *Entrance requirements:* For master's and doctorate, minimum GPA of 3.0. Additional exam requirements/recommendations for international students: Required—TOEFL, TWE. *Faculty research:* Genetics; soils; tree improvement, development, reproduction, physiology, and biotechnology; insect ecology; entomology.

University of New Hampshire, Graduate School, College of Life Sciences and Agriculture, Department of Natural Resources, Durham, NH 03824. Offers environmental conservation (MS); forestry (MS); soil science (MS); water resources management (MS); wildlife (MS). Part-time programs available. *Faculty:* 40 full-time. *Students:* 25 full-time (11 women), 31 part-time (21 women), 5 international. Average age 32. 74 applicants, 38% accepted, 16 enrolled. In 2003, 13 degrees awarded. *Degree requirements:* For master's, thesis or alternative. *Entrance requirements:* For master's, GRE General Test. Additional exam requirements/recommendations for international students: Required—TOEFL (minimum score 550 paper-based; 213 computer-based); Recommended—TSE. *Application deadline:* For fall admission, 4/1 for domestic students; for winter admission, 12/1 for domestic students. Applications are processed on a rolling basis. Application fee: $50. Electronic applications accepted. Tuition, area resident: Full-time $7,070. *Expenses:* Tuition, state resident: full-time $10,605. Tuition, nonresident: full-time $17,430. Required fees: $15. *Financial support:* In 2003–04, 3 fellowships, 15 research assistantships, 12 teaching assistantships were awarded. Career-related internships or fieldwork, Federal Work-Study, scholarships/grants, and tuition waivers (full and partial) also available. Support available to part-time students. Financial award application deadline: 2/15. *Unit head:* Dr. William H. McDowell, Chairperson, 603-862-2249, E-mail: tehoward@cisunix.unh.edu. *Application contact:* Linda Scogin, Administrative Assistant, 603-862-3932, E-mail: natural.resources @unh.edu.

The University of Tennessee, Graduate School, College of Agricultural Sciences and Natural Resources, Department of Forestry, Wildlife, and Fisheries, Program in Forestry, Knoxville, TN 37996. Offers MS. *Degree requirements:* For master's, thesis or alternative. *Entrance requirements:* For master's, GRE General Test, minimum GPA of 2.7. Additional exam requirements/recommendations for international students: Required—TOEFL. Electronic applications accepted.

University of Toronto, School of Graduate Studies, Life Sciences Division, Faculty of Forestry, Toronto, ON M5S 1A1, Canada. Offers M Sc F, MFC, PhD. *Faculty:* 40 full-time (5 women). *Students:* 98 full-time (39 women), 2 part-time, 20 international. 75 applicants, 71% accepted. In 2003, 18 master's, 5 doctorates awarded. *Degree requirements:* For master's, thesis, oral thesis/research paper defense, comprehensive exam; for doctorate, thesis/dissertation, oral defense of thesis. *Entrance requirements:* For master's, bachelor's degree in a related area, minimum B average in final year (M Sc F), final 2 years (MFC); resumé, 3 letters of reference; for doctorate, writing sample, minimum A– average, master's in a related area, 3 letters of reference, resumé. *Application deadline:* For fall admission, 2/1 priority date for domestic students, 4/15 priority date for international students. Application fee: $90 Canadian dollars. Tuition, nonresident: full-time $4,185. International tuition: $10,739 full-time. *Financial support:* Career-related internships or fieldwork available. *Unit head:* Rorke Bryan, Dean, 416-978-5752, Fax: 416-978-3834, E-mail: r.bryan@utoronto.ca. *Application contact:* Marilyn Wells, Registrar, 416-978-5751, Fax: 416-978-3834, E-mail: marilyn.wells@utoronto.ca.

University of Vermont, Graduate College, School of Natural Resources, Program in Forestry, Burlington, VT 05405. Offers MS. *Students:* 12 (6 women); includes 1 minority (Hispanic American) 15 applicants, 47% accepted, 4 enrolled. In 2003, 5 degrees awarded. *Degree requirements:* For master's, thesis. *Entrance requirements:* For master's, GRE General Test. Additional exam requirements/recommendations for international students: Required—TOEFL. *Application deadline:* For fall admission, 3/1 for domestic students. Applications are processed on a rolling basis. Application fee: $25. *Expenses:* Tuition, state resident: part-time $362 per credit hour. Tuition, nonresident: part-time $906 per credit hour. *Financial support:* Research assistantships, teaching assistantships available. Financial award application deadline: 3/1. *Faculty research:* Forest resource management. *Unit head:* Dr. J. Shane, Chairperson, 802-656-2620. *Application contact:* D. Wang, Coordinator, 802-656-2620.

University of Washington, Graduate School, College of Forest Resources, Seattle, WA 98195. Offers forest economics (MS, PhD); forest ecosystem analysis (MS, PhD); forest engineering/forest hydrology (MS, PhD); forest products marketing (MS, PhD); forest soils (MS, PhD); paper science and engineering (MS, PhD); quantitative resource management (MS, PhD); silviculture (MFR); silviculture and forest protection (MS, PhD); social sciences (MS, PhD); urban horticulture (MFR, MS, PhD); wildlife science (MS, PhD). *Degree requirements:* For master's, thesis (for some programs), registration; for doctorate, thesis/dissertation, comprehensive exam (for some programs), registration. *Entrance requirements:* For master's and doctorate, GRE, minimum GPA of 3.0. Additional exam requirements/recommendations for international students: Required—TOEFL. Electronic applications accepted. *Faculty research:* Ecosystem analysis, silviculture and forest protection, paper science and engineering, environmental horticulture and urban forestry, natural resource policy and economics.

University of Wisconsin–Madison, Graduate School, College of Agricultural and Life Sciences, Department of Forest Ecology and Management, Madison, WI 53706-1380. Offers forest science (MS, PhD); forestry (PhD). *Accreditation:* SAF. Part-time programs available. *Faculty:* 16 full-time (1 woman). *Students:* 48 full-time (23 women), 7 part-time (5 women); includes 9 minority (1 African American, 7 Asian Americans or Pacific Islanders, 1 Hispanic American), 13 international. Average age 32. 42 applicants, 10% accepted, 3 enrolled. In 2003, 5 master's, 5 doctorates awarded. *Degree requirements:* For master's, thesis (for some programs); for doctorate, thesis/dissertation. *Entrance requirements:* For master's and doctorate, GRE. Additional exam requirements/recommendations for international students: Required—TOEFL. *Application deadline:* For fall admission, 8/30 for domestic students; for spring admission, 12/31 priority date for domestic students. Applications are processed on a rolling basis. Application fee: $45. Electronic applications accepted. Tuition, area resident: Full-time $7,593; part-time $476 per credit. Tuition, nonresident: full-time $22,824; part-time $1,430 per credit. Required fees: $292; $38 per credit. Part-time tuition and fees vary according to course load and reciprocity agreements. *Financial support:* In 2003–04, 36 research assistantships with full tuition reimbursements (averaging $17,430 per year) were awarded; fellowships with full tuition reimbursements, career-related internships or fieldwork, Federal Work-Study, institutionally sponsored loans, health care benefits, and unspecified assistantships also available. Support available to part-time students. *Faculty research:* Forest and landscape ecology, forest biology, wood and fiber science, social forestry, recreation resources. Total annual research expenditures: $3.5 million. *Unit head:* Raymond P. Guries, Chair, 608-262-0449, Fax: 608-262-9922, E-mail: rpguries@wisc.edu. *Application contact:* Diane Walton, Program Assistant, 608-262-9975, Fax: 608-262-9922, E-mail: dwalton@wisc.edu.

Utah State University, School of Graduate Studies, College of Natural Resources, Department of Forest, Range, and Wildlife Sciences, Logan, UT 84322. Offers ecology (MS, PhD); forestry (MS, PhD); range science (MS, PhD); wildlife biology (MS, PhD). Part-time programs available. *Faculty:* 22 full-time (4 women), 17 part-time/adjunct (3 women). *Students:* 55 full-time (21 women), 16 part-time (9 women), 7 international. Average age 24. 42 applicants, 33% accepted, 10 enrolled. In 2003, 8 master's, 2 doctorates awarded. *Degree requirements:* For master's and doctorate, thesis/dissertation. *Entrance requirements:* For master's and doctorate, GRE General Test, minimum GPA of 3.0. Additional exam requirements/recommendations for international students: Required—TOEFL. *Application deadline:* For fall admission, 6/15 for domestic students; for spring admission, 10/15 for domestic students. Applications are processed on a rolling basis. Application fee: $50 ($60 for international students). *Expenses:* Tuition, state resident: part-time $270 per credit hour. Tuition, nonresident: part-time $946 per credit hour. Required fees: $173 per credit hour. *Financial support:* In 2003–04, 14 research assistantships with partial tuition reimbursements (averaging $13,600 per year) were awarded; fellowships, teaching assistantships, career-related internships or fieldwork, Federal Work-Study, and institutionally sponsored loans also available. *Faculty research:* Range plant ecophysiology, plant community ecology, ruminant nutrition, population ecology. Total annual research expenditures: $3.5 million. *Unit head:* Dr. David W. Roberts, Interim Head, 435-797-2503, Fax: 435-797-3796, E-mail: ggriffeth@cnr.usu.edu. *Application contact:* Gaye Griffeth, Staff Assistant, 435-797-2503, Fax: 435-797-3796, E-mail: ggriffeth@cnr.usu.edu.

Virginia Polytechnic Institute and State University, Graduate School, College of Natural Resources, Department of Forestry, Blacksburg, VA 24061. Offers forest biology (MF, MS, PhD); forest biometry (MF, MS, PhD); forest management/economics (MF, MS, PhD); industrial forestry operations (MF, MS, PhD); outdoor recreation (MF, MS, PhD). *Faculty:* 22 full-time (1 woman). *Students:* 38 full-time (15 women), 30 part-time (17 women); includes 1 minority (Asian American or Pacific Islander), 6 international. Average age 30. 67 applicants, 69% accepted, 24 enrolled. In 2003, 12 master's, 3 doctorates awarded. *Entrance requirements:* For master's and doctorate, GRE General Test. Additional exam requirements/recommendations for international students: Required—TOEFL (minimum score 550 paper-based; 213 computer-based). *Application deadline:* Applications are processed on a rolling basis. Application fee: $45. Electronic applications accepted. Tuition, area resident: Full-time $6,039; part-time $336 per credit. Tuition, nonresident: full-time $9,708; part-time $539 per credit. Required fees: $905; $130 per credit. *Financial support:* In 2003–04, 30 research assistantships with full tuition reimbursements (averaging $15,443 per year), 4 teaching assistantships with full tuition reimbursements (averaging $12,623 per year) were awarded. Career-related internships or fieldwork, Federal Work-Study, scholarships/grants, and unspecified assistantships also available. Financial award application deadline: 4/1. *Unit head:* Dr. Harold E. Burkhart, Head, 540-231-6952, Fax: 540-231-3698, E-mail: burkhart@vt.edu. *Application contact:* Sue Snow, Information Contact, 540-231-5483, Fax: 540-231-3698, E-mail: suesnow@vt.edu.

Virginia Polytechnic Institute and State University, Graduate School, College of Natural Resources, Department of Wood Science and Forest Products, Blacksburg, VA 24061. Offers forest products marketing (MF, MS, PhD); wood science and engineering (MF, MS, PhD). *Faculty:* 13 full-time (1 woman). *Students:* 13 full-time (2 women), 5 part-time (2 women); includes 1 minority (African American), 3 international. Average age 29. 13 applicants, 54% accepted, 4 enrolled. In 2003, 5 master's, 1 doctorate awarded. *Entrance requirements:* For master's and doctorate, GRE General Test. Additional exam requirements/recommendations for international students: Required—TOEFL (minimum score 550 paper-based; 213 computer-based). *Application deadline:* Applications are processed on a rolling basis. Application fee: $45. Electronic applications accepted. Tuition, area resident: Full-time $6,039; part-time $336 per credit. Tuition, nonresident: full-time $9,708; part-time $539 per credit. Required fees: $905; $130 per credit. *Financial support:* In 2003–04, 12 research assistantships with full tuition reimbursements (averaging $12,173 per year), 2 teaching assistantships with full tuition reimbursements (averaging $10,686 per year) were awarded. Career-related internships or fieldwork, Federal Work-Study, scholarships/grants, and unspecified assistantships also available. Financial award application deadline: 4/1. *Faculty research:* Wood chemistry, wood engineering, wood composites, wood processing, forest products marketing/management, recycling. *Unit head:* Dr. Paul M. Winistorfer, Head, 540-231-8854, Fax: 540-231-8176, E-mail: pstorfer@vt.edu. *Application contact:* D. Garnard, Information Contact, 540-231-8853, Fax: 540-231-8176, E-mail: garnandd@vt.edu.

West Virginia University, Davis College of Agriculture, Forestry and Consumer Sciences, Division of Forestry, Program in Forest Resource Science, Morgantown, WV 26506. Offers PhD. *Students:* 19 full-time (8 women), 5 part-time (1 woman), 3 international. Average age 33. 8 applicants, 38% accepted. In 2003, 4 degrees awarded. *Degree requirements:* For doctorate, thesis/dissertation, comprehensive exam. *Entrance requirements:* For doctorate, GRE, minimum GPA of 3.0. Additional exam requirements/recommendations for international students: Required—TOEFL. *Application deadline:* For fall admission, 6/15 priority date for domestic students, 6/15 priority date for international students; for winter admission, 9/15 for domestic students; for spring admission, 12/15 for domestic students. Applications are processed on a rolling basis. Application fee: $45. *Expenses:* Tuition, state resident: full-time $4,332. Tuition, nonresident: full-time $12,442. *Financial support:* In 2003–04, 15 research assistantships were awarded; teaching assistantships, career-related internships or fieldwork, Federal Work-Study, institutionally sponsored loans, and tuition waivers (full and partial) also available. Financial award application deadline: 2/1; financial award applicants required to submit FAFSA. *Faculty research:* Impact of management on wildlife and fish, forest sampling designs, forest economics and policy, oak regeneration. Total annual research expenditures: $900,000. *Unit head:* Ray R. Hicks, Coordinator, 304-293-2941 Ext. 2424, Fax: 304-293-2441, E-mail: rhicks3@wvu.edu.

West Virginia University, Davis College of Agriculture, Forestry and Consumer Sciences, Division of Forestry, Program in Forestry, Morgantown, WV 26506. Offers MSF. *Students:* 13 full-time (3 women), 4 part-time; includes 1 minority (Hispanic American), 1 international. Average age 29. 25 applicants, 40% accepted. In 2003, 6 degrees awarded. *Degree requirements:* For master's, thesis. *Entrance requirements:* For master's, GRE, minimum GPA of 3.0. Additional exam requirements/recommendations for international students: Required—TOEFL. *Application deadline:* For fall admission, 6/15 priority date for domestic students, 6/15 priority date for international students; for winter admission, 9/15 for domestic students; for spring admission, 12/15 for domestic students. Applications are processed on a rolling basis. Application fee: $45. *Expenses:* Tuition, state resident: full-time $4,332. Tuition, nonresident: full-time $12,442. *Financial support:* In 2003–04, 12 research assistantships, 1 teaching assistantship were awarded. Federal Work-Study, institutionally sponsored loans, and tuition waivers (full and partial) also available. Financial award application deadline: 2/1; financial award applicants required to submit FAFSA. *Faculty research:* Health and productivity on Appalachian forests, wood industries in Appalachian forests, role of forestry in regional economics. Total annual research expenditures: $900,000. *Unit head:* Ray R. Hicks, Coordinator, 304-293-2941 Ext. 2424, Fax: 304-293-2441, E-mail: rhicks3@wvu.edu.

Yale University, Graduate School of Arts and Sciences, Department of Forestry and Environmental Studies, New Haven, CT 06520. Offers environmental sciences (PhD); forestry (PhD). *Students:* 43 full-time (22 women); includes 6 minority (5 Asian Americans or Pacific Islanders, 1 Hispanic American), 9 international. 97 applicants, 10% accepted, 8 enrolled. In 2003, 4 degrees awarded. *Degree requirements:* For doctorate, thesis/dissertation. *Entrance requirements:* For doctorate, GRE General Test. *Application deadline:* For fall admission, 1/2 for domestic students. Application fee: $80. *Expenses:* Tuition: Full-time $25,600; part-time $6,400 per term. *Financial support:* Fellowships, Federal Work-Study and institutionally sponsored loans available. Support available to part-time students. *Unit head:* Dean, School of Forestry and Environmental Studies, 203-432-5109. *Application contact:* Admissions Information, 203-432-2770.

See in-depth description on page 805.

Yale University, School of Forestry and Environmental Studies, New Haven, CT 06511. Offers MES, MF, MFS, DFES, PhD, JD/MES, MBA/MES, MBA/MF, MES/MA, MES/MPH, MF/MA. *Accreditation:* SAF (one or more programs are accredited). Part-time programs available. Terminal master's awarded for partial completion of doctoral program. *Degree requirements:* For doctorate, thesis/dissertation. *Entrance requirements:* For master's and doctorate, GRE General Test. Expenses: Contact institution. *Faculty research:* Ecosystem science and management, coastal and watershed systems, environmental policy and management, social ecology and community development, conservation biology.

See in-depth description on page 805.

Natural Resources

Ball State University, Graduate School, College of Sciences and Humanities, Department of Natural Resources, Muncie, IN 47306-1099. Offers MA, MS. *Faculty:* 11. *Students:* 13 full-time (9 women), 2 part-time (1 woman), 5 international. Average age 25. 12 applicants, 92% accepted, 5 enrolled. In 2003, 8 degrees awarded. *Entrance requirements:* For master's, GRE General Test. Application fee: $25 ($35 for international students). *Expenses:* Tuition, state resident: full-time $5,748. Tuition, nonresident: full-time $14,166. *Financial support:* In 2003–04, 2 research assistantships with full tuition reimbursements (averaging $8,441 per year), 5 teaching assistantships with full tuition reimbursements (averaging $8,441 per year) were awarded. Career-related internships or fieldwork also available. Financial award application deadline: 3/1. *Faculty research:* Acid rain, indoor air pollution, land reclamation. *Unit head:* Hugh Brown, Chairman, 765-285-5780, Fax: 765-285-2606, E-mail: hbrown@bsu.edu.

Colorado State University, Graduate School, College of Natural Resources, Department of Geosciences, Fort Collins, CO 80523-0015. Offers earth resources (PhD); geology (MS), including geomorphology, hydrogeology, petrology/geochemistry and economic geology, sedimentology, structural geology. Part-time programs available. *Faculty:* 9 full-time (4 women), 2 part-time/adjunct (0 women). *Students:* 19 full-time (6 women), 17 part-time (7 women); includes 1 minority (American Indian/Alaska Native), 3 international. Average age 31. 56 applicants, 46% accepted, 8 enrolled. In 2003, 6 master's, 2 doctorates awarded. *Degree requirements:* For master's and doctorate, thesis/dissertation, registration. *Entrance requirements:* For master's and doctorate, GRE General Test, minimum GPA of 3.0. Additional exam requirements/recommendations for international students: Required—TOEFL (minimum score 550 paper-based; 213 computer-based). *Application deadline:* For fall admission, 2/1 priority date for domestic students, 2/1 priority date for international students. Applications are processed on a rolling basis. Application fee: $50. Electronic applications accepted. *Expenses:* Tuition, state resident: full-time $4,156. Tuition, nonresident: full-time $14,762. Required fees: $205. Tuition and fees vary according to course load, campus/location, program and reciprocity agreements. *Financial support:* In 2003–04, fellowships (averaging $3,800 per year), research assistantships with partial tuition reimbursements (averaging $14,400 per year), teaching assistantships with full tuition reimbursements (averaging $10,206 per year) were awarded. Career-related internships or fieldwork, Federal Work-Study, institutionally sponsored loans, scholarships/grants, and traineeships also available. Financial award application deadline: 2/15. *Faculty research:* Snow, surface, and groundwater hydrology; fluvial geomorphology; geographic information systems; geochemistry; bedrock geology. Total annual research expenditures: $407,835. *Unit head:* Dr. Judith L. Hannah, Head, 970-491-5662, Fax: 970-491-6307, E-mail: jhannah@cnr.colostate.edu. *Application contact:* Barbara Holtz, Staff Assistant, 970-491-5662, Fax: 970-491-6307, E-mail: barbh@cnr.colostate.edu.

Cornell University, Graduate School, Graduate Fields of Agriculture and Life Sciences, Field of Natural Resources, Ithaca, NY 14853-0001. Offers aquatic science (MPS, MS, PhD); environmental management (MPS); fishery science (MPS, MS, PhD); forest science (MPS, MS, PhD); resource policy and management (MPS, MS, PhD); wildlife science (MPS, MS, PhD). *Faculty:* 43 full-time. *Students:* 73 full-time (31 women); includes 10 minority (1 African American, 2 American Indian/Alaska Native, 5 Asian Americans or Pacific Islanders, 2 Hispanic Americans), 14 international. 107 applicants, 22% accepted, 18 enrolled. In 2003, 16 master's, 6 doctorates awarded. *Degree requirements:* For master's, thesis (MS), project paper (MPS); for doctorate, thesis/dissertation, comprehensive exam. *Entrance requirements:* For master's and doctorate, GRE General Test, 2 letters of recommendation. Additional exam requirements/recommendations for international students: Required—TOEFL (minimum score 550 paper-based; 213 computer-based). *Application deadline:* ; for spring admission, 10/30 for domestic students. Applications are processed on a rolling basis. Application fee: $60. Electronic applications accepted. *Expenses:* Tuition: Full-time $28,630. One-time fee: $50 full-time. *Financial support:* In 2003–04, 63 students received support, including 11 fellowships with full tuition reimbursements available, 27 research assistantships with full tuition reimbursements available, 25 teaching assistantships with full tuition reimbursements available; institutionally sponsored loans, scholarships/grants, health care benefits, tuition waivers (full and partial), and unspecified assistantships also available. Financial award applicants required to submit FAFSA. *Faculty research:* Ecosystem-level dynamics, systems modeling, conservation biology/management, resource management's human dimensions, biogeochemistry. *Unit head:* Director of Graduate Studies, 607-255-2807, Fax: 607-255-0349. *Application contact:* Graduate Field Assistant, 607-255-2807, Fax: 607-255-0349, E-mail: nrgrad@cornell.edu.

Duke University, Graduate School, Department of Environment, Durham, NC 27708. Offers natural resource economics/policy (AM, PhD); natural resource science/ecology (AM, PhD); natural resource systems science (AM, PhD). Part-time programs available. *Faculty:* 35 full-time. *Students:* 64 full-time (31 women); includes 7 minority (3 African Americans, 1 Asian American or Pacific Islander, 3 Hispanic Americans), 18 international. 151 applicants, 16% accepted, 15 enrolled. In 2003, 1 master's, 7 doctorates awarded. Terminal master's awarded for partial completion of doctoral program. *Degree requirements:* For doctorate, variable foreign language requirement, thesis/dissertation. *Entrance requirements:* For master's and doctorate, GRE General Test. Additional exam requirements/recommendations for international students: Required—IELT (preferred) or TOEFL. *Application deadline:* For fall admission, 12/31 for domestic students. Application fee: $75. *Expenses:* Tuition: Full-time $23,280; part-time $835 per unit. *Financial support:* Fellowships, research assistantships, teaching assistantships, Federal Work-Study available. Financial award application deadline: 12/31. *Unit head:* Kenneth Knoerr, Director of Graduate Studies, 919-613-8002, Fax: 919-684-8741, E-mail: nmm@duke.edu.

Duke University, Nicholas School of the Environment and Earth Sciences, Durham, NC 27708-0328. Offers coastal environmental management (MEM); environmental health and security (MEM); environmental science and policy (PhD); environmental toxicology, chemistry, and risk assessment (MEM); forest resource management (MF); global environmental change (MEM); resource ecology (MEM); resource economics and policy (MEM); water and air resources (MEM). PhD offered through the Graduate School. *Accreditation:* SAF (one or more programs are accredited). Part-time programs available. Terminal master's awarded for partial completion of doctoral program. *Degree requirements:* For master's, thesis (for some programs); for doctorate, thesis/dissertation. *Entrance requirements:* For master's, GRE General Test, previous course work in biology or ecology, calculus, statistics, and microeconomics; computer familiarity with word processing and data analysis; for doctorate, GRE General Test. Additional exam requirements/recommendations for international students: Required—TOEFL (minimum score 550 paper-based; 213 computer-based). Electronic applications accepted. Expenses: Contact institution. *Faculty research:* Ecosystem management, conservation ecology, earth systems, risk assessment.

See in-depth description on page 787.

Georgia Institute of Technology, Graduate Studies and Research, College of Engineering, School of Chemical and Biomolecular Engineering, Paper Science and Engineering Program, Atlanta, GA 30318-5794. Offers MS, PhD. *Accreditation:* SACS/CC. *Faculty:* 33 full-time (1 woman), 13 part-time/adjunct (1 woman). *Students:* 38 full-time (8 women); includes 12 minority (9 Asian Americans or Pacific Islanders, 3 Hispanic Americans). 40 applicants, 50% accepted, 10 enrolled. In 2003, 5 master's awarded, leading to business/industry 100%, 2 doctorates awarded, leading to business/industry 100%. Terminal master's awarded for partial completion of doctoral program. *Degree requirements:* For master's, thesis/dissertation; for doctorate, thesis/dissertation, comprehensive exam. *Entrance requirements:* For master's and doctorate, GRE, minimum GPA of 3.0. *Application deadline:* For fall admission, 2/1 for domestic students. Applications are processed on a rolling basis. Application fee: $50. Electronic applications accepted. *Expenses:* Tuition, state resident: part-time $1,925 per semester. Tuition, nonresident: part-time $7,700 per semester. Required fees: $434 per semester. Full-time tuition and fees vary according to program. *Financial support:* In 2003–04, 10 fellowships with tuition reimbursements (averaging $20,000 per year) were awarded *Application contact:* Janice Whatley, Academic Advisor, 404-894-2877, Fax: 404-894-2866, E-mail: jwhatley@chbe.gatech.edu.

Humboldt State University, Graduate Studies, College of Natural Resources and Sciences, Programs in Natural Resources, Arcata, CA 95521-8299. Offers MS. *Faculty:* 26 full-time (3 women), 5 part-time/adjunct (1 woman). *Students:* 57 full-time (32 women), 35 part-time (13 women); includes 10 minority (1 African American, 4 Asian Americans or Pacific Islanders, 5 Hispanic Americans), 2 international. Average age 30. 65 applicants, 52% accepted, 22 enrolled. In 2003, 21 degrees awarded. *Degree requirements:* For master's, thesis or alternative. *Entrance requirements:* For master's, appropriate bachelor's degree, minimum GPA of 2.5. Additional exam requirements/recommendations for international students: Required—TOEFL. *Application deadline:* Applications are processed on a rolling basis. Application fee: $55. *Expenses:* Tuition, state resident: full-time $2,539. *Financial support:* Fellowships, career-related internships or fieldwork and Federal Work-Study available. Support available to part-time students. Financial award application deadline: 3/1; financial award applicants required to submit FAFSA. *Faculty research:* Spotted owl habitat, presettlement vegetation, hardwood utilization, tree physiology, fisheries. *Unit head:* Dr. Gary Hendrickson, Coordinator, 707-826-4233, E-mail: thiesfel@humboldt.edu.

Iowa State University of Science and Technology, Graduate College, College of Agriculture, Department of Natural Resource Ecology and Management, Ames, IA 50011. Offers animal ecology (MS, PhD), including animal ecology, fisheries biology, wildlife biology; forestry (MS, PhD). *Faculty:* 23 full-time, 7 part-time/adjunct. *Students:* 36 full-time (13 women), 7 part-time (2 women), 8 international. 44 applicants, 36% accepted, 12 enrolled. In 2003, 6 master's, 4 doctorates awarded. *Median time to degree:* Master's–2.7 years full-time; doctorate–4.5 years full-time. *Degree requirements:* For master's, thesis (for some programs); for doctorate, thesis/dissertation. *Entrance requirements:* For master's and doctorate, GRE General Test. Additional exam requirements/recommendations for international students: Required—TOEFL (paper score 547; computer score 210) or IELTS (score 6). *Application deadline:* For fall admission, 1/1 priority date for domestic students, 1/1 priority date for international students; for spring admission, 9/1 priority date for domestic students, 9/1 priority date for international students. Application fee: $30 ($70 for international students). Electronic applications accepted. Tuition, nonresident: part-time $560 per credit. Required fees: $38 per unit. *Financial support:* In 2003–04, 35 research assistantships with full and partial tuition reimbursements (averaging $17,496 per year), 4 teaching assistantships with full and partial tuition reimbursements (averaging $17,496 per year) were awarded. *Unit head:* Dr. J. Michael Kelly, Chair, 515-294-1166. *Application contact:* Lyn Van De Pol, Information Contact, 515-294-6148, E-mail: lvdp@iastate.edu.

Iowa State University of Science and Technology, Graduate College, Interdisciplinary Programs, Program in Biorenewable Resources and Technology, Ames, IA 50011. Offers MS, PhD. *Students:* 3 full-time (0 women). 12 applicants, 100% accepted, 4 enrolled. *Entrance requirements:* For master's and doctorate, GRE General Test (international applicants). Additional exam requirements/recommendations for international students: Required—TOEFL (paper score 550; computer score 213) or IELTS (score 6.5). *Application deadline:* For fall admission, 1/1 priority date for domestic students, 1/1 priority date for international students. Application fee: $30 ($70 for international students). Tuition, nonresident: part-time $560 per credit. Required fees: $38 per unit. *Financial support:* In 2003–04, 1 research assistantship with full and partial tuition reimbursement (averaging $16,632 per year) was awarded *Unit head:* Dr. Brent Shawles, Chair, Supervising Committee, 515-294-6555, E-mail: brtgrad@iastate.edu. *Application contact:* Tonia McCarley, Program Coordinator, 515-294-6555, E-mail: brtgrad@iastate.edu.

Louisiana State University and Agricultural and Mechanical College, Graduate School, College of Agriculture, School of Renewable Natural Resources, Baton Rouge, LA 70803. Offers fisheries (MS); forestry (MS, PhD); wildlife (MS); wildlife and fisheries science (PhD). *Faculty:* 30 full-time (0 women). *Students:* 56 full-time (12 women), 16 part-time (7 women); includes 42 minority (1 American Indian/Alaska Native, 41 Hispanic Americans), 27 international. Average age 30. 34 applicants, 50% accepted, 11 enrolled. In 2003, 20 master's, 9 doctorates awarded. *Degree requirements:* For master's and doctorate, thesis/dissertation. *Entrance requirements:* For master's, GRE General Test, minimum GPA of 3.0; for doctorate, GRE General Test, MS, minimum GPA of 3.0. Additional exam requirements/recommendations for international students: Required—TOEFL (minimum score 550 paper-based; 213 computer-based). *Application deadline:* For fall admission, 1/25 priority date for domestic students, 5/15 priority date for international students. Applications are processed on a rolling basis. Application fee: $25. Electronic applications accepted. *Expenses:* Tuition, state resident: part-time $337 per hour. Tuition, nonresident: part-time $577 per hour. *Financial support:* In 2003–04, 2 fellowships (averaging $18,750 per year), 50 research assistantships with partial tuition reimbursements (averaging $15,766 per year), 2 teaching assistantships with partial tuition reimbursements (averaging $16,375 per year) were awarded. Federal Work-Study also available. Financial award application deadline: 4/15; financial award applicants required to submit FAFSA. *Faculty research:* Forest biology and management, aquaculture, fisheries biology and ecology, upland and wetlands wildlife. Total annual research expenditures: $7,325. *Unit head:* Dr. Bob G. Blackmon, Director, 225-578-4131, Fax: 225-578-4227, E-mail: bblackmon@agctr.lsu.edu. *Application contact:* Dr. Allen Rutherford, Coordinator of Graduate Studies, 225-578-4187, Fax: 225-578-4227, E-mail: druther@lsu.edu.

See in-depth description on page 789.

McGill University, Faculty of Graduate and Postdoctoral Studies, Faculty of Agricultural and Environmental Sciences, Department of Natural Resource Sciences, Montréal, QC H3A 2T5, Canada. Offers agrometeorology (M Sc, PhD); entomology (M Sc, PhD); forest science (M Sc, PhD); microbiology (M Sc, PhD); neotropical environment (M Sc, PhD); soil science (M Sc, PhD); wildlife biology (M Sc, PhD). *Faculty:* 18 full-time (1 woman). *Students:* 69 full-time, 2 part-time. 51 applicants, 37% accepted, 15 enrolled. In 2003, 12 master's, 4 doctorates awarded. *Degree requirements:* For master's and doctorate, thesis/dissertation. *Entrance requirements:* For master's, minimum GPA of 3.0; for doctorate, M Sc, minimum GPA of 3.0. Additional exam requirements/recommendations for international students: Required—TOEFL (paper score 550; computer score 213) or IELTS (paper score 6). *Application deadline:* For fall admission, 6/1 for domestic students, 3/1 for international students; for winter admission, 10/15 for domestic students; for spring admission, 2/15 for domestic students. Applications are processed on a rolling basis. Application fee: $60 Canadian dollars. Electronic applications accepted. Tuition, area resident: Full-time $1,668. *Expenses:* Tuition, state resident: full-time $4,173. Tuition, nonresident: full-time $9,468. Required fees: $1,081. *Financial support:* In 2003–04, 2 fellowships with partial tuition reimbursements (averaging $8,000 per year), 34 teaching assistantships were awarded. Institutionally sponsored loans also available. *Faculty research:* Toxicology, reproductive physiology, parasites, wildlife management, genetics. *Unit head:* Dr. Benoit Côté, Chair, 514-398-7952, Fax: 514-398-7990, E-mail: coteb@nrs.mcgill.ca. *Application contact:* Marie Kubecki, Graduate Student Coordinator, 514-398-7991, Fax: 514-398-7990, E-mail: kubecki@nrs.mcgill.ca.

Memorial University of Newfoundland, School of Graduate Studies, Interdisciplinary Program in Oil and Gas Studies, St. John's, NL A1C 5S7, Canada. Offers MOGS. Part-time programs available. *Entrance requirements:* For master's, undergraduate degree with minimum B standing in an oil and gas cognate discipline, minimum 5 years employment experience in the oil and gas sector. *Application deadline:* For fall admission, 2/15 for domestic students; for winter admission, 8/15 for domestic students. Application fee: $40. Tuition and fees charges are reported in Canadian dollars. *Expenses:* Tuition, state resident: part-time $733 Canadian dollars per semester. Tuition, nonresident: part-time $953 Canadian dollars per semester.

Required fees: $194 Canadian dollars per year. Tuition and fees vary according to degree level and program. *Unit head:* Gerrit Maureau, Director, 709-737-2017, E-mail: gmaureau@mun.ca. *Application contact:* Dr. Alex Faseruk, Graduate Officer, 709-737-8005, E-mail: afaseruk@mun.ca.

Montana State University–Bozeman, College of Graduate Studies, College of Agriculture, Department of Land Resources and Environmental Sciences, Bozeman, MT 59717. Offers land rehabilitation (interdisciplinary) (MS); land resources and environmental sciences (MS, PhD). Part-time programs available. *Faculty:* 13 full-time (1 woman), 2 part-time/adjunct (1 woman). *Students:* 13 full-time (9 women), 48 part-time (28 women); includes 1 minority (American Indian/Alaska Native), 2 international. Average age 32. 22 applicants, 73% accepted, 12 enrolled. In 2003, 12 master's, 1 doctorate awarded. *Degree requirements:* For master's, thesis (for some programs), comprehensive exam, registration; for doctorate, thesis/dissertation, comprehensive exam, registration. *Entrance requirements:* For master's and doctorate, GRE General Test. Additional exam requirements/recommendations for international students: Required—TOEFL (minimum score 550 paper-based; 213 computer-based). *Application deadline:* For fall admission, 7/15 priority date for domestic students, 5/15 priority date for international students; for spring admission, 12/1 priority date for domestic students, 10/1 priority date for international students. Applications are processed on a rolling basis. Application fee: $50. Electronic applications accepted. *Expenses:* Tuition, state resident: full-time $3,907; part-time $163 per credit. Tuition, nonresident: full-time $12,383; part-time $516 per credit. Required fees: $890; $445 per term. Tuition and fees vary according to course load and program. *Financial support:* Application deadline: 3/1; Total annual research expenditures: $4 million. *Unit head:* Dr. John Wraith, Interim Head, 406-994-4605, Fax: 406-994-3933, E-mail: jwraith@montana.edu.

North Carolina State University, Graduate School, College of Natural Resources and College of Agriculture and Life Sciences, Program in Natural Resources, Raleigh, NC 27695. Offers MNR, MS. *Faculty:* 20 full-time (3 women). *Students:* 34 full-time (17 women), 18 part-time (8 women); includes 3 minority (1 African American, 1 Asian American or Pacific Islander, 1 Hispanic American), 1 international. Average age 29. 24 applicants, 79% accepted. In 2003, 11 degrees awarded. *Degree requirements:* For master's, thesis optional. *Entrance requirements:* For master's, GRE. *Application deadline:* For fall admission, 6/25 for domestic students, 3/1 for international students; for spring admission, 11/25 for domestic students, 7/15 for international students. Application fee: $45. *Expenses:* Tuition, state resident: part-time $396 per hour. Tuition, nonresident: part-time $1,895 per hour. *Financial support:* In 2003–04, 19 research assistantships with tuition reimbursements (averaging $4,482 per year), 3 teaching assistantships with tuition reimbursements (averaging $4,098 per year) were awarded. Fellowships with tuition reimbursements *Unit head:* Dr. Robert C. Abt, Director of Graduate Programs, 919-515-7563, Fax: 919-515-8149, E-mail: bob_abt@ncsu.edu. *Application contact:* Dr. Michael G. Wagger, Director of Graduate Programs, 919-515-4269, Fax: 919-515-2167, E-mail: michael_wagger@ncsu.edu.

The Ohio State University, Graduate School, College of Food, Agricultural, and Environmental Sciences, School of Natural Resources, Columbus, OH 43210. Offers soil science (MS, PhD). Part-time programs available. *Faculty:* 61. *Students:* 45 full-time (26 women), 10 part-time (7 women); includes 2 minority (1 African American, 1 Hispanic American), 8 international. 54 applicants, 35% accepted. In 2003, 15 master's, 3 doctorates awarded. *Degree requirements:* For master's, thesis optional. *Entrance requirements:* For master's, GRE General Test. *Application deadline:* For fall admission, 8/15 for domestic students. Applications are processed on a rolling basis. Application fee: $40 ($50 for international students). *Expenses:* Tuition, state resident: full-time $7,233. Tuition, nonresident: full-time $18,489. *Financial support:* Fellowships, research assistantships, teaching assistantships, Federal Work-Study, institutionally sponsored loans, and unspecified assistantships available. Support available to part-time students. *Faculty research:* Environmental education, natural resources development, fisheries and wildlife management. *Unit head:* Dr. Gary W. Mullins, Director, 614-292-8522, Fax: 614-292-7432, E-mail: mullins.2@osu.edu. *Application contact:* Dr. David L. Johnson, Graduate Studies Committee Chair, 614-292-9803, Fax: 614-292-7432, E-mail: johnson.46@osu.edu.

Oklahoma State University, Graduate College, College of Agricultural Sciences and Natural Resources, Stillwater, OK 74078. Offers M Ag, M Bio E, MS, Ed D, PhD. Part-time programs available. *Faculty:* 233 full-time (37 women), 13 part-time/adjunct (2 women). *Students:* 149 full-time (62 women), 208 part-time (71 women); includes 19 minority (5 African Americans, 10 American Indian/Alaska Native, 1 Asian American or Pacific Islander, 3 Hispanic Americans), 158 international. Average age 30. 213 applicants, 58% accepted. In 2003, 79 master's, 32 doctorates awarded. *Degree requirements:* For doctorate, thesis/dissertation. *Entrance requirements:* Additional exam requirements/recommendations for international students: Required—TOEFL. *Application deadline:* Applications are processed on a rolling basis. Application fee: $25 ($50 for international students). Electronic applications accepted. *Expenses:* Tuition, state resident: full-time $3,752; part-time $118 per credit hour. Tuition, nonresident: full-time $10,346; part-time $393 per credit hour. Tuition and fees vary according to course load. *Financial support:* In 2003–04, 245 students received support, including 227 research assistantships (averaging $13,541 per year), 29 teaching assistantships (averaging $12,480 per year); fellowships, career-related internships or fieldwork, Federal Work-Study, and tuition waivers (partial) also available. Support available to part-time students. Financial award application deadline: 3/1. *Unit head:* Dr. Samuel E. Curl, Dean, 405-744-5398, Fax: 405-744-5339, E-mail: securl@okstate.edu.

Purdue University, Graduate School, College of Agriculture, Department of Forestry and Natural Resources, West Lafayette, IN 47907. Offers aquaculture, fisheries, aquatic science (MSF); aquaculture, fisheries, aquatic sciences (MS, PhD); forest biology (MS, MSF, PhD); natural resources and environmental policy (MS, MSF); natural resources environmental policy (PhD); quantitative resource analysis (MS, MSF, PhD); wildlife science (MS, MSF, PhD); wood science and technology (MS, MSF, PhD). *Faculty:* 28 full-time (3 women), 3 part-time/adjunct (1 woman). *Students:* 67 full-time (28 women), 3 part-time (all women); includes 3 minority (1 African American, 2 Hispanic Americans), 24 international. Average age 30. 44 applicants, 23% accepted, 9 enrolled. In 2003, 7 master's, 6 doctorates awarded. *Degree requirements:* For master's and doctorate, thesis/dissertation. *Entrance requirements:* For master's and doctorate, GRE General Test, minimum B+ average in undergraduate course work. Additional exam requirements/recommendations for international students: Required—TOEFL. *Application deadline:* For fall admission, 1/5 for domestic students; for spring admission, 9/15 for domestic students. Applications are processed on a rolling basis. Application fee: $55. Electronic applications accepted. *Financial support:* In 2003–04, 10 research assistantships (averaging $15,259 per year) were awarded; fellowships, teaching assistantships, career-related internships or fieldwork and scholarships/grants also available. Support available to part-time students. Financial award application deadline: 1/5; financial award applicants required to submit FAFSA. *Faculty research:* Wildlife management, forest management, forest ecology, forest soils, limnology. Total annual research expenditures: $200,000. *Unit head:* Dr. Robert K. Swihart, Interim Head, 765-494-3590, Fax: 765-494-9461, E-mail: rswihart@purdue.edu. *Application contact:* Kelly Garrett, Graduate Secretary, 765-494-3572, Fax: 765-494-9461, E-mail: kgarrett@purdue.edu.

See in-depth description on page 795.

State University of New York College of Environmental Science and Forestry, Faculty of Construction Management and Wood Products Engineering, Syracuse, NY 13210-2779. Offers environmental and resources engineering (MPS, MS, PhD). *Faculty:* 7 full-time (1 woman). *Students:* 6 full-time (0 women), 13 part-time (3 women); includes 1 minority (African American), 4 international. Average age 31. 7 applicants, 71% accepted, 2 enrolled. In 2003, 2 master's, 2 doctorates awarded. *Degree requirements:* For master's, thesis (for some programs), registration; for doctorate, thesis/dissertation, comprehensive exam, registration. *Entrance requirements:* For master's and doctorate, GRE General Test, minimum GPA of 3.0. Additional exam requirements/recommendations for international students: Required—TOEFL (minimum score 550 paper-based; 213 computer-based). *Application deadline:* For fall admission, 2/1 priority date for domestic students, 2/1 priority date for international students; for spring admission, 11/1 priority date for domestic students, 11/1 priority date for international students. Applications are processed on a rolling basis. Application fee: $50. Tuition, area resident: Part-time $288 per credit hour. Tuition, nonresident: part-time $438 per credit hour. Required fees: $300; $5 per credit hour. $18 per semester. One-time fee: $25 full-time. *Financial support:* In 2003–04, 8 students received support, including 1 fellowship with full tuition reimbursement available (averaging $9,446 per year), 1 research assistantship with full tuition reimbursement available (averaging $11,000 per year), 3 teaching assistantships with full tuition reimbursements available (averaging $9,446 per year); career-related internships or fieldwork, Federal Work-Study, institutionally sponsored loans, scholarships/grants, health care benefits, and unspecified assistantships also available. Financial award applicants required to submit FAFSA. Total annual research expenditures: $225,325. *Unit head:* Dr. Robert W. Meyer, Chair, 315-470-6835, Fax: 315-470-6879. *Application contact:* Dr. Dudley J. Raynal, Dean, Instruction and Graduate Studies, 315-470-6599, Fax: 315-470-6879, E-mail: esfgrad@esf.edu.

Texas A&M University, College of Agriculture and Life Sciences, Department of Forest Science, College Station, TX 77843. Offers forestry (MS, PhD); natural resources development (M Agr). Part-time programs available. *Faculty:* 8 full-time (4 women). *Students:* 14 full-time (3 women), 10 part-time (3 women), 11 international. Average age 27. 15 applicants, 60% accepted, 8 enrolled. In 2003, 1 master's, 3 doctorates awarded. Terminal master's awarded for partial completion of doctoral program. *Degree requirements:* For master's, thesis (for some programs); for doctorate, thesis/dissertation. *Entrance requirements:* For master's and doctorate, GRE General Test. Additional exam requirements/recommendations for international students: Required—TOEFL. *Application deadline:* For fall admission, 3/1 for domestic students; for spring admission, 11/1 priority date for domestic students. Applications are processed on a rolling basis. Application fee: $50 ($75 for international students). Electronic applications accepted. *Expenses:* Tuition, state resident: full-time $3,420. Tuition, nonresident: full-time $9,084. Required fees: $1,861. *Financial support:* In 2003–04, fellowships with partial tuition reimbursements (averaging $15,000 per year), 7 research assistantships with partial tuition reimbursements (averaging $15,000 per year), 5 teaching assistantships with partial tuition reimbursements (averaging $15,000 per year) were awarded. Career-related internships or fieldwork and institutionally sponsored loans also available. Support available to part-time students. Financial award application deadline: 3/1; financial award applicants required to submit FAFSA. *Faculty research:* Expert systems, geographic information systems, economics, biology, genetics. *Unit head:* Dr. C. T. Smith, Professor and Head, 979-845-5033, Fax: 979-845-6049, E-mail: tat-smith@tamu.edu. *Application contact:* Dr. Carol Loopstra, Associate Head for Research and Graduate Studies, 979-862-2200, Fax: 979-845-6049, E-mail: c-loopstra@tamu.edu.

Texas A&M University, College of Agriculture and Life Sciences, Department of Rangeland Ecology and Management, College Station, TX 77843. Offers natural resource development (M Agr); rangeland ecology and management (M Agr, MS, PhD). *Faculty:* 11 full-time (0 women). *Students:* 41 full-time (21 women), 28 part-time (7 women); includes 4 minority (2 Asian Americans or Pacific Islanders, 2 Hispanic Americans), 17 international. Average age 31.Terminal master's awarded for partial completion of doctoral program. *Degree requirements:* For master's, thesis optional; for doctorate, thesis/dissertation. *Entrance requirements:* For master's and doctorate, GRE General Test. Additional exam requirements/recommendations for international students: Required—TOEFL. *Application deadline:* For fall admission, 3/1 for domestic students; for spring admission, 8/1 priority date for domestic students. Applications are processed on a rolling basis. Application fee: $50 ($75 for international students). Electronic applications accepted. *Expenses:* Tuition, state resident: full-time $3,420. Tuition, nonresident: full-time $9,084. Required fees: $1,861. *Financial support:* In 2003–04, research assistantships (averaging $12,566 per year), teaching assistantships (averaging $12,200 per year) were awarded. Fellowships, career-related internships or fieldwork, scholarships/grants, and unspecified assistantships also available. Support available to part-time students. Financial award application deadline: 4/1; financial award applicants required to submit FAFSA. *Faculty research:* Plant ecology, restoration ecology, watershed management, integrated resource management, information technology. *Unit head:* Dr. Robert E. Whitson, Head, 979-845-5579, Fax: 979-845-6430, E-mail: r-whitson@tamu.edu. *Application contact:* Dr. Jennifer E. Funkhouser, Graduate Advisor, 979-845-5579, Fax: 979-845-6430, E-mail: j-funkhouser@tamu.edu.

Texas A&M University, College of Agriculture and Life Sciences, Department of Recreation, Park and Tourism Sciences, College Station, TX 77843. Offers natural resources development (M Agr); recreation and resources development (M Agr); recreation, park, and tourism sciences (MS, PhD). *Faculty:* 11 full-time (0 women). *Students:* 42 full-time (29 women), 8 part-time (6 women); includes 1 minority (Hispanic American), 25 international. Average age 28. 35 applicants, 43% accepted. In 2003, 6 master's, 4 doctorates awarded. *Degree requirements:* For master's, thesis (for some programs), internship and professional paper for M Agr; for doctorate, thesis/dissertation. *Entrance requirements:* For master's and doctorate, GRE General Test. Additional exam requirements/recommendations for international students: Required—TOEFL. *Application deadline:* For fall admission, 4/15 for domestic students; for spring admission, 10/15 priority date for domestic students. Applications are processed on a rolling basis. Application fee: $50 ($75 for international students). Electronic applications accepted. *Expenses:* Tuition, state resident: full-time $3,420. Tuition, nonresident: full-time $9,084. Required fees: $1,861. *Financial support:* In 2003–04, 5 research assistantships, 16 teaching assistantships were awarded. Fellowships, career-related internships or fieldwork, institutionally sponsored loans, and scholarships/grants also available. Financial award application deadline: 4/15; financial award applicants required to submit FAFSA. *Faculty research:* Administration and tourism, outdoor recreation, commercial recreation, environmental law, system planning. *Unit head:* Dr. Joseph T. O'Leary, Head, 979-845-5412, Fax: 979-845-0446, E-mail: joleary@rpts.tamu.edu. *Application contact:* Marguerite M. Van Dyke, Graduate Recruitment Coordinator, 979-845-5412, Fax: 979-845-0446, E-mail: mvandyke@rpts.tamu.edu.

Université du Québec à Montréal, Graduate Programs, Program in Earth Sciences, Montreal, QC H3C 3P8, Canada. Offers geology-research (M Sc); mineral resources (PhD); non-renewable resources (DESS). Part-time programs available. *Faculty:* 16 full-time (2 women), 16 part-time/adjunct (1 woman). *Students:* 51 full-time (9 women), 15 international. 18 applicants, 56% accepted. In 2003, 7 master's, 4 doctorates awarded. Terminal master's awarded for partial completion of doctoral program. *Median time to degree:* Of those who began their doctoral program in fall 1995, 90% received their degree in 8 years or less. *Degree requirements:* For master's, thesis (for some programs); for doctorate, thesis/dissertation. *Entrance requirements:* For master's, appropriate bachelor's degree or equivalent, proficiency in French. *Application deadline:* Applications are processed on a rolling basis. Application fee: $50. *Financial support:* In 2003–04, fellowships (averaging $5,000 per year), research assistantships (averaging $4,000 per year), teaching assistantships (averaging $1,000 per year) were awarded. Scholarships/grants also available. *Faculty research:* Economic geology, structural geology, geochemistry, Quaternary geology, isotopic geochemistry. *Unit head:* Alfred Jaouich, Director, 514-987-3000 Ext. 3378, Fax: 514-987-7749, E-mail: jaouich.alfred@uqam.ca. *Application contact:* Micheline Lacroix, Admissions Officer, 514-987-3000 Ext. 3370, Fax: 514-987-7749, E-mail: lacroix.micheline@uqam.ca.

University of Alberta, Faculty of Graduate Studies and Research, Department of Renewable Resources, Edmonton, AB T6G 2E1, Canada. Offers agroforestry (M Ag, M Sc, MF); conservation biology (M Sc, PhD); forest biology and management (M Sc, PhD); land reclamation and remediation (M Sc, PhD); protected areas and wildlands management (M Sc, PhD); soil science (M Ag, M Sc, PhD); water and land resources (M Ag, M Sc, PhD); wildlife ecology and management (M Sc, PhD). Part-time programs available. *Faculty:* 26 full-time (4 women), 22 part-time/adjunct (3 women). *Students:* 63 full-time (33 women), 50 part-time (20 women), 14 international. 122 applicants, 24% accepted, 22 enrolled. In 2003, 16 master's, 8 doctorates awarded. *Median time to degree:* Of those who began their doctoral program in fall 1995,

Natural Resources

University of Alberta (continued)

100% received their degree in 8 years or less. *Degree requirements:* For master's, thesis (for some programs); for doctorate, thesis/dissertation, comprehensive exam. *Entrance requirements:* For master's, 2-3 years of relevant professional experiences, minimum GPA of 3.0; for doctorate, minimum GPA of 3.0. Additional exam requirements/recommendations for international students: Required—TOEFL (minimum score 550 paper-based; 213 computer-based). *Application deadline:* For fall admission, 7/1 priority date for domestic students, 6/1 priority date for international students. Applications are processed on a rolling basis. Application fee: $0. Electronic applications accepted. Tuition charges are reported in Canadian dollars. Tuition, nonresident: full-time $3,921 Canadian dollars. International tuition: $7,113 Canadian dollars full-time. *Financial support:* In 2003–04, 63 students received support, including 21 research assistantships with partial tuition reimbursements available (averaging $2,800 per year), 28 teaching assistantships with partial tuition reimbursements available (averaging $1,900 per year); scholarships/grants and unspecified assistantships also available. *Faculty research:* Natural and managed landscapes. Total annual research expenditures: $6.1 million. *Unit head:* Dr. John R. Spence, Chair, 780-492-1426, Fax: 780-492-4323, E-mail: john.spence@ualberta.ca. *Application contact:* Sandy Nakashima, Graduate Program Secretary, 780-492-2820, Fax: 780-492-4323, E-mail: sandy.nakashima@ualberta.ca.

University of Alberta, Faculty of Graduate Studies and Research, Program in Business Administration, Edmonton, AB T6G 2E1, Canada. Offers international business (MBA); leisure and sport management (MBA); natural resources and energy (MBA); technology commercialization (MBA). *Accreditation:* AACSB. Part-time and evening/weekend programs available. *Faculty:* 77 full-time, 20 part-time/adjunct. *Students:* 131 full-time (56 women), 109 part-time (51 women). Average age 29. 525 applicants, 30% accepted, 90 enrolled. In 2003, 114 degrees awarded. *Median time to degree:* Master's–2 years full-time, 4 years part-time. *Degree requirements:* For master's, thesis or alternative. *Entrance requirements:* For master's, GMAT. Additional exam requirements/recommendations for international students: Required—TOEFL (minimum score 600 paper-based; 250 computer-based). *Application deadline:* For fall admission, 4/30 priority date for domestic students, 4/30 priority date for international students. Applications are processed on a rolling basis. Application fee: $0. Electronic applications accepted. Tuition charges are reported in Canadian dollars. Tuition, nonresident: full-time $3,921 Canadian dollars. International tuition: $7,113 Canadian dollars full-time. *Financial support:* Fellowships, research assistantships, teaching assistantships, career-related internships or fieldwork, scholarships/grants, health care benefits, and unspecified assistantships available. *Faculty research:* Natural resources and energy/management and policy/family enterprise/international business/healthcare research management. Total annual research expenditures: $1 million. *Unit head:* Dr. Vikas Mehrotra, Associate Dean, 780-492-3946, Fax: 780-492-7825, E-mail: vikas.mehrotra@ualberta.ca. *Application contact:* Joan A. White, Secretary, 780-492-3679, Fax: 780-492-2024, E-mail: joan.white@ualberta.ca.

The University of Arizona, Graduate College, College of Agriculture and Life Sciences, School of Natural Resources, Natural Resources Studies, Tucson, AZ 85721. Offers MS, PhD. *Faculty:* 10 full-time (1 woman). *Students:* 31 full-time (15 women), 12 part-time (5 women), 3 international. Average age 34. 16 applicants, 44% accepted, 5 enrolled. In 2003, 3 master's, 3 doctorates awarded. *Degree requirements:* For master's, thesis/dissertation; for doctorate, thesis/dissertation, comprehensive exam. *Entrance requirements:* For master's and doctorate, GRE General Test, minimum GPA of 3.0, 3 letters of recommendation. Additional exam requirements/recommendations for international students: Required—TOEFL (minimum score 550 paper-based; 213 computer-based). *Application deadline:* For fall admission, 8/1 priority date for domestic students, 12/1 priority date for international students. Applications are processed on a rolling basis. Application fee: $50. *Expenses:* Tuition, state resident: part-time $196 per unit. Tuition, nonresident: part-time $326 per unit. *Financial support:* Fellowships, research assistantships, teaching assistantships, scholarships/grants, health care benefits, tuition waivers (partial), and unspecified assistantships available. *Faculty research:* Global carbon markets and carbon sequestration, integrated watershed management and policy, conservation biology, landscape planning, wildlife conservation and management. *Unit head:* Dr. Mitchel P. McClaran, Chair, 520-621-7264, Fax: 520-621-8801, E-mail: mcclaran@u.arizona.edu. *Application contact:* Cheryl L. Craddock, Academic Coordinator, 520-621-7260, Fax: 520-621-8801, E-mail: ccraddoc@email.arizona.edu.

University of Arkansas at Monticello, School of Forest Resources, Monticello, AR 71656. Offers MS. Part-time programs available. *Degree requirements:* For master's, thesis, comprehensive exam. *Entrance requirements:* For master's, GRE General Test, minimum GPA of 2.7. Additional exam requirements/recommendations for international students: Required—TOEFL (minimum score 550 paper-based; 213 computer-based). *Faculty research:* Geographic information systems/remote sensing, forest ecology, wildlife ecology and management.

University of Connecticut, Graduate School, College of Agriculture and Natural Resources, Department of Natural Resources Management and Engineering, Field of Natural Resources Management and Engineering, Storrs, CT 06269. Offers natural resources (MS, PhD). *Faculty:* 11 full-time (1 woman). *Students:* 21 full-time (5 women), 5 part-time (3 women), 7 international. Average age 30. 15 applicants, 40% accepted, 4 enrolled. In 2003, 4 degrees awarded. Terminal master's awarded for partial completion of doctoral program. *Degree requirements:* For master's, comprehensive exam; for doctorate, thesis/dissertation. *Entrance requirements:* For master's, GRE General Test, GRE Subject Test. Additional exam requirements/recommendations for international students: Required—TOEFL (minimum score 550 paper-based; 213 computer-based). *Application deadline:* For fall admission, 2/1 priority date for domestic students, 2/1 priority date for international students; for spring admission, 11/1 for domestic students, 10/1 for international students. Applications are processed on a rolling basis. Application fee: $55. Electronic applications accepted. *Expenses:* Tuition, state resident: part-time $3,860 per semester. Tuition, nonresident: part-time $9,036 per semester. *Financial support:* In 2003–04, 18 research assistantships with full tuition reimbursements, 2 teaching assistantships with full tuition reimbursements were awarded. Fellowships, Federal Work-Study, scholarships/grants, health care benefits, and unspecified assistantships also available. Financial award application deadline: 2/1; financial award applicants required to submit FAFSA. *Application contact:* John Clausen, Chairman, Graduate Admissions, 860-486-0139, Fax: 860-486-5408, E-mail: john.clausen@uconn.edu.

University of Florida, Graduate School, College of Agricultural and Life Sciences, School of Forest Resources and Conservation, Gainesville, FL 32611. Offers MFRC, MS, PhD, JD/MFRC, JD/MS, JD/PhD. Part-time programs available. *Faculty:* 33. *Students:* 51 full-time (29 women), 15 part-time (3 women); includes 5 minority (1 African American, 1 American Indian/Alaska Native, 2 Asian Americans or Pacific Islanders, 1 Hispanic American), 20 international. Average age 24. 101 applicants, 35% accepted. In 2003, 12 master's, 5 doctorates awarded. *Degree requirements:* For master's, project (MFRC), thesis defense (MS); for doctorate, thesis/dissertation, qualifying exams, defense. *Entrance requirements:* For master's and doctorate, GRE General Test, minimum GPA of 3.0. Additional exam requirements/recommendations for international students: Required—TOEFL. *Application deadline:* For fall admission, 6/1 for domestic students; for spring admission, 10/1 for domestic students. Applications are processed on a rolling basis. Application fee: $20. Electronic applications accepted. *Expenses:* Tuition, state resident: part-time $205 per credit hour. Tuition, nonresident: part-time $775 per credit hour. *Financial support:* In 2003–04, 3 fellowships with full tuition reimbursements, 31 research assistantships with full tuition reimbursements, 2 teaching assistantships with full tuition reimbursements were awarded. Federal Work-Study and institutionally sponsored loans also available. Support available to part-time students. *Faculty research:* Forest biology and ecology, agroforestry and tropical forestry, forest management, economics, and policy, natural resource education and ecotourism. *Unit head:* Dr. Tim White, Director, 352-846-0850, Fax: 352-392-1707, E-mail: tlwhite@ufl.edu. *Application contact:* Dr. George M. Blakeslee, Graduate Coordinator, 352-846-0845, Fax: 352-392-1707, E-mail: gb4stree@ufl.edu.

University of Georgia, Graduate School, School of Forest Resources, Athens, GA 30602. Offers MFR, MS, PhD. *Faculty:* 48 full-time (3 women). *Students:* 121 full-time (36 women), 23 part-time (7 women); includes 7 minority (4 African Americans, 2 Asian Americans or Pacific Islanders, 1 Hispanic American), 29 international. 65 applicants, 48% accepted. In 2003, 37 master's, 6 doctorates awarded. *Degree requirements:* For master's, thesis (MS); for doctorate, one foreign language, thesis/dissertation. *Entrance requirements:* For master's and doctorate, GRE General Test. *Application deadline:* For fall admission, 7/1 for domestic students; for spring admission, 11/15 for domestic students. Application fee: $50. Electronic applications accepted. *Expenses:* Tuition, state resident: part-time $161 per hour. Tuition, nonresident: part-time $690 per hour. One-time fee: $435 part-time. *Financial support:* Fellowships, research assistantships, teaching assistantships, unspecified assistantships available. *Unit head:* Dr. James M. Sweeney, Interim Dean, 706-542-2866, Fax: 706-542-2281, E-mail: jsweeney@smokey.forestry.uga.edu. *Application contact:* Dr. Barry D. Shiver, Graduate Coordinator, 706-542-3009, Fax: 706-542-8356, E-mail: shiver@smokey.forestry.uga.edu.

University of Guelph, Graduate Program Services, Ontario Agricultural College, Department of Land Resource Science, Guelph, ON N1G 2W1, Canada. Offers atmospheric science (M Sc, PhD); environmental and agricultural earth sciences (M Sc, PhD); land resources management (M Sc, PhD); soil science (M Sc, PhD). Part-time programs available. *Faculty:* 19 full-time (5 women), 3 part-time/adjunct (0 women). *Students:* 47 full-time (24 women), 3 part-time; includes 1 African American, 6 Asian Americans or Pacific Islanders, 2 Hispanic Americans, 2 international. Average age 28. 24 applicants, 46% accepted. In 2003, 9 master's, 4 doctorates awarded. *Degree requirements:* For master's and doctorate, thesis/dissertation. *Entrance requirements:* For master's, minimum B- average during previous 2 years; for doctorate, minimum B average during previous 2 years. Additional exam requirements/recommendations for international students: Required—TOEFL (minimum score 550 paper-based; 213 computer-based). *Application deadline:* For fall admission, 7/1 priority date for domestic students, 5/1 priority date for international students; for winter admission, 10/1 for domestic students; for spring admission, 3/1 for domestic students. Applications are processed on a rolling basis. Application fee: $75 Canadian dollars. Electronic applications accepted. Tuition and fees charges are reported in Canadian dollars. Tuition, nonresident: full-time $3,440 Canadian dollars. International tuition: $5,432 Canadian dollars full-time. Required fees: $753 Canadian dollars. *Financial support:* In 2003–04, 30 students received support, including 40 research assistantships (averaging $16,500 Canadian dollars per year), 15 teaching assistantships (averaging $3,800 Canadian dollars per year); fellowships, scholarships/grants also available. *Faculty research:* Soil science, environmental earth science, land resource management. Total annual research expenditures: $2.1 million Canadian dollars. *Unit head:* Dr. S. Hilts, Chairman, 519-824-4120 Ext. 52447, Fax: 519-824-5730, E-mail: shilts@uoguelph.ca. *Application contact:* Dr. T. J. Gillespie, Graduate Coordinator, 519-824-4120 Ext. 54276, Fax: 519-824-5730, E-mail: tgillesp@lrs.uoguelph.ca.

University of Hawaii at Manoa, Graduate Division, College of Tropical Agriculture and Human Resources, Department of Natural Resources and Environmental Management, Honolulu, HI 96822. Offers MS, PhD. Part-time programs available. *Faculty:* 23 full-time (3 women), 8 part-time/adjunct (2 women). *Students:* 22 full-time (12 women), 3 part-time (1 woman); includes 4 minority (all Asian Americans or Pacific Islanders), 7 international. Average age 34. 36 applicants, 67% accepted, 13 enrolled.Terminal master's awarded for partial completion of doctoral program. *Median time to degree:* Doctorate–7 years full-time. *Degree requirements:* For master's, thesis or alternative; for doctorate, thesis/dissertation. *Entrance requirements:* For master's and doctorate, GRE, minimum GPA of 3.0 in last 4 semesters. Additional exam requirements/recommendations for international students: Required—TOEFL. *Application deadline:* For fall admission, 3/1 for domestic students, 1/15 for international students; for spring admission, 9/1 for domestic students, 8/1 for international students. Applications are processed on a rolling basis. Application fee: $50. *Expenses:* Tuition, state resident: full-time $4,464; part-time $186 per credit hour. Tuition, nonresident: full-time $10,608; part-time $442 per credit hour. Tuition and fees vary according to program. *Financial support:* In 2003–04, 7 research assistantships (averaging $15,746 per year), 5 teaching assistantships (averaging $14,089 per year) were awarded. Fellowships, career-related internships or fieldwork and tuition waivers (full and partial) also available. *Faculty research:* Bioeconomics, natural resource management. *Unit head:* Dr. Samir El-Swarfy, Chairperson, 808-956-6708, Fax: 808-956-2811.

University of Illinois at Urbana–Champaign, Graduate College, College of Agricultural, Consumer and Environmental Sciences, Department of Natural Resources and Environmental Science, Champaign, IL 61820. Offers MS, PhD. *Faculty:* 47 full-time (5 women), 1 part-time/adjunct (0 women). *Students:* 130 full-time (54 women); includes 5 minority (2 Asian Americans or Pacific Islanders, 3 Hispanic Americans), 38 international. 138 applicants, 22% accepted, 26 enrolled. In 2003, 24 master's, 8 doctorates awarded. *Degree requirements:* For master's and doctorate, thesis/dissertation. *Entrance requirements:* For master's and doctorate, GRE, minimum GPA of 3.0. *Application deadline:* For fall admission, 2/1 for domestic students. Applications are processed on a rolling basis. Application fee: $40 ($50 for international students). Electronic applications accepted. *Expenses:* Tuition, state resident: full-time $6,692. Tuition, nonresident: full-time $18,692. *Financial support:* In 2003–04, 7 fellowships, 79 research assistantships, 10 teaching assistantships were awarded. Tuition waivers (full and partial) also available. Financial award application deadline: 2/15. *Unit head:* Wesley M. Jarrell, Head, 217-333-2770, Fax: 217-244-3219. *Application contact:* Mary Lowry, Resident Specialist, 217-244-5761, Fax: 217-244-3219, E-mail: lowry@uiuc.edu.

University of Maine, Graduate School, College of Natural Sciences, Forestry, and Agriculture, Department of Forest Management and Forest Ecosystem Science, Orono, ME 04469. Offers forest resources (PhD); forestry (MF, MS). *Accreditation:* SAF (one or more programs are accredited). Part-time programs available. *Students:* 37 full-time (12 women), 12 part-time (5 women), 12 international. Average age 30. 21 applicants, 81% accepted, 8 enrolled. In 2003, 9 master's, 4 doctorates awarded. *Degree requirements:* For master's, thesis; for doctorate, one foreign language, thesis/dissertation. *Entrance requirements:* For master's and doctorate, GRE General Test. Additional exam requirements/recommendations for international students: Required—TOEFL. *Application deadline:* For fall admission, 2/1 for domestic students. Applications are processed on a rolling basis. Application fee: $50. Electronic applications accepted. *Expenses:* Tuition, state resident: part-time $235 per credit. Tuition, nonresident: part-time $670 per credit. Tuition and fees vary according to course load. *Financial support:* In 2003–04, research assistantships with tuition reimbursements (averaging $13,500 per year), teaching assistantships with tuition reimbursements (averaging $12,276 per year) were awarded. Fellowships, career-related internships or fieldwork, Federal Work-Study, and institutionally sponsored loans also available. Financial award application deadline: 3/1. *Faculty research:* Forest economics, engineering and operations analysis, biometrics and remote sensing, timber management, wood technology. *Unit head:* Dr. David Field, Chair, 207-581-2856, Fax: 207-581-2858. *Application contact:* Scott G. Delcourt, Associate Dean of the Graduate School, 207-581-3218, Fax: 207-581-3232, E-mail: graduate@maine.edu.

University of Maine, Graduate School, College of Natural Sciences, Forestry, and Agriculture, Department of Plant, Soil, and Environmental Sciences, Orono, ME 04469. Offers biological sciences (PhD); ecology and environmental sciences (MS, PhD); forest resources (PhD); horticulture (MS); plant science (PhD); plant, soil, and environmental sciences (MS); resource utilization (MS). *Students:* 20 full-time (14 women), 8 part-time (5 women); includes 1 minority (Asian American or Pacific Islander), 2 international. Average age 31. 12 applicants, 42% accepted, 5 enrolled. In 2003, 2 degrees awarded. *Entrance requirements:* For master's and doctorate, GRE General Test. Additional exam requirements/recommendations for international students: Required—TOEFL. *Application deadline:* Applications are processed on a rolling basis. Application fee: $50. Electronic applications accepted. *Expenses:* Tuition, state resident: part-time $235 per credit. Tuition, nonresident: part-time $670 per credit. Tuition and fees vary according to course load. *Financial support:* In 2003–04, 9 research assistantships with tuition reimbursements (averaging $12,180 per year) were awarded; teaching assistantships, scholarships/grants, tuition waivers (full and partial), and unspecified assistantships also available. *Unit head:* Dr. M. Susan Erich, Chair, 207-581-2938, Fax: 207-581-3207. *Application contact:* Scott G. Delcourt, Associate Dean of the Graduate School, 207-581-3218, Fax: 207-581-3232, E-mail: graduate@maine.edu.

University of Maryland, College Park, Graduate Studies and Research, College of Agriculture and Natural Resources, Department of Natural Resource Sciences and Landscape Architecture, Natural Resource Sciences Program, College Park, MD 20742. Offers MS, PhD. *Students:* 34 full-time (20 women), 6 part-time (3 women); includes 4 minority (2 African Americans, 1 Asian American or Pacific Islander, 1 Hispanic American), 8 international. 38 applicants, 53% accepted. In 2003, 1 master's, 1 doctorate awarded. *Degree requirements:* For master's, thesis optional; for doctorate, thesis/dissertation. *Entrance requirements:* For master's, GRE General Test, minimum GPA of 3.0, 3 letters of recommendation; for doctorate, GRE General Test. *Application deadline:* For fall admission, 5/1 for domestic students, 2/1 for international students; for spring admission, 10/1 for domestic students, 6/1 for international students. Applications are processed on a rolling basis. Application fee: $50. Electronic applications accepted. *Expenses:* Tuition, state resident: part-time $349 per credit hour. Tuition, nonresident: part-time $602 per credit hour. *Faculty research:* Wetland soils, acid mine drainage, acid sulfate soil. *Application contact:* Trudy Lindsey, Director, Graduate Enrollment Management Services, 301-405-4190, Fax: 301-314-9305, E-mail: tlindsey@gradschool.umd.edu.

University of Michigan, School of Natural Resources and Environment, Ann Arbor, MI 48109-1115. Offers industrial ecology (Certificate); landscape architecture (MLA, PhD); resource ecology and management (MS, PhD), including natural resources and environment (PhD), resource ecology and management (MS); resource policy and behavior (MS, PhD), including natural resources and environment (PhD), resource policy and behavior (MS); spatial analysis (Certificate). MLA, MS, PhD, and JD/MS offered through the Horace H. Rackham School of Graduate Studies. *Accreditation:* ASLA (one or more programs are accredited); SAF (one or more programs are accredited). *Degree requirements:* For master's, thesis or alternative, thesis, practicum, or group project; for doctorate, thesis/dissertation, oral defense of dissertation, preliminary exam, comprehensive exam, registration. *Entrance requirements:* For master's, GRE General Test; for doctorate, GRE General Test, master's degree. Additional exam requirements/recommendations for international students: Required—TOEFL (paper score 560; computer score 220) or IELTS. Electronic applications accepted. *Expenses:* Tuition, state resident: full-time $7,463. Tuition, nonresident: full-time $13,913. Full-time tuition and fees vary according to course load, degree level and program. *Faculty research:* Ecology, environmental policy, landscape architecture, climate change, Great Lakes, sustainable systems.

The University of Montana–Missoula, Graduate School, College of Forestry and Conservation, Missoula, MT 59812-0002. Offers ecosystem management (MEM, MS); fish and wildlife biology (PhD); forestry (MS, PhD); recreation management (MS); resource conservation (MS); wildlife biology (MS). *Faculty:* 34 full-time (4 women). *Students:* 158 full-time (44 women), 49 part-time (22 women); includes 3 minority (2 American Indian/Alaska Native, 1 Hispanic American), 16 international. 175 applicants, 35% accepted, 46 enrolled. In 2003, 28 master's, 5 doctorates awarded. *Degree requirements:* For doctorate, thesis/dissertation. *Entrance requirements:* For master's and doctorate, GRE General Test. Additional exam requirements/recommendations for international students: Required—TOEFL (minimum score 575 paper-based; 213 computer-based). *Application deadline:* For fall admission, 1/31 for domestic students; for spring admission, 8/31 priority date for domestic students. Applications are processed on a rolling basis. Application fee: $45. *Expenses:* Tuition, state resident: full-time $1,848; part-time $221 per credit. Tuition, nonresident: full-time $4,880; part-time $333 per credit. Required fees: $2,200. *Financial support:* In 2003–04, 25 research assistantships with tuition reimbursements, 12 teaching assistantships with full tuition reimbursements were awarded. Fellowships, career-related internships or fieldwork and Federal Work-Study also available. Financial award application deadline: 3/1; financial award applicants required to submit FAFSA. Total annual research expenditures: $6.7 million. *Unit head:* Dr. Perry Brown, Dean, 406-243-5521, Fax: 406-243-4845, E-mail: pbrown@forestry.umt.edu.

University of Nebraska–Lincoln, Graduate College, College of Agricultural Sciences and Natural Resources, Lincoln, NE 68588. Offers M Ag, MA, MS, PhD. *Degree requirements:* For doctorate, thesis/dissertation, comprehensive exam. *Entrance requirements:* Additional exam requirements/recommendations for international students: Required—TOEFL. Electronic applications accepted. *Faculty research:* Environmental sciences, animal sciences, human resources and family sciences, plant breeding and genetics, food and nutrition.

University of New Hampshire, Graduate School, Interdisciplinary Programs, Doctoral Program in Natural Resources and Earth Science, Durham, NH 03824. Offers earth and environmental science (PhD), including geology, oceanography; natural resources and environmental studies (PhD). *Faculty:* 72 full-time. *Students:* 45 full-time (14 women), 18 part-time (7 women); includes 1 minority (Asian American or Pacific Islander), 17 international. Average age 38. 23 applicants, 70% accepted, 6 enrolled. In 2003, 5 degrees awarded. *Degree requirements:* For doctorate, thesis/dissertation. *Entrance requirements:* For doctorate, GRE if from a non U.S. university. Additional exam requirements/recommendations for international students: Required—TOEFL (minimum score 550 paper-based; 213 computer-based); Recommended—TSE. *Application deadline:* For fall admission, 4/1 for domestic students. Applications are processed on a rolling basis. Application fee: $50. Electronic applications accepted. Tuition, area resident: Full-time $7,070. *Expenses:* Tuition, state resident: full-time $10,605. Tuition, nonresident: full-time $17,430. Required fees: $15. *Financial support:* In 2003–04, 5 fellowships, 15 research assistantships, 5 teaching assistantships were awarded. Federal Work-Study, scholarships/grants, and tuition waivers (full and partial) also available. Financial award application deadline: 2/15. *Faculty research:* Environmental and natural resource studies and management. *Unit head:* Dr. John D. Aber, Chairperson, 603-862-3045. *Application contact:* Dr. Alison Magill, Administrative Assistant, 603-862-4098, E-mail: nress.phd.program@unh.edu.

University of Northern British Columbia, Office of Graduate Studies, Prince George, BC V2N 4Z9, Canada. Offers community health science (M Sc); disability management (MA); education (M Ed); first nations studies (MA); gender studies (MA); history (MA); interdisciplinary studies (MA); international studies (MA); mathematical, computer and physical sciences (M Sc); natural resources and environmental studies (M Sc, MA, MNRES, PhD); political science (MA); psychology (M Sc, PhD); social work (MSW). Part-time and evening/weekend programs available. Postbaccalaureate distance learning degree programs offered (no on-campus study). *Students:* 293 full-time (187 women), 77 part-time (62 women). 290 applicants, 31% accepted, 80 enrolled. In 2003, 61 master's, 2 doctorates awarded. *Degree requirements:* For master's and doctorate, thesis/dissertation. *Entrance requirements:* For master's, GRE, minimum B average in undergraduate course work; for doctorate, candidacy exam, minimum A average in graduate course work. *Application deadline:* For fall and spring admission, 2/15; for winter admission, 9/15 for domestic students. Applications are processed on a rolling basis. Application fee: $50 ($250 for international students). *Expenses:* Tuition, state resident: full-time $2,272. *Financial support:* In 2003–04, 4 fellowships (averaging $7,750 per year), 250 research assistantships (averaging $12,000 per year), 60 teaching assistantships (averaging $8,000 per year) were awarded. Career-related internships or fieldwork, institutionally sponsored loans, and scholarships/grants also available. Support available to part-time students. Financial award application deadline: 2/15. *Unit head:* Dr. Robert W. Tait, Dean of Graduate Studies, 250-960-5726, Fax: 250-960-5362, E-mail: tait@unbc.ca. *Application contact:* Susan Deevy, Graduate Studies Officer, 250-960-6336, Fax: 250-960-6330, E-mail: deevys@unbc.ca.

University of Oklahoma, Graduate College, College of Engineering, School of Petroleum and Geological Engineering, Program in Petroleum Engineering, Norman, OK 73019-0390. Offers natural gas engineering (MS); petroleum engineering (MS). Part-time programs available. Postbaccalaureate distance learning degree programs offered. *Students:* 63 full-time (7 women), 66 part-time (2 women); includes 4 minority (2 African Americans, 2 Hispanic Americans), 90 international. 57 applicants, 63% accepted, 34 enrolled. In 2003, 35 degrees awarded. *Degree requirements:* For master's, industrial team project or thesis. *Entrance requirements:* For master's, bachelor's degree in engineering, letter of recommendation, minimum GPA of 3.0 during final 60 hours of undergraduate course work. Additional exam requirements/recommendations for international students: Required—TOEFL (minimum score 550 paper-based; 213 computer-based). *Application deadline:* For fall admission, 6/1 priority date for domestic students, 4/1 priority date for international students; for spring admission, 11/1 for domestic students, 9/1 for international students. Applications are processed on a rolling basis. Application fee: $25 ($75 for international students). *Expenses:* Tuition, state resident: full-time $2,774; part-time $116 per credit hour. Tuition, nonresident: full-time $9,571; part-time $399 per credit hour. Required fees: $953; $33 per credit hour. Full-time tuition and fees vary according to course level, course load and program. *Financial support:* In 2003–04, 8 students received support; research assistantships with partial tuition reimbursements available, teaching assistantships with partial tuition reimbursements available, career-related internships or fieldwork and unspecified assistantships available. Financial award application deadline: 4/15; financial award applicants required to submit FAFSA.

University of Rhode Island, Graduate School, College of the Environment and Life Sciences, Department of Environmental and Natural Resource Economics, Kingston, RI 02881. Offers resource economics and marine resources (MS, PhD). In 2003, 15 master's, 1 doctorate awarded. *Degree requirements:* For master's, thesis optional; for doctorate, thesis/dissertation. *Entrance requirements:* For master's and doctorate, GRE General Test. Additional exam requirements/recommendations for international students: Required—TOEFL. *Application deadline:* For fall admission, 4/15 for domestic students. Applications are processed on a rolling basis. *Expenses:* Tuition, state resident: full-time $4,338; part-time $281 per credit. Tuition, nonresident: full-time $12,438; part-time $704 per credit. Required fees: $1,840. *Unit head:* Dr. James Anderson, Chairperson, 401-874-2471. *Application contact:* Dr. Tim Tyrrell, Graduate Admissions Committee, 401-874-2472, Fax: 401-782-4766, E-mail: renri@uriacc.uri.edu.

University of Wisconsin–Stevens Point, College of Natural Resources, Stevens Point, WI 54481-3897. Offers MS. Part-time programs available. *Faculty:* 26 full-time (1 woman), 5 part-time/adjunct (1 woman). *Students:* 24 full-time (17 women), 31 part-time (17 women); includes 2 minority (1 African American, 1 American Indian/Alaska Native), 1 international. In 2003, 38 degrees awarded. *Degree requirements:* For master's, thesis or alternative. *Entrance requirements:* For master's, GRE. *Application deadline:* For fall admission, 3/15 for domestic students; for spring admission, 11/15 for domestic students. Applications are processed on a rolling basis. Application fee: $45. *Expenses:* Tuition, state resident: full-time $4,842; part-time $269 per credit. Tuition, nonresident: full-time $15,452; part-time $858 per credit. Required fees: $524; $53 per credit. *Financial support:* Research assistantships, teaching assistantships, career-related internships or fieldwork, Federal Work-Study, and unspecified assistantships available. Support available to part-time students. Financial award application deadline: 5/1; financial award applicants required to submit FAFSA. *Faculty research:* Wildlife environmental education, fisheries, forestry, policy and planning. *Unit head:* Dr. Christina Thomas, Associate Dean, 715-346-2853, Fax: 715-346-3624.

University of Wyoming, Graduate School, College of Agriculture, Department of Renewable Resources, Laramie, WY 82070. Offers entomology (MS, PhD); rangeland ecology and watershed management (MS, PhD), including soil sciences (PhD), soil sciences and water resources (MS), water resources. *Faculty:* 22 full-time (1 woman). *Students:* 20 full-time (7 women), 10 part-time (3 women), 7 international. 8 applicants. In 2003, 11 master's, 3 doctorates awarded. *Degree requirements:* For master's, thesis (for some programs); for doctorate, 2 foreign languages, thesis/dissertation. *Entrance requirements:* For master's and doctorate, GRE General Test, minimum GPA of 3.0. *Application deadline:* For fall admission, 6/1 for domestic students; for spring admission, 12/1 priority date for domestic students. Applications are processed on a rolling basis. Application fee: $40. *Expenses:* Tuition, state resident: part-time $142 per credit hour. Tuition, nonresident: part-time $408 per credit hour. Required fees: $134 per semester. Tuition and fees vary according to course load, campus/location, program and student level. *Financial support:* In 2003–04, 8 students received support, including 8 research assistantships with full tuition reimbursements available (averaging $10,062 per year); career-related internships or fieldwork and Federal Work-Study also available. Financial award application deadline: 3/1. *Faculty research:* Plant control, grazing management, riparian restoration, riparian management, reclamation. *Unit head:* Dr. Thomas L. Thurow, Head, 307-766-2263, Fax: 307-766-6403, E-mail: thurow@uwyo.edu. *Application contact:* Kimm Mann-Malody, Office Assistant, Sr., 307-766-2263, Fax: 307-766-6403, E-mail: kimmmann@uwyo.edu.

University of Wyoming, Graduate School, College of Arts and Sciences, Department of Geography, Program in Rural Planning and Natural Resources, Laramie, WY 82070. Offers community and regional planning and natural resources (MP). *Faculty:* 1 full-time (0 women), 2 part-time/adjunct (0 women). *Students:* 2 full-time (0 women), 5 part-time (3 women). 4 applicants, 100% accepted. In 2003, 2 degrees awarded. *Degree requirements:* For master's, thesis or alternative. *Entrance requirements:* For master's, GRE General Test, minimum GPA of 3.0. *Application deadline:* For fall admission, 2/15 for domestic students. Applications are processed on a rolling basis. Application fee: $40. *Expenses:* Tuition, state resident: part-time $142 per credit hour. Tuition, nonresident: part-time $408 per credit hour. Required fees: $134 per semester. Tuition and fees vary according to course load, campus/location, program and student level. *Financial support:* In 2003–04, 1 teaching assistantship with full and partial tuition reimbursement was awarded; career-related internships or fieldwork and Federal Work-Study also available. Financial award application deadline: 3/1. Total annual research expenditures: $10,400. *Unit head:* Dr. John Allen, Chair, Department of Geography, 307-766-3311, Fax: 307-766-3294, E-mail: geography-info@uwyo.edu.

Utah State University, School of Graduate Studies, College of Natural Resources, Interdisciplinary Program in Natural Resources, Logan, UT 84322. Offers MNR. *Students:* 6 full-time (1 woman), 1 (woman) part-time, 1 international. Average age 30. 5 applicants, 40% accepted, 1 enrolled. In 2003, 3 degrees awarded. *Entrance requirements:* For master's, GRE General Test, minimum GPA of 3.0. Additional exam requirements/recommendations for international students: Required—TOEFL. *Application deadline:* For fall admission, 2/15 for domestic students; for spring admission, 10/15 priority date for domestic students. Applications are processed on a rolling basis. Application fee: $50 ($60 for international students). *Expenses:* Tuition, state resident: part-time $270 per credit hour. Tuition, nonresident: part-time $946 per credit hour. Required fees: $173 per credit hour. *Faculty research:* Ecosystem management, human dimensions, quantitative methods, informative management. Total annual research expenditures: $4 million. *Application contact:* Dr. Raymond D. Dueser, Associate Dean, 435-797-2445, Fax: 435-797-2448, E-mail: nradvise@cc.usu.edu.

Virginia Polytechnic Institute and State University, Graduate School, College of Natural Resources, Blacksburg, VA 24061. Offers MF, MNR, MS, PhD. *Faculty:* 57 full-time (6 women). *Students:* 98 full-time (33 women), 53 part-time (26 women); includes 5 minority (2 African Americans, 1 American Indian/Alaska Native, 1 Asian American or Pacific Islander, 1 Hispanic American), 16 international. Average age 30. 146 applicants, 51% accepted, 45 enrolled. In 2003, 34 master's, 6 doctorates awarded. *Entrance requirements:* Additional exam requirements/recommendations for international students: Required—TOEFL. *Application deadline:* Applications are processed on a rolling basis. Application fee: $45. Electronic applications accepted. Tuition, area resident: Full-time $6,039; part-time $336 per credit. Tuition, nonresident: full-time $9,708; part-time $539 per credit. Required fees: $905; $130 per credit. *Financial support:* In 2003–04, 65 research assistantships with full tuition reimbursements (averaging $14,438 per year), 15 teaching assistantships with full tuition reimbursements (averaging $11,704 per year) were awarded. Career-related internships or fieldwork, Federal Work-Study, scholarships/grants, health care benefits, and unspecified assistantships also available. *Unit head:* Dr. Gregory N. Brown, Dean.

Washington State University, Graduate School, College of Agricultural, Human, and Natural Resource Sciences, Department of Natural Resource Sciences, Pullman, WA 99164. Offers MS,

Natural Resources

Washington State University (continued)
PhD. *Faculty:* 11 full-time (2 women), 3 part-time/adjunct (0 women). *Students:* 7 full-time (3 women), 5 part-time (3 women), 1 international. In 2003, 3 degrees awarded. *Degree requirements:* For master's, oral exam, thesis optional; for doctorate, thesis/dissertation, oral exam. *Entrance requirements:* For master's and doctorate, GRE General Test, minimum GPA of 3.0. Additional exam requirements/recommendations for international students: Required—TOEFL. *Application deadline:* For fall admission, 3/1 for domestic students; for spring admission, 10/1 for domestic students. Applications are processed on a rolling basis. Application fee: $35. *Expenses:* Tuition, state resident: full-time $6,278; part-time $314 per hour. Tuition, nonresident: full-time $15,514; part-time $765 per hour. Required fees: $444. Full-time tuition and fees vary according to campus/location, program and student level. Part-time tuition and fees vary according to course load. *Financial support:* In 2003–04, 8 research assistantships with full and partial tuition reimbursements, 1 teaching assistantship with full and partial tuition reimbursement were awarded. Career-related internships or fieldwork, Federal Work-Study, institutionally sponsored loans, tuition waivers (partial), and unspecified assistantships also available. Financial award application deadline: 4/1; financial award applicants required to submit FAFSA. *Faculty research:* Restoration ecology, effects habitation mule due morality. Total annual research expenditures: $414,056. *Unit head:* Dr. Keith A. Blatner, Chair, 509-335-4499. *Application contact:* Robert R. Clausen, Administrator, 509-335-6166.

Washington State University, Graduate School, College of Sciences, Programs in Environmental Science and Regional Planning, Program in Environmental Science and Regional Planning, Pullman, WA 99164. Offers environmental and natural resource sciences (PhD); environmental science (MS). *Faculty:* 4 full-time (0 women), 2 part-time/adjunct (0 women). *Students:* 22 full-time (13 women), 7 part-time (2 women); includes 2 minority (1 American Indian/Alaska Native, 1 Hispanic American), 4 international. In 2003, 17 degrees awarded. *Degree requirements:* For master's, oral exam, thesis optional; for doctorate, oral exam, written exam. *Entrance requirements:* For master's and doctorate, minimum GPA of 3.0. Additional exam requirements/recommendations for international students: Required—TOEFL. *Application deadline:* For fall admission, 3/1 for domestic students. Applications are processed on a rolling basis. Application fee: $35. *Expenses:* Tuition, state resident: full-time $6,278; part-time $314 per hour. Tuition, nonresident: full-time $15,514; part-time $765 per hour. Required fees: $444. Full-time tuition and fees vary according to campus/location, program and student level. Part-time tuition and fees vary according to course load. *Financial support:* In 2003–04, 3 research assistantships with full and partial tuition reimbursements, 8 teaching assistantships with full and partial tuition reimbursements were awarded. Federal Work-Study, institutionally sponsored loans, and tuition waivers (partial) also available. Financial award application deadline: 4/1; financial award applicants required to submit FAFSA. *Application contact:* Coordinator, 509-335-8536, Fax: 509-335-7636, E-mail: esrp@wsu.edu.

West Virginia University, Davis College of Agriculture, Forestry and Consumer Sciences, Division of Resource Management, Program in Natural Resource Economics, Morgantown, WV 26506. Offers PhD. Part-time programs available. *Students:* 7 full-time (4 women), 3 part-time (2 women); includes 1 minority (Asian American or Pacific Islander), 7 international. Average age 34. 18 applicants, 56% accepted. In 2003, 4 degrees awarded. *Degree requirements:* For doctorate, thesis/dissertation. *Entrance requirements:* For doctorate, GRE General Test. Additional exam requirements/recommendations for international students: Required—TOEFL. Application fee: $45. *Expenses:* Tuition, state resident: full-time $4,332. Tuition, nonresident: full-time $12,442. *Financial support:* In 2003–04, 4 research assistantships, 1 teaching assistantship were awarded. Federal Work-Study, institutionally sponsored loans, and tuition waivers (partial) also available. Financial award application deadline: 2/1; financial award applicants required to submit FAFSA. *Unit head:* Dr. Gerard E. D'Souza, Graduate Coordinator, 304-293-4832 Ext. 4471, Fax: 304-293-3740.

Range Science

Colorado State University, Graduate School, College of Natural Resources, Department of Forest, Rangeland, and Watershed Stewardship, Program in Rangeland Ecosystem Science, Fort Collins, CO 80523-0015. Offers MS, PhD. *Faculty:* 10 full-time (0 women), 1 part-time/adjunct (0 women). *Students:* 9 full-time (5 women), 24 part-time (10 women); includes 2 minority (both American Indian/Alaska Native), 4 international. Average age 32. 23 applicants, 48% accepted, 6 enrolled. In 2003, 6 master's, 2 doctorates awarded. *Degree requirements:* For master's, thesis or alternative; for doctorate, thesis/dissertation. *Entrance requirements:* For master's and doctorate, GRE General Test, minimum GPA of 3.0. Additional exam requirements/recommendations for international students: Required—TOEFL. *Application deadline:* For fall admission, 2/1 for domestic students. Applications are processed on a rolling basis. Application fee: $50. Electronic applications accepted. *Expenses:* Tuition, state resident: full-time $4,156. Tuition, nonresident: full-time $14,762. Required fees: $205. Tuition and fees vary according to course load, campus/location, program and reciprocity agreements. *Financial support:* In 2003–04, 3 fellowships (averaging $12,000 per year), 14 research assistantships with full tuition reimbursements (averaging $14,000 per year), 2 teaching assistantships with full tuition reimbursements (averaging $9,720 per year) were awarded. Career-related internships or fieldwork, Federal Work-Study, and traineeships also available. Support available to part-time students. *Faculty research:* Disturbed land restoration, range animal nutrition and behavior, simulation modeling, natural resource planning, riparian ecology. Total annual research expenditures: $1 million. *Application contact:* Kelley Mathers, Graduate Coordinator, 970-491-4994, Fax: 970-491-6754, E-mail: kmathers@cnr.colostate.edu.

Kansas State University, Graduate School, College of Agriculture, Department of Agronomy, Manhattan, KS 66506. Offers crop science (MS, PhD); range management (MS, PhD); soil science (MS, PhD); weed science (MS, PhD). Part-time programs available. *Faculty:* 63 full-time (11 women). *Students:* 40 full-time (13 women), 12 part-time (5 women); includes 12 minority (3 African Americans, 5 Asian Americans or Pacific Islanders, 4 Hispanic Americans). 26 applicants, 92% accepted, 5 enrolled. In 2003, 11 master's, 7 doctorates awarded. Terminal master's awarded for partial completion of doctoral program. *Degree requirements:* For master's, thesis or alternative, oral exam; for doctorate, thesis/dissertation, preliminary exams. *Entrance requirements:* For master's, minimum GPA of 3.0 in B.S. For doctorate, minimum GPA of 3.5 in masters program, transcripts. Additional exam requirements/recommendations for international students: Required—TOEFL. *Application deadline:* For fall admission, 2/1 for domestic students; for spring admission, 10/1 for domestic students. Applications are processed on a rolling basis. Application fee: $0 ($25 for international students). Electronic applications accepted. *Expenses:* Tuition, state resident: part-time $155 per credit hour. Tuition, nonresident: part-time $428 per credit hour. Required fees: $11 per credit hour. *Financial support:* In 2003–04, 34 research assistantships (averaging $15,264 per year), 6 teaching assistantships with partial tuition reimbursements (averaging $2,763 per year) were awarded. Institutionally sponsored loans and scholarships/grants also available. Support available to part-time students. Financial award application deadline: 3/1; financial award applicants required to submit FAFSA. *Faculty research:* Plant breeding, weed science, environmental soil science, crop and water management, range science. Total annual research expenditures: $3 million. *Unit head:* Dr. David B. Mengel, Head, 785-532-6101, Fax: 785-532-6094, E-mail: dmengel@ksu.edu. *Application contact:* Dr. Gerard Kluitenberg, Director, 785-532-7215, E-mail: gjk@ksu.edu.

Montana State University–Bozeman, College of Graduate Studies, College of Agriculture, Department of Animal and Range Sciences, Bozeman, MT 59717. Offers MS, PhD. Part-time programs available. *Faculty:* 13 full-time (3 women), 5 part-time/adjunct (2 women). *Students:* 5 full-time (2 women), 18 part-time (10 women); includes 1 minority (American Indian/Alaska Native), 1 international. Average age 28. 10 applicants, 70% accepted, 6 enrolled. In 2003, 7 degrees awarded. *Degree requirements:* For master's, comprehensive exam, registration; for doctorate, thesis/dissertation, comprehensive exam, registration. *Entrance requirements:* For master's and doctorate, GRE General Test. Additional exam requirements/recommendations for international students: Required—TOEFL (minimum score 550 paper-based; 213 computer-based). *Application deadline:* For fall admission, 7/15 priority date for domestic students, 5/15 priority date for international students; for spring admission, 12/1 priority date for domestic students, 10/1 priority date for international students. Applications are processed on a rolling basis. Application fee: $50. Electronic applications accepted. *Expenses:* Tuition, state resident: full-time $3,907; part-time $163 per credit. Tuition, nonresident: full-time $12,383; part-time $516 per credit. Required fees: $890; $445 per term. Tuition and fees vary according to course load and program. *Financial support:* In 2003–04, 12 students received support, including 6 research assistantships with partial tuition reimbursements available (averaging $12,000 per year), 1 teaching assistantship with partial tuition reimbursement available (averaging $12,000 per year); scholarships/grants and unspecified assistantships also available. Financial award application deadline: 3/1; financial award applicants required to submit FAFSA. *Faculty research:* Range nutrition, genetics, reproductive physiology, range ecology, livestock management, invasive species management. Total annual research expenditures: $2 million. *Unit head:* Dr. Michael Tess, Head, 406-994-5610, Fax: 406-994-5589, E-mail: mwtess@montana.edu.

New Mexico State University, Graduate School, College of Agriculture and Home Economics, Department of Animal and Range Sciences, Las Cruces, NM 88003-8001. Offers animal science (M Ag, MS, PhD); range science (M Ag, MS, PhD). Part-time programs available. *Faculty:* 17 full-time (1 woman), 7 part-time/adjunct (0 women). *Students:* 33 full-time (15 women), 12 part-time (6 women); includes 12 minority (3 American Indian/Alaska Native, 9 Hispanic Americans), 6 international. Average age 29. 27 applicants, 63% accepted, 11 enrolled. In 2003, 4 master's, 4 doctorates awarded. *Degree requirements:* For master's, thesis, seminar; for doctorate, thesis/dissertation, research tool. *Entrance requirements:* For master's, minimum GPA of 3.0 in last 60 hours of undergraduate course work (MS); for doctorate, minimum graduate GPA of 3.2. *Application deadline:* For fall admission, 7/1 for domestic students; for spring admission, 11/1 for domestic students. Applications are processed on a rolling basis. Application fee: $30 ($50 for international students). Electronic applications accepted. *Expenses:* Tuition, state resident: full-time $2,670; part-time $151 per credit. Tuition, nonresident: full-time $10,596; part-time $481 per credit. Required fees: $954. *Financial support:* In 2003–04, 5 research assistantships, 17 teaching assistantships were awarded. Federal Work-Study also available. Support available to part-time students. Financial award application deadline: 3/1. *Faculty research:* Reproductive physiology, ruminant nutrition, nutrition toxicology, range ecology, wildland hydrology. *Unit head:* Dr. Mark Wise, Head, 505-646-2514, Fax: 505-646-5441, E-mail: mawise@nmsu.edu.

North Dakota State University, The Graduate School, College of Agriculture, Food Systems, and Natural Resources, Department of Animal and Range Sciences, Fargo, ND 58105. Offers animal science (MS, PhD); natural resources management (MS, PhD); range science (MS, PhD). *Degree requirements:* For master's and doctorate, thesis/dissertation. *Entrance requirements:* For master's and doctorate, GRE General Test. Additional exam requirements/recommendations for international students: Required—TOEFL. Tuition, nonresident: full-time $4,071. Required fees: $493. *Faculty research:* Reproduction, nutrition, meat and muscle biology, breeding/genetics.

Oregon State University, Graduate School, College of Agricultural Sciences, Department of Rangeland Resources, Corvallis, OR 97331. Offers M Agr, MAIS, MS, PhD. *Faculty:* 18 full-time (3 women). *Students:* 13 full-time (3 women), 4 part-time, 5 international. Average age 31. In 2003, 2 master's, 1 doctorate awarded. Terminal master's awarded for partial completion of doctoral program. *Degree requirements:* For master's, thesis (for some programs); for doctorate, thesis/dissertation. *Entrance requirements:* For master's and doctorate, GRE, minimum GPA of 3.0 in last 90 hours. Additional exam requirements/recommendations for international students: Required—TOEFL. *Application deadline:* For fall admission, 6/1 for domestic students; for spring admission, 12/15 for domestic students. Applications are processed on a rolling basis. Application fee: $50. *Expenses:* Tuition, state resident: full-time $8,139; part-time $301 per credit. Tuition, nonresident: full-time $14,376; part-time $532 per credit. Required fees: $1,227. *Financial support:* Research assistantships, career-related internships or fieldwork, Federal Work-Study, and institutionally sponsored loans available. Support available to part-time students. Financial award application deadline: 2/1. *Faculty research:* Range ecology, watershed science, animal grazing, agroforestry. *Unit head:* Dr. William C. Krueger, Head, 541-737-1615, Fax: 541-737-0504, E-mail: william.c.krueger@orst.edu. *Application contact:* Dr. Paul S. Doescher, Head Adviser, 541-737-1622, Fax: 541-737-0504, E-mail: paul.s.doescher@orst.edu.

Sul Ross State University, Division of Agricultural and Natural Resource Science, Program in Range and Wildlife Management, Alpine, TX 79832. Offers M Ag, MS. Part-time programs available. *Degree requirements:* For master's, thesis (for some programs). *Entrance requirements:* For master's, GRE General Test, minimum undergraduate GPA of 2.5 in last 60 hours.

Texas A&M University, College of Agriculture and Life Sciences, Department of Rangeland Ecology and Management, College Station, TX 77843. Offers natural resource development (M Agr); rangeland ecology and management (M Agr, MS, PhD). *Faculty:* 11 full-time (0 women). *Students:* 41 full-time (21 women), 28 part-time (7 women); includes 4 minority (2 Asian Americans or Pacific Islanders, 2 Hispanic Americans), 17 international. Average age 31.Terminal master's awarded for partial completion of doctoral program. *Degree requirements:* For master's, thesis optional; for doctorate, thesis/dissertation. *Entrance requirements:* For master's and doctorate, GRE General Test. Additional exam requirements/recommendations for international students: Required—TOEFL. *Application deadline:* For fall admission, 3/1 for domestic students; for spring admission, 8/1 priority date for domestic students. Applications are processed on a rolling basis. Application fee: $50 ($75 for international students). Electronic applications accepted. *Expenses:* Tuition, state resident: full-time $3,420. Tuition, nonresident: full-time $9,084. Required fees: $1,861. *Financial support:* In 2003–04, research assistantships (averaging $12,566 per year), teaching assistantships (averaging $12,200 per year) were awarded. Fellowships, career-related internships or fieldwork, scholarships/grants, and unspecified assistantships also available. Support available to part-time students. Financial award application deadline: 4/1; financial award applicants required to submit FAFSA. *Faculty research:* Plant ecology, restoration ecology, watershed management, integrated resource management, information technology. *Unit head:* Dr. Robert E. Whitson, Head, 979-845-5579, Fax: 979-845-6430, E-mail: r-whitson@tamu.edu. *Application contact:* Dr. Jennifer E. Funkhouser, Graduate Advisor, 979-845-5579, Fax: 979-845-6430, E-mail: j-funkhouser@tamu.edu.

Texas A&M University–Kingsville, College of Graduate Studies, College of Agriculture and Home Economics, Program in Range and Wildlife Management, Kingsville, TX 78363. Offers MS.

Degree requirements: For master's, thesis or alternative, comprehensive exam. *Entrance requirements:* For master's, GRE General Test, minimum GPA of 3.0. Additional exam requirements/recommendations for international students: Required—TOEFL.

Texas Tech University, Graduate School, College of Agricultural Sciences and Natural Resources, Department of Range, Wildlife, and Fisheries Management, Lubbock, TX 79409. Offers fisheries science (MS, PhD); range science (MS, PhD); wildlife science (MS, PhD). Part-time programs available. *Faculty:* 13 full-time (0 women). *Students:* 39 full-time (15 women), 10 part-time (4 women); includes 1 minority (Hispanic American), 11 international. Average age 30. 17 applicants, 47% accepted, 7 enrolled. In 2003, 14 master's, 2 doctorates awarded. *Degree requirements:* For master's and doctorate, thesis/dissertation. *Entrance requirements:* For master's and doctorate, GRE General Test. Additional exam requirements/recommendations for international students: Required—TOEFL (minimum score 550 paper-based; 213 computer-based). *Application deadline:* Applications are processed on a rolling basis. Application fee: $50 ($60 for international students). Electronic applications accepted. *Expenses:* Tuition, state resident: full-time $3,312. Tuition, nonresident: full-time $8,976. Required fees: $1,745. Tuition and fees vary according to program. *Financial support:* In 2003–04, 34 students received support, including 27 research assistantships with partial tuition reimbursements available (averaging $10,699 per year), 6 teaching assistantships with partial tuition reimbursements available (averaging $11,200 per year); Federal Work-Study and institutionally sponsored loans also available. Support available to part-time students. Financial award application deadline: 5/1; financial award applicants required to submit FAFSA. *Faculty research:* Use of fire on range lands, waterfowl, upland game birds and playa lakes in the southern Great Plains, reproductive physiology in fisheries, conservation biology. Total annual research expenditures: $1.2 million. *Unit head:* Dr. Ernest B. Fish, Chairman, 806-742-2841, Fax: 806-742-2280. *Application contact:* L. Jeannine Moerbe, Graduate Secretary, 806-742-2825, E-mail: jeannine.moerbe@ttu.edu.

The University of Arizona, Graduate College, College of Agriculture and Life Sciences, School of Natural Resources, Program in Rangeland Ecology and Management, Tucson, AZ 85721. Offers MS, PhD. *Faculty:* 9 full-time (1 woman). *Students:* 5 full-time (3 women), 4 part-time (2 women). Average age 30. 3 applicants, 0% accepted. In 2003, 4 degrees awarded. *Degree requirements:* For master's, thesis/dissertation; for doctorate, thesis/dissertation, comprehensive exam. *Entrance requirements:* For master's and doctorate, GRE General Test, minimum GPA of 3.0, 3 letters of recommendation. Additional exam requirements/recommendations for international students: Required—TOEFL (minimum score 550 paper-based; 213 computer-based). *Application deadline:* For fall admission, 8/1 priority date for domestic students, 12/1 priority date for international students. Applications are processed on a rolling basis. Application fee: $50. *Expenses:* Tuition, state resident: part-time $196 per unit. Tuition, nonresident: part-time $326 per unit. *Financial support:* Research assistantships, teaching assistantships, career-related internships or fieldwork, scholarships/grants, health care benefits, tuition waivers (partial), and unspecified assistantships available. *Faculty research:* Criteria for defining, mapping, and evaluating range sites; methods of establishing forage plants on southwestern range lands; plants for pollution and erosion control, beautification, and browse. *Unit head:* Dr. George Ruyle, Chair, 520-621-1384, Fax: 520-621-8801, E-mail: gruyle@ag.arizona.edu. *Application contact:* Cheryl L. Craddock, Academic Coordinator, 520-621-7260, Fax: 520-621-8801, E-mail: ccraddoc@email.arizona.edu.

University of California, Berkeley, Graduate Division, Group in Range Management, Berkeley, CA 94720-1500. Offers MS. *Faculty:* 18 full-time (6 women), 2 part-time/adjunct (1 woman). *Students:* 7 (2 women); includes 2 minority (1 African American, 1 American Indian/Alaska Native). 3 applicants, 100% accepted, 3 enrolled. In 2003, 1 degree awarded. *Degree requirements:* For master's, thesis, registration. *Entrance requirements:* For master's, GRE General Test, minimum GPA of 3.0. Additional exam requirements/recommendations for international students: Required—TOEFL. *Application deadline:* For fall admission, 12/17 for domestic students. Application fee: $60. International tuition: $12,491 full-time. Required fees: $5,484. *Financial support:* In 2003–04, 4 students received support, including 2 fellowships (averaging $10,000 per year), 2 research assistantships with full tuition reimbursements available (averaging $12,000 per year); unspecified assistantships also available. Financial award application deadline: 12/17; financial award applicants required to submit FAFSA. *Faculty research:* Grassland and savannah ecology, wetland ecology, oak woodland classification, wildlife habitat management. *Unit head:* Barbara H. Allen-Diaz, Chair, 510-642-7125, Fax: 510-643-5098, E-mail: ballen@nature.berkeley.edu. *Application contact:* Sue Baumgartner, Student Affairs Officer, 510-642-6410, Fax: 510-642-4034, E-mail: espmgradproginfo@nature.berkeley.edu.

University of Idaho, College of Graduate Studies, College of Natural Resources, Department of Rangeland Ecology and Management, Moscow, ID 83844-2282. Offers MS, PhD. *Students:* 7 full-time (6 women), 2 part-time (1 woman), 2 international. Average age 38. *Degree requirements:* For doctorate, thesis/dissertation. *Entrance requirements:* For master's, minimum GPA of 2.8; for doctorate, minimum undergraduate GPA of 2.8, 3.0 graduate. *Application deadline:* For fall admission, 8/1 for domestic students; for spring admission, 12/15 for domestic students. Application fee: $55 ($60 for international students). *Expenses:* Tuition, state resident: full-time $3,348. Tuition, nonresident: full-time $10,740. Required fees: $540. *Financial support:* Research assistantships, teaching assistantships available. Financial award application deadline: 2/15. *Unit head:* Dr. Karen L. Launchbaugh, Head, 208-885-6536.

See in-depth description on page 803.

University of Idaho, College of Graduate Studies, College of Natural Resources, Program in Forestry, Wildlife, and Range Sciences, Moscow, ID 83844-2282. Offers PhD. *Degree requirements:* For doctorate, thesis/dissertation. *Entrance requirements:* For doctorate, minimum undergraduate GPA of 2.8, 3.0 graduate. *Application deadline:* For fall admission, 8/1 for domestic students; for spring admission, 12/15 for domestic students. Application fee: $55 ($60 for international students). *Expenses:* Tuition, state resident: full-time $3,348. Tuition, nonresident: full-time $10,740. Required fees: $540. *Financial support:* Fellowships, research assistantships, teaching assistantships available. Financial award application deadline: 2/15. *Application contact:* Dr. Ali Moslemi, Graduate Coordinator, 208-885-6126.

University of Wyoming, Graduate School, College of Agriculture, Department of Renewable Resources, Laramie, WY 82070. Offers entomology (MS, PhD); rangeland ecology and watershed management (MS, PhD), including soil sciences (PhD), soil sciences and water resources (MS), water resources. *Faculty:* 22 full-time (1 woman). *Students:* 20 full-time (7 women), 10 part-time (3 women), 7 international. 8 applicants. In 2003, 11 master's, 3 doctorates awarded. *Degree requirements:* For master's, thesis (for some programs); for doctorate, 2 foreign languages, thesis/dissertation. *Entrance requirements:* For master's and doctorate, GRE General Test, minimum GPA of 3.0. *Application deadline:* For fall admission, 6/1 for domestic students; for spring admission, 12/1 priority date for domestic students. Applications are processed on a rolling basis. Application fee: $40. *Expenses:* Tuition, state resident: part-time $142 per credit hour. Tuition, nonresident: part-time $408 per credit hour. Required fees: $134 per semester. Tuition and fees vary according to course load, campus/location, program and student level. *Financial support:* In 2003–04, 8 students received support, including 8 research assistantships with full tuition reimbursements available (averaging $10,062 per year); career-related internships or fieldwork and Federal Work-Study also available. Financial award application deadline: 3/1. *Faculty research:* Plant control, grazing management, riparian restoration, riparian management, reclamation. *Unit head:* Dr. Thomas L. Thurow, Head, 307-766-2263, Fax: 307-766-6403, E-mail: thurow@uwyo.edu. *Application contact:* Kimm Mann-Malody, Office Assistant, Sr., 307-766-2263, Fax: 307-766-6403, E-mail: kimmmann@uwyo.edu.

Utah State University, School of Graduate Studies, College of Natural Resources, Department of Forest, Range, and Wildlife Sciences, Logan, UT 84322. Offers ecology (MS, PhD); forestry (MS, PhD); range science (MS, PhD); wildlife biology (MS, PhD). Part-time programs available. *Faculty:* 22 full-time (4 women), 17 part-time/adjunct (3 women). *Students:* 55 full-time (21 women), 16 part-time (9 women), 7 international. Average age 24. 42 applicants, 33% accepted, 10 enrolled. In 2003, 8 master's, 2 doctorates awarded. *Degree requirements:* For master's and doctorate, thesis/dissertation. *Entrance requirements:* For master's and doctorate, GRE General Test, minimum GPA of 3.0. Additional exam requirements/recommendations for international students: Required—TOEFL. *Application deadline:* For fall admission, 6/15 for domestic students; for spring admission, 10/15 for domestic students. Applications are processed on a rolling basis. Application fee: $50 ($60 for international students). *Expenses:* Tuition, state resident: part-time $270 per credit hour. Tuition, nonresident: part-time $946 per credit hour. Required fees: $173 per credit hour. *Financial support:* In 2003–04, 14 research assistantships with partial tuition reimbursements (averaging $13,600 per year) were awarded; fellowships, teaching assistantships, career-related internships or fieldwork, Federal Work-Study, and institutionally sponsored loans also available. *Faculty research:* Range plant ecophysiology, plant community ecology, ruminant nutrition, population ecology. Total annual research expenditures: $3.5 million. *Unit head:* Dr. David W. Roberts, Interim Head, 435-797-2503, Fax: 435-797-3796, E-mail: ggriffeth@cnr.usu.edu. *Application contact:* Gaye Griffeth, Staff Assistant, 435-797-2503, Fax: 435-797-3796, E-mail: ggriffeth@cnr.usu.edu.

Water Resources

Albany State University, College of Arts and Sciences, Department of History, Political Science and Public Administration, Albany, GA 31705-2717. Offers community and economic development (MPA); criminal justice (MPA); fiscal management (MPA); general management (MPA); health administration and policy (MPA); human resources management (MPA); public policy (MPA); water resource management and policy (MPA). Part-time programs available. *Degree requirements:* For master's, thesis, comprehensive exam. *Entrance requirements:* For master's, GRE General Test, minimum GPA of 2.5. Electronic applications accepted. *Faculty research:* Transportation, urban affairs, political economy.

Albany State University, School of Business, Albany, GA 31705-2717. Offers water policy (MBA). *Accreditation:* ACBSP. Part-time and evening/weekend programs available. Postbaccalaureate distance learning degree programs offered (no on-campus study). *Degree requirements:* For master's, comprehensive exam. *Entrance requirements:* For master's, GMAT, minimum GPA of 2.5. Electronic applications accepted. *Faculty research:* Economic impacts, employment opportunities, instructional technology.

Colorado State University, Graduate School, College of Engineering, Department of Civil Engineering, Fort Collins, CO 80523-0015. Offers bioresource and agricultural engineering (MS); bioresource and agriculture engineering (PhD); environmental engineering (MS, PhD); hydraulics and wind engineering (MS, PhD); structural and geotechnical engineering (MS, PhD); water resources planning and management (MS, PhD); water resources, hydrologic and environmental sciences (MS, PhD). Part-time programs available. *Faculty:* 36 full-time (3 women). *Students:* 80 full-time (28 women), 112 part-time (17 women); includes 6 minority (4 Asian Americans or Pacific Islanders, 2 Hispanic Americans), 73 international. Average age 32. 229 applicants, 54% accepted, 46 enrolled. In 2003, 35 master's, 10 doctorates awarded. Terminal master's awarded for partial completion of doctoral program. *Degree requirements:* For master's, thesis or alternative; for doctorate, thesis/dissertation. *Entrance requirements:* For master's and doctorate, GRE General Test, minimum GPA of 3.0. Additional exam requirements/recommendations for international students: Required—TOEFL. *Application deadline:* For fall admission, 3/1 priority date for domestic students, 3/1 priority date for international students; for spring admission, 8/1 priority date for domestic students, 8/1 priority date for international students. Applications are processed on a rolling basis. Application fee: $50. Electronic applications accepted. *Expenses:* Tuition, state resident: full-time $4,156. Tuition, nonresident: full-time $14,762. Required fees: $205. Tuition and fees vary according to course load, campus/location, program and reciprocity agreements. *Financial support:* In 2003–04, 19 fellowships (averaging $1,500 per year), 47 research assistantships (averaging $12,186 per year), 18 teaching assistantships (averaging $12,006 per year) were awarded. Federal Work-Study, institutionally sponsored loans, and traineeships also available. *Faculty research:* Hydraulics, hydrology, water resources, infrastructure, environmental engineering. Total annual research expenditures: $7.8 million. *Unit head:* Sandra Woods, Head, 970-491-5049, Fax: 970-491-7727, E-mail: woods@engr.colostate.edu. *Application contact:* Laurie Howard, Student Adviser, 970-491-5844, Fax: 970-491-7727, E-mail: lhoward@engr.colostate.edu.

Colorado State University, Graduate School, College of Natural Resources, Department of Forest, Rangeland, and Watershed Stewardship, Program in Watershed Science, Fort Collins, CO 80523-0015. Offers MS. Part-time programs available. *Faculty:* 5 full-time (1 woman), 2 part-time/adjunct (1 woman). *Students:* 13 full-time (7 women), 17 part-time (6 women), 1 international. Average age 29. 48 applicants, 44% accepted, 9 enrolled. In 2003, 12 degrees awarded. *Degree requirements:* For master's, thesis, registration. *Entrance requirements:* For master's, GRE General Test, minimum GPA of 3.0. Additional exam requirements/recommendations for international students: Required—TOEFL. *Application deadline:* For fall admission, 2/1 for domestic students. Applications are processed on a rolling basis. Application fee: $50. Electronic applications accepted. *Expenses:* Tuition, state resident: full-time $4,156. Tuition, nonresident: full-time $14,762. Required fees: $205. Tuition and fees vary according to course load, campus/location, program and reciprocity agreements. *Financial support:* In 2003–04, 1 fellowship (averaging $2,500 per year), 10 research assistantships with partial tuition reimbursements (averaging $13,000 per year), 4 teaching assistantships with full tuition reimbursements (averaging $9,720 per year) were awarded. Career-related internships or fieldwork, Federal Work-Study, institutionally sponsored loans, and scholarships/grants also available. Financial award application deadline: 2/15. *Faculty research:* Land use hydrology, water quality, watershed planning and management, snow hydrology, hillslope-wetland hydrology. Total annual research expenditures: $800,000. *Unit head:* Dr. John D. Stednick, Program Leader, 970-491-7248, Fax: 970-491-6307, E-mail: jds@cnr.colostate.edu. *Application contact:* Barbara Holtz, Staff Assistant, 970-491-5662, Fax: 970-491-6307, E-mail: barbh@cnr.colostate.edu.

Duke University, Nicholas School of the Environment and Earth Sciences, Durham, NC 27708-0328. Offers coastal environmental management (MEM); environmental health and security (MEM); environmental science and policy (PhD); environmental toxicology, chemistry, and risk assessment (MEM); forest resource management (MF); global environmental change (MEM); resource ecology (MEM); resource economics and policy (MEM); water and air resources (MEM). PhD offered through the Graduate School. *Accreditation:* SAF (one or more programs are accredited). Part-time programs available. Terminal master's awarded for partial completion of

Water Resources

Duke University (continued)
doctoral program. *Degree requirements:* For master's, thesis (for some programs); for doctorate, thesis/dissertation. *Entrance requirements:* For master's, GRE General Test, previous course work in biology or ecology, calculus, statistics, and microeconomics; computer familiarity with word processing and data analysis; for doctorate, GRE General Test. Additional exam requirements/recommendations for international students: Required—TOEFL (minimum score 550 paper-based; 213 computer-based). Electronic applications accepted. Expenses: Contact institution. *Faculty research:* Ecosystem management, conservation ecology, earth systems, risk assessment.

See in-depth description on page 787.

Iowa State University of Science and Technology, Graduate College, College of Liberal Arts and Sciences, Department of Geological and Atmospheric Sciences, Ames, IA 50011. Offers earth science (MS, PhD); geology (MS, PhD); meteorology (MS, PhD); water resources (MS, PhD). *Faculty:* 17 full-time. *Students:* 28 full-time (13 women), 7 part-time (2 women); includes 1 minority (African American), 19 international. 24 applicants, 38% accepted, 6 enrolled. In 2003, 12 master's, 1 doctorate awarded. *Median time to degree:* Master's–2.9 years full-time. *Degree requirements:* For master's, thesis (for some programs); for doctorate, thesis/dissertation. *Entrance requirements:* For master's and doctorate, GRE General Test. Additional exam requirements/recommendations for international students: Required—TOEFL (paper score 530; computer score 197) or IELTS (score 6.0). *Application deadline:* For fall admission, 2/15 for domestic students. Applications are processed on a rolling basis. Application fee: $30 ($70 for international students). Electronic applications accepted. Tuition, nonresident: part-time $560 per credit. Required fees: $38 per unit. *Financial support:* In 2003–04, 20 research assistantships with full and partial tuition reimbursements (averaging $15,432 per year), 11 teaching assistantships with full and partial tuition reimbursements (averaging $15,432 per year) were awarded. Fellowships, scholarships/grants, health care benefits, and unspecified assistantships also available. *Unit head:* Dr. Carl E. Jacobson, Chair, 515-294-4477.

Iowa State University of Science and Technology, Graduate College, Interdisciplinary Programs, Program in Water Resources, Ames, IA 50011. Offers MS, PhD. *Students:* 18 full-time (4 women), 4 part-time (2 women); includes 2 minority (both African Americans), 10 international. In 2003, 7 master's, 1 doctorate awarded. *Degree requirements:* For master's and doctorate, thesis/dissertation. *Entrance requirements:* Additional exam requirements/recommendations for international students: Required—IELTS or TOEFL. *Application deadline:* For fall admission, 1/1 priority date for domestic students, 1/1 priority date for international students. Application fee: $30 ($70 for international students). Electronic applications accepted. Tuition, nonresident: part-time $560 per credit. Required fees: $38 per unit. *Financial support:* In 2003–04, 13 research assistantships with partial tuition reimbursements (averaging $16,632 per year), 3 teaching assistantships with partial tuition reimbursements (averaging $15,432 per year) were awarded. Scholarships/grants, health care benefits, and unspecified assistantships also available. *Unit head:* Dr. William Crumpton, Supervisory Committee Chair, 515-294-4752, Fax: 515-294-9573.

The Johns Hopkins University, Zanvyl Krieger School of Arts and Sciences, The Morton K. Blaustein Department of Earth and Planetary Sciences, Baltimore, MD 21218-2699. Offers geochemistry (MA, PhD); geology (MA, PhD); geophysics (MA, PhD); groundwater (MA, PhD); oceanography (MA, PhD); planetary atmosphere (MA, PhD). *Faculty:* 14 full-time (1 woman), 1 (woman) part-time/adjunct. *Students:* 23 full-time (10 women); includes 2 minority (both Hispanic Americans), 10 international. Average age 25. 48 applicants, 21% accepted, 5 enrolled. In 2003, 5 master's, 3 doctorates awarded. *Median time to degree:* Of those who began their doctoral program in fall 1995, 99% received their degree in 8 years or less. *Degree requirements:* For doctorate, thesis/dissertation, registration. *Entrance requirements:* For master's and doctorate, GRE General Test. Additional exam requirements/recommendations for international students: Required—TOEFL (minimum score 600 paper-based; 250 computer-based). *Application deadline:* For fall admission, 1/15 priority date for domestic students, 1/15 priority date for international students. Application fee: $55. Electronic applications accepted. *Expenses:* Tuition: Full-time $28,730; part-time $1,490 per course. Part-time tuition and fees vary according to course load, campus/location and program. *Financial support:* In 2003–04, 4 fellowships, 13 research assistantships, 7 teaching assistantships were awarded. Federal Work-Study and institutionally sponsored loans also available. Financial award application deadline: 4/15; financial award applicants required to submit FAFSA. Total annual research expenditures: $2.3 million. *Unit head:* Dr. Peter Olson, Chair, 410-516-4659, Fax: 410-516-7933, E-mail: epschair@jhunix.hcf.jhu.edu. *Application contact:* Carol Spangler, Academic Program Assistant, 410-516-7034, Fax: 410-516-7933, E-mail: cspangler@jhu.edu.

Montclair State University, The Graduate School, College of Science and Mathematics, Department of Earth and Environmental Studies, Program in Geoscience, Upper Montclair, NJ 07043-1624. Offers geoscience (MS); water resource management (Certificate). Part-time and evening/weekend programs available. *Faculty:* 12 full-time (0 women), 7 part-time/adjunct. *Students:* 1 (woman) full-time, 7 part-time (1 woman), 1 international. 8 applicants, 63% accepted, 3 enrolled. In 2003, 8 degrees awarded. *Degree requirements:* For master's, thesis or alternative, comprehensive exam. *Entrance requirements:* For master's, GRE General Test, 2 letters of recommendation. Additional exam requirements/recommendations for international students: Required—TOEFL (minimum score 550 paper-based; 213 computer-based). *Application deadline:* Applications are processed on a rolling basis. Application fee: $60. *Expenses:* Tuition, state resident: full-time $8,771; part-time $323 per credit. Tuition, nonresident: full-time $10,365; part-time $470 per credit. Required fees: $42 per credit. Tuition and fees vary according to degree level and program. *Financial support:* In 2003–04, research assistantships with full tuition reimbursements (averaging $5,000 per year); Federal Work-Study, scholarships/grants, and unspecified assistantships also available. Support available to part-time students. Financial award application deadline: 3/1; financial award applicants required to submit FAFSA. *Unit head:* Dr. Duke Ophori, Adviser, 973-655-7558, E-mail: ophorid@mail.montclair.edu.

Nova Scotia Agricultural College, Research and Graduate Studies, Truro, NS B2N 5E3, Canada. Offers agriculture (M Sc), including air quality, animal behavior, animal molecular genetics, animal nutrition, animal technology, aquaculture, botany, crop management, crop physiology, ecology, environmental microbiology, food science, horticulture, nutrient management, pest management, physiology, plant biotechnology, plant pathology, soil chemistry, soil fertility, waste management and composting, water quality. Part-time programs available. *Faculty:* 38 full-time (5 women), 13 part-time/adjunct (1 woman). *Students:* 46 full-time (27 women), 21 part-time (13 women); includes 13 minority (10 African Americans, 2 American Indian/Alaska Native, 1 Asian American or Pacific Islander). 45 applicants, 58% accepted, 16 enrolled. In 2003, 11 degrees awarded, leading to university research/teaching 18%, continued full-time study36%, business/industry 9%, government 27%. *Median time to degree:* Master's–2.25 years full-time, 4 years part-time. *Degree requirements:* For master's, thesis, candidacy exam. *Entrance requirements:* For master's, B.Sc. honors degree, minimum GPA of 3.0. Additional exam requirements/recommendations for international students: Required—TOEFL (minimum score 580 paper-based; 237 computer-based), Michigan English Language Assessment Battery. *Application deadline:* For fall admission, 6/1 for domestic students, 4/1 for international students; for winter admission, 11/15 for domestic students; for spring admission, 2/28 for domestic students. Applications are processed on a rolling basis. Application fee: $70. *Expenses:* Tuition, state resident: full-time $6,270. Tuition, nonresident: full-time $9,270. Required fees: $402. Tuition and fees vary according to student level. *Financial support:* In 2003–04, 63 students received support, including research assistantships (averaging $15,000 per year), teaching assistantships (averaging $900 per year); career-related internships or fieldwork, scholarships/grants, and unspecified assistantships also available. *Faculty research:* Organogenesis, somatic embryogenesis, composting, sustainable agriculture, ecotoxicology. Total annual research expenditures: $2 million. *Unit head:* Jill L. Rogers, Manager, 902-893-6360, Fax: 902-893-3430, E-mail: jrogers@nsac.ns.ca. *Application contact:* Marie Law, Administrative Assistant, 902-893-6502, Fax: 902-893-3430, E-mail: mlaw@nsac.ns.ca.

Rutgers, The State University of New Jersey, New Brunswick/Piscataway, Graduate School, Program in Environmental Sciences, New Brunswick, NJ 08901-1281. Offers air resources (MS, PhD); aquatic biology (MS, PhD); aquatic chemistry (MS, PhD); atmospheric science (MS, PhD); chemistry and physics of aerosol and hydrosol systems (MS, PhD); environmental chemistry (MS, PhD); environmental microbiology (MS, PhD); environmental toxicology (PhD); exposure assessment (PhD); fate and effects of pollutants (MS, PhD); pollution prevention and control (MS, PhD); water and wastewater treatment (MS, PhD); water resources (MS, PhD). *Faculty:* 62 full-time (12 women), 6 part-time/adjunct (1 woman). *Students:* 50 full-time (23 women), 57 part-time (27 women); includes 7 minority (1 African American, 4 Asian Americans or Pacific Islanders, 2 Hispanic Americans), 37 international. Average age 32. 110 applicants, 11% accepted, 8 enrolled. In 2003, 9 master's, 4 doctorates awarded. Terminal master's awarded for partial completion of doctoral program. *Degree requirements:* For master's, thesis or alternative, oral final exam, comprehensive exam; for doctorate, thesis/dissertation, thesis defense, qualifying exam, comprehensive exam. *Entrance requirements:* For master's and doctorate, GRE General Test. Additional exam requirements/recommendations for international students: Required—TOEFL. *Application deadline:* For fall admission, 3/1 for domestic students; for spring admission, 11/1 for domestic students. Applications are processed on a rolling basis. Application fee: $50. Electronic applications accepted. *Expenses:* Tuition, state resident: full-time $10,030. Tuition, nonresident: full-time $14,202. *Financial support:* In 2003–04, 10 fellowships with full tuition reimbursements (averaging $19,000 per year), 34 research assistantships with full tuition reimbursements (averaging $16,400 per year), 3 teaching assistantships with full tuition reimbursements (averaging $14,300 per year) were awarded. Career-related internships or fieldwork and Federal Work-Study also available. Financial award application deadline: 1/15; financial award applicants required to submit FAFSA. *Faculty research:* Atmospheric sciences; biological waste treatment; contaminant fate and transport; exposure assessment; air, soil and water quality. Total annual research expenditures: $5.7 million. *Unit head:* Dr. Barbara Turpin, Director, 732-932-9540, Fax: 732-932-8644, E-mail: env_gradpgm@envsci.rutgers.edu. *Application contact:* Dr. Paul J. Lioy, Graduate Admissions Committee, 732-932-0150, Fax: 732-445-0116, E-mail: plioy@eohsi.rutgers.edu.

South Dakota School of Mines and Technology, Graduate Division, Joint PhD Program in Atmospheric, Environmental, and Water Resources, Rapid City, SD 57701-3995. Offers PhD. *Students:* 3 full-time (1 woman), 9 part-time (2 women); includes 1 minority (American Indian/Alaska Native), 3 international. In 2003, 2 degrees awarded. *Degree requirements:* For doctorate, thesis/dissertation. *Entrance requirements:* For doctorate, GRE General Test, GRE Subject Test. Additional exam requirements/recommendations for international students: Required—TOEFL, TWE. *Application deadline:* For fall admission, 6/15 for domestic students; for spring admission, 10/15 for domestic students. Applications are processed on a rolling basis. Application fee: $35. Electronic applications accepted. *Expenses:* Tuition, state resident: part-time $109 per credit hour. Tuition, nonresident: part-time $323 per credit hour. Required fees: $100 per credit hour. *Financial support:* In 2003–04, 5 research assistantships with partial tuition reimbursements (averaging $23,500 per year) were awarded; teaching assistantships with partial tuition reimbursements *Unit head:* Dr. Andrew Detwiler, Chair, 605-394-2291. *Application contact:* Brenda Brown, Secretary, 800-454-8162 Ext. 2493, Fax: 605-394-5360, E-mail: graduate_admissions@silver.sdsmt.edu.

See in-depth description on page 313.

South Dakota State University, Graduate School, College of Engineering, Joint PhD Program in Atmospheric, Environmental, and Water Resources, Brookings, SD 57007. Offers PhD. Postbaccalaureate distance learning degree programs offered (minimal on-campus study). *Degree requirements:* For doctorate, thesis/dissertation, preliminary oral and written exams. *Entrance requirements:* Additional exam requirements/recommendations for international students: Required—TOEFL (minimum score 525 paper-based). Expenses: Contact institution.

See in-depth description on page 313.

State University of New York College of Environmental Science and Forestry, Faculty of Environmental Studies, Syracuse, NY 13210-2779. Offers environmental and community land planning (MPS, MS, PhD); environmental and natural resources policy (PhD); environmental communication and participatory processes (MPS, MS, PhD); environmental policy and democratic processes (MPS, MS, PhD); environmental systems and risk management (MPS, MS, PhD); water and wetland resource studies (MPS, MS, PhD). Part-time programs available. *Faculty:* 8 full-time (4 women), 10 part-time/adjunct (8 women). *Students:* 40 full-time (24 women), 26 part-time (16 women); includes 4 minority (2 African Americans, 1 Asian American or Pacific Islander, 1 Hispanic American), 25 international. Average age 32. 72 applicants, 61% accepted, 19 enrolled. In 2003, 25 master's, 3 doctorates awarded. *Degree requirements:* For master's, thesis (for some programs), registration; for doctorate, thesis/dissertation, comprehensive exam, registration. *Entrance requirements:* For master's and doctorate, GRE General Test, minimum GPA of 3.0. Additional exam requirements/recommendations for international students: Required—TOEFL (minimum score 550 paper-based; 213 computer-based). *Application deadline:* For fall admission, 2/1 priority date for domestic students, 2/1 priority date for international students; for spring admission, 11/1 priority date for domestic students, 11/1 priority date for international students. Applications are processed on a rolling basis. Application fee: $50. Tuition, area resident: Part-time $288 per credit hour. Tuition, nonresident: part-time $438 per credit hour. Required fees: $300; $5 per credit hour. $18 per semester. One-time fee: $25 full-time. *Financial support:* In 2003–04, 25 students received support, including 16 fellowships with full and partial tuition reimbursements available (averaging $9,446 per year), 5 research assistantships with full and partial tuition reimbursements available (averaging $10,000 per year), 7 teaching assistantships with full and partial tuition reimbursements available (averaging $9,446 per year); career-related internships or fieldwork, Federal Work-Study, institutionally sponsored loans, scholarships/grants, health care benefits, and unspecified assistantships also available. Support available to part-time students. Financial award applicants required to submit FAFSA. *Faculty research:* Environmental education/communications, water resources, land resources, waste management. Total annual research expenditures: $237,610. *Unit head:* Dr. Richard Smardon, Chair, 315-470-6636, Fax: 315-470-6915, E-mail: rsmardon@syr.edu. *Application contact:* Dr. Dudley J. Raynal, Dean, Instruction and Graduate Studies, 315-470-6599, Fax: 315-470-6978, E-mail: esfgrad@esf.edu.

State University of New York College of Environmental Science and Forestry, Faculty of Forest and Natural Resources Management, Syracuse, NY 13210-2779. Offers environmental and natural resource policy (MS, PhD); environmental and natural resources policy (MPS); forest management and operations (MF); forestry ecosystems science and applications (MPS, MS, PhD); natural resources management (MPS, MS, PhD); quantitative methods and management in forest science (MPS, MS, PhD); recreation and resource management (MPS, MS, PhD); watershed management and forest hydrology (MPS, MS, PhD). *Faculty:* 28 full-time (5 women). *Students:* 48 full-time (18 women), 26 part-time (10 women); includes 2 minority (1 African American, 1 Hispanic American), 14 international. Average age 32. 47 applicants, 57% accepted, 14 enrolled. In 2003, 35 master's, 5 doctorates awarded. *Degree requirements:* For master's, thesis (for some programs), registration; for doctorate, thesis/dissertation, comprehensive exam, registration. *Entrance requirements:* For master's and doctorate, GRE General Test, minimum GPA of 3.0. Additional exam requirements/recommendations for international students: Required—TOEFL (minimum score 550 paper-based; 213 computer-based). *Application deadline:* For fall admission, 2/1 priority date for domestic students, 2/1 priority date for international students; for spring admission, 11/1 priority date for domestic students, 11/1 priority date for international students. Applications are processed on a rolling basis. Application fee: $50. Tuition, area resident: Part-time $288 per credit hour. Tuition, nonresident: part-time $438 per credit hour. Required fees: $300; $5 per credit hour. $18 per semester. One-time fee: $25 full-time. *Financial support:* In 2003–04, 43 students received support, including 9 fellowships with full and partial tuition reimbursements available (averaging $9,446 per year), 15 research assistantships with full and partial tuition reimbursements available (averaging $10,000 per year), 14 teaching assistantships with full and partial tuition reimbursements available (averaging $9,446 per year); career-related internships or fieldwork, Federal Work-Study, institutionally sponsored loans, scholarships/grants, health care benefits, and unspecified assistantships also available. Financial award applicants required to submit FAFSA. *Faculty research:* Silviculture recreation management, tree improvement, operations management, economics. Total annual research expenditures: $1.9 million. *Unit head:* Dr. Chad P. Dawson, Chair, 315-470-6536, Fax: 315-470-6535, E-mail: cpdawson@esf.edu. *Application contact:* Dr. Dudley J. Raynal, Dean, Instruction and Graduate Studies, 315-470-6599, Fax: 315-470-6978, E-mail: esfgrad@esf.edu.

The University of Arizona, Graduate College, College of Agriculture and Life Sciences, Department of Soil, Water and Environmental Science, Tucson, AZ 85721. Offers MS, PhD. *Faculty:* 18 full-time (2 women). *Students:* 58 full-time (28 women), 15 part-time (7 women); includes 8 minority (2 African Americans, 2 Asian Americans or Pacific Islanders, 4 Hispanic Americans). Average age 32. 29 applicants, 52% accepted, 9 enrolled. In 2003, 6 master's, 3 doctorates awarded. *Degree requirements:* For master's, thesis; for doctorate, one foreign language, thesis/dissertation. *Entrance requirements:* Additional exam requirements/recommendations for international students: Required—TOEFL. *Application deadline:* For fall admission, 3/1 for domestic students. Applications are processed on a rolling basis. Application fee: $50. *Expenses:* Tuition, state resident: part-time $196 per unit. Tuition, nonresident: part-time $326 per unit. *Financial support:* In 2003–04, 5 students received support, including research assistantships (averaging $16,000 per year), teaching assistantships (averaging $16,000 per year); Federal Work-Study, institutionally sponsored loans, scholarships/grants, and tuition waivers (full and partial) also available. Financial award application deadline: 5/1. *Faculty research:* Plant production, environmental microbiology, contaminant flow and transport. Total annual research expenditures: $2.8 million. *Unit head:* Dr. Jeffery C. Silvertooth, Head, 520-621-7228, Fax: 520-621-1647, E-mail: silver@ag.arizona.edu. *Application contact:* Judi Ellwanger, Graduate Coordinator, 520-621-1646, Fax: 520-621-1647, E-mail: ellwangr@ag.arizona.edu.

The University of Arizona, Graduate College, College of Engineering, Department of Hydrology and Water Resources, Tucson, AZ 85721. Offers hydrology (MS, PhD); water resources engineering (M Eng). Part-time programs available. *Faculty:* 30. *Students:* 61 full-time (20 women), 23 part-time (8 women); includes 4 minority (2 American Indian/Alaska Native, 2 Hispanic Americans), 28 international. Average age 32. 58 applicants, 76% accepted, 16 enrolled. In 2003, 19 master's, 8 doctorates awarded. *Median time to degree:* Of those who began their doctoral program in fall 1995, 100% received their degree in 8 years or less. *Degree requirements:* For master's and doctorate, thesis/dissertation. *Entrance requirements:* For master's, GRE General Test, minimum undergraduate GPA of 3.0; for doctorate, GRE General Test, minimum undergraduate GPA of 3.2, 3.4 graduate. Additional exam requirements/recommendations for international students: Required—TOEFL. *Application deadline:* For fall admission, 4/30 for domestic students, 12/1 for international students. Applications are processed on a rolling basis. Application fee: $50. *Expenses:* Tuition, state resident: part-time $196 per unit. Tuition, nonresident: part-time $326 per unit. *Financial support:* In 2003–04, 3 fellowships with partial tuition reimbursements (averaging $15,000 per year), 42 research assistantships with partial tuition reimbursements (averaging $17,074 per year), 5 teaching assistantships with partial tuition reimbursements (averaging $8,537 per year) were awarded. Institutionally sponsored loans, scholarships/grants, health care benefits, and unspecified assistantships also available. Financial award application deadline: 1/31. *Faculty research:* Subsurface and surface hydrology, hydrometeorology/climatology, applied remote sensing, water resource systems, environmental hydrology and water quality. Total annual research expenditures: $7.5 million. *Unit head:* Dr. Victor R. Baker, Head, 520-621-7120, E-mail: baker@hwr.arizona.edu. *Application contact:* Teresa Thompson, Academic Advising Coordinator, 520-621-3131, Fax: 520-621-1422, E-mail: programs@hwr.arizona.edu.

University of Florida, Graduate School, College of Agricultural and Life Sciences, Department of Soil and Water Science, Gainesville, FL 32611. Offers M Ag, MS, PhD. Part-time programs available. *Faculty:* 53. *Students:* 62 full-time (24 women), 16 part-time (2 women); includes 6 minority (3 African Americans, 3 Hispanic Americans), 33 international. 27 applicants, 78% accepted. In 2003, 11 master's, 1 doctorate awarded. Terminal master's awarded for partial completion of doctoral program. *Degree requirements:* For master's, thesis optional; for doctorate, thesis/dissertation. *Entrance requirements:* For master's and doctorate, GRE General Test, minimum GPA of 3.0. Additional exam requirements/recommendations for international students: Required—TOEFL. *Application deadline:* For fall admission, 6/1 for domestic students; for spring admission, 9/14 for domestic students. Applications are processed on a rolling basis. Application fee: $20. Electronic applications accepted. *Expenses:* Tuition, state resident: part-time $205 per credit hour. Tuition, nonresident: part-time $775 per credit hour. *Financial support:* In 2003–04, 33 students received support, including 24 research assistantships, 2 teaching assistantships; fellowships, career-related internships or fieldwork, Federal Work-Study, institutionally sponsored loans, and unspecified assistantships also available. Support available to part-time students. *Faculty research:* Environmental fate and transport of pesticides, conservation, wetlands, land application of nonhazardous waste, soil/water agrochemical management. *Unit head:* Dr. K. Ramesh Reddy, Chair and Graduate Research Professor, 352-392-1803 Ext. 341, Fax: 352-392-3399, E-mail: krr@ufl.edu. *Application contact:* Dr. Nicholas B. Comerford, Graduate Coordinator and Professor, 352-392-1951 Ext. 248, Fax: 352-392-3902, E-mail: nbc@mail.ifas.ufl.edu.

University of Illinois at Chicago, Graduate College, College of Liberal Arts and Sciences, Department of Earth and Environmental Sciences, Chicago, IL 60607-7128. Offers crystallography (MS, PhD); environmental geology (MS, PhD); geochemistry (MS, PhD); geology (MS, PhD); geomorphology (MS, PhD); geophysics (MS, PhD); geotechnical engineering and geosciences (PhD); hydrogeology (MS, PhD); low-temperature and organic geochemistry (MS, PhD); mineralogy (MS, PhD); paleoclimatology (MS, PhD); paleontology (MS, PhD); petrology (MS, PhD); quaternary geology (MS, PhD); sedimentology (MS, PhD); water resources (MS, PhD). *Faculty:* 9 full-time (2 women). *Students:* 18 full-time (7 women), 5 part-time (1 woman); includes 3 minority (1 African American, 1 American Indian/Alaska Native, 1 Asian American or Pacific Islander), 11 international. Average age 29. 15 applicants, 27% accepted, 4 enrolled. In 2003, 2 degrees awarded. *Degree requirements:* For master's and doctorate, thesis/dissertation. *Entrance requirements:* For master's and doctorate, GRE General Test, minimum GPA of 3.75 on a 5.0 scale. Additional exam requirements/recommendations for international students: Required—TOEFL. *Application deadline:* For fall admission, 5/15 for domestic students, 2/1 for international students; for spring admission, 11/1 for domestic students, 7/15 for international students. Applications are processed on a rolling basis. Application fee: $40 ($50 for international students). Electronic applications accepted. *Expenses:* Tuition, state resident: part-time $941 per semester. Tuition, nonresident: part-time $2,338 per semester. *Financial support:* In 2003–04, 16 students received support; fellowships with full tuition reimbursements available, research assistantships with full tuition reimbursements available, teaching assistantships with full tuition reimbursements available, Federal Work-Study, scholarships/grants, traineeships, tuition waivers (full), and unspecified assistantships available. Financial award application deadline: 3/1; financial award applicants required to submit FAFSA. *Unit head:* Neil Sturchio, Head, 312-996-3154. *Application contact:* Peter Doran, Director of Graduate Studies, 312-413-7275, E-mail: pdoran@uic.edu.

University of Kansas, Graduate School, School of Engineering, Department of Civil, Environmental, and Architectural Engineering, Lawrence, KS 66045. Offers architectural engineering (MS); civil engineering (MCE, MS, DE, PhD); construction management (MCM); environmental engineering (MS, PhD); environmental science (MS, PhD); water resources science (MS). Part-time and evening/weekend programs available. *Faculty:* 27. *Students:* 42 full-time (12 women), 108 part-time (28 women); includes 5 minority (2 African Americans, 2 American Indian/Alaska Native, 1 Hispanic American), 25 international. Average age 30. 119 applicants, 48% accepted, 30 enrolled. In 2003, 31 master's, 3 doctorates awarded. *Degree requirements:* For master's, thesis or alternative, exam; for doctorate, thesis/dissertation, comprehensive exam. *Entrance requirements:* For master's, GRE, minimum GPA of 3.0; for doctorate, GRE, minimum GPA of 3.5. Additional exam requirements/recommendations for international students: Required—TOEFL, Michigan English Language Assessment Battery. *Application deadline:* For fall admission, 7/1 for domestic students, 7/1 for international students; for spring admission, 12/1 for domestic students, 12/1 for international students. Applications are processed on a rolling basis. Application fee: $55 ($60 for international students). Electronic applications accepted. *Expenses:* Tuition, state resident: full-time $3,745. Tuition, nonresident: full-time $10,075. Required fees: $574. *Financial support:* In 2003–04, 18 research assistantships with full and partial tuition reimbursements (averaging $11,073 per year), 10 teaching assistantships with full and partial tuition reimbursements (averaging $9,540 per year) were awarded. Fellowships, career-related internships or fieldwork also available. Financial award application deadline: 4/1. *Faculty research:* Structures (fracture mechanics), transportation, environmental health, water resources, engineering materials. Total annual research expenditures: $2.2 million. *Unit head:* Thomas E. Mulinazzi, Chair, 785-864-3766, Fax: 785-864-5631, E-mail: tomm@ku.edu. *Application contact:* Bruce McEnroe, Graduate Director, E-mail: mcenroe@ku.edu.

University of Minnesota, Twin Cities Campus, Graduate School, College of Agricultural, Food, and Environmental Sciences, Department of Soil, Water, and Climate, Minneapolis, MN 55455-0213. Offers MS, PhD. *Faculty:* 28 full-time (1 woman), 8 part-time/adjunct (0 women). *Students:* 26 full-time (12 women), 2 part-time (both women); includes 1 African American, 6 Asian Americans or Pacific Islanders, 4 Hispanic Americans. Average age 25. 19 applicants, 58% accepted, 9 enrolled. In 2003, 5 degrees awarded. *Median time to degree:* Master's–2.5 years full-time. *Degree requirements:* For master's, thesis or alternative; for doctorate, thesis/dissertation. *Entrance requirements:* For master's and doctorate, GRE General Test, minimum GPA of 3.0. Additional exam requirements/recommendations for international students: Required—TOEFL (minimum score 550 paper-based; 213 computer-based). *Application deadline:* For fall admission, 6/15 for domestic students; for spring admission, 10/15 for domestic students. Applications are processed on a rolling basis. Application fee: $55 ($75 for international students). Electronic applications accepted. *Expenses:* Tuition, state resident: full-time $3,681; part-time $614 per credit. Tuition, nonresident: full-time $7,231; part-time $1,205 per credit. *Financial support:* In 2003–04, 2 fellowships with full tuition reimbursements (averaging $17,000 per year), 24 research assistantships with full and partial tuition reimbursements (averaging $16,000 per year), 2 teaching assistantships with full tuition reimbursements (averaging $16,000 per year) were awarded. Federal Work-Study, scholarships/grants, health care benefits, tuition waivers (full), and unspecified assistantships also available. Support available to part-time students. *Faculty research:* Soil water and atmospheric resources, soil physical management, agricultural chemicals and their management, plant nutrient management, biological nitrogen fixation. *Unit head:* Dr. Edward A. Nater, Head, 612-625-9734, Fax: 612-625-2208, E-mail: enater@umn.edu. *Application contact:* Dr. Deborah L. Allan, Professor and Director of Graduate Studies, 612-625-3158, Fax: 612-625-2208, E-mail: dallan@umn.edu.

University of Missouri–Rolla, Graduate School, School of Materials, Energy, and Earth Resources, Department of Geological Sciences and Engineering, Program in Geology and Geophysics, Rolla, MO 65409-0910. Offers geochemistry (MS, PhD); geology (MS, PhD); geophysics (MS, PhD); groundwater and environmental geology (MS, PhD). Part-time programs available. *Faculty:* 8 full-time (1 woman). *Students:* 26 full-time (10 women), 3 part-time (1 woman); includes 2 minority (1 African American, 1 Hispanic American), 10 international. Average age 31. 26 applicants, 65% accepted, 3 enrolled. In 2003, 13 master's, 4 doctorates awarded. *Median time to degree:* Master's–1.5 years full-time, 5.3 years part-time; doctorate–5 years full-time, 7 years part-time. *Degree requirements:* For master's and doctorate, thesis/dissertation. *Entrance requirements:* For master's, GRE General Test, GRE Subject Test, minimum GPA of 3.0 in last 4 semesters; for doctorate, GRE General Test, GRE Subject Test. Additional exam requirements/recommendations for international students: Required—TOEFL. *Application deadline:* For fall admission, 7/1 for domestic students; for spring admission, 12/1 for domestic students. Applications are processed on a rolling basis. Application fee: $50. Electronic applications accepted. *Expenses:* Tuition, state resident: full-time $5,871. Tuition, nonresident: full-time $13,114. Required fees: $820. Tuition and fees vary according to course load. *Financial support:* In 2003–04, 23 students received support, including 22 fellowships with full tuition reimbursements available (averaging $13,250 per year), 16 research assistantships with partial tuition reimbursements available (averaging $13,250 per year); teaching assistantships with partial tuition reimbursements available, Federal Work-Study and institutionally sponsored loans also available. Support available to part-time students. Financial award application deadline: 3/1; financial award applicants required to submit FAFSA. *Faculty research:* Economic geology, geophysical modeling, seismic wave analysis. Total annual research expenditures: $272,086.

University of Nevada, Las Vegas, Graduate College, College of Science, Program in Water Resources Management, Las Vegas, NV 89154-9900. Offers MS. Part-time programs available. *Faculty:* 6 part-time/adjunct (1 woman). *Students:* 4 full-time (1 woman), 9 part-time (3 women); includes 1 minority (Hispanic American), 1 international. 8 applicants, 63% accepted, 5 enrolled. *Degree requirements:* For master's, thesis, comprehensive exam. *Entrance requirements:* For master's, GRE Subject Test, minimum GPA of 3.0. Additional exam requirements/recommendations for international students: Required—TOEFL (minimum score 550 paper-based; 213 computer-based). *Application deadline:* For fall admission, 6/15 for domestic students, 5/1 for international students; for spring admission, 11/15 for domestic students, 10/1 for international students. Application fee: $60 ($75 for international students). *Expenses:* Tuition, state resident: part-time $115 per credit. Tuition, nonresident: part-time $242 per credit. Required fees: $8 per semester. Tuition and fees vary according to course load. *Financial support:* In 2003–04, 1 research assistantship with partial tuition reimbursement (averaging $10,000 per year) was awarded. Financial award application deadline: 3/1. *Unit head:* Dr. Charalambos Papelis, Director, 702-895-3262. *Application contact:* Graduate College Admissions Evaluator, 702-895-3320, Fax: 702-895-4180, E-mail: gradcollege@ccmail.nevada.edu.

University of New Brunswick Fredericton, School of Graduate Studies, Faculty of Engineering, Department of Civil Engineering, Fredericton, NB E3B 5A3, Canada. Offers construction engineering and management (M Eng, M Sc E, PhD); environmental engineering (M Eng, M Sc E, PhD); geotechnical engineering (M Eng, M Sc E, PhD); groundwater/hydrology (M Eng, M Sc E, PhD); materials (M Eng, M Sc E, PhD); pavements (M Eng, M Sc E, PhD); structures (M Eng, M Sc E, PhD); transportation (M Eng, M Sc E, PhD). Part-time programs available. *Degree requirements:* For master's, thesis; for doctorate, thesis/dissertation, qualifying exam. *Entrance requirements:* For master's and doctorate, minimum GPA of 3.0. Additional exam requirements/recommendations for international students: Required—TOEFL, TWE. *Faculty research:* Steel and masonry structures, traffic engineering, highway safety, centrifuge modeling, transport and fate of reactive contaminants, durability of marine concrete.

University of New Hampshire, Graduate School, College of Life Sciences and Agriculture, Department of Natural Resources, Durham, NH 03824. Offers environmental conservation (MS); forestry (MS); soil science (MS); water resources management (MS); wildlife (MS). Part-time programs available. *Faculty:* 40 full-time. *Students:* 25 full-time (11 women), 31 part-time (21 women), 5 international. Average age 32. 74 applicants, 38% accepted, 16 enrolled. In 2003, 13 degrees awarded. *Degree requirements:* For master's, thesis or alternative. *Entrance requirements:* For master's, GRE General Test. Additional exam requirements/recommendations for international students: Required—TOEFL (minimum score 550 paper-based; 213 computer-based); Recommended—TSE. *Application deadline:* For fall admission, 4/1 for domestic students; for winter admission, 12/1 for domestic students. Applications are processed on a rolling basis. Application fee: $50. Electronic applications accepted. Tuition, area resident: Full-time $7,070. *Expenses:* Tuition, state resident: full-time $10,605. Tuition, nonresident: full-time $17,430. Required fees: $15. *Financial support:* In 2003–04, 3 fellowships, 15 research assistantships, 12 teaching assistantships were awarded. Career-related internships or fieldwork, Federal Work-Study, scholarships/grants, and tuition waivers (full and partial) also available. Support available to part-time students. Financial award application

Water Resources

University of New Hampshire (continued)

deadline: 2/15. *Unit head:* Dr. William H. McDowell, Chairperson, 603-862-2249, E-mail: tehoward@cisunix.unh.edu. *Application contact:* Linda Scogin, Administrative Assistant, 603-862-3932, E-mail: natural.resources @unh.edu.

University of New Mexico, Graduate School, Program in Water Resources, Albuquerque, NM 87131-2039. Offers MWR. Part-time programs available. *Faculty:* 1 (woman) part-time/adjunct. *Students:* 18 full-time (11 women), 28 part-time (15 women); includes 10 minority (1 American Indian/Alaska Native, 1 Asian American or Pacific Islander, 8 Hispanic Americans). Average age 34. 25 applicants, 76% accepted, 15 enrolled. In 2003, 8 degrees awarded. *Degree requirements:* For master's, thesis, comprehensive exam. *Entrance requirements:* For master's, minimum GPA of 3.0 during last 2 years of undergraduate work, 3 letters of reference, letter of intent. *Application deadline:* For fall admission, 7/13 for domestic students; for spring admission, 11/13 for domestic students. Application fee: $40. *Expenses:* Tuition, state resident: full-time $1,802; part-time $152 per credit hour. Tuition, nonresident: full-time $6,135; part-time $513 per credit hour. Tuition and fees vary according to program. *Financial support:* In 2003–04, 20 students received support, including 7 research assistantships (averaging $3,605 per year) Financial award application deadline: 3/1; financial award applicants required to submit FAFSA. *Faculty research:* Sustainable water resources, transboundary water resources, economics, water law. Total annual research expenditures: $16,207. *Unit head:* Dr. Michael E. Campana, Director, 505-277-7759, Fax: 505-277-5226, E-mail: aquadoc@unm.edu. *Application contact:* Jennifer Honey, Administrative Assistant II, 505-277-7759, E-mail: jhoney@unm.edu.

University of Oklahoma, Graduate College, College of Engineering, School of Civil Engineering and Environmental Science, Program in Environmental Science, Norman, OK 73019-0390. Offers air (M Env Sc); environmental science (PhD); groundwater management (M Env Sc); hazardous solid waste (M Env Sc); occupational safety and health (M Env Sc); process design (M Env Sc); water quality resources (M Env Sc). Part-time programs available. *Students:* 17 full-time (13 women), 6 part-time (3 women); includes 6 minority (2 African Americans, 3 American Indian/Alaska Native, 1 Asian American or Pacific Islander), 5 international. 17 applicants, 65% accepted, 5 enrolled. In 2003, 3 degrees awarded. Terminal master's awarded for partial completion of doctoral program. *Degree requirements:* For master's, oral exams; for doctorate, thesis/dissertation, oral, and qualifying exams, comprehensive exam. *Entrance requirements:* For master's, minimum GPA of 3.0; for doctorate, minimum graduate GPA of 3.5. Additional exam requirements/recommendations for international students: Required—TOEFL (minimum score 600 paper-based). *Application deadline:* For fall admission, 4/1 priority date for domestic students, 4/1 priority date for international students; for spring admission, 11/1 for domestic students, 9/1 for international students. Applications are processed on a rolling basis. Application fee: $25 ($75 for international students). *Expenses:* Tuition, state resident: full-time $2,774; part-time $116 per credit hour. Tuition, nonresident: full-time $9,571; part-time $399 per credit hour. Required fees: $953; $33 per credit hour. Full-time tuition and fees vary according to course level, course load and program. *Financial support:* In 2003–04, 8 students received support; fellowships, research assistantships with partial tuition reimbursements available, teaching assistantships with partial tuition reimbursements available, scholarships/grants available. Financial award application deadline: 3/1; financial award applicants required to submit FAFSA. *Application contact:* Susan Williams, Graduate Programs Specialist, 405-325-2344, Fax: 405-325-4217, E-mail: srwilliams@ou.edu.

University of Vermont, Graduate College, School of Natural Resources, Program in Water Resources, Burlington, VT 05405. Offers MS. *Students:* 7 (4 women). 21 applicants, 29% accepted, 3 enrolled. In 2003, 3 degrees awarded. *Entrance requirements:* For master's, GRE General Test. Additional exam requirements/recommendations for international students: Required—TOEFL. *Application deadline:* For fall admission, 3/1 for domestic students. Applications are processed on a rolling basis. Application fee: $25. *Expenses:* Tuition, state resident: part-time $362 per credit hour. Tuition, nonresident: part-time $906 per credit hour. *Financial support:* Application deadline: 3/1. *Unit head:* Dr. A. McIntosh, Director, 802-656-2620. *Application contact:* D. Wang, Coordinator, 802-656-2620.

University of Wisconsin–Madison, Graduate School, Gaylord Nelson Institute for Environmental Studies, Water Resources Management Program, Madison, WI 53706-1380. Offers MS. Part-time programs available. *Faculty:* 1 full-time (0 women), 49 part-time/adjunct (14 women). *Students:* 15 full-time (12 women), 4 part-time (all women); includes 1 minority (African American) Average age 29. 33 applicants, 70% accepted, 8 enrolled. In 2003, 9 degrees awarded. *Degree requirements:* For master's, practicum. *Entrance requirements:* For master's, GRE General Test. Additional exam requirements/recommendations for international students: Required—TOEFL (minimum score 550 paper-based; 213 computer-based). *Application deadline:* For fall admission, 2/1 for domestic students, 2/1 for international students; for spring admission, 10/15 for domestic students, 10/15 for international students. Application fee: $45. Electronic applications accepted. Tuition, area resident: Full-time $7,593; part-time $476 per credit. Tuition, nonresident: full-time $22,824; part-time $1,430 per credit. Required fees: $292; $38 per credit. Part-time tuition and fees vary according to course load and reciprocity agreements. *Financial support:* In 2003–04, 9 students received support, including 1 fellowship with full tuition reimbursement available (averaging $14,400 per year), 2 teaching assistantships with full tuition reimbursements available (averaging $11,260 per year); research assistantships, career-related internships or fieldwork, Federal Work-Study, scholarships/grants, health care benefits, unspecified assistantships, and project assistantships also available. Financial award application deadline: 1/2. *Faculty research:* Geology, hydrogeology, water chemistry, limnology, oceanography. *Unit head:* Frederick W. Madison, Chair, 608-263-4004, Fax: 608-262-2273, E-mail: fredmad@wisc.edu. *Application contact:* James E. Miller, Associate Student Services Coordinator, 608-263-4373, Fax: 608-262-2273, E-mail: jemiller@wisc.edu.

University of Wyoming, Graduate School, College of Agriculture, Department of Renewable Resources, Laramie, WY 82070. Offers entomology (MS, PhD); rangeland ecology and watershed management (MS, PhD), including soil sciences (PhD), soil sciences and water resources (MS), water resources. *Faculty:* 22 full-time (1 woman). *Students:* 20 full-time (7 women), 10 part-time (3 women), 7 international. 8 applicants. In 2003, 11 master's, 3 doctorates awarded. *Degree requirements:* For master's, thesis (for some programs); for doctorate, 2 foreign languages, thesis/dissertation. *Entrance requirements:* For master's and doctorate, GRE General Test, minimum GPA of 3.0. *Application deadline:* For fall admission, 6/1 for domestic students; for spring admission, 12/1 priority date for domestic students. Applications are processed on a rolling basis. Application fee: $40. *Expenses:* Tuition, state resident: part-time $142 per credit hour. Tuition, nonresident: part-time $408 per credit hour. Required fees: $134 per semester. Tuition and fees vary according to course load, campus/location, program and student level. *Financial support:* In 2003–04, 8 students received support, including 8 research assistantships with full tuition reimbursements available (averaging $10,062 per year); career-related internships or fieldwork and Federal Work-Study also available. Financial award application deadline: 3/1. *Faculty research:* Plant control, grazing management, riparian restoration, riparian management, reclamation. *Unit head:* Dr. Thomas L. Thurow, Head, 307-766-2263, Fax: 307-766-6403, E-mail: thurow@uwyo.edu. *Application contact:* Kimm Mann-Malody, Office Assistant, Sr., 307-766-2263, Fax: 307-766-6403, E-mail: kimmmann@uwyo.edu.

DUKE UNIVERSITY

Nicholas School of the Environment and Earth Sciences

Programs of Study

The Nicholas School has a commitment to education and research addressing an area of vital concern—the quality of the Earth's environment and the sustainable use of its natural resources. The Nicholas School is built on the belief that finding workable solutions to environmental issues requires the viewpoints of more than one discipline.

With facilities at Duke's Durham campus and the Duke Marine Laboratory within the Outer Banks on the North Carolina coast, the Nicholas School is organized around program areas and research centers rather than traditionally structured departments. The centers serve to focus interdisciplinary research and educational activity on a variety of national and international environmental issues.

The Nicholas School's faculty members specialize in an array of disciplines, with particular strengths in global change, ecosystem science (forest and wetlands), coastal ecosystem processes, environmental health (responses to toxic pollutants), and environmental economics and policy. Through joint faculty appointments and research, the School is affiliated with Duke's Departments of Biology, Biological Anthropology and Anatomy, Cell Biology, Chemistry, Economics, and Statistics; the School of Engineering; and Duke University Medical Center. Joint-degree programs are offered with the School of Law, Fuqua School of Business, the Terry Sanford Institute of Public Policy, and the Master of Arts in Teaching program.

Students may earn a Master of Environmental Management (M.E.M.) or Master of Forestry (M.F.) degree through the Nicholas School of the Environment and Earth Sciences. These are two-year professional degrees that require 48 units of credit. A one-year, 30-unit M.F. program is available for students who have a Bachelor of Science in Forestry from an accredited forestry school. A reduced-credit option is also available through the Senior Professional Program for students who have at least five years of related professional experience; this option requires a minimum of 30 units and one semester in residence.

The Ph.D. is offered through the Graduate School of Duke University and is appropriate for students planning careers in teaching or research. The M.S. degree may be awarded as part of a Ph.D. program.

Course work and research for the School's professional degrees are concentrated in seven program areas: coastal environmental management, environmental health and security, forest resource management, global environmental change, resource ecology, environmental economics and policy, and water and air resources. In addition, faculty members at the Nicholas School's Marine Laboratory offer opportunities for course work and research in the basic ocean sciences, marine biology, environmental and human health sciences, and marine biotechnology.

Research Facilities

The Nicholas School is headquartered in the Levine Science Research Center, an interdisciplinary, state-of-the-art facility that is fully equipped to meet the technical demands of modern teaching and research. The center's fiber-optic networking systems give students access to high-performance computing at Duke and around the world. Students also have access to an online reference network linking all libraries at Duke University, North Carolina State University, and the University of North Carolina at Chapel Hill. The 8,000-acre Duke Forest lies adjacent to the campus and in two neighboring counties. A phytotron with fifty controlled-growth chambers and greenhouses is available for plant research.

The Marine Laboratory in Beaufort, North Carolina, is a complete residential research and teaching facility with modern laboratories, computer facilities, and an extensive library. It is the home port for the 135-foot oceanographic research vessel *Cape Hatteras* and the 57-foot coastal ocean research and training vessel *Susan Hudson.*

Financial Aid

Scholarships, fellowships, assistantships, and student loans are available from a variety of sources, and many students receive financial aid. The Nicholas School maintains its own career services office to assist students in finding paid internships and permanent employment.

Cost of Study

Tuition is $25,254 per year full-time and $968 per unit part-time in 2004–05. A health fee of $524 is required.

Living and Housing Costs

Most graduate and professional students live off campus and many share rent with 1 or 2 roommates. Rent for apartments and houses in Durham varies widely; students can expect to pay from $400 to $700 monthly. Living costs in Beaufort are comparable. A limited amount of on-campus housing is also available on the Durham campus.

Student Group

Approximately 200 students are enrolled in the Nicholas School of the Environment, and 50 are in the Department of the Environment of the Graduate School. The ratio of men to women is approximately equal. The School draws students with undergraduate degrees from liberal arts colleges and research universities and from international locations. While prior work experience is not a requirement for admission, it is highly valued.

Location

Durham (population 198,000), Raleigh, and Chapel Hill form an urban area known as the Research Triangle of North Carolina. Area residents enjoy annual outdoor festivals and numerous other events in drama, music, dance, and the visual arts. The Atlantic Ocean and the Blue Ridge Mountains are each within several hours' drive. The Marine Laboratory is located 180 miles east, on Pivers Island within North Carolina's Outer Banks, adjacent to the historic town of Beaufort (population 5,000).

The University and The School

Noted for its magnificent Gothic architecture and its academic excellence, Duke is among the smallest of the nation's leading universities, having a total enrollment of about 11,000. Its spacious campus is bounded on the east by residential sections of Durham and on the west by the Duke Forest.

The Nicholas School of the Environment and Earth Sciences was established in 1991, but its roots date back to 1938. Duke's Department of Geology was added to the School in 1997. The Nicholas School is the only private graduate school of forestry, environmental studies, and marine sciences in the country. Its professional forestry program has been continuously accredited by the Society of American Foresters since 1938.

Applying

Most students are admitted for fall matriculation. Applications must be received by February 1 for priority consideration. Those received after the priority deadline are considered if space is available. Applications for spring are considered on a space-available basis; the deadline is October 15. GRE scores are required. Applicants for federal financial aid must submit a Free Application for Federal Student Aid (FAFSA).

Applicants interested only in research or summer courses at the Marine Laboratory should direct their first inquiry to the Admissions Office, Duke University Marine Laboratory.

Individuals interested in M.S. or Ph.D. degrees in earth or ocean sciences through the School's Division of Earth and Ocean Sciences should see the separate listing under Geology Directory of this guide.

Correspondence and Information

Enrollment Services Office
Nicholas School of the Environment
and Earth Sciences
Duke University
Box 90330
Durham, North Carolina 27708-0330
Telephone: 919-613-8070
E-mail: envadm@duke.edu
World Wide Web: http://www.nicholas.duke.edu

Admissions Office
Duke University Marine Laboratory
Nicholas School of the Environment
and Earth Sciences
Duke University
135 Duke Marine Lab Road
Beaufort, North Carolina 28516-9721
Telephone: 252-504-7502
E-mail: hnearing@duke.edu
World Wide Web: http://www.nicholas.duke.edu

Duke University

THE FACULTY AND THEIR RESEARCH

William H. Schlesinger, Dean, Nicholas School of the Environment and Earth Sciences; Ph.D., Cornell, 1976. Global biogeochemistry, particularly the role of soils in global element cycles.

Core Faculty/Durham

Paul A. Baker, Ph.D., California, San Diego (Scripps), 1981. Geochemistry and diagenesis of marine sediments and sedimentary rocks and their desposital history.
Alan E. Boudreau, Ph.D., Washington, 1986. Understanding the crystallization of large layered intrusions with particular attention on the Archean Stillwater complex in Montana.
Norman L. Christensen, Ph.D., California, Santa Barbara, 1973. Effects of disturbance on plant populations and communities, patterns of forest development, remote sensing of forest change, fire ecology.
James S. Clark, Ph.D., Minnesota, 1988. Factors responsible for ecosystem patterns and how they respond to long-term changes in the physical environment, especially fire.
Bruce Hayward Corliss, Ph.D., Rhode Island, 1978. Cenozoic paleoceanography and studies of marine microfossils and deep-sea sediments.
Thomas Crowley, Ph.D., Brown, 1976. Study of past climates—patterns and nature of climate change and their relevance to understanding present climate change and future projections of climate change.
Richard T. Di Giulio, Ph.D., Virginia Tech, 1982. Aquatic toxicology; metabolism, modes of action, and genotoxicity in aquatic animals; development of biochemical responses as biomarkers of environmental quality.
Jonathan H. Freedman, Ph.D., Yeshiva (Einstein), 1986. Molecular biology and toxicology, molecular mechanisms regulating an organism's response to environmental stress.
Peter K. Haff, Ph.D., Virginia, 1970. Quantitative modeling techniques, including computer simulation, to describe and predict the course of natural geological processes that occur on the surface of the Earth.
Patrick N. Halpin, Ph.D., Virginia, 1995. Landscape ecology, GIS and remote sensing and international conservation management.
Gary S. Hartshorn, Ph.D., Washington (Seattle), 1972. Tropical forest dynamics, biodiversity conservation, dominance-diversity patterns, and sustainable forest management.
Robert G. Healy, Ph.D., UCLA, 1972. Natural resource, land-use, and environmental policy; reconciling Third World development with environmental quality and sustainable use of natural resources; tourism policy.
Gabriele Hegerl, Ph.D., Ludwig-Maximilians (Germany), 1992. Natural variability of climate, changes in climate due to natural and anthropogenic changes in radiative forcing.
David E. Hinton, Ph.D., Mississippi, 1969. Environmental toxicology and effects assessment in aquatic organisms.
Robert B. Jackson, Ph.D., Utah State, 1992. Ecosystem functioning and feedbacks between global change and the biosphere.
Jeffrey A. Karson, Ph.D., SUNY at Albany, 1977. Structural and tectonic analysis of rift and transform plate boundaries.
Prasad S. Kasibhatla, Ph.D., Kentucky, 1988. Anthropogenic emissions on atmospheric composition and reactivity on marine and terrestrial ecosystems.
Gabriel G. Katul, Ph.D., California, Davis, 1993. Hydrology and fluid mechanisms in the environment.
Richard F. Kay, Ph.D., Yale, 1973. The evolutionary history of the order primates, including further documenting the fossil history of Neotropical monkeys.
Robert O. Keohane, Ph.D., Harvard, 1966. Role of international institutions, including international environmental regimes; how such institutions become effective in promoting concern about the environment.
Emily M. Klein, Ph.D., Columbia, 1989. The geochemistry of ocean ridge basalts using diverse tools of major and trace element and isotropic analysis.
Randall A. Kramer, Ph.D., California, Davis, 1980. Environmental economics, economic valuation of environmental quality, quantitative analysis of environmental policies.
Seth W. Kullman, Ph.D., California, Davis, 1996. Molecular toxicology, with an emphasis on the biochemical and molecular mechanisms of cellular response to environmental pollutants.
Michael L. Lavine, Ph.D., Minnesota, 1987. Sensitivity and robustness of Bayesian analyses, statistical issues in energy and environmental studies, Bayesian nonparametrics, spatial statistics.
Edward D. Levin, Ph.D., Wisconsin, 1984. Basic neurobiology of learning and memory, neurobehavioral toxicology, and the development of novel therapeutic treatments for cognitive dysfunction.
Elwood A. Linney, Ph.D., California, San Diego, 1973. Signal transduction during embryogenesis.
Daniel A. Livingstone, Ph.D., Yale, 1953. The circulation and chemical composition of lakes, particularly in Africa, and how the distribution and abundance of organisms are affected by them.
M. Susan Lozier, Ph.D., Washington (Seattle), 1989. Mesoscale and large-scale ocean dynamics. Research approach ranges from the application of numerical models to the analysis of observational data with the focus on the testing and development of theory.
Lynn A. Maguire, Ph.D., Utah State, 1980. Application of simulation modeling and decision analysis in natural resource management; endangered species; conservation biology; conflict resolution.
Peter E. Malin, Ph.D., Princeton, 1978. Tectonics, seismic wave propagation and earthquakes with current focus on central California.
Marie Lynn Miranda, Ph.D., Harvard, 1990. Natural resource and environmental economics with interdisciplinary, policy-oriented perspectives.
A. Brad Murray, Ph.D., Minnesota, 1995. Surficial processes and patterns, including rivers and a range of desert, Arctic, and alpine phenomena.
Ram Oren, Ph.D., Oregon State, 1984. Physiological ecology and its application to quantifying water, nutrient, and carbon dynamics in forest ecosystems.
Orrin H. Pilkey, Ph.D., Florida State, 1962. Basic and applied coastal geology, focusing primarily on barrier island coasts.
Stuart L. Pimm, Ph.D., New Mexico State, 1974. Conservation biology and the impact of human interactions on the survival of species.
Lincoln F. Pratson, Ph.D., Columbia, 1993. Role of sedimentary processes in shaping continental margins.
Kenneth H. Reckhow, Ph.D., Harvard, 1977. Water-quality modeling and applied statistics, decision and risk analysis for water-quality management, uncertainty analysis and parameter estimation in water-quality models.
James F. Reynolds, Ph.D., New Mexico State, 1974. International efforts on land degradation in arid and semiarid regions of the world.
Curtis J. Richardson, Ph.D., Tennessee, 1972. Wetland ecology, ecosystem analysis, soil chemistry/plant nutrition relationships, phosphorus cycling, effects of pollutants on biogeochemical cycling in ecosystems.
Daniel D. Richter, Ph.D., Duke, 1980. Forest ecosystem ecology, biogeochemistry of acid soils, soil and watershed management in the humid temperate zone and the tropics.
Stuart Rojstaczer, Ph.D., Stanford, 1988. The role of fluid in crustal processes with particular interest in geologic hazards, subsidiary interest in the development of new techniques to determine elastic and fluid flow properties of the Earth in situ.
Erika Sasser, Ph.D., Duke, 1999. The evolving shape of environmental regulation of business and the impact of private, voluntary governance mechanisms on environmental outcomes.
Martin D. Smith, Ph.D., California, Davis, 2001. Natural resource economics, modeling linkages between economic behavior and biophysical processes.
John W. Terborgh, Ph.D., Harvard, 1963. Tropical ecology and biogeography, adaptive strategies of plants and animals, conservation biology.
Jerry J. Tulis, Ph.D., Illinois, 1965. Occupational and environmental biohazards, indoor air quality, waste management.
Dean L. Urban, Ph.D., Tennessee, 1986. Landscape ecology, forest ecosystem dynamics, application of simulation models to assess forest response to land-use practice and climatic change.
Jonathan B. Wiener, J.D., Harvard, 1987. Interplay of science, economics, and law in addressing environmental and human health risks.

Core Faculty/Beaufort

Richard T. Barber, Ph.D., Stanford, 1967. Thermal dynamics and ocean basin productivity.
Celia Bonaventura, Ph.D., Texas, 1968. Structure-function relationships of macromolecules; biotechnology.
Joseph Bonaventura, Ph.D., Texas, 1968. Marine biomedicine, protein structure-function relationships.
Larry B. Crowder, Ph.D., Michigan State, 1978. Marine ecology and fisheries oceanography.
Richard B. Forward Jr., Ph.D., California, Santa Barbara, 1969. Physiological ecology of marine animals.
William W. Kirby-Smith, Ph.D., Duke, 1970. Ecology of marine-freshwater systems.
Michael K. Orbach, Ph.D., California, San Diego, 1975. Application of social and policy sciences to coastal and ocean policy and management.
Joseph S. Ramus, Ph.D., Berkeley, 1968. Algal ecological physiology, estuarine dynamics, biotechnology.
Andrew J. Read, Ph.D., Guelph, 1989. Biology and conservation of small cetaceans.
Daniel Rittschof, Ph.D., Michigan, 1975. Chemical ecology of marine organisms.

LOUISIANA STATE UNIVERSITY

School of Renewable Natural Resources

Programs of Study

The School of Renewable Natural Resources (SRNR) offers Master of Science (M.S.) degrees in forestry, wildlife, and fisheries and Doctor of Philosophy (Ph.D.) degrees in forestry and in wildlife and fisheries science. M.S. degrees require a minimum of 30 hours of course work, a research thesis, and a final comprehensive oral exam. Ph.D. degrees require 48 hours of course work beyond a B.S., qualifying and general examinations, and an original dissertation.

Programs of study are designed by each candidate and his/her graduate adviser and advisory committee. Areas of study include aquaculture, fisheries science, fish biology, conservation ecology, wildlife science, forest biology, forest resource management, forest economics, biometrics, industrial forestry operations, forest products operations, forest products marketing and management, wood science, and engineering. The SRNR has established close working relationships with landowners, industry, nonprofit conservation groups, and federal and state agencies. Natural resource commodities contribute more than $3.5 billion to Louisiana's annual economy. The economic and ecological importance of natural resources and the comprehensive nature of the SRNR provide students with a rich environment for graduate studies.

Research Facilities

The SRNR is housed in a comprehensive educational and research complex that includes twenty-eight research laboratories as well as office space for both faculty members and graduate students. The LSU AgCenter Aquaculture Research Station, one of the largest in the U.S., has 150 research ponds totaling more than 100 water acres. Graduate students have access to microcomputer laboratories, a mainframe computer, photographic and digital interpretation systems, and microcomputer-based geographic information systems.

Financial Aid

Applicants with excellent academic credentials are eligible to compete for a limited number of research and teaching assistantships, which are awarded annually. Outstanding applicants are eligible to compete for a Gilbert Foundation Fellowship. Assistantship and fellowship awards range from $14,000 to $20,000 per year. International students from underrepresented countries are eligible for tuition remission through the Graduate School Tuition Award. Rockefeller Scholarships, which award $1000 per year, are available to Louisiana students and to out-of-state students after they establish residency. Most students are funded from faculty-generated research grants. For additional information, students should visit the financial aid Web site (http://gradlsu.gs.lsu.edu/asstfaid.htm).

Cost of Study

Tuition and fees for full-time resident graduate students (9 or more hours) are $1714 per semester, and nonresidents' tuition and fees are $4364. For students awarded graduate assistantships, nonresident fees are waived. In fall 2003, LSU implemented a three-year plan to waive tuition for all students on graduate assistantships. During year one (2003–04), graduate teaching and research assistants were given a one-third tuition waiver, followed by a two-thirds waiver in the second year (fall 2004) and a full waiver after year three (fall 2005).

Living and Housing Costs

Off-campus housing information is available from http://www.theadvocate.com. Information on campus housing and dining plans can be found at http://appl003.lsu.edu/slas/reslife.nsf/index.

Student Outcomes

Graduates of the School of Renewable Natural Resources are employed in a wide variety of natural resource professions, including those in private industry, government agencies, and academic and other U.S. and international nongovernmental organizations. Recent graduates are employed with the U.S. Army Corps of Engineers, U.S. Fish and Wildlife Service, U.S. Geological Survey, USDA Forest Service, Nature Conservancy, numerous state fish and game and natural resource agencies, and universities worldwide.

Location

LSU is located in Baton Rouge, Louisiana, 75 miles northwest of New Orleans on the banks of the Mississippi River. Baton Rouge, the state capital, has a population of 600,000 and is in the heart of Cajun country. The area has a subtropical climate—winters are mild and summers are warm. Louisiana is known as the "Sportsman's Paradise" because of the expansive aquatic habitats, including the Atchafalaya River basin, which is the largest deep-water swamp in the United States.

The University and The School

Louisiana State University was founded in 1860 as Louisiana's land-grant university. It has grown to have an enrollment of 34,000 students and has become one of the top seventy research universities in the United States. Since the first graduate degree was awarded in 1869, LSU has awarded more than 7,000 Ph.D. and 39,000 master's degrees in more than 130 graduate degree programs. LSU has a tradition in natural resource teaching and research, beginning with its first forestry class in 1911 to the current School of Renewable Natural Resources. Today, research and teaching programs in the SRNR include forestry, forest products, wildlife, fisheries, and aquaculture.

Applying

All applicants for admission to the SRNR must have a B.S. degree from an accredited institution, be acceptable to the graduate faculty, and have an identified major professor. Each applicant must submit official Graduate Record Examinations (GRE) scores, official transcripts, and letters of recommendation. International students must also submit a minimum Test of English as a Foreign Language (TOEFL) score of 550 (paper-based) or 213 (computer-based). These materials are used to rank and select applicants and to award assistantships.

Applicants may be granted regular admission with a GPA of at least 3.0 on all undergraduate and any graduate course work already completed. Students with an undergraduate GPA of 2.55 or below are not considered for admission into any graduate program in the SRNR.

Online applications are available at http://gradlsu.gs.lsu.edu. This site provides links to general Graduate School information and other information on graduate admissions. The General Catalog, which is the official document on policies, deadlines, and information, can be found at http://aaweb.lsu.edu/catalogs/2004. The LSU Schedule of Class not only contains class and final exam schedules but also includes the academic calendar, graduate deadlines, registration information, and fee schedules.

Correspondence and Information

Dr. D. Allen Rutherford
Coordinator of Graduate Studies and Research
119 Renewable Natural Resources Building
Louisiana State University
Baton Rouge, Louisiana 70803
Telephone: 225-578-4187
Fax: 225-578-4227
E-mail: druther@lsu.edu
World Wide Web: http://www.rnr.lsu.edu

Louisiana State University

THE FACULTY AND THEIR RESEARCH

Fisheries

William E. Kelso, Professor; Ph.D. Virginia Tech. Natural fisheries, fisheries management, fish-habitat interactions, fish biology and ecology.

Megan LaPeyre, Adjunct Assistant Professor; Ph.D., Louisiana State. Wetland fisheries ecology, plant ecology, wetland ecology, coastal marsh management.

D. Allen Rutherford, Professor; Ph.D., Oklahoma State. Natural fisheries, stream habitats and lotic fish assemblages, watershed management practices, ecology of larval and juvenile fishes.

Aquaculture

John Hargreaves, Associate Professor; Ph.D., Louisiana State. Crustacean aquaculture and ecology, production-associated water quality, aquatic ecology.

Charles G. Lutz, Professor; Ph.D., Louisiana State. Fisheries extension.

Robert C. Reigh, Professor; Ph.D., Texas A&M. Fish and crustacean nutrition, feed development, feeding techniques.

Robert P. Romaire, Professor; Ph.D., Louisiana State. Crustacean aquaculture, crawfish production, water-quality management.

Terrance R. Tiersch, Professor; Ph.D., Memphis State. Genetic improvement of aquaculture organisms, molecular genetics, hybridization, polyploidy, cryopreservation.

Forestry

Quang V. Cao, Associate Professor; Ph.D., Virginia Tech. Mensuration, forest biometrics.

Jim L. Chambers, Professor; Ph.D., Missouri. Forest ecology, tree physiology.

Sun Joseph Chang, Professor; Ph.D., Wisconsin–Madison. Forest economics, wood products utilization and marketing.

Thomas J. Dean, Associate Professor; Ph.D., Utah State. Quantitative silviculture, production ecology, stand dynamics.

Hallie Dozier, Assistant Professor; Ph.D., Florida. Forest and natural resource ecology, ecology and management of biological invasions, urban forestry, extension.

Richard Keim, Assistant Professor; Ph.D., Oregon State. Hydrology of forested wetlands and watersheds; management of bottomland and coastal forests; ecosystem restoration; large woody debris; hydrological interactions between forests, soils, and the atmosphere.

Zhijun Liu, Associate Professor; Ph.D., Michigan State. Tree physiology, cultivation of medicinal plants, micropropagation.

Michael Stine, Associate Professor; Ph.D., Michigan State. Genetic improvement, molecular biology, tissue culture of southern trees.

Yi-Jun Xu, Assistant Professor; Ph.D., Göttingen. Hydrologic and biogeochemical processes and modeling.

Forest Products

Cornelius de Hoop, Associate Professor; Ph.D., Texas A&M. Environmental safety and business in forest products.

Todd F. Shupe, Associate Professor; Ph.D., Louisiana State. Wood science, silvicultural and genetic influences on the properties and qualities of wood and wood composites.

W. Ramsay Smith, Professor; Ph.D., Berkeley. International trade in forest products, wood physics.

Richard Vlosky, Professor; Ph.D., Penn State. Domestic and international wood products marketing, technology applications to improve wood products business competitiveness.

Qinglin Wu, Associate Professor; Ph.D., Oregon State. Wood drying, wood moisture relationships, hygroscopic shrinkage and swelling of wood, wood composite materials to economic development, value-added products opportunities.

Wildlife

Alan D. Afton, Adjunct Associate Professor; Ph.D., North Dakota. Avian behavioral ecology and bioenergetics, ecological aspects of avian migration, waterfowl ecology and management.

Michael J. Chamberlain, Assistant Professor; Ph.D., Mississippi State. Wildlife management, geographic information systems.

Sammy King, Adjunct Assistant Professor; Ph.D., Texas A&M. Wetland wildlife management and ecology, bottomland hardwood management.

Craig A. Miller, Assistant Professor; Ph.D., Penn State. Human dimensions, renewable natural resource policy.

J. Andrew Nyman, Assistant Professor; Ph.D., Louisiana State. Wetland wildlife management, wetland ecology, coastal marsh management.

Frank C. Rohwer, Associate Professor; Ph.D., Pennsylvania. Avian ecology, reproductive ecology, wildlife ecology, conservation biology, population biology.

Philip Stouffer, Associate Professor; Ph.D., Rutgers. Conservation ecology, wildlife ecology, population ecology.

Vernon L. Wright, Professor; Ph.D., Washington State. Population dynamics, sampling, problems in natural resource management, biometrics, wildlife damage management.

MICHIGAN TECHNOLOGICAL UNIVERSITY

School of Forest Resources and Environmental Science Graduate Program in Forest Ecology and Management

Programs of Study

The School of Forest Resources and Environmental Science (FRES) at Michigan Technological University (MTU) offers degrees in three different program areas: forest ecology and management (M.S. in forestry, applied ecology, or forest ecology and management and Master of Forestry (M.F.)), forest science (Ph.D.), and forest molecular genetics and biotechnology (M.S. and Ph.D.).

Forest ecology and management research covers a wide range of issues from conservation biology to managing forests for sustainable production of timber, wildlife, and clean water. Through MTU's graduate program, students acquire knowledge and skills necessary for successful career development in either the public or private sector as forest managers, ecologists, consultants, researchers, or educators. Current research in forest science includes biogeochemistry and nutrient cycling (with concentrations in belowground ecology and root growth, carbon sequestration and organic matter decomposition, impact of climate change, and soil biology), forest ecology and protection, (with concentrations in community ecology, entomology, fire ecology/management, and pathology), forest productivity (with concentrations in ecophysiology, growth and yield, optimization and modeling, and silviculture and vegetation dynamics), natural resource policy and social dimensions, remote sensing and geographic information systems, soil ecology, wetland ecology, and wildlife ecology (with concentrations in conservation biology, forest biodiversity, ornithology, and wildlife management).

A Peace Corps master's international program is also offered in the School and is designed for students interested in international environmental issues at the community level. It is open to students from any undergraduate major. Students in the program have undergraduate degrees in anthropology, botany, biology, exercise and health physiology, fine arts, forestry, geography, geology, math and computer science, music, philosophy, and other fields. MTU offers the ability to combine a high-quality graduate education with Peace Corps service. The curriculum blends traditional forestry, ecosystem science, and international development work. Michigan Tech is also able to provide support to students in the field that is not available to the typical Peace Corps volunteer. More information is available at http://peacecorps.mtu.edu.

Research Facilities

Capitalizing on this diverse geographical area, many of Michigan Tech's graduate programs stress a field-oriented, hands-on approach. MTU also has excellent laboratory facilities that complement its field research and add to its excellent graduate programs in molecular genetics and biotechnology.

The School of Forest Resources and Environmental Science has a 50,000-square-foot addition to the Ecosystem Sciences Building, which doubled the amount of space for teaching and research laboratories and added additional graduate student offices and study space. Many of these new facilities are dedicated to belowground ecology, remote sensing, forested wetlands, and landscape ecology. The School also houses state-of-the-art molecular biology and microarray functional genomics instrumentation, which enables studies of population genetics and biodiversity using molecular tools. A new stable isotope laboratory enables cutting-edge research in nutrient cycling and trophic studies. Graduate students in FRES can also take advantage of several well-equipped laboratories in GIS/remote sensing at Michigan Tech through an interdisciplinary Remote Sensing Institute. The U.S. Forest Service North Central Research Station maintains a research laboratory on the Michigan Tech campus, where its scientists teach graduate courses and collaborate closely with faculty members and students on the ecology of belowground ecosystems. The School also has a 4,547-acre research forest (Ford Forest) for research and education. Physical facilities are designed to accommodate programs of education, research, and service. Modern dormitory and related facilities provide year-round housing capability for 94 people. A dining hall, four classrooms, a large conference/meeting room, and office buildings provide support facilities.

Prospective graduate students are encouraged to contact individual faculty members directly to investigate potential openings in their research programs and should visit the School's Web site.

Financial Aid

Financial aid is available to a limited number of qualified full-time students in the form of fellowships, research assistantships, and teaching assistantships. Aid packages include a stipend, tuition, and some student fees. The stipend for M.S. candidates is currently $4415 per semester and for Ph.D. candidates, $5126 per semester. In addition, a health insurance supplement is provided by the University. Tuition and most student fees are covered as well. Funding may be available on a competitive basis for students to travel to professional conferences.

Cost of Study

Tuition for full-time graduate students (resident and nonresident) for the 2004–05 academic year is $3888 per semester; engineering and computer science majors pay $4288 per semester. All students are responsible for a student activity fee of approximately $135 per semester. Health insurance is required for all graduate students; the supplement is subject to financial aid status.

Living and Housing Costs

Michigan Tech residence halls have accommodations for single students, and applications may be obtained from the Director of Residential Services. For married students, Michigan Tech has one- and two-bedroom furnished apartments; applications may be obtained from the manager of Daniell Heights Apartments. Because the cost of housing is subject to change, representative costs are not stated. There is also off-campus housing available in the surrounding community. *Yahoo! Internet Life* lists the overall cost of living index for Houghton at 83 (the national average is 100). Prospective students should consult the Web site at http://list.realestate.yahoo.com/realestate/neighborhood/main.html for more information.

Student Group

Michigan Tech has about 6,610 students in residence, 672 of whom are graduate students. The School of Forest Resources and Environmental Science typically has 70 graduate students.

Location

Michigan Tech is located in Houghton in Michigan's scenic Keweenaw Peninsula. The Keweenaw stretches about 70 miles into Lake Superior, and the surrounding area is perfect for any outdoor activity imaginable. The campus is a 15-minute walk from downtown Houghton; public transportation is available from the cities of Houghton and Hancock. Houghton has been listed as the safest college town in Michigan and was ranked eight out of 467 nationwide in the report, "Crime at College: Student Guide to Personal Safety." The Houghton County Memorial Airport (CMX) serves the area with direct flights to Minneapolis via Northwest Airlink; Marquette K. I. Sawyer International Airport (SAW), approximately a 2-hour drive from Houghton, serves the area with direct flights to Detroit.

The University

Michigan Tech was founded in 1885 as the Michigan Mining School to serve the nation's first major mining enterprises focussed on copper and iron. Several name changes tracked the growth and diversification of the institution, and it was named Michigan Technological University in 1964. Today, the University offers a full range of associate, bachelor's, master's, and doctoral degrees in the sciences, engineering, forestry, business, communication, and technology. MTU has been rated one of the nation's "Top Ten" best buys for science and technology by *U.S. News & World Report.*

Applying

Application materials may be requested from the School via e-mail; online applications are also accepted through the University Web site at http://www.mtu.edu/apply/. Completed application materials are reviewed as they are received in the department. Required materials include application, original transcripts, and three letters of recommendation. A form for the letters can be found at the School's Web site. All applicants must take the GRE General Test, and applicants whose native language is not English must take the TOEFL.

Correspondence and Information

Dr. Margaret R. Gale, Dean and Graduate School Coordinator
School of Forest Resources and Environmental Science
Michigan Technological University
1400 Townsend Drive
Houghton, Michigan 49931-1295
Telephone: 906-487-2352
800-WOODS-MI (966-3764; toll-free)
Fax: 906-487-2915
E-mail: mrgale@mtu.edu
World Wide Web: http://forest.mtu.edu

Michigan Technological University

THE FACULTY AND THEIR RESEARCH

Kimberly D. Brosofske, Research Assistant Professor (Forest Ecology and Management). Landscape ecology. (e-mail: kdbrosof@mtu.edu)

Andrew J. Burton, Research Assistant Professor (Forest Ecology and Management). Forest ecology, forest soils, belowground carbon and nutrient cycling, responses of forests to global change, root ecology and physiology. (telephone: 906-487-2566; e-mail: ajburton@mtu.edu)

Victor B. Busov, Assistant Professor (Forest Molecular Genetics and Biotechnology). Tree functional genomics, activation tagging for functional gene discovery in trees; hormonal regulation of tree growth and development, micro-RNA's role in regulation of woody plant development. (telephone: 906-487-1728; e-mail: vbusov@mtu.edu)

David J. Flaspohler, Associate Professor (Forest Ecology and Management). Conservation biology, ornithology-reproductive ecology and forest management, forest and open land songbird habitat use and demography, amphibian ecology, tropical ecology. (telephone: 906-487-3608; e-mail: djflaspo@mtu.edu)

Alex Friend, Research Ecologist/Adjunct Faculty (Forest Service). Forest ecosystem ecology, physiological ecology and belowground studies. (telephone: 906-482-6303; e-mail: afriend@fs.fed.us)

Robert E. Froese, Assistant Professor (Forest Ecology and Management). Forest biometrics, growth and yield, forest vegetation modeling, spatial modeling of forest resources. (telephone: 906-487-2723; e-mail: froese@mtu.edu)

Margaret R. Gale, Professor (Forest Ecology and Management), Dean, and Graduate School Coordinator. Wetlands ecology, management effects on wetlands, community ecology, root ecology. (telephone: 906-487-2352; e-mail: mrgale@mtu.edu)

Christian Giardina, Research Ecologist/Adjunct Faculty (Forest Service). Biotic and abiotic controls on productivity and belowground carbon cycling in forests; forest and nutrient response to harvest and prescribed and wildfire. (telephone: 906-482-6303; e-mail: cgiardina@fs.fed.us)

Kathleen E. Halvorsen, Associate Professor (Forest Ecology and Management). Sociology of natural resources, natural resource and environmental policy, ecosystem management. (telephone: 906-487-2824; e-mail: kehalvor@mtu.edu)

Scott A. Harding, Research Assistant Professor (Forest Molecular Genetics and Biotechnology). Plant cell biology, tree physiology, and molecular basis of tree development and adaptation of biotic and abiotic stresses. (telephone: 906-487-2912; e-mail: sahardin@mtu.edu)

Chandrashekhar P. Joshi, Associate Professor (Forest Molecular Genetics and Biotechnology). Plant molecular genetics, genetic engineering of cellulose and lignin in trees, regulation of gene expression during fast growth, tree genomics and forest bioinformatics. (telephone: 906-487-3480; e-mail: cpjoshi@mtu.edu)

Martin F. Jurgensen, Professor (Forest Ecology and Management) and Director of Graduate Studies. Forest soils/soil biology; management effects on soil chemical, physical, and microbiological properties; nutrient cycling in forest ecosystems; soil properties/forest productivity relationships; acid rain impacts on northern hardwood forest. (telephone: 906-487-2206; e-mail: mfjurgen@mtu.edu)

David F. Karnosky, Professor (Forest Ecology and Management and Forest Molecular Genetics and Biotechnology). Forest genetics/forest biotechnology; larch breeding, micropropagation, and genetic engineering of fast-growing trees; air pollutant impacts on genetic composition of forest ecosystems; mechanisms for differences in air pollution tolerance. (telephone: 906-487-2898; e-mail: karnosky@mtu.edu)

John S. King, Assistant Professor (Forest Ecology and Management). Carbon and nutrient cycling in forest ecosystems, forest water balances, effects of global change on forests, tropical ecology, tropical forestry, sustainable development, tree allometry (telephone: 906-482-6303; e-mail: jsking@mtu.edu)

Peter E. Laks, Professor (Forest Science). Wood preservation, the development of low mammalian toxicity wood preservatives based on agricultural chemistries, the use of chemical additives to improve the properties of wood composites, phytochemistry. (telephone: 906-487-2364; e-mail: plaks@mtu.edu)

Eric Lilleskov, Research Ecologist/Adjunct Faculty (Forest Service). Forest ecology, mycorrhizal fungal ecology, soil microbial communities and ecosystem function. (telephone: 906-482-6303; e-mail: elilleskov@fs.fed.us)

Ann L. Maclean, Associate Professor (Quantitative Forest Science). Remote sensing, digital image processing, geographic information systems (GIS), spatial analysis and modeling. (telephone: 906-487-2030; e-mail: amaclean@mtu.edu)

Linda M. Nagel, Assistant Professor (Forest Ecology and Management). Silviculture, forest vegetation dynamics, physiological processes of forest stand structures, tree ecophysiology. (telephone: 906-487-2812; e-mail: lmnagel@mtu.edu)

Blair D. Orr, Associate Professor (Forest Ecology and Management, Quantitative Forest Service, and Loret Miller Ruppe Peace Corps Master's International Program). International forestry (particularly arid areas in developing countries), economic modeling of forest management and industries. (telephone: 906-487-2291; e-mail: bdorr@mtu.edu)

Rolf O. Peterson, Professor (Forest Ecology and Management). Ecology and population dynamics of mammals, carnivore ecology, predator-prey relationships, wolf-prey dynamics and other ecological studies at Isle Royal National Park. (telephone: 906-487-2179; e-mail: ropeters@mtu.edu)

James B. Pickens, Professor (Quantitative Forest Science). Management science, harvest scheduling, operations research, mathematical models. (telephone: 906-487-2218; e-mail: jpickens@mtu.edu)

Kurt S. Pregitzer, Professor (Forest Ecology and Management). Forest ecology, biogeochemical cycling, forest productivity, global changes and ecosystem science. (telephone: 906-487-2396; e-mail: kspregit@mtu.edu)

Sari C. Saunders, Research Assistant Professor (Forest Ecology and Management). Landscape ecology. (e-mail: scsaunde@mtu.edu)

Andrew Storer, Assistant Professor (Forest Ecology and Management). Forest insect ecology; insect/fungus/plant interactions in forest ecosystems; impacts of exotic species on forest ecosystems; interactions among fire, insects, and disease in forests; urban forest health. (telephone: 906-487-3470; e-mail: storer@mtu.edu)

Chung-Jui Tsai, Associate Professor (Forest Molecular Genetics and Biotechnology). Forest biotechnology, molecular biology, lignin biosynthesis, tissue culture and transformation of woody plants, genetic manipulation of tree growth and wood formation. (telephone: 906-487-2914; e-mail: chtsai@mtu.edu)

John A. Vucetich, Research Assistant Professor (Forest Ecology and Management). Demographic and genetic aspects of population biology, conservation of endangered and recovering species, ecological modeling, trophic interactions, wildlife biology. (telephone: 906-487-1711; e-mail: javuceti@mtu.edu)

Leah M. Vucetich, Research Assistant Professor (Forest Ecology and Management and Forest Molecular Genetics and Biotechnology). Genetics and demography of small, isolated populations; mercury in terrestrial ecosystems; Isle Royale ecology. (telephone: 906-487-1234; e-mail: lmvuceti@mtu.edu)

Christopher R. Webster, Assistant Professor (Forest Ecology and Management). Quantitative ecology, forest management, silviculture. (telephone: 906-487-3618; e-mail: cwebster@mtu.edu)

MICHIGAN TECHNOLOGICAL UNIVERSITY

School of Forest Resources and Environmental Science
Forest Science

Programs of Study The School of Forest Resources and Environmental Science (FRES) at Michigan Technological University (MTU) offers degrees in three different program areas: forest ecology and management (M.S. in forestry, applied ecology, or forest ecology and management and Master of Forestry (M.F.)), forest science (Ph.D.), and forest molecular genetics and biotechnology (M.S. and Ph.D.).

Forest science research covers a wide range of issues, from conservation biology to managing forests for sustainable production of timber, wildlife, and clean water. Through MTU's graduate program, students acquire knowledge and skills necessary for successful career development in either the public or private sector as forest managers, ecologists, consultants, researchers, or educators. Current research in forest science includes biogeochemistry and nutrient cycling (with concentrations in belowground ecology and root growth, carbon sequestration and organic matter decomposition, impact of climate change, and soil biology), forest ecology and protection, (with concentrations in community ecology, entomology, fire ecology/management, and pathology), forest productivity (with concentrations in ecophysiology, growth and yield, optimization and modeling, and silviculture and vegetation dynamics), natural resource policy and social dimensions, remote sensing and geographic information systems, soil ecology, wetland ecology, and wildlife ecology (with concentrations in conservation biology, forest biodiversity, ornithology, and wildlife management).

The Peace Corps master's international program is designed for students interested in international environmental issues at the community level and is open to students from any undergraduate major. Students in the program have undergraduate degrees in anthropology, botany, biology, exercise and health physiology, fine arts, forestry, geography, geology, math and computer science, music, philosophy, and other fields. MTU offers the ability to combine a high-quality graduate education with Peace Corps service. The curriculum blends traditional forestry, ecosystem science, and international development work. Michigan Tech is also able to provide support to students in the field that is not available to the typical Peace Corps volunteer. More information is available at http://peacecorps.mtu.edu.

Research Facilities Capitalizing on this diverse geographical area, many of Michigan Tech's graduate programs stress a field-oriented, hands-on approach. MTU also has excellent laboratory facilities that complement its field research and add to its excellent graduate programs in molecular genetics and biotechnology.

The School of Forest Resources and Environmental Science has a 50,000-square-foot addition to the Ecosystem Sciences Building, which doubled the amount of space for teaching and research laboratories and added additional graduate student offices and study space. Many of these new facilities are dedicated to belowground ecology, remote sensing, forested wetlands, and landscape ecology. The School also houses state-of-the-art molecular biology and microarray functional genomics instrumentation, which enables studies of population genetics and biodiversity using molecular tools. A new stable isotope laboratory enables cutting-edge research in nutrient cycling and trophic studies. Graduate students in FRES can also take advantage of several well-equipped laboratories in GIS/remote sensing at Michigan Tech through an interdisciplinary Remote Sensing Institute. The U.S. Forest Service North Central Research Station maintains a research laboratory on the Michigan Tech campus, where its scientists teach graduate courses and collaborate closely with faculty members and students on the ecology of belowground ecosystems. The School also has a 4,547-acre research forest (Ford Forest) for research and education. Physical facilities are designed to accommodate programs of education, research, and service. Modern dormitory and related facilities provide year-round housing capability for 94 people. A dining hall, four classrooms, a large conference/meeting room, and office buildings provide support facilities.

Prospective graduate students are encouraged to contact individual faculty members directly to investigate potential openings in their research programs and should visit the School's Web site.

Financial Aid Financial aid is available to a limited number of qualified full-time students in the form of fellowships, research assistantships, and teaching assistantships. Aid packages include a stipend, tuition, and some student fees. The stipend for M.S. candidates is currently $4415 per semester and for Ph.D. candidates, $5126 per semester. In addition, a health insurance supplement is provided by the University. Funding may be available on a competitive basis for students to travel to professional conferences.

Cost of Study Tuition for full-time graduate students (resident and nonresident) for the 2004–05 academic year is $3888 per semester; engineering and computer science majors pay $4288 per semester. All students are responsible for a student activity fee of approximately $135 per semester. Health insurance is required for all graduate students; the supplement is subject to financial aid status.

Living and Housing Costs Michigan Tech residence halls have accommodations for single students; applications may be obtained from the Director of Residential Services. For married students, Michigan Tech has one- and two-bedroom furnished apartments; applications may be obtained from the manager of Daniell Heights Apartments. Because the cost of housing is subject to change, representative costs are not stated. There is also off-campus housing available in the surrounding community. *Yahoo! Internet Life* lists the overall cost of living index for Houghton at 83 (the national average is 100). Prospective students should consult the Web site at http://list.realestate.yahoo.com/realestate/neighborhood/main.html for more information.

Student Group Michigan Tech has about 6,610 students in residence, 672 of whom are graduate students. The School of Forest Resources and Environmental Science typically has 70 graduate students.

Location Michigan Tech is located in Houghton in Michigan's scenic Keweenaw Peninsula. The Keweenaw stretches about 70 miles into Lake Superior, and the surrounding area is perfect for any outdoor activity imaginable. The campus is a 15-minute walk from downtown Houghton; public transportation is available from the cities of Houghton and Hancock. Houghton has been listed as the safest college town in Michigan and was ranked eight out of 467 nationwide in the report, "Crime at College: Student Guide to Personal Safety." The Houghton County Memorial Airport (CMX) serves the area with direct flights to Minneapolis via Northwest Airlink; Marquette K. I. Sawyer International Airport (SAW), approximately a 2-hour drive from Houghton, serves the area with direct flights to Detroit.

The University Michigan Tech was founded in 1885 as the Michigan Mining School to serve the nation's first major mining enterprises focused on copper and iron. Several name changes tracked the growth and diversification of the institution, and it was named Michigan Technological University in 1964. Today, the University offers a full range of associate, bachelor's, master's, and doctoral degrees in the sciences, engineering, forestry, business, communication, and technology. MTU has been rated one of the nation's "Top Ten" best buys for science and technology by *U.S. News & World Report.*

Applying Application materials may be requested from the School via e-mail; online applications are also accepted through the University Web site at http://www.mtu.edu/apply/. Completed application materials are reviewed as they are received in the department. Required materials include the application, original transcripts, and three letters of recommendation. A form for the letters can be found at the School's Web site. All applicants must take the GRE General Test, and applicants whose native language is not English must take the TOEFL.

Correspondence and Information

Dr. Margaret R. Gale
Dean and Graduate School Coordinator
School of Forest Resources and Environmental Science
Michigan Technological University
1400 Townsend Drive
Houghton, Michigan 49931-1295
Telephone: 906-487-2352
800-WOODS-MI (966-3764; toll-free)
Fax: 906-487-2915
E-mail: mrgale@mtu.edu
World Wide Web: http://forest.mtu.edu

Michigan Technological University

THE FACULTY AND THEIR RESEARCH

Kimberly D. Brosofske, Research Assistant Professor (Forest Ecology and Management). Landscape ecology. (e-mail: kdbrosof@mtu.edu)

Andrew J. Burton, Research Assistant Professor (Forest Ecology and Management). Forest ecology, forest soils, belowground carbon and nutrient cycling, responses of forests to global change, root ecology and physiology. (telephone: 906-487-2566; e-mail: ajburton@mtu.edu)

Victor B. Busov, Assistant Professor (Forest Molecular Genetics and Biotechnology). Tree functional genomics, activation tagging for functional gene discovery in trees; hormonal regulation of tree growth and development, micro-RNA's role in regulation of woody plant development. (telephone: 906-487-1728; e-mail: vbusov@mtu.edu)

David J. Flaspohler, Associate Professor (Forest Ecology and Management). Conservation biology, ornithology-reproductive ecology and forest management, forest and open land songbird habitat use and demography, amphibian ecology, tropical ecology. (telephone: 906-487-3608; e-mail: djflaspo@mtu.edu)

Alex Friend, Research Ecologist/Adjunct Faculty (Forest Service). Forest ecosystem ecology, physiological ecology and belowground studies. (telephone: 906-482-6303; e-mail: afriend@fs.fed.us)

Robert E. Froese, Assistant Professor (Forest Ecology and Management). Forest biometrics, growth and yield, forest vegetation modeling, spatial modeling of forest resources. (telephone: 906-487-2723; e-mail: froese@mtu.edu)

Margaret R. Gale, Professor (Forest Ecology and Management), Dean, and Graduate School Coordinator. Wetlands ecology, management effects on wetlands, community ecology, root ecology. (telephone: 906-487-2352; e-mail: mrgale@mtu.edu)

Christian Giardina, Research Ecologist/Adjunct Faculty (Forest Service). Biotic and abiotic controls on productivity and belowground carbon cycling in forests; forest and nutrient response to harvest and prescribed and wildfire. (telephone: 906-482-6303; e-mail: cgiardina@fs.fed.us)

Kathleen E. Halvorsen, Associate Professor (Forest Ecology and Management). Sociology of natural resources, natural resource and environmental policy, ecosystem management. (telephone: 906-487-2824; e-mail: kehalvor@mtu.edu)

Scott A. Harding, Research Assistant Professor (Forest Molecular Genetics and Biotechnology). Plant cell biology, tree physiology, and molecular basis of tree development and adaptation of biotic and abiotic stresses. (telephone: 906-487-2912; e-mail: sahardin@mtu.edu)

Chandrashekhar P. Joshi, Associate Professor (Forest Molecular Genetics and Biotechnology). Plant molecular genetics, genetic engineering of cellulose and lignin in trees, regulation of gene expression during fast growth, tree genomics and forest bioinformatics. (telephone: 906-487-3480; e-mail: cpjoshi@mtu.edu)

Martin F. Jurgensen, Professor (Forest Ecology and Management) and Director of Graduate Studies. Forest soils/soil biology; management effects on soil chemical, physical, and microbiological properties; nutrient cycling in forest ecosystems; soil properties/forest productivity relationships; acid rain impacts on northern hardwood forest. (telephone: 906-487-2206; e-mail: mfjurgen@mtu.edu)

David F. Karnosky, Professor (Forest Ecology and Management and Forest Molecular Genetics and Biotechnology). Forest genetics/forest biotechnology; larch breeding, micropropagation, and genetic engineering of fast-growing trees; air pollutant impacts on genetic composition of forest ecosystems; mechanisms for differences in air pollution tolerance. (telephone: 906-487-2898; e-mail: karnosky@mtu.edu)

John S. King, Assistant Professor (Forest Ecology and Management). Carbon and nutrient cycling in forest ecosystems, forest water balances, effects of global change on forests, tropical ecology, tropical forestry, sustainable development, tree allometry (telephone: 906-482-6303; e-mail: jsking@mtu.edu)

Peter E. Laks, Professor (Forest Science). Wood preservation, the development of low mammalian toxicity wood preservatives based on agricultural chemistries, the use of chemical additives to improve the properties of wood composites, phytochemistry. (telephone: 906-487-2364; e-mail: plaks@mtu.edu)

Eric Lilleskov, Research Ecologist/Adjunct Faculty (Forest Service). Forest ecology, mycorrhizal fungal ecology, soil microbial communities and ecosystem function. (telephone: 906-482-6303; e-mail: elilleskov@fs.fed.us)

Ann L. Maclean, Associate Professor (Quantitative Forest Science). Remote sensing, digital image processing, geographic information systems (GIS), spatial analysis and modeling. (telephone: 906-487-2030; e-mail: amaclean@mtu.edu)

Linda M. Nagel, Assistant Professor (Forest Ecology and Management). Silviculture, forest vegetation dynamics, physiological processes of forest stand structures, tree ecophysiology. (telephone: 906-487-2812; e-mail: lmnagel@mtu.edu)

Blair D. Orr, Associate Professor (Forest Ecology and Management, Quantitative Forest Service, and Loret Miller Ruppe Peace Corps Master's International Program). International forestry (particularly arid areas in developing countries), economic modeling of forest management and industries. (telephone: 906-487-2291; e-mail: bdorr@mtu.edu)

Rolf O. Peterson, Professor (Forest Ecology and Management). Ecology and population dynamics of mammals, carnivore ecology, predator-prey relationships, wolf-prey dynamics and other ecological studies at Isle Royal National Park. (telephone: 906-487-2179; e-mail: ropeters@mtu.edu)

James B. Pickens, Professor (Quantitative Forest Science). Management science, harvest scheduling, operations research, mathematical models. (telephone: 906-487-2218; e-mail: jpickens@mtu.edu)

Kurt S. Pregitzer, Professor (Forest Ecology and Management). Forest ecology, biogeochemical cycling, forest productivity, global changes and ecosystem science. (telephone: 906-487-2396; e-mail: kspregit@mtu.edu)

Sari C. Saunders, Research Assistant Professor (Forest Ecology and Management). Landscape ecology. (e-mail: scsaunde@mtu.edu)

Andrew Storer, Assistant Professor (Forest Ecology and Management). Forest insect ecology; insect/fungus/plant interactions in forest ecosystems; impacts of exotic species on forest ecosystems; interactions among fire, insects, and disease in forests; urban forest health. (telephone: 906-487-3470; e-mail: storer@mtu.edu)

Chung-Jui Tsai, Associate Professor (Forest Molecular Genetics and Biotechnology). Forest biotechnology, molecular biology, lignin biosynthesis, tissue culture and transformation of woody plants, genetic manipulation of tree growth and wood formation. (telephone: 906-487-2914; e-mail: chtsai@mtu.edu)

John A. Vucetich, Research Assistant Professor (Forest Ecology and Management). Demographic and genetic aspects of population biology, conservation of endangered and recovering species, ecological modeling, trophic interactions, wildlife biology. (telephone: 906-487-1711; e-mail: javuceti@mtu.edu)

Leah M. Vucetich, Research Assistant Professor (Forest Ecology and Management and Forest Molecular Genetics and Biotechnology). Genetics and demography of small, isolated populations; mercury in terrestrial ecosystems; Isle Royale ecology. (telephone: 906-487-1234; e-mail: lmvuceti@mtu.edu)

Christopher R. Webster, Assistant Professor (Forest Ecology and Management). Quantitative ecology, forest management, silviculture. (telephone: 906-487-3618; e-mail: cwebster@mtu.edu)

PURDUE UNIVERSITY

Department of Forestry and Natural Resources

Programs of Study

The Department of Forestry and Natural Resources offers graduate study leading to the degrees of Master of Science, Master of Science in Forestry, and Doctor of Philosophy in aquaculture, fisheries and aquatic sciences, forest biology (ecology, tree physiology, soils, and silviculture), natural resource and environmental policy, quantitative resource analysis (forest economics, biometry, operations research, and GIS and remote sensing), wildlife science (conservation biology, genetics, physiology, and community ecology), and wood science and technology. Graduate programs in the department are supported by courses and personnel throughout the University. This broad-based support and departmental expertise gives students the opportunity to design a program and pursue studies in their areas of specialization.

The Master of Science in Forestry and the Master of Science are research-oriented degrees that prepare the individual for employment in his or her area of specialization or may provide background to continue for the Ph.D. degree. Completion of an M.S. usually requires two years of intensive study. An oral and/or written exam is given near the end of the program by the graduate advisory committee. The Ph.D. is a research degree that prepares candidates for employment in teaching and research and is available to outstanding students who demonstrate ability for scholarly work and original research. Course and foreign language requirements depend on student needs and are at the discretion of their graduate advisory committee. Written and oral exams are given by an examining committee after completion of formal course work. An oral defense of the research is required upon completion of the dissertation. The graduate faculty is actively involved in research designed to increase benefits derived from natural resources, promote more efficient management and utilization of forest resources, and protect environmental values.

The department is committed to expanding the scientific understanding of natural resources and coordinates its efforts with other campus units in the social, biological, and physical sciences. Internationally, the department participates in cooperative research and educational agreements with other universities or agencies in Australia, China, India, Indonesia, Brazil, Sweden, and Costa Rica and has research involvements in European, African, Latin American, Pacific Rim, and Caribbean countries.

Research Facilities

The department operates laboratories for research in aquaculture, fisheries biology, forest biology, soils, tree physiology, wildlife ecology, wildlife nutrition, wildlife physiology, wood science, and spatial data analysis. Off-campus facilities include Martell Memorial Forest, John S. Wright Forestry Center, the Purdue Wildlife Area, other department properties, and many holdings managed by state and federal agencies and private companies. Wildlife and fish-holding facilities supply controlled environments for physiological and nutritional research. Special equipment for wood science includes an MTS testing system with computer-aided data acquisition, a 30-kip universal testing machine, and a computer-controlled testing machine for performance testing of furniture structures. General woodworking equipment in the shop is complemented by a Thermwood Model 40 CNC router. Computing facilities are located throughout the department. Statistical software, including SPSS, SAS, and IMSL, is fully supported. The spatial data processing laboratory supports GPS, GIS, and remote sensing research. Equipment includes Windows XP computers, scanner, large-format plotter, and GPS receivers. Major software supported are ArcGIS, ArcView, Imagine, IDRISI, SLIPS, and KHOROS.

Financial Aid

Graduate teaching and research assistantships are available on a competitive basis to qualified students. For 2003–04, stipends for entry-level twelve-month assistantships are approximately $15,259 to $17,518, depending on students' qualifications, degree level, and appointment time. Fellowships are also available from the University and the School of Agriculture. The department provides funds for each student to attend one major meeting per year. Tuition is waived for students who receive stipends.

Cost of Study

Tuition for 2003–04 was $5860 per year for Indiana residents and $17,640 per year for nonresidents. Tuition is waived each semester for students who receive stipends, with the exception of approximately $502 for domestic students and $552 for international students.

Living and Housing Costs

Estimated yearly costs for a single student living on campus were about $8850 in 2003–04. This included room, board, books, supplies, and miscellaneous expenses. Housing costs for married students ranged from $500 to $1000 per month. Off-campus housing costs vary widely.

Student Group

Graduate enrollment in the School of Agriculture is 493, with 70 in the Department of Forestry and Natural Resources. Forty-four percent of graduate students in the department are women, and 40 percent are international students. Most receive a stipend or other financial assistance and are provided desk and office space. Seminars and orientation sessions foster professional and social relationships among students.

Student Outcomes

Employment includes a wide variety of positions in government, industry, organizations, and academia. Typical agency positions include forestry, recreation, wildlife, fisheries, and economics specialists for state agencies, as well as similar positions with federal agencies such as the Forest Service and Fish and Wildlife Service. Private-industry employers include environmental consulting firms, furniture manufacturers, wood products manufacturers, timber companies, and aquaculture producers. Doctoral graduates also hold faculty positions at colleges and universities.

Location

Purdue is in West Lafayette, across the Wabash River from Lafayette. The two cities' population exceeds 140,000. The area is served by airport, bus, and train facilities and is near I-65. Purdue is 65 miles northwest of Indianapolis and 126 miles southeast of Chicago. West Lafayette is a pleasant community with excellent medical facilities, parks, community theater and dance, a symphony, and art museums.

The University and The Department

Founded in 1869, Purdue is a "Big Ten" land-grant university. It enrolls more than 37,000 students on its West Lafayette campus and 30,000 on regional campuses. Approximately 2,100 faculty members teach and engage in research on the 650-acre main campus. The department, founded in 1914, is accredited by the Society of American Foresters, and its faculty represents a wide range of expertise in the natural resource sciences.

Applying

Applications are accepted at any time, but applicants requesting financial aid should return completed applications by January 5 (for fall) and September 15 (for spring). Notification of admission is made by April 15. A nonrefundable fee of $55 must accompany the formal application. GRE scores are required of all applicants. Students from non-English-speaking countries must furnish TOEFL scores with their applications.

Correspondence and Information

Graduate Secretary
Department of Forestry and Natural Resources
Purdue University
West Lafayette, Indiana 47907-2061
Telephone: 765-494-3572
Fax: 765-494-9461
E-mail: gradrep@fnr.purdue.edu
World Wide Web: http://www.fnr.purdue.edu

Purdue University

THE FACULTY AND THEIR RESEARCH

Dennis C. Le Master, Professor and Head; Ph.D., Washington State, 1974. Resource economics and policy.

Shorna Broussard, Assistant Professor, Ph.D., Oregon State, 2000. Forest resources; social and political impacts of natural resource management; environmental and natural resource policy; educational program evaluation; natural resource management and decision making; examining aspects of human behavior related to contemporary problems of management.

Paul B. Brown, Professor; Ph.D., Texas A&M, 1987. Aquatic animal nutrition; aquaculture.

Daniel L. Cassens, Professor; Ph.D., Wisconsin–Madison, 1973. Wood utilization; primary and secondary wood processing; resource policy as it relates to wood products manufacturing and industry education.

William R. Chaney, Professor; Ph.D., Wisconsin–Madison, 1969. Tree physiology; growth and development; plant growth regulation.

J. Andrew DeWoody, Assistant Professor, Ph.D., Texas Tech, 1997. Genetics; population genetics; molecular ecology and evolution.

John B. Dunning Jr., Associate Professor; Ph.D., Arizona, 1986. Wildlife ecology; community and population ecology; animal behavior; conservation biology.

Carl A. Eckelman, Professor; Ph.D., Purdue, 1968. Wood products; furniture design and engineering.

Richard L. Farnsworth, Associate Professor; Ph.D., Berkeley, 1979. Development of GIS-based and Internet-based multiple objective decision support systems for state and federal resource managers, watershed groups, and agricultural producers; assessment of state and federal conservation programs.

Rado Gazo, Associate Professor; Ph.D., Mississippi State, 1994. Wood products manufacturing, industrial engineering aspects, including modeling, simulation, and quality improvement.

Andrew R. Gillespie, Professor; Ph.D., Purdue, 1988. Silviculture; agroforestry; international forestry.

Eva Haviarova, Assistant Professor and Manager, Wood Research Laboratory; Ph.D., Purdue, 2000. Wood science and technology.

Harvey A. Holt, Professor; Ph.D., Oregon State, 1970. Industrial weed science; vegetation management for forests and rights-of-way; tree growth regulators; urban forestry and arborculture.

William L. Hoover, Professor; Ph.D., Iowa State, 1977. Forest economics and marketing; timber tax; investment strategies; economics of property rights, wood-based product design, rural economic development, and social forestry.

Michael O. Hunt, Professor; Ph.D., North Carolina State, 1970. Structural wood-base composite materials; damage accumulation; nondestructive testing; wood in historic restoration.

Douglass F. Jacobs, Assistant Professor; Ph.D., Oregon State, 2001. Forest tree regeneration; nursery management; root architecture; forest tree improvement; plant mineral nutrition; drought resistance; photosynthesis.

Richard Meilan, Associate Professor; Ph.D., Iowa State, 1990. Physiology and molecular biology; forest biology.

Charles Michler, Adjunct Assistant Professor; Ph.D., Ohio State, 1985. Plant physiology and biochemistry. Clonal propagation of fine hardwoods; genetic modification; genetic control of economic traits in hardwoods.

Walter L. Mills Jr., Associate Professor; Ph.D., Purdue, 1980. Management/economics; application of decision-support systems, expert systems, and GIS in forest ecosystem management; physical and financial risk of forest ecosystem management.

John W. Moser Jr., Professor; Ph.D., Purdue, 1967. Forest biometrics; growth and yield, quantitative methods and application of computers.

George R. Parker, Professor; Ph.D., Michigan State, 1970. Forest ecology; long-term dynamics of forest ecosystems and plant population response to disturbance.

Bryan C. Pijanowski, Associate Professor; Ph.D., Michigan State, 1991. Zoology.

Paula M. Pijut, Adjunct Assistant Professor; Ph.D., Ohio State, 1988. Plant physiology.

Vicki Poole, Research Specialist in Hydrology; M.S., Purdue, 1985.

Phillip E. Pope, Professor; Ph.D., Virginia Tech, 1974. Forest soils; nutrient dynamics of forest ecosystems; soil restoration; hardwood regeneration and plantation management.

Linda Prokopy, Assistant Professor; Ph.D., North Carolina at Chapel Hill, 2002. Natural resource planning.

Olin E. Rhodes Jr., Professor; Ph.D., Texas Tech, 1991. Wildlife ecology and genetics; genotoxicology.

Guofan Shao, Associate Professor; Ph.D., Chinese Academy of Sciences, 1989. Remote sensing, geographic information systems, forest modeling, landscape ecology.

Anne Spacie, Professor; Ph.D., Purdue, 1975. Stream ecology; water quality; toxic substances; limnology; watershed studies.

Trent M. Sutton, Assistant Professor, Ph.D., Virginia Tech, 1997. Fisheries sciences; inland fisheries management; applied ecology of fishes; fish population dynamics; biology and conservation of Great Lakes fishes.

Robert K. Swihart, Professor; Ph.D., Kansas, 1985. Wildlife ecology; behavioral/ecological approaches to wildlife damage control; plant-animal interactions; population dynamics of mammals in fragmented landscapes.

Harmon P. Weeks Jr., Professor; Ph.D., Purdue, 1974. Wildlife ecology and physiology; herbivore feeding strategies and sodium relationships; fitness in songbirds nesting on man-made structures; fragmentation, edge, and vertebrate populations.

Keith E. Woeste, Adjunct Assistant Professor; Ph.D., California, Davis, 1994. Genetics; hardwood tree genetics; forest tree breeding and crop improvement; seed orchard establishment and performance and disease resistance; heritability estimates for traits such as juvenile growth and figure; use of molecular markers to improve breeding program efficiency, identify QTL, and delineate seed zones; dispersal and gene flow in natural walnut and cherry stands; effect of timber harvesting on genetic diversity.

Professional and Technical Staff

Philip L. Anderson, Property Supervisor.

Don Carlson, Woodlands Forester; B.S., Purdue, 1995. Forestry.

Ed Hopkins, Computer Software Specialist; B.S., Purdue, 1970. Electrical engineering technology.

Brian MacGowan, Extension Wildlife Specialist; M.S., Purdue, 1998. Wildlife science.

Rita L. McKenzie, Urban Forester; M.S., Purdue, 1997. Urban forestry.

Brian K. Miller, Wildlife Extension Specialist and Coordinator of Marine Advisory Services, Illinois-Indiana Sea Grant Program; Ph.D., Purdue, 2003. Forest and agricultural wildlife management.

Taj Mohammad, Laboratory Manager, Forest Biology and Molecular Tree Physiology; Ph.D., Panjab (India), 1982. Organic chemistry.

Lisa Murfitt, Genomics Laboratory Manager; M.S., Purdue, 2002. Molecular biology.

Ronald Rathfon, Regional Extension Forester; M.S., Virginia Tech, 1990. Forest soils and hardwood silviculture.

Noel Rizutto, Manager, Aquculture Research Facility; M.S., South Florida, 2002. Zoology.

John R. Seifert, Regional Extension Forester; M.S.F., Missouri, 1978. Seedling quality and hardwood regeneration; vegetation management; hardwood silviculture.

Gerald A. Stillings, Senior Analyst/Manager FNR Computer Service; M.S., Purdue, 1985.

Sally Weeks, Manager, Dendrology Laboratory; M.S., Purdue, 2001. Forestry and natural resources.

Rod N. Williams, Vertebrate Curator and Coordinator of Laboratory Instruction; M.S., Purdue, 1998.

Keith A. Wilson, Manager, Aquaculture Research Facility; B.S., Purdue, 1992.

UNIVERSITY OF IDAHO

College of Natural Resources
Department of Fish and Wildlife Resources

Programs of Study

The College of Natural Resources (CNR), one of ten colleges at the University of Idaho (UI), offers a Doctor of Philosophy (Ph.D.) in natural resources, with an emphasis in fishery resources or wildlife resources, and a Master of Science (M.S.) thesis option or Master of Science nonthesis option in fishery resources or wildlife resources.

The Department of Fish and Wildlife Resources is one of the leading programs in the nation in fishery and wildlife resources. Fishery and wildlife resources deal with the application of principles of biology and ecology to the understanding of how fish and wildlife populations interact with each other and with their environment, which includes humans. The research mission of the department is to attain new knowledge and to understand natural resources, their interrelationships, and their uses. The objectives of the research program are to obtain knowledge of the environment and to develop management alternatives that can assist in the conservation of resources while meeting society's needs. The dissemination of this knowledge through publications, continuing education, and other channels of communication is an essential departmental function.

Graduate students spend on average 2½ to 3 years in the M.S. programs, while doctoral candidates spend four to five years working on their degree. Students work closely with their major professors to develop and complete their research programs.

Research Facilities

The U.S. Geological Survey's Idaho Cooperative Fish and Wildlife Research Unit is housed in the department. The Aquaculture Research Institute also provides important research opportunities for graduate studies in fishery resources and aquaculture.

The fisheries laboratories include the University of Idaho (UI) Fisheries Wet Labs; Aquaculture Research Laboratory, a 4,000-square-foot wet lab with pass-through water supply; Fish Culture Laboratory, a 1,200-square-foot wet lab with recirculating water supply; Ornamental Fish Laboratory with 10-, 15-, and 55-gallon aquaria; and the Hagerman Fish Culture Experiment Station Research Facility, which houses two major research centers: the Center for Sustainable Aquaculture and the Center for Salmonid and Other Freshwater Species at Risk. Other labs include the Geographic Information System (GIS) Laboratory and genetics research facilities, such as the Laboratory of Ecological and Conservation Genetics (LECG) and the Genetic Research Laboratory in the Aquaculture Research Institute. The LECG is a core-facility lab located in the College of Natural Resources and is equipped with an ABI Prism 377XL Automated Sequences and Genetic Data Analysis Center for top-of-the-line sequence verification, fragment analysis, paternity testing, species identification, and other genetic tasks.

In addition, departmental faculty members and students have access to the University Experimental Forest, a 7,200-acre forest 25 miles from campus; the McCall Field Campus, located on Payette Lake in the mountains of west-central Idaho; the Clark Fork Field Campus in northern Idaho; and the Taylor Ranch Wilderness Field Station in the heart of the Frank Church "River-of-No-Return" Wilderness.

The University of Idaho Library and the Washington State University Library are both available to UI students.

Financial Aid

Graduate students accepted into the Department of Fish and Wildlife Resources are normally provided a research assistantship along with a research project. The current research assistantship (20 hours per week) pays $13.62 per hour for a master's student and $15.53 per hour for a Ph.D. student. Each semester the department needs teaching assistants for courses. Students already enrolled are considered for these positions and paid at the same level as research assistants. Seventy-seven percent of full-time graduate students are supported by research or teaching assistantships.

Cost of Study

For 2004–05, full-time graduate fees are $2086 per semester for Idaho residents with an additional $4010 per semester for nonresidents. Resident students enrolled part-time pay $205 per credit; nonresidents pay an additional $123 per credit for part-time course work. Full-time fees are charged for 8 credits or more. Fees are subject to change.

Living and Housing Costs

Graduate student housing is available through the University. Apartments range in size from efficiencies to four-bedroom units. Potential graduate students are advised to reserve housing early. Off-campus housing lists are available at http://www.asui.uidaho.edu.

Student Group

The faculty members look for applicants who have a previous degree in the sciences with a GPA of 3.0 or better, high GRE scores, field work experience, and strong letters of recommendation.

Currently, the department's graduate student population includes 95 Master of Science and Doctor of Philosophy degree students.

Student Outcomes

Graduates often find employment with state and federal agencies, engineering and environmental consulting firms, nonprofit organizations, private conservation organizations, and academic institutions.

Approximately 95 percent of the graduates are employed in the field of their choice. Recent graduates have gone on to such positions as unit scientist for the South Dakota Cooperative Fish and Wildlife Research Unit, research biologist for the Minnesota Department of Natural Resources, nongame biologist for the Idaho Department of Fish and Game, endangered species biologist for the U.S. Fish and Wildlife Service, biologist for the Point Reyes Bird Observatory, and research wildlife ecologist for the Wildlife Conservation Society.

Location

Moscow, a community of 20,000 located in the Idaho panhandle with farmland changing colors with the seasons, provides easy access to northern Idaho's mountains, lakes, and rivers. Cultural and recreational activities include the world-class Lionel Hampton Jazz Festival, art galleries, movie theaters, live theater and music performances, NCAA Division I-A athletics, and an eighteen-hole golf course.

The Department

The Department of Fish and Wildlife Resources is one of the five academic departments of the College of Natural Resources and consists of 16 faculty members, 4 departmental staff members, 2 research associates, 5 postdoctoral fellows, and 15 project staff members. The 220 undergraduates and 95 graduate students keep the department very active. For the faculty members there is a constant juggle with teaching, advising, conducting research, and committee work.

Applying

The department follows the College of Graduate Studies guidelines for applying to the program. The deadline for the fall semester is July 1; for the spring semester, November 1; and for the summer session, April 1. Students who wish to apply for a departmental assistantship should consult with the department regarding the process and deadline date, which may be earlier than the application deadline.

Correspondence and Information

Karla Makus, Administrative Assistant
Department of Fish and Wildlife Resources
CNR Room 105
University of Idaho
P.O. Box 441136
Moscow, Idaho 83844-1136

Telephone: 208-885-4006
Fax: 208-885-9080
E-mail: fish_wildlife@uidaho.edu
World Wide Web: http://www.cnr.uidaho.edu/fishwild

University of Idaho

THE FACULTY AND THEIR RESEARCH

Jeffrey H. Braatne, Assistant Professor; Ph.D. (botany), Washington, 1989. Stream and riparian ecology.

Kenneth D. Cain, Assistant Professor; Ph.D. (animal sciences), Washington State, 1997. Aquaculture, fish disease, fish health, immunology, host/pathogen relationships.

Jim L. Congleton, Associate Professor; Ph.D. (marine biology), California, San Diego (Scripps), 1970. Disease resistance in fish/immunology, stress physiology, comparative physiology of wild and hatchery salmonids.

Brian Dennis, Professor; Ph.D. (ecology), Penn State, 1982. Statistical ecology, biometrics (biological stats), mathematical modeling.

Edward O. Garton, Professor; Ph.D. (ecology), California, Davis, 1976. Dynamics/management of bird/mammal populations, population estimation, modeling/simulation of population processes, forest bird ecology, large mammal ecology.

George W. LaBar, Professor; Ph.D. (zoology), Montana State, 1970. Fisheries management and ecology, predator/prey interactions, bioenergetic modeling.

Wayne Melquist, Research Associate Professor; Ph.D. (wildlife resources), Idaho, 1981. Carnivore biology and predator-prey relationships, impacts of highways and other linear developments on wildlife movements and survival, ecology of furbearers and factors important to their management, conservation and management of threatened and endangered species, raptors and their management.

Christine M. Moffitt, Research Associate Professor; Ph.D. (fisheries biology), Massachusetts, Amherst, 1979. Biology, health and management of anadromous fish, aquaculture chemicals, host-parasite interactions.

Christopher A. Peery, Assistant Research Professor; Ph.D. (fisheries resources), Idaho, 1995. Riverine and stream fish behavior and migrations, fish energetics, effects of altered systems on fish populations, fish conservation and recovery, aquatic ecosystem studies, large river ecology.

Janet L. Rachlow, Assistant Professor; Ph.D. (ecology, evolution, and conservation biology), Nevada, Reno, 1997. Wildlife ecology and management, large mammal ecology, conservation biology.

John T. Ratti, Research Professor; Ph.D. (wildlife ecology), Utah State, 1977. Avian ecology (birds), waterfowl ecology/management, upland bird ecology, research design/techniques, wetland ecology, habitat analysis.

Kerry P. Reese, Professor; Ph.D. (wildlife), Utah State, 1983. Upland game bird ecology/management, waterfowl and wetland ecology, avian ecology and habitat relationships.

Dennis L. Scarnecchia, Professor; Ph.D. (fisheries), Colorado State, 1983. Salmon and trout research, paddlefish research, Atlantic salmon, population dynamics, community ecology in large rivers.

J. Michael Scott, Professor; Ph.D. (zoology), Oregon State, 1973. Reserve identification selection and design, bird ecology/management, habitat relationships, translocation strategies, recovery of endangered species, Hawaiian forest birds.

Lisette P. Waits, Assistant Professor; Ph.D. (genetics), Utah, 1996. Conservation biology, conservation genetics, molecular ecology.

R. Gerald Wright, Professor; Ph.D. (systems ecology), Colorado State, 1972. Wildlife management in national parks/wilderness, ungulate ecology and habitat use, resolution of ecological problems, natural resource data management and GIS, human dimensions of wildlife.

UNIVERSITY OF IDAHO

Department of Forest Products

Programs of Study

The Department of Forest Products offers Bachelor of Science (B.S.), Master of Science (M.S.), and Doctor of Philosophy (Ph.D.) degree programs pertinent to efficient, environmentally sensitive, and sustainable use of forest resources. Graduate students and faculty members are involved in a wide range of research projects, including business management; forest engineering; road design and engineering; forest products manufacturing; wood pellet technology; inorganic bonded wood and fiber composites; measurement of dry kiln emissions; sawmill and logging simulation; affordable housing; timber harvesting technology; mill operations; veneer and composite technology; computer detection of flaws in scanned logs; small-diameter timber utilization; designing, engineering, and testing wood structures; and stress-wave analysis of lumber. Faculty members also work in coordination with the Bureau of Business and Economic Research at the University of Montana and the Wood Materials and Engineering Laboratory at Washington State University.

Research Facilities

The Forest Products Wood Research Laboratory is equipped for projects involving kiln drying, mechanical property testing, adhesives evaluation, composites manufacturing and testing, and chemical analysis. In addition, the Department uses testing equipment located at the Wood Materials and Engineering Laboratory located at Washington State University in Pullman, Washington, just 8 miles away. Many projects are also conducted on the University of Idaho Experimental Forest, industrial forest lands, and with individual wood manufacturers in the region.

Financial Aid

Graduate assistantships, typically involving 20 hours of work per week, are available in the form of teaching assistantships in which graduate students participate in the delivery of undergraduate courses. Research assistantships are also available. They allow graduate students to conduct research in several funded research projects. Financial aid is also available through the Federal Perkins Loan Program and work-study grants. The Student Financial Aid Office can provide information and applications.

Cost of Study

For 2003–04, full-time graduate fees were $2086 per semester for Idaho residents; nonresidents paid an additional $4010. Resident students who enrolled part-time paid $205 per credit; nonresident part-time students paid an additional $123 per credit. There is no additional fee charged to nonresidents for credits during the summer session. Full-time fees are charged for 8 credits or more. Fees are subject to change.

Living and Housing Costs

Graduate student housing is available through the University for $346 to $629 per month for apartments ranging in size from efficiencies to four-bedroom units. Potential graduate students are advised to reserve housing early. Off-campus housing lists are available at http://www.asui.uidaho.edu.

Student Group

Most graduate students enter the programs with B.S. degrees, typically in wood science, forestry, or engineering. Students with degrees in other areas may need to supplement their undergraduate education prior to beginning their research. Most graduate students are full-time and are provided with some type of financial aid, usually in the form of graduate assistantships. There are 3 women graduate students and 8 international students.

Student Outcomes

Most of the graduates holding master's degrees work for the wood products industry in positions with major industrial landowners, wood products manufacturers, and equipment manufacturers. For example, many forest products graduates are now in charge of quality control or technical services for large wood products manufacturing companies. The Ph.D. graduates often seek faculty positions, although several are in charge of wood research laboratories or research and development departments in industry.

Location

Moscow, located in the Idaho panhandle among the rolling hills of the Palouse, is an agricultural and recreational area and is the cultural center of the region. Local music and theater productions have received international acclaim. Skiing and lake and river sports are within easy drives. Spokane is 88 miles north, and Seattle and Portland are each 6 hours west.

The Department

The University of Idaho has a relatively small department (80 undergraduates, 6 faculty members, and 14 graduate students) with strong industry contacts, offering a personalized program for each student. The undergraduate curriculum is accredited by the Society of Wood Science and Technology (SWST), and there are many active student members of SWST and the Forest Products Society (FPS). In addition, many of the graduate students participate in the regional and national conferences, usually by presenting their research results.

Applying

Potential graduate students may apply for the degree program through the University of Idaho Graduate Admission Office. Each applicant must provide a brief statement of objectives, which provides additional background for selecting candidates and assigning faculty advisers. All graduate students are considered for one of the many graduate assistantships. Students wishing to apply for a departmental assistantship should consult with the department regarding the process and deadline date, which may be earlier than the application deadline date. For additional information, or to inquire about specific programs, prospective graduate students should contact:

Correspondence and Information

Dr. Thomas Gorman, P.E., Professor and Department Head
Department of Forest Products
P.O. Box 441132
University of Idaho
Moscow, Idaho 83844-4266
Phone: 208-885-7402
Fax: 208-885-4406
E-mail: tgorman@uidaho.edu
World Wide Web: http://www.cnr.uidaho.edu/forp

University of Idaho

THE FACULTY AND THEIR RESEARCH

Richard L. Folk, Assistant Professor; Ph.D., Idaho, 1991. Wood drying, energy from wood.
Thomas M. Gorman, Professor; Ph.D., SUNY at Syracuse, 1987. Mechanical properties of lumber, log construction.
Han-Sup Han, Assistant Professor; Ph.D., Oregon State, 1997. Timber harvesting.
Harry W. Lee, Emeritus Assistant Professor; Ph.D., Idaho, 1983. Timber harvesting.
Armando G. McDonald, Associate Professor; Ph.D., York, 1993. Wood composites, polymer chemistry.
Steven R. Shook, Assistant Professor; Ph.D., Washington (Seattle), 1997. Wood products marketing.
Francis G. Wagner, Professor; Ph.D., Mississippi State, 1982. Wood drying, primary manufacturing.

UNIVERSITY OF IDAHO

College of Natural Resources
Department of Forest Resources

Programs of Study

The Department of Forest Resources offers graduate programs leading to the Master of Science (thesis and nonthesis options) and Doctor of Philosophy with a major in natural resources (administered at the College level for all departments). Graduate programs are offered in most areas of specialization in forest resources, including policy, growth and yield, expert systems, community forestry, ecology/ecosystem processes, extension, fire ecology/management, genetics/tree improvement/ecogenetics, hydrology/watershed management, mensuration/inventory, nursery management, remote sensing/GIS, silviculture, sociology of natural resources, forest ecosystem management/sustainable forestry, tree physiology, restoration/conservation biology, environmental studies/management, regeneration, entomology/pathology.

The M.S. degree requires an oral presentation in addition to the written thesis or professional paper. A written examination is an option of the graduate committee. Most M.S. programs take two to three years to complete, depending on the student's background and the amount of field work/number of seasons required to complete the research. Doctoral candidates are expected to have an understanding of the principles of resource management in areas other than that chosen as a specialization. There is only one major for the Ph.D. degree (natural resources); however, dissertation topics are selected from disciplinary areas within the student's academic home department. (The single designation for the major is in keeping with the College's philosophy of integrated resource management.) Doctoral programs normally take three to five years to complete, depending on background and dissertation research. Doctoral students are expected to have completed a master's degree with a thesis. All Ph.D. students must spend at least one semester at the University of Idaho campus in Moscow and serve one semester as a teaching assistant.

Research Facilities

The 7,000-acre Experimental Forest on Moscow Mountain provides a real-world field environment to conduct a wide variety of graduate research projects. Some research sites in the Experimental Forest have several decades of data. There are a wide variety of forest habitat types as well as past and current management regimes. There are also many opportunities for field work on USDA Forest Service lands in the region and with Forest Service Experimental Forests, such as at Priest Lake in northern Idaho. There are new remote sensing and GIS facilities with complementary Windows NT (sixteen machines) and UNIX networks, a large fileserver (140 Gb), color output, GPS equipment, and the latest remote sensing and GIS software (ERDAS, ENVI, Arc/Info, Arcview). Other laboratory facilities include a mass spectrometer for analysis of stable isotopes, field ecophysiology instruments, and state-of-the-art facilities for molecular genetic analysis of wildland plants, including an ABI377 Automated DNA Sequencer.

Financial Aid

The department has a limited number of teaching assistantships. Applicants with strong quantitative skills are especially encouraged. In addition, most full-time graduate students secure a research assistantship during at least part of their graduate studies. Individual faculty members regularly post available assistantships and also work with new students to secure assistantships in the student's area of research interest. There are specific scholarships in nursery management and remote sensing. Financial aid is also available through the Federal Perkins Loan Program and work-study grants. The Student Financial Aid Office can provide information and applications.

Cost of Study

For 2004–05, full-time graduate fees are $2086 per semester for Idaho residents; nonresidents pay an additional $4010 per semester. Resident students enrolled part-time pay $205 per credit; nonresidents pay an additional $123 per credit for part-time study. Full-time fees are charged for 8 credits or more.

Living and Housing Costs

Graduate student housing is available through the University for $462 to $684 per month for apartments that range in size from efficiencies to four-bedroom units. Graduate students are advised to reserve housing early. Off-campus housing lists are available at http://www/asui.uidaho.edu.

Student Group

There are 50–55 graduate students in the department. About two thirds come from all over the United States and one third are international students. One third are women, one third are Ph.D. candidates, and about 60 percent are full-time. Graduate students come from a wide variety of educational institutions and have a wide variety of backgrounds, such as biology, botany, genetics, ecology, environmental science, political science, economics, wildlife, recreation, and wood products as well as traditional forestry.

Student Outcomes

Department graduates have an excellent record of employment. One hundred percent of Ph.D. graduates and more than 90 percent of M.S. graduates have achieved employment in their field according to recent employment surveys. Graduates are working in environmental and other types of consulting firms, the forest industry, state and federal land management agencies, and universities and as staff for professional organizations and a variety of nongovernmental organizations, including The Nature Conservancy.

Location

Moscow, located in the Idaho panhandle among the rolling hills of the Palouse, is an agricultural and recreational area and is the cultural center of the region. Local music and theater productions have received international acclaim. Skiing and lake and river sports are within easy drives. Spokane is 88 miles north, and Seattle and Portland are each 6 hours west. Moscow is located near a wide variety of forest ecosystems.

The Department

The Department of Forest Resources is a group of faculty members and students working on complex forest resource problems that vary from basic to applied sciences; genetic to landscape scales; biophysical to socioeconomic sciences; and ecological processes to forest management. Graduates think critically, ask the tough questions, accept ambiguity and trade-offs in decision making, and can live and work as professionals in an era when society has many conflicts about the values, products, and services that are important in forest ecosystems.

Applying

Applicants are required to submit a completed application form, two letters of recommendation, a statement of career objectives, a completed Area of Emphasis form, official GRE scores, and official transcripts. International applicants must also submit the TOEFL scores with a 550 or better.

The departmental deadline is the date by which the complete application file should be received by the department. Applicants must submit all materials to the Graduate Admissions Office early enough to allow at least four weeks' processing time *before* the departmental deadlines, which are as follows for domestic students: fall semester, July 1; spring semester, November 1; summer session, April 1. For international students, the deadlines are fall semester, June 1; spring semester, October 1; summer session, March 15.

Students applying for a departmental assistantship should consult with the department regarding the process and the deadline date, which may be earlier than the other application deadlines.

Correspondence and Information

Department of Forest Resources
College of Natural Resources
University of Idaho
P.O. Box 441133
Moscow, Idaho 83844-1133
Telephone: 208-885-4266
Fax: 208-885-4406
E-mail: fores@uidaho.edu
World Wide Web: http://www.its.uidaho.edu/forres/

University of Idaho

THE FACULTY AND THEIR RESEARCH

Steven J. Brunsfeld, Professor; Ph.D., Washington State, 1990. Ecology/ecosystem processes, genetics/tree improvement/ecogenetics, restoration/conservation biology.
Stephen P. Cook, Assistant Professor; Ph.D., North Carolina State, 1985. Forest entomology, forest ecosystem management/sustainable forestry, environmental studies/management, remote sensing/sensing/geographic information systems.
Lauren Fins, Professor; Ph.D., Berkeley, 1979. Forest ecosystem management/sustainable forestry, genetics/tree improvement/ecogenetics.
Jo Ellen Force, Professor and Department Head; Ph.D., Ohio State, 1978. Administration/policy, international forestry, land use planning, sociology of natural resources.
Paul E. Gessler, Associate Professor; Ph.D., Australian National University, 1996. Ecology/ecosystem processes, environmental studies/management, forest ecosystem management/sustainable forestry, hydrology/watershed management, international forestry, remote sensing/geographic information systems.
Charles R. Hatch, Professor and Vice President for Research and Graduate Studies; Ph.D., Minnesota, 1971. Growth and yield modeling, forest measurements.
Kathleen L. Kavanagh, Associate Professor; Ph.D., Oregon State, 1993. Ecology/ecosystem process, environmental studies/management, forest ecosystem management/sustainable forestry/regeneration, restoration/conservation biology, silviculture, tree physiology.
Timothy E. Link, Assistant Professor; Ph.D., Oregon State, 2001. Ecology/ecosystem processes/modeling, hydrology/watershed management.
Gary E. Machlis, Professor; Ph.D., Yale, 1979. Sociology of natural resources.
Ronald L. Mahoney, Extension Professor; Ph.D., Idaho, 1981. Ecology/ecosystem processes, extension, forest ecosystem management/ sustainable forestry, regeneration, silviculture.
John D. Marshall, Professor; Ph.D., Oregon State, 1985. Ecology/ecosystem processes, environmental studies/management, tree physiology.
Penelope Morgan, Professor; Ph.D., Idaho, 1984. Ecology/ecosystem processes, environmental studies/management, fire ecology/ management, forest ecosystem management/sustainable forestry, restoration/conservation biology, silviculture.
A. George Newcombe, Assistant Professor; Ph.D., Guelph, 1988. Forest pathology, genetics/tree improvement/ecogenetics.
Jay O'Laughlin, Professor; Ph.D., Minnesota (St. Paul), 1980. Administration/policy.
Andrew P. Robinson, Assistant Professor; Ph.D., Minnesota, 1998. Forest biometrics, growth and yield/mensuration/inventory/process modeling, tree physiology, ecology/ecosystem processes/modeling.
Molly W. Stock, Professor; Ph.D., Oregon State, 1972. Computer-aided forest management.
David L. Wenny, Professor; Ph.D., Idaho, 1981. Nursery management, regeneration, silviculture.

UNIVERSITY OF IDAHO

College of Natural Resources
Department of Rangeland Ecology and Management

Programs of Study

The department offers the Master of Science in rangeland ecology and management and a Ph.D. through College auspices. The department specializes in an ecological approach to the study and management of lands where the vegetation is predominantly composed of grasses, grasslike plants, forbs, or shrubs, commonly termed rangeland. The research and teaching expertise of the faculty covers several major areas of rangeland science and management, including community ecology, landscape ecology, foraging behavior, fire ecology, restoration ecology, grazing management, ecophysiology, riparian ecology, and livestock-wildlife relations.

Research Facilities

Individual faculty members conduct directed study, with the research location dictated by the objectives of the study. Locations include College facilities, such as the LA Sharp Experimental Area in southern Idaho; public lands in cooperation with agencies such as the Agricultural Research Service, Forest Service, or Bureau of Land Management; and private lands. In addition, the University of Idaho (UI) libraries contain approximately 2.5 million items, including more than 12,000 serial titles. The main library recently completed a major expansion and renovation.

Financial Aid

Many departments offer teaching assistantships or research assistantships, which include a waiver of nonresident tuition. Information on assistantships may be obtained directly from the director of graduate studies. Financial aid is also available through the Federal Perkins Loan Program, the Federal Stafford Student Loan Program, and work-study grants. Information and applications can be provided by the Student Financial Aid Office.

Cost of Study

For 2004–05, full-time graduate fees are $2086 per semester for Idaho residents, with an additional fee of $4010 per semester for nonresidents. Resident students enrolled part-time pay $205 per credit; nonresidents pay an additional $123 per credit for part-time study. There is no additional fee charged to nonresidents for credits taken during the summer session. Full-time fees are charged for 8 credits or more. Fees are subject to change.

Living and Housing Costs

Graduate student housing is available through the University from $346 to $629 per month for apartments ranging in size from efficiencies to four-bedroom units. Potential graduate students are advised to reserve housing early. Off-campus housing lists are available at http://www.asui.uidaho.edu.

Student Group

Total graduate enrollment at UI for fall 2001 was 2,230 students: 1,545 on the main campus in Moscow and 685 at UI's Coeur d'Alene, Boise, and Idaho Falls instructional centers and through the Outreach Programs. UI enrolls students from all fifty states and from seventy-eight other countries, providing cultural diversity as part of its educational mission.

Student Outcomes

In 1995–99, 26 of 28 students (93 percent) earning a graduate degree found professional positions at or shortly after graduation.

Location

Moscow is located in the Idaho panhandle among the rolling hills of the Palouse. It is an agricultural and recreational area and is the cultural center of the region. Local music and theater productions have received international acclaim. Skiing and lake and river sports are within easy drives. Spokane is 88 miles to the north, and Seattle and Portland are each 6 hours to the west.

The University and The Department

The University of Idaho was created in 1889, a year before Idaho became a state. UI is a publicly supported, comprehensive land-grant institution with principal responsibility in Idaho for performing research and granting the Ph.D. degree. More than 750 faculty members participate in teaching and research. In addition to the accreditation of individual programs, the University is accredited by the Northwest Commission on Colleges and Universities. The Department of Rangeland Ecology and Management is the only department in the College of Natural Resources and one of only a few in the University with a named professorship: The Heady Professorship of Range Ecology.

Applying

The Department of Rangeland Ecology and Management requires that a complete application form, two letters of recommendation, a statement of purpose, a complete area of emphasis form, application fee, GRE scores, and official transcripts be sent to the Graduate Admissions Office. International applicants must take the TOEFL and achieve a score of 550 or better. The deadlines for domestic applicants are July 1 (fall), November 1 (spring), and April 1 (summer). The deadlines for international applicants are June 1 (fall), October 1 (spring), and March 15 (summer). Students applying for departmental assistantships should consult with the department regarding the process and deadline date, which may be earlier than the application deadline date.

Correspondence and Information

Dr. Karen Launchbaugh
Department of Rangeland Ecology and Management
College of Natural Resources
University of Idaho
Moscow, Idaho 83844-4266
Telephone: 208-885-6536
Fax: 208-885-4406
E-mail: range@uidaho.edu
World Wide Web: http://www.cnr.uidaho.edu/range/graduate.htm

University of Idaho

THE FACULTY AND THEIR RESEARCH

Karen L. Launchbaugh, Associate Professor and Department Chair; Ph.D., Utah State. Animal nutrition and behavior, grazing management.

Jeffrey Braatne, Assistant Professor; Ph.D., Washington (Seattle). Riparian and stream ecology management.

Stephen C. Bunting, Heady Professor: Ph.D., Texas Tech. Range ecology, fire ecology, landscape ecology.

John E. Ehrenreich, Emeritus Professor; Ph.D., Iowa State. Range ecology, agroforestry, international forestry.

Minoru Hironaka, Emeritus Professor; Ph.D., Wisconsin. Range ecology, community ecology, range classification.

Kendall L. Johnson, Emeritus Professor; Ph.D., Colorado State. Shrubland ecology and management, range extension.

James L. Kingery, Associate Professor: Ph.D., Idaho. Forest range relationships, rangeland rehabilitation.

Ronald Robberecht, Professor; Ph.D., Utah State. Ecophysiology, autecology, range ecology.

Kenneth D. Sanders, Professor; Ph.D., Texas Tech. Range extension, grazing management, range improvements.

YALE UNIVERSITY

School of Forestry & Environmental Studies

Programs of Study

The School of Forestry & Environmental Studies offers master's degrees in environmental management (M.E.M.), environmental science (M.E.Sc.), forest science (M.F.S.), and forestry (M.F.) as well as one-year master's degree programs (M.E.M. and M.F.) for experienced environmental professionals. Joint degrees can be pursued at Yale in developmental economics, divinity, international relations, law, management, and public health. Joint programs with Vermont Law School and Pace Law School have also been established. In addition, students have the opportunity to continue their studies through the Graduate School of Arts and Sciences in a Ph.D. program.

Course work and research opportunities are concentrated in areas of faculty research, which currently encompass the following broad foci: ecology, ecosystems, and biodiversity; forest science and management; policy, economics, and law; industrial environmental management; coastal and watershed systems; health and environment; urban ecology and sustainable design; global change, science, and policy; and social ecology of conservation and development.

While curricula of study in all master's programs are sufficiently flexible to accommodate varying backgrounds and career aspirations, they are partially structured to ensure professional competence and maximum exposure to the diverse offerings of the School and Yale's other departments and professional schools. Programs of study leading to all degrees consist of lecture courses, seminars, and individual and group projects. No formal thesis is required for the master's degrees, but all programs require a master's group project or other capstone experience. Students pursuing doctoral degrees are assigned a faculty committee and are required to successfully complete written and oral qualifying examinations as well as defend their dissertation.

Research Facilities

The School's seven buildings house laboratories, controlled-environment rooms, a greenhouse, computer labs, and other research facilities. The forestry library in Sage Hall has holdings of more than 130,000 volumes and 326 periodicals. Approximately 800 other serial publications are received. This library is part of the Yale University library system. Field instruction and research are conducted on the more than 10,000 acres of Yale forests located in northeastern Connecticut, southwestern New Hampshire, and Vermont. Private and public land across the United States and in Puerto Rico is also available.

Financial Aid

Every effort is made to enable qualified students to attend the School, regardless of their financial circumstances. Financial aid is awarded on the basis of need, academic merit, and available resources. Approximately two thirds of the student body receive financial aid in the form of loans, work-study, and/or scholarships. All applicants are encouraged to complete and submit the F&ES financial aid application by February 14. U.S. citizens and permanent residents applying to a master's program who are requesting financial aid must also submit the Free Application for Federal Student Aid (FAFSA) by February 14. Applicants are also encouraged to investigate external sources of aid.

Cost of Study

The 2004–05 tuition for master's degree programs is $23,850. Two-year master's students must pay full tuition for two years, regardless of the number of courses they take. Doctoral students must pay full tuition for four years and may remain on continuing registration status for only two years thereafter. Most doctoral students receive a University fellowship that covers the costs of the first four years of tuition and health insurance and includes a stipend during the academic year, but they must pay a nominal continuing registration fee thereafter. The School reserves the right to revise tuition as it deems appropriate.

Two-year master's students must participate in a required three-week summer training module in technical skills, for which they are charged an instructional expense fee of $900 (which may be revised at any time).

For 2004–05, student expenses also include $1300 for hospitalization coverage and $1060 for books and supplies. Materials fees charged by other schools and departments in the University are additional.

Living and Housing Costs

University housing is available for a limited number of single students and for married students. Most students live off campus. A single student can expect living expenses of approximately $11,400 for a nine-month period. A single student in the summer module program should anticipate living expenses of approximately $900 for a three-week period.

Student Group

The total graduate enrollment at Yale is 5,000. Approximately 220 master's students and 75 Ph.D. students are enrolled in the School of Forestry & Environmental Studies. Students come from diverse educational, geographical, and national backgrounds. Thirty percent of the students come from forty-three countries around the world.

Location

Yale University is located in New Haven, Connecticut, a harbor city of approximately 127,000, which is situated on Long Island Sound, midway between New York City and Boston. Known for its theater life and its distinct neighborhoods, New Haven also permits easy access to harbor, beach, and mountain areas.

The University and The School

Yale University is a private institution, founded in 1701 under the leadership of a group of Congregational ministers. Today it continues its early tradition of liberal education and community service. Yale is noted for the high quality of its theater productions, art galleries, and libraries as well as for its renowned educational and research facilities.

For more than 100 years, the Yale School of Forestry & Environmental Studies has prepared students for important positions of environmental leadership in the United States and throughout the world. Graduates of this interdisciplinary program assume influential roles in government, business, nongovernmental organizations, public and international affairs, research, and education. In 1973, the name of the School was changed to include environmental studies to reflect the broadening of its programs. The School's professional forestry programs are accredited by the Society of American Foresters.

Applying

Applications for the master's and Ph.D. degree programs must be postmarked by January 14 and January 3, respectively. Notification of acceptance to the master's program is made by April 1. There is a $70 online application fee or a $90 paper application fee for master's programs. Official scores on the GRE General Test are required of all applicants. Students for whom English is a second language must submit a TOEFL score as part of their application to any of the programs offered by the School. For more information, interested students should visit http://www.yale.edu/environment.

Correspondence and Information

For master's programs:
Emly McDiarmid
Director of Admissions
Yale School of Forestry
& Environmental Studies
205 Prospect Street
New Haven, Connecticut 06511
E-mail: emly.mcdiarmid@yale.edu

For Ph.D. programs:
Dr. Xuhui Lee
Director of Doctoral Programs
Yale School of Forestry
& Environmental Studies
205 Prospect Street
New Haven, Connecticut 06511
E-mail: xuhui.lee@yale.edu

Elisabeth Barsa
Doctoral Program Administrator
Yale School of Forestry
& Environmental Studies
205 Prospect Street
New Haven, Connecticut 06511
E-mail: elisabeth.barsa@yale.edu

Yale University

THE FACULTY

(All phone numbers listed below are in Area Code 203.)

Shimon C. Anisfeld, Lecturer and Associate Research Scientist in Environmental Chemistry and Water Resources; Ph.D. Telephone: 432-5748, e-mail: shimon.cohen-anisfeld@yale.edu.
Mark S. Ashton, Professor of Silviculture and Forest Ecology; M.F., Ph.D. Telephone: 432-9835, e-mail: mark.ashton@yale.edu.
James W. Axley, Professor of Architecture; M.Arch., Ph.D. E-mail: james.axley@yale.edu.
Michelle L. Bell, Assistant Professor of Environmental Health; M.S.E., Ph.D. Telephone: 432-9869, e-mail: michelle.bell@yale.edu.
Gaboury Benoit, Professor of Environmental Chemistry, Professor of Environmental Engineering, Co-Director of the Hixon Center for Urban Ecology, and Director of the Center for Coastal and Watershed Systems; Ph.D. Telephone: 432-5139, e-mail: gaboury.benoit@yale.edu.
Graeme Pierce Berlyn, Professor of Anatomy and Physiology of Trees; Ph.D. Telephone: 432-5142, e-mail: graeme.berlyn@yale.edu.
Ruth Elaine Blake, Assistant Professor of Geology and Geophysics, Department of Geology and Geophysics; Ph.D. Telephone: 436-3420, e-mail: ruth.blake@yale.edu.
Garry D. Brewer, Frederick K. Weyerhaeuser Professor of Resources Policy and Management, joint appointment with School of Management; Ph.D. Telephone: 432-6379, e-mail: garry.brewer@yale.edu.
William Richard Burch Jr., Frederick C. Hixon Professor of Natural Resource Management and Professor, Institution for Social and Policy Studies; Ph.D. Telephone: 432-5119, e-mail: william.burch@yale.edu.
Adalgisa Caccone, Senior Scientist in Ecology and Evolutionary Biology, Department of Ecology and Evolutionary Biology; Ph.D. Telephone: 432-5259, e-mail: adalgisa.caccone@yale.edu.
Ann Camp, Lecturer in Stand Dynamics and Forest Health; M.F.S., Ph.D. Telephone: 436-3980, e-mail: ann.camp@yale.edu.
Carol Carpenter, Lecturer in Natural Resource Social Science and in Anthropology; Ph.D. Telephone: 432-7530, e-mail: carol.carpenter@yale.edu.
Benjamin Cashore, Assistant Professor of Sustainable Forestry Management and Chair, Program of Forest Certification; Ph.D. Telephone: 432-3009, e-mail: benjamin.cashore@yale.edu.
Marian R. Chertow, Assistant Professor of Industrial Environmental Management; Director, Program on Solid-Waste Policy; and Director, Industrial Environmental Management Program; M.P.P.M., Ph.D. Telephone: 432-6197, e-mail: marian.chertow@yale.edu.
Timothy W. Clark, Adjunct Professor of Wildlife Ecology and Policy; Ph.D. Telephone: 432-6965, e-mail: timothy.w.clark@yale.edu.
Lisa M. Curran, Associate Professor of Tropical Resources and Director, Tropical Resources Institute; Ph.D. Telephone: 432-3772, e-mail: lisa.curran@yale.edu.
Michael Donoghue, G. Evelyn Hutchinson Professor of Ecology and Evolutionary Biology, Department of Ecology and Evolutionary Biology, and Curator of Botany, Yale Peabody Museum; Ph.D. E-mail: michael.donoghue@yale.edu.
Amity Appell Doolittle, Program Director, Tropical Resources Institute, and Lecturer in Social Change and the Environment; M.E.S., Ph.D. Telephone: 432-3660, e-mail: amity.doolittle@yale.edu.
Michael Roger Dove, Professor of Social Ecology and of Anthropology; Ph.D. Telephone: 432-3463, e-mail: michael.dove@yale.edu.
Paul Alexander Draghi, Lecturer in Forest History and Director, Information and Library Systems; Ph.D. Telephone: 432-5115, e-mail: paul.draghi@yale.edu.
Menachem Elimelech, Llewellyn West Jones Professor of Environmental Engineering and of Chemical Engineering, Faculty of Engineering; Ph.D. Telephone: 432-2789, e-mail: menachem.elimelech@yale.edu.
Roger Ely, Assistant Professor of Chemical Engineering, Faculty of Engineering, Ph.D. Telephone: 432-2218, e-mail: roger.ely@yale.edu.
Daniel C. Esty, Professor of Environmental Law and Policy; Clinical Professor, Law School; Director, Center for Environmental Law and Policy; and Director,Yale World Fellows Program; M.A., J.D. Telephone: 432-6256, e-mail: daniel.esty@yale.edu.
Robert Eugene Evenson, Professor of Economics, Department of Economics; Ph.D. Telephone: 432-3626, e-mail: robert.evenson@yale.edu.
Jonathan Feinstein, Professor of Economics, School of Management; Ph.D. Telephone: 432-5975, e-mail: jonathan.feinstein@yale.edu.
Gordon T. Geballe, Lecturer in Urban Ecology and Associate Dean, Student and Alumni Affairs; Ph.D. Telephone: 432-5122, e-mail: gordon.geballe@yale.edu.
Bradford S. Gentry, Lecturer in Sustainable Investments and Co-Director, Yale-UNDP Collaborative Program on the Urban Environment; J.D. Telephone: 432-9374, e-mail: bradford.gentry@yale.edu.
Mary Helen Goldsmith, Professor of Molecular, Cellular, and Developmental Biology, Department of Molecular, Cellular, and Developmental Biology; Ph.D. E-mail: mary.goldsmith@yale.edu.
Thomas Eldon Graedel, Professor of Industrial Ecology, of Chemical Engineering, of Geology and Geophysics and Director, Center for Industrial Ecology; Ph.D. Telephone: 432-9733, e-mail: thomas.graedel@yale.edu.
Timothy G. Gregoire, J. P. Weyerhaeuser Jr. Professor of Forest Management and Associate Dean, Academic Affairs; Ph.D. Telephone: 432-9398, e-mail: timothy.gregoire@yale.edu.
Arnulf Grübler, Professor in the Field of Energy and Technology; Ph.D. E-mail: arnulf.grubler@yale.edu.
Stephen Robert Kellert, Tweedy/Ordway Professor of Social Ecology and Co-Director, Hixon Center for Urban Ecology; Ph.D. Telephone: 432-5114, e-mail: stephen.kellert@yale.edu.
Nathaniel Keohane, Assistant Professor of Economics, School of Management; Ph.D. E-mail: nathaniel.keohane@yale.edu.
Brian Leaderer, Susan Dwight Bliss Professor of Public Heath and Professor and Head, Division of Environmental Sciences, Department of Epidemiology and Public Health; Ph.D. Telephone: 785-2880, e-mail: brian.leaderer@yale.edu.
Xuhui Lee, Associate Professor of Forest and Micrometeorology; Ph.D. Telephone: 432-6271, e-mail: xuhui.lee@yale.edu.
Reid J. Lifset, Associate Research Scholar; Associate Director, Industrial Environmental Management Program; and Editor-in-Chief, *Journal of Industrial Ecology;* M.S., M.P.P.M. Telephone: 432-6949, e-mail: reid.lifset@yale.edu.
Erin T. Mansur, Assistant Professor of Environmental Economics, jointly appointed with the School of Management; Ph.D. Telephone: 432-6233, e-mail: erin.mansur@yale.edu.
Robert Mendelsohn, Edwin W. Davis Professor of Forest Policy and of Economics and Professor in the School of Management; Ph.D. Telephone: 432-5128, e-mail: robert.mendelsohn@yale.edu.
Florencia Montagnini, Professor in the Practice of Tropical Forestry; Ph.D. Telephone: 436-4221, e-mail: florencia.montagnini@yale.edu.
William Nordhaus, A. Whitney Griswold Professor of Economics, Department of Economics; Ph.D. Telephone: 432-3598, e-mail: william.nordhaus@yale.edu.
Chadwick Dearing Oliver, Pinchot Professor of Forest Policy and Director, Global Institute for Sustainable Forestry; M.F.S., Ph.D. Telephone: 432-7409, e-mail: chad.oliver@yale.edu.
Sheila Cavanagh Olmstead, Assistant Professor of Environmental Economics; M.P.Aff., Ph.D. Telephone: 432-6274, e-mail: sheila.olmstead@yale.edu.
Jeffrey Powell, Professor of Ecology and Evolutionary Biology, Department of Ecology and Evolutionary Biology; Ph.D. E-mail: jeffrey.powell@yale.edu.
Peter A. Raymond, Assistant Professor of Ecosystem Ecology; Ph.D. Telephone: 432-0817, e-mail: peter.raymond@yale.edu.
James E. Saiers, Associate Professor of Hydrology; Ph.D. Telephone: 432-5121, e-mail: james.saiers@yale.edu.
Oswald J. Schmitz, Professor of Population and Community Ecology; Director, Doctoral Studies; and Director; Center for Biodiversity Conservation and Science; Ph.D. E-mail: oswald.schmitz@yale.edu.
James C. Scott, Eugene Mayer Professor of Political Science; Professor of Anthropology; and Director, Program in Agrarian Studies, Yale Center for International and Area Studies; Ph.D. Telephone: 436-4091, e-mail: james.scott@yale.edu.
Thomas G. Siccama, Professor in the Practice of Forest Ecology and Director, Field Studies; Ph.D. Telephone: 432-5140, e-mail: thomas.siccama@yale.edu.
David K. Skelly, Associate Professor of Ecology; Ph.D. Telephone: 432-3603, e-mail: david.skelly@yale.edu.
Ronald B. Smith, Professor of Geology and Geophysics and of Mechanical Engineering, Department of Geology and Geophysics, and Director, Yale Center for Earth Observation; Ph.D. Telephone: 432-3129, e-mail: ronald.smith@yale.edu.
James Gustave Speth, Professor and Dean, Practice of Environmental Policy and Sustainable Development; M.Litt., J.D. Telephone: 432-5109, e-mail: gus.speth@yale.edu.
Stephen Stearns, Edward P. Bass Professor of Ecology and Evolutionary Biology, Department of Ecology and Evolutionary Biology; Ph.D. E-mail: stephen.stearns@yale.edu.
Fred Strebeigh, Lecturer in Environmental Writing; B.A. Telephone: 432-2250, e-mail: fred.strebeigh@yale.edu.
Karl Turekian, Benjamin Silliman Professor of Geology and Geophysics, Department of Geology and Geophysics, and Director, Yale Institute for Biospheric Studies; Ph.D. E-mail: karl.turekian@yale.edu.
John Peter Wargo, Professor of Environmental Risk Analysis and Policy and of Political Science and Director, Environment and Health Initiative; Ph.D. Telephone: 432-5123, e-mail: john.wargo@yale.edu.
Andrew Willard, Lecturer in Natural Resource Policy. E-mail: andrew.willard@yale.edu.
Eric Worby, Assistant Professor of Anthropology; Ph.D. E-mail: eric.worby@yale.edu.

APPENDIXES

Institutional Changes Since the 2004 Edition

Following is an alphabetical listing of institutions that have recently closed, moved, merged with other institutions, or changed their names or status. In the case of a name change, the former name appears first, followed by the new name.

Academy of Art College (San Francisco, CA): name changed to Academy of Art University

Bethel College (St. Paul, MN): name changed to Bethel University.

Bluffton College (Bluffton, OH): name changed to Bluffton University.

Canadian Bible College (Calgary, AB): merged with Canadian Theological Seminary to form Alliance University College.

Caribbean University College (Bayamón, PR): name changed to Caribbean University.

Concordia University (St. Paul, MN): name changed to Concordia University, St. Paul.

Coppin State College (Baltimore, MD): name changed to Coppin State University.

DeVry Institute of Technology (Chicago, IL): name changed to DeVry University.

DeVry Institute of Technology (Columbus, OH): name changed to DeVry University.

DeVry Institute of Technology (Decatur, GA): name changed to DeVry University.

DeVry Institute of Technology (Irving, TX): name changed to DeVry University.

DeVry Institute of Technology (Long Beach, CA): name changed to DeVry University.

DeVry Institute of Technology (Phoenix, AZ): name changed to DeVry University.

DeVry Institute of Technology (Pomona, CA): name changed to DeVry University.

DeVry University-Keller Graduate School of Management (Oakbrook Terrace, IL): name changed to DeVry University.

The Dr. William M. Scholl College of Podiatric Medicine at Finch University of Health Sciences (North Chicago, IL): name changed to The Dr. William M. Scholl College of Podiatric Medicine at Rosalind Franklin University of Medicine and Science.

Fairmont State College (Fairmont, WV): name changed to Fairmont State University.

Ferris State University (Big Rapids, MI) merged with Kendall College of Art and Design (Grand Rapids, MI) to form Kendall College of Art and Design of Ferris State University.

Finch University of Health Sciences/The Chicago Medical School (North Chicago, IL): name changed to Rosalind Franklin University of Medicine and Science.

Georgian Court College (Lakewood, NJ): name changed to Georgian Court University.

Grand Rapids Baptist Seminary of Cornerstone University (Grand Rapids, MI): name changed to Grand Rapids Theological Seminary of Cornerstone University.

Holy Names College (Oakland, CA): name changed to Holy Names University.

Jewish Theological Seminary of America (New York, NY): name changed to The Jewish Theological Seminary.

Kendall College of Art and Design (Grand Rapids, MI): merged with Ferris State University (Big Rapids, MI)to form Kendall College of Art and Design of Ferris State University.

Mary Washington College (Fredericksburg, VA): name changed to University of Mary Washington.

Mount Saint Mary's College and Seminary (Emmitsburg, MD): name changed to Mount Saint Mary's University.

Ohio State University-Lima Campus (Lima, OH): name changed to The Ohio State University at Lima.

Ohio State University-Mansfield Campus (Mansfield, OH): name changed to The Ohio State University–Mansfield Campus.

Ohio State University-Marion Campus (Marion, OH): name changed to The Ohio State University at Marion.

Ohio State University-Newark Campus (Newark, OH): name changed to The Ohio State University–Newark Campus.

Picower Graduate School of Molecular Medicine (Manhasset, NY): name changed to North Shore-Long Island Jewish Graduate School of Molecular Medicine.

Plattsburgh State University of New York (Plattsburgh, NY): name changed to State University of New York at Plattsburgh.

Point Park College (Pittsburgh, PA): name changed to Point Park University.

RAND Graduate School of Policy Studies (Santa Monica, CA): name changed to Frederick S. Pardee RAND Graduate School.

Saint Mary University (Leavenworth, KS): name changed to University of Saint Mary.

School of the Museum of Fine Arts (Boston, MA): name changed to School of the Museum of Fine Arts, Boston.

Shepherd College (Shepherdstown, WV): name changed to Shepherd University.

Southeast Institute of Oriental Medicine (Miami, FL): name changed to Acupuncture and Massage College.

State University of New York at Albany (Albany, NY): name changed to University at Albany, State University of New York.

State University of New York College of Technology at Utica/Rome (Utica, NY): name changed to State University of New York Institute of Technology.

Tai Sophia Institute (Laurel, MD): name changed to Tai Sophia Institute for the Healing Arts.

Thunderbird, The American Graduate School of International Management (Glendale, AZ): name changed to Thunderbird, The Garvin School of International Management.

Troy State University (Troy, AL): name changed to Troy University.

Troy State University Dothan (Dothan, AL): name changed to Troy University Dothan.

Troy State University Montgomery (Montgomery, AL): name changed to Troy University Montgomery.

Union College (Schenectady, NY): name changed to The Graduate College of Union University.

The University of Health Sciences (Kansas City, MO): name changed to Kansas City University of Medicine and Biosciences.

Westminster Theological Seminary in California (Escondido, CA): name changed to Westminster Seminary California.

Abbreviations Used in the Guides

The following list includes abbreviations of degree names used in the profiles in the 2005 edition of the guides. Because some degrees (e.g., Doctor of Education) can be abbreviated in more than one way (e.g., D.Ed. or Ed.D.), and because the abbreviations used in the guides reflect the preferences of the individual colleges and universities, the list may include two or more abbreviations for a single degree.

Degrees

A Mus D	Doctor of Musical Arts
AC	Advanced Certificate
AD	Artist's Diploma
ADP	Artist's Diploma
Adv C	Advanced Certificate
Adv M	Advanced Master
AGSC	Advanced Graduate Specialist Certificate
ALM	Master of Liberal Arts
AM	Master of Arts
AMRS	Master of Arts in Religious Studies
APC	Advanced Professional Certificate
App Sc	Applied Scientist
Au D	Doctor of Audiology
B Th	Bachelor of Theology
C Phil	Certificate in Philosophy
CAES	Certificate of Advanced Educational Specialization
CAGS	Certificate of Advanced Graduate Studies
CAL	Certificate in Applied Linguistics
CALS	Certificate of Advanced Liberal Studies
CAMS	Certificate of Advanced Management Studies
CAPS	Certificate of Advanced Professional Studies
CAS	Certificate of Advanced Studies
CASPA	Certificate of Advanced Study in Public Administration
CASR	Certificate in Advanced Social Research
CATS	Certificate of Achievement in Theological Studies
CBHS	Certificate in Basic Health Sciences
CBS	Graduate Certificate in Biblical Studies
CCJA	Certificate in Criminal Justice Administration
CCMBA	Cross-Continent Master of Business Administration
CCSA	Certificate in Catholic School Administration
CE	Civil Engineer
CEM	Certificate of Environmental Management
CG	Certificate in Gerontology
CGS	Certificate of Graduate Studies
Ch E	Chemical Engineer
CHSS	Counseling and Human Services Specialist
CIAMBA	Cohort Option Information Age Master of Business Administration
CIF	Certificate in International Finance
CITS	Certificate of Individual Theological Studies
CME	Clinical Master of Education
CMH	Certificate in Medical Humanities
CMM	Master of Church Ministries
CMS	Certificate in Ministerial Studies Certificate in Museum Studies
CNM	Certificate in Nonprofit Management
CP	Certificate in Performance
CPASF	Certificate Program for Advanced Study in Finance
CPC	Certificate in Professional Counseling Certificate in Publication and Communication
CPH	Certificate in Public Health
CPM	Certificate in Public Management
CPS	Certificate of Professional Studies
CSD	Certificate in Spiritual Direction
CSE	Computer Systems Engineer
CSS	Certificate of Special Studies
CTE	Certificate of Technologies of Education
CTS	Certificate of Theological Studies
CURP	Certificate in Urban and Regional Planning
D Arch	Doctor of Architecture
D Ed	Doctor of Education
D Eng	Doctor of Engineering
D Engr	Doctor of Engineering
D Env	Doctor of Environment
D Env M	Doctor of Environmental Management
D Jur	Doctor of Jurisprudence
D Law	Doctor of Law
D Litt	Doctor of Letters
D Med Sc	Doctor of Medical Science
D Min	Doctor of Ministry
D Min PCC	Doctor of Ministry, Pastoral Care, and Counseling
D Miss	Doctor of Missiology
D Mus	Doctor of Music
D Mus A	Doctor of Musical Arts
D Mus Ed	Doctor of Music Education
D Phil	Doctor of Philosophy
D Ps	Doctor of Psychology
D Sc	Doctor of Science
D Sc D	Doctor of Science in Dentistry
D Th	Doctor of Theology
D Th P	Doctor of Practical Theology
DA	Doctor of Arts
DA Ed	Doctor of Arts in Education
DAOM	Doctorate in Acupuncture and Oriental Medicine
DAST	Diploma of Advanced Studies in Teaching
DBA	Doctor of Business Administration
DBS	Doctor of Buddhist Studies
DC	Doctor of Chiropractic
DCC	Doctor of Computer Science
DCD	Doctor of Communications Design
DCL	Doctor of Comparative Law
DCM	Doctor of Church Music
DCN	Doctor of Clinical Nutrition
DCS	Doctor of Computer Science
DDN	Diplôme du Droit Notarial
DDS	Doctor of Dental Surgery
DE	Doctor of Education Doctor of Engineering
DEIT	Doctor of Educational Innovation and Technology
DEM	Doctor of Educational Ministry
DEPD	Diplôme Études Spécialisées
DES	Doctor of Engineering Science
DESS	Diplôme Études Supérieures Spécialisées

DFA	Doctor of Fine Arts
DFES	Doctor of Forestry and Environmental Studies
DGP	Diploma in Graduate and Professional Studies
DH Sc	Doctor of Health Sciences
DHA	Doctor of Health Administration
DHCE	Doctor of Health Care Ethics
DHL	Doctor of Hebrew Letters Doctor of Hebrew Literature
DHS	Doctor of Human Services
DHSc	Doctor of Health Science
DIBA	Doctor of International Business Administration
Dip CS	Diploma in Christian Studies
DIT	Doctor of Industrial Technology Doctor of Information Technology
DJ Ed	Doctor of Jewish Education
DJS	Doctor of Jewish Studies
DM	Doctor of Management Doctor of Music
DMA	Doctor of Musical Arts
DMD	Doctor of Dental Medicine
DME	Doctor of Manufacturing Management Doctor of Music Education
DMFT	Doctor of Marital and Family Therapy
DMH	Doctor of Medical Humanities
DML	Doctor of Modern Languages
DMM	Doctor of Music Ministry
DN Sc	Doctor of Nursing Science
DNS	Doctor of Nursing Science
DO	Doctor of Osteopathy
DPA	Doctor of Public Administration
DPC	Doctor of Pastoral Counseling
DPDS	Doctor of Planning and Development Studies
DPE	Doctor of Physical Education
DPH	Doctor of Public Health
DPM	Doctor of Plant Medicine Doctor of Podiatric Medicine
DPS	Doctor of Professional Studies
DPT	Doctor of Physical Therapy
Dr DES	Doctor of Design
Dr PH	Doctor of Public Health
Dr Sc PT	Doctor of Science in Physical Therapy
DS	Doctor of Science
DS Sc	Doctor of Social Science
DSJS	Doctor of Science in Jewish Studies
DSL	Doctor of Strategic Leadership
DSM	Doctor of Sacred Music Doctor of Sport Management
DSN	Doctor of Science in Nursing
DSW	Doctor of Social Work
DTL	Doctor of Talmudic Law
DV Sc	Doctor of Veterinary Science
DVM	Doctor of Veterinary Medicine
EAA	Engineer in Aeronautics and Astronautics
ECS	Engineer in Computer Science
Ed D	Doctor of Education
Ed DCT	Doctor of Education in College Teaching
Ed M	Master of Education
Ed S	Specialist in Education
Ed Sp	Specialist in Education
Ed Sp PTE	Specialist in Education in Professional Technical Education
EDM	Executive Doctorate in Management
EDSPC	Education Specialist
EE	Electrical Engineer
EJD	Executive Juris Doctor
EM	Mining Engineer
EMBA	Executive Master of Business Administration
EMCIS	Executive Master of Computer Information Systems
EMHA	Executive Master of Health Administration
EMIB	Executive Master of International Business
EMPA	Executive Master of Public Affairs
EMS	Executive Master of Science
EMTM	Executive Master of Technology Management
Eng	Engineer
Eng Sc D	Doctor of Engineering Science
Engr	Engineer
Env E	Environmental Engineer
Ex Doc	Executive Doctor of Pharmacy
Exec Ed D	Executive Doctor of Education
Exec MBA	Executive Master of Business Administration
Exec MIM	Executive Master of International Management
Exec MPA	Executive Master of Public Administration
Exec MPH	Executive Master of Public Health
Exec MS	Executive Master of Science
FIAMBA	Flexible Option Information Age Master of Business Administration
GBC	Graduate Business Certificate
GBE	Graduate Business Certificate in Ethics
GCE	Graduate Certificate in Education
GDPA	Graduate Diploma in Public Administration
GDRE	Graduate Diploma in Religious Education
GEMBA	Global Executive Master of Business Administration
Geol E	Geological Engineer
GMBA	Global Master of Business Administration
GPD	Graduate Performance Diploma
GSS	Graduate Special Certificate for Students in Special Situations
HS Dir	Director of Health and Safety
HSD	Doctor of Health and Safety
IMA	Interdisciplinary Master of Arts
IMBA	International Master of Business Administration
IMM	International Master's in Management
ITMA	Master of Instructional Technology
JCD	Doctor of Canon Law
JCL	Licentiate in Canon Law
JD	Juris Doctor
JSD	Doctor of Juridical Science Doctor of Jurisprudence Doctor of the Science of Law
JSM	Master of Science of Law
L Th	Licenciate in Theology
LL B	Bachelor of Laws
LL CM	Master of Laws in Comparative Law
LL D	Doctor of Laws
LL M	Master of Laws
LL M CL	Master of Laws in Comparative Law
LL M T	Master of Laws in Taxation
M Ac	Master of Accountancy Master of Accounting Master of Acupuncture
M Ac OM	Master of Acupuncture and Oriental Medicine

M Acc	Master of Accountancy Master of Accounting
M Acct	Master of Accountancy Master of Accounting
M Accy	Master of Accountancy
M Actg	Master of Accounting
M Acy	Master of Accountancy
M Ad	Master of Administration
M Ad Ed	Master of Adult Education
M Adm	Master of Administration
M Adm Mgt	Master of Administrative Management
M Adv	Master of Advertising
M Aero E	Master of Aerospace Engineering
M Ag	Master of Agriculture
M Ag Ed	Master of Agricultural Education
M Agr	Master of Agriculture
M Anesth Ed	Master of Anesthesiology Education
M App Comp Sc	Master of Applied Computer Science
M App St	Master of Applied Statistics
M Appl Stat	Master of Applied Statistics
M Aq	Master of Aquaculture
M Ar	Master of Architecture
M Arch	Master of Architecture
M Arch E	Master of Architectural Engineering
M Arch H	Master of Architectural History
M Arch UD	Master of Architecture in Urban Design
M Bio E	Master of Bioengineering
M Biomath	Master of Biomathematics
M Bus Ed	Master of Business Education
M Ch	Master of Chemistry
M Ch E	Master of Chemical Engineering
M Chem	Master of Chemistry
M Cl D	Master of Clinical Dentistry
M Cl Sc	Master of Clinical Science
M Co E	Master of Computer Engineering
M Comp E	Master of Computer Engineering
M Coun	Master of Counseling
M Cp E	Master of Computer Engineering
M Dent	Master of Dentistry
M Dent Sc	Master of Dental Sciences
M Des	Master of Design
M Des S	Master of Design Studies
M Div	Master of Divinity
M E Com	Master of Electronic Commerce
M Ec	Master of Economics
M Econ	Master of Economics
M Ed	Master of Education
M Ed T	Master of Education in Teaching
M En	Master of Engineering
M En S	Master of Environmental Sciences
M Eng	Master of Engineering
M Eng Mgt	Master of Engineering Management
M Eng Tel	Master of Engineering in Telecommunications
M Engr	Master of Engineering
M Env	Master of Environment
M Env Des	Master of Environmental Design
M Env E	Master of Environmental Engineering
M Env Sc	Master of Environmental Science
M Ext Ed	Master of Extension Education
M Fin	Master of Finance
M Fr	Master of French
M Geo E	Master of Geological Engineering
M Geoenv E	Master of Geoenvironmental Engineering
M Geog	Master of Geography
M Hum	Master of Humanities
M Hum Svcs	Master of Human Services
M Kin	Master of Kinesiology
M Land Arch	Master of Landscape Architecture
M Lit M	Master of Liturgical Music
M Litt	Master of Letters
M Man	Master of Management
M Mat SE	Master of Material Science and Engineering
M Math	Master of Mathematics
M Med Sc	Master of Medical Science
M Mgmt	Master of Management
M Mgt	Master of Management
M Min	Master of Ministries
M Mtl E	Master of Materials Engineering
M Mu	Master of Music
M Mu Ed	Master of Music Education
M Mus	Master of Music
M Mus Ed	Master of Music Education
M Nat Sci	Master of Natural Science
M Nurs	Master of Nursing
M Oc E	Master of Oceanographic Engineering
M Pharm	Master of Pharmacy
M Phil	Master of Philosophy
M Phil F	Master of Philosophical Foundations
M Pl	Master of Planning
M Pol	Master of Political Science
M Pr A	Master of Professional Accountancy
M Pr Met	Master of Professional Meteorology
M Prob S	Master of Probability and Statistics
M Prof Past	Master of Professional Pastoral
M Ps	Master of Psychology
M Psych	Master of Psychology
M Pub	Master of Publishing
M Rel	Master of Religion
M Sc	Master of Science
M Sc A	Master of Science (Applied)
M Sc AHN	Master of Science in Applied Human Nutrition
M Sc BMC	Master of Science in Biomedical Communications
M Sc CS	Master of Science in Computer Science
M Sc E	Master of Science in Engineering
M Sc Eng	Master of Science in Engineering
M Sc Engr	Master of Science in Engineering
M Sc F	Master of Science in Forestry
M Sc FE	Master of Science in Forest Engineering
M Sc Geogr	Master of Science in Geography
M Sc N	Master of Science in Nursing
M Sc OT	Master of Science in Occupational Therapy
M Sc P	Master of Science in Planning
M Sc Pl	Master of Science in Planning
M Sc PT	Master of Science in Physical Therapy
M Sc T	Master of Science in Teaching
M Soc	Master of Sociology
M Sp Ed	Master of Special Education
M Stat	Master of Statistics
M Sw E	Master of Software Engineering
M Sw En	Master of Software Engineering
M Sys Sc	Master of Systems Science
M Tax	Master of Taxation

M Tech Master of Technology
M Th Master of Theology
M Th Past Master of Pastoral Theology
M Tox Master of Toxicology
M Trans E Master of Transportation Engineering
M Vet Sc Master of Veterinary Science
MA Master of Administration
Master of Arts
MA Comm Master of Arts in Communication
MA Ed Master of Arts in Education
MA Ed Ad Master of Arts in Educational Administration
MA Ext Master of Agricultural Extension
MA Islamic Master of Arts in Islamic Studies
MA Min Master of Arts in Ministry
MA Missions Master of Arts in Missions
MA Past St Master of Arts in Pastoral Studies
MA Ph Master of Arts in Philosophy
MA Ps Master of Arts in Psychology
MA Psych Master of Arts in Psychology
MA Sc Master of Applied Science
MA Th Master of Arts in Theology
MA(R) Master of Arts (Research)
MAA Master of Administrative Arts
Master of Applied Anthropology
Master of Arts in Administration
MAAA Master of Arts in Arts Administration
MAAE Master of Arts in Applied Economics
Master of Arts in Art Education
MAAT Master of Arts in Applied Theology
Master of Arts in Art Therapy
MAB Master of Agribusiness
MABC Master of Arts in Biblical Counseling
Master of Arts in Business Communication
MABE Master of Arts in Bible Exposition
MABL Master of Arts in Biblical Languages
MABM Master of Agribusiness Management
MABS Master of Arts in Biblical Studies
MABT Master of Arts in Bible Teaching
MAC Master of Accounting
Master of Addictions Counseling
Master of Applied Communications
Master of Arts in Communication
Master of Arts in Counseling
MACAT Master of Arts in Counseling Psychology: Art Therapy
MACC Master of Arts in Christian Counseling
MACCM Master of Arts in Church and Community Ministry
MACCT Master of Accounting
MACE Master of Arts in Christian Education
MACFM Master of Arts in Children's and Family Ministry
MACH Master of Arts in Church History
MACL Master of Arts in Classroom Psychology
MACM Master of Arts in Christian Ministries
Master of Arts in Church Music
Master of Arts in Counseling Ministries
MACN Master of Arts in Counseling
MACO Master of Arts in Counseling
MACP Master of Arts in Counseling Psychology
MACS Master of Arts in Christian Service
MACSE Master of Arts in Christian School Education
MACT Master of Arts in Christian Thought
MACTM Master of Applied Communication Theory and Methodology
MACY Master of Arts in Accountancy
MAD Master in Educational Institution Administration
Master of Art and Design
MADH Master of Applied Development and Health
MADR Master of Arts in Dispute Resolution
MADS Master of Animal and Dairy Science
MAE Master of Aerospace Engineering
Master of Agricultural Economics
Master of Architectural Engineering
Master of Art Education
Master of Arts in Economics
Master of Arts in Education
Master of Arts in English
Master of Automotive Engineering
MAEd Master of Arts Education
MAEE Master of Agricultural and Extension Education
MAEM Master of Arts in Educational Ministries
MAEN Master of Arts in English
MAEP Master of Arts in Economic Policy
MAES Master of Arts in Environmental Sciences
MAESL Master of Arts in English as a Second Language
MAET Master of Arts English Teaching
MAF Master of Arts in Finance
MAFLL Master of Arts in Foreign Language and Literature
MAFM Master of Accounting and Financial Management
MAFS Master of Arts in Family Studies
MAG Master of Applied Geography
MAGP Master of Arts in Gerontological Psychology
MAGU Master of Urban Analysis and Management
MAH Master of Arts in Humanities
MAHA Master of Arts in Humanitarian Assistance
Master of Arts in Humanitarian Studies
MAHCM Master of Arts in Health Care Mission
MAHL Master of Arts in Hebrew Letters
MAHN Master of Applied Human Nutrition
MAHRM Master of Arts in Human Resources Management
MAHS Master of Arts in Human Services
MAIB Master of Arts in International Business
MAICS Master of Arts in Intercultural Studies
MAIDM Master of Arts in Interior Design and Merchandising
MAIM Master of Arts in Intercultural Ministry
MAIPCR Master of Arts in International Peace and Conflict Management
MAIR Master of Arts in Industrial Relations
MAIS Master of Accounting and Information Systems
Master of Arts in Intercultural Studies
Master of Arts in Interdisciplinary Studies
Master of Arts in International Studies
MAIT Master of Administration in Information Technology
MAJ Master of Arts in Journalism
MAJ Ed Master of Arts in Jewish Education
MAJCS Master of Arts in Jewish Communal Service
MAJE Master of Arts in Jewish Education
MAJS Master of Arts in Jewish Studies
MAL Master in Agricultural Leadership
MALA Master of Arts in Liberal Arts
MALD Master of Arts in Law and Diplomacy
MALER Master of Arts in Labor and Employment Relations
MALL Master of Arts in Liberal Learning
MALM Master of Arts in Leadership Evangelical Mobilization

MALS Master of Arts in Liberal Studies
MAM Master of Acquisition Management
Master of Agriculture and Management
Master of Applied Mathematics
Master of Applied Mechanics
Master of Arts in Management
Master of Arts in Ministry
Master of Arts Management
Master of Avian Medicine
MAMB Master of Applied Molecular Biology
MAMC Master of Arts in Mass Communication
Master of Arts in Ministry and Culture
MAME Master of Arts in Missions/Evangelism
MAMFC Master of Arts in Marriage and Family Counseling
MAMFCC Master of Arts in Marriage, Family, and Child Counseling
MAMFT Master of Arts in Marriage and Family Therapy
MAMM Master of Arts in Ministry Management
MAMS Master of Applied Mathematical Sciences
Master of Arts in Ministerial Studies
Master of Arts in Ministry and Spirituality
Master of Associated Medical Sciences
MAMT Master of Arts in Mathematics Teaching
MAN Master of Applied Nutrition
MANM Master of Arts in Nonprofit Management
MANT Master of Arts in New Testament
MAO Master of Arts in Organizational Psychology
MAOE Master of Adult and Occupational Education
MAOL Master of Arts in Organizational Leadership
MAOM Master of Acupuncture and Oriental Medicine
Master of Arts in Organizational Management
MAOT Master of Arts in Old Testament
MAP Master of Applied Psychology
Master of Arts in Planning
Master of Public Administration
Masters of Psychology
MAP Min Master of Arts in Pastoral Ministry
MAPA Master of Arts in Public Administration
MAPC Master of Arts in Pastoral Counseling
MAPE Master of Arts in Political Economy
MAPM Master of Arts in Pastoral Ministry
MAPP Master of Arts in Public Policy
MAPPS Master of Arts in Asia Pacific Policy Studies
MAPS Master of Arts in Pastoral Counseling/Spiritual Formation
Master of Arts in Pastoral Studies
Master of Arts in Professional Studies
MAPW Master of Arts in Professional Writing
MAR Master of Arts in Religion
Mar Eng Marine Engineer
MARC Master of Arts in Rehabilitation Counseling
Master of Arts in Religious Communication
MARE Master of Arts in Religious Education
MARL Master of Arts in Religious Leadership
MARS Master of Arts in Religious Studies
MAS Master of Accounting Science
Master of Actuarial Science
Master of Administrative Science
Master of Advanced Study
Master of Aeronautical Science
Master of American Studies
Master of Applied Science
Master of Applied Statistics
Master of Archival Studies
MASA Master of Advanced Studies in Architecture
MASAC Master of Arts in Substance Abuse Counseling
MASD Master of Arts in Spiritual Direction
MASE Master of Arts in Special Education
MASF Master of Arts in Spiritual Formation
MASL Master of Arts in School Leadership
MASLA Master of Advanced Studies in Landscape Architecture
MASM Master of Arts in Special Ministries
Master of Arts in Specialized Ministries
MASMED Master of Arts in Science and Mathematics Education
MASP Master of Applied Social Psychology
Master of Arts in School Psychology
MASPAA Master of Arts in Sports and Athletic Administration
MASS Master of Applied Social Science
Master of Arts in Social Science
MAST Master of Arts Science Teaching
MAT Master of Arts in Teaching
Master of Arts in Theology
Master of Athletic Training
Masters in Administration of Telecommunications
Mat E Materials Engineer
MATCM Master of Acupuncture and Traditional Chinese Medicine
MATDE Master of Arts in Theology, Development, and Evangelism
MATE Master of Arts for the Teaching of English
MATESL Master of Arts in Teaching English as a Second Language
MATESOL Master of Arts in Teaching English to Speakers of Other Languages
MATF Master of Arts in Teaching English as a Foreign Language/Intercultural Studies
MATFL Master of Arts in Teaching Foreign Language
MATH Master of Arts in Therapy
MATI Master of Administration of Information Technology
MATL Master of Arts in Teaching of Languages
Master of Arts in Transformational Leadership
MATM Master of Arts in Teaching of Mathematics
MATS Master of Arts in Theological Studies
Master of Arts in Transforming Spirituality
MATSL Master of Arts in Teaching a Second Language
MAUA Master of Arts in Urban Affairs
MAUD Master of Arts in Urban Design
MAUM Master of Arts in Urban Ministry
MAURP Master of Arts in Urban and Regional Planning
MAW Master of Arts in Writing
MAWL Master of Arts in Worship Leadership
MAWS Master of Arts in Worship/Spirituality
MAWSHP Master of Arts in Worship
MAYM Master of Arts in Youth Ministry
MB Master of Bioinformatics
MBA Master of Business Administration
MBA-EP Master of Business Administration–Experienced Professionals
MBA-PE Master of Business Administration–Physician's Executive
MBAA Master of Business Administration in Aviation
MBAE Master of Biological and Agricultural Engineering
Master of Biosystems and Agricultural Engineering
MBAH Master of Business Administration in Health
MBAi Master of Business Administration–International

MBAIM Master of Business Administration in International Management
MBAPA Master of Business Administration–Physician Assistant
MBATM Master of Business in Telecommunication Management
MBC Master of Building Construction
MBE Master of Bilingual Education
Master of Biomedical Engineering
Master of Business Education
MBET Master of Business, Entrepreneurship and Technology
MBIOT Master of Biotechnology
MBIT Master of Business Information Technology
MBMSE Master of Business Management and Software Engineering
MBOL Master of Business and Organizational Leadership
MBS Master of Basic Science
Master of Behavioral Science
Master of Biblical Studies
Master of Biological Science
Master of Biomedical Sciences
Master of Bioscience
Master of Building Science
Master of Business Studies
MBSI Master of Business Information Science
MBT Master of Biblical and Theological Studies
Master of Biomedical Technology
Master of Business Taxation
MC Master of Communication
Master of Counseling
MC Ed Master of Continuing Education
MC Sc Master of Computer Science
MCA Master of Arts in Applied Criminology
Master of Commercial Aviation
MCALL Master of Computer-Assisted Language Learning
MCAM Master of Computational and Applied Mathematics
MCC Master of Computer Science
MCCS Master of Crop and Soil Sciences
MCD Master of Communications Disorders
Master of Community Development
MCE Master in Electronic Commerce
Master of Christian Education
Master of Civil Engineering
Master of Civil Engineering
Master of Construction Engineering
Master of Continuing Education
Master of Control Engineering
MCEM Master of Construction Engineering Management
MCH Master of Community Health
MCHS Master of Clinical Health Sciences
MCIS Master of Communication and Information Studies
Master of Computer and Information Science
Master of Computer Information Systems
MCIT Master's of Computer and Information Technology
MCJ Master of Criminal Justice
MCJA Master of Criminal Justice Administration
MCL Master of Canon Law
Master of Civil Law
Master of Comparative Law
MCM Master of Christian Ministry
Master of Church Management
Master of Church Ministry
Master of Church Music
Master of City Management
Master of Community Medicine
Master of Construction Management
Master of Contract Management
Masters of Corporate Media
MCMS Master of Clinical Medical Science
MCP Master in Science
Master of City Planning
Master of Community Planning
Master of Counseling Psychology
MCPD Master of Community Planning and Development
MCR Masters in Clinical Research
MCRP Master of City and Regional Planning
MCRS Master of City and Regional Studies
MCS Master of Christian Studies
Master of Combined Sciences
Master of Communication Studies
Master of Computer Science
MCSE Master of Computer Science and Engineering
MCSL Master of Catholic School Leadership
MCSM Master of Construction Science/Management
MCTE Master of Career and Technology Education
MCTP Master of Communication Technology and Policy
MCVS Master of Cardiovascular Science
MD Doctor of Medicine
MDA Master of Development Administration
Master of Dietetic Administration
MDE Master of Developmental Economics
Master of Distance Education
MDR Master of Dispute Resolution
MDS Master of Defense Studies
Master of Dental Surgery
ME Master of Education
Master of Engineering
Master of Entrepreneurship
Master of Evangelism
ME Sc Master of Engineering Science
MEA Master of Educational Administration
Master of Engineering Administration
MEAP Master of Environmental Administration and Planning
MEC Master of Electronic Commerce
MECE Master of Electrical and Computer Engineering
Mech E Mechanical Engineer
MED Master of Education of the Deaf
MEDS Master of Environmental Design Studies
MEE Master in Education
Master of Electrical Engineering
Master of Environmental Engineering
MEEM Master of Environmental Engineering and Management
MEENE Master of Engineering in Environmental Engineering
MEEP Master of Environmental and Energy Policy
MEERM Master of Earth and Environmental Resource Management
MEH Master in Humanistics Studies
MEHS Master of Environmental Health and Safety

MEHWE	Master of Engineering in Hazardous Waste Engineering
MEL	Master of Educational Leadership
MEM	Master of Ecosystem Management
	Master of Electricity Markets
	Master of Engineering Management
	Master of Environmental Management
	Master of Marketing
MEME	Master of Engineering in Manufacturing Engineering
	Master of Engineering in Mechanical Engineering
MEMS	Master of Engineering in Manufacturing Systems
MENVEGR	Master of Environmental Engineering
MEP	Master of Engineering Physics
	Master of Environmental Planning
MEPC	Master of Environmental Pollution Control
MEPD	Master of Education–Professional Development
MEPM	Master of Environmental Policy and Management
	Master of Environmental Protection Management
MER	Master of Employment Relations
MES	Master of Education and Science
	Master of Engineering Science
	Master of Environmental Science
	Master of Environmental Studies
	Master of Environmental Systems
	Master of Special Education
MESM	Master of Environmental Science and Management
MET	Master of Education in Teaching
	Master of Educational Technology
	Master of Engineering Technology
	Master of Entertainment Technology
	Master of Environmental Toxicology
Met E	Metallurgical Engineer
METM	Master of Engineering and Technology Management
MEVE	Master of Environmental Engineering
MF	Master of Finance
	Master of Forestry
MFA	Master of Financial Administration
	Master of Fine Arts
MFAC	Master of Fine Arts in Computing
MFAS	Master of Fisheries and Aquatic Science
MFAW	Master of Fine Arts in Writing
MFC	Master of Forest Conservation
MFCC	Marriage and Family Counseling Certificate
	Marriage, Family, and Child Counseling
MFCS	Master of Family and Consumer Sciences
MFE	Master of Financial Engineering
	Master of Forest Engineering
MFG	Master of Functional Genomics
MFHD	Master of Family and Human Development
MFM	Master of Financial Mathematics
MFMS	Masters in Food Microbiology and Safety
MFP	Master of Financial Planning
MFPE	Master of Food Process Engineering
MFR	Master of Forest Resources
MFRC	Master of Forest Resources and Conservation
MFS	Master of Family Studies
	Master of Food Science
	Master of Forensic Sciences
	Master of Forest Science
	Master of Forest Studies
	Master of French Studies
MFSA	Master of Forensic Sciences Administration
MFT	Master of Family Therapy
	Master of Food Technology
MFWS	Master of Fisheries and Wildlife Sciences
MG	Master of Genetics
MGA	Master of Government Administration
MGD	Master of Graphic Design
MGE	Master of Gas Engineering
	Master of Geotechnical Engineering
MGH	Master of Geriatric Health
MGIS	Master of Geographic Information Science
MGP	Master of Gestion de Projet
MGS	Master of General Studies
	Master of Geosciences
	Master of Gerontological Studies
	Master of Global Studies
MH	Master of Humanities
MH Sc	Master of Health Sciences
MHA	Master of Health Administration
	Master of Healthcare Administration
	Master of Hospitality Administration
MHCA	Master of Health Care Administration
MHCI	Master of Human-Computer Interaction
MHE	Master of Health Education
MHE Ed	Master of Home Economics Education
MHHS	Master of Health and Human Services
MHI	Master of Health Informatics
MHIS	Master of Health Information Systems
MHK	Master of Human Kinetics
MHL	Master of Health Law
	Master of Hebrew Literature
MHM	Master of Hospitality Management
MHMS	Master of Health Management Systems
MHP	Master of Health Physics
	Master of Heritage Preservation
	Master of Historic Preservation
MHPA	Master of Heath Policy and Administration
MHPE	Master of Health Professions Education
MHR	Master of Human Resources
MHRD	Master in Human Resource Development
MHRDL	Master of Human Resource Development Leadership
MHRIM	Master of Hotel, Restaurant, and Institutional Management
MHRIR	Master of Human Resources and Industrial Relations
MHRLR	Master of Human Resources and Labor Relations
MHRM	Master of Human Resources Management
MHROD	Master of Human Resources and Organization Development
MHRTA	Master in Hotel, Restaurant, Tourism, and Administration
MHS	Master of Health Sciences
	Master of Health Studies
	Master of Hispanic Studies
	Master of Homeland Security
	Master of Humanistic Studies
MHSA	Master of Health Services Administration
	Master of Human Services Administration
MI	Master of Instruction
MI Arch	Master of Interior Architecture
MI St	Master of Information Studies
MIA	Master of Interior Architecture
	Master of International Affairs
MIAA	Master of International Affairs and Administration

MIB	Master of International Business
MIBA	Master of International Business Administration
MICM	Master of International Construction Management
MID	Master of Industrial Design Master of Industrial Engineering Master of Interior Design Master of International Development
MIE	Master of Industrial Engineering
MIE Mgmt	Master of Industrial Engineering Management
MIJ	Master of International Journalism
MILR	Master of Industrial and Labor Relations
MIM	Master of Information Management Master of International Management
MIMLAE	Master of International Management for Latin American Executives
MIMS	Master of Information Management and Systems Master of Integrated Manufacturing Systems
MIP	Master of Infrastructure Planning Master of Intellectual Property
MIPP	Master of International Policy and Practice Master of International Public Policy
MIR	Master of Industrial Relations Master of International Relations
MIS	Master of Industrial Statistics Master of Information Science Master of Information Systems Master of Integrated Science Master of Interdisciplinary Studies Master of International Service Master of International Studies
MISKM	Master of Information Sciences and Knowledge Management
MISM	Master of Information Systems Management
MIT	Master in Teaching Master of Industrial Technology Master of Information Technology Master of Initial Teaching Master of International Trade
MITA	Master of Information Technology Administration
MITE	Master of Information Technology Education
MITM	Master of International Technology Management
MITO	Master of Industrial Technology and Operations
MJ	Master of Journalism Master of Jurisprudence
MJ Ed	Master of Jewish Education
MJA	Master of Justice Administration
MJPM	Master of Justice Policy and Management
MJS	Master of Judicial Studies Master of Juridical Science
ML Arch	Master of Landscape Architecture
MLA	Master of Landscape Architecture Master of Liberal Arts
MLAS	Master of Laboratory Animal Science
MLAUD	Master of Landscape Architecture in Urban Development
MLBLST	Master of Liberal Studies
MLD	Master of Leadership Development Master of Leadership Studies
MLE	Master of Applied Linguistics and Exegesis
MLER	Master of Labor and Employment Relations
MLERE	Master of Land Economics and Real Estate
MLHR	Master of Labor and Human Resources
MLI	Master of Legal Institutions
MLI Sc	Master of Library and Information Science
MLIS	Master of Library and Information Science Master of Library and Information Studies
MLM	Master of Library Media
MLRHR	Master of Labor Relations and Human Resources
MLS	Master of Legal Studies Master of Liberal Studies Master of Library Science Master of Life Sciences
MLSP	Master of Law and Social Policy
MLT	Master of Language Technologies
MM	Master of Management Master of Ministry Master of Missiology Master of Music
MM Ed	Master of Music Education
MM Sc	Master of Medical Science
MM St	Master of Museum Studies
MMA	Master of Marine Affairs Master of Media Arts Master of Musical Arts
MMAE	Master of Mechanical and Aerospace Engineering
MMAS	Master of Military Art and Science
MMB	Master of Microbial Biotechnology
MMBA	Managerial Master of Business Administration
MMC	Master of Competitive Manufacturing Master of Mass Communications Master of Music Conducting
MMCM	Master of Music in Church Music
MMCSS	Masters of Mathematical Computational and Statistical Sciences
MME	Master of Manufacturing Engineering Master of Mathematics for Educators Master of Mechanical Engineering Master of Medical Engineering Master of Mining Engineering Master of Music Education Mater of Mathematics Education
MMF	Master of Mathematical Finance
MMFT	Master of Marriage and Family Therapy
MMG	Master of Management
MMH	Master of Management in Hospitality Master of Medical History Master of Medical Humanities
MMIS	Master of Management Information Systems
MMM	Master of Manufacturing Management Master of Marine Management Master of Medical Management
MMME	Master of Metallurgical and Materials Engineering
MMP	Master of Marine Policy Master of Music Performance
MMPA	Master of Management and Professional Accounting
MMQM	Master of Manufacturing Quality Management
MMR	Master of Marketing Research
MMRM	Master of Marine Resources Management
MMS	Master of Management Science Master of Marine Science Master of Marine Studies Master of Materials Science Master of Medical Science Master of Medical Science Master of Medieval Studies Master of Modern Studies
MMSE	Master of Manufacturing Systems Engineering Master of Science in Systems Engineering

MMT	Master in Marketing Master of Music Teaching Master of Music Therapy Masters in Marketing Technology
MMus	Master of Music
MN	Master of Nursing Master of Nutrition
MN Sc	Master of Nursing Science
MNA	Master of Nonprofit Administration Master of Nurse Anesthesia
MNAS	Master of Natural and Applied Science
MNE	Master of Network Engineering Master of Nuclear Engineering
MNL	Master in International Business for Latin America
MNM	Master of Nonprofit Management
MNO	Master of Nonprofit Organization
MNPL	Master of Not-for-Profit Leadership
MNPS	Master of New Professional Studies
MNR	Master of Natural Resources
MNRES	Master of Natural Resources and Environmental Studies
MNRM	Master of Natural Resource Management
MNS	Master of Natural Science
MOA	Maître d'Orthophonie et d'Audiologie
MOD	Master of Organizational Development
MOGS	Master of Oil and Gas Studies
MOH	Master of Occupational Health
MOL	Master of Organizational Leadership
MOM	Master of Manufacturing Master of Oriental Medicine
MOR	Master of Operations Research
MOT	Master of Occupational Therapy
MoTM	Master of Technology Management
MP	Master of Physiology Master of Planning
MP Ac	Master of Professional Accountancy
MP Acc	Master of Professional Accountancy Master of Professional Accounting Master's of Public Accounting
MP Aff	Master of Public Affairs
MP Th	Master of Pastoral Theology
MPA	Master of Physician Assistant Master of Professional Accountancy Master of Professional Accounting Master of Public Administration Master of Public Affairs
MPA-URP	Master of Public Affairs and Urban and Regional Planning
MPAC	Masters in Professional Accounting
MPAD	Master of Public Administration
MPAID	Master of Public Administration and International Development
MPAP	Master of Public Affairs and Politics
MPAS	Master of Physician Assistant Science Master of Physician Assistant Studies Master of Public Art Studies
MPC	Master of Pastoral Counseling Master of Professional Communication
MPD	Master of Product Development
MPDS	Master of Planning and Development Studies
MPE	Master of Physical Education
MPEM	Master of Project Engineering and Management
MPH	Master of Public Health
MPHE	Master of Public Health Education
MPHTM	Master of Public Health and Tropical Medicine
MPIA	Master of Public and International Affairs
MPL	Master of Pastoral Leadership
MPM	Master of Pastoral Ministry Master of Pest Management Master of Practical Ministries Master of Project Management Master of Public Management
MPNA	Master of Public and Nonprofit Administration
MPP	Master of Public Policy
MPPA	Master of Public Policy Administration Master of Public Policy and Administration
MPPM	Master of Public and Private Management Master of Public Policy and Management
MPPPM	Master of Plant Protection and Pest Management
MPPUP	Master of Public Policy and Urban Planning
MPRTM	Master of Parks, Recreation, and Tourism Management
MPS	Master of Pastoral Studies Master of Perfusion Science Master of Political Science Master of Preservation Studies Master of Professional Studies Master of Public Service
MPSA	Master of Public Service Administration
MPSRE	Master of Professional Studies in Real Estate
MPT	Master of Pastoral Theology Master of Physical Therapy
MPVM	Master of Preventive Veterinary Medicine
MPW	Master of Professional Writing Master of Public Works
MQF	Master of Quantitative Finance
MQM	Master of Quality Management
MR	Master of Recreation
MRC	Master of Rehabilitation Counseling
MRCP	Master of Regional and City Planning Master of Regional and Community Planning
MRD	Master of Rural Development
MRE	Master of Religious Education
MRED	Master of Real Estate Development
MRLS	Master of Resources Law Studies
MRM	Master of Rehabilitation Medicine Master of Resources Management
MRP	Master of Regional Planning
MRRA	Master of Recreation Resources Administration
MRS	Master of Religious Studies
MS	Master of Science
MS Acct	Master of Science in Accounting
MS Accy	Master of Science in Accountancy
MS Admin	Master of Science in Administration
MS Aero E	Master of Science in Aerospace Engineering
MS Ag	Master of Science in Agriculture
MS Arch	Master of Science in Architecture
MS Arch St	Master of Science in Architectural Studies
MS Bio E	Master of Science in Bioengineering Master of Science in Biomedical Engineering
MS Biol	Master of Science in Biology
MS Bm E	Master of Science in Biomedical Engineering
MS Ch E	Master of Science in Chemical Engineering
MS Chem	Master of Science in Chemistry
MS Cp E	Master of Science in Computer Engineering
MS Eco	Master of Science in Economics
MS Econ	Master of Science in Economics
MS Ed	Master of Science in Education

MS El	Master of Science in Educational Leadership and Administration
MS En E	Master of Science in Environmental Engineering
MS Eng	Master of Science in Engineering
MS Engr	Master of Science in Engineering
MS Env E	Master of Science in Environmental Engineering
MS Exp Surg	Master of Science in Experimental Surgery
MS Int A	Master of Science in International Affairs
MS Mat E	Master of Science in Materials Engineering
MS Mat SE	Master of Science in Material Science and Engineering
MS Met E	Master of Science in Metallurgical Engineering
MS Metr	Master of Science in Meteorology
MS Mgt	Master of Science in Management
MS Min	Master of Science in Mining
MS Min E	Master of Science in Mining Engineering
MS Mt E	Master of Science in Materials Engineering
MS Nsg	Master of Science in Nursing
MS Otal	Master of Science in Otalrynology
MS Pet E	Master of Science in Petroleum Engineering
MS Phr	Master of Science in Pharmacy
MS Phys	Master of Science in Physics
MS Phys Op	Master of Science in Physiological Optics
MS Poly	Master of Science in Polymers
MS Psy	Master of Science in Psychology
MS Pub P	Master of Science in Public Policy
MS Sc	Master of Science in Social Science
MS Sp C	Master of Science in Space Science
MS Sp Ed	Master of Science in Special Education
MS Stat	Master of Science in Statistics Master of Science in Statistics
MS Surg	Master of Science in Surgery
MS Tax	Master of Science in Taxation
MS Tc E	Master of Science in Telecommunications Engineering
MS(R)	Master of Science (Research)
MS-ASE	Master of Science in Applied Science Education
MSA	Master of School Administration Master of Science Administration Master of Science in Accountancy Master of Science in Accounting Master of Science in Administration Master of Science in Agriculture Master of Science in Anesthesia Master of Science in Architecture Master of Science in Aviation Master of Sports Administration
MSA Phy	Master of Science in Applied Physics
MSAA	Master of Science in Astronautics and Aeronautics
MSAAE	Master of Science in Aeronautical and Astronautical Engineering
MSABE	Master of Science in Agricultural and Biological Engineering
MSACC	Master of Science in Accounting
MSaCS	Master of Science in Applied Computer Science
MSAE	Master of Science in Aeronautical Engineering Master of Science in Aerospace Engineering Master of Science in Agricultural Engineering Master of Science in Applied Economics Master of Science in Architectural Engineering Master of Science in Art Education
MSAH	Master of Science in Allied Health
MSAIS	Master of Science in Accounting Information Systems
MSAM	Master of Science in Applied Mathematics
MSAOM	Master of Science in Agricultural Operations Management
MSAS	Master of Science in Administrative Studies Master of Science in Architectural Studies
MSAT	Master of Science in Advanced Technology
MSB	Master of Science in Bible Master of Science in Biology Master of Science in Business
MSBA	Master of Science in Business Administration
MSBAE	Master of Science in Biological and Agricultural Engineering Master of Science in Biosystems and Agricultural Engineering
MSBC	Master of Science in Building Construction
MSBE	Master of Science in Biomedical Engineering
MSBENG	Master of Science in Bioengineering
MSBIS	Master of Science in Business Information Systems
MSBIT	Master of Science in Business Information Technology
MSBM	Master of Sport Business Management
MSBME	Master of Science in Biomedical Engineering
MSBMS	Master of Science in Basic Medical Science
MSBS	Master of Science in Biomedical Sciences
MSC	Master of Science in Commerce Master of Science in Communication Master of Science in Computers Master of Science in Counseling Master of Science in Criminology
MSCC	Master of Science in Christian Counseling
MSCD	Master of Science in Communication Disorders Master of Science in Community Development
MSCE	Master of Science in Civil Engineering Master of Science in Clinical Epidemiology Master of Science in Computer Engineering Master of Science in Continuing Education
MSCEE	Master of Science in Civil and Environmental Engineering
MSCET	Master of Science in Computer Education and Technology
MSCF	Master of Science in Computational Finance
MSCHE	Master of Science in Chemical Engineering
MSCI	Master of Science in Clinical Investigation Master of Science in Curriculum and Instruction
MSCIS	Master of Science in Computer and Information Systems Master of Science in Computer Information Systems
MSCIT	Master of Science in Computer Information Technology
MSCJ	Master of Science in Criminal Justice
MSCJA	Master of Science in Criminal Justice Administration
MSCM	Master of Science in Conflict Management Master of Science in Construction Management
MScM	Master of Science in Management
MSCP	Master of Science in Clinical Psychology Master of Science in Counseling Psychology
MSCPharm	Master of Science in Pharmacy
MSCRP	Master of Science in City and Regional Planning Master of Science in Community and Regional Planning
MSCS	Master of Science in Computer Science Master of Science in Construction Science

MSCSD Master of Science in Communication Sciences and Disorders
MSCSE Master of Science in Computer Science and Engineering
Master of Science in Computer Systems Engineering
Master of Science in Control Systems Engineering
MSCTE Master of Science in Career and Technical Education
MSD Master of Science in Dentistry
Master of Science in Design
MSDD Master of Software Design and Development
MSDM Master of Design Methods
MSDR Master of Dispute Resolution
MSE Master of Science Education
Master of Science in Education
Master of Science in Engineering
Master of Software Engineering
Master of Structural Engineering
MSE Mgt Master of Science in Engineering Management
MSECE Master of Science in Electrical and Computer Engineering
MSED Master of Sustainable Economic Development
MSEE Master of Science in Electrical Engineering
Master of Science in Environmental Engineering
MSEH Master of Science in Environmental Health
MSEL Master of Science in Executive Leadership
Master of Studies in Environmental Law
MSEM Master of Science in Engineering Management
Master of Science in Engineering Mechanics
Master of Science in Environmental Management
MSENE Master of Science in Environmental Engineering
MSEO Master of Science in Electro-Optics
MSEP Master of Science in Economic Policy
MSES Master of Science in Engineering Science
Master of Science in Environmental Science
Master of Science in Environmental Studies
MSESM Master of Science in Engineering Science and Mechanics
MSET Master of Science in Engineering Technology
MSETA Master of Science in Educational Technology Administration
MSETM Master of Science in Engineering and Technology
Master of Science in Environmental Technology Management
MSEV Master of Science in Environmental Engineering
MSEVH Master of Science in Enviromental Health and Safety
MSF Master of Science in Finance
Master of Science in Forestry
Master of Social Foundations
MSFA Master of Science in Financial Analysis
MSFAM Master of Science in Family Studies
MSFCS Master of Science in Family and Consumer Science
MSFE Master of Science in Financial Engineering
Master of Science in Financial Engineering
MSFM Master of Financial Management
MSFOR Master of Science in Forestry
MSFP Master of Science in Financial Planning
MSFS Master of Science in Financial Sciences
Master of Science in Forensic Science
MSFT Master of Science in Family Therapy
MSGC Master of Science in Genetic Counseling
MSGFA Master of Science in Global Financial Analysis
MSGL Master of Science in Global Leadership
MSH Master of Science in Health
Master of Science in Hospice
MSHA Master of Science in Health Administration
MSHCA Master of Science in Health Care Administration
MSHCI Master of Science in Human Computer Interaction
MSHCPM Master of Science in Health Care Policy and Management
MSHCS Master of Science in Human and Consumer Science
MSHE Master of Science in Health Education
MSHES Master of Science in Human Environmental Sciences
MSHFID Master of Science in Human Factors in Information Design
MSHFS Master of Science in Human Factors and Systems
MSHP Master of Science in Health Professions
MSHR Master of Science in Human Resources
MSHRM Master of Science in Human Resource Management
MSHROD Master of Science in Human Resources and Organizational Development
MSHS Master of Science in Health Science
Master of Science in Health Services
Master of Science in Health Systems
MSHSA Master of Science in Human Service Administration
MSHT Master of Science in History of Technology
MSI Master of Science in Instruction
MSIA Master of Science in Industrial Administration
MSIAM Master of Science in Information Age Marketing
MSIB Master of Science in International Business
MSIDM Master of Science in Interior Design and Merchandising
MSIDT Master of Science in Information Design and Technology
MSIE Master of Science in Industrial Engineering
Master of Science in International Economics
MSIEM Master of Science in Information Engineering and Management
MSIM Master of Science in Information Management
Master of Science in Investment Management
MSIMC Master of Science in Integrated Marketing Communications
MSIR Master of Science in Industrial Relations
MSIS Master of Science in Information Science
Master of Science in Information Systems
Master of Science in Interdisciplinary Studies
MSISE Master of Science in Infrastructure Systems Engineering
MSISM Master of Science in Information Systems Management
MSIST Master of Science in Information Systems Technology
MSIT Master of Science in Industrial Technology
Master of Science in Information Technology
Master of Science in Instructional Technology
MSITM Master of Science in Information Technology Management
MSJ Master of Science in Journalism
Master of Science in Jurisprudence
MSJE Master of Science in Jewish Education
MSJFP Master of Science in Juvenile Forensic Psychology

MSJJ	Master of Science in Juvenile Justice
MSJPS	Master of Science in Justice and Public Safety
MSJS	Master of Science in Jewish Studies
MSK	Master of Science in Kinesiology
MSL	Master of School Leadership Master of Science in Limnology Master of Studies in Law
MSLA	Master of Science in Landscape Architecture Master of Science in Legal Administration
MSLD	Master of Science in Land Development
MSLP	Master of Speech-Language Pathology
MSLS	Master of Science in Legal Studies Master of Science in Library Science Master of Science in Logistics Systems
MSLT	Master of Second Language Teaching
MSM	Master of Sacred Music Master of School Mathematics Master of Science in Management Master of Science in Mathematics
MSMA	Master of Science in Marketing Analysis
MSMAE	Master of Science in Materials Engineering
MSMC	Master of Science in Marketing Communications Master of Science in Mass Communications
MSME	Master of Science in Mechanical Engineering
MSMFE	Master of Science in Manufacturing Engineering
MSMGEN	Master of Science in Management and General Engineering
MSMIS	Master of Science in Management Information Systems
MSMIT	Master of Science in Management and Information Technology
MSMM	Master of Science in Manufacturing Management
MSMO	Master of Science in Manufacturing Operations
MSMOT	Master of Science in Management of Technology
MSMP	Master of Science in Molecular Pathology
MSMS	Master of Science in Management Science
MSMSE	Master of Science in Manufacturing Systems Engineering Master of Science in Material Science and Engineering Master of Science in Mathematics and Science Education
MSMT	Master of Science in Management and Technology Master of Science in Medical Technology
MSN	Master of Science in Nursing
MSN(R)	Master of Science in Nursing (Research)
MSN-OB	Master of Science in Nursing-Organizational Behavior
MSNA	Master of Science in Nurse Anesthesia
MSNE	Master of Science in Nuclear Engineering
MSNS	Master of Science in Natural Science
MSOD	Master of Science in Organizational Development
MSOES	Master of Science in Occupational Ergonomics and Safety
MSOL	Master of Science in Organizational Leadership
MSOM	Master of Science in Organization and Management Master of Science in Oriental Medicine
MSOR	Master of Science in Operations Research
MSOT	Master of Science in Occupational Technology Master of Science in Occupational Therapy
MSP	Master of School Psychology Master of Science in Pharmacy Master of Science in Planning Master of Speech Pathology
MSP Ex	Master of Science in Exercise Physiology
MSPA	Master of Science in Physician Assistant Master of Science in Professional Accountancy
MSPAS	Master of Science in Physician Assistant Studies
MSPC	Master of Science in Professional Communications Master of Science in Professional Counseling
MSPE	Master of Science in Petroleum Engineering Master of Science in Physical Education
MSPG	Master of Science in Psychology
MSPH	Master of Science in Public Health
MSPHN	Master of Science in Public Health Nursing
MSPHR	Master of Science in Pharmacy
MSPM	Master of Science in Professional Management
MSPNGE	Master of Science in Petroleum and Natural Gas Engineering
MSPS	Master of Science in Pharmaceutical Science Master of Science in Psychological Services
MSPT	Master of Science in Physical Therapy
MSR	Master of Science in Radiology Master of Science in Rehabilitation Sciences
MSRA	Master of Science in Recreation Administration
MSRC	Master of Science in Resource Conservation
MSRE	Master of Science in Religious Education
MSRED	Master of Science in Real Estate Development
MSRLS	Master of Science in Recreation and Leisure Studies
MSRMP	Master of Science in Radiological Medical Physics
MSRS	Master of Science in Recreational Studies
MSS	Master of Science in Sociology Master of Science in Software Master of Social Science Master of Social Services Master of Sports Science Master of Strategic Studies
MSSA	Master of Science in Social Administration
MSSE	Master of Science in Software Engineering
MSSEM	Master of Science in Systems and Engineering Management
MSSI	Master of Science in Strategic Intelligence
MSSL	Master of Science in Strategic Leadership
MSSLP	Master of Science in Speech-Language Pathology
MSSM	Master of Science in Systems Management
MSSPA	Master of Science in Student Personnel Administration
MSSR	Master of Science in Social Research
MSSS	Master of Science in Safety Science Master of Science in Systems Science
MSSW	Master of Science in Social Work
MST	Master of Science in Taxation Master of Science in Teaching Master of Science in Technology Master of Science in Telecommunications Master of Science in Transportation Master of Science Teaching Master of Science Technology Master of Systems Technology
MSTC	Master of Science in Telecommunications

MSTE	Master of Science in Telecommunications Engineering Master of Science in Transportation Engineering
MSTIM	Master of Science in Technology and Innovation Management
MSTM	Master of Science in Technical Management Master of Science in Technology Management
MSTOM	Master of Science in Traditional Oriental Medicine
MSUD	Master of Science in Urban Design
MSUESM	Master of Science in Urban Environmental Systems Management
MSVE	Master of Science in Vocational Education
MSW	Master of Social Work
MSWE	Master of Software Engineering
MSWREE	Master of Science in Water Resources and Environmental Engineering
MSX	Master of Science in Exercise Science
MT	Master of Taxation Master of Teaching Master of Technology Master of Textiles
MTA	Master of Arts in Teaching Master of Tax Accounting Master of Teaching Arts Master of Tourism Administration
MTCM	Master of Traditional Chinese Medicine
MTD	Master of Training and Development
MTE	Master in Educational Technology Master of Teacher Education
MTEL	Master of Telecommunications
MTESL	Master in Teaching English as a Second Language
MTHM	Master of Tourism and Hospitality Management
MTI	Master of Information Technology
MTIM	Masters of Trust and Investment Management
MTL	Master of Talmudic Law
MTLM	Master of Transportation and Logistics Management
MTM	Master of Technology Management Master of Telecommunications Management Master of the Teaching of Mathematics
MTMH	Master of Tropical Medicine and Hygiene
MTOM	Master of Traditional Oriental Medicine
MTP	Master of Transpersonal Psychology
MTPW	Master of Technical and Professional Writing
MTS	Master of Teaching Science Master of Theological Studies
MTSC	Master of Technical and Scientific Communication
MTSE	Master of Telecommunications and Software Engineering
MTT	Master in Technology Management
MTX	Master of Taxation
MUA	Master of Urban Affairs
MUD	Master of Urban Design
MUEP	Master of Urban and Environmental Planning
MUP	Master of Urban Planning
MUPDD	Master of Urban Planning, Design, and Development
MUPP	Master of Urban Planning and Policy
MUPRED	Masters of Urban Planning and Real Estate Development
MURP	Master of Urban and Regional Planning Master of Urban and Rural Planning
MUS	Master of Urban Studies
Mus Doc	Doctor of Music
Mus M	Master of Music
MVPH	Master of Veterinary Public Health
MVT Ed	Master of Vocational and Technical Education
MVTE	Master of Vocational-Technical Education
MWC	Master of Wildlife Conservation
MWPS	Master of Wood and Paper Science
MWR	Master of Water Resources
MWS	Master of Women's Studies
Nav Arch	Naval Architecture
Naval E	Naval Engineer
ND	Doctor of Naturopathic Medicine Doctor of Nursing
NE	Nuclear Engineer
NPMC	Nonprofit Management Certificate
Nuc E	Nuclear Engineer
Ocean E	Ocean Engineer
OD	Doctor of Optometry
OTD	Doctor of Occupational Therapy
PD	Professional Diploma
PDD	Professional Development Degree
PE Dir	Director of Physical Education
PED	Doctor of Physical Education
PGC	Post-Graduate Certificate
Ph L	Licentiate of Philosophy
Pharm D	Doctor of Pharmacy
PhD	Doctor of Philosophy
PhD Otal	Doctor of Philosophy in Otalrynology
Phd Surg	Doctor of Philosophy in Surgery
PhDEE	Doctor of Philosophy in Electrical Engineering
PM Sc	Professional Master of Science
PMBA	Professional Master of Business Administration
PMC	Post Master's Certificate
PMS	Professional Master of Science
PPDPT	Postprofessional Doctor of Physical Therapy
PSD	Professional Studies Diploma
PSM	Professional Master of Science
Psy D	Doctor of Psychology
Psy M	Master of Psychology
Psy S	Specialist in Psychology
Psya D	Doctor of Psychoanalysis
Re D	Doctor of Recreation
Re Dir	Director of Recreation
Rh D	Doctor of Rehabilitation
S Psy S	Specialist in Psychological Services
SAS	School Administrator and Supervisor
Sc D	Doctor of Science
Sc M	Master of Science
SCCT	Specialist in Community College Teaching
ScDPT	Doctor of Physical Therapy Science
SD	Doctor of Science
SJD	Doctor of Juridical Science
SLPD	Doctor of Speech-Language Pathology
SLS	Specialist in Library Science
SM	Master of Science
SM Arch S	Master of Science in Architectural Studies
SM Vis S	Master of Science in Visual Studies
SMBT	Master of Science in Building Technology
SP	Specialist Degree
Sp C	Specialist in Counseling
Sp Ed	Specialist in Education
Sp Ed As	Specialist in Administrative Supervision

Sp Sch Psych	Specialist in School Psychology
SPCM	Special in Church Music
Spec	Specialist's Certificate
Spec M	Specialist in Music
SPEM	Special in Educational Ministries
SPS	School Psychology Specialist
Spt	Specialist Degree
SPTH	Special in Theology
SSP	Specialist in School Psychology
STB	Bachelor of Sacred Theology
STD	Doctor of Sacred Theology
STL	Licentiate of Sacred Theology
STM	Master of Sacred Theology
TDPT	Transitional Doctor of Physical Therapy
Th D	Doctor of Theology
Th M	Master of Theology
V Ed S	Vocational Education Specialist
VMD	Doctor of Veterinary Medicine
WEMBA	Weekend Executive Master of Business Administration
WMBA	Web-based Master of Business Administration
XMBA	Executive Master of Business Administration

INDEXES

In-Depth Descriptions and Announcements

Directories and Subject Areas in Books 2–6

Following is an alphabetical listing of directories and subject areas in Books 2–6. Also listed are cross-references for subject area names not used in the directory structure of the guides, for example, "Arabic (*see* Near and Middle Eastern Languages)."

Multilingual and Multicultural Education—Book 6
Museum Education—Book 6
Museum Studies—Book 2
Music—Book 2
Music Education—Book 6
Music History (*see* Music)
Musicology (*see* Music)
Music Theory (*see* Music)
Music Therapy (*see* Therapies—Dance, Drama, and Music)
Native American Studies (*see* American Indian/Native American Studies)
Natural Resources—Book 4
Natural Resources Management (*see* Environmental Management and Policy; Natural Resources)
Naturopathic Medicine—Book 6
Near and Middle Eastern Languages—Book 2
Near and Middle Eastern Studies—Book 2
Near Environment (*see* Family and Consumer Sciences; Human Development)
Neural Sciences (*see* Biopsychology; Neuroscience)
Neurobiology—Book 3
Neuroendocrinology (*see* Biopsychology; Neuroscience; Physiology)
Neuropharmacology (*see* Biopsychology; Neuroscience; Pharmacology)
Neurophysiology (*see* Biopsychology; Neuroscience; Physiology)
Neuroscience—Book 3
Nonprofit Management—Book 6
North American Studies (*see* Northern Studies)
Northern Studies—Book 2
Nuclear Engineering—Book 5
Nuclear Medical Technology (*see* Clinical Laboratory Sciences/Medical Technology)
Nuclear Physics (*see* Physics)
Nurse Anesthesia—Book 6
Nurse Midwifery—Book 6
Nurse Practitioner Studies (*see* Advanced Practice Nursing)
Nursery School Education (*see* Early Childhood Education)
Nursing—Book 6
Nursing and Healthcare Administration—Book 6
Nursing Education—Book 6
Nutrition—Book 3
Occupational Education (*see* Vocational and Technical Education)
Occupational Health (*see* Environmental and Occupational Health; Occupational Health Nursing)
Occupational Health Nursing—Book 6
Occupational Therapy—Book 6
Ocean Engineering—Book 5
Oceanography—Book 4
Oncology—Book 3
Oncology Nursing—Book 6
Operations Research—Book 5
Optical Sciences—Book 4
Optical Technologies (*see* Optical Sciences)
Optics (*see* Applied Physics; Optical Sciences; Physics)
Optometry—Book 6
Oral and Dental Sciences—Book 6
Oral Biology (*see* Oral and Dental Sciences)
Oral Pathology (*see* Oral and Dental Sciences)
Organic Chemistry—Book 4
Organismal Biology (*see* Biological and Biomedical Sciences; Zoology)
Organizational Behavior—Book 6
Organizational Management—Book 6
Organizational Psychology (*see* Industrial and Organizational Psychology)
Organizational Studies—Book 6
Oriental Languages (*see* Asian Languages)
Oriental Medicine—Book 6
Oriental Studies (*see* Asian Studies)
Orthodontics (*see* Oral and Dental Sciences)
Osteopathic Medicine—Book 6
Painting/Drawing (*see* Art/Fine Arts)
Paleontology (*see* Geology)
Paper and Pulp Engineering—Book 5
Paper Chemistry (*see* Chemistry)
Parasitology—Book 3
Park Management (*see* Recreation and Park Management)
Pastoral Ministry and Counseling—Book 2
Pathobiology—Book 3
Pathology—Book 3
Peace Studies (*see* Conflict Resolution and Mediation/Peace Studies)
Pediatric Nursing—Book 6
Pedodontics (*see* Oral and Dental Sciences)
Performance (*see* Music)
Performing Arts (*see* Dance; Music; Theater)
Periodontics (*see* Oral and Dental Sciences)
Personnel (*see* Human Resources Development; Human Resources Management; Organizational Behavior; Organizational Management; Organizational Studies)
Petroleum Engineering—Book 5
Pharmaceutical Administration—Book 6
Pharmaceutical Chemistry (*see* Medicinal and Pharmaceutical Chemistry)
Pharmaceutical Engineering—Book 5
Pharmaceutical Sciences—Book 6
Pharmacognosy (*see* Pharmaceutical Sciences)
Pharmacology—Book 3
Pharmacy—Book 6
Philanthropic Studies—Book 2
Philosophy—Book 2
Philosophy of Education (*see* Foundations and Philosophy of Education)
Photobiology of Cells and Organelles (*see* Botany and Plant Biology; Cell Biology)
Photography—Book 2
Photonics—Book 4
Physical Chemistry—Book 4
Physical Education—Book 6
Physical Therapy—Book 6
Physician Assistant Studies—Book 6
Physics—Book 4
Physiological Optics (*see* Physiology; Vision Sciences)
Physiology—Book 3
Planetary Sciences—Book 4
Plant Biology—Book 3
Plant Molecular Biology—Book 3
Plant Pathology—Book 3
Plant Physiology—Book 3
Plant Sciences—Book 4
Plasma Physics—Book 4
Plastics Engineering (*see* Polymer Science and Engineering)
Playwriting (*see* Theater; Writing)
Podiatric Medicine—Book 6
Policy Studies (*see* Educational Policy; Energy Management and Policy; Environmental Management and Policy; Public Policy and Administration; Strategy and Policy; Technology and Public Policy)
Political Science—Book 2
Polymer Science and Engineering—Book 5
Pomology (*see* Agricultural Sciences; Botany and Plant Biology; Horticulture; Plant Sciences)
Population Studies (*see* Demography and Population Studies)
Portuguese—Book 2
Poultry Science (*see* Animal Sciences)
Power Engineering—Book 5
Preventive Medicine (*see* Public Health; Community Health)

Directories and Subject Areas in This Book